THE 1902 EDITION OF

THE SEARS, ROEBUCK CATALOGUE

With an Introduction by

CLEVELAND AMORY

BOUNTY BOOKS · NEW YORK

See Publisher's Note following Introduction
for explanation of missing pages.

This 1986 edition is published by Bounty Books,
distributed by Crown Publishers, Inc.,
by arrangement with Crown Publishers, Inc.,
225 Park Avenue South, New York, New York 10003

Printed and Bound in the United States of America

Library of Congress Cataloging-in-Publication Data

The 1902 edition of the Sears, Roebuck catalogue.

1. Manufactures—Catalogs.
I. Sears, Roebuck and Company.
TS199.A16 1986 973.91'1 86-6162
ISBN 0-517-00922-6

hh gg ff ee

1. Manufacturers—Catalogs.

INTRODUCTION

A glance through the pages of this catalogue provides a view of the American scene at the turn of the century with an excitement and an accuracy that would defy the most eminent historian. Published in the spring of 1902, the catalogue mirrors the dreams and needs of Americans at a time when life was less complex than it is today, when a rural economy was still dominant and vast numbers of people were moving westward.

For each of us this catalogue will hold a different meaning. Some will recall those early twentieth-century years with a special nostalgia reserved for those who spent them as youths. Some will recall stories their parents and grandparents told about the "good old days" of the horse and buggy, the village blacksmith, and the gaslight. All, including those whose forebears were city folk or from the "old country," will find the catalogue an endless source of information, diversion, and entertainment.

Richard Warren Sears, the original founder of Sears, Roebuck and Co., was a master of psychology and provided in his catalogue a wealth of knowledge along with a good bit of hard-sell-copy to help gain the attention of his readers and convert them to loyal customers.

Consider, for example, the detailed descriptions of watch movements on page 25, and the explanation of terms used in describing watch movements that fills all of page 26. Note also the fascinating explanation of how gold-filled watch cases and rings were made (pages 27 and 71). Three pages (688, 689, 691) are devoted to intensive coverage of windmills—very important items at a time when electricity was still in its infancy—and the way they work.

And throughout the catalogue Sears editorialized. On page 151 he offered telegraph instruments and recommended that "to those who are about to start in life, either ladies or gentlemen, there is nothing at the present time which offers better inducements than telegraphy. The smallest salaries paid are about $35 per month." Sears, whose business career included some time as a railroad telegrapher, obviously had reason for his strong feelings about the value of telegraphy. He went on to explain that many operators had risen to high positions and larger incomes elsewhere after starting in this field. (Possibly he meant himself.)

The decline, since 1902, in the value of the American dollar is clearly illustrated as one goes through the thousands upon thousands of items offered. See page 175 for a description of a handsome piano, guaranteed for twenty-five years and priced at only $98.50; see page 180 for a solid-oak home organ for only $22.00; or see page 722 for a drop-head sewing machine guaranteed for twenty years and priced at only $10.45!

A view of the drug pages provides strong documentation of the conditions that led to the passing of the federal Pure Food and Drugs Act of 1906. Offered along with other similarly presented items are a Sure Cure for the Tobacco Habit (page 441), Dr. Rose's Arsenic Complexion Wafers (page 447), and White Ribbon Secret Liquor Cure (page 451). And "no matter what the cause may be or how severe your trouble is, Dr. Hammond's Nerve and Brain Pills will cure you" (page 443).

For those who think the marriage manual is an innovation of the present-day sexual revolution, there is Dr. Hood's *Plain Talks*, including a thirty-two-page pamphlet of "Female Productive Organs" and "many chapters devoted to sexual immorality and numerous interesting subjects concerning marriage and the sexual relations" (page 245).

One could go on and on picking out interesting offerings to talk about, ranging from *G. & C. Merriam's Webster'sUnabridged Dictionary*, bound in full sheepskin and indexed, and priced at only $5.00 (about one-tenth of today's price for a clothbound edition) because "publishers sacrifice profits in order to drive out inferior so-called unabridged dictionaries which trade on the honored name of Webster" (page 24) to the statement about buggies on page 362 that "We have no dull season. By keeping factories going all year 'round we prepare for rush of orders when vehicle season opens and also greatly reduced costs." Obviously, the Sears management that followed was astute enough to reduce production in time when the horseless carriage began to make its presence felt.

Of historical note to the advertising fraternity in particular is the charge of 50 cents for this catalogue. Another edition was issued when customers not on a "preferred" list ordered it at $1.00 in a special clothbound version with a brilliant red cover. (Six hundred thousand copies of the Sears catalogue were distributed in the spring of 1902.) Sears attempted to convince his customers that they were saving money by paying for his catalogue, but apparently he was not overly successful. Subsequent catalogues were again offered free!

—Cleveland Amory

Publishers' note regarding this Bounty Edition:

We have retained the continuity and flavor of the original, but in order to keep within a useful format of over 700 pages, we have omitted those pages which were mostly repetitious. Nevertheless, where we believed the present-day interest in a particular section was great enough for preservation in its entirety, such as the Gun Section, we did preserve it. The index that follows page 534 will guide you to specific items you may wish to find. Owing to our deletions, an occasional offering may not be found, but those items will almost certainly be few. You will notice an occasional running head that appears to be cut off. This was caused by bad trimming of the original catalogue.

Index *follows page 534*

OUR MAMMOTH CATALOGUE CONTAINS OVER 100,000 ILLUSTRATIONS AND QUOTATIONS, MAILED TO ANY ADDRESS ON RECEIPT OF 50 CENTS.

WE SELL EVERYTHING BY MAIL ORDER ONLY, TO OUR TWO MILLION CUSTOMERS ALL OVER THE WORLD.

68-96 FULTON, ST.
73-87 N. DESPLAINES, ST.
1-31 WAYMAN, ST.
74-88 N. JEFFERSON, ST.

CHICAGO,

OUR REFERENCES. SEE PAGES 12 AND 13. We refer by special permission to The National City Bank of New York City, Capital and Surplus, $15,700,000.00; and the Metropolitan National Bank and The Corn Exchange National Bank of Chicago, Combined Capital and Surplus of $6,000,000.00.

READ THE BANK LETTERS ON PAGE 12. Also note our reference by permission to the leading bankers in every country on the globe.

Kind Friend:--This big catalogue has been made so thoroughly complete in every department that it is intended to be used for ordering goods and for reference, season after season.

This one book, if preserved, can be used for sending us orders and for reference for several years, for it has been made thoroughly complete in every department. The prices quoted are the very lowest Chicago wholesale prices, with all advertising expense deducted. If you should order from this book two or three years hence and there has been any reduction in the price of the goods ordered by you, we will give you the benefit of the lower prices and return the difference to you in cash.

Understand, as long as you preserve this catalogue you can use it either for reference or for sending orders to us, always with the understanding that the goods are guaranteed to be perfectly satisfactory to you or your money will be returned to you, and where any prices have been reduced you will get the benefit of the reduction without notice, and the difference will be returned to you in cash.

We have departed from the long established and universally adopted policy of all other catalogue houses that sell goods from catalogues, circulars, booklets, samples or by mail order, and wholly in the interest of our customers and lower prices, we are making a charge to cover the first cost of every catalogue or booklet we publish. It is today and it has, for all time, been the custom with all catalogue houses, every kind of institution selling goods by mail order, to issue various catalogues, booklets, samples, etc., and mail them postpaid to any address either free, on application, or for a very small fraction of their cost. The amount of money that is annually wasted in the vast amount of printed matter, in the thousands of tons of paper that are annually printed up into catalogues and booklets, and the thousands of yards of cloth of all kinds that is cut up into samples, the enormous amount of postage paid to circulate this matter into every one of the over 70,000 postoffices, the amount of money that is expended for all this, that goes into the hands of people who never buy one penny's worth of goods, would represent a figure so large, so colossal, as would stagger almost any buyer or seller.

All this expense, all this wasted advertising that goes to the people who do not buy is paid for by the people who do buy. Every penny expended in printed matter, postage, and samples is accounted for as an item of wasted advertising expense and added to the selling price of the goods, and when you buy an article from a

(over)

catalogue or mail order house that supplies catalogues, samples or booklets free or for a fraction of their cost,you will pay an extra price to cover a number of samples, catalogues and booklets that have been mailed to people who never buy.

We believe it is time to discontinue asking our customers to pay us money for something they have never received. If we have sent out a large number of catalogues to people who have never bought from us, we do not believe we have any right to charge you any part of that expense by adding it to the selling price of the goods you order from us.

This catalogue, like our different sample booklets, costs us money the same as our merchandise costs us money, and if a party wishes our catalogue,the only way we can furnish it to him in fairness to our customers is to ask him to pay us the cost price of the book; then if he never buys we are not the loser, but by reason of his having paid for the catalogue we have not been compelled to add any catalogue advertising expense to our selling prices and he can buy from us at a much lower price than he can buy from any other house. Then our old customers who buy from us regularly, season after season, will have no reason to complain of our going to a big expense to furnish catalogues free, or for a fraction of their cost to people who do not buy and adding this expense to our selling price. Under our system it has all been deducted.

The prices quoted in this catalogue are for the cost of the goods bought in large quantities for cash, our economical handling expense, and our one small percentage of profit added, but not one penny for wasted catalogue, booklet or sample circulation.

We do not compete with other houses on the price of catalogues and sample booklets, no more do other houses attempt to compete with us on the prices we make on merchandise.

We accept all orders with the understanding that if any goods ordered from us are not perfectly satisfactory when received, they can be returned to us at our expense and we will immediately return your money, together with any freight or express charges you may have paid. We make you perfectly secure and sell to you at much lower prices than any other house. In order to do this we must get paid for our catalogues and samples, we must ask our customers to send the full amount of cash with their order (this saves clerical expense in our house and saves the customer from 25 to 75 cents collection express charges). We must ask our customers to send no order amounting to less than 50 cents. Getting paid for all catalogues and samples, receiving cash in full with all orders, thus doing away with clerical expense and filling no small orders under 50 cents, we make a big saving and we give you the benefit of every penny saved in the incomparably low prices quoted in this book.

In presenting this catalogue, we wish to warn our customers against impostors, who knowing we make the lowest prices of any house in the world, travel about the country claiming to represent us, soliciting orders and collecting money. All such people are frauds and should be treated as such, for there is no one outside of our store either in Chicago or elsewhere who is authorized to solicit an order or collect one dollar for our account.

On the basis of far more value for your money than you can get elsewhere, made possible by our getting paid for our catalogues and samples (thereby saving the great waste incurred by the old time methods), and deducting this expense from our selling prices, and by our getting cash in full with all orders, we earnestly speak for your trade.

Yours very truly,

A4342 SEARS, ROEBUCK & CO.

CONSUMERS GUIDE
No. 111
FOR 50 CENTS
WE MAIL THIS BOOK TO ANY ADDRESS

OUR ONLY TERMS ARE CASH WITH ORDER.

WE REQUIRE ALL ORDERS TO BE ACCOMPANIED BY ASH FOR THE FULL AMOUNT OF THE ORDER. We ac- ɜept your order and your money, guaranteeing the goods to reach you in due time and in perfect condition, and if they are not **perfectly satisfactory** to you when received, you can return them to us at our expense of freight or express charges both ways and we will immediately return your money.

IN ORDER TO MAINTAIN OUR INCOMPARABLY LOW PRICES, prices which, quality considered, are not and cannot be met by any other house, we are compelled to ask our customers to invariably send cash in full with their orders, always with the understanding that we accept your money only subject to the goods reaching you in perfect condition and being in every way satisfactory to you; otherwise we will take them back at our xpense, and immediately return your money to you.

WE HAVE ABOLISHED ALL C. O. D. TERMS in the interest of lower prices, bigger values and better service, and hereafter no orders will be accepted to be shipped C. O. D.

NO GOODS WILL BE SENT BY FREIGHT WITH DRAFT ON BILL OF LADING FOR COLLECTION, no goods on open account; but for standard merchandise at lower prices than any other house can make, our terms will be alike to one and all, namely, **cash in full with order, safe delivery and satisfaction guaranteed.**

WE HAVE NO DISCOUNTS. We sell for cash only and the prices quoted in this catalogue are absolutely net, from which there is no discount whatever, **and our prices and terms are alike to one and all, namely, net cash, as quoted in this book, cash in full to accompany all orders.**

NO REDUCTION OR CONCESSION OF ANY KIND will be made to any retail dealer, jobber or broker. Whether you order one or one thousand, the prices and terms are the same for they are already figured as low as it is possible to quote.

WHY WE ASK CASH IN FULL WITH ALL ORDERS.

WE HAVE DISCONTINUED MAKING C. O. D. SHIPMENTS; discontinued shipping by freight with draft on bill of lading for collection; discontinued shipping on open account or on any terms other than cash in full with orders, solely in the interest of our customers, with a view to naming still lower prices, giving greater values than ever before.

GOODS SHIPPED ON ANY TERMS OTHER THAN CASH IN FULL WITH ORDER MEANS EXTRA EXPENSE BOTH TO THE BUYER AND SELLER. It means an extra cost to us in additional clerical work, in the handling and collecting of the money, and it means an extra charge to the buyer that the express companies always make for collecting and returning the money to us.

BY ABOLISHING THE C. O. D. SYSTEM WE MAKE A BIG SAVING in our clerical expense which immediately comes off the selling price and is shown in the low prices quoted in this catalogue, and we save you the expense of collection charges and return of money to us on every C. O. D. shipment.

ANY HOUSE THAT SHIPS GOODS BY EXPRESS C. O. D., subject to examination, or by freight with draft on bill of lading for collection payable after goods are received, or on open account, whether a cash deposit accompanies the order or not, incurs an expense in the handling of such orders that makes it impossible to furnish their customers the same values we quote on the upwards of 100,000 items in this catalogue.

THE POLICY OF OUR HOUSE is to adopt such business methods as will make it possible to give the greatest possible value for every dollar sent us by our customers, and to this end we are endeavoring to eliminate every item of unnecessary expense commonly incurred by other houses and in every case giving our customers the benefit of every penny of saving by quoting lower prices than ever before.

BY GETTING 50 CENTS FOR OUR BIG CATALOGUE, thus doing away with nearly all advertising expense, we have effected a very great saving which has changed our selling prices accordingly. By accepting no orders for less than 50 cents, we effect another saving which helps to reduce our selling prices. Now by abolishing our C. O. D. draft on bill of lading, and open account terms of shipment and asking everyone to send cash in full with their orders we do away with all C. O. D. clerical and collection expense and effect a net saving to us which we give you the benefit of in still lower prices and as a result name you prices on the upwards of 100,000 items listed in this catalogue, much lower than you can possibly get elsewhere.

OUR OLD CUSTOMERS KNOW OUR REPUTATION for fair and honorable dealing, know it is perfectly safe to send any amount of money to us in advance. They know we will ship the goods exactly as ordered. We guarantee them to reach their destination in perfect condition and to prove entirely satisfactory oı we will immediately return the money sent us and pay transportation charges on the goods both ways. They know if they send us too muc

DO NOT FAIL TO GIVE SIZE, COLOR, WEIGHT, ETC., IF REQUIRED, WHEN WRITING YOUR ORDE

the difference will be returned to them at once; if the price y article or articles has been reduced they will get the benefit .nout notice and the difference will be immediately returned to .nem in cash. They know it is just as safe to place their money in our hands as in the strongest national banks of the country. They know that we take all the risk, guarantee the goods to please, guarantee safe delivery, and are always ready and willing to return any money sent us.

TO THOSE WHO HAVE NOT AS YET DEALT WITH US, and therefore may not be acquainted with our methods and our reputation and financial standing, as a positive guarantee of your security in sending us any amount of money with your order; as a guarantee that the goods will be sent to you promptly, that they will reach you in perfect condition, that they will be found entirely satisfactory to you, or your money will be immediately returned to you; as a guarantee that any money sent to us is as safe in our hands as in the hands of any bank in the land, we call your attention to the two bank letters, as reproduced on page 12 of this book, one the Metropolitan National Bank of this city, with a capital and surplus of three million dollars, and one the Corn Exchange National Bank of this city with a capital and surplus of three million dollars.

WE REFER TO THESE TWO CHICAGO BANKS BY SPECIAL PERMISSION, as well as to the largest bank in the United States, the National City Bank of New York City, (see page 13), with a capital and surplus of fifteen million seven hundred thousand dollars, and any one so desiring is at liberty to send their money and order to any of these banks with instructions not to turn it over to us unless they know us to be thoroughly reliable.

OUR COMMERCIAL AND FINANCIAL STANDING is established in every country on the globe. On page 12 we give the names of some of the largest banking and financial houses in all the different countries in the world with whom we have the special privilege of referring our customers.

WE ARE AUTHORIZED AND INCORPORATED UNDER THE LAWS OF THE STATE OF ILLINOIS with a cash capital and surplus of over Two Million Dollars. We have over three million customers located in every town and community in the United States and we refer to any of our customers, to any bank, commercial agency, business house or resident of Chicago. We employ nearly 3,000 clerks, own and occupy entire the building in which our business is conducted, a building that covers an entire city block, fronting on four streets, Fulton, Desplaines, Wayman and Jefferson. Our financial and commercial standing is so thoroughly established in every section of the United States that we feel confident that no one will hesitate when ordering merchandise to send cash in full with their order, especially when they know by doing so they not only save the express charges for collection and return of money to us, but they also buy the goods at a lower price than we could afford to sell them if we were to continue shipping goods on C. O. D. terms.

NO ORDER WILL BE ACCEPTED FOR LESS THAN 50 CENTS.

AS A MATTER OF ECONOMY, both to our customers and to ourselves, we do not fill single orders for less than 50 cents. The postage or express charges usually makes small orders under 50 cents unprofitable to purchasers, or at least much more expensive than to order amounts for 50 cents or more.

We make this exception: In the case of needed repairs, attachments, or supplies, such as needles for our sewing machines, parts of guns, etc., etc., which can be secured only from us, we will fill the order no matter how small it may be.

IF YOU WISH TO ORDER ANY ARTICLE COSTING LESS THAN 50 CENTS, SELECT ONE OR MORE NEEDED ITEMS, increasing the amount of your order to 50 cents or more. In this way you will effect a big saving and materially reduce the express charges.

TO MAKE ORDERING BY MAIL VERY PROFITABLE to our customers we especially urge that you make your orders as large as possible. Orders of from $2.00 to $5.00 or more are always very much more profitable than smaller orders, for the express or freight charges are in this way very greatly reduced. It always pays even if you have to get some friend or neighbor to join with you to make up an order of from $2.00 to $5.00 or more and include enough heavy goods to make a profitable freight shipment of 50 to 100 pounds. In this way you reduce the transportation charges on each item to next to nothing. You then pay the exact same freight charges which your storekeeper must pay on the goods he sells.

ON THE BASIS OF FAR GREATER VALUE FOR YOUR MONEY than you can possibly get elsewhere, lower prices than any other house does or can make, the best possible service, every item ordered guaranteed to reach you in perfect condition and give satisfaction or your money to be immediately returned to you, with all charges paid by us, on our binding guarantee to protect you in every way on every dollar sent us, wholly in your own interest we ask you to kindly conform to our terms and always send cash in full with your order.

Paragraph A.

ABOUT OUR PRICES.

HOW WE CAN UNDERSELL ALL OTHER CONCERNS.

SECTION 1. BY REASON OF OUR ENORMOUS OUTPUT OF GOODS we are able to make contracts with representative manufacturers and importers for such large quantities of merchandise that we can secure the lowest possible prices, and in some lines our trade has been so large, as, for example, in vehicles, stoves, cloaks, tailoring, guns, revolvers, etc., that we have been able to equip our own factories and foundries, thus saving you even the manufacturer's profit; but whether the goods are manufactured by ourselves or bought direct in large quantities, we add the smallest percentage of profit possible to the actual cost to us, and on this economic, one small profit plan, direct from manufacturer to consumer, you can buy a large percentage of the merchandise we handle, direct from us at less than your storekeeper at home can buy in quantities.

BY CHARGING 50 CENTS FOR EVERY CATALOGUE, by asking payment in advance for every samp'e booklet and special catalogue, we practically eliminate all the advertising expense, do away with an enormous expense of wasted catalogues and free samples which go into the hands of thousands who never buy, but are merely asked for out of curiosity. This enormous expense, which all other catalogue houses who furnish their catalogues and sample booklets free or for a fraction of their cost, must add to their selling price, but in our case this is all deducted, and as a result, you will find prices in this book not to be found in any other catalogue published.

WE EMPLOY THE MOST COMPETENT BUYERS that money can obtain, men who are experts and have a life long experience in their particular lines. Our established reputation for buying everything in enormous quantities gives our buyers inside track with all the largest manufacturers, thereby giving us the benefit of first choice in the markets. Manufacturers who are overstocked often come to us and offer their goods for a big discount for cash, knowing that we have a larger outlet for merchandise than any other concern. For this reason many articles in this catalogue are quoted at less money than the actual cost to produce. No matter how cheap we buy, we give our customers the benefit, for we feel that our bargains are our customers' bargains.

SECTION 2. WE BUY AND SELL FOR CASH, and having no bad debts, no traveling men's expenses, no expenses for collecting, securing the manufacturers' lowest spot cash prices, we can sell goods at a smaller margin of profit than any other business house could do and still exist.

WE MAKE NO REDUCTIONS IN OUR PRICES. To those who are inclined to write us for a reduction from the prices quoted in this catalogue, we wish to state that we cannot afford to make any reduction or concession, whether you order in large or small quantities. The price quoted on each and every article in this catalogue is as low as we can possibly make it, and it is out of the question to reduce these prices still further; and we earnestly believe a careful comparison of our prices with those of any other concern will convince you that we can furnish you better goods for less money than you can obtain from any other house in the United States.

ALL PRICES ARE SUBJECT TO THE FLUCTUATION OF THE MARKET. The prices quoted in this book are correct, according to market conditions at the date the catalogue is printed, and our wants have been anticipated as far as possible by contract, goods in stock, etc.; but when our stock on hand is sold or when a contract expires and the market conditions at that time are such that we are compelled to pay more money for the goods, we reserve the right to advance our prices without notice, charging you the difference the advance represents, only the difference in cost to us. The necessity for advancing prices very rarely happens, but as a protection to us, at the extremely low prices we are making, we must reserve this right, and this space is used to inform everyone of the right so reserved. If prices decline so that we are able to buy any goods to fill orders at lower prices than those printed in this catalogue, you will always get the benefit of such prices and the difference will be returned to you in cash.

AS THE TENDENCY IS FOR LARGER CONTRACTS, larger purchases, closer buying, the history of our house and our records show that **we reduce prices and return the difference in cash ten times** where we make an advance and ask more money once; but for our protection the right to recognize advances and declines must be and is reserved.

IN THIS CATALOGUE you will find only such goods listed as we can save you money on, goods that can be delivered anywhere in the United States for less money than they can be bought at your local dealer's. The amount of money that we can save you over the prices you pay at home varies from 15 to 50 per cent, according to the nature of the goods but there is not an item quoted in this entire catalogue on which the saving is not worth taking into consideration, to say nothing of the fact that our goods are, as a rule, of a higher grade than those carried by the average storekeeper or catalogue house.

THE ILLUSTRATIONS AND DESCRIPTIONS IN THIS CATALOGUE can be depended upon. We aim to illustrate and describe every article with the strictest accuracy. Most all of the illustrations are made from photographs taken direct from the article. They are such as enable you to order intelligently; in fact, with our assortment, correct illustrations and accurate descriptions, you can order from this catalogue with the same ease, confidence and security as though you were personally in our store selecting the goods yourself.

Paragraph B.

ABOUT OUR RELIABILITY.

WE ARE AUTHORIZED AND INCORPORATED under the laws of the State of Illinois, with a cash capital and surplus of over Two Million Dollars paid in full. We refer by special permission to the Metropolitan National Bank and Corn Exchange National Bank of Chicago, the National City Bank and the German Exchange Bank of New York, (see facsimile copies of letters from these banks on page 12), to any commercial agency or to any express or railroad company, or any reliable business house or financial institution in Chicago. Should you write for information to any of the references given be sure to enclose a 2-cent stamp for reply. **Our customers are our best references.** As we have thousands of customers in every state and territory, you will no doubt find one of them a neighbor, who can explain to you how thoroughly we live up to all our representations and how carefully we watch the interests of our customers, and we take the most pleasure in referring to our thousands of satisfied customers.

OUR EMPLOYES ARE INSTRUCTED to treat every customer at a distance exactly as they would like to be treated were they in the customer's place and the customer in ours. If you favor us with your patronage we will do everything in our power to merit your trade, and no matter how small your order may be it will receive the same prompt and careful attention as if it were ever so large. The courteous and careful attention we pay to our customers invites their continued patronage and we consider that a satisfied customer is the best advertisement that a firm can have.

WE EMPLOY NO AGENTS. This catalogue is our sole and only representative. We have no agents, and anyone representing himself as such is a fraud. Our customers deal direct with us through this catalogue. Thus the farmer, miner, mechanic, business man, in fact, anyone can send us his order and save all the profit the agent or local storekeeper would make.

THE POLICY OF OUR HOUSE. We hold it as the keynote and the fundamental principle of this business that the consumer should not be called upon to pay more than one small profit over and above the actual cost of any kind of merchandise. We contend that it is not legitimate and in accordance with modern business methods for the farmer, the clerk, the mechanic or the laborer, to pay one-half the price of any article in excessive profits, profits of the manufacturer, the jobber, the wholesaler and the retailer; to give out his hard earned money, won by honest toil, for something that adds nothing to the intrinsic value of the goods, but is only a useless expense caused by faulty business methods. The money received by the consumer for his labor is the actual value of his labor. The price of goods in the ordinary store is not the actual value of the goods, but is the price on an inflated basis, a price made by an endless and excessive chain of profits. We believe it is therefore unjust and unreasonable for the consumer to exchange the money received for his labor, which is the true and actual value of his labor, for the goods he needs at the fictitious prices usually asked for such goods. It is an unfair plan.

FOR THESE REASONS and for these reasons alone, we commend this catalogue to the careful consideration of all buyers. If you think we are right in our belief that the consumer should not pay more than the actual cost of goods, with only enough added to cover the expense of conducting a business on the most economical plan, and to allow for one fair profit, we then solicit your patronage. If lower prices than any other concern can quote are any inducement, then we say, send us your orders. If a scrupulous and painstaking honesty, if strictly correct representations, religious like in their fidelity to truth, are worthy principles, then you need not hesitate to trust us; "your money back for anything not satisfactory, transportation charges refunded also" is sufficient guarantee, then you can safely trade with us.

Paragraph C.

HOW TO ORDER.

Please refer to the sample order on page 13. **This illustrates an order** made out on one of our regular order blanks.

Always keep well supplied with our order blanks, **as it is more convenient** for you to make out your order on our regular order blanks than in any other way. If out of them at any time, drop us a postal card and we will be pleased to send you some. Fill out our order blank as shown in the sample order on page 13.

Whether you write your order on our regular order blank or letter paper instead, **be sure to observe the following instructions:**

Always sign your full name (Christian name and surname).

Write your name in full, clearly and distinctly.

Give your postoffice, county and state, and your shipping point, if different from the postoffice.

Always give catalogue number in full (write every figure and letter in the catalogue number), description and price of each article ordered.

Always try to mention the number or name of the catalogue or circular from which your order is taken, and be sure to give the size, color, weight and measurements when ordering anything where either is required.

We must have your correct size or measurements for such goods as hats, shoes, clothing, ladies' ready made dresses, cloaks, and the size and color of everything that has size and color.

Be sure to enclose your money with your order and state plainly in your order how much money you enclose and in what form. Sending us money in one envelope and your order in another causes delay and confusion in our office, as they become separated in the mails. For instructions on how to send money see **paragraph F.**

Be sure you have followed our rules carefully about enclosing the proper amount of money with the order, including enough to pay postage if the goods are to be sent by mail, and insurance fee if to be sent by insured mail.

Be sure your name and address is written plainly and in full, that your shipping directions are plainly stated, that the exact amount of money enclosed is plainly stated, that you have given us catalogue number, price, description, correct size and measurements and you will seldom if ever have any delay or inconvenience. By carefully observing these rules you will avoid errors and loss of time by our having to write you for further information.

AFTER WRITING AN ORDER, please compare it with these rules, check it over closely and see if you have written your order correctly.

IF YOU WISH TO REFER TO ANY MATTER not concerning the order, be sure to write it on a separate sheet. Do not write about it on your order sheet, though you may enclose it in the same envelope with your order. Our orders and letters are handled in separate and distinct departments, and we ask you therefore please do not fail to observe this rule.

ALWAYS TRY TO WRITE REMARKS CONCERNING YOUR ORDER on the same sheet with the order. This will prevent the possibility of such remarks or instructions being separated from the order. Should you have occasion to write us concerning an order which you have already sent us, do not fail to mention the date on which your letter was mailed, also state the nature and value of your remittance and the name and address as given in your order. This information will enable us to promptly locate the matter you refer to.

Paragraph D.

ABOUT OMISSIONS.

ALL ORDERS FOR MERCHANDISE are accepted by us with the understanding that we will use every reasonable effort to promptly ship every item exactly as ordered, and in order to make this possible we carry in stock, constantly, merchandise to the value of more than two million dollars, and if we do not have the goods in stock we invariably buy them in Chicago if we can, even if we are compelled to pay more than we get for them, rather than delay an order or withhold shipment of any part of an order. But it sometimes happens that on an order including several items of merchandise there may be one or two items that are not in stock and cannot be had in Chicago, usually for the reason that the manufacturers are behind with their orders, have met with some accident or there has been some unusual delay in transportation.

DO NOT FAIL TO GIVE SIZE, COLOR, WEIGHT, ETC., IF REQUIRED, WHEN WRITING YOUR ORDER,

WE THEREFORE ACCEPT ALL ORDERS with the understanding that we reserve the right when unable to ship every item, to cancel that portion of the order which we cannot ship promptly, filling the balance of the order, and returning to the customer in cash the amount for the item or items cancelled. We make this explanation so that anyone ordering merchandise from us, and receiving the goods with one or more items missing, and receiving by mail his money returned for the omitted items, will understand that the reason for omitting is that the goods are not in stock and cannot be had in Chicago. Where an omission for the above reason is necessary we usually send a letter telling when we expect to have a stock of the missing goods, so that the customer may renew his order if he so desires.

UNDERSTAND, it seldom happens that we are unable to fill an order complete and exactly as given, but out of the many thousands of orders we receive every day, there are always a few (a very small number) on which items must be cancelled, and we make this explanation in our catalogue so that none of our customers need misunderstand our position.

Paragraph E.

ABOUT SUBSTITUTION.

WE ARE BITTERLY OPPOSED TO SUBSTITUTING one article for another unless instructed to do so by the customer. We believe, except in rare cases, it is very presuming on the part of any house receiving an order for one kind of goods to send another, without first having the written consent of the customer to do so. There are, however, exceptions where we take upon ourselves the responsibility of substituting, and with reference to this we make the following explanation:

IF A PARTY SENDS US AN ORDER and there is some article in that order which we have not in stock and cannot get in Chicago, but we have the same kind of an article in a higher grade, we then take the liberty of sending the higher grade at the price of the lower grade, sacrificing our profit rather than to disappoint the customer. A customer ordering a watch may call for a 7-jeweled Elgin or Waltham movement and we may not have one in stock, and there may not be one in the Chicago market, in which case we would consider ourselves justified in taking the liberty of substituting a higher grade in an 11 or 15-jeweled Elgin or Waltham movement, but always at the price of the cheaper one ordered, taking the loss ourselves for the difference in price. This is an example. The same would apply on hundreds of items in our stock, but only in cases where in our judgment the customer can only be the better pleased by reason of such action on our part. However, even this kind of substitution we admit is presuming on our part, and when such substitution is made it must be understood it is done entirely at our risk, and with the understanding that if our action is not entirely satisfactory to the customer, he is at liberty to return the goods at our expense of transportation charges both ways and his money is to be immediately returned to him.

Paragraph F.

HOW TO SEND MONEY.

REMIT BY POSTOFFICE MONEY ORDER, express money order, bank draft, cash or stamps. We do not accept revenue stamps, foreign stamps and due stamps, as they are of no value to us. Do not send them.

POSTAGE STAMPS in amounts exceeding $1.00 will be accepted only at a discount of five per cent (5%), or ninety-five cents on the dollar. If you order an article priced at $2.00 and send stamps you should send $2.10. If a $3.00 article you should send $3.15 in stamps. We are compelled to dispose of all surplus stamps at a discount of from 2 per cent to 5 per cent and besides there is an extra expense in handling stamps, and our very small profit will not admit of this expense. We advise remitting by postoffice or express money order, but will accept postage stamps in any amount at 95 cents on the dollar. As an accommodation to our customers we will accept postage stamps at the face value in amounts less than $1.00.

WE RECOMMEND THE POSTOFFICE OR EXPRESS MONEY ORDER SYSTEMS, because they are inexpensive, of less trouble and safe. Besides this, if the money order should get lost or miscarry, your loss will be made good.

DO NOT UNDER ANY CIRCUMSTANCES send money or stamps in a letter except by registered mail. If sent by open mail the letter may never reach us, and in such a case a great amount of trouble and inconvenience is caused, as well as the loss you sustain. **If you prefer to remit by registered mail, we advise the use of two envelopes, one inside the other,** and the outer one carefully and securely sealed. **Do not send gold or silver coin that is defaced,** as light weight coins are worth no more than bullion and bullion is less than the face value of the coin.

TO INSURE SAFETY always register a letter containing money. Be sure to state in your order plainly how much cash you enclose and in what form. You need not be afraid of sending too much, as we always refund when too much money is sent.

Paragraph G.

METHODS OF SHIPMENT.

We can ship goods by mail (**see paragraph H about mail shipments**), by express (see paragraph I about express shipments), by freight, (see paragraph K about freight shipments). If left to our judgment we will ship goods in the manner which will be the least expensive to our customers. In all cases transportation charges are to be paid by the customer.

Paragraph H.

MAIL SHIPMENTS.

The mail service affords a convenient method for the transportation of merchandise of small weight and considerable value to points that are distant from express or railroad offices. On all orders to be shipped by mail we require sufficient money extra to pay postage and insurance or registration, when same is desired. There are three methods of shipping goods by mail:

SECTION 1. OPEN MAIL, which is so called because only the regular amount of postage, according to the classification of goods, is paid and the customer must assume all risk. We do not recommend sending goods by open mail, for if the package is lost or stolen, neither we or the customer have any recourse. In sending goods by open mail the customer must assume all risk.

SECTION 2. INSURED MAIL. This we consider the best and safest method of shipping by mail. The following is the rate, in addition to the regular postage. For a package valued at $5.00 or under, 5 cents each. For a package valued at $10.00 or under, 10 cents each. For each additional $5.00 in value, 5 cents extra. In case of loss, we duplicate the shipment on receipt of affidavit that goods were not received. We advise insuring everything of value. Insurance is usually less than the cost of registering. If you want your mail package insured be sure to write "**Insure**" in your order, and in addition to your remittance for the order be sure to add enough money to pay postage and insurance fee. To secure adjustment it is necessary to make prompt notification of the failure to receive package.

SECTION 3. REGISTERED MAIL, so called because in such cases the postoffice authorities keep a record of the transaction and are thus enabled to trace your shipment. The amount required to register a package is 8 cents in addition to the regular postage.

A PACKAGE SHIPPED BY MAIL CANNOT EXCEED 4 POUNDS, but any number of packages may be sent at one time, each weighing four pounds or less. If you live at a great distance from the express office, it might be more convenient to send an order by mail in two or more packages, each weighing four pounds. **One book can be sent by mail, no matter what its weight. The rate is ½-cent per ounce.**

THE RATE ON MERCHANDISE BY MAIL IS 1 CENT PER OUNCE, on books and printed matter, ½ cent per ounce, and you should allow, in addition to the weight of an article, from one to five ounces for packing material, according to size of package shipped. So far as possible we have given the packed weight under each description.

IF YOU ARE NOT SURE AS TO THE WEIGHT OF THE ARTICLE, be sure to enclose enough money for postage; if you send too much we will refund balance.

EXPLOSIVES, POISONOUS OR INFLAMMABLE ARTICLES cannot be mailed under any circumstances whatever.

LIQUIDS OVER 4 OUNCES CANNOT BE SENT BY MAIL.

SECTION 4. PROFITABLE MAIL SHIPMENTS. ARTICLES SUCH AS WATCHES, JEWELRY and other valuable merchandise of light weight, make profitable mail shipments. In all cases where other goods are not ordered at the same time, we advise that such articles can be sent by mail economically.

CERTAIN MEDIUM PRICED GOODS, which, being weighty, cost considerable postage for transportation, should, if possible, be ordered in connection with other needed articles, sufficient to make up express or freight shipment, thus reducing the transportation charges to one-quarter or one-eighth of the postage rate and effecting a far greater saving for you.

WITH THE EXCEPTION OF ARTICLES OF SMALL WEIGHT and of some value, sending goods by mail is by far the most expensive means of transportation, but even in cases where the postage may seem out of proportion to the value of the goods, the cost of the goods with the postage added is usually less than if purchased at the local dealer's and frequently the article wanted is not handled by them at all, while our immense stock of merchandise will supply your demands.

Paragraph I.

EXPRESS SHIPMENTS.

HOW TO FIGURE EXPRESS CHARGES, SEE PAGES 7 TO 11.

SHIPPING GOODS BY EXPRESS is an absolutely safe method of transportation and offers the advantages of quick service. It is the most profitable method of shipping goods when the weight is less than 20 pounds. Frequently a customer is in a hurry for certain goods and is willing to pay the extra cost of express charges over freight, the money we save him making it profitable on such shipments instead of buying the goods at home.

IF YOU HAVE NO AGENT at your station, all express shipments will be carried to the nearest town where there is an agent. If there is no agent at your station always state in your order at what station you prefer to receive your goods.

A RECOMMENDATION THAT WILL SAVE YOU MONEY. If you live at a far distant point and wish to order some article of merchandise which would weigh about 20 pounds and amount to $6.00 or less, on which the express charges would be from $1.25 to $2.75, and you require nothing further from our catalogue at the time, show the book to your friends, let them add articles they may be in need of and the shipment can go by freight at about the same cost per 100 pounds as by express for 20 pounds, your proportion of the transportation charges being then about 60 cents.

Paragraph K.

FREIGHT SHIPMENTS.

FOR FREIGHT CLASSIFICATION AND FREIGHT RATES, SEE PAGES 7 to 11. Heavy, bulky merchandise, such as agricultural implements, household goods, furniture, groceries, hardware, etc., can be shipped most profitably by freight. When a shipment weighs 100 pounds or more, the railroad companies will charge only for the actual number of pounds.

HOW TO SAVE MONEY ON FREIGHT SHIPMENTS. Railroad companies usually charge no more for 100 pounds than they do for 20 pounds. While the extremely low prices at which we sell our merchandise would make even a small order by freight profitable, as you would certainly be getting the goods cheaper than you could possibly buy them through your local dealer, at the same time it would be a considerable saving of money if you could make up a larger order, either of your own wants or club together with your neighbors, as the freight charges will amount to comparatively very little more. The saving that may be effected by anticipating your wants and sending one large order instead of five or six smaller orders at different times is quite an item, and therefore should be taken into consideration by our customers.

YOU MUST PAY THE FREIGHT OR EXPRESS CHARGES, but it will amount to very little as compared with what you will save in the price.

IF YOU HAVE NO AGENT AT YOUR SHIPPING POINT, freight charges must be prepaid. If you do not know what the freight charge will amount to be sure and allow liberally for same. If you send more than actual amount required we will immediately refund the difference. If you have an agent at your station it is not necessary to prepay charges, as they are the same whether paid by you or by us, as our system of checking rates insures for our customers almost absolute correctness in transportation charges.

OVERCHARGES IN TRANSPORTATION. Whenever a customer suspects an overcharge on the part of the transportation company, we will be pleased to give same our most prompt and careful attention in his behalf, if he will send us the expense bill received from the agent, after he has paid the charges. Complaints for overcharges are very few, as our system of checking the rates on freight and express shipments, insures for our customers almost absolute correctness in transportation charges.

Paragraph L.

INFORMATION ABOUT GOODS SHIPPED DIRECT FROM THE FACTORY.

IN ORDER TO GIVE OUR CUSTOMERS THE VERY LOW PRICES WE DO, prices based on the actual cost to manufacture, cost of material and labor only, with but our one small percentage of profit added, prices much lower than they could possibly get elsewhere, we find it necessary to ship many heavy goods direct from the factory where they are made, and in doing this we save the freight on the goods into our warehouse in Chicago, the cartage, handling and other expenses incident to merchandise passing through the store in Chicago, and we give our customers every particle of the benefit of this saving in our extremely low prices. Wherever the catalogue states the goods are shipped from the factory, the prices quoted are for these goods delivered on board the cars at the factory and the customer pays the transportation charges from the factory. In many cases, the freight from the factory will be less than from Chicago, the factory being nearer to the purchaser. In some cases the factory will be at a greater distance than Chicago, in which case there will be an additional freight beyond the Chicago rate; but even in such cases the saving to you is very great, for if we were to ship the goods to you ourselves we would be compelled to add the freight to Chicago to all the goods, and to this add the expense of handling to and from the railroad, in and out of our store and other expenses incident to general handling of merchandise in the city.

IT SOMETIMES HAPPENS that a customer orders several articles in one order that are shipped from different factories. For instance, he may order a buggy to be shipped from our factory in Southern Michigan, a stove to be shipped from our factory in Central Ohio, a windmill that will be shipped from our factory in Southern Wisconsin. In this case we would be compelled to make three different shipments. The goods would go direct to our customer from the three different factories, but there would be no extra freight charge by reason of the three shipments, as each shipment would weigh more than 100 pounds and would therefore entitle the customer to the same freight per hundred pounds as if the shipments were all made together.

WHILE THE GREATER PART OF OUR GOODS ARE CARRIED IN STOCK IN OUR STORE AND WAREHOUSES IN CHICAGO, and this factory shipment information does not apply to small or general merchandise, we have found it necessary to make factory shipments on many heavy and bulky articles, purely in the interests of our customers, in order to give our customers the greatest possible value for their money, to enable us to deliver the goods to them at our one small percentage of profit direct from the manufacturer to the consumer, and your attention is called to the explanation that is always made in the catalogue regarding any article that is to be shipped from the factory, that you may understand that the freight is to be paid by the purchasers from the factory direct, and also that you will understand our reason for this method of handling certain merchandise.

WE FREQUENTLY RECEIVE ORDERS which include merchandise, a part of which is to be shipped direct from the factory and part direct from our store. For example: A man may order a buggy and a harness. The buggy will be shipped from the factory, the harness from the store. He may order a stove and some stove furniture, cooking utensils, etc. The stove would be shipped direct from the foundry and the cooking utensils from the store.

WHEN AN ORDER INCLUDES SUCH HEAVY GOODS as we ship direct from the factory (in order to make the low price), and other goods which we ship direct from our store, if that portion of the order which is to be shipped direct from our store is a profitable shipment (see Paragraph M about unprofitable shipments), we make two shipments; the stove, buggy or other heavy shipment going direct from the factory, the balance from our store. But it sometimes happens that that portion of the order to be shipped from our store would not be a profitable shipment. It may be for a few cooking utensils, amounting to $1.00 or $2.00, or a very low priced harness of $5.00 or $6.00, or $1.00 or $2.00 worth of miscellaneous merchandise, on which the freight charges would amount to more than the saving, or difference between our price and the price at which the customer could buy in his own town. In such cases of unprofitable shipment we use our very best judgment, and where we deem that portion of the order that is to go from our house an unprofitable shipment, we cancel that portion of the order and return the amount to our customer in cash for the goods canceled.

AS A FURTHER EXAMPLE: The customer may order a parlor suite for $15.00 to $20.00, which we ship from the factory, and may include with his order one chair for 90 cents, which we ship from the house. This one chair (except to nearby points), would be considered an unprofitable shipment. On such an order we would take the liberty of cancelling the order for the chair, returning the 90 cents to the customer at once, and we would ship the parlor suite to him direct from the factory by freight, with a letter of full explanation for our action. This article is intended to explain our methods of treating special orders only in the interest of the customers.

Paragraph M.

ABOUT UNPROFITABLE SHIPMENTS.

WE FREQUENTLY RECEIVE ORDERS which we term "unprofitable" shipments, which means that the shipment would not be profitable to our customer. For example: A party living far distant may order a dollar's worth of sugar to go by express. The express charges would equal the cost of the sugar. We occasionally get an order for heavy hardware, the order amounting to perhaps less than $5.00. The goods weigh 100 pounds. We are asked to ship them by express. This is usually an "unprofitable" shipment. An order for a single pair of heavy cheap boots to go a great distance by express, or for very bulky woodenware or furniture or other merchandise, might be what we term an "unprofitable" shipment.

WE WOULD ADVISE OUR CUSTOMERS to study the freight and express rates as given on the following pages, for we do not wish you to send us a dollar for anything unless we can save you money on the purchase.

ORDERS THAT WOULD BE UNPROFITABLE to ship by mail or express may be very profitable when sent by freight, but as one hundred pounds is usually carried by freight for the same charge as ten pounds, by adding other merchandise to your order, either for yourself or by getting your neighbors to join you in making up a large order, **you can make the shipment very profitable.**

Paragraph N.

CLUB ORDERS.

TO EQUALIZE OR REDUCE THE COST OF TRANSPORTATION, we advise the sending of club orders. Anyone can get up a club. Simply have your neighbors or friends send their orders in with yours and advise us to ship all to one person by freight. If each customer writes his order under his own name, it will be a very easy matter for us to keep each one's goods separate, and the freight charges will be next to nothing when shared by several persons.

IF YOU LIVE AT A FAR DISTANT POINT and wish to order some article or articles of merchandise, which, together, would weigh about twenty pounds, the value of which may be $5.00 or less, and you find that the express charges will be from $1.25 to $2.75, and there is nothing further in our catalogue that you require at the time, show this catalogue to your friends. Let your friends add twenty, thirty or forty pounds, even fifty or seventy-five pounds of goods, then the goods can go by freight at about the same rate as the express charges.

Paragraph O.

HOW TO RETURN GOODS.

BEFORE RETURNING THE GOODS to us in any manner, we would ask that you communicate with us in regard to them, as we are frequently able to adjust matters in a manner that will avoid the delay occasioned by return of goods.

INVOICE NUMBER. Be sure to mention your invoice number when returning goods.

NEVER RETURN GOODS BY EXPRESS if the weight is more than twenty-five pounds, as it is cheaper to send heavy packages by freight. **When you return goods by express or freight** be sure to enclose in the package your letter of instructions and particulars. **Don't forget** we must always have your invoice number. **Never write us** about a shipment and omit the invoice number. **Don't forget** that a letter containing full instructions should be in all express and freight shipments returned. **Don't forget** we must have your full name and address, exactly as given in the original shipment, in order to properly adjust any matter pertaining to an order returned.

WHEN RETURNING A PACKAGE BY MAIL, write your name, address and invoice number plainly in the upper left hand corner, providing you do not have one of the labels which we furnish when we know goods are to be returned. **Send us by separate mail the particulars and instructions.**

DO NOT ENCLOSE WRITTEN MATTER of any kind in mail packages, as by so doing you are liable to a fine of $10.00 and double letter rate postage.

THE UNITED STATES POSTAL LAWS AND REGULATIONS require that all packages of merchandise sent in the mails must be wrapped or enveloped in such a manner that their contents may be readily examined by the postmaster without destroying the wrapper. **Never seal packages returned by mail,** but tie them securely with twine.

DO NOT FAIL TO REGISTER MAIL PACKAGES WORTH $2.00 OR MORE. Merchandise is sometimes lost when sent by open mail. A package can be registered for 8 cents and if necessary can be traced. Do not enclose money with merchandise returned by mail.

Paragraph P.

ABOUT DELAYED SHIPMENTS.

IF YOU HAVE SENT US AN ORDER FOR GOODS and you think it is time they should have arrived, before writing us concerning the delay please consider the following:

While we are willing and glad to answer all kinds of inquiries, to make every possible kind of research, to quickly look up and trace any shipment said to have been delayed, we are daily in receipt of hundreds of letters claiming that goods have been delayed, when the orders have been filled by us with all possible promptness, and have been handled by the railroad or express companies with their usual dispatch. The investigation simply shows the customer is impatient and has not allowed sufficient time for the order to reach us, we to fill the order and the express company to deliver the goods.

WE FILL ALL ORDERS with the greatest possible dispatch consistent with proper care and safety. It requires from two to six days after your order is received for us to ship goods. Where goods are ordered that have to be made to order or finished after received, such as tailoring, upholstered furniture, vehicles, etc., additional time must be allowed. Goods shipped direct from our factory, such as stoves, sewing machines, furniture and a few other heavy items, require from five to ten days to make shipment, add to this the necessary time for the express company or railroad company to carry the goods to you and you will seldom, if ever, be disappointed in the arrival of your goods.

BEFORE WRITING us concerning goods ordered or before calling for them at your railroad station, first consider if you have allowed ample time for your order to reach Chicago, the required time for us to fill same, as above stated, and for the railroad or express company to carry it to you. If you will always do this, allowing liberal time, bearing in mind that express and railroad companies sometimes delay goods a few days after they receive them, you will seldom, if ever, have occasion to write us concerning a delay.

IN CASE, HOWEVER, an order should be delayed beyond the time above referred to, and you write us, do not fail to mention the date on which you mailed your order, the name and address as given in the original order, the value and nature of the cash you sent, and, if possible, give us your invoice number, for if you received from us a postal card acknowledging the receipt of the order, you will find the invoice number on the card mailed you.

ABOUT MISTAKES. If we make a mistake in filling your order, kindly give us a chance to correct it. We try to fill every order absolutely correct; but errors sometimes creep in. They do in all business houses. You will always find us willing to correct ours. Do not fail to write us in case of an error, otherwise we may never know of it.

CHANGE OF ADDRESS. We would kindly request our customers to **immediately advise** us concerning any **change of address,** as we keep our records according to states and towns, and should you order from one town and then write from another, we would be compelled to send for further information before we could adjust the matter in question.

Paragraph Q.

ABOUT UNNECESSARY CORRESPONDENCE.

WHILE WE EMPLOY OVER ONE HUNDRED STENOGRAPHERS for the accommodation of our customers, and are willing and glad to answer all letters and furnish any special information that may be desired, we daily receive hundreds of letters of inquiry about things that are plainly answered in this catalogue, hundreds of letters which might be avoided, saving loss of time and unnecessary expense.

IT IS VERY SELDOM NECESSARY TO WRITE US, asking what the freight or express charge will be on any article to any point, for, from the weights given under each description and from the express and freight rates shown on pages 7 to 11, you can calculate very closely what the freight or express will amount to and save the time and trouble of writing for this information.

OUR OLD CUSTOMERS rarely ever have occasion to write us, asking what the freight or express will be on any article, and new customers will hardly ever have occasion to if they will refer to pages 7 to 11.

LETTERS CONCERNING SHIPMENTS CAN OFTEN BE AVOIDED. We receive hundreds of letters every day from parties who have ordered and have not allowed sufficient time for the order to reach us, the goods to be packed and shipped and for the goods to reach them. (**See Paragraph P.**) **Never write about a shipment until ample time has been allowed for the goods to reach you.** We receive hundreds of letters asking for prices or special prices on articles on which the price is plainly printed in this catalogue. All such letters are unnecessary, for it only means an answer again referring you to the catalogue.

WE RECEIVE HUNDREDS OF LETTERS DAILY from people who ask us if we can't make changes in the goods as advertised, that they want the same thing or things with slight changes. This is all irregular and could not be furnished excepting at an advanced price, and we have found it impracticable to make any such changes, and to all such inquiries we can save you the time and trouble by saying that no changes can be made from those made plain in this catalogue.

Paragraph R.

INSTALLMENT PLAN OR PARTIAL PAYMENT.

WE RECEIVE HUNDREDS OF LETTERS asking for prices on certain goods, especially on organs, pianos and other goods that run into money, from parties who wish to buy on the installment plan and to make settlement in notes. All these inquiries can be avoided for the reason that our only terms are cash, we never extend time, we open no accounts nor allow goods to be sold on the installment plan.

Paragraph S.

ABOUT CLAIMS FOR DAMAGE.

WE CAREFULLY PACK AND DELIVER ALL OUR GOODS in good condition on board the cars, either in Chicago or at the factory, as made plain in this catalogue. We accept a receipt from the railroad company for the goods in good order, and it very rarely happens that any goods that we pack and ship reach their destination in bad order.

IF IT SHOULD EVER HAPPEN that any article reaches you marred, scratched, broken or in any way defective, be sure to have the railroad agent make a notation of such defect on the freight receipt (expense bill) he gives you. You can then present your claim for damage to the railroad agent from whom you received the goods, it being his duty at that end to take the matter up with the officials of that road and collect for you any damage that may have occurred.

WHILE THE PROPER PLACE FOR TAKING UP ANY CLAIMS FOR DAMAGE on goods in transit, either by freight or express, is through the agent who delivers the goods, the trouble, delay and expense of writing us to do this can also be avoided. We, however, guarantee the goods we ship to reach you in the same perfect condition they leave us, and to be satisfactory to you in every way, and if you find them damaged in transit and you accept them and the agent hesitates to take and collect your claim for damage, you can write us enclosing your receipt (expense bill) for the freight charges paid the agent, with the agent's written notation on the expense bill, stating what the damage is, and we will take the matter up at this end, collect the damage and send the money to you.

WHILE WE HAVE a large corps of stenographers and corresponding clerks in our employ, whose duty it is to promptly and courteously answer all inquiries and give all desired information, in order to maintain our extremely low prices the cost of conducting our business must be cut down to the very minimum, and to do this our customers are especially requested before writing us concerning freight rates, claims, delays, or before asking us for information of any kind, to carefully consult this catalogue, and if they will do this they will find in nine cases out of ten the information can be had or the adjustment of damage made, without going to the trouble or writing us or putting us to the expense of corresponding on the subject.

FREIGHT AND EXPRESS RATES.

THE FOLLOWING TABLE IS TO VARIOUS POINTS IN EVERY STATE AND TERRITORY . . . . . .

HOW TO FIGURE FREIGHT CHARGES

SEE PAGE 11 for list of articles and their class, then find the weight of the desired article (which we aim to give underneath its description in this catalogue), and if not given you can estimate the weight very closely. Find the rate in following table under its class, and multiply the rate by the weight, and you have the freight charges sufficiently correct for your information.

THE RAILROADS have what is called a **MINIMUM FREIGHT CHARGE**, meaning the least amount of money they will haul a freight shipment for, no matter how little it weighs. **In the first column we quote the minimum freight charge or explain how it is made up.**

Note 1. THE MINIMUM CHARGE to towns covered by Note 1 is the same as for 50 pounds at the rate under the class to which the article belongs, provided it is not less than 50 cents.

Note 2. SAME AS NOTE 1, provided it is not less than 75 cents.

Note 3. THE MINIMUM CHARGE to towns covered by Note 3 is the same as for 100 pounds at the rate under the class to which the article belongs.

IT IS NOT NECESSARY to write us for freight and express rates, as the following tables and the instructions we herewith give will show just what the freight and express rates are to different points in the United States and Canada. Take the nearest town to your own in the table below, and the freight rate to your town will be almost, if not exactly, the same for 100 pounds.

EXPRESS CHARGES. In the following table are given the express rates for 100 pounds, but for shipments weighing less than that see page 10. Freight is the cheapest way to ship orders weighing 20 pounds or more. Make your order for 100 pounds, if possible, and get the benefit of the minimum charge, as shipments weighing from 20 to 100 pounds usually cost no more than 20 pounds. Where two rates are shown, add them together to figure the charges on packages weighing 7 pounds or under. For packages weighing more than 7 pounds, figure the charges at each rate separately, and then add these amounts for the total.

NO MATTER HOW FAR AWAY you may live, we can still save you money on your purchases. **DISTANCE IS NO DRAWBACK.** Remember, your local dealer must pay the exact same rate of freight that you pay on the goods, and this cost of freight he must add to the cost of the goods when he figures his selling price. But our prices on practically everything in this catalogue are so very much lower than the same quality of goods can be had from smaller concerns, that after you pay all transportation charges, even to very distant points, we can save you money

	Min. freight charge	1st class freight per 100 lbs	2d class freight per 100 lbs	3d class freight per 100 lbs	4th class freight per 100 lbs	5th class freight per 100 lbs	6th class freight per 100 lbs	Express per 100 lbs
ALABAMA—								
Birmingham	Note 1	$1 19	$1 03	$0 83	$0 64	$0 55	$0 42	$ 3 75
Brewton	Note 3	1 51	1 27	1 04	85	78	71	4 00
Dadeville	Note 2	1 82	1 54	1 23	99	84	65	4 50
Decatur	Note 1	1 19	1 03	83	64	55	42	3 25
Gadsden	Note 1	1 47	1 26	1 06	85	71	58	3 75
Mobile	$ 1 10	1 10	90	75	58	47	41	4 00
Montgomery	Note 1	1 38	1 26	1 03	80	67	53	3 75
Ozark	Note 3	1 96	1 68	1 43	1 11	93	76	4 75
Randolph	Note 1	1 67	1 45	1 23	99	85	64	4 00
Tuscaloosa	Note 1	1 48	1 28	1 04	81	70	54	4 00
Whatley	Note 1	1 80	1 53	1 26	99	82	70	4 25
ARIZONA—								
Benson	$3 01	3 42	3 01	2 66	2 10	......	......	10 75
Duncan	2 71	2 99	2 68	2 49	2 29	......	......	9 50
Flagstaff	3 40	3 90	3 40	2 70	2 10	......	......	10 50
Holbrook	3 25	3 74	3 35	2 70	2 10	......	......	10 25
Phœnix	3 25	3 72	3 25	2 90	2 30	......	......	12 50
Prescott	3 25	3 72	3 25	2 90	2 30	......	......	12 00
Seligman	3 40	3 90	3 40	2 70	2 10	......	......	10 75
Solomanville	3 02	3 28	3 02	2 71	2 30	......	......	10 60
Tucson	3 05	3 52	3 05	2 70	2 10	......	......	11 50
Yucca	3 40	3 90	3 40	2 70	2 10	......	......	11 00
Yuma	3 05	3 52	3 05	2 70	2 10	......	......	11 50
ARKANSAS—								
Daleville	Note 3	1 37	1 19	99	75	......	......	3 75
Fort Smith	Note 3	1 30	1 06	87	65	......	......	4 00
Fayetteville	Note 3	1 42	1 21	1 00	74	......	......	3 75
Knobel	Note 3	1 08	87	68	53	......	......	2 75
Little Rock	Note 3	1 20	1 01	77	55	......	......	3 50
Morrillton	Note 3	1 37	1 14	93	69	......	......	3 75
Newport	Note 3	1 07	86	67	55	......	......	3 25
Pine Bluff	Note 3	1 20	1 01	77	55	......	......	3 50
Texarkana	Note 3	1 30	1 15	99	88	......	......	4 00
Van Buren	Note 3	1 30	1 06	87	65	......	......	4 00
Warren	Note 3	1 42	1 24	1 05	85	......	......	4 00
BRITISH COLUMBIA—								
Arrowhead	$3 54	3 89	3 24	2 59	1 89	......	......	$5 25- 6 00
Field	3 17	3 52	2 94	2 36	1 72	......	......	5 25- 4 75
Trail	3 50	3 80	3 32	2 79	2 32	......	......	11 50- 1 25
Kamloops	3 69	4 04	2 91	2 68	1 95	......	......	5 25- 6 50
Lytton	3 83	4 18	3 47	2 76	2 00	......	......	5 25- 7 25
Manaimo	2 65	3 05	2 65	2 25	1 95	......	......	12 00- 1 00
Three Forks	3 45	3 80	3 32	2 79	2 32	......	......	5 25- 7 00
Vancouver	2 65	3 05	2 65	2 25	1 95	......	......	12 00- 6 00
Yale	3 89	4 24	3 51	2 79	2 02	......	......	5 25- 7 50
CALIFORNIA—								
Bakerfield	2 85	3 80	3 38	2 70	2 10	......	......	11 50
Fresno	2 85	3 50	2 08	2 65	3 10	......	......	11 50
Los Angeles	2 60	3 00	2 60	2 20	1 90	......	......	11 50
Needles	3 40	3 90	3 40	2 70	2 10	......	......	11 50
Redding	2 85	3 61	3 16	2 70	2 32	......	......	12 50
Sacramento	2 60	3 00	2 60	2 20	1 90	......	......	11 50
San Bernardino	2 85	3 34	2 90	2 46	2 13	......	......	11 50
San Diego	2 60	3 00	2 60	2 20	1 90	......	......	11 50
San Francisco	2 60	3 00	2 60	2 20	1 90	......	......	11 50
Santa Cruz	2 85	3 21	2 79	2 37	2 05	......	......	12 25
Yreka	3 65	4 00	3 50	2 80	2 20	......	......	13 50
COLORADO—								
Alamosa	1 70	3 17	2 60	2 03	1 57	......	......	6 00- 2 00
Cripple Creek	1 36	2 70	2 26	1 83	1 52	......	......	7 50
Denver	75	2 05	1 65	1 25	97	......	......	6 00
Eagle	2 09	3 56	2 99	2 31	1 83	......	......	6 00- 2 75
Grand Junction	2 25	3 10	2 65	2 15	1 75	......	......	8 00
Greeley	75	2 05	1 65	1 25	97	......	......	6 00
Gunnison	1 75	3 20	2 65	2 10	1 72	......	......	8 00
Kit Carson	50	1 99	1 65	1 25	97	......	......	5 50
La Junta	50	2 05	1 65	1 25	97	......	......	6 00
Mancos	2 75	4 25	3 65	2 97	2 42	......	......	6 00- 4 00
Montrose	2 05	3 50	2 95	2 30	1 82	......	......	6 00- 3 00
Pueblo	75	2 05	1 65	1 25	97	......	......	6 00
Sterling	50	1 81	1 58	1 25	97	......	......	5 50
Trinidad	75	2 05	1 65	1 25	97	......	......	6 00
CONNECTICUT—								
Bridgeport	82	82	71	55	39	33	......	3 00
Canaan	82	82	71	55	39	33	......	3 00
Hartford	82	82	71	55	39	33	......	3 00
New Haven	82	82	71	55	39	33	......	3 00
New London	82	82	71	55	39	33	......	3 00
New Melford	82	82	71	55	39	33	......	3 00
Putnam	82	82	71	55	39	33	......	3 00
Willimantic	82	82	71	55	39	33	......	3 00
DELAWARE—								
Dover	75	75	65	50	35	30	......	2 90
Farmington	75	75	65	50	35	30	......	3 00
Middleton	75	75	65	50	35	30	......	2 90
Newark	73	73	63	48	33	28	......	2 25
Wilmington	73	73	63	48	33	28	......	2 25
DIST. OF COLUMBIA—								
Langdon	72	72	62	47	32	27	......	2 25
Washington	72	72	62	47	32	27	......	2 25

	Min. freight charge	1st class freight per 100 lbs	2d class freight per 100 lbs	3d class freight per 100 lbs	4th class freight per 100 lbs	5th class freight per 100 lbs	6th class freight per 100 lbs	Express per 100 lbs.
FLORIDA—								
Careyville	Note 3	$1 70	$1 40	$1 07	$0 94	$0 87	$0 80	$4 50
Gainesville	Note 1	1 91	1 64	1 44	1 23	1 05	85	5 50
Jacksonville	Note 1	1 35	1 14	1 00	87	73	58	5 00
Key West	$1 00	1 65	1 42	1 25	1 07	93	76	7 00
Pensacola	1 10	1 10	90	75	58	47	41	4 25
Punta Gorda	Note 2	2 37	2 05	1 75	1 56	1 34	1 09	6 50
Sebastian	Note 2	2 29	1 98	1 68	1 49	1 28	1 08	6 50
Tallahassee	Note 2	2 19	1 88	1 63	1 41	1 23	1 03	5 25
Tampa (all rail)	Note 2	1 85	1 57	1 34	1 19	1 01	85	6 00
Tampa (rail and water: via. Mobile)	$1 35	1 47	1 24	1 08	93	78	63	....
GEORGIA—								
Albany	Note 1	1 67	1 43	1 21	98	82	67	4 75
Atlanta	Note 1	1 47	1 26	1 06	85	71	58	3 75
Brunswick	Note 1	1 35	1 14	1 00	87	73	58	4 50
Cairo	Note 2	1 95	1 61	1 26	1 11	1 00	82	5 25
Columbus	Note 1	1 47	1 26	1 06	85	71	58	4 50
Folkston	Note 2	1 67	1 43	1 26	1 11	79	61	5 25
Macon	Note 1	1 47	1 26	1 06	85	71	58	4 25
Quitman	Note 2	2 03	1 72	1 35	1 21	86	67	5 25
Rome	Note 1	1 47	1 26	1 06	85	71	58	3 75
Savannah	Note 1	1 35	1 14	1 00	87	73	58	5 00
Stillmore	Note 2	1 99	1 73	1 52	1 33	1 11	88	5 00
Valdosta	Note 1	1 96	1 67	1 41	1 09	93	74	5 50
Warrenton	Note 2	1 77	1 53	1 31	1 07	89	71	4 50
Waycross	Note 1	1 75	1 50	1 32	1 16	96	75	5 00
IDAHO—								
American Falls	$2 40	3 30	2 80	2 20	1 82	......	......	8 75
Boise City	2 40	3 30	2 80	2 45	2 02	......	......	10 00
Gem	3 10	3 60	3 10	2 60	2 10	......	......	10 00
Idaho Falls	2 40	3 30	2 80	2 20	1 82	......	......	8 00
Ketchum	2 65	3 55	3 05	2 45	2 07	......	......	10 00
Moscow	3 10	3 60	3 10	2 60	2 10	......	......	10 00
Mountain Home	2 40	3 30	2 80	2 45	2 02	......	......	10 00
Pocatello	2 40	3 30	2 80	2 20	1 82	......	......	8 00
Spencer	2 40	3 30	2 80	2 20	1 82	......	......	8 00
ILLINOIS—								
Belvidere	25	35	29	24	7	......	......	75
Cairo	25	59	48	39	25	......	......	2 00
Danville	25	30	25	20	14	......	......	1 00
Freeport	25	40	32	24	18	......	......	1 00
Joliet	25	22	19	15	10	......	......	50
Litchfield	25	47	38	29	23	......	......	1 50
Milan	25	46	37	29	22	......	......	1 00
Mt. Vernon	25	50	40	30	25	......	......	1 50
Peoria	25	40	32	24	18	......	......	1 00
Quincy	25	47	38	29	22	......	......	1 25
Springfield	25	47	38	29	22	......	......	1 00
Toledo	25	47	38	29	20	......	......	1 50
INDIANA—								
Bedford	37	37	32	24	16	13	......	1 25
Connersville	39	39	33	25	17	14	......	1 50
Elkhart	25	25	22	20	13	09	......	75
Evansville	40	40	34	25	17	15	......	1 75
Ft. Wayne	29	29	25	20	14	11	......	75
Goshen	25	25	22	20	13	09	......	75
Indianapolis	32	32	27	22	14	12	......	1 25
Lafayette	30	30	25	20	13	10	......	90
New Albany	40	40	34	25	17	15	......	1 50
Terre Haute	32	32	27	22	14	12	......	1 25
Valparaiso	25	15	13	12	10	08	......	50
INDIAN TERRITORY—								
Atoka	50	1 50	1 29	1 07	95	......	......	3 75
Checotah	50	1 38	1 18	90	66	......	......	3 50
Eufaula	50	1 41	1 21	92	70	......	......	3 75
Kiowa	50	1 50	1 29	1 01	86	......	......	3 75
Red Fork	50	1 30	1 10	85	60	......	......	4 00
Vinita	50	1 25	1 03	83	60	......	......	3 25
Wagoner	50	1 30	1 10	85	60	......	......	3 50
Wewoka	50	1 50	1 29	1 00	84	......	......	4 00
IOWA—								
Alta	25	80	65	45	32	......	......	2 00
Audubon	25	80	65	45	32	......	......	2 00
Bedford	25	80	65	45	32	......	......	2 00
Bode	25	75	63	44	31	......	......	2 00
Burlington	25	47	38	29	22	......	......	1 25
Carroll	25	79	64	44	31	......	......	2 00
Cedar Rapids	[illegible]	58	47	35	24	......	......	1 50
Centerville	25	68	57	40	29	......	......	1 75
Council Bluffs	25	80	65	45	32	......	......	2 00
Davenport	25	46	37	29	22	......	......	1 25
Des Moines	25	68	57	40	29	......	......	1 75
Hamburg	25	80	65	45	32	......	......	2 00
Keokuk	25	47	38	29	22	......	......	1 25
Mason City	25	63	53	42	26	......	......	1 75
Muscatine	25	47	38	29	22	......	......	1 25
Ottumwa	25	61	50	36	26	......	......	1 75
Waterloo	25	60	50	40	25	......	......	1 75
Waukon	25	60	50	40	25	......	......	....
Webster City	25	72	60	42	29	......	......	2 00

	Min. freight charge	1st class freight per 100 lbs	2d class freight per 100 lbs	3d class freight per 100 lbs	4th class freight per 100 lbs	5th class freight per 100 lbs	6th class freight per 100 lbs	Express per 100 lbs
KANSAS—								
Atchison	$0 25	$0 80	$0 65	$0 45	$0 32	.....	.....	$2 00
Council Grove	50	1 29	1 05	80	60			3 25
Dodge City	50	1 67	1 43	1 16	92			4 50
Ft. Scott	50	97	81	60	43			2 75
Garnett	50	1 07	88	66	47			3 00
Great Bend	50	1 46	1 23	95	73			4 00
Hartland	50	1 74	1 49	1 22	97			5 00
Leavenworth	25	80	65	45	32			2 00
Leoti	50	1 70	1 46	1 18	92			4 75
Mankato	50	1 33	1 13	85	64			3 50
Meade	50	1 70	1 45	1 15	93			4 75
Norton	50	1 52	1 29	1 05	84			4 00
Sawyer	50	1 57	1 34	1 05	82			4 25
Topeka	50	1 09	89	64	47			2 75
Wichita	50	1 40	1 18	91	70			3 75
Winfield	50	1 43	1 21	94	73			3 75
KENTUCKY—								
Ashland	45	45	39	30	21	$0 18	$0 15	2 00
Burnside	Note 1	93	78	66	48	43	37	2 75
Campbellsville	Note 3	1 06	90	74	60	52	47	2 25
Frankfort	Note 1	66	57	45	34	31	27	2 00
Henderson	48	48	41	30	22	18	15	2 00
Louisville	41	41	35	26	18	15	12	1 50
Maysville	44	44	38	29	20	17	14	2 00
Owensboro	48	48	41	30	22	18	15	2 00
Paducah	60	60	50	40	25	22	18	2 50
Paris	Note 1	68	59	46	32	29	25	2 00
Versailles	Note 1	71	62	50	39	35	30	2 00
LOUISIANA—								
Alexandria	Note 3	1 30	1 10	92	78	58	.....	4 75
Baton Rouge	1 10	1 10	90	75	58	47	41	3 25
Crowley	Note 3	1 43	1 22	98	82	65	.....	5 00
Kentwood	50	1 39	1 13	95	78	65	57	4 25
Lake Charles	Note 3	1 30	1 10	92	75	56	.....	4 75
Many	50	1 50	1 29	1 09	1 00	77		5 00
Monroe	Note 3	1 30	1 10	92	78	.....		4 25
Morgan City	1 29	1 29	1 11	89	75			4 50
Moreauville	1 50	1 50	1 29	1 09	1 00	77		5 85
New Orleans	1 10	1 10	90	75	58	47	41	3 75
Ponchatoula	50	1 40	1 13	95	78	65	57	4 25
Shreveport	Note 3	1 30	1 10	92	78	58		4 25
Tangipahoa	50	1 39	1 13	95	78	65	57	4 25
Winnsboro	1 35	1 73	1 45	1 25	1 02	83	74	5 00
MAINE—								
Augusta	1 07	94	81	64	45	38	.....	3 00
Alfred	82	82	71	55	39	33	.....	2 90
Bangor	1 07	98	85	65	47	40	.....	3 25
Brownville Junction	1 07	1 07	91	72	51	43	.....	3 75
Caribou	1 70	1 70	1 35	1 05	84	56	.....	4 35
Eastport	1 07	1 07	91	72	51	43	.....	4 00
Kennebunk	1 07	89	77	61	44	38	.....	2 75
Lowelltown	1 07	1 07	91	72	51	43	.....	3 75- 60
Ludlow	1 44	1 44	1 18	92	71	51	.....	4 00
Portland and Lewiston	82	82	71	55	39	33	.....	3 00
Rockland	1 07	94	81	64	45	48	.....	3 25
Skowhegan	1 07	1 02	89	69	49	41	.....	3 25
MANITOBA—								
Binscarth	1 81	2 16	1 80	1 46	1 09	.....		4 50- 2 50
Gladstone	1 67	2 02	1 69	1 36	1 02			5 50- 60
Pilot Mound	1 47	1 82	1 53	1 24	95			4 50- 1 00
Pipestone	1 76	2 11	1 77	1 42	1 06			5 50- 90
Starbuck	1 24	1 59	1 34	1 09	84			4 50- 1 00
Winnipeg	1 18	1 53	1 29	1 05	81			5 00
MARYLAND—								
Annapolis	80	80	70	53	38	32		2 50
Baltimore	72	72	62	47	32	27		2 25
Brandywine	75	75	65	49	34	29		2 75
Elkton	73	73	63	48	33	28		2 75
Finksburg	72	72	62	47	32	27		2 75
Frederick	72	72	62	47	32	27		2 25
Germantown	72	72	62	47	32	27		2 25
Hagerstown	72	72	62	47	32	27		2 25
Port Tobacco	75	75	65	49	34	29		2 75
Roaring Point	75	75	65	50	35	30		3 00
MASSACHUSETTS—								
Ashley Falls	82	82	71	55	39	33	.....	3 00
Barnstable	82	82	71	55	39	33	.....	2 50- 75
Bellingham Jct	82	82	71	55	39	33	.....	2 90
Boston	82	82	71	55	39	33	.....	2 50
Graniteville	82	82	71	55	39	33	.....	2 50
Hinsdale	82	82	71	55	39	33	.....	2 50
Jefferson	82	82	71	55	39	33	.....	2 75
Lakeville	82	82	71	55	39	33	.....	2 50- 60
New Bedford	82	82	71	55	39	33	.....	3 00
Provincetown	82	82	71	55	39	33	.....	2 50- 75
Springfield	82	82	71	55	39	33	.....	2 50
Templeton	82	82	71	55	39	33	.....	2 75
Worcester	82	82	71	55	39	33	.....	2 50
MICHIGAN—								
Adrian	35	35	30	23	15	13	.....	1 25
Alba	53	53	45	34	26	20	.....	2 00
Alpena	55	55	45	35	26	20	.....	2 40
Bay City	37	37	32	24	16	13	.....	1 75
Boyne Falls	53	53	45	34	26	20	.....	2 00
Cheboygan	55	55	45	35	26	20	.....	2 50
Detroit	37	37	32	24	16	13	.....	1 25
Emmett	37	37	32	24	16	13	.....	1 50
Grand Rapids	33	33	29	22	15	12	.....	1 25
Kalamazoo	30	30	26	21	14	11	.....	75
Lansing	36	36	31	23	16	13	.....	1 25
Manistee	47	47	41	31	23	18	.....	1 75
Ishpeming	25	30	50	40	28	22	.....	1 75
Paris	42	42	36	27	19	16	.....	1 50
Petoskey	53	53	45	34	26	20	.....	2 00
Roscommon	55	55	45	35	26	20	.....	2 25

	Min. freight charge	1st class freight per 100 lbs	2d class freight per 100 lbs	3d class freight per 100 lbs	4th class freight per 100 lbs	5th class freight per 100 lbs	6th class freight per 100 lbs	Express per 100 lbs
MINNESOTA—								
Albert Lea	$0 25	$0 60	$0 50	$0 40	$0 25	.....	.....	$2 00
Audubon	25	1 30	1 10	85	60	.....	.....	3 75
Crookston	50	1 40	1 18	92	65	.....	.....	$0 80- 3 25
Duluth	25	65	55	44	28	.....	.....	2 25
Edgerton	25	86	70	49	38	.....	.....	2 25
Farris	50	1 24	1 01	83	61	.....	.....	2 00- 1 75
Hallock	50	1 64	1 38	1 12	85	.....	.....	2 00- 2 50
Mankato	25	65	55	43	27	.....	.....	2 00
Marshall	25	85	72	55	40	.....	.....	3 00
Menahga	50	1 22	1 03	81	58	.....	.....	2 00- 1 75
Milan	25	90	77	64	43	.....	.....	3 00
Minneapolis	25	60	50	40	25	.....	.....	2 00
Moorhead	25	1 30	1 10	85	60	.....	.....	4 00
Redwood Falls	25	70	56	45	34	.....	.....	2 75
Tower	50	1 10	94	78	57	.....	.....	3 25
Winona	25	50	42	33	23	.....	.....	1 75
MISSISSIPPI—								
Ackerman	50	1 25	1 02	82	70	$0 57	$0 51	3 75
Holly Spring	50	1 09	93	77	64	51	44	3 10
Jackson	50	1 18	99	80	67	56	49	3 75
Meridian	1 18	1 18	99	80	67	56	49	4 00
Mississippi City	Note 3	1 67	1 40	1 13	90	77	68	4 25
Natchez	1 10	1 10	90	75	58	47	41	3 75
Ocean Springs	Note 3	1 67	1 40	1 13	90	77	68	4 25
Port Gibson	1 18	1 18	98	83	66	55	49	4 10
Roxie	50	1 57	1 26	1 06	86	62	54	4 25
State Line	50	1 56	1 40	1 20	94	76	62	4 00
Vicksburg	1 10	1 10	90	75	58	47	41	3 75
West Point	50	1 25	1 02	82	70	57	48	3 50
MISSOURI—								
Charleston	Note 3	1 12	88	74	61	.....	.....	2 40
Chicopee	50	1 60	1 30	95	75	.....	.....	4 00
Chillicothe	25	80	65	45	32	.....	.....	2 00
Clinton	50	90	72	50	37	.....	.....	2 50
Hannibal	25	47	38	29	22	.....	.....	1 25
Independence	50	80	65	45	32	.....	.....	2 00
Jefferson City	50	71	58	42	29	.....	.....	2 00
Kahoka	25	52	43	32	23	.....	.....	1 50
Kansas City	25	80	65	45	32	.....	.....	2 00
Kirkwood	50	61	50	38	32	.....	.....	1 90
Osceola	50	90	72	50	37	.....	.....	2 75
Paris	50	63	49	37	26	.....	.....	1 75
Poplar Bluff	Note 3	1 22	96	79	62	.....	.....	2 60
Richards	50	97	81	60	43	.....	.....	2 75
Rolla	50	1 05	85	64	54	.....	.....	2 50
Springfield	50	90	72	50	37	.....	.....	3 00
St. Louis	35	52	43	34	28	.....	.....	1 50
St. Joseph	25	80	65	45	32	.....	.....	2 00
MONTANA—								
Big Timber	2 25	2 90	2 50	2 02	1 67	.....	.....	7 75
Billings	2 45	2 85	2 45	1 98	1 65	.....	.....	7 00
Butte	2 40	3 10	2 65	2 15	1 75	.....	.....	8 00
Chinook	1 98	2 54	2 23	1 79	1 53	.....	.....	2 00- 5 25
Dillon	2 40	3 10	2 65	2 15	1 75	.....	.....	8 00
Glasgow	1 61	2 24	1 86	1 56	1 26	.....	.....	5 00- 2 00
Glendive	1 51	2 15	1 76	1 46	1 19	.....	.....	5 50
Great Falls	2 30	2 95	2 55	2 05	1 70	.....	.....	8 00
Helena	2 40	3 10	2 65	2 15	1 75	.....	.....	8 00
Kalispell	2 56	3 27	2 81	2 31	1 90	.....	.....	2 00- 7 00
Livingston	2 30	2 95	2 55	2 05	1 70	.....	.....	8 00
Missoula	2 50	3 20	2 75	2 25	1 85	.....	.....	9 00
Neihart	2 76	3 45	3 01	2 43	2 01	.....	.....	2 00- 6 75
NEBRASKA—								
Ainsworth	50	1 57	1 33	1 06	82	.....	.....	3 75
Alliance	50	1 81	1 58	1 25	97	.....	.....	5 00
Battle Creek	50	1 28	1 07	77	56	.....	.....	3 00
Beaver City	50	1 48	1 28	1 03	82	.....	.....	4 00
Chadron	50	1 90	1 64	1 34	1 03	.....	.....	4 75
Chappell	50	1 81	1 58	1 25	97	.....	.....	4 75
Cody	50	1 68	1 45	1 15	91	.....	.....	4 25
Crawford	50	2 02	1 76	1 43	1 17	.....	.....	4 75
Duncan	50	1 17	99	73	53	.....	.....	3 00
Grant	50	1 63	1 41	1 16	94	.....	.....	4 50
Hastings	50	1 31	1 11	83	62	.....	.....	3 50
Hemingford	50	1 85	1 62	1 31	1 01	.....	.....	5 00
Imperial	50	1 63	1 41	1 16	91	.....	.....	4 50
Lincoln	50	85	70	49	36	.....	.....	2 25
Loup City	50	1 45	1 23	96	75	.....	.....	3 75
Nelson	50	1 31	1 11	83	62	.....	.....	3 50
Ogallala	50	1 63	1 41	1 16	91	.....	.....	4 50
Omaha	25	80	65	45	32	.....	.....	2 00
O'Neill	50	1 43	1 18	89	68	.....	.....	3 25
Pawnee	50	89	74	53	40	.....	.....	2 75
Thedford	50	1 58	1 36	1 10	86	.....	.....	4 25
Valentine	50	1 64	1 41	1 11	87	.....	.....	4 00
NEVADA—								
Austin	4 32	4 82	4 32	3 62	3 02	.....	.....	13 00
Carson	3 65	4 15	3 65	2 95	2 35	.....	.....	12 25
Elko	3 40	3 90	3 40	2 70	2 10	.....	.....	11 50
Eureka	3 65	4 20	3 70	3 00	2 40	.....	.....	13 00
Hawthorne	3 65	4 90	4 40	3 70	3 10	.....	.....	13 50
Reno	3 40	3 90	3 40	2 70	2 10	.....	.....	11 50
Toana	3 40	3 90	3 40	2 70	2 10	.....	.....	11 50
Winnemucca	3 40	3 90	3 40	2 70	2 10	.....	.....	11 50
NEW BRUNSWICK—								
Chatham	1 05	1 05	90	72	54	46	.....	1 25- 3 50
Clarendon	95	95	83	66	49	42	.....	1 25- 3 25
Fredericton	1 09	1 09	95	76	57	48	.....	1 25- 3 25
Grand Falls	95	95	83	66	49	42	.....	1 25- 3 25
Moncton	95	95	83	66	49	42	.....	1 25- 3 50
Woodstock	1 13	1 13	98	78	59	50	.....	1 25- 3 25
NEW HAMPSHIRE—								
Berlin	82	82	71	55	39	33	.....	3 50
Colebrook	82	82	71	55	39	33	.....	3 75
Conway	82	82	71	55	39	33	.....	3 00
Dover	1 07	89	77	61	44	30	.....	2 50
Enfield	82	82	71	55	39	33	.....	3 00
Keene	83	83	71	55	39	33	.....	2 75
Laconia	82	82	71	55	39	33	.....	2 90
Manchester	82	82	71	55	39	33	.....	2 50
Plymouth	82	82	71	55	39	33	.....	3 25
Portsmouth	82	82	71	55	39	33	.....	2 50
Suncook	82	82	71	55	39	33	.....	2 75
Wing Road	82	82	71	55	39	33	.....	3 25

	Min. freight charge	1st class freight per 100 lbs	2d class freight per 100 lbs	3d class freight per 100 lbs	4th class freight per 100 lbs	5th class freight per 100 lbs	6th class freight per 100 lbs	Express per 100 lbs
NEW JERSEY—								
Bridgeton	$0 80	$0 80	$0 70	$0 55	$0 40	$0 35	....	$2 50
Chatsworth	80	80	70	55	40	35	....	2 75
Lafayette	75	75	65	50	35	30	....	2 75
Middletown	80	80	70	55	40	35	....	2 75
Morristown	75	75	65	50	35	30	....	2 50
Mullica Hill	78	78	68	53	38	33	....	2 50
Newark	75	75	65	50	35	30	....	2 50
Oxford Furnace	75	75	65	50	35	30	....	2 50
Pleasantville	80	80	70	55	40	35	....	2 75
Pompton	75	75	65	50	35	30	....	2 75
Somerville	75	75	65	50	35	30	....	2 50
NEW MEXICO—								
A'buquerque	1 96	2 32	2 06	1 88	1 67	....	....	7 25
Carlsbad	2 12	2 12	1 90	1 73	1 62	....	....	6 75
Clayton	75	2 05	1 65	1 25	97	....	....	6 75
Las Vegas	1 61	2 32	2 06	1 88	1 62	....	....	7 25
Lordsburg	2 46	2 72	2 46	2 27	2 07	....	....	8 75
Raton	1 00	2 24	1 79	1 37	1 06	....	....	6 50
Roswell	1 67	2 32	2 06	1 88	1 67	....	....	6 75
Santa Fe	1 90	2 32	2 06	1 88	1 67	....	....	7 25
Socorro	1 96	2 32	2 06	1 88	1 67	....	....	7 25
Wingate	2 84	3 18	2 84	2 60	2 10	....	....	9 00
NEW YORK—								
Albany	72	72	63	48	34	29	....	2 25
Big Moose	82	82	71	55	39	33	....	3 00
Boston Corners	82	82	71	55	39	33	....	2 75
Buffalo	45	45	39	30	21	18	....	1 75
Canton	82	82	71	55	39	33	....	3 00
Cortland	60	60	52	40	28	24	....	2 25
Delhi	98	98	84	65	47	39	....	3 00
Elmira	65	65	56	43	30	26	....	2 25
Fort Edward	97	91	79	61	45	38	....	2 75
Hastings (Oswego Co.)	68	68	59	45	32	21	....	2 50
Lake Placid	94	94	82	65	47	....	....	3 55
Lyons	60	60	52	40	28	24	....	2 00
Malone	82	82	71	55	39	33	....	3 15
New York	75	75	65	50	35	30	....	2 50
North Creek	1 11	1 11	95	75	57	50	....	3 75
Nunda	56	56	48	37	26	22	....	2 40
Plattsburg	1 04	1 04	90	69	50	44	....	3 25
Poughkeepsie	75	75	65	50	35	30	....	2 50
Rochester	56	56	48	37	26	22	....	2 00
Saranac Lake	82	82	71	55	39	33	....	3 15
Warsaw	56	56	48	37	26	22	....	2 00
Watertown	75	75	65	50	35	30	....	2 75
Whitehall	82	82	71	55	39	33	....	3 00
NORTH CAROLINA—								
Belhaven	97	1 22	1 03	83	59	49	$0 41	3 50
Charlotte	Note 1	1 40	1 20	95	70	60	47	4 00
Clinton	Note 1	1 40	1 20	95	70	60	49	4 00
Fayetteville	Note 1	1 40	1 20	95	70	58	45	4 00
Goldsboro	Note 2	1 33	1 13	89	64	52	41	3 75
Goldston	Note 1	1 40	1 20	95	70	60	47	4 25
Greensboro	Note 1	1 33	1 13	89	64	55	43	3 75
Halifax	Note 1	1 32	1 12	89	64	55	43	3 50
Hertford	$0 97	1 02	87	67	47	39	32	3 25
Mount Airy	Note 1	1 43	1 22	97	76	67	54	4 25
Newbern	Note 1	1 10	93	74	56	48	39	4 25
Newport	Note 1	1 27	1 09	85	61	53	42	4 50
Raleigh	Note 1	1 33	1 13	89	64	55	43	4 00
Salisbury	Note 1	1 40	1 20	95	70	60	47	3 75
Shelby	Note 1	1 52	1 32	1 07	82	68	54	4 50
Wadesboro	Note 1	1 40	1 20	95	70	60	47	4 50
Washington	Note 1	1 10	93	74	56	48	39	3 50
Wilkesboro	Note 1	1 43	1 22	97	71	61	48	4 00
Wilmington	Note 1	1 27	1 07	87	62	52	39	4 25
NORTH DAKOTA—								
Aneta	$0 50	1 55	1 31	1 02	73	....	....	$2 00- 2 40
Bismarck	50	1 80	1 52	1 24	97	....	....	4 75
Bottineau	50	1 82	1 54	1 25	98	....	....	2 00- 3 00
Carrington	50	1 65	1 39	1 12	82	....	....	4 50
Cooperstown	50	1 52	1 28	1 00	71	....	....	4 50
Dickinson	50	2 02	1 65	1 36	1 10	....	....	5 25
Ellendale	25	1 32	1 15	85	62	....	....	3 50
Fargo	25	1 30	1 10	85	60	....	....	3 50
Grand Forks	50	1 40	1 18	92	65	....	....	4 25
Hannah	50	1 77	1 50	1 22	95	....	....	2 00- 3 00
Jamestown	50	1 55	1 31	1 02	7[illegible]	....	....	4 25
Lakota	50	1 62	1 37	1 11	83	....	....	2 00- 2 75
Medora	50	2 07	1 69	1 39	1 14	....	....	5 50
Minot	50	1 75	1 49	1 21	95	....	....	5 00
Pembina	50	1 68	1 42	1 16	87	....	....	4 50
St. John	50	1 80	1 52	1 24	97	....	....	2 00- 3 00
Wahpeton	25	1 20	1 00	80	55	....	....	3 50
NOVA SCOTIA—								
Berwick	1 18	1 18	1 02	81	61	51	....	4 50- 75
Hopewell	95	95	83	66	49	42	....	1 25- 4 00
Mulgrove	95	95	83	66	49	42	....	1 25- 4 25
North Sidney	1 03	1 03	90	72	54	46	....	1 25- 4 50
Oxford Jct.	95	95	83	66	49	42	....	1 25- 3 75
Pictou	95	95	83	66	49	42	....	1 25- 4 00
Truro	95	95	83	66	49	42	....	1 27- 3 75
Yarmouth	1 32	1 32	1 14	91	67	58	....	2 50- 75
OHIO — Bellefontaine	37	37	32	24	16	13	....	1 50
Bucyrus	39	39	33	25	17	14	....	1 50
Caldwell	45	45	39	30	21	18	....	2 00
Canton	41	41	35	26	18	15	....	1 50
Chillicothe	44	44	38	29	19	17	....	1 75
Cincinnati	40	40	34	25	17	15	....	1 50
Cleveland	41	41	35	26	18	15	....	1 50
Columbus	41	41	35	26	18	15	....	1 50
Coshocton	44	44	38	29	19	17	....	1 75
Dayton	40	40	34	25	17	15	....	1 50
Defiance	33	33	29	22	15	12	....	1 00
Georgetown	45	45	39	30	21	18	....	1 95
Greenville	39	39	33	25	17	14	....	1 25
Hillsboro	44	44	38	29	19	17	....	1 75
Jobs	45	45	39	29	21	18	....	2 00
Laura	39	39	33	25	17	14	....	1 50
Lima	37	37	32	24	16	13	....	1 25
Logan	45	45	39	29	21	18	....	1 75
Marion	39	39	33	25	17	14	....	1 25
Ottawa	37	37	32	24	16	13	....	1 25
Portsmouth	45	45	39	30	21	18	....	2 00
Steubenville	45	45	39	30	21	18	....	1 75
Toledo	37	37	32	24	16	13	....	1 25
Xenia	40	40	34	25	17	15	....	1 50
Youngstown	44	44	38	29	19	17	....	1 50

	Min. freight charge	1st class freight per 100 lbs	2d class freight per 100 lbs	3d class freight per 100 lbs	4th class freight per 100 lbs	5th class freight per 100 lbs	6th class freight per 100 lbs	Express per 100 lbs
OKLAHOMA TER.—								
Alva	$0 50	$1 50	$1 29	$1 07	$0 88			$4 25
Calumet	50	1 50	1 29	1 07	89			4 25
El Reno	50	1 50	1 29	1 00	84			4 25
Guthrie	50	1 50	1 29	1 00	84			4 00
Kingfisher	50	1 50	1 29	1 00	84			4 25
Newkirk	50	1 50	1 27	97	76			4 00
Oklahoma	50	1 50	1 29	1 00	84			4 00
Tecumseh	50	1 55	1 34	1 05	89			4 50
Woodward	50	1 50	1 29	1 07	95			4 75
ONTARIO—								
Haliburton	78	78	67	51	37	$0 31	....	$1 25- 1 50
Kingston	68	68	59	45	32	27	....	2 75
London	45	45	39	30	21	18	....	1 85
Mattawa	1 09	1 09	95	75	58	49	....	1 25- 2 00
Ottawa	75	75	65	50	35	30	....	3 00
Parry Sound	1 02	1 02	90	71	53	....	....	1 25- 1 50
Toronto	45	45	39	30	21	18	....	1 25- 1 00
OREGON—								
Arlington	3 10	3 60	3 10	2 60	2 10			11 00
Baker City	3 10	3 60	3 10	2 60	2 10			10 00
Elgin	3 10	3 60	3 10	2 60	2 10			10 00
Eugene	2 85	3 50	3 02	2 59	2 26			12 25
Heppner	3 10	3 60	3 10	2 60	2 10			11 75
Huntington	2 85	3 80	3 25	2 65	2 22			10 00
La Grande	3 10	3 60	3 10	2 60	2 10			10 00
Lebanon	2 85	3 45	2 96	2 53	2 20			12 00
Leland	3 10	3 60	3 10	2 60	2 10			13 00
Medford	3 10	3 60	3 10	2 60	2 10			13 00
Monmouth	3 35	3 38	2 92	2 48	2 15			12 00
Pendleton	3 10	3 60	3 10	2 60	2 10			10 00
Portland	2 60	3 00	2 60	2 20	1 90			11 50
Roseburg	3 10	3 60	3 10	2 60	2 10			13 00
Salem	2 85	3 10	2 70	2 30	2 00			12 00
Sheridan	2 85	3 34	2 89	2 45	2 11			12 00
PENNSYLVANIA—								
Allentown	73	73	63	48	33	28	....	2 50
Bedford	72	72	62	47	32	27	....	3 00
Blairsville	53	53	45	34	24	21	....	2 25
Driftwood	72	72	62	47	32	27	....	3 00
Erie	45	45	39	30	21	18	....	2 00
Gettysburg	72	72	62	47	32	27	....	2 25
Harrisburg	72	72	62	47	32	27	....	2 25
Huntingdon	72	72	62	47	32	27	....	2 75
Jackson Center	44	44	38	29	19	17	....	2 10
Larabee	56	56	48	37	26	....	....	2 25
Lewisburg	72	72	62	47	32	27	....	2 50
Nanticoke	73	73	63	48	33	28	....	2 50
New Castle	44	44	38	29	19	17	....	1 75
Philadelphia	73	73	63	48	33	28	....	2 25
Pittsburg	45	45	39	30	21	18	....	1 75
Pottsville	73	73	63	48	33	28	....	2 50
Reading	73	73	63	48	33	28	....	2 25
Scranton	73	73	63	48	33	28	....	2 50
Sharpsville	44	44	38	29	19	17	....	1 75
Tionesta	45	45	39	30	21	18	....	2 10
Towanda	73	73	63	48	33	28	....	2 50
Uniontown	50	50	43	33	23	20	....	2 00
Wellsboro	72	72	62	47	32	27	....	2 25
Williamsport	72	72	62	47	32	22	....	2 50
QUEBEC—								
La Belle	93	93	81	64	46	39	....	1 25- 2 25
Megantic	1 15	1 15	1 01	82	61	52	....	3 75
Montreal	75	75	65	50	35	30	....	3 25
Quebec	89	89	76	59	42	36	....	3 75
Richmond	82	82	71	55	39	33	....	1 25- 2 00
Sherbrooke	82	82	71	55	39	33	....	3 50
Sorel	87	87	76	59	43	42	....	1 25- 2 00
St. Jean Port Joli	93	93	81	64	47	40	....	1 25- 2 50
Waltham	97	97	84	66	48	40	....	1 25- 2 00
RHODE ISLAND—								
Bristol	82	82	71	55	39	33	....	2 50- 40
Greene	82	82	71	55	39	33	....	3 00
Pascoag	82	82	71	55	39	33	....	3 00
Providence	82	82	71	55	39	33	....	2 50
Slocumville	82	82	71	55	39	33	....	3 00
Westerly	82	82	71	55	39	33	....	3 00
Wickford Junction	82	82	71	55	39	33	....	3 00
SOUTH CAROLINA—								
Abbeville	Note 1	1 56	1 41	1 11	84	70	$0 62	4 50
Aiken	Note 1	1 56	1 41	1 11	84	70	59	5 00
Beaufort	Note 1	1 35	1 14	1 00	87	73	58	5 50
Charleston	Note 1	1 35	1 14	1 00	87	73	58	4 75
Columbia	Note 1	1 47	1 26	1 06	82	68	56	4 50
Florence	Note 1	1 51	1 37	1 09	82	67	54	4 50
Georgetown	Note 1	1 32	1 13	93	67	55	43	5 25
Greenville	Note 1	1 56	1 41	1 11	84	70	62	4 50
Greenwood	Note 1	1 56	1 41	1 11	84	70	62	4 50
Hampton	Note 2	1 84	1 58	1 38	1 19	99	79	5 50
Lancaster	Note 1	1 47	1 27	1 02	1 77	64	51	4 50
Ridgeway	Note 1	1 56	1 34	1 11	83	70	56	4 50
Spartanburg	Note 1	1 56	1 41	1 11	84	70	62	4 50
Sumter	Note 1	1 57	1 37	1 09	82	76	54	5 00
SOUTH DAKOTA—								
Aberdeen	$0 25	1 25	1 05	75	56	....	....	3 25
Armour	25	1 10	95	74	50	....	....	3 00
Belle Fourche	75	2 35	2 05	1 63	1 32	....	....	5 75
Canton	25	83	68	47	34	....	....	2 50
Chamberlain	25	1 25	1 08	80	55	....	....	3 25
Deadwood	75	2 25	1 95	1 60	1 32	....	....	5 75
Edgemont	50	2 04	1 78	1 43	1 19	....	....	6 00
Eureka	25	1 40	1 15	90	67	....	....	3 50
Gettysburg	25	1 35	1 10	85	65	....	....	3 25
Huron	25	1 24	1 05	75	51	....	....	3 25
Millbank Jct.	25	98	82	68	44	....	....	3 25
Mitchell	25	1 05	94	68	47	....	....	2 75
Pierre	25	1 30	1 10	80	60	....	....	3 25
Rapid City	75	2 16	1 90	1 55	1 28	....	....	5 50
Redfield	25	1 25	1 05	75	56	....	....	3 25
Sisseton	25	1 10	90	70	50	....	....	3 25
Spearfish	50	2 35	2 05	1 69	1 42	....	....	6 25
Vermilion	25	89	73	51	37	....	....	2 50
Watertown	25	1 00	85	65	46	....	....	3 25
Wolsey	25	1 25	1 05	75	52	....	....	3 25
Yankton	25	91	73	51	37	....	....	2 50

	Min. freight charge	1st class freight per 100 lbs	2d class freight per 100 lbs	3d class freight per 100 lbs	4th class freight per 100 lbs	5th class freight per 100 lbs	6th class freight per 100 lbs	Express per 100 lbs
TENNESSEE—								
Allens Creek	Note 3	$1 42	$1 24	$1 01	$0 81	$0 70	$0 66	$3 75
Bristol	$0 84	84	72	55	39	33	27	3 75
Charleston	Note 1	1 50	1 29	1 08	86	73	57	3 50
Chattanooga	Note 1	1 16	99	82	64	55	42	3 00
Clarksville	Note 1	81	70	56	43	36	30	2 65
Clinton	Note 2	1 32	1 14	95	74	63	49	3 50
Greenfield	$0 50	91	75	60	49	37	34	2 75
Knoxville	Note 1	1 16	99	82	64	55	42	3 50
Jackson	$0 50	1 03	85	70	57	42	39	2 90
Manchester	Note 3	1 38	1 22	1 00	79	69	63	3 50
Memphis	$0 85	85	65	55	43	37	31	3 00
Parsons	Note 3	1 36	1 17	93	73	58	49	3 25
Sparta	Note 3	1 53	1 37	1 14	93	80	72	3 50
TEXAS—								
Abilene	Note 3	1 50	1 29	1 09	1 00	.....	.....	5 50
Amarillo	Note 3	1 60	1 38	1 17	1 07	.....	.....	5 50
Austin	Note 3	1 50	1 29	1 09	1 00	.....	.....	5 25
Beaumont	Note 3	1 50	1 29	1 09	1 00	.....	.....	5 25
Canadian	Note 3	1 56	1 34	1 13	1 04	.....	.....	5 25
Corpus Christi	Note 3	1 50	1 29	1 09	1 00	.....	.....	6 50
Dallas	Note 3	1 50	1 29	1 09	1 00	.....	.....	4 25
Denison	Note 3	1 50	1 29	1 09	1 00	.....	.....	3 75
El Paso	Note 3	1 62	1 42	1 27	1 20	.....	.....	7 00
Henrietta	Note 3	1 50	1 29	1 09	1 00	.....	.....	4 50
Houston	Note 3	1 50	1 29	1 09	1 00	.....	.....	5 25
Kerrville	Note 3	1 57	1 36	1 15	1 03	.....	.....	6 50
Laredo	Note 3	1 62	1 42	1 27	1 20	.....	.....	6 75
Llano	Note 3	1 50	1 29	1 09	1 00	.....	.....	6 00
Lufkin	Note 3	1 50	1 29	1 09	1 00	.....	.....	5 25
Palestine	Note 3	1 50	1 29	1 09	1 00	.....	.....	5 00
Pecos	Note 3	1 86	1 58	1 40	1 30	.....	.....	6 75
Port Lavaca	Nota 3	1 50	1 29	1 09	1 00	.....	.....	5 75
San Angelo	Note 3	1 57	1 36	1 15	1 03	.....	.....	6 00
San Antonio	Note 3	1 50	1 29	1 09	1 00	.....	.....	5 75
Sanderson	Note 3	1 87	1 59	1 41	1 31	.....	.....	7 00
Seymour	Note 3	1 50	1 29	1 09	1 00	.....	.....	5 25
Sierra Blanca	Note 3	1 87	1 59	1 41	1 31	.....	.....	6 75
Spofford	Note 3	1 62	1 41	1 23	1 15	.....	.....	6 75
Waco	Note 3	1 50	1 29	1 09	1 00	.....	.....	4 75
UTAH—								
Belknap	$2 73	3 60	3 13	2 61	2 19	.....	.....	9 00
Bingham Jct	2 25	3 10	2 65	2 15	1 75	.....	.....	8 00
Cache Jct	2 40	3 30	2 80	2 20	1 82	.....	.....	8 00
Colton	2 25	3 10	2 65	2 15	1 75	.....	.....	8 00
Echo	2 25	3 10	2 65	2 15	1 75	.....	.....	8 00
Ephraim	2 50	3 30	2 83	2 31	1 89	.....	.....	8 25
Fairfield	2 50	3 35	2 89	2 37	1 95	.....	.....	8 50
Frisco	2 78	3 65	3 18	2 66	2 24	.....	.....	10 50
Kelton	3 40	3 90	3 40	2 70	2 10	.....	.....	10 25
Milford	2 73	3 60	3 13	2 61	2 19	.....	.....	10 25
Nephi	2 50	3 30	2 83	2 31	1 89	.....	.....	8 75
Ogden	2 25	3 10	2 65	2 15	1 75	.....	.....	8 00
Salt Lake City	2 25	3 10	2 65	2 15	1 75	.....	.....	8 00
VIRGINIA—								
Abingdon	84	84	72	55	39	33	.....	3 75
Alexandria	72	72	62	47	32	27	.....	2 50
Basic	72	72	62	47	32	27	.....	3 00
Big Stone Gap	Note 1	1 20	1 03	83	70	63	.....	3 25
Clarksville	Note 1	1 27	1 08	33	56	48	.....	3 50
Emporia	.....	1 22	1 04	82	55	47	.....	3 50
Farmville	$0 72	72	62	47	32	27	.....	3 50
Fredericksburg	72	72	62	47	32	27	.....	2 85
Harrisonburg	72	72	62	47	32	27	.....	2 50
Lexington	72	72	62	47	32	27	.....	2 75
Lynchburg	72	72	62	47	32	27	.....	3 25
Martinsville	Note 1	1 15	98	75	50	43	.....	4 00
New Castle	$0 84	84	72	55	38	31	.....	3 25
Old Point Comfort	72	72	62	47	32	27	.....	2 75
Orange	72	72	62	47	32	27	.....	3 00
Pleasant Valley	72	72	62	47	32	27	.....	2 50
Pulaski City	84	84	72	55	39	33	.....	3 25
Richmond	72	72	62	47	32	27	.....	3 00
Riverton	72	72	62	47	32	27	.....	2 75
Salem	72	72	62	47	32	27	.....	3 25
Suffolk	72	72	62	47	32	27	.....	3 75
Swordscreek	84	84	72	55	39	33	.....	3 25
Virginia City	84	84	72	55	39	33	.....	3 25
West Point	72	72	62	47	32	27	.....	3 00
VERMONT—								
Bradford	82	82	71	55	39	33	.....	3 25
Brattleboro	82	82	71	55	39	33	.....	2 75
Burlington	82	82	71	55	39	33	.....	3 25
Cavendish	82	82	71	55	39	33	.....	3 00
Essex Jct	82	82	71	55	39	33	.....	3 25
Greensboro	82	82	71	55	39	33	.....	3 25
Hartford	82	82	71	55	39	33	.....	3 10
Leicester	82	82	71	55	39	33	.....	3 25
Montpelier	82	82	71	55	39	33	.....	3 25
North Bennington	82	82	71	55	39	33	.....	2 75
Rutland	82	82	71	55	39	33	.....	3 00
South Londonderry	82	82	71	55	39	33	.....	2 75
St. Albans	82	82	71	55	39	33	.....	3 25
St. Johnsbury	82	82	71	55	39	33	.....	3 25
WASHINGTON—								
Anacortes	2 60	3 00	2 60	2 20	1 90	.....	.....	12 00
Chehalis	2 60	3 00	2 60	2 20	1 90	.....	.....	11 50
Colfax	3 10	3 60	3 10	2 60	2 10	.....	.....	$2 00- 8 00
Connell	3 10	3 60	3 10	2 60	2 10	.....	.....	10 00
Coulee City	3 10	3 60	3 10	2 60	2 10	.....	.....	10 50
Dayton	3 10	3 60	3 10	2 60	2 10	.....	.....	10 00
Easton	3 10	3 60	3 10	2 60	2 10	.....	.....	11 00
Hoquiam	2 60	3 00	2 60	2 20	1 90	.....	.....	12 00
Kalama	2 60	3 00	2 60	2 20	1 90	.....	.....	11 50
Meyers Falls	3 35	4 14	3 62	3 09	2 55	.....	.....	2 00- 9 50
New Whatcom	2 60	3 00	2 60	2 20	1 90	.....	.....	12 00
North Yakima	3 10	3 60	3 10	2 60	2 10	.....	.....	11 00
Olympia	2 60	3 00	2 60	2 20	1 90	.....	.....	11 50
Pasco	3 10	3 60	3 10	2 60	2 10	.....	.....	10 00
Snohomish	2 60	3 00	2 60	2 20	1 90	.....	.....	11 50
South Bend	2 60	3 00	2 60	2 20	1 90	.....	.....	12 00
Spokane	3 10	3 60	3 10	2 60	2 10	.....	.....	10 00
Tacoma	2 60	3 00	2 60	2 20	1 90	.....	.....	11 50
Walla Walla	3 10	3 60	3 10	2 60	2 10	.....	.....	10 00
Wallula	3 10	3 60	3 10	2 60	2 10	.....	.....	10 00
Wenatchee	3 10	3 60	3 10	2 60	2 10	.....	.....	2 00- 9 00
WEST VIRGINIA—								
Beverly	$0 97	$0 84	$0 72	$0 56	$0 40	$0 34	.....	$3 25
Charleston	45	45	39	30	21	18	.....	2 50
Clarksburg	57	57	49	38	26	18	.....	2 25
Dingess	84	84	72	55	39	33	.....	2 50
Grafton	57	57	49	38	26	21	.....	2 00
Harpers Ferry	72	72	62	47	32	27	.....	2 25
Hinton	72	72	62	47	32	27	.....	3 00
Martinsburg	72	72	62	47	32	27	.....	2 25
Parkersburg	45	45	39	30	21	18	.....	2 00
Parsons	97	90	76	60	41	35	.....	3 25
Ripley Landing	45	45	39	30	21	18	.....	2 25
Romney	77	77	66	50	34	29	.....	2 25
Spencer	67	67	58	45	32	27	.....	2 25
Wheeling	45	45	39	30	21	18	.....	1 75
WISCONSIN—								
Ashland	25	65	55	44	28	.....	.....	2 00
Athens	25	60	50	40	25	.....	.....	2 00
Beloit	25	37	30	24	18	.....	.....	75
Cameron	25	65	55	44	28	.....	.....	1 75
Chelsea	25	60	50	40	25	.....	.....	2 00
Chippewa Falls	25	60	50	40	25	.....	.....	1 75
Fond du Lac	25	40	33	28	20	.....	.....	1 00
Grand Rapids	25	50	42	33	23	.....	.....	1 50
Green Bay	25	43	36	29	20	.....	.....	1 25
Hudson	25	60	50	40	25	.....	.....	1 75
Hurley	25	65	55	44	28	.....	.....	2 00
Lancaster	25	50	42	33	23	.....	.....	1 50
Madison	25	40	35	26	18	.....	.....	1 00
Manitowoc	25	30	25	21	16	.....	.....	1 10
Milwaukee	25	25	20	15	12	.....	.....	60
Mineral Pt	25	46	38	30	21	.....	.....	1 25
Mondovi	50	60	50	40	25	.....	.....	1 75
Oconto	25	43	36	29	23	.....	.....	1 50
Pembine	25	60	50	40	25	.....	.....	1 50
Prairie du Chien	25	50	42	33	23	.....	.....	1 50
Prentice	25	60	50	40	25	.....	.....	2 00
Richland Center	25	50	42	33	23	.....	.....	1 50
Rhinelander	25	60	50	40	25	.....	.....	1 75
Sparta	25	50	42	33	23	.....	.....	1 50
Spooner	25	65	55	44	28	.....	.....	2 00
Sturgeon Bay	50	43	36	29	23	.....	.....	1 75
Wabeno	25	60	50	40	25	.....	.....	1 75
Wausau	25	58	48	37	23	.....	.....	1 75
WYOMING—								
Casper	75	2 70	2 35	1 90	1 55	.....	.....	6 00
Cheyenne	75	2 05	1 65	1 25	97	.....	.....	6 00
Cokeville	2 40	3 30	2 80	2 20	1 82	.....	.....	8 00
Dana	2 03	2 95	2 43	1 87	1 49	.....	.....	7 75
Evanston	2 25	3 10	2 65	2 15	1 75	.....	.....	8 00
Gillette	50	2 70	2 35	1 90	1 55	.....	.....	7 00
Green River	2 25	3 10	2 65	2 15	1 75	.....	.....	8 00
Hanna	2 00	2 91	2 40	1 85	1 47	.....	.....	7 50
Laramie	1 70	2 56	2 10	1 64	1 29	.....	.....	6 75
Lusk	75	2 45	2 01	1 55	1 22	.....	.....	5 25
Medicine Bow	1 95	2 85	2 35	1 81	1 43	.....	.....	7 50
Rawlins	2 14	3 09	2 54	1 94	1 56	.....	.....	8 00
Sheridan	50	2 70	2 35	1 90	1 55	.....	.....	7 00
Wamsutter	2 25	3 10	2 65	2 08	1 70	.....	.....	8 00
Wheatland	1 16	2 45	2 01	1 55	1 22	.....	.....	6 50

HOW TO FIGURE EXPRESS CHARGES.

Refer to above table for the express rate per 100 pounds to the nearest town in your state, then refer to the same rate per 100 pounds in the table below, and you can tell exactly what the express charges will be on a package weighing from 1 to 25 pounds, 50 pounds or 100 pounds from Chicago to your station. For example: Express rate for 100 pounds to Fargo, N. D., is $4.00; 5 pounds would cost 65 cents.

When two rates are shown figure the charges for 7 pounds or less, at combined rates; if over 7 pounds figure at separate rates and add both charges together.

100 pounds	1 pound.	2 pounds.	3 pounds.	4 pounds.	5 pounds.	7 pounds.	10 pounds.	15 pounds.	20 pounds.	25 pounds.	50 pounds.
$0.40	$0.25	$0.25	$0.25	$0.25	$0.25	$0.25	$0.25	$0.25	$0.25	$0.25	$0.30
.50	.25	.25	.25	.25	.25	.30	.30	.30	.30	.35	.45
.60	.25	.25	.25	.25	.25	.30	.30	.30	.30	.35	.45
.75	.25	.25	.25	.30	.30	.35	.35	.35	.35	.40	.55
1.00	.25	.25	.30	.30	.35	.35	.40	.40	.45	.50	.70
1.25	.25	.25	.30	.30	.40	.40	.45	.50	.55	.60	.90
1.50	.25	.25	.30	.35	.40	.45	.50	.60	.65	.70	1.00
1.75	.25	.25	.35	.40	.45	.50	.55	.60	.70	.75	1.00
2.00	.25	.25	.40	.45	.50	.55	.60	.70	.80	.90	1.00
2.50	.25	.30	.45	.50	.55	.65	.75	.80	.90	1.00	1.25
3.00	.25	.30	.45	.55	.65	.70	.75	.85	1.00	1.10	1.50
3.50	.25	.30	.45	.60	.65	.75	.90	1.00	1.15	1.25	1.75
4.00	.25	.30	.45	.60	.65	.75	.90	1.00	1.15	1.30	2.00
4.50	.25	.30	.45	.60	.70	.85	1.00	1.10	1.25	1.50	2.25
5.00	.25	.30	.45	.60	.70	.90	1.00	1.15	1.30	1.50	2.50
6.00	.25	.30	.45	.60	.70	.95	1.15	1.35	1.65	1.85	3.00
7.00	.25	.30	.45	.60	.75	1.00	1.20	1.50	1.75	2.00	3.50
8.00	.25	.30	.45	.60	.75	1.00	1.25	1.60	2.00	2.25	4.00
9.00	.25	.30	.45	.60	.75	1.00	1.35	1.75	2.00	2.50	4.50
10.00	.25	.30	.45	.60	.75	1.00	1.50	2.00	2.50	3.00	5.00
11.00	.25	.30	.45	.60	.75	1.00	1.50	2.00	2.50	3.25	5.50
12.00	.25	.30	.45	.60	.75	1.00	1.50	2.15	2.75	3.50	6.00
13.00	.30	.35	.45	.60	.80	1.00	1.50	2.15	2.75	3.50	6.50
14.00	.30	.35	.45	.60	.80	1.10	1.50	2.15	2.85	3.50	7.00
15.00	.35	.40	.50	.65	.85	1.15	1.65	2.35	3.00	3.75	7.50
16.00	.35	.40	.50	.65	.85	1.15	1.65	2.50	3.20	4.00	8.00
17.00	.35	.45	.55	.75	.90	1.25	1.75	2.60	3.40	4.25	8.50
18.00	.35	.45	.60	.75	.95	1.40	1.80	2.75	3.60	4.50	9.00
20.00	.40	.50	.60	.80	1.00	1.50	2.00	3.00	4.00	5.00	10.00

If you cannot figure the freight or express charges from above tables, ask your agent; he will be pleased to furnish them, if not write us and we will give you all the information you desire.

Express or freight charges add next to nothing to the cost of goods you order from us compared with what you will save in price.

One order will convince you that it is just as convenient and far more economical to buy goods direct from us than from a local store.

FREIGHT CLASSIFICATION.

1 stands for First Class.
2 stands for Second Class.
3 stands for Third Class.
4 stands for Fourth Class.
5 stands for Fifth Class.
6 stands for Sixth Class.
1¼ stands for 1¼ times First Class.
1½ stands for 1½ times First Class.
D1 stands for Double First Class.
2½ stands for 2½ times First Class.
3T1 stands for 3 times First Class.
4T1 stands for 4 times First Class.

THE RAILROADS CHARGE FOR FREIGHT ACCORDING TO ITS CLASSIFICATION. For example: Stoves take 3rd class rate. By referring to pages 7 to 10 you will find the 3rd class rate to the nearest town in your state. Multiply the weight of the article (which you can get from our catalogue or estimate pretty closely) by the rate, and you will be able to figure the freight charges almost to the cent. If the following list does not contain the article you want, you can as a rule use the rate on some article of a similar nature.

THE CLASSIFICATION ON SOME ARTICLES IS DIFFERENT, to different sections of the country. For example: Hardware takes 2nd class rate to the western and southern states, and 3rd class to the eastern states. Hay presses take 2nd class rate to the western states, 3rd class to the eastern states and 4th class to the southern states.

REMEMBER, WE ALWAYS PACK AND SHIP OUR GOODS IN A MANNER THAT SECURES FOR YOU THE LOWEST FREIGHT CHARGES.

WEST. The railroads running west, northwest and southwest from Chicago, use the western classification. Use the classification in column marked "WEST" if you live in any of the following states: Arizona, Arkansas, British Columbia, California, Colorado, Idaho, Illinois, Indian Territory Iowa, Kansas, Louisiana, Mexico, Minnesota, Missouri, Montana, Nebraska, Nevada, New Mexico, North Dakota, Oklahoma Territory, Oregon, South Dakota, Texas, Utah, Washington, Wisconsin, Wyoming.

EAST. The railroads running east and northeast from Chicago, use the eastern classification. Use the classification in column marked "EAST" if you live in any of the following states: Connecticut, Delaware, District of Columbia, Indiana, Maryland, Maine, Massachusetts, Michigan, New Brunswick, New Hampshire, New Jersey, New York, Nova Scotia, Ohio, Ontario, Pennsylvania, Quebec, Rhode Island, Vermont, Virginia, West Virginia.

SOUTH. The railroads running south and southeast from Chicago, use the southern classification. Use the classification in column marked "SOUTH" if you live in any of the following states: Alabama, Florida, Georgia, Kentucky, Mississippi, North Carolina, South Carolina, Tennessee.

ARTICLES	CLASS West	East	South
Advertising Matter	1	1	2
Ammunition	1	2	1
Animal Food	3	3	4
Anvils	4	4	5
Artists' Materials	1	1	1
Asbestos Building Felt	4	4	3
Axes	2	3	4
Axles	3	4	6
Baby Carriages	1½	1½	1
Bags, Burlap	3	3	6
Bags, Cotton	2	2	5
Barb Wire	4	5	6
Bar Iron	4	5	6
Baskets	D-1	D-1	D-1
Bath Brick	4	4	5
Beans	3	4	5
Beds, Folding	1½	1½	2
Bed Slats	3	3	3
Bedsteads	2	2	2
Bee Hives	3	3	6
Bells	3	3	2
Bellows	1	1	1
Bicycles	D-1	1½	1½
Binding Twine	2	3	3
Blackboards	2	3	2
Blankets	1	1	1
Blinds	3	1	4
Blowers	1	2	2
Bob Sleds	1	1	
Bodies, Buggy, Finished	1½	2½	1½
Bodies, Buggy, Unfinished	1½	1½	3
Boilers	2	2	3
Bone, Ground	4	4	6
Book Cases	1½	1½	1½
Books	1	1	1
Boots and Shoes	1	1	1
Bows, Felloes, Singletrees, Spokes, Hubs and Rims, Unfinished	3	3	5
Brooms	1	1	1
Brushes	1	1	1
Buggies.....(See Vehicles)			
Buggy Tops	1½	1½	1½
Building Felt	3	4	6
Building Paper	3	4	6
Bureaus	1	1	2
Cameras	D-1	1	2
Candles	4	4	4
Candy	3	3	5
Canned Goods	4	4	4
Cant Hooks	3	2	2
Carriages...(See Vehicles)			
Carpets	1	1	1
Carts, Road	1½	D-1	1½
Castings	4	4	5
Cement	4	4	6
Cereals	3	5	6
Chains	4	4	5
Chairs, Bamboo, Rattan, Reed or Willow	3T1	3T1	3T1
Chairs, Cane Seat	1½	2½	1
Chairs, Upholstered	D-1	2½	1½
Chairs, Wood Seat	1½	D-1	1
Cheese	2	3	3
Chiffoniers	1	1	2
Churns	2	2	2
Cigars and Cigarettes	1	1	1
Cloaks	1	1	1
Clocks	1	1	1
Clothing	1	1	1
Cobbler's Outfit	2	2	2
Cod Fish	4	5	5
Coffee	4	4	5
Coffins	1	1	1
Commodes	1	1	2
Condensed Milk	4	3	3
Corn Planters	2	3	2
Corn Shellers	2	3	2
Corrugated Iron	4	4	6
Cots	3	2	3

ARTICLES	CLASS West	East	South
Couches	1½	1½	1½
Crackers	2	2	4
Crockery	2	3	2
Crowbars	4	4	6
Cultivators	2	3	3
Cupboards	2	1½	1
Cutters (Sleighs)	2½	3T1	
Decoy Ducks	2	1	3
Desks	1	1	1
Dishes	2	3	2
Door Hangers	3	4	2
Door Screens	1	1	2
Doors	3	3	4
Doors, Glazed	3	1	4
Doubletrees	3	3	2
Dried Fruits	3	3	4
Drugs	1	1	1
Drums	4T1	3T1	3T1
Dry Goods	1	1	1
Earthenware	2	2	2
Electric Batteries	1	1	1
Electrical Goods	1	1	1
Engines	2	2	3
Evaporators, Fruit	3	2	1
Explosives	D-1	D-1	D-1
Fanning Mills	1	1	1
Feed Cookers	3	1	3
Feed Cutters	2	2	3
Felt, Building	3	4	6
Fence Wire, Barb and Smooth	4	5	6
Fencing	3	4	5
Fertilizers	4	4	6
Firearms	1	1	1
Fish, Canned	4	4	4
Fish, Pickled or Salted	4	5	6
Flax Meal	4	5	3
Flour	4	5	6
Food, Animal or Poultry	3	3	4
Forges	2	2	3
Forks	2	3	3
Freezers	1	1	3
Fruit, Canned	4	4	4
Fruit, Dried	3	3	4
Fruit Evaporators	1½	2	1
Fruit Jars	3	3	3
Galvanized Iron	4	5	6
Gas for Calcium Lights	1	3	1
Gas Machines	1	D-1	2
Gasoline Stoves	1	3	2
Gears, Running	1½	1	
Generators, Gas	1	D-1	2
Glassware	2	3	2
Granite and Enameled Ware	2	2	2
Graphophones	D1	1	1
Grease, Axle	4	4	6
Grindstone Frames	3	4	3
Grindstones	4	4	6
Grits	4	5	4
Gunpowder	D-1	D-1	D-1
Guns, Revolvers, etc	1	1	1
Hall Trees	D1	1	1½
Hammocks	1	1	1
Hardware	2	3	2
Harness and Saddles	1	1	1
Harrows	2	3	4
Hay Presses	2	3	4
Heaters, Tank	3	2	3
High Explosives	D-1	D-1	D-1
Hinges	3	4	2
Hoes	2	3	3
Hollow-ware	3	3	3
Hominy	4	5	6
Horse and Mule's Shoes	4	4	6
Horse Powers	2	3	2
Hullers, Pea	1	1	2
Ice Cream Freezers	1	1	3
Incubators	1	1	1
Iron Pipe	4	5	6

ARTICLES	CLASS West	East	South
Iron Tires	3	4	6
Kettles	3	3	4
Ladders	2	2	1
Lamps	1	1	2
Lard	4	4	5
Lasts	3	2	2
Lawn Mowers	2	3	1
Lime	4	4	6
Linseed Meal	4	5	3
Lounges	1½	1½	1
Lye	3	4	5
Machines, Sewing	1	1	1
Machines, Sewing, Drop Head	1	1	2
Magic Lanterns	D-1	1	1
Mandrels	4	3	5
Matting	1	1	2
Mattresses	1	1½	1½
Meats, Cured	4	4	6
Mills, Cider, Cob, Corn and Cane	2	2	4
Mirrors	1	1	1
Molasses in bbls	4	4	5
Molasses, in cans, kegs or kits	4	4	4
Mowers	2	3	3
Musical Instruments	D-1	1½	1
Nails	4	5	6
Notions	1	1	1
Nuts, edible	2	2	2
Oars	1	3	3
Oat Meal	4	5	6
Oil	3	3	3
Oil Cake Meal	4	5	3
Oil Cloth	1	2	2
Organs	1	1	1
Oyster Shells	4	4	6
Pails	2	1	1
Paint, in Barrels	4	4	5
Paint, in Cans or Pails	4	3	4
Paper Hangings	1	2	3
Pea Hullers	1	1	2
Phonographs	D1	1	1
Pianos	1	1	1
Planters	2	3	2
Plow Points and Shares	3	4	6
Plows	2	3	4
Plumbing Material	2	2	2
Poles, Buggy, Carriage or Wagon. Finished	1	1	1
Unfinished	1	3	1
Presses, Cider and Cotton	2	2	4
Printed Matter	1	1	2
Pumps	1	2	4
Queensware	2	4	2
Refrigerators	2	2	2
Rice	4	4	6
Road Carts	1½	D1	1½
Rolled Oats	4	5	6
Roofing	3	4	6
Rope	3	3	3
Rope, Wire	3	3	5
Rubber Goods	1	1	1
Saddlery	1	1	2
Sad Irons	4	4	4
Safes	3	4	3
Salt	4	4	6
Sash	3	1	4
Sash Weights	4	5	6
Sash, Window	3	1	4
Saws	1	2	2
Scales	2	3	2
Scientific Instruments	D-1	1	1
Screen Doors or Windows	1	1	2
Screens	1	1	1
Seats, Carriage and Buggy	2	1	2
Sewing Machines	1	1	1
Sewing Machines, Drop Head	1	1	2
Shafts, Carriage and Buggy	1½	D-1	1

ARTICLES	CLASS West	East	South
Shot	4	4	2
Sideboards	1	1	1
Skeins	3	4	3
Sleds, Bob	1	1	
Sleighs	2½	3T1	
Soap	4	4	6
Soap Powder	4	4	5
Sofas	D-1	D-1	1½
Sporting Goods	1	1	1
Spring Wagons.........(See Vehicles)			
Starch	3	4	3
Stationery	1	1	1
Stereopticons	D-1	1	1
Stove Furniture	3	3	3
Stove Linings	3	4	4
Stove Pipe	D-1	D-1	D-1
Stove Pipe, Iron	3	4	4
Stoves	3	3	3
Sugar	4	4	5
Sulkies	3T1	D-1	
Surreys.....(See Vehicles)			
Swage Blocks	3	3	5
Syrup	4	4	4
Syrup in Barrels	4	4	6
Tables	3	2	2
Tanks, Galvanized Iron (Set Up)	D-1	1½	1
Tanks, Galvanized Iron (Knocked Down)	4	2	2
Tanks, Iron	D-1	3	3
Tanks, Wooden (Knocked Down)	3	3	6
Tank Heaters	2	2	3
Tents and Poles	1	1	2
Tinware	2	3	3
Tire Shrinkers	3	2	2
Tire Upsetters	3	2	2
Tire Benders	3	3	2
Tobacco	1	1	2
Tools	2	2	2
Tools in Chest	1	1	2
Tops, Buggy	1½	1½	1½
Toys	1	1	1
Trunks	1	1½	1
Tubs	1	1	3
Twine	2	3	3
Varnish in Cans	1	2	2
Varnish in Wood	3	3	3
Vehicles, such as Buggies, Carriages, Surreys, Spring Wagons:			
Crated under 30 inches in height	1½	1¼	1
Crated under 50 inches in height	1½	D-1	1½
Crated over 50 inches in height	1½	3T1	D-1
Vinegar	4	3	5
Vises	2	3	3
Wagon Jacks	2	2	3
Wagons, Farm	1	1	4
Wall Paper	1	2	3
Washing Machines	1	2	2
Wash Stands	1	1	2
Wheelbarrows	2	1	3
Wheels, Wagon or Buggy	1	1	2
Wheels, Wagon or Buggy, Unfinished	1	1	3
Wind Mills	2	3	3
Window Screens	1	1	1
Wine	1	1	1
Wire Fencing	3	4	5
Wire Rope	3	3	5
White Lead	4	4	4
Woodenware	2	1	3
Wringers	2	2	2

WHAT OUR BANKERS SAY.

№ 3179.

E. G. Keith, President
Wm. J. Watson, Vice President.

Capital $2,000,000.
Surplus $1,000,000.

H. H. Hitchcock, Cashier
Edward Dickinson, Asst. Cashier

The Metropolitan National Bank
OF CHICAGO.

October 24, 1901.

TO WHOM IT MAY CONCERN:

We take pleasure in testifying to the responsibility of Sears, Roebuck & Company, of this city, who are incorporated under the laws of the State of Illinois and have a fully paid up capital and surplus of over $2,000,000. They are one of the leading business houses of our city, occupying commodious quarters and employing in the neighborhood of three thousand people. The officers and stockholders of the company are well and favorably known to us, command our full confidence, and we believe will carry out in a satisfactory manner any engagements made by them.

We commend them to the business public, feeling sure that any dealings with the company will be of an entirely satisfactory nature.

Yours very truly,

H. H. Hitchcock

ERNEST A. HAMILL, PRESIDENT
CHARLES L. HUTCHINSON, VICE PRESIDENT
D. A. MOULTON, VICE PRESIDENT
ROBERT M. ORR, VICE PRESIDENT

FRANK W. SMITH, CASHIER
B. C. SAMMONS, ASS'T CASHIER
J. EDWARD MAASS, ASS'T CASHIER

NO. 5106

THE CORN EXCHANGE NATIONAL BANK
OF CHICAGO.

CAPITAL $2,000,000.
SURPLUS $1,000,000.

October 30th, 1901.

To Whom It May Concern:

We take pleasure in recommending Messrs. Sears, Roebuck & Company, of Chicago. The firm has a paid up capital and surplus of over Two Million Dollars and enjoys the highest credit with its Chicago Banks, of which this bank is one. We do not hesitate to state our good opinion of the house and its officers, and feel sure that it is worthy the confidence of the public.

Very truly yours,

Frank W. Smith
Cashier.

In writing to either of the above Banks as to our reliability, be sure to enclose a 2-cent stamp for reply.

WE REFER CUSTOMERS IN FOREIGN COUNTRIES TO THE FOLLOWING WELL KNOWN BANKING AND OTHER FINANCIAL INSTITUTIONS:

ANTWERP, BELGIUM,
R. Berns.
BANGKOK, SIAM,
Windsor & Co.
BERLIN, GERMANY,
Dresdner Bank.
BOMBAY, INDIA,
Latham & Co.
BUENOS AYRES, ARGENTINE REPUBLIC,
London and Brazilian Bank.
CAIRO, EGYPT,
E. Raiss & Co.
CAPE TOWN, SOUTH AFRICA,
Standard Bank of South Africa.
CHRISTCHURCH, NEW ZEALAND,
J. M. Heywood & Co.
CHRISTIANA, NORWAY,
H. Heitmann & Son.
Messrs. Tho. Joh. Hoftye & Son.
COPENHAGEN, DENMARK,
Ove Haugsted.
Private Bank of Copenhagen.
EAST LONDON, SOUTH AFRICA,
Angus W. Newman.
GENOA, ITALY,
Russian Bank for Foreign Trade.
HAMBURG, GERMANY,
Dresdner Bank.
Wulkow & Cornelsen.
HOBART,
A. F. Strutt & Co.
HONG KONG, CHINA,
MacEwen, Frickel & Co.
HONOLULU, HAWAIIAN ISLANDS,
Bishop & Company.
JOHANNESBURG, SOUTH AFRICA,
Peycke & Son.
Standard Bank of South Africa.
KOBE, JAPAN,
A. Cameron & Co.
T. A. Christenson & Co.
LISBON, PORTUGAL,
London and Brazilian Bank.
LIVERPOOL, ENGLAND,
G. W. Wheatley & Co.
LONDON, ENGLAND,
G. W. Wheatley & Co.
Union Bank of London, (Limited).
MADRAS, INDIA,
Oakes & Co.
MELBOURNE, AUSTRALIA,
Bank of New Zealand.
MEXICO CITY, MEXICO,
Bank of London and Mexico.
NAGASAKI, JAPAN,
Holme, Ringer & Co.
ODESSA, RUSSIA,
Russian Bank for Foreign Trade.
PARIS, FRANCE,
G. W. Wheatley & Co.
Munroe & Company.
RIO JANEIRO, BRAZIL,
London and Brazilian Bank.
ROTTERDAM, HOLLAND,
Rotterdamsche Bank.
SHANGHAI, CHINA,
Lane, Crawford & Co.
SIDNEY, NEW SOUTH WALES,
Duguid & Co.
SINGAPORE, INDIA,
T. Gosling & Co.
STOCKHOLM, SWEDEN,
Sundsvalls Enskilda Bank.
ST. PETERSBURG, RUSSIA,
Russian Bank for Foreign Trade.
VERA CRUZ, MEXICO,
Bank of London and Mexico.
VIENNA, AUSTRIA,
Kais. Kon. Priv. Oesterreichische Landerbank.
WELLINGTON, AUSTRALIA,
Bank of New Zealand.
WELLINGTON, NEW ZEALAND,
South British Forwarding Com'y.

The National City Bank of New York.

CAPITAL FULLY PAID, $ 10,000,000
SHAREHOLDERS' LIABILITY, $ 10,000,000
SURPLUS & UNDIVIDED PROFITS $ 5 700,000
CABLE ADDRESS "CITIBANK"

New York

We also refer by special permission to the largest bank in the United States, The National City Bank of New York, with a capital and surplus of Fifteen Million, Seven Hundred Thousand Dollars.

THIS IS AN EXACT COPY OF AN ORDER WRITTEN ON OUR REGULAR ORDER BLANK.

A CAREFUL STUDY OF EACH POINT WILL AID YOU IN MAKING YOUR OWN ORDER.

A2929

ORDER BLANK OF SEARS ROEBUCK AND CO

73-87 N. Desplaines St.
74-88 N. Jefferson St.
68-96 Fulton St.
1-31 Wayman St.
CHICAGO, ILL.

OUR ONLY TERMS ARE CASH WITH THE ORDER. WE GUARANTEE ENTIRE SATISFACTION OR IMMEDIATELY RETURN YOUR MONEY. WE DO NOT ACCEPT ORDERS FOR LESS THAN 50 CENTS. OUR REASONS ARE EXPLAINED IN THE INTRODUCTORY PAGES OF OUR LARGE CATALOGUE.

HOW TO ORDER.

NOTICE TO CUSTOMERS. { Don't fail to read the instructions on this blank before ordering, as a careful observance of our rules will greatly aid us in filling your orders in a satisfactory manner, AND BE SURE TO MENTION, IN SPACE PROVIDED BELOW, THE NUMBER OF CATALOGUE, CIRCULAR, OR NAME OF PAPER FROM WHICH YOU SELECT YOUR GOODS.

PLEASE SEND TO June 3 1902 (Date of this order.)

NAME William Johnson (Write very plainly and always sign your full christian name.)

POSTOFFICE Fort Niobrara

STREET AND NUMBER

COUNTY Cherry STATE Nebr.

BELOW GIVE SHIPPING POINT IF DIFFERENT FROM POSTOFFICE.

NAME (Give name here only when shipment is to be made to another party. If to yourself, leave name blank.)

SHIPPING POINT Valentine

COUNTY Cherry STATE Nebr

RAILROAD CO. F. E. & M. V. EXPRESS CO.

If you will leave method of shipment to our judgment we will ship to best advantage and by cheapest way possible. However if you prefer to state how you want goods shipped put an X in proper space below. READ OUR RULES on pages 1 to 5 of our large catalogue.

FREIGHT	X
EXPRESS	
SPEC'L PREPAID EXPRESS	
INSURED MAIL	
REGISTERED MAIL	

TO INSURE SAFETY, ALWAYS REGISTER A LETTER CONTAINING CURRENCY.

Be sure to state *how much* cash you enclose and in *what form*, by filling in proper spaces below.

ENCLOSED FIND	DOLLARS	CENTS
Draft or Check		
Postoffice Order	10	11
Express Money Order		
S., R. & Co.'s Check		
S., R. & Co.'s Credit Draft	1	60
Currency		
Postage Stamps (In amounts exceeding $1.00 we accept postage stamps only at a discount of 5 per cent, or at 95 cents on the dollar, as explained in our large catalogue, page 3, paragraph G.)		
TOTAL	11	71

Is there a Freight Agent at Your Shipping Point? Yes (State Yes or No)

If there is no freight agent at your shipping point, you must send extra money enough to prepay freight charges. When too much money is sent we always refund the balance. See Paragraph K.

ORDERS TO BE SENT BY MAIL MUST BE ACCOMPANIED BY CASH IN FULL, WITH EXTRA FOR POSTAGE AND INSURANCE.

AFTER WRITING YOUR ORDER, CHECK IT OVER CLOSELY TO SEE THAT YOU HAVE WRITTEN DOWN CORRECT CATALOGUE NUMBERS, QUANTITIES, NAME OF ARTICLES WANTED AND CORRECT PRICES.

WHEN ORDERING GOODS, ALWAYS GIVE SIZE, COLORS, ETC., TO AVOID ERRORS AND LOSS OF TIME.

OUR STOCK IS ARRANGED IN THE SAME ORDER AS OUR CATALOGUE QUOTATIONS. PATRONS WILL THEREFORE GREATLY FACILITATE THE HANDLING OF ORDERS BY TRYING, AS FAR AS POSSIBLE, TO ARRANGE THE ARTICLES ORDERED AS THEY ARE IN THE CATALOGUE, OR AT LEAST TO COLLECT ALL GOODS OF A CLASS TOGETHER.

THESE GOODS ARE SELECTED FROM CATALOGUE NUMBER OR NAME 111 CIRCULAR PAPER

Number of article in Catalogue.	Quantity desired.	NAME OF ARTICLES WANTED	Sizes, Colors, etc.	Price of each, or per dozen: Dollars	Cents	Extend totals here and then add this column: Dollars	Cents
3R394	1	Book Modern Blacksmithing			68		68
4R2114	1	Goldfilled Bracelet		2	00	2	00
6R401	1	Long Range Winner gun 12 gauge 30 in.		3	98	3	98
7R117	10	pounds Spcl Grade Roasted Coffee		—		2	10
7R1751	100	Bars SR & Co's Family Laundry Soap		—		2	95
						11	71
		This is only a fac-simile order					

NOTE. IF ANY OF ABOVE GOODS ARE OUT OF STOCK MAY WE SUBSTITUTE? Yes

IF SO KINDLY MENTION SECOND AND THIRD CHOICE Use your best judgment

SEE OTHER SIDE OF THIS ORDER BLANK FOR INSTRUCTIONS ON HOW TO TAKE MEASUREMENTS OF EVERY LINE OF WEARING APPAREL.

If You Do Not Use This Order Blank at Once, Preserve it for Future Use, *AS WE CAN FILL ORDERS* better and quicker if written on our regular order blanks, and they are *MORE CONVENIENT FOR YOU.* *We will be only too glad to send you a new supply when these are gone, if you will drop us a postal card, or will include them in your next order.*

NOTE THAT CATALOGUE NUMBER IS WRITTEN OUT IN FULL. DO NOT FAIL TO WRITE EVERY LETTER AND FIGURE IN THE CATALOGUE NUMBER.

SEND FOR OUR Grocery Price List.

FOR ONLY 15 CENTS (stamps taken), we mail our big 32-page price list (issued every two months), for one year to any address. We revise our Grocery Price List every two months to follow the lowest Chicago wholesale prices, and to give our customers the benefit of the very lowest prices at which the highest grade goods can be bought for at wholesale. Prices of groceries are always fluctuating so rapidly, many articles advancing and declining from month to month, that it is impossible to quote our complete line of groceries in this, our general catalogue, which holds good for one year; but we ask all who want our complete list with the **LATEST WHOLESALE MARKET QUOTATIONS**, to send us 15 cents in stamps and let us send them our Grocery Price List, revised every two months, for the entire year. **Our Grocery Price List will keep you posted on the LOWEST CHICAGO WHOLESALE PRICES on everything in groceries, will show you exactly how much your local grocer has to pay for everything he buys and will show you how you can save from $1.00 to $5.00 on nearly every bill of groceries you buy, depending upon the amount, and from $50.00 to $100.00 a year on all the groceries you use.**

We quote on the following pages the most staple articles in groceries, which we invite you to include in making up your order for other merchandise, especially if your order is small and you want to make it large enough to make it a freight order and thus get the benefit of the lowest cost of transportation.

WHY WE MAKE A SMALL CHARGE FOR OUR GROCERY PRICE LIST.

THE EXTREMELY LOW PRICES at which we quote everything in the grocery line, prices that are always as low as the lowest Chicago wholesale prices, and on some goods even less than wholesale, are figured so close that we have found it necessary to cut out and eliminate every unnecessary expense. Our large 32-page Grocery Price List which we issue every two months, is a book that costs us nearly 8 cents to print and mail, and if we sent hundreds of thousands of them out free of charge, many of them to curious people who have no intention of buying, it would mean a big expense to us that we would be compelled to add to our selling prices. In other words, to maintain our extremely close prices, **in order to sell on this very narrow margin of profit, we cannot afford the extra expense of printing and mailing thousands of free catalogues, a large percentage of which do not do us any good.** We make this charge of 15 cents solely in the interests of our customers, simply to protect them on prices. We do not think it is fair to raise our prices and make our customers pay a certain percentage more for their groceries simply to pay for the free catalogues sent to curious people. Of course we could do as many other mail order houses do, **we could send out free catalogues and figure the expense of these catalogues in making our selling prices.**

These are only a few items from the different lines in our Grocery Department.
EVERY LINE OF GOODS IS COMPLETE IN THE 32-PAGE SPECIAL GROCERY CATALOGUE
WHICH COSTS 15 CENTS A YEAR.

IF YOU SEND US AN ORDER FOR GROCERIES and find that you save from $1.00 to $5.00 on the single order, depending upon the amount of the bill, the few cents we ask to cover the expense of the price list amounts to nothing as compared to the $1.00 to $5.00 saved on the groceries. **You can save $50.00 to $100.00 a year by sending to us for your groceries,** as we quote prices on the very highest grade of groceries against which no house can possibly compete. **Don't fail to send us 15 cents** (stamps taken) **together with your name and address and receive our Grocery Price List for a full year.** If you do not care to send us 15 cents send us 3 cents for a sample copy. You can then compare our prices on all groceries with the prices named by your local dealer or by any other mail order house; and you will find a big difference in our favor.

LOOK OVER THE FOLLOWING PAGES CAREFULLY, make up and send us a trial order for groceries. We will surprise you with the astonishingly fine quality goods we furnish and the money we can save you. When you order other merchandise from this catalogue, include what you need in groceries and get the benefit of lowest freight rates.

ABOUT THESE PRICES. There may be a slight variation in the market on these goods at the time your order is received, but we will give you the benefit of the lowest wholesale Chicago market price on that day. We make this plain, for we must protect ourselves against advances; but we also protect our customers. In case of a decline, we refund the difference in cash without notice.

TEA.

	By the chest, per lb.	20-lb. caddy, per lb.	10-lb. caddy, per lb.	Less than 10 pounds, per lb.
Japan—Sun Dried (Uncolored).				
No. 7R12 Extra choicest	40c	42c	44c	46c
No. 7R13 Extra choice selected leaf	37c	39c	41c	43c
No. 7R14 Choice	33c	35c	37c	39c
No. 7R15 Bargain	31c	33c	35c	37c
JAPAN BASKET FIRED, BLACK.				
No. 7R20 Extra choicest	46c	48c	50c	52c
No. 7R21 Extra choice	39c	41c	43c	45c
No. 7R22 Choice	37c	39c	41c	43c
No. 7R23 Bargain	35c	37c	39c	41c
Japan—Siftings.				
No. 7R30 Best grade	20c	22c	23c	24c
No. 7R31 Best grade Japan dust	19c	21c	22c	23c
New Tea Siftings.				
No. 7R34 Extra choicest siftings. 1-pound air-tight packages. 80 lbs. in chest	22c	22c	23c	24c
Gunpowder—Moyune.				
No. 7R38 Extra choicest	46c	48c	50c	52c
No. 7R39 Extra choice	38c	40c	42c	44c
No. 7R40 Choice	36c	38c	40c	42c
No. 7R41 Good	31c	33c	35c	37c
Imperial Green.				
No. 7R45 Extra choicest	35c	37c	39c	41c
YOUNG HYSON—MOYUNE.				
No. 7R50 Extra choicest	48c	50c	52c	54c
No. 7R51 Extra choice	37c	39c	41c	43c
No. 7R52 Choice	32c	34c	36c	38c
No. 7R53 Good	29c	31c	33c	35c
Green Japan.				
No. 7R55 Extra choicest	45c	47c	49c	51c
No. 7R56 Extra choice	41c	43c	45c	47c
No. 7R57 Choice	31c	33c	35c	37c
Oolong—Formosa.				
No. 7R60 Extra choice	43c	45c	47c	49c
No. 7R61 Choice	38c	40c	42c	44c
No. 7R62 Good	35c	37c	39c	41c
No. 7R63 Very fair quality	33c	35c	37c	39c
English Breakfast—Moning Congou.				
No. 7R68 Extra choicest	47c	49c	51c	53c
No. 7R69 Choicest	45c	47c	49c	51c
No. 7R70 Choice	38c	40c	42c	44c
No. 7R71 Good	32c	34c	36c	38c

We quote a more complete line of teas in our Special Grocery Catalogue. Send 15 cents for a year's subscription.

Our $3.75 Tea Offer.

For $3.75 we furnish 10 pounds of our own specially selected high grade tea in a 10-pound tin canister.

Be sure to state the kind of tea wanted.

No. 7R5 Our special price for 10-lb. canister...$3.75

Our $2.00 Tea Offer.

For $2.00 we furnish 5 pounds of our own specially selected high grade tea in a 5-pound tin canister. Be sure to state the kind of tea wanted

No. 7R6 Our special price for 5-pound canister.......$2.00

A full line of green coffee listed in our special grocery list.

Coffees—Roasted.

	10 lbs. and up, per lb.	Per lb.
No. 7R100 Mocha, genuine	$0.23	$0.24
No. 7R101 Peaberry extra Mocha	.19	.20
No. 7R102 Mandahling Java	.27	.28
No. 7R103 Old Government Java	.26	.27
No. 7R104 African Java	.20	.21
No. 7R105 Mocha and Java Blend	.22	.23
No. 7R106 Golden Santos, extra	.18	.19
No. 7R107 Choice Santos	.15	.16
No. 7R108 Our Special Blend	.18	.19
No. 7R109 Select Rio	.13	.14
No. 7R110 Santos and Rio	.10½	.11½
No. 7R115 Peaberry	.17	.18

No. 7R117 **For $2.10 we will furnish 10 pounds of this our own special grade of roasted coffee,** complete with large enameled covered 10-pound tin canister. Price for 10-pound can........$2.10

No. 7R118 **For $1.10 we will furnish 5 lbs. of this our own special grade of roasted coffee,** complete with large enameled covered 5-lb. tin canister. Price........$1.10

Crushed Java Coffee Compound.

No. 7R140 **Java Coffee Compound;** crushed excellent favored drink. Drums of 100 pounds, per pound, 12½c; drums of 50 pounds, per pound, 13c; less than 50 pounds, per pound........14c

Cereal Coffees.

No. 7R144 **Postum Cereal,** 1 dozen 20-ounce packages, in case. Per case, $2.25; per package........21c

No. 7R145 **Caramel Cereal,** 25 1-pound packages in case. Per case, $3.05; per package........14c

Chicory and Coffee Essence.

No. 7R146 **Chicory,** five papers to pound, per pound........5c

Full case, 65 pounds, per pound........4¼c

No. 7R147 **English Chicory,** bulk, per pound..6c

50-pound drum, per pound........5½c

No. 7R148 **Coffee Essence,** Hummel's, in tin cans, 6 dozen in a box, per box........$1.40

Per dozen, 25c; each........2½c

Cocoa.

	Full box. Per lb.	Less than full box. Per tin
No. 7R149 **Wilbur's Breakfast,** ½-pound tins, 6 pounds in box	$0.42	$0.23
No. 7R151 **Baker's Breakfast,** ½-pound tins, 6 pounds in box	.45	.24
No. 7R153 **Epps' Homeopathic,** ½-pound tins, 7 pounds in box	.40	.21
No. 7R155 **Van Houten's,** ½-pound tins, 12 pounds in case	.88	.45
No. 7R156 **Van Houten's,** 1-pound tins, 12 pounds in case	.78	.80
No. 7R157 **Colonial,** ½-pound tins, 6 pounds in case	.40	.21

Cocoa Shells.

No. 7R163 **Sears, Roebuck & Co.'s.** Finest quality. 1-pound package........7c

Chocolate.

12-pound Boxes.

	Box. Per lb.	Per lb.
No. 7R169 **Sears, Roebuck & Co.'s Acme Premium Chocolate**	$0.29	$0.30
No. 7R170 **Wilbur's Premium**	.32	.34
No. 7R171 **Paramount, Vanilla,** sweet, ½-pound	.30	.31
No. 7R172 **Crescent Sweet,** 5 cakes to pound	.20	.22
No. 7R174 **German Sweet,** ¼-pound packages	.21	.23
No. 7R175 **Baker's Premium**	.29½	.32
No. 7R176 **Baker's,** 10-lb. cakes, for bakers' use. (We do not sell less than 10-pound cakes)		.24
No. 7R177 **Royal Sweet Chocolate,** ¼-pound packages	.20	.22

Cocoanut.

No. 7R180 Price, for 1-pound package........21c

MOLASSES—Continued from preceding page.

Doris New Orleans Molasses.

For Cooking and Baking.

This is a prime, new, open kettle, full grain, extra stock molasses. We guarantee this grade to give satisfaction in all cases.

No. 7R1415 50-gallon barrels, per gallon...$0.28
30-gallon ½-barrels, per gallon... .30
10-gallon jacket can, per can... 3.50
5-gallon jacket can, per can... 1.85
2½-gallon jacket can, per can... 1.10
1-gallon tin can, each... .45

Seroco Fancy New Orleans Molasses.

For Cooking and Baking.

We offer our Extra Fancy New Orleans Molasses, the best on the market, heaviest weight, fullest stock, at the following special low prices:

No. 7R1416 50-gallon barrels, per gallon....$0.39
30-gallon ½-barrels, per gallon... .41
10-gallon jacket cans, per can... 4.60
5-gallon jacket cans, per can... 2.40
2½-gallon jacket cans, per can... 1.25
1-gallon tin can, each... .54

Maple Syrup.

We guarantee our Maple Syrup to be absolutely pure.

No. 7R1420 Pure New Hampshire Maple Syrup. 50-gallon barrel, per gallon...$0.92
30-gallon ½-barrel, per gallon. .94
10-gallon jacket can, per can.. 9.90
5-gallon jacket can, per can.. 5.05
1-gallon tins, each... 1.10
½-gallon tins, each... .60
Quart tins, each... .32

Pure Ohio Maple Syrup.

No. 7R1429 10-gallon jacket cans...$8.50
5-gallon jacket cans... 4.75
1-gallon tins... .95
½-gallon tins... .55

Maple Syrup, in Bottles.

No. 7R1432 Quarts, handsome bottle, extra fine goods. Per dozen bottles...$3.75
Per bottle... .35

Honey.

No. 7R1435 Pure White Clover Honey, Strained. 1-gallon cans, ½ dozen in case. Per dozen...$15.50
Each... 1.35

Extracted Honey.

No. 7R1437 Glass Tumblers, not pure, 1-pound each... Doz. $1.00 Each $0.09
No. 7R1438 Glass Jars, pure, 1-pound each... 2.0_ .20

Cheese.

In our Special Grocery List we list a full and complete line of Domestic and Imported Cheese.

Seroco Brand Full Cream Cheese.

No. 7R1440 The illustration gives you an idea of the appearance of this cheese. The cakes are 10 inches square by 2¼ inches deep, each one has 10 creases, marking it off into 10 1-pound sections. Guaranteed absolutely full cream and the very best obtainable. We do not sell less than one 10-pound cheese.

Price, per 10-pound cheese...$1.50

No. 7R1443 Young America, full cream, about 10 pounds each. Per pound... 12c

CRACKERS.

We list a most complete line of crackers and bakery goods in our Special Grocery List. Send 15 cents for a years' subscription.

20-Pound Box of Crackers, 99 Cents.

As a special, we are offering the finest butter, soda and oyster crackers on the market, in 20-pound wooden boxes, at 99 cents, the same class of goods that dealers sell at 10 cents per pound.

No. 7R1460 Price, for 20-lb. box Soda Biscuits, 99c
Price, for 20-lb. box Oyster Biscuits... 99c
Price, for 20-lb. box Butter Biscuits... 99c

CANDY.

Send for our Special Grocery List, in which we list a full line of candy of every description.

No. 7R1550 Chicago Mixed Candy.
Price per 30-pound pail...$2.25
Price, per 5-pound box... .40

No. 7R1551 Columbia Mixed Candy.
Price, per 30-pound pail... 2.95
Price, per 5-pound box... .55
Price, per 2-pound box... .28

No. 7R1552 Kindergarten Mixed Candy.
Price, per 30-pound pail... 2.85
Price, per 5-pound box... .53
Price, per 2-pound box... .25

No. 7R1553 Gum Drops.
Price, per 30-pound pail... 1.75
Price, per 5-pound box... .32

No. 7R1554 Licorice Gum Drops.
Price, per 30-pound pail... 3.00
Price, per 5-pound box... .55

No. 7R1555 French Mixed Candy.
Price, per 30-pound pail... 4.60
Price, per 5-pound box... .85
Price, per 2-pound box... .38
Price, per 1-pound box... .20

See next column.

CANDY—(Continued).

Clear Goods and Cut Goods.		5-pound box
No. 7R1556	Sour Balls	$0.52
No. 7R1557	Lemon Drops	.52
No. 7R1558	Moss Squares	.52
No. 7R1559	Horehound Squares	.52
No. 7R1560	Lemon Squares	.52
No. 7R1561	Jackson Balls	.59
No. 7R1562	Lady Kisses	.52
No. 7R1563	Mint Kisses	.52
No. 7R1564	Lemon Kisses	.52
No. 7R1565	Molasses Mint Kisses	.52
No. 7R1566	Fruit Drops	.52
No. 7R1567	Rock and Rye Drops	.52
No. 7R1568	Fruit Squares	.52
No. 7R1569	Mint Balls	.52
No. 7R1570	Cinnamon Balls	.59
No. 7R1571	Wine Balls	.59
No. 7R1572	Gooseberries	.59
No. 7R1573	Chicago Marbles	.59

We do not sell less than a full box of above.

No. 7R1574 Ambrosia Delicious Chocolate Creams and Bonbons. Price, per 5-pound box, $1.75
Price, per 2-pound box... .75
Price, per 1-pound box... .39

No. 7R1575 Ambrosia Molasses Golf Chips.
Price, per 5-pound box...$1.35
Price, per 2-pound box... .60
Price, per 1-pound box... .33

No. 7R1576 Fancy Opera Mixed.
Price, per 5-pound box... 1.75
Price, per 2-pound box... .75
Price, per 1-pound box... .39

No. 7R1577 Chocolate Ice Cream Bars.
Price, per box of 100 bars... .69

No. 7R1578 Chocolate Creams.
Price, per 5-pound box (no less sold)... .73

No. 7R1579 Java Chocolate Creams, assorted flavors. Price, per 5-pound box... 98c
Price, per 2-pound box... 55c
Price, per 1-pound box... 29c

No. 7R1580 Fancy Caramels.
Price, per 5-pound box, assorted... 60c
Price, per 2½-pound box, one flavor only... 40c

No. 7R1585 Great Drive in Fancy Stick Candy.
Price, per 30-pound pail, per pound... 8½c
Price, 3-pound box for... 30c

No. 7R1591 French Mottoes.
Price, per 5-pound box... 79c

No. 7R1592 Ice Cream Drops.
Price, per 5-pound box... 64c

No. 7R1593 Marshmallows.
Price, per 5-pound box... 67c

No. 7R1594 Cream Wafers.
Price, per box containing 100 wafers... 69c

No. 7R1595 Old Fashioned Arabian Gum Drops.
Price, per 5-pound box... 64c

No. 7R1596 Cranberry Dips.
Price, per 5-pound box... 63c

No. 7R1597 Royal Creams.
Price, per 5-pound box, assorted only... 63c

No. 7R1598 Chocolate Bars.
Price per box of 100 bars, assorted flavors... 64c

No. 7R1602 Marshmallow Bananas.
Price, per box, about 5 pounds... 64c

No. 7R1610 American Mint Lozenges, white.
Price, per 5-pound box... 59c

No. 7R1611 Wintergreen Lozenges, pink and white. Price, per 5-pound box... 59c

No. 7R1612 Conversation Lozenges, assorted.
Price, per 5-pound box... 64c

No. 7R1620 Rock Candy, white, best quality.
Price, per 5-pound box... 59c

No. 7R1622 Rock Candy, assorted colors.
Price, per 5-pound box... 59c

No. 7R1625 Japanese Cocoanut.
Price, per box containing 100 strips... 54c

No. 7R1635 Cream Dips, assorted flavors.
Price, per 5-pound box... 69c

No. 7R1636 Assorted Bonbons.
Price, per 5-pound box...$1.10

No. 7R1661 Maple Creams.
Price, per 5-pound box... 59c

No. 7R1665 Strawberry Creams.
Price, per 5-pound box... 59c

No. 7R1670 Flippi Cream Almonds. This is a popular candy, a little larger than a pecan nut, almond center with a heavy coat of pure sugar flavored with vanilla. Price, per 5-pound box... 75c

No. 7R1675 Spanish Peanut Stick.
Price, per box of 100 bars... 64c

No. 7R1676 Jelly Squares, crystallized.
Price, per 5-pound box... 59c

No. 7R1677 Jelly Fruit Beans. Price, per 5-pound box... 50c

Shelled Nuts.

No. 7R1678 Almonds, Jordan, shelled.
Price, 5-pound box, per pound... 47c
Price, less quantities, per pound... 49c

No. 7R1679 Almonds, Taragona, shelled.
Price, 5-pound box... 35c
Price, less quantities, per pound... 37c

No. 7R1680 Peanuts, Spanish, shelled, green.
Price, 100-pound box, per pound... 7½c
Price, less quantities, per pound... 8½c

No. 7R1681 Peanuts, shelled and salted, guaranteed fresh roasted.
Price, 50-pound box, per pound... 9¼c
Price, per 5-pound box,... 50c
Price, per 2-pound box... 22c

REMEMBER . .

Our lines of GROCERIES are complete in our big 32-page GROCERY PRICE LIST, revised and issued every 60 days. Send 15 cents for a year's subscription to this Price List and

SAVE MONEY ON YOUR GROCERY PURCHASES.

Nuts.

No. 7R1684 Almonds, Taragona soft shell.
Price, 50-lb. box, per lb... 16c
Less quantities, per lb... 17c

No. 7R1685 Almonds, California, paper shell.
Price, 50-lb. box, per lb... 17c
Less quantities, per lb... 18c

No. 7R1686 Brazils, or Cream Nuts.
Price, 50-lb. box, per lb... 14c
Less quantities, per lb... 15c

No. 7R1690 Filberts, new crop.
Price, 50-lb. box, per lb... 13c
Price, less quantities, per pound... 14c

No. 7R1691 Walnuts, California, soft shell, new crop. Price, 50-pound box, per pound... 14c
Price, less quantities, per pound... 15c

No. 7R1692 Walnuts, California, hard shell, new crop. Price, 50-pound box, per pound... 12c
Price, less quantities, per pound... 13c

No. 7R1693 Pecans, new crop.
Price, 50-pound box, per pound... 12c
Price, less quantities, per pound... 13c

No. 7R1694 Peanuts, No. 1 green, Virginia.
Price, 50-pound box, per pound... 6c
Price, less quantities, per pound... 7c

No. 7R1695 Peanuts, No. 1 roasted, Virginia.
Price, 50-pound box, per pound... 7c
Price, less quantities, per pound... 8c

Mixed Nuts.

No. 7R1696 Mixed Nuts, fine selection, new crop.
Price, 50-pound box, per pound... 13c
Price, less quantities, per pound... 14c

No. 7R1697 Mixed Nuts, S., R. & Co.'s Christmas brand, new crop and a fine selection, put up in 5-pound cartons, including a polished nutcracker.
Price, per 5-pound box... 75c

Chewing Gum.

We do not sell less than full box.

No. 7R1699 Adams' Black Jack Gum, 5 sticks in package, 20 packages in box. Price, per box... 55c

No. 7R1700 Adams' New York Rubber Gum, 400 pieces in a box. Price, per box... 59c

No. 7R1701 Adams' Pepsin Tutti Frutti Gum, 5 squares to the bar, 2 bars to the package, 20 packages to the box. Price, per box... 59c

No. 7R1703 Beeman's Pepsin Gum, 5 pieces to package, 20 packages to box. Price, per box... 62c

No. 7R1704 Yankee Spruce Gum, 5 pieces to package, 20 packages to box. Price, per box... 60c

No. 7R1706 White's Yucatan Gum, 5 pieces to package, 20 packages to box. Price, per box... 55c

No. 7R1707 Ripe Fruit Gum, 20 5-cent packages in box. Price, per box... 55c

No. 7R1708 Primley's California Fruit, 20 5-cent packages in box. Price, per box... 59c

No. 7R1709 Kiss Me Gum, 20 5-cent packages in box. Price, per box... 55

If by mail, postage extra, per box, 15 cents.

Cracker Jack.

No. 7R1710 Price, per case of 24 packages..$0.82
Price, per case of 50 packages... 1.55
Price, per case of 100 packages... 2.85

We do not break cases.

LAUNDRY SOAPS.

Sears, Roebuck & Co.'s Celebrated Family Laundry Soap.

For only $2.95 for a box of 100 bars, a little less than 3 cents a bar, we offer our celebrated Sears, Roebuck & Co.'s Family Laundry Soap as the equal of laundry soaps that sell everywhere at 5 cents a bar, and even more. At our $2.95 price per box of 100 bars we feel confident we are giving such value in laundry soap as is offered by no other house.

Our special family laundry soap is put up for us under contract by one of the best soap manufacturers in Chicago, a manufacturer who sells the same soap under another name at almost double our price. The cost of our family soap is figured on very large quantities, on the basis of the actual cost of the material and the labor, to which we add the narrowest kind of a margin of profit, making our Family Laundry Soap the special leader of our soap department. Our Family Laundry Soap is an extra thick bar, convenient shape, hard pressed and rubbed. It is made of selected material, it is strictly first class in every respect, and there is no ingredient in its manufacture that will harm the most delicate fabric. It is a laundry soap that will help to make the laundry work much lighter. Every bar is put up under our binding guarantee, and if you do not find this soap equal to any soap you can buy from your storekeeper at home at 4, 5 and 6 cents per bar, you can return it to us at our expense and we will refund your money.

At our special $2.95 price for a box of 100 bars, you will make a saving of at least 50 per cent.

No. 7R1751 Our special price, per box of 100 bars...$2.95
Price, for 30 bars... .93
Price, for single bar... .03¼

Soaps continued on next page.

Standard Navy Plug Tobacco.

No. 7R2281 Standard Navy Plug Tobacco. 28-pound butts, per pound........37c
14-pound butts, per pound........37c
Less quantity, 14-ounce plug........35c

Battle Ax Plug.

No. 7R2283 Battle Ax Plug. 28-pound butts, per pound........36c
14-pound butts, per pound........36c
Less quantity, 14-ounce plug........34c

FINE CUT CHEWING TOBACCO.

S., R. & Co.'s Bed Rock.

No. 7R2290 S., R. & Co.'s Bed Rock. Our special price in 10-pound pails, per pound........31c

S., R. & Co.'s Manila Girl.

No. 7R2291 S., R. & Co.'s Manila Girl. Our special price, in 10-pound pails, per pound........35c

S., R. & Co.'s Beats All.

No. 7R2292 S., R. & Co.'s Beats All. Our special price, per pound, in 10-pound pails........39c

S., R. & Co.'s Mayflower.

No. 7R2293 S., R. & Co.'s Mayflower. Our special price, per pound, in 10-pound pails........42c

S., R. & Co.'s Honey Dew.

No. 7R2294 S., R. & Co.'s Honey Dew. Our special price, per pound, in 10-pound pails........44c

S., R. & Co.'s Maple Leaf.

No. 7R2295 S., R. & Co.'s Maple Leaf. Price, per pound, in 10-pound pails........49c

Sweet Burley Fine Cut.

No. 7R2296 Sweet Burley Fine Cut. Price, per pound, in 5-pound pails or 1-pound drums........44c

Sterling Fine Cut.

No. 7R2298 Sterling Fine Cut. Our price, in 10-pound pails, per pound........44c

Big Havana.

No. 7R2307 Big Havana. Price, full case of 10 pounds, per pound........27c
Price, less quantity (six packages), per lb........28c

Smoking Tobacco

Hard Times Smoking.

No. 7R2308 Hard Times Smoking. Price, in full case of 20 pounds, per pound........26c
Price, less quantity, per pound........27c

Valley Smoker.

No. 7R2309 Valley Smoker. Price, in full case, 25 pounds, per pound........25c
Price, less quantity, per pound........26c

Beck's Hunting Smoking Tobacco.

No. 7R2310 Beck's Hunting Smoking Tobacco. Price, per pound, any quantity........36c

THESE PRICES are as low as your local dealer pays when he buys, and we save you all his profit.

Seroco Cigar Clippings.

No. 7R2312 Seroco Cigar Clippings. Price, per pound, any quantity........32c

Sweet Clippings.

No. 7R2313 Sweet Clippings. Price, per pound, any quantity........26c

Sweet Kentucky Smoking.

No. 7R2314 Sweet Kentucky Smoking. Price, per pound, any quantity........25c

Plow Boy Smoking.

No. 7R2316 Plow Boy Smoking. Price, per pound, any quantity........36c

Duke's Mixture.

No. 7R2317 Duke's Mixture. Price, 1⅜-ounce packages, per pound........36c

Briar Pipe Smoking.

No. 7R2318 Briar Pipe Smoking. Per pound, 35c

Corn Cake Smoking.

No. 7R2319 Corn Cake Smoking. Price, per pound (including pipe)........23c

Yum Yum Smoking.

No. 7R2320 Yum Yum Smoking. Per pound, 37c

Fashion Cut Plug Smoking.

No. 7R2323 Fashion Cut Plug Smoking. Price, per pound........37c

Genuine Durham Bull.

No. 7R2330 Genuine Durham Bull.
Price, 1-pound cloth bags, per pound........54c
Price, ½-pound cloth bags, per pound........59c
Price, 3⅓-ounce cloth bags, per pound........61c
Price, 1⅜-ounce cloth bags, per pound........63c
Price, small 5-cent trial packages, each........4c

Seal of North Carolina, Granulated.

No. 7R2335 Seal of North Carolina, Granulated.
Price, 1⅜-ounce cloth bags, per pound........59c
Price, 3⅓-ounce cloth bags, per pound........58c
Price, 8-ounce cloth bags, per pound........54c
Price, 1-pound wood drum........46c

Mail Pouch Smoking.

No. 7R2339 Mail Pouch Smoking. Price, per pound........38c

Sweet Tip Top Smoking.

No. 7R2341 Sweet Tip Top Smoking. Per lb., 36c

Old Tip Top Smoking.

No. 7R2342 Old Tip Top Smoking. Per pound, 34c

Badger Fancy Smoking.

No. 7R2345 Badger Fancy Smoking. Per pound (8 or 16-oz. packages)........31c

Peerless Smoking.

No. 7R2346 Peerless Smoking. It is put up in packages of either 1-lb., ½-lb. or 3⅓-oz., as desired. Per pound........33c

INCLUDE GROCERIES with your order; get the benefit of the freight rates, a cheap means of transportation, and make all the saving that is possible.

Seal of North Carolina Cut Plug.

No. 7R2348 Seal of North Carolina Cut Plug.
16-ounce wood drums, per pound........58c
8 ounce wood drums, per pound........63c
1⅜ or 3⅓-ounce pouches, per pound........67c
1⅜ or 3⅓-ounce foil packages, per pound........67c

Myrtle Navy Cut Plug.

No. 7R2349 Myrtle Navy Cut Plug. 3⅓-ounce pouches, per pound........41c

Golden Sceptre Smoking.

No. 7R2350 Golden Sceptre Smoking. 1-pound tins, per pound........$0.95
½-pound tins, per pound........1.05
3⅓-ounce tins, per pound........1.10
1⅜-ounce tins, per pound........1.20

The Whale.

No. 7R2351 The Whale. Per pound, including pipe........25c

Snuff.

Per lb.
No. 7R2352 Maccaboy, 2, 5 and 10-lb. jars..$0.50
1-pound jars........ .55
No. 7R2353 Rappee, 2, 5 and 10-lb. jars........ .50
1-pound jars........ .55
No. 7R2354 Norrkoping, 2, 5 and 10-lb. jars .50
1-pound jars........ .55
No. 7R2355 Garrett's Scotch Snuff, 1-oz. tins. Per dozen, 70c; each........ .06

W., R. & Co.'s Improved Butter Color.

No. 7R2155 Large, $1.00 size, per bottle........80c
Medium, 50-cent size, per bottle........38c
Small, 25-cent size, per bottle........18c

Butter Paper.

No. 7R2157 Manila Waxed Butter Paper, grease proof. 12x18 inches. Per ream of 480 sheets...39c
9x12 inches, per ream of 480 sheets........14c

Parchment Dairy Paper.

Cut in the sizes as quoted and put up in packages of 1,000 sheets.

No. 7R2159

Size	Price, 1,000 sheets	Price, 5,000 sheet
6x 6	$0.29	$1.40
8x 8	.58	2.83
9x 9	.78	3.74
8x11	.81	3.92
9x12	.88	4.25
10x10	.90	4.30
12x12	1.18	5.60

Kerosene Oil.

No. 30R2490 In full barrels of 52 gallons. Price, per gallon........10½c
No. 30R2491 Price for 10-gallon can, including the can free (can alone costs us 50 cents)........$1.70

S., R. & Co.'s Family Safety Kerosene Oil.

Guaranteed in any state; gives beautiful white light. Finest oil made.
No. 30R2492 Price for barrel, per gallon....11½c
No. 30R2493 Price for 10-gallon can, including the can free (can alone costs us 50 cents)........$1.30

Gasoline.

No. 30R2512 Stove Gasoline, 74 degrees; deodorized, barrels only, per gallon........12c
No. 30R2513 Engine Gasoline, barrels only, per gallon........12c

READY MIXED PAINTS AT THE LOWEST POSSIBLE PRICES.

WE MAKE A SPECIALTY OF READY MIXED PAINTS. Our special prices of 45 to 98 cents a gallon, for ready to use mixed paints, are based on the actual cost of material and labor, with but our one small percentage of profit added. We are selling the very highest grade of ready mixed paints for less money than your dealer pays for his paint when he buys it at wholesale. We have an arrangement with one of the largest makers of best ready mixed paints, a year around contract by which we take practically all the ready mixed paint this factory turns out. We offer it to our customers on the basis of manufacturer's cost, with one narrow percentage of profit added.

OUR QUALITY GUARANTEE. Every gallon of ready mixed paint is put out under our own and the manufacturer's binding guarantee. We guarantee our prepared paint to give better satisfaction as to durability and lasting appearance than any other mixed paint on the market.

YOU CAN SELECT THE COLOR WANTED from the description given here with perfect satisfaction, but if you want to see the exact shade, send us 2 cents for our paint color book. On receipt of a 2-cent stamp, we will mail to anyone our handsome paint color book, showing the actual colors and shades of the different paints we furnish—house, roof, fence, barn, floor, buggy, etc. Our paint color book is handsomely gotten up, showing actual samples of all the different shades of all the different kinds of paint. It is an expensive book to get up and we ask 2 cents from each applicant as an evidence of good faith and to prevent thousands from sending out of mere curiosity, which would mean a big expense to us and which would compel us to add to our selling prices on paint.

YOU CAN SELECT THE COLOR WANTED FROM THE DESCRIPTION GIVEN HERE WITH PERFECT SATISFACTION, BUT IF YOU WANT TO SEE THE EXACT SHADE, SEND US 2 CENTS FOR OUR PAINT COLOR BOOK.

No. 30R2692 **READY MIXED HOUSE PAINTS.** Always order by color number as well as catalogue number. We furnish in the following different colors:

201 French Gray
202 Lavender
203 Straw
204 Pea Green
205 Light Drab
206 Canary
207 Lemont Stone
208 Pearl
209 Beaver
210 Pink
211 Milwaukee Brick
212 Quaker Drab
213 Nile Green
214 OliveDrab
215 Cream
216 Fawn
217 Pure Blue
218 Buff
219 Terra Cotta
220 Apple Green
221 Leather Brown
222 Pure Gray
223 Light Blue
224 Maroon
225 Bronze
226 Willow Green
227 Drab
228 Olive
229 Red
230 Brown
231 French Yellow
232 Myrtle Green
233 Lead
234 Vermilion
235 Light Stone
236 Emerald Green
240 Yellow Stone
242 Light Slate
244 Sky Blue
250 Azure Blue
IW Inside White
OW Outside White
Blk Black

SPECIAL PRICES FOR OUR READY MIXED LIQUID PAINT.

READY MIXED HOUSE PAINTS, ALL COLORS, excepting Nos. 232, 234 and 236.
1-quart cans, each........$0.28
2-quart cans, each........ .53
1-gallon cans, each........ .98
5-gallon buckets, per gallon.. .95
10-gallon kegs, per gallon.....$0.93
25-gallon half barrels; per gallon........ .88
50-gallon barrels, per gallon.. .85

No. 232 Myrtle Green.
Per quart........$0.50
2 quarts........ .95
1 gallon........ 1.80

No. 236 Emerald Green.
Per quart........$0.50
2 quarts........ .95
1 gallon........ 1.80

No. 234 Vermilion.
Per quart........$0.65
2 quarts........ 1.20
1 gallon........ 2.35

ROOF, FENCE AND BARN PAINT AT 45 TO 60c A GALLON.

At 45 to 60 cents a gallon we furnish roof, fence and barn paint in the following colors:

700 Oxide Red, 710 Lead Color, 720 Drab, 730 Yellow, 740 Brown, 750 Maroon,

No. 30R2710 Our special prices as follows: 1-gallon cans, per gallon, 60c; 5-gallon kegs, per gallon, 55c; 25-gallon barrels, per gallon, 50c; 50-gallon barrels, per gallon, 45c.

SEND A 2-CENT STAMP FOR THE HANDSOME COLOR BOOK OF EVERYTHING IN PAINTS IN ACTUAL SAMPLES AND COLORS.
OUR PAINT COLOR BOOK TELLS THE PRICES ON EVERYTHING IN OILS, VARNISHES, PAINT BRUSHES, ETC., SEND 2 CENTS FOR IT.

WATCH, DIAMOND AND JEWELRY DEPARTMENT.

WE CALL SPECIAL ATTENTION to our very complete lines of Watches, Diamonds and Jewelry, goods that will appeal to the most refined taste. There is perhaps no other merchandise in which so much reliance must be placed upon the dealer. Confidence must be had when buying watches and jewelry, and to inspire that degree of confidence in us we guarantee every item as represented or we will cheerfully refund your money.

IN WATCHES ESPECIALLY we acknowledge no competition. Our watch department is the largest and most complete in the world, and our prices by reason of our purchasing power are the lowest of any, quality considered.

SEARS, ROEBUCK & CO.'S Special Watch Movements are the perfection of mechanical skill, made especially for us after our own original design and in such large quantities that we get them at a price which enables us to sell them to you at what other dealers very often ask for cheap and unreliable watches.

WE WANT YOUR ORDERS FOR EVERYTHING IN THE WATCH, DIAMOND AND JEWELRY LINE.

OUR GUARANTEE

With every gold filled, silver or solid gold watch we give a certificate of guarantee. With gold filled watches the certificate guarantees the case to wear and keep its color for two, five, twenty or twenty-five years, and the movement to be an accurate timekeeper for five years. This guarantee is given in addition to the guarantee which is fitted in the back of the watch case. As to the value of our guaranty, we will refer you to the first page of this book under the head of OUR RELIABILITY.

TERMS

Our only terms are cash with the order. While in the interests of economical business methods we require the full amount of cash with the order, as explained in the introductory pages of this catalogue, we stand ready to immediately refund the money including transportation charges for anything that does not prove entirely satisfactory and fully as represented. You run no risk whatever in sending cash with your order.

OUR PRICES

In Watches and Jewelry we buy EVERYTHING direct from the manufacturers in large quantities for spot cash. As we sell for cash, having no bad debts, we are satisfied to sell at prices which the retailer pays, and, on a large per cent of goods, for much less money.

MAIL SHIPMENTS

We recommend sending Jewelry, Watches, etc., by mail, as it is perfectly safe and far the cheapest. Postage is 1 cent per ounce. A watch packed for shipment weighs from 6 to 8 ounces; chains, rings and other small articles of jewelry about 2 ounces. Packages amounting to $1.00 or over should be registered, which costs 8 cents extra. We guarantee the safe delivery of all registered mail packages. Be sure to send enough for postage, and if any balance remains we will return it to you.

ENGRAVING

We charge for engraving in script on jewelry, watches, etc., 2½ cents per letter; in old English, small, 5 cents per letter; small script monograms on jewelry, etc., from 25 to 75 cents. In writing orders when goods are to be engraved, write or draw plain letters, so as to avoid mistakes. We cannot exchange goods after they have been engraved.

REGARDING ENGRAVINGS ON WATCH CASES

It sometimes happens that we are out of the exact engraving on watch case ordered, but we aim to carry exact designs. When the exact engraving cannot be had, we always have a very similar one, which we will take the liberty of sending rather than delay your order. **It being understood, you can return same if not perfectly satisfied.**

WATCH REPAIRING

We have a thoroughly equipped mechanical department, which is fitted with all of the latest tools and appliances for the repairing of all kinds of watches. We have a large force of thoroughly skilled watchmakers under the supervision of a very competent foreman, and any watch sent to us for repairs will receive very careful and prompt attention. We do not solicit for watch repair work, but are willing to accommodate our customers who wish to have work done in a thoroughly first class manner. Our charges are about one-half what is usually charged by the retail dealers, but the work will be done in a very superior manner. We cannot give an accurate estimate of the cost of repairs without a thorough examination. Our charges are merely enough to cover cost of manufacture and labor. None but a thoroughly competent watchmaker should ever take a watch to pieces, for the chances are that he will ruin it.

YOU CAN MAKE MONEY SELLING WATCHES, ETC.

For when you can buy them for the same, or less money than the retail dealer who sells on from 30 to 100 per cent profit and has large expenses in the way of rent, clerk hire, fuel, light, etc., you can readily see that you could undersell him and still make a handsome profit for yourself.

DESCRIPTION OF THE MOVEMENTS WE LIST.

TO SAVE SPACE BY AVOIDING REPETITION WE have adopted the following as the best method of describing movements.

18-Size Elgin, Waltham and Hampden Movements.

THE SETH THOMAS MOVEMENTS. Nickel damaskeened. Seven jeweled. They have safety pinion and compensation balance. They are made by the old reliable Seth Thomas Clock Co.

THE SEVEN JEWELED WALTHAM has exposed pallets, nickel plates, cut expansion balance, patent Breguet hairspring, hardened and tempered in form, highly finished oval regulator, polished and gilded index plate.

THE SEVEN JEWELED ELGIN has quick train, right angle escapement in hunting, straight line escapement in open face, exposed pallets, cut expansion balance, Breguet hairspring, polished oval steel regulator, nickel index, dust ring, nickel damaskeened plates.

THE FIFTEEN JEWELED ELGIN has quick train, right angle escapement in hunting, straight line escapement in open face, exposed pallets, cut expansion balance, Breguet hairspring, polished oval regulator, nickel index, dust ring, nickel damaskeened plates.

THE FIFTEEN JEWELED WALTHAM has exposed pallets, cut expansion balance, patent Breguet hairspring, hardened and tempered in form, highly finished oval regulator, nickel plates, polished and gilded index plate.

THE SEVENTEEN JEWELED ELGIN is adjusted to temperature, quick train, straight line escapement, exposed pallets, compensating balance, Breguet hairspring, micrometric regulator, sunk second dial, dust band and gilt plates.

THE SEVENTEEN JEWELED WALTHAM has exposed pallets, compensating balance, adjusted to temperature, patent Breguet hairspring, hardened and tempered in form, patent micrometric regulator and gilt plates.

THE G. M. WHEELER ELGIN has 17 jewels, gilded settings, adjusted to temperature, quick train, straight line escapement, exposed pallets, compensating balance, Breguet hairspring, micrometric regulator, sunk second dial, dust ring, nickel damaskeened plates.

THE P. S. BARTLETT WALTHAM has 17 jewels (settings), exposed pallets, compensating balance, adjusted to temperature, patent Breguet hairspring, hardened and tempered in form, patent micrometric regulator, and nickel plates.

DUEBER GRAND HAMPDEN. NICKEL. 17 jewels in composition settings, adjusted, Breguet hairspring, micrometric regulator, compensating balance, bright flat screws, elegantly engraved and damaskeened, Arabic or Roman dial, red marginal figures, moon hands.

THE APPLETON, TRACY & CO. WALTHAM has 17 ruby jewels, gold settings, jewel pin set without shellac, double roller escapement, steel escape wheel, exposed pallets, compensating balance in recess, adjusted to temperature and three positions, patent Breguet hairspring, hardened and tempered in form, patent micrometric regulator, tempered steel safety barrel, exposed winding wheels, double sunk dial and nickel plates.

THE B. W. RAYMOND ELGIN has 17 ruby jewels, gold settings, adjusted to temperature, isochronism and positions, quick train, straight line escapement with steel escape wheel, exposed pallets, compensating balance, Breguet hairspring, micrometric regulator, patent recoiling click, double sunk dial, dust ring, damaskeened plates, carefully timed, nickel plates, finely finished throughout.

THE NEW RAILWAY HAMPDEN. NICKEL. Has 17 fine ruby jewels in solid gold settings, micrometric regulator, compensating balance, gold screws, accurately adjusted to temperature, isochronism and position, Breguet hairspring, mean time screws, patent center pinion, center jeweled, elegantly engraved and damaskeened, fleur-de-lis hands and first quality Hampden mainspring.

THE No. 150 GRADE ELGIN has 21 ruby jewels, gold settings, adjusted to temperature, isochronism and positions, quick train, straight line escapement with steel escape wheel, pallet arbor and escape pinion cone pivoted and cap jeweled, exposed pallets, compensating balance, Breguet hairspring, micrometric regulator, patent recoiling click, double sunk glass enamel dial, dust ring, engraving inlaid with gold, frosted and damaskeened nickel plates, closely timed and elaborately finished.

FATHER TIME. Open face or hunting. 21 fine ruby jewels, gilded settings, adjusted to temperature, isochronism and positions, quick train, straight line escapement with steel escape wheel, exposed pallets, compensating balance, Breguet hairspring micrometric regulator, open face, with patent recoiling click, double sunk dial, dust ring, damaskeened plates, carefully timed and finely finished throughout.

THE VERITAS. NICKEL. Has 23 extra fine ruby jewels, raised gold settings, open face lever set only, adjusted to temperature, isochronism and positions, quick train with gold wheels, straight line double roller escapement with steel escape wheel, poised pallet and fork, pallet arbor and escape pinion cone pivoted and cap jeweled, exposed pallets, compensating balance, Breguet hairspring, micrometric regulator, patent safety barrel with spring box rigidly mounted on bridge, barrel arbor pivots running in jewels, display winding work, patent recoiling click, patent self-locking setting device, double sunk glass enamel dial, dust ring, plates beautifully damaskeened, carefully timed, and parts finely finished throughout.

THE VERITAS. 21-jeweled, same as the above less two jewels.

THE JOHN HANCOCK HAMPDEN, 21 JEWELED. NICKEL. Has 21 fine ruby and sapphire jewels in gold settings, escapement cap jeweled, compensating balance, gold screws, adjusted to temperature, isochronism and position, Breguet hairspring, mean time screws, new model stud, patent micrometric regulator, bright bevel head screws, patent center pinion, polished steel work, double sunk glass enamel dial, finely damaskeened and finished throughout, gold lettering.

THE VANGUARD WALTHAM has 21 diamond and ruby jewels, both balance pivots running on diamonds, raised gold settings, jewel pin set without shellac, double roller escapement, steel escape wheel exposed pallets, compensating balance in recess, adjusted to temperature, isochronism and five positions, patent Breguet hairspring, hardened and tempered in form, embossed gold patent micrometric regulator tempered steel safety barrel, exposed winding wheels, elaborately finished nickel plates with gold lettering, plate and jewel screws gilded, steel parts chamfered, double sunk dial.

THE CRESCENT STREET WALTHAM has 21 fine ruby jewels, gold settings, jewel pin set without shellac, double roller escapement, steel escape wheel, exposed pallets, compensating balance in recess, adjusted to temperature, isochronism and five positions, patent Breguet hairspring, hardened and tempered in form, patent micrometric regulator, tempered steel safety barrel, exposed winding wheels, double sunk dial and nickel plates.

THE SPECIAL RAILWAY HAMPDEN has 23 extra fine ruby and sapphire jewels, solid gold settings, barrel arbor and center staff jeweled with the finest of sapphires, escapement cap jeweled, conical pivots, finely graduated micrometric regulator, compensating balance, gold screws, Breguet hairspring, mean time screws, new model stud, accurately adjusted to temperature, isochronism and position, patent centerpinion, bevel head gilt screws, highly polished steel work, fine double sunk glass enameled dial, best fleur-de-lis hands, elegantly engraved and damaskeened in two colors, gold lettering and nickel plates.

The Waltham 16-Size Movements.

THE SEVEN JEWELED No. 610 GRADE has cut expansion balance, Breguet hairspring, hardened and tempered in form, exposed winding wheels, tempered steel safety barrel, nickel plates.

THE FIFTEEN JEWELED No. 620 GRADE has patent micrometric regulator, compensating balance, safety pinion, patent Breguet hairspring, hardened and tempered in form, exposed winding wheels, polished and red gilded center wheel, jeweled settings, nickel plates.

THE ROYAL WALTHAM has 17 jewels, red gold settings, exposed pallets, compensating balance, adjusted to temperature, patent Breguet hairspring, hardened and tempered in form, patent micrometric regulator, tempered steel safety barrel, exposed winding wheels, nickel plates, red gold center wheel.

THE RIVERSIDE WALTHAM has 17 fine ruby jewels, raised gold settings, double roller escapement, steel escape wheel exposed pallets, compensating balance, adjusted to temperature and three positions, patent Breguet hairspring, hardened and tempered in form, patent micrometric regulator, tempered steel safety barrel, exposed winding wheels, nickel plates red gold center wheel.

THE RIVERSIDE MAXIMUS, NICKEL, has 21 diamond and ruby jewels, two pairs diamond caps, both balance pivots running on diamonds, raised gold settings jewel pin set without shellac, double roller escapement, exposed pallets, compensation balance, accurately adjusted to temperature, isochronism and five positions and carefully timed, patent Breguet hairspring, hardened and tempered in form, patent micrometric regulator, tempered steel safety barrel, exposed winding wheels, gold train, fine glass hand painted, dial of most modern and artistic design.

The Elgin 16-Size Movements.

THE SEVEN JEWELED Nos. 210 AND 211 GRADE has quick train, straight line escapement, exposed pallets, cut expansion balance, Breguet hairspring, polished steel regulator, display winding work, patent self-locking setting device, dust ring, nickel damaskeened plates.

THE FIFTEEN JEWELED Nos. 210 AND 211 GRADE has quick train, straight line escapement, exposed pallets, cut expansion balance, Breguet hairspring, micrometric regulator, display winding work, patent recoiling click, patent self-locking setting device, dust ring, nickel damaskeened plates.

THE SEVENTEEN JEWELED Nos. 241 AND 244 GRADE has gilded settings, adjusted to temperature, quick train with gold center wheel, straight line escapement, exposed pallets, compensating balance, Breguet hairspring, micrometric regulator, display winding work, patent recoiling click, patent self-locking setting device, sunk second glass enamel dial, dust ring, nickel damaskeened plates.

THE SEVENTEEN JEWELED Nos. 154 AND 160 GRADE has gilded settings, adjusted to temperature, quick train with gold center wheel, straight line escapement, exposed pallets, Breguet hairspring, micrometric regulator, display winding work, patent recoiling click, patent self-locking setting device, sunk second glass enamel dial, dust ring, damaskeened plates, thoroughly well finished.

THE SEVENTEEN ROSY RUBY JEWELED Nos. 155 AND 161 GRADE has gold settings, adjusted to temperature, isochronism and positions, quick train with gold wheels, straight line escapement with steel escape wheel, exposed pallets, compensating balance, Breguet hairspring, micrometric regulator, display winding work, patent recoiling click, patent self-locking setting device, double sunk glass enamel dial, dust ring, engraving inlaid with gold, frosted and damaskeened plates, carefully timed and finely finished throughout.

THE TWENTY-ONE EXTRA FINE RED RUBY JEWELED Nos. 156 AND 162 GRADE has raised gold settings, adjusted to temperature, isochronism and positions, quick train with gold wheels, straight line escapement with steel escape wheel, pallet arbor and escape pinion, cone pivoted and cap jeweled, exposed pallets, compensating balance, Breguet hairspring, micrometric regulator, display winding work, patent recoiling click, patent self-locking setting device, double sunk glass enamel dial, dust ring, beautifully damaskeened plates, closely timed and thoroughly first quality finish throughout.

12-Size Movements.

THE Nos. 232 AND 234 GRADE ELGIN has 7 jewels, quick train, straight line escapement, exposed pallets, cut expansion balance, Breguet hairspring, polished steel regulator, display winding work, patent recoiling click, patent self-locking setting device, sunk second glass, enamel dial, dust ring, nickel plates, damaskeened plates.

THE No. 210 GRADE WALTHAM has 7 jewels, exposed pallets, cut expansion balance, patent Breguet hairspring, hardened and tempered in form, tempered steel safety barrel, nickel plates, exposed winding wheels.

THE No. 187 AND 191 GRADE ELGIN has 15 jewels (settings), quick train with gold center wheel, straight line escapement, exposed pallets, cut expansion balance, Breguet hairspring, micrometric regulator, patent safety barrel with spring box rigidly mounted on bridge, display winding work, patent recoiling click, patent self-locking setting device, sunk second glass, enamel dial, dust ring, nickel damaskeened plates.

THE No. 220 GRADE WALTHAM has 15 jewels (settings), exposed pallets cut expansion balance, patent Breguet hairspring, hardened and tempered in form, patent micrometric regulator, tempered steel safety barrel, exposed winding wheels, nickel plates.

THE No. 188 AND 192 GRADE ELGIN has 17 jewels (raised gilded settings), adjusted to temperature, quick train with gold center wheel, straight line escapement, exposed pallets, compensating balance, Breguet hairspring, micrometric regulator, patent safety barrel with spring rigidly mounted on bridge, display winding work, patent recoiling click, patent self-locking setting device, sunk second glass, enamel dial, dust ring, nickel damaskeened plates.

ROYAL GRADE WALTHAM has 17 jewels (settings), exposed pallets, compensating balance, adjusted to temperature, patent Breguet hairspring, hardened and tempered in form, patent micrometric regulator, tempered steel safety barrel, exposed winding wheels, nickel plates.

THE RIVERSIDE GRADE WALTHAM has 17 fine ruby jeweled gold settings, double roller escapement, exposed pallets, compensating balance, adjusted to temperature and three positions, patent Breguet hairspring, hardened and tempered in form, patent micrometric regulator, tempered steel safety barrel, exposed winding wheels, nickel plates.

THE Nos. 189 AND 193 ELGIN GRADE has 19 rosy ruby jeweled raised gold settings, adjusted to temperature, isochronism and positions, quick train with gold wheels, straight line escapement with steel escape wheel, exposed pallets, compensating balance, Breguet hairspring, micrometric regulator, patent safety barrel with spring box rigidly mounted on bridge, barrel arbor pivots running in jewels, display winding work, patent recoiling click, patent self-locking setting device, sunk second glass enamel dial, dust ring, frosted and nickel damaskeened plates, engraving inlaid with gold.

THE RIVERSIDE MAXIMUM GRADE WALTHAM has 21 diamond and ruby jewels, two pairs diamond caps, both balance pivots running on diamonds, raised gold settings, jewel pin set without shellac, double roller escapement, exposed pallets, compensating balance, accurately adjusted to temperature, isochronism and five positions and carefully timed, patent Breguet hairspring, hardened and tempered in form, patent micrometric regulator, tempered steel safety barrel, exposed winding wheels, gold train, nickel plates, fine glass hand painted dial of most modern and artistic design. The superior construction of this movement adapts it to the most exacting service.

THE Nos. 190 AND 194 ELGIN GRADE has 23 extra fine red ruby jeweled raised gold settings, adjusted to temperature, isochronism and positions, quick train with gold wheels, straight line escapement with steel escape wheel, pallet arbor and escape pinion cone, pivoted and cap jeweled, exposed pallets, compensating balance, Breguet hairspring, micrometric regulator, patent safety barrel with spring box rigidly mounted on bridge, barrel arbor pivots running in jewels, display winding work, patent recoiling click, patent self-locking setting device, sunk second glass enamel dial, dust ring, nickel plates beautifully damaskeened and parts finely finished throughout.

6-Size Movements.

THE SEVEN JEWELED SETH THOMAS MOVEMENTS are two-thirds plate, nickel, damaskeened. They have patent pinion and compensating balance.

THE SEVEN JEWELED WALTHAM "Y" GRADE has exposed pallets, cut expansion balance, patent Breguet hairspring, hardened and tempered in form, tempered steel safety barrel, nickel plates.

THE SEVEN JEWELED ELGIN No. 206 GRADE has quick train, straight line escapement, exposed pallets, cut expansion balance, Breguet hairspring, polished steel regulator, nickel damaskeened plates.

THE ELEVEN JEWELED HAMPDEN No. 206 GRADE has composition settings, patent center pinion, sunk second dial, bright flat screws, elegantly engraved and damaskeened nickel plates, fine moon hands and regular Hampden mainspring.

THE FIFTEEN JEWELED WALTHAM "Y" GRADE has settings, exposed pallets, cut expansion balance, patent Breguet hairspring, hardened and tempered in form, tempered steel safety barrel, nickel plates.

THE FIFTEEN JEWELED ELGIN No. 216 GRADE has settings, quick train, straight line escapement, exposed pallets, cut expansion balance, Breguet hairspring, polished steel regulator, nickel damaskeened plates.

THE SIXTEEN ROSY RUBY JEWELED ELGIN No. 168 GRADE has raised gilded settings, adjusted to temperature, quick train with gold wheels, straight line escapement with gold escape wheel, exposed pallets, compensating balance, Breguet hairspring, micrometric regulator, sunk second glass enamel dial, engraving inlaid with gold, frosted and damaskeened nickel plates, finely finished throughout.

0-Size Movements.

THE SEVEN JEWELED ATLAS MOVEMENT has anchor escapement, cut expansion balance, lever set.

THE SEVEN JEWELED ELGIN No. 269 GRADE has quick train, straight line escapement, exposed pallets, cut expansion balance, Breguet hairspring, display winding work, patent recoiling click, patent self-locking setting device, polished steel regulator, dust ring, nickel damaskeened plates.

THE SEVEN JEWELED WALTHAM No. 61 GRADE has exposed pallets, cut expansion balance, patent Breguet hairspring, hardened and tempered in form, tempered steel safety barrel, nickel plates.

THE ELEVEN JEWELED ELGIN No. 224 GRADE has settings, quick train, straight line escapement, exposed pallets, cut expansion balance, Breguet hairspring, polished steel regulators, patent safety barrel with spring box rigidly mounted on bridge, display winding work, patent recoiling click, patent self-locking setting device, sunk second dial, dust ring, nickel damaskeened plates.

THE FIFTEEN JEWELED ELGIN No. 223 GRADE has settings, quick train, straight line escapement, exposed pallets, cut expansion balance, Breguet hairspring, polished steel regulator, nickel damaskeened plates.

THE FIFTEEN JEWELED WALTHAM No. 65 GRADE has settings, exposed pallets, cut expansion balance, patent Breguet hairspring, hardened and tempered in form, tempered steel safety barrel, nickel plates.

THE SIXTEEN RUBY JEWELED WALTHAM, LADY WALTHAM GRADE, has settings, exposed pallets, compensating balance, adjusted to temperature, patent Breguet hairspring, hardened and tempered in form, patent micrometric regulator, tempered steel safety barrel, nickel plates.

THE SEVENTEEN RUBY JEWELED WALTHAM RIVERSIDE GRADE has raised gold settings, exposed pallets, compensating balance, adjusted to temperature and position, patent Breguet hairspring, hardened and tempered in form, patent micrometric regulator, tempered steel safety barrel and nickel plates.

DESCRIPTION OF SEARS, ROEBUCK & CO.'S 6, 16 AND 18-SIZE MOVEMENTS.

18-SIZE, SOLID NICKEL THROUGH AND THROUGH, 17 jewels, adjusted. Full plate, fancy solid gold damaskeened finish, five pair gold settings, compensation full double cut expansion balance wheel, adjusted to isochronism and position, patent micrometer regulator, genuine ruby jeweled pin, highly polished beveled edged screws, fully protecting dust band, safety pinion, double sunk, white enameled dial and sunk second hand dial. The superior construction of this movement adapts it to the most exacting service.

16-SIZE, SOLID NICKEL, FANCY GOLD DAMASKEENED FINISH, consisting of three separate bridges, viz., barrel, train and balance bridges, very artistically arranged. 17 genuine ruby jewels, in solid gold settings. Exposed to view winding apparatus, the steel parts of which are highly polished and chamfered; patent micrometer regulator, five pairs of extra solid gold settings and gold train, genuine ruby pallet jewels visible to view, and ruby roller jewel, patent safety center pinion and barrel. Compensation, double cut, full expansion balance wheel, adjusted in accordance to variations of the temperature, fully protecting dust band, double sunk, genuine hard French enamel dial. This movement will excel the highest grade movements on the market.

6-SIZE, NICKEL, VERY ELABORATELY DESIGNED, damaskeened finish, 17 jewels, full compensation balance wheel, patent safety center pinion, ruby roller and patent escapement, blue beveled edge, highly polished screws. Movement consists of three separate bridges, very artistically arranged, plain white, hard enameled dial and fancy blue steel hands.

Explanation of the Terms

USED IN THE DESCRIPTION OF

Watch Movements

On the Preceding Page.

TO ASSIST OUR CUSTOMERS....

In making an intelligent selection of a movement best suited to their requirements, and that they may know exactly what they are buying, we give below an explanation of terms used on preceding page.

REMEMBER that the numbers which are always engraved on watch movements have **nothing to do with our catalogue number,** or the manufacturers' number, which indicates the grade. Every movement is numbered consecutively, and you **will find no two movements made by the same factory that have the same number.**

JEWELS **are not used to add to the intrinsic value of a movement,** as is supposed by many, but for the purpose of **equalizing and reducing friction,** which will reduce the variation, and cause the pivots and bearings to wear much longer, and thus **retain the good qualities of the movement** for an indefinite length of time. **They are made of garnet or ruby.** The ruby, being harder and more expensive, is used only in the higher grade movements. A great deal depends on the quality and perfect finish of the jewels.

In movements of lower grade than fifteen jewels, the jewels are used in places where there is the most friction.

With the seven-jeweled grade, the pivots of the balance wheel each run in a jewel, and, in addition to this, is used what is called cap jewels, which serve as bearings for the ends of the balance pivots, which are made with conical instead of square shoulders, and the ends of the pivots rest on the cap jewels, instead of the shoulders resting on the hole jewels. By this method the friction can be equalized, and the watch keep the same rate, whether on its face, edge or back. Two jewels are used in the pallet, which operates on the 'scape wheel, and one, called the roller jewel, is set in the roller table, which is under the balance wheel on the balance staff.

In the fifteen-jeweled grade, seven jewels are used in the escapement and eight plate jewels are used, four of which are set in the upper plate and the other four on the opposite pivots on the lower plate.

In the seventeen-jeweled grade, the jewels are distributed as in the fifteen, with the addition of one for each pivot of the center wheel.

In the twenty-one-jeweled grade, the jewels are distributed as in the seventeen-jeweled grade, with the addition of two cap jewels each for the pallet and 'scape wheel.

THE COMPENSATION BALANCE **is made of a combination of hammer hardened brass and steel,** in such proportions as to compensate for the variations in temperature. The brass is used on the outside and steel on the inside. The brass being softer than steel is more sensitive to ranges of temperature, and as the rim of the balance wheel is cut in two places, and the balance wheel has but two arms, it leaves each half of the rim attached at the end and leaves the other ends of the rim free to be influenced by the expansion or contraction of the brass on the outside of the rim. A small balance wheel used with the same hairspring would run much faster than a large balance wheel. At a high temperature the entire balance wheel would naturally expand in bulk and consequently run slower. But, with the compensation balance, while the entire bulk of the balance wheel expands, the expansion of the brass on the outside of the rim is greater than the steel on the inside, consequently it throws the loose end of the rim of the balance wheel in toward the center of the wheel, thus making the circumference enough smaller to compensate for the increased volume.

By the results of experience it is possible to make these wheels by machinery, so nearly correct, that the rate is sufficiently close for all ordinary purposes. For closer rate the balance wheel must be adjusted to temperature.

ADJUSTMENT. **There are three kinds of adjustments which affect the rate of a watch.** These are used in the finer timepieces, such as those of railroad men, sailors and others, who require a timepiece which can be depended on for a very close rate. The adjustment of a movement requires the most skill at the hands of a workman of any of the departments of watchmaking. Adjustments are perfected only by experiment and a great deal of careful hand labor on each individual movement.

The first adjustment is that of heat and cold. Every compensation balance is provided with screws in the rim of the balance wheel, by the use of which the adjustment of heat and cold may be changed by the workman. **The movement is tested in an ice box or in an oven,** and if it does not keep the same rate in both extremes of temperature, as well as the average temperature, the screws in the balance wheel are shifted to or from the loose end of the balance rim, so as to bring about the desired results.

The second adjustment is position. The watch must keep the same rate when lying on its face, on its back, or on the edge with pendant up, pendant down, three and nine up. This adjustment is accomplished by having the jewels in which the balance pivot rests, of the proper thickness in proportion to the diameter of the pivot, and at the same time it must equal the surface on the end of the pivot, which rests on the cap jewel; also the balance wheel, as well as pallet and 'scape wheel, must be perfectly poised. A wheel is perfectly poised when the pivots can be supported on two flat surfaces, perfectly smooth and polished, and the wheel placed in any position, when it will remain exactly as it is placed. If it is not perfectly poised, the heaviest part of the wheel will always turn to the point immediately under the lines of support.

The third adjustment is that of isochronism. This is the result of careful calculation and experiments in the way of selecting a hair spring of the exact proportions, as to length, strength, etc., which will cause the balance wheel to give the same length of arc of rotation, when the mainspring is wound full up, as it does when nearly run down. The natural tendency is for the watch to run slower when nearly run down than it does when wound full up. This is why your watchmaker will sometimes tell you to always wind your watch at the same time every day. This adjustment overcomes this serious difficulty. While the variations from that cause are not sufficient to be of any consequence in a watch for ordinary use, it is very important with very fine timepieces.

THE PATENT REGULATOR **is a device which is used on all gent watches of high grade,** for the purpo of assisting in the finer manipulation of the regulator. It is so arranged th the regulator can be moved the shortest possible distance, without fear moving it too far. They always have a fine graduated index attached, whi makes it possible to see just how much the regulator has been moved.

THE MAINSPRING **in general use on the ordinary grade watches known as the flat hairspring.** A great deal pends on the form and temper of any style hairspring, in order that may retain its elasticity and give the best result. **The Breguet ha spring** is an improvement over the flat hairspring and is used on high gra watches. The inside coil of any hairspring is attached to what is callec colleton the balance staff, and the end of the outside coil of the hairspri is attached to a stud, which is held firmly by a screw in the balance whe bridge. Two small pins, with the end of each fastened to a projection in th regulator, clasp the outer coil of the hairspring a short distance from wher it is fastened in the stud. If the regulator is moved toward "S," these pir called guard pins, are moved toward the stud, which lengthens the h spring and allows the balance wheel to make a longer arc of rotation, wh causes the watch to run slower, because it requires a longer time for wheels to perform the longer arcs. When the regulator is moved towards these pins are moved from the stud, which shortens the hairspring makes shorter the arcs of the balance wheel, thus causing the movemen run fast. It sometimes happens that the next coil to the outside one, fro heavy jar, will catch between these guard pins, which will shorten length of the hairspring just one round, causing a gaining rate of about one hour per day. When such does occur, the hairspring can be easily released by the aid of a pin, and it will resume its former rate. Under such conditions your local jeweler is very apt to tell you that the watch needs a new hairspring, which is not true.

THE BREGUET HAIRSPRING is a recent improvement which accomplishes two objects. It prevents the liability of the hairspring catching on the guard pins, and at the same time there is no lateral or side motion given to the balance wheel, as the expansion is equal all around, owing to the fact that the outside coil of the spring is bent up and turned around, so as to pass near the center and across to opposite side and is attached to the stud above the level of the body of the spring.

THE PATENT OR SAFETY PINION **is now used in most of the American watches,** and was invented for the purpose of protecting the train from reaction caused by breakage of the mainspring, which is liable to happen in any grade of watch at any time, without apparent cause; sometimes from over winding. It is the pinion of the center staff with which the barrel (the hollow wheel which contains the mainspring) engages.

In case the mainspring breaks, the recoil and backward action given to the main wheel disengages the pinion from the center staff and allows it to turn freely on the staff.

When solid pinions are used, balance staffs, jewels, teeth of wheels and other parts have been seriously damaged by the breaking of the mainspring. The patent pinion prevents all such accidents.

FULL PLATE **movements are those on which usually the balance wheel only is exposed to view.**

THREE-QUARTER PLATE **movements are those which have a portion of the upper plate cut away,** so as to expose a portion of the train wheels, pallet, etc. Three-quarter plate is used mostly on 16, 6 and 0-size movements.

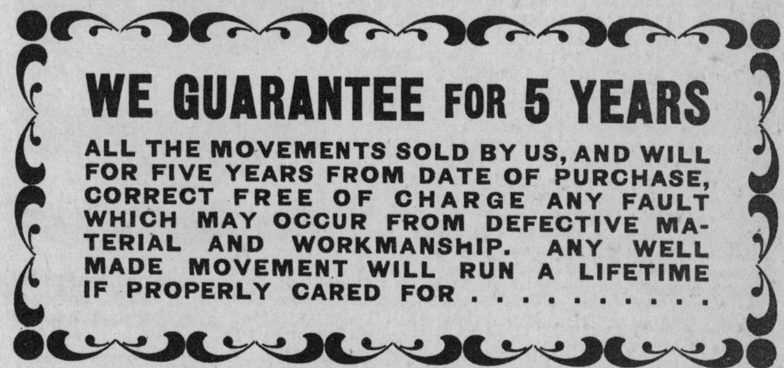

WE GUARANTEE FOR 5 YEARS
ALL THE MOVEMENTS SOLD BY US, AND WILL FOR FIVE YEARS FROM DATE OF PURCHASE, CORRECT FREE OF CHARGE ANY FAULT WHICH MAY OCCUR FROM DEFECTIVE MATERIAL AND WORKMANSHIP. ANY WELL MADE MOVEMENT WILL RUN A LIFETIME IF PROPERLY CARED FOR . . . .

REMEMBER **that your watch should not run longer than one and one-half years without having the old oil cleaned off and fresh oil applied. This must be done at the expense of the purchaser.**

The balance wheel of all modern watches makes 18,000 beats or revolutions per hour; 432,000 per day, or 157,788,000 per year. An engine or sewing machine will be oiled several times per day, but we have known people to carry a watch for ten years without having it cleaned or fresh oil applied.

Usually, a movement thus treated is of no value, being entirely worn out. Take good care of your watch if you wish it to perform its duty properly, for it is a very delicate machine. Our charge for cleaning and oiling is 75 cents. The regular retail price is $1.50.

WE CAN FURNISH ANY MOVEMENT OR CASE MADE. IF YOU DO NOT FIND IN OUR CATALOGUE WHAT YOU WANT, WRITE US.

HOW GOLD FILLED CASES ARE MADE

AS GOLD FILLED CASES have become so popular in the past thirty years, and there is so little known by the general public of the relative proportions of the different materials that enter into their construction and the methods employed in making them, we feel that it will be interesting to our customers and their friends to know more about such an important industry. **With every line that we handle and list** in our catalogue, we make ourselves thoroughly familiar with the manner in which the goods are made, and the **quality and proportion of each kind of material** which enters into their construction. It is very necessary for us to do this in order to protect the interests of our customers, for their interests are our own.

WE EMPLOY MEN IN EACH DEPARTMENT who are thoroughly familiar with the construction of the goods they handle, know where to look for **weak and strong** points, and are **thoroughly competent to judge** and to protect the interests of both our customers and ourselves from being **imposed upon by fraudulent concerns** whose only object is to make up cheap, showy goods and market them to the unsuspecting public in competition with goods of real merit, which, if bought right, can be owned for the same or even less than the shoddy goods. We can say without fear of contradiction that the average merchant does not employ competent people, and even himself is not a practical man. Let us repeat that **we leave nothing undone** to thoroughly understand and know the merits of everything we sell.

THERE ARE AT THE PRESENT TIME eleven watch case factories in the United States, with a **daily average of about 4,500 filled cases, or 1,498,500 per year.** Most of the watch case factories in operation at the present time are reputable makers who have been established a great many years, and have proved by the experience of over a quarter of a century that gold filled cases, when properly made, are not only theoretically but practically a success, and have given their owners entire satisfaction.

WE MIGHT SAY that it has been our good fortune and pleasure to have had the privilege of examining a great many gold filled watch cases which have been in constant use from 20 to 30 years, and, **without exception, we found all of those which were made by reputable concerns to be in good condition** and to all appearances equal to solid gold cases. (Of course, the joints were somewhat loose from wear, which is a natural consequence with any watch case.) Even though the first filled cases were satisfactory as to wear and appearance, improved machinery and **years of experience have made it possible to turn out cases at a very low price,** which for style and appearance are far superior to a solid gold case and for wear are all that could be wished for.

The following article, together with accompanying illustrations, will give the reader a good general idea of how gold filled cases are made.

THE FIRST OPERATION is to prepare a sheet of material which is composed of two plates of gold with a plate of hard composition metal between. **Instead of rolling all three plates out** to the required thickness before soldering them together (which would be a very difficult operation and attended with unsatisfactory results, such as uneven thickness of the plates, not being soldered well together, etc.) the material is made ready, as shown in Figure 1, by taking one piece of gold about 4 inches long by 2 inches wide, and another of the same width and length but thinner for the inside of the case, as there is no wear on the inside. Now, a piece of hard composition metal the same width and length is placed between the two pieces of gold, and after placing a few bits of hard gold solder between the plates **the three are put into a furnace** heated at a very high heat by a charcoal fire and a hot air blast. The solder soon melts, and all three of the original pieces of metal are in one solid **piece as seen in Fig. 1.**

Fig. 1.

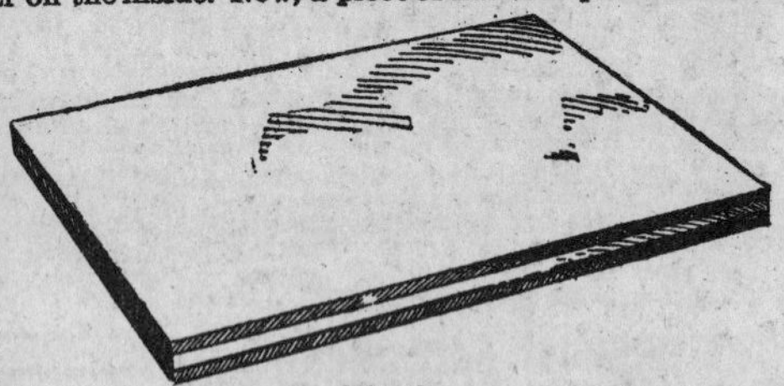
Fig. 2.

This piece is passed between adjustable hard steel rollers, which are brought closer together by a set screw after each time the plate has been passed through until it is reduced to a thin sheet a little less than 1/16 of an inch in thickness. Fig. 2 represents a plate after having been passed through several times. By this method all three of the original sheets are reduced proportionately equal so that neither the gold nor the composition metal will be thicker in one place than another.

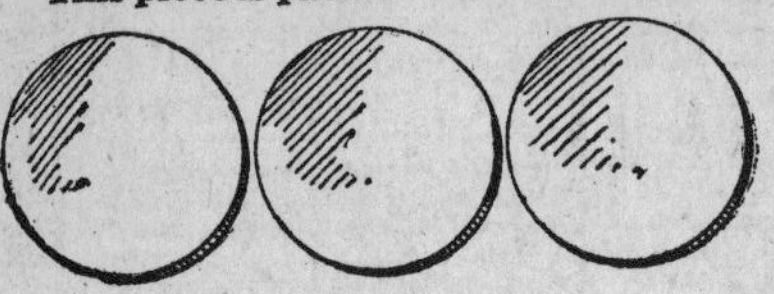
Fig. 3.

Fig. 4.

The next operation is to cut the plate into strips of such width as to accommodate the different parts of the case, which are free to be stamped out by large automatic rotary presses. The back, front and cap of the cases are stamped out in a circular plate **as shown in Fig. 3,** and the piece of the strip that is left is **represented by Fig. 4.** Cuts are about one-third size.

By a single operation these round plates are forced into a steel die in a large rotary press which turns up the edges all round so as to give it a bowl shaped appearance, **as shown in Fig. 5.** In another operation the edges are turned down, **as shown in Fig. 6,** which is called the snap.

Fig. 5.

Fig. 6.

The next step is to place the piece thus shaped into a sectional hard **steel concave die.** On the inside is operated **with very heavy pressure** a small hard steel polished roller **(see Fig. 8)** which forces the metal into the die in all parts, which shapes the piece to conform to the style of case which is being made. If the case is to have corrugated edges, or Star vermicilli work, or heavy engraving, it is formed in this die. This operation also shapes the inside edges of the piece so as to form the snap **as seen in Fig. 7.**

Fig. 7.

The piece thus shaped is put on the head of a lathe and the inside edge turned out a little with a sharp tool to make it snap and fit perfectly on the center of the case. After this is done a rotary cutter propelled at a high speed is run across one edge to cut the seat for the joint (hinge). Two pieces of gold joint wire about ⅜ of an inch in length (joint wire is made in sticks about 4 inches in length with a small hole running the entire length, and is cut into pieces of the required length with a saw) is placed in the seat cut by the tool and bound in place with fine wire. **Some bits of fine hard gold solder are then laid over the crevice and the pieces are held in a gas** jet which is stimulated by an air blast. The solder is melted and secures the joints, after which the binding wire is taken off. **A piece of solid gold** is soldered on in the same way on the edge of the back of case to form the thumb piece.

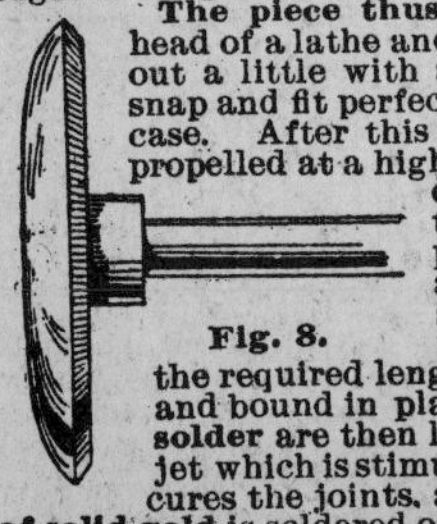
Fig. 8.

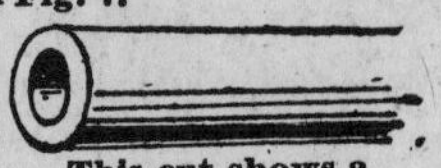
This cut shows a Section of Joint Wire Enlarged.

The center of the case is made by taking a strip of stock (prepared in the same way as described in the first part of this article), about ¾ of an inch wide by **about 7 inches long (see Fig. 9),** which is bent in a circle and the ends soldered so as to form a band or ring a little over two inches in diameter. This piece is placed in a sectional die **(see Fig. 10)** which is held securely in a very heavy frame. **A small hard polished roller** is rolled on the inside of the ring with very heavy pressure until the metal comes in contact with every part of the die. The inside of the die is made in the exact shape of the outside of center of case so that when the metal has been well pressed in, it is shaped complete **as seen in Fig. 12.** The rough edges on the inside are now turned out (on the lathe) to the standard size to fit the movement.

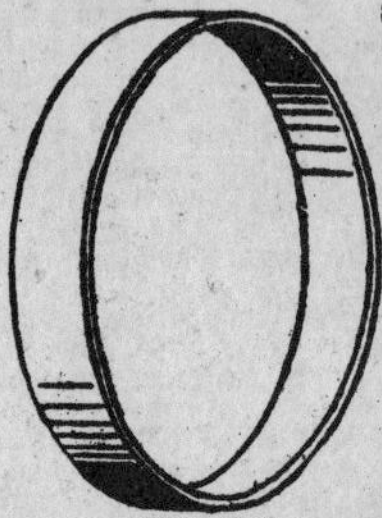
Fig. 9.

Fig. 10.

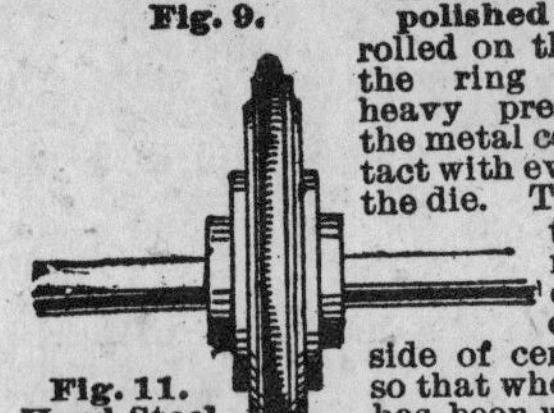
Fig. 11. Hard Steel Roller Used on Inside of Die.

The seats for the joints are milled out and joints soldered on as described above, except that one piece of joint wire instead of two are put on. The pendant **(see Fig. 13)** is made by forcing a small piece of stock into a die. A small concave seat is cut in the center **(Fig. 12)** to receive it, and it is bound in place and soldered on with gold solder.

The pendant bow (usually called the ring) is made of solid gold. The bezel (crystal ring) is made in much the same way as the center. All the joints (hinges) are now filed and broached so as to fit perfectly, **the case springs** are secured in their places and the different parts of the case are fitted together.

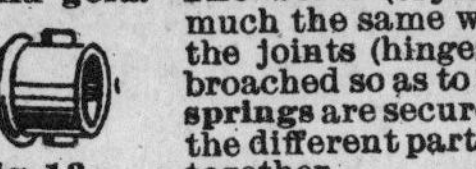

Fig. 13.

Fig. 12.

The next operation is to engrave the case, which is done by hand with a small tool about 5 inches in length **(see Fig. 14),** which is held as seen in **Fig. 15.** Engraving is very fine work and requires years of practice as well as natural ability to master the art. **After** the engraving is done the case is polished inside and out on cotton buff wheels from 1 to 5 inches in diameter, which run at the rate of about **3,000 revolutions per minute** and are saturated with alcohol and red rouge (very fine powdered oxide of iron). The case is now washed carefully, put in a soft cotton bag and is **ready for the market.**

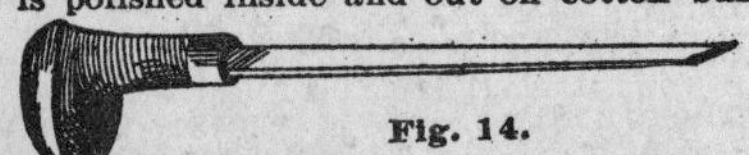
Fig. 14.

Fig. 15.

GRADES OF GOLD. For the benefit of those of our customers who are not familiar with what is meant by **10, 14 or 18-karat gold,** we make the following explanation: **24 is taken as a basis.** For 14-karat gold, fourteen twenty-fourths of the composition is pure gold and ten twenty-fourths is alloy. **For 10-karat,** ten twenty-fourths is pure gold while fourteen twenty-fourths is alloy.

RAISED COLORED GOLD ORNAMENTATION is mentioned in different parts of our Watch and Jewelry department. Gold can be made in many different colors by using different kinds of metal for alloy. **Pure gold is bright yellow;** gold of a reddish color is made by using copper for alloy; **very light colored gold** is made by using silver for alloy; **green gold is made** with light alloys and colored by a chemical treatment. A white metal is also used in raised colored decorations, **which is platinum, and when pure it will not tarnish or corrode.**

WATCHMAKERS' TOOLS ....AND MATERIALS

THE NUMEROUS INQUIRIES we have received from time to time have induced us to list a line of watchmakers' and jewelers' tools. For want of space we can illustrate only the most useful and desirable, and have been compelled to reduce the cuts in order to illustrate what we do. The goods, however, are all of standard make and size, **and of the best quality.** If there is anything you want that you do not find illustrated, send us your order, enclosing market price for same, and give an accurate description. If you do not know what the cost is, be sure to enclose enough, and we will return what is left. **We guarantee our prices to be as low as any,** and you will find that we always furnish goods at lowest wholesale prices. We will be glad, however, to quote you if you desire prices before ordering.

WHEN ORDERING MATERIAL FOR REPAIRS, ALWAYS SEND A SAMPLE IF POSSIBLE.

If not, fully describe the size and make of watch or clock for which parts are intended. When ordering materials you will save both time and trouble by making a remittance of sufficient funds to cover all possible charges for cost of goods and mailing. We will always refund any balance left after paying cost of goods and mailing.

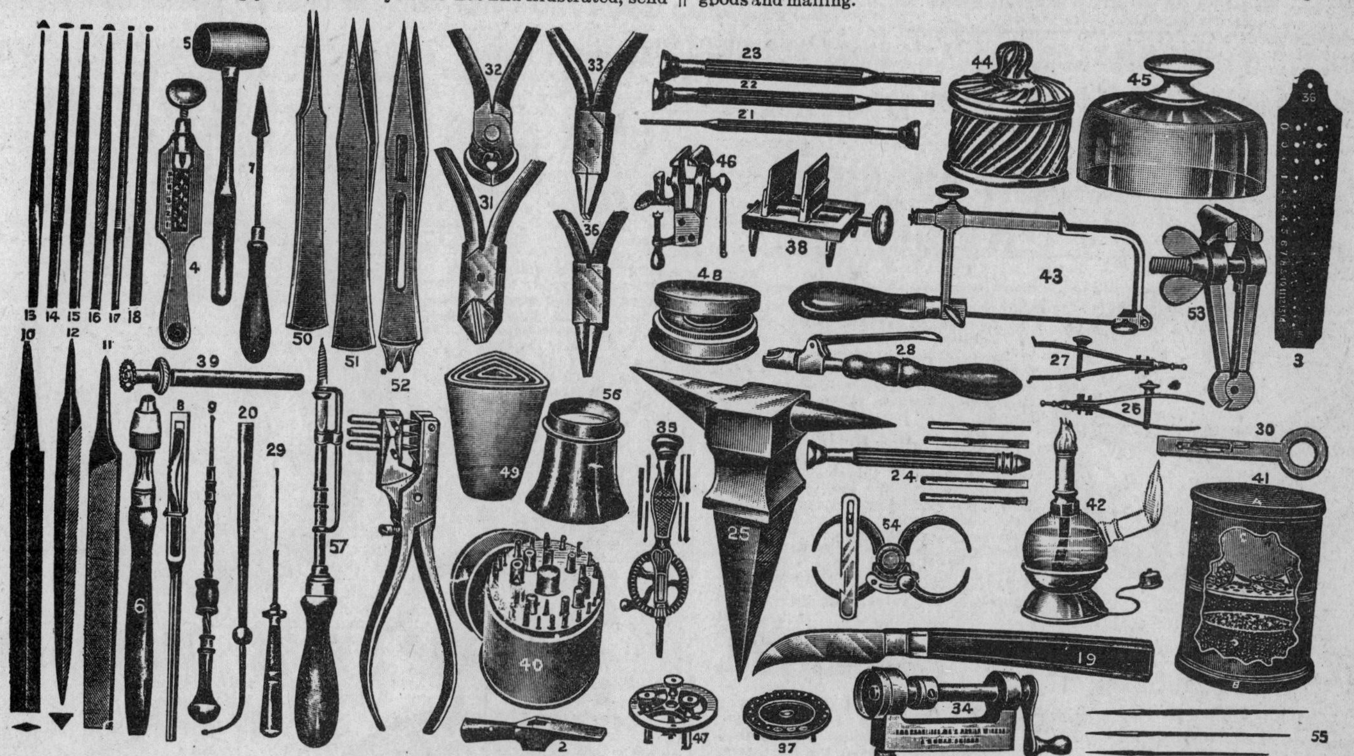

No.			
44	Alcohol cups	each	$0.35
25	Anvil (jewelers')	each	.75
100	Blow Pipes, common brass	each	.25
20	Blow Pipes, with balls	each	.30
101	Blow Pipes, nickel plated, with ball	each	.50
19	Bench Knife (jewelers')	each	.50
102	Buffs, Chamois or Felt, round or flat	each	.20
103	Brushes, watch or clock	each	.30
104	Burnishers, jewel	each, 25c to	.75
55	Broaches, Stubb's best quality, assorted sizes from No. 75 to No. 40	per dozen	1.00
6	Broach Handle, adjustable	each	.25
106	Broaches, Swiss make	per dozen	.25
26	Caliper, pinion, plain	each	.25
109	Caliper, regular	each	.30
54	Caliper, nickel plated, with bar and screw	each	.65
153	Clock Screwdriver	each	.28
110	Clock wire bender	each	.20
111	Countersinks, per set of three		1.00
113	Countersinks, adjustable handle, per set		.75
49	Crucibles, per set of four		.35
48	Cups, Oil, for watch or clock	each	.20
114	Drills, common	per dozen	.36
116	Drills, Stock, common	each	.50
117	Drill Bow, to use with above stock	each	.20
9	Drill Stock, patent spiral	each	.60
35	Drill Stock, patent guard	each	1.00
41	Drying Box	each	1.25
39	Escape Wheel Holder	each	.40
56	Eyeglass, Watchmakers', common	each	.30
118	Eyeglass, Watchmakers', with coil spring		.50
119	Files, round or square, small	each	.18
10	File, knife	each	.35
13	Files, needle, three-cornered	each	.15
14	Files, needle, knife	each	.15
15	Files, needle, oblong	each	.15
16	Files, needle, one-half round	each	.15
17	Files, needle, square	each	.15
18	Files, needle, round	each	.15
12	Files, three-cornered, 3⅛-inch	each	.30
11	Files, flat, regular	each	.35
121	Files, screw head	each	.25
120	Files, rounding and entering	each	.35
123	Gauge, Degree, nickel plated, with rule,	each	1.00
2	Hammers, according to size	each, 40c to	.75
124	Hammer Handles, ebony	each	.25
125	Hands, Watch, per pair, 10c;	per doz. pair	.50
126	Hands, Second, each, 5c	per dozen	.30
128	Hands, Clock	per pair, 5c; per doz.	.30
129	Handles, adjustable, for graver or small files	each	.15
130	Handles, adjustable, for medium files,	each	.25
131	Jeweling Tools, Swiss, in box	each	1.50
132	Jewelers' Cement, per bottle	each	.25
30	Jewel Pin Setter	each	.88
134	Jeweling Tool, complete	each	1.50
135	Keys, Watch	per dozen	.25
136	Keys, Watch, wind any watch	each	.20

No.			
137	Keys, Watch, for bench use	each	$0.50
138	Keys, iron or brass, for clocks	each	.10
42	Lamps, Alcohol, patented, large	each	1.75
139	Lamps, Alcohol, faceted glass	each	.88
140	Mainsprings, Watch	each, 10c; per doz.	1.20
141	Mainsprings, Clock, 1-day	each	.15
142	Mainsprings, Clock, 8-day	each	.45
150	Mainspring Punch, improved	each	1.25
34	Mainspring Winder	each	1.50
5	Mallet, Jewelers'	each	.20
47	Movement Holder	each	.75
143	Oil, Watch or Clock	per bottle	.20
29	Oiler, Watch	each	.15
144	Oil Stone, best Arkansas, in box	each	1.00
145	Pin Slide, common medium	each	.35
146	Pin Vise, hollow handle	each	.75
151	Punch, Mainspring, English	each	.75
1	Punch, Mainspring, (3 punches)	per set	1.25
40	Punches, set of 24, with hollow stake, in hardwood box	complete set	1.25
36	Pliers, round	each	.65
33	Pliers, flat	each	.65
31	Pliers, Stubb's best side cutting	each	1.00
32	Pliers, cutting, regular Swiss	each	.65
38	Poising Tool	each	.85
28	Roller Remover	each	.75
30	Ruby Pin Setter	each	.60
57	Screw Holder and Driver combined	each	.75

No.			
37	Screw Holder	each	$0.30
3	Screw Plate, 36 holes		.95
23	Screwdriver, large	each	.25
22	Screwdriver, Watch, medium	each	.25
21	Screwdriver, Watch, small	each	.25
24	Screwdriver, Watch, adjustable, 4 sizes,	set	.60
8	Second Hand Holder, nickel plated	each	.40
153	Stake, Riveting, hard steel	each	.25
43	Saw Frame, Swiss, extra quality, nickel plated	each	1.10
154	Saws for above	per dozen	.15
7	Soldering copper	each	.20
157	Soldering fluid, per bottle	each	.25
158	Solder, silver	per package	.25
159	Solder, gold	per package	1.00
4	Screw Stock and Dies	per set	2.00
50	Tweezers, fine	each	.35
51	Tweezers, medium	each	.35
52	Tweezers and hand raiser combined	each	.45
46	Vise, Bench	each	.70
53	Vise, Hand	each	.75
45	Watch Cover Glass	each	.35
161	Watch Glasses, hunting style	each	.10
162	Watch Glasses, per ½ dozen of one number		.15
163	Watch Glasses, assorted	per gross	2.50
164	Watch Glasses, thick, open face, fitted,	each	.20
165	Watch Glasses, thick open face,	per dozen	.40
166	Watch Keys, Birch's	each	.20

OUR COMPLETE WATCH TOOL SET, PRICE $10.00.

THE TOOLS AND IMPLEMENTS we herewith illustrate are the most necessary in the equipment of a watchmaker's kit. Every one of them performs important work, making it absolutely necessary to have at least as great a selection as we illustrate in our complete set. The material of our tools is made of the very finest procurable; the most expert toolmakers, skilled in their art, the only ones employed in the production of this merchandise. **EACH TOOL goes through a rigid inspection before leaving our establishment,** so that we are assured of them being received by our customers in perfect condition. Our mechanics here who do our watch work use our own manufacture of tools and the work done by us is excelled by none. **This set for $10.00 consists of 36 separate and distinct pieces.** Any man of average mechanical skill can learn to rectify the majority of causes that make a watch stop. The set not alone includes tools necessary for watch repairing, but likewise includes a complete set of tools for silverware, jewelry and clock repairing. **We know that you would not fail to be pleased with your purchase if you conclude to favor us with an order for one of these wonderful watchmakers' and jewelers' sets.**

No. 4R1 Complete Tool Set, $10.00.

No. 4R1 Price for complete set, including text book........ **$10.00**

94 CENTS AND UPWARDS FOR AMERICAN WATCHES.

NICKEL, METAL, ELECTRO PLATE, SILVER, GOLD FILLED AND SOLID GOLD WATCHES AT PRICES HERETOFORE UNKNOWN.

OUR PRICES - - - Are Prices Unknown to Others. A Great Saving to Buyers.

SWEEPING REDUCTIONS ON EVERYTHING IN THIS DEPARTMENT

MADE POSSIBLE BY LARGER PURCHASES AND LARGER CONTRACTS THAN EVER BEFORE, MEANS LOWEST PRICES EVER QUOTED BY US OR ANY OTHER HOUSE.

REMEMBER WE ARE ALWAYS READY TO REFUND YOUR MONEY IF OUR GOODS ARE NOT FOUND AT ALL TIMES AS REPRESENTED.

LOOK CAREFULLY AT OUR BARGAIN PAGES of watches scattered through this department. Every bargain page is a money saving, money making surprise.

No. 4R2

94-CENT AMERICAN WATCH.

94c

No. 4R2

Far better than ever and yet only 94 cents.

A gentleman's stem wind watch for 94 cents.

This is a **nickel plated metal watch,** stem wind and stem set, regular 18-size, **open face case. A patent lever** movement, and runs 30 to 36 hours with one winding.

Guaranteed American made and a very good timekeeper; movement is strong in construction, and will stand much rougher usage than a finer and higher priced watch.

Remember your boy with one of these 94-cent watches. Nothing will please him better. **94 cents** is little money and **far less money** than the watch can be bought for elsewhere.

Consider the price, only 94 cents.

ONLY $1.69

Only 500 left. This spring we sold 1,000 at $1.79. We will close the balance out at $1.69. A $3.00 stem wind watch for only $1.69.

How We Can Do It. We bought a large number of these watches nearly two years ago, before the change in tariff, and we got the lot at the **lowest price ever known.** Case is gents' full 18-size, open face, heavy nickel plated, highly polished, stem wind and stem set.

Movement—A nickel cylinder escapement, and while we do not guarantee it, they keep very good time. **It's a boy's pride,** and as our price is only **$1.69, get your boy a watch. $1.69** will be our **special price** until our stock is entirely exhausted.

No. 4R3

$1.69

No. 4R3

$2.40 ALASKA SILVER ALL-AMERICAN OPEN FACE WATCH.

No. 4R6

$2.40

$2.40 FOR AN AMERICAN STEM WIND AND STEM SET **nickel movement and American case, we believe is a lower price than was ever before quoted by any house in any quantity,** and making this price of **$2.40** on an all-American watch, one that can be guaranteed for time and for wear, we feel sure will insure us an immense trade. For this reason we have contracted with the manufacturer for a very large number of these watches, which alone makes it possible for us to make this **$2.40 price.**

UNDERSTAND, IN THIS WATCH AT $2.40 you have both in the case and in the movement a strictly up to date American Watch, one that is guaranteed for wear, guaranteed for timekeeping qualities, and such a watch as has never before been shown at anything like the price.

ALASKA SILVER CASE.

THIS HANDSOME CASE AS ILLUSTRATED is what is known as **ALASKA SILVER.** It is a composition of several metals, giving the watch the appearance of coin silver; and in fact, it is in appearance and in every way except intrinsic value the equal of coin silver. **It will wear and retain its coin silver color for a lifetime.** It is handsomely finished as shown in illustration, in a **CORRUGATED PATTERN** with fancy heavy beaded edge. **It is open face, full 18-size, stem wind and stem set,** and is fitted with a **heavy bevel edge crystal.**

AT $2.40 WE FURNISH THIS CASE COMPLETE WITH MOVEMENT in what we call snap back and snap bezel. The front and back snap on.

MOVEMENT. WE FURNISH IN THIS WATCH AT OUR SPECIAL PRICE OF $2.40 a 7-jeweled solid nickel stem wind and stem set movement. These movements are made by the Trenton Watch Co., of Trenton, N. J., for export trade. Some are stamped Pan-American; some are stamped Riverside, and some are stamped Trenton. **Every movement is guaranteed by the manufacturers for five years,** and they issue a five-year guarantee **with the watch.**

OUR SPECIAL AND HERETOFORE UNHEARD OF PRICE OF $2.40 COMMENDS THIS WATCH to all those who require a reliable timepiece and American case that will not tarnish, for very little money, and **$2.40** is a price based on the actual cost to produce, with but our one small profit added.

NO. 4R8 SAME WATCH AS ABOVE, with the case hinged in front and snap back, $2.50.

We recommend this hinged or jointed front case at $2.50.

The 10 cents additional which we charge you is the exact difference in the cost to us, and we believe the watch is well worth the difference.

No. 4R8 Our special price..**$2.50**

$4.95

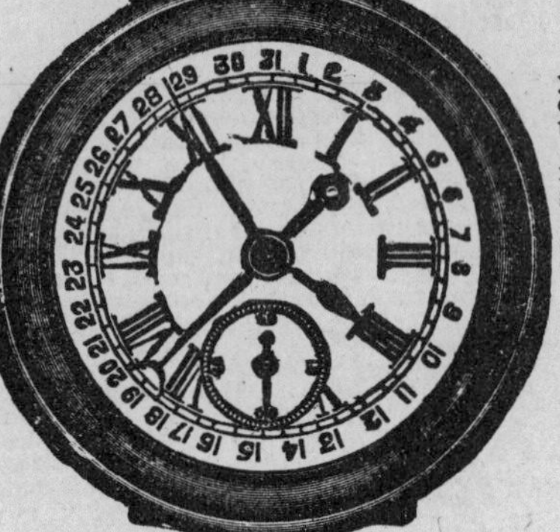

No. 4R4

SWISS CALENDAR WATCH

If you own one of these watches you will not find it necessary to consult an almanac or ask anyone to tell you the day of the month.

The case is nickel plated, and fitted with a heavy beveled edge glass.

The movement is imported, stem wind and stem set, jeweled, cylinder escapement, hard enameled dial, and in addition to being complete in every respect as a timekeeper, it has a

COMPLETE CALENDAR

which works automatically, always indicating correctly the day of the month.

No. 4R4 Price..........**$4.95**

SOLID SILVER, GOLD FILLED AND GUN METAL MOON CALENDAR WATCH.

This watch is made in Switzerland and is a mechanical wonder, but at the same time is offered at a price which is within the reach of all.

The case is **solid silver,** beautifully engraved, and fitted with heavy beveled edge glass.

The movement is stem wind and stem set, patent lever escapement, jeweled bearings, and in addition to being a complete timepiece, it is also a **COMPLETE CALENDAR, indicating the day of the week, day of the month, month of the year, and the changes of the moon.** At the same time it is so simple that it is not more liable to get out of order than an ordinary watch. It is fully guaranteed by both the manufacturers and ourselves.

We can furnish it in open face only.

No. 4R10 Solid silver..**$8.65**

No. 4R16 Gun metal, same as above..........**$6.00**

No. 4R17 Gold filled, 20 years guaranteed......**$18.50**

$8.65

No. 4R10

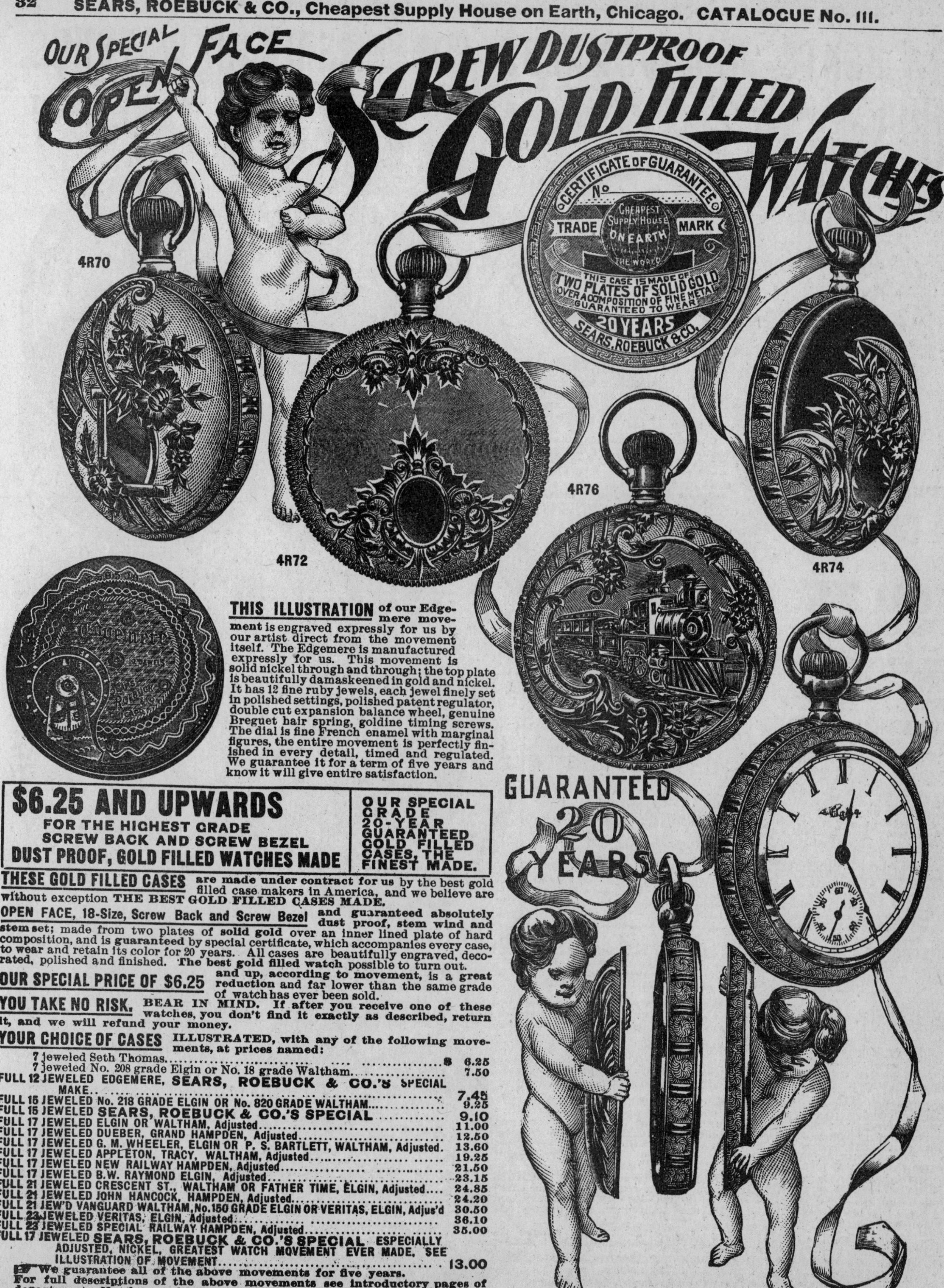

THIS ILLUSTRATION of our Edgemere movement is engraved expressly for us by our artist direct from the movement itself. The Edgemere is manufactured expressly for us. This movement is solid nickel through and through; the top plate is beautifully damaskeened in gold and nickel. It has 12 fine ruby jewels, each jewel finely set in polished settings, polished patent regulator, double cut expansion balance wheel, genuine Breguet hair spring, goldine timing screws. The dial is fine French enamel with marginal figures, the entire movement is perfectly finished in every detail, timed and regulated. We guarantee it for a term of five years and know it will give entire satisfaction.

$6.25 AND UPWARDS

FOR THE HIGHEST GRADE SCREW BACK AND SCREW BEZEL

DUST PROOF, GOLD FILLED WATCHES MADE

OUR SPECIAL GRADE 20-YEAR GUARANTEED GOLD FILLED CASES, THE FINEST MADE.

THESE GOLD FILLED CASES are made under contract for us by the best gold filled case makers in America, and we believe are without exception THE BEST GOLD FILLED CASES MADE.

OPEN FACE, 18-Size, Screw Back and Screw Bezel and guaranteed absolutely dust proof, stem wind and stem set; made from two plates of solid gold over an inner lined plate of hard composition, and is guaranteed by special certificate, which accompanies every case, to wear and retain its color for 20 years. All cases are beautifully engraved, decorated, polished and finished. The best gold filled watch possible to turn out.

OUR SPECIAL PRICE OF $6.25 and up, according to movement, is a great reduction and far lower than the same grade of watch has ever been sold.

YOU TAKE NO RISK. BEAR IN MIND. If after you receive one of these watches, you don't find it exactly as described, return it, and we will refund your money.

YOUR CHOICE OF CASES ILLUSTRATED, with any of the following movements, at prices named:

7 jeweled Seth Thomas	$ 6.25
7 jeweled No. 208 grade Elgin or No. 18 grade Waltham	7.50
FULL 12 JEWELED EDGEMERE, SEARS, ROEBUCK & CO.'S SPECIAL MAKE	7.45
FULL 15 JEWELED No. 218 GRADE ELGIN OR No. 820 GRADE WALTHAM	9.25
FULL 15 JEWELED SEARS, ROEBUCK & CO.'S SPECIAL	9.10
FULL 17 JEWELED ELGIN OR WALTHAM, Adjusted	11.00
FULL 17 JEWELED DUEBER, GRAND HAMPDEN, Adjusted	12.50
FULL 17 JEWELED G. M. WHEELER, ELGIN OR P. S. BARTLETT, WALTHAM, Adjusted	13.60
FULL 17 JEWELED APPLETON, TRACY, WALTHAM, Adjusted	19.25
FULL 17 JEWELED NEW RAILWAY HAMPDEN, Adjusted	21.50
FULL 17 JEWELED B.W. RAYMOND ELGIN, Adjusted	23.15
FULL 21 JEWELED CRESCENT ST., WALTHAM OR FATHER TIME, ELGIN, Adjusted	24.85
FULL 21 JEWELED JOHN HANCOCK, HAMPDEN, Adjusted	24.20
FULL 21 JEW'D VANGUARD WALTHAM, No. 150 GRADE ELGIN OR VERITAS, ELGIN, Adjus'd	30.50
FULL 23 JEWELED VERITAS, ELGIN, Adjusted	36.10
FULL 23 JEWELED SPECIAL RAILWAY HAMPDEN, Adjusted	35.00
FULL 17 JEWELED SEARS, ROEBUCK & CO.'S SPECIAL ESPECIALLY ADJUSTED, NICKEL, GREATEST WATCH MOVEMENT EVER MADE, SEE ILLUSTRATION OF MOVEMENT	13.00

☞ We guarantee all of the above movements for five years.

For full descriptions of the above movements see introductory pages of department. No charges for repairs on watches or clocks will be allowed unless our written consent is first secured in advance.

OUR SPECIAL GOLD FILLED HUNTING CASES

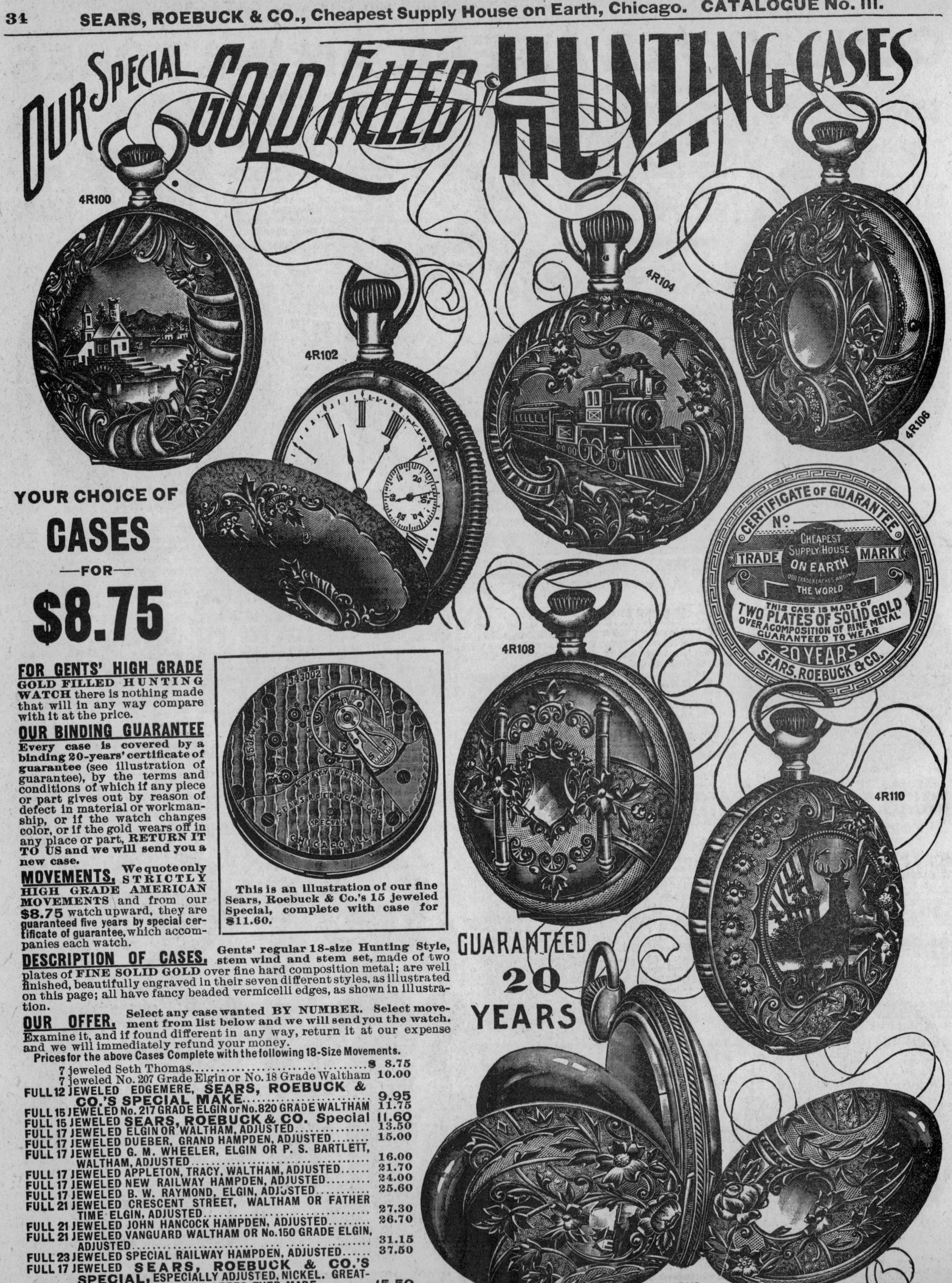

This is an illustration of our fine Sears, Roebuck & Co.'s 15 jeweled Special, complete with case for $11.60.

YOUR CHOICE OF

CASES

—FOR—

$8.75

FOR GENTS' HIGH GRADE GOLD FILLED HUNTING WATCH there is nothing made that will in any way compare with it at the price.

OUR BINDING GUARANTEE Every case is covered by a binding 20-years' certificate of guarantee (see illustration of guarantee), by the terms and conditions of which if any piece or part gives out by reason of defect in material or workmanship, or if the watch changes color, or if the gold wears off in any place or part, **RETURN IT TO US** and we will send you a new case.

MOVEMENTS. We quote only **STRICTLY HIGH GRADE AMERICAN MOVEMENTS** and from our **$8.75** watch upward, they are guaranteed five years by special certificate of guarantee, which accompanies each watch.

DESCRIPTION OF CASES. Gents' regular 18-size Hunting Style, stem wind and stem set, made of two plates of **FINE SOLID GOLD** over fine hard composition metal; are well finished, beautifully engraved in their seven different styles, as illustrated on this page; all have fancy beaded vermicelli edges, as shown in illustration.

OUR OFFER. Select any case wanted **BY NUMBER.** Select movement from list below and we will send you the watch. Examine it, and if found different in any way, return it at our expense and we will immediately refund your money.

Prices for the above Cases Complete with the following 18-Size Movements.

7 jeweled Seth Thomas	$ 8.75
7 jeweled No. 207 Grade Elgin or No. 18 Grade Waltham	10.00
FULL 12 JEWELED EDGEMERE, SEARS, ROEBUCK & CO.'S SPECIAL MAKE	9.95
FULL 15 JEWELED No. 217 GRADE ELGIN or No. 820 GRADE WALTHAM	11.75
FULL 15 JEWELED SEARS, ROEBUCK & CO. Special	11.60
FULL 17 JEWELED ELGIN OR WALTHAM, ADJUSTED	13.50
FULL 17 JEWELED DUEBER, GRAND HAMPDEN, ADJUSTED	15.00
FULL 17 JEWELED G. M. WHEELER, ELGIN OR P. S. BARTLETT, WALTHAM, ADJUSTED	16.00
FULL 17 JEWELED APPLETON, TRACY, WALTHAM, ADJUSTED	21.70
FULL 17 JEWELED NEW RAILWAY HAMPDEN, ADJUSTED	24.00
FULL 17 JEWELED B. W. RAYMOND, ELGIN, ADJUSTED	25.60
FULL 21 JEWELED CRESCENT STREET, WALTHAM OR FATHER TIME ELGIN, ADJUSTED	27.30
FULL 21 JEWELED JOHN HANCOCK HAMPDEN, ADJUSTED	26.70
FULL 21 JEWELED VANGUARD WALTHAM OR No. 150 GRADE ELGIN, ADJUSTED	31.15
FULL 23 JEWELED SPECIAL RAILWAY HAMPDEN, ADJUSTED	37.50
FULL 17 JEWELED SEARS, ROEBUCK & CO.'S SPECIAL, ESPECIALLY ADJUSTED, NICKEL. GREATEST WATCH MOVEMENT OFFER EVER MADE (See illustration of movement.)	15.50

For Full Description of above Movements, see introductory pages to this Department.

COIN SILVER AMERICAN WATCHES

$6.55 TO $37.13

FOR A HEAVY, STRONG, SUBSTANTIAL WATCH CASE to thoroughly protect the watch movement there is nothing superior to a coin silver watch case properly constructed. These requirements the watches listed on this page thoroughly fulfill, and which we sell at a price other dealers are forced to pay for them.

A large number of persons prefer carrying a silver watch instead of a solid gold, gold filled or plated. That class of customers we keep closely in mind when purchasing our stock of solid coin silver cases, searching the market carefully to secure the finest grade of silver, the highest character of workmanship in construction and finish; and take pleasure in recommending the celebrated Fahys' and Dueber Watch Cases.

$6.75 TO $39.25

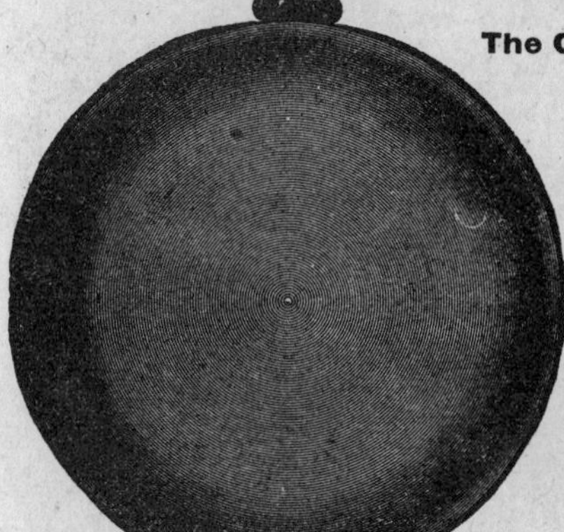

The Cases are Fitted with an extra double thick crystal, beveled edge, giving the watch that double strength which makes an open face watch so popular in the minds of the general public.

NO CHARGES FOR REPAIRS ON WATCHES OR CLOCKS WILL BE ALLOWED UNLESS OUR WRITTEN CONSENT IS FIRST SECURED IN ADVANCE.

No. 4R120 3-ounce Fahys' Open Face, dust proof, screw back and bezel coin silver case.
No. 4R122 4-ounce Case, same as above.
At 30 cents more than prices quoted we can supply any of the above beautifully hand engraved.

No. 4R124 3-ounce Dueber Open Face, dust proof, gold jointed case.
No. 4R126 4-ounce Case, same as above.
At 30 cents more than prices quoted we can supply any of the above beautifully hand engraved.

No. 4R128 3-ounce Hunting, gold joint, plain case.
No. 4R130 4-ounce Case, same as above.
No. 4R133 5-ounce Case, same as above.
At 60 cents more than prices quoted we can supply any of the above beautifully hand engraved.

This shows the SEARS, ROEBUCK & CO.'S SPECIAL 17 JEWELED MOVEMENT GREATEST VALUE EVER OFFERED.

WE FIT THESE CASES WITH THE FOLLOWING 18-SIZE MOVEMENTS.	4R120 4R124	4R128 4R139	4R122	4R126	4R136 4R140	4R130	4R138 4R144	4R133
7 Jeweled Seth Thomas	$ 6.55	$ 6.75	$ 7.00	$ 7.45	$ 7.55	$ 7.75	$ 8.20	$ 9.50
7 Jeweled 208 Grade Elgin or No. 18 Grade Waltham	7.80	8.00	8.25	8.70	8.80	9.00	9.45	10.75
Full 12 Jeweled EDGEMERE, SEARS, ROEBUCK & CO. SPECIAL MAKE	7.75	7.95	8.20	8.65	8.75	8.95	9.40	10.70
Full 15 Jeweled 218 Grade Elgin or 820 Grade Waltham	9.55	9.75	10.00	10.45	10.55	10.75	11.20	12.50
Full 15 Jeweled SEARS, ROEBUCK & CO. SPECIAL	9.40	9.60	9.85	10.30	10.40	10.60	11.05	12.35
Full 17 Jeweled Elgin or Waltham, Adjusted	11.30	11.50	11.75	12.20	12.30	12.50	12.95	14.25
Full 17 Jeweled Dueber Grand, Hampden, Adjusted	12.80	13.00	13.25	13.70	13.80	14.00	14.45	15.75
Full 17 Jeweled G. M. Wheeler, Elgin or P. S. Bartlett, Waltham, Adjusted	13.99	14.13	14.65	14.70	14.80	15.00	15.45	16.75
Full 17 Jeweled Appleton, Tracy, Waltham, Adjusted	19.64	19.78	20.28	20.28	20.36	20.50	20.75	22.40
Full 17 Jeweled New Railway, Hampden, Adjusted	21.80	22.00	22.25	22.70	22.80	23.00	23.45	24.75
Full 17 Jeweled B. W. Raymond, Elgin, Adjusted	23.54	23.68	24.18	24.18	24.26	24:40	24.65	26.30
Full 21 Jeweled Crescent St., Waltham or Father Time, Elgin, Adjusted	25.24	25.38	25.88	25.88	25.96	26.10	26.35	28.00
Full 21 Jeweled John Hancock, Hampden, Adjusted	24.50	24.70	24.95	25.40	25.50	25.10	26.15	27.45
Full 21 Jeweled Vanguard, Waltham; 150 Grade Elgin, or Veritas, Elgin, Adjusted	30.89	31.03	31.53	31.53	31.60	31.75	32.00	33.65
Full 23 Jeweled Veritas, Elgin, Adjusted	36.49	36.63	37.13	37.13	37.21	37.35	37.60	39.25
Full 23 Jeweled Special Railway, Hampden, Adjusted	35.30	35.50	35.75	36.20	36.30	36.50	36.95	38.25
Full 17 Jeweled SEARS, ROEBUCK & CO., especially adjusted, nickel, greatest watch movement offer ever made. (See illustration of movement.)	13.30	13.50	13.75	14.20	14.30	14.50	14.95	16.25

$7.55 TO $37.60

THIS CASE FITTED WITH OUR 12 JEWELED EDGEMERE MOVEMENT AT $8.75

THIS IS OUR NEW GENTS' REGULAR 18-SIZE MOVEMENT. SEARS, ROEBUCK & CO'S. SPECIAL.

Made expressly for us. It is full 15 jeweled, handsomely damaskeened, patent regulator and escapement, safety pinion, jewels set in settings and is one of the best high grade movements on the market. We guarantee it for a term of five years.

The Edgemere Movement Has 12 Fine Ruby Jewels.

$7.55 TO $37.60

No. 4R136 3-ounce Fahys' Open Face, dust proof, screw back and bezel, gold inlaid case. Prices of watch listed above.
No. 4R138 4-ounce Case, same as above.

No. 4R139 Dust Proof, screw bezel, solid back.

No. 4R140 3-ounce Fahys' Open Face, dust proof, screw back and bezel, gold inlaid case. Prices of watch listed above.
No. 4R144 4-ounce Case, same as above.

12 AND 16-SIZE THIN MODEL SOLID GOLD WATCHES.

AT $23.75 OR $26.50 OPEN FACE OR HUNTING STYLE. The latest 12-size solid gold 14-karat, warranted United States Assay; case fitted with a genuine Elgin or Waltham 7-jeweled grade movement; GUARANTEED AN ACCURATE TIMEKEEPER FOR A TERM OF 5 YEARS. THE 12-SIZE WATCH IS THE LATEST SIZE MADE, it is the smallest gentlemen's size, a size larger than the largest ladies' size, and the most popular size used in our large cities.

IF YOU DESIRE A SMALL SIZE WATCH, one that does not weigh down your pocket, one that is not bulky and is an assured timekeeper, BUY THE LATEST 12-SIZE WATCH.

PRICES POSITIVELY LESS THAN WHOLESALE.

OUR 10-JEWELED EDGEMERE MOVEMENT FITTED IN ANY ONE OF THESE 14-KARAT SOLID GOLD 12-SIZE CASES at $23.70 to $37.45, means a price equal to 40 per cent less than your local dealer asks for an inferior watch.

AT $26.45 we offer our solid gold 16-size latest model watch, fitted with our new 10-jeweled Edgemere movement.

$26.45 IS THE PRICE OF THE WATCH COMPLETE.

REMEMBER: We carry nothing but 14-karat quality in our solid gold cases.

12-SIZE HUNTING AND OPEN FACE WATCHES.

14-Karat Solid Gold Watches.

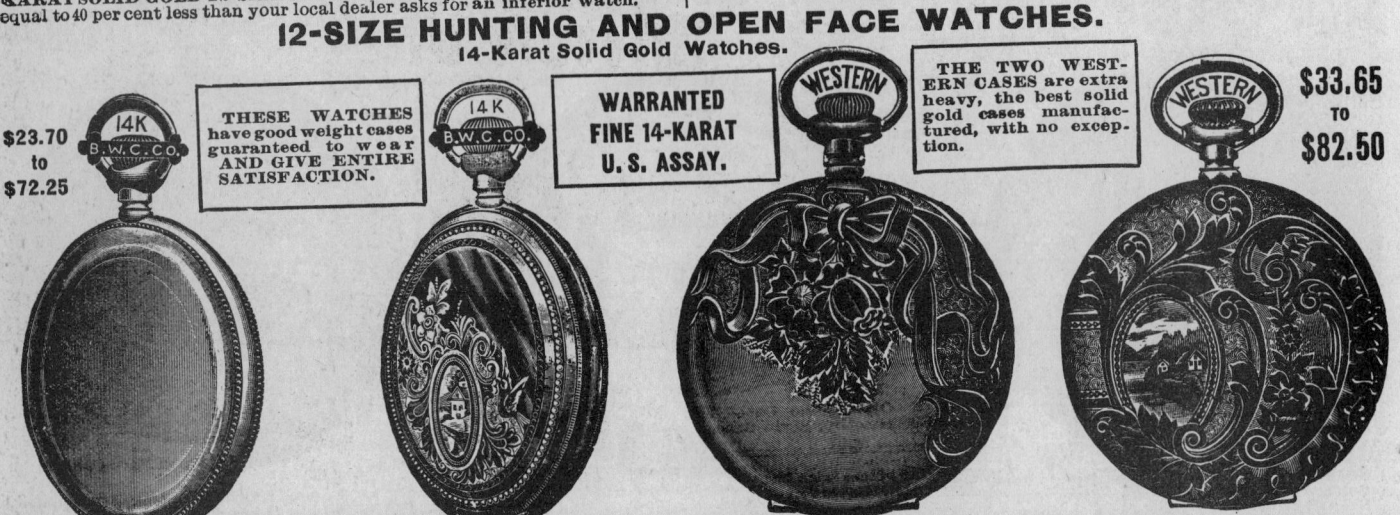

$23.70 to $72.25

THESE WATCHES have good weight cases guaranteed to wear AND GIVE ENTIRE SATISFACTION.

WARRANTED FINE 14-KARAT U. S. ASSAY.

THE TWO WESTERN CASES are extra heavy, the best solid gold cases manufactured, with no exception.

$33.65 TO $82.50

Plain or Engine Turned.
No. 4R262 Hunting Style.
No. 4R263 Open Face.

No. 4R264 Hunting Style.
No. 4R265 Open Face.

No. 4R266 Hunting Style.
No. 4R267 Open Face.

No. 4R268 Hunting Style.
No. 4R269 Open Face.

WE FIT THESE CASES WITH THE FOLLOWING 12-SIZE MOVEMENTS. WARRANTED FOR 5 YEARS	PRICE OF COMPLETE WATCH.						
	No. 4R263 Open Face	No. 4R262 Hunting No. 4R265 Open Face	No. 4R264 Hunting	No. 4R267 Open Face	No. 4R269 Open Face	No. 4R266 Hunting	No. 4R268 Hunting
7 Jeweled No. 232 and 234 Grade Elgin or 210 Grade Waltham	$23.75	$25.00	$26.50	$31.00	$33.70	$36.00	$37.50
Full 10 JEWELED EDGEMERE, SEARS, ROEBUCK & CO.'S SPECIAL MAKE	23.70	24.95	26.45	30.95	33.65	35.95	37.45
Full 15 jeweled No. 187 or 191 Grade Elgin or 220 Grade Waltham	26.75	28.00	29.50	34.00	36.70	39.00	40.50
Full 17 jeweled No. 188 Grade Elgin or Royal Waltham, adjusted	30.75	32.00	33.50	38.00	40.70	43.00	44.50
Full 17 jeweled Riverside Waltham, adjusted	36.75	38.00	39.50	44.00	46.70	49.00	50.50
Full 19 jeweled No. 189 or 193 Grade Elgin, adjusted	40.55	41.30	42.25	46.30	49.00	50.80	51.55
Full 21 jeweled Riverside Maximus, Waltham, adjusted	65.85	66.60	67.60	71.60	74.30	76.10	76.85
Full 23 jeweled No. 190 or 194 Grade Elgin, adjusted	71.50	72.25	73.25	77.25	79.95	81.75	82.50

16-SIZE HUNTING THIN MODEL 14-KARAT SOLID GOLD CASES.

$30.70 AND UPWARD

$27.20 AND UPWARD

It took us four years to perfect our "Sears, Roebuck & Co.'s Special" Movement. We would be satisfied with nothing less than a masterpiece.

$25.20 AND UPWARD

This is Our New 16-Size Sears, Roebuck & Co.'s Special 15-Jeweled Movement. See the description. It is full 15-jeweled, set in settings, solid gold plated, Roman color, beautifully finished, patent pinion and escapement, high grade finish throughout, guaranteed for five years.

No. 4R278 Extra Heavy Weight.

No. 4R280 Plain or Engine Turned. Medium Weight.

No. 4R282 Medium Weight.

WE FIT THESE CASES WITH THE FOLLOWING 16-SIZE MOVEMENTS.	PRICE OF COMPLETE WATCH.		
	No. 4R282	No. 4R280	No. 4R278
7 Jeweled American made movement	$ 25.20	$ 27.20	$ 30.70
7 Jeweled No. 210 Grade Elgin or No. 610 Grade Waltham	26.50	28.50	32.00
FULL 10 JEWELED EDGEMERE, SEARS, ROEBUCK & CO.'S SPECIAL MAKE	26.45	28.45	31.95
FULL 15 JEWELED No. 247 GRADE ELGIN OR No. 620 GRADE WALTHAM	30.00	32.00	35.50
FULL 15 JEWELED SEARS, ROEBUCK & CO.'S SPECIAL	28.50	30.50	34.00
FULL 17 JEWELED ELGIN No. 241 GRADE, OR THE No. 630 GRADE WALTHAM, ADJUSTED	32.50	34.50	38.00
FULL 17 JEWELED ROYAL WALTHAM, ADJUSTED	34.50	36.50	40.00
FULL 17 JEWELED ELGIN, No. 154 GRADE, ADJUSTED	38.00	40.00	43.50
FULL 17 JEWELED RIVERSIDE WALTHAM, ADJUSTED	40.50	42.50	46.00
FULL 17 JEWELED ELGIN, No. 155 GRADE, ADJUSTED	42.00	44.00	47.50
FULL 21 JEWELED ELGIN, No. 156 GRADE, OR RIVERSIDE MAXIMUS, WALTHAM, ADJUSTED	67.00	69.00	72.50
FULL 17 JEWELED SEARS, ROEBUCK & CO.'S SPECIAL, especially adjusted, Nickel, greatest Watch Movement ever offered. See Illustration of movement	32.00	34.00	37.50

We Guarantee all of the Above Movements for a Term of Five Years.

OUR 16-SIZE SOLID SILVER, SILVERINE AND GOLD FILLED WATCHES.

A SOLID SILVER CASE FITTED WITH AN AMERICAN MADE movement for $5.30. You can save 25 to 35 per cent by buying your watches from us. Why not get a watch that is reliable in every respect. We give you our written, binding guarantee with every watch we sell to be as represented. The 16-size watch is a size smaller than the popular 18-size. It does not weigh down your vest; it fits the pocket; it's the gentleman's size. The correct size for your young son. It's the doctor's size watch; in fact, it pleases all and is adapted for all.

WE HAVE REDUCED THE PRICES so that we will sell thousands of them. You need not buy until you have investigated. Price these watches at the jewelry store; don't buy unless you find what we say is true: 35 to 50 per cent cheaper than what they ask. Order one of these watches, we will ship to you by express or mail, mail is the cheaper way, and if not as described and not as you expected, return it and we will refund you your money. You take no risk in ordering goods from us.

$3.85 TO $51.12

REFER TO PRICE LIST BELOW.

16-SIZE SILVER AND SILVERINE CASES.

If Goods Prove not Satisfactory return and we will exchange or cheerfully refund your money. We desire satisfied customers.

$4.30 TO $51.50

No. 4R375 Silverine. Screw Back and Screw Bezel.
No. 4R377 Solid Silver, same as above.

No. 4R379 Solid Silver, Hunting Style, Gold Ornamented, Hand Engraved, Fancy Center.

No. 4R381 Silverine, Jointed Back and Front.
No. 4R383 Solid Silver, same as above.

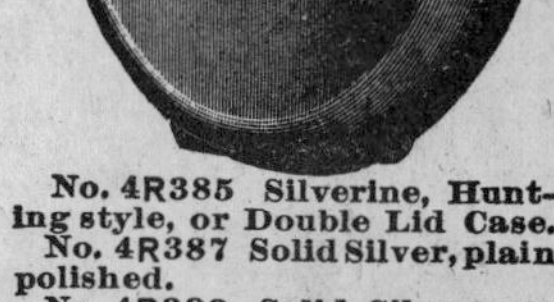

No. 4R385 Silverine, Hunting style, or Double Lid Case.
No. 4R387 Solid Silver, plain polished.
No. 4R390 Solid Silver, engine turned.

SPECIAL 16-SIZE

We fit these cases with the following 16-Size movements.	No. 4R375 No. 4R381 Silverine	No. 4R385 Silverine	No. 4R377 Solid Silver	No. 4R383 Solid Silver	No. 4R387 No. 4R390 Solid Silver	No. 4R379 Solid Silver
7 Jeweled American Made Movement	$3.85	$4.30	$5.30	$5.95	$6.20	$ 8.45
7 Jeweled 210 or 211 Grade Elgin or 610 Grade Waltham	5.57	5.95	6.75	7.25	7.50	9.75
Full 10 Jeweled EDGEMERE, SEARS, ROEBUCK & CO.'S SPECIAL MAKE	5.10	5.55	6.55	7.00	7.40	9.65
Full 15 Jeweled 248 or 247 Grade Elgin or 620 Grade Waltham	9.52	9.90	10.70	11.10	11.20	13.25
Full 15 Jeweled SEARS, ROEBUCK & CO.'S SPECIAL	7.15	7.60	8.60	9.25	9.50	11.75
Full 17 Jeweled No. 244 GRADE ELGIN or No. 630 GRADE WALTHAM, Adjusted	12.32	12.70	13.50	13.90	14.00	16.00
Full 17 Jeweled ROYAL WALTHAM, Adjusted	14.57	14.95	15.75	16.15	16.25	18.25
Full 17 Jeweled ELGIN, No. 160 GRADE, Adjusted	18.52	18.90	19.70	20.10	20.20	22.20
Full 17 Jeweled RIVERSIDE WALTHAM, Adjusted	21.32	21.70	22.50	22.90	23.00	25.00
Full 17 Jeweled ELGIN, No. 161 GRADE, Adjusted	23.00	23.38	24.18	24.58	24.68	26.70
Full 21 Jeweled ELGIN, No. 162 GRADE or RIVERSIDE MAXIMUS WALTHAM, Adjusted	51.12	51.50	52.30	52.70	52.80	54.80
Full 17 Jeweled SEARS, ROEBUCK & CO.'S SPECIAL, especially adjusted, Nickel, greatest watch movement ever offered. (See illustration of movement.)	11.15	11.60	12.60	13.25	13.50	15.75

GENTS' 16-SIZE Hunting and Open Face, 20-YEAR GOLD FILLED WATCHES.

$6.45 TO $16.50

$10.45 for the highest grade 16-size hunting, 20-year, guaranteed gold filled case, complete with a 10 jeweled Edgemere Movement means a great saving to you—a price much lower than is made by any other house.

$7.70 for your choice of cases in open face, fitted with a genuine 12 jeweled Edgemere Movement.

Guaranteed Highest Grade Gold Filled Case and accompanying each case is a Binding, 20-Year Guarantee, by the terms and conditions of which, if the case wears through or changes its color within 20 years we will replace it free of charge.

$6.45 TO $16.50

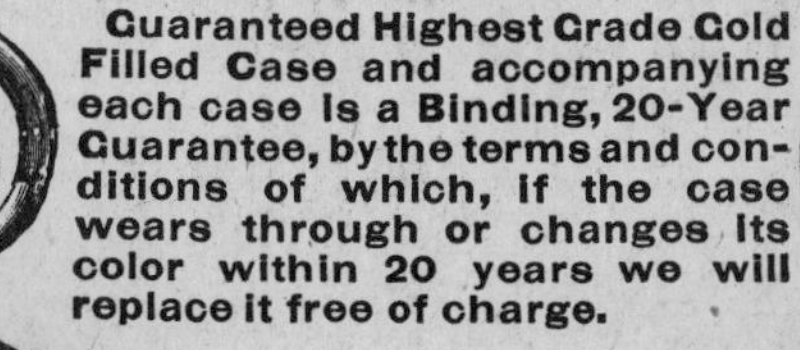

NEVER BEFORE in the history of the watch case business has the small or 16-size case sold so well as at the present time.

WE CONTROL The product of the factory on these 16-size Hunting, 20-year Gold Filled Cases, which alone makes it possible for us to make this incomparably low price.

No. 4R391 16-size, 20-year guaranteed, gold filled at $9.20 and up. Hunting style.
No. 4R392 20-year guaranteed gold filled, at $6.45 and up, 16-size, open face, screw back and screw bezel.

No. 4R394 Your choice of these highest grade, 16-size hunting cases, with movement at $9.20 and up.
No. 4R396 16-size, open face, screw back and screw bezel, 20-year guaranteed, gold filled, $6.45 and up.

No. 4R398 $9.20 and up, according to movement. The highest grade 16-size, 20-year, gold filled hunting style.
No. 4R400 16-size, open face, screw back and screw bezel, 20-year guaranteed, gold filled, $6.45 and up.

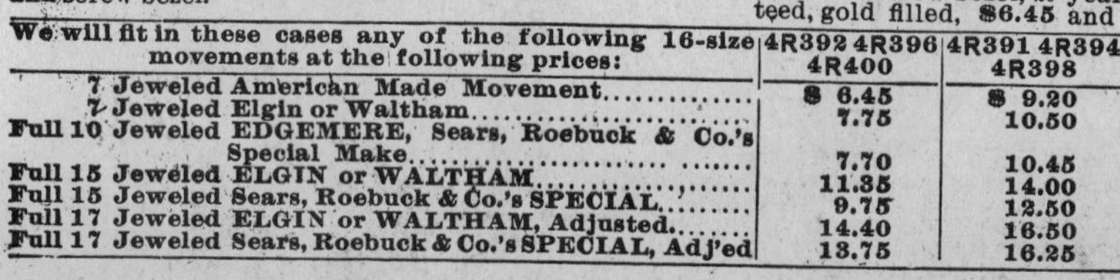

We will fit in these cases any of the following 16-size movements at the following prices:	4R392 4R396 4R400	4R391 4R394 4R398
7 Jeweled American Made Movement	$ 6.45	$ 9.20
7 Jeweled Elgin or Waltham	7.75	10.50
Full 10 Jeweled EDGEMERE, Sears, Roebuck & Co.'s Special Make	7.70	10.45
Full 15 Jeweled ELGIN or WALTHAM	11.35	14.00
Full 15 Jeweled Sears, Roebuck & Co.'s SPECIAL	9.75	12.50
Full 17 Jeweled ELGIN or WALTHAM, Adjusted	14.40	16.50
Full 17 Jeweled Sears, Roebuck & Co.'s SPECIAL, Adj'ed	13.75	16.25

Any of these 16-size, Hunting, highest grade 20-year, gold filled cases furnished complete with full 15 jeweled Sears, Roebuck & Co.'s special 16-size for $12.50. Open face for $9.75.

$10.45 BUYS A WATCH

You pay your dealer at least $25.00 for. This movement is strictly high grade, guaranteed by special certificate for five years. With care will last a lifetime.

Our Special Ladie's Gold Filled Watches
Guaranteed 20 Years.
4R625
4R627
4R640
4R639
4R629
4R637
4R635
4R631
4R633
CERTIFICATE OF GUARANTEE
No.
CHEAPEST SUPPLY HOUSE ON EARTH
TRADE MARK
THIS CASE IS MADE OF TWO PLATES OF SOLID GOLD OVER A COMPOSITION OF FINE METAL GUARANTEED TO WEAR
20 YEARS
SEARS, ROEBUCK & CO.
OUR PRICE IS
$8.50
No Retail Dealer Can Sell These Watches.
We control the entire product of the factory for these CASES in both Ladies' and Gents' Size.
EVERY CASE MADE TO OUR OWN SPECIFICATIONS AND DESIGNS, under contract by one of the largest and most reliable watch case manufacturers in America; a concern whose enviable reputation for the manufacture of the highest grade gold filled cases is A GUARANTEE FOR QUALITY.
WE SAVE YOU ONE-HALF IN PRICE. Our price to you is based on the actual cost of material and labor, with only our one small percentage of profit added. YOU SAVE THREE PROFITS and own the watch on the basis of actual cost to make by placing your order in our hands.
WE MAKE THE PRICE AND PROTECT YOU BY A BINDING GUARANTEE.
DESCRIPTION OF CASES. Made of two plates of solid gold over fine hard composition metal, are thoroughly well made in every respect and beautifully engraved. They are warranted by certificate of guarantee, which accompanies every case (see copy of guarantee in picture) to wear and retain their color for TWENTY YEARS. So far as finish, quality and design are concerned there is nothing made that will surpass them. You must not get the impression on account of the low price that they have an appearance of cheapness, for such is not the case. They are in appearance, style, finish, durability and service equal to any case made.
MANY CUSTOMERS of ours own one of these watches. They are satisfied in every way. We know you would be. We know by actual test exactly what these goods are and so can conscientiously recommend them to you.
This is a Picture taken direct from our 6-size
SEARS, ROEBUCK & CO.
15 Jeweled Movement,
a movement we can guarantee to give entire satisfaction.
Price........................ $10.75
Fitted in any case illustrated here.
NICKEL
7 jeweled Seth Thomas.. $ 8.50
7 jeweled, No. 206 Grade Elgin or "Y" Grade Waltham...... 9.50
FULL 11 JEWELED EDGEMERE, SEARS, ROEBUCK & CO.'S SPECIAL MAKE 9.45
FULL 15 JEWELED SEARS, ROEBUCK & CO.'S SPECIAL 10.75
FULL 15 JEWELED, No. 216 GRADE ELGIN OR "V" GRADE WALTHAM.... 11.00
FULL 17 JEWELED SEARS ROEBUCK & CO.'S SPECIAL, ESPECIALLY MADE........ 12.50
CONSIDER OUR GUARANTEE. Every case covered by special certificate of guarantee for twenty years. Every movement guaranteed for five years, and so covered by a binding guarantee.

OUR LADIES' NEW O-SIZE, 20-YEAR, GOLD FILLED WATCHES AT $8.00 AND UPWARDS ARE THE GREATEST VALUES EVER OFFERED IN THE HIGHEST GRADE GOLD FILLED WATCHES IN THIS SMALL SIZE...

$8.00 FOR LADIES' HIGHEST GRADE O-SIZE GOLD FILLED WATCH.

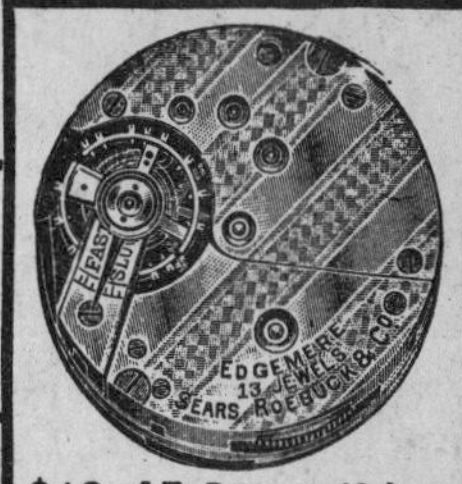

$10.45 Buys our 13 jeweled Edgemere, fitted in any of these high grade cases you may select.

YOUR CHOICE OF CASES with 7 jeweled Atlas movement for $8.00. Select any case illustrated on this page, the price is the same; twelve different patterns to select from, and all the latest style.

NEVER BEFORE were such high grade gold filled watches offered for so little money. **Our $8.00 price is made possible by reason of our taking the entire output of the factory to get the lowest manufacturing cost,** to which we add our one small percentage of profit.

THESE LADIES' O-SIZE CASES are made by one of the largest and most reliable watch case manufacturers in America, made from two heavy plates of solid gold over an inner plate of hard composition metal and are guaranteed by special certificate of guarantee to wear for 20 years. Cases are ladies' 0-size, one size smaller than regular 6-size, the most popular, stylish and handsome size made, they are beautifully engraved and decorated, have the latest style antique bow and winding crown, are stem wind and stem set hunting.

OUR PROTECTIVE OFFER: IF, AFTER YOU EXAMINE THE WATCH YOU GET, you do not find it in EVERY WAY just as represented and warranted, return it to us, and we will REFUND YOU THE PURCHASE PRICE.

No charges for repairs on watches or clocks will be allowed unless our written consent is first secured in advance.

THE EDGEMERE IS OUR LATEST MOVEMENT BARGAIN.

$8.00 IS THE LOWEST PRICE EVER KNOWN ON SUCH A WATCH.

YOU HAVE YOUR CHOICE OF CASES.

No. 4R680

No. 4R682

This is the exact picture of the 17 Jeweled Waltham Movement.

No. 4R684

No. 4R686

YOU CAN MAKE MONEY SELLING THESE WATCHES.

THE GREATEST WATCH VALUES IN THE WORLD.

SELECT THE MOVEMENT AS QUOTED BELOW.

No. 4R688

No. 4R690

This is the picture of our 15 jeweled Waltham O-size.

EVERY CASE WARRANTED FOR TWENTY YEARS.

No. 4R692

No. 4R694

OUR O-SIZE EDGEMERE MOVEMENT HAS 13 FINE RUBY JEWELS.

Description of Suffolk Movement.

JEWELERS ASK 50 PER CENT MORE FOR THESE WATCHES.

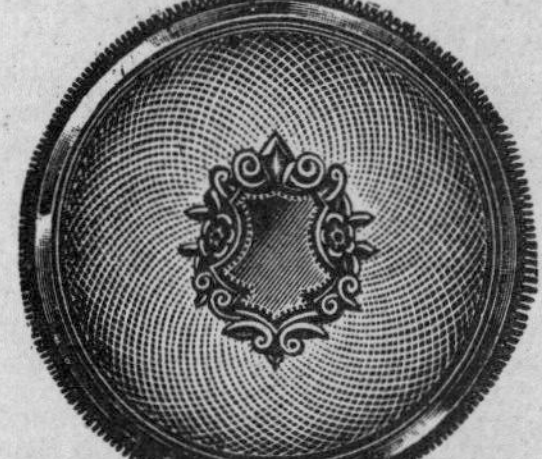

No. 4R696

No. 4R698

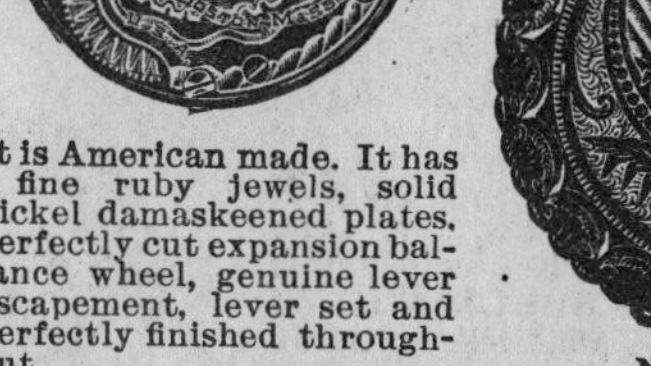

It is American made. It has 7 fine ruby jewels, solid nickel damaskeened plates, perfectly cut expansion balance wheel, genuine lever escapement, lever set and perfectly finished throughout.

No. 4R700

No. 4R702

WE CAN FIT THESE MOVEMENTS IN ANY OF THE ABOVE CASES.

7 jeweled Atlas	$ 8.00
7 jeweled Suffolk	9.50
7 jeweled, No. 269 Grade Elgin or No. 61 Grade Waltham	10.50
Full 13 jeweled Edgemere, SEARS, ROEBUCK & CO.'S special make	10.45
Full 11 jeweled No. 224 Grade Elgin	$11.75
Full 15 jeweled No. 223 Grade Elgin or No. 65 Grade Waltham	13.50
Full 16 jeweled Waltham, Adjusted	15.50
Full 17 jeweled No. 204 Grade Elgin, Adjusted	16.50
Full 17 jeweled Riverside Waltham	25.15

WE GUARANTEE ANY ONE OF THE ABOVE MOVEMENTS FOR FIVE YEARS.

This is the picture made direct from the photograph of the 15-jeweled 400-size Hampden Movement.

"THE FOUR HUNDRED"

Smallest American Watch Made. Handsomest Ladies' Watch Made

IN 14-KARAT SOLID GOLD AND 14-KARAT GOLD FILLED. GUARANTEED FOR 25 YEARS' WEAR.

$17.00 AND $19.50 for 14-karat Solid Gold Cases, according to movement.

HIGHEST GRADE GOLD FILLED MODEL. Made by the Great Dueber Watch Case Co., at Canton, Ohio, from extra heavy plates of 14-karat solid gold over an inner plate of hard composition metal, and is guaranteed to wear for 25 years. A written binding 25 years' certificate of guarantee signed by John C. Dueber himself accompanies each case, by the terms and conditions of which if the case wears through or changes color within 25 years it will be replaced with a new one FREE OF CHARGE.

$11.50 AND $14.50 is our special offer, according to grade of movement for gold filled.

THE DUEBER "400"-SIZE is the exact size as illustrated; all the rage in large cities; very dainty, very handsome and just as durable, just as accurate as the largest sizes.

THESE "400"-SIZE CASES are stem wind and stem set hunting cases, elaborately engraved, decorated and ornamented as shown in illustrations, made with the latest style handsome antique bow.

WHEN YOU BUY A WATCH FROM US you are protected in every respect. We guarantee it to you to be in every way as represented. If not found so after a most thorough examination, RETURN IT AT OUR EXPENSE and we will cheerfully refund your money.

IN 14-KARAT SOLID GOLD you have a watch second to none. They have just been put on the market and are meeting with great success.

DON'T PAY RETAIL PRICES for watches when you can buy the latest "400"-size complete with a 7 jeweled movement for $11.50.

Remember, for 50 cents less than price quoted we can furnish open face case.

No. 4R776 14-K. filled.
No. 4R778 14-K. solid gold.

12 cents will carry one of these watches anywhere in the U. S. by registered mail.

No. 4R780 14-K. filled.
No. 4R782 14-K. solid gold.

Any name engraved on these cases at the rate of 2½ cents per letter.

No. 4R784 14-K. filled.
No. 4R786 14-K. solid gold.

We advocate the 15 jeweled grade movement.

No. 4R788 14-K. filled.
No. 4R790 14-K. solid gold.

No. 4R792 14-K. filled.
No. 4R794 14-K. solid gold

These cases are hand engraved and hand chased

No. 4R796 14-K. filled.
No. 4R798 14-K. solid gold.

The higher the grade the more accurate the time.

No. 4R800 14-K. filled.
No. 4R802 14-K. solid gold.

$14.50, with 15 jeweled Hampden movement.

No. 4R804 14-K. filled.
No. 4R806 14-K. solid gold.

No. 4R808 14-K. filled.
No. 4R810 14-K. solid gold.

Solid gold case fitted with 15 jeweled movement, $19.50.

No. 4R812 14-K. filled.
No. 4R814 14-K. solid gold.

WE FIT THESE CASES WITH THE FOLLOWING 400-SIZE MOVEMENTS:

SOLID GOLD—Prices for complete watch:
Full 7 Jeweled Molly Stark Hampden Movement.. $17.00
Full 15 Jeweled Hampden Movement.......... 19.50

GOLD FILLED—Prices for complete watch:
Full 7 Jeweled Molly Stark Hampden Movement.. $11.50
Full 15 Jeweled Hampden Movement.......... 14.50

ALL OF THE ABOVE MOVEMENTS WE GUARANTEE FOR A TERM OF FIVE YEARS.

NAPOLEON GOLD FILLED CASES.

GUARANTEED FOR A TERM OF TEN YEARS.

CUT PRICES.

NEVER BEFORE HAS A 10-YEAR GOLD FILLED CASE been offered at the price we are asking. The very latest sizes shown here. 16-size, 12-size in Open Face or Hunting style and 0-size. The latest gentlemen's size, boys' size and ladies' size. The Napoleon Case is manufactured by the celebrated Illinois Watch Case Company, of Elgin, Ill., manufacturers of the Elgin Giant and Elgin Commander gold filled cases.

$6.35 for a gentlemen's 16-size gold filled watch, hunting style, fitted with an American made movement, a price unheard of before. Our $6.00 price for this 0-size 10-karat 10-year gold filled case fitted with the celebrated 7 jeweled Atlas movement means a saving to you of no less than 50 per cent.

REMEMBER our liberal offer holds good with any of the watches you may select. If goods are not found as represented, return them and we will refund your money.

$6.00 TO $7.35

No. 4R816 16-Size Hunting.
No. 4R817 Open Face, Screw Back and Bezel.

	4R816	4R817
With 7 Jeweled American Made Movement	$6.35	$6.00
With 7 Jeweled Elgin or Waltham Movement	7.35	7.00
With 12 Jeweled Edgemere Movement	7.30	6.95

$7.95 TO $8.35

No. 4R818 12-Size Hunting.
No. 4R819 Open Face, Screw Back and Screw Bezel.

	4R818	4R819
With 7 Jeweled Elgin or Waltham Movement	$8.35	$8.00
With 10 Jeweled Edgemere Movement	8.30	7.95

$6.00 TO $8.45

No. 4R820 0-Size.

With 7 Jeweled Atlas Movement	$6.00
With 7 Jeweled Suffolk Movement	7.50
With 7 Jeweled Elgin or Waltham Movement	8.50
With 13 Jeweled Edgemere Movement	8.45

THE MOVEMENTS.

We guarantee any of the above movements for a term of five years against defect in material or workmanship.

LADIES' IMPORTED CHATELAINE WATCHES

NICKEL, SOLID GOLD, SILVER, GUN METAL and ENAMEL.

PRICE OF EACH COMPLETE

WE ALWAYS LEAD IN... STYLES and PRICES. THAT'S WHAT BRINGS OUR ...SUCCESS...

OUR TERMS ARE CASH ..WITH THE ORDER.. But we guarantee satisfaction or refund your money.

BUY WATCHES AND JEWELRY OF A FIRM THAT HAS A GOOD FINANCIAL STANDING.

No charges for repairs on watches or clocks will be allowed unless our written consent is first secured in advance.

No. 4R856 Ladies' Nickel Open Face Chatelaine Watch. Case is plain polished, and same size as illustrated; is stem wind and stem set, has an imported cylinder escapement movement, and is a good timekeeper. Price....................$3.25

No. 4R858 Ladies' Open Face Silver Chatelaine Watch. Size of watch, same as illustrated. Case is of solid silver, beautifully engraved and perfectly finished in every detail. Movement is a fine imported 7-jeweled Swiss cylinder one, stem wind and stem set. The extra fine finish and jeweling of this watch insures excellent timekeeping qualities. Price......................$4.00

No. 4R860 Ladies' Solid Silver, Engraved, Open Face Chatelaine Watch. Is stem wind, pendant set, has fine quality 7-ruby jeweled imported cylinder escapement movement with second hand. This watch is finished better and has heavier case than No. 4R858, and has second hand. Price..........................$4.25

No. 4R864 Solid Gold. Same as above. Price....................$10.00

No. 4R862 Ladies' Solid Silver Hunting Chatelaine Watch. Is stem wind and stem set and fitted with a fine 7 ruby jeweled imported cylinder escapement movement. Case is full engraved. Watch is a good timekeeper. Price..............$4.56

No. 4R866 Solid Gold. Same as above. Price.........$12.50

We are always Up to Date. The very Latest

GUN METAL WATCH

A BARGAIN AT $2.75

No. 4R868

No. 4R868 Gentlemen's or Ladies' Size Gun Metal Watch for $2.75. Is made of fine oxidized gun metal and will wear a lifetime; especially adapted for modest people. The movement has cylinder escapement and is finely jeweled. It is manufactured in Switzerland. We would especially recommend this watch to those desiring a cheap and durable watch, and for the price quoted it is a wonderful bargain. Price............$2.75

No. 4R869 Ladies' Size. Same style. About one-half the size of illustration. Price.....$2.75

We Guarantee to Satisfy you or Refund Money.

No. 4R870

No. 4R870 Our Latest Genuine French Enameled Chatelaine Watch, for $8.00. The case is gold filled, beautifully enameled in either blue, ruby red or green. The chatelaine matches the watch. The movement is an imported one, made in Switzerland, perfectly trued and adjusted; we guarantee it to give entire satisfaction. The picture is two-thirds size of watch.

At $8.00 for the complete outfit, case, chatelaine and watch you have a bargain at least 33⅓ per cent cheaper than any local jeweler could possibly sell it. Price......................$8.00

If by mail, postage extra, 16 cents.

LADIES' SOLID SILVER O-SIZE WATCHES.

OPEN FACE OR HUNTING STYLE.

...THE... PICTURE shows the EXACT SIZE..

No. 4R873 Open Face.
No. 4R874 Hunting Style.

AN AMERICAN MADE WATCH in this small size, made of silver, has been wanted by thousands of ladies. So as to make our catalogue complete, so as to positively quote all kinds and styles of watches, we show here the **smallest silver American watch made. These cases are solid silver through and through,** hand engraved; they have the antique bow, the entire case is perfectly finished in every respect. They are stem wind and pendant set. **We guarantee the movement for a term of five years, and the case will last your natural lifetime.** We fit these cases with the following movements at prices quoted:

7 Jeweled Atlas..........................	$5.75
7 Jeweled Suffolk........................	7.25
7 Jeweled Elgin or Waltham............	8.25
13 Jeweled Edgemere....................	8.20
15 Jeweled Elgin or Waltham............	11.25

PHOTOGRAPHS ON WATCH CASES AND DIALS.

An ever present reminder of your relatives or friends, in the form of a photograph on the dial or back cap of your watch, at a trifling expense. The work is done by the Photographic Enamel Process, and is as perfect in detail and finish as the best cabinet photographs, and with ordinary care will last forever. It is an excellent place to carry a **picture of the baby, your wife or husband, or your sweetheart.** No extra charge for group if the pictures are all on same photo. When group picture is wanted and pictures are on separate photographs, add $1.40 for each extra figure. Send us your watch by mail or express, carefully packed in a small strong box, well wrapped in some very soft material (cotton batting or similar substance is best) together with a photo to copy from (size makes no difference). As soon as the work is done we will return the watch and picture uninjured. It usually requires about a week after we get the watch and picture to complete the work.

We are doing a great deal of this work, which has in every case given most excellent satisfaction. We have received many letters and testimonials speaking in the highest terms, and that the work was far nicer than they could have expected, and that they could not find words to express their appreciation and thanks. The work can be done on any kind or size of watch. Gold or gold filled are the best for cap work, but it makes no difference for dial work. Be sure to state whether you want the picture on the dial or on the cap.

Sample A.
The above is a sample of dial work. Price... .75c

Sample B.
The above is a sample of work on the cap in back of watch. Price, $1.30.

SOLID GOLD 14-KARAT AND 10-KARAT GENTLEMEN'S VEST CHAINS.

WE SELL OUR CHAINS FOR EXACTLY WHAT THEY ARE. We guarantee them to be exactly as represented. They are solid gold through and through; every part and piece of them is of the same quality. Gold chains have always been a leader with us. We believe that a gold chain, like a diamond, sold at the remarkably low figures we make, is one of the greatest advertisements we could possibly have. We sell our gold chains at but a slight advance over the actual cost of gold.

BUY A SOLID GOLD CHAIN and you are making an investment. You can always realize nearly what you paid for it as old metal. Anybody will buy old gold. A chain such as we describe will last you your entire lifetime; it cannot be worn out; you can use it for an heirloom in your family; your son's son can own it; it never will look shabby, it is always elegant yet genteel.

POSTAGE ON GENTLEMEN'S VEST CHAINS, 3 cents; 8 cents extra for registered or insured mail.

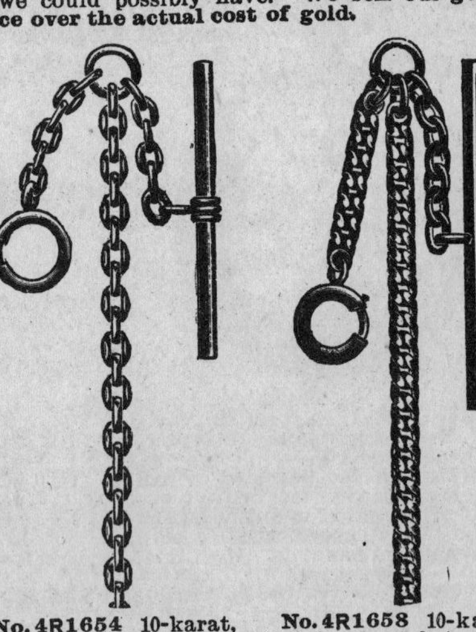

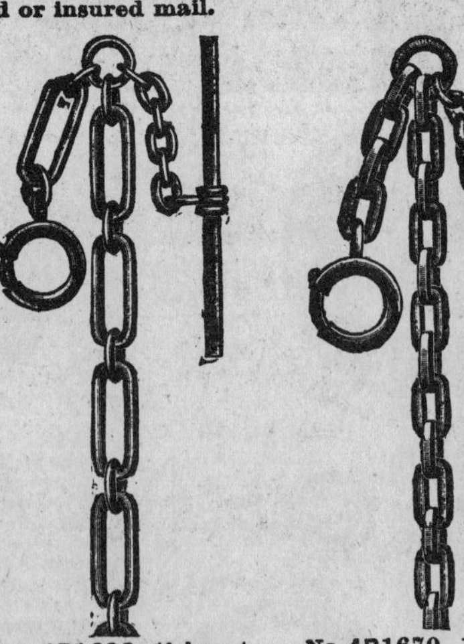

No. 4R1650 10-karat, 10 inches long, between 5 and 6 pwt. Price..$4.65
No. 4R1652 14-karat, 10 inches long, between 5 and 6 pwt. Price..$6.35

No. 4R1654 10-karat, 10 inches long, between 5 and 6 pwt. Price..$5.65
No. 4R1656 14-karat, 10 inches long, between 6 and 7 pwt. Price..$8.45

No. 4R1658 10-karat, 10 inches long, between 7 and 8 pwt. Price..$7.35
No. 4R1660 14-karat, 10 inches long, between 8 and 9 pwt. Price, $10.95

No. 4R1662 10-karat, 10 inches long, between 7 and 8 pwt. Price..$5.90
No. 4R1664 14-karat, 10 inches long, between 7 and 8 pwt. Price..$8.45

No. 4R1666 10-karat, 10 inches long, between 6 and 7 pwt. Price..$6.00
No. 4R1668 14-karat, 10 inches long, between 7 and 8 pwt. Price..$8.50

No. 4R1670 10-karat, 10 inches long, between 8 and 9 pwt. Price..$7.50
No. 4R1672 14-karat, 10 inches long, between 9 and 10 pwt. Price, $10.90

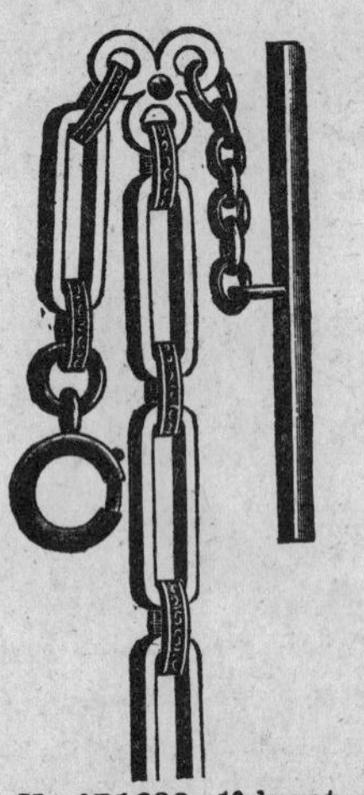
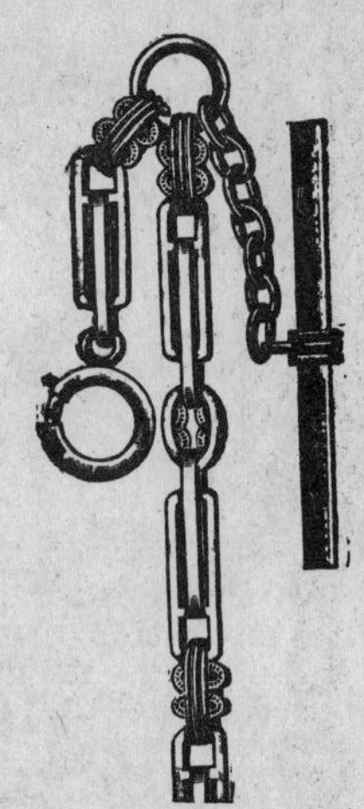

No. 4R1674 10-karat, 12 inches long, between 18 and 19 pwt. Price, $14.25
No. 4R1676 14-karat, 12 inches long, between 20 and 21 pwt. Price, $19.00

No. 4R1678 10-karat, 12 inches long, between 19 and 20 pwt. Price, $15.00
No. 4R1680 14-karat, 12 inches long, between 21 and 22 pwt. Price, $21.00

No. 4R1682 10-karat, regulation length.
Price..............$8.25
Without charm..6.50
No. 4R1684 14-karat, regulation length.
Price..........$12.00
Without charm 9.50

No. 4R1686 10-karat, regulation length.
Price..............$8.25
Without charm.. 6.50
No. 4R1688 14-karat, regulation length.
Price..........$12.00
Without charm 9.50

No. 4R1690 10-karat, 10 inches long, between 12 and 13 pwt. Price, $10.50
No. 4R1692 14-karat, 12 inches long, between 15 and 16 pwt. Price, $15.25

No. 4R1694 10-karat, 12 inches long, between 13 and 14 pwt. Price, $10.50
No. 4R1696 14-karat, 12 inches long, between 14 and 15 pwt. Price, $14.25

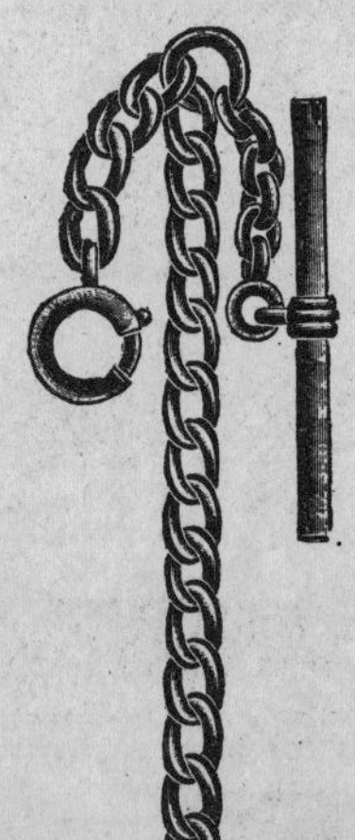
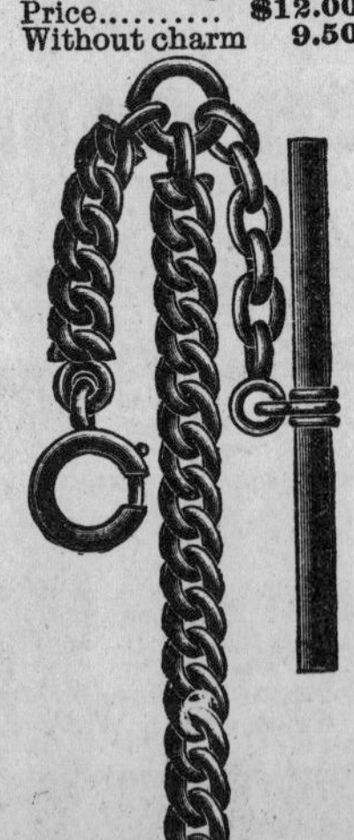

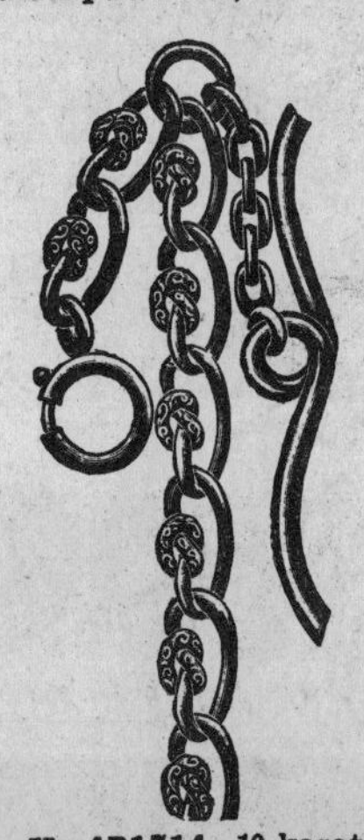
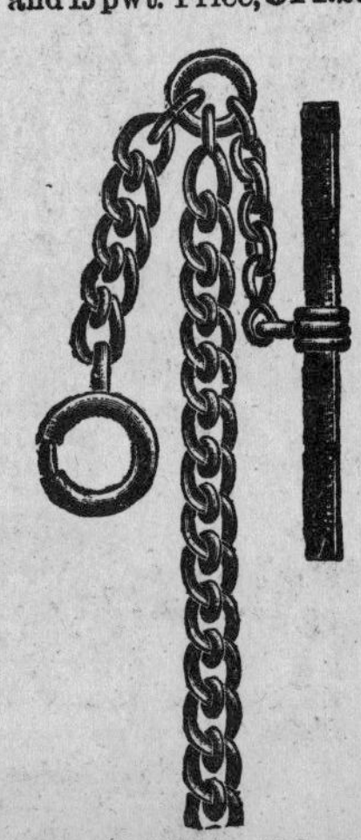

No. 4R1698 10-karat, 12 inches long, between 14 and 15 pwt. Price, $11.25
No. 4R1700 14-karat, 12 inches long, between 16 and 17 pwt. Price, $16.15

No. 4R1702 10-karat, 10 inches long, between 6 and 7 pwt. Price..$6.50
No. 4R1704 14-karat, 10 inches long, between 7 and 8 pwt. Price..$8.45

No. 4R1706 10-karat, 12 inches long, between 23 and 24 pwt. Price, $18.00
No. 4R1708 14-karat, 12 inches long, between 25 and 26 pwt. Price, $24.75

No. 4R1710 10-karat, 12 inches long, between 15 and 16 pwt. Price, $12.00
No. 4R1712 14-karat, 12 inches long, between 17 and 18 pwt. Price, $17.25

No. 4R1714 10-karat, 12 inches long, between 15 and 16 pwt. Price, $12.00
No. 4R1716 14-karat, 12 inches long, between 17 and 18 pwt. Price, $17.25

No. 4R1718 10-karat, 12 inches long, between 14 and 15 pwt. Price, $10.50
No. 4R1720 14-karat, 12 inches long, between 16 and 17 pwt. Price, $16.15

GENTS' GOLD FILLED CHAINS, TWO AND THREE STRANDS.

FOR A CHAIN THAT IS MADE EXCEPTIONALLY STRONG AND HAS GREAT WEARING DURABILITY, WE RECOMMEND THESE CHAINS. THE FRONT AND BACK OF SLIDES ARE SOLID GOLD, THE CHAINS THEMSELVES GOLD FILLED AND GUARANTEED. THE BAR, SWIVEL AND CHARM ATTACHMENTS ARE FINISHED AS ELEGANTLY AS ANY OTHER PART OF THE CHAIN.

No. 4R1728 Two-strand Curb, very heavy, engraved slide and tips. Price, each........ $3.50

No. 4R1730 Two-strand Rope Chain, gold filled, warranted for 20 years. Engraved slide. Price, each........ $3.45

No. 4R1732 Two-strand Rolled Gold Plated, guaranteed for 6 years. Engraved tips and slide. Price, each........ $1.85

No. 4R1734 Three-strand Rolled Gold Plated Curb Chain, engraved tips and slide. Warranted for 6 years. Price, each........ $2.25

No. 4R1736 Three-strand Gold Filled Curb Chain, hand engraved slide. Guaranteed for 20 years. Price, each........ $3.50

No. 4R1738 Three-strand Curb Chain, hand engraved slide and tips. Guaranteed for 20 years. Price, each........ $4.15

No. 4R1740 Three-strand Curb Chain, hand engraved slide and tips, gold filled. Guaranteed for 20 years. Price, each........ $4.18

No. 4R1742 Two-strand Curb, with tips and slide. solid sterling silver. Price, each........ $2.75
No. 4R1743 White Metal, as above. Price, each........ .40

No. 4R1746 Alternate Polished and Fancy Trace Links. Solid silver. Price, each........ $1.75
No. 4R1748 Solid white metal. Price, each........ .30

No. 4R1750 Curb Chain, with tips. Solid sterling silver. Price, each........ $1.70
No. 4R1751 White Metal, same as above. Price, each........ .20

No. 4R1754 Fancy Rope Pattern, solid sterling silver. Price, each........ $2.50
No. 4R1756 Solid white metal. Price, each........ .35

No. 4R1760 Silk Vest Chain, gold filled mountings. Length, 12 inches. Price, each........ 75c

No. 4R1766 Silk Vest Chain, fancy braided, gold filled mountings. Length, 7 inches. Price, each........ 85c

No. 4R1762 Silk Vest Chain, three strands, gold filled mountings. Length, 9 inches. Price, each........ 85c

No. 4R1768 Silk Vest Chain, gold filled mountings. Length, 9 inches. Price, each........ $1.25

No. 4R1764 Silk Vest Chain, gold filled mountings. Length, 11 inches. Price, each........ 70c

No. 4R1770 Silk Vest Chain, gold filled mountings. Length, 9 inches. Price, each........ $1.20

We are not in position to quote prices on this guard made to order.

No. 4R1775 Fancy Woven Hair Vest Guard, 8½ inches long, with very fancy gold filled mountings. Price, each........ $1.35

GOLD FILLED AND ROLLED PLATED MOUNTED FOBS.

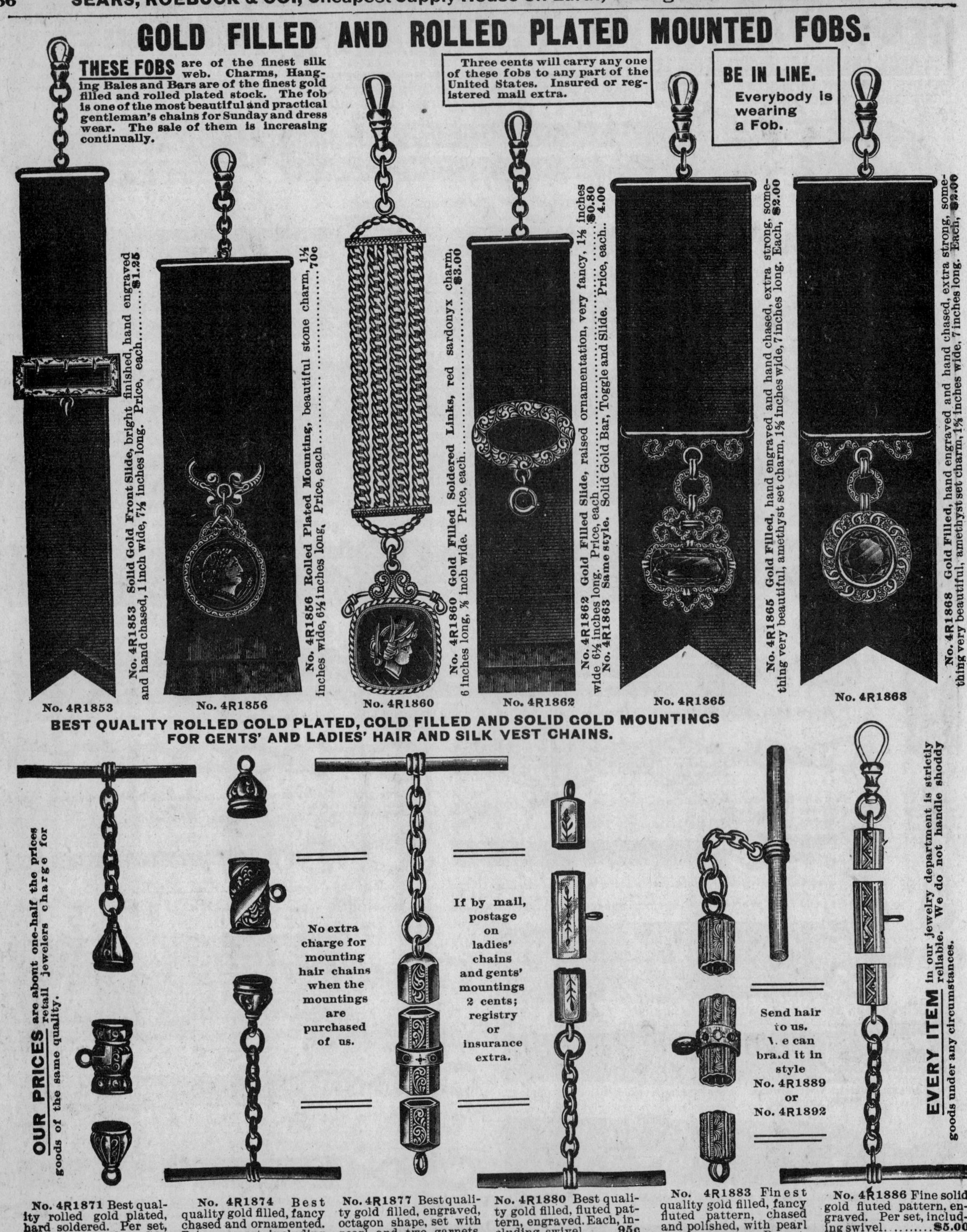

THESE FOBS are of the finest silk web. Charms, Hanging Bales and Bars are of the finest gold filled and rolled plated stock. The fob is one of the most beautiful and practical gentleman's chains for Sunday and dress wear. The sale of them is increasing continually.

Three cents will carry any one of these fobs to any part of the United States. Insured or registered mail extra.

BE IN LINE. Everybody is wearing a Fob.

No. 4R1853 Solid Gold Front Slide, bright finished, hand engraved and hand chased, 1 inch wide, 7½ inches long. Price, each........$1.25

No. 4R1856 Rolled Plated Mounting, beautiful stone charm, 1½ inches wide, 6½ inches long. Price, each..................70c

No. 4R1860 Gold Filled Soldered Links, red sardonyx charm, 6 inches long, ⅞ inch wide. Price, each..................$3.00

No. 4R1862 Gold Filled Slide, raised ornamentation, very fancy, 1⅛ inches wide 6½ inches long. Price, each..................$0.80
No. 4R1863 Same style. Solid Gold Bar, Toggle and Slide. Price, each.. 4.00

No. 4R1865 Gold Filled, hand engraved and hand chased, extra strong, something very beautiful, amethyst set charm, 1⅝ inches wide, 7 inches long. Each, $2.00

No. 4R1868 Gold Filled, hand engraved and hand chased, extra strong, something very beautiful, amethyst set charm, 1⅝ inches wide, 7 inches long. Each, $2.00

No. 4R1853 — No. 4R1856 — No. 4R1860 — No. 4R1862 — No. 4R1865 — No. 4R1868

BEST QUALITY ROLLED GOLD PLATED, GOLD FILLED AND SOLID GOLD MOUNTINGS FOR GENTS' AND LADIES' HAIR AND SILK VEST CHAINS.

OUR PRICES are about one-half the prices retail jewelers charge for goods of the same quality.

No extra charge for mounting hair chains when the mountings are purchased of us.

If by mail, postage on ladies' chains and gents' mountings 2 cents; registry or insurance extra.

Send hair to us. We can braid it in style No. 4R1889 or No. 4R1892

EVERY ITEM in our jewelry department is strictly reliable. We do not handle shoddy goods under any circumstances.

No. 4R1871 Best quality rolled gold plated, hard soldered. Per set, including swivel.....70c

No. 4R1874 Best quality gold filled, fancy chased and ornamented. Price, per set, including swivel..................70c

No. 4R1877 Best quality gold filled, engraved, octagon shape, set with pearl and two garnets. Per set, including swivel..................$1.10

No. 4R1880 Best quality gold filled, fluted pattern, engraved. Each, including swivel.......95c

No. 4R1883 Finest quality gold filled, fancy fluted pattern, chased and polished, with pearl and two garnets. Per set, including swivel...$2.25

No. 4R1886 Fine solid gold fluted pattern, engraved. Per set, including swivel.........$5.00

No. 4R1889 Hair chain braided to order, in two pieces like above. Each..$1.00

No. 4R1892 Hair chain made to order, two pieces, like above. Each..$1.50

BEST QUALITY NECK CHAINS, SOLID GOLD, GOLD FILLED AND GENUINE AMBER.

OUR NECK CHAINS ARE REGULATION LENGTH, 12 TO 13 INCHES, all have soldered links, making them serviceable, and particularly adapted for babies and children. The gold filled chains are warranted for a term of 20 years. The solid gold chains we guarantee to be solid gold through and through and to wear a lifetime. In fact, they could be used as an heirloom in a family. It will be noted that the prices are extremely low. Many of the designs are our own, and cannot be duplicated elsewhere.

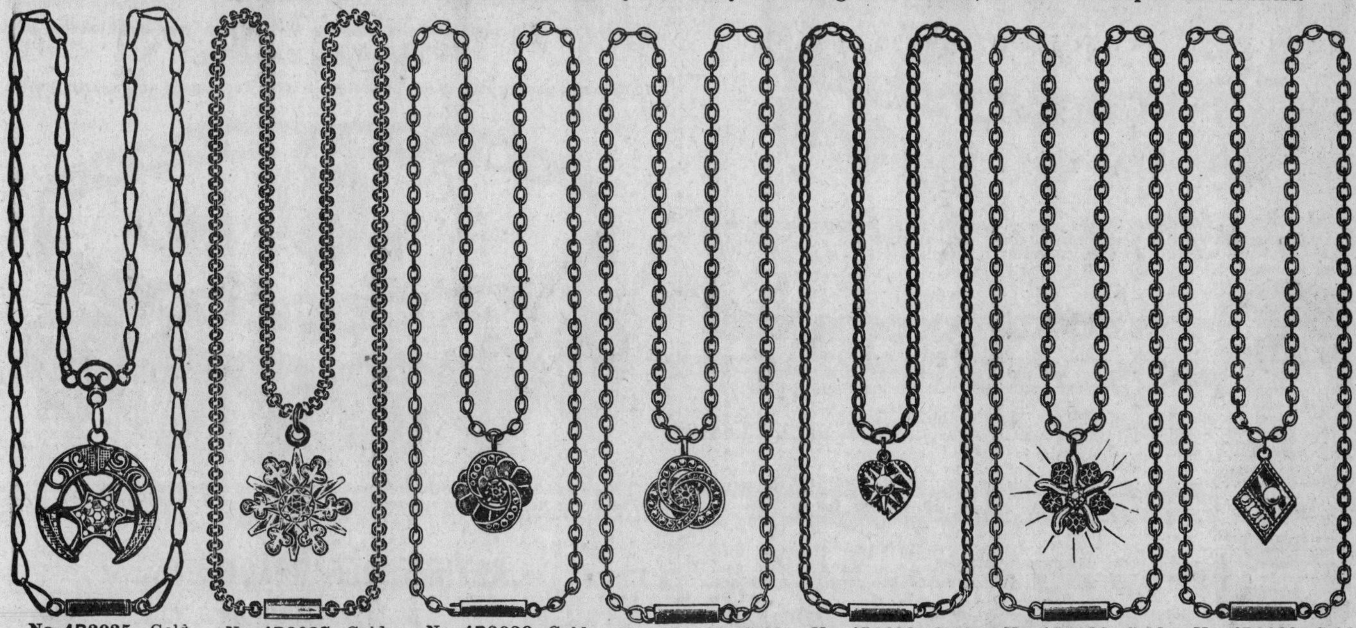

No. 4R2025 Gold filled chain, fancy crescent and star pendant, set with large white brilliant. Price.........$1.45

No. 4R2027 Gold filled chain, with colored gold ornamented charm, set with stone. Price.........$1.65

No. 4R2029 Gold filled chain, fancy Roman colored gold pendant, set with ruby doublet stone. Price.........$1.50

No. 4R2031 Gold filled chain, fancy Roman colored gold pendant set with almandine stone. Price.........$1.40

No. 4R2033 Gold filled chain, fancy heart pendant, set with genuine opal. Price.........$1.60

No. 4R2036 Gold filled chain, fancy pendant set with 5 ruby doublets and 1 white stone. Price.........$1.68

No. 4R2039 Gold filled chain, fancy pendant set with 3 pearls, 1 genuine opal. Price...$1.70

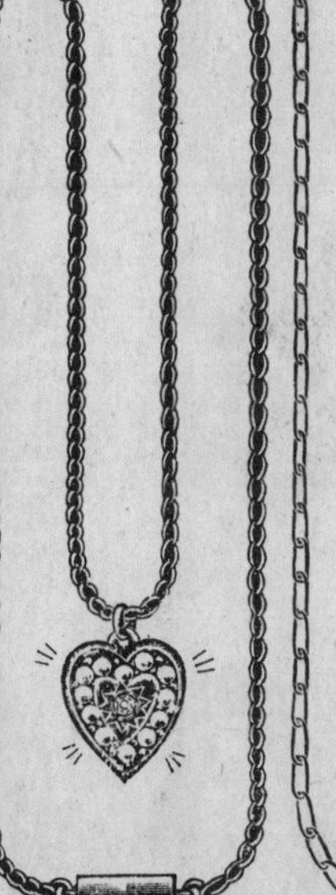

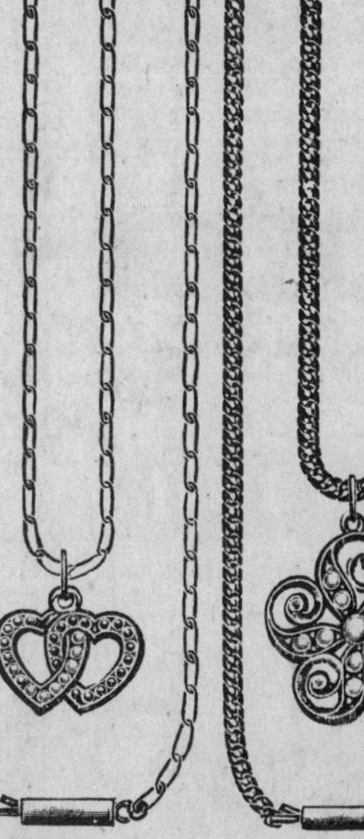

No. 4R2041 Solid gold chain, Roman finished, fancy links, solid gold, satin finished, heart pendant. Price...........$2.00

No. 4R2043 Solid gold chain, plain soldered traced links, fancy pendant, set with 6 pearls and 1 ruby center. Each.........$3.50

No. 4R2045 Solid gold, woven wire chain, with solid gold Roman finished gold heart, set with 12 pearls and 1 real diamond. Price..$5.40

No. 4R2047 Solid gold, fancy plain soldered traced links, double heart pendant set with 13 turquoise and 15 pearls. Each.........$4.50

No. 4R2049 Solid gold, very heavy plain soldered curb links, bright cut finish pendant set with 11 pearls. Each.........$5.25

No. 4R2051 Solid gold soldered rope chain, fancy pendant, Roman finish, bright cut engraving set with 1 genuine opal. Each....$4.75

No. 4R2052 Solid gold, very heavy soldered balloon links, extra strong, very fancy pendant set with 4 pearls and 1 large amethyst. Each.........$6.00

No. 4R2053 Solid gold, Roman finish, soldered traced links, three heart pendants, each set with turquoise. This chain is particularly adapted for babies and children. Each...$2.50

No. 4R2054 Genuine Amber Bead Necklace. This is a genuine amber bead necklace of fine quality, strung on linen cord. The beads are beautifully cut and very transparent. It is thought by many that amber, when worn as a necklace, acts as a preventive against colds, sore throat and the contagious diseases to which children are subject. They are very light and make a beautiful and inexpensive necklace. Price.......................................$1.25

Postage on neck chains 3 cents, 8 cents for registered mail extra.

SOLID GOLD, GOLD FILLED AND SOLID STERLING SILVER BRACELETS.

No. 4R2078 Child's or Baby Bracelet, gold filled, bright finished, the very latest engraved bangles, soldered links. Price, each........**$1.75**

No. 4R2081 Child's or Baby Bracelet, sterling silver, same as above, bright finished. Price, each........**$1.25**

No. 4R2083 Misses' Gold Filled Bracelet, plain polished links, with raised ornamented and polished lock, length 5 inches. Each........**60c**

No. 4R2086 Solid Sterling Silver, same as above. Each........**60c**

No. 4R2089 Solid Gold, roman color, same as above. Each........**$3.00**

No. 4R2090 Solid Silver through and through, soldered links, hand chased and hand engraved, one of the very latest effects. Price, each........**$2.60**

No. 4R2097 Gold Filled Bracelet, best quality, fancy chased links, raised, ornamented and polished lock. Each **$2.00**

No. 4R2098 Same style, solid gold. Each....15.00

No. 4R2099 Gold Filled Bracelet, best quality, with fancy chased links, raised, ornamented and polished lock. Each........**$2.45**

No. 4R2103 Solid Sterling Silver, same style as above. Each.... 1.75

No. 4R2104 Same style, solid gold. Each....... 6.50

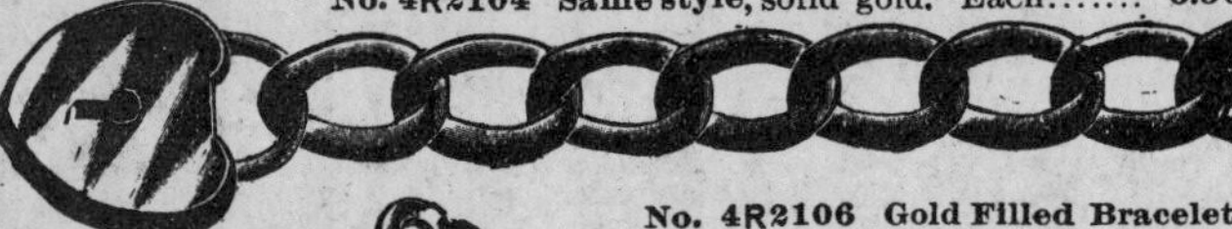

No. 4R2106 Gold Filled Bracelet, best quality, plain polished links and lock. Each........**$2.25**

No. 4R2109 Gold Filled Bracelet, best quality, flattened links, fancy chased, raised, ornamented and polished lock. Each........**$2.90**

No. 4R2113 Solid Sterling Silver Bracelet, flattened chased links, raised, ornamented and satin lock. Each........**$2.55**

No. 4R2114 Gold Filled Bracelet, bright polished square hand chased links, something novel; raised, ornamented, polished lock. Each........**$2.00**

No. 4R2115 Solid Silver Bracelet. Same as above, but not chased links; plain satin finished lock. Ea. **$2.25**

No. 4R2119 Fancy Gold Filled, hand chased, hand engraved, soldered throughout, raised ornamented lock, the very latest pattern. Price, each........**$2.75**

No. 4R2120 Gold Filled Bracelet, loose curb flattened links with chased center, with raised, ornamented and polished lock. Each........**$1.75**

AT $2.75 OUR No. 4R2122 IS A WONDERFUL BARGAIN.

WE OWN THIRTY GROSS OF THESE BRACELETS BOUGHT AT A VERY LOW PRICE : : : :

We give you this opportunity to own one at less than your local jeweler pays for the same thing of the jobber.

If by mail, postage on these bracelets, extra, 3c; registry and insurance extra.

No. 4R2122 Solid Silver Bracelet, hand engraved and hand chased, six solid silver heart pendants, each set with turquoise and opal. Price, for complete bracelet........**$2.75**

NETHERSOLE BRACELETS.

No. 4R2153 Gold Filled, bright polished embossed hearts. Each.....**$1.95**

No. 4R2156 Sterling Silver, plain polished, embossed hearts. Each......**$1.25**

No. 4R2157 Baby size, same as above......**85c**

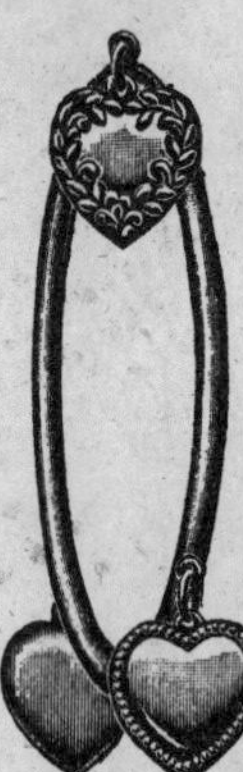

No. 4R2159 Sterling Silver, bright polished, embossed hearts. Each........**68c**

No. 4R2161 Sterling Silver, hand chased, hand embossed. Each **90c**

No. 4R2162 Baby size, same as above **45c**

No. 4R2163 Sterling Silver, bright twist. Each........**65c**

No. 4R2164 Baby size, same as above......**45c**

No. 4R2165 Sterling Silver, embossed fancy. twist, extra heavy Each........**85c**

No. 4R2168 Sterling Silver, hand engraved, hand chased, bright polished. Each......**$1.75**

No. 4R2169 Gold Filled, same as above. Each **$2.50**

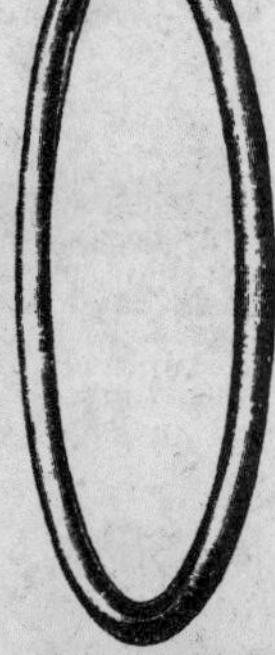

No. 4R2174 Sterling Silver, light weight, plain polish, bright finish. Each..... ...**65c**

If by mail, postage extra, 3 cents.

GOLD FILLED RINGS

AND HOW..... GOLD FILLED RINGS .....ARE MADE

We have given in the front part of this department an article explaining the manner in which gold filled cases are made, and as we offer you here a page of gold filled rings, we believe it would be interesting to you and much more satisfactory before making a purchase of a gold filled ring to know just how they are made. It would seem to the average person and even a mechanic that it would be a difficult problem to completely envelop a piece of hard composition metal with solid gold, and at the same time turn out and place the goods on the market at such a low price. The operation, however, is very easy when it is understood. To start with, a piece of solid gold tube from 1½ to 2 inches in diameter is taken and the hole on the inside made perfectly smooth, after which a piece of hard, fine composition metal is placed on the inside of the tube so as to fit the opening perfectly. Some fine gold solder is now placed in the crevice and the whole is inserted in the furnace. As soon as the two pieces are heated sufficiently the solder flows into the crevice, after which it is removed from the furnace, and after it is cold the two original pieces are o e.

One end of this piece is then hammered and drawn out, so as to make it a little smaller, after which it is inserted in what is called the draw plate, which is a long steel plate with a num er of holes in it of such shape as the pieces which it is desired to make. These holes are graduated in size, at one end being very large and at the other end small. The piece of material to be worked on is inserted in the large hole first, and with a pair of tongs it is drawn through; this reduces the piece, when it is again hammered at the end to make it small enough to be inserted in the next smaller hole and in turn drawn through this. (All kinds of wire for whatever purpose it may be intended is drawn in the same manner. Sometimes a wire will be drawn in this manner to a mile or more in length). The edges of the holes are all polished so as not to scrape, but to press the metal. This drawing hardens the metal to such an extent that after drawing it through several times it would break easily. It is then annealed by inserting it in the fire and allowing it to cool gradually. After the piece has been drawn out to the required shape and size, one end is bent around a steel mandrel until it has formed a circle of the size the ring is to be made. It is then cut off at the proper place and both ends are carefully surfaced in order to bring them together and make a perfect joint, and on this joint is placed some fine gold solder and the ring inserted in a furnace sufficiently heated to cause the solder to flow into the joint. The ring is then polished carefully on a cotton buff wheel with tripoli and rouge, after which it is ready for the market. Solid gold rings are made in the same manner with th exception of the composition metal on inside.

The market is flooded with cheap brass rings which are electro gold plated, and are called rolled plate or rolled gold plate, and which are utterly worthless. In gold filled rings we handle nothing but the very best. The gold used is 14-karat, and will wear an indefinite length of time, and is guaranteed to give entire satisfaction.

SEE OUR PRICES ON

BEST QUALITY 14-KARAT GOLD FILLED RINGS.

WILL BE FURNISHED IN SIZES 5 TO 11

If by Mail, Postage on Rings, 2 Cents Extra.

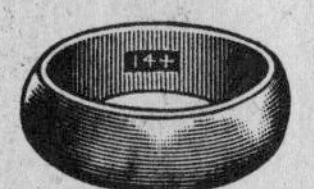

No. 4R2238 Plain oval band. Each......60c

No. 4R2241 Plain oval band. Each......95c

No. 4R2244 Plain oval band. Each ...$1.30

No. 4R2247 Plain oval band. Each....$1.65

No. 4R2250 Plain flat band. Each....$1.30

No. 4R2253 Plain flat band. Each....$1.70

No. 4R2256 Flat band chased. Each....80c

No. 4R2259 Flat band chased. Each....75c

No. 4R2262 Flat band chased. Each....80c

No. 4R2265 Flat band, fancy engraved and embossed. Each.........$1.00

No. 4R2268 Flat band, fancy engraved and embossed. Each.........$1.30

No. 4R2271 Flat band, engraved and embossed. Each..$1.40

No. 4R2274 Flat band, fancy engraved and embossed. Each.........$1.55

No. 4R2277 Flat band, fancy engraved and embossed. Each........$1.70

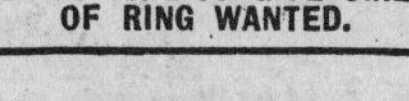
DON'T FAIL TO GIVE SIZE
OF RING WANTED.

SECOND QUALITY GOLD FILLED RINGS.

FOR THE PRICE NOTHING BETTER ON THE MARKET.

No. 4R2280 Plain oval band. Each......45c

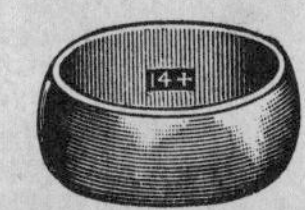

No. 4R2283 Plain oval band. Each......60c

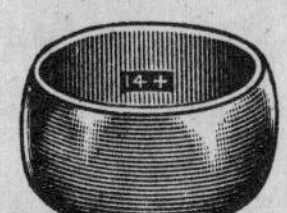

No. 4R2286 Plain oval band. Each......80c

No. 4R2289 Plain oval band. Each......$1.00

No. 4R2292 Plain flat band. Each... .90c

No. 4R2295 Plain flat band. Each....$1.00

No. 4R2298 Flat band chased. Each....60c

No. 4R2301 Flat band chased. Each....55c

No. 4R2304 Flat band chased. Each....60c

No. 4R2307 Flat band chased. Each ...55c

No. 4R2310 Flat band chased. Each....70c

No. 4R2313 Flat band chased. Each....75c

No. 4R2316 Flat band chased. Each....85c

No. 4R2319 Flat band chased. Each.. .95c

SILVER, GOLD FILLED AND SOLID GOLD THIMBLES.

IF BY MAIL, POSTAGE EXTRA, 2 CENTS.

DON'T FAIL TO GIVE SIZE OF RING WANTED.

No. 4R2322 Solid silver. Each........15c

No. 4R2323 Solid silver, heavy. Each........25c

No. 4R2325 Solid silver, beautifully engraved. Each........45c

No. 4R2326 Solid silver, hand engraved. Each........35c

No. 4R2329 Gold filled, warranted. Each........50c

No. 4R2331 Gold filled, engraved, warranted. Each.....$1.00

No. 4R2332 Solid 10-karat gold. Each.....$1.95

No. 4R2335 Solid 14-karat gold. Each.....$3.75

GENUINE DIAMONDS IN SOLID GOLD RINGS, MOUNTINGS, SCARF PINS AND EARRINGS

AT EXTREMELY LOW PRICES.

WE ARE AMONG THE LARGEST BUYERS OF DIAMONDS IN THE COUNTRY. We make the rings in which we set them. Our machinery for manufacturing the mountings is the most modern and our labor the most skilled. For these reasons we are able to quote this very high grade of diamond jewelry at the remarkably low figures listed below. These are genuine rose cut diamonds and will undoubtedly more than meet your expectation; the only difference is that the rose is a flat bottom diamond instead of running to a point. The mountings are made of solid gold through and through, and we wish particularly to emphasize that if these goods are not entirely satisfactory and if the values do not meet with your expectation, you are at liberty to return them to be exchanged for other goods or your money refunded. Diamond jewelry will only be shipped by express, registered mail or insured mail. **IF BY MAIL, POSTAGE EXTRA, 4 CENTS; REGISTRATION OR INSURANCE EXTRA.**

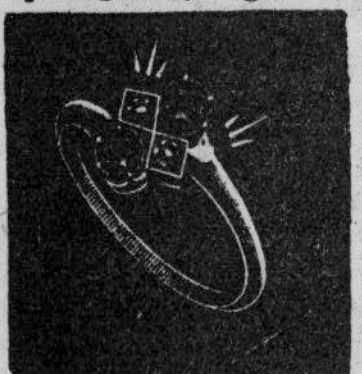

No. 4R3053
2 rose diamonds
2 garnets
Each........$2.75

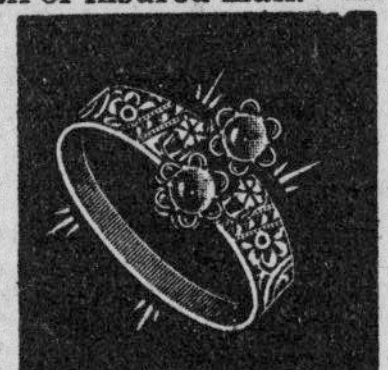

No. 4R3056
2 very fine rose diamonds and 2 fire opals
Each........$4.25

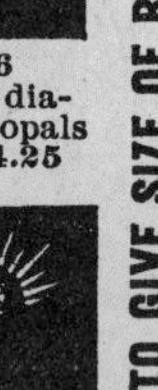
DON'T FAIL TO GIVE SIZE OF RING WANTED.

No. 4R3059
2 very fine rose diamonds and 2 large fire opals
Each........$7.50

No. 4R3060
3 fine rose diamonds
fancy mounting
Each........$6.50

DON'T FAIL TO GIVE SIZE OF RING WANTED.

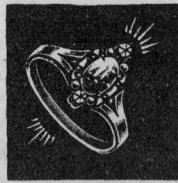

No. 4R3066
6 very fine rose diamonds and 1 fire opal
Each........$8.25

No. 4R3068
1 diamond
fancy mounting
Each..........$3.75

No. 4R3071
2 fine rose diamonds
2 emeralds
Each........$4.10

No. 4R3074
2 fine rose diamonds
1 large opal
Each........$5.75

No. 4R3077
2 fine rose diamonds
1 almandine
Each........$4.95

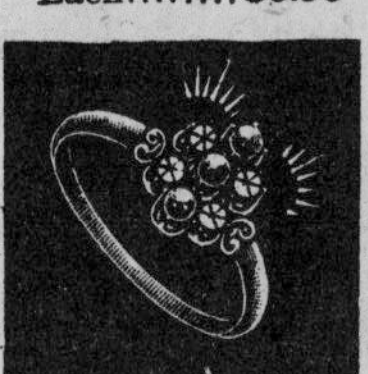

No. 4R3080
4 fine rose diamonds
3 fire opals
Each........$6.85

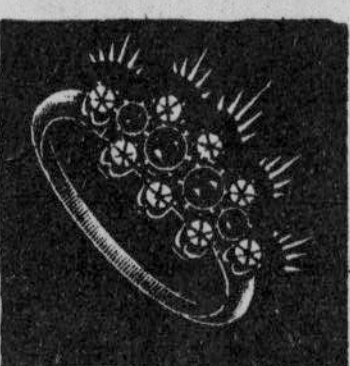

No. 4R3083
8 fine rose diamonds
4 almandines
Each........$9.95

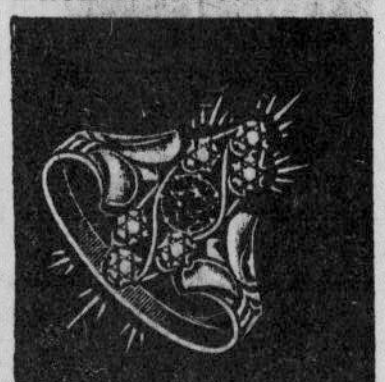

No. 4R3086
6 very fine rose diamonds and 1 emerald doublet
Each..........$7.50

No. 4R3089
6 rose diamonds
turquoise center
Each......$1.50

No. 4R3092
6 rose diamonds
emerald center
Each......$2.75

No. 4R3095
8 rose diamonds
ruby center
Each......$5.95

No. 4R3098
4 rose diamonds
ruby center
Each......$1.50

No. 4R3101
12 rose diamonds
very pretty
Each......$3.75

No. 4R3104
12 rose diamonds
turquoise center
Each......$5.25

No. 4R3107
15 rose diamonds
very fine
Each......$6.75

No. 4R3110
12 rose diamonds
ruby center
Each......$6.50

No. 4R3113
1 rose diamond, Roman setting.
Per pair........$3.00

No. 4R3116
6 rose diamonds, turquoise center
Per pair........$3.00

No. 4R3119
6 rose diamonds, opal center
Per pair........$5.75

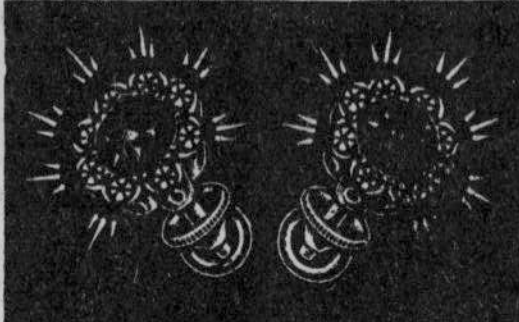

No. 4R3122
8 rose diamonds, emerald center
Per pair........$7.[illegible]

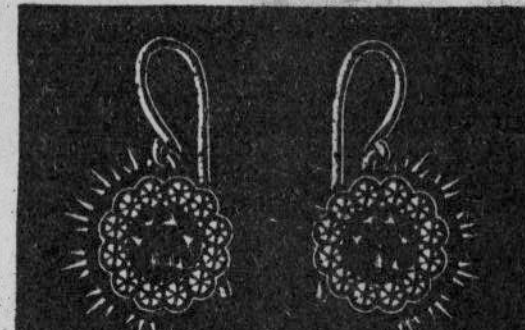

No. 4R3125
12 rose diamonds, ruby center
Per pair........$7.50

GOLD HEADED CANES.

GUARANTEED BEST QUALITY GOLD HEADED CANES, MOUNTED ON FINE POLISHED GENUINE EBONY STICKS.

CASH IN FULL MUST BE SENT WITH YOUR ORDER.

$3.50 to $14.00.

No. 4R3128 Round head, raised ornamentation and hand engraved, plain polished top, ⅝-inch stick, 10-karat gold. Each..............$4.45

No. 4R3131 Round head, fancy raised ornamentation and hand engraved, plain polished top, ⅝-inch stick, 14-karat gold. Each...$6.95

No. 4R3133 Polo crook, beautiful raised ornamentation and head engraved, polished ends, ⅝-inch stick 10-karat. Each..............$9.95
No. 4R3134 Same in 14-karat. Each..............$14.00

No. 4R3138 Round head, raised ornamentation and hand engraved, plain polished top, ⅝-inch stick, 10-karat gold. Each..............$3.50

Any of the above mountings can be engraved with any name or inscription in script at 2½ cents per letter, or old English at 5½ cents per letter.

CANES CANNOT GO BY MAIL.

FINE GOLD FILLED GENTS' CHARMS, SET WITH MOST POPULAR COLORED STONES.

We have selected many new and novel designs this year in this very popular gents' chain ornament. The stones when so set are securely fastened, thereby preventing the loss of setting. The finish is nearly as good as solid gold, and we can conscientiously recommend a gift of this sort, when but a small amount of money is to be expended upon same for a gentleman. Orders always promptly and carefully filled. The postage on any charm listed would be 3 cents; insurance or registry extra.

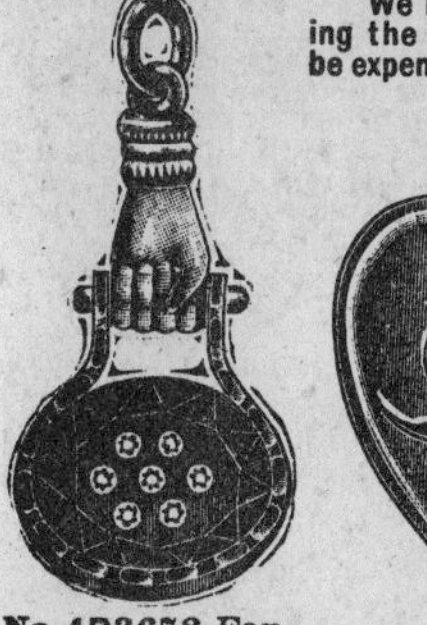
No. 4R3678 Fancy swinging bale, topaz set with seven brilliants. Price........ 40c

No. 4R3681 Bright polished, two brilliants and two emeralds, hand engraved. Price... $1.00

No. 4R3684 Fancy engraved, genuine stone set. Price.. 85c

No. 4R3687 Painted Dog's Head, cornelian stone back. Price.. 25c

No. 4R3690 Fancy mounting, engraved stone setting........ 45c

No. 4R3693 Compass, fancy mounting, no toy, but scientifically accurate. Price ... $1.50

No. 4R3696 Lantern charm, ruby glass. Price....... 50c

No. 4R3697 Very fancy extra fine, four brilliants and one ruby. Price........... $2.25

No. 4R3699 Fancy mounting, engraved, cornelian setting... 75c

No. 4R3702 Fancy mounting, engraved stone setting. Price............ 45c

No. 4R3705 Fancy bale, engraved stone setting. Price..... 75c

No. 4R3708 Fancy stone setting. Price............ 25c

No. 4R3711 Bicycle Lamp, set with brilliant, emerald and ruby. Price.. 40c

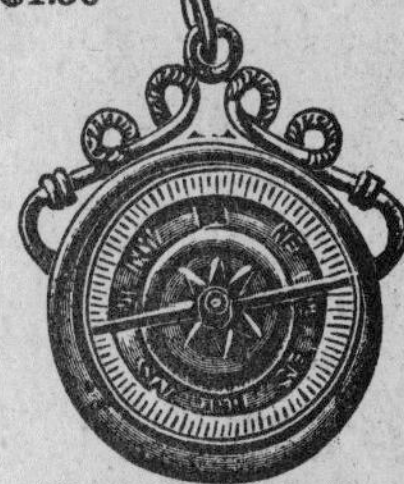
No. 4R3712 Compass, extra fine, fancy mounting. Price, $1.45

No. 4R3714 Agate barrel, fancy mounting. Price.............. 65c

No. 4R3717 Anvil charm, stone mounted base. Price........ 30c

No. 4R3720 Genuine stone, very fancy hand cut intaglio. Price............ $1.15

No. 4R3723 Fine Compass. Price........ 45c

No. 4R3726 Anchor. Price........... 50c

No. 4R3729 Extra fine, four brilliants and one genuine opal. Price..... $2.50

No. 4R3732 Extra fine hand engraved, three brilliants and one genuine opal. Price.. $2.75

No. 4R3733 Fancy Horse Shoe and Horse. Price................ 90c

No. 4R3735 Fancy mounted Horse's Head, stone base. Price............... 65c

No. 4R3738 Compass. Price..... 25c

No. 4R3741 Mail Pouch. Price, 40c

No. 4R3744 Fancy engraved, genuine stone set. Price.. 85c

No. 4R3747 Compass. Price 35c

No. 4R3750 Fancy mounting, bright polish, Pointer Dog. Price............. 45c

No. 4R3753 Fancy genuine stone, hand cut intaglio. Price.... 80c

No. 4R3756 Fancy mounting, painted setting. Price.......... 30c

No. 4R3759 Chased Horse, ruby eyes. Price 75c

No. 4R3762 Bicycle charm. Price...... 50c

No. 4R3765 Model of Locomotive finely executed. Price.................. 95c

No. 4R3768 Compass, fancy mounting, very accurate. Price.......... 85c

No. 4R3771 Chased roman collar Heart. Price.. 30c

No. 4R3774 Engraved, with brilliant setting. Price... 35c

No. 4R3777 Team of Horses, well finished. Price............... 70c

No. 4R3780 Hand Carved Horse, heavy gold plated, with ruby eyes. Price.......................... $1.85

No. 4R3783 Genuine stone, hand cut intaglio. Price.......... 90c

No. 4R3786 Fancy engraved with three stones. Price...... 55c

No. 4R3789 Revolver, revolving barrel. Price............................ 40c

FINEST QUALITY LOCKETS.

GOLD, GOLD FILLED AND ROLLED PLATE.

No. 4R3825 Plain polished heart, set with 2 brilliants and 1 ruby doublet. Price, each..$1.25

No. 4R3828 Bright polished, hand engraved edge, set with opal. Each......80c

No. 4R3831 Bright polished, hand engraved, set with 5 brilliants and 1 genuine opal. Price, each..$1.35

No. 4R3834 Gold front, hand engraved. Each..........40c

No. 4R3837 Gold front, hand engraved, three stone settings. Each............55c

No. 4R3843 Gold front, fancy mounting, hand engraved. Each............75c

No. 4R3846 Gold front, hand engraved, four stone settings. Each...........60c

No. 4R3849 Plain satin finished, brilliant center. Each............68c

No. 4R3852 Gold front, bright polished, hand engraved, baled, very fancy. Price, each..$1.15

No. 4R3855 Gold front, raised gold ornaments, brilliant center. Each....85c

No. 4R3858 Raised ornamentation, brilliant center. Each..........$1.05

No. 4R3861 Gold front, gold ornamentation. Each.........$1.20

No. 4R3864 Gold front, satin finish, five fancy stone sets. Each.........$1.25

No. 4R3867 Locket, engraved. Each...........60c

No. 4R3870 Locket, engraved Horseshoe, brilliant setting. Each...........75c

No. 4R3873 Locket, engraved, brilliant setting. Each............75c

No. 4R3876 Gold front, gold ornamentation. Each............75c

No. 4R3888 Gold front, fancy border, almandine setting. Each.........$1.40

No. 4R3891 Gold front, hand engraved, swinging bale. Each......98c

No. 4R3894 Gold front, raised gold ornaments, brilliant center. Each..$1.20

No. 4R3900 Locket, solid gold front, sapphire, ruby, and brilliants, hand engraved. Each, $1.85

No. 4R3903 Fancy mounting, raised ornamentation. Engraved stone setting. Ea..$1.40

No. 4R3906 Solid gold front, Roman finish, baled, fancy stone set. Each.........$1.48

No. 4R3912 Very heavy, raised ornamentation, solid gold front, engrav'd, baled. Each.......$1.56

No. 4R3915 Solid gold front, fancy border, 5 almandine sets. Each..$1.65

No. 4R3918 Solid gold front, hand engraved, fancy mounting, 8 fancy sets. Each.... $1.75

No. 4R3924 Solid gold front, fancy border, engraved, 4 almandines, 1 pearl. Each........ $1.75

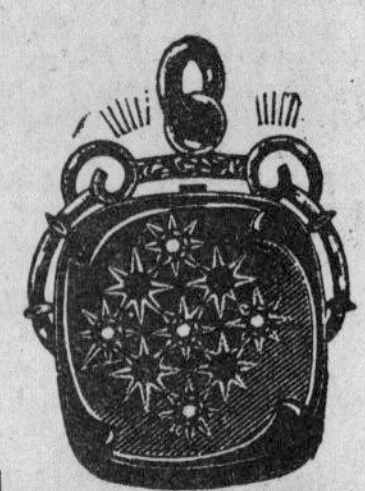
No. 4R3927 Solid gold front, engraved, baled, 9 fancy stone sets. Each....$2.25

SOLID GOLD LOCKETS.

MONOGRAMS ENGRAVED For 35c to 75c Extra.

POSTAGE ON LOCKETS . . . . . . 3 CENTS EXTRA.

No. 4R3930 Satin finished, hand engraved, for two pictures. Each...$1.35

No. 4R3933 Satin finished, hand engraved, for two pictures. Each..$1.50

No. 4R3936 Satin finished, hand engraved, star set with opal, for one picture. Each...... $2.75

No. 4R3939 Satin finished, hand engraved, for two pictures. Each..$2.50

No. 4R3942 Bright polished, hand engraved, fancy baled, for two pictures. Each........$3.50

No. 4R3945 Satin finished star with diamond spark, for one picture. Each..........$3.50

No. 4R3948 Satin finished, hand engraved star, set with 5 pearls and 1 ruby doublet, for one picture. Each....$3.85

No. 4R3949 Satin finished, plain, for one picture. This locket is beautified by a monogram. Each....... ..$4.00

No. 4R3951 Roman satin finished, plain, for one picture. This locket is beautified by a monogram. Each......... $5.00

No. 4R3952 Satin finished, raised rococo border, one picture. Each $4.50

No. 4R3953 Satin finished, raised colored gold ornamentation, two pictures. Each... ......$5.65

4R3956 is adapted for a monogram.

No. 4R3956 Satin finished, plain, extra heavy, two pictures. Each..........$5.65

No. 4R3960 Satin finished, raised colored gold ornamentation. Two pictures. Each... $6.75

No. 4R3965 Satin finished, raised colored gold ornamentation, two pictures. Each..............$6.75

SECRET SOCIETY AND EMBLEM CHARMS.

GOLD AND GOLD FILLED.

THESE CHARMS are manufactured of the best materials procurable. The enamel is guaranteed a hard enamel, and will not chip or wear off. Warranted to give absolute satisfaction in every particular. Our success as a mercantile firm was only accomplished by honest methods and honest dealings. We know that if you buy once from us you will always be a steady customer.

POSTAGE ON CHARMS, 3 CENTS EXTRA.

No. 4R3975 Blue enameled, gold filled, Masonic. Price.....$1.25
No. 4R3978 Same as above, solid gold. Price.....$3.75

No. 4R3981 Gold filled, Masonic and Odd Fellows. Price.........$1.15
No. 4R3984 Same as above, solid gold. Price........ $4.00
No. 4R3985 Solid gold, Masonic only. Price.........$2.75

No. 4R3987 Gold filled, enameled and engraved Independent Order of Foresters. Price.....$1.00
No. 4R3990 Same as above, solid gold. Price.$7.50

No. 4R3993 Gold filled, enameled, Knights of Pythias. Price.........$1.25
No. 4R3996 Same as above, uniformed rank. Price...$1.25

No. 4R3999 Gold filled, enameled and engraved, G. A. R. Price....$1.35
No. 4R4000 Same as above, ¾ size. Price .90c
No. 4R4002 Same as above, solid gold. Price..........$12.00

No. 4R4005 Gold filled, enameled and engraved, Independent Order of Odd Fellows. Price...$1.50
No. 4R4008 Same as above, solid gold. Price.......$12.00

No. 4R4011 Gold filled, enameled and engraved, Sons of Veterans. Price........85c
No. 4R4013 Same as above, solid gold. Price. $4.50

No. 4R4016 Rolled plate, hard enameled, Ancient Order United Workmen. Price 35c
No. 4R4019 Same style, Masonic. Price............35c
No. 4R4022 Same style, Independent Order of Odd Fellows. Price............35c
No. 4R4025 Same style, Knights of Pythias, Price...35c

No. 4R4028 Pearl emblem, onlaid, filled mounting, Independent Order of Foresters. Price. 45c
No. 4R4031 Same style, Woodmen of America. Price, 45c
No. 4R4034 Same style, Maccabees. Price............45c
No. 4R4037 Same style, Ancient Order United Workmen. Price.............45c
No. 4R4038 Same style, Woodmen of the World. Price, 45c

No. 4R4040 Pearl, gold filled emblem, Modern Woodmen. Price............65c
No. 4R4043 Same style, Masonic. Price............65c
No. 4R4046 Same style, Knights of Pythias. Price..65c
No. 4R4049 Same style, Odd Fellows. Price...........65c
No. 4R4050 Same style, Woodmen of the World. Price, 65c
No. 4R4051 Same style, Foresters of America. Price, 65c

No. 4R4052 Gold filled, hard enameled and engraved, Improved Order of Red Men. Price.......75c
No. 4R4055 Same style G. A. R. Price............75c
No. 4R4058 Same style, Odd Fellows. Price............75c
No. 4R4061 Same style, Catholic Order of Foresters. Price............75c

No. 4R4064 Gold filled, enameled, Odd Fellows Encampment. Price.....85c
No. 4R4067 Same style as above. Odd Fellows. Price..85c
No. 4R4070 Same style, Ancient Order of United Workmen. Price............85c
No. 4R4073 Same style, Masonic. Price..... ......85c

No. 4R4076 Gold filled emblem, set in black onyx, Masonic. Price.........$1.00
No. 4R4079 Same style, Odd Fellows. Price.........$1.00
No. 4R4082 Same style, Knights of the Maccabees. Price.........$1.00
No. 4R4085 Same style, Royal Arcanum. Price...$1.00

No. 4R4088 Gold filled, hard enameled and engraved, Junior Order United American Mechanics. Price.........$1.50
No. 4R4091 Same style, Knights of Pythias. Price $1.50
No. 4R4094 Same style, Modern Woodmen. Price...$1.50
No. 4R4097 Same style, Odd Fellows. Price.........$1.50

No. 4R4103 Solid gold, hard enameled and engraved, Ancient Order United Workmen. Price.....$3.75

No. 4R4106 Solid gold, hard enameled, engraved, Odd Fellows. Price....$2.75
No. 4R4109 Same style, Masonic. Price............$2.75
No. 4R4110 Same style, Knights of Pythias. Price...$2.75

No. 4R4112 Solid gold, Masonic thirty-second degree. Price.$2.00

No. 4R4115 Daughters of Rebekah, solid gold. Price.....$3.00

No. 4R4117 Solid gold, hard enameled, engraved, Eastern Star. Price......$3.35

No. 4R4119 Solid gold, enameled, Knights of Pythias. Price $2.00

No. 4R4121 Solid gold, enameled, Odd Fellows. Price.$2.00

No. 4R4123 Solid gold hard enameled, engraved, Odd Fellows Encampment. Price.$3.75

No. 4R4125 Solid gold. Masonic. Price.....$5.00
No. 4R4126 As above, stone center. Price..$4.00
No. 4R4127 Same as above, gold filled. Ea..$1.35

No. 4R4129 Solid gold, enameled, Knights of Pythias. Price.........$7.00
No. 4R4131 Same as above, gold filled. Price..... ...$1.45

No. 4R4133 Solid gold, hard enameled, engraved, Knights of Pythias. Price.........$9.90

No. 4R4135 Solid gold, hard enameled, engraved, Knights of the Maccabees. Price.........$9.00
No. 4R4137 Same style, Knights Templars, solid gold. Price.........$8.00

No. 4R4139 Solid gold, extra heavy, enameled colors, hand engraved. Price.......$12.00

No. 4R4141 Solid gold, enameled, hand engraved. Odd Fellows. Price.........$9.00

No. 4R4143 Extra heavy, black onyx 10 rubies, 5 diamonds. Price.......$21.96

GENTLEMEN'S SOLID GOLD AND GOLD FILLED CUFF BUTTONS.

FOR A SMALL SUM OF MONEY THE GOODS LISTED ON THIS PAGE ARE VERY APPROPRIATE GIFTS FOR GENTLEMEN.

These goods are made from the highest grade of material and guaranteed to us by the manufacturer. We in turn guarantee them to give you thorough satisfaction.

POSTAGE ON CUFF BUTTONS, 3 CENTS EXTRA. REGISTRATION, 8 CENTS.

No. 4R4378 Fancy inlaid stone. Per pair........25c

No. 4R4381 Fancy hand painted setting, fancy border. Pair 25c

No. 4R4384 Raised ornamentation, hand chased. Per pair. 35c

No. 4R4387 Raised ornamentation, hand chased. Per pair. 35c

No. 4R4390 Raised ornamentation, hand chased. Per pair. 35c

No. 4R4393 Polished and engraved. Per pair........32c

No. 4R4396 Raised ornamentation and engraved. Pair, 40c

No. 4R4399 Raised ornamentation and engraved. Per pair........45c

No. 4R4400 Raised ornamentation and engraved. Per pair........50c

No. 4R4403 Hand engraved intaglio, very neat and durable, stone set. Pr. 50c

No. 4R4406 Raised ornamentation, hand chased, bright and Roman finish. Pr. 60c

No. 4R4409 Raised and colored gold, ornamented and engraved. Pair....95c

No. 4R4412 Hand engraved intaglio, very neat and durable. stone set. Pr. 65c

No. 4R4415 Rolled plate, bright finish, hand engraved. Per pair........60c

No. 4R4418 Raised ornamentation, bright and Roman finish. Per pair .60c

No. 4R4421 Solid gold front, hand engraved. Per pair........70c

No. 4R4424 Raised ornamented and engraved. Per pair........75c

No. 4R4427 Solid gold front, hand engraved. Per pair........70c

No. 4R4430 Solid gold front, fancy border, plain center. Per pair........95c

No. 4R4433 Raised ornamentation, bright polish. Per pair........55c

No. 4R4436 Raised ornamentation, bright and Roman finish. Per pair..75c

No. 4R4439 Solid gold front, hand engraved, fancy border, bright finish. Per pair........88c

No. 4R4442 Solid gold front, hand engraved, bright finish. very fine. Per pair......$1.15

No. 4R4445 Solid gold front, bright and Roman finish, hand engraved, very elegant. Pair ...$1.35

No. 4R4448 Solid gold front, bright and Roman finish, hand engraved, very elegant. Pair....$1.25

No. 4R4451 Solid gold front, bright and Roman finish, hand engraved, very elegant. Pair....$1.55

No. 4R4454 Pearl, gold band ornamentation. Per pair..35c

No. 4R4457 Solid gold front, bright and Roman finish, hand engraved, very elegant. Pair....$1.43

No. 4R4460 Ladies or boys' solid gold fronts, hand engraved. Per pair.....75c

No. 4R4463 Ladies' or boys', solid gold fronts, hand engraved. Per pair.....75c

No. 4R4466 Solid gold front, satin finished, hand engraved. Per pair $1.50

Engraving 5c per letter, large script.

No. 4R4469 Solid gold, satin finished. Per pair......$2.50

Engraving 5c per letter, Old English.

No. 4R4471 Solid gold, satin finished. Per pair......$2.50

No. 4R4475 Solid gold, polished center. Per pair......$3.85

No. 4R4478 Solid gold, satin finished. Per pair......$4.50

SOLID GOLD DUMB BELL PATTERN CUFF LINKS.

No. 4R4480 Solid gold, raised ornamentation. Per pair. ...$1.65

No. 4R4482 Solid gold, raised ornamentation. Per pair.....$1.90

No. 4R4485 Solid gold, raised ornamentation. Per pair.....$2.00

No. 4R4486 Solid gold, set with fire opal. Per pair......$2.20

Engraving 5c per letter for large script.

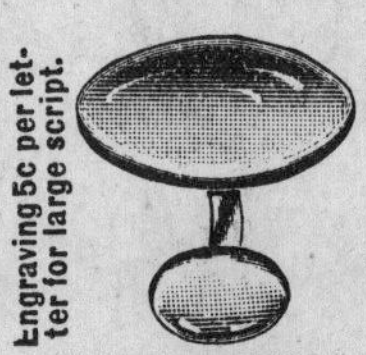

No. 4R4489 Solid gold, made heavy. Per pair......$2.40

Engraving 5c per letter for Old English.

No. 4R4491 Solid gold, raised ornamentation, set with fire opal. Per pair.....$2.50

No. 4R4495 Solid gold, raised ornamentation, extra strong. Per pair......$2.50

No. 4R4500 Solid gold, raised ornamentation, extra strong. Per pair......$3.70

No. 4R4503 Solid gold, raised ornamentation, bright finish. Per pair......$2.75

No. 4R4506 Solid gold, set with genuine rose diamond. Per pr., $3.40

No. 4R4510 Solid gold, set with genuine rose diamond. Per pr., $4.25

No. 4R4513 Solid gold, colored ornamentation, extra heavy. Per pr. $4.25

No. 4R4516 Solid gold, with extra large genuine rose diamond. Per pr., $6.00

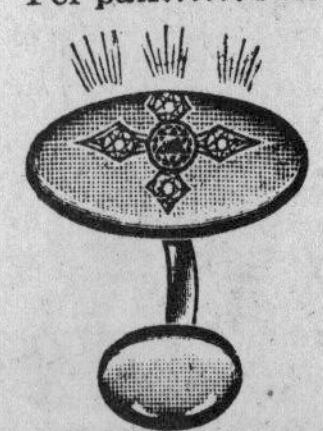

No. 4R4518 Solid gold, set with 4 rose diamonds and 1 garnet. Per pair, $7.35

BEST QUALITY STUDS AND COLLAR BUTTONS.

. . . In Solid Gold, Gold Filled and Rolled Plate . . .

WE HAVE ADDED to our line of stud sets a very handsome gold filled line for negligee shirts. This stud set 's made on the same plan as a small collar button, but is especially adapted for negligee shirt fronts. The designs we have selected are the ones used by our swell dressers in all large cities; simple but neat patterns.

COLLAR BUTTONS we quote are the most staple patterns made. We have endeavored to list a complete line. The quality we know will give absolute satisfaction. Orders for these goods will receive our most prompt and very careful attention.

OUR SOLID GOLD single stone set studs are the nobbiest and most fashionable on the market, genuine stones being used, most brilliant and finest cut to be found, firmly set in solid gold settings, the same way as a diamond is set.

WE GUARANTEE THEM TO YOU IN EVERY PARTICULAR.

The spiral used on these studs is double strength; in fact, we are proud of our line of studs, knowing the entire satisfaction they give.

If by mail, postage extra, 2 cents; registration 8 cents extra.

SOLID GOLD SINGLE STONE SET STUDS.

No. 4R4652 Genuine opal. Each. $1.35

No. 4R4655 Genuine opal. Each. $1.60

No. 4R4658 Ruby doublet. Each.. $1.60

No. 4R4661 Emerald doublet. Each..... $1.60

No. 4R4664 Ruby doublet. Each.. $1.25

No. 4R4667 Emerald doublet. Each..... $1.75

No. 4R4670 Sapphire doublet. Each...... $1.90

No. 4R4673 Almandine stone. Each....., $1.95

No. 4R4676 Pearl front. Rolled plate back, separable. Per set...20c

No. 4R4679 Pearl front. Rolled plate back, separable. Per set....30c

No. 4R4682 Carbuncle set. Rolled plate back, separable. Per set....35c

No. 4R4685 Carbuncle set. Gold filled back, separable. Per set....50c

No. 4R4688 Gold front engraved. Gold filled back, separable. Per set....50c

No. 4R4691 Pearl front, gold ornamentation, hand engraved, separable. Per set 60c

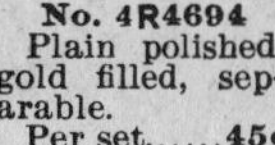

No. 4R4694 Plain polished, gold filled, separable. Per set......45c

No. 4R4697 Negligee gold filled, solid posts, raised ornamentation. Per set......45c

No. 4R4700 Gold filled solid posts, negligee. Per set......45c

No. 4R4703 Gold filled, raised ornamentation, separable. Per set....40c

No. 4R4706 Gold filled, ruby, turquoise, and pearl set, separable. Per set....85c

No. 4R4709 Gold filled, bright and satin finish, ruby set, separable. Per set....75c

No. 4R4712 Gold filled, ruby set, separable. Per set....55c

No. 4R4715 Gold filled, set with rubies, separable. Per set....70c

No. 4R4718 Gold filled, set with pearls, separable. Per set....75c

No. 4R4721 Solid gold heads, set with rubies, separable. Per set...$1.25

No. 4R4724 Solid gold heads, raised ornamentation, separable. Per set...$1.50

No. 4R4727 Gold filled, set with opals, separable. Per set.....50c

SOLID GOLD COLLAR BUTTONS.

No. 4R4730 Ball top, medium. Each.......... 90c

No. 4R4733 Ball top, high. Each...$1.00

No. 4R4736 Flat top, low. Each....90c

No. 4R4739 Flat top, medium. Each..........95c

No. 4R4742 Flat top, high. Each..$1.00

No. 4R4745 Lever top, medium. Each..........80c

No. 4R4748 Lever top, large. Each....$1.10

No. 4R4751 Lever pointer. Each...$1.10

GOLD FILLED COLLAR BUTTONS.

Flat Top. No. 4R4754 Rolled plate. Each....10c No. 4R4757 Gold filled. Each....25c

Ball Top. No. 4R4760 Rolled plate. Each...10c No. 4R4763 Gold filled. Each...25c

Lever Pearl Back. No. 4R4766 Rolled plate. Each.........15c

Lever Medium. No. 4R4769 Rolled plate. Each...10c No. 4R4772 Gold filled. Each...25c

Lever High. No. 4R4775 Rolled plate. Each...10c No. 4R4778 Gold filled. Each...25c

Lever Pointer. No. 4R4781 Rolled plate. Each...10c No. 4R4784 Gold filled. Each...25c

Separable. No. 4R4787 Gold filled. Each.......15c

Separable No. 4R4790 Gold filled. Each..........15c

SCARF, STICK PINS AND HAT PINS. SOLID GOLD, GOLD FILLED AND ROLLED PLATE.

POSTAGE ON SCARF PINS AND STICK PINS, 2 CENTS; HAT PINS, 3 CENTS. INSURANCE OR REGISTRY EXTRA.

No. 4R5006 Three star balls. Each....20c

No. 4R5009 Anchor, pearl set. Each....20c

No. 4R5012 Chased, Roman finished, emerald center. Each........20c

No. 4R5015 Chased with ruby center. Each......25c

No. 4R5018 Tiffany setting, white stone. Each 27c

No. 4R5024 Tiffany setting, white stone. Each....40c

No. 4R5027 Cluster, four rubies, 4 white stones, 1 pearl. Each......40c

No. 4R5036 Pearl, 2 brilliants. Each....25c

No. 4R5039 Three garnets. Each....35c

No. 4R5042 1 brilliant, bright polished fan. Each....40c

No. 4R5051 Fancy 5 brilliants, 1 sapphire. Each....50c

No. 4R5054 3 pearls, 1 genuine seashell. Each....48c

No. 4R5060 Bright ornaments, opal center. Each....45c

No. 4R5066 Horseshoe, 9 brilliants. Each....50c

No. 4R5069 Horseshoe, 7 rubies, 8 brilliants. Each. $1.00

No. 4R5072 Cluster, 14 brilliants, 8 rubies, 1 pearl Each....85c

No. 4R5075 Battle Axe, blue enamel, 2 rubies, 1 brilliant. Each....36c

No. 4R5081 Horseshoe and arrow, 9 pearls. Each....75c

No. 4R5083 Fly, 3 pearls, 1 fancy stone. Each....40c

No. 4R5093 Fancy, bright finish, pearl center. Each....40c

SOLID GOLD SCARF PINS

No. 4R5100 Solid Gold Heart, almandine center. Each....80c

No. 4R5103 Solid Gold, bright polished, emerald setting. Each....85c

No. 4R5107 Solid Gold, hand eng'ved, genuine opal. Each..$1.10

No. 4R5113 Solid gold, ruby and emerald setting. Each..$1.30

No. 4R5116 Solid gold, very fancy, bright polished, 13 pearls Each..$1.35

No. 4R5125 Solid gold 1 emerald, sapphire and ruby setting. Each..$1.25

No. 4R5128 Solid gold, bright finish, genuine opal center. Each..$1.50

No. 4R5131 Solid gold, very fancy, amethyst, 3 brilliants. Each. $1.60

No. 4R5143 Solid gold, Fancy Bird, 4 pearls, 1 ruby. Each. $1.25

No. 4R5146 Solid gold 13 brilliants, ruby center. Each. $1.50

No. 4R5152 Solid gold, bright cut and engraved, almandine center. $1.90

No. 4R5155 Solid gold Fancy Sickle, 2 turquoise, 2 pearls. Each. $2.00

No. 4R5158 Solid gold, bright finish, large genuine fire opal. Each, $3.25

No. 4R5161 Solid gold, bright finish, knot, emerald set. Each, $1.10

No. 4R5164 Solid gold, bright finish, Roman, colored rope. Each, $1.15

No. 4R5167 Solid gold, bright finish, almandine center and 4 genuine fire opals. $1.20

No. 4R5173 Solid gold, bright finish, star and crescent, 6 pearl sets. Each $1.45

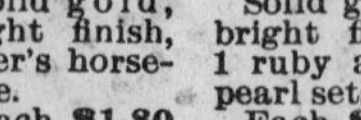
No. 4R5176 Solid gold, bright finish, racer's horseshoe. Each, $1.80

No. 4R5182 Solid gold, bright finish, 1 ruby and 4 pearl sets. Each, $2.10

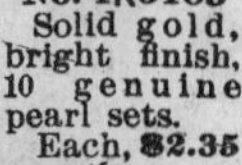
No. 4R5185 Solid gold, bright finish, 10 genuine pearl sets. Each, $2.35

GOLD FILLED HAT PINS.

No. 4R5191 Very fancy rolled plated, 6 white stone settings, fancy stone center. Each, 35c

No. 4R5192 Gold filled, very fancy, hard enameled in colors. Each.............50c

No. 4R5193 Gold filled, very fancy, set with 13 white stones and 1 large amethyst. Ea., 55c

No. 4R5194 Gold filled, very fancy cluster, set with 17 emeralds and 12 white stones. Each, 60c

No. 4R5195 Gold filled, very fancy, Roman color, set with 20 emeralds and 14 brilliants. Each............ $1.25

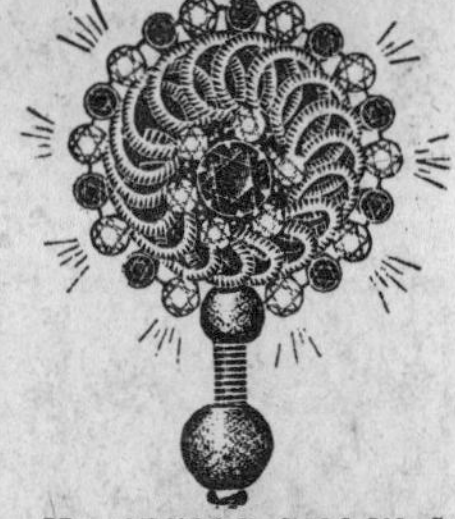
No. 4R5196 Gold filled, Roman finished vibrating top, 2 large rubies, 22 fine cut brilliants and 6 small rubies. Each, $1.60

No. 4R5197 Gold filled fancy ball, Roman finish, set with 8 pearls and 1 large ruby center. Each...............65c

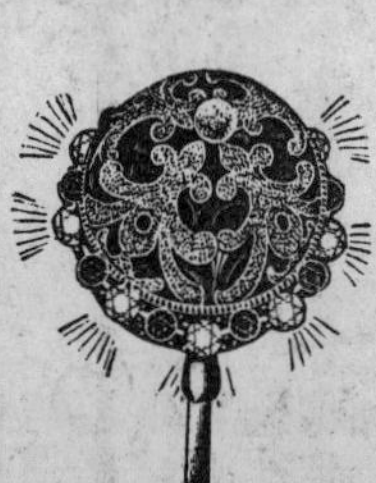
No. 4R5198 Gold filled fancy ball, Roman finish, set with 9 emeralds and 9 brilliants. Each.............90c

No. 4R5199 Gold filled, satin finished ball, set with 20 emeralds and 20 fine cut brilliants, very attractive. Each..$1.15

No. 4R5200 Gold filled, fancy cube, set with 6 large turquoise and 36 fine cut brilliants. The very latest design. Ea., $1.50

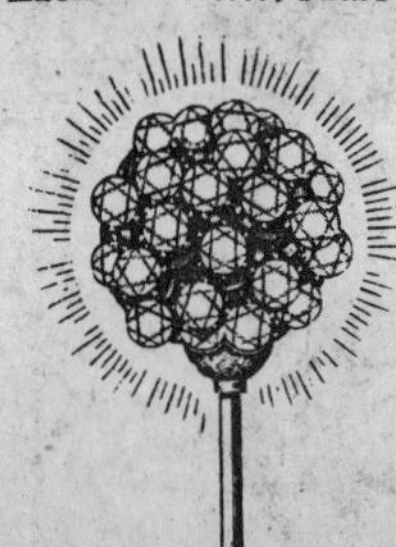
No. 4R5201 Gold filled ball, Roman finished vibrating top, set with 36 fine large cut brilliants. Each......$1.60

No. 4R5202 Gold filled, set with 6 large sapphires and 43 brilliants. Each $1.75

BEST QUALITY SOLID GOLD, GOLD FILLED, JET MOURNING AND SOLID GOLD FRONT, ENGRAVED LACE PINS, BEAUTY PINS AND SETS.

BEAUTY PINS ARE MEETING WITH UNIVERSAL SUCCESS AS THE BEST IDEAS FOR WAIST OR SKIRT ORNAMENTS. BOTH USEFUL AND ORNAMENTAL.

If by Mail, Postage, 2 Cents; Registered Mail, 8 Cents Extra.

No. 4R5203 Solid gold front. Each.........30c

No. 4R5212 Solid gold front, engraved, 1 garnet. Each 45c

No. 4R5219 Jet Lace Pin, polished and fancy engraved. Price..30c

No. 4R5220 Polished Jet Lace Pin, with small gold ornament set with real pearl. Price.......... ....75c

No. 4R5206 Gold filled, 1 garnet. Each......35c

No. 4R5215 Gold front, engraved, 1 sapphire, 1 brilliant, 1 garnet. Each........................95c

No. 4R5224 Gold filled, fancy, 2 garnets. Each..60c

No. 4R5209 Gold filled, fancy. Each........35c

No. 4R5216 Jet Lace Pin, polished ball in flower Price..75c

No. 4R5227 Solid gold front, engraved. Each..$1.30

CHILD'S BIB AND BABY PINS, ETC.

No. 4R5230 Gold filled, 2 brilliants, 1 garnet. Each.............................20c

No. 4R5233 Solid gold front, engraved. Per pair................40c

No. 4R5236 Gold front, raised ornamented ends. Per pair................55c

No. 4R5251 Solid gold, Roman color, set with 3 real pearls. Per pair.....$2.50

No. 4R5239 Solid gold front, engraved. Per pair................65c

No. 4R5254 Solid gold, Roman color, raised ornamentation. Per pair..$2.00

No. 4R5242 Solid gold front, engraved. Per pair................70c

No. 4R5257 Fine solid gold, polished center, beaded edges. Per pair......$1.45

No. 4R5245 Solid gold front, 1 garnet, 1 pearl, 1 sapphire. Per pair......85c

No. 4R5248 Solid gold, Roman color, hand engraved. Per pair.....$1.00

No. 4R5260 Fine gold filled Pin Set, fancy raised ornamentation. Each.............90c

No. 4R5263 Fine gold filled Pin Set, raised ornamentation. Each..65c

No. 4R5266 Solid gold Pin Set, fancy raised ornamentation. Each........................$3.50

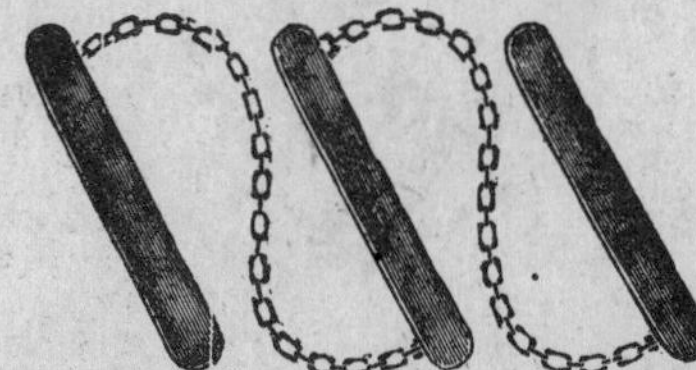

No. 4R5269 Solid gold front Pin Set, satin finished. Each $1.50

No. 4R5272 Solid gold front Pin Set, fancy pattern, engraved, satin finished. Each...............$1.65

No. 4R5275 Solid gold front engraved Pin Set, 1 garnet, 1 pearl, 1 sapphire. Each..............$1.60

BEAUTY OR WAIST PIN SETS. SOLD IN SETS OF SIX ONLY.

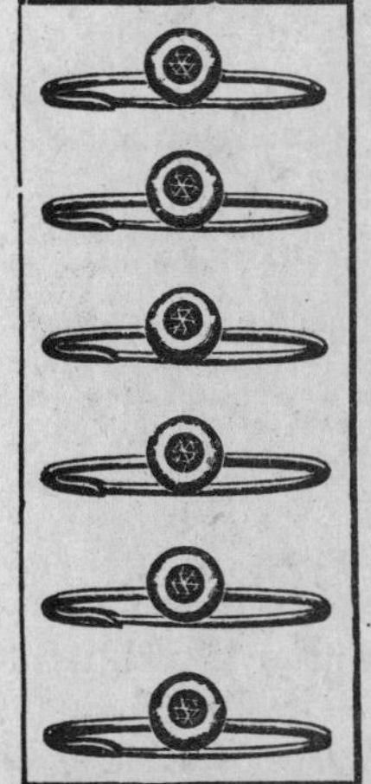

No. 4R5278 Beauty Pin Sets, gold filled, bright polished, set with red or blue stones. Price, per set.......50c

No. 4R5281 Beauty Pins, fancy center, Roman and bright finish, gold filled, set with turquoise. Price, per set,98c

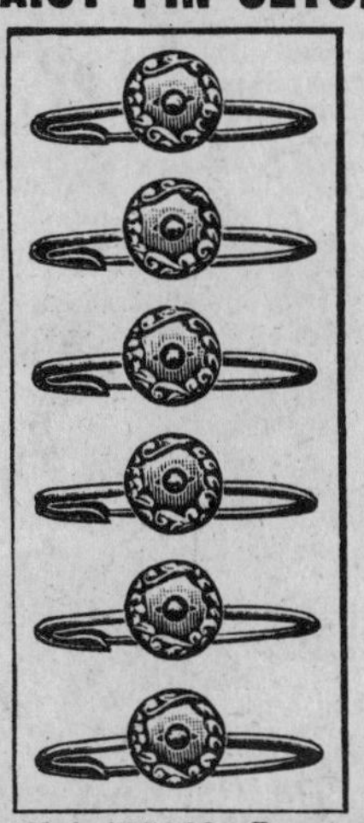

No. 4R5283 Beauty Pins, fancy raised center, set with turquoise, Roman and bright finish, gold filled. Set....$1.00

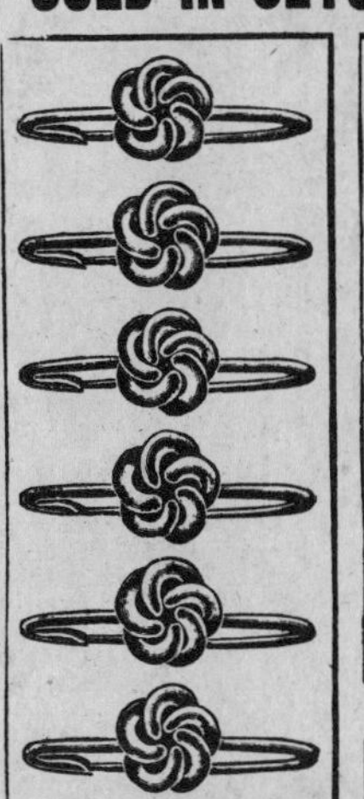

No. 4R5287 Beauty Pins, fancy raised center, knot pattern, bright finish, gold filled. Price, per set....$1.25

No. 4R5290 Beauty Pins, fancy embossed pattern, set with garnets, Roman finish, gold filled. Price, per set ...$1.30

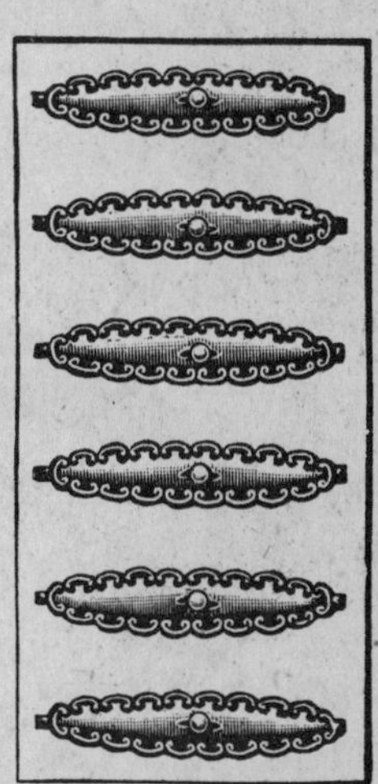

No. 4R5293 Beauty Pins, fancy rococo border, Roman finish, set with pearls, gold filled. Price, per set....$1.35

STERLING SILVER NOVELTIES.

THE DEMAND HAVING INCREASED TO SUCH A WONDERFUL EXTENT THAT NECESSITATED OUR PUTTING IN A MUCH LARGER LINE OF THESE GOODS,

we have with care selected such novelties as are most appropriate for a gift or personal use. In making a gift, we believe that it is always better to give a useful article, so in selecting these novelties we have endeavored to buy only such articles as have utility. All these goods are made of the finest sterling silver, and the prices quoted, it will be noted, are extremely low. It will be seen that the articles—that is a great many of them—can be used as a gift for either a lady or gentleman, as a birthday or holiday present. Bear in mind that our novelties are all 925-1000 fine. The engraving is hand engraved, and the chasing, hand chased. They are sufficiently heavy to be well able to stand continual usage. If you buy once we know that you will continue to be frequent patrons of our firm. If goods are not exactly as described we always cheerfully refund money.

No. 4R5827 Sterling Silver Button Hook, 7¾ inches long. Price........98c
If by mail, postage extra, 5 cents.

No. 4R5829 Sterling Silver Paper Cutter, 7¾ inches long, fine pearl blade. Price............(If by mail, postage extra, 4 cents)....................$1.10

No. 4R5831 Sterling Silver Tooth Brush, 7½ inches long. Price..70c
If by mail, postage extra, 3 cents.

No. 4R5833 Sterling Silver Curling Iron, length, 7 inches. Price..70c
If by mail, postage extra, 6 cents.

No. 4R5835 Sterling Silver Paper Cutter, 6¾ inches long. Price...............(If by mail, postage extra, 4 cents).............85c

No. 4R5837 Sterling Silver Manicure File, 6 inches long. Price......(If by mail, postage extra, 4 cents)........90c

No. 4R5839 Sterling Silver Button Hook, 5½ inches long. Price......(If by mail, postage extra, 3 cents).......40c

No. 4R5841 Sterling Silver Letter Seal, length, 3 inches. Any letter cut, 15 cents extra. (If by mail, postage extra, 4 cents) Price............70c

No. 4R5843 Sterling Silver Letter Opener, 4¾ inches long. Price..35c
If by mail, postage extra, 3 cents.

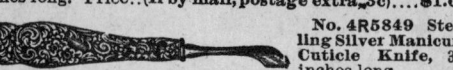

No. 4R5845 Sterling Silver Paper Cutter, 4¼ inches long. Price......(If by mail, postage extra, 3 cents).......80c

No. 4R5847 Sterling Silver Pocket Mustache Comb, 4 inches long. Price..(If by mail, postage extra, 3c)....$1.00

No. 4R5849 Sterling Silver Manicure Cuticle Knife, 3¾ inches long. Price......(If by mail, postage extra, 3 cents).........50c

No. 4R5851 Sterling Silver Mounted Corkscrew, length of handle, 6 inches; length of screw, 3½ inches. Price....(If by mail, postage extra, 10 cents).....$2.00

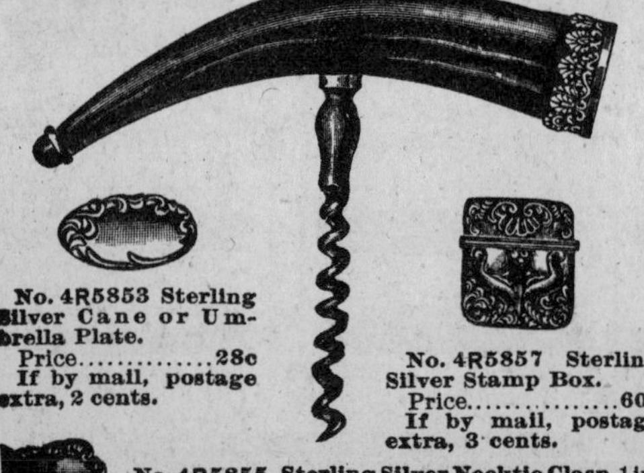

No. 4R5853 Sterling Silver Cane or Umbrella Plate. Price..............28c
If by mail, postage extra, 2 cents.

No. 4R5857 Sterling Silver Stamp Box. Price...............60c
If by mail, postage extra, 3 cents.

No. 4R5855 Sterling Silver Necktie Clasp, 1 in. long. Price.(If by mail, postage extra, 3c)..40c

No. 4R5859 Sterling Silver Paper Cutter, 8½ inches long. Price.....$1.10
If by mail, postage extra, 5 cents.

No. 4R5861 Sterling Silver Shoe Horn, 7½ inches long. Price.........$1.05
If by mail, postage extra, 6 cents.

No. 4R5864 Sterling Silver Coat Hanger, 2 inches long. (If by mail, postage extra, 2 cents) Price..........50c

No. 4R5866 Sterling Silver Hat Mark, 2 inches long. (If by mail, postage extra, 2 cents) Price...........35c

No. 4R5869 Sterling Silver Desk Knife, 5 inches long. Price.....(If by mail, postage extra, 3 cents)..........95c

No. 4R5871 Sterling Silver Ink Eraser, 5¼ inches long. Price....(If by mail, postage extra, 3 cents)..........95c

No. 4R5873 Sterling Silver Manicure File, 5½ inches long. Price...45c
If by mail, postage extra, 3 cents.

No. 4R5867 Sterling Silver Embroidery Scissors, length, 4 inches. Price.....(Postage extra, 4c)......95c

No. 4R5875 Sterling Silver Scissors, length, 5½ inches. Price.............................$1.10
If by mail, postage extra, 4c.

No. 4R5877 Sterling Silver Nail Polisher, 3½ inches long, Price.........65c
If by mail, postage extra, 4 cents.

No. 4R5879 Sterling Silver Baby Ring, 1¼ inches in diameter, silver bells, pearl ring. Price..........80c
If by mail, postage extra, 3 cents.

No. 4R5881 Sterling Silver Stamp Box. Price................68c
If by mail, postage extra, 3 cents.

No. 4R5883 Sterling Silver Needle Emery. Price.........28c
If by mail, postage extra, 3c.

No. 4R5885 Sterling Silver Baggage Check, very heavy. Ea..48c
If by mail, postage extra, 3c.

No. 4R5887 Sterling Silver Mounted Pocket Mirror, 2 inches in diameter. Price...............................35c
If by mail, postage extra, 3c.

No. 4R5889 Necktie Clasp, ¾ inch long. Price.34c
If by mail, postage extra, 3 cents.

No. 4R5891 Sterling Silver Nail File, in box, length, 3 inches. Price...(If by mail, postage extra, 3 cents)....70c

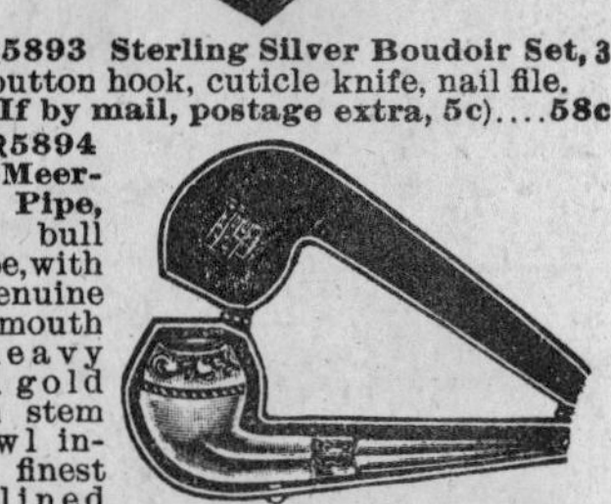

No. 4R5893 Sterling Silver Boudoir Set, 3 pieces—button hook, cuticle knife, nail file. Price...(If by mail, postage extra, 5c)....58c

No. 4R5894 Genuine Meerschaum Pipe, straight, bull dog shape, with 3-inch genuine amber mouth piece, heavy chased gold band on stem and bowl inlaid, in finest plush lined chamois covered case. Price, each....$5.[illegible]
If by mail, postage extra, 5 cents.

The Articles Illustrated and Described

On this page cover an assortment from which a most desirable present may be selected for

WEDDING, BIRTHDAY OR CHRISTMAS

Sterling Silver Folding Corkscrew.

No. 4R5897 Sterling Silver Folding Corkscrew. Screw can be set in handle. 2¾ inches long when folded. Price.....................$1.50
If by mail, postage extra, 5 cents.

STERLING SILVER NOVELTIES

No. 4R5953 Sterling Silver Glove Set, consisting of five pieces, box 5x4 inches. Price, complete set, $1.75
If by mail, postage extra, 10 cents.

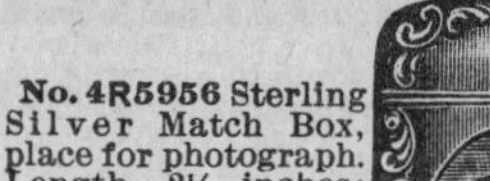

No. 4R5956 Sterling Silver Match Box, place for photograph. Length, 2½ inches; width, 1½ inches. Price........$2.25
No. 4R5959 Same in silver plated. Price...........80c
If by mail, postage extra, 3 cents.

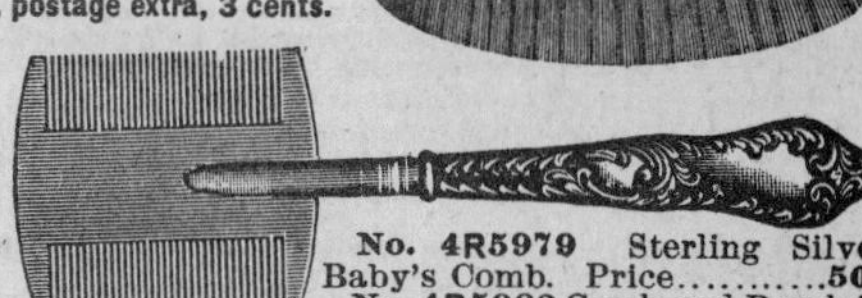

No. 4R5978 Sterling Silver Baby's Hair Brush. Price..................70c
If by mail, postage extra, 3 cents.

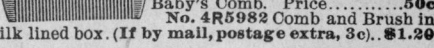

No. 4R5979 Sterling Silver Baby's Comb. Price..........50c
No. 4R5982 Comb and Brush in silk lined box. (If by mail, postage extra, 3c)..$1.29

No. 4R5962 Sterling Silver Match Box. Price..$1.25

No. 4R5965 Sterling Silver Match Box. Price..$1.00
If by mail, postage extra, 3 cents.

No. 4R5968 Sterling Silver Match Box. Price..$1.10

No. 4R5971 Sterling Silver Match Box. Price. $1.20
If by mail, postage extra, 3 cents.

No. 4R5974 Sterling Silver Match Box, extra heavy. Price.. ....$1.30

No. 4R5983 Sterling Silver Baby's Ring, one bell. Price..........75c

No. 4R5986 Sterling Silver Horseshoe key ring. Price.. .....58c
If by mail, postage extra, 2 cents.

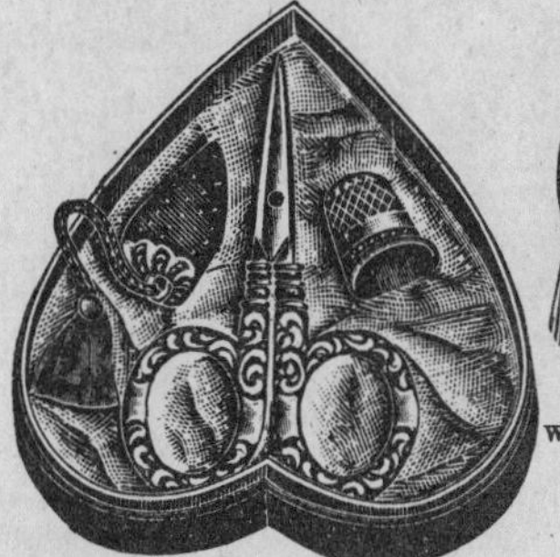

No. 4R5989 Sterling Silver Embroidery Set, 3 pieces. Price... (If by mail, postage extra, 6 cents)....$1.20

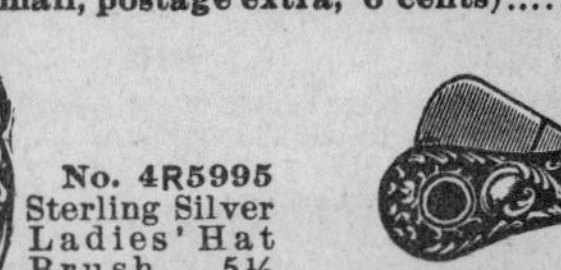

No. 4R5992 Sterling Silver Brush, 6¼ inches long, 1½ inches wide. Price. ....(If by mail, postage extra, 6 cents)........$2.25

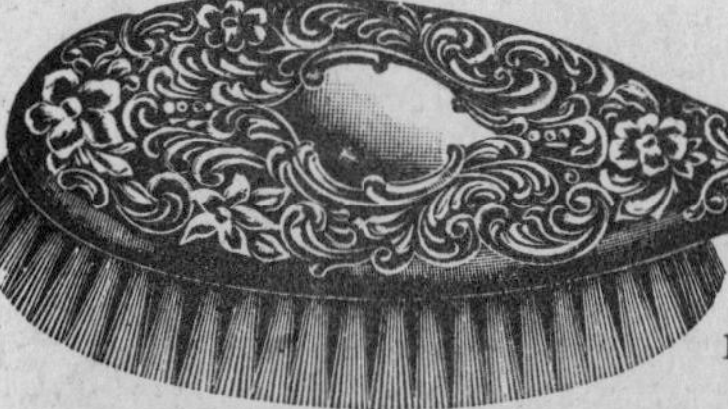

No. 4R5999 Sterling Silver Hair Brush, 7¾ inches long. Price...$2.75
If by mail, postage extra, 6 cents.

No. 4R5995 Sterling Silver Ladies' Hat Brush, 5¼ inches long. Price, $1.25
If by mail, postage extra, 4 cents.

No. 4R5998 Sterling Silver Pocket Cigar Cutter, 1¼ inches long. Price...............65c
If by mail, postage extra, 3 cents.

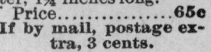

No. 4R6000 Sterling Silver Comb, 7½ inches long, to match brush. Price..$1.25
If by mail, postage extra, 3 cents.
Can furnish set complete in box, silk lined. No extra charge for box.

No. 4R6012 Sterling Silver Silk Bobbin for winding silk. Price...............58c
If by mail, postage extra, 3 cents.

No. 4R6014 Sterling Silver Mounted Garters, fine silk web, plaid effect, something nobby. Price, per pair, $1.40
If by mail, postage extra, 6 cents.

No. 4R6001 Sterling Silver Stocking Darner, 5½ inches long. Price......50c

No. 4R6004 Sterling Silver Table Bell, 4 inches long. Price.........$1.10

No. 4R6007 Sterling Silver Baby Rattle. Length, 5 inches. Price..........$1.10
If by mail, postage extra, 5 cents.

No. 4R6010 Sterling Silver Book Mark. Price.... ...25c
If by mail, postage extra, 2c.

No. 4R6016 Sterling Silver Mounted Garters, set with handsome ruby, fine silk web. Very handsome. Price..........$2.00
If by mail, postage extra, 6 cents.

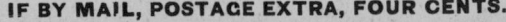

LADIES' GOLD FILLED AND SILVER FILLED BUCKLES

CUT PRICES—Positively Figured at Less Than Wholesale.

BE IN STYLE buy a buckle from us and you will own the latest style, the best quality and the biggest bargain for the money. We will save you 25 to 30 per cent by buying these buckles. We get them in gross lots, where others purchase them in dozens; we, therefore, command the price. They are made of the **highest quality stock.** The stone setting selected from the best, and the designing done by the most skilled artists.

FOUR CENTS will carry one of our sash buckles to any part of the United States of America.

THE ROSE GOLD AND FRENCH GRAY FINISH is the latest id in the finishing buckles. Its effect is unsurpassed; it is both rich and attractive, yet mode it fills a long felt want. Both old and young can use it and be in good tas Any costume would be improved by one of our buckles—either a walki dress or a ball room gown.

THEY ARE BEING WORN EVERYWHERE by the ladies in all o cosmopolitan cities; the are more than a fad; they have become a necessity. Your costume is no complete without one of our latest ideas in a sash buckle.

No. 4R6028 Sash Buckle, rose finish, gold filled. Price 65c
No. 4R6031 Sash Buckle, same style as above, gray silver filled. Price.....55c

No. 4R6034 Sash Buckle, rose finish, gold filled. Price..................65c
No. 4R6037 Sash Buckle, same style as above, gray silver filled. Price......55c

No. 4R6040 Sash Buckle, fancy raised ornamentation, rose finish, gold filled. Price..................70c
No. 4R6043 Sash Buckle, same style as above, French gray, silver filled. Price..................60c

No. 4R6046 Sash Buckle, very rich design in raised ornamentation, rose finish, gold filled. Price........75c
No. 4R6049 Sash Buckle, same style as above, French gray, silver filled. Price..................60c

No. 4R6052 Sash Buckle, extra size; select design rich raised ornamentation rose finish; gold filled. Price..............$1
No. 4R6055 Sash Buc same style as above, g silver filled. Price......

No. 4R6058 Sash Buckle, Roman gold filled, set with eight turquoise, eight emeralds and two rubies. Very gorgeous effect. Price..................$1.40

Four cents will carry any buckle to any part of the United States of America.

No. 4R6061 Sash Buckle, very rich embossed design, rose gold finish, set with six turquoise and one large center stone, gold filled. Price 50c
No. 4R6062 Sash Buckle, same as above, French gray finish, silver filled. Price..................75c

No. 4R6064 Sash Buckle, Roman finish, beautifully ornamented, set with eight small rubies and two large center ones. Price..................$1.10

Four cents will carry any one of these to any part of the United States of America.

No. 4R6067 Sash Buckle, very tractive sash buckle, gold filled, or mented rose colored gold finish, ric embossed latest design. Parisian portation. Price..................$1
No. 4R6068 Sash Buckle, same above, silver filled, French gray ished. Price..................$1.

No. 4R6070 Sash Buckle, gold filled, rose finish, very artistic, set with sixty-one turquoise. French design. Price..................$1.00
No. 4R6073 Sash Buckle, same as above, silver filled, French gray finished. Price..................90c

No. 4R6076 Sash Buckle, gold filled, richly embossed, rose gold finished, set with four rubies, newest design, Parisian importation. Price....$1.25
No. 4R6079 Sash Buckle, same as above, set with four emeralds, silver filled, French gray finish. Price.$1.10

No. 4R6082 Sash Buckle, gold filled, Roman finish, set with fourteen turquoise, richly embossed, very artistic and attractive, French design. Price..................$1.05

Four cents extra by mail.

No. 4R6085 Sash Buckle, gold rose gold finish, new departure, so thing artistic, beautifully embos the latest craze. Price..........
No. 4R6088 Sash Buckle, sam above, silver filled, oxidized. Price ....

No. 4R6091 Sash Buckle, silver filled, rococo border, French gray finish, attractive design, set with large fancy center stone. Price............65c

No. 4R6094 Sash Buckle, in black for mourning. Price..................55c

No. 4R6097 Sash Buckle, gold filled, Roman fin set with seventeen rubies, something very attracti one of the latest ideas. Price..........5
No. 4R6100 Sash Buckle, same as above, silv filled, French gray finish. Price..........5

No. 4R6101 Sash Buckle, Parisian importation, richly embossed, rococo border, fine bas relief in center, gold filled, rose colored finish. Price..................68c
No. 4R6104 Sash Buckle, same as above, silver filled, oxidized. Price.........58c

No. 4R6107 Sash Buckle, gold filled, rose gold finish, beautifully embossed, double dragon design, something new. Price........40c
No. 4R6110 Sash Buckle, same as above, silver filled, French gray finish. Price..................40c

No. 4R6113 Sash Buckle, very latest, dragon effect, gold filled, rose colored finish, French idea. Price..................$1.00
No. 4R6116 Sash Buckle, same as above, silver filled, oxidized. Price. 95c

No. 4R6119 Sash Buckle, gold plated, Roman colored, richly embossed. Price.40c
No. 4R6122 Sash Buckle, same as above, silver plated, French gray finish. Price..................40c

No. 4R6125 Sash Bu gold plated, fancy eme Roman finish, set with s amethysts. Price........
No. 4R6128 Sash Bu silver plated, French finished. Price..........

IF BY MAIL, POSTAGE EXTRA, FOUR CENTS.

SOLID GOLD PENS AND PEARL HOLDERS.

MADE UNDER CONTRACT FOR US. THE SPECIFICATIONS ARE CARRIED OUT IN EVERY DETAIL.

JR PENS AND HOLDERS. THE BEST ON THE MARKET. We know what is best in a pen and we know what is not. The manufacturer, lowing the exact details of our contract, produces for us, at a price cheaper by 25 per nt, pens that are worth 50 per cent more than the best pen sold by others. Pens are ade first to write with. This is the great idea in making them. Our pens write. They ill wear. We have them made of solid gold through and through, heavy and well temered. The points of every one of them are tipped with genuine iridium (sometimes called liamond pointed). Iridium, a very hard metal, being applied at the writing point of a en, gives it a wearing period of practically a lifetime. It costs many more times the rice of gold, but a small amount is necessary to tip the points. The pearl sticks, gold lled holders and noses are made and selected from the best stock to be purchased. y one of our pens and holders and you will not alone have a pen that will write, but will write well, d practically forever. **WE WARRANT EACH ONE OF THEM.**

AT 10 OR 25 CENTS EXTRA WE WILL FURNISH A FINE HINGED PEN BOX.

10 cents moroccoine covered, 25 cents for a genuine silk plush covered, lined with plush, with any pen you select.

BEST QUALITY SOLID GOLD PEN IN GOLD FILLED AND EBONY DESK HOLDER.

		No. 1 Pen.	No. 2 Pen.	No. 3 Pen.	No. 4 Pen.	No. 5 Pen.	No. 6 Pen.	No. 7 Pen.
4R6178	10-karat gold Pen with Holder	$0.60	$0.65	$0.70	$0.75	$0.90	$1.00	$1.20
4R6181	16-karat gold Pen with Holder	.70	.75	.90	1.00	1.15	1.25	1.50

BEST QUALITY SOLID GOLD PEN IN GOLD PLATED AND EBONY SLIDE HOLDER.

		No. 1 Pen.	No. 2 Pen.	No 3 Pen.	No. 4 Pen.	No. 5 Pen.	No. 6 Pen.	No. 7 Pen.
4R6184	10-karat gold Pen with Holder	$0.80	$0.85	$0.95	$1.00	$1.15	$1.35	$1.50
4R6187	16-karat gold Pen with Holder	90	.95	1.15	1.25	1.40	1.60	1.80

BEST QUALITY GOLD PEN IN GOLD FILLED AND PLAIN PEARL DESK HOLDER.

		No. 1 Pen.	No. 2 Pen.	No. 3 Pen.	No. 4 Pen.	No. 5 Pen.	No. 6 Pen.
4R6190	10-karat gold Pen with Holder	$0.75	$0.90	$0.95	$1.10	$1.35	$1.55
4R6193	16-karat gold Pen with Holder	.85	1.00	1.15	1.35	1.60	1.80

SOLID GOLD PEN IN BEST QUALITY GOLD FILLED AND PLAIN PEARL SLIDE HOLDER.

		No. 1 Pen.	No. 2 Pen.	No. 3 Pen.	No. 4 Pen.	No. 5 Pen.	No. 6 Pen.
o. 4R6196	10-karat gold Pen with Holder	$1.00	$1.15	$1.20	$1.40	$1.50	$1.70
o. 4R6199	16-karat gold Pen with Holder	1.10	1.25	1.40	1.65	1.75	2.00

SOLID GOLD PEN IN BEST QUALITY GOLD FILLED AND FANCY TWIST CUT PEARL DESK HOLDER.

		No. 1 Pen.	No. 2 Pen.	No. 3 Pen.	No. 4 Pen.	No. 5 Pen.	No. 6 Pen.
4R6202	10-karat gold Pen with Holder	$0.95	$1.10	$1.25	$1.40	$1.60	$1.80
4R6205	16-karat gold Pen with Holder	1.05	1.25	1.45	1.65	1.85	2.05

SOLID GOLD PEN IN BEST QUALITY GOLD FILLED AND FANCY ONE-HALF TWIST CUT PEARL DESK HOLDER.

		No. 1 Pen.	No. 2 Pen.	No. 3 Pen.	No. 4 Pen.	No. 5 Pen.	No. 6 Pen
R6208	10-karat gold Pen with Holder	$0.95	$1.10	$1.25	$1.40	$1.60	$1.80
R6211	16-karat gold Pen with Holder	1.05	1.25	1.45	1.65	1.85	2.05

SOLID GOLD PEN IN BEST QUALITY GOLD FILLED AND FANCY TWIST CUT PEARL DESK HOLDER.

		No. 1 Pen.	No. 2 Pen.	No. 3 Pen.	No. 4 Pen.	No. 5 Pen.	No. 6 Pen.
6214	10-karat gold Pen with Holder	$1.00	$1.15	$1.30	$1.45	$1.65	$1.85
6217	16-karat gold Pen with Holder	1.10	1.30	1.50	1.70	1.90	2.10

SOLID GOLD PEN IN BEST QUALITY GOLD FILLED AND TWIST PEARL SLIDE HOLDER.

		No. 1 Pen.	No. 2 Pen.	No. 3 Pen.	No. 4 Pen.	No. 5 Pen.	No. 6 Pen.
4R6220	10-karat gold Pen with Holder	$1.20	$1.40	$1.50	$1.60	$1.85	$1.95
4R6223	16-karat gold Pen with Holder	1.30	1.50	1.75	1.85	2.10	2.20

SOLID GOLD PEN IN BEST QUALITY GOLD FILLED AND RUSTIC CUT PEARL DESK HOLDER.

		No. 1 Pen.	No. 2 Pen.	No. 3 Pen.	No. 4 Pen.	No. 5 Pen.	No. 6 Pen.
o. 4R6226	10-karat gold Pen with Holder	$0.95	$1.10	$1.25	$1.40	$1.60	$1.80
o. 4R6229	16-karat gold Pen with Holder	1.05	1.25	1.45	1.65	1.85	2.05

No. 4R6230

DESK SET

Consisting of Pearl Paper Cutter and Pearl Handled Penholder and Solid Gold 16K No. 1 Pen.

Cutter and Penholder made to match, ornamented with gold filled wire work.

No. 4R6230 Price, with box complete.....**$2.00**

We guarantee all goods sold by us to give entire satisfaction. You run no risk whatever. Our terms are cash with order.

If by mail, postage extra, 3c; registry or insurance extra. Be sure to state how much is inclosed for postage, and follow instructions in front of book.

PAUL E. WIRT FOUNTAIN PENS.

BEFORE LISTING A LINE OF FOUNTAIN PENS we have thoroughly investigated the mechanism of all makes, and have spared no pains to place at the disposal of our customers, **the finest fountain pens manufactured.** The construction of these pens is of such a simple and practical kind that it is utterly impossible for one of them to become out of order, and cause more trouble to the writer and destroy more copy than the entire thing is worth, instead of being a convenience making it in reality an absolute inconvenience.

THE PAUL E. WIRT FOUNTAIN PEN stands at the head without a peer. It is most simple and practical in construction as to operation and beauty of workmanship. Their popularity rests upon the fact that their ink feed device is the most perfect and simplest ever discovered. Do not buy inferior imitations, but get the original, genuine article. They are elegant, simple, clean and durable; every fountain is fitted with a 14-karat solid gold pen. Each one is warranted by the manufacturers, and we guarantee them to you personally to be the finest and most practical pen made.

No. 4R6253 Chased case, slip nozzle, medium length, fitted with No. 2 fine, medium or stub gold pen. Price..$1.10
No. 4R6256 Chased case, medium length, regular nozzle, fitted with No. 2 fine, medium or stub gold pen. Price..$1.20

No. 4R6259 Taper case, regular size, chased, fitted with No. 3 fine, medium or stub gold pen. Price..$1.95
No. 4R6262 Taper case, chased, regular size, gold mounted, fitted with No. 3 fine, medium or stub gold pen. Price........ $2.75

No. 4R6265 Hexagon, regular plain case, fitted with No. 3 fine, medium gold or stub pen. Price........$2.50
No. 4R6268 Regular hexagon, special size case, fitted with No. 4 fine, medium or stub gold pen. Price..$2.75
No. 4R6271 Regular hexagon, special size thick case, fitted with No. 5 fine, medium or stub gold pen. Price........$3.00

No. 4R6274 Regular size case, gold mounted, fitted with No. 3 fine, medium or stub gold pen. Price........$2.25
No. 4R6274½ Extra size case, gold mounted, fitted with No. 4 size pen. Price........$2.40

No. 4R6275 Ladies' pen, gold mounted, fine chased taper case, fitted with No. 2 fine, medium or stub gold pen. Price........$3.00
No. 4R6276 Ladies' pen, full gold and silver mounted, thin taper case, fitted with fine, medium or stub gold pen. Price........$3.75

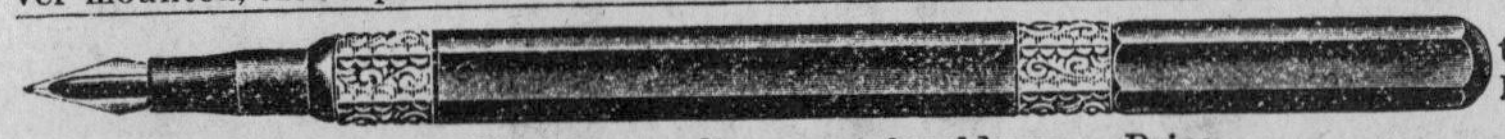

No. 4R6277 Hexagon case, regular size, gold trimmed, fitted with No. 3 fine, medium or stub gold pen. Price........$3.00
No. 4R6280 Hexagon case, gold mounted, special size thick case, fitted with No. 4 fine, medium or stub gold pen. Price........$3.50
No. 4R6283 Hexagon case, gold mounted, extra special size thick case, fitted with No. 5 fine, medium or stub gold pen. Price....... 4.00

No. 4R6308 Gold Filled, Fancy Chased Magic Pencil. Price........95c
When closed the pencil is about one-half the length as seen above.

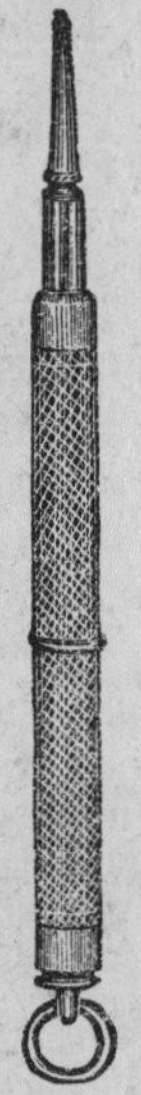

No. 4R6315 Rolled Gold Plated Screw Pencil. Price, 25 cents. When not in use the point is drawn inside the case by simply turning the top. Toothpick of the same style can be furnished at same price.

SOLID GOLD, GOLD FILLED AND STERLING SILVER PENS, PENCILS, HOLDERS AND PICKS.

No. 4R6286 Solid Sterling Silver Holder, beautifully chased and tapered, very pretty and stylish. Price........ $1.15

Gold Filled and Ebony Telescopic Holder, with best quality iridium pointed Pens.
No. 4R6290 10-karat Pen with Holder, No. 3 Pen, $0.95; No. 4 Pen, $1.00; No. 5 Pen, $1.20; No. 6 Pen, $1.40; No. 7 Pen, $1.55.
No. 4R6291 16-karat Pen with Holder, No. 3 Pen, 1.15; No. 4 Pen, 1.25; No. 5 Pen, 1.45; No. 6 Pen, 1.65; No. 7 Pen, 1.85.

No. 4R6292 Gold Filled, Improved Telescopic Pen Holder and Combined Screw Pencil. When it is desired to use the pencil the pen can be slid back into the holder by means of a band on the outside, and the pencil can be brought into position.
16-karat Pen with Holder, No. 3 Pen, $1.70; No. 4 Pen, $1.95; No. 5 Pen, $2.10; No. 6 Pen, $2.45.

No. 4R6298 Fine Gold Filled, Fancy Chased, Cut Stone Head Toothpick. Price........85c

No. 4R6295 Fine Gold Filled, Fancy Chased Toothpick and Ear Spoon. Price........$1.25
Nos. 4R6295 and 4R6298 are made of fine gold filled throughout, and are exceptional value for the money. The Pick and Ear Spoon can be drawn inside of the case when not in use.

No. 4R6298

DESK SET.

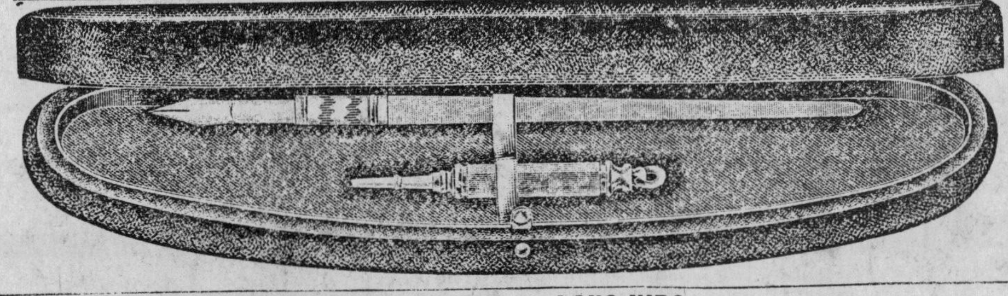

No. 4R6300 Desk Set, consisting of pearl pen, pencil and plush covered and lined box. Pen is solid gold, 16-karat, No. 1 size; pencil is pearl with gold filled trimmings.

Price, for complete set,

$2.50

If by mail, postage 4 cents. Registry extra.

GOLD PENS REPOINTED for 30 cents each. 2 cents extra for mail charges.

LONG NIBS. **STUBS.**

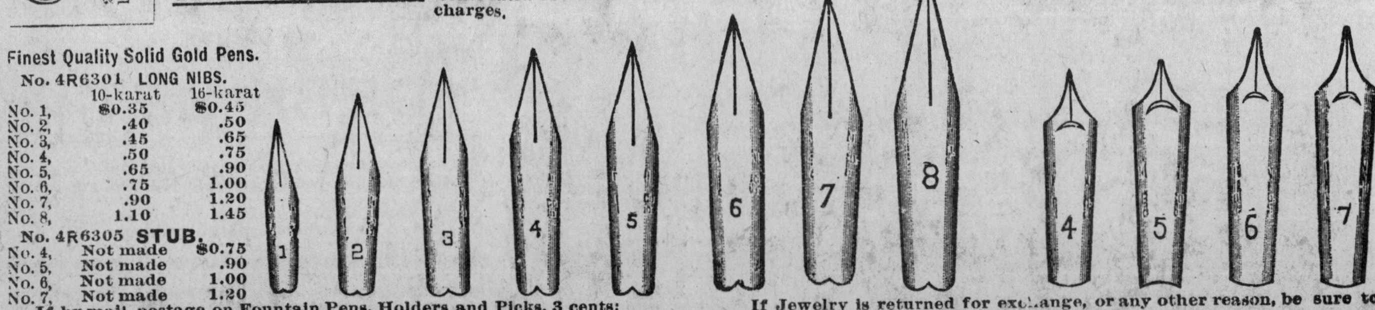

Finest Quality Solid Gold Pens.

No. 4R6301 LONG NIBS.

	10-karat	16-karat
No. 1,	$0.35	$0.45
No. 2,	.40	.50
No. 3,	.45	.65
No. 4,	.50	.75
No. 5,	.65	.90
No. 6,	.75	1.00
No. 7,	.90	1.20
No. 8,	1.10	1.45

No. 4R6305 STUB.

No. 4,	Not made	$0.75
No. 5,	Not made	.90
No. 6,	Not made	1.00
No. 7,	Not made	1.20

If by mail, postage on Fountain Pens, Holders and Picks, 3 cents; registry or insurance extra.

If Jewelry is returned for exchange, or any other reason, be sure to follow instructions in front part of this book.

ALASKA SILVERWARE—A NEW DISCOVERY.

THE CHEAPEST AND BEST FLAT WARE MADE The Alaska silverware is not plated, but is the same solid metal through and through, and will hold the same color as long as there is any portion of the goods left. Do not be deceived by any dealer who undertakes to sell you any of the numerous imitations of this ware, that are sold on the market for more money than we ask for the genuine. **The genuine Alaska Silverware can be had only of us.**

Before taking hold of this new discovery we left nothing undone to thoroughly investigate the properties of this metal, and to test the same in every conceivable manner, to satisfy ourselves that it was all that it was represented to be. After having made all sorts of experiments, and it stood all tests, we made a contract with the factory to handle the goods. It has now been about two years since we began to handle this line, and it has not only proved from experiment to be as represented, but with two years of actual service in the hands of many thousands of our customers, who send us the most flattering recommendations in praise of these goods, and with the rapidly increasing sales, we feel that we cannot recommend it too highly.

The metal is very dense and tough, is almost as white as genuine silver, takes a beautiful polish and requires no care, as does silver plated ware. You can scrape kettles or pots, or subject it to any kind of service without fear of damage.

We have this year added a beautiful engraved pattern, which is equal in appearance and artistic finish to any of the best silver plated or solid silver goods on the market. The engravings are as fine as can be made, the handles of an oval shape, and will be furnished at only a slight advance over the prices of the plain pattern. The immense quantities of these goods we handle, and the condition of our contract direct with the factory, puts us in a position to furnish this genuine Alaska Silverware at a slight advance over cost to manufacture.

Hereafter all these Goods, except the Knives, will be Stamped "Sears, Roebuck & Co.'s Alaska Silverware."

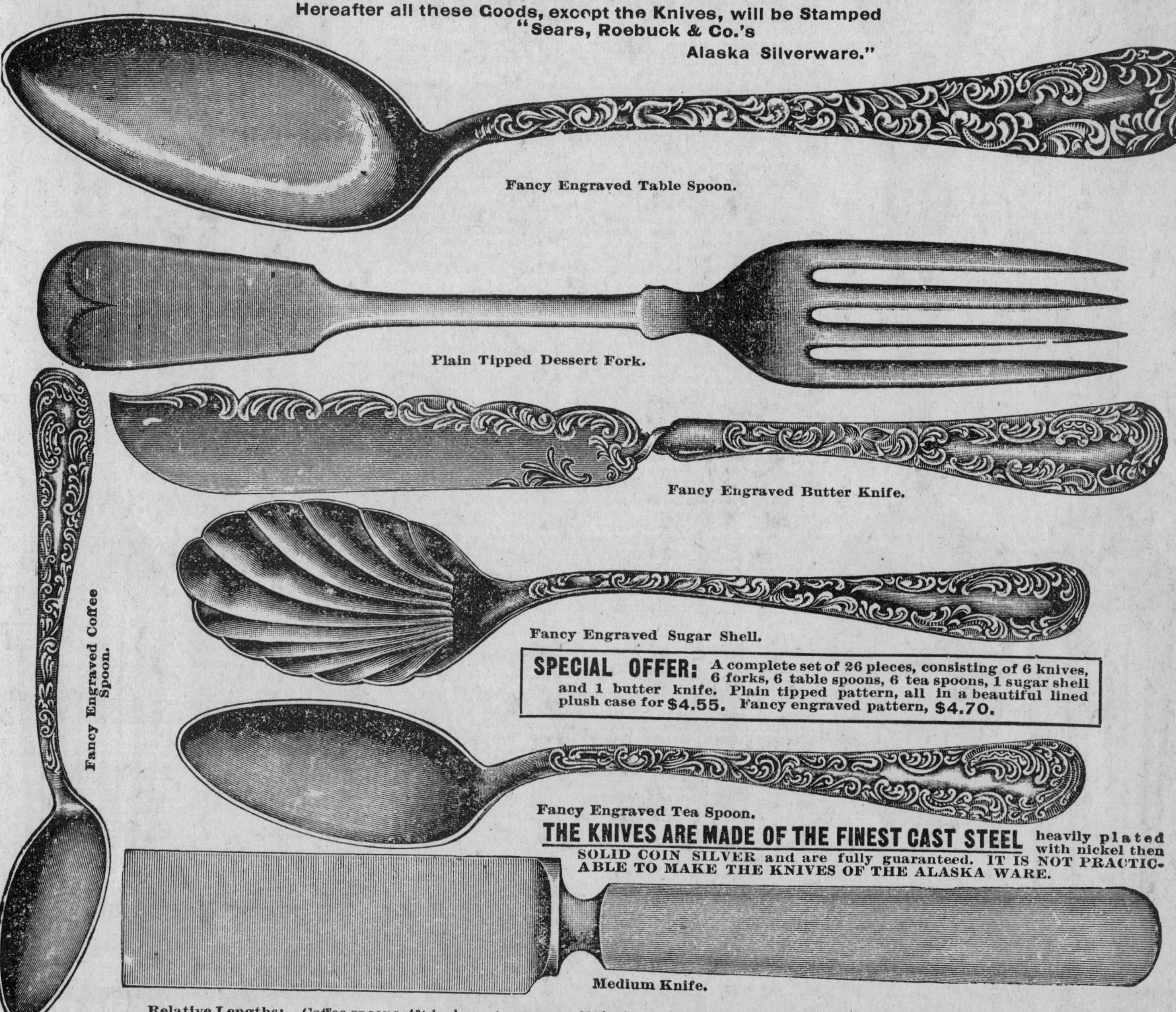

Fancy Engraved Table Spoon.

Plain Tipped Dessert Fork.

Fancy Engraved Butter Knife.

Fancy Engraved Coffee Spoon.

Fancy Engraved Sugar Shell.

SPECIAL OFFER: A complete set of 26 pieces, consisting of 6 knives, 6 forks, 6 table spoons, 6 tea spoons, 1 sugar shell and 1 butter knife. Plain tipped pattern, all in a beautiful lined plush case for **$4.55.** Fancy engraved pattern, **$4.70.**

Fancy Engraved Tea Spoon.

THE KNIVES ARE MADE OF THE FINEST CAST STEEL heavily plated with nickel then SOLID COIN SILVER and are fully guaranteed. IT IS NOT PRACTICABLE TO MAKE THE KNIVES OF THE ALASKA WARE.

Medium Knife.

Relative Lengths: Coffee spoons, 4⅜ inches; tea spoons, 6¾ inches; dessert spoons, 7½ inches; table spoons, 8¼ inches; dessert forks, 7 inches; medium forks, 7½ inches; dessert knives, 8 inches; medium knives, 9 inches; sugar shells, 5¾ inches; butter knives, 7 inches.

OUR SPECIAL PRICES.

Any of these goods can be sent by mail on receipt of price and additional amount named to pay postage.

Plain tipped pattern like fork above.

No. 5R6500	Coffee Spoons	set of ½ dozen,	$0.51
No. 5R6502	Tea Spoons	set of ½ dozen,	.51
No. 5R6504	Dessert Spoons	set of ½ dozen,	.85
No. 5R6506	Table Spoons	set of ½ dozen,	1.02
No. 5R6508	Medium Forks (regular size)	set of ½ dozen,	1.02
No. 5R6510	Dessert Forks	set of ½ dozen,	.85
No. 5R6512	Plain Handle Dessert Knives	set of ½ dozen,	1.10
No. 5R6514	Plain Handle Medium Knives	set of ½ dozen,	1.25
No. 5R6516	Sugar Shells	each,	.15
No. 5R6518	Butter Knives	each,	.15

Fancy engraved pattern like all but the fork above.

No. 5R6520	Coffee Spoons	set of ½ dozen,	$0.56
No. 5R6522	Tea Spoons	set of ½ dozen,	.56
No. 5R6524	Dessert Spoons	set of ½ dozen,	.90
No. 5R6526	Table Spoons	set of ½ dozen,	1.07
No. 5R6528	Medium Forks (regular size)	set of ½ dozen,	1.07
No. 5R6530	Dessert Forks	set of ½ dozen,	.99
No. 5R6532	Sugar Shells	each,	.16
No. 5R6534	Butter Knives	each,	.16

Postage on the above goods, if to go by mail, will be extra per half dozen as follows: On coffee spoons, 5 cents; tea spoons, 6 cents; dessert spoons or forks, 12 cents; table spoons or medium forks, 15 cents; dessert or medium knives, 18 cents; and sugar shells or butter knives, 2 cents each. It is cheaper to send them by express, if you have an express office near by.

The standard of quality and finish of the above goods **are guaranteed** by the manufacturer to us, and we guarantee them to our customers. You run no risk whatever in purchasing this ware, for if you do not find them to be exactly as represented, they can be returned to us and your money will be refunded. Be sure to state catalogue number and pattern wanted when you order.

REMEMBER WE SEND WITH THIS SET A BEAUTIFUL PLUSH COVERED SILK LINED CASE TO HOLD IT.

OUR OWN SPECIAL HIGH GRADE TRIPLE SILVER PLATED TABLEWARE.

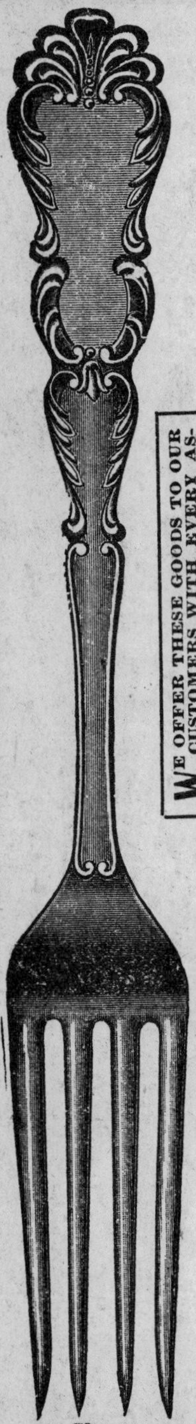

IN ORDER THAT WE MAY GIVE OUR CUSTOMERS such value in strictly high grade silverware as they could not possibly get elsewhere, we have had made by one of the largest and most reliable silverware manufacturers in America, an immense quantity of strictly high grade triple plated silver knives, forks and spoons.

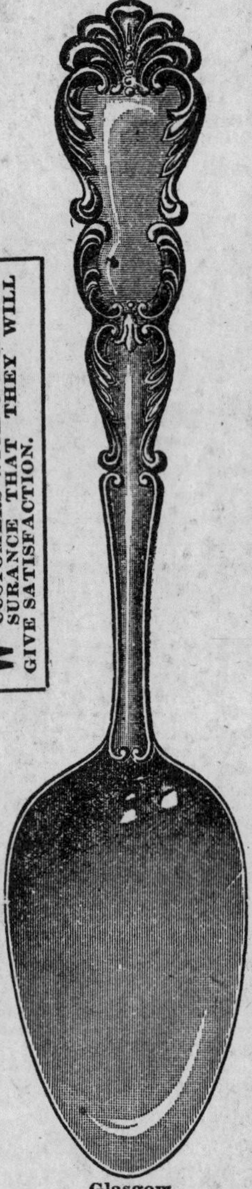

THE SILVERWARE is made after our specifications and each piece contains a larger amount of silver than is used on any other standard plated ware on the market.

THE DISPOSITION OF MANUFACTURERS has been to cheapen this class of goods and yet hold it at a higher price, and in order that our customers might have the very best, we have gotten these goods out under our own specifications; we know just the amount of silver that goes on every piece, we know we are perfectly safe in issuing a binding guarantee and we are able to make the price based on the actual cost of material and labor, with but our one small percentage of profit added, which will mean a great saving to our customers.

IF YOU BUY OUR SPECIAL BRAND WARE you will get the best plated ware that money can buy. The silver that goes into the plating of these goods is $\frac{925}{1000}$ fine and is the highest grade used in silverware.

DIFFERENT FROM ALMOST ALL OTHER SILVERWARE, our silverware is made by a manufacturer of long experience in the manufacture of gold filled watch cases and is made on the same principle as gold filled watch cases are made, and while we term it silver triple plated it is really silver filled. It is made from two heavy plates of coin silver over a base of hard metal, is a goods there is practically no wear out to.

OUR FIRST CONTRACT WITH THE MANUFACTURER for this class of goods was made nearly a year ago, and the enormous sale we have had the past season has warranted us in making preparation for a much larger supply the coming season, and in doing this we have been able to reduce the cost of production and we give you the benefit of this great reduction in the prices we quote you in this catalogue, which are much lower than we were able to quote last season.

WE ADVISE YOU BY ALL MEANS in ordering tableware to select our own special grade. You get infinitely more value for your money than you can in any other grade made. In advertising the other known grades of silverware we are compelled to pay the manufacturer a large profit and of course we in turn must get from you the cost to us with our one small profit added, which compels us to ask 50 per cent more for other grades inferior to our own.

WE OFFER THESE GOODS TO OUR CUSTOMERS WITH EVERY ASSURANCE THAT THEY WILL GIVE SATISFACTION.

THESE ARE HIGH GRADE, RELIABLE GOODS, and our prices are much below what is usually asked for equal grades.

...THE SECURITY WE OFFER YOU...

If you find after examination these goods are not as described and warranted, you are at liberty to return them and we will cheerfully refund your money.

This is the great value page of our silverware department. We expect more advertising from this page than any other page in our jewelry department. We are giving such values in these goods as has never before been attempted; we know every customer who receives any of our special brand silverware will be so well pleased with it that he will recommend our house to his friends and we will receive more orders from his neighborhood.

		Tipped Per doz.	Glasgow Per doz.
5R6625	Tea Spoons.....Extra Plate	$1.75	$1.85
5R6626	Tea Spoons.....Triple Plate	2.40	2.55
5R6627	Dessert Spoons.Extra Plate	3.10	3.45
5R6628	Dessert Spoons.Triple Plate	4.00	4.60
5R6629	Table Spoons...Extra Plate	3.45	4.00
5R6630	Table Spoons...Triple Plate	4.80	5.15
5R6633	Medium Forks..Extra Plate	3.45	3.75
5R6634	Medium Forks..Triple Plate	4.80	5.15
5R6636	Dessert Forks..Extra Plate	3.10	3.45
5R6637	Dessert Forks..Triple Plate	4.00	4.60
5R6639	Sugar Shell, Extra Plate, each	.30	.35
5R6642	Butter Knives, Triple Plate	.35	.40

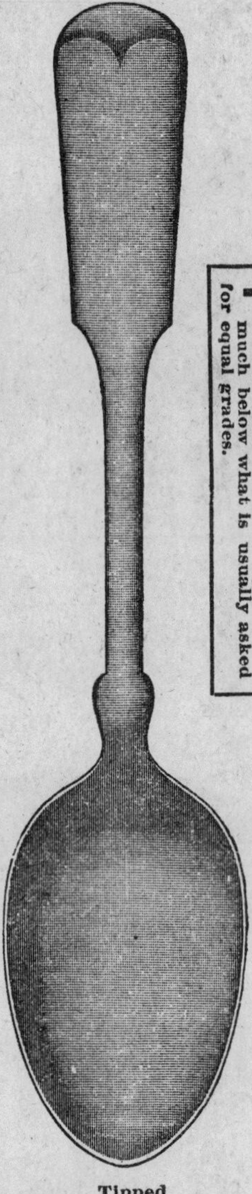

Glasgow

Glasgow

Tipped

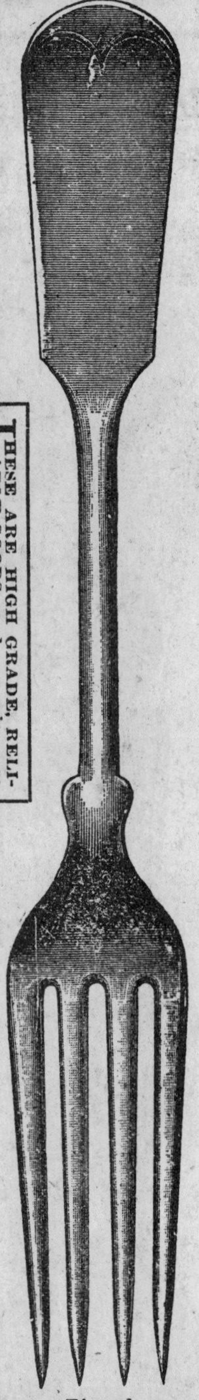

Tipped

OUR BINDING GUARANTEE. We guarantee every piece of our special brand silverware to be the highest grade silverware on the market regardless of price, we guarantee it to outwear any other silver plated wear on the market, and we hold ourselves in readiness to make good with new any silverware that proves defective by reason of material or workmanship.

OUR SPECIAL REDUCED PRICES. At $1.75 per dozen we furnish tea spoons superior to anything you can buy from your dealer at home at double the price; at $3.10 we quote dessert spoons superior to anything you can buy from your dealer at home at $5.00; for $3.45 we furnish table spoons superior to anything you can buy from your dealer at home at $6.00; at $2.60 we furnish knives the equal of knives that retail everywhere at $5.00 to $6.00.

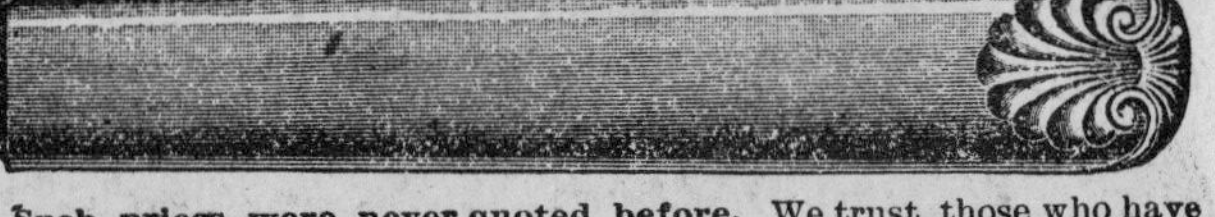

Such prices were never quoted before. We trust those who have not already supplied themselves with this high grade ware will take advantage of this most extraordinary offer.

No. 5R6645 Shell Medium Knives, per dozen $2.85

No. 5R6647 Shell Medium Forks, per dozen........................$2.85

No. 5R6649 Plain Medium Knives, per dozen $2.60

No. 5R6652 Plain Medium Forks, per dozen..........................$2.60

...C. ROGERS & BROS.' FINE SILVER PLATED WARE...

A GREAT REDUCTION IN C. ROGERS & BROS.' PLATED SILVERWARE PRICES.

THERE CAN BE NO QUESTION as to the quality of these goods. Ask your jeweler or any other authority and he will tell you there is NONE BETTER. We positively are offering you THE BEST AT PRICES ABOUT ONE-HALF of what others are asking. We guarantee this ware in every particular. All special pieces such as jelly servers, pie servers, pie knives, sugar shells, butter knives, berry spoons and cold meat forks HAVE ALL SEPARATE SILK LINED BOXES. Postage extra as quoted below.

..A.. HANDSOME NEW DESIGN

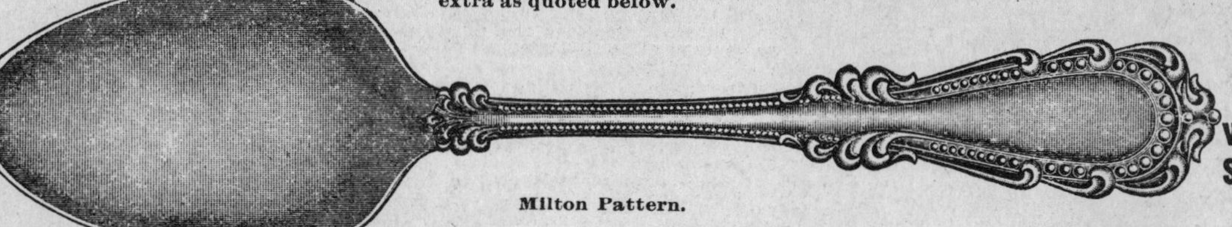

Milton Pattern.

..THE.. WELL KNOWN SILVERWARE

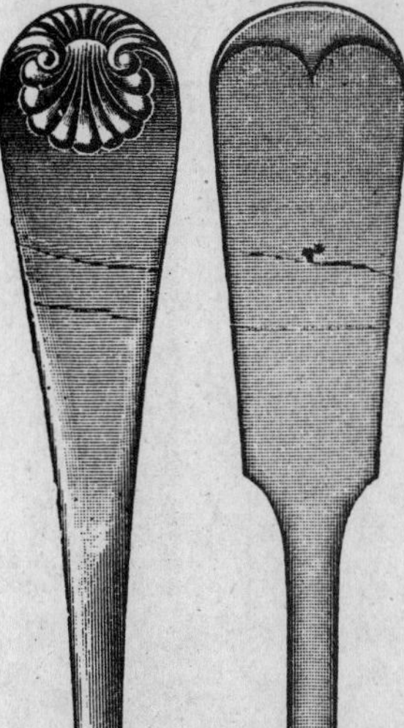

Shell. Tipped.

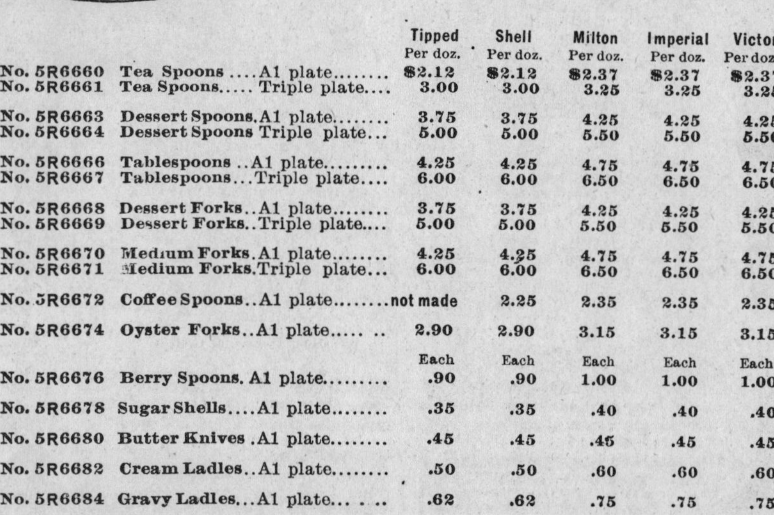

	Tipped Per doz.	Shell Per doz.	Milton Per doz.	Imperial Per doz.	Victor Per doz.
No. 5R6660 Tea Spoons ....A1 plate........	$2.12	$2.12	$2.37	$2.37	$2.37
No. 5R6661 Tea Spoons..... Triple plate....	3.00	3.00	3.25	3.25	3.25
No. 5R6663 Dessert Spoons.A1 plate........	3.75	3.75	4.25	4.25	4.25
No. 5R6664 Dessert Spoons Triple plate...	5.00	5.00	5.50	5.50	5.50
No. 5R6666 Tablespoons ..A1 plate.........	4.25	4.25	4.75	4.75	4.75
No. 5R6667 Tablespoons...Triple plate....	6.00	6.00	6.50	6.50	6.50
No. 5R6668 Dessert Forks..A1 plate........	3.75	3.75	4.25	4.25	4.25
No. 5R6669 Dessert Forks..Triple plate....	5.00	5.00	5.50	5.50	5.50
No. 5R6670 Medium Forks.A1 plate........	4.25	4.25	4.75	4.75	4.75
No. 5R6671 Medium Forks.Triple plate....	6.00	6.00	6.50	6.50	6.50
No. 5R6672 Coffee Spoons..A1 plate........	not made	2.25	2.35	2.35	2.35
No. 5R6674 Oyster Forks..A1 plate..... ..	2.90	2.90	3.15	3.15	3.15
	Each	Each	Each	Each	Each
No. 5R6676 Berry Spoons. A1 plate.........	.90	.90	1.00	1.00	1.00
No. 5R6678 Sugar Shells....A1 plate........	.35	.35	.40	.40	.40
No. 5R6680 Butter Knives .A1 plate........	.45	.45	.45	.45	.45
No. 5R6682 Cream Ladles..A1 plate........	.50	.50	.60	.60	.60
No. 5R6684 Gravy Ladles...A1 plate... . ..	.62	.62	.75	.75	.75

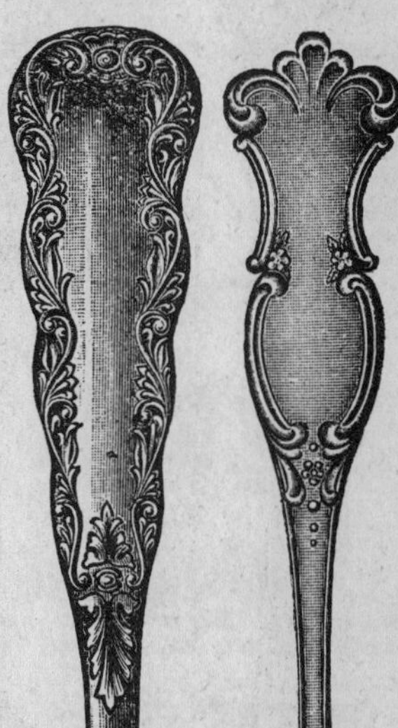

Imperial. Victor.

THESE GOODS PUT UP EACH IN SATIN LINED CASE.

ILLUSTRATIONS SHOWN HEREON ARE REDUCED SIZE.

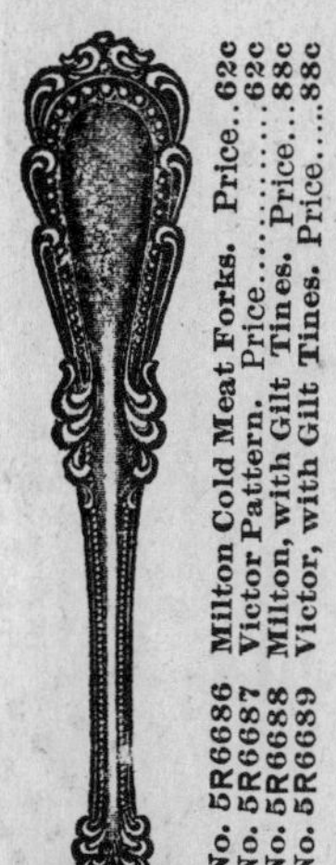

No. 5R6686 Milton Cold Meat Forks. Price..62c
No. 5R6687 Victor Pattern. Price.....62c
No. 5R6688 Milton, with Gilt Tines. Price....88c
No. 5R6689 Victor, with Gilt Tines. Price....88c

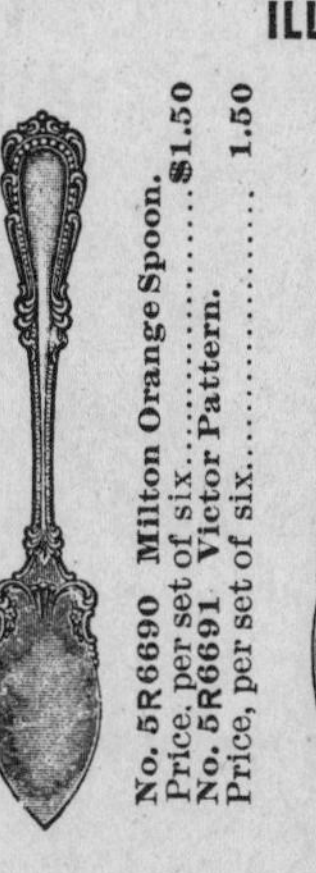

No. 5R6690 Milton Orange Spoon. Price, per set of six..........$1.50
No. 5R6691 Victor Pattern. Price, per set of six..........1.50

No. 5R6692 Milton Jelly Server. Price, each..........75c
No. 5R6693 Victor Pattern. Price, each..........75c

No. 5R6694 Milton Pie Server. Price, each..........$1.50
No. 5R6695 Victor Pattern. Price, each..........1.50

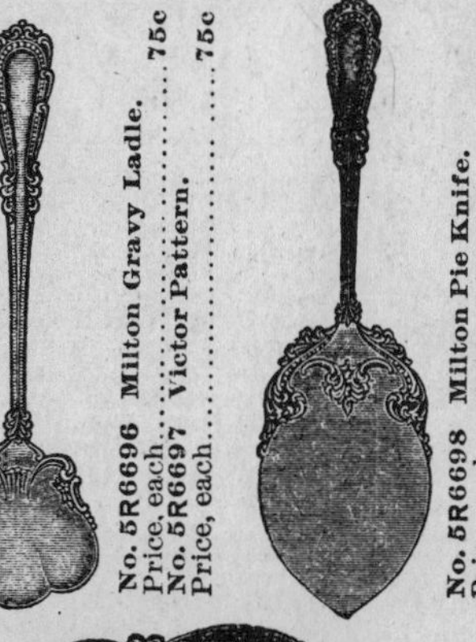

No. 5R6696 Milton Gravy Ladle. Price, each..........75c
No. 5R6697 Victor Pattern. Price, each..........75c

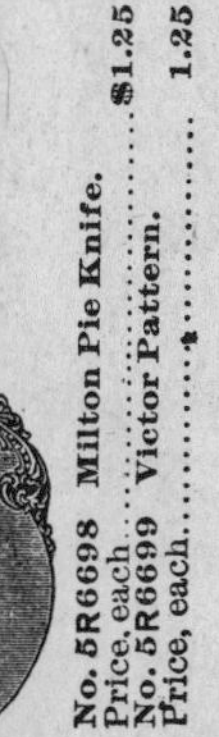

No. 5R6698 Milton Pie Knife. Price, each..........$1.25
No. 5R6699 Victor Pattern. Price, each..........1.25

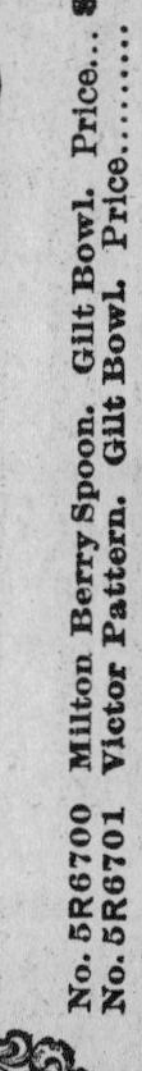

No. 5R6700 Milton Berry Spoon. Gilt Bowl. Price...$1.40
No. 5R6701 Victor Pattern. Gilt Bowl. Price.......1.40

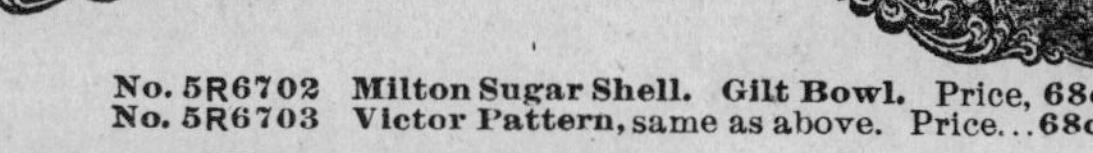

No. 5R6702 Milton Sugar Shell. Gilt Bowl. Price, 68c
No. 5R6703 Victor Pattern, same as above. Price...68c

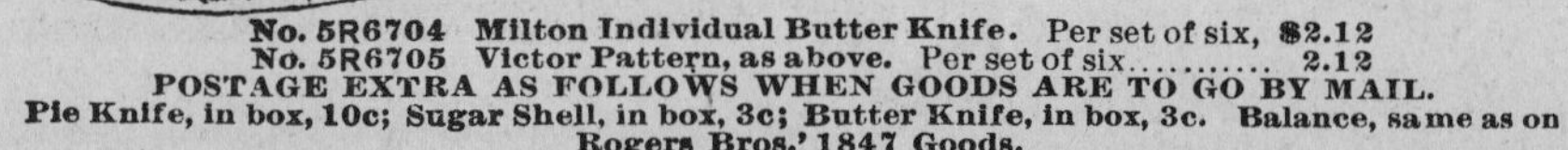

No. 5R6704 Milton Individual Butter Knife. Per set of six, $2.12
No. 5R6705 Victor Pattern, as above. Per set of six........... 2.12

POSTAGE EXTRA AS FOLLOWS WHEN GOODS ARE TO GO BY MAIL.
Pie Knife, in box, 10c; Sugar Shell, in box, 3c; Butter Knife, in box, 3c. Balance, same as on Rogers Bros.' 1847 Goods.

C. ROGERS & BROS.' FINE SILVER PLATED WARE IN SILK LINED BOXES.

BUY ROGERS' MAKE SILVERWARE and you have the best manufactured. C. Rogers & Bros. are one of the oldest established makers. The quality of their product is beyond question. The base of all their goods, with the exception of their steel plated line, is of a fine 21 per cent nickel, a material that has

THE SAME COLOR AS SOLID SILVER.

This base is heavily plated with pure silver, thus making their line positively one of the most enduring and HIGHEST GRADE MANUFACTURED.

No. 5R6717 Windsor Carving Set, etched handles. Price, per set........ $3.00
No. 5R6720 Plain Carving Set, same as above. Price, per set........ $2.75

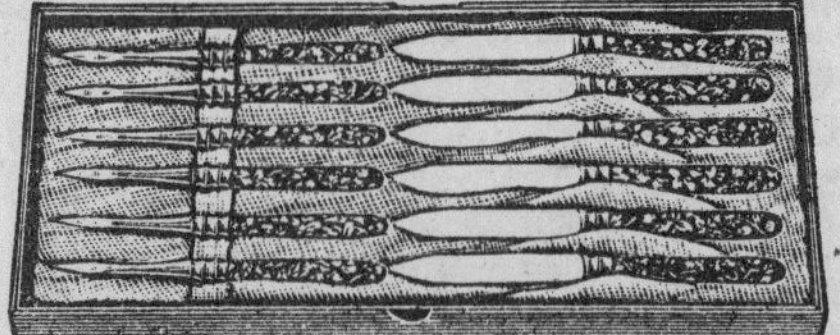

No. 5R6722 Windsor Fruit Set, six fruit knives and six nut picks, etched handles. Price....... $2.50

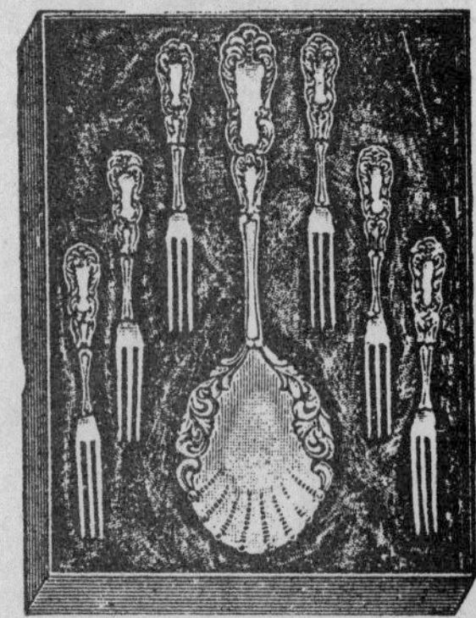

No. 5R6730 Regent Berry Set, six forks and one spoon. Price.. $2.75

No. 5R6724 Regent Child Set. Price, per set........ 98c

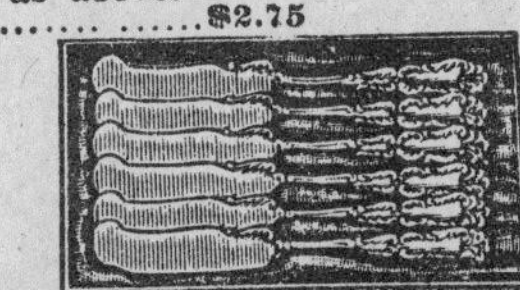

No. 5R6726 Regent Individual Butter Spreaders, set of six. Price.... $2.12

No. 5R6728 Regent Orange Set, pearl handled knife. Price........ $1.50

POSTAGE EXTRA, AS FOLLOWS, when goods are sent by mail: Coffee Spoons and Tongs in box, 6 cents; Berry Sets, 7 cents; Salad Sets, 6 cents; Fruit Sets, 25 cents; Butter Spreaders, per set 6 cents; Orange Sets, 6 cents; Child's Sets, 7 cents; Jelly Servers, Berry Spoons, Cake Servers, Gravy Ladles, 5 to 6 cents.

No. 5R6732 Regent Coffee Spoons, set of six. Price........ $1.50

No. 5R6734 Regent Coffee Set, six spoons and one pair sugar tongs, set complete. Price........ $2.12

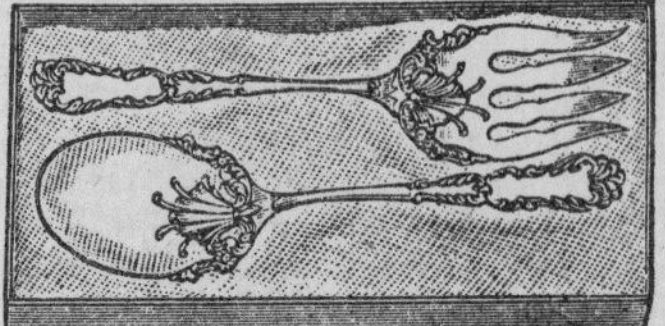

No. 5R6736 Regent Salad Set, fork and spoon. Price...... $2.25

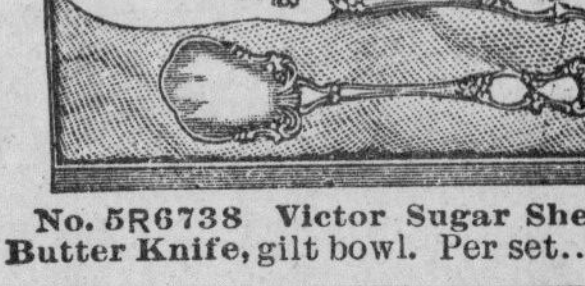

No. 5R6738 Victor Sugar Shell and Butter Knife, gilt bowl. Per set.. $1.00

No. 5R6746 Regent Cake Server, gilt bowl. Each........ $1.54
No. 5R6747 Regent Cake Server, plain. Each........ $1.16

No. 5R6740 Victor Gravy Ladle, gilt bowl. Each........ 85c

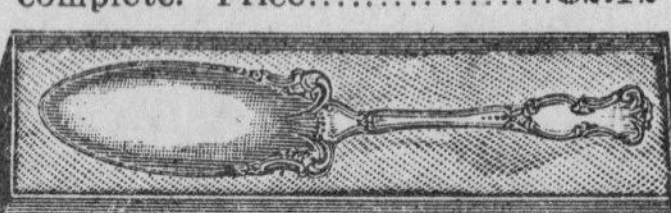

No. 5R6742 Victor Jelly Server, gilt bowl. Each........ $1.00

No. 5R6744 Regent Berry Spoon, gilt bowl. Each........ $1.35

No. 5R6748 Newton Pattern Child's Set, pearl handled knife, three pieces in set. Price, per set........ $1.65

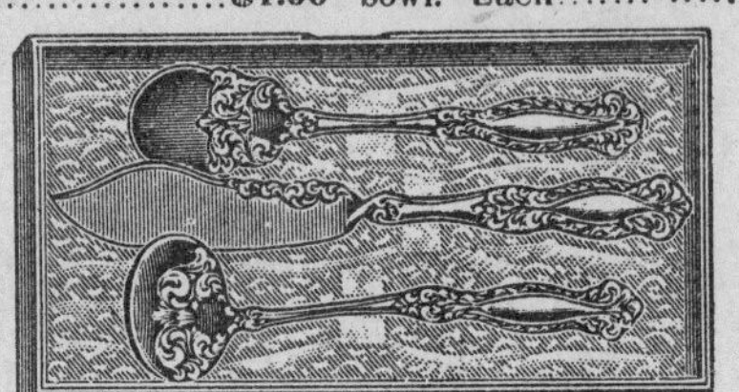
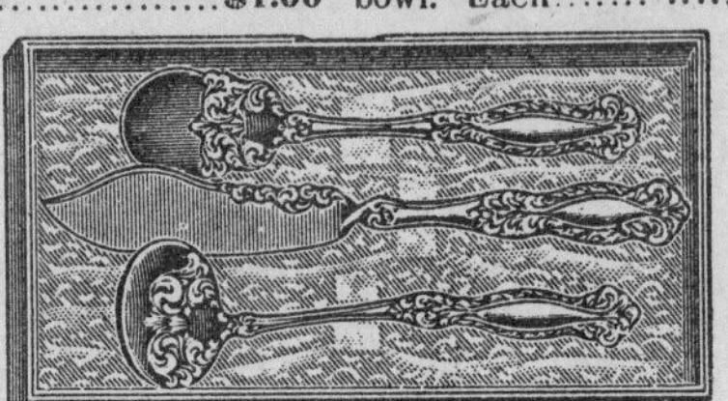
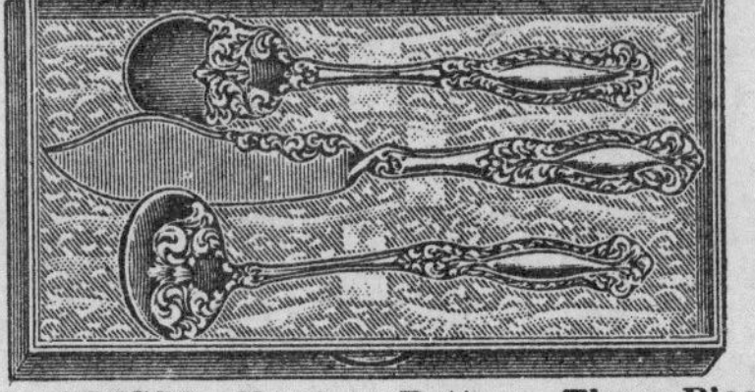

No. 5R6752 Newton Pattern Three-Piece Set, consisting of sugar shell, cream ladle and butter knife, gold bowls and blade. Price, per set........ $2.20

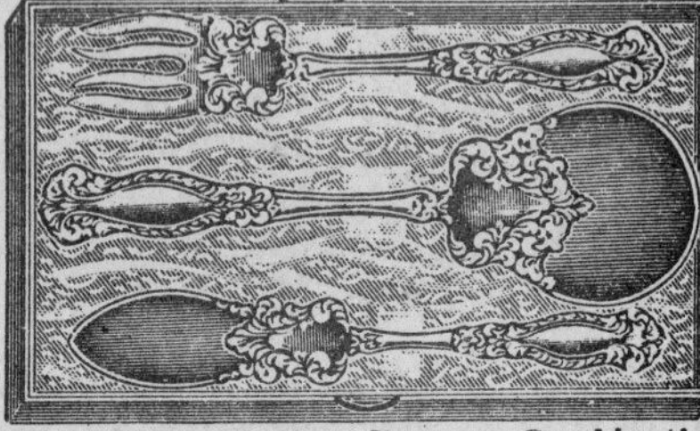

No. 5R6754 Newton Pattern Combination Three-Piece Set, berry spoon, jelly server and cold meat server, gold bowls and blades. Price, per set........ $3.25

No. 5R6750 Newton Pattern Cold Meat Server, gold tines. Price, each........ 88c

C. ROGERS & BROS.' KNIVES AND FORKS.

Per doz.

No. 5R6756 Med. Knives, plain...... $3.25
No. 5R6758 Med. Forks, plain...... $3.25
No. 5R6760 Dessert Knives, plain...... $3.15
No. 5R6762 Dessert Forks, plain...... $3.15

No. 5R6764 Med. Knives, shell...... $3.35
No. 5R6766 Med. Forks, shell...... $3.35
No. 5R6768 Dessert Knives, shell...... $3.25
No. 5R6770 Dessert Forks, shell...... $3.25

No. 5R6772 Med. Knives, fancy...... $3.35
No. 5R6774 Med. Forks, fancy...... $3.35
No. 5R6776 Dessert Knives, fancy .. $3.25
No. 5R6778 Dessert Forks, fancy...... $3.25

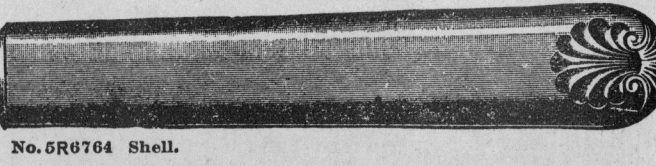

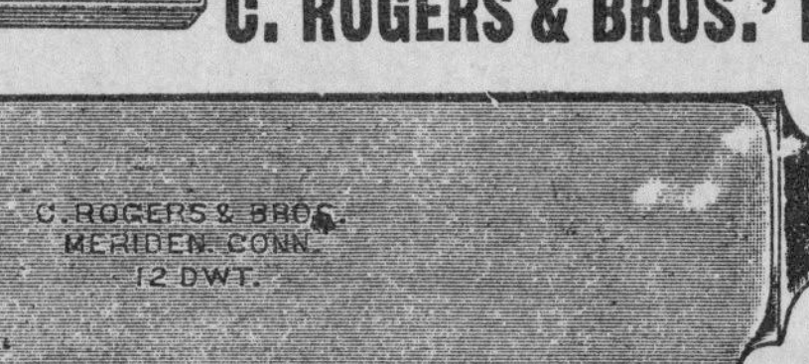

No. 5R6756 Plain.

No. 5R6764 Shell.

C. ROGERS & BROS.
MERIDEN. CONN.
12 DWT.

No. 5R6772 Fancy.

THE NAME IS A GUARANTEE FOR THE QUALITY.

WE CANNOT RECOMMEND THESE GOODS TOO HIGHLY.

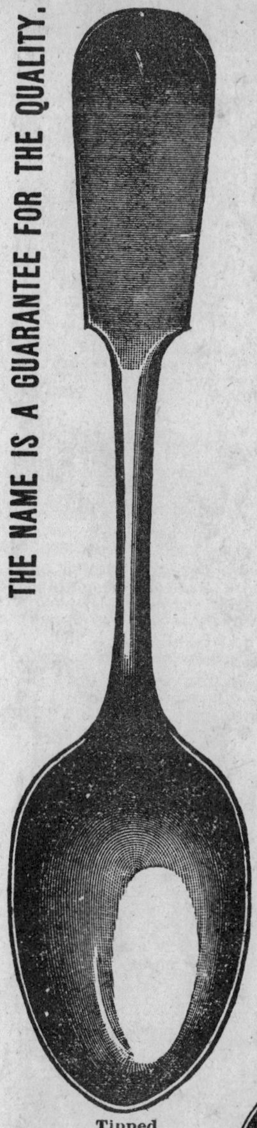

WE HANDLE A COMPLETE LINE OF

ROGERS BROTHERS' 1847 GOODS

But our space will not permit us to list more than a portion of the same. We, however, have represented one of each style of nearly all the styles in which these goods are made, which includes the very

LATEST AND BEST PATTERNS

We list the goods in two grades, namely, what is known as the A1 plate and the triple plate; the latter of which is the better of the two. Bear in mind that the goods which we quote and describe are exactly as represented. We do not substitute other make of goods, as many unscrupulous firms do.

If by mail, postage extra,
½-dozen Tea Spoons.......8c
½-dozen Dessert Spoons.......10c
½-dozen Dessert Forks.......10c

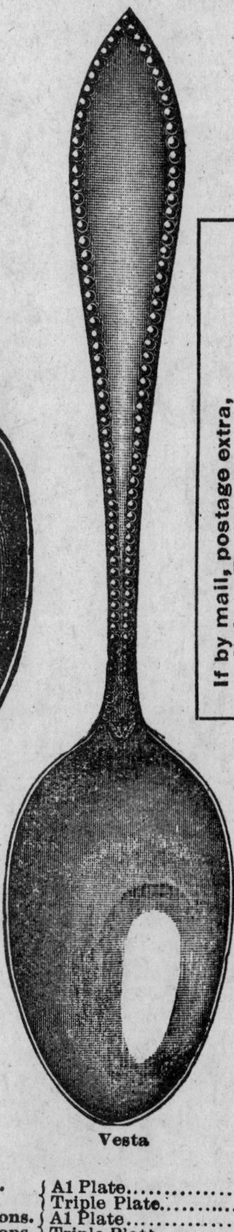

If by mail, postage extra,
½-dozen Table Spoons.......15c
½-dozen Medium Forks.......12c
½-dozen Coffee Spoons.......5c

If by mail, postage extra,
Sugar Shells, each.......3c
Butter Knives, each.......3c

Tipped

Shell

Vesta

Columbia

Berkshire

Lotus

THESE GOODS HAVE A REPUTATION THE COUNTRY OVER FOR QUALITY AND DURABILITY.

YOU WILL FIND THE GENUINE AND CELEBRATED ROGERS BROS.' 1847 SILVERWARE IN THE FINEST HOMES EVERYWHERE.

PRICES PER DOZEN.

No.	Article	Grade	Tipped	Shell	Vesta	Columbia	Berkshire	Lotus
No. 5R6792	Tea Spoons.	A1 Plate	$2.29	$2.29	$2.56	$2.56	$2.56	$2.56
No. 5R6793	Tea Spoons.	Triple Plate	3.24	3.24	3.51	3.51	3.51	3.51
No. 5R6794	Dessert Spoons.	A1 Plate	4.05	4.05	4.59	4.59	4.59	4.59
No. 5R6795	Dessert Spoons.	Triple Plate	5.40	5.40	5.94	5.94	5.94	5.94
No. 5R6796	Dessert Forks.	A1 Plate	4.05	4.05	4.59	4.59	4.59	4.59
No. 5R6797	Dessert Forks.	Triple Plate	5.40	5.40	5.94	5.94	5.94	5.94
No. 5R6798	Table Spoons.	A1 Plate	4.59	4.59	5.13	5.13	5.13	5.13
No. 5R6799	Table Spoons.	Triple Plate	6.48	6.48	7.02	7.02	7.02	7.02
No. 5R6800	Medium Forks.	A1 Plate	4.59	4.59	5.13	5.13	5.13	5.13
No. 5R6801	Medium Forks.	Triple Plate	6.48	6.48	7.02	7.02	7.02	7.02
No. 5R6802	Coffee Spoons.	A1 Plate	not made	2.43	2.54	2.54	2.54	2.54
No. 5R6804	Sugar Shells.	A1 Plate only. Price, each	.36	.36	.40	.40	.40	.40
No. 5R6806	Butter Knife.	A1 Plate only. Price, each	.45	.45	.48	.48	.48	.48

No. 5R6808 Portland Jelly Knife, in lined box.
Price, each, 82c
If by mail, postage extra, 3 cents.

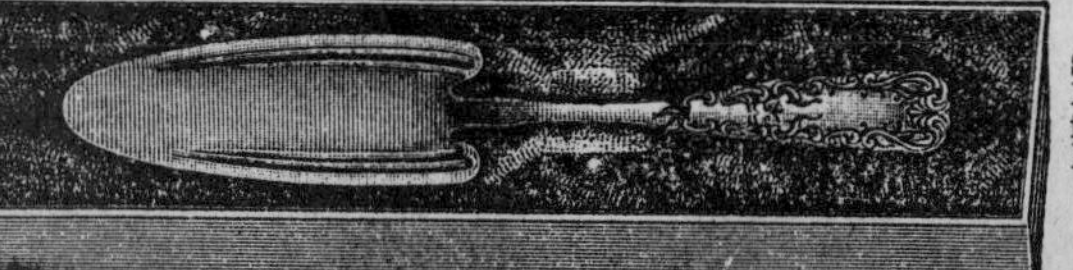

No. 5R6810 Savoy Long Pickle Fork, in lined box.
Price, each, 60c
If by mail, postage extra, 3 cents.

BEST QUADRUPLE PLATED SILVERWARE—CUPS AND NAPKIN RINGS.

THE BEST MONEY CAN BUY. EACH PIECE IS WARRANTED TO BE EXACTLY AS REPRESENTED.

THIS WARE IS QUADRUPLE PLATED with pure silver on genuine Britannia metal. Britannia metal is a white composition metal, same color as silver, hard and durable. It will not corrode and is without question the best metal used in hollow silver plated ware.

SEE THE PRICES WE ARE QUOTING. Examine our designs. If not found the very latest patterns, if our ware is not the very best and the quotations the cheapest of any, don't buy.

No. 5R7119 Child's Cup, bright finished, gold lined, beaded and embossed; height, 2¾ inches. Price........$1.75

No. 5R7122 Child's Cup, satin finished, gold lined, hand engraved; height, 3 inches. Price..................$1.50

No. 5R7125 Child's Cup, plain, bright finished, gold lined; height, 3 inches. Price..................$1.40

No. 5R7128 Child's Cup, satin finished, hand engraved, gold lined; height, 3 inches. Price..................$1.40

No. 5R7132 Child's Cup, satin finished, hand engraved, gold lined; height, 3 inches. Price..................$1.35

No. 5R7135 Child's Cup, plain, bright finished, beaded borders, gold lined; height, 2 inches. Price..........$1.30

No. 5R7138 Child's Cup, satin finished, hand engraved, gold lined; height, 2½ inches. Price..................$1.10

No. 5R7140 Child's Cup, satin finished, hand engraved, gold lined; height, 3 inches. Price..................$1.00

No. 5R7143 Child's Cup, satin finished, hand engraved, gold lined; height, 2¾ inches. Price..................90c

No. 5R7146 Child's Cup, satin finished, hand engraved, gold lined; height, 2½ inches. Price..................50c

No. 5R7148 Child's Cup, satin finish, gold lined, engraved; height, 3 inches; ornamented border and handle, something beautiful. Each..................$2.25

No. 5R7151 Cup and Saucer, engraved, gold lined, satin finish. Each..................$2.75

No. 5R7154 Mustache Cup and Saucer, very fancy saucer, gold lined, engraved and ornamented border, satin finish. Each..................$3.50

No. 5R7155 Mustache Cup and Saucer, gold lined, beautifully hand engraved and satin finished. Each..................$4.50

Postage extra on plain band napkin rings, boxed, ready for shipment, 4 cents; fancy rings, toothpick holders and cups, about 8 cents; cups and saucers, about 12 cents. Silverware takes first class express and freight rates. See front of book for further instructions.

NAPKIN RINGS
FROM
15 CENTS TO $1.65.

No. 5R7160 Napkin Ring, satin finish, engraved, figure of man; height, 3 inches. Each.................. 95c

No. 5R7163 Napkin Ring, figure of a dog, satin finish, hand engraved; height, 3¼ inches. Each..................$1.10

No. 5R7166 Napkin Ring, hand engraved, satin finish, gold lined. Each..................$1.65

No. 5R7169 Napkin Ring, satin finish, hand engraved Each.....15c

No. 5R7172 Napkin Ring, plain, hand chased. Each.........30c

No. 5R7175 Napkin Ring, hand engraved, bare foot boy; gold lined, satin finish. Each, $1.40

No. 5R7176 Napkin Ring. Very fancy, hand engraved; height, 2¾ in. Each..........75c

No. 5R7181 Child's Napkin Ring, plain, hand chased. Each.......20c

No. 5R7184 Napkin Ring, satin finish, engraved "Father." Each..50c

No. 5R7187 Napkin Ring, satin finish, engraved "Mother." Each..50c

No. 5R7190 Napkin Ring, satin finish, and engraved, extra scroll design. Each..........65c

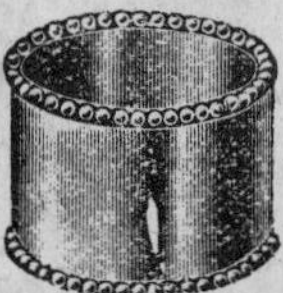

No. 5R7192 Napkin Ring, satin finish, hand engraved, fancy border. Each..........55c

No. 5R7194 Napkin Ring, satin finish, hand engraved Each..........45c

No. 5R7196 Napkin Ring, satin finish, hand engraved, fancy border Each........75c

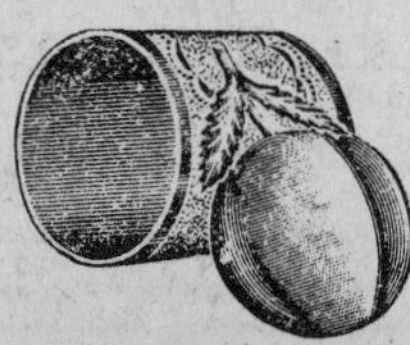

No. 5R7198 Fancy Napkin Ring, satin finished, engraved; height, 2¼ inches; fancy base. Each..................75c

No. 5R7200 Fancy Napkin Ring; height, 2¼ inches; hand engraved, raised ornamented base. Each........85c

No. 5R7202 Fancy Napkin Ring; height, 3 inches; satin finish, engraved, carved man and dog. Each..........$1.00

No. 5R7204 Fancy Napkin Ring, satin finish, engraved, fancy base; height, 2 inches. Each..........$1.25

No. 5R7206 Fancy Napkin Ring, satin finish, hand engraved; height, 3 inches. Each..................80c

OUR $4.95 INITIAL SILVERWARE SET.

FOR $4.95 we offer a 26-piece set of silverware, engraved with any initial, complete with case, the equal of anything you can buy anywhere at three times the price.

NO RISK IN ORDERING ONE OF THESE SETS. Examine and compare it. If you have not a bargain, return it and we will refund your money. This is an offer not made by others. We know our goods; we know you will be delighted with your purchase, and we have no fear of it being returned. Express charges will amount to next to nothing as compared with what you will save in price. The express charges will average for 500 miles, 35 cents; 1,000 miles, 50 cents. Greater or less distance in proportion.

THIS SET CONSISTS OF 6 full size table spoons as illustrated, each spoon engraved on the handle with any initial desired, as shown in illustration; 6 tea spoons as illustrated, each spoon engraved on the handle with any initial desired, as shown in illustration; 6 full size forks as illustrated, each fork engraved on the handle with any initial desired, as illustrated; 1 sugar shell, 1 butter knife and 6 heavy silver plated knives.

IN ADDITION TO THE 26 PIECES of silverware as illustrated, we furnish this handsome plush covered and fancy blue lined case. Case is 12 inches long, 10 inches wide and 2 inches deep, nicely finished with a fancy metal clasp and so divided as to just hold the 26 pieces in position, as shown in illustration, so that when the tableware is not in use it can be kept in perfect condition in the case, as illustrated.

No. 5R7300

No. 5R7300

No. 5R7300

THIS SOLID SILVER METAL is the nearest approach in composition metal for tableware to the pure coin silver that has ever been attained. This composition silver is one solid metal through and through, guaranteed to retain its perfect silver color and to wear forever.

IT WILL NEVER TARNISH. It is stronger than silver; more springy; you can scour it with a brick; you cannot harm it.

THIS SILVER COMPOSITION METAL is made by a process known only to the manufacturer of these sets, who supplies them to us in immense quantities; is in appearance, finish and every way (except intrinsic value) equal to coin silver. In appearance it cannot be told from solid coin silver, it must be examined by an expert to detect the difference.

FOR A CHRISTMAS PRESENT, birthday present, wedding present, for a gift to a friend or a gift for any purpose, nothing is more suitable, nothing at the price will be more appreciated, nothing could be more appropriate than this, **our 26-piece set with initial engraved on every piece, except the six knives, all for $4.95.**

AT $4.95 WE FURNISH THIS 26-PIECE SET of initial silverware complete with case as the greatest value ever offered in this class of goods; in fact, our $4.95 price is based on the actual cost to us in immense quantities for cash, with but our one small percentage of profit added. We know if you order this case of silverware from us you will be so well pleased with it that you will show it to your friends, recommend our house and other orders will follow from your neighbors.

DO NOT COMPARE THIS, our composition silver initial ware, with any of the cheap plated ware that is offered in cases. We could furnish a 26-piece set of cheap silver plated ware with a cheap case similar to the cases that are being furnished by some houses at $1.50 to $2.00, but we believe our customers want a higher grade of goods and we have received so many letters of commendation for this class of goods the past two seasons that we have decided to increase our contracts and offer the goods in sets of twenty-six pieces at even a lower price than we have ever before been able to sell the same class of goods without the case.

BEST QUALITY QUADRUPLE PLATED SILVERWARE.

Is plated with pure silver on fine solid white metal, and warranted.

THESE GOODS WERE SELECTED AS BEING APPROPRIATE FOR WEDDING, BIRTHDAY OR CHRISTMAS PRESENTS.

No. 5R7353 Shaving Mug and Brush to match, richly engraved, satin finished, mug gold lined. Price, complete....$4.00
No. 5R7354 Mug alone, as above. Each..............$2.25
Shipping weight, 1½ to 2 lbs.

No. 5R7356 Shaving Mug; something neat, new and novel, satin finished, beaded top border, fancy handle, top lifts out and is used for the soap, the bottom for hot water. Each..........$1.75
Shipping weight, 1½ to 2 lbs.

No. 5R7359 Jewel Box, satin finished, hand engraved. Height, 2½ inches; length, 4½ inches. Each..............75c
Shipping weight, 1½ to 2 lbs.

No. 5R7362 Fancy Box, raised ornamentations, satin finish. Each.......... $1.15
Shipping weight, 1½ to 2 lbs.

No. 5R7363 Soap Box, 4 inches long, bright polished, raised ornamentation, gold lined. Each..............$1.80
Shipping weight, 1½ to 2 lbs

No. 5R7368 Cigar Box, ornamented base and lid, satin finished throughout. Very appropriate gift for gentlemen. Each. (Shipping weight, 1½ to 2 lbs.) $6.25

No. 5R7371 Jewel Box, hand engraved, satin lined, satin finished, burnished throughout. Height, 2¼ inches; length, 7 inches. Each..$3.75
Shipping weight, about 3 pounds.

No. 5R7374 Chafing Dish, ebony trimmings, bright nickel finish, capacity, 3 pints. Complete. $3.95
Shipping weight, about 10 lbs.

No. 5R7377 Stamp Box, raised ornamented border and top, satin finished.
Each....... $1.00
If by mail, postage extra 4 cents.

No. 5R7381 Smoking Set, satin finish, hand engraved, gold lined. Height, 3¼ ins.; 8½-inch tray. Price, complete. $1.25
Shipping weight, about 2 pounds.

No. 5R7383 Curling Set, burnished throughout. Length, 5¾ inches. Very serviceable.
Each...................................$2.90
Shipping weight, about 3 pounds.

No. 5R7386 Flask; capacity, ¾-pint, satin finish, with screw top.
Each....................$1.90
Shipping weight, about 2 pounds.

No. 5R7389 Flask; finely embossed, bright finish, hard metal collapsible cup. Height, 6 inches. Each $4.25
Shipping weight, about 2 pounds.

No. 5R7392 Ice Pitcher, and engraved and chased, polished and satin finished. Each..$2.95
Shipping weight, about 10 lbs.

No. 5R7393 Mustard Pot, plain polished glass bowl. Price, each, $1.20
Shipping weight, about ½ pound.

No. 5R7397 Sugar Dredge, hand engraved, satin finished, fancy chased handle. Height, 4½ inches. Each................$2.25
Shipping weight, about 1½ lbs.

No. 5R7401 Ink Stand; beautifully embossed base, flint crystal bottle; height, 2½ inches; width, 5½ inches.
Each....................95c
Shipping weight, about 2 pounds.

No. 5R7404 Ink Stand; fancy top and base, flint crystal bottle; height, 2½ inches; width, 3 inches.
Each...................50c
Shipping weight, about 2 pounds.

No. 5R7407 Ink Set; embossed base and top, cut glass bottle; height, 4 inches. Each.......$2.00
Shipping weight, about 3 lbs.

No. 5R7410 Writing Set; cut glass bottles, very fancy tops; length, 6½ inches; satin finished. Each.................$4.50
Shipping weight, about 3 pounds.

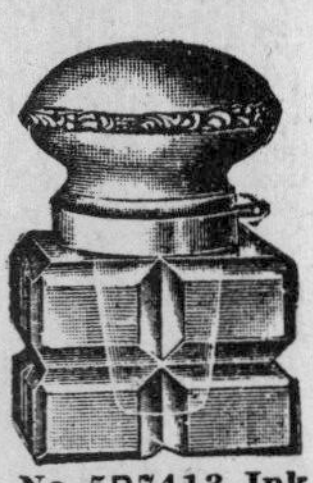

No. 5R7413 Ink Stand; cut glass; heavy silver top; height, 3¾ inches.
Each......$1.75
Shipping weight, about 2 lbs.

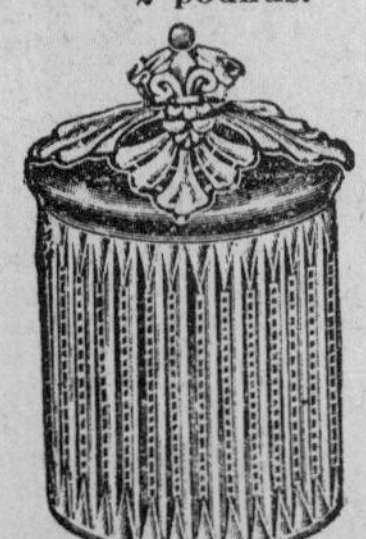

No. 5R7416 Cigar Jar; fancy gold filled top, ornamented in enamel; jar of white crystal; height, 7 in.; diameter, 3¾ in.
Each.............$2.00

No. 5R7419 Tobacco Jar; satin finish; imported Bohemian glass, fitted with patent moistener; height, 6½ inches.
Each..............$1.95

No. 5R7422 Puff Jar; fancy gold filled top, ornamented with enamel; height, 3¾ in.; diameter, 5 inches. Each.......65c

No. 5R7425 Puff Jar; gold filled top, ornamented in enamel; height, 4½ in.; diameter, 3½ inches.
Each..............$1.15

No. 5R7428 Tobacco Jar; latest idea, gold filled; height, 7½ in.; diam., 6 in. Each....$1.50

No. 5R7431 Perfume Bottle; fancy gold filled, hard enameled in colors, bottle of pressed flint crystal; height, 4½ in.
Each.........$1.75
Shipping weight, about 2 lbs.

Shipping weight of Nos. 5R7416, 5R7419, 5R7422, 5R7425 and 5R7428, ABOUT 3 POUNDS.

...OUR CLOCK DEPARTMENT...

NO CHARGES FOR REPAIRS ON WATCHES OR CLOCKS WILL BE ALLOWED UNLESS OUR WRITTEN CONSENT IS FIRST SECURED IN ADVANCE. . . . .

IN CLOCKS WE REPRESENT ALL OF THE OLDEST AND MOST RELIABLE MAKERS who have built up a reputation for their goods by making only such clocks as they could guarantee. We list clocks made by the following concerns, namely: **Waterbury Clock Company**, Waterbury, Conn.; **New Haven Clock Company**, New Haven, Conn.; **Ansonia Clock Company**, Ansonia, Conn., and the **Seth Thomas Clock Company**, Thomaston, Conn. Bear in mind that the Waterbury Clock Company has **no connection whatever** with the Waterbury Watch Company; it is a very much older concern.

EVERY CLOCK THAT WE SELL IS GUARANTEED by the manufacturers and **we warrant them** to our customers. Any clock bought from us that is not in every way satisfactory can be returned and it **WILL BE EXCHANGED OR THE MONEY REFUNDED.**

WE SELL OUR CLOCKS AT EXTREMELY LOW PRICES. It must be understood **that you are buying wholesale**, thereby avoiding the retailer's profit. Do not think that the shipping charges will advance our prices to anywhere near the price you would have to pay your retail dealer, because he likewise must pay express charges and must add same to the cost of the clock when he sells it to you. We wish you to **investigate the matter yourself and be convinced that we can save you from 30 to 50 per cent on clocks.**

ORDER ONE OF THESE CLOCKS and if after you have examined it you do not find it in every particular as described, return it and we will cheerfully refund your money. **Our terms are cash with the order.**

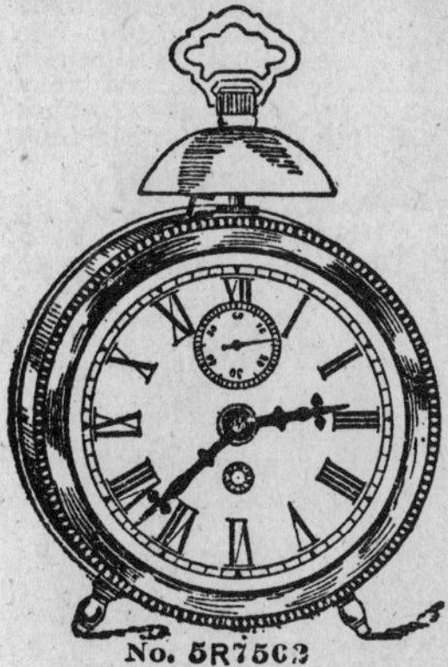
No. 5R7502

No. 5R7500 Imported. Nickel Alarm Clock, 4-inch dial, similar to No. 5R7502, a very good timekeeper.
No. 5R7500 Each............65c
Shipping wt., 2 lbs.

No. 5R7502 Beacon. Nickel Alarm Clock; height, 6¼ inches; width, 4¼ inches; 4-inch dial; made by the celebrated **New Haven Clock Company**; lever movement; best grade nickel clock made; warranted.
No. 5R7502 Each............72c
Shipping wt., 2 lbs.

SEARS, ROEBUCK & CO.'S SPECIAL.

No. 5R7514 Sears, Roebuck Special. Nickel Alarm Clock. Height, 6¼ inches; dial, 4 inches; made expressly for us by one of the largest clock companies in the United States. It goes through a thorough inspection before leaving the factory and again before leaving our establishment by one of our expert watchmakers; a clock we can conscientiously recommend to you as being everything that an alarm clock should be.
No. 5R7514 Each............................80c
Shipping weight, 2 pounds.

CELEBRATED PARKER ALARM CLOCK.

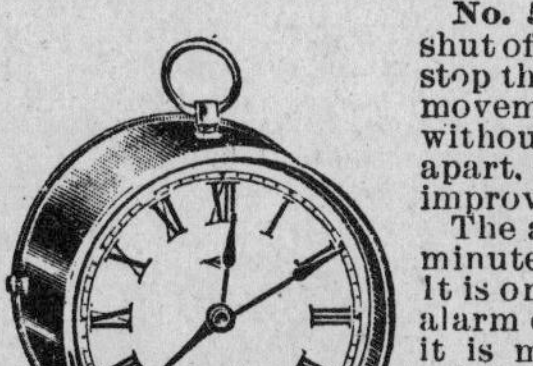

No. 5R7516 It has the shut off attachment: you can stop the alarm at will. The movement can be taken out without taking the clock apart, one of the very latest improvements.

The alarm runs nearly five minutes with one winding. It is one of the most perfect alarm clocks on the market; it is manufactured by the celebrated **Parker Clock Co.**, of Meriden, Conn. The name of Parker on any clock is a guarantee of perfection. Height of clock, 4½ inches; depth of clock 3½ inches.
No. 5R7516 Price **$1.20**
Shipping weight, boxed, about 2 pounds.

No. 5R7504 Beacon Luminous. Nickel Alarm Clock, with luminous dial; height 5½ inches; width 4¼ inches; 4-inch dial; manufactured by the New Haven Clock Company of New Haven, Conn.; best grade lever movement.
No. 5R7504 Each.. .... 85c
Shipping wt., 2 lbs.

NOTE—The dial on above clock is luminous, and will show distinctly the time in the dark. The darker it is the brighter it glows.

No. 5R7504

BEAUTIFUL OXIDIZED ALARM CLOCK FOR $2.50

No. 5R7518

No. 5R7518 The New Long Alarm Clock rings from 20 to 30 minutes, but can be switched off any minute desired. This clock will not tip over; no battery necessary; absolutely no trouble. **The case is finished in superfine oxidized copper,** hand engraved and hand chased, in fact, making an ornament that would grace any parlor mantelpiece. Height, 10 inches; dial, 5 inches; movement manufactured by the celebrated **Seth Thomas Clock Company**, and is

GUARANTEED TO GIVE : : ABSOLUTE SATISFACTION IN EVERY RESPECT: : : :

Runs 36 hours with one winding. The steel parts are fish oil hardened, brass parts highly wrought by hand, full conical pivots, patent pinions, agate drawn hairspring, agate drawn main spring, thoroughly timed and adjusted by two expert mechanics, one at the factory and one at our establishment, assuring our customers it being received in perfect condition. **It is a clock longed for by thousands.** It fills a long felt want. If not exactly as described in every particular return it and we will refund the amount deposited or remitted.
No. 5R7518 Price. **$2.50**
Shipping weight, 2 pounds.

No. 5R7509

No. 5R7509 "MustGet Up." Nickel Alarm Clock; height, 5⅞ inches; dial, 4½ inches; made by the Waterbury Clock Company. This clock has very large bell on the back of the clock; the alarm runs five minutes with one winding; can be made to run a short, medium, long, or extra long time, and can be stopped at pleasure.
No. 5R7509 Ea..**$1.40**
No. 5R7510 As above, spasmodic, alarms every ½-minute for 15 minutes.
Each.............**$1.40**
Shipping wt., 2 lbs.

No. 5R7512 The Fly Alarm Calendar. Height, about 6½ inches; dial, 4 inches; one-day clock with calendar and alarm, manufactured by the New Haven Clock Company. Movement, very fine grade lever; a clock that we know will give entire satisfaction in every respect; has fine large nickel alarm bell on top, entire clock beautifully burnished, the calendar very finely adjusted, and thoroughly inspected before leaving our establishment, has extra long alarm ring or can be regulated by winding apparatus for short ring.

No. 5R7512

No. 5R7512 Each...92c
Shipping weight, 2 pounds.

A $3.00 CLOCK FOR $1.10.

BRONZE $1.10 **..GILT.. $1.25**

Sears, Roebuck & Co.'s **SEROCO.** A clock such as has never been offered before for the money. This beautiful bronze clock, solid metal through and through, standing 12 inches high and 9½ inches broad, weighing when boxed about 7 lbs., at the unheard of price of **$1.10 in bronze, $1.25 in full gilt.** The movement is a fine lever escapement movement, oil tempered steel parts and hand wrought brass parts, conical pivots, the hair spring agate drawn; runs for 36 hours with one winding; in fact, a movement that we guarantee to give absolute satisfaction. The case is a masterpiece, representing the emblems of Hope and Plenty, Hope being represented by a heroic figure of a woman with Greek drapery, resting her hand upon a cornucopia that represents Plenty. The base of the clock is made up of three graceful scrolls meeting at a base upon which the figure of Hope stands. The parts are brought out by hand engraving and hand chasing and burnishing. A beautiful wreath of roses in strong relief connects the two designs, that of Hope and Plenty. To sell this clock at this unheard of low price, a price that does not represent one-half its true value, we had to contract with the factory that makes them in such large quantities that the price of a single one is practically lost sight of. The design was executed by ourselves and is copyrighted. **It cannot be procured elsewhere.** If the clock is not the greatest bargain that you have ever seen or heard of, and if it does not in every way, shape and manner come up to our description and thoroughly satisfy you, return it to us and we will refund you the entire amount of your remittance.

No. 5R7520

No. 5R7520 Price, in bronze...**$1.10**
No. 5R7521 Price, in gilt...**1.25**
Shipping weight, 7 pounds.

FINE CABINET CLOCKS.

MANUFACTURED BY THE GREATEST CLOCK MAKERS IN THE WORLD.

WE GUARANTEE EACH AND EVERY ONE OF THEM IN EVERY PARTICULAR, AND IF GIVEN THE CARE THAT ALL CLOCKS SHOULD HAVE, WILL LAST A LIFETIME.

This 8-Day Clock for $2.00.

THE RICHALD is made by the Waterbury Clock Co., in either oak or walnut as desired. It runs eight days with one winding, it stands 22 inches high, has 6-inch dial, strikes the hours and half hours on a wire bell. Case is beautifully carved and perfectly made in every detail.
No. 5R7525 Price, $2.00
No. 5R7526 With alarm. Price, $2.30
No. 5R7527 With cathedral gong, no alarm. Price, $2.30
No. 5R7528 With cathedral gong and alarm. Price, $2.60

Special Value For $2.90.

No. 5R7546 THE VULCAN. Height, 23½ inches; dial, 6 inches. Very fine movement. Manufactured and guaranteed by the Ansonia Clock Company. Frame hand engraved and carved, rich top ornamentation, highly polished throughout. Walnut only.
No. 5R7546 Price $2.90
No. 5R7547 With alarm. Price $3.15

Nothing Finer for $4.00. Our Price, $2.50.

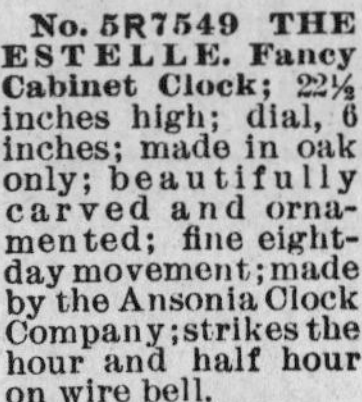

No. 5R7549 THE ESTELLE. Fancy Cabinet Clock; 22½ inches high; dial, 6 inches; made in oak only; beautifully carved and ornamented; fine eight-day movement; made by the Ansonia Clock Company; strikes the hour and half hour on wire bell.
No. 5R7549 Price $2.50
No. 5R7549½ With alarm. Price $2.80
No. 5R7550 With gong. Price $2.70

Very Latest and Best Design for $2.00.

No. 5R7552 THE VESTA. Latest pattern Cabinet Clock in solid oak or walnut as desired; case finely ornamented with decorated glass; height of clock 22 inches; dial, 6 inches; fine eight-day movement, guaranteed to keep accurate time; manufactured by the celebrated Waterbury Clock Company; strikes the hour and half hour on a wire bell.
No. 5R7552 Price $2.00
No. 5R7553 With alarm. Price $2.30
No. 5R7554 With cathedral gong. Price $2.30

This Choice Bargain at $3.15.

Another rare specimen of clock perfection manufactured by the Celebrated Waterbury Clock Co.

No. 5R7555 This clock not alone gives you the time for eight days with one winding, but likewise gives you the date of the month, the temperature of the weather and the condition of the atmosphere, having barometer and thermometer attachments, as shown in the picture, and likewise strikes the hour and half-hour. This clock can be supplied in either oak or walnut. It stands 27 inches high; weighs, boxed ready for shipment, about 17 pounds; dial is 6 inches in diameter. The movement, one of the best manufactured, **is warranted an accurate timekeeper and we guarantee it to give entire satisfaction.** The pendulum is exposed, the glass is beautifully decorated, and we believe it is one of the choicest of choice bargains we are offering this season.
No. 5R7555 Price of clock complete $3.15

THE ELDENAN Eight Day Clock, suitable for the office, workshop or the house. It has a complete calendar attachment, showing the days of the month. It strikes the hours and half hours on a wire bell. The case stands 22 inches high, beautifully embossed, is made in either oak or walnut by the Waterbury Clock Co. and is guaranteed an accurate timepiece. The glass is handsomely decorated. The pendulum is a fancy one.
No. 5R7556 Price, $2.70
No. 5R7557 Same with cathedral gong. Price $3.00

THE DUKE Cabinet Clock, made by the Waterbury Clock Co., in either oak or walnut. It runs eight days with one winding, it strikes the hours and half-hours on a wire bell. The case stands 22 inches high, is beautifully carved and ornamented. The dial is 6 inches in diameter. This clock is warranted to give entire satisfaction.
No. 5R7562 Price, $2.50
No. 5R7563 With cathedral gong $2.80
No. 5R7563½ With alarm attach't $2.80

No. 5R7564 THE QUEENSLAND. Handsome Cabinet Clock in oak or walnut, as desired; latest design; fancy carved and ornamented case; height, 22 inches; dial, 6 inches; eight-day movement; guaranteed by the Waterbury Clock Company, strikes the hour and half hour on wire bell.
No. 5R7564 Price $2.60
No. 5R7565 With alarm. Price $2.85
No. 5R7566 With gong. Price $2.75

Our $2.65 Cabinet Clock.

No. 5R7567 THE FLORIDA. One of the most complete clocks ever offered to the public. It has an eight-day movement, guaranteed by the Waterbury Clock Company. Strikes the hour and half-hour on a wire bell. It also has thermometer and barometer attachment. The case is of solid oak or walnut, as desired; beautifully carved, with ornamented door and fancy glass. The pendulum is likewise ornamented and very fancy. Stands 22 inches high and has a six-inch dial.
No. 5R7567 Price $2.65
No. 5R7568 With alarm. Price 3.00
No. 5R7569 With cathedral gong. Price 2.85

A Bargain for $3.65.

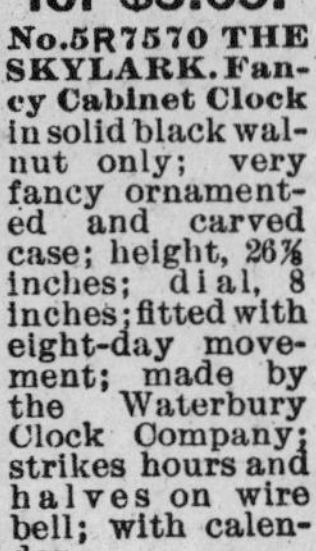

No. 5R7570 THE SKYLARK. Fancy Cabinet Clock in solid black walnut only; very fancy ornamented and carved case; height, 26⅞ inches; dial, 8 inches; fitted with eight-day movement; made by the Waterbury Clock Company; strikes hours and halves on wire bell; with calendar.
No. 5R7570 Price $3.65
No. 5R7571 With cathedral gong. Price, $3.95

Our $5.20 King Clock Would Retail for $10.00.

No. 5R7573 THE KING. A very fancy Cabinet Clock in black walnut only. Fancy carved, with bronze ornaments and fancy French sash. Height, 24½ inches; dial, 6 inches; with eight-day movement; made by the Ansonia Clock Company; strikes hours and halves, with fancy pendulum.
No. 5R7573 Price $5.20
No. 5R7574 With cathedral gong. Price $5.40

A Handsome Parlor Clock, $4.50.

No. 5R7576 THE PRETOX. Very fancy Parlor Clock. Can furnish in either oak, walnut or mahogany, as desired. It is 24 inches high; has a six-inch dial, finely carved case, plate glass mirrors and cupids at sides. Has an eight-day movement and strikes the hour and half-hour on wire bell. Manufactured by the Waterbury Clock Co.
No. 5R7576 Price $4.50
No. 5R7577 With alarm. Price $4.80
No. 5R7578 With gong. Price $4.80

The Mantel Clocks on this page weigh, boxed, from 22 to 30 pounds. Compare our prices with those you would have to pay in your own town at your retail jeweler's, if you wish to know how much you can save by buying of us. No charges for repairs on Watches or Clocks will be allowed unless our written consent is first secured in advance.

OUR NEW ACME QUEEN CATHEDRAL GONG CLOCK PRICE CUT TO $5.75

LAST YEAR WE SOLD THIS CLOCK FOR $6.90, BUT ON ACCOUNT OF IMMENSE SALES WE WERE ENABLED TO GIVE A LARGER O:DER, AND PAYING SPOT CASH WE WERE ABLE TO CUT THE COST THIS AMOUNT. WE ARE GIVING YOU THE ADVANTAGE OF IT . . . .

FROM THIS LARGE ILLUSTRATION, which is engraved by our artist direct from a photograph, you can form some idea of the appearance of this clock and figure, but it must be seen to be appreciated.

No. 5R7600

AT $5.75 we furnish this clock complete with handsome bronze figure, exactly as illustrated. At $4.75 we furnish the clock only, without the bronze figure. Order this clock, and if you do not find it all and even more than we claim for it, such a clock as you could not buy elsewhere even at double the price, you can return it to us at our expense and we will cheerfully refund your money. At $5.75 we offer this big, handsome clock, complete, with large bronze figure as illustrated, as the greatest value we have ever offered in a high grade cathedral gong 8-day clock.

THIS OUR SPECIAL $5.75 CLOCK complete with figure, is a clock that we believe combines the good qualities of all high grade Waterbury mantel clocks, with the defects of none. This clock is covered by a binding guarantee, and if any piece or part gives out by reason of defect in material or workmanship, or for some reason the clock fails to run accurately, it can be returned at our expense and we will cheerfully refund your money.

AS A GIFT, A WEDDING, A BIRTHDAY OR AN ENGAGEMENT PRESENT,

you cannot select anything more appropriate. One of these clocks will be beautiful as well as ornamental, and will last a generation. Nothing handsomer for mantel ornamentation; nothing more useful than our $5.75 Acme Queen Parlor Clocks.

WHILE WE OFFER MANY RARE BARGAINS in our clock department, offer them at the manufacturers' lowest prices, prices as low, and in many cases even lower than dealers can buy in quantities, this our Special Acme Queen Cathedral Gong 8-day clock, complete with figure, at $5.75 is the greatest clock value in our catalogue, and we recommend this clock in preference to all others. It is a handsome clock for mantel or shelf; for an ornament for the home there is no clock made that will compare with it at anything like the price; as a timekeeper there is nothing better.

GENERAL DESCRIPTION.

SIZE—Height of clock, including figure, 20 inches; clock only, 11½ inches; figure only, 8½ inches. Length of clock at base, 17½ inches; length of clock at top, 15 inches. Diameter of dial, 5½ inches. Length of bronze figure, 9 inches.

This large, handsome bronze, marbleized metal clock is made in two colors, black and green, in imitation of black and Mexican onyx, and it so closely resembles the genuine Mexican onyx that it cannot be detected except by an expert. Better than the genuine onyx, it can be cleaned with a damp cloth without injury and is guaranteed never to warp or crack. This is an eight-day clock—runs eight days with one winding—and strikes the hours and half hours upon a perfect cathedral gong.

This clock stands on large handsome bronze feet. It is ornamented with lion head bronze side ornaments, heavy bronze panel ornaments and bronze center ornaments. It is furnished with a handsome Mosaic dial in heavy gilt, 5½ inches in diameter. This clock is one of the highest grade made by the Waterbury Company. It has blued steel hands, the movement is highly polished wrought brass. All steel parts are oil tempered. Has the latest improved regulator and pinions, safety barrel and escapement. Weight, boxed ready for shipment, 25 pounds.

No. 5R7600 Price, Acme Queen Cathedral Gong Clock.......... .... $5.75

OUR PARLOR SPECIAL FOR $3.75

THIS CLOCK AS ILLUSTRATED FOR $3.75 is about one-half what you would pay your local dealer for the same sized clock. A clock as beautifully ornamented, sold by the clock companies to the retail dealers for $4.25. We have made a purchase of an immense quantity; the entire clock is manufactured expressly for us by the renowned Waterbury Clock Company, located at Waterbury, Connecticut, and each and every one of them is thoroughly guaranteed in every respect and we warrant them to give entire satisfaction.

FROM THIS LARGE ILLUSTRATION ON THE RIGHT, we have tried to give you some idea of the appearance of this handsome parlor special clock, and while this picture accurately presents it,

YOU MUST SEE AND EXAMINE THE CLOCK TO APPRECIATE THE VALUE WE ARE OFFERING.

DESCRIPTION OF CASE.

THIS CLOCK CASE IS MADE OF WOOD, covered with a secret preparation in imitation of black marble. This clock, wiped with a damp cloth at intervals, will always keep as new. It is guaranteed not to chip, warp or wear off and always retains its appearance of genuine black Italian marble.

THE CLOCK IS ORNAMENTED with four handsome gold plated scrolls. It stands upon beautiful metal feet made to match the balance of the scroll work. The dial of the clock is one of the very latest productions, being fancy rococo embossed pattern. The numerals are Arabic ones. Height of clock is 12½ inches; width of clock, 9¾ inches; depth of clock, 4½ inches.

DESCRIPTION OF MOVEMENT.

THE MOVEMENT FITTED IN THIS CASE is one of the Waterbury guaranteed movements, runs eight days with one winding. It is made of the finest tempered steel and hand wrought brass; it strikes the hour on a cathedral gong and the half hour on a brass bell. You can always know the time without seeing the clock. The hands are very fine hand sawed blue steel of the Fleur de Lis pattern.

This clock, boxed ready for shipment, weighs about 15 pounds.

No. 5R7615 Remember, our price for this beautiful clock is but . . . $3.75

NO CHARGES FOR REPAIRS ON WATCHES OR CLOCKS WILL BE ALLOWED UNLESS OUR WRITTEN CONSENT IS FIRST SECURED IN ADVANCE.

No. 5R7615

Regular Eight-Day Clock with Perpetual Calendar Attachment for $6.40.

No. 5R7627 This clock is manufactured by the celebrated Waterbury Clock Company. Can be supplied in either oak or walnut. Stands 28¼ inches high. Is an eight-day clock and strikes the hour and half hour on a cathedral gong. **It has the calendar attachment,** as shown on the lower dial, which is a perpetual one, marking even the leap years without having to be reset. The dials are 8 inches in diameter, making it possible to see either time or date at a considerable distance. This clock is particularly adapted for dining rooms, libraries and offices, although it can be used anywhere where a clock is necessary. **The movement used in this clock runs for eight days with one winding.** We warrant it to be an accurate timekeeper and one of the best movements ever placed on the market. The parts are made of finely wrought brass and oil tempered steel, making it not alone most accurate for time keeping, but gives it great durability. **The case is beautifully hand carved and embossed.** In fact, a rare specimen of the cabinet maker's art. The glass in the door is decorated in black and gold, completing the rich appearance of the entire clock. This clock would bring in the average retail store no less than $10.00. See our price, **$6.40. We absolutely guarantee it to give entire satisfaction.** Weight, boxed for shipment, about 25 pounds.

No. 5R7627 Price............................**$6.40**

$3.15 Buys a Calendar Clock with Barometer and Thermometer.

No. 5R7631 CALENDAR EIGHT-DAY CLOCK with thermometer and barometer. This clock has been one of the greatest bargains that we have ever been able to offer to our customers. We buy them in immense quantities for spot cash, and the price at which we offer them will save you, we believe, fully 50 per cent over the prices asked by retail dealers. The clock will be furnished with solid black walnut or antique oak case, as desired, **beautifully carved and ornamented.** The height is 24 inches with dial 6 inches. The movement is one of the **best made, and is warranted to be an accurate timekeeper;** has a complete calendar attachment which works automatically and always indicates correctly the day of the month. It has a perfect thermometer on one side and on the other a barometer. The barometer always indicates the condition of the atmosphere and always correctly foretells the probabilities of the weather. It is eight-day and strikes the hour and half hour on a wire bell. We cannot furnish it with alarm; in fact, an alarm should not be used on a cabinet clock. This clock will last a lifetime if properly cared for and we will guarantee satisfaction in every respect. Weight of clock, boxed ready for shipment, 17 pounds.

No. 5R7631 Price.....**$3.15**

A $10.00 Eight-day Clock with Cathedral Gong for $5.65.

No. 5R7634 SENECA. Oak or walnut as desired. This clock is one of the productions of the Waterbury Clock Company, and will keep time as well as any regulator manufactured. It has an eight-day movement of polished brass that is tested and examined thoroughly before leaving the factory and tested again before leaving our establishment. It strikes the hour and half hour upon a cathedral gong. 6-inch dial. Height of entire clock is 33⅜ inches. Has a fine wood pendulum, so it is not affected by heat or cold, and we believe this clock is second to none in style. Weight, boxed, 17 pounds.

No. 5R7634 Price............................**$5.65**

Special Price, $5.15 — Second to none at the price.

No. 5R7636 CUCKOO CLOCK. Case is made of German oak or walnut, ornamented with inlaid ash, ebony and mahogany. Beautifully hand carved throughout, strikes the hour and half-hour on a gong, the cuckoo appears and calls at the same time. Height of clock, 21 inches; width, 14 inches. The movement is made in the Black Forest, Germany, of the finest tempered steel and polished brass, finely finished and adjusted, guaranteed to be a good time keeper. The two weights are copper finished iron ones and the hands and figures are of bleached white bone. One of the most artistic ornaments for a parlor ever made. Weight, boxed, 25 pounds.

No. 5R7636 Price............................**$5.15**

German Cuckoo Clock. Our Special Price, $7.55.

No. 5R7640 CUCKOO. Case made of German oak or walnut, hand carved bird top, hand carved oak leaves. The entire carving on this clock is done by hand by the natives of the Schwarzwald, Germany, and is especially fine and artistic. The figures are accurate and lifelike. The **movement is made of the very finest tempered steel and highly wrought brass.** It is finely finished and perfectly adjusted. The weights are copper finished iron ones. The hands and figures are bleached white bone. **It strikes the hour and half hour on a gong, a cuckoo appears and calls at the same time.** Height, 18 inches; width, 14 inches. Weight, boxed, 20 pounds.

No. 5R7640 Price............................**$7.55**

No. 5R7643 The New Parker Pedestal Alarm Clock with shut off attachment. Height of clock, 6 inches; width of dial, 3¼ inches. **By this late shut off improvement you can stop the alarm in an instant without interfering with the running of the clock.** Clock boxed ready for shipment, weighs about 2½ pounds.

No. 5R7643 Price.....**$1.45**

Octagon Lever. Oak, walnut or cherry veneered octagon case or round nickel case. Movement is patent lever, is made by the Waterbury Clock Company, and is a good reliable time piece. This clock is especially desirable for offices, schools, churches, etc.; one-day, with 4-inch dial, time only.

Nos. 5R7646 and 5R7649

No. 5R7646 Price............................**$1.30**

No. 5R7649 One-day, 6-inch dial, time only. Weight, boxed, 25 pounds. Price............**$1.95**

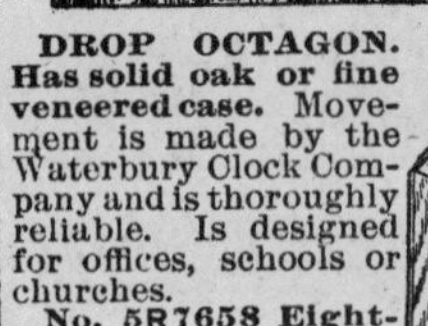

Seth Thomas. This is the genuine old reliable Seth Thomas Weight Clock, made by the Seth Thomas Clock Company, of Thomaston, Conn. The case has rosewood or walnut finish, with one day weight strike movement; height 25½ inches.

No. 5R7651 Price.....**$4.70**

No.5R7653 With eight-day weight strike movement; height 29½ inches. Weight, boxed, 37 pounds.

No. 5R7653 Price.....**$6.85**

DROP OCTAGON. Has solid oak or fine veneered case. Movement is made by the Waterbury Clock Company and is thoroughly reliable. Is designed for offices, schools or churches.

No. 5R7658 Eight-day, 10-inch dial; time only. Price......**$2.95**

No. 5R7661 Eight-day, 10-inch dial; time only, with calendar. Price...........**$3.25**

No. 5R7664 Eight-day, 10-inch dial; strikes hours and halves, with calendar. Price...........**$3.80**

No. 5R7667 Eight-day, 12-inch dial; time only. Weight, boxed, 25 pounds. Price,**$3.70**

Nos. 5R7658 to 5R7673

No.5R7670 Eight-day, 12-inch dial; strikes hour and half hour. Price. **$3.70**

No. 5R7673 Eight day, 12-inch dial; time only, with calendar. Price,**$3.40**

NOTE—The height of the clocks with 10-inch dial is 21 inches; 12-inch dial, 23½ inches.

No. 5R7676

No. 5R7676 Regulator. Has solid oak or handsome veneered and very fine finished case. Height, 32 inches, with 12-inch dial; has very fine eight-day movement, with calendar; made by the Waterbury Clock Company, has wood pendulum rod, which is not affected by changes of temperature, and is a very fine time piece; makes a very fine office clock or regulator. Weight, boxed, 28 pounds.

No. 5R7676 Price............................**$5.00**

Our $1.60 Porcelain Clock.

No. 5R7700 THE DAINTY. A beautiful porcelain case with gilt and fancy coloring and painted decorations. It is 5½ inches high, 6 inches wide with dial 2 inches in diameter, fitted with a bevel glass and a very fancy gilt sash. The movement is a one-day guaranteed lever, manufactured by the Waterbury Clock Company. One of the most dainty little clocks that we have ever had the pleasure of listing in our catalogue. Weight, boxed, 15 pounds.

No. 5R7700 Price........................$1.60

Elegantly Decorated Porcelain Clock for $6.15.

No. 5R7706 This clock is manufactured by the Waterbury Clock Co., of Waterbury, Conn. Clock stands 11⅛ inches high, with a width of 9½ inches. The case is French imported porcelain, beautifully decorated in gilt, with a ground color of either green, red or blue. The face of the clock is beautifully decorated, illustrating sprays of violets in their natural tints. The base of this clock is represented by four dragon claws, likewise handsomely gilded and colored, making a finish to the clock that is surpassed by none. The movement is a highly polished one; steel parts made of oil tempered steel, hair spring and mainspring both agate drawn, thoroughly timed and adjusted before leaving the factory, and again before leaving our establishment. The dial of this clock is 4¼ inches, with ornamented gilt sash, Arabic numerals and American ivory finished dial. Strikes the hours and half hours upon cathedral gong. Weight, boxed, 20 to 25 pounds.

No. 5R7706 Price........................$6.15

$7.00 Webster Mantel Clock.

At $7.00 the Webster Mantel Clock, made of bronze, by the Waterbury Clock Co. This clock runs eight days, strikes the hours and half-hours on a deep toned cathedral gong. Stands 12¼ inches high; width, 14¾ inches; dial, 4¼ inches. As a parlor ornament this grand clock is unsurpassed; the design a masterpiece, executed by master artists. The carving is elaborate and well defined, the figure is life like; in fact, we cannot by words or illustration half do justice to this our great Webster clock bargain. Weight, boxed ready for shipment, about 30 pounds.

No. 5R7707 Price........................$7.00

No. 5R7708 Same as above, done in rich roman gold plate. Price........................$9.00

$5.80 Buys a $9.00 Marbleized Clock.

No. 5R7709 A genuine marbleized case, imitation of Italian green onyx, manufactured by the Waterbury Clock Co., of Waterbury, Conn. This clock stands 10¾ inches high; width, 14 inches. The case of this clock is covered by a new preparation, a very close imitation of the celebrated marble of Italy. It is green in color and makes a most attractive ornament. Movement is eight-day, solid brass, and steel parts polished and tempered, and guaranteed in every respect by the manufacturers. The dial is 5¼ inches, with fancy brass fret work in the center, and French rococo sash. Strikes the hours on cathedral gong and the half hours on brass bell. Weight, boxed, from 20 to 25 pounds.

No. 5R7709 Price........................$5.80

Our $4.15 Iron Clock.

No. 5R7712 THE TWEED. The case of this very handsome clock is cast of fine grained iron. It is polished and enameled to the highest degree. It is almost impossible to tell it from a genuine marble clock. Manufactured and guaranteed by the New Haven Clock Company. Has a beautiful 6-inch dial with fancy figures. On the front of the clock there is a hand cut scroll and on the sides are ornamental griffins made of bronze. It rests upon bronze feet. Eight-day movement and strikes the hours and half hours on a gong. Weight, boxed, 20 to 25 pounds.

No. 5R7712 Price........................$4.15

Our $3.50 Eight-Day Clock.

Our Duchess. The case is handsomely enameled wood with gilt ornaments and gilt engravings. An exact duplicate of a French marble pattern and is manufactured by the Waterbury Clock Co. It runs eight days and strikes the hours on a deep toned cathedral gong, and the half hours on a metal bell. Has handsome 5½-inch dial with ornamented sash. Height, 10⅝ inches; width, 12⅛ inches. Weight, boxed, 20 to 24 pounds.

No. 5R7713 Price........................$3.50

A Special $5.30 Bargain.

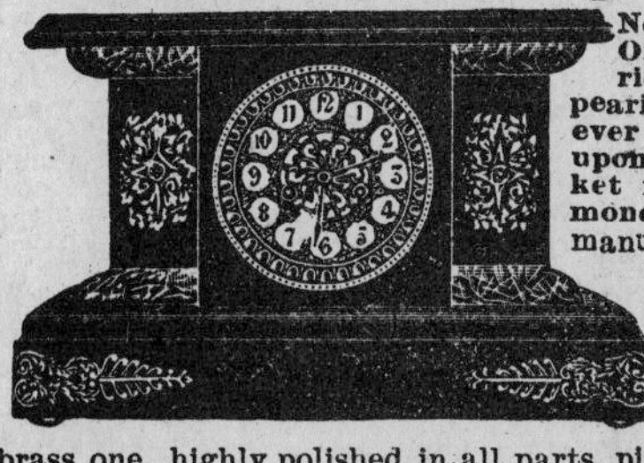

No. 5R7718 One of the richest appearing clocks ever placed upon the market for the money. It is manufactured and guaranteed by the Waterbury Clock Co. The movement is a brass one, highly polished in all parts, pivots, hair spring and main spring of the finest tempered steel, and guaranteed to be an accurate timekeeper. It strikes the half hours upon a brass bell, beautifully toned, and the hours upon a cathedral gong. The height is 10¾ inches, width 16⅓ inches. It is handsomely embellished by gilt ornaments and marbleizing, and would last a lifetime if taken care of. The dial of this clock is one of the most beautiful in the market and is 5¼ inches in diameter. Arabic numerals, and a French rococo sash. Color of the clock is black, being an imitation of black marble. A soft cotton cloth keeps this clock renewed for years. Weight, boxed, 20 to 25 pounds.

No. 5R7718 Price........................$5.30

Handsome Iron Clock for $4.85.

No. 5R7721 THE GEORGIANA. A very handsome iron clock with columns of marbleized iron on each side. Has beautiful rich gilt scroll engravings on the front of clock. The dial is a very handsome gilt French effect with fancy ornamented hands. Has beautiful raised ornamented iron feet. The entire clock is thoroughly polished and enameled to represent black marble. Eight-day movement; strikes the hours and half hours on a cathedral gong. Height, 10⅞ inches; width, 14⅛ inches; dial, 6 inches. Weight, boxed, 20 to 25 pounds.

No. 5R7721 Price........................$4.85

NOTE. **Porcelain clocks on this page weigh, boxed, about 20 pounds, enameled iron clocks, 22 to 37 pounds, and marbleized wood 15 to 19 pounds.**

$4.50 Buys a $7.00 Walnut Clock.

No. 5R7723 THE CORINTHIAN. A very handsome walnut frame, hand engraved and handcarved height of clock, 18½ inches; 14 inches wide; dial, 5½ inches in diameter. Has a cathedral gong, a half-hour slow striking arrangement. The movement is an eight-day, guaranteed by the Ansonia Clock Co. This clock has a very handsome American perforated dial. Weight, boxed, 20 to 25 pounds.

No. 5R7723 Price........................$4.50

Our $6.50 Mantel Clock.

The Levue Mantel Clock, manufactured by the Waterbury Clock Co., and is guaranteed to give entire satisfaction. This clock runs eight days with one winding, strikes the hours on a cathedral gong and the half hours on a metal bell. Clock is 11 inches high and 13⅛ inches wide; the dial 4½ inches in diameter, dial sash handsomely ornamented. The case is a beautiful design in black enameled iron, with bronze columns, column caps and bases, feet and massive ornament below the dial, done in fine gilt. Weight, boxed ready for shipment, 20 to 25 pounds.

No. 5R7725 Price........................$6.50

Rare Value for $8.75.

No. 5R7729 THE STOCKWELL. Very handsome iron case, black enameled and polished to represent marble. It is trimmed with beautiful scrolls of gilt trimmings with raised and chased ornamentations constituting the scrolls. The height of the clock is 10½ inches; width 13½ inches; dial 5 inches. The dial has a beautiful border of French design. The movement is an eight-day movement with a half hour gong striking attachment. Made by the Ansonia Clock Company. Weight, boxed, 20 to 25 pounds.

No. 5R7729 Price........................$8.75

A $12.50 Clock for $7.30.

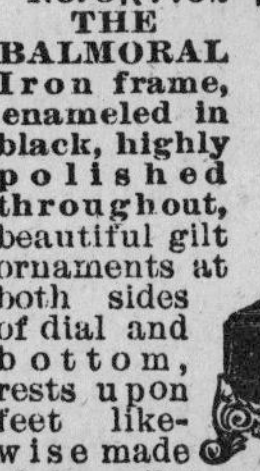

No. 5R7732 THE BALMORAL Iron frame, enameled in black, highly polished throughout, beautiful gilt ornaments at both sides of dial and bottom, rests upon feet likewise made of fine gilt bronze, richly chased and ornamented. Height of clock, 10⅜ inches; width, 15¾ inches; dial, 6 inches. We can supply either pearl or white dial as desired. Movement is an eight-day movement, strikes the hours and half hours upon a cathedral gong. Manufactured and guaranteed by the New Haven Clock Company. Weight, boxed, 20 to 25 lbs.

No. 5R7732 Price........................$7.30

SPECTACLES AND EYEGLASSES.

WE PARTICULARLY CAUTION OUR CUSTOMERS against buying the very cheap grades of spectacles or eyeglasses. The lenses of these cheap goods are made of very poor material, are improperly cut, and almost certain to do untold injury to the eyes. An injury to your clothes can be mended or repaired, but **an injury to the eyes may never be cured.**

THE PROPER READING DISTANCE for ordinary print is from 12 to 14 inches. If it is necessary to hold the reading nearer the eye than this, glasses for near sight are required. If it is necessary to hold the reading more than 12 to 14 inches away from the eye, glasses are required for far sight. Practically everybody should wear glasses after reaching the age of forty years, as the eyes at this time commence to be far sighted, and the longer the wearing of glasses is put off the harder it will be to remedy the trouble. **Near sightedness** is also very common, especially among young people, and should never be neglected, as this trouble is so easily and perfectly relieved by proper eyeglasses or spectacles.

TYPE FOR TESTING THE EYES.

60

The smallest size letters on this card should be read easily at fifteen inches from the eye. If you cannot do so you should wear spectacles. It does not pay to buy cheap spectacles.

52

They distort the rays of light, disturb the angles of vision, cause pain and discomfort and injure the eyesight. When it is necessary to hold work or reading matter farther than fifteen inches from the eyes

44

in order to see distinctly, it is a sure sign of failing vision, and much annoyance, discomfort and pain will be prevented

40

by having a pair of glasses fitted. Pain in the eyes when wearing spectacles is usually caused

36

either by improperly fitted lenses, or from the centres of the lenses not corresponding with

32

the centres of the eyes. To be perfect, a lens must be made with highly polished surfaces

26

of accurate curvatures. Our crystalline lenses are the best in the market.

22

They are made from the clearest and finest material obtainable

20

AND ARE WARRANTED TO BE OF ABSOLUTELY

18

PERFECT CONSTRUCTION.

16

BUY NO OTHER KIND.

13

CRYSTALLINE

11

LENSES

10

ARE THE

8

B E S T

30F

R E D

40F

O P

50F

N

Give the catalogue number of the style of Spectacles or Eyeglasses that you want, and answer very carefully the following questions.

When ordering spectacles or eyeglasses of any kind to be sent by mail, include 5 cts. extra for postage.

Instructions for Testing the Eyes.

No. 1. What is your age?
No. 2. Have you ever worn glasses before, and if so, how long and what number were they?
No. 3. Do your eyes stand out prominently or are they sunken?
No. 4. Do your eyes become tired after slight use?
No. 5. Does the light hurt your eyes?
No. 6. How long is it since your sight began to fail?
No. 7. Do you suffer from headaches or pain over the eyes?
No. 8. Can you see well at a distance without glasses?
No. 9. Do you desire glasses for reading or for seeing at a distance?
No. 10. Can you read test type No. 30F at a distance of 20 feet without glasses? If not, what number can you see at this distance?
No. 11. What is the number of the **smallest type** that you can easily and distinctly read, when holding this page at a distance of 12 inches from the eyes, without glasses?
No. 12. What is the **greatest possible distance** at which you can easily and distinctly read paragraph No. 26, without glasses?

If you desire SPECTACLES answer the following three questions:

No. 13. What is the distance between the pupils (A to B)?
No. 14. What is the width of nose at base (C to D)?
No. 15. What is the distance between the temples (E to F)?

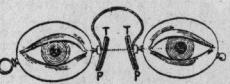

If you desire EYEGLASSES answer the following four questions.

No. 16. What is the width of nose (T to T)?
No. 17. What is the width of nose (P to P)?
No. 18. Is the bridge of your nose prominent or flat?
No. 19. What is the distance from the center or pupil of one eye to the center or pupil of the other eye?

OUR $1.90 GOLD FILLED SPECTACLES.

For $1.90 we furnish these fine gold filled Riding Bow Spectacles as the equal of Riding Bow Spectacles that are furnished by opticians at $6.00 to $12.00. **10-YEARS' GUARANTEE.** Every pair of our special $1.90 gold filled Riding Bow Spectacles is put out under our binding 10-years' guarantee, and if they wear through, tarnish or in any way change color or give out by reason of defect in material or workmanship within ten years, we will replace or repair them free of charge. The gold filled frame is one of the **highest grade gold filled frames made.** It is genuine gold filled, made of gold filled stock, two plates of heavy fine solid gold over an inner plate of hard composition metal, beautifully polished and finished, neatly adjusted, the highest grade gold filled frames made.

This illustration will give you an idea of the appearance of our special $1.90, 10-year guaranteed, gold filled Riding Bow Spectacles. They are made with broad nose piece; they are fitted with the very finest quality of crystalline lenses, accurately adjusted. The lenses are carefully selected to your eye test and order. We send these glasses out with the understanding that if they are not perfectly satisfactory in every way they can be returned to us at our expense and we will return your money.

No. 20R100 Our special price, per pair.......... $1.90

Riding Bow Spectacles.

The Riding Bow Spectacles, known also as Hook Bow, are to be preferred in all cases where the glasses are to be worn constantly, or nearly so. The shape of the temples prevents the spectacles falling off, and also keeps the lenses more exactly in the proper position all the time.

No. 20R110 Steel Spectacles, riding bow temples, finely tempered, with good quality lenses. Each..35c

No. 20R113 Best Grade Steel Spectacles, the very best riding bow steel spectacle made, nickel plated, finely finished, perfectly tempered, and warranted in every respect. These spectacles are fitted with **the finest quality crystalline lenses**, carefully ground and accurately adjusted. Price, each............72c

No. 20R115 Alumnico Spectacles, riding bow temples, light and well finished, with fine periscopic lenses. Alumnico is a composition metal in weight and color exactly like aluminum. **Warranted not to tarnish.** Price, each.......................... $1.00

No. 20R125 Solid Gold Spectacles, riding bow temples, perfection joints, highly polished and fitted with the finest accurately centered crystalline lenses. Price, 14-karat, $3.30; 10-karat......$2.98

Straight Temple Spectacles.

With Round Eye Wire.

Straight Temple Spectacles are most suitable for those who wear glasses for near work only, and therefore remove them frequently from the eyes.

No. 20R131 Steel Spectacles, straight temples, finely tempered, with good quality lenses. Each..35c

No. 20R135 Best Grade Steel Spectacles, the best straight temple steel spectacle that can be manufactured, full nickel plated, perfectly tempered, elegantly finished, both frame and lenses guaranteed in every way. These spectacles are fitted with the very best quality of **accurately ground crystalline lenses**, carefully adjusted. Price, each...............69c

No. 20R136 Alumnico Spectacles, straight temples, light and well finished, silvery color, warranted not to tarnish, with fine periscopic lenses. Ea..$1.00

No. 20R140 Gold Filled Spectacles, straight temples, finest quality; **warranted for ten years**; with fine crystalline lenses. Price.............$1.90

No. 20R145 Solid Gold Spectacles, straight temple bows, perfection joints, highly polished, heavy weight; fitted with the finest accurately centered crystalline lenses. Price, 14-K..$3.45; 10-K.....$3.20

RIMLESS SPECTACLES.

No. 20R126 Rimless or Skeleton Spectacles with riding bow temples, the latest and most stylish spectacle made. Light and elegant in appearance, and **very popular among people who want the best.** The mounting is the very best grade, 10-karat gold filled, finely finished and equal in wear and appearance to solid gold. Our rimless spectacles are fitted with the very finest crystalline lenses, the very best lenses that can be made, lenses that are accurately adjusted, highly polished and guaranteed in every respect. Every pair in fine morocco case.

Price, each................................$2.20

Cable Riding Bow Spectacles.

In the Cable Riding Bow frames the temples are slightly larger than the regular style, and owing to their peculiar construction are extremely flexible and thus very comfortable to the wearer.

No. 20R150 Alumnico Spectacles, Cable riding bow temples, very best quality, light and durable, of a silvery color, warranted not to tarnish; with fine periscopic lenses. Price......**$1.20**

No. 20R155 Gold Filled Spectacles, Cable riding bow temples, finest quality, warranted for ten years, with fine crystalline lenses. Price......**$2.10**

Bifocal Lenses.

Cut shows appearance of Bifocal Lens. We recommend Bifocal Lenses in cases where spectacles are required for both near and distant vision. **We furnish these lenses in the style known as cemented bifocal lenses,** which are the latest, best and most satisfactory style made. **Any of the spectacles or eyeglasses** in this cataolgue can be furnished with bifocal lenses for **50 cents extra;** for example, spectacle No. 20R136, the regular price of which is **$1.00,** would be **$1.50** with bifocal lenses.

Flexible Guard Eyeglasses.

The Flexible Guard Eyeglasses are generally preferred when glasses are not constantly worn, as they are easily adjusted to the nose.

No. 20R160 Alumnico Eyeglasses, flexible cork lined guards, and oval spring, light and of silvery color, will not tarnish, fitted with finest periscopic lenses. Price......**75c**

No. 20R165 Gold Filled Eyeglasses, flexible cork lined guards and oval spring, warranted for ten years, fitted with finest crystalline lenses. Price......**$1.25**

Offset Guard Eyeglasses.

The Offset Guard Eyeglasses are used exclusively when glasses are worn constantly, as they are specially adapted to remain in a fixed position.

No. 20R170 Alumnico Eyeglasses, offset guards cork or shell lined, round hoop spring, light and of silvery color, warranted not to tarnish, fitted with finest periscopic lenses. Price......**75c**

No. 20R175 Gold Filled Eyeglasses. Offset guards either cork or shell lined, round hoop spring warranted for ten years, fitted with finest crystalline lenses. Price......**$1.25**

Rimless Eyeglasses.

No. 20R177 Rimless or Skeleton Eyeglasses. Best quality 10-karat gold filled mountings, warranted for ten years. Offset guards either cork or shell lined, round hoop spring, and fitted with extra grade accurately centered crystalline lenses, with gold filled mountings, ten years' guarantee. Price......**$1.65**

Colored Spectacles and Eyeglasses.

Colored Lens Spectacles and Eyeglasses are made without magnifying power and therefore do not assist the sight, being intended only to protect the eyes from strong light. They are a very great comfort to those whose eyes are weak, and do much to preserve the sight.

No. 20R210 Colored Spectacles, steel frame, riding bow temples, coquille lenses, common quality. **Smoke or blue.** Price......**20c**

No. 20R212 Colored Spectacles, best quality steel frame, riding bow temples, extra fine quality coquille lenses. Smoke or blue. Price......**45c**

No. 20R223 Colored Eyeglasses, fine quality steel frame, plain guards, first quality coquille lenses. Smoke or blue. Price......**45c**

IF YOU ALLOW OUR EXPERT OPTICIANS TO FIT YOU WITH GLASSES, YOU WILL RECEIVE BETTER SERVICE THAN YOU WOULD GET ELSEWHERE, NOT TO MENTION THE BIG SAVING IN PRICE....

SEE PRECEDING PAGE FOR FULL INSTRUCTIONS.

Scenery or Shooting Spectacles.

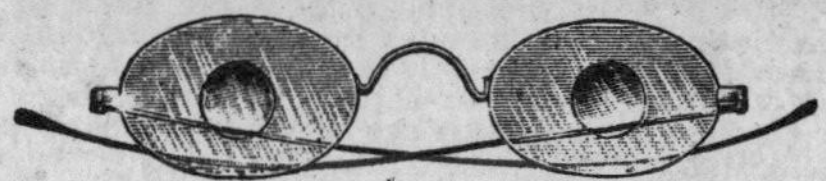

Nos. 20R230 to 20R234.

While these spectacles are commonly known as shooting spectacles they are largely used by tourists in looking at scenery, especially where the light is bright and dazzling or when the ground is covered with snow, which reflects the light and tires the eyes. **The peculiar amber tint of the lenses, not only improves the view but enables one to see more plainly at a distance,** and is very pleasant and soothing to the eye. **The lenses are known as diaphragm lenses,** being sanded or ground in such a manner as to exclude the view except through the clear circle in the center of each lens.

No. 20R230 Shooting Spectacles, steel frames, straight temples, good quality, nickel plated, amber tinted diaphragm lenses. Price......**16c**

No. 20R231 Shooting Spectacles, steel frames, straight temples, best quality, finely tempered with bronze finish. Best amber tinted diaphragm lenses. Price......**36c**

No. 20R232 Shooting Spectacles, steel frames, same as cut, but with **riding bow temples,** fine quality, extra finish with amber tinted diaphragm lenses. Price......**28c**

No. 20R234 Shooting Spectacles, steel frames, straight temples, best quality, finely tempered and extra finish, with best grade smoke tinted diaphragm lenses. Price......**42c**

If by mail, postage extra, each, 5 cents.

Goggles.

The use of Goggles as a protection to the eyes from light, dust, etc., is so common and well known that no comment upon them is necessary.

Nos. 20R240 and 20R241.

No. 20R240 Goggles, ordinary quality, wire gauze with common smoke, blue, green or white glasses. Price......**8c**

No. 20R241 Goggles, good quality, wire gauze, velvet bound edges, with smoke, blue or white glasses. Each pair in cloth bound box. Price......**20c**

No. 20R243 Goggles, steel frame, velvet bound, finely finished, with stiff nose piece and tempered riding bow temples. Extra fine wire gauze and highest grade light smoke lenses. Each pair in fine leather case. Price......**98c**

If by mail, postage extra, each, 5 cents.

Eye Protectors.

These eye protectors, being extremely light and also well ventilated, are very comfortable, and as a protection against excessive light, blinding storms of sleet, snow or rain, floating cinders, mud, dust, flying sparks, the chaff of harvest field and thrashing machine, are unexcelled. They are used by wheelmen, street carmen, railroadmen, stone cutters, quarrymen, millers, harvesters, in fact by all who are in any way exposed to the danger of injuring the eyes.

No. 20R248 Celluloid Eye Protector, well made from the best transparent celluloid, felt bound, in white, blue or green. Price, including case......**16c**

If by mail, postage extra, 2 cents.

No. 20R249 Mica Eye Protector. Made of selected mica, substantially constructed and bound with corrugated felt. This Eye Protector is hinged at the center, thus folding into small space, and is made in either smoke, blue or white glass.

Price, with morocco case......**20c**

If by mail, postage extra, each, 2 cents.

Spectacle and Eyeglass Cases.

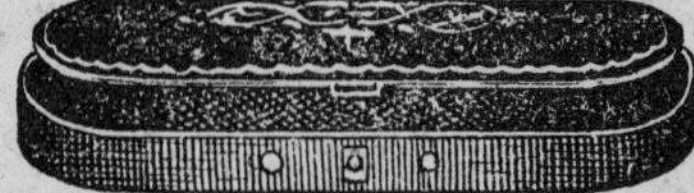

No. 20R255 Papier Mache. With hinged cover and inlaid metal design. For riding bow spectacles. Strong, handsome and durable. Each......**24c**

No. 20R256 Papier Mache. With inlaid metal design, a very strong and handsome case, open end only; for straight temple spectacles. Each......**22c**

EYEGLASS CORDS AND CHAINS.

No. 20R260 Eyeglass Cord, pure silk, light weight, with bead slide. Each......**3c**

No. 20R261 Eyeglass Cord, pure silk, fine quality and extra strong, with bead slide. Each......**5c**

If by mail, postage extra, each, 2 cents.

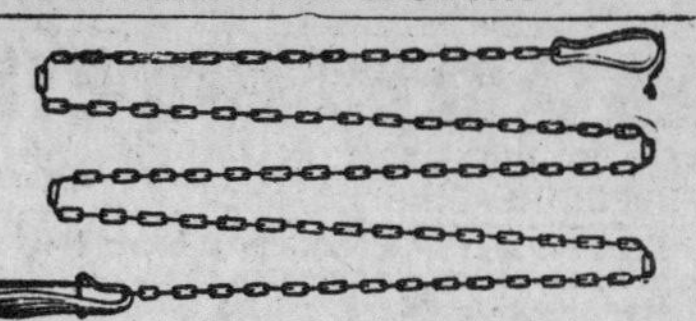

Nos. 20R265 to 20R269.

No. 20R265 Eyeglass Chain, gold plated, with snap and hook. Each......**38c**

No. 20R267 Eyeglass Chain, fine quality, gold filled, fully guaranteed. Each......**63c**

No. 20R269 Eyeglass Chain, extra fine quality, solid gold. Each......**$1.42**

If by mail, postage extra, each, 4 cents.

Nos. 20R273 to 20R277

No. 20R273 Eyeglass Hook, black enameled steel. Each......**7c**

No. 20R275 Eyeglass Hook, fine quality gold filled. Each......**15c**

No. 20R277 Eyeglass Hook, solid gold, extra quality. Each......**62c**

If by mail, postage extra, each, 2 cents.

No. 20R280 Eye Shade, metal rim, with leather bound edges. Each......**10c**

No. 20R281 Eye Shade, metal rim, transparent green celluloid, light and comfortable. Each......**15c**

If by mail, postage extra, each, 4 cents.

READING GLASSES

are very desirable for reading fine print, and as they are strong magnifiers and give a large range of vision they are very restful to the eyes and especially desirable for old people. They are also used for looking at photographs and other pictures, as they bring out the detail and add greatly to the beauty of the picture, the principle being the same as the graphoscope.

Powerful Burning Glasses.

Any of these reading glasses are powerful sun or burning glasses, readily setting fire to light materials such as paper, shavings, dry leaves, etc. The larger the glass the greater its burning power is.

German Reading Glasses.

These glasses, Nos. 20R335 to 20R339 are fitted with first quality lenses, nickel plated frames and black enameled handles.

Nos. 20R335 to 20R339

No. 20R335 German Reading Glass, 2¼ inches in diameter. Price......**24c**

If by mail, postage extra 12 cents.

No. 20R336 German Reading Glass, 2¾ inches in diameter. Price......**38c**

If by mail, postage extra, 14 cents.

No. 20R337 German Reading Glass, 3¼ inches in diameter. Price......**65c**

If by mail, postage extra, 18 cents.

No. 20R338 German Reading Glass, 4 inches in diameter. Price......**78c**

If by mail, postage extra, 20 cents.

No. 20R339 German Reading Glass, 5 inches in diameter. Price......**$1.47**

If by mail, postage extra, 25 cents.

Best Grade Reading Glasses.

Nos. 20R345 to 20R349

These glasses, Nos. 20R345 to 20R349, are the highest grade manufactured, with strongly made nickel plated frames, and wood handles, finished in black enamel, high magnifying power. Better or more powerful glasses than these are not manufactured.

No. 20R345 Reading Glass, 2 inches in diameter Price......**35c**

If by mail, postage extra, 12c.

No. 20R346 Reading Glass, 2¼ inches in diameter. Price......**48c**

If by mail, postage extra, 14c.

No. 20R347 Reading Glass, 3 inches in diameter. Price......**63c**

If by mail, postage extra, 17c.

No. 20R348 Reading Glass, 4 inches in diameter. Price......**$1.24**

If by mail, postage extra, 20c.

No. 20R349 Reading Glass, 5 inches in diameter. Price......**$1.76**

If by mail, postage extra, 25 cents.

Pearl Handle Reading Glass.

No. 20R350 The handle of this beautiful Reading Glass is made of brilliant iridescent oriental pearl, the rim is finely gold plated and the lens is best grade manufactured. Diameter, 3½ inches. The handsome appearance and fine quality make it especially suitable for a birthday or Christmas gift. Price......**$2.58**

If by mail, postage extra, 20 cents.

$27.85 BUYS OUR COMPLETE OPTICIANS' OUTFIT, A BIG MONEY MAKER.

WE HAVE RECEIVED IN THE PAST SUCH A LARGE NUMBER OF ORDERS from our customers, individuals, dealers and those about to embark in the optical business, for different items from this department—lenses, test charts, eyeglass frames and other sundries that go to make up an opticians' stock or regular outfit—that we have decided to make up for the convenience of our customers a complete outfit that would include everything necessary for this work.

AS A RESULT OF MUCH CARE IN SELECTION, with a view of providing everything that is necessary for the business, without articles that would entail unnecessary expense, including all the items that professional opticians use, and that should be used to fit eyes successfully, we have gotten up this very complete opticians' outfit, and considering the quality, are able to offer it at a surprisingly low price.

BY MAKING UP THESE OUTFITS, in large quantities, buying the individual items each from the largest manufacturer in that particular line, placing our order for the season's output at one time, we secure the lowest manufacturing price, and with every outfit exactly alike, figuring the total cost of the items that go to make up 5,000 complete outfits, adding our one small percentage of profit on this total volume of business, which makes the profit on each single outfit exceedingly small, so little as to be almost imperceptible, we are able to name the astonishingly low price of $27.85.

$27.85 IS OUR PRICE FOR THE COMPLETE OUTFIT, exactly as illustrated and described, including everything necessary for testing the eyes and fitting spectacles correctly, including even a special text book, a book of instructions, a complete opticians' guide which gives full information, and with it anyone will be able to carry on the work successfully. If you bought this outfit at regular retail prices, or if each item were bought separately, it would cost you more than double our price.

EVERY ITEM INCLUDED in this outfit is strictly high grade, every article is put out under our binding guarantee for quality, we guarantee the outfit the greatest value ever offered in this line, and if you order one of these outfits and do not find it entirely satisfactory, exactly as we represented it to be, or if you find that it does not include everything necessary to start this business and carry it on successfully, you may return the outfit to us and we will immediately return your money.

No. 20R375
ORDER BY NUMBER

No other business offers the opportunity for realizing as large profits on so small an investment.

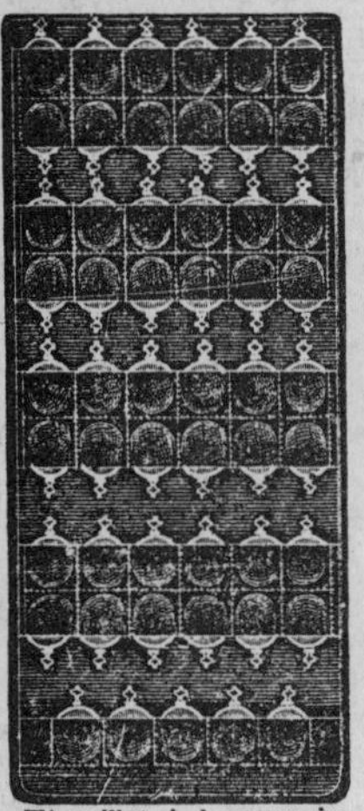
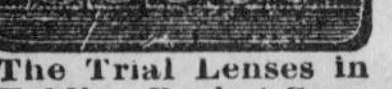
The Trial Lenses in Folding Pocket Case.

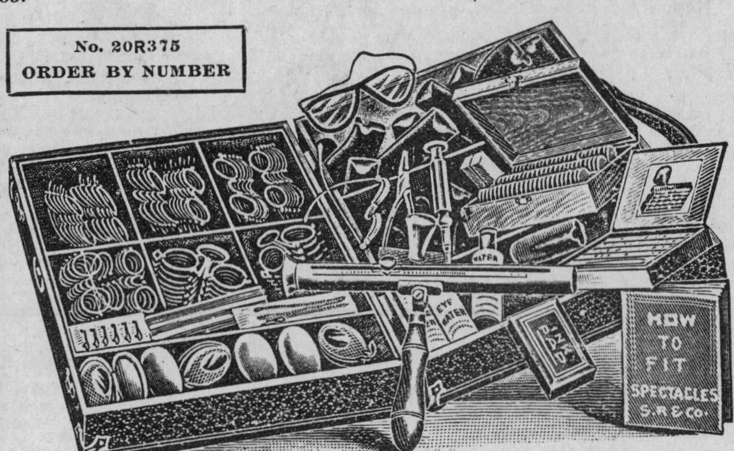

The Complete Outfit.

Carrying Case Closed.

LARGE PROFITS IN SELLING SPECTACLES.

IT IS A WELL KNOWN FACT that opticians make very large profits and it is perfectly right that they should do so, as the customer who buys a pair of spectacles not only pays for the goods that he actually receives, but he also pays for the labor and skill required in fitting the spectacles.

NO PREVIOUS EXPERIENCE REQUIRED.

WITH OUR OUTFIT and with the special information we furnish, spectacle fitting becomes a simple and easy matter. We include with our **Big Opticians' Outfit** a complete book of instructions, giving **special inside information** on the testing of eyes and the fitting of spectacles. With our outfit and our special book of instructions the correct fitting of spectacles is an easy business to learn. No long and difficult study is required, everything is perfectly simple and easy. Within forty-eight hours after receiving one of these outfits you will know more about the spectacle business than your local optician or jeweler, and **you can start right into a pleasant and profitable profession.**

OUR OPTICIANS' OUTFIT

CONTAINS EVERTHING NECESSARY for starting in the spectacle business, all the apparatus for testing eyes, including a set of **extra quality trial lenses** contained in a fine folding pocket case, a high grade optometer for testing the eyes, an assortment of test types and charts. In addition to the apparatus for testing the eyes, we include **a complete line of spectacle goods,** such as spectacle frames, eyeglass frames, lenses, goggles, eye protectors, silk cords, eyeglass hooks, spectacle cases, etc. In short, **everything you will need.** The actual retail value of the stock included with this outfit **is several times the price we ask for the complete outfit.**

THE OPTICAL BUSINESS IS PLEASANT because you are independent. You are not subject to any individual, company, corporation or community. You have no boss or bosses; you conduct the business to suit yourself. You travel in good style, stop in good hotels. Everywhere you are respected and looked up to by the communities you visit, and are placed in an assured position, commercially and socially, with the best people with whom you come in contact.

WHY WE ARE ABLE TO SELL THIS BIG OUTFIT FOR $27.85.

WE BUY EACH AND EVERY ONE of the various items direct from the manufacturers under special contracts in immense quantities, we assemble and pack the outfits ourselves, and have thus reduced the cost to the lowest possible figure. Moreover, we do not depend on the actual sale of these outfits for our profit, as we feel certain that after you have once started into the spectacle business you will build up a big trade and be constantly in the market for more spectacle frames, lenses and other optical goods, so that our first sale will be but a small portion of the business that we will do with you in the near future.

OUR OPTICIANS' OUTFIT is put up in a fine black seal grain carrying case, with nickel trimmings. This case is provided with lock and key in addition to two snap locks. It is divided into fourteen separate compartments, thus allowing space for all the various items of the outfit.

THIS CARRYING CASE presents an exceedingly neat and attractive appearance, and this neat, attractive appearance will tend to make a very favorable impression upon the customers with whom you come in contact.

FOR $27.85 WE OFFER YOU THE LARGEST THE MOST COMPLETE AND THE BEST OPTICIANS' OUTFIT ON THE MARKET.

The Equal of Outfits Sold by Others at from $60.00 to $75.00.

LIST OF ARTICLES COMPRISING OUR OPTICIANS' OUTFIT:

48 EXTRA QUALITY TRIAL LENSES, for testing. Mounted in nickel plated and gold plated steel rims.
1 Blank Disc. 1 Blue Glass.
1 Stenopaic Slit. 1 Smoked Glass.
1 Ground Glass.
1 Fine Quality Folding Pocket Case; to contain the trial lenses, blank disc, stenopaic slit, blue glass, smoke glass and ground glass.
1 Fine Nickel Plated Trial Frame, for use while testing the eyes.
1 **IMPROVED PATENT TUBULAR OPTOMETER, for testing the eye and measuring defects of sight.**
2 Test Charts, with type for both near and distant vision.
1 Opticians' Screwdriver.
1 Opticians' Pliers.
½ dozen Alumnico Eyeglass Frames, with cork lined flexible guards.
½ dozen Roman Alloy Eyeglass Frames (look like solid gold), with flexible guards, cork lined.
1 dozen Steel Eyeglass Frames, with cork lined flexible guards.
½ dozen Alumnico Spectacle Frames, with straight temples.
1 dozen Steel Spectacle Frames, with straight temples.
½ dozen Alumnico Spectacle Frames, with riding bow temples.
½ dozen Roman Alloy Spectacle Frames (look like solid gold), with riding bow temples.
½ dozen Colored Spectacles, with smoke and blue coquille lenses, assorted.
½ dozen Shooting Spectacles, with amber tinted diaphragm lenses.
½ dozen Wire Gauze Goggles, with smoke, clear and green lenses assorted.
72 **CRYSTALLINE SPECTACLE LENSES, extra fine quality, with polished edges, assorted numbers, including every focus needed, all packed in polished hardwood lens box.**
1 Patent Celluloid Eye Shield.
½ dozen Silk Eyeglass Cords.
½ dozen Black Enamel Eyeglass Hooks.
1 Gold Plated Eyeglass Chain.
2 dozen fine Leather Spectacle Cases.
2 dozen fine Leather Eyeglass Cases.
3 **BOTTLES DR. WALTER'S FAMOUS EYE WATER, a positive remedy for all cases of weak or inflamed eyes.**
1 Copy **HOW TO FIT SPECTACLES. A complete opticians' guide, giving full information regarding the testing of eyes and the proper adjusting of spectacles, also a special confidential wholesale price list of spectacle frames, lenses and other optical goods that you will need in this business.**

No. 20R375 Our Complete Opticians' Outfit, including everything mentioned above, and just as shown in our three illustrations. Price........ **$27.85**

Our 75-Cent Dust Protector.

No. 20R400 Against dust it **is the greatest protector ever made.** For threshers, grain men, millers, farmers and everyone whose duties call him into dusty places. It's worth a **thousand times its cost** as a protection to the lungs, to the general health and comfort. **Thousands of men are saved from consumption** by the use of this protector. It **protects the nose and mouth** from the intrusion of dust which is so injurious to the head and lungs. **No miller, grain buyer, thresher or farmer is safe without one.** They afford perfect protection with perfect ventilation. **Made of fine metal,** handsomely nickel plated, bound with chamois skin, adjustable to anyone by strong elastic band, absolutely indestructible and worth a **thousand times the trifling cost** as a safeguard to health. Each protector comes packed in a neat box with full instructions for use. Our special price each....................75c
If by mail, postage extra, each, 5 cents.

Conversation Tubes.

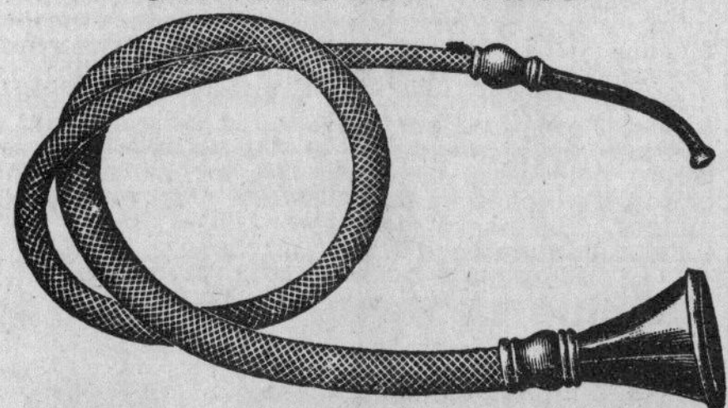

These Tubes are adapted to more obstinate cases of deafness, are very finely constructed throughout, lined with a peculiar spiral wire, which, although admitting of great flexibility, keeps the tube fully distended in any position.

No. 20R410 Conversation Tube, 3 feet in length, fine quality flexible mohair, hard rubber ends. Price.... (If by mail, postage extra, 8c)..$1.40

No. 20R412 Conversation Tube, highest grade, flexible mohair, tapered tube, 3 feet in length, hard rubber mountings. Suitable for the most obstinate cases of deafness. Price..............$1.65
If by mail, postage extra, 15 cents.

No. 20R414 Conversation Tube. Same size and style as No. 20R412 but covered with best grade black silk. Price..............................$1.89
If by mail, postage extra, 15 cents.

Hearing Horns.

These horns are exactly the same as those advertised by many dealers at prices ranging from $8.00 to $15.00 each. These London Hearing Horns are constructed of light metal upon an entirely new principle. They may be carried in the pocket and when in use are easily concealed in the hand. **They are designed for the use of those who are only moderately deaf** and enable one to hear not only an ordinary conversation but **sounds at a distance** as well, making them suitable for use anywhere—at home, in church, or public entertainments.

Made in Two Sizes, with Black Oxidized Finish.

No. 20R420 London Hearing Horn, medium size, 2½ inches in length. Price, each..............$1.29
If by mail, postage extra, 5 cents.

No. 20R421 London Hearing Horn, large size, 4 inches in length. Price, each.....................$1.35
If by mail, postage extra, 8 cents.

Your money will be promptly refunded if the horn does not give entire satisfaction.

Miss Greene Hearing Horn.

No. 20R425 This is a new device, being an improvement in shape over all other Tin Trumpets, and is more easily carried. The sound receiving end is flat oval shape, 5½ inches in diameter by 1½ inches in depth. Its peculiar formation is especially adapted to gather in sounds and convey them audibly and distinctly to the ear; is one of the best arrangements for conversation or public speaking; can be held to the ear without raising the hand; made of metal, in two pieces, japanned black.
Price..$1.32

OPERA GLASSES.

There is probably no other branch of optical goods on which we are able to save our customers as much money as in the line of opera glasses. Opera glasses are sold by retail dealers everywhere at enormous profits compared to the actual manufacturing and importation cost of the goods. There is also no other line in which poor quality can be so easily disguised beneath a handsome appearance as in optical goods of every description. **OUR OPERA GLASSES ARE MADE FOR US UNDER CONTRACT AND IMPORTED DIRECT FROM THE VERY BEST PARIS MAKERS, whose names alone guarantee the quality, and selling them at our usual small percentage above the actual manufacturing cost, we are enabled to make such low prices as no dealer can possibly compete with. Every opera glass we catalogue is put out under our binding guarantee for quality, perfect material, perfect workmanship, better lenses, higher definition and better finish in every way than opera glasses sold by others at 50 per cent more money.**

Our $1.75 Opera Glass.

No. 20R450 This is a good practical glass, made with a good quality achromatic lenses, 1⅛ inches in diameter; covered with black morocco leather; draw tubes and trimmings are black. It is an excellent instrument for so little money, an opera glass that will compare favorably with those usually offered at $3.50 and $4.00. Comes complete with handsome silk lined black morocco leather case.
Price..$1.75
If by mail, postage extra, 16 cents.

A Genuine LeMaire Opera Glass, Only $4.00.

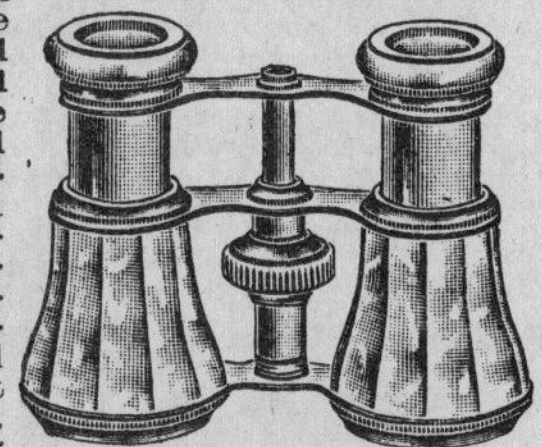

No. 20R455 We offer the genuine LeMaire Opera Glass, perhaps the very best make on the market, for only $4.00, the lowest price ever made on a genuine LeMaire instrument. This opera glass is covered with fine black morocco leather; it has the best black enameled tubes and trimmings and the finest achromatic lenses, 1⅝ inches in diameter. It is perfect in operation, will not work loose or get out of adjustment easily. The name LeMaire is a guarantee for quality, and if you desire a strictly high grade glass, **where every cent of the cost is put into the lenses and substantial make, without going into fancy finish or fancy trimmings, this is the glass to buy.** By importing these goods direct from the maker in Paris we are able to offer it complete in a fine morocco leather, silk lined case for only..........................$4.00
If by mail, postage extra, 18 cents.

Our Best Opera Glass, $6.85.

No. 20R460 We offer this beautiful Pearl and Gold Opera Glass as the equal of any pearl opera glass sold, regardless of price. A beautiful instrument, optically perfect, of elegant design, perfect workmanship and fitted with the very best achromatic lenses. All metal parts, draw tubes and trimmings are heavily gold plated, guaranteed not to tarnish. The body is covered with the finest Oriental and iridescent pearl. Has pearl tops and pearl focusing screw. It is a size that is suitable for either lady or gentleman, and is the most popular size and style of opera glass made. **We offer this handsome, gold and pearl, finest achromatic lens opera glass as the equal of those sold in the large jewelry stores in this and other metropolitan cities at double the price.** It is such a glass as will not be found in the smaller jewelry stores throughout the country at any price. It comes complete with a handsome silk lined genuine morocco leather carrying case, with a patent lock clasp.
Our price.......................................$6.85
If by mail, postage extra, 18 cents.

Our $4.29 Pearl Opera Glass.

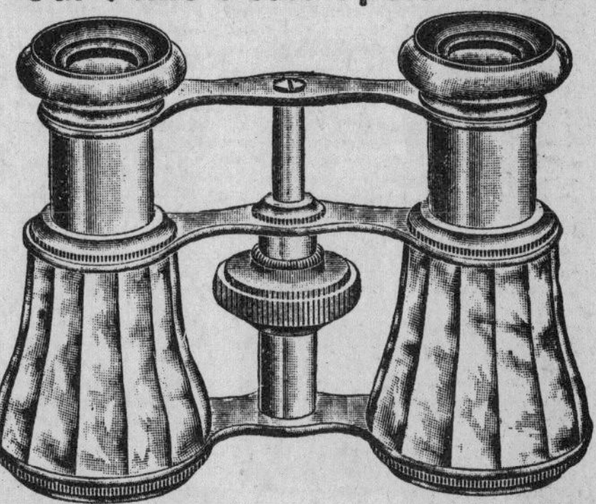

No. 20R465 This is the greatest value we are able to offer in the line of a strictly high grade pearl opera glass. This glass is fitted with the finest achromatic lenses, 1⅛ inches in diameter. It is a strictly high grade instrument, and in material and trimming is equal to glasses sold at two and three times the price. Handsomely covered with beautiful Oriental pearl. The tubes and trimmings are handsomely gold plated, warranted to keep its luster. It makes an ideal gift, and one that will be greatly appreciated by the recipient. Comes complete in a handsome silk lined morocco leather carrying case, and we offer it at a price slightly above the actual importing cost. Price only.....................$4.29
If by mail, postage extra, each, 18 cents.

Our $7.25 Genuine Jena Aluminum Opera Glass.

The newest production in the line of opera glasses, the highest grade glass we handle.

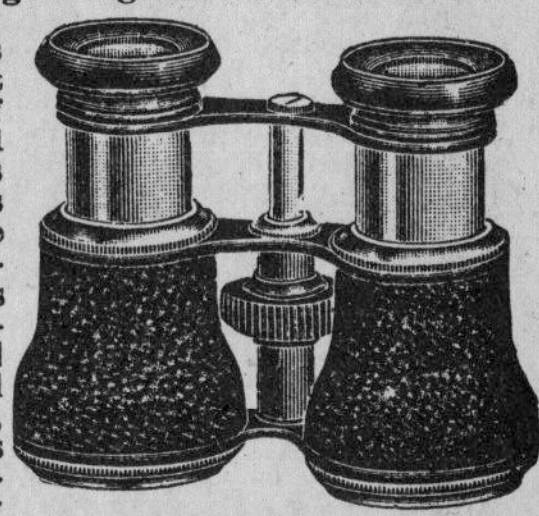

No. 20R470 Aluminum Opera Glasses have come into great favor on account of their lightness and durability. This genuine Jena glass is the highest grade aluminum instrument. The lenses are 1¼ inches in diameter, are ground from the celebrated Jena special glass, the finest glass known for optical instruments. Every genuine Jena glass is stamped on the cross bar "The Jena Special." All metal parts are made of aluminum, the lightest metal known, takes a beautiful finish and is highly polished, has the appearance of silver and is extremely durable. The tops of the glasses and the cross bars are finished in black enamel. The body is covered with fine black morocco leather. The draw tubes and trimmings are finished in the natural highly polished silvery color of the aluminum. **This is the most practical opera glass to buy.** It is large size, very powerful large lenses, large eye pieces, best construction, best possible workmanship throughout. While this glass is not as showy as the fancy pearl finished glasses, yet the silvery aluminum finish makes a handsome contrast to the black morocco and black enamel, and really forms a beautiful instrument. Comes complete with fine silk lined morocco leather carrying case, with patent lock spring. Price..........................$7.25
If by mail, postage extra, each, 17 cents.

Our $8.90 Enameled Opera Glass, with Lorgnette Handle.

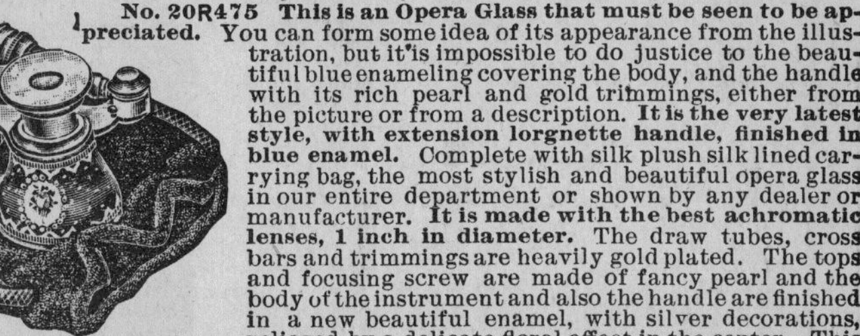

$8.90

No. 20R475 This is an Opera Glass that must be seen to be appreciated. You can form some idea of its appearance from the illustration, but it's impossible to do justice to the beautiful blue enameling covering the body, and the handle with its rich pearl and gold trimmings, either from the picture or from a description. **It is the very latest style, with extension lorgnette handle, finished in blue enamel.** Complete with silk plush silk lined carrying bag, the most stylish and beautiful opera glass in our entire department or shown by any dealer or manufacturer. **It is made with the best achromatic lenses, 1 inch in diameter.** The draw tubes, cross bars and trimmings are heavily gold plated. The tops and focusing screw are made of fancy pearl and the body of the instrument and also the handle are finished in a new beautiful enamel, with silver decorations, relieved by a delicate floral effect in the center. This floral effect consists of a delicate design of flowers in natural colors enclosed within a border of light blue jewels, giving the most exquisite effect to the entire instrument. The extension handle is 8 inches long when extended, 4 inches long when closed. When not in use it folds conveniently behind the glasses. **Each glass complete in a silk plush, silk lined bag, with silk cords.** As a gift of any sort for a sister, wife, mother or sweetheart, nothing will compare at the price, nothing makes the handsome appearance or carries the intrinsic value, nothing would be more highly appreciated than a pair of these new, stylish, enameled opera glasses. No. 20R475 Our price, complete as illustrated and described..................$8.90

FIELD GLASSES.

We have this season made contracts with the best known and most famous makers of field glasses in Paris and Germany to furnish us with the largest quantity of high grade field glasses ever purchased by any one house. We succeeded in inducing the manufacturers to figure the cost to us on a basis of the actual cost of material and labor. To this price, figured on actual shop cost, we add simply our one small percentage of profit, and as a result we offer in our cheapest field glass at $3.95, an instrument for which you would pay the ordinary optician from $8.00 to $10.00. In our highest grade field glasses such as the famous LeMaire or our new Jena Special Glass, we offer for only $11.95 and $12.95 instruments which have heretofore been sold at from $20.00 to $35.00. Even our cheapest field glass is fitted with achromatic lenses, and well made. We do not carry in stock at all nor offer for sale the cheap non-achromatic glasses advertised by many dealers; such instruments are worthless and dear at any price. Following the usual custom we indicate the size of our fiel l glasses by giving the diameter of the object glasses, that is the large lenses, in lignes, the French unit of measurement for optical instruments.

Our $3.95 Delmar Field Glass.

No. 20R500 For $3.95 we furnish this Delmar Field Glass fitted with genuine achromatic lenses, bars, draw tubes and trimmings finished in black and body covered in black morocco leather. We offer this Delmar Field Glass as the equal of field glasses sold by retail dealers at prices ranging from $8.00 to $10.00. **The Delmar Field Glass** measures 6 inches high when closed, and 7¼ inches when extended. The object glasses are 24 lignes in diameter and the weight is 17 ounces. **Magnifying power four times.**

Price, complete with leather case and strap. **$3.95**

If by mail, postage extra, 40 cents.

$6.95 Buys a $15.00 Field Glass.

No. 20R510 This Field Glass is provided with first quality achromatic lenses, carefully fitted, the draw tubes are finished in dead black and the trimmings are in bright black enamel and nickel plate. Although possessing no higher magnifying power than the Delmar Field Glass, the lenses are of better quality, thus giving finer definition and greater clearness. Workmanship and materials throughout are first class. **Our $6.95 Field Glass** measures 5¾ inches high when closed, 7¼ inches when extended. The diameter of the object glasses is 24 lignes, the magnifying power is five times and the weight is 22 ounces. Price, complete with leather case and strap.......... ....**$6.95**

If by mail, postage extra, 42 cents.

Jointed Bar Field Glass for $7.75.

No. 20R515 The distinctive feature of this field glass is the jointed cross bars, permitting the instrument to be adjusted so that the barrels will be exactly the same distance apart as the eyes of the user. Our jointed bar field glass is provided **with ten superior achromatic lenses,** carefully ground and accurately fitted. The magnifying power is five times, with extra fine definition. This field glass measures 5¼ inches high when closed and 6½ inches when extended. Diameter of object glasses, 21 lignes. Weight, 21 ounces. **If by mail, postage extra, 42c.**

Price, complete, with case and strap..........**$7.75**

High Grade Tourist's Field Glass for $6.90.

No. 20R525 This is an exceptionally fine field glass, designed especially for tourists or those who expect to carry a field glass to a considerable extent, its small size and light weight making it very desirable. Our high grade tourist's field glass is fitted with the **best achromatic lenses,** very carefully ground, accurately fitted and adjusted. The finish throughout is extra fine, the trimmings, cross bars and draw tubes are the best quality black enamel, the covering is the best grade of fine morocco leather, and the workmanship throughout is the best. **The extra high grade lenses of our Tourist Field Glass are noted for their definition and clearness; the magnifying power is four times.** Our Tourist Field Glass measures only 4 inches high when closed, and 5¾ inches when extended, the draw tubes being extra long in proportion to the size of the instrument. The weight is 16 ounces, and the object glasses are 19 lignes in diameter. Price, complete with case and strap...**$6.90**

If by mail, postage extra, 30 cents.

Exceptional Value at $9.90.

No. 20R530 We offer our $9.90 Field Glass as the equal of any $25.00 field glass on the market, a strictly high grade, serviceable field glass that we know will give perfect satisfaction. Our $9.90 field glass is made expressly for us under contract by one of the best field glass makers in Paris; it is made of the very best materials throughout and every one is sold under a binding guarantee. The lenses used in our $9.90 field glass are the finest quality specially ground achromatic, accurately adjusted, of high magnifying power and fine definition. The finish throughout is perfect, the trimmings, cross bars and tops in black enamel, the draw tubes oxidized in black, and the covering the best grade of morocco leather. **Our $9.90 Field Glass is substantially constructed,** the workmanship is the best, it is a glass that will stand rough handling, a glass that is built for practical purposes and it is a glass that we can absolutely guarantee to give satisfaction. Our **$9.90** field glass measures 5⅛ inches high when closed, 6¾ inches when extended. The weight is 25 ounces. The magnifying power is five times.

Price, complete with case and strap..........**$9.90**

If by mail, postage extra, 47 cents.

Genuine LeMaire Field Glass for $11.95.

No. 20R535 This Genuine LeMaire Field Glass, made in the famous LeMaire Optical Works, Paris, is offered by us at the heretofore unheard of price of $11.95, actually less than the net wholesale cost to the ordinary dealer in optical goods. The name LeMaire on a field glass is universally recognized as a guarantee of good quality. The workmanship on our LeMaire Field Glass is the best, only the finest materials are used, and the construction is optically perfect. All metal parts are finished in fine bright black enamel, and the covering, fitted with the utmost care without seam or visible joint, is the best morocco leather. **Only the finest high power achromatic lenses are used in the LeMaire Field Glass,** lenses that are noted for their clearness and fine definition. The magnifying power is six times. The dimensions are: 5 inches high when closed, 6¼ inches when extended. Weight, 28 ounces. The object glasses are 26 lignes in diameter. **Understand, our special $11.95 price is for the genuine LeMaire Field Glass, the large size, with 26 ligne object glasses,** exactly the same as sold at retail for $25.00 to $30.00.

Price, complete with case and strap.........**$11.95**

If by mail, postage extra, 46 cents.

Only $12.95 for Our Highest Grade Genuine Jena Special Field Glass.

No. 20R560 This large illustration, engraved by our artist direct from a photograph, will give you an idea of the appearance of our JENA SPECIAL FIELD GLASS. The lenses of this field glass are ground from the famous Jena Special optical glass, made in the Jena glass factory in Germany. The sole object of this remarkable factory is the production of new and special kinds of glass for optical purposes. One of their latest productions is a glass especially suited to the requirements of field glass lenses.

It is from **this special new glass,** this latest result of the experiments and investigations of the most skilled and scientific glass makers of Europe, that the lenses for our Jena Special Field Glasses are ground. They are ground by the most skilled lens grinders, they are fitted with the utmost care, and they are accurately adjusted. **These lenses combine, to a degree never before attained, the highest power with the most marvelous definition and clearness.**

We offer the Jena Special Field Glass not merely as the equal of glasses sold by other dealers at several times our price, but we offer it **as absolutely the best field glass that can be obtained at any price.** We sell this glass under a positive guarantee, and if you do not find it superior to any field glass to which you may compare it, you may return it at our expense and we will refund your money.

Bear in mind that our special $12.95 price is for the large size Jena Special Field Glass with lenses 26 lignes in diameter. This Field Glass measures 6 inches high when closed and 7⅝ inches when extended, weighs 33 ounces, and the magnifying power is seven times. The draw tubes, cross bars, tops and trimmings are all finished in fine black enamel and the covering is the best grade of morocco leather.

Price, complete with fine case and strap....**$12.95**

No. 20R561 OUR JENA SPECIAL ALUMINUM FIELD GLASS. Exactly the same as our No. 20R560, **except that all metal parts are made of aluminum,** thus reducing the weight and adding to its handsome appearance. The highly polished draw tubes are finished in the natural silvery color of aluminum, all trimmings are finished in black and the covering is morocco leather. Weight, only 18 ounces.

Price, complete with case and strap........**$16.90**

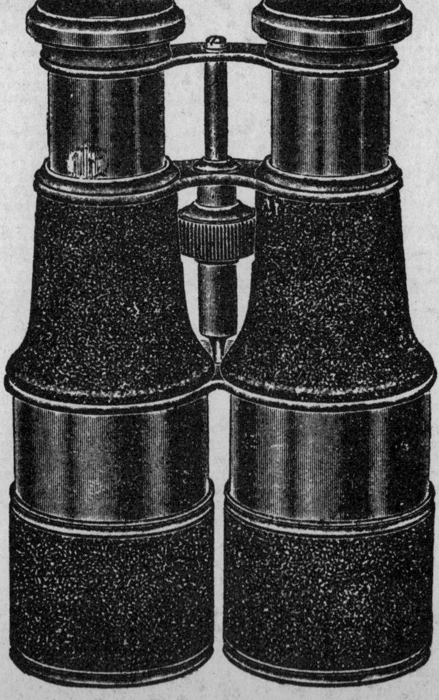

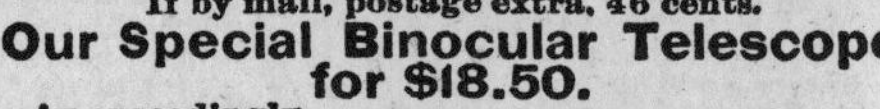

Our Special Binocular Telescope for $18.50.

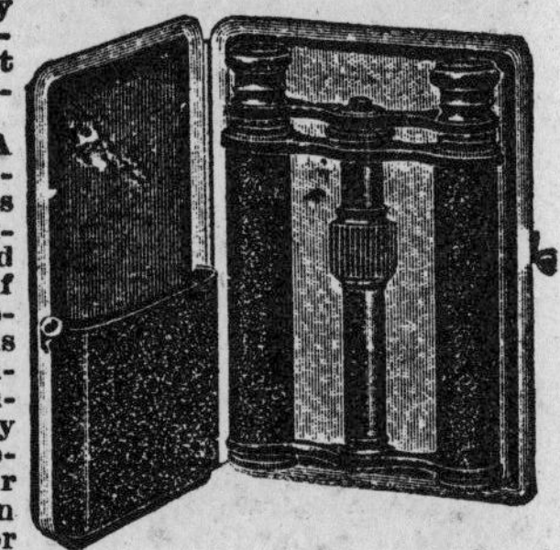

An exceedingly small and compact instrument of high magnifying power.

No. 20R565 A special arrangement made this season with Maxim, the noted Paris maker of Binocular Telescopes, enables us to offer this superb little instrument for only $18.50. Our special Binocular Telescope is an ideal glass for tourists, farmers, hunters, ranchmen, stockmen or anyone requiring a powerful instrument which at the same time **is small in size, light and compact. Our special Binocular Telescope weighs only nine ounces and is so compact that it may be carried in the coat pocket as easily as a pocketbook, yet has a magnifying power of nine times, or one-half again as high a power as the best field glasses.** Our illustration shows the glass in the fine silk lined morocco leather pocket case, which is included without extra charge. **When closed our Special Binocular Telescope measures only 4¼ inches high, the distance from side to side is only 3½ inches and the barrels are only ¾ of an inch in diameter. The length when extended for use is 6¾ inches.** The lenses with which our Special Binocular Telescope is fitted are the best quality achromatic, accurately fitted and adjusted. The magnifying power is nine times and the definition is exceptionally fine. Price complete with morocco pocket case just as shown in the cut, **$18.50**

If by mail, postage extra, 20 cents.

SPY GLASSES AND TELESCOPES.

THE SPY GLASSES AND TELESCOPES **which we handle are intended for practical purposes, are made with fine achromatic lenses, well finished and accurately fitted. Every spy glass or telescope described on this page is guaranteed to be a perfect instrument,** the best of its kind, and if not found exactly as represented and perfectly satisfactory in every respect, may be returned to us at our expense and money will be refunded. Our high grade spy glasses and telescopes, **all made with fine achromatic lenses, with brass bodies and brass draw tubes,** should not be compared with the cheap instruments advertised by some dealers, or with the trashy goods used as premiums, etc. These instruments are manufactured expressly for us by the leading manufacturers in Paris, every one is carefully tested and examined by our expert optician before shipping, and we absolutely guarantee every spy glass or telescope which we sell. We indicate the sizes of these telescopes by giving the diameter of the front lens or object glass in lignes (the French unit of measurement). Eleven lignes are equal to about one inch.

THE VALUE OF A SPY GLASS **or telescope is dependent upon the actual magnifying power, and also upon the quality of the lenses.** It is the quality of the lenses that determines the definition—that is, the power to clearly distinguish details. So important is the quality known as definition, that an instrument with extra high grade lenses may be even more **effective** than another instrument of actually greater magnifying power, but poorer lenses. For example: Our Bardou Rifle Range Telescope, although magnifying only 33 times, is a more effective telescope than an ordinary instrument having a magnifying power of 40 or 50 times. Our telescopes described under Nos. 20R600 to 20R603 inclusive, are fitted with first quality achromatic lenses; our Nos. 20R615, 20R640, and 20R650 to 20R656, are fitted with extra quality achromatic lenses, and the Bardou Rifle Range Telescope has absolutely the best lenses it is possible to manufacture.

GENUINE

BARDOU & SON

RIFLE RANGE TELESCOPE

FOR

$16.50

No. 20R675 The Bardou Rifle Range Telescope represents the highest degree of perfection attained in telescope making. The firm of Bardou & Son, Paris, enjoy the reputation of producing the finest telescopes in the world, and this instrument was especially designed by Bardou & Son for the French government, which desired an extra good glass for military purposes. Both ends of the Bardou Rifle Range Telescope are protected by leather caps, which at the same time afford a means of attaching the shoulder strap for convenience in carrying; the barrels are finished in dead black, a great improvement over the usual highly burnished brass draws, which soon tarnish. The body of the Bardou Rifle Range Telescope is covered with the best grade smooth horsehide leather, with black oxidized draw tubes and trimmings, fine quality horsehide leather caps for each end, and shoulder strap. The Bardou Rifle Range Telescope is fitted with absolutely the best achromatic lenses made, giving great clearness and fine definition.

We guarantee the Bardou Rifle Range Telescope to show a bullet mark at a distance of half a mile, in clear atmosphere. The diameter of the object glass is 22 lignes, the length when closed is 11 inches, when extended 36 inches. **The power is 33 times.**
Price, complete **$16.50**
If by mail, postage extra, 60 cents.

No. 20R676 Astronomical Eye Piece for Bardou Rifle Range Telescope, increasing the power to 50 diameters, thus making it an extra fine instrument for observing the sun, moon and stars. Price..**$3.00**
If by mail, postage extra, 10 cents.

Delmar Achromatic Spy Glasses.

The Delmar Spy Glasses (made in four sizes) are fitted with first quality achromatic lenses, carefully and accurately fitted. They are provided with a slide cover to protect the smaller lens or eye piece, and a brass cap to protect the front lens or object glass. The draw tubes are made from the best quality brass tubing highly burnished, fitted and adjusted with the utmost care. All trimmings are of lacquered brass and the bodies are covered with fine black morocco leather. Every Delmar Telescope is made in four sections, thus closing to about one-third its total length, for convenience in carrying, and we include with each one a good leatherized linen case.

The Delmar Spy Glass, partly extended.

No. 20R600 Delmar Spy Glass, diameter 10 lignes; length closed 4½ inches; extended 13 inches; magnifying power 10 times. Price..............(**If by mail, postage extra, 10 cents**)................ **$1.45**

No. 20R601 Delmar Spy Glass, diameter 12 lignes; length closed 5 inches; extended 14 inches; magnifying power 12 times. Price..............(**If by mail, postage extra, 12 cents**)................ **$1.65**

No. 20R602 Delmar Spy Glass, diameter 14 lignes; length closed 6¼ inches; extended 16¼ inches; magnifying power 16 times. Price ....(**If by mail, postage extra, 16 cents**)................ **$2.20**

No. 20R603 Delmar Spy Glass, diameter 16 lignes; length closed 8 inches; extended 22 inches; magnifying power 20 times. Price..............(**If by mail, postage extra, 20 cents**)................ **$3.25**

Our Pocket Spy Glass.

No. 20R615 The special feature of this Spy Glass is the extra quality lenses and the rounded, nickel plated caps fitted to each end. These caps not only enhance the appearance of the instrument, but make it **dust proof,** thus protecting the lenses and making it very convenient to carry in the pocket. Our Pocket Spy Glass is fitted with **extra quality** achromatic lenses, the draw tubes are of burnished brass, caps nickel plated, and the body finely covered with the best morocco leather. **Extra fine workmanship and finish throughout.** Length when closed, 6¾ inches; when extended, 16¾ inches; magnifying power, 20 times. Price..............................(**If by mail, postage extra, 16 cents**)................ **$2.90**

Telescopes with Sunshade.

Partly Extended.

These Telescopes are made by the same maker who furnishes us with the Delmar Spy Glasses and the workmanship and quality throughout is practically the same as in the Delmar instruments, but they are of larger size and are provided with an additional feature known as a sun shade. This consists of a lacquered brass sleeve, which can be extended forward in such a manner as to shade the object glass from the direct rays of sunlight. These instruments are fitted with first quality achromatic lenses, burnished brass draw tubes, lacquered brass trimmings, morocco leather covering, carefully and accurately made and guaranteed throughout.

No. 20R625 Sun Shade Telescope, diameter 18 lignes; length, closed, 10 inches; extended, 30 inches; magnifying power 25 times. Price..............(**If by mail, postage extra, 25 cents**)................ **$4.25**

No. 20R626 Sun Shade Telescope, diameter, 22 lignes; length, closed, 10½ inches; extended, 37 inches; magnifying power 30 times. Price..............(**If by mail, postage extra, 45 cents**)................ **$6.90**

Our Black Beauty Telescope.

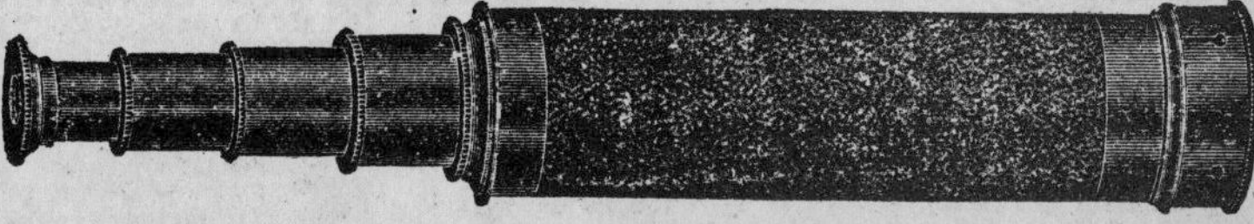

No. 20R640 We have had this Telescope especially designed for us by the leading telescope maker of Paris, and offer it this season for the first time. The most distinctive feature in the appearance of this splendid instrument is the dead black oxidized finish throughout. All brass parts, draw tubes and trimmings are perfectly black, a finish which is not only pleasing in appearance, but is also permanent and entirely free from liability to tarnish. Our **Black Beauty Telescope** is provided with extra quality achromatic lenses, carefully and accurately fitted, the workmanship and finish throughout is the best that can be produced, and every one is guaranteed to be optically perfect. **The eye piece of our Black Beauty Telescope is fitted with an adjustable dark glass,** thus making the instrument suitable for observations of the sun. The spots on the sun, the mountains of the moon, the larger satellites of Jupiter, double stars, and many other interesting features of the heavenly bodies are readily seen with this instrument. The diameter of the object glass is 19 lignes, the length when closed is 9¾ inches, when extended 30 inches. The magnifying power is 25 times.
Price, complete..............(**If by mail, postage extra, 25 cents**)................ **$6.67**

OUR SPECIAL MAHOGANY TELESCOPES.

GENUINE PARIS MADE TELESCOPES.
EXTRA LARGE SIZE, THE FINEST ACHROMATIC LENSES.

Nos. 20R650 to 20R656

No. 20R650 22-Ligne Mahogany Telescope. This telescope, which has a **magnifying power of 40 diameters,** is a fine instrument for ordinary or terrestrial observations, and by reason of the **extra high grade lenses,** which give great clearness and fine definition, affords excellent views of the sun, moon and other heavenly bodies, showing distinctly the sun's spots, the craters on the moon's surface, the satellites of Jupiter, Saturn's rings, etc. Length, closed, about 11½ inches; extended, about 36 inches, **five sections.** Weight, 2½ pounds. It is only by importing these telescopes in great quantities direct from the maker in Paris that we are enabled to sell them at this extremely low price. **Diameter of object glass, 22 lignes; finely polished mahogany body, burnished brass draw tubes and lacquered brass trimmings.** Provided with an **adjustable dark glass in eye piece for observation of the sun, and fitted with finest quality of achromatic lenses of high power and fine definition.**
Price..............(**If by mail, postage extra, 45 cents**)................ **$7.50**

No. 20R651 Mahogany Telescope, same as No. 20R650, but provided with an additional astronomical eye piece, thus affording two powers, one of 40 times for ordinary observations, and one of 75 times for observations of the heavenly bodies. Price, complete **$11.75**
If by mail, postage extra, 55 cents.

No. 20R655 25-Ligne Mahogany Telescope. In general appearance, style of construction, workmanship and quality of lenses, this instrument is the same as our 22-ligne telescope, No. 20R650, but it is of much larger size, having an object glass 25 lignes in diameter and measuring, closed, 12½ inches; extended, 41 inches. The eye piece is provided with adjustable dark glass for astronomical observations. The magnifying power is 45 times. The beautifully polished piano finish mahogany body of this telescope contrasted with the brilliantly burnished brass draw tubes and the darker trimmings in lacquered brass, gives it a very beautiful appearance. The extra quality lenses, the fine workmanship and high grade materials used makes this telescope a most desirable instrument in every respect.
Price.. **$11.50**
Too heavy to send by mail.

No. 20R656 Mahogany Telescope, same as No. 20R655, but provided with an additional astronomical eye piece, thus affording two powers, one of 45 times for ordinary observations, and one of 100 times for viewing the sun, moon and stars. Price, complete.. **$15.90**
Too heavy to send by mail.

MICROSCOPES.

Tripod Microscope.

No. 20R710 Tripod Microscope, adapted to a variety of uses where a short focus and high magnifying power is desirable. The focus is adjustable by means of a screw, has a strong compact frame 1⅜ inches in diameter, standing on three legs, with very strong double lenses. Each......25c

If by mail, postage extra, 5c.

Seed Microscope.

No. 20R716 Cage or Seed Microscope, 1¼ inches high by 1⅛ inches in diameter, has strong lenses, nickel plated mounting with glass body, is used for the examination of seeds, grain, live bugs or insects, etc. Each....19c

If by mail, postage extra, 5 cents.

Combination Microscope.

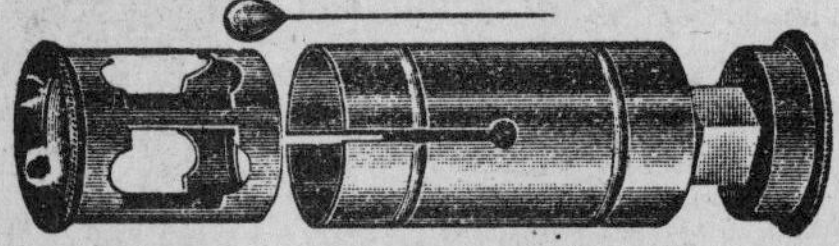

No. 20R719 Combination Microscope with lacquered brass case, 2 inches in length, has two lenses, one of very high power, the other of medium power; is especially adapted for the pocket. Price, including one insect holder, each..........................19c

If by mail, postage extra, 5 cents.

Folding Magnifying Glasses.

No. 20R721 Folding Magnifying Glass, nickel plated with folding handle. The handle of this glass folds over the lens, affording it protection, thus adapting it for pocket use; has a strong lens ¾-inch. Price, each, 20c

If by mail, postage extra, each, 3 cents.

Prospector's Magnifying Glass.

No. 20R725 Prospector's Magnifying Glass, heavy, well finished hard rubber case, two lenses 1 inch and 1½ inches in diameter, of high magnifying power. Strong and durable. **Especially adapted to the use of mineral prospectors.** Being designed by a mining expert of long experience, and made expressly for us by one of the best optical manufacturers in the world. Price............$1.95

If by mail, postage extra, 5 cents.

Linen Testers.

No. 20R727 Linen Tester, a folding pocket magnifier, especially designed for use in counting the number of threads to the inch in linen or other fabrics, and also adapted to general use as a magnifying glass, folds very compactly, finished in lacquered brass. Price..........19c

If by mail, postage extra, 3 cents.

No. 20R729 Linen Tester, same as No. 20R727, but with better lens, more powerful and finely nickel plated. Price..(If by mail, postage extra, 4c)..48c

Single Lens Magnifiers.

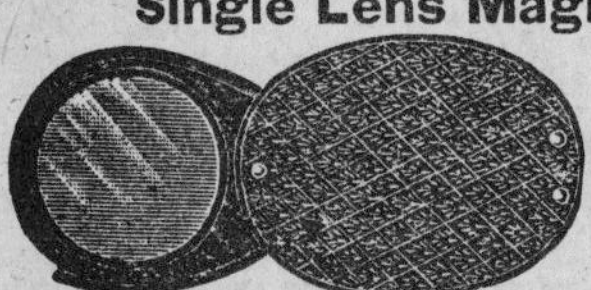

Made with extra fine quality magnifying glasses, powerful, mounted in well finished hard rubber folding cases.

No. 20R731 Diameter of lens, ¾ inch. Price...18c
No. 20R732 Diameter of lens, 1¼ inch. Price...35c
No. 20R733 Diameter of lens, 2 inch. Price...68c

Double Lens Magnifiers.

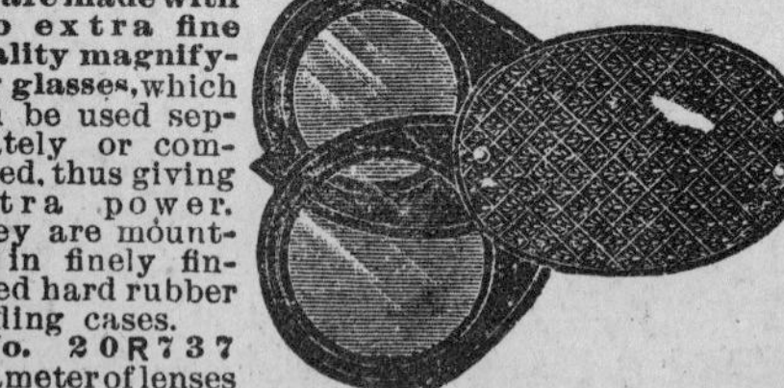

These Magnifiers are made with two extra fine quality magnifying glasses, which can be used separately or combined, thus giving extra power. They are mounted in finely finished hard rubber folding cases.

No. 20R737 Diameter of lenses ⅝ inch and ¾ inch. Price............36c
No. 20R738 Diameter of lenses, ⅞ inch and 1 inch. Price............42c
No. 20R739 Diameter of lenses, 1⅛ inch and 1¼ inch. Price............62c
No. 20R740 Diameter of lenses, 1¼ inch and 1⅜ inch. Price............85c

Triple Lens Magnifiers.

These are the most powerful instruments made in this style of construction, having three extra fine quality magnifying glasses, which can be used separately or all together, as desired, thus giving a range of power. The three lenses used together form an extra powerful magnifier. Mounted in finely finished hard rubber cases.

No. 20R746 Diameter of lenses, ½, ⅝ and ¾ inch. Price............43c
No. 20R747 Diameter of lenses, ⅝, ¾ and ⅞ inch. Price............57c
No. 20R748 Diameter of lenses, ¾, ⅞ and 1 inch. Price............72c

Watchmakers' Eyeglasses.

A Very Convenient Form of Magnifying Glass.

No. 20R760 Watchmakers' Eyeglass, with hard rubber mounting, 2-inch to 4-inch focus, same as used by all watchmakers. Price, each............19c

If by mail, postage extra, 5 cents.

No. 20R762 Watchmakers' Eyeglass, with hard rubber mounting and spring to go around the head for holding the glass to the eye, 2 to 4-inch focus. Price, each............39c

If by mail, postage extra, 5 cents.

No. 20R764 Watchmakers' Eyeglass, hard rubber mounting, with two lenses, giving two strengths and two lengths of focus, very powerful. Each..47c

If by mail, postage extra, 5 cents.

Coddington Magnifiers.

Coddington Magnifiers are well known for their excellent finish, compactness and high magnifying power. They are especially adapted to the use of mineral prospectors, as well as all other purposes where a strong magnifying glass is required.

No. 20R775 Diameter ⅝ inch. Price......$0.60
No. 20R776 Diameter 1 inch. Price...... .90
No. 20R777 Diameter 1⅜ inches. Price.... 1.00

FOLDING CODDINGTON MAGNIFIERS.

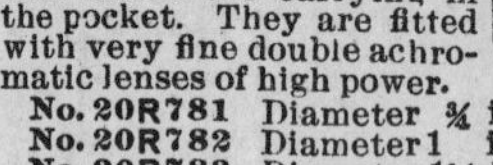

These Coddington Magnifiers are made with folding metal cases, nickel plated, making them very convenient for carrying in the pocket. They are fitted with very fine double achromatic lenses of high power.

No. 20R781 Diameter ¾ inch. Price......$0.90
No. 20R782 Diameter 1 inch. Price...... 1.10
No. 20R783 Diameter 1¼ inch. Price...... 1.35
No. 20R784 Diameter 1⅜ inch. Price...... 1.55

Our Gem Microscope.

No. 20R805 This little instrument is designed especially for beginners in this fascinating study, and its simplicity, compact form and low price make it a very popular style. It is substantially made of brass throughout, stands 6 inches high, has one eye piece and one objective giving a magnifying power of 20 diameters. Between the stage a mirror is provided for illumination of transparent objects. **The Gem Microscope** has sufficient power to render the minute objects in mineral, animal and vegetable life distinctly visible and will prove a source of enjoyment and profitable instruction.

Price, complete in polished wood case........$1.95

Our Household Microscope.

No. 20R810 Our Household Microscope is designed especially for those who wish a well made and easily handled microscope at a very moderate price and is of sufficient power for investigating the minute animal and vegetable life by which we are surrounded. This microscope stands 7½ inches high, has sliding adjustment for focusing, is provided with concave mirror for illumination of transparent objects from below, and in addition has a convex condensing lens, with ball and socket mounting, which can be adjusted to any desired angle for illumination of opaque objects from above. **Our Household Microscope is provided with a divisible objective, giving powers of 30, 50 or 80 diameters.** Our Household Microscope is constructed from brass, with the exception of the base and pillar, which are made from cast iron and finished in black enamel.

Price, complete in polished wood case........$4.90

Our Students' Microscope.

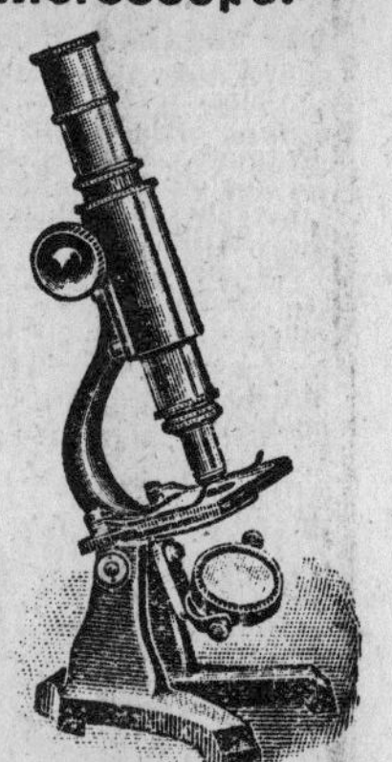

No. 20R815 Our Students' Microscope, is of the style of construction known as the American Model, **and is strongly constructed of brass,** with heavy iron base, provided with rack and pinion movement for focusing, revolving diaphragms for regulating the amount of light, concave mirror for illuminating transparent objects, and steel clips for holding objects in position. Provided with a separable objective, giving powers of 50 to 200 diameters, and each instrument comes complete in fine polished hardwood box. A fine instrument for home use, school work or scientific investigation.

Price..............$13.75

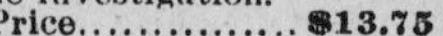

Our $17.85 College Microscope.

No. 20R820 This microscope is constructed throughout, with the exception of the base, from brass, finely finished and lacquered. The base, which is extra broad and heavy enough to give great stability to the instrument, is constructed from cast iron with black enamel finish. The mirror is both plane and concave and can be swung to any angle either above or below the stage. **Our College Microscope** is fitted with a 1-inch Huyghenian eye piece and a ⅝ and ⅙ divisible objective. The coarse adjustment is accomplished by a fine diagonal rack and pinion movement, and the fine adjustment by a microscopic screw located at base of arm and working in a hardened steel nut. Everything in connection with this instrument is strictly high grade; the materials used throughout are the best and it is just as carefully constructed and just as accurately adjusted as the highest priced instruments. Price, complete, with fine polished hardwood case..........................$17.85

Professional Microscope, $29.40.

No. 20R830 Made of brass throughout, highly polished and lacquered, complete in the smallest details of construction. The base, made of cast iron, finished in black enamel, is large and heavy, making the instrument very stable and steady at any angle of inclination. **The coarse adjustment** is operated by a very fine diagonal rack and pinion movement, and the **fine adjustment** is operated by a micrometer screw.

The draw tube is nickel plated, **graduated in millimeters,** and is adjustable in the cloth lined sleeve of the main tube. **The mirror** is so mounted that it may be swung to any obliquity, either above or below the stage; **the stage** is provided with a **fine iris diaphragm.**

Our Professional Microscope is provided with a DOUBLE NOSE PIECE, for instantly changing objectives and is provided with two extra high grade objectives, a ⅔-inch and ⅙-inch, and the best quality 1-inch Huyghenian eye piece. With the objectives furnished with this instrument any kind of pathological or histological work and urinary analysis may be accomplished, and will detect tuberculosis germs and some other easily recognizable forms. This microscope is of large size, standing from 13 to 15½ inches high according to tube length. With the objectives which we furnish, a range of magnifying power from 96 to 540 diameters is available. Price, complete, in fine polished hardwood case..........................$29.40

Our $\frac{1}{12}$-Inch Objective.

No. 20R845 Our $\frac{1}{12}$-Inch Oil Immersion Objective, an extra high grade objective, for bacteriological or other work requiring very high power. Used in connection with our Professional Microscope it gives a magnifying power of from 1,060 to 1,500 diameters, according to tube length used. Made with society screw, and can therefore be used with any standard microscope.

Price, in case, with bottle of cedar oil..........................$25.90

Pocket Compasses.

No 20R1010 **Pocket Compass**, open face, bevel edge glass, paper dial, brass case, watch style, with ring.
Diameter, 1 inch. Each........................12c
Diameter, 1½ inches. Each........................18c
Diameter, 2 inches. Each........................22c
If by mail, postage extra, each, 4 cents.

No. 20R1013 **Pocket Compass**, open face, heavy bevel edged glass, silvered metal dial, brass case, watch style, with ring, diameter 1¾ inches. Price........................38c
If by mail, postage extra, 4 cents.

No. 20R1015 **Pocket Compass**, watch style, open face, brass case, with ring, silvered metal dial, heavy bevel edged glass and sliding stop; diameter, 1¾ inches. Price............43c
If by mail, postage extra, 4 cents.

No. 20R1017 **Pocket Compass**, brass case with cap cover, no ring, paper dial. Diameter, 1½ inches, each 21c; diameter, 2 inches, each........................24c
If by mail, postage extra, on each size, 4 cents.

No. 20R1020 **Pocket Compass**, fine brass case with milled edge, heavy beveled glass, cap cover, silvered metal dial with full divisions, jeweled cap to needle, and sliding stop.
Diameter, 1¾ inches, each........................72c
Diameter, 2⅛ inches, each........................82c
Diameter, 2⅝ inches, each........................92c
If by mail, postage extra, on each size, 5 cents.

No. 20R1023 **Pocket Compass.** Finely made nickel plated case, silvered metal dial, with full divisions, English bar needle, jeweled, automatic stop (the pressure of the cover raises the stop), heavy bevel edge glass with slip cover.
Diameter, 2⅜ in...$1.95
Diameter, 2⅞ in... 2.45
If by mail, postage extra, on each size, 8 cents.

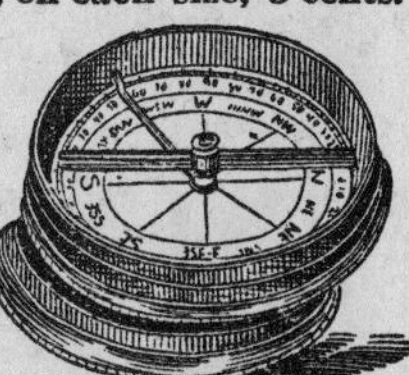
No. 20R1023

No. 20R1027 **Pocket Compass, with strong brass case**, slip cover, jeweled English bar needle, silvered metal dial, marked with double degrees and raised circle division to level of needle. Heavy bevel edged glass and automatic stop. Diameter, 3 inches. **Strong, substantial and well made in every respect.** Price........................$1.98
If by mail, postage extra, 12 cents.

POCKET COMPASS WATCH STYLE

No. 20R1030 **Pocket Compass**, brass case with ring, watch style, making it very convenient for carrying in the pocket, **hinged cover**; silvered metal dial, with full circle divisions; **jeweled cap** to needle, slide stop, strongly made throughout, will last a lifetime. Exceptional value at this price, guaranteed to give absolute satisfaction, and can be depended upon at all times and conditions.
Diameter, 1¾ inches. Price, each........................88c
Diameter, 2 inches. Price, each........................98c
If by mail, postage extra, on either size, 6 cents.

No. 20R1035 **Wood Case Compass**, polished mahogany, 3 inches square, hinged cover, silvered metal dial, automatic stop.
Price........................67c
If by mail, postage extra, 7 cents.

No. 20R1037 **Wood Case Compass**, polished mahogany, 2¾ inches square, hinged cover, silvered metal dial with **full circle division, jeweled English bar needle**, automatic stop.
Price........................98c

Nos. 20R1035 to 20R1041 **If by mail, postage extra, 7c**

No. 20R1041 **Wood Case Compass**, polished mahogany, 2¾ inches square, hinged cover, silvered metal dial, **full circle divisions raised to level of needle**, jeweled English bar needle, automatic stop.
Price........................$1.38
If by mail, postage extra, 7 cents.

Pocket Compass for $1.95.

No. 20R1050 **Pocket Compass.** Watch shape, with **spring** hinged cover, **dust proof**, silvered metal dial with full circle divisions, **jeweled English bar needle**, with automatic stop, **nickel plated case**, heavy beveled glass. Diameter, 2 inches. A very fine compact little instrument. Price........................$1.95
If by mail, postage extra, 7 cents.

No. 20R1050

Woodman's Compass.

No. 20R1053 **Woodman's Compass.** Double thick oxidized case with hinged cover, **made for rough service.** Jeweled English bar needle with automatic stop, silvered metal dial with **full circle divisions, raised to level of needle.** Heavy bevel edge glass. Weight, 9½ ounces. **Best possible materials and workmanship.** Price......$3.20
If by mail, postage extra, 14c.

Sun Dial Compass.

No. 20R1056 **Sun Dial Compass.** Watch style, nickel plated case, with hinged cover, silvered metal dial with full circle divisions, jeweled needle and automatic stop, 2 inches in diameter. A folding sun dial is attached to the glass cover of this compass, and when the sun is shining will indicate the time with a fair degree of accuracy. A very handsome little instrument.
Price........................$2.50
If by mail, postage extra, 6c.

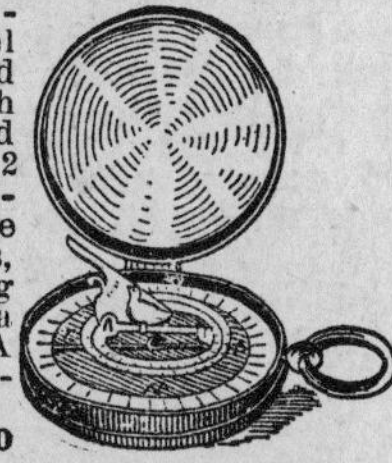
No. 20R1056

Folding Sight Compasses.

For Guides, Woodmen, Architects, Builders, Surveyors, etc.

No. 20R1150 **Folding Sight Compass**, with 2-inch needle, **hooked sights** (for hanging compass on a line), jeweled English bar needle, full circle divisions raised to level of needle, silvered metal dial. Each one in velvet lined morocco case with hinged cover. Diameter, 3¼ inches. A serviceable instrument for retracing lines once surveyed.
Price........................$3.00
If by mail, postage extra, 15 cents.

No. 20R1152 **Folding Sight Compass**, same as No. 20R1150, but with 2⅝-inch needle. Diameter, 4 inches.
Price........................$3.75
If by mail, postage extra, 20 cents.

No. 20R1160 **Folding Sight Compass**, with nickel plated case, watch style, silvered metal dial, full circle divisions raised to level of needle, 1⅛-inch jeweled English bar needle. Diameter, 2 inches. Suitable for same purpose as No. 20R1150 and more convenient for carrying in pocket.
Price........................$3.25
If by mail, postage extra, 8c

No. 20R1162 **Folding Sight Compass**, same as No. 20R1160 but with 1⅝-inch needle. Diameter, 2⅝ inches.
Price........................$3.50
If by mail, postage extra, 10 cents.

No. 20R1164 **Folding Sight Compass**, same as No. 20R1160, but with 1½-inch needle. Diameter, 2¾ inches. Price........................$4.20
If by mail, postage extra, 12 cents.

Surveyors' Compasses.

No. 20R1175 **Surveyors' Compass**, with folding sights, 2½-inch needle, same general style and quality as No. 20R1150, but provided with ball and socket joint and Jacob staff mountings, contained in neat strong wood box.
Price, complete............$5.60
If by mail, postage extra, 20 cents.

No. 20R1178 **Surveyors' Compass**, folding sights, 3½-inch needle, ball sockets, with Jacob staff mountings, in neat, strong wood box. Each............$7.05
If by mail, postage extra, 30 cents.

No. 20R1180 **Surveyors' Compass**, folding sights, 3½-inch needle, ball and socket joint with two levels, Jacob staff mountings, in neat, strong wood box.
Price, each........................$9.20
If by mail, postage extra, 50 cents.

Surveyors' Compasses.

No. 20R1187

No. 20R1185 **Surveyors' Compass**, folding sights, 4⅛-inch needle, ball and socket joint, with two levels, Jacob staff mountings, in neat, wood box.
Price, each........................$10.40

No. 20R1187 **Tripod with Jacob staff** top for the above compass, metal shoes. Price, each....$2.35

No. 20R1190 **Jacob staff** with metal shoe to stick in the ground, for use with the above compass instead of tripod.
Price, each........................88c

SURVEYORS' VERNIER COMPASSES.

No. 20R1195 **Vernier Compass** for surveyors, folding sights, two levels, 3½-inch needle, in neat strong wood box. Weight complete with tripod, 7 pounds; weight without tripod, 2½ pounds.
Price, complete......$18.50
Price, without tripod 14.50

No. 20R1198 **Vernier Compass** with folding sights, two levels, 4½-inch needle, in neat strong wood box. Weight complete, 7¼ pounds, weight without tripod, 3 pounds.
Price, complete......$20.50
Price, without tripod 16.50

OUR $34.50 SURVEYORS' VERNIER COMPASS.

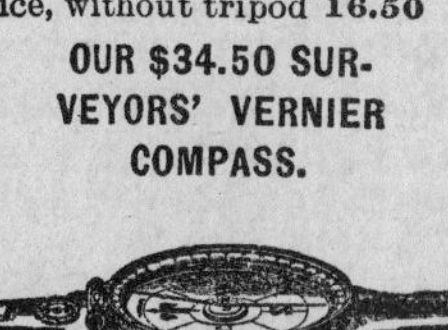
No. 20R1199

No. 20R1199 **Surveyors' Vernier Compass**, high grade, two straight levels, 5-inch needle. Jacob staff mountings, with ball and socket joint, brass cover, outkeeper. Vernier under the glass for adding or subtracting the magnetic variations of the needle, sights graduated for taking angles of elevations and depressions sights detachable but very firm; is a strictly high grade instrument, all packed complete without tripod, in a substantial mahogany box with lock and strap for carrying.
Price........................$34.50
Price, with regular tripod........................39.20

NOTE—The Jacob staff mountings for our No. 20R1199 compass include a metal shoe for the bottom of the staff, and the mounting of the compass has a socket to receive the other end of the staff.

GIVE CATALOGUE NUMBER IN FULL WHEN YOU WRITE YOUR ORDER

Surveyors' Chains.

Genuine Chesterman Measuring Chains, recognized the world over as the best chains made.

Standard of Accuracy.

It is only by importing these goods in large quantities direct from Chesterman & Co., Sheffield, England, that we are enabled to quote the following extremely low prices.

No. 20R1250 **Iron Chain**, made of best iron wire, with two oval rings between links, brass swivel handles, brass tallies.

Length,	2 poles	4 poles	50 feet	100 feet
Price,	$1.60	$2.50	$1.80	$2.75

No. 20R1255 **Steel Chain**, made of best cast steel wire, hardened, tempered and polished, two oval rings between links, brass swivel handles and brass tallies.

Length,	2 poles	4 poles	50 feet	100 feet
Price,	$2.45	$4.50	$2.65	$5.00

No. 20R1260 **Brazed Steel Chain**, same as No. 20R1255, but with all joints brazed, making a solid chain. **The best chain made.**

Length,	2 poles	4 poles	50 feet	100 feet
Price,	$4.00	$7.50	$4.25	$7.75

NOTE—The 2-pole and 4-pole chains are divided into links and tallied every link. The 50 feet and 100 feet chains are divided into feet and tallied every 10 feet.

No. 20R1270 **Arrows or Marking Pins**, iron, 15 inches long, in sets of eleven. Per set........55c

No. 20R1271 **Arrows or Marking Pins**, steel, best grade, 15 inches long, in sets of eleven.
Price, per set........................85c

STEREOSCOPES

24c

STEREOSCOPES AND VIEWS NEVER WERE MORE POPULAR THAN AT THE PRESENT TIME.

With the large assortment of views which we list, there is an endless amount of entertainment to be obtained from an outfit of this kind, at a very small expense. We do not list the cheapest line of stereoscopes made, for we cannot conscientiously recommend them to our customers.

YOU CAN MAKE BIG MONEY SELLING THESE STEREOSCOPES AND VIEWS.

Our 36-cent views readily bring $1.00 per dozen. Our colored views, for which we ask you only 54 cents, will sell easily for $1.50, and our best grade views should never be sold at retail for less than $3.00 per dozen. Our 24-cent stereoscopes sell like hot cakes at from 75 cents to $1.00 each.

STEREOSCOPES.

No. 20R1310 Stereoscope, cherry frame, fine quality medium sized lenses, patent folding handle, nicely varnished hood. Price....................24c

If by mail, postage extra, 30 cents.

No. 20R1315 Stereoscope, cherry frame, large lenses of first quality, patent folding handle, handsomely figured cherry hood, nicely varnished. Price....................36c

If by mail, postage extra, 30 cents.

No. 20R1320 Stereoscope, walnut frame, extra large lenses of finest quality, patent folding handle, finely varnished hood. **First quality throughout.** Price....................60c

If by mail, postage extra, 30 cents.

No. 20R1325 Stereoscope, walnut frame, extra large lenses of finest quality, patent folding handle, **polished tulip wood hood,** first quality throughout. Price....................82c

If by mail, postage extra, 30 cents.

No. 20R1330 Stereoscope, frame, handle and hood made of **polished rosewood,** finest quality pure white glass lenses extra large size, patent folding handle, **nickel plated trimmings,** finest quality throughout—in fact, **the best Stereoscope made.** Price....................$1.87

If by mail, postage extra, 30 cents.

Stereo-Graphoscopes.

These instruments are made upon a new principle by means of which they may be adjusted for either regular stereoscopic views or ordinary single photographs simply by reversing the lenses. They thus combine in one instrument both a stereoscope and a graphoscope.

No. 20R1343 Stereo Graphoscope, good lenses of medium size, wood screw handle, cherry frame, polished cherry hood. Price..40c

If by mail, postage extra, 25 cents.

No. 20R1347 Stereo-Graphoscope, fine lenses of large size, patent folding handle, cherry frame, polished cherry hood. Price..........56c

If by mail, postage extra, 25 cents.

No. 20R1349 Stereo-Graphoscope, large size lenses of highest grade, patent folding handle, polished cherry hood, nickel plated trimmings first quality throughout. Price....................82c

If by mail, postage extra, 25 cents.

Views in Norway, Sweden and Denmark.

No. 20R406 We have this season succeeded in obtaining some fine stereoscopic views taken in Norway, Sweden and Denmark. Our assortment of these Swedish, Danish and Norwegian subjects is very large, the subjects are all very interesting, and the views are strictly high grade, finished in the best possible style.

No. 20R1400 Stereoscopic Views from Norway. Price, per dozen....................79c

No. 20R1401 Stereoscopic Views from Sweden. Price, per dozen....................79c

No. 20R1402 Stereoscopic Views from Denmark. Price, per dozen....................79c

If by mail, postage extra, per dozen, 6 cents.

OUR 36-CENT STEREOSCOPIC VIEWS.

These are **genuine photographic views,** made from negatives upon photographic paper and mounted on good cards.

If by mail, postage extra, per dozen, 6 cents.

From the Sporting Series.

No. 20R1410 World's Fair Series. The White City in all its glory, and choice views along the Midway Plaisance. Price, per dozen..........36c

No. 20R1412 American Picturesque Series. A beautiful collection of subjects illustrating the picturesque features of the American continent. Price, per dozen..........36c

No. 20R1414 Sporting Series. Choice views illustrating camp life, hunting and fishing scenes, game, etc. Price, per dozen..........36c

No. 20R1416 American Cities Series. Glimpses of streets, parks, public buildings, etc., in the principal cities of America. Price, per dozen..........36c

No. 20R1418 Yellowstone Park Series. Beautiful views showing the canons, geysers, hot springs and wonderful rock formations. Price, per dozen....36c

No. 20R1420 Foreign Picturesque Series, showing Old World scenery. Price, per dozen..........36c

No. 20R1422 Antiquities Series. Showing the old ruins of ancient days. Price, per dozen..........36c

No. 20R1424 Foreign Cities Series. Glimpses of interesting points in the great cities of Europe. Price, per dozen....................36c

No. 20R1426 Comic Series. Comical scenes photographed from life. Price, per dozen..........36c

Colored Views 54 cents per Dozen.

If by mail, postage extra, 6 cents per dozen.

No. 20R1435 Yellowstone Park Series. Beautiful **colored** views, spouting geysers, brilliant deposits from hot springs, mountains, cliffs and rivers. Price, per dozen....................54c

No. 20R1437 American Picturesque Series. Beautifully **colored** views, showing the most picturesque places throughout our country. Price, per doz..54c

No. 20R1439 Foreign Picturesque Series. Beautifully colored views illustrative of the grandest scenery of Europe. Price, per dozen..........54c

No. 20R1441 Comic Series Beautifully colored views, various comical scenes, child life, amusing situations, etc., all photographed from life. Price, per dozen..........54c

From the Comic Series.

Our Highest Grade Views.

We take great pleasure this season in introducing for the first time this magnificent line of Stereoscopic Views. They are unquestionably the finest ever placed upon the market, being printed on Aristotype paper from original retouched negatives only, handsomely mounted on heavy cards, and finished in the highest style of the photographer's art. **We confidently recommend them to those desiring only the best** that can be produced, and at our price of only 81 cents per dozen, they represent most exceptional value.

Furnished in four different series, as follows:

No. 20R1455 Yellowstone National Park, a magnificent series of pictures taken in this world famous region, canons, spouting geysers, castled rocks, terraces and boiling springs, towering mountains, wonderful rock formations and beautiful waterfalls. Nearly 200 different subjects. Price, per dozen..........81c

From the Yosemite Series.

No. 20R1457 Yosemite Valley and Big Trees, a series of beautiful views exhibiting in a most striking manner the varied scenes of California's marvelous wonderland. Price, per dozen....................81c

No. 20R1459 Sporting Views. This splendid collection of hunting, fishing and camp life scenes, all photographed direct from life, will be especially interesting to those who appreciate the pleasures of rod or gun. They bring back memories of pleasant days in the woods, on the marshes or along some shady stream, revive the memories of dead camp fires, and anticipate the pleasures of days to come. Over 200 different subjects. Price, per dozen.... 81c

From the Comic Views.

No. 20R1461 Comic Views. In addition to scores of the most humorous and laughter provoking scenes, all photographed direct from life, this series contains some of the choicest views of child life, showing the little ones engaged in their various and amusing occupations and pretty bits of scenery caught with the artist's camera. A very popular series with over 250 different subjects. Price, per dozen....................81c

No. 20R1475 Spanish-American War Views. A splendid collection of views made during our late war, showing our soldiers in camp and on the march, camp life scenes, portraits of the prominent officers and statesmen, Spanish and American battleships, in fact the finest collection of views that were made during the war. These views are strictly high grade, printed from original retouched negatives and form a splendid souvenir of our latest triumphs in arms. Price, per dozen....................95c

If by mail, postage extra, per dozen, 8 cents.

Religious Subjects.

No. 20R1485 Life of Christ Set. Twelve splendid views portraying in the most vivid manner the story of our Savior's life before and after the crucifixion. Price, per set.....48c

No. 20R1486 The Crucifixion Set. Twelve splendid views, representing the Nativity, Early Life, Crucifixion and Resurrection of Christ. Price, per set....................48c

No. 20R1487 Life of Christ Set. Same as No. 20R1485, but **beautifully hand colored.** Price, per set....................60c

No. 20R1488 The Crucifixion Set, same as No. 20R1486, but **beautifully hand colored.** Price, per set....................60c

If by mail, postage extra, per dozen, 6 cents.

PHOTOGRAPHY

FOR PLEASURE
AND FOR PROFIT.....

OFFERS A COMBINATION OF ADVANTAGES WHICH WE BELIEVE LEADS ANY OTHER LINE OF MERCHANDISE.

OUR ONLY TERMS

......ARE......

Cash With the Order.

OUR STRAIGHT CASH WITH ORDER TERMS help to enable us to make these low prices BY REASON OF CUTTING OUT THE EXPENSE ATTENDANT UPON C. O. D. SHIPMENTS, and these terms also effect a greater saving to our customers, as they do not have the additional expense of the return charges on the money necessary on a C. O. D. shipment.

WHILE WE REQUIRE CASH IN FULL WITH THE ORDER and do not deviate from these terms under any circumstances,

OUR CUSTOMERS DO NOT RUN THE SLIGHTEST RISK

in complying with these terms, for if any goods purchased, either in this or any other department, do not prove entirely satisfactory and exactly as we represent them in this catalogue, all that is necessary is to return the goods to us and your money, including what you paid for transportation charges, will be promptly returned to you.

OUR CAMERA DEPARTMENT has established a reputation. We are known throughout the country by the large camera manufacturers as the largest handlers of cameras in the United States. We have the reputation among the users of photographic goods of selling cameras and supplies at lower prices than any other concern. **THESE GOODS FORMERLY** were sold at much higher prices. They have been sold on a basis of long list prices, long profits, and prices that include a big expense attendant upon office, traveling, selling and collecting expenses. We have changed all this. We have made a contract with one of the largest camera makers in the country, a maker located at Rochester, N. Y. Our contract is the largest ever made by any one house for high grade cameras, and the manufacturer has figured the goods to us on the net basis of the cost of material and labor with all these other expenses eliminated. As a result, we offer in our cheapest folding camera, the Delmar, at $3.75, such a camera as you would pay your dealer at home $8.00 to $10.00 for. We offer in our very highest grade camera, the Seroco Long Focus Reversible Back Camera, at $15.90, a camera the equal of cameras that retail as high as $30.00.

OUR GUARANTEE. As the astonishingly low prices which we quote in this department may lead some to question the high quality of our goods, we put out every camera under our own binding guarantee as to quality of material, construction and workmanship. WE GUARANTEE EVERY CAMERA TO BE STRICTLY HIGH GRADE, exactly as represented, and if you do not find it in every way satisfactory, simply return it to us and we will return your money together with the express charges you paid.

COMPLETE INSTRUCTIONS IN PHOTOGRAPHY

OUR NEW 112-PAGE MANUAL.

A SPECIAL FEATURE OF OUR PHOTOGRAPHIC OUTFITS IS THE BOOK, "COMPLETE INSTRUCTIONS IN PHOTOGRAPHY," WHICH IS INCLUDED

FREE OF CHARGE WITH EVERY CAMERA OR COMPLETE OUTFIT.

THIS BOOK WAS WRITTEN EXPRESSLY FOR US by one of the most expert photographers in the United States; a man who has spent fifteen years in making photographs, teaching photography, and selling photographic merchandise to both amateur and professional photographers. The experience thus gained, not only in the actual processes of photography, but in contact with other photographers—with amateurs and with beginners—enables him to appreciate and to understand, better than anyone else, the difficulties met with and the errors made by beginners. This experience enables him to understand just what the beginner wants to know, enables him to make it plain and simple, and the success which is attending the efforts of those who are already using "Complete Instructions in Photography" is the best proof we can offer as to its value. **COMPLETE INSTRUCTIONS IN PHOTOGRAPHY** tells secrets of the trade never before published; gives valuable information heretofore possessed only by a few professional photographers; GIVES DOZENS OF VALUABLE FORMULAS OR RECIPES; tells you how to make your own developers, your own solutions of all kinds; tells you how to determine the correct amount of exposure, how to save plates which are wrongly exposed, how to make good portraits, how to make blue paper, how to dry a negative in five minutes, HOW TO MAKE MONEY IN PHOTOGRAPHY, how to avoid all the troubles sometimes met with by beginners, how to select a camera; tells all about a hundred other things which we haven't space to mention here.

REMEMBER, There is no other book like it. It was written expressly for us. It is published only by us, and can be secured only from us. **IT COSTS YOU NOTHING.**

ANSWERS ALL YOUR QUESTIONS.
SOLVES ALL YOUR DIFFICULTIES.
ANTICIPATES ALL YOUR TROUBLES.
MAKES PHOTOGRAPHY EASY.

Indispensable to the Beginner. Invaluable to the Advanced Photographer.

WE INCLUDE IT FREE OF CHARGE with every camera which we sell. If you already have an outfit and desire a copy of the book, we will include it free of charge with an order for photographic supplies amounting to $2.50 or more (provided you state in your order that you desire it). We do not sell this book. We had it written and publish it exclusively for the benefit of our customers, but in order to protect ourselves against actual loss, we are obliged to give it only to those who send us an order for at least $2.50 worth of photographic goods, and state in their order that a copy of "Complete Instructions in Photography" is desired.

THE PERFECTION JR. CAMERA AND COMPLETE PHOTOGRAPHIC OUTFIT

$7.50 OUTFIT FOR $2.69

FOR 3½x3½ PICTURES.

...THE PERFECTION Jr. CAMERA.

A HIGH GRADE AND THOROUGHLY PRACTICAL CAMERA, made up in the most popular and convenient form and adapted to any class of work which the average amateur desires to do, but at the same time offered by us at **nearly one-half the prices** asked by other concerns for goods of equal merit. **There is nothing to get out of order,** as they are constructed in the **simplest possible form,** having no unnecessary springs, catches or adjustments to get out of order and annoy the owner or create a source of expense.

THE PERFECTION JR. CAMERAS are manufactured by one of the best and most reputable camera manufacturers. They are made under a binding contract to comply with our specifications and are sold only by us. **THE LENSES ARE ACHROMATIC** of the highest grade, being made of both crown and flint optical glass. (Lenses made of a single piece of glass will not give a sharp focus, as the light rays are reflected in such a way that rays of different color focus at different distances from lenses.) They are ground and set for a **Universal Focus** and need no adjustment even when pictures are to be taken at different distances. **THE UNIVERSAL FOCUS LENS is a special feature of advantage,** anything in the picture up to within a few feet of the camera, or any distance in the background, being in focus, that is, **sharp and clear. THE SHUTTER** is one of the most simple, but is thoroughly practical and is equally adapted to both **snap shot and time exposures.** It is well made and finished in every respect and has no complications to get out of order. **THE VIEW FINDER** is an important feature of these cameras, for it shows the operator an exact copy of the picture as it will appear when finished, and makes it an easy matter to get the subject to be photographed in the proper position on the plate. **THE COVERING is artistic, neat, has the seal grain finish,** same as used in the highest priced cameras; is creased on all corners; has a handle for carrying, and thoroughly finished in every respect. **THE SIZE,** 3½x3½, is the most popular one for amateur work with the single exception of the 4x5. **GLASS PLATES ONLY** are used in The Perfection Jr. for making negatives, and we recommend them as being much better and easier to handle than films. **All of the material** used for these cameras is **the same as used by professional photographers,** which places the amateur in a position to do the very best of work. **THE DEVELOPING AND FINISHING OUTFIT** is the most complete and convenient outfit ever offered in this size, and includes **everything necessary for making pictures** and finishing them complete, mounted on cards. **SIZE AND WEIGHT: The Perfection Jr. Camera** measures 4¾x5⅛x7¼ inches, and weighs 18 ounces. The camera has space in the back for three double plate holders, making the carrying capacity six plates. **"Complete Instructions in Photography"** is furnished with this outfit, and even if you have never taken a picture you will be able to make good photographs from the start.

THE PERFECTION JR. OUTFIT CONTAINS:

1 Perfection Jr. Camera. 1 Metal Dark Room Lamp. 1 Tray for Developing Plates. 1 Tray for Fixing Plates. 1 Tray for Toning Prints. 1 Printing Frame. 1 Measuring Glass. 1 Print Roller for smoothing down the prints when mounted. 1 Paste Brush for mounting. ½ doz. Dry Plates for making negatives. 1 doz. Sheets Sensitized Paper. 1 doz. Embossed Border Cards for mounting the pictures. 1 Package Dry Developer, (makes 8 oz. of solution). 1 Package Dry Toner, (makes 8 oz. of solution), 1 Package Hypo, for fixing negatives and prints. 1 Jar Prepared and Scented Mounting Paste. 1 Copy "Complete Instructions in Photography."

The Camera alone if purchased from the regular retail dealers would cost you $4.00, and the complete developing and material outfit as listed above would cost at least $3.50, making the total value of the Perfection Jr. Camera and outfit at retail $7.50. Our policy of purchasing each of the items composing these outfits direct from the manufacturers, having them made expressly for us in enormous quantities, enables us to offer you the complete outfit for actually less than the retail dealer can buy it for.

No. 20R2040 The Perfection Jr. Camera and Complete Developing and Material Outfit and one double dry plate holder as described above. **$2.69**

No. 20R2041 The Perfection Jr. Camera with one double dry plate holder, but without the complete outfit **$1.68**

No. 20R2042 Extra Double Plate Holders. Each .... **.35**

If by mail, postage extra, 5 cents.

A MOUNTED SAMPLE PICTURE TAKEN WITH THE PERFECTION JR. CAMERA BY AN AMATEUR PHOTOGRAPHER WILL BE MAILED TO ANY ADDRESS FREE OF CHARGE.

THE SEROCO MAGAZINE CAMERA.

$4.95 BUYS THE SEROCO MAGAZINE CAMERA.

FOR 4x5 PICTURES.

THE LATEST, THE BEST and the SIMPLEST MAGAZINE CAMERA YET CONSTRUCTED

BETTER THAN OTHER MAGAZINE CAMERAS SOLD AT PRICES FROM $10.00 TO $12.00.

$4.95 FOR THE SEROCO MAGAZINE CAMERA is a price made possible only by a very special contract which we succeeded in making with the best magazine camera maker in this country, the same maker who designed all of the best magazine cameras on the market, up to the present time; and our Seroco Magazine Camera is his latest design, representing his latest and best ideas, the culmination of years of practical experience, embodying improvements over all other magazine cameras.

THE SEROCO MAGAZINE CAMERA

does away entirely with plate holders, as 12 PLATES CAN BE PUT INTO THE CAMERA AT ONCE, and exposed one after another as desired.

LOADING AND UNLOADING. In this respect our Seroco Magazine Camera is an improvement over all other magazine cameras, as any or all of the exposed plates may be removed at any time without disturbing those remaining.

THE SHUTTER. The shutter of this camera is always set, there being no levers to pull, and no buttons to turn. It is not only the most simple, and therefore the least liable to get out of order, but it is also the most effective and the most easily operated shutter on the market.

BULB RELEASE. The shutter of the Seroco Magazine Camera is operated by a bulb and tube, thus preventing any possible jarring of the camera, which is so often a cause of failure especially in time exposures. **One pressure of the rubber bulb makes the exposure and the shutter resets itself automatically.** When desired the rubber bulb may be instantly detached and the shutter operated in the usual manner by the finger.

DIAPHRAGMS. A set of diaphragms or stops is provided, permitting the use of different sized openings in order to adapt the exposure to varying degrees of light. In connection with the diaphragms is a cut-off by means of which the opening may be entirely closed, and any possibility of premature or accidental exposures entirely prevented.

OPERATION The operation of the Seroco Magazine Camera is the acme of simplicity. One pressure of the bulb makes the exposure, and a one-fourth turn of a button places the next plate in position, and this is all—two movements, the camera does the rest.

REGISTER. The automatic register, located in plain view on top of the camera, shows at a glance at any time the exact number of plates that have been exposed and the number that are still left in the camera.

LENSES. Every lens used in the Seroco Magazine Camera is carefully tested by an expert optician before being fitted to the camera, and again tested after it is in the camera before it leaves the factory. It is a single achromatic lens of the type known as the combination Meniscus, being composed of two pieces of glass, one a flint, the other a crown, perfectly cemented together with an invisible cement. **We positively guarantee every lens used in our Seroco Magazine Cameras to be optically perfect.**

PLATE DROPPING DEVICE. The Seroco Magazine Camera is the first magazine camera and the only magazine camera that has a perfect device for dropping the exposed plates. It is so constructed that it is absolutely positive in its action and it is impossible to drop more than one plate at a time. This is a feature which will be especially appreciated by those who have used other magazine cameras.

No. 20R2046 THE 4X5 SEROCO MAGAZINE CAMERA. PRICE $4.95

The 4x5 DELMAR CAMERA

With Complete Developing and Material Outfit for Taking 4x5 Cabinet Size Pictures. Less than Half Regular Prices. A $10.00 Complete Outfit for $3.68

CATALOGUE No. 20R2050.

INCLUDES EVERYTHING NEEDED TO MAKE AND FINISH FIRST CLASS PICTURES.

THE IMMENSE SALE OF THESE most popular cameras and outfits has made it possible for us to place very large contracts with the manufacturers of the Cameras, and by purchasing the **chemicals by the barrel,** and the other materials by the thousands of each, and by assembling and boxing the outfits by the thousands, being satisfied with a very small percentage of profit, we are able to **CUT THE PRICE IN TWO,** while other concerns still insist on selling with large profits, which has always been the custom in the photographic line, with the result that they sell small quantities of goods and charge their patrons double what they should.

LAST SPRING WE MADE IMPROVEMENTS in this outfit which so increased the cost that we were obliged to **RAISE THE PRICE TO $5.45.** Now, however, we have been able to make such advantageous arrangements with manufacturers, owing to the still large quantities used, that in spite of the universal increase in value of raw materials, we can again offer the outfit with **all the latest improvements,**

THE BEST OUTFIT WE HAVE EVER SOLD, AT THE ORIGINAL AND UNEQUALED PRICE OF **$3.68**

THE SIZE AND STYLE OF THE DELMAR 4x5 is by far the most popular on the market, and this statement will be better appreciated when we say that we believe at least seven out of ten of all the amateur Cameras sold are of this same size and style; while it takes a 4x5 cabinet size picture, its outside dimensions are only 6x7x8½ inches, and it weighs but 34 ounces. **One Double Plate Holder** for two plates is included with each Camera, and there is space in the Camera for two extra holders, giving a capacity for six plates.

THE LENS is what is known as the **Meniscus Achromatic,** and is the finest universal focus lens made; in fact is the same grade and quality as used in Cameras which sell as high as **$10.00 to $15.00.** It has great depth of focus, which gives full and sharp detail to objects at a distance as well as to those which are near by.

THE SHUTTER IS AUTOMATIC AND ALWAYS SET, BEING OPERATED BY A SPRING

in connection with a very ingenious device; is very simple, with no complicated parts to get out of order, but so perfect in its arrangement that it can be instantly changed for either snap shot or time exposures.

THE VIEW FINDERS form a part of the Camera, and not only are they of invaluable assistance in locating and centering the objects to be photographed, but they add much to its artistic appearance.

SIMPLICITY. **The ease of manipulation is one of the best features of this outfit. Remember, the shutter is always set,** you don't have to turn any buttons or push any levers before making an exposure, operations which are very apt to be forgotten or wrongly executed in the excitement of the moment, and **you don't have to focus each time a picture is made** as the lens is of universal focus, **always ready.** With other cameras many a fine picture is lost because of the delay in setting the shutter, focusing, etc. In the meantime the subject is gone or the scene is changed, **but the Delmar Camera is always ready.**

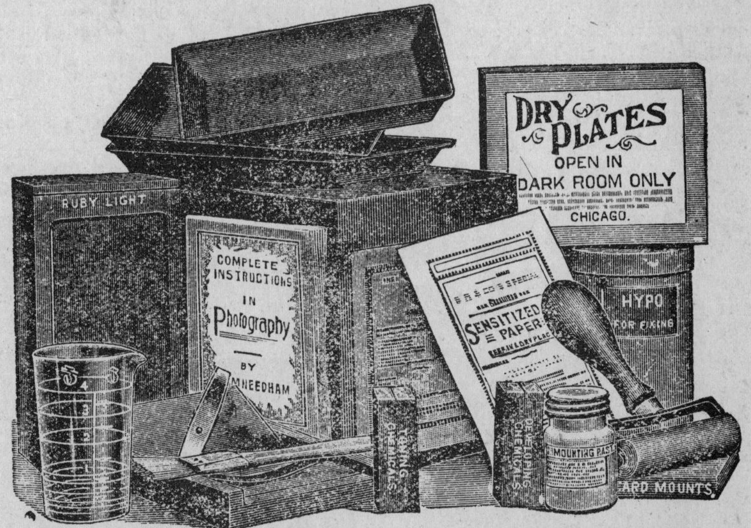

Think seriously of the opportunity to possess a Camera and Complete Outfit for making 4x5 pictures for the small sum of $3.68, and then ask yourself

WHAT WOULD AFFORD MORE PLEASURE

than to own a Photographic Outfit, with which you could as the opportunities present themselves, take the pictures of your friends and relatives, brothers and sisters; the pets, such as dogs, cats and horses; the home, both inside and out; pretty landscapes, buildings and places of interest seen while traveling; and especially the picture of the baby in all its cute and amusing positions. It will not be fully realized, until after years, what treasures have been secured in the way of pictures of friends, and places or things of interest.

THE CAMERA AS AN ASSISTANT IN BUSINESS PLAYS A PROMINENT PART AND WILL RENDER VALUABLE SERVICE.

If you have real estate, horse, buggy or almost anything that you wish to sell, take pictures of it and put them in conspicuous places, or mail them to prospective buyers and you will be most sure to make the sale.

THE COMPLETE OUTFIT CONTAINS:

- 1 **4x5 Delmar Camera, with double plate holder.**
- 1 Metal dark room lamp.
- 1 Tray for Developing Plates.
- 1 Tray for Fixing Plates.
- 1 Tray for Toning Prints.
- 1 Print roller for smoothing down the mounted prints.
- 1 Paste Brush.
- 1 Graduated Glass for Measuring Liquids.
- ½ Dozen Dry Plates.
- 1 Dozen Card Mounts with fancy embossed borders.
- 1 Package Concentrated Dry Developer (makes 8 ounces of solution).
- 1 Package Concentrated Dry Toner (makes 8 ounces of solution).
- 1 Dozen sheets Sensitized Paper.
- 1 Printing Frame.
- 1 Package Hypo for fixing Negatives and Prints.
- 1 Jar of fine Scented Photo Mounting paste.
- 1 **Copy of Complete Instructions in Photography.**

Everything in the outfit is the best that can be secured.

THE DELMAR CAMERA, like the **Perfection Junior,** is the simplest and by far the most popular and convenient form of amateur Camera. It is made of the best seasoned material throughout, is strong, well made in every respect and has absolutely **no complicated parts to get out of order.**

THE DELMAR CAMERA has a beautiful **black seal grain finished covering,** has leather handle for carrying, and two tripod sockets for attaching a tripod when desired, for either perpendicular or horizontal pictures.

DRY PLATES ONLY are used in the Delmar Cameras. The dry plates for negatives are much easier to develop and print from than films, and as dry plates only are used by professional photographers, it is evident that they are the best.

THE REASON WHY **we list the most popular Cameras with Developing and Material Outfits** is that nearly every purchaser wants a complete outfit, but unless they have had previous experience they would not know what to order, and then by making up the outfits by the thousand, we can sell them much lower.

No. 20R2050 The 4x5 Delmar Camera, with one double plate holder and complete developing, finishing and material outfit, as described above, ... $3.68

NOTE.—If you have no express office near you, we can, by making several packages of this outfit, ship same by mail, the postage required being $1.50.

No. 20R2051 The 4x5 Delmar Camera, with one double plate holder, but without the developing, finishing and material outfits............ ..$2.48
If by mail, postage extra, 50 cents.

No. 20R2052 Extra Double Plate Holders. With pressed board slides each, 34c; with hard rubber slides, each.......................................44c
If by mail, postage extra, 6 cents.

SEE FOLLOWING PAGES FOR EXTRA SUPPLIES, SUCH AS DRY PLATES, SENSITIZED PAPER, DEVELOPERS, TONERS, ETC. ANY OF THE SUPPLIES LISTED IN THIS CATALOGUE ARE SUITABLE FOR THE DELMAR CAMERA.

A SAMPLE PICTURE TAKEN WITH THE DELMAR CAMERA BY AN AMATEUR PHOTOGRAPHER WILL BE MAILED TO ANY ADDRESS UPON APPLICATION.

OUR DELMAR FOLDING CAMERA FOR $3.75, FOR 4x5 PICTURES

A VERY HIGH GRADE. RELIABLE FOLDING CAMERA, DESIGNED FOR 4x5 PICTURES, AT AN EXTREMELY LOW PRICE.

The Delmar Folding Camera is made for us under contract by one of the best camera makers in America. It is made from the very best materials throughout, it is simple in construction (following our printed rules a child can operate it), and it TAKES A PICTURE 4X5 INCHES, THE MOST POPULAR SIZE.

Carrying case.

Camera open.

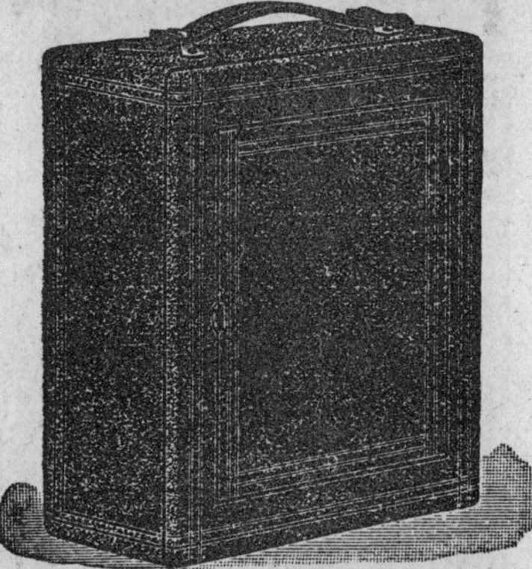

Camera closed.

THE WOOD used is solid mahogany, with fine piano finish, the metal parts are of lacquered brass, and the bellows are the best grade of red leather. The outside of the camera is covered with a fine quality black morocco leather, with seal grain finish.

THE SHUTTER is so constructed that it may be used for either time or instantaneous exposures, and is so simple in construction and operation that it is practically impossible for it to get out of order. The Delmar Folding Camera is provided with spring actuated ground glass focusing screen, a very desirable feature, especially when the most careful and accurate work is desired. It is also provided with an accurate focusing scale, by means of which the camera can be instantly focused when desired without using the ground glass screen. This camera has rising and falling front, enabling the operator to control the relative amount of sky and foreground. It is fitted with a set of diaphragms for regulating the intensity of illumination and bringing both near and distant objects into sharp focus at the same time. **THE VIEW FINDER,** which is conveniently located on the bed of the camera, is reversible, making the camera available for either upright or horizontal pictures. **THE LENS,** which is the most important part of a camera, is an extra high grade single achromatic of the Meniscus type of extra large size, manufactured expressly for the Delmar Folding Camera by the Bausch & Lomb Optical Company, who are universally recognized as the makers of the highest grade photographic lenses in the world. This lens is extra rapid, making it especially suitable for instantaneous exposures, and at the same time it possesses great depth of focus and is guaranteed to cover the entire plate sharply to the extreme corners. The Delmar Folding Camera is suitable for either interior or outdoor work. It will take snap shots, interiors, flashlights, portraits, landscapes or buildings. In fact, is suitable for general all around work.

ITS SMALL SIZE combining compactness, light weight and simplicity, with ease of operation, makes it a favorite with bicyclists and travelers. When closed this camera measures only 2½x5⅜x6¼ inches; the carrying case measures only 2⅞x6½x10¾ inches, and the total weight of the camera, carrying case and one double plate holder is only 40 ounces.

FREE INSTRUCTION BOOK. With the Delmar Folding Camera at $3.75 we furnish, without charge, our new 112 page manual, COMPLETE INSTRUCTIONS IN PHOTOGRAPHY. This book can be obtained only from us; there is no other book like it and it is the only instruction book ever written which enables the beginner in photography to take, develop and finish perfect pictures without any previous experience whatever. With our instruction book as a guide, failure is practically impossible.

FOR $1.20 EXTRA we will include a big developing, printing and material outfit, same as described under No. 20R2895.

REMEMBER, that the camera only, with the carrying case and one double plate holder, is $3.75; and if you desire the developing, finishing and material outfit also, the total cost is $4.95.

BE SURE TO GIVE CATALOGUE NUMBER and name of Camera when you order.

No. 20R2058 The Delmar Folding Camera, with carrying case and one double plate holder. Price........ **$3.75**

No. 20R2059 The Delmar Folding Camera, with carrying case, one double plate holder, as above described, and complete developing, finishing and material outfit, as described under No. 20R2895. Price........ **4.95**

SEE PAGE 145 for prices on extra plate holders.

OUR NEW KENWOOD FOLDING CAMERA.

AT $4.98 FOR THE 4x5 SIZE

AT $7.90 FOR THE 5x7 SIZE

Camera closed.

Camera open.

Carrying case.

OUR SPECIAL $4.98 AND $7.90 PRICES for the Kenwood Folding Camera are based on the actual cost of material and labor, with but our one small percentage of profit added, and are the lowest prices ever made for cameras of this grade.

OUR ILLUSTRATIONS, engraved by the artist direct from photographs of the camera, will give you some idea of the appearance of our handsome Kenwood Folding Camera; the one illustration showing the camera fully extended and ready for use, another showing the camera closed, and the third illustration showing the appearance of the camera and plate holders when in the carrying case.

OUR KENWOOD FOLDING CAMERA represents one of the very latest styles for 1901. It embodies all the most up to date features of all high grade folding cameras, with the defects of none. With the Kenwood Folding Camera you can accomplish any results and do any kind of work that can be done with other cameras at from three to five times our prices, and as we include without extra charge a copy of our new 112-page manual, COMPLETE INSTRUCTIONS IN PHOTOGRAPHY, the making of perfect pictures with this camera is a simple matter, even for those without the slightest previous experience or knowledge of photography. The Kenwood Folding Camera is constructed throughout of selected Honduras mahogany, with highly polished piano finish. It is covered with heavy seal grain black morocco leather of the best quality, the bellows are made of an excellent quality of red leather, lined with absolutely light proof black gossamer cloth. The trimmings and all metal parts are finely finished and highly polished, thus making an exceedingly handsome appearance in contrast with the dark, rich finish of the mahogany woodwork.

THE VIEW FINDER IS REVERSIBLE and the camera is fitted with two tripod sockets, thus making it available for either vertical or horizontal pictures, both when used with a tripod or when used as a hand camera. The Kenwood Folding Camera is made with rising and falling front for regulating the relative amount of sky and foreground. It is provided with a ground glass focusing screen for careful and accurate work, and this ground glass is protected from injury when not in use by a hinged panel. An accurate focusing scale is carefully adjusted and enables the user to focus the camera instantly when it is not desirable to use the ground glass. **SHUTTER.** We use in our Kenwood Folding Camera the Gem automatic shutter, one of the latest productions of the celebrated Bausch & Lomb Optical Company, and introduced this season for the first time. It is entirely automatic in its action, requiring only a pressure of the bulb to make any kind of exposure desired. It is so arranged that it may be set for either instantaneous, time or bulb exposures, thus covering the entire range of adjustments, the same as possessed by the very highest priced shutters on the market. **LENSES.** The lenses used in our Kenwood Folding Camera are made expressly for this camera by the Bausch & Lomb Optical Company and are the highest grade of single achromatic lenses which this manufacturer turns out. They possess great depth of focus, covering the plate sharply to the extreme corners, work very rapidly, producing sharp, clear pictures with fine detail.

OUR SPECIAL $4.98 AND $7.90 PRICES include the Kenwood Folding Camera complete with lens, automatic Gem shutter, carrying case and one double plate holder.

PRICES.

GIVE NAME OF CAMERA, CATALOGUE NUMBER AND SIZE WHEN YOU ORDER.

No. 20R2064 The 4x5 Kenwood Folding Camera, complete as above stated. Price........ **$4.98**

No. 20R2066 The 5x7 Kenwood Folding Camera, complete as above stated. Price........ **7.90**

SEE PAGE 145 for prices on extra plate holders.

WE OFFER THE

SEARS SPECIAL FILM CAMERAS

as the equal of other Film Cameras sold at from $8.00 to $12.00.

THE SEARS SPECIAL FILM CAMERAS

AT $3.60 AND $5.70.

WE HAVE THIS SEASON closed a contract with the leading manufacturer of Film Cameras, which enables us to furnish the highest grade film cameras at prices heretofore unknown in the camera business.

OUR FILM CAMERAS are manufactured exclusively for us; they are made under contract that calls for the very best materials, the very best of

ACHROMATIC LENSES.........

and the most perfect workmanship throughout.

THEY ARE EQUIPPED with all the latest improvements and we can guarantee them in every way, both as to materials, workmanship and picture making qualities.

...OUR...

FILM CAMERAS

use the

CARTRIDGE SYSTEM OF DAYLIGHT LOADING FILMS

and they may be loaded and unloaded in broad daylight.

FILM CARTRIDGES are unbreakable; their weight and bulk as compared with glass plates is practically nothing; the results obtained are in every way equal to pictures made upon glass plates, and one-half dozen film cartridges, each sufficient for twelve pictures, may be carried in the pocket without inconvenience.

THE No. 1 SEARS SPECIAL FILM CAMERA, for 3½x3½ pictures. Weight, 20 ounces.
Measurements, 4¼x4½x5½ inches. Capacity, six exposures.
No. 20R2116 Price........ $3.60

THESE PRICES DO NOT INCLUDE FILMS.

THE SEARS SPECIAL FILM CAMERAS represent a type of camera that is complete in itself, with no removable parts. They are fitted with the finest high grade fixed focus achromatic lenses, and are provided with a set of three diaphragms.

THE SHUTTER is suitable for both time and instantaneous exposures, and the speed may be regulated in accordance with the brightness of the light.

EACH OF THESE FILM CAMERAS is provided with an automatic registering device, which shows at a glance exactly how many pictures have been taken and how many unexposed films remain in the camera.

THE SEARS SPECIAL FILM CAMERAS are provided with brilliant view finders and tripod sockets. The covering is the best quality of black morocco leather, and all metal parts are finely nickel plated.

THE No. 2 SEARS SPECIAL FILM CAMERA, for 4x5 pictures. Weight, 28 ounces.
Measurements, 5x5¾x6½ inches. Capacity, twelve exposures.
No. 20R2118 Price........ $5.70

THESE PRICES DO NOT INCLUDE FILMS.

FILMS FOR THE SEARS SPECIAL FILM CAMERAS. This Film is put up in light-tight rolls, or cartridges, all ready to go into the camera, and may be put in at any time or place in broad daylight.

No. 20R2125 Daylight Loading Film Cartridge, for six exposures, 3½x3½. Price........ 26c
If by mail, postage extra, 3 cents.

No. 20R2126 Daylight Loading Film Cartridge, for twelve exposures, 3½x3½. Price........ 52c
If by mail, postage extra, 4 cents.

No. 20R2127 Daylight Loading Film Cartridge, for six exposures, 4x5. Price........ 39c
If by mail, postage extra, 4 cents.

No. 20R2128 Daylight Loading Film Cartridge, for twelve exposures, 4x5. Price........ 78c
If by mail, postage extra, 5 cents.

$11.98 BUYS THE COMPLETE PERFECTION VIEWING OUTFIT

FOR 5 x 7 PICTURES.

No. 20R2135

ORDER BY NUMBER.

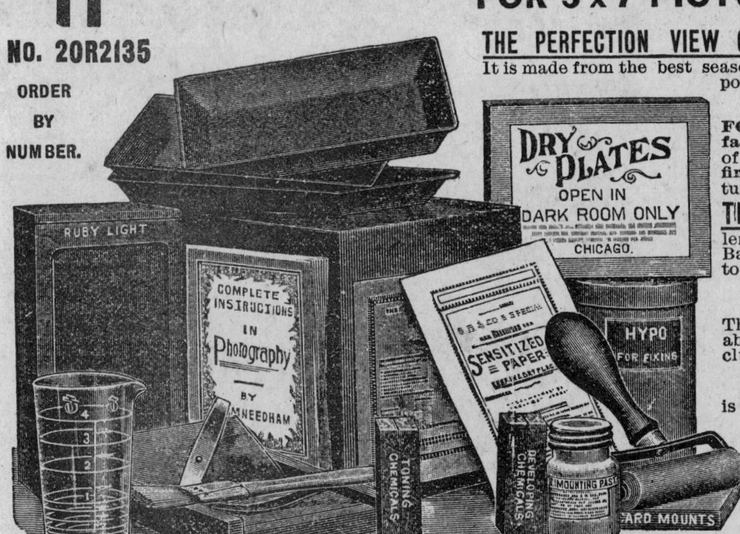

THE PERFECTION VIEW CAMERA is a thoroughly up to date, well made, substantial camera. It is made from the best seasoned mahogany, finely finished and highly polished, and all metal parts are nickel plated.

THE PERFECTION VIEW CAMERA FOLDS UP COMPACTLY, has rising and falling front for adjusting relative amount of sky or foreground, and is provided with a first class swing back, a very valuable feature, especially when photographing buildings.

THE LENS is our Monarch Single Achromatic, a strictly high grade lens, manufactured especially for us by the Bausch & Lomb Optical Co., and guaranteed to be

The Best Single Achromatic Lens that can be made.

The Monarch Single Achromatic Lens is suitable for general all around photography including landscapes, groups, portraits, etc.

THE PERFECTION VIEW CAMERA is made with REVERSIBLE BACK, thus permitting the camera to be used for either vertical or horizontal pictures without changing its position on the tripod.

THE BELLOWS is made from the very best quality of black gossamer cloth of double thickness and is cone shaped. Both the cone shaped bellows and the reversible back are features which have never before been offered except in high priced cameras.

SOLID MAHOGANY CAMERA WITH FINE ACHROMATIC LENS, CARRYING CASE, TRIPOD, PLATE HOLDER, AND COMPLETE DEVELOPING, FINISHING AND MATERIAL OUTFIT.

THE COMPLETE OUTFIT CONTAINS:

- 1 5x7 Perfection Viewing Camera, with Monarch Achromatic Lens, Sliding Tripod, Canvas Carrying Case, and one Double Plate Holder.
- 1 Metal Ruby Lamp.
- 3 Compressed Fiber Trays for developing, fixing and toning.
- 1 8-ounce Measuring Glass.
- 1 5x7 Printing Frame.
- 1 4-inch Ruler.
- 1 2-inch Paste Brush.
- 2 Dozen Sensitized Paper.
- 1 Dozen Dry Plates.
- 25 Card Mounts.
- 1 Package Concentrated Developer.
- 1 Package Concentrated Toning and Fixing Solution.
- 1 Package Hypo.
- 1 Tube of Paste.
- 1 Fine Gossamer Focus Cloth.
- 1 Copy of "Complete Instructions in Photography."

No. 20R2135 The Complete Perfection Viewing Outfit. Price, $11.98

No. 20R2136 Extra Plate Holders for Perfection View Camera. Price, each........ .55

IF YOU WISH TO SEE THE STYLE and quality of work that can be done with the Perfection Viewing Camera we will be pleased to mail you a sample picture made with this Camera, upon receipt of 10 cents.

THE PERFECTION VIEWING CAMERA makes pictures 5x7 inches; the most popular size both for professional and amateur purposes.

THE TRIPOD is our best quality sliding tripod, thoroughly substantial and rigid.

REMEMBER $11.98 includes the entire outfit just as listed and described. There are no extras to buy before you can commence work. The outfit contains absolutely everything necessary for starting into a pleasant and good paying business.

SUCCESS IS CERTAIN, even though you have never had the slightest experience in photographic work. You will be able to turn out good pictures right from the start, as our new 112-page Instruction Book, which we include absolutely free with every one of these outfits, makes everything so plain and easy that failure is practically impossible.

THE EMPIRE STATE PHOTOGRAPHIC OUTFIT

WITH COMPLETE DEVELOPING, FINISHING AND MATERIAL OUTFITS.

EVERYTHING NEEDED for the BEST AMATEUR or PROFESSIONAL WORK.

A... SAMPLE PICTURE Made with the **5x7 Size Empire State Outfit....** will be **MAILED** upon receipt of **10c.**

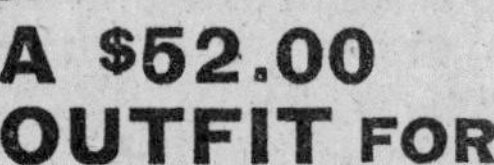

A $52.00 OUTFIT FOR $23.37

RAPID RECTILINEAR LENS, DOUBLE VALVE UNICUM SHUTTER.

The Empire State Camera

3 Sizes: 5 x7, 6½x8½, 8 x10

THE SPECIAL ADVANTAGES of the EMPIRE STATE CAMERA are many, as it is capable of any class of work that can be done with any view or portrait camera. It is constructed throughout from **thoroughly seasoned Honduras mahogany**, and all metal parts are of polished brass. **FOCUSING** is accomplished quickly and easily by **a fine rack and pinion movement.** The bed is hinged and folds completely under the camera, thus permitting the use of **very short focus or wide angle lenses,** if desired. **THE FRONT** has a **rising and falling movement,** enabling the operator to regulate the relative amount of sky or foreground at will. **THE SWING BACK,** which is pivoted at the center, can be quickly adjusted to any desired angle and securely clamped into position by turning a milled head screw. **THE BACK is reversible,** and may be changed instantly from upright to horizontal pictures, without disturbing the camera. The holder is inserted between the spring actuated ground glass and the camera back, and the **slide may be drawn from either side, top or bottom,** a great advantage when working in confined situations. **THE LENS** is our **double rapid rectilinear, possessing great depth of focus, giving the finest detail and the most brilliant definition.** As it is perfectly rectilinear and works very rapidly, it is splendidly adapted to **instantaneous work, groups and portraits, and is unexcelled for landscapes or buildings.**

THE UNICUM SHUTTER is one of the features of this outfit, being a wonderfully ingenious piece of mechanism. It is constructed of bronze metal, practically dust proof, and the shutter blades are made of thin, hard rubber, thus avoiding the danger of rust to which metal blades are subject. **THE IRIS DIAPHRAGM,** with which this shutter is provided, is also made from thin sheets of hard rubber, of the most perfect construction, and affording the best known means for regulating the size of stop or diaphragm. **With one pressure of the bulb the Unicum shutter gives automatic exposures of from $\frac{1}{100}$ of a second to one full second.** With the indicator set at B, a pressure of the bulb opens the shutter which remains open until the pressure is released, a very convenient and accurate method of making short time exposures. With the indicator set at T, the first pressure of the bulb opens the shutter and it remains open until the bulb is again pressed, the best known method for long time exposures.

The Unicum Shutter.

THE COMPLETE EMPIRE STATE PHOTOGRAPHIC OUTFIT CONTAINS:

- 1 Empire State Camera, with double Rapid Rectilinear Lens, Double Valve Unicum Shutter, Sliding Tripod, one Double Plate Holder, and Canvas Carrying Case.
- 1 Heavy Printing Frame.
- 1 Cone Shaped Graduate for measuring liquids.
- 1 Print Roller for smoothing down prints.
- 1 Heavy 2-inch Paste Brush.
- 1 Dozen Dry Plates.
- 1 Fine Metal Dark Room Lamp, with oil burner.
- 1 Compressed Fiber Tray for developing.
- 1 Compressed Fiber Tray for toning.
- 1 Compressed Fiber Tray for fixing.
- 2 Dozen Sheets Sensitized Paper.
- 25 Card Mounts.
- 1 8-oz. Bottle Concentrated Developer.
- 1 8-ounce Bottle Concentrated Toning and Fixing Solution.
- 1 8-ounce Bottle Intensifier for weak negatives.
- 1 Package Hypo for fixing negatives or prints.
- 1 Jar Photo Mounting Paste.
- 1 Fine Gossamer Focus Cloth.
- 1 Copy "Complete Instruction in Photography."

Taking the 5x7 size as an example, the camera alone, if purchased at retail, would cost $17.00, the lens $15.00, the shutter $9.00, the tripod $2.25, and the developing, finishing and material outfit about $8.80, making the total retail value of the entire outfit over $52.00.

...OUR SPECIAL PRICES...

Complete Outfits with Rectilinear Lenses and Unicum Shutters.

No. 20R2200 The 5x7 Empire State Photographic Outfit, consisting of camera, rapid rectilinear lens, Unicum shutter, tripod, plate holder and complete outfit, as described above. Price.........**$23.37**

No. 20R2201 The 6½x8½ Empire State Photographic Outfit, consisting of camera, rapid rectilinear lens, Unicum shutter, tripod, plate holder and complete outfit, as described above. Price....**$29.95**

No. 20R2202 The 8x10 Empire State Photographic Outfit, consisting of camera, rapid rectilinear lens, Unicum shutter, tripod, plate holder and complete outfit, as described above. Price.........**$34.38**

COMPLETE OUTFITS WITHOUT SHUTTER.

No. 20R2207 Empire State Photographic Outfits, complete, just as described above, with Seroco rapid rectilinear lens, **but without shutters.**

Prices, 5x7, **$19.92**; 6½x8½, **$26.65**; 8x10, **$30.82**

COMPLETE OUTFITS WITH ACHROMATIC LENSES.

No. 20R2212 Empire State Photographic Outfits. For the benefit of those who do not desire to invest in the complete outfit with rectilinear lens and Unicum shutter, we can furnish the Empire State Outfits complete, just as described above, **but without shutters** and with our **Monarch single achromatic lens,** instead of the double rectilinear lens, at the following prices:

Prices, 5x7, **$17.92**; 6½x8½, **$19.95**; 8x10, **$24.33**

From the profits made with the outfit, the double rapid rectilinear lens and Unicum shutter can be easily added later.

PRICES ON CAMERAS ONLY.

No. 20R2216 We also furnish the Empire State Cameras, without lens, shutter, tripod or outfit, at the following prices:

Size	Price	Size	Price
5 x 7	$10.50	10x12	$22.35
6½x 8½	11.75	11x14	23.35
8 x10	13.00	14x17	34.67

These prices include canvas case and one plate holder.

$52.00 WORTH OF GOODS... FOR $23.37

EXTRA PLATE HOLDERS. **No. 20R2220 The plate holder used with the Empire State Camera is beyond question the most efficient, most easily handled and best made holder on the market. In fact, it is one of the features of the outfit.** We advise the purchase of a number, as the more holders you have the more plates you can carry at a time.

Size	Price	Size	Price
5 x7	$0.54	10x12	$1.58
6½x8½	.90	11x14	2.25
8 x10	1.13	14x17	3.15

TELEGRAPH INSTRUMENTS.

To those who are about to start in life, either ladies or gentlemen, there is nothing at the present time which offers better inducements than telegraphy. The smallest salaries paid are about $35.00 per month, but the salaries usually paid are from $50.00 to $125.00 per month and many even get much more. Besides, the only inducements are not the salary alone, for it opens the way to other and more expansive fields of work.

A large number of the high officials of railroad companies who command salaries from $15,000.00 to $50,000.00 per year started as telegraph operators. Thomas A. Edison, the wonderful inventor, who owns over 600 patents and is immensely wealthy, began as a telegraph operator.

Those who are not familiar with telegraphy are liable to believe that it is something mysterious and difficult to learn, but this is a mistake. It is very easy to learn, can be thoroughly mastered in from two to six months, and with a reasonable amount of care and application it can be learned at home and after a little experience the practice can be made very interesting by constructing a short line between two or more houses, which can be done at a very small expense; all that is necessary is to carefully follow the instructions laid down in the instruction book.

Our Complete Learner's Telegraph Outfit.

PRICE $1.65

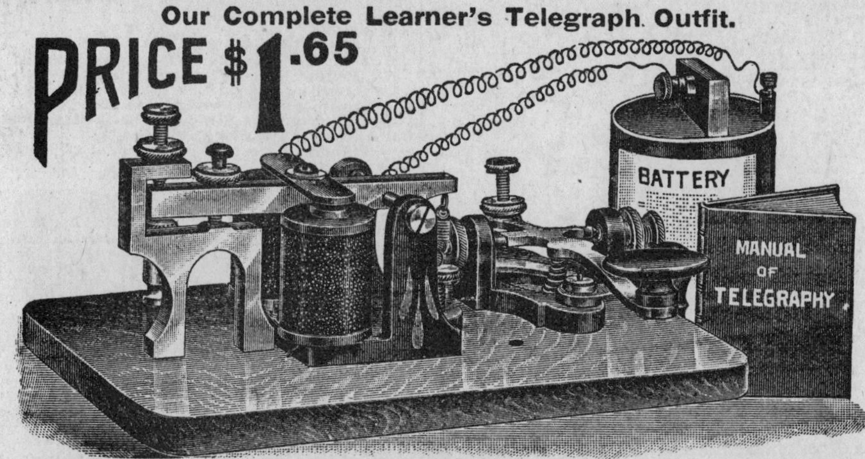

No. 20R4415

For $1.65 we furnish a LEARNER'S COMPLETE TELEGRAPH OUTFIT, consisting of key and sounder, working battery, wire and Manual of Telegraphy (a complete instruction book), a regular $5.00 outfit. **Use this outfit,** follow the instructions and you will soon become a telegraph operator. Positions are open for operators on railroads, everywhere at $40.00 to $60.00 per month.

THIS OUTFIT as illustrated, **consists of a full size key and sounder,** mounted on a polished cherry base. Comes complete with full size battery, with wire and chemicals, all ready for work. Key has nickel bar, latest thumbscrew adjustment, best rubber hand hold and cut out, platinum points, carefully adjusted. Sounder has covered magnets wound to 4 ohms resistance, polished brass sounding bar and frame; thumbscrew adjustment connections. **A thoroughly serviceable and practical LEARNER'S TELEGRAPH OUTFIT.**

INSTRUCTION BOOK. **The instruction book, or Manual of Telegraphy,** furnished with this outfit gives full instructions how to read and write by the Morse system, the alphabet, figures, punctuation, etc.; teaches you how to send and receive messages, teaches you everything pertaining to telegraphy, enables you, by carefully following the instructions and using the outfit in practice, by your own efforts to become an expert telegraph operator.

No. 20R4415 Learner's Telegraph Outfit, complete as described above. Price, each............**$1.65**

4-Ohm Learner's Instrument.

No. 20R4426 4-Ohm Learner's Instrument, exactly the same as the instrument included with outfit No. 20R4415, but without battery or connecting wire. Price, each..............................**$1.48**

20-Ohm Learner's Instrument.

No. 20R4427 20-Ohm Learner's Instrument, full size sounder and key, mounted on polished cherry base, magnets wound to 20 ohms resistance. **This instrument is intended for long distance work,** and can be used on lines **one-half mile or more** in length. Price, each..............**$1.90**

Extra High Grade Private Line Instruments.

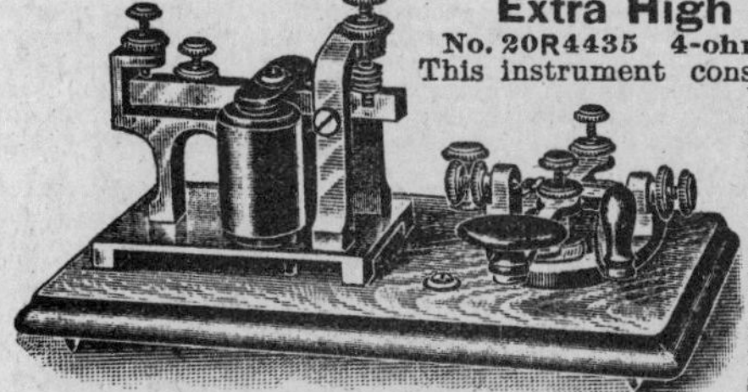

No. 20R4435 4-ohm Private Line Instrument, for practice or short lines. This instrument consists of an extra high grade sounder and fine steel lever key, mounted on highly polished mahogany base. Materials and workmanship are the best. **The sounder magnets are wound to 4 ohms resistance** and covered with polished hard rubber, the sounding bar is made from aluminum, and for tone, loudness and quick action is unsurpassed. The fine steel lever key, has solid trunnion, hardened platina points, and thumbscrew trunnion adjustments. Price, each........................**$3.25**

No. 20R4436 20-ohm Private Line Instrument, exactly the same as No. 20R4435, except that the sounder magnets are wound to 20 ohms resistance, making the instrument suitable for long distance work. Can be used on lines one-half mile or more in length. Price, each..**$3.90**

THE OMNIGRAPH.

An Automatic Learner's Telegraph Instrument.

THE OMNIGRAPH is a High Grade Telegraph Instrument that will tick off messages, containing all the letters in the Morse alphabet, absolutely correct and at any speed. **The Dots, Dashes and Spaces can be both seen and heard, and it makes learning both easy and interesting.** Did you ever stop to think how you learned to talk? You learned by hearing other people talk; telegraphy is the same as language, and by simply listening to the Omnigraph as it ticks off the **characters of the Morse alphabet** you will very quickly memorize them and be able to read messages as well as an experienced operator. The Omnigraph consists of a regular sounder and key mounted on a polished mahogany base, and between the sounder and a key is an exceedingly ingenious mechanical device called the transmitter, operated by a small crank. **This transmitter enables the Omnigraph to do, what no other telegraph instrument will do,** that is, send you messages, in the most perfect manner, at any speed and at any time, and by simply listening to these messages you can learn the alphabet and with a little practice **become an expert operator in less time than by any other method.** Any kind of a battery can be used for operating the Omnigraph, but we especially recommend a dry cell battery such as our No. 20R4615. One cell is sufficient to operate the Omnigraph, but if two are used the sound is louder and clearer. **The Omnigraph can also be operated with the key in the ordinary manner just the same as any telegraph instrument.** We include sufficient wire with each instrument to connect with the battery. **No battery is included with the Omnigraph.**

No. 20R4445 Price, each..**$3.37**

Steel Lever Keys.

No. 20R4448 Steel Lever Key, legless. This is the standard Western Union Key, of the **latest and most improved type,** the lever and trunnions being made of solid steel, nickel plated, instead of brass, as in the old type of instrument. The same strength is secured with much lighter weight and the liability of loose trunnions completely avoided. This is without doubt **one of the handsomest and best working keys on the market.** Its adoption by the **Western Union Company** is certainly a sufficient recommendation for it. Price, each........................**$1.45**

If by mail, postage extra, 10 cents.

No. 20R4449 Steel Lever Key, with legs. A standard Western Union key, just the same in general construction, material, workmanship and efficiency as the preceding style, but made with two legs, which go through the table, connection thus being made from below. Price, each........................**$1.38**

Aluminum Lever Sounder

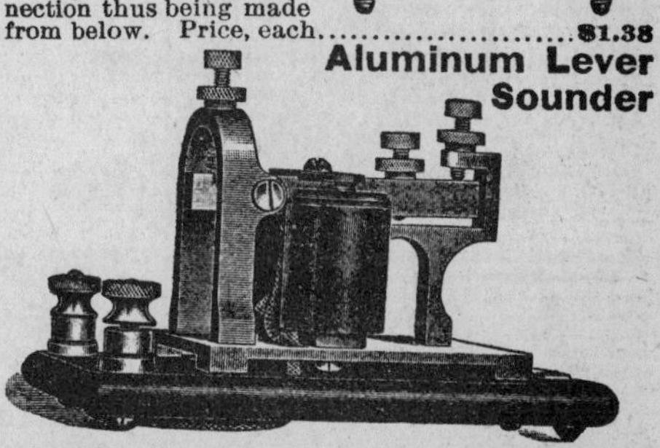

Our New Aluminum Lever Giant Sounders excel all other sounders in tone, loudness and quick action, being in every respect the finest and best sounders made. The sounding bar is made from **aluminum,** the balance of the instrument is of brass, and the magnets are covered with polished hard rubber. The base is of highly polished mahogany, and the entire instrument is finished with the most careful attention to details and appearance.

Special attention is directed to the way in which the wooden base is connected to the instrument, an open space being left between the wood and the metal, which greatly increases the sound and improves the tone. **The Western Union Telegraph Co. has thousands of these sounders in use on their main lines,** a fact which in itself speaks for their quality.

No. 20R4460 Aluminum Lever Giant Sounder, as described and illustrated above, with magnets wound to **4 ohms** resistance, for lines one-quarter mile or less in length. Price, each...............**$1.98**

No. 20R4461 Aluminum Lever Giant Sounder, as described and illustrated above, with magnets wound to **20 ohms** resistance, for lines one-half mile or more in length. Will work on lines up to fifty miles in length. Price, each........................**$2.28**

BATTERIES.

Batteries for Telegraph Instruments.

When only one instrument is used, simply for practice, a dry cell battery, such as we describe under No. 20R4615 **is the most convenient and best battery to use. But when a complete line with two or more instruments is established the only suitable battery is the gravity,** described under Nos. 20R4575 and 20R4576. If the dry cell battery is used on a line complete with two or more instruments, it will very quickly become exhausted, but the gravity battery will last for months.

Gravity Battery.

The Gravity Battery is a closed circuit battery which is used for telegraphic work, and can also be used for operating electric bells, small motors, etc., but is not so desirable for such work on account of evaporation and the necessity for renewing the battery more often.

No. 20R4575 Gravity Battery, cell complete, size 5x7, weight about 5 pounds. Each........................**47c**

No. 20R4576 Gravity Battery, cell complete, size 6x8, weight about 7 pounds. Each..................**55c**

No. 20R4578 Battery Jar, glass, 5x7. Each..**18c**

No. 20R4580 Battery Jar, glass, 6x8. Each..**20c**

No. 20R4582 Zinc, for 5x7 battery. Each....**20c**

No. 20R4584 Zinc, for 6x8 battery. Each....**26c**

No. 20R4586 Copper, for 5x7, or 6x8 battery. Each...**8c**

No. 20R4588 Blue Vitriol, per pound.........**8c**

JUVENILE MAGIC LANTERN OUTFITS

The young people not only derive great pleasure from giving MAGIC LANTERN EXHIBITIONS, but the business training which they gain in all the various details connected with the management of an entertainment, putting up advertising posters, **selling tickets**, etc., gives them ideas of the rudiments of **money making** which starts them on the highway to business success. REMEMBER that each outfit is complete, containing

A FINE MAGIC LANTERN, A SPLENDID ASSORTMENT OF COLORED VIEWS, A LARGE SUPPLY OF ADVERTISING POSTERS, PLENTY OF TICKETS.

INTERESTING, INSTRUCTIVE AND PROFITABLE.

You will easily make the original cost of the outfit in your first exhibition; after that it's all profit.

The Home Magic Lantern Outfits.

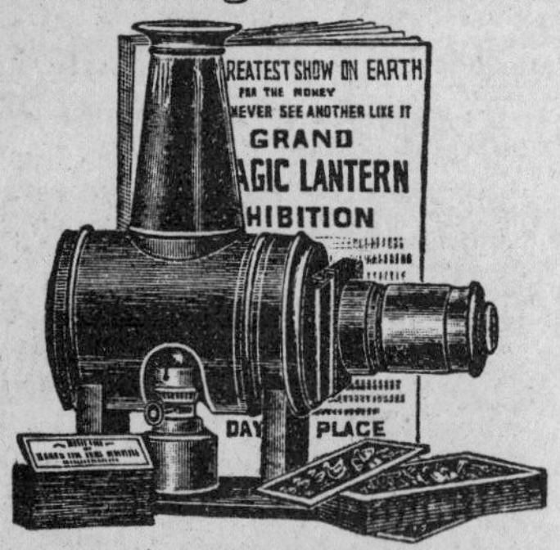

Our illustration gives a very exact idea of the general appearance and construction of the Home Magic Lantern. The body of this lantern is made of metal, japanned in black, **handsomely decorated in gilt,** and mounted on wood baseboard. Burns ordinary kerosene or coal oil.

No. 20R5020 The Home Magic Lantern Outfit No. 1, with **Home Magic Lantern** as described above, using slides $1\frac{3}{8}$ inches wide and magnifying pictures to about **1 foot in diameter.** The complete outfit contains lantern, **6 colored slides,** three to four pictures on each slide, **25 advertising posters and 25 admission tickets.** Price, complete..**59c**

No. 20R5023 Home Magic Lantern Outfit No. 2, same as No. 20R5020, but using slides $1\frac{3}{8}$-inches wide, **magnifying pictures to 2 feet and including 12 colored slides** instead of 6. Price, complete......**$1.28**

No. 20R5026 Home Magic Lantern Outfit No. 3, same as No. 20R5020, but using slides 2 inches wide, magnifying pictures to about 3 feet in diameter. Price, complete..**$1.98**

The Brilliant Magic Lantern Outfits.

The Brilliant Magic Lanterns are very handsome instruments of the upright style, finely finished in brass, bronze and nickel plate, with the body of the lantern enameled in bright red. They are provided with **double convex condensing lens** and finely ground projecting lens. In addition to the regular long glass slides, these lanterns also use a slide in the form of **a round disc with six views.** Each lantern contained in neat wood box with handle.

No. 20R5040 The Brilliant Magic Lantern Outfit No. 1, with Brilliant Magic Lantern as described above, **using slides 1⅜ inches wide,** and magnifying pictures to about 2 feet in diameter. **The complete outfit consists of lantern, six long glass colored slides, three to four views on each slide, three glass discs with six colored views on each disc, twenty-five advertising posters and twenty-five admission tickets.**
Price, complete..**$1.90**

No. 20R5041 Brilliant Magic Lantern Outfit No. 2, same as No. 20R5040, but **using slides 1¾ inches wide,** magnifying pictures to about 3 feet in diameter. Price, complete..............................**$2.98**

No. 20R5042 Brilliant Magic Lantern Outfit No. 3, same as No. 20R5040, but **using slides 2 inches wide,** magnifying pictures to about 4 feet in diameter. Price, complete..**$3.75**

The Gem Magic Lantern.

The Gem Magic Lantern, our best grade lantern, is finely finished in Russia sheet iron, lacquered, with brass lens tube and trimming. **The Gem Lantern is provided with a pair of convex condensing lenses,** and finely ground projection lens, and has blue glass window in door to protect the eyes from the dazzling light. The lamp with which the Gem lantern is fitted is of the duplex or double burner style, giving a very brilliant illumination. Burns ordinary kerosene or coal oil. **A fine instrument for parlor exhibitions.**

No. 20R5050 The Gem Magic Lantern Outfit No. 1, with Gem Magic Lantern as described above, using slides **2 inches wide** and magnifying pictures to about 3 feet in diameter. The complete outfit consists of **the lantern, twelve colored slides, three to four pictures on each slide, one comic slip slide, one movable scenery slide, one brilliantly colored chromotrope or artificial fireworks slide, fifty large advertising posters, and fifty admission tickets.** Price, complete..............................**$4.95**

No. 20R5051 The Gem Magic Lantern Outfit No. 2, same as No. 20R5050, but **using slides 2⅜ inches wide,** magnifying pictures to about 4 feet in diameter. Price, complete..................**$5.95**

No. 20R5052 The Gem Magic Lantern Outfit No. 3, same as No. 20R5050, but **using slides 2¾ inches wide,** magnifying pictures to about 5 feet in diameter. Price, complete..................**$6.75**

Extra Chimneys and Wicks.

We can furnish glass chimneys and wicks to fit the magic lanterns described on this page at the following prices:

No. 20R5055 Chimney to fit any of the Home or Brilliant Magic Lanterns. Price, each, any size..**10c**
If by mail, postage extra, 6 cents.

No. 20R5056 Wicks, to fit any of our magic lanterns. Price, six for..**5c**

N. B.—When ordering chimneys or wicks be sure to state which lantern they are to fit.

Colored Slides.

Plain Colored Slides.

No. 20R5060 These slides are all highly colored and each slide has from three to four views. They are put up in packages of one dozen slides and each package contains an assortment of both comic and scenic views. **We cannot sell less than one package,** and we are unable to furnish any special subjects.

Width	Price
$1\frac{3}{8}$ inches, package of 1 dozen	$0.20
1⅜ inches, package of 1 dozen	.30
$1\frac{5}{8}$ inches, package of 1 dozen	.36
1¾ inches, package of 1 dozen	.51
2 inches, package of 1 dozen	.64
2⅜ inches, package of 1 dozen	.85
2¾ inches, package of 1 dozen	1.11

Comic Movable Slides.

No. 20R5063 These pictures are painted in bright colors on glass slips, which slide in metal frames, each slide containing two comic views. **Very amusing effects are produced** by suddenly slipping the second view into the place of the first. Put up in packages of one dozen slides each.

Width, inches	Price, per pkg. of 1 dozen	Width, inches	Price, per pkg. of 1 dozen
1⅜	60c	2	$1.08
$1\frac{5}{8}$	67c	2⅜	1.28
1¾	92c	2¾	1.48

The Brilliant Slides.

No. 20R5066 The most economical slides made, printed on celluloid and affording a class of pictures never before offered in anything but high priced slides. Made in one size only, 2 inches wide, but can be used in any lantern using slides 2 inches or wider. If your lantern uses slides 2⅜ or 2¾ inches wide, we will include, **for 8c extra,** a small wooden carrier by means of which you can use these **Brilliant Slides.** Each series of the **Brilliant Slides** contains 12 slides, three pictures on each slide, making a total of **36 views in each series.** Order by series.

Series		Price
A	**Noted Places Around the World**	**36c**
B	**Miscellaneous Views, mostly very comic.**	**36c**
H	**Old and New Testament Bible Views**	**36c**
I	**Comic, each good for a laugh**	**36c**
M	**American and Foreign Scenery**	**36c**

All the Brilliant Slides are 2 inches wide and not made in any other size.

If by mail, postage extra, per set, 1 cent.

Chromotropes.

No. 20R5069 These Slides, known also as **artificial fireworks,** consist of two glass discs, painted in bright colors in radiating geometrical patterns, which are revolved in opposite directions by means of the small crank, producing a **very brilliant effect.** Several different patterns of each size can be furnished.

Width	Price
Width, $1\frac{3}{8}$ inches; price, each	**25c**
Width, 1¾ inches; price, each	**30c**
Width, 2 inches; price, each	**33c**
Width, 2⅜ inches; price, each	**36c**
Width, 2¾ inches; price, each	**39c**

Genuine Photographic Slides.

Spanish-American War. A Trip Across the Continent. Our Heroes' Return.

We are able to offer this season for the first time the following series of actual photographic views, all popular and up to date subjects, in sizes suitable for use with our Juvenile Magic Lanterns. By making up these slides in great quantities, and putting four views on a slide, we are able to furnish them at astonishingly low prices. Heretofore real photographic slides could be obtained only in the regular professional size, suitable only for use with the large professional stereopticons; they were made with only one view on a slide, and cost from 35 cents to 50 cents per view. **Each set of our genuine photographic slides contains twelve slides, and there are four views in each slide, making a total of forty-eight views in every set. With every set we include a printed lecture, giving a complete description of every view.**

The Spanish-American War.

No. 20R5080 A splendid set of forty-eight views, illustrating the most interesting features of the late war between the United States and Spain. Portraits of prominent officers, battleships, camp life, battle scenes, etc. Twelve slides in the set, four views on each slide, making a total of forty-eight views.

Width	Price
Width, $1\frac{3}{8}$ inches; price, per set, with lecture,	**$1.13**
Width, 2 inches; price, per set, with lecture,	**1.35**
Width, 2⅜ inches; price, per set, with lecture,	**2.48**
Width, 2¾ inches; price, per set, with lecture,	**2.93**

Sold only in sets. We cannot sell less than a set.

Our Heroes' Return.

No. 20R5085 This interesting set of views is also descriptive of events in connection with the war, but deals more particularly with happenings after peace was declared. It contains some splendid views of battleships, pictures of the Dewey parade in New York, soldiers on the way home, distinguished generals, naval parade, etc. All actual photographs from life. Twelve slides in the set, four views on each slide, forty-eight views in all.

Width	Price
Width, $1\frac{3}{8}$ inches; price, per set, with lecture,	**$1.13**
Width, 2 inches; price, per set, with lecture,	**1.35**
Width, 2⅜ inches; price, per set, with lecture,	**2.48**
Width, 2¾ inches; price, per set, with lecture,	**2.93**

Sold only in sets. We cannot sell less than a set.

A Trip Across the Continent.

No. 20R5090 This exceedingly popular set is a series of photographic views, illustrating points of interest throughout the United States, prominent buildings, magnificent scenery in the Yellowstone Park, at Niagara, and in the Yosemite Valley, views of Washington, D. C., and other cities. Twelve slides in the set, four views on each slide, forty-eight views in all.

Width	Price
Width, $1\frac{3}{8}$ inches; price, per set, with lecture,	**$1.13**
Width, 2 inches; price, per set, with lecture,	**1.35**
Width, 2⅜ inches; price, per set, with lecture,	**2.48**
Width, 2¾ inches; price, per set, with lecture,	**2.93**

Sold only in sets. We cannot sell less than a set.

NOTE—These photographic slides can be used with any of our Juvenile Lanterns, except Nos. 20R5020 and 20R5040. Note in the description of the lanterns the size of slide used, and select the corresponding size in these photographic slides.

DRAWING INSTRUMENTS AND MATERIALS.

Mechanical drawing or draughting is an accomplishment, the value of which can hardly be overestimated. For the mechanic, the artist, or for anyone at all interested in the manual arts, architecture, civil engineering, mining, surveying, bridge building or any of these kindred sciences, a knowledge of mechanical drawing is not only of great assistance, but is absolutely essential. Mechanical drawing is a study that can easily be self taught. It does not require any artistic ability or previous knowledge of drawing to become proficient, and the time and effort spent in acquiring it will be fully repaid.

In this line of drawing sets the instruments are made of brass, and nickel plated. The exceedingly low prices quoted upon these sets, place them within the reach of all who desire to learn draughting.

NICKEL PLATED INSTRUMENTS IN SETS.

Our 19-Cent Compass Set.

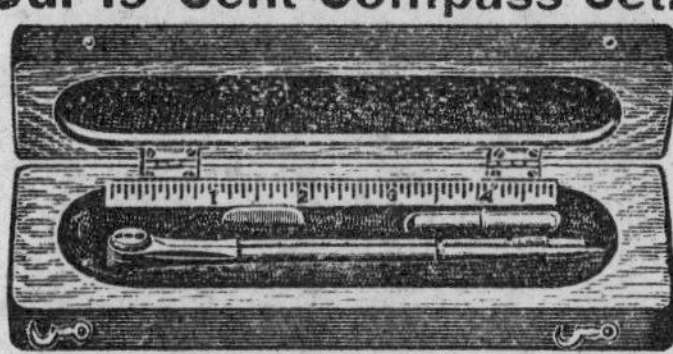

No. 20R5500 Amateur Compass Set containing: 4½-inch Dividers with pencil point, Case of Leads, Key for adjusting Dividers. Contained in velvet lined wood box. Price....19c

If by mail, postage extra, 5 cents.

54 Cents for This Amateur Set.

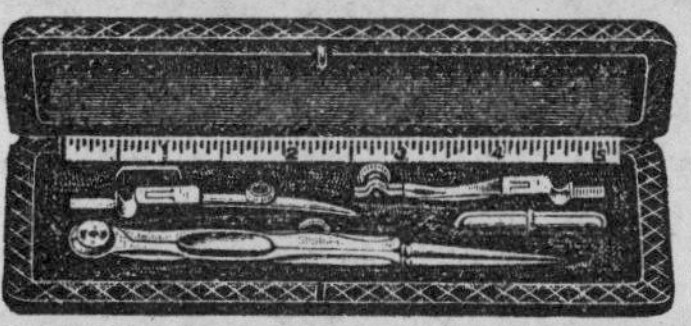

No. 20R5505 Amateur Drawing Set, containing: 4½-inch Dividers, with both pen and pencil points, Metal Protractor, Rule, Case of Leads, Key for adjusting Dividers. Better quality than the preceding set, and contained in velvet lined leatherette case. Price....54c

If by mail, postage extra, 6 cents.

Our School Set at 68 Cents.

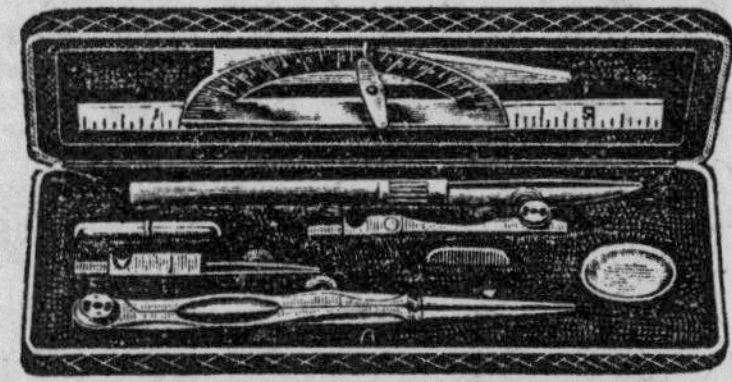

No. 20R5510 School Drawing Set, containing: 4½-inch Dividers, with both pen and pencil points, 4¾-inch Ruling Pen, 5-inch Graduated Rule, Case of Leads, Metal Protractor, Key for adjusting Dividers. Well made and contained in velvet lined leatherette pocket case. Price....68c

If by mail, postage extra, 8 cents.

A Good Set for 78 Cents.

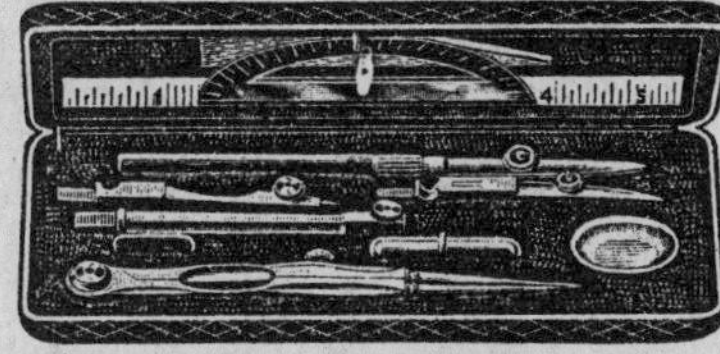

No. 20R5515 School Drawing Set, containing: 5-inch Dividers, with both pen and pencil points, 5-inch Ruling Pen, 5-inch Graduated Rule, Metal Protractor, Case of Leads, Key, Small Wood Triangle, Lengthening Bar for Dividers. Contained in velvet lined leatherette case. Price....78c

If by mail, postage extra, 8 cents.

98 Cents Buys This Scholars' Set.

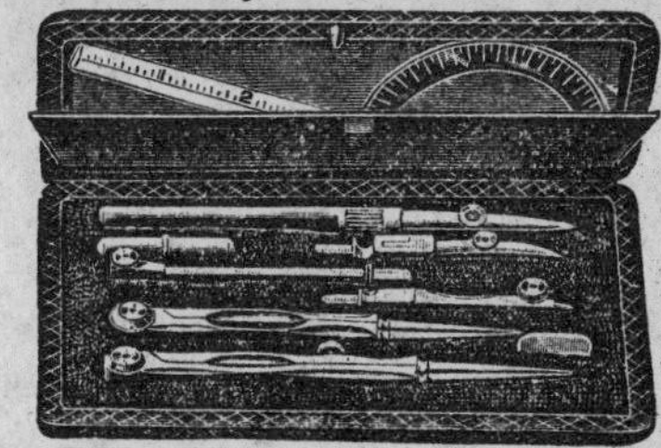

No. 20R5520 Scholars' Drawing Set, consisting of: 4½-inch Plain Dividers, Lengthening Bar for Compasses, Graduated Rule, Case of Leads, Small Wood Triangle, 5-inch Compasses, with both pen and pencil points, 4¾-inch Ruling Pen, Metal Protractor, Key. Contained in a handsome velvet lined leatherette case. Price....98c

If by mail, postage extra, 14 cents.

Set With Spring Bow Pen for $1.45.

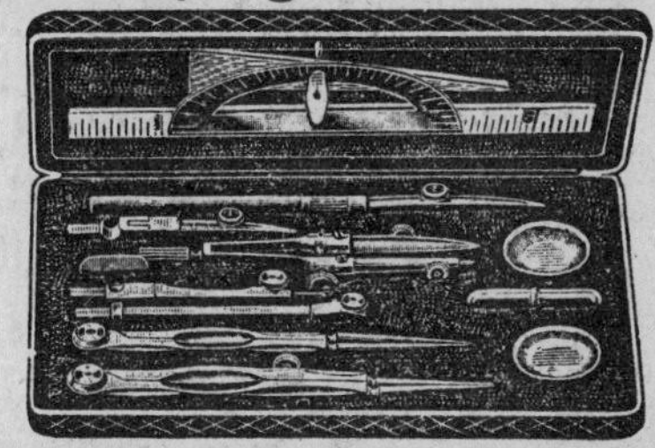

No. 20R5525 Our Special Drawing Set, consisting of: 4½-inch Plain Dividers, 4½-inch Compasses, with both pen and pencil points, Lengthening Bar for compasses, 4¾-inch Ruling Pen, 3½-inch Spring Bow Pen, Metal Protractor, Graduated Rule, Case of Leads, Key. Handsomely finished and contained in durable velvet lined leatherette case. Price...$1.45

If by mail, postage extra, 17 cents.

FINE GERMAN SILVER INSTRUMENTS IN SETS.

In the following sets the instruments are constructed from German silver and the best English steel. Both dividers and compasses are made with patent handles.

Exceptional Value at $2.69.

No. 20R5530 Fine German Silver Drawing Set, consisting of:
- 5-inch Plain Dividers.
- 5½-inch Compasses with pen and pencil points.
- 5½-inch Ivory Handle Ruling Pen with joint.
- Lengthening Bar for Compasses.
- Box of Leads and Key.

These well made instruments are contained in genuine leather velvet lined pocket case. Price....$2.69

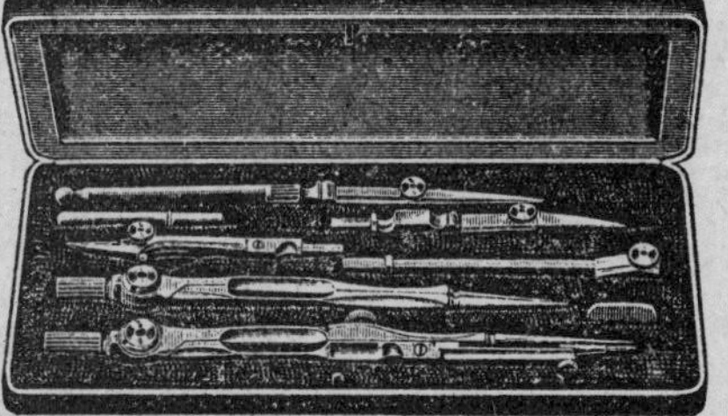

If by mail, postage extra, 15 cents.

A High Grade Set for $2.98.

No. 20R5535 Fine German Silver Drawing Set, consisting of:
- 5½-inch Ruling Pen with joint.
- 5-inch Plain Dividers.
- 5½-inch Compasses with pen and pencil points.
- Lengthening Bar for Compasses.
- 3½-inch Steel Spring Bow Pen.
- Box of Leads and Key.

Contained in genuine leather velvet lined pocket case. Fully meets the requirements for use in manual training schools or elementary work in engineering colleges. Price....$2.98

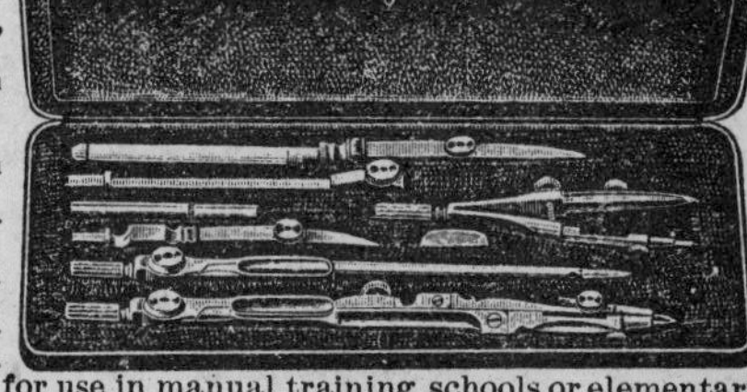

If by mail, postage extra, 18 cents.

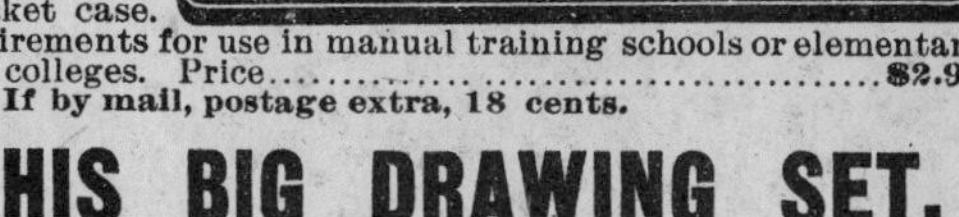

$4.98 BUYS THIS BIG DRAWING SET.

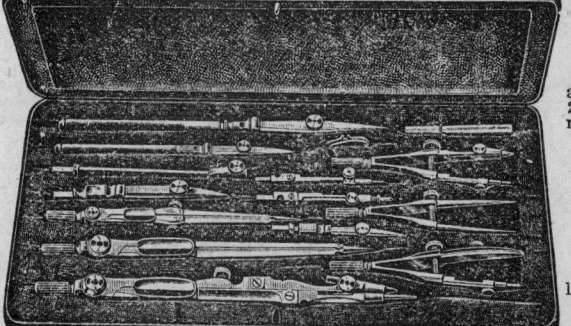

No. 20R5540 Fine German Silver Drawing Set. The instruments contained in this set are the same high grade of German silver and English steel construction as those of set No. 20R5535, but the number of pieces is greater, in fact the set includes everything that would be required for the most advanced work. The set consists of:

- **5½-inch Plain Dividers.**
- **3¾-inch Compasses with pen and pencil points.**
- **Needle Points for 3¾-inch Compasses.**
- **5½-inch Compasses, with pen and pencil points.**
- **Needle Point for 5½-inch Compasses.**
- **4-inch Ruling Pen with joint.**
- **5½-inch Ruling Pen with joint.**
- **3½-inch Steel Spring Bow Pen.**
- **3½-inch Steel Spring Bow Pencil.**
- **3½-inch Steel Spring Bow Dividers.**
- **Lengthening Bar for Compasses.**
- **Box of Leads and Key.**

This very complete set is contained in a fine leather pocket case of the regular style, velvet lined. Price....$4.98

If by mail, postage extra, 22 cents.

WONDERFUL VALUE AT $5.95.

No. 20R5545 SUPERIOR GERMAN SILVER DRAWING SET. The instruments of this set are made from the finest grade of hard German silver, carefully tempered and highly finished. The tongues of the joints, needle points and other steel parts are made from the best English steel finely tempered and hardened. Both the dividers and compasses are made with the famous pivot joint, universally accepted by draughtsmen as the most desirable joint made. **A set that will wear a life time.** The following instruments are included:

- **4¼-inch Ruling Pen with spring.**
- **5-inch Ruling Pen with spring.**
- **5-inch Hair Spring Dividers, with pivot joint.**
- **5½-inch Compasses, pivot joint, with pen, pencil and needle points.**
- **Lengthening bar for compasses.**
- **3½-inch Spring Bow Dividers, with metal handle.**
- **3½-inch Spring Bow Pencil, with metal handle.**
- **3½-inch Spring Bow Pen, with metal handle.**
- **Box of leads.**

This elegant set is contained in our new style **folding pocketbook case,** made of genuine seal grain morocco leather, and lined with silk velvet. Price....(If by mail, postage extra, 20 cents)....$5.95

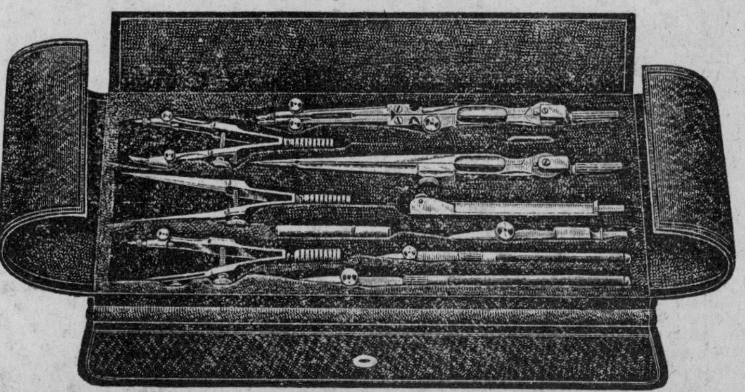

DEPARTMENT OF PUBLIC ENTERTAINMENT OUTFITS AND SUPPLIES.

Our experience in the past has proved that public exhibition work is extremely profitable and, with comparatively small investment, affords to the exhibitor an opportunity for realizing very large profits, and in addition opens up to him a line of business that is pleasant as well as invaluable in the development and building up of a successful business man.

THIS DEPARTMENT is maintained for the information of those who contemplate entering the exhibition field, or those who having done so, desire to "stay in front" and keep their exhibition outfits up to date and consequently successful, and with ability, energy and push, be the means of enabling the exhibitor to accumulate a fortune.

PUBLIC EXHIBITION WORK has never been brought to the same state of perfection as now. Our outfits are entirely new, are founded on the newest kind of intensely interesting, new and up to date subjects. Upon application we will send selections from the many hundred testimonials we have received bearing upon the same subject.

IN THESE PAGES we shall describe outfits for public exhibition work such as have never been brought together before, at lower prices than other dealers could offer them, and of a quality which it is impossible to surpass.

THE WONDERFUL GRAPHOPHONE TALKING MACHINE in its newest and most approved type, is the giant-voiced marvel of the present century

THE STEREOPTICON PANORAMIC EXHIBITION portrays illustrations of strange lands, men and countries, the varied beauties and grandeur of our own land, and illustrations of the all absorbing topics of the day. We aim to emulate the example of the great metropolitan daily, and to illustrate on canvas the important events of the day.

ILLUSTRATED SONGS. The present most effective method of illustrating the popular songs of the day by means of stereopticon pictures, showing the various scenes and incidents as they are described in the song itself, is new and has proved a most wonderful success wherever exhibited.

THE UNRIVALLED EDISON KINETOSCOPE, moving picture machine, giving a pictorial presentation, not lifelike merely, but apparently life itself, with every movement, every action and every detail brought so vividly before the audience that it becomes difficult for them to believe that what they see before them can be other than nature's very self.

NO PREVIOUS EXPERIENCE NECESSARY, no ability as a public speaker required. Some of our most successful entertainers had never spoken in public before.

For the convenience of those who do not know what constitutes a complete exhibition outfit and to assist them in making their selection we draw attention to a few

COMPLETE EXHIBITION OUTFITS.

These are only a few out of the many outfits which we offer, and are intended principally as suggestions and means of guidance in arriving at the price of an outfit. We have divided these outfits under three heads: GRAPHOPHONE CONCERT ENTERTAINMENTS, PANORAMIC STEREOPTICON EXHIBITIONS, and ANIMATED PICTURE OUTFITS. All of these are provided with beautifully illustrated advertising matter and admission tickets. All are complete in every respect and ready to go at once to work. If you are undecided as to exactly what you need, write us for advice which is always at your command. Let us know what changes you would prefer to make on these outfits and we will quote you prices on them altered to suit your requirements. Any two or all three of these types may be satisfactorily combined to make up a high grade outfit, and posters advertising the combined attraction will be furnished free with each order.

Graphophone Concert Entertainments.

Our leader for exhibition work is our $23.75 Talking Machine Outfit, made up as follows:

- 1 Gem Graphophone, complete with loudest reproducing diaphragm and set of hearing tubes for two persons.
- 1 large amplifying horn, complete with stand.
- 24 high grade electrically recorded musical and talking records.
- 1,000 highly illustrated advertising posters.
- 1,000 admission tickets.
- 1 rubber printing outfit for filling in dates.

COMPLETE FOR $23.75

See full description of outfit on page 157.

Our Mammoth Graphophone Grand Peerless Talking Machine Outfit includes:

- 1 Graphophone Grand complete, using mammoth 5-inch cylinder records, extra loud aluminum reproducer, recorder, shaving knife and recording horn.
- 1 42-inch amplifying brass horn, complete with stand.
- 12 5-inch cylinder records.
- 1 handsome leatherette case for carrying records.
- Posters. Tickets. Rubber Printing Outfit. } In same quantities as our $23.75 outfit.

COMPLETE FOR $75.00

See full description of outfit on page 159.

Our New Regal Flat Disc, Unbreakable Record Outfits. Our newest machine and, owing to its portability and the indestructible nature of its equipment, is destined to be the unrivaled concert outfit of the future, includes:

- 1 Regal Concert Graphophone, with latest patent combined reproducer and concert sound box.
- 1 22-inch amplifying horn.
- 2 dozen 10-inch Climax unbreakable disc records.
- Posters. Tickets. Rubber printing outfit. } Same as preceding outfits.

COMPLETE FOR $65.00

See full description of outfit on page 164.

Panoramic Stereopticon Exhibitions.

Our Complete Professional Panoramic Stereopticon Lecture Exhibition Outfit is made up as follows:

- 1 High Grade Enterprise Stereopticon, complete with best imported projecting and condensing lenses and carrying case for same.
- 1 generator and burner outfit, complete for acetylene gas.
- 52 magnificent stereopticon slides. Select any of our standard set.
- 1 polished wood case, for views.
- 1 12x12 screen.
- 1,000 illustrated advertising posters.
- 2,000 admission tickets.
- Rubber printing outfit, for filling in dates, etc.

COMPLETE FOR $53.00

See full description of outfit on page 165.

Our New Hydro-Carbon Light and Leader Lantern. A perfect lighting and projecting outfit.

- 1 high grade stereopticon with 4½ inch condensing lenses, ½ size adjustable projection lens and double slide carrier.
- 1 beautifully finished leather carrying case, with nickel corners and trimmings, and lock and key.
- 1 hydro-carbon outfit complete, including tank, burner, pressure gauge, pump and mantels.
- 1 light fiber case with straps for carrying same.

COMPLETE FOR $59.50

With the above outfit the song illustrator or traveling lecturer is fitted with the acme of perfection in the way of both stereopticon and light. We also furnish the leader lantern complete without hydro-carbon outfit, fitted either with calcium burner or electric arc lamp, complete with the same for $45.00.

OUR TERMS ARE CASH WITH THE ORDER.

We require cash with all orders as fully explained on pages 1 and 2.

Animated Moving Picture Outfits.

Our complete moving picture outfit, fitted with arc lamp for attaching to electric current, films, stereopticon slides and all other requisites for high grade animated moving picture entertainment.

- 1 combined 1901 model Edison Kinetoscope with stereopticon, fitted with arc lamp and rheostat.
- 1 12x12 screen.
- 1 set of stereopticon views, 25 in number, customer's selection.
- 300 feet of best selected film.
- 500 posters.
- 1,000 tickets.
- Rubber printing outfit, for filling in dates and places of giving entertainment.

COMPLETE FOR $160.50

If it is desired to substitute calcium or oxy-hydro light instead of electricity, the additional cost of the outfit will be as follows:

1 No. 40 gas making outfit	$40.00
Chemicals and high test gasoline, for generating oxygen and hydrogen gas, also lime for producing calcium light, a sufficient supply to last for two weeks' entertainment	6.00
Total	$46.00
Adding the cost of the moving picture outfit, as given above	160.50
Grand total of outfit equipped for calcium light	$206.50

COMPLETE FOR $206.50

Moving Picture Outfit with Hydro-Carbon Light, suitable for small halls and school houses:

- 1 1901 Edison Kinetoscope, without calcium burner or arc lamp.
- 1 hydro-carbon outfit complete.
- Set of 52 selected stereopticon slides. 1 12x12 screen.
- 4 50-foot moving picture films.

COMPLETE FOR $171.50

WE GUARANTEE every machine, apparatus and appliance sold by us to be exactly as represented, to work perfectly and to give perfect satisfaction.

DO NOT LET THIS MONEY MAKING OPPORTUNITY PASS AND WHEN IT IS TOO LATE, SAY, "I AM SORRY I DID NOT TAKE HOLD OF IT."

OUR TALKING MACHINE DEPARTMENT.

THE GRAPHOPHONE, OR TALKING MACHINE, has proved itself in the past, and we believe always will be a most successful and popular entertainer. The novelty and wonder of the natural reproduction of the human voice as well as band and instrumental music insures preliminary interest, and the performance itself is so wonderfully realistic and the actual reproduction of speech and music of such a quality as could not otherwise be heard.

IT REPRODUCES with startling accuracy the productions of the most noted bands, orchestras, vocalists and public speakers and the songs, music or conversation of self or friends. The capabilities of the Graphophone are not confined to the reproduction of regular factory made records, but, when provided with a recording diaphragm, they will record and reproduce any words spoken to it, or song sung to it, and such records may be preserved and reproduced at any time.

AS A MONEY MAKER or as a home entertainer it has no equal. It is one of the most wonderful of all inventions, and yet its construction is so extremely simple that it causes the observer to wonder that its basic principle did not lead to its discovery long ago.

RECENT IMPROVEMENTS, simplicity of construction, replacing the expensive electric motors with the simple but practical spring motor, automatic machinery for their manufacture, making them in very large quantities, etc., has enabled us to make arrangements with the manufacturers whereby we can now offer this most wonderful little machine, complete with all the necessary accessories, at a price which not only brings them within the easy reach of those of small means, who wish to give public entertainments, but they can be owned by almost any family as a source of home amusement.

The Perfect Musical and Talking Machine. Tried, Tested and Guaranteed. A Public Entertainer of Unrivaled Merit and a Mint of Money for the Exhibitor.

AS A MONEY MAKER THE GRAPHOPHONE HAS NO EQUAL.

OUR LEADER, THE NEW GEM GRAPHOPHONE TALKING MACHINE.

YOU CAN MAKE $5.00 TO $25.00 every evening by giving public exhibitions in halls, churches, school houses, etc., at 15 to 25 cents admission, or by using with hearing tubes and charging 5 cents for each individual.

No. 21R1 Gem Graphophone, with two hearing tubes and concert horn, but without oak base and carrying case...... **$10.00**

No. 21R2 Gem Graphophone, with two hearing tubes, concert horn and handsome oak carrying case with handle, as illustrated...... **$12.00**

Above price does not include records. Price of our best musical and talking records is $5.00 per dozen or 50 cents each when ordered in less than dozen quantities.

FROM THE ILLUSTRATION, engraved by our artist direct from a photograph of the outfit, you can form a good idea of the appearance of this, OUR SPECIAL OFFER $23.75 PROFESSIONAL TALKING MACHINE EXHIBITION OUTFIT, but you must see and compare it with other graphophone outfits to appreciate the real value we are offering.

COMPLETE OUTFIT $23.75

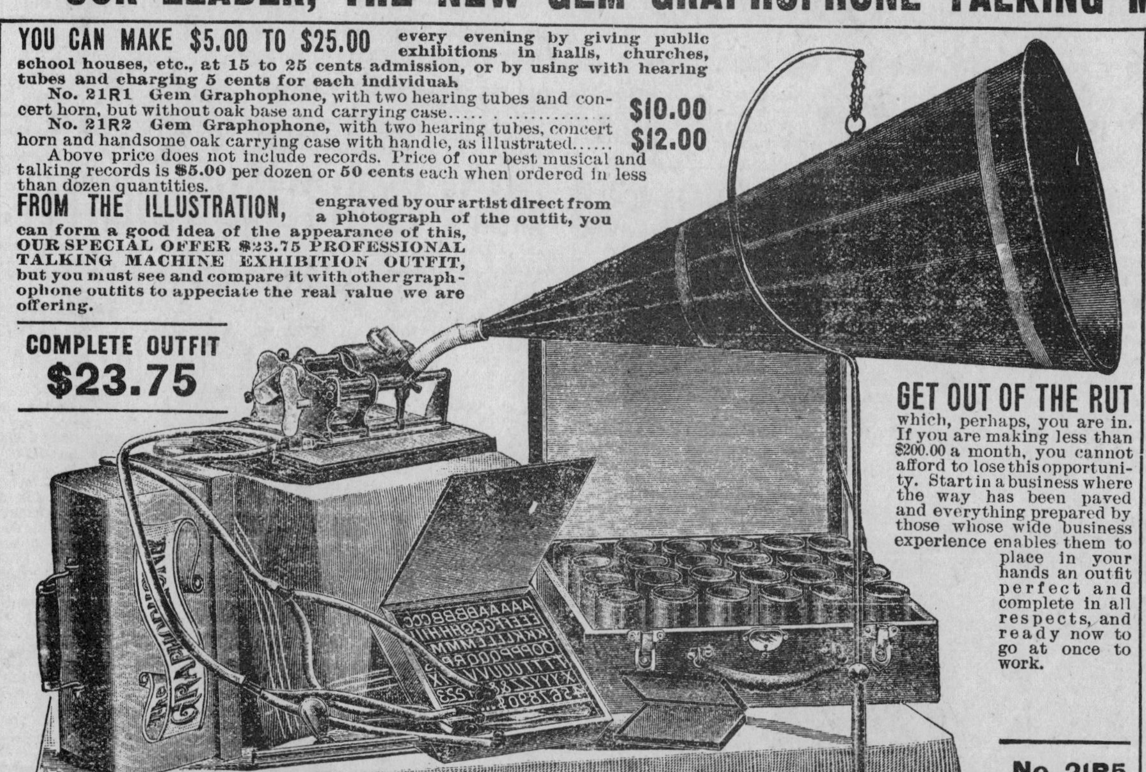

GET OUT OF THE RUT which, perhaps, you are in. If you are making less than $200.00 a month, you cannot afford to lose this opportunity. Start in a business where the way has been paved and everything prepared by those whose wide business experience enables them to place in your hands an outfit perfect and complete in all respects, and ready now to go at once to work.

No. 21R5
Order by Number.

THE GEM GRAPHOPHONE IS A CONCERT SIZE MACHINE and an exceedingly handsome one, thoroughly well made in every respect, and perfectly finished. It is provided with a powerful spring motor, guaranteed not to get out of order. The gears and pinions are machine cut, insuring perfect accuracy of action. It is provided with governor and tension screw, which effectually regulates the speed. Runs two pieces with one winding. Has the latest automatic, extra loud, aluminum reproducer; new style, extra long bearing record mandrel. The machine is substantially mounted on a handsome oak base, with highly finished bent oak cover, furnished with convenient clamps securing cover to base and carrying handle. It is equipped with all the latest improvements, all the up to date points of all high grade graphophones made, with the defects of none. No lighter, more portable, more durable, handsomer or louder graphophone was ever offered; far superior and not to be compared with the old style machines.

ABOVE ALL DO NOT DELAY to take advantage of the most liberal offer ever made on the most complete and perfect talking machine outfit ever gotten together. Every detail of the outfit has been carefully prepared and considered, every item is guaranteed to give satisfaction, and we feel safe in guaranteeing absolute success. Remember, $23.75 is a special offer price; $23.75 is a price that has never been made before on a concert exhibition graphophone and complete outfit such as we are now offering; $23.75 is a price that is intended to secure your order at once; it is a price based on the actual cost of material and labor, with only our one small percentage of profit added; a price that will not be made by any other concern on a complete high grade outfit; a price that means a saving to you on such an outfit of fully one-half.

NEW IMPROVED GEM TALKING MACHINE EXHIBITION OUTFIT. For those who wish to secure one of our new improved Gem Talking Machines for exhibition purposes, we have made up an exhibition outfit. We furnish the following complete outfit which includes everything needed as follows: For only $23.75 we now offer a complete Talking Machine Exhibition Outfit, including our new large Concert Exhibition Graphophone with the new 26-inch Amplifying Horn. A larger, better and more complete Talking Machine Outfit than has ever been offered before at a great deal more money. No. 21R5 Graphophone Outfit Complete:

No. 21R2 Gem Graphophone, the popular and perfectly finished Gem Graphophone described above.
1 Automatic extra loud Aluminum Reproducer.
24 best Musical or Talking Records, your own selection.
1,000 Advertising Posters, large size (14x21 inches).
2,000 Admission Tickets.
1 Rubber Printing Outfit, with movable type for filling in date, place where exhibition is to be given, etc.
1 Large Japanned Tin Amplifying Horn, 26 inches in length, with supporting stand.
1 Instruction Book, complete, with information about operating the outfit, making engagements ahead, etc.

No. 21R5 OUTFIT ALL FOR $23.75

The carrying case in which records are shown in this illustration is not included with the outfit, but it can be purchased for only $3.25 extra.

THE LATEST AND THE GREATEST, THE COLUMBIA GRAND.

USES 5-INCH CYLINDER RECORDS. APPLICATION OF NEW PRINCIPLE IN RECORDING AND REPRODUCING. ABSOLUTE PERFECTION ATTAINED AT LAST.

THE MONEY MAKER OF THE AGE. Will pay for itself in one week. The graphophone has been developed step by step, until today the Columbia Grand stands upon the pinnacle of perfection. Perfectly reproduces the human voice. Just as loud, just as clear, just as sweet. Duplicates instrumental music with perfect fidelity, tone and brilliancy. The Columbia Grand fills the largest auditorium or concert hall, and never fails to charm all who hear it.

IT IS THE TALKING MACHINE LONG LOOKED FOR, bringing the singer, the musician and the orchestra into the audible presence of the listener. Those familiar with other types, but who have never listened to the Graphophone Grand, have no conception of its wonders. Even those who are familiar with the marvels accomplished by sound reproducing mechanism, on first hearing the Grand are amazed by the absolute naturalness, the full volume and tone perfection of the reproduced sound, which seem almost beyond belief. It is the real sound, resonant and vibrant, and can be heard as far and even farther than the original.

THE PRICE OF THIS MACHINE IS LOW, considering its unique character and the marvelous results which can be obtained from it in sound reproduction. When first produced, this machine sold readily for $100. We are now able to offer for the first time, the same machine, of the same sterling qualities, the same loudness and beauty of tone, the same wonderfully vibrant and clear reproduction, for the unapproachable price of $50.00, while the 5-inch cylinder records will be furnished for $1.00 each.

No. 21R180 The Columbia Grand. Price $50.00

THIS PRICE INCLUDES MACHINE COMPLETE WITH HANDSOME OAK CABINET

1 Automatic reproducing diaphragm, guaranteed to give the loudest and clearest result obtainable, furnished with genuine sapphire reproducing ball.
1 New style "Perfect" automatic recorder.
1 Shaving knife with adjustable lever carriage for paring or cleaning records, so that they may be used over and over again, and one especially adapted brass horn for recording work.

THUS EQUIPPED the machine at this price is ready for use either in making new records or reproducing those already made. It is furnished with heavy spring motor, which will last a lifetime, the most careful attention has been paid to every detail and it is properly described as THE MOST HANDSOME, MASSIVE AND PERFECTLY FINISHED MUSICAL INSTRUMENT OF THIS DESCRIPTION EVER FURNISHED.

THE SUCCESS OF THE COLUMBIA GRAND has been demonstrated in New York, Washington and Chicago, in some cases to an audience composed of 2,000 people, with the most satisfactory results, even to those in the remote corners of the hall, the reproduction being heard as loudly and plainly as by those in the front seats.

No. 21R180 Order by Number.

For reproducing and concert work we recommend a larger horn. Actually accomplishes what has heretofore been deemed the impossible.

Picture represents machine with small recording horn only.

FOR EXHIBITION WORK THE COLUMBIA GRAND IS WITHOUT A PEER.

NOT ONLY AS A TALKING MACHINE, BUT IN ITS POWER OF ENTERTAINING AND AMAZING AN AUDIENCE, AND ABOVE ALL AS A MONEY GETTER, it cannot at the present time be equaled by any other entertainment feature now before the public.

OUR ADVICE TO WOULD-BE EXHIBITORS IS THAT NO ENTERTAINMENT OUTFIT which has so far been placed on the market is the equal of the Columbia Grand in the three great requisites for a beginner: of simplicity, portability and money producing power.

FOR ONLY $75.00 WE NOW OFFER OUR COMPLETE GRAND PEERLESS TALKING MACHINE EXHIBITION OUTFIT.

Including Columbia Grand, with our own special 42-inch Amplifying Horn, the greatest, the loudest, the most complete and perfect talking machine outfit ever assembled. One suitable for the largest metropolitan opera house, and which has drawn crowds in cities of such magnitude as New York, Chicago and Washington. With this our new Graphophone Grand Peerless Exhibition Outfit we furnish the Columbia Graphophone Grand No. 21R180, complete in every respect as above described. One 42-inch monster amplifying brass horn, doubling or tripling the volume of sound which can be obtained even from this wonderfully loud and brilliant machine, and one finely nickel plated adjustable horn stand for supporting the amplifying horn. Twelve 5-inch cylinder grand records, each one guaranteed a master and subjected to thorough examination and test before placed in stock. One handsome leatherette case (as shown in cut), for safely carrying and caring for the grand records. 500 mammoth grand posters for advertising work. 1,000 admission tickets, 500 adults and 500 children. One hand rubber stamp for filling in dates and place of exhibition.

OUR PEERLESS COLUMBIA GRAND ENTERTAINMENT OUTFIT No. 21R181 COMPLETE FOR ONLY

$75.00 No. 21R181 Order by Number.

FROM THIS ILLUSTRATION . . . engraved by our artist direct from a photograph of the outfit, some idea can be obtained of its magnitude and completeness. But no one who has seen only the ordinary standard graphophones and outfits, can appreciate the real merit and value we are offering.

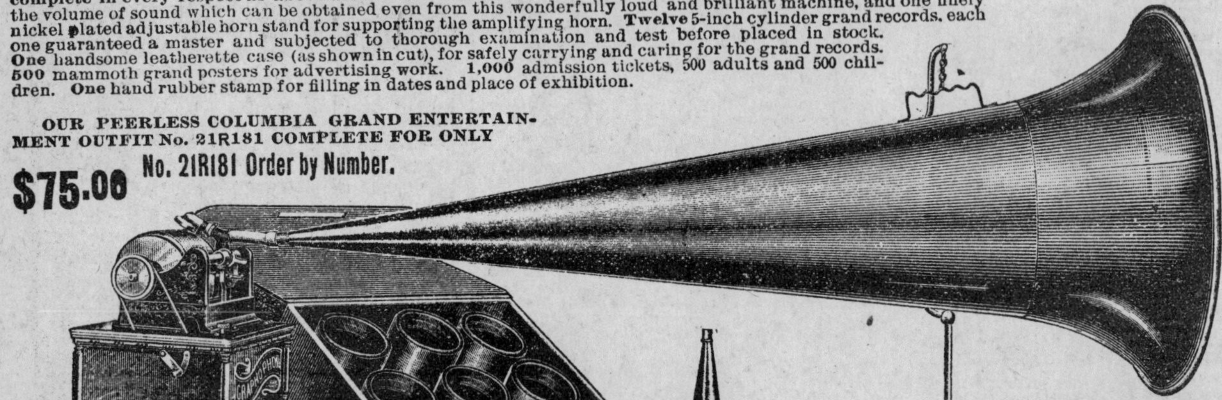

WE MUST ASK CASH WITH YOUR ORDER.

You save the extra charges the express companies make on C. O. D. shipments, and you run no risk whatever in sending cash with your order, for if everything is not satisfactory and just as we represent it, you are at liberty to return it to us and we will immediately RETURN YOUR MONEY.

AN UNSURPASSED OPPORTUNITY PRESENTS ITSELF to those who are first in the field, of making not only big wages, but a small fortune in an easy, honorable and pleasant manner. The records furnished by us with these machines are incomparable. Price, each $1.00

EVERY EXHIBITOR can now have an entertainer on hand which sings, talks and plays with the same volume of tone as the best professional artists in the world.

ORIGINAL RECORDS can be made on this machine very easily and this has proved a most attractive exhibition feature. A record can be made in the hearing of the audience and at once reproduced. This feature is novel, startling and effective. The Grand type of talking machines is supplied with the same record making device as those used by professional record makers.

A GRAPHOPHONE GRAND FOR $25.00

THE COMBINATION GRAPHOPHONE GRAND,

INTERCHANGEABLE

using on one machine both large (G) cylinders and small (P) cylinders, marks

THE MOST IMPORTANT IMPROVEMENT IN TALKING MACHINES

that has ever been perfected. It is so constructed that on one machine either the grand records, which are 5 inches in diameter, or the small standard P records can be used.

IT IS INVALUABLE

for those who already have a supply of small or standard records, and who, while desirous of adding a grand equipment, do not wish to sacrifice the records they already have.

PORTABILITY. It is the lightest talking machine playing the grand or large records, weighing less than 16 pounds.

A NEW TYPE, A NEW IDEA, A MECHANICAL WONDER, A MUSICAL PRODIGY, uses Grand records and small ones; plays all records made for any type of talking machine.

THE NEW COMBINATION INTERCHANGEABLE GRAPHOPHONE GRAND.

CHEAPNESS
PORTABILITY
BEAUTY

STRENGTH OF CONSTRUCTION
ADAPTABILITY and the new
SPEED REGULATOR and INDICATOR

are the leading characteristics of this wonderful mechanical innovation in the talking machine field, combining the leading features and advantages of every known type of machine.

CHEAPNESS. We were the first to order from the manufacturers of the new INTERCHANGEABLE GRAPHOPHONE GRAND (before it was even placed upon the market), an enormous number of these wonderful instruments, enabling us to offer it to our customers at a price exactly one-half of what a machine of the Grand type was ever offered before. For $25.00 we can make you the owner of a machine which will play small records as well as any graphophone made, and will produce the grandest musical results from the mammoth giant voiced 5-inch cylinder grand records.

BEAUTY. As will be seen from the photographic reproduction, this is a most beautiful instrument, finished in high art oak, cabinet, and every part finished with the most exact and scrupulous care.

STRENGTH. It is fitted with machine cut gears, is propelled by a powerful spring, has governor and screw for regulating the speed and as shown is provided with quarter sawed oak top attached to the base by safety hooks and has a handle for carrying. With proper care it will last a lifetime.

ADAPTABILITY. With simple interchange of mandrels, it can be used for either large or small records. It is provided with a recording as well as reproducing diaphragm, therefore records can be made on the machine by the operator and reproduced at will.

THE PUBLIC HAS BEEN WAITING FOR THIS, THE GREATEST VALUE FOR THE LEAST MONEY EVER ADVERTISED.

Order by number and at once. The factory cannot keep pace with its orders. We have a large stock, however, and will be able to take care of our customers for some time.

A GRAND MACHINE COMPLETE FOR $25.00.

EXHIBITION WORK. This is the machine which the exhibitors have long looked for, combining the essential points already referred to of economy, portability and ability to use either class of records. We have prepared a very special outfit which we offer for the consideration of would be exhibitors and guarantee that equipped with this outfit, he cannot fail of success and it would be at most the matter of a few days before he has made the entire price of his outfit.

No. 21R190 Our Latest Graphophone (uses Grand records)...$25.00

No. 21R191 OUR SPECIAL COMBINATION INTERCHANGEABLE GRAND CONCERT OUTFIT CONTAINS THE FOLLOWING ITEMS:

1 No. 21R190 Combination Interchangeable Graphophone Grand with extra grand mandrel, standard mandrel for P records, recorder and reproducer.
12 standard new process P records, vocal or instrumental.
12 mammoth giant voiced 5-inch cylinder records, vocal or instrumental.
Our special 30-inch Clarion spun brass horn with handsome nickel plated stand.
500 handsome and attractive advertising posters.
1,000 admission tickets; 500 for adults and 500 for children.
1 rubber printing outfit for filling in dates and places of entertainment.

No. 21R191 A complete outfit for only........................$48.50

By using No. 21R190, the New Type Interchangeable Grand Machine, we are able to offer our customers something entirely new.

OUR GREAT ILLUSTRATED GRAPHO COMBINED OUTFIT.

No. 21R195
ORDER BY NUMBER.

PICTURES IN SONGS ......AND...... SONGS IN PICTURES

Complete Outfit, $119.50

FOR RENDERING AND ILLUSTRATING POPULAR SONGS OF THE DAY.

From "'Mid the Green Fields of Virginia."

AT THE PRESENT TIME ILLUSTRATED SONGS are the most popular means of entertaining the public and have been immensely successful in the various theaters in all the larger cities. The dramatic effect produced by illustrating the song in this manner is very marked and all audiences become greatly enthused over the vivid combination of the two. The views consist of pictures representing the most important incidents related in the song and are projected by the stereopticon. They are all hand painted and in each instance taken from life models, and when shown with the stereopticon, enlarged to life size, are exceedingly realistic.

THE GRAPHOPHONE GRAND furnishes the music, delighting the ear, and the pictures are vividly projected onto the screen in view of the audience at the same time; while the comparative cheapness of this, the newest type of Grand machine, combined with its unapproachable musical excellence, enable us to place the outfit within the reach of our customers at a price hitherto unheard of.

From "The Girl I Loved in Sunny Tennessee."

THE ILLUSTRATED GRAPHOPHONE GRAND AND POPULAR SONG COMBINATION CONSISTS OF THE FOLLOWING ITEMS:

THE COMBINATION GRAPHOPHONE GRAND INTERCHANGEABLE, described at the head of this page, equipped with our mammoth 42-inch brass amplifying horn and stand, so as to obtain the largest volume of sound possible from this wonderful instrument.

SIX 5-INCH CYLINDER MAMMOTH GRAND RECORDS, three of which will correspond with the three sets of illustrated song slides included with this outfit.

TWELVE P OR STANDARD RECORDS of regular size for general entertainment purposes. NOTE—Both these types of records can be used on the same machine.

THE ENTERPRISE STEREOPTICON. Highest grade professional stereopticon obtainable, with finest imported achromatic lens (money cannot purchase a more perfect instrument.) Projects a 10x10-foot picture brilliantly and perfectly on the screen and equipped with the HYDRO-CARBON LIGHT, the most perfect and brilliant illuminant procurable for stereopticon illumination. Provides a light of 500 candle power and projects a picture on the screen so clearly and brilliantly that the result can only be described as perfection attained at last.

ONE 12X12-FOOT SCREEN for projecting scenes upon.

BEAUTIFULLY ILLUSTRATED SONG SLIDES. Three sets, each illustrating a modern song or ballad played at the same time from one of the records included with the graphophone equipment. The sets of song slides can be selected from the list found on page 168 of this catalogue, and each set will contain not less than twelve artistically hand colored views posed for from life models, and vividly illustrating the different points of the song in the most artistic and highly finished manner.

500 ESPECIALLY PREPARED POSTERS, advertising the combined attraction, and 1,000 ADMISSION TICKETS, 500 for adults and 500 for children. We also include one handsome Rubber Hand Stamping Outfit, with movable interchangeable letters and figures for filling in dates and places of giving public entertainments. NOTE—We especially direct attention to the fact that the outfit is furnished with the brilliant Hydro-Carbon Light; this completely removes it from the class of outfits suitable only for small entertainments in schools and country halls, but places the exhibitor in a position to give these entertainments anywhere, and with perfect confidence to make engagements in theaters and opera houses in the largest cities.

NO EFFORT HAS BEEN SPARED to make this the most perfect combined outfit ever prepared, presenting the most novel musical attraction of the day. It includes a projecting machine with highest grade of lens which cannot be surpassed, and offers attractions similar to those which are proving nightly successful in most of the leading metropolitan theaters throughout the country.

THIS IS OUR LEADER IN ILLUSTRATED WORK and no combination has so far been made up which will prove such a money maker. No outfit can so easily be kept new and up to date, and none can more thoroughly enthuse and delight an audience.

MOVING PICTURE EFFECTS. This entire outfit has been made up with a special view to the AFTER ADDITION of moving picture effects. This can be done at any time very cheaply, as the entire outfit, stereopticon and light is calculated to do high class moving picture work in combination with the moving picture machine itself, which can be procured and added to the outfit at any time.

No. 21R195 Illustrated Grapho Grand and Popular Ballad Combination, complete for........................$119.50

DISC GRAPHOPHONE WITH HARD UNBREAKABLE RECORDS.

THE DEMAND ON THE PART OF EXHIBITORS AND THOSE WHO HAVE OCCASION TO TRAVEL OR MOVE THEIR MACHINE MUCH FROM PLACE TO PLACE, FOR A GRAPHOPHONE USING THE FLAT DISC UNBREAKABLE RECORDS, MUST BE RECOGNIZED

WE ARE NOW IN A POSITION to offer a Flat Disc Unbreakable Record Machine which possesses all the merits claimed by any machine of this description, and has most effectually eliminated the drawbacks and inferior effects which have so far rendered this most convenient form of machine below the musical standard of the machines using wax cylinders. We refused to handle this type **until we were sure we could offer an instrument which would reproduce instrumental, vocal and musical utterances with perfect**

FIDELITY, BRILLIANCY LOUDNESS AND CLEARNESS.

OUR ABSOLUTE GUARANTEE **is binding on any graphophone of any kind and we guarantee our customers the privilege of returning unsatisfactory goods.**

THE BEST KNOWN, **the largest and most successful builders of talkin machines and records have at our request and unde our instructions been experimenting along the line of flat disc machines foı months past.** The first attempts were not satisfactory; too much like the old style hard disc machine with which the market was flooded, and which combined almost every demerit of a talking machine and possessed only the merit of portability and of using unbreakable records. These features have been kept prominently to the forefront in all experiments, and our efforts have been centered on combining them with the same sonorous, loud, clear and musical tone which has distinguished the wonderful type of Graphophone Grands which have lately been so enormously successful. **We are now glad to be able to announce to our customers perhaps the most important step which has ever been taken in the presentation of**

A PERFECT TALKING MACHINE WITH UNBREAKABLE RECORDS.

THE REGAL GRAPHOPHONE GRAND uses the hard 10-inch concert records, **affording a volume of purity and tone unequalled by any other instrument. For concert work, unapproachable; for volume and purity of tone, unrivaled; for loudness, clearness and brilliancy, unequaled.**

THE REGINA GRAPHOPHONE is especially designed to use either the flat **disc 7-inch unbreakable record or the 10-inch concert record with equal facility and the same admirable results;** a combination never attempted before in any type of flat disc talking machine, and securing a result which is practically

TWO MACHINES IN ONE.

In placing orders for these machines and records, you may be quite certain that they are the finest goods in their class which have ever been placed upon the market; and in this branch, as in all others of the talking machine industry, we intend to and will lead all competitors in variety of types and selection, as well as in the quality of the instrument offered.

THE REGAL GRAPHOPHONE **is not only the best concert machine on the market using the unbreakable records,** but, as shown in the illustration drawn direct from a photograph, is a most beautiful instrument, **massive in proportion and handsome in appearance.** The mechanism is contained in a handsomely designed quarter sawed highly polished oak cabinet made up in appropriate and decorated design supported at corners by Gothic pillars and beautifully fluted, ornamented solid base, supported on solid rubber cushions to prevent reverberation and secure resonance of sound. Ornamented metal carrying handle, heavy solid steel bed to support records providing for absolutely true running of the record and preventing any variation of sound. All exposed metal parts, speed adjuster, arm holder, horn support and sound box highly nickel plated.

THE MECHANISM **of the machine is well nigh perfect and it is** equipped with scientifically designed spring motor of the most thorough and substantial construction, assuring regular and reliable action, and running three of the large 10-inch concert records with each winding. All gears are machine cut and simplicity and durability are considered in every detail. It is made as accurately as a scientific instrument and will appeal to all users of talking machines as much for its mechanical perfections as for any other reason. The ease with which the spring motor is accessible so that it may be oiled, examined and inspected at any time is demonstrated by the cut below which shows the machine open and ready for examination. The cost of repairs, if any should be needed, is thus reduced to a minimum.

THE RESULTS **obtained from the machines and records in the way of sound reproduction are unbelievable.** Seated in the largest hall or auditorium its vibrant, resonant and perfectly musical tones can be heard by the audience in the most remote part of the auditorium; nor are its loud and brilliant tones its only or principal merit, **perfect accuracy in reproduction, perfect fidelity to the original and perfect quality of musical tone** are rendered with an instrument which it is absolutely necessary to hear before its wonderful qualities can be fully appreciated.

Showing Mechanism and Ease of Access.

THE EQUIPMENT **consists of case and mechanism already described; steel bed plate for records with nickel holder; tension screw for regulating tune and speed; break for stopping and controlling the revolution of the disc, which acts directly on the governor; twenty-two-inch amplifying horn, steel body and burnished brass bell; beautiful nickel plated ornamented stand and carrying arm** for horn, extra loud vibrant combined **sound box and reproducer** constructed on entirely new principles and guaranteed to insure a volume and purity of tone unapproachable by any other talking machine using the hard disc records; handsome leatherette cover and carrying case, absolutely protecting the machine when not in use from dust, etc., and rendering it compact for transportation so that it may be easily carried in one hand **For exhibition this machine has never been equaled.** The instrument itself is so well and substantially made that it can be carried from place to place without the slightest danger of breakage or derangement. **The unbreakable disc records are contained in a case made for the purpose,** and the entire outfit of Concert Grand size can readily be carried by a boy without fatigue.

THE REGAL **is especially designed for the 10-inch record,** and with this record will reproduce the greatest volume of sound. The smaller 7-inch disc, however, can be run on the machine as well.

No. 21R200 Regal machine with concert sound box, elegant piano finish, ornamental cabinet, 21-inch steel body, burnished brass amplifying horn, 200 needles and needle case. Price....... **$40.00**

TO THE PROFESSIONAL EXHIBITOR. **The work of public exhibition with a talking machine is pleasant and remunerative.** Many of our customers who have started in the past with but a small talking machine have had such success as to realize an ample competency. All that is required to make this business more successful than ever is the addition of novelty which this instrument affords, **greater portability** so that it may be removed readily from place to place, eliminating all danger of breakage and harm either to records or machine in transportation, **absolute perfection in the quality of tone, loudness and clearness of enunciation and the perfection of musical harmony.** All these have been brought together in the **"Regal"** as the perfection instrument for successfully engaging in exhibition business.

NO EXPERIENCE IS NECESSARY **to operate an outfit of this description. No previous experience** is necessary to operate the Regal Graphophone and to begin public exhibition work at once. You will have something new to show the people and something which, at comparatively trifling expense, can always be kept new, always fresh and always up to date.

OUR INSTRUCTIONS **give complete information how to operate the outfit successfully,** how to make engagements, hire halls, etc. and enable anyone without previous experience to make from $10.00 to $50.00 a day every working day in the year.

No. 21R220 Regal Complete Exhibition Outfit for up to date exhibitors and money makers consists of the following items:

Our new Concert Regal Graphophone, specially designed for using the Climax 10-inch concert record, enclosed in handsome oak carrying case and furnished with our new and strictly patented combined reproducing and concert sound box with highly nickel plated standard and supporting arm for amplifying horn..........

Two dozen highest grade Climax unbreakable Disc Records..........

One Handsome Leatherette Carrying and Covering Case

One 22-inch Amplifying Horn, steel body, and brightly burnished brass bell..........

Substantially finished and exceedingly handsome carrying case which will accommodate four dozen records........

Handsomely illustrated advertising posters, 14x21 inches, 1,000 admission tickets for adults and children, one rubber printing outfit..........

A "GRAND" OUTFIT COMPLETE FOR ONLY **$65.00**

WE ABSOLUTELY GUARANTEE **the Regal and Regina machines for loudest reproduction, perfect mechanism, handsome appearance, and will keep them in repair free of charge to the customer for one year from date of sale.**

THE REGINA **corresponds with the description of the Regal machine except that the case is somewhat plainer and less ornamental.** The same care is given to the mechanism and the same attention to each and every detail. It is specially designed for the smaller 7-inch record, and will run three of such records with each winding. **The large 10-inch concert record can, however, be used on the Regina machine,** thus for the first time offering two machines in one.

No. 21R205 Regina, this machine with same equipments. Price.......... **$20.00**

REGINA GRAPHOPHONE **using unbreakable Flat Disc records running either the Climax 10-inch record or the 7-inch Acme record,** for home and family purposes is a high grade and perfect talking machine, smaller and less ornamental than the Regal machine, but will run either large or small records.

HOME OUTFITS **We suggest the following as a perfect outfit for home purposes,** a beautiful gift for one member of the family to make to another and an incomparable present for Christmas or the holiday season. Possesses every advantage of a perfect high priced organ or piano and places the finest vocal and instrumental selections absolutely in the hands of a beginner who has not had and does not require one hour's previous experience. It will provide a home entertainment and delight yourself, family and friends, keeping you in touch with the best and latest music and in a month more than repay its first cost.

No. 21R221 Our family Regina Outfit complete will consist of the following:

One Regina Flat Disc Graphophone..........

Twelve Acme 7-inch Unbreakable Records..........

Three Climax 10-inch Grand Concert Records..........

ALL FOR **$28.00**

IN EVERY DETAIL OF CONSTRUCTION, **in superiority of mechanism and in quality of reproduction, the Regal and Regina possess innumerable points of superiority over every other flat disc talking machine on the market. Run three records with one winding, no other machine runs more than one. The record bed fits on a conical standard,** entirely preventing any rocking motion. Constructed in such a way that **the mechanism is easily accessible for all purposes. The stop brake or lever works directly on the internal governor mechanism** instead of on the bed plate as in other machines, thus preventing the injurious jar of instantly stopping the record plate while in motion.

CLIMAX RECORDS **The Climax Records are the highest achievement in the production of sound records for disc machines. They are** suitable not only to our own machines, the Regal and Regina, but for any other machine now on the market using disc records. Two sizes, the Climax, ten inches, the Acme, seven inches.

Both the Climax and Acme Records can be used on the Regina as well as the Regal machine.

These records are most conveniently carried in a very handsome record carrying case and occupy the smallest appreciable space.

No. 21R210	Climax Records, 10-inch, per dozen, $10.00; each..........	$1.00
No. 21R211	Acme Records, 7-inch, per dozen, $5.00; each..........	.50
No. 21R215	Climax 10-inch record carrying case..........	3.00
No. 21R216	Acme 7-inch record carrying case..........	2.00

SEND TO US for FULL LIST of CLIMAX and ACME RECORDS.

OUR SPECIAL STEREOPTICON LECTURE DEPARTMENT.

DO YOU WISH TO MAKE MONEY WITH LITTLE EFFORT?

Pleasant and honorable employment. Short hours and little effort. No soliciting and no goods to sell.

OUR REGULAR ILLUSTRATED STEREOPTICON OUTFITS ARE OFFERED FOR $53.00,

and represent the greatest bargain in the way of an exhibition outfit ever gotten up.

Projects a clear and Brilliant Picture 10 feet square.

PROFESSIONAL LECTURE OUTFIT FOR ONLY

$53.00

No. 21R230

This illustration is made from a photograph of the Stereopticon as it appears in operation.

TO THOSE WHO ARE NOT SATISFIED with their present occupation, to those whose income is perhaps less than $1,000 per year, we direct attention to the unrivaled opportunities presented by our special lecture outfits. Place your order for one of these special outfits. Your first week's work will more than pay for this investment, your first evening's work may pay for it.

NO PREVIOUS EXPERIENCE or no ability as a public speaker is required, as the description of the view is printed and can be read while they are shown with the stereopticon.

A comparatively small investment will enable you to make a start.

THE STEREOPTICON provided with this outfit is the Enterprise Stereopticon with the Seroco Acetylene Light. It is the highest grade of lantern made.

WE FURNISH WITH THE STEREOPTICON OUTFIT

52 MAGNIFICENT TRANSPARENT PHOTOGRAPHIC VIEWS,
1 POLISHED WOOD CASE FOR THE VIEWS,
1 SEROCO GENERATOR AND SIMPLEX BURNER FOR ACETYLENE ILLUMINATION,
1 SPECIAL HIGH POWER SINGLE STEREOPTICON,
1 CARRYING CASE FOR STEREOPTICON,
1 LARGE WHITE SCREEN (120 square feet),
1 LECTURE, BOUND IN BOOK FORM,
1,000 LARGE ILLUSTRATED ADVERTISING POSTERS,
2,000 EXHIBITION ADMISSION TICKETS,
1 PRINTING OUTFIT FOR FILLING IN DATES, ETC.,
1 BOOK OF INSTRUCTIONS.

No. 21R230 ALL FOR...$53.00

The above complete Stereopticon outfit includes any 52 slides or views which the customer may select of which twelve will be colored, and forty plain; the selection of a larger number of slides will only very slightly increase the cost in proportion, and the coloring of a larger number would also, if desired, be provided for at a small increase.

WHILE THE CHOICE OF LECTURES AND VIEWS is left exclusively to our customers' discretion, we are sometimes asked to advise as to which is the most popular set for present purposes. We think that now and for some time to come the PAN-AMERICAN EXPOSITION with lecture, possesses attractive qualities superior to any other. The exposition is exciting national interest, and thousands of intelligent people throughout the country, who were unable to attend personally would eagerly seize the opportunity of witnessing a well selected and artistic lecture set of this description, which would convey a realistic idea of the actual appearance of the most interesting scenes of this wonderful fair. This subject presents drawing capabilities and insures an audience to an extent which must not be overlooked by exhibitors.

WHEREVER IT IS POSSIBLE we would strongly advise the exhibitor to add to this Pan-American set, our special set of fifteen slides describing the

ASSASSINATION OF PRESIDENT McKINLEY,

which are proving the most attractive of special lecture feature ever offered.

THE SET OF McKINLEY ASSASSINATION SLIDES include realistic views of the assassination, of the assassin himself, taken within ten minutes of his capture by the police, and beautiful illustrations of the funeral cortege, in fact, a complete illustrated history of the most terrible tragedy of the present century. The love and respect in which the President was held by all classes of people, of all shades of politics, will insure the success of this addition to an outfit.

No. 21R238 Set of Pan-American slides with lecture and view box, complete, forty slides plain and twelve colored.................................$16.00

This or any other of our regular lecture sets described on the next two pages is included in our special stereopticon lecture outfit at our price of.................................$53.00

No. 21R239 Set of descriptive slides, illustrative of the assassination of President McKinley, fifteen in number, all colored, with graphic lecture and description of the tragedy.................................$7.50

This set of President McKinley slides can be used in connection with the Pan-American at the additional price of $7.50, and in fact will form a very valuable addition to any set which customer may select.

The following are some of the many additional lecture sets which are placed at the customers disposal for selection, any of which will insure success, and all of which will be found fully described in the following pages.

PATRIOTIC AND MARTIAL.

No. 21R231 Spanish-American War and the Philippines, illustrated.
No. 21R232 Cuba, The Maine and the Cuban War.
No. 21R233 The Boer-English War and Scenes in South Africa.

RELIGIOUS AND INSTRUCTIVE.

No. 21R234 Shadows of a Great City.
No. 21R235 Passion Play Series.
No. 21R237 Life of Christ on Earth.
No. 21R240 Around the World in Eighty Minutes.

TRAVEL AND EXPOSITIONS.

No. 21R236 Scenes in Paris and the Exposition.
No. 21R238 Pan-American Exposition.
No. 21R241 Scenes in the Philippines and our New Possessions.

SPECIAL COPYRIGHTED SUBJECTS.

No. 21R242 Passing of the Indian.
No. 21R243 Life Under a Circus Tent.
No. 21R244 Chicago Stock Yards, or from Hoof to Market.

For further information on these lecture sets consult full descriptions on the next two pages.

No. 21R238 PAN-AMERICAN EXPOSITION.

The "Plaza."

OUR LEADING and most popular lecture set at the present time. The exposition just completed in Buffalo has proved to be one of the features of the present decade, and while millions have attended, there are still millions whose inability to do so does not detract from their interest in the subject. An exhibitor who purchases this set makes no mistake. The negatives were made by our special commissioner, and the entire set is of great artistic beauty and merit. The set consists of 54 slides, 12 colored and 42 plain. It is included in our regular stereopticon outfit for $53.00.

No. 21R238 Set of 54 slides alone, without stereopticon, 12 colored and 42 plain, including high grade lecture descriptive of each subject and of the exposition in general. Price........ **$15.50**

No. 21R239 ASSASSINATION OF PRESIDENT McKINLEY.

IN RESPONSE to almost numberless requests for lecture set on this subject, we have had a special set of descriptive slides made up at great expense which we believe will not only be of the most enthralling interest at the present time but will always remain a valuable memento of the sad event whereby the nation was deprived of its president under circumstances so afflicting and grieving to every American citizen. The range of subjects is complete, covering almost every leading scene and incident in connection with the tragedy. Send for full descriptive circular.

The Assassin Czolgosz.

No. 21R239 Fifteen slides in this special set, all colored with lecture. Price........ **$7.50**

No. 21R241 THE PHILIPPINES AND OUR NEW POSSESSIONS.

WHILE THE WAR, which has been raging for so long a time in the Philippines, was practically ended by the surrender of Aguinaldo, more interest than ever now exists in the Philippine Islands, and in our New Possessions near adjacent. Recognizing this fact, and that a set of views descriptive of the scenery, native customs, and other interesting incidents of our new territory, would be of more value than one devoted entirely to the war, we have secured a very large number of valuable photographic negatives, taken by the government commissioner appointed for the purpose.

No. 21R241 The Philippine Islands and Our New Possessions Lecture. Set, complete, including 52 views and all attachments, as described on preceding page........ **$53.00**

Set of Slides, "The Philippines," 12 colored and 40 plain........ **16.00**

No. 21R240 AROUND THE WORLD IN EIGHTY MINUTES.

PARTICULAR ATTENTION is directed to this, one of the best and most standard lecture sets ever prepared, consisting of eighty views, describing a complete trip around the globe. With this wonderful selection of choice views the exhibitor can give his patrons a big run for their money, as he takes them with him on a trip around the world and imparts information which it has cost thousands of dollars to secure. Five hundred posters only supplied with this outfit.

No. 21R240 Price, complete, with stereopticon and lecture including eighty slides, of which 60 are plain and 20 colored........ **$62.50**

Set of Slides, "Around the World," 80 slides, 20 colored and 60 plain........ **25.00**

No. 21R242 THE PASSING OF THE INDIAN.

THIS IS ONE OF THE LATEST and best of stereopticon view sets. Something entirely out of the ordinary, something which you can be sure has not been shown throughout the country and worked to death by other exhibitors, something which will be recognized wherever you go as entirely new, and therefore of interest to everyone.

THE EXTINCTION of this once powerful race is a subject worthy of most careful consideration, and excellent food for wholesome thought.

No. 21R242 The Passing of the Indian. Stereopticon outfit, including 50 views, 40 plain and 12 colored........ **$53.00**

Price of 50 slides, including view box and lecture........ **16.00**

No. 21R243 LIFE UNDER A CIRCUS TENT.

NEW STEREOPTICON view set just out. A winner and a big money maker. All the world loves the circus, but all the world does not get the opportunity of seeing the biggest and finest circus and menageries, which visit only the largest points. This set of views shows both circus and menagerie, from actual negatives and will be found intensely interesting to both old and young. This set consists of 52 views, 12 plain and 40 colored, and is furnished with 250 beautifully printed colored advertising posters, a sample of which will be sent on request.

No. 21R243 Life Under a Circus Tent, stereopticon outfit complete, including 52 views and 250 posters, printed in several different colors........ **$53.00**

Set of "Circus" slides, 12 colored and 40 plain........ **16.00**

No. 21R244 THE CHICAGO STOCK YARDS, OR FROM HOOF TO MARKET.

Killing Cattle.

WHILE THERE MAY BE subjects more interesting to one or the other than this particular one, there is no subject of such general interest throughout the country as the method of conducting the wonderful packing houses at the Chicago Stock Yards. The largest and best of these was selected by us for this purpose, and a complete and valuable set of 55 slides, showing the entire workings and method of a modern packing house from the time of the shipping of the animals, their reception at the stock yards, the slaughtering, curing, saving and inspecting, the manner in which the by-products are utilized, and numerous other matters of interest in connection with the work, which are not within the space at present at our disposal.

No. 21R244 Price of stereopticon lecture complete, with 55 slides, of which 12 are colored, special........ **$53.00**

Price of 55 slides, including view box and lecture, 12 slides colored, 43 uncolored........ **$16.00**

The Pens.

DEPARTMENT OF MOVING PICTURE OUTFITS.

THIS IS UNDOUBTEDLY THE MOST NOVEL, THE MOST INTERESTING AND THE MOST POPULAR FORM OF PUBLIC ENTERTAINMENT WHICH IS NOW BEING PRESENTED AND ONE WHICH OFFERS A WIDER FIELD AND GREATER RETURNS FOR THE MONEY INVESTED THAN ANY OTHER SPECIES OF PUBLIC ENTERTAINMENT.

THE MOVING PICTURE APPARATUS, although used in combination with the stereopticon, must not be confounded with it. The Magic Lantern or Stereopticon shows merely the stationary pictures with which all have been familiar for years, the moving picture machine, however, is of comparatively recent invention, and projects moving pictures lifelike and of life size upon a screen or canvas. It undoubtedly represents the highest branch in the art of photography and illuminated picture projections and brings before the eye an exact and life size reproduction, with all the accompanying effects of light, shadow and expression. We have always been in the forefront of dealers in handling this type of outfit. We have made a study of this branch of the exhibition business. For the past three years the manager of this department has come in personal contact with more exhibitors, has corresponded with a larger number of successful operators than probably any man in the United States. We know what is needed to build up a successful exhibition. We place our knowledge and our experience at the disposal of any purchaser or prospective purchaser absolutely free of charge. We advise him to the best of our ability whether he does or does not purchase an outfit, and we are able to assist him in his final selection by pointing out to him outfits which will make his success certain, and subjects for his exhibition which will insure him an audience wherever he advertises, and guarantee him in successfully entertaining them.

WE GUARANTEE EVERY MACHINE, every outfit which we send out. We have an established reputation in this line to support. Those who have dealt with us do not require any assurance of this, but to those who have not, we say, that any outfit sent out by us can be thoroughly tested, tried and examined at the customer's house and if not exactly as represented, up to standard and capable of the most effective work, we not only permit but we ask that you return it to us within a reasonable time from its receipt and we will refund whatever money you have paid for it.

MOVING OR ANIMATED PICTURES are just as popular and even more so than ever before. They possess a merit which increases their popularity every time they are shown, and they are, by this time, so well advertised that the mere announcement of a moving picture entertainment is sufficient to bring out every entertainment lover or frequenter of this class of exhibitions.

THE MOVING PICTURE OUTFIT may be shortly described as made up of three principal items outside of the small and less considered accessories; these are, first: The moving picture machine or apparatus itself, upon which the most depends and in the choice of which the frankest and most careful advice is offered to our patrons, and an absolute guarantee given with the machine. Without a high grade projecting instrument, such as we furnish, the most talented operator can do nothing, and the small amount saved by purchasing an inferior or lower grade machine is money worse than wasted; it is not only thrown away, so far as the moving picture outfit is concerned, but tends to bring the entire exhibition into disrepute owing to its inferiority. Irrespective of price entirely, we have always endeavored to present, for our customers' consideration, the best instrument procurable, and we are pleased to announce that in the Edison Improved Kinetoscope, 1901 model, combined with stereopticon, we are able to furnish our customers with the highest grade of instrument for projecting both moving and stationary pictures which ingenuity, time, effort and experiment have ever produced.

The Edison Projection Kinetoscope.

"THE MOST PERFECT MOVING PICTURE MACHINE EVER MADE.

Presents a sharp, clear and brilliant picture, and is entirely free from flicker or unsteadiness. The only projecting machine which, according to recent legal decisions, is safe for an exhibitor to operate or to have in his possession.

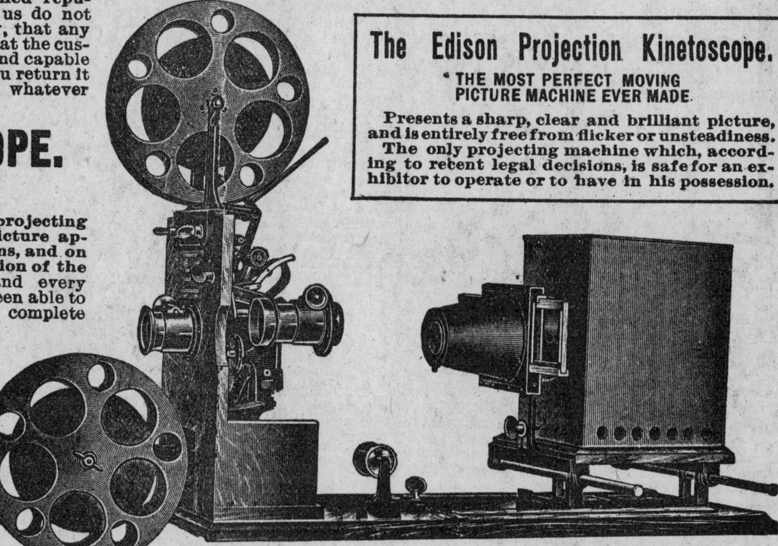

THE EDISON 1901 KINETOSCOPE.

(IMPROVED MODEL.)

THIS SEASON we shall handle the Edison Kinetoscope for projecting moving pictures exclusively. The moving picture apparatus is known as one of the greatest of the Edison inventions, and on it the Wizard of Originality has spent much time in the perfection of the present type of machine, embodying every improvement and every convenience which science, mechanical skill and research have been able to add to the first invention. The machine is handsome, durable and complete in every detail.

PORTABILITY. Weighs, when fully equipped, only 55 pounds, and can be packed in one case or can be packed in an ordinary trunk and shipped as baggage.

SIMPLICITY. The machine is easily set up and operated; every instrument is accompanied by full directions. An amateur can operate it as well as a professional.

SCIENTIFIC ACCURACY. Every detail has been so carefully planned that the result is a steady and brilliant picture, and any scratching or injury to the films is reduced to a minimum.

SIZE OF PICTURE. The size of the picture which can be projected with this machine is unlimited; it depends only upon the distance at which it is set from the screen. Twelve hundred feet of film can be used on this machine at one time in one continuous roll.

SUPERIORITY OF CONSTRUCTION. The machine is constructed at the Edison factory, under the immediate supervision of the inventor, a statement which assures as near an approach to perfection as is mechanically possible. It includes many devices and many improvements which until the present year were entirely unknown.

THE FRAMING DEVICE, which is new to this machine, is simple and strikingly effective. By merely adjusting a lever the entire mechanism which holds the film is moved up and down, enabling the operator to frame his film in the fraction of a second.

NO RISK OF HARASSING LITIGATION. The United States court has handed down a decision holding that the Edison Manufacturing Company is entitled to claim priority of patent on moving picture machines and films.

THE EDISON 1901 KINETOSCOPE is the best. It is the perfected model which gives the best results, and is the only machine with which the exhibitor can, in view of recent legal decision, be free from harassing litigation.

No. 21R400 1901 Edison Projecting Kinetoscope and Combined Stereopticon, furnished with electric arc lamp and rheostat for reducing current. Price... **$105.00**

No. 21R401 1901 Model Kinetoscope and Combined Stereopticon, with latest type of calcium burner and rubber adjustment to make connections for calcium light. Price........ **105.00**

No. 21R402 Kinetoscope Front for adding the Edison moving picture feature to any stereopticon or professional magic lantern. Price........ **75.00**

No. 21R405 Improved Take Up Device, for rewinding film; can be attached to any Edison Kinetoscope, if desired. Price........ **10.00**

WE ARE EXCLUSIVE DEALERS IN THE EDISON MACHINE AND FILMS.

THREE REASONS which now make it more than ever profitable for the exhibitor to start out with a moving picture machine are: **FIRST,** The improved machine will add efficiency and improve the outfit to an extent that has hardly yet been realized. **SECOND,** The slightly increased cost will, in many instances, prevent incompetent persons from entering the field, thus deterring those who could and would successfully handle an exhibition of this kind. **THIRD,** The mechanical perfection obtained in the construction of this machine is such as to insure its being always in order and no annoying inconvenience from break down or for repairs need be feared.

FILMS FOR PROJECTION OF MOVING PICTURES.

NEXT TO THE INSTRUMENT for projecting moving pictures, the film which contains the pictures themselves is the most important item. The film is a long celluloid tape usually about 50 feet, with a series of photographs taken at the rate of forty every second, in order to produce the animated movement for passing rapidly before the projecting lens at the same rate of speed from the beginning to the end of the film, thus reproducing all the movements which were in view when the picture was taken.

For Each Subject a Separate Film is Necessary.

THE FILMS which we handle are exclusively made in the Edison laboratory, and the results obtained surpass anything which has hitherto been produced. A complete revolution in the printing and development departments, the employment of an entirely new process, and the care exercised in scrutinizing and inspecting every film before it is sent from the factory, has resulted in a clearness of definition and a mellow tone, which although long sought for by leading exhibitors, has never been obtained before.

SEE NEXT PAGE for description of various lights used in Moving Picture Work.

WE CARRY SO LARGE A STOCK of these films on hand to fill orders as promptly as received, that it is well nigh impossible to give a detailed list in this place. We publish, however an elegant booklet containing names and description of the latest films. We supplement this list with monthly statements of all new films as they are taken, and upon receipt of postal card we will send free of cost this list and will place name upon our mailing list, so that our customers may keep posted in regard to the latest subjects. **A few of the many subjects at present on hand, which will suffice to indicate the wide range we cover, are as follows:**

Set of films descriptive of the sublime representation of the Passion Play as given at Oberammergau, Bavaria, of most intense interest not only to churches and religious bodies, but to all classes of people.

Films descriptive of scenes and incidents in connection with the assassination of our late president, Wm. McKinley. The events which transpired at the Buffalo Fair, the funeral cortege in that city, the lying in state at Washington and the interment at Canton.

The Life and Daily Happenings to a Fireman, faithfully portrayed in the wonderful series of unequaled moving picture films.

Pan-American Exposition at Buffalo is reproduced by another set of films.

Our Railway Series shows trains in motion, limited express trains at full speed, etc.

War Films are immensely popular at the present time. The Boer-British war, the war in the Philippines and the Chinese war are all admirably illustrated by our special sets, made up for the purpose.

Yacht Racing and Ocean Scenes are also thoroughly illustrated, including the recent victory of the Columbia over the Shamrock.

The Funeral of Victoria, the late English Queen.

Camp Incidents, Indian Dances and Customs, and Panoramic Scenes of Niagara Falls, while lighter subjects are represented by comic scenes of the most amusing description, graceful dances, exciting horse races and the latest representation of mystical, magical and sensational films.

The Light or Illuminant used for the Projection of Moving Pictures.

A MUCH MORE POWERFUL LIGHT IS REQUIRED FOR THE PROJECTION OF MOVING PICTURE FILMS THAN FOR THE STEREOPTICON OR STATIONARY PICTURES. THERE ARE ONLY THREE LIGHTS WHICH CAN BE USED TO PRODUCE A SATISFACTORY PROJECTION OF MOVING PICTURES; THESE ARE: FIRST, ELECTRICITY; SECOND, CALCIUM LIGHT; THIRD, THE NEW HYDRO-CARBON LIGHT.

ELECTRIC ARC LIGHT

Is the best artificial light which can be used for projection purposes, due not only to its brilliancy, but as it radiates from a small point, there is no loss of light.

AN ARC LIGHT cannot be made from a battery, but must be taken from a current where a dynamo is used. It is only practically available in the larger towns and cities. The average exhibitor therefore cannot make much use of electric light. In cases however, where only occasional exhibitions are given in towns where access can be had to an electric current, **our new electric arc lamp is invaluable and should form part of every equipment.**

THE ILLUSTRATION given on this page, **taken from photograph, shows the new model arc lamp which** is used with the combined Edison Kinetoscope and Stereopticon. It combines every improvement and convenience, the carbons may be set at any angle and adjusted by feed screws either at top or rear of the lamp.

No. 21R410 Electric Arc Lamp for connection with electric current. Price..**$8.00**

THE RHEOSTAT.

WHEN USING AN ARC LAMP WITH AN INCANDESCENT ELECTRIC CURRENT it is necessary to use a rheostat to convert a low tension current into an arc lamp. Our special Excelsior Rheostat is light, strong, tightly wound and thoroughly adjustable and adaptable to circuits of from 55 to 110 volts. **Illustration shows our Excelsior Rheostat ready to connect up. Can be used for alternating or direct currents, and can be operated by any one.**

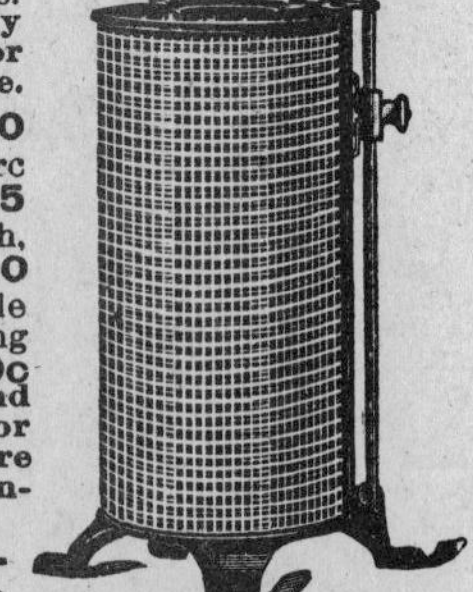

No. 21R411 Excelsior Rheostat complete **$5.00**

No. 21R412 Carbons for using in electric arc lamp, price, per hundred, ⅜-inch diameter...**$2.75**

No. 21R413 Large size carbons, diameter ⅝-inch, price, per hundred..............................**$4.10**

No. 21R414 Insulated electric light wire, flexible wire with heavy corded insulation for making electric light connections, price, per foot........**10c**

The arc lamp and carbons with rheostat and flexible wire constitute all that is necessary for projecting by means of electric light where there is already an established current with which connection can be made.

N. B.—We equip the combined Edison Kinetoscope and Stereopticon with arc lamp, and also with Excelsior Rheostat, free of charge.

OXY-HYDRO GAS OR LIME LIGHT.

THIS IS THE SECOND AND MOST EFFICIENT LIGHT for the projection of moving pictures, and the one on which exhibitors in smaller towns where electricity is not available are compelled to rely upon almost entirely. Calcium or lime light is in general use by exhibitors, advertising and theatrical companies who require a powerful light for projection purposes. It is produced, as is known, by burning oxygen and hydrogen gases combined on a lime pencil, **and is familiarly known as the "exhibitors stand-by."**

The necessary oxygen and hydrogen gases may be obtained in two ways. By purchasing of the calcium light companies, who store it in steel tanks under pressure, and ship to different points as directed, customer paying a deposit in order to insure return of the tanks which remain the property of the calcium light company. The expense of using oxygen and hydrogen light in this manner is about $1.50 per night. It is cheaper and in many ways more satisfactory to use an apparatus for generating the oxygen and hydrogen gases for which purpose we list the only portable calcium light outfit **constructed on practical and scientific principles.**

THIS ILLUSTRATION describes our new improved calcium light and gas making apparatus for stereopticon or moving picture machine provided with the latest improved **non-explosive saturator**, by the use of which the exhibitor is enabled to make his own gas at a cost of about one-fourth of ready made gas, and is also independent of calcium light companies, avoids delay in shipment and many other annoying circumstances.

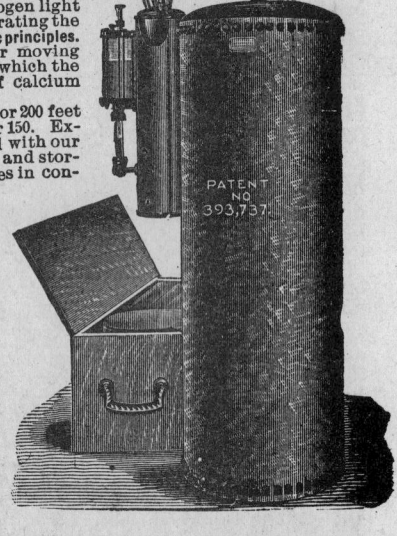

CONNECT HOSE WITH BURNER.

PATENT NO 393,737.

THE PERFECTION OXYGEN JET FOR CALCIUM LIGHT.

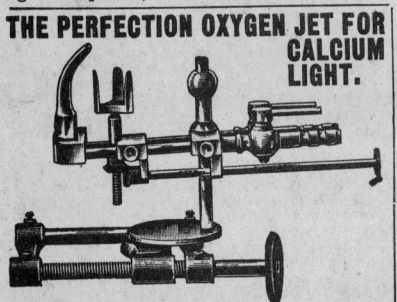

These jets are very carefully made and yield the minimum intensity of illumination and give a uniform light without hissing.

No. 21R415 Perfection oxygen jet with swing or stand. Price....................**$8.00**

WE MANUFACTURE THESE OUTFITS in two sizes, one tested for 200 feet of gas and the other for 150. Except for the size both outfits are exactly similar, and each is provided with our latest non-explosive saturator. They consist of the gas making outfit and storage tanks, the improved saturator, retort and all necessary appliances in connection with it. It has brass valves and connections, all of which are polished; the large tanks weigh 53 pounds and will hold sufficient gas for three hours; the small tank is of the same material and weighs about 40 pounds, and holds sufficient gas for about two hours.

No. 21R420 Small tank portable gas making outfit complete **$40.00**

No. 21R421 Same outfit complete with large tank.......... **45.00**

These outfits possess many points of superiority over gas in ready made tanks. You can make your own gas at one-fourth the expense, and to those who expect to show in small towns, the calcium light apparatus is indispensable. **Produces about 700 candle power,** and is the only efficient, satisfactory substitute for electricity in moving picture work. Both the small and large tank outfits are provided with a pressure gauge showing the amount of oxygen gas in the cylinder at any time.

HYDROGEN GAS IS PRODUCED FROM A SATURATOR. We use our new improved non-explosive saturator for the purpose, the only safe reliable and scientific one made, provided with glass gauge, regulating valve and reserve supply tank.

THE HYDROGEN GAS is produced by the evaporation of 88-test gasoline stored in the saturator of reserve tank, and the glass gauge not only shows when the proper amount of liquid is in the saturator, but also serves as a by-pass, mixing and agitating the gasoline whereby the evaporation is considerably increased.

IT IS ALMOST IMPOSSIBLE to have any trouble with a saturator of this description. Send for circular devoted to the description of this apparatus, and which will give you all possible information.

NEW HYDRO-CARBON LIGHT, OR BRIGHT WHITE LIGHT.

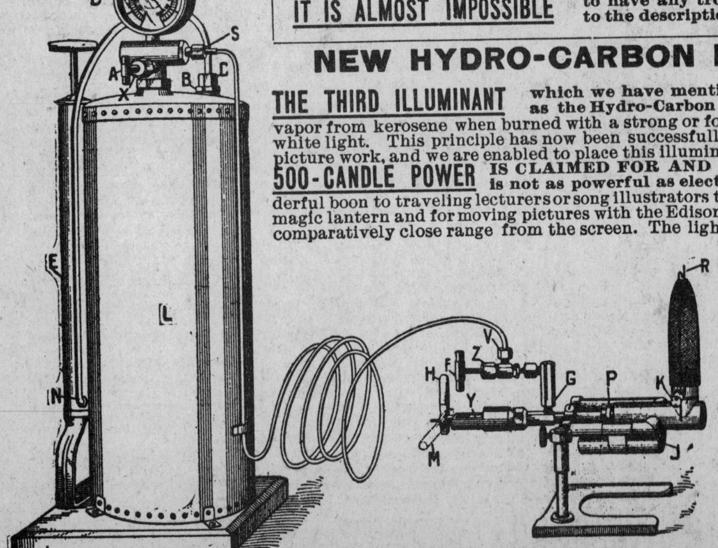

THE THIRD ILLUMINANT which we have mentioned in connection with the projection of moving pictures, is known as the Hydro-Carbon Light. The discovery was made a few years ago, that the hydro-carbon vapor from kerosene when burned with a strong or forced draft under proper conditions, produces an intensely brilliant, pure white light. This principle has now been successfully applied to a portable outfit suitable for both stereopticon and moving picture work, and we are enabled to place this illuminant before our customers the first, as usual, of any dealers in a similar line.

500-CANDLE POWER IS CLAIMED FOR AND DEMONSTRATED BY THIS WONDERFUL LIGHT, and while this is not as powerful as electricity or calcium, it is sufficiently strong to constitute it the most wonderful boon to traveling lecturers or song illustrators that has yet been brought out. It can be used with any regular professional magic lantern and for moving pictures with the Edison kinetoscope in cases where exhibitions are given in a small room and at a comparatively close range from the screen. The ligh produced is nearly white and intensely brilliant. The expense of operating is almost nominal, a gallon of oil lasting twelve hours and making the running expense less than one cent per hour.

THE LIGHT IS FREE FROM FLICKER or disagreeable odor, absolutely safe and reliable, and easy to handle, so that it can be used by an operator without previous experience. It is so light in weight that it can be carried in the hand, and the material used (ordinary kerosene), can be obtained in any small town or cross roads in the country, and not only in this country but all over the world. The light is obtained by placing about three gallons of kerosene in a stout steel cylinder, this is vaporized by the action of compressed air into the vaporizer, and under a strong draft is burned on a regular Welsbach mantle. By means of a pump the air is compressed in the cylinder to the proper point, and the apparatus is ready for immediate use.

No. 21R430 Hydro-Carbon Light outfit, including tank, burner, pressure gauge, pump and six mantles........................**$25.00**

No. 21R431 Light fiber case with straps for carrying outfit.. **2.00**

Extra mantles, each.. **.15**

WRITE FOR SPECIAL CIRCULAR DESCRIPTIVE OF THE NEW HYDRO-CARBON LIGHT.

Sears Roebuck & Co.
INCORPORATED
Musical Goods Department
We call particular attention to this, our very complete department of . . . . . .
PIANOS, ORGANS AND OTHER
MUSICAL INSTRUMENTS
WE BELIEVE a comparison will show that this department carries the most complete line of only strictly high grade goods, and at prices below any kind of competition.
MUSICAL FURNISHINGS, INSTRUCTION BOOKS, SUPPLIES, ETC.

We have revolutionized the piano and organ business. We have made it possible for our customers to buy a piano or an organ, a strictly high grade instrument, at less than one-half the price at which such instruments have been sold, at even less than any retail dealer can buy at wholesale.

OUR ORGANS AND PIANOS are made for us by the largest and most reputable makers of high grade instruments in the country, concerns whose reputation for the manufacture of only strictly high grade instruments is a guarantee for quality. There is perhaps no other article of merchandise in which poor quality can be as easily disguised as in the putting together of pianos and organs. For this reason it is essential in buying these goods to have the guarantee of a reliable house back of them.

WE CONSIDER QUALITY FIRST. It is our aim to market only the very finest instruments, goods that will be a lasting and standing advertisement for us in any home, and every care is taken that only high grade materials enter into their construction. Every piece and part is carefully selected; every detail is inspected, and we can conscientiously say that our pianos and organs represent the highest standard of musical construction.

FROM OUR AMERICAN HOME PIANO at $98.50 to our highest grade Artists' Cabinet Grand at $155.00, we offer the very best pianos it is possible to produce, at prices which mean a saving over what such instruments are sold for by retail dealers throughout the country, of at least 50 per cent. Our organs from our Happy Home organ at $22.00 to our Imperial Grand instrument at $48.50, represent the same high standard of quality as our pianos and the same wonderful saving in price.

OUR ILLUSTRATIONS AND DESCRIPTIONS can be depended upon as being strictly accurate. Remember that our only salesman is this catalogue. We have no local agent to talk up the goods, but depend solely upon our catalogue illustrations and descriptions, the high standard of quality we maintain, the extremely low prices we quote, the saving we can make for anyone who intends to buy a musical instrument, and our established reputation everywhere for responsibility. However, if you can come to Chicago, we would be pleased to satisfy you personally of the values we are offering. **If you have any friends in Chicago to whom you can write, we would be very glad to have them come and examine our instruments and then write to you if they believe it is to your interest to place your order with us.**

DO NOT PAY YOUR LOCAL DEALER or an agent two or three times our price for a piano or an organ. Do not buy an instrument on time and pay a cash deposit that alone would buy a better instrument from us, and then pay a big balance on installments. It would be more for your interest, if it is necessary, for you to borrow the money and pay 6 per cent interest and send us your order for one of our high grade instruments, rather than pay a local dealer or an agent two to three times the price, get a poor instrument and incur the responsibility of time payments.

WE GUARANTEE
OUR PIANOS AND ORGANS
FOR 25 YEARS.

Our written binding 25 years' guarantee accompanies every instrument, during which time if any piece or part gives out by reason of defective material or workmanship we will replace it free of charge. With care our instruments will last a lifetime.

ABOUT FREIGHT. We can effect such a big saving for you in this department that the freight is a small item; besides, it is no more than the freight your dealer or agent would be compelled to pay if you order through him. **Organs or pianos are accepted by railroad companies at first class freight rates.** Under each description we give the weight of the instrument, and if you will refer to the freight rates in the front of the book, for the first class rate for 100 pounds to the nearest point in your state, you can calculate almost exactly what the freight will amount to.

WHILE WE REQUIRE the full amount of the price to be sent with the order, as our only terms are cash with the order, you will not run the slightest risk by complying with these terms. If after the instrument is received, examined, compared with other instruments, even after you have used the instrument for one year, if you do not find it perfectly satisfactory, exactly as we have represented it to be, if you are not perfectly satisfied with your purchase and the money we have saved you, even after a year has expired, you are at liberty to return the instrument to us and we will immediately return your money, including what you paid for transportation charges.

TO THOSE WHO ARE NOT ACQUAINTED with us or do not know us by reputation, it may seem like some little risk to send quite a sum of money away for such a purchase, and if you have any doubt whatever or hesitate to send us your order on our only terms—cash with the order—send your money first to any bank, business house or express company in this city with instructions not to turn it over to us until you are satisfied from their report that we are perfectly responsible and reliable. **Look on page 12 of this Catalogue and see what our bankers say regarding us.** Ask any of your friends or neighbors about us. We have more than two million customers in all parts of the country and are sure you will find our customers among your friends and neighbors. Ask them if they consider us responsible. Ask them if they would advise your sending us your order, for we are willing to abide by their decision.

OUR GUITARS, MANDOLINS, VIOLINS, band instruments, other musical instruments and musical merchandise, **we guarantee the highest grade American made, warranted never to crack or split, perfect scale, sweetest tone and best instruments made.** The manufacturer, every dealer concedes, is the best maker of guitars and mandolins in America. Our violins and band instruments are made under contract for us by the leading manufacturers, and we import from the most noted European makers, and in every case our prices are based on the actual cost, freight, duty and our one small profit added, and our prices in many cases will be found less than one-half the prices charged by retail dealers. Many musical instruments we sell to our customers for less than the average retail dealer can buy them for even at wholesale.

SUPPLIES for our pianos and organs, such at strings, reeds, springs, etc., can be procured at any time, without cost, no matter when ordered. A perfect record is kept of each instrument manufactured, enabling us to send properly fitting parts when needed.

REMEMBER, OUR TERMS ARE CASH WITH THE ORDER, BUT WE GUARANTEE COMPLETE SATISFACTION OR REFUND YOUR MONEY.

OUR NEW AMERICAN HOME UPRIGHT PARLOR GRAND PIANO

OUR FACTORY TO CONSUMER PRICE $98.50

WITH EVERY PIANO WE ISSUE A WRITTEN, BINDING, 25 YEARS' GUARANTEE.

SUCH VALUE WAS NEVER KNOWN BEFORE

MARVEL OF MARVELS. A PERFECT PIANO. GUARANTEED TO LAST A LIFETIME.

ONLY CONSIDER, a full size piano, mahogany or burl walnut finish, for $98.50. Retail dealers ask from $175.00 to $250.00 for same grade.

WE SEND FREE with each piano a handsome stool and complete instruction book. If you want to buy a good, durable piano at a low price, you cannot do better than to send us your order for this our New American Home at $98.50. REMEMBER, it costs you absolutely nothing if not entirely satisfactory and exactly as represented by us. No one can make a fairer offer than this.

OUR BINDING 25-YEARS' GUARANTEE

WE ISSUE A WRITTEN BINDING 25 YEARS' GUARANTEE, by the terms and conditions of which, if any piece or part gives out by reason of defect in material or workmanship, we will replace it FREE OF CHARGE. THIS IS THE LONGEST, STRONGEST AND MOST BINDING GUARANTEE GIVEN WITH ANY PIANO.

WHY PAY A RETAIL DEALER OR PIANO AGENT $200.00 OR $300.00 FOR A PIANO NO BETTER THAN THIS OUR NEW AMERICAN HOME AT $98.50?

WE GIVE YOU EVERY PROTECTION WHEN YOU PURCHASE A PIANO OF US. OUR 25 YEARS' GUARANTEE IS AS BINDING AS A GOVERNMENT BOND.

No. 12R1 Our $98.50 New American Home Piano, Engraved from a Photograph.

DESCRIPTION

SIZE OF PIANO: Height, 4 feet 7 inches; width, 2 feet 3 inches; length, 61 inches; weight, boxed for shipment, about 800 pounds.

THE CASES of these pianos are very pleasing in design, and made of carefully selected hard rock maple, beautifully finished in mahogany or fancy burl walnut. These finishes are so cleverly made that it is with difficulty that you can tell them from the natural wood. This is especially true of our mahogany finish, while the burl walnut is a perfect copy of the natural French burl walnut.

THE ACTION is of a very durable construction, otherwise we could not guarantee our instruments, as we do, for twenty-five years. It is made of well selected material, the hammers and felts being of a superior quality. Has perfect and simple adjustment to take up all possible wear; is very responsive and pleasing to the touch.

THE WREST PLANK OR PIN BLOCK is made of several veneers of hard maple, with the grain running in different directions. This makes the tuning pin sit firmly in the wood, and renders frequent tuning unnecessary. This wrest plank is securely bolted to our composition metal frame, and its construction makes twisting, warping or otherwise pulling out of shape impossible.

SCALE. Full size, 7⅓ octaves, overstrung bass, three strings to each note, except wound bass strings. Double cap hammers. The scale is perfectly even and the touch is fine and perfectly repeating.

THE TONE is of course the most important consideration when selecting a piano, at least it is one that should receive careful thought, and in this piano we have used our very best endeavors to produce an instrument at a low figure that would not be lacking in this respect. We can therefore guarantee this instrument to possess a tone that is full, round and powerful, at the same time sweet and melodious.

IF YOU WILL REFER TO THE FREIGHT RATES in the front of the book you can tell almost exactly what the freight on this piano will be to your railroad station, and thus save the time and trouble of writing to us for an estimate of freight.

OUR HOME FAVORITE PIANO-ORGAN.

No. 12R12 Order by Number.

$59.45 OUR A GRADE HOME FAVORITE PIANO-ORGAN . .

is 4 feet 10½ inches long, 4 feet 7½ inches high, 2 feet 1½ inches deep; has 7⅓ octaves of keys and four sets of reeds divided as follows: 4⅔ octaves diapason, 2⅔ octaves melodia, 4⅔ octaves vox celeste, 2⅔ octaves principal, base and treble coupler—176 reeds in all. Furnished complete with a handsome stool and complete instruction book.

No. 12R14 Order by Number.

OUR AA GRADE HOME FAVORITE PIANO-ORGAN . . $64.95

is the same as our A Grade, but has in addition a saxophone set of reeds, making a total of

FIVE SETS OF REEDS—214 IN ALL.

A complete instruction book and handsome stool furnished free with this organ.

ORDER BY NUMBER. Shipping weight, 400 pounds.

WHY OUR ORGANS ARE A SUCCESS.

They embody to the greatest extent the essentials of a perfect organ. In

APPEARANCE, Equal to a piano.

CONSTRUCTION, Simplest mechanism of any organ made.

TONE, Most nearly resembles that of a pipe organ.

CAPACITY FOR MUSIC. All classes can be executed same as on piano.

PEDAL ARRANGEMENT. Compared with it, the old pedal board is ridiculous.

VARIETY OF EXPRESSION, Unequaled, and not necessary to stop playing to change stops.

WE GUARANTEE THIS ORGAN.... FOR 25 YEARS

OUR SOLE AND ONLY PLEA FOR YOUR ORDER IS A BETTER INSTRUMENT AT A MUCH LOWER PRICE THAN YOU CAN GET ELSEWHERE.

OUR TERMS are alike to one and all—CASH WITH ORDER. Remember, we guarantee satisfaction or refund money.

IN APPEARANCE THE CASE EXACTLY RESEMBLES AN UPRIGHT PIANO.

IS HANDSOMELY CARVED AND EXCELS MOST PIANOS IN BEAUTY AND DESIGN. WE CAN FURNISH THIS ORGAN IN BEAUTIFUL WALNUT OR A RICH MAHOGANY VENEER, AS DESIRED.

THE FINISH is hand polished and rubbed, thus producing a luster seen only on the best pianos. All styles have the **full extension music desk,** also the **double fold grand fall board.**

VARIETY OF TONE. The method of constructing the case, combined with a specially constructed reed board, qualifies the tone, causing it to differ from all reed organs, and giving it a delicacy with power that is wonderful and only equaled in resonating quality by the pipe organ. Like on the pipe organ also, the player can vary the tone and render the most beautiful effects and pleasing contrasts without stopping the music, by means of our wonderful yet simple method of controlling the action, while the seven and one-third octave keyboard and responsive touch of our organs give them **the same capacity for music as a piano.**

DURABILITY. In lasting qualities these instruments excel any reed organ in the market, as a most casual examination will show. The cases, keys, actions, veneered bellows and sounding boards, etc., are all of the highest grade materials and construction throughout, with absolute freedom from the slightest imperfection, while the great value of our improvements, in addition to the advantages they afford, is that they are all in the line of simplicity and replace features that are objectionable and the cause of trouble in other organs.

EASY OPERATION. This is an extremely important point that cannot receive too much attention from the purchaser. What satisfaction is there, however handsome and sweet toned the organ, if the touch tires the fingers, the treadles tire the feet, and the action is not easily controlled so as to give variety and effect to the music? It is in this very feature that **our piano-organs are so far beyond all comparison,** with their new and special improvements of touch, pedal arrangement, bellows and action control. First, in regard to

TOUCH we claim perfection. The keys respond with extraordinary quickness and elasticity, having none of the slow, stiff movement so common in organs, as we use the best reeds that speak quickly.

PEDAL ARRANGEMENT. The patented pedal arrangement has largely contributed to the remarkable success of our organs. The nickel pedals with guard are precisely like those of a piano, and have the exact leverage necessary to conform to the movement of the feet. **Thus a small child is able to sustain the full power of the organ with ease.**

THE BELLOWS. The bellows, being unusually large and powerful, produce a full tone the entire length of the keyboard and also lessen the work of pumping. The bellows and sounding boards are made of three thicknesses of lumber glued together, the grain of each thickness running in contrary direction, thus making impossible any shrinkage or splitting. The rubber bellows cloth is manufactured especially for us, none of the grades in the market for this purpose being durable. The bellows are the life of the organ, and of the thousands of organs made by us, we have never heard of a single bellows becoming imperfect.

OUR HAPPY HOME ORGAN, $22.00

GRADE B, CASH IN FULL WITH ORDER, $22.00.

No. 12R17 OUR $22.00 ORGAN IS FULL SIZE eight stops, five octaves, two knee swells, three sets of reeds. CASE—SOLID OAK, FINISHED ANTIQUE, OR BLACK WALNUT.

No. 12R17 Our special price, in Grade B.....$22.00
No. 12R18 Our special price, in Grade A. See description below, only.....27.00

Our grade B which we offer at $22.00 is full size, five octaves, three sets of reeds, one set of 25 Diapason, one set of 37 Melodia and one set of 37 Celeste, double octave couplers. Eight stops as follows: Diapason, Dulciana, Melodia, Celeste, Bass Coupler, Treble Coupler, Diapason Forte and Principal Forte. Two Knee Swells. **The price quoted is for the organ carefully boxed and delivered free on board the cars in Chicago. Shipping weight, 325 pounds.**

DESCRIPTION OF CASE. Height, 65 inches; length, 44 inches; width, 23 inches. We furnish this organ either in solid-oak or black walnut finish as desired. It is a neat and elegant design, beautifully ornamented as shown in illustration, and is given a high finish. **This Special Happy Home Organ** which we quote at **$22.00** in our Grade B will compare favorably with anything you can buy in your local market at more than double the price. We are able to offer it at this heretofore unheard of price of $22.00 only by reason of our contracting with the manufacturer for large quantities and on a spot cash basis. **If you buy this organ from us at $22.00** you are buying it on the basis of the actual cost of material and labor, with only one small profit added. We do not guarantee this organ, but offer it with a view to showing what it is possible for us to supply for the home at a price below any competition. It is the best bargain we have to offer and you get it for even less than your local dealers can buy in quantities.

No. 12R18 DESCRIPTION OF OUR A GRADE HAPPY HOME ORGAN AT $27.00. For those who wish a more powerful action we have finished our Happy Home Organ in what we term our A Grade, which we furnish at $27.00. Our A Grade Organ, which we quote at $27.00, will compare favorably with anything in your local market at $40.00. At $27.00 you are buying it for less than your local dealers can buy in quantities. This organ has an additional set of 24 principal reeds, making it much more powerful, and contains in all 11 stops, including Diapason, Dulciana, Melodia, Celeste, Cremona, Bass Coupler, Treble Coupler, Diapason Forte, Principal Forte, Vox Humana, Grand Organ and Knee Swell, 122 reeds in all. We would advise you, by all means, to pay the $5.00 difference and secure the A Grade. The $5.00 difference we charge you is the difference in cost to us and should be taken advantage of.

DO NOT OVERLOOK OUR WRITTEN BINDING GUARANTEE. WE GUARANTEE THIS ORGAN FOR TWENTY-FIVE YEARS, AND ISSUE THE LONGEST, STRONGEST AND MOST BINDING GUARANTEE GIVEN WITH ANY ORGAN. SHIPPING WEIGHT, 325 POUNDS.

No. 12R17

No. 12R17 Order by Number.

THE BILHORN TELESCOPE ORGAN

FOR SCHOOL ROOMS, AT YOUR HOMES, WHEREVER MUSIC IS WANTED, IN PRICE THE CHEAPEST.

YOU NEED IT EVERYWHERE. Our "49-note" (four-octave) organ is rapidly supplanting more expensive instruments in Churches everywhere. **Our Telescope Organ is adapted for use under all circumstances, in places where there is no instrument, or where portability is desired.**

IT IS THE ONLY PERFECT FOLDING ORGAN. We challenge competition of workmanship, and we claim: 1st—In size, the smallest. 2d—In appearance, the neatest. 3d—In traveling, the handiest. 4th—In shipping, the strongest. 5th—In carrying, the lightest. 6th—In wet weather, the safest. 7th—In folding, the quickest. 8th—In tone, the sweetest. 9th—In volume, the most powerful. **BEST OF ALL.**

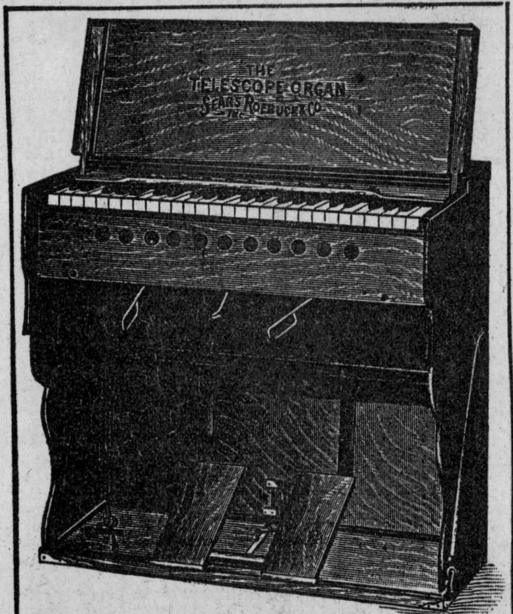

CASE—The case is built of choice 3-ply oak veneering, ¼ inch thick, thus making it light, durable and far more resonant than the old way of making organ cases.

TRIMMINGS—The outside trimmings, including hinges, screws, corners, etc., are of brass, with high nickel polish. This gives the organ a fine appearance and prevents the metal parts from rusting in damp or salty climates.

KEYS—The keys are regular organ width. They are overlaid with XX celluloid, and are like all other first class piano or organ keys.

BELLOWS—The bellows is one of our special features. It is very easily operated, of great power, is made of 3-ply select stock, and will never crack, split or leak. The rubber sheeting used is of the very best quality. It will stand the test of any climate and strain of any reasonable usage.

LININGS—Special attention has been given this part and only the best material obtainable used.

TONE—This most essential quality has been carefully considered and the result is a rich, mellow tone, highly satisfactory to the most musical cultured ear. The full organ gives sufficient power to lead a thousand voices in song, while with the mutes a tone soft, clear and sweet can be produced.

FINISH—The finish is strictly first class, only the very best material being used. All organs are well filled, coated and recoated with best body varnish, hand rubbed and highly polished; giving a smooth, hard and durable surface.

PEDALS—The pedals are large enough for a man's foot. They are neatly covered with oilcloth, and so arranged that when the organ opens they instantly spring into place, and in folding the organ they adjust themselves. They are neat in design and substantial.

BOOK REST—The book rest will accommodate sheet music or any sized song books.

SPRINGS—The air chamber valves and springs are of the same style and quality used in larger organs costing from $150.00 to $200.00.

APPEARANCE—When folded the organ has the appearance of a neat sample case, and is secure against dust, rain, snow or mice. They can easily be carried with one hand.

HANDLES—The handles are cushioned with rubber, and so arranged that they are convenient for one or two persons.

Our 39-note, double reed Diapason and Flute, ranging from F below the bass staff to G above the treble.
Shipping weight, 50 pounds.

	Size: When Open	Size: When Closed
Width	15 inches.	11 inches.
Height	35½ inches.	16 inches.
Length	23½ inches.	23½ inches.

Carrying weight, only 28 pounds.

No. 12R19 Our Special Price - - - - $21.50

Our 49-note, double reed Diapason and Flute, ranging from C below the bass staff, to C above the treble.
Shipping weight, 60 pounds.

	Size: When Open	Size: When Closed
Width	15 inches.	11 inches.
Height	35½ inches.	16 inches.
Length	29 inches.	29 inches.

Carrying weight, only 32 pounds.

No. 12R20 Our Special Price - - - - $24.75

OUR ACME QUEEN PARLOR ORGAN, $27.45.

WE CHALLENGE any and all competition to produce the equal of this ELEGANT HIGH CLASS ORGAN at anything like our DIRECT FROM FACTORY PRICE.

No. 12R22 ORDER BY NUMBER

DESCRIPTION OF OUR ACME QUEEN ORGAN.

DIMENSIONS—The height is 72 inches, the length is 42 inches and the width is 23 inches. You will observe by these dimensions that it is large, full size and in this respect equal to anything your retail dealer ordinarily carries in stock.

SHIPPING WEIGHT—The weight of this organ, boxed for shipment, is about 350 pounds. We box and pack our organs with great care, paying special attention to this detail, so that the instrument may reach you in perfect condition, not marred in any way, shape or manner.

THE FREIGHT on the organ will be very little compared with what we save you. See first class freight rates as given in front of book. In most instances the freight to any point within 200 miles would be about $1.50; 500 miles, $2.25; 1,000 miles, $5.00, and so on, and when you compare the $20.00 to $30.00 saving with the small freight charges, you can readily see that there is no comparison whatever.

COMPLETE IN EVERY RESPECT.

ACTION—The action of this high grade Acme Queen Organ consists of the celebrated Newell reeds, which are used only in the highest grade instruments. This organ is fitted with **Hammond's Couplers and Vox Humana**, also the best Dolge felts, leather, etc.

This organ has five octaves, eleven stops, two octave couplers, one toning swell, one grand organ swell, four sets of orchestral toned resonatory high quality reeds, one set exquisitely pure and sweet Melodia reeds, 37 in all, one set of 37 charmingly brilliant Celeste reeds, one set of 24 rich, mellow, smooth, Diapason reeds, one set of 24 pleasing, soft, melodious, Principal reeds; **a total of 122 reeds.**

NAMES OF THE ELEVEN STOPS—Diapason, Principal, Dulciana, Melodia, Celeste, Cremona, Bass Coupler, Treble Coupler, Diapason Forte, Principal Forte and Vox Humana.

THE CASE—It is difficult from the illustration, even large as the one shown, or from a general description to give you an idea of the beauty of this case. **It is one of the handsomest ever used on any organ at anything like the price.** We furnish it only in solid oak, handsomely finished, beautifully carved and ornamented. It is especially constructed to develop the acoustic properties of the organ, forming a qualifying chamber, **which gives a pipe like quality to the tone hitherto unattained in the finest reed organs.** Special attention has been given to the seasoning of the wood of which this organ is constructed, so that it is not subject to climatic changes. It is highly finished, has a **10x14 inch French bevel plate mirror,** nickel plated pedal frames and every modern improvement.

THE BELLOWS—The bellows used in this action are made of the best rubber cloth and of 3-ply bellows stock, and the finest sheepskin leather in the valves.

THE TONE—The tone is one of the most important qualities in any organ and with our Acme Queen the tone is faultless. The depth and breadth of the sounding chamber is exactly proportioned, so as to give beauty to the tone without sacrificing the sweetness. This, together with the finely tempered metal used in the reeds, **secures a purity of tone which can only be equaled by the soft pipe of the church organ.**

We are safe in saying that in no other organ manufactured have these pipe like qualities been procured. The special feature in the action of our Acme Queen Organ will be found only in organs of this manufacture.

Do you hesitate to send cash with your order? Read what we say about cash terms on page 1.

$27.45 BUYS THE ORGAN

and we are bound to please you or the organ is shipped back to us and you get

ALL YOUR MONEY RETURNED.

25 YEARS' GUARANTEE.

FREE...

With this organ we present you FREE and ship with it, a fine ORGAN STOOL and a very complete and valuable INSTRUCTION BOOK.

GREAT VIOLIN BARGAINS.

...OUR ENTIRE LINE OF VIOLINS...

has been carefully selected by our violin expert, who has devoted his entire life to the study of violins, and we can safely state that we believe every instrument to be the greatest bargain ever offered and the finest value for the money which can be procured in this or any other country.

With Each Violin We Furnish Free a Nice Violin Bow, a Set of Strings and a Valuable Instruction Book.

SHIPPING WEIGHT, 7 POUNDS.

Our $2.45 Stradivarius Model.

No. 12R212 This violin is Stradivarius model, made of specially selected wood; beautifully varnished, reddish color, highly finished. Possessing a tone very seldom found in violins at very much higher prices. Such a violin as we offer herewith retails everywhere at $8.00 to $10.00.

No. 12R212 Our special price..**$2.45**

Our Special $3.45 Conservatory Violin.

No. 12R214 Our Special $3.45 Conservatory Violin. This violin is modeled after the original Stradivarius violin, an instrument which is perhaps more popular than any other, and which is copied more largely by the best violin makers of Europe than any other. This violin is handsomely finished throughout, fitted with solid ebony fingerboard and tailpiece. It is reddish brown in color, beautifully shaded and handsomely polished. **Do not purchase until you have seen and tried this violin.**

No. 12R214 Our special price..**$3.45**

A Genuine Maggini Violin for $4.75.

No. 12R216 For quality and power of tone this is one of the finest violins we have ever offered at the price. A genuine Maggini model, being a direct copy of violins by that great maker. Made of selected and seasoned wood, beautifully varnished, reddish brown in color, highly polished. It is trimmed with solid ebony fingerboard and tailpiece. Like the renowned Maggini violins, it has double inlaid purfling, giving it a distinguished and handsome appearance. **A violin that readily sells at retail for $15.00 to $20.00.**

No. 12R216 Our special price..**$4.75**

Our Stainer Model for $5.65.

No. 12R218 The Stainer model is much sought after by all players of the violin on account of this model producing an exceptionally sweet and powerful tone. This violin has best quality ebony trimmings, is handsomely varnished, highly polished, and well finished in every respect. You should not fail to examine this instrument before deciding to purchase elsewhere.

No. 12R218 Our special price..**$5.65**

The Amati Copy for $6.35.

No. 12R220 The Amati Violins are noted for their usually sweet quality of tone. Specially desirable for parlor playing. They are among the finest instruments known to violin players. The violin, as shown in the illustration, has a beautiful curly maple back and sides, carefully selected top of fine old wood, maple neck and scroll. The varnish is the regular rich Amati color, highly polished, and the ebony trimmings are of the best quality. **A violin which has always been considered a rare bargain.**

No. 12R220 Our special price..**$6.35**

Our $6.95 Genuine Stradivarius Model.

No. 12R222 These violins are made expressly for us by one of the greatest makers in Europe, and are offered at our one small percentage of profit as the greatest value we can offer. It has a two-piece maple back, beautifully flamed, as shown in illustration. Top of resonant spruce, especially selected; reddish brown varnish, beautifully shaded, in imitation of an old violin. Neck and scroll are made of curly maple to correspond with the back and sides. The fingerboard, tailpiece and pegs are of best quality solid ebony.

No. 12R222 Our special price..**$6.95**

FOR VIOLIN FURNISHINGS AND STRINGS, SEE PAGE 214.
FOR FOLIOS AND INSTRUCTION BOOKS, SEE PAGES 220 to 224.

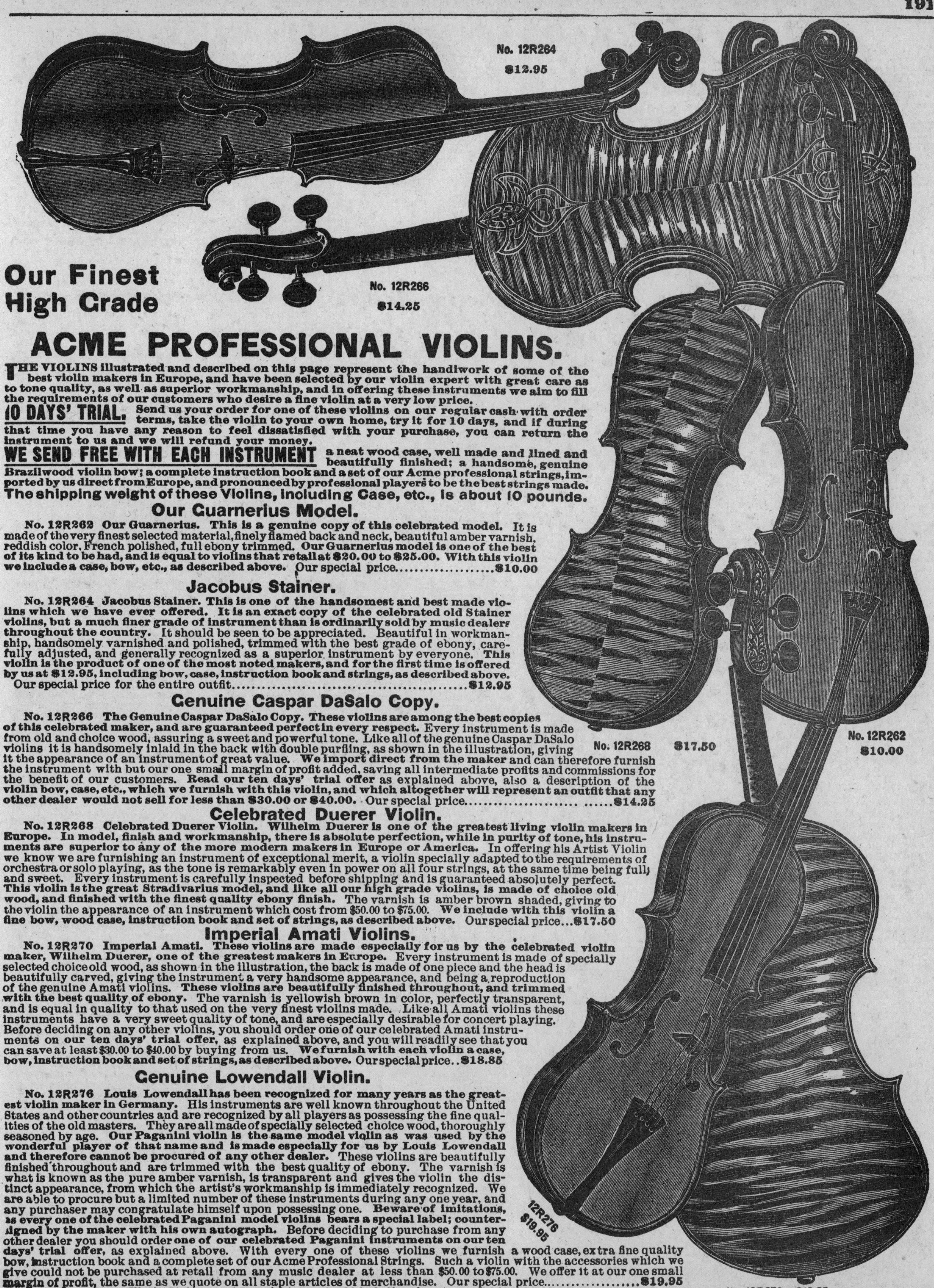

Our Finest High Grade

ACME PROFESSIONAL VIOLINS.

THE VIOLINS illustrated and described on this page represent the handiwork of some of the best violin makers in Europe, and have been selected by our violin expert with great care as to tone quality, as well as superior workmanship, and in offering these instruments we aim to fill the requirements of our customers who desire a fine violin at a very low price.

10 DAYS' TRIAL. Send us your order for one of these violins on our regular cash with order terms, take the violin to your own home, try it for 10 days, and if during that time you have any reason to feel dissatisfied with your purchase, you can return the instrument to us and we will refund your money.

WE SEND FREE WITH EACH INSTRUMENT a neat wood case, well made and lined and beautifully finished; a handsome, genuine Brazilwood violin bow; a complete instruction book and a set of our Acme professional strings, imported by us direct from Europe, and pronounced by professional players to be the best strings made.

The shipping weight of these Violins, including Case, etc., is about 10 pounds.

Our Guarnerius Model.

No. 12R262 Our Guarnerius. This is a genuine copy of this celebrated model. It is made of the very finest selected material, finely flamed back and neck, beautiful amber varnish, reddish color, French polished, full ebony trimmed. **Our Guarnerius model is one of the best of its kind to be had, and is equal to violins that retail at $20.00 to $25.00. With this violin we include a case, bow, etc., as described above.** Our special price....................**$10.00**

Jacobus Stainer.

No. 12R264 Jacobus Stainer. This is one of the handsomest and best made violins which we have ever offered. It is an exact copy of the celebrated old Stainer violins, but a much finer grade of instrument than is ordinarily sold by music dealers throughout the country. It should be seen to be appreciated. Beautiful in workmanship, handsomely varnished and polished, trimmed with the best grade of ebony, carefully adjusted, and generally recognized as a superior instrument by everyone. **This violin is the product of one of the most noted makers, and for the first time is offered by us at $12.95, including bow, case, instruction book and strings, as described above.** Our special price for the entire outfit....................**$12.95**

Genuine Caspar DaSalo Copy.

No. 12R266 The Genuine Caspar DaSalo Copy. These violins are among the best copies of this celebrated maker, and are guaranteed perfect in every respect. Every instrument is made from old and choice wood, assuring a sweet and powerful tone. Like all of the genuine Caspar DaSalo violins it is handsomely inlaid in the back with double purfling, as shown in the illustration, giving it the appearance of an instrument of great value. **We import direct from the maker** and can therefore furnish the instrument with but our one small margin of profit added, saving all intermediate profits and commissions for the benefit of our customers. **Read our ten days' trial offer as explained above, also a description of the violin bow, case, etc., which we furnish with this violin, and which altogether will represent an outfit that any other dealer would not sell for less than $30.00 or $40.00.** Our special price......................**$14.25**

Celebrated Duerer Violin.

No. 12R268 Celebrated Duerer Violin. Wilhelm Duerer is one of the greatest living violin makers in Europe. In model, finish and workmanship, there is absolute perfection, while in purity of tone, his instruments are superior to any of the more modern makers in Europe or America. In offering his Artist Violin we know we are furnishing an instrument of exceptional merit, a violin specially adapted to the requirements of orchestra or solo playing, as the tone is remarkably even in power on all four strings, at the same time being full and sweet. Every instrument is carefully inspected before shipping and is guaranteed absolutely perfect. **This violin is the great Stradivarius model, and like all our high grade violins, is made of choice old wood, and finished with the finest quality ebony finish.** The varnish is amber brown shaded, giving to the violin the appearance of an instrument which cost from $50.00 to $75.00. **We include with this violin a fine bow, wood case, instruction book and set of strings, as described above.** Our special price...**$17.50**

Imperial Amati Violins.

No. 12R270 Imperial Amati. These violins are made especially for us by the celebrated violin maker, Wilhelm Duerer, one of the greatest makers in Europe. Every instrument is made of specially selected choice old wood, as shown in the illustration, the back is made of one piece and the head is beautifully carved, giving the instrument a very handsome appearance, and being a reproduction of the genuine Amati violins. **These violins are beautifully finished throughout, and trimmed with the best quality of ebony.** The varnish is yellowish brown in color, perfectly transparent, and is equal in quality to that used on the very finest violins made. Like all Amati violins these instruments have a very sweet quality of tone, and are especially desirable for concert playing. Before deciding on any other violins, you should order one of our celebrated Amati instruments on our ten days' trial offer, as explained above, and you will readily see that you can save at least $30.00 to $40.00 by buying from us. **We furnish with each violin a case, bow, instruction book and set of strings, as described above.** Our special price..**$18.85**

Genuine Lowendall Violin.

No. 12R276 Louis Lowendall has been recognized for many years as the greatest violin maker in Germany. His instruments are well known throughout the United States and other countries and are recognized by all players as possessing the fine qualities of the old masters. They are all made of specially selected choice wood, thoroughly seasoned by age. **Our Paganini violin is the same model violin as was used by the wonderful player of that name and is made especially for us by Louis Lowendall and therefore cannot be procured of any other dealer.** These violins are beautifully finished throughout and are trimmed with the best quality of ebony. The varnish is what is known as the pure amber varnish, is transparent and gives the violin the distinct appearance, from which the artist's workmanship is immediately recognized. We are able to procure but a limited number of these instruments during any one year, and any purchaser may congratulate himself upon possessing one. **Beware of imitations, as every one of the celebrated Paganini model violins bears a special label; countersigned by the maker with his own autograph.** Before deciding to purchase from any other dealer you should order **one of our celebrated Paganini instruments on our ten days' trial offer,** as explained above. With every one of these violins we furnish a wood case, extra fine quality bow, instruction book and a complete set of our Acme Professional Strings. Such a violin with the accessories which we give could not be purchased at retail from any music dealer at less than $50.00 to $75.00. We offer it at our one small margin of profit, the same as we quote on all staple articles of merchandise. Our special price..................**$19.95**

Violin Strings and Furnishings of all kinds listed on pages 214 and 215.

OUR SPECIAL BARGAINS IN VIOLIN OUTFITS.

IN ADDITION to our very complete assortment of violins, shown and described on the preceding pages, we have a line of complete violin outfits, made up under the direct supervision of the manager of our musical department, who is a musician and fully acquainted with the demands of all classes of violinists.

We offer these COMPLETE OUTFITS to ARTISTS, AMATEURS and PROFESSIONALS alike.

TO CONVINCE THE PURCHASER that we are offering these outfits at an unusually **low price**, we specify exactly the articles as selected from our stock, showing at the same time the regular retail prices and also our special outfit price. To anyone who contemplates buying a violin the accessories which we offer in these outfits are always necessary.

THE OUTFITS **are selected from our own stock, which is a guarantee of their high quality, and every instrument we carry is vouched for by the manufacturers of the highest grade violins in the world.**

FOR THE BEGINNER ESPECIALLY **we recommend these complete Violin Outfits.** They include just what is necessary, and by buying the outfit together you save considerable over the prices of the separate items.

WE CHALLENGE COMPETITION ON THE QUALITY AND LOW PRICE OF OUR VIOLIN OUTFITS......

OUTFIT No. 12R300

$3.75 BUYS A REGULAR $10.20 OUTFIT.

	Regular Retail Price
THIS OUTFIT IS THE BEST VALUE FOR THE MONEY EVER OFFERED. Anyone desiring a complete outfit for general use should not fail to see and examine our famous bargain. The outfit contains one of our **Genuine Stradivarius Model Violins,** made of old wood, curly maple back and sides, top of seasoned pine, selected especially for violins, edges inlaid with purfling, best quality ebony finished trimmings....	$ 8.00
1 Genuine Brazil Wood Bow, ebony frog with inlaid dots.	.75
1 Case of Marbleized Pasteboard, imported direct from Europe for our trade..........	.40
1 Full Set of Strings..........	.25
1 Piece of Rosin, good quality..........	.05
1 Instructor, simplest and most complete instruction book published..........	.50
1 Lettered Fingerboard Chart, can be adjusted to any violin without changing the instrument, a valuable guide for beginners..........	.25
Total value of outfit. (Shipping weight, 7 pounds)....	$10.20
OUR SPECIAL OUTFIT PRICE,	**$3.75**

Send $3.75 with your order and we will send you this outfit by express, and if you do not find it the greatest bargain you ever saw or heard of, and entirely satisfactory in every respect, return it at our expense and we will cheerfully refund your money.

OUTFIT No. 12R304

A REGULAR $12.50 OUTFIT FOR $5.50.

	Regular Retail Price
Everyone will recognize at once that in this outfit they will secure a violin of exceptionally good qualities, being the **celebrated Maggini model,** which has been so much sought after by the world's greatest violinists. The violin is one which produces a very powerful tone of beautiful quality. This violin is made of curly maple back and sides, beautifully varnished and highly polished. Characteristic of the Maggini violin, it has double purfling around the edges. The trimmings are splendid quality, the fingerboard and tailpiece being of solid ebony. The neck is curled maple and is nicely finished..........	$10.00
The outfit includes also	
1 Genuine Brazil Wood Bow with good quality hair and ebony frog..........	1.00
1 Imported Marbleized Pasteboard Case.......	.40
1 Set of Strings, good quality..........	.25
1 Large Piece of Rosin..........	.10
1 Complete Instruction Book, one of the best instruction books published..........	.50
1 Fingerboard Chart which can be adjusted to the violin without changing the instrument, and has proven a valuable guide for beginners..........	.25
Total value of outfit..........	$12.50

Shipping weight, 7 pounds.

This outfit could not be procured from any other dealer at less than the prices stated above and is furnished by us only at **our special complete outfit price of.......... $5.50**

HIGH GRADE AMATEUR OUTFIT FOR $7.85.

OUTFIT No. 12R308

THIS OUTFIT **we have made up especially for the requirements of players who would like to procure a first class violin with accessories for less than $10.00.** We can recommend it in every respect as being equal to outfits which could not be purchased from other dealers **at less than from $18.00 to $20.00.**

The outfit contains

	Regular Retail Price
1 Genuine **Stradivarius Model Violin,** made expressly for us by one of the best makers in Europe. It is made of specially seasoned old wood, giving the instrument an unusually mellow and sweet tone. The violin is beautifully finished throughout and fitted with the best ebony fingerboard, tailpiece and pegs. It is reddish brown in color, beautifully shaded and handsomely polished...	$12.00
The Bow which we furnish with this outfit is a first class Brazil wood bow with ebony frog, German silver trimmed and German silver button..........	$1.50
The Case is of solid wood, handsomely lined, and has lock, handle and hooks..........	1.50
1 Set of our Acme Strings..........	.75
1 Piece Rosin..........	.10
1 Instruction Book..........	.50
1 Fingerboard Chart, which has proven valuable to both amateur and artist alike..........	.25
1 Tuning Pipe, giving the proper pitch to which the instrument should be tuned..........	.25
Total value of outfit. (Ship'ing weight 10 lbs.)	$16.85
Our special outfit price, complete..........	$7.85

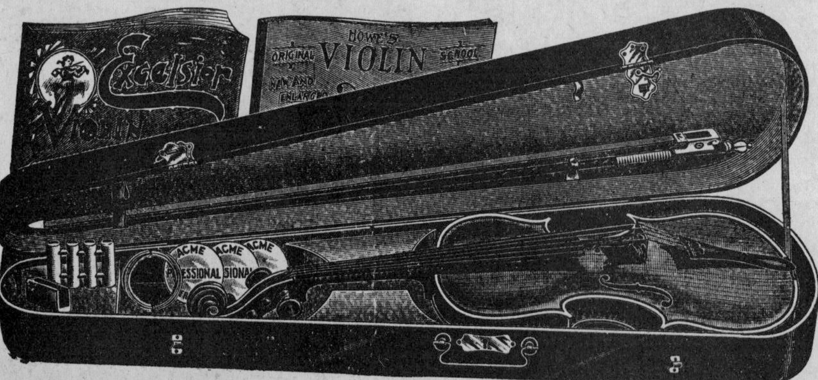

OUTFIT No. 12R316

SPECIAL HIGH GRADE PROFESSIONAL.

A $30.00 OUTFIT FOR $15.00.

	Regular Retail Price
1 Special High Grade **Genuine Stradivarius Model Violin,** an instrument remarkably superior in every respect, made of specially selected curly maple back and sides, resonant spruce top, a rich color of varnish beautifully shaded and handsomely polished. The trimmings are of the very best quality of solid ebony, making the instrument durable and much sought after by professionals. The tone is full and strong and suited to all requirements..........	$20.00
1 Vuillaume Model Bow, genuine snakewood with carved ivory frog..........	4.00
1 Solid Wood Case, provided with lock, handle and spring clasps, lined throughout inside with red flannel..........	2.75
1 Piece Genuine Gustave Barnadel Rosin, the best manufact'd. Imported by us direct from France	.25
1 Howe's Original Violin School, complete in every respect, and teaches how to play correctly	.75
1 Set of our Acme Professional Strings, imported direct from Europe..........	.85
1 Fingerboard Chart, which is valuable to beginners and advanced players alike..........	.25
1 Set Violin Tuning Pipes, invaluable to the beginner, as it aids him in tuning his instrument accurately..........	.65
1 Book of Choice Violin Music..........	.50

Shipping weight, 10 pounds.

Such an outfit as described above could not be purchased from your local dealer, nor, in fact, any other dealer, at less than $30.00 to $40.00.

OUR SPECIAL OUTFIT PRICE COMPLETE.......... $15.00

...OUTFIT... No. 12R318 OUR HIGHEST GRADE ARTIST OUTFIT WONDERFUL ...VALUE...

BY SPECIAL ARRANGEMENT with the celebrated violin maker, Louis Lowendall, of Berlin, Germany, we have been able to procure a limited number of his high grade instruments for this special outfit. His violins are sought after by the greatest players in the world, as they possess all the qualifications of a fine violin. Anyone desiring to purchase an instrument could do no better than toorder one of these outfits.

IN MAKING UP THIS OUTFIT we have endeavored to include a combination of instrument and equipment such as has never been offered by any concern in the world and which cannot be duplicated by any music dealer at anything like the price at which we offer it. The outfit includes:

	Regular Retail Price
1 Special High Grade Genuine Louis Lowendall Violin, Stradivarius Model, made of specially selected curly maple back and sides, choice old resonant spruce top, highest grade solid ebony trimmings. The tone is of the superior quality, found only in the Lowendall violins. NOTE—Every instrument bears the label, countersigned by Louis Lowendall with his own autograph. (Beware of imitations.)	$50.00
1 Tourte Model Bow, with full German silver trimmings and best quality Brazil wood	5.00
1 Solid Wood Case, Exposition Shape, full flannel lined, provided with lock and spring clasp	3.50
1 Piece of Genuine Gustave Barnadel Rosin, the best manufactured, and imported by us direct from France	.25
1 Instruction Book, complete in every respect and teaches how to play correctly	1.00
1 Set of Acme Professional Strings, imported by us direct from Europe	.85
1 Latest Patent Violin Chin Rest, used by most players	1.50
1 Fingerboard Chart, which is valuable to beginners and advanced players	.25
1 Set of Violin Tuning Pipes, by the aid of which the instrument can be tuned accurately	.50
1 Violin Mute, required when playing soft music	.15
1 Choice Collection of violin music	.50
Total value of outfit	$63.50

SHIPPING WEIGHT, 10 POUNDS.

The above outfit could not be procured from your local dealer, nor any music dealer at less than $50.00 to $75.00. Our special price, complete..........**$19.85**

FINGERBOARD CHART.

With each Violoncello or Double Bass we give free of charge one of these fingerboard charts. They are of great value to either beginner or professional player, for they tell at a glance the proper place to press the strings to produce the note desired. Beginners can become proficient in a very short time, with the assistance of this chart. It can be firmly gummed to the fingerboard, and in no way interferes with the tone or playing of the instrument.

...VIOLONCELLOS...

OUR LINE OF VIOLONCELLOS includes only the productions of the best manufacturers. We quote the instruments both with peg head and with patent head. **In tone, model and finish these violoncellos have no superior at any price. OUR LIBERAL GUARANTEE. If any violoncello proves defective** in workmanship or material, it may be returned to us at our expense, and we will cheerfully refund your money. **Weight, packed for shipment, about 45 pounds.**

Our $9.25 Violoncello with Patent Head.

No. 12R400 Our $9.25 High Grade Violoncello. This Violoncello at $9.25 **is excellent value,** being made of good model and material, and the best care used in its construction and finish. We furnish it complete with perfect fitting canvas bag, violoncello bow, a piece of fine rosin in pasteboard case, and a **complete instruction book,** and the instrument is ready to play as soon as received by you. Special price..**$9.25**

No. 12R406 **At $11.20** we offer a violoncello which will compare very favorably with **anything** ordinarily carried in retail stores and for which **retail** dealers will ask from $15.00 to $18.00. This instrument is of excellent quality and **has handsome inlaid edges which add very greatly to its general appearance.** It has patent head as shown in illustration. **It is fitted with a complete set of the best strings, and with it are furnished free a perfect fitting canvas bag, a handsome violoncello bow,** an extra large piece of fine rosin and **a valuable instructor,** by the use of which anyone can learn to play the violoncello **without the aid of a teacher.**
Our special price..**$11.20**

No. 12R412 At $12.95 we offer a Violoncello which will seldom, if ever, be sold by retail dealers at less than $25.00, and found in the finest retail stores in large cities. **It has beautiful inlaid edges,** a decoration which adds wonderfully to the handsome appearance of the instrument; **superior in quality and material, fine workmanship and superb tone. It has best peg head, the pegs and fingerboard being made of solid ebony,** is furnished complete with a perfect fitting canvas bag, valuable instruction book, a handsome violoncello bow and a large piece of excellent rosin.
Our special price..........................**$12.95**

No. 12R414 Same description as our No. 12R412, only fitted with best quality brass plate patent head. Our special price.........**$14.95**

Our Highest Grade Violoncello with Peg or Patent Head.

No. 12R420 This is an instrument which must be seen, examined and tested in order to fully appreciate all its merits. **This Violoncello** is extra fine quality, beautifully polished. **Solid ebony trimmings throughout,** including the solid ebony fingerboard and solid ebony tailpiece. **The peg head is the very best which is manufactured and the material used in the body is such as is found only in the highest grade instruments. It is made by expert workmen,** and the construction is such that it produces a tone such as you would naturally expect only from instruments which retailers sell at from $25.00 to $30.00. We also include a perfect fitting canvas bag, valuable instruction book, a violoncello bow, and a large piece of our best rosin in pasteboard box, so that the instrument is ready to play as soon as received. Our special price..........................**$15.45**

No. 12R422 Same description as our No. 12R420 but fitted with best quality patent head on brass plates. Price..**$17.85**

DOUBLE BASS VIOLS.

Buying as we do these desirable instruments in quantities from the leading manufacturer, we offer them with the assurance that they will compare favorably with the very finest that are made, in fact, there is no line of double bass viols manufactured which is superior in tone and workmanship to these which we quote and illustrate on this page. These instruments are furnished complete with a **splendid double bass bow** and **complete instructor. Each instrument is packed with great care, and when ready to ship, weighs 125 pounds.**

Our $18.95 One-Half Size Double Bass Viol.

No. 12R450 At $18.95 we offer a four string Double Bass Viol, one-half size, with bow, and complete instruction book. **This double bass viol is** of the very best model, is dark red shaded, **very highly polished,** and is superior quality **in every respect.** Best patent head. Our special **price.........$18.95**

Our $20.50 Four String Bass Viol.

No. 12R454 Our One-Half Size Double Bass Viol with four strings at $20.50 will compare favorably with any double bass viol on the market **offered by retail dealers at from $28.00 to $30.00.** This instrument has the best iron patent head, is red brown in color, **is beautifully polished and of excellent quality.** The workmanship employed on this instrument is of the very best. Furnished complete with strings, **double bass bow and a complete instructor,** by the use of which **anyone** with any taste for music **whatever may** learn to play without the aid of a teacher. Our special price....**$20.50**

Our Three-Quarter Size Double Bass Viol.

No. 12R462 A High Grade Three-Quarter Size Double Bass Viol for $19.50. This double bass **has four** strings finest iron patent head and is beautifully shaded and colored. **In finish it is wonderfully fine, being highly polished throughout. In model and quality it is decidedly superior and possesses a remarkably fine tone, a tone which you will ordinarily find possessed only by the most expensive instruments. Complete, with excellent double bass bow, and a valuable instruction book.**
Our special price, each.......**$19.50**

$22.85 Double Bass Viol.

Three-Quarter Size.

No. 12R466 This Double Bass Viol has four strings, high grade iron patent head, solid ebony fingerboard. **The inlaid purfling is very handsome** and adds greatly to the attractiveness of the instrument, giving it the appearance of the most expensive and highest priced viols on the market. **A particularly fine model and possesses a tone which is superior to the instruments ordinarily carried by retail dealers at any price. We furnish free with each instrument, a good double bass bow,** and complete instruction book.
Our special price, each.......**$22.85**

OUR GUITARS are made for us by one of the best manufacturers of guitars and mandolins in America. Every instrument is guaranteed true in scale, and is constructed with a view of obtaining both quality of tone and power. We have endeavored to furnish different styles of finish, and thereby be able to please everyone. The wonderful value we are offering can be best appreciated after an inspection of the guitar, and you should not order elsewhere before sending for one of our guitars on approval.

SHIPPING WEIGHT, 12 POUNDS.

WE GIVE WITH EVERY GUITAR A VALUABLE INSTRUCTION BOOK, a full set of Glendon strings, a fingerboard chart, by the aid of which anyone can learn to play without a teacher, and one of our celebrated Magic Capo d'Astros as illustrated and described on page 216.

THE TROUBADOUR.

No. 12R602 An instrument of surprising quality and tone, mahogany finished, highly polished, inlaid around sound hole, fingerboard accurately fretted with raised frets and inlaid position dots. Has metal tailpiece and genuine American patent head. A complete and desirable outfit, including extras as above. No other concern can duplicate it at anything like our price.

No. 12R602 Price, standard size...$2.45

THE EDGEMERE.

No. 12R604 This guitar is made of solid quarter sawed oak, fully guaranteed. Has beautiful fancy wood inlaid around sound hole and top edge, with celluloid bound top edge and has a fancy inlaid strip in back. Fingerboard is made of rosewood, accurate in scale, raised frets, and position dots. American screw patent head and nickel plated metal tailpiece. We furnish free with this instrument the extras described above and when you receive this instrument, we ask you to compare it with any instrument sold by other dealers at from $8.00 up.

No. 12R604 Price...$3.75

No. 12R606 Guitar is exactly the same as No. 12R604, described above, but has handsome rosewood finish highly polished instead of oak.

No. 12R606 Price...$3.75

THE MARLOWE.

No. 12R610 This guitar is made of genuine mahogany. Has mahogany neck, rosewood fingerboard, accurate in scale, raised frets and inlaid position dots. Has handsome inlaying around sound hole, and celluloid bound and inlaid top edge. Best American made brass patent head and nickel plated metal tailpiece. This guitar has a beautiful quality of tone and in appearance will equal instruments that other dealers sell at $10.00 and $12.00. We include free the extras as described above.

No. 12R610 Price...$5.45

THE ACME.

Our 20th Century Bargain.

No. 12R614 Nothing like it ever offered before at the price. Back and sides of selected quarter sawed oak. Top of Eastern spruce. Edges inlaid with variegated woods and bound with celluloid. Beautiful inlaid strip in back and around sound hole. Neck of genuine Spanish cedar, highly polished. Fingerboard of rosewood, accurately fretted and guaranteed true in scale. Inlaid position dots, nickel plated tailpiece, the latest style. Best American made screw patent head. The finish of the entire guitar is of the best quality, highly polished throughout. The tone is sweet and powerful and equal to guitars sold by other dealers at twice our price. We give free with this guitar the extras described above.

No. 12R614 Price...$6.95

No. 12R616 The same guitar as No. 12R614, but concert size.

No. 12R616 Price...$7.65

THE KENMORE.

No. 12R620 A beautifully made solid rosewood guitar, with top of selected Eastern spruce. Finest French polish. Genuine mahogany neck. Fingerboard accurate in scale, with raised frets and inlaid position dots. Inlaid strip in back and beautiful inlaying around sound hole. American made patent head. Tone equal to the best guitar made. This guitar outfit includes the extras described above.

No. 12R620 Price...$8.75

No. 12R622 Same guitar as No. 12R620, as described above, but concert size.

No. 12R622 Price...$9.50

For Guitar Strings and Furnishings see pages 214 to 216.
For Folios and Instruction Books, see pages 220 to 224.

MADE
ESPECIALLY FOR US

By One of The Most Celebrated Makers of Guitars in America,

and whose instruments are used largely by professional players and teachers in all parts of the world. They are made of selected material, thoroughly seasoned. **Latest and most approved models, accurate in scale and perfect in tone.**

GUARANTEED FOR ONE YEAR

AGAINST WARPING OR CRACKING.

These guitars are strung with our Celebrated Acme Professional Strings, consisting of silk wound basses and superior quality gut strings.

WITH EACH GUITAR WE SEND A COMPLETE BOOK OF GUCKERT'S CHORDS and a set of our Celebrated Acme Professional Strings.

WE PACK THESE INSTRUMENTS IN A LIGHT, STRONG BOX, which insures their reaching you in perfect condition. Shipping weight, about 7 pounds.

THE ARON.

Fancy mahogany, highly polished, egdes inlaid with beautiful variegated woods and bound with celluloid, figured inlay around sound hole and strip in back, top of selected Eastern spruce, mahogany neck, rosewood fingerboard, inlaid pearl position dots, rosewood veneered head, best American screw patent head.

No. 12R650 Our special price, standard size..$ 9.95
No. 12R652 Same as No. 12R650, in concert size. Our special price.................. 11.45

THE JULIEN.

Best quality rosewood back and sides, with top of resonant Eastern spruce; elaborate inlaying around sound hole and front edge and handsome inlaid strip in back; both edges bound in celluloid. Neck of solid mahogany; best quality ebony fingerboard, with beautiful pearl position marks. The head has rosewood veneer on front and back and best quality American made screw patent head. A wonderful instrument, highly finished and rich and powerful in tone.

No. 12R656 Our special price, standard size........................$12.75
No. 12R658 Same as No. 12R656, concert size........................ 14.00
No. 12R660 Same as No. 12R656, grand concert size.................. 15.25

THE RICHARD.

Highly polished carefully selected rosewood back and sides, with fine quality Eastern spruce; elaborate ornamental inlay around sound hole and edges, and celluloid binding on both edges. Handsome inlaid strip in back, choice mahogany neck, head of which has rosewood veneer on front and back. Convex fingerboard of ebony, elaborately inlaid with pearl position marks. Bone nut and saddle and best quality American screw patent head. This guitar retails elsewhere at $30.00.

No. 12R664 Our special price, standard size.......$15.50
No. 12R666 Same as No. 12R664, concert size....... 16.75
No. 12R668 Same as No. 12R664, grand concert size 18.25

THE SEROCO.

Our Highest Grade Guitar—Nothing Better Made.

This guitar is made of the very finest quality of specially selected rosewood and only the most resonant extra seasoned choice Eastern spruce is used for the top, which is inlaid around sound hole and edges with colored wood and a broad strip of pearl, as shown in the illustration. Top and back edges are bound with white celluloid; handsome inlaid strip of variegated wood in back; convex ebony fingerboard, richly inlaid with pearl in fancy designs; edges of the fingerboard bound with white celluloid; the best grade of mahogany is used in the neck and the head is veneered on front and back with rosewood, finished to a point on the back, giving the head of the instrument a handsome appearance from the back as well as the front. The machine head is the best that can be made, and the guitar is highly polished and finished throughout as perfectly as the best mechanics can make it. Nothing better in the market. This guitar is strung with our best Acme professional strings and we include an extra full set; also a first class perfect fitting canvas leather bound case and a valuable instruction book, making an outfit which retails regularly at $40.00 to $50.00. **Satisfaction guaranteed or money refunded.**

No. 12R672 Our special price, standard size...$18.75
No. 12R674 Same as No. 12R672, concert size... 20.50
No. 12R676 Same as No. 12R672, grand concert. 23.00

For Guitar Strings and Furnishings, see pages 214 and 216.
For Folios and Instruction Books, see pages 220 to 224.

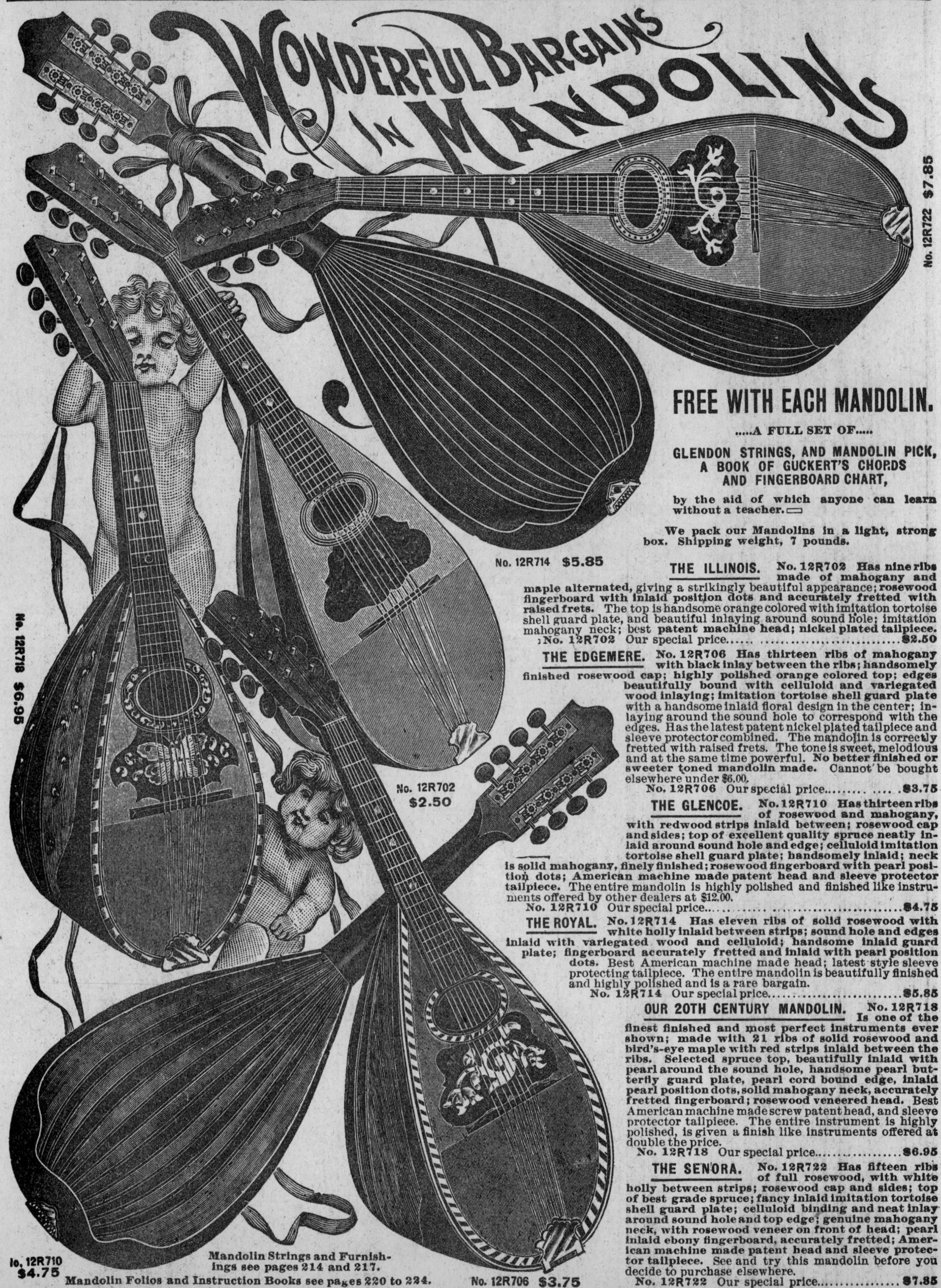

FREE WITH EACH MANDOLIN.

.....A FULL SET OF.....

GLENDON STRINGS, AND MANDOLIN PICK, A BOOK OF GUCKERT'S CHORDS AND FINGERBOARD CHART,

by the aid of which anyone can learn without a teacher.

We pack our Mandolins in a light, strong box. Shipping weight, 7 pounds.

THE ILLINOIS. No. 12R702 Has nine ribs made of mahogany and maple alternated, giving a strikingly beautiful appearance; rosewood fingerboard with inlaid position dots and accurately fretted with raised frets. The top is handsome orange colored with imitation tortoise shell guard plate, and beautiful inlaying around sound hole; imitation mahogany neck; best patent machine head; nickel plated tailpiece.
No. 12R702 Our special price.......................................$2.50

THE EDGEMERE. No. 12R706 Has thirteen ribs of mahogany with black inlay between the ribs; handsomely finished rosewood cap; highly polished orange colored top; edges beautifully bound with celluloid and variegated wood inlaying; imitation tortoise shell guard plate with a handsome inlaid floral design in the center; inlaying around the sound hole to correspond with the edges. Has the latest patent nickel plated tailpiece and sleeve protector combined. The mandolin is correctly fretted with raised frets. The tone is sweet, melodious and at the same time powerful. No better finished or sweeter toned mandolin made. Cannot be bought elsewhere under $6.00.
No. 12R706 Our special price..................$3.75

THE GLENCOE. No. 12R710 Has thirteen ribs of rosewood and mahogany, with redwood strips inlaid between; rosewood cap and sides; top of excellent quality spruce neatly inlaid around sound hole and edge; celluloid imitation tortoise shell guard plate; handsomely inlaid; neck is solid mahogany, finely finished; rosewood fingerboard with pearl position dots; American machine made patent head and sleeve protector tailpiece. The entire mandolin is highly polished and finished like instruments offered by other dealers at $12.00.
No. 12R710 Our special price.......................................$4.75

THE ROYAL. No. 12R714 Has eleven ribs of solid rosewood with white holly inlaid between strips; sound hole and edges inlaid with variegated wood and celluloid; handsome inlaid guard plate; fingerboard accurately fretted and inlaid with pearl position dots. Best American machine made head; latest style sleeve protecting tailpiece. The entire mandolin is beautifully finished and highly polished and is a rare bargain.
No. 12R714 Our special price..............................$5.85

OUR 20TH CENTURY MANDOLIN. No. 12R718 Is one of the finest finished and most perfect instruments ever shown; made with 21 ribs of solid rosewood and bird's-eye maple with red strips inlaid between the ribs. Selected spruce top, beautifully inlaid with pearl around the sound hole, handsome pearl butterfly guard plate, pearl cord bound edge, inlaid pearl position dots, solid mahogany neck, accurately fretted fingerboard; rosewood veneered head. Best American machine made screw patent head, and sleeve protector tailpiece. The entire instrument is highly polished, is given a finish like instruments offered at double the price.
No. 12R718 Our special price..................$6.95

THE SENORA. No. 12R722 Has fifteen ribs of full rosewood, with white holly between strips; rosewood cap and sides; top of best grade spruce; fancy inlaid imitation tortoise shell guard plate; celluloid binding and neat inlay around sound hole and top edge; genuine mahogany neck, with rosewood veneer on front of head; pearl inlaid ebony fingerboard, accurately fretted; American machine made patent head and sleeve protector tailpiece. See and try this mandolin before you decide to purchase elsewhere.
No. 12R722 Our special price..................$7.85

Mandolin Strings and Furnishings see pages 214 and 217.
Mandolin Folios and Instruction Books see pages 220 to 224.

GREAT Banjo Values

No. 12R808 $2.85

No. 12R804 $2.25

BANJOS.

WE FURNISH

FREE WITH EVERY BANJC

(Except the $1.75 Instrument),

one set of Glendon strings; one instruction book of chords, and one lettered fingerboard chart which is invaluable to beginners.

Our $1.75 Banjo.

No. 12R800 **The Banjo under this number has the shell made of maple,** with nickel band; the neck is finished in imitation cherry; has 10-inch calfskin head, with **six screw brackets. At $1.75 we consider this banjo a wonder.** However, we would not recommend it, but would suggest sending for one of our better grades, which we guarantee. Cash in full must accompany order.

No. 12R800 Our special price........................**$1.75**
Weight, boxed, about 7 pounds.

Our Special $2.25 and $2.85 Banjos.

No. 12R804 **As shown in the illustration, has a genuine nickel shell,** wood lined. The neck is stained in imitation cherry, with **seven nickel plated hexagon brackets.** Has genuine calfskin head, 10 inches in diameter.

No. 12R804 Our special price........................**$2.25**
Weight, boxed, about 10 pounds.

No. 12R808 We offer exceptional value in this. It has 10-inch head, nickel shell, wood lined, a carefully fitted and well made neck, imitation mahogany, **raised frets,** accurately fretted; nine nickel plated hexagon brackets; fine quality calfskin head.

No. 12R808 Our special price........................**$2.85**

Our Edgemere Banjo at $3.95.

No. 12R812 **This is an 11-inch Banjo, with genuine nickel shell,** wood lined; has seventeen nickel plated hexagon brackets, **raised frets; has birch neck** finished in imitation mahogany.

No. 12R812 Our special price........................**$3.95**
Weight, boxed, about 12 pounds.

Our Leader at $5.75.

No. 12R816 **This Banjo has a genuine nickel shell, 11-inch** calfskin head; has wired edges, heavy nickel plated strainer hoops and twenty-one nickel plated brackets. The fingerboard is accurately fretted; has raised frets and is inlaid with pearl position dots; birch neck, highly polished. Retails regularly at $9.50.

No. 12R816 Our special price........................**$5.75**
Weight, boxed, about 12 pounds.

A $12.00 Instrument for $6.90.

No. 12R820 **In offering this Banjo** we enable good **players to secure a first class instrument at a low price.** Send for it and after you have tried it for ten days you may return it if not found as represented, and your money will be refunded. Has an extra heavy nickel rim, 11-inch best quality calfskin head. Both edges of the rim are wired; has an extra heavy strainer hoop, twenty-one nickel plated brackets with protection nuts; highly polished cherry neck; ebony fingerboard, inlaid with pearl position dots; ebony pegs, patent tailpiece, and is strung with good quality strings.

No. 12R820 Our special price........................**$6.90**
Weight, boxed, about 12 pounds.

Wonderful Value for $7.95.

Your Retail Dealer would ask you $15.00 for this sam Instrument.

Our Factory to Consumer Plan gives you an opportunity be the possessor of an instrument such as artists use. In worl manship, finish and tone, it is that of a **$15.00** instrument.

No. 12R824 **This Banjo has a genuine nickel shell, selecte maple rim,** the edges of which are wired; the head is the bes quality opaque, 11 inches in diameter; has twenty-five nicke plated brackets with an extra heavy rabbeted strainer hoop. Th neck is made of selected birch, very highly polished, has an ebony fingerboard beautifully inlaid with pearl and metal ebony pegs, and patent tailpiece. A metal stay piece is used on the neck which prevents it from coming loose.

No. 12R824 Our special price........................**$7.95**
Weight, boxed, about 12 pounds.

A full line of Banjo Furnishings listed on page 217.
Banjo Folios on pages 220 to 224.

THE AUTOHARP

THE AUTOHARP has become one of the **MOST POPULAR** of small instruments. This popularity is well deserved. Thousands are in use and the sale keeps on increasing at a wonderful rate. **REASONS WITHOUT NUMBER** exist for the universal demand for these high class instruments. **SIMPLICITY:** There are no complicated parts, no mechanism that requires the skilled hand to operate. Anyone—whether he has musical ability or not, can play it with very little practice, and play it well. **MUSICAL QUALITY:** Thousands testify to its sweetness of tone, which equals that of the highest grade piano. The most difficult productions may be played on it, while as an accompaniment for the voice it has no superior. **CHEAPNESS.** Never before has it been possible for the house to be graced with high class music at so small an expense. The prices which we name enable the poorest to possess an instrument which will produce the sweetest music and give just as much pleasure as would a high priced piano.

TEN DAYS' TRIAL. Use the Autoharp ten days in your own home and if during that time you have any reason to be dissatisfied, return it to us and WE WILL RETURN YOUR MONEY.

WE REQUIRE CASH IN FULL TO BE SENT WITH ALL ORDERS.

THESE ARE OUR ONLY TERMS. Cash with the order, but our customers do not run the slightest risk in sending cash with order, for if anything is not entirely satisfactory, we will immediately return the money, including what you paid for transportation charges.

OUR MUSICAL INSTRUMENTS have a reputation all over the country. Ask your neighbors their opinion of our musical goods. Our instruments will be found in nearly every town in the states,
AND THEY ARE OUR BEST ADVERTISEMENTS.

Our $1.75 Autoharp.

No. 12R900 Our $1.75 Autoharp. It has 20 strings, 3 bars, and produces 3 chords. With this instrument the simpler airs and chords may be played. **The best steel strings are furnished and the tone is remarkably sweet.** Without a single exception, every purchaser has been delighted with this autoharp, and would not part with it at any price if another could not be secured.

No. 12R900 Our special price.................. $1.75

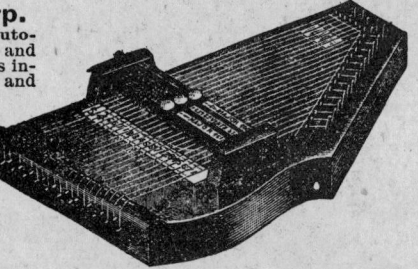

Weight, packed for shipment, 6 pounds.

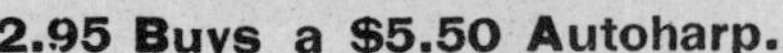

$2.95 Buys a $5.50 Autoharp.

$2.95

No. 12R902 Our $2.95 Autoharp has 23 strings, 5 bars and produces 5 chords. **The possibilities of this beautiful instrument are unbounded, and while but little practice is needed for the beginner to play nicely, constant practice will enable the performer to produce very difficult music.** We give a complete instructor free with each Autoharp.

No. 12R902 Our special price..... $2.95

Weight, packed for shipment, 7 pounds.

Our Special Autoharp for $4.95.

No. 12R904 For $4.95 **we offer an Autoharp that is entirely new,** strictly first class in workmanship, and susceptible to wonderful manipulation in the hands of a musician, whether **artist or amateur.** This special Autoharp is complete **with 32 strings and is fitted with 8 bars,** producing as many different chords. The range of different music is very great, and the **possibilities of the instrument are beyond that of any other of similar construction and much higher price.** We furnish **a very complete instruction book free,** and with its use anyone can in a short time **become a skillful performer** on this most charming of all instruments. **We also furnish free with each Autoharp, a ring for playing, music rack, tuning hammer** and selections of Autoharp music.

No. 12R904 Our special price, complete.................. $4.95

Weight, packed for shipment, 9 pounds.

$6.45 for the New Style Autoharp.

No. 12R906 Autoharp is the very latest product of the manufacturer, and is destined to become the most popular style of their entire list. **It has 37 strings and 12 chord bars; these bars are placed closely together, making the manipulation of them exceedingly easy;** they produce the major chords of C, D, G and F, with their relative minors. **It is strung and tuned in a perfect chromatic scale,** making it possible to pick out any tune or melody. **The finish is beautiful; highly polished ebony finish;** altogether a handsome, useful, musical instrument.

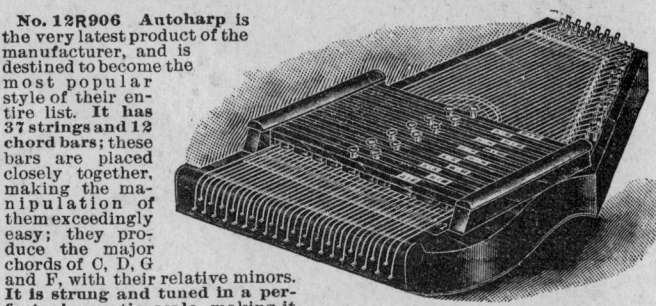

No. 12R906 Our special price.................................. $6.45

Weight, packed for shipment, 10 pounds.

Our Highest Grade Concert Autoharp for $10.85.

...A... BEAUTIFUL INSTRUMENT

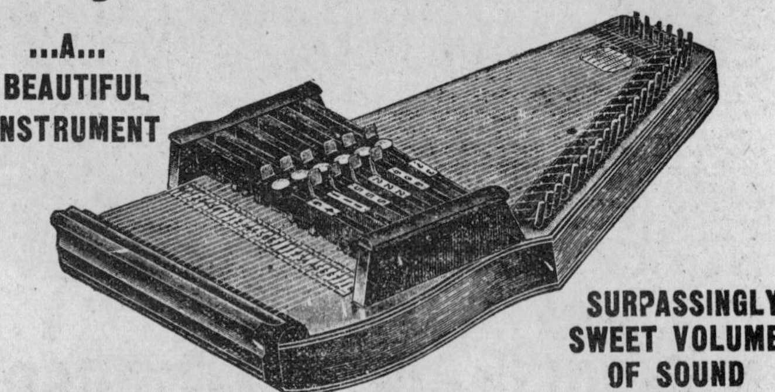

SURPASSINGLY SWEET VOLUME OF SOUND

No. 12R910 **This beautiful Concert Autoharp** is one of the most desirable of all stringed instruments made. The manufacturers of the world renowned autoharp have taken **special pains with this particular style** to make it the best that high class material and expensive skilled mechanics can make it. **It has 32 strings and 6 bars with shifters, producing 16 chords,** as follows: F, C, G, D major, 5 minor and 1 seventh. With this instrument, anyone with sufficient skill and practice can produce any music, however difficult. It is suitable **for all classes of music, sacred, classical or popular.** It is suitable **for accompaniment to the voice,** suitable to be played in connection with other musical instruments. It is unusually handsome, having the **finest inlaid edges, imitation rosewood top,** and all complete. It is polished and finished equal to the finish of a **high grade piano.** We include free with this instrument a fine black wood autoharp case, flannel lined, a case which would retail at $2.50. Complete with **instruction book, strings, music and music rack.**

No. 12R910 Our special price for the outfit........................ $10.85

Weight, packed for shipment, about 16 pounds.

Our $3.45 Mandolinetto.

No. 12R912 The body is 10 inches long, 7½ inches wide, made of maple, finished in imitation rosewood, **light colored spruce top, with celluloid bound top edge, figured wood inlaying around sound hole,** gutta percha guard plate, imitation mahogany neck, with rosewood finish and pearl position dots, brass screw patent head, nickel plated tailpiece and sleeve protector. **We include, without extra charge,** one genuine tortoise shell mandolin pick, and one complete mandolin instruction book. Regular price, $10.00.

No. 12R912 Our special price.................................. $3.45

Shipping weight, about 7 pounds.

No. 12R914 Same style as No. 12R912, only made of solid rosewood, with selected Eastern spruce top, celluloid bound edges, top and back, inlaying around sound hole, gutta percha guard plate, mahogany neck, solid ebony fingerboard, position dots of pearl, best quality American patent head, nickel plated tailpiece and sleeve protector combined. We include **free of charge** a genuine tortoise shell pick and complete instruction book.

No. 12R914 Our special price.................................. $6.25

Our $6.95 Banjo-Mandolin.

$6.95 buys this beautiful instrument. One that is seldom found in retail stores except at 50 to 75 per cent more than our direct from factory price.

No. 12R916 This instrument in appearance is just like a banjo, but is only about 22 inches long, has a 7-inch calfskin head, German silver rim, double wired edge, wood lined, 16 brackets, chased strainer hoop, mahogany neck, 14 inches long, ebony fingerboard, inlaid with pearl position dots, ebony veneered headpiece, nickel plated tailpiece and sleeve protector, and the genuine patent keys. **We furnish this instrument** complete, with a genuine tortoise shell pick and mandolin instruction book, which is the proper instructor to use. Any other dealer would ask $20.00.

No. 12R916 Our special price.................................. $6.95

Shipping weight, 9 pounds.

Mandolinetto and Banjo-Mandolin Cases.

No. 12R917 Mandolinetto Case, canvas-leather bound and flannel lined. Each.................................. 85c

No. 12R918 Banjo-Mandolin Case, canvas-leather bound, flannel lined. Each.................................. 90c

COLUMBIA ZITHERS.

THE COLUMBIA IS A SIMPLIFIED GERMAN ZITHER AND REQUIRES NO TEACHING. **Our method of instruction is so easy that anyone can learn to play the instrument in a very short time.** The base notes are tuned in groups of chords. This is a very attractive feature, as one has the various chords of the key ready to be plucked without effort. As an accompaniment to the voice these chords are invaluable. In connection with the violin, piano and other musical instrument, the Columbia is delightful. **It rewards individual skill more than any other harp in existence.** We have produced a musical instrument which charms alike the home circle and the concert audience. Every instruction book contains a list of music arranged for the instrument in figures easily comprehended. Our repertoire contains nearly **everything published in the popular music of the day,** besides all the standard music which has won the hearts of generation after generation.

CAUTION—Do not confuse the Columbia Zither with anything in the harp line. It is not a harp, but a zither—an instrument upon which can be played any class of music, and it is without an equal.

The Columbia Zither, Only $1.75.

No. 12R920 The Columbia Zither illustrated herewith, is 11 inches wide by 19½ inches long, made of maple, finished in imitation ebony, highly polished, has 31 strings, which produce the scale and chords of key of C, also a chart attached, which gives the number and letter of each string. An instruction book, music rack and tuning key free with each instrument. Our special price **$1.75**

Shipping weight, 9 pounds.

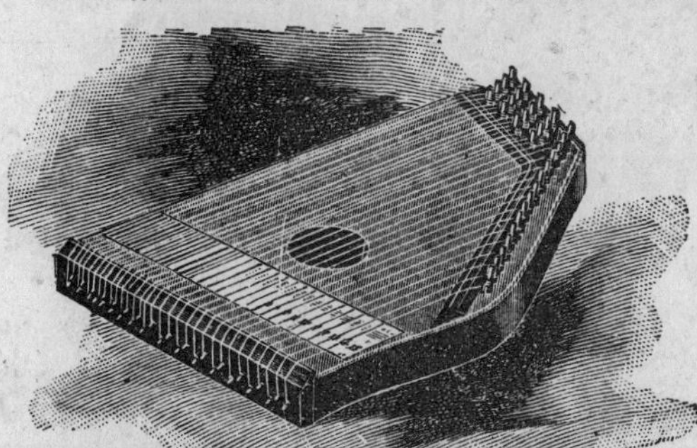

Columbia Zither Special No. 2¼ at $2.00.

No. 12R922 Columbia Zither No. 2¼ Special, similar in appearance to No. 12R920 but, as shown in the illustration, is finished in imitation ebony. It is beautifully decorated and highly polished, and somewhat larger in size, being 20 inches long by 13 inches wide, has 31 strings, arranged so as to produce scale and chords of key of C. Chart attached to instrument showing number and letter of every string, also arm rest over hitch pins to afford protection to the sleeve. Instruction book, pick and tuning hammer accompany each instrument. Our price **$2.00**

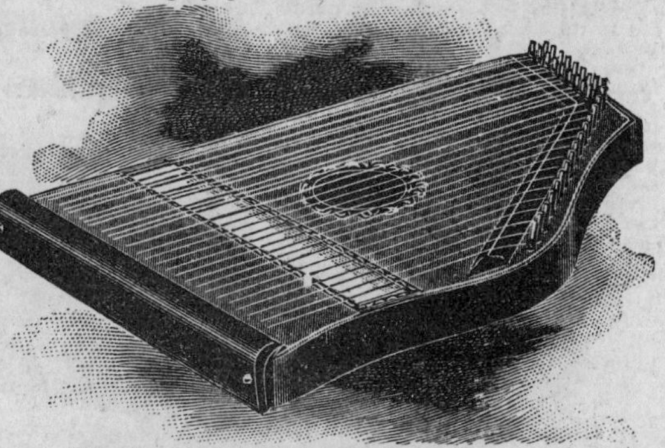

Shipping weight, 10 pounds.

Only $2.90 for a Regular $5.00 Instrument.

No. 12R924 Columbia Zither, is 20 inches long by 14 inches wide; finished in imitation ebony, with gilt striping, highly polished; has 38 strings, so arranged as to produce the chords and scales with the relative minor of the key of C and F; has nickel plated damper, also arm rest over hitch pins.

NOTE.

With this instrument we give, besides an instruction book, pick and key, three charts for beginners, which will enable anyone to play the instrument in five minutes. An invaluable addition.

Our special price ... **$2.90**

Shipping weight, 10 pounds.

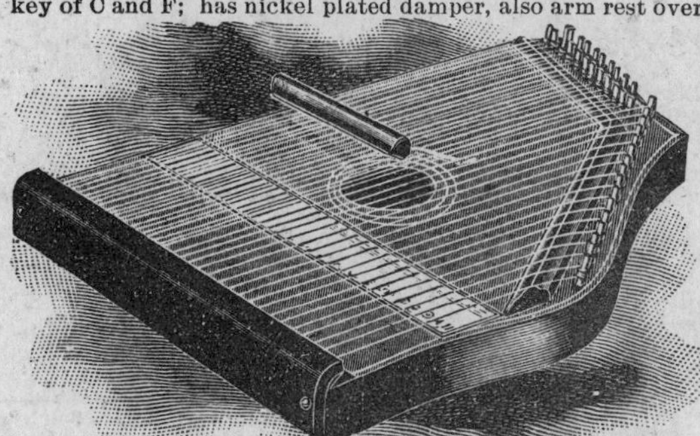

A $7.50 Columbia Zither for $3.95.

No. 12R926 This Columbia Zither is 21½ inches long by 16 inches wide, finished in imitation ebony with beautiful decalcomanie decorations, piano polished; 47 strings, arranged so as to produce six chords, comprising the scales and major and minor chords of the keys of C and F; has nickel plated damper, also arm rest over hitch pins. Instruction book, pick and tuning key with each instrument.

Our special price.... **$3.95**

Shipping weight, 14 pounds.

MANDOLIN-GUITAR-ZITHER.

THREE INSTRUMENTS COMBINED AT THE PRICE OF ONE.

THE WONDER OF THE AGE.

THE DEWEYLIN HARP, the greatest musical instrument that has ever been placed before the public. The Mandolin, Guitar and Zither, three of the sweetest toned instruments, are combined in this Harp, which is so simply constructed that anyone may become master of it in a very short time, without the aid of a teacher. No picks or rings are required to play the instrument, a patent keyboard being used instead. As you will see in the illustration, the instrument is made after the style of the Guitar-Zither, having treble strings on which the air is played and accompaniment strings for the accompaniment. The keyboard, which is placed over the strings, is the one great feature with which the mandolin effect is produced. The keys, which are made of ebony, placed on spiral springs, extend through the cover or keyboard, which is mounted on rubber rollers actuated by springs on the ends, which, when moved rapidly, trill the strings, imitating the mandolin perfectly; in fact, a better trill can be made than with the hand. This improvement also keeps the instrument in better tune, as the strings are picked evenly at all times. The accompaniment, or guitar effect, is produced with the left hand by picking the strings, which are arranged in chords. **Any chord or chords of the key of the instruments may be made as well as thirds and sixths.** The wonderful simplicity of this instrument, together with the numbered music which is published for it, makes it the greatest novelty of the musical world. **An instruction book and a tuning hammer accompany each instrument.**

$3.45

A Bargain at $3.45.

No. 12R940 A Deweylin Harp, made of selected material, ebonized with fancy decorated hand rest, exactly as shown in the illustration. Has 31 strings, part of which are so arranged as to produce 4 chords, as follows: G, C and F major and G 7th. Packed in neat pasteboard box with instruction book and tuning key.

Weight, packed for shipment, 9 lbs.

Our special price....... **$3.45**

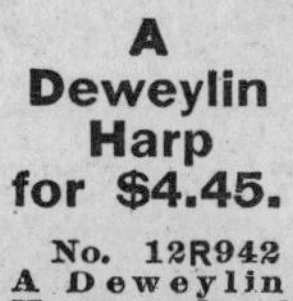

A Deweylin Harp for $4.45.

No. 12R942 A Deweylin Harp, made of selected material, beautifully ebonized and decorated with decalcomanie ornamentations around the edges; has 41 strings, which are so arranged as to give 15 tones and 6 half tones on the keyboard, the balance arranged so as to produce five chords: C, G, F, D, and A major. Packed in a neat pasteboard box with instruction book and tuning key.

Weight, packed ready for shipment, 12 pounds.

Our special price........ **$4.45**

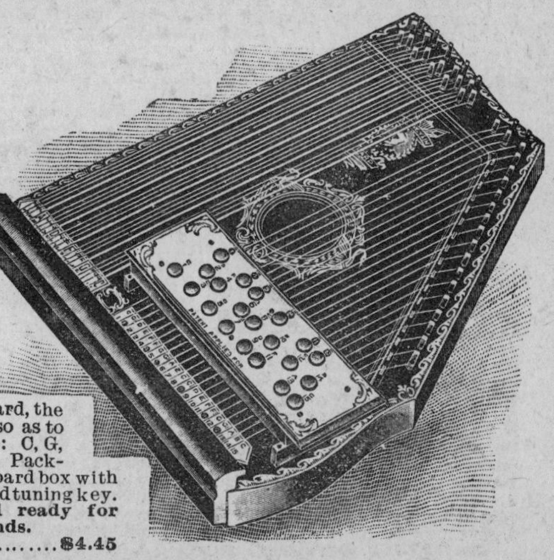

THE ZITHO-HARP

IS A NEW OVERSTRUNG INSTRUMENT OF EXTRAORDINARY BEAUTY AND ELEGANCE, PRODUCING A TONE WHICH FOR SWEETNESS, PURITY AND RESONANCE FAR EXCELS ANY AND ALL INSTRUMENTS OF ITS CLASS

IS A DOUBLE INSTRUMENT having two distinct parts, one for the treble or melody, played with the right hand, the other for the bass or accompaniment, arranged in harmonic groups or chords, played with the left hand. The great feature of the Zitho-Harp is the crossing at right angles of the bass and accompaniment strings over the melody strings and over the center of the sounding board and sounding hole, an entirely new arrangement found in no other instrument, making it not only easier and more convenient to play, but adding a beauty and fullness to the tone such as has never been approached on any stringed instrument. The artistic and handsome design of the Zitho-Harp permitting of a large, deep sounding chest, accounts partly for the great volume of tone of which this instrument is capable.

The beautiful and sympathetic blending of the crossed vibrations thus produced is something wonderful.

OUR SPECIAL PRICE . . . $2.75

No. 12R944 Style D. Dimensions, 19x19 inches, 33 strings. Finished in ebony, handsomely decorated; 17 melody strings, with 2 sharps; 4 chords, C, D, F, G. Shipping weight, 10 pounds.

THIS, TOGETHER WITH THE NATURAL AND EASY POSITION enjoyed by the performer, both hands being supported by rests, makes the Zitho-Harp truly a great favorite and "the ideal of the new century."

A MODEL SELF INSTRUCTOR with a fine variety of instrumental and vocal selections, played either by notes or figures, is given free with every instrument. The system used is so simple and easy that anyone, young or old, can learn to play without a teacher.

TO BE FULLY APPRECIATED IT MUST BE SEEN AND HEARD, AND WE PREFER TO LET THE ZITHO-HARP SPEAK FOR ITSELF

No. 12R946 Style E. Dimensions, 19x19 inches, 41 strings. Finished in ebony, handsomely decorated. 21 melody strings with 6 sharps; 5 chords, C, G, F, D, A. Shipping weight, 12 pounds.

OUR SPECIAL PRICE, $3.45

MUSIC BOXES

SELF-ACTING—AUTOMATIC—CYLINDER. These boxes are made by the best manufacturer in Switzerland, the home of the music box. It is a recognized fact that the originator and best makers of musical boxes are the Swiss people. In presenting this line to our customers, we have made a very careful selection from the catalogue of one of the best known Swiss makers, and know we are offering an assortment that is unsurpassed. Every box is made with the greatest care, and the comb and mechanism being firmly attached to the bottom (the sounding board) of the beautifully finished cases, brings forth the best possible quality of tone—that sweet, delightful tone so peculiar to the Swiss box. The mechanism is simple and will not get out of order, unless tampered with. A drop of oil occasionally in the worm of the governor keeps them running nicely, and each box is furnished with a safety catch that makes serious accidents impossible.

No. 12R948 This box measures 4½x3¼x2¼ inches; is a perfect little musical instrument. It plays two tunes. The case is highly finished in natural wood. The mechanism winds with a key, and can be started and stopped by a small lever on the front of the box. Shipping weight, 16 ounces.
Our special price............................$1.95

No. 12R950 The music box as shown in illustration is 5¼ inches long, 3¼ inches wide and 2¼ inches high. The case is made of walnut, beautifully polished and highly finished. The cylinder is 2¼ inches long; the comb has 36 teeth, plays three tunes. **It is wound with a key and changes automatically.** Shipping weight, 19 ounces.
Our special price............................$3.45

No. 12R952 This box is the same as No. 12R950, shown in the illustration; the same size and finish, but plays four tunes.
Our special price..........(Shipping weight, 19 ounces.)...........$3.95

No. 12R954 This box is made in imitation rosewood, highly polished and handsomely decorated. The box is 3½ inches long, 7 inches wide, 5¼ inches high. Has a 3½-inch cylinder. It plays six tunes and has a tune indicator, showing which selection is being played. **It is operated by a strong steel spring;** it is wound up by a lever handle; is also provided with two levers which enable you to have the box repeat any tune and the other lever to stop or start the music. The mechanism is covered by a glass lid to protect it from dust. **This box is a great bargain at the price at which we offer it.** Shipping weight, 12 pounds.
Our price........................$6.20

No. 12R956 This box is the same description as No. 12R954, but is somewhat larger. It has a 4½-inch cylinder and plays eight tunes; it is in every other detail the same as No. 12R954. Shipping weight, 15 pounds. Price....$7.95

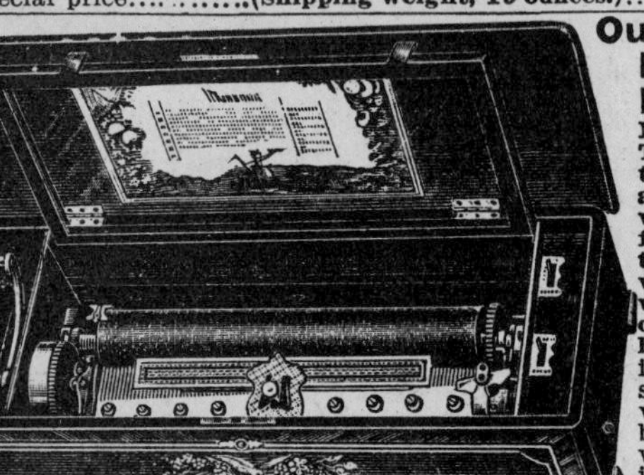

Our $24.95 Music Box.

No. 12R958 This box is the largest and finest box which we furnish and is the most wonderful value ever offered in this line. The case is of handsome rosewood veneer, with beautiful white wood inlaying, highly polished and finished.

The box is 24x9½x6½ inches. The cylinder is 11 inches in length and plays 12 complete and different tunes. The tone is exceptionally pleasing, and with the new auto-zither attachment a surprising and delightful change in tune can be made. This can be used at will by the simple moving of a lever and a very pretty effect can be secured. **PLAYS 12 TUNES.**

The box is operated by a very large strong spring; which is wound up by a lever handle. There are also two levers, one to enable you to repeat any tune desired and which can be repeated as many times as you wish, the other lever to start and stop the box. **Our price on this box is considerably less than what other dealers are obliged to ask as we import all of our Swiss boxes direct and list them at our usual one small percentage of profit.**

No. 12R958 Our price..$24.95
Shipping weight, 45 pounds.

Symphonion Music Boxes. American Manufacture.

These boxes are fitted with indestructible interchangeable metal tune discs. With each music box we give six discs free of charge, and additional discs can be purchased at a very small cost.

Our $7.95 Symphonion.

Size: 8½ inches long, 7¾ inches wide, 6½ inches high. Disc, 5¾ inches in diameter.

No. 12R960 This Symphonion Music Box shown in the illustration is a perfect musical instrument and the best of its kind to be had in the market.

The case is **finished in mahogany only,** nicely polished. The comb contains 40 steel tongues. Price, including six discs...**$7.95**
Shipping weight, 15 pounds.
Extra discs, each..........................10c
If by mail, postage extra, each, 4 cents.

Our Leader at $10.45.

No. 12R970 The case is made of thoroughly seasoned wood, and is finished in imitation mahogany. The comb has 41 steel tongues. A large number of selections are made for this box. Complete lists furnished on application. **We include with this box six discs.** Shipping weight, 24 pounds.
Size, 11¾ inches long, 10 inches wide, 7 inches high. Diameter of Discs, 7¾ inches.
Our special price...................$10.45
Extra discs, your own selection, each .18
If by mail, postage extra, each, 10 cents.

THE ANGELICA ORGAN INCLUDING 3 ROLLS OF MUSIC FOR $5.95.

Hundreds of dollars may be spent in music lessons, and the learner then not be able to produce sweeter music than can be obtained from this remarkably desirable organ. Like our Gem Roller Organ, no knowledge of music is necessary. By turning the handle the music is played, and hence you can see that the action is simplicity itself. **Any child can play it**—no musical ability at all is required. Many have heard this instrument without seeing it, and have judged that the music was produced by a **high grade church organ.** This instrument is the greatest and latest improvement over the old style organette. It has 14 reeds and the case is made of black walnut molding and cover, with real leatherette sides. **The entire case is beautifully finished** and makes a pleasing and elegant ornament for any home, whether it is that of the rich or poor. The case is 12½ inches long, 10 inches high and 9½ inches wide. The music is produced by perforated paper, which is rolled on spools. **We can furnish this music in all the latest airs,** old time melodies, dance music, church music and almost anything that may be desired. We furnish three rolls of music free with the Angelica. We have printed lists of extra music which can be had on application. This list, as stated above, includes all varieties, sacred, German, Norwegian, Swedish and Spanish music, as well as popular airs and dance music. The Angelica can be used in the ballroom or as an accompaniment for the voice. **A complete list of tune sheets, containing from one to four tunes, furnished on application.** Music rollers for Gem and Concert Roller Organs, cannot be used on the Angelica.

No. 12R972 Our special price, each, including three rolls of music........ ....(Shipping weight, 11 pounds.)...............$5.95

OUR GEM ROLLER ORGAN — $3.25 — OUR LEADER.

THE GREATEST VALUE EVER OFFERED IN A MUSICAL INSTRUMENT. PRICE REDUCED FROM $4.20 TO $3.25. This reduction was made possible by our contracting for the entire output of the factory which makes this wonderful little instrument, AND NO DEALER IS ABLE TO FURNISH YOU A GEM ORGAN AT AS LOW A PRICE AS WE QUOTE IT.

THE GEM ORGAN is distinctly a musical instrument of excellent quality; substantially made by the best manufacturers of this class of goods in the United States. **It is so simply constructed that a child can operate it.** The music is obtained from a roller, which has teeth or pins like those of the cylinder of a regular Swiss music box. These pins operate on valve keys and the roller is turned by a gear which also works the bellows. **The reeds used are the same as those used in regular cabinet parlor organs and the tone is therefore similar to that of a regular cabinet parlor organ.**

WE CAN FURNISH any kind of music, including Sacred, Spanish, German, Norwegian, popular airs and all of the latest up to date selections. These rollers cost less than the ordinary sheet music and therefore afford you the pleasure of playing or hearing all of the most desirable compositions of the day with but little expense.

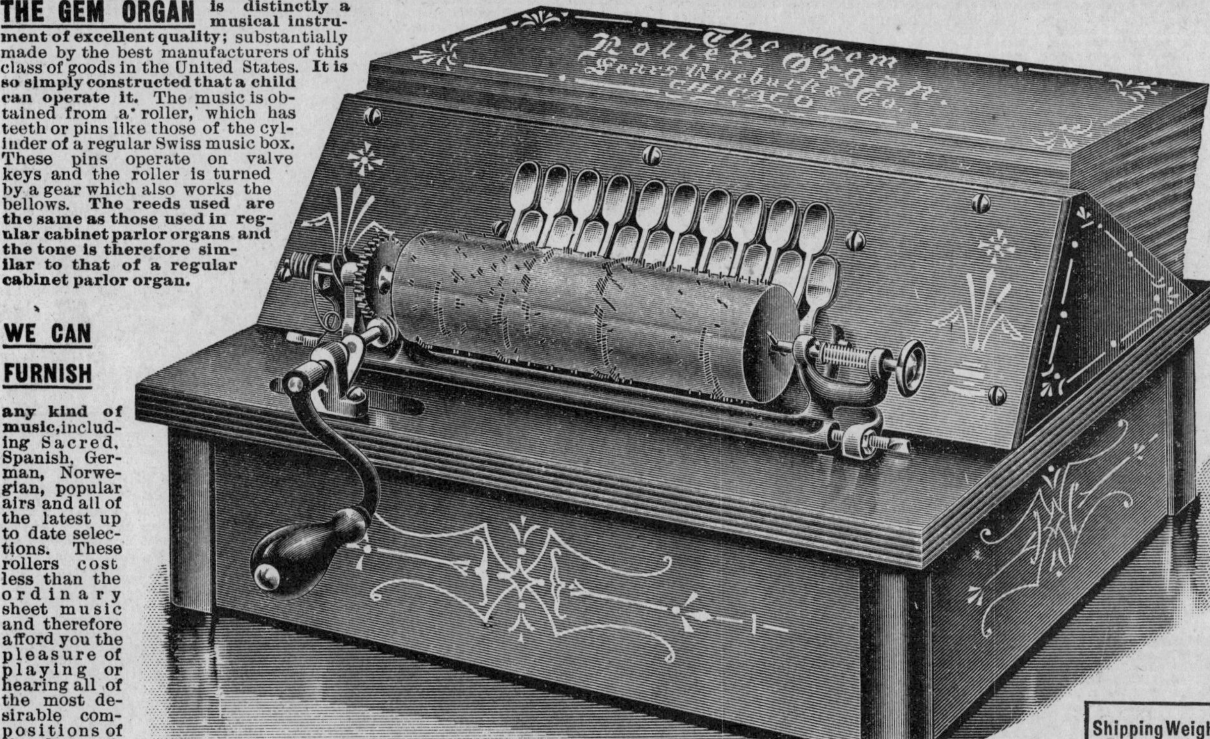

THE CASE of the Gem Roller Organ is made of imitation dark walnut; is 16 inches long, 14 inches wide and 9 inches high.

THE INSTRUMENT... is durable and you can secure as many rolls and as many different kinds of music as you desire. We list below some of the best known and most desirable selections taken from our entire collection, and the complete list is furnished with every organ.

Our special price for the **GEM ROLLER ORGAN** including THREE ROLLERS is

$3.25

Shipping Weight, 12 Pounds.

When ordering be sure to order by number. No. 12R985

WE FURNISH THREE ROLLERS FREE WITH EACH ORGAN AT $3.25.

Complete List of the Best Rollers for Gem and Concert Roller Organs.

Series No. 12R986 Order by Number.
OUR SPECIAL PRICE, PER DOZEN, $2.16; EACH..................18 Cents.
If by mail, postage extra, each, 6 cents.

SACRED MUSIC.

1 The Sweet Bye and Bye
2 Nearer, my God, to Thee
3 I Need Thee Every Hour
4 From Greenland's Icy Mountains
5 Duke Street
6 Onward Christian Soldiers
11 Sicilian Hymn
12 Hold the Fort
13 Just as I am
14 America
15 Antioch
18 He Leadeth Me
19 I Love to Tell the Story
20 The Home Over There
22 Almost Persuaded
23 Where Is My Boy Tonight
24 Bringing in the Sheaves
25 Let the Lower Lights be Burning
26 Only an Armor Bearer
27 I Will Sing of My Redeemer
29 Pull for the Shore
30 Precious Name
32 Hark, the Herald Angels Sing
36 Pleyel's Hymn
37 Zion
39 Abide With Me
42 Even Me
43 Watchman Tell Us of the Night
45 Federal Street
59 Portuguese Hymn
60 Wellesley
62 Come Ye Disconsolate
65 What a Friend We Have in Jesus
67 Rock of Ages
68 Sweet Hour of Prayer
70 Greenville
71 Old Hundred
72 Pass Me Not
73 Jesus, Lover of My Soul
78 Beulah Land
81 We Shall Meet Beyond the River
85 I am Praying for You
88 Whosoever Will
90 All the Way My Saviour Leads Me
91 Rescue the Perishing
92 Follow On [There
603 Knocking, Knocking, Who is
634 Shall we Gather at the River

POPULAR SONGS, DANCES.

101 Waltz—Les Roses [Fly
103 When the Swallows Homeward
104 The Blue Alsatian Mountains
106 The Soldiers' Joy
107 When the Leaves Begin to Fade
108 Sweet Violets
109 Marching Through Georgia
111 Waltz, My Queen
112 Old Uncle Ned
113 Austrian National Hymn
115 Climbing up the Golden Stairs
118 Meet Me in the Lovely Twilight
119 Vienna Polka
121 Old Folks at Home
122 Sailors' Hornpipe
123 Home, Sweet Home
124 The Marseillaise Hymn
126 Auld Lang Syne
131 In the Gloaming
132 The Dreamland Waltz
134 Marble Halls
137 Miserere, from Il Trovatore
138 The Parade March
141 Mignonette Polka
144 Nellie Gray
146 Annie Laurie
149 The Last Rose of Summer
150 Waltz—German Hearts
152 See-Saw Waltz
153 Polka—On the Wing
155 The Beautiful Blue Danube
156 Listen to the Mocking Bird
157 Then You'll Remember Me
159 Tyroler and Child
161 The Blue Bells of Scotland
162 The Wearing of the Green
164 The Campbells are Coming
165 The Minstrel Boy
166 Little Old Log Cabin
173 Darling Bessie of the Lea
183 The Flyaway Galop
184 Tyrolian Song
186 Oft in the Stilly Night
190 Yankee Doodle
194 The Golden Slippers
195 The Quilting Party
196 Waltz Song, Love Comes
197 Polka—Ah there
198 The Cadets' March
200 I
201 II
202 III Gay Life Quadrilles
203 IV
204 V
205 Dixie
207 The Arkansas Traveler
209 The Kiss Waltz
212 When You and I Were Young
213 College Hornpipe
217 Medley Jig
226 Bring Back My Bonnie to Me
229 Tramp, Tramp
230 Don't Be Angry With Me, Darling
233 Poor Old Dad
234 Waltz—Cricket on the Hearth
237 I'll Remember You, Love
238 Put My Little Shoes Away
240 Her Bright Smile Haunts Me Still
243 Money Musk
244 Scotch Lassie Jean
246 The Irish Washerwoman
247 The Devil's Dream
251 I'll Take You Home Again
254 Jennie, the Flower of Kildare
256 The Little Fishermaiden
262 Old Black Joe
263 Flow Gently, Sweet Afton
266 Killarney
268 Comin' Thro' the Rye
270 Massa's in de Cold Ground
272 Grandfather's Clock
273 The Star Spangled Banner
275 Maryland, my Maryland
277 Hail Columbia
278 Juanita
279 Red, White and Blue
280 Tenting on the Old Camp Ground
282 There is a Tavern in the Town
283 The Old Oaken Bucket
293 You Never Miss the Water
297 St. Patrick's Day
298 Miss McLeod's Reel
301 The Girl I Left Behind Me
309 Down Went McGinty
329 Love's Old Sweet Song
335 Little Annie Rooney, Waltz
336 Sweetbrier Waltz
337 Take Back the Heart
347 Good Luck Mazurka
349 Dairy Maid Waltz
351 Flee as a Bird
363 Only a Dream of My Mother
368 Schottische—Little Beauty
374 Some Day I'll Wander Back Again
375 Take Me Back to Home & Mother
390 The Battle Cry of Freedom
392 Come Back to Erin
394 Bonnie Dundee
399 John Brown
406 Schottische—Always Smiling
407 Waltz—Loves' Dreamland [Deep
410 Why Did They Dig Ma's Grave so
416 Captain Jinks
420 Schottische—Happy-go-Lucky
421 My Mother's Old Red Shawl
423 Polka—Peep-o-day
443 Oh My Darling Clementine
444 Galop—Jolly Brothers
446 Manhattan Polka
450 Clayton's Grand March
452 Fresh Life, Waltz
453 Galop—Little Fairy
456 Racquet Waltz
457 Waltz—Estudiantina
476 Silver Threads Among the Gold
480 General Grant's Grand March
487 Lullaby from Erminie
516 Maggie Murphy's Home
517 Mary and John
577 The High School Cadets' March
578 The Skirt Dance
1001 The Tourist's March
1003 Won't You Be My Sweetheart
1004 The Bowery
1005 Jennie Riley
1006 Two Little Girls in Blue
1009 The Washington Post March
1010 Daisy Bell
1012 Wot Cher
1016 The Miner's Dream of Home
1017 Then You Wink the Other Eye
1019 Molly and I and the Baby
1020 Little Alabama Coon [Wow
1027 Daddy Wouldn't Buy a Bow-
1028 Oh! Mr. Porter [Moon
1030 In Love With the Man in the
1036 Sweet Marie
1038 The Sidewalks of New York
1039 The Fatal Wedding [Yard
1050 I Don't Want to Play in Your
1052 My Pearl Is a Bowery Girl
1053 Ben Bolt
1054 The Honeymoon March
1058 Just Tell Them That You Saw Me
1059 Only One Girl in the World for Me
1061 The Sunshine of Paradise Alley
1063 We Were Sweethearts, Nell and I
1064 Mother was a Lady
1065 Up the Street, March
1066 March—Cosmos
1069 My Old Kentucky Home
1070 The Darkies' Dream
1071 Sweet Rosie O'Grady
1083 Hot Time in the Old Town
1084 Bombasto March, Two Step
1085 Dora Dean
1086 There'll Come a Time
1087 All Coons Look Alike to Me
1088 Blue Eyes
1089 Wizard of the Nile, March
1090 On the Banks of the Wabash
1096 Stars and Stripes Forever, March
1097 Alice, Where Art Thou
1098 Warmest Baby in the Bunch
1099 Sweet Spirit Hear my Prayer
1100 Sunny Side Clog
1101 She was Bred in Old Kentucky
1102 Break the News to Mother
1107 Georgia Camp Meeting
1112 Hello, Ma Baby
1113 High Born Lady
1114 Smoky Mokes
1115 Eli Green's Cake Walk
1116 Whistling Rufus
1117 Just as the Sun Went Down
1118 Just One Girl
1119 Zenda Waltzes
1120 Home to Our Mountains
1121 Narcissus
1122 Intermezzo Rusticana

ACCORDIONS.

OUR ACCORDIONS are made by three of the most famous European makers. We handle nothing but strictly high grade goods, and in this class of instruments are prepared to save you fully one-half in price. **Our instruments are made for us under contract** with the greatest care, and our prices are based on the actual cost to produce, duty, transportation, and our one small profit added. **There are many imitations on the market**, but for strictly high grade, first quality instruments of highest standard of reputation our prices are far below any competition. **We include free a most complete and valuable instruction book** with each accordion. With its aid anyone may become proficient in the use of this charming instrument.

Our $2.25 Leader.

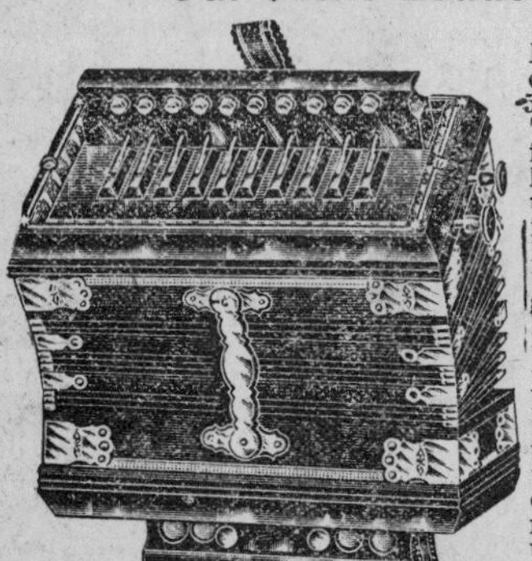

No. 12R1002 It is 10¼ inches high by 5 inches wide. The case is imitation mahogany beautifully polished, with light green panels with gilt border handsomely wound with white celluloid; has ten nickel keys, two stops and two sets of extra quality reeds, with triple bellows, with nickel patent corners on bellows folds; nickel corners and clasps. Our special price........................$2.25
Weight, boxed, about 9 pounds.

$3.10 Buys a $6.00 Accordion.

No. 12R1004 We offer this Accordion in competition with any instrument you can buy elsewhere at from $6.00 to $8.00. This accordion is 13 inches in height, 6¼ inches in width has beautiful ebonized case, fancy cut corners, handsome gilt ornaments on corners and top. Beautifully gilt beading around same. Has two stops and two sets of reeds. Open action. Nickel corners and clasps. Double bellows. Price........................$3.10
Weight, boxed, about 12 pounds.

The Empress.

No. 12R1008 The illustration gives but a fair idea of the beauty of this instrument. It is 8 inches in height by 6½ in. in width, with **beautiful ebonized moldings**, light blue panels, double bellows, variegated colors, **nickel bound around the front and back frames, two stops, two sets of reeds, ten nickel keys**, nickel corners and clasps, leather straps. Our special price........................$3.85
Weight, boxed, about 9 pounds.

Our $4.65 Accordion.

No. 12R1012 This is our Empress Tremolo Accordion, fitted with the latest improved tremolo attachment, easily controlled, by the thumb of the right hand. This tremolo acts equally well with the draw or pull of the bellows. 12⅛ in. high, 6½ in. wide. Double bellows, two sets of reeds, excellent tone and a serviceable, durable accordion. Our price............$4.65
Weight, packed for shipment, 12 pounds.

No. 12R1016 This double row or two-key Accordion is 11¼ inches in height, 6¾ inches in width. The case is made of **beautiful ebonized wood, highly polished**; eight full double bellows, nickel corners and clasps, has nineteen nickel keys, two stops and two sets of **extra broad steel bronze reeds**; a better accordion was never offered by any house. Our special price........................$5.95
Weight, boxed, about 15 pounds.

No. 12R1018 Same description as No. 12R1016, but **has twenty-one keys.** Our special price......$6.95
Weight, boxed for shipment, 18 pounds.

No. 12R1022 The Empress Professional Instrument. Broad mahogany molded frames, mahogany panels and keys. The frame and panels are ornamented with handsome gilt and nickel ornaments. Clasps and corners fully nickel plated. Sunken open key board, double ribbed bellows, ten keys, eight stops, four sets of reeds, tuned in chords. **Complete instruction book free.**
Our special price........................$7.50
Weight, packed, 18 pounds.

OUR ACME PROFESSIONAL ACCORDIONS.

THE FINEST ACCORDIONS MADE. **Manufactured expressly for us by the greatest maker of accordions in Europe. Strictly high grade in every respect.** Specially selected material. Broad hand made steel reeds, producing a rich, full and powerful tone. These accordions have the patent **Hercules 10-fold bellows**, so constructed that the brass corners do not pinch the folds of the bellows which therefore are smooth and easy to play. By a special arrangement the leather underneath the metal corners becomes absolutely airtight. **Every accordion is guaranteed and may be returned if not found entirely satisfactory and your money will be refunded in full.**

The Gem.

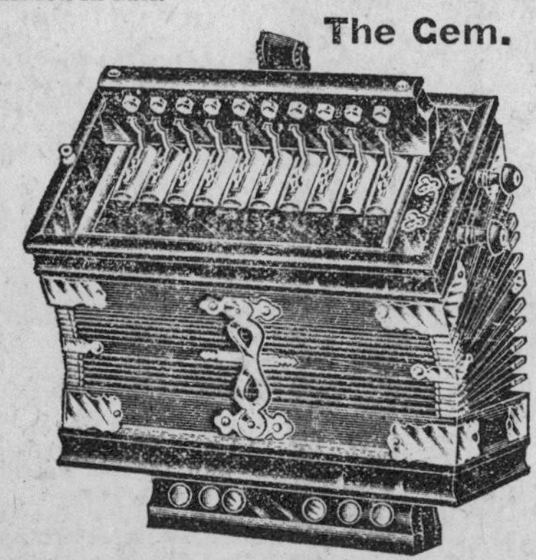

No. 12R1052 This Accordion is 11x7 inches, has highly polished ebonized case, decorated with nickel trimmings, patent keyboard, 10-fold bellows. **An exceptionally fine instrument.** Sells regularly at $8.00. Price........................$4.45
Shipping weight, 10 pounds.

No. 12R1054 This Acme Professional Accordion is 11x7 inches. Has highly finished ebonized case with nickel trimmings, 10-fold leather bound air tight bellows, with patent brass corners, same as illustration of No. 12R1052 above, but with three stops and three sets of broad hand made steel reeds.
Our special price........................$4.95

Little Giant.

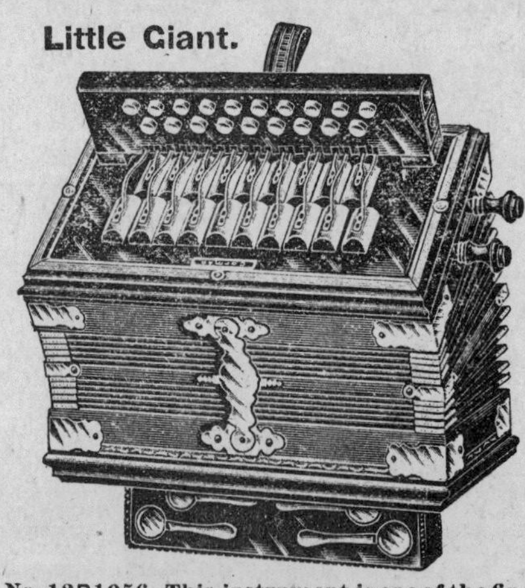

No. 12R1056 This instrument is one of the finest accordions we have ever sold. It is handsome in appearance, having mahogany moldings, sunken ebonized keyboard, 10-fold air tight Hercules bellows, two stops, two sets of reeds, 17 keys, gilt valves, patent keyboard. Regular retail price, $12.00.
Our special price........................$6.65
Shipping weight, 12 pounds.

No. 12R1058 Same Accordion as No. 12R1056, but has 19 keys. Our special price............$7.45
Shipping weight, 13 pounds.

The Hercules.

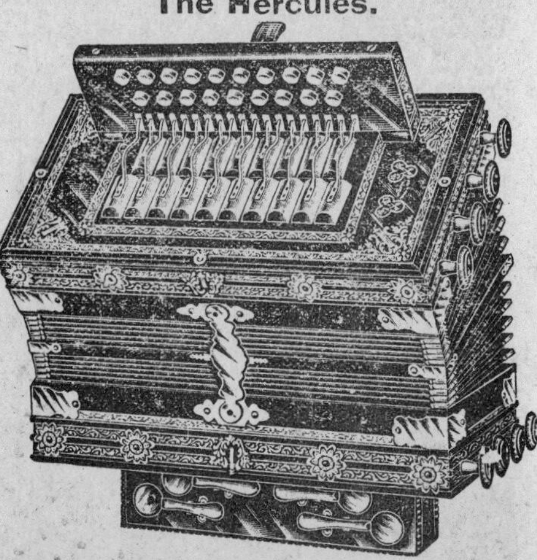

No. 12R1070 This Accordion is very large, being 14½ by 8 inches; has highly polished ebonized case, handsomely decorated with golden transfers. Stars on the moldings, gilt valves, German silver buttons; has 19 keys, 8 stops and 4 basses; 10-fold bellows, leather bound. Has an unusually rich, full and powerful tone. Regular retail price, $18.00. Our special price....(**Shipping weight, 20 lbs.**)....$11.85

No. 12R1074 This Accordion is exactly like No. 12R1070, but has 21 keys. Our special price...$12.75
Shipping weight, 20 pounds.

Harmonicas.

No. 12R2877 Made especially for us by the greatest manufacturer in Europe. Has ten single holes, white metal reed plates with good quality steel reeds, accurately tuned, easy blowing. Our special price, each 7c
If by mail, postage extra, 4 cents.

No. 12R2878 Genuine Bohm Professional Harmonica, has ten single holes and twenty best quality brass reeds. **Best value for money ever offered.** Brass plates, nickel covers. Our price, each.............................10c
If by mail, postage extra, each, 4 cents.

No. 12R2879 Genuine Ludwig Harmonica, Richter Pattern Harmonica, has ten single holes, twenty reeds, accurately tuned; brass plates and nickel covers. Our price, each..11c
If by mail, postage extra, each, 4 cents.

If by mail, postage extra, each, 7 cents.

No. 12R2881 Genuine Ludwig Harmonica, Richter Pattern. Double sided Harmonica with ten holes and twenty reeds on each side; brass plates and nickel covers. Our price, each..... ..21c

No. 12R2883 Genuine Ludwig Favorite Concert Harmonica, Richter Pattern. Harmonica has twenty double holes, forty brass reeds, heavy brass reed plates and fancy nickel covers; has very powerful tone; specially fine value. Our price, each..32c
If by mail, postage extra, each, 8 cents.

No. 12R2890 Sousa's Band is 4 inches long, 1 inch wide; has ten holes and twenty brass reeds; heavy brass reed plates; handsome nickel covers. The best harmonica ever offered at the price, **retails regularly at 35 cents.** Our special price........18c
If by mail, postage extra, 6 cents.

No. 12R2892 Sousa's Band is 4¾ inches long, 1¼ inches wide; has twenty holes; forty brass reeds; heavy brass reed plates and fancy nickel covers. **The tone is powerful and of excellent quality. A regular concert harp.** Our special price........32c
If by mail, postage extra, 8 cents.

If by mail, postage extra, each, 4 cents.

No. 12R2903 The M. Hohner Harmonica, one of the best known and best liked harmonicas made; ten single holes, best reeds and brass reed plates. Nickel covers. Price, each.............................15c

No. 12R2904 A Special Hohner Harmonica, with ten double holes, forty excellent reeds, brass reed plates and nickel covers. Price, each.......35c
If by mail, postage extra, each, 7 cents.

No. 12R2906 Hohner Harmonica. A double instrument of powerful and pleasing tone. Has ten double holes on each edge, twenty double holes in all; eighty very fine reeds, brass reed plates, nickel covers. Our special price...................... ...80c
If by mail, postage extra, 8 cents.

Brass Band Harmonica.

The King of all Harmonicas.

No. 12R2907 The finest instrument of its kind in the world. Made by a most celebrated manufacturer. For purity and volume of tone **this harmonica has no equal. The reeds** are made of the finest bell metal and are extremely sensitive, producing a remarkably smooth tone. **The covers are flaring** at the back and are made of solid brass, heavily nickel plated and are consequently of unusual strength, thus protecting the reeds perfectly. Accurately tuned to concert pitch. **The Brass Band Harmonica** has ten double holes, forty bell metal reeds, brass reed plates and extension ends. It is in high favor with professional and amateur alike. We include a **handsomely wood lined case,** as shown in the illustration. Retails for $1.00 and is worth every cent of it. Price, each..65c
If by mail, postage extra, each, 8 cents.

No. 12R2914 Same Harmonica as No. 12R2907, but has ten holes and twenty reeds, and comes packed in neat pasteboard case. Price, each ....(If by mail, postage extra, each, 6 cents).............19c

No. 12R2916 Bohm's Jubilee Harmonica. Harmonica has ten single holes, twenty brass reeds, mounted on heavy brass reed plates, nickel covers. Made in imitation of organ pipes, producing an exceptionally nice quality of tone.
Our special price, each.................................18c
If by mail, postage extra, each, 5 cents.

No. 12R2918 Bohm's Sovereign Harmonica. A rare bargain in harmonicas. This harmonica is 5½ inches long and 1¼ inches wide; has sixteen double holes and thirty-two steel bronze reeds, heavy metal reed plates and beautiful fancy nickel covers.
Our special price, each...................................19c
If by mail, postage extra, each, 8 cents.

No. 12R2925 Angel's Clarion. Manufactured by C. H. Weiss, maker of the celebrated Brass Band Harmonica. This Harp resembles the brass band clarion in some respects, but is so constructed as to produce a peculiar, vibrating, organ like tone not found in any other harmonica. It has twenty-eight holes, with twenty-eight brass reeds and mounted on heavy brass reed plates. Has the clarion pipe and nickel covers. Every harmonica player should own one of these harps. Our special price, each..................(If by mail, postage extra, each, 8 cents)...................35c

The Brass Band Clarion.

The Wonder Harmonica of the Age. A New Invention in Harmonicas.

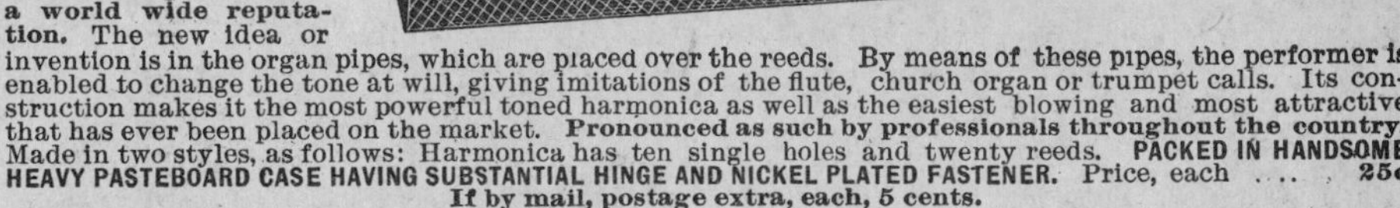

No. 12R2940 The Clarion Brass Band Harmonica, manufactured by C. H. Weiss, the celebrated manufacturer of the Brass Band Harmonica. Although a novelty, the **sales have been enormous, greatly exceeding those of any harmonica heretofore known.** The illustration will give you an idea of the appearance of this wonder instrument. The brass reed plates and bell metal reeds are the same as those used in the **Celebrated Brass Band Harmonica, which has gained such a world wide reputation.** The new idea or invention is in the organ pipes, which are placed over the reeds. By means of these pipes, the performer is enabled to change the tone at will, giving imitations of the flute, church organ or trumpet calls. Its construction makes it the most powerful toned harmonica as well as the easiest blowing and most attractive that has ever been placed on the market. **Pronounced as such by professionals throughout the country.** Made in two styles, as follows: Harmonica has ten single holes and twenty reeds. **PACKED IN HANDSOME HEAVY PASTEBOARD CASE HAVING SUBSTANTIAL HINGE AND NICKEL PLATED FASTENER.** Price, each 25c
If by mail, postage extra, each, 5 cents.

No. 12R2941 Clarion Brass Band Harmonica, concert or large size, has ten double holes and forty reeds; packed in handsome pasteboard case. Price, each...................................55c
If by mail, postage extra, each, 8 cents.

Tremolo Concert.

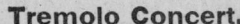

No. 12R2942 Tremolo Concert Harmonicas are made by And's Koch, sixteen double holes, 7¼ inches in length, 2 inches wide, two reeds to each hole, sixty-four reeds in all. Brass reed plates and nickel plated covers. Our special price..................65c
If by mail, postage extra, 6 cents.

No. 12R2943 Same as No. 12R2942, except larger, has twenty double holes, eighty reeds in all.
Our special price.......................................70c
If by mail, postage extra, 7 cents.

No. 12R2944 Our special Ph. Brunnbauer instrument for $1.15. Worth $2.00. One of the most powerful toned harmonicas made. **Beautiful gilt and fancy enameled covers, decorated with flowers,** etc. Best brass reed plates, finest reeds, thirty-two double holes. Will produce the **most exquisite music in the hands of an expert player.** Our price, each...(If by mail, postage extra, 8 cents). $1.15

No. 12R2945 Is the same genuine Ph. Brunnbauer make as above described, but has forty double holes. Our special price, each $1.30
If by mail, postage extra, 9 cents.

Harmonophone.

The Latest Novelty in Harmonicas—A Wonder of Tone.

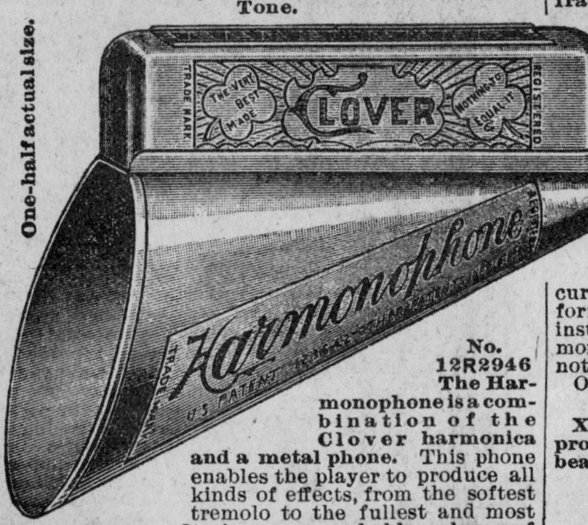

No. 12R2946 **The Harmonophone** is a combination of the Clover harmonica and a metal phone. This phone enables the player to produce all kinds of effects, from the softest tremolo to the fullest and most sonorous tones. It gives a **remarkable volume of music,** increasing it just as the metal horn of a phonograph increases the sounds. **The phone acts as a sounding board, taking up every tone, however faint, and giving it remarkable richness and purity.** This phone is attached to the mouth organ by metal clamps and can be attached or detached instantly. The player operates the Harmonophone in the same manner as an ordinary harmonica, but places the right hand over the open end of the phone, and by moving the hand produces the marvelous effects above quoted. Our special price, any key..38c
If by mail, postage extra, 10 cents.

Grand Concert Harmonophone.

No. 12R2947 Same as No. 12R2946, large concert size, 20 holes double, 40 reeds. Price.............70c
If by mail, postage extra, 12 cents.

No. 12R2948 **Genuine Richter Bell Harmonica, with bell. The best quality of reeds is used in this instrument;** 10 single holes, brass reed plates, German silver covers, extended ends, 1 bell.
Our price, each.............. 25c
If by mail, postage extra, 6 cents.

No. 12R2949 Our Special Concert Harmonica, with bells. Best quality; 10 double holes, with 40 reeds; brass reed plates, fancy engraved German silver covers, 2 bells. Weight, 7 ounces.
Our special price, each..............50c
If by mail, postage extra, 7 cents.

No. 12R2950 Koch's Concert Bell Harmonica, 40 reeds, 10 double holes and nickel plated covers. Full concert harmonica of powerful tone. The bells are of good quality, well made and supplied with strong, durable strikers, producing a really sweet and musical ring. Our special price..............70c
If by mail, postage extra, 8 cents.

No. 12R2951 Same as No. 12R2950, with 20 reeds, 1 bell. Our special price................35c
If by mail, postage extra, 6 cents.

Brass Band Bell Harmonica.

No. 12R2952 The Brass Band Bell Harmonica is made by the celebrated manufacturer of other brass band harmonicas and is of the same high grade as all other brass band harmonicas. It has 10 double holes, 40 reeds, accurately tuned and mounted on heavy brass reed plates. **The bells are of the very best quality and not of that flimsy construction so often found in other grades of bell harmonicas.** The tone of this instrument is unusually powerful and of beautiful quality and when used together with the bells produces a striking effect.
No. 12R2952 Our special price, each.........75c
If by mail, postage extra, 8 cents.

No. 12R2953 **Harmonica Pouches** or pocket cases, made of **best calf leather with nickel plated frame** with clasp. To hold **10-hole Richter model.** Our special price, each..................8c
No. 12R2954 Same, to hold 10-hole Concert Harmonica. Our special price, each 12c
If by mail, postage extra, 2 cents.

Excelsior Harmonica Holder.

No. 12R2956 Simplicity of construction, easy and quick to adjust, durable. No hooks to tear one's clothes, no rubber to lose its elasticity, but two springs which instantly adjust themselves to any sized harmonica, thus firmly securing the same, so that the performer is at liberty to use any other instrument to accompany the harmonica at the same time. When not in use, it may be folded to a small compass.
Our special price..................................30c
If by mail, postage extra, 14 cents.

Xylophones, made of maple, on a frame. Each bar producing a different tone, when struck with the beater.

No. 12R3066 Fifteen maple bars, as illustrated, letter C to C; fifteen notes, key of C; on frame; excellent quality and tone. Each.....................95c
No. 12R3068 Twenty-five maple bars, ten extra bars for chromatic scale, letter F to F, key of F; on frame. Fine quality. Each......................$3.75

Bones or Clappers.

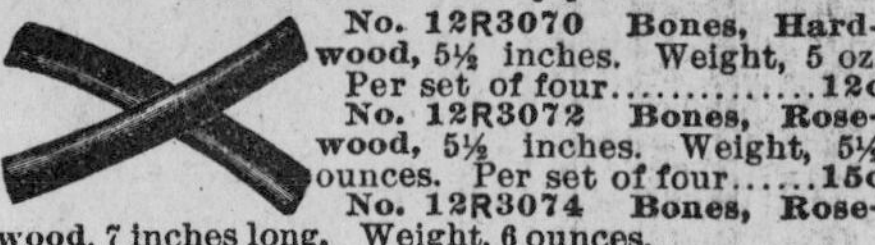

No. 12R3070 Bones, Hardwood, 5½ inches. Weight, 5 oz. Per set of four..............12c
No. 12R3072 Bones, Rosewood, 5½ inches. Weight, 5¼ ounces. Per set of four......15c
No. 12R3074 Bones, Rosewood, 7 inches long. Weight, 6 ounces.
Per set of four..................................20c
No. 12R3076 Bones, Solid Ebony, 5½ inches. Weight, 6 ounces. Per set of four............25c
No. 12R3078 Bones, Solid Ebony, 7 inches long. Weight, 7 ounces.
Per set of four..................30c
No. 12R3080 Clappers. Made of Walnut, with patent steel spring and lead clappers. Per set of two.....10c

Triangles.

No. 12R3084 4-inch nickeled steel, with hammer. Weight, 7 oz. Each.25c
No. 12R3086 6-inch nickeled steel, with hammer. Weight, 9 oz. Each.25c
No. 12R3088 7-inch nickeled steel, with hammer. Weight, 12 oz. Each.30c
No. 12R3090 8-inch nickeled steel, with hammer. Weight, 15 oz. Each.40c

Tambourines.

No. 12R3096 7-inch maple rim, with tacked sheepskin head and three sets of jingles. Weight, 10 ounces.
Per dozen, **$3.00;** each..............................25c
No. 12R3098 Same, with 8-inch head. Weight, 12 ounces. Per dozen, **$3.60;** each.......................30c
No. 12R3100 Same, with 10-inch head. Weight, 14 ounces. Per dozen, **$4.20;** each.......................35c
No. 12R3102 Maple painted rim, 8-inch tacked calfskin head, nine sets of jingles. Weight, 16 ounces.
Each..65c
No. 12R3104 Maple painted rim, 10-inch tacked calfskin head, twelve sets jingles. Weight, 19 ounces.
Each..88c
No. 12R3106 Maple rim, very strong and durable, 10-inch calfskin head, fastened with metal band without tacks, three sets jingles. Weight, 16 ounces. Each.........................80c

Salvation Army Tambourines.

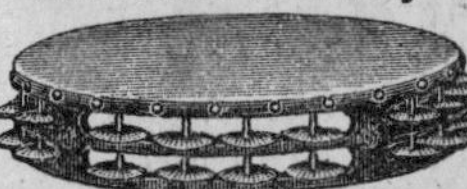

No. 12R3109 10-inch Maple Hoop, fancy painted and ornamented, 28 sets brass jingles, calfskin head fastened with brass tacks. Our special price.....................**$1.45**
No. 12R3111 Same as No. 12R3109, but with 32 sets of jingles. Our special price......................**$1.95**

Dulcimers.

No. 12R3118 Dulcimers of American manufacture, neatly decorated, fine finish, chromatically strung, can be tuned so as to play easily in all keys, and is the most complete instrument of the kind produced. We include one pair of dulcimer beaters and complete instruction book. **Shipping weight, about 40 pounds.**
Our price..**$13.85**

Ocarinas.

Fiehn's Vienna Make.

NO BETTER OCARINAS can be had at any price than these **genuine imported instruments.**

WE IMPORT THESE DIRECT FROM EUROPE and own them at prices enabling us to offer them to you at about **what your dealer himself pays.**

THESE INSTRUMENTS ARE EASILY BROKEN and must be packed with care. **We guarantee that each Ocarina leaves our hands in perfect condition.**

No.	Key of	Each	No.	Key of	Each
12R3120	C, Soprano	$0.14	12R3131	A*b*, Alto	$0.33
12R3121	B*b*, Soprano	.14	12R3132	G, Alto...	.35
12R3122	A, Soprano.	.14	12R3133	F, Alto...	.43
12R3123	G, Soprano.	.17	12R3134	E, Alto...	.65
12R3124	F, Soprano..	.17	12R3135	E*b*, Alto..	.70
12R3125	E, Soprano..	.19	12R3136	D, Bass...	.70
12R3126	E*b*, Soprano	.19	12R3137	C, Bass...	1.05
12R3127	D, Alto.....	.23	12R3138	B*b*, Bass..	1.25
12R3128	C, Alto.....	.25	12R3139	A, Bass...	1.30
12R3129	B*b*, Alto....	.28	12R3140	A*b*, Bass..	1.75
12R3130	A, Alto.....	.30	12R3141	G, Bass...	1.90

No. 12R3146 Quartettes; 1st and 2d Tenor, 1st and 2d Bass, per set.......................**$2.95**
Sopranos, weight, 4-oz.; Altos, 14-oz.; Bass, 26-oz.; Contra Bass, 40-oz.
A sheet of instructions with each instrument showing exactly how it is played.

Jews' Harps.

The Jews' Harps which we list below are made by the best maker in America, and are known as the genuine E. L. American Jews' Harps and are not to be compared with the many inferior harps on the market. They are all made of white metal frames and have brass tipped tongues. If you are thinking of ordering a Jews' Harp it will pay you to buy our genuine E. L. Harp. They will outlast six of the ordinary harps offered for sale by other dealers.

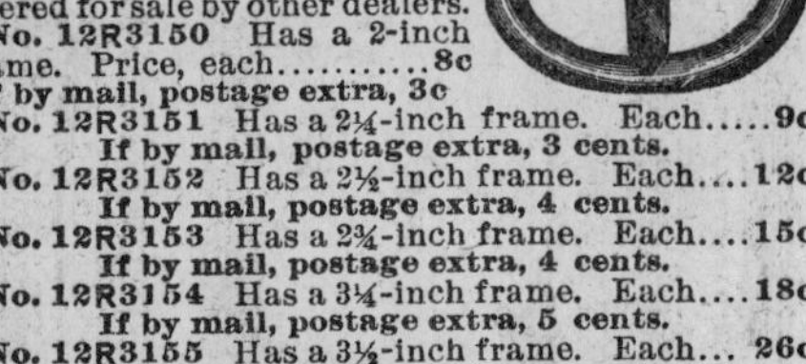

No. 12R3150 Has a 2-inch frame. Price, each...........8c
If by mail, postage extra, 3c
No. 12R3151 Has a 2¼-inch frame. Each.....9c
If by mail, postage extra, 3 cents.
No. 12R3152 Has a 2½-inch frame. Each....12c
If by mail, postage extra, 4 cents.
No. 12R3153 Has a 2¾-inch frame. Each....15c
If by mail, postage extra, 4 cents.
No. 12R3154 Has a 3¼-inch frame. Each....18c
If by mail, postage extra, 5 cents.
No. 12R3155 Has a 3½-inch frame. Each... 26c
If by mail, postage extra, 5 cents.
No. 12R3156 Has a 3¾-inch frame. Each....32c
If by mail, postage extra, 6 cents.
No. 12R3157 Jumbo Harp. Has a 4¼-inch frame. Each.......................................39c
If by mail, postage extra, 6 cents.

Tuning Forks.

New standard or low pitch.

No. 12R3180 Steel, A or C, philharmonic. Each, 9c
No. 12R3181 Nickel plated steel, A or C, superior quality. Each..........................20c
No. 12R3182 Blued steel, A or C, superior quality. Each..........................30c

Tuning Pipes.

New standard or high pitch.

No. 12R3190 German silver, keys of A and C combined, extra fine quality in white metal boxes. Each......................9c
No. 12R3192 Same, keys of C and G combined. Each..........................9c
For violin, mandolin and guitar tuners, see pages containing Violin, Mandolin, Guitar and Banjo Furnishings.

Piano Tuning Hammers.

No. 12R3201 Long rosewood handle with extension rod of steel, double head with oblong holes, and single head with star holes. Extra quality, warranted. Each........................**$1.50**

Metronomes.

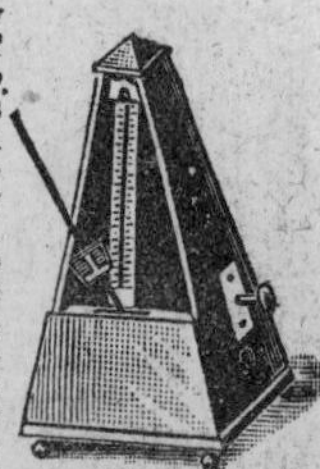

The Metronome is used by students of music, especially of the piano, to indicate the tempo or time. The upright rod moves backward and forward like an inverted pendulum, the movement being actuated by a spring which is wound up with a key. The time is indicated both to eye and ear, the movement being in sight and ticking similar to a clock. **The time is regulated fast or slow by the sliding weight on the pendulum, while the latter has a graduated scale. This is an invaluable instrument for pupils of the piano and organ especially.**
No. 12R3202 Metronome, solid mahogany, fixed key, without bell, Maelzel system. Each.......**$1.85**
No. 12R3204 **Same, with bell.** Each. 2.75

ON THE PRECEDING PAGE we call the attention of everyone interested in band instruments to our celebrated Marceau instruments that we have run with such success for several years, the instruments that have built up our trade among musicians, that have given us a reputation among amateur and professional band players alike for supplying the best instruments to be found in this market at anything like our prices; and for the first season we present on this and the opposite page a complete line of what we consider, and what professional bandsmen everywhere will recognize, as a still higher grade of instruments, a still better instrument for volume and beauty of tone, finish and ease of operation, the line of BRASS BAND INSTRUMENTS MADE BY M. DUPONT, OF PARIS, FRANCE, and for which we have secured the sole and exclusive agency for the United States.

WE HAVE secured the agency of the United States for the WORLD RENOWNED

DUPONT BAND INSTRUMENTS,

THE HIGHEST OF ALL HIGH GRADE BRASS BAND INSTRUMENTS.
The genuine well known DUPONT make, the very acme of excellence in brass band instrument manufacture.

WE HAVE BEEN ENCOURAGED TO PLACE THIS LINE OF INSTRUMENTS BEFORE OUR CUSTOMERS by reason of the instant success and universal satisfaction of the celebrated Marceau instruments, and as it is our constant endeavor to make our lines as complete as possible, to give our customers the benefit of the very highest grade goods it is possible to produce in any department of merchandise,

WE HAVE SECURED AND ACCEPTED THE SALE OF THIS DUPONT MAKE.

OUR PRICES are extremely moderate, while these instruments are the highest grade in the world. It is possible to buy higher priced instruments from retail dealers, but it is not possible to buy better instruments. We sell Dupont Band Instruments on the same small margin of profit that we sell other and less expensive goods, and for this reason our prices on this, the finest line of instruments made, compare favorably with the prices asked by dealers generally for inferior makes of instruments. The prices of many other makes of band instruments are so enormously high mostly by reason of expensive engraving, which adds nothing to the actual value of the instrument.

HOW THE WORLD RENOWNED DUPONT BAND INSTRUMENTS ARE MADE.

THE BRASS the most important feature, is of the very best quality. So much depends upon the tempering of the brass and in the Dupont instruments the brass is tempered just to that point which makes it absolutely perfect as a medium for the transmission of vibration and sound. This point has been arrived at by years of experience. The tubing is rolled until it is practically seamless, and gradually increases in size from the mouthpiece to the bell, with no abrupt turn. This gives every instrument a most graceful shape. There are no sharp turns even in passing through the valves, nor from the valves into the valve slides and back. These two effects make it possible for the amateur to produce quite as good tone as the professional performer.

THE VALVES are without fault, and there is no valve made that will operate more quickly or lightly. The valve tube is quite heavy, which is necessary to afford proper protection from any pressure or blow to which it might be subjected. This point is very important and valuable, as any musician will readily understand that the least indentation or impression made upon this part renders the instrument useless, as no passage can be rendered with any degree of rapidity and accuracy. The valve piston is made of pure German silver and is carefully ground into the valve tube, making it perfectly air tight and with the least possible friction. Perfect cleanliness, freedom from all oil, and proper lubrication with saliva make these valves the very best that are made, and will admit of the execution of the most rapid and difficult passages with perfect freedom, clearness and distinctiveness of each and every note.

EXTRA PRECAUTION is taken in making the joints so that they are very strong, perfectly air tight and that no obstruction is left upon the inside of the tube that would hinder the passage of air. Very neat and attractive reinforcing bands are used at the end of each valve slide, which not only adds to the appearance of the instrument, but makes those parts much stronger and less liable to become dented. All instruments are heavily braced at all points where any possibility of bending or breaking might occur. The bell upright instruments have a heavy reinforcement at the lower bend, which affords protection when the instrument is set upon the floor.

THE MODEL OF THESE INSTRUMENTS is the result of much study with respect to appearance as well as to the shape that would allow the best possible results musically. The Valve Trombones are the new long model and are indeed handsome instruments, the tone of the B♭ Tenor being of exceptional quality and brilliancy and its tone can hardly be distinguished from the rich tones of the Slide Trombone. Each instrument is provided with a silver plated mouthpiece and a very strong music rack. The B♭ Cornets are furnished with an A set piece for use in orchestra or solo playing. The C Cornet, which is intended for playing Church, Sunday School and all vocal music without transposition, is provided with a B♭ Crook, which makes it equally as useful in brass bands as in Church or Sunday School.

We furnish these instruments in four different styles of finish:

- Finish No. 1—Highly polished brass.
- Finish No. 2—Highly burnished nickel plate.
- Finish No. 3—Triple silver plate, satin finish.
- Finish No. 4—Triple silver plate, burnished.

SEE PRICE LIST ON ☞ OPPOSITE PAGE.

When ordering be sure to state which finish is desired.

FOR AMATEUR OR PROFESSIONAL we cannot recommend any band instruments more highly than this, the DUPONT line. We feel positive that any one who orders one of these instruments and appreciates a fine instrument will be delighted with his purchase. We sell these goods as we do everything quoted in this catalogue, under the guarantee that if they do not prove perfectly satisfactory and exactly as we represent them to be, we will immediately refund the money. We direct the attention of everyone interested in band instruments to this unsurpassed line. Those who are organizing bands cannot do better than to make their selection from these pages, if they desire the most satisfactory and lasting high grade instruments. The individual player who wants to own the finest instrument made will make no mistake to select a DUPONT.

UNDERSTAND, every DUPONT instrument is put out under our binding guarantee to give perfect satisfaction, or we stand ready to immediately refund your money.

TEN DAYS' TRIAL. ANY DUPONT INSTRUMENT WHICH DOES NOT PROVE ENTIRELY SATISFACTORY AFTER A TRIAL OF TEN DAYS CAN BE RETURNED AND MONEY WILL BE REFUNDED.

PRICE LIST.

IN ORDERING BE SURE AND STATE FINISH WANTED.

Dupont Eb Cornet.

No. 12R3250
Finish No. 1........................$ 8.25
Finish No. 2........................ 9.25
Finish No. 3........................ 13.95
Finish No. 4........................ 14.55

Dupont Bb Cornets.

No. 12R3252 Single water key.
Finish No. 1........................$ 9.45
Finish No. 2........................ 10.45
Finish No. 3........................ 15.25
Finish No. 4........................ 16.70

No. 12R3254 Double water key with A set piece and C attachment.
Finish No. 1........................$14.45
Finish No. 2........................ 15.45
Finish No. 3........................ 20.30
Finish No. 4........................ 22.25

No. 12R3256 A Cornet for Leaders. Double water key. Ornamented trimmings, very heavily braced. A cornet for artists and professionals.
Finish No. 1........................$15.45
Finish No. 2........................ 16.45
Finish No. 3........................ 21.45
Finish No. 4........................ 23.35

Dupont C Cornet.

No. 12R3258 Single water key.
Finish No. 1........................$ 9.85
Finish No. 2........................ 10.85
Finish No. 3........................ 15.75
Finish No. 4........................ 17.65

Dupont Altos.

No. 12R3270 Solo alto, bell front.
Finish No. 1........................$13.30
Finish No. 2........................ 15.20
Finish No. 3........................ 22.55
Finish No. 4........................ 26.65

No. 12R3272 Bell upright.
Finish No. 1........................$13.35
Finish No. 2........................ 15.25
Finish No. 3........................ 22.60
Finish No. 4........................ 26.70

No. 12R3274 Concert Alto in key of F, with slides for **Eb, D and C. French Horn Model.** May be used in orchestra as well as in brass bands.
Finish No. 1........................$31.85
Finish No. 2........................ 33.95
Finish No. 3........................ 41.90
Finish No. 4........................ 44.55

Dupont Bb Tenor.

No. 12R3276 Bell upright.
Finish No. 1........................$14.85
Finish No. 2........................ 17.35
Finish No. 3........................ 25.20
Finish No. 4........................ 30.25

Dupont Bb Baritone.

No. 12R3278 Bell upright.
Finish No. 1........................$17.95
Finish No. 2........................ 20.70
Finish No. 3........................ 29.65
Finish No. 4........................ 35.10

Dupont Basses.

No. 12R3279 **Bb Bass.** Bell upright.
Finish No. 1........................$20.55
Finish No. 2........................ 23.80
Finish No. 3........................ 35.85
Finish No. 4........................ 42.65

No. 12R3280 **Eb Bass.** Bell upright.
Finish No. 1........................$26.15
Finish No. 2........................ 29.90
Finish No. 3........................ 43.15
Finish No. 4........................ 53.65

No. 12R3282 **Eb Contra Bass.** Bell upright. **Extra large size.**
Finish No. 1........................$28.45
Finish No. 2........................ 32.40
Finish No. 3........................ 50.65
Finish No. 4........................ 58.15

Dupont Trombones.

No. 12R3290 **Eb Alto Valve Trombone.** Bell front.
Finish No. 1........................$13.40
Finish No. 2........................ 15.30
Finish No. 3........................ 22.65
Finish No. 4........................ 26.75

No. 12R3292 **Bb Tenor Valve Trombone.** Bell front.
Finish No. 1........................$14.70
Finish No. 2........................ 17.20
Finish No. 3........................ 25.05
Finish No. 4........................ 30.10

No. 12R3294 **Bb Baritone Valve Trombone.** Bell front.
Finish No. 1........................$17.90
Finish No. 2........................ 20.65
Finish No. 3........................ 29.60
Finish No. 4........................ 34.95

No. 12R3296 **Eb Alto Slide Trombone.**
Finish No. 1........................$ 8.25
Finish No. 2........................ 10.25
Finish No. 3........................ 14.55
Finish No. 4........................ 16.60

No. 12R3298 **Bb Tenor Slide Trombone.**
Finish No. 1........................$ 9.35
Finish No. 2........................ 11.35
Finish No. 3........................ 15.65
Finish No. 4........................ 17.75

BAND OF 6	BAND OF 7	BAND OF 8	BAND OF 9	BAND OF 10	BAND OF 11
1 Eb Cornet. 1 Bb Cornet. 1 Eb Alto. 1 Bb Tenor. 1 Bb Baritone. 1 Eb Bass.	1 Eb Cornet. 2 Bb Cornets. 1 Eb Alto. 1 Bb Tenor. 1 Bb Baritone. 1 Eb Bass.	1 Eb Cornet. 2 Bb Cornets. 2 Eb Altos. 1 Bb Tenor. 1 Bb Baritone. 1 Eb Bass.	1 Eb Cornet. 2 Bb Cornets. 2 Eb Altos. 2 Bb Tenors. 1 Bb Baritone. 1 Eb Bass.	1 Eb Cornet. 3 Bb Cornets. 2 Eb Altos. 2 Bb Tenors. 1 Bb Baritone. 1 Eb Bass.	1 Eb Cornet. 4 Bb Cornets. 2 Eb Altos. 2 Bb Tenors. 1 Bb Baritone. 1 Eb Bass.
BAND OF 12	**BAND OF 13**	**BAND OF 14**	**BAND OF 15**	**BAND OF 16**	**BAND OF 17**
1 Eb Cornet. 4 Bb Cornets. 2 Eb Altos. 2 Bb Tenors. 1 Bb Baritone. 1 Bb Bass. 1 Eb Bass.	1 Eb Cornet. 4 Bb Cornets. 3 Eb Altos. 2 Bb Tenors. 1 Bb Baritone. 1 Bb Bass. 1 Eb Bass.	1 Eb Cornet. 5 Bb Coruets. 3 Eb Altos. 2 Bb Tenors. 1 Bb Baritone. 1 Bb Bass. 1 Eb Bass.	1 Eb Cornet. 5 Bb Cornets. 3 Eb Altos. 2 Bb Tenors. 1 Bb Baritone. 1 Bb Bass. 2 Eb Basses.	1 Eb Cornet. 5 Eb Cornets. 3 Eb Altos. 2 Bb Tenors. 2 Bb Baritones. 1 Bb Bass. 2 Eb Basses.	1 Eb Cornet. 6 Bb Cornets. 3 Eb Altos. 2 Bb Tenors. 2 Bb Baritones. 1 Bb Bass. 2 Eb Basses.

We can furnish any of the above instruments ARTISTICALLY ENGRAVED and with GOLD BELL at a very slight additional expense. PRICES FURNISHED UPON APPLICATION.

Zobo Brass Musical Instruments.

Anybody can play, anybody can buy; brilliant martial and orchestral music at small cost; best and cheapest sacred music. The Zobo Musical Instruments are the latest addition to the Zobo, and are rapidly becoming the most popular amusement in the novelty and musical way, as the tone is produced by singing into them. Anyone can play them without any difficulty, and produce good music or many imitations if so desired; with **Zobo Brass Band Instruments** a brass band can be organized with men or boys who have no knowledge of musical instruments whatever, but with a few rehearsals are capable of rendering brilliant music, and producing instrumental effects possible hitherto to none but the best brass band and orchestra.

The Zobo.

No. 12R3307 The Zobo is the simplest musical instrument made. **No trouble to learn.** Place your lips to the instrument, make a noise on one end, and the pleasing music is emitted from the other. Made of maple, with metal ring.
Price, each....(If by mail, postage extra, 2c)...8c
No. 12R3308 Zobo Cornetto is like the Zobo, but has a small brass horn attached to mouthpiece.
Price, each...(If by mail, postage extra, 4c)...16c

Zobo Cornet.

No. 12R3309 The Zobo Cornet, as illustrated, is made of brass and is attached to the Zobo as shown. Gives the voice an exact imitation of the cornet. Each....60c
If by mail, postage extra, each, 15 cents.

Alto Cornet.

No. 12R3312 As shown in cut. Same as No. 12R3309, but much larger in size, being 15 inches long with a 6-inch bell; is used to play a second part alto or second tenor in a quartette. Our special price..............85c
If by mail, postage extra, each, 25 cents.

Zobo Professional Cornet.

No. 12R3313 The Latest Zobo Instrument, looks precisely like a regular cornet as played by professionals. Has three working plungers. 11 inches long, 5½-inch bell. Our special price...$1.35
If by mail, postage extra, each, 15 cents.
No. 12R3314 Zobo Professional Alto. Looks exactly like No. 12R3313 but in alto size.
Price, each. (If by mail, postage extra, 25c).$1.45

Zobo Saxophone.

No. 12R3315 Twenty-one inches long with 6-inch bell, as shown in cut. Is used for playing first bass in a quartette or zobo band.
Our special price. $1.15
Shipping weight, 7 pounds.

Zobo Trombone.

No. 12R3317 Zobo Trombone, is 26 inches long, 5-inch bell; when fully extended with slide, 34 inches long. Used for baritone voice. Price, each...$2.45
Weight, boxed ready for shipment, about 7 lbs.

Zobo Bass.

No. 12R3318 As shown in cut, 21 inches high, 9-inch bell; used for bass voice, solo, quartette or zobo band. Our special price..........$2.95
Shipping weight, 10 pounds.

Zobo Vibrators.

No. 12R3322 Vibrators for Zobo in packages of one dozen. Our special price, per dozen...............5c
If by mail, postage extra, each, 1 cent.
Instruction Book with each band outfit free.

Zobo Instructor.

No. 12R3326 Zobo Instructor for Zobo band instruments contains the rudiments of music, scales and exercises for the different voices for soloists, quartettes and zobo bands, by Otto Langey.
Price, each...(If by mail, postage extra, 3c)...19c

Zobo Quartette.

No. 12R3327 Zobo Quartette consists of cornet, alto cornet, saxophone and bass horn. A full set of four instruments, as described above, including an instruction book, all packed in a wooden case.
Price, each..(Shipping weight, 20 pounds)..$5.60

Zobo Bands.

In making up Zobo Bands any number of instruments can be used in the combination, according to requirements. With larger organizations it is desirable to add a snare and bass drum. The combination depends largely upon whether the voices are mixed or all male voices. We are prepared to furnish full particulars, upon application, giving information concerning the most desirable combination for any brass band.

BUGLES.

Officer's Bugle.

No. 12R3329 The Officer's Bugle, made of brass and finely finished, key of C; weight, boxed, about 5 pounds. Our special price... $1.25
No. 12R3330 Same, finely nickel plated. Our special price..........................$1.75

Cavalry Bugle

No. 12R3334 Cavalry Bugle, brass, key of F; weight, boxed, 6 pounds. Our special price $1.95
No. 12R3335 Same, nickel plated..$2.45

No. 12R3334

Artillery Bugle.

No. 12R3338 Artillery Bugle, brass, key of G; weight, boxed, 6 pounds.
Price....$2.35
No. 12R3339 Same, finely nickel plated. Price....$2.95

No. 12R3338

Infantry Bugle.

No. 12R3341 Infantry Bugle; brass; key of C with B flat crook; weight, boxed, 6 pounds.
Price....$1.95
No. 12R3342 Same, nickel plated.
Price.. . $2.65

No. 12R3341

Hunting Horns.

No. 12R3345 Hunting Horns; brass; one turn, Each.......... ....70c
No. 12R3346 Hunting Horns; brass; three turns.
Each...............$1.15

Regulation U. S. Cavalry Trumpet. Key of F.

No. 12R3347 Is made of brass, with tuning slide.
Our price..
......$2.95
No. 12R3348 Same, nickel plated..........................$3.45
Weight, boxed, 8 pounds.

Fifes.

Key of B Flat and C only. Instruction Book, 12c.
Shipping weight, 8 ounces.
BE SURE TO STATE KEY WANTED.

No. 12R3358 Key of B Flat or C; solid rosewood; brass ferrules. Each. 25c
No. 12R3359 Key of B Flat or C; cocoa wood; German silver. Each.............................30c
No. 12R3361 Key of B Flat or C; solid ebony; nickel plated ferrules. Each 55c
No. 12R3362 Key of B Flat or C; solid ebony; long metal ferrules. **Crosby model;** extra fine quality. Each..80c

Nickel Plated Fifes.

Shipping weight, 10 ounces.

No. 12R3364 Key of B Flat or C. Nickel plated, with raised finger holes, with gutta percha embouchure. Each.......................... ....85c

Our Special Acme Hand Made Fife

Shipping weight, 12 ounces.

No. 12R3365 Metal nickel plated, strictly high grade Fife for professional players. Made in two pieces. Easy blowing, perfect in scale. None better made. Our special price, each..................$1.25

Nightingale Flageolets.

Shipping weight, 6 ounces.
BE SURE TO STATE KEY WANTED.

No. 12R3366 Nightingale Flageolets, as shown above, made of seamless brass tubing. A reliable and well made instrument, accurately tuned, and must not be compared with cheap imitations. A sheet of instructions with each instrument. Furnished in any of the following keys: B, C, D, E, F, G.
Our special price, each..............................22c
No. 12R3367 Same as above, only nickel plated.
Our special price 24c

Atlas Fifes.

No. 12R3368 Atlas Fifes, made of cast metal, nickel plated, are of French manufacture and imported by us direct from France. An exceptionally well made instrument, accurately tuned and superior to the ordinary metal flageolets generally offered. Come only in key of D. Our special price.........33c
If by mail, postage extra, 8 cents.

Flageolets.

Shipping weight, 10 ounces.

In Pasteboard Boxes.
No. 12R3372 Key of D, Boxwood; black; 1 key. Each..$1.20
No. 12R3373 Key of D, Grenadilla; German silver trimmed; 1 key. Each.................................$1.25
No. 12R3375 Key of D, Grenadilla; German silver trimmed; 4 keys. Each $2.00
No. 12R3376 Key of D, Grenadilla; German silver trimmed; 6 keys. Each..............................$2.35

Atlas Flageolets.

No. 12R3378 Atlas Flageolets, made of cast metal, nickel plated, are of French manufacture and imported by us direct from France. Is an exceptionally well made instrument, accurately tuned in key of D. Our special price.................................39c
If by mail, postage extra, 12 cents.

Piccolo-Flageolets.

Shipping weight, 12 ounces.

With extra mouthpiece; can be played **either as a piccolo or as a flageolet.** In pasteboard boxes.
No. 12R3382 Key of D, Boxwood; German silver trimmed; 1 key. Each.............................$1.50
No. 12R3383 Key of D, Grenadilla; German silver trimmed; 5 keys. Each...........................$2.25
No. 12R3384 Key of D, Grenadilla; German silver trimmed; 6 keys. Each $2.45

Atlas Piccolos.

No. 12R3390 Atlas Piccolos, made of cast metal, nickel plated, mouthpiece opening at side, and so constructed that anyone can play it accurately; tuned in key of D. Are of French manufacture and imported by us direct from France.
Our special price...49c
If by mail, postage extra, 11 cents.

Multiflutes.

No. 12R3391 Multiflute, the latest French novelty. Is a combination instrument. It is made of cast metal, nickel plated, and has three distinct mouthpieces, as shown in the illustration. The instrument is of French manufacture and imported by us direct from France. It is accurately tuned in key of D, and is easy to play. Our special price.....................65c
If by mail, postage extra, 16 cents.

Piccolos.

Shipping weight, 6 to 8 ounces.

No. 12R3392 Cocoa wood, one key, German silver trimmed, in pasteboard box. Key of D or E flat.
Price, each 45c
No. 12R3393 Cocoa wood, with one key and tuning slide, German silver trimmed, in pasteboard box. **Key of D or E flat.** Each.........................65c
No. 12R3394 Grenadilla wood, with tuning slide and four keys, German silver trimmed, in pasteboard box. **Key of D or E flat.** Each.............$1.15
No. 12R3395 Grenadilla wood, with tuning slide, six keys, German silver trimmed, cork joints, in pasteboard box. **Key of D or E flat.** Each...$1.60

Meyer Pattern Piccolo.

ANYONE KNOWING THE VALUE OF PICCOLOS will acknowledge the wonderful superiority of the **MEYER PICCOLOS.** The one shown in the illustration below is offered as a select example of the **highest grade Meyer pattern piccolo it is possible to make.**

No. 12R3396 Grenadilla, ivory head, six keys, with slide cork joints and German silver trimmed, in fine velvet lined morocco case, as shown in illustration. **Key of D or E flat.**
Price, each..$4.65
Shipping weight, 15 ounces.

FOR FIFE AND FLUTE MOUTHPIECES, SEE PAGE 218.

FLUTES.

No. 12R3428 Genuine cocoa, German silver trimmed, with tuning slide and one key, in pasteboard case. Shipping weight, about 12 ounces. Each..........$1.65

No. 12R3430 Grenadilla wood, German silver trimmed, with tuning slide, four keys, in pasteboard case. Shipping weight, about 12 ounces. Each..........$2.35

No. 12R3432 Grenadilla wood, with tuning slide, cork joints, six keys, German silver caps and trimmings, in pasteboard case. Shipping weight, about 16 ounces. Each....$3.15

No. 12R3434 Grenadilla wood, with tuning slide, cork joints, eight keys, German silver caps and trimmings, in neat pasteboard case. **Shipping weight, 16 ounces.**
Our special price..........$4.00

No. 12R3436 Grenadilla wood, with tuning slide, cork joints, eight keys, German silver caps and trimmings **and metal embouchure**, in pasteboard case. **Shipping weight, about 16 ounces.** Each..........$4.50

No. 12R3438 Genuine Meyer Model Flute, key of D, eight keys, grenadilla wood, with tuning slide, cork joints, **in fine morocco case**, as shown, velvet lined, **with joint caps, grease box**, swab, pads and screwdriver. **Weight, 26 ounces.** Our special price..........$6.95

No. 12R3440 Genuine Meyer Model Flute, key of D, **ten keys, grenadilla wood**, with tuning slide and cork joints. In fine morocco case, velvet lined, as shown, complete with **joint caps, grease box, swab, pad and screwdriver. Shipping weight, 26 ounces.**
Our special price.......... $9.50

Genuine Meyer Model Flute for $14.45.

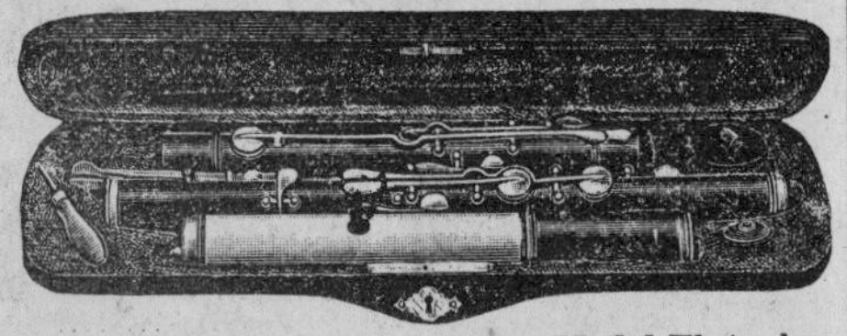

No. 12R3442 Genuine Meyer Model Flute, key of D; ten keys, grenadilla wood, with tuning slide, cork joints and genuine ivory head, as illustrated above. **In fine velvet lined morocco case**, with joint caps, grease box, swab, pads and screwdriver. **Weight, 26 ounces.** Our special price.......$14.45

IMPORTANT.

Proper care must be taken of clarionets, flutes piccolos and similar wooden instruments. They are liable to crack or check at any time through carelessness on the part of the owner or user. They are susceptible to **changes of atmosphere**, and especially so when damp from usage or otherwise. Always after using they **should be wiped dry**, inside and outside, and **rubbed with sweet oil**. No music dealer will be responsible **for checking or cracking.**

Genuine Martin Clarionets....

IMPORTED BY US DIRECT FROM THE CELEBRATED MAKER, J. B. MARTIN, OF PARIS, FRANCE.

STRICTLY HIGH GRADE CLARIONETS.

WE EXAMINE EACH INSTRUMENT **with scrupulous care, and we warrant every one to leave our house in perfect condition.**

Can be furnished in the following Keys: A, B Flat, C, D, E Flat.

DO NOT FAIL TO STATE KEY WANTED WHEN ORDERING CLARIONET OR TRIMMINGS.

Celebrated Albert System.

Made of grenadilla wood, with **cork joints, thirteen German silver keys**, two rings and German silver trimmed. **Weight, 20 ounces.**

No. 12R3450 Our special price, each..........$11.95

Albert System as illustrated; made of grenadilla wood, with cork joints, fifteen German silver keys (extra Bb and C sharp), two rings, German silver trimmed. **Weight, 23 oz.**

No. 12R3452 Our special price, each..........$14.75

CYMBALS.

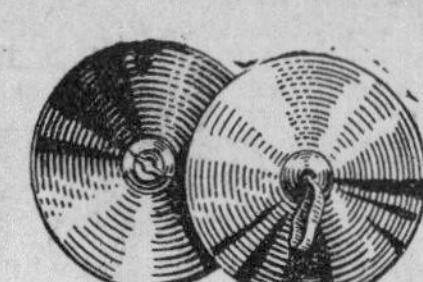

No. 12R3460 10-inch Brass Cymbals, with leather handles. Weight, 35 ounces. Per pair..........$1.20

No. 12R3461 11-inch Brass Cymbals, with leather handles. Weight, 40 ounces. Per pair..........$1.35

No. 12R3462 12-inch Brass Cymbals, with leather handles. Weight, 45 ounces. Per pair..........$1.45

No. 12R3463 13-inch Brass Cymbals, with leather handles. Weight, 50 ounces. Per pair..........$1.65

No. 12R3464 Turkish Cymbals, 8-inch, composition metal, with leather handles. Weight, 35 ounces. Per pair..........$4.00

No. 12R3466 Turkish Cymbals, 12-inch, composition metal, with leather handles, weight 65 ounces. Per pair..........$8.10

ACME PROFESSIONAL DRUMS.

To meet the ever increasing demand for high class Tenor and Bass Drums, we take pleasure in offering to our customers our line, descriptions of which will be found below.

The **shell, hoops, heads and trimmings** are all of special quality, **warranted extra select, and put** together by skilled workmen, whose knowledge is the result of years of experience. We consequently offer prospective purchasers a line of drums that must not be compared with the cheap, dingy instruments found in ordinary music stores or by competitive houses. In fact, few retailers outside of large cities carry a stock of drums. The retailers must send away to some wholesale house. The advantage of buying from us is very apparent, for you get such goods direct from the factory.

We shall **be glad to name a special price on quantities to clubs.** In writing, always state the exact style and number of instrument you want. If you do not find described herein just what you need, write us. **Additional supplies for drum corps, such as fifes, piccolos, drum major's batons, etc.,** will be found in this catalogue. **Many imitations of these pattern drums are now on the market.** Bear in mind that price alone does not make a bargain. Quality must be just as great a consideration. Through our factory to consumer plan we **combine quality and price** in a degree of economic perfection never before seen. We claim the best goods at the least money, and only ask a fair chance to back up every assertion.

THE ACME PROFESSIONAL SNARE OR TENOR DRUMS. Prussian Pattern.

Weight, packed, about 15 pounds.

No. 12R3470 Has 14-inch maple shell, 6 inches high; seven rods, white metal plated hooks and trimmings, six snares, one calfskin head, one pair rosewood sticks. Our special price..........$4.80

No. 12R3472 Has 16-inch maple shell, is 6 inches high with eight rods and hoops of maple, finished in imitation rosewood or ebony, with trimmings **of white metal, plated**, best quality calfskin head, eight rawhide snares.
Our special price, including one pair of rosewood sticks..........$5.45

No. 12R3474 The same style of drum as No. 12R3472, with brass shell. Our special price....$5.50

No. 12R3476 The same drum as No. 12R3472, but has two best quality calfskin heads. Our special price, including one pair of rosewood sticks........$5.90

No. 12R3478 Same drum as No. 12R3472, but has brass shell, and two best quality calfskin heads. Our special price, including one pair rosewood sticks..$5.95

No. 12R3480 Has 16-inch shell, is 6 inches high with **eight patent rods**, hoops of maple, decorated with fancy decalcomanie ornamentation, trimmings of white metal plated, best of calfskin heads, **eight rawhide snares.**
Our price, including one pair of rosewood sticks, $6.10

No. 12R3482 Same description as No. 12R3480, with the **exception of the shell, which is made of brass.**
Our special price, including one pair of rosewood sticks..........$6.15

OUR ACME PROFESSIONAL TENOR OR SNARE DRUMS.

Regulation Pattern. **Weight, packed, about 15 pounds.**

No. 12R3488 This is the regulation pattern with a shell 14 inches in diameter, made of bird's-eye maple, varnish finish, 8 inches high, cord hooks, with 7 braces. The hoops are of maple, finished in imitation ebony or rosewood, best of calfskin heads, **6 snares, new pattern snare strainer.**
Our special price, including one pair of sticks $4.95

No. 12R3490 Regulation pattern, but with a 16-inch shell, 9½ inches high, made of bird's-eye maple with maple hoops, finished in ebony or rosewood. Shell has fine varnish finish, **eight braces, best calfskin heads, new pattern snare strainers.** Our special price, including one pair of rosewood sticks..........$5.85

No. 12R3492 The same description as No. 12R3490, but has a shell made of rosewood, fine varnish finished.
Our special price..........$5.85

ACME PROFESSIONAL BASS DRUMS.

Weight, packed, about 50 pounds.

Following descriptions are for the regulation pattern bass drums. **We can furnish the Prussian pattern in same size at same price.** Prussian pattern bass drums are all 9½ inches high.

No. 12R3502 Bird's-Eye Maple Shell, finished in natural color, 24 inches in diameter, cord hooks, 10 inches high, has eleven braces, **made of best Italian hemp cord**, strung over the improved pattern cord hook. Has one calfskin and one sheepskin head. Our special price, including one buckskin head stick..$7.95

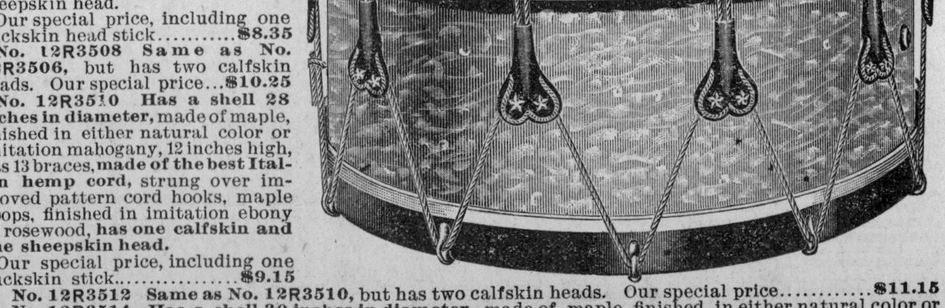

No. 12R3504 Same as No. 12R3502, but has two calfskin heads. Our special price.....$8.95

No. 12R3506 Has a shell 26 inches in diameter, made of maple, finished in either natural color or imitation mahogany, 11 inches high, has 12 braces, **made of best Italian hemp cord**, strung over improved pattern cord hooks, maple hoops, finished in imitation ebony or rosewood, has one calfskin and one sheepskin head.
Our special price, including one buckskin head stick..........$8.35

No. 12R3508 Same as No. 12R3506, but has two calfskin heads. Our special price...$10.25

No. 12R3510 Has a shell 28 inches in diameter, made of maple, finished in either natural color or imitation mahogany, 12 inches high, has 13 braces, **made of the best Italian hemp cord**, strung over improved pattern cord hooks, maple hoops, finished in imitation ebony or rosewood, **has one calfskin and one sheepskin head.**
Our special price, including one buckskin head stick..........$9.15

No. 12R3512 Same as No. 12R3510, but has two calfskin heads. Our special price..........$11.15

No. 12R3514 Has a shell 30 inches in diameter, made of maple, finished in either natural color or imitation mahogany, 12 inches high, has 14 braces, **made of the best Italian hemp**, strung over improved cord hooks, maple hoops, finished in imitation ebony or rosewood, has one calfskin and one sheepskin head. Shipping weight, boxed, 65 pounds. Our special price, including one buckskin head stick..........$10.15

No. 12R3516 Same as No. 12R3514, but has two calfskin heads. Our special price..........12.20

Eclipse Broad Rim Mouthpieces.

This Mouthpiece is similar to the Austin model, but has a very wide rim; is extensively used on long marches, parades and several days' continuous playing; made only for B flat cornet.

No. 12R5871 B flat Cornet....................85c

Our Acme Professional Mouthpieces.

SPECIAL HAND MADE.

We make up these mouthpieces for Eb and Bb cornets. When ordering be sure to send an impression of the tube where the mouthpiece is to enter.

No. 12R5872 Eb Cornets, small surface for lips, large bore. Especially recommended for playing with ease on the upper register.
Our special price....................90c

No. 12R5874 Same as No. 12R5872, but for Bb cornet. Our special price....................95c

Music Racks for Band Instruments.

No. 12R5884 Band Instrument Music Rack, brass, fit any band instrument excepting slide trombone; improved pattern, with square wire shank, three separate prongs. Shipping weight is 6 ounces. Each....................34c

No. 12R5886 Same as No. 12R5884, nickel plated. Shipping weight, 6 ounces. Each.44c

No. 12R5888 Bass Drum Music Rack, improved pattern, three separate prongs, with plate, brass. Shipping weight, 6 ounces. Each....................66c

No. 12R5890 Same as No. 12R5888, nickel plated. Shipping weight, 6 ounces. Each....................84c

No. 12R5892 Snare Drum Music Rack, improved pattern, three separate prongs, with plate. Brass. Shipping weight, 6 ounces. Price....................66c

No. 12R5894 Same as No. 12R5892. Nickel plated. Shipping weight, 6 ounces. Each.........84c

No. 12R5898 Clarionet Music Rack, nickel plated, with adjustable ring, three separate prongs. (Be sure to give key of clarionet.) Shipping weight, 6 ounces. Each....................64c

No. 12R5900 Piccolo and Fife Music Rack, three separate prongs, has strap to buckle on arm, brass, improved pattern. Shipping weight, 6 ounces. Each....................$1.00

No. 12R5902 Slide Trombone Music Rack, improved pattern, with extra long shank, brass. Shipping weight, 6 ounces. Each....................60c

No. 12R5904 Same as No. 12R5902. Nickel plated. Shipping weight, 6 ounces. Each.......65c

Band Instrument Mutes.

No. 12R5910 Improved Model Cornet Mute, made of brass, plain. Shipping weight, 10 ounces.
Price, each..........70c

No. 12R5912 Same, brass, finely nickel plated. Shipping weight, 10 ounces.

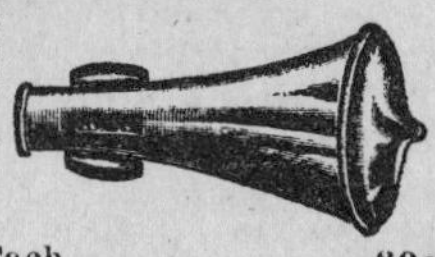

Each....................80c
If by mail, postage extra, 10 cents.

Music Stands.

No. 12R5920 Our Special Umbrella Pattern Folding Music Stand, made of iron, handsomely japanned. Folds up into small compass. Shipping weight, 43 ounces.
Price, each..............30c

No. 12R5924 Same, nickel plated. Shipping weight, 43 ounces.
Price, each..............70c

Music Stand Cases.

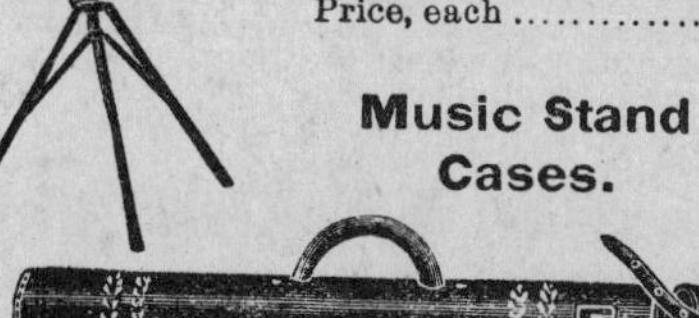

No. 12R5926 Our Best Music Stand Case is made of sole leather and is exactly like the illustration above. It is made for folding iron stands such as we quote above. Shipping weight, 18 ounces.
Our special price, each.....................80c

Student's Music Pad.

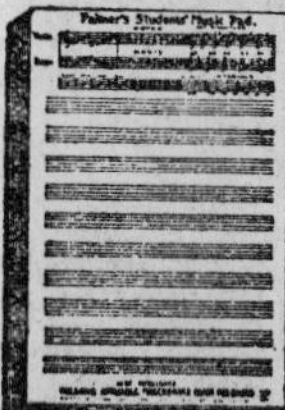

No. 12R5930 One Hundred Sheets of Ruled Music Paper, put up in the form of a pad, suitable for music students. Each sheet shows all signatures used in writing music, which serve as a great aid to composers.
Our special price....................15c
If by mail, postage extra, 8 cents.

GIVE CATALOGUE NUMBER IN FULL WHEN YOU WRITE YOUR ORDER

Music Blank Books.

These books are well bound and are made of good quality paper, ready ruled for writing music. Size, 7½x9½ inches.

No. 12R5940 6 staves, 40 pages....................14c
No. 12R5941 8 staves, 24 pages....................16c
No. 12R5942 8 staves, 40 pages....................13c
No. 12R5943 8 staves, 64 pages....................19c
If by mail, postage extra, per book, 4 cents.

Music Paper.

Super Royal Music Paper. Size, 10¼x13¼ inches.
No. 12R5947 10 staves, octavo.
No. 12R5948 12 staves, octavo, or oblong.
No. 12R5949 12 staves, octavo, for vocal or piano.
No. 12R5950 14 staves, octavo, or oblong.
Price, per quire (24 sheets)....................25c
If by mail, postage extra, per quire, 11 cents.

Gummed Paper.

No. 12R5952 French Gummed Paper, for mending sheet music. Per sheet....................10c

Ruling Pens.

No. 12R5956 Ruling Pens, with five lines for drawing staff. Each....................10c

Steel Pens.

No. 12R5962 Steel Pens, with three points, for writing music, special make, with L. & H. brand. Per dozen....................18c

Music Rolls, Bags and Folios.

No. 12R6001 This is made of beautiful imitation seal grain leather, has leather handle strap and buckle. Size, unrolled, 14½x15 inches. Price....................35c
If by mail, postage extra, 6 cents.

No. 12R6003 A very fine imitation seal grain leather roll; has leather handle, wide strap and fancy buckle. We furnish this roll in either orange or black. Our special price........50c
If by mail, postage extra, 6 cents.

No. 12R6005 Solid case leather, with strap and buckle, strap handle, neatly hand tooled and finished. Size, unrolled 14½x15 inches. Our special price....................70c
If by mail, postage extra, 6 cents.

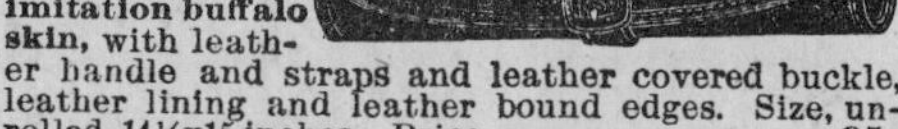

No. 12R6007 Perfect imitation of high grade alligator, cloth lined, leather bound, 1¼-inch strap, leather handle, Japan buckle. Size, unrolled, 14½x15 inches.
Our special price....................85c
If by mail, postage extra, 6 cents.

No. 12R6009 A very handsome leather roll in imitation buffalo skin, with leather handle and straps and leather covered buckle, leather lining and leather bound edges. Size, unrolled, 14½x15 inches. Price....................95c
If by mail, postage extra, 5 cents.

No. 12R6015 Seal grain leather, broad strap buckle; leather lined; leather bound edges. Size, unrolled, 15x15¼ inches. Our special price.....$1.10
If by mail, postage extra, 7 cents.

Music Bags.

No. 12R6023 Music Bag, made in fine imitation seal grain leather. Leather handles and strap, 15 inches long and 6½ inches high. Exactly like illustration.
Price..........75c
If by mail, postage extra, 7 cents.

No. 12R6025 Music Bag. Perfect imitation alligator, 15 inches wide, 12 inches high. Will hold full size sheet music without folding or rolling. Has strong strap handles, reaching entirely around the bag, which adds greatly to its strength and durability.
Price..$1.45

If by mail, postage extra, 12 cents.

REMEMBER our terms are CASH WITH ORDER. We guarantee satisfaction or refund your money.

Music Folios.

No. 12R6030 Music Folio, cloth back, black morocco paper sides, Music in gilt on side. Each....................57c

No. 12R6032 Music Folio, as illustrated, bound in full cloth back and sides, assorted colors, Music and flowers in gilt and black.
Each....................95c

No. 12R6034 Music Folio, bound in seal leather back and sides. Music in elaborate raised oxidized letters.
Each....................$1.89

No. 12R6030

Piano and Organ Stools.

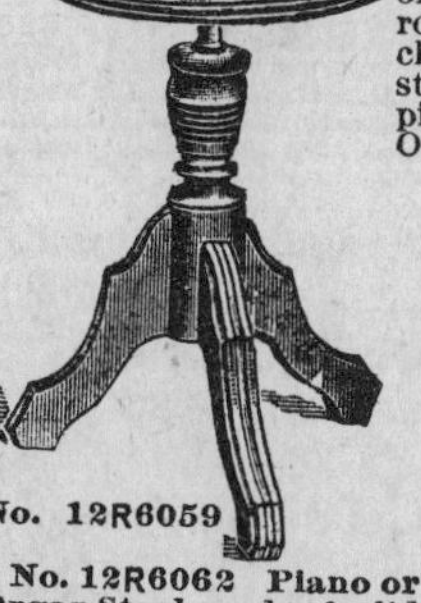
No. 12R6059

No. 12R6059 Piano or Organ Stool, made of solid oak or in ebony or walnut finish, round polished top, 13½ inches in diameter; three legs, strong and well made. Shipping weight, about 20 pounds.
Our special price, each..75c

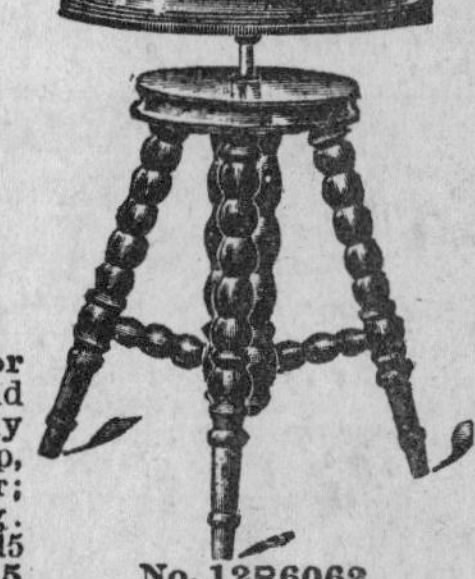
No. 12R6062

No. 12R6062 Piano or Organ Stool, made of solid oak, walnut or mahogany finish, round polished top, 13½ inches in diameter; three legs, very strong. Shipping weight, about 15 pounds. Price......$1.15

No. 12R6064

Our $1.75 Piano or Organ Stool.

No. 12R6064 Organ or Piano Stool, 13½x16 inches seat, covered with durable mohair plush, maroon or crimson, plain or embossed covering, dark rosewood finish legs' adjustable seat, Weight, 25 pounds. packed. Our special price....................$1.75

Special Value at $1.45.

No. 12R6068 Piano or Organ Stool, made of solid oak or in ebony, walnut, mahogany, rosewood, burl walnut or Circassian walnut finish, nicely polished round top, 13½ inches in diameter; three legs, with brass feet and glass balls; shipping weight about 25 pounds. Our price.$1.45

No. 12R6070 Same description as No. 12R6068, but with four legs.
Our special price, $1.70
Solid walnut...... 2.90

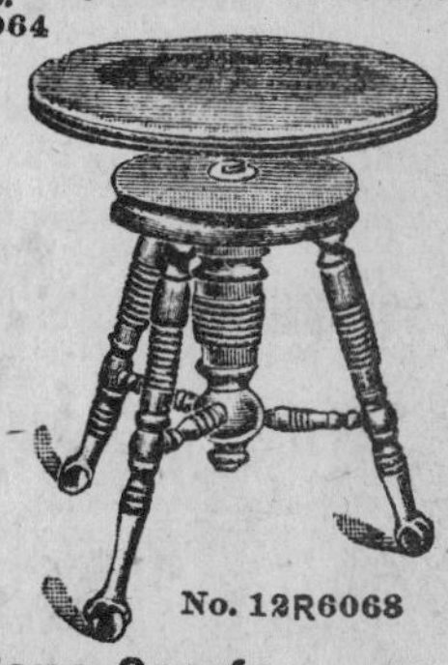
No. 12R6068

Upright Piano Scarfs.

No. 12R6081 Special Heavy Damask Scarf, in assorted colors and patterns, with extra heavy silk fringe, draped in two places. Shipping weight, about 20 ounces. Our special price....................$1.95

No. 12R6083 Fine Figured China Silk Scarf, in assorted colors and patterns with heavy all silk fringe draped in two places. Shipping weight, 5 ounces.
Our special price....................$2.15

No. 12R6085 Special Fine Silk Damask Scarf, in assorted colors and patterns, with heavy silk fringe, draped in two places. Shipping weight, about 15 ounces. Our special price....................$2.35

No. 12R6087 Fine Velours Scarf, in assorted colors and patterns, with extra heavy silk fringe, draped in two places. Shipping weight, 20 oz. Price......$2.65

No. 12R6089 Extra Fine Velours Scarf, in assorted colors and patterns, with extra heavy silk fringe, draped in two places. Shipping weight, about 20 ounces. Our special price....................$2.95

BOOK DEPARTMENT

WE PRESENT TO YOUR NOTICE THIS MOST COMPLETE BOOK DEPARTMENT, AND IF INTERESTED IN ANYTHING IN THIS LINE WE BELIEVE IT WILL PAY YOU TO CAREFULLY READ THE FOLLOWING PAGES.....

NOTE THE ILLUSTRATIONS AND DESCRIPTIONS AND PARTICULARLY THE PRICES.

WE FURNISH ONLY SUCH BOOKS AS ARE QUOTED ON THIS AND THE FOLLOWING PAGES.

OUR ONLY TERMS ARE CASH WITH THE ORDER.

WE GUARANTEE EVERYTHING IN THIS DEPARTMENT to be exactly as represented, to give entire satisfaction, **OR WE WILL IMMEDIATELY RETURN YOUR MONEY.**

ABOUT MAIL SHIPMENTS. WHEN BOOKS ARE TO BE SENT BY MAIL BE SURE TO ENCLOSE ENOUGH EXTRA TO PAY POSTAGE. If you send too much we will immediately return the balance, but if you do not send enough we will be compelled to hold your order and write for the balance. DO NOT OVERLOOK THE NECESSARY POSTAGE IN ORDERING BOOKS BY MAIL.

OUR CLUB ORDER SYSTEM COMMENDS ITSELF TO BOOK BUYERS, for you will observe in looking over this catalogue that we have been able to figure our prices so low on many of the books that we can quote them to you at but little more than the cost of postage. For example, **our Argyle Series**, beautiful cloth bound books at 14 cents each, postage, 11 cents per volume.

It is therefore much cheaper to have books shipped by express or freight, **freight being preferable.** The transportation cost per volume is then reduced to next to nothing. **To take advantage of the lowest transportation rate,** it is desirable to make up a freight order. This you can do by getting your friends and neighbors to join with you and make up a club order.

We always advise our readers to make their book orders large enough that we may ship by freight, but if one or more books are wanted by mail, the postage extra must be included.

AGRICULTURAL WORKS.

AT A SAVING OF 50 PER CENT.

Under this heading we list Books on Butter, Cheese Making and the Dairy, Etc.

The Amateur's Practical Garden Book.

Contains the simplest directions for the growing of the commonest things about the house and garden. By C. E. Hunn. 250 pages; illustrated.
No. 3R150 Our price..........................70c
If by mail, postage extra, 12 cents.

American Gardener's Assistant.

By Thos. Bridgeman. Contains practical directions for the cultivation of vegetables, flowers, fruit trees and grape vines. Illustrated. Size, 5½x7½ inches. Cloth.
No. 3R152 Our price..........................80c
If by mail, postage extra, 12 cents.

Book of The Farm;
Or the Handbook of Husbandry.

Contains practical information in regard to buying or leasing a farm, fences and farm buildings, farming implements, drainage, plowing, rotation of crops. Illustrated. Size, 5⅛x7⅛ inches. Cloth.
No. 3R156 Our price..........................75c
If by mail, postage extra, 15 cents.

Butter and Butter Making.

By Willis P. Hazard. How to color butter, milking and care of milk, skimming, churning, etc. Illustrated. Paper cover.
No. 3R158 Our price..........................20c
If by mail, postage extra, 3 cents.

Canning and Preserving.

By Mrs. S. T. Rorer. How to can and preserve fruits and vegetables; and, also, the best method of making marmalades, fruit butter and jellies, catsups, pickling. Oil cloth. Size, 5¼x7½ inches.
No. 3R166 Our price..........................50c
If by mail, postage extra, 6 cents.

Cheese Making.

By J. H. Monrad. A short manual for farm cheese makers in cheddar, goudar, Danish export (skim cheese), French cream cheese, sour milk cheese, etc. Paper.
No. 3R172 Our price..........................38c
If by mail, postage extra, 3 cents.

Flower Gardening.

By Thomas Bridgeman. A valuable book for amateur or inexperienced gardeners. 166 pages. Illustrated. Size, 5¼x7½ inches. Cloth.
No. 3R178 Our price..........................58c
If by mail, postage extra, 8 cents.

Gardening for Profit.

By Peter Henderson. The only standard and authentic work of the kind published. Illustrated. Cloth. Size, 5½x7½ inches.
No. 3R182 Our price..........................$1.18
If by mail, postage extra, 14 cents.

Irrigation and Drainage.

By F. H. King. This book deals in a most clear and helpful way with immediately practical problems from the farmer's, fruit grower's and gardener's standpoint. Cloth.
No. 3R188 Our price..........................$1.12
If by mail, postage extra, 14 cents.

Kitchen Gardening.

By Thomas Bridgeman. Contains instructions for the planting and care of all kinds of vegetables. Illustrated. Size, 5¼x7½ inches. Cloth.
No. 3R194 Our price..........................42c
If by mail, postage extra, 8 cents.

Pasteurization and Milk Preservation.

By J. H. Monrad. With a complete chapter on selling milk. 70 illustrations; paper covers. Size, 5½x7½ inches. **If by mail, postage extra, 3 cents.**
No. 3R202 Our price..........................38c

Potato Culture.

By C.C. Carpenter. This book has only been completed after years of experience. Mr. Carpenter has made a specialty of potato culture. He has carefully considered the suggestions of many seed growers, and is thoroughly convinced that there is a great lack of practical information among the average farmers upon this subject. Paper.
No. 3R206 Price..........................15c
If by mail, postage extra, 2 cents.

ARCHITECTURE.

American Architecture; or, Every Man a Complete Builder.

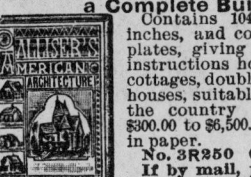

Contains 104 pages; size, 11x14 inches, and consists of large 9x12 plates, giving detailed plans and instructions how to build seventy cottages, double houses, brick block houses, suitable for all sections of the country and costing from $300.00 to $6,500.00 each, etc. Bound in paper.
No. 3R250 Our price..........65c
If by mail, postage extra, 11 cents.

Barn Plans and Out Buildings.

250 illustrations. Bound in cloth. Size, 5½x7½ inches. Contains ideas, hints, suggestions, plans, etc., for the construction of barns and out buildings, by practical writers. A few chapters are devoted to the economic erection and use of grain houses, cattle and sheep barns, corn, smoke and ice houses, pig pens, granaries, etc.
No. 3R256 Our price..........................80c
If by mail, postage extra, 12 cents.

Complete Housebuilder, with Hints on Building.

Contains 50 plans and specifications of dwellings, barns, churches, public buildings, etc. Adapted to all conditions of town and country, with accurate estimates of material and cost. Where to and how to build, and thousands of other subjects pertaining to material, help, etc. Bound in paper.
No. 3R264 Price..................17c
If by mail, postage extra, 2 cents.

Ideal Homes.

Latest and best book of its kind published. Complete in two volumes, illustrating 91 new houses, summer cottages, churches, barns and lumber sheds, etc., ranging in price from $550.00 to $6,500.00 each, giving all the comforts and convenience, and suited to every taste, location, want, etc. If you contemplate building or altering and adding to your present home, you ought to have a copy of this book. The illustrations are printed from the best halftone cuts on enameled paper. Size, 7½x10½ inches.
No. 3R270 Our price, for two volumes, complete..........................75c
If by mail, postage extra, 12 cents.

Gould's Carpenters' and Builders' Assistant and Woodworkers' Guide.

An invaluable book. Fourth revised edition, containing 36 plates, fully described; also, tables of the strength of materials, length of brace where the run is given, and length of run where the brace is given. Technical terms used by carpenters, etc. By L. D. Gould. Bound in cloth.
No. 3R276 Our price........$1.75
If by mail, postage extra, 15 cents.

Palliser's New Cottage Homes.

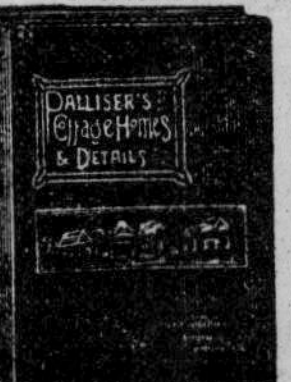

Containing 160 new and original designs for cottages costing from $75.00 to $7,500.00 each, giving all the comforts and conveniences, and suited to every taste, location, want, etc. Fifty new designs for city brick block houses; 12 new designs for stable and carriage houses: 1,500 detailed drawings, covering the whole range of interior finish and exterior construction and ornamentation of plans; fences, summer houses, pavilions, conservatories, out buildings, etc. Bound in cloth, leather back. Size, 11x14 inches. Retail price, $4.00.
No. 3R300 Our price..........................$2.75
If by mail, postage extra, 28 cents.

Palliser's Useful Details.

Palliser's Useful Details. These details are, without exception, the best and cheapest lot of working drawings that have ever been offered to the workman. The whole series of 40 plates contain something like 1,100 separate designs. Bound in paper; portfolio style, 14x22 inches.
No. 3R302 Our price..........................$1.40
If by mail, postage extra, 16 cents.

Practical Carpentry.

Guide to the correct working and laying out of all kinds of carpenters' and joiners' work; with the solutions of the various problems in hip roofs, gothic work, centering, splayed work, joints and joining, hinging, dovetailing, mitering, timber splicing, hopper works, skylights, raising mouldings, circular work, etc. Illustrated, over 300 engravings. Bound in cloth, gilt.
No. 3R306 Our price..............73c
If by mail, postage extra, 12 cents.

Reed's House Plans for Everybody.

It gives an estimate on the quantity of every article used in the construction and the cost of each article at the time the building was erected or the design made. Illustrated, handsomely bound in cloth, black and gold. Size, 5½x7½ inches.
No. 3R316 Our price..........................79c
If by mail, postage extra, 13 cents.

Stair Building Made Easy.

Simple, plain, and may be learned in an hour. A full and clear description of the art of building the bodies, carriages and cases for all kinds of stairs and steps, together with illustrations showing the manner of laying out stairs, forming treads and risers, building cylinders, preparing strings; with instructions for making carriages for common platform, dog-legged and winding stairs. Bound in cloth, gilt.
No. 3R320 Our price..........................70c
If by mail, postage extra, 10 cents.

The Steel Square and Its Uses.

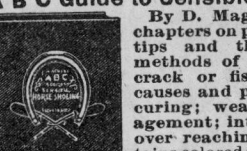

By Fred T. Hodgson. Part First. This is the only work on the steel square and its uses published. It is thorough, clear and exhaustive, and easily understood. Illustrated with 75 wood cuts. Bound in cloth. Size, 5½x7 inches.
No. 3R324 Cloth. Our price....70c
If by mail, postage extra, 10 cents.

The Steel Square and Its Uses.

By Fred T. Hodgson. Part Second. A companion volume to part first. With the two books any carpenter can solve every problem. Retail price, $1.00. **If by mail, postage extra, 10 cents.**
No. 3R328 Our price..........................70c

BOOKS ON BLACKSMITHING.

A B C Guide to Sensible Horseshoeing.

By D. Magner. Containing chapters on principles of shoeing, tips and thin shoes, simple methods of curing any case of crack or fissure of toe; corns, causes and practical methods of curing; weak heels, their management; interfering, clicking or over reaching, stumbling. Contains colored plates and other illustrations. Size, 5½x7½ inches. Cloth.
No. 3R390 Our price........65c
If by mail, postage extra, 10c.

Modern Blacksmithing.

Contains elementary rules for practical horseshoeing and wagon making, with rules, tables and receipts, useful to manufacturers, machinists, well drillers, engineers, liverymen, blacksmiths, wagonmakers, horseshoers, farmers, etc. By J. G. Holmstrom. This valuable work is written by a man of thirty years' practical experience; all subjects carefully and correctly explained, strictly devoid of technical terms. Size, 5½x7½ inches.
No. 3R394 Cloth. Illustrated. Our price.....68c
No. 3R396 Half morocco. Illustrated. Price, 98c
If by mail, postage extra, 12 cents.

GUNS.

Gunsmith's Manual.

Describes all forms of guns and pistols, tells how to fit up a shop, something about gun cleaning, general gunsmithing, the style tools required and how to make them, the work bench, etc. Fully illustrated. Contains 400 pages. Bound in cloth.
No. 3R616 Price..............................$1.38
If by mail, postage extra, 14 cents.

HOROLOGY.

We quote only the latest, best and most complete books on watchmaking, watch repairing, etc., published.

American Watchmaker and Jeweler.

By Henry G. Abbott. An encyclopedia for the horologist, jeweler, gold and silversmith. Contains hundreds of private recipes and formulas compiled from the best and most reliable sources. Complete directions for using all the latest tools, attachments and devices for watchmakers and jewelers. 367 pages. Illustrated with 288 engravings.
No. 3R634 Bound in cloth. Price, 98c
If by mail, postage extra, 12 cents.

Watch Repairing.

By N. B. Sherwood. Contains descriptions of the bench and its accessories, the vise and oilstone, lathe appliances, the depthing tool, expanding the web of a wheel, the spreading tool and its use, opening the regulator, roller remover, replacing broken teeth, polishing pivots, hard tempering, etc.
No. 3R640 Illustrated. Our price..............26c
If by mail, postage extra, 3 cents.

BOOKS ON HYPNOTISM, PALMISTRY, PHYSIOGNOMY, ASTROLOGY.

Complete Palmist.

By Niblo. A practical guide to the study of chirognomy and chiromancy. Adapted from the works of the world's most renowned palmists. **Your past history and future destiny are written upon the palm of your hand.** Bound in cloth; illustrated. Retail price, $2.00.
No. 3R654 Our price.....95c
If by mail, postage extra, 18 cents.

Descriptive Mentality.

A New Book on Physiognomy, Phrenology and Palmistry. Illustrated with over 600 original drawings by Prof. Holmes W. Merton. The most accurate, comprehensive and clearest book on the subjects ever published. One by comparing his own hands with the drawings and illustrations in this volume can read his own nature and destiny as portrayed by those signs, lines and meanings that are present in their hands. Retail price, $1.50.
No. 3R658 Our special price. 95c
If by mail, postage extra, 14 cents.

Faciology.

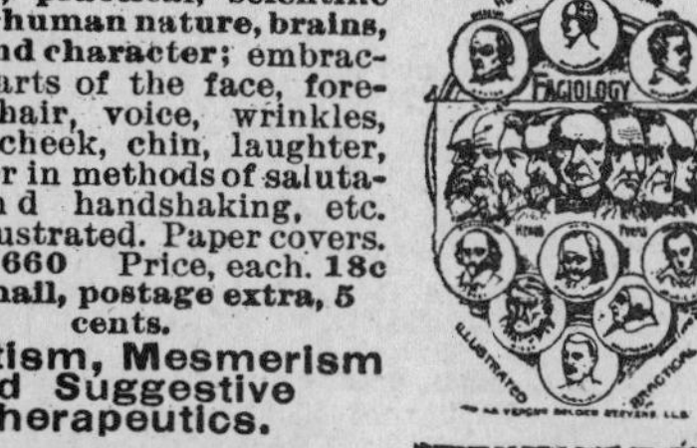

A new, practical, scientific work on human nature, brains, forms and character; embracing all parts of the face, forehead, hair, voice, wrinkles, mouth, cheek, chin, laughter, character in methods of salutation and handshaking, etc. Fully illustrated. Paper covers.
No. 3R660 Price, each. 18c
If by mail, postage extra, 5 cents.

Hypnotism, Mesmerism and Suggestive Therapeutics.

A complete system of method, application and use; everything that is known in the art and practice of Mesmerism and Mental Healing. Prepared for the self instruction of beginners as well as for the use of advanced students and practitioners. Every subject fully and systematically explained by Prof. L. W. DeLaurence, the World's famous Hypnotist and Magnetic Healer. Illustrated with pictures taken from life. Nothing problematical is given; but facts gained from personal experience of many years by the author in the successful practice of Hypnotism, Mesmerism, Suggestive Therapeutics and Magnetic Healing. Bound in cloth, decorated cover, illustrated.
No. 3R670 Our price..............................67c
If by mail, postage extra, 12 cents.
No. 3R672 Bound in paper, decorated cover, illustrated. Our price..............................30c
If by mail, postage extra, 3 cents.

Medical Hypnosis.

Medical Hypnosis. Physician's edition; new and enlarged. **By L. W. DeLaurence.** Especially prepared for medical students and practitioners. Eighteen full page illustrations, taken from life.
No. 3R674 Price, each..............................$1.15
If by mail, postage extra, 14 cents.

Practical Chirosophy; or Science of the Hand.

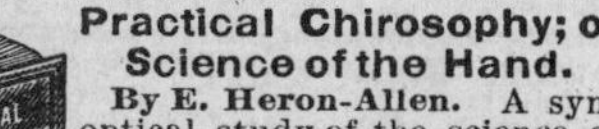

By E. Heron-Allen. A synoptical study of the science of the hand. Illustrated. Bound in cloth. Retail price, 75 cents.
No. 3R678 Our price.....49c
If by mail, postage extra, 6 cents.

Treatise on Phrenology.

By Prof. Wm. Windsor, LL.D., Ph. D. All subjects appertaining to the head are fully explained. Also the following subjects: Approbativeness, Firmness, Conscientiousness, Hope, Faith, Veneration, Benevolence, Imitation, Individuality, Eventuality, Constructiveness, Matrimony, the trades to which one is adapted, and thousands of other subjects.
No. 3R686 Bound in paper. Price..............20c
If by mail, postage extra, 5 cents.

Twentieth Century Guide to Palmistry.

By Zanzigs. All discoveries, investigation and researches of centuries summed up in this practical book. There is no trait, no characteristic, no inherited tendency that is not marked on the palm of the hand and can be traced with unerring accuracy by following the principles and instructions laid down in this book. Illustrated with 86 fine engravings.
No. 3R690 Bound in paper. Our price 17c
If by mail, postage extra, 3 cents.
No. 3R692 Bound in cloth. Our price........65c
If by mail, postage extra, 10 cents.

Were You Born Under a Lucky Star?

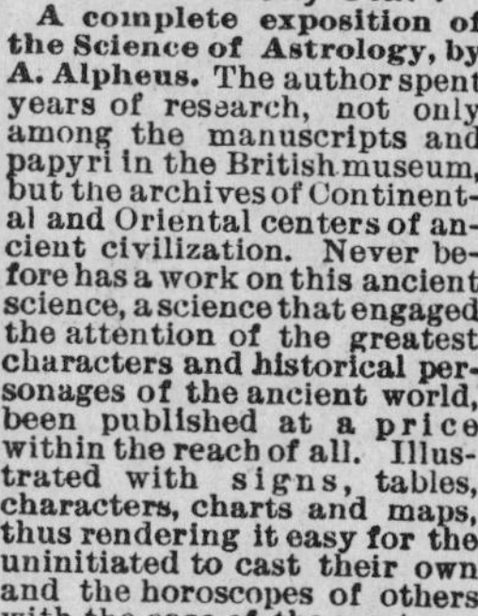

A complete exposition of the Science of Astrology, by A. Alpheus. The author spent years of research, not only among the manuscripts and papyri in the British museum, but the archives of Continental and Oriental centers of ancient civilization. Never before has a work on this ancient science, a science that engaged the attention of the greatest characters and historical personages of the ancient world, been published at a price within the reach of all. Illustrated with signs, tables, characters, charts and maps, thus rendering it easy for the uninitiated to cast their own and the horoscopes of others with the ease of the most experienced. Bound in cloth.
No. 3R694 Our price..............................75c
If by mail, postage extra, 11 cents.

LIQUORS.

Including Books on the Art of Compounding Liquors, Wines, Mixing Cocktails, Fancy Drinks, Etc.

Art of Blending and Compounding Liquors and Wines.

By Joseph Fleischman. Showing how all the leading and favorite brands of whiskies, brandies and other liquors and wines are prepared for the trade by rectifiers, etc., at the present time, with complete and correct recipes for making all the ingredients, flavorings, etc. Cloth. Size, 5½x7½ inches.
No. 3R710 Our price..............................$1.40
If by mail, postage extra, 12 cents.

Complete Buffet Manual, or How to Mix Fancy Drinks.

The need of an up to date book treating on this subject has been a long felt want. We earnestly believe that this want is now supplied with this book, and we trust the reader, if he becomes the practitioner, will enjoy the beverages after following the directions, as much as the author did in preparing this handy little volume.
No. 3R714 Paper covers. Our price.........17c
If by mail, postage extra, 3 cents.
No. 3R716 Cloth. Our price..................35c
If by mail, postage extra, 6 cents.

GIVE CATALOGUE NUMBER IN FULL WHEN YOU WRITE YOUR ORDER

BOOKS ON MAGIC, PUZZLES, PARLOR AMUSEMENTS.

Including Sleight of Hand, Conjuring, Shadow Entertainments, Ventriloquism, etc.

Card Tricks and Sleight of Hand.

By Prof. R. Kunard. Every card trick known is fully exposed by explicit directions and carefully prepared illustrations, among which are the following: The animated card, dealing five from the bottom, causing a chosen card to appear at any given number in the pack; method of dealing one's self all the trumps in Whist; how to palm a card, producing a particular card from the pack without seeing it; vanishing a card from the pack and finding it elsewhere, and thousands of other subjects too numerous to mention.
No. 3R740 Bound in paper. Our price........17c
No. 3R742 Bound in cloth. Our price........35c
If by mail, postage extra, paper, 3c; cloth, 5c.

Herrmann's Conjuring for Amateurs.

A practical treatise on the art of performing modern tricks, by Prof. Herrmann. Great care has been exercised by the author to include only such tricks as have never before appeared in print. Coins, cards, silk hat, handkerchiefs, balls, are introduced in the many programmes offered, thus affording an endless variety from which to select for parlor or stage entertainments.
No. 3R750 Bound in paper. Our price........17c
If by mail, postage extra, 14 cents.
No. 3R752 Bound in cloth. Our price ... .35c
If by mail, postage, extra, 5 cents.

Keller's Variety Entertainments.

By Prof. Keller. A collection of original laughable skits on conjuring. Physiognomy, juggling, performing feats, wax workings, panoramas, phrenology, phonography, second sight, lightning calculator, ventriloquism and spiritualism, etc.
No. 3R756 Bound in paper. Our price...........17c
If by mail, postage extra, 4c
No. 3R758 Bound in cloth. Our price 35c
If by mail, postage extra, 5c

Magical Experiments.

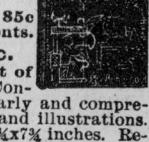

By Arthur Good. Contains 200 amusing, popular, scientific experiments for the recreation of old and young. Illustrated. Bound in cloth. Size, 8¼x6 inches. Retail price, $2.50.
No. 3R760 Our price..............85c
If by mail, postage extra, 16 cents.

Modern Magic.

A practical treatise on the art of conjuring. By Prof. Hoffmann. Contains 318 illustrations. Tricks clearly and comprehensively explained by diagrams and illustrations. 563 pages. Bound in cloth. Size, 5¾x7¾ inches. Retail price, $2.00. **If by mail, postage extra, 14 cents.**
No. 3R764 Our price..............................98c

More Magic.

By Prof. Hoffmann. A companion volume to Modern Magic, but more advanced. Exposes all sleight of hand tricks; including cards, handkerchief, hat, egg, stage and miscellaneous tricks. Bound in cloth. Size, 5½x7½ inches. Retail price, $2.00.
No. 3R766 Our price..............................98c
If by mail, postage extra, 14 cents.

Practical Ventriloquism.

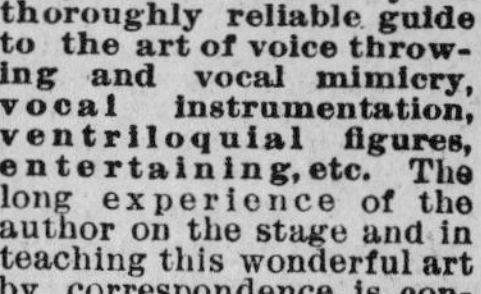

By Robert Ganthony. A thoroughly reliable guide to the art of voice throwing and vocal mimicry, vocal instrumentation, ventriloquial figures, entertaining, etc. The long experience of the author on the stage and in teaching this wonderful art by correspondence is conclusive evidence that by a little application to the fundamental principles laid down in this book and by constant practice after acquiring the two or three simple rules, you can become an adept in the art. Fully illustrated.
No. 3R774 Paper. Our price..........................18c
If by mail, postage extra, 1 cent.
No. 3R776 Cloth. Our price..........................35c
If by mail, postage extra, 5 cents.

Macaulay's Essays and Poems.

These books comprise all his most prominent works, including Critical Works, Historical and Miscellaneous Essays and Poems. **New revised edition.** These volumes are extra large, averaging about **800 pages to the volume. Bound in cloth,** stamped in gold, and have gilt tops. The size of each volume is 5½x7½ inches.

No. 3R2130 Our price, per set..................**78c**
If by mail, postage extra, per set, 35 cents.

Life of Dwight Lyman Moody.

The greatest evangelist of the 19th century. Contains a history of his youth, his first mission work, his labors in Great Britain, New York, Chicago, etc. Also fourteen illustrations. Size, 5½x7½ inches.

No. 3R2134 Bound in cloth. Our price.......**38c**
If by mail, postage extra, 12 cents.

Memorial Edition of Ingersollia.

Gems of thought from the lectures, speeches and conversations of the late Col. Robert G. Ingersoll, including his speech nominating James G. Blaine, Dream of the War, Gods and Devils, His Last Poem, Oration at His Brother's Grave, Heaven and Hell, etc., together with biographical sketch and record of his death. Contains 352 pages, printed from clear type, bound in cloth, stamped in silver.

No. 3R2138 Our special price..................**75c**
If by mail, postage extra, 10 cents.
No. 3R2140 Bound in paper. Our price.......**18c**
If by mail, postage extra, 2 cents.

COOK BOOKS AND WORKS ON ETIQUETTE.

American Pure Food Cook Book and Household Economist.

A $3.00 Up to Date Cook Book for 85 cents. This work treats in an authentic manner on everything pertaining to the kitchen, what to eat and how to select and cook it; also a chapter on the health, treating on such subjects as the sick room, home sanitation, food for the sick, care of children, advice to mothers, household remedies, etc.

Part I of this work contains especially tested recipes, including soups, fish, poultry and game, beef, veal, lamb and mutton, sweetbreads and sauces, eggs and omelets, salads and salad dressings, vegetables, potatoes, entrees, bread and thousands of other dishes, etc.

Part II contains 20 special chapters on home economics, food for the sick, care of children, health, suggestions and household remedies, the bath, proper clothing, toilet articles and recipes, etc. **Illustrated.**

No. 3R2190 Our price..........................**85c**
If by mail, postage extra, 26 cents.

Chafing Dish Recipes.

By Mrs. Olive A. Cotton. The only complete work on this subject published. Embraces the history of the chafing dish; practical suggestions; soups, sauces, oysters and clams, crustaceans, fish, meats, chicken and turkey, birds and game, eggs, cheese, vegetables, mushrooms, miscellaneous menus—**190 distinct recipes.** Attractively bound in cloth.

No. 3R2194 Our price.........................**48c**
If by mail, postage extra, 7 cents.

Encyclopedia of Etiquette.

A book of manners for everyday use. What to do, what to say, what to write, what to wear. The most complete, authentic, and best book on the subject published. Embraces introductions, calls, dinners, table manners, balls, weddings, theater and opera parties, correspondence, garden parties, etc. Beautifully illustrated with halftone engravings.

No. 3R2196 Bound in cloth. Our price......**$1.45**
If by mail, postage extra, 18 cents.

Etiquette.

By Agnes H. Morton, B. O. Most manuals are obviously inadequate to the needs of the great mass "who dwell within the broad zone of the average." For this large class **a book that gives information as to the essential points of correct behavior** in social life—points equally applicable to the rich and to the poor—is the ideal manual. And such a book is this volume.

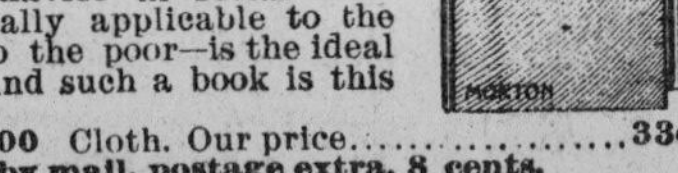

No. 3R2200 Cloth. Our price...................**33c**
If by mail, postage extra, 8 cents.

Everyday Cook Book.

5,000 to be closed out at 25c each. Cyclopedia of Practical Recipes. By Miss E. Neill. Economical, reliable, excellent. 315 pages. Bound in oilcloth. Size, 5½x7½ inches.

No. 3R2206 Our special price...**25c**
If by mail, postage extra, 12 cents.

Up to date Cookery with Directions for Carving and Table Etiquette. Contains many useful practical recipes not found in any other book. Bound in heavy paper covers.

No. 3R2208 Our price..............................**14c**
If by mail, postage extra, 6 cents.

Housekeepers'-Handy Book of Universal Information and Encyclopedia of Practical Recipes.

A BOOK FOR EVERY DAY, WEEK AND MONTH IN THE YEAR.

The most complete, authentic, reliable and best recipe book published. The only complete ready reference book which is specially adapted to the home. It embraces every known subject of value pertaining to housekeeping, such as cooking, what to eat and how to prepare it, care of the health, teeth and complexion, how to remove freckles, sunburn, etc. Contains a valuable collection of practical recipes for farmers, dairymen, dyers, druggists, tanners and family generally, also chapters on christian names and their meanings, language of flowers, postage rates and thousands of other subjects too numerous to mention.

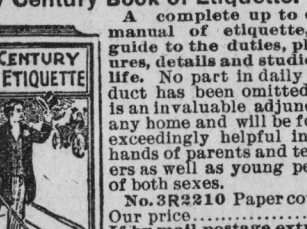

No. 3R2209 Paper covers. Price............**25c**
If by mail, postage extra, 4 cents.
No. 3R2209½ Cloth. Price....................**48c**
If by mail, postage extra, 12 cents.

New Century Book of Etiquette.

A complete up to date manual of etiquette, or guide to the duties, pleasures, details and studies of life. No part in daily conduct has been omitted. It is an invaluable adjunct to any home and will be found exceedingly helpful in the hands of parents and teachers as well as young people of both sexes.

No. 3R2210 Paper covers. Our price..............**18c**
If by mail, postage extra, 2c
No. 3R2212 Cloth. Our price..........**35c**
If by mail, postage extra, 5c

Ladies' and Gentlemen's Etiquette.

A complete manual of the manners and dress of American society. Containing forms of letters, invitations, acceptances and regrets. By E. B. Duffey. Artistically bound in cloth. Size, 5½x7½ inches.

No. 3R2218 Our price.......**42c**
If by mail, postage extra, 12 cents.

A Manual of Etiquette.

35c for a 75c Book. With Hints on Politeness and Good Breeding. By Daisy Eyebright. An admirable little book containing **sensible talks about etiquette for home, visiting, traveling,** dinner parties, evening entertainments; social intercourse, dress, letter writing, etc. Bound in cloth. **Size, 5¼x7 inches.**

No. 3R2222 Our price..............................**35c**
If by mail, postage extra, 10 cents.

Twentieth Century Cook Book and Practical Housekeeping.

$3.00 Book for 85 cents.

In this, the latest Cook Book, we have the fruit of centuries of investigation and improvements in all lines of housekeeping. It is the latest and best book on the subject yet published. Everything contained in it is practical, and out of the three or four thousands recipes, the greater majority will be found serviceable in any of the American homes. It contains 816 large octavo pages, elegantly printed and fully illustrated. Bound in white oil cloth, with marble edges and embossed with handsome designs. **If by mail, postage extra, 30 cents.**

No. 3R2230 Price.........................**85c**

The Original White House Cook Book.

Only 65 Cents.

Authentic and unabridged edition by Hugo Ziemann and Mrs. F. L. Gillette. The art of cooking in its latest perfection. By special arrangements with the publishers we are able to offer this household compendium at less than actual cost to produce; **contains over 600 household recipes, nothing relating to practical housekeeping is omitted.** Embraces cooking, toilet and household recipes, menus, dinner giving, table etiquette, care of the sick, health suggestions, facts worth knowing, and thousands of other subjects too numerous to mention. **This book has been prepared with great care.** Every recipe has been tried and tested, and can be relied upon as one of the best of its kind. It is comprehensive, filling completely the requirements of housekeepers of all classes. It is pre-eminently **the book for the housekeeper;** it is the standard of excellence. Handsomely bound, enameled cloth, illustrated.

No. 3R2238 Our special price................**65c**
If by mail, postage extra, 28 cents.

Woman Beautiful; Or the Art of Beauty Culture.

By Mme. Qui Vive.

Contains articles on the complexion, care of the hair, the hands, eyes, teeth, thin and plump girls. How to remove tan, sunburn and freckles, facial eruptions and blackheads, etc.

No. 3R2242 Bound in paper. Price...............................**18c**
If by mail, postage extra, 4 cents.
No. 3R2250 Bound in cloth. Price..........................**55c**
If by mail, postage extra, 12 cents.

WORKS OF FICTION.

In ordering be sure to allow the extra additional money if the books are to go by mail.

BEST FICTION OF THE DAY.

New popular copyright books at from 30 to 50 per cent less than retail prices.

Boy, A Sketch.

By Marie Corelli. In Boy, Miss Corelli is at her best. The story is told with charming simplicity of style. Bound in cloth.

No. 3R2300 Our price..............................**$1.08**
If by mail, postage extra, 11 cents.

David Harum.

By Edward Noyes Westcott. A story of American life. True, strong and thoroughly alive with humor. The spirit of the book is congenial and wholesome, and the love story is in keeping with it. Bound in cloth.

No. 3R2304 Our price..........................**$1.07**
If by mail, postage extra, 12 cents.

The Funny Side of Politics.

By George S. Hilton. A book original and new. It gives many amusing stories told in the House and Senate in Washington. It is replete with anecdotes of many living politicians. Bound in cloth.

No. 3R2308 Our price..................................**80c**
If by mail, postage extra, 12 cents.

Gal's Gossip.

For Men Only. By Arthur M. Binstead. A series of letters from Maude to her Cousin Madge. New and original. Nothing like them has ever before appeared. They are the richest and best collection of letters published. Cloth bound.

No. 3R2310 Our price..................................**55c**
If by mail, postage extra, 7 cents.

Gentleman from Indiana.

By Booth Tarkington. A love story and study of life in the Middle West. Illustrated. Cloth.

No. 3R2312 Our price.... ....**$1.05**
If by mail, postage extra, 12 cents.

Janice Meredith.

By Paul Leicester Ford. Not to have read this great novel of the Revolution is to have missed a great historical romance. The story grips the attention from the first and holds it steadily by the triple force of its love story, its mystery element and its spicy charm of style. Cloth.

No. 3R2314 Price.........**$1.03**
If by mail, postage extra, 12 cents.

John Henry.

Something new. A regular side splitter, and as good as Billy Baxter. It contains John Henry at the Theater, in Street Car, on Literature, Playing Pool, Progressive Euchre, Would-Be Actor, etc. Illustrated. Bound in cloth.

No. 3R2316 Our price..................................**48c**
If by mail, postage extra, 8 cents.

King of Honey Island.

By Maurice Thompson, author of "Alice of Old Vincennes." The events take place when the War of 1812 was at high tide. The scene is made on the Gulf coast near New Orleans. The story throughout is complete with dramatic adventure.

No. 3R2317 Bound in cloth. Our price.....**$1.10**
If by mail, postage extra, 12 cents.

The Maid of Maiden Lane.

By Amelia E. Barr. A story of love in Old New York, or "New Amsterdam," as it was then called. The quaint experiences and love affairs of this antirevolutionary maiden are told with all the charm of this gifted authoress. Cloth.

No. 3R2318 Our price..................................**$1.05**
If by mail, postage extra, 12 cents.

Dr. Hood's Plain Talks About Nature, Sexual Physiology, Natural Relations of the Sexes, Civilization, Love and Marriage.

You cannot get along without a copy. Worth its weight in gold. A common sense medical adviser. No man or woman who anticipates a bright future and wishes to enjoy married life in its fullest sense can afford to be without a copy of this valuable work. It is the largest, latest, most complete and authentic and best medical guide ever published. **Here are answered in plain language a thousand questions that occur in the minds of both young and old,** but about which they feel a delicacy in consulting their physician. Many chapters are devoted to sexual immorality and numerous interesting subjects concerning marriage and the sexual relations, which make it a superior guide to the actions of men and women both in and out of marriage. Contains an **exhaustive treatment** of all sexual considerations, distinctive traits of the sexes, developments of the sexual organs, also the following:

Influence on Civilization—The beginning of civilization, influence of the sexual organs thereon; early polygamy induced compulsory monogamy; encouragement of prostitution by the ancients; as it is in Japan; the concealed wormwood that embitters social life.

Sexual Isolation—Male and female elements in all nature; the universal attraction between the two; the sexual characteristics of different persons explained; effects of sexual isolation upon females in factories; upon old maids; the temptations of young men, etc.

Prostitution—Its moral and physical effects; how disease is generated; is prostitution necessary; the cause of prostitution; how girls are seduced; where reform should commence.

Prevention of Conception—A valuable lesson for those who would enjoy higher and better love.

Unhappy Marriages—Destroys the tone of the nervous system; effects on offspring.

Duties of Married Life—What is perfect happiness? Why are so many marriages a failure?

Diseases of Women—How caused; unwillingness of women to become mothers; diseases of the organs of generation, etc.

Pregnancy—Rules of conduct during pregnancy; diseases of pregnancy; cause, treatment and cure; preventions of pregnancy, etc.

It covers thousands of other subjects among which are valuable suggestions to those contemplating marrying, factors to be considered in entering the marriage relations; physical basis of marriage; the time to marry; the wedding tour, etc.; jealousy, sexual indifference; subject of prevention; food for pregnant women; philosophy of childbirth; barrenness and excessive child bearing. **Adorned with hundreds of illustrations reproducing the vital organs,** anatomy of men and women, blood disorders, ear, eye and throat diseases, etc. **This work is supplemented by a 32-page pamphlet, placed in a pocket inside the back cover of the book.** This pamphlet contains twenty-nine special plates, illustrating the female productive organs, each plate being fully described. It also contains many chapters devoted to prescriptions for common ailments and emergencies, table of poison antidotes; full and accurate directions for treating wounds, injuries; rules of health, hygiene, etc. **Bound in art cloth, printed in two colored inks, marble edge.**

No. 3R3530 Subscription price, $5.00; our special price **(If by mail, postage extra, 38 cents.) $1.25**

Koradine.

By Alice B. Stockham. Although a charming story, by gradual sequence develops a philosophy of life, teaching that bodily health is possible to all, that physical ailments may be prevented and relieved; at the same time it gives the art of true living and the power to meet every difficulty. It is one of the rarest books in the literature of today. All parents should read it; all teachers should read it; all young folks and children should read it. Cloth.

No. 3R3532 Price....**(Postage extra, 13c)....70c**

A Manual of Nursing.

By Victoria White, M. D. Recently revised by Dr. M. P. Jacobi. **This is one of the most complete and authentic works of the kind ever published. Attractively bound in boards, cloth back.**

No. 3R3534 Our price............................**70c**

If by mail, postage extra, 10 cents.

The Ladies' New Medical Guide.

New edition. By Dr. S. Pancoast. An instructor, counselor and friend in all delicate and wonderful matters peculiar to women. Fully explaining the nature and mystery of the reproductive organs in both sexes; **love, courtship, marriage, pregnancy, labor and childbirth, with the causes, treatment and symptoms of all their own special diseases and diseases of children.** Illustrated. Bound in one large volume. Cloth. Size, 5¾x8 inches. **If by mail, postage extra, 20 cents.**

No. 3R3538 Our price............................**89c**

Physical Life of Woman.

Advice to the maiden, wife, and mother. A new edition revised to the latest date, with a life of the author. This is the only work on the delicate topic **of woman recommended for popular reading by the most distinguished physicians,** eminent divines, prominent educators, leading medical journals, and the press generally. Size, 5½x7¾ inches. Cloth.

No. 3R3540 Our price.....**85c**

If by mail, postage extra, 12 cents.

A True Guide to Marriage.

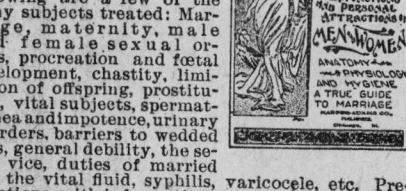

A book for adults, married or single, and parents. This book takes the ground that children have a right to be well born. It is a standard treatise on sexual physiology and is just such a book as is needed for self-instruction. Written in language that can be readily understood. The following are a few of the many subjects treated: Marriage, maternity, male and female sexual organs, procreation and fœtal development, chastity, limitation of offspring, prostitution, vital subjects, spermatorrhea and impotence, urinary disorders, barriers to wedded bliss, general debility, the secret vice, duties of married life, the vital fluid, syphilis, varicocele, etc. Prescriptions, with information as to the curing of all urinary diseases and disorders enumerated above, are given in plain language, easily understood by any druggist. Fully illustrated.

No. 3R3545 Bound in paper. Price............**35c**

If by mail, postage extra, 5 cents.

No. 3R3547 Bound in cloth. Price............**55c**

If by mail, postage extra, 12 cents.

Transmission of Life.

Counsels on the nature and hygiene of the masculine functions. New edition revised and enlarged. Cloth, gilt back and sides. Size, 5½x7¾ inches.

No. 3R3554 Our price.....................**85c**

If by mail, postage extra, 12 cents.

True Manhood.

The secret of power. A manual of science and guide to health, strength and purity. **By E. R. Sheppherd.** Reveals physiological facts and uncovers truth with a chaste and gentle hand. This work is devoted to the presentation of facts which are eagerly sought by all boys verging upon manhood. It describes the origin, growth, powers and possibilities of the individual life as well as its relation to other lives. Cloth.

No. 3R3558 Price..........**75c**

If by mail, postage extra, 11 cents.

Till the Doctor Comes.

By George H. Hope, M. D., M. R. C. S. E. Contains chapters on the sick room, nurses and nursing, medicine chests, burns and scalds, bleeding from the nose and how to stop it, broken elbow, foot, ankle, hip, thigh and how to doctor same; poisoning and its effect, embracing arsenic, acids, snake bite, chloride of tin and zinc, copper, prussic acid, etc. Bound in boards, cloth back.

No. 3R3560 Our price............................**70c**

If by mail, postage extra, 5 cents.

Tokology.

Special Cut Price only $1.48.

A book for every woman. By Alice B. Stockham, M. D. This is unquestionably the most valuable work of the kind published. The author, in sympathy with the needs of her sex, discusses at length, with strength and purity, physical questions of the greatest importance. Complete, plain and specific directions for the care of a woman during the entire term of pregnancy, including baths, diet, exercise, clothing and medical treatment. Explicit lessons are given for her management **during and after confinement. Plain instructions for the care of an infant, its clothing, bathing, nursing, etc., are given.**

No. 3R3564 Bound in cloth. Our price....**$1.48**

No. 3R3566 Bound in morocco. Our price. **1.90**

If by mail, postage extra, 21 cents.

POETRY.

American Patriotism Poems.

Patriotic and stirring verse by great poets and writers of today on the American wars and kindred subjects. Edited by R. L. Paget. While favorite poems relating to the earlier wars of America are well represented in this collection, the greater part of the book is naturally at this time devoted to the verse which helped us to **"make the history" of the War with Spain.** Verse which springs from the heart of the nation, of which a great deal deserves to be and is certain to become standard. Size, 5x7 inches. Cloth.

No. 3R3600 Our price...**75c**

If by mail, postage extra, 11 cents.

Lord Byron's Complete Works.

Newstead Edition. The complete dramatic and poetical works of Lord Byron, with illustrated life of the poet, embodying many fresh and interesting incidents of Byron's life, and with notes and references to his poems and writings. Beautifully illustrated with 13 full page engravings. Complete in one volume, containing 720 pages.

No. 3R3604 Our price cloth............**$1.15**

No. 3R3606 Bound in full American Russia, gold back and sides, gilt edge, library style. Price, **$1.95**

If by mail, postage extra, 24 cents.

Classic Gems of Prose and Poetry.

This remarkable volume contains a vast collection of choice literature selected from the works of the world's greatest authors, including Shakespeare, Lytton, Emerson, Hugo, Spencer, Holmes, Scott, Carlyle, Bryant, James Whitcomb Riley, Byron, Bunyan, Ruskin, Irving, Poe, Thackeray, Dickens, Burns, Browning, Garfield, Wordsworth, Longfellow, Tennyson, Lowell, Will Carlton, David Swing and hundreds of others. Beautifully illustrated with numerous full page engravings. Size of volume, 10x7¼x1¼ inches.

No. 3R3614 Our price............................**70c**

Weight, packed for shipment, 3¼ pounds.

See page 4 for postal rates.

Kipling's Poems.

Edited with introductory essays by Wallace Rice. This volume contains all the verses of Mr. Kipling originally printed in "Departmental Ditties" and "Barrack Room Ballads." Contains also "The Recessional." Gilt top, cloth, stamped in gold on front and back covers, printed on laid paper. Size, 5½x7½ inches.

No. 3R3622 Our price......**75c**

If by mail, postage extra, 12 cents.

ENCYCLOPEDIAS AND REFERENCE BOOKS.

The student particularly and the reader generally is at a constant loss without the valuable aid of one or more complete and reliable works of reference. In the following well selected line of such books will be found the most desirable ever published. These are offered to you in many cases at half the price they are usually sold at by retail dealers. The saving in dollars and cents is only equaled by the wonderful satisfaction the high quality of our books invariably gives. We especially wish to direct your attention to The New Century and the Universal Encyclopedias and G. & C. Merriam's Latest Edition of Webster's Unabridged Dictionary, only $5.00. These books are the latest, most complete, authentic, and best works of the kind in existence.

ONLY $5.00—LESS THAN ONE-HALF PRICE—for G. & C. Merriam Company Authorized Copyright Edition of Webster's Unabridged Dictionary. We have closed the largest book deal on record, enabling us to offer the regular authorized and authentic G. & C. Merriam Company edition of Webster's Dictionary of the English Language for only $5.00, indexed. By purchasing a stupendous quantity of this great standard authority of the English language, involving thousands upon thousands of dollars, we can now positively give our customers the real authentic unabridged dictionary with all its modern improvements and high standard of manufacture for only **$5.00.** This unheard of reduction is the result of a desire of the publishers to sacrifice profits in order to drive out inferior so called unabridged dictionaries, which now trade upon the honored name of Webster. Their desire is to effectually and forever stop misrepresentation and foul practices on the masses of people by representing the photographic re-print dictionaries as the original unabridged.

The G. & C. Merriam Company's edition of Webster's Unabridged Dictionary is acknowledged all over the English speaking world as the standard authority of the English language. A standard authority of the United States Supreme Court; of State Supreme Courts; The United States Government Printing Office. Warmly commended by college presidents, State superintendents of schools and other educators. **Bear in mind that the book we are selling is not a special edition of inferior manufacture, but the original 1900 edition.** We guarantee it to be identical in point of material used and manufacturing just exactly as it always was.

It is bound in full law sheep, with patent index, contains 2,012 large quarto pages, printed on fine, strong paper, of a durable quality, with thousands of illustrations distributed throughout the text, 3,000 classified illustrations additional; four color plates; a history of the English language; complete key to pronunciation, with diacritical marks on every page; the principles of pronunciation with explanations of the key; orthography and rules for spelling, charts of abbreviations used, metric system of weights and measures; explanatory and pronouncing vocabularies of names, places, persons and things, of modern geographical names, common Christian names, with vocabularies of Scripture proper names, Greek and Latin proper names; pronouncing gazetteer of the world, biographical dictionary, tables of quotations, rules, phrases, proverbs, etc., from the Latin and foreign languages; abbreviations, contractions and arbitrary signs used in writing and printing.

For years the G. & C. Merriam Co. edition has been sold at $8.50 for the plain and $9.25 for the indexed, and we had long since given up hope of ever being able to supply our customers with this standard authority of the English language, authentic and authorized edition, for less than the combination price. This is a golden opportunity, and opportunities are only made golden by their infrequent appearance. This is your golden opportunity, and if you wish to take advantage of this phenomenal purchase, we suggest that you get your order in early. Size, 5x10x12 inches.

No. 3R3730 Bound in full sheep with patent index, only........ **$5.00**
Weight, packed for shipment, 12 pounds.

Grimm-Webster German-English, English-German Dictionary.

Illustrated. This is the most complete and reliable German-English Dictionary published. It contains all words in both languages except such as are rare, purely technical or obsolete. Bound in stiff cloth, stamped in silver. Indexed.
No. 3R3780 Our special price........ **30c**
If by mail, postage extra, 8 cents.

Hill's Educator and Complete Library of Reference.

Contains Loisette's System of Memory Culture, Business and Legal Forms, Stocks and Dividends, Railroads and Transportation, Tariff and Civil Service, Colored Charts of History and Statistics, Medicine and Hygiene, Labor Saving and Ready Reference Tables. Poultry, Horses, Cattle, Swine, Sheep, etc. Also a collection of more than 2,000 formulas and suggestions for all trades and occupations; Size of volume, 11x9x2¼ inches. Profusely illustrated. Bound in cloth, colored edges, library style. Weight, 4¼ pounds. Retail price, $5.00.
No. 3R3792 Our price........ **$1.50**
Bound in half Russia leather, marble edges, library style. Retail price, $6.00.
No. 3R3793 Our price........ **$1.90**
If by mail, postage extra, 32 cents.

Hill's German-English and English-German Dictionary.

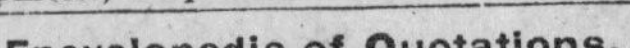

Vest pocket edition. Bound in full leather, gilt edges.
No. 3R3796 Our price........ **35c**
No. 3R3797 Bound in cloth. Price........ **20c**
French-English and English-French Dictionary; vest pocket edition. Bound in full leather, gilt edges, gold stamp.
No. 3R3798 Our price........ **35c**
No. 3R3799 Bound in cloth. Price........ **20c**
If by mail, postage extra, each 3 cents.

Nuttall's Standard Dictionary of the English Language.

Complete edition. Containing a vocabulary of new words and scientific terms, besides much tabulated and interesting matter. This book is unquestionably the handiest and one of the best dictionaries published.
No. 3R3811 Bound in cloth. Size, 5¾x8¼ inches. Retail price, $1.50; our price........ **75c**
No. 3R3812 Same style as No. 3R3811 but with patent index. Retail price, $2.00; our price........ **95c**
If by mail, postage extra, 18 cents.

Commercial Calculator.

A book that should be in the hands of every student, farmer, commercial and business man.

Ropp's Commercial Calculator. Saves labor, time and money; simple, rapid, reliable; adapted to all kinds of business, trades and professions. The only work of its kind **that has survived the test of time and acquired a national reputation.**
No. 3R3738 Bound waterproof leatherette.... **12c**
If by mail, postage extra, each, 3 cents.
No. 3R3740 Fine colored cloth, with pocket.... **27c**
No. 3R3742 Elegant leather, with pocket, silicate slate and account book. Each........ **65c**
No. 3R3744 Fine seal grain, gilt edges with pocket, silicate slate and account book........ **85c**
If by mail, postage extra, each, 6 cents.

Encyclopedia of Quotations.

A Treasury of Wisdom, Wit and Humor, Odd Comparisons, Proverbs; contains 1,400 subjects, 931 authors, 10,300 quotations, compiled and arranged by Adam Woolever, 530 pages. Cloth. Size, 9½x7x2¼ inches.
No. 3R3776 Our price........ **83c**
If by mail, postage extra, 24 cents.

Cassell's Dictionaries.

No. 3R3750 Cassell's French-English English-French Dictionary. Contains 1,232 pages. Bound in cloth. Retail price, $1.50; our price........ **$1.10**
If by mail, postage extra, per volume, 16 cents.
No. 3R3752 Cassell's German-English English-German Dictionary. Contains 1,102 pages. Bound in cloth. Retail price, $1.50; our price........ **$1.10**
If by mail, postage extra, per volume, 16 cents.
No. 3R3754 Cassell's Latin-English English-Latin Dictionary. Contains 927 pages. Bound in cloth. Retail price, $1.50; our price........ **$1.10**
If by mail, postage extra, 16 cents.

A Complete Dictionary of Synonyms and Antonyms.

No. 3R3764 By Rt. Rev. Samuel Fallows, A. M., D. D. Size, 5¼x7½ inches. Cloth. Retail price, $1.00; our price........ **85c**
If by mail, postage extra, 10 cents.

Contains also an appendix embracing a dictionary of Briticisms, Americanisms, colloquial phrases, etc., in current use; the grammatical uses of prepositions, and prepositions discriminated; a list of homonyms and homophonous words; a collection of foreign phrases, and complete list of abbreviations and contractions used in writing and printing.

"This is unquestionably one of the most valuable books that has come to our table. To those who desire to write and speak English with elegance and accuracy, it is indispensable."

New Century Encyclopedia.

A superb reference library covering the entire range of human knowledge, invention and discoveries up to the present day. Designed especially for the student, the teacher and the busy man. **This work presents in attractive form all the great facts in every department of human knowledge:** Art, science, biography, geography, history, geology, astronomy, navigation, physiology, explorations, botany, agriculture, commerce, finance, zoology, chemistry, electricity, law, theology, Arctic explorations, electrical science, X ray, political economy, natural history, flying machines, air ships, and in the field of recent events gives a detailed account of the Boxers in China, the Philippine War and the capture of Aguinaldo by Gen. Funston, the war in South Africa, special articles on the Nicaraguan canal project, Cuba and the Cuban constitution, Porto Rico, the Hawaiian and Samoan Islands, the Hague peace treaty; in fact, embraces every subject of importance, new and old, in the world. It gives the new 1900 census, population of every incorporated town and city of over 5,000 inhabitants in the United States. In method the work is unique—clear and concise in stating facts—no long articles on theory; everything presented from a practical standpoint. Everything is arranged alphabetically, and the longer articles are carefully outlined and arranged with subheadings to make ready reference easy and rapid.

No. 3R3734 Complete in two volumes, handsomely bound in cloth, imitation leather back and corners, marble edge, library style. Weight, packed for shipment, 8 pounds. Our special price........ **$2.35**
No. 3R3736 Popular one-volume edition, cloth, otherwise same as No. 3R3734. Weight, packed for shipment, 7½ pounds. Price........ **$1.60**

$5.95 Buys this $20.00 Library. Chambers' Encyclopedia, 15 volumes.

New popular edition. Rewritten and revised. A complete work of reference on Art, Science, History, Literature, Music, Biography, Geography, etc., with a very large addition upon topics of special interest to American readers. **The latest American census given in full,** in connection with other matters of national importance, including the Spanish-American War. Printed on good paper from new type-set plates, durably bound in cloth. Size of volumes, **5½x7½ inches. Complete in 15 volumes.**
No. 3R3762 Our price........ **$5.95**

$9.98 BUYS THIS MAGNIFICENT $50.00 LIBRARY.

UNIVERSAL ENCYCLOPEDIA.

THIS WORK treats authoritatively every subject of interest to any class of persons. Biographies of men and women up to 1899 are given, as well as the stories of the lives of great leaders of past centuries. The growth of the nations, discoveries in science and great inventions are treated exhaustively, as well as thousands of questions on historical, scientific and philosophical subjects.

THIS IS PRE-EMINENTLY THE ENCYCLOPEDIA for the business man and scholar. A thousand questions arise which it will answer reliably, and without any doubt or delay. It will assist the boys and girls in their various school studies; it will equip the rising youth for their chosen vocations in life. It will solve the difficulties of the adult worker, and will entertain and enlighten all by a concurrent use with the reading and discussion of the affairs of the outer world.

A COMPLETE WORLD EMBRACING TEXT BOOK of History, Geography and the Sciences, with the most exhaustive and masterly treatments of Astronomy, Architecture, Engineering, Etymology, Mechanics, Law, Medicine, Literature, Navigation, Exploration, Banking, Insurance, etc.; articles on the Roentgen X Rays, Tesla's Oscillator, the Vitascope and similar inventions. Special articles on the Navy, Coast Defenses, Currency, Arbitration, Postal Savings Banks and kindred subjects have been furnished for the work by official experts. Sports and recreations of all sorts, such as Baseball, Golf, Billiards, Horse Racing, etc., are presented by specialists.

THE DEFENSIVE AND AGGRESSIVE resources of the United States are authoritatively discussed under navy, army, coast defenses, submarine boats, artillery, gun making, etc.

RECENT HISTORY and statistics of all countries are given in detail. Of Greece and Turkey, for instance, there is given not only their present industrial and financial standing, but also their commerce, shipping, means of communication and naval and military resources.

THERE ARE ELABORATE ARTICLES ON CUBA and her war with Spain; Venezuela and the Monroe doctrine; matters of political significance concerning Canada and South Africa; the annexation of the Hawaiian Islands; a full history of the Japan-China war; a full history of the recent Spanish-American war, with biographies of the men who took the chief parts therein; full accounts of our new possessions—the Philippines and Porto Rico; and also of the gold fields of Alaska and the Klondike.

IT CONTAINS DESCRIPTIONS of American cities, with a history of their origin and growth, as well as accurate information of their situation, population, resources, etc.

NOTHING OF OLD WORLD INTEREST has been omitted, and due reference has been made to all grand personages and events which have made the history of America the admiration of the world.

A REVELATION in journalism and literature. The greatest literary offer ever conceived.

A SUPERIOR REFERENCE LIBRARY

Covering the entire range of human knowledge, inventions, discoveries, etc., up to the present date.

THIS IS THE very latest GENERAL REFERENCE WORK published. Contains a complete history of the

SPANISH-AMERICAN WAR

biography of Admiral Dewey, the hero of Manila, biography of Aguinaldo, of Gomez, Cervera, Hobson, and in fact all the heroes of the late war.

Weight, packed for shipment, 46 pounds.

THIS SET CONSISTS OF TWELVE large octavo volumes, containing over 25,000 columns of reading matter. It has thousands of illustrations and diagrams to explain the text of articles, and the geographical features are enhanced by 100 colored maps, showing the chief countries of the world, with a special map of every state in the Union, corrected and revised to date.

No. 3R3802 Bound in fine English silk cloth, with special design in gold and colored inks. Retail price, $50.00. Our price........ $ 9.98
No. 3R3803 Bound in fine sheepskin, with special embossed design, leather labels, marbled edges. Retail price, $60.00. Our price........ 14.50

Imperial Atlas of the World.

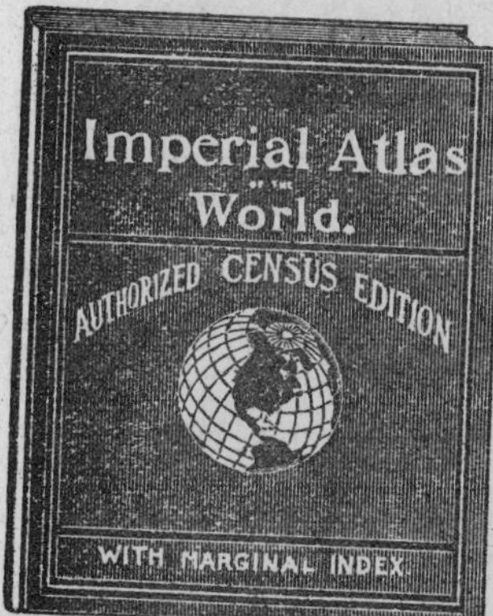

Authorized census edition. Latest, most complete, authentic and best atlas published, containing the 1900 census, maps of every country, and special county maps of each state in the United States, maps of large cities, and historical matter pertaining to information, historical events, discoveries, explorations and inventions (chronologically arranged), all the countries of the world, their geographical topography, general products, etc. A brief historical, descriptive, statistical and political review of the states and territories of the United States. An entirely new edition, revised and corrected up to date.

No. 3R3804 Our special price.............$1.35
If by mail, postage extra, 24 cents.

Illustrated German and French Dictionaries, for 75 Cents.

New, complete and reliable, containing all words in both languages, except such as are rare, purely technical or obsolete. Illustrated. Cloth. Size, 5¼x7½ inches.

German-English and English-German. Retails at $1.25.
No. 3R3808 Our price....75c
French-English and English-French. Retail price, $1.25.
No. 3R3810 Our price.............75c
If by mail, postage extra, 15 cents.

It tells just what to do and how to do it. A full compendium of indispensable information and instructions in the most useful mechanical trades. Embraces the following subjects: Carpentry; paints and how they are prepared, mixed and applied, giving full and plain information about colors, tints; also about graining, staining on glass or wood; lettering, glazing, paper hanging, etc., fancy and ornamental furniture and cabinet articles; full instructions on horse shoeing; manufacture of plain, fancy, and medicinal soaps, syrups, creams, pastes, ices, candies, etc.; plain and explicit instructions for the making and baking the various varieties of bread, crackers, cakes, pies and pastry. No other twelve books ever published treats of so many of the trades or contain in any one of them information so thoroughly practical in character. 885 pages. Bound in cloth. Size, 2x6¼x8¾ inches.

No. 3R3814 Our special price.............98c
If by mail, postage extra, 23 cents.

Law at a Glance.

A complete work, embracing every known subject, among which are the following: Affidavits, agents, agreements, arbitration, assignments, power of attorneys, bankruptcy, bills of lading, exchange and sale, chattel mortgages, co-partnership, corporations, damages, debts, deeds, frauds, forms of guarantee, injunction, injury, insolvency, insurance, judgment, sales, husband and wife—their relations, divorce, losses, etc. Size, 5½x7¼ inches. Bound in cloth.

No. 3R3815 Our price........... 65c
If by mail, postage extra, 12 cents.

Business Pointers.

A complete commercial instructor and counselor. It embraces everything known in the commercial world, beginning with general business principles, penmanship, correspondence, commercial papers, banking, law forms of legal business, bookkeeping, commercial arithmetic, large amount of valuable miscellaneous information for merchants, mechanics and farmers. The following subjects are fully treated: Contracts, Co-operation, Guarantees, Insurance, Landlord and Tenants, Farm Leases, Letters of Credit, Mortgages, Naturalization, Partnership, Passports, Patents and Copyrights, Rights and Obligations of Parents and Children. The practical value of this convenient volume can hardly be estimated. On the desk of an accountant, in the hands of the merchant, contractor, mechanic, business men of every class, as also the farmer, the book will prove a ready counselor and ready guide. No intelligent business man can afford to be without the information it furnishes. Much unpleasant litigation is the result of ignorance concerning the proper forms of legal business and points of commercial laws. Bound in cloth. Illustrated.

No. 3R3816 Our special price............ ....85c
If by mail, postage extra, 14 cents.

Special Subscription Edition

THEODORE ROOSEVELT.

A live portrayal of the youngest president, depicting his entire career in all its phases—as a school boy, student, politician, rancher, hunter, soldier, governor and president, etc. A work of sterling and enduring worth. Beautifully illustrated; contains over 400 pages.

No. 3R3817 Cloth, embossed, library edition, our special price.............98c
No. 3R3818 Handsome gift edition in half russia, gold top, marbled sides. Our price.............$1.35
If by mail, postage extra, each, 22 cents.

Shakespeare's Complete Works only $1.25.

A saving of from 50 to 60 per cent. Authentic and unabridged edition. The illustration will give you some idea of the appearance of these books. You can only form an idea of the wonderful value which we are giving, by personal examination. Printing and binding are strictly first class, paper is of superior quality and the binding of an excellent library cloth. Size of each volume, 5x7½ inches. Retail price, $5.75.

No. 3R4354 Our special cut price..........$1.25

Weight, packed for shipment, 10 pounds.

No. 3R4356 Another Edition of Shakespeare's Complete Works in four volumes. Cloth bound. Size, 5½x7¼ inches. Our special price..........90c

Weight, packed for shipment, 8 pounds.

SPECIAL BARGAINS IN STANDARD SETS.

78 CENTS BUYS REGULAR $3.50 5-VOLUME STANDARD SETS. We have purchased from the leading publishers in the United States and England a few thousand sets of standard 5-volume books, which we will close out at less than the actual cost to produce. This low price is made possible by reason of immense cash contract orders, and we are giving our customers the benefit of this purchase.

Cooper's Leather Stocking Tales.

Complete in five volumes for only 78 cents. An entirely new edition, printed from large, clear type, on extra quality of paper and handsomely bound in cloth, consisting of the following: The Deerslayer, The Pathfinder, The Prairie, The Pioneers, and The Last of the Mohicans. Size of volumes, 5⅛x7⅛ inches. Put up in paper boxes and published to retail at $3.50.

No. 3R4360 Our special cut price..........78c

Weight, packed for shipment, 8 pounds.

Cooper's Sea Tales.

By J. Fenimore Cooper, author of Leather Stocking Tales. Complete in five volumes. Uniform in size, with Leather Stocking Tales. Comprising the following: Red Rover, The Pilot, Wing and Wing, Water Witch, and The Two Admirals. A handsome library edition.

No. 3R4364 Our special cut price for the five volumes..........78c

Weight, packed for shipment, 8 pounds.

Hall Caine's Complete Works.

The only 5-volume edition of Hall Caine's works published. Uniformly bound in cloth. Printed on extra quality of paper, from new type set plates. Comprising the following: The Bondman, The Shadow of a Crime, Son of Hagar, The Deemster, She's All the World to Me.

No. 3R4370 Our spec'l cut price. 78c

Weight, packed for shipment, 8 lbs.

Rosa N. Carey's New 5-Volume Edition.

Comprising Aunt Diana, Averil, Esther, Merle's Crusade and Our Bessie. Uniformly bound in cloth, printed from clear new type. Library edition. Size of volume, 5⅛x7⅛ inches.

No. 3R4373 Our special cut price for the five volumes..........78c

Weight, packed for shipment, 8 pounds.

Marie Corelli's Complete Works. 78 Cents.

Five volumes, embracing Ardath, Romance of Two Worlds, Thelma, Vendetta and Wormwood. Uniformly bound in cloth, printed from large, clear type. Size of volumes, 5½x7¼ inches. Published to retail at $3.50.

No. 3R4382 Our special cut price for the set of five volumes, only..........78c

Weight, packed for shipment, 8 pounds.

Ralph Waldo Emerson's Works.

Uniformly bound in cloth, handsome library edition, in five volumes, embracing the following: English Traits; Essays, first series; Essays, second series; Representative Men and Poems. Size, 5⅛x7⅛ inches. Published to retail at $3.50.

No. 3R4385 Our special cut price for complete set of five volumes..........78c

Weight, packed for shipment, 8 pounds.

Nathaniel Hawthorne's Works.

New Edition. The set embraces: Grandfather's Chair, Blithedale Romance, House of the Seven Gables, Scarlet Letter and Twice Told Tales. Bound in popular style for the first time and published to sell at $3.50. Weight, packed for shipment, 8 lbs.

No. 3R4388 Our special cut price for the set..78c

G. A. Henty's Works.

Embracing: By Right of Conquest, True to the Old Flag, Under Drake's Flag, With Lee in Virginia, and With Wolfe in Canada. Uniformly bound in cloth. Size, 5⅛x7⅛ inches.

No. 3R4391 Our special cut price for the complete set..........78c

Weight, packed for shipment, 8 pounds.

Mary J. Holmes' Works.

Five of her most popular and well-known books: English Orphans, Homestead on the Hillside, Lena Rivers, Meadowbrook, Tempest and Sunshine. The sale of these five books exceeds by one-half million the sale of any author's works, perhaps, since the beginning of book-making. There is a steady and constantly increasing demand, and appreciating this fact, and with a desire to give our customers real book bargains, we induced the publishers to make this particular five volume set. They are uniformly bound in cloth, stamped in gold.

No. 3R4394 Our special cut price, for the complete set, five volumes..........78c

Weight, packed for shipment, 8 pounds.

Rudyard Kipling's Works.

Consisting of In Black and White, Phantom Rickshaw, Plain Tales from the Hills, Soldiers Three and The Light that Failed. Size of volumes, 5⅛x7⅛ inches. Uniformly bound in cloth. Published to retail at $3.50. Weight, packed for shipment, 8 lbs.

No. 3R4397 Our cut price, for complete set.... 78c

Longfellow's Complete Works.

New 5-volume edition. Bound in silk ribbed cloth, printed from new, large, clear type, comprising Evangeline, Golden Legend, Hiawatha, Hyperion and Book of Poems. Size of volumes, 5⅛x7⅛ inches. Retail price, $3.50.

No. 3R4400 Our special cut price, for complete set.... 78c

Weight, packed for shipment, 8 pounds.

Oliver Optic's Works.

New edition, uniformly bound in cloth, embracing All Aboard, The Boat Club, Now or Never, Poor, But Proud, Try Again. Size of volumes, 5⅛x7⅛ inches.

No. 3R4403 Our cut price, for complete set... 78c

Weight, packed for shipment, 8 pounds.

Capt. Mayne Reid's Works.

Consisting of Child Wife, Death Shot, Rifle Rangers, Scalp Hunters and Free Lances. Uniformly bound in cloth, printed on extra quality of paper. Size of volume, 5⅛x7⅛ inches.

No. 3R4407 Our special cut price, for complete set, five volumes..........78c

Weight, packed for shipment, 8 pounds.

John Ruskin's Works.

New 5-Volume Edition, embracing Ethics of the Dust, Morning in Florence, Queen of the Air, Sesame and Lilies, and St. Mark's Rest. Attractively bound in cloth. Size of volume, 5⅛x7⅛ inches.

No. 3R4410 Our cut price for five volumes...78c

Weight, packed for shipment, 8 pounds.

Robert Louis Stevenson's Works.

Uniformly bound in cloth, library style, embracing Dr. Jekyll and Mr. Hyde, Master of Ballantrae, Misadventures of John Nicholson, New Arabian Nights and Treasure Island. Size of volume, 5⅛x7⅛ inches. Weight, packed for shipment, 8 lbs.

No. 3R4413 Our special cut price for complete set of five volumes..........78c

Jules Verne's Works.

New Edition, consisting of Claudius Bombarnac, Michael Strogoff, The Texan's Revenge, Twenty Thousand Leagues Under The Sea, and The Tour of the World in Eighty Days. Attractively bound in cloth. Size of volume, 5⅛x7⅛ inches.

No. 3R4416 Our special cut price for complete set..........78c

Weight, packed for shipment, 8 pounds.

NEW POPULAR SETS AT CUT PRICES.

Cloth. Gold stamped. Size of volume, 5½x7½ in.

Works of Mrs. Alexander.

Complete in five volumes, consisting of the following: Blind Fate, Crooked Path, Snare of the Fowler, Broken Links and Mona's Choice.

No. 3R4430 Our special price..........60c

Weight, packed for shipment, 7 pounds.

Charlotte M. Braeme's Works.

Consisting of Dora Thorne, Earl's Atonement, Her Martyrdom, Duke's Secret and Golden Heart.

No. 3R4432 Price, per set of five volumes.. 60c

Weight, packed for shipment, 7 pounds.

Frances Hodgson Burnett's Works.

Complete in five volumes. Embracing Kathleen, Pretty Polly Pemberton, Theo. Lindsay's Luck, Quiet Life. Weight, packed for shipment, 7 lbs.

No. 3R4434 Our price, per set of five volumes. 60c

Alexander Dumas' D'Artagnan Romances.

Complete in six volumes, embracing Three Guardsmen, Vicomte de Bragelonne, Man in the Iron Mask, Twenty Years After, Louise de la Valliere, and Son of Porthos.

No. 3R4436 Price, per set of six volumes......69c

Weight, packed for shipment, 8 pounds.

Works of E. Marlitt.

New edition, embracing Gold Elsie, Princess of the Moor, Second Wife, Old Mam'selle's Secret, Owl's Nest. Weight, packed for shipment, 7 lbs.

No. 3R4438 Special price, per set of five vols.. 75c

W. Clark Russell's Works.

Complete in five volumes. Embracing Frozen Pirate, My Danish Sweetheart, Master Rockefeller's Voyage, Marriage at Sea, and Strange Elopement.

No. 3R4440 Price, per set of five volumes..... 65c

Weight, packed for shipment, 7 pounds.

Sir Walter Scott's Works.

Complete in six volumes, embracing Fortunes of Nigel, Ivanhoe, Old Mortality, Guy Mannering, Kenilworth, Waverly.

No. 3R4442 Price for complete set, six volumes. 75c

Weight, packed for shipment, 8 pounds.

EXCELSIOR SERIES OF 2-VOLUME SETS.

Cloth bound. Size of volume, 5½x7½ inches.

History of Our Own Time.

By Justin McCarthy.

No. 3R4470 Our price, per set of two volumes. 68c

Weight, packed for shipment, 3 pounds

The Mysteries of Paris.

By Eugene Sue. New large type edition. Complete in two volumes.

No. 3R4472 Our price, per set of two volumes. 75c

Weight, packed for shipment, 30 ounces.

Tom Brown's School Days, and Tom Brown at Oxford.

By Thomas Hughes. New edition.

No. 3R4474 Price, per set of two volumes..... 60c

Weight, packed for shipment, 36 ounces.

Victor Hugo's Masterpiece, Les Miserables, for only 78 Cents.

This complete and unabridged library edition contains Les Miserables, complete in two volumes. Printed on fine calendered paper from new plates, averaging 650 pages to the book. Size of each volume 5⅜x8 inches. Weight, packed for shipment, 36 ozs.

No. 3R4476 Price, per set of two volumes..... 78c

The Wandering Jew.

By Eugene Sue. Complete in two volumes. Handsomely bound in cloth. Library style. Size of volume, 5⅛x7⅛ inches. Weight, packed for shipment, 36 ozs.

No. 3R4478 Price, per set of two volumes... 65c

Testaments, Prayer Books, Hymnals, Etc.

THESE BOOKS ARE THE PRODUCT of one of the GREATEST AND BEST KNOWN BIBLE PUBLISHERS in the world. In PRINTING AND BINDING they are UNEXCELLED, and the purchaser of any book quoted below will be ASTONISHED AT THE WONDERFUL VALUE WE ARE ABLE TO OFFER at such remarkably low prices. In ordering, be sure to give catalogue number, and when books are to go by mail do not fail to enclose the necessary extra postage.

Testaments.

No. 3R4634 Bound in linen cloth, limp, cut flush, sprinkled edges. Retail price, 15c; our price, each...**6c**
If by mail, postage extra, 3 cents.

No. 3R4636 Bound in leatherette, cut flush, round corners, red edges. Size, 2⅝x3¾ inches. Retail price, 20c; our price, each.(If by mail, postage extra, 4 cents)..**12c**

No. 3R4638 French morocco, limp, round corners, red under gold edges. Ruby, 48mo. Size, 2¾x4 inches. Retail price, 40c; our price...**20c**

No. 3R4640 French morocco, improved divinity circuit, round corners, red under gold edges. Retail price, 60c; our price...**30c**
If by mail, postage extra, 4 cents.

No. 3R4642 Imitation ivory, gold, silver and illuminated floral sides, round corners, gilt edge, rims and clasp, full gilt leather back. Price...**50c**

Large Type Testaments for Old People.

Size, 5¼x8½ inches.

No. 3R4644 Bound in morocco, grain cloth, embossed sides, round corners, red edges. Retail price, 90c; our price...**60c**
If by mail, postage extra, 14 cents.

No. 3R4646 Bound in French morocco, limp, linen lined, round corners, red under gold edges. Retail price, $1.50; our price...**95c**
If by mail, postage extra, 13 cents.

Testament with Book of Psalms.

Ruby, 48mo. Size, x¼23¾ inches.

No. 3R4650 French morocco, round corners, red under gold edges. Retail price, 40c; our price...**30c**

No. 3R4652 French morocco, improved divinity circuit, cloth lined, round corners, red under gold edges. Retail price, 60c; our price...**40c**
If by mail, postage extra, 6 cents.

No. 3R4654 Large Type Testament and Psalms. Size, 5¼x8¼ inches. Bound in morocco grain cloth; embossed sides; limp; round corners; red burnished edges. Retail price, 95c; our price...**75c**
If by mail, postage extra, 16 cents.

No. 3R4656 Large Type Testament and Psalms. Bound in French morocco; limp; linen lined; round corners; red under gold edges. Size, 5¼x8½ inches. Price........(If by mail, postage extra, 16 cents)....**$1.05**

Red Letter New Testament.

No. 3R4670 The Red Letter New Testament is an innovation that has long been vaguely wished for, but which has only in the present day found practical expression in its actual production. Every word spoken by our Lord printed in red. It is absolutely free from typographical imperfections of any kind. Beautifully bound in American levant, soft and flexible, with overlapping edges, red under gold. For home reading, pocket use, or church and Sunday school work it is an ideal Testament. A more exquisite gift cannot be conceived, nor one that will afford more genuine satisfaction and more intense pleasure. Our special price, each...**98c**
If by mail, postage extra, 10 cents.

Prayer Books and Hymnals in Sets.

Minion, 48mo. Size, 2⅝x4 inches. Prayer book according to the new standard. The Hymnal revised and enlarged. Combination sets. Prayer and Hymnal. Printed on fine white paper.

No. 3R4678 Skytogen leatherette, gilt title and cross on sides, gilt title on backs, round corners, gilt edge. Retail price, $1.60; our price...**75c**

No. 3R4682 French morocco, limp, blind frame, round corners, gilt edge. Retail price, $2.00; our price...**98c**

No. 3R4686 Cloth, blind frame, gilt title on cover, gilt ornate I. H. S., square corners, plain edges. Retail price, $1.25; our price...**50c**

No. 3R4690 Seal grain, gilt I. H. S., round corners, red under gold edges, gold roll. Retail price, $2.50; our price...**$1.45**
If by mail, postage extra, 6 cents.

No. 3R4692 French morocco, limp, blind frame, blind cross, round corners, gilt edges. Retail price, $2.50; our price...**$1.65**

No. 3R4694 French calf, limp, gilt ornate I. H. S., round corners, red under gold edges. Retail price, $3.00; our price...**$1.90**

No. 3R4696 Leopard grain Persian, padded, gilt cross or I. H. S., and gilt title on side, round corners, red under gold edge, gold roll. Price..**$2.00**

No. 3R4698 German Seal, flexible limp antique, leather lined, round corners, red under gold edge. Retail price, $3.00; our price...**$1.75**
If by mail, postage extra, 16 cents.

Catholic Prayer Books.

Child's Catholic Prayer Books. Approved by His Eminence Cardinal Gibbons and Most Rev. Archbishop Ryan. New and complete, large, clear type edition, with 36 illustrations of the Mass. Contains 288 pages. Size, 2¼x3⅝ inches.

No. 3R4730 Fine black cloth, gilt side tamp. Price...**12c**

No. 3R4732 French seal, limp, round corners, gilt edges. Price...**30c**

No. 3R4736 Handsomely bound in celluloid, leather back, new flower design, gilt edges, nickel rim and clasp. Retail price, $1.00. Our price...**55c**
If by mail, postage extra, each, 4 cents.

Key of Heaven.—Gift Edition.

With beautiful Cross of Pearl in front cover.

No. 3R4740 48mo. With Epistles and Gospels. Size, 2¼x3¾ inches. Contains 575 pages. Beautifully bound in German calf, padded, round corners, fancy gold side stamping, gold edges, beautiful cross of pearl, and indulgence prayer inside of front cover. Price, each.(If by mail, postage extra, 6 cents)..**$1.25**

Catholic Key of Heaven.

Catholic Prayer Books. With Epistles and Gospels. 615 pages, 32mo. Size, 3¼x4½x⅞ inches. A pocket manual of small and compact size, containing all the principal prayers, litanies, way of the cross and other devotions that are in daily use. It may be justly regarded as one of the most complete pocket prayer books ever offered to the Catholics of this country.

No. 3R4742 Extra fine black satin cloth. Retail price, 45c; our price...**20c**

No. 3R4744 French, duplex, padded, morocco grain leather, red under gold edges. Retail price, $2.00; our price...**95c**
If by mail, postage extra, 7 cents.

No. 3R4746 German morocco, limp, round corners, fancy gold I. H. S. in center, red under gold edges. Retail price, $1.40; our price...**65c**

No. 3R4748 Persian calf, padded, fancy gold and silver center stamp, round corners, red under gold edges. Retail price, $2.00. Our price...**$1.10**
If by mail, postage extra, each, 5 cents.

Vest Pocket Prayer Books. (Catholic.)

No. 3R4754 With Epistles and Gospels. Contains 364 pages. 9/16 inch thick. Bound in French morocco, limp, round corners, red under gold edges. Retail price, 60c; our price...**35c**

No. 3R4756 Bound in French seal, limp, round corners, red under gold edges. Retail price, 75c; our price...**45c**

No. 3R4758 Bound in polished crocodile, limp, round corners, red under gold edges, extra rich designs. Retail price, $1.50; our price...**80c**
If by mail, postage extra, each, 5 cents.

Prayer Books in Two-Volume Sets. (Catholic.)

We save you from 40 to 60 per cent on this class of books. WE BUY THEM DIRECT FROM THE PUBLISHER at lowest possible prices, and our price to you is the same, with but our one small profit added.

Key of Heaven, 32mo. Size, 3½x4½ inches. Epistles and Gospels Separate.

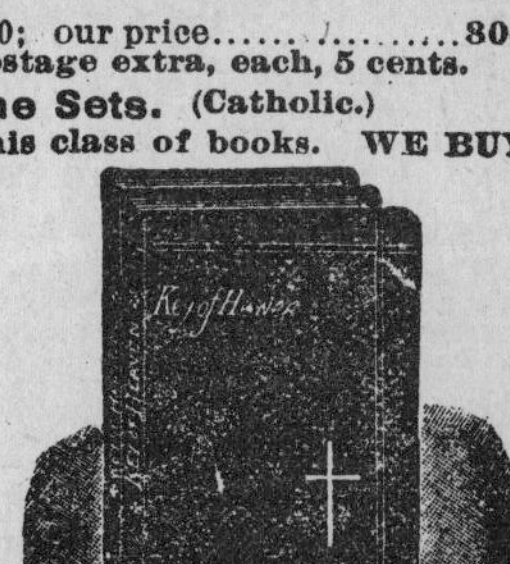

No. 3R4762

No. 3R4760 French seal, limp, round corners, red under gold edges. Retail price, $2.25; our price, per set...**95c**

No. 3R4762 French Calf, limp, round corners, red under gold edges. Retail price, $2.50; our price, per set...**$1.30**

No. 3R4764 Venetian seal, limp, round corners, red and gold edges, gold roll. Retail price, $3.50; our price, per set...**$1.85**

No. 3R4766 Persian, duplex, padded, seal grain panel, smooth border, round corners, red and gold edges. Retail price, $3.50; our price, per set..**$2.25**
If by mail, postage extra, each, 10 cents.

Just Published. A new, beautifully illustrated Teachers' Catholic Bible, large type edition. Translated from the Latin Vulgate. Compared with the Hebrew, Greek and other editions in divers languages. Contains the Old Testament first published by the English College at Duay, A. D. 1609. The New Testament first published by the English College at Rheims, A. D. 1582, with annotations, references, historical and chronological index. This Bible was published only after repeated requests from clergymen, laymen and Sunday school teachers. The utmost care has been exercised in the compilation. Printed from large, clear, new type on fine white paper; strength, excellence, durability, combine to place it far in advance of any Bible heretofore published in America.

No. 3R4774 Bound in fine cloth, gilt back title, blind cross on side, round corners, red edges, illustrated. Our special price...**75c**
If by mail, postage extra, 24 cents.

No. 3R4776 Bound in French morocco, limp, gilt back and side title, round corners, red under gold edges, illustrated. Our price...**$1.40**
If by mail, postage extra, 24 cents.

No. 3R4780 Bound in Imperial seal, divinity circuit (overlapping edges), gilt back and side title, red under gold edges, illustrated. Our price...........(If by mail, postage extra, 24 cents)...**$1.75**

FAMILY BIBLES.

AT FROM $1.10 TO $6.75 we are offering a line of Family Bibles such as are offered by retail dealers and agents at more than double our prices.

WE DESIRE ESPECIALLY to call your attention to the self pronouncing Family Bibles, which are acknowledged by ministers, Bible students and ablest critics to be superior to any other Bibles published.

STRONG, HANDSOME AND DURABLE BINDINGS, magnificently executed engravings, fine paper, thorough excellence in manufacture, more recent and instructive features and Bible aids, more maps, illustrations, tables and collateral matter, etc.

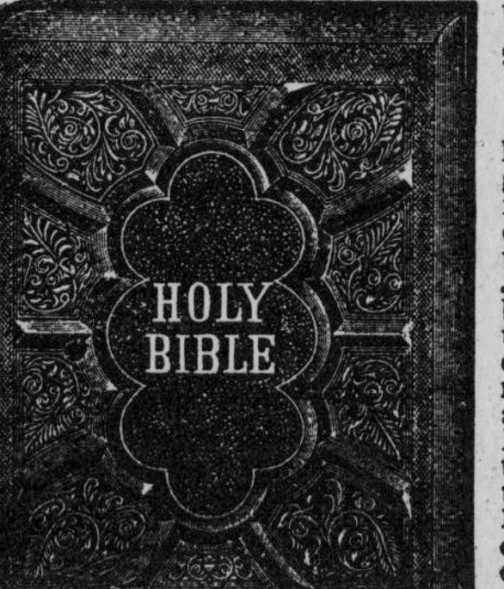

$1.10 for this Splendid Family Bible.

Family Bible. Bound in imitation leather; back and side titles stamped in gold and with gold edges; printed from clear, new type on an extra quality of fine paper. Size, 10x12¼x2 inches. Contains the Old and New Testament, King James' text, origin and history of the books of the Bible, pronouncing dictionary of proper names, department of references, with maps and illustrations, marriage certificate and record, temperance pledge and triumphal entry, new Lord's Prayer, pictorial title, colored title and eight magnificent Dore illustrations, chronological index to the Holy Bible, according to recent chronologists. Brown's Complete Concordance of the Old and New Testaments. Weight, packed for shipment, 6½ pounds. Retail price, $3.50.

No. 3R4792 Our special price...**$1.10**

No. 3R4794 Genuine Leather Bound Edition, beautifully illustrated, otherwise same as No. 3R4792. Our price...**$1.75**

$3.98 for This Elegant Bible.

BOOK STORES ASK $6.00 TO $8.00.

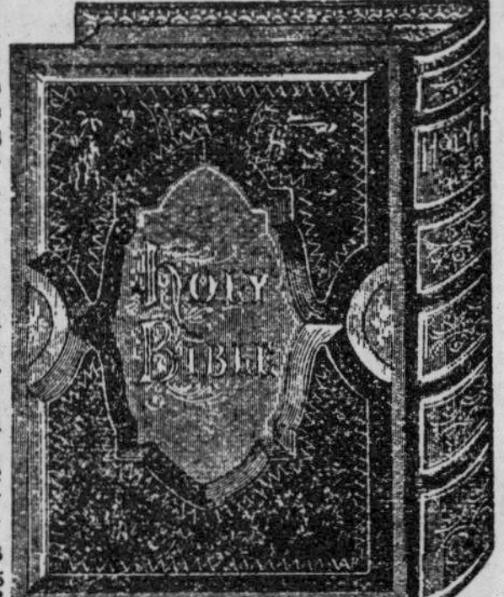

Shows in simple form all changes, additions and omissions made by the revisers of the Old and New Testaments, and enables readers to see at a glance wherein the two versions differ. The King James Version is the basis. This Bible contains in addition to the Combination Text, which is printed from extra large, new, clear type on a good quality of paper, the following features: Marginal references, many multi-colored plates, including presentation plates, ten colored parable plates, ten commandments and Lord's Prayer, the Israelitish tabernacle and sacred furniture; colored maps of Palestine, marriage certificate, family record, family temperance pledge, etc; Household Dictionary of the Bible by Wm. Smith, LL. D., Smith's History of the Books of the Bible, Natural History of the Bible by Rev. A. H. Thompson, A. M., Biography and History of the Holy Apostles; scenes and incidents in the Life of Christ; Proverbs of Solomon, St. Paul's journeys, path of Jesus, Babylonian, Grecian, Persian and Roman empires, Hoffman Gallery of Original New Testament Illustrations, printed in colors with descriptions. Cruden's complete Concordance and life of Alexander Cruden, 4,000 questions and answers on the Old and New Testament. Bound in American morocco, calf finish, raised panel sides, beautifully ornamented with emblematical designs, embossed in gold with gold edges. Size of Bible when closed, 10¼ wide by 12⅛ long. Retail price, $10.00.

No. 3R4796 Our price to you..**$3.98**

Weight, packed for shipment, 13 pounds.

$2.75 for This Illustrated $6.50 Family Bible.

AGENTS SELL THESE THROUGHOUT THE COUNTRY AT TWO AND THREE TIMES THE PRICE.

Family Bible. Contains the Old and New Testaments; self pronouncing dictionary of proper names; 2 colored and 16 full page Dore engravings; numerous Biblical illustrations; chronological index to the Holy Bible; giving years when remarkable events occurred and passages wherein they are recorded, a summary of its contents and many valuable aids and helps to Bible students; illuminated marriage certificate and family record of marriages, births and deaths; alphabetical table of proper names in the Old and New Testaments; history of the books of the Bible; **48 magnificent full page illustrations;** illuminated title, etc. Handsomely bound in American morocco. Raised panel. Gold sides and title. Printed from clear, new type on an extra quality of fine paper. Size, 10¾x12⅛x2¾ inches. Weight, packed for shipment, 13 pounds.

Retail price, $6.50.

No. 3R4800 Our price..............**$2.75**

New Combination Padded Family Bible, $2.98.

SUCH VALUE IN BIBLES WAS NEVER BEFORE OFFERED.

Self pronouncing, showing in simple form, all changes, additions and omissions made by the revisers of the Old and New Testaments, arranged in parallel columns, enabling the writer to see at a glance wherein the two versions differ. The King James version is the basis and this version is read straight along from the text, while the revised version is read from the text in combination with the foot notes. The text is comformable to that of the University of Oxford and Cambridge, with a complete concordance of the Psalms of David in meter. **Contains in addition to the Combination Text,** which is printed from large, new, clear type on extra quality paper, the following features: Marginal references, History of the Bible, marriage certificate, family record, many halftone and other illustrations, etc. Size, 10x12⅛x2¼ inches. Bound in American morocco, padded sides, gold side title and gold edges. Retail price, $8.00.

No. 3R4804 Our price................**$2.98**

Weight, packed for shipment, 13 pounds.

Magnificent Family Bible for $4.25.

A REALLY BEAUTIFUL WORK.

Containing the origin and history of the Books of the Bible, department of reference; with maps and illustrations; marriage certificate and record for marriages, births and deaths; temperance pledge and triumphal entry; beautifully illustrated presentation page; 24 magnificent Dore illustrations; story of the books of the Old Testament; Biblical antiquities (illustrated), and Old Testament scenes; Psalms; Brown's Concordance; gallery of Scripture illustrations; two steel engravings; Hoffman's gallery of colored illustrations. Handsomely bound in red sheepskin leather, padded, round corners. Printed from clear, new type on an extra quality of fine paper. Size, 10x12⅛x3 inches. Weight, packed for shipment, 11½ pounds. Retail price, $8.00.

No. 3R4808 Our price........ **$4.25**

Only $3.75 for This Magnificent $8.00 Family Bible.

New self pronouncing combination edition. Illustrated with two colored and 24 full page Dore engravings, history of the books of the Bible illustrated with 48 full page engravings, complete concordance to the Holy Scripture, Psalms of David in meter, chronological index to the Holy Bible, complete history of the Bible with a summary of its contents and many valuable aids and helps to Bible students; self-pronouncing edition of Smith's Bible Dictionary, illustrated; natural history; ancient coins, trees, plants, flowers and fruits of the Bible, birds, etc., illustrated; illuminated marriage certificate. family record, etc. Size, 9x12x2⅛ inches. Handsomely bound in American calf, padded sides, round corners, full gold edges.

No. 3R4812 Our special price......**$3.75**

Weight, packed for shipment, 13 pounds.

$4.95 Buys This Magnificent $12.00 Self Pronouncing, Combination Family Bible.

Beautifully bound in Persian morocco, padded sides, round corners, red under gold edges. This Bible shows in simple form all changes, additions and omissions made by the revisers of the Old and New Testament, and contains in addition to the Combination Text the Proverbs of Solomon and the Parables of Our Lord illustrated, beautiful stories for the young with 72 illustrations; 10 multi-colored parable plates; 4 superb halftone engravings in gold and colors; Jewish Worships, Tabernacle and Vestments; Holy Apostles' with descriptions; Sacred Biography of the Holy Apostles and the Evangelists; 8 pages of maps of the Bible land; 6 beautiful steel and 32 full page Dore engravings; Cruden's Concordance; Smith's Bible Dictionary; Ancient Coins of the Bible; History of the Religious Denominations of the World and many valuable tables and helps to the Bible student, etc. Size, 10x12⅛x3 inches. Bound in Persian morocco, padded, round corners, red under gold edges.

No. 3R4816 Our special price..**$4.95**

Weight, packed for shipment, 15 pounds.

Combination Self Pronouncing Family Bible, Only $6.65.

A SPLENDID EDITION.

This Magnificent Bible contains in addition to the combination text—which is printed from extra large, new, clear type on fine paper—marginal references; many colored illustrations, including illustrated presentation page, ten colored parable illustrations, ten commandments and Lord's Prayer in colors, the Israelites' tabernacle, sacred furniture; beautiful colored maps of Palestine; marriage certificate; family record; family temperance pledge; Smith's Bible Dictionary; history of the Bible; natural history; biography and history of the Holy Apostles, scenes and incidents in the life of Christ; Proverbs of Solomon; St. Paul's journeys; path of Jesus; Grecian, Persian and Roman empires; Hoffman's Gallery of Original New Testament Illustrations, printed in colors; Cruden's complete Concordance and his Life, also 4,000 questions and answers on the Old and New Testaments. **Size, 10x12½x3 inches. Beautifully bound in genuine Turkey morocco,** antique gold and carmine design, English style, carmine under gold edges.

No. 3R4820 Retail price, $14.00; our special price **$6.65**

Weight, packed for shipment, 15 pounds.

A Superb Self Pronouncing Combination Family Bible, Only $5.25.

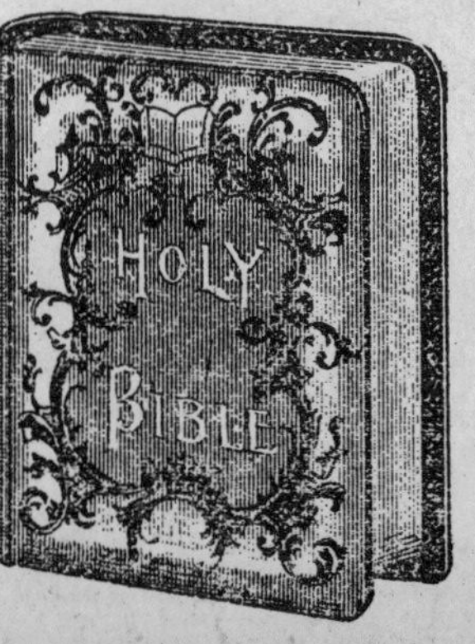

This Magnificent Family Bible contains the authorized and revised versions of both the Old and the New Testaments, arranged in parallel columns, line for line; marginal references; marriage certificate and family record; history of the books of the Bible; the ten commandments and our Lord's Prayer, illuminated; biographical sketch of the translators, the reformers and martyrs; a gallery of seventy-two Scriptural illustrations and descriptions of the Israelites' Tabernacle; Life of our Lord and Savior; cities and towns of the Bible; colored maps of Palestine; ancient and modern Jerusalem; Proverbs of Solomon; St. Paul's journeys; Grecian, Persian and Roman empires; Hoffman's gallery of Original New Testament Illustrations.

Size, 9¼x12½x3¼ inches. Bound in French morocco, padded sides, round corners, gold edges.

No. 3R4822 Our special price.... **$5.25**

Weight, packed for shipment, 17 pounds.

STATIONERY DEPARTMENT.

WE INCLUDE HEREIN AN ASSORTMENT OF WRITING PAPER, TABLETS, PAPETERIES AND GENERAL STATIONERY, superior to that found in ordinary retail stores.

POSTAGE ON THIS CLASS OF GOODS IS ONE CENT PER OUNCE. It will be wise for you to include such items as you may need in this line with your express or freight order of heavy goods, in which case the carrying charges on the stationery will be reduced to a minimum. We are well prepared to take care of complete grammar and high school supplies. We are quoting school ink, blackboards, erasers and school supplies at from 40 to 60 per cent lower than manufacturers. It will pay you to investigate before placing your orders elsewhere.

BLANK BOOKS.

No. 3R5100 Cap Folio, bound in slate duck, imitation Russia corners, spring back, hubs, green edges, paged, ruled in journals, single entry and double entry ledgers, cash and records. Size, 9x13 inches.

No. pages each	Price each
250	$0.60
300	.75
400	.90
500	1.15

No. 3R5104 Crown Folio, containing extra heavy white wove paper, black cloth sides, Russia back and corners, green edges, sewed strongly on bands, paged, ruled in day books, D. E. and S. E. ledgers, records and long day. Size, 9½x14 inches.

Price, per book, 150 pages........38c
Price, per book, 200 pages........52c
Price, per book, 250 pages........68c
Price, per book, 300 pages........82c
Price, per book, 400 pages........95c

No. 3R5108 Cap Folio. Size, 8¼x13 inches. Full bound canvas, Russia leather corners, loose back, strongly sewed on bands and well stayed, extra quality of white paper. Ruled in day books, cash, journal, record, S. and D. E ledger. Indexed.

Pages	200	300	400	500	600	800	1,000
Prices	42c	55c	68c	75c	85c	98c	$1.15

No. 3R5112 Cap Folio. Standard banner, containing fine grade of white wove paper, bound in slate duck, Russia corners, spring back, hubs, paged, ruled with unit lines in day books, journal, record, S. E. and D. E. ledgers. Size, 9x13 inches.

Price, per book, 250 pages........$0.80
Price, per book, 300 pages.........90
Price, per book, 350 pages........1.10
Price, per book, 400 pages........1.30
Price, per book, 500 pages........1.60

Bookkeeping Blanks.

No. 3R5114 For practice in schools and colleges, excellent quality white paper, blank book finish, colored press board covers, 38 pages to book. Size, 8½x14 inches; weight, each, 8 ounces, ruled as follows: Day books, record, journal, cash book, D. E. ledger, and trial balance. **Always mention kind of ruling wanted.**

Price, each........7c

Hotel Registers.

No. 3R5116 Crown Folio, three-quarter bound, American Russia red leather back and corners, green cloth sides, spring back, hubs, marbled edges, containing heavy white wove paper. Size, 9½x14⅝ inches.

No. of pages, each	250	300	400	500	600
Price, per book	$1.60	$1.90	$2.25	$2.75	$3.10

Complete Account Book and Weather Record.

And Valuable Information for Farmers, Stock Breeders, Dairymen, Poultry Raisers, Etc.

No. 3R5123 The only book of its kind in existence. It embraces separate account departments, itemized and consolidated for all general products and stocks, orchard, dairy, garden, hay, seed, cotton, etc., together with ruled forms, printed and descriptive headings for every department, also valuable information, such as exemption laws in all states, legal forms, something about landlords and the privileges of tenants, bills payable and receivable, how to rent farms, interest laws in United States, a short, concise interest rule, also information as to how many bushels of seed to the acre, a correct table of the different varieties of seed, showing the quantity of each required to plant an acre, also the number of trees that can be planted on an acre of ground and just how deep to plant various crops, such as wheat, corn, etc. **Handsomely bound in cloth.** Retail price, $2.50; our price........$1.50

If by mail, postage extra, 16 cents.

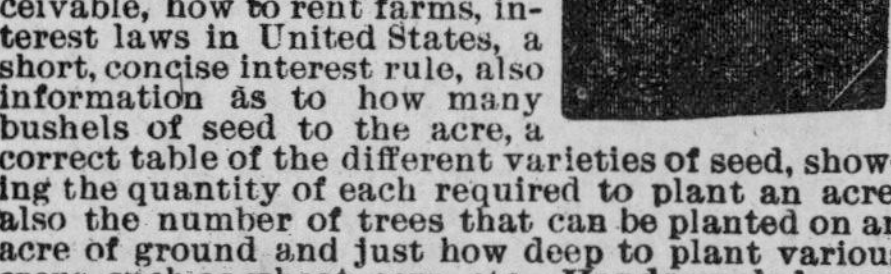

Scrap Albums.

No. 3R5124 Scrap Album. New handsome scrap album with embossed cover, assorted designs, containing 36 leaves. Size, 10½x11¾ inches. Weight, packed for shipment, 13 ounces. Price, each...25c

No. 3R5128 Scrap Album. New handsome scrap album with embossed cover, assorted designs stamped in colored ink and gold, containing 60 leaves. Size, 10½x12 inches. Weight, packed for shipment, 2½ pounds. Price, each........55c

Twentieth Century Scrap Book.

20th Century Scrap Book. Newest, latest and best way of preserving clippings. Hold three times the capacity of the old style scrap book. It embodies a new idea, simple and valuable. One clipping overlaps another. (See illustration). They can be easily raised with the finger, both sides can be seen. Used by editors, architects, actors, platform speakers, musicians, lawyers and business men. Size, 9x11, contains 50 pages, cloth bound.

No. 3R5130 Our price........75c
No. 3R5132 Size, 11x16, contains 50 pages, cloth bound. Our price........$1.25

Scrap Books.

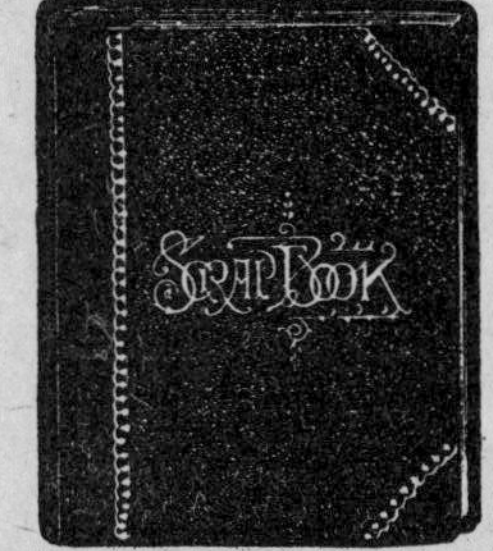

No. 3R5131 Scrap Book, containing finest grade of manila paper, roan back and corners, gold lines, comb marbled paper sides; 7¼x9¼ inches; 152 pages. Price..50c

No. 3R5133 Scrap Book, crown folio, containing best grade of manila paper, dark blue, roan back and corners, gold lines and marbled edges; paper sides; 10x14½ inches; 184 pages. Price........75c

Memorandum Books.

	Size	No. pages	Price each
No. 3R5136 Memorandum Book, 32mo, ruled cross bar, side opening	2¼x3¼	80	6c
No. 3R5138 Memorandum Book, cap, long 12mo, ruled cross bar, end opening	5⅜x2¼	80	9c
No. 3R5140 Memorandum Book, cap, long 12mo, ruled cross bar, end opening	5⅜x2¼	120	10c
No. 3R5142 Memorandum Book, cap, 24mo, ruled cross bar, bound in imitation Russia leather, turned-in gilt edges, side opening	2½x4½	80	10c
No. 3R5144 Memorandum Book, cap, 8vo, bound in imitation Russia leather, turned-in gilt edges, ruled in dollars and cents, side opening	3⅝x6	180	20c
No. 3R5146 Memorandum Book, cap, 12mo, bound in imitation seal, ruled cross bar, side opening, turned-in gilt edges	5x3 in.	144	18c
No. 3R5148 Memorandum Book, bound in leatherette, turned-in gilt edges, gilt stamp on side, ruled in dollars and cents, side opening	3⅝x6 in.	180	12c

Books—Pocket Receipt.

No. 3R5152 Best grade, pressed board cover, cloth back with stub, perforated. Size, 2½x7 inches. Contains 50 leaves. Weight, 4 ounces.

Price, each........4c

Books—Rent Receipts.

No. 3R5154 Rent Receipt Book, pressed board cover, cloth back, perforated, containing 50 receipts. Size, 3¼x11 inches. Weight, 5 ounces.

Price, each........7c

Books—Draft.

No. 3R5156 Drafts. Best pressed board cover, cloth back, perforated. Contains 50 receipts, 100 pages. Size, 3¼x11 inches. Weight, 5 ounces

Price, each........7c

Books—Note.

No. 3R5158 Notes. Pressed board covers, cloth back, perforated. Size, 3¼x11 inches. Contains 50 leaves, 100 pages. Weight, 6 oz. Price, each........7c

Books—Standard Letter Copying.

No. 3R5160 Copying Book. Half-bound, sheep back and corners, black cloth sides, containing best quality of white paper; patent index. Size, 10½x12¼ inches. Price, each, 500 pages........$0.75
700 pages........95
1000 pages........1.35

Copying Press Sheets (Cloth).

No. 3R5162 Made of heavy white best grade cotton fabric; non-shrinkable; rubber interwoven. Will last a lifetime.

Sheets, size 9x11, each........10c
Sheets, size 10x12, each........12c
Sheets, size 10x14, each........15c

Malleable Iron Letter Press.

Malleable Iron Letter Press, highly enameled in black. Our copying presses are warranted against imperfections in material and workm'ship.

No. 3R5164 Size of follower, 10x12½ inches. Our special price........$3.75

No. 3R5168 Size of follower, 10x15 inches. Our special price........$4.50

No. 3R5172 Size of follower, 11x16 inches. Our special price....$7.35

Order Books.

No. 3R5190 Order Book, contains extra white paper, full canvas bound, 300 pages, with name "Order Book" stamped on cover. Our price, each..40c

No. 3R5194 Order Book, full bound canvas, strong and neatly made, ruled in dollars and cents, containing 500 pages fine white paper. Size, 6½x15 inches. Our price, each........50c

No. 3R5198 Order Book. Size 8½x12⅝ bound in canvas, ruled in dollars and cents; contains 500 pages extra quality white paper. Our price, each..45c

No. 3R5210 Pocket Order Book, bound in full canvas, cut flush, contains 96 leaves of extra fine white paper, ruled in dollars and cents. Size, 4x6¾ inches. Our price, each........8c

If by mail, postage extra, each, 3 cents.

Pass Books.

No. 3R5212 Press Board Cover Pass Books. Printed in black and gold. Handsome design; good white paper. Size, 6¼x8¾ inches. Contains 40 leaves. Our price, two for........5c

No. 3R5214 Crown 8vo. Size, 3¾x6⅛ inches. Contains 20 leaves. Our price, three for........5c

No. 3R5216 Butchers' Pass Books. Cap, 8vo, canvas press board covers, contains 40 leaves extra white paper. Size, 3⅝x3⅞. Our price, three for 10c

No. 3R5218 Grocers' Press Board Cover Pass Books. Printed in black fancy design. Size, 3¾x5⅝ inches. Price, two for........5c

Scale Books.

No. 3R5224 Fairbank Standard Scale Book. Size, 8½x11 inches. Containing 500 weigh forms. Printed on an extra quality of good paper, with stubs attached. Bound in heavy board, marble paper sides and cloth back. Very durable. Our price, each...25c

No. 3R5226 Howe Standard Scale Book. Size, 8½x11 inches. Very durable. Bound in heavy boards, cloth backs. Contains 500 weigh forms. Printed on a very good quality of paper, with stubs attached. Our price, each........25c

No. 3R5228 The United States Standard Scale Books. Size, 8½x11 inches. Durably bound in boards; marble sides; cloth back. Contains 500 weigh forms. Printed on a good quality of paper, with stubs attached. Our price, each........25c

INK AND PENCIL TABLETS.

The following well selected line of Ink and Pencil Tablets are made by one of the largest manufacturers in the United States, and are guaranteed first quality. Always include tablets and boxed paper in your freight and express orders. Owing to their weight they make unprofitable mail shipments.

Tablets.

No. 3R5238 The Lion. Artistic design in delicate colors; **contains extra grade pencil paper.** Permanently bound and perforated. **Ruled.** Size, 6x9 inches. 240 pages.

Price, six for........20c
Weight per tablet, 10 ounces.

No. 3R5244 The Gray Eagle. An artistic design in colors. Permanently bound; perforated. Extra quality of finest pencil paper, ruled. Contains 280 pages (140 leaves). Size, 6x9 inches. Weight, packed, 12 ounces.

Price, five for.20c

No. 3R5248 Blossoms. Contains a beautifully finished white pencil paper; artistic lithographed covers in colored inks. Permanently bound. Ruled. Size, 8x10 inches. 250 pages (150 leaves). Weight, packed for shipment, 11 ounces.

Price, three for........15c

Society Stationery.

No. 3R5428 Feather Weight Society Stationery. Contains one quire of pure white, rice finish, octavo paper for foreign correspondence, with envelopes to match. Size, 5x6½ inches. Weight, packed for shipment, 4 ounces.
Our price, each..............21c

Warwick.

No. 3R5436 Pure fabric octavo note paper, with baronial envelopes to match; banded and tied with silk ribbon; put up in heavy box, stamped in gold. Size, 5¼x6½ inches. Weight, packed for shipment, 14 ounces.
Price, per box..............27c

Society Correspondence.

No. 3R5456 Silk Moire. Selected Society Correspondence. New patented paper, silk water lined, very best grade, pure white paper, banded and tied with silk ribbon. Size of paper, 6x5 inches. Weight, packed for shipment, 14 ounces.
Our price, each...........30c

No. 3R5460 Contains one quire of pure white paper and envelopes, banded and tied with ribbon. Put up in a very attractive telescopic case, covered with decorated paper and tied with silk ribbon. Size, 7x5½x2 inches. Weight, packed for shipment, 16 ounces. Price..............38c

No. 3R5462 Beautifully shaped box, the feature being the cut down sides, which show both the paper and envelopes on both sides of the middle partition, and telescope cover. Contains two quires and two packs of **highest grade velvet finish 60-pound octavo size note paper.** Both envelopes and paper tied with crinkled silk. Size of sheet, 4½x7 inches. Weight, packed for shipment, 28 ounces. Retail price, $1.00; our price...............65c

Ladies' Art Stationery.

Including Initial Seal, Sealing Wax and Candles.

No. 3R5464 First Quality Cream Wove. Smooth Note Paper, with baronial envelopes to match, unruled; 50 envelopes and 50 sheets of paper in cabinet style box, together with three sticks of sealing wax and half dozen wax candles. When ordering, be sure and give letter wanted on initial seal. Size of sheets, 4½x7 inches. Weight, 19 ounces. Per box........60c

PAPETERIES IN FANCY BOXES.

Nothing More Appropriate for Birthday, Wedding, Christmas and New Year Presents.
If by mail, postage, 1 cent per ounce.

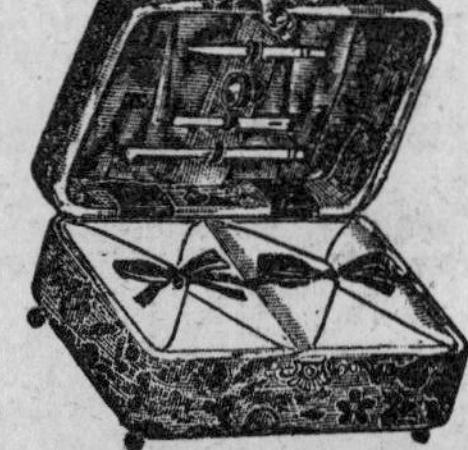

No. 3R5480 Fancy Plush Work Box. With ball feet; cover lined with sateen and fitted with bodkin, crochet hook, thimble, stiletto; filled with one quire of cream white wove paper, with envelopes to match, tied with silk ribbon. Size of box, 3x4½x5¼ inches. Weight, packed for shipment, 23 ounces.
Price, each.........98c

No. 3R5494 Photo Cabinet. Beautiful Photo Box with medallion, cover lined with white satin, filled with cream wove, octavo note paper, with envelopes to match, tied with silk ribbon. Box fitted with ball feet and hinges and nickel clasp. Size, 5¼ x 8 inches. Weight, packed for shipment, 22 ounces.
Price, each 75c

Handkerchief Boxes.

No. 3R5496 Contains first quality cream wove octavo note paper, with Baronial envelopes to match. Put up in a wooden box, covered with a beautiful lithographed top. Size of paper, 4½x6 inches. Weight, packed for shipment, 18 ounces.
Price, per box..........55c

No. 3R5504 Celluloid Handkerchief Box. With medallion on outside cover, sateen lined cover, containing extra quality of writing paper, with envelopes to match. Size of box, 6x6¾ inches. Weight, packed for shipment, 18 ounces.
Price...65c

Glove Box.

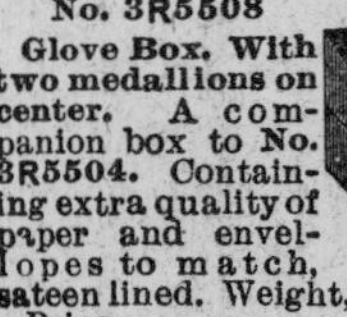

No. 3R5508 Glove Box. With two medallions on center. A companion box to No. 3R5504. Containing extra quality of paper and envelopes to match, sateen lined. Weight, packed for shipment, 18 ounces.
Price $0.65
Per set, Glove and Handkerchief.......... 1.15

Fancy Plush Work Box.

No. 3R5515 Fancy Plush Work Box. Cover lined with sateen. Contains crochet hook, thimble, bodkin and stiletto. Also ne quire of cream wove square note paper with envelopes to match, tied with silver cord. Ball feet. Size, 8x2¼x5¼ inches. Weight, packed for shipment, 18 ounces.
Price................53c

Regret Cards.

No. 3R5518 25 cards and 25 envelopes; put up in an artistically shaped box; cards of the best grade heavy white stock, gilt edges. Weight, 9 ounces.
Price, per box......25c
No. 3R5520 Regret Cards. 25 cards and 25 envelopes; put up in an artistically shaped box, plain edges. Weight, 9 ounces. Price, per box....20c

Juvenile Stationery.

No. 3R5525 Juvenile Box of Fine Stationery, artistically shaped, containing one quire of smooth white paper, ruled, with envelopes to match. Weight, 10 ounces. Size, 4½x3¾ inches.
Price, per box..................11c

Fancy Work Box.

No. 3R5528 Fancy Plush Work Box, for children, containing extra white cream wove paper, tied with silk cord, with envelopes to match, crochet hook, bodkin and stiletto. Weight, packed for shipment, 8 ounces.
Price, each..............25c

Plain Visiting Cards.

No. 3R5532 Visiting Cards. Superfine Satin Finished, highest quality. Size, 2¼x3¼ inches; put up 50 cards to the package.
Per package 9c
If by mail, postage per pack of 50 cards, 5c.

BEST SCHOOL INKS.

By special arrangements with one of the largest ink manufacturers in America we are able to offer a No. 1 first quality school ink at from 25 to 50 per cent lower than school supply establishments. The boards of education, superintendents, secretaries and principals of schools will find it to their advantage to consider our prices before placing orders elsewhere.

We guarantee this ink to be an absolutely pure, easy flowing, writing fluid.

No. 3R5540 Price for a 3-gallon keg, filled with best school ink..............................$1.25
No. 3R5542 Price for a 5-gallon keg, filled.. 1.60
No. 3R5544 Price for a 10-gallon keg, filled.. 2.98
No. 3R5546 Price for a 20-gallon keg, filled.. 5.98

GIVE CATALOGUE NUMBER IN FULL
WHEN YOU WRITE YOUR ORDER

Dann's Blue Black Writing Fluid.

Dann's Inks, Mucilages and Pastes are the best made. Guaranteed first quality. It is very unprofitable to ship inks, mucilages, etc., by mail. Always enclose a supply to go in your freight or express orders with other goods.

An Ideal Ledger Ink, rich in color, smooth in flow, absolutely permanent. Best made.

No. 3R5548 2-ounce wide mouth cylinder bottle. Price, each........4c
No. 3R5549 4-ounce round bottle. Price, each.....................8c
No. 3R5550 ½-pints, with patent pourout. Price, each..............18c
No. 3R5552 Pints, with patent pourout. Price, each..............30c
No. 3R5554 Quarts, with patent pourout. Price, each..55c
Unmailable on account of weight.

Dann's New Carmine (Red) Writing Fluid.

This Ink has great brilliancy; does not affect and is not affected by steel pens.
No. 3R5558 Fast Red Fluid. Very brilliant. 1½-ounce. Wide mouth cylinder. Black milled top. Price, each...............................4c
No. 3R5560 Put up in a wide mouth cylinder, 2-ounce bottles. Price, each........................7c
No. 3R5562 ½ pints. Light glass with hard rubber stopper. Price, each.......................40c
Unmailable on account of weight.

Dann's Best Black Ink.

No. 3R5564 2-ounce glass bottles. Price, per bottle.......4c
If by mail, postage and tube extra, each, 8c.
No. 3R5565 4-ounce bottles. Per bottle.........................7c
No. 3R5566 ½-pint bottles, with spouts. Per bottle......18c
No. 3R5568 Pint bottles, with spouts. Per bottle............30c
No. 3R5570 Quart bottles, with spouts. Per bottle.......50c
Unmailable on account of weight.

Dann's Premium Raven Black Ink.

No. 3R5578 4-ounce wide mouth cylinders. Price, 4-ounce stand...........8c
No. 3R5582 ½-pints. With hard rubber stopper. Price, per ½-pint.........22c
Unmailable on account of weight.

Dann's Writing and Copying Ink.

Blue Black. Easy flow and makes perfect copies.
No. 3R5590 4-ounce wide mouth cylinders. Price, each...........................8c
No. 3R5592 ½-pints, with hard rubber tops. Price, each.......................30c
No. 3R5594 Pint bottles, with patent pourouts. Price, each..40c
No. 3R5596 Quart bottles, with patent pourouts. Price, each.......................................75c
Unmailable on account of weight.

Dann's Green Ink.

No. 3R5599 2-ounce round stands, enameled tops. Per bottle...........8c
Unmailable on account of weight.

Ink Powders.

No. 3R5604 Put up in wooden boxes. Each box contains enough powder to make **one pint of good ink;** blue, green, purple, red and black. **In ordering, be sure to give the color.**
Per box...9c
If by mail, postage extra, per box, 2c.

Dann's Gloss Black Ink.

No. 3R5610 Best Aniline Ink. For ornamental penmanship, card writing, engraving, etc. Writes a beautiful gloss black. Dries quickly. Excellent for school and home use. Put up in 1¼-ounce wide mouth cones. Price, each..6c
If by mail, postage and tube extra, 8 cents.

Japanese Gold Ink.

No. 3R5614 Japanese Gold Ink, for corresponding, designing, decorating, etc.; **a brilliant gold ink which writes fluently with a common steel pen;** in ½-ounce bottles; weight (packed for mailing), 2 ounces.
Per bottle..9c
If by mail, postage extra, 5 cents.
No. 3R5616 1-ounce bottle Gold Ink. Price...15c
If by mail, postage extra, 5 cents.

Indelible Ink for Marking Linens.

No. 3R5620 Indelible Ink, for marking linen, silk and cotton with a common pen; **no preparation is required.** It becomes deep black when dry.
Per 1-dram...................................15c
Per 1-ounce bottle...........................50c
Per 1-pint bottle, for hotels, laundries, etc. Price...........................$1.20
If by mail, postage and tube extra, 10 cents.

Dann's Indelible Ink.

No. 3R5624 Writes dark, changes to deep black and is permanent; put up in a practical bottle, with stretcher for holding fabric while marking, and pen and penholder in decorated tin box.
Weight, packed, 4 ounces. Price...................19c
If by mail, postage extra, 3 cents.

Flexible Prepared Glue.

The Strongest Glue on the Market. Requires a little heat before using, therefore making it stronger by not being cut with acids or other ingredients to keep it liquid. Has no offensive odor, and age does not weaken it; water not being used in manufacturing it, therefore does not evaporate or absorb, consequently it does not dry up. Always retains its flexibility and strength.

No. 3R5630 1-oz. bottles. Each.......... 7c
No. 3R5634 2-oz. bottles. Each.......... 12c
If by mail, postage and tube, extra, 10 and 12c.
No. 3R5636 ½-pint tin cans. Each........ $0.20
No. 3R5638 1-pint tin cans. Each........ .38
No. 3R5640 1-quart tin cans. Each........ .56
No. 3R5642 1-gallon cans. Each........ 1.75
Unmailable on account of weight.

Dann's Best Mucilage.

No. 3R5648 Dann's Best Mucilage, flat cylinder stand, flint glass. 2-ounce bottle.
Price, each........................5c
No. 3R5650 Dann's Best Mucilage, 3½-ounce bottle. Each. 8c
If by mail, postage extra, 8 cents.
No. 3R5654 Dann's Best Mucilage, ½-pint flint glass bottles with hard rubber tops.
Price, each....................30c
No. 3R5660 Dann's Best Mucilage. 1-pint glass bottles with hard rubber tops. Price, each. 45c
No. 3R5662 Dann's Best Mucilage. 1-quart flint glass bottles with hard rubber tops. Price, each..........................69c
Unmailable on account of weight.

Dann's Photo Library Paste.

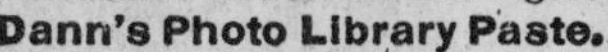

Dann's Photo Library Paste. This paste embodies the latest results of advanced chemical research in the Department of Adhesives. It has a beautiful white color and is delightfully perfumed.

No. 3R5664 1-ounce collapsible tubes, without brush. Price, each..4c
No. 3R5666 2-ounce tube, with patented brush attached.
Price, each....................8c
No. 3R5668 3-ounce collapsible tubes, without brush. Price, each, 10c
No. 3R5670 3-ounce tube, with patented brush attached. Price, each. 15c
If by mail, postage extra, per tube, 3c
No. 3R5672 4-ounce jar, with nickel screw cap. Price, each..............15c
No. 3R5674 2-ounce cylinder, flint glass, with cap and brush. Price, each..........5c
Shipping weight, 12 ounces. Shipping weight of tube, 5 ounces.

INKSTANDS.

The New Gardner Inkstand.

No. 3R5690 Guaranteed dust proof, non-evaporating, supplies just enough ink, keeps the ink always fresh, made of heavy pressed glass, with embossed hard rubber front. Size, 2½x2½ inches. Price, each..............................45c
Weight, packed for shipment, 12 ounces.

Smith's Automatic Inkstand.

No. 3R5694 Always ready for use, automatically inks the pen, leaving all surplus ink, and does not soil the fingers. Moulding and evaporation are impossible. Fitted with dip cup stem, admitting the ink at the side instead of the bottom. Completely air tight; 3 inches square; weight, 22 ounces.
Price..............................98c
No. 3R5696 Automatic Inkstand. Size, 2x2 inches. Otherwise same as No. 3R5694. Price...70c

Genuine Wrought Iron Leaf Shape Inkstands.

No. 3R5698 Genuine Wrought Iron Leaf Shape Inkstands. 2¾ inches high, base 4½ inches, fitted with 1½-inch square glass well. Weight, packed for shipment, 12 ounces. Our price, each..............15c

Library Inkstand.

No. 3R5702 Library Inkstand. An attractive library ink stand, new style, made of solid wood, highly finished, fitted with 1½-inch glass bottle and pen rack. Our price, each, 17c
If by mail, postage extra, 9 cents.

SATISFACTION GUARANTEED.

SEE PAGE 1 OF THIS CATALOGUE AND LEARN WHAT IT MEANS.

Automatic Inkstand.

No. 3R5708 New Patent Automatic Inkstand, made with a hardwood polished base; top and ends are brass and steel, finely nickeled; contains two receptacles for ink also one each for pens and postage stamps; always closed; prevents evaporation and keeps out the dust; suitable for a mantel, parlor or library. Our special price. 55c
Weight, packed for shipment, 16 ounces.

$1.00 Library Inkstand For Only 35c.

No. 3R5716 Enameled Inkstand, containing two heavy flint glass bottles, mounted on an iron rack; size, 4¾x4 inches.
Our special price......35c
Weight, packed for shipment, 20 ounces.

Handy Inkstand.

No. 3R5717 Handy Inkstand, finished in bronze, iron cover and case; heavy flint glass bottle, 3 inches high; base, 3½x3½ inches. Weight, packed, 20 ounces. Each ..20c

No. 3R5718 Beautiful Fancy Shape Iron Inkstand, fitted with 7-inch base, suitable for holding pens, penholders, stamps, etc. 4½-inches square glass ink well with removable cover. 2¼ inches high. Weight, packed for shipment, 16 ounces. Our price, each..................28c

No. 3R5722 Fancy Shape Office or Library Inkstand. Made of genuine hand forged wrought iron, leaf pattern, 4 inches high, 5½-inch base, fitted with 1½-inch glass ink well with loose cap cover. Weight, packed for shipment, 16 ounces.
Our price, each..............35c

No. 3R5726 Common Sense Inkstand for commercial and general use. No evaporation; no spilling of ink. The most practical and useful inkstand made; 2 inches high; weight, packed, 6 ounces.
Price, each..........................9c

No. 3R5730 Beautiful Fancy Rose and Leaf Pattern Library Inkstand. 4 inches high; 5-inch base; fitted with 1¾-inch cut glass ink well, with removable cover. Weight, packed for shipment, 16 ounces. Our price..............98c

No. 3R5750 New Fancy Safety Pocket Inkstand. Guaranteed non-leakable. Covered with imitation leather. Celluloid top trimmings. 1½ inches in diameter. Price, each..........25c
If by mail postage extra, 5 cents.

No. 3R5754 My Diary. A book shape leather covered box, containing a safety ink well, non-leakable, pocket size.
Price, each................30c
If by mail, postage extra, 5 cents.

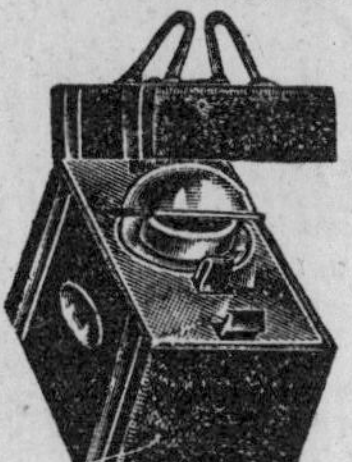

No. 3R5760 New Fancy Pocket and Travelers' Safety Inkstand. Leather suit case pattern, 2¼ inches long, 1¾ inches wide. A very desirable gift. Price, each..........35c
If by mail, postage extra, 5 cents.

No. 3R5764 Fancy Guitar Shaped Pocket Inkstand. Leather bound, imitation nickel trimmings, 3½ inches long, ¾ inch deep. A very desirable birthday or Christmas present.
Price, each..................................40c
If by mail, postage extra, 5 cents.

Paper Weight.

No. 3R5770 An attractive **Paper Weight,** ebonoid finish. Extra heavy **sterling trimmings.** Size, 2¼x2 inches. Price, each......................40c
If by mail, postage extra, 5 cents.

Calendar Stand and Memorandum Pad.

No. 3R5774 Shows the days and months of the year plainly marked on every leaf and has an extra large memorandum writing space. This stand occupies less desk space than any other stand on the market. Base is neat, firm and ornamental. Our price for stand, complete, with pad,
Price............50c
Weight, packed for shipment, 1½ pounds.

Leather Writing Companions.

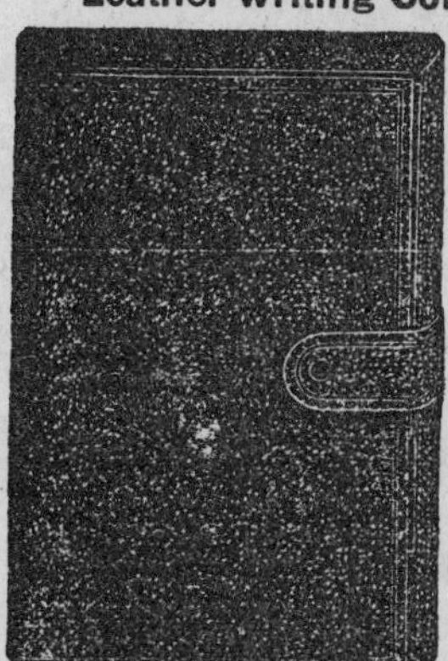

No. 3R5776 Leatherette, imitation seal, strap with button lock, gusseted pocket inside of flap, pen, and large box compartment for stationery, screw cap inkstand. Size, 6¾x10⅜ inches. Weight, packed, 20 ounces.
Price........55c
No. 3R5780 Leather, imitation seal, strap with button lock, gusseted pocket with two envelope pockets, pen and large box compartment for stationery, and silvered spring catch inkstand. Size, 8x12 inches. Weight, packed, 2 pounds.
Price..................................$1.40
No. 3R5782 Leather, cape goat morocco, assorted colors, strap with button lock, gusseted pocket with two envelope pockets, pen and large box compartment for stationery, and silvered spring catch inkstand. Size, 8x12 inches. Weight, packed, 2 pounds. Price.................................$1.90
No. 3R5784 Leather, imitation seal, leather strap, with large nickel lock and key, gusseted pocket with two envelope pockets, pen and large box compartment for stationery, and silvered spring catch inkstand. Size, 8x12 inches. Weight, packed, 2 pounds. Price..................................$1.65

SEND A 2-CENT STAMP for WALL PAPER SAMPLE BOOK and save money on your wall paper.

SEND 5 CENTS for samples of BOYS' and CHILDREN'S CLOTHING. We are offering wonderful values this season.

Scholars' Writing Desk Boxes.

No. 3R5794 Scholars' Companion. A desk shaped box; lined; fitted with inkstand and spaces for penholders, pencils, rubber erasers, writing paper, etc. Size, closed, 6½x9¼x2⅜ inches. Weight, packed for shipment, 30 ounces.
Price, each..........40c

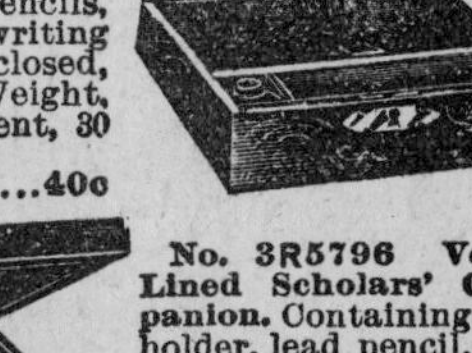

No. 3R5796 Velvet Lined Scholars' Companion. Containing penholder, lead pencil, rubber eraser. Size, 10x7x3½ inches. Otherwise same as No. 3R5794. Weight, packed for shipment, 2½ pounds.
Price, each.........50c

No. 3R5798 Large Size Scholars' Companion. Made of imported, decorated wood; velvet lined, gold border; size, 12x8x4 inches. Otherwise, same as No. 3R5794.
Weight, packed for shipment, 3¼ pounds.
Price, each....75c

Fountain Pens, Stylographics.

No. 3R6014 Eagle Fountain Pen assortment, contains one fountain pen, three extra vials, and one dozen extra pens, **in neat compartment box. A complete, popular and useful outfit.** Weight, packed, 5 ounces. Per box.....**18c**
If by mail, postage extra, 5 cents.

No. 3R6018 Fountain Pen only, without assortment. Price, each.....................................**8c**
No. 3R6020 Fountain Pen Filler, for fountain pen use; straight glass with seamless rubber bulb. Price, each.....................................**4c**
If by mail, postage extra, 2 cents.

No. 3R6024 Eagle Fountain Pen, black enamel finish, hexagon shape, nickel cap, containing glass vial filled with ink, to which is attached the feeder holding a noncorrosive pen; the most complete, useful and finest fountain pen made. Price, each...**10c**
If by mail, postage extra, 3 cents.
No. 3R6026 Glass Vials, filled with ink, for use in **Nos. 3R6018, 3R6020,** fountain pens.
Price, per dozen.....................................**23c**
We do not sell less than one dozen.
If by mail, postage extra, per dozen, 6 cents.

No. 3R6028 Fountain Pen, black enamel finish, round, with imitation gilt band. Containing glass vial filled with ink ready for use. The most complete, useful and cheapest fountain pen made. Guaranteed to give absolute satisfaction.
Our price, each.....................................**15c**
If by mail, postage extra, 3 cents.

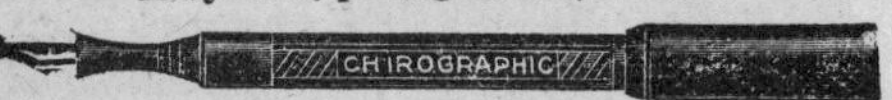

No. 3R6031 Chirographic Fountain Pen, fitted with solid gold pen, absolutely perfect, guaranteed non-leakable. Each pen put up in a strong box with glass filler and instructions. Price, each....**60c**
If by mail, postage extra, 3 cents.

Excello Fountain Pen.

No. 3R6032 Guaranteed 14-karat solid gold pen. The new feeding device is the simplest and most perfect yet produced, composed of but a single piece of hard rubber, so constructed as to produce the necessary flow, which is automatically regulated by the act of writing. No complicated parts to get out of order. Each pen put up in a strong box with glass filler and instructions. Our price, each....**89c**
If by mail, postage extra, 5 cents.

$1.10 Non-Leakable Fountain Pen.

No. 3R6034 Correspondent Fountain Pen, fitted with a 14-karat gold pen and chased hard rubber barrel; absolutely perfect, guaranteed non-leakable. The construction and internal mechanism are of the most improved and highest order, both as to quality and workmanship. Made with latest patented detachable reservoir which unscrews from the bottom and not from the top like the old style pens. Each pen put up in a strong box with glass filler and instructions. Retail price, $2.50; our price....**$1.10**
If by mail, postage extra, 3 cents.

$1.50 Non-Leakable Gold Fountain Pen.

No. 3R6038 Same as No. 3R6034, but handsomely ornamented with heavy 18-karat gold bands. Price.....................................**$1.50**
If by mail, postage extra, 5 cents.

Stylographic Pen.

No. 3R6042 Stylographic Pen, made of hard vulcanite. The flow of ink is produced and regulated by a gold needle with a spring attached, and a platinum point. This is the best and most practical stylographic pen made. Each pen packed in a separate box with glass filler and directions.
Our special price.....................................**60c**
If by mail, postage extra, 8 cents.

Automatic Pencils.

No. 3R6050 Sterling Silver Propel and Repel Pencil, with ring. Corrugated pattern. A new and attractive novelty, 2¾ inches long. Retail price, 30c; our price, each.....................................**20c**
If by mail, postage extra, 2 cents.

No. 3R6054 Eagle Automatic Pencil, stop gauge, with copying ink lead, which writes black and copies green; length, 5 inches. Price, each..............**7c**
No. 3R6058 Copying Ink Leads for the above pencil; three leads in metallic box.
Price, per box.....................................**7c**
If by mail, postage extra, 2 cents.

Automatic Pencils and Novelties.

No. 3R6060 Eagle Automatic Pencils, with violet ink lead, 4⅛ inches long. Price, each.........**4c**
No. 3R6062 Copying Ink Leads, violet for the above; three leads in box. Price, each..............**4c**
If by mail, postage extra, 2 cents.

Reversible Combination Pen and Pencil.

No. 3R6066 Eagle Combination Pen and Pencil. Neat in appearance, convenient and practical. Fitted with lead pencil, rubber eraser and steel pen. Highly polished barrel. Price, three for.............**10c**
If by mail, postage extra, on three, 2 cents.

Combination Sliding Penholder and Pen.

No. 3R6070 Combination Sliding Penholder and Pen; pencil with rubber eraser and protector. Nickel, highly finished. Price, each.....................**5c**
If by mail, postage extra, 2 cents.

No. 3R6074 Propel-Repel Pencil. Nickel. Containing extra grade of No. 2 lead, with ring for attaching to band, cord and programs.
Our price, each.....................................**25c**
If by mail, postage extra, 2 cents.
No. 3R6076 Extra Leads for No. 3R6074. Per box of three.....................................**5c**
If by mail, postage extra, 2 cents.

No. 3R6080 Eagle Patent Cigar Cutter, fitted with 3½-inch extra fine grade lead pencil and rubber eraser; **a most convenient article for smokers.**
Price, each.....................................**7c**
If by mail, postage extra, 3 cents.

No. 3R6090 Magic Automatic Combination Knife and Pencil Sharpener. The easiest knife in the world to open; no stiff joints, consequently no broken thumb nails. The blade moves out or in when pressure is applied on the end opposite the blade, according as that end is held down or up; the blade entirely concealed in the case, is effectually protected from dirt and rust. Highly polished, black handle, gilt stamped. Price, each.....................................**20c**
If by mail, postage extra, 3 cents.

Eagle Magic Knife.

No. 3R6096 Eagle Magic Knife, with nickeled spiral handle and blade, which moves in or out when pressure is applied to the cap; length, open, 5 inches. Price, each.....................................**8c**
If by mail, postage extra, 1 cent.

Eagle School Compass.

No. 3R6104 Eagle School Compass, most practicable and useful article for schools, colleges, etc., fitted with a 7-inch polished cedar pencil No. 2.
Price, per dozen, 48c; each.....................................**4c**
If by mail, postage extra, 2 cents.

Eagle Compass and Divider.

No. 3R6108 Eagle Compass and Divider, reliable in its work and useful for school children, mechanics, artists, draftsmen and architects; **a child can readily and** freely use it; nicely nickel plated, regulated by spring and screw adjustment, each in neat box, with nickel box containing six extra leads. Weight, packed, 3 ounces. Price, each.....................**18c**
If by mail, postage extra, 4 cents.

Rubber Erasers.

No. 3R6112 Faber's Combined Ink and Pencil Eraser, wood center, best quality erasive rubber.
Price, each.....................................**7c**
If by mail, postage extra, 3 cents.

S., R. & Co. Oblong Rubber Eraser.

No. 3R6114 Cabinet Bevel Point Oblong Rubber Eraser. Silk finish, superior quality, small size.
Price, per dozen, 10c; six for.....................**5c**
If by mail, postage extra, for six, 3 cents.
No. 3R6116 Cabinet Eraser, silk, medium size.
Price, per dozen, 30c; two for.......................**5c**
If by mail, postage extra, for two, 3 cents.

Cartridge Eraser.

No. 3R6118 A novel and popular style. Containing first quality erasive rubber for ink or pencil. Mounted in a highly polished nickel shell.
Price, per dozen, 60c; each.....................................**5c**
If by mail, postage extra, 2 cents.

Faber's Circular Eraser.

No. 3R6120 Faber's Circular Eraser, for typewriter ink or pencil. **The circular is very convenient,** giving a sharp continuous edge for use until worn out.
Price, per dozen, 48c; each....**4c**
If by mail, postage extra, 2 cents.

Ink and Pencil Eraser.

No. 3R6122 Combined Ink and Pencil Eraser, superior quality, beveled ends.
Price, each.....................................**4c**
Per dozen.....................................**48c**
If by mail, postage extra, 2 cents.

Columbia Eraser.

No. 3R6124 Columbia Eraser, made of red, white and blue rubber of first quality, specially adapted for school work.
Price, per dozen, 40c; three for.....................**10c**
If by mail, postage extra, for three, 4 cents.

Rubber Bands.

No. 3R6126 Assortment of superior quality Rubber Bands, for office and home use, packed in a box 1⅞x3½x6¼ inches. Weight, 6 ounces. Per box....**25c**
If by mail, postage extra, 7 cents.
No. 3R6128 Gray Thread Bands. No. 8 size, ⅞ inch long; one gross in a box; we do not sell less than a box.
Price, per box (144)........**9c**
If by mail, postage extra, 3 cents.

No. 3R6130 Gray Thread Bands. No. 10 size, 1¼-inches long; one gross in a box. We do not sell less than a box.
Price, per box (144), **10c**
If by mail, postage extra, 4 cents.

No. 3R6132 Gray Thread Bands. No. 12 size, 1⅝ inches long; one gross in a box. We do not sell less than a box. Price, per box (144)......**13c**
If by mail, postage extra, 5 cents.

No. 3R6134 Gray Thread Bands, No. 14 size, 2 inches long; one gross in a box. We do not sell less than a box. Price, per box (144)..............**16c**
If by mail, postage extra, 5 cents.

No. 3R6138 Gray Rubber Bands, ¼-inch wide.
No. 000¼, length, 3 inches. Price, per dozen.....**8c**
No. 0000¼, length, 3½ inches. Price, per dozen....**9c**
We do not sell less than one dozen.
If by mail, postage extra, 3 cents.

No. 3R6140 Gray Rubber Bands, ½-inch wide.
No. 00½, length, 2½ inches. Four for..............**5c**
No. 000½, length, 3 inches. Three for..............**5c**
No. 0000½, length, 3½ inches. Three for..............**5c**
No. 3R6142 Gray Rubber Bands, ¾-inch wide.
No. 000¾, length, 3 inches. Three for..............**5c**
No. 0000¾, length, 3½ inches. Four for..............**10c**
If by mail, postage extra, for three, 4 cents.

The Myograph.

No. 3R6148 Myograph. Made from superior spring brass, nickel plated, with penholder and pen attached. Prevents the finger movement and develops the muscular movement in writing. Keeps pen and hand in correct position. Prevents writers' cramp. Price, each..**12c**
If by mail, postage extra, 3 cents.

Penholders.

If by mail, postage extra, on three, four or five penholders, extra, 3 cents.

Open.

Closed.

No. 3R6158 Eagle Arrow Pocket Penholder, dust proof, metal. By pressing the cap or top it will release the pen and bring it in position ready for use; a reverse action closes the pen (as shown in illustration). Finished in black japanned handle. Price, each..........8c

No. 3R6160 Straight Handled Penholder, accommodation tips, for school use. Price, per doz., 3c

No. 3R6162 Japanned Swell Penholder, cedar handle, highly finished nickel tip, best quality and high dip; color finish in black, red and natural. Medium size. Price, per dozen, 30c; two for..........5c

No. 3R6166 Crown Penholder, taper highly finished cedar wood handle, with patented hard rubber tip. Price, per dozen, 60c; each..........5c

No. 3R6168 Cork Penholder, taper finished, in black, rosewood and natural polish. The cork tip is very agreeable and easy to the touch; does not tire the fingers. Price, per dozen, 60c; each..........5c

No. 3R6170 Oblique Penholder. Medium size, polished cedar handle, natural or japanned finish. The tip that holds the pen is adjustable, thereby allowing the pen to be used at any angle. **A favorite with expert penmen and card writers.** Price, per dozen, 48c; each..........4c

No. 3R6172 Pen-Ejecting Holder, long taper swell polished cedar handle with a corrugated hard rubber tip. By sliding the rubber tip back it readily ejects the pen without soiling the fingers. Price, per dozen, 48c; each..........4c

No. 3R6174 Sears, Roebuck & Co.'s Natural Finished Penholder, with red rubber sleeve which prevents the ink from staining fingers; long taper handles. Price, per dozen, 60c; each..........5c

No. 3R6176 Glass Writing Pen. Twisted glass for point in nickeled barrel. Black enameled holder. Price, each..........9c

If by mail, postage extra, 2 cents.

Stylus and Shading Pens.

No. 3R6180 Steel Point Stylus, for writing on manifold paper, nickel mounted, black japanned, taper handle. Price, each..........8c

AUTOMATIC SHADING PEN

No. 3R6190 Automatic Shading Pens, for engrossing, fancy lettering, card writing, etc.

Nos.	0	1	2	3	4	5
Width,	1/16 in.	1/8 in.	3/16 in.	1/4 in.	3/8 in.	1/2 in.

Price, each..........10c

No. 3R6192 No. 6, 5/8-inch wide. Each..........12c

No. 3R6194 No. 8, 7/8-inch wide. Each..........12c

If by mail, postage extra, 1 cent.

Ink for Automatic Shading Pens.

No. 3R6198 Shading Pen Ink, prepared especially for use with automatic shading pens; in wide mouth, round, flint glass 1½-ounce bottles. Colors, red, violet, blue, green, black or gold. Per bottle, 10c

If by mail, postage and mailing tube extra, 13c.

Book on Pen Lettering and Designs.

No. 3R6200 For the student, teacher and artist. Contains instructions, alphabets, mottoes, display and business cards, beautiful and elaborate designs, monograms, hat and book marks, Christmas, New Year and calling cards; also many halftone engravings. Handsomely bound in paper covers with an artistic design. Our price..........98c

If by mail, postage extra, 6 cents.

Pencil Holder.

No. 3R6210 "Dove" Nickel Pencil Holder, made to fit any pocket. Each..........7c

If by mail, postage extra, 2 cents.

Pencil Holders.

No. 3R6212 "Handy" Pencil Holder, leatherette, plush lined, with metal spring, will hold four pencils. Each..........7c

If by mail, postage extra, 2 cents.

No. 3R6216 "Au Fait." Latest Improved Pencil Holder; can be attached to pocket, suspenders or trouser band; nickel plated. Has double barrel which may be adjusted to hold any size lead pencil, pen holder or fountain pen. Leather clamp securely attaches holder to garment. Each..........7c

If by mail, postage extra, 2 cents.

New Acme Pencil Sharpener.

No. 3R6220 With double edge blade. When one edge becomes dull the blade can be reversed, thus there is an equivalent of two blades with each sharpener. Combines simplicity with perfection. One of the most valuable and practical pencil sharpeners in the market. Each..........20c

If by mail, postage extra, 3 cents.

No. 3R6224 Extra blades for the Acme Pencil Sharpener. Price, each..........8c

If by mail, postage extra, 2 cents.

20th Century Pencil Sharpener.

No. 3R6230 A new, practical pencil sharpener. The case is of solid metal, affording a certain firmness and steadiness to the hand when in use. Blade is held in position by screws, which can be worked with the aid of any implement. Requires no adjusting, always ready for use. Each..........9c

If by mail, postage extra, 3 cents.

Steel Ink Erasers and Envelope Openers.

No. 3R6238 Steel Ink Erasers, cocoa wood handles, with spear point. Length, 5 inches. Each, 30c

If by mail, postage extra, 2 cents.

Brush Ink Eraser.

No. 3R6242 Steel Brush Ink Eraser, consists of a number of very fine steel wires in the shape of a brush with bone tip for smoothing paper after erasing. Each..........18c

If by mail, postage extra, 2 cents.

Initial Seals.

No. 3R6248 Initial Seal, for sealing wax; length 2⅛ inches, black enameled handle, nickel metal die with rustic initial letter. Our special price, each..........7c

No. 3R6250 Initial Seal, for use with sealing wax; length, 3 inches; black enameled handle, nickeled metal die with Old English initial letter. Our price, each..........11c

If by mail, postage extra, 3 cents.

Sealing Wax.

No. 3R6256 Sanford's No. 2 Red Express Sealing Wax; four 4-ounce sticks to pound or eight 2-ounce sticks to pound. Per 4-ounce stick..........11c

Per lb. (either size), 30c; per 2-oz. stick..........5c

No. 3R6264 Perfumed Sealing Wax, for use in fine correspondence; five sticks in box. Weight per box, 5 ounces. Per box..........20c

If by mail, postage extra, 5 cents.

STEEL PENS.

The cuts show exact size of pens. We quote a varied line and warrant every one to be the best that can be found. Not less than a ¼ gross of any kind sold.

If by mail, postage on all pens extra, per ¼ gross, 3 cents.

Esterbrook Steel Pens.

No. 3R6280 "Bank" (No. 14), bronze finish, medium point, **an excellent and popular pen for business use.** Per ¼ gross..........14c

No. 3R6282 "Short Nib Engrossing," or Stub (No. 161 F), bronze finish, medium fine stub. **Very popular.** Per ¼ gross..........16c

STEEL PENS—Continued.

No. 3R6284 "Judge's Quill" (No. 312), gray finish, fine point stub; a large engrossing pen, very popular. Per ¼ gross..........17c

No. 3R6286 "School" (444), bronze finish, medium fine; **largely used in the public schools.** Per ¼ gross..........12c

Spencerian Steel Pens.

No. 3R6288 "College" (No. 1), point fine, elastic, and action perfect, **largely used by the best penmen in this country.** Per ¼ gross..........25c

Gillott's Steel Pens.

No. 3R6290 "Magnum Quill" (No. 601 E. F.), extra fine point, for fine and ordinary writing, very popular for general use. Per ¼ gross..........25c

No. 3R6292 "Double Elastic" (No. 604 E. F.), extra fine point. The original double elastic pen, **a favorite with professors of penmanship and teachers in business colleges.** Per ¼ gross..........20c

Eagle Pens.

No. 3R6294 Ledger (No. 470), extra fine point, suitable for business and general use; **flexible, bronze and gray finish.** Per ¼ gross..........18c

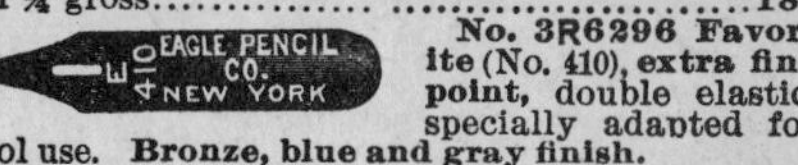

No. 3R6296 Favorite (No. 410), **extra fine point, double elastic, specially adapted for school use. Bronze, blue and gray finish.** Per ¼ gross..........13c

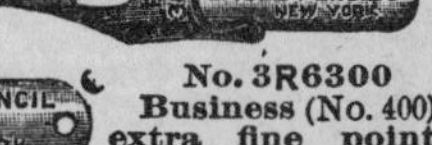

No. 3R6298 Ladies' Falcon (No. 30), **small size, gray finish.** Per ¼ gross..........15c

No. 3R6300 Business (No. 400), **extra fine point, gray finished,** recommended to business men as an easy writer. Per ¼ gross..........18c

Pliable Pens.

No. 3R6302 Pliable (No. 170), **medium fine point, gray finish, very popular school pen.** Per ¼ gross..........13c

No. 3R6304 Eagle Falcon (No. 10), medium point, gray finish, an excellent pen for general business purposes. Per ¼ gross..........12c

School Pens for Vertical Writing.

No pressure is required in using this pen, and it will not scratch or spatter, and writes with all the freedom of a lead pencil.

No. 3R6310 Vertical Steel Pen (No. 1), for vertical writing, medium point. Particularly recommended for use in primary classes. Per ¼ gross..........16c

Vertical Steel Pens.

No. 3R6312 Vertical Steel Pen (No. 2), **medium fine point.** For use in Intermediate classes. Per ¼ gross..........16c

No. 3R6314 Vertical Steel Pen (No. 4), extra fine point. For advanced or high classes. Per ¼ gross..........16c

Pantagraph for Enlarging Purposes.

No. 3R6330 Made of hardwood. A simple mechanical apparatus, which without any instruction enables one to enlarge portraits, using ordinary cabinet sized pictures. Maps, ornamental designs, music, monograms and patterns can be enlarged or reduced to any size by the use of this instrument. Price, each..........12c

If by mail, postage extra, 12 cents.

No. 3R6332 Has very neat and substantial trimmings, clean cut figures a finely finished and satisfactory instrument. Price, in box, each..........35c

No. 3R6336 Brass mounted, with brass elbow joint wheel, pencil holder and movable point; polished black figures. Price, in box, each..........$1.25

No. 3R6338 Heavily mounted, with nickel plated elbow joint wheel, pencil holder and exchangeable point; finely polished black figures. Price, in box, each..........$1.90

Instructions Accompanying Each.

If by mail, postage extra, 12 cents.

SEND 5 CENTS FOR SAMPLES OF MEN'S CLOTHING.

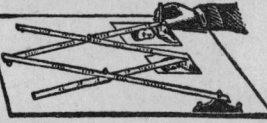

PHOTO STANDS AND HOLDERS.

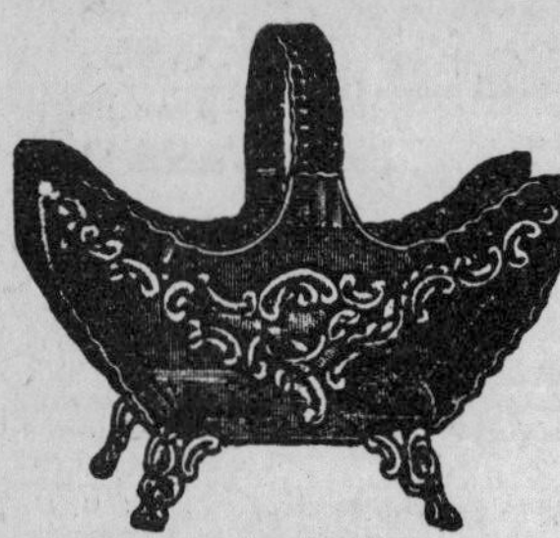

New Attractive Photo Stand. Beautiful design. Sides made of brilliant color transparent celluloid with notched and crinkled gilded edges; celluloid handle; genuine satin lined bottom; neatly trimmed with fancy colored finished metal ornaments and corner feet. Size, 3x7⅝x7⅝ ins.

No. 3R6842 Price.................................65c

If by mail, postage extra, 14 cents.

Our 9-Cent Photo Holder.

Fancy Photograph Holder. Made of imported papier mache, beautifully decorated, fitted with glass. Size, 7½x9 inches.

No. 3R6846 Our price,....9c

If by mail, postage extra, 5 cents.

Celluloid Photo Frame.

Photograph Frame. Made of beautiful tinted celluloid, elegantly set off at sides with wide, rich gilt bands, edges turned back and tied with silk cord and tassel, easel back. Size, 6⅛x8⅜ inches.

No. 3R6848 Price, 12c

If by mail, postage extra, 5 cents.

Aluminum Photo Frame.

Fancy Aluminum Photo Frame, with frosted surface, crinkled border, holds one cabinet size photo, hand painted, easel back. Size, 5⅞x8¾ inches.

No. 3R6850 Price....20c

If by mail, postage extra, 5 cents.

Our 25-Cent Photo Holder.

Fancy Photo Holder, nickel trimmed, beautifully decorated, fitted with glass. Size, 6½x8½ inches.

No. 3R6860 Our price, each..........................25c

If by mail, postage extra, 10c

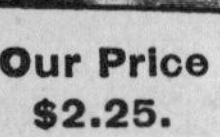

Our Price $2.25. Worth $5.00.

Automatic Photographic Case. Large size. Fine black seal grained case, heavily padded cover, handle hand tooled and well finished, oxidized metal catch and hinges, lined with fine quality satin, divided into two compartments for panel size photographs. Size, closed, 4⅜x7¾x10⅛ inches.

No. 3R6864 Weight, packed for shipment, 3 pounds. Price..................................$2.25

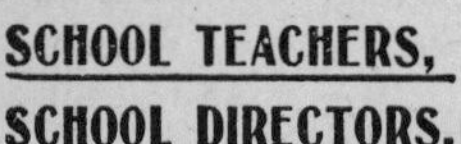

SCHOOL TEACHERS, SCHOOL DIRECTORS, and those on the Board of Education are directed to our very low prices on

SCHOOL INKS and BLACKBOARD ERASERS

in quantity. We are selling the best grades of ink in 3, 5, 10 and 20-gallon kegs at much lower prices than can be secured elsewhere. On all kinds of school supplies our prices are below competition of any kind.

FANCY COLLAR, CUFF, GLOVE AND HANDKERCHIEF CASES, SMOKERS' OUTFITS, SHAVING AND DRESSING CASES FOR MEN.

The fancy goods quoted below are most desirable gifts for men.

Collar and Cuff Cases.

Imitation Seal Grained Leather Collar and Cuff Box, fitted with finished metal pocket on cover for collar and cuff buttons, pins, etc.; separate compartments for collars and cuffs, durable and lasting, 5⅝ inches high, 6¼ inches in diameter.

No. 3R6880 Special price.................55c

Weight, packed for shipment, 1½ pounds.

Horseshoe, Novelty Shape, Full Celluloid Collar and Cuff Box. Made of brilliant colored transparent celluloid, crinkled edge cover with large horseshoe design, gilded extension base, separate compartments for collars and cuffs. Size, 5⅛x6⅛x6⅜ inches.

No. 3R6882 Our special price..........69c

Weight, packed for shipment, 1½ pounds.

An Attractive, Square Shape Collar and Cuff Box, made of tinted celluloid, cover heavily raised and embellished in gilt with fine design of words "Collars and Cuffs," ornamented with leaves and branches, open corner of front side turned back and neatly trimmed with gold finished metal ornaments, metal feet; divided into two compartments, satin lined. Size, 6⅞x6⅞x6⅞ ins.

Weight, packed for shipment, 18 ounces

No. 3R6886 Price..............................$1.40

FANCY NECKTIE CASES.

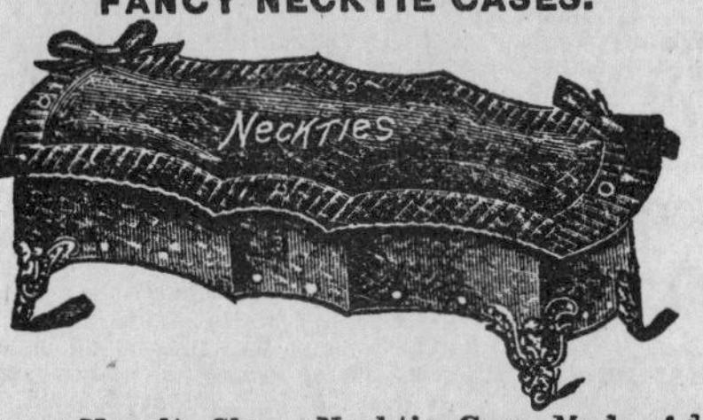

Fancy Novelty Shape Necktie Case. Made of delicately tinted, transparent celluloid; double raised cover with crinkled edges; handsomely set off with an elaborate design and fancy lettering in gilt; tied with ribbon bows, gros grained sateen lining, fancy metal corner feet. Size, 2⅞x4¼x11⅛ inches.

No. 3R6892 Price, each...........................53c

Weight, packed for shipment, 16 ounces.

98 Cents for This Beautiful $2.00 Celluloid Necktie Case.

Artistic Shape, Delicately Tinted, Satin Finished, Celluloid Necktie Case. Double raised covers with gilded crinkled edge; elegantly hand painted gold and floral decorations and fancy lettering on cover, fancy built up sides with open, gilded, crinkled corners, metal feet, sateen lining. Size, 3⅛x3⅞x13¼ inches.

No. 3R6896 Our price..........................98c

Weight, packed for shipment, 18 ounces.

$2.95 Buys A $3.50 Fancy Shaving Case.

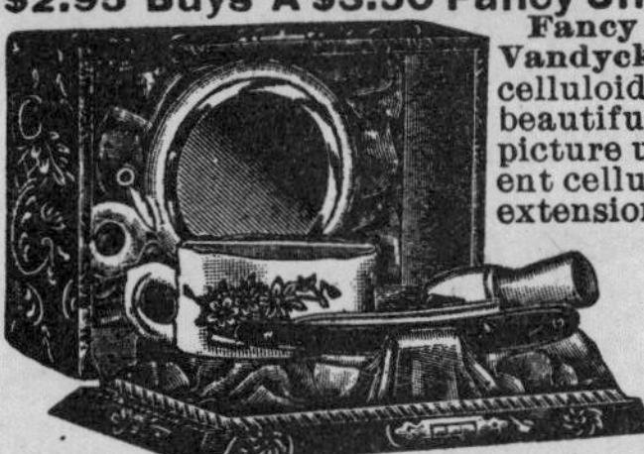

Fancy shaped case, Vandyck effect, full celluloid over top with beautiful lithographed picture under transparent celluloid on center, extension base, sateen lined. Contains a shaving mug, an excellent razor, lather brush and adjustable ring handle bevel plate mirror. Size, 3⅞x6⅝x8¾ inches.

No. 3R6910 Price..................................$2.95

Weight, packed for shipment, 2¼ pounds.

$1.98 for This Beautiful Dressing Case.

Roll Up Dressing Case, made of fine black seal grain leather, bound and stitched round edges. Closes with nickel spring catch. Interior has two infolding flaps and is lined throughout with fine piggra in lining. **Contains polished solid wood back hair brush,** nickel soap box, screw cap odor bottle and glass case holding a bone handled tooth brush. Size, open, 12¼x16⅛ inches; closed, 2x4⅝x7¾ in.

No. 3R6914 Our special price.......... ....$1.98

Weight, packed for shipment, 1½ pounds.

Our $3.45 Dressing Case.

Dresser Roll Up Case, made of fine heavy black seal grain leather, bound and stitched. Closes with a strap and covered with buckle, is leather lined throughout, has four infolding flaps, and is provided with pocket. **Contains a fine set of ebonized fittings,** tooth brush in glass case, solid back hair brush, screw cap odor bottle, nickel soap box, manicure scissors, shoe buttoner, file, wide comb and mirror. Size, open, 1½x7x16¼ inches; closed, 2¼x5⅝x8⅝ inches.

No. 3R6916 Our special price...............$3.45

Weight, packed for shipment, 2½ pounds.

ARTISTS' MATERIALS.

The well selected line quoted on this and the following pages will meet the approval of every artist. These goods are chosen because they are the highest grade made.

Artists' Tube Paints, Oil Colors.

Finely prepared colors for artists. Our tube paints are prepared from carefully selected pigments. The system employed in their manufacture is such that it secures that firm consistency and firmness of texture required by artists. Put up in collapsible tubes.

No. 3R7100 Single tube, class A, price each....5c

If by mail, postage per doz., single tubes, 18 cents.

No. 3R7104 Double tube, class A, price each...8c

If by mail, postage per doz., double tubes, 26 cents.

Always specify colors and size of tubes desired.

Am. Vermilion
Antwerp Blue
Asphaltum
Bitumen
Blue Black
Bone Brown
Brown Pink
Brown Ochre
Burnt Roman Ochre
Burnt Sienna
Burnt Umber
Caledonian Brown
Cappah Brown
Carmine Lake
Cremnitz White
Chrome Green, Light
Chrome Green, Medium
Chrome Green, Deep
Chrome Yellow Light
Chrome Yellow, Medium
Chrome Yellow, Deep
Chrome Yellow, Orange
Crimson Lake
Chinese Blue
Cologne Earth
Emerald Green
Flake White
Gamboge
Ivory Black
Indian Lake
Indian Red
Indigo
Italian Pink
King's Yellow
Light Red
Lamp Black
Magenta
Mauve
Megilp
Mummy
Naples Yellow, Light
Naples Yellow, Medium
Naples Yellow, Deep
Neutral Tint
New Blue
Oxford Ochre
Olive Tint
Orpiment
Payne's Gray
Permanent Blue
Purple Lake
Prussian Blue
Raw Sienna
Raw Umber
Roman Ochre
Rose Lake
Rose Pink
Sap Green
Scarlet Lake
Silver White
Sugar of Lead
Terre Verte
Transparent Gold Ochre
Vandyke Brown
Venetian Red
Verdigris
Verona Brown
Yellow Lake
Yellow Ochre
Zinnabar Green, Light
Zinnabar Green, Medium
Zinnabar Green, Deep
Zinc White

Gold Enamel.

No. 3R7464 Chinese Gold Enamel. Unmixed. An excellent substitute for gold leaf, for gilding and decorating purposes, produces a smooth gold surface and will neither rub nor tarnish. Each outfit contains a vial of powder, a bottle of mixed liquid, cup and brush. Price, small size....................14c

No. 3R7470 Chinese Gold Enamel. Large size. Contains gold powder, liquid, brush and cup. Can be used on furniture, frames, albums, statues, glasses, ceilings, centerpieces, flower pots, bedsteads, earthenware, etc. Each..25c

Favorite Gold Enamel.

No. 3R7472 Decorates anything and everything. It is used on furniture, frames, slippers, shoes, bicycles, baby carriages, baskets, tables, chairs, railings, artificial flowers, albums, statues, bric-a-brac, glasses, bottles, ornamental candles, gas fixtures, ceilings, centerpieces, garden sticks, flower pots, ink stands, clocks, grates, iron bedsteads, sewing machines, earthenware, etc. Can be washed with soap and water.

No. 3R7472 Price, per box..... ..20c

If by mail, postage and tube extra, per box, 16 cents.

Star Enamel.

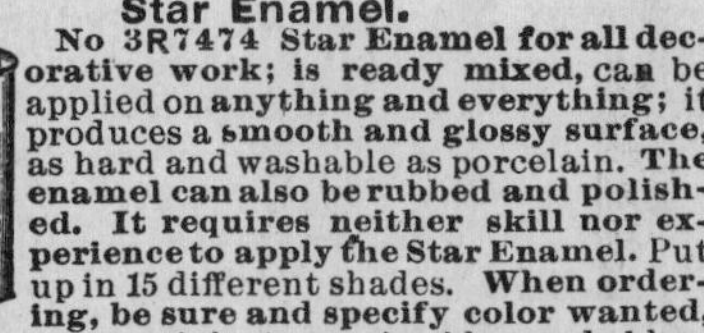

No 3R7474 **Star Enamel for all decorative work; is ready mixed, can be applied on anything and everything; it produces a smooth and glossy surface, as hard and washable as porcelain. The enamel can also be rubbed and polished. It requires neither skill nor experience to apply the Star Enamel.** Put up in 15 different shades. **When ordering, be sure and specify color wanted,** white, ivory, rose, pink, turquoise blue, pale blue, light green, yellow, orange, vermilion, cardinal red, oak brown, maroon, black, moss green and dark green. 1-pint can, 40c; ¼-pint can..............20c

If by mail, postage and tube, ¼-pint cans, extra, per can, 16 cents.

Larger sizes unmailable on account of weight.

Gold Paint.

No. 3R7480 For gilding ornamental candles and all kinds of waxwork, gilding fancy baskets, frames and every variety of woodwork, gilding metallic ornaments, gilding albums, stationery and all kinds of paper work, gilding dancing shoes and all kinds of leather work, gilding gas fixtures, gilding theatrical properties. **Put up in attractive, highly polished wooden boxes.**

No. 3R7480 Price, per box....................15c

If by mail, postage extra, per box, 5 cents.

Perfection Adding Machine.

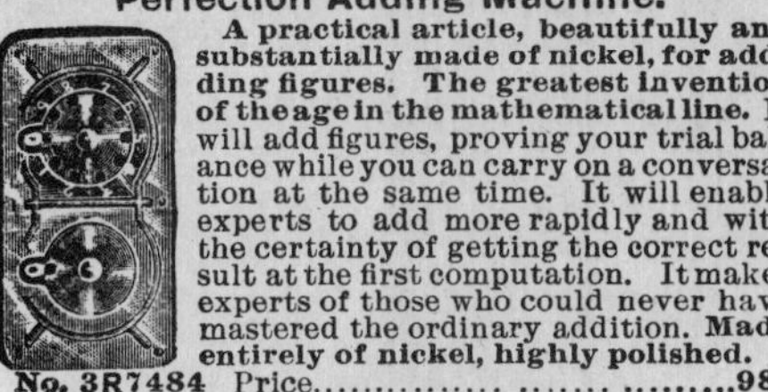

A practical article, beautifully and substantially made of nickel, for adding figures. The greatest invention of the age in the mathematical line. It will add figures, proving your trial balance while you can carry on a conversation at the same time. It will enable experts to add more rapidly and with the certainty of getting the correct result at the first computation. It makes experts of those who could never have mastered the ordinary addition. **Made entirely of nickel, highly polished.**

No. 3R7484 Price.......................98c

If by mail, postage extra, 5 cents.

The Little Gem Typewriter.

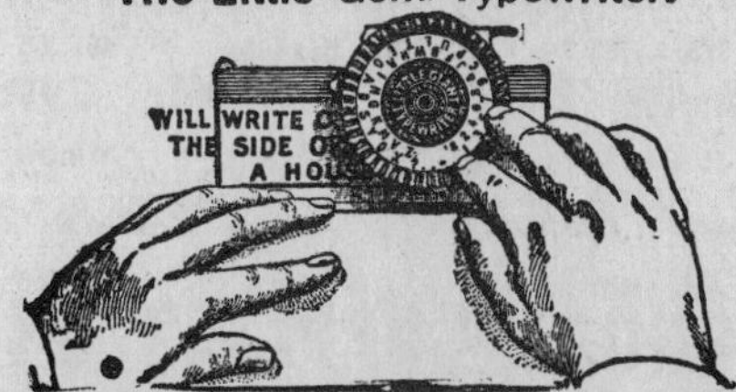

No. 3R7488 A practical machine for the household, and a kindergarten instructor of merit. Simple of operation, adjustable to single or double spacing, easily inked, and may be used to write on a book, package, or any other object as well as ordinary typewriter paper. Price, each..............75c

If by mail, postage extra, 15 cents.

Practical Typewriter.

A strong handsome steel nickel plated typewriter, suitable for business and private use. Made on entirely new principles, easily understood and operated. Has roller feed with spring adjustment, full line of characters, bell, large and small letters, writing always in sight; positive and perfect alignment; will take any width of paper.

No. 3R7490 Our special price...................$3.75

Weight, packed for shipment, 5 pounds.

New Improved Simplex Typewriter.

Takes full width paper, easily operated, substantially made, has full range of characters. Typewriter is mounted on a reversible polished wood base, which, when reversed, forms cover of a handsome hardwood carrying case with nickel handle. Weight, packed for shipment, 28 ounces.

No. 3R7494 Our price....................$2.70

If by mail, postage extra, 28 cents.

New Improved American Typewriter for Only $7.95.

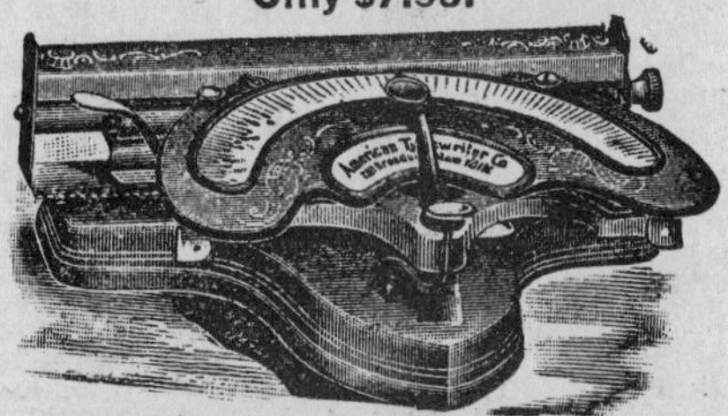

Scientifically constructed of cold rolled steel, brass and base of annealed iron. It prints directly from the type. Leaves a clear-cut impression. **The alignment is perfect and permanent. The writing is always in sight,** so corrections and insertions are made with ease and accuracy and thus it is perfectly adapted to making statements of accounts and other tabulating. **The operating is very simple. The feed is especially adapted to holding envelopes and postal cards,** which can be handled with the same rapidity as with the $100.00 machines. There are 73 characters, including capitals, small letters, figures and punctuation marks. Packed in a handsome metal case, with mahogany finished base.

No. 3R7508 New American Typewriter....$7.95
No. 3R7512 Ink for duplicating, per bot'e.. .25
No. 3R7514 Extra rollers required for each color..... ...... .52

Visible Writing Machine.

$22.50 buys this magnificent thoroughly up to date Visible Typewriter.

It is the production of fifteen years' experience, and is unquestionably the best and most thoroughly up to date low priced, Universal keyboard, visible typewriter on the market. Writing in sight is a self evident advantage. The carriage is extremely light and counter balanced. It is so well composed and connected with the shift key that the action is extremely light. Fitted with Universal keyboard of 27 keys, and writes altogether 81 characters. The speed of the Universal bar is so great that no operator, however rapid, could possibly reach its limit. Every key has a uniform depression and absolutely equal leverage. It takes paper up to 8¾ inches wide and writes a line 7½ inches. **The paper feed and release is most simple and effective,** marginal stop is positive and convenient, bell trip which could not be easier to handle, carriage release, which is simplicity itself; in fact, the entire machine is not only perfection, perfectly perfected, but simplicity, simply simplified.

No. 3R7520 Our special cut price.........$22.50

Weight, unpacked, 10½ pounds.

Typewriter Supplies.

No. 3R7524 Typewriter Ink. Put up in 1-ounce bottles. Price, per bottle....................15c

If by mail, Postage, including wooden case, extra, 12 cents.

No. 3R7528 Typewriter Ribbons for the Chicago, Munson, Smith Premier, Oliver, Caligraph, Remington and other standard machines. When ordering, be sure to state whether **blue, green, black or copying ribbon is wanted;** also give name of machine. Weight, packed for shipment, 4 ounces. Price, each....................69c

If by mail, postage extra, 4 cents.

No. 3R7532 Typewriter Oil. Best quality. Weight, packed for shipment, 10 ounces. Price, per bottle, 15c

If by mail, postage extra, 10 cents.

No. 3R7534 Typewriter Cleaning Brush. Weight, packed for shipment, 3 ounces. Price, each......20c

If by mail, postage extra, 3 cents.

TYPEWRITER SUPPLIES—Continued.

Typewriter Paper. Matchless Brand, for all standard typewriters. 500 sheets to the ream. We do not break reams.

No. 3R7536 Size, 8½x11 inches, plain white paper. Price, per ream....................60c

No. 3R7540 Size, 8½x13 inches, plain white paper, Price, per ream....................65c

No. 3R7542 Size, 8½x10 inches, plain white paper, Price, per ream....................50c

No. 3R7544 Size, 8½x10 inches, linen laid, extra quality paper. Price, per ream....................75c

No. 3R7546 Size, 8½x13 inches, linen laid, extra quality paper. Price, per ream....................85c

No. 3R7550 Typewriter Carbon Paper for manifold work and copying purposes. Size, 8x13 inches, price, per sheet, 4c; 8½x10 inches, per sheet.......3c

Rubber Type Outfits.

This picture illustrates the style in which all our Type is packed. Represents our 5A6a font of Solid Rubber Type, containing 285 separate pieces, including letters, figures, quads, spaces, and tweezers. Our number 2A3a font contains 150 letters, figures, nickel plated tweezers, also pad.

AAaaaBBbbbCCcccDDddd12

No. 3R7578 2A3a font of Type, solid rubber, containing 150 pieces. Same style as above illustration, including a two-line holder 3 inches long, ink and pad. Put up in a box 4x8½ inches.

Price.......................60c

If by mail, postage extra, 10 cents.

No. 3R7580 5A6a font of Rubber Type. Same style type as No. 3R7578, but contains 285 pieces, including a four-line holder 3 inches long.

Price, each....................$1.15

If by mail, postage extra, 15 cents.

AAAAAaaaaaaB3

No. 3R7582 5A6a font of Solid Rubber Type, containing 285 pieces, including a four-line holder 3 inches long. This outfit is especially convenient for the business man, can be used for stamping cards, envelopes, letter heads and miscellaneous printing. Put up in a box size 4x6¼ in. Price....$1.30

If by mail, postage extra, 15 cents.

AAAAAAAAAAABBBB

No. 3R7586 Superior Rubber Type Outfit, 5A6a font, containing eleven printers' alphabets (5A6a) of type, four sets of figures, two large and two small, punctuation marks, dollar and percentage signs, stars and brackets for fancy work, tweezers, improved self inking pad, and type holder for setting up four lines of matter. In addition to the eleven alphabets or letters, the outfit contains the following sign words and sentences: "&," "and," "For Sale," "From," "Return in 10 days to." **This is the most complete business outfit made. Price, $1.75**

If by mail, postage extra, 20 cents.

AAaaaBBbbbCCcccDD12

No. 3R7588 Success Rubber Type Outfit, 2A3a contains five printers' alphabets (2A3a) of type, two sets of figures, bottle of indelible ink, one line holder and ink pad, tweezers, quads, etc. Price, 35c

If by mail, postage extra, 5 cents.

AAaaaBBbbbCCcccDDddd12

No. 3R7590 Special Printing Card Outfit, 2A3a font, containing 150 pieces, is especially convenient for printing calling cards, stationery, etc. Put up in a box, size 4x3½ inches. Price....................65c

If by mail, postage extra, 10 cents.

AAaaaBBbbbCCcccDDddd€

No. 3R7592 Linen Markers' Rubber Type Outfit, 2A3a font. Containing five printers' alphabets, large and small letters of Old English type, punctuation marks, type for fancy work, pad, one line holder and pair of tweezers. Price....................45c

If by mail, postage extra, 10 cents.

AAaaaBBbbbCCcccDD112

No. 3R7594 Business Printing Outfit, 5A6a font, contains 285 pieces, complete with 4-line holder 3 inches long. Price....................$1.35

If by mail, postage extra, 15 cents.

No. 3R7596 2A3a font of type, same style type as shown under No. 3R7594, **containing 185 pieces,** 2-line holder 3 inches long. Price....................65c

If by mail, postage extra, 10 cents.

REFER TO FREIGHT AND EXPRESS RATES

in the front of this catalogue,

And You Can Calculate Just what the Transportation Charges will Amount to.

Our $5.95 Improved Self Inking Press and Complete Outfit.

No. 3R7916 (No. 11) Comes complete with two rollers, two fonts of standard long type, and the press is substantially mounted on a cherry base. **The outfit consists of two complete fonts of type, each font complete with letters, figures, punctuation marks, spaces and quads, each font in a separate box, divided into compartments the same as regular cases used by practical printers;** assortment of cards, furniture, ink, etc., and full directions for operating the press, type setting, taking care of the press and materials. **This press prints a form 2½x4 inches. Weight of press and outfit, boxed for shipment, 18 pounds.** Press stands 10 inches high and 15 inches wide, with the lever extended.

Our special price, for the press and outfit.... **$5.95**

Price for press only, without type, etc........ **4.45**

Our $15.80 Professional Printing Press and Outfit.

No. 3R7920 (No. 12) Prints a form 4½x6¼ inches. Consists of our new improved self inking press, with two inking rollers and inking table; four fonts of type, one 6-inch steel composing stick for setting type, one set of gauge pins, one pair of tweezers, big assortment of furniture, complete set of quoins, one shooting stick for locking up the form, one planer for planing down the form and getting the face of the type even, one oil can, supply of ink, etc. Stands 15 inches high, 23 inches wide. **The complete outfit weighs 80 pounds and is without question one of the best built and easiest working printing presses made.** Mounted on a handsome cherry base.

Our price for the complete outfit............ **$15.80**

Price for press only, without type or extra supplies.................. **12.80**

No. 3R7924 (No. 13) Prints a form 5½x8 inches. Weight of the press and outfit, boxed, 125 pounds. Complete with five fonts of type, composing stick, planer, furniture, leads and ink, chase, oil can, set of iron quoins, shooting stick and wrench. Our $21.70 press is made in the exact same manner as our $15.80 press described above, with the exception that it is one size larger, and will do a greater variety of work, printing a form up to 5½x8 inches in size. This is a size press that will get out circulars and will even print a small newspaper, a small book or magazine. Full directions are sent with every press and outfit.

Price for the press and outfit................ **$21.70**

Price for press only, without type or supplies **16.95**

Our $29.90 New, Large, Self Inking Printing Press and Outfit.

No. 3R7928 (No. 14) Prints a form 6x9 inches. Comes complete with two ink rollers, walnut delivery table, hand roller, oil can, set of iron quoins, furniture, leads, shooting stick, gauge pins, ink and seven complete fonts of type. The principle of the operation of our $29.90 press is the same as our smaller and cheaper self inking presses, with the exception of the location of the hand lever. The platen has gripper pins, and with the gauge pins no difficulty will be experienced in securing a perfect make-ready, and neat, clean and perfect work will be turned out. The inking table is especially full size, carries a good supply of ink, revolves at every impression and insures a thorough inking of the form. **We furnish seven complete fonts of type,** all standard sizes and standard varieties, two rollers, etc. Weight of the complete outfit packed for shipment, 125 pounds.

Our price for the press and complete outfit..**$29.90**

Price for press only, without type, etc...... **25.25**

Our $34.98 Pilot Job Printing Press.

Prints a form 6½x10 inches. The most improved, latest and best cheap job printing press made. Strong, easily operated and thoroughly practical. No other press has attained such popularity. Simple in construction, light running and strongly built. A time saver, as many jobs of cards, envelopes, stationery and other work can be put on this press and completed in less time than would be consumed in making ready on ordinary job presses. The illustration will give you a general idea as to its appearance. It is the best and strongest self inking printing press built on the most improved lines, made of the very best material that can be secured, put together by skilled mechanics. It is operated by means of a large, powerful hand lever, working from the side, requiring very little exertion to operate it. The body of the press, the hand lever, the chase and roller arms are solid castings throughout. Made of extra hardened steel. The roller is made of the very best genuine composition, mounted on a steel shaft. The inking table is full size, carries a good supply of ink, revolves at every impression, presenting a new supply to the roller, insuring a thorough inking of the form. The delivery table is a great convenience. It keeps your work right at hand and in the best possible condition. Made of select polished walnut, attached to the press. Furnished complete with one set of rollers, wrench and chase.

No. 3R7930 Pilot Job Printing Press. Our special price.......................... **$34.98**

Extra Supplies for our Special Pilot Job Press.

No. 3R7934 Roller Mold.................. **$2.00**
No. 3R7936 Roller Stocks, each.............. **.35**
No. 3R7937 Rollers, cast, each.............. **.40**
No. 3R7938 Spider Chase...................... **.75**
No. 3R7939 Hand Roller....................... **.50**

MATERIALS FOR PRINTING PRESSES.

Printing Ink, Sizing and Varnish.

No. 3R7940 2-ounce cans, black......... ......**15c**
2-ounce cans, blue, purple or green.............. **20c**
2-ounce cans, red or yellow...................... **20c**
2-ounce can, printers' varnish................... **15c**
2-ounce gold sizing.... .... **20c**
1-ounce gold bronze.............................. **20c**
1-ounce silver bronze............................ **20c**

Gold size is to be used in place of ink. Sprinkle the bronze over the printing done, to produce gold letters. By using silver bronze, silver letters are produced.

Letter, Note, Bill and Statement Heads.

No. 3R7946 Note Heads. Best superfine wove white paper; size, 5⅛x8½ inches; 5 lbs. to the ream.

Price, per ream of 5 pounds, **50c**; per pound....**12c**

No. 3R7947 Royal Packet Note Heads. Best white wove paper; size, 6x9¼ inches; 7 lbs. to the ream.

Price, per ream of 7 pounds, **90c**; per pound....**15c**

No. 3R7948 Letter Heads. Containing same quality of paper as No. 3R7947, size, 8½x11 inches; 10 pounds to the ream.

Price, per ream of 10 pounds, **$1.50**; per lb.....**17c**

No. 3R7949 Letter Heads. Containing first quality white wove bond paper; size, 8½x11 inches; unruled. Price, per pound........................**18c**

No. 3R7950 Bill Heads. Size, 8½x4⅜ inches; 3,000 sheets to the ream; one-sixth ream in a package; ruled one side.

Price, per ream of 3,000 sheets................**$1.60**
Price, per package of 500 sheets................ **.40**

No. 3R7951 Bill Heads. Size, 8½x7 inches; 2,000 sheets to the ream; ruled one side.

Price, per ream of 14 pounds, **$1.55**; per one-quarter ream...**45c**

No. 3R7952 Bill Heads. Size, 8½x9½ inches; 1,500 sheets to the ream; ruled one side.

Price, per ream of 14 pounds, **$1.65**; per one-third ream..**60c**

No. 3R7953 Bill Heads. Size, 8½x14 inches; 1,000 sheets to the ream; put up in one-half ream packages; ruled one side.

Price, per ream of 14 pounds, **$1.70**; per one-half ream..**90c**

No. 3R7954 Statements. Size, 5½x8½ inches; 1,000 sheets to the ream; put up in one-half ream packages.

Price, per ream of 5 pounds, **50c**; per one-half ream..**35c**

No. 3R7955 Typewriter Carbon Paper. For manifold work; size, 8x13 inches.

Price, per box of 100 sheets, **$1.98**; per dozen, **20c**; per sheet..**3c**

Gummed Paper for Labels, Pasters, Etc.

No. 3R7964 An Extra Quality of Imported Gummed Paper, most satisfactory to use for labels, pasters, etc. Every sheet full gummed and full size.

White. Size, 17x22, per 100 sheets, **$1.75**; per 10 sheets...**20c**

White. Size, 18x23, per 100 sheets, **$2.60**; per 10 sheets...**28c**

Yellow, Green or Pink. Size, 20x25, per 100 sheets, **$2.25**; per 10 sheets..............................**25c**

We do not sell less than 10 sheets.

Blank Cards.

The following prices are for the very best grades of China, Bristol, Enamel and plain white blank cards. These cards are put up 100 in a package. We do not break packages.

Postage, per 100, on sizes 4, 5, 9 and 10, 4 cents; on sizes 11 and 12, 9 cents: on sizes 13 and 14, 14 cents.

No. 3R7968 White Extra Finish 2-Ply Cardboard. For general purposes.

For Presses No.	4	5	9	10	11	12	13	14
Per 100...............	4c	5c	7c	7c	7c	9c	10c	11c
Per 500...............	15c	20c	25c	25c	25c	40c	40c	50c
Per 1000..............	25c	35c	45c	45c	45c	70c	75c	90c

100 sheets, 22x28 inches, **$1.75.**

No. 3R7970 Heavy White 6-Ply Cardboard. For extra fine work.

Presses No.	4	5	9	10	11	12	13	14
Per 100....	9c	10c	11c	$0.14	$0.14	$0.20	$0.22	$0.30
Per 500....	40c	40c	50c	.55	.55	.85	.90	1.10
Per 1000....	70c	75c	90c	1.00	1.00	1.50	1.70	2.00

100 sheets, 22x28 inches, **$3.75.**

No. 3R7980 Colored Cardboard. 3-ply No. 1 Bristol. For high grade work. Assorted: Blue, gray, yellow, pink, etc.

For Presses No.	4	5	9	11	10	12	13	14
Per 100.........	7c	8c	9c	10c	10c	$0.12	$0.15	$0.18
Per 500.........	30c	35c	40c	45c	45c	.55	.65	.75
Per 1000.........	45c	55c	70c	80c	80c	1.00	1.10	1.25

100 sheets, 22x28 inches, **$4.50.**

METAL TYPE FOR PRESSES.

Over each specimen line is given first, the number of font by which to order; second, the number of A, or a in the font; third, price of the font. With every font is included quads and spaces, enough for card work. **Figures are included in every font.** The number of A designates the proportionate size of a font; there is not an equal number of every letter; of certain letters most used the number is equal to A, but of others proportion varies according to use in general printing. **Our type is made to work on any press.**

No. 3R7988 5A 6 point 58c
A NEAT LETTER FOR JOB PRINTING 1901

No. 3R7990 5A 6 point 53c
A BEAUTIFUL TYPE FOR SMALL JOB WORK 1234567890

No. 3R7992 5 A 6 point 63c
A POPULAR LETTER FOR CARDS 12345

No. 3R7994 5A 5a 6 point 93c
EVERYTHING Comes to Him Who Waits 9012

No. 3R7996 6A 10a 6 point 90c
S., R. & CO.'S Large Mail Order Business 34567

No. 3R7998 5A 10a 6 point 88c
DON'T THINK you can get along without this face 891234

No. 3R8000 5A 5a 6 point 98c
GOSPEL Meetings Well Attended 56789

No. 3R8002 5A 10a 8 point 85c
A BREVIER ROMAN IS Indispensable for all sorts of book and job printing. 1234

No. 3R8004 5A 8 point 53c
ALL OUR GOODS ARE THE VERY BEST 23468790

No. 3R8006 5A 8 point 58c
WE LEAD THE WORLD 123456

No. 3R8008 5A 8 point 53c
YOUR NEIGHBORS LIKE THIS TYPE 123456

No. 3R8010 5A 8 point 58c
WE SELL EVERYTHING MADE 1234567890

No. 3R8012 5A 5a 8 point 73c
CHEAPEST Supply House on Earth 0123456789

No. 3R8014 5A 8 point 68c
MAIL ORDER HOUSE CHICAGO ILL 34567

No. 3R8016 5A 5a 8 point 83c
A NEAT Letter for Job Printing 0123456789

No. 3R8018 5A 5a 8 point 75c
GREAT Display of Fine Shoes 70832

No. 3R8020 5A 5a 8 point 70c
The Finest Goods on the Market For Sale 03605

No. 3R8022 5A 10 point 45c
LETTER WRITER PRINT 1234567

No. 3R8024 5A 10 point 70c
THE GARDEN CITY 1072

No. 3R8026 5A 5a 10 point 83c
ORDER a Printing Outfit 431908

No. 3R8028 5A 10 point 58c
OUR TRADE REACHES AROUND THE WORLD 1901

No. 3R8030 3A 5a 12 point $1.15
See Our Special Price List 29857

No. 3R8032 3A 5a 18 point $2.00
Good Setter for Visiting Cards 24

No. 3R8034 4A 18 point $1.00
SCHOOL SUPPLIES 946

No. 3R8036 3A 18 point $1.20
ADVERTISING 160

No. 3R8038 3A 5a 18 point $1.70
WE SELL Everything 15098

No. 3R8040 4A 24 point $1.65
ADVERTISING 24703

BRASS RULES.

No. 3R8042 Price, per foot, 9c

No. 3R8044 Price, per foot, 9c

GIVE CATALOGUE NUMBER IN FULL WHEN YOU WRITE YOUR ORDER

NEW 1902 BICYCLES AT $8.95 TO $15.75

AT FROM $8.95 TO $15.75, according to grade, we furnish men's and women's bicycles in the very latest models for 1902, bicycles brought strictly up to date, embodying all the new improvements, all the new 1902 features.

$15.75 for our highest grade bicycle, one of the highest grade wheels made, the celebrated Napoleon and Josephine, three-crown nickel jointed wheel, complete with highest grade equipment, including the celebrated Morgan & Wright double tube pneumatic tires.

$12.75 for the celebrated high grade, flush joint, Elgin King and Queen Bicycles, improved for 1902, handsomer and better than ever before and fitted with high grade equipment, including high grade guaranteed Seroco single tube tires.

$10.95 for the famous Kenwood Bicycle in either gents' or ladies' style, new and improved for 1902, well equipped throughout, including our high grade, guaranteed Seroco single tube tires.

$8.95 for the Ladies' Edgemere bicycle, the new 1902 model, fitted with a good standard equipment and offered at $8.95, in competition with bicycles that sell generally at double the price. The Edgemere Bicycle can be furnished only in ladies' drop curved frame, as illustrated on this page. We have been unable to secure any Gents' Edgmere Bicycles. The $8.95 Edgemere Wheel we can furnish only in a ladies' drop curve frame.

OUR REPUTATION as the largest dealers in bicycles in America, selling direct to the rider, is so well known, so thoroughly established in every community, that we do not feel it is necessary to dwell at length on the many advantages we have or on the incomparable values we always furnish.

LAST SEASON we sold about one-quarter of all the wheels made and sold in America. Our sales for 1901 were between 90,000 and 100,000 bicycles, while the estimated production and total sales for this country was approximately 400,000. It will thus be seen that we practically control the bicycle situation, make the price, and for like quality undersell by far any and all competition.

OUR BINDING GUARANTEE. With every bicycle we issue a written binding guarantee, guaranteeing every piece and part of the material and workmanship that enters into the construction of the wheel. We give the strongest kind of a guarantee as to quality.

TIRE GUARANTEE. For the season of 1902 we will use the celebrated Morgan & Wright double tube pneumatic bicycle tires on our highest grade wheels, the $15.75 Napoleon and Josephine, and every tire is covered by the manufacturers (Morgan & Wright) binding association guarantee, guaranteeing the tire perfect, and if any tire proves defective or unsatisfactory in any way it can be returned to us or to Morgan & Wright at any time within thirty days from date of purchase and it will be repaired or replaced with a new tire. Everyone knows the Morgan & Wright tire with fair usage will give the very best of satisfaction and last from three to five years.

THE SEROCO SINGLE TUBE GUARANTEED TIRE is furnished with all other bicycles, with the Edgemere, Kenwood, and Elgin King and Queen. These tires are made for us under contract by one of the best makers in the country. Every tire is guaranteed to be perfect in every respect, and if any tire proves defective in any way or unsatisfactory it can be returned to us at any time within thirty days and it will be repaired or replaced with a new tire. A Seroco tire with care will give the best of satisfaction and last for several years.

OUR TEN DAYS' FREE TRIAL OFFER. Anyone ordering a bicycle from us can give the bicycle ten days' trial (any ordinary usage), and if for any reason they become dissatisfied with the bicycle at any time within ten days, they can return it to us at our expense of express charges both ways, and we will immediately return the money sent us, together with the express or freight charges that have been paid.

OUR TERMS OF SHIPMENT. We have arranged our terms on bicycles the same as all other classes of merchandise. The full amount of cash must always accompany the order, but you can send your order and money to us with the understanding and agreement between us, that the bicycle must reach you in perfect condition and if it is not perfectly satisfactory when received, or after given ten days trial (with ordinary usage), you are at liberty to return it to us at our expense of express or freight charges both ways and we will immediately return your money.

WE FEEL THAT OUR COMMERCIAL AND FINANCIAL STANDING is now so thoroughly established in every section, the bank references and other references we give, which are referred to on the introductory pages of this catalogue, are such as to warrant us in asking our customers to invariably send us the full amount of cash with their orders. In asking that cash in full accompany all orders, we reduce the clerical expense in our house, and the expense of collecting money, and we can therefore make you a lower price on bicycles and save you the express charges on return of money to us, of from 25 to 50 cents, which the express companies would charge for collecting and returning the money to us.

WE HAVE ABOLISHED OUR C. O. D. SYSTEM solely in the interests of our customers that we may be able to furnish them better values than ever before, better values than any house can furnish that makes C. O. D. shipments, and with the further purpose of doing away with this extra 25 to 50 cent expense to the customers which the express companies always ask for C. O. D. shipments.

UNDERSTAND, you take no risk in sending your money to us for you are always protected by the strongest kind of a guarantee and your money is always ready for you, if the goods do not reach you in perfect condition and are not found in every way satisfactory to you.

$8.95 BUYS THE LADIES' 1902 MODEL EDGEMERE BICYCLE

AT $8.95 we furnish this new 1902 model Edgemere Bicycle in the very latest style handsome drop curve frame, as illustrated, complete with dress and chain guards. We can furnish this bicycle in ladies' drop curve frame, as illustrated, only, we being unable to furnish the Edgemere in gents' style.

THE MANUFACTURER of the Edgemere bicycle disposed of his entire stock of wheels. The gents' wheels were sold in small lots, distributed among different wholesale dealers, but we purchased the entire stock of ladies' wheels thus securing the ladies' wheel only, in this style.

WHILE WE CAN FURNISH the Edgemere only in the ladies' style, as illustrated, it being a 22-inch frame and made extra strong throughout it is suitable for man or woman, boy or girl, and while a handsome and perfect ladies' bicycle it is especially adapted for a boy's bicycle, for boys from 12 years of age and over.

AT $8.95 we furnish this ladies' Edgemere Bicycle, fully equipped, including the high grade Seroco guaranteed pneumatic tires, good grade pedals, handle bar, saddle, tools and tool bag, and all complete with dress and chain guards.

FIGURING THE TIRES as worth at least $3.50, we get for the wheel complete without tires, only $5.45, a price that you can readily understand does not cover the cost of production, the first cost of material and labor. We bought this big lot of Ladies' Edgemere Bicycles, closing out the manufacturer's entire stock at our own special close-out offer price, and to this first cost we added our one small percentage of profit, naming the heretofore unheard of price of $8.95. 50 to 75 cents will carry this bicycle by express to nearly any point within 500 miles of Chicago.

SEND US $8.95, state color of enamel and gear wanted, and we will send you the bicycle with the understanding that if it is not perfectly satisfactory when received you can return it to us at our expense, and we will immediately return your money.

UNDERSTAND, accompanying every bicycle is the strongest kind of written binding guarantee, guaranteeing every piece and part, including the Seroco pneumatic tires. While we require the full amount of cash to accompany all orders, you take no risk, for we agree to return your money at once if you are not perfectly satisfied.

From the above illustration, engraved from a photograph, you can get a very good idea of the general appearance of this, our $8.95 new 1902 model Ladies' Edgemere Bicycle. The Edgemere is handsomely finished throughout and is fitted with highly nickel plated sprockets, which come in an assortment of new and handsome designs.

THIS BICYCLE is made with 22-inch frame, 1⅛-inch tubing; gear, 68 to 80 inches; enameled in black, green or maroon as desired, and weighs all on, about 28 pounds. It is nicely finished, all usual bright parts nickel plated, complete with equipments, including Seroco single tube guaranteed tires, and is put out UNDER OUR BINDING GUARANTEE.

$10.95 BUYS THE CELEBRATED 1902 MODEL GENTS' KENWOOD BICYCLE

REDUCED from our last year's price of $13.75, a reduction of $2.80, and the bicycle improved in every respect, brought strictly up to date, the lastest in every feature for this season, the equal of bicycles that sell generally at about double the price, the Kenwood bicycle is too well known to require a lengthy description. It has always been known and sold as a strictly high grade wheel.

IT WAS FIRST INTRODUCED at a retail price of $125.00. The next season it sold for $100.00, the next season for $75.00, and the following season we took the output of the factory and named what was considered an astonishingly low price of $16.75. Last season we sold it for $13.75. This year we bring it out with all the new 1902 improvements and name the heretofore unheard of price of $10.95.

UNDERSTAND, every Kenwood Bicycle is covered by the strongest kind of a written binding guarantee. The equipment throughout is high grade, including our Seroco guaranteed single tube pneumatic tires, high grade pedals, saddle and handle bars, everything first class. Every piece and part guaranteed.

WE ARE THE SOLE SELLING AGENTS FOR THE KENWOOD BICYCLE.

For the last three seasons we have had control of this wheel, and it could be had only from us. Formerly it was sold through specially appointed agents, and always at the highest price.

THE KENWOOD WHEEL was awarded diplomas, medals and blue ribbons at the World's Fair. Since that date, and especially since we came into control of this wheel, we have aimed to keep it in the very first rank of up to date high grade wheels, and we therefore urge that you do not compare it with any of the many cheap bicycles that are being advertised at prices ranging from $15.00 to $20.00.

OUR 10 DAYS' FREE TRIAL AND GUARANTEE OFFER. While we require the full amount of cash, $10.95, to accompany your order, as we have, solely in the interest of our customers, discontinued making any shipments of any kind of merchandise C. O. D. subject to examination, we will accept your order and your money, $10.95, guaranteeing the bicycle to reach you in the same perfect condition it leaves us, **also guaranteeing it to prove entirely satisfactory to you, and giving you the further and special privilege of using the bicycle ten days,** and if at any time during the ten days you become dissatisfied with your purchase for any reason whatever, you can return the bicycle to us at our expense of express or freight charges both ways, and we will immediately return your $10.95.

YOU CAN SAVE FROM $10.00 TO $20.00 by ordering your bicycle from us as against buying it from your dealer at home. You will find the freight charges will amount to next to nothing as compared to what you will save in price. Bicycles properly crated for shipment weigh about 50 pounds and the freight on a bicycle averages about 50 cents for 500 miles, greater or lesser distances in proportion. **If you have any doubt of our ability to furnish you a much better wheel than you can buy elsewhere at anything approaching the price we offer, make inquiry among your friends and neighbors.**

WE SOLD NEARLY 100,000 BICYCLES LAST SEASON ALONE. As by far the largest dealers in bicycles in America, certainly our wheels are ridden by some of your own friends in your own neighborhood. Ask them how they are pleased with the bicycles they bought from us last season and how much money we saved them, and then consider our bicycles have been improved for 1902 and the prices have been materially reduced, our Kenwood selling at $10.95, $2.80 lower than ever before.

THE KENWOOD IS KNOWN BY THE NAME PLATE. Since 1890 the one name plate, as illustrated, stamped Kenwood as the highest of high grade wheels. The Kenwood wheel that was awarded the highest diploma at the World's Fair bears this name plate and trade-mark. Any imitation of this registered name plate of the celebrated Kenwood Wheel is intended to deceive. **Only the Kenwood, the original, high grade, up to date wheel, bears this mark.**

Kenwood
CHICAGO.

WE ASK YOU TO SEND the full amount of cash, $10.95, with your order. We know some houses offer to ship bicycles C. O. D. subject to examination, the same as we did last season, but this incurs an extra expense to you, as they must ask more for their wheels in order to defray the extra expense of handling C. O. D. orders, and the express companies will make an extra charge to you of 25 to 50 cents for collecting and returning the money.

WE BELIEVE our reputation is so thoroughly established, even in your own neighborhood, that you will not hesitate to send the full amount of money with your order, thus securing the lowest possible price and avoiding the express charges made for returning the money on C. O. D. orders.

$10.95

No. 19R5
ORDER BY NUMBER

The above illustration, engraved by our artist from a photograph, gives you an idea of the appearance of our new 1902 model high grade Kenwood Bicycle, reduced from last year's price of $13.75 to the present astonishingly low price of $10.95.

THIS WHEEL goes to you under our binding guarantee covering every piece and part that enters into it, including the high grade Seroco tires. At this price it is shipped to you with the understanding that if it is not satisfactory you have the privilege at any time within ten days to return it at our expense, your money to be immediately returned to you.

GENERAL DESCRIPTION

FRAME—Our $10.95 Gents' Kenwood Bicycle comes in either 22 or 24-inch frame, as desired. We especially recommend the 24-inch frame, for this is the frame used on most all bicycles. The frame is made from the very highest grade 1⅛-inch seamless tubing, flush at every joint, including rear braces, latest flush connection at seat post.

UPPER BRACES—The upper braces are made from ¾-inch cold drawn diamond tubing, bent very narrow at seat post cluster. The lower braces are made from ⅝-inch cold drawn tubing, tapering.

WHEELS—Wheels are made from selected material. They are 28 inches in diameter, 32 spokes in front, 36 in rear. The frames are the very best rock elm, seasoned and steamed. The wheels are highly finished throughout.

CRANKS—The cranks are the latest up to date model, made with 7-inch throw. Made from drop forgings, handsomely finished, heavily nickel plated and highly polished.

SPROCKET—Every $10.95 Kenwood has the very latest 1902 sprocket; new shape, adjustable, made from the very finest drop steel forgings, heavily nickel plated and highly polished.

HUBS—The $10.95 Kenwood has high grade barrel hubs turned from solid bar steel, fitted with ¼ and 3/16-inch balls, with ball retainers complete. The hub cones are made from the very best tool steel, tempered to a straw color. Hubs are highly polished and heavily nickel plated.

FINISH—The $10.95 Kenwood is given an extra fine finish. The enameling is done by the best known process. All usual parts are heavily nickel plated on copper, highly polished. The frames come enameled in black or maroon, as desired.

TOOL BAG AND TOOLS—Our $10.95 Kenwood is furnished with a heavy solid leather tool bag, highly polished and finished, complete with best set of bicycle tools, including wrench, oiler, pump and quick tire repair outfit.

PEDALS—The $10.95 Kenwood is furnished with strictly high grade pedals, full ball bearing, heavily nickel plated inside and out, and highly polished.

HANDLE BARS—The $10.95 Kenwood has a high grade ⅞-inch diamond steel tubing seamless handle bar, 20 inches wide, drop or upturned as desired, fitted with best leather grips.

SADDLE—The $10.95 Kenwood is equipped with a strictly high grade fair leather padded saddle, extra well finished, and one of the best saddles on the market.

TIRES—We equip the $10.95 Kenwood complete with highest grade Seroco single tube pneumatic tires, tires that are covered by the strongest Association guarantee.

GEAR—72 to 96 inches as desired. An unusual demand may prevent sending exact gear wanted, but we shall always send the nearest possible size.

WEIGHT—All on, about 28 pounds.

$10.95 FOR OUR NEW 1902 MODEL LADIES' KENWOOD BICYCLE

For $10.95 a reduction from last year's price of $14.25, $3.30 lower than ever before, we offer this new improved high grade bicycle in ladies' drop curve frame as illustrated. Like the gents' Kenwood, illustrated and described on the preceding page, the ladies' Kenwood has always ranked among the highest of high grade wheels. It was awarded special diplomas at the World's Fair in 1893, kept strictly up to date from that time until the present. It retailed first at $125.00, then at $100.00, then at $75.00, when it came into our control and sold by us at $16.75. Last season we sold it for $14.25, and this year it is reduced to the heretofore unheard of price of $10.95.

THE KENWOOD BICYCLE was built in Chicago more than ten years ago by one of the best makers in America, and has been kept strictly up to date. Nothing but high grade material has been used in its construction, and it should not be in any way compared with the many cheap bicycles on the market that are being advertised at prices ranging from $12.00 to $20.00.

IF YOU ARE NOT ACQUAINTED with the Kenwood Bicycle, with its superiority over cheaply made wheels, ask your friends and neighbors. Last season we sold nearly 100,000 bicycles, a large percentage of which were high grade Kenwood bicycles. Surely some of them are being ridden by your own friends in your own neighborhood. Look at their Kenwood Bicycle, consider that the wheel is improved for this season, brought strictly up to date, and offered at a lower price than ever before, only $10.95.

The above illustration is a small reproduction of the large diploma awarded the Kenwood Bicycle at the World's Fairin Chicago in 1893. As the Kenwood Wheel was awarded this special diploma, medals and blue ribbons, it has every since held its position, keeping strictly up to date as one of the highest grade wheels. The original World's Fair diploma is on file in our store.

OUR BINDING GUARANTEE.

With every Ladies' Kenwood Bicycle we furnish a written binding guarantee, the strongest guarantee issued with any bicycle. The guarantee covers every piece and part, including high grade Seroco single tube tires with which the Kenwood is equipped.

WE BELIEVE with our reputation for fair and honorable dealing thoroughly established in every community in the United States, that it is proper for us to ask our customers to send the full amount of cash with their orders, since by doing so we can sell them goods at lower prices and save them the express charges of from 25 cents to 50 cents on every shipment, which express companies always charge for collecting and returning the money to us.

OUR 10 DAYS' FREE TRIAL OFFER.

While we require cash in full to accompany all orders, and have, in the interest of low prices and economy to our customers, discontinued shipping any goods C. O. D. subject to examination, under any circumstances, if you will send us your order for a Ladies' Kenwood Bicycle, enclosing $10.95, we will send the bicycle to you by freight or express, guaranteeing it will satisfy you in every way, that you will find it a much better bicycle than you could buy elsewhere even at a higher price, and if for any reason you are not perfectly satisfied with it after having used the bicycle ten days, you can return it to us at our expense of freight charges both ways, and we will immediately return your $10.95.

TO SHOW THE CONFIDENCE we have in our bicycles and the value we are giving, we suggest if you are about to buy a bicycle from your dealer at home or from any other house in Chicago or elsewhere, that when you send for a bicycle of another make you send for ours at the same time and compare them side by side; if you are not convinced that our wheel is better in quality and lower in price, you can return our bicycle at our expense and we will immediately return your money.

$10.95

No. 19R7
Order by Number.

From the above illustration, engraved by our artist from a photograph, you can form some idea of the appearance of this our new 1902 model, drop frame, Ladies' Kenwood Bicycle, a bicycle we offer at $10.95 in competition with bicycles that sell generally at about double the price.

GENERAL DESCRIPTION

FRAME—The frame is 22 inches high, handsome drop curved shape, made from 1⅛-inch high grade seamless flush tubing.

WHEELS—The wheels are made from the very best material procurable. They are 28 inches in diameter, 32 spokes in front wheel, 36 in rear. The rims are the best rock elm seasoned and steamed, will never warp, split or crack. The wheels are highly finished throughout.

CRANKS—The cranks are the latest 1902 model, one piece, made from drop forgings, heavily nickel plated and highly polished.

HANGER CONES—The hanger cones are made from the finest tool steel tubing, tempered to a straw color.

PEDALS—The Kenwood is furnished with extra high grade full ball bearing pedals, heavily nickel plated and highly polished.

SADDLE—The Kenwood is furnished with a strictly high grade fair leather padded saddle, extra well finished, and one of the best saddles ever made.

TOOLS AND TOOL BAG—The Ladies' $10.95 Kenwood is furnished with a heavy, solid leather tool bag, highly polished and finished. It comes complete with the best set of bicycle tools, including wrench, oiler, pump and quick tire repair kit.

GEAR—68 to 80 inches, as desired. Unusual demand may prevent sending exact gear, but we always send the nearest possible size.

SPROCKETS—The sprockets are the very latest 1902 pattern, assorted designs, made from finest drop forgings, heavily nickel plated and highly polished.

HANDLE BAR—The Kenwood has the very finest ⅞-inch diamond seamless steel tubing handle bars, extra wide, drop or upturned, as desired, heavily nickel plated and highly polished, fitted with the latest style nickel ferrules, with leather grips.

TIRES—With our $10.95 Ladies Kenwood we furnish our celebrated Seroco single tube guaranteed tires, one of the best single tube pneumatic bicycle tires made; tires that are covered by the regular Association thirty days' guarantee, and with care will last many seasons.

HUBS—The Ladies' $10.95 Kenwood has high grade barrel hubs turned from solid bar steel, fitted with ¼ and $\frac{3}{16}$-inch balls, with ball retainers complete. The hub cones are made from the very best tool steel, tempered to a straw color. The hubs are highly polished and heavily nickel plated.

EXPANDERS—The Kenwood is furnished with the latest style expander in seat post and handle bar for adjusting and fastening the seat post and handle bar in any position.

CHAIN—With the Kenwood is furnished a high grade steel link chain, tempered to a straw color and beautifully finished.

FINISH—The Kenwood is given an extra fine finish. The enameling is done by the best known process. All usual parts are heavily nickel plated on copper and highly polished. Comes enameled in black, green or maroon as desired.

EQUIPMENT—At $10.95 we furnish the bicycle fully equipped, complete with pedals, saddle, handle bar, tools and tool bag, mud and dress guard. Every bicycle goes out under our binding guarantee.

$15.75 FOR OUR NEW 1902 NAPOLEON.

$15.75 BUYS OUR HIGHEST GRADE BICYCLE, THE HIGHEST OF HIGH GRADE, THE FULL THREE-CROWN NICKEL JOINTED, NICKEL HEAD, FLUSH JOINT NAPOLEON.

MORGAN & WRIGHT'S highest grade double tube, season guaranteed pneumatic bicycle tires, extra high grade, finely finished ball bearing pedals, high grade adjustable handle bar; extra high grade full padded saddle, heavy finished leather tool bag, complete set of high grade tools including quick tire repair outfit, the best of everything throughout, in the highest grade bicycle shown by any maker for the season of 1902, and all for $15.75.

SPECIAL POINTS OF EXCELLENCE over all other bicycles and found only in our $15.75 Napoleon and Josephine Bicycles.

THREE CROWNS—The strongest, handsomest, smoothest and best finished bicycle frame connections made, rear stay crown, rear fork crown, front crown. FLUSH JOINTS—Flush joints throughout, including three-crown, seat post cluster, front and bottom stays, the strongest re-inforced flush joint frame connection made. NICKEL CROWNS—The three nickel crowns, flush seat post cluster, steering head, rear brace ends and front fork ends are heavily nickel plated on copper, highly polished and beautifully finished; guaranteed without exception the handsomest, strongest and altogether the best bicycle frame used on any bicycle for 1902. THE LATEST 1902 ONE-PIECE HANGER—including one of the handsomest heavily nickel plated front sprockets made; all sprockets come exactly as illustrated. THE LATEST 1902 EXPANDER IN SEAT POST AND HANDLE BAR for adjusting seat post and handle bar to any position. EVERY NEW, UP TO DATE FEATURE FOR 1902 IN OUR $15.75 NAPOLEON AND JOSEPHINE, combining the good features and high grade marks of all high grade wheels with the defects of none, none of the ear marks of cheapness common to bicycles that are being sold generally at $15.00 to $30.00. MORGAN & WRIGHT TIRES—The Morgan & Wright double tube pneumatic bicycle tires have gained such a reputation among high grade bicycle tires, they have become so generally recognized as the highest grade, longest lived, most resilient, the least liable to give trouble and the easiest tire to repair if out of order, punctured or otherwise, that we have decided to equip all our $15.75 Napoleon and Josephine Bicycles with only the genuine Morgan & Wright double tube, season guaranteed, highest of high grade tires, thus bringing the equipment of the $15.75 Napoleon up to the very highest standard of quality.

WE RECOMMEND the Napoleon and Josephine Bicycles above all others, and while our $10.95 Kenwood is a thoroughly reliable wheel, the equal of bicycles that sell generally at more than double the price, and our Elgin King and Queen, the new 1902 handsomely decorated red head bicycles at $12.75, are strictly high grade, guaranteed in every way and equal to bicycles that sell at double the price, we especially recommend our highest of high grade, Napoleon and Josephine, our $15.75 bicycles, which we put out under our binding guarantee as the equal of any bicycles on the market regardless of price.

DO NOT COMPARE the Napoleon and Josephine with any of the many cheap bicycles now being advertised and sold by dealers generally. It can only be compared with the highest grade bicycles made. The Napoleon and Josephine bicycles have been manufactured for years and always sold at the very highest price. THEY HAVE STOOD THE TEST OF SERVICE. They were originally sold only through exclusive agents, one in each town, and always sold at the highest price for the highest grade wheels. Ask your friends and neighbors about the Napoleon. Thousands were sold before we secured control of these bicycles, and in the past two seasons we have sold about 50,000 of these wheels. They have gone into almost every town in the United States. Surely some are being ridden by your friends and neighbors. We know if you can see one of our three-crown nickel joint Napoleons and can ask the owner what he thinks of it, you will have no other.

OUR BINDING GUARANTEE. With every Napoleon and Josephine Bicycle at $15.75, we issue the strongest kind of a written binding guarantee, covering every piece and part that goes into the bicycle, including the strongest Association binding guarantee for the Morgan & Wright pneumatic tube tires with which the Napoleon and Josephine Bicycles are equipped. While we have discontinued shipping bicycles or other merchandise C. O. D., WE MAKE YOU **THIS TEN DAYS' FREE TRIAL OFFER:**

SEND US $15.75 for either a Napoleon or Josephine Bicycle, state height of frame, color of frame, and gear wanted, and we will send the bicycle to you, guaranteeing it to reach you in perfect condition, guaranteeing it to prove entirely satisfactory, and give you the further privilege of giving the bicycle ten days' trial, during which time if you become dissatisfied with your purchase for any reason, you can return the bicycle to us at our expense of express or freight charges both ways, and we will immediately return your $15.75. Our reputation at home and abroad, the references we furnish, the strong endorsements furnished by the banks in Chicago and New York with whom we do business, our standing among our customers in your own neighborhood, we feel justifies us in asking our customers to send the full amount of cash with their orders and thus save the 25 cents to 50 cents express charges for the return of the money to us, and secure a lower price than we could possibly give if we continued making C. O. D. shipments, always knowing that we will return their money at once if they are not perfectly satisfied.

NOTE—This wheel is strictly a three-crown frame, flush at every joint, flush seat post cluster, nickel plated at every joint, nickel head, nickel around crowns, nickel rear fork ends, nickel front fork end, latest one-piece hanger, highest of high grade in every piece and part, and offered at only $15.75, a price that barely covers the cost of material and labor with but our one small percentage of profit added.

$15.75

No. 19R15

ORDER BY NUMBER.

From the above illustration, engraved by our artist from a photograph, you can form some idea of the appearance of our new 1902 model $15.75 up to date Napoleon Bicycle.

DETAILED DESCRIPTION.

FRAME—The frame is 22 or 24 inches, as desired, made of the highest grade 1⅛-inch seamless tubing, the very finest 1902 connections. All connections made from finest drop forgings and steel. Three-crown frame, flush at every joint, the highest grade, handsomest, smoothest and strongest full flush joint frame shown by any maker for 1902.

WHEELS—The highest grade wheels made. The very best piano wire swaged spokes, full finish, very fine hubs, hubs turned from bar steel highly polished, heavily nickel plated and accurately trued. Full ball bearing with the latest patent ball retainers.

RIMS—The rims are the highest grade, handsomely striped, full seasoned non-warpable full finish rims, such as are used only on the highest grade of wheels made.

REAR FORKS—The latest 1902 three-crown pattern, latest design fork and stays, tapering and continuous, flush at every point.

BEARINGS—The very highest grade bearings, made from tool steel, carefully tempered to straw color, highly polished and finished, ball bearing and latest patent ball retainers at every point.

FRONT FORKS—Crown, drop forgings, finest seamless tubing side fork; crown and fork ends, heavily nickel plated on copper and highly polished.

HANGER—Latest 1902 one-piece hanger, beautifully finished, runs in finest steel bearings, made ball bearing throughout, latest patent ball retainers.

SPROCKETS—Sprockets are the latest 1902 design of sprockets, exactly as shown in illustration above, beautifully and neatly shaped pattern, heavily nickel plated and beautifully polished.

TIRES—Morgan & Wright highest grade double tube season guaranteed pneumatic bicycle tires. We wish to call your special attention to the fact that the Napoleon and Josephine Bicycles are fitted only with these now generally recognized highest of high grade tires made, the longest lasting, the least liable to get out of repair and the easiest tire to repair when injured by puncture or otherwise. Every tire is covered by our own and the manufacturer's (Morgan & Wright) binding season guarantee. With care these tires will last five years at least.

GEAR—Geared regular 72 to 96 inches, as desired.

SADDLE—Strictly high grade full padded fair leather saddle.

NICKEL HEAD—The head is the handsomest, all flush joint bicycle head made, shortened to the latest 1902 design, nickel plated throughout, the entire head being heavily nickel plated on copper, highly polished and beautifully finished.

HANDLE BARS—We equip the $15.75 Napoleon with our special high grade, extra wide, full adjustable handle bars, a bar that can be instantly adjusted to any position, as desired, complete with special high grade leather grips.

PEDALS—On the $15.75 Napoleon we use a special high grade pedal, heavily nickel plated the pedal turned from bar steel, accurately adjusted and full ball bearing.

FINISH—All connections heavily nickel plated on copper, nickel plated at every joint, as illustrated. The three crowns nickel plated, fork ends, head and arch crown, the whole made perfectly flush at every part, including flush seat post cluster. The frame is enameled by the best known process, either **black or maroon**, as desired, beautifully striped and without doubt the handsomest bicycle on the market regardless of price. In ordering be sure to state color of enamel desired.

OUR $15.75 1902 MODEL JOSEPHINE BICYCLE.

THE JOSEPHINE IS THE LADIES' MODEL OF OUR HIGHEST GRADE WHEEL. THE GENTS' OF THE SAME GRADE IS KNOWN AS THE NAPOLEON. THE LADIES', THE DROP CURVED FRAME WITH DRESS AND CHAIN GUARDS, AS ILLUSTRATED BELOW, IS KNOWN AS THE JOSEPHINE.

IT IS OUR THREE-CROWN flush nickel jointed bicycle, the highest of high grade, the best wheel we sell, a bicycle which is fitted with Morgan & Wright highest grade double tube pneumatic bicycle tires, the highest grade equipment throughout and offered with all the latest improvements, all the new 1902 features, at the actual cost of material and labor, with but one small percentage of profit added, less than dealers can buy in any quantity, only $15.75.

THE NAPOLEON AND JOSEPHINE BICYCLES require little or no description, they are already so well known among the highest of high grade wheels. They have been made for the last ten years by one of the best bicycle makers in America, at a factory in which only the very best of material has been used, only the most skilled mechanics employed, and turned out always as **the equal of any bicycle made regardless of price,** and until we secured control of the output and reduced the selling price to the actual cost to build with but our one small percentage of profit added, the Napoleon and Josephine bicycles could be had only from retail agents, one especially appointed agent in each town or city, and there only at the top notch price, the highest price asked for high grade wheels.

AS THE LARGEST DEALERS in bicycles in America, selling more bicycles direct to the consumer than all other catalogue or mail order houses combined, consuming as we do about one-quarter of the bicycle production of this country, controlling the output of the factory in which our bicycles are made, basing our selling prices on the actual cost of material and labor, with but our one small percentage of profit added, we can furnish you in our new 1902 model three-crown nickel joint Ladies' Josephine Bicycle, at $15.75, such a bicycle as you could not buy elsewhere at less than about double the price.

OUR BINDING GUARANTEE With every Josephine bicycle at $15.75, equipped with the highest grade Morgan & Wright double tube pneumatic bicycle tires, we issue the strongest written, binding guarantee, covering every piece and part that enters into the construction of the bicycle, including the strongest kind of a season guarantee, a guarantee binding upon the manufacturers and ourselves.

OUR TEN DAYS' TRIAL OFFER. While we require the full amount of cash to accompany your order, $15.75, we accept your money and order with the understanding that the bicycle is guaranteed to reach you in the same perfect condition it leaves us, and if at any time within the ten days you become dissatisfied with your purchase you are at liberty to return the bicycle to us, at our expense of express or freight charges both ways, and we will immediately return your money.

While our Kenwood Bicycle at $10.95 is a thoroughly reliable wheel, covered by our binding guarantee, and the Elgin King and Queen at $12.75 are strictly high grade, flush joint, ball bearing bicycles, the equal of bicycles which sell at double the price, we especially urge that our customers select our finest wheels, the three-crowned nickel joint Napoleon and Josephine, the best bicycles on the market, complete with highest grade equipment throughout, including the celebrated Morgan & Wright double tube pneumatic bicycle tires, which we sell at $15.75 in competition with bicycles that sell generally at more than double the price.

No. 19R17
Order by Number.

From the above illustration, engraved by our artist from a photograph, you can get some idea of this our new 1902 Model Ladies' Three-Crown Nickel Joint One-Piece Hanger $15.75 Josephine Bicycle. Every bicycle is furnished exactly as illustrated. All sprockets exactly alike, flush at every joint, with every high grade up to date 1902 feature, a bicycle the equal of any bicycle on the market regardless of price.

DETAILED DESCRIPTION.

FRAME—The very latest designed 1902 model of a ladies' drop frame in three-crown construction, as illustrated. Certainly the handsomest, strongest and highest grade ladies' frame ever offered. Made of 1⅛-inch cold drawn seamless steel tubing, 22 inches high, reinforced and well brazed at every joint; flush at all connections, the steering head, the front, upper rear and lower rear crowns, seat post cluster, both rear and front fork tips are heavily nickel plated and beautifully finished.

WHEELS—The wheels are of the highest grade, made only of the very finest swaged piano wire spokes, full finished, rims are made from carefully selected, non-warpable, seasoned hickory, the highest grade on the market.

HUBS—The hubs are the highest grade, made from selected steel, turned from solid bar steel, heavily nickel plated, ball bearing throughout, accurately adjusted and fitted with the highest grade ball retainers.

BEARINGS—The Josephine is equipped with the highest grade bearings made, all turned from solid bar tool steel, tempered to a straw color, highly finished, accurately adjusted and gauged, ball bearing at every part, with latest patent ball retainers.

HANDLE BAR—We use the latest adjustable handle bars, with internal expander, which can be adjusted to any position desired. They are extra wide, heavily nickel plated on copper, and fitted complete with the best quality leather grips.

FRONT FORKS—Latest handsome crown fork, made from hollow drop forgings, 1902 Josephine design, finest seamless tubing fork sides, crown and fork tips heavily nickel plated on copper.

REAR FORKS—The latest 1902 three-crown pattern, handsomely shaped and finished, made flush at joints. The crowns are heavily nickel plated on copper, both upper and lower.

SADDLE—The saddle is strictly high grade, full padded, fair leather in ladies' design, one of the best saddles made.

HANGER—The very latest 1902 one-piece hanger, handsomely designed, nicely finished, heavily nickel plated and fitted with finest ball bearings.

THE TIRES—The tires are the celebrated Morgan & Wright highest grade double tube pneumatic tires, tires covered by the strongest season guarantee, bicycle tires that are known everywhere as the highest of high grade, that will undoubtedly wear longer and give better satisfaction than any bicycle tire on the market.

SPROCKET—The very latest 1902 sprocket exactly as shown in illustration, made from the finest steel, handsomely finished, heavily nickel plated and highly polished.

PEDALS—The pedals are extra high grade, made from the finest tool steel highly nickel plated inside and out, highly polished and true to gauge, and full ball bearing.

EXPANDERS—Both seat post and handle bar are fitted with latest internal expander, thus doing away with all bolts and nuts.

FINISH—All connections are heavily nickel plated on copper. The flush cluster seat post, the joints and the three crowns, the rear fork ends, the arch crown and the front fork ends are heavily nickel plated on copper, making one of the handsomest bicycles shown by any maker. The frame comes enameled in either black or maroon as desired, enameled by the best known process, neatly striped and finished, and are without doubt the handsomest bicycles shown this season.

EQUIPMENT—At $15.75 we equip the Josephine bicycle with the very highest grade equipment; with Morgan & Wright tires, high grade adjustable handle bar, high grade saddle, pedals, tools, tool bag and quick tire repair outfit, and the bicycle comes complete with mud and dress guards. It weighs, all on, about 28 pounds, and at our $15.75 price is furnished carefully crated, delivered on board cars at Chicago. We guarantee it to reach you in the same perfect condition it leaves us, and give you the privilege of a ten days' trial, and if for any reason you become dissatisfied with it within the ten days, you can return it to us at our expense of freight charges both ways, and we will immediately return your money.

For one of the finest Ladies' Wheels made, a bicycle embodying all the up to date features for 1902, such a bicycle as you could not buy elsewhere at double the price, we especially urge that you order our $15.75 Josephine.

OUR ACME WONDER JUVENILES.

OUR $10.75 BICYCLE. NEW 1902 MODEL. FOR BOYS FROM 7 TO 12 YEARS OF AGE.

AT $10.75 we offer the highest grade Boys' Bicycle made, the equal of bicycles that others sell at double the price. Our $10.75 price is based on the actual cost of material and labor, with but our one small percentage of profit added, the lowest price ever quoted on a

Strictly High Grade Guaranteed Bicycle for Boys.

No. 19R69
Select Size and Order by Number.

EQUIPMENT. These bicycles, made especially for boys from 7 to 12 years of age, carry the highest grade equipment, including the same tire that we use on our highest grade adults' wheels, the celebrated Seroco single tube pneumatic tire, covered by the regular association 30 days' guarantee, a tire that with care will last many seasons.

TEN DAYS' TRIAL OFFER. While we require you to send cash with your order, we give you the privilege of a ten days' trial of the bicycle, during which time if you have any reason to feel dissatisfied with your purchase, simply return the bicycle to us and we will immediately return your money including transportation charges.

OUR GUARANTEE. Every bicycle is covered by our binding guarantee, covering every piece and part that enters into the wheel. We guarantee the material perfect, and if not so the wheel can be returned to us at once and your money will be cheerfully refunded.

DESCRIPTION.

TWO SIZES—Be careful in ordering. The small size, for boys from 7 to 9 years of age, has a 16-inch frame, the wheels being 24 inches; specify Catalogue No. 19R69. The large size, for boys 10 to 12 years old, has an 18-inch frame with 26-inch wheels, and should be ordered from Catalogue No. 19R71.

TIRES—The celebrated Seroco single tube.

PEDALS—Ball bearing rat trap.

CHAIN—High grade 3/16-inch chain.

HANDLE BAR—High grade raised steel handle bar, full nickel plated, full finished, complete with leather grips.

From the above illustration, engraved by our artist from a photograph, you can form a very good idea of the appearance of this handsome new 1902 Model $10.75 Bicycle for Boys.

NOTE—The 16-inch frame is for boys from 7 to 9 years of age. The 18-inch frame is for boys from 10 to 12 years of age.

SADDLE—Special high grade Juvenile saddle.

GEAR—Every wheel geared to 60 inches.

HANGER—We use the very latest 1902 style Juvenile hanger, the strongest, best finished and nicest hanger used on a boys' wheel.

SPROCKETS—We use handsome sprockets, latest 1902 style, both front and rear; highly finished, heavily nickel plated and polished; assorted designs.

ENAMEL—Frames are enameled either maroon or black; elegantly finished. All usual bright parts are highly nickeled.

At our special $10.75 price, we include a fine leather tool bag, complete with wrench, oiler, pump and tire repair outfit.

No. 19R69 Boys' bicycle, 16-inch frame with 24-inch wheels, for boys 7 to 9 years of age............ **$10.75**

No. 19R71 Boys' bicycle, 18-inch frame with 26-inch wheels, for boys 10 to 12 years of age............ **$10.75**

OUR $10.75 NEW 1902 MODEL DROP FRAME GIRLS' BICYCLE FOR GIRLS FROM 7 TO 12 YEARS OF AGE.

THIS SPECIAL $10.75 BICYCLE is the highest grade bicycle made for girls. Made of the highest grade material, by skilled mechanics, equipped with the highest grade equipment, including the celebrated single tube guaranteed Seroco tire, and offered at our special $10.75 price, at a price based on the actual cost of material and labor, with but our one small percentage of profit added.

THIS IS THE EXACT SAME BICYCLE as our special $10.75 boys' wheel, with the exception of the girls' style of drop curved frame.

YOU WILL NOTE we furnish these wheels with 16-inch frame for girls from 7 to 9 years of age, 18-inch frame for girls from 10 to 12 years of age. The price is the same. In ordering be sure to note the different size frames to accommodate the different ages.

UNDERSTAND, every bicycle is covered by a binding guarantee as to quality of material and workmanship. Every pair of tires is covered by our regular guarantee.

TEN DAYS' TRIAL OFFER. While we require you to send cash with your order, we give you the privilege of a ten days' trial of the bicycle, during which time, if you have any reason to feel dissatisfied with your purchase, simply return the bicycle to us and we will immediately return your money, including transportation charges.

$10.75

No. 19R74
Select Size and Order by Number.

..DESCRIPTION..

This bicycle is exactly the same as the boys' bicycle, with the exception of the drop curved frame. The frames are 16 or 18 inches high, made from highest grade tubing, nicely enameled, nicely finished, made extra strong in every part. The wheels are 24 or 26 inches in diameter, strictly high grade. We use high grade, full finished spokes, non-warpable hickory rims. Hubs are strictly high grade, drawn from bar steel, full finished, heavily nickel plated, ball bearing throughout, with ball retainers.

TIRES—Tires are the celebrated Seroco single tube pneumatic tires, fully guaranteed. Tires come complete with quick tire repair outfit.

From the above illustration, engraved by our artist from a photograph, you can form some idea of the appearance of our handsome new model, $10.75 bicycle, the 1902 wheel, but you must see, examine and compare this bicycle with bicycles offered by other houses at greatly advanced prices to appreciate the extraordinary value we are offering.

SADDLE—We use a special high grade Juvenile saddle.

HANDLE BAR—We furnish a strictly high grade steel, raised handle bar, heavily nickel plated, highly finished, complete with leather grips.

BEARINGS—We use strictly high grade bearings, drawn from bar steel, full finished, accurately gauged and adjusted, tempered to a straw color, highly finished and fully guaranteed.

CHAIN—We use a high grade 3/16-inch chain, the best chain used on any juvenile wheel.

PEDALS—We use high grade combination pedals, full ball bearing, heavily nickel plated and highly finished.

HANGER—We use the very latest 1902 hanger.

SPROCKETS—Sprockets are the latest style for 1902, made from the very best steel, highly polished, heavily nickel plated and beautifully finished, assorted designs.

GEAR—Geared to 60 inches.

EQUIPMENT—You get in this wheel the very highest grade equipment, the same high grade equipment that goes on our highest grade ladies' wheel, including the very best Seroco tires, finest nickel plated handle bars, ball bearing pedals, extra quality saddle, tool bag, quick repair outfit, wrench and oiler.

ENAMEL—Enameled in either black or maroon, as desired, handsomely finished, all usual parts heavily nickel plated on copper.

No. 19R74 Girls' 16-inch drop frame bicycles, with 24-inch wheels, for girls 7 to 9 years of age............ **$10.75**

No. 19R78 Girls' 18-inch drop frame bicycle, with 26-inch wheels, for girls 10 to 12 years of age............ **$10.75**

Boys' All Steel Velocipedes.

Give the boy all the fun he wants at the expense of a few pennies.

We show an all steel velocipede that will stand a "heap of racket" on the part of the restless youth. **There are no nuts or bolts in the head connections to rattle or come loose.** It is adjustable and can be taken apart in shipping. The coil spring in seat does not sag or get out of repair. **We use the best drive wheel made** in this velocipede. The manner in which the fork and backbone are secured to head and axle is a new method **far superior to any other, and makes them doubly strong.** The handle is of one piece and stationary. The frames are made of malleable iron. Made both with steel tires or rubber tires. Prices as follows:

STEEL TIRES.

No. 19R501 Front wheel, 16 inches $1.35
No. 19R502 Front wheel, 20 inches 1.75
No. 19R503 Front wheel, 24 inches 2.15
No. 19R504 Front wheel, 26 inches 2.25

RUBBER TIRES.

No. 19R505 Front wheel, 16 inches $2.50
No. 19R506 Front wheel, 20 inches 3.00
No. 19R507 Front wheel, 24 inches 3.45
No. 19R508 Front wheel, 26 inches 3.95

Tricycles.

Notwithstanding the immense popularity of the bicycle, the tricycle still remains in favor. Many parents prefer them for their children by reason of their safety, convenience, and the ease with which they can be run by the little girl or boy. The tricycle which we illustrate is made for girls or boys from two to seven years. **They are constructed with especial care,** and will stand the abuse they very frequently receive. They are very easy running and handsomely finished. The improved spring seat takes all vibration, and being upholstered in plush and furnished with back, makes riding easy and comfortable. Frame is enameled black. Quoted with iron tire wheels or C plate rubber tire wheels. The following are our special prices:

IRON TIRE WHEELS.

No. 19R509 Rear wheels, 18 inches $2.95
No. 19R510 Rear wheels, 20 inches 3.75
No. 19R511 Rear wheels, 22 inches 4.45

RUBBER TIRE WHEELS.

No. 19R512 Rear wheels, 18 inches $4.45
No. 19R513 Rear wheels, 20 inches 5.45
No. 19R514 Rear wheels, 22 inches 6.95

OUR KENWOOD SINGLE TUBE TIRES AT $3.50 PER PAIR.

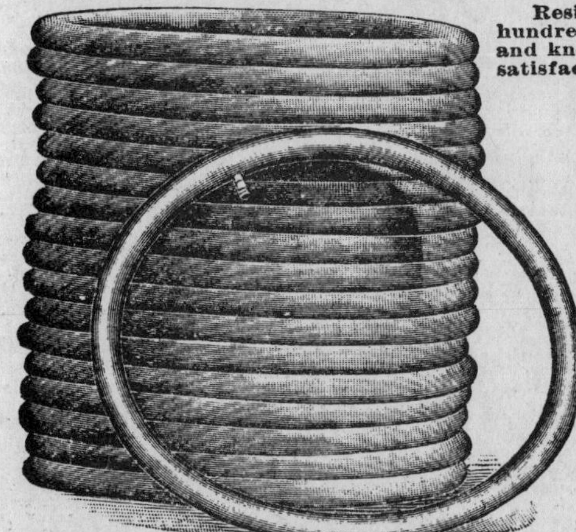

Resilient, speedy and durable. We have sold over one hundred thousand pairs of these justly celebrated tires and know by experience that they have given universal satisfaction to all of our customers that have used them. Inasmuch as our bicycle business is beyond question the largest business of its kind in the world, our purchasing power is so strong that for the coming year we have been enabled to make a most satisfactory contract, involving several hundred thousand dollars, whereby we practically control the output of this celebrated tire, which is made by one of America's largest and most thoroughly equipped tire factories, a factory that is fitted with the latest and most improved labor saving machinery, with a plant giving them exceptional facilities, together with a large force of thoroughly trained mechanics.

The chief consideration whereby we were enabled to make such a favorable contract was, that we agreed to accept the delivery of the tires as fast as they could be made, and particularly during the dull months of fall and winter, thus enabling the factory to run continually and, therefore, on a most economical basis. While we could easily ask a dollar or two more per pair, we are content to give our customers the benefit of this advantageous purchase by simply adding our one small percentage of profit. A brief description of these tires is as follows, viz.: The inner wall or air chamber is constructed of the finest quality of Para rubber, upon which layer after layer of wear-resisting fabric is alternately amalgamated with further layers of a fine quality of rubber until the outer wall is reached, the latter being composed of a quality of rubber stock especially selected for its durability, and then cured in mechanically perfect steel molds. It would be impossible in this limited space to thoroughly explain the countless operations and manifold tests to which these tires are subjected before being offered for sale, but we can truthfully say that in the history of our previous bicycle experience we have never been able to offer such a remarkably good value at the price stated.

WE GUARANTEE EACH AND EVERY TIRE TO BE ABSOLUTELY FREE FROM ANY IMPERFECTIONS, either of material or workmanship, in accordance with the regular Association guarantee, and we will cheerfully repair or replace any tire claimed defective, providing the same is sent us prepaid for our examination within thirty days from date of sale. **This does not apply to punctures or damage caused by neglect or wear.**

With each complete pair of tires we include a first class hand pump and a single tube repair kit, but neither are furnished with single tire.

The sizes and prices of the Kenwood tires are as follows:

No. 19R70 28x1⅝ inches. Price, per pair $3.50
No. 19R71 26x1½ inches. Price, per pair 3.25
No. 19R72 24x1½ inches. Price, per pair 3.00

TIRES.

WHEN ORDERING TIRES To assist us in filling your orders for tires intelligently, be careful in giving us the correct size. **When in doubt read the following instructions,** and you will make no mistake. Notice our diagram, showing manner of taking measurement, following these directions:

A wheel measuring 20¼ inches, requires a 24-inch tire.

A wheel measuring 22¼ inches, requires a 26-inch tire.

A wheel measuring 24½ inches, requires a 28-inch tire.

Or, measuring a wheel with an inflated tire, measure from the ground to the top of tire, which will give the measurement needed, such as 24, 26 or 28 inches.

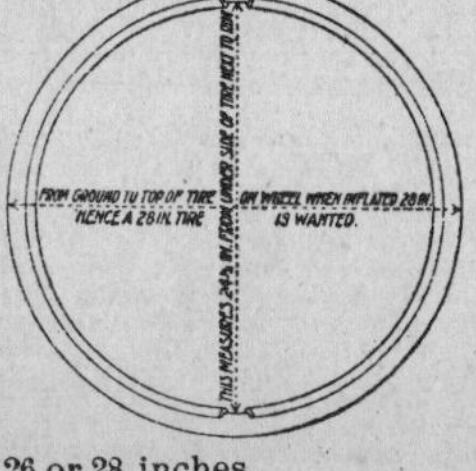

Morgan & Wright's Plain Double Tube Tires.

Too well known to require special notice here. Prices quoted do not include pump or repair kit.

No. 19R30 Style S. Size, 28x1⅛ inches. Price, per pair $3.95
No. 19R31 Style D. Size, 28x1⅝ inches. Price, per pair $3.95
No. 19R32 Style X. Size, 28x1⅝ inches. Price, per pair $3.95
No. 19R33 Style G. Size, 26x1½ inches. Price, per pair $3.50
No. 19R34 Style G. Size, 24x1½ inches. Price, per pair 3.50
No. 19R35 Style G. Size, 20x1½ inches. Price, per pair 3.50
No. 19R39 Cataplaro Tires (formerly known as Plank Road, Cactus or Export Tandem). Sizes, 28x1¼ or 1⅝ or 1¾ inches. Price, per pair 4.50

Parts of Morgan & Wright Double Tube Tires.

CASINGS.

No. 19R43 Cataplaro Casings, 28x1⅝ inches. Price, each $1.75
If by mail, postage extra, each, 40 cents.
No. 19R44 M. & W. Road Casings, 28x1⅝ inches. Price, each $1.58
If by mail, postage extra, each, 32 cents.

INNER TUBES.

No. 19R45 Morgan & Wright 28-inch plain inner tube. Price, each 60c
No. 19R51 Morgan & Wright 26-inch plain inner tube. Price, each 60c
No. 19R52 Morgan & Wright 24-inch plain inner tube. Price, each 60c
If by mail, postage extra, each, either size, 13 cents.

VALVES AND PARTS.

No. 19R46 Morgan & Wright Valve and Stem, complete. Price, each 10c
If by mail, postage extra, each, 2 cents.
No. 19R47 Morgan & Wright Metal Valve only. Price, each 7c
If by mail, postage extra, each, 2 cents.
No. 19R48 Morgan & Wright Rubber Stem only. Price, each 4c
If by mail, postage extra, each, 2 cents.

SINGLE TUBE VALVES.

No. 19R64 Shoe Valve for Single Tube Tires. Price, each 12c
If by mail, postage extra, each, 3 cents.

Morgan & Wright's Single Tube Tires.

We quote only the principal sizes, less pump and kit.

No. 19R49 Sizes, 28x1⅛ or 1⅝ inches. Price, per pair $4.25

Dunlop Detachable Tires.

Note that we quote separate prices for tires and rims, as the latter are not included in price of tires. Rims come drilled 32 and 36 holes only. Natural finish. A pump and repair kit is included free with every complete pair of tires, but not otherwise.

No. 19R60 Dunlop Tires. 28x1⅝ inches. Per pair ... $8.00
No. 19R61 Inner Tube, 28x1⅝ inches, with valve. Price, each $1.35
If by mail, postage extra, each 15 cents.
No. 19R62 Casings, 28x1⅝ inches. Price, each $2.85
If by mail, postage extra, each, 35 cents.
No. 19R63 Dunlop Wood Rims, 28x1⅝ inches. Price, per pair $1.25
If by mail, postage extra, per pair, 45 cents.

G. & J. Detachable Tires.

Note that prices are quoted separately for tires and rims. Rims are natural finish, and come drilled with 32 and 36 holes. Pump and repair kit furnished only with complete pair of tires.

No. 19R75 G. & J. Tires, 28 x1⅝ inches. Per pair $8.50
No. 19R76 Inner Tubes, 28x 1⅝ inches, with valve. Price, each $1.25
If by mail, postage extra, each, 15 cents.
No. 19R77 Casings, 28x1⅝ inches. Price, each $3.15
If by mail, postage extra, each, 34 cents.
No. 19R78 G. & J. Rims, 28x1⅝ inches. Price, per pair $1.25
If by mail, postage extra, per pair, 45 cents.
No. 19R79 G. & J. Hand Pump. Each 20c
If by mail, postage extra, each, 6 cents.
No. 19R80 G. & J. Valve. Each 15c
If by mail, postage extra, each, 3 cents.

Our Guaranteed Single Tube Tires at $2.75 per Pair.

These tires are thoroughly well made and every tire guaranteed to be perfect both in material and workmanship. They are cheap only in price and we can recommend them as being very satisfactory. Made only in standard road size, viz.: 28x1⅝ inches. At this price we include a pump and repair kit.

No. 19R16 Price, per pair $2.75

Unguaranteed Single Tube Tires.

These are the tires largely used by other houses in trying to compete with the more reliable tires offered by us; and while we sell the tires separately, we will not guarantee them, nor use them on any of our bicycles. The tires come only in the 28x1⅝ size, and at the price quoted we do not supply pump or repair kit.

No. 19R14 Unguaranteed Single Tube Tires. Price, per pair $2.25

Hartford Tires.

Hartford Tires of the single tube variety, require no extended description. A pump and repair kit furnished with every complete pair, but not with single tires.

No. 19R102 Hartford Tires No. 80, 28x1⅝ inches. Price, per pair $6.50
No. 19R103 Hartford Tires No. 77, 28x1⅝ inches. Price, per pair $5.95
No. 19R104 Hartford Tires No. 70, 28x1⅝ inches. Price, per pair $4.95

GIVE CATALOGUE NUMBER IN FULL WHEN YOU WRITE YOUR ORDER

Coaster Hub and Brake.

We know of no bicycle invention introduced within recent years that possesses as many advantages as the modern and latest improved coaster hub and brake. Its true worth cannot be described within the limits of our short space, but we will briefly explain that our coaster hub and brake consists of a mechanically perfect rear bicycle hub, somewhat heavier than the ordinary hub because within the barrel and flange are contained the coasting and braking device. The arm on left side is to be fastened to rear fork. In operation, our brake is positively the most safe and at the same time the most simple device now before the public, and must not be confounded with the many freak hubs and others of faulty construction with which many competing houses endeavor to delude the public. A coaster hub and brake is wanted for two reasons, coasting, as a means of pleasure, and a brake to probably save life and limb; consequently, when one wants a brake **it is wanted badly.** A few cents, therefore, should not be allowed to influence a decision in favor of a cheap article. A slight withholding of pressure upon the pedals will release the pull on chain and give a free rear wheel, enabling the rider to coast without losing control of his pedals at all. The action of back pedaling immediately and automatically locks the rear wheel, consequently the bicycle must come to a stop, either gradual or sudden, at the will of the rider. **Our celebrated coaster hub and brake will fit any bicycle,** and purchasers can have the same put into their rear wheel by any local repair man. The size of the sprockets that we can furnish is 8, 9 and 10-tooth for $\frac{3}{16}$-inch chain. Unless otherwise specified, we will send a 9-tooth sprocket.

No. 19R40 Coaster Hub and Brake. Each..**$3.45**

We are prepared to furnish rear wheels (less tire), fitted with our coaster hub and brake, as follows:

No. 19R42 Rear wheel for ordinary tire. Price, each.......................................**$4.95**

No. 19R43 Rear wheel with G. & J. or Dunlop rim, fitted with coaster and brake. Each....**$5.45**

It is very essential that care be taken in giving specifications for wheels as above. (Extra charge for steel rims.)

Our Railroad Attachment.

This is the most practical and durable device of its kind on the market, and consists of three braces made of steel tubing that telescope for convenience in carrying, together with a steel wheel with flanges, the running surface of which is covered with rubber, also the necessary clamps for attaching the braces to the bicycle. Our illustration plainly indicates the manner of attachment, which is so simple that anyone can attach or detach the device within the space of a very few minutes, and when not needed for use on the railroad track the parts can be taken down and placed in the cloth carrying case, which we furnish with every attachment, and the same can then be securely fastened to the bicycle when the latter is used on the wagon roads. This attachment is not confined to any certain size of track, but is adjustable for either standard or narrow gauge tracks or street car tracks. The parts are substantially made and intended for honest wear, nicely enameled in black and weigh 9 pounds. We have found this device to be very popular with railroad and telegraph men, particularly in the West, although it is adapted for use by anyone, and the parts will fit a lady's bicycle as readily as a man's bicycle.

No. 19R99 Railroad Attachment. Price..**$8.50**

Padded Saddles.

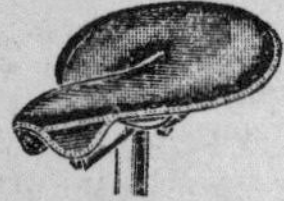

Thoroughly up to date, well padded, made of well tanned leather; supplied with a finely nickeled spring and clamp.

No. 19R115 Gents' Saddle. Price, each.......................**45c**

No. 19R116 Ladies' Saddle. Price, each......**45c**

If by mail, postage extra, each, 30 cents.

Christy Anatomical Saddles.

Aluminum base; hair padding; maroon leather top, making a very comfortable saddle; made in both ladies' and gents'.

No. 19R121 Gents' Saddle. Price, each.......................**$1.25**

No. 19R122 Ladies' Saddle. Price, each...**$1.25**

If by mail, postage extra, each, 40 cents.

The Naber Saddle with Torsional Spring.

Its perfection is due to the action of the double torsional spring, which by twisting, not springing, takes up and exhausts all the jars, jolts and roughness found on country roads thus doing away with most of this disagreeable feature of bicycling. It is made of first class material and makes an ideal saddle for lady riders.

No. 19R130 Gents' Naber Saddle, each....**$1.00**

No. 19R131 Ladies' Naber Saddle, each...**$1.00**

If by mail, postage extra, each, 38 cents.

The Rubberneck Saddle.

Its special feature is a patented rubber cushion, honeycombed with air cells, which is placed between the steel base and the leather covering which serves as the top. The material and workmanship is of the best and the saddle will commend itself to many riders. Made in two styles, ladies' and gents'.

No. 19R142 Gents' Road Saddle, each......**$1.50**

If by mail, postage extra, 32 cents.

No. 19R143 Ladies' Road Saddle, coil springs, each.......................................**$1.50**

If by mail, postage extra, 32 cents.

Gents' Wheeler Saddle.

Made of the finest oak tanned leather, on a wood base, having the new "high back" feature; a very popular saddle.

No. 19R160 Gent's Wheeler Saddle. Price, each.......**70c**

If by mail, postage extra, 30 cents.

Our Leader Pedals.

Elegant in design, first class in finish and fully guaranteed. Broken parts will be cheerfully replaced if sent to us prepaid. Made in standard size with ½-inch, 20-thread pedal pins. Mated right and left. **Always state catalogue number of style desired.**

No. 19R180 Men's Rat Trap Pedals. Per pair.**35c**

If by mail, postage extra, per pair, 24 cents.

No. 19R181 Men's Combination Pedals. Per pair.....(**Postage extra, per pair, 25 cents**).......**45c**

No. 19R182 Ladies' Combination Pedals. Per pair.....(**Postage extra, per pair, 25 cents**)......**45c**

Our Ideal Pedals.

Made extra heavy, handsomely nickel plated, of a very new and neat design. Made in rat trap or combination. Pedal pins are ½-inch, 20-thread, right and left.

No. 19R193 Gents' Rat Trap Pedals. Per pair............**75c**

If by mail, postage extra, per pair, 22 cents.

No. 19R194 Gents' Combination Pedals. Price, per pair..................................**85c**

If by mail, postage extra, per pair, 25 cents.

No. 19R195 Ladies' Combination Pedals. Price, per pair.....................................**85c**

If by mail, postage extra, per pair, 25 cents.

The Empire Pedal.

An extra fine pedal, construction similar to above, but made of a little finer stock and more elaborate in finish. Side plates are of a very handsome design. Made both in rat trap and combination styles. Pedal pins ½-inch by 20-thread, right and left.

No. 19R206 Gents' Rat Trap Pedals. Price, per pair.......................................**90c**

If by mail, postage extra, per pair, 22 cents.

No. 19R207 Gents' Combination Pedals. Price, per pair....................................**$1.00**

If by mail, postage extra, per pair, 24 cents.

Combination Stirrup Pedals.

A combination of the well known stirrup toe clip with the newest form of pedal, making a splendid rest for the feet in pedaling, giving additional advantages in hill climbing. **Made of the very finest steel obtainable, elegantly nickel plated, all parts being particularly well made. Every pedal is fully guaranteed as to material and workmanship.** Pedal pins are ½ inch, 20 threads. Leather tops are adjustable, can be quickly changed to fit a large or a small foot.

No. 19R208 Combination Stirrup Pedals. Price, per pair.......................................**$1.35**

If by mail, postage extra, per pair, 25 cents.

Universal Pedal Rubbers.

Snap on to any make of pedal without the use of screws, bolts or plates, and do not rattle. Four rubbers constitute the set.

No. 19R219 Pedal Rubbers. Price, per set.......................................**15c**

If by mail, postage extra, 5 cents.

TOOL BAGS.

Our Pocket Tool Bag.

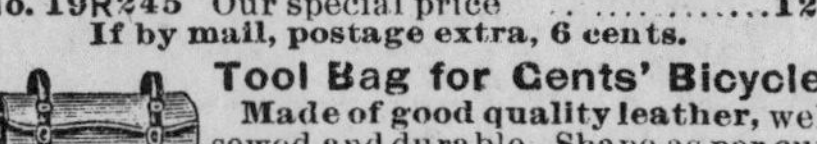

Made to fit coat pocket, or by using the straps furnished with every bag, can be attached to bicycle. Made of black pebble leather.

No. 19R245 Our special price **12c**

If by mail, postage extra, 6 cents.

Tool Bag for Gents' Bicycle.

Made of good quality leather, well sewed and durable. Shape as per cut.

No. 19R249 Our special price.......................**18c**

If by mail, postage extra, 8 cents.

Triangular Tool Bag.

Made of fine quality of grain leather, shape as per cut, clasp fastening, nicely embossed and an ornament to any wheel.

No. 19R257 Our special price...**34c**

If by mail, postage extra, 10 cents.

Fine Leather Bag.

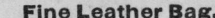

Excellent quality, large and roomy, thoroughly well made of oak tanned leather, nicely embossed, fastened with patent clasps. This is a fine bag.

No. 19R268 Tool Bag. Price, each...........**25c**

If by mail, postage extra, 8 cents.

Ladies' Pistol Pocket Tool Bag.

Made of finest oak tanned leather, beautifully embossed, clasps to match with straps to attach to bicycle frame.

No. 19R271 Ladies' Tool Bag. Price, each..................................**29c**

If by mail, postage extra, 9 cents.

Bicycle Tourist's Case.

Made in triangular shape as per our cut. This case is made of heavy pressboard, covered with canvas and linen lined. The cover is fastened with patent clasps, and straps are provided for attaching to frame. It will fit any 24-inch diamond frame and most of the 22-inch frames, unless the latter have very short heads.

No. 19R276 Tourist Case. Price, each.......**59c**

Another case, same description as above, but made stronger and more substantial, and better adapted for regular use.

No. 19R280 Tourist Case. Price, each.......**85c**

Bicycle Lamps.

In making your selection kindly bear in mind that our oil lamps are made to burn common kerosene or coal oil, obtainable everywhere. The new gas lamps require calcium carbide (Catalogue No. 19R364), which can be purchased in all bicycle stores or ordered from us.

NOTE—All lamps are guaranteed to be perfect when sold, and we will credit or exchange same when delivered to us in same perfect and unused condition as when shipped, but we cannot accept for credit or exchange lamps that have been used.

The Arc Light Gas Lamp.

A strictly high grade lamp at a popular price, Made entirely of brass, handsome in design, elegantly nickel plated, free from any intricate mechanism. **The lamp burns the loose form of carbide,** every particle being consumed, doing away with waste. The valve and gasway is straight, permitting instant cleansing. Has parabolic reflector, large lens, and gives a very powerful light. Bracket with every lamp, adjustable to fit any make of bicycle.

No. 19R336 The Arc Light Gas Lamp. Price, each....(**Postage extra, 30 cents**)....**$1.25**

The Columbia Automatic Gas Lamp.

This lamp is positively automatic. The size of flame can be instantly regulated by a gas valve, and it is impossible to flood the carbide chamber with water. On that account it is more economical than others, and the carbide charge can be repeatedly used until entirely exhausted. Having a large lens, a parabolic reflector, a long candle flame, it is able to throw a most powerful stream of light. The bracket accompanying every lamp is adjustable to every possible degree, and enables the rider to attach lamp to either fork or steering head.

No. 19R339 Columbia Automatic Gas Lamp. Price, each.....(**Postage extra, 28 cents**)....**$1.29**

The Searchlight Gas Lamp.

Beautifully made of brass, every wearing part reinforced. A handsome design, every part so accurately made as to insure absolute perfection. The only lamp made that can be instantly taken apart for cleansing; has removable dome, top body, tip holder, lens and reflector—all of the very finest construction. **The lamp burns loose carbide,** has needle valve for regulating flow of water, and gives such a powerful light as to rightly deserve its name, "Searchlight." The bracket supplied with lamp is adjustable to fit any bicycle.

No. 19R343 Searchlight Gas Lamp. Price, each....(**Postage extra, 40 cents**)....**$1.75**

The Banner Gas Lamp.

A beautiful lamp, made of brass, elegantly finished. It has a powerful reflector, with large burner and 3-inch lens, throwing a wonderful volume of light. Height, 7¼ inches. Weight, 21 ounces. The lamp is provided with an adjustable bracket to fit different diameters of tubing. The construction allows of positively automatic control—simply turn on the water, light your gas, and let it alone—as the amount of water feed is regulated by the quantity of gas consumed.

No. 19R348 Banner Gas Lamp. Price.....**$1.50**

If by mail, postage extra, 38 cents.

The Bundy Lamp.

New model—no cartridges—many improvements made over last year's model, being now constructed for the use of loose carbide. Made of brass, highly nickel plated, has two finely cut colored jewels, removable parabolic reflector, large double convex lens and fishtail burner. Carbide chamber is larger than formerly, and when filled with carbide the lamp will burn for five hours. Every lamp is supplied with a substantial bracket, permitting instant and positive adjustment.

No. 19R351 Bundy Gas Lamp. Price.....**$1.49**
If by mail, postage extra, 37 cents.

The Electro Gas Lamp.

Made entirely of brass and aluminum; small in size, only 6 inches high, weight 16 ounces, still it has a large carbide chamber for burning loose carbide. The reflector is very large, of the parabolic type, the burner of lava, gives a large flat flame, insuring a brilliant light far in front of the rider. The bracket accompanying every lamp is adjustable for either fork or steering head.

No. 19R356 Electro Gas Lamp. Price, each **$1.98**
If by mail, postage extra, 30 cents.

The 20th Century Gas Headlight.

Burns any loose carbide six to eight hours with one charge. aluminum parabola reflector, which spreads a wonderful light. A brass carbide holder accompanies every lamp, together with full directions for handling same. New adjustable lamp bracket, to fit either head or fork.

No. 19R359 20th Century Gas Headlight.
Price..(**If by mail, postage extra, 38 cents**)..**$2.25**

Calcium Carbide.

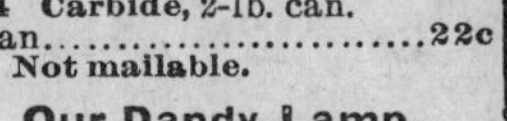

For use in Acetylene Gas Bicycle Lamps. ½-inch size, packed in airtight tin cans containing 2 pounds.

No. 19R364 Carbide, 2-lb. can.
Price, per can..**22c**
Not mailable.

Our Dandy Lamp.

The best cheap oil lamp made. Entirely of brass, handsomely nickel plated, no solder to melt, no parts to fall apart while riding. Burns kerosene oil, is five inches high and easily kept clean.

No. 19R368 Our Dandy Lamp.
Price, each....................**65c**
If by mail, postage extra, 18 cents.

The Banner Oil Lamp.

Made of brass, riveted wherever there are joints, burns kerosene. Has a hinged front door, wick locking device. Oil fount is removable and reversible. This is a thoroughly satisfactory lamp in every respect.

No. 19R372 Banner Lamp.
Price, each.....................**$1.35**
If by mail, postage extra, 25 cents.

The 20th Century Headlight.

This well known bicycle lamp does not need much description. It is smaller, lighter, and simpler than ever, many improvements being made for 1902, but all with a view to increasing its already great light giving capacity. It has the parabola reflector, self locking wick, **cannot jar out.** Rigid bracket, adjustable to fit any angle on fork or head; also has a bail handle, for use as a hand lantern. **Burns kerosene.**

No. 19R376 20th Century Oil Lamp.
Price.(**If by mail, postage extra, 27 cents**)..**$1.59**

The Searchlight Oil Lamp.

Burns kerosene oil; positively the finest lamp of this kind ever constructed for bicycle use. Every metal part of the lamp is made of brass with beautiful embossing, the exterior being elegantly nickel-plated. The oil fount, or bottom, is reversible, so that lamp can be attached to either fork or to steering head. It has a double front lens, while the reflector is detachable and covered with a glass so as not to tarnish. The bracket supplied with each lamp is adjustable, so as to fit on any part of bicycle, either on the front fork or on the head.

No. 19R380 Searchlight Oil Lamp. Each..**$1.75**
If by mail, postage extra, 30 cents.

Handle Bars.

Drop or raised, with expander, made of best tubing, 20 inches wide. Our bars are all with ⅞-inch stem, which is standard, as used on nearly all bicycles; we cannot supply any other size. All bars nicely nickel plated and fitted with good grips, securely cemented.

No. 19R420 Raised bar. Price, each..........**55c**
If by mail, postage extra, 25 cents.
No. 19R421 Down turn bar. Price, each.....**55c**
If by mail, postage extra, 25 cents.
Without grips, deduct 10 cents.

Adjustable Handle Bar.

Sometimes called "Reversible Bar." Made of best steel tubing, with patent forged stem. By loosening bolt, the bar can be instantly changed from a drop to a raised position, or vice versa. Made only 20 inches wide, ⅞-inch expander stem, and fitted with good grips, securely cemented.

No. 19R427 Adjustable Bar. Price, each....**60c**
If by mail, postage extra, each, 28 cents.
Without grips, deduct 10 cents.

Our 12-Cent Bell.

Electric stroke, large gong 2 inches in diameter. Made of pure bell metal. Strong steel base and reliable double screw fastening. **It is handsomely nickel plated** and a beautiful bell at a very low price.

No. 19R487 Price, each........................**12c**
If by mail, postage extra, each, 8 cents.

Fancy Bell.

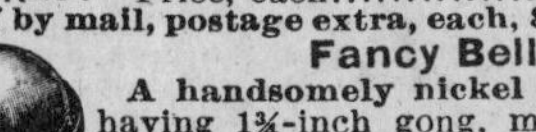

A handsomely nickel plated bell, having 1¾-inch gong, made of pure bell metal. The gong has beaded edge, with ribbon border and rotary electric movement.

No. 19R490 Ribbon border bell.
Price, each..................................**15c**
If by mail, postage extra, 8 cents.

Bell with Enameled Flag Top.

This Bell is handsomely designed, having a 2-inch gong, made of pure bell metal, with the national emblem enameled thereon. The entire bell is handsomely nickel plated and has the rotary electric movement.

No. 19R494 Flag Bell, electric movement. Price, each................................**22c**
If by mail, postage extra, 8 cents.

Decorated Bell for 20 Cents.

A beautiful bell, with gong made from pure metal. Base and all movement parts made of brass, every part being elegantly nickel plated. This bell has that celebrated rotary electric movement, so pleasant to the ear, and is a beauty.

No. 19R497 Decorated Bell. Price, each...**20c**
If by mail, postage extra, each, 8 cents.

Anchor and Shield Bell.

A very pretty design, 1¾ inch gong, with the shield handsomely enameled in colors, all other parts being finely nickel plated. This bell has rotary electric movement.

No. 19R499 Anchor and shield bell. Price, each................**24c**
If by mail, postage extra, 8 cents.

The Continuous Ringing Bell.

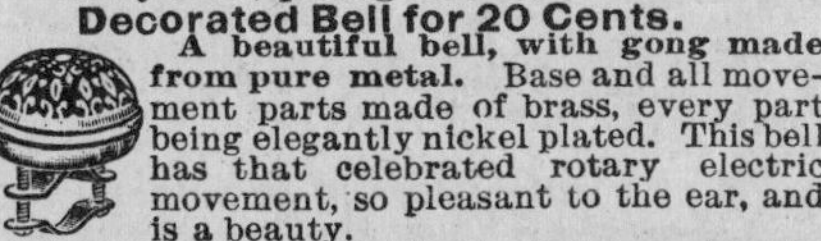

This Bell works like a watch; by turning the gong to the right, you wind up the continuous ringing mechanism; by simply pressing the lever, the bell will ring for any desired length of time. Gong is of the beaded pattern, 2⅜-inch diameter, made of pure bell metal, base of steel fastened to handle bar by a double screw clamp. All parts elegantly nickel plated, and an ornament to any bicycle.

No. 19R502 Continuous Ringing Bell.
Price, each...**33c**
If by mail, postage extra, each, 12 cents.

Continuous Ringing Bell, with Flag Top.

In appearance this bell resembles our No. 19R502, shown above, only that it is larger, having a 2⅝-inch gong, and the top is also handsomely enameled showing the national emblem in natural colors. The mechanism is ratchet electric, continuous ringing, and makes a beautiful bell.

No. 19R506 Continuous Ringing Flag Bell. Price, each.......................**40c**
If by mail, postage extra, 12 cents.

Solid Brass Bicycle Lock.

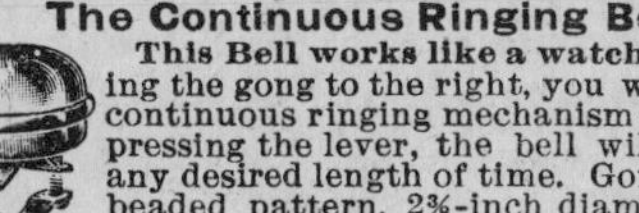

The cheapest good brass lock ever sold at this low price, thoroughly well made, of new design.

No. 19R560 Brass Bicycle Lock. Each,**7c**
If by mail, postage extra, 3 cents.

Sprocket Lock.

A very handsome appearing lock, steel case, black finish, shackle of brass. Well made and a most remarkable bargain at our price.

No. 19R563 Sprocket Lock.
Price, each.......................**11c**
If by mail, postage extra, each, 3 cents.

Yale Sprocket Lock.

Brass spring shackle steel case, finished ivory black. Actual size 2⅝ inches, two keys.

No. 19R567 Yale Sprocket Lock.
Price, each..............................**18c**
If by mail, postage extra, each, 4 cts.

A Newly Designed Sprocket Lock.

Every rider needs a lock. This one is intended to be attached to front sprocket, thereby locking same securely, which makes it impossible for anyone to ride the bicycle in the owner's absence. This style is new, lock is neat and elegantly finished, made of real bronze.

No. 19R570 Sprocket Lock. Each..**17c**
If by mail, postage extra, each, 4 cents.

New Model Sprocket Lock.

A new design. Very handsomely finished, black body with brass shackle. A lock that will recommend itself.

No. 19R574 New Model Sprocket Lock.
Price, each.................................**17c**
If by mail, postage extra, 4 cents.

Bicycle Lock, with Chain.

A chain lock is desired by many riders, and we herewith offer one that fills the bill, and is not too heavy for the pocket when not in use. Has steel case, black finish, brass shackle and chain, with one key.

No. 19R577 Lock and Chain.
Price, each.......................**20c**
If by mail, postage extra, 5 cents.

Cyclists' Watch Chain.

Emblematic of the wheel, being made of bicycle chain links and to which is attached a miniature sprocket. Handsomely nickel plated and a useful novelty.

No. 19R580 Cyclists' Watch Chain. Price.. **15c**
If by mail, postage extra, 3 cents.

BICYCLE WHISTLES.

No. 19R608 The Gem Whistle; gives a soft, loud alarm, a favorite whistle. Price, with chain........**14c**
If by mail, postage extra, each, 5 cents.

Single Tube Whistles.

No. 19R611 Single Tube Whistle; the strongest and shrillest whistle in use. The slightest effort is all that is required to use it. Price.................................**15c**
If by mail, postage extra, each, 4 cents.

The Security Cyclometer.

No. 19R614 The Security Cyclometer for 28-inch wheels. Positively the most durable cyclometer ever presented to the rider. It fits around the barrel of front hub between the flanges and cannot be knocked or broken off in falls. The interference pin is placed on inside of fork, out of danger. Its mechanism is perfect, with a total register of 10,000 miles. It is finely nickel plated and thoroughly first class in every way.

Price, each..**64c**
If by mail, postage extra, each, 3 cents.

The Veeder Cyclometer.

No. 19R617 The Veeder Cyclometer registers 10,000 miles and repeats. So well known to the riding public as to require no special introduction. It is the original barrel cyclometer, very neat and compact, as well as being thoroughly reliable. **Weighs but 1 ounce.** It is both dust and waterproof, finely nickel plated, every instrument being carefully tested at factory. **Furnished for 28-inch wheels.** Price, each.........................**62c**
If by mail, postage extra, each, 3 cents.

Veeder Double Barrel Cyclometer.

No. 19R620 The Veeder Double Barrel Cyclometer is practically two cyclometers set side by side. One registers to 10,000 miles and repeats. The other is a trip cyclometer, and registers 100 miles; but at any moment may be set back to "0," enabling the rider to ascertain his mileage for any trip or hour. Furnished for 28-inch wheels. Price, each...................................**$1.20**
If by mail, postage extra, each, 5 cents.

Pumps.

No. 19R648 "A very windy Pump," made of good, strong material, and will **last two or three seasons. The favorite** style and size. **Single action,** including hose connection which will fit all modern valves, having a universal inside thread. Each..**9c**
If by mail, postage extra, each, 4 cents.

Our 29-Cent Giant Foot Pump.

No. 19R652 The Giant Foot Pump, will not rust or corrode. Positively the best foot pump ever sold at this price. Sold in many retail stores at double our price. Made of brass, finely nickel plated. Barrel 1¼x12 inches, with a powerful plunger, large wood handle, a pump that will inflate a tire in a jiffy. Hose has a swivel connection that will fit all modern valves having a universal inside thread. You make no mistake in buying this pump.

Price, each...**29c**
If by mail, postage extra, each, 27 cents.

The Giant Pocket Foot Pump.

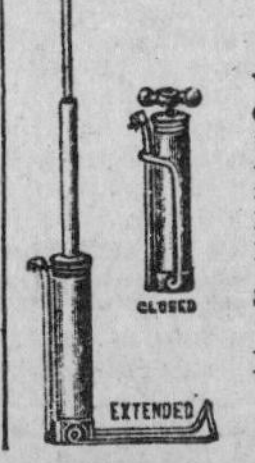

A combination hand or foot pump, very powerful. Our cut shows pump extended for use as a foot pump, also when telescoped ready to carry in pocket. Made of seamless brass, finely nickel plated. Size when closed, 6½ inches; extended, 15½ inches. **Has universal valve connection to fit any standard tire.**

No. 19R660 Giant Pocket Foot Pump. Price, each...................**39c**
If by mail, postage extra, 10 cents.

Large Foot Pump.

This Pump is adapted for heavy work, has 18-inch barrel, hose with universal thread connection. Is strong enough to inflate carriage or vehicle tires.

No. 19R664 Pump. Price, each....49c

If by mail, postage extra, 39 cents.

Handy Strap Carrier.

Consisting of two russet leather straps, each 26 inches in length, provided with adjustable leather lined spring clips. The straps can be used to attach packages to handle bars or on bicycle frame. Being light and small, they can be easily rolled up and carried in the pocket, if desired.

No. 19R700 Price, per pair....................16c

If by mail, postage extra, 8 cents.

Canvas Parcel Carrier.

A favorite bag, made of canvas, with double thickness in flap, which fastens with patent clasps. The bag is attached to handle bar with two leather lined spring clasps. As the bag has ample width it has a large capacity and will be found very useful. Size, 12x9x3 inches. Postage extra, 10 cents.

No. 19R703 Canvas Parcel Carrier. Each...24c

Pocket Parcel Carrier.

Positively the neatest and lightest carrier made. It consists of a black netted bag, extra wide at bottom, with a double elastic band at top, which fastens securely to any shape handle bar, by means of two spring clasps. As there is no frame used in its construction, it can be instantly adjusted to any width and it will accomodate any reasonably sized package. When not in use, it can be rolled up and carried in the pocket or tool bag.

No. 19R706 Pocket Parcel Carrier. Price..21c

If by mail, postage extra, 5 cents.

Camera Carrier.

Made of heavy steel wire, nickel plated, with extra long straps. This makes an ideal carrier for cameras, valises or heavy packages. It can be instantly attached to handle bars or removed at will.

No. 19R710 Camera Carrier. Price, each...........35c

If by mail, postage extra, 16 cents.

The Fairy Child's Seat.

Adapted for use on either ladies or gents' bicycles, extremely light and does not interfere with the adult rider. The supporting wire rods follow the shape of handle bar and steering head, and securely fastened with but one buckle. Perfectly safe for children of ordinary weight.

No. 19R718 Fairy Child's Seat. Price, each...............98c

Our Triumph Oiler.

In this oiler we present one of the neatest patterns on the market, well made, nicely nickel plated and just the right size to go in tool bag.

No. 19R742 Triumph Oiler. Price, each......4c

If by mail, postage extra, each, 2 cents.

Perfect Pocket Oiler.

No. 19R746 Perfect Pocket Oiler. The cleanest and handsomest pocket oiler in the world. Price...................15c

If by mail, postage extra, each, 2 cents.

Adjustable Coasters.

No. 19R760 Adjustable Foot Rests or Coasters; very light, but strong and neat in design. When not in use can be folded against the side of the fork, out of your way. Price, per pair.................11c

If by mail, postage extra, each, 6 cents.

Combination Lamp Brackets.

Combination Lamp Bracket, for head of frame or fork, is an up to date original accessory; unique in design, simple in construction, hence easily adjusted, light, durable, made and finished in the best possible manner. Nickeled steel.

No. 19R770 Price, each..........15c

If by mail, postage extra, each, 4 cents.

Cork Grips.

Our lucky purchase is your gain. Only 7 cents per pair while they last. Made of the best material that can be secured, with nickel plated ferrule tips. You can afford to secure a new pair of grips while these last, for they are excellent value for the money.

No. 19R790 Cork Grips, with nickel tips, per pair, 7c

If by mail, postage extra, per pair, 4 cents.

Leather Grips.

These Grips are made from genuine sole leather and are certainly the most durable grips made. Made in ⅞-inch size only.

No. 19R798 Leather Grips. Price, per pair....7c

If by mail, postage extra, per pair, 5 cents.

Fancy End Cork Grips.

With enameled ends nicely inlaid, as per our illustration, made for ⅞-inch size only, and with maroon or black tips.

No. 19R800 Fancy Cork Grips. Price, per pair, 14c

If by mail, postage extra, per pair, 7 cents.

Aluminum Chain Guards.

These are real aluminum, not to be confounded with the many cheap makeshifts now on the market. They are an ornament to any bicycle, and are sure to accomplish their purpose, to prevent lady riders falling on account of skirts becoming caught in chain. Always state for what size front sprocket.

No. 19R840 Aluminum Guard, medium size, for 19-tooth sprockets. Price, each...............$1.55

If by mail, postage extra, 32 cents.

No. 19R841 Aluminum Guard, for 23-tooth front sprockets. Price, each $1.55

If by mail, postage extra, 32 cents.

The Automatic Chain Brush.

Overcomes all trouble arising from dirty chain. It consists of a pair of first quality bristle brushes, clamped in a nickeled steel frame and so adjusted that bristles are in constant contact with chain. Always with you. Fits all makes of bicycles. No friction. Bristles will last the average rider from one to two years and may be readily replaced.

No. 19R860 Price, each, complete...........25c

If by mail, postage extra, each, 6 cents.

No. 19R861 Extra Bristles. Price, per set.....8c

If by mail, postage extra, per set, 2 cents.

Burlington Mud Guard.

Improved for 1902, the lightest, most durable mud guard made. Made of rubber cloth, rolls up small enough to go into tool bag. Just the thing to protect the enamel of your bicycle. It saves many times its cost, in that you don't have to clean your bicycle so often, and it saves the enamel.

No. 19R884 Mud Guard. Price, each........20c

If by mail, postage extra, 3 cents.

Automatic Rear Wheel Brake.

This Brake is attached to the lower rear forks as indicated in illustration. Any rider can place it in position. It acts as a positive brake as soon as the rider back pedals, as that action straightens the lower reach of the chain, which in turn operates on the brake roller, and thus the spoon is applied to the tire. This brake is perfect, nicely nickel plated, removable at will, and ought to be on every bicycle. Don't fail to send for one. Postage extra, 18 cents.

No. 19R900 Automatic Brake. Price, each..98c

Handle Bar Buffer.

The Rubber Handle Bar Buffer goes on over frame and prevents your handle bar from knocking off the enamel. Every cyclist should have one.

No. 19R910 Our special price, each.6c

If by mail, postage extra, 3 cents.

Patent Trouser Guard.

Patent Trouser Guard, a neat and handy device for saving the trousers from dirt and grease; can be carried in the vest pocket or worn around the legs under the trousers when not in use.

No. 19R916 Patent Trouser Guard. Per pair..1c

If by mail, postage extra, per pair, 3 cents.

Saddle Clamp.

Well and strongly made, will fit any two-spring saddle. Nicely nickel plated.

No. 19R926 Price, each 7c

If by mail, postage extra, 3 cents.

Bicycle Screwdriver.

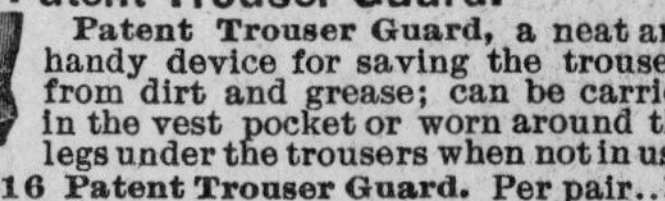

Made of steel, twisted in serpentine shape, useful for many purposes; has a 2-inch blade.

No. 19R936 Steel Screwdriver. Price, each...2c

If by mail, postage extra, 2 cents.

S., R. & Co.'s Bicycle Wrench.

Every rider needs a good wrench for his tool bag. This wrench is made of best quality steel, hardened jaws, handsomely nickel plated.

No. 19R940 Bicycle Wrench. Price, each.....9c

If by mail, postage extra, 6 cents.

Drop Forged Bicycle Wrench.

Made heavier than our cheaper wrench. Drop forged, with hardened jaws; suitable for all purposes possible for a small wrench. Finely nickel plated. Will fit in any regular size tool bag.

No. 19R950 Wrench. Price, each...........14c

If by mail, postage extra, 8 cents.

Bicycle Tire Brush.

Made of Russian bristles. Will clean both tire and edges of rim at same time. A most useful article for the rider, as it prevents the soiling of hands or clothes. Brush can be readily cleaned with hot or cold water and is then as good as new.

No. 19R954 Bicycle Tire Brush. Each.......19c

If by mail, postage extra, 10 cents.

Chain Brush.

Chain Brush for cleaning chain and sprockets, made of pure bristles. The very thing for muddy chains and sprockets.

No. 19R960 Chain Brush. Price, each.......10c

If by mail, postage extra, 8 cents.

Pincers for Inserting Plugs.

These pliers are made for inserting plugs in single tube tires, but are also found useful for many other purposes.

No. 19R964 Plug Pliers. Price, each.........4c

If by mail, postage extra, 5 cents.

The Perfect Nipple Grip.

Made of the best drop forged steel, jaws case hardened. The only tool that will budge obstinate nipples; will last indefinitely and will not wear off the square edge of nipples.

No. 19R980 Perfect Nipple Grip. Each......33c

If by mail, postage extra, 6 cents.

Handy Nipple Grip.

Fits the pocket and tool bag, is nicely nickel plated and a very handy little article, needed by every rider.

No. 19R984 Handy Nipple Grip. Price, each.........................8c

If by mail, postage extra, 2 cents.

Adjustable Stirrup Toe Clips.

Adjustable Stirrup Toe Clips. Latest 1902 model. The one-piece leather cover can be quickly adjusted to fit a large or small foot.

No. 19R988 Adjustable Stirrup Toe Clips. Price, per pair..........................30c

If by mail, postage extra, per pair, 10 cents.

Thiem's Toe Clips.

Thiem's Toe Clips, are made of crucible wire. The foot cannot slip from the pedal with this clip, and nothing but a severe accident will put it out of shape. Use only screwdriver to apply to pedal.

No. 19R992 Theim's Toe Clips. Per pair.....14c

If by mail, postage extra, per pair, 10 cents.

Ideal Toe Clips.

These Toe Clips are made of the best spring steel, of handsome design, nickel plated in the best manner. They are easy to get into and afford great purchase in hill climbing.

No. 19R994 Ideal Toe Clips. Price, per pair..........................10c

If by mail, postage extra, per pair, 10 cents.

The Standard Toe Clips.

The Standard Toe Clips are made of tempered steel and are a very popular clip. Fit any pedal. No fast riding without them.

No. 19R996 Standard Toe Clip. Price, per pair........................9c

Postage extra, per pair, 10 cents.

Bicycle Frames for Repair Orders.

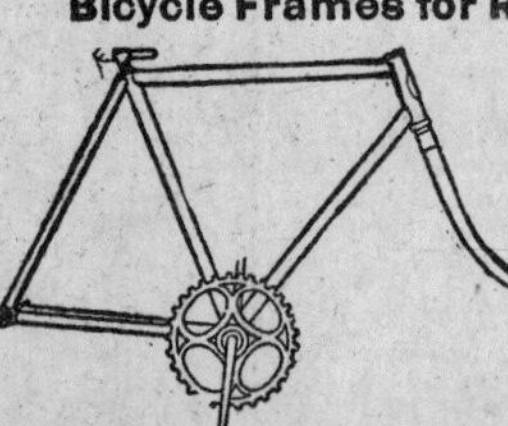

We are frequently called upon to assist our customers in obtaining repairs for bicycles made by defunct concerns, and as such calls will constantly increase, we have made arrangements to supply a stripped frame and fork of modern design to fill such orders, that our customers may purchase such frame and fork and with assistance of his old wheels, tires, saddle and handle bar may have practically a new and good bicycle instead of being compelled to buy an entirely new machine. We have seen instances where repairs on a frame or hanger have cost our customers as much as our price for frame, and at that rate they still had nothing but a second hand frame. In such cases it would be economy to buy one of the frames we quote below. We can only supply 22 and 24-inch men's frames and only the regular 22-inch ladies' frames. At our quotations we include the main frame, front fork, head cups and cones, hanger cups and cones, crank and sprocket, also seat post. On the ladies' frames we include the dress and chain guards. The usual bright parts are highly nickel plated, while the frames proper are nicely enameled either in black or maroon.

No. 19R1020 Gents' 22-inch frame and fork..$4.95

No. 19R1021 Gents' 24-inch frame and fork..4.95

No. 19R1022 Ladies' 22-inch frame and fork..5.45

L. C. SMITH BREECH LOADING SHOTGUNS

IN PRESENTING TO OUR CUSTOMERS the L. C. Smith Shotguns, manufactured by the Hunter Arms Company, Fulton, New York, we do so, knowing that these guns possess a high standard of merit; are very popular and have as many friends among the shooting classes as any guns yet produced.

THE SPECIAL FEATURES of the L. C. Smith Guns consist of their being built on symmetrical lines, nicely balanced, systematically bored for hard shooting and made from the finest material money can buy.

ALL THE EMPLOYEES of the Hunter Arms Company are classed as skilled mechanics of a high order and with a wide experience in gun manufacture.

THE L. C. SMITH GUNS have the popular nitro cross bolt lock which takes up wear and prevents the gun from becoming loose and shaky. All have elegantly tapered and matted ribs, finely case hardened frame and locks, nicely checkered stock and fore end, polished and blued mountings, straight grain walnut stock, and are first class in every way.

SHOOTING QUALITIES. The shooting qualities of the L. C. Smith are recognized by the professional sportsmen everywhere as the highest of high grades, the greatest possible penetration, the best target that any gun can make and every gun is carefully tested to target, to penetration and to accuracy in all parts before it leaves the factory.

THE L. C. SMITH is made on the very latest principles. It is extra strong at every point, devoid of all complicated mechanism, has the best known mechanical movement for cocking tumblers and strikers; easy to manipulate. The bolting joint check and extractor mechanism are the best known to gun making. The cocking mechanism on the hammerless gun is composed of but two pieces, with no springs, pins or screws.

THE L. C. SMITH hammer and hammerless guns are made from the very best material that money can buy. Only skilled mechanics are employed. There is probably no more popular gun among trap and professional shooters than the L. C. Smith. It has stood the crucial test of years of constant service at the trap and in the field, and it is so strong and so perfect in its action that we have yet to learn of one which has become loose or shaky, and many of them have a record of over one hundred thousand shots, and this is most remarkable when it is considered that the most powerful charges of nitro powder are common to this class of shooting, and this most extraordinary record fully substantiates the claim that the Smith gun is constructed on thoroughly sound mechanical principles, as no gun, no matter how finely made, can stand the test of everyday use unless the metal is properly distributed, the bearings large and well supported and the locking device of the most substantial character.

FINISH. The L. C. Smith Guns are given the highest possible finish and they are put out at our special inside prices in competition with guns that sell everywhere at 50 to 100 per cent more money.

THE L. C. SMITH GUNS are made by the Hunter Arms Company, of Fulton, New York. They have earned a reputation as among the

VERY HIGHEST OF HIGH GRADE AMERICAN HAMMERLESS SHOTGUNS.

27.75

No. 6R26
Order by Number.

Our Special Inside Price, $27.75

THE ABOVE ILLUSTRATION, engraved from a photograph, will give you some idea of the appearance of the No. 00 grade L. C. Smith hammerless gun. We furnish the L. C. Smith in the various grades as illustrated hereon.

ON OUR SPECIAL No. 00 GRADE illustrated above, we name a very low price, the lowest price ever made on an L. C. Smith hammerless shotgun, and if you wish a genuine L. C. Smith gun at an extremely low price, we would recommend the gun above illustrated and described.

BY OUR SPECIAL ARRANGEMENT with the manufacturer we can quote a price on this gun based on the actual cost of material and labor at the factory, with but one small percentage of profit added.

THE ABOVE ILLUSTRATION will give you a good idea of the appearance of this, our special No. 00 grade L. C. Smith double barrel hammerless shotgun, but you must see it, examine it and compare it with other high grade guns.

THIS OUR No. 00 GRADE is built on the very latest lines for this season. It is made with new Armor high grade steel barrels; both barrels full choke bored and fully tested; tested for nitro powder. It has a very fine imported English walnut stock, beautifully finished; half pistol grip, fancy checkered and well finished; it has the latest top break; it comes in either 30 or 32-inch barrels; fancy case hardened locks; automatic safety block; heavy breech; narrow muzzles, nicely tapered matted rib, with all the latest improvements. Weighs from 7½ to 8 pounds.

The above illustration is of the New Armor Steel Smith Hammerless Gun. English walnut pistol grip stock checkered, and checkered fore end, case hardened locks, automatic safety block, heavy breech, narrow muzzles with all the latest improvements, guaranteed for nitro as well as black powders.

No. 6R26 No. 00 grade, 12-gauge, 30 or 32-inch barrels, 7½ to 8 pounds. OUR SPECIAL PRICE **$27.75**

No. 6R28 Same as No. 6R26, with patent automatic ejector, 12-gauge, 30 or 32-inch barrels, 7½ to 8 pounds. MADE TO SPECIAL ORDER. OUR SPECIAL PRICE **37.50**

Damascus Barrels,
BORED FOR NITRO POWDER.

No. 6R32

No. 6R32 No. 0 grade Damascus barrels, imported walnut stock, pistol grip, rubber butt plate, case hardened lock plates and action, plain finished but a good gun, every one warranted. 12-gauge, 30 or 32-inch barrels; 7½ to 8 pounds. OUR SPECIAL PRICE **$31.70**

No. 6R34 No. 0 grade. Same as No. 6R32 with patent automatic ejector, 12-gauge. MADE TO SPECIAL ORDER. OUR SPECIAL PRICE, **$40.50**

2-Blade Damascus Barrels,
BORED FOR NITRO POWDER.

No. 6R36

No. 6R36 No. 1 grade, fine 2-blade Damascus steel barrels, imported walnut stock, pistol grip and fore end, rubber butt plate, hardened lock plates and action. Plain line engraving, but well made and desirable, and just as good a shooter as a higher priced gun. 12-gauge, 30 or 32-inch barrels; 7½ to 8 pounds. OUR SPECIAL PRICE **$40.50**

No. 6R38 Same as No. 6R36, with automatic ejector. 12 or 16-gauge. MADE TO SPECIAL ORDER. OUR SPECIAL PRICE... **50.62**

3-Blade Damascus Barrels,
BORED FOR NITRO POWDER.

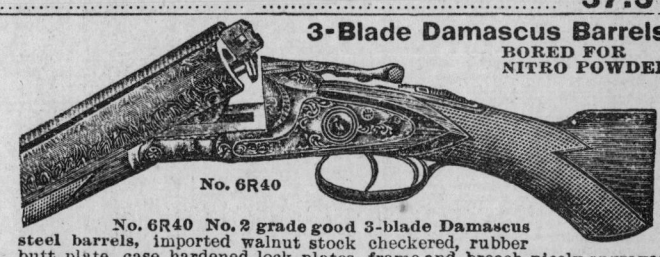

No. 6R40

No. 6R40 No. 2 grade good 3-blade Damascus steel barrels, imported walnut stock checkered, rubber butt plate, case hardened lock plates, frame and breech nicely engraved, finely finished, 12-gauge, 30 or 32-inch barrels; 7½ to 8 pounds. OUR SPECIAL PRICE **$54.00**

No. 6R42 No. 2 Grade, same as No. 6R40, with patent automatic ejector. Made to Special Order. OUR SPECIAL PRICE **$64.12**

Special High Grade L. C. Smith Guns.
12-gauge, 30 or 32-inch barrels, 7½ to 8 lbs. Bored for nitro powder. Illustration of No. 6R44 or No. 3 Grade L. C. Smith.

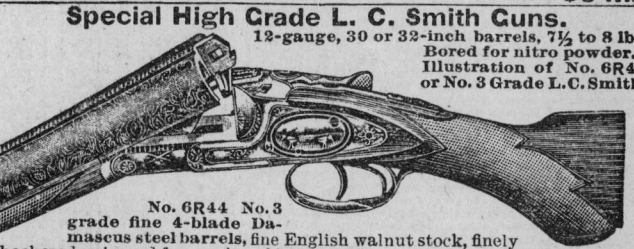

No. 6R44 No. 3 grade fine 4-blade Damascus steel barrels, fine English walnut stock, finely checkered grip and fore end, rubber butt plate, case hardened locks, frame and breech handsomely engraved and finely finished in 12-gauge. OUR SPECIAL PRICE **$67.50**

No. 6R46 No. 3 grade, same as No. 6R44, with automatic ejector in 12 or 16-gauge. MADE TO SPECIAL ORDER. OUR SPECIAL PRICE **$77.62**

NOTICE.

Nos. 6R36, 6R38, 6R40 and 6R42 can also be had with Special Crown Steel Barrels to special order. This would incur some little delay, however. If you wish the Crown Steel Barrels mention it when you order. The price will be the same as for Damascus barrels.

Nos. 6R36, 6R38, 6R40 and 6R42 in 10-gauge, 30 or 32-inch barrels, 8½ to 10 pounds, to special order, same price as 12-gauge.

On Guns made to special order we require full amount of cash with the order and if made according to order CANNOT BE RETURNED UNDER ANY CIRCUMSTANCES.

WE MAKE NO CHARGE FOR BOXING GUNS FOR SHIPMENT.

NOTICE.

Nos. 6R44 and 6R46 can be furnished with special nitro steel barrels, to special order, at the same price as Damascus barrels.

Nos. 6R44 and 6R46, in 10-gauge, to special order, 30 or 32-inch barrels; 8½ to 9½ pounds, same price as 12-gauge.

The L. C. Smith Pigeon Gun.

No. 6R48 The L. C. Smith Pigeon Gun, finest blued finish crown steel barrels, straight grip, highly finished and engraved; bored for nitro powder and made especially for trap shooting, beautifully balanced and made in the highest art of gun making; finely checkered English stock and fore end, matted rib, 2½ to 3-inch drop for trap shooting, 12-gauge, 30 or 32-inch barrels, 7½ to 8 lbs. MADE TO SPECIAL ORDER. OUR SPECIAL PRICE **$84.37**

No. 6R50 L. C. Smith Pigeon Gun, same as No. 6R48, in 12-gauge, with automatic ejector. MADE TO SPECIAL ORDER. OUR SPECIAL PRICE **$94.50**

AT $15.75 IT IS THE WORLD'S WONDER

No. 6R54 Order by Number.

$15.75 buys the now justly celebrated, high grade, Chicago Long Range Wonder, Double Barrel Breech Loading Hammerless Shotgun, as illustrated hereon, a double barrel, hammerless gun, which in gun making is indeed the "World's Wonder."

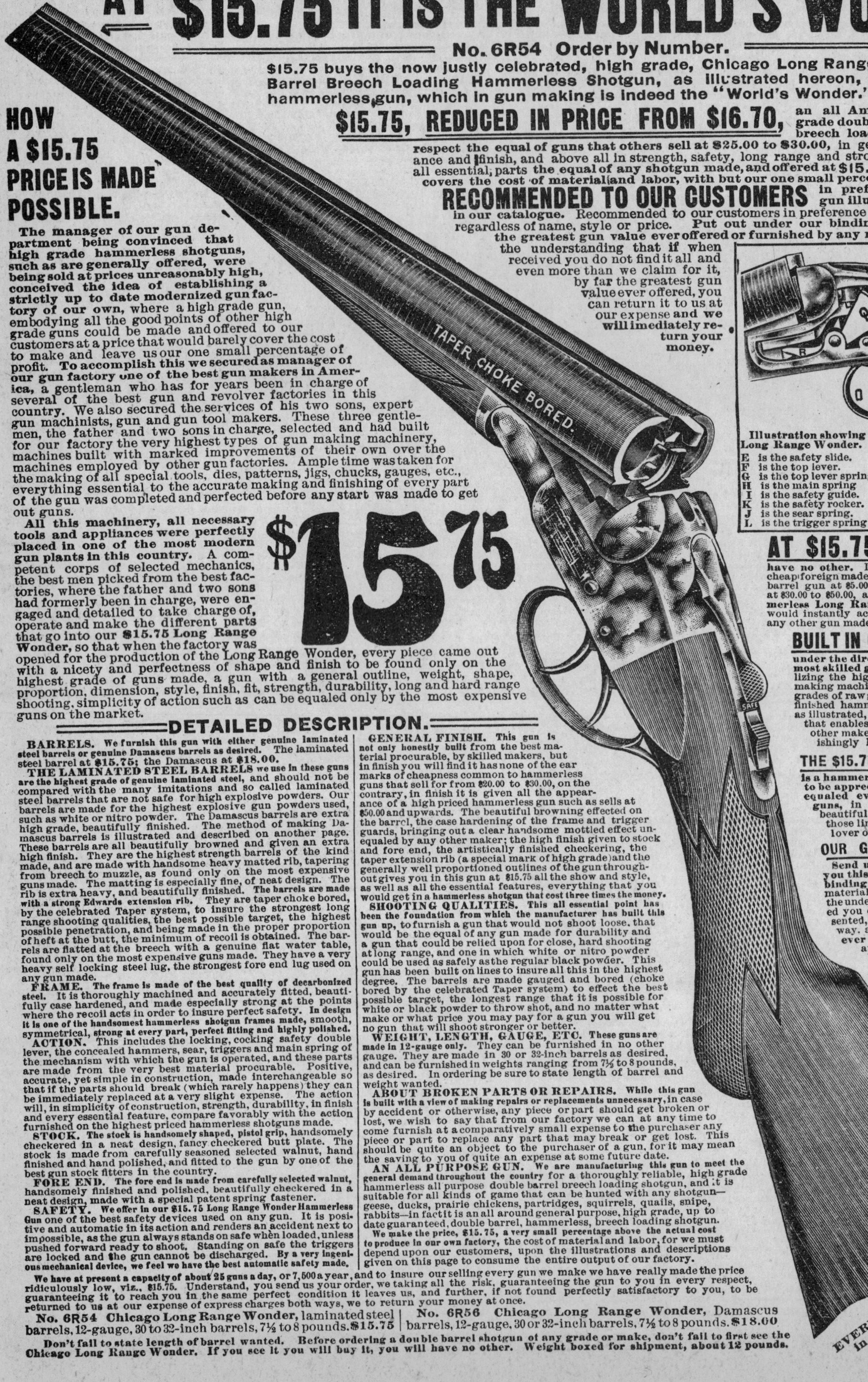

$15.75, REDUCED IN PRICE FROM $16.70, an all American strictly high grade double barrel, hammerless, breech loading shotgun, in every respect the equal of guns that others sell at $25.00 to $30.00, in general outline, appearance and finish, and above all in strength, safety, long range and strong shooting, in fact in all essential parts the equal of any shotgun made, and offered at $15.75, a price that barely covers the cost of material and labor, with but our one small percentage of profit added.

RECOMMENDED TO OUR CUSTOMERS in preference to any other gun illustrated and described in our catalogue. Recommended to our customers in preference to any other gun made, regardless of name, style or price. Put out under our binding guarantee as by far the greatest gun value ever offered or furnished by any maker, sold to you with the understanding that if when received you do not find it all and even more than we claim for it, by far the greatest gun value ever offered, you can return it to us at our expense and we will imediately return your money.

HOW A $15.75 PRICE IS MADE POSSIBLE.

The manager of our gun department being convinced that high grade hammerless shotguns, such as are generally offered, were being sold at prices unreasonably high, conceived the idea of establishing a strictly up to date modernized gun factory of our own, where a high grade gun, embodying all the good points of other high grade guns could be made and offered to our customers at a price that would barely cover the cost to make and leave us our one small percentage of profit. **To accomplish this we secured as manager of our gun factory one of the best gun makers in America,** a gentleman who has for years been in charge of several of the best gun and revolver factories in this country. We also secured the services of his two sons, expert gun machinists, gun and gun tool makers. These three gentlemen, the father and two sons in charge, selected and had built for our factory the very highest types of gun making machinery, machines built with marked improvements of their own over the machines employed by other gun factories. Ample time was taken for the making of all special tools, dies, patterns, jigs, chucks, gauges, etc., everything essential to the accurate making and finishing of every part of the gun was completed and perfected before any start was made to get out guns.

All this machinery, all necessary tools and appliances were perfectly placed in one of the most modern gun plants in this country. A competent corps of selected mechanics, the best men picked from the best factories, where the father and two sons had formerly been in charge, were engaged and detailed to take charge of, operate and make the different parts that go into our **$15.75 Long Range Wonder,** so that when the factory was opened for the production of the Long Range Wonder, every piece came out with a nicety and perfectness of shape and finish to be found only on the highest grade of guns made, a gun with a general outline, weight, shape, proportion, dimension, style, finish, fit, strength, durability, long and hard range shooting, simplicity of action such as can be equaled only by the most expensive guns on the market.

$15.75

TAPER CHOKE BORED.

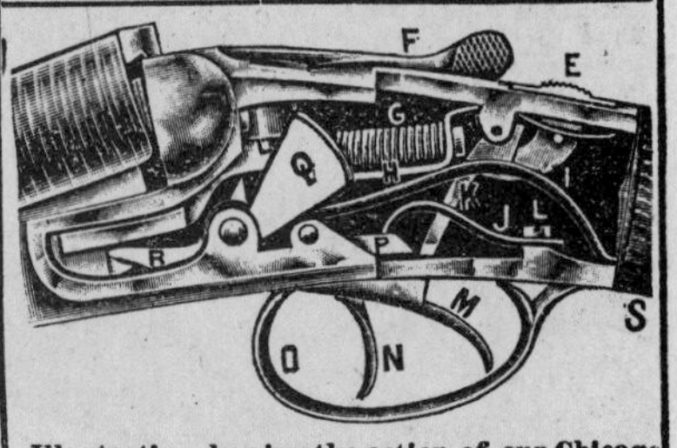

Illustration showing the action of our Chicago Long Range Wonder.

E	is the safety slide.	M	is the left trigger.
F	is the top lever.	N	is the right trigger.
G	is the top lever spring.	O	is the guard.
H	is the main spring	P	is the sear.
I	is the safety guide.	Q	is the hammer.
K	is the safety rocker.	R	is the cooking lever
J	is the sear spring.	S	is the stock.
L	is the trigger spring screw.		

AT $15.75 we know we are offering a hammerless gun that once seen, you would have no other. If you are about to select a cheap foreign made gun at $10.00 to $20.00, a single barrel gun at $5.00 to $15.00 or a high priced gun at $30.00 to $50.00, and could first see our **Hammerless Long Range Wonder at $15.75,** you would instantly accept this gun in preference to any other gun made.

BUILT IN OUR OWN FACTORY

under the direct supervision of one of the most skilled gun makers in America, utilizing the highest types of automatic gun making machinery, buying only the highest grades of raw gun material, we produce the finished hammerless, double barrel shotgun as illustrated, at a net shop or factory cost that enables us to undersell almost any other maker by half, and quote the astonishingly low price of **$15.75.**

THE $15.75 LONG RANGE WONDER

is a hammerless gun that must be seen to be appreciated, a gun that is seldom equaled even by the most expensive guns, in its perfect proportion, in its beautiful case hardened finish, in all those lines so much appreciated by the lover of a fine hammerless shotgun.

OUR GUARANTEE OFFER.

Send us $15.75 and we will send you this gun by express under our binding guarantee for quality, for material and workmanship, and with the understanding that if when received you do not find it exactly as represented, perfectly satisfactory in every way, and the **greatest gun value ever offered,** you can return it to us at our expense of express charges both ways and we will immediately **return your money.**

THIS ILLUSTRATION which is engraved from a photograph taken direct from our **$15.75 Chicago Long Range Wonder,** will give you some idea of the appearance of this handsome gun, but it must be seen and compared with other hammerless shotguns to appreciate the value we are giving.

DETAILED DESCRIPTION.

BARRELS. We furnish this gun with either genuine laminated steel barrels or genuine Damascus barrels as desired. The laminated steel barrel at **$15.75;** the Damascus at **$18.00.**

THE LAMINATED STEEL BARRELS we use in these guns are the highest grade of genuine laminated steel, and should not be compared with the many imitations and so called laminated steel barrels that are not safe for high explosive powders. Our barrels are made for the highest explosive gun powders used, such as white or nitro powder. The Damascus barrels are extra high grade, beautifully finished. The method of making Damascus barrels is illustrated and described on another page. These barrels are all beautifully browned and given an extra high finish. They are the highest strength barrels of the kind made, and are made with handsome heavy matted rib, tapering from breech to muzzle, as found only on the most expensive guns made. The matting is especially fine, of neat design. The rib is extra heavy, and beautifully finished. **The barrels are made with a strong Edwards extension rib.** They are taper choke bored, by the celebrated Taper system, to insure the strongest long range shooting qualities, the best possible target, the highest possible penetration, and being made in the proper proportion of heft at the butt, the minimum of recoil is obtained. The barrels are flatted at the breech with a genuine flat water table, found only on the most expensive guns made. They have a very heavy self locking steel lug, the strongest fore end lug used on any gun made.

FRAME. The frame is made of the best quality of decarbonized steel. It is thoroughly machined and accurately fitted, beautifully case hardened, and made especially strong at the points where the recoil acts in order to insure perfect safety. **In design it is one of the handsomest hammerless shotgun frames made,** smooth, symmetrical, **strong at every part, perfect fitting and highly polished.**

ACTION. This includes the locking, cocking safety double lever, the concealed hammers, sear, triggers and main spring of the mechanism with which the gun is operated, and these parts are made from the very best material procurable. Positive, accurate, yet simple in construction, made interchangeable so that if the parts should break (which rarely happens) they can be immediately replaced at a very slight expense. The action will, in simplicity of construction, strength, durability, in finish and every essential feature, compare favorably with the action furnished on the highest priced hammerless shotguns made.

STOCK. The stock is handsomely shaped, pistol grip, handsomely checkered in a neat design, fancy checkered butt plate. The stock is made from carefully seasoned selected walnut, hand finished and hand polished, and fitted to the gun by one of the best gun stock fitters in the country.

FORE END. The fore end is made from carefully selected walnut, handsomely finished and polished, beautifully checkered in a neat design, made with a special patent spring fastener.

SAFETY. We offer in our $15.75 Long Range Wonder Hammerless Gun one of the best safety devices used on any gun. It is positive and automatic in its action and renders an accident next to impossible, as the gun always stands on safe when loaded, unless pushed forward ready to shoot. Standing on safe the triggers are locked and the gun cannot be discharged. **By a very ingenious mechanical device, we feel we have the best automatic safety made.**

GENERAL FINISH. This gun is not only honestly built from the best material procurable, by skilled makers, but in finish you will find it has none of the ear marks of cheapness common to hammerless guns that sell for from $20.00 to $30.00, on the contrary, in finish it is given all the appearance of a high priced hammerless gun such as sells at $50.00 and upwards. The beautiful browning effected on the barrel, the case hardening of the frame and trigger guards, bringing out a clear handsome mottled effect unequaled by any other maker; the high finish given to stock and fore end, the artistically finished checkering, the taper extension rib (a special mark of high grade) and the generally well proportioned outlines of the gun throughout gives you in this gun at $15.75 all the show and style, as well as all the essential features, everything that you would get in a **hammerless shotgun that cost three times the money.**

SHOOTING QUALITIES. This all essential point has been the foundation from which the manufacturer has built this gun up, to furnish a gun that would not shoot loose, that would be the equal of any gun made for durability and a gun that could be relied upon for close, hard shooting at long range, and one in which white or nitro powder could be used as safely as the regular black powder. This gun has been built on lines to insure all this in the highest degree. The barrels are made gauged and bored (choke bored by the celebrated Taper system) to effect the best possible target, the longest range that it is possible for white or black powder to throw shot, and no matter what make or what price you may pay for a gun you will get no gun that will shoot stronger or better.

WEIGHT, LENGTH, GAUGE, ETC. These guns are made in 12-gauge only. They can be furnished in no other gauge. They are made in 30 or 32-inch barrels as desired, and can be furnished in weights ranging from 7½ to 8 pounds, as desired. In ordering be sure to state length of barrel and weight wanted.

ABOUT BROKEN PARTS OR REPAIRS. While this gun is built with a view of making repairs or replacements unnecessary, in case by accident or otherwise, any piece or part should get broken or lost, we wish to say that from our factory we can at any time to come furnish at a comparatively small expense to the purchaser any piece or part to replace any part that may break or get lost. This should be quite an object to the purchaser of a gun, for it may mean the saving to you of quite an expense at some future date.

AN ALL PURPOSE GUN. We are manufacturing this gun to meet the general demand throughout the country for a thoroughly reliable, high grade hammerless all purpose double barrel breech loading shotgun, and it is suitable for all kinds of game that can be hunted with any shotgun— geese, ducks, prairie chickens, partridges, squirrels, quails, snipe, rabbits—in fact it is an all around general purpose, high grade, up to date guaranteed, double barrel, hammerless, breech loading shotgun.

We make the price, $15.75, a very small percentage above the actual cost to produce in our own factory, the cost of material and labor, for we must depend upon our customers, upon the illustrations and descriptions given on this page to consume the entire output of our factory.

We have at present a capacity of about 25 guns a day, or 7,500 a year, and to insure our selling every gun we make we have really made the price **ridiculously low, viz., $15.75.** Understand, you send us your order, we taking all the risk, guaranteeing the gun to you in every respect, guaranteeing it to reach you in the same perfect condition it leaves us, and further, if not found perfectly satisfactory to you, to be returned to us at our expense of express charges both ways, we to return your money at once.

No. 6R54 Chicago Long Range Wonder, laminated steel barrels, 12-gauge, 30 to 32-inch barrels, 7½ to 8 pounds. **$15.75**

No. 6R56 Chicago Long Range Wonder, Damascus barrels, 12-gauge, 30 or 32-inch barrels, 7½ to 8 pounds. **$18.00**

Don't fail to state length of barrel wanted. Before ordering a double barrel shotgun of any grade or make, don't fail to first see the Chicago Long Range Wonder. If you see it you will buy it, you will have no other. Weight boxed for shipment, about 12 pounds.

EVERY LITTLE POINT is studied in this gun to make it in all essential points the equal of any gun made, regardless of price, a shotgun we can recommend above all others.

REMINGTON NEW MODEL DOUBLE BARREL SHOTGUNS.

AT $20.00, $23.00 and $25.00 we furnish the latest New Model, Highest Grade, Guaranteed Double Barrel Breech Loading Hammer Shotguns.

At $25.00, $35.00 and $45.00 we furnish the Highest Grade Automatic Remington Double Barrel Hammerless Shotguns.

AT $40.00 and $50.00 we furnish the very latest Self Acting Automatic Ejector Remington Double Barrel Hammerless Shotguns.

OUR TEN DAYS' FREE TRIAL OFFER. We give you the privilege of ordering any Remington gun, giving it 10 days' trial, during which time you can compare it as to shooting qualities, strength, durability and finish with any gun made, and if you are not perfectly satisfied with your purchase, you are at liberty to return the gun to us at our expense, and we will immediately return all the money you have sent us. All we ask is that you keep the gun in perfect condition.

WE ARE HEADQUARTERS for the Remington double barrel hammer and hammerless self-ejecting shotguns. We buy them direct from the manufacturers, the Remington Arms Company of Ilion, New York, under contract in immense quantities for cash, at a price based on the actual cost to produce, to which our one small percentage of profit is added, making it possible for you to get the highest grade Remington gun direct from us for even less than your dealer can buy in quantities.

$20.00 FOR OUR LATEST MODEL Double Barrel Remington Shotgun. $20.00 is our price for this the latest double barrel barlock, pistol grip Remington hammer shotgun. How much we save you in price you can tell by comparing our prices with those asked by others.

THE BINDING GUARANTEE. Every Remington gun is covered by a binding guarantee. It is made on the very latest principles, from the best material that can be secured, by skilled mechanics, and if any piece or part gives out by reason of defect in material or workmanship it will be replaced free of charge. Every Remington gun that goes out of our place is put to a careful test, both as to target, penetration and strength at every point, and each gun bears a tag showing the target that each gun made in its test before shipping.

OUR REMINGTON GUNS are all the very latest model. There is not an old style or old model gun in our stock; all made on the very latest lines. They embody every improvement, are up to date, and in comparing our prices with others please bear in mind that we not only save you the difference in price, but we give you the very latest up to date, targeted, tested and guaranteed stock.

From the above illustration engraved from a photograph, you can form some idea of the appearance of this our special $20.00 barlock double barrel Remington shotgun. This special $20.00 gun is built on the very latest lines for this season, up to date in every piece and part.

DESCRIPTION—The barrels are made by the Remington Arms Company from blued barrel steel, elegantly finished, tested to the highest test and guaranteed in every respect. **STOCK**—The stock is a fine walnut stock, made of thoroughly seasoned selected black walnut, correctly shaped, nicely finished, full pistol grip, handsomely decorated, made with fancy butt plate. **LOCKS**—This gun is fitted with Remington Arms Company decarbonized steel bar action locks, made from the very best material that money can buy, thoroughly tested, accurately fitted and adjusted. **ACTION**—Our $20.00 Remington has the strongest, most simple and nearest perfect action of any similar gun on the market, built with a deep matted extension rib, with two heavy automatic locking bolts; extra heavy, well finished breech; low circular hammers; latest style top snap break; all parts are made interchangeable; the fore end is automatic, self acting; beautifully checkered finish. The gun is built extra strong at every part, made and bored for nitro or black powder.

FOR LONG RANGE SHOOTING, for ducks, geese and other large game, we recommend the 10-gauge Remington as one of the very best long range shooting guns made, and if you order our $20.00 Remington gun and you do not find it as a shooter, the equal of any gun made, regardless of price, you are at liberty to return it to us at our expense and we will refund your money.

OUR $20.00 REMINGTON GUNS come in 12-gauge; weigh 7½ to 8 pounds; length of barrel 30 or 32 inches, as desired, 10-gauge guns come in 32-inch barrels and weigh 8¾ to 9¾ pounds.

OUR $20.00 REMINGTON GUNS are furnished with choke bored barrels, bored on the best principles with a view to securing the most perfect long range target possible.

No. 6R63 Our No. 1 grade furnished with fine decarbonized steel barrels, as described and illustrated above, 10 or 12-gauge........ **$20.00**

No. 6R65 Our No. 2 grade, same as No. 6R63, but with fine laminated steel barrels. 12-gauge, 30 or 32-inch barrels, 7½ to 8 pounds; or 10-gauge, 32-inch barrels, 8¾ to 9¾ pounds. Our special price........ **23.00**

No. 6R67 Our No. 3 grade, same as No. 6R63, but with fine two-blade Damascus barrels. 12-gauge, 30 or 32 inch barrels, 7½ to 8 pounds; or 10-gauge, 32-inch barrels, 8¾ to 9¾ pounds. Our special price........ **25.00**

REMINGTON DOUBLE BARREL HAMMERLESS SHOTGUNS.

AT $25.00, $35.00, $40.00, $45.00 AND $50.00.

AT $25.00, $35.00 AND $45.00 we offer the highest grade Damascus Steel Barreled Remington Hammerless Shotguns as illustrated and described.

AT $40.00 AND $50.00 we offer the Remington high grade Automatic Self Ejector Remington Hammerless Shotguns as illustrated and described.

OUR SPECIAL PRICES OF $25.00 TO $50.00 are the lowest prices ever quoted for these high grade guns, and we honestly believe the Remington double barrel hammerless shotgun in any grade is, in shooting qualities and in point of construction, general workmanship, finish and durability, in fact, in every essential point, the equal of any gun made, regardless of price.

OUR SPECIAL $25.00, $35.00, $40.00, $45.00 and $50.00 PRICES are prices based on the actual cost under large season contract, with but our one small percentage of profit added, prices that guarantee to you a saving of all the profit your dealer would make and more.

THE REMINGTON HAMMERLESS GUNS are strong and durable. The mechanism is very simple, hence it cannot get out of order. In opening the gun, the fore end engages with the cocking levers, which raises the hammers to full cock, when the sears drop into position. The gun can be taken apart or put together with one or both hammers cocked or uncocked. This obviates trouble or the use of special tools in assembling, and does away with the snapping of hammers, or putting the gun away cocked, as required in some actions. The hammers can be let down without snapping, by breaking down the gun, pushing forward the safety slide and closing the action as the triggers are pulled. The cocking mechanism is so arranged that before the gun can be opened sufficiently to admit of a shell being inserted in the chamber

BOTH HAMMERS ARE COCKED AND TRIGGERS ARE LOCKED AUTOMATICALLY.......

From the above illustration, engraved from a photograph, you can form a very good idea of the appearance of the highest of high grade Remington Double Barrel, Hammerless, Self Acting, Automatic Shell Ejecting Shotguns which we quote at $40.00 and $50.00, and without the automatic ejector, at $25.00, $35.00 and $45.00.

OUR BINDING GUARANTEE Every Remington gun is sent out under our binding guarantee, and if any piece or part gives out by reason of defect in material or workmanship, we will repair or replace it FREE OF CHARGE.

THE AUTOMATIC EJECTOR is composed of hammer, sear, center sear, main and sear springs, and is cocked by the action of the extractor when closing the gun. It is operated when the gun is fired by the main spring moving forward and lifting the ejector sear out of the ejector hammer notch. This allows the ejector hammer to fall on the center sear where it remains until the gun is nearly opened, when the joint check engages with the center sear and raises it out of the ejector hammer notch. Then the ejector hammer, moving forward, strikes the ejector stem, causing the fired shell to be expelled from the gun.

QUALITY OF MATERIAL. The Remington Hammerless Guns are made from the best material money can buy. The stock, the barrels, the locks, the working parts, the trimmings and the finishings are from the very best material that can be procured, and only the most skilled mechanics are employed. The fittings are perfection, they are done with all the accuracy of the finest watch mechanism. The action is simple, accurate, strong and almost everlasting.

SHOOTING QUALITIES. The Remington Hammerless Shotgun is in shooting qualities, without doubt, the equal of any gun made, regardless of price. There is no gun made that will give a better target, greater penetration, that will kill game at longer range than will the Remington shotguns. They are made by a concern who have had the experience of years; they embody every high point of perfection in every high grade gun, with the defects of none.

AT $25.00 TO $50.00 according to grade, these guns all come with fine steel and Damascus barrels as illustrated, all are choke bored to secure the very best possible target and penetration, all have fine imported English walnut stocks, full pistol grip, beautifully finished, polished, and checkered; fancy rubber butt plate, fancy checkered fore end, very finest case hardened frame and mountings, latest patent automatic safety, genuine Purdy fore end snap; fore end is beautifully finished and handsomely decorated; extension rib with nitro bite, flat matted rib, and the automatic ejectors on the $40.00 and $50.00 grades are the equal of any ejectors made.

No. 6R66 K grade has fine Decarbonized steel barrels, plain English walnut stock, plain finish without automatic ejector, 12-gauge, 30 or 32-inch barrels, 7½ to 8 pounds. Our special price.... **$25.00**

No. 6R68 A grade, two stripe Damascus barrels, plain finish, English walnut stock, without ejector, 12-gauge, 30 or 32-inch barrels, 7½ to 8 pounds. Our special price........ **35.00**

No. 6R70 AE grade, two stripe Damascus steel barrels, fine line engraving, with automatic ejector, 12-gauge, 30-inch barrels, 7½ to 8 pounds. Our special price........ **40.00**

No. 6R72 B grade, extra quality fine three stripe Damascus barrels, fine line engraving, extra fine imported English walnut stock, without ejector, 12-gauge, 30-inch barrels, 7½ to 8 pounds. Our special price........ **$45.00**

No. 6R74 BE grade, with extra quality three stripe Damascus barrels, fine line engraving, extra fine imported English walnut stock, with automatic ejector, 12-gauge, 30-inch barrels, 7½ to 8 pounds. Our special price........ **50.00**

ON GUNS MADE TO SPECIAL ORDER WE REQUIRE FULL AMOUNT OF CASH WITH THE ORDER, AS ON ALL OTHER MERCHANDISE, AND IF MADE ACCORDING TO YOUR ORDER THEY CANNOT BE RETURNED UNDER ANY CIRCUMSTANCES. WE DO NOT CHARGE FOR BOXING GUNS.

ITHACA NEW MODEL HAMMER AND HAMMERLESS SHOTGUNS

At $21.00, $25.00, $26.50, $33.00, $36.50 and $37.50, we offer the new improved, latest and highest grade ITHACA HAMMER AND HAMMERLESS SHOTGUNS

The New Improved Ithaca Hammer Gun in fine English stub twist barrel, for $21.00; in fine damascus steel barrels, $25.00
The Ithaca Hammerless Gun at $26.50, $33.00 and $37.50, according to grade.
The New Improved High Grade Ithaca Automatic Ejector Hammerless Gun at $36.50.

OUR SPECIAL INSIDE $21.00 TO $37.50 PRICES ON ITHACA GUNS are the lowest prices ever named. They are prices based on the actual cost under season contract direct from the factory, with but our one small percentage of profit added, prices as low if not lower than your dealer could buy in quantities.

OUR BINDING GUARANTEE. Every Ithaca gun is covered by a binding guarantee, by the terms and conditions of which if any piece or part gives out by reason of defect in material or workmanship we will replace or repair it free of charge. The Ithaca guns are manufactured by the Ithaca Gun Company, of Ithaca, New York. They are made on the latest and most improved mechanical lines. Only the best of material is used, only skilled mechanics are employed. They build a strictly high grade gun, extra strong in every piece and part, perfect in action, accurately gauged and adjusted, price for price the equal of any gun made.

SHOOTING QUALITIES. The Ithaca gun is recognized as one of the strongest shooters in the market. For target and penetration it is really a marvel. The Ithaca heavy 10-gauge gun for extra long range shooting for big game, such as geese, turkeys, etc., is one of the most favorite guns among professional sportsmen.

OUR FREE TRIAL OFFER. So confident are we of our ability to furnish you with an Ithaca gun which will not only be lower in price but will be a better shooter than you would be likely to get elsewhere, that we are willing to send you any Ithaca gun on our regular terms, with the understanding that if at any time during the ten days' thorough trial, test and comparison you have any reason to be dissatisfied with your purchase, you can return the gun to us at our expense and we will cheerfully return the money you have sent us. All we ask is that you keep the gun in perfect condition.

UNDER OUR CONTRACT every Ithaca gun that comes into our house must be tested at the factory as to target, penetration, fit, finish, quality of material, action, etc., and the gun must not only be perfect in every part but must produce a certain target and a certain penetration, and attached to each gun must be the manufacturer's tag which shows the result of such test, and this tag remains attached to the gun until it reaches you. In addition, every gun is tested by an inspector in our gun department and found accurate in sight, range, target, drop, penetration, equalization, finish and action, and the result is that if you get an Ithaca gun from us you get one that is perfect in every respect, you get one from which every point of the slightest imperfection has been culled out and thrown back.

WE ARE HEADQUARTERS FOR ITHACA GUNS.

We are the recognized general selling agents to the consumer. We name the lowest price the factory ever named, give you the benefit of all the profit the wholesaler and retailer would make in our special $21.00 to $37.50 prices.

OUR NEW IMPROVED UP TO DATE ITHACA HAMMER GUN FOR $21.00.

FOR $21.00 We offer this the very latest model ITHACA HAMMER GUN, a gun with all the up-to-date improvements, with all the latest changes and additions effected, brought right up to date.

From the above illustration engraved from a photograph, you can form a very good idea of the appearance of this the new improved Ithaca Double Barrel Breech Loading Hammer Gun which we quote at $21.00.

This extra strong, compact, adjusted, perfect hanging, strong shooting arm is, as before stated, made of the best of materials. It has the simplest and best locking device known, it has the latest low circular hammers, latest fancy finished top lever break, swinging over the hammers when cocked, it is made self-compensating, self-acting and automatic in adjustment, made to take up wear at every point, so adjusted as never to get loose or shaky. It has the latest steel Edwards' extended matted rib; it has a finely finished walnut stock, with full pistol grip, handsomely checkered. It has the best grade case hardened lock plates, with fine blue mountings. The guns come all choke bored to give the longest possible range, the most uniform close pattern and the greatest possible penetration. All guns are made with fancy rubber butt plate, they have a fancy checkered finished fore end. Bored for nitro or black powder.

No. 6R75 Fine English stub twist barrels, 12-gauge, 30 or 32-inch barrels; weight, 7½ to 8¼ pounds. Our special price.......... **$21.00**

No. 6R75½ Fine English stub twist barrels, 10-gauge, 32-inch barrels; weight, 9 to 9¾ pounds. Our special price.......... **21.00**

No. 6R77 Fine Damascus barrels, 12-gauge, 30 or 32-inch barrels; weight, 7½ to 8¼ pounds. Our special price.......... **$25.00**

No. 6R77½ Fine Damascus barrels, 10-gauge, 32-inch barrels; weight, 9 to 9¾ pounds. Our special price.......... **25.00**

WHEN ORDERING GIVE LENGTH, GAUGE AND WEIGHT YOU PREFER. 16-gauge, 28 or 30-inch barrels, made to special order (cash with order), same price as 10 or 12-gauge.

$26.50 ..TO.. $37.50 THE NEW IMPROVED ITHACA HAMMERLESS SHOTGUNS... FOR 1902.

The new model 1902 and at $26.50; it is wonderful gun value. NO BETTER SHOOTING GUN ever made by anyone at any price. Every gun covered by binding guarantee. Greatly improved. The best hammerless gun ever turned out for the money.

No. 6R80

We are able to offer the Ithaca Hammerless Gun at $26.50, a gun which has retailed at $40.00 and upwards and wholesaled at $30.00 to $35.00. The prices we name are based on factory cost, the actual cost of material and labor with our one small profit added; with all the unnecessary expenses for advertising, salesmen, bad debts, etc., omitted. We give you full gun value for your money.

THE ACCOMPANYING ILLUSTRATION is engraved from a photograph and will give you some idea of the general appearance of the **Ithaca Hammerless Gun.** This gun is too well known to require comment from us. It is bored for nitro and black powders. Barrels can be put on and taken off same as hammer gun, whether gun is cocked or not. Locks are rebounding, automatic safety, can be changed to independent by a touch of the thumb for rapid firing. All have pistol grip, all have extension rib, all choke bored, all finely finished and greatly improved for this season. All have matted ribs. The stub twist barrels used on these guns are better than laminated or cheap Damascus barrels. 30-inch barrel, 12-gauge, weighs 7½ to 8 pounds; 32-inch weighs 7¾ to 8¼ pounds.

No. 6R76 Our 1 P. grade, **fine English stub twist barrels,** American walnut stock, pistol grip checkered, line engraving, 12-gauge, 30 or 32-inch barrels. Price.......... **$26.50**

No. 6R78 Our 1½ grade, **fine Damascus steel barrels,** English walnut stock, pistol grip checkered, 12-gauge, 30 or 32-inch barrels. Our price.......... **$33.00**

No. 6R78½ Our 1½ grade; 10-gauge, 30 or 32-inch barrels; weight 8½ to 9 pounds. Price.......... **33.00**

No. 6R80 Our 2 grade, **fine Damascus barrels,** English walnut stock, pistol grip checkered, engraved, 12-gauge, 30 or 32-inch barrels; weight, 7½ to 8¼ pounds. Price.......... **$37.50**

10 or 16-gauge, same price as 12-gauge. Made to special order.

THE NEW ITHACA EJECTOR HAMMERLESS GUN,

LATEST EJECTOR. $36.50

No. 6R82

THIS ILLUSTRATION IS ENGRAVED FROM A PHOTOGRAPH OF THE NEW ITHACA EJECTOR HAMMERLESS GUN,

and will give you an idea of the appearance of this gun. The Ithaca Gun is so well known that it is unnecessary for us to make a full description of every detail. **The New Ejector** in addition to having all of the advantages of the Ithaca Hammerless Gun, has the **new automatic ejector,** made expressly for this gun, and **is more simple than any other ejector on the market.** That it works direct on the extractor and is all contained in the lug makes it less complicated, and therefore less likely to get out of order. It is made of tool steel and is not only more durable, but is stronger and more positive than the other ejectors, which are made more complicated.

No. 6R82 Our 1 P. E. grade, fine English stub twist barrels, with checkered walnut pistol grip stock, 12-gauge, 30-inch barrels; weight, 7½ to 8 pounds. Our special price.......... **$36.50**

WE CHARGE YOU NOTHING FOR BOXING GUNS FOR SHIPPING.

ON ANY GOODS NOT DESCRIBED OR LISTED IN THIS CATALOGUE AND MADE TO ORDER, WE MUST ASK CASH IN FULL WITH ORDER, AS ON ALL OTHER MERCHANDISE, AND IF MADE AS ORDERED, THEY CANNOT BE RETURNED UNDER ANY CIRCUMSTANCES.

NEW IMPROVED BAKER BREECH LOADING SHOTGUNS

AT $22.50, $24.00, $32.00, $37.50 AND $60.00, WE OFFER THE CELEBRATED BAKER DOUBLE BARREL BREECH LOADING SHOTGUNS, THE VERY LATEST UP TO DATE MODELS, THEIR NEW IMPROVED GUNS, UNDER OUR BINDING GUARANTEE.

WE ARE HEADQUARTERS for the new improved Baker Hammer and Hammerless Shotguns. We are general selling agents to the consumer. Under our arrangements with the manufacturer we are able to quote you prices based on the cost of material and labor, with but our one small percentage of profit added, a price as low as any dealer can buy in quantities, **a price that will mean a saving to you of from $5.00 to $15.00 on a gun.**

THE NEW IMPROVED HAMMER AND HAMMERLESS Baker Breech Loading Shotguns are made for us under contract by the Baker Gun and Forging Company of Batavia, New York. They are made from strictly high grade material on the most improved lines of gun making. They embody the good points of all strictly high grade American guns. They are among the most durable, strongest shooting and best finished guns on the market.

ORDER A BAKER GUN FROM US and we will send it to you with the understanding and agreement that if it is not in every way perfectly satisfactory, if you are not convinced that you are saving from 20 to 30 per cent in price, you can return the gun to us at our expense of express charges both ways and we will return your money. **All we ask is that you keep the gun in perfect condition.**

WE CHALLENGE COMPETITION IN OUR GUN DEPARTMENT. Our prices by comparison will be found below those of any other dealer. We handle only strictly high grade goods, such as we can afford to guarantee, and if you want to save money on your gun purchase you cannot do better than to make your selection from these pages.

DON'T BUY A GUN OF ANY KIND UNTIL YOU HAVE GOTTEN OUR PRICE. If you are thinking of buying a breech loading shotgun, before patronizing your dealer at home or before sending to any other house, write to us. We are prepared to give such values in high grade shotguns as can be had from no other house. We not only give you the benefit of a lower price than you can get elsewhere, but we give a uniformly higher grade of goods, for every American gun in our stock is given a thorough test as to penetration and target, a careful test and inspection as to accuracy, fit and finish, and every gun must come up to the highest mark of perfection before it leaves our house.

OUR NEW IMPROVED UP TO DATE $22.50 BAKER BREECH LOADING SHOTGUNS ....

FOR $22.50 we offer this high grade double barrel breech loading hammer shotgun as the best hammer breech loader ever turned out by **THE BAKER GUN AND FORGING COMPANY.**

OUR CONTRACT CALLS FOR THE VERY BEST WORK the makers can possibly furnish, best in every piece and part and every gun must be covered by a **WRITTEN BINDING GUARANTEE.**

They claim for this gun even pattern, powerful shooting, and in durability, simplicity and long range shooting, the equal of any gun made, regardless of price.

The above illustration, engraved from a photograph, will give you an idea of the appearance of this, our new improved, up to date, high grade Baker Hammer Gun, which we quote at $22.50.

THIS GUN IS MADE WITH ENGLISH STEEL TWIST BARRELS, very latest bar lock, cross bite extension rib, fancy checkered pistol grip, fancy English walnut stock, fancy rubber butt plate, low circular hammers, solid strikers, rebounding locks, latest top snap break, interchangeable parts throughout, choke bored to make the very best possible target at longest possible range, unless otherwise ordered. This is a very handsome, plain, richly finished, well balanced gun, made with compensating fore end, cannot get loose and shaky in the hinge joint; in fact, just the gun for business, and at a moderate price. Bored for NITRO or BLACK POWDER.

No. 6R83 12-gauge, 30 or 32-inch barrels, 7½ to 8¾ pounds. Our price, **$22.50** | No. 6R85 10-gauge, 32-inch barrels, 8½ to 9¾ pounds. Our price... **$22.50**

THE IMPROVED BAKER HAMMERLESS SHOTGUNS

Manufactured by the **BAKER GUN AND FORGING CO.,** Batavia, New York.

THE BATAVIA LEADER, $24.00.
Bored for Nitro Powder.

MADE IN 12-GAUGE ONLY.

The above illustration will give you an idea of the appearance of our high grade Baker gun. This gun was one of our best sellers the past season, and has given excellent satisfaction.

THIS GUN IS SO WELL KNOWN that it is needless to go into a lengthy description of it. The BAKER GUNS have always had a good reputation for hard shooting qualities, simple mechanism and durability, and we do not hesitate to offer these guns as good values, and guns which will give entire satisfaction. **All Baker Guns are choke bored for close, hard shooting.**

No. 6R86 Batavia Leader, twist barrel, top snap, automatic safety lock, pistol grip checkered, compensating checkered fore end, cross bite matted extension rib, 12-gauge, 30-inch, 7½ to 8 pounds. Our special price....... **$24.00**

No. 6R88 Model B grade is furnished with fine stub twist barrels. The rib is matted, the frame, guard, lock plates and lever are handsomely engraved. The stocks are of imported walnut, fully checkered in neat designs. This gun is carefully fitted and adjusted throughout, making a strong and durable weapon capable of withstanding hard work. 12-gauge, 30-inch, 7½ to 8 pounds. Factory price, $40.00. Our special price....... **$32.00**

No. 6R90 Model A grade is furnished with a fine quality four-blade Damascus barrel. The rib is matted, the frame, guard, lock plates and lever are elaborately engraved. The stocks are of selected Circassian walnut. The checkering is laid out in handsome patterns and is of a high class workmanship. The A grade gun is a beautiful and serviceable arm, 12-gauge, 30-inch barrels, 7½ to 8 pounds. Factory price, $50.00. Our special price....... **$37.50**

No. 6R92 Paragon Grade. Fine Damascus barrels, beautifully engraved, fine English walnut stock, matted rib, handsomely checkered stock and fore end made to special order, and equal to any $100.00 gun made. 12-gauge, 30 or 32-inch barrels, 7¼ to 8 pounds. Factory price, $80.00. Our special cash with order price....... **$60.00**

PARKER HAMMERLESS SHOTGUNS.

MADE BY PARKER BROTHERS, MERIDEN, CONN.

THE PARKER GUNS are too well known and too famous to require an elaborate or exhaustive description. They are considered the standard at the trap and in the field and we cannot recommend them too highly. **OUR TERMS ON PARKER GUNS ARE THE SAME AS ON ALL OTHER GUNS. ALL ARE BORED FOR NITRO OR BLACK POWDER.**

PARKER HAMMER GUNS are not carried in stock and must be made to special order, and if made as ordered they cannot be returned under any circumstances. It requires from four to eight weeks to execute an order for Parker Hammer Guns.

PRICES ON PARKER HAMMERLESS GUNS.

No. 6R110 DH grade has very fine Damascus barrels, very fine imported walnut stock, fine checkering and engraving, 12-gauge only. 30-inch barrels, 7½ to 8 pounds. Our special price....... **$72.75**
No. 6R114 GH grade, fine Damascus barrels, fine imported stock, nicely engraved, 12-gauge only, 30-inch barrels, 7½ to 8 lbs. Special price, **58.20**
No. 6R116 PH grade, fine English twist barrels, fine American stock, line engraving, 12-gauge only, 30-inch barrels, 7½ to 8 lbs. Special price **48.75**
No. 6R118 VH grade, Vulcan steel barrels, fine American stock, plain frame, 12-gauge only, 30 or 32-inch barrels, 7½ to 8 lbs. Special price **36.75**

WHY GUN BARRELS BURST, AND DONT'S TO SHOOTERS WHO USE NITRO POWDER

REGULAR LOADS OF STANDARD NITRO POWDERS do not produce a greater strain than similar loads of good black powder, and while they will give a greater force than cheap black powders, they have less bursting strain than the fine grain high grades of black powder. By observing the following rules you will have no trouble or accidents.

Don't vary from the directions and loads, on the powder can, when loading Nitro Powder. Don't accidentally put two loads in the same shell. **Don't** use rags or tow for wadding. **Don't** put more than one cardboard wad over the powder, but fill up with Black Edge or other felt wads. Use one thin card wad over the shot. **Don't** crimp the shell more than a quarter of an inch. **If** your shell is not full add soft wads over the powder. **Don't** ram the powder hard. Always look through the barrels before loading to see that there is nothing in them. **Don't** ram the wad edgeways into the powder. **Don't** load nitro shotgun powder in rifle cartridges. **Don't** put the muzzle in water especially in very cold weather when a coating of ice may form inside the barrel. **Don't** shoot buckshot in a choke bored gun. **Don't** rest the muzzle in snow, ground or mud. **Don't** carry your shells in the same pocket with small coins. **Don't** lay gun in a wagon uncovered.

FOLLOW THESE INSTRUCTIONS and you will never have a burst gun barrel. When loading shells try to get into the habit of putting a wad over the shell after you put in the powder. This will remind you which shell already has powder and you will not accidentally get two charges in the same shell.

A loose wad over the shot has been known to bulge a barrel. All guns as a rule, are tested by the makers. Gun barrels usually burst at the **breech** or chamber when caused by an overload of nitro powder, and at or near the **muzzle** when caused by some obstruction inside the barrel. We have never heard of a gun barrel bursting from black powder unless there was some obstruction inside the barrel, such as mud, snow, sand, a wad, leaves, a cleaning rag or the muzzle being held in water. We advise every shooter to always look through the barrels before loading. If you burst a gun barrel don't blame the maker of the gun, but stop and trace the cause and you will probably find you can trace it to one of the foregoing rules. Leading, inside of the barrels, is sometimes caused by using chilled shot with black powder or a poor grade of black powder and soft or chilled shot. To shooters who have guns bored for black powder and wish to use nitro powder in them, we advise using a wad one size larger than they use for black powder.

WE MAKE NO CHARGE FOR BOXING GUNS FOR SHIPMENT, SOME HOUSES DO.

THE NEW DAVIS HAMMER AND HAMMERLESS GUNS.

THE DAVIS HAMMERLESS GUN FOR . . . $19.50

No. 6R130

Best quality twist barrels, choke bored, extension matted rib, double bolt, one on the lug of barrel and nitro cross bolt through extended rib, patent fore end. **Full pistol grip stock,** stock and fore end checkered. All parts nicely fitted. Cocks by the opening of barrels, and by the action of closing them the sears and triggers are both blocked by a positive motion, **thus avoiding all danger from jarring off or prematurely pulling off,** by trigger or otherwise, and is **absolutely safe.** Safety can be used as automatic or independent, a very desirable feature for rapid firing. Gun can be put together or taken apart with hammers in any position, **and without any extra operation.** Hammers may also be let down without snapping, which is always preferable. **Fine twist barrels,** American walnut stock.

No. 6R130 12-gauge, 30 and 32-inch barrels, 7½ to 8 pounds.
Our price.......... **$19.50**

Weight, packed for shipment, about 15 pounds.

SEE OUR PRICES FOR LOADED SHELLS.

$15.75 BUYS THE DAVIS DOUBLE BARREL BREECH LOADING SHOTGUN.

Made by N. R. DAVIS & SON, Assonnet, Mass.

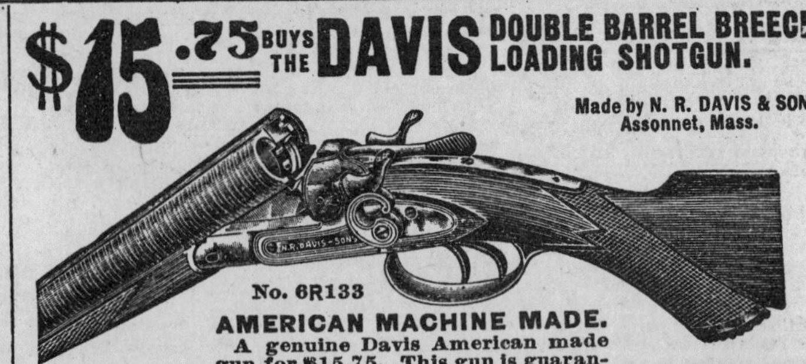

No. 6R133

AMERICAN MACHINE MADE.

A genuine Davis American made gun for $15.75. **This gun is guaranteed by the manufacturer to be equal in material and workmanship to any $25.00 gun on the market.** The illustration is engraved from a photograph and will give you some idea of the appearance of this gun. **Bar rebounding locks,** strongest and most simple lock made, double bolt, one on the lug and a cross bolt on the rib. **The barrels are genuine twist, double thickness** over shell chamber, fine selected imported walnut stock, fancy checkered full pistol grip, **fancy rubber butt plate,** latest style low circular hammers, best and latest top snap break, strong, long extension rib, large firing pins, case hardened mountings, choke bored.

No. 6R133 12-gauge, 30 or 32-inch barrels, 7¼ to 8 pounds. State length wanted. Our special price.......... **$15.75**

We have a few of these in 10-gauge, with 30-inch barrels, 8¾ to 9½ pounds, same price as 12-gauge. **Weight, packed for shipment, 14 pounds.**

HOW OUR BELGIUM GUNS ARE TESTED BY THE BELGIAN GOVERNMENT.

All our Belgian guns are tested by the government of Belgium in the following manner: After the barrels are first made and before they are brazed together, reamed or chambered, they are sent to the government proof house where a plug is screwed into the breech of the barrel and it is loaded with 11 drams of good quality black powder and a bullet weighing 1 ounce. **After this test they** are brazed together and tested again with 7 drams of good black powder and a bullet weighing 1 ounce. After this second test is made the frame, or breech, is fitted to the barrels and they are tested for the third time with 6⅛ drams of powder and 1⅛ ounces of shot. You will see that the test is very severe and each and every Belgium gun which we sell, from the cheapest to the best, is put through this same test, so if you buy a Belgium gun of us you are assured that you are getting a gun which has been thoroughly tested for Sears, Roebuck & Co. with more powder and more shot than you can possibly put into a shell. In order to put such a heavy charge into the barrels the government must load from the muzzle and any gun you buy from us is safe, as you will see by the foregoing rigid tests.

OUR LINE OF IMPORTED DOUBLE BARREL SHOTGUNS.

OUR LINE OF IMPORTED GUNS is very extensive and embraces the products of some of the best European makers. We recognize no competition in this line, and a comparison of our prices with those of other houses will convince you that we have none. We aim to handle only thoroughly first class goods, guns that will stand service and give the best satisfaction, and every gun we offer is warranted in every respect.

In our line of imported guns we would call your attention to our **Double Barrel Breech Loader,** our **T. Barker,** our **Special Greener Action Guns,** and our high grade machine guns. We are in a **position to make you prices on this class of goods at least 25 per cent below any competition, and if you will** favor us with your order we know you will be so well pleased that you will not only give us your future orders, but recommend our house to your friends.

SEE OUR PRICES FOR LOADED SHELLS.

IN ORDERING SHOTGUNS you will avoid delay and annoyance both for yourself and for us by ordering by catalogue number, and state name of gun. Where a choice is given, always **STATE GAUGE, LENGTH OF BARRELS, WEIGHT** desired, and **GIVE ALL PARTICULARS** with care. You will then **be sure to get what you want, and exactly as you want it, for you leave nothing for us to chance or guess.**

$7.45

AN EXTENSION RIB GUN . . . . 10, 12 and 16-Gauge.

No. 6R237

OUR $7.45 BACK ACTION GUN.

We offer you a high grade, imported double barrel shotgun at $7.45 which cannot be duplicated elsewhere for less than $10.00 to $12.00. We import these guns direct. Every gun is a direct blow at monopoly. The result is you buy a gun for less than one-half the retail price, 20 to 40 per cent cheaper than other houses advertise, and far below the price you would pay for a poorer gun from other houses. **We guarantee every gun to have barrels of best Raleigh steel.**

The above illustration, engraved from a photograph, will give you an idea of the appearance of this gun. Weight, packed for shipment, 14 pounds.

DESCRIPTION—Double barrel breech loader, top lever snap action rebounding back action locks, **walnut stock,** case hardened lock plates and mountings, **shell extractor, twist finish barrels** and fancy butt plate, nicely checkered stock and fore end, Raleigh steel barrels.

No. 6R237 10-gauge, 32-inch barrels, 8½ to 9¼ pounds. State weight wanted. Our special price..........
No. 6R237¼ 12-gauge, 30 or 32-inch barrels, 7½ to 8 pounds. State length wanted. Our special price..........
No. 6R237½ 16-gauge, 28 or 30-inch barrels, 6½ to 7 pounds. State length wanted. Our special price.......... **$7.45**

OUR HIGHLY ENGRAVED DIANA STYLE BREECH SHOTGUN

30 OR 32-INCH, $8.95

38-INCH, $11.10

38-INCH BARRELS - -	$11.10
32-INCH BARRELS - - -	8.95
30-INCH BARRELS - -	8.95

ENGRAVED LOCKS, MATTED RIB, TOP SNAP, 12-GAUGE ONLY, PISTOL GRIP, PATENT FORE END.

CASE HARDENED FRAME, 30, 32 OR 38-INCH BARRELS.

WE CHARGE YOU NOTHING FOR BOXING AND PACKING GUNS FOR SHIPMENT.

No. 6R238

This cut, engraved from a photograph, will give you some idea of the gun. All our Belgium guns are thoroughly tested for safety and we have no hesitation in saying that they are superior to any guns in the market. Don't buy guns known as seconds when you can buy first quality guns of us. This gun has top snap, two blade Damascus finished Raleigh steel barrels, Diana style breech, rebounding back action locks, pistol grip stock, matted extension rib, checkered pistol grip and patent fore end, latest style nitro firing pins, circular hammers, fancy butt plate, highly engraved locks; in fact, a very superior gun.

No. 6R238 12-gauge, 30 or 32-inch barrels, 7½ to 8 pounds. Mention length of barrel which you desire. Our special price.......... **$8.95**
No. 6R239 12-gauge, 38-inch barrels, 8 to 8¾ pounds. Our special price.......... **11.10**
Mention length of barrel which you prefer. Weight, packed for shipment, about 14 pounds.

OUR CELEBRATED SAM HOLT GUNS FOR $9.40.

FOR $9.40 WE OFFER YOU THE **GENUINE BAR LOCK DOUBLE BARREL BREECH LOADER...**

CASE HARDENED MOUNTINGS.

EXTENSION RIB. BAR LOCKS.

10 and 12-Gauge Only.

THIS IS A LOWER PRICE than most houses in this country ask for a back action lock double barrel breech loader. All these guns have been put through the Belgian government rigid test, and for strength, durability and finish they are superior to any bar lock guns ever offered by any other house at

20 to 40 per cent more money

$9.40

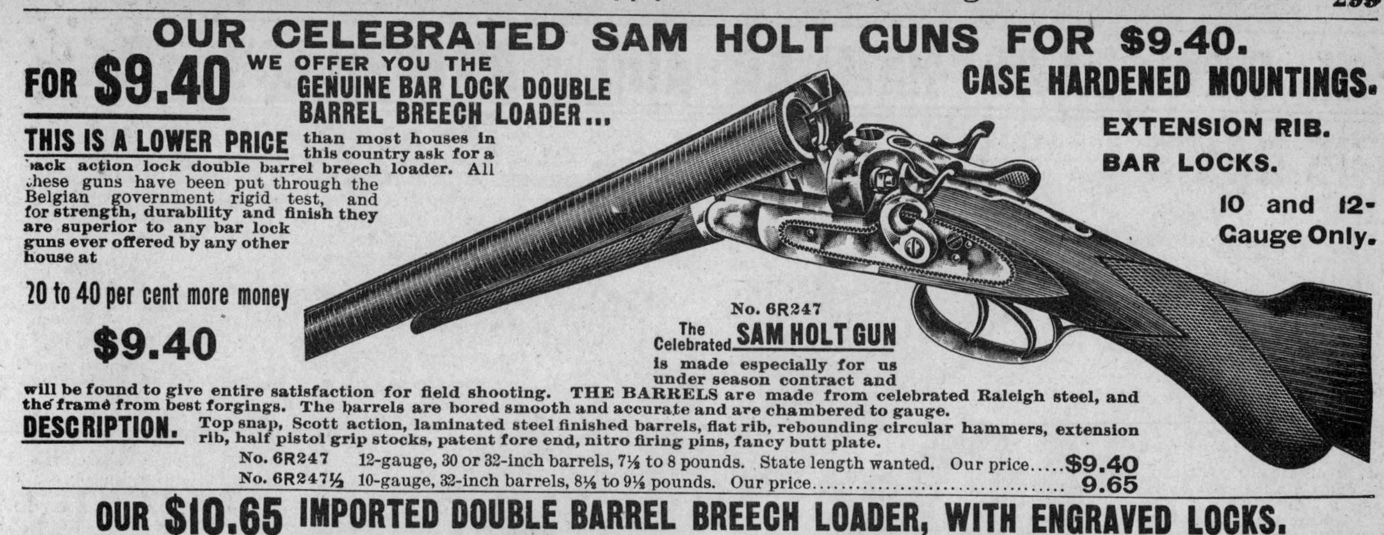

No. 6R247

The Celebrated **SAM HOLT GUN** is made especially for us under season contract and will be found to give entire satisfaction for field shooting. THE BARRELS are made from celebrated Raleigh steel, and the frame from best forgings. The barrels are bored smooth and accurate and are chambered to gauge.

DESCRIPTION. Top snap, Scott action, laminated steel finished barrels, flat rib, rebounding circular hammers, extension rib, half pistol grip stocks, patent fore end, nitro firing pins, fancy butt plate.

No. 6R247 12-gauge, 30 or 32-inch barrels, 7½ to 8 pounds. State length wanted. Our price.....**$9.40**

No. 6R247½ 10-gauge, 32-inch barrels, 8¾ to 9¼ pounds. Our price.................................... **9.65**

OUR $10.65 IMPORTED DOUBLE BARREL BREECH LOADER, WITH ENGRAVED LOCKS.

MADE IN 12-GAUGE ONLY.

....CASE HARDENED MOUNTINGS....

EXTENSION RIB. ENGRAVED LOCKS.

$10.65

FOR $10.65 we offer you the genuine **BAR LOCK DOUBLE BARREL BREECH LOADER**

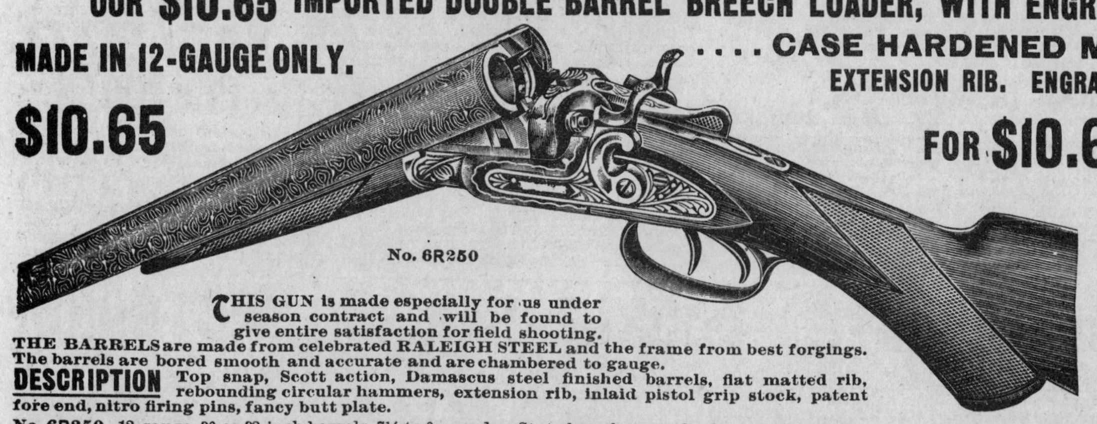

No. 6R250

THIS IS A LOWER PRICE than most houses in this country ask for a back action lock double barrel breech loader. All these guns have been put through the Belgian government rigid test, and for strength, durability and finish they are superior to any bar lock guns ever offered by any other house and present a handsome appearance.

THIS GUN is made especially for us under season contract and will be found to give entire satisfaction for field shooting.

THE BARRELS are made from celebrated RALEIGH STEEL and the frame from best forgings. The barrels are bored smooth and accurate and are chambered to gauge.

DESCRIPTION Top snap, Scott action, Damascus steel finished barrels, flat matted rib, rebounding circular hammers, extension rib, inlaid pistol grip stock, patent fore end, nitro firing pins, fancy butt plate.

No. 6R250 12-gauge, 30 or 32-inch barrels, 7½ to 8 pounds. State length wanted. Our special price........................**$10.65**

OUR FIVE GREAT LEADERS IN STRICTLY HIGH GRADE GUARANTEED AMERICAN GUNS, NEW FOR THIS YEAR.

WE OFFER YOU THESE NEW HIGH GRADE guaranteed American guns at prices $10.22, $10.95, $12.67, $13.42, and $15.87 as the equal of any gun you can buy anywhere at double the money.

YOU CANNOT AFFORD to buy a cheap gun when you can get a strictly high grade, genuine American machine made, double barrel, breech loading gun, in durability, accuracy and penetration the equal of any Belgian gun made, regardless of price, and as low as $10.22.

THESE SPECIAL GUARANTEED AMERICAN GUNS are worth a dozen cheap guns. Different from the cheap gun, which others would ask you from $15.00 to $20.00 for, our five guaranteed American guns are bored for white powder, while it is exceedingly dangerous to use white powder in a cheap gun; different from the cheap gun that scatters, has poor penetration and is poorly bored. The American guns are choke bored by the very best known system, they shoot close, they have a penetration and a target equal to any gun made, regardless of price.

THE VAST DEMAND WE HAVE HAD FOR GUNS at prices ranging from $10.22 to $15.87, and which we have heretofore been compelled to supply with guns that are not equal to American guns, has induced us to look for a manufacturer who would build a line of strictly high grade, thoroughly well made, guaranteed guns, at prices that would admit of our competing in price with the Belgian guns. We found a manufacturer who was willing to accept a contract with us on this class of goods. We placed our contract with him for this year to build these special guns on specifications furnished by us from the best material that money could buy. Guns that we guarantee for durability and shooting qualities the equal of any American guns on the market, and by reason of taking the entire capacity of the factory during this year we were enabled to reduce the cost of construction to where we could, by adding one very small profit, name prices of $10.22 to $15.87 in competition with cheap Belgium made guns.

OUR BINDING GUARANTEE. With every one of these American guns we issue a guarantee. We guarantee the gun to be made of the best material, to be American made by the latest machine process, all parts to be accurate and true to gauge and interchangeable, guarantee the gun for durability, for shooting qualities, penetration and pattern, and if not found so the gun can be returned to us at our expense and we will cheerfully refund your money.

IF YOU WILL REFER TO THE EXPRESS RATES IN FRONT OF BOOK you can tell almost exactly what the express charges on any gun will be to your station. The express will amount to nothing compared to the big saving in price.

THESE GUNS, PACKED FOR SHIPMENT, WEIGH ABOUT 12 TO 14 POUNDS.

MORE THAN 55,000 OF THESE GUNS NOW IN USE, AND ALL SOLD WITHIN FIVE YEARS.

OUR NEW $10.22 AMERICAN GUN.

FOR $10.22 WE OFFER A GENUINE BAR LOCK ALL AMERICAN high grade guaranteed gun as the equal of any double barrel breech loading gun on the market at double the price.

YOU CANNOT AFFORD TO BUY AN IMPORTED Belgium gun at any price when for $10.22 you can get this genuine American made gun, a gun combining the good points of all strictly high grade guns and the defects of none.

FROM THE ILLUSTRATION, engraved from a photograph, you can form some idea of the appearance of this our strictly high grade $10.22 American made gun. These guns are made with the very best steel frames, hardened steel locks and parts, all beautifully case hardened, all made by machinery and interchangeable. The gun is bored by the latest Taper system, the same as is used on the highest grade work made, bored for nitro or black powder. The left barrel is full choke bored, the right barrel cylinder bored.

WE GUARANTEE THIS GUN in durability and shooting qualities, the equal of any American gun made, regardless of price.

No. 6R259

THIS GUN IS MADE WITH THE LATEST TOP SNAP, has genuine armory steel barrels, has the strongest kind of a bar lock, and locks are rebounding, barrels are made round at breech, the gun is fitted with the latest concave circular hammers, nitro firing pins, strong Edwards' extension rib; it has nicely checkered and capped full pistol grip, has full matted rib, latest patent fore end, and fancy butt plate.

OUR SPECIAL $10.22 PRICE IS BASED ON THE ACTUAL COST OF MATERIAL AND LABOR with but our one small percentage of profit added. It is the lowest price ever made on a strictly high grade American gun.

No. 6R259 12-gauge, 30 or 32-inch barrels, weight, 7½ to 8 pounds. Our special price...................................**$10.22**

NOTICE—On any goods not described or listed in this catalogue and bought for your convenience, we must ask cash in full with the order, as on any other goods, and they cannot be returned under any circumstances. We make no charge for boxing and packing guns for shipment.

OUR $10.95 DOUBLE BARREL AMERICAN BAR LOCK WONDER

FOR $10.95 we offer this strictly high grade A1 American extra strong full pistol grip American Double Barrel Breech Loading Shotgun, as the superior of any imported machine made gun sold generally at $20.00 to $30.00, and the first time a strictly high grade bar lock choke bored genuine laminated steel breech loading genuine American gun was ever offered at anything like the price.

GENUINE LAMINATED STEEL.

TAPER CHOKE BORED

WHERE THE GUN IS MADE.

THIS GUN is made for us under contract by a large New England maker, a manufacturer who has gained the reputation for the manufacture of

STRICTLY HIGH GRADE breech loading shotguns, guns that are made and offered in competition with other American guns that sell at double the price. Only skilled mechanics are employed.

EVERY PIECE AND PART THAT ENTERS INTO THIS GUN IS MADE TRUE TO GAUGE AND IS INTERCHANGEABLE.

$10.95

SEE ILLUSTRATION. From this large illustration, engraved by our artist from a photograph taken direct from our $10.95 American Bar Lock Wonder Double Barrel Breech Loading Shotgun, you can get some idea of its appearance, yet it is a gun you must see and compare with other guns to appreciate. It is the greatest American gun bargain ever offered by any house in double barrel breech loading guns.

IT IS BUILT ON THE VERY LATEST APPROVED LINES FOR THIS SEASON. HAS ALL THE

LATEST UP TO DATE FEATURES.

NOTHING HAS BEEN SPARED TO MAKE IT WHAT IT SHOULD BE FOR

SERVICE AND DURABILITY.

$10.95

BORED FOR NITRO POWDER

GENERAL DESCRIPTION.

BARRELS. The barrels are genuine laminated steel. They are made on the most approved process. Every barrel, before leaving the factory, is thoroughly tested with nitro (white and black) powder, tested to the greatest possible strain. These barrels are choke bored on the latest taper system, with a view to giving the most perfect target, the greatest possible penetration, to insure long range effect such as can be had only from the highest grade American guns made.

FINISH OF BARRELS. These barrels are given an extra fine finish and polish. The illustration will give you some idea of the effect worked out on the coloring process, the barrels being browned, colored and decorated by the latest barrel coloring process.

RIB. The rib to these barrels is handsomely finished, beautifully matted, perfectly leveled and comes with a heavy genuine Edwards' lock extension rib.

EXTRACTOR. These barrels are fitted with the very latest shell extractor, as illustrated; positive in its action.

EXTRA HEAVY BOLTS. These barrels are fitted with extra heavy bolts, made very strong, thus insuring perfect lock and a strength from which the gun, even with the use of white or black powder, can not give out or wear loose or shaky.

LENGTH OF BARREL. The American Wonder comes with either 30 or 32-inch barrels, as desired. In ordering, be sure to state whether you wish 30 or 32-inch barrels.

WEIGHT. The American Wonder is made to weigh from 7½ to 8 pounds.

AMERICAN WONDER FRAME. This gun is made with one of the heaviest, strongest and most durable steel gun frames made. The frames are extra heavy, strong in every part, extra well finished, case hardened and handsomely colored. They have the latest nitro firing pins, handsomely shaped; perfect acting top snap break, neat circular hammers, very strong genuine bar lock, with steel hardened interchangeable parts perfectly finished.

STOCK. The stock is made from carefully selected straight grained walnut, thoroughly seasoned. It is perfectly shaped. The maker of these guns employs only the most expert stock makers. The stock is fitted to the frame by an automatic stock fitting machine that insures a perfect fit and the frame and stock are so constructed at the point of construction as to insure the strongest kind of a stock where many guns are weakened. This stock is full pistol grip with a handsome rubber cap on grip. The grip is handsomely checkered, as illustrated. Stock comes with handsomely ornamented butt plate.

FORE END. Our $10.95 American Wonder is fitted with the Edwards' automatic fore end, made of selected walnut, handsomely checkered as illustrated, beautifully finished, self locking in its application.

GAUGE. These guns come in 12-gauge only, but in shooting qualities, penetration, pattern and for long range work they are the equal of any ordinary 10-gauge American gun. For all kinds of game for which a shotgun in used this American Wonder is perfectly suited.

HOW WE MAKE THE PRICE SO LOW.

While a thoroughly reliable genuine American Double Barrel Breech Loading gun has never been sold at anything beginning to approach our special $10.95 price, determined that we would get out a genuine American gun at as low or a lower price than the very inferior machine made foreign or Belgian gun could be sold, we took the matter of manufacturing this high grade gun up with the celebrated New England gun maker, figuring how by running a certain branch of his factory at its utmost capacity, the price of a reliable gun might be greatly reduced. We found by employing the very highest type of automatic working machinery for making the different parts, by buying the raw material, including the drop forgings, steel, walnut, etc., in large quantities, and by running the factory to its utmost capacity, the actual factory cost, the cost of material and labor could be reduced even below what we ourselves or the manufacturer had any idea of reaching and to this net factory cost, the cost of material and labor, we add our one small percentage of profit and name you the heretofore unheard of price of $10.95.

THE BARRELS ON THESE GUNS are all Genuine Laminated Steel, and not Imitation Laminated Steel as sold by some houses. We guarantee them just as represented or money refunded.

NO OTHER HOUSE will give you such a guarantee on a gun at the price which we offer you this gun, and it is certainly the best value offered by any house in the United States.

SAFETY AND DURABILITY. First, in considering hard long range shooting, extra penetration, extra target, the question of strength, durability and safety has not been overlooked, and while it is not safe to use white or nitro powder in any cheap foreign made guns or many of the cheap American guns manufactured, this gun is built for shooting any white powder of proper load that can be safely used in any of the highest priced American guns made. It has been built extra strong, of the best material, strongly locked, strongly reinforced, especially strong where many guns are weak, all with a view of giving you a gun that will be always safe, always reliable; a gun that will last for years and give the very best of satisfaction.

SHOOTING QUALITIES. Too much cannot be said for the shooting qualities of our $10.95 Wonder. Nothing has been spared to make this gun in shooting quality the equal of any gun made, regardless of price. The gun was in every part designed by one of the best and most practical gun makers in this country. It was designed after considering all the strong points for shooting work of all other American guns and has been built with a view of embodying the strong features of other double barrel breech loading American guns with the defects of none. If a strong point, one that would add to the target or penetration, anything that would help for long range shooting was found in another American gun, it has been applied in this, so that we feel perfectly safe in assuring the purchaser that he will find in this gun a gun that will equal if not outdo in strength and shooting qualities any other gun he has ever used.

ORDER BY NUMBER.

No. 6R260 Our American Bar Lock Wonder, 12-gauge, 30 or 32-inch barrels, 7½ to 8 pounds. State length wanted. Our special price........ **$10.95**

THE NEW AMERICAN DOUBLE BARREL BREECH LOADER, $12.67

MADE IN 10 AND 12-GAUGE ONLY

30 OR 32-INCH BARRELS.

WEIGHT, 12-GAUGE, 7½ TO 8 LBS.

THIS GUN HAS GENUINE DAMASCUS BARRELS AND IS STRICTLY OF AMERICAN MAKE.

No. 6R263

HAS TOP SNAP, genuine Damascus steel barrels, bar rebounding locks, barrels round at breech, concave circular hammers, nitro firing pins, Edwards' extension rib, nicely checkered full pistol grip stock and fore end, flat matted rib, patent fore end, fancy butt plate, left barrel full taper choke bored, right barrel cylinder bored. Made in 10 or 12-gauge, 30 or 32-inch barrels. State length you prefer, if you have a preference.

NOTICE—The lock parts of these guns are hardened. The screws and top lever parts, also the lock parts and hammers, being made by machinery, are practically interchangeable.

Weight, packed for shipment, about 12 pounds.

THE BARRELS on these guns are all genuine Damascus, and not imitatio Damascus as sold by some houses. We guarantee them just as represented money refunded. No other house will give you such a guarantee on a gun at th price which we offer you this gun and it is certainly the best value offered by an house in the United States.

No. 6R263 12-gauge, 30 or 32-inch barrels; weight, 7¼ to 8 pounds. Our special price.........
No. 6R263½ 10-gauge, 30 or 32-inch barrels; weight, 8¼ to 8¾ pounds. Our special price......... $12.67

OUR SPECIAL HIGH GRADE AMERICAN GUN WHICH WE QUOTE AT $13.42

WE KNOW IN OUR FIVE HIGH GRADE AMERICAN GUNS we are offering such value as was never before offered, such guns as you could not get elsewhere at less than double the price. We know you would be so well pleased with any one of these guns you order that you would show it to your friends, recommend our house and we will be sure to receive more orders from your neighborhood.

THE GUN IS MADE OF THE VERY BEST MATERIAL THROUGHOUT. It has a strong steel frame, beautifully case hardened steel parts and locks. Every part in this gun is machine made and interchangeable.

THIS GUN HAS THE LATEST TOP SNAP BREAK, fancy laminated steel barrels, strongest bar rebounding locks, barrels are flattened at breech, known as water table; has the very latest concave circular hammers, the best nitro firing pins, Edwards' full extension rib, capped full fancy pistol grip, handsome checkered walnut stock and fore end, full matted rib. It is fitted with the Deeley & Edge patent fore end, has a fancy rubber butt plate; the left barrel is full taper choke bored, and the right barrel cylinder bored.

BORED FOR NITRO POWDER.

ORDER BY NUMBER.

Shipping weight, about 13 pounds.

The above illustration shows our New High Grade Special $13.42 American Made Gun.

THE BARRELS on these guns are all genuine laminated steel and not imitation laminated steel, as sold by some houses. We guarantee them just as represented or money refunded.

NO OTHER HOUSE will give you such a guarantee on a gun at the price which we offer you this gun and it is certainly the best value offered by any house in the United States.

THIS GUN IS HANDSOMELY HAND ENGRAVED AND DECORATED; it is a gun the equal of American guns that sell everywhere at double the price; there is no better shooting gun or stronger gun made at any price.

No. 6R264 We furnish this gun in 12-gauge with 30 or 32-inch barrels; weight, 7¼ to 8 pounds. Price.................. $13.42

OUR VERY FINEST SPECIAL MADE AMERICAN GUN FOR $15.87

FOR $15.87 WE OFFER THE HIGHEST GRADE GUN made by the manufacturer on our contract for this year. For $15.87 we have endeavored to furnish you a gun on the basis of the actual cost of material and labor, with but our one small profit added, that will combine the good points of every strictly high grade gun made, with the defects of none. For $15.87 we offer you a gun under our binding guarantee as the equal in all essential parts of any gun made, regardless of price. For strength, for safety, for shooting qualities, penetration, pattern, and all, we guarantee this gun equal to any gun made.

$15.87

ORDER ONE OF THESE GUNS and after you receive it, compare it with any gun you can buy from your dealer at home for double the money, and if it is not equal in every way, return it to us and we will immediately return your money.

FROM THIS ILLUSTRATION, ENGRAVED FROM A PHOTOGRAPH, you can form some idea of the gun we are offering for $15.87. This is a strictly high grade American gun. It has the strongest kind of a steel frame, and the locks, screws, levers and all parts are made of the finest case hardened steel. All are made true to gauge by automatic machinery and are practically interchangeable.

MADE IN 12-GAUGE ONLY.

THIS $15.87 GUN IS MADE WITH THE LATEST TOP SNAP BREAK, has genuine Damascus steel barrels, has the very best made bar rebounding locks, barrels are flattened at breech, known as water table; is fitted with the very latest concave circular hammers, has the very best nitro firing pins, is made with an Edwards' strong full extension rib, which is neatly decorated, has a full fancy capped pistol grip, handsomely decorated; fine walnut stock and fore end, is fitted with the celebrated Deeley & Edge patent fore end, has a fancy rubber butt plate; the gun is elaborately engraved by hand.

CONSIDER, FOR $15.87 YOU GET A GENUINE AMERICAN MADE GUARANTEED DOUBLE BARREL BREECH LOADING SHOTGUN, fitted with the very finest genuine Damascus steel barrels, choke bored by the celebrated Taper system, bored for white or nitro powder; you get a gun covered by a binding guarantee to the effect that it is in all essential parts the equal of any gun made, regardless of price. For $15.87 we furnish this gun in 12-gauge, 30 or 32-inch barrels, a gun weighing 7½ to 8 pounds.

WE ESPECIALLY RECOMMEND THIS OUR HIGH GRADE GUN AT $15.87. We guarantee every penny extra you pay in selecting this our highest grade gun goes into the work. The difference of $10.22 for our cheapest guaranteed American gun and this at $15.87 is the exact difference in cost to us. It is represented by the difference in the cost of material and labor.

WE GUARANTEE THAT IF YOU ORDER THIS GUN FOR $15.87 you will find it equal to any gun you can buy elsewhere for twice the money equal in all essential parts to any gun at any price. Don't let anyone persuade you into buying an imitation Damascus barrel gun, offered by other houses. This gun is guaranteed to have genuine Damascus barrels or money refunded. Shipping weight, about 13 pounds.

No. 6R265 12-gauge, 30 or 32-inch barrels; weight, 7¼ to 8 pounds. Our special price............ $15.87

WE CHARGE NOTHING FOR BOXING AND PACKING GUNS FOR SHIPMENT—SOME HOUSES DO.

OUR DIANA PATTERN BREECH LOADER FOR $10.18.

EQUAL TO ANY $15.00 BELGIUM GUN ON THE MARKET...

12-GAUGE ONLY.
See Our Prices for Loaded Shells.

A Genuine BAR LOCK GUN ...WITH... TWO-BLADE DAMASCUS FINISH BARRELS,

Blued at breech, matted doll's head extension rib, fancy butt cap, full pistol grip, stock and fore end handsomely checkered.

No. 6R269 **$10.18**

ONE OF OUR BEST SELLERS.

THE ABOVE ILLUSTRATION is engraved from a photograph, and will give you some idea of the gun. It is one of our best selling Belgium guns and has all modern improvements. It has engine turned rib, rebounding bar locks, pistol grip, patent fore end, nicely checkered stock and fore end, circular hammers, bored smooth inside, latest nitro firing pins, case hardened frame and lock plates, blued mountings, a good sound honest gun and one that will please you. This gun and all our other Belgium guns are thoroughly tested by the Belgian government before we get them. The celebrated Raleigh steel barrels are used in this gun. A breech loader boxed will weigh about 14 pounds.

No. 6R269 12-gauge only, 30 or 32-inch barrels, 7½ to 8¼ pounds. Our special price.......**$10.18**

ON GUNS MADE TO SPECIAL ORDER WE REQUIRE FULL AMOUNT OF CASH WITH ORDER, AND IF MADE TO YOUR ORDER THEY CANNOT BE RETURNED UNDER ANY CIRCUMSTANCES.

$7.00 Lefeaucheaux Action Gun.

We offer you the Celebrated Lefeaucheaux Action, double barrel shotgun at **$7.00**, a better grade than is generally sold in this make, and yet the price is lower than the price made by others.

$7.00

GIANT ACTION. 12-Gauge Only.

No. 6R275

The Celebrated Lefeaucheaux Action, no stronger action made, guaranteed the best gun of this make in the market, **with Hawley blued decarbonized steel barrels,** back action locks, checkered grip, bottom lever, 30 or 32-inch barrels, 12-gauge, weight, 7¼ to 8 pounds.

No. 6R275 12-gauge, 30 or 32-inch barrels; weight, 7½ to 8 lbs. Our special price.......**$7.00**

Our Little Ladies' Breech Loading Double Barrel Shotgun, 44-Caliber.

$11.14

44-Caliber Shotgun

No. 6R276

This gun is especially designed for ladies or boys who want a gun which does not kick, and which is effective for squirrels, birds or small game. 44-caliber, smooth bored; is the nicest little double barrel gun yet produced. It makes a fine present for a lady or boy who likes to hunt. It has top snap, twist finished barrels, rebounding locks, pistol grip stock, patent fore end, nitro firing pins, and makes a good quail gun. It is made in 44-caliber, 25-inch barrels and weighs about 4 pounds.

No. 6R276 Our special price.......**$11.14**

50 Shot Cartridges (No. 6R2517) for this gun.......**.75**

These cartridges come 50 in a box, loaded with No. 8 shot. Weight, packed for shipment, about 9 pounds.

$10.67 Buys a Regular $15.00 Gun.

THIS GUN IS MADE IN EUROPE by one of the oldest and most reliable makers there, and we offer it for the first time at the remarkably low price of **$10.67. Don't be deceived** by anyone into buying any of the many cheap imitations.

Made in 12-Gauge Only.

$10.67

No. 6R280

The above illustration, engraved from a photograph, will give you some idea of the appearance of this gun. **Complete bar locks,** top snap break, engraved lock plates, the best made, **finest two-blade Damascus finished steel barrels,** rebounding hammer, strong matted extension rib, pistol grip, selected walnut stock, finely checkered fore end, **strong nitro firing pins,** fancy butt plate. 12-gauge, 30 or 32-inch barrel as desired; weight, 7½ to 8 pounds.

No. 6R280 Price.....(Weight, packed, about 13 pounds).....**$10.67**

Compare our prices with other houses and you will find none can compete with us.

$21.40

Giant 8-Gauge Goose Gun. 36-inch Barrels.

Our 8-Gauge Goose Gun for Long-Range Shooting. Strong French action. The illustration represents our new 8-gauge Lefeaucheaux Breech Loading Gun. Bottom lever, genuine laminated steel barrels, best double key fore end, pistol grip stock, case hardened frame, fancy butt plate, rebounding locks, checkered grip; made for long range shooting. **Our 8-gauge Goose Gun is made especially for us under contract, and nothing but the best material and the best barrels are used in the construction of this gun.** We realized the importance of having guns intended for 8-gauge charges, strong at every point, and we have covered these points in the manufacture of these goose guns.

No. 6R282 **The Giant Goose Gun.** Made 8-gauge, 36-inch barrels; weight, 12 to 14 pounds. Our special price.......**$21.40**

CELEBRATED GREENER ACTION BREECH LOADING SHOTGUN.... $14.85

$14.85 BUYS A $25.00 GUN.

The barrels of this gun are made of Wilson's best steel...........

WEIGHT, PACKED IN BOX, ABOUT 14 POUNDS.

12-GAUGE ONLY

DESCRIPTION.

THIS GUN HAS TOP SNAP BREAK, the best break made, **very beautiful Damascus finished barrels,** bar action, rebounding locks, fancy pistol grip, patent fore end, extension rib, the **celebrated Greener cross bolt** with engraved locks, nicely checkered stock and fore end, **left barrel modified choke, right barrel cylinder bored.** Bar lock, fancy cap on pistol grip, fancy butt plate. **Gun comes 12-gauge only, 30 or 32-inch barrels, weighs 7½ to 8 lbs.** We cannot recommend this gun too highly, and we are extremely anxious to receive your order for one of them, for we know it will mean the sale of many more. There is nothing in the market at anything like the price. **Under our system of one small profit direct from the manufacturer to the consumer, you will own this gun for less money than your local dealer can buy it in quantities.**

No. 6R285

This gun is one we have imported from Europe, at a price which is less than half the price charged by retail dealers for guns of this quality. You will find this gun equal to anything on the market at any price. There is no better shooting gun made.

No. 6R285 12-gauge only. 30 or 32-inch barrels, 7½ to 8 pounds. Our special price.......**$14.85**

SOME HOUSES CHARGE FOR PACKING AND BOXING GUNS. WE DON'T.

NOTICE. On any goods not described or listed in this catalogue and bought for your convenience, or made to special order, cannot be returned under any circumstances if sent as ordered.

SEND GOODS BY FREIGHT. We advise sending goods by freight, as it is cheaper than by express. If you order a gun or a rifle, and you include enough needed goods from our big catalogue to make a shipment of 50 to 100 pounds, the entire shipment will be very near as cheap by freight as the gun alone would cost you by express. When shipping 50 to 100 pounds or more by freight, it makes the freight charges cost practically next to nothing on each item.

OUR HIGHLY ENGRAVED DIANA STYLE BREECH, DOUBLE BARREL BREECH LOADER FOR ONLY $10.90

MADE IN 12-GAUGE ONLY.

$10.90

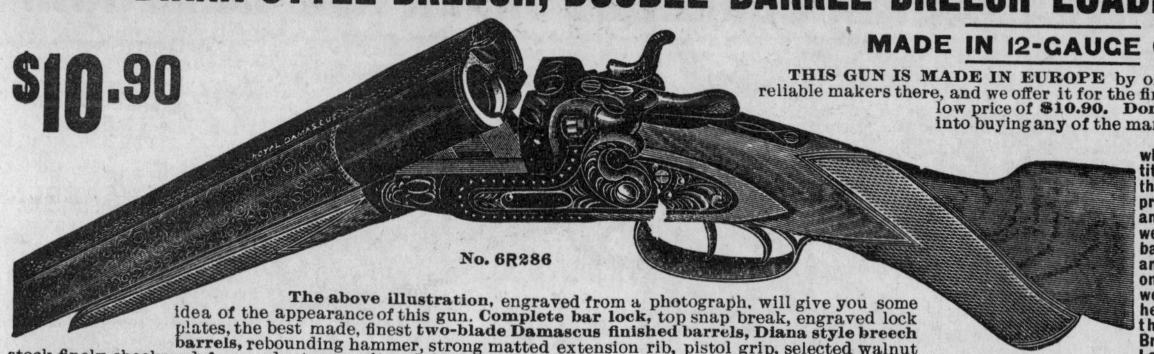

No. 6R286

THIS GUN IS MADE IN EUROPE by one of the oldest and most reliable makers there, and we offer it for the first time at the remarkably low price of **$10.90. Don't be deceived** by anyone into buying any of the many cheap imitations.

By reason of a large contract, which we have made for a quantity of these guns, we have gotten the manufacturer to figure the price down to the lowest point, and by paying cash for the goods we were able to obtain them based on the actual cost of labor and material, and by adding our one small percentage of profit, we are enabled to name you this heretofore unheard of price on the highly engraved Diana Style Breech, Double Barrel Breech Loading Shotgun.

The above illustration, engraved from a photograph, will give you some idea of the appearance of this gun. **Complete bar lock**, top snap break, engraved lock plates, the best made, finest two-blade **Damascus finished barrels, Diana style breech barrels**, rebounding hammer, strong matted extension rib, pistol grip, selected walnut stock, finely checkered fore end, **strong nitro firing pins**, fancy butt plate. 12-gauge, 30 or 32-inch barrels as desired. Weight, 7½ to 8 pounds. **A neat, well made and attractive looking gun. Weight, packed, about 13 pounds.**

FOR $10.90 we offer you this genuine bar lock, highly engraved breech loader, which retails anywhere in this country at 20 to 40 per cent more money.

ALL THESE GUNS are tested by the Belgian Government to stand the rigid Government test, and all guns have the celebrated Raleigh steel barrels.

No. 6R286 12-gauge, 30 or 32-inch barrels, 7½ to 8 pounds, price **$10.90**

THE CELEBRATED THOMAS BARKER DOUBLE BARREL BREECH LOADING SHOTGUN FOR $10.40

Made in 16-gauge, 6½ to 7 lbs. 30-inch barrels.

20-gauge, 6¼ to 6¾ lbs. 30-inch barrels.

10, 12, 16 OR 20-GAUGE.

$10.40

Made in 12-gauge, 7½ to 8¼ lbs. 30 or 32-inch barrels.

10-gauge, 8½ to 9¼ lbs. 32-inch barrels.

This illustration will give you some idea of the appearance of this gun.

DESCRIPTION.

Top snap twist finish barrels, bar action, rebounding locks, matted rib, full checkered pistol grip stock, circular hammers, patent fore end, nitro firing pins, fancy butt plate, left barrel choke bored, right barrel cylinder bored, doll's head extension rib bored smooth and true, inlaid pistol grip. A first class gun in every respect. **A first class shooter. None better.** They come in 10, 12, 16 and 20-gauge (the price is the same for all gauges). One of the best guns made for field shooting.

No. 6R289

OVER 50,000 NOW IN USE.

Weight, packed, about 13 pounds.

No. 6R289 Price, each. See the sizes above and give gauge and length wanted **$10.40**

T. BARKER GUN FOR $11.40.

ROYAL DAMASCUS FINISH.

$11.40

OVER 50,000 NOW IN USE.

$11.40

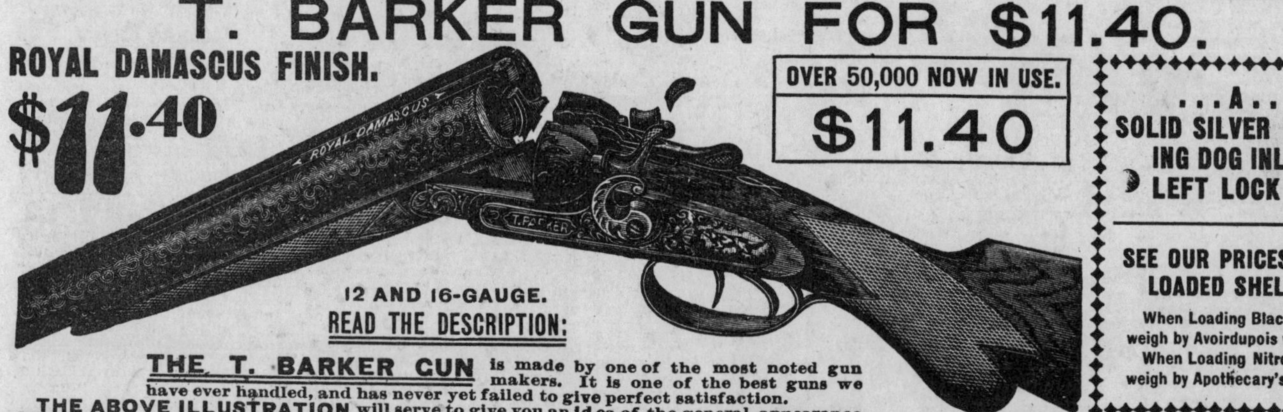

...A... SOLID SILVER HUNTING DOG INLAID IN LEFT LOCK ....

SEE OUR PRICES FOR LOADED SHELLS.

When Loading Black Powder weigh by Avoirdupois weight.
When Loading Nitro Powder weigh by Apothecary's weight.

12 AND 16-GAUGE.

READ THE DESCRIPTION:

THE T. BARKER GUN is made by one of the most noted gun makers. It is one of the best guns we have ever handled, and has never yet failed to give perfect satisfaction.

THE ABOVE ILLUSTRATION will serve to give you an idea of the general appearance of this gun, which is very handsome in appearance, and a first class shooter. It has **Royal Damascus finished barrels**, made from Wilson's celebrated steel, with fine matted rib. The latest patent top lever break. **Low circular rebounding hammers** below the line of sight. **Beautifully engraved locks and action.** The lock plates being inlaid with a **silver hunting dog**, which, together with the beautiful hand engraving gives this gun the fine appearance rarely found in high priced guns. **The stock is of fine walnut**, full checkered pistol grip with inlaid cap, and full checkered patent fore end; fancy butt plate. **Strong, durable action** with two through lumps, shell extractor, Morgan extension rib, **and all improvements of the high priced guns.**

No handsomer gun made.

No better gun for all purposes.

OUR BIG LEADER. This gun would retail at **$25.00** from regular stores. We furnish them in 12 or 16-gauge, as desired. **Weight, packed for shipment, 13 pounds.**

No. 6R292 12-gauge, 30 or 32-inch barrels, 7½ to 8 pounds. Our price, **$11.40**

No. 6R292¼ 16-gauge, 30-inch barrels, 6¾ to 7 pounds. Our price.... **$11.40**

PITTING OF GUN BARRELS.

We frequently have complaints from some customers saying that their gun or rifle barrels have become pitted (or spotted) inside, and we wish to inform our customers that this is not the fault of the material from which gun barrels are made, nor is it the fault of the gun maker; it is usually caused by carelessness or neglect on the part of the owner of the gun.

If you wish to prevent your gun barrels from becoming pitted, do no leave any burnt powder inside, especially burnt nitro powder. Burnt nitro powder is extremely severe on steel and iron.

When 10, 12 or 16-gauge barrels become pitted, it necessitates having them re-bored and re-polished, which costs from $1.50 to $5.00, according to the condition of the barrels. As we are not responsible for pitting of gun barrels, we must charge for re-boring and re-polishing same.

Always clean and oil the gun or rifle barrels after shooting, and if you wish to put the gun up for several months, put a coating of gun grease inside of the barrels and keep it in a dry place. As a rule pitting does not hurt the shooting qualities of a gun.

HOW DAMASCUS GUN BARRELS ARE MADE.

D A B C

The above cut illustrates, as near as possible, how the Damuscus gun barrels are made. The three strips, A, B and C, each consist of from 40 to 60 layers of iron and steel welded together into one square strip, then they are twisted (D) while hot and rewelded into one strip about ⅜-inch wide, and ⅛-inch thick: the object being that if any one of these numerous layers of iron or steel has a flaw, the welding process entirely eliminates the flaw. After these numerous layers of iron and steel are twisted and rewelded into one strip, the strip is twisted around a mandrel and welded together as shown in the cut.

These barrels are all made by hand by skilled mechanics who have spent years in learning this art. They cannot be made by machinery. When a barrel is made from three strips it is called three-stripe Damascus, when made from two strips it is called two-stripe Damascus, and when made from one strip it is called laminated steel. The more strips used in making the barrel, the finer is the figure of the barrel, and the more costly to make.

HOW TO AVOID DELAY.

We carry a stock valued at about Two Million Dollars, and aim to keep this stock up, but it sometimes happens that we receive orders in one day from every part of the United States for the same single item, which exhausts the stock temporarily. It also sometimes happens that one of our factories fails in business, has labor strikes, can't make goods as fast as we sell them, and, while we try as far as possible to deal with reliable factories, we cannot guarantee to furnish goods under these conditions, but we always try to do the best we can for our customers. **If you can give us a second or third choice when we are out of an article, it will avoid delay in shipping your order.**

WE MAKE NO EXTRA CHARGE FOR BOXING AND PACKING GUNS. SOME HOUSES DO.

OUR $17.10 BELGIAN COMBINED RIFLE AND SHOTGUN.

THIS ILLUSTRATION OF OUR COMBINED RIFLE AND SHOTGUN is an engraving made by our artist direct from the gun itself and is a very excellent reproduction of this handsome field piece. For hunters who find use for both shotgun and rifle, this gun is par excellence, relieves one of the necessity of carrying two guns, is thoroughly well made by the best European manufacturer, accurate, reliable, and thoroughly satisfactory in every respect. The rifle barrel shoots cartridge No. 6R2432.

EQUAL TO $25.00 AND $30.00 GUNS.

OUR $17.10 BELGIAN COMBINED RIFLE AND SHOTGUN is a gun equal to what retail gun stores offer for $25.00 to $30.00; it is such a gun value as has never before been offered. In appearance one of the handsomest guns made. Combines every strictly high grade feature, easily handled. A gun that cannot get out of order, a gun that will last a lifetime.

EVERY $17.10 GUN we put out will be a big advertisement for us. Everyone who sees the gun will admire it; every true sportsman will appreciate its splendid qualities, and every dealer in sporting goods will realize the wonderful value we are offering in this fieldpiece at only $17.10. On this basis we solicit your order, feeling confident we will give you such a gun at the price as cannot be duplicated elsewhere.

$17.10

38-55 CALIBER RIFLE BARREL.

12-GAUGE SHOTGUN BARREL.

No. 6R308

This combined shotgun and rifle has a 38-55 caliber rifle barrel and a 12-gauge shotgun barrel, side by side, as shown in the illustration. It has top snap, the barrels are laminated finish, complete with back action locks, rebounding hammers, extension rib and pistol grip. Has the celebrated Spring patent fore end and nitro firing pins. It has matted rib, handsomely ornamented butt plate and circular hammers. The sights are the best rifle front and rear sights.

IN OFFERING THIS GUN AT $17.10 we are saving you the profits and expenses of the jobber and retailer and being large importers ourselves are able to furnish the gun to you at importers' prices, which means that the gun costs our customers about the same that the wholesale dealer has to pay for it. This gun will seldom if ever retail at less than $25.00 to $28.00, and even a higher price will be asked by many dealers who have little competition. Weight, boxed for shipping, about 15 pounds.

No. 6R308 12-gauge shotgun barrel, 38-55 caliber rifle barrel, 30-inch, about 8¼ to 8¾ pounds. Our special price.......................... **$17.10**

OUR NEW BELGIAN DOUBLE BARREL BREECH LOADING SHOTGUN, $13.87

12-GAUGE ONLY.

$13.87

BARRELS MADE FROM WILSON'S BEST STEEL.

DEELEY & EDGE FORE END.

No. 6R310

AT $13.87 WE OFFER a strictly high grade Belgian shotgun as shown in this illustration. While this picture is drawn by our artist, and the cut is made direct from the gun itself, it does not give a perfect idea of the wonderful value which we are offering at the low price named above. This shotgun is one of the latest guns on the market, bought by our European buyer because of its manifest excellence and wonderful value, and offered to our customers at importers' prices, representing a saving of from 33⅓ to 40 per cent.

THIS BEAUTIFUL GUN is furnished in 12-gauge only, has fine two blade Boston finished Damascus barrels, rebounding bar locks, matted extension rib, circular hammers and pistol grip. The stock is made of the very best selected walnut and, as shown in the illustration, the gun has the celebrated Deeley & Edge fore end. It is complete with nitro firing pins, fancy butt plate, case hardened locks and breech. Our buyer was able to secure another lot of these high grade guns. In view of the fact that we are quoting this gun in our catalogue, which goes to 700,000 customers, it will be well worth your while to send your order at once, for after this consignment is gone we doubt whether others can be secured before six months or a year. While they last they will be offered at the extremely low price named above.

No. 6R310 12-gauge, 30 or 32-inch barrels, 7½ to 8 pounds. Weight, packed for shipping, about 13 pounds. Our special price................ **$13.87**

OUR SPECIAL $5.65 DOUBLE BARREL MUZZLE LOADER.

$5.65

No. 6R324 Has laminated steel finished barrels, filed patented breech, case hardened back action lock plates, fancy carved stock as shown in the cut, wood ramrod, German silver escutcheons, iron butt plate, blued mountings. The above cut is made from a photograph by our artist and we consider this the best value ever offered for the money. Made in 12 or 14-gauge, 32 or 34-inch barrels, 7½ to 8 pounds. Weight, packed for shipping, about 13 pounds. Our special price........................ **$5.65**

THE BELGIAN MUZZLE LOADING DOUBLE BARREL SHOTGUN ...FOR $6.98

No. 6R331

These guns are imported direct from Belgium, and all have the Belgian Government test same as our Breech Loaders.

No. 6R331 Has genuine patent breech, genuine twist barrels, case hardened bar lock plates, checkered pistol grip stock, wood ramrod, German silver escutcheons, iron butt plate, case hardened and blued mountings. The cut is made from a photograph of the gun and is an exact cut. This is our best grade muzzle loading double gun and is made in 12 and 14-gauge, 32 or 34-inch barrels. Weight, 7½ to 8 pounds. Weight, packed for shipping, about 13 pounds. Price... **$6.98**

TO LOAD SHELLS. If you load your own shells and put one card wad and two black edge and then another cardboard wad over the powder and one card wad over the shot, it takes 1¼ pounds of black powder, 6¼ pounds of shot, 200 black edge wads and 300 cardboard wads to load 100 shells with 3 drams of powder and 1 ounce of shot.

A CUT DOWN MUSKET FOR $2.75.

We have secured a few more Cut Down Muskets, which we will close out at $2.75 each. There are only a few of these guns left on the market, and when these are gone there will be no more, at any price. They are good shooters for general use.

No. 6R347

No. 6R347 The above illustration shows the exact appearance of our Special $2.75 Cut Down Musket, made from U. S. Springfield Musket Model, 1863. Altered to shotgun, front action lock, case hardened mountings and lock, blued barrel, steel rod. For quality of material, shooting qualities and durability, this guns is too well known to require any comment from us. Weight, packed for shipping, about 13 pounds. Price..... **$2.75**

OUR 16-GAUGE AUTOMATIC EJECTOR SINGLE GUN, $4.90.

Decarbonized Armory Steel Barrels.

16-gauge only. 30 or 32-inch barrels. Weight, about 6½ lbs.

OUR $4.90 16-gauge Ejector Single Gun is fitted with decarbonized steel barrel, pistol grip stock, walnut fore end, bored smooth and true to gauge, choke bored for field shooting and has fancy but plate. The hammer is hung in the center so as to strike the cartridge square. The automatic ejector device is very strong and simple and cannot get out of order. The barrel is detachable, making it convenient to carry the gun apart in a Victoria style gun case. The stock is made of selected walnut, pistol grip, fancy butt, rebounding lock, top snap break. The frame and trigger guard are case hardened and beautifully finished. 16-gauge, 30 or 32 inch barrel. Shell is thrown out automatically when you open the gun. State length of barrel wanted.

No. 6R400 Weight, boxed for shipping, 10 pounds. Our price... **$4.90**

$3.98 BUYS THE LONG RANGE WINNER

AT $3.98 reduced from $5.50 the price of a year ago, and reduced from $4.45 the price of last season, we offer the genuine Long Range Winner as one the highest grade automatic, shell ejecting, single barrel breech loading shotguns made.

$3.98 barely covers the cost of material and labor in our own gun factory with but our one small percentage of profit added. It is lower than dealers can buy in any quantity, a gun the equal of guns that retail everywhere at from $7.00 to $10.00.

OUR GUARANTEE AND REFUND OFFER.

SEND US $3.98 (we require cash in full to accompany all orders, with the understanding that we return your money at once if you are not perfectly satisfied), and we will send this gun to you by express, guaranteeing it to reach you in perfect condition, guaranteeing every piece and part that enter into the construction of the gun to be absolutely perfect, guaranteeing the working parts to be perfect in every respect, and if you do not find it so, if you are not perfectly satisfied with the gun, if you do not find it the equal of any automatic single barrel long range gun, the equal of guns that retail at $7.00 to $10.00, you can return the gun to us at our expense of express charges both ways and we will immediately return your money.

COMPARE THIS OUR $3.98 LONG RANGE WINNER with any of the single barrel, automatic shell ejecting, breech loading guns on the market, those catalogued by other houses at $4.50 to $6.00, those that retail generally at $7.00 to $10.00, and if you do not find our Long Range Winner at $3.98, the equal of any other shell ejecting breech loader, you can return the gun to us at our expense of express charges both ways and we will immediately return your money.

HOW WE MAKE THE PRICE *$3.98.*

WE OWN THE FACTORY in which these guns are made and control the entire output. The cost to us is gotten down to merely the cost of the raw material and labor, and to this we add our one small percentage of profit, naming the heretofore unheard of price of $3.98. This gun is made in our own factory at Worcester, Mass., and the factory is in charge of one of the best single gun makers in the world, and we believe under his management, utilizing the modern machinery we do, that we produce a better automatic shell ejecting single barrel shotgun at a lower cost than any other factory.

WE MAKE AND FINISH MORE BARRELS of this kind than any other maker, thus reducing the cost. On the cost of barrels alone there is a saving to us in the cost of every gun over other manufacturers of about 50 cents. Where nearly all makers of single guns import the barrels, the barrels being made in Belgium, we make our barrels in our own factory from solid bars of genuine Wilson welded steel. To make the barrels we buy the highest grade of genuine Wilson welded steel in solid bars of about 12 foot lengths. We cut this steel up into lengths of 30 and 32 inches, and in a new improved automatic barrel boring machine we bore two barrels at a time, and by this process we not only reduce the cost of the barrels about 50 cents each, but we furnish a higher grade, truer, stronger, better finish, and hence a better shooting barrel than is furnished on any single gun made.

BY OUR SYSTEM each barrel is choke bored for strong and long range shooting, made and bored to shoot either white, nitro or black powder, is more highly polished, better finished and blued than any similar gun on the market. We have installed special machinery for making every screw, every piece and every part for the milling, cutting, polishing, shaping, making and fitting of stock, the most economical and finest case hardening plant, everything combined to turn out a perfect gun at the very minimum of cost, and to this actual cost we add our one small percentage of profit, and quote the ridiculously low price of $3.98.

WE LOCATED OUR SINGLE GUN FACTORY at Worcester as a matter of economy and efficiency of labor. Worcester, Mass., is located in the very center of the gun and revolver making industry of America. Within a short radius of our factory, nearly all the American gun and revolver factories are located, hence we have the most skilled labor concentrated and always at our disposal. The supply usually being in excess of the demands of other factories, we are able to build this gun at a lower wage scale at Worcester than at any other point in the country.

ALL THIS HELPS TO MAKE POSSIBLE OUR SPECIAL $3.98 PRICE.

WILSON'S WELDED STEEL.

TAPER CHOKE BORED

$3.98

SPECIAL POINTS OF EXCELLENCE.

We claim for the Long Range Winner, superiority over other single barrel guns, especially on the following points: First, genuine Wilson's welded steel barrels, choke bored, and finished in our own factory, smoother, stronger and better than other makers furnish.

AUTOMATIC SHELL EJECTOR, stronger, more sure, and less liable to get out of order than any other single barrel shell ejecting device made.

LOCKING BOLT. The heaviest, strongest and best locking bolt used on any single gun.

FRAME AND ACTION. The strongest, handsomest, most simple, neatest and best finished frame and action used on a single barrel ejector.

SHOOTING QUALITIES. Above all we claim for our $3.98 Long Range Winner, the best shooter of any single barrel gun of this type on the market. Our barrels and frames are made, and the gun is hung in a way that insures a better target at longer range than you will get from any single barrel gun you can buy from any other house at $1.00 to $3.00 more money.

UNDERSTAND, we accept your order and money with the agreement to immediately return your money to you and pay the express charges both ways if the gun is not found perfectly satisfactory.

$3.98

ILLUSTRATION SHOWS THE ACTION OF OUR LONG RANGE WINNER.

T is the Hammer.
U is the Top Lever.
V is the Top Lever Spring.
W is the Locking Bolt.
X is the Main Spring.
Y is the Trigger Spring.
Z is the Trigger.
G is the Stock.
1 is the Extractor Cam Spring.
2 is the Extractor Cam.
3 is the Extractor Hook.
4 is the Fore End.
5 is the Trigger Guard.

NOTE THE ILLUSTRATION. From this large illustration, engraved by our artist from a photograph taken direct from the gun, showing the ejector and action automatically throwing the shell from the gun, you can form a good idea of the general finish and style of this our $3.98 Long Range Winner, but it is a gun you must see and compare with other guns to appreciate the value we are offering.

ABOUT THE EXPRESS CHARGES

The gun weighs packed for shipment about 10 pounds, and you will find the express charges will amount to next to nothing as compared with what we will save you in price. The express charges will average for 300 miles, 40 cents; for 500 miles, 50 to 65 cents; 1,000 miles and upwards, 75 cents to $1.00.

OUR $3.98 GUN weighs about 6½ pounds, making a light gun to carry, very convenient and at the same time one of the strongest shooting guns made, and in this respect is more convenient than a double barrel gun, for it is in shooting qualities equal to a double barrel gun that would weigh from 8 to 10 pounds.

Weight, packed for shipment, about 10 pounds.

DETAILED DESCRIPTION.

BARREL. The barrel is made from the highest grade of extra refined, thoroughly tested genuine Wilson's welded steel, choke bored by the celebrated Taper system. Each barrel is blued, decarbonized finish, fitted with automatic shell ejector, one of the strongest positive motions, perfect working automatic shell ejectors made, so constructed that when you open the gun the empty or discharged shell is automatically thrown clear from the gun.

The illustration shows the action of the shell as it is being automatically ejected. By this device there is no stopping to remove the shell by hand, it being thrown clear from your way ready to receive the new loaded shell. This makes possible very rapid firing, in fact, you can load and unload very much faster than with the ordinary extractor gun. The device is only appreciated by those who have used automatic shell ejecting guns, and such people would have no other, in fact with this single barrel automatic shell ejecting gun you shoot almost as rapidly, and do almost the same execution that you can accomplish with a double barrel hammer breech loading shotgun.

FRAME. The $3.98 Long Range Winner has one of the very strongest solid steel frames, made extra heavy, reinforced at all parts, nicely shaped, perfectly finished. It is given a handsome mottled finish on the outside. It has the latest rebounding hammer, positive springs, the very latest top snap break. The gun is the latest type of take-down or detachable model. By simply removing the thumbscrew the barrel and fore end can be detached from the frame.

STOCK. This gun is fitted with an extra quality, thoroughly seasoned straight grain walnut stock, with pistol grip as illustrated, and the stock is fitted with a fancy butt plate. The fore end is of selected straight grained seasoned black walnut.

GENERAL FINISH. This gun is gotten up to present a more symmetrical, shapely and in every way a better general appearance than the ordinary single barrel gun. With its neat stock, handsome butt plate, beautifully decarbonized frame and trimmings, highly finished blued barrel, nicely proportioned parts and fittings throughout, even at our special $3.98 price it is one of the handsomest single guns on the market.

GAUGE. This gun comes in 12-gauge only, and being made and bored for white or black powder, made extra strong throughout, the gun is suitable for any kind of shooting where any shotgun can be used, suitable for game, geese, ducks, chickens, partridge, quail, snipe, rabbit, squirrel, etc.

LENGTH OF BARREL. The barrel is either 30 or 32 inches in length as desired. When ordering be sure to state the length of barrel wanted.

No. 6R401 ORDER BY NUMBER.

No. 6R401 Long Range Winner, 12-gauge, 30 or 32-inch barrel. Our special price, **$3.98**

THE NEW WHITE POWDER WONDER, $4.10.

ONLY $4.10 FOR A GENUINE AMERICAN MADE NITRO POWDER BREECH LOADER. $4.10 is the LOWEST PRICE ever made on a breech loading gun made to shoot white powder. The manufacturer guarantees this gun the equal of any gun made in shooting qualities and OUR SPECIAL PRICE of $4.10 is based on the actual cost to make, with but our one small percentage of profit added. Don't buy a cheap gun. Order this and if you don't find it the greatest value for $4.10 in a single barrel breech loader you have ever seen, return it at our expense and we will refund your money.

The strongest single gun made. Barrels are made of Wilson's best welded steel. Choke bored. Makes a good target. Will shoot any kind of smokeless or black powder.

THE NEW WHITE POWDER WONDER is a gun that will stand any load. We have had a large quantity of these guns made especially for us and can now supply those of our customers who desire an extra strong gun for nitro powder, and adapted to heavy loads for long range shooting. This gun is gotten up expressly for heavy shooting and will stand any proper load, having a double reinforced breech, and made of the finest quality of steel, imported expressly for them. The barrel fits squarely in the frame and is bolted by a special device, which makes it impossible for it to become shaky. They have a fine walnut pistol grip stock with top lever break. The barrel and mountings are of the finest blued finish. The breech of this gun being very thick, gives the barrel a beautiful taper which is seldom seen even on high priced guns.

WE FULLY GUARANTEE this gun for either smokeless or blake powder, and for those who desire a gun for heavy shooting, we recommend the White Powder Wonder. All are choke bored, bored on the taper system. Our sale of these guns has been constantly increasing, and we have made a contract this year for twice as many guns as we sold last year, and by increasing our contract we were able to make a slight reduction in the cost of manufacture, and we give you the benefit of this reduction.

12-GAUGE ONLY.

No. 6R413 12-gauge only, 30 or 32-inch barrel; weight, 6¼ to 6½ pounds. Mention length wanted. Weight, packed for shipment, about 10 pounds. Our special price........ **$4.10**

OUR $4.40 NEW WHITE POWDER WONDER EJECTOR.

OUR $4.40 PRICE is made possible by reason of our building this gun in our own factory. We started the manufacture of these guns with a view of giving our customers something better than the regular grade of single barrel guns turned out by factories generally. We started our own factory that we might produce a gun free from all the weak points of the many guns that are being manufactured under competitive conditions that compel the manufacturer to slight vital parts in order to meet the price made by other makers.

WE HAVE SUCCEEDED in turning out in our New White Powder Wonder Ejector, a gun combining the good points of all strictly high grade guns with the defects of none, and yet on a basis of the actual manufacturing cost, the cost of material and labor with but our one small percentage of profit added. We can offer this gun

AT ONLY $4.40, much less than inferior single guns are being sold generally.

AT $4.40, a reduction of $1.50 from our last year's price of $5.90, we offer the New Improved White Powder Wonder Ejector, a gun with all the very latest 1902 improvements brought right up to date, a high class automatic shell ejector breech loading single barrel shotgun, built to combine the good points of every strictly high grade single barrel shotgun made, with the defects of none, at a price much lower than ever before known, a price that barely covers the cost of material and labor with but our one small percentage of profit added, one of the highest of high grade single barrel shotguns. We especially recommend to you for your consideration our New 1902 Model White Powder Wonder Automatic Ejecting Single Barrel Loading Shotgun at only $4.40.

No. 6R414 Order by Number.

FROM THE ILLUSTRATION, engraved by our own artist from a photograph, taken direct from our $4.40 New White Powder Wonder Ejector, you can form some idea of the appearance of this gun, but you must see this gun, examine it, compare it with others, must put it to the test of its shooting qualities, compare its target, penetration, long range, killing effect, to realize fully what we have, from our own factory, from the material we ourselves control, from the workmanship we put on the gun by employing the very finest automatic machinery, attained in this justly termed, New White Powder Wonder Ejector;

THE ONLY WHITE POWDER EJECTOR AMERICAN GUN OFFERED AT ONLY $4.40.

SPECIAL POINTS OF SUPERIORITY in the New Model White Powder Wonder over the many other single guns made: Wilson's highest grade full welded steel barrel, bored for black or white nitro powder, choke bored by the celebrated taper system; more perfect and more positive action; stronger built and lock mechanism; highest grade automatic shell ejector made; greater strength, accuracy and better finished frame; interchangeable and better finished parts; longer range, better target and more carefully tested. All these very essential points in the shooting and lasting qualities of a gun go to make our New Model White Powder Wonder Ejector superior to any of the regular factory made ejectors now on the market.

BROKEN PARTS ALWAYS REPLACED. If by accident or otherwise any part should get broken or become lost, being interchangeable they can be readily replaced and can always be had from us at a very nominal charge.

OUR BINDING GUARANTEE. Every New White Powder Wonder Ejector offered at $4.40, is sent out under our binding guarantee, by the terms and conditions of which if any piece or part gives out by reason of defect in material or workmanship within one year from date of purchase, we will replace or repair it free of charge.

DETAILED SPECIFICATIONS. Wilson's welded steel barrel; choke bored by the celebrated taper system; very finest automatic ejector, heavy bolted, self locking, self compensating, interchangeable parts, reinforced frame, beautifully case hardened; barrel detachable from frame; rebounding hammer, latest top snap break, fine selected straight grain pistol grip walnut stock, fancy butt plate to stock.

Weight, packed for shipment, about 10 pounds.

No. 6R414 Automatic Ejector, Wilson's steel barrel, case hardened frame, 12-gauge only, 30 or 32-inch barrel. State length wanted. Our special price........ **$4.40**

OUR GOLD MEDAL WONDER, WITH GENUINE TWIST BARREL, $4.60.

FOR $4.60 WE OFFER YOU A GENUINE TWIST BARREL AMERICAN MADE SINGLE BARREL BREECH LOADER, BORED FOR NITRO OR BLACK POWDER.

WE HAVE JUST CONSUMMATED A LARGE CONTRACT with one of the largest manufacturers in this country, and by taking his entire output for a term of years, we are able to offer you this heretofore unheard of price on an American made Single Barrel Breech Loader with GENUINE TWIST BARRELS.

THE GOLD MEDAL WONDER Single Barrel Breech Loader is made from the best material that money can buy, made by the latest improved machinery by skilled mechanics, bored on the latest improved principles, all leading parts being made to gauge are interchangeable, the springs of the best quality steel, best quality walnut stock, fancy butt plate and walnut fore end.

FROM THE ILLUSTRATION engraved by our artist from a photograph taken direct from the gun, you can form some idea of the appearance of the new

GOLD MEDAL WONDER SINGLE BARREL BREECH LOADING SHOTGUN.

OUR BINDING GUARANTEE. We guarantee this gun to the extent that if any piece or part gives out by reason of defect in material or workmanship, we will replace it free of charge at any time within one year. The barrel is guaranteed to be genuine twist or money refunded.

We furnish the Gold Medal Wonder Single Barrel Breech Loading Shotgun with GENUINE TWIST BARREL in 12-gauge only; 30 or 32-inch; weighs, 6¼ to 6½ pounds.

DESCRIPTION—It is fitted with a top snap break, rebounding hammer, walnut pistol grip stock and fore end. The mountings are beautifully finished, made extra strong at all essential points, and the gun is so constructed that the barrel may be taken from the frame by unscrewing the thumbscrew at the side of the frame, and the gun is bored on the taper choke system, giving the best penetration possible.

THE PRICE which we name on this gun is, as far as we can learn, lower than any dealer can buy a similar gun in quantities, and it represents the actua cost of material and labor with one small percentage of profit added. Weight, packed for shipment, about 10 pounds.

No. 6R420 Our Gold Medal Wonder with genuine twist barrel, 12-gauge, 30 or 32-inch barrel. Mention length wanted. Our special price..... **$4.60**

OUR WORLD'S CHALLENGE EJECTOR, WITH GENUINE TWIST BARREL $4.90

FOR $4.90 WE OFFER THE WORLD'S CHALLENGE EJECTOR SINGLE BARREL BREECH LOADER WITH GENUINE TWIST BARREL.

WE HAVE JUST CLOSED A CONTRACT for a very large quantity of these guns, and by reason of this contract we are enabled to make our customers the heretofore unheard of price of $4.90, which we confidently believe is a lower price than has ever been made by any other house on a gun of equal quality, with genuine twist barrels.

OUR BINDING GUARANTEE.

This gun is covered by a binding guarantee, by reason of which, if any part gives out through any defect in material or workmanship within one year, we will replace it free of expense to you.

EACH AND EVERY ESSENTIAL PART is made to gauge and interchangeable, and the gun is made from the best material, by the most improved machinery and by the best mechanics obtainable for this class of work. The barrel is bored on the latest improved taper system, which gives the best possible penetration for field or water fowl shooting.

DESCRIPTION: Our World's Challenge Ejector has a genuine twist barrel, the best quality walnut pistol grip stock, beautifully case hardened frame, walnut fore end, top lever, rebounding hammer, fancy butt plate, and is bored for either nitro or black powder.

IT IS ONE OF THE BEST and closest shooting single barrel shotguns made, and will shoot any proper load of smokeless or black powder.

THE BARRELS on these guns are all genuine twist and not imitation twist as sold by some houses. We guarantee them just as represented or money refunded.

NO OTHER HOUSE will give you such a guarantee on a gun at the price which we offer you this gun, and it is certainly the best value offered by any house in the United States.

OUR WORLD'S CHALLENGE EJECTOR is fitted with an automatic shell ejector, which throws out the empty shell after it has been fired and the gun is ready for reloading. By having an automatic shell ejector gun, you can load and shoot a single barrel gun very nearly as quick as a double barrel gun. **Weight, packed for shipping, about 10 lbs.**

No. 6R422 **Our World's Challenge Ejector** is made in 12-gauge only, 30 or 32-inch barrel; weight, 6¼ to 6½ pounds. **Mention length wanted.** Our special price.... **$4.90**

NEW FOREHAND SINGLE BARREL HAMMERLESS GUN, $6.87

WE HAVE ALL THE GUNS THAT HAVE BEEN FINISHED SPECIALLY FINE AND PUT TO THE SEVEREST TEST OF PATTERN, PENETRATION AND ACTION.

Made by the Forehand Arms Co. The finest, the best single breech loading shotgun made. Retails everywhere at $12.00 and upward. Our special drive price, **$6.87.** Best, safest, most durable single barrel shotgun made. **Top snap break, pistol grip,** patent snap fore end, **automatic action, with an absolute safety catch to lock the trigger to prevent accidental discharge,** simple in construction, perfectly safe and made of the very best material, **choke bored,** finest blued steel barrel, using brass or paper shells, center fire, 12-gauge, 30 or 32-inch barrel; weight 7 pounds.

We guarantee the shooting qualities of this gun fully equal to any 12-gauge gun made.

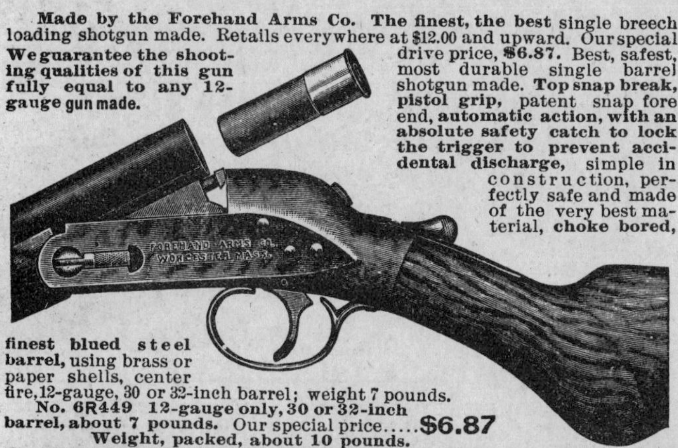

No. 6R449 12-gauge only, 30 or 32-inch barrel, about 7 pounds. Our special price..... **$6.87**
Weight, packed, about 10 pounds.

OUR CLUB HAMMERLESS GUN, $5.45.

Weight, packed, about 10 lbs. **$5.45** **Our Special Club Hammerless Shotgun.**

CHOKE BORED
BORED FOR NITRO POWDER.

No. 6R488 ORDER BY NUMBER.

Our New Club. This gun is made specially for us by one of the most reliable manufacturers in the country, and is intended to supply those of our customers who desire a good hammerless single gun for a small amount of money. **We consider this the best hammerless gun that can possibly be made for the money,** after having taken great pains in making our selections, in order to obtain only the guns that we can **guarantee and recommend to our customers.** It has a rolled steel blued barrel, Scott top lever break, case hardened frame, checkered pistol grip stock, fancy butt plate, and is choke bored. A good close shooter for general purposes. The barrel is made from the best grade of Wilson steel.

No. 6R488 12-gauge, 30 and 32-inch barrel, 6½ to 7 pounds. **State length wanted. Our special price**.......... **$5.45**

No. 6R488¼ 16-gauge, 30 and 32-inch barrel, 6½ pounds. **State length wanted. Our special price**.......... **5.45**

NOTICE—The Hopkins & Allen Single Barrel Ejector Shotguns, take down style, which we sold at $6.00, are no longer to be had, as the factory was entirely destroyed by fire and we have sold out all we had.

The New Improved Trap Hammerless Single Barrel Gun with Genuine Twist Barrel for $6.25.

Don't Buy a Gun at Retail, Until After You Have Consulted this Catalogue.

Fine Twist Barrel. Taper Choke Bored. 12 or 16-Gauge.

ORDER BY NUMBER

THIS HAMMERLESS TRAP GUN AT $6.25 Like all our Single Barrel Shotguns, is made especially for us, under contract; all especially selected stock; all carefully targeted and fully guaranteed.

The New Trap Hammerless Single Breech Loading Gun, made by the celebrated Crescent Fire Arms Company, is one of the best shooting single guns made. It has fine twist barrel, rebounding lock, pistol grip stock and checkered fore end; combines all the late improvements of the best guns, and is intended to perfectly satisfy those who desire a very close shooting, single, hammerless gun. They are all taper choke bored; 12 and 16-gauge only.

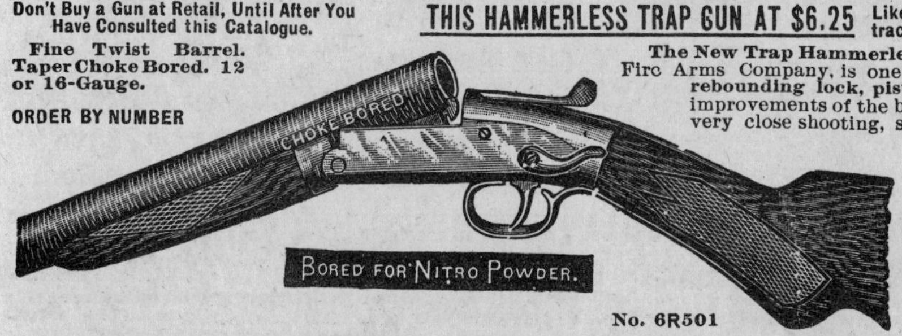

No. 6R501

THE HIGHEST GRADE TRAP SINGLE GUN. This gun is made specially for us under contract. **Every gun tested for perfect target and penetration.**

COMPARE OUR SINGLE TRAP GUN with any other and you will find it better finished, better made, will make a better target and a better penetration than any other trap gun on the market.

QUALITY CONSIDERED, you will save 25 per cent by buying this gun from us. **These guns make an average target of 275 pellets in 30-inch circle at 40 yards. Load used, 3¼ drams black powder, 1⅛ ounces No. 8 shot. Weight, packed in box, 10 lbs.**

No. 6R501 12-gauge, 30 or 32-inch barrel, weight about 7 pounds. State length wanted. Our special price.......... **$6.25**

No. 6R502 16-gauge, 30-inch barrel, weight about 6¾ pounds. Our special price.......... **6.25**

Our New Crescent Genuine Twist Barrel Take Down Gun, with all Modern Improvements. 16-Gauge Only.

Our New Crescent Twist Single Barrel Gun is one of the best single guns made. This gun is made by the reliable **Crescent Fire Arms Co.,** whose name alone is a sufficient guarantee for the quality of this gun. **It has fine twist steel barrel, center hammer, patent top lever break, pistol grip stock, rebounding hammer, fancy butt plate, and is choke bored.** These new guns as now made for us, leave out absolutely nothing that is to be desired in a first class single gun, **as they are a combination of every real improvement of merit.** The barrels used are of steel twist of the best quality, imported especially for them. These guns make an average target of 250 pellets in a 30-inch circle at 40 yards. Load used, 3¼ drams black powder, 1⅛ ounces of No. 8 shot.

No. 6R505 **16-gauge, 30-inch barrel, 6½ pounds.** Our special price.......... **$5.40**

BEWARE OF IMITATIONS.

Weight, packed in box, about 10 pounds.

Some houses charge for packing and boxing guns. We don't.

READ THE DESCRIPTION.

$5.40

CHOKE BORED
BORED FOR NITRO POWDER.

No. 6R505 Order by Number.

RUSTED AND DAMAGED GUNS. **Do not return to us a gun, revolver or rifle which is rusted, pitted or has the finish worn off, for we have no way of selling these guns. If you have a gun, revolver or rifle which needs repairing, first write us fully describing the article, and what is broken and we may be able to send you the part necessary, thus saving the express charges on the gun both ways.**

SINGLE BARREL SHOTGUNS.

OUR NEW 36-INCH BARREL, AUTOMATIC EJECTOR, SINGLE BARREL BREECH LOADER, $5.95.

In response to the many inquiries for a 36-inch, 12 or 16-gauge Single Barrel Breech Loading Shotgun, we have had some special barrels made and are now able to furnish a single barrel gun with 36-inch barrels for our southern and western trade.

As all 12 and 16-gauge guns are usually made in 30 and 32-inch barrels, all makers have their machinery arranged and set for the 30 and 32-inch barrels only, and will not go to the expense of changing the machinery for making and handling 36-inch barrels; we have gone to this expense and now offer you 36-inch single barrel, breech loading guns in 12 and 16-gauge for only

$5.95

BORED FOR NITRO POWDER.

WILSON'S WELDED STEEL.

No. 6R510

These Special 36-inch Barrel Guns are made OF BEST MATERIAL THROUGHOUT, with automatic shell ejectors, made on the latest improved principle, choke bored by the latest taper system, fine quality of walnut stock, and fore end nicely finished; and bored for nitro or black powder.

ORDER BY NUMBER.

The automatic ejector device is very strong and simple and less liable to get out of order than any other device known.

The frame is made from the best material that money can buy; the barrel from Wilson's best quality welded steel, and we consider it one of the best guns that was ever put upon the market.

The frame and trigger guard are case hardened and beautifully finished; all are made with pistol grip walnut stocks. The hammer is hung in the center of the frame so as to strike the shells squarely; and the gun can be taken down by removing the patent fore end screw key. Weight, packed in box, for shipping, about 12 pounds.

No. 6R510 12 or 16-gauge, 36-inch barrels, weight about 7 to 7½ pounds, blued steel barrels, pistol grip stock, rebounding hammer, patent top snap action, fancy butt plate, automatic shell ejector. State gauge wanted. Our special price............ $5.95

THE GENUINE REMINGTON SEMI-HAMMERLESS, SINGLE BARREL BREECH LOADING SHOTGUN.

Special Price, **$7.50**

No. 6R515

BEWARE OF IMITATIONS.
All Genuine Remington Guns Bear the Name . . . . . : REMINGTON ARMS CO., ILION, N. Y.

Handsome and Well Made. Can You Match It?

OUR SPECIAL PRICE IS $7.50.
IT RETAILS FOR $12.00.

The Remington Semi-Hammerless Single Barrel Breech Loading Shotgun, top lever break, the best break made, blued armory steel barrel, choke bored, side cocking lever, case hardened frame and butt plate, pistol grip stock, rebounding lock. The material, finish and shooting qualities are the same high standard as the Remington double barrel gun. Every gun is warranted perfect and a strong shooter. They are all put to a test before leaving the factory and none are allowed to go out until a perfect pattern has been shown. You take no risk in buying the old and reliable Remington.

No. 6R515 12-gauge only; 30 or 32-inch barrel; 6 to 6½ pounds. Our special price............ $7.50

BEWARE OF IMITATIONS. Many houses are selling guns that are similar, but not genuine We guarantee our guns to be as represented or money refunded. Weight, packed in box, about 10 pounds.

THE DAVENPORT SINGLE BARREL 8 AND 10-GAUGE GOOSE GUNS, $16.50 AND $13.00.

AT $16.50 FOR 8-GAUGE AND $13.00 FOR 10-GAUGE we will furnish you the celebrated Davenport Goose Guns. These guns are made especially for us and all guns are

TESTED BEFORE THEY LEAVE OUR STORE.

COMPARE OUR GOOSE GUNS WITH ANY OTHER, and you will find them better made and better finished than any goose guns on the market.

No. 6R518 8-Gauge Davenport Single Barrel Gun, adapted to heavy shooting. A very popular goose gun for long range, hard shooting. All parts made with a view to securing a strong, lasting gun. Choke bored, fine laminated barrel, 36 inches long; weight, 10 pounds.
Our special price............ $16.50

No. 6R520 10-Gauge Davenport Single Barrel Gun, adapted to heavy shooting. A very popular goose gun for long range, hard shooting. All parts made with a view to securing a strong, lasting gun. Choke bored, fine laminated barrel, 36 inches long; weight, 9 pounds.
Our special price............ $13.00

The Best Low Priced Gun for Long Range Shooting Ever Made.

FOR GEESE AND LARGE GAME.

8-GAUGE	10-GAUGE
$16.50	$13.00

OUR NEW TAKE DOWN SINGLE BARREL SHOTGUN, ONLY $4.35.

12 OR 16-GAUGE

$4.35

OUR NEW TAKE DOWN Single Barrel Breech Loading Gun, American made, with rolled blued steel barrel, pistol grip, oiled walnut stock and fore end, top lever break, rebounding lock with direct firing pin. Hammer in center of frame.

BARREL IS BORED FROM SOLID METAL, WITH MODERATE CHOKE FOR GENERAL SHOOTING.

All working parts made of the best drop forged steel and machine fitted. An excellent shooting gun for a small amount of money.

No. 6R530 12-Gauge, 30 or 32-inch barrel; weight, about 6½ pounds. Our special price............ $4.35

No. 6R530¼ 16-Gauge, 30-inch barrel only; weight, about 6¼ pounds. Our special price............ 4.35

Weight, packed, about 10 pounds.

OUR REVOLUTIONARY FLINT LOCK MUSKET FOR ONLY $2.65.

$2.65

F shows where flint is placed.

We have succeeded in obtaining a limited quantity of revolutionary Flint Lock Muskets. These muskets have a 37-inch blued barrel, and weigh 9 pounds, fitted with three steel bands and a steel ramrod.

They have been cleaned and refinished. It has been supposed that there were no more of these flint lock muskets to be had, but our European buyer succeeded in finding a small lot of them in Belgium and has sent them on to us.

This Revolutionary Musket is not only a good antique relic, but it may also be used as a shotgun, by first loading the gun, then raising the hammer and placing some powder in the powder pan. The gun is then ready to shoot. When you pull the trigger, the flint ignites the powder by striking the pan cover and producing sparks.

Do not fail to place your order as early as possible, because the supply is limited and liable to become exhausted. When you have one of these flint lock muskets you can show your friends the kind of gun that our grandfathers and great grandfathers used to shoot before caps and cartridges were invented. All you need for shooting this musket is powder and shot. The gun does the rest.

No. 6R540 Our special price for this revolutionary flint lock musket, only............ $2.65
Weight, packed ready for shipment, about 14 pounds.

NOTICE. On any goods not described or listed in this catalogue and bought for your convenience, we must ask cash in full with the order, the same as on our other merchandise, and they cannot be returned under any circumstances if made as ordered. We make no charge for boxing and packing guns. Some houses do.

SEND GOODS BY FREIGHT. We advise sending goods by freight as it is cheaper than by express. If you order a gun or a rifle, and you include enough needed goods from our big catalogue to make a shipment of 50 to 100 pounds, the entire shipment will be very near as cheap by freight as the gun alone would cost by express. When shipping 50 to 100 pounds or more by freight, it makes the freight on each item cost practically next to nothing.

WINCHESTER REPEATING SHOTGUNS.

$17.82

ILLUSTRATION OF WINCHESTER REPEATING SHOTGUN, MODEL 1897.

EVERY WINCHESTER SHOTGUN we sell is carefully selected and tested for target, pattern and penetration, so if you buy a Winchester Gun from us you can depend on getting as perfect and strong a shooter as there is made. The best gun made for ducks, chickens, partridges, etc., as you can fire much more rapidly than with any double barreled gun; besides the penetration of these guns is simply wonderful. WEIGHT OF 12-GAUGE, PACKED FOR SHIPMENT, ABOUT 15 POUNDS.

Model 1897. Latest Repeating Shotgun Made.

THIS GUN IS KNOWN AS THE WINCHESTER PUMP GUN.

Model of 1897. Winchester Repeating Shotgun. Shoots six times without reloading. Retails at $25.00; our special price... **$17.82**

THE HIGHEST GRADE, MOST PERFECT, BEST WORKING AND LOWEST PRICE REPEATING SHOTGUN MADE.

Choke Bored. No. 6R550 Order by Number **Choke Bored.**

Best gun made for ducks, chickens or partridges. No stronger shooting gun made; has wonderful penetration and makes a perfect pattern. Operated by sliding forearm below the barrel. When the hammer is down the backward and forward motion of this slide unlocks and opens the breech lock, ejects the cartridge or fired shell and replaces it with a fresh cartridge. The construction of the arm is such that the hammer cannot fall on the firing pin and strike the cartridge until the breech block is in place and locked fast; while the hammer stands at the full cock notch the gun is locked against opening. In this position the firing pin must be pushed forward to open the gun. When the hammer stands at half cock, the gun is locked both against opening and pulling the trigger.

To load the magazine turn the gun with the guard upward, lay the cartridge on the underside of the carrier and push it into the magazine.

Finest quality, patent rolled steel barrels, fine selected walnut stock, pistol grip; length of stock, 13 inches; drop of stock, 2¾ inches; weight, 7¾ pounds, shoots six times without reloading.

No. 6R550 12-gauge, 30 or 32-inch barrel. Mention length wanted. Our special price.. **$17.82**

No. 6R555 Winchester Brush Gun. 12-gauge, 26-inch barrel, magazine holds four cartridges. A fine gun for buckshot. Our price **$19.24**

The Brush gun is simple in construction, very few parts and not liable to get out of order. Most rapid action made, cylinder bored to do the best shooting possible with buckshot.

Weight, packed in box, about 14 pounds.

Winchester Take Down Shotguns.

WONDERFUL VALUE FOR $19.24.

$19.24 FOR WINCHESTER latest model Take Down, six shot repeater 12-gauge shotgun. Is a shooter equal to any $100.00 gun. We target every gun and they are carefully inspected before leaving our place. Greatest shotgun value ever offered. Order this gun and if you do not find it equal to any gun made, regardless of price, return it at our expense. Our $19.24 price we guarantee the lowest wholesale price to dealers.

$19.24 TO $33.50

The Winchester Take Down Repeating Shotgun is the popular model, 1897, with a strong, simple, serviceable and handy take down system applied to it. This gun may be taken apart and put together again as quickly and easily as a double barrel shotgun and carried in a Victoria case, packed in a trunk or rolled up in camp beddings. The system used is similar to that used on Winchester take down rifles, and has been thoroughly tested and found to be faultless.

No. 6R560 12-gauge, 30 or 32-inch barrel of rolled steel. Weight, 7¾ pounds. Mention length wanted. Our price........ .... **$19.24**

No. 6R562 16-gauge, 28-inch barrel. Our special price... .... **19.24**

No. 6R565 Winchester Take Down Brush Gun. 12-gauge, 26-inch rolled steel barrel, cylinder bored. Price... .... **20.67**

No. 6R570 Winchester Take Down Trap Gun. 12-gauge, 30-inch barrel, fancy walnut stock, checkered; straight grip, fancy walnut fore end, checkered. Price.................................. .... **$33.50**

Weight, packed in box, about 14 pounds.

BRUSH GUNS ARE CYLINDER BORED.

A FEW WORDS ABOUT TWIST BARRELS.

Some of our customers order twist barrels and when they receive laminated steel they object, so we will explain the difference in these barrels. Many years ago there were three leading style barrels made; namely, twist, laminated steel and Damascus. The twist was a very coarse figure, the laminated steel a finer figure and much more expensive than the twist, and the Damascus still more expensive. By improved methods in manufacture and by making large quantities the makers were able to reduce the cost of laminated steel to the same price as the twist barrels and laminated steel barrels became the popular barrels. Laminated steel barrels are really better barrels and have a finer figure than twist barrels.

SEE OUR PRICES FOR LOADED SHELLS.

We charge nothing for boxing and packing guns. Some houses do.

The Winchester Lever Action Repeating Shotgun.

MODEL 1901. No. 6R575

No better shooting gun made. The barrel can be examined and cleaned from the breech. The magazine and carriers hold five cartridges, which, with the one in the chamber, makes six at the command of the shooter. The forward and backward motion of the finger lever, which can be executed while gun is at shoulder, throws out empty shells, raises a new cartridge from magazine and puts it into the barrel. The gun is then ready to be fired. Finest quality rolled steel barrels, case hardened frame and pistol grip, walnut stock. All guns are full choked, and no gun will be sent out that will not make a perfect target. The standard gun will have a stock 12¾ inches in length and 2⅝ inches drop. Any variation from standard length or drop will be charged for extra.

Six Shooter. Retails at $30.00. Our price, $21.37. Order by number.

No. 6R575 10-gauge, 32-inch barrel. Weight, 9 pounds.

Our special price............(Not made in 12-gauge).................. **$21.37**

MARLIN TAKE DOWN SHOTGUNS, $17.25.

The Marlin Take Down Repeating Shotgun, model 1898, can be taken apart and put together very quickly and easily. Made in 12-gauge, 30-inch barrel only. Weight, about 7 pounds. Barrel made of blued steel choke bored, guaranteed for nitro powder. Pistol grip stock. This gun has been tried and thoroughly tested by the best shooters in the country and found to be perfect in every detail. Magazine holds five shells, and one in the chamber, making six shots.

No. 6R580 Factory price, $24.00; our special price, 12-gauge, 30-inch barrel only..(Weight, packed in box, about 14 pounds.).. **$17.25**

Fancy Marlin Take Down Repeating Shotgun for $28.00.

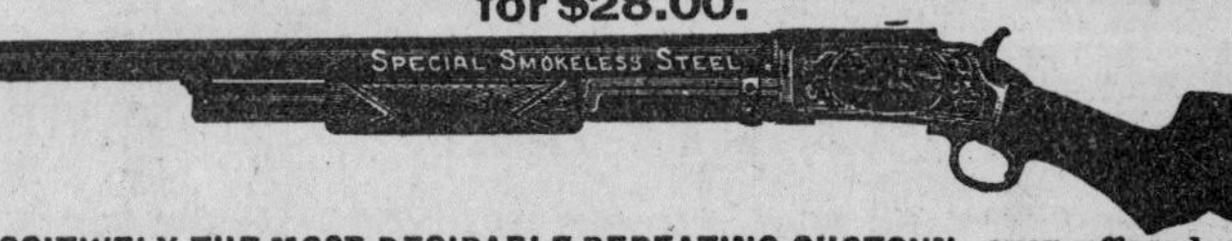

POSITIVELY THE MOST DESIRABLE REPEATING SHOTGUN ever offered, a marvel for accuracy, penetration and as perfectly balanced a gun as has ever been put on the market. It is a take down model, six-shot, the very latest design, convenient in every respect, no possible complications in the take down apparatus, a gun that every true sportsman would like to own.

THIS SPECIAL MARLIN SHOTGUN has a special smokeless steel barrel of the finest quality. The stock and fore end are made of specially selected fancy figured walnut and have an extra fine finish. The stock and fore end are beautifully checkered by hand. The illustration is too small to show the handsome engraving on the lock, or other features which make it one of the most attractive fire arms on the market. We doubt if any such gun as this can be secured from retail dealers at less than $50.00; in fact it is a new model which will be found in scarcely any but the very largest retail stores in large cities.

No. 6R586 C grade. Our special price in 12-gauge, 30-inch barrel, 7¼ pounds, full choke bored.. **$28.00**

OUR GENUINE $10.00 PALMER RIFLE FOR ONLY $2.70

FOR $2.70 we offer you this genuine Palmer Rifle, with twenty rounds of cartridges, fitted with first quality walnut stock, best quality steel barrel, strong breech block, safety attachment, leaf sight. Made from the best material that money can buy, the locks, guard and trimmings case hardened, bored and rifled for strong hard shooting. Made originally for the U. S. government and costs about $10.00 to build.

THE SAFETY DEVICE. The Palmer Rifle is fitted with a safety device, so that you cannot pull the trigger until the gun is loaded and ready to shoot, making it one of the safest rifles conceivable. At a forced sale we bought a large quantity of these rifles for cash, and by adding our one small percentage of profit to the cost, including twenty rounds of ammunition, we are able to make you this extremely low price of $2.70 for the GENUINE PALMER RIFLE.

THE PALMER RIFLE has a 20-inch steel rifled barrel, shoots 56-50 caliber Spencer cartridges, which can be had from us or any first class hardware or sporting goods house, weighs about 5½ pounds, and we offer them, while our stock lasts, at $2.70, including twenty rounds of cartridges with each rifle. It is just the kind of a rifle to have on the farm, in the woods or in camp, and it will kill any kind of game, such as bear, deer, mountain lion, etc.

No. 6R650 Our Palmer Rifle, caliber 56-50, 20-inch barrel, with twenty rounds of cartridges, for only.............................. **$2.70**

Weight, packed for shipment, about 12 pounds.

FLOBERT RIFLES.

NOTE—WE DO NOT RECOMMEND NOR GUARANTEE FLOBERT RIFLES. Buy a good rifle. It will pay in the end. We recommend Nos. 6R665 and 6R666. We think No. 6R665 is the best value for the money.

This rifle is made for BB caps, has side extractor, bright mountings, octagon barrel, varnished stock, 22-inch barrel, and will not shoot 22-caliber cartridges. Weighs about 4½ lbs. Cannot be sent by mail.
No. 6R655 Our special price.. **$1.60**

Our $2.25 Remington System Flobert Rifle.

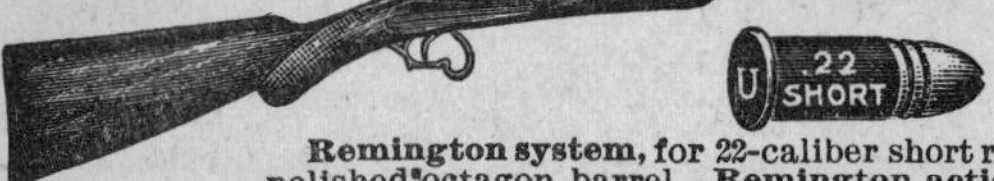

Remington system, for 22-caliber short rim fire cartridges, polished octagon barrel, **Remington action,** trigger guard, light barrel, rifled, oiled stock, dark mountings, fine checkered pistol grip, 22-inch barrel. Weighs about 4½ pounds.
No. 6R657 Our special price, cash with order.......................... **$2.25**

Warnant System Flobert Rifle.

22-CALIBER
$2.60 and $2.80.

Warnant or Springfield action, polished **medium heavy octagon barrel, pistol grip, fancy butt, trigger guard, checkered stock, dark mountings. 22-inch barrel.** Weight, about 4¾ lbs. Uses 22-caliber short or long rim fire cartridge.
No. 6R658 Our special price, cash with order.......................... **$2.60**
No. 6R659 Same as above, but heavier and 24-inch barrel, well made and well finished. The safest rifle for boys.
Our special cash with order price.. **$2.80**

No. 6R663 New Model Warnant Action, oiled walnut stocks, checkered pistol grip, **24-inch octagon barrel, 32-caliber, short rim fire, shell extractor, barrel very finely finished.** Weight, 6½ pounds.

32-CALIBER
$2.85.

Our special cash with order price.......... **$2.85**

THE NEW PIEPER RIFLE FOR $2.55.

With Remington Action.

Patented 1897.

THE BEST BOYS' RIFLE MADE FOR SQUIRREL AND SMALL GAME.

The New Pieper Rifle. Patented 1897. This is the best Boys' Rifle made. It fills a long felt want, and is first class in every respect. **This rifle has the celebrated Remington action,** which is the best action used. **It is entirely machine made. All parts are interchangeable,** which is a great advantage. **It shoots accurately, is adapted to and will shoot either 22-caliber long or short cartridge, or BB caps,** has 20-inch finely rifled octagon barrel. Weighs about 3¾ pounds. **Just the rifle for squirrels, rabbits and small game.** Don't buy a cheap rifle when you can get a genuine Pieper for $2.55.
No. 6R665 Our special price.................................. **$2.55**

THE STEVENS' CRACK SHOT TAKE DOWN RIFLE FOR $2.95.

FOR $2.95 we furnish you the **STEVENS' CRACK SHOT RIFLE** which is well worth **$5.00.** This is a strictly American made rifle, smooth, well bored and well rifled, all the working parts are of steel and interchangeable, and if any part breaks we can furnish you another part to replace it. **Why buy a hand made Flobert, which no house can guarantee, when you can buy the CRACK SHOT, which is guaranteed and made by one of the best rifle makers in the country. It will pay you in the end to buy a CRACK SHOT RIFLE.** This rifle has in addition to its many good features, a safety catch on the frame behind the hammer, so that the rifle can't be accidentally discharged by children, or any one else, until you press the safety catch back with your thumb. **This feature has never appeared on any cheap rifle before and is a great point in favor of the STEVENS CRACK SHOT RIFLE.**

The CRACK SHOT RIFLE will shoot accurately and is chambered to take a BB cap or 22-caliber short cartridge. We recommend using only 22-caliber short cartridges in it. It has a blued steel barrel, solid breech block, as shown in illustration, and can easily be taken apart by unscrewing the screw in front of the guard. **We guarantee the stock to be of the best American walnut. The CRACK SHOT has 20-inch barrel and weighs about 4 lbs.**
No. 6R666 Our special price.. **$2.95**

No. 6R677½ML We have a few Sharps Linnen Rifles taking the Linnen Cartridge, caliber 52. These rifles are not quite new, having been used in the government service during the Civil War. We are unable to obtain any Linnen Cartridges for these rifles, but they can be used as a muzzle loader by using musket caps, barrel is 22 inches long, well rifled. They make a strong and good muzzle loader and we offer them while our stock lasts at only..........(Weight packed for shipping, about 15 pounds) **$1.65**

OUR NICHOLSON REVOLVING RIFLE.

22-CALIBER, $2.25

This revolving rifle is made similar to a hinge pistol. The barrel hinges on the forearm, as shown in the cut, and the cylinder is intended to be revolved by hand, having a cylinder stop which stops the cylinder on a line with the barrel. When shooting, always keep the left hand back of the revolving cylinder. The Nicholson Revolving Rifle is intended to shoot 22-caliber short rim fire cartridges, or 22-caliber shot cartridges. This is one of the best revolving rifles ever offered for the price.

For $2.25 we are offering for the first time a revolving boys' rifle, 22-caliber, 7-shot; barrel, 8¼ inches long; entire length 32 inches; with nickel plated mountings, dark wood stock, metal butt plate; weight, about 2¼ pounds.

No. 6R667 Our Nicholson Revolving Rifle, 22-caliber. Weight, 2½ pounds. Entire length, 32 inches. Our special price.............. **$2.25**

Quackenbush Improved Nickel Plated Air Gun,

$4.50

No. 1 Rifle. 21-100-caliber. Full length, 36 inches. Shoots darts and slugs. Each gun is neatly boxed, with six patent darts, six paper targets, 100 slugs, together with a combined claw and wrench. The gun can be instantly taken apart for the convenience of carrying in trunk or valise.
No. 6R669 Our special price.................... **$4.50**
Weight, 4½ pounds. Cannot be sent by mail.

Darts, Slugs, Etc.

No. 6R670 21-100 Darts for Quackenbush rifle. Per dozen....... **.30**
No. 6R670½ 17-100 Darts for Daisy and other air rifles. Per dozen............ **.25**
No. 6R671 21-100 Felted Slugs for Quackenbush rifle. Per 100............ **.08**

Quackenbush Junior Safety Rifle, $3.60.

$3.60

The Quackenbush Junior Safety Rifle has a fine steel nickel plated skeleton stock, which can be easily detached for carrying in small 18-inch space. Blued barrels, finely rifled. Whole length, 32 inches. Weight, 4 pounds, 22-caliber, rim fire only. Safe, accurate **and reliable, and fully warranted by the manufacturers. Guaranteed good shooters.**
No. 6R672 Our special price.............................. **$3.60**

Our $3.65 Improved Quackenbush Bicycle Rifle.

JUST THE RIFLE FOR CYCLISTS.

Perfectly accurate, all steel, beautifully finished and can be used either as a rifle or pistol. Breech system same as that used on the **Quackenbush safety rifle.** The skeleton stock can be moved in and out quickly and is held firmly when in place. The form of stock and pistol grip are such that the rifle comes to the shoulder, hand and eye, **as conveniently as any rifle. Each rifle is tested before leaving the works.** Shoots 22-short, 22-long, 22-long rifle or 22-shot cartridges.
No. 6R673 22-caliber, whole length 27 inches, closed 16 inches, 12-inch barrel. Weight, 31 ounces. Each..... .... **$3.65**

Quackenbush Safety Cartridge Rifle, $3.90 and $4.15

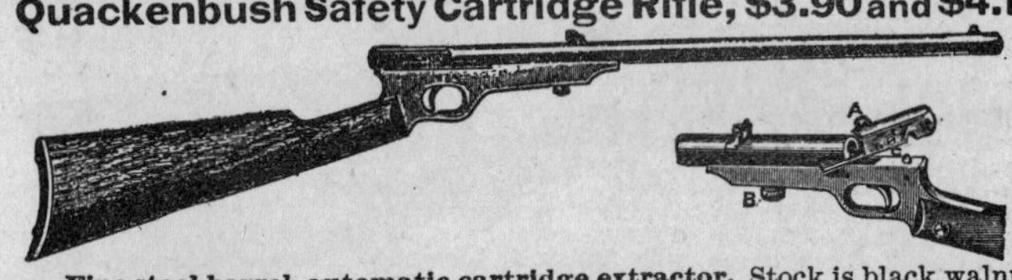

Fine steel barrel, automatic cartridge extractor. Stock is black walnut, handsomely finished, and so fastened to the barrel that the two may be easily and quickly separated, making the arm **handy to carry in a trunk, valise or package.** The barrel is blued, and parts are well and **durably nickeled,** except the breech block, which is case hardened in color. **Whole length, 33 inches,** 18-inch barrel, **22-caliber for regular rim fire,** BB or long and short cartridges. Plain open sights, as shown in illustration. Weight, about 4½ pounds. **Guaranteed good shooters.**
No. 6R674 Our special price with 18-inch barrel.... **$3.90**
No. 6R676 Our special price with 22-inch barrel.... **4.15**

This $12.00 Sharps Rifle for $2.90.

$2.90

For $2.90 we offer you this genuine Sharps Rifle with twenty rounds of 50-caliber Government Standard Central Fire Cartridges.

These rifles were originally made for the United States Government, and made to pass the most careful government inspection, and made at a cost of $12.00 for the rifle alone, and this is the identical rifle which we are offering you as the best rifle value ever offered by any house in this country. **The Sharps Rifle is too well known to require an exhaustive description.** It is made from the very best materials that money can buy, made true and accurate in every detail, has the best quality rifle steel barrel, the finest quality walnut stock, fitted with graduated leaf sight, as shown in illustration, and made to kill any kind of game, such as bear, deer moose, etc. **We bought a large lot of these rifles at a forced sale on our own cash terms,** and by adding our one small percentage of profit, we are able to offer you this handsome Sharps Rifle with 20 cartridges **for only $2.90**
No. 6R677 Sharps Rifle, with 22-inch barrel, weight about 7¾ pounds, taking caliber 50-70 central fire cartridges. Our special price **$2.90**
No. 6R4294½ Loading Tools, 50-70 caliber for this rifle, per set **1.75**

THE GENUINE REMINGTON NEW MODEL TAKE DOWN RIFLE. No. 4, Single Shot.

AT $5.00 we offer the No. 4 Remington Rifle; every gun carefully tested and made Take Down. WE GUARANTEE EVERY REMINGTON RIFLE we sell to be tested to target, perfect in every way and superior to regular stock goods.

22 and 32-calibers. RIM FIRE.

These are the Genuine Remington Rifles. Don't buy imitations offered by many houses. They are worthless.

Oiled walnut stock, case hardened frame and mountings, open front and rear sights. As finely rifled as any rifle in the market, and made of the very best rifle material. Perfectly accurate, and every one warranted. No better or longer range rifles made of these calibers. Warranted as represented.

No. 6R678 22-caliber, rim fire, 22½-inch octagon barrel. A fine little rifle and an accurate shooter. Weight, 4½ pounds, rifle butt. Take Down model. Our special price.......... $5.00

No. 6R680. 32-caliber, rim fire, 24-inch octagon barrel. Weight, 4½ pounds, rifle butt. Our special price.......... 5.00

OUR NEW No. 6 REMINGTON TAKE DOWN RIFLE, $3.75.

The New Remington No. 6 Take Down Rifle is placed upon the market with the view of giving the best possible value at a low price. This new No. 6 Remington Rifle is made from the best material that money can buy, and the shooting quality is of a high order, and each rifle is bored and rifled with the same accuracy and precision that follows the entire line of Remington rifles which have become famous for their shooting qualities. These rifles are made in 22-caliber only, and shoot the 22-caliber short cartridges.

No. 6R681 Remington Rifle No. 6, 22-Caliber. 20-inch round barrel, weight 3¼ pounds, walnut stock and fore end, case hardened frame, Take Down model. Our special price $3.75

THE GENUINE REMINGTON RIFLE. No. 2. 5½ to 6 Lbs. For $7.50.

22 and 32-Caliber Rim Fire. 32 and 38-Caliber Center Fire. New Model. Single Shot. With Octagon Barrel.

Case hardened frame, walnut stock, rifle butt plate, steel octagon barrel, fitted with sporting front and rear sights. The ejector used in this rifle automatically throws the shell out of the chamber. **We handle only the Genuine Remington Rifles. We do not handle the Imitation Remington Rifles. They are worthless.**

Remington No. 2, Fine Target Rifle.

No. 6R682 22-caliber rim fire, using 22 long or short cartridge, 24-inch octagon barrel. Weight, 5½ to 6 lbs. Our special price.......$7.50

No. 6R684 32-caliber, rim fire, using long or short rim fire cartridges, 26-inch octagon barrel. Weight, 5¾ to 6 lbs. Price...... 7.50

No. 6R685 32-caliber, center fire, taking 32-20 Winchester central fire cartridge, 26-inch barrel. Price.......... 7.50

No. 6R687 38-caliber, center fire, taking 38-40 Winchester central fire cartridge, 28-inch barrel. Price.......... 7.50

The Famous Kentucky Ballard Rifle for $2.65.

We have secured a limited quantity of these famous Kentucky Ballard Rifles, and while they last we are offering them to our customers for the heretofore unheard of price of $2.65.

$2.65

These rifles have been bought at a forced sale, and were it not for this fact, we would not be able to sell them at less than from $10.00 to $12.00. They are all made from the best of material that money can buy, all parts are made true to gauge, and the barrels are of the finest quality of steel. The stock and fore end are of black walnut. The frame is made of the best drop forging and is case hardened. The barrels are well rifled for accurate shooting, and all the rifles are fitted with a leaf sight for short or long range shooting. **The Kentucky Ballard Rifle** takes a 44-caliber long, rim fire cartridge, and this rifle has always been considered a strong, wicked shooter, as the cartridge contains 28 grains of powder and a 220-grain bullet. We can always furnish ammunition for this rifle. **Why buy a cheap rifle when you can get a rifle worth from $10.00 to $12.00 for the small sum of $2.65?** A rifle that will give you satisfaction in every way for strong shooting, one which has a solid Ballard breech block, and a rifle which will cost you about a fourth of the actual cost of manufacture.

No. 6R690 The Kentucky Ballard Rifle, with 22-inch round barrel; weight, about 7 pounds. Our special price.......... $2.65

No. 6R2364 Price, per box of 50 cartridges for this rifle.......... .60

Stevens' Favorite Rifle, Detachable Barrel, $5.00

STEVENS' ENTIRE LINE will be found in this catalogue at prices lower than can be had from any other house. **OUR PRICES ON STEVENS' RIFLES are for the highest grade tested goods and our prices are based on the actual cost to produce, with but our one small profit added.**

$5.00

THE FAVORITE.

Is guaranteed as well finished and rifled a barrel as found in the most costly rifles. Entirely new model. The barrel is held to stock by a set screw, and easily separated or put together. Rifling and quality of barrel same as the higher cost rifle. **Case hardened frame, walnut stock, finely finished, warranted accurate, all rim fire, the 22-caliber, using long or short, the 25-caliber using 25-caliber Stevens' rim fire and the 32-caliber using 32-caliber long or short rim fire cartridges; 22-inch barrel; weight, 4½ lbs.**

No. 6R706 25-caliber rim fire, with open sights. Our price..$5.00

No. 6R707 32-caliber, with open sights. Our special price....... 5.00

No. 6R708 22-caliber rim fire, with open sights. Our price.... 5.00

Lyman's Combination Rear and Ivory Bead Front Sights may be fitted to the Favorite at $3.25 extra, to pay for sights and fitting.

Stevens' New Pocket Rifle, $7.50 and $8.44.

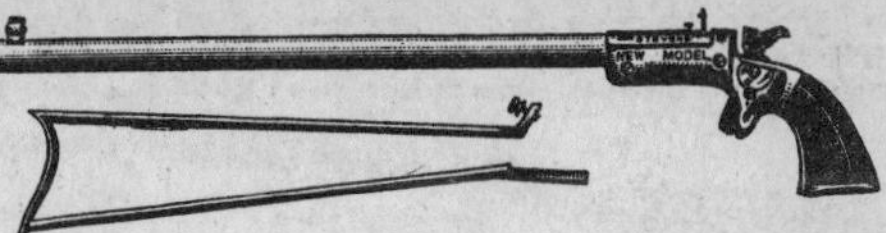

A Fine Target or Squirrel Rifle. Good for 100 yards. Latest model, 22-caliber, rim fire, shoots short cartridge or BB caps.

No. 6R716 12-inch barrel, weight, 2¼ lbs. Our special price.....$7.50

No. 6R717 15-inch barrel, weight, 2½ lbs. Our special price.... 8.44

Stevens' Latest Ideal Rifle, 7 to 7¼ Pounds.

STEVENS IDEAL No44 — **$8.25**

This rifle meets the demand for a reliable and accurate rifle at a moderate price. It is recommended by us and fully guaranteed by the maker. Half octagon barrel, oiled walnut stock and forearm, rifle butt, sporting rear and Rocky Mountain front sights, 7 to 7¼ lbs.

No. 6R718 22-caliber, 24-inch barrel. Weight, 7 pounds. Price.....$8.25
No. 6R719 25-caliber, Stevens rim fire. 24-inch barrel. Price...... 8.25
No. 6R720 25-20-caliber, Stevens center fire, 26-inch barrel. Price.. 8.25
No. 6R721 32-40-caliber, center fire. 26-inch barrel. Price.......... 8.25

Extra length of barrel to special order 75 cents per inch. Lyman's Combination Rear Sight, extra **$2.20.** Lyman's Ivory Bead Front Sight, extra, **70 cents. For fitting sights, extra, 25 cents.**

OUR SPENCER 8-SHOT REPEATING RIFLE FOR ONLY $3.65.

$3.65

25 CARTRIDGES 56-52 CALIBER SPENCER

For $3.65 we offer you the Genuine Spencer 8-shot Repeating Rifle with 25 rounds of ammunition. This rifle could not be manufactured today for three times the price.

We have bought a large lot of these rifles at a forced sale at our own price, and in order to give our customers the benefit of our purchase, we have added our one small percentage of profit to the cost of this rifle, and are able to make you the unheard of price of **$3.65 for this Spencer 8-shot Repeating Rifle,** fitted with graduated leaf sight. The Spencer Repeating Rifle is loaded from the butt plate. Turn the magazine tube to the right, take it out, place seven cartridges in the magazine and one in the chamber, replace the tube and you can shoot eight times without reloading. **This is the lowest price ever made on a repeating rifle.** These rifles shoot the 56-52 caliber rim fire Spencer cartridges, shoot hard and strong, and we would advise you to send your order early as we will be unable to get any more of these rifles at anything like the price after our present stock is sold. The cartridges for this rifle can always be had from us or any first class hardware or gun store. **The Spencer Repeating Rifle** has a fine steel barrel 22 inches long, sound walnut stock, weighs about 8¼ pounds, and the cartridges for this rifle cannot be reloaded. This rifle has a steel frame and is so constructed with a cut off in front of the trigger that you can use it as a repeater or single shot rifle. Turn the cut off a quarter turn and it becomes a single shot rifle instead of a repeater. **Order by number.** Weight, packed in box for shipment, with 25 cartridges about 16 pounds.

No. 6R722 Spencer Repeating Rifle with 25 rounds of ammunition. Our special price.......... $3.65

The Latest New Winchester 22-Caliber Rifle.

$3.75

The New Winchester Single Shot, Model 1900, is the latest creation of the Winchester Repeating Arms Company, and enables us to place upon the market a rifle bearing the name of the Winchester Arms Company, **at the extremely low price of $3.75.** This rifle is made with the same high grade shooting qualities which follow the Winchester rifles all through their line. Each and every rifle is tested and targeted before it leaves the factory, just the same as their higher priced single shot and repeating rifles are. The rifle is guaranteed to shoot as well as any 22-caliber rifle made and is adapted to the 22-short or 22-long rim cartridges. 18-inch round barrel, 12¾-inch stock, 2¾-inch drop and fitted with plain open sights. **This rifle cannot be furnished any other way.** In order to take out the breech block, take the barrel off the stock, press down the extractor with a lead pencil or nail and the breech block immediately comes out through the back of the barrel. The rifle can be taken apart in an instant, so that it can be carried in a trunk or a grip by simply unscrewing the thumbscrew on the fore end.

No. 6R723 Our special price, 18-inch barrel, weight 3 pounds..$3.75

Colt's New Lightning Magazine Rifles.

Manufactured by **Colt's Patent Fire Arms Manufacturing Company,** Hartford, Conn. Constructed upon entirely new principles. The workmanship is of the same high standard as that of other arms manufactured by this company. **The old shell is ejected and new cartridge inserted by a sliding motion of forearm,** and can be done with the left hand. It is convenient and rapid. Every rifle warranted, the **22-caliber are rim fire and half magazine;** using cartridges No. 6R2336 or 6R2338, plain fore end and plain open sights, all others have sporting rear sights, plain fore end and are center-fire with full magazine, using same cartridges as the Winchester rifles of same caliber

No. 6R724 22-caliber, 24-inch octagon barrel, 15-shot, weight 5¾ lbs..$10.20
No. 6R727 32-caliber, 26-inch round barrel, 15-shot, weight 7½ lbs.. 11.50
No. 6R729 38-caliber, 26-inch round barrel, 15-shot, weight 7¼ lbs.. 11.50
No. 6R730 38-caliber, 26-inch octagon barrel, 15-shot, weight 7¼ lbs.. 12.50
No. 6R731 44-caliber, 26-inch round barrel, 15-shot, weight 7¼ lbs.. 11.50
No. 6R732 44-caliber, 26-inch octagon barrel, 15-shot, weight 7¼ lbs.. 12.50

TESTING RIFLES FOR ACCURACY.

When testing rifles for accuracy, sit down while firing, and rest the muzzle, securing a solid rest for the arms and body. In this way, extreme accuracy can be obtained suitable for testing the rifle. Do not, in any case, attempt to get accuracy by screwing the rifle in a vise. No reliable results can be obtained in that way, and even an accurate rifle will shoot wild.

Always keep the barrel cleaned and oiled when not in use. This prevents pitting in the bore of the rifle.

MARLIN REPEATING RIFLES.

ALL ARMS OF THIS MAKE have solid top frames and eject at the side. The solid top keeps out rain, snow, twigs, pine needles, alkali, dust, sand, etc., and protects the head of the shooter from any accident. The side ejection is much more convenient than the old fashioned systems that throw the shell into your face, fill your nostrils and eyes with smoke and gas and generally interferes with a quick second or third shot. All barrels are exactly the same as Ballard Target Rifle Barrels, made by the Marlin Co. and

SO LONG RECOGNIZED AS THE STANDARD OF ACCURACY THROUGHOUT THE WORLD.

THE MARLIN RIFLE, TAKE DOWN MODEL 1897.

$12.10 AND $13.50

FOR EXTRAS SEE BELOW.

The New Marlin Model '97, Take Down Rifle, is the latest 22-caliber arm on the market. This rifle is practically the model '92 with the addition of the "take down" feature and many other valuable improvements. It has a finely tapered barrel and a neat rubber butt plate; the receiver is made of special steel, used in the high power smokeless rifles, and is finely case hardened. This rifle is very easily cleaned; by simply removing the side plate (by use of the thumbscrew for the purpose) makes ready access to the inside of this rifle. It comes in 22-caliber only, **shooting either the short, long or long rifle cartridges.**

No. 6R734 Octagon barrel, 24-inch, weight, 5¾ lbs. Price.....**$13.50**
No. 6R735 Round barrel, 24-inch, weight, 5½ lbs. Price..... **12.10**

THE NEW MARLIN REPEATING RIFLES. MODEL 1892.

ILLUSTRATION SHOWS ROUND BARREL.

...22-CALIBER RIM FIRE.
...32-CALIBER RIM FIRE...
32-CALIBER CENTER FIRE...

The Model 1892 Rifles have BLUED FRAMES.

MODEL 1892.
Illustration shows rifle with plate off, showing interior of works.

In one and the same rifle, without adjusting, may be used any or all of the following rim fire cartridges: 22-short, 22-long, and 22-long rifle. This is the only repeater that will do this. Other systems require two or three rifles to do the same work. 22-short cartridges are accurate up to 100 feet, 22-long up to 150 feet, 22-long rifle up to 600 feet. The Marlin is the only repeater using the long rifle cartridge, and is guaranteed to shoot any of these cartridges as accurately as any arms made. **This model takes entirely to pieces without tools,** allowing of perfect cleaning.

No. 6R740 Octagon barrel, 22-caliber, 24-inch, 6 pounds. The magazine holds 25 short 22-caliber cartridges, 20 long 22-caliber cartridges or 18 long rifle 22-caliber cartridges...**$11.25**
No. 6R741 Round barrel, 22-caliber, 24-inch barrels, 6 pounds **10.40**
No. 6R742 Octagon barrel, 32-caliber, 24-inch. The magazine holds 18 short or 15 long cartridges, 6¼ pounds..................... **11.25**
No. 6R743 Round barrel, 32-caliber, 24-inch barrel, 6¼ lbs.... **10.40**

All 32-caliber rifles sent out with two firing pins. This rifle is so made that in the same rifle may be used 32-short rim fire, 32-long rim cartridges, and by changing the firing pin 32-short center fire and 32-long center fire. This ammunition is cheap, and as compared to repeaters using the 32-20 cartridge will save the entire cost of the rifle on first 2,000 cartridges. The ammunition is what costs. Get the only repeater made for these cheap cartridges. **FOR EXTRAS SEE BELOW.**

TAKE DOWN RIFLES IN ANY OF THE ABOVE CALIBERS MADE TO SPECIAL ORDER, EXTRA, $3.50. FOR FITTING LYMAN SIGHTS ALLOW 25 CENTS EXTRA.

THE NEW MARLIN SAFETY REPEATING RIFLES. MODEL 1894.

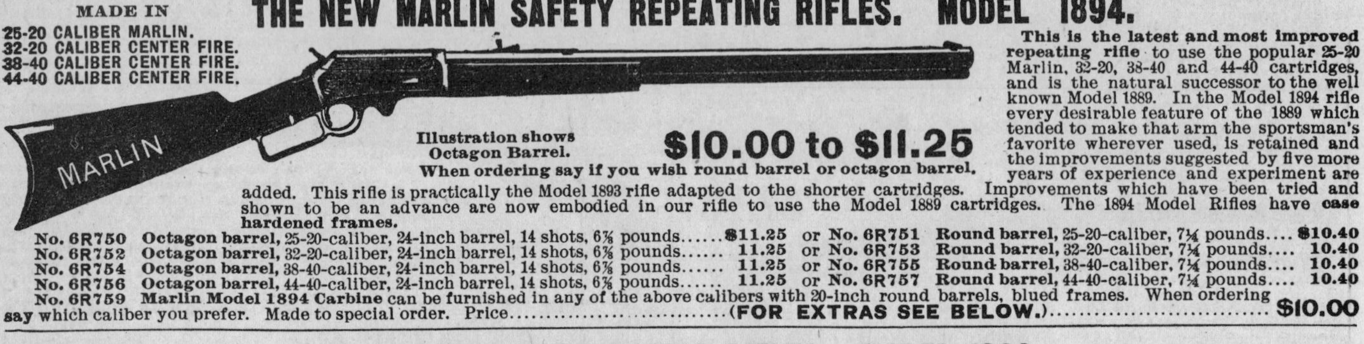

MADE IN
25-20 CALIBER MARLIN.
32-20 CALIBER CENTER FIRE.
38-40 CALIBER CENTER FIRE.
44-40 CALIBER CENTER FIRE.

Illustration shows Octagon Barrel.

$10.00 to $11.25

When ordering say if you wish round barrel or octagon barrel.

This is the latest and most improved repeating rifle to use the popular 25-20 Marlin, 32-20, 38-40 and 44-40 cartridges, and is the natural successor to the well known Model 1889. In the Model 1894 rifle every desirable feature of the 1889 which tended to make that arm the sportsman's favorite wherever used, is retained and the improvements suggested by five more years of experience and experiment are added. This rifle is practically the Model 1893 rifle adapted to the shorter cartridges. Improvements which have been tried and shown to be an advance are now embodied in our rifle to use the Model 1889 cartridges. The 1894 Model Rifles have **case hardened frames.**

No. 6R750 Octagon barrel, 25-20-caliber, 24-inch barrel, 14 shots, 6¾ pounds......**$11.25** or **No. 6R751** Round barrel, 25-20-caliber, 7¼ pounds.... **$10.40**
No. 6R752 Octagon barrel, 32-20-caliber, 24-inch barrel, 14 shots, 6¾ pounds...... **11.25** or **No. 6R753** Round barrel, 32-20-caliber, 7¼ pounds.... **10.40**
No. 6R754 Octagon barrel, 38-40-caliber, 24-inch barrel, 14 shots, 6¾ pounds...... **11.25** or **No. 6R755** Round barrel, 38-40-caliber, 7¼ pounds.... **10.40**
No. 6R756 Octagon barrel, 44-40-caliber, 24-inch barrel, 14 shots, 6¾ pounds...... **11.25** or **No. 6R757** Round barrel, 44-40-caliber, 7¼ pounds.... **10.40**
No. 6R759 Marlin Model 1894 Carbine can be furnished in any of the above calibers with 20-inch round barrels, blued frames. When ordering say which caliber you prefer. Made to special order. Price..............................**(FOR EXTRAS SEE BELOW.)**.................................. **$10.00**

THE NEW MARLIN REPEATING RIFLES. MODEL 1893.

MADE IN
32-40 CALIBER.
38-55 CALIBER.
25-36 CALIBER.
30-30 CALIBER.

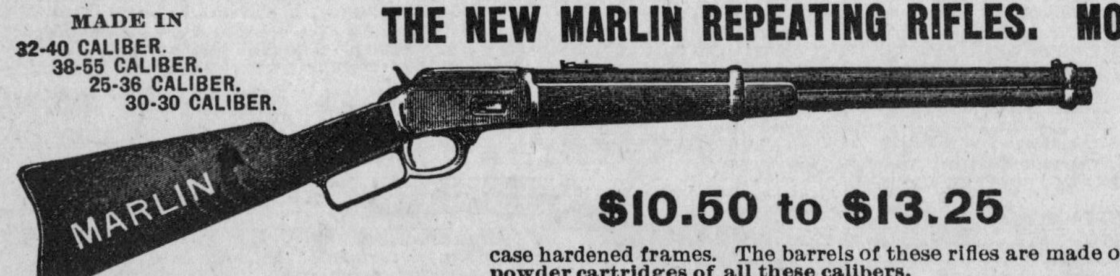

$10.50 to $13.25

This model is similar in principle to the 1894 Model, and is made in response to the many demands for a rifle in 25-36, 30-30, 32-40 and 38-55 calibers. It is the only repeater on the market using 25-36 caliber cartridges. These rifles have exactly the same barrels as were used in the famous Ballards. The standard length of barrel is 26 inches, and a rifle with octagon barrels of this length weighs about 7½ pounds. This weight, we believe, will be found about right for hunting purposes. All rifles of this model have case hardened frames. The barrels of these rifles are made of special smokeless steel. **We can furnish smokeless powder cartridges of all these calibers.**

No. 6R760 Octagon barrel, 25-36 Marlin, 26-inch, 7¾ lbs., 10 shots. **$13.25**
No. 6R761 Round barrel, 25-36 Marlin, 26-inch, 8 lbs., 10 shots.. **12.75**
No. 6R762 Octagon barrel, 32-40 Marlin, 26-inch, 7¾ lbs., 10 shots.. **11.70**
No. 6R763 Round barrel, 32-40 Marlin, 26-inch, 8 lbs., 10 shots.. **10.85**
No. 6R764 Octagon barrel, 38-55 Marlin, 26-inch, 7¾ lbs., 10 shots.. **11.70**
No. 6R765 Round barrel, 38-55 Marlin, 26-inch, 8 lbs., 10 shots.. **10.85**
No. 6R766 Octagon barrel, 30-30 Smokeless Marlin, 26-inch, 7¾ lbs., 10 shots... **13.25**

No. 6R767 Round barrel, 30-30 Smokeless Marlin, 26-inch, 8 lbs., 10 shots.. **$12.75**

Extras of all kinds of this model, except set triggers.

No. 6R768 CARBINES. Marlin, 32-40 or 38-55-caliber, 20-inch, round barrel, 7 shots, 6¾ lbs. Made to special order. State caliber... **10.50**
No. 6R769 Carbine, 30-30 Smokeless (nickel steel) 20-inch, round barrel, 7 shots, 6¾ lbs. Made to special order. State caliber... **12.00**

EXTRAS. **The following come under the head of extras and when any of these features are added to Marlin rifles they cost extra as follows:**

On Models	1892	1893	1894	1895	1897
Selected straight grip stock and fore end....	$4.25	$4.25	$4.25	$4.25	$4.25
Selected straight grip stock and fore end, checkered........................	6.50	6.50	6.50	6.50	6.75
Selected pistol grip stock and fore end..........	6.50	6.50	6.50	6.50	6.75
Selected pistol grip stock and fore end, checkered......................	9.75	9.75	9.75	9.75	9.75
Extra selected pistol grip stock and fore end, checkered and extra finished..............	12.75	12.75	12.75	12.75	12.75
Plain walnut pistol grip stock and fore end, checkered................................	$3.75	$3.75	$3.75	$3.75	$3.75
Matting barrels..	3.75	3.75	3.75	3.75	3.75
Shortening or lengthening butt stock or changing drop.....	6.50	6.50	6.50	6.50	6.50
Leaving off rear sight slot..........................	1.00	1.00	1.00	1.00	1.00
Extra length of barrel for every 2 inches.	1.50	1.50	1.50	1.50	1.50

Engraving from $5.00 up, according to quality and style.
For fitting Lyman Sights on any of the above rifles, 25 cents extra.
SET TRIGGERS CANNOT BE FURNISHED ON MARLIN RIFLES.

WE MAKE NO EXTRA CHARGE FOR BOXING RIFLES AND GUNS. SOME HOUSES DO.

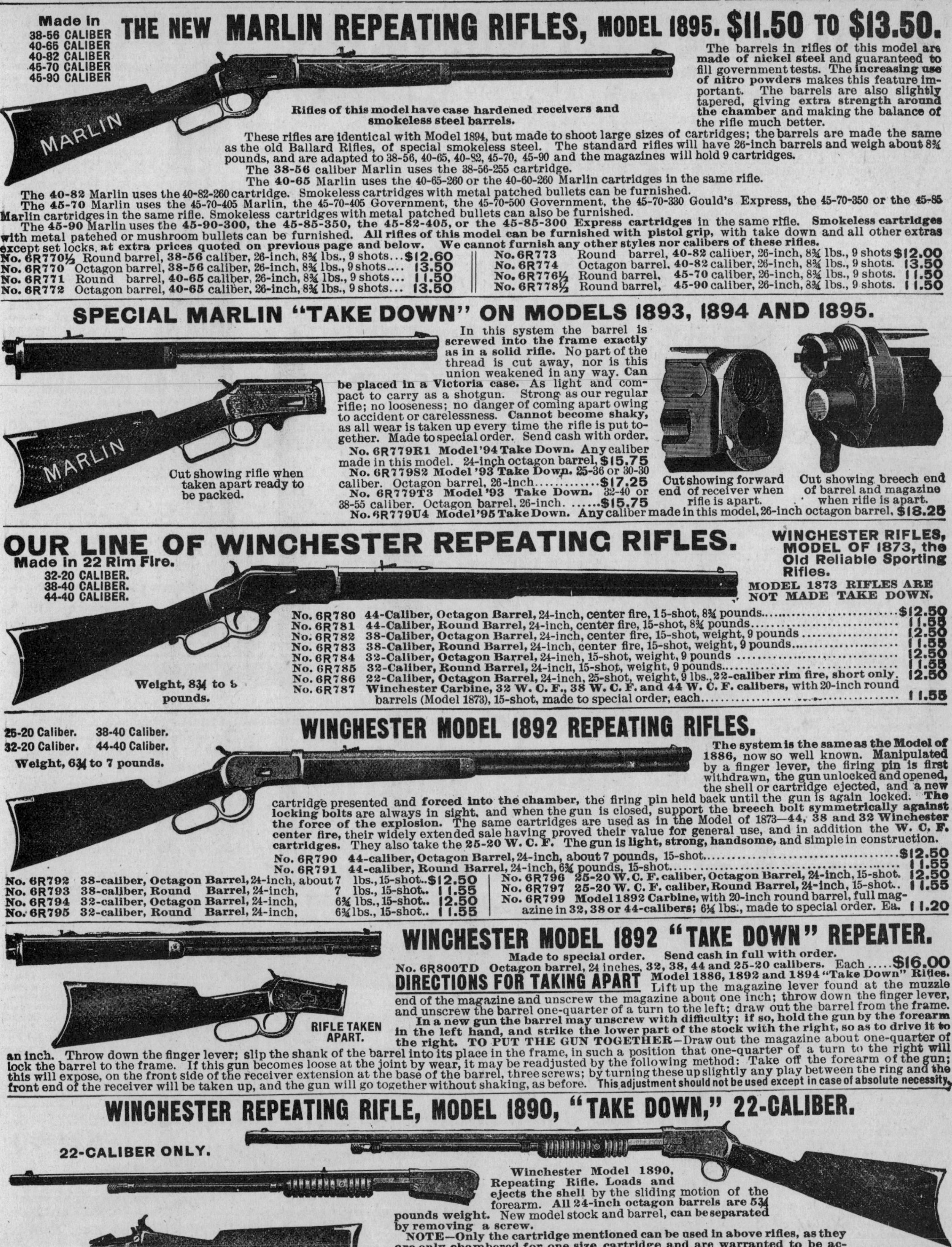

THE NEW MARLIN REPEATING RIFLES, MODEL 1895. $11.50 TO $13.50.

Made in
38-56 CALIBER
40-65 CALIBER
40-82 CALIBER
45-70 CALIBER
45-90 CALIBER

Rifles of this model have case hardened receivers and smokeless steel barrels.

The barrels in rifles of this model are made of nickel steel and guaranteed to fill government tests. The increasing use of nitro powders makes this feature important. The barrels are also slightly tapered, giving extra strength around the chamber and making the balance of the rifle much better.

These rifles are identical with Model 1894, but made to shoot large sizes of cartridges; the barrels are made the same as the old Ballard Rifles, of special smokeless steel. The standard rifles will have 26-inch barrels and weigh about 8¾ pounds, and are adapted to 38-56, 40-65, 40-82, 45-70, 45-90 and the magazines will hold 9 cartridges.

The 38-56 caliber Marlin uses the 38-56-255 cartridge.

The 40-65 Marlin uses the 40-65-260 or the 40-60-260 Marlin cartridges in the same rifle.

The 40-82 Marlin uses the 40-82-260 cartridge. Smokeless cartridges with metal patched bullets can be furnished.

The 45-70 Marlin uses the 45-70-405 Marlin, the 45-70-405 Government, the 45-70-500 Government, the 45-70-330 Gould's Express, the 45-70-350 or the 45-85 Marlin cartridges in the same rifle. Smokeless cartridges with metal patched bullets can also be furnished.

The 45-90 Marlin uses the 45-90-300, the 45-85-350, the 45-82-405, or the 45-85-300 Express cartridges in the same rifle. Smokeless cartridges with metal patched or mushroom bullets can be furnished. All rifles of this model can be furnished with pistol grip, with take down and all other extras except set locks, at extra prices quoted on previous page and below. We cannot furnish any other styles nor calibers of these rifles.

No. 6R770½ Round barrel, 38-56 caliber, 26-inch, 8¾ lbs., 9 shots... $12.60
No. 6R770 Octagon barrel, 38-56 caliber, 26-inch, 8¾ lbs., 9 shots... 13.50
No. 6R771 Round barrel, 40-65 caliber, 26-inch, 8¾ lbs., 9 shots... 11.50
No. 6R772 Octagon barrel, 40-65 caliber, 26-inch, 8¾ lbs., 9 shots... 13.50
No. 6R773 Round barrel, 40-82 caliber, 26-inch, 8¾ lbs., 9 shots $12.00
No. 6R774 Octagon barrel, 40-82 caliber, 26-inch, 8¾ lbs., 9 shots. 13.50
No. 6R776½ Round barrel, 45-70 caliber, 26-inch, 8¾ lbs., 9 shots. 11.50
No. 6R778½ Round barrel, 45-90 caliber, 26-inch, 8¾ lbs., 9 shots. 11.50

SPECIAL MARLIN "TAKE DOWN" ON MODELS 1893, 1894 AND 1895.

Cut showing rifle when taken apart ready to be packed.

In this system the barrel is screwed into the frame exactly as in a solid rifle. No part of the thread is cut away, nor is this union weakened in any way. Can be placed in a Victoria case. As light and compact to carry as a shotgun. Strong as our regular rifle; no looseness; no danger of coming apart owing to accident or carelessness. Cannot become shaky, as all wear is taken up every time the rifle is put together. Made to special order. Send cash with order.

No. 6R779R1 Model '94 Take Down. Any caliber made in this model. 24-inch octagon barrel, $15.75

No. 6R779S2 Model '93 Take Down. 25-36 or 30-30 caliber. Octagon barrel, 26-inch............ $17.25

No. 6R779T3 Model '93 Take Down. 32-40 or 38-55 caliber. Octagon barrel, 26-inch. $15.75

Cut showing forward end of receiver when rifle is apart.

Cut showing breech end of barrel and magazine when rifle is apart.

No. 6R779U4 Model '95 Take Down. Any caliber made in this model, 26-inch octagon barrel, $18.25

OUR LINE OF WINCHESTER REPEATING RIFLES.

Made in 22 Rim Fire.
32-20 CALIBER.
38-40 CALIBER.
44-40 CALIBER.

WINCHESTER RIFLES, MODEL OF 1873, the Old Reliable Sporting Rifles.

MODEL 1873 RIFLES ARE NOT MADE TAKE DOWN.

Weight, 8¾ to 9 pounds.

No. 6R780 44-Caliber, Octagon Barrel, 24-inch, center fire, 15-shot, 8¾ pounds........ $12.50
No. 6R781 44-Caliber, Round Barrel, 24-inch, center fire, 15-shot, 8¾ pounds........ 11.55
No. 6R782 38-Caliber, Octagon Barrel, 24-inch, center fire, 15-shot, weight, 9 pounds........ 12.50
No. 6R783 38-Caliber, Round Barrel, 24-inch, center fire, 15-shot, weight, 9 pounds........ 11.55
No. 6R784 32-Caliber, Octagon Barrel, 24-inch, 15-shot, weight, 9 pounds........ 12.50
No. 6R785 32-Caliber, Round Barrel, 24-inch, 15-shot, weight, 9 pounds........ 11.55
No. 6R786 22-Caliber, Octagon Barrel, 24-inch, 25-shot, weight, 9 lbs., 22-caliber rim fire, short only. 12.50
No. 6R787 Winchester Carbine, 32 W. C. F., 38 W. C. F. and 44 W. C. F. calibers, with 20-inch round barrels (Model 1873), 15-shot, made to special order, each........ 11.55

WINCHESTER MODEL 1892 REPEATING RIFLES.

25-20 Caliber. 38-40 Caliber.
32-20 Caliber. 44-40 Caliber.
Weight, 6¾ to 7 pounds.

The system is the same as the Model of 1886, now so well known. Manipulated by a finger lever, the firing pin is first withdrawn, the gun unlocked and opened, the shell or cartridge ejected, and a new cartridge presented and forced into the chamber, the firing pin held back until the gun is again locked. The locking bolts are always in sight, and when the gun is closed, support the breech bolt symmetrically against the force of the explosion. The same cartridges are used as in the Model of 1873—44, 38 and 32 Winchester center fire, their widely extended sale having proved their value for general use, and in addition the W. C. F. cartridges. They also take the 25-20 W. C. F. The gun is light, strong, handsome, and simple in construction.

No. 6R790 44-caliber, Octagon Barrel, 24-inch, about 7 pounds, 15-shot........ $12.50
No. 6R791 44-caliber, Round Barrel, 24-inch, 6¾ pounds, 15-shot........ 11.55
No. 6R792 38-caliber, Octagon Barrel, 24-inch, about 7 lbs., 15-shot.. $12.50
No. 6R793 38-caliber, Round Barrel, 24-inch, 7 lbs., 15-shot.. 11.55
No. 6R794 32-caliber, Octagon Barrel, 24-inch, 6¾ lbs., 15-shot.. 12.50
No. 6R795 32-caliber, Round Barrel, 24-inch, 6¾ lbs., 15-shot.. 11.55
No. 6R796 25-20 W. C. F. caliber, Octagon Barrel, 24-inch, 15-shot. 12.50
No. 6R797 25-20 W. C. F. caliber, Round Barrel, 24-inch, 15-shot.. 11.55
No. 6R799 Model 1892 Carbine, with 20-inch round barrel, full magazine in 32, 38 or 44-calibers; 6¼ lbs., made to special order. Ea. 11.20

WINCHESTER MODEL 1892 "TAKE DOWN" REPEATER.

RIFLE TAKEN APART.

Made to special order. Send cash in full with order.

No. 6R800TD Octagon barrel, 24 inches, 32, 38, 44 and 25-20 calibers. Each..... $16.00

DIRECTIONS FOR TAKING APART

Model 1886, 1892 and 1894 "Take Down" Rifles. Lift up the magazine lever found at the muzzle end of the magazine and unscrew the magazine about one inch; throw down the finger lever, and unscrew the barrel one-quarter of a turn to the left; draw out the barrel from the frame. In a new gun the barrel may unscrew with difficulty; if so, hold the gun by the forearm in the left hand, and strike the lower part of the stock with the right, so as to drive it to the right. TO PUT THE GUN TOGETHER—Draw out the magazine about one-quarter of an inch. Throw down the finger lever; slip the shank of the barrel into its place in the frame, in such a position that one-quarter of a turn to the right will lock the barrel to the frame. If this gun becomes loose at the joint by wear, it may be readjusted by the following method: Take off the forearm of the gun; this will expose, on the front side of the receiver extension at the base of the barrel, three screws; by turning these up slightly any play between the ring and the front end of the receiver will be taken up, and the gun will go together without shaking, as before. This adjustment should not be used except in case of absolute necessity.

WINCHESTER REPEATING RIFLE, MODEL 1890, "TAKE DOWN," 22-CALIBER.

22-CALIBER ONLY.

Winchester Model 1890, Repeating Rifle. Loads and ejects the shell by the sliding motion of the forearm. All 24-inch octagon barrels are 5¾ pounds weight. New model stock and barrel, can be separated by removing a screw.

NOTE—Only the cartridge mentioned can be used in above rifles, as they are only chambered for one size cartridge and are warranted to be accurate and reliable.

RIFLE TAKEN APART.

No. 6R804 For 22-caliber, rim fire, short only, 15-shot, octagon barrel. Our special price $10.25
No. 6R806 For 22-caliber, rim fire, long only, 12-shot, octagon barrel. Our special price. 10.25
No. 6R808 For 22-caliber, rim fire, special Winchester cartridges, No. 6R2344, octagon barrel. 10-shot. Our special price........ 10.25

For fitting Lyman Sights on any of the above rifles, 25 cents extra. We box and pack guns free of cost to you. Some houses charge extra for this.

WINCHESTER SINGLE SHOT RIFLES.

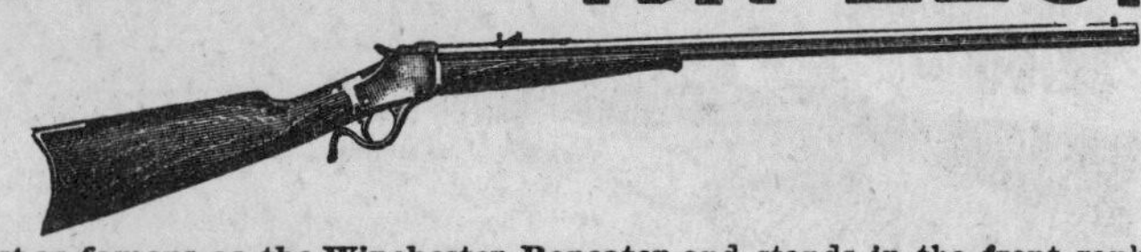

THE WINCHESTER RIFLES HAVE AN ESTABLISHED REPUTATION.

THE BEST EVERYWHERE.

OUR LINE OF WINCHESTER GOODS IS VERY COMPLETE AND LOWER PRICES CANNOT BE FOUND ANYWHERE.

ALTHOUGH THIS RIFLE IS A RECENT PRODUCTION, it has become almost as famous as the Winchester Repeater and stands in the front rank with the very best target rifles of this and other countries. This gun has the old Sharp's breech block and lever, and is as safe and solid as a Sharp's. The hammer is centrally hung, but drops down with the breech block when the gun is opened, and is cocked by the closing movement. It can also be cocked by hand. This arrangement allows the barrel to be wiped and examined from the breech. In our line everything has been done to make the gun pleasing to the eye. All of these guns have case hardened lock plates and dark walnut stock. Other styles and calibers made to special order. Every rifle warranted perfect and accurate. The double set locks are adjustable by a little screw in rear of trigger, and can be set to pull as desired or not used at all. Pushing the rear trigger forward places it in the hair pull notch, same as working a double trigger. All rifles have sporting rear sights.

No.	Barrel	Weight	Trigger	Caliber	Price	No.	Barrel	Weight	Trigger	Caliber	Price
6R810	Octagon, 24-in.	7 lbs.	Plain	22-long or 22-long rifle rim....	$10.69	6R819	Octagon, 30-in.	9 lbs.	Plain	38-55 Marlin central fire......	$10.69
6R811	Octagon, 26-in.	7 lbs.	Plain	22-long or 22-long rifle rim....	11.40	6R820	Octagon, 30-in.	9 lbs.	Set	38-55 Marlin central fire.....	12.13
6R812	Octagon, 26-in.	7 lbs.	Plain	32-rim, short or long..........	10.69	6R821	Octagon, 30-in.	9½ lbs.	Plain	40-60 Winchester central fire.	10.69
6R813	Octagon, 26-in.	7 lbs.	Plain	22-Winchester central fire...	10.69	6R824	Octagon, 30-in.	9½ lbs.	Plain	45-70 Winchester central fire.	10.69
6R814	Octagon, 28-in.	7 lbs.	Plain	25-20 Winchester single shot..	10.69	6R825	Octagon, 30-in.	9½ lbs.	Plain	40-65 Winchester central fire.	10.69
6R815	Octagon, 28-in.	7 lbs.	Plain	32-20 Winchester central fire.	10.69	6R826	Octagon, 26-in.	9½ lbs.	Plain	45-90 Winch'r C. F., model '86	10.69
6R816	Octagon, 30-in.	9 lbs.	Plain	32-40 Marlin central fire......	10.69	6R828	Special Round 30-in.	9 lbs.	Plain	30 U. S. Army Smokeless......	14.25
6R818	Octagon, 28-in.	8½ lbs.	Plain	38-40 Winchester central fire..	10.69						

Any additional changes from the above styles will have to be made to order and cause a delay of from one to four weeks.

WINCHESTER RIFLES, MODEL 1894. 32-40, 38-55, ALSO THE NEW 30-30 CALIBER AND 25-35 CALIBERS.

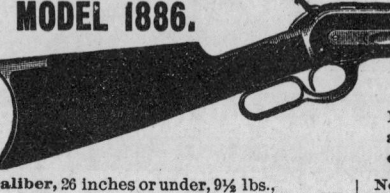

No. 6R830 Octagon barrel, 32-40-caliber, 26-inch, 10-shot, 7½ pounds....$12.50

No. 6R831 32-40-caliber, Round barrel, 26-inch, 10-shot, 7¼ pounds.......... 11.55

No. 6R832 38-55-caliber, Octagon barrel, 26-inch, 10-shot, 7½ pounds.......... 12.50

No. 6R833 Round barrel, 38-55-caliber, 26-inch, 10-shot, 7¼ pounds.......... 11.55

No. 6R836 Octagon or round barrel, 30-caliber Winchester smokeless cartridges, 26-inch, 10-shot, 7¾ pounds 14.75

No. 6R838 Octagon or round barrel, 25-35 Winchester smokeless cartridges, 26-inch, 10-shot, 7¾ pounds..... 14.75

NOTICE. For Take Down Rifle, Model 1894, add $3.50 to above prices in any caliber. These are made to special order. Be sure to say which style barrel you wish.

EXTRAS ON RIFLES.

All deviations from standard styles and sizes involve a large proportional outlay for hand labor, and when ordered will be subject to the following charges.
For additional length of barrel and magazine, add to price 75 cents per inch; and on model 1886, add $1.00 per inch.
Extra for single set triggers on model 1873, $2.00.
Extra for plain walnut pistol grip stock not checkered, $2.50.
Extra for fancy walnut pistol grip stock and fore end checkered, $12.00.
Extra for Sling straps and swivels, $1.50 per set.

FOR FITTING LYMAN SIGHTS ON ANY OF THE ABOVE RIFLES, 25 CENTS EXTRA.

WINCHESTER RIFLES. MODEL 1886.

Model . . . 1886.
Weighs 9 to 9½ pounds.

This is an illustration of Winchester Rifles Nos. 6R850 to 6R865, and NOT FURNISHED Take Down at prices quoted. For Take Down in any of the following calibers add $3.90 to round barrel and $2.90 to octagon barrel rifles; these are made to special order.

No. 6R850 Octagon Barrel, 40-82-caliber, 26 inches or under, 9½ lbs., 260-grain bullet, 8-shot.......... $14.97

No. 6R852 Octagon Barrel, 45-70-caliber, 26 inches or under, 9¼ lbs., 405-grain bullet, using a regular government cartridge, 8-shot.. .... 14.97

No. 6R853 Round Barrel, 45-70-caliber, 26 inches or under, 9 lbs..... 13.90

No. 6R856 Octagon Barrel, 38-56-caliber, 26 inches, 9½ lbs., 9-shot.. 14.97

No. 6R858 Octagon Barrel, 40-65-260-caliber, 26 in., 9½ lbs., 9-shot. $14.97

No. 6R865 Model 1886, Carbine can be furnished 22 inches, round barrel, in any of the above calibers to special order at.......... 13.55

NOTICE—The standard length of barrel will be 26 inches. Guns taking the 45-70 cartridge will have the sporting leaf sight, and all others the sporting rear sight. Each rifle will be accompanied by a cleaning rod free. Set triggers, made to special order, $2.25 extra.

THE WINCHESTER BOX MAGAZINE SPORTING RIFLE. MODEL 1895.

30-Caliber Army. 5 Shots.

This is the Gun that Shoots Two Miles.

Velocity, 2,400 Feet Per Second.

THE WINCHESTER BOX MAGAZINE SPORTING RIFLE is the first Box Magazine Lever Action gun put on the market, and is one of the strongest shooting guns ever invented. The velocity of a bullet fired from this rifle is 2,400 feet per second. The penetration of this gun is demonstrated by a trial at the factory, at which place the rifle shot through fifty-eight pine boards, ⅞-inch each. It is light in weight, handsome, safe, swift and sure. The moving parts are few and strong. It carries five shots in the magazine. The disposition of the magazine and parts is such that the gun can be readily used as a single loader, keeping the loads in the magazine in reserve. This gun is adapted to smokeless cartridges only, and will shoot either the steel jacketed or soft point bullets. The soft point gives the best satisfaction for large game shooting. The barrel of the 30-caliber army is of nickel steel, and comes only in 28-inch, and only round barrels can be furnished.

No. 6R877 30-caliber army, 28-inch round barrel. This rifle will shoot a metal patched bullet through 58 pine boards ⅞-inch thick. Our price, $17.82

FOR FITTING LYMAN SIGHTS ON ANY OF THE MODEL 1895 RIFLES, 50 CENTS EXTRA.

Any additional changes from the above styles will have to be made to order and cause a delay of from one to four weeks.

SAVAGE HAMMERLESS REPEATING RIFLES.

$21.50

The Savage is a hammerless rifle made on scientific principles and is one of the most powerful shooting rifles yet produced. A steel boiler plate ⅜-inch thick has been perforated by a bullet—caliber .303—fired from a Savage rifle at a distance of thirty feet and it will penetrate 35 pine boards ⅞-inch thick.

VELOCITY 2,000 FEET PER SECOND.

Powerful Shooters.

.303 FOR SAVAGE RIFLE SMOKELESS

No. 6R882 Savage Hammerless Repeating Rifle. Simple in construction, light in weight. Ejects shells from side. Length of barrel, 26 inches; weight, 8 pounds. Magazine holds five cartridges. Velocity, 2,000 feet per second. Our special price, with octagon barrel.......... $21.50

No. 6R883 Savage Repeating Rifle, for 30-30 caliber smokeless cartridges. 26-inch octagon barrels. Weight, about 8 pounds. Price.......... 21.50

WE BOX and EXAMINE ALL GUNS CAREFULLY BEFORE SHIPPING AND GUARANTEE SATISFACTION.
WE CHARGE YOU NOTHING FOR BOXING RIFLES FOR SHIPMENT—SOME HOUSES DO.

OUR 50-CALIBER SPRINGFIELD GOVERNMENT BREECH LOADING RIFLE, $2.90

WITH LEAF SIGHT AND 20 ROUNDS OF AMMUNITION

$2.90

FOR $2.90 we offer you this Genuine Springfield Government Breech Loading Rifle with 20 rounds of ammunition for each rifle. This rifle cost originally from $12.00 to $14.00 to produce. They were made by the United States Government and bear the Government Stamp. At a forced sale we bought a large lot of these for cash, and are able to offer you one of the best made rifles possible for only $2.90. These are the Genuine Springfield Breech Loading Rifles taking the 50-70 Caliber Government Center Fire Cartridges, and any of our customers who have been in the Civil War will know that there are no better rifles made at any price, for these are the same rifles that were used in our Civil War.

These Genuine Springfield Rifles have 36-inch steel barrels; the empty shell is thrown out when you open the breech block, ready for a new cartridge; they are fitted with sling swivels; the very best quality walnut stock; have the finest quality steel barrels; can be had with or without bayonets at the same price in case some of our customers wish to use them for G. A. R. purposes; will kill all kinds of game, and our special $2.90 price is within the reach of everybody. You cannot afford to be without a rifle at this price, and we would advise you to send your order early as we anticipate a heavy sale on these rifles and cannot get any more after these are sold. **Order by number.**

No. 6R885 Our Springfield Breech Loading Rifle, with 20 rounds of ammunition........................ **$2.90**
Weight, packed in a box ready for shipment, about 18 pounds.

No. 6R4294½ Loading Tools for this rifle, 50-70 caliber. Per set........................ **$2.10**
We charge you nothing for boxing and packing rifles. Some houses do.

RUSTED AND DAMAGED GUNS AND RIFLES. **Do not return to us a gun, revolver or rifle which is rusted, pitted or has the finish worn off, for we have no way of selling these guns.** If you have a gun, revolver or rifle which needs repairing, first write us, fully describing the article and what is broken and we may be able to send you the part necessary, thus saving the express charges on the gun both ways.

30-30-160 Winchester | 30-30-160 Winchester

This illustration shows bullet
BEFORE SHOOTING | AFTER SHOOTING

...A FEW WORDS ABOUT RIFLES AND RANGES OF CARTRIDGES...

Our customers frequently ask us: What is the range of such and such cartridge? This is a difficult question to answer, because some may mean the range to kill game and others may mean the flight of the bullet. The killing range would depend upon what kind of game you wish to kill and where the bullet hits the game. In former years, hunters used large caliber rifles, such as 45-70, 40-82, 50-70, etc., for deer and other large game. At the present time they use small caliber rifles and smokeless cartridges, and get the same results. For instance, the **30-30 Marlin** and **30-30 Winchester** cartridges with soft point bullets, as shown in the cut, are effective and accurate up to 1,500 and 2,000 yards. The **25-35** and **25-36 smokeless cartridges** are effective up to 1,000 or 1,200 yards, while the **30-caliber Army** is accurate up to 2,000 yards. It is difficult to see any game at 500 yards, and a man becomes invisible at 1,000 to 1,500 yards. **For hunting purposes we recommend soft point bullets in smokeless cartridges, as the point expands on hitting the game.** Full metal patched bullets are liable to go right through the game and they do not produce the shock that soft point bullets do. All governments are beginning to use full metal patched bullets in war, as they do not tear or shatter the bones of a man when hit, but disable him, unless he is struck in a vital place. **It must be remembered that when a bullet leaves the rifle, it revolves in its flight, and it really bores a hole through the object.**

BLACK POWDER CARTRIDGES. **RIM FIRE—22-caliber short, are accurate to 35 yards; 22-caliber long, to 50 yards, and 22-caliber long rifles, to 200 yards in good rifles. CENTRAL FIRE—32-20, 32-40, 38-40, 44-40, etc., are accurate and good for 200 to 500 yards. 38-56, 32-40, 38-55, etc., are good for 300 to 600 yards, and 25-35, 30-30, 45-70 government and 50-70 government, are good for 1,000 yards.**

NOTICE—WHEN ORDERING SIGHTS, GIVE NAME AND NUMBER AND CALIBER OF RIFLE.

...LYMAN SIGHTS...

In ordering sights be sure to state the kind of rifle, also the model and caliber in order to insure a perfect fit.

The above cut shows how game appears to the hunter when using the Lyman Patent Combination Rear Sight. It resembles a ring or hoop and the object is that it is not necessary to get a real fine sight, as is the case with open sights, in order to get the game. When the game is seen in the ring or hoop you generally get it.

Lyman's Patent Combination No. 1 Rear Sights.

No. 6R1005 Lyman's Patent Combination Rear Sight. Anyone can attach it to the tang of the rifle in a few minutes with the assistance of a screwdriver. When ordering, state the name of your rifle, also the caliber and model of same, as these sights are made to fit each particular model and caliber of rifle. In other words, one sight will not do for any rifle, but we furnish them for nearly all styles of rifles on the market. Our special price........................ **$2.20**
Extra for fitting sight to rifle........................ **.25**
If by mail, postage extra, 6 cents.

No. 6R1007 No. 21 Receiver Sight, for use only on the models 1886 and 1895 Winchester and the models 1893 and 1895 Marlin. Intended for rifles having long firing bolts, which prevents the use of No. 6R1005 sight. Price........................ **$2.75**
For fitting this sight to rifle we make an extra charge of 50 cts.

Patent Ivory Front Sights.

No. 6R1008 No. 26, Patent Ivory Front Sight, to be used only with No. 6R1007 and will fit only model 1895 Winchester Rifles. It will not fit any other rifle. Price....... **45c**

No. 6R1009 No. 20, Ivory Bead Jack Front Sight, for quick shooting. Good for shooting when the light is poor. Price.............. **70c**

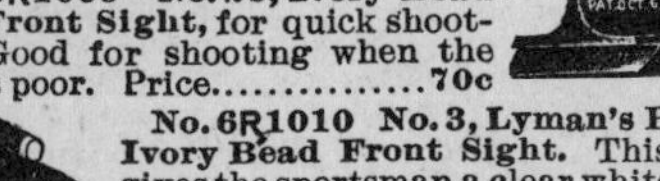

No. 6R1010 No. 3, Lyman's Patent Ivory Bead Front Sight. This sight gives the sportsman a clear white bead which can be seen distinctly against any object in the woods or in the bright sunlight. Price........................ **70c**
If by mail, postage extra, 3 cents.

No. 6R1012 No. 4, Lyman's Patent Improved Ivory Front Hunting Sight. This sight is better than the bead sight for a hunting rifle. **The ivory is so well protected by the surrounding metal that there is no danger of its being injured.** Price........................ **35c**
If by mail, postage extra, 3 cents.

Lyman's Patent Ivory Shotgun Sights.

No. 6R1014 Lyman's Patent Ivory Shotgun Sight with reamer. Front and rear, for double barrel guns only. State whether front or rear is wanted. Price, per pair 70c; each, **35c**
If by mail, postage extra, 2 cents.

No. 6R1015 No. 5, Lyman's Patent Combination Ivory Front Sight. One cut shows the sight on the barrel and the other with the globe turned up and the ivory turned down. Price, each.. **70c**
If by mail, postage extra, 3 cents.

No. 6R1022 No. 14, Excellent Spirit Level, which can be used in place of a blank piece. Price................ **70c**
If by mail, postage extra, 3 cents.

Lyman's Rear Leaf Sight.

No. 6R1028 No. 6, one leaf is a bar with a triangular ivory center, the other is a wide open V crotch. Price, each........................ **70c**
If by mail, postage extra, 2 cents.

No. 6R1030 No. 12, Blank Piece to replace the crotch sight which is usually on the barrel when the rifle is purchased and which should always be removed when peep sights are used.
Price....(If by mail, postage extra, 3 cents)...**18c**

In ordering rifle sights, be sure and state the maker's name, model and caliber of your rifle.

Winchester Graduated Peep Sights.

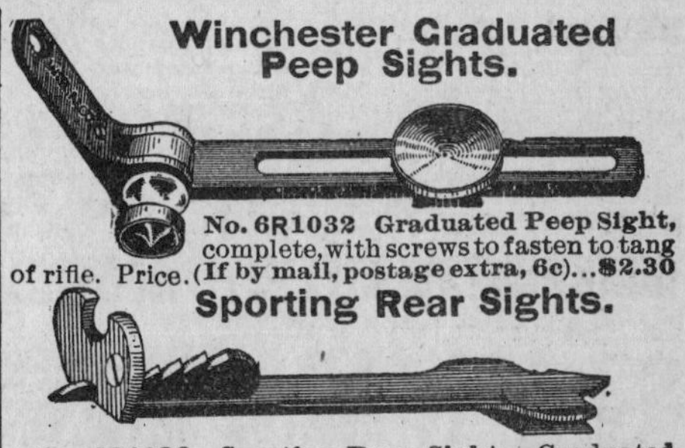

No. 6R1032 Graduated Peep Sight, complete, with screws to fasten to tang of rifle. Price. (If by mail, postage extra, 6c)... **$2.30**

Sporting Rear Sights.

No. 6R1036 Sporting Rear Sight. Graduated from 50 to 300 yards. Price........................ **60c**
If by mail, postage extra, 3 cents.

No. 6R1042 Sporting Front Sight. Price........................ **23c**
If by mail, postage extra, 2 cents.

No. 6R1046 Knife Blade Front Sight. German silver or ivory blade. Price................ **45c**
If by mail, postage extra, 2 cents.

Beach Combination Sights.

As open.

At globe.

No. 6R1047 Price.......... **70c**
If by mail, postage extra, 3c.

No. 6R1048 Rocky Mountain Front Sight. Price.. **44c**
If by mail, postage extra, 3c.

The Barger Shotgun Sights.

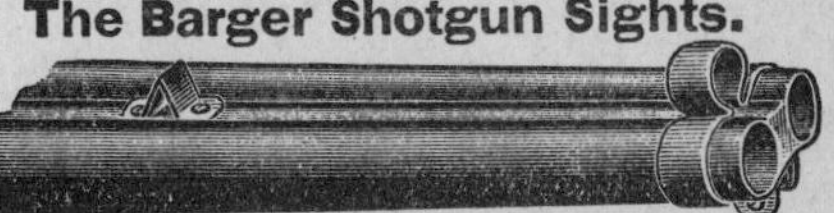

Barger Sight. Here is what you have been looking for ever since you have been shooting a shotgun. We have just placed our order for a large lot of these sights, and we know that nearly everyone who shoots a shotgun wants this sight as soon as they know it is made.

The Barger Sight is made exactly on the same principle as the **Globe front sight** for a rifle; it is made of steel, nicely blued and the sight is so made that it is adjustable to nearly all double barrel guns and they are also made for single barrel shotguns. The sights are intended to be adjusted at the muzzle as shown in this cut, and by the use of these sights any one may become an expert shot at the trap or in the field. They are made of good quality steel, and can be adjusted to the muzzle of any gun in a few seconds. **When ordering say if they are wanted for single or double barrel guns.**

Sights for single or double barrel shotguns. Mention gauge of gun, as a 12-gauge will not fit a 10-gauge gun.
No. 6R1049 Price, each........................ **50c**
If by mail, postage extra, 2 cents.

$2.95 BUYS OUR AUTOMATIC REVOLVER.

AT $2.95 we offer you from our own revolver factory, in Worcester, Mass., an automatic shell ejecting 32 or 38-caliber revolver, under our guarantee that it is superior in every way to automatic revolvers of other makes that sell at much higher prices. We established our own revolver factory at Worcester, Mass., for the sole purpose of turning out a uniformly higher grade revolver than those usually furnished by other makers, and yet at a cost to us that would enable us to supply our customers at a lower price than we could possibly supply other makes.

MAKERS HAVE, in our judgment, for several years, been asking too much money for revolvers. There has been too much profit to the manufacturer and too much profit to the retail dealer, and it was with a view of changing this condition, getting a lower cost and a lower price to our customers, and a better made revolver, that we have established our own revolver factory.

THE CUSTOMER who reads this description can have little idea of the effort and outlay of money necessary to produce such a revolver for $2.95. From the time the manager of this department conceived the idea of building a factory and making our own revolvers, for nearly two years, we have been busy with a large force of men making special machines, getting out designs, making dies, jigs, gauges, tools, etc., before the first revolver could be produced.

IT HAS REQUIRED nearly two years time, a large force of mechanics and a big outlay of money to first build the equipment necessary to produce the finished revolver at the price. We are now fully equipped. Our revolver factory, like one of our gun factories, is also located in Worcester, Massachusetts, is in charge of one of the best revolver makers in the country. We have one of the most, if not the most modern, up to date revolver making plants in America. We have every facility for turning out the neatest, handsomest, most up to date design, best finished and best shooting revolver on the market and at the very lowest possible cost, and our special $2.95 price to you represents the net cost to us with but our one small percentage of profit added.

IF YOU WANT A REVOLVER you will find far greater value in one of our own make, one of the revolvers illustrated on this page, than in any other revolver made. This we positively guarantee. We will accept your order with the understanding that if the revolver is not perfectly satisfactory when received, if you are not convinced that it is the greatest revolver value offered by any house and in every way equal, and in many ways superior, to revolvers that sell at double the price, you can return it to us at our expense of express charges both ways and we will immediately return your money.

$2.95

If by mail, postage extra, 17 to 24 cents.

FROM THE ILLUSTRATION, engraved by our artist from a photograph of the revolver, you can get some idea of the general appearance of the revolver. This illustration is life size, and shows the exact size of the 32 caliber revolver, just as it appears in the photograph, yet you must see, examine and compare the revolver with others to appreciate what we are turning out, and how much you save by sending your order to us.

WE HAVE ENDEAVORED to make this revolver superior to the regular line of automatic revolvers, not only in what we consider a handsomer design, a neater and better shape, a more beautiful outline, but we believe we have the best shell extracting device, the best cylinder catch and barrel latch, the simplest, strongest and best self-cocking action, that is produced on any revolver made regardless of price, and if you order one of these revolvers we leave it to you to be the judge.

IN OUR NICKELING AND BLUING DEPARTMENT we believe we get a finer finish than is furnished on other revolvers. We have endeavored in this respect to turn out a revolver unexcelled, if equaled by any other revolver made.

THESE REVOLVERS are made from the very finest decarbonized steel procurable. The cylinders are neatly fluted, the barrels are bored true to gauge and full rifled. They have the latest style high rib, as illustrated, are accurately sighted, made with handsome monogram rubber handle, neatly shaped trigger guard, trigger and hammer, a compact, well made and well finished automatic revolver, built with a view to combining the good qualities of all automatic revolvers with the defects of none and yet offered at a price lower than offered by any other concern, a price that barely covers the cost of material and labor, with but our one small percentage of profit added, only $2.95.

No. 6R1161 32-caliber, 3-inch barrel, nickel plate finish, rubber handle. Price........ $2.95
No. 6R1162 38-caliber, 3-inch barrel, nickel plate finish, rubber handle. Price........ 2.95
No. 6R1163 32-caliber, 3-inch barrel, blued steel finish. Price..... 3.35
No. 6R1164 38-caliber, 3-inch barrel, blued steel finish. Price..... 3.35
Extra for pearl stock for any of above revolvers, $1.00.

$3.40 FOR OUR HAMMMERLESS AUTOMATIC REVOLVER.

AT $3.40 WE OFFER this Hammerless Automatic Shell Ejecting Revolver, in 32 or 38-caliber, built in our own factory and guaranteed superior in every respect to hammerless revolvers of other makes that sell at much higher prices.

THIS HAMMERLESS REVOLVER at $3.40 like our special $2.95 Automatic Hammer Revolver, illustrated above, is built in the same factory—a factory we own and control at Worcester, Mass.—and our special $3.40 price barely covers the cost of material and labor with but our one small percentage of profit added. It is made from the same materials on the same machines by the same skilled labor as our $2.95 revolver above described. It differs only in that it is hammerless instead of a hammer revolver.

OUR BINDING GUARANTEE AND REFUND OFFER. Order one of our own revolvers at our special price, and we will send it to you with the understanding that if it is not perfectly satisfactory when received, you can return it to us at our expense of express charges both ways, and we will immediately return your money. Further, we guarantee every piece and part that goes into these revolvers, and if any revolver proves defective when received, in any piece or part, it can be returned to us at our expense of express charges both ways, and we will exchange it for another or your money will be refunded at your option.

IN EVERY DETAIL, in the making of the barrel, frame, cylinder and stock, this is the exact same type of a revolver as our special $2.95, above illustrated and described. It is gotten out with a view of giving our customers the highest type of a hammerless revolver it is possible to make, yet at the very minimum price, a price much lower than you can buy elsewhere.

$3.40

THIS ILLUSTRATION IS THE EXACT LIFE SIZE of our 32-caliber revolver, engraved by our artist direct from a photograph of the revolver, and from it you can get a general idea of the outlines and style of the revolver, and we believe you will agree with us that it carries a distinctiveness in beauty of design and general style, and above all, we guarantee it to excel in workmanship and general finish any revolver on the market approaching it in price.

IF YOU ARE IN THE MARKET FOR A REVOLVER of any kind, we especially urge that you select either this $3.40 hammerless or our $2.95 hammer revolver, above described, on the condition that if when received you do not consider it better than other makes at much higher prices, return it at our expense and we will immediately return your money.

WHY WE RECOMMEND THE HAMMERLESS REVOLVER OVER ALL OTHERS. We especially recommend that you select this our hammerless revolver at $3.40 in preference to the hammer revolver at $2.95. We recommend this additional outlay of 45 cents in the interest of safety. There is no hammer revolver that can be carried with absolute safety to the owner, for, the hammer being exposed, a fall, stumble or other accident that may bring the horn of the hammer immediately in contact with a rigid surface is liable to drive the hammer onto the cartridge and discharge the revolver. Such accidents are not infrequent with hammer revolvers, whereas it could not happen with a hammerless revolver; the trigger being protected by a guard and the revolver being hammerless, there is no possibility of accidental discharge.

WHILE THE PROFIT IS EXACTLY THE SAME TO US whether you order a hammerless revolver or a hammer revolver, for the above reasons we especially recommend that you order the hammerless in place of the hammer revolver.

WE FURNISH THIS REVOLVER in either nickel plate or steel blued, in either 32 or 38-caliber, either fancy rubber or handsone pearl handles, as desired, at the following prices:

No. 6R1171 32-caliber, 3-inch barrel, nickel plate finish. Price.... $3.40
No. 6R1172 38-caliber, 3-inch barrel, nickel plate finish. Price.... 3.40
No. 6R1173 32-caliber, 3-inch barrel, blued steel finish. Price..... 3.80
No. 6R1174 38-caliber, 3-inch barrel, blued steel finish. Price..... 3.80
Extra for pearl stock for any of the above revolvers, $1.00
If by mail, postage extra, 17 to 24 cents.

While we especially urge THE PURCHASE OF A REVOLVER MADE IN OUR OWN FACTORY, AS ILLUSTRATED AND DESCRIBED ON THE OPPOSITE PAGE, WE SHOW ON THIS AND THE FOLLOWING PAGES, A COMPLETE LINE OF ALL THE WELL KNOWN MAKES, AND AT PRICES LOWER THAN YOU CAN BUY ELSEWHERE.

WE OFFER YOU ALL THE STANDARD MAKES of Revolvers at manufacturers' lowest prices. When you get our price you are getting the manufacturers' price with only our one small profit added, and owning the revolver for less money than any dealer can buy in quantities. For this coming season we have many special bargains to offer, as our contracts with the different manufacturers have been so very large that we are able to make the very closest prices, and a comparison of our prices with those of any other concern will convince you there is a saving of 25 to 35 per cent.

IN ORDERING SINGLE REVOLVERS we advise sending by mail. This can be done by enclosing enough extra money to cover postage. The postage is 1 cent per ounce, or fraction thereof. We advise sending enough to cover insurance or registry fee as well as postage.

CASH IN FULL MUST BE SENT WITH YOUR ORDER.

YOU RUN NO RISK, for if the revolver is not satisfactory return it to us and we will refund your money. Express offers a safe method of sending revolvers.

Our New Model Double Action Revolvers, $1.50 and $1.60.

All full nickel plated and checkered rubber handle, steel rifled barrels, forged parts, and made from the best material that money can buy.

32 and 38-caliber.

No. 6R1183 32-caliber, rim fire, 2½-inch barrel. Weight, 16 ounces Using cartridge No. 6R2352.
Our price....................$1.60

No. 6R1185 32-caliber, center fire, 2½-inch barrel. Weight, 16 oz. Using cartridge No. 6R2377. 5 or 6 shot; nickel plated; rubber handles; octagon barrel.
Our price....................$1.60

No. 6R1186 38-caliber, center fire, 2½-inch barrel. Weight, 16 oz. Using cartridge No. 6R2388. 5-shot; full nickel plated; rubber handles; octagon barrel.
Our price....................$1.50

Extra for pearl stock for any of above revolvers.
Our price....................$1.10

If by mail, postage extra, 20 cents.

NOTICE—SEE OUR PRICES FOR CARTRIDGES

For 20 cents extra we will send any revolver on this page by open mail, postpaid. For 28 cents extra we will send by registered mail, postpaid or prepaid express.

Our $1.90 and $2.10 Revolvers.

THESE REVOLVERS ARE STRICTLY FIRST CLASS IN EVERY RESPECT, and made especially for us under season's contract. The quality of material and workmanship is the best. All have rifled barrels and are good shooters; all 5-shot. These are not toys, but good guns. No one can meet our prices on these goods.

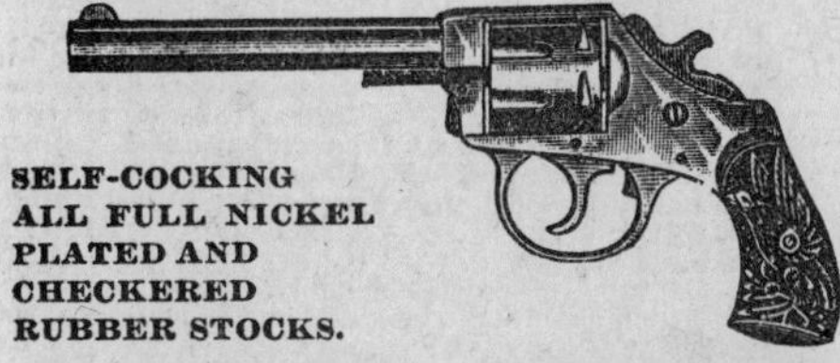

SELF-COCKING ALL FULL NICKEL PLATED AND CHECKERED RUBBER STOCKS.

No. 6R1189 32-caliber, center fire, 4½-inch barrel. Weight, 16 ounces. 5 or 6-shot. Using cartridge No. 6R2377. Our price....................$1.90
Extra for pearl stocks....................1.10

No. 6R1190 38-caliber, center fire, 4½-inch barrel. Weight, 16 ounces. 5-shot. Using cartridge No. 6R2388. Our price....................$1.90

No. 6R1191 32-caliber, center fire, 6-inch barrel. Weight, 17 ounces. 5 or 6-shot. Using cartridge No. 6R2377. Our price....................$2.10
Extra for pearl stocks....................1.10

No. 6R1192 38-caliber, center fire, 6-inch barrel. Weight, 18 ounces. 5-shot. Using cartridge No. 6R2388. Our price....................$2.10
Extra for pearl stocks....................1.10

If by mail, postage extra, 20 to 27 cents.

Our $1.65 Double Action Revolver.

Forehand & Wadsworth New Double Action, Self Cocking Revolver, full nickel plated, rubber stock, rifled barrel, safe and reliable, accurate, rebounding locks, parts are interchangeable.

No. 6R1195 32-caliber, 2½-inch octagon barrel; using cartridge No. 6R2377. Weight, 15 ounces. 6-shot.
Our price....................$1.65

No. 6R1196 38-caliber, 2½-inch octagon barrel, 5-shot; using cartridge No. 6R2388. Weight, about 15 ounces. Our price....................$1.65

If by mail, postage extra, 20 cents.

Our $1.67 Double Action Revolver.

No. 6R1197 Forehand & Wadsworth safety hammer, double action revolver, full nickel plated, rubber stock, rifled barrel, rebounding lock, safe, reliable and accurate, 32-caliber, 2½-inch octagon barrel, 6-shot, using cartridge No. 6R2377. Weight, 15 ounces. Our price......$1.67

No. 6R1198 38-caliber, 2½-inch octagon barrel, 5-shot, using cartridge No. 6R2388. Weight, 15 ounces.
Our price....................$1.67

If by mail, postage extra, 20 cents.

These goods are genuine, and new from the factory. Beware of imitations and shop worn goods, which are sold for less money by some firms. We handle nothing but first class goods.

The Forehand Perfection Automatic 5-Shot Revolver for $3.10.

Forehand Perfection Automatic, small frame, rebounding lock, positive stop on cylinder, and hammer blocked, same as in other Forehand Automatics. Accidental discharge impossible.

32-Caliber only.

Using cartridge No. 6R2377. Weighs but 13 ounces. A fine pocket revolver. Full length, 7¼ inches.

No. 6R1205 32-caliber, 3-inch, nickel plated $3.10

No. 6R1207 32-caliber, 3-inch, blue steel frame and barrel. Price....................$3.50

If by mail, postage extra, 17 cents.

Our $3.10 Forehand Automatic.

32 and 38-Caliber.

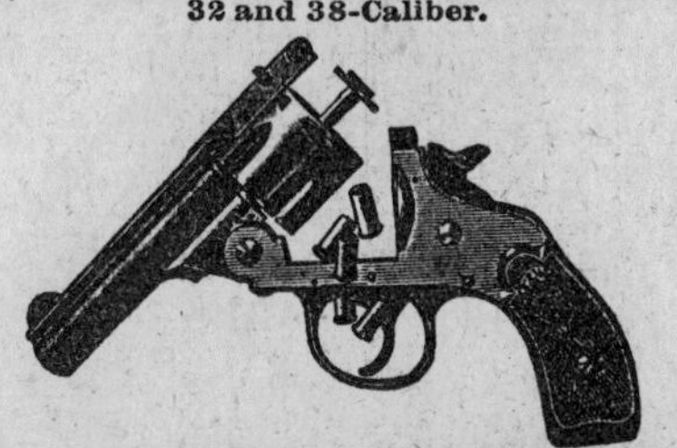

The Celebrated Forehand & Wadsworth Automatic Revolver for $3.10; a revolver that retails at from $5.00 to $6.00. The very latest improved model, automatic shell extractor, rebounding locks, double action, self cocking, simple and accurate, interchangeable parts made from drop steel forgings. The frame is cast steel, no malleable iron about it; nickel plated throughout; fancy rubber stock, every revolver is fully warranted; length of barrel, 3¼ inches, weight, 17 ounces; entire length, 7¾ inches. The fact that we sold more of these revolvers during the last year than ever before is evidence of the general satisfaction they give.

No. 6R1219 32-caliber nickel plated, taking Smith & Wesson center fire cartridges, 5-shot, using cartridge No. 6R2377. Our price........$3.10

No. 6R1221 32-caliber, blued finish.... 3.50

No. 6R1222 38-caliber, nickel plated, taking Smith & Wesson center fire cartridges, 5-shot. Using cartridge No. 6R2388. Our price........$3.10

No. 6R1224 38-caliber, blued finish.
Our price.................... 3.50

If by mail, postage extra, 24 cents.

HOW TO AVOID DELAY.

We carry a stock valued at about two million dollars, and aim to keep this stock up, but it sometimes happens that we receive orders in one day from every part of the United States for the same single item, which exhausts the stock temporarily. It also sometimes happens that one of our factories is destroyed by fire. Sometimes it happens that one of our factories fails in business, has labor strikes, can't make goods as fast as we can sell them, etc., and while we try as far as possible to deal with reliable factories, we cannot guarantee to furnish goods under these conditions, but we always do the best we can for our customers. If you can give us a second choice when we are out of an article it will avoid delay in shipping your order.

Forehand Automatic 5-inch Barrel Revolver, $3.60.

32 and 38-caliber.

Taking same cartridges as the Smith & Wesson Double Action Revolvers.

Forehand Automatic. Same as No. 6R1219 but with 5-inch barrel. These are made with the same care, skill and accuracy as the other Forehand revolvers.

No. 6R1225 32-caliber, nickel plated, 5-inch $3.60
No. 6R1227 32-caliber, blued, 5-inch....... 4.00
No. 6R1226 38-caliber, nickel plated, 5-inch 3.60
No. 6R1228 38-caliber, blued, 5-inch....... 4.00

If by mail, postage extra, 27 cents.

Our $3.60 Forehand Hammerless.

SMALL FRAME.

32 and 38-Caliber.

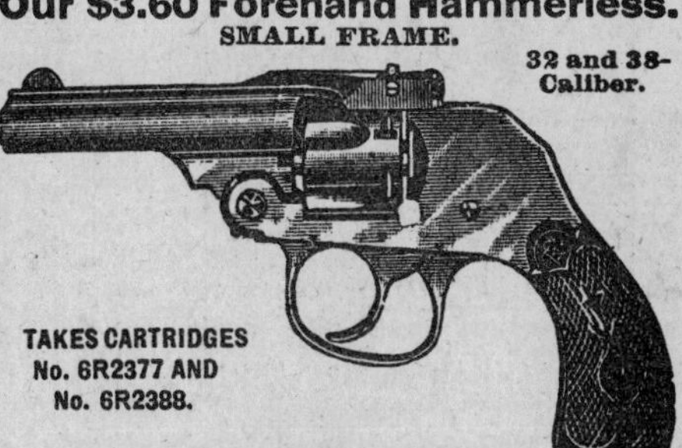

TAKES CARTRIDGES No. 6R2377 AND No. 6R2388.

We offer you at $3.60 a hammerless revolver which has never been retailed at less than $6.00. No other house will meet our price. Make a comparison and decide for yourself. This is the celebrated Forehand & Wadsworth new style hammerless revolver, made by Forehand Arms Co. No better revolver made. Automatic shell extractor, double action, self cocking, rebounding lock, absolutely safe catch to lock hammer, made of best material, beautifully finished throughout, accurate and reliable. All center fire, nicely nickel plated throughout, uses Smith & Wesson center fire cartridges, 32-caliber, 5-shot; 38-caliber, 5-shot; using cartridge No. 6R2377 and No. 6R2388.

No. 6R1241 32-caliber, nickeled. Our price. $3.60
No. 6R1243 32-caliber, blued. Our price... 4.00
No. 6R1242 38-caliber, nickeled; using cartridge No. 6M2388. Our price.............. 3.60
No. 6R1244 38-caliber, blued. Our price.. 4.00

If by mail, postage extra, 17 to 24 cents.

Forehand Hammerless, with 5-inch Barrel, $4.10.

5-INCH BARREL.

No. 6R1245 32-caliber, nickeled; 5-inch barrel.
Our price....................$4.10
No. 6R1247 32-caliber, blued; 5-inch barrel.
Our price....................$4.50
No. 6R1246 38-caliber, nickeled; 5-inch barrel.
Our price....................$4.10
No. 6R1248 38-caliber, blued; 5-inch barrel.
Our price....................$4.50

If by mail, postage extra, 28 cents.

SEND GOODS BY FREIGHT.

We advise sending goods by freight, as it is cheaper than by express.

If you order a gun or rifle, and you include enough needed goods from our big catalogue to make a shipment of 50 to 100 pounds, the entire shipment will be very near as cheap by freight as the gun alone would cost by express. When shipping 50 to 100 pounds or more by freight it makes the freight charges cost practically next to nothing on each item.

Iver Johnson Small Frame Automatic Revolver, $3.10.

32 and 38-Caliber.

The Iver Johnson Automatic Safety Hammer Revolver, double action, **self cocking, 5-shot, 13 and 18 ounce weight**, 3-inch barrel, finely nickel plated, neatly finished. Every one warranted. All take center fire Smith & Wesson cartridges.

No. 6R1253 32-caliber, 3-inch barrel, nickel plated. Weight about 13 ounces. Each........**$3.10**
No. 6R1255 32-caliber, 3-inch barrel, blued finish. Weight about 13 ounces. Each........**$3.50**
No. 6R1254 38-caliber, 3¼-inch barrel, nickel plated. Weight about 18 ounces. Each........**$3.10**
No. 6R1256 38-caliber, 3¼-inch barrel, blued finish. Weight about 18 ounces. Each........**$3.50**
Pearl Stocks extra, 32-caliber, $1.10; 38-caliber, $1.25
If by mail, postage extra, 17 to 24 cents.

Iver Johnson Hammerless Automatic Revolver, $3.60.

32 and 38-Caliber.

The above illustrated revolver is the celebrated Iver Johnson automatic hammerless double action; high grade finish, fine adjustments. Its trigger locking device makes it one of the safest revolvers to carry in the pocket. Automatic self ejector, **rebounding lock, safety trigger locking device,** chambered cylinder, rifled barrel. **Smith & Wesson** small frame, 5-shot, weighs 13 oz., length of barrel, 3 inches; revolver that retails at from $7.00 to $10.00.

No. 6R1321 32-caliber nickel plated. Weight about 13 ounces. Our price........**$3.60**
No. 6R1323 32-caliber, blued. Our price.. **4.00**
No. 6R1322 38-caliber, 3¼-inch barrel, nickel plated. Weight about 18 ounces. Our price...**$3.60**
No. 6R1324 38-caliber, blued, 3¼-inch barrel. Our price........**$4.00**
If by mail, postage extra, 17 to 24 cents.
Pearl Stocks, 32-caliber, $1.10 extra; 38-caliber, $1.25 extra.

The Stevens' New Model Tip Up Pistol.

22-caliber only. 3½-inch barrel.

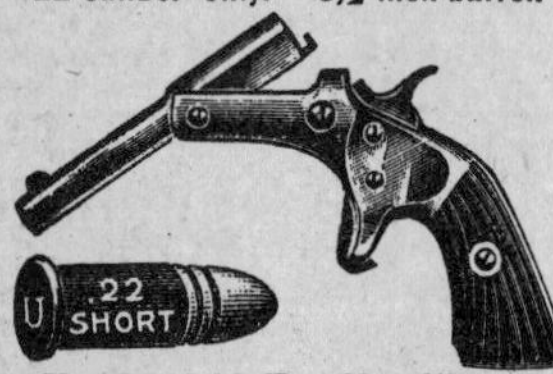

Stevens' Single Shot Pistol. Tip up barrel, nickel plated finish, 3½-inch barrel, 22-caliber only, rim fire. No better material put in rifles. A fine target pistol. Rifled barrel and well made throughout.

No. 6R1343 For 22-caliber short cartridges. Price........**$1.95**
If by mail, postage extra, 15 cents.

Stevens' Diamond Model Target Pistol.

The Celebrated Stevens' Target Pistol, the best pistol made for fine, close shooting. It has fine blued barrel, nickel plated frame, rosewood stock, 6-inch tip up barrel; fitted with fine globe and peep target sights, 22-caliber, rim fire. Shoots either 22 long rifle or 22 short cartridges; good for 50 yards. **22-caliber. 6-inch barrel.**

No. 6R1344 Our price........**$3.95**
No. 6R1345 The same pistol but with open sights as shown in the cut will cost........$4.00
If by mail, postage extra, 17 cents.

Remington Derringers.

This is the genuine Remington Double Derringer. Don't buy imitations. The Remington Double Derringer, 41-caliber rim fire, **checkered rubber stock; length of barrels 3 inches; entire length of pistol is 5 inches; nickel plated.**

No. 6R1347 Price, nickel plated........**$5.00**
No. 6R1348 Same, blued. Price........ **5.10**
Pearl handles, extra........ 1.25
If by mail, postage extra, 24 cents.

Harrington & Richardson's Young America, Ladies' Revolver.

Double Action, Reduced Size, 22-Caliber, Rim Fire.

No. 6R1354

$1.62 AND $2.52

Young America.

Full nickel plated, 22-caliber, 7 shot, 2-inch Rifled octagon barrel.

No. 6R1352 22-caliber, rubber stocks, 7 oz..**$1.62**
No. 6R1354 With pearl handles........ **2.52**
The Young America can be carried in the vest pocket as conveniently as a watch, and is designed especially for ladies' use.
If by mail, postage extra, 13 cents.

Harrington & Richardson's Young America, Self Cocker.

Reduced Size, 32-Caliber, Double Action, Rifled Barrel, Central Fire.

$1.60 AND $2.50

32-caliber only.

Young America.

Full nickeled, rubber stocks, 5-shot, 2-inch rifled octagon barrel, 9 ounces. Takes the 32-caliber S. & W. cartridge, No. 6R2377.

No. 6R1355 32-caliber, central fire........**$1.60**
No. 6R1357 32-caliber, with pearl stocks.... **2.50**
If by mail, postage extra, 15 cents.

SEE OUR PRICES FOR CARTRIDGES.

Harrington & Richardson's Young America, Safety Hammer Self Cocker.

Reduced Size, Full Nickeled. Rubber Stocks, 5-Shot Rifled Barrel with Safety Hammer.

$1.70 AND $2.60

32-caliber only.

The Young America.

Safety hammer, 32-caliber, central fire only, 2-inch barrel.
Takes 32-caliber S. & W. cartridge, No. 6R2377.

No. 6R1359 32-caliber, central fire, 9 oz....**$1.70**
No. 6R1361 With pearl handles........ **2.60**
If by mail, postage extra, 15 cents.

Harrington & Richardson's Vest Pocket Self Cocker.

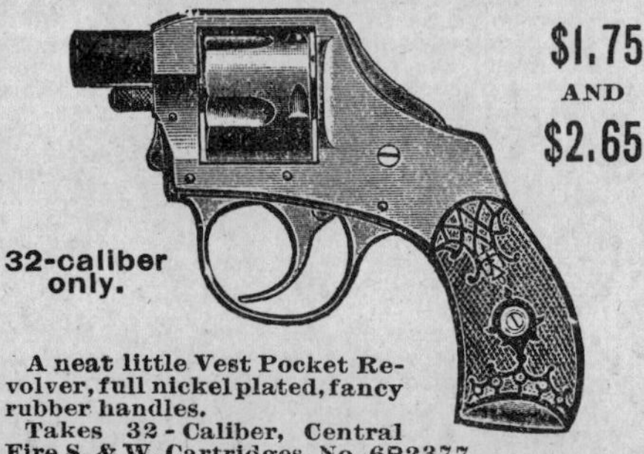

$1.75 AND $2.65

32-caliber only.

A neat little Vest Pocket Revolver, full nickel plated, fancy rubber handles.
Takes 32-Caliber, Central Fire S. & W. Cartridges, No. 6R2377.

Made to carry in the vest pocket, with 1⅛-inch round barrel. Weight, 8½ ounces.

No. 6R1363½ With rubber handles; our special price........**$1.75**
No. 6R1365½ With pearl handles; special price........ **2.65**
If by mail, postage extra, 14 cents.

On any goods not described or listed in this catalogue and made to order we must ask cash in full with order, the same as on our other merchandise, and if made as ordered, they cannot be returned under any circumstances.

Harrington & Richardson's Young America, Target Revolver.

Double Action, Reduced Size, 22-Caliber, Rim Fire, with 6-inch Rifled Barrel.

Young America

$2.40 and $3.30

Full nickeled, rubber or pearl stocks, 7-shot, 6-inch rifled octagon barrel.

No. 6R1368 22-caliber, 7-shot, 6-inch barrel, rim fire, rubber handles, 8-ounce........**$2.40**
No. 6R1369 The same, with pearl handles. **$3.30**
This is the only 22-caliber, 7-shot, target pistol on the market and we were the first to offer it to our customers. **If by mail, postage extra, 16 cents.**

Harrington & Richardson's New Model Premier 22-Caliber, 3-inch Barrel.

ILLUSTRATION OF No. 6R1372

The "Premier" is automatic shell ejecting, small frame, 7-shot, and is adapted to 22-caliber short or long rim fire cartridges. The working parts are drop forged. This is a fine 22-caliber automatic revolver. The frame, cylinder and barrel are steel, hammer rebounding, automatic shell ejector, rubber stocks. Full nickel plated or blued finish, rifled barrel. This is a good pocket size revolver.

No. 6R1370 22-caliber, 7 shot, 3-inch barrel, nickel plated, weight, 12½-ounces, with rubber handle. Our price........**$3.10**
No. 6R1371 22-caliber, 7 shot, 3-inch barrel, blued finish, weight, 12½-oz., with rubber handle........ **3.50**
No. 6R1372 22-caliber, 7 shot, 3-inch barrel, nickel plated, weight, 13-oz. with pearl handle, **4.10**
No. 6R1373 22-caliber, 7 shot, 3-inch barrel, blued finish, weight, 13-oz. with pearl handle. Our special price........ **4.50**
If by mail, postage extra, 20 cents.

Harrington & Richardson's New Model Premier 22-Caliber, 5-inch Barrel.

$3.60 AND $4.00

It is automatic shell ejecting, small frame, 7-shot, and is adapted to 22-caliber, short or long rim fire cartridges. The working parts are drop forged. This is a fine 22-caliber automatic revolver. The frame, cylinder and barrel are steel, hammer rebounding, automatic shell ejector, rubber stocks, rifled barrel. Full nickel plated or blued finish.

No. 6R1374 22-caliber, 7-shot, 5-inch barrel, nickel plated; weight, 14 oz., with rubber handle......**$3.60**
No. 6R1375 22-caliber, 7-shot, 5-inch barrel, blued finish, weight, 14 oz., with rubber handle **4.00**
Extra for pearl handles........ **1.00**
If by mail, postage extra, 22 cents.

Harrington & Richardson's New Model Premier 32-Caliber, Central Fire.

$3.10 AND $4.10

The Premier is automatic shell ejecting, small frame, 5-shot, and is adapted to 32-caliber Smith & Wesson central fire cartridges. The working parts are drop forged. This is a fine 32-caliber automatic revolver with rifled barrel. The frame, cylinder and barrel are steel, hammer rebounding, automatic shell ejector, rubber stocks. Full nickel plated, with 3-inch barrel, and makes a good pocket size revolver.

No. 6R1377 32-caliber, 5-shot, 3-inch barrel, nickel plated, weight, 12¼ oz. Our price........**$3.10**
No. 6R1379 32-caliber, 5-shot, 3-inch barrel, nickel plated, weight, 12¼ oz., with pearl handle **4.10**
If by mail, postage extra, 18 cents.

SEE FOLLOWING PAGES FOR

AMMUNITION.

OUR PRICES ARE THE VERY LOWEST.

The Genuine Harrington & Richardson's Automatic Revolvers.

$3.10 32 and 38-Caliber.

Over 3,000,000 Harring on & Richardson Revolvers now in use.

Our $3.10 Automatic.

This revolver would retail in any first class gun store at from $5.00 to $6.00. The celebrated **Harrington & Richardson's Improved Automatic**, self extracting, double action, self cocking revolver, modeled on the Smith & Wesson pattern, beautifully nickel plated, rubber stock, as accurate and durable as any revolver on the market, and equal to the Smith & Wesson in shooting. Weight, 18½ ounces, 3¼-inch barrel.

No. 6R1385 32-caliber, nickel plated, center fire. Using cartridge No. 6R2377. Our price........ **$3.10**
No. 6R1387 32-caliber, blued finish, center fire. Using cartridge No. 6R2377. Our price......... **$3.50**
No. 6R1386 38-caliber, nickel plated, center fire. Using cartridge No. 6R2388. Our price........ **$3.10**
No. 6R1388 38-caliber, blued finish, center fire. Using cartridge No. 6R2388 Our price.......... **$3.50**
Extra for pearl stocks on any of the above.. **1.10**
If by mail, postage extra, 22 cents.

WHEN ORDERING REVOLVERS ALWAYS GIVE CATALOGUE NUMBER, CALIBER AND LENGTH OF BARREL.

Our Harrington & Richardson's Automatic with 5-inch Barrel, $3.60.

Made on the same principle as the regular automatic, but has a long barrel, 5 inches in length. Expressly designed for carrying in a holster and belt. **This is one of the best medium priced revolvers made.** Has good rifle barrel and comes in nickel plated or blued finish.

No. 6R1391 32-caliber, nickel plated, 5-inch barrel. Our price.......... **$3.60**
No. 6R1393 32-caliber, blued finish, 5-inch barrel Our price.......... **$4.00**
No. 6R1392 38-caliber, nickel plated, 5-inch barrel. Our price.......... **$3.60**
No. 6R1394 38-caliber, blued finish, 5-inch barrel. Our price.......... **$4.00**
Extra, for pearl stocks on any of above..... **1.10**
If by mail, postage extra, 27 cents.

The New Harrington & Richardson Automatic Bayonet Revolver.

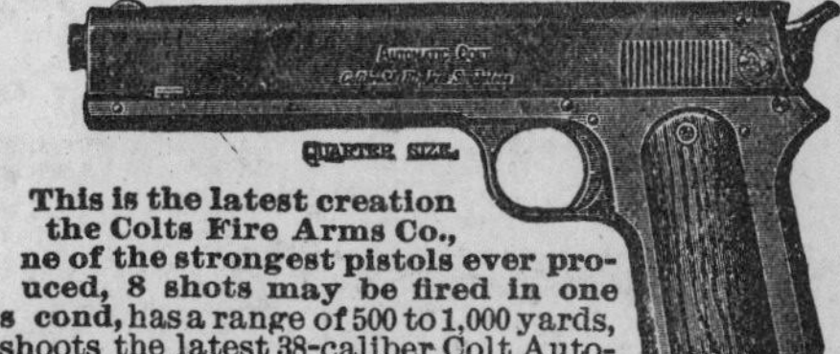

Made in 38-caliber only, using the same cartridges as the Smith & Wesson Revolvers.

In response to the many inquiries for a bayonet revolver, we are pleased to say that we can now furnish this article.

The Harrington & Richardson's New Automatic Bayonet Revolver is made in 38-caliber only, with 4-inch barrel, the bayonet extending 2½ inches forward of the muzzle. They are handsomely nickel plated, all working parts are steel and case hardened, and the bayonet is so constructed that it can be folded under the barrel instantly when desired. **When open the bayonet is securely locked. This revolver is fitted with nicely checkered rubber stocks, but can be furnished with pearl stocks when so desired.** It is well rifled and thoroughly well made throughout. All parts are interchangeable, so that if you accidentally break any part, it can be duplicated at small cost.

No. 6R1396 38-caliber, 4-inch barrel, 18 ounces. Nickel plated. Our special price.......... **$4.65**
Extra for pearl stocks.......... **1.10**
If by mail, postage extra, 27 cents.

WHILE OUR ONLY TERMS ARE CASH WITH ORDER,

you do not run the slightest risk, for if anything is not perfectly satisfactory when received return it to us and we will immediately refund your money, including what you paid for transportation charges.

Harrington & Richardson's Automatic Police Revolver.

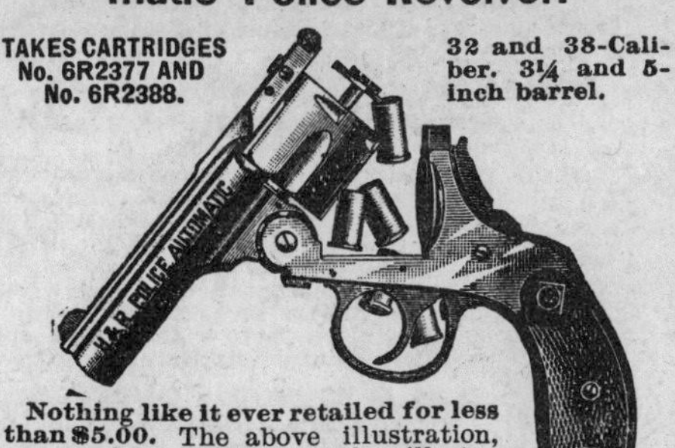
TAKES CARTRIDGES No. 6R2377 AND No. 6R2388.
32 and 38-Caliber. 3¼ and 5-inch barrel.

Nothing like it ever retailed for less than $5.00. The above illustration, engraved from a photograph, will give you some idea of the appearance of this gun. It is the **celebrated Harrington & Richardson police**, automatic, safety hammer, double action, self cocking, **automatic shell extractor**, fancy rubber stock, full nickel plated, center fire, rifle barrel, 32 or 38-caliber; using cartridge Nos. 6R2377 and 6R2388.

No. 6R1401 32-caliber, nickel plated, 6-shot, 3¼-inch barrel, 18 ounces. Our price.......... **$3.10**
No. 6R1403 32-caliber; blued finish. Our price.......... **$3.50**
No. 6R1402 38-caliber, nickel plated, 5-shot, 3¼-inch barrel, 18-ounces; using cartridge No. 6M2388. Our price.......... **$3.10**
No. 6R1404 38-caliber; blued finish, 3¼-inch barrel, 5-shot. Our price.......... **$3.50**
No. 6R1405 32-caliber, 5-inch barrel, 6-shot, 19 ounces, nickeled. Our price.......... **$3.60**
No. 6R1406 38-caliber, 5-inch barrel, 5-shot, 19 ounces, nickeled. Our price.......... **$3.60**
Extra for pearl stocks on any of the above. 1.10
If by mail, postage extra, 24 cents.

Harrington & Richardson's Hammerless Revolvers.

32 or 38-Caliber, Adapted to S. & W. Cartridges.

$3.60

Patented, Oct. 4, 1887. May 14, 1889. April 2, 1896. April 7, 1897.

This is Harrington & Richardson's latest production. The great demand for hammerless revolvers has prompted them to make a hammerless revolver of fine quality and workmanship, small and light and always ready to shoot. The revolvers have automatic shell ejectors, forged parts, steel barrels and rubber stocks. The 32-caliber has a small light frame, making them a good convenient pocket size. They are full nickel plated or blued and are adapted to 32 and 38-caliber S. & W. cartridges.

No. 6R1411 Price of 32-caliber, 5 shot, 3-inch barrel, 13-ounce central fire, nickel plated.......... **$3.60**
No. 6R1413 Price of 32-caliber, 5 shot, 3-inch barrel, 13-ounce central fire, blued finish...... **4.00**
No. 6R1412 Price of 38-caliber, 5 shot, 3¼-inch barrel, 18-ounce central fire, nickel plated **3.60**
No. 6R1414 Price of 38-caliber, 5 shot, 3¼-inch barrel, 18-ounce central fire, blued finish. **4.00**
Pearl handles on any of the above revolvers will cost extra.......... 1.10
If by mail, postage extra, 18 to 24 cents.

Harrington & Richardson's Hammerless Revolvers, 5-Inch Barrel.

32 or 38-Caliber, Adapted to S. & W. Cartridges.

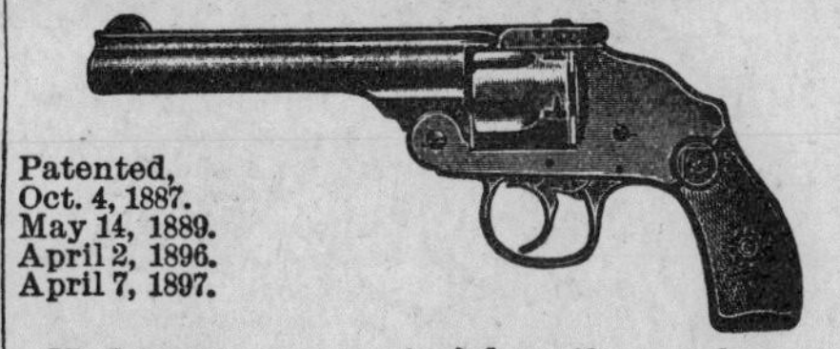

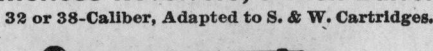

Patented, Oct. 4, 1887. May 14, 1889. April 2, 1896. April 7, 1897.

Made on the same principle as the regular automatic hammerless, but has a long barrel, 5 inches in length. Expressly designed for a belt revolver. It is made in nickel plated and blued finish, has a good rifled barrel and takes the same cartridges as the Smith & Wesson revolvers.

No. 6R1415 Price of 32-caliber, 5 shot, 5-inch barrel, 15-ounce central fire, nickel plated,........ **$4.10**
No. 6R1417 Price of 32-caliber, 5 shot, 5-inch barrel, 15-ounce central fire, blued finish. **4.50**
No. 6R1416 Price of 38-caliber, 5 shot, 5-inch barrel, 21-ounce central fire, nickel plated **4.10**
No. 6R1418 Price of 38-caliber, 5 shot, 5-inch barrel, 21-ounce central fire, blued finish, **4.50**
Pearl handles on any of the above revolvers will cost extra.......... 1.10
If by mail, postage extra, 22 to 28 cents.

Our 16th Century Flint Lock Pistol for Only $2.75.

F is the flint.
C is cover of powder pan.

For $2.75 we offer you our special Flint Lock Pistol. Many people supposed that there were no more of these revolvers to be had, but our European buyer succeeded in finding a small lot of them in Europe, and has sent them to us.

We are always on the lookout for anything that interests our customers, and if you are collecting relics we know that this 16th Century Pistol will go along with your other antiquities.

This, our special flint lock pistol, is one which our grandfathers and great grandfathers used to shoot before the advent of modern arms.

Do not think because we offer these pistols cheap, that they can only be used as an ornament, for if you desire you can shoot the pistol; shoot it the same as you would a muzzle loading gun.

The pistol has a 14-gauge barrel, 9 inches long and weighs 2¾ pounds, and is loaded from the muzzle the same as an ordinary muzzle loading gun.

After loading, place a little powder in the powder pan, close down the pan cover (C) to prevent the powder from falling out, pull the hammer to full cock, fire. The flint (F) ignites the powder by sparks caused by striking the pan cover. This pistol has a bright polished barrel, walnut stock, is brass mounted, and has a good, strong, substantial lock.

Do not fail to place your order as early as possible, because the supply is limited and at the present time we do not know of any more to be had anywhere. Show the boys the kind of a pistol which our grandfathers used to shoot, before gun caps were invented.

No. 6R1430 Our special flint lock pistol, 9-inch barrel, 14-gauge, weight 2¾ pounds, our special price.......... **$2.75**

OUR $4.50 FRONTIER REVOLVER.

This Frontier Revolver is offered as the BEST strong shooting arm made at a medium low price. The best revolver for the money for frontier use This large, strong shooting and well finished revolver retails everywhere at from $6.00 to $8.00.

$4.50
TAKES CARTRIDGE No. 6R2409.

5½-inch barrel, 6-shooter, **fine engraved rubber stock, 44-caliber, center fire, full nickel plated or blued finished. This revolver is adapted to 44-caliber Winchester cartridges,** so that a person having a rifle need not change ammunition, but can use the same cartridges in both. Weight, 35 ounces.

No. 6R1434 Our price, nickel plated...... **$4.50**
No. 6R1436 The same revolver blued finish **5.00**
If by mail, postage extra, 40 cents.

Colts Automatic Pistol only $18.50

QUARTER SIZE.

This is the latest creation the Colts Fire Arms Co., ne of the strongest pistols ever prouced, 8 shots may be fired in one s cond, has a range of 500 to 1,000 yards, shoots the latest 38-caliber Colt Automatic high pressure cartridge, and has a velocity of 1,300 feet per second.

In placing this pistol on the market, we predict an advent in pistols, for this pistol is made on entirely different principles from revolvers, the magazine is in the handle, and it has no cylinder, whereby it differs from revolvers. **To operate this pistol, place seven cartridges in the magazine, and one in the chamber, raise the hammer, and all you have to do after that is to pull the trigger, for the pistol cocks itself after every shot is fired** by its own recoil, ejects the cartridge which has been fired, places a new cartridge in the chamber, and is ready to shoot again as soon as you are ready to pull the trigger, in other words, the pistol shoots, raises the hammer, ejects the empty shell, replaces another shell in the chamber, about as fast as you can pull the trigger. If you keep your finger on the trigger, the entire eight loads may be fired as fast as you can pull the trigger.

No. R1440 Colts Automatic Pistol, using 38-caliber Colts Automatic high pressure smokeless cartridges, 6-inch barrel, blued finish, eight shooter; weight, 32 ounces: range, 500 to 1,000 yards; has the force of a rifle. Our special price.... **$18.50**

NOTICE. **Owing to the heavy advance in prices on revolvers at the different factories, and which are liable to go much higher, Our Prices are Subject to Change Without Notice.**

Place your orders early, while our present stock lasts, as these prices apply only to stock on hand.

$5.50 AND $5.90

No. 6R1480

TAKES No. 6R2409 CARTRIDGES

If by registered mail, 45 cents extra.

THE IMPORTED AUTOMATIC DOUBLE ACTION REVOLVER.

IMITATION OF SMITH & WESSON.

This cut, engraved from a photograph by our artist, will give you some idea of the revolver.

It is central fire, and has 5½-inch barrel, finished in blued or nickel plated. Made in 44-caliber only.

It has rebounding hammer, rubber stock, weighs 35 ounces and is automatic shell ejecting.

This revolver takes the same cartridge as the Winchester Rifle, 44-caliber, (No. 6R2409) so that a man who has a 44-caliber rifle can use the same ammunition in both the rifle and this revolver. We have contracted for a large lot of these revolvers so as to get the price so we can sell them with our one small percentage of profit at these figures.

PRICES OF IMPORTED AUTOMATIC REVOLVER

No. 6R1480 44-caliber, rubber stock, 5½-inch barrel, nickeled finish. Our special price $5.50
No. 6R1481 44-caliber, rubber stock, 5½-inch barrel, blued finish. Our special price $5.90

Colt's New Service Double Action Revolver.

45-Caliber.

The New Service Double Action Revolvers, jointless solid frame, combined with simultaneous ejector, using 45-caliber Colt's double action cartridges; 5½ or 7½-inch barrel. Blued finish only. Weight, about 2 pounds.

No. 6R1561 45-caliber, 5½-inch barrel, blued finish. Each $15.40
No. 6R1563 45-caliber, 7½-in. bbl., blued. 15.40

We carry only blued finish in stock, but can supply nickel plated to special order, and must be shipped from factory, when wanted in nickel plated.

Pearl Stocks, extra $5.50

If by mail, postage extra, 44 cents.

COLT'S REVOLVERS.

MADE BY THE COLT'S FIRE ARMS CO., HARTFORD, CONN.

Colt's New Pocket Revolver.

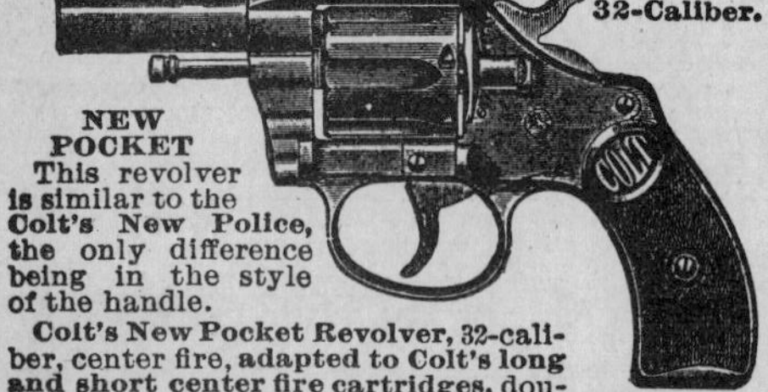

32-Caliber.

NEW POCKET

This revolver is similar to the Colt's New Police, the only difference being in the style of the handle.

Colt's New Pocket Revolver, 32-caliber, center fire, adapted to Colt's long and short center fire cartridges, double action, self cocking, jointless solid frame with simultaneous extractor. Weight, about 14 ounces. Nickel plated and blued finish.

No. 6R1500 32-caliber, 3½-inch barrel, nickel plated. Each $11.00
No. 6R1501 32-caliber, 3½-in. bbl., blued 11.00
Pearl stocks, extra 1.60

If by registered mail, postage extra, 25 cents.

Colt's New Police Revolver.

32-Caliber.

32-Caliber Colt's New Police Double Action Side Ejecting Revolver, jointless solid frame combined with simultaneous ejector, using the 32 short or 32 long Colt double action, center fire cartridges. This is the revolver adopted by the New York City police. Length of barrel, 4 inches.

No. 6R1511 32-caliber, blued finish, 4-inch barrel. Price $12.10
Pearl stocks, extra 3.00

If by mail, postage extra, 40 cents.

Colt's New Navy Revolver.

Cut showing the revolver open. 38 and 41-Caliber.

This Revolver has been adopted by the U. S. navy, and every one has to pass a rigid inspection.

Colt's New Navy double action, self cocking, automatic shell ejecting revolver, rubber stock, beautifully finshed, finest material, length about 12½ inches; six shooter; weight, 2 pounds; nickel plated or blued.

Colt's New Navy.

No. 6R1520 38-cal., 4½-in. bbl., nickel plated $13.20
No. 6R1521 38-caliber, 4½-in. bbl., blued... 13.20
No. 6R1522 38-cal., 6-in. bbl., nickel plated. 13.20
No. 6R1523 38-caliber, 6-in. bbl., blued.... 13.20
No. 6R1524 41-cal., 4½-in. bbl., nickel plated 13.20
No. 6R1525 41-caliber, 4½-in. bbl., blued... 13.20
No. 6R1526 41-cal., 6-in. bbl., nickel plated. 13.20
No. 6R1527 41-caliber, 6-in. bbl., blued.... 13.20
Pearl Stocks, extra 3.00

If by mail, postage extra, 40 cents.

SEE OUR NEW PRICES ON..... **AMMUNITION**

We are selling the very best guaranteed Ammunition at lower prices than ever before.

THE LOWEST PRICES QUOTED BY ANY FIRM.

Colt's Double Action Revolver.

38 and 41-Caliber.

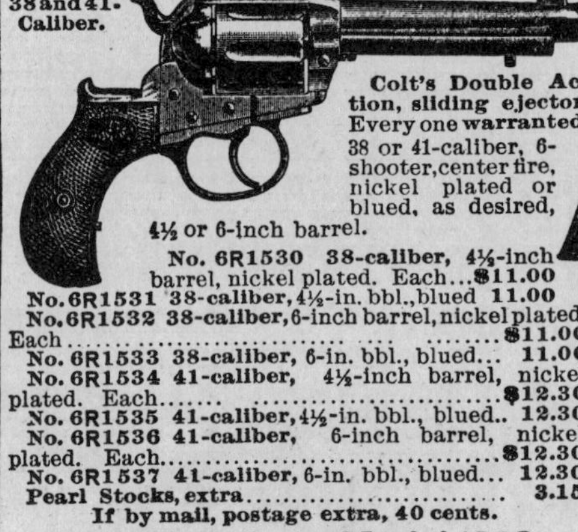

Colt's Double Action, sliding ejector. Every one warranted. 38 or 41-caliber, 6-shooter, center fire, nickel plated or blued, as desired, 4½ or 6-inch barrel.

No. 6R1530 38-caliber, 4½-inch barrel, nickel plated. Each ...$11.00
No. 6R1531 38-caliber, 4½-in. bbl., blued 11.00
No. 6R1532 38-caliber, 6-inch barrel, nickel plated. Each $11.00
No. 6R1533 38-caliber, 6-in. bbl., blued.... 11.00
No. 6R1534 41-caliber, 4½-inch barrel, nickel plated. Each $12.30
No. 6R1535 41-caliber, 4½-in. bbl., blued.. 12.30
No. 6R1536 41-caliber, 6-inch barrel, nickel plated. Each $12.30
No. 6R1537 41-caliber, 6-in. bbl., blued... 12.30
Pearl Stocks, extra 3.15

If by mail, postage extra, 40 cents.

Colt's New Army Model 1892.

38 and 41-Caliber.

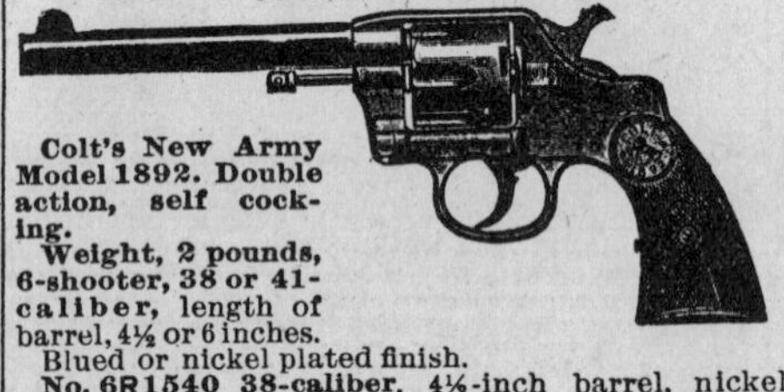

Colt's New Army Model 1892. Double action, self cocking. Weight, 2 pounds, 6-shooter, 38 or 41-caliber, length of barrel, 4½ or 6 inches. Blued or nickel plated finish.

No. 6R1540 38-caliber, 4½-inch barrel, nickel plated. Each $13.20
No. 6R1541 38-caliber, 4½-in. bbl., blued. 13.20
No. 6R1542 38-caliber, 6-inch barrel, nickel plated. Each $13.20
No. 6R1543 38-caliber, 6-in. bbl., blued... 13.20
No. 6R1544 41-caliber, 4½-inch barrel, nickel plated. Each $13.20
No. 6R1545 41-caliber, 4½-in. bbl., blued. 13.20
No. 6R1546 41-caliber, 6-inch barrel, nickel plated. Each $13.20
No. 6R1547 41-caliber, 6-in. bbl., blued.. 13.20
Pearl Stocks, extra 3.00

If by mail, postage extra, 40 cents.

Colt's Double Action Army Revolver.

44 and 45-Caliber.

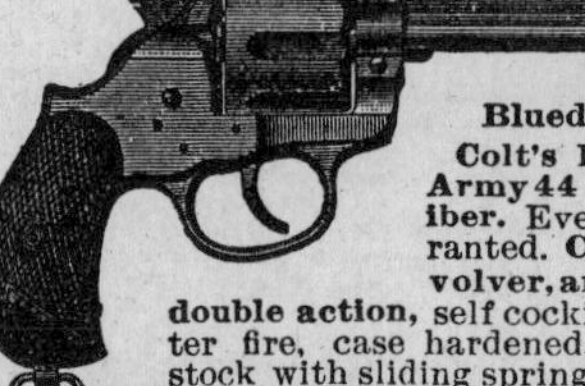

Blued finish only.

Colt's Double Action Army 44 and 45-caliber. Every one warranted. Colt's revolver, army size double action, self cocking, center fire, case hardened, rubber stock with sliding spring ejector. Blued finish barrel, 5½ or 7½ inches long; 44 and 45-caliber; 6-shooter.

No. 6R1551 44-caliber, 5½-inch barrel, blued finish. Each $14.30
No. 6R1553 44-caliber, 7½-inch barrel, blued finish. Each $14.30
No. 6R1555 45-caliber, 5½-inch barrel, blued finish. Each $14.30
No. 6R1557 45-caliber, 7½-inch barrel, blued finish. Each $14.30
Pearl Stocks, extra 4.25

We can furnish these revolvers in nickel plated, but they would not be regular in our stock, and we ship these from the factory when ordered nickel plated.

If by mail, postage extra, 44 cents.

Colt's Single Action Army, Frontier and Target Revolver.

32, 41, 44 and 45-Caliber.

This is the old reliable Cowboys' Gun, and our special price is $13.20 for all calibers. Blued finish only. Colt's single action, 6-shooter, rubber stock, solid frame, the best quality and finish; warranted perfect and accurate in every detail. Barrel 5½ or 7½ inches; entire length 12½ inches; 32, 41, 44 or 45-caliber, as desired. We can furnish these in blued finish.

The 32-caliber takes the 32-caliber Winchester cartridge No. 6R2384. The 41-caliber takes the 41-caliber Colt's C. F. cartridge No. 6R2401. The 44-caliber is called The Frontier and takes the 44-caliber Winchester C.F. cartridge No. 6R2409, and the 45-caliber takes the Colt's 45-caliber C. F. cartridges No. 6R2413.

When ordering say which length barrel you prefer.

No. 6R1571 32-20-caliber, 5½-in. bbl., blued $13.20
No. 6R1573 32-20-caliber, 7½-in. bbl., blued 13.20
No. 6R1575 41-caliber, 5½-in. bbl., blued... 13.20
No. 6R1577 41-caliber, 7½-in. bbl., blued... 13.20
No. 6R1579 44-40-caliber, 5½-in. bbl., blued 13.20
No. 6R1581 44-40-caliber, 7½-in. bbl., blued 13.20
No. 6R1583 45-caliber, 5½-inch barrel, blued finish. Each $13.20
No. 6R1585 45-caliber, 7½-inch barrel, blued finish. Each $13.20
Pearl Stocks, extra 5.35

If by mail, postage extra, 44 cents.

Nickel plated finish furnished to special order, and shipped from factory.

Colt's Special Pearl Handle Revolver

Single Action Frontier.

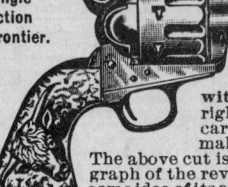

This is our special Cowboy's Six Shooter with pearl handles. The right handle has an Ox Head carved in raised design and makes a handsome revolver. The above cut is engraved from a photograph of the revolver and will give you some idea of its appearance. Blued finish.

When ordering say which length barrel you prefer.

No. 6R1587 32-20-caliber, 5½-inch barrel. $22.00
No. 6R1589 32-20-caliber, 7½-inch barrel. 22.00
No. 6R1591 44-40-caliber, 5½-inch barrel. 22.00
No. 6R1593 44-40-caliber, 7½-inch barrel. 22.00

The above may be had in 41 and 45-calibers to special order, cash with order.

Colt's Single Action Bisley Model Revolver.

45-Caliber.

The Colt's Bisley Model Revolver is patterned after the Single Action Army Revolver, but has a longer handle, a different shape hammer, and the lock work is somewhat different, and it makes a good smooth working revolver. The frame is case hardened, and the barrel and cylinder are blued. This revolver embodies all the high grade workmanship of the famous Colt's revolvers. We carry this revolver regularly in 45-caliber, using 45-caliber Colt's cartridges, but we can furnish it to special order (cash with order) to take the 45 Colts, 38-40 and 44-40 caliber rifle cartridges.

No. 6R1610½ 32-20-caliber, 5½-inch barrel, blued finish. Weight, 40 ounces. Price, each $13.20
No. 6R1611½ 32-20-caliber, 7½-inch barrel, blued finish. Weight, 40 ounces. Price, each $13.20

If by mail, postage extra, 45 cents.

NOTICE—On any goods not described or listed in this catalogue and bought for your convenience, cash in full must accompany order as on all other merchandise, and they cannot be returned under any circumstances.

GENUINE SMITH & WESSON REVOLVERS.

Smith & Wesson Side Ejecting Revolver.

Solid Frame, side ejecting, rebounding lock, rubber stock, blued or nickel plated; weight, 19 ounces; 3¼, 4¼ and 6-inch barrel; 6 shot, using 32-caliber S. & W. long cartridge No. 6R2376. A fine, strong shooting revolver with a solid steel frame.

No. 6R1702 32 caliber 3¼-inch barrel, nickel plated $10.50
No. 6R1703 32 caliber 3¼-inch barrel, blued finish. 10.50
No. 6R1704 32 caliber 4¼-inch barrel, nickel plated 10.75
No. 6R1705 32 caliber 4¼-inch barrel, blued finish. 10.75
No. 6R1706 32 caliber 6 -inch barrel, nickel plated $11.25
No. 6R1707 32 caliber 6 -inch barrel, blued finish 11.25
First Quality Pearl Stocks, extra 1.25
If by mail or prepaid express, 20 to 30 cents extra.

Model 1899 Smith & Wesson Military and Police Revolver.

Double action, center fire, 6-shot; with solid frame; swing-out cylinder and hand ejecting mechanism; weight, 30 ounces; 5 and 6½-inch barrel; blued or nickeled frame; using 38-caliber long Colt DA cartridge No. 6R2392. **This revolver is Smith & Wesson's latest creation and is a revolver that is built for business.** It will withstand hard usage and has a movable firing pin on the nose of the hammer, which absolutely closes the firing pin hole and prevents any possible gas from going back of the frame. It is highly recommended for target shooting, and made in blued or nickeled finish. Weight, 1¾ to 2 pounds.

No. 6R1714 Our special price, with 5 -inch barrel, nickel plated $14.00
No. 6R1715 Our special price, with 5 -inch barrel, blued finish. 14.00
No. 6R1716 Our special price, with 6½-inch barrel, nickel plated 14.50
No. 6R1717 Our special price, with 6½-inch barrel, blued finish.. 14.50
First Quality Pearl Stocks, extra 2.25
If by mail, postage extra, 40 cents.
Smith & Wesson Revolvers are not made for 32-20 or 38-40 cartridges.

FOR PEARL STOCKS, with ox head carved on the right hand side, add $4.00 to the price of pearl. Cash in full must accompany all orders.

The Genuine Smith & Wesson Double Action Revolvers.

These revolvers are warranted genuine Smith & Wesson. Manufactured by Smith & Wesson, Springfield, Mass. **Self cocking, double action,** automatic shell extractor, fine rubber stocks, nickel plated or blued finish. Made of the finest material that money can buy and the workmanship is equal in finish to that of any ordinary watch. If you want the best work for your money buy a Smith & Wesson.

DOUBLE ACTION REVOLVERS.

No. 6R1720 32-caliber, 5-shot, 3 -inch barrel, nickel plated...... $10.75
No. 6R1721 32-caliber, 5-shot, 3 -inch barrel, blued finish 10.75
No. 6R1722 32-caliber, 5-shot, 3½-inch barrel, nickel plated. 10.75
No. 6R1723 32-caliber, 5-shot, 3½-inch barrel, blued 10.75
No. 6R1726 32-caliber, 5-shot, 6 -inch barrel, nickel plated 11.75
No. 6R1727 32-caliber, 5-shot, 6 -inch barrel, blued 11.75
No. 6R1730 38-caliber, 5-shot, 3¼-inch barrel, nickel plated...... 11.75
No. 6R1731 38-caliber, 5-shot, 3¼-inch barrel, blued 11.75
No. 6R1732 38-caliber, 5-shot, 4 -inch barrel, nickel plated...... 12.00
No. 6R1733 38-caliber, 5-shot, 4 -inch barrel, blued 12.00
No. 6R1734 38-caliber, 5-shot, 5 -inch barrel, nickel plated 12.25
No. 6R1735 38-caliber, 5-shot, 5 -inch barrel, blued 12.25
No. 6R1736 38-caliber, 5-shot, 6 -inch barrel, nickel plated...... 12.75
No. 6R1737 38-caliber, 5-shot, 6 -inch barrel, blued 12.75
First Quality Pearl stocks for 32 or 38-caliber, extra 1.25
Any of the above by mail or prepaid express, 20 to 30 cents extra.

SMITH & WESSON FRONTIER DOUBLE ACTION—44-caliber.

No. 6R1746 44-Caliber, Frontier, 6-shot, 6-inch barrel, chambered for 44-caliber Winchester cartridges, nickel plated $14.50
No. 6R1747 44-Caliber, Frontier, 6-shot, 6-inch barrel, chambered for 44-caliber Winchester cartridges, blued finish 14.50
First Quality Pearl handles on 44-caliber revolvers, extra 2.50
If by mail, postage extra, 40 to 50 cents.

Smith & Wesson Hammerless Revolvers.

The GENUINE SMITH & WESSON HAMMERLESS.

Made by Smith & Wesson, Springfield, Mass. Latest type, new model hammerless, automatic shell ejector, patent safety catch self locking rebounding locks, double action, blued or nickel plated finish. This is positively the best hammerless revolver made. "A thing of beauty is a joy forever." If you own one of these revolvers you are certain to own one of the best revolvers made and one which always has a market value.

PRICES OF THE S. & W. HAMMERLESS.

No. 6R1752 32-caliber, 3 -inch barrel, nickel plated $11.75
No. 6R1753 32-caliber, 3 -inch barrel, blued finish 11.75
No. 6R1754 32-caliber, 3½-inch barrel, nickel plated 11.75
No. 6R1755 32-caliber, 3½-inch barrel, blued finish 11.75
No. 6R1760 38-caliber, 3¼-inch barrel, nickel plated 12.75
No. 6R1761 38-caliber, 3¼-inch barrel, blued finish 12.75
No. 6R1762 38-caliber, 4 -inch barrel, nickel plated 13.00
No. 6R1763 38-caliber, 4 -inch barrel, blued finish 13.00
No. 6R1764 38-caliber, 5 -inch barrel, nickel plated 13.25
No. 6R1765 38-caliber, 5 -inch barrel, blued finish 13.25
No. 6R1766 38-caliber, 6 -inch barrel, nickel plated 13.75
No. 6R1767 38-caliber, 6 -inch barrel, blued finish 13.75
First Quality Pearl Stocks, extra 1.25
If by mail, postage extra, 18 to 30 cents. ☞ See our prices on cartridges.

NOTICE—On any goods not described or listed in this catalogue and made to order, we must ask cash in full with the order, the same terms as apply on other items, and they cannot be returned under any circumstances.

RUSTED AND DAMAGED GUNS.

Do not return to us a gun, revolver or rifle which is rusted, pitted or has the finish worn off, for we have no way of selling these guns. If you have a gun, revolver or rifle which needs repairing, first write us fully, describing the article and what is broken, and we may be able to send you the part necessary, thus saving the express charges on the gun both ways.

The New Model King Air Rifle, Single Shot.

Our King Rifles we Guarantee the Highest Grade Made.

68 Cents.

All metal, **nickel plated,** shoots BB shot. Length of barrel 19 inches, length over all 34 inches. Weight, 2 pounds. **The New Model King Air Rifle shoots common BB shot** accurately and with sufficient force to go through ¾-inch soft pine. **The barrel and all working parts can be easily removed** by simply unscrewing the metal cap on front part of gun, a feature when seen that must be appreciated, as it makes the removal of shot that are sure to become lodged in all muzzle loading air guns a very simple and easy matter. **Each gun is sighted with movable sights.**

No. 6R1832 Our special price for the single shot 68c
No. 6R1833 The New King Repeater. Same style as King single shot. This is one of the best Repeating Air Rifles on the market, and **shoots 152 times at one loading.** Our special price $1.10
If by mail, postage extra, 44 cents.

The Improved Daisy Air Rifle for 73 Cents.

Our 73-cent Daisy is the most perfect little all metal gun ever shown. Shoots No. 18-100 darts and BB shot.

Made entirely of metal and wood, nickel plated, latest improved pattern; length of barrel, 19 inches; **total length, 30 inches.** Weight, 2 pounds. Is now fitted **with globe sights,** each rifle carefully tested before leaving factory. This is the latest model improved Daisy Air Rifle. Shoots shot or darts.

No. 6R1835 Our special price, with skeleton wood stock 73c
If by mail, postage extra, 48 cents.
DARTS. For prices of darts see Quackenbush Air Rifles.

The New Rapid. The Latest Air Rifle, 95 Cents.

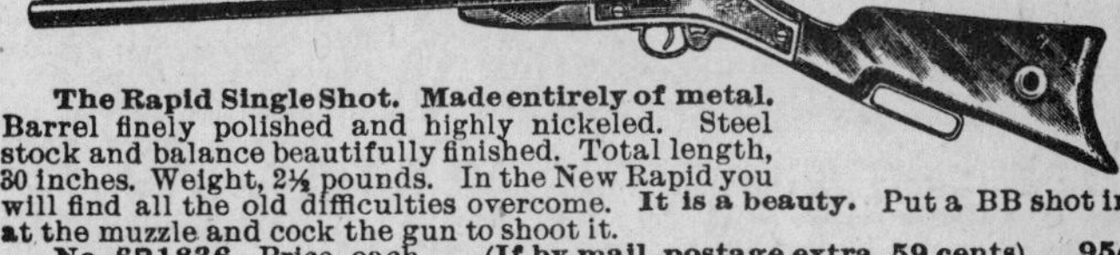

The Rapid Single Shot. Made entirely of metal. Barrel finely polished and highly nickeled. Steel stock and balance beautifully finished. Total length, 30 inches. Weight, 2¼ pounds. In the New Rapid you will find all the old difficulties overcome. **It is a beauty.** Put a BB shot in at the muzzle and cock the gun to shoot it.

No. 6R1836 Price, each.....**(If by mail, postage extra, 59 cents)**....95c

Our Sheet Steel Single Shot Air Rifle, 66 Cents.

This Air Rifle is constructed of sheet metal, has a nicely nickel plated barrel and frame, wood stock and will shoot the ordinary BB air rifle shot. In order to load the gun, first drop a BB shot into the barrel, then cock the gun until you hear the trigger click, and the gun is ready to shoot. The total length of the Steel Air Rifle is 30 inches, and weighs about 2 pounds, and the above illustration, which is engraved from a photograph, will give you a general idea of its appearance.

No. 6R1842 Our special price on this Steel Single Shot Air Rifle.....66c
If by mail, postage extra, 36 cents.

Our New Rival Single Shot Air Rifle, 67 Cents.

The Rival Single Shot Air Rifle is the latest thing in air rifles. The frame and barrel are made of sheet steel; **no castings to break.** This rifle is made to shoot a BB shot as accurately and with as much force as any air rifle made. The barrel and frame are nickel plated, the stock is made of good seasoned wood and the rifle is cocked by the well known hinge system, and almost any boy can operate it. The above cut is engraved from the rifle and will give you some idea of it. **Each gun is sighted and tested before it leaves the factory.** The entire gun is 34 inches long and weighs about 2 pounds.

No. 6R1844 Our special price 67c
If by mail, postage extra, 44 cents.

The Columbian 1,000-Shot Air Rifle, $1.40.

The Columbian 1,000-Shot Air Rifle, as now made, with improved lock parts and magazine, is an air rifle which will give universal satisfaction. The loading device is very similar to that of the old model air rifle, that by pushing the sleeve forward you fill the magazine with BB shot, and to operate the rifle, hold the gun in the left hand, turn the muzzle toward the ceiling, throw the lever forward, same as you would with the Winchester rifle, and the gun loads itself. **Every time you throw the lever you put a shot in the barrel,** it is best to shoot after you load the gun, or you will get several pellets in the barrel. **Should an imperfect shot get into the barrel,** it can easily be removed by cocking the gun and inserting a wire from the muzzle, which pushes the shot into the chamber from which it can be easily removed. **The Columbian Repeating Air Rifle** will hold about 1,000 pellets of BB shot in the magazine, and can be shot repeatedly until the magazine is empty. The entire length of the **Columbian 1,000-Shot Air Rifle** is 34½ inches; the barrel is nickel plated and the frame is japanned; the stock is a good seasoned hardwood. **The gun weighs about 4¼ pounds.** It looks like a Winchester, works like a Winchester and pleases the boys.

No. 6R1846 Our special price.......**(Cannot be sent by mail)**......$1.40

NOTICE—On any goods not described or listed in this catalogue and made to order, we must ask cash in full with the order, the same terms as apply on other items, and they cannot be returned under any circumstances

LOADED SHOTGUN SHELLS.

IN DIRECTING YOUR ATTENTION to our line of loaded shotgun shells in the different sizes of shells and loads, both in black and smokeless powder, the highest grade of loaded shotgun shells made, we wish to plainly state that in offering these shells we are not restrained by the makers as to the price at which we can sell them. We are not called upon to enter into an agreement to sell them at exorbitant prices. We have not by any agreement placed ourselves in a position where we are compelled to take an exorbitant profit from our customers.

THE AMERICAN ASSOCIATION LOADED SHOTGUN SHELLS are supplied by the manufacturers only to such houses as will enter into an agreement to charge what we consider an exorbitant price for the goods. For example, they will furnish us 12-gauge shotgun shells, loaded with three drams of black powder and one ounce shot at a net price of $1.21 per hundred; only on condition that we will not print a price in our catalogue less than $1.66 per hundred. This makes a profit of about $4.50 on 1,000 shells, and they exact about the same ratio of difference between their selling price to us and the price at which they will permit us to print in our catalogue on their entire line of all grades and sizes of loaded shotgun shells and metallic cartridges for revolvers, rifles, etc., and if we decline to ask such exorbitant profits and print such high prices they flatly refuse to sell us the goods, and any catalogue house or other concern who prints these prices which these companies exact are in our opinion taking om their customers an unfair and unjust profit.

WE HAVE NEARLY THREE MILLION CUSTOMERS in the United States and we do not believe that one of them would care to buy a shotgun, revolver or rifle shell or cartridge made by a company who sell their oods only on condition that such big profits be added to their selling price, emanding that the man who uses the goods (at least in our judgment) must pay for them more than they are worth.

OUR BLACK AND SMOKELESS POWDER LOA ED SHELLS come packed 25 shells in a paper box, 20 boxes or 500 shells in a case. A case of 500 12-gauge shells weighs about 65 pounds; a case of 500 10-gauge shells weighs about 75 pounds.

TO GIVE YOU A BETTER MACHINE LOADED SHELL than you can possibly get elsewhere, to give you higher grade of metallic cartridges for revolvers and rifles than you can possibly get elsewhere and to furnish them to you at honest prices, prices based on the actual cost to make, material and labor with but our one small percentage of profit added, we have arranged for a supply of shells, metallic cartridges and ammunition, the highest of high grade, which we put out under our binding guarantee as to quality, and we urge you in behalf of honest merchandising to at least give our ammunition a trial, and call your attention to our position, which in spite of concerted effort to maintain high prices, we are prepared to supply you the highest grade of goods at lower prices than ever before.

OUR LOADED SHOTGUN SHELLS in both smokeless and black powder are made for us under contract by one of the best makers in America, a manufacturer who heretofore has manufactured a loaded shell in limited quantities for special trade where only extra high grade goods were wanted, for trap shooters, market shooters, semi-professional sportsmen, etc. These goods have always commanded extra high prices, but feeling forced in behalf of our customers to give them a very high grade of ammunition and at lower prices than we cared to allow others to dictate us to ask, we arranged with this manufacturer to largely increase his manufacturing capacity to accommodate our needs, and in doing this we made an arrangement whereby we could be supplied on the basis of the actual cost of material and labor with a very small manufacturing profit to which we add our one small percentage of profit, and for strength, sure fire, penetration, pattern, shape, cleanliness of action, in fact in every essential point, we guarantee our loaded ammunition, and especially our shotgun shells to be superior to any machine loaded shells on the market regardless of price.

IN THE LOADING OF OUR SHELLS only the most approved and highest type of machinery is employed. The even pressure of the powder is perfectly controlled in the loading, the even pressure of the wadding on the powder is unmatchable, the quality of the wadding, the quality of the shot has been carefully observed, and if you will send us an ord , no matter how small, we assure you you will use no other than our speci l loaded shells.

WE ADVISE THAT YOU ASK YOUR FRIENDS to join with you and order these shells by the case or by the thousand and ship them by freight, so as to save you the express charges which are always considerably higher than freight charges.

Our Line of Black Powder Loaded Shells.

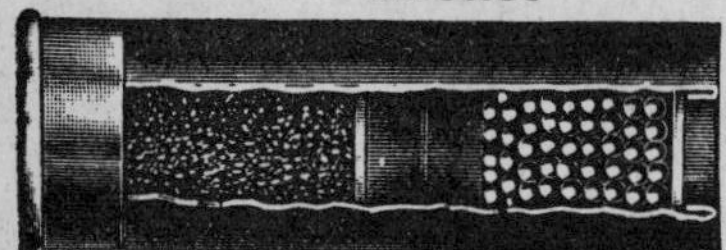

We have all our shells loaded especially to our order with the best quality of black powder, the best quality and style of wadding, the best quality of shot by one of the best shell loading companies.

Order No. 6R2212 12-GAUGE. LOADED WITH BLACK POWDER.

Load No.	Drams of Powd'r	Ounces of Shot	Size of Shot	Price per box of 25 Shells	Price per 100 Shells
206 208 200	3	1	6 8 10	34c	$1.35
214 216 218	3	1 1/8	4 6 8	35c	$1.40
232 234 235 236 237 238	3 1/4	1 1/8	2 4 5 6 7 8	36c	$1.43
264 266 268	3 1/2	1 1/8	4 6 8	37c	$1.45
28B	3 3/4	1 1/8	BB	40c	$1.60
5B	3 1/2	1 1/8	5 Buck	45c	$1.80

Order No. 6R2210 10-GAUGE. LOADED WITH BLACK POWDER.

Load No.	Drams of Powd'r	Ounces of Shot	Size of Shot	Price per box of 25 Shells	Price per 100 Shel
120	4	1 1/8	10	39c	$1.5
134 136 138	4 1/4	1 1/8	4 6 8	40c	$1.59
152 154	4 1/2	1 1/8	2 4	45c	$1.80
19BB	5	1 1/8	BB	45c	$1.80

Order No. 6R2216 16-GAUGE. LOADED WITH BLACK POWDER.

Load No.	Drams of Powd'r	Ounces of Shot	Size of Shot	Price per box of 25 Shells	Price per 100 Shells
416	2 3/4	1	6	35c	$1.40
418	2 3/4	1	8	35c	1.40

Order No. 6R2220 20-GAUGE. LOADED WITH BLACK POWDER.

Load No.	Drams of Powd'r	Ounces of Shot	Size of Shot	Price per box of 25 Shells	Price per 100 Shells
4206	2 1/2	7/8	6	34c	$1. 5
4208	2 1/2	7/8	8	34c	1. 5

Black Powder Hand Loaded Shells.

To any of our customers, who wish any specially loaded shells not mentioned in this catalogue, we will load by hand, the same loads as mentioned in this catalogue, but we will be obliged to charge 20 per cent extra for this work; for instance, if you wish specially loaded shells 3 drams of black powder, and 1 ounce of shot, we will be obliged to charge 20 per cent more for the hand loaded than for the machine loaded shells, which we describe in this catalogue.

For any special loads of buckshot we cannot load less than 25 at a time, and we must charge for these, with black powder, $1.25 per box of 25 shells.

OUR SMOKELESS POWDER LOADED SHELLS.

We have done considerable experimenting with medium and high priced smokeless loaded shells, and as far as pattern, carrying power, and penetration are concerned, we find that by shooting the medium grade smokeless shells, and the high priced grade smokeless shells, in the same guns, the pattern, penetration and carrying power is almost identical and we therefore abandon all high grade and high priced smokeless powder loaded shells, believing that we should not ask our customers to pay any more for high priced goods than is necessary when the medium priced goods answer the same purpose.

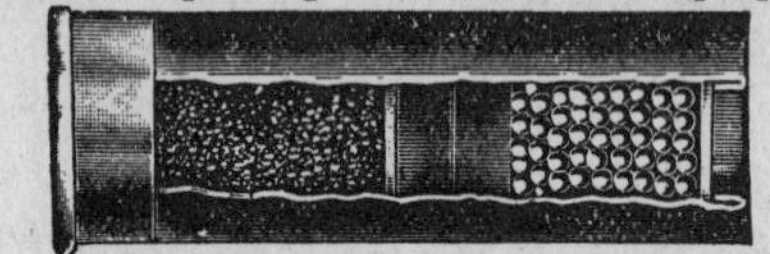

LOADED WITH SMOKELESS POWDER. No. 6R2232 12-GAUGE.

Load No.	Drams of Powder	Weight of Shot	Size of Shot	Price per box of 25 Shells	Price per 100 Shells
x 6-706 x 6-708 x 6-700	3	1 oz.	No. 6 No. 8 No. 10	44c	$1.75
x 7-762 x 7-764 x 7-766 x 7-768	3	1 1/8 oz.	No. 2 No. 4 No. 6 No. 8	46c	$1.83
x 8-772 x 8-774	3	1 1/4 oz.	No. 2 No. 4	48c	$1.90

No. 6R2230 10-GAUGE.

Load No.	Drams of Powder	Weight of Shot	Size of Shot	Price per box of 25 Shells	Price per 100 Shells
x 11-817 x 11-818 x 11-819	3 1/4	1 1/8 oz.	No. 7 No. 8 No. 9	50c	$1.99
x 14-832 x 14-834 x 14-836	3 1/2	1 1/4 oz.	No. 2 No. 4 No. 6	53c	$2.12

No. 6R2236 16-GAUGE.

Load No.	Drams of Powder	Ounces of Shot	Size of Shot	Price per box of 25 Shells	Price per 100 Shells
x20x616 x20x618	2 1/2	1	6 8	44c	$1.75

No. 6R2238 8-GAUGE. HAND LOADED.

Load No.	Drams of Powder	Ounces of Shot	Size of Shot	Price per box of 25 Shells	Price per 100 Shells
8BB	5 1/2	1 1/2	BB	$1.25	$12.50

LOADED METALLIC PISTOL AND RIFLE CARTRIDGES.

IN DIRECTING YOUR ATTENTION to our line of loaded metallic cartridges, in all the different sizes for revolvers, rifles, etc., on the following pages, we wish to state that the same price restriction condition that covers the sale of the American Association loaded or empty shotgun shells applies also to loaded metallic cartridges. The manufacturers of these metallic cartridges are willing to supply us at their lowest prices only on condition that we print certain selling prices, which in our judgment are too high, and which would compel us to ask from our customers what we would consider an exorbitant profit. For example: They will sell us 22-caliber short rim fire metallic cartridges for 21 cents per hundred only on condition that we will not print a price on these cartridges in our catalogue lower than 29c per hundred. This is about 40 per cent profit, and they exact about the same proportionate ratio of difference between their selling price to us and the price at which they will allow us to print on their entire line of metallic cartridges, and no house who buys goods from these makers, must print prices any lower than the selling prices fixed by the manufacturers, prices which in our judgment are exorbitant and entirely unfair to the customer.

DETERMINED THAT OUR CUSTOMERS shall have the highest grade of metallic cartridges, and at prices not restricted by any maker, prices based on the actual cost of material and labor with but a one small honest profit added, we have discontinued the sale of the American Association cartridges and call to your attention our special line of metallic cartridges which we offer as the highest grade cartridges made, cartridges combining all the good points of all cartridges with the defects of none. These metallic cartridges are made for us under contract, by a manufacturer who with fifteen years of experience in the making of metallic cartridges, turns out what we believe to be (and what we believe our customers will say when they use them) the highest grade cartridge made. And in the making and the loading the manufacturer employs the very highest type of machinery, the finest grades of carefully tested ammunition, a line of cartridges which for sure fire, shape, smoothness, accuracy, and above all, penetration are unexcelled, if indeed equaled by any other cartridge made.

AMONG OUR THREE MILLION CUSTOMERS we believe there are few, if any, who would want to buy a cartridge made by a manufacturer who undertakes to dictate at what price the goods shall be sold, especially when he says we must sell at a price which in our judgment means an exorbitant profit, and when we give you the opportunity of buying the highest g ade of cartridges at prices that are not controlled, prices that only pay one small percentage of profit above the cost to us, we believe that you will favor us with your orders, and will lend your kind influence in our behalf in interesting your friends and neighbors in our metallic cartridges, our loaded shotgun shells and other ammunition.

WHERE ANY MANUFACTURER UNDERTAKES TO DICTATE TO US at what prices we must sell his goods, and refuses to supply us unless we follow the prices laid down by the manufacturer, if in our judgment these prices are exorbitant and means the taking of an unfair profit from our customers, it shall be our policy in the millions of catalogues we print, that reach the hands of a very large percentage of the buying public in the United States, to make a plain statement of the facts to our people, and give them the opportunity of discriminating between goods on which the selling price is not controlled by the manufacturer as against goods which the manufacturer endeavors to control the retail selling price.

LOADED METALLIC CARTRIDGES.

COMPARE OUR RRICES WITH OTHER HOUSES.
REMEMBER OUR TERMS ARE CASH WITH ORDER.

WE CAN FURNISH ALL KINDS OF CARTRIDGES NOT ON THIS LIST AT LOWEST MARKET PRICES. Cartridges can be shipped with other goods by express or freight, but cartridges cannot be sent by mail, because they are explosive. Prices subject to change without notice. Our ammunition is always fresh. We sell large quantities, consequently have no old stock on hand.

EXPLOSIVES CANNOT BE SENT BY MAIL.

RIM FIRE CARTRIDGES.

EXPLOSIVES CANNOT BE SENT BY MAIL.

No. 6R2331 No. 6R2332 No. 6R2336 No. 6R2338 No. 6R2340 No. 6R2344

No. 6R2342 No. 6R2346 No. 6R2348 No. 6R2350 No. 6R2351 No. 6R2352 No. 6R2353

No. 6R2354

No. 6R2356

No. 6R2357

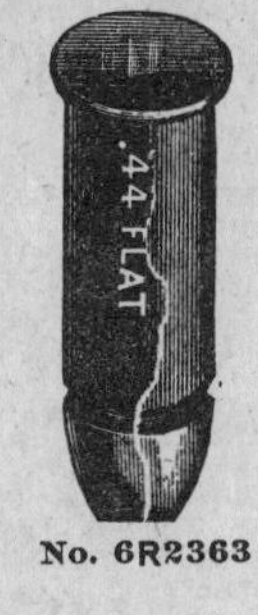
No. 6R2363

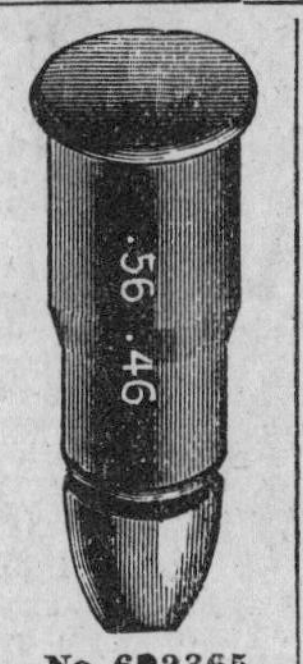
No. 6R2365

No. 6R2367

No. 6R2360

OUR TERMS ARE CASH WITH ORDER.

WE HAVE NO OLD, SHOP WORN AMMUNITION WHICH SOME HOUSES OFFER A FEW CENTS BELOW OUR PRICES. OUR AMMUNITION IS FRESH AND LOADED WITH FIRST CLASS POWDER.

No.	Caliber	Grains of Powder	Grains of Lead	Weight per 100	Price for 50	Price for 100
6R2331	B. B. Caps	....	21	7 oz.	....	$0.16
6R2332	C. B. Caps	....	24½	8 oz.	... .	.20
6R2336	22 Short	3	30	9 oz.	$0.12	.24
6R2338	22 Long	5	29	11 oz.	.14	.28
6R2340	22 Long Rifle	5	40	14 oz.	.14	.28
6R2342	22 Ex. Long	6	40	15 oz.	....	.43
6R2344	22 Winchester	7	45	18 oz.	.22	.43
6R2346	25 Stevens	11	65	29 oz.	.35	.70
6R2348	30 Short	6	55	20 oz.	.22	.43
6R2350	30 Long	9	55	21 oz.	.25	.50
6R2351	32 Ex. Short	6	55	20 oz.	.25	.50
6R2352	32 Short	9	82	27 oz.	.24	.48
6R2353	32 Long	13	90	30 oz.	.28	.55
6R2354	32 Ex. Long	20	90	33 oz.	.40	.80
6R2356	38 Short	18	130	43 oz.	.38	.76
6R2357	38 Long	21	148	48 oz.	.43	.86
6R2360	41 Short	13	130	40 oz.	.38	.75
6R2361	41 Long	16	130	43 oz.	.43	.85
6R2363	44 Flat	28	200	64 oz.	.57	1.14
6R2364	44 Long Ballard	28	220	4½ lbs.	.60	1.20
6R2365	56-46 Spencer	45	330	6½ lbs.	.95	1.90
6R2366	56-50 Spencer	45	350	7 lbs.	.95	1.90
6R2367	56-52 Spencer	45	386	7 lbs.	.95	1.90
6R2368	56-56 Spencer	45	350	6¾ lbs.	.95	1.90

Our price is the same for a box as it is for 1000.

Our Terms are Cash with Order.

Explosives cannot be sent by mail.

CENTRAL FIRE PISTOL AND RIFLE CARTRIDGES.

Our Terms are Cash with Order.

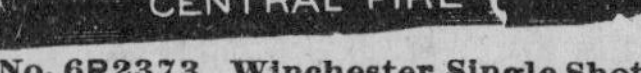

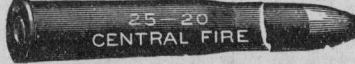

No. 6R2371 No. 6R2373 Winchester Single Shot. No. 6R2374 No. 6R2382

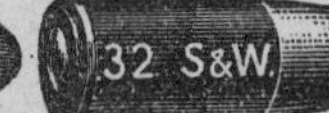

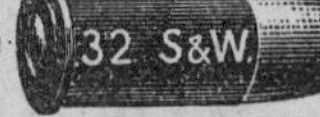

No. 6R2376 Hand Ejector. No. 6R2377 No. 6R2378 No. 6R2380 No. 6R2381 No. 6R2375 Model 1894.

No. 6R2383 No. 6R2384 No. 6R2388 No. 6R2389 Target No. 6R2391

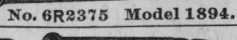

OUR TERMS ARE CASH WITH ORDER.

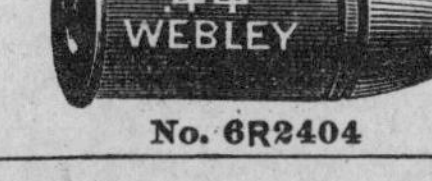
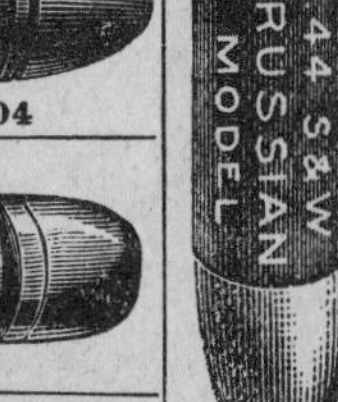

No. 6R2404

No. 6R2406

No. 6R2396 No. 6R2401

No. 6R2397 No. 6R2405

No. 6R2407 No. 6R2413

No. 6R2409 No. 6R2411

No. 6R2408

WE HANDLE ONLY FRESH AMMUNITION DIRECT FROM THE FACTORY, LOADED WITH FIRST CLASS POWDER.

No.	Caliber	Grains of Powd'r	Grains of Lead	Weight per 100	Price for 50	Price for 100
6R2371	22 Winchester S. S.	13	45	1½ lbs.	$0.54	$1.07
6R2373	25-20 Winchester S. S.	19	86	2½ lbs.	.68	1.35
6R2374	25-20 Winchester, '92	17	86	2½ lbs.	.57	1.14
6R2375	25-20 Marlin	17	86	2½ lbs.	.57	1.14
6R2376	32 S. &. W. Long	13	98	2¼ lbs.	.45	.90
6R2377	32 Smith & Wesson	9	85	1½ lbs.	.39	.78
6R2378	32-44 S. & W. Target	10	85	2 lbs.	.71	1.42
6R2379	32-44 S. & W. Gallery	4½	55	1½ lbs.	.68	1.35
6R2380	32 Short Colts Revolver.	9	82	1½ lbs.	.39	.78
6R2381	32 Long Colts Revolver.	13	90	2 lbs.	.43	.85
6R2382	32 Ex. Long	20	105	2½ lbs.	.68	1.35
6R2383	32 Colts Rifle	20	100	3 lbs.	.57	1.14
6R2384	32-20 Winchester	20	115	3 lbs.	.57	1.14
6R2385	32-20 Marlin	20	100	3 lbs.	.57	1.14
6R2386	32-30 Remington	30	125	3¼ lbs.	.94	1.87
6R2387	32 Ideal	25	150	3½ lbs.	.75	1.50
6R2388	38 Smith & Wesson	14	145	3¼ lbs.	.48	.96
6R2389	38-44 S. & W. Target	20	146	3½ lbs.	.86	1. 72
6R2391	38 Short Colts	18	130	3 lbs.	.48	.96
6R2392	38 Long Colts	19	150	3¼ lbs.	.52	1.03
6R2396	38-40 Winchester	40	180	4½ lbs.	.68	1.35
6R2397	38-40 Colts N. L	38	180	4½ lbs.	.68	1.35
6R2398	38-40 Marlin	40	180	4½ lbs.	.68	1.35
6R2400	41 Short Colts	14	160	3¼ lbs.	.54	1.07
6R2401	41 Long Colts	21	200	4¼ lbs.	.62	1.24
6R2404	44 Webley	18	200	4 lbs.	.59	1.17
6R2405	44 S. & W. Am	25	205	4¼ lbs.	.68	1.35
6R2406	44 S. & W. Russian	23	255	5 lbs.	.71	1.42
6R2407	44 Evans, Old Model	28	215	4½ lbs.	.83	1.65
6R2408	44 Colts Revolver	23	210	4¼ lbs.	.71	1.42
6R2409	44-40 Winchester	40	200	5 lbs.	.68	1.35
6R2411	44-40 Colts N. L	40	217	5 lbs.	.68	1.35
6R2412	44-40 Marlin	40	217	5 lbs.	.68	1.35
6R2413	45 Colts Revolver	40	250	5½ lbs.	.79	1.57

Our price is the same for a box as it is for 1000. We always give the lowest prices.

COMPARE OUR PRICES WITH OTHER HOUSES. NONE CAN COMPETE WITH US.

CENTER FIRE MILITARY AND SPORTING CARTRIDGES. ....LOADED WITH BLACK POWDER.

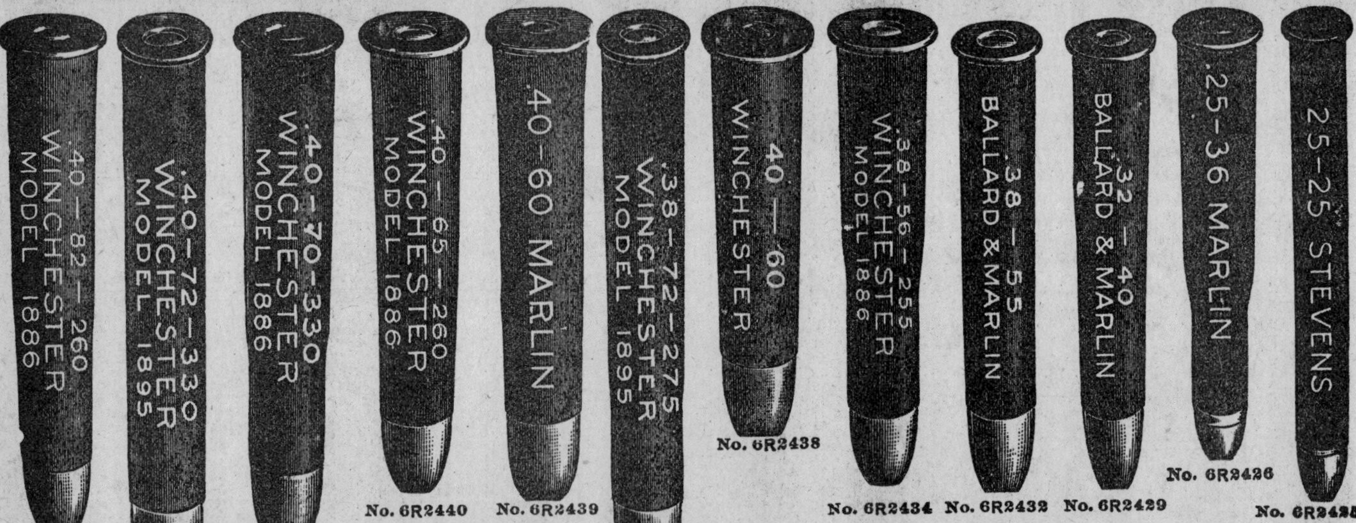

No. 6R2458 No. 6R2455 No. 6R2451 No. 6R2440 No. 6R2439 No. 6R2436 No. 6R2438 No. 6R2434 No. 6R2432 No. 6R2429 No. 6R2426 No. 6R2425

CASH IN FULL MUST ACCOMPANY ALL ORDERS.

ALL THESE CARTRIDGES HAVE LEAD BULLETS ONLY.

EXPLOSIVES CANNOT BE SENT BY MAIL.

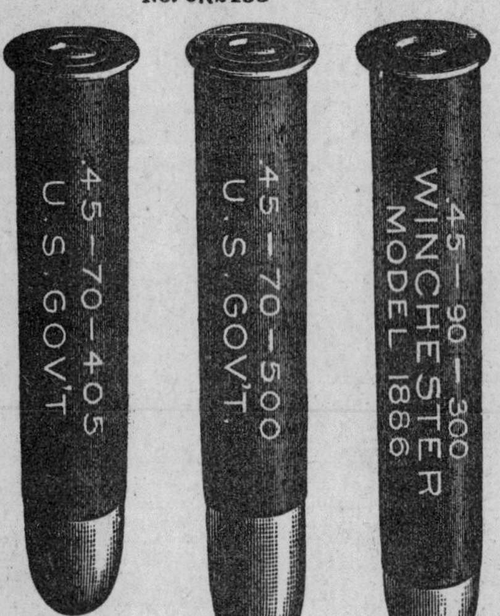

No. 6R246 No. 6R2474 No. 6R2480 No. 6R2490

COMPARE OUR PRICES WITH OTHER HOUSES

NONE CAN COMPETE WITH US

PRICES:

No.	Caliber	Grains of Powd'r	Grains of Lead	Weight per 100	Price for 20	Price for 100
6R2429	32-40 Ballard & Marlin..	40	165	6 lbs	.42	2.06
6R2430	32-40 Marlin S. Range....	13	98	5½ lbs	.44	2.18
6R2432	38-55 Marlin.	55	255	7 lbs	.51	2.52
6R2433	38-55 Ballard & Marlin.. Short Range..........	20	155	6⅛ lbs	.54	2.66
6R2434	38-56 Winchester.........	56	255	8 lbs	.51	2.52
6R2435	38-70 Winchester, '86......	68	255	8¼ lbs	.58	2.82
6R2436	38-72 Winchester, '95......	72	275	9 lbs	.55	2.74
6R2437	40-60 Colts.	60	260	8⅛ lbs	.51	2.52
6R2438	40-60 Winchester..........	62	210	7⅛ lbs	.51	2.52
6R2439	40-60 Marlin...............	60	260	8 lbs	.51	2.52
6R2440	40-65 Winchester, '86......	65	260	8 lbs	.51	2.52
6R2451	40-70 Winchester, '86......	70	330	10 lbs	.58	2.90
6R2454	40-70 Sharp's Patched....	70	330	10 lbs	.62	3.06
6R2455	40-72 Winchester, '95......	72	330	10 lbs	.57	2.82
6R2458	40-82 Winchester, '86......	82	260	9½ lbs	.56	2.76
6R2459	40-85 Ballard Patched...	85	370	10⅛ lbs	.77	3.82
6R2462	40-110 Winchester Ex.....	110	260	12 lbs	1.23	6.12
6R2464	45-60 Winchester, '76......	62	300	9 lbs	.51	2.52
6R2466	45-70-405 Government....	70	405	10½ lbs	.54	2.67
6R2468	45-70 Armory..............	5	140	6 lbs	.49	2.42
6R2470	45-85 Marlin Necked.....	85	285	8½ lbs	.57	2.83
6R2472	44-77 Sharp Necked	77	405	10½ lbs	.68	3.36
6R2474	45-70-500 Government....	70	500	12¼ lbs	.58	2.90
6R2476	45-75 Winchester.........	75	350	10 lbs	.54	2.67
6R2480	45-90 Winchester..........	90	300	10 lbs	.55	2.75
6R2490	50-70 Government........	70	450	11⅛ lbs	.57	2.83
6R2492	50-95 Winchester Ex.....	95	312	10 lbs	.62	3.06

SHOT CARTRIDGES.

Loaded with shot instead of ball. For use in rifles and revolvers.

No.	Caliber	Weight per 100	Price per 50	Price per 100
6R2510	22 Rim Fire.........	¾ lb	$0.27	$0.54
6R2511	32 Long, R. F.......	1¼ lbs	.55	1.09
6R2512	32 C. F. S. & W.......	1½ lbs	.42	.84
6R2513	32 C. F. Winch......	2¼ lbs	.62	1.24
6R2514	38 C. F. Winch......	3½ lbs	.70	1.40
6R2515	38 C. F. S. & W.....	2½ lbs	.52	1.04
6R2516	44 C. F. Winch......	4 lbs	.70	1.40
6R2517	44 C. F. XL.........	5 lbs	.75	1.50
6R2518	56 Spencer........	7 lbs	1.05	2.10

French Pin Fire Pistol Cartridges.

44-caliber. 38-caliber. 32-caliber.

No. 6R2521 7 M.M. for pistols, per box of 50, weight, 18 ounces.......................................45c

No. 6R2522 9 M.M. for pistols, per box of 50, weight, 22 ounces.......................................55c

No. 6R2523 12 M.M. for pistols, per box of 50, weight, 24 ounces.......................................75c

Primed Empty Rifle and Pistol Shells.

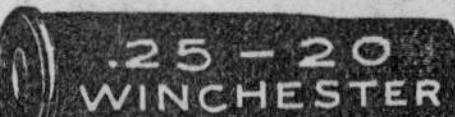

These Shells have the primer, but have no powder and bullets.

No. 6R2524 Sold in any quantity, from one box to a thousand. All center fire. Shells cannot be sent by mail. Order by number, caliber, model of gun and style. Small sizes come 50 in a box. Sporting rifle and military sizes come 20 in a box.

Style	Caliber	Weigh per 100	Price per 100
A	22 Winchester, single shot.....	1 lb	$0.90
B	25-20 Winchester, single shot.	1 lb	1.20
C	25-20 Marlin and Winchester..	1 lb	.90
D	32 Smith & Wesson............	¾ lb	.60
E	32 Long, Smith & Wesson......	1 lb	.68
F	32-44 Smith & Wesson, gallery	1 lb	1.00
G	32-44 Smith & Wesson, target..	1 lb	1.00
H	32-20 Winchester	1¼ lbs	.90
I	32-20 Marlin	1¼ lbs	.90
J	38 Smith & Wesson......	1 lb	.70
K	38-44 Smith & Wesson, gallery	1 lb	1.20
L	38-44 Smith & Wesson, target..	1 lb	1.20
M	38 Long, Colts.................	1¼ lbs	.75
N	38-40 Winchester...............	1½ lbs	1.00
O	38-40 Marlin....................	1½ lbs	1.00
P	41 Long Colts..................	1 lb	.80
Q	44 Smith & Wesson, Russian...	1½ lbs	.95
R	44-40 Winchester...............	1½ lbs	1.00
S	44-40 Marlin..................	1½ lbs	1.00
T	44 Webley.....................	1 lb	.80
U	44 Evans' New Model..........	1¼ lbs	1.10
V	45 Colts	1¼ lbs	1.05

No. 6R2525 Sporting Rifle and Military Sizes:

Style	Caliber	Weight per 100	Price per 100
AA	25-35 Winchester...............	2¼ lbs	$1.50
BB	25-36 Marlin....................	2¼ lbs	1.50
CC	30-30 Winchester...............	2½ lbs	1.80
DD	30-40 U. S. Army................	3 lbs	2.00
EE	32-40 Marlin & Ballard.........	2¼ lbs	1.50
FF	38-55 Marlin & Ballard.........	2¼ lbs	1.80
GG	38-56 Winchester...............	2¼ lbs	1.80
HH	38-72 Winchester...............	3 lbs	2.40
II	40-65 Winchester...............	2¾ lbs	1.80
JJ	40-82 Winchester...............	3 lbs	2.40
KK	45-70-405 Government..........	3 lbs	2.20
LL	45-70-500 Government..........	3 lbs	2.20
MM	45-90 Winchester...............	3¼ lbs	2.40
NN	50-110 Winchester..............	4 lbs	3.00
OO	50-70 Government...............	3¾ lbs	2.25

We can furnish other sizes for old rifles to special order. If possible, when ordering, send a sample shell which has been fired, when ordering other styles.

Blank Cartridges.

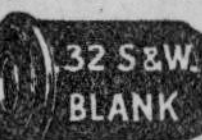

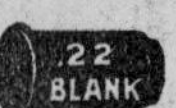

No. 6R2526 Primed with regular powder charge, but without bullets. Weight per box of 50, ¾ to 1¼ lbs. **Order by number and style.**

Style
- A 22-caliber, rim fire, per 100.......................$0.15
- B 32-caliber, rim fire, per box of 50............... .14
- C 32-caliber, S. & W. blanks, per 100............ .55
- D 38-caliber, S. & W. blanks, per 100 .... .70
- E 44-caliber, W. C. F., model '73, per 100.......1.43

30-30-170 Bullet.
Before Shooting.

30-30-170 Bullet.
After Shooting.

These Styles Bullets are not loaded with Black Powder.

SMOKELESS CARTRIDGES.

Metallic Cartridges, loaded with Smokeless Powder, are all the same shape and size as regular Black Powder Cartridges.

THESE TWO CUTS SHOW A SOFT POINT BULLET BEFORE AND AFTER SHOOTING. The soft point bullets have a metal patch or jacket to the point and when the bullet strikes it spreads at the point, as shown in the cut. **The full metal patched bullets have a metal jacket covering the entire bullet and keep their shape after shooting. We recommend soft point bullets for hunting purposes, but for powerful shooting, full metal patched are better;** for instance, a 30-caliber Army metal patched bullet will go through 58 pine boards, ⅞-inch thick, 15 feet from the muzzle of the rifle. A 30-caliber Winchester will go through 35 boards ⅞-inch thick in the same distance, while a lead bullet would go through only about one-half as many boards.

DON'T LOAD SHOTGUN SMOKELESS POWDER INTO CARTRIDGE SHELLS. **In fact, we advise using only factory loaded smokeless cartridges. Factory loaded ammunition is safe, but we have heard of rifles bursting** **BY LOADING SHOTGUN SMOKELESS POWDER IN RIFLE CARTRIDGES. Our terms are cash with order.**

Cartridges cannot be sent by mail.

No. 6R2535

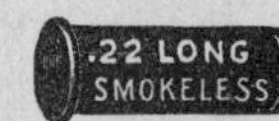

No. 6R2539

No. 6R2541

RIM FIRE SMOKELESS COME WITH LEAD BULLETS ONLY.

No.	Caliber	Grains of Powd'r	Grains of Lead	Weight per 100	Price for 50	Price for 100
6R2535	22 Short	1½	30	10 oz.	$0.15	$0.30
6R2537	22 Short Hollow Point	1½	27	9 oz.	.17	.33
6R2539	22 Long	2½	35	12 oz.	.22	.44
6R2541	32 Extra Short	2$\frac{1}{10}$	55	10 oz.	.36	.72

CENTRAL FIRE SMOKELESS CARTRIDGES. RIFLE AND PISTOL SIZES.

NOTICE.—L. means Lead Bullet, S. P. means Soft Point Bullet and M. P. means Metal Patched Bullet.

All Smokeless Cartridges are the same style and size as Black Powder Cartridges. Cartridges cannot be sent by mail.

No. 6R2551

No. 6R2581

No. 6R2557—For Single Shot only.

No. 6R2566

No. 6R2553

No. 6R2584

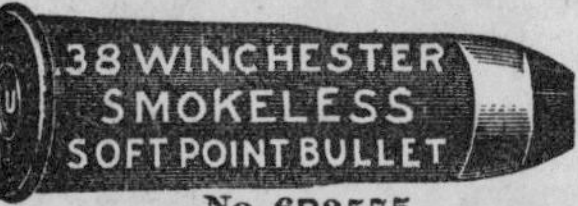

No. 6R2575

No. 6R2589

No. 6R2580

No. 6R2565

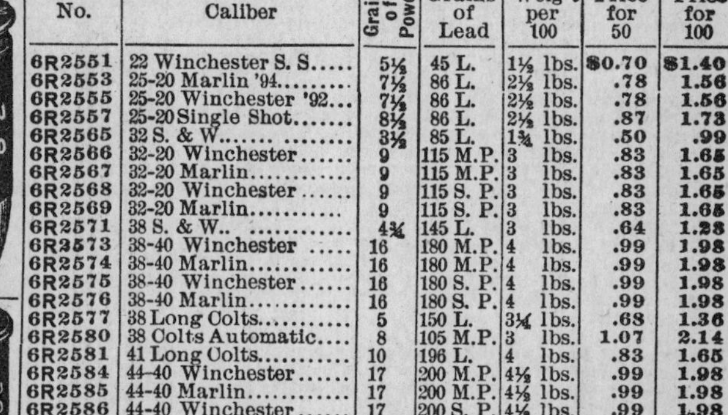

No.	Caliber	Grains of Powd'r	Grains of Lead	Weig't per 100	Price for 50	Price for 100
6R2551	22 Winchester S. S.	5½	45 L.	1½ lbs.	$0.70	$1.40
6R2553	25-20 Marlin '94	7½	86 L.	2½ lbs.	.78	1.56
6R2555	25-20 Winchester '92	7½	86 L.	2½ lbs.	.78	1.56
6R2557	25-20 Single Shot	8½	86 L.	2½ lbs.	.87	1.73
6R2565	32 S. & W.	3½	85 L.	1¾ lbs.	.50	.99
6R2566	32-20 Winchester	9	115 M.P.	3 lbs.	.83	1.65
6R2567	32-20 Marlin	9	115 M.P.	3 lbs.	.83	1.65
6R2568	32-20 Winchester	9	115 S. P.	3 lbs.	.83	1.65
6R2569	32-20 Marlin	9	115 S. P.	3 lbs.	.83	1.65
6R2571	38 S. & W.	4¾	145 L.	3 lbs.	.64	1.28
6R2573	38-40 Winchester	16	180 M.P.	4 lbs.	.99	1.98
6R2574	38-40 Marlin	16	180 M.P.	4 lbs.	.99	1.98
6R2575	38-40 Winchester	16	180 S. P.	4 lbs.	.99	1.98
6R2576	38-40 Marlin	16	180 S. P.	4 lbs.	.99	1.98
6R2577	38 Long Colts	5	150 L.	3¼ lbs.	.68	1.36
6R2580	38 Colts Automatic	8	105 M.P.	3 lbs.	1.07	2.14
6R2581	41 Long Colts	10	196 L.	4 lbs.	.83	1.65
6R2584	44-40 Winchester	17	200 M.P.	4½ lbs.	.99	1.98
6R2585	44-40 Marlin	17	200 M.P.	4½ lbs.	.99	1.98
6R2586	44-40 Winchester	17	200 S. P.	4½ lbs.	.99	1.98
6R2587	44-40 Marlin	17	200 S. P.	4½ lbs.	.99	1.98
6R2589	45 Colts	10	255	5½ lbs.	1.01	2.02

ALL OUR AMMUNITION IS FRESH FROM THE FACTORY AND LOADED WITH FIRST CLASS POWDER.

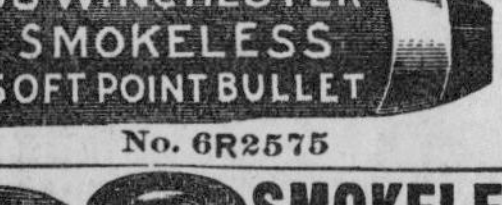

SMOKELESS SPORTING RIFLE AND MILITARY CARTRIDGES.

All smokeless cartridges are the same style and size as black powder regular cartridges.

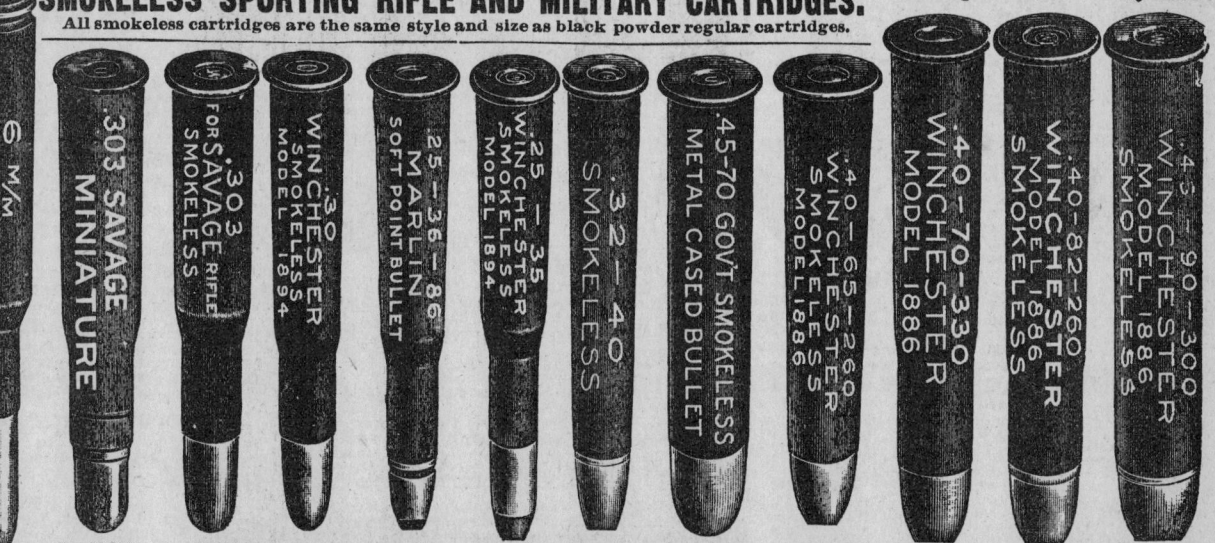

Cartridges cannot be sent by mail.

Smokeless.

No. 6R2613 No. 6R2612 No. 6R2611 No. 6R2608 No. 6R2605 No. 6R2603 No. 6R2601 No. 6R2619 No. 6R2639 No. 6R2631 No. 6R2633 No. 6R2637 No. 6R2641

NOTICE.

L. means Lead Bullet.
M. P. means Metal Patched Bullet.
S. P. means Soft Point Bullet.

No. 6R2625

No. 6R2624

No.	Caliber	Grains of Powd'r	Grains of Lead	Weig't per 100	Price for 20	Price for 100
6R2600	25-35 Winchester	23	117 M. P.	4¼ lbs	$0.59	$2.88
6R2601	25-35 Winchester	23	117 S. P.	4¼ lbs	.59	2.88
6R2602	25-36 Marlin	23	117 M. P.	4¼ lbs	.59	2.88
6R2603	25-36 Marlin	23	117 S. P.	4¼ lbs	.59	2.88
6R2605	30-30 Winchester	30	160 M. P	6 lbs	.67	3.32
6R2607	30-30 Winchester	30	160 S. P.	6 lbs	67	3.32
6R2608	303 Savage	30	180 M. P.	6¼ lbs	.67	3.32
6R2609	303 Savage	30	180 S. P.	6¼ lbs	.67	3.32
6R2611	303 Savage Miniature	5½	100 L.	5 lbs	.53	2.62
6R2612	6 M. M., U. S. Navy	....	112 M. P.	6 lbs	.88	4.37
6R2613	30 U. S. Army	37	220 M. P.	7½ lbs	.88	4.37
6R2614	30 U. S. Army	37	220 S. P.	7½ lbs	.88	4.37
6R2615	30-30 Marlin	30	160 M. P.	6 lbs	.67	3.32
6R2616	30-30 Marlin	30	170 S. P.	6 lbs	.67	3.32
6R2617	30 Winchester Short Range	6	100 L.	5¼ lbs	.53	2.62
6R2618	30 Marlin, Short Range	6	100 L.	5¼ lbs	$0.53	$2.62
6R2619	32-40 Marlin	17	165 M. P.	5½ lbs	.56	2.80
6R2620	32-40 Marlin	17	165 S. P.	5½ lbs	.56	2.80
6R2623	38-55 Marlin & Winchester	19	255 M. P.	7 lbs	.70	3.49
6R2624	38-55 Marlin & Winchester	19	255 S. P.	7 lbs	.70	3.49
6R2626	38-56 Winchester	25	255 S. P.	8 lbs	.70	3.49
6R2630	38-72 Winchester, '95	25	275 S. P.	9 lbs	.75	3.76
6R2632	40-65 Winchester, '86	27	260 S. P.	7½ lbs	.70	3.50
6R2633	40-70 Winchester, '86	28	330 M. P.	9 lbs	.75	3.75
6R2637	40-82 Winchester, '86	33	260 M. P.	8 lbs	.75	3.75
6R2638	40-82 Winchester, '86	33	265 S. P.	8 lbs	.75	3.75
6R2639	45-70-405 Government	29	405 M. P.	10 lbs	.74	3.67
6R2640	45-70 Government	29	405 S. P.	10 lbs	.74	3.67
6R2641	45-90 Winchester	37	300 M. P.	9 lbs	.75	3.75
6R2647	50-110 Winchester, '86	43	300 M. P.	10 lbs	.96	4.80

WE HANDLE ONLY FRESH AMMUNITION LOADED WITH BEST GRADES OF POWDER.

A Few Words About Gun Wads.

There is considerable difference of opinion among shooters about the best method of loading shells, with reference to the wadding. We have gone into this matter extensively and our experience is as follows; That if you place one cardboard wad next to the powder, then use one or two of ¼-inch black edge wads (according to the length of the shell), after this put another cardboard wad over the black edge wads, then put in your shot and a thin cardboard wad over the shot, leaving about ¼-inch of the shell to be crimped, you will get as good results as you will from any fancy loading, all other things being equal. **When loading with nitro powder** it is a good plan to put a thin cardboard wad next to the powder, then you may use either one or two of ¼-inch black edge or may use one or two dry felt wads (wads which contain no lubricant), either one of these will produce good results. **The object of putting in a cardboard wad next to the powder,** is that the powder will not tear the felt wad badly as the cardboard wad protects the felt wad. **The object of placing a thin cardboard wad next to nitro powder** is to prevent the nitro powder from absorbing the lubricant of the felt wads which is said to deteriorate the force of the powder. In our opinion the above methods of loading will give you a good average result. Should you not get good results from these two methods, the fault is not with your loading, but with the boring of your gun barrel. **The main scientific principles in shooting is to confine the gas generated by the burning powder behind the shot;** if loading as above mentioned does not give the proper pattern we advise you to try one size larger felt wads. For instance, if you do not get good results with No. 12 black edge wads, try No. 11 wads, for it sometimes happens that the diameter of one gun barrel is a mere trifle larger than another. **If you are doing rapid shooting,** enough so as to cause the barrel of your gun to become heated, bear in mind that this heating process expands the bore of the gun, though not enough to notice it with the naked eye, still enough to impair the shooting qualities. If you have ever so fine a gun and the gun barrel becomes heated, do not blame the gun, if you do not get good patterns, this is caused by the expansion of the barrels through heat.

Cardboard Wads.

Made from Specially Prepared Cardboard.

No. 6R3300 Cardboard Wads, to be used next to the powder, but may be used over the shot also. Weight, about 1¼ pounds per 1000.

	Per box of 250	Per 1000
7 or 8-gauge wads..	5½c	21c
9 or 10-gauge wads....	5c	18c
11 to 20-gauge wads....	4c	15c

If by mail, postage extra, box, 5c.

No 6R3320 Thin Cardboard Wads to use over the shot, weight about 1 pound per 1000. Made from specially prepared paper.

	Per box of 250	Per 1000
9 or 10-gauge.......	5c	18c
11 to 20-gauge.......	4c	15c

If by mail, postage extra, box, 5c

Black Edge Wads, ⅛ Inch Thick.

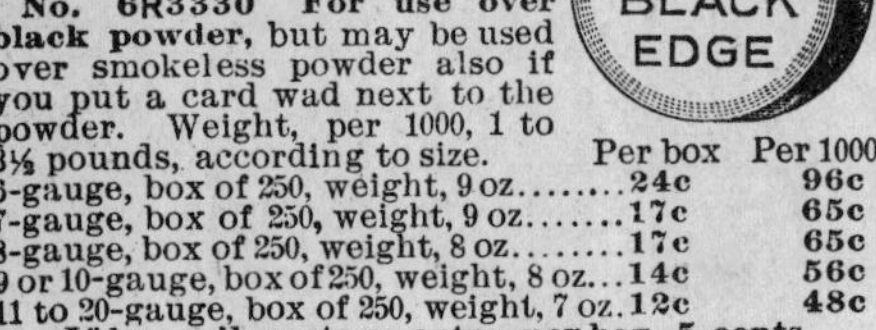

No. 6R3330 For use over black powder, but may be used over smokeless powder also if you put a card wad next to the powder. Weight, per 1000, 1 to 3½ pounds, according to size.

	Per box	Per 1000
6-gauge, box of 250, weight, 9 oz.......	24c	96c
7-gauge, box of 250, weight, 9 oz.......	17c	65c
8-gauge, box of 250, weight, 8 oz.......	17c	65c
9 or 10-gauge, box of 250, weight, 8 oz...	14c	56c
11 to 20-gauge, box of 250, weight, 7 oz.	12c	48c

If by mail, postage extra, per box, 5 cents.

Black Edge ¼-inch Wads.

No. 6R3340 For use over black powder, but may be used over smokeless powder also if you put a card wad next to the powder. Weight, per 1000, 2½ pounds. Packed 250 in a box.

	Per box	Per 1000
9 or 10-gauge..................	22c	85c
11 or 12-gauge..................	18c	72c

If by mail, postage extra, per box, 13 cents.

Black Edge Wads, ⅜ Inch Thick.

No. 6R3350 Black Edge Wads, ⅜ inch thick, for use over black powder, but may be used over smokeless also. One of these is equal to three of the ⅛-inch wads. 125 in a box.

	Per box	Per 1000
9 or 10-gauge..................	28c	$2.20
11 or 12-gauge...	25c	2.00

If by mail, postage extra, per box, 14 cents.

NOTICE—In 12-gauge brass shells, use 10-gauge wads. In paper shells, use wads the same size as shell. **Always put the wad down to place flat and evenly, otherwise the shooting quality of your gun will be greatly impaired.**

Nitro Felt Wads.

Made of elastic felt, soft and pliable, unlubricated, perfectly dry and free from all greasy matter, for use over nitro powder. 125 in a box, ⅛, ¼ and ⅜ inch thick.

			Per box	Per 1000
No. 6R3360	⅛-inch	9 or 10-gauge	7c	56c
		11 or 12-gauge	6c	48c
No. 6R3370	¼-inch	9 or 10-gauge	11c	84c
		11 or 12-gauge	9c	72c

If by mail, postage extra, per box, 10 cents.

Pink Edge Felt Wads, ⅛ Inch Thick.

No. 6R3410 For use over black powder, but may be used over smokeless powder if you put a card wad next to the powder. Weight per 1000, 1¾ to 3 pounds, according to size. These wads come 250 in a box.

	Per Box	Per 1000
6-gauge, pink edge, per box of 250.......	35c	$1.40
7-gauge, pink edge, per box of 250.......	30c	1.20
8-gauge, pink edge, per box of 250.......	30c	1.20
9 or 10-gauge, pink edge, per box of 250,	25c	1.00
11 to 20-gauge, pink edge, per box of 250,	20c	.80

If by mail, postage extra, per box, 10 cents.

Pink Edge Felt Wads, ¼ Inch Thick.

No. 6R3420 For use over black powder, but may be used over smokeless powder if you put a card wad next to the powder. 250 in a box.

	Per box	Per 1000
11 or 12-gauge..	25c	$1.00
9 or 10-gauge..	30c	1.20

If by mail, postage extra, per box, 12 cents.

White Felt Wads, ⅜ Inch Thick.

No. 6R3430 For use over black powder, but may be used over smokeless powder if you put a card wad next to the powder. One of these is equivalent to three ⅛-inch wads. Weight, per 1000, 5 to 6 pounds. 125 wads in a box.

	Per box	Per 1000
7-gauge, box of 125....................	40c	$3.20
8-gauge, per box of 125....................	40c	3.20
9 or 10-gauge, per box of 125....................	30c	2.40
11, 12, 16, 20-gauge, per box of 125...	28c	2.20

If by mail, postage extra, per box, 18 cents.

SMOKELESS POWDERS.

A FEW VALUABLE POINTERS ABOUT NITRO POWDERS.

1—**Don't guess at the quantity; measure it with a good measure and you won't have anything to regret afterwards. It is weighed by apothecary weight.**

2—**Use wads enough to confine the gas produced by the explosion, or there will not be force enough to carry the shot.**

3—**Don't use a too heavy load of nitro powder; it's not good for the gun.**

NOTICE—Be careful in loading nitro powders. Don't deviate from the directions on the powder can.

NOTICE—Smokeless powder is only half as heavy as black powder; for instance, if you have a 1-pound black powder can you will fill it with one-half pound of smokeless powder.

SCHULTZE Smokeless Powders.

This is one of the very best and safest of nitro powders. Can be loaded with a black powder and shot measure.

Schultze Powders for shotguns, very little smoke.

No. 6R3501 1 pound can (actual weight ½ pound.)..................54c

No. 6R3502 10-pound can (actual weight 5 pounds.).................$4.86

Follow the directions on can for loading.

E. C. Smokeless Powder.

E. C. Shotgun Powder, little or no smoke. It is becoming more popular every year.

No. 6R3505 1 pound can (actual weight ½ pound). Price, per can.................................. 54c

No. 6R3506 10-pound can (actual weight 5 pounds). Price, per can..................................$4.86

Great care must be taken in loading these powders to obtain the best results. Directions on each can.

The great advantage of Du Pont's Smokeless, Schultze and E.C. Powders over common powders is the fact that there is much less recoil and no smoke to prevent seeing game or target for second shot.

NOTICE. Don't load shotgun powder in rifle cartridges. When loading smokeless powder by weight, use an apothecary scale, which weighs 5,750 grains to the pound.

DU PONT Smokeless or Nitro Powder.

The Du Pont Smokeless Nitro Powder is a fine grain, hard powder, safe and reliable. It may be loaded the same as black powder, except the quantity should be less; use paper shells only. If you use a regular black powder measure, load in 16-gauge 2 to 2½ drams; in 12-gauge 2½ to 3 drams; in 10-gauge 2¾ to 3¼ drams. This is one of the most satisfactory nitro powders.

No. 6R3510 12½-pound can, equal in bulk to 25 pounds of black powder.............................$11.88

No. 6R3511 6¼-pound can, equal in bulk to 12½ pounds of black powder.............................$6.09

No. 6R3512 3½-pound can, equal in bulk to 6¾ pounds of black powder.............................$3.10

No. 6R3513 ½-pound can, equal in bulk to 1 pound of black powder.............................54c

NOTICE—All nitro or smokeless powder can be shipped by express or freight, either alone or with other goods.

Du Pont's Smokeless Rifle Powder.

No. 6R3514 Du Pont's Smokeless Rifle Powder, No. 1, for rifle cartridges from 25-20 to 45-90; see directions for loading with each can. This powder is put up in 1-pound cans only.

Price, per can (actual weight, ½ pound).......**$1.00**

No. 6R3515 Du Pont's Smokeless Rifle Powder, No. 2, for all pistol cartridges and rifle cartridges 38-40 and 44-40; directions with can, 1-pound cans only. Price, per can (actual weight, ½ lb.).....**$1.00**

No. 6R3518 Du Pont's Smokeless Special, for 30-caliber rifles. 1-pound can (actual weight, ½ lb).**$1.25**

BLACK POWDER.

Du Pont Rifle and Shotgun Black Powder.

Our Special Prices for Du Pont's Special Powder ought to induce every buyer of powder to give us his order. **OUR LOW PRICES are based on actual cost to manufacture with but our one small profit added.**

THIS DU PONT'S POWDER IS GUARANTEED, you can get nothing better in black powder for all around use.

Remember we are absolutely headquarters for these powders and they are made specially for us. Cheap powders do not give good penetration and are liable to lead the inside of the gun, but these powders are made from the best ingredients which go into the manufacture of powder.

This powder is made especially for us from the best grades of refined saltpetre, willow or elder charcoal, refined sulphur and nitre.

Don't buy cheap powder which gives poor penetration. Pay a few cents more and get better satisfaction.

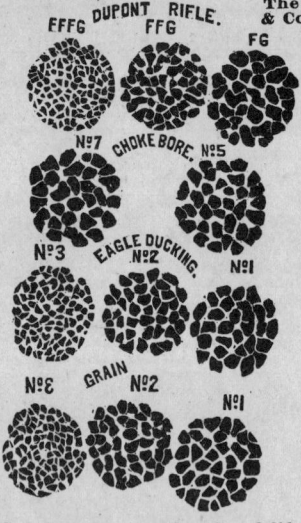

The Messrs. Du Pont & Co. are the oldest powder makers and have the most extensive works in the country. We consider their powder the best. Every pound warranted good and clean. In air tight metallic kegs; Fg is coarse; FFg is medium and FFFg is fine grain. (See cut.) When ordering state which grain you prefer.

PRICES.

No. 6R3530 In F, FF or FFF grain, per 25-lb. keg.......**$4.00**

No. 6R3532 In F, FF or FFF grain, per 12½-lb. keg.......**$2.25**

No. 6R3534 In F, FF or FFF grain, per 6¼-lb. keg.......**$1.25**

No. 6R3536 In F, FF or FFF grain, per 1-lb. can.........**30c**

Cut showing size of grains of different powders. Hazard Powder same price as Du Pont.

Powder cannot be sent by express. It must be sent by freight on regular powder trains. Freight charges on powder are double first class.

THERE ARE 256 DRAMS OF BLACK POWDER TO THE POUND IF YOU WISH TO LOAD YOUR OWN SHELLS.

Du Pont Choke Bore Black Powder.

Excellent powder made especially for choke bored guns. See illustration.

No. 6R3540 Kegs, Nos. 5 or 7 grain, 25 lbs..**$5.00**

No. 6R3542 ½-kegs, Nos. 5 or 7 grain, 12½ lbs. **2.75**

No. 6R3544 ¼-kegs, Nos. 5 or 7 grain, 6¼ lbs. **1.50**

No. 6R3546 1-lb. cans, Nos. 5 or 7 grain.... **.35**

NOTE—We furnish Hazard powder in the same numbers and same size kegs at the same price as Du Pont's when desired. Hazard powder is good.

Du Pont Eagle Duck.

This is the very finest grade of black powder.

No. 6R3550 Kegs, Nos. 1, 2 or 3 grain, 25 lbs.**$8.00**

No. 6R3552 ½-kegs, Nos. 1, 2 or 3 grain, 12½ pounds.......... **4.25**

No. 6R3554 ¼-kegs, Nos. 1, 2 or 3 grain, 6¼ pounds.......... **2.25**

No. 6R3556 1-lb cans, Nos. 1, 2 or 3 grain... **.45**

Powder cannot be shipped by express, but must be sent in separate kegs or cases and marked "gunpowder," and sent by freight on regular powder trains. Freight charges are double first class **rates** on powder.

Du Pont's Special V. G. P. Brand.

No. 6R3560 The New Trap Powder—black, moist, quick, clean and strong (not a nitro).

6¼-pound kegs.....**$1.25** 12½-pound kegs.....**$2.25**

Special Blasting Powder.

No. 6R3565 Du Pont Blasting Powder. In ordering state for what purpose it is wanted.

Price, per 25-pound keg.............................**$1.6**

DO NOT CUT, TEAR OR MUTILATE THIS CATALOGUE. Order by number and we will know just what is wanted. **Preserve this book carefully. IT IS YOUR GUIDE TO ECONOMICAL BUYING.**

Our No. 1 Victor Blasting Machine.

In response to a great many inquiries for blasting machines, we have investigated the matter, and concluded to handle the No. 1 Victor Blasting Machine.

This machine is fitted with two posts from which to make the connection of electric fuze for blasting purposes.

The No. 1 Victor Blasting Machine has a capacity of firing five to eight holes in one instant.

To operate this machine place the electrical fuzes in the dynamite cartridge, the same as you would an ordinary cap and fuse. If blasting two or more holes connect the fuzes with connecting wire, and after the various holes are connected (like illustration above), attach one of the leading wires from one post to first fuze, then attach the other leading wire from the post to the last fuze wire, as shown in illustration, then pull up the handle of the blasting machine to the arrow point, after it is up press the handle down quickly with all the force you can, and this action will discharge all the cartridges in one instant. One-half a turn of the crank handle should produce a discharge of all the cartridges. The No. 1 Victor Blasting Machine is a dynamo electric machine and does not need to be recharged with electricity.

No. 6R3566½ No. 1 Victor Blasting Machine, capacity, five to eight holes. Our special price, $15.00

Electric Fuzes to be Used in Connection with the Victor Blasting Machine.

When using these fuzes it is not necessary to have blasting caps. The fuses are inserted in the dynamite cartridge the same as a blasting cap. The above cut shows a fuze in a dynamite cartridge.

Always use the fuze 2 feet longer than the hole in which you put the dynamite cartridge; for instance, if you wish to blast at the bottom of a 4-foot hole, use a 6-foot fuze. These fuzes come 50 in a box, and we cannot sell less than a box of a size. Order by number and length.

Prices on Electrical Fuzes.

No. 6R3568		
4 feet Fuzes	$2.70	per 100
6 feet Fuzes	3.20	per 100
8 feet Fuzes	3.68	per 100
10 feet Fuzes	4.16	per 100
12 feet Fuzes	4.65	per 100

Leading Wire.

Leading Wire comes in coils of 500 feet to the coil. We cannot sell less than a coil.

No. 6R3569 Our special price per coil of 500 feet....$4.00

Connecting Wire. Where you wish to blast more than one hole the fuzes are connected by this connecting wire. We do not sell less than one pound.

No. 6R3569½ Price, per pound....32c

DYNAMITE AND BLASTING SUPPLIES.

Dynamite is, in our opinion, far superior to any other agent for removing stumps.

When a stump is in hard clay soil, place the dynamite under the stump if possible. When the stump is in sandy soil use an auger as shown in cut, a 2-inch wood auger is preferable. When the ground is frozen is the best time to blow out stumps with dynamite. Please note that dynamite freezes at 42 degrees Fahrenheit.

To those who are not familiar with handling dynamite, we will, on application, mail a booklet giving full information.

Dynamite comes in cartridge shape 8 inches long by 1¼ inches diameter, and a 25-pound case contains 48 to 51 cartridges. A 50-pound case contains 98 to 102 cartridges. Order by catalogue number and per cent number.

Dynamite is put up only 25 and 50 pounds in a case. We can only sell one kind in a case and not less than a case of a kind. It must be shipped alone from the factory by freight. Cannot be shipped with other goods.

No. 6R3570	
No. 3x 30 per cent nitroglycerine, per pound,	13 c
No. 2b 35 per cent nitroglycerine, per pound,	13½c
No. 2 40 per cent nitroglycerine, per pound,	14 c
No. 2x 45 per cent nitroglycerine, per pound,	14¾c
No. 2xx50 per cent nitroglycerine, per pound,	15½c
No. 1 60 per cent nitroglycerine, per pound,	17 c
No. 1xx75 per cent nitroglycerine per pound,	19¼c

Nos. 4, 4x and 3 are suitable for clay, shell rock, frozen earth, and in quarries where rock is split but not shattered.

Nos. 3x, 2c, 2b and 2 for ores, stumps, ice and moderately hard work.

Nos. 2x and 2xx for hard rock, etc.

Nos. 1 and 1xx for very hard rock, ores, iron and submarine blasting.

BE CAREFUL

TO WRITE EVERY LETTER AND FIGURE IN THE CATALOGUE NUMBER.

BLASTING CAPS, ETC.

We cannot sell less than a box of 100.

No. 6R3590 Blasting Caps, quadruple force, per 100....$0.85

No. 6R3592 Blasting Caps, quintriple, per 100, 1.00

Caps cannot be shipped with dynamite. Must go separately by freight.

Store your caps away from the dynamite, and do not carry them with dynamite. Keep them in separate places.

ACME COMBINATION FUSE CUTTER AND CRIMPER.

No. 6R3594 Fuse Cutter and Crimper combined, for crimping cap to fuse, and the leg is intended to make a hole in the cartridge to insert the cap. Price....45c

Safety Fuze.

Order by number and state kind wanted.

No. 6R3596 Safety fuse in 50 foot coils.

Cotton fuze, for dry work, per 1000 feet	$2.90
Single tape fuze, for damp ground, per 1000 feet,	3.50
Double tape fuze, for wet work, per 1000 feet	4.70
Triple tape fuze, for under water, per 1000 feet,	5.70

SHOT AND BAR LEAD.

Subject to market changes without notice.

Buck Shot: 8, 7, 6, 5, 4, 3, 2, 1

Drop Shot: 12, 11, 10, 9, 8, 7, 6, 5, 4, 3, 2, 1, B, BB, BBB, 0, 00, 000

WE CANNOT SELL SHOT IN 5-LB. SACKS AT 25-LB. SACK RATE

Chilled and dropped shot in sacks of 5 pounds and 25 pounds at lowest market rates. We do not sell less than a sack. The price of shot fluctuates so much that we cannot quote permanent prices. Prices are subject to change without notice.

No. 6R3601 Drop shot, all sizes, 1 to 12, per 25-lb. sack, $1.60

No. 6R3603 Drop shot, all sizes, 1 to 12, per 5-lb. sack....40c

No. 6R3605 Chilled shot, all sizes, 2 to 10, per 25-lb. sack, $1.90

No. 6R3607 Chilled shot, all sizes, 2 to 10, per 5-lb. sack....45c

No. 6R3609 Buckshot, sizes, B to No. 8, 25-lb. per sack. $1.90

No. 6R3611 Buckshot, sizes B to No. 8, per 5-lb. sack....44c

In case of fluctuation chilled shot is always 40 cents higher in 25-lb. sacks, and 5 cents higher in 5-lb. sacks than drop shot. We will always bill shot at the lowest market rates.

No. 6R3613 Bar lead for running bullets at market price; average price about 7 cents per pound.

No. 6R3615 BB Shot in 1-lb. packages for air rifles. Per pound....10c

We always bill at lowest market prices.

We guarantee lowest market price on cartridges, shells, primers, powder, shot, etc.

Prices subject to change without notice.

RELOADING TOOLS.

Winchester's Lever Reloading Tools, including Bullet Molds—Complete Set.

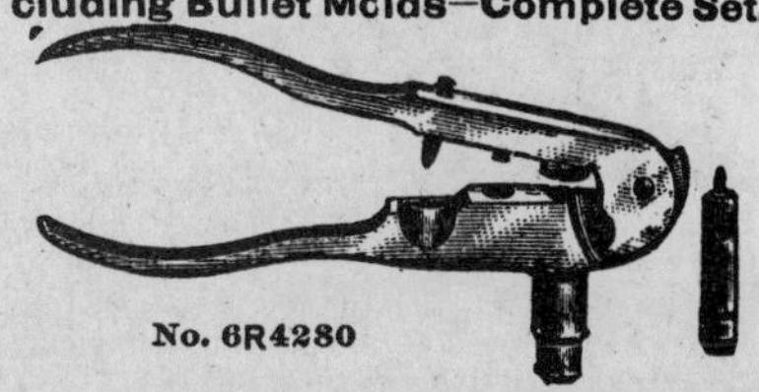

No. 6R4280

A set of implements comprises the reloading tool, a bullet mold and charge cup. The reloading tool removes the exploded primer and fastens ball in the shell, at the same time swaging the entire cartridge to the exact form and with absolute safety. Bullet molds have wood handles. Blued, finished and polished. Perfect in every respect.

No. 6R4280	Per set
22-caliber, center fire, Winchester, single shot.	$1.75
25-20 caliber, center fire, Winchester single shot	1.75
25-20 caliber, center fire, Winchester model '92	1.75
32-20 caliber, center fire, Winchester M.73 & 92	1.75
32 caliber, Smith & Wesson	1.75
38 caliber, Smith & Wesson	1.75
38-40 caliber, Winchester M 73 and mod. 92	1.75
38-90 caliber, Winchester Express	2.40
44 caliber, center fire, Webley	1.75
44-40 caliber, Winchester M 73 and mod. 92	1.75
40-90 caliber, Sharp's patched straight	2.40
40-70 caliber, Ballard patched ball	2.40
40-110 caliber, Winchester Express	2.40
44 caliber, S. & W., Russian	1.75
44 caliber, S. & W., American	1.75
50-95 caliber, Winchester Express	2.40
No. 6R4281 Reloaders, only 22 to 44-caliber	1.05
No. 6R4282 Reloaders, only from 40-90 to 45-60 caliber, each	1.35
No. 6R4283 Bullet Molds, any caliber, each	.82
No. 6R4284 Brass charge cups, each	.10

Order by number and mention caliber and name of rifle when ordering tools.

If by mail, postage extra, per set, 42 and 45 cents.

Winchester Model 1894 Reloading Tools, Including Bullet Mold and Complete Set; Reloads and Resizes the Shells.

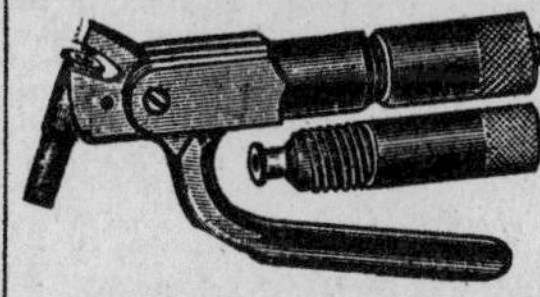

Winchester 1894 Model Tool, including bullet mold with wood handles. A complete set. Reloads and resizes the shell. Weight, 3¼ pounds. Polished, blued finish. Perfect in every respect.

No. 6R4286 Order by number and give caliber and name of rifle.

	Per set
25-35 Winchester, without bullet mold	$1.55
30-30 Winchester, without bullet mold	1.55
30-40 U. S. Army, without bullet mold	1.55
303 caliber Savage, without bullet mold	1.55
If by mail, postage extra, 40 cents.	
32-40 caliber Winchester, complete	2.09
38-55 caliber Winchester, complete	2.09
38-56 caliber Winchester, complete	2.09
38-70 caliber Winchester, complete	2.09
38-72 caliber Winchester, complete	2.09
40-60 caliber Winchester, complete	2.09
40-65 caliber Winchester, complete	2.09
40-70 caliber Winchester, complete	2.09
40-72 caliber Winchester, complete	2.09
40-82 caliber Winchester, complete	2.09
45-60 caliber Winchester, complete	2.09
45-70 caliber Government, 405 complete	2.09
45-70 caliber Government, 500 complete	2.09
45-75 caliber Winchester, complete	2.09
45-90 caliber Winchesters, complete	2.09
45-70-330 Hollow Ball, complete	2.35
50-70 Government, complete	2.09
50-95 Winchester Express, complete	2.45
50-110 Winchester Express, complete	2.45

If by mail, postage extra, per set, 56 cents.

TO PRESERVE SHELLS, always wash them out with hot soap suds or hot soda water as soon after shooting as possible.

IDEAL Combined Reloading Tools, No. 1.

All parts necessary to load the cartridge and make bullets are combined in this one tool.

No. 6R4288 Any caliber. State caliber wanted.

	Per set
22-caliber, center fire, Winchester S. S.	$1.47
32-caliber, short, center fire	1.47
32-caliber, long, center fire, outside lubricant	1.47
32-caliber, Smith & Wesson	1.47
32-caliber, Smith & Wesson, long	1.47
32-caliber, extra long, center fire	1.47
38-caliber, short, center fire	1.47
38-caliber, long, outside lubricator, center fire	1.47
38-caliber, extra long, center fire	1.47
38-caliber, Smith & Wesson center fire	1.47
41-caliber, short, Colt's D. A. pistol, center fire	1.47
41-caliber, long, Colt's outside lubricant, center fire	1.47

If by mail, postage extra, per set, 23 cents.

Note—If you want to load S. & W. cartridges buy S. & W. tools. No other tool will load them.

No. 3 IDEAL Tools.

No. 6R4290 The No. 3 is a reloader only, and has no bullet mold. This tool is intended to go with the Perfection or cylindrical mold for those who wish to cast special bullets. It is made in all the popular sizes, including 30-30 Winchester and Marlin, 30-caliber Army, and furnished to special order only. Send cash with order and state size wanted.

Price for reloader without mold....$2.00

Price in caliber 303 Savage....2.25

No. 4 IDEAL Tool.

All parts necessary to load the cartridge and cast bullets are combined in this one tool. State which caliber is wanted.

No. 6R4291 Ideal Tools.	Per set
25-20 caliber, Winchester single shot	$1.72
25-20 caliber, Marlin Rifle. or Winchester	1.72
32 caliber, Winchester Rifle, Model '92 and '73	1.72
32 caliber, Colt's Lightning Rifle	1.72
32-20 caliber, Marlin	1.72
38-40 caliber, Winchester Model '73 and '92	1.72
38-40 caliber, Marlin or Colt's Rifles	1.72
44-40 caliber, Winchester Model '73 and '92	1.72
44-40 caliber, Marlin or Colt's Rifles	1.72
44 caliber, S. & W. Russian Model	1.72
44 caliber, S. & W. American model	1.72
45 caliber, Colt's Pistol	1.72

If by mail, postage extra, per set, about 28 cents.

NOTICE. For information on casting bullets, etc., send 3 cents to pay the postage on our handbook of useful information.

No. 6 IDEAL Tool.

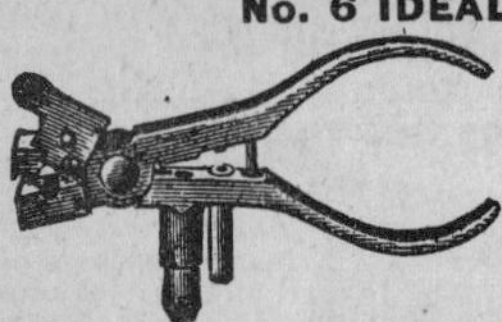

No. 6R4294 Ideal Reloading Tools, complete with bullet mold. This tool contains all the necessary appliances to make bullets, decap and recap shells, cast, load and seat the bullets, and is without doubt the best tool made. State caliber wanted.

25-36-caliber, Marlin. Per set... $2.05
25-35 Winchester. Per set... 2.05
30-30-caliber, Marlin. Per set... 2.05
30-30 Winchester. Per set... 2.05
32-40 Ballard and Marlin. Per set... 2.10
38-55 Marlin. Per set... 2.10
38-56 Winchester & Colts. Per set... 2.10
40-60 Winchester. Per set... 2.10
40-60 Colt & Marlin. Per set... 2.10
40-65 Winchester. Per set... 2.10
40-82 Winchester. Per set... 2.10
44 Evans' new model. Per set... 2.10
If by mail, postage extra, per set, 32 cents.
45-60 Winchester. Per set... 2.10
45-70 405 Government. Per set... 2.10
45-70 500 Government. Per set... 2.10
45-85 285 Marlin. Per set... 2.10
45-90 Winchester. Per set... 2.10
50-70 Government. Per set... 2.10
If by mail, postage extra, per set, about 39 cents.

We can furnish any other caliber in the Ideal Tools that are made, and tools not quoted in this catalogue will have to be made specially, and cannot be returned if sent as ordered. We ship them from the factory.

No. 8 IDEAL Tool.

No. 6R4295 This tool is practically the same as No. 6, but is made to load the new inside lubricant cartridges, which have a V shaped cavity at the base. This tool will not load the old style outside lubricant cartridges.

32-caliber, long, Colts, inside lubricant. Per set. $2.60
38-caliber, long, Colts, inside lubricant. Per set. 2.60
41-caliber, long, Colts, inside lubricant. Per set. 2.60
If by mail, postage extra, 36 cents.

Shell Reducer and Resizer.

No. 6R4296 Shell Reducer and Resizer for any size from 32-40, and larger, to resize shells which have become bulged. Each... $1.37
Order size wanted. If by mail, postage extra, 15c.

TO LUBRICATE BULLETS. Dip the bullets in lubricant and set them on a board till lubricant is hard in the grooves. Good lubricant can be made from beef tallow with enough vaseline to soften it, or pure vaseline with enough paraffin to harden it. Never use fat which has salt or acid in it. It is liable to rust or pit the barrel.

IDEAL BULLET MOLDS.

Be sure and give the size wanted, also give the name of rifle or revolver.

For all sporting and military size cartridges, of regular weight bullets. For special bullets see Nos. 6R4304 and 6R4305. 1 part tin (or solder) and 40 parts of lead makes a good bullet. If bullet is too soft add more tin. These molds are all made specially and we require cash with order, the same as for our other goods.

No. 6R4300 To make grooved bullets, each, $0.76
No. 6R4301 To make express bullets, each, 1.70
Give caliber of mold when ordering.

No. 6R4304 The Perfection Mold. This mold is intended for making grooved bullets of different weights in the same mold. For instance, the 25-20 mold will cast 25-20, 25-36, 25-35, etc. It is not made for sharp pointed nor hollow base bullets. State caliber wanted. Price, each... $2.40
If by mail, postage extra, 15 cents.

No. 6R4305 The Cylindrical Mold will do the same work as the Perfection, but for patched bullets instead of grooved bullets. Made in 25, 32, 38, 40 and 45 calibers. State caliber wanted. Price, each.. $2.40

When ordering bullet molds give the exact size wanted or send sample bullet or empty shell by mail. For postage rate, see page 4.

No. 6R4307 Ideal Dipper for running bullets. Each... 37c

If by mail, postage extra, 7 cents.

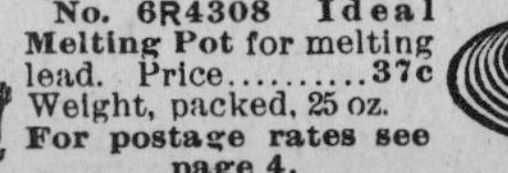

No. 6R4308 Ideal Melting Pot for melting lead. Price... 37c
Weight, packed, 25 oz.
For postage rates see page 4.

Melting Pot. Cut ⅙ size.

No. 6R4309 Adjustable Cover. Cover to fit any stove for Ideal Melting Pot, 37c
Weight, packed, 24 ounces.
For postage rate see page 4.

Melting Ladles.

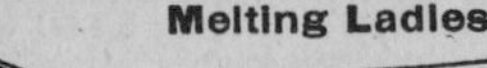

Weight, 1 to 2½ pounds. Ladles, for melting lead, etc.

	Each
No. 6R4311 3-inch diameter bowl, weight, 12 oz..	20c
No. 6R4312 4-inch diameter bowl, weight, 24 oz..	30c
No. 6R4313 5-inch diameter bowl, weight, 36 oz..	40c
No. 6R4314 6-inch diameter bowl, weight, 42 oz..	50c

If by mail, postage extra, per ounce, 1 cent.

Cast Steel Wad Cutters.

Be sure and give gauge wanted.

No. 6R4318 7 and 6 gauge, 80c
No. 6R4319 9 and 8 gauge, 18c
No. 6R4320 10 to 20 gauge, 15c
No. 6R4321 Any size pistol or rifle, 22 to 50-caliber. Mention caliber wanted. Price... 35c
If by mail, postage extra, 5 cents.

THESE SPECIAL RELOADING TOOLS ARE THE HIGHEST GRADE. OUR PRICE WILL SAVE YOU 30 PER CENT.

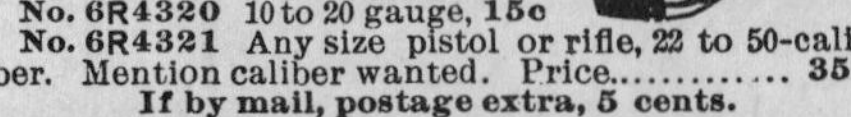

A Recapper and Decapper, Shell Extractor and Rammer, All in One.

33 Cents for Complete Set.

The Ideal Shell Pocket Loader, including funnel and base, bronze finish, compact and handy to carry in the pocket, recaps and decaps and seat wads. Weight, 4 ounces. See above cut.

No. 6R4322 Each, 16-gauge... 33c
No. 6R4323 Each, 12-gauge... 33c
No. 6R4324 Each, 10-gauge... 33c
If by mail, postage extra, 6 cents.

Ideal Hand Closer.

Our Special Price, 19 Cents.

The Ideal Hand Shell Closer for paper shells; handy to carry in pocket; always ready for use. Weight, 6 ounces.

No. 6R4325 16-gauge, each... 19c
No. 6R4326 12-gauge, each... 19c
No. 6R4327 10-gauge, each... 19c
Weight, packed, 6 ounces. If by mail, postage extra, 6 cents.

Shell Loaders.

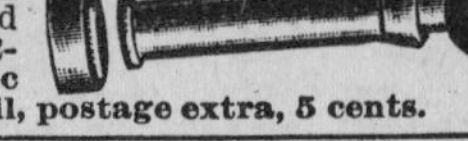

No. 6R4330 Wine Colored Loader. Polished nickel spun tube. 10 and 12-gauge. Price, each... 12c
14, 16 and 20-gauge. Price, each... 14c
If by mail, postage extra, 4 cents.

NOTE—The decapper, or expelling pin, will be found in all loaders by taking the knob off the rammer—see illustration.

No. 6R4331 **Applewood Loaders.** Polished nickel spun tube. 10 and 12-gauge. Price, each... 9c
If by mail, postage extra, 2 cents.

No. 6R4335 Barclay Loader, with inside spring wad starter, 10 and 12-gauge. Each... 38c
If by mail, postage extra, 5 cents.

8-GAUGE RELOADING IMPLEMENTS.

These tools are of the very best quality and are the only style made for this gauge.

No. 6R4338 Cocobolo Loader, with tube and extracting pin. 8-gauge only... 45c
If by mail, postage extra, 5 cents.

No. 6R4339 Shell Crimper, best quality, 8-gauge only. Each... $1.45
If by mail, postage extra, 28 cents.

The Paragon Recappers.

No. 6R4350 Japanned Recapper, neat and handy, 10 and 12-gauge, Weight, 2 oz. Price, each. 7c

No. 6R4351 16 and 20-gauge. Each... 8c
If by mail, postage extra, 3 cents.

Remington Recapper and Decapper.

No. 6R4353 Remington Decapper and Recapper. 10, 12 or 16-gauge. Each... 45c

Be sure and give gauge wanted when ordering decappers and recappers or implement sets. If by mail, postage extra, 10 cents.

The Common Sense Decapper and Recapper.

No. 6R4355 The Common Sense Decapper and Recapper is first class in every respect, nickel plated shell post, cocobolo handle. **A simple, convenient and effective implement,** decapping and recapping the cartridge shell, doing its work easily, rapidly and perfectly. Misfires will be avoided by its use. **If you haven't a Common Sense De and Recapper, don't find fault if your gun misfires.**

Price, 12-gauge, $1.00; 10-gauge... $1.00
If by mail, postage extra, 17 cents.

Eureka Paper Shell Crimper.

No. 6R4356 Paper Shell Crimper, dark japanned, 10, 12, 16 and 20-gauge. State gauge wanted; a crimper will crimp only one gauge.
Each... 25c
Weight, packed, 16 ounces. For postage rate see page 4.

Paragon Paper Shell Crimper.

No. 6R4357 Paper Shell Crimper, dark japanned, with expelling pin, 10 and 12. State gauge wanted.
Price, each, 10 or 12-gauge... 29c
Price, each, 16 or 20-gauge... 30c
Weight, packed, 17 ounces. For postage rate see page 4.

Bronze Paper Shell Closer.

No. 6R4358 Our Acme Paper Shell Closer, gold bronzed, cocobolo handle, expelling pin; a good, strong closer. 10 or 12-gauge. Each... 50c
Weight, packed, 17 ounces. For postage rate see page 4.

No. 6R4358½ Paper Shell Crimper, best quality, for 14, 16 or 20-gauge only... 60c
If by mail, postage extra, 17 cents.
To produce perfect crimp turn fast and feed slowly.

The New Ideal Diamond Square or Round Crimp Closer.

No. 6R4360 The New Improved Diamond Ideal Square Crimper. New straight feed lever, with steel grip. The only tool that will **crimp every shell alike,** no matter what variations of load may be. The only tool having an **automatic plunger,** that prevents the end of the shell from spreading over the wad. **All wearing parts and cups are of steel.** The best crimper ever made; 10, 12 and 16-gauge only. **State gauge wanted.** Order by number. Price, each... $1.55

Showing style of square crimp.

If by mail, postage extra, 32 cents.

No. 6R4361 The New No. 3 B. G. I. Handy Crimper, with reversible crimp, making either the oval or square crimp with the same tool; **a good, strong and durable article. State gauge of shell you wish to crimp. A 10-gauge crimper will not crimp a 12-gauge.** 10 or 12-gauge only. Price... $1.40
If by mail, postage extra, 3 cents.

Gun Cleaning Implements.

No. 6R4365 Cleaning Rods, applewood, patent brass joints, and three implements, swab, scratch brush and wiper. 10, 12, 16-gauge. Weight, packed, 13 ounces. Price, per set... 27c
If by mail, postage extra, 13 cents.

Our Cocobolo Cleaning Rod.

No. 6R4366 Our Fancy Cocobolo Jointed Cleaning Rod is made in three joints as shown in the above illustration. It is made of cocobolo wood, with nickel plated joints and trimmings, universal thread for implements which takes any of the standard swabs, slots, or wire scratch brushes. The rod when joined is 37 inches long, and when disconnected, each joint is 13 inches long. **It is a very handsome cleaning rod, and each rod is accompanied by a wire scratch brush, wool swab and and a slotted wiper.** Our special price for this handsome cleaning rod, 55c
If by mail, postage extra, 13 cents.

Ferris Gun Cleaner.

No. 6R4370 The Celebrated Ferris Gun Cleaner. The best cleaner on the market. It can be attached to jointed cleaning rods. 10 or 12-gauge. Excellent for removing lead or burnt powder from the barrel. Price, each... 38c
If by mail, postage extra, 5 cents.

Brass Wire Brush.

10, 12, 16 and 20 Gauge.

No. 6R4371 Brass Wire Brush for removing lead caking and rust spots; **can be attached to any jointed rod;** 10, 12, 16 and 20-gauge. Order by gauge, as one brush will fit but one gauge. Price, each... 43c
If by mail, postage extra, 2 cents.

Our Pioneer Gun Cleaner.

No. 6R4373 Made of **springy wood, with universal thread** to fit any jointed cleaning rod, and it comes with brass screen wire cloth, which is one of the best lead removers known. It is also slotted so it may be used for oiling guns. 10 and 12-gauge.
Price, each, with screen cloth............ ......35c
If by mail, postage extra, 4 cents.

No. 6R4375 No. 6R4376 No. 6R4377

No. 6R4375 Wool Swab, to fit jointed rod; brass shank, universal thread, 10 and 12-guage. Each...5c
If by mail, postage extra, 4 cents.

No. 6R4376 Flannel Wiper to fit jointed rod; made of brass, double slotted, universal thread, 10, 12 and 16-gauge. Each..........................9c
If by mail, postage extra, 4 cents.

No. 6R4377 Wire Scratch Brush; brass shank, steel wire, universal thread, **to fit jointed rods;** 10, 12 and 16-gauge. Price, each.........................4c
If by mail, postage extra, 4 cents.

ALWAYS WRITE CATALOGUE NUMBER IN FULL.

The Hartness Brass Cleaner.

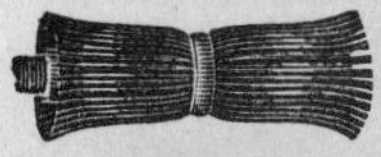

No. 6R4378½ Hartness Brass Cleaner for removing lead from inside of barrel. Cuts both ways for choke bored guns. Fits jointed cleaning rods, 10 or 12 gauge.
Price, each...30c
If by mail, postage extra, 3 cents.

The Tomlinson Gun Cleaner.

No. 6R4379 The Tomlinson Gun Cleaner for Shotguns; wire gauze cleaner; this is the best cleaner on the market; fits any standard jointed cleaning rod, 10 or 12-gauge. Each...65c
If by mail, postage extra, 3 cents.

The A B C Shotgun Cleaner.

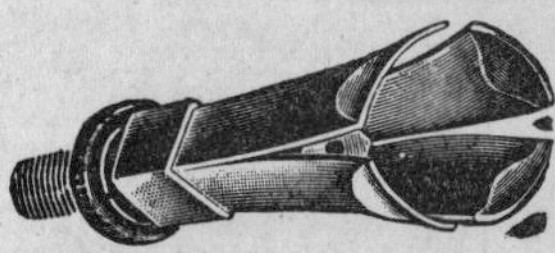

No. 6R4380 This is the latest and one of the best shotgun cleaners made. It has broad, sharp blades covering the entire circumference of gun barrel, which instantly cuts out all lead and burnt powder. Is made of brass, nickeled, will not harm the finest barrel. When used for holding cloth for wiping, and brass strainer cloth for burnishing, it is the finest burnisher made. Constant use only makes it sharper. Turning thumb nut adjusts it to 10 or 12-gauge.
Price, each, nickel plated.........................43c
If by mail, postage extra, 4 cents.

Shell Extractor.

No. 6R4383 The Universal Shell Extractor will extract any shell from 8 to 22-caliber. Nickel plated. Each......14c **If by mail, postage extra, 1 cent.**

Wormers.

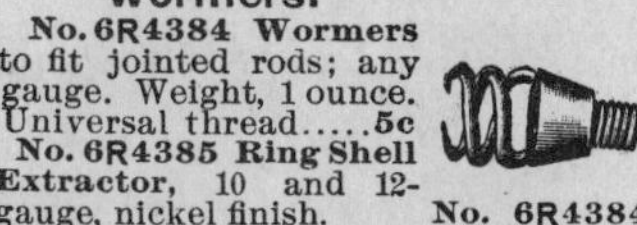

No. 6R4384 Wormers to fit jointed rods; any gauge. Weight, 1 ounce. Universal thread.....5c
No. 6R4385 Ring Shell Extractor, 10 and 12-gauge, nickel finish. No. 6R4384
No. 6R4385 Weight, 1 ounce. Each..............7c
No. 6R4385½ Ring Shell Extractor, for 14, 16 or 20-gauge only. **State gauge wanted**............8c
If by mail, postage extra, 1 cent.

Powder and Shot Measure.

No. 6R4388 Powder and Shot Measure combined; apple wood handle, polished nickel finish; the same measure will answer for powder or shot.
Price, each..9c
If by mail, postage extra, 3 cents.

Micrometer Powder and Shot Measure.

No. 6R4389 May be adjusted to the fractional part of a grain of powder.
May be used either for black or nitro powder, from 2½ to 4¾ drams dry powder, and 1 to 2½ ounces shot.
Each..(**If by mail, postage extra, 3 cents**)....30c

No. 6R4390 Twisted Wire and Bristle Revolver Brushes. State caliber when ordering. Comes in 22, 32, 38 and 44-caliber. Price, each..............6c
If by mail, postage extra, 1 cent.

Rifle Cleaning Rods.

No. 6R4391 Twisted wire, bristle brush on end, 22-caliber. Price, each...... ....8c
If by mail, postage extra, 5 cents.

No. 6R4393 Our Folding Pocket Screwdriver, with square shape nipple wrench for musket nipples.
Price, each.......................4c
If by mail, postage extra, 2 cents.

No. 6R4394 Our Folding Pocket Screwdriver, with U shape nipple wrench for musket nipples.
Price,each...... ... .4c
If by mail, postage extra, 2 cents.

Brass Rifle Brushes.

22 to 50 Caliber.

No. 6R4396 Brass Wire Brush to fit **No. 6R4398** rods. Brass shank especially made for cleaning rust and burnt powder out of rifles. 22, 30, 32, 38, 40, 44, 45 and 50 calibers. State caliber wanted. Each..........................18c
If by mail, postage extra, each, 2 cents.

Brass Cleaning Rods, 43 Cents.

No. 6R4398 Four-jointed Brass Cleaning Rods; can be carried in the pocket. This rod has a revolving handle so the brush or cleaning rag follows the rifling grooves. State caliber wanted.

22-caliber	.43c	32-caliber	.43c
30-caliber	.43c	45-caliber	.43c
38-caliber	.43c	44-caliber	.43c
50-caliber	.43c		

If by mail, postage extra, each, 7 cents.

U. S. Government Cleaner.

No. 6R4400 Consists of a bristle brush and slotted wiper, with detachable cord and weight for dropping through barrel; a separate slotted wiper for drawing through a dry cloth and for oiling. The No. 6R4396 brush may be used with this cleaner. 22, 32, 38 or 45-caliber. Each..........................33c
If by mail, postage extra, each, 2 cents.

GUN IMPLEMENT SETS.

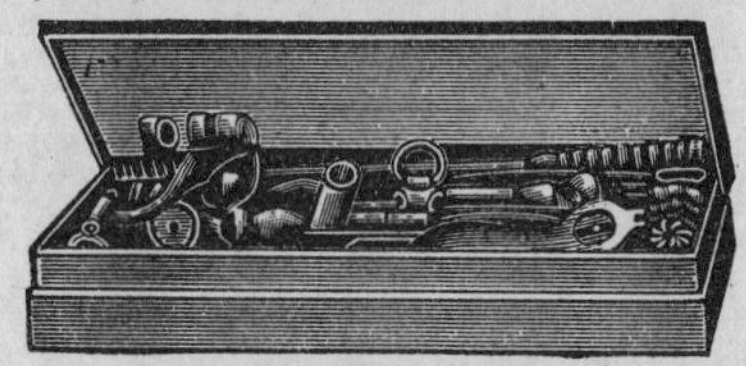

No. 6R4401 Our 7-piece Set. The Complete Gun Implement Set contains 7 articles, embracing **loader, paper shell crimper, recapper and decapper, shell extractor, powder and shot measure, a cleaning rod with implements, and a loading block which holds 20 shells.** This set comes in a strong pasteboard box, neatly divided into compartments for each article, and each implement is made of good material and recommends itself. to every owner of a breech loading shotgun. **The best ever offered for the money.** Size of box, 5x13 inches. Price, per set, best quality, 10, 12, 16 or 20-gauge. Weight about 2½ pounds. State gauge wanted. Price..........**$1.55**

No. 6R4402 Our 6-piece Set, price, per set, medium quality, but with fine cocobolo, jointed rod. 10,12, 16 and 20-gauge, without loading block. Weight, 2 pounds. State gauge wanted. Price......... **$1.25**

No. 6R4403 Our 6-piece Set; good everyday quality, 10, 12, 16 or 20-gauge; **consists of loader, closer, recapper, extractor, powder and shot measure, applewood jointed rod with implements.** Weight, 2 pounds. **State gauge wanted.** Price..**80c**

NOTE—Don't say there is no decapper in these sets. Remove the knob from the rammer and you will find it. Wad cutters do not come with tools.

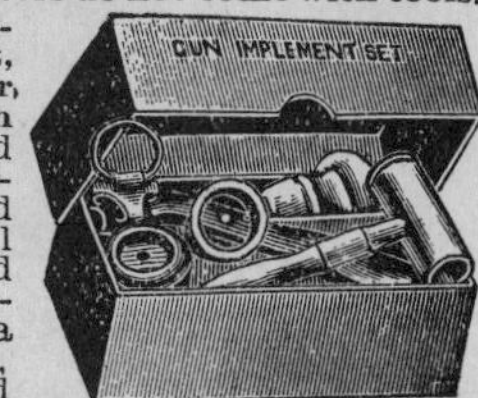

No. 6R4405 Our 5-piece Reloading Set, consisting of **rammer, and decapper with base block,** nickeled loading tube and recapper, ring extractor and patent paper shell crimper, graduated powder and shot measure, all inclosed in a strong paper box, making a neat and convenient set of tools; 16 or 20-gauge. Per set..**43c**
No. 6R4406 10 or 12-gauge. Price, per set....**43c**
If by mail, postage extra, 20 cents.

No. 6R4407 Our 4-piece Set; for brass shells only, consists of loader, powder and shot measure, ring extractor and recapper, in 10 or 12-gauge only.
Price, per set..18c
No. 6R4408 16 or 20-gauge. Price. per set...**24c**
If by mail, postage extra, 10 cents.
NOTE—Reloading sets do not include wad cutters. They cost extra when wanted.

Shell Loading Block.

Our deep New Model of 1900 block. Made of white wood, holes bored with shoulder to fit the entire length of shell. The top of hole is reamed out to act as a wad starter; **shell does not come within one-half inch of top of block;** shells cannot bulge or break down. Just the thing to load shells for the Smith or Parker guns, or where wads larger than the shell are required. Weight, 3 pounds.
No. 6R4410 Holding 50 12-gauge shells........**90c**
No. 6R4411 Holding 50 10-gauge shells.......**90c**
If by mail, postage extra, 50 cents.

No. 6R4413 Loading Block, holding 20 shells; depth of block, 1 inch; 10 or 12-gauge. State gauge wanted.
Price 40c
If by mail, postage extra, 10 cents.

Powder Flasks.

No. 6R4416 Holding 8 ounces black powder, with cord, common top. Ea.**24c**
No. 6R4417 Holding 12 ounces black powder, with cord, common top. Ea.**48c**
No. 6R4418 Holding 16 ounces black powder, with cord, common top. Ea.**60c**
If by mail, postage extra, 6 to 9 cents.

Leather Shot Pouches.

No. 6R4420 Plain leather with lever charger for holding 2½ to 3 pounds shot. Each...45c
No. 6R4421 Fancy leather with lever charge for holding 2½ to 3 pounds shot. Each...**60c**
No. 6R4422 Shot Belt Irish Charger, to hang over the shoulder; we have a few left. Each.... **25c**

Our Blackbird Expert Target Trap, $5.50.

This Blackbird Target Trap is the latest improved trap, combining all the good points of all traps with the defects of none. This trap is neat in appearance, has no surplus cast iron, no complicated machinery, handles the targets gently, gives an even, steady flight and is adjustable to elevations, angles and tension; is 21 inches long and 15 inches high. The Blackbird Trap which we quote at $5.50 is made by expert mechanics, will throw any standard target, and we think there will be less breakage with this trap than any other trap made.
No. 6R4428 Our special price...............**$5.50**
Weight, packed for shipment, 25 pounds.

Our Blackbird Targets. Per Thousand, $3.75.

As a result of a manufacturer's many years' practical experience in target making, we are now able to furnish you the Blackbird Targets. These targets are made in black color, with a yellow colored stripe round the edge, present a larger surface to the shooter, and their flight is steady and even and measure 4¼ inches in diameter. The inside of the rim is reinforced, which, in a measure, prevents breakage in transit. The Blackbird Targets are packed 500 in a barrel, and the shipping weight is about 270 pounds to the thousand. These Blackbird Targets may be thrown from any standard single or magazine trap.
No. 6R4429 Our special price, per 1000 targets..**$3.75**

SHOOTING GALLERY TARGETS.

Round Steel Face Plain and Figure Targets. Figure springs up and rings bell when bull's eye is hit; can be reset with rope from the shooting stand.

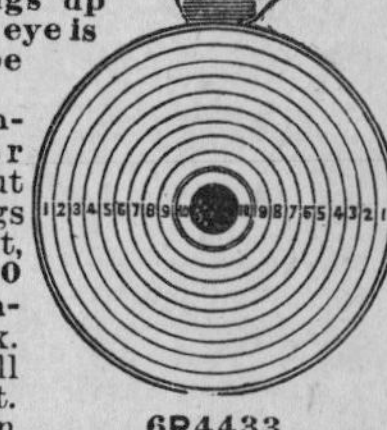

6R4433

No. 6R4431 12-inch diameter, heavy, for 22-caliber cartridges. Steel face without the bird figure, but a bell rings when bull's eye is hit. Weight, 12 pounds. Each........**$2.00**
No. 6R4433 12-inch diameter, steel faced, ¼-inch thick. Bird is thrown up and bell rings when bull's eye is hit. For cartridges not larger than 22-long. Weight, 12½ pounds. Each...........**$2.50**

The Latest and Best Target Made—Our Special White Flyer.

NOTE OUR PRICES **of $2.00 for 500, $4.00 for 1000, and you will observe our price is below all others. Our terms are cash with order.**

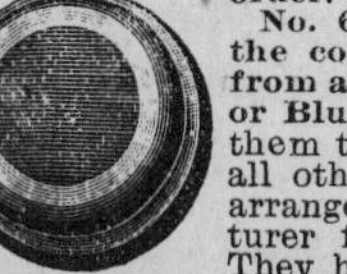

No. 6R4436 This is no doubt **the coming target, and will fly from any trap taking the Empire or Blue Rock pigeon.** We believe them to be superior in quality to all other targets, and have made arrangements with the manufacturer for an enormous quantity. They having a white rim, make a lighter colored target than the others, which will be a great advantage on dark days. **Try a barrel of White Flyers and you will surely want more.** Weight, per barrel (500 targets), 148 pounds.
Price, per 1000, **$4.00**; per barrel (500).......**$2.00**
Our terms are cash with order.

Expert Blue Rock Trap.

$6.40 for the Expert Blue Rock Trap is a great reduction in price, made possible by a very large purchase we recently made. **At $6.40** you will be owning this trap for less money than any dealer can buy it. **Our $6.40 Expert** we guarantee the best all-around trap on the market. One that is used generally by clubs and trapshooters.

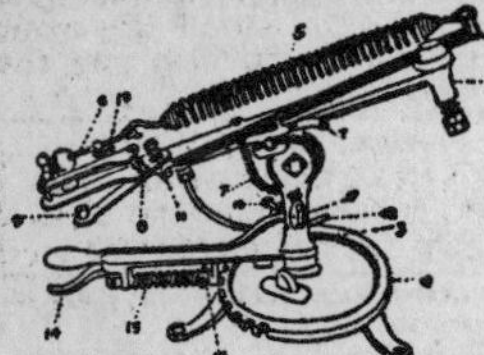

No. 6R4438 The New Expert Blue Rock Trap, so well known by all trap shooters and considered the best trap on the market. These traps will throw either the Blue Rock or White Flyer targets. Weight, 35 lbs. Price, each...**$6.40**

OUR SPECIAL BLUE ROCK TARGETS.

We have these Blue Rock Targets specially made so that if only two or three pellets strike them they will break. Send cash with order. Weight, per barrel, 130 pounds.

No. 6R4440 { Price, per barrel (500)........**$2.38** { Price, per 1000........**4.75**

Our Special Blue Rock Extension Trap.

White Flyers Work Just as Well as other Targets in Blue Rock Traps.

No. 6R4449 Blue Rock Extension Trap. Weight, 25 pounds. Each.......**$4.85**

POLICE EQUIPMENTS.

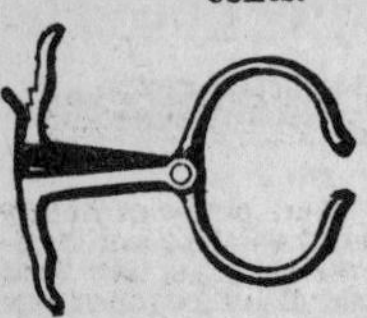

Perfect Twisters.

No. 6R4450 Chain Twister, nicely finished with locking handle. Price, each.......**90c**
If by mail, postage extra, 5 cents.

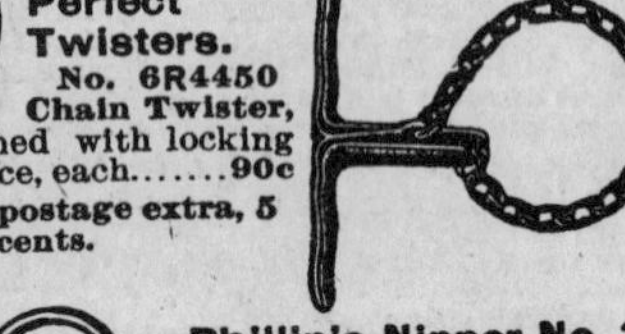

Phillip's Nipper No. 3.

No. 6R4451 Phillip's Nipper, nicely finished and nickel plated, locks with a spring catch on the handle. Price, each..............**90c**
If by mail, postage extra, 6 cents.

Thomas' Nipper No. 4.

No. 6R4452 Thomas' Nippers, nicely finished and nickel plated. This nipper locks automatically when it is put on the prisoner's wrist. Price, each..............**$1.75**
If by mail, postage extra, 8 cents.

Double Lock Detective's Handcuffs.

These handcuffs are adjustable to any size wrist and lock automatically, but they cannot be unlocked without a key. They are made of forged steel, strong and durable.

No. 6R4453 No. 10. Nicely polished and finished. Price, per pair..............**$3.50**
No. 6R4454 No. 11. Nicely polished and nickel plated. Price, per pair..............**$4.00**
If by mail, postage extra, 20 cents.

Tower's Permanent Lock Handcuffs.

These handcuffs lock with a key and are adjustable to any size wrist. They are made of forged steel, are light, and used generally by detectives and other officers of the law.

No. 6R4455 No. 60. Nicely polished and finished. Price, per pair..............**$3.50**
No. 6R4456 No. 61. Nicely polished and nickel plated. Price, per pair..............**$4.00**
If by mail, postage extra, 16 cents.
No. 6R4459 Extra Keys for Handcuffs. Price, each..............**28c**
If by mail, postage extra, 1 cent.

Patrolman's Rosewood Club.

No. 6R4457 Patrolman's Rosewood Day Club, 14 inches long. Price, each, **45c**
If by mail, postage extra, 13 to 16 cents.

Police Slung Shots and Billies.

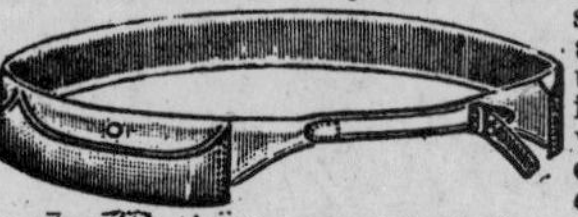

No. 6R4472 Braided Leather Slung Shot, made of the best material, cannot be equalled for the price. Each..............**20c**
If by mail, postage extra, 6 cents.

No. 6R4472

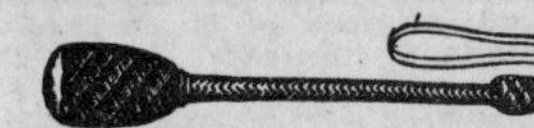

No. 6R4473 Plaited Billy, leather covered head. Weight, about 7 ounces. Each..............**19c**

No. 6R4475 Braided Leather Billy, plaited and loaded with shot, made of the best material and **cannot be equaled for the price.** Length, 9½ inches. Weight about 9 ounces. Each..............**50c**
If by mail, postage extra, 9 cents.

No. 6R4477 Russet Leather Billy, 8¼ inches long, with sliding leather handle, filled with shot, sewed down the side and well made. Weight, about 12 ounces. Price, each..............**75c**
If by mail, postage extra, 12 cents.

Money Belts.

No. 6R4495 Money Belts. Made of soft chamois skin; to be worn around the waist, under the clothing; the safest way to keep money. It is soft and comfortable, and made with three compartments. Price, each..............**44c**
If by mail, postage extra, 3 cents.
No. 6R4496 Money Belts. Made of soft tanned horsehide; same style as above. Strong and durable. Price, each..............**58c**
No. 6R4497 Money Belts, made of soft drilling cloth, which is tough and strong and not affected by perspiration in warm weather. Price, each..............**35c**
If by mail, postage extra, 3 cents.

No. 6R4498 Money and Gold Dust Belts. Four inches wide; made of the very finest oil tanned calfskin; very soft and pliable; will never get stiff and is **just the thing to carry money or gold dust in;** it is double stitched all around; made with three compartments; the center pocket is eight inches long; the two end pockets are five inches long, each; the outside cover folds over very closely and is fastened by snap buttons. **This is the finest belt on the market for the purpose.** Each..............**85c**
If by mail, postage extra, 4 cents.

Recoil Pads.

Give length of butt end plate.

No. 6R4503 Rudolph's Popular Recoil Pad. Solid leather, with lacing; will not become loose; with padded butt to protect the shoulder. Give length of butt plate when ordering. Price, each....**44c**
If by mail, postage extra, 10 cents.

No. 6R4503

No. 6R4504 The Climax Rubber Recoil Pad, Made entirely of rubber; well padded and will fit any gun, its elasticity keeping it in position and preventing the shock of the recoil doing injury to the shoulder. They come in three sizes. No. 2 is 5 inches long; No. 3 is 5¼ inches long and No. 4 is 5½ inches long. Give length of butt plate when ordering. Price, each..**28c**
No. 6R4504
If by mail, postage extra, 5 cents.

No. 6R4505 The Acme Pure Red Rubber Recoil Pad. The best pad in the market. Give length of heel plate on gun for which you want the pad. They come in 3 sizes: No. 2 is 5 inches long; No. 3 is 5¼ inches long and No. 4 is 5½ inches long. Price, each..............**65c**
If by mail, postage extra, 7 cents.

Heike's Hand Protector.

No. 6R4510 Heike's Hand Protector, for shotgun barrels; a protection from cold barrels or hot barrels, made of spring steel, morocco leath'r covered. **A necessity to trap shooters.** It slips over the barrels and comes for 10 or 12-gauge guns. State gauge wanted. Each..............**65c**
If by mail, postage extra, 3 cents.

No. 6R4512 The Universal Leather Cheek Pad, to lace on gun stock for protection of the cheek. Will fit any gun stock. Made of soft russet leather, oil tanned, making it soft and pliable, and is chamois lined. Each..............**50c**
If by mail, postage extra, 5 cents.

Our Arkansaw Bowie Knife.

No. 6R4515 Bowie Knife, buckhorn handle, 6-inch steel clip blade, leather sheath, with loop to attach to belt; entire length, 11 inches. Price..........**75c**
No. 6R4516 Bowie Knife, with 7-inch blade. Price, each, with leather sheath..............**85c**
No. 6R4517 Bowie Knife, with 8-inch blade. Price, each, with leather sheath..............**95c**
If by mail, postage extra, 10 cents.

Our Montana Hunting Knives.

No. 6R4518 Our Montana Hunting Knife, nicely checkered handle, 6¼-inch blade, leather sheath with loops to attach to a belt. The best hunting knife on the market for the money. Price, each.. (If by mail, postage extra, 9c)...**65c**

Deer Foot Hunting Knives.

No. 6R4519 Hunting Knife, deer foot handle, 6-inch clip blade, leather sheath, nickel bolster and hilt. Price, each..............**$1.25**
No. 6R4520 Hunting Knife, deer foot handle, 7-inch clip blade, best steel, leather sheaths. with loop to attach to belt, nickel bolster and hilt.........**$1.50**
If by mail, postage extra, 12 cents.

Sportsmen's Folding Lock Blade Knife.

No. 6R4521 S., R. & Co.'s Sportsmen's Folding Lock Blade Knife, with 3⅝-inch (scimiter) blade of finest steel, and 4½-inch genuine deer foot handle making the entire length, when open, 8¼ inches. It has **dagger hilt, with German silver bolster, patent lock,** which holds the blade either open or closed, and a corkscrew in the handle. **Just the knife for camping.** Price, each..............**$1.45**
If by mail, postage extra, 12 cents.

Pearl and Stag Handle Daggers.

No. 6R4523 Our Finest Quality Ladies' Dagger This is a little beauty with the very finest quality of steel in blade. Length of blade, 4 inches, both edges sharp, with **beautiful pearl handle and dagger hilt, furnished with fancy leather sheath.** This is the finest quality of a **dirk knife,** and the metal is warranted. Our special price, only...**$1.25**
If by mail, postage extra, 8 cents.
No. 6R4524 Same as No. 6R4523, but with stag handle instead of pearl handle. Our special price..............**75c**

No. 6R4530 Leather Hunting Knife Sheaths. 6-inch..**20c** 8-inch..**28c** 7-inch..**24c** 9-inch..**32c**
If by mail, postage extra, 4 cents.
No. 6R4531 Leather Belts, for knife sheaths, 1¼ inches wide. Price...(Postage extra, 8 cents)...**25c**

Hunters' Axes.

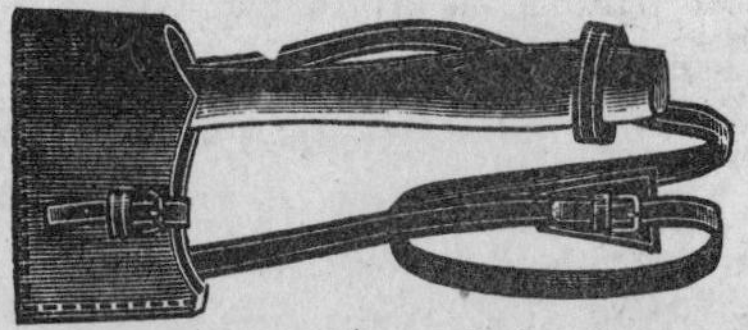

No. 6R4533 Hunters' Axe, with handle, extra cast steel blade, weight, 1¾ pounds; with heavy russet leather sheath, as per cut. A very convenient tool; makes a light axe or a heavy hatchet for putting up tents, etc., when camping. Price, each, with carrying sheath..............**85c**

The Marble Safety Pocket Hatchet.

No. 6R4534 The Marble Safety Pocket Hatchet, is made of the finest grade tool steel, handsomely polished, with hard rubber handle, fastened by three screws on each side, and safety guard to go over the edge of the hatchet when not in use, and it may be folded back into the handle when you wish to use the hatchet. One of the neatest little hatchets on the market. The entire length of this hatchet is 11 inches and weighs 23 ounces. Our special price..............**$1.75**

Pocket Oilers.

"PERFECT" POCKET OILER

SELF-CLOSING VALVE (OPENED)

No. 6R4540 The C. & D. Perfection Gun Oiler the best and handiest gun and revolver oiler on the market. Each......(Postage extra, 2 cents).....**17c**

GUN OIL, ETC.

Winchester Gun Grease, put up by the Winchester Repeating Arms Company.

No. 6R4543 The Winchester Gun Grease is the best rust preventer manufactured. It has been in use in their factory for years. For any steel or polished iron surface, and for inside or outside of gun or rifle barrels, it has no equal. Put up in neat metallic tubes.
Price, per tube..........10c

No. 6R4546 S., R. & Co.'s Sperm Gun Oil; put up exclusively for guns, gunlocks and fine machinery, removes rust and will not gum; 2-oz. bottles. Price, per bottle....8c
If by mail, postage extra, 8 cents.

Our Pocket Flask, ½ Pint Size.

No. 6R4556 Our Pocket Drinking Flask, made of glass and covered with leather, has a screw top lined with cork to prevent leaking and is made in half-pint size only. Our special price....80c
If by mail, postage extra, 10 cents.

BIRD CALLS.

No. 6R4560 Allen's Latest Improved Wood Duck Caller, the most natural toned, easiest blowing. Used in the field by the best duck shooters in America. Each..........35c

No. 6R4563 Duck Calls, B. G. I. with rosewood mouthpiece, horn tip. Good quality. Price, each..........22c

No. 6R4565 Turkey Calls, horn tip with rosewood mouthpiece, calls by sucking into it. Each..........25c
If by mail, postage extra, each, 3 cents.

Snipe Call.

No. 6R4567 Snipe Calls, made of best horn and a perfect snipe call. Each....18c
If by mail, postage extra, each, 2 cents.

No. 6R4570 Fuller's Metallic Wild Goose Caller. Very good, Each..........75c
If by mail, postage extra, 5 cents.

The Improved Surprise Whistle.

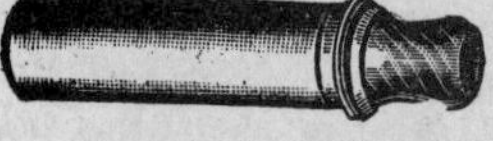

No. 6R4572 The Surprise Whistle the loudest and best dog call in the market. By squeezing in the bulb at the end you can regulate the sound and produce any effect from purling or muffled notes up to a great swelling, booming, piercing note. A good snipe or plover call also. Price, each..........14c
If by mail, postage extra, 2 cents.

Horn and Celluloid Whistles.

The Celluloid Dog Call, or Whistle. A loud one, made in fancy colors and a neat looking whistle.
No. 6R4573 Large size. Price, each, 15c
If by mail, postage extra, 2 cents.

Horn Whistle, loud and shrill and leaves no bad taste in the mouth.
No. 6R4574 Small size. Price, each..........15c
No. 6R4575 Medium size. Price, each..........20c
No. 6R4576 Large size. Price, each..........25c
If by mail, postage extra, 2 cents.

Barnum's Patent Game Carrier. Model 1900.

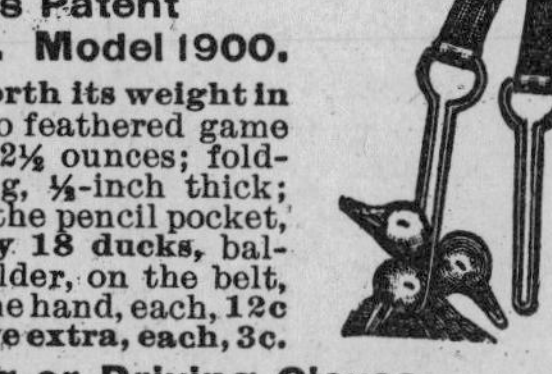

No. 6R4580 Worth its weight in gold; a blessing to feathered game shooters; weight, 2½ ounces; folded, 8½ inches long, ¼-inch thick; can be carried in the pencil pocket, yet holds securely 18 ducks, balanced on the shoulder, on the belt, gun barrel, or in the hand, each, 12c
If by mail, postage extra, each, 3c.

Hunting or Driving Gloves.

These Gloves are made of soft, pliable leather, with first finger and thumb as shown in illustration. They are so made that one can pull the trigger with the first finger, or when through shooting the four fingers can be put in the body of the mit. **They have gauntlet cuffs,** as shown in illustration, to keep the wrists warm, and are made lined with flannel or unlined for fall, winter and spring hunting or driving.
No. 6R4582 Price, per pair, unlined..........65c
No. 6R4583 Price, per pair, lined..........80c
If by mail, postage extra, 8 cents.

Decoy Ducks.

In making these decoys great care has been used to select only sound white cedar for their construction and to secure a perfect balance. They are light, substantial and naturally painted. Assortments: Mallard, canvas back, red head, blue bill, teal, pin or sprig tails. Weight, per dozen, 35 to 40 pounds. They will not sink if you shoot them. $2.00 and $2.95 per dozen. Each dozen contains 8 drakes and 4 females. We cannot furnish them any other way except by special order, which causes delay. Decoys below these prices cannot be properly made and painted to look natural. For highest grade Wood Decoy Ducks, this is a special reduction in price. **A PRICE BELOW ANY COMPETITION.**

No. 6R4595 No. 1 our best decoy ducks, nicely painted in natural colors, with glass eyes, per doz...$2.95
No. 6R4596 No. 3 good decoy ducks, nicely painted in natural colors but with painted eyes, per doz. $2.00
No. 6R4597 Cords and anchors for decoys, per dozen..........40c

Collapsible Ducks.

No. 6R4600 Collapsible Canvas Decoy. A good imitation of the natural duck. Made of best canvas, beautifully painted in natural colors, waterproofed, inflated with air, and when not in use the air can be let out and ducks folded. Weight, 4 ounces, each. Packed one dozen in a neat wooden box, 2¾x9 inches. **We sell in any quantity.** Mallards, red heads, canvas backs and blue bills. Per dozen, $5.45

Canvas Collapsible Geese.

No. 6R4602 Canvas Geese Decoys, made of best sea island domestic canvas, covered with **waterproof dressing, painted exactly like a wild goose.** They are not affected by heat or cold and will last almost indefinitely. **They are very easily inflated,** and when the air is let out can be packed in a very small space. Weight, per dozen, packed, 12 pounds. Price, per dozen..........$11.75
If by mail, postage extra, each, 20 cents.

The Acme Folding Canvas Duck.

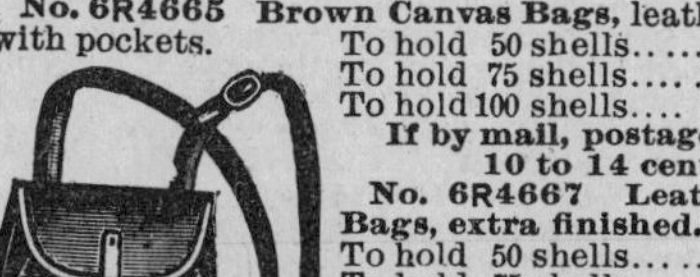

No. 6R4604 The New Acme Folding Canvas Decoy Mallard is very simple in construction. Mounted on a wood base, with wire frame. The best collapsible duck on the market. The inflated canvas ducks are useless when punctured with shot but this duck still keeps its shape, even though there were several holes through the canvas. Packed one dozen in a neat wooden carrying case, complete with cords and anchors. Per dozen..$4.00
If by mail, postage extra, each, 20 cents.

Shell Bags for Carrying Loaded Shells.

No. 6R4665 Brown Canvas Bags, leather bound, with pockets.
To hold 50 shells..........30c
To hold 75 shells..........33c
To hold 100 shells..........35c
If by mail, postage extra, 10 to 14 cents.

No. 6R4667 Leather Shell Bags, extra finished.
To hold 50 shells..........$0.95
To hold 75 shells..........1.10
To hold 100 shells..........1.25
If by mail, postage extra, 12 to 23 cents.

No. 6R4668 Extra Heavy Brown Colored Canvas Shell Bag, bound with red leather, 2 pockets, extra shoulder piece, handsome and durable.
Each
To hold 50 shells..........60c
To hold 75 shells..........65c
To hold 100 shells..........75c
If by mail, postage extra, 11 to 20 cents.

Bedells' Patent Game Skirt.

No. 6R4670 Bedells' Patent Special Game and Cartridge Holder, heavy russet leather belt with game hooks, double leather shoulder straps, heavy brown canvas skirt with pockets to carry 100 shells, and hooks attached all around for carrying game conveniently. The best game and cartridge holder for field shooting in the market. Each..........$1.25
If by mail, postage extra, 26 cents.

OUR GUN AND RIFLE COVERS.

We have selected the following line of gun and rifle covers and placed a large season contract for them so as to enable us to give you the best possible value for the least amount of money in this line of goods. When you order a gun cover from us you are getting it at a price based on the actual cost of material and labor with only our one small percentage of profit added. **You will assist us materially when ordering these goods, if you will give us the name of your gun or rifle, also length of barrel, and advise us whether it is a single barrel, double barrel, repeating shotgun or rifle for which you want the cover;** this will enable us to furnish you the exact cover you wish without any delay.

NOTICE.
8-oz. canvas means a yard weighs 8 oz.
10-oz. canvas means a yard weighs 10 oz.
12-oz. canvas means a yard weighs 12 oz.
The more ounces to the yard, the heavier the canvas.

Mention length of barrel and name of gun or rifle when ordering a gun cover.

Our Special 8-Ounce Cover, 35 Cents.

No. 6R4690 Brown 8-oz. Canvas Gun or Rifle Cover, leather bound all around, with leather handle, cotton flannel lined, full length. For 24 to 32-inch barrel. Each..........35c
If by mail, postage extra, 15 cents.
Give length of barrel, and name of gun or rifle when ordering a cover.

Our 45-Cent Leather Bound Cover.

No. 6R4695 Rifle and Gun Cover, best 8-oz. brown canvas, leather bound, leather sling, cotton flannel lined, best quality, for 24 to 32-inch barrel. Mention length of barrel when ordering and say if you wish it for a rifle or shotgun. Each..........45c
If by mail, postage extra, 13 cents.

Special Value for 70 Cents.

No. 6R4698 Heavy Tan 18-oz. Duck Cover, for magazine rifles. Full leather bound, with heavy sole leather lock and muzzle protector, with handle and sling, for 24 to 32-inch barrels. Price, each..........70c
Give name of rifle and length of barrel when ordering. If by mail, postage extra, 16 cents.

Our $1.50 Leather Rifle and Shotgun Cover

Give name of rifle or shotgun and length of barrel when ordering.

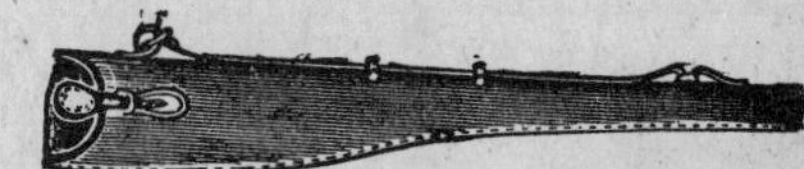

No. 6R4701 Soft Leather Cover, made of heavy soft russet bag leather, with combined sling and handle. Bright trimmings, for magazine rifles. For 24 to 32-inch barrels; give length of barrel and name of gun or rifle when ordering; absolutely waterproof and a good one. Price, each..........$1.50
If by mail, postage extra, 25 cents.

Rifle and Carbine Sheath.

No. 6R4703 Rifle and Carbine Sheath, best russet leather, for Winchester carbines and models 1873, 1876 and 1886 rifles. These sheaths are not full length covers, but are intended for carrying rifle on saddle, leaving stock of rifles exposed, to be easily grasped.
Weight, for carbines, 13 oz.; model '73, 16 oz.; models '76 and '86, 26 oz. State if wanted for carbine or rifle when ordering. Each..........$1.25
If by mail, postage extra, 30 cents.

Our 90-Cent Duck Gun Case.

Victoria Style.
No. 6R4706 Heavy 18-oz. tan duck, waterproof leather bound, with straps and tool pocket, leather lock and muzzle protector, flannel lined for 30 or 32-inch barrels. Price, each..........90c
If by mail, postage extra, 32 cents.

Our Victoria Gun Case, $1.10.

No. 6R4707 Victoria Gun Case, heavy 18-oz. waterproof canvas, reinforced with leather lock and muzzle protector with pocket for cleaning rod; also shell bag to hold 50 shells. The most complete cover offered to sportsmen and trap shooters; for 30 or 32-inch barrels. State length wanted. Price, each..........$1.10
If by mail, postage extra, 35 cents.

Our California Style Gun Case, 80 Cents.

No. 6R4710 Heavy tan 18-oz. duck, flannel lined with tool pocket, sling and handle, leather muzzle protector, California leg of mutton shape, for 30 or 32-inch barrels. This cover is adapted to Lefaucheaux action guns as well as other breech loading guns. The ordinary Victoria cases will not take Lefaucheaux action guns. State length wanted. Price, each 80c

No. 6R4712 Tan colored duck for take down shotguns without rod pocket, 8-ounce canvas, 30 or 32 inches. Give length of barrel. Price, each 45c

No. 6R4713 Tan colored duck for take down shotguns with rod pocket, made of 8-ounce canvas, 30 or 32 inches. Give length of barrel. Price, each... ...55c

No. 6R4714 Folding Gun Case. Heavy 18-oz. tan colored canvas, reinforced ends, leather muzzle protector, with sling strap and handle. Price, each... ....85c

Our 18-oz. Canvas Victoria Rifle Case for Take Down Rifles, Only 75 Cents.

No. 6R4716 Heavy 18-oz. tan duck, with lock and muzzle protector, rod pocket on the side, Victoria style, flannel lined, well made. This case is made for the take down rifles only, namely, Model '92, Model '93, Model '94, Model '90, Model '86. Give length of barrel and model and name of rifle when ordering. Each....75c

IF YOU OWN A FINE GUN it pays to have a sole leather cover, as it protects the gun from bruises, dents, etc., when carrying it in a wagon, etc.

Our Sole Leather Victoria Gun Case, $1.90 and $2.25.

No. 6R4725 Victoria Gun Case, made of heavy russet leather; embossed, double stitched; making it very strong and durable; 30 and 32-inch. State length wanted. Without rod pocket. Our price....$1.90

No. 6R4726 Same as No. 6R4725, but with rod pocket on one side for 30 or 32-inch. State length wanted. Our special price....$2.25

English Victoria Gun Cases, $2.75.

Leg of Mutton Shape.

No. 6R4731 English Victoria Gun Case, leg of mutton shape, oak tanned, sole leather, flannel lined, fancy trimmings, handle and sling, lock buckle, name plate, the best case on the market for the money. For 30 or 32 inch barrels. State length wanted. Our special price....$2.75

Our Oak Tanned Russet Case, Only $3.25.

No. 6R4733 English Victoria, Leg of Mutton Shape Gun Case, made of oak tanned russet colored sole leather, brass trimmings with lock buckle and name plate, handle and sling, a beauty; for 30 or 32-inch barrels. Flannel lined. State length wanted. Each....$3.25

No. 6R4734 The same case, but made for two sets of barrels, 30 or 32-inch. State length wanted. Our special price....$4.25

Our Orange Leather Case, $3.75.

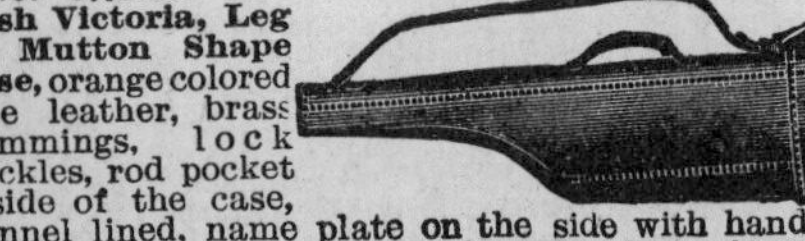

No. 6R4735 English Victoria, Leg of Mutton Shape Case, orange colored sole leather, brass trimmings, lock buckles, rod pocket inside of the case, flannel lined, name plate on the side with handle and sling for 30 or 32 inch barrels. State length wanted. Our special price....$3.75

Our Olive Sole Leather Case, Only $3.95.

No. 6R4737 Our Olive Green Color Leg of Mutton Case, brass trimmings, flannel lined, lock buckle, with tool pocket, handle and sling. **A very handsome case, with name plate, for 30 or 32-inch barrels.** State length wanted. Price $3.95

Our Finest Sole Leather Case, Hand Made.

No. 6R4740 English Victoria, Leg of Mutton Style, Sole Leather Case, made of the finest chestnut or oak sole leather, with fine brass trimmings, and lock buckle, handle and sling; very strong and durable; flannel lined, name plate. This case is made by hand, and none but the best workmen are employed, and no better case can be made regardless of price; for 30 and 32-inch; give length of barrel in ordering. Our price, flannel lined....$4.75

No. 6R4742 Same, lined with chamois skin. 5.50

Shell Boxes.

No. 6R4747 Sole Leather Shell Boxes, tin lined, with compartments, nickel plated trimmings; holding 200 shells. Weight, 5 pounds. Each....$3.00

Our Line of Revolver Holsters.

By taking advantage of the leather market and laying in a supply of leather before the advance, we are enabled to make you the following prices. **When you order holsters of us you are buying** them on our system of one small percentage of profit, from the maker to the consumer, and we are sure that you will agree with us, that quality considered, **our prices are below any competition.** When ordering holsters, **always give the name of your revolver, length of barrel, and caliber,** to enable us to give you the exact size, for these holsters vary in size, according to caliber and length of barrel.

Pistol Holsters.

No. 6R4754 Russet Leather Pocket Holster (as adopted by police officers), made of **russet leather,** for 3½-inch barrel, 32 and 38-caliber. Made to wear in the hip pocket; and it keeps the revolver handle up; always ready for use. Ea. 26c

If by mail, postage extra, 6 cents. Mention length of barrel and caliber when ordering.

Embossed Leather Flap Holster

No. 6R4756 Flap Pistol Holster, with loop and flap, similar to cut, heavy russet leather, 32 or 38 caliber, 3½ to 4-inch barrel. State length wanted. Each....30c

If by mail, postage extra, 5 cents.

Embossed Flap Holsters.

Mention length of barrel and caliber when ordering.

No. 6R4757 Flap Pistol Holster, with loop for belt, made of russet leather, 38, 44 or 45 caliber, 4½ to 5½-inch barrels. State length wanted. Price, each 35c

No. 6R4758 38, 44 or 45-caliber, 6 and 7½-inch barrel for frontier revolvers. State length wanted. Each....45c

If by mail, postage extra, 7 cents.

The Rubber Holster is rust proof, and being soft and pliable, **it is the best and most convenient holster ever made to carry a revolver in the pocket.** Will hold revolvers with 3½-inch barrel, or shorter.

No. 6R4759 Rubber Pocket Holster, with steel clasps to fasten on the outside of the pocket so you can pull out the revolver and the holster will remain in the pocket. Mention caliber wanted. **Not made for 5 and 6-inch barrel revolvers.**

Style A is for 32-caliber, for 3½-inch barrel....24c
Style B is for 38-caliber, for 3½-inch barrel....28c
Style C is for 44-caliber, for 4-inch barrel....33c

If by mail, postage extra, 4 cents.

The Chicago Pistol Pocket.

No. 6R4760 Is made of soft pliable leather and is intended for the pocket but can be used on a belt by cutting two slits down ½ in. from the top on one side. Made in 22, 32 or 38-caliber. Mention caliber wanted. Price, each 14c

If by mail, postage extra, 3 cents.

Embossed Mexican Open Top Holsters.

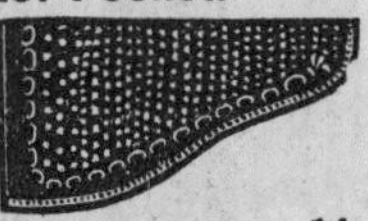

No. 6R4761 Pistol Holster, with loop for belt; **heavy russet leather,** 32 and 38-caliber 3¼-inch to 4-inch barrel; state length wanted. Price, each....21c

If by mail, postage extra, 4 cents.

Embossed Mexican Open Top Holsters.

No. 6R4762 Pistol Holster, with loop for belt; **best russet leather,** 32 or 38 caliber, 4½ to 5-inch barrel. Mention length of barrel wanted. Each....24c

If by mail, postage extra, 5 cents.

No. 6R4763 Pistol Holster, with loop for belt; best russet leather, 44 and 45-caliber, 4½ to 5½-inch barrel. Mention length of barrel. Each....30c

No. 6R4764 Pistol Holster, with loop for belt; best russet leather, 44 and 45-caliber, 6 to 7½-inch barrel. Mention length of barrel wanted. Each...35c

Embossed Leather Mexican Olive Holsters, 45 to 65 Cents.

No. 6R4765 Mexican Olive Holster, best leather, heavy and durable, 32 or 38-caliber, 3½-inch barrel. Price, each....45c

Style A, 44 to 45-caliber, 4½ to 5½-inch barrel. Each..55c

Style B, 44 to 45-caliber, 6 to 7½-inch barrel. Each 65c

If by mail, postage extra, 6 cents.

NOTE—Always state length of barrel on your pistol; also the caliber.

No. 6R4767 The Cowboy Holster. Made of heavy russet tanned leather; hand embossed work; made to match in color and style our **Cowboy Sheath.** The best holster on the market. All hand work. **When ordering give the length of the barrel of your revolver.**

No. A Price, 38-caliber, 4-inch....$1.10

No. B Price, 38 and 44-caliber, 5 or 6-inch....$1.25

No. C Price, 44 and 45-caliber, 7½-inch....$1.40

If by mail, postage extra, 11 cents.

The Texas Shoulder Holster.

No. 6R4768 The Texas Shoulder Holster, with breast and shoulder strap, nicely embossed, to wear under coat, on the left side, as shown in cut, for quick action. **Made of fine soft russet leather,** any caliber or length of barrel.

Style A, 38-caliber, 3½ or 4½-inch....60c
Style B, 38-caliber, 6-inch....65c
Style C, 44-caliber, 4½ or 5½-inch....70c
Style D, 44-caliber, 6 or 7½-inch....75c

If by mail, postage extra, 6 cents.

Always state caliber and length of barrel and name of revolver when ordering, if you are in a hurry for your goods, and then it will not be necessary to write you for size.

Our Holster and Cartridge Belts.

We would like to have you compare our line of belts with any line offered by any other house, and, quality considered, we think you will find that our prices are equal to those paid by the largest dealers. **OUR LEATHER GOODS ARE THE BEST IN THE MARKET.**

Plain Leather Belts and Cartridge Belts.

No. 6R4771 Belts only, russet leather, 1¼-inch wide, line embossed, without loops for cartridges. Length, 32 to 40 inches. Give length wanted. Each...(If by mail, postage extra, 5 cents) ...19c

No. 6R4772 Belts only, russet leather, nicely embossed edge, with loops for cartridges; 32, 38, 41 and 44-caliber, 1½ inches wide, plain roller buckle, 30 to 40 inches long. Give length and caliber wanted. Each...(If by mail, postage extra, 5 cents) ...30c

No. 6R4773 Belts only, fine russet leather, nicely embossed edge, with loops for cartridges; 32, 38, 44 and 45-caliber, 2¼ inches wide, large nickel plated buckle, 32 to 40 inches long. Give length and caliber. Each...(If by mail, postage extra, 10 cents)...55c

Combination Cartridge and Money Belts.

No. 6R4774 Mexican Combined Cartridge and Money Belt. Made of the very best soft russet leather; belt, 3 inches wide; soft and pliable and will not get hard and crack; neatly embossed. Mention caliber wanted.

Style A. 32 or 38-cal., give waist measure. Price, 90c
Style B. 44-caliber, give waist measure. Price, 90c
Style C. 45-caliber, give waist measure. Price, 90c
Style D. 50-caliber, give waist measure. Price, 90c

Don't forget to state caliber wanted, also waist measure.

If by mail, postage extra, 15 cents.

No. 6R4775 The Cowboy Combined Cartridge and Money Belt. Made of heavy russet tanned leather; strong and durable; nicely embossed, designed to match our Cowboy Scabbard and Holster; 38, 44 and 45-caliber. Mention caliber wanted, and give waist measure. Price, each $1.15

If by mail, postage extra, 18 cents.

Canvas and Web Cartridge Belts.

Made of heavy web with loops for cartridges. A very strong and durable belt, not impaired by any kind of weather. Mention caliber wanted when ordering.

No. 6R4776 Web Belts, for rifle and pistol cartridges; 32, 38, 44 or 45-caliber. Price, each.......45c

If by mail, postage extra, 17 cents.

Shell Belts for Shotgun Shells.

8, 10, 12 and 16-Gauge.

No. 6R4786 Canvas Shell Belts; 10, 12, 16 and 20-gauge, with shoulder strap. Mention gauge wanted.
Price, each.............25c

If by mail, postage extra, 6 cents.

No. 6R4787 Russet Leather Shell Belt; nicely embossed, with shoulder strap; for 10, 12, 16 and 20-gauge. Mention gauge wanted. Price, each.....50c

If by mail, postage extra, 10 cents.

No. 6R4788 Russet Leather Shell Belt; with shoulder strap; for 8-gauge only.
Price, each.......................................65c

If by mail, postage extra, 16 cents.

The New Anson Mills Woven Shell Belts.

No. 6R4791 In these belts the loops are woven into the belts, making them very strong and durable in all kinds of weather; 10, 12 and 16-gauge, with shoulder strap and game hooks. Mention gauge wanted. Price, each......................$1.25

If by mail, postage extra, 22 cents.

No. 6R4793 Same as above, without shoulder straps and game hooks, for 44 or 45-caliber cartridges. Mention caliber wanted.
Our special price...............................$1.25

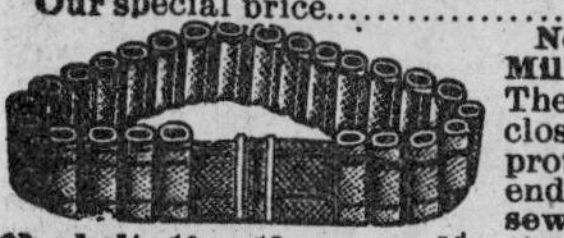

No. 6R4794 Anson Mills Hunters' Belt. The loops are woven, closed at the bottom, protecting the crimped end of the shell; no sewing whatever on the belt; 10 or 12-gauge. Mention gauge wanted.
Price, each......................................75c

If by mail, postage extra, 20 cents.

Grass Suits. Reduced to 90 cents.

90c PER SUIT is our price, and thousands are now being worn by sportsmen everywhere.

No. 6R5112 For wild goose, duck and all kinds of shore bird shooting; made of long tough imported marsh grass into cape coat with hood. They weigh less than four pounds, are convenient to wear and shoot from. Make good waterproofs in rainy weather, are easily packed and carried. Hunters appreciate the value of these suits, as no blind or bough house is necessary when shooting on marshes. Weight, about 5 pounds.
Single suits, each..................................90c

NOTICE: On any goods not described or listed in this catalogue and bought for you or made to order, we must not only ask cash in full with the order, but they cannot be returned under any circumstances, if sent as ordered.

HOW TO AVOID DELAY.

We carry a stock valued at about Two Million Dollars, and aim to keep this stock up; but it sometimes happens that we receive orders in one day from every part of the United States for the same single item, which exhausts the stock temporarily. It also sometimes happens that one of our factories fails in business, has labor strikes, can't make goods as fast as we sell them, and, while we try as far as possible to deal with reliable factories, we cannot guarantee to furnish goods under these conditions, but we always try to do the best we can for our customers. **If you can give us a second or third choice, when we are out of an article it will avoid delay in shipping your order.**

OUR HUNTING CLOTHING

OWING TO THE ANTICIPATED ADVANCE IN THE COST OF CANVAS, we have made arrangements with one of the largest manufacturers of this line of goods, and placed our season contract early in order to take advantage of the lowest possible prices on canvas, corduroy and leather, and by adding our uniformly one small percentage of profit to the actual cost of material and labor, we can offer you canvas and corduroy hunting clothing

LOWER THAN ANY OTHER HOUSE,

quality taken into consideration.

IN ORDERING state the number of inches around the body at breast under the arms or say what size dress coat you wear.

Our Best Canvas Hunting Coat, $3.75.

No. 6R5135 Our Very Best Quality Hunting Coat, made of the very best quality 12-ounce army duck, dead grass color, double stitched throughout, lined throughout the entire back with good quality 8-ounce army duck, sleeves lined with Walker's sateen, corduroy collar and corduroy cuffs, with adjustable sleeves, reinforced leather shoulder pieces, leather bound throughout, including the pocket flaps; silk crow feet stitching at the pockets and silk stitched buttonholes. The pockets are made on the let-in principle, same as a dress coat, which is very neat, and the game pockets are made so as to be accessible from the front and under the armpits, as shown in illustration. This is our best hunting coat, has seven outside pockets, and two spacious game pockets, with best quality of horn buttons, and no pains have been spared to make this hunting coat as good as any hunting coat can be made. It comes in sizes of 36 to 46 inches. Give chest measure when ordering.
Our special price only...................................$3.75

If by mail, postage extra, 60 to 75 cents.
12-ounce canvas weighs 12 ounces to the yard.

Regular Special Value Coat, for $1.85.

No. 6R5139 Hunting Coat, made of 10-oz. duck, dead grass color, drill lined, corduroy collar and adjustable cuffs, shoulders reinforced, double stitched throughout, five outside shell pockets, with flaps, reinforced, three game pockets with entrance from front edge and back seams, fancy stitching around entrance to game pockets. Sizes of chest measure from 36 to 46. Give chest measure when ordering.
Price, each............$1.85

If by mail, postage extra, 35 to 45 cents.

Our Leather Bound $2.25 Hunting Coat.

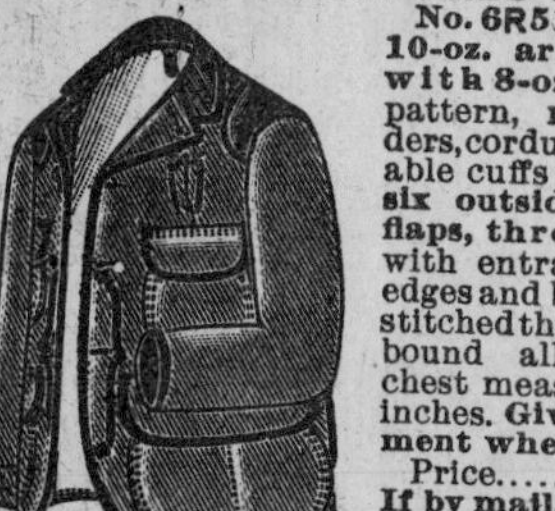

No. 6R5141 Best quality 10-oz. army duck, lined with 8-oz. army duck, full pattern, reinforced shoulders, corduroy collar, adjustable cuffs corduroy lined, **six outside pockets with flaps, three game pockets** with entrance from front edges and back seam, double stitched throughout; leather bound all around. Sizes, chest measure, from 36 to 46 inches. **Give chest measurement when ordering.**
Price...................$2.25

If by mail, postage extra, 45 to 55 cents.

Our Waterproof Mackintosh Hunting Coat, $2.20.

No. 6R5142 We have had a great many inquiries for a Mackintosh Hunting Coat and have induced one of the large mackintosh manufacturers to make for us a hunting coat of dead grass color. As a rule manufacturers of mackintoshes do not care to vary from their standard line of goods, but in order to accommodate us this maker has done so, and we can now **offer you a first class mackintosh hunting coat, dead grass color, at $2.20.**

Our Mackintosh Waterproof Hunting Coat is made double stitched, lined three quarter in the back, fly and back pockets for game; adjustable sleeves, six outside pockets, reinforced at all vital places, and weighs about 3½ pounds. These coats are made in sizes 36 to 44 inches, and when ordering give chest measure.
Our special price..$2.20

If by mail, postage extra, each, 55 to 60 cents.

Our $1.40 Hunting Coat.

No. 6R5143 Hunters' Coat made of 8-oz. duck (a yard of this canvas weighs 8 ounces), drill lined, dead grass color, corduroy collar, adjustable cuffs, **five outside pockets, three game pockets,** with entrance from front edges and back seams, shoulders reinforced, double stitched, three buttons. Sizes, chest measure, from 36 to 46 inches. **Give chest measurement when ordering.**
Price, each...............$1.40

If by mail, postage extra, 35 to 45 cents.

No. 6R5145 Exactly the same as No. 6R5143, but **leather bound all around.** Sizes, chest measure from 36 to 46. Price, each..$1.60

If by mail, postage extra, 35 to 45 cents.

No. 6R5147 Made of heavy drill, dead grass color, five outside pockets, two inside pockets. Sizes, chest measure, 36 to 46 inches. **Give chest measure when ordering.** Each..58c

If by mail, postage extra, 20 to 35 cents.

Our Boys' Hunting Coats, $1.45.

No. 6R5150 We have had so many calls for Boys' Hunting Coats that we were persuaded to put in a line of these in 32 and 34 inches (chest measure). They are made of 10-ounce canvas with five outside pockets, two game pockets, corduroy collars, and made up in first class style same as our regular men's coats. **Give chest measure when ordering.** Our special price..$1.45

If by mail, postage extra, 28 to 34 cents.

DON'T FORGET TO give measurement on Hunters' Clothing. Ten ounce canvas weighs 10 ounces to the yard.

Our $2.85 Corduroy Coat.

No. 6R5152 Is made of good quality corduroy, mouse color, well stitched, flaps over pockets, four outside pockets, two inside game pockets of large size, lined with drilling, reinforced shoulders. A dandy for the money, made in 36, 38, 40, 42 and 44 inches chest measure. Give chest measure when ordering.
Our special price, $2.85

If by mail, postage extra, 35 to 42 cents.

Hunting Vests.

No. 6R5155 Hunting Vest, with loops for cartridges. Made of 8-ounce duck, unlined; holds about 36 shells. Sizes, from 34 to 44 inches; 10 or 12-gauge. **Give chest measure when ordering.**
Price...............................73c

If by mail, postage extra, 12 to 18 cents.

Our 58-Cent Hunting Vest, made of Heavy 8-ounce Duck.

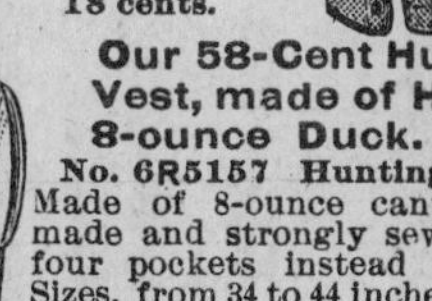

No. 6R5157 Hunting Vest. Made of 8-ounce canvas, well made and strongly sewed, with four pockets instead of loops. Sizes, from 34 to 44 inches. **Give chest measure when ordering**
Price, each.....................58c

If by mail, postage extra, 12 to 18 cents.

Hunting Pants.

No. 6R5158 Hunting Pants. Made of 8-ounce duck; dead grass color, with four patch pockets. Sizes, from 28 to 40 inches waist measure. **Give waist measure and leg measure of inseam when ordering.**
Price.................73c

If by mail, postage extra, 25 to 30 cents.

No. 6R5159 Duck Hunting Pants. Made of 10-ounce army duck, dead grass color, business style. "Cut-in" front and back pockets. Sizes, from 28 to 40 inches, waist measure. **Give waist measure and leg measure of inseam when ordering.** Each..............................$1.20

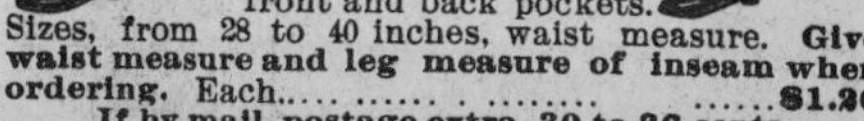

If by mail, postage extra, 30 to 36 cents.

Corduroy Hunting Suit.

No. 6R5172 Corduroy Coat, made of best imported drab mouse color corduroy, sateen lined, seven outside pockets, three game pockets, **adjustable sleeves.** The finest corduroy coat made. Sizes, 36 to 44 chest measure. Price..........$5.95
If by mail, postage extra, 60 to 75 cents.

No. 6R5174 Corduroy Vest. Business style with pockets, to match above coat. **Give chest measure when ordering.** Price.......$2.75

No. 6R5175 Corduroy Pants. Business style. To match above coat. **Give waist measure and inseam of leg when ordering.**
Price..........$3.50
If by mail, postage extra, 30 to 38 cents.

OIL TANNED HORSEHIDE CLOTHING.

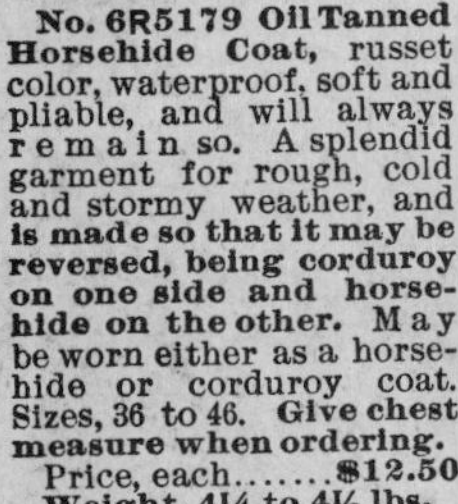

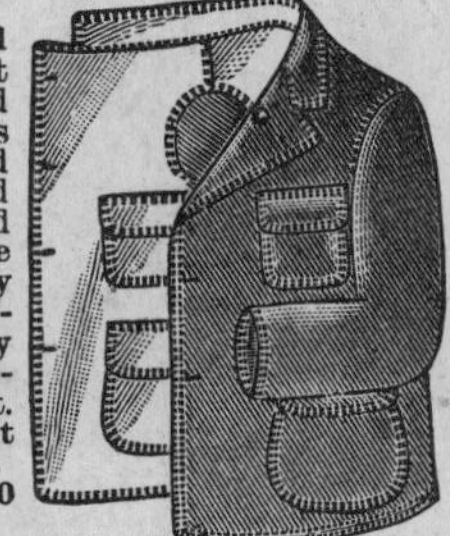

No. 6R5179 Oil Tanned Horsehide Coat, russet color, waterproof, soft and pliable, and will always remain so. A splendid garment for rough, cold and stormy weather, and **is made so that it may be reversed, being corduroy on one side and horsehide on the other.** May be worn either as a horsehide or corduroy coat. Sizes, 36 to 46. **Give chest measure when ordering.**
Price, each.......$12.50
Weight, 4¼ to 4½ lbs.

Our Reversible Leather and Corduroy Hunting Coat, $6.90.

For $6.90 we furnish this Hunting Coat, made of tan colored soft tanned pliable leather on one side and mouse colored corduroy on the reverse side, double stitched at all essential places, three pockets on the leather side and three pockets on the reverse or corduroy side, making six pockets in all. This is one of the best coats ever offered by any house, and for rainy or stormy weather it is by far the best, warmest and most useful coat ever made; it can be worn in stormy weather with the leather side out, and in clear weather it may be worn with the corduroy side out, making a nice neat dressy coat, a coat which will please you. **Weight, about 4¼ pounds.** These coats come in 36, 38, 40, 42 and 44-inch chest measure. **Give measurement of chest when ordering.**

No. 6R5180 Our reversible leather and corduroy hunting coat. Our special price..........$6.90

Horsehide Vests and Pants.

No. 6R5182 Horsehide Vest, with pockets, cassimere lined; business style, not reversible. Sizes, 34 to 46. **Give chest measure when ordering.**
Price, each..........$4.50

No. 6R5183 Horsehide Pants, business style, not reversible, cassimere lined. **Give waist measure and inseam of leg measure when ordering.** Per pair.......$7.50

Chamois Shirt.

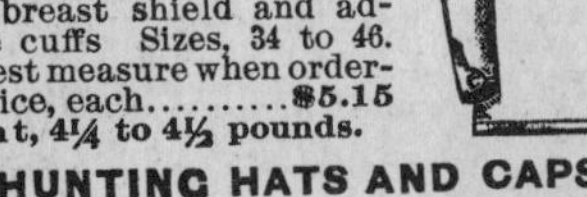

No. 6R5184 Chamois Shirt, a very comfortable garment, and a perfect protection in rough weather. Made of French chamois skin, flannel lined, with a breast shield and adjustable cuffs. Sizes, 34 to 46. Give chest measure when ordering. Price, each..........$5.15
Weight, 4¼ to 4½ pounds.

HUNTING HATS AND CAPS.

No. 6R5189 Canvas Cape Cap, made of 8-ounce duck, dead grass color, single stiff visor, full cape, flannel lined, an excellent rough weather cap. **State size wanted.**
Each..........35c
If by mail, postage extra, 7 cents.

No. 6R5190 Made of 8-ounce duck, dead grass color, double stiff visor, taped seams. **State size wanted.**
Each..........30c
If by mail, postage extra, 7 cents.

Hunting Hats and Caps.

No. 6R5191 Made of 8-ounce duck, dead grass color, stiff brim, solar style, a cool hat, ventilated. **State size wanted.** Each......48c
If by mail, postage extra, 7 cents.

No. 6R5192 Made of 8-ounce duck, dead grass color, round top, taped seams, double stitched, stitched brim. State size wanted. Each.......36c
If by mail, postage extra, 7 cents.

No. 6R5193 Same style made of good quality corduroy, light drab color, with taped seams. **State size wanted.** Each..........65c
If by mail, postage extra, 7 cents.

No. 6R5194 Made of imported corduroy, drab color, flat top, taped seams, brim lined with sateen. State size wanted.
Each..........64c
If by mail, postage extra, 7 cents.

No. 6R5195 Made of heavy imported corduroy, Windsor style, silk finish, sateen lined. An excellent winter cap. State size, wanted. Each..........66c
If by mail, postage extra, 7 cents.

Our $1.35 Klondike Cap.

No. 6R5197 The greatest winter cap made. Just the thing for farmers, teamsters and the Klondike. Made of heavy duck, lined with soft tanned sheepskin with the wool left on, with flap over face and strap and buckles; large visor, green lined, to protect the eyes, with nose protector. The best cap on the market to protect you from extreme cold weather. State size wanted.
Price, each..........$1.35
If by mail, postage extra, 20 cents.

Our Hunting and Riding Leggings.

We have taken great pains to select a line of leggings both canvas and leather, which we can sell at popular prices and which give entire satisfaction to our customers for hunting and other purposes. We have sold many thousand pairs of leggings for horseback riding, walking through wet grass, farm work and hunting, and our leggings have always given satisfaction. When ordering leggings always give the measurement around the calf of the leg, outside of the pants about 7 inches below the knee, so we can insure you a perfect fit.

For Hunting Boots and Shoes, see Index.

No. 6R5200

No. 6R5200 Wiley's Army Style Leggings. These leggings being of the army pattern and 15 inches long, are very comfortable, and are particularly adapted to long walks for those who travel long distance. They are made of **heavy 18-ounce canvas, brown, waterproof**, with grommets and hooks to lace all the way. **In ordering send size around calf, 7 inches below knee.** Price, per pair....47c
If by mail, postage extra, 12 cents.

No. 6R5202

No. 6R5202 Men's Knee Leggings, heavy 10-ounce canvas, tan color, to buckle, leather bound top and bottom.
Price, per pair..........45c

No. 6R5203 Same style as No. 6R5202, **but made of 24-ounce waterproof duck**, with double seams, leather bound top and bottom. The best buckle legging for wet weather and snow.
Price, per pair..........85c

No. 6R5205 Men's Knee Leggings, made of 8-ounce tan color duck, to lace, leather bound top and bottom. Per pair.35c

No. 6R5205

No. 6R5207 Men's Knee Leggings, made of 24-ounce tan color duck, to lace, leather bound top and bottom, a very fine legging and waterproof.
Price, per pair..........80c

No. 6R5215 Men's Leggings to lace, made of 12-ounce tan colored duck.
Price, per pair..........48c

No. 6R5220 Our Blanket Lined Mackintosh Leggings, to lace. This legging is made as near waterproof as possible from covert cloth of brownish color lined with blanket cloth, leather bound top and bottom. A warm, well made legging.
Our special price, per pair..........88c
If by mail, postage extra, 18 to 20 cents.

Be sure to give calf measure outside of pants, about 7 inches below the knee. Usually the measure is 15 to 17 inches.

DON'T FAIL TO GIVE MEASUREMENT AROUND CALF OF LEG, 7 INCHES BELOW THE KNEE.

Men's Thigh Leggings.

No. 6R5222

No. 6R5222 Men's Thigh Leggings, made of best quality 18-ounce waterproof brown canvas, leather bound **top** and bottom, **buckle to knee, lace to thigh, extra long.** Price, per pair...87c
If by mail, postage extra, 30 cents.

Our 92-Cent Thigh Leggings.

No. 6R5226 Men's Thigh Leggings, made of best **quality 18-ounce waterproof brown canvas**, with spring steel fastening below knee, lace to thigh. Full leather bound, easily **and quickly put on. One of the most popular leggings we have.** Give calf measure wanted.
Price, per pair..........92c
If by mail, postage, extra, 30 cents.

No. 6R5226

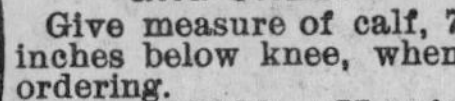

No. 6R5230 Men's Canvas Knee Leggings, made of heavy 15-ounce tan colored **duck**, with steel spring fastener, **leather** bound top and bottom; a fine legging.
Price, per pair..........63c
If by mail, postage extra, 25 cents.

No. 6R5230

Men's Fine Leather Leggings for $1.20 and $1.25.

Give measure of calf, 7 inches below knee, when ordering.

No. 6R5232 Men's Leather Knee Leggings, Napoleon style, made of fine grain leather, black color with steel spring fastener.
Price, per pair.....$1.25

No. 6R5236 Men's Fine Grain Leather Knee Leggings, Napoleon style, to lace, black color.
Price, per pair....$1.20
If by mail, postage extra, 25 cents.

No. 6R5232 No. 6R5236

NOTICE—**10-ounce canvas means a yard will weigh 10 ounces, 15-ounce canvas means a yard will weigh 15 ounces, etc.**

Dog Couplers.

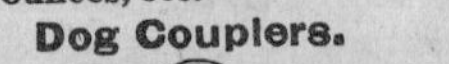

No. 6R5326 Dog Couplings, polished steel, **large** ring in center, snap hook on each end, two swivels **to** couple a young dog to an old one while training.
Price, each..........25c
If by mail, postage extra, 6 cents.

Our Hand Made Dog Whips.

No. 6R5340 Whips, hand braided russet leather, snap on handle, small size and durable.
Price, each..........40c

No. 6R5342 The Never Break Whip, same as No. 6R5340, but much heavier, making a good lead as well as whip, can be folded into small compass and carried in pocket.
Price, each..........60c

No. 6R5344 The Never Break Whip, 12-plait braided leather, with leather loop on end, loaded butt, strong and durable.
Price, each..........80c
If by mail, postage extra, 8 cents.

DOG MUZZLES.

NOTICE—**When ordering Dog Muzzles please give measurement around the dog's neck and around mouth, ½-inch from the tip of the nose, and the length from tip of the nose to the top of head where the strap goes around his neck, and you will assist us in fitting the muzzle.**

Safety.

Dog Muzzles, tinned iron wire, with strap to buckle around the neck. Made to cover nose and mouth. Give measure as above mentioned.

No. 6R5345 Small size.......18c
No. 6R5346 Large size.......22c
If by mail, postage extra, 7 cents.

Leather Strap Dog Muzzle.

Leather Strap Dog Muzzle, to buckle around neck and buckles to take up length around head if too large. Give measure when ordering.

No. 6R5347 Small size.
Price, each..........30c
No. 6R5348 Large size.
Price, each..........40c
If by mail, postage extra, 4 cents.

LAWN TENNIS GOODS, ETC.

Tennis Nets.

No. 6R6633 Tennis Nets, 27x3 feet, 12-thread. Weight, packed, 31 ounces. Each........68c
No. 6R6634 Tennis Nets, 36x3 feet, 15-thread. Weight, packed, 36 ounces. Each........$1.00
No. 6R6635 Tennis Nets, 42x3 feet, 15-thread. Weight, packed, 36 ounces. Each........$1.25
No. 6R6637 Tennis Nets, 42x3 feet, 15-thread, canvas bound. Each........$1.75
No. 6R6638 Tennis Nets, 42x3 feet, 21-thread, canvas bound. Each........$2.25
No. 6R6639 Back Stop Net to prevent balls from rolling out of grounds. 50x8 ft., 12-thread. Each.$2.25

OUR VICTOR LINE OF TENNIS RACKETS.

All our Rackets are made by the best of American manufacturers, and are guaranteed the best on the market. We do not guarantee rackets against breaking after being used.

No. 6R6650 The Lenox, No. 355. A strong, well made racket. Has good sized head. The best racket on the market for the money. Price, each........85c
No. 6R6651 The Comet, No. 354. Full sized head, good frame. A very popular racket at a popular price. A big seller. Price, each........$1.60
No. 6R6652 The Belle, No. 353. The best medium priced racket made. Built on popular lines, full size, strong frame, strung with a good quality of gut. **Buy this racket and you will get your money's worth.** Price, each........$2.00
No. 6R6653 The Victor Tournament No. 352 Racket. Frame made of well seasoned ash, reinforced throat, fine quality oriental gut, checkered grip handle. An excellent racket. Price......$3.25
No. 6R6655 Our Victor Special, No. 351. This racket is made on a new and approved model. Frame of selected second growth ash, well seasoned. Handle of mahogany with gun stock checking, and throat strongly reinforced, strung with best English gut. **Very durable and handsome.** Each....$4.25
If by mail, postage extra, each, 16 cents.

LAWN TENNIS BALLS.

No. 6R6658 Regulation Newport Finals, No. 350A........30c
No. 6R6659 Victor Championship Tennis Balls, No. 350........40c
If by mail, postage extra, 3 cents.

OUR SPECIAL CROQUET SETS.

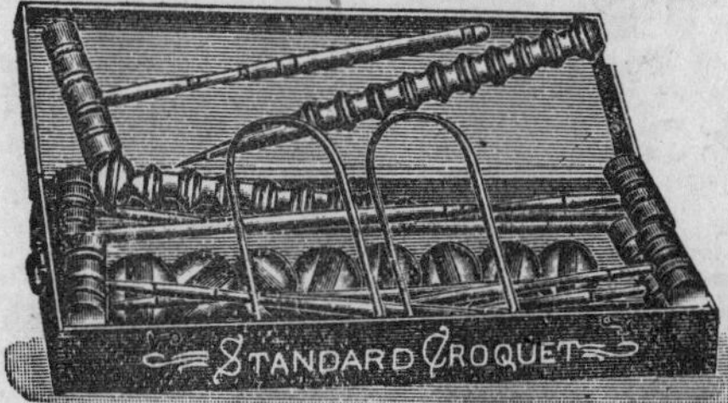

No. 6R6678

No. 6R6670 Four-ball Croquet Set, four plain mallets, hardwood varnished balls and stakes, ten arches in neat box with hinged cover. Weight, about 13 pounds. Price........55c
No. 6R6672 Same as No. 6R6670 with eight balls and eight mallets in dovetailed box with hinged cover. Weight, about 22 pounds. Price........75c
No. 6R6674 Eight-ball Croquet Set, painted and striped, eight mallets and eight balls, of neat design, two large fancy stakes, heavy arches. **An excellent set at a low price.** Weight, about 24 pounds...$1.25

$1.50 Buys a Regular $3.00 Croquet Set.

No. 6R6676 Eight-ball Croquet Set, handsome, maple, with eight fancy striped mallets, handles and balls, two elegant fancy stakes, **heavy pointed arches**, superior workmanship and materials in every part. Weight, about 25 pounds........$1.50

Our Finest Croquet Set Complete For $2.60.

No. 6R6678 Our Best Eight-ball Croquet Set, shellac finish, eight fancy balls, eight striped ebonized and bronzed mallets, handles and balls **beautifully finished**, painted and striped, two **elegantly beaded stakes**, heavy arches with sockets; **an elegant set.** Weight, about 27 pounds. Price........$2.60

GIVE CATALOGUE NUMBER IN FULL
WHEN YOU WRITE YOUR ORDER.

BOXING GLOVES. Our Special Leader.

Our Department of Boxing Gloves is strictly up to date. You will find gloves to suit all tastes, for either amateur or professional. These gloves are selected by an expert, who is posted on this class of goods. They are all and more than we claim for them, and are all guaranteed the best that can be had for the money. **We send free a copy of the Marquis of Queensbury Rules with every set. A set consists of four gloves, two pairs, packed in a box.**

No. 6R6800 Boys' size, made of oiled tanned kid leather ecru color, stuffed with good quality short hair, ventilated palm, laced wristband, good shape; a well made and durable glove. Weight, per set, about 26 ounces.
Per set of four gloves........85c

No. 6R6801 Youths' size. Made of wine colored kid leather, soft and pliable, stuffed with good quality curled hair; stitched fingers, laced wristband, ventilated palm. Weight, per set, about 34 ounces.
Per set of four gloves..$1.10

No. 6R6802 J. Simon's Men's Size Standard Pattern. Made of ecru kid leather, stuffed with good quality short hair, ventilated palm, laced wristband, drill lined. Weight, per set, about 46 ounces.
Per set of four gloves........$1.10

No. 6R6803 Our Snyder Glove. Men's Standard Pattern, Improved. Made of claret colored California Napa leather with padded finger ends, ventilated palm, split and laced wrist, stuffed with good quality curled hair, drill lined. Weight, per set, about 46 ounces.
Per set of four gloves........$1.25

No. 6R6804 Corbett Pattern. Red back with ecru palm and wrist, ventilated palm, drill lined, laced wristband; stuffed with good quality curled hair. Weight, per set, about 46 ounces.
Per set of four gloves........$1.50

No. 6R6805 Corbett Pattern. Made of wine colored kid leather, serge lining, stitched fingers, ventilated palm, split wrist with laced wristband and padded cuffs; stuffed with best quality curled hair. Weight, per set, about 50 ounces.
Per set of four gloves........$1.65

No. 6R6806 Corbett Pattern. Made of selected green California Napa leather, with fingers, serge lining, laced wrist, ventilated palm; stuffed with best quality curled hair. Weight, per set, about 48 ounces. Per set of four gloves...$1.75

No. 6R6807 Corbett Pattern. Made of selected wine color kid, back and wrist tan color, palm of selected kid, stitched fingers, ventilated palm, split wrist with lacing wristband, serge lining; stuffed with best quality curled hair, stitched fingers, double stitched throughout. Weight, per set, about 48 ounces.
Per set of four gloves........$2.75

No. 6R6808 H. A. Steele's Corbett Pattern. Made of selected especially tanned wine color kid, laced wrist, padded cuffs, leather bound; best serge lining, ventilated palm, stuffed with extra quality curled hair, stitched fingers, double stitched throughout. Weight, per set, about 48 ounces.
Per set of four gloves........$3.00

Wonderful Value at $3.25 Per Set.

No. 6R6810 Geo. Stoll's Corbett Pattern. Made of selected French kid, tan brown color, with grip across center of palm, lined throughout, stitched fingers, double stitched with silk, laced wrist, leather binding, wrist with padded cuffs, ventilated palm; stuffed with best quality curled hair. Weight, per set, about 48 ounces.
Per set of four gloves.....$3.25

No. 6R6812 Barry Pattern. Made of selected especially tanned French kid leather, green color, with grip in center, thumb well padded on top, affording absolute protection, leather lined and leather binding, laced wrist with tape laces, wrist extra padded, roll hand sewed; stuffed with extra quality curled hair, double stitched throughout with silk. Weight, per set, about 48 ounces. Per set of four gloves........$3.75

No. 6R6813 Our Forster Pattern men's size. Made of best claret colored California kid leather, with grip in center and toe pad, ventilated palm, best serge lining, laced wrist, leather binding; stuffed with best quality curled hair, double stitched with silk throughout. A good sparring glove. Weight, per set, about 48 ounces.
Per set of four gloves........$2.00

Our Highest Grade Glove at $3.65 Per Set.

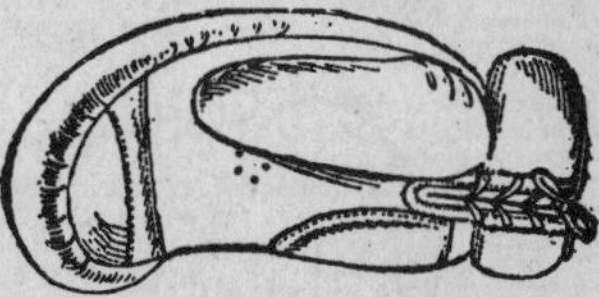

No. 6R6814 A Quality. Fitzsimmons Pattern with California thumb. Made of selected French kid leather, green color, with grip and side or heel pad, leather lined and leather binding, laced wrist with tape laces, wrist made with extra padded roll, hand sewed; stuffed with extra quality curled hair, double stitched throughout with silk. Weight, per set, about 52 ounces. Per set........$3.65
We can furnish this glove in 5 or 6-ounce to order, at the same price as the regular gloves.

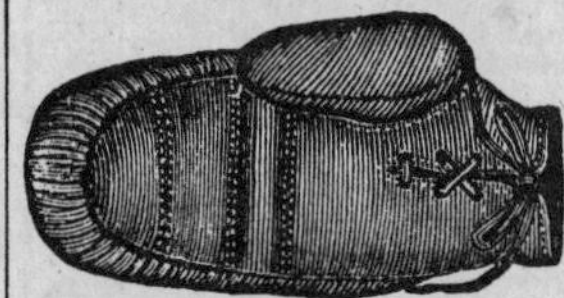

No. 6R6815 Our Hoerstal Pattern Professional Fighting Glove. Made of selected green California Napa leather, with grip in center and toe pad, ventilated palm, lined throughout, laced and leather bound wrist; stuffed with very best quality curled hair, made extra strong for hard usage, double stitched with linen thread, made in 6-ounce only. Weight, per set, about 45 ounces.
Per set of four gloves........$2.10

Our Perfect Striking Bag Platform, $4.65

From the accompanying illustration, engraved by our artist direct from the platform, you can form some idea of our Perfect Striking Bag Platform.

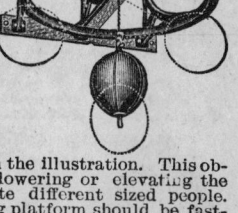

This platform is made of selected ash, well braced by three iron brackets, and the center tube is so constructed that the bag may be raised or lowered by simply turning the thumbscrew, as shown in the illustration. This obviates the necessity of lowering or elevating the platform to accommodate different sized people. The Perfect punching bag platform should be fastened so that the ring will be about 6¾ feet from the floor, this height will accommodate the average person. **This is the latest thing in a punching bag platform,** and constitutes a rigid, adjustable platform, one which can be used by man or boy without changing the position when once fastened against the wall.
No. 6R6819 Our special price on the **Perfect Punching Bag Platform** (this price does not include the punching bag), only........$4.65
Weight, crated for shipment, about 85 pounds.

HANDLE THIS CATALOGUE CAREFULLY...
AND PRESERVE IT FOR
READY REFERENCE.

STRIKING BAGS.

Our line of bags is the most complete and the finest in the market. All are carefully tested before they are put in stock. Our bags all have the best grade of bladder that money can buy. The buyer of a bag wants a strong, substantial article that can be relied on and a rubber inside that will not burst the first time it is used. All our bags are lined to keep their original shape. 33-inch is the regulation size. **Prices include the bag and bladder, complete, with a piece of rope and screw eye.**

Single End Bags.

No. 6R6825 Made of gold tan with strong loop. Single end, good, desirable and strong, 30-inch circumference when inflated. Weight, complete, about 10 ounces. Price, with bladder..**$1.15**

No. 6R6828 Made of Craven tan leather, with strong loop, very good, strong bag, 33-inch circumference when inflated. Weight, complete, about 12 ozs. Price, with bladder..............**$1.35**

No. 6R6829 Best quality claret colored, soft tanned leather, strong loop, triple seams, making an extra strong bag, one of the best sellers, 33-inch circumference when inflated. Weight, complete, about 14 ounces. Price, each, with bladder............**$1.50**

No. 6R6830 Best quality Craven olive tan leather, strong loop, welted seams, a fine bag and very fast, 33-inch. Weight, complete, about 12 ounces. Price, each, with bladder..................**$1.75**

No. 6R6835 Oil tan satin calf, a good, strong, lasting bag. A good article, retails for $3.50. 33-inch circumference when inflated. Weight, complete, about 14 ounces. Our price, with bladder.....**$2.20**

No. 6R6836 Oil tan horsehide bag, very strong and tough. Professional bag; made up first class in every respect; very fast, and the finest bag made, 33-inch circumference when inflated. Weight, complete, 14 ounces. Price, with bladder..........**$2.45**

If by mail, postage extra, 20 to 25 cents.

DOUBLE END BAGS.

Here is a line of double end bags which are lively, good and can be put up anywhere where you can put in two screw eyes. Illustration shows a bag put up in a doorway. Bore a 1-inch hole in your door sill, turn a screw eye into it so it will be below the sill and out of the way; fasten a hook to the elastic cord and hook it to the screw eye, and you can take down the bag or put it up in a few seconds any time. **These prices include the bag, bladder, a piece of rope, two screw eyes, and a piece of elastic cord.**

No. 6R6845 Made of gold tan with strong loop. Double end, good, desirable and strong, 30-inch circumference when inflated. Weight, complete, about 14 ounces. Price, with bladder, rope and elastic cord....**$1.35**

No. 6R6846 Best quality claret colored, soft tanned leather, strong loop, triple seams, making an extra strong double end bag, and one of the best sellers; 33 inches circumference when inflated. Weight, complete, about 14 ounces. Price, with bladder, rope and elastic cord....**$1.75**

No. 6R6847 Oil tan satin calf, a good, strong, lasting bag. A good article, retails for $4.00. 33-inch circumference when inflated. Weight, complete, about 15 ounces. Price, with bladder, rope and elastic cord....**$2.45**

If by mail, postage extra, 22 to 27 cents.

Our Pear Shape Bag.

This is the latest thing in punching bags. The Pear Shape Bag has no loop but the rope comes through the top of the bag and is so made that the strain is on all sections of the bag instead of one place. The top and bottom are stitched by hand and the bag is built to withstand constant use—in fact the bag is built for work.

No. 6R6848 Made of sheepskin, plain seams, canvas lined, wine color, 30-inch circumference when inflated. Weight, complete, 11 ounces. Each, with bladder..**$1.40**

No. 6R6849 Fine quality goatskin, olive green color, napa tanned, bound lips, eyeleted, lace holes, welted triple seams, canvas lined, 33 inches circumference when inflated. Weight, complete, 11 ounces. Price, each, with bladder..................**$1.85**

No. 6R6850 Fine quality satin calfskin. Craven tan color, bound lips, eyeleted lace holes, welted seams, canvas lined, weight 9 to 12 ounces, 34 inches in circumference when inflated, hand stitched top and bottom, with very best quality of rubber bladder that can be had, just the bag for professional bag punchers. Weight, complete, 11 ounces. Price, each, with bladder..................**$2.50**

If by mail, postage extra, 22 cents.

ELASTIC FLOOR ATTACHMENTS.

No. 6R6851 Elastic Floor Attachments for Double End Bags, made of elastic and covered with braided cotton and used for attaching the bottom of the bag to the floor. Price, each..............**22c**

If by mail, postage extra, 5 cents.

Rubber Striking Bag Bladders.

No. 6R6852 10-inch Bladders, made of pure para rubber, for 30-inch striking bags. Price, each..............**50c**

No. 6R6853 12-inch Bladders for bags 33 inches. Price, each..............**60c**

If by mail, postage extra, 5 cents.

No. 6R6854 Striking Bag Swivel. The latest out; has all improvements, and **none of the defects of the old swivel.** Rope can be taken out without unscrewing from platform and permits bag to be knocked in any direction without twisting rope. Price, each..............**83c**

If by mail, postage extra, 5 cents.

Striking Bag Knuckle Gloves.

No. 6R6855½ The Celebrated Frazer Striking Bag Knuckle Glove, small, neat, made of the best oil tanned horsehide, heavily padded, thus making a complete protection for the knuckles. Per pair..............**40c**

If by mail, postage extra, 5 cents.

Maple Indian Clubs.

No. 6R6856 Sold in pairs only and made of the best first quality rock maple, and finely polished. Weight given is the weight on each club. If you order one pair 1-pound clubs you get two 1-pound clubs, etc.

Each club weighs	Per pair
½ pound	13c
¾ pound	15c
1 pound	17c
1½ pounds	20c
2 pounds	23c
3 pounds	37c
4 pounds	44c
5 pounds	55c

When ordering state which weight you wish.

WOOD DUMB BELLS.

No. 6R6857 Wood Dumb Bells, made of polished maple, of best quality and nicely polished.

Weight	½ lb.	¾ lb.	1 lb.	2 lbs.	3 lbs.	4 lbs.
Per pair	13c	15c	17c	23c	37c	45c

Mention the weight you wish when ordering.

Striking Bag Mitts.

No. 6R6858 Striking Bag Mitt, made of kid, with grip in center, padded back, elastic wristband. This is the only punching bag glove to use for bag punching. Price, per pair....**65c**

If by mail, postage extra, 10 cents.

Iron Dumb Bells.

No. 6R6859 Our Iron Dumb Bells are cast from pure gray iron, and are very much stronger and more durable than those ordinarily sold, which are usually made from scrap iron, tin, etc., and are very brittle and break easily. We make them in weights as follows: 1, 2, 3, 4, 5, 6, 8, 10, 12, 14, 15, 20 and 25 lbs. These are the weights of each dumb bell. Sold by the pound. Mention weight you wish when ordering. Price, per pound..............**4c**

Quoits.

No. 6R6860 Japanned Iron Quoits, made of malleable iron; 4½ inches diameter, the weight, per set of four is 7½ pounds. Price, per set..........**40c**

5½ inches diameter, the weight, per set of four is 11½ pounds. Price, per set..............**60c**

6 inches diameter, the weight, per set of four is 13 pounds. Price, per set..............**75c**

Basket Balls.

No. 6R6862 Victor Official Basket Ball, made of the best English grain leather, 30½ to 31 inches circumference, the best basket ball made. Our special price........**$4.00**

If by mail, postage extra, 30c

No. 6R6863 Our College Basket Ball, made of the best American grain leather, regulation size, well made and durable. Our special price........**$2.75**

If by mail, postage extra, 28c.

No. 6R6864 Pure rubber gum bladders for basket balls. Price, each..............**65c**

If by mail, postage extra, 3 cents.

Basket Ball Goals.

No. 6R6868 Basket Ball Goals, made of iron frame with cotton netting, suitable to fasten against a fence or wall. Price, per pair..............**$3.50**

Exercising or Swinging Rings.

No. 6R6869 Wooden Rings, three pieces, made of walnut and maple glued together. Price, per pair..................**50c**

If by mail, postage extra, 11 cents.

Horizontal Bars.

Weight, 4½ to 6 pounds.

No. 6R6870 Made of the best quality second-growth straight grain hickory, square ends.

4 feet long, each,	**$1.25**	5½ feet long, each,	**$2.00**
4½ feet long, each,	1.50	6 feet long, each,	2.25
5 feet long, each,	1.75		

Trapeze Bars.

No. 6R6871 Made of the best second growth hickory. Straight grain. Without ropes. **Weight, 2 to 3½ pounds.**

	Each		Each
2½ ft. Bar	**$1.25**	3½ ft. Bar	**$1.75**
3 ft. Bar	1.50		

Common Sense Exercisers.

NO HOME IS COMPLETE WITHOUT IT. Convenient, perfect working, the latest and best on the market and our special price of 34 cents will surely commend it.

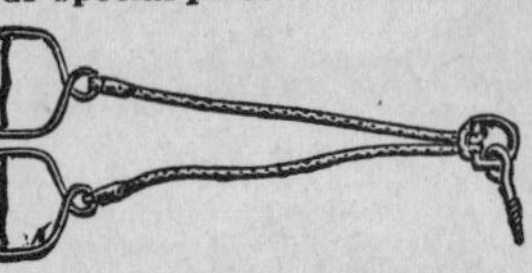

No. 6R6872 Our New Common Sense Exerciser, made of heavy elastic cord, the latest and cheapest exerciser yet produced, can be put up in any part of the room. Our price, complete..............**34c**

If by mail, postage extra, 12 cents.

Whiteley Exercisers.

The Whiteley is conceded by all leading gymnasts to be the best exerciser that has ever been produced. Every muscle of the human body may be developed with this simple machine. It is small and compact—can be hung up on any door frame. Is absolutely noiseless. **Is made of elastic cords, running through three cone bearing pulleys.** All parts guaranteed.

No. 6R6873 Made of elastic cord with wood pulleys, plain handles and foot attachment. Our special price..............**$1.65**

If by mail, postage extra, 22 cents.

No. 6R6874 Made of elastic cord with metal pulleys running in brass bushings, enameled handles with foot attachment. Our special price....**$2.45**

If by mail, postage extra, 30 cents.

No. 6R6875 Made of elastic cord with fancy decorated metal pulleys, nickel plated trimmings, enameled handles with foot attachment. Our special price..............**$3.15**

If by mail, postage extra, 30 cents.

GOLF CLUBS AND BALLS.

THE VICTOR GOLF CLUBS.

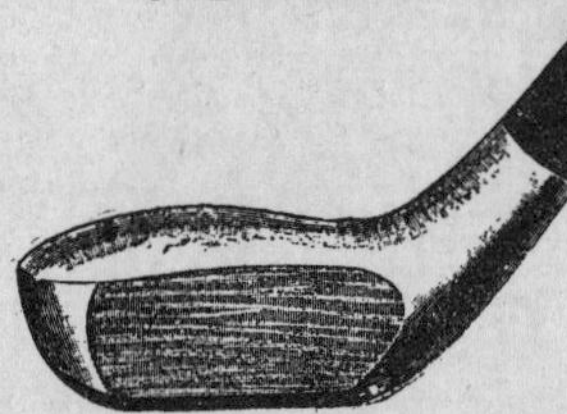

Made of selected grade of dog wood, with second growth hickory shafts, made on approved models, and very desirable clubs in every respect. Order by catalogue number and style number.

No. 6R6876 Style No. 701, Bulger Driver, each, **$1.25**; style No. 705, Bulger Brassey, each.....**$1.25**

The Country Club brand Golf Club. Style No. 801, Bulger Driver, each, **$1.00**; style No. 805, Bulger Brassey, each..............**$1.00**

VICTOR IRON GOLF CLUBS.

Made of hand forged heads, straight grain, second growth hickory shafts; rights only. The shafts are made to balance properly by Scotch makers, who are also expert players.

	Each
No. 6R6877 Style No. 707, Cleek Club	**$1.25**
Style No. 708, Lofting Iron Club	1.25
Style No. 709, Niblick Club	1.25
Style No. 710, Gun Metal Putter Club	1.25
Style No. 712, Mashy Club	1.25
Style No. 715, Mid-Iron Club	1.25

GOLF BALLS.

Made of gutta percha rubber, thoroughly seasoned and perfect in flight. We handle only these two styles. Try them. **They are all right.**

No. 6R6878 Our Practice Ball, per dozen........$2.70

No. 6R6879 Our Craig Park Ball, per dozen..$3.50

If by mail, postage extra, each, 2 cents.

Ten Pins and Balls.

No. 6R6880 League Model Ten Pins. Made of best material, nicely finished.
Per set of ten pins.........$2.90

No. 6R6881 Ten Pin Balls. Made of selected lignum vitæ wood, carefully turned.

Diam., 4 inch. Price, each, $0.70
Diam., 4½ inch. Price, each, .75
Diam., 5 inch. Price, each, 1.10
Diam., 5½ inch. Price, each, 1.25

Diameter	Price, each	Diameter	Price, each
6 inch	$1.50	7½ inch	$2.50
6½ inch	1.75	8 inch	2.75
7 inch	2.00	8½ inch	3.25

Finger holes in balls 25 cents extra.

Mention size of thumb and finger holes wanted and how far apart must the holes be.

No. 6R6882 Regulation Ball with finger holes, 27 inches circumference. Weight, 18 pounds. Adopted by the American Bowling League. Price, each, $4.25

Baseball Goods.

Baseballs.

No. 6R6885 The Victor League Ball, made entirely by hand; double covered, best Para rubber center; the best ball that can be produced; specially prepared two-piece horsehide cover, stitched with heavy linen thread, makes this the strongest ball on the market; the specifications of the National League are rigidly followed. **Guaranteed to hold its shape for nine innings. No better ball made at any price.**
Our special price...(Postage, each, 7 cents)....90c

No. 6R6886 For those who wish the Spalding League Balls, we have them at, each..........$1.15

No. 6R6887 Our National Association, made of best materials exactly in accordance with approved specifications. A regular dollar ball. Each ball in a separate box and sealed. Each....................70c

No. 6R6888 Our Intercollegiate, a ball made for amateurs and minor leagues, and recommended by various leagues throughout the country. Each..75c

No. 6R6889 Our High School League. A high grade ball, regulation size, will keep its shape under heavy batting. We recommend it. Each........45c

No. 6R6890 Our Pitcher's Pride. A beauty, has horsehide cover, well made; each in a separate box, sealed. Each.......................................25c

No. 6R6892 Our Little Victor, the best ball ever offered for the money, well made. Each..........10c

No. 6R6893 Our Star, an extra well made ball for the money. Not an ordinary ball, but well worth twice our price. Each.................................5c

Baseball Bats.

No. 6R6915 Professional Model Bat, made of best quality second growth wide grain ash. Guaranteed the best bat on the market. Each................55c

No. 6R6916 Made of fine quality ash. An excellent medium grade bat. Men's sizes. Each...35c

No. 6R6917 Good quality ash. Men's sizes. An extra good bat at a low price. Each.............25c

No. 6R6918 Boys' Professional Bat. 31 inches long. Made of selected ash. Each....................20c

No. 6R6919 Boys' Favorite. A good strong, well finished bat. Each.................................10c

No. 6R6920 Boys' 27-inch Bat. A daisy for the money. Each......................................5c

Baseball Mitts.

No. 6R6925 Victor Professional Mitt, made of the highest grade drabhorsehide. This mitt is designed especially for professionals and embodies suggestions received from many of the league catchers. Workmanship the best, material the best. Has patent thumb strap and patent lace. The patent thumb strap forms and keeps a deep pocket in the mitt, thus you buy a mitt that is already broken in. **No better mitt made at any price.** Price, each...(Postage, 38 cents)....$5.00

Baseball Mitts.

No. 6R6927 Our Victor Cleveland Mitt. We believe this mitt superior to any $5.00 mitt that was ever put on the market. The front is of best quality horsehide and the back and trimmings are of calf. Has the patent strap and lace, same as our $5.00 mitt. Made on lines of the professional mitts. Our special price.......$3.75
Postage, 40 cents.

No. 6R6928 Our Amateur League Mitt is made of selected calfskin throughout, double stitched, reinforced, made with full crescent palm, leather bound around the edges, with deep pocket in the palm, a mitt that measures 10¼ inches long, 9½ inches wide, and one that is made after the improved pattern of the professional league catcher's mitt. **This is a genuine calfskin mitt and one that will give satisfaction and service. Postage, 40 cents.**
Our special price..$2.75

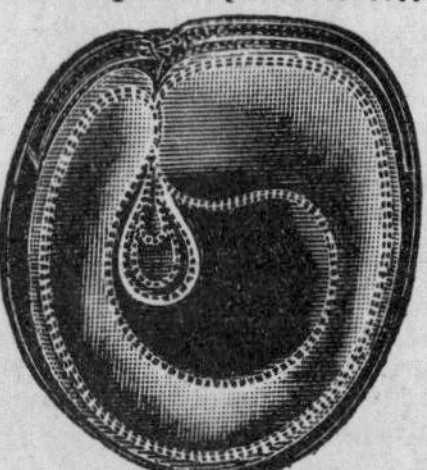

No. 6R6931 Our Commercial League Men's Mitt, made of fine quality especially tanned selected calf, heavily padded cup shaped palm, with crescent pad; extension quirk, double stitched all around. A fine mitt for little money. Must be seen to be appreciated.
Our special price.$2.25
Postage, extra, 32 cents.

No. 6R6932 S., R. & Co.'s Chelsea Mitt, palm made of genuine horsehide and fingers of selected sheepskin, reinforced thumb; crescent pad, forming a pocket, well stuffed and well finished, full size. An excellent mitt for semi-professional games. Price, $1.75
Postage, extra, 30 cents.

No. 6R6933 S., R. & Co.'s Men's Buck Mitt, palm made of selected quality buckskin, back made of goatskin, with fingers, thumb reinforced and thong stitched, well finished and well padded. This mitt is patterned after the professional mitt and is an ideal amateur mitt.
Price, each...................$2.00
Postage, extra, 30 cents.

No. 6R6935 S., R. & Co.'s Amateur Medium Size Mitt, palm is made of tan calf leather, crescent pad, sheep skin back, well made and well finished, cup shaped palm. A fine mitt, well stuffed.
Price, each............$1.45
Postage, extra, 28 cents.

No. 6R6937 S., R. & Co.'s Medium Size Mitt, palm of good quality buck leather, soft tanned, back of colt's skin, reinforced thumb, cup shaped palm, crescent pad. Each.................$1.25
Postage, extra, 25 cents.

No. 6R6938 S., R. & Co.'s Medium Size Men's Mitt, sheepskin finished palm, back of tan color leather, reinforced thumb. Price, each..........75c

No. 6R6939 S., R. & Co.'s Large Size Youths' Mitt, made of yellow or red leather, well padded, worth 75 cents. Our price...............................40c

No. 6R6940 Sears, Roebuck & Co.'s Youths' Mitt, made of selected tan leather, with fingers well padded. **A good strong mitt. Each, 35c**

No. 6R6941 Boys' Mitt, made of leather palm, canvas back and leather fingers, well padded. A bargain for............20c

No. 6R6942 Boys' Canvas Mitt, made of canvas throughout; a good, cheap mitt for boys; well stuffed. Price, each...10c

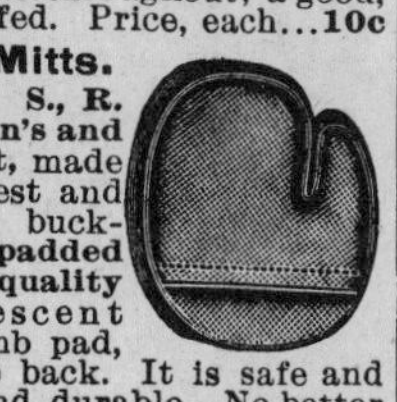

Baseman's Mitts.

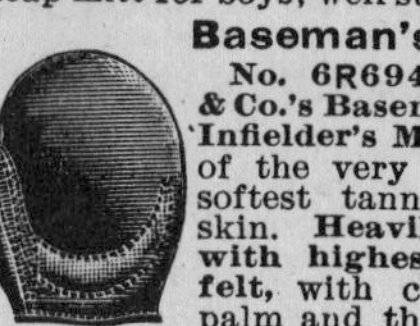

No. 6R6943 S., R. & Co.'s Baseman's and Infielder's Mitt, made of the very best and softest tanned buckskin. **Heavily padded with highest quality felt,** with crescent palm and thumb pad, welt seam, leather bound, lace back. It is safe and easy fitting. Very strong and durable. No better mitt made. Our special price...........................$1.25
If by mail, postage extra, each, 10 cents.

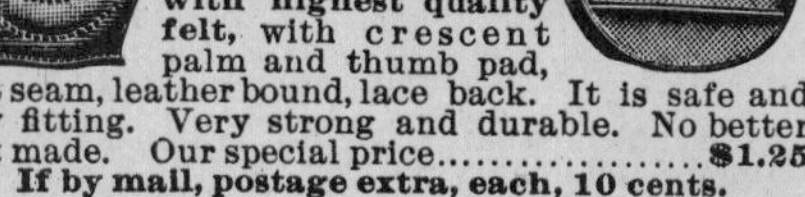

No. 6R6946 S., R. & Co.'s Special Boys' Baseman's Mitt is made of fine quality Yucatan goatskin, oil tanned, extra well padded. **Full leather lined and bound all around. The best** youths' baseman's mitt in the market.
Price...50c
If by mail, postage extra, each, 4c.

Baseman's and Fielder's Gloves.

No. 6R6954 Our Victor Professional Baseman's Glove. Made of horsehide; heavily padded; crescent pad extending in a semicircle around palm, making a deep pocket, correctly padded. **The best glove on the market.**
Price, each..................$1.95
Postage, extra, 12 cents.

No. 6R6956 Baseman's and Infielder's Glove, made of good quality buckskin, crescent palm, heavily padded; a medium priced professional glove and a good one. Our price.$1.27
Postage extra, 12 cents.

No. 6R6958 Our Chicago Glove, men's size, made of Napa tanned horsehide; well padded, with finger tips; crescent padded palm. Leather finger tips will be popular this season.
Price, each..................$1.00

No. 6R6960 Made of Napa tanned ecru leather; felt lined, heavily padded palm, leather bound; button wrist. Price, 60c

No. 6R6961 Made of gold tanned ecru leather; felt padded palm and fingers, leather bound edges, button wristband.
Our special price 40c

Boys' Fielder's Gloves.

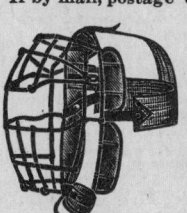

No. 6R6964 S., R. & Co.'s Youths' Infielder's Glove, made of finest oil tanned sheepskin; **heavily padded.** Leather bound all around; button fastener. **A regular boys' professional glove.** Our special price........35c
If by mail, postage extra, each, 3 cents.

Our 18c Boys' Glove.

No. 6R6966 S., R. & Co.'s Boys' Infielder's Glove; made of fine tan colored sheepskin, **palm felt lined and padded;** well stitched seams; button or elastic fastener. Our special price 18c
If by mail, postage extra, each, 3 cents.

BASEBALL CATCHER'S MASKS.

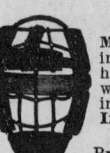

No. 6R6974 Patent Neck Protecting Mask, has an extension at bottom giving absolute **protection to the neck** without interfering in the least with the movements of the head. The wire is of the **best annealed steel,** is extra heavy and covered with black enamel to prevent the reflection of light. The **padding is filled with goat hair** and faced with finest imported dogskin, which, being impervious to perspiration, always remains **soft and pliant** to the face. Each................$2.25
If by mail, postage extra, 30 cents.

No. 6R6975 Men's Professional League Mask. Black enameled wire of $\frac{5}{32}$ and $\frac{3}{32}$-inch diameter, which prevents the reflection of the light; temple and cheek pads, with head and chin pieces; weight, 24 ounces; an A1 quality mask; 10½ inches long, 7½ inches wide. A very strong mask.
Our special price.....$1.75
If by mail, postage extra, each, 29 cents.

No. 6R6977 Men's Professional League Mask. Black enameled wire of $\frac{5}{32}$ and $\frac{3}{32}$-inch diameter, which prevents the reflection of the light; temple and cheek pads, with head and chin pieces; weight, 22 ounces; an A1 quality mask; 10½ inches long, 7½ inches wide. A very strong mask.
Our special price..............$1.50
If by mail, postage extra, each, 27 cents.

No. 6R6978 Men's Professional Mask. Black enameled wire, $\frac{5}{32}$-inch in diameter; temple and cheek pads; head and chin pieces; well made; weight, 18 ounces; 10 inches long, 7 inches wide. Price, each.......$1.00
If by mail, postage extra, each, 22c.

No. 6R6980 Men's Amateur Mask. Bright wire, $\frac{5}{32}$-inch in diameter temple and cheek pads; nicely finished; weight, 11 ounces; 10 inches long, 7 inches wide. Price, each..........50c
If by mail, postage extra, each, 14c.

No. 6R6983 Youths' Mask. Bright wire, $\frac{3}{32}$-inch in diameter; temple and cheek, pads; nicely finished; weight, 6 ounces; frame, 10 inches long, 6 inches wide. Price, each.....................35c
If by mail, postage extra, each, 9c.

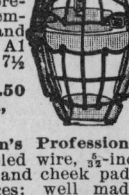

No. 6R6984 Boys' Mask. Bright wire, $\frac{3}{32}$-inch in diameter; temple and cheek pads; nicely finished; weight, 4 ounces; frame, 9 inches long, 5 inches wide.
Price, each..18c
If by mail, postage extra, each, 6 cents.

Patent Body Protectors, 84c to $6.00.

No. 6R6990 Our Special Professional League Body Protector, made of the very best rubber, inflated with air; light, pliable, and does not interfere with movements of the wearer. When not in use air may be let out and the protector rolled into a small package. Our price. **$6.00**

No. 6R6991 Our Special Amateur Body Protector, inflated with air, similar to our league, but has fewer air compartments. It is made with the same care as our professional and all are warranted perfect when they leave our store. Our special price **$4.00**

No. 6R6992 Our Boys' Body Protector, made of canvas, well stuffed and quilted, same shape as our league but smaller for boys. Our special price... **84c**

No. 6R6993 Our Men's Body Protector, made of canvas, stuffed and quilted. Price, each....... **$1.20**

Special League Shoe Plates.

(Patented.)

Our Special League Plates are made of the finest tempered steel and the strength increased.

6R6996

No. 6R6996 Special Hand Forged Steel Toe Plates. Price, per pair.................. **40c**

No. 6R6997 Special Hand Forged Steel Heel Plates. Price, per pair... **40c**

If by mail, postage extra, per pair, 3 cents.

6R6997

League Shoe Plates.

No. 6R6998 League Toe Plates, best quality steel. Per pair.............. **20c**

If by mail, postage extra, 3 cents.

No. 6R6999 League Heel Plates, best quality steel. Per pair.............. **20c**

If by mail, postage extra, 3 cents.

6R6999

Boys' Amateur Shoe Plates.

No. 6R7001 Amateur Shoe Plates, fine steel for boys' shoes. Per pair.... **9c**

If by mail, postage extra, 3 cents.

6R7001

Score Books—Club Sizes.

Pocket Sizes.

No. 6R7029 Paper Cover, for 7 games. Each... **10c**

No. 6R7030 Board Cover, for 22 games. Each... **25c**

No. 6R7032 Score Cards. Per dozen........... **25c**

If by mail, postage extra, each, 2 to 12 cents.

Baseball Caps.

Made in Chicago or Boston styles. When ordering say which style you prefer and mention color wanted. Baseball clothing is all made to order and cannot be returned if sent as ordered.

No. 6R7035 Best Athletic Worsted Flannel, in white, navy blue, maroon and gray colors; give hat size, or measure by inches.

Price, each.............. **75c**

Boston Style.

No. 6R7036 Medium Athletic Worsted Flannel, in navy blue, maroon and pearl gray colors; give hat size or measure by inches.

Price, each.............. **55c**

No. 6R7037 Athletic Cotton Fabric, in blue gray or mixed gray colors; give size of hat or measure by inches. Price, each.......... **45c**

Chicago Style.

No. 6R7038 Cotton Fabric, in brown, blue or white color only; give hat size or measure by inches.

Price, each...................... **25c**

If by mail, postage extra, 6 to 10 cents.

Baseball Belts.

No. 6R7040 Special Worsted Web Belts, in red, blue, black or navy colors; leather lined, 2½ inches wide; large nickel plated buckle. Price, each. **75c**

No. 6R7040

No. 6R7041 Special Worsted Web Belts, in red, blue, black or navy colors; 2½ inches wide, with 2 buckles. Each....... **45c**

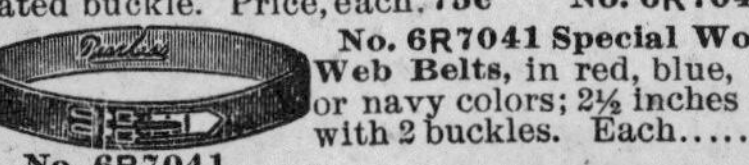

No. 6R7041

No. 6R7042 Special Cotton Web Belt, in red, blue, black or navy colors; 2½ inches wide, with one plain buckle.

Price, each.................. **20c**

Mention color wanted. No. 6R7042

If by mail, postage extra, 3 cents.

Baseball Stockings.

No. 6R7050 Heavy, all Wool Ribbed Stockings, in maroon, navy blue and black colors. **Mention size wanted.**

Per pair...................... **90c**

No. 6R7051 Medium Weight Wool Ribbed, in maroon, navy blue and black colors. **Mention size wanted.**

Per pair...................... **70c**

No. 6R7052 Medium Weight Wool Ribbed Stockings, cotton feet. Maroon, navy blue and black colors only. **Mention size wanted.** Per pair... **50c**

No. 6R7053 Heavy Cotton Ribbed Stockings; black color only. **Mention size wanted.** Per pair...................... **25c**

If by mail, postage extra, 5 to 8 cents.

Baseball Shoes.

No. 6R7057 Our Men's Amateur Special Baseball Shoes; best kangaroo calfskin, steel plates riveted to heel and sole, best oak soles, flexible and equal to any $5.00 shoes made. Sizes, 6 to 11, in C, D and E width. State size and width wanted. Weight, about 24 ounces. Per pair.................. **$2.15**

If by mail, postage extra, per pair, 36 cents.

See our shoe department for a complete line of baseball, football and running shoes, quoted at lowest wholesale prices.

Baseball Shirts.

Baseball Shirts are made to order and **cannot be returned if sent as ordered.** When ordering give neck measure and length of arm from collar button back of the neck to wrist when arm is bent in the shape of a letter L, from the shoulder forward. It takes four to six days to make shirts. Send 5c. for our sample cards of uniform material, or if you don't have time to do so, mention color you prefer, and give us a second choice, in case we are temporarily out of one color, when we receive your order. **Lettering on shirts cost 5 cents per letter, and each letter is about 3 inches long. Don't get too many letters, or they will not go on the front. Say if you wish laced front or button front.** We always send button front when you do not mention which you prefer.

No. 6R7060 Best Athletic Worsted Flannel, in white, navy blue, maroon and gray colors. Give measurement.

Each.......................... **$2.75**

No. 6R7061 Medium Grade Athletic Worsted Flannel, in navy blue, maroon and pearl gray colors. Give measurement. Each........... **$2.00**

No. 6R7062 Best Cotton Athletic Fabric, in blue gray or mixed gray colors. Give measurement.

Each........................... **$1.50**

No. 6R7063 Ordinary Cotton Fabric, in brown, blue or white color only. Give measurement. Each..... **$1.00**

For letters on shirts, add 5 cents per letter.

If by mail, postage extra, 15 cents.

Baseball Pants.

Baseball Pants are made to order. **Send cash with the order.** All our baseball pants are **heavily padded and quilted and come with elastic bottom.** When ordering, give waist and length measure. Pants should go below the knee, about 4 to 6 **inches.**

NOTICE—Many players are using football pants for baseball games, claiming they are stronger though they don't look quite as well.

No. 6R7066 Best Athletic Worsted Flannel, in white, navy blue, maroon and gray colors. Give measurement. Per pair..... **$2.75**

No. 6R7067 Medium Grade Athletic Worsted Flannel, in navy blue, maroon or pearl gray colors. Give measurement. Per pair. **$2.00**

No. 6R7068 Best Cotton Athletic Fabric, in blue gray or mixed gray colors. Give measurement.

Per pair...................... **$1.50**

No. 6R7069 Ordinary Cotton Fabric, in brown, blue or white color only. Give measurement.

Per pair..**(If by mail, postage extra, 25c)**... **$1.25**

BASEBALL UNIFORMS, Complete.

These Uniforms have to be made to order and cannot be returned if sent as ordered.

It takes from four to ten days to make up these uniforms, according to the number of orders we have on hand, when your order is received. Send 5c. for our sample card showing quality of flannels and colors, also measuring blanks showing how to measure for uniforms.

OUR UNIFORMS are made up in the following manner. The pants are heavily padded and quilted, with elastic bottoms. Taped bottoms may be furnished if wanted. Our **shirts** are made in button fronts or may be had with laced front if wanted. **Caps** may be had in Chicago style on cheap suits and Chicago or Boston style, as desired, on the two best grade suits. **Belts** may be had in red, blue, black, or navy colors. **Wool stockings** come in navy blue, maroon and black colors only. Cotton stockings come in black color only. **A complete uniform** consists of shirt, pants, cap, belt, and stockings.

No. 6R7080 Ordinary Cotton Fabric Shirt, Pants and Cap in brown, blue or white color, cotton web belt and black cotton stockings. Price, per suit.................. **$2.75**

No. 6R7081 Best Cotton Athletic Fabric Shirt, Pants and Cap, in blue gray or mixed gray combination color, cotton web belt, and black cotton stockings. Price, per suit...................... **$3.75**

No. 6R7082 Medium Grade Athletic Worsted Flannel Shirt, Pants and Cap, in navy blue, brown and pearl gray colors, worsted belt and medium weight wool stockings, in maroon, navy blue or black color. Price, per suit...................... **$5.25**

No. 6R7083 Best Athletic Worsted Flannel Shirt, Pants and Cap, in white, navy blue, maroon and gray colors, worsted web belt, and heavy wool stockings in maroon, navy or black colors. As good a suit as you can get anywhere at $10.00 to $15.00.

Price, per suit.............................. **$7.50**

GRAIN LEATHER Association Round Footballs.

No. 6R7084 The Victor Official Association Football. Made of the best imported English grain leather, welted seams, regulation 27-inch balls, best quality bladder, with lacing needle and pump.

Price, each..................... **$3.75**

No. 6R7085 The High School Association Football; made of best American oil tanned grain leather; hand sewed; laced opening, regulation. 27-inch circumference. Price each.................. **$2.10**

If by mail, postage extra, 15 cents.

No. 6R7086 Best Oiled Tanned Leather, 24-inch for boys........................... **$1.35**

The Victor Rugby Football, Oval Pattern.

No. 6R7087 The Victor Intercollegiate Official Rugby Football. Made of best imported grain leather, with all possible stretch removed. **The highest grade football on the market, guaranteed;** has lacing needle and pump.

Each, with bladder.. **$3.50**

If by mail, postage extra, 12 cents.

No. 6R7088 Rugby Football. Made of best American oil tanned leather, canvas lined, to keep its shape, extra strong, regulation, No. 5 size, with bladder. A fine bag for a little money. Price, each, **$1.50**

If by mail, postage extra, 20 cents.

No. 6R7089 Best American oil tanned leather, 24-inch, for boys. Price.......................... **$1.15**

Football Bladders.

For Association Footballs.

No. 6R7090 For 27-inch Ball. Each.................. **55c**

Rugby Bladders.

Our bladders are all the best grade. We do not carry cheap bladders. They are worthless.

No. 6R7091 For regulation ball. Each.................. **50c**

If by mail, postage extra, 8 to 12 cents.

Association Style.

No. 6R7092 American Round Rubber Footballs. These footballs are inflated through the key. When inflated turn key to right to close the valve. **Order by number.**

No. 1, 6-inch diameter.... **34c**
No. 2, 7-inch diameter.... **44c**
No. 3, 8-inch diameter.... **49c**
No. 4, 9-inch diameter.... **54c**
No. 5, 10-inch diameter.... **64c**
No. 6, 11-inch diameter.... **69c**

If by mail, postage extra, 7 to 12 cents.

No. 6R7093 Extra keys for football. Each............ **5c**

If by mail, postage extra, 1c

Football Inflaters.

No. 6R7094 Pocket Football Inflaters, nickeled tubes, for pumping up bladders. **(If by mail, postage extra, 4c)**.... **15c**

No. 6R7096 Our Best Football Inflater. Made similar to a bicycle foot pump, and is the most powerful football and punching bag inflater made. It inflates a football and punching bag to its full capacity.

Price, each...**(If by mail, postage extra, 15c)**.... **40c**

FOOTBALL GOODS.

Football Jackets, Full Sleeves.

These jackets are made to order. Send cash with the order.

No. 6R7100 Made of white twilled drilling, laced front, well sewed, a good boys' jacket; give chest measure under the arms. Price, each........... **50c**

No. 6R7101 Made of 8-ounce white duck, laced front, reinforced with double seams at important places; give chest measure under the arms.

Price, each................. **75c**

No. 6R7104 Made of 10-ounce brown colored duck, laced front, reinforced with double seams; give chest measure under the arms.

Price, each........................... **$1.00**

Send 3 cents for sample card of football suits.

Sleeveless Football Jackets.

These jackets are made to order. Send cash with the order.

No. 6R7107 Made of white twilled drilling, laced front, well sewed, a good boys' jacket; give chest measurement under the arms.

Price, each.................... **40c**

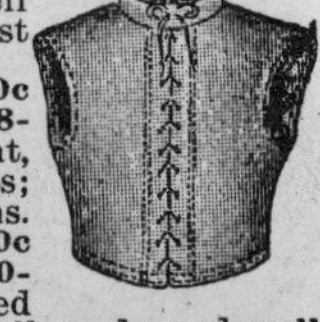

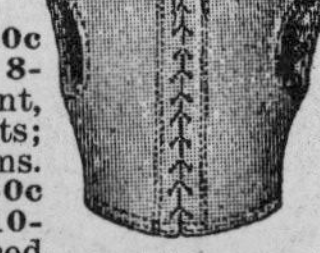

No. 6R7108 Made of good 8-ounce white duck, laced front, double seams at important points; give chest measure under the arms.

Price, each **50c**

No. 6R7109 Made of good 10-ounce brown colored duck, laced front, double seam reinforced, well made and well finished; give chest measure under the arms.

Price, each.................................. **75c**

Send 3c for a sample card of football material.

Football Pants.

These pants are made to order and cannot be returned if sent as ordered.

The front and hips of all our pants are padded and quilted in the most approved manner, and all have elastic bottoms.

No. 6R7116 Made of white twilled drilling, laced front, half quilted; give waist measure. Price, per pair..........60c

No. 6R7117 Made of white 8-ounce duck, laced front, cross quilted, well made; give waist measure.
Price, per pair...........90c

No. 6R7118 Made of brown colored 10-ounce duck, laced front, full cross quilted, well made and well finished; give measure. Postage, 28 to 36 cents. Price, per pair..$1.25

Send 3c for a sample card of football material.

Don't forget these goods must be made to order, so allow us four to ten days' time, according to the number of orders we have on hand when yours reaches us.

NOTICE—If your opponents tackle your center rush by the loops of his pants, cut off the loops and sew the pants and jacket together.

For a Complete Line of Football Shoes, see Our Shoe Department. Exceptional Values Offered in this Line of Goods.

FOOTBALL SUNDRIES.

Victor Nose Mask.

No. 6R7121 Made of finest Rubber. Gives absolute protection to nose and teeth. Price, each....................$1.50
If by mail, postage extra, 10 cents.

Head Harness.

Head Harness, specially intended to protect the head and ears; made of oil-tanned horsehide, padding for ears of soft material and open in center allowing same to entirely surround ear and rest on head without pressing ear or obstructing hearing.

No. 6R7122 Style A Harness protecting head only.......................................$1.75

No. 6R7123 Style B Harness protecting head and both ears................................ 2.00
If by mail, postage extra, 10 cents.

Shin Guards.

No. 6R7124 Shin Guards, made of light weight canvas, padded and stiffened with rattan, very substantial, double stitched all around and quilted.

Price, per pair, 9 inches long, for boys...48c

No. 6R7125 Price, per pair, 12 inches long, for men..........................72c
If by mail, postage extra, 7 cents.

NOTE—For Football Stockings, Belts, etc., see Baseball List.

ATHLETIC ELASTIC BANDAGES.

Elastic Elbow Bandage.

Best made. They are excellent as a support or for sprains. In ordering, give circumference above and below elbow and state whether intended for light or strong pressure.

No. 6R7127 Cotton thread and elastic, each..........$1.15 Elbow.

No. 6R7128 Silk thread and elastic, each... 1.35
If by mail, postage extra, 2 cents.

Elastic Knee Cap Bandages.

The best thing made for a sprained knee. In ordering, give circumference below knee, at knee, and just above knee, and state if light or strong pressure is desired.

No. 6R7131 Cotton thread and elastic, each, $1.15

No. 6R7132 Silk thread and elastic, each... 1.35
If by mail, postage extra, 2 cents.

Ankle Bandage.

Excellent as an Ankle Support and for a Sprained Ankle. In ordering, give circumference around ankle and over instep, and state if light or strong pressure is desired.

No. 6R7133 Cotton thread and elastic, each...............$1.15

No. 6R7134 Silk thread and elastic, each..................... 1.35
If by mail, postage extra, 2 cents.

Ankle.

Wrist Bandage.

Suitable as a wrist support and excellent for sprained wrist. In ordering, give circumference around smallest part of wrist, and state whether for **light or strong pressure.**

No. 6R7135 Cotton thread and elastic, each..60c

No. 6R7136 Silk thread and elastic, each.....75c
If by mail, postage extra, 2 cents.

Supporters and Bandages.

Improved Morton Supporters. Our price, 20 and 43 cents. Made of Canton flannel, lace front. Each supporter in separate box.

No. 6R7139 Improved Morton. Each..........................20c

No. 6R7141 Elastic on sides and back. Each.....(If by mail, postage extra, 3 cents).......43c

Our Elastic Combination Jockey Strap Suspensory.

This Ideal Jockey Strap Suspensory is made entirely of elastic woven material, is free from buckles and buttons; the waist and thigh loop being all made of the same material makes it a neat, comfortable fitting combination jockey strap suspensory.

The material used in its construction is cotton and elastic, the weave is open, affording a certain degree of elasticity and at the same time making it a comfortable fitting article, with the pressure evenly distributed and no danger of the circulation being impaired. It can be washed in lukewarm water, with castile soap, without danger of injuring the elastic.

For swimming, athletic exercises, bicycle riding, etc., this Jockey Strap Suspensory has no equal. Give waist measure when ordering, and we will fit you every time. **If by mail, postage extra, 10 cents.**

No. 6R7142 Our special price only............75c

Elastic Bandages.

This bandage is **light, porous and easily applied.** The pressure can be applied wherever necessary and quickly secured by inserting end under the last fold.

No. 6R7143 Width, 2¼ inches, 5 yards long (when stretched). Each 40c

No. 6R7144 Width, 3 inches, 5 yards long (when stretched). Each **(If by mail, postage extra, 3c.)** 60c

Leather Wrist Supporter.

A perfect support and protection to the wrist. Invaluable to baseball, tennis and cricket players or in any game where the strain is on the wrist.

No. 6R7146 In domestic grain leather, tan or black. Each. 21c
If by mail, postage extra, 2c.

The Hackey Ankle Supporter.

Patented May 24, 1887.

Relieves pain immediately, cures a sprain in a short time and prevents turning of the ankle. Made of fine, soft leather, and is worn over stocking, lacing very tight in center, loose at top and bottom. The shoe usually worn can be used. Mention the size shoe you wear when ordering.

No. 6R7150 Hackey Supporter.
Per pair....**(If by mail, postage extra, 3c)**........75c

Fencing Foils and Sticks.

Weight, 24 to 32 ounces per pair.

No. 6R7175 No. 1 Fencing Foils, with steel blades, iron mounted Fig. 8 guard, corded handle. Our special price, per pair..................98c

No. 6R7176 No. 2 Fencing Foils, with Solingen steel blades, iron mounted, Fig. 8 guard, leather handles. Our special price, per pair...........$1.75

No. 6R7177 No. 3 Fencing Foils, best Solingen steel blades, nickle plated bell guard or hilt, leather wound handles. Our special price, per pair....$2.65
If by mail, postage extra, 25 cents.

Athletic and Swimming Suits.

Our full sleeve and quarter sleeve shirts for all athletic purposes are the highest grade, and the same that are adopted by the highest sporting authorities, and quality considered, are now offered at the lowest prices ever known.

Our standard colors will be black and navy blue, but we are prepared to furnish, on special orders, white, maroon or other solid colors, or stripes, if wanted. Any deviation from the standard colors, however, is liable to cause a few days' delay. When ordering, be sure to give the measure around the chest for shirts, and measure around waist for pants and tights. Our full fashioned garments are knitted to shape and not cut and stitched. No house can compete with us on them.

Full Sleeve Shirts.

No. 6R7188 Full Sleeve Shirts, full fashioned, made of the **best worsted,** seamless, perfect fitting, black or navy blue color. Give chest measure.
Price, each.... ... .$2.75
If by mail, postage extra, 15 cents.

No. 6R7189 Full Sleeve Fine Worsted Shirt, medium quality, black or navy blue color. Give chest measure.
Price, each...$1.75
If by mail, postage extra, 12 cents.

No. 6R7190 Full Sleeve Fine Cotton Shirt, black or flesh color. Give chest measure. Price, each, 50c
If by mail, postage extra, 10 cents.

Quarter Sleeve Shirts.

No. 6R7195 Quarter Sleeve Shirts, full fashioned, made of **best worsted,** solid colors, seamless, made in black or navy blue. Sizes, 26, 28, 30, 32, 34, 36, 40 and 42 inches chest measure. Give chest measure when ordering.
Our special price, each.........$2.00
If by mail, postage extra, 15 cents.

No. 6R7195

No. 6R7196 Quarter Sleeve Shirts. Medium quality worsted, solid colors, seamless, made in black or navy blue. Give chest measure when ordering.
Our special price, each...................................$1.50
If by mail, postage extra, 12 cents.

No. 6R7197 Cotton Shirt, quarter sleeve, good quality. Made in solid colors of black or navy blue. Give chest measure when ordering. Price, each **(If by mail, postage extra, 10 cents.)**......35c

Full Length Tights.

No. 6R7199 Full Length Tights, full fashioned, made seamless of **best worsted,** in solid colors of black or navy blue. Give waist measure.
Our special price, per pair........$2.75
If by mail, postage extra, 12 cents.

No. 6R7200 Full Length Tights, made of **medium grade worsted,** in solid colors of black or navy blue. Give waist measure when ordering.
Price, per pair.......................$2.25
If by mail, postage extra, 10 cents.

No. 6R7201 Full Length Cotton Tights, in solid colors of black or flesh color. Give waist measurement when ordering. Price, per pair...........80c
If by mail, postage extra, 8 cents.

Athletic Knee Tights.

No. 6R7202 Made of best quality of worsted, seamless, in solid colors of black or navy blue. Give waist measure when ordering. Per pair.....$2.00

No. 6R7203 Made of medium grade worsted in solid colors of black or navy blue. Give waist measure.
Price, per pair........................$1.25

No. 6R7204 Cotton Tights. Good quality cotton tights, made in solid colors of black or navy blue. Give waist measure. Price, per pair 30c
If by mail, postage extra, 6 to 10c.

Velvet Puff Trunks.

No. 6R7206 Beautiful velvet puff trunks, made of the finest velvet, full puff, either black, navy, green or maroon color for theatrical or athletic exhibitions. Price, per pair.80c
Postage, extra, per pair, 7 cents.

BATHING SUITS.

Our One-Piece Best Cotton Bathing Suit is made like a Union Suit (with buttons in front). It is like an ordinary shirt and knee pants, but all in one piece, made in solid colors and fancy stripes, and ranging in size from 32 to 44 inches chest measure. When ordering give chest measure.

No. 6R7208 Cotton One-Piece Suit, in solid color black or navy blue; give chest measure.
Price.......................................75c

No. 6R7210 Cotton One-Piece Suit, in fancy stripes, assorted patterns; give chest measure.
Price...................................$1.00

No. 6R7212 Cotton OnePiece Suit. Same as No. R7210, for boys, 24 to 32-inch chest. Price........75c
If by mail, postage extra, 12 cents.

Our Ladies' Two-Piece Bathing Suits.

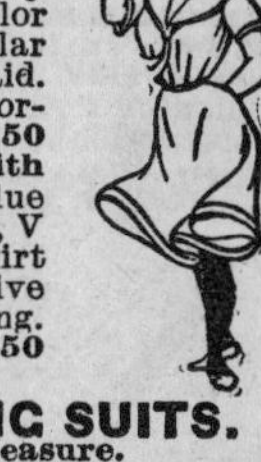

No. 6R7214 Ladies' Union Suit with skirt, made from good quality navy blue cotton fabric, with sailor collar, blouse effect, with the collar and skirt trimmed with white braid. Give waist and bust measure when ordering. Our special price per suit.$2.50

No. 6R7215 Ladies' Union Suit with skirt, made from good quality blue mohair or brilliantine, sailor collar, V shape front, the collar and skirt trimmed with braid, button front. Give waist and bust measure when ordering.
Our special price.......................$3.50
Postage, 30 to 35 cents.

TWO-PIECE BATHING SUITS.

Give Chest and Waist Measure.

No. 6R7216 Two-piece Bathing Suit, consisting of quarter sleeve shirt and knee pants, made in black or navy blue colors. Price, per suit............98c

No. 6R7217 Same, in stripes. Price, per suit.$1.50

No. 6R7218 Two-Piece Bathing Suit, medium grade worsted in black or navy blue colors only, give chest and waist measure. Price, per suit..(In stripes, extra, 25c).....$2.75
If by mail, postage extra, 15 cents.

Our Swimming Trunks.

Our Cotton Swimming Trunks, made up in assorted designs of stripes with draw string; assorted sizes for men or boys. When ordering, give waist measure.

No. 6R7219 Our Men's Swimming Trunks, our special price, per pair, 25c

No. 6R7220 Our Boys' Swimming Trunks. Our special price, per pair, 20c
If by mail, postage extra, 5 cents.

Peerless Hammock Spreader.

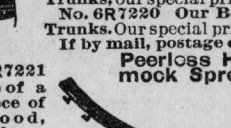

No. 6R7221 Is made of a solid piece of hardwood, bent bow shape, with hooks on its lower edge.
Price, each.......................................8c
If by mail, postage extra, 12 cents.

Hammock Ropes.

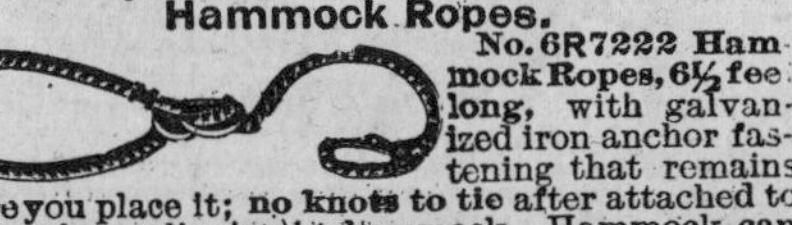

No. 6R7222 Hammock Ropes, 6½ feet long, with galvanized iron anchor fastening that remains where you place it; **no knots to tie after attached to hammock, no slipping in hammock.** Hammock can be raised and lowered in an instant. Each..........8c
If by mail, postage extra, 6 cents.

OUR LINE OF HAMMOCKS.

WHEN HANGING A HAMMOCK ALWAYS HANG IT SO THAT HEAD WILL BE HIGHER THAN THE FOOT.

The most select line of Hammocks ever placed on the market. We have selected this line of Hammocks with a view to giving our customers the best possible value for their money. SEE OUR PRICES.

Mexican Woven Hammock, 80 Cents.

No. 6R7231 Mexican Woven Hammock, made of sisal twine, fancy assorted colors. Entire length, 12 feet 6 inches; length of bed, 6 feet. Rope edge. Weight, 3 lbs. Price, without spreaders, each.....80c

Canvas Hammocks.

No. 6R7234

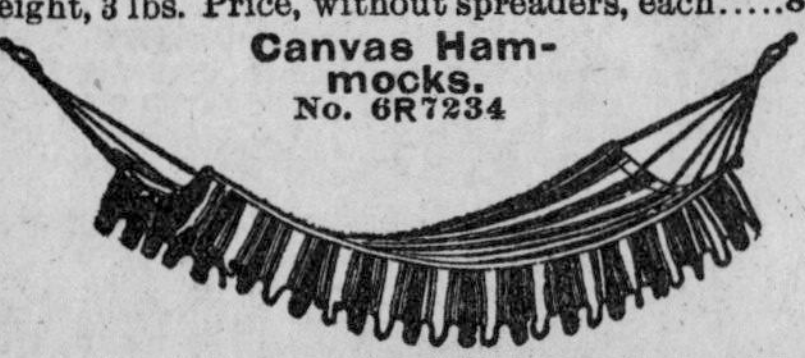

This is the latest thing in Hammocks. These hammocks are made of canvas throughout, are very strong and durable, and we predict a large sale for them. They are made of 8-ounce canvas and will surely become popular. The bed is about 7 feet long and 3 feet wide, and they are similar to hammocks used in the U.S.Navy. All have spreaders at each end.

No. 6R7232 Made of 8-ounce canvas, spreader at each end, without valance. Price, each.........85c

No. 6R7233½ Made of striped canvas, fancy stripes, spreader at each end, without valance. Price, each.....................................$1.10

No. 6R7234 Made of striped canvas, fancy stripes, spreader at each end, with valance. Price, each.....................................$1.40

Weight, 4 pounds.

Open Weave Cotton Hammocks, 55c.

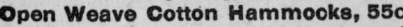

No. 6R7235 Open Weave Cotton Hammocks. Fine cotton weave, quarter color, with fancy colored stripes. Size of bed, 6½ feet long, 3 feet wide. **Strong and durable;** without pillow or spreader. A good hammock for children. Weight, 2 pounds. Our special price.................................55c

Cotton Weave Hammock with Pillow and Spreader, 85 Cents.

No. 6R7237 Cotton Hammock, with close woven body, of the best cotton weave, **full fancy colors, with spreader and pillow.** Size of bed, 6½ feet long, 3 feet wide. A hammock that sells regularly at $1.25 to $1.50. Weight, 3½ pounds. Our special price, with fancy pillow and spreader.........................85c

Canvas Weave Hammock with Pillow and Spreader, $1.25.

No. 6R7239 Hammock. Made of closest fancy canvas weave, in full fancy bright colors. **Made with three-ply warps,** with fancy colored pillow and spreader. **A very strong hammock.** Retails from $1.75 to $2.00. Size of bed, 6½ feet long, 3 feet wide. Weight, 4 lbs. Our special price..$1.25

Special Value with Fringe Valance for $1.15.

No. 6R7241 Cotton Hammock, close excelsior weave, with short fancy fringe valance; full fancy bright colors; with pillow and spreader. Size of bed, 6½ feet long, 3 feet wide. **A first class hammock in every respect.** Sells regularly at $1.50. **Weight,** 5 pounds. Our special price...........$1.15

Our Leader $2.25 Value for $1.50.

No. 6R7242 Hammocks, fine excelsior weave with deep woven valance with fringe, full fancy bright colors, with one spreader and one pillow. Size of bed, 6½ feet long, 3 feet wide. A beauty for the money. Weight, about 4½ lbs. Our special price, $1.50

Our Damask Weave Hammock, $2.05.

No. 6R7243 Our Big Leader Hammock, made in **figured fancy weave, damask pattern, full fancy fluted valance,** with fringe and scroll pattern. One strong spreader at head, **with fancy pillow,** also one short wood spreader at the foot. Size of bed, 40x80 inches. One of the most beautiful hammocks ever placed on the market. Strong and durable, and one which generally sells at retail for $3.00. Weight, 6½ pounds. Our special price.........$2.05

Our Canvas Weave Hammock, $2.75.

No. 6R7245 Hammock, extra heavy, fancy close canvas weave, fine fancy bright colors, extra deep fluted valance with fancy tufted pillow, heavy strong spreader. One short wood bar at the foot. Size of bed, 40x84 inches. **This is a large size hammock, strong, durable and very showy.** Weight, 9 pounds. Our special price $2.75

Our Damask Pattern Tufted Pillow Hammock, $2.55.

No. 6R7248 Our Large Size, Tufted Pillow Hammock. This hammock is made in full fancy colors, strong spreader and detachable, tufted pillow at one end with extra wood bar as shown in the illustration, full deep valance at the sides. Size of bed, 40x82 inches. The pillow is made so that it can be easily detached if not desired, **and we consider this one of the best bargains which we offer in hammocks.** Weight, 10 pounds.

Our special price for this full size hammock, $2.55

Close Woven Baby or Child's Hammock, 50 Cents.

No. 6R7255 Child's Hammock, cotton cord open mesh. Entire length from end to end, 6 feet 6 inches; bed 4½ feet long. **Strong, well made and durable;** just the thing for the baby. Weight, 16 ounces. Price, each...50c

Our Portable Swinging Hammock Chair, 85 Cents.

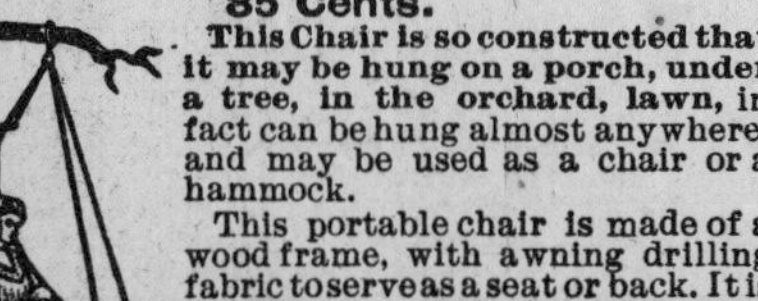

This Chair is so constructed that it may be hung on a porch, under a tree, in the orchard, lawn, in fact can be hung almost anywhere, and may be used as a chair or a hammock.

This portable chair is made of a wood frame, with awning drilling fabric to serve as a seat or back. It is 45 inches long, 25 inches wide, and weighs about 7 pounds. It is adjusted to different positions by drawing in or letting out ropes and tieing knot when in the position desired.

No. 6R7258 Our special price on this Portable Hammock Chair, only.................................85c

Hammock Hooks.

No. 6R7266 Screw Hammock Hooks, tinned, $\frac{7}{16}$-inch diameter, to screw in. Price, each...............5c

If by mail, postage extra, 3 cents.

No. 6R7267 Plate Hammock Hooks, tinned, $\frac{7}{16}$-inch in diameter to fasten with screws. Price, each...........................6c

If by mail, postage extra, 3 cents.

LAWN SWINGS, $3.50 and $4.25

For Children and Adults.

This is the best Lawn Swing on the market. It is made of hard pine and gum wood, with connections well bolted and well braced, painted in red color, and after they are started the swinging is continued by pressing the feet on the footboard. It is great fun for the children, and adults will find them quite comfortable.

No. 6R7271 Adult's size, about 8½ feet high. The seat is 20 inches wide, which is wider than the ordinary chair and will hold two grown persons or four children. Weight, about 100 lbs. Price, each..$3.50

No. 6R7272 Large size, 10 feet high, seat 30 inches wide, large enough to seat four adults or six children. Weight, about 150 pounds. Price, each.........$4.25

We can furnish larger swings to special order for public amusements, such as picnic groves, etc., from 8 to 16 feet high, made extra strong for rough use, if wanted.

Our Acme Folding Lawn Settee, 86c.

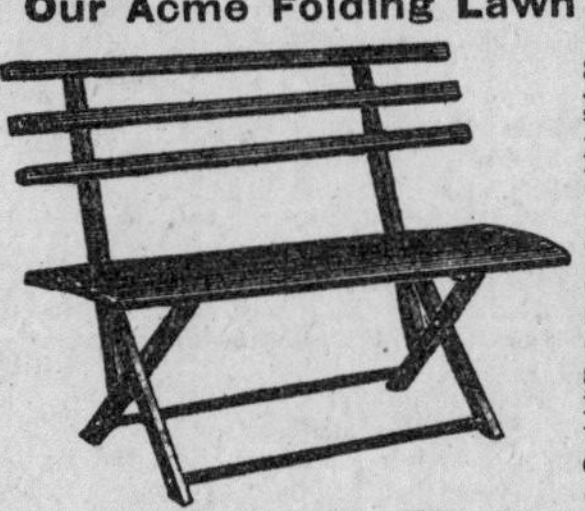

No. 6R7274 For 86 cents we offer you our Acme Lawn Settee, made of selected wood, painted in a bright attractive color and constructed on substantial principles. This lawn settee is made so it may be folded up and set away during the winter or it may be left on a porch as desired. The acme lawn settee is a very useful and desirable article and will recommend itself to our customers, in fact it requires no care or attention and saves many times its value in the wear and tear of regular household furniture. Our acme lawn settee, 3½ feet long, painted. Weight, 20 pounds. At our special price...............86c

The Chicago Folding Porch Chair.

No. 6R7278 The Chicago Folding Porch Chair. All joints riveted and may be folded when not in use. Weighs about 10½ pounds and the back may be adjusted to various angles for comfort. All have arm rests and high back are easily carried about and saves the household furniture.

Price, each. ...84c

REPAIR PARTS FOR FLOBERT RIFLES.

NOTICE—These parts are not fitted. They are in a filed state and must be fitted by a gunsmith or mechanic. If possible send us the broken part and we will try to match it as near as we can.

Flobert Breech Blocks.

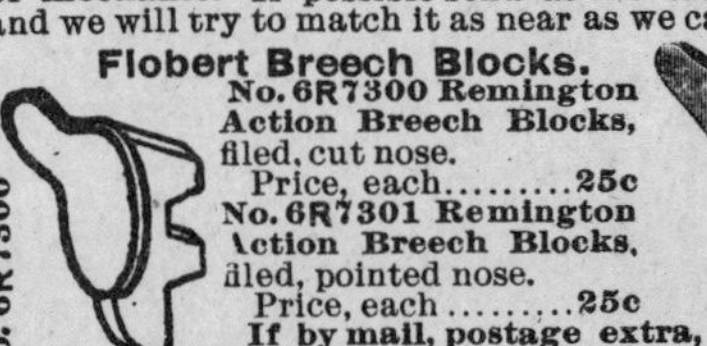

No. 6R7300 Remington Action Breech Blocks, filed, cut nose. Price, each.........25c

No. 6R7301 Remington Action Breech Blocks, filed, pointed nose. Price, each.........25c

If by mail, postage extra, 2 cents.

Warnant Breech Blocks.

No. 6R7303 For light Warnant action Floberts, weighing about 4½ pounds, not fitted. Each.35c

No. 6R7304 For heavy Warnant Floberts, weighing about 6 pounds, not fitted. Price, each. 35c

If by mail, postage extra, 6 cents.

Improved Warnant Breech Blocks.

No. 6R7305 For light improved Warnant action, like our No. 6R658, not finished. Price, each.........40c

No. 6R7306 For heavy improved Warnant action, like our No. 6R659 or No. 6R663, not finished. Price, each...45c

If by mail, postage extra, 5 cents.

FISHING TACKLE DEPARTMENT.

Our Fishing Tackle Department for this season will contain the most complete assortment of high grade tackle on the market. We have dropped all the cheap grades and hereafter will not carry anything but good tackle. We guarantee everything we sell in this department to be exactly as represented and of the best quality. Do not compare our goods with the cheap grades. Descriptions of goods may be just alike, but when you come to compare the goods themselves you will find great difference. ANY TACKLE BOUGHT FROM US MAY BE RETURNED AT OUR EXPENSE IMMEDIATELY IF YOU FIND IT NOT AS REPRESENTED, PROVIDED YOU RETURN IT IN PERFECT CONDITION.

JAPANESE RODS.

We are offering our customers this season a line of Japanese jointed rods which we believe are better value than you can get from any other house in the United States, quality considered. We have departed from the regular rule of offering our customers common wood rods when we are able to offer them this season genuine Japanese rods at only a trifle more than common wood rods would cost.

We have endeavored to get most of this line of Japanese rods all fitted with solid reel seat and zylonite butt, which makes a very attractive and expensive looking rod, and by placing a large contract for these goods, we were able to get the cost of manufacture down to the lowest point, and by adding our one small percentage of profit we are able to give you such value as we believe you cannot get anywhere else in the United States.

Male Bamboo Two-Piece Rod, 7 to 8 Feet, 13 Cents.

No. 6R8595 Two-Piece Jointed Male Bamboo Rod, 7 to 8 feet. Price, each......13c
If by mail, postage extra, 6 cents.

Male Bamboo Three-Piece Rod, 9½ to 10½ Feet, 22 Cents.

No. 6R8596 Three-Piece Jointed Male Bamboo Rod, 9½ to 10½ feet. Price......(If by mail, postage extra, 17 cents).....22c

Japanese Two-Piece Rod, 7½ to 8½ Feet, 19 Cents.

No. 6R8597 Two-Piece Japanese Rod, natural color, double telescope ferrules, ringed for line, about 7½ to 8½ feet. Price, each......19c
If by mail, postage extra, 8 cents.

Japanese Two-Piece Rod with Zylonite Butt, 7 to 8 Feet, 45c.

No. 6R8600 Two-Piece Japanese Rod, about 7½ feet long, fitted with nickel plated telescope ferrules, solid reel seat above the grip, black zylonite butt, tie guides for lines made of mottled Japanese cane. One of the best rods on the market for the money. Weight, about 12 ozs. Our special price....(If by mail, postage extra, 14 cents)....45c

Japanese Three-Piece Rod with Zylonite Butt, 8½ to 9 Ft., 60c

No. 6R8602 Three-Piece Japanese Rod, about 8½ to 9 feet long, nickel plated telescope ferrules, solid reel seat above the grip, black zylonite butt, tie guides for the lines made of mottled Japanese cane, one of the best rods on the market for the money. Weight, about 13 ozs. Our special price......(If by mail, postage extra, 15 cents)......60c

Japanese Four-Piece Rod, with Zylonite Butt, about 14 Ft., 98c.

No. 6R8604 Four-Piece Japanese Rod, about 14 feet long, fitted with nickel plated telescope ferrules, solid reel seat above the grip, black zylonite butt, tie guides for lines made of mottled Japanese cane, the best long rod on the market for the money. Weight, about 24 ounces. A good rod to fish from the shore. Our special price only......98c
If by mail, postage extra, 26 cents.

Four-Piece Calcutta Trunk Rod, about 8 Feet, 85 Cents.

No. 6R8606 Four-Piece Calcutta Trunk Rod, 7½ to 8 feet long, nickel plated telescope ferrules, strong tie guides for lines, solid reel seat above the grip; zylonite butt, made of genuine mottled Calcutta cane, nickel plated trimmings. Each piece is 24 inches long, so it may be carried in a trunk or grip. Our special price......85c
If by mail, postage extra, 12 cents.

Calcutta Four-Piece Trolling Rod, 15 to 16 Feet, $1.08.

No. 6R8607 Four-Piece Calcutta Bamboo Rod, double telescope ferrules, ringed for lines, with butt cap and reel bands. Length, 15 to 16 feet. Weight, about 3 pounds. Price, each......$1.08

LANCEWOOD RODS.

There are about thirty to fifty styles of Lancewood rods, manufactured by the various makers, and each style necessitates a change in equipment, machinery, etc., and by reducing the number of styles of our Lancewood Rods, we are able to save the expense of these changes, which expense is necessarily added to the rods when so many styles are handled by one house. We have decided to reduce the number of styles of Lancewood Rods in order to handle a few styles and manufacture them with the least possible expense. By doing this we were able to reduce the cost of our Lancewood Rods, and we give you the benefit of this reduction by pricing the following line of rods, based on our reduced cost, adding our one small percentage of profit.

St. Croix River Lancewood Fly Rods, 10 to 10½ Feet, $1.05.

No. 6R8616 Our St. Croix River Lancewood Fly Rod, made in three pieces, with an extra tip, genuine lancewood throughout, nickeled mountings and raised telescope ferrules. Silk wound tie guides and silk whippings at each mounting. Solid reel seat below hand. Zylonite corrugated grip. Length, about 10 to 10½ feet. Put up in neat partitioned cloth bag. Weight, about 9 ounces. A fine looking rod. Price, each......(If by mail, postage, extra 12 cents)......$1.05

Twin Lakes Lancewood Bass Rods, 8½ to 9 Feet, $1.00.

No. 6R8621 Twin Lakes Lancewood Bass Rod, made of genuine lancewood throughout; three pieces, with an extra lancewood tip, nickeled mountings, raised telescope ferrules, silk wound tie guides and silk wrappings at mountings, solid reel seat above grip, with corrugated zylonite butt. Length, about 8½ to 9 feet. Weight, about 14 ounces. Put up in neat partitioned cloth bag. A fine looking rod and one which will please you.
Price, each......$1.00
If by mail, postage extra, 18 cents.

Combination Bass and Fly Trunk Rod, $1.75.

No. 6R8624 This Rod is made of first quality lancewood, has four pieces when made into a bass rod and five pieces when made into a fly rod. It may be used as a fly rod as well as a bass rod. When the fly rod is assembled it makes the rod measure 9 feet, and when assembled as a bass rod, it measures about 7½ feet. The bass fly tip is interchangeable with the third joint of the fly rod, making it a combination rod. The pieces are about 25 inches long, the rod has the reel seat above the hand, is silk wound at short intervals, has shouldered ferrules, standing spiral line guides, nickel plated ferrules and trimmings, corrugated zylonite black and white butt, and one of the most convenient rods on the market. Weight, 13 ounces.
Our special price for this combination rod......$1.75
If by mail, postage extra, 16 cents.

Two-Piece Lancewood Bass Rod, about 5½ Feet, $2.10.

No. 6R8625 Our Two-Piece Lancewood Bass Rods, about 5½ feet long, nickel plated telescope ferrules, silk wound at intersections, tie guides for lines, solid reel seat above the grip, zylonite butt, nickel trimmings, silk wound, put up in a neat cloth bag, with an extra tip. Weight of rod, about 7 ounces, for boat casting.
Our special price only......$2.10
If by mail, postage extra, 12 cents.

The Beaverkill, a Very Fine Lancewood Fly Rod, $4.25.

No. 6R8626 Our Special Beaverkill Lancewood Fly Rod, made up with solid reel seat below the hand, German silver mountings all engraved or milled to make a very handsome appearance. It has solid anti-friction guides, windings of black and red, beautifully clustered. Put up in three joints with an extra tip on a wood form covered with velvet. We cannot recommend these rods too highly. They are perfection. Ordinarily retail at $10.00. Weight, 8 ounces. Length, 8½ feet.
Our price......$4.25
If by mail, postage extra, 20 cents.

Lake George Special Lancewood Bass Rod, with Agate Tip, $4.65.

No. 6R8627 Our Lake George Fine Special Lancewood Bait Casting Rod, with solid reel seat above hand, German silver mountings, all engraved or milled to make a very handsome appearance. It has anti-friction trumpet guides, agate tip, windings of black and red, beautifully clustered. Put up in three joints with an extra tip on a wood form covered with velvet. We cannot recommend these rods too highly. They are perfection. Ordinarily retail for $10.00. Weight, 8 ounces. Length, 6½ feet. The short rod is the coming bait casting rod. Our price......$4.65
If by mail, postage extra, 18 cents.

Our Celebrated Greenheart Rods, 6½ Feet, $1.90.

This Celebrated Greenheart Rod is made very much on the same principle as a split bamboo od, from a wood, known as Greenheart, which is usually imported from Spain and Italy, and is noted for its strength and durability. It is considered the strongest and best wood known for use in fish rods, and in color it is a greenish brown. They are having a large sale and are well liked.

No. 6R8628 Our Greenheart Bass Rod, nickel plated telescope ferrules, cork grip, alternate silk wrappings, nickel plated mountings, solid reel seat above the grasp, three pieces and an extra tip 6½ to 7 feet long.
Our special price......$1.90
If by mail, postage extra, 20 cents.

OUR TERMS ARE **CASH WITH ORDER**

but we guarantee satisfaction or refund your money.

Our Two-Piece Muskallonge and Trolling Rods.

No. 6R8629 Made of Lancewood, two joints, for heavy trolling, zylonite butt, full nickel plated telescope ferrules and mountings, extra heavy mountings, with double guides on tip, zylonite grasp. Put up in partitioned cloth bag, length 7 feet. Strong and good. Price, each.................**$2.40**
If by mail, postage extra, 28 cents.

Our Three-Piece Muskallonge Rods.

No. 6R8629½ Muskallonge and Trolling Rod, extra heavy, made of selected lancewood with zylonite grasp and full nickel plated mountings, 8 feet long, three-piece with an extra tip, welded telescope ferrules and double guides. Put up in partitioned cloth bag, has grasp above and below hand. Price, each.................**$3.40**
If by mail, postage extra, 34 cents.

OUR SPLIT BAMBOO RODS.

This illustration will give you as near as it is possible an idea of how a split bamboo rod is made. At first the bamboo cane is split in a sort of triangle shape, as shown in illustration, and then six pieces are tapered and glued together, forming a hexagonal shape. This is where the rod derives its name—Split Bamboo—(the bamboo is split and glued together). After this the grip and reel seat is attached, then the rod is whipped or bound with silk, the ferrules and guides are attached, the rod is polished and varnished and it is ready for the market. The above illustration is intended to show the six pieces as they are separated and glued together.

NOTE—Our line of Split Bamboo Rods consists of the very best quality. We have taken great care in selecting our rods for the coming season, and our stock is the very best that can be obtained. Our prices on these rods are lower than any retail dealer can possibly sell them, so do not judge the quality by the price. We guarantee them exactly as represented or money refunded. Ten years ago a split bamboo rod could not be bought under $7.00 to $10.00. We can now sell them from 85 cents up. This is made possible by our large contract and the small profit we ask above the cost of labor and material.

Our Climax Split Bamboo Bass Rods, 8 to 9 Feet, 85 Cents.

No. 6R8630 Solid reel seat above the hand. This rod is one that we are **making a run on at an exceedingly low price and are positive the rod cannot be duplicated for twice the amount anywhere in the country. Split and glued bamboo bass rods, nickel plated telescope ferrules, silk wound line guides, with alternate silk wrappings, nickeled mountings, three pieces, with an extra tip. Put up on a wooden form in a cloth bag.** About 8 to 9 feet long. Weight, about 11 ounces. Our special price.................**85c**
If by mail, postage extra, 20 cents.

Our Acme Split Bamboo Fly Rod, 9½ to 10 Feet, 90 Cents.

No. 6R8634 Solid reel seat below the hand. This rod is the same quality as our Climax, except that the reel seat is below the hand for trout and light fishing. Has silk wound ring guides, with wrappings of fine silk every few inches; solid reel seat and nickel plated telescope ferrules and mountings. Length, about 9½ to 10 feet. Weight, about 11 ounces. **Worth $1.75 anywhere. Comes in three pieces with an extra tip on a wood form and in a cloth bag.** Our special price, each.................**90c**
If by mail, postage extra, 19 cents.

Our Chautauqua Lake Split Bamboo Bass Rod, About 7 Feet Long, $1.50.

No. 6R8640 Solid reel seat above the hand. Made of the **best quality selected bamboo,** split and glued, hexagonal, with silk wound line guides, **cork butt, nickel plated telescope ferrules and mountings; short, heavy, strong and durable. A first class bait casting rod, put up in three pieces with an extra tip on a covered wood form. Length, about 7 to 7½ feet. Weight, about 8 ounces.** The short rod is the coming rod for bait casting. Worth $2.75 anywhere. Our special price, with cork grasp.................**$1.50**
If by mail, postage extra, 17 cents.

Our Special Wilowemock Split Bamboo Fly Rod, 9½ to 10 Feet, $1.65.

No. 6R8641 Solid reel seat below the hand. This rod is made of special selected bamboo, hexagonal in shape, with close wrappings of colored silk, full nickel plated telescope ferrules and mountings, cork grasp. Put up in three pieces with an extra tip on a fine covered wood form and in a neat bag. Length, about 9½ to 10 feet. A rod that retails at $3.00 in stores.
Our special price.................**$1.65**
If by mail, postage extra, 18 cents.

Our Fox River Split Bamboo Bass Rod, 6 Feet Long, $2.78.

For $2.78 we offer you our Fox River Bamboo Trunk Fishing Rod, made of six pieces selected bamboo, split and glued together, with solid reel seat, standing line guides, fancy silk wrappings at short intervals, nickel plated mountings, shouldered ferrules and swelled butt. The bamboo is strengthened at the reel seat by extra inlaying of cedar, making it very strong and durable. **The rod comes in three pieces with an extra tip,** so that if you break one tip you may have the other one at your command; put up on a nicely covered wood form. Each piece is about 25 inches long, and when the rod is put together the entire length is about 6 feet, and weighs 8 ounces. This is undoubtedly one of the best bait casting rods to be had for the money, all fine bait casting rods are now made 5½ to 6½ feet long.

No. 6R8667 Our Genuine Fox River Bamboo Bait Casting Rod, about 6 feet long, with corrugated black and white celluloid butt for boat casting.
Our special price....**(If by mail, postage extra, 17 cents)**.................**$2.78**

Our Special Rio Grande High Grade Split Bamboo Fly Rod, 9 to 10 Feet Long, $2.76.

For $2.76 we offer you our Special Rio Grande High Grade Split Bamboo Fishing Rod, made of six pieces selected bamboo, split and glued together, with solid real seat, ring line guides, fancy silk wrappings at short intervals, nickel plated mountings, shouldered ferrules and swelled butt. The bamboo is strengthened at the reel seat by extra inlaying of cedar at the butt, making it very strong and durable. **The rod comes in three pieces with an extra tip,** so that if you break one tip you may have the other one at your command; put up on a covered wood form. Each piece is about 36 inches long, and when the rod is put together the entire length is about 9 to 10 feet, and weighs 8 ounces. This is undoubtedly one of the best bait casting rods to be had for the money.

No. 6R8669 Our Rio Grande Split Bamboo Fly Rod, about 9 to 10 feet long, with corrugated black and white celluloid butt. Our special price..**$2.76**
If by mail, postage extra, 17 cents.

THE GENUINE BRISTOL STEEL FISHING RODS. Warranted.

We offer the genuine Bristol Steel Fishing Rods with the assurance that there are no better rods made at any price. These rods are patented by the makers and no steel rods are genuine except these. Do not buy any imitations which infringe upon these rods, and at the price we offer these **Genuine Bristol Steel Rods** you cannot afford to buy anything but the genuine article. All rods are warranted by the makers for one year and if any piece or part gives out by reason of defect in material or workmanship it will be repaired or replaced free of cost to you. Keep a drop of oil on joints to prevent corrosion.

Steel Telescope Fly and Bass Rods, 9½ Feet Long.

No. 6R8670 Steel Telescope Bass Rods, 9 feet 6 inches in length, full nickel mounted, with solid reel seat above the hand. Line runs through the center of the rod. When telescoped the rod is 32 inches in length, all inclosed within the butt length, as shown in illustration. Weight, each, 11¾ ounces. With celluloid handle. Our special price.................**$3.00**
If by mail, postage extra, 15 cents.

Steel Telescope Fly Rod, 9½ Feet Long.

No. 6R8672 Same style as above, but with reel seat below the hand for trout fishing. Line runs through the center of the rod. When telescoped, the rod is 32 inches in length. All inclosed within the butt length. Weight, 11¾ ounces. With celluloid handle. Our special price.................**$3.00**
If by mail, postage extra, 15 cents.

Our High Grade 10-Foot Jointed Steel Fly Rod.

No. 6R8674 Steel Fly Rod, 10 feet long, full nickel mounted, **with solid reel seat below the hand.** This rod is jointed and fitted with two-ring German silver tie guide and one-ring German silver fly tip. Is made with three pieces and handle; each joint being 38 inches long. **Does not telescope.** Weight, 9½ ounces. With celluloid wound handle. Our special price.................**$3.95**
If by mail, postage extra, 13 cents.

The Genuine Henshall 8½-Foot Jointed Steel Brass Rod.

No. 6R8676 Full nickel mounted, with solid reel seat above the hand. This rod is jointed and fitted with two-ring German silver tie guides and German silver three-ring tip. Is made with three pieces and handle; each joint being 32 inches long. **Does not telescope. This rod is the best bass or pickerel rod made.** Weight, 10 ounces. With celluloid wound handle. Our special price.................**$3.96**
If by mail, postage extra, 15 cents.

The Genuine Expert 6½-Foot Jointed Steel Bass Rod.

No. 6R8680 The Expert Steel Bait Casting Rod, 6¼ feet long, full nickel mounted, with **solid reel seat above the hand.** This rod is jointed and fitted with two-ring German silver tie guides and German silver three-ring tip. It is made with three pieces and handle; the joints are 24 inches long. This is a fine rod for long casts and for heavy work. **Does not telescope.** Weight, 8¼ ounces. With celluloid wound handle. Our special price.................**$3.97**
If by mail, postage extra, 13 cents.

Genuine Bristol 5½-Foot Jointed Steel Bait Casting Rod.

No. 6R8687 The New Bristol Steel Bait Casting Rod, 5½ feet long, German silver trumpet guides and German silver double hole tip. This rod is intended for those who prefer a short rod, **which is rapidly becoming more popular,** being more readily handled and not so severe on the wrist. This rod does not telescope and is fitted with celluloid handle. Weight, 8¾ ounces. Our special price.................**$4.65**
If by mail, postage extra, 13 cents.

No. 6R8688 The New Bristol Steel Bait Casting Rod, 5½ feet long, with agate tip and one agate guide, the other guides are German Silver, trumpet style. This rod is intended for those who prefer a **short rod, which is rapidly becoming more and more popular,** being more readily handled and not so severe on the wrist. This rod does not telescope and is fitted with celluloid handle. Weight, 8¾ ounces. Our special price.................**$5.50**
If by mail, postage extra, 13 cents.

Stamped Sheet Steel Boats.

These boats are made of eight plates of galvanized sheet steel, riveted and doubly seamed, making them strong, light and durable. They have the advantage over wooden boats in that they do not become water logged when exposed to the sun, can be easily transported from place to place, are always ready for use and for hunting purposes have no superior.

They are modeled after the whaleback steamers of the Christopher Columbus type, the bottom is dish shaped, and can be used in shallow water, over grass, reeds, etc., and each boat has an air chamber sufficient in size to float four men on the upturned boat, should it happen to capsize, making it practically a perfect, non-sinkable boat. At each end there is a hole through the air chamber from top to bottom of the boat, which can be used either to anchor the boat with a pole or attach a temporary sail. The boats are all painted a dead grass color, and with an additional coat of paint from time to time the boats should last a good many years.

No. 6R8703 The "GET THERE" Sheet Metal Hunting Boat, 14 feet long, 36-inch beam, 14 inches deep at the top of combing. The cock pit is 9 feet long and the boat weighs about 80 pounds.

Our special price, with one pair of oars, one long or short paddle, one seat and one hickory slat bottom.......................................**$17.50**

No 6R8704 "BUSTLE" Sheet Metal Hunting Boat is almost identically the same as the **"Get There"** except the air chambers are on the side of the boat instead of the ends, making it 10 inches wider than the **"Get There,"** and is a little more steady in the water. Our special price, with one pair of oars, one long or short paddle, one hickory slat bottom and one seat.............................**$24.50**

Extra seats, each.......................................**.75**

Our Special Folding Canvas Boat, at $19.50

and $24.60.

From the above illustration, engraved by our artist from a photograph, you can form some idea of our special canvas waterproof folding boats.

These boats are made from heavy duck, prepared by a flexible waterproof process, so they will not crack when folded, and are made in two sizes, 8 and 12 feet long. Our 8-foot boat is calculated to be a hunting boat, and for one person only. Our 12-foot boat is calculated to hold three persons safely; and as they draw only 4 inches of water, these boats can float in very shallow streams.

Our $19.50 and $24.60 canvas folding boats are constructed with bent wood ribs instead of common iron ribs, which rust easily, made of heavy army duck that will last a long time and not crack, and are built to our special order by a maker who has had twenty-five years' experience in canvas boat building—some boats which he built fifteen years ago being still in use. As these boats weigh only 35 to 45 pounds, they can be easily carried from one lake to another, may be shipped by express or freight at a very small expense, while a regular full length boat of any kind nearly always has a high classification of freight rate on account of it taking up so much room in a freight car.

No. 6R8706 Our 8-foot Canvas Boat. 36 inches wide, 11 inches deep amidship, with jointed bottom board, side boards, gunwale, one stool, one pair of 6½-foot copper tipped jointed oars. Designed for one person only. Weight complete, about 35 pounds.

Our special price.......................................**$19.50**

No. 6R8708 Our 12-foot Canvas Boat. 33 inches wide, 12 inches deep amidship, 15 inches deep at stem and stern, with jointed bottom board, jointed side boards, jointed gunwale, one stool, one pair of jointed 6½-foot copper tipped oars. Designed for three persons, who weigh, all told, not over 600 pounds, and draws about 4 inches of water. Very steady in the water. Wgt. complete, about 40 lbs. Price..**$24.60**

Each boat comes put up in a cloth bag so that it may be easily handled.

The Genuine Feather Light Reel, $1.36.

This Reel has a removable balance spool, as shown in illustration, which **makes it very handy for cleaning same.** Has drag **steel click and steel spindle** and is made in fine oxidized finish. The reel is 2¾ inches in diameter and ⅝ inch wide, for trout or bass fishing.

No. 6R8722 60 yards. Price, each..........**$1.36**

If by mail, postage, extra, 10 cents.

Our Mascot Multiplying Reel, 65 Cents.

No. 6R8730 This is one of the very best double multiplying reels on the market. It is full nickel plated, with balance handle, double screw-off oil cap, one of the easiest and smoothest running reels on the market, the bearings being of steel. They have back sliding click and drag. Every reel is stamped Mascot.

No. D, 80 yard reel. Our special price............**65c**

If by mail, postage extra, 15 cents.

No. 6R8736 Our Chicago Single Action, raised pillar, riveted brass reel. A strong and durable reel, without click. 25 yards. Price..................**10c**

If by mail, postage extra, 4 cents.

Our Orleans Reel, single action, raised pillar, riveted brass reel. **A very strong and durable reel with click.**

No. 6R8737 25 yards, Price.......................**15c**

No. 6R8738 60 yards, Price.......................**20c**

If by mail, postage extra, 6 cents.

Double multiplying raised pillar, balance handle, screwed connections, lacquered brass reel, with patent **adjustable slide drag** and back sliding click, polished bearings.

No. 6R8740 40 yards, **45c**
No. 6R8741 60 yards. **55c**
No 6R8742½ 80 yards..........**65c**

If by mail, postage extra, 9 cents.

Our double multiplying raised pillar, balance handle, screwed connections, full nickel plated reel, with patent adjustable slide drag and back sliding click, polished bearings.

No. 6R8743 40 yards. **60c**
No. 6R8744½ 60 yards..........**.70c**
No. 6R8745 80 yards. **80c**

If by mail, postage extra, 9 cents.

Our Polished Rubber Cap Reel, double multiplying **raised pillar,** balance handle, screwed connections, **nickel plated reels,** with patent adjustable slide drag and back sliding click.

No. 6R8746 40 yds., **65c**
No. 6R8747 60 yds., **75c**
No. 6R8748 80 yds.. **85c**

If by mail, postage extra, 9 cents.

Our Quadruple Reel has round disc, balance handle, screwed brass connections, with **fine steel pivots in bronzed bushed bearings,** patent adjustable slide drag, back sliding click, and nickel plated.

No. 6R8750 40 yards.......................**$1.25**
No. 6R8751 60 yards.......................**1.40**
No. 6R8752 80 yards.......................**1.65**

If by mail, postage extra, 13 cents.

Our Acme Trout Reel is single action, extra fine quality screwed **hard rubber reels** with flush balance handle, bushed bearings and back sliding click, **nickel plated.** For trout and fly fishing.

No. 6R8753 40 yards...**75c**
No. 6R8754 60 yards..**85c**

If by mail, postage extra, 10 cents.

Our Genuine Pennell Reel made especially for us. Each reel is carefully tested for smooth running and careful adjustment before leaving the factory. Don't buy imitations when you can get genuine goods at the same price or even less. We guarantee these to be the genuine Pennell quadruple reels, the best reels for bass fishing or trolling.

Our Quadruple Pennell Round Disc Reel is fitted with adjustable sliding click and drag steel pivots, bridge over cogs; **one of our leaders.** This is a high grade reel, and one that we are offering at a very low price; and made of the best material possible, handsomely nickel plated, balance handle and constructed for all fishermen who are looking for a **fine looking reel at a low figure.**

No. 6R8755 40 yards size.......................**$1.75**
No. 6R8756 60 yards size.......................**2.00**
No. 6R8757 80 yards size.......................**2.25**
No. 6R8758 100 yards size.......................**2.40**

If by mail, postage extra, 15 cents.

The Celebrated Pennell Rubber Plate and Nickeled Quadruple Reel, $2.75.

The Celebrated Pennell Patent Compensating Quadruple Reel, **finest quality throughout,** one of the best reels made, **with steel pinion and pivots. Rubber plate and nickel plated metal bands** incasing the rubber, which protects same from any breakage. **It has steel pivots in bushed bearings, bridge over pinions, balance handle, back sliding click, front drag, screw-off oil cap.** These reels have the finest reputation for **perfection and smoothness of action. They are strictly high grade reels** and cannot be purchased at retail for double our price. They positively compare with the finest quadruple reels made.

No. 6R8759 80 yards. Our special price, each, **$2.75**
No. 6R8760 100 yards. Our special price, each. **3.00**

If by mail, postage extra, 15 cents.

The above reels sell on this market at from $5.00 to $7.50 each.

Our Celebrated Tournament Agate Cap Quadruple Pennell Reels for $3.00.

We offer you for the first time in the history of the fishing tackle business a 60-yard Quadruple Agate Cap Reel with balance handle, round disc, wide spool fitted with click and drag, all parts made true, to run with the least possible friction. The discs and agate caps are milled, making a very handsome appearance, handsomely nickel plated, screw connections, adjustable slide click and drag. **These celebrated reels have the genuine agate caps, which makes them smooth and free running,** and by reason of a large contract we were able to obtain a price which admits of our selling the 60-yard reel at the exceptionally low price of **$3.00.** Many people have said that we could not place a reel with genuine agate bearings upon the market at three times the price we are asking you, but we give you our **binding guarantee** that these reels have the genuine agate bearings or money refunded.

No. 6R8762½A Our 60-yard agate bearing Pennell reel, only.......................**$3.00**

No. 6R8763½A Our 80-yard agate bearing Pennell reel, only.......................**3.25**

If by mail, postage extra, 15 cents.

Our Celebrated Rubber Cap, Agate Quadruple Pennell Reels for $3.90.

At $3.90 we offer you an 80-yard Rubber Cap Quadruple Genuine Agate Reel, with balance handle, round disc, wide spool fitted with click and drag, all parts made true, to run with the least possible friction. All are handsomely nickel plated, screw connections, adjustable sliding click and drag. **These celebrated reels have the genuine agate caps, which makes them smooth and free running,** at the exceptionally low price of **$3.90. OUR BINDING GUARANTEE.**—We guarantee these reels to have the genuine agate bearings or money refunded.

No. 6R8765½A Our 80-yard agate bearing Pennell reel, only.......................**$3.90**

No. 6R8766½A Our 100-yard agate bearing Pennell reel, only.......................**4.15**

If by mail, postage extra, 14 cents.

Our Round Plate Multiplying Reel, 70 Cents to $1.00.

We offer for the first time a Round Plate Reel at a popular price. This reel is excellent value and must be seen to be appreciated. Every reel is carefully tested before leaving the factory. Our round disc reel is fitted with balance handle, round plate, screw oil cups, adjustable sliding click and drag and all are handsome nickel plated. Double multiplying and nicely finished. Order by number and state size wanted.

No. 6R8768 40 yards size. Price, each....**$0.70**
No. 6R8769½ 60 yards size. Price, each.... **.80**
No. 6R8770 80 yards size. Price, each.... **.90**
No. 6R8771 100 yards size. Price, each... **1.00**

If by mail, postage extra, 12 to 18 cents.

Our Pennell-Vom Hofe Quadruple Reel, $2.25.

This is the latest high grade reel on the market, combining all the good points of the Vom Hofe and Pennell reels. Each and every reel is tested to gauge, accuracy and smooth running qualities before leaving the factory, and for casting or trolling these reels have no equal. Our Pennell-Vom Hofe reel has the new 1⅛-inch wide spool, is quadruple multiplying, fitted with accurate steel pivots, handsomely nickel plated and knurled adjustable click and drag, special handle and adjusting pivot cap. Made in 80 and 100-yard size only.

No. 6R8772 80-yard size. Price, each.......**$2.25**
No. 6R8773 100-yard size. Price, each.......**2.50**

If by mail, postage extra, 12 to 18 cents.

No. 6R8964 Bucktail Bass Flies. The wings are made from the hair of a buck's tail, the bodies are pure silk, ribbed with tinsel and are tied on Nos. 2-0, 1-0, 1 and 2 hollow point sproat hooks, made in the following styles: Buck, fawn, doe, king buck, or queen doe. State size hooks wanted. Each......12c

No. 6R8965 Bucktail Trout Flies. Made the same as the **Bucktail Bass Fly,** but smaller, tied to Nos. 4, 6 and 8 Trout hooks. **One of the best luring flies** on the market for trout and other small gamy fish. Give size hooks wanted in ordering. Price, each....................9c

If by mail, postage extra, 2 cents.

SIZES OF SPOON BAITS.

NOTE 2. The spoons of spoon baits come in various lengths, and the following is a list showing the length of the spoon on baits from No. 1 to 8. They may vary a trifle either way, for no two manufacturers make them exactly alike.

Nos.	1	2	3	4	4½	4¾	5	6	7	8
Length, in.,	1	1⅛	1¼	1½	1⅝	1⅞	2⅛	2⅜	2½	2⅝

Artificial Spoon Baits for Bass.

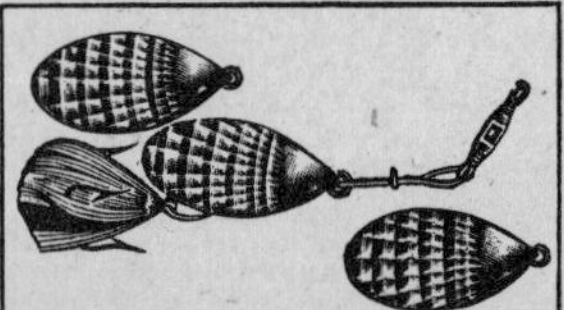

We have selected the best and most used baits, all of which we can recommend.

No. 6R8966 Is a fluted trolling spoon, which should please the most fastidious fisherman. This bait has three spoons, brass, nickeled and coppered, which are interchangeable. You can take off one spoon and put on another in a few seconds. This is one of the best baits on the market. Made in sizes Nos. 3, 4, 5, 6 and 7; sizes are same as other spoon baits. See Note 2 for sizes. Price of bait, with two extra spoons, in any size (mention size you prefer).........15c

If by mail, postage extra, 2 cents.

American Spinner Bait.

No. 6R8967 Best Plated Spoon, one-half hammered, best material and a rapid spinner, for bass, pickerel, etc. Nos. 2, 3, 4, 5 and 6. See Note 2 for sizes. Our special price, each..........15c

If by mail, postage extra, 2 cents.

Fluted Spoon Bait for Bass.

No. 6R8968 Fluted Trolling Spoon, full nickel plate, inside painted red, same shape spoon as Skinner's and same size hook, treble hook and fly; a first class spoon bait.

Nos.	1	2	3	4	4½	4¾	5	6	7	8
Size, inches.	1	1⅛	1¼	1½	1⅝	1⅞	2⅛	2⅜	2½	2⅝

Nos. 1, 2, 3, 4, 4½, 4¾, price, each..........10c
Nos. 5, 6, 7 and 8, price, each..........12c

If by mail, postage extra, 2 cents.

Skinner's Spoon Bait for Bass.

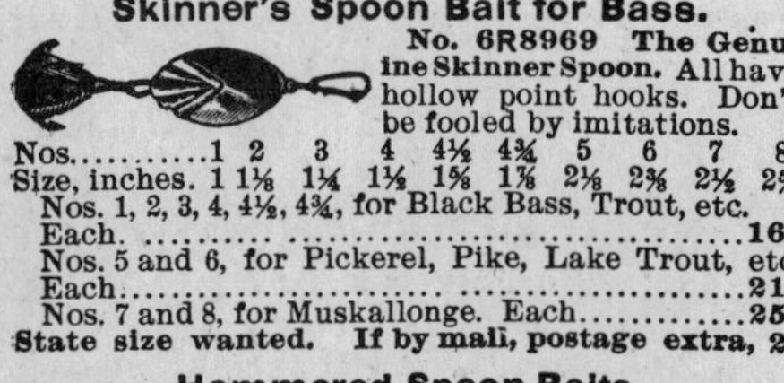

No. 6R8969 The Genuine Skinner Spoon. All have hollow point hooks. Don't be fooled by imitations.

Nos.	1	2	3	4	4½	4¾	5	6	7	8
Size, inches.	1	1⅛	1¼	1½	1⅝	1⅞	2⅛	2⅜	2½	2⅝

Nos. 1, 2, 3, 4, 4½, 4¾, for Black Bass, Trout, etc. Each..........16c
Nos. 5 and 6, for Pickerel, Pike, Lake Trout, etc. Each..........21c
Nos. 7 and 8, for Muskallonge. Each..........25c

State size wanted. If by mail, postage extra, 2c

Hammered Spoon Baits.

In ordering, state what kind of fishing wanted for.

No. 6R8970 Nickel Plated Spoon, feathered treble hook. One of the most successful baits in the market. For For sizes see Note 2. These come in Nos. 1, 2, 3, 4, 5, 6. Price, each..........8c

If by mail, postage extra, 2 cents.

No. 6R8971 Black Bass Spinners, finely plated, with swivel, revolving spoon, feathered hooks. State size wanted.

Nos.	1	2	3	4	5	6
Length of spoons, inches..	½	¾	1	1⅛	1⅜	1½
Each						8c

If by mail, postage extra, 2 cents.

Lightning Ball Bait.

No. 6R8972 Ball Bait, good nickel plated spoons, feathered treble hook. No. 1, smallest for small bass; largest ones for pickerel, pike and muskallonge. Nos. 1, 2, 3, 4, 5 and 6. Mention size wanted. For sizes see Note 2. Price, each..........15c

If by mail, postage extra, 2 cents.

No. 6R8973 Tinned Pickerel Bait, with swivel, an extra fine bait. Size 1 to 7. Mention size wanted. For sizes see Note 2. Each..........9c

If by mail, postage extra, 2 cents.

The Maloney Weedless Bass Hook.

No. 6R8975 This is the latest and most practical weedless hook on the market. It is so made that it is weighted so when casting for bass, the frog is always right side up. They are made in sizes 2-0, 3-0, 4-0 and 5-0. See page 349 for sizes and state size wanted. Price, each..........10c

If by mail, postage extra, 1 cent.

Skinner's Casting Spoon.

No. 6R8977 The Skinner Casting Spoon is very popular, being among the **best killing bass bait** on the market. It makes an **excellent trout catcher** when baited with a small worm. Comes in two sizes.

No. 1 With 1-inch spoon. Price, each..........12c
No. 2 With 1¼-inch spoon. Price, each..........12c

If by mail, postage extra, 2 cents.

The Muskallonge or Tarpon Baits.

The herculean strength of this bait will tell its own story to the fisherman in the pursuit of large gamy fish. For the **St. Lawrence, the western lakes and rivers,** and the coast of Florida they will fill the bill to perfection.

No. 6R8978 Fine Nickel Plated Spoon, treble hook, feathered, very best material, 2⅝-inch spoon, for 10 to 25 lb. fish. Each.20c
3¼-inch spoon, for 20 to 100 lb. fish. Each..25c

If by mail, postage extra, 3 cents.

Hammered Muskallonge or Tarpon Spoon.

No. 6R8979 Same as No. 6R8978, but hammered. Sizes in length are same.
2⅝-inch spoon..........19c
3¼-inch spoon..........24c

The Payson's Weed Guard Hook.

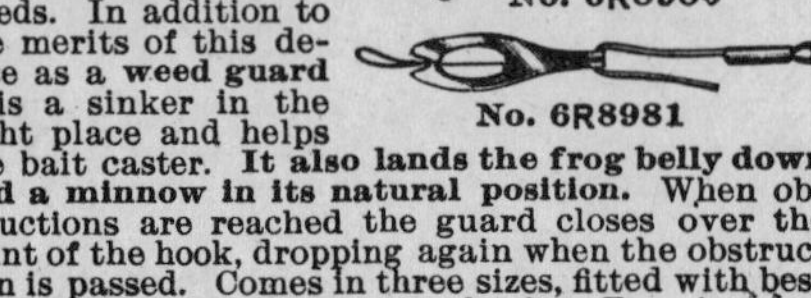

No. 6R8980

No. 6R8981

The Payson's Weed Guard Hook will not foul in the thickest weeds. In addition to the merits of this device as a weed guard it is a sinker in the right place and helps the bait caster. **It also lands the frog belly down and a minnow in its natural position.** When obstructions are reached the guard closes over the point of the hook, dropping again when the obstruction is passed. Comes in three sizes, fitted with best Carlisle hook, and two extra hooks. For sizes see cut of hooks on page 349.

No. 6R8980 2-0, 4-0 or 7-0. Price, each..........20c
No. 6R8981 The New Reversible, 2-0 or 4-0. Price, each (mention size of hook wanted)..........22c

If by mail, postage extra, 2 cents.

Sea Spinner.

No. 6R8982 Light Running and Interchangeable with eye spoons. The best bait made for casting a minnow, frog or pork rind. Brass, nickel plated on heavy treble gut loop.

Nos.	2	3	4
Length of blade, inches	1⅜	1⅛	1
Size of small hook	2	3	4
Size of large hook on the end	4-0	3-0	2-0
Price, each			12c

Shell Casting Spoon.

No. 6R8984 Spoon is brass, nickel plated, on sproat hook, twisted piano wire with gut loop. No. 1 is smallest size; No. 4 is largest size. Nos. 1, 2, 3 and 4, sizes of spoon same as Skinner's Baits. Each..........9c

If by mail, postage extra, 3 cents.

Nickel Kidney Bait.

No. 6R8985 Nickel Plated Kidney Baits, with bright feathered hooks. Spoons same size as Skinner's Baits No. 6R8969. Mention size wanted.

Nos. 1 to 7. Price, each..........9c

If by mail, postage extra, 3 cents.

Coburg Muskallonge Bait.

No. 6R8987 The Great Washington and Oregon Bait. Brass nickel plated, with bright hooks; 3¼-blade. Each..........21c

If by mail, postage extra, 3 cents.

Coburg Bass and Pickerel Bait.

No. 6R8989 The Celebrated Coburg Bait is now one of the most popular on the market. Blade is brass, nickel plated with bright hooks and swivel. Mention size wanted. For sizes see Note 2. Nos. 1 to 7, each..........15c

If by mail, postage extra, 3 cents.

Our Spinning Coachman.

No. 6R8991 First quality, with 1⅛-inch coppered or nickel plated spoon. No 1 hook tied with double gut, nickel plated box swivel. Each bait comes with a Coachman and two other popular bass flies mounted on a handsome enameled card. One of the **best bass baits on the market.** Price, each......20c

If by mail, postage extra, 2 cents.

Our Special Lowe's Star Bait.

No. 6R8993 Oval shape, finished in two colors the **lower half gold and the upper half silver plated.** Feathered treble hook, box swivel. An extra fine bait for Bass, Muskallonge and large, gamy fish. Try this bait. Nearly every customer who tries them buys more.

Numbers.	3-0	2-0	1-0	1	2	4	6
Length blade, inch	3¼	3	2¾	2¼	2	1⅝	1
Price, each	50c	40c	40c	35c	35c	28c	25c

If by mail, postage extra, 3 cents.

The Ghost.

No. 6R8997 The Ghost is constructed on entirely new principles. In every way superior to all other trolling baits. May be trolled slowly on the surface, or by using heavy sinker may be trolled at any depth desired; the rotary motion may be regulated by changing the fins. No. 1 is the bass killer, large size. No. 3 is the striped bass killer.

No. 3 is the smallest size, 1¼-inch spinner and extra treble hook. Price, each..........30c
No. 1 is the largest size, 2⅜-inch spinner, weedless fly gang and extra treble hook. Price, each......40c

If by mail, postage extra, 2 cents.

Our Phantom Minnows.

No. 6R9008 One of the most successful baits made. The body is made of silk, waterproofed, nicely mounted, assorted in blue, silver and brown colors. We claim our Phantom Minnows equal to any upon the market, regardless of price. Mention length of minnow wanted when ordering.

Inches long	2	2¼	2¾	3	3¼	4	4¼
Price, each	25c	26c	27c	28c	29c	32c	40c

If by mail, postage extra, 3 to 7 cents.

Imported Rubber Baits.

No. 6R9010 Large crawfish, soft rubber about 3 inches long.
Each.....(If by mail, postage extra, 3 cents)...23c

Shrimp Bait.

No. 6R9012 Shrimps, about 2 inches long.
Each..........20c
If by mail, postage extra, 3 cents.

Helgamites.

No. 6R9014 Helgamite or Dobson soft rubber, with swivel. Each..19c
If by mail, postage extra, 3 cents.

Our Special Fly Minnows.

No. 6R9015 Fly Minnow, 1¼ inches long, a good imitation of a minnow.
Each..........14c
If by mail, postage extra, 2 cents.

No. 6R9016 Grub Bait, an excellent imitation of a grub worm. No. 1 hook.
Price, each.....6c
If by mail, postage extra, 1 cent.

No. 6R9019 Grasshopper, soft rubber, 1⅜ inches long, quite natural. Each..........12c
If by mail, postage extra, 1 cent.

OUR TENT DEPARTMENT.

How to Pitch a Tent.

Having unrolled the tent in the exact position you want it to be when up, place the ridge pole, rounded side up, inside the tent, and on a line with the large eyelet holes, which are in the center of the roof; then insert the uprights in the holes bored in the ridge pole, and let the pikes in the upright pole come through the top of the tent. If a fly is used let the pikes also go through that, in precisely the same way as the tent; then take hold of the uprights and raise tent and fly together; secure the corner guys first and then the others between them. **Do not drive the pegs straight,** but angling; they hold very much better in this way. The tent being now up and guys all adjusted so that they bear equal strain, then proceed to dig a V-shaped trench all around the tent, about three inches deep; **this will insure you a dry floor at all times. Do not take the tent down when wet or even damp. Heat and dampness are the cause of mildew,** which destroys more tents than all other causes combined.

SPECIAL NOTICE—If you are interested in other styles of tents not listed in this catalogue, we invite your correspondence. Quotations given on application, and at bottom prices. **We can meet your expectation.** Tents are made to order and **cannot be returned if sent as ordered.** We can fill orders in two to four days after we receive the order. Send two cents for samples of canvas which goes into our tents.

"A," or Wedge Tents.

Weight, without poles, 18 to 40 lbs.; weight of poles, 14 ounces to the foot in length. When POLES are not wanted with TENTS deduct 1½ cents per running foot from these prices. The following prices include poles:

Order No.	Length and Breadth	Height	Price, 8-oz. Duck	Price, 10-oz. Duck	Price, 12-oz. Duck
No.	7 x 7 ft.	7 ft.	$3.15	$3.65	$ 4.85
6R10340	7 x 9 ft.	7 ft.	3.75	4.40	5.85
	9 x 9 ft.	7 ft.	4.10	4.90	6.50
12-oz.	9½x12 ft.	7½ft.	5.15	6.00	8.05
	12 x14 ft.	9 ft.	7.40	8.70	11.65

Miners' Tents.

Weight, without poles, 17 to 30 pounds; poles, 13 ounces per foot in length.

Tents cannot be returned if sent as ordered. Send for samples of canvas which goes into our tents.

No. 6R10342		Price, Complete with Pole.		
Size of Base	Height	8-oz. Single Filling Duck	10-ounce Duck	12-ounce Duck
7 feet x 7 feet	7 ft.	$2.25	$2.52	$3.50
9 feet x 9 feet	8 ft.	3.30	3.80	5.25
12 feet x12 feet	9 ft.	5.00	5.75	8.00

Refreshment Tents.

Oblong or Refreshment Tent, made of plain white duck; not striped, as shown in illustration. Price includes poles. pins, guy ropes, etc., **complete ready to set up.** Illustration shows front open; the front may be closed or stretched out in front for an awning or taken off altogether, as it is put on with hooks for these changes. **An 8-ounce stripe, blue or brown, is the same price as 10-ounce double filling white duck.**

No. 6R10344

Size	Height Wall	Height Center	8-oz. White Duck	10-oz. White Duck	12-oz. White Duck
9x14	6 ft.	10 ft.	$10.70	$12.08	$12.76
9x16½	6 ft.	10 ft.	12.00	13.60	14.50
9x19	6 ft.	10 ft.	13.30	15.12	16.12
12x19	6 ft.	11 ft.	14.65	16.75	18.24
12x21½	6 ft.	11 ft.	17.60	20.10	22.00
14x21¼	6 ft.	11 ft.	18.00	19.58	22.84
14x23½	6 ft.	11 ft.	22.20	25.44	28.60

Tents Without Poles, 5 per cent Less Than Above Prices.

REFRESHMENT TENT TOPS.

These prices are for the top only without walls for temporary use at picnics, for dancing platforms in groves, etc., where no wall is needed. These tops are all made to order and cannot be **returned.**

No. 6R10346 (Prices are without wall.)

Size	Height Center	8-oz. White Duck	10-oz. White Duck	12-oz. Double Filling Duck
9x14	10 ft.	$ 6.45	$ 7.00	$ 8.60
9x16½	10 ft.	7.35	7.95	9.95
9x19	10 ft.	8.25	9.00	11.20
12x19	11 ft.	9.25	10.15	12.95
12x21½	11 ft.	11.40	12.50	15.97
14x21½	11 ft.	11.80	13.02	16.82
14x23½	11 ft.	14.80	16.40	21.45

The above prices include everything complete, except walls, ready for putting up. Where 8-ounce stripe is wanted the price will be the same as 12-ounce double filling. **Tents without poles, 5 per cent less than above prices.**

Wall Tents. These are the best style tents for all general purposes, such as camping, golfing, to use as an out house, summer kitchen, etc. We can furnish tents in large or small quantities on short notice generally. Our tents are the best quality, they are all full size, and all have a good "pitch" to roof, to turn rain, and all made in a durable and substantial manner. Tents cannot be returned, as they have to be made to order. We warrant them to be exactly as represented. **In ordering, give catalogue number, length, breadth and price. We can make to order all kinds of tents, canopies, etc. Send for samples of canvas which goes into our tents.**

No. 6R10350 Wall Tent.

We give weights of tents with poles below on 8-ounce tents. 10-ounce will weigh about ⅛ more and 12-ounce about ¼ more than 8-ounce. **The weights may vary slightly, as poles do not always run alike.**

No. 6R10350

Length and Breadth	Height Wall	Height Pole	Weight, 8-ounce	Price, with Poles, Pegs, Guys, Guy Ropes, etc. Complete, ready to set up.		
Feet	Feet	Feet	Lbs.	8-oz. Duck	10-oz. Duck	12-oz.. Duck
7 x 7	3	7	35	$ 4.00	$ 4.75	$ 6.10
7 x 9	3	7	40	4.75	5.50	7.30
9 x 9	3	7½	45	5.47	6.40	8.50
9½ x 12	3	7½	50	6.25	7.60	10.00
9½ x 14	3	7½	60	7.32	8.55	11.35
12 x 12	3½	8	70	7.65	9.00	11.87
12 x 14	3½	8	75	8.65	10.10	13.40
12 x 16	3½	8	90	9.60	11.20	14.90
12 x 18	3½	8	100	10.70	12.45	16.50
14 x 14	4	9	105	10.30	12.05	16.10
14 x 16	5	9	100	11.35	13.30	17.75
14 x 18	4	9	125	12.70	14.90	19.50
14 x 20	4	9	110	14.05	16.40	21.50
14 x 24	4	9	115	15.90	18.40	24.05
16 x 16	5	11	125	14.05	16.55	22.10
16 x 18	5	11	135	15.45	18.20	24.10
16 x 20	5	11	145	17.05	19.90	26.10
16 x 24	5	11	155	19.40	22.60	29.50
16 x 30	5	11	160	23.45	27.40	35.75
16 x 35	5	11	165	26.30	30.70	40.10
18 x 18	5	11	170	17.75	20.80	27.60
18 x 20	5	11	175	19.50	22.70	29.85
18 x 24	5	11	180	21.80	25.45	33.20
18 x 30	5	11	240	26.10	30.45	39.95
18 x 35	5	11	290	29.05	33.90	44.50

Where higher wall is wanted, add 5 per cent of the cost of the tent for each 6 inches extra height of wall.

Poles and pins are included in above prices. Prices on any size of wall tent, not mentioned above, given on application; **we can furnish any style of tent wanted.**

A tent fly makes an extra movable or double roof to a tent, and affords a greater protection from sun and rain, and can be made to serve as an awning, either in front or rear of tent. **They are not really necessary, and are not included in prices of tents,** but we can furnish them, if ordered, at one-half the price of tents of corresponding size and quality; for instance, a fly for a 7x7, 8-oz. tent, costs $2.00 extra.

When tent poles are not wanted with tents, deduct 5 per cent from above prices of tents. Tents cannot be returned when made to order.

Photographers' Tents.

Tents cannot be returned, as they are made to order. It takes two to four days to fill tent orders.

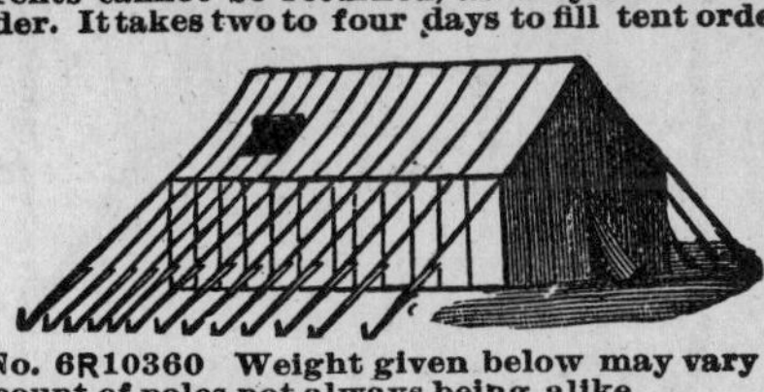

No. 6R10360 Weight given below may vary on account of poles not always being alike.

Size	Weight of 8-oz. Lbs.	Pole	Wall	Price, complete, without dark room		
				8-oz. single fill'g duck	10-oz. single filling duck	10-oz. double filling duck
12x16 ft.	135	11 ft.	6 ft.	$14.16	$15.80	$18.96
12x21 ft.	155	11 ft.	6 ft.	17.28	19.92	23.52
12x24 ft.	175	11 ft.	6 ft.	19.20	22.08	25.92
14x16 ft.	195	12 ft.	6 ft.	15.84	18.72	22.50
14x21 ft.	220	12 ft.	6 ft.	19.20	22.08	26.64
14x24 ft.	230	12 ft.	6 ft.	20.88	24.24	28.80
14x28 ft.	240	12 ft.	6 ft.	23.76	27.60	32.64
16x18 ft.	250	13 ft.	6 ft.	18.72	21.84	26.16
16x24 ft.	260	13 ft.	6 ft.	23.04	26.85	31.92
16x28 ft.	270	13 ft.	6 ft.	26.16	30.48	36.24
16x30 ft.	275	13 ft.	6 ft.	27.08	32.64	38.88

Prices on tents include poles, pins, guy ropes, etc. Tents above are complete, **ready to set up. If poles are not wanted deduct 5 per cent from above prices. Dark rooms extra, 6x6 feet, $5.50; 4½x4½** feet, **$4.75.** Our dark rooms are **made of same material,** same weight and color as the tent—**all white.** We make the room only; the artist can darken it to suit his own taste. Some use black silesia, some yellow, orange or red muslin, etc.

Quotations on other sizes on application and at bottom prices.

Prices on stable tents, stable tops, Sibley tents, canopy tops without wall, photographers' tents, square hip-roof tents, or any other style, given on application and at bottom prices.

Stockmen's Bed Sheets.

For herders who are compelled to sleep in a tent or on the ground, or they may be used as sod covers. Weight, 10 to 22 pounds. **Fitted with snaps and rings or eyelets** as may be ordered. **When ordering say if you wish snaps and rings or eyelets. Made to order of very best heavy white duck, and cannot be returned if sent as ordered.**

No.	Feet	13-oz.	15-oz.	18-oz.
6R10362	6x12	$2.62	$3.18	$3.41
	6x14	3.04	3.67	3.96
	6x15	3.27	3.93	4.22
	6x18	3.90	4.70	5.05
	7x12	3.06	3.65	4.03
	7x14	3.51	4.21	4.65
	7x15	3.77	4.52	5.00
	7x18	4.44	5.34	5.92
	8x12	3.79	4.57	4.98
	8x14	4.38	5.26	5.78
	8x18	5.61	6.78	7.42

Rubber Blankets.

Owing to the heavy demand for Rubber Blankets for camping purposes and for sleeping on the ground in wet weather, we have gotten up a variety of these blankets to supply the wants of any who may want a **first class waterproof rubber blanket to afford absolute protection from rain and wet weather.**

No. 6R10364 Our Luster Sheeting Rubber Blanket is made of fine quality rubber, lined with sheeting. Size, 45x70 inches. Price, each........**$1.10**

No. 6R10366 Our Fleece Lined Blanket is made of the very best rubber, with fine fleece lining; gotten up especially for hunters and prospectors who are compelled to sleep on the **damp ground and out doors in rainy weather. Positively the finest rubber blanket in the market.** Waterproof and large, with eyelets. Size, 54x96 inches.

Our special price, each..........................**$2.75**

When you send us your order, you save all the profit of the wholesaler, jobber and retailer. You pay only one small profit above the manufacturing cost.

Paulins or Stack and Machine Covers.

Weight, from 15 to 100 lbs.; 16x14, 10 to 26 lbs.; 14x20, 25 to 30 lbs.; 20x20, 38 to 45 lbs.

No. 6R10370 White duck. Always state size wanted when ordering. Prices quoted on application on sizes not mentioned here. **These goods are not tents, but paulins or stack covers. Paulins are made to order and cannot be returned. Write for samples of canvas which goes into our covers.**

Size, Feet	8-oz. Duck	10-oz. Duck	12-oz. Duck
10x16	$ 2.27	$ 2.80	$ 4.09
10x18	2.57	3.15	4.68
12x14	2.48	3.06	4.38
12x16	2.92	3.51	5.20
12x18	3.20	3.94	5.85
12x20	3.59	4.40	6.43
14x16	3.80	4.64	6.27
14x18	4.25	5.25	7.02
14x20	4.75	5.85	7.83
14x24	5.70	7.00	9.47
16x16	4.35	5.30	7.16
16x18	4.90	6.00	8.07
16x20	5.43	6.63	9.00
16x24	6.50	7.99	10.76
18x20	6.10	7.48	10.10
18x24	7.34	8.97	12.09
18x28	8.56	10.48	14.10
18x30	9.16	11.23	15.10
20x24	8.15	9.95	13.44
20x36	12.23	14.95	20.12
24x30	12.23	14.95	20.17
24x40	16.28	19.94	26.91
24x50	20.35	24.92	33.63

Stack covers have short ropes, BUT NO POLES; machine and **merchandise covers** have eyelets around side. Any other size furnished on short notice. Prices on application. **Stack Covers cannot be returned.**

Binder Covers.

No. 6R10371 Weight, 6½ to 7¼ lbs. Fitted to cover the binder and not the whole machine. Will fit any binder. 5x16 feet. Made of white 8 and 10-oz. duck. Price, each, 8-ounce, **$1.60**; 10-ounce, **$1.85**

Black Oiled or Tarpaulin Wagon Covers.

These covers, although black and called tarpaulins, have no tar in their composition. Our waterproof dressing is an oil preparation and **is entirely free from anything calculated to rot or burn the canvas,** but adds to the durability of the cover, being impervious to water and very soft and pliable. It will neither rot nor mildew from damp, nor break from being too hard. **They are invaluable to all persons who are shipping and receiving goods** that are liable to be damaged by wet weather. In ordering give catalogue number, size and price. Weight, 9 to 28 lbs. 6x12, 12 lbs.; 6x9, 9 lbs.; 7x12, 16 lbs.; 7x14, 19 lbs.

No.	Size	Price	Size	Price	Size	Price
6R 10375	6x 8 ft.	$2.36	7x 9 ft.	$3.15	8x10 ft.	$4.10
	6x 9 ft.	2.62	7x10 ft.	3.51	8x12 ft.	4.91
	6x10 ft.	2.90	7x12 ft.	4.20	8x14 ft.	5.72
	6x12 ft.	3.51	7x14 ft.	4.91	8x16 ft.	6.58
	6x14 ft.	4.09	7x16 ft.	5.61	9x14 ft.	6.58

Prices given on other sizes upon application.

White Duck Emigrant Wagon Covers

No. 6R10380 Wagon Covers, white duck. Always give size when ordering. Weight given is on 8-oz covers. **10-oz. weighs ⅛ more and 12-oz. about ¼ more than 8-oz.**

Size, Feet	Lbs.	8-oz. Duck	10-oz. Duck	12-oz. Duck
10x10	7	$1.60	$2.05	$3.15
10x12	7½	2.00	2.45	3.75
10x14	7¾	2.30	2.90	4.30
10x15	8	2.45	3.10	4.75
10x16	9	2.65	3.35	5.03
11x13	9	2.40	3.00	4.55
11x15	10	2.75	3.50	5.30
11x18	13	3.40	4.20	6.40
12x15	20	3.15	3.90	5.90
12x16	25	3.40	4.35	6.30
12x20	30	4.15	5.15	7.85

Comstock Malleable Iron Tent Pegs.

They last a lifetime. Cannot be broken.

No. 6R10387 Short Peg, 8¾ inches long. Weight, about 4⅛ ounces. Price, per dozen................**50c**

No. 6R10388 Long Peg, 13½ inches long. Weight, about 7¼ ounces. Price, per dozen............ **.70c**

Our Family Compartment Tents.

Our Family Compartment Tents are designed for camping parties or families, or parties where ladies desire separate rooms. The rooms are divided by sheeting of the same height as the wall. The tent top, sides and wall are canvas, and the rooms are on each side of the tent, while the center forms a dining room. The front wall may be raised to form an awning, as shown in the cut, or may be left as a wall, as you may desire. The prices of these tents include poles, pegs, guy ropes and sheeting to use as partitions. **Tents are made especially to order and cannot be returned if made as ordered. When ordering give catalogue number and size wanted.**

No. 6R10389

Size of Tent Feet	Height of Wall, Feet	Height of Pole, Feet	Number of Bed Rooms	Size of Each Side Room, Feet	Size of Dining room Feet	Price, 10-oz. Double Filling	Price, 12-oz. Double Filling
9 x16½	6	10	2	5½x9	5½x 9	$19.90	$22.50
9 x19	6	10	2	6 x9	6½x 9	22.06	24.69
12 x19	6	11	4	6 x6	7 x12	25.56	29.06
12 x21½	6	11	4	6 x7	7½x12	27.75	31.69
14 x21½	6	12	4	7 x7	7½x14	30.62	34.75
14 x23½	6	12	4	7 x7	9½x14	32.62	37.94
16½x23½	6	13	4	8¼x8¼	7 x16½	37.94	42.19
16½x26	6	13	4	8¼x8¼	10 x16	40.00	45.05
16½x28	6	13	4	8¼x8¼	12 x16	42.62	48.56

Hay Cock Covers.

To cover hay for preserving it from the weather and prevent wind from blowing it away.

No.	Size	Price each 8-oz. Duck	Price each 10-oz. Duck
6R10392	3 x3 feet	30c	40c
	3½x3½ feet	40c	50c
	5 x5 feet	50c	60c
	6 x6 feet	60c	80c
	7 x7 feet	70c	95c

Waterproof Ponchos.

No. 6R10394 Our Luster Ponchos, made of finest quality rubber, lined with fine sheeting and has hole in center, covered with heavy flap. By using this hole and **drawing the blanket over the head, it forms a large rubber cape, protecting the entire body.** It is absolutely waterproof and may also be used as a rubber blanket. Size, 45x72 inches. Weight, 3½ pounds.

Price, each.................. ...**$1.25**

Arctic Sleeping Bags.

The Improved, made of heavy, waterproof tan colored duck, lined with sheepskin, with the wool left on; inside of sheepskin lining is a heavy drill lining that can be taken out and cleaned **at any time.** Large enough to cover any man entirely. **Can cover up "head and ears,"** and still have plenty of air. Loops on sides, so that **it can be hung up with ropes if desired.** With these bags all beds and bedding can be dispensed with. It rolls up into small package, so that it can be fastened to a saddle or "packed on back." **The best bed ever invented for outdoor sleeping or tent camping.** Weight, about 20 pounds.

No. 6R10396 Price, each..... ....**$12.00**

Our Sportsmen Carryall Bag, $2.79.

No. 6R10398 We furnish our genuine 24-ounce standard duck, leather bound, with leather handles, leather flap with strap to lock carryall bag. These bags are made on the same principle as a mail bag, all the seams being leather bound, with a handle on each end and another strap to take up the bag in case you do not wish to fill it entirely. This carryall bag is made for camping and outing purposes, also for exploring expeditions, to carry whatever articles are necessary for such purposes. The carryall bag comes 31 inches long, 22 inches wide, and is shaped so it will be small at the top and 7 inches deep at the bottom, and you will be astonished how many necessary articles you can stow away in this bag. The handles at each end are intended so that if you put goods in of a weight too heavy for one man to carry, two men can carry it, and it can also be checked as baggage on railroad trains. Weight, about 4½ pounds.

No. 6R10398 Our special price for this carryall bag, with a lock and key, ready for use, only..**$2.79**

Camp Chairs and Stools.

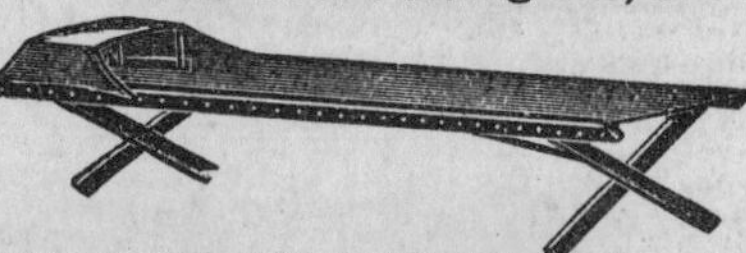

No. 6R10431 Canvas Top Camp Stool, well made. Weight, 2¾ pounds.

Price, each..............**20c**

No. 6R10432 Canvas Top Camp Chair, same as No. 6R10431, with back. Weight, 3¾ pounds. Price, each..**30c**

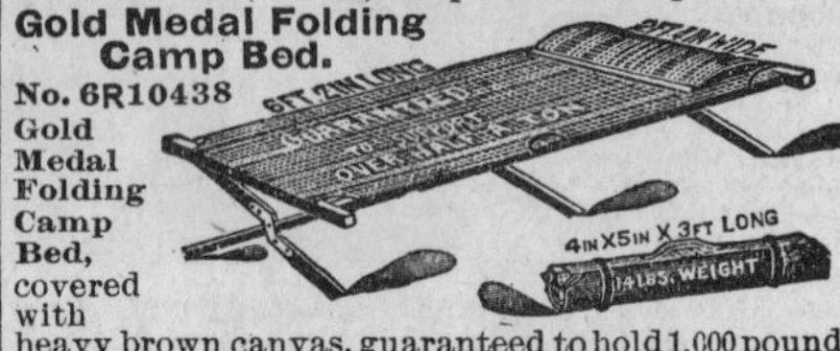

No. 6R10433 Our Chicago Canvas Seat Camp Stool is so made that it may be folded in to look like a short, round piece of wood; 24 inches long, 1¾ inches diameter. It is one of the handiest chairs to take along on outings, etc.

Price, each..............................**22c**

If by mail, postage extra, 22 cents.

The U. S. Folding Cot, $1.75.

The U.S. Folding Cot. Just the thing **for camping purposes, covered with either white or brown 10-ounce duck.** This is the lightest, strongest and most compact folding cot made. It has the only practical pillow ever put on a cot. Length, 6 feet, 3 inches. Width, 29 inches. Dimensions, when folded and ready for shipment, 6 feet, 3 inches by 5 inches by 2 inches. Weight, 15 pounds.

No. 6R10435 Price, complete with pillow...**$1.75**

No. 6R10436 Price, complete without pillow **1.50**

Gold Medal Folding Camp Bed.

No. 6R10438 Gold Medal Folding Camp Bed, covered with heavy brown canvas, guaranteed to hold 1,000 pounds. With pillow. Size, folded, 3 feet long by 5 inches square. Weight, about 16 pounds. Price, each..**$2.00**

Camping Outfits Complete at $4.45 and $5.75.

Cut of kit unpacked.

No. 6R10455 Pat. March 10, '96

No. 6R10455 Wilson's Kamp Kook's Kit. Just the thing for camping out. 53 pieces. Fire jack, two boilers suitable for using as an oven, fry pan, coffee pot and all utensils and tableware for a party of six. **Everything first class.** Boilers are made of 26-gauge smooth steel. **The entire kit nests in small space,** and when packed ready for shipment makes a package 14½x 10½x8 inches, **all nested together and can be firmly locked up by** ordinary padlock. Weight, complete, 20 pounds.

Price, complete............**$5.75**

No. 6R10456 20-piece set, containing the fire jack and complete apparatus without the tableware.

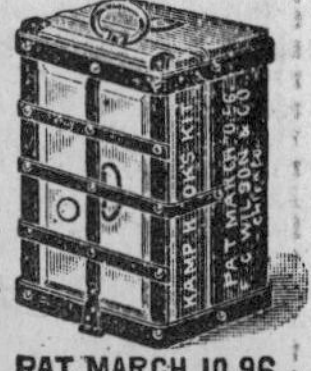

PAT. MARCH 10.96.

No. 6R10455 Cut of kit packed for shipment.

Price.........**$4.45**

Vehicle, Harness ...and Saddlery DEPARTMENTS.

FROM OUR OWN FACTORIES located at Brighton, Ohio, and Kalamazoo, Mich., we offer for this season, a higher grade of vehicle work than we have ever before been able to show; better made and better finished work throughout than will be offered by any other house, better than anything handled by the local implement and carriage dealer, a class of work such as is offered only in the best city repositories, and there at fancy prices. Our two factories are located where we can take advantage of the lowest possible prices for the highest grades of material that enter into the construction of the different styles, where we can secure the highest class of mechanical skill at the least possible expense, where the finest work can be made with the greatest economy.

OUR OWN MAKE. All road wagons, top and open buggies, surreys and phaetons are now built in our own factories under the care of our own superintendents, and we are this season better fitted than ever before to furnish strictly first class material, workmanship and finish that is characteristic of our own make, causing so much demand for vehicles built by us. We have made contracts with reputable manufacturers that build first class work to furnish our wagons, trucks, etc., and by agreeing to take enormous quantities of each style, we can name prices lower than your local dealer can procure the same work. You can readily see how it is possible for us to do this, for we buy ten carloads where a regular dealer buys one. **WE KNOW WHAT WE BUY.** Every farm wagon, truck, spring wagon, etc., built outside our own shop, is carefully inspected by our own inspectors before shipment is made and so confident are we that every job is correct that we issue

OUR ONE YEAR BINDING GUARANTEE

with each vehicle listed in our catalogue. This guarantee covers every part of the vehicle, and should any piece give out through defective material or workmanship **during a period of one year from date of sale, we will replace it free of charge.**

OUR TRIAL OFFER. So confident are we of our ability to furnish you a better rig for less money than you can buy elsewhere, that we extend this offer to everyone: Select any rig shown in this catalogue, we will send it to you on our regular terms; (cash with the order), you can give it ten days' thorough trial, during which time you can compare it with any rig you can get from your dealer at home or from any dealer or maker anywhere, and if at any time during the ten days you, for any reason, become dissatisfied with our rig, if at the expiration of ten days, you are not still satisfied that you have gotten more value from us than you could get from anyone else, **you are at liberty to return the rig to us at our expense of freight charges both ways, and we will immediately refund your money.**

FACTORY DELIVERY. The prices we quote on our vehicles are the prices crated and delivered on board the cars at the factories, and not at our place of business in Chicago. The saving in handling goes a long way to help us to name these extremely low prices. It should be understood that the price is always the price delivered at the factory, from which point you must pay the freight, **but you will find the freight will amount to next to nothing as compared with what you will save in price.**

IT WILL BE USELESS TO ASK FOR ANY REDUCTION IN PRICE ON ANY VEHICLE.

On our own work, the work we make in our own factories at Kalamazoo, Mich., and Brighton, Ohio, we could easily meet almost any view as to reduction in price by taking it out of the cost of the rig if we were so inclined, but this we will not do.

OUR ONLY TERMS ARE CASH WITH THE ORDER. We require cash in full with all orders and we know our customers will cheerfully comply with these terms when they realize it is to their own interest to do so. Read carefully our reasons for asking cash with all orders on the first page of this catalogue. Read our bank references on pages 12 and 13. Remember we guarantee entire satisfaction in every transaction or refund your money.

ABOUT THE FREIGHT.

MOST OF THE RAILROAD COMPANIES accept vehicles by freight at one and one-half times first class. In some cases it is two times first class, and as the shipping weight is estimated under each vehicle, and the first class freight rate for one hundred pounds from Chicago to the different points in all the different states **is listed in the front part of this catalogue**, you can calculate very closely what the freight will amount to on any vehicle to your place.

TO MAKE SURE YOU CAN ASK YOUR LOCAL FREIGHT AGENT, OR, IF YOU WISH YOU CAN WRITE TO US AND WE WILL BE PLEASED TO SEND YOU A FREIGHT ESTIMATE FROM THE FACTORY TO YOUR NEAREST RAILROAD STATION ON SUCH A RIG AS YOU WANT.

OUR PRICES are for vehicles at our factories, and in every case customer pays the freight from the factory to his railroad station.

WE CANNOT BE UNDERSOLD. If you will compare the prices listed in this catalogue with those of local dealers and other catalogue houses, you will readily realize the exceptional values we are offering this season. Prices of springs, steel tires, iron, wheels, etc., have advanced, in fact there is hardly a part of a vehicle that has not advanced in cost of raw material. Our buyers are always on the lookout for these advances, and with our large cash resources were able to place large contracts for our stock before the advance took place, and we secured most all our material **at prices far below those that the average manufacturer will be able to secure them. Our prices cannot be equaled, quality considered;** however it is possible by using a lower grade of wheels, a cheaper body, cheaper grade of upholstering and cheaper paints to produce a vehicle at the same price as ours, but for a strictly high class, reliable vehicle as shown and described in this catalogue, **we defy competition.** We could build vehicles such as are usually sold by most dealers and catalogue houses, but we have a reputation of furnishing nothing but first class material and workmanship in all our work, and we do not desire to compete with the shoddy class of goods that flood the market each year; **besides, you know each and every piece of material we use is covered by OUR ONE YEAR BINDING GUARANTEE. It is not for the profit on the one vehicle we may sell you that we are working,** but we are in the business to stay, and we try and build each vehicle so that it will not only please you, but will be a lasting advertisement in your community, and bring us orders from your friends. **We will not ship a job that we know is not just as represented and described,** for we know it would ruin the reputation we have gained—namely, **"MANUFACTURERS OF HIGH GRADE VEHICLES AT LOWEST PRICES."**

OUR WHEELS DO NOT WABBLE. Wheels that wabble are the first sign of a cheaply constructed vehicle. We recognize that the most vital part of a vehicle is the wheels and we take special pains to see that each wheel is given the proper dish to enable it to stand the rough usage it may be subjected to.

NOTE OUR PROCESS. We buy nothing but the finest wheels that can be procured for the money, and we put on our own tires. After welding the tires in proper sizes they are placed in an improved automatic tire furnace, and are kept continually revolving until they are at a blue heat. This expands every part of the tire instead of just one portion, as is the custom of most manufacturers. While at a blue heat, fully expanded, they are placed on the wheels and run through a patent tire evener, which sets the tire on the rim of the wheel so that no part projects more than another, but makes it the same all around. The tire is then cooled off in water, which contracts and gradually gives the wheel the proper dish, which is the most important part of a wheel and makes a wheel last twice as long and bear twice the load of the old machine method of putting the tires on cold and dishing at the same time. **The wheel is next put on a machine for boring the hub for the boxing and this machine is so constructed that each hub is bored at the right angle, and it would be impossible to furnish a wheel bored on this machine that was not exactly true. The wheel is now ready for the boxing,** which has previously been covered with a thick coat of white lead. We place the wheel on the hydraulic press and the boxing under a pressure of twenty-five tons is forced into the hub. This press is automatic and cannot be stopped till the boxing has been driven just so far and reverses at the proper place so that no boxing can be driven further than another. **This insures a solid hub and tight boxing far superior to the old sledge hammer method of driving boxes. We use every automatic machine and every improvement in the market,** and this insures for our customers wheels that will outwear two sets of the regular wheels usually furnished on jobs sold by most local dealers and jobbers, and our tires won't need resetting nearly as often.

THE GEAR. Next in importance to the wheels we consider the gear, and here is how we put it up. The wood parts, such as wood axle caps, spring bars and reaches are carefully selected hickory. We cement the axle caps or beds to the axle, using the best English waterproof cement, and they are then clamped down till the cement is perfectly hard and well set. We then put them on a sand belt, where they are sanded down to a perfectly smooth surface. **The axles and wood caps are then thoroughly primed with lead and oil and allowed to stand till perfectly dry before the clips are put on.** This insures a perfect axle and the water cannot get in and crack the paint, as you so often notice on cheap work. The reaches are then braced and connected to the axles with Norway iron braces and clips, and front axle is fitted with full circle fifth wheel, having king bolt back of axle. When our high grade oil tempered springs are attached we have a gear to correspond with our wheels, **and a complete running gear we guarantee to last and outwear any gear built on the same proportions.** So on all the way through, we exercise great care; we finish the body, upholster the seat and back, build the top, everything complete, and watch every detail with the one end in view, namely to produce a vehicle that will be better value for your money than you can obtain elsewhere and one that will be a lasting advertisement for us.

JUST COMPARE the general build and finish with a job purchased from other catalogue houses or your local dealer, and you will readily see why there is so great a demand for our work built in our own factories.

THE RESULT IS that last year we nearly doubled the sales of the previous year, and as every vehicle sold last year was carefully inspected and built, we feel that each job will be the means of securing more orders for us and we anticipate a vehicle business this season that will far exceed our past sales. **WE ARE READY FOR IT.** In order to take care of this demand for our work, we have fitted both our Brighton, Ohio, and Kalamazoo, Mich., factories with every improvement and automatic labor saving device known to the vehicle trade, and have greatly increased our capacity, till now we have two of the best regulated factories in the United States with a combined output that will take care of our increasing business.

WE HAVE NO DULL SEASON. Years of experience in the vehicle business has enabled us to assemble in this catalogue a line of up to date, stylish vehicles that meets the demand of the farmer, doctor, liveryman, peddler and business men in general; no matter what your calling, we have a vehicle to suit you. In furnishing a regular line, and being able from past experience to list vehicles that we know will sell, we can keep our factories running the year around, having no dull season, and as we build each style vehicle in large lots, running through our factories immense stock of wheels, gears, bodies, tops, etc., we not only prepare ourselves for the rush of orders when the vehicle season opens, **but are able to greatly reduce the cost of output.**

WE CANNOT MAKE CHANGES. It is impossible for us to make any changes in our work and can furnish them only as described, but you will note we give you choice in some cases where it can be done without increasing the cost or delaying the order. For the benefit of the few who may not be able to find in our regular line a job that will suit, **we are listing a special job under catalogue No. 11R809,** and you will note that we give you a choice or selection in most every part; and while we will furnish this vehicle almost any way you may desire, we will have to start same through our factory after the order is received and cannot furnish as cheap or quickly as our regular line.

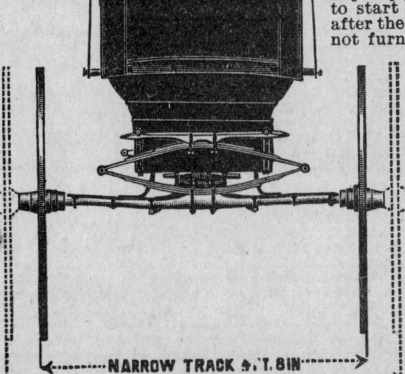

NARROW TRACK 4 FT. 8 IN.
WIDE TRACK 5 FT. 2 IN.

WE USE THE CELEBRATED GOODYEAR RUBBER TIRES.

BE SURE TO STATE WIDTH OF TRACK. With the exception of a few special track vehicles, as noted in our catalogue, all vehicles are furnished either in the 4 feet 8 inches, narrow, or 5 feet 2 inches, wide track, as desired.

THE ABOVE ILLUSTRATION shows the method of measuring track same being distance from outside to outside of rear wheels on the ground.

OUR $22.35 ROAD WAGON.

DON'T FAIL TO STATE WIDTH OF TRACK
$22.35

No. 11R3

$22.35 IS OUR LOWEST PRICE for a reliable road wagon. Road wagons could be sold closer, and it would be possible for us to build a road wagon that we might sell at $16.00 to $17.00; but believing our customers are entitled to reliable work, believing we would be robbing our customers by using cull wheels, cheap material and cheap finish; believing that this, **our cheapest rig,** should be a substantial one—**a wagon that will give service, a wagon that will satisfy our customers**—we offer only such a wagon, **and this at $22.35,** barely covers the cost to build—the cost of material and labor—with but our small percentage of profit added. You will find this road wagon better than any road wagon you can buy elsewhere at the price; and if not so, you are at liberty to return it to us at our expense of freight charges both ways and we will cheerfully return your money. It is stylish, light, strong and convenient. It is unusual value for the price offered.

GENERAL DESCRIPTION.

BODY—The body is 22 inches wide, 52 inches long, made of carefully selected stock, screwed, glued and plugged. The corners are braced with corner angle irons. The seat is large and roomy, with lazy back.

GEAR—The axles are 15/16-inch double collar steel.

TRIMMINGS—Seat cushion and back upholstered in a good quality imitation leather, nicely tufted and buttoned, and finished in a workmanlike manner. Good quality straight dash, hung on steel frame securely braced and bolted to the body. Toe carpet, whipsocket, toerail, anti-rattlers, washers and wrench. Shafts full ironed and trimmed.

WHEELS—Sarven's patent, sixteen spokes to the wheel, made of selected hickory stock, with ⅞-inch oval edge steel tires, extending over the rim, protecting the felloe.

No. 11R3 Price, complete with shafts.......................................**$22.35**

Shipping weight, about 300 pounds.

Shipped from Kalamazoo, Michigan, or Brighton, Ohio, from which point the customer must pay the freight.

OUR $23.95 ROAD WAGON.

No other factory can touch us in this line of work, at the price we offer it, quality considered.

No. 11R9

GENERAL DESCRIPTION.

BODY—The body is Corning style, made of carefully selected material. The sills are of Pennsylvania ash, the panels are of air seasoned poplar; corners are mitered with hardwood posts, panels are glued, screwed and plugged. Solid panel spring back.

SPRINGS—Oil tempered, best grade end springs, made from spring steel carefully tested. They are strong, easy riding.

WHEELS—Sarven's patent, full bolted, ⅞-inch tires; with oval edge tire; height of wheels 38 inches front, 42 inches rear; well finished and fully guaranteed.

GEAR—The gear is made of second growth hickory thoroughly ironed with wrought and Norway iron. Axles beds cemented and clipped to axles; wrought iron full bearing fifth wheel; strong reaches well ironed and braced with wrought iron stay braces.

TRIMMINGS—Seat cushion and back upholstered with imitation leather or standard grade of body cloth as desired. The upholstering is nicely tufted and buttoned.

PAINTING—Body, black, with neat striping; seat raisers, seat and back panel finished to match; gear, dark green or red.

TRACK—4 feet 8 inches or 5 feet 2 inches. State width required when ordering.

No. 11R9 Price, all complete.......................................**$23.95**

EXTRAS.

Pole in place of shafts..	1.25
Both pole and shafts..	3.00
Genuine leather upholstering..	1.50

Shipping weight, about 400 pounds.

Shipped from our factory at Brighton, Ohio, or Kalamazoo, Michigan, from which point the customer pays the freight.

NO CHARGES FOR REPAIRS on vehicles will be allowed unless our written consent is first secured in advance.

DOUBLE BRACED SHAFTS YOU DO NOT FIND ON MOST FACTORY JOBS, BUT WE FURNISH THEM ON ALL OUR BUGGIES.

OUR NEW $27.75 OPEN BUGGY.

DON'T FAIL TO STATE WIDTH OF TRACK
$27.75

No. 11R15

SOLD UNDER OUR BINDING GUARANTEE and the price quoted is for buggy delivered on board the cars at the factory at Brighton, Ohio, or Kalamazoo, Michigan, from which point you must pay the freight.

GENERAL DESCRIPTION.

BODY—19 or 22 inches wide, as desired, by 54 inches long. It is built of high grade, carefully selected material, thoroughly well ironed, strongly braced, bolted and stayed.

TRIMMINGS—Seat, cushion and back are trimmed with the best grade Keratol leather or standard green body cloth as desired. Handsome carpet, has lined side panels, nickel dash rail, nickel rope arm rail, seat rail and handles, rubber drill boot, anti-rattlers, toe-rail, wrench, washers, whipsocket and shafts with lightning coupler.

GEAR—15/16-inch refined steel perfectly trued, with axle beds fitted, clipped and bolted to axles. Reaches are heavily ironed, braced and bolted with stay rods. Fifth wheel is full bearing.

WHEELS—The wheels are Sarven's patent, 38 inches front, 42 inches rear, full bolted; ¾ or ⅞-inch, made of select hickory stock, fitted with an oval edged steel tire, rounded and crimped. Can furnish 40-inch front and 44-inch rear wheels if ordered.

PAINTING—Body, black; gear, dark green or red, as desired, with suitable striping.

SPRINGS—The springs we use on this job are made of the best oil tempered refined steel. We can furnish either elliptic end springs as illustrated or Brewster side bar springs when ordered.

TRACK—Narrow, 4 feet 8 inches, or wide, 5 feet 2 inches.

No. 11R15 Price, complete as above.......................................**$27.75**

EXTRAS.

Pole with neckyoke and whiffletree complete in place of shafts.....	1.25
Both pole and shafts..	3.00
Genuine leather trimming in place of cloth or Keratol leather.....	1.50
¾-inch rubber tires..	12.45
⅞-inch rubber tires..	13.45
Armstrong single leaf spring..	1.50

Shipping weight, about 400 pounds.

OUR SPECIAL $28.95 ACME OPEN BUGGY.

DON'T FAIL TO STATE WIDTH OF TRACK
$28.95

No. 11R21

GENERAL DESCRIPTION.

BODY—25 inches wide by 52 inches long. The sills of the frame are made of selected ash, seasoned and rabbeted, so that the floor of the body rests on the inner edge of the sill; corners mortised. Body panels are made of seasoned poplar. All screw heads are countersunk. The corners of the body are mitered and slightly rounded. Nickel plated body rail around top of the body, running from seat posts full around body, securely bolted to the side of body sill.

SEAT—35 inches wide across the top cushion. Full spring back with solid panel back, highly painted and finished the same as body.

SPRINGS—Elliptic end springs, oil tempered, made of the very best refined crucible steel. Hickory spring bars supporting full, strong body loops, securely bolted to springs with wrought iron clips and bolts.

GEAR—15/16-inch, double collar, swaged, steel axles. Axle beds cemented, clipped and bolted to axles. Double reach running full length from fifth wheel to axle.

WHEELS—Sarven's patent, sixteen spokes, full bolted between every spoke; ⅞ or 1-inch tires, as ordered, with oval edge protecting the rims of the wheels; 38-inch front and 42-inch rear, or 40-inch front and 44-inch rear, as ordered,

TRIMMINGS—Seat cushion and back upholstered with dark green broadcloth, whipcord or Keratol leather; full button tufted, upholstered in a first class manner, by first class workmen. Leather dash hung on steel frame, securely braced and bolted to body, mounted with nickel line rail. Full length carpet, whipsocket, toerail, anti-rattlers, washers and wrench.

PAINTING—Lower panel of body in black with line stripes, as shown in illustration. Neatly striped with double fine lines. Gear, dark green or red, as desired.

TRACK—4 feet 8 inches or 5 feet 2 inches. State size required.

No. 11R21 Price, fitted with best steel tires..............................	**$28.95**
Price, fitted with ¾-inch best Goodyear rubber tires..................	41.40
Price, fitted with ⅞-inch best Goodyear rubber tires..................	42.40

EXTRAS.

Genuine leather trimmings instead of cloth..............................	1.50
Pole complete in place of shafts..............................	1.25
Both pole and shafts..............................	3.00

Shipping weight, about 400 pounds.

Shipped from Kalamazoo, Mich., from which point customer pays the freight.

$34.95 THE WONDER OF THE BUGGY WORLD. $34.95

LEATHER QUARTER TOP BUGGY.

AT $34.95 WE ARE ABLE TO GIVE YOU A GENUINE LEATHER QUARTER TOP BUGGY, THE EQUAL OF WHICH CANNOT BE SECURED OR PRODUCED OUTSIDE OF OUR FACTORY. . . . . .

THIS BUGGY CANNOT BE CLASSED with the cheap top buggies usually sold by dealers for **$40.00 or $45.00, as it is surely a wonder and must be seen to be appreciated.** Everyone who has purchased one of these buggies found it more than they expected and it is only by making this a standard, running it through our factories in large quantities and building it at times when other factories are compelled to shut down, having no dull season in our own factories, **that we can sell you this handsome leather quarter top buggy for $34.95.** If we built this buggy in small lots, as most factories do, we could not produce it for less than $40.00 or $45.00.

EVERY PIECE OF MATERIAL entering into the construction of this buggy is carefully selected and covered by our ONE YEAR BINDING GUARANTEE, and should any piece or part of this our wonder buggy give out through defective material or workmanship during a period of one year from date of sale, we will replace it free of expense to you.

PRICES OF MATERIAL HAVE ADVANCED, and buggies will cost the manufacturers more to build this year; but we were on the lookout and placed our contracts before the advance took place, and with our large cash resources bought immense quantities of material, enabling us to offer you at last season's prices, this **OUR $34.95 BUGGY, THE ACKNOWLEDGED LEADER.**

IN ORDER TO GIVE YOU SUCH A LOW PRICE on this leather quarter top buggy, we built them all alike, and we cannot change a bolt, nut or any part no matter how small and insignificant it may appear to you. It is a standard pattern, each and every part is run through our factories in thousand lots and by boring, tiring and fitting the boxes in 1,000 sets of wheels at one time, by running through our trimming and painting shops 1,000 bodies and building 1,000 tops, each and every one alike, **we are able to produce this buggy at a price far below anything you can secure from any other source.**

SO CONFIDENT ARE WE OF OUR ABILITY to furnish you this leather quarter top buggy, built to meet with your approval, that we give you the privilege of ordering same and trying it ten days, and if in that time, after comparing it with other leather quarter top buggies, even buggies sold by dealers at 25 to 50 per cent more money, you do not find it equal or better and exactly as represented and described, **you can return same and we will refund your money, together with any freight charges you have paid.**

WE SET THE PACE, others follow. Last season our $34.95 wonder buggy was a surprise to the dealers and manufacturers as well as our customers, but now that material costs a great deal more they wonder more than ever how we do it.

WE ARE THE ACKNOWLEDGED LEADERS

and feel confident that this buggy cannot be equaled. However, it may be possible to produce a buggy to meet this price, but they will have to reduce the quality by using cheaper wheels, bodies, steel, upholstering, etc., **but we cannot afford and do not care to compete with this class of work.**

WE HAVE AN ENVIABLE REPUTATION for furnishing high grade buggies at low prices, and this we mean to maintain.

ORDER AND YOU WILL SAVE MONEY.

Last year we made over 5,000 customers just as happy as this one by sending them a $34.95 Wonder Buggy.

Stewart, Iowa.
Sears, Roebuck & Co.,
Chicago, Ill.

Gentlemen:—The buggy I received from you for **$34.95** I could not get here for less than $75.00. The $7.95 harness sent with it I could not buy here for less than $15.00. The freight charges total were $5.21. I am thoroughly satisfied with same.

B. ABRAMS.

SPECIAL TO LIVERY TRADE, CARRIAGE TRADE AND BLACKSMITHS.

Hundreds of carriage dealers, liverymen and blacksmiths order these buggies at our special $34.95 price set them up in their shop or stable, mark them with large figures "$50.00" and sell from one to six a month, adding from $25.00 to $50.00 to their income every month. Dealers, livery trade, blacksmiths, wagon makers, traders, merchants, farmers and others make money buying our special $34.95 top buggy to sell again, to sell at $50.00 and upwards.

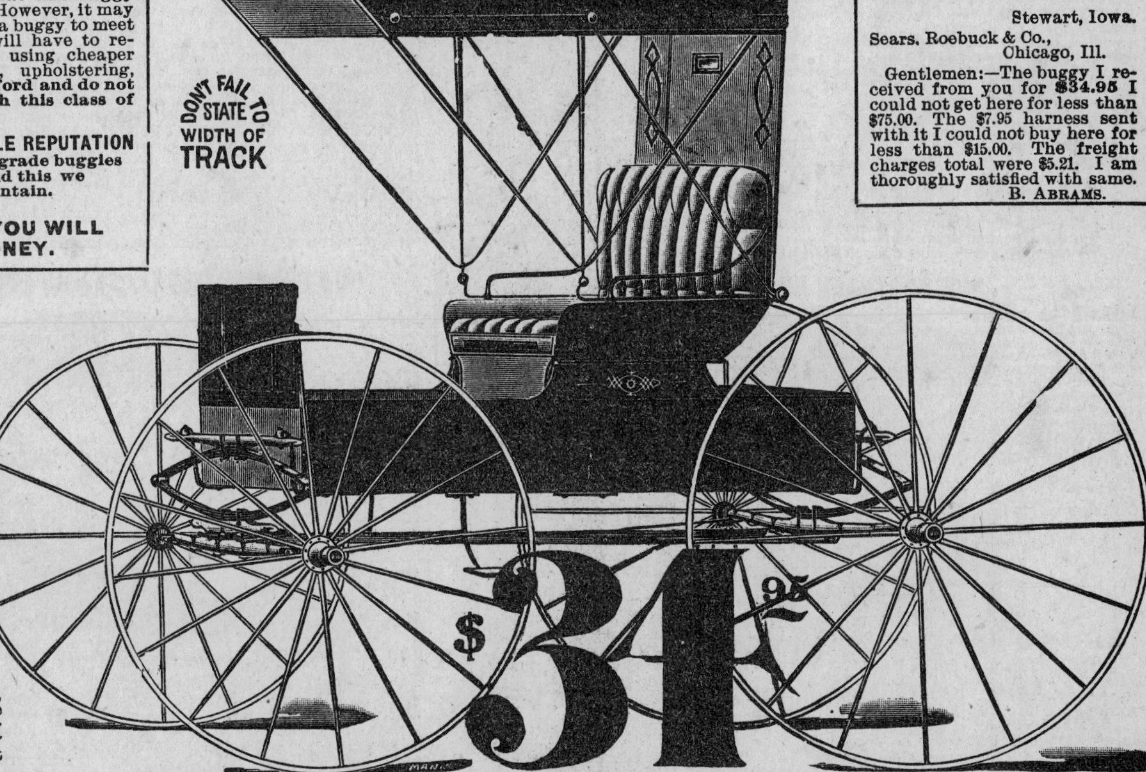
DON'T FAIL TO STATE WIDTH OF TRACK
$34.95

No. 11R215

DETAILED DESCRIPTION.

BODY—This handsome piano box body is made of selected wood, thoroughly seasoned, finished with round corners, convex risers. The body is double braced and reinforced at sides and corners, ironed full length on bottom and top. The seat has high side panels, solid panel back, made of four-ply built-up stock, double braced and reinforced at corners and bottom. We use only the very best air seasoned wood, and in building it up it is mitered, glued, screwed and plugged. We believe this body is as well built as any piano box body made regardless of price.

WHEELS—In this $34.95 buggy we use wheels made of selected hickory stock, full finished, full bolted between every spoke; Sarven's patent hub; boxes set by hydraulic pressure in white lead; every wheel true; tires set hot, the only reliable way of setting tires so as not to injure wheels. We use the highest grade full crimped extended edge steel tires. The wheels on our $34.95 buggy will outwear one-half dozen sets of cheap cull wheels. The wheels are ⅞-inch, standard size.

TOP—Three-bow top, exactly as illustrated, **leather quarters and back stays.** Quarters are cut very deep and made of good quality full finished leather. Roof made of Star A brand waterproof black rubber; back of best black rubber imitation leather; side curtains of black enameled drill. The top is made with a heavy valance front and rear, sewed on. Top is lined with a good quality green cloth top lining, ornamented with fancy sewing and trimming; hold-up straps in rear; metal trimmed window in back. We use the very best grade of black enameled bow sockets; best grade of wrought iron rails; a good, substantial, well built buggy top.

SPRINGS—In this $34.95 buggy we use high grade, full sweep elliptic end springs, the same grade of springs as are used on the highest grade buggies made.

GEAR—This gear is made of good selected hickory and Norway iron; selected gear wood throughout; double reach, ironed full length; best axles clipped to axle bed with Norway iron clips; genuine Anderson full circle fifth wheel.

UPHOLSTERING—Our $34.95 rig is upholstered either in dark green body cloth or genuine leather, as desired (leather $1.50 extra). We use the very best full tempered steel springs in cushion and back. Cushion and back are handsomely button tufted, as illustrated; seat ends are full padded; a strictly standard grade of trimming.

PAINTING—We paint this buggy in a thoroughly substantial manner. Body is painted black; gear, dark Brewster green, with suitable striping. The body is rubbed out with pumice stone and water. We use nothing but the very best paints, oils and varnishes, and we put on a body of finish which insures a lasting and durable finish.

NO. 11R215 At our special **$34.95 price we furnish this rig complete,** with top, side curtains, toe carpet, panel carpet, wrench, anti-rattlers and double braced shafts, with quick shifting shaft couplers. Extra for pole with neckyoke and whiffletree complete in place of shafts, **$1.20**; extra for both pole and shafts, **$3.00.** At our special **$34.95 price we furnish the buggy exactly as illustrated, exactly as described, delivered on board the cars at** our factory in Southern Ohio or Kalamazoo, Mich., **from which point you must pay the freight.** The buggy weighs (crated for shipment) from 450 to 500 pounds, **and the freight will amount to next to nothing as compared with what you will save in price.**

OUR $36.95 EASY RIDING SIDE SPRING BUGGY.

DONT FAIL TO STATE WIDTH OF TRACK
$36.95

No. 11R221

GENERAL DESCRIPTION.

BODY—22 inches wide by 54 inches long. Can furnish Corning body if ordered.

GEAR—Axles are 15/16-inch, made of the best refined steel, double collar fantail. Gear is fitted with the long side springs, as illustrated, run from front to rear. We attach to the gear the celebrated quick shifting shaft coupler.

WHEELS—Sarven's patent, high grade. Front wheels, 38 or 40 inches high; rear wheels, 42 or 44 inches high, as desired. ⅞ or 1-inch tread.

TRIMMINGS—Cushion and back are upholstered with 14-ounce English wool faced cloth or Keratol leather, padded and lined seat ends, spring cushion and spring back, fancy tufted, as illustrated, worsted toe carpet, carpet lined panels.

PAINTING—Body painted black; gear, dark Brewster green, artistically striped. Red gear if ordered.

TOP—Leather quarter top, quarter cut deep, with leather back stay, padded and lined; three-bow, rubber roof and back curtain. Can furnish four bows if ordered.

TRACK—Narrow, 4 feet 8 inches, or wide, 5 feet 2 inches, as desired.

No. 11R221 Price, with steel tires.......... $36.95
Price, with ⅞-inch best Goodyear rubber tires.......... 50.40
Price, with 1-inch best Goodyear rubber tires.......... 52.45

EXTRAS.

Pole, neckyoke and whiffletree in place of shafts.......... 1.25
Both pole and shafts.......... 3.00
Leather roof and back curtain in place of rubber roof and back curtain 3.50
Genuine leather upholstering.......... 1.50

We ship from Brighton, Ohio. **Weight, about 500 pounds.**

OUR SOUTHERN BEAUTY, $38.25.

DONT FAIL TO STATE WIDTH OF TRACK
$38.25

No. 11R227

GENERAL DESCRIPTION.

BODY—Piano body, 19x54 inches; concave risers and convex seat panels; seat 24x16 inches; stylish and of handsome proportions.

GEAR—Axles 15/16-inch; double collar fantail steel, with axle caps cemented, sanded and clipped. Three and four-leaf elliptic end springs with Bailey body loops. Can furnish Armstrong single leaf spring when ordered.

WHEELS—Are Sarven's patent, well seasoned hickory, with full bolted steel tires, regular ⅞-inch tread, 38-inch front, 42-inch rear (can furnish 40-inch front and 44-inch rear when ordered).

TOP—Two and one-half bow handy top as illustrated, but will furnish regular three-bow top when ordered. Quarters are deep cut leather with leather backstays and rubber roof.

UPHOLSTERING—We use a fine grade of fancy colored Keratol leather in our Southern Beauty, and upholstered in latest style as shown in illustration. Can furnish cloth cushion and back if ordered.

PAINTING—Body, black with artistic decorations and striping as shown, gear, carmine with neat striping. Can furnish rosewood body when ordered.

TRIMMINGS—Oxidized nickel dash rail, hub bands, seat handles and prop nuts, quick shifting shaft coupler.

TRACK—Either 4 foot 8-inch or 5 foot 2-inch track, as ordered.

No. 11R227 Price, as described at Brighton or Kalamazoo factory, $38.25

EXTRAS.

Genuine leather upholstering.......... 1.50
Full leather top.......... 3.00
Pole in place of shafts.......... 1.50
Both pole and shafts.......... 3.00
⅞-inch rubber tires.......... 13.45

Weight, crated for shipment, about 500 pounds.

OUR NEW MODEL $40.00 BUGGY.

DONT FAIL TO STATE WIDTH OF TRACK
$40.00

No. 11R233

GENERAL DESCRIPTION.

BODY—Body 22 inches wide by 54 inches long, bottom measurement. Full round corners to seat and body. Can furnish 19-inch body if desired.

GEAR—1500-mile axle, 15/16-inch fantail; reaches are ironed full length and braced with wrought iron stay braces, rear circle fifth wheel, three-plate elliptic spring in front and four-plate in rear, quick shaft coupler.

WHEELS—Sarven's patent wheels, screwed rims, full bolted. Front wheels, 38 or 40 ins. high; rear wheels, 42 or 44 ins. high; tired with ⅞ or 1-in. steel tires.

UPHOLSTERING—The buggy is upholstered in a 14-ounce imported wool dyed green body cloth, high solid panel back. Full padded seat ends.

PAINTING—Body black, neatly and modestly striped; gear, dark Brewster green with appropriate striping. Can furnish carmine gear if desired.

MOUNTING—Fancy nickel dash rail, Brussels toe carpet, front panels of body lined with Brussels carpet.

TOP—Three bow, leather quarters; top is lined throughout with a good quality of head lining, lined back curtain. Can furnish four-bow top if desired.

No. 11R233 Price, fitted with best steel tires.......... $40.00
Price, fitted with ⅞-inch best Goodyear rubber tires.......... 53.45
Price, fitted with 1-inch best Goodyear rubber tires.......... 55.50

EXTRAS.

Full leather top in place of leather quarter.......... 3.00
Pole complete in place of shafts.......... 1.25
Both pole and shafts.......... 3.00
Leather cushion and back.......... 1.50

Shipped from Brighton, Ohio, or Kalamazoo, Mich. **Weight, about 500 lbs**

OUR SPECIAL MODEL $43.95 LIVERY BUGGY.

DONT FAIL TO STATE WIDTH OF TRACK
$43.95

No. 11R239

GENERAL DESCRIPTION.

BODY—23 inches wide by 54 inches long. Full concave seat risers, full convex seat panels, heavy oval edge irons, full rounded corners to seat and body; heavily braced in corners, made extra strong throughout.

GEAR—1500-mile axle with dust proof collar. The axles are 1 1/16-inch, special weight for livery trade, made from the finest refined axle steel, fantailed; wood caps are extra weight. Heavy reaches ironed full length with extra heavy wrought iron, full braced and full bolted, quick shaft coupler.

WHEELS—Sarven's patent, special selected heavy stock, bolted throughout. Front wheels are 38 or 40 inches high, rear wheels, 42 or 44 inches high. They are 1-inch tread and fitted with 5/16-inch, crimped edge steel tires.

TOP—Large heavy leather quarter top. Top has patent curtain fasteners, extra heavy No. 1 metal bow sockets, extra heavy wrought iron joints, rails and stays, three or four-bow as ordered.

UPHOLSTERING—This heavy livery buggy is upholstered in standard body cloth. No. 1 extra heavy deep buffed leather cushion and back, $1.50 extra.

PAINTING—Body is painted black; gear, dark Brewster green, with appropriate striping. Can furnish carmine gear if desired.

No. 11R239 Price, fitted with best steel tires.......... $43.95
Price, fitted with ⅞-inch best Goodyear rubber tires.......... 57.40
Price, fitted with 1-inch best Goodyear rubber tires.......... 59.45

EXTRAS.

Pole complete in place of shafts.......... 1.25
Both pole and shafts.......... 3.00
Deep buffed leather upholstering in place of cloth.......... 1.50

Shipped from our Ohio or Michigan factory. **Weight, about 525 pounds.**

OUR VERY FINEST.... ACME ROYAL TOP BUGGY $54.90

IF YOU ARE IN THE MARKET for a high class buggy, one that is usually sold for $80.00 to $100.00 by local dealers and others, we ask you to read carefully the detailed description of this our very finest Acme Royal Top Buggy.

THIS BUGGY IS NOT TO BE COMPARED with the class of buggies that usually sell from $55.00 to $65.00, but is made of a carefully selected material, and we offer you in this buggy better value than is possible to secure elsewhere.

OFFERED $100.00 FOR HIS BUGGY.

Below is an extract from a letter we received; we have hundreds of such letters from satisfied customers.

"I want to thank you for the splendid buggy you sent me. I have several times been offered $100.00 cash for it, but I did not purchase for sale. Everyone admires it."
Your friend, G. D. WILKINSON, M.D.,
Giddings, Texas.

GUARANTEED ONE YEAR.

And with care will outwear any two buggies usually sold at $100.00.

WE DEFY ANYONE TO FURNISH A BETTER BODY AND FINISH THAN WE PUT ON OUR ACME ROYAL BUGGY.

Nothing but finest grade oils and varnishes used, giving a lasting finish and luster, and our buggy will look better after one year than the ordinary buggy will look after 30 days use.

READ THE DESCRIPTION OF PAINTING.

THIS BUGGY......

Never fails to please the most exacting.

WE COULD NOT BUILD IT BETTER.

DON'T FAIL TO STATE WIDTH OF TRACK

No. 11R269

...DETAILED DESCRIPTION...

BODY—Body is 22 inches wide by 54 inches long. Seat is 27x16 inches. Concave seat risers and convex seat panels. Seat ironed with oval edge irons. Full rounded corners on body and seat. Swell seat panels, rounded front to cushion, high seat panels. The sills of seat and body are made of the best seasoned white ash; corner posts, toothpick braces and seat frame of the best seasoned white ash; body panels and seat panels made of selected well seasoned poplar. Body is glued, clamped, plugged and screwed, braced throughout, and highly finished. There is no better buggy body made.

GEAR—We use in this our highest grade gear, the celebrated Anderson gear, made with 1500-mile axle, with dustproof collar. The axles are $\frac{15}{16}$-inch, fantail, swaged, made of the best refined steel. We use the very best waterproof cement in cementing our wood caps to the axles. They are then clamped and put on the sand belt, smoothing them off and giving them a smooth finish; they are then primed with lead and oil, and allowed to stand a sufficient time to become thoroughly dry; then the clips are put on, full clipped and full bolted, thus giving them good priming under the clips. The gear woods are of the highest grade selected second growth hickory, carefully finished. The gear is ironed throughout with Norway iron. Full length reaches; reaches ironed full length, braced and bolted. We use the highest grade 36-inch open head elliptic, oil tempered steel springs, full finished, three-plate front and four-plate rear. We use the celebrated Robinson full circle fifth wheel. The gear is furnished with the high grade quick shaft couplers, for the instantaneous changing of the shafts to pole or pole to shafts, and body is hung on Bailey body loops.

WHEELS—Dodson celebrated brand of Sarven's patent wheels, a strictly high grade, guaranteed wheel, made of well seasoned hickory, made with full screwed rims; comes in either Sarven's patent or compressed band wood hub, as desired. They are full bolted between each spoke. Front wheels are 38 or 40 inches high; rear wheels, 42 or 44 inches high. Can furnish compressed band wood hub if desired.

TRIMMINGS—Cushion and back trimmed with very fine, heavy 16-ounce, all wool dyed green body cloth. Cushion is fitted up with box frame. Staple and Handford open coil springs in cushion and back. The pattern of cushion and back is diamond biscuit as illustrated; full lined seat panels, leather covered seat handles, leather boot, rubber covered step pads, heavy enameled leather dash, full length velvet carpet, full swell cushion in front, the back is very high; in fact, this job is upholstered in the highest style of the art, and if you do not find it a better job of upholstering than you have ever seen offered by anyone else you can return the rig to us and we will return your money. Machine buffed leather trimming, in place of cloth, furnished at $2.00 extra.

TOP—Full leather quarter top, made of strictly No. 1 machine buffed leather, extra well finished. The top is made extra high, extra wide and extra deep, with extra deep heavy quarters. Has solid leather valance front and rear. The valance is raised in the center, bound by hand and sewed to the top by hand. The top is lined throughout with a heavy dark green wool head lining, heavy lined rubber back curtain. The back stays are solid No. 1 leather, full padded and lined with heavy green cloth. The top is fitted with a heavy double strength glass curtain light, Higgin's patent curtain fasteners, leather covered prop nuts, very fancy enameled steel bow sockets, finest quality joints, rails and trimmings. Top comes complete with full length back and side curtains. Top is made from the best material that can be secured, only the most skilled mechanics are employed, and it is such a top as you will not find on any buggy outside of buggies that sell at double the price in repositories in large cities. Three-bow; can furnish four-bow if ordered.

PAINTING—This buggy is painted in the highest style of the art; body jet black, without striping. The body and seat are built up with twelve coats of filler, rough stuff, color and varnish, and is given a finish you will find on nothing but the very finest work in the best repositories. The gear is painted dark green, with double lines of glazed carmine striping. We could save several dollars in the painting of this rig, but with a view of giving our customers the best painted job it is possible to turn out, nothing but the very best of oils, varnish and colors have been used. Every rig is given ample time in paint shop; only the most skilled mechanics are employed. We turn out the finest buggy we make painted in a manner to insure lasting service and every satisfaction. We can furnish carmine gear if ordered.

TRACK—This buggy comes in narrow track, 4 feet 8 inches, or wide track, 5 feet 2 inches, as desired.

SHAFTS—We furnish this rig with double braced shafts, made from selected second growth hickory, ironed, braced and bolted throughout with the best Norway iron, extra well finished; metal tips, leather trimmed 30 inches back with heavy enameled leather, bound in the best possible manner; such shafts as you will find only on the very finest buggies.

The special price quoted is for the buggy crated and delivered on board the cars at our factory either in Brighton, Ohio, or Kalamazoo, Michigan, and the freight will amount to next to nothing as compared with what you save in price.

No. 11R269 Price, for buggy as illustrated, fitted with best steel tires	**$54.90**
Price, fitted with ¾-inch Goodyear rubber tires	67.35
Price, fitted with ⅞-inch Goodyear rubber tires	68.35
Price, fitted with 1-inch Goodyear rubber tires	70.40
Extra for leather side curtains	3.75
Extra for machine buffed leather upholstering in cushion and back, in place of cloth	2.00
Extra for pole with neckyoke and whiffletree, complete in place of shafts	2.00
Extra for both pole and shafts	3.00
Extra for full leather top	3.00

Weight, crated for shipment, 450 to 500 pounds.

OUR $39.85 CANOPY TOP WAGON.

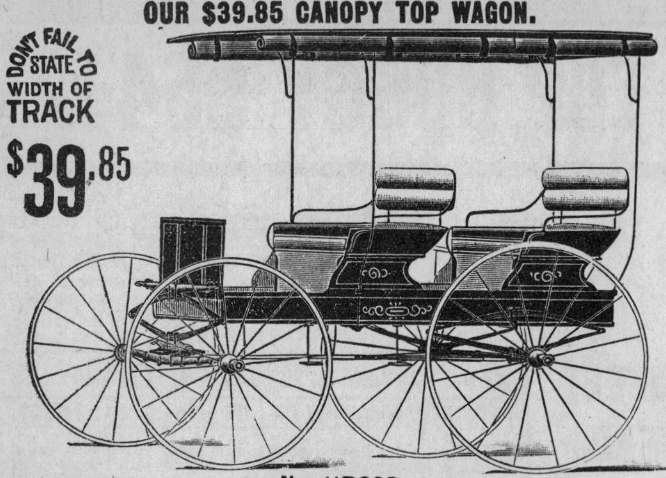

No. 11R603

GENERAL DESCRIPTION.

SEATS—Two removable seats with lazy back, as shown in illustration. The seats are roomy, high mounted on a good, substantial, hardwood seat raiser, well braced, well finished, and can be detached without removing the top.

SPRINGS—Elliptic front end spring securely bolted to hickory spring bar and to hickory head block, with two strong rear elliptic springs, all made of good grade spring steel.

BODY—The body is 6 feet long, 38 inches wide outside, ironed and well finished, making an easy riding, good appearance, general purpose vehicle.

GEAR—Axles are 1-inch front, 1⅛-inch rear, made from best grade axle steel, with hickory axle bed cemented, clipped and bolted.

WHEELS—Wheels are Sarven's patent, ⅞-inch, tired with 1¼-inch best steel tires, guaranteed to be a good grade of selected air seasoned hickory stock.

TOP—The top is well made, light and strong, neat in appearance, attached to four steel curved upright rods with four curved brazed tension top braces. Fitted with full length side and back roll up curtains, wrench, anti-rattlers and shafts.

TRACK—4 feet 8 inches or 5 feet 2 inches. State width required.

No. 11R603 Price, all complete....$39.85

EXTRAS.

Both pole and shafts complete	3.00
Pole in place of shafts	1.25
Genuine leather trimming in place of imitation leather	3.00

Shipping weight, about 800 pounds.

Shipped from factory in Southern Ohio, from which point the customer pays the freight.

We buy this wagon from a reliable manufacturer in Ohio, and the rate is the same as from our Brighton, Ohio, factory.

OUR $43.95 CANOPY TOP RIG.

$43.95
DON'T FAIL TO STATE WIDTH OF TRACK

No. 11R609

GENERAL DESCRIPTION.

BODY—The body is 61 inches long, 27 inches wide, made from good selected well seasoned material, full ironed and full finished, making an easy riding, good appearing general purpose rig.

TOP—The top is well made, well finished, light and strong, attached to four steel curved upright rods with four-angle tension top braces, with full length side and back curtains, wrench, anti-rattlers and shafts.

SEATS—The seats are strong and roomy, and can be detached without removing the top. They are very comfortable, substantial, well braced and well finished.

GEAR—The axles are $1\frac{1}{16}$-inch, fantailed, double collar, best axle steel, with hickory axle bed cemented, clipped and bolted.

WHEELS—The wheels are Sarven's patent, ⅞ or 1-inch; height, 38 inches front and 42 inches rear.

SPRINGS—Elliptic 1½-inch end springs, four or five-plate, made from good spring steel, securely clipped to hickory spring bar, axle bed and hickory head block.

TRACK—4 feet 8 inches or 5 feet 2 inches. State width required.

No. 11R609 Price, all complete....$43.95

EXTRAS.

Both pole and shafts complete	3.00
Pole with neckyoke and whiffletree in place of shafts	1.50
Full leather cushions and back	3.00

Shipping weight, crated, about 800 pounds.

We buy this job in large quantities from a reputable manufacturer in Ohio. The freight is the same as when shipped from Brighton.

NO CHARGES FOR REPAIRS ON VEHICLES WILL BE ALLOWED

UNLESS OUR WRITTEN CONSENT IS SECURED IN ADVANCE.

OUR $46.90 FARMERS' CANOPY TOP SURREY.

All purpose Farmers' Carriage.
$46.90
DON'T FAIL TO STATE WIDTH OF TRACK

No. 11R615

GENERAL DESCRIPTION.

BODY—5 feet 10 inches long by 25 inches wide on the bottom; a good, long, roomy body. The body is made of seasoned lumber; fitted with heavy sliding phaeton seats and with high panel backs. The rear seat, while made to take out, is securely fastened to the rear canopy top standard, to make the seat very secure. The sides of the body are full ironed, full bolted, full braced, and double stayed and reinforced at the joints.

UPHOLSTERING—Cushions and backs in both seats are trimmed in cloth, biscuit pattern, full buttoned finish. Full springs in seat, spring back, full padded, full lined seat ends. Full length carpet in body, enameled tan curved dash and canopy top.

WHEELS—Sarven's patent; sixteen spokes to the wheel. Good hickory stock; a thoroughly honest, well built wheel. Heavy Sarven's steel hub bands. The wheels are bolted between each spoke. Wheels heavily tired, crimped and rounded throughout. Front wheel, 38 inches high, rear wheel, 42 inches high; 1-inch rims.

GEAR—A good heavy balance spring, substantial well made gear, $1\frac{1}{16}$ inches. The gear is ironed throughout with good heavy iron, double reaches ironed full length with heavy iron.

TRACK—Narrow, 4 feet 8 inches; wide, 5 feet 2 inches.

PAINTING—Body is painted dark green with black seat panels; gear, dark green, neatly striped.

WHEEL AXLES—The axles are double collars, swaged, made of a fine axle steel. Fitted to the axles are heavy hickory axle caps, which are fastened with heavy wrought iron clips and bolts.

SPRINGS—Good heavy substantial elliptic end springs, four-leaf in front and five-leaf in rear; good heavy circle fifth wheel, king bolt in rear of axle.

No. 11R615 Price, complete at our factory at Brighton, Ohio, or Kalamazoo, Mich....$46.90

EXTRAS.

Pole complete in place of shafts	1.25
Both pole and shafts	3.00
Genuine leather in place of cloth	4.00

Weight, crated for shipment, about 700 pounds.

OUR $53.75 FARMERS' LEATHER QUARTER EXTENSION TOP SURREY.

No. 11R621

Order by number.

No. 11R621

THIS HANDSOME SURREY is a companion to our No. 11R615, and is built on the same lines of proportion, finished, upholstered and trimmed exactly like our No. 11R615. The same general description applies, only that this job is fitted with a genuine leather quarter extension top.

No. 11R621 Price, without fenders, at our factory at Brighton, Ohio, or Kalamazoo, Mich....$53.75

EXTRAS.

Pole in place of shafts	1.25
Both pole and shafts	3.00
Genuine leather in place of cloth	4.00
Fenders as shown in illustration	2.75

Weight, crated for shipment, about 700 pounds.

OUR NEW ACME MODEL SURREY, $58.90.

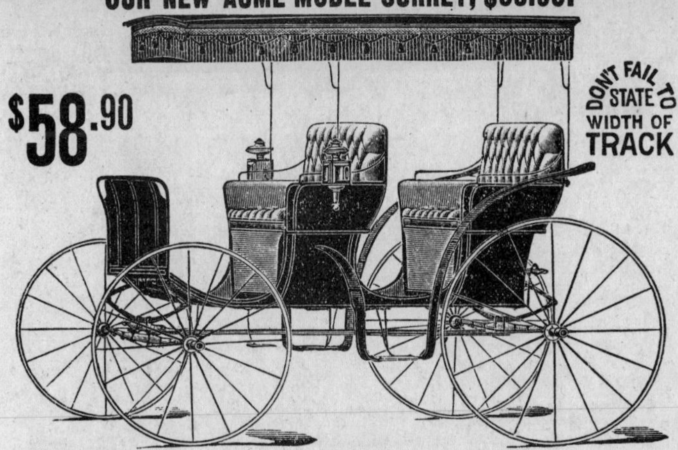

No. 11R627

GENERAL DESCRIPTION.

BODY—5 feet 10 inches long, 26 inches wide. High seat panels, high solid phaeton spring backs of seats with round corners.

GEAR—Axles, $1\frac{1}{16}$-inch, double collar, fantail, swaged, made of selected axle steel. Full sweep elliptic springs, four-plate front, five-plate rear. Double reaches, ironed full length, full back circle fifth wheel. Quick shifting shaft coupler.

WHEELS—Sarven's patent wheels, full bolted between each spoke. Front wheel 38 inches high, rear wheel 42 inches high, 1-inch tread.

UPHOLSTERING—Upholstered in 14-ounce English dark green body cloth, padded, lined, seat ends latest style diamond piped patent biscuit tufting.

TOP—Full canopy top, trimmed throughout with a good fringe, with full length side and back curtains, oil burning lamps.

PAINTING—Body painted dark green with nonpareil green pillars. Gear is painted dark coach or Brewster green, handsomely trimmed.

TRACK—Narrow, 4 feet 8 inches; or wide, 5 feet 2 inches, as desired.

No. 11R627 Price, fitted with best steel tires.......... $58.90
Price, fitted with 1-inch best Goodyear rubber tires.......... 74.40

EXTRAS.

Full leather cushion, leather backs and seat linings.......... $3.50
Pole in place of shafts.......... 1.50
Both pole and shafts.......... 3.50

Weight, crated, about 750 pounds.

Shipped from Brighton, Ohio, or Kalamazoo, Mich. Customer pays freight.

OUR ACME MODEL $63.90 CUT UNDER CANOPY TOP SURREY.

$63.90
DON'T FAIL TO STATE WIDTH OF TRACK

No. 11R633

GENERAL DESCRIPTION.

BODY—Body is good size, 5 feet 10 inches long, 26 inches wide on the bottom. Iron seat rods run down through the sills. Seats are made with extra high seat panels, full rounded, as illustrated.

GEAR—Heavy Anderson surrey gear, $1\frac{1}{16}$-inch double collar, fantail, steel axles, swaged and finished. Full oil tempered elliptic springs, four-plate front and five-plate rear; a heavy single surrey reach, heavily ironed full length and full bolted; Robinson full back circle fifth wheel; kingbolt in rear of axle. Quick shifting coupler.

UPHOLSTERING—Cushions and backs trimmed in 14-ounce English wool faced green body cloth, biscuit tufted cushions with diamond and pipe pattern back, as illustrated. Seat ends are padded and lined, soft coil springs in backs and cushions, full worsted carpet, heavy enameled leather dash.

TOP—A good, strong, substantial canopy top. Four steel standards, full braced and well built. Top is trimmed with a good quality head fringe, top lined with good quality lining, furnished complete with full length side and back curtains. Oil burning lamps.

WHEELS—Sarven's patent; full bolted between each spoke. Front wheel 34 inches high, rear wheel 42 inches high; 1-inch tread, tired with a heavy, round edge, full crimped steel tire.

PAINTING—The body is painted dark green, with nonpareil green pillars and black moldings, giving it a very beautiful, yet modestly rich effect. Gear is painted dark Brewster green, handsomely striped and trimmed.

TRACK—Narrow, 4 feet 8 inches; or wide, 5 feet 2 inches, as desired.

No. 11R633 Price, fitted with best steel tires.......... $63.90
Price, fitted with 1-inch best Goodyear rubber tires.......... 79.40

EXTRAS.

Pole in place of shafts.......... 1.50
Both pole and shafts.......... 3.50
Heavy leather cushions and back in place of cloth.......... 3.50

Weight, crated, about 825 pounds.

Shipped from Brighton, Ohio, or Kalamazoo, Mich. Customer pays freight.

OUR ACME MODEL $64.90 EXTENSION TOP SURREY.

$64.90
DON'T FAIL TO STATE WIDTH OF TRACK

No. 11R639

GENERAL DESCRIPTION.

BODY—5 feet 10 inches long by 26 inches wide on bottom. The seats are high solid phaeton seats, heavy high rounded panels, extra high rounded panel backs.

WHEELS—The wheels are Sarven's patent with heavy steel bands. They are 1-inch, tired with heavy steel tires, rounded and crimped. Front wheel is 38 inches high and rear wheel 42 inches high.

GEAR—Anderson surrey gear, built heavy, strong and firm, and well finished. The axles are $1\frac{1}{16}$-inch double collar, fantail, swaged. Extra heavy, elliptic end springs, four-plate in front and five-plate in rear; full circle Robinson fifth wheel, with kingbolt in rear of axle. Quick shifting shaft coupler.

UPHOLSTERING—Cushions and backs trimmed in 14-ounce English wool faced green body cloth, padded and lined seat ends. Soft coil springs in cushions and backs. Oil burning lamps.

PAINTING—Dark coach green body with nonpareil pillars, black molding. Gear, dark green, handsomely striped.

TOP—Leather quarter extension top. The quarters and stays are extra deep and extra long and cut from genuine heavy buffed leather.

TRACK—Narrow, 4 feet 8 inches; or wide, 5 feet 2 inches, as desired.

No. 11R639 Price, fitted with best steel tires.......... $64.90
Price, fitted with ⅞-inch best Goodyear rubber tires.......... 78.35
Price, fitted with 1-inch best Goodyear rubber tires.......... 80.40

EXTRAS.

Leather cushions and backs in place of cloth.......... 4.00
Pole complete in place of shafts.......... 1.50
Both pole and shafts.......... 3.50

Weight about 800 pounds.

Shipped from Brighton, Ohio, or Kalamazoo, Mich.

OUR NEW ACME MODEL CUT UNDER EXTENSION TOP SURREY.

$69.95
DON'T FAIL TO STATE WIDTH OF TRACK

No. 11R645

GENERAL DESCRIPTION.

BODY—Latest style cut under extension body. Body is good size, 5 feet 10 inches long by 26 inches wide on the bottom. The seats are heavy high paneled surrey seats, full rounded.

GEAR—This gear is built on a $1\frac{1}{16}$-inch double collar, fantail, swaged axle. One long cut under surrey reach, heavily ironed full length; full circle fifth wheel. End springs, four-plate in front and five-plate in rear; kingbolt in rear of axle. Quick shifting shaft coupler.

WHEELS—They are 1-inch tread; Sarven's patent, with heavy steel bands; The tires are extra heavy, rounded edge, full crimp steel tires, full bolted. The front wheel is 34 inches high, rear wheel 42 inches high.

UPHOLSTERING—Upholstered in a 14-ounce English wool faced dark green body cloth. Seat ends full padded and full lined, soft coil springs in back and cushions. Oil burning lamps.

TOP—Extra high, extra wide and extra deep extension leather quarter top. Quarters and stays cut extra large and from genuine leather.

PAINTING—This body is painted a dark green with black pillars; the gear is a dark Brewster green, neatly striped.

TRACK—Narrow, 4 feet 8 inches, or wide, 5 feet 2 inches, as desired.

No. 11R645 Price, fitted with best steel tires.......... $69.95
Price, fitted with ⅞-inch best Goodyear rubber tires.......... 83.40
Price, fitted with 1-inch best Goodyear rubber tires.......... 85.45

EXTRAS.

Leather cushions and backs in place of cloth.......... $4.00
Pole complete in place of shafts.......... 1.50
Both pole and shaft.......... 3.50

Weight, crated, about 825 pounds.

Shipped from Brighton, Ohio, or Kalamazoo, Mich.

OUR $116.40 EXTENSION TOP CABRIOLET.

$116.40
With Best Steel Tires.
$139.40
With 1-inch Rubber Tires.
DON'T FAIL TO STATE WIDTH OF TRACK
Understand, it is covered by our binding guarantee. We guarantee it to reach you in perfect condition.

No. 11R675

GENERAL DESCRIPTION.

BODY—Body is large, roomy and strong, and at the same time artistic in proportions; latest style cut under, thoroughly ironed and braced. We could not furnish a better body as every detail is studied and watched carefully and we know there is not a more stylish, well proportioned body on the market. Front seat is 33 inches wide by 16 inches deep, with 10-inch solid panel spring back; rear seat is 35 inches wide by 19 inches deep, with 15-inch solid panel spring back. Body measures 29 inches wide, bottom measurement.

GEAR—On this cabriolet we furnish a strong hand made gear, all wood parts being selected second growth hickory; front axles fitted with wood cap, cemented and clipped to axle; rear axle coached. Single bent reach, ironed and braced. 1500-mile long distance axle, fitted with felt pad and dustproof collar.

WHEELS—Highest grade selected second growth hickory wheels, screwed rims, front 34, rear 44 inches, 1 or 1⅛-inch tread, Sarven's patent regular, but will furnish compressed band wood hub when ordered.

SPRINGS—Best oil tempered, full elliptic springs, one in front, two in rear; made of the best refined spring steel.

UPHOLSTERING—Style as shown in illustration, with heavy dark green body cloth, light colored whipcord or No. 1 machine buffed leather, as desired. Cushions and backs fitted with springs. If not specified in your order we will use our judgment in kind of upholstering.

TOP—We furnish a handsome, well proportioned leather quarter top on this job; quarter deep cut buffed leather with leather back stays padded and lined.

PAINTING—This job is given our regular Acme Royal piano finish; body, black with belts and neat striping to match color of gear. Gear painted black, Brewster green, New York red or sultan red, as desired. Comes regular with green gear, unless otherwise ordered.

This cabriolet is furnished regular with fine oil burning lamps and pole.

No. 11R675 Price, fitted with best steel tires.......................$116.40
Price, with canopy top in place of leather quarter top.......... 112.90

EXTRAS.

Both pole and shafts... 3.50
1-inch rubber tires.. 23.00
1⅛-inch rubber tires... 27.00

We use a specially constructed rubber tire on this job.
When desired, we will omit the pole and furnish shafts at same price.
Shipping weight, about 900 pounds. Shipped from Brighton, Ohio.

OUR $49.75 REGULAR JUMP SEAT BUGGY.

No. 11R803

DETAILED DESCRIPTION.

BODY—Made throughout of the best selected seasoned poplar and ash, corners mitered, glued, screwed, plugged and secured with corner irons; 25 inches wide by 54 inches long.

SEATS—Seats are roomy and comfortable; high panel spring back on rear seat; front seat folds down flat on bottom of body; back seat moves forward and is exactly the same as a one-seated buggy.

SPRINGS—Hung on Brewster side bar springs; gear hung to carry a load evenly balanced on springs and gear when either one or two seats are used.

TRIMMINGS—Front and rear seats upholstered in tant leather or all wool dark green cloth; body carpet, good grade. No. 1 patent leather dash, hung on a steel frame, securely bolted to body; whipsocket, toerail, anti-rattlers, washers and wrench, storm apron; shafts nicely leather trimmed and well ironed.

GEAR—1$\frac{1}{16}$-inch double collar, swaged and fantailed, made of refined steel with axle caps cemented and clipped to axles with Norway iron clips and bolts. Full circle fifth wheel. Reaches ironed full length, bolted and braced with wrought iron stay braces.

WHEELS—Sarven's patent, 1-inch steel oval edge tires; height, 38 inches front and 42 inches rear. Made of selected second growth hickory and fully warranted.

PAINTING—Body, black, nicely gold striped; gear, dark Brewster green or carmine, neatly striped.

TOP—Four bows; full heavy weight first quality rubber, inside of top and back stays lined with dark green wool cloth, leather valance, stitched; sewed on.

TRACK—4 feet 8 inches or 5 feet 2 inches.

No. 11R803 Price, with heavy rubber top.............................$49.75
Price, with machine buffed leather quarter top....................... 52.75
Price, with machine buffed full leather top.......................... 55.75

EXTRAS.

Both pole and shafts complete.. 3.00
Pole with neckyoke and whiffletree in place of shafts................ 1.50
1⅛-inch axles and wheels... 2.50
Genuine leather upholstering... 2.50

Delivered free on board cars at the factory in Brighton, Ohio.
This buggy will weigh, crated for shipment, about 650 pounds.

No. 11R804 Same description as No. 11R803, only hung on two elliptic end springs. Price...$49.75

No. 11R805 Same description as No. 11R803, only hung on three springs, one in front and two in rear. Price..................................$50.75

$57.75—BUILT TO ORDER—$57.75.

If you do not find in our regular line just what you want, perhaps we can build this job to suit you.

We have to run this job through our factories one at a time, which adds greatly to the cost of production, and we must have time to build it, as it is built up after your order is received.

Covered by our One-Year Binding Guarantee.

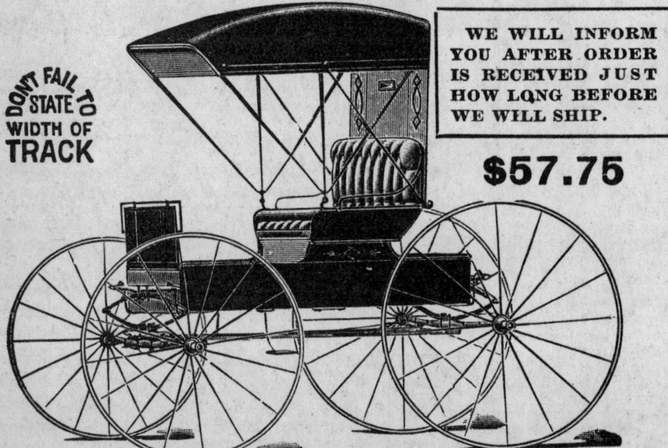

WE WILL INFORM YOU AFTER ORDER IS RECEIVED JUST HOW LONG BEFORE WE WILL SHIP.

$57.75

No. 11R809

GENERAL DESCRIPTION.

Note the choice we give on this buggy.

BODY—19, 22 or 23 inches wide by 54 inches long, concave seat risers and convex panels; screwed, glued and plugged; well seasoned material, with full length body loops, well ironed and braced. Piano box, as illustrated, or Corning body if ordered.

GEAR—Axles $\frac{15}{16}$-inch, 1500-mile long distance, with felt pad dust proof bell collar; refined steel; all wood parts carefully selected second growth hickory, fully ironed and braced, with wrought and Norway iron. Quick shifting shaft couplers.

SPRINGS—Oil tempered, full sweep elliptic end springs, as shown in illustration, with wood spring bar. If ordered, will give you choice of the following: Brewster side bar, or Brewster side bar in combination with coil springs; elliptic end springs, with Bailey body loops or longitudinal springs; Armstrong single leaf end spring, with or without longitudinal spring.

WHEELS—Sarven's patent or compressed band wood hub, as desired; $\frac{38}{42}$, $\frac{36}{40}$, or $\frac{40}{44}$, as ordered, with ¾, ⅞ or 1-inch tread. All wheels made of carefully selected second growth hickory, with screwed rims. Tires fitted hot, full bolted between every spoke.

UPHOLSTERING—We will upholster this job in Keratol leather, dark green body cloth, or light colored whipcord, as ordered, any style shown in our catalogue; comes regular as shown, if not otherwise specified. Solid panel back, with springs in cushion and backs.

TOP—Three or four-bow leather quarters, cut deep, with heavy rubber roof and back curtain, lined, good grade head lining to correspond with color of upholstering. Can furnish two and one-half or three and one-half bow handy top when ordered. Can furnish good quality rubber top, in place of leather quarter, if desired

PAINTING—Comes regular with body black, gear dark Brewster green; can stripe body and gear, if desired. Can furnish gear painted carmine, New York red, black, or coach green. Fancy seat risers when ordered.

TRIMMINGS—Comes regular with full length carpet and lined panels, shafts, wrench, anti-rattler dash, whipsocket, storm apron and rubber boot. Can furnish with or without nickel mountings, with or without rubber padded steps.

No. 11R809 Price, as described, on cars at Brighton, Ohio, or Kalamazoo, Michigan....................$57.75

EXTRAS.

Pole in place of shafts.............................$ 1.50
Both pole and shafts................................. 3.00
Genuine leather upholstering......................... 1.50
Full leather top..................................... 3.50
Leather side curtains................................ 3.50
Leather covered bow sockets.......................... 2.50
Leather boot... 1.00
Rubber dust hood.....................................$1.25
1⅛-inch wheels....................................... 2.00
Brake.. 5.00
¾-inch Goodyear rubber tires......................... 12.45
⅞-inch Goodyear rubber tires......................... 13.45
1-inch Goodyear rubber tires......................... 15.50

Shipping weight, about 500 pounds.

You must give us full set of specifications on this "Built-to-Order Buggy," and allow for all extras.

OUR $29.95 THREE-SPRING HANDY WAGON.

No. 11R1003

GENERAL DESCRIPTION.

BODY—The body is 28 inches wide and 6 feet long, outside measurement, having two full sized seats; is well ironed throughout; both seats are made removable; seats are made with good, comfortable wide backs, as illustrated.

GEAR—The gear is made with 1-inch axle in front, 1⅛-inch axle in rear.

WHEELS—⅞-inch Sarven's patent, ¾-inch steel tires.

SPRINGS—The springs are 1¼-inch, oil tempered elliptic.

PAINTING—It is well painted and artistically striped. Body, black; gear, dark green; or, if desired, body and gear oak grained without extra charge.

At $29.95 we offer this Three-Spring Handy Wagon, delivered on board the cars at the factory in Southern Ohio, as the equal of three-spring wagons that retail at $45.00 to $50.00; two-seat, light, three-spring, handy wagon at $29.95 is offered at **the lowest price at which a reliable three-spring wagon can be built.**

At our special $29.95 price we furnish this rig complete, trimmed in imitation leather, and with wrench, anti-rattlers and shafts. Track, 4 feet 8 inches or 5 feet 2 inches. State width required.

No. 11R1003 Our special price.......................................**$29.95**

EXTRAS.

Pole with neckyoke and whiffletree complete in place of shafts......	1.50
Both pole and shafts....................................	3.00
Brake...	4.00

Weight, crated, about 700 pounds.

We buy this wagon in Southern Ohio; freight rates the same as from Brighton, Ohio.

OUR $34.95 THREE-SPRING WAGON.

$34.95
DON'T FAIL TO STATE WIDTH OF TRACK

No. 11R1009

GENERAL DESCRIPTION.

BODY—The body is 7 feet long and 32 inches wide, with panels 8 inches deep. This body is extra strong, having side and end sills 3¼x1⅛ inches, mortised with a 2¾-inch center sill, running full length, mortised in the cross sill; drop end gate.

SPRINGS—In this, our three-spring gear, the springs are made by D. W. Schuler & Son, of the best oil tempered spring steel, thoroughly tested. Front spring, 1⅜-inch, four-leaf; rear spring, 1¼-inch, four-leaf.

GEAR—The axles are 1$\frac{1}{16}$-inch, double collar, made of the best refined steel, with axle beds cemented, clipped and bolted to axles. The rear axle is coached, front axle is full fantailed, full bearing, short turn fifth wheel. Heavy double reaches, well ironed, full length, braced and bolted with wrought iron stay braces.

WHEELS—The wheels are Sarven's patent, best air seasoned, selected second growth hickory; 1-inch tire, full bolted to rims between each spoke.

SEATS—Two high back solid panel seats, as illustrated. They are large and roomy, removable, and ironed throughout with best Norway iron.

TRIMMINGS—Seat and back cushions are nicely upholstered with the long wear genuine whipcord, imitation leather, or genuine leather. Genuine leather is $3.00 extra.

PAINTING—Body, black or Brewster green, nicely decorated; gear, green or carmine, neatly striped.

No. 11R1009 Price, complete.......................................**$34.95**

EXTRAS.

Canopy top with full length side and back curtains................	12.00
Brake...	4 00
Both pole and shafts....................................	3.00
Seat and back cushions upholstered with genuine leather..........	3.00
Pole in place of shafts..................................	1.50

Weight, complete, crated for shipment, about 800 pounds.

Shipped from Eastern Ohio or Kalamazoo, Mich., from which point the customer pays the freight.

OUR WAGONS STAND HARD TESTS.

SECANE, Delaware Co., Pa., October 17, 1901.

SEARS, ROEBUCK & CO., Chicago, Illinois.

In regard to your spring wagon will say that we drove the wagon from Lebanon, Ky., to Denver, Colo., crossing the Ozark Mountains in Missouri. Then back to Brookfield, Mo., and from there to Florida, crossing the Cumberland Mountains in Tennessee and Alabama; and from Florida to Pennsylvania, crossing the Sand Mountain in Alabama. The wagon carried from 700 to 800 pounds all the time. We never broke anything and was not out a cent for repairs, only having the hind tires shrunk. We bought the wagon in June, 1900.

Yours truly, SHERMAN ECKER.

OUR $35.95 COMBINATION PLATFORM SPRING WAGON.

$35.95
DON'T FAIL TO STATE WIDTH OF TRACK

No. 11R1015

GENERAL DESCRIPTION.

BODY—The body is 7 feet long and 32 inches wide, with panels 8 inches deep. This body is extra strong, having side and end sills 3¼x1⅛ inches, mortised, with a 2¾-inch center sill, running full length, mortised in the cross sill. Drop end gate.

SEATS—In this wagon we furnish two high back, solid panel seats, as illustrated. They are large and roomy, removable, and ironed throughout with best Norway iron.

SPRINGS—In this, our half platform gear, the springs are made by D. W. Schuler & Son, of the best oil tempered spring steel, thoroughly tested. Front spring 1⅜ inches, four-leaf; rear spring 1¼ inches, four-leaf.

GEAR—The axles are 1$\frac{1}{16}$-inch, double collar, made of the best refined steel, with axle beds cemented, clipped and bolted to axles. The rear axle is coached, front axle is full fantailed, full circle bearing, short turn fifth wheel. Heavy double reaches, well ironed, full length, braced and bolted with wrought iron stay braces.

WHEELS—The wheels are Sarven's patent, best air seasoned, selected second growth hickory. 1-inch tires, full bolted to rims between each spoke.

TRIMMINGS—Seat and back cushions are nicely upholstered with the long wear genuine whipcord, imitation leather or genuine leather. Genuine leather $3.00 extra.

PAINTING—Body, black or Brewster green, nicely decorated; gear, green or carmine, neatly striped.

No. 11R1015 Price, complete.......................................**$35.95**

EXTRAS.

Canopy top with full length side and back curtains................	12.00
Brake...	4.00
Both pole and shafts....................................	3.00
Seat and back cushions upholstered in genuine leather............	3.00
Pole in place of shafts..................................	1.50

Weight complete, crated for shipment, about 800 pounds.

Shipped from Eastern Ohio or Kalamazoo, Mich., from which point the customer pays the freight.

$59.60 HEAVY THREE-SEAT FULL PLATFORM WAGON.

No. 11R1021

We have a large demand for these wagons among liverymen, who use it for carrying six or more passengers, or for carrying one or two passengers with several trunks or sample cases. It is also used very largely in the far West.

At $59.60 we furnish this heavy, three-seat full platform wagon, delivered on board the cars at the factory in Southern Ohio, from which point the customer pays the freight.

GENERAL DESCRIPTION.

BODY—Body is made of the very best selected material. Solid ash sills, well ironed, glued, screwed and plugged. It is 8 feet 6 inches long and 3 feet 2 inches wide. Has a drop end gate with snap lock springs. We furnish three large roomy seats with full backs, as shown in illustration.

GEAR—1¼-inch double collar steel axles. Full circle fifth wheel. All clips are of the best wrought and Norway iron.

WHEELS—Sarven's patent hub, made of selected hickory, fully warranted; 1¼-inch oval edge tires.

SPRINGS—Full platform, coupled together with equalizing shackles, strong and durable, having a capacity of 1,800 pounds, and will carry more on good roads.

TRIMMINGS—Seat cushions and backs upholstered with Evans' enameled finished leather, nicely tufted. Seat cushions have full length falls to bottom of buggy.

PAINTING—Body, black; gear, dark Brewster green, or carmine, as ordered.

TRACK—4 feet 8 inches or 5 feet 2 inches. In ordering, give track required.

No. 11R1021 This wagon comes complete with pole, neckyoke and whiffletree, for.......................................**$59.60**

EXTRAS.

Canopy top complete with full rolled up side and back curtains....	12.00
Genuine machine tufted leather cushions and backs................	8.00
Brake...	4.00

Shipping weight, about 950 pounds.

Shipped from Southern Ohio. Freight rates same as from our Brighton, Ohio, factory.

READ CAREFULLY ON PAGE 362, HOW OUR RIGS ARE BUILT.

OUR $36.90 HALF-PLATFORM SPRING DELIVERY WAGON.

WITH FLARING SIDEBOARDS.

$38.90 WITH HIGH SEAT. $36.90 AS ILLUSTRATED. DON'T FAIL TO STATE WIDTH OF TRACK

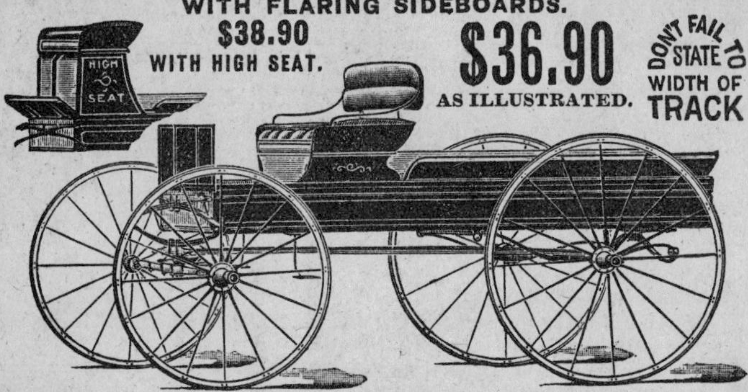

No. 11R1027

This is a strong, well built, well ironed, well finished wagon. Guaranteed by the manufacturers and by us.

GENERAL DESCRIPTION.

BODY—The body is 7 feet long, 36 inches wide, with drop hinged end gate, snap spring fasteners; fitted regularly with one seat with cushion and double roll upholstered lazy back as illustrated. The body is well ironed, well braced, well bolted and hung on a good, strong, well finished gear.

SPRINGS—Half-platform rear springs, with elliptic end spring.

GEAR—The axles are 1⅛-inch, double collar, made or the best refined steel with hickory axle bed, cemented, steel clipped and bolted. Fitted with a full bearing fifth wheel; good reaches, well ironed, braced and bolted with wrought iron stay braces.

WHEELS—Sarven's patent, 1⅛-inch, made of good selected air seasoned hickory stock, fully warranted.

TRIMMINGS—Seat and lazy back are upholstered in good wear imitation leather.

PAINTING—This wagon is well painted. Body, black with suitable striping; gear, green or red, as desired. Lettered to order when so requested at 5 cents per plain letter, or 10 cents per gold letter. Furnished with substantial, well ironed shafts, anti-rattlers, wrench and washers.

TRACK—4 feet 8 inches or 5 feet 2 inches. State width required.

No. 11R1027 Price, all complete, at factory in Southern Ohio **$36.90**
Price of wagon with high seat extra, as illustrated **38.90**

EXTRAS.

Brake	4.00
Pole with neckyoke aud whiffletree in place of shafts	1.50
Both pole and shafts complete	3.00

For same style wagon as above with 1¼-inch axles and 1¼-inch Sarven's patent wheels, extra heavy 1½-inch springs, complete with shafts, add $7.00 to the above prices.

We can furnish this wagon in a lighter build—1-inch axles, hung on three elliptic springs, body 6 feet long by 31 inches wide, for $34.95.

Weight, crated for shipment, about 800 pounds.

Shipped from the factory at Brighton, Ohio; customer pays freight.

OUR $56.90 RURAL MAIL DELIVERY WAGON.

$56.90 DON'T FAIL TO STATE WIDTH OF TRACK

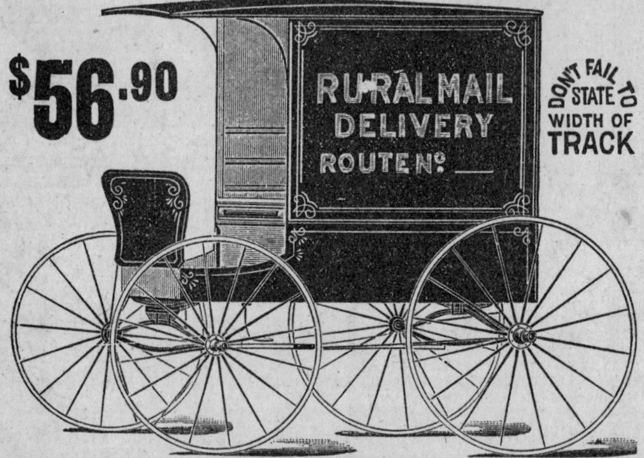

No. 11R1033

GENERAL DESCRIPTION.

BODY—The body is 5 feet 9 inches long and 3 feet wide, outside measure; is paneled on the lower side 15 inches up, and has 17-inch tail gate, heavy, well finished duck sides and roof, with moldings all around edges; rubber roll-up curtain at the rear end, heavy duck; well tufted, well finished, good wearing cushion, with a good, substantial, well braced, well ironed dashboard.

WHEELS—Sarven's patent or wood hub, 38 and 42 inches high, 1$\frac{1}{16}$-inch hickory spokes with screws in rims at each side of spokes; 1 by ¼-inch best steel tires, projecting over the rims and full bolted between each spoke.

AXLES—The axles are 1 inch, made of the best axle steel, drop forged double collar, half patent.

SPRINGS—The springs are four-leaf, half patent, 1¼ inches wide, made of best oil tempered spring steel in combination with the drop forged axle, allowing the bed to be dropped much lower than is possible with the ordinary springs—ideal for this wagon, for this purpose. Short turn full bearing fifth wheel.

Shipped from Southern Ohio. **Shipped as a standing top; cannot be knocked down.**

No. 11R1033 Price, all complete **$56.90**

EXTRAS.

Pole in place of shafts	1.50
Both pole and shafts	3.00
Brake complete	4.00
Genuine leather upholstering in place of duck	2.50

Lettering, as shown, extra. Plain letters, each, 5 cents; gold finished letters, 10 cents each.

Weight, about 400 pounds; weight, crated for shipment, about 550 pounds; capacity, 600 pounds.

OUR $59.75 PONTIAC SPECIAL MILK WAGON.

$59.75 DON'T FAIL TO STATE WIDTH OF TRACK

No. 11R1035

GENERAL DESCRIPTION.

BODY—Body is made from the best seasoned wood. It is 7 feet long, 2 feet 10 inches wide. It is a complete knock down body, put together with twelve iron rods. It stands only 27 inches from the ground and will turn around in a circle of 12 feet.

DOORS—This rig is fitted with steel patent sliding doors with glass panel in upper half of door. Front is fitted with solid panel at bottom and swinging glass panel at top; front sides fitted with glass panels or white enamel oil duck. This rig is fitted with our own patent short turn wrought iron fifth wheel.

AXLES—Axles come regularly 1-inch, of the best crucible steel, double collar. For $4.00 extra we can furnish a heavier gear throughout with a 1⅛-inch axle. If 1⅛-inch axles are wanted, be sure to state so and include $4.00.

PAINTING—This rig is painted in the very best manner. Body, dark blue or dark green, with vermilion striping; gear, wine color, nicely striped. The carrying capacity of this wagon is 700 pounds.

TRACK—4 feet 8 inches or 5 feet 2 inches. State width required.

WHEELS—Wheels are No. 1 grade Sarven's patent or compressed band. They are well bolted, round edge tires, extra thick, crimped and bolted between each spoke.

No. 11R1035 Price, complete **$59.75**

EXTRAS.

1⅛-inch axles	4.00
Brake	4.00
Both pole and shafts	3.00
Pole in place of shafts	1.50

Weight, crated for shipment, about 800 pounds.
Shipped from Southern Michigan.

OUR $59.85 SPECIAL GROCERY WAGON.

$59.85 DON'T FAIL TO STATE WIDTH OF TRACK

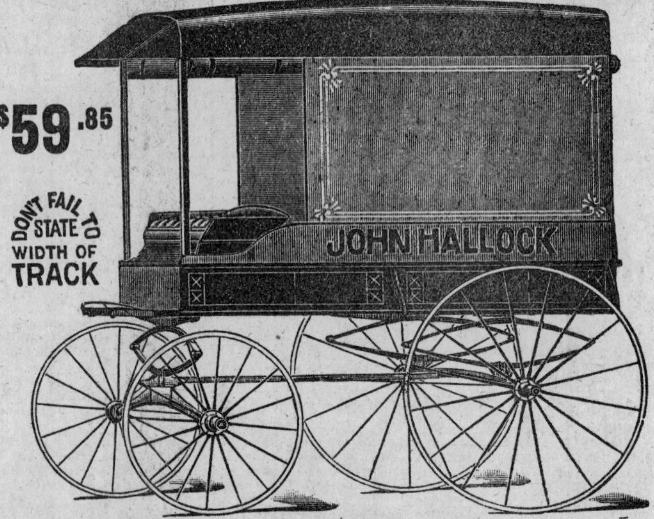

No. 11R1039

GENERAL DESCRIPTION.

BODY—The body is 5 feet 9 inches long, 3 feet 3 inches wide, outside measurement; drop hinged end gate with snap spring fasteners, hardwood bolted sills, hardwood stringers, fully iron angled and corner braced, strong and durable.

GEAR—The axles are 1⅛-inch best axle steel; front axle arched, cemented and clipped to hickory axle bed; rear axle the same size, with springs, block mounted and double clipped. The reaches are fully ironed and truss braced. The body is hung to carry up level when loaded.

WHEELS—The wheels are Sarven's patent; full 1⅛-inch oval edged best steel tires.

SPRINGS—Elliptic, six-leaf, 1¼-inch front ribbed spring, four-leaf 1¼-inch rear ribbed springs, made of the best oil tempered spring steel. The front spring is securely bolted to the head block, double clipped and bolted to hardwood strong body spring bar; rear springs are double bolted to axle, hardwood wide cross body brace.

TRIMMINGS—Sides and rear curtain are extra quality, standard, well wearing curtain material; a good, substantial, long wearing seat cushion. The front end and top have a gradual slope with a scoop weather hood.

PAINTING—The body is well painted, neatly striped and decorated. The gear is painted to correspond. The wagon complete is nicely finished.

CAPACITY—800 to 1,000 pounds.

WEIGHT—About 600 pounds, all complete.

No. 11R1039 Price, complete **$59.85**

EXTRAS.

Pole in place of shafts	1.50
Both pole and shafts complete	3.00
Brake	4.00

Shipping weight, securely crated, about 700 pounds.

Shipped from Southern Ohio, from which point the customer pays the freight.

No. 11R1203

OUR FAMOUS SEARS WAGON

HIGHEST GRADE FARM WAGON BUILT.

$39.70 TO $46.30 AS ILLUSTRATED, WITHOUT BRAKE.

OFFERED AT A PRICE based on the actual cost of material and labor, the best farm wagon built, shipped from the best factory in Indiana. We have agreed with the manufacturer not to use his name, but it is a wagon that sells everywhere under its own name at $5.00 to $15.00 more than any other standard wagon.

FURNISHED in wide or narrow track, as desired, either stiff or drop tongue, any width tire. If you want wider than regular tire add to the price of the wagon $2.00 for each one-half inch wider than regular; that is, if you want a 2-inch tire on wagon you will add $2.00 to price of wagon; if you want box brake, add $2.50; gear brake, add $4.00.

At these special prices we furnish these wagons delivered free on board the cars in Indiana. Customer pays freight.

Number	Size of skein	Height of wheels		Length of bed outside	Width of bed		Height of bed		Size of tires	Carrying capacity	Weight, complete (about)	Price, complete		Weight of gear (about)	Price for gear only	
		Front	Hind		Narrow track	Wide track	Lower side	Top side				Cast skeins	Steel skeins		Cast skeins	Steel skeins
11R1203	2½x 8 in.	3 ft. 8 in.	4 ft. 6 in.	10 ft.	3 ft. 2 in.	3 ft. 6 in.	11 in.	7 in.	1⅜x7/16 in.	1,500 lbs.	800 lbs.	$39.70	$42.55	520 lbs.	$30.70	$33.55
	2¾x 8 in.	3 ft. 8 in.	4 ft. 6 in.	10 ft.	3 ft. 2 in.	3 ft. 6 in.	12 in.	8 in.	1½x½ in.	2,000 lbs.	860 lbs.	41.35	44.65	575 lbs.	31.90	35.25
	3 x 9 in.	3 ft. 8 in.	4 ft. 6 in.	10 ft. 6 in.	3 ft. 2 in.	3 ft. 6 in.	12 in.	10 in.	1½x9/16 in.	2,500 lbs.	975 lbs.	43.25	46.55	695 lbs.	33.80	37.10
	3¼x10 in.	3 ft. 8 in.	4 ft. 6 in.	10 ft. 6 in.	3 ft. 2 in.	3 ft. 6 in.	14 in.	10 in.	1½x9/16 in.	3,800 lbs.	1,050 lbs.	44.65	48.45	740 lbs.	34.50	38.30
	3½x11 in.	3 ft. 8 in.	4 ft. 6 in.	10 ft. 6 in.	3 ft. 2 in.	3 ft. 6 in.	14 in.	12 in.	1⅝x⅝ in.	4,800 lbs.	1,100 lbs.	46.30	51.05	800 lbs.	35.95	40.65

Extra for box brake, as shown in cut........................$2.50
Extra for gear brake........................4.00
Extra for stiff tongue instead of drop tongue........................1.65
Extra for boot and box........................1.20
Extra for both pole and shafts........................5.00
(We can furnish, when so desired, shafts in place of pole, at same price.)

Extra for any depth of lower box desired at an additional charge per inch........................$0.35
Extra for any depth of top box desired at an additional charge per inch........................ .20
Extra for any length box, per foot or fractional foot........................ .85
Extra for bows and staples, per set of five........................ .90
Extra for second spring seat, if desired........................2.60

THE ABOVE EXTRAS ARE LISTED IN CONNECTION WITH OUR FAMOUS SEARS WAGON, AND CAN ONLY BE FURNISHED AT ABOVE PRICES WITH A COMPLETE WAGON OR GEAR.

OUR $29.95 ONE-HORSE SOLID STEEL AXLE WAGON.

$29.95 to $40.60 AS ILLUSTRATED.

THIS IS THE BEST SINGLE WAGON ON THE MARKET

Extra for pole in place of shafts........................$2.50
Extra for both pole and shafts........................4.50

AT OUR SPECIAL $29.95 and $40.60 PRICES we furnish this wagon complete with double box, spring seat and shafts. Box Brake........................$2.50 extra.
Gear Brake........................$3.50

No. 11R1209

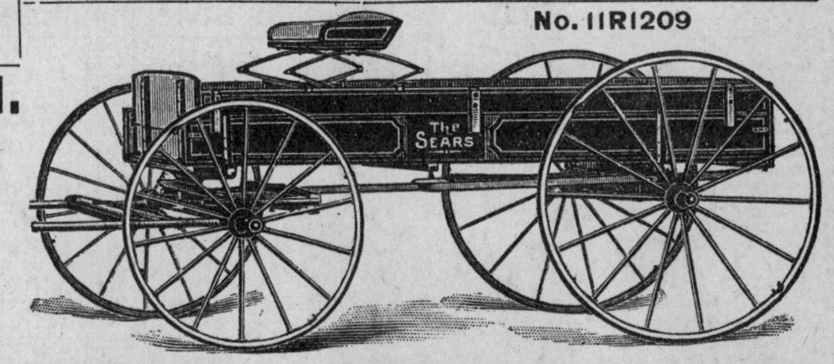

Number	Steel axles		Height of wheels		Dimensions of bed, outside measure				Capacity	Weight, complete	Price, complete	Price of running gear
	Size of arms	Size of tires	Front	Hind	Length	Width of N. T.	Width of W. T.	Depth				
11R1209	1¼x7½ in.	1¼x5/16 in.	3 ft. 6 in.	4 ft.	7 ft. 10 in.	3 ft.	3 ft. 4 in.	9 in.	1,500 lbs.	500 lbs.	$29.95	$24.75
	1⅜x8 in.	1⅜x⅜ in.	3 ft. 6 in.	4 ft.	8 ft. 6 in.	3 ft.	3 ft. 4 in.	10 in.	2,000 lbs.	650 lbs.	33.90	28.50
	1½x8½ in.	1¼x½ in.	3 ft. 6 in.	4 ft.	9 ft.	3 ft.	3 ft. 4 in.	10 in.	2,500 lbs.	750 lbs.	40.60	34.50

BE SURE TO GIVE WIDTH OF TRACK, NARROW OR WIDE.
PRICE FOR ABOVE ONE-HORSE WAGON IS FOR WAGON DELIVERED ON BOARD CARS IN INDIANA. CUSTOMER PAYS FREIGHT.
Third top box, depth 6 inches, on any size wagon, $2.50. We furnish the third top box in depth as high as 15 inches at 40 cents for each additional inch over 6 inches.

No. 11R1215

OUR GIANT HANDY WAGON.

Our Giant Handy Wagon is popular because of its everlasting wearing qualities and general convenience. In the harvest field it saves high loading; it is ideal in drawing logs, rails, and for general service around the farm, and on the road, in fact, everywhere. It is less expensive than any other wagon of the same capacity. It can scarcely be overloaded. Furnished according to size from our factory in Western Illinois, shipped knocked down and freighted under the same classification as the ordinary farm wagon. The wagon is guaranteed by the manufacturer and by us to be just as represented in every piece and part. We catalogue it this season at a close price, cash in full with order, to accommodate our regular customers. The customer pays the freight from the factory.

SIZE AND PRICE OF METAL WAGONS AS SHOWN IN ILLUSTRATION.

No.	Wheels	Tires	Carrying Capacity, 4,000 lbs.		Carrying Capacity, 6,000 lbs.		Carrying Capacity, 8,000 lbs.	
			Weight	Price	Weight	Price	Weight	Price
11R1215	22x28 in.	4x⅜ in.	525 lbs.	$22.20	625 lbs.	$27.30	700 lbs.	$32.40
	26x32 in.	4x⅜ in.	555 lbs.	23.05	660 lbs.	28.15	800 lbs.	34.15
	28x34 in.	4x⅜ in.	580 lbs.	23.30	690 lbs.	28.40	820 lbs.	36.60
	30x36 in.	4x⅜ in.	590 lbs.	23.90	700 lbs.	29.00	840 lbs.	37.55
	32x38 in.	4x⅜ in.	620 lbs.	24.75	720 lbs.	29.85	850 lbs.	39.25
	34x40 in.	4x⅜ in.	640 lbs.	25.60	740 lbs.	30.70	870 lbs.	40.90
	36x42 in.	4x⅜ in.	660 lbs.	26.45	760 lbs.	31.50	890 lbs.	42.65
	38x44 in.	4x⅜ in.	680 lbs.	27.35	780 lbs.	32.45	910 lbs.	44.40

If Tires on Wheels are One-Half Inch Thick Add Forty Pounds to the Weight.

EXTRAS.

If tires ½-inch thick are wanted, add........................$1.20
If tires 5 inches wide are wanted, add........................1.20
If tires 6 inches wide are wanted, add........................2.50
If tires 7 inches wide are wanted, add........................3.80
If tires 8 inches wide are wanted, add........................$5.10
If neckyoke, single and doubletree are wanted, add........................1.60
If brake is wanted, add........................3.00

All sizes obtainable are quoted in the above table. In ordering be particular to give the size of wheels required, width of tires, carrying capacity and width of track, 4 feet 6 inches or 5 feet, and send with your order the full amount of money.

This wagon comes with pole complete as shown in illustration, without whiffletree or neckyoke. If desired, we can send it fitted with shafts instead of pole at same price.

PRICE FOR EXTRAS APPLY ONLY WHEN FURNISHED IN CONNECTION WITH A REGULAR ORDER FOR WAGON, AS EXTRAS ARE NOT SOLD SEPARATELY AT THE PRICES QUOTED

AN IDEAL WAGON BOX.

No. 11R1221 Owing to the constant demand from our customers for a thoroughly well made wagon box, we have decided to catalogue one at a price but little in advance of the factory cost. We can furnish this substantial, well built, well finished box, guaranteed as represented, at our factory in Indiana, at the following factory prices:

Be careful to give exact measurements between standards on bolster.

Our 10-foot 6-inch box with bottom bed, 14 inches deep; top box, 12 inches deep, to fit bolsters 38 or 42 inches between standards, for........................$9.85
For bottom box, 15 inches deep, and top box, 13 inches deep, add........................ .45
For third or tiptop box, 9 inches high, no irons on edge, add........................1.75

For high grade spring seat, two heavy leaf springs, add........................$1.85
If a lazy back is desired, add........................ .20
For box brake attached, add........................1.80

WE DO NOT SELL EITHER BOTTOM OR TOP BOX SEPARATELY. We furnish extras at the above prices only when ordered in connection with a complete box. Customer pays freight from our factory in Indiana.

OUR FULTON SPECIAL ROAD CART, $9.75.

Our FULTON SPECIAL ROAD CART is made throughout of CAREFULLY SELECTED MATERIAL. EVERY PIECE and PART COVERED by our BINDING GUARANTEE.

The workmanship is first class, and the illustration shows the cart just as it will appear when you have received it at your freight station.

The wheels are Sarven's patent, 46 inches high, 1-inch oval edge steel tires. The cart is very strong and thoroughly well made, nicely finished in wine color; carrying capacity, two passengers. All wood parts, seat and spring block are made of carefully selected seasoned timber; shafts, cross bar and shaft circle are of select hickory; 1-inch double collar steel axle, square at shoulders, octagon in center, hung so as to be perfectly balanced on long, easy riding, oil tempered springs. Seat 30 inches wide from rail to rail, long bent seat arm. Made in either width of track, narrow, 4 feet 8 inches, or wide, 5 feet 2 inches. **In ordering state width of track required.**

No. 11R1045 Price, cash in full with order **$9.75**

EXTRAS.

We can hang this cart on coil springs instead of the long elliptic springs for..... **$1.00**

We can furnish tight foot rack, if desired, for.......... **.65**

The price quoted is for the cart delivered free on board the cars at Chicago. Customer pays the freight.

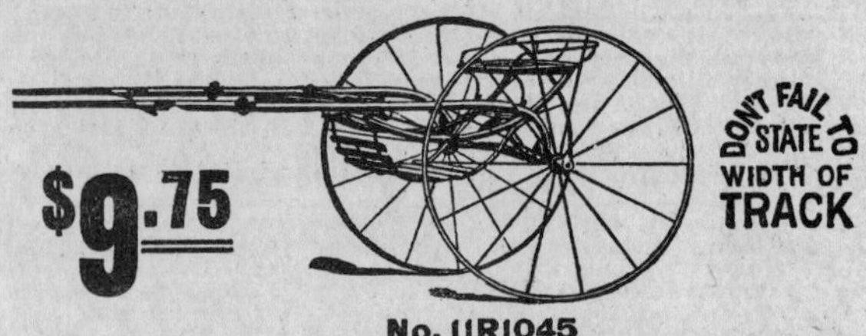

$9.75
DON'T FAIL TO STATE WIDTH OF TRACK

No. 11R1045

The weight of the cart, ready for shipment, is about 150 pounds.

Department of Cutters.

OUR CUTTERS are built at our own factory under the supervision of our own foreman, finished in our own finishing rooms, and we are able to guarantee them exactly as represented.

WE BUILD FOUR STANDARD STYLES, including an up to date bob sleigh, each the latest model for the coming season. We are able to make these remarkable prices by building cutters on the long run plan, using the latest automatic labor saving machines, avoiding changes in style and finish, bringing the price of manufacturing to the lowest notch, making direct factory shipments to the customers at the actual factory cost with but a single manufacturing profit added, selling them $5.00 to $10.00 less than retail prices.

DO NOT WRITE US FOR OTHER STYLES, peculiar finish, or special upholstering except as provided in the extras. Our prices will not allow changes; we are not in the market to supply anything else; our season's output will be finished and ready before the snow flies. **We are prepared to make prompt shipments of either style, but we cannot supply other styles at any price.**

ORDERS FROM MIDDLEMEN, jobbers or implement dealers generally, will be promptly handled at the exact same price and terms as quoted. All of our cutters are sold under our vehicle binding guarantee, sold at the actual factory cost, with but a small factory working profit added.

Each cutter is fitted, finished and trimmed as described. Our remarkable prices are possible only by avoiding changes in style, changes in trimming, changes in painting, etc.

OUR $16.95 PORTLAND CUTTER.

IN FIXING THE PRICE we do not provide for the jobber, the traveling salesman, or the local agent, but we make shipment direct to the customer, pricing this sleigh at the actual factory cost, adding but a single manufacturing profit.

No. 11R1403 Body is made of the best air seasoned selected material, solid panels, guaranteed not to split, warp or crack. Gear is made of selected second growth hickory; double bent knees. Braces, bolts and clips best grade Norway iron. Higgins' best grade hardened steel shoes; seat upholstered in the best possible manner with 14 ounce dark green broadcloth, with spring back and spring cushion. Cushions are removable. Painting is first class, highly polished and neatly ornamented; body, black, neatly striped; gear, Brewster green; nickel plated arm rails and dash rail with steps, nicely trimmed.

No. 11R1403 Price, complete with shafts.......... **$16.95**
Extra for pole in place of shafts.......... **1.25**
Extra if trimmed in plush in place of broadcloth.......... **1.50**
Shipped direct from our factory at Kalamazoo, Mich., from which point the customer pays the freight. Shipping weight, crated, about 200 pounds.

OUR $19.90 IMPERIAL PORTLAND.

THIS OUR SPECIAL $19.90 **Portland Cutter, is the latest in design for this season.** It is modeled after the original Ideal Portland; built from thoroughly seasoned and carefully selected materials. We are furnishing for $19.90 a cutter that cannot be had elsewhere for less than $5.00 to $8.00 more money.

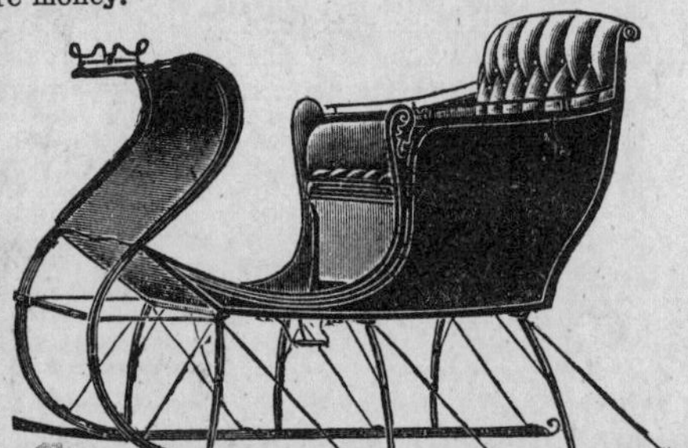

No. 11R1409 Body is large, roomy and comfortable; made with high panels and extra high back; made of the best air seasoned timber, solid panels. All joints are reinforced, screwed, glued and plugged. Gear is made of the best selected second growth hickory; double bent knees. Braces, bolts and clips from the best Norway iron. Higgins' best grade hardened steel shoes, securely bolted to runners. Painted in the highest style of the art, highly polished, neatly striped and ornamented. Body black, striped in gold bronze and carmine. Gear, Brewster green, striped in gold bronze. Seat upholstered in heavy 14-ounce English green broadcloth. Full spring back and spring cushion; cushions are removable; curved dash with side wings and nickel plated dash rail. Nickel plated arm rails; neat foot steps and nicely trimmed shafts.

No. 11R1409 Price, complete with shafts.......... **$19.90**
Extra for pole in place of shafts.......... **1.25**
Extra if trimmed in plush in place of broadcloth.......... **1.50**
Shipped direct from our factory at Kalamazoo, Michigan, from which point the customer pays the freight. Shipping weight, crated, about 200 pounds.

Prices on Vehicles are Subject to Advance Without Notice.

The steel market is such that we are looking for higher prices in springs, axles, wheels, etc. Buggies may cost from $1.00 to $3.00 more to build; surreys, $3.00 to $5.00 more. We will fill orders at printed prices as long as our material on hand lasts; if it is then higher we will claim the right to advance our prices to cover the exact difference of cost of material to us.

OUR $22.50 FINEST STANHOPE PORTLAND CUTTER.

OUR FINEST CUTTER the New Stanhope Portland at **$22.50,** made in our own factory at Kalamazoo, Mich. Latest in design, latest in finish, thoroughly up to date; offered in competition with cutters that will sell everywhere at $30.00 to $40.00.

No. 11R1415 This, our finest Stanhope Cutter, has a very large body, beautifully designed; solid panels, extra high side panels, with "O G" shaped, handsomely hand carved effect; curved bracket front and round molding; special constructed and steam curved wing dash, elegantly proportioned with wings on side and mounted with nickel plated dash rail. Gear made throughout of the best selected air seasoned material; second growth hickory double bent knees; ornamented steps; Higgins' best grade hardened steel shoes, securely bolted to runners. Painted in the best manner known, tastily striped and ornamented, dark green panels, and dash with black molding handsomely striped; Brewster green gear, with gold bronze striping. Seat upholstered in the highest style of the art with heavy green English broadcloth. Full spring cushion and spring back. Cushions are removable. Nickel plated arm rails; nicely trimmed shafts.

No. 11R1415 Price, complete with shafts.......... **$22.50**
Extra for pole in place of shafts.......... **1.25**
Extra if trimmed in plush in place of broadcloth.......... **1.50**
Shipped direct from our factory at Kalamazoo, Mich., from which point customer pays freight.
Shipping weight, crated about 200 pounds.

OUR $46.90 RUSSIAN BOB SLEIGH.

No. 11R1421 Our Russian beauty combines elegance and comfort, is strictly high grade throughout, is such a sleigh as is usually sold from the boulevard city repositories at from $65.00 to $80.00.

Our Russian two-seat beauty is built at our own factory, built and finished during our dull season in the carriage trade, and shipped direct to our customer from our factory finishing rooms.

The gear is made of select seasoned second growth stock, full bent raves, not sawed. Heavy steel shoes, with wrought iron fancy scroll braces, with Norway iron clips, rivets and bolts throughout, strong and durable. Wide, roomy, comfortable body, twenty-four inches high, built in solid, thirty-six inches wide, deep sides. One-piece panels, thoroughly glued, screwed and plugged. Double sweep easy back, shaped for comfort and elegance. Bent curved front, with handsome flaring wing dash, mounted with fine nickel screen with artistic body panels. Spring backs and cushion, richly upholstered with imported English broadcloth. The body panels are painted green, moldings black, artistically decorated. Gear, dark Brewster green, striped to harmonize with the body.

We make no changes in this high grade sleigh whatever; it is the latest model; it is our two-seated cutter bargain, built to discount competition in any market. We positively cannot change the finish or the upholstering to accommodate anyone. We do not build any other style two-seated sleigh. **The price is the same whether one or one dozen is ordered at one time, or a carload to a dealer at the same price. Remember, on this two-seated high grade cutter, one style and one finish only.**

No. 11R1421 Price, complete with shafts.......... **$46.90**
Extra for pole in place of shafts.......... **1.50**
Shipped from our own factory at Kalamazoo, Mich., from which point the customer pays the freight.
Shipping weight, crated, about 400 pounds.

HARNESS DEPARTMENT.

WE INVITE ATTENTION to our very complete Harness and Saddlery Department. On this line of goods we undersell the retail dealer by a big margin, as in most cases our prices to you are less than the prices at which manufacturers and jobbers sell to the ordinary retail dealer. It is no exaggeration for us to say that WE CAN SAVE YOU FROM 35 TO 50 PER CENT on these goods, besides giving you a LARGER assortment and a BETTER grade of merchandise than is found in the regular harness stores in other towns.

WE HANDLE THE VERY BEST OF HARNESS that is possible to be made. Our harness is made of the very best of high grade leather with fine trimmings. Our single and double buggy harness is of the very latest styles and the trimmings the very best nickel composition or Davis rubber trimmings. Our Farm, Team and Concord Harness is of the very best that can be made, and we invite the closest comparison of quality and price.

OUR ONLY TERMS ARE CASH WITH THE ORDER. We have discontinued C. O. D. shipments purely in the interest of our customers in order to do away with an expense, which saving permits us to make lower prices than ever, as fully explained on page 1 of this catalogue. Our Harness and Saddlery Goods are fully guaranteed by us. We know they are reliable and just as we describe them. If you order anything from this department and it does not prove entirely satisfactory in every particular, simply return it to us and we will return your money pleasantly, together with what you paid for transportation. Our motto is: "Entire satisfaction or your money back."

NOTICE. WE WILL MAKE ANY CHANGE you want in any of our team harness you may order from our catalogue, and only charge you what it costs us to make such changes, except where we say no changes made. ALWAYS STATE the parts you want in place of the ones which are listed with the harness. ALWAYS STATE the size of collar wanted when ordering the harness with collars or in ordering sweat pads; if you want a harness without the collar always state the size of hames it will require to fit your collar. ALWAYS STATE the kind of checks wanted, whether overchecks or side checks. IF YOU DO NOT STATE the kind of check wanted, we will send you overcheck. ALWAYS STATE the style of the harness you want, whether single or double, also the kind of trimmings, whether XC, nickel or imitation rubber. ALWAYS STATE the weight of your horse. Give us the measurement of your horse around girth where saddle or pad work, and from gig saddle to horse's tail. The size of bridle from bit ring to bit ring over the head, and state style of horse, if long ranged or short chunky horse.

HARNESS DEALERS, LIVERY MEN, everyone interested in these goods, is invited to compare our prices with what they have been paying for equal goods. Many goods we list dealers can buy from us at less money than they have been paying jobbers and wholesalers. Look carefully over our very complete line of blankets, fly nets, dusters, robes, etc. Nowhere will you find as complete an assortment, nowhere will you be able to match our low prices.

NOTE. EXTRAS: Russet Hand Parts on any harness over $8.00, 25 cents extra. Extra for Buckles on Crupper on Single Harness, 15 cents; Double Harness, 30 cents.

WE MAKE NO CHARGE FOR BOXING, CRATING, PACKING OR CARTAGE, BUT DELIVER ALL GOODS AT ANY EXPRESS OFFICE OR FREIGHT DEPOT IN CHICAGO FREE OF CHARGE.

Single Breast Collar Buggy Harness.

WE MAKE NO CHANGES IN THIS HARNESS.

Our $4.37 Harness

This Harness is large enough for a 900 to 1200-pound horse.

No. 10R1

Bridle, ⅝-inch checks, patent leather blinds, flat winker brace and check reins, ring bit, fancy front and rosettes, overcheck or side reins, as desired; **lines**, ¾-inch flat, all black, to loop in bit; **breast collar**, folded and stitched; **saddle**, 2½-inch, enameled cloth bottom, doubled and stitched bearers; **shaft tugs**, 1-inch with ⅝-inch buckles and ¾-inch bellyband billets; **bellyband**, ⅝-inch flat; **breeching**, folded and stitched, ⅝-inch flat hip strap, ¾-inch turn back, lapped and stitched to crupper pieces, folded crupper, docks sewed on breeching straps, ¾-inch; **traces**, 1-inch doubled and stitched to breast collar. This single buggy harness comes in full XC trimmings, imitation hand sewed. **Shipping weight, 12 pounds.**

No. 10R1 Price.........**$4.37**

Our Texas Single Harness, $4.90.

Our $4.90 Harness

This harness is full size; a cheaper harness must be made smaller size. This harness will be large enough for a 900 to 1200-pound horse. Don't buy a cheaper single harness than this one. We don't make any changes in this harness.

Bridle, ⅝-inch checks, patent leather blinds, flat winker brace and check reins, ring bit, fancy front and rosettes; overcheck or side reins, as desired; **lines**, ¾-inch flat, all black, to loop in bit; **breast collar**, folded and stitched; **gig saddle**, 2¼-inch, enameled cloth bottom, doubled and stitched bearers; **shaft tugs**, 1-inch with ⅝-inch buckles and ¾-inch bellyband billets; **bellyband**, ⅝-inch flat; **breeching**, folded and stitched, ⅝-inch flat hip strap, ¾-inch turn back, lapped and stitched to crupper pieces, folded crupper, docks sewed on breeching straps, ¾-inch; **traces**, 1-inch doubled and stitched to breast collar. This single buggy harness comes in full XC trimmings, imitation hand sewed.

No. 10R5 Price (Weight, about 12 lbs.)....**$4.90**

No. 10R10 Same as the description of No. 10R5 with the exception of collar and hames in place of breast collar, kip collar, any size, traces attached to hames. Price.........**$6.25**

State size of collar wanted. **Weight, about 18 lbs.**

Our Georgia Single Harness, $7.69.

This harness is large enough for 900 to 1200-pound horse.

Bridle, ⅝-inch overcheck, box loops, round winker stay, initial letter rosette; **breast collar**, folded with wide layer and box loops; **traces**, 1-inch, double and stitched, round edge; **breeching**, folded with wide layer; **side straps**, ¾-inch; **hip strap**, ⅝-inch; **turn back**, ¾-inch, round crupper; **saddle**, 2½-inch, single strap, all leather skirts and bottom, patent leather jockey; **bellyband**, Griffith style; **lines**, ⅞x1-inch, all black loop in bit; XC trimmings throughout. This harness will fit 900 to 1200-pound horse.

No. 10R15 Price.........**$7.69**

No. 10R20 Same as the description of No. 10R15 with the exception of collar and hames in place of breast collar, 3½-pound iron hames, box loop, hame tugs, kip collars, 1-inch trace, double and stitched with round edge. Price.........**$8.69**

Weight, about 22 pounds.

Our Vicksburg Single Harness.

Shipping Weight, 20 pounds.

This harness will fit 900 to 1200-pound horse.

Bridle, ⅝-inch overcheck, box loops, round winker stay or side rim; **breast collar**, folded, with layer, box loops; **traces**, 1⅛-inch, doubled and stitched; **breeching**, folded with layer, side straps ⅝-inch, hip strap ⅝-inch, turnback ¾-inch, round crupper sewed on; **saddle**, 3-inch, iron jockey, harness leather skirts, leather bottom, double and stitched shaft rig; **bellyband**, Griffith style only; **lines**, ⅞-inch, all black, to loop bit. Trimming XC or japanned. This harness made for 900 to 1200-pound horses.

No. 10R25 Our special price.........**$7.92**

Will furnish this harness extra large for 1400-pound horses add, extra.........**$1.00**

Add extra for buckle on crupper.........**15c**

No. 10R30 Same style harness as No. 10R25, only made in nickel trimming with **Patent Leather Jockey** saddle, selected quality leather, and smooth hames throughout, always sent with overcheck (unless ordered flat side rein).

Price, for nickel trimmed harness.........**$8.75**

Our Ashby Single Harness with Collar and Hames, $8.97.

For 900 to 1200-pound horse.

Bridle, ⅝-inch box loop check, patent leather blinds, round winker brace, overcheck or side rein; **lines**, ⅞-inch, all black, to loop in bit; **traces**, 1⅛-inch doubled and stitched, round edge finish, 3¼-pound hames, iron hame, full japanned on japanned harness and full XC plate on XC harness; **hame tug** with box loop; **breeching** folded with layer, ⅝-inch single hip strap, ⅝-inch side strap and ¾-inch back strap, with crupper sewed on; **gig saddle**, 2¼-inch single strap skirt, leather bottom with iron jockey; **bellyband flat**, Griffith style only; **collar**, full kip. We do not make any changes in this harness, only furnish it as described above. This harness made in one size only for 900 to 1200-pound horse.

No. 10R35 Our special price with collar....**$8.97**

Weight, boxed, about 35 pounds.

Our Iowa Single Harness.

$8.95

For 900 to 1200-pound horse.
Weight, boxed, 23 pounds.

Lines, a very important point about this harness is 1-inch black line, loop in bit; **extra good stock**; **gig saddle**, extra good single strap, harness leather skirt, with heavy bearer and shaft tug; **bellyband** folds Griffith style, ⅝-inch hip strap, ⅝-inch side strap, ¾-inch turnback scalloped, with round crupper sewed on; **breast collar**, folded with heavy straight layer and box loops; **breeching**, folded with heavy straight layer double and stitched breeching brace; **traces**, the most important part of this harness, are 1⅛ inches by 6 feet long, extra good stock, well made, smooth round edge to buckle in breast collar; **bridle**, ⅝-inch box loops, round winker brace, patent leather blind, overcheck or side rein, fancy front and **initial letter rosette**; **trimmings, fine nickel or Davis imitation rubber.**

No. 10R40 Price, as illustrated.........**$8.95**

Add extra for russet hand parts.........**.25**

Add extra for buckle on crupper.........**.15**

Will make this harness extra large for 1400 to 1600-pound horse add, extra.........**$2.00**

A Regular $25.00 Harness FOR ONLY $11.88

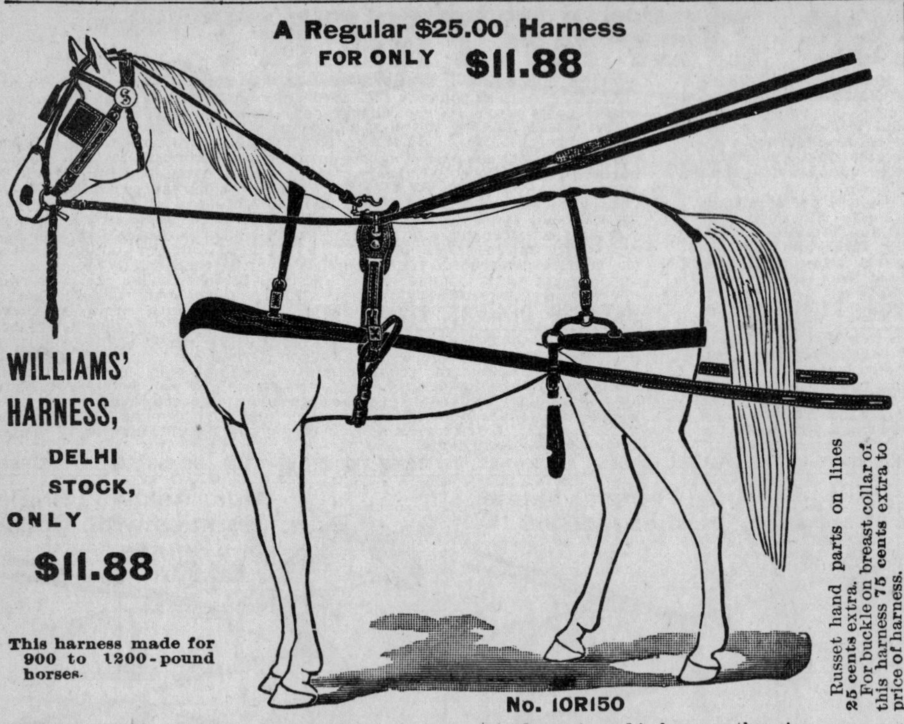

WILLIAMS' HARNESS, DELHI STOCK, ONLY $11.88

This harness made for 900 to 1200-pound horses.

No. 10R150

Russet hand parts on lines 25 cents extra.
For buckle on breast collar of this harness 75 cents extra to price of harness.

GENUINE DELHI LEATHER in every strap, the highest grade stock used in harness, there is no wear out to it. **You can't buy better at any price. Highest grade trimming** throughout; the harness is made by **WILLIAMS**, maker of the best single strap work on the market.

Bridle, ⅝-inch, patent leather blinds, box loops, round winker stay, layer on crown, overcheck with nose piece or round side reins, **initial rosettes**; **breast collar**, extra wide, V shaped; **traces**, 1¼-inch single strap, stitched to breast collar with scalloped points; **breeching**, 1⅜-inch; **side straps**, ⅝-inch; **hip strap**, ¾-inch; **turnback**, ⅞ inch, scalloped with round crupper sewed on; **saddle**, 3-inch, single strap, swell padded patent leather jockey, harness leather skirts, leather bottom; **bellybands**, wide single strap, Griffith style; **lines**, ⅞x1⅛-inch black hand parts with spring billets; **hitch rein**, ⅝-inch, with snap. Made plain, smooth round edge; **trimmings**, nickel or Davis rubber.

No. 10R150 Our special price, nickel trimmings **$11.88**
No. 10R155 Our special price, genuine rubber trimmings **13.88**

No. 10R160 **Williams' Fancy Brass Harness**, same style as No. 10R150 made with **brass trimming throughout, yellow bridle front and yellow beaded gig saddle.** Stitching on blinds and pad is yellow. This makes a very handsome harness trimmed in brass. **Nobby and very stylish.**
Our special price **$13.25**
Add extra for double hip strap breeching **1.00**

No. 10R165 **Williams' Fancy Brass Collar and Hame Harness**, made with **half patent leather collar, full plated brass hames, 1¼-inch traces riveted to hames**, balance of trimming fine brass, same as No. 10R160, with **double hip strap breeching**. This is a very handsome single strap surrey harness.
Our special price, with collar and hames **$16.25**

Open or blind bridle with this harness. Shipping weight, about 30 pounds.

Our Single Strap Buggy Harness.

Single Strap, $9.95

Bridle, ⅝-inch, overcheck, box loops, round winker stay, nose band over check; **breast collar**, shaped extra wide; **traces**, 1¼-inch, stitched to breast collar; **breeching**, 1⅜-inch; side strap, ⅝-inch; hip strap, ¾-inch; turnback, ⅞-inch; scalloped, round crupper; **saddle**, 3-inch, strap, pad, patent leather jockey, harness leather skirts, leather bottom; **bellyband**, Griffith style; **lines**, 1-inch, to loop in; **trimmings**, nickel or imitation rubber.
No. 10R195 Our price **$9.95**
Weight, 18 pounds.

Our Madison Single Strap Single Harness.

The Finest $7.65 Single Strap Harness Ever Made.

This harness made for 900 to 1200-pound horses.

Bridle, ⅝-inch, patent leather winkers, box loop checks, over check or side reins, as desired; **breast collar**, 1⅜-inch, heavy stock; **traces**, 1⅛-inch, heavy stock; **breeching**, 1½-inch; **side strap**, ¾-inch; **hip strap**, ⅞-inch; **turnback**, ¾-inch, scalloped, with round crupper sewed on; **saddle**, 2½-inch, single strap harness leather skirts, leather bottom; **bellybands**, Griffith style; **lines**, ⅞-inch, all black, nickel or imitation rubber trimmings throughout.
No. 10R200 Price **$7.65**
Add extra for collar and hames in place of breast collar **2.00**
Add extra for buckle on crupper .... **.15**
Weight, about 21 pounds.

Our Ohio Single Buggy Harness.

Collar and Hames.

$12.50

Weight, about 35 lbs., boxed.

This harness made for 900 to 1250-pound horses.

Bridle, ⅝-inch box loop cheek, patent leather blinds, round winker brace, fancy front, (overcheck with nose band or side rein), (blind or open bridle), initial rosette, tie strap; **lines**, extra good line, ⅞-inch front with spring billet, 1⅛-inch hand parts (black); **gig saddle**, fine single strap harness leather skirts, leather bottom, double and stitched shaft bearer and shaft tug; **bellyband** folded (Griffith style or old style); **breeching**, folded with layer ⅝-inch single hip strap, ¾-inch back strap with round crupper sewed on ⅝-inch side strap; **traces**, 1⅛-inch, 6 feet long, raised round edge finish; **collar and hames**, fine kip collar, buggy size, buckle top, Dixon hame, japanned body, nickeled terret, box loop hame tug.
No. 10R170 Price of harness complete with collar **$12.50**
Add extra for buckle on crupper .... **.15**
Add extra for double hip strap breeching **1.75**
Add extra for 3-inch full laced saddle **2.00**
Add extra for russet hand parts **25c**

Our Lexington Single Strap Track or Buggy Harness.

$9.00

No. 10R180

This harness made for 900 to 1200-pound horses.

Bridle, ⅝-inch, overcheck, patent leather blinds, box loops, round winker stays, layer on crown, side rein or overcheck, **initial rosettes**; **breast collar**, 1¾-inch; **traces**, 1⅛-inch, stitched to breast collar; **breeching**, 1⅜-inch; **side straps**, ⅝-inch; **hip strap**, ⅝-inch; **turnback**, ¾-inch, scalloped, with round crupper sewed on; **saddle**, 2½-inch, single strap, patent leather jockey, harness leather skirt, enameled leather bottom; **bellybands**, Griffith style; **lines**, 1-inch black buckle or billet ends or to loop in bit. Harness all made plain, with single edge crease. Nickel or imitation rubber trimmings throughout.
No. 10R180 Price **$9.00**
Add extra for collar and hames, with traces attached to hames, in place of breast collar, with three holes in back end **2.00**
Add extra for full patent leather saddle in place of single strap gig saddle .... **.95**
Add extra for buckle on crupper .... **.15**
Add extra for russet hand parts .... **.25**
This harness will be made extra large, for 1400 and 1600-pound horse, for $2.00 extra to price of harness.
Weight, boxed, about 22 pounds.

Our Reno Single Strap Buggy Harness, $10.80

COLLAR AND HAMES.

No. 10R205

This harness made for 900 to 1250-pound horses.

Bridle, ⅝-inch, box loop check, patent leather blinds, round winker stay, overcheck with nose band or side rein, with layer on crown piece, initial rosettes and tie strap; **lines**, ⅞-inch front, with 1-inch black hand parts to loop in bit; **breeching**, 1⅜-inch single strap, with scalloped and raised point, doubled and stitched breeching brace, ⅝-inch single hip strap, ⅞-inch side strap, ⅞-inch scalloped and stitched back strap, with flaxseed cruppers sewed on; **hames**, 3½-pound iron hames, made with 1¼-inch single strap traces, with safe riveted to hames, 6 feet 4 inches long; **gig saddle**, 3-inch single strap, harness leather skirt, swell patent leather jockey, leather bottom, doubled and stitched bearer, box loop shaft tug, flat bellyband, Griffith style or old style, kip collar. **A fine single strap harness, with collar and hames.** Made in nickel and imitation rubber only. We do not make any changes whatever in this harness. Only sold as listed above.
No. 10R205 Our price complete with collar. **$10.80**
If wanted less collar, deduct .... **.85**
Add extra for buckle on crupper .... **.15**
Add extra for full laced saddle **2.00**
Add extra for russet hand part on lines .... **.25**
Weight, about 27 pounds, boxed.

Our Iowa Spring Wagon Harness.

XC Trimming, $20.95
Nickel Trimming, $21.98
Brass Trimming, $22.00

Spring Wagon Harness is made of extra quality Dundee Oak leather, well selected; special care is taken to have them light and very strong, making a light spring wagon harness and also a light farm harness. The best is always the cheapest. Size of harness for 900 to 1200-pound horses.

Trimmings, XC, brass and nickel. Two tie and spread straps; **bridles**, ¾-inch box loop, round rein and winker stay, sensible or square blinds (will send sensible blinds, unless ordered square); **hames**, low top wood hame with breast rings; line ring on XC harness will be XC, brass on brass harness, nickel on nickel harness; **hame tugs**, made with box loop and Champion trace buckle; **pads**, swell pad, leather bottom, single strap skirts, double and stitched bearer (will make the skirts with inside trace), loop if wanted (but must state inside loop on pad); **turnbacks**, ⅝-inch scalloped and stitched with round crupper to buckle on; ⅝-inch hip strap; **bellybands**, folded; **traces**, extra good, 1¼-inch by 6½ feet, double and stitched, raised with cockeye, made without cockeye if wanted; **lines**, a very important part of this harness, are 1-inch by 18 feet long; good and strong; **breast straps**, 1¼-inch with buckle, snap and slides, 1¼-inch martingales; ¾-inch collar snaps.

No. 10R670 XC Harness, no collars....... **$20.95**
No. 10R675 Nickel Harness, no collars.... **21.98**
No. 10R680 Brass Harness, no collars..... **22.00**
Add extra for breeching with ¾-inch double hip straps and ⅝-inch side straps.................. **4.75**

Be sure and state the size of hames wanted to fit collars. Weight, boxed, about 70 pounds.

Chain or Plow Harness.

$12.45 Will fit 900 to 1200-pound horse.

Bridles, ⅞-inch, Jenny Lind or Sensible blinds; **hames**, varnished, iron overtop, hook; **back bands**, 3½-inch leather with leather loops. **bellybands**; 1¼-inch with loop ends; **back straps**, 1¾-inch, running from ring on hip to the hames with 1⅛-inch hip trap; **traces**, 7-foot chains with 30-inch leather piping; **lines**, ⅞-inch by 15 feet, with snaps; **breast straps**, with 1½-inch breast strap, slides and snaps.

There are no hitching straps included with the harness, or pole straps. The price of the harness is without collars. For prices on collars see collar page. Weight, boxed, about 60 pounds.

No. 10R805 Double Harness, no collars...**$12.45**

Special Team or Plow Harness. $13.50

Full Size for Horses weighing 1200 pounds.

Bridles, ⅞-inch Concord blind or Jenny Lind, flat rein, flat winker brace; **hames**, black iron, overtop; **pads**, flat with 1¼-inch billets; **back straps**, 1¼-inch; **hip straps**, 1-inch with folded crupper; **traces**, 1½-inch, 4 feet 6 inches, double and stitched with 3½-foot stage chain; **lines**, good selected stock, ⅞-inch by 15 feet, wire snap; **breast straps**, with snap and slides; **martingales**, 1¼-inch, no collar strap; **tie straps**.

Don't buy small size harness, as you cannot use them. Our $13.50 harness is full size.

No. 10R810 Price, without collars.................. **$13.50**
Add extra for 1¾-inch traces.............................. **1.00**

Weight, boxed, about 45 pounds.

Our Special Farm Harness, $17.25.

Weight, about 45 pounds. Full size for 900 to 1200-pound horses.

No. 10R815

Bridles, ¾-inch flat rein, round winker brace and sensible blind; **hames**, iron overtop clip and staple, made with breast ring; **traces**, double and stitched, 1½ inches wide and 4½ feet long, with 3½ feet stage chain; traces riveted to hames; **breeching**, folded body, 1-inch double and stitched layer, 1½-inch back straps running to hames, ⅞-inch double hip straps, ⅝-inch double side straps to snap to ring on trace or under horse in martingale; **pads**, flat body with 1¼-inch billets; **lines**, 1 inch wide, 15 feet long, with snaps; **breast straps**, 1½ inches, with snaps and slide. Collar straps running from collar to bellyband, 1¼ inches. Hitching reins and spread straps included with this harness.

No. 10R815 Price of harness, without collars, **$17.25**
Add extra for 1¾-inch traces................ **1.00**

Single Goat or Dog Harness.

Red Leather, Fire Department Style.

$2.70

No. 10R830

Weight, about 3 pounds.

Bridle, ½-inch with bit to snap; **breast collar**, 1¼-inch flat with plain layer point; **traces**, 1-inch, flat, sewed to breast collar; **saddle**, 2-inch, flat, no tree, full lined, with loose ring terrets; **shaft tugs**, ⅝-inch; **hip strap**, ½-inch; **bellyband**, double with snaps; **side straps**, ⅝-inch; **turnback**, ⅝-inch, plain with safe; **breeching**, 1¼-inch, flat with plain layer point; **lines**, ⅝-inch, to snap in bit.

No. 10R830 Price, per set.......................... **$2.70**
No. 10R835 Double Goat Harness, same style as No. 10R830. Price, per set for two goats...... **$6.00**

Oklahoma Flat Pad Team Harness. $15.97

For 900 to 1200-pound horse.

Bridles, ⅞-inch, sensible blinds; **hames**, black, iron overtop; **pads**, flat, folded, 1¼-inch billets; **back straps**, 1¼-inch, hip straps 1-inch; **traces**, 1½-inch, 5 feet 10 inches, double and stitched; **lines**, ⅞-inch, 15 feet, with snaps; **breast straps**, 1½-inch, with slides and snaps; **pole straps**, 1½-inch. **A good flat pad team harness. Weight, about 40 pounds.**

No. 10R840 Our price, without collars... **$15.97**
Add extra for 1¾-inch traces..................... **1.00**

For prices on collars, see collar page.

Double Farm Harness.

$21.75

Size of harness for 900 to 1200-pound horses.

Bridle, ¾-inch short check, open bridle, with nose band and chin strap, with ring; bit strap; ⅝-inch flat rein and tie strap (or blind bridle if wanted); **hames**, steel clad ball top XC hame clip and staple; **traces**, 1½-inch double and stitched, clip cockeye, folded hame tug, riveted to hame, Champion trace buckle, 1¼-inch bellyband billets, with folded bellyband; **lines**, fine selected Dundee oak leather, ⅞-inch by 18 feet, with snap; **pads**, heavy folded pad, with 1¼-inch layer and round loop; pad to buckle to trace buckle; **hip and back straps**, 1¼-inch back strap, run from hip strap to hame through loop on pad; 1-inch hip strap sewed in Cooper trace carriers, with tug loop; **breast straps**, 1½-inch, with snap and slides; **pole straps**, 1½-inch, with collar strap, spread strap and rings. **For prices of collars, see collar page.**

No. 10R845 Price, without collars...... **$21.75**
Add extra for team breeching, No. 10R2490.. **3.05**
Add extra for 1¾-inch traces..................... **1.00**
Add extra for double hip strap breeching, No. 10R2475.. **3.75**
Add extra for hook and terret pad.......... **1.60**
Add extra for large harness, for 1400 to 1600-pound horse,................................ **2.00**

Will make any change of hames at difference in price. **Weight, 60 pounds.**

Our Danville Farm Harness, $22.95.

NOTICE—Made in slip tug, if wanted, at same price. Weight, boxed, about 85 pounds.

Size of harness for 900 to 1200-pound horses.

Bridle, ¾-inch short check bridle, with nose band and bit strap. Concord blind, round winker brace, round side check and tie strap; **lines**, 1-inch by 18 feet, with snaps **traces**, 1½ inch trace, double and stitched, with cockeyes sewed in, 6 feet long; **hames**, XC iron overtop, with Hayden hold back, 1½-inch clip hame tug, champion trace buckle, folded bellyband, breast straps, 1½ inches, with snaps and slides; pole straps, 1½ inches with collar strap; **pads**, folded body, 1¼ layer, with perfection tree hook and terret to buckle in hame tug; **hip straps**, 1-inch hip and back strap, with folded crupper to buckle on.

No. 10R850 Price, complete, without collars **$22.95**
Add extra for 1¾-inch traces.............................. **1.00**
Add extra for breeching to buckle on hip straps **3.05**
Add extra for breeching with double hip strap, **4.10**

Our Bismarck Concord Farm Harness, $25.75.

Weight, boxed for shipment, about 80 pounds

Full size harness for 900 to 1200-pound horses.

Bridles, ¾-inch long check, Concord blinds, round winker brace, spotted face piece, round reins and tie strap with snap; **lines**, well selected line leather, 1 inch by 18 feet long; **traces**, fine Dundee trace leather, 1½-inch double and stitched point, 2¼-inch single strap body, with cockeye sewed in; **hame and hame tugs**, No. 6 oiled Concord bolt hame, fine **lace box loop hame tugs**, Champion trace buckle, 1¼-inch bellyband billet and heavy folded bellyband; **hip and back straps**, selected leather, 1-inch hip and back straps, sewed in Cooper trace carrier, with trace loop to buckle on hip strap; **pads**, our special hook and terret pad, folded body, turtle bottom, with D-ring on side, with short market strap to trace buckle. One of the finest pads on the market; **breast and pole straps**, 1½-inch breast strap, with snap and slides; 1½-inch pole strap, with collar strap; spread strap and ring, tie strap and roller breast strap snap.

No. 10R855 Our special price, **less collars**............................ **$25.75**
Add extra for 1¾x2½-inch traces.... **$1.50**
Add extra for 1½-inch by 20-foot lines........... **.65**
Add extra for team breeching No. 10R2490..... **3.05**
Add extra for double hip strap breeching, No. 10R2475... **$4.45**
Add extra for collar No. 10R3480 each.......... **2.95**

Will furnish good double and stitched trace at same price.

Our Buffalo Heavy Concord Truck Harness, $27.98.

No. 10R940

Bridles, ⅝-inch long cheek, spotted face piece, Concord blinds, round winker brace, flat rein; **lines**, fine selected Dundee oak leather, 1-inch wide and 18 feet long, with snaps; **hames**, oiled Concord bolt hames with brass balls; **traces**, heavy selected stock, double and stitched, 1½-inch, with heel chain, 1¼-inch bellyband, billet and heavy folded bellyband, traces made as shown in cut; **breeching**, heavy folded body, with 1¼-inch layer, 1-inch side strap running to hame, 1-inch double hip strap, 1-inch side strap to snap in pole strap ring under horse; **breast straps**, 1½-inch with roller snaps; **pole straps**, made Chicago style. This harness is full size for 1,000 to 1,250-pound horses.

No. 10R940 Our special price, **without collars**, per set........ **$27.98**

Add for Extras to Price of Harness.

Add extra for 1¾-inch traces........ **$1.50**
Add extra for 2-inch traces........ **2.25**
Add extra for 1⅛-inch by 20-foot lines........ **.65**
Add extra for No. 10R2485 breeching in place of breeching on harness........ **1.60**
Add extra for harness large enough for 1,400 to 1,600-pound horse........ **2.00**
For price on collars, see collar page.
Our No. 10R3480 curled hair face collars, each add........ **2.95**

Weight, boxed, about 88 pounds.

Montana Concord Harness, $29 97

This harness is largely used in Montana, Oregon, Idaho, Utah, and, in fact, all the western states.

No. 10R950

How this harness is made. This harness is made with great care, with extra heavy fine Concord pad, stuffed bottom; brass loop on pad with buckle and billet end to buckle into trace buckle. **Made to be used on bolt hames. Quality of leather.** Leather used in this harness is our **fine Delhi oak tanned leather. Stock is well selected, carefully cut and blacked, and we think it is equaled by none and superior to all other grades of harness leather** for this particular style and grade of harness.

Bridles, ⅝-inch box loop, Concord blinds, spotted face piece, heavy front, round winker brace, ⅞-inch flat rein to throw over hame; **hames**, No. 6 oiled Concord bolt hame, lace box loop hame tug, Champion trace buckle, 1¼-inch bellyband billet, heavy folded bellyband; **pads**, fine Concord pad, stuffed bottom, **brass** loop on top of pad; **traces**, fine selected Dundee oak leather, 1½-inch double and stitched point, 2¼-inch single strap body with cockeye sewed in; **breeching**, heavy folded body, with wide layer, 1¼-inch back strap to run through loop on pad to hame, ⅞-inch double hip strap, ⅞-inch side strap to snap under horse in pole strap ring; **lines**, selected line leather, well made, 1-inch by 18 feet, with snap; **breast straps**, 1½ inches, with roller snap, pole strap 1½ inches, with collar strap, spread strap and ring, tie strap. This harness is full size for 1,000 to 1,250-pound horses. **Extra large harness** for 1,400 to 1,600-pound horses will cost you **$2.00 extra.**

No. 10R950 Our special price, **without collars**........ **$29.97**
Add extra for brass ball hame No. 10R3801, brass trimmed bridles, brass buckle shields, balance of harness full japanned trimmed........ **$3.50**
Add for 1¾ inches by 2¼ inches single strap body trace........ **$1.50**
Add for 2 inches by 2¾ inches single strap body trace........ **$2.25**
Add for toggle on trace in place of cockeye........ **.50**
Weight, about 85 pounds, boxed for shipment.
For price on collars, see collar page.
Our No. 10R3480 collar, each........ **$2.95**

DEPARTMENT OF SADDLES.

IN OUR SADDLE DEPARTMENT WE HAVE ENDEAVORED TO SHOW EVERYTHING IN THE SADDLE LINE, INCLUDING ALL THE VERY LATEST STYLES AND MOST DESIRABLE GOODS.

OUR SADDLES are all made by the largest and most reliable manufacturers in the country, concerns whose reputation for the manufacture of the **HIGHEST GRADE WORK is everywhere recognized.**

IF YOU BUY YOUR SADDLES FROM US you will be sure not only of getting lower prices than you could possibly get elsewhere, **but the best grade work on the market.**

OUR SADDLE TRADE HAS GROWN until we are now among the largest dealers in this line in this country. **We are daily shipping saddles** to almost every state and territory in the Union, as well as foreign countries. **The low prices we offer** and the quality of goods we handle, commend our line to your favorable consideration.

ABOUT OUR PRICES. We advertise hand made saddles at from **$1.85 upward,** and we believe a careful comparison of our prices with those of any other concern will convince you that we can save you from 25 to 50 per cent in price. The freight or express charges will amount to next to nothing as compared with what you will save in price.

WE ARE EXTREMELY ANXIOUS TO RECEIVE YOUR ORDER, not so much for the little profit there is in it for us as for the good it will do us as an advertisement, and will endeavor to send you a saddle with which you will be so well pleased that your friends will also order from us.

OUR LINE OF STOCK SADDLES we believe is the handsomest line on the market, and the prices certainly are below any possible comparison. Our Western and Southwestern trade has been so very large that we have felt justified in making very extensive preparations in the stock saddle line for the coming season, and if you are in the market for this class of goods, we are sure that one trial order will convince you that you cannot afford to place your orders elsewhere.

MEN'S SADDLES.

No. 10R1300 For $1.85 we offer a Morgan Saddle, which you would pay your retailer double the price for. This saddle comes in **fair or black leather,** as desired. 13-inch tree, Morgan horn, hide covered, stirrup leathers are ⅝-inch, **girth is from super cotton,** stirrups 3-inch wood. Our $1.85 saddle has been advertised extensively and **a large number have been sold in every state,** and from everywhere we are receiving the most flattering testimonials. **The sale of one of these saddles almost invariably leads to the sale of more. If you favor us with your order we can guarantee that you will be thoroughly satisfied with the saddle received.** The saddle weighs about 5 lbs. Our price... **$1.85**

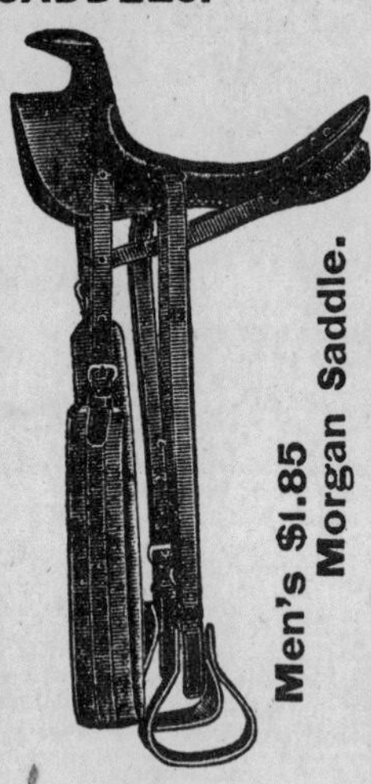

Men's $1.85 Morgan Saddle.

Men's $4.20 Morgan Saddle.

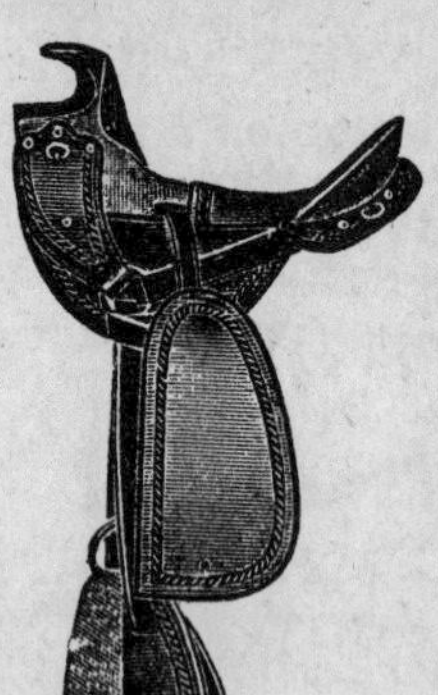

No. 10R1305 This Saddle is made of russet or black leather, as desired, 13-inch tree.

Genuine hide covered Morgan horn.

Seat is half leather covered, has 1⅛-inch tie straps, 1-inch stirrup leather, with large fancy fenders; 4-inch soft woven hair cinch.

Leather covered wood stirrups. This is a single cinch rigged saddle. Weight, about 9 pounds. Our special price.. **$4.20**

Men's $3.75 Morgan Saddle.

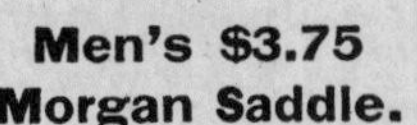

No. 10R1310 This Saddle is made from russet or black leather, as desired, has a 13-inch Muley Morgan hide covered tree, half leather covered seat, 1⅛-inch tie strap, 1-inch stirrup leathers, with large fancy fenders, 4-inch soft woven hair cinch, wood stirrups. We can furnish this saddle stamped or carved, as desired.

A regular single cinch rigged saddle. Weight, about 8 pounds.

Our price........ **$3.75**

Men's $6.55 Batesville Saddle.

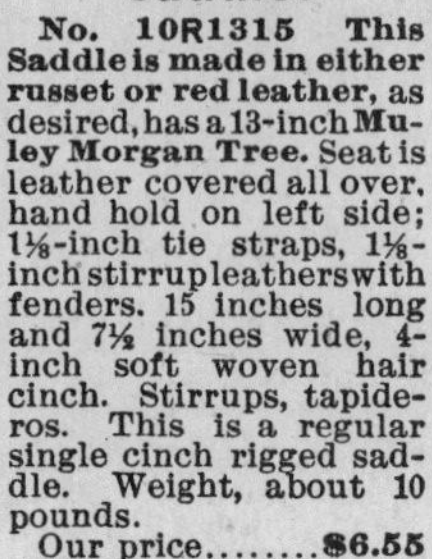

No. 10R1315 This Saddle is made in either russet or red leather, as desired, has a 13-inch **Muley Morgan Tree.** Seat is leather covered all over, hand hold on left side; 1⅛-inch tie straps, 1⅛-inch stirrup leathers with fenders. 15 inches long and 7½ inches wide, 4-inch soft woven hair cinch. Stirrups, tapideros. This is a regular single cinch rigged saddle. Weight, about 10 pounds.

Our price........ **$6.55**

Shipping weight, 22 pounds.

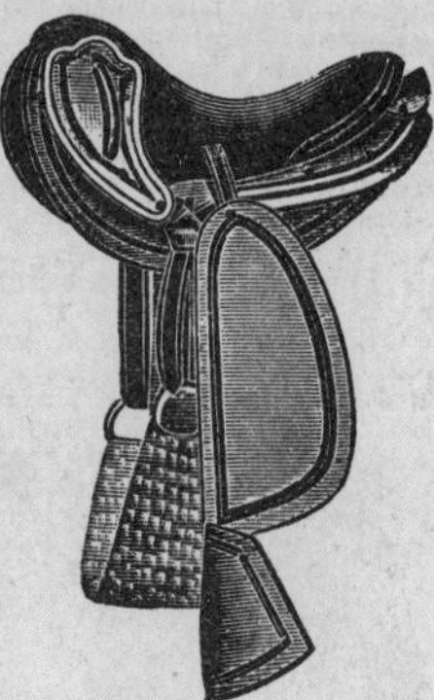

McClellan Black Saddle, $4.70.

No. 10R1320 Tree, 14-inch black hide covered, **stirrup strap** 1-inch with 2½-inch covered stirrup, 3½-inch cotton cinch with leather safe; leather skirt, a good, cheap saddle, man size only. **All black leather.**

Price, each...... **$4.70**

Add extra for Finder on stirrup strap... **$1.60**

Shipping weight, about 10 pounds.

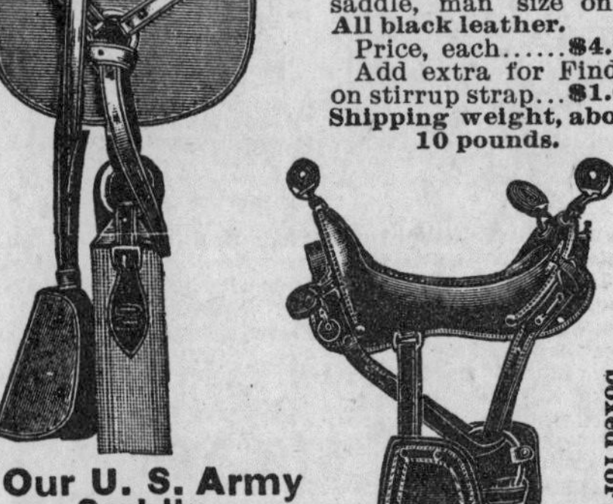

Our U. S. Army Saddle.

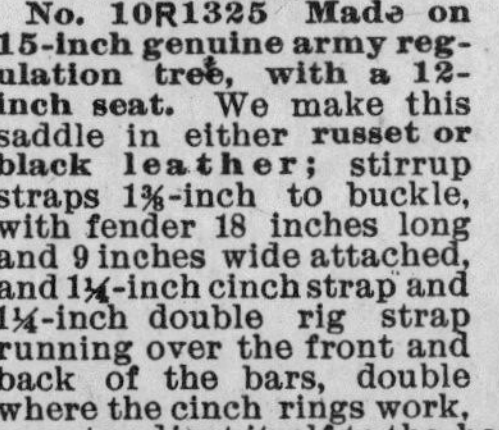

No. 10R1325 Made on 15-inch genuine army regulation tree, with a 12-inch seat. We make this saddle in either **russet or black leather;** stirrup straps 1⅜-inch to buckle, with fender 18 inches long and 9 inches wide attached, and 1¼-inch cinch strap and 1¼-inch double rig strap running over the front and back of the bars, double where the cinch rings work, so as to adjust itself to the horse, which will allow the girth to be set forward or back, as the rider wishes; **20-strand cinch with wool lined chase;** stirrup, 4-inch regulation, with 9½-inch tap. The saddle is rigged with mantle straps, as shown in cut. **This saddle has all the brass trimmings, the same as all army saddles.** This saddle is made with an opening in the seat of 1½ inches the full length of seat, in center of the tree. The covering on saddle is stitched by hand, making it a first class saddle, as used by the regular army.

Weight of saddle, 16 pounds; boxed for shipment, 30 pounds.

Price of saddle, with mantle straps........ **$16.50**
Price of saddle, without mantle straps..... **15.50**

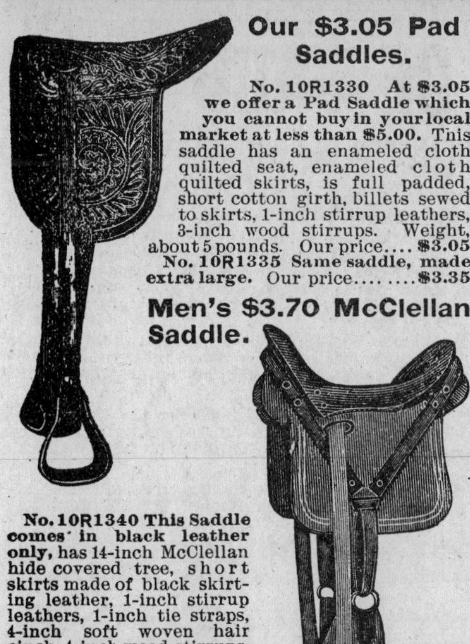

Our $3.05 Pad Saddles.

No. 10R1330 At $3.05 we offer a Pad Saddle which you cannot buy in your local market at less than $5.00. This saddle has an enameled cloth quilted seat, enameled cloth quilted skirts, is full padded, short cotton girth, billets sewed to skirts, 1-inch stirrup leathers, 3-inch wood stirrups. Weight, about 5 pounds. Our price.... $3.05

No. 10R1335 Same saddle, made extra large. Our price.......$3.35

Men's $3.70 McClellan Saddle.

No. 10R1340 This Saddle comes in black leather only, has 14-inch McClellan hide covered tree, short skirts made of black skirting leather, 1-inch stirrup leathers, 1-inch tie straps, 4-inch soft woven hair cinch, 4-inch wood stirrups. **This is a regular single cinch rigged saddle.** Weight, about 8 pounds; boxed for shipment, 18 lbs.

Our price............$3.70

Men's $2.50 Plain English Saddle.

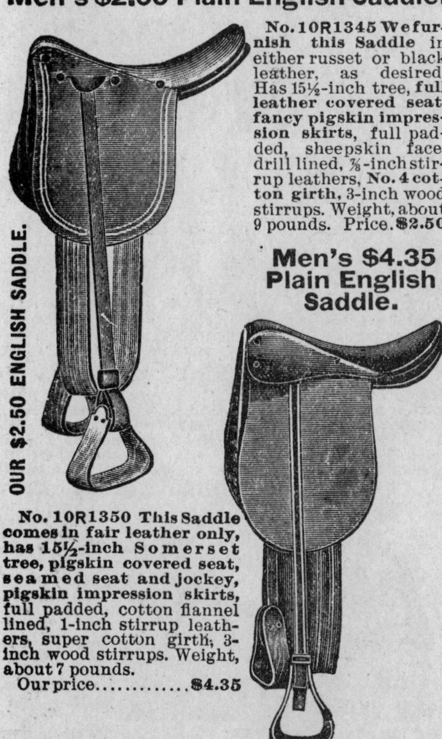

No. 10R1345 We furnish this Saddle in either russet or black leather, as desired. Has 15½-inch tree, **full leather covered seat, fancy pigskin impression skirts,** full padded, sheepskin face, drill lined, ⅞-inch stirrup leathers, **No. 4 cotton girth,** 3-inch wood stirrups. Weight, about 9 pounds. Price. $2.50

Men's $4.35 Plain English Saddle.

No. 10R1350 This Saddle comes in fair leather only, has 15½-inch Somerset tree, pigskin covered seat, seamed seat and jockey, pigskin impression skirts, full padded, cotton flannel lined, 1-inch stirrup leathers, super cotton girth, 3-inch wood stirrups. Weight, about 7 pounds.

Our price............$4.35

Our Plain Leather Mosby Saddle, $7.95.

No. 10R1355 Our Special All Leather Covered Mosby Saddle, made on the 14-inch genuine Mosby tree, solid leather seat, a round hand loop on near side, leather underskirts, leather jockeys, 1¼-inch stirrup straps with large fender attached, 3-inch wood stirrup leather covered or hooded stirrup, cotton strand, Texas girth to tie with 1¼-inch side straps. **This is a strictly first class Mosby Saddle.** Weight, about 9 pounds; boxed, 20 pounds.

Our special price.......$7.95

Special Mosby Saddle.

No. 10R1360 Sears, Roebuck & Co.'s Special Mosby Saddle made on a 14-inch Mosby tree seating, fine calfskin skirting in fancy stitch, stirrup leathers, 1¼ inch with heavy fender. This saddle has large skirts and jockey. Tie straps, 1⅛ inches and heavy cording strand Texas girth, 4-inch wood Texas stirrup; is a strictly high grade Mosby saddle. We are making a leader of it at our special price, of..................$9.90

Weight, 10 pounds; boxed for shipment, 20 pounds.

Our $10.25 English Saddle.

No. 10R1365 Our Handsome Full Quilted English Shaftoe, black enameled leather saddle, **made on a genuine 16-inch Somerset tree.** Made of fine enameled leather, **handsomely quilted.** Skirts full enamel leather quilted knee and thigh puff; full pad and leather faced; stirrup leathers 1⅛ inches, with enamel leather covers to prevent chafing; **extra heavy cotton girth** and XC metal stirrups. This is one of the **most stylish** saddles for a gentleman, and handled only by us. **You will find,** if you order a saddle from us, you will get such value in **material, workmanship and general finish** as you cannot possibly get elsewhere at within 50 per cent of the price.

For $10.25 we offer this handsome English Saddle as the most perfect saddle of the kind ever shown at anything like the price. Our price..........$10.25

11 pounds net, 24 pounds boxed for shipment.

Our Large Ferguson Saddle.

For 200 to 250-Pound Men.

No. 10R1370 This Saddle is made on a 16-inch Mosby tree, Cheyenne rolled cantle, full leather covered seat, single cinch rig; skirts 22 inches long, 14 inches wide, cut on circle. Stirrup straps, 2 inches wide to buckle, 4 feet long, double reinforced at stirrup, with fender 10¾ inches wide and 20 inches long attached. Tie straps 1⅛ inches wide, and 4 feet long. Cinch, 4½ inches, 3-ply heavy cotton belting web, 4-inch Texas wood stirrup. This saddle is made out of the very finest quality of russet saddle skirting, and is suitable for a man weighing 200 to 250 pounds. Weight of saddle, 16 lbs.; boxed, 26 lbs.

Price of saddle....$12.50

$8.95. Somerset Saddle.

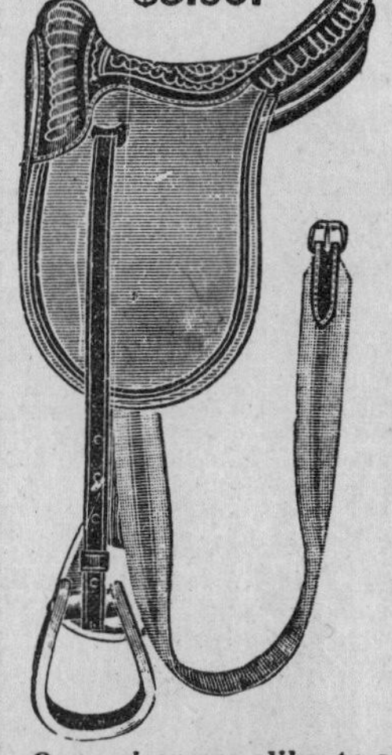

No. 10R1375 This Saddle is made on a spring seat tree with spring bars, will adjust itself with the movement of the horse and rider; size of skirt, 21 inches from center of saddle to bottom of skirt, 11½ inches wide; **made on a 16-inch tree, with hogskin improved skirts,** seating of calfskin finely quilted with a heavy roll in front and back, stirrup leather 1-inch made of good solid stock, with a 4-inch wood bolt stirrup, padding of sheepskin, drill lined, girth an extra quality of cotton, making a very stylish and durable saddle. Weight net, 9 pounds. Boxed for shipment, 20 pounds.

Our price.... $8.95

Our prices are alike to all. We do not give the largest merchant ordering in the largest quantities one cent advantage in price over the man who orders a single item.

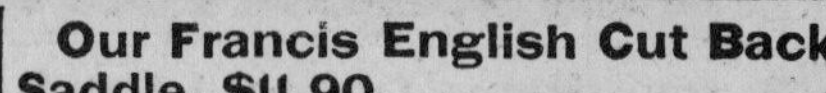

Our Francis English Cut Back Saddle, $11.90.

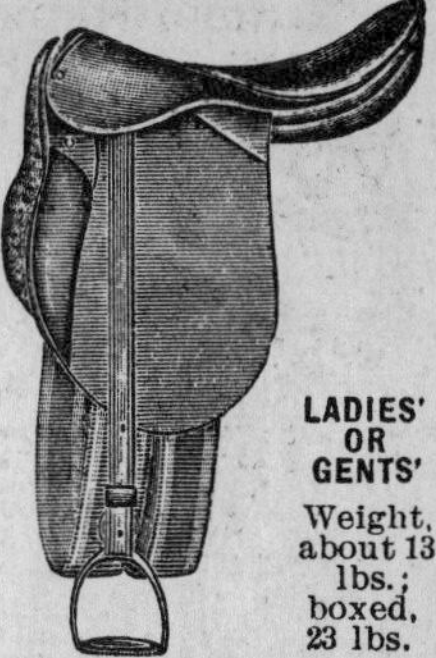

LADIES' OR GENTS'

Weight, about 13 lbs.; boxed, 23 lbs.

No. 10R1380 Made on a 17-inch English cut back tree, with patent stirrup bars. This stirrup bar will let the stirrup strap loose in case of accident. Serge lined pad, very soft on the horse's back. Stirrup leathers, 1⅛-inch, with iron stirrups. 2½-inch double worsted girth, hogskin seating, seam jockey, hogskin skirt, with knee and thigh puff. A strictly first class saddle. **This saddle can also be used for a ladies' stride saddle.** Our special price. $11.90

Our Hyde Park Gents' Saddle, $16.50.

Weight, about 13 lbs.; boxed, 24 lbs.

No. 10R1385 Fine English Cut Back Gents' or Ladies' Saddle, with patent stirrup bars. This stirrup bar will let the stirrup strap loose in case of accident. Heavy serge lined pad, 1⅛-inch stirrup leathers, with iron stirrups; 3-inch double worsted girth, fancy pigskin seat, seam jockey, fancy pigskin skirt, with knee and thigh puff. **This is a very fine, extra well made and durable saddle,** having one of the best English trees. This is the finest gents' English cut back saddle we make.

Our special price.........$16.50

Our Lexington Spring Bar Somerset Saddle, $13.25.

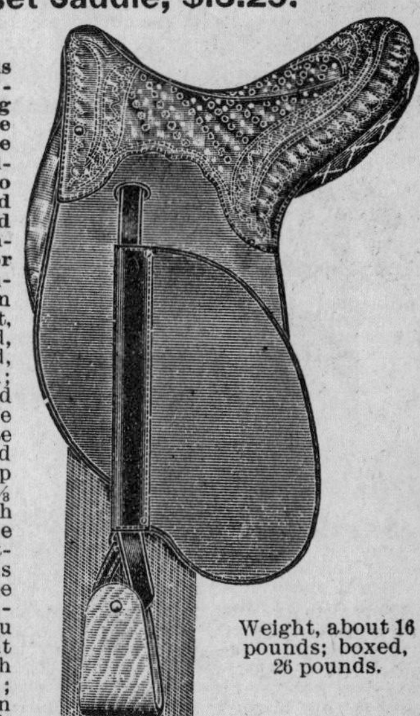

Weight, about 16 pounds; boxed, 26 pounds.

No. 10R1386 This Saddle is made on a 17-inch spring bar tree, the best tree made to adjust itself to the rider and horse and make it comfortable for both. Genuine calfskin quilted seat, hand raised, star stitched, with roll; very soft and easy to the rider; white linsey lined pad; stirrup leathers 1⅛ inches with large pipe fender attached. This fender can be easily removed if you do not want to ride with fenders; heavy cotton corded girth and 4-inch Texas wood bolt stirrup. **This saddle has a large sale throughout the South. A strictly first class, high grade, spring bar saddle.**

Price, each..........$13.25

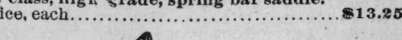

Men's McClellan Saddles at $7.60.

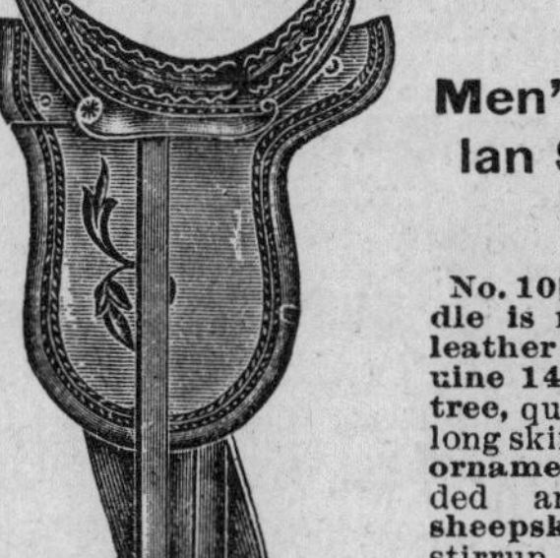

No. 10R1390 This Saddle is made in russet leather only, has a genuine 14-inch McClellan tree, quilted seat, fancy long skirts, stamped and ornamented, bars padded and lined with sheepskin. Has 1-inch stirrup leathers, double super cotton girths, leather covered stirrups.

Weight, about 10 pounds.

Our price.......$7.60

Weight, packed for shipment, 21 pounds.

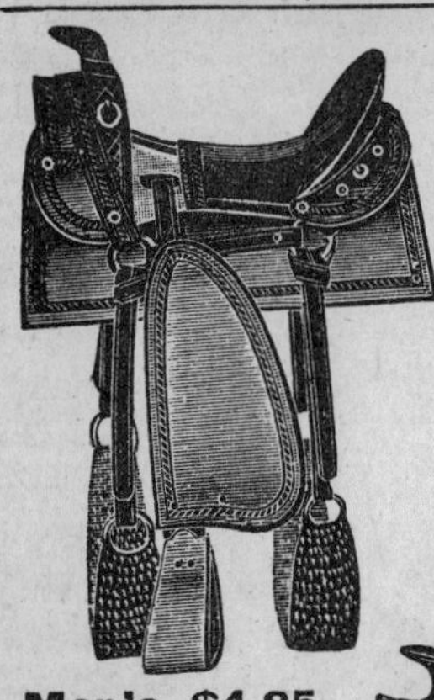

Our Special $6.30 Stock Saddle

No. 10R1395 13-inch Morgan tree, hide covered. 21-inch skirts, 1⅛-inch stirrup leathers to buckle, with fenders 14 inches long, 7½ inches wide, 1⅛-inch tie straps, 4-inch woven soft hair cinches, 3-inch wood stirrups. **This is a good substantial well made saddle.** Weight, about 11 pounds; boxed for shipment, 21 pounds.
Our price.. **$6.30**

Men's $4.85 Morgan Saddle.

No. 10R1400 This Saddle is made of russet leather. It has a 13-inch hide covered Morgan tree; 1-inch stirrup leathers with fenders 13 inches long and 7 inches wide; 1-inch tie straps; **solid woven hair cinches;** wood stirrups. **This is a double cinch rigged saddle.** Weight, about 10 pounds.
Our price... ...**$4.85**

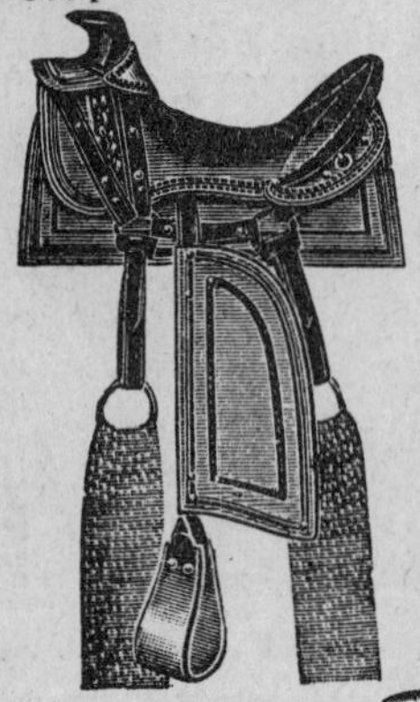

Men's $5.75 Morgan Saddle.

No. 10R1405 This Saddle is made of russet saddle leather; has a Morgan tree, unlined skirts, 4-inch cinches; 1-inch stirrup leathers with fenders; 14 inches long, 6¼ inches wide; 1-inch tie straps; **solid woven hair cinches; very strong wood stirrups.** Weight, about 11 pounds.
Our price........**$5.75**

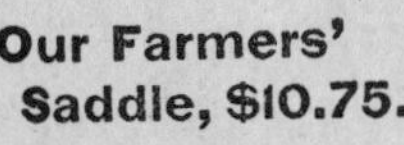

Our Farmers' Saddle, $10.75.

No. 10R1410
Our Farmers' Saddle, made on 15-inch solid fork, army tree, hide covered; leather seat, 1¼-inch long stirrup strap with fenders attached, 4-inch wood stirrup, leather covered; 1¼-inch tie strap, soft hair cinch, a man's saddle single cinch. Weight, about 16 pounds, net; boxed for shipment, 30 pounds.
Price, each.....**$10.75**

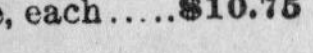

STOCK SADDLES.

Our Missouri Saddle, $8.60.

No. 10R1415 Our Special Missouri Saddle, made on 14-inch steel fork, hide covered tree. Skirts 21 inches long, good solid stock unlined, with bars of tree lined with wool sheepskin. Stirrup leather, 1½-inch to buckle; fender, 14 inches long and 8 inches wide; tie straps, 1 inch; 4-inch cotton cinches, 4-inch Texas wood stirrups. Weight, about 15 pounds; boxed for shipment, 30 lbs.
Our special price, **$8.60**

Our Popular $8.95 Saddle.

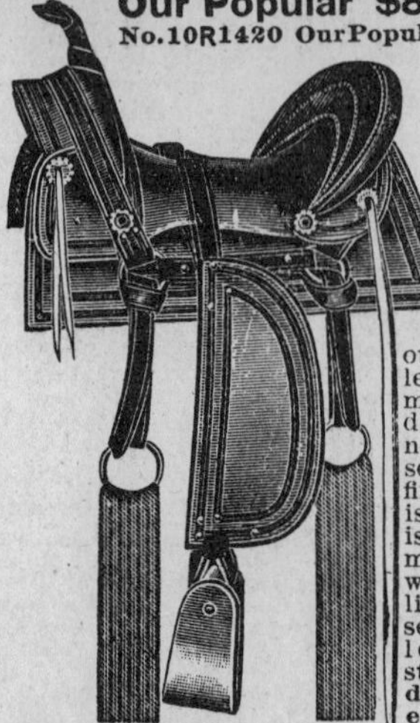

No. 10R1420 Our Popular Saddle is made on a thoroughly first class steel fork tree with high horn. This tree is made for general purposes for all kinds of ordinary use and will stand a great deal of rough work. The leather used in the making of this saddle is a fine oil tanned, skirting well selected and nicely finished. The tree is 14½ inches (this is the only size we make this saddle), with 22½-inch unlined skirts. The seating is of solid leather fancy stamped. **The saddle is made with edged creasing throughout,** with steel strainer and roll cantle, 1½-inch stirrup straps, with large fenders attached, size 15 inches long, 7 inches wide. It is double rig to tie with 1⅛-inch tie straps and 4-inch woven cinches and 4-inch Texas wood stirrups. Weight of saddle, about 16 pounds; packed for shipment, about 30 pounds. **We can highly recommend this saddle as being one of the best cheap stock saddles we handle and is sure to give excellent service.** Price, with unlined skirts............**$8.95**

No. 10R1425 The same saddle made with sheepskin wool lined skirts. Price...................**$9.85**

Gunnison Saddle. $11.90

No. 10R1430 Our Gunnison Stock Saddle. We have lately improved this saddle by making it on a new steel fork Gunnison tree, hide covered 14½-inch tree. The leather used in this saddle is a fine quality oil tanned skirting, well selected and well finished. The stirrup, fender and jockey are fancy stamped. The saddle is made with 22½-inch skirts and lined with an extra quality wool sheepskin, with steel strainer and roll cantle, raised and beaded gullet, 1½-inch stirrup straps to buckle, with large fenders attached. Size of fender 16 inches long, 7 inches wide, 1¼-inch latigo straps to tie on a double cinch rig, genuine Mexican strong hair cinches and 3-inch California wood stirrup, leather bottom. **This saddle is one of our leading sellers** and when compared with other saddles of like price, you will find it superior in quality of material and in workmanship. Weight, 20 pounds, net, and 45 pounds boxed for shipment. Price.... ...**$11.90**

Our Prescott Steel Fork Stock Saddle, $14.95.

Weight, about 20 pounds.

Weight, boxed for shipment, about 35 lbs.

No. 10R1432 Made on a 14-inch steel fork tree, hide covered, with 22½-in. wool lined skirts, extended full seat, bound cantle. Seat and jockey in one piece. A very roomy saddle. Stirrup leathers 1¾-in. to lace, with fenders 14x7 inches wide attached. Tie straps 1¼ in. long on the inner side to tie, and 1⅛ in. to buckle on the off side. 20-strand gray California hair cinches; 5-inch Texas bolted bar stirrup. The saddle skirting used in this saddle is a very choice selection of California oil skirting, heavily oiled. Our special price, **$14.95**

Our Special Green River Steel Fork Saddle. $19.95.

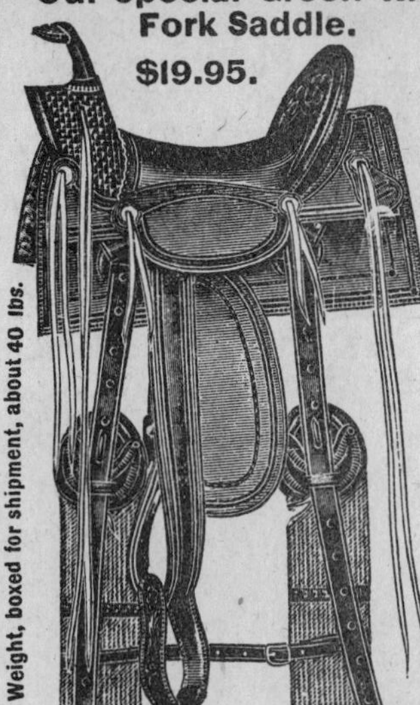

Weight, boxed for shipment, about 40 lbs.

No. 10R1434 Made on a 15-in. Green River tree. 24-inch wool lined skirts, full extended seat, bound cantle. Seat and jockey in one piece. A good roomy saddle. Hand stamped gullet; stirrup leathers 3 in. wide, with fenders 16 in. long and 8¼ in. wide attached. Steel leather covered stirrup, 1⅝-inch tie straps, 6 feet long to buckle on the near side and 1⅜ in. to buckle on the off side. 20-strand white angora hair cinches, with wool lined chafes and connecting straps. Heavy California oil skirting, well selected. Particular attention paid to parts of this saddle where heavy wear and great strain is required. **This saddle is a leader of leaders, and has no equal at our special low price.** Price, **$19.95**

Our Helena Steel Fork Saddle. $11.59.

Weight, 16 lbs.

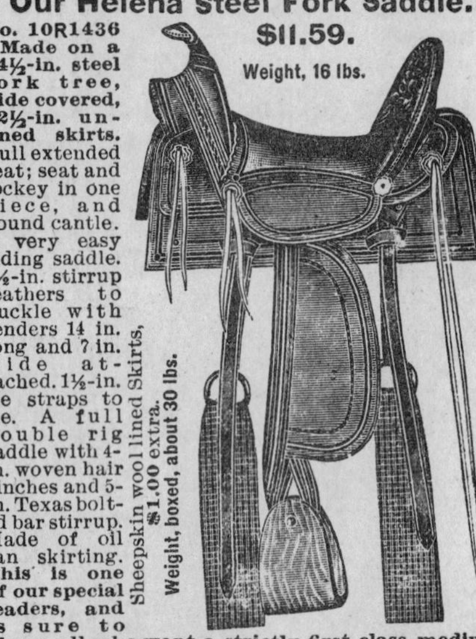

Sheepskin wool lined Skirts, $1.00 extra.
Weight, boxed, about 30 lbs.

No. 10R1436 Made on a 14½-in. steel fork tree, hide covered, 22½-in. unlined skirts. Full extended seat; seat and jockey in one piece, and bound cantle. A very easy riding saddle. 1½-in. stirrup leathers to buckle with fenders 14 in. long and 7 in. wide attached. 1⅛-in. tie straps to tie. A full double rig saddle with 4-in. woven hair cinches and 5-in. Texas bolted bar stirrup. Made of oil tan skirting. **This is one of our special leaders, and is sure to please all who want a strictly first class medium priced steel fork saddle.** Our special price..**$11.59**

Our Special Milford Steel Fork Saddle. $11.19

Weight. 16 lbs.

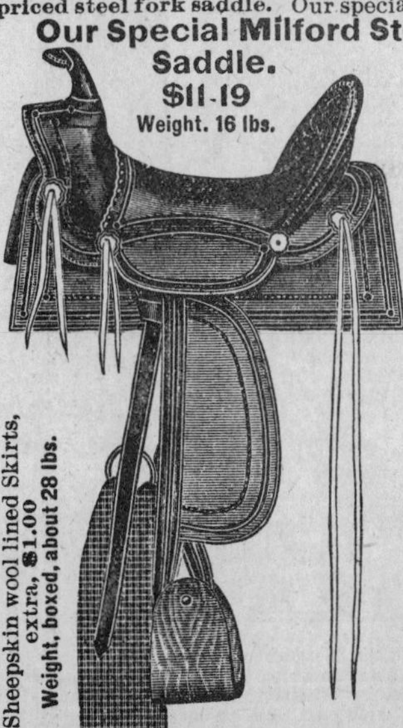

Sheepskin wool lined Skirts, extra, $1.00
Weight, boxed, about 28 lbs.

No. 10R1438 Made on a 14½ inch Milford tree, hide covered, and good steel fork. 22½ inch unlined skirts, full extended seat and bound cantle. Seat and jockey in one piece. This is a very roomy and easy riding saddle. Stirrup leathers 1⅛ inch to buckle, with fenders 14 inch long and 7 inch wide attached. Single cinch under rig saddle. 1¼-inch tie straps; 5-inch solid woven hair cinches; 5 inch Texas bolted bar stirrup. Made in bound or roll cantle. Will always send bound cantle unless ordered roll cantle. This saddle is made of oil tan skirting. It is one of the biggest sellers in our line. Full cinch saddle with seat and jockey in one piece. Our special price..................**$11.19**

Winfield Special Stock Saddle.

No. 10R1440

$17.59

Made out of selected oil tan Oregon saddle skirting. All parts of saddle are given special attention where extra heavy strain is required. Made on a 15-inch Winfield steel fork tree, hide covered, with 24-inch sheepskin wool lined skirts. Full extended seat; seat and jockey in one piece. Steel strainer and bound cantle. Stirrup leathers 2-inch to lace, with fenders 15 inches long and 8 inches wide attached. Tie straps 1⅛-inch on near side to tie and 1¾-inch to buckle on the off side; 20 strand white Angora hair cinches; wool lined chafes and connecting straps; leather covered steel stirrups. **We will make this saddle in roll cantle if wanted, but will always send bound cantle unless otherwise ordered.** A strictly up to date good saddle, a saddle that would sell for $5.00 to $8.00 more than our special price. **Weight, about 25 pounds; boxed, 35 pounds.**

Our price.......................................$17.59

Casper Big Heavy Stock Saddle.

THIS SADDLE IS LARGE SIZE AND WILL FIT A MAN 200 TO 250 POUNDS.

$26.90

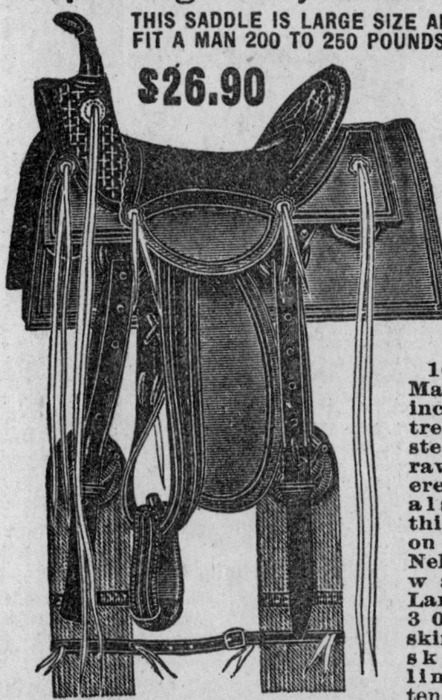

No. 10R1442

Made on a 17-inch Visalia tree, heavy steel fork, raw hide covered. We will also make this saddle on a 17-inch Nelson tree if wanted. Large heavy 30-inch skirts; sheepskin wool lined. Extended full seat; bound cantle; seat and jockey in one piece. This is an extra large, roomy saddle, for a big heavy stout rider. 3-inch stirrup leathers to lace with extra heavy steel leather covered stirrups. Large heavy fender 18 inches long, 9½ inches wide, attached. Heavy 20-strand white hard hair cinches; wool lined chafes and connecting straps. 1⅝-inch tie straps 7 feet long on the inner side to buckle and 2 inches long on the off side to buckle. We will make any changes in cinches wanted on this saddle; either all cotton or back band webbing cinches, but will send cinches listed regular with the saddle unless otherwise specified. We will also make this saddle in roll cantle if wanted. Remember, this saddle is made of an extra quality of fine Oregon heavy oil skirting, with full extended seat; seat and jockey in one piece. This saddle is made with lariat strap on the off side and head string on the inner side. Weight of this saddle is about 38 pounds. **This saddle will sell in most places from $45.00 to $65.00, and at our low price it is a special bargain.**

Price.......................................$26.90

IF YOU WILL REFER

to the freight rates in the front of the book you can tell almost exactly what the freight on these saddles will be to your railroad station, and thus SAVE THE TIME AND TROUBLE of writing to us for an estimate of freight.

Our Kit Carson Cowboy Saddle.

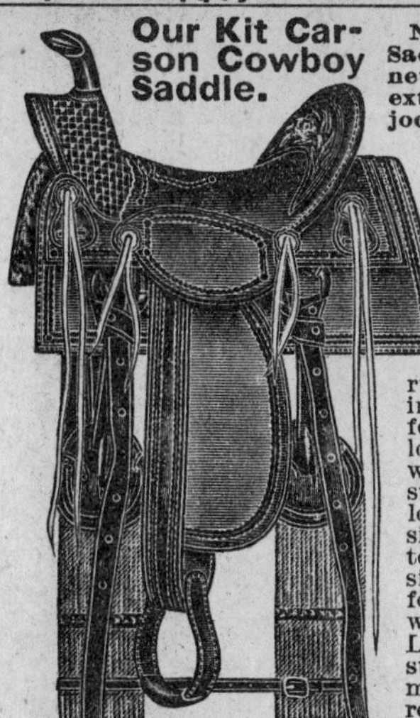

No. 10R1445 This Saddle is strictly new, made with full extended seat and jockey in one piece. Made on a 15-inch new San Juan tree, steel fork and hide covered. This is one of the new San Juan trees. 25-inch sheepskin lined skirts. Stirrup leathers 2½ inches to lace with fenders 16 inches long and 8½ inches wide attached. Tie straps, 1½ inches long on the near side and 1¾ inches to buckle on the off side. Cinches, California strand, white Angora hair. Leather covered steel stirrups, made in bound or roll cantle. Will always send bound cantle unless ordered roll cantle. Fine quality of saddle skirting. **Every part of the saddle is well selected and well finished. Strictly high grade throughout.** Weight, about 28 pounds.

Our special price.......................................$20.90

Our Olympia Heavy High Grade Cowboy Saddle.

$31.85

No. 10R1447 This is a strictly new saddle, made with full extended seat, with bucking roll. Bound cantle. Made on a high grade 15½-inch Portland tree. **Steel fork, and hide covered.** The Portland is new and one of the best high grade trees made, and is sure to please all who want a strictly high grade saddle. 28½-inch wool lined skirts; 3-inch stirrup leathers to lace, with fenders 18x9 inches attached. 1⅝-inch tie straps on the near side and 1¾-inch to buckle on the off side. Cinches, white hard hair, California strand, with leather chafes and connecting straps. XC Turner's Malleable Iron Stirrups. Weight of this saddle about 32 pounds. Made in bound or roll cantle. **Will always send bound cantle unless order calls for roll cantle.** Remember, this saddle is made of a very fine selection of oil tan skirting. Great pains is taken in selecting the different straps and parts of this saddle, having them cut and highly finished. **This saddle will range with all high grade stock saddles through the West.** Our special price.......$31.85

Our Jefferson Riding Saddle.

No. 10R1449 Made on a 14½-inch. Missouri steel fork tree, hide covered, with skirts 22½ inches long, felt lined. Stirrup leathers 1¾ inches to buckle with fenders 14½ inches long by 7 inches wide. Tie straps 1¼ inches to tie; leather covered cinch ring; soft gray hair cinches, 4-inch wood Texas stirrup, with bolt bar. **Bound cantle and full seat; seat and jockey in one piece.** Weight, about 20 lbs. Also made with roll cantle, if wanted, but will always send bound cantle unless ordered roll cantle. Price, each.......$12.85

Our Cheyenne Cowboy Saddle.

$19.90

No. 10R1451 A new and strictly up to date saddle, made of extra fine quality of oiled russet skirting leather on a strictly high grade 15-inch Hidalgo steel fork rawhide covered tree. This is one of the finest steel fork trees there is made for this grade of saddle. Narrow and rangey. Skirts 26 inches, round cornered sheepskin wool lined. Stirrup leathers 2½ inches wide to lace with fenders 16 inches long by 8 inches wide attached. Tie straps 1½ inches to tie. California strand white hard hair cinch. Single rig saddle, 2-inch wood brass bound stirrup; bound cantle, loop seat. **Made in roll cantle if wanted, but will always send bound cantle unless ordered roll cantle.** Weight of saddle, 25 pounds. Heavy oiled russet saddle skirting. Our special price.......................................$19.90

Our Pocatello Cowboy Saddle.

$21.82

WEIGHT, ABOUT 28 POUNDS. BOXED, 38 POUNDS.

No. 10R1453 This Saddle is something new and strictly up to date. Made on a 16-inch Oregon steel fork tree, hide covered. 26½-inch sheepskin wool lined skirts; stirrup leathers 3 inches to lace with fenders 17 inches long by 9 inches wide attached. Tie straps 1⅛ inches on near side, extra long, and 1¾ inches to buckle on off side. The girths are white Angora hair, California strand. 2-inch ox bow stirrups. Roll cantle. Extended full seat; seat and jockey in one piece. Weight of saddle about 28 pounds. **We will also make this saddle in bound cantle if so desired, but will always send roll cantle unless otherwise ordered.** The skirting used in this saddle is strictly high grade quality, well selected and finished. Oiled russet saddle kirting throughout. Our special price......$21.82

Our Special Kiowa Stock Saddle.

No. 10R1454 This Saddle is made on an improved Kiowa tree 14½ inches, steel fork and hide covered. Has the latest improved bars and is a very good easy riding saddle tree. The saddle is made of russet tanned oiled skirting. Roll cantle. The skirts, 22 inches long and 11½ inches wide, sheepskin wool lined. Stirrup leather, 1⅝ inches to buckle, with fender 8 inches wide and 14 inches long attached. Tie straps on the off side 1⅛ inches to buckle, 1⅜ inches on the near side to buckle; 15 strand soft hair cinches with leather chafes and tongues with connecting straps. Bent wood stirrups with leather bottom. This is one of the great bargains in our line. **Weight of saddle, about 22 pounds.** Price.......................................$12.95

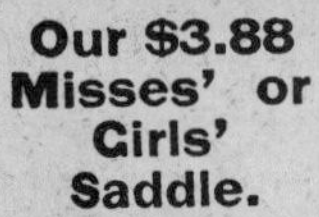

Our $3.88 Misses' or Girls' Saddle.

No. 10R1560 This Saddle is made on a 15½-inch English tree.

Skirts, Fancy Pigskin Impression.

Carpet seating pad, full English drill lined, ¾-inch stirrup leather, 3-inch super-cotton girth.

Weight, about 8 pounds.

Price..............$3.88

XC PLATED SHOE STIRRUP.

Our Special. The Princess Side Saddle.

OUR SPECIAL PRICE. $9.47

No. 10R1565 Tree. The tree used in the manufacture of this our special Princess Side Saddle, is a strictly first class Ruwart tree, with bars of saddle padded with sheep skin, so as to be soft and easy on the horse's back. **Leather. The leather used in the manufacture of this saddle is of the very finest selection of russet skirting,** highly polished well finished edges, leather tanned expressly for saddles and guaranteed to be superior to leather used in a great many other saddles at a great deal higher price than our special price, $9.47, on this saddle. **Seating. The seating of this saddle is of the finest quality of buckskin,** handsomely ornamentally stitched, making a very soft and easy cushion. This saddle is made with large jockey on back, the skirting is handsomely stamped four pieces, pigskin impression body, extra heavy 1¾-inch leather surcingle with ¾-inch stirrup strap, fine buckskin impression hooded stirrup, leather bottomed, lined with sheepskin, leaping horns seamed and buckskin lined, heavy double under rigging with woven hair cinches with 1½-inch tie straps on each side. **We want your order for this saddle,** not so much for the small amount of profit there is in it for us, **but because we know that you will be well satisfied with this saddle and it will be a great advertisement for us.** If you order this saddle and do not find it the greatest bargain you have ever seen for the money, you can return it to us at our expense and we will refund you the money paid for this saddle.

No. 10R1565 Our special price on this saddle $9.47

Weight, about 16 pounds; boxed for shipment, 30 pounds.

Our Special South-West Side Saddle, $14.00.

No. 10R1567 This Saddle is made of oiled California skirting, double rigged seamed leaping horn, made on the western style tree, and heavy rolled cantle, the same as man's heavy stock saddle. The tree used in this saddle is the genuine Ruwart tree; skirts, wool lined, 12⅛ inches wide and 28 inches long on the near side and 12½ inches wide and 23½ inches long on the off side, with pocket 5½x8½ inches on the off side. The illustrations will show both sides of this saddle. The seat is all leather covered, seat basket stamped pattern, hand stitched solid rolled cantle. Makes a very firm, strong, durable side saddle. Stirrup straps, ⅞-inch, with 2½-inch hooded, wool lined stirrup; cinches, 20-strand white Angora hair, with tongs; 1¼-inch buckle tie strap on the off side and 1½-inch buckle tie straps on the near side. This is one of our special leaders for 1902.

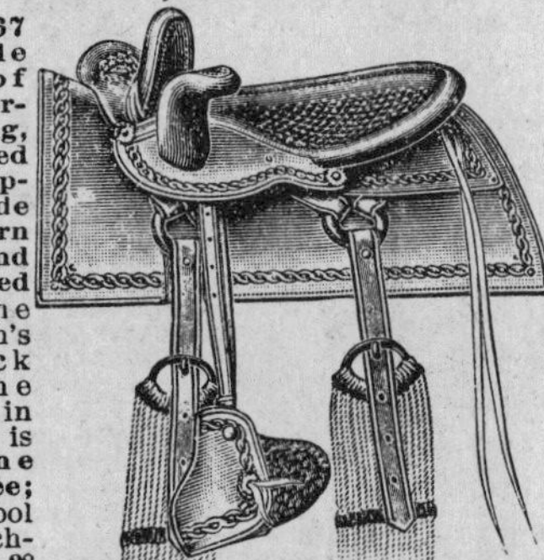

Price of this saddle............................$14.00

Weight, about 21 pounds; boxed, 35 pounds.

Sears, Roebuck & Co.'s Special Iowa Side Saddle.

The Greatest Value Ever Offered for the Money.

OUR SPECIAL PRICE, $6.95

No. 10R1580 Our Special Iowa Side Saddle, made on 18-inch Ruwart tree, skirts fancy stamped pigskin impression with fancy figured seating. Has heavy padded bars so as not to hurt the horse, 1⅛-inch tie strap on cinches, ¾-inch stirrup leathers with metal shoe stirrup, 4-inch soft woven hair cinches and seamed buckskin lined leaping horn. An extra good double cinch ladies' side saddle.

Price, each........$6.95

Weight, about 14 lbs.

Add extra for changes of stirrup on any saddle the difference in price of stirrups on page 419.

Ladies' $4.25 Saddle.

No. 10R1585 This Saddle is made of russet leather, has an 8-inch Ruwart tree, pigskin impression skirts, seating of figured carpet, with roll. Pad, bars padded, duck lining, hair stuffed. 1⅛-inch tie strap, ¾-inch stirrup leather, 4-inch soft woven hair cinch. Stirrup is an XC plated shoe. **Horn is carpet lined.** Price..$4.25

Weight of saddle, about 11 lbs.

Ladies' $5.42 Saddle.

Weight of saddle, about 12 lbs.

No. 10R1590 This Saddle is made of russet leather, has an 18-inch Ruwart tree, skirts pigskin, with fancy impression; seating of figured carpet with leather roll. Pad, bars padded, duck lining, hair stuffed, 1½-inch tie straps, ¾-inch stirrup leathers, 2½-inch corded cotton girth, 4-inch woven soft hair cinch. XC plated shoe stirrup. **Horn leather lined and leather faced.** Our price.......$5.42

Our Special Alice Improved Southern Side Saddle.

No. 10R1592 Made on the improved 18-inch Ruwart tree, with roll. Fine plush seating, plush leg fender and plush trimmed skirt. The skirt on this saddle is 18 inches wide and 15 inches deep, which is very large, and protects ladies' dresses. Soft, gray hair cinches. A double rig side saddle, with iron slipper stirrup strap; sheepskin padded bars; soft and easy on the horse's back. This is an entirely new and handsome side saddle. Satchel hook on off side.

Weight, boxed, about 25 lbs.

Price, without leaping horn.........$7.97

Price, with leaping horn........................8.55

Our Bessie Texas Side Saddle.

No. 10R1593 Made on improved Ruwart tree, with velvet carpet seating. Roll seat and velvet carpet leg fender. A very rich and tasty side saddle. The skirt is 16½ inches wide and 13½ inches deep. Heavy cotton strand Texas girth, double cinch Texas side saddle; sheepskin padded bars. Satchel to hook on off side. A strictly up to date rich looking side saddle. Made only without leaping horn. Oiled tan California skirting throughout.

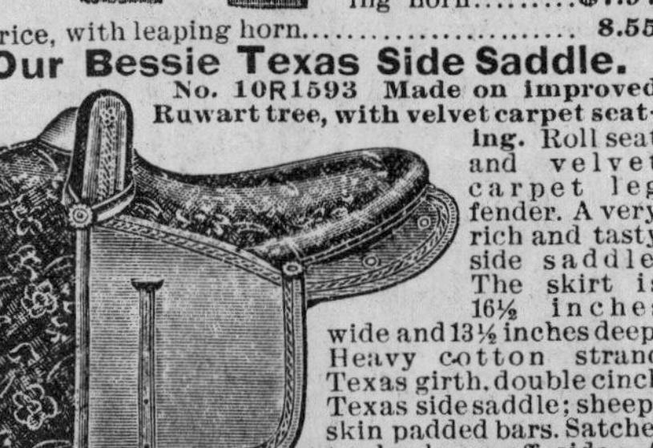

Weight, boxed, about 23 lbs.

Price, each......$6.55

Our Great Western Special Cow Girl Saddle.

$14.25

Weight, boxed for shipment, about 25 pounds.

No. 10R1595 This Side Saddle is made on genuine 18-inch Ruwart tree; extra strong seating of fine skirting leather or genuine buckskin quilted skirts; extra heavy 24-inch underskirt, with wide fender, wool lined underskirt; tie strap, 1½ inch by 5½ feet long and 1⅝ inch to buckle on the other side; Tapidero stirrup, wool lined; heavy seamed leaping horn; extra heavy covered rings buckle girths, with leather chafe and connecting strap; front girth heavy cotton string and back girth heavy cotton web. Nothing like this saddle ever sold before at this low price.

Our special price...............................$14.25

Our Improved Western Side Saddle, $13.25.

No. 10R1600 This is an Improved Western Style Side Saddle, and one of the best on the market. It is made on an 18-inch Ruwart tree, skirts are of California skirting, plain, underskirts square wool lined. Seating of genuine buckskin ornamentally stitched, has ⅞-inch stirrup leather. Cinches, 20-strand gray **California hair.** 1¼-inch tie straps, **leaping horn genuine buckskin seamed.** A regular double cinch rigged saddle.

Our price.......(Weight, 19 pounds).........$13.25

Our Special Colorado Stock Side Saddle.

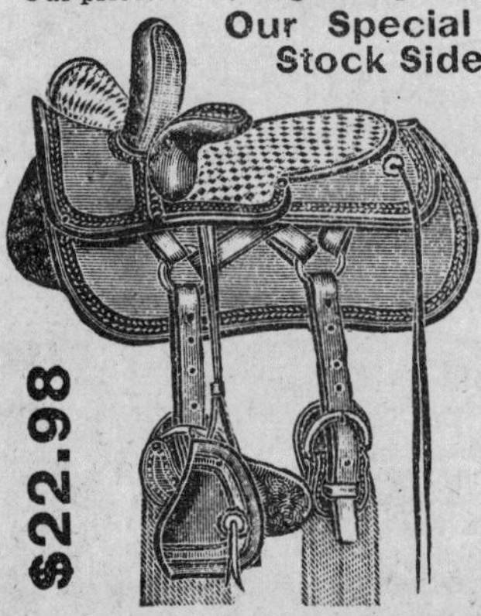

$22.98

No. 10R1605 Sears, Roebuck & Co.'s Special Cow-Girl Colorado Stock Side Saddle made on an 18-inch Ruwart rawhide covered tree, heavy ironed and one of the best trees on the market. Seating and jockey of the saddle are in one piece with hood to lace and the leaping horn is handsomely hand stamped in diamond patterns. Skirts extra heavy oil tanned skirting, round cornered, 27 inches long and 15 inches wide with sheepskin lining. The rigging you will notice on the saddle is our sawbuck style with covered rings, the lap of each strap is sewed by hand, making it very firm and strong, short buckle cinch strap on near side and long buckle cinch strap on off side, wood stirrups, leather bottom and large tapideros wool lined. Cinches: the front cinch is made of soft woven hair with wool lined chafes and buckle ring with connecting strap. This is a strictly high grade Western Saddle, and we guarantee it in every respect, in style, quality of leather and workmanship. Our special price........$22.98

Weight, about 20 pounds; boxed, 40 pounds.

Our Greeley Pack Saddle.

No. 10R1798 The demand for a strictly first class pack saddle has caused us to make this, our Greeley pack saddle. Made on a first class Greeley tree, double rig and tie straps 1¼-inch, with 1-inch hip and pack strap, web breast collar and web breeching with double cinch girth and extra cinch girth for pack. We only handle this saddle as shown in illustration, double rig only. Our special price on this extra fine Greeley Pack Saddle............ ....$4.70

No. 10R1799 Calfskin Bucking Roll. This roll can be put on any saddle. Made to order only. State the number of saddle you want the roll to fit. Price, each, $1.45
Weight, ½ pound.

No. 10R1800 Flat Snaffle, flat head and reins, solid crown piece, leather front. Made of good russet leather, with XC bar buckles and XC two-ring port bit and ⅝-inch curb strap.
¾-inch, each............$0.80
⅞-inch, each........ .90
1-inch, each........ 1.00
Weight, about 24 ounces.

No. 10R1803 Flat Snaffle, flat russet leather head and reins, with XC bar buckles, head stall and reins sewed into a full cheek XC snaffle bit.
¾-inch, each..........$1.10
⅞-inch, each.......... 1.20
Weight, about 16 ounces.

No. 10R1805 Flat Snaffle, extra fine russet leather, all hand sewed flat checks and reins, imitation leather covered or XC bar buckles, XC port bit with curb strap.
¾-inch, each..........$1.25
⅞-inch, each.......... 1.33
1-inch, each.......... 1.45
Weight, about 31 ounces.

Sidney Lucas Racing Bridle.

Made of the finest russet bridle leather, carefully selected and well finished, with close plate silver buckles; cheeks and rein made to loop in bit. Made in two sizes.
No. 10R1807 ¾-inch cheek, with 1-inch rein, without bit. Each$1.95
No. 10R1809 ⅞-inch cheek, with 1⅛-in. rein, without bit. Each$2.25
Add for large ring steel racing bit........75c
Weight, 12 ounces.

Halter Riding Bridle.

No. 10R1810 Our Fawn Web Halter Riding Bridle, adjustable crown piece and nose band, chin strap, front and throat latch, web and reins, complete with bit. Weight, 1½ lbs. Price, each..50c

Flat Pelham Bridle.

No. 10R1811 Superfine Flat Pelham Bridle, choice russet leather, **all hand sewed,** flat head stall with two reins, leather covered English buckles, nickel bit and curb strap.
¾-inch, each... ....$2.05
⅞-inch, each.......... 2.25
Weight, about 32 ozs.

Our Pony Bridle.

No. 10R1812 Our Shetland Pony Bridle, flat, with bar buckles, solid crown piece, with throat latch and cheeks to buckle on. Nickel buckles and full snaffle bit. ⅝-inch bridle and reins 4½ feet long. Made in russet or black. Price, each.....95c
Weight, 1 pound.

$2.95 Round Pelham Bridle.

No. 10R1813 Round Pelham. Superfine round russet leather bridle, round cheeks, front and two round reins, narrow loops, leather covered buckles, fine nickel port bit and curb strap.
Each..................$2.95
Weight, about 32 ounces.
No. 10R1815 Same style as No. 10R1813, only single rein in place of double rein. Price, each.......$2.20

Our Stallion Lead Bridle.

No. 10R1816 Our Stallion Lead Bridle, made of russet or black leather, 1-inch check, fancy front and 1¼-inch by 13-foot lead with round stopper on end. Buckle and billet on the other, XC buckle. Without bit, price, each, $2.05
No. 10R1817 1¼-inch throughout, nickel buckles. Without bit, price, each, $2.45
See page 420 for price on bits.
Weight, about 30 ounces.

New Stallion Bridle

No. 10R1818 Our Special Norman Stallion Bridle. Made of fine russet leather, brass buckles, scallop and inlaid cheeks, front and nose band, 13-foot lead rein with chain and round stopper. This is a very fine russet stallion bridle.
Price of bridle, less bit..................$4.00
Weight, 2½ pounds.

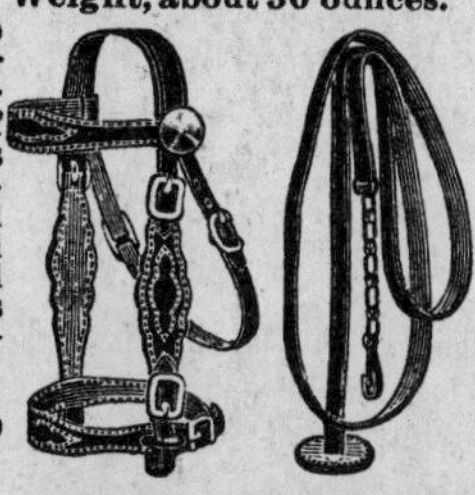

Cowboy Bridles.
Made of Oiled Russet Leather.

Weight, about 33 oz.

No. 10R1819 With double head stall to buckle on top, reins 5 feet long, to loop in bit. XC bar buckles, port bit and curb strap ⅝-inch.
Each................................90c
No. 10R1820 ⅞-inch bridle with bit. Price, each....98c

No. 10R1821 Made of heavy Oregon oiled tanned leather, ¾-inch double head stall to buckle on top, ¾-inch reins 6 feet long, to loop in bit. XC buckles, port bit and curb strap. Without bit............$0.90
Price, with bit 1.00
No. 10R1822 ⅞-inch bridle with bit. Price, each..$1.10
Weight, about 1½ pounds.

No. 10R1823 Made extra heavy and strong, Oregon oiled tanned leather, ⅞-inch double head stall to buckle on top, ⅞-inch reins, 6 feet long, XC buckles and curb strap.
Without bit, each.........$1.35
With XC port bit.......... 1.45
With blued Texas port bit...................... 1.48
Weight, about 1½ pounds.

No. 10R1825 Extra fine and durable. Made of Oregon oiled tanned leather, ⅞-inch double head stall to buckle on top, ⅞-inch reins, 6 feet long; **nickel buckles and box loops throughout.** Ends of reins laced with buckskin. Each without bit, $1.85; with blued Texas port bit $2.00
With nickel plated California bit with rein chains $3.60
Weight, about 1¾ pounds.

No. 10R1827 Extra heavy Oregon oiled tanned leather. 1-inch double head stalls to buckle on top; 1-inch reins, 6 feet long, laced at ends with buckskin. **Heavy fringed front, fringed slide loops on checks and throat latch.** ⅝-inch curb strap. Nickel buckles. Without bit, each...$2.15
No. 10R1829 With blued Texas port bit, each....$2.25
No. 10R1830 With nickel Texas port bit, each $2.35
Weight, about 2¼ pounds.

Williams Special Short Cheek Halter Riding Bridle.

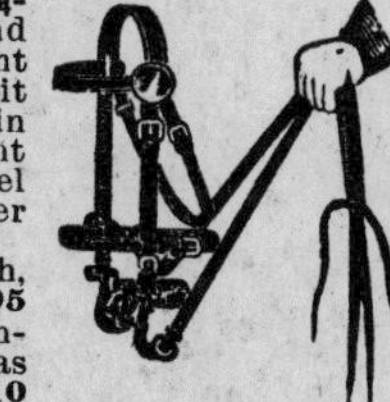

Made of russet leather, ¾-inch cheek, ¾-inch nose band and chin strap, ¾-inch front and throat latch, ¾-inch bit strap, ¾-inch reins to loop in bit, 6 feet long with light curb strap, made with nickel bent heel buckles and leather loops.
No. 10R1831 Price, each, without bit..............$1.95
No. 10R1833 Price, complete with blue port Texas bit........................$2.10
Weight, 2 pounds.

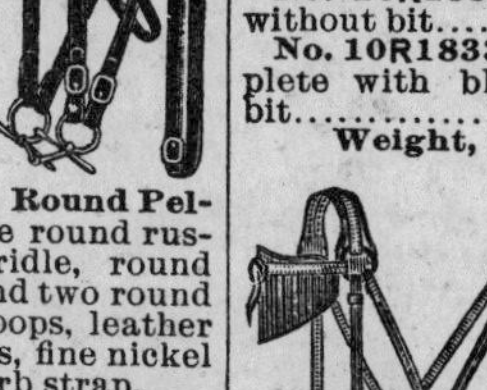

No. 10R1835 Fringed Front Bridle. This **Bridle** is made with long, heavy bridle rein **with quirt end, double checks ⅞-inch** to buckle in bit and ring on crown piece, **heavy fringed front,** sewed in **ring** on crown piece, crown has wide scallop **chafe** with layer, making one of the best of **Cowboy Bridles.**
Without bit, each.... $1.65
Weight, about 2 pounds.

Hand Braided Cowboy Bridles.

This Bridle is made from fine calfskin leather, tanned expressly for fine bridles. **The bridle is made with a double crown piece and front** and single rein with **braided knots and frills.** A **heavy** double braided front and rosettes. **The price of the bridle is without bit.** 12 oz.
No. 10R1837 Four-plait double check and single rein. **Weight, about 8 oz.** Without bit, each......$2.15
No. 10R1839 Six plait, double check and single rein. Without bit, each.............................$2.75

Our Special Mexican Cowboy Fine Diamond Braided Bridle, made of extra fine oil tanned **calfskin,** 8-plait, double head, double check and double front with fancy rosettes; extra braided billets, self adjusting crown piece, **fancy braided knots and frills, extra fine long braided rein with round loop and romal or quirt end.** The finest fancy diamond braided bridle ever offered to our many customers. Equal if not superior to bridles which retail at $12.00 to $15.00. Weight, 1½ lbs.
No. 10R1841 Our special price, without bit, $6.95
No. 10R1843 Same style of bridle as No. 10R1841, **only six-plait.** Price, each, without bit........$4.50

Riding Martingales.

No. 10R1845 Made of russet leather, with neck strap. XC center bar buckles and rings.
Weight, about 8 oz. Each....35c
No. 10R1847 Same as above, made of oiled leather. Each....40c
No. 10R1849 Heavy russet leather, with flat neck strap. XC or imitation leather covered buckles and rings. **Weight, about 8 ounces.** Each.............................55c
No. 10R1851 Extra fine russet leather, with neck strap, round forks, balance flat. Imitation leather covered buckles and rings. **Weight, about 8 ounces.** Each.......$1.00
No. 10R1853 Round russet leather forks and neck straps, with flat body piece. Leather covered English buckles and rings.
Weight, about 9 ounces. Each...........................$1.50

Driving Martingale.

No. 10R1855 Our Fine Black Leather Driving Martingale, made with buckle and billet on lower end and two black rubber rings, fine round edge finish.
Price, each..47c
Weight, about 8 ounces.

Driving Martingale.

No. 10R1860 Our Fine Driving Martingale, made of black leather, round jaw piece with buckle and billet, round body martingale runs from bellyband to bit. Price, each, 65c
Weight, ½ pound.

Buggy Bridles.

No. 10R1895 Our ⅝-inch cheap Buggy Bridle (no box loop), overdraw check, or side rein, patent leather blind, flat winker brace, XC buckles throughout. Price, ea., 90c
No. 10R1897 Our ⅝-inch box loop check, patent leather blind, round winker brace, XC trimmings, over check or side rein.
Price, each................$1.45
No. 10R1899 Same bridle as described in No. 10R1897, only nickel or Davis rubber trimming, **with initial rosette. Weight, about 2¼ lbs.**
Price, each...................$1.65

No. 10R1897

No. 10R1900 Our fine ⅝-inch box loop check, grain patent leather blind, round winker brace, over draw check with nose band or side rein, nickel or Davis rubber trimmings, **initial rosette,** good bit.
Price.........................$1.85
No. 10R1901 Same style bridle as No. 10R1900, only a much finer quality, better made, ⅝-inch box loop check, extra fine, patent leather blind, nickel or Davis rubber trimmings, long layer on crown piece, over draw check with nose band or side rein, round winker braces, **initial rosette. Weight, about 2¼ pounds.**
Price, each.............$1.95

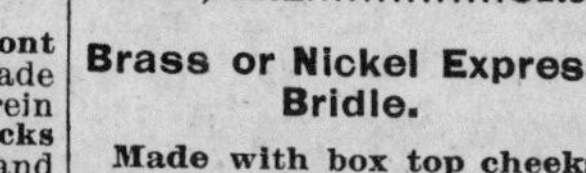

Brass or Nickel Express Bridle.

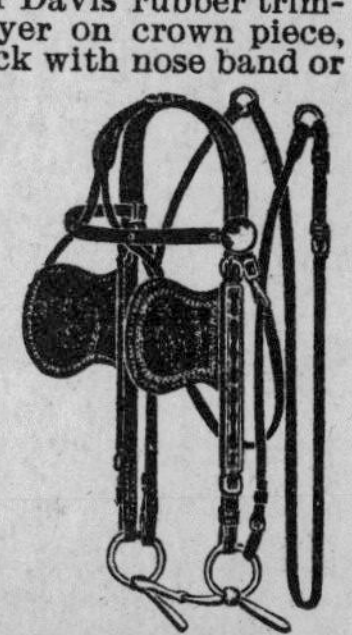

Made with box top cheeks, sensible blind, round winker brace, brass or nickel band front, **long round rim.** This bridle is for single express or spring wagon harness.
No. 10R1902 Price, ¾-inch bridle, each................$2.35
Weight, about 3 pounds.

83 Cents Buys a $1.50 Rawhide Halter.

No. 10R2019 We show in the cut an illustration of our special grade five-ring riveted Rawhide Halter. This halter is extra good quality, very heavy and well made, complete with tie straps. Size, 1 inch. Weight, about 28 ozs.
Our special price, each.....83c

No. 10R2021 Five-ring riveted Rawhide Halter, complete with tie straps, same as illustrated and described above, but 1¼ inches wide. Weight, about 40 ounces.
Price, each.......................$1.08

Our 37-Cent Cow Halter.

No. 10R2023 This is a heavy 1-inch leather cow halter, is easy on head, does not chafe around horns. The best cow halter made. Weight, about 1 pound. Price, each..............37c

Halter Ropes.

No. 10R2035 Made of ½-inch sisal rope, 8 feet long, extra strong, taper to point, with loop braided. Weight, about 4 ounces. Price, per dozen, $1.08; each....9c

Halters and Ties.

No. 10R2037 Covert's Cattle Tie, ½-inch jute rope, full length. Price, each..11c
Weight, about 8 ounces.

No. 10R2039 Covert's Horse Tie, ½-inch jute rope.
Price, each..............15c
Weight, about 12 ounces.

No. 10R2041 Round Rope Halter, ⅝-inch sisal.
Price, each.....11c
Weight, about 12 ounces.

No. 10R2043 Braided Rope Halter, fancy woven.
Price, each....12c
Weight, about 12 ounces.

Heavy Leather Neck Halters.

No. 10R2045 Solid Leather Neck Halter, 1-inch neck strap, 1-inch stale. Price, each..............55c
Weight, about 15 ounces.

No. 10R2047 1¼-inch Neck Strap, 1-inch stale. Weight, about 16 ounces. Price, each...............64c

No. 10R2049 1½-inch Neck Strap, 1¼-inch stale. Weight, about 18 ounces. Price, each..............75c

Riding Bridle Reins.

No. 10R2051 Flat Reins, riveted. XC plate, center bar buckles. Each, ¾-inch, 35c; 1-inch, 50c

No. 10R2053 Same as No. 10R2051, better quality reins. Price.......75c
Weight, about 8 ounces.

Open Bridle Cheeks.

No. 10R2055 Our Round Bridle Cheeks, made with buckle and billet, used for making open bridle. For one horse. Weight, about 4 ozs. Price, per pair, 50c

No. 10R2057 Our ⅝-inch Box Loop Open Bridle Cheek, used for making open bridle, fine fancy stamped box loop.
Price, per pair, for one horse..............................69c
Weight, about 6 ounces.

Check Reins.

For Single and Double Buggy Harness.

No. 10R2059 Over Checks, 3 buckles, 2 billets, nickel or Davis rubber buckles. Each........63c

No. 10R2061 Better quality. Same as No. 10R2059......75c

Weight, about 8 ozs.

Side Checks.

No. 10R2062 Side Checks, ⅝-inch billets, nickel or Davis rubber buckles and rings. Each......57c
Weight, about 11 ounces.

No. 10R2063 ¾-inch Team Side Checks. Weight, about 12 ounces. Price, each...............65c

Single Driving Lines.

Flat for single buggy harness.

No. 10R2065 Single Flat Driving Lines, ⅞-inch front, 1-inch russet or black leather hand parts. Length, 12 feet 6 inches. Price............$1.45
Weight, about 30 ounces.

No. 10R2067 Single Flat Driving Lines, ⅞-inch fronts, with billets to buckle in bits, 1⅛-inch russet or black leather hand parts. All hand made. Weight, about 32 ounces. Price.................$1.90

Loops or Rein Holder.

No. 10R2080 Russet Leather Rein Holder, folded, double stitched layer, nickel loops. Can be attached to any driving lines. Per pair..63c

Double Driving Lines.

Double Driving Lines. Flat for double buggy harness.

No. 10R2090 Flat Double Driving Lines, ⅞-inch front with 1-inch russet or black leather handle parts, nickel buckles. Length, 14 feet. Per set, $2.40

No. 10R2093 Flat Double Driving Lines, ⅞-inch front, with 1⅛-inch russet or black leather hand parts sewed to checks. Nickel or Davis rubber buckles. Length, 14 feet. Per set.................$3.00

No. 10R2095 Web Team Lines, made from 1-inch heavy russet web, with snap, made in one length and used for farm or general team work.
Price, per set, 20 feet, $1.60; 18 feet..........$1.25

Double Team Lines.

Our B Grade Black Leather Team Lines made with bar rein buckles, per set for two horses:

No. 10R2150 ⅞-in. wide,	15 ft.	18 ft.	20 ft.	22 ft.
Weight, about, pounds.....	3	3¼	3¾	3¾
Price, per pair..............	$1.87	$2.25	$2.50	$2.97
No. 10R2155 1-in. wide,				
Weight, about, pounds....	3¾	4	4¼	4½
Price, per pair..............	2.10	2.40	2.75	3.19

A Grade Team Lines.

Our A Grade Black Leather Team Lines, genuine hand made from selected stock, roller buckles, Per set for two horses:

No. 10R2160 ⅞-in.	15 ft.	18 ft.	20 ft.	22 ft.	28 ft.
Weight, about, pounds,	3	3¼	3¾	3¾	
Price, per pair......	$2.06	$2.36	$2.55	$2.80	$3.58
No. 10R2165 1-in.					
Weight, about, lbs.	3¾	4	4¼	4½	
Price, per pair.....	2.31	2.50	2.76	2.90	3.95

Our AA Grade Team Lines.

Our Extra Heavy AA Grade, Hand Made Lines, from choice selected stock, with roller buckles. Per set for two horses:

No. 10R2170 1⅛ inches wide.	18 ft.	20 ft.	22 ft.
Weight, about, pounds......	4½	5¼	5½
Price, per pair................	$3.00	$3.25	$3.50

S., R. & Co.'s Special Round Team Lines.

No. 10R2175 Our Extra Fine Round Check Team Lines, made with Ring and Short Bit Strap, 1 inch by 18 feet. Hand parts sewed on. This is a good pair of lines for team work. Price, per set, for 2 horses, $3.95

No. 10R2176 Price, per set, for 20-foot line.. 4.25

S., R. & Co.'s Special Square Check Lines.

No. 10R2180 Same style of lines as above, only square check in place of round check, 1 inch by 20 feet. Hand parts sewed on.
Price, per set, for two horses...................$4.05

Hand Made Hame Straps.

No. 10R2300 Hame Straps. This hame strap is hand made, of fine oak stock, 21 inches long, with roller buckles and two leather loops. Made in sizes:

Size, inches..........	¾	⅞	1	1¼
Price, each.........	8c	10c	11c	18c

Weight, each, 4 ounces.

No. 10R2305 Hame Straps, made with twin loop, made from good heavy leather. 21 inches long. Price, each, 1-inch, 11c; ⅞-inch..........10c

No. 10R2310 Same as above, only 30-inches long. Price, each, 1-inch, 14c; ⅞-inch...........................11c

No. 10R2315 Rawhide Hame Straps, best quality oil tanned rawhide. Each, 1-inch, 14c; ⅞-inch..12c

Spread Strap and Ring.

No. 10R2317 Spread Strap and Ring for team harness, made with twin loop and one slide loop with good ring. Weight, about 2 ounces. Price, each..14c

Spreader Straps.

No. 10R2321 Leather Spreader Straps, without rings or loops, with ⅝-inch buckle, 24 inches long, black leather. Each........................10c

Skate Straps.

No. 10R2325 S., R. & Co. Special Skate Strap, made of Dundee oak leather, with roller skate buckle made in three lengths.

Length, inches.....	18	21	24
Price, per pair	5c	6c	7c
Price, per doz. pair	60c	72c	84c

Halter or Hitching Straps.

No. 10R2327 Black Leather Hitching Strap, 7 feet long, ¾-inch wide, with German snaps riveted on.

Size, inches..........	⅝	¾	⅞	1	1¼
Weight, about, ounces..	6	7	8	8	12
Price, each...........	19c	23c	27c	33c	42c

No. 10R2329 With buckles.

Size, inches...........	¾	⅞	1	1¼
Weight, about, ounces...	7	8	8	12
Price, each............	27c	30c	38c	45c

Our Special Surface Tanned Rawhide Halter Strap.

No. 10R2331 This Halter Strap is made of extra fine quality of oil tanned rawhide leather, is soft and pliable, easy to tie, and is extra strong, 7 feet long, cut and twisted loop.

Size, inches.....	1	1¼	1½
Wt., about, oz..	7	8	9
Price, each...	35c	45c	53c

Breast Straps.

No. 10R2332 Team Breast Strap, made for a cheap team farm harness, two 1½-inch pieces sewed together with buckle snaps on each end, with slide.
Price, each.......................39c
Weight, about 1½ pounds.

Breast Strap Made With Twin Loop.

Our Team Breast Strap, made of good heavy leather 1¼ inches wide, with twin loop. Full length breast straps.

No. 10R2333 1¼-inch. Price, each...............40c
Weight, about 10 ounces.

No. 10R2334 1½-inch. Price, each.............46c
Weight, about 12 ounces.

Hand Made Breast Straps.

Our fine hand made team Breast Strap, made with two heavy leather loops. Heavy roller buckle, 4 feet, 8 inches long.

No. 10R2335 1½-inch. Price, each...................49c
No. 10R2336 1¾-inch. Price, each...................53c
No. 10R2337 2 -inch. Price, each....................64c
Weight, each, 18 ounces.

Double and Stitched Buggy Neckyoke Strap.

Our Special Double and Stitched Neckyoke Strap. This is extra strong, well made, 3 feet, 4 inches long, double loop and buckle. The best kind of strap for safety to parties in buggy and carriage. Made in two sizes. Weight, about 12 ounces.

No. 10R2338 Size, 1¼-inch. Price, each......60c
No. 10R2339 Size, 1½-inch. Price, each......80c

Buggy Neckyoke Strap.

Our Single Strap Neckyoke Strap. Dundee oak leather, 1¼ inches wide, 3 feet, 4 inches long, for neckyoke on double buggy.

No. 10R2340 Weight, about ½ pound. Price .45c

Pole Strap or Martingale.

Made of extra heavy leather, with roller buckle and loop on one end, and loop and ring on the other, made in three sizes. NO COLLAR STRAP.

No. 10R2345 1½-inch. Price, each..................44c
No. 10R2347 1¾-inch. Price, each..................49c
No. 10R2349 2 -inch. Price, each...................57c
Weight, each, 15 ounces.

S., R. & Co.'s Chicago Truck Martingale.

This is our Heavy Martingale made of fine Dundee oak leather, single strap body running from belly-band to collar, and short heavy strap running from ring on body to neckyoke, or chain, made in three sizes and the best martingale or pole strap for heavy trucking we make.

	1½-inch	1¾-inch	2-inch
No. 10R2351 Price, each	92c	$1.08	$1.28

No. 10R2353 Same style as above, only double and stitched body, 1½ inches wide only, with wool lined shape. Price each.................................$1.75

The price is for single martingale for one horse. If you want a pair, for two horses, order two.

S., R. & Co.'s Special Heavy Team Housing.

No. 10R2375 Made of two pieces of harness leather stitched together. Leather layer on center, with curved top front, stitched around holes. The housing is left solid, so you will be able to make the hole for your hames where you want it. Size of housing 16 inches long from center by 12¾ inches wide at bottom. This is the best solid leather team housing on the market. Weight, about 8½ pounds each. Price, each..$3.00

No. 10R2377 Price, per pair.............................6.00

We will put brass block letters on this housing for you as follows: 1½-inch letters. Price, each....12c
1¼-inch letters. Price, each...............................10c

Pole Strap or Martingale with Collar Strap.

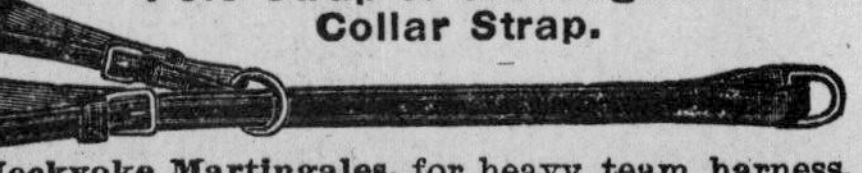

Neckyoke Martingales, for heavy team harness, buckled loop at one end, ring at the other end, choke ring stitched on; 24-inch collar strap with buckle. When ordering, give number of article desired.

No. 10R2378 1½-inch. Price, each 58c
No. 10R2379 1¾-inch. Price, each...............65c
Weight, about 18 ounces.

Harness Oils.

No. 10R4680 Eureka Harness Oil. Makes the leather soft and glossy and prevents the harness cracking. Put up in lithographed cans with screw top.

Gallon can, 50c; ½-gallon can.......35c
Quart can, 20c; pint can 12c
Weight, pints, 1 lb.; quarts, 2¼ lbs.; ½ gallon, 4 lbs.; 1 gallon, 7½ lbs.

Acme Black Edge Ink.

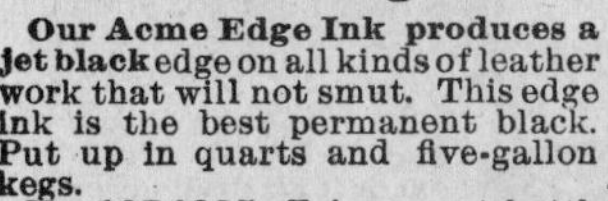

Our Acme Edge Ink produces a jet black edge on all kinds of leather work that will not smut. This edge ink is the best permanent black. Put up in quarts and five-gallon kegs.

No. 10R4685 Price, quart bottle, each $0.10
Price, 5-gallon keg, each.............. 1.45
Weight, about 2¾ pounds.

Acme Harness Soap.

No. 10R4690 Our Special Acme Harness Soap is made by the finest chemist in the country. It is soft; will clean and soften harness to perfection. **A genuine oil soap.** Lathers freely and keeps in any climate. Put up in tin boxes ready for use. Made up in ½-pound, pound, 2¼ and 5-pound cans.

Price, ½-pound can, each..........................11c
Price, 1-pound can, each..........................16c
Price, 2¼-pound can, each.........................35c
Price, 5-pound can, each..........................70c

Acme Harness Dressing.

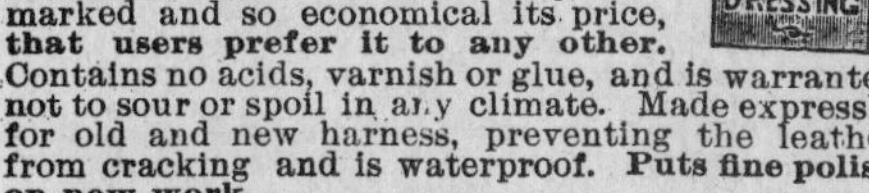

No. 10R4695 Acme Harness Dressing **is considered the best dressing made in the country,** where the user of Acme Dressing has been able to judge side by side with other dressings of standard makes. Its excellency is so marked and so economical its price, **that users prefer it to any other.** Contains no acids, varnish or glue, and is warranted not to sour or spoil in any climate. Made expressly for old and new harness, preventing the leather from cracking and is waterproof. **Puts fine polish on new work.**

Price, half-pint cans, each.......................13c
Price, pint cans, each............................19c
Price, quart cans, each...........................35c
Weight about: ½ pint, 10 ounces; 1 pint, 20 ounces; 1 quart, 2½ pounds.

Genuine Bickmore Gall Cure.

The genuine gall cure, for all kinds gall, wire cuts, all kinds of sores on horses and cattle. Furnished in three sizes.

No. 10R4696 Price, per doz. $1.75; 2-oz. box each...15c
No.10R4697 Price, per doz. $3.50; 6-oz. box,ea.30c
No.10R4698 Price, per doz. 7.00; 16-oz. box,ea.59c

No. 10R4700 Acme Gall Cure, guaranteed to cure saddle gall, collar gall, collar bunches, scratches, cuts, calks, bruised heel, speed cracks, quarter cracks, contracted feet, old sores of all kinds on horses or cattle, and sure cure for sore teats on cows. No one can afford to be without a box of Acme Gall Cure.

Price, per doz., $1.56; 3-ounce boxes, each.....13c
Price, per doz., 2.76; 8-ounce boxes, each.....23c

A Leader at 60 Cents.

No. 10R4800 The Herald. It is a new clipper and a **leader.** The plates are detachable and interchangeable; has two thumb nuts **and tension springs; no wrench needed to adjust this clipper.** It takes the place of the cheap clippers which we formerly imported. Weight, 14 ounces.

Price, each..60c

The Lenox Clipper for 85 Cents.

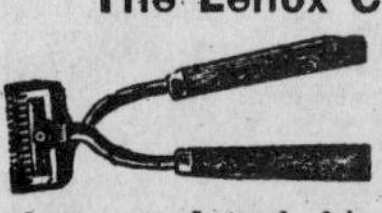

No. 10R4805 The Lenox. This is a standard clipper **and a great favorite with horsemen;** has bright **red handles; it is well finished and attractive.** Cutting plates are detachable and interchangeable. Weight, 20 ounces.

Price, each.......................................85c
Price, top plates, each...........................30c
Price, bottom plates, each........................45c

The Leader Clipper for 75 Cents.

No. 10R4815 Our 75-cent **Leader Fetlock or Dog Clipper,** made of extra fine tool steel plates, well ground and polished, wide mill teeth, handsomely nickel plated, fine piano steel spring. **A strictly first class clipper.** Dealers sell for $1.50.

Our special price, each...........................75c
Weight, about 8 ounces.

Our $1.00 Newmarket Clipper.

No. 10R4820 The Newmarket Clipper. It is carefully constructed, **handsome in appearance,** has bright red handles; there is no clipper made so well known to professional horse clippers as the **Newmarket pattern; the name sells it.** All parts are detachable and interchangeable. Weight, 18 ounces. Price, each.$1.00

Top plates, 72c; bottom plates....................80

$1.50 Buys the O.K. Horse Clipper.

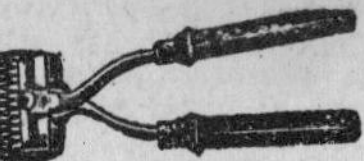

No. 10R4825 The O. K. No. 62. Our old reliable; nickel plated; **an excellent cutter,** bright polished handles, and **has had the lead of all other clippers for several seasons.** Cutting plates detachable and interchangeable. Weight 20 ounces. Price, each...............$1.50

Top plates, 80c; bottom plates................ 1.10

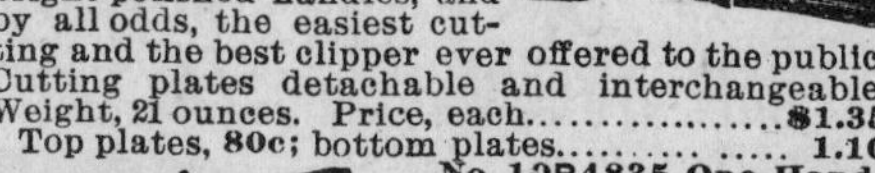

No. 10R4830 The B.B. (Ball Bearing). New this season. Has anti-friction ball bearings, finest nickel finish, bright polished handles, and by all odds, the easiest cutting and the best clipper ever offered to the public. Cutting plates detachable and interchangeable. Weight, 21 ounces. Price, each..................$1.35

Top plates, 80c; bottom plates................ 1.10

No. 10R4835 One-Handed Horse or Dog Clipper. For trimming about the ears and fetlocks requires a keen cutting one-handed clipper with strong elastic spring. You will find this is the one that is sought after. Plates detachable and interchangeable. Weight, 12 ounces. Each.$1.00

Extra springs, each .... .10

The parts of all our Clippers are interchangeable and can be promptly duplicated.

NOTE—When ordering clippers, plates for an old clipper, state the name of your clipper that is stamped in plate and the number that is stamped on plate. Then we can tell if the ones we send you will fit or not; or send your old one with your order.

Singeing Lamp.

No. 10R4840 Sears, Roebuck & Co.'s Special Singeing Lamp. By the use of this lamp you will give new life to the hair of horses and cattle. The lamp is also used for removing hair from horses' ears or other places where you cannot use clippers. Every farmer and liveryman should have one of these, our special lamps. Used with kerosene oil, and wide wick furnished complete with each lamp. No farm or stable is complete without a singeing lamp.

Price, each.....(**Weight, 7 ounces**)..........$1.00

Our Montana Special Sheep Shearing Machine.

This machine is considered one of the best by a great many of the large sheep growers throughout the United States and Australia.

In offering this special Montana machine to our many customers who are raising a great many sheep and want to avail themselves of the opportunity of getting a machine to shear their sheep that will prove sadsfactory to them, this machine will save time and save any injury to the sheep in shearing. It does not require a practical man to run this Special Montana Clipping Machine. A book of full instructions is shipped with every machine which shows the position that the sheep will be in.

The machine consists of a large wheel which is perfectly true and gear is enclosed in a stationary frame and drives a hardened steel cut pinion. The pinion shaft is even with a small turn balance wheel, which, running at a high speed, makes the machine run perfectly steady at all times. The cutters are of an improved pattern and are so made that they will easily penetrate in any kind of wool that grows no matter how dense or fine. The number of sheep, this machine will cut without sharpening the knives depends much on the condition the sheep are in and how much grit or sand there may be in the fleece.

All farmers who raise sheep and shear them should not be without one of the Improved Montana Machines, or some other good sheep shearing machine, as you get longer wool and your sheep will never be injured in shearing. You will save the price of the machine in two weeks. **Weight, boxed, 70 pounds.**

No. 10R4844 Price of the machine, with four pair of sheep knives..............................$14.70

No. 10R4845 Price of machine with three pair of sheep knives, and one pair horse knives.. 14.75

Add for extra cutting handle.................. 7.00
Add for extra knives, per pair................ 1.00

Add extra for belt wheel, which you can attach to the machine on the crank bar and run the machine by power. The 8-inch pulley is substituted for the crank handle. You can run the machine with any kind of power with a 1-inch flat belt to transmit the power to the machine.

Price of belt wheel, extra............................$1.50

Our New Illinois Swing Clipper.

No. 10R4863 The very latest and best improved machine on the market. The machine suspended from ceiling by rope which passes through a screw eye, free end is passed under eccentric pulley journaled in the frame, which locks at any point desired by letting go the rope. Large balance heel, flexible shaft, good cutting knives, turns ery easy, any one can work this machine, complete with one cutting head.

Price, each....................................$7.85
Top plates, each................................ .90
Bottom plates, each............................ 1.45
Extra cutting heads, to attach to machine.. 2.35
Weight, about 36 pounds.

The Acme Hand Power Clippers.

We endeavor to show in the illustration our high grade Horse Clippers, and the cut will give you some idea of the appearance of this, the **best machine of the kind manufactured.** It is made by a manufacturer who makes a specialty of this class of machinery and who has been making the **best clippers** for the last thirty or forty years. This machine is **complete with ball bearing cutters.** It is the only machine in the market that has an **all steel tempered** flexible staff with riveted joints. It is the only high grade ball bearing machine manufactured. It is very light running, easily handled, takes up little room and performs every service required of it. We furnish **vibrating cutters with each machine.** It is complete and ready for use. **Every blacksmith** should own one of these machines, and can make big money by doing work for other people. **Farmers can make the machine pay** for itself renting it to neighbors. We furnish one extra cutting head with this machine.

No. 10R4865 Our special price...............$17.25
Weight, packed for shipment, 75 pounds.

Extra cutters, **$3.00;** top plates, **$1.00;** bottom plates, **$1.50** each for above clipping machine. **All machines should have two extra set of cutters.**

Our Dakota Horse Clipper, $10.75.

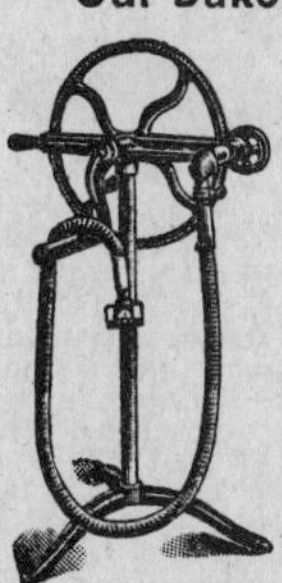

The picture represents one of the latest and most perfect Horse Clipping Machines on the market. This is a new pattern, strictly up to date, with all the latest improvements that are used in high priced machines. It has many advantages over others which will readily recommend themselves to the user. First, it has a **positive driving mechanism,** and the operator knows that when he turns the handle of the drive wheel that the knife will cut, because there is no belt to slip, and no extra motions required to do the work. The next special feature is the knives, which are held together by one set screw, so that it is impossible to tighten one end of the blades tighter than the other, as the set screw works in the center and tightens the full blade evenly. The large drive wheel is machined all over, the teeth are milled from solid metal, and engaged in a hard steel pinion. the small balance wheel revolving at a great speed completely equalizes the motion, completely closed and dust proof; this machine is equipped with flexible shaft attached to the machine and cutting head. We believe in presenting this our latest improved Dakota Clipping Machine to our customers that we are offering them a machine that will be hard to duplicate anywhere, with our special improvements, and you will find the cutting qualities of this machine equal to any of the very best high grade machines on the market.

No. 10R4881 Our price of this machine with one set of knives complete...............$10.75

No. 10R4883 For extra knives to attach to the clipping head, price per pair.............2.25

NOTICE—To sharpen sheep shearing knives or horse clipping plates: Take a very fine piece of emery cloth, stretch securely over a smooth surfaced board, and tack it down. Rub your sheep shearing knives or clipper plates face down perfectly flat, and rub them eight or ten good quick rubs and you will sharpen the teeth very quick. This will save you sending your plates away to be sharpened as you can repeat this process very often during the day. **Weight, boxed, 75 pounds.**

Curry Combs.

A horse well curried not only looks sleek and attractive, but his health is greatly improved by keeping his skin clean and pliable. Careful grooming saves much feed.

Weight of Curry Comb, from 4 to 15 ounces.

No.10R4900 6-Bar Open Back Curry Comb. Japanned iron, wood handle. Weight, about 4 ounces.

Each..............3c
Per dozen ... .36c

Curry Combs continued on following page.

CURRY COMBS.

No.10R4905 8-Bar Japanned Open Back Curry Comb. Wood handle with double brace running over top of comb. Weight, about 10 ounces.
Each....................8c
Per dozen.......96c

No. 10R4910 6-Bar Lacquered Steel Curry Comb. Black enameled handle, strongly riveted on. Heavy knockers. Best cheap comb on the market. Weight, about 10 ozs.
Price, per dozen, **$1.20**; each....................10c

No. 10R4913 Barnes Solid Brass Closed Back Curry Comb. 6 bars, solid shank, riveted through handle. A fine solid brass curry comb. Same style as No. 10R4910. Price, each....................20c

No. 10R4915 6-Bar Open Back Steel Curry Comb. Strongly riveted, wood handle, **well made and a bargain.** Weight, about 10 ounces
Each....................6c
Per dozen....................72c

Mane and Curry Comb Combined.

No.10R4920 Mane and Curry Comb combined. Lacquered steel, 6 bars, with comb on top for carding the horse's mane. Enameled handle. **Extra value for the money.** Weight, about 11 ounces. Per dozen, **$1.44**; each....................12c

No. 10R4925 S., R. & Co.'s Special Improved Wire Grasp Open Back Curry Comb. Made of roll steel, solid end pieces with wire handles and steel shank riveted through handle. Six bars. Fine lacquered finish.
Each....................7c
Per dozen....................84c

No. 10R4930 Our Improved Closed Back Fine Rolled Steel, extra fine lacquered finish, six bars, closed back, wire grasp handles and steel shank riveted through handle. Price, per dozen, **$1.08**; each....... ..9c

Special 10-Cent Open Back Curry Comb.

No. 10R4935 S., R. & Co.'s Improved Extra Fine Wire Grasp Open Back Curry Comb. Made of fine rolled steel, extra fine lacquered finish. Eight bars with riveted end pieces, wire grasp and steel shank riveted through handle.
Price, per dozen, **$1.20**; each....................10c

No. 10R4937 Solid Brass Open Back Curry Comb. Wire shank riveted through handle. The best open back brass curry comb made. Same style as No. 10R4935. Our special price, each....................12c

Fine Forged Steel Curry Combs.

No.10R4940 Fine Forged Steel Curry Combs. 8 bars, solid blued backs, enamel wood handle, wrought shank running through handle, **and extra strong brace and knockers.** This is beyond a doubt the best curry comb ever offered for the money. Weight, about 15 ounces. Price, per dozen, **$2.16**; each....................18c

Self Cleaning Curry Combs.

No. 10R4945 The Self Cleaning Curry Comb. A great favorite with all who have used it, 8 bars, japanned iron, wood handle, strongly riveted. **Will give satisfaction.** Weight, about 15 ounces.
Each....................$0.19
Per dozen....................2.28

No. 10R4950 Our Perfection Black Grasp 6-bar Japanned Steel Curry Comb, with mane comb riveted through handle. Weight, about 12 ounces.
Price, each..10c

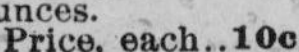

Fancy Brass Curry Comb.

No. 10R4953 Kittie Fancy Brass Curry Comb, Same style as No. 10R4950. 6 bars. solid brass, wire shank riveted through handle; main comb a very fine solid brass curry comb. Weight, about 12 ounces.
Price, each....................15c

The Humane Curry Comb.

No. 10R4955 The Humane Curry Comb. This is the only comb fit to use on horses' legs or on clipped or short haired horses. **It is impossible to hurt a horse with it.** It is also **the best thing ever produced for a cattle cleaner.** Weight, each, 6 ounces.
Price, per dozen, 1.20; each....................10c

Circular Spring Steel Curry Combs.

No. 10R4960 Circular Steel Spring Curry Combs. Three complete circles of steel, working independent of each other, attached to an iron back by a hinged joint, wood handles; **a good solid comb.**
Price, per dozen, **$1.44**; each....................12c
Weight, each, 10 ounces.

Horse Curry Cards.

No. 10R4965 Large, 3½ x8¼ inches, first quality.
Each....................7c
Per dozen....................84c
No. 10R4970 Small, 3½ x5½ inches. Each.........6c
Per dozen....................72c
Weight, each, 8 ounces.

HORSE BRUSHES.

We guarantee our line of Palmetto, Rice Root and leather back Horse Brushes strictly high grade, our bristle brushes, the finest and the very best that labor and quality of material can produce. Our bristle brushes are of the very best.

No. 10R5000 Mexican Rice Root Horse Brushes, wood back and strap, 3 inches wide and 7 inches long. Weight, 8 ounces.
Price, per dozen, **$1.08**; each.9c

No. 10R5005 Our Tampico Wood Back Horse Brush, 2¾ inches wide and 7 inches long. Three rows of mixed Tampico, leather strap. Weight of brush, 8 ounces. Same style as No. 10R5000.
Price, per dozen, **$1.20**; each....................10c

No. 10R5010 Our Special Palmetto Horse Brush, 2¼ inches wide by 7 inches long. Leather strap. Three rows of heavy Palmetto, 1⅛ inches long. Same style as No. 10R5000. Weight of brush, 8 ounces.
Price, per dozen, **$1.80**; each....................15c

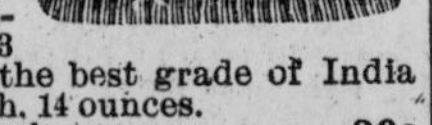

No. 10R5015 Sears, Roebuck & Co.'s India Fiber, wood back with pointed ends horse brush. Fiber 1⅛ inches long, the size of brush 2¾ by 10 inches. Weight of brush 9 ounces. Strictly first class.
Price, per dozen, **$1.80**; each....................15c

No. 10R5020 Our special Mexican Rice Root, pointed ends horse brush. A good quality of rice root 2 inches long; outside row consists of 32 bunches of rice root, heavy wood back pointed ends, 2⅛ by 10 inches. Weight of brush 9 ounces. Same style as No. 10R5015. Price, per dozen, **$1.92**; each......16c

No.10R5025 Sears, Roebuck & Co.'s special mixed Rice Root and India Fiber, which prevents the root from breaking off, thick heavy body of brush 2 inches long. Same style as No. 10R5015. Double back, screw top, 3 inches wide and 10 inches long. Highly polished. Weight 12 ounces.
Price, per dozen, **$2.28**; each....................19c

No. 10R5040 Sears, Roebuck & Co.'s Special Wood Back Palmetto Horse Brush, 8 inches long, 2⅛ inches wide, with five rows of strictly pure palmetto fiber 1⅛ inches long. A strictly first class brush in every respect. Without strap. Weight of brush, 9 ounces.
Price, per dozen, **$1.80**; each....................15c

No. 10R5050 Our Heavy Wood Back, India fiber horse brush, same style as the "Ruf and Redy," 2 inches long India fiber. Size of brush, 8½ inches long and 3¼ inches wide, with leather strap. Weight of brush, 12 ounces.
Price, per dozen, **$2.16**; each....................18c

No. 10R5055 Sears, Roebuck & Co.'s Special Tiger Brand, solid wood back, heavy tampico brush, 1⅛ inches long, very black and heavy. Size of brush, 3⅜ by 8½ inches, heavy leather strap. Same style as No. 10R5050. Weight of brush, 14 ounces.
Price, per dozen, **$2.28**; each....................19c

No. 10R5060 Sears, Roebuck & Co.'s Special Solid Palmetto, 1⅛ inches long, heavy solid wide back, 8 inches long by 3 inches wide, with a heavy leather strap. This brush is equal to, if not superior to any palmetto brush we list. Same style as "Ruf and Redy" and No. 10R5055. Weight of brush, 10 ounces.
Price, per dozen, **$3.00**; each....................25c

No. 10R5070 Sears, Roebuck & Co.'s Special Grade of India Fiber Horse Brush, 1¾ inches long, double wood back, screw top, highly polished, 10½ inches long by 3 inches wide; pointed ends; the best grade of India fiber brush. Weight of brush, 14 ounces.
Price, per dozen, **$2.40**; each....................20c

Our High Grade Horse Brushes

No. 10R5075 Sears, Roebuck & Co.'s Double Wood Back, Rice Root Brush, rice root 2 inches long. Size of brush, 10 inches long and 2¾ inches wide, polished top, pointed ends. Extra quality and extra grade of rice root throughout. Same style as No. 10R5070. Weight of brush, 10 ounces. Price, each..........25c

No. 10R5080 Our Special Mixed Rice Root Center, India Fiber Outside. Pointed Ends Horse Brush. Length of root, 2 inches. Size of brush, 10 inches long, 2¾ wide, double screw top. The mixed rice root and India fiber wears better and longer and not so apt to break as a strictly all rice root brush. Same style as No. 10R5070. Weight of this brush, 12 ounces.
Price, per dozen, **$3.12**; each....................26c

No. 10R5090 Sears, Roebuck & Co.'s special quality extra high grade Rice Root Horse Brush. Size of brush, 10 inches long and 2¾ inches wide; double polished top, pointed ends, leather thumb and finger guards. A strictly high grade brush Weight of brush, 12 ounces.
Price, per dozen, **$4.20**; each....................35c

No. 10R5095 Our extra fine quality of Rice Root Horse Brush. Pointed ends, double polished back; size of brush, 10½x2¾ inches; thumb and finger leather guards, highest grade of strictly first class rice root. This is a highly finished horse brush. Weight of brush, 12 ounces. Same style as No. 10R5090.
Price, per dozen, **$5.40**; each....................45c

No. 10R5096 Our Crawford Leather Back Horse Brush. This brush is made with dark mixed tampico center, with two rows of white tampico on the outside, making a fifteen-row brush. The brush is made about 9 inches long and 4½ inches wide, with good leather strap. Weight, 9 ounces, A good leather back horse brush. Price, each....................30c

No. 10R5097 Our Evansville Leather Back Horse Brush. One row of white tampico outside and nine rows of good mixed tampico center; a good eleven-row tampico horse brush; good, solid leather back; 9 inches long and 4½ inches wide, with good heavy strap; stitched all around with good heavy thread. Weight, 10 ounces. Price, each..........35c

No. 10R5098 Our Syracuse Leather Back Horse Brush. Made of fifteen rows of extra quality mixed gray tampico, solid leather back, extra wide band, shaped leather strap, well stitched with a heavy thread, flexible back; 9 inches long and 5 inches wide. The best 45-cent leather back horse brush made. A big seller. Price, each....................45c

Lincoln Army Brush.

No. 10R5099 Leather Back Horse Brush. Made with flexible leather back. The back is stitched with wire. Fifteen rows of mixed tampico and bristle. Outside row of gray bristle; body of brush extra fine quality of gray tampico. Looks like an all-bristle brush. A good flexible leather back army brush. Weight, 10 ounces; size, 9 inches long and 4¼ inches wide. Price, each....................65c

Leather Back Horse Brush.

No. 10R5109 Leather back, oval shape, Tampico center. Size of brush 9 inches long, 4⅛ inches wide, with leather strap, length of Tampico 1 inch. Extra good cheap brush. Weight of brush, 12 ounces.
Price, each....................60c

No. 10R5110 Oval Shape Horse Brush, warranted all bristles, oval face, 15 rows of sewed stub bristles. Size of brush, 9 inches, 4 inches wide, leather strap. Same style as No. 10R5109. Weight of brush, 10 ounces.
Price, each....................75c

No. 10R5115 Special extra quality all black bristles, oval face, heavy leather strap. Size of brush, 9 inches long, 4¼ inches wide, heavy leather back. Extra good cheap brush. Weight of brush, 12 ounces. Same style as No. 10R5109. Price, each..........90c

No. 10R5120 Our Fine Quality of Mixed Bristle Brush, flat face, fine quality of mixed black and brown bristles, flexible back, leather strap and leather back. Size of brush, 9 by 4⅛. Weight of brush, 10 ounces. Same style as No. 10R5109.
Price, each....................$1.00

No. 10R5125 Our Special All Gray Bristle Oval Face Horse Brush. Leather back, leather strap. Size of brush, 4¼ by 9 inches. Weight of brush, 12 ounces.
Price, each....................$1.40

No. 10R5130 Sears, Roebuck & Co.'s Special All Black Bristle Horse Brush. 19 rows of black bristles. Flat face. Size of brush, 9 inches long, 4½ inches wide. Same style as No. 10R5125. Weight of brush, 10 ounces. Price, each....................$1.50

No. 10R5135 Sears, Roebuck & Co.'s special warranted all black bristle, leather back and leather handle. 19 rows of bristles. Flat face. Size of brush, 9 inches long and 4½ inches wide. Same style as No. 10R5125. Weight of brush, 12 ounces, packed in single box. Price, each....................$2.00

No. 10R5140 Sears, Roebuck & Co.'s Special Warranted All White Bristle Oval Faced Brush 19 rows of bristle, adjustable strap, leather back. Size of brush, 9 by 4½ inches. Extra fine horse brush. Weight of brush, 12 ounces, packed in single box. Price..........$2.25

Extra Quality Leather Back Horse Brush.

The Finest on the Market.

No. 10R5145 Our Special All White Russia Bristle Brush; 21 rows of bristles, oval face, heavy leather strap, leather back, 9 inches long and 4½ inches wide. Strictly first class white bristle horse brush. Weight of brush, 12 ounces, packed in single box. Price, each....................$2.75

S., R. & Co.'s Horse Brushes.

No. 10R5150 Sears, Roebuck & Co.'s heavy sole leather flexible top, flat face, strictly all pure white bristles 1 inch long, heavy leather strap, large hand room, solid leather back, 8½ inches long, 4⅜ inches wide, and 21 rows of white bristles. Weight of brush 12 ounces, packed in single box. One of our high grade horse brushes. Price, each....................**$3.00**

No. 10R5150

No. 10R5155 Sears, Roebuck & Co.'s special solid leather, flexible back, heavy leather strap, fine quality of yellow Russia bristle. Length of bristles 1⅛-inch, 19 rows, flat face. Weight of brush, 12 ounces. Size, 8½x4⅜ inches. A strictly first class brush. Packed in single box. Price, each....................**$3.25**

No. 10R5155

No. 10R5160 Sears, Roebuck & Co.'s Extra, extra fine warranted all white, pure Russia bristle. 21 rows, solid leather, flexible back, leather hand loop. The best horse brush on the market, flat face, 1-inch bristles. Size of brush, 8⅜ inches long, 4½ inches wide. Best brush we can offer to our trade. Weight, 12 ounces, packed in single box. Price, each....................**$3.50**

No. 10R5160

Stable or Street Broom.

This is made with **14-inch wood back, four rows rattan splints.** Should be used in every stable. Furnished with or without handle.

No. 10R5165 Price of broom, each....................45c

No. 10R5170 Price of handle each....................4c

No. 10R5165

Our Acme Klar Broom.

No. 10R5175

Made with **heavy wood back,** the brush part made of **fine Klar fiber.** The brush will **last for years.** The price of broom is without handle.

No. 10R5175 Price of broom, each....................50c

No. 10R5180 Price of handle, each....................4c

Jockey Cap With Tie for $1.15.

No. 10R5200 Our Special Fine Satin Jockey Caps. These caps are made on the very latest improved patterns, good fore piece, and any size wanted. The driver's cap is made without a draw string. When ordering cap be sure and state color and size wanted. Price, each....................**$1.15**

Our $1.10 Driver's Cap.

No. 10R5202 Our Special Jockey Cap. Made of extra fine quality fancy colored satin, with extra draw string, so as to adjust the size of cap. When ordering cap be sure and state colors wanted, and also state the **size.** Price, each....................**$1.10**

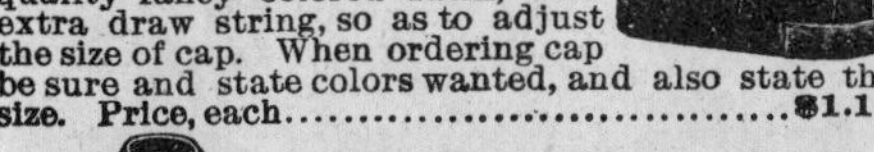

Driver's Jacket for $4.85.

No. 10R5205 Our Special Driver's Jacket. Made of any color satin that you want. Made up with standing collar button front, **well made and finished throughout.** State the waist measure and also the measurement of the coat you wear. **We will make the jacket out of any color satin. Always state the color and size of the jacket your driver wears.**

Price, each....................**$4.85**

Jockey Blouse or Jacket.

No. 10R5206 Our Special Jockey Blouse. Made of any color fancy satin wanted. This blouse is made with a draw string to tie around the waist. Short standing collar. **Well made, handsomely finished,** with button front. Always state the size of the coat the jockey wears, and give us the length of the sleeve from shoulder to wrist. We will make the jackets any color of fine satin wanted. **Always state the color, and size of coat your jockey wears.** Our jockey blouse jackets and caps are of the very finest quality, and such as are furnished at double the price we ask for them. Our special price for this jockey blouse, each....................**$4.95**

Jockey Riding Boots.

No. 10R5220 Our Special Hand Made Jockey Boot. This boot is made of a very light strong, calfskin, hand stitched, **and strictly hand turned boot throughout.** It is always the cheapest to buy a strictly first class boot. We handle no other. **Boots are made to order only,** and if sent as ordered cannot be returned. Be sure and state size of boot your jockey wears. We can furnish boots in from three to four days on receipt of order.

Price, per pair....................**$7.50**

It will be to your interest to look over our line of Turf Goods as illustrated. We have made a special effort to offer this year the best line of these goods ever put on the market. They are strictly guaranteed in regard to quality and workmanship, and you will notice that they are made especially in three sizes. **Be sure and state the size wanted when ordering.**

Our Common Ankle Boot.

No. 10R5300 Our Common Ankle Boot, made of heavy leather cup shaped pad in top, with one strap. Weight per pair, 6 ounces.

Price, each....................9c

Price, per pair....................18c

If by mail, postage extra, 6 cents.

Our Fine Two-Strap Ankle Boot.

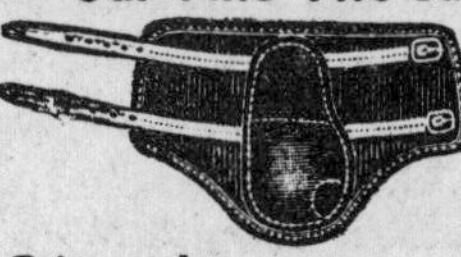

No. 10R5305 Our Fine Two-Strap Ankle Boot, made of fine leather, cup shaped, kersey cloth, leather bound. Weight per pair, 8 ounces.

Price, each....................24c

Price, per pair....................48c

If by mail, postage extra, 8 cents.

Our Fine Calfskin Ankle Boot.

No. 10R5310 Our Fine Calfskin Ankle Boot, made with heavy cupped body, lined with fine calfskin, two straps. Weight, per pair, 10 oz.

Price, each....................30c

Price, per pair....................60c

If by mail, postage extra, 10 cents.

S., R. & Co.'s Fine Scalper Boot.

No. 10R5315 S., R. & Co.'s Fine Scalper Boot. Made of fine boot leather, calfskin pad top, one strap, rubber lined, spur strap to buckle. Weight, per pair, 12 ounces.

Price, per pair....................**$1.50**

If by mail, postage extra, 12 cents.

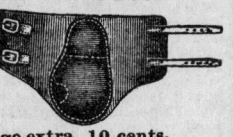

S., R. & Co.'s Front and Side Scalper Boot.

No. 10R5320 S., R. & Co.'s Front and Side Scalper. This boot is made of fine boot leather, one strap, with buckle spur strap, kersey lined top and side. The best front and side scalper in the market. Weight, per pair, 13 ounces. Our special price, per pair..**$1.90**

If by mail, postage extra, 13 cents.

No. 10R5321 Our Special White Felt Scalper Boot. The scalper is made with an **extra quality of white wool felt, full front and side protection.** One strap and buckle spur strap. This is a very fine, light, neat scalping boot. **A big seller.** Weight, per pair, 3 ounces. Price, per pair....................**$1.97**

If by mail, postage extra, 15 cents.

S., R. & Co.'s Russet Coronet Boot.

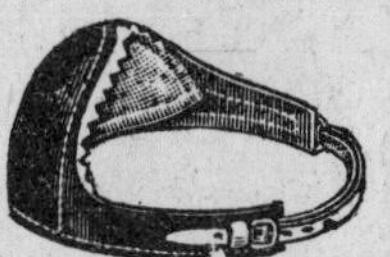

No. 10R5325 S., R. & Co.'s Russet Coronet Boot. This boot is made of fine boot leather, felt lined, one strap, an extra fine coronet boot for pacing horse; weight, per pair, 3 ounces.

Price, per pair....................**$1.75**

If by mail, postage extra, 10 cents.

S., R. & Co.'s Cross Firing Pacers' Quarter Boot.

No. 10R5330 S., R. & Co.'s Cross Firing Pacers' Quarter Boot. Made high on inside, two strap, calfskin lined, rubber brace in back. The finest cross firing pacer quarter boot made, neat and good. Try a pair. Weight, per pair, 14 ounces.

Price, per pair....................**$2.75**

If by mail, postage extra, 20 cents.

S., R. & Co.'s Low Cut Quarter Boot.

No. 10R5335 S., R. & Co.'s Low Cut Quarter Boot. One strap, with spur strap, felt lined; one of the best boots made. This is a special with us. Weight, 12 ounces.

Price, per pair....................**$1.50**

If by mail, postage extra, 14 cents.

No. 10R5336 Our Special White Felt Low Cut One-Strap Quarter Boot. This boot is made of a very fine quality of all wool white felt, well cupped and shaped, and one of the nicest light, low, one strapped quarter boots we make. **Leather lined heel,** which makes it strong. Weight, per pair, about 3 ounces. Price, per pair....................**$1.70**

If by mail, postage extra, 15 cents.

S., R. & Co.'s Bell Quarter Boot.

No. 10R5340 S., R. & Co.'s Fine Calfskin Roll Bell Quarter Boot, made of fine russet boot leather, lined with calfskin, with roll top billet and loop fasteners. Made in three sizes: small, medium and large. Weight, per pair, 10 ounces.

Price, per pair....................**$2.90**

If by mail, postage extra, 12 cents.

S., R. & Co.'s Bell Quarter Boot.

No. 10R5345 S., R. & Co.'s Bell Quarter Boot. This boot is made of the best of russet boot leather, billet and loop fasteners, half lined, with wool top. This is one of the best bell quarters on the market. Weight, per pair, 16 ounces.

Price, per pair....................**$3.00**

If by mail, postage extra, 16 cents.

Three-Strap Quarter Boot.

No. 10R5350 S., R. & Co.'s Three-Strap Quarter Boot. This quarter boot is made of fine boot leather, calfskin lined, three-strap, well braced and shaped at bottom; this boot can be washed with soap. Weight, per pair, 12 ounces.

Price, per pair....................**$2.65**

If by mail, postage extra, 12 cents.

Our One-Strap Pacing Quarter Boot.

No. 10R5351 This boot is made out of the very best of russet tan boot leather and lined with an extra quality of calf lining, with high inside protection or pacing attachment. This boot is a big seller and for a one-strap, low, close-fitting quarter, with inside protection, is one of the best boots on the market. Made in large, medium and small sizes. Weight, per pair, about 8 ounces. Price, per pair....................**$2.35**

If by mail, postage extra, 15 cents.

Our Special White Compressed Felt Quarter Boot.

No. 10R5352 Made the same style of boot as No. 10R5351, low cupped quarter, with high inside protection. This boot is made with one pulley strap reinforced leather heel which gives it extra strength. This white felt, low, fitting quarter, with inside protection, is a very desirable boot and one that is used a great deal. Weight per pair, about 4 ounces.

Per pair..(**If by mail, postage extra, 15c**)..**$2.65**

Two-Strap Quarter Boot.

No. 10R5355 S., R. & Co.'s Two-Strap Quarter Boot, made of fine boot stock, calfskin lined, lower draw strap, top buckle strap, an extra fine low quarter boot.

Weight, per pair, 8 ounces.

Price, per pair....................**$2.45**

If by mail, postage extra, 14 cents.

Riveted Hinge Quarter Boot.

No. 10R5360 S., R. & Co.'s Riveted Hinge Quarter Boot. This boot is made of fine boot leather, elkskin lined, one of our best quarter boots, made in three sizes, two straps, lower draw strap. Weight per pair, 10 oz.

Price, per pair....................**$2.65**

If by mail, postage extra, 15 cents.

Back Hinge Quarter Boot.

No. 10R5365 S., R. & Co.'s Back Hinge Quarter Boot, two-strap, lower draw strap, made of the latest style elk skin lined, you can not buy better than we will send you. Weight, per pair, 10 oz.

Price, per pair....................**$2.65**

If by mail, postage extra, 15 cents.

S. R. & Co.'s Plain Shin Boot.

No. 10R5370 S., R. & Co.'s Plain Shin Boot. Full padded shin, calfskin lined, three strap. An extra fine shin boot. Weight, per pair, 6 oz.

Price, per pair....................**$1.15**

If by mail, postage extra, 10 cents.

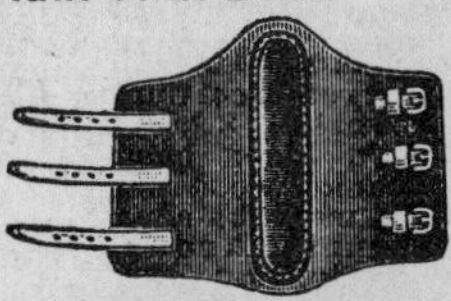

S., R. & Co.'s Shin and Ankle Boot.

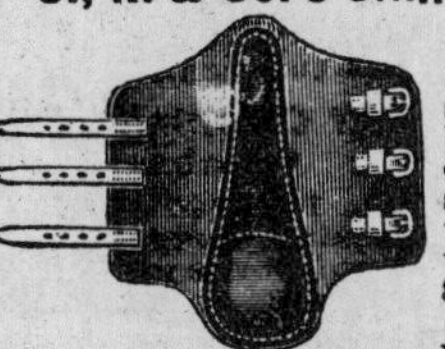

No. 10R5380 S., R. & Co.'s Shin and Ankle Boot. Made of fine russet leather, cupped bottom, padded shin, calfskin lined, three strap. This boot can be washed with soap and water. Weight, per pair, 8 ounces.

Our special price, per pair....................**$1.50**

If by mail, postage extra, 10 cents.

Shin, Ankle and Tendon Boot.

No. 10R5385 S., R. & Co.'s Shin, Ankle and Tendon Boot. This is our fine shin, ankle and tendon boot, made **of fine russet boot leather, calfskin lined, extra fine tendon, elastic strap. There is no better boot made than this one. If not** satisfactory return at our expense. Weight, per pair, 8 ounces.

Per pair..(**If by mail, postage extra, 14c**)..**$3.85**

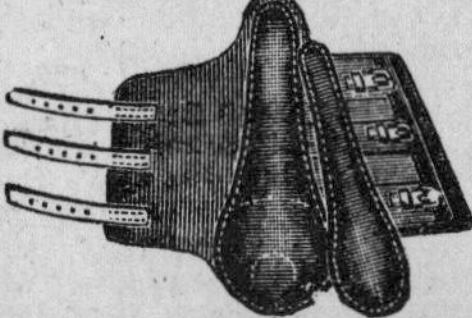

S., R. & Co.'s Knee Boot.

No. 10R5390 S., R & Co.'s Knee Boot, made of fine black boot leather, felt lined, with pad in top, two-strap. This is an extra good knee boot, and one we know you will be pleased with. Weight, per pair, 8 ounces.
Price, per pair..........$1.50
If by mail, postage extra, 10 cents.

Our Special White Felt Knee Boot.

No. 10R5391 Made the same style as No. 10R5390, only made out of white felt, which makes it a very easy and light knee boot. This boot is used largely on horses who are not extra hard hitters, and who want a light easy protection. This white felt knee boot fills that want. Strictly first class with one buckle and strap and one arm strap. Weight, per pair, about 6 ounces. Price, per pair......$1.75

S., R. & Co.'s Fine Knee Boot.

No. 10R5395 S., R. & Co.'s Fine Knee Boot, made in russet boot leather, calfskin lined, small pad in top, one strap top and long arm straps. This is the best knee boot that can be made. If you order this boot and are not satisfied that it is what we say it is, return at our expense. Weight, per pair, 9 ounces. Per pair...$3.00
If by mail, postage extra, 14 cents.

Poultice Boots.

No. 10R5400 Made of heavy harness leather, extra heavy leather bottom, riveted on. Small, medium or large sizes.
Each, $1.47

Trotting Balls.

No. 10R5405 Rubber Trotting Balls. Weight, per string, 7 ounces.
Per string..........$0.12
Per dozen strings.. 1.32

Roy Wilkes Special Quarter Boot.

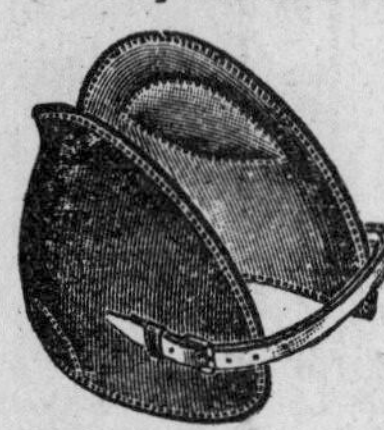

No. 10R5410 Made of fine russet boot leather, calfskin lined, high inside, extra pad, very close fitting, one pulley strap; considered by all horsemen one of the finest one-strap Pacing Quarter Boots on the market. This boot has, without a doubt, had the largest sale of any quarter boot ever made; made in three sizes, small, medium and large. Weight, per pair, 8 ounces.
Price, per pair..........$3.00
If by mail, postage extra, 12 cents.

Be sure to state the size boot wanted. We shall always send medium size where size is omitted.

Our Improved Quarter Boot.

No. 10R5415 Calfskin lined, double strap, and has an independent purchase strap encircling the hoof, which holds the boot in the proper position without binding or resting on the horse's quarter. This is pronounced by all horsemen to be one of the best and lightest of close fitting quarter boots; an excellent boot for trotters and pacers. Weight, per pair, 8 ounces.
Price, per pair..........$2.75
If by mail, postage extra, 12 cents.

Mane Combs.

No. 10R5420 Brown Horn Mane Combs, extra quality. Size, 2¾x4½ inches. Weight, each, 2 ounces.
Price, per dozen, $1.32; each, 11c

Derby Bandages, Fine Double and Single Cotton and Red and White Flannel Bandages.

No. 10R5437 S., R. & Co.'s Fine White Cotton Derby Bandage, with long tie. This is the finest cotton bandage, made in three lengths.

Length	2 yards	2½ yards	3 yards
Weight, ounces	8	10	14
Price, per set	29c	37c	45c

Heavy Cotton Derby Bandage. This bandage is made of extra quality of fine knitting yarn, 4½ inches wide, two bandages 2½ yards long for the fore legs, and two bandages 3 yards long for the hind legs, put up in sets in nice package. This is a double knitted bandage, well made. Weight per set, packed in box, 20 ounces.
No. 10R5438 Price, per set..........70c

Bandages.

Our Special Single Web Cotton Bandage. This bandage is made of a fine quality of knitting yarn, woven single, which binds closely and never slips. They do not stretch or string out, and are very elastic in width, allowing plenty of play and give at the joints. This bandage is considered one of the best that can be used on trotting or running horses. Put up in sets of four bandages, and in two colors, white and natural gold. Two bandages for the fore legs 2½ yards long, and two bandages for the hind legs, 3 yards long. Width of bandage, 4 inches. Horsemen generally favor this style of sets, as the hind leg requires a longer bandage than the fore leg.
No. 10R5439 Neat fawn or brown color. Weight, boxed, 20 ounces. Price, per set..........80c
No. 10R5441 Plain white bandage. Weight, boxed, 20 ounces. Price, per set..........65c
Our Special Flannel Bandage. Made of a very fine quality of flannel, single width, 4½ inches wide, used by veterinary surgeons and also on running horses, where they want a strictly high grade extra fine bandage. Our flannel bandages are put up in sets, two bandages 2½ yards long, and two bandages 3 yards long, for front and hind legs. These bandages are furnished in all white or all red flannel.
No. 10R5442 All white flannel bandage. Weight, 12 ounces boxed. Price, per set..........90c
No. 10R5443 Fine red flannel bandage. Weight boxed, 12 ounces. Price, per set..........95c
Our Special Raw Silk Rubbing Cloths. Made of a good quality of raw silk toweling stock, loosely woven, and well made. Size of cloth, 27 inches wide, 31 inches long. Weight, 6 ounces.
No. 10R5444 Price, each....45c

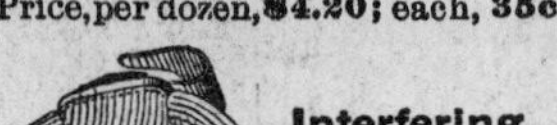

Rubbing Cloths.

No. 10R5445 Genuine Imported Ashton's Salt Sacks for rubbing cloths; full size; best quality.
Weight, 1¾ pounds.
Price, per dozen, $4.20; each, 35c

Interfering Device.

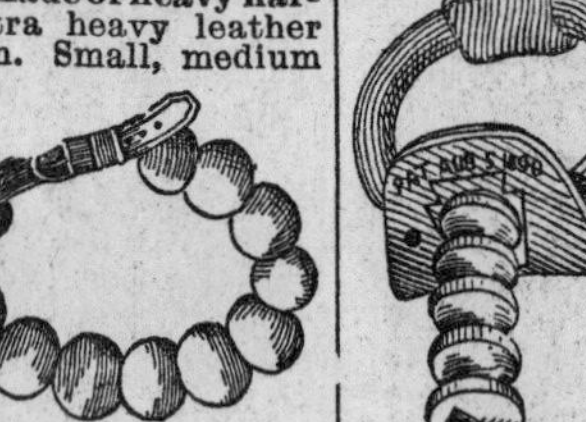

No. 10R5450 This device has been used for some time, has never failed to stop the most obstinate case of interfering, and in most cases can be dispensed with after ten days to two weeks. They will spread the colt's gait and make him a wide traveler. Every horseman will understand the merits of them when seen.
Weight, each 4 ounces.
Price, per pair, 50c; each..........25c
If by mail, postage extra, 8 cents.

Anderson's Quarter Boot.

No. 10R5455 Anderson's Special Back Hinge Quarter Boot. The body of the boot is made with a low shaped, well cupped quarter, with the upper part attached in back, with wide rawhide hinge. **The upper part of quarter is lined with fine calfskin with rolled top.** Rawhide pulley strap on the lower quarter, and rawhide single strap with rubber tubing on the upper quarter. This quarter boot is pronounced by leading horsemen throughout the country to be absolutely the best hinge quarter boot for protecting hard hitters and upper cuts of any boot made. **Made of the very best solid boot leather and very light.** Weight, per pair, 9 ounces. Made small, medium and large. Be sure to state the size wanted. Price, per pair, $2.75
No. 10R5456 Anderson's Pacing Boot. Same style of boot as listed above and shown by cut only, made for pacers, with high inside to protect cross firing; otherwise the same style of boot as above. Weight, per pair, 10 ounces. Price, per pair....$2.75

Pacing Quarter Boot.

No. 10R5460 Our Pacing Quarter Boot made close fitting, double strap, high inside to **protect cross firing,** lined with French calfskin, easy to keep clean and gives the best of satisfaction as a pacing boot. Made with **aluminum heel plate which** protects the inside and outside of the boot. Moisture will not affect it. **These heel plates do not rust or make the boot any heavier.** It gives the boot no chance to wear out at the heel where they always give out after a few weeks' wear. **All horsemen prefer this boot.** Weight, about 12 ounces.
Our special price, per pair..........$3.75
Aluminum heel plates extra, so as to put on any quarter boot, sold in pairs only. Weight, about 3 oz.
We do not break pairs. Price, per pair..........$1.00
No. 10R5462 Close Fitting Quarter Boot, with heel plate, same as No. 10R5460, without pacing attachment. Weight, about 10 oz. Price, per pair, $3.50

Our Special Felt Soaking Boot.

No. 10R5465 Made of extra heavy double felt with Sponge Frog Pad, buckle toe and buckle and billet, round pad. This is the finest soaking boot we handle; you can make a horse's foot very soft and take all soreness out by using this boot. Weight, 8 ounces.
Price, each..........$1.40

Shoe Boil Roll.

No. 10R5470 Shoe Boil Roll, made of heavy web, composite stuffing, buckle and billet. The best shoe boil roll we handle. Weight, 20 ounces. Price, each..........79c

Calking Roll.

No. 10R5475
Made with a soft inner roll, with buckle and billet. This roll will prevent the horse from calking himself with his shoes.
Weight, 20 oz. Price, each..$1.50

Knee and Arm Boot.

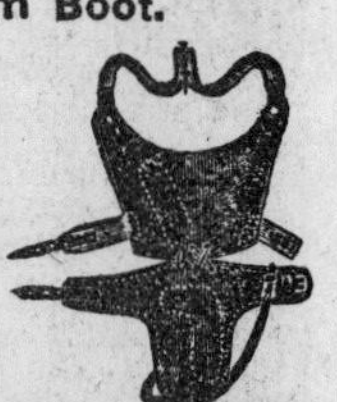

No. 10R5480 Russia Calf Knee and Arm Boot. Arm padded, soft and close fitting. This style of boot has a large sale, and we highly recommend it as the best knee and arm boot on the market. Complete with suspenders made of fine quality russet boot leather, fine finish, handsomely made, light and strong. Weight, 12 ounces.
Per pair..........$5.75

Star Pointer Knee and Arm Boot.

No. 10R5495 Russet leather body, padded arm, wool felt lined, with suspender. Protects the knee on hard hitters. Weight, about 10 ounces.
Price, per pair...$3.50
We do not break pairs.
No. 10R5496 Our Special Star Pointer White Felt Knee and Arm Boot. Made of a good quality of compressed felt, compressed top, **cupped knee and close fit.** This knee and arm boot is made with suspender attachment double strap, makes a very fine **light knee and arm boot.** This style of boot is used and recommended by the very best drivers throughout the country. Weight, per pair, about 9 ounces. Price, per pair..........$3.65

Our Safety Skelper and Speedy Cut.

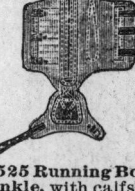

No. 10R5500 For hard hitters, with full protection. Made of russet boot leather, rawhide leather straps, padded speedy cut. A high grade boot. Weight, 14 ounces. Price, per pair, $3.75
We do not break pairs.

Elastic Stocking.

No. 10R5505 Our Special Black Elastic Stocking, made to lace. For running horses. It strengthens and supports weak ankles. This is a strictly first class article.
Weight, 8 ounces.
Price, per pair...$3.75

Running Boots.

No. 10R5510 Hock, Shin, Ankle and Speed Cut. Calfskin leather wrapper with rawhide billets. A strictly first class, high grade article. Weight, 15 ounces.
Price, per pair..........$6.75
We do not break pairs.

No. 10R5515 Running Boot, improved pattern running heel, calfskin wrapper, elastic buckle piece, rawhide billets. A smooth and well finished boot. Weight, 6 ounces.
Price, per pair..........$3.75

No. 10R5520 Running Boot. Cut down and heel boot combination. Calfskin wrapper, rawhide billets, rubber buckle piece. Russet boot leather, well made and finely finished. Weight, 11 ounces.
Price, per pair..........$5.65

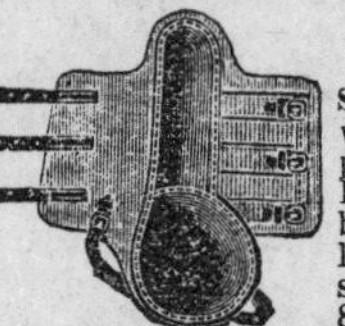

No. 10R5525 Running Boot' Shin and ankle, with calfskin wrapper. Ankle extension, protecting the back of ankle. Rawhide billets. Rubber buckle piece. Russet boot leather. Well made and handsomely finished boot. Weight, 8 oz. Price, per pair....$4.15

No. 10R5530 Running Boot. Shin and ankle, with calfskin wrapper. Elastic side, russet boot leather, rawhide billets. A strictly first class running boot. Weight, 6 ounces.
Price, per pair..........$3.75

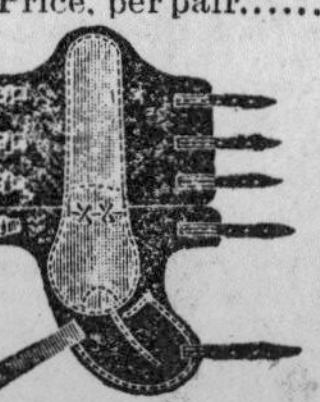

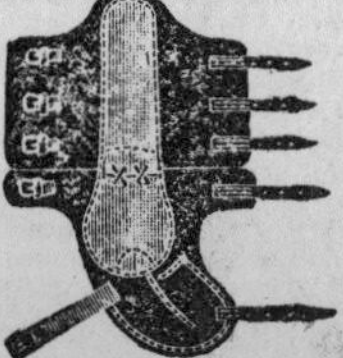

No. 10R5535 Running Boot, Shin, Ankle and Speedy Cut Hind Leg Boot, calfskin leather wrapper with rawhide billets russet leather body. A strictly first class boot. Weight, 12 oz.
Price, per pair..........$4.50
We do not break pairs.

Hickory Whip Stocks.

No. 10R6120 White Hickory Whip Stock.

Length, feet	3½	4	4½	5
Price, each	8c	9c	10c	11c

Our Special Cowles Whip Stock.

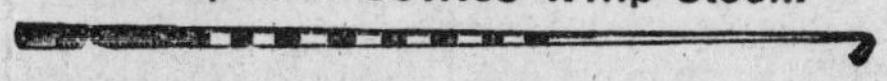

No. 10R6125 Made of fine hand shaved hickory, with eight nickel ferrules and 10-inch leather covered handle, with leather loop. These stocks when mounted with nickel ferrules produce one of the handsomest articles in the whip stock line. Tastefully and carefully selected. Buckskin keeper, tightly wound with black thread. Made ¾-inch at the butt and tapers to point. Plain wood color.

Length of stock	4 ft.	4½ ft.	5 ft.	5½ ft.	6 ft.
Each	44c	45c	46c	47c	60c

Whip Crackers.

No. 10R6133 Whip Crackers, half silk and half cotton. 7 inches long. Price, per dozen....13c

No. 10R6135 Whip Crackers, all silk, best quality. 7 inches long. Per dozen......23c

We do not break dozens.

No. 10R6140 Cotton Whip Crackers, 7 inches long. Price, per dozen..........5c

Rawhide Riding Whip.

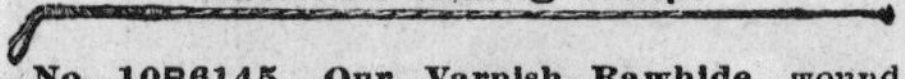

No. 10R6145 Our Varnish Rawhide, wound leather handle, leather button and loop, 3 feet long. Price, each..........18c

Fancy Rawhide Whip.

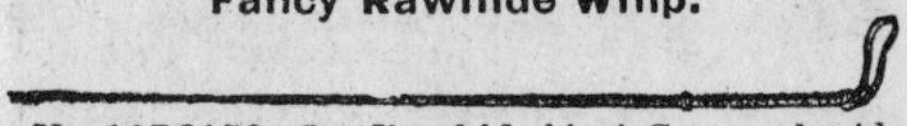

No. 10R6150 Our Rawhide black German braided cover, **fancy basket handle,** two braided buttons, japanned capped, fancy plaited **wrist loop,** English loop. Price, each..........35c

No. 10R6155 Our Extra Heavy Whalebone Riding Whip, imitation gut, extra heavy, plaited through, six-stitch head button, braided loop, japanned cap, half silk snap. One of the best riding whips made. Price, each..........73c

Fine Bone Riding Whip.

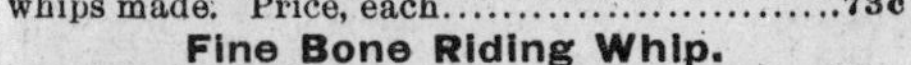

No. 10R6160 Our Fine Bone Riding Whip, black star finish, two six-stitch buttons, japanned cap, half silk English snap, 3 feet long. Price, each..........56c

Imitation Gut Riding Whip.

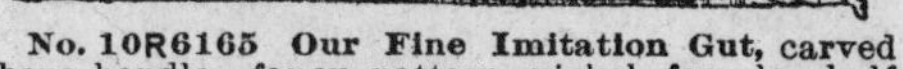

No. 10R6165 Our Fine Imitation Gut, carved bone handle, fancy pattern, nickel ferrule, half English snap, silk tassel. A very handsome riding whip. Price, each..........85c

Weight, about 3 ounces.

Solid Leather Team Whip.

No. 10R6170 Our XX oiled leather body, calf point, out seamed. The cheapest leather team whip made.

Length, feet	5	6	7
Price, each	37c	47c	57c

No. 10R6175 Our Oiled, Tanned, Covered XXXX Team Whip, buck stitched cover, fine braided buck point, two braided buttons and hand loop.

Length, feet	4	4½	5	5½	6
Price, each	45c	50c	54c	59c	63c

Boys' Drovers' Whip.

No. 10R6180 Our Boys' Drover Whip, 6-plait, oiled kip, made with wood handle, 9 inches long, lash strongly wired on, California style. **Weight, 16 ounces.**

Length, feet	6	7	8
Price, each	36c	43c	50c

No. 10R6185 Our fine 8-plait Oiled Kip, leather with calf point and handsome laced fastener, with revolving handle. **Weight, 20 ounces.**

Length, feet	9	10	12
Price, each	80c	87c	98c

Jacksonville Drovers' Whip.

No. 10R6190 Our Fine Drovers' Whip. Jacksonville knot, 8-plait, oiled kip leather body with buck point. One of the best whips made. One of our leaders.

Length, feet	9	10	12	14
Price, each	94c	$1.05	$1.15	$1.29

Weight, 21 ounces.

No. 10R6195 A Fine Drovers' Whip, Jacksonville knot, shot loaded, heavy 8-plait, oiled kip body, with extra fine buck point. This whip will prove very satisfactory. **Notice price. Weight, 22 ounces.**

Length, feet	10	12	14
Price, each	$1.15	$1.27	$1.40

GIVE CATALOGUE NUMBER IN FULL
WHEN YOU WRITE YOUR ORDER

Improved Rotary Jacksonville Drovers' Whip.

This Whip is the most perfect drover whip on the market, light and easily handled, wrought iron bolt center, with maple wood revolving handle, made in three styles, as follows:

No. 10R6201 California style, fine 8-plait latigo body, with buck point. **Not shot loaded.**

Length, feet	10	12	14
Price, each	$1.00	$1.25	$1.50

No. 10R6202 Shot loaded, California style, 8-plait latigo body, buck point.

Length, feet	10	12	14
Price, each	$1.25	$1.40	$1.60

No. 10R6203 Shot loaded, California style, 10-plait body, buck point.

Length, feet	10	12	14
Price, each	$1.50	$1.67	$1.90

Our Drover and Quirt whips are made of the finest whip leather.

WE ALWAYS QUOTE THE LOWEST PRICE.

S., R. & Co.'s Australian Cattle Whip.

Made with adjustable double loop fastener, revolving handle, shot loaded, **warranted not to break down at handle or break the shot sack,** can be easily repaired when worn out, or if you break the handle, you can put it in yourself. This is the best cattle whip made. Made in **calfskin, buckskin, rawhide. Leather tanned expressly for fine cattle whips.** Order by number and state number of feet long.

No. 10R6210 8-plait Calf Australian Cattle Whip.

Length, feet	10	12	14
Price, each	$1.88	$2.05	$2.23

No. 10R6215 12-plait Calf Australian Cattle Whip.

Length, feet	10	12	14
Price, each	$2.15	$2.30	$2.45

No. 10R6220 8-plait Genuine Buckskin Australian Cattle Whip.

Length, feet	10	12	14
Price, each	$2.05	$2.25	$2.40

No. 10R6225 12-plait Genuine Buckskin Australian Cattle Whip.

Length, feet	10	12	14
Price, each	$2.30	$2.45	$2.65

No. 10R6230 8-plait Oiled Rawhide Australian Cattle Whip.

Length, feet	10	12	14
Price, each	$2.15	$2.35	$2.55

No. 10R6235 12-plait Oiled Rawhide Australian Cattle Whip.

Length, feet	10	12	14
Price, each	$2.40	$2.58	$2.75

Weight, about 24 ounces.

Nebraska Quirt.

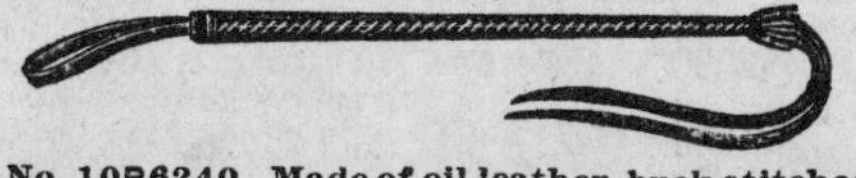

No. 10R6240 Made of oil leather, buck stitched solid leather body, 15 inches long. Total length of quirt, 30 inches. **Weight, 8 ounces.** Price, each..........27c

Texas Quirt.

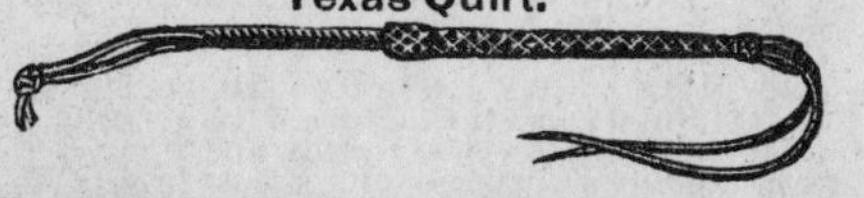

No. 10R6250 Made with braided body, iron spike handle, leather hand loop, two-braided knots. Length of body, 16 inches; total length of quirt, 30 inches. **Weight, 8½ ounces.** Price, each..........30c

San Antonio Quirt.

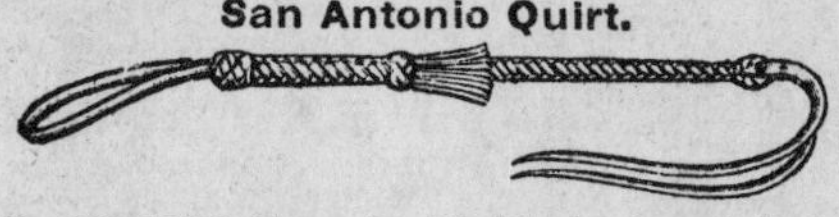

No. 10R6255 Fancy braided body, four plaits fine calfskin, two braided knots and frill. Length of body, 18 inches: total length of quirt, 33 inches. **Weight, about 6 ounces.** Price, each..........35c

Oklahoma Quirt.

No. 10R6260 Made of 8-plait calf, shot loaded body, fancy braided quirt, three braided knots and frills. Length of body, 20 inches; total length of quirt, 33 inches. **Weight, about 16 ounces.** Price, each..........50c

Benson Quirt.

No. 10R6265 Made of 8-plait calf lace leather, solid braided body, rtwo baided knots, shot loaded. Length of body, 17 inches; total length of quirt, 31 inches. With leather loop. **Weight of quirt about 10 ounces.** Price, each..........65c

Mexican Quirt.

No. 10R6270 Made of 8-plait calf lace leather. Iron spike, heavy braided knots, leather hand loop. Length of body, 19 inches; total length of quirt, 34 inches. **Weight, about 12 ounces.** Price, each..........75c

Elko Quirt.

No. 10R6275 Made of fancy checkered 12-plait braided calfskin, two-braided knots and frills, leather hand loop. Length of body, 18 inches; total length of quirt, 31 inches. **Weight, about 12 ounces.** Price, each..........95c

Dallas Quirt.

No. 10R6280 Made of 12-plait buckskin, shot loaded body, fancy braided corded handle, 3-braided knots and frills. Length of body, 20 inches; total length of quirt, 33 inches. **Weight, about 16 ounces.** Price, each..........$1.00

Milford Quirt.

No. 10R6285 Made of 8-plait genuine rawhide body, braided handle, braided hand loop, shot loaded body. Length of body, 19 inches; total length of quirt, 36 inches. **Weight, about 14 ounces.** Price, each..........$1.58

Our Western Mule Skinner.

No. 10R6290 Made of fine latigo leather body, buck stitched, braided buckskin point, heavy braided knot, shot loaded. The best mule skinner on the market. Price, each, as follows:

6 feet..$1.15 7 feet..$1.30
6½ feet.. 1.20 7½ feet.. 1.35

Weight, about 25 ounces.

Saddle Strings and Lacing for Heading.

No. 10R7500 No. 1 Rawhide Lace or Whang Leather, oiled and tanned. One side measures from 7 to 18 square feet. Per square foot..........27c

No. 10R7505 Belt Lacing or Saddle Strings, cut from No. 1 oak tanned rawhide or whang leather, put up in bunches of 50 feet each.

Per bunch, ⅜-inch..........53c
Per bunch, ½-inch..........68c
Per bunch, ⅝-inch..........90c

Steel Thong Awls.

No. 10R7510 A very handy tool for mending harness and repairing belts and heavy strap work of any kind. Made very strong, with round handles. Length of awl, 7 inches. Price, each..........21c

Weight, 8 ounces.

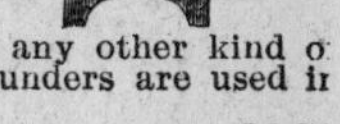

No. 10R7515 Sears, Roebuck & Co.'s Special Nine Hole Rounder, used for rounding up winker braces, bridle fronts, bridle reins or round lines, or any other kind of round leather work. These rounders are used in bench vise, with thumb bolt. Our special price, each..........$2.70

Harness Makers' Collar Awls.

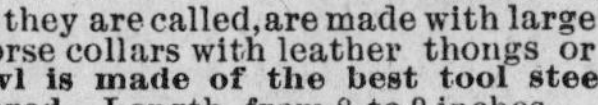

No. 10R7520 Drawing Awls or Collar Awls, as they are called, are made with large eye for sewing horse collars with leather thongs or whangs. **The awl is made of the best tool steel, highly tempered.** Length, from 8 to 9 inches. Price, each..........30c

Weight, 4 ounces.

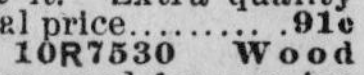

No. 10R7525 Williams' Single-Handed Spoke Shave, used for trimming traces, round reins and all kinds of leather work. Strictly first class. No leather worker's kit complete without it. Extra quality fine tool steel knife. Our special price..........91c

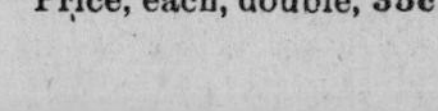

No. 10R7530 Wood Creaser, used for creasing the edge of straps, and putting a smooth edge on them. **Weight, 3 ounces.** Price, each, double, 35c; single..........25c

Single Edge Creaser.

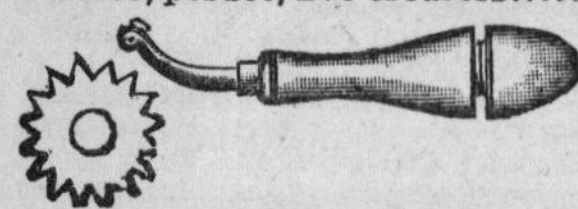

No. 10R7535 Sears, Roebuck & Co.'s Special Steel Single Edge Creaser, made of fine tool steel; round handle. Sizes Nos. 1, 2, 3, 4 and 5. Be sure and state size wanted. Price, each....$0.37
Price, per set, five creasers........................ 1.75

No. 10R7540 Our Fine Hollow Overstitching Carriage, with screw cap, or top. One that you can change the wheels by removing the thumbscrew and put in any size wheel you wish to use, from 5 to 12-inch. Price of carriage without wheels, each, 79c

No. 10R7545 Wheels for the above, extra. **Be sure and state the number of stitches you want to the inch when ordering wheels.** We carry in stock sizes from 5 to 12 to the inch. Each.........29c

Leather Gauge Knife.

No. 10R7550 This is the best hollow iron handle gauge knife in the market. Will cut from ⅛ to 4 inches in width. It is the same knife used by all practical harness makers.
Price, each..................95c

No. 10R7555 Our Improved Draw Gauge, made with iron frame, rosewood handle with three rivets with improved finger guard. Set-screw at knife and bar. All harness makers want this one.
Price, each..$1.25
If by mail, postage extra, 18 cents.

No. 10R7560 Osborne's Fine Strap End Punches, used by all harness makers in cutting the ends of straps round. Made in sizes from ½ inch to 1½ inches. Be sure and state the size wanted. Price each....$0.74
Price, per set, ½, ⅝, ¾, ⅞, 1, 1⅛, 1¼, 1½ inches, 5.75

No. 10R7565 Our Fine Osborne Straight Channelers, used for channeling any leather work where you wish to cover up the stitching such as hame tug, traces, bridle checks, etc., made with sliding blade. Price, each........86c

No. 10R7570 Our Fine Osborne Round Channeler, used for channeling all kinds of round work, such as round lines, bridle checks, winker brace, grip handles, etc.
Price, each..$1.26
Weight, 4 ounces.

No. 10R7575 S., R. & Co.'s French Edger used for raising leather laps, such as back strap breeching layers, or points on traces for breast collar. Very fine Osborne tool, made in sizes 0, 1, 2, 3, 4, 5, 6, 7 and 8. Be sure and state size wanted.
Our special price, each..............................$0.37
Furnished in sets (8) tools. Price, per set... 2.75

Harness Makers' Edging Tool.

No. 10R7580 A very handy tool for removing the sharp corners of any new strap work. Made 5 inches long, nicely polished.
Price, each...13c
Weight, 3 ounces.

No. 10R7585 Stationary Finishing or Overstitch Wheels. Fine octagon carriage used for setting up stitches or finishing work after it is stitched. Sizes from 5 to 10 inches. Price, each.....................63c

No. 10R7590 Stationary Pricking Wheels in fine octagon carriage, used for tracing leather work for stitching. Sizes from 5 to 10 inches.
Price, each..........(Weight, 7 ounces).......49c

Harness Makers' Round Knife.

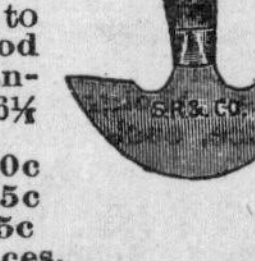

No. 10R7595 Made of the best tool steel, elegantly tempered to take a very sharp edge. **Rosewood Handles. Every one is guaranteed.** Blades measure 5, 6, 6½ inches.
5 inches. Price, each........60c
6 inches. Price, each........65c
6½ inches. Price, each.......75c
Weight, 5 ounces.

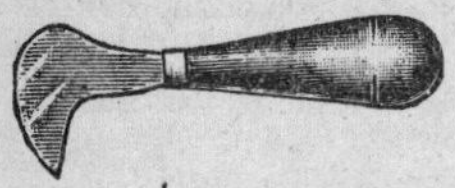

No 10R7600 Our Fine Head Knife, a knife that everyone working in leather goods should have; made of the finest tool steel with rosewood handle. Price, each.....(Weight, 4 ounces).....45c

Square Point Trimming Knife.

No. 10R7605 Our Fine Square Point Trimming Knife. Round handle with a fine blade made from fine tool steel. Price, each..(Weight, 3 ounces).10c

No. 10R7610 Osborne's Fine Tool Steel Bag Punches, used for punching buckle holes of all descriptions. By the use of this punch, you will never have a bad buckle hole. All harness makers should have them. Made in sizes from ⅛ to 1 inch. Price, each..68c
From 1⅛ to 1½, price, each..............................95c
Furnished in sets of (7) punches. Price, per set..$5.00

No. 10R7615 S., R. & Co.'s Special Scratch Compass made of extra fine tool steel and with set screw, used for scratching work to sink the stitches, such as trace hame tug, blinds or pads. Weight, 4 ounces. Each...74c

Osborne's Patent Awl Handles.

No. 10R7620 This handy little tool has a large sale, and is considered one of the most convenient articles to have about the premises. The awls are held securely in place by a metal cap, which screws tightly on the socket of the awl. **You can change the awls at any time without breaking them.** The prices quoted below do not include the awls, simply the handles and wrench. A small iron wrench, nicely adjusted, fits the cap and goes with each handle. **Weight, 4 ounces.**
Price, per dozen, $1.92; each....................16c

Write for prices on Creasing Machine and Creasing Rolls. Prices on all kinds of Saddlery Tools quoted on application.

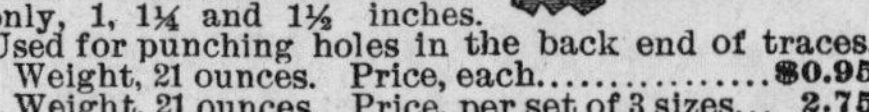

No. 10R7635 Osborne's Trace End Punch, made of extra fine quality of tool steel, to be used with mallet and lead. Made in three sizes only, 1, 1¼ and 1½ inches. Used for punching holes in the back end of traces.
Weight, 21 ounces. Price, each..................$0.95
Weight, 21 ounces. Price, per set of 3 sizes... 2.75

Special Blind Irons.

No. 10R7645 Sears, Roebuck & Co.'s Special Square Blind Irons, to be used with the square dies, made of extra fine rolled iron. Size 4x4 inches, and weight about 3 pounds per set.
Price, per set of four.....................6c
Per dozen sets..............................72c

No. 10R7655 Sears, Roebuck & Co.'s Special Concord Blind Irons, made of fine rolled iron, common size, 3½ pounds, to be used with blind dies.
Price, per set of four.....................6c
Per dozen sets..............................72c

Osborne's Special Improved Splitting Machine.

No. 10R7656 This machine is made with a lever handle which raises and lowers the roller and regulates the splitting of the strap. There is an extra brass rod above the blade which does not let the strap split only as raised by the roller, and it is very hard to cut a strap in two when splitting. This is considered by all harness makers the best bench splitting knife made. This knife is sold only in the one size, 6 inch. Weight, 7 pounds.
Price, each...$6.00

Leather Splitting Machine.

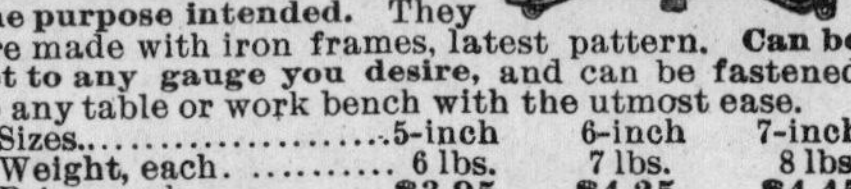

No. 10R7660 The Genuine Osborne Splitting Knife, which has a wide reputation and is considered **the best article in the market for the purpose intended.** They are made with iron frames, latest pattern. **Can be set to any gauge you desire,** and can be fastened to any table or work bench with the utmost ease.

Sizes	5-inch	6-inch	7-inch
Weight, each	6 lbs.	7 lbs.	8 lbs.
Price, each	$3.95	$4.25	$4.45

We can make you prices on larger machines, from 8 to 12 inches, upon application.

Our Fine Chase Splitting Knife.

No. 10R7665 Made for harness, saddle and belt makers; the only machine that **will split a strap without cutting the strap in two.** The blade is made of fine tool steel with **a roller on top and bottom.** The gauge is set by the two wheels at top. Weight, 30 pounds.

	8-inch	10-inch	12-inch
Price, each	$7.50	$9.00	$10.50

No. 10R7670 Our Fine Lignum Vitæ Slickers, made in one solid piece and pronounced by all harness and saddle makers much better than glass slickers because they will not get broken.
Weight, 9 ounces. Price, each.........................42c

No. 10R7675 Sears, Roebuck & Co.'s Special Harness Repair Outfit. By using this harness mender you are your own harness maker. Put up in a nice box, with lid, consisting of one strong leather clamp, a ball of wax, ball of thread, one round punch, one sewing awl handle, a package of needles, and one paper of copper rivets and burrs. The outfit put up in a wooden box weighs about 10 pounds. Price, 74c

No. 10R7680 Our Fine Steel Rein Trimmer, with fine round handle, used by all workers in leather when making all kinds of rounds, such as round lines, winker braces, grip handles and cruppers.
Weight, about 2 ounces. Price, each....................67c

No. 10R7685 Harness Needles, 25 in paper, assorted sizes, from 0 to 4.
Per paper...............................9c

No. 10R7690 Wax. Per ball...............................1c

Harness Thread.

No. 10R7695 Harness Thread, best No. 10 H. B. thread, natural linen color, 2-oz. balls. Per ball...9c

No. 10R7700 No. 10 H. B. Super Thread, wound on tubes; waste by snarling or tangling prevented. Natural linen color, 2-ounce balls.
Per lb. (8 balls), 96c; per ball..12c

No. 10R7705 No. 12 H. B. Devonshire Thread, wound on tubes, natural linen color, 2-ounce balls.
Per lb. (8 balls), $1.12; per ball.14c

No. 10R7710 Harness Awl Blades, to be used in extra handles. Per dozen.......22c

No. 10R7715 Common Wood Awl Handles, with ferrule.
Per dozen..........................17c

No. 10R7720 Genuine Collar Needle, used to sew or repair old collars, to be used with collar palm. Price....15c

No. 10R7721 Sacking Needles, Each..........3c

No. 10R7725 Collar Palms, used to repair old collars or make new ones, and something every farmer should have. Price, each.........65c

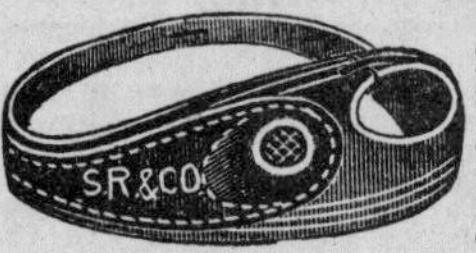

No. 10R7730 S., R. & Co.'s Special Sailor Palm, made of fine kip leather body, **palm covered with rawhide and thimble attached, used for making sails or other canvas work.** Each...25c

Harness Horse.

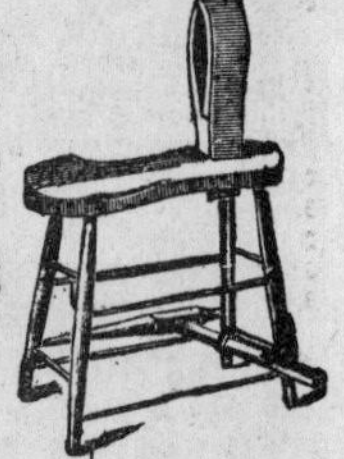

No. 10R7740 Harness Makers' Stitching Horse. This is something every horse owner should have. Any man can do his own repairing and save his time, as well as his money. Made of good sound wood.
Price for stitching horse with jaw strap..................$2.60
Without jaw strap....... 2.35
Weight, 18 pounds.

Stitching Horse Attachment.

No. 10R7745 Coopers' Moline to be used in making round lines, around bridle fronts, or around reins on bridle or any other class of round leather work. By the use of this attachment you are able to hold your round in the proper position to stitch, fastened to the jaws on the stitching horse by a set screw. Weight, 16 ounces.
Our special price, each..........................65c

LEATHER.

NOTE—Owing to the uncertainty of the leather and hide market, the prices on these goods are subject to change without notice.

No. 10R7750 Hemlock Tanned Black Harness Leather, B grade, whole side only; sides weighing from 17 to 21 pounds.
Price, per pound.........................34c

No. 10R7755 No. 1 Hemlock Black Harness Leather, extra quality; weight, per side, from 17 to 22 pounds. Price, per pound..........................35c

No. 10R7760 Pure Oak Harness Leather, good B grade, whole sides only; sides weigh from 17 to 22 pounds. Price, per pound..........................36c

No. 10R7765 Extra Quality No. 1 Oak Tanned Leather, black; weight, per side, from 17 to 2. pounds. Price, per pound..........................38c

No. 10R7770 Russet Leather Sheep Skins, good, large size, for blacksmiths' and lumbermen's aprons, etc. Price, each.........................$1.30

No. 10R7775 Sheep Skins, tanned with the wool on, used for lining saddles, harness breeching and breast collars, extra large. Price, each........$1.35

NOTE—All of our different grades of Harness Leather are selected from packers' steer hides.

Ladies' Stirrups.

No. 10R7780 Ladies' Metal Shoe Stirrups for side saddle, XC plated. Weight, 8 ounces.
Each..............11c

No. 10R7785 Ladies' Metal Stirrups (men's pattern) XC plate. Weight, 5 ounces.
Each...............7c

No. 10R7780 — No. 10R7790

No. 10R7790 Same, XC plate, men's size. Weight, 6 ounces. Price, each..........................10c

No. 10R7795 Ladies' Slipper Stirrup for side saddle, sole or shank, is of steel, covered with leather stitched on, **heavy hog skin vamp, strong iron swing, comfort and security combined.** Weight, 12 ounces. Price, each..........................66c

Men's Wood Stirrups.

No. 10R7800 Boys' size, common wood, two rivets. Per pair..........8c

No. 10R7805 Men's size, 2½-inch, common wood, two rivets. Per pair ...9c

No. 10R7810 Men's size, common, 3-inch, wood, two rivets. Per pair.........10c

No. 10R7815 Our Heavy Texas Wood Stirrup, made of extra quality of wood with bolted center, suitable for all kinds of saddles. Made in sizes, 4-inch, 14c; 5-inch, 16c; 6-inch............20c
Weight, about 2 pounds.

No. 10R7800

No. 10R7815

No. 10R7820 S., R. & Co.'s Special Ox-bow Stirrup, made of best quality of choice white ash timber, making one of the most durable and desirable stirrups on the market. Made for 2 and 3-inch stirrup straps. Per pair.....23c

No. 10R7825 Same style as No. 10R7820 of ox-bow stirrups, heavy brass bound, made to take 2½ and 3-inch stirrup leathers. Made of white ash, extra quality. Price, per pair,.........75c
Weight, per pair, 3 pounds.

No. 10R7820

No. 10R7830 Our Special Heavy Cowboys' Metal Stirrup, made of extra quality of gray iron with bar large enough to take 2½ and 3-inch stirrup leathers; a stirrup that is in great demand throughout the Western country. XC plate.
Price, per pair.........74c
Weight, per pair, 2¼ pounds.

No. 10R7830

Metal Stirrups.

No. 10R7835 S., R. & Co.'s Special Brass Bound Stirrup, has an extra fine shape allowing the foot to set flat in the bottom of the stirrup, with stirrup roller large enough to take 2½ and 3-inch stirrup leathers. A stirrup that will give universal satisfaction. Made in sizes 2½ and 3½ inches at bottom width.
Price, per pair.........70c
Weight, per pair, 3½ pounds.

No. 10R7835

No. 10R7840 Our Fine Steel Leather Covered Stirrups, with extra heavy leather bottom and leather covered roller, making one of the best stirrups that can be used on heavy stock saddles. Price, per pair.........$1.20
Weight, about 2¼ pounds.

No. 10R7840

No. 10R7845 S., R. & Co.'s Special Ladies' Hooded Stirrup, made with 2½-inch wood stirrup leather bottom, fancy top, wool lined, oiled leather, fancy rosette. Strong and durable Price, each ..70c
Weight, about 12 oz.

No. 10R7845

No. 10R7850 Our Fine Common 2½-inch Wood Stirrup, with common russet leather tap, suitable for any kind of a boys' or men's saddle.
Price, per pair..48c

10R7850

No. 10R7855 S., R. & Co.'s Heavy Covered Wood Stirrup, made of fine russet oil tanned leather. Extra heavy, suitable for any kind of saddle. Bar will take stirrup strap from 1 to 2 inches
Price, per pair...........84c
Weight, per pair, about 3 lbs.

No. 10R7855

No. 10R7860 Our Common Eagle Bill Tapidero, made of oil tanned leather, edge creasing, seamed front with layer and nickel rosette with lace string, on a good heavy wide stirrup.
Price, per pair.........$1.75
Weight, per pair, about 3½ lbs.

No. 10R7865 S., R. & Co.'s Special Eagle Bill Tapideros, made of fine Oregon oil tanned leather with 5-inch wide Texas stirrup, fancy edge stamping, reinforced front with two rosettes and tie strings, making one of the very best tapideros in our line. **Weight, per pair, about 4 pounds.** Price, per pair.........$1.95

No. 10R7860

No. 10R7867 Our Special Cowboy Eagle Bill Tapideros. This special tapideros is made pug nose, with layer doubled and stitched, and long pointed eagle bill points. Three sizes. 6 double scalloped fancy leather rosettes, made on 3-inch California pattern stirrup, Leather bottom and bar. This is one of the best Eagle Bill taps made. Strictly first class. Suitable for any of our high grade saddles. Made in three sizes, 12, 14 and 16-inch.

12-inch Tap.	Weight, 3¾ lbs.	Price, per pair $2.20
14-inch Tap.	Weight, 4 lbs.	Price, per pair 2.47
16-inch Tap.	Weight, 4¼ lbs.	Price, per pair 2.75

The tap will match our large heavy stock saddles. State size wanted.

Spurs.

Spurs are quoted by the pair; make no mistake.

We do not break pairs, as they are made right and left.

Our stock of spurs is the most complete, and we are prepared to serve you better and cheaper than any other concern.

No. 10R8000

No. 10R8000 English Pattern XC Plate Spurs.
Light Weight, 4 ounces. Per pair.........15c
Medium. Weight, 7 ounces. Per pair.........20c
Extra heavy. Weight, 9 ounces. Per pair.........25c

No. 10R8005 English Pattern Spur, solid brass, extra heavy, oval heel band, ⅝-inch rowel shank, ⅞-inch steel plate rowel, regular military style, without straps. Weight, about 4 ounces. Per pair.........23c

No. 10R8005

No. 10R8010 Eureka Spurs, wide steel heel band and nickel plated 1¼-inch malleable rowel, two buttons without straps.
Weight, about 6 ounces.
Per pair.........22c

No. 10R8010

No. 10R8015 Mexican Spurs, fine steel, chased, filled, engraved and ornamented, chain and trinkets, 1½-in. rowel. Weight, about 12 ounces. Per pair.....30c

No. 10R8020 Same style spur as No. 10R8015, only made with 2⅞-inch rowel. Weight, 14 ounces.
Price, per pair.........49c

No. 10R8015

No. 10R8025 S., R. & Co.'s Special English Spur, made of malleable iron, XC plated, with spur strap.
Weight, 5 ounces. Per pair...30c

No. 10R8030 S., R. & Co.'s Fine Heavy Brass English Spur, made of solid brass, highly polished, with spur strap.
Weight, 5 ounces. Per pair...33c

No. 10R8025

No. 10R8035 California Spur. Hand forged steel, nickeled and chased, leather lined, 2-inch rowel, without strap, one button and chain. Weight, about 15 ounces.
Per pair.........$2.25

10R8035

We do not break pairs spurs.

10R8040

No. 10R8040 California Spur, hand forged steel, nickeled and chased, leather lined, 2½-inch rowel, without strap, one button, chain and trinkets. Weight, about 16 ounces. Per pair, $2.65
We do not break pairs spurs.

No. 10R8045 California New Patent Steel Spur, with chains, burnished and engraved, solid, medium weight heel band, 1⅝-inch rowel. Weight, about 15 ounces.
Per pair.........85c
We do not break pairs spurs.

10R8045

No. 10R8050 Same style as No. 10R8045 spur only made with 2¼-inch rowel, with bells. Weight, 16 ounces. Price, per pair.........90c

Army Officers' Spurs.

No. 10R8055 Military Spur and Spur Strap, spur is made out of gun metal, highly polished, with chain and spur strap. This is a regular army officers' spur. The finest and best made. Sold in pairs only, complete, as shown in cut.
Weight, 12 ounces. Per pair $1.95
We do not break pairs spurs.

Regulation Military Bit.

No. 10R8060 Hand Forged Steel Regular Pattern No. 3 U. S. Military Bit. This is strictly first class in every particular. Made in burnished or blued.
Weight, 15 ounces. Each..$2.00

No. 10R8065 Nickel plated 2.35

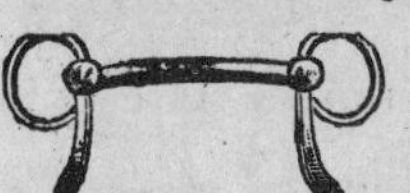

No. 10R8070 Our X C Plate Stiff Mouth Driving Bit, made of malleable iron.
Weight, 8 ounces. Each 10c

No. 10R8075 Same style of bit as No. 10R8070, only full japanned finish, stiff mouth. Weight, 8 oz; each 10c

No. 10R8080 Our XC Plate Jointed Mouth Driving Bit, made of fine malleable iron, strong. Price, each......10c

No. 10R8085 Same style of bit as No. 10R8080, only all black finish. Jointed mouth. good, strong bit. Weight, 8 ounces. Price, each 10c

Nickel Driving Bit.

No. 10R8090 Our Fine Nickel Driving Bit, made of good malleable iron and fine nickel finish. Jointed or stiff. Weight, 8 ounces. Price, each.........15c

No. 10R8095 Our Fine Pony Bit, same style as No. 10R8080, jointed or stiff; 4½-inch mouth.
Price, each nickel plate, 14c; XC plate,.........10c
Weight, 6 ounces.

Buckeye Safety Bit.

No. 10R8100 Made with three-ring cheek, loose bar, solid mouth or jointed large size. This bit is one of the best team bridle bits made, as it will be easy on a horse or severe at the same time providing it is necessary. Made in XC plate only. (Will always send solid mouth unless ordered jointed.)
Weight, 16 ounces. Price, each.........25c

Fine Military Steel Watering Bit.

No. 10R8105 Steel mouth, jointed, with snaps in rings to snap in halter or rings. This bit can be used on any kind of short check bridle. Made in blued finish only.
Weight, 9 ounces. Price, each...50c

Fine Nickel Spanish Bit.

No. 10R8110 Made with swivel ring saber bent cheek, medium high port and curb chain, ornamented check. Nickel plated only. Price, each..59c
Weight, 15 ounces.

Our Special Leather Mouth Driving Bit.

No. 10R8115 Made of solid leather mouth, flexible large ring, lined with leather, and chin strap. This is an extra fine bit, one that is used by a great many drivers. Made only in solid leather mouth, not jointed.
Our special price, each, $1.00
Weight, 5 ounces.

Our Special Colorado Bit.

No. 10R8116 This Bit is made with loose jointed cheeks, port mouth bar with roller, one of the best port bits in our line. Fine nickel plated only.
Weight, 15 ounces. Price, each....79c

Williams' Special Low Port Swivel Ring Bar Bit and Connecting Cheek Bars.

No. 10R8117 This Bit is made with very low port with roller; the roller can be taken out if not wanted. Fine cast steel bit; blued finish. Price, each.........$1.20
Weight, 16 ounces.

No. 10R8118 Williams' Hand Forged Steel Bit, blued finish only, the best made. Same style as No. 10R8117. Weight, 17 ounces. Price, each..$2.75

Our Improved Low Port Nickel Bit.

No. 10R8119 So many call for low port bits that we had this extra good nickel bit made; very strong and well finished. Weight, 10 ounces. Each..73c

Our California Patent Spade Mouthed Cowboy Bit.

No. 10R8121 This Bit is made of malleable iron, fancy filed and chased cheek, port with roller and side braces. 8-inch rein chain and extra chin chain connecting cheeks of bit. This bit is a big seller, a good strong serviceable bit for hard mouthed horses. **Weight, each, 20 ounces.**
Price, each.........75c

King Nickel Driving Bit.

No. 10R8125 Made jointed or stiff, half cheek snaffle, Ben Lane cheek, small loops for overcheck. Fine nickel plated only. We always send jointed unless ordered stiff. Weight, 12 ounces. Price, each......35c

Racine Nickel Driving Bit.

No. 10R8130 Made with solid mouth bar, half cheek snaffle. This is one of the best nickel driving bits on the market, and one that we have a very large sale on. Stiff or jointed. We always send jointed unless ordered stiff. Weight, 8 ounces. Price, each.........15c

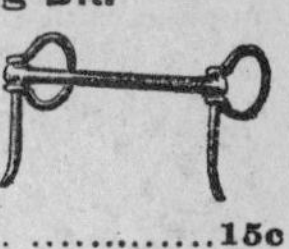

Dexter Driving Bit.

No. 10R8135 This is the finest Forged Steel Driving Bit we handle. Large, heavy cheeks, large, heavy tapered mouthpiece, jointed or stiff, as wanted. The best of nickel plating, and one thing about a bridle that should be the very best is the bit. We recommend this as being the best, most handsome and solid driving bit we handle. Weight, 14 ounces. Price, each 50c

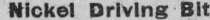

COTTON AND LEATHER FLY NETS.

...WE DIRECT SPECIAL ATTENTION THIS SEASON TO OUR MOST COMPLETE AND LOWEST PRICED LINE OF COTTON AND LEATHER FLY NETS.

We have made very special and advantageous contracts for these goods, and can confidently say that our prices admit of no competition. Our nets are all strictly high grade, they are full size, strong, durable, first quality, well made nets, and the prices at which we offer them are less than the same goods are sold to jobbers.

Cotton Cord Mesh Team Net.

55 Cents

No. 10R9000 Our Cotton Cord Team Net. Body, neck and ear tips; diamond knotted mesh, woven center bar; neck part snaps to body; fancy colored body, border and tassels. **An extra good cheap mesh net.** Weight, 1¾ pounds per pair.
Price, each.....$0.55
Price, per pair, for two horses.....1.10

Cotton Cord Mesh Team Net.

69 Cents

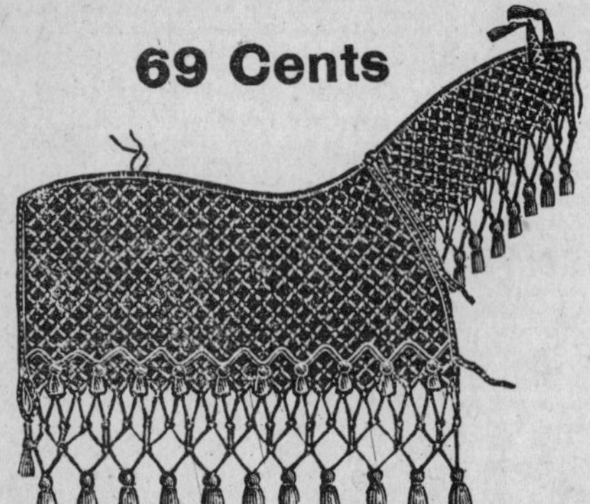

No. 10R9005 Our Special Cotton Cord Team Net. Diamond knotted mesh, heavy cord, woven center bar; body, neck and ear tips; neck snaps to body; 1½-inch mesh. **A good everyday team net. Made in two patterns.** Pattern No. 1, black body, lemon border and black tassels. Pattern No. 2, green body, lemon border, red tassels. Weight, per pair, 2¼ pounds. Price, each.....$0.69
Price, per pair, for two horses.....1.38

Cotton Mesh Team Net.

85 Cents

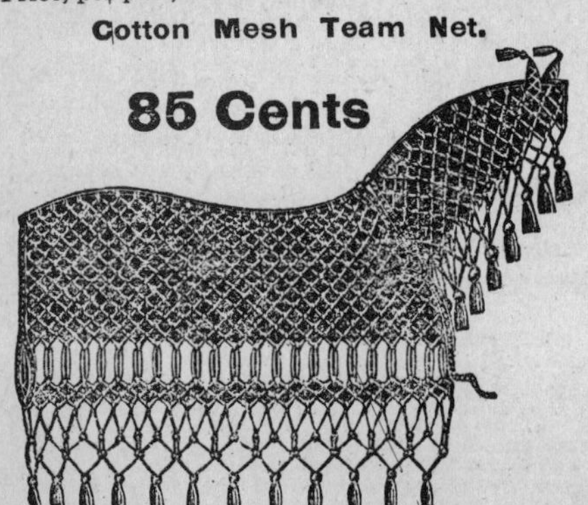

No. 10R9010 Sears, Roebuck & Co.'s Special Heavy Single Cord Mesh Net. Body, neck and ear tips; neck snaps to body; fancy braid end bars, large size net, woven center bar, 1½-inch diamond knotted mesh. **Made in two patterns.** Pattern No. 1, red body, green border and lemon tassels. **A very handsome net.** Pattern No. 2, old gold body, salmon border and white tassels. **A good everyday team or light wagon net.** Weight, per pair, 3 pounds.
Price, each.....$0.85
Price, per pair, for two horses.....1.70

Cotton Cord Team Net.

90 Cents

No. 10R9015 Our Variegated Center Cotton Cord Team Net. Made up very fancy, with diamond knotted mesh body, neck and ear tips, woven center bar, neck snaps to body, two rows of tassels. **A high grade cotton team net, suitable for spring wagon use. Made in two color patterns.** Pattern No. 1, old gold body, green center and red tassels; pattern No. 2, black body, lemon center and purple tassels. **A rich looking team net.** Weight, per pair, 2¼ pounds. Price, each.....$0.90
Price, per pair, for two horses.....1.80

Our Heavy Double Cord Team Net.

$1.10

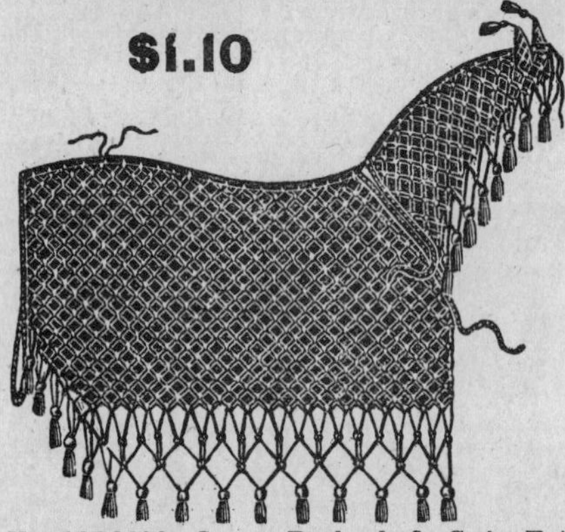

No. 10R9020 Sears, Roebuck & Co.'s Extra Heavy Double Cord Team Net. Double diamond mesh and double knotted body. A full double corded net throughout. **This is the heaviest double cord team net made.** Large size deep body net. Body, neck and ear tips, woven center bar and detachable neck. **We make this net in two color patterns, viz:** Pattern No. 1, red and lemon cord doubled, knotted together, with white trimmings; pattern No. 2, black and lemon cord, body knotted together, with olive trimmings. Braided end bars. Two row tassels. Weight, per pair, 4 pounds.
Price, each.....$1.10
Price, per pair, for two horses.....2.20

Our Fine White Miller Shaft Net.

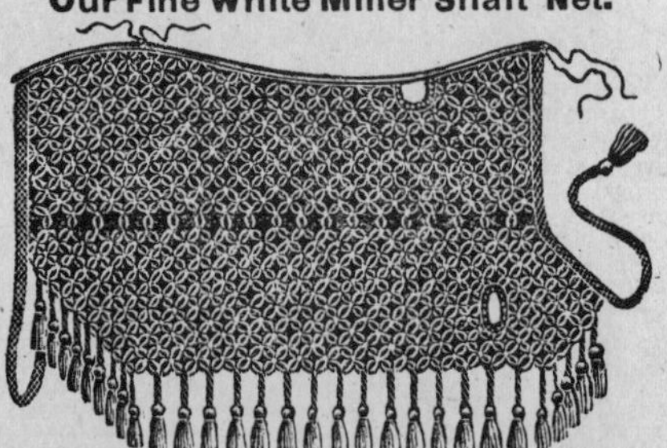

Sears, Roebuck & Co.'s Fine White Miller Net, made of hard twisted English cord. Hand made knots, fancy braided end bars, with long handsome tassels, fancy hand made shell mesh. This is the finest all white net made. Large and small mesh body net. Weight, each 2 pounds.
No. 10R9100 Large mesh. Price, each.....$1.75
No. 10R9105 Small mesh. Price, each.....2.10
Neck pieces for above net, extra.....1.00

Our Single Mesh Buggy Net.

70 Cents

No. 10R9110 Our Single Fancy Mesh Net, made of fancy color cotton cord, diamond mesh. Braided center bar, body and neck, with ear tip. Weight, 14 ounces. Price, each.....70c

Our Silver Morn Shaft Net.

80 Cents

No. 10R9115 Our Silver Morn Single White Mesh Buggy or Shaft Net, made of all white cotton cord. Braided center bar; diamond mesh body, neck and ear tips. Neck snaps to body. A good all white single net. Weight, 16 ounces. Price, each.....80c

Our Belle Single Shaft Net.

95 Cents

No. 10R9120 Our Belle Single Fancy Color Mesh Buggy or Shaft Net, fancy braided center bar, body and neck, with ear tips. Neck snaps to body. Color of net, red, green and yellow. Weight, 14 ounces.
Price, each.....95c

Our Alma Wilton Shaft Net.

$1.15

No. 10R9125 Our Alma Wilton Fancy Color Single Cotton Mesh Net, made of fine hard twisted cotton cord, diamond mesh, hand knotted. Braided center bar, body and neck, with ear tips. Neck snaps to body. Black, lemon and red or old gold, with red and green and red tassels. Weight, 16 ounces.
Price, each.....$1.15

S., R. & Co.'s Extra Heavy Upper Leather Body and Breast Team Net.

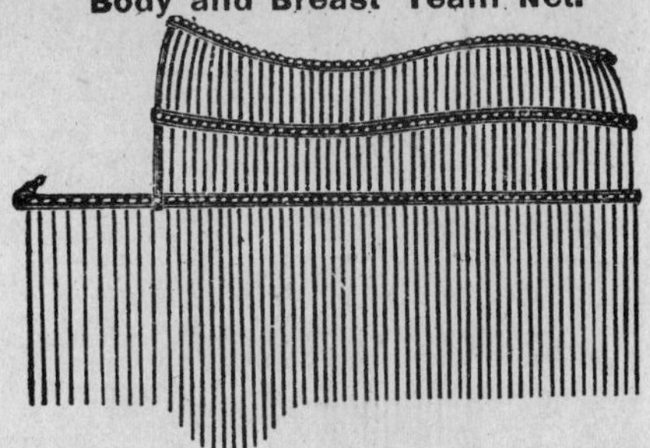

No. 10R9065 Sears, Roebuck & Co.'s Extra Heavy Body and Breast Team Net; ⅞-inch harness leather bars, long body net, hame bar, extra long strings over shoulders and fore leg, body about 5½ feet long. **The best heavy upper leather body and breast net made.** Price is for one horse.

Strings......	50	60	70
Weight, lbs.	3	3½	4½
Price, each.	$2.50	$2.84	$3.17

Our Iowa Special Upper Leather Team Net.

No. 10R9070 Made of waxed upper leather string, cut good and heavy, and extra long; ⅞-inch harness leather bars and hame bars, body and neck with lower bars full length of horse and around breast, making breast piece. This net is about 7¼ feet long from head to tail, with long string over shoulder and fore leg. **This is our medium weight net. A high grade upper leather team net.** Made in three sizes. Price is for one horse.

	72 strings	84 strings	100 strings
	Weight, 3½ lbs.	Weight, 4 lbs.	Weight, 4½ lbs.
Price, each,	$2.58	$2.95	$3.29

S., R. & Co.'s Heavy Upper Leather Jumbo Net.

The heaviest and best upper leather net made. 7-foot body string, 8-foot string over-shoulder and hind legs.

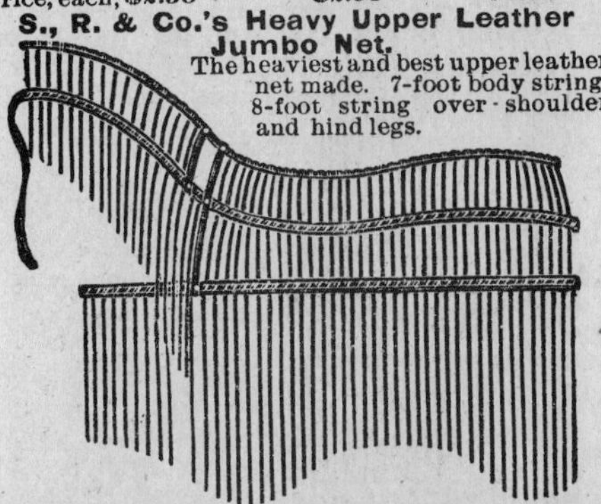

No. 10R9075 Our Heavy Upper Leather Jumbo Team Net is the heaviest and best team net made. **Strings are cut ¼ inch wide, extra long strings at front and hind leg, 1 inch harness leather bar, three bars run to head and 2 bars around breast. Net 7 feet 4 inches long, extra strong and well made. The price is for one horse.**

	72 strings	84 strings	100 strings
Weight, lbs..............	6¼	7½	8½
Price, each............	$3.55	$3.85	$4.15

S., R. & Co.'s Extra Heavy Jumbo Upper Leather Body and Breast Team Net.

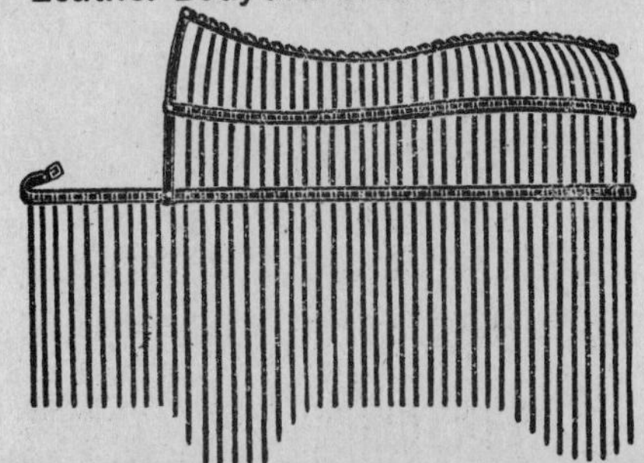

No. 10R9080 This is the best net we can make, cut five strings to inch. Extra long at fore and hind legs, 1-inch bar, 5½ feet net from hame to tail. The price is for one horse. The strings are extra heavy; 7 foot long in body, with 8-foot string over shoulder and hind legs.

	60 Strings	70 Strings
Weight, lbs............	6	7
Price, each............	$3.64	$3.95

PLAIN AND FANCY LAP ROBES.

We take great pride in the completeness of this department, as well as in the fact that we have succeeded in making lower prices for our customers than in any past season. The manager of this department has selected these goods with the greatest care to secure the best styles and qualities. Taking price and grade into consideration, these values are unapproachable. While you can get some idea of the pattern of each robe from the small illustration we show,

YOU MUST SEE THE ROBES IN THEIR FULL SIZE, COLOR AND DESIGN TO APPRECIATE THEIR FULL BEAUTY.

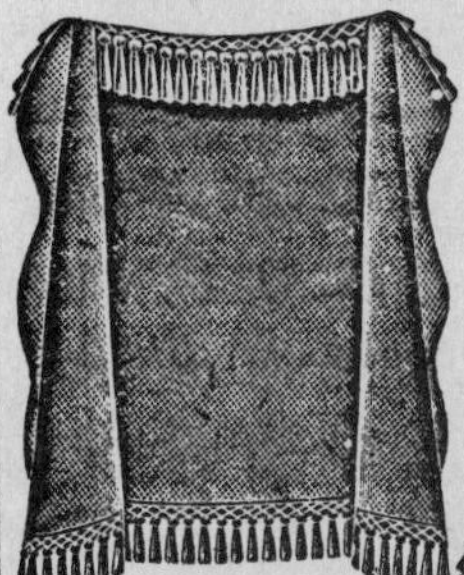

Plain Linen Robe.

No. 10R10025 Our Plain Imported German Linen Lap Robe. Knotted fringe, perfectly plain center, large size, medium weight. A strictly high class linen buggy robe at a low price. Weight of robe, 16 ounces. Size of robe, 50x60 inches.
Price, each.......$1.00

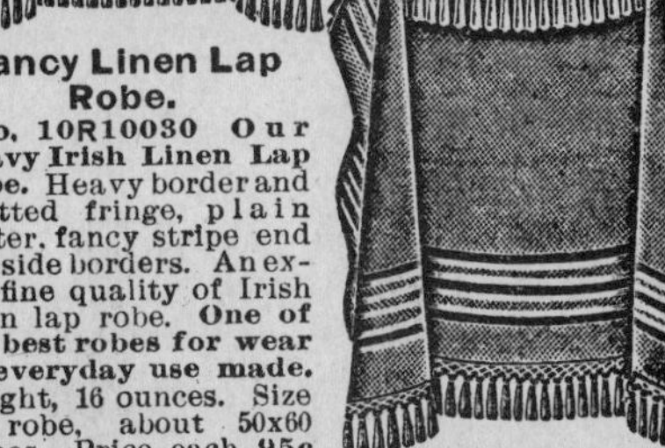

Fancy Linen Lap Robe.

No. 10R10030 Our Heavy Irish Linen Lap Robe. Heavy border and knotted fringe, plain center, fancy stripe end and side borders. An extra fine quality of Irish linen lap robe. **One of the best robes for wear or everyday use made.** Weight, 16 ounces. Size of robe, about 50x60 inches. Price, each..95c

No. 10R10035 Our Fancy Stripe German Lap Robe, with knotted fringe, fancy plaid border, fancy pink striped body and handsome pink border. This is positively the richest and most handsome lap robe made. **Being all linen, it will wash and look as nice as new. This robe is pronounced by all to be the handsomest linen lap robe on the market.** Size of robe, about 50x60 inches. Worth $3.00. Weight, 18 ounces. Price, each..............................$1.50

Linen Lap Robe.

No. 10R10040 S., R. & Co.'s Extra Heavy Irish Linen Buggy Robe. Plain linen body, with white woven stripes through body and white woven border. This robe is extra large size and very firmly woven. Weight of robe, 16 ounces. **This is positively one of the best linen lap robes we handle. It would retail at your home dealers for $1.75 or $2.00.** Size of robe, about 50x60 inches.
Our special price..$1.00

Checked Linen Buggy Robe, 55c.

No. 10R10005 Fancy Striped Border Linen Buggy Robe with plain fringed ends. A good linen robe. Weight of robe, 10 ounces. Size of robe, 48x60 inches. Linen robes are easy to wash and always look clean and nice.
Price, each.........55c

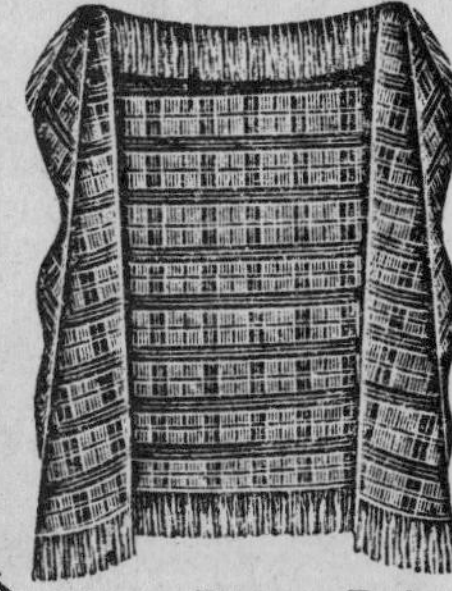

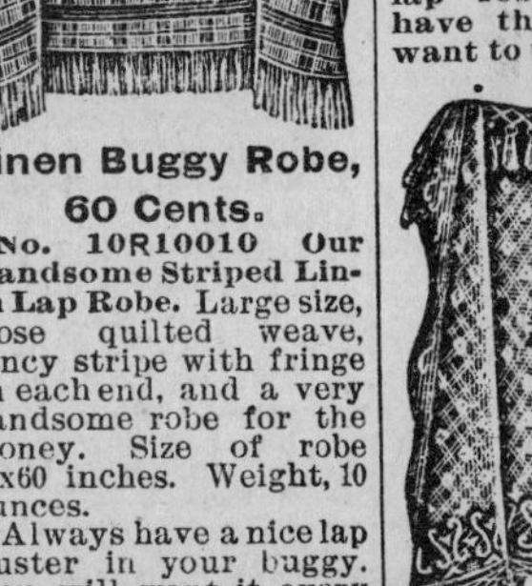

Linen Buggy Robe, 60 Cents.

No. 10R10010 Our Handsome Striped Linen Lap Robe. Large size, close quilted weave, fancy stripe with fringe on each end, and a very handsome robe for the money. Size of robe 50x60 inches. Weight, 10 ounces.

Always have a nice lap duster in your buggy. You will want it every day.
Price, each........ 60c

Striped Linen Buggy Robe, 95c.

No. 10R10015 Our Linen Lap Robe with fancy stripe and headings; ground, natural color, plain fringe on each end. Size of robe, 50x60 inches. Weight, 10 ounces.

We show the best line of summer lap dusters on the market for buggy use.
Our special low price, 95c

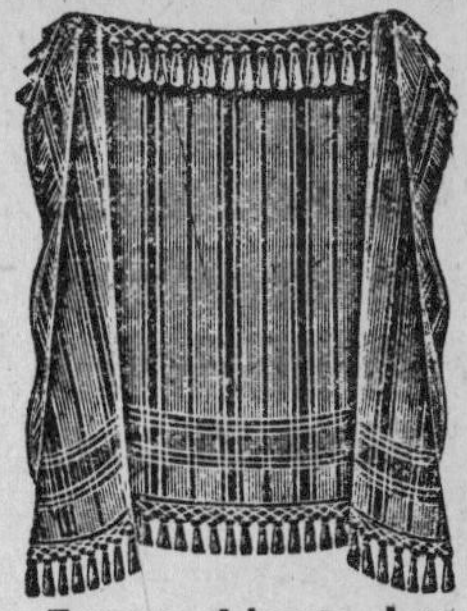

Fancy Linen Lap Robe, 90c.

No. 10R10020 S., R. & Co.'s Special Fancy Pattern Linen Lap Robe. Knotted fringe, heavy striped border, fancy vine center stripes. Makes a very handsome buggy duster or fancy table cover by working the outline of flowers with fancy colored yarns. Pronounced by all ladies the handsomest pattern in linen robes made. Extra large size. Weight, 14 ounces. Size of robe, about 50x60 inches.
Price, each 90c

Our Light Summer Buggy Lap Robe, 30 Cents.

No. 10R10200 Made of fancy woven Momie cloth, fancy stripe; plain fringe, fancy color; plain center. Weight, 7 ounces. Size of robe, 48x60 inches.
Price, each..........30c

Our lap robes of all kinds are the greatest value ever offered and are sure to please you.

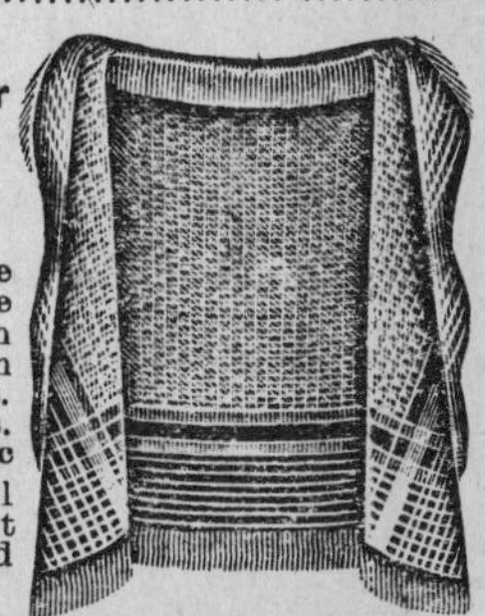

Our Fancy Dotted Momie Duster, 40 Cents.

No. 10R10205 Fancy border, plain fringe, with spray of flowers in center of duster. Extra Jacquard fancy woven body; a very durable lap robe and a big seller. Would retail at 75 cents. Size, 48x56 inches.
Weight, 10 ounces.
Our special price...40c

NOTICE—Our line of summer lap robes are the very latest styles and colors.

Our Plain Center Momie Duster, 50 Cents.

No. 10R10210 Fancy plaid, double weave body, scroll border, knotted fringe on each end. A very durable buggy duster. Size, 48x56 inches. Weight, about 10 ounces. Assorted fancy patterns.
Price, each.........50c

NOTICE—Order your lap robes early and have them when you want to use them.

Our Special Momie Duster or Buggy Lap Robe, 65c.

No. 10R10215 Fancy double weave body, handsomely dropped weave headings, with fancy border, knotted fringe and very pretty design embroidered center, with very fine blending colors, extra fine spotted weave pattern. Size of robe, 48x56 inches. Weight, about 12 ounces.
Price, each..........65c

Plain Green Double Plush Robes, $1.15 to $3.95.

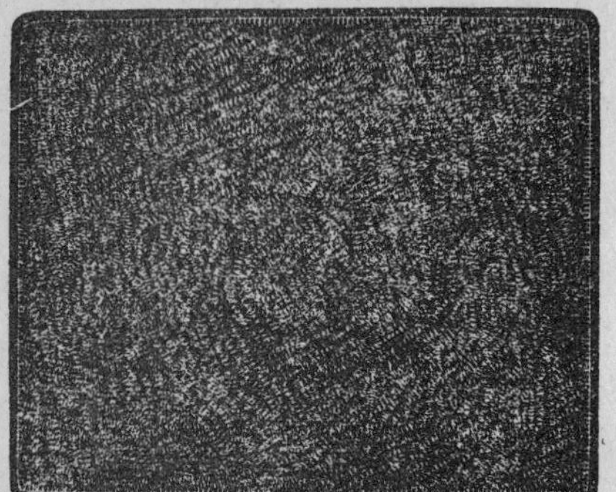

No. 10R10464 Our Gray and Fancy Color Single Plush Buggy Robe. This robe is made of soft gray and colored plush stock, bound around edges. Size, 48x60 inches. Weight, about 3 pounds.
Price, each, gray, **$1.00; fancy color........$1.15**

No. 10R10465 Our Plain Double Green Plush Carriage Robe. Plain green pattern on one side and plain black on the other side. A very handsome, stylish and well made plush robe. Size of robe, 48x60 inches. Weight of robe, about 5 pounds.
Price, each..**$1.95**

No. 10R10467 Sears, Roebuck & Co.'s Special Extra Heavy Green Double Plush Lap Robe. Plain green on one side and black on the other. This is an extra quality of fine plush robe. Size, 50x60 inches. Weight, 5½ pounds. The best kind of a robe for everyday use. Always looks neat and clean.
Price, each..**$2.25**

No. 10R10469 Sears, Roebuck & Co.'s Extra Heavy Double Green Plush Robe. Superfine quality of plain green silk plush on one side and handsome shade of black on the other side. Double extra large. Size, 56x74 inches. Weight, 8½ pounds. This is the largest, handsomest and most durable double green plush robe we handle. One of the best sellers in our line. Price, each..........................**$3.95**

Plush Robe, Rubber Face, $1.90 and $2.30.

No. 10R10473 Sears, Roebuck & Co.'s Special Heavy, Rubber Lined Waterproof Lap Robe. This robe is made with a fine plush back, facing of rubber, made for all kinds of stormy weather. **Can be used with either plush or rubber side up.** Size, 48x60 inches. Weight, about 5¾ lbs. Price, each....**$1.90**

No. 10R10475 Sears, Roebuck & Co.'s Special Plush Lined, Rubber Faced, Storm Lap Robe. This lap robe is made of an extra quality of rubber facing and superfine plush back. **Nothing better ever made in a storm lap robe.** Size, 48x60 inches. Weight, about 6 pounds. For extra quality, our special price..**$2.30**

Our Indiana Double Plush Robe.

No. 10R10476 This Robe is made of dark colored plush body, fancy red and yellow border, wolf head center with fancy red and green leaf effect. Size, 48x60 inches, and weight, 5 pounds. This is one of the cheap double plush robes, and yet the kind of plush robe that sells at retail for $3.50 to $4.00. Fancy pattern one side and plain black the other.
Price, each..**$2.65**

American Buffalo Robes are the Best, $5.50 to $7.50.

Retail everywhere at $10.00 and upwards.

The World's Best Robe. This Robe is made of a very fine quality of imported brown wool, having a knit body with this wool carefully woven in. The appearance of the robe is like the old buffalo robe of the plains; has a very curly face. The robe, when finished, has a very soft and pliable effect, being lined with black astrakhan cloth lining, such as fine astrakhan capes are made out of, with an inner lining of rubber cloth, which makes the robe absolutely wind and waterproof. This robe, when wet from snow or rain, will dry quickly and never has the hard effect of the old buffalo robe from the fact that there is no hide to get dry and hard. It has a very handsome felt pinked border edge. We can fully recommend it to our customers as a strictly first class article of the very finest quality. We make this robe in three sizes:

	Size, inches	Weight, lbs.	Each
No. 10R10478	54x52	8	$5.50
No. 10R10479	54x62	10	6.50
No. 10R10480	54x72 or extra large	11½	7.50

Pug Dog Center Plush Robe, $2.77.

No. 10R10491 Our Pug Dog Center Plush Robe. This robe is a fine double plush robe. The pattern of the robe is two pug dogs and basket center, with a light shaded brown fancy border. This is one of the handsomest patterns in the cheap Madelia center plush robes. Size, 48x60 inches. Weight, 5 pounds.
Price, each..**$2.77**

Our Redfield Double Plush Dog Center Robe, $2.95.

No. 10R10495 This Robe is made with black plush on one side and fancy plush on the other. Yellow dog head with red circle and yellow and brown ornamental frame. This is an extra fine handsome double plush robe. Size, 48x60 inches. Weight, about 5 pounds. Price, each..........................**$2.95**

THE ILLUSTRATIONS will give you some idea of the patterns of these plush robes, but you must see and examine them, feel the texture, note the make and finish to fully appreciate the value we are offering.

Horse Head Plush Robe, $2.99.

No. 10R10496 Our Horse Head Center Robe. This robe is rather on a dark color, being a very dark green ground work with fancy border, and a large horse head as center piece. Size, 48x60 inches. Weight, 5½ pounds. Our special price.........**$2.99**

Tiger Center Plush Robe, $3.35.

No. 10R10498 Our Bengal Tiger Center Plush Robe. A very large pattern of a tiger in the center with glass eyes, shaded brown border. Color of tiger is brown with striped body. Size, 48x60 inches. Weight, about 5 pounds. Our special price.............**$3.35**

Our Richmond Fancy Double Plush Robe.

No. 10R10500 Plain black plush on one side and fancy figured pattern on the other. Dark and light stock used in making this robe. Fancy red and yellow, with ornamental flowers of green. A very fine, handsome, light double plush robe. Panel or slash from corner to corner, double in red. Size of robe, 48x60 inches. Weight, 5½ pounds. This robe would retail at $4.75. Our special price........**$3.15**

Buffalo Center Plush Robe, $3.79.

No. 10R10501 Our Special Buffalo Center Plush Robe. This robe is made of fine quality of plush with four buffalo pattern center, light shaded green border. Buffalos are light and dark brown. This robe has had a very large sale, it is not an extra loud pattern, but very handsome. Size of robe, 48x60 inches. Weight, about 5 pounds. Price.......**$3.79**

Our Aberdeen Sweat Blanket, Superfine All Wool, $6.00 and $6.70.

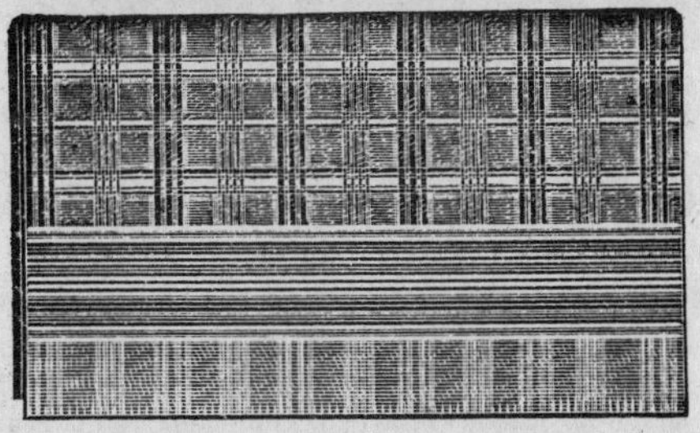

No. 10R11040 Our Special Aberdeen Sweat Blanket. This sweat blanket is made of the very finest superfine all wool blanket stock, in fancy plaid patterns, very firm, hard twisted warp. This is one of the very best all wool blankets that can be made. Size, 90x96 inches. Weight, 4 lbs. Price..$6.00

No. 10R11045 Our Heavy Aberdeen Sweat Blanket, made extra heavy out of finest wool stock. Size, 90x96 inches. Weight, 6 pounds. Price, each..$6.70

No. 10R11050 Our Special Long Hood to match our Aberdeen Sweat Blanket.
Each.....(Same style as Keystone Mack).....$4.35

Our Special Texas Minnie Superfine All Wool Cooling Blanket $3.75, $4.25.

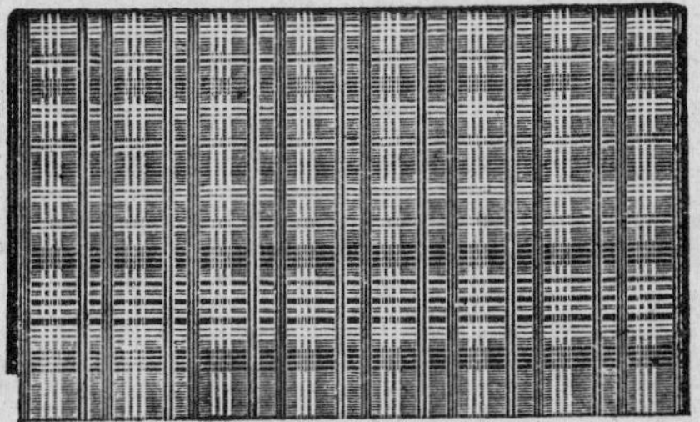

No. 10R11051 Our Special Texas Minnie Superfine All Wool Cooling Blanket, made in fancy plaid patterns, fast colors. The very finest all wool blanket stock, firmly twisted, heavily gigged, with hard twisted warp, making the best all wool cooling blanket on the market.
Size, 84x90 inches, Weight, 2½ pounds.
Price, each..$3.75
Size, 90x96 inches. Weight, 2¾ pounds.
Price, each.. 4.25

No. 10R11053 Long Cooling Hoods to match Texas Minnie Cooling Blanket.
Price, each..(Same style as Keystone Mack).$3.00

Short Cooling Hoods—Fancy Plaid or All White.

No. 10R11070 Made of the same quality fine all wool blanket stock, throat handsomely bound, eye and ear holes, a strictly up to date short hood, about 30 inches long. Weight, 18 ounces.
Price.....$1.54

No. 10R11072 Our fancy short white wool sweating hood, made of an extra quality of all white wool blanket, bound all round, and buttons on side of neck; bound ear and eye holes. This short, white hood is used for sweating purposes mostly. A large seller and great value. A strictly up to date white sweating hood. Weight, 18 ounces.
Price, each..$1.95

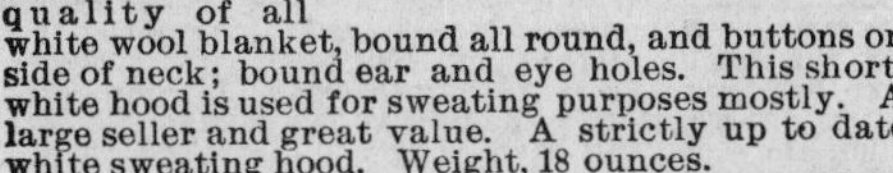

Long Sweat Hoods—Fancy Plaid or All White.

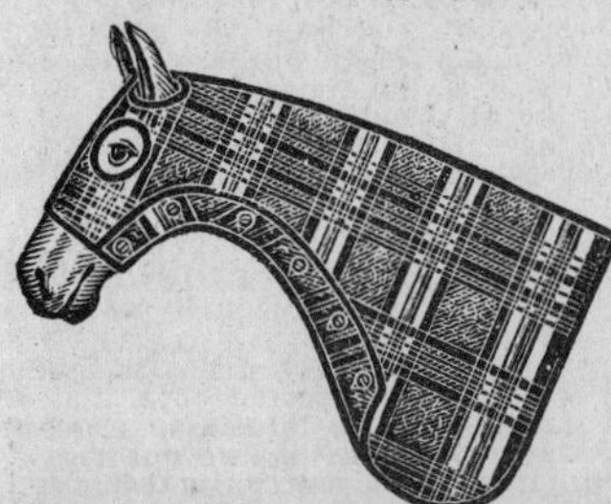

No. 10R11073 Our Long Hood Keystone Mack, only a very much finer quality all-wool blanket stock, eye, ear and button holes, handsomely bound with an extra heavy binding of black braid, making one of the best long hoods on the market. Weight, 38 ounces.
Price, each..$2.49

Throat Hoods—Fancy Plaid or All White.

No. 10R11074 Made of fine wool plaid, an extra quality all wool blanket stock, handsomely bound with a very heavy braid, long strap to buckle.
Price, each..........83c

No. 10R11076 Our special white wool throat hood with bound eye holes, and long strap and buckle. This throat hood being made in all white wool is used principally for sweater. Weight, 8 ounces. Price, each........................95c

Our Long White Wool Sweat Hood.

No. 10R11077 Made of fine, all white wool blanket, extra long, button on side of neck, bound all round; bound ear and eye holes. This special, long, white hood is one of the best that we make and is used for sweating purposes mostly. Weight of hood, 32 ounces. Same style as No. 10R11073.
Price, each..$4.00

Fancy Plaid Duck Blanket and Long Hood and Plain Burlap Suit.

$1.67 $1.47

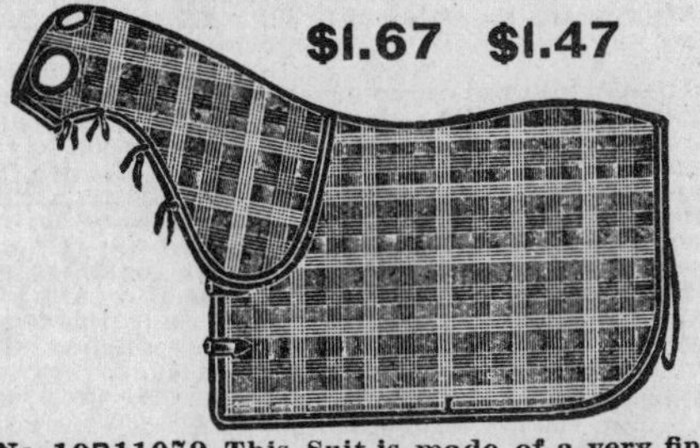

No. 10R11079 This Suit is made of a very fine Scotch plaid duck, bound all round with boot web binding, two buckle straps in front with long hood to match to tie under throat, with bound eye and ear holes to match. This makes a very light, cool, duck stable suit, and one there is a large demand for, made with two corded surcingles. The surcingles can be removed if not wanted, but the suit will be sent with surcingle. For 900 to 1200-pound horse. Weight, 2½ pounds.
Price of suit, blanket and hood..................$1.67

No. 10R11081 Our Special Plain 10-Ounce Burlap Suit, Blanket and Long Hood. Made the same style as the plaid duck suit only of plain burlap, bound all round with boot web binding, and long hood to match made to tie under throat, with two heavy corded surcingles that can be removed if not wanted. A very cool, strong summer stable suit. This style of suit is a big seller. For 900 to 1200-pound horse. Weight, 2½ pounds.
Price, per suit, blanket and hood..................$1.47

Running Suit.

$2.50 $3.75

No. 10R11083 Sidney Lucas Special Fine Linsey Running Suit. This suit is one solid blanket, made in fancy plaid patterns, fine, firmly woven linsey cloth. Used only on running horses. Ties in front and under throat. Weight, 3 lbs. Price, per suit, $2.50

No. 10R11085 Golden Age Special Linsey Two-Piece Suit, consists of blanket and long hood, made the same style as DuBois Mare. Very fine quality fancy plaid Linsey cloth, making one of the best two-piece suits on the market. The blanket and hood both tie. Weight, 3½ pounds. Price, per suit..$3.75

Fine Cooling Blanket with Long Hood.

$5.75

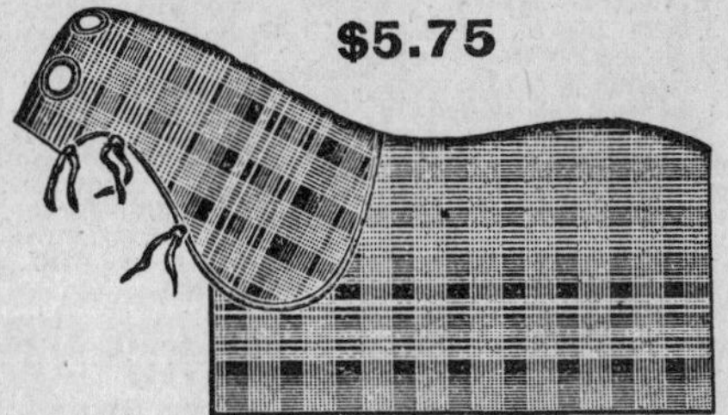

No. 10R11087 This Suit is made with a 90x96 inch 3-pound cooling blanket, brown and white checked and drab plaid, with long hood to match. This hood ties under the throat, with bound ear and eye holes. The suit would weigh about 5 pounds. This is a very fine, light, cooling suit, for which there is a large demand. Price of suit, with blanket and long hood..$5.75

No. 10R11089 Our California Cooling Suit Made with a 90x96 inch 3-pound, fancy plaid cooling blanket and long hood to match. The hood ties under the throat, with bound ear and eye holes. This is the very finest fancy plaid wool cooling suit we make. It is in the AA grade and is considered the very best, and is sure to please all who want a strictly up to date, fancy cooling suit. Weight of suit about 5½ pounds. Same style as No. 10R11087.
Price, per suit, for blanket and hood..........$6.99

Our Gibson Fawn Cooling Suit.

$4.75

No. 10R11091 Made of fawn blankets with two wide surcingles and long fawn hood to button. This blanket will prove to be an exceptional bargain in quality and price. Absolutely one of the best stable suits made. A horse will dry off under this suit. Pronounced by horsemen to be the **best, strongest, warmest and most durable.** For 900 to 1200-pound horse. Price of blanket and hood, $4.75
Price, hood only, each........................ 2.00
Weight of blanket, 6½ pounds; weight of hood, 3 pounds.

Our S., R. & Co.'s Special Fancy Drop Box Weave Handsome Trimmed Horse Suit.

$12.00

No. 10R11093 This Suit is made with woven cloth layer, braided, fancy ornamented surcingle pockets. Blanket is made with a folded breast to button; long hood is made to button under throat; with bound eye and ear holes. This is one of the handsomest suits than can be made out of a drop box blanket. The cut represents this suit exactly. This suit would sell at retail at $15.00 to $18.00. For 900 to 1200-pound horse. Price of suit.........$12.00
Weight of suit, 6½ pounds.

Our Fancy Wool Drop Box Weave Kentucky Horse Suit.

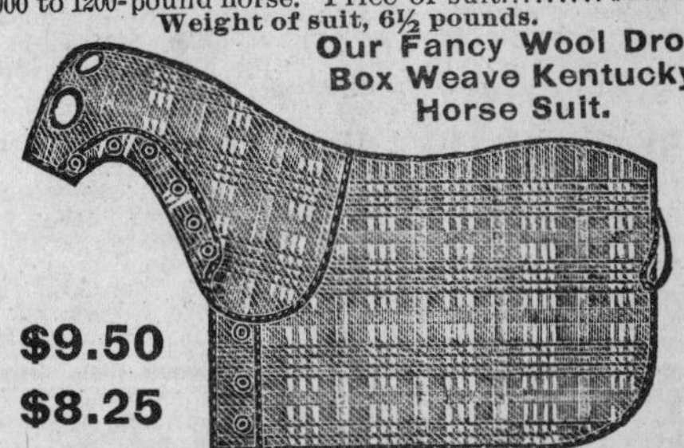

$9.50
$8.25

No. 10R11095 Made of fancy plaid blanket with a folded and buttoned breast, long hood to match, buttoned under throat, bound ear and eye holes. This is one of the big sellers in horse suits. Strictly up to date, fancy, durable and well made, a suit that would retail at $12.00 to $14.00.
Our special price for blanket and long hood..$9.50
Weight of suit, about 6½ pounds.

Special Du Bois Wool Suit.

No. 10R11097 S., R. & Co.'s Special Du Bois Wool Suit, made with long hood and blanket to button. Buttonholes bound with chamois skin, bound all around with extra heavy fine quality black braid; blanket made of the very finest extra superfine all wool blanket stock, woven in fancy patterns, very new designs, making the very best horse suit on the market. Size of blanket, 32x72 inches. Size of long hoods, 50 inches. Price, per suit.................$8.25
Weight of suit, about 6½ pounds.

ABOUT FREIGHT AND EXPRESS CHARGES.

It is seldom necessary to write to us and ask what the freight and express will amount to. The weight of almost every item is given under the description. If you will refer to pages 7 to 10 you can get the rate of freight or express to a point near you in your state which will be almost; if not exactly, the same rate as to your nearest railroad station. From this you can calculate almost exactly what the freight or express will amount to on any shipment to your town, and you will find it will amount to next to nothing as compared to what you will save in price. By noting the weight and the express or freight rates you can tell almost exactly what the cost of transportation will be and save the trouble and delay of writing to us for this information.

Do You Want to... EARN MONEY? A Large Income to All Interested.

FOR YEARS WE WERE OBLIGED TO DECLINE ALL OFFERS FROM OUR FRIENDS TO ASSIST US IN THE INTRODUCTION AND SALE OF THE WELL KNOWN HOUSEHOLD REMEDIES WHICH WE HAVE PLACED UPON THE MARKET WITH SUCH UNPRECEDENTED SUCCESS.

THE MERITS OF THESE REMEDIES having popularized them to such an extent that the demands for local distributing privileges have of late increased enormously, we have now made arrangements which enable us to supply a large number of our Household Remedies at prices never heard of before, special prices which are made for advertising purposes only, regardless of the retail selling price, regardless of the actual cost of production.

THE FACILITIES OF OUR DRUG DEPARTMENT and chemical laboratories having been increased and improved during the past few years so extensively as to make them the best equipped medical laboratories in existence, we are today in a position to manufacture the highest grade of medicinal preparations at the lowest cost of production, and consequently can furnish these remedies at prices lower than either druggist or jobber can buy standard remedies of recognized merit.

FACTS AND FIGURES. TO ILLUSTRATE:—Certain well known and widely advertised sarsaparillas, for instance, sell at $8.00 a dozen to the druggist and $7.20 to the jobber, while our Dr. Hammond's Sarsaparilla, guaranteed the best on the market, is furnished by us under this special offer at $4.80 per dozen. A good celery compound costs the druggist $8.75 per dozen. The jobber must pay $7.73 for it, but we can supply our celebrated Celery Malt Compound, a most superior remedy, at the astonishingly low price of only $4.50 per dozen. THINK OF IT! You can obtain from us our Standard Household Remedies for almost one-half the price the druggist or jobber must pay for such medicines when buying from other houses.

PLEASE DO NOT MAKE THE ERROR of forming the conclusion that because other remedies are sold for considerably higher prices that they must be better. We guarantee each and every one of our preparations, and will back up every medicine that we place upon the market to be strictly as represented and to do all that is claimed for it. We guarantee that at these exceedingly low prices quoted on quantities of our Household Remedies we will furnish in all cases the same high grade medicines as we have supplied to our customers for years and the merit of which has been fully demonstrated.

ASSURE YOURSELF A VERY LARGE INCOME by securing the distributing privileges for our Household Remedies in your locality. EVERYBODY NEEDS THEM AND USES THEM. We sell, of course, single bottles or packages at special prices, but we allow a liberal discount to those ordering certain remedies in quantities. In many instances you will be in a position to dispose of these medicines at retail prices, for, if the parties would send for a single bottle and pay postage or expressage on same, it would often make the cost higher than the regular retail price. On the other hand, the transportation charges on a few dozen medicines by freight would be very little, if any more than on a single bottle by express, so that you can order in quantities without increasing the very low dozen prices to any extent. A remedy the retail price of which is $1.00 per bottle, when ordered in dozen lots costs you only 40 cents per bottle, and, even if you sell each bottle for 20 cents less that the retail price you could still make 100 per cent profit.

REALIZING THAT SINCE THE DEMAND for our remedies has increased and grown to such large proportions in every section of the country and the disappointment experienced by thousands of persons who often wish to obtain these remedies quickly when needed and who cannot always wait until they send to Chicago, and for the medicine to arrive, we conceived this plan of establishing distributing centers in each locality to overcome this difficulty, to give everybody an opportunity to secure Sears, Roebuck & Co.'s Celebrated Household Remedies in their own neighborhood and without any unnecessary delay.

WE DO NOT ASK YOU TO CANVASS from house to house and urge people to buy our medicines. This is not necessary. We only expect you to supply the large demand that has been created to make it convenient for the sick to get their medicines from you to save delay, as they cannot get our remedies at drug stores. We never sell to drug stores. This does not require any extra effort on your part and yet it will pay you well. All that is really required is that you inform your friends and neighbors that you have these medicines on hand, and that they can get them from you. This alone will bring you a large extra income on the sale of our remedies, and you will be favoring many sick people by delivering to them promptly what they want and must have, and for which they would otherwise have to wait several days, during which time they would suffer unnecessarily.

UNDER THIS NEW ARRANGEMENT, you carrying a supply of our remedies, you can afford sick people the means of immediate relief. Although the furnishing of our remedies to others will add considerable to your earnings, the fact that you can help and minister to the sick, that you can promptly allay pain, that you can aid the ailing in hastening their cure, will be a source of still greater gratification and satisfaction to you.

TO THOSE WHO HAVE THE TIME AND INCLINATION to undertake the distribution of our remedies on a larger scale, our quantity prices offer a chance of a lifetime. With no investment to speak of, they can start in the medicine business, and within a very short time build up a trade for themselves that would yield them an income larger than they could obtain by devoting their time to any other line of work. The standard quality and merit of these remedies being highest, the prices for same positively the lowest, your profits being very large, you can make big money by taking advantage of this special proposition, and without assuming even the slightest risk on your part.

QUANTITY PRICES WE WILL ALLOW ONLY ON SUCH ARTICLES WHERE THE DOZEN PRICE IS HEREIN QUOTED.

ON ANY MEDICINE OR ARTICLE on which the price per dozen is not indicated, we positively can make no reduction, whether you order in single or dozen lots. Do not ask us to deviate from this rule. We can make no exception whatever. When we are in a position to offer an article at a quantity price, such article will be added to this list and all notified of this fact strictly in accordance with our well known policy of fair and businesslike treatment to all trading with our house.

WE WILL ACCEPT no order at a quantity price unless a full dozen is ordered to be shipped at one time, but you need not order a dozen of each kind. You can, if you prefer, order a half dozen each of two kinds or a quarter dozen each of four kinds, and you will be entitled to quantity prices just the same, as long as you order altogether a dozen bottles or packages of medicine on which quantity prices are quoted. This is the only exception we make in our entire catalogue in making a reduction in price for quantity. We make this exception as a matter of accommodation to our customers to induce some one in every neighborhood to carry a small stock of our great remedies, and thus have the opportunity of relieving the afflicted without delay.

DO NOT DELAY in securing the distributing privileges for Our Household Remedies to cover your locality if you are interested. Thousands of our customers have during the past few years requested such privileges when we were not in a position to grant their request. They will now, no doubt, quickly take advantage of the opportunity afforded. Only a limited number of distributing centers will be established, sufficient to take care of each locality in a proper manner. When this point has been reached, we reserve the right of withdrawing our special quantity prices, which will then be available only to those who have started the sale of our Household remedies prior to that date and who may then continue to order at these special prices as long as they remain in effect.

DRUG DEPARTMENT.

OUR DRUG DEPARTMENT IS IN CHARGE OF A COMPETENT CHEMIST AND REGISTERED PHARMACIST, who has had long experience both in this country and Europe in compounding drugs and chemicals. He has strict instructions to examine thoroughly every article received in this department, to note its quality and freshness, to apply tests to ascertain its strength and purity and to reject everything that does not come up to full standard required by the drug inspectors of the United States government.

OUR PRESCRIPTION DEPARTMENT. OUR PRESCRIPTION DEPARTMENT IS UNDER THE DIRECT CHARGE OF ONE OF THE MOST ABLE CHEMISTS AND PHARMACISTS IN THIS COUNTRY. Every prescription is compounded with the greatest care, only the very best drugs are used and yet we are able to save our customers in nearly all cases more than one-half in price. If you will send your doctor's prescription or any other prescription to us, you can rest assured it will be given professional care. There will not be any substitutions such as local druggists are compelled to make for want of certain drugs, it will be compounded in the most scientific manner and returned to you immediately at a saving in price on an average of more than one-half.

ABOUT STANDARD PATENT REMEDIES. WE CARRY IN STOCK AT ALL TIMES almost every known patent remedy, every remedy of merit, every remedy that is now being or has ever been advertised to any extent, and our price to you is the lowest wholesale prices on such remedies. We can usually save you from 25 to 50 per cent on any patent medicine of any kind. If there is a known remedy wanted and you do not find it in our catalogue, send your order to us. If it is a dollar article it will be perfectly safe for you to send 75 cents, if it is a 50-cent remedy, it will be perfectly safe for you to send 40 cents. Be sure and send enough. We will fill your order immediately and if you have overpaid us we will return the balance of the money with your order. It will pay you handsomely to order any patent remedies from us. You will be saving all the profit your druggist would make and more.

OUR OWN SPECIAL REMEDIES. IN THIS DEPARTMENT we have endeavored to show a very complete line of our own special remedies, remedies that we have had prepared from prescriptions furnished by the world's highest medical authority. They are prepared in our own laboratory from the very best material that can be obtained, they are to the best of our knowledge the best known remedies for the different ailments for which they are intended, they are prepared without regard to expense that our customers can get the very best that money can buy.

We are daily receiving testimonials from every state and territory telling us of the wonderful cures effected by our many special remedies.

IN SENDING US YOUR ORDER for anything in the line of drugs, chemicals or toilet supplies, you are not only sure of effecting a big saving in price, but you have the additional advantage of obtaining the best and purest goods in this line, a grade of drugs and chemicals better than is carried by the average retail dealer, a far superior and larger stock than the regular retail druggist can afford to carry, and you are assured the attention of an experienced chemist, a graduate physician, one who has made the specialty of drugs and chemicals his life-long study.

REGARDING SPIRITUOUS LIQUORS. WE DO NOT DEAL IN SPIRITUOUS LIQUORS OF ANY KIND. We do not believe in the traffic and we allow no liquors to go out of our house, and same are only used for medicinal purposes as may be required in our laboratory for compounding remedies that could not be manufactured in any other way. We call the attention of our customers to this fact for the reason that we constantly receive inquiries with reference to prices on various kinds of liquors, and we wish it to be understood that we not only do not deal in spirituous liquors, but we are not in sympathy with the traffic.

POISONOUS, INFLAMMABLE OR EXPLOSIVE MATERIALS CANNOT BE MAILED.

Sure Cure for the Tobacco Habit.

Retail price .... 50c and $1.00
Our price, 50c size, each $0.40
Our price, 50c size, per dozen 3.60
Our price, $1.00 size, each .... .75
Our price, $1.00 size, per dozen 6.60

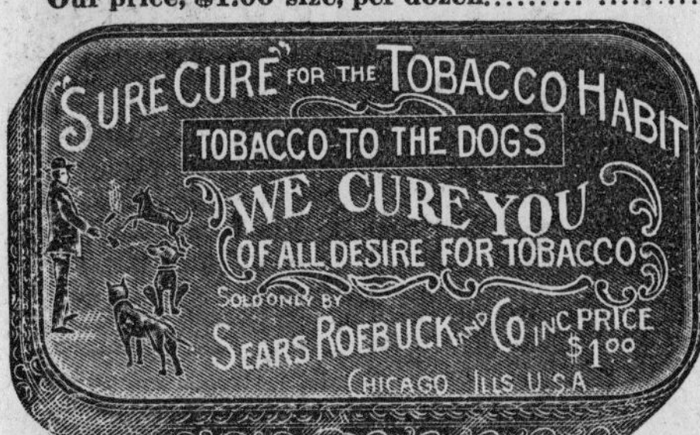

WE CURE YOU This is nature's own remedy, entirely harmless. It cures because it builds up and fortifies, rejuvenates the weak and unstrung nerves caused by over indulgence in this poisonous weed. It stops the craving for tobacco by supplying instead a healthy nerve tonic and strengthener; it does more, it eradicates the poisonous nicotine from the system which has accumulated from long continued use of tobacco. Nicotine is a virulent poison and the chief ingredient of tobacco. It is the cause of all the nervous troubles and general debility of smokers. Our sure cure will destroy the effects of this nicotine, chase it from the system and make weak men strong again, and impotent men gain weight and vigor, make the old feel young again. It satisfies the craving for tobacco, and its use brings great health, increasing the appetite for food, strengthens the stomach, enriches and purifies the blood, giving good general health. It is not a drug; it can be chewed the same as tobacco, or taken dissolved in coffee or hot water. It is not only a sure cure for the tobacco habit, but also one of the best tonics for sexual weakness ever made. Give it a trial and be convinced

> You can cure yourself and others from the tobacco habit. Order a supply at our special quantity prices. You can sell them easily at a good profit.

No. 8R1 Price, regular size box, per dozen, $3.60; each 40c
No. 8R2 Price, large box, per dozen, $6.60; each 75c
If by mail, postage extra, per box, small, 2 cents; large, 4 cents.

Somone, for Sweet, Refreshing Sleep.

Retail price $1.50
Our price, each $0.67
Our price, per dozen 6.00

A RELIABLE REMEDY FOR SLEEPLESSNESS. We ask any of our customers who may be troubled with insomnia, who cannot sleep at night, to give this valuable remedy a trial. No matter from what cause the sleeplessness arises, a sound sleep will be procured by its use, and you will awake in the morning refreshed, strengthened and cheerful; no bad effects from its use. We guarantee it to contain no opium, morphine or poisonous narcotics of any kind whatever. It is a vegetable preparation composed of herbs soothing and healing to the entire system. It can be used in safety by the weakest and most delicate and is a boon to those of nervous dispositions. A single dose will strengthen and invigorate them and cause them to forget their troubles. Ladies troubled with nervous spells should always have a bottle at hand. A dose or two in time will save them many hours of agony and serious discomfort and often prevent total collapse of the nervous system. It has a marvelous effect on those afflicted with nervous prostration, acting like magic in restoring the nerves to their normal condition and causing a strong healthy feeling to prevail throughout the whole body. It quiets the nervous excitement and muscular trembling caused by the excessive use of liquor, and acts as an antidote to the liquor habit. Full directions accompany each bottle how to use it both for sleeplessness and nervous troubles.

> DO NOT FAIL TO INCLUDE THIS REMEDY IN YOUR QUANTITY ORDER. THOUSANDS OF PATIENTS NEED IT AND BUY IT.

No. 8R5 Price, per dozen bottles, $6.00; each 67c
Cannot be sent by mail on account of weight.

Mexican Headache Cure.

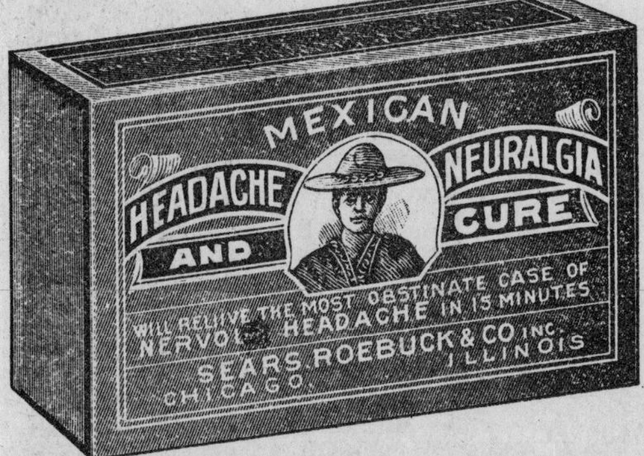

Retail price 25c
Our price, each .. $0.17
Our price, per doz. 1.50

A SPLITTING HEADACHE CURED IMMEDIATELY by our positive Headache and Neuralgia Cure. Almost everyone is more or less troubled with a headache at some time or other. Some persons are hardly ever free from them, and suffer martyrdom. We confidently say to our customers that it is not necessary to suffer longer than the time it takes to get a package of our Mexican Headache Cure. We positively guarantee relief within fifteen minutes after the first dose has been taken. Rarely is a second dose required except in very obstinate cases. No matter from what cause, whether a nervous headache, or from the stomach, or a severe case of neuralgia, we guarantee complete relief. It is perfectly harmless, no bad results follow its use. Give it a trial when you suffer, and you will be sure to speak of us as your friends.

> Who does not suffer from headaches occasionally? You can sell this cure to everybody you meet. Many customers who are now in charge of a distributing point for our orders are sending twelve dozen orders at one time..........

No. 8R8 Price, per box $0.17
Per dozen boxes 1.50
If by mail, postage extra, per box, 2 cents.

German Liquor Habit Cure.

Retail price .... 50c and $1.00
Our price, 50c size, each $0.42
Our price, 50c size, per dozen 3.60
Our price, $1.00 size, each .... .75
Our price, $1.00 size, per dozen 6.60

Every Man Can be Permanently Cured of the Habit or Desire for Intoxicating Drink of Any Kind.

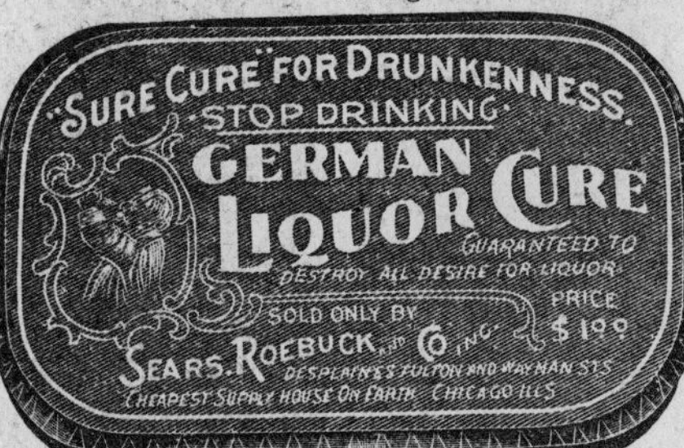

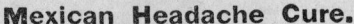

WE GUARANTEE A COMPLETE CURE. Our remedy is perfectly harmless, none of the bad effects produced by many so-called liquor cures so widely advertised. That drunkenness is a disease that can be cured by medicine, just the same as other diseases can, is a fact becoming well known. Thousands of cases have been cured by this medicine; in fact, its wonderful curative properties are now well known throughout the entire world. We bring this cure within the reach of everyone. It is now not necessary to go to an institute for treatment; home treatment is just as successful. The impression has been cultivated by interested parties that cures could not be effected except by hypodermic injections, but nothing is more absurd. Any medicine taken into the stomach will be as effective as if used hypodermically. No medicine has had such a wonderful success in this age of progress as Our Liquor HabitCure. It creates an appetite for food instead of liquor, it stimulates the whole system to healthy action, it quiets nervous excitement, vertigo, muscular trembling and all the dangerous effects of excessive use of liquor. It improves the appetite and digestion and regulates the bowels. It is, in fact, a perfect cure for the drink habit.

> YOU CAN SELL LARGE QUANTITIES OF THIS REMEDY. IT WILL ALWAYS DO THE WORK, AND RECOMMENDS ITSELF WHEREVER USED.

We urge everyone who have accustomed themselves to the excessive use of liquor, and who wish to stop the practice, to send for even a small box as a trial. We know our remedy will cure you. We are sure that after using a few doses you will feel the craving for liquor disappearing and a warm healthy glow spreading from the stomach over the whole system; you will have a desire for food instead of whisky. This will be the commencement of the cure, and if you will follow it up faithfully for a few months it will effect a permanent cure. When you have used a small box, we know you will send for more to thoroughly complete the cure.

No. 8R11 Price, small box containing 24 doses, per dozen, $3.60; each. 42c
No. 8R12 Price, large box containing 48 doses, per dozen, $6.60; each. 75c
If by mail, postage, extra, per box, small, 2 cents; large, 4 cents.

Cure for the Opium and Morphia Habit.

Retail price $1.50
Our price, each $0.67
Our price, per dozen 6.00

WE HERE OFFER A PERFECTLY SAFE AND RELIABLE CURE to those addicted to the habit of using opium or morphia in any form or manner whatever. We guarantee this preparation to be absolutely harmless, to contain no poisonous narcotics. Can be taken freely without producing any of the deleterious effects on the system, such as are caused by the use of opium and morphia. Immediately on taking a dose of this remedy a calming and soothing effect is produced. It acts as a tonic to the nerves; its use will completely destroy that terrible craving for morphine in those who are victims to the deadly habit of taking these poisonous drugs, and free them from their bondage, restoring their health and making them feel like living again. A dose can be taken whenever a craving for morphia or opium exists; it will act at first as a perfect substitute, rendering the patient independent of these poisonous drugs, and after continued use for a short period the nerves will become strong and the general health improved, so that the remedy can be taken at longer intervals and soon altogether discontinued; then the cure is complete.

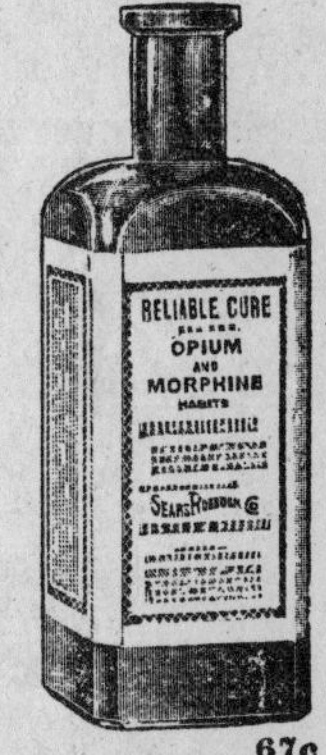

No. 8R15 Price, per dozen bottles, $6.00; each 67c
Cannot be sent by mail on account of weight.

Fat Folks, Take Dr. Rose's Obesity Powders and Watch the Result.

Retail price 75c
Our price, each $0.50
Our price, per dozen 4.20

TOO MUCH FAT is a disease and a source of great annoyance to those afflicted. It impairs the strength and produces fatty degeneration of the heart, and sudden death results. All people who have obesity are troubled with sluggish circulation and labored action of the heart. The patient feels lazy and burdensome. There is a sluggish condition of the whole system; they are not exactly sickly, there is a feeling that all is not right. Nervousness, rheumatism, headache, dropsy and kidney diseases are frequent complications of obesity, and, more cause to be alarmed, the heart is always affected. Send at once for a box of Dr. Rose's Obesity Cure. It will reduce corpulency in a safe and agreeable manner, perfectly harmless. No bad results follow its use, as is the case with many of the much advertised cures. Explicit directions and valuable information for fat folks enclosed in each box.

> A boon to fat people who will be glad to obtain this remedy at home when they know you keep it on hand ....

No. 8R18 Price, per dozen boxes, $4.20; per box 50c
If by mail, postage extra, per box, 2 cents.

)r. Worden's Female Pills for All Female Diseases.

Retail price.. 50c
Our price, per box......................................$0.35
Our price, per dozen boxes..............................3.00

'his is acknowledged as one of the GREATEST REMEDIES of the age.

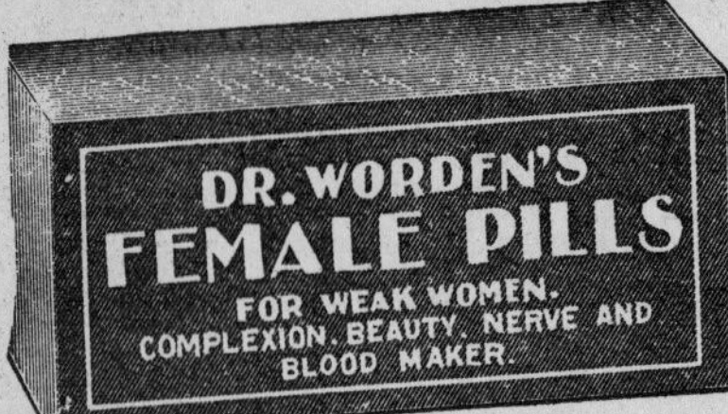

A GREAT BLOOD purifier and nerve tonic. Cures all diseases arising from a poor and wasted condition of the blood, such as pale and sallow complexion, general weakness of the muscles, loss of appetite, depression of spirits, lack of ambition, anæmia, chlorosis or green sickness, palpitation of the heart, shortness of breath on slight exertion, coldness of hands and feet, swelling of the feet and limbs, pain in the back, nervous headache, dizziness, ›ss of memory, feebleness of will, ringing in the ears, early decay. ALL 'ORMS OF FEMALE WEAKNESS—leucorrhœa, tardy or irregular periods, uppression of the menses, hysteria, locomotor ataxia, partial paralysis, ciatica, rheumatism, neuralgia. Cures all diseases depending on vitiated umors in the blood, causing scrofula, swelled glands, fever sores, rickets, ip joint diseases, hunchback, acquired deformities, decayed bones, chronic rysipelas, consumption of the bowels and lungs. In invigorating the blood ystem when broken down by overwork, worry, iseases, excesses and indiscretions of living, his is a most wonderful medicine.

> One of our best sellers. Women who have used these pills will gladly recommend them to others. They will increase your sales and profits immensely. . . . . .

HESE FEMALE PILLS are not a purgative medicine; they are not a cure-ll. They contain nothing that could injure the ıost delicate system but act upon the diseases ependent upon poor and watery blood or a achectic state of that fluid.

'OMEN CAN BE BEAUTIFUL, their complexion perfect, nervous ›stem normal, circulation perfect. All weak-ess and disease removed by taking these pure vegetable pills. Thousands f women have been cured by using Dr. Worden's Pills, after all other emedies and physicians had failed.

'E GUARANTEE A CURE. One single box will furnish great relief. Six boxes are usually sufficient to cure cases that are not of o long standing, while ten to twelve boxes will cure any case for the treat-ıent of which these pills are prepared. We positively guarantee to cure ny case of female weakness if the treatment is proceeded with in a sys-ematic manner, and for a reasonable length of time.

No. 8R39 Our special price, per dozen boxes, $3.00; per box..........35c
If by mail, postage extra, per box, 2 cents.

Cathartic Pills, Only 10 Cents per Box.

Retail price.. 25c
Our price, per box...................................$0.10
Our price, per dozen boxes.............................90

HIS IS THE OLD FASHIONED UGAR COATED CATHARTIC PILL ' the U. S. Pharmacopœia, the ıme as Ayer's, Brandreth's, ıynes' and other much adver-ˌsed pills. They act principally . the liver, and move the bowels ntly without griping. These lls are carefully prepared from esh vegetable extracts, and can be thoroughly relied upon. For this reason ıey are much superior to many others sold at double their price.

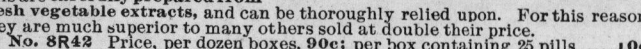

No. 8R42 Price, per dozen boxes, 90c; per box containing 25 pills.....10c
If by mail, postage extra, per box, 2 cents.

Wonderful Little Liver Pills.

Retail price.......................................25c
Our price, each....................................$0.13
Our price, per dozen...............................1.00

ıtirely vegetable in their composition. These wonderful little pills operate without disturbance to the system, diet or occupation.

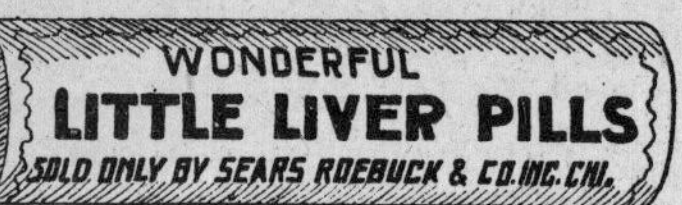

CONSTIPATION, that most hideous and deathly demon of sickness, is an easy enough thing to cure if you will only persist in taking proper treatment. It is one of the commonest troubles and often thought to be a very little thing. Yet we say that nine-tenths of human sickness is due to this one thing. When the bowels do not move ɡularly the natural drainage tract in the human system is dammed up, ɛcomposition ensues and poisonous gases and liquids are carried all rough the system. The result is jaundice, torpid liver, biliousness, llow skin, indigestion, foul breath, coated tongue, loss of appetite, mples, belching foul gases, blotches, boils, dizziness, headache, cramps, lic, etc. You can easily avoid all these troubles and keep your system re and healthy by taking from time to time one or two of our WONDER-L LITTLE LIVER PILLS. Some of our customers call them "LITTLE ANTS," they are so small in size and so easy to swallow, yet so effective l mild in their operation. Whenever your stomach, liver and bowels get t of order take one or two of our LITTLE WONDERS and notice the ick effect and great relief you will experience. Keep a box always beside u. Use them occasionally and you will always feel well and look the ture of health.

No. 8R45 Price, per dozen boxes, $1.00; each.......................13c
If by mail, postage extra, per box, 2 cents.

Do You Sneeze? Camphor Pills.

Retail price..............................25c and $1.00
Our price, 25c size, each.......................$0.18
Our price, 25c size, per dozen....................1.50
Our price, $1.00 size, each.........................50
Our price, $1.00 size, per dozen..................4.80

'E BEEN LONG USED BY THE OLD SCHOOL PHYSICIANS, a remedy for cold in the head, cramps, colic, diarrhœa and olera morbus and other annoying troubles resulting from catch-gcold. Also for menstrual colic. A bottle of these pills ought be carried in the pocket continually by those who are travel-ɡ, or outside most of the day exposed to all weathers. Though ry effective in performing cures, they are small and can be con-niently kept in the vest pocket.

No. 8R48 Price, regular size, per dozen $1.50; each.................18c
If by mail, postage, extra, small, 2 cents.

Large size (containing four times as much as small ones). Price, per dozen, .80; each..........(If by mail, postage extra, large, 16 cents.)..........50c

Dr. Hammond's Nerve and Brain Pills.

GUARANTEED THE HIGHEST GRADE ON THE MARKET.

A BOON FOR WEAK MEN.

Retail price...$1.00
Our price, each...$0.60
Our price, per dozen.....................................6.00

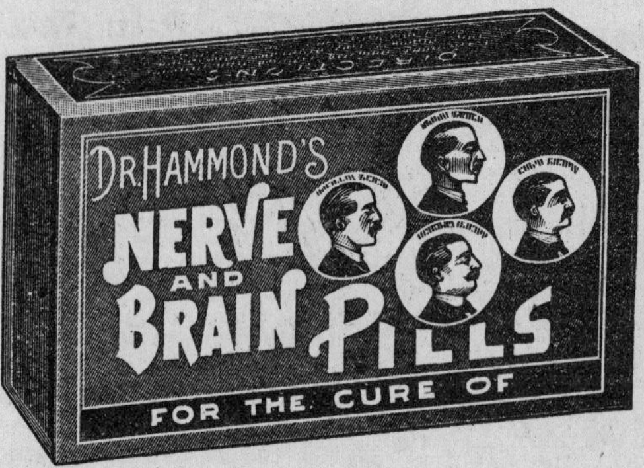

SIX BOXES POSITIVELY GUARANTEED TO CURE ANY DISEASE for which they are intended. This will cure you if you feel generally miserable or suffer with a thousand and one indescribable bad feelings, both mental and physical, among them low spirits, nervousness, weariness, lifelessness, weakness, dizziness, feeling of fullness like bloating after eating, or sense of goneness or emptiness of stomach in morning; flesh soft and lacking firmness, headache, blurring of eyesight, specks floating before the eyes, nervous irritability, poor memory, chilliness, alternating with hot flushes; lassitude, throbbing, gurgling or rumbling sensations in bowels, with heat and nipping pains occasionally; palpitation of heart, short breath on exertion, slow circulation of blood, cold feet, pain and oppression in chest and back, pain around the loins, aching and weariness of the lower limbs, drowsiness after meals but nervous wakefulness at night, languor in the morning, and a constant feeling of dread, as if something awful was going to happen.

IF YOU HAVE ANY OF THESE SYMPTOMS our NERVE AND BRAIN PILLS will cure you. No matter what the cause may be or how severe your trouble is, DR. HAMMOND'S NERVE AND BRAIN PILLS will cure you. These pills have a remarkable effect on both old and young. They cannot be equaled by any other medicine as a cure for impotency, spermatorrhœa, night sweats, emissions, varicocele (or swollen veins), weakness of both brain and body arising from excesses and abuses of any kind. They will tone up the whole nervous system, no matter how much worn out, overworked or depressed you may be; the weak and timid young man made strong and bold again; they will give youthful vigor and a new lease of life to the old.

BEWARE OF QUACK DOCTORS who advertise to scare men into paying money for remedies which have no merit. Our Nerve and Brain Pills are compounded from a prescription of one of the most noted German scientists, and are the same as have been used in German hospitals for years with marvelous success. HOW TO CURE YOURSELF and full and explicit directions are enclosed with every box. All orders and inquiries concerning these pills will be treated confidentially, and all shipments made in plain sealed package.

ONLY $3.00 FOR SIX BOXES. Enough to cure almost any case, no matter how severe, no matter how long standing, whether old or young, no matter from what cause. Send us $3.00 and we will send you six boxes by return mail, postpaid, in plain sealed package, with full instructions.

If you need these pills don't delay. This is the first time the American people have had an opportunity of getting the genuine Dr. Hammond's Pills, and the first time they have been sold anywhere at anything like our price.

No. 8R51 Price, per dozen boxes, $6.00; each...........................60c
If by mail, postage extra, per box, 2 cents.

Our Famous Blood Pills.

A WONDERFUL PURIFIER.

Retail price.....................50c
Our price, each...............$0.22
Our price, per dozen.........1.80

For men and women that require a nerve tonic, blood purifier or builder.

Over one hundred thousand sold last year, which shows what is thought of these pills when known. Others sell them at 50 cents per box.

FOR FEMALE TROUBLE they are an unfailing remedy, and guaranteed far superior to any other pills on the market at any price. They give tone to the whole system, making the eyes bright, the cheek rosy, and, through strength and buoyancy, the step is firm and elastic.

OUR BLOOD PILLS can be taken according to directions without any danger, by either sex, and if carefully followed will give quick results and permanent relief. Weakness, poor, thin blood, giving a sallow or pale complexion, loss of appetite, chlorosis or green sickness, pain in the back, palpitation of the heart, nervous headaches, suppression of menses, leucorrhœa, tardy or irregular periods, hysteria, paralysis, and all diseases resulting from humors in the blood, which cause erysipelas, sores, swellings, and even consumption, also in cases where the system is broken down by overwork of mind or body, or from excesses and indiscretions of living.

THE EFFECT IS WONDERFUL. These pills are not of a cathartic nature; they do not, nor are they intended to purge. They are intended to act on the blood, and supply what is needed in restoring the tone and lacking constituents, stimulating to activity the sluggish system.

FOR WOMEN in case of suppression of menses, leucorrhœa or whites, chlorosis, anæmia, locomotor ataxia, a quick and permanent cure can be effected; in fact, it is the greatest remedy known.

FOR MEN these pills stand without a rival, and should be used in all cases where the patient is suffering from a tainted condition of the blood. They have proved especially valuable in the treatment of blood and skin diseases, and as a rule are prescribed by the most successful physicians in cases of eczema and blood poison. A similar class of pills retails everywhere from 50 cents to $1.00, but they cannot be compared with our famous Blood Pills, which are the grandest prescription in existence for restoring the blood to a natural, healthy and normal condition.

No. 8R54 Price, per dozen boxes, $1.80; each...........................22c
If by mail, postage extra, per box, 2 cents.

Dr. Rose's French Arsenic Complexion Wafers.

Retail price....................50c and $1.00
Our price (50 treatments), per box....................$0.35
Our price (50 treatments), per dozen boxes.................... 3.30
Our price (100 treatments), per box.................... .67
Our price (100 treatments), per dozen boxes.................... 6.00

PERFECTLY HARMLESS when used in accordance with our directions, it possesses the "Wizard's Touch" in producing, preserving and enhancing beauty of form and person in male and female by surely developing a transparency and pellucid clearness of complexion, shapely contour of form, brilliant eyes, soft and smooth skin, where by nature the reverse exists.

THE GREAT TROUBLE HITHERTO has been how to make this beautifying principle safely available and at the same time avoid what is detrimental and injurious. Arsenical solutions have utterly failed, and until a recent discovery by a French physician and chemist, the internal administration of arsenic has been attended with more or less danger as well as disappointing results. In the direction for which they are intended their effect is simply magical, the most astounding transformation in personal appearance being brought about by their steady use. Even the coarsest and most repulsive skin and complexion, marred by freckles and other disfigurements, slowly changes into an unrivaled purity of texture, free from any spot or blemish whatever; the pinched features become agreeable, the form angular gradually transforms itself into the perfection of womanly grace and beauty. Used by men the favorable results are the same. All danger is averted in these complexion wafers, prepared by our experienced chemist, and the remedy taken in the manner directed on each box is absolutely innocuous, while the peculiar virtues of the remedy remain unimpaired and intact. Taken as directed the wafers will be found a positive, safe and magical specific for all sorts of skin troubles, unsightliness and imperfections, being in reality the only beautifier of the complexion, skin and form known. Guaranteed a sure cure for freckles, moth, blackheads, pimples, vulgar redness, rough, yellow or muddy skin, and other facial disfigurements are permanently removed and a deliciously clear complexion and rounding up of angular forms assured.

Every lady a possible buyer of this celebrated complexion preparation and beautifier. Regular size, also large size boxes, can be sold constantly at a very good profit.

LADIES, YOU CAN BE BEAUTIFUL. No matter who you are, what your disfigurements may be, you can make yourself as handsome as any lady in the land by the use of our French Arsenic Wafers. We recommend ordering one dozen large boxes and then carefully follow our directions.

No. 8R99 Our price, per dozen boxes, $3.30; per box of 50 treatments... 35c
No. 8R100 Our price, per dozen boxes, $6.00; per box of 100 treatments, 67c
If by mail, postage extra, per box, small, 2 cents; large, 3 cents.

The Genuine German Herb Laxative Tea.

Retail price....................25c
Our price, each....................$0.16
Our price, per dozen.................... 1.50

A HARMLESS VEGETBALE REMEDY and a positive cure for constipation, with no bad after effects. It is composed of herbs and roots familiar to the peasant of Germany, especially those who nurse the sick. Through irregular living, poorly cooked food, improper habits of eating, nearly all persons are suffering more or less from constipation and the resultant sick headaches; although there may be a daily movement of the bowels, there is still much fecal matter adhering to the intestines and poisoning the blood. Our Herb Tea, made of the simple, harmless herbs, will, when taken regularly for a short time, thoroughly cleanse the stomach and bowels of all unclean matter. The blood becomes purified and the person greatly improved in health.

No. 8R102 Price, per dozen, $1.50; per box....................16c
If by mail, postage extra, per box, 4 cents.

Blackberry Balsam.

Retail price....................50c
Our price, each....................$0.22
Our price, per dozen.................... 1.80

A REMEDY which should be kept constantly on hand. The poorest in the land can afford it at only 22 cents a bottle. It will prevent serious illness if used promptly, and often be the means of saving life. It is a pleasant, safe, speedy and effectual remedy for Dysentery, Diarrhoea, Looseness, Asiatic Cholera, Cholera Morbus, Cholera Infantum, Summer Complaint, Colic, Cramps, Griping Pains, Sour Stomach, Sick and Nervous Headache, Pain or Sickness of the Stomach, Vomiting, Restlessness and Inability to Sleep, Wind in the Stomach and Bowels, Hysterics, and for all bowel affections. We have received thousands of certificates from physicians, clergymen and families of the first respectability bearing the strongest testimony in its favor.

Our Blackberry Balsam is a household remedy in the fullest sense of the name, and will be found helpful for the above named symptoms in infants, children and adults.

No. 8R103 Price, per dozen, $1.80; per bottle..22c
If by mail, postage and tube extra, 16 cents.

Every Mother Who Has Used It, Proclaims Castroline Better than Castoria.

1100 Drops for Only 18 Cents.

Retail price....................$0.35
Our price, each....................$0.18
Our price, per dozen.................... 1.80

KEEP YOUR CHILDREN HEALTHY and cheerful by using Castroline only. You need not have any other medicine in the house for your children. It is unquestionably the best thing for infants and children the world has ever known. It is harmless, and children like it. It gives them health and may save their lives. Mothers keep it beside you, and you will always have something absolutely safe, pleasant to take, and the acme of perfection as a child's medicine for every ailment they are subject to.

CASTROLINE WILL DESTROY WORMS, allay fever, prevent vomiting, cures diarrhoea and wind colic, relieves teething troubles. Cures constipation and flatulency. It assimilates the food, regulates the stomach and bowels, and gives to the child a healthy and natural sleep. When your baby cries give it a dose of CASTROLINE, its effect will be soothing to the baby and pleasant to you. It contains neither morphine nor opium nor any other narcotic property. It is much superior to the so-called soothing syrups which are being advertised daily. It will cause the baby to sleep when fretful, giving the mother her much needed rest. One size bottle only.

No. 8R106 Price, per dozen, $1.80; per bottle....................18c
If by mail, postage and tube extra, per bottle, 16 cents.

Reliable Worm Syrup and Worm Cakes.

Retail price, each....................50c
Our price, each....................$0.22
Our price, per dozen.................... 1.80
Our price for Worm Cakes, per box.................... .20
Our price for Worm Cakes, per doz. boxes.................... 1.50

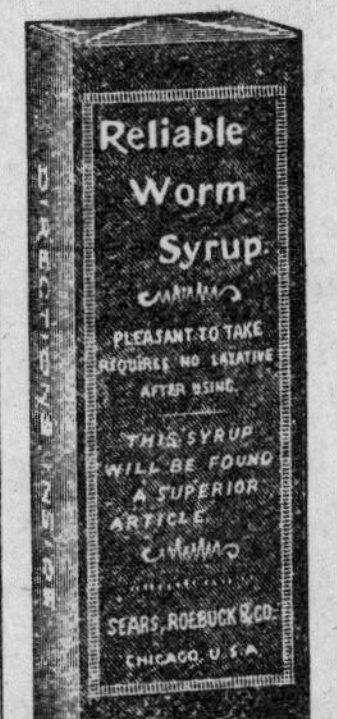

YOU CAN SAVE YOUR CHILDREN from much suffering and in many cases save their lives. No other disease is so fatal to children as worms. Unfortunately they are seldom free from them, and as the symptoms resemble those of almost every other complaint, they often produce alarming effects without being suspected. Worms are not only a cause of disease in themselves, but by their irritation aggravate all other diseases, wandering from one part of the body to another, winding themselves up into large balls, obstructing the bowels and frequently the throat, causing convulsions and too often death.

OUR RELIABLE WORM SYRUP effectually destroys the worms and removes the nest in which their young are deposited. It moves the bowels very gently; the worms being to a greater or less extent dissolved by the action of the medicine, can scarcely be recognized in the stools, but the improvement in the health of the child will be sufficient evidence of the beneficial effects of the medicine.

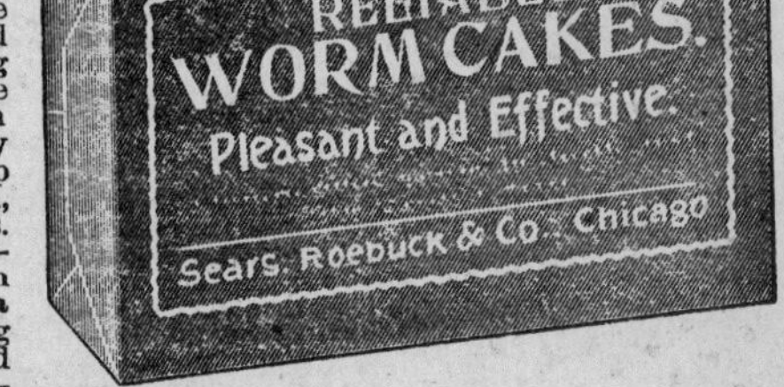

EVERY MOTHER ought to have a bottle of the syrup or a box of the cakes always in the house. The syrup and the cakes are the same medicine in different forms. The syrup is more pleasant to the taste and more suitable for very young children. The cakes can be given to older people; even adults can be benefited by using them, as grown up folks, as well as children, often suffer from worms. These reliable worm medicines are not only worm destroyers, but act as a general tonic, destroying sourness of the stomach and producing a healthy appetite. Mothers, keep your children healthy.

No. 8R109 Worm Syrup. Price, per dozen bottles, $1.80; per bottle..22c
If by mail, postage and tube extra, per bottle, 16 cents.
No. 8R112 Worm Cakes. Price, per dozen boxes, $1.50; per box......20c
If by mail, postage extra, per box, 2 cents.

Electric Liniment.

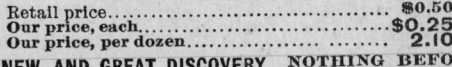

Retail price....................$0.50
Our price, each....................$0.25
Our price, per dozen.................... 2.10

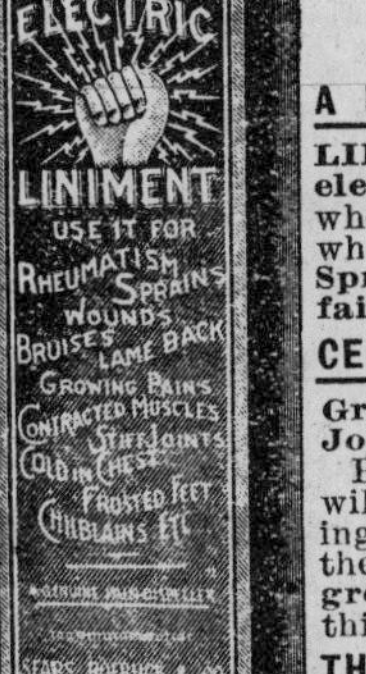

A NEW AND GREAT DISCOVERY. NOTHING BEFORE HAS BEEN KNOWN LIKE IT. By a newly discovered process this liniment is electrically charged by a powerful current of electricity, whereby the ingredients undergo a powerful change, which, when applied to the most severe cases of Rheumatism, Sprains and Bruises, effects immediate relief. It never fails in its Magical Effect.

CERTAIN CURE FOR Rheumatism, Cuts, Sprains, Old Sores, Wounds, Corns, Galls, Bruises, Growing Pains, Contracted Muscles, Lame Back, Stiff Joints, Frosted Feet, Chilblains, etc.

Persons suffering from partial paralysis of arms and legs will be rendered great benefit by its use, frequently regaining complete use of these members; also an application to the Throat and Chest and externally for Lung Trouble great relief will be experienced by rubbing the chest with this, the most penetrating liniment in the world. TRY IT.

THERE IS NO LINIMENT that will equal our Electric Liniment in quality. Needed in every home. Thousands of families will positively use no other liniment at any price. You can sell hundreds of bottles quickly.

No. 8R115 Price, per dozen, $2.10; per bottle....................25c
If by mail, postage and tube extra, per bottle, 16c

Wine of Life VIN VITAE Wine of Life

Retail Price, per bottle, $1.25

Our Price, 69 Cents.

A NEW AND PERFECT TONIC STIMULANT FOR THE TIRED, WEAK AND SICK OF ALL CLASSES. A RENEWER OF ENERGY, A STIMULANT FOR THE FATIGUED, A STRENGTHENER FOR THE WEAK, AN EFFECTIVE AND AGREEABLE FOOD FOR THE BLOOD, BRAIN AND NERVES.

NOT A MEDICINE, BECAUSE IT IS DELIGHTFUL TO THE TASTE AND TO THE STOMACH . . . . . .

NOT MERELY A STIMULANT, BUT A GENUINE TONER AND STRENGTHENER

A Tonic which we find is as yet Unequaled.

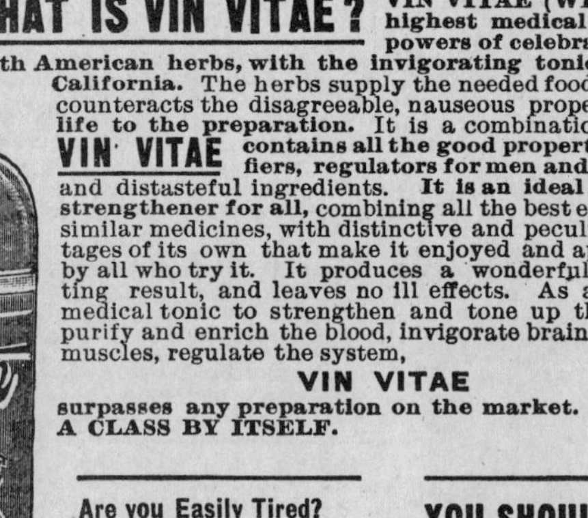

WHAT IS VIN VITAE? VIN VITAE (WINE OF LIFE) is a preparation combining through highest medical skill the curative, healing and strengthening powers of celebrated vegetable elements, procured from medicinal South American herbs, with the invigorating tonic effects of the purest and finest wines of sunny California. The herbs supply the needed food strength for the blood and nerves, the wine element counteracts the disagreeable, nauseous properties of the herbs and gives just the right fire and life to the preparation. It is a combination producing a wonderful medical tonic.

VIN VITAE contains all the good properties of all the well known sarsaparillas, blood purifiers, regulators for men and women, nerve tonics, etc., without their disagreeable and distasteful ingredients. It is an ideal tonic and strengthener for all, combining all the best elements of similar medicines, with distinctive and peculiar advantages of its own that make it enjoyed and appreciated by all who try it. It produces a wonderful exhilarating result, and leaves no ill effects. As a pleasant medical tonic to strengthen and tone up the nerves, purify and enrich the blood, invigorate brain, body and muscles, regulate the system,

VIN VITAE

surpasses any preparation on the market. IT IS IN A CLASS BY ITSELF.

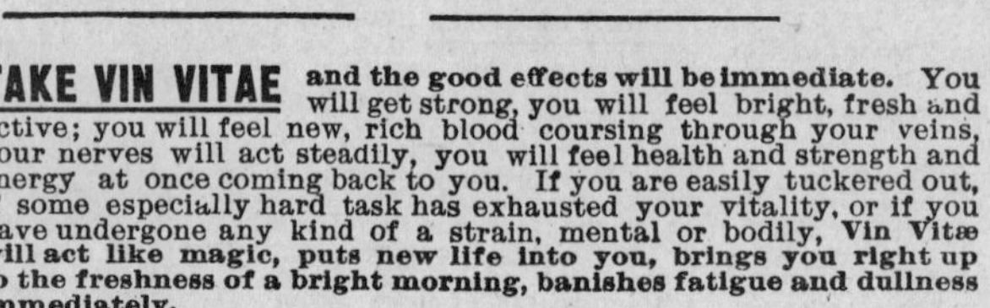

Are you Easily Tired?
Do you Sleep Badly?
Are you Nervous?
Do you Feel Exhausted?
Have you Lost your Appetite?
Is your Stomach Weak?
Are you Thin?
Is your Circulation Poor?
Are you Weak, either constitutionally or from recent sickness?

YOU SHOULD TAKE VIN VITAE REGULARLY IF YOU MUST ANSWER **YES** TO ANY ONE OF THESE QUESTIONS.

TAKE VIN VITAE and the good effects will be immediate. You will get strong, you will feel bright, fresh and active; you will feel new, rich blood coursing through your veins, your nerves will act steadily, you will feel health and strength and energy at once coming back to you. If you are easily tuckered out, if some especially hard task has exhausted your vitality, or if you have undergone any kind of a strain, mental or bodily, Vin Vitæ will act like magic, puts new life into you, brings you right up to the freshness of a bright morning, banishes fatigue and dullness immediately.

No. 8R118
Price, per bottle........69c

69 CTS.

Vin Vitae gives health and strength.

VIN VITAE is agreeable to the taste and acceptable to the most delicate stomach. For tired nerves in men and women, exhaustion, overwork, weakness, nervous trouble, weak stomach, or dyspepsia, loss of sleep, nervous trouble of any kind, for those recovering from a period of sickness, for all who feel tired, weak, worn out, Vin Vitæ, taken according to directions, acts with quick and wonderful results. It puts new blood into the veins, new life into the body, it fills every nerve cell with vibration and energy, renews wasted tissues, gives one the power to do double the ordinary amount of work without fatigue.

VIN VITAE MAKES WOMEN STRONG. Weak women, easily tired, worn out by ordinary household duties, should take Vin Vitæ, the Wine of Life, regularly as a tonic. Women sufferers from the diseases and troubles peculiar to their sex will realize more benefit from the strengthening and tonic effects of Vin Vitæ than from most of the "female regulators," extensively advertised, put together. It is a wonderful tonic for ailing and suffering women. Vin Vitæ is giving thousands of women health, beauty and freedom from the dragging pains which have made their lives so miserable. Those terrible backaches, headaches, aching sides and limbs, that torture some women have every month, that make women old before their time, disappear if Vin Vitæ is taken as a tonic regulator. Vin Vitæ corrects all derangements peculiar to the sex, regulates the system, stops the pains, tones up the nervous organism, brightens the eye, clears the complexion, rounds out the figure and restores health.

WHAT DOES VIN VITAE DO FOR CHILDREN? Delicate children, undeveloped, puny boys and girls should be given Vin Vitæ regularly. It builds up the growing system, gives needed nourishment to the muscles, makes bone and tissue. Children with delicate stomachs, unable to retain the strong and nauseous children's preparations with which the market is flooded, accept Vin Vitæ with a relish. It is a splendid medicinal tonic for children.

69c BUYS A LARGE BOTTLE OF VIN VITAE. The illustration shows the appearance of the bottle, except that it is a large, full size bottle, containing a commercial pint, a quantity sufficient for all ordinary cases. Vin Vitæ is handsomely put up in keeping with the splendid preparation that it is.

VIN VITAE is compounded in our own laboratory, under the direction of our own skilled chemists, after a strict formula, to which we have the exclusive right. Every ounce is carefully tested for strength and purity, so that we can offer it to our customers with our highest recommendation, under our binding guarantee, as the finest tonic wine stimulant, the most pleasant and powerful strengthener and rejuvenator. It can be taken with perfect safety. It is recommended by every physician who has made a test of it, and if it is subjected to analysis it will be found to contain only the best and purest ingredients, products that are noted for their stimulating, nourishing and strengthening properties, combined in such a way as to form a most agreeable tasting and effective preparation.

FOR LACK OF APPETITE, general lassitude, worn out nerves, Vin Vitæ is just what is needed. It improves the appetite, assists digestion, purifies and enriches the blood, carries life and strength direct to every nerve and fiber in the body, and induces a vigor and tone that ordinary medicines would never give.

DON'T FAIL TO ORDER ONE BOTTLE as a sample of this splendid, perfect preparation. We offer it on its merits, offer it to our customers as a perfect preparation. We urge everyone who is in need of a tonic to try Vin Vitæ. We offer it feeling positive that if you try it you will be more than pleased with its agreeable and strengthening effects, and

YOU WILL NOT FAIL TO RECOMMEND VIN VITÆ TO YOUR FRIENDS AND NEIGHBORS

OUR GUARANTEE AND CHALLENGE OFFER.

Order a bottle of Vin Vitæ, take it according to directions, and if you do not feel greatly improved within a few days, if you do not feel that it renews your energy, soothes the nerves, improves the digestion, induces restful sleep, brings back former strength; in fact, if you do not find that it does you more good than any medicinal tonic you have ever tried,

SEND IT BACK AND WE WILL PROMPTLY REFUND YOUR MONEY.

ALMOST EVERYONE NEEDS A TONIC AT SOME TIME OR OTHER

Keep a supply of Vin Vitae on hand.

YOU WILL FIND A CONSTANT DEMAND FOR IT.

No. 8R118 Our special price per bottle for Vin Vitæ, the Wine of Life........$0.69
Price, per dozen bottles........6.60

WHITE RIBBON SECRET LIQUOR CURE

Makes Them Stop Drinking Forever.

Drunkards Cured Without their Knowledge. Cured to Stay Cured.
Regular retail price..$2.50
Our price, complete box, 30 treatments........................$1.10
Our price, complete box, 30 treatments, per dozen..............9.60

THE GREATEST MEDICAL DISCOVERY OF THE AGE. White Ribbon Secret Liquor Cure, only **$1.10 per box, 30 complete treatments,** saves thousands from that awful monster drink; snatches thousands from a life of disease, poverty and degradation, releases man from the bondage of whisky, reforms the most abandoned drunkard as well as preventing the whisky habit from taking a hold on only moderate drinkers.

WHITE RIBBON SECRET LIQUOR CURE is odorless, colorless and tasteless; a powder that can be given secretly in tea, coffee or food, and by its action on the system positively removes all taste, desire or craving for intoxicating liquors. **Anyone can give the powder, no preparation required, absolutely no danger.** Can be given to any man, young or old, without his knowledge, and whether he is a regular drinker or only a mild tippler it abolishes all desire for liquor and stops the terrible habit in due time and forever. **White Ribbon Secret Liquor Cure** stays the weak and flagging nerves, the mind becomes clear, the brain active, the flush of the face subsides, the step becomes steady, new health and strength is imparted, a higher moral tone is upheld; in a word, it makes him a man among men.

DRUNKENNESS IS A DISEASE and must be fought and counteracted by proper medical methods the same as any other disease. The desire for liquor once established, the system requires its stimulus, and unless this appetite is counteracted it must be satisfied and the victim is powerless against its demands. Pledges and prayers often prove powerless after the appetite for intoxicants is once established. The system craves liquor with an insatiable demand that the average strength of the drinker cannot resist, and every time this desire is satisfied it means that the next time it comes on with redoubled force.

SEND FOR A BOX OF THE WONDERFUL WHITE RIBBON SECRET LIQUOR CURE, give it according to directions, a small powder in his tea or coffee. He cannot tell any difference, but it will work just the same. The effect will surprise and delight you. You will soon notice the improvement. The remedy will not only stop drinking but it will produce a positive dislike for liquor. The normal health will return, eyes become bright, step elastic, appetite good, sleep sound and natural—**he is a saved man.**

CAN THERE REALLY BE A CURE FOR DRUNKENNESS, or is it a habit that cannot be shaken off but grows stronger every day? **No, drunkenness is curable.** Drunkenness is a disease more than a habit and as such is subject to treatment. If the proper medical elements necessary to counteract the effect of liquor and destroy the appetite for it are combined, there is no reason why it is not curable. **White Ribbon Secret Liquor Cure is just such a preparation.** The most successful and perfect secret liquor cure ever manufactured. It is made expressly for us according to the celebrated original formula in our possession and we know just what it is and can offer it to our customers with every assurance that they will receive the genuine Secret Liquor Habit Cure. It is prepared in the form of this odorless and tasteless powder so that **it can be given secretly without the patient's knowledge.**

IN OUR WHITE RIBBON SECRET LIQUOR CURE, whisky has found its conqueror. The habit goes down in defeat when pitted against the power of our remedy, and the thanks of the thousands of the rescued follow our preparation wherever it is introduced.

MAKE AN EFFORT TO SAVE THEM! Have you a loved one, a husband, a father, brother or son, or even a friend who is afflicted with this terrible curse or who is, perhaps, taking the first steps in a downward career. Do not delay your effort, do not fail to send for a box of the White Ribbon Secret Liquor Cure, do not allow anything to prevent you from giving our honest and efficient treatment a trial. If you could see the grateful letters we have received from women and men everywhere testifying to the good our treatment has done them, you would not hesitate to send your order at once. **Remember, the price is only $1.10 per box (30 complete treatments). Full directions sent with each box. Medicine is sent in plain sealed package. All correspondence confidential. Remember, White Ribbon Secret Liquor Cure positively cures drunkenness.**

No. 8R151 Our special price, per dozen, **$9.60**; per box............**$1.10**
If by mail, postage extra, 12 cents.

The Household Disinfectant and Deodorizer.

Retail price, pints..........................50c
Our price, pints.............................$0.20
Our price, pints, per dozen...................2.00
Our price, quarts.............................30
Our price, gallon.............................90

A Powerful Germicide, Deodorant, Disinfectant and Antiseptic.

ESPECIALLY USEFUL in disinfecting rooms where patients suffering from contagious diseases have been lying. **Bedding, carpets, clothes, furs and all furnishings** of the sick room contaminated by the germs of cholera, diphtheria, scarlet fever, la grippe, tuberculosis, erysipelas, etc., are readily, easily and cheaply disinfected by simply sprinkling with Household Deodorizer. **Comes in concentrated form.**

We here offer to our customers the most powerful disinfectant, deodorizer and antiseptic known to science. It is non-poisonous, and when diluted with water, it is the cheapest disinfectant ever offered to the public. Can be used to disinfect drains, sinks, gullies, urinals, water closets, farm yards and buildings, chicken pens, rabbit hutches, bird cages, cattle trucks, slaughter houses, stables, kennels, ash barrels, garbage cans. It kills all disease germs and should be used for general disinfecting purposes. It is also one of the best insecticides; will destroy fleas on dogs and other animals, lice on chickens, cures mange on animals, makes an excellent and cheap sheep dipping; will also protect animals from the torment of flies, mosquitoes, midges, gnats, etc. It will also destroy insects on plants and trees without any injury to the plants or trees themselves, and destroy weeds on garden paths.

It will purify the air wherever it is used, remove all foul smells, destroying all germs and pests of every kind. One pint will make from one to five gallons according to the purpose required. It mixes readily with water. Agreeable and pleasant to use by the most delicate.

Household Deodorizer is made of chemical agents which combine with compounds causing odors, entirely destroying all disease germs. It is the best general disinfectant known. Rapid, does not injure material and there is no danger of fire. Sprinkle freely. Saturate clothes and hang in rooms. Place in open saucers and you may be sure all germs have been destroyed. **Full directions with each bottle.**

No. 8R154 Price, pints, per dozen, **$2.00**; each..........................20c
Quart..........................30c
Gallon..........................90c

A very convenient manner of applying the Household Disinfectant and Deodorizer is by using a sprayer or atomizer, which we can furnish at a special price of 40 cents each. Unmailable on account of weight.

Dr. Lyon's Celebrated Skin Ointment.

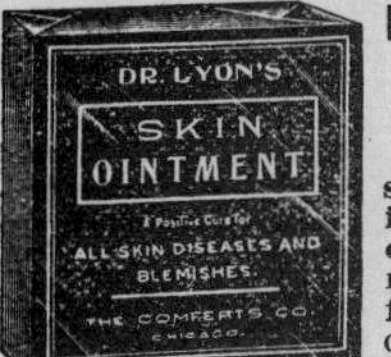

Retail price..........................50c
Our price, each.......................$0.29
Our price, per dozen...................2.70

A positive cure for all skin diseases and blemishes and superior to every other skin ointment in the market, and furnished by us at less than one-half its selling value. This skin ointment is guaranteed to cure all eruptive and skin diseases, pimples, blotches, boils, eczema, salt rheum, erysipelas, ringworms or any scaly or scabby eruptions, often healing cracked or rough skin on the hands, face or any part of the body by a single application. We are in a position to furnish this grand cure for skin diseases and blemishes for only 29 cents a box. You could obtain no remedy that is better or can equal it in healing qualities if you were to pay $1.00 per package.

No. 8R157 Dr. Lyon's Skin Ointment.
Price, per dozen, **$2.70**; per box............**29c**
If by mail, postage extra, 3 cents.

Dr. Lyon's Skin Ointment is another preparation that is needed by thousands of sufferers. This remedy is already well known in every section of the country, and those that have tried it will accept no other ointment under any circumstances. You will find a ready sale for this article and it will yield you a good profit.

Boracetine.

Retail price..........................35c and $1.00
Our price, regular size, per dozen, $1.80; each..........20c
Our price, large size, per dozen, $5.40; each..........56c

The Marvelous New Medicine for general household usage pronounced by many superior to Listerine or any similar preparation.

BORACETINE is an absolutely safe and powerful antiseptic made from vegetable antiseptic essences and benzo and boric acid, acts as a preventive medicine; is swift and certain in the destruction of living particles, microbes, etc., which form contagion. It does not irritate and may be applied to the most delicate tissues. For sponging and bathing all sick persons and especially in typhoid conditions it is unequaled by any other preparations as regards effects and results. The faithful use of Boracetine in catarrh establishes prompt relief and a satisfactory relief, and even in chronic cases of catarrh of nose or throat the parts if sprayed with Boracetine night and morning will feel its immediate effect in a cooling and refreshing manner overcoming the sore and sometimes inflamed condition of the tissues, and in time will effect a cure, not excepting the most stubborn chronic cases of this character. Boracetine has proven itself successful in the treatment of female troubles, and local applications will always result in prompt relief and in removing the difficulty in a short time. As a mouth and throat wash, also as a gargle, for the treatment of eczema, cuts and bruises, it is acknowledged to be the very best remedy. Should be used as a toilet antiseptic, also after shaving. In the sick room when sprinkled upon furniture and clothing it will impart an agreeable odor, refreshing to the patient and those in attendance. There is really no more valuable general remedy than Boracetine, the great antiseptic household remedy. It is not a luxury, but a necessity for every home.

No. 8R160 Regular size bottle, per dozen, **$1.80**; each..............**20c**
Large bottle, commercial pints, per dozen, **$5.40**; each..............**56c**
If by mail, regular size bottle, postage and tube extra, 14 cents. Large size unmailable.

Egyptian Pile Cure.

Retail price..........................$1.00
Our price, each.......................$0.42
Our price, per dozen...................4.20

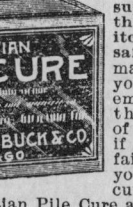

A scientifically prepared pile remedy in suppository form, soothing, healing and for the most effective curing of both blind, itching or bleeding piles. Instant relief, safe in its action, permanent in its cure. No matter what you may have employed for the treatment of this trouble, if all else has failed to afford you relief and cure, you should send for the Egyptian Pile Cure at once. You may have the same experience as have thousands of other sufferers troubled with different forms of this ailment, that is, you will find that the Egyptian Pile Cure will not only promptly relieve, but establish a cure in due time. The remedy having been prepared in the form of suppositories, admits of easy and convenient application, and will in this manner thoroughly reach the affected parts, and by its prompt healing action will prove more satisfactory than almost any mode of treatment of piles. The preparation is furnished in regular $1.00 size boxes, which we, however, supply to our customers at the exceedingly small price of only 42 cents per box.

No. 8R163 Egyptian Pile Cure. Price, per dozen, **$4.20**; per box.....**42c**
If by mail, postage extra, 3 cents.

An extraordinary good seller. Don't omit to include in your quantity order a large supply of Egyptian Pile Cure. There are millions of men and women requiring this remedy, and as it is almost the only sure cure for piles, you can readily understand that you can dispose of very large quantities of same. The margin of profit on this remedy is very large. . .

OUR OWN COUGH CURE.

SOLD UNDER A POSITIVE GUARANTEE.

Retail price..50c and $1.00
Our price, 50-cent size, each........................$0.35
Our price, 50-cent size, per dozen........................3.00
Our price, large $1.00 size, each........................59
Our price, large $1.00 size, per dozen........................5.40

NEGLIGENCE ON THE PART OF PARENTS, negligence on your own part, very often permits serious sickness to overtake the children or yourself when a little caution, a trifling expense, would have saved all the worry, trouble and not infrequently spared a dear life. We positively believe that there is among household remedies none that can prevent slight indispositions and serious illness so quickly, providing it is kept on hand, not sent for after the trouble has already developed to a certain degree, and also providing you secure the right preparation, a remedy that will not only relieve, but positively cure. We mean **OUR OWN COUGH CURE.**

WE RECOMMEND OUR OWN COUGH CURE knowing that it is without question the only cough remedy that will act quickly and at the same time is perfectly safe. What we recommend, however, still more is that you under no consideration delay ordering this remedy until you actually need it. **Order it at once, see that you have a supply of same always on hand,** so that it can be administered the moment the first signs of a cough are apparent. **A few doses will then do the work,** will prevent the cough from developing into bronchitis, pleurisy, pneumonia and other diseases of the lungs and pulmonary organs.

THERE IS DANGER indicated in the slightest cough. Don't neglect it. You owe it to yourself, to your relatives and friends to have the best means, that is Our Own Cough Cure, ready at hand as soon as the cough makes its appearance. We cannot express it too strongly. We can't point out the danger too forcibly, and again ask you to consider the consequences of neglecting the first symptoms of a cough, and the necessity of immediate treatment to prevent the cough from developing into something worse, something that cannot be easily cured, something that may finally lead into consumption—incurable.

There is no city, no town, no hamlet, nor a single household where you cannot sell Our Own Cough Cure. Everyone needs this remedy and will keep it on hand. You will need large quantities of both sizes. Be sure and order enough. . . . . . .

OUR OWN COUGH CURE is not only the best to stop the cough immediately, it is not only the best cough remedy for infants and children, it is practically the only safe and sure cure where a cough has become chronic; and we know of no medicine in existence that will do what **Our Own Cough Remedy does in chronic cases,** affording relief, always promptly allaying the inflammation of the bronchial tubes, and by its healing influence upon the organs that are always affected in such cases, it will gradually restore them to normal and healthy functions and assist in removing the chronic condition within the shortest possible time.

OUR OWN COUGH CURE is sold under a positive guarantee to be non-poisonous, to possess all the elements necessary for preventing the development of a cough and where it has already taken hold of the patient to quickly cure it. We personally guarantee it to be perfectly safe and harmless and to be the only cough remedy in existence that we can conscientiously recommend as being not only the cheapest but the best that can be produced. We supply Our Own Cough Cure in two sizes, the regular 50-cent size for **35 cents,** the large $1.00 size for **59 cents.**

DO NOT FAIL to include in your next order a supply of Our Own Cough Cure. You should never be without it. It is one of the greatest sickness preventers—a life saver.

No. 8R166 Price, per dozen, regular **50c** size, **$3.00**; each..........**35c**
No. 8R167 Price, per dozen, regular **$1.00** size, **$5.40**; each..........**59c**

OUR TWENTY-MINUTE COLD CURE.

NEVER FAILS.

Retail price..$0.25
Our price, each........................$0.17
Our price, per dozen........................1.50

OUR TWENTY-MINUTE COLD CURE is not only what its name implies, but a gentle laxative and a powerful tonic. It acts gently on the bowels without griping, induces the liver to healthy action and assists in restoring your general health. It is a splendid tonic for the nervous system, and if once used you will never be without it. It promptly cures colds, la grippe, headache and all the symptoms usually present in a severe cold.

YOU MAY SIT IN A DRAFT, or get your feet wet, may become chilled and soon notice that the pores are stopped up, perhaps a slight fever starts, you begin to snuffle. These are the signs of your getting down with a cold. This is the time to use our Cold Cure. Use one or two doses, follow it up by another dose or two in twenty minutes, and you have cured your cold in its incipiency. There is no good reason why you should suffer with a cold for days, for weeks. There is absolutely no reason why you should take any chances of having the cold proceed and perhaps get down with a more serious disease after letting the cold reach a stage where it will require the services of a physician on account of development of a very dangerous disease.

Don't forget that Our Twenty-Minute Cold Cure is a hot seller. It is an extraordinary low priced remedy, and yields you a big profit. It can conveniently be carried by the patient and will always be ready for use.

TWENTY MINUTES' TREATMENT with our Cold Cure will be sufficient to stop the cold, to prevent it from getting any further. A few doses of this grand preparation taken right at the beginning of the first symptoms of a cold will do the work. Don't wait a day or even an hour. Take Our Cold Cure at once. Promptness is the important part.

HAVE OUR COLD CURE in the house and if away from home carry a box with you in your vest pocket. The remedy is supplied in tablet form, in neat boxes, convenient to be carried in that manner. Nothing else will be needed to prevent a cold. **Our Twenty-Minute Cold Cure will save all the dangerous results of a cold.** All that is necessary is that you take it in time. In cases where the cold has already become seated before our cold cure could be obtained and used, be sure and get same as quickly as possible, use it in accordance with directions supplied with the remedy, and in connection with it Our Own Cough Cure, and you may feel assured that the combination of these two medicines will break up and cure the most severe cold and cough in the very shortest time.

No. 8R170 Our Twenty-Minute Cold Cure. Per dozen, **$1.50**; each..**17c**

Our Homeopathic Remedies.

Twelve bottles of different Homeopathic Remedies, your own selection, only........................$1.50
A nice black cloth covered Medicine Case and Instruction Sheet free.

OUR HOMEOPATHIC SPECIFICS are prepared under the supervision of an old experienced homeopathic physician. Great care is taken in preparing them according to the rules laid down by the **highest authorities on homeopathy,** and only the purest drugs used. Every one of the following specifics is a **special cure** for the disease named on it. **Adults take 6 pellets children from 1 to 3 according to age,** and from two to four doses are to be taken every day, according to the severity of the case. We ask the special attention of all our customers to these **high grade remedies.** If you have them near at hand, we guarantee they will **save you many a doctor's bill,** and what is of more consequence, quickly relieve any suffering member of the family and ward off more serious sickness.

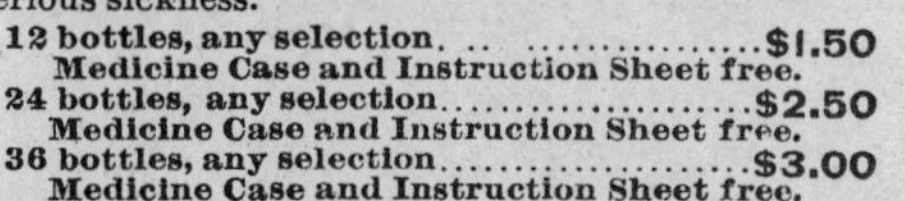

12 bottles, any selection........................$1.50
Medicine Case and Instruction Sheet free.
24 bottles, any selection........................$2.50
Medicine Case and Instruction Sheet free.
36 bottles, any selection........................$3.00
Medicine Case and Instruction Sheet free.

A SPECIAL OFFER. As an inducement to give these remedies a thorough trial, we will allow you to select 12 cures, including the 60-cent ones. Make your own selection, one or more of any kind, and we will put them in a neat case such as we represent here and only charge you $1.50. **No family can afford to neglect this great offer.**

A 12-Box Case will save you many dollars doctor's bills in a year and may save your life. **No family should be without a case of our Homeopathic Remedies.**

No.		Usual Price	Our Price
No. 8R245	Cures rheumatism or rheumatic pains	$0.25	$0.15
No. 8R247	Cures fever and ague, intermittent fever, malaria, etc.	.25	.15
No. 8R249	Cures piles, blind or bleeding, external or internal	.25	.15
No. 8R251	Cures ophthalmia, weak or inflamed eyes	.25	.15
No. 8R253	Cures catarrh, influenza, cold in the head	.25	.15
No. 8R255	Cures whooping cough, spasmodic cough	.25	.15
No. 8R259	Cures asthma, oppressed or difficult breathing	.25	.15
No. 8R261	Cures fevers, congestions, inflammations	.25	.15
No. 8R263	Cures worm fever or worm diseases	.25	.15
No. 8R265	Cures colic, crying and wakefulness of infants teething	.25	.15
No. 8R267	Cures diarrhoea of children and adults	.25	.15
No. 8R269	Cures dysentery, griping, bilious colic	.25	.15
No. 8R271	Cures cholera, cholera morbus, vomiting	.25	.15
No. 8R273	Cures coughs, colds, bronchitis	.25	.15
No. 8R275	Cures toothache, faceache, neuralgia	.25	.15
No. 8R277	Cures headache, sick headache, vertigo	.25	.15
No. 8R279	Cures dyspepsia, indigestion, weak stomach	.25	.15
No. 8R281	Cures suppressed or scanty menses	.25	.15
No. 8R283	Cures leucorrhoea, or profuse menses	.25	.15
No. 8R285	Cures croup, hoarse cough, difficult breathing, laryngitis	.25	.15
No. 8R287	Cures salt rheum eruptions, erysipelas	.25	.15
No. 8R289	Cures ear discharge, earache	.25	.15
No. 8R291	Cures scrofula, swellings, ulcers	.25	.15
No. 8R293	Cures general debility, physical weakness, brain fag.	.25	.15
No. 8R295	Cures dropsy, fluid accumulations	.25	.15
No. 8R297	Cures seasickness, nausea, vomiting	.25	.15
No. 8R299	Cures kidney disease, gravel, calculi	.25	.15
No. 8R301	Cures nervous debility, vital weakness	1.00	.60
No. 8R303	Cures sore mouth and canker	.25	.15
No. 8R305	Cures urinary incontinence, wetting bed	.25	.15
No. 8R307	Cures painful menses, pruritus	.25	.15
No. 8R309	Cures diseases of the heart, palpitation	1.00	.60
No. 8R311	Cures epilepsy, St. Vitus' dance	1.00	.60
No. 8R313	Cures sore throat, quinsy or ulcerated sore throat	.25	.15
No. 8R315	Cures chronic congestions, headache	.25	.15
No. 8R317	Cures grip and chronic colds	.25	.15

If by mail, postage extra, per case, 26 cents; per bottle, 2 cents.
Only $1.50 for a case of 12 bottles, your own selection. Take our warning notice; don't be without them.

Homeopathic Medicines.

WE ARE PREPARED TO FURNISH ANYTHING in the line of Homeopathic Supplies, and guarantee them to be full strength and fresh condition. We mention a few of the more prominent. We will be pleased to furnish information on homeopathic medicines if you are in doubt as to what to order. We will also send a copy of **Halsey's Manual** (152 pages), **a complete homeopathic treatise, free on request. When ordering the following remedies please specify what form you wish them in—pills, powder, discs or liquid.**

Name	Strength	Name	Strength	Name	Strength
Aconite	3x	Cuprum met	3x	Mercurius viv	3x
Antimon. crud	3x	Digitalis	2x	Natrum mur	6x
Apis mel	3x	Drosera	2x	Nitric acid	6x
Arnica	3x	Dulcamara	3x	Nux vomica	3x
Arsenic alb	3x	Eupatorium p'r	1x	Opium	3x
Baptisia	1x	Ferrum phos	3x	Phosphorus	3x
Belladonna	3x	Gelsemium	1x	Phosphorus aci	3x
Bryonia alba	3x	Glonoine	3x	Phytolacca	0
Calcarea carb	3x	Graphites	6x	Podophyllin	3x
Cantharis	3x	Hamamelis	1x	Pulsatilla	3x
Carbo veg	3x	Hepar sulph. tr	3x	Rhus tox	3x
Caulophyllum	1x	Hydrastis	1x	Sanguinaria	2x
Causticum	3x	Hyoscyamus	3x	Secale cor	1x
Chamomilla	3x	Ignati	3x	Sepia	3x
China	2x	Iodium	3x	Silicea	6x
Chinin, arsen	2x	Ipecac	3x	Spigelia	3x
Cimicifuga	1x	Kali bichr	3x	Spongia	3x
Cinna	2x	Lachesis	6x	Staphysagria	3x
Cocculus	3x	Lycopodium	3x	Sulphur	3x
Coffea crud	3x	Mercurius bnod	3x	Tartar emetic	3x
Colchicum	3x	Mercurius corr	3x	Veratrum alb	3x
Colocynthis	3x	Mercurius sol	3x		

Halsey's Cases.

12 one-dram vials of above listed remedies with case and instructions... **$0.85**
12 two-dram vials of above listed remedies with case and instructions... **1.50**
No. 8R330 ¼-ounce vials each, 10c; by mail........................**15c**
No. 8R332 ½-ounce vials each, 15c; by mail........................**20c**
No. 8R334 1 -ounce vials each, 20c; by mail........................**25c**
No. 8R336 2 -ounce vials each, 40c; by mail........................**45c**

SEE NEXT PAGE FOR HALSEY'S SPECIALTIES.

DYES

The Finest Household Colors in the World are the Seroco Stainless Dyes.

ALL COLORS.

There are any number of household dyes on the market, but if you will try them all you will find that the Seroco Dyes are the very best. These dyes are made in our own laboratory and are guaranteed by us. They are so simple a child can use them. Will not stain the hands or the vessel in which they are used. Our Seroco Dyes will dye cotton, silk and wool in the same bath. They wash as well as dye and are the only absolutely antiseptic dyes on the market. They dye a beautiful fast, permanent and fadeless color. Many dollars can be saved by using them. Old, worn and faded dresses and ribbons, feathers, etc., made to look new and fresh again. We can send any color or shade you desire. Come put up in envelopes, each containing a separate dye, **with full directions for use.** Send sample that you want matched or state the color you wish.

No. 8R475 Price, each....8c

If by mail, postage extra, each, 2 cents.

We can furnish cheaper dyes to compete with the cheap dyes that are universally sold, as follows, but we recommend our Seroco:

No. 8R480 German Dyes. all colors. Price, each....5c

No. 8R485 Angel Dainty Dyes, all colors. Price, each....6c

No. 8R490 Standard Dyes, all colors. Price, each....7c

If by mail, postage extra, each, 2 cents.

Cleanit Liquid.

The only preparation that removes fresh paint, grease, oils, syrup, beer or wine stains from carpets, dress goods, silks and all kinds of clothing, etc., without injury to the finest fabric. It leaves the goods soft and clean, free from marks or creases. It also removes all gloss or shine caused by wear, restoring the natural luster. A preparation that is indispensable in every household.

No. 8R495 Price for 4-ounce bottle....15c

Price for 8-ounce bottle....25c

Price for 16-ounce bottle....40c

Unmailable on account of weight.

The Daisy Fly Killer.

The best fly killer known. It is a beauty. Will not injure or soil anything. Will effectually kill flies in a room. **Harmless to persons.** Will last all the season. It is cheaper than fly paper. **Clean, neat, ornamental. Try it.**

No. 8R500 Price, only....15c

If by mail, postage extra, 9 cents.

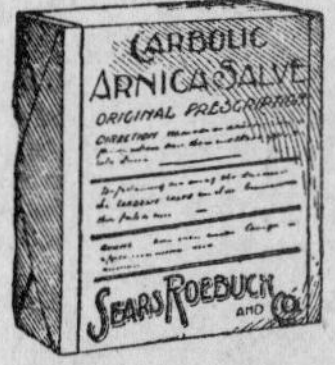

Arnicated Carbolic Salve.

The best in the world for burns, flesh wounds, chilblains, boils, felons, sores, piles, ulcers and fever sores. Excellent for salt rheum, eczema, and ringworm.

No. 8R503

Price, per box....18c

If by mail, postage extra, per box, 3 cents.

Our Mexican Gulf Sea Salt.

For taking a genuine ocean bath at home. We have found this salt remarkable for strengthening the nerves and muscles. Toughens the skin, makes it clear and healthy, renders it impervious to skin troubles **and we can highly recommend it in the physical development of both adults and children. We put it up.**

No. 8R506 10-pound bags, each, 25c; 5-pound bags, each....15c

China Cement.

Sears, Roebuck & Co.'s China Cement. The best cement for mending galss. china, ivory, shell, marble, fur, terra cotta, meerchaum, porcelain, plaster paris, wool, alabaster and leather. Does the work well and quickly.

No. 8R509 Price, per bottle....12c

If by mail, postage and tube extra, 8 cents.

Castor Oil.

Cold pressed and almost tasteless.

No. 8R512 2-oz. bottles, each....8c

4-oz. bottles, each....12c

1-pt. bottles, each....25c

If by mail, postage and tube extra, 16 cents. Large, unmailable.

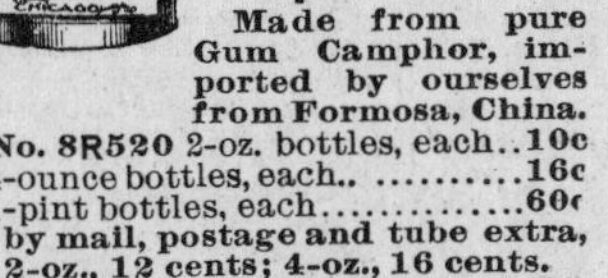

Olive Oil (Sweet Oil).

This is a fine oil imported by us from olive vineyards in Italy, for either internal or external use. Any one wishing to use an absolutely pure olive oil should send for this.

No. 8R515

2-oz. bottles, each....7c

4-oz. bottles, each....10c

½-pt. bottles, each, 17c

If by mail, postage and tube extra, 16 cents. Pints, unmailable.

Spirits of Camphor.

Made from pure Gum Camphor, imported by ourselves from Formosa, China.

No. 8R520 2-oz. bottles, each....10c

4-ounce bottles, each....16c

1-pint bottles, each....60c

If by mail, postage and tube extra, 2-oz., 12 cents; 4-oz., 16 cents. Pints unmailable account weight.

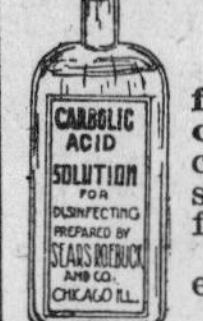

Tincture of Arnica.

We are careful to make this of great strength from recently picked Arnica Flowers, thereby getting the full virtues of the herb. The value of Arnica is well known as an application to bruises, sprains, cuts, swellings, etc., but to secure any benefit it is necessary to have a strong, well prepared tincture **such as ours.**

No. 8R523 4-oz. bottles, each....14c

½-pint bottles, each....22c

1-pint bottles, each....40c

($3.00 per gallon.)

If by mail, postage and tube extra, 16 cents. Larger, unmailable on account of weight.

Camphorated Oil.

An excellent article for rubbing on children and grown up persons' chests and throats in cases of croup, difficulty in breathing, sore throat, coughs. A small quantity of pure spirits of turpentine added to it will increase its effectiveness in many cases.

No. 8R526 8-oz. bottles, 28c; 4-oz. bottles....18c

Postage and tube extra, 4-ounce bottle, 16 cents. 8-ounce bottle unmailable on account of weight.

Spirits of Turpentine.

Pure, for internal or external use. When you wish to use turpentine as a medicine whether internally or externally, **always get a pure article,** never use the common oil of turpentine that is generally sold for mixing with paints. **We sell the pure.**

No. 8R529 4-ounce bottles, each....9c

8-ounce bottles, each....12c

16-ounce bottles, each....20c

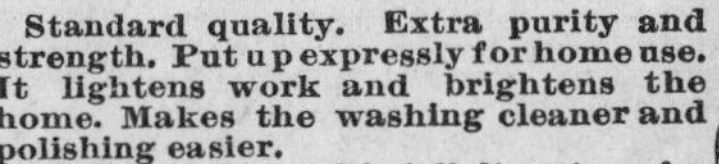

Glycerine.

Warranted absolutely pure. Can be used either externally or internally.

No. 8R532 2-ounce bottles, each....9c

4-ounce bottles, each....12c

½-pound bottles, each....17c

1-pound bottles, each....28c

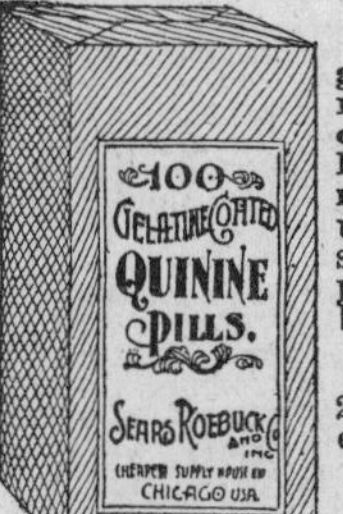

Petroleum Jelly.

This is another name for Pure Vaseline or Cosmoline, and other titles given to it. It is one of the most valuable and also the most harmless and simple articles to have at hand in cases of bruises, cuts, burns, chaps, roughness of the skin, etc. For convenience, we put it in 2-oz. screw top glass jars.

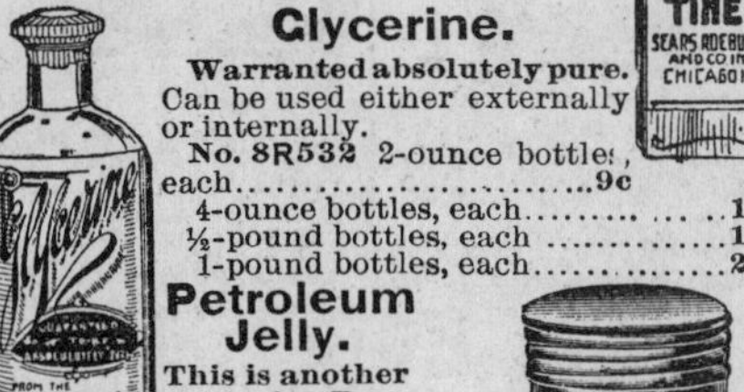

No. 8R535 Price, 2-ounce glass jars....4c

1-pound cans, each....17c

If by mail, postage extra, each, small, 8 cents; large, 20 cents.

Carbolized Petroleum Jelly.

This is the same as the above, with the addition of pure carbolic acid, which increases to a great extent its powers of healing.

No. 8R538 2-ounce bottles, each....10c

1-pound cans, each....30c

If by mail, postage extra, each, small, 8 cents; large, 20 cents.

Seidlitz Powders.

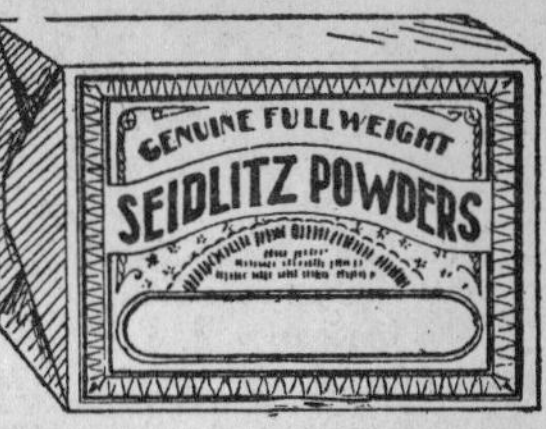

We always make our Seidlitz Powders fresh when we receive the order for them. Most of the powders bought in stores are worthless from being kept too long; they lose their strength. **We guarantee all Seidlitz Powders we send out to be made from pure materials and full strength.** Put up in tin boxes, containing in each 10 blue and 10 white papers.

No. 8R541 Price, each box....16c

If by mail, postage extra, per box 5 cents.

Carbolic Acid.

A saturated solution of Carbolic Acid for disinfecting purposes, destroying contagion, cleansing purposes, etc. Excellent for keeping away disease, destroying bad smells. Put up expressly for household use.

No. 8R544 Price, 1-pound bottles, each....18c

Unmailable on account of weight.

Ammonia.

Standard quality. Extra purity and strength. Put up expressly for home use. It lightens work and brightens the home. Makes the washing cleaner and polishing easier.

In pint bottles, with full directions for using in the laundry, for the toilet, and for cleaning glass, crockery, paint, taking out stains, etc.

No. 8R547 Price, per bottle....7c

Unmailable on account of weight.

Quinine Pills.

Two grains each, sugar or gelatine coated. We have made a special contract with one of the best known and largest manufacturers of quinine pills in the world to supply us with these pills made full strength and with absolutely pure quinine. Put up in wooden boxes containing 25 pills.

No. 8R550 Price, per box..12c

Also, bottles containing 100 2-grain pure quinine pills, either gelatine or sugar coated.

No. 8R553 Per bottle....22c

If by mail, postage extra, per box of 25, 2 cents; for bottle of 100, 8 cents.

Genuine Witch Hazel Extract.

Buy Direct and Save All Retail Profits.

We can save you money, save you one-half on anything in this line, and guarantee highest grade goods on the market. Our Extract of Witch Hazel, you will find even better than Pond's Extract, a universal all healing remedy. Should be in every household, useful for sore throat, hemorrhage, wounds, sprains, bruises, sore eyes, stiff joints, burns, and in nearly every accident that one can have. We guarantee this to be pure, full strength and such as is not often found in retail stores. Our price is so low that every family can afford to keep a supply in their homes. Look at our prices.

No. 8R556

½-pint bottle, retail price, 40c; our price....12c

1-pint bottle, retail price, 50c; our price....22c

1-quart bottle, retail price, $1.00; our price....33c

½-gallon, retail price, $1.75; our price....60c

1-gallon, retail price, $2.50; our price....95c

Unmailable on account of weight.

Rat Killer.

The Great Vermin Destroyer.

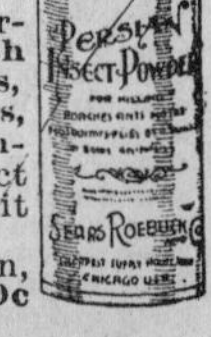

The most efficient poison for rats, mice, cockroaches, ants, flies, squirrels, crows, bed bugs, and all kinds of troublesome vermin. This is a sure destroyer. Rats and mice do not die in the house after eating it, but go outside for air and water.

No. 8R559 Price per box....11c

If by mail, postage extra, per box, 4 cents.

Insect Powder.

A true Dalmatian Insect Powder, warranted free from all adulterations. Fresh and strong. Sure death to bed bugs, **croton bugs, potato bugs, cockroaches, fleas, ice, moths, flies, ants and all insects.** This article is very much subject to adulteration. Buy from us and get it pure.

No. 8R562 Price, put up in ¼-pound tin, boxes, 10c; 1-pound boxes, each....30c

Insect Powder Gun.

For using the above powder.

No. 8R565 Price, each 5c

If by mail, postage extra, ea., 7c.

Large or Jumbo Powder Gun holds ¼-lb. of powder, button and spout screw off. Large opening for filling.

No. 8R568 Price, each............18c

No. 8R568

If by mail, postage extra, each, 6 cents.

Strangle Food.

"IT'S KILLING" KREMBS' STRANGLE FOOD SURE DEATH TO COCKROACHES, BED BUGS, MOTHS, LICE

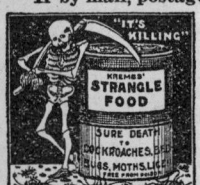

The surest and quickest death to bugs. It instantly strangles. Kills cockroaches, bedbugs, croton bugs, ants, moths, fleas, lice and all other vermin. Harmless to man, beast or bird.

No. 8R571 Price, per can....................22c

If by mail, postage extra, per can, 8 cents.

A Few Handy Pocket Goods.

In Screw Top Air Tight Glass Vials.

Aromatic Cachou Lozenges for perfuming the breath. Make a delicious confection.

No. 8R574 Each....................7c

Silver Cachous, for perfuming the breath. Vest pocket size.

No. 8R576 Each....................7c

Chlorate Potash Tablets. 5 grains each. For sore throat, hoarseness, etc.

No. 8R578 Each....................7c

No. 8R574

Soda Mint Tablets, for sour stomach, flatulency, nausea, etc.

No. 8R580 Each....................7c

Bronchial Troches, for coughs, colds, sore throat, hoarseness.

No. 8R582 Each....................7c

Licorice Lozenges, pure, very soothing to the throat and bronchial tubes.

No. 8R584 Each....................7c

Slippery Elm Lozenges. Demulcent for roughness in the throat and irritating cough.

No. 8R586 Each....................7c

Paregoric Tablets. Each tablet equals 15 drops of paregoric; dose 1 to 4 according to age.

No. 8R588 Each....................7c

All of the above tablets furnished at 65c per pound in bulk.

Pepsin tablets. Made from pure pepsin, for dyspepsia, indigestion, etc.

No. 8R590 Per bottle....................15c

Trix for the breath.

No. 8R592 Per package....................3c

Sen-Sen.

No. 8R594 Per package....................3c

If by mail, postage extra, per bottle, 2 cents.

Compound Licorice Powder.

This is a well known gentle laxative, pleasant to take. Children take it readily. It has an effective and healing action on the bowels. We prepare it carefully, according to the instructions of the German Pharmacopœia.

No. 8R597 4-ounce package, 20c; 8-ounce package, 35c; 1-pound package....................60c

NURSERY DEPARTMENT.

Borated Talcum Baby Powder.

For the toilet and nursery. Preserves, softens and whitens the skin. For chafing it is an excellent powder. Absorbs moisture and keeps the skin cool and soft. Nicely perfumed and put up in handsomely decorated metal boxes, with sprinkler top.

No. 8R600 Price, per box...........8c

If by mail, postage extra, per box, 4 cents.

No. 8R603 Excelsior Borated and Perfumed Talcum Powder. Tin boxes.

Price, each....................5c

If by mail, postage extra, per box, 4 cents.

Baby Soothing Syrup.

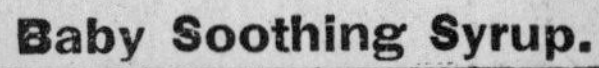
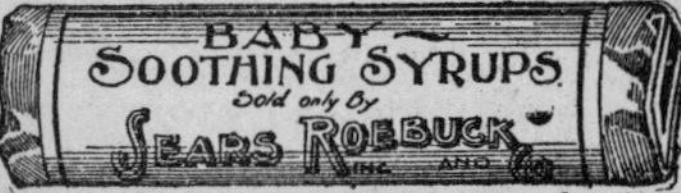

A blessing to parents, harmless and effectual in soothing and quieting children of any age. We guarantee it to contain no opium or morphine; prepared from simple herbs and has a wonderful effect in soothing and quieting a child who may be cross, no matter from what reason. A remedy for colic, excellent during teething time.

No. 8R606 Price, per bottle....................15c

If by mail, postage and tube, extra, 12 cents.

Rubber Teething Rings.

No. 8R612

No. 8R609 Rubber Teething Rings, seamless, full size, best white rubber.

Price, each..........3c

No. 8R612 Rubber Teething Rings, full size, seamless best black rubber. Price, each...4c

No. 8R615 Bone Teething Ring, 1¾ inches, nicely finished.

Price, each..........4c

No. 8R618 Vegetable Ivory Teething Ring. Teething ring of real vegetable ivory and large seamless black rubber nipple

Price, each.........10c

No. 8R621 New Style Rubber Teething Ring, with one hard and one soft nipple, a great favorite with babies.

Price, each........ 20c

If by mail, postage extra, each, 2 cents.

Nursery Bottle Fittings.

Best quality, all complete, in white, black or maroon.

No. 8R624 Price, each....................5c

Nursing Flasks.

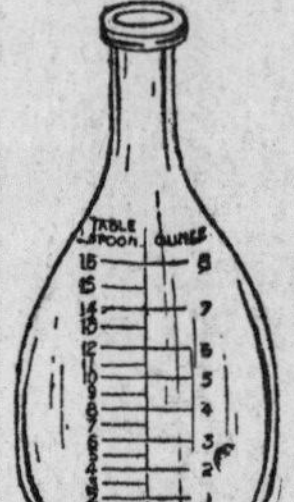
No. 8R627

Graduated to hold 8 ounces, oval shape with sloping sides. No corners, therefore easy to clean.

No. 8R627 Price, each.........6c

Weight, 14 oz.

Plain Nursing Bottle.

No. 8R630 Plain Nursing Bottle, for tube fittings.

Each....................5c

If by mail postage extra, each, 14 cents.

THE EMPIRE

No. 8R630

Rubber Nipples.

Rubber Nipples for tube fittings. White, black and maroon.

No. 8R633 Price, per dozen, 20c; each......2c

Rubber Nipples to fit over bottle. White, black or maroon.

No. 8R636 Price, per dozen, 25c; each......3c

Rubber Nipples, Davidson's patent. Black, white or maroon. To fit over bottle.

No. 8R639 Price, per dozen, 30c; each.. .. 3c

Health Nipples. Made from the finest Para rubber; is constructed so that the infant can obtain a strong hold and renders nursing easy.

No. 8R642 Price, per dozen, 45c; each......4c

PAT'D. APL-10-88.

Mizpah Valve Nipple. Making nursing easy. Allows the food to flow easily. Prevents colic.

No. 8R645 Price, per dozen, 50c; each......5c

If by mail, postage extra, per dozen, 6 cents; each, 1 cent.

Nursing Bottles.

Nursing Bottles. Burr patent white rubber fittings.

No. 8R648 Price, each.........8c

If by mail, postage extra, each, 15 cents.

S., R. & Co.'s Complete Nurser.

S., R. & Co. Nurser No. 1. Fitted with white, black or maroon fittings. Complete with two brushes in each box. Weight, 16 oz

No. 8R651 Price, each.......... 17c

Glass Nipple Shields.

Glass Nipple Shield with white rubber nipple and bone guard.

No. 8R654 Price, each....8c

If by mail, postage extra, each, 8 cents.

Glass Nipple Shield with long flexible rubber tube, mouth guard and rubber nipple.

No. 8R657 Price, each....................10c

Weight, 8 ounces.

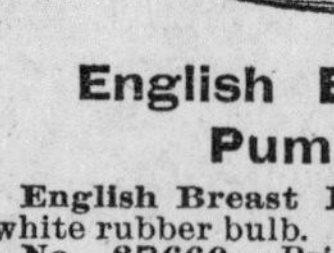

English Breast Pump.

English Breast Pump, with white rubber bulb. One in box.

No. 8R660 Price, each...16c

If by mail, postage extra, each, 8 cents.

Toilet Powder Puffs.

No. 8R663 For ladies' and infants' use. Satin tops, ivory handle. Price, each....................15c

If by mail, postage extra, each, 2 cents.

Puff Boxes.

Celluloid, in ivory, pink or blue. Very light and handsome.

No. 8R666 Each.......... 40c

White metal, handsome covers, ornamental tops.

No. 8R669 Each.......... 22c

If by mail, postage extra, each, 8 cents.

Favorite Foot Powder.

This is the excellent powder for the feet adopted by the German army for the use of the infantry. It is particularly beneficial to those inclined to perspiration. For destroying bad odors and giving comfort to sore feet nothing like it has hitherto been put on the market. A little shaken in the shoes keeps the feet comfortable at all times.

No. 8R672 Price, per box....................12c

If by mail, postage extra, per box, 3 cents.

Japanese Loofah Flesh Brush.

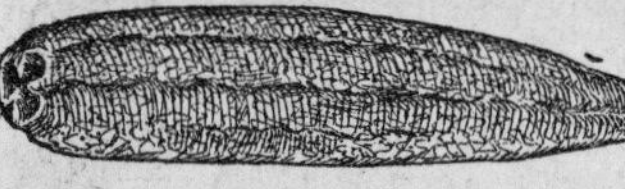

The Loofah is a fibrous part of a gourd that grows in the south of Japan. Its health giving properties, when used as a flesh brush or sponge, have been known to the Japanese for ages. In England, where they have been used for some years, they are rapidly taking the place of the ordinary sponge for bath purposes. Their use gives a healthy glow to the body, removes all accumulations from the pores of the skin, increases the circulation of the blood, and leaves a pleasant sensation. DIRECTIONS: The loofah may be used as a sponge just as it is, or to make it a trifle more handy, soak in water until it expands full size; cut lengthwise and remove the inner substance so that the loofah opens out like a cloth.

No. 8R675 Price....................9c

If by mail, postage extra, each, 3 cents.

Loofah Bath Mitten.

Loofah front with Turkish toweling back. The best bath mitten in the market.

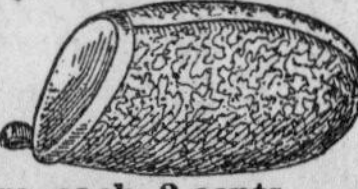

No. 8R678 Price.....20c

If by mail, postage extra, each, 2 cents.

Loofah Bath Brush.

Try one and satisfy yourself, that: 1st. It is the best bath brush made. 2d. It is light, cheap and durable. 3d. It is very porous and easily dried. 4th. It is a pleasant and perfect friction brush. 5th. It is nature's own medicine. 6th. It is recommended by all as the best sanitary and hygienic brush known for the bath.

No. 8R681 Price....................18c

If by mail, postage extra, each, 8 cents.

Sponges.

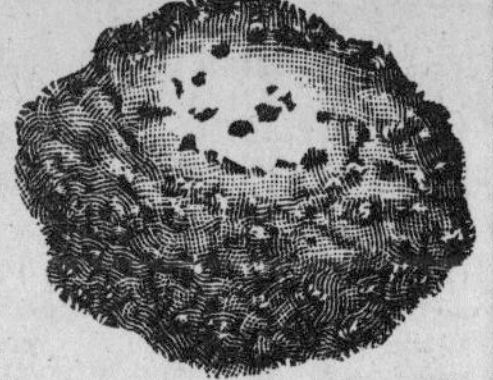

Very fine, "small eye" sponge. For surgical and nursery use.

No. 8R684 Price ea., 6c

Small Toilet Sponge, for toilet use or can be used in shaving.

No. 8R687 Price ea., 6c

Medium size sheep's wool sponges, tough and durable.

No. 8R690 Price, each........................12c

Large Toilet Sponge, suitable for the bath.

No. 8R693 Price, each..............................18c

No. 8R696 Large Size Sheep's Wool Sponges. A very durable sponge. Price, each..............22c

No. 8R699 Cleaning Sponges. When wet they are about 15 to 24 inches in circumference. Suitable for carriage, wood work, etc. Price, each........10c

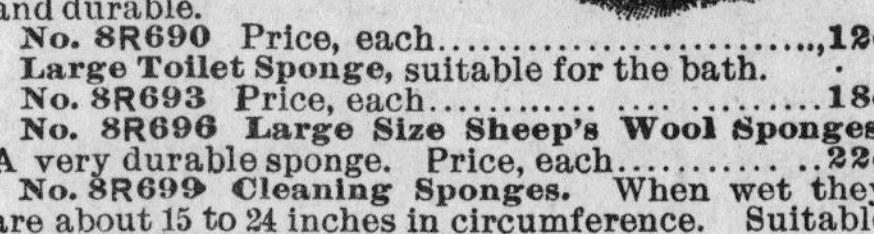

No. 8R702 Ladies' Silk Sponges, very fine, regular form. Each....20c

No. 8R705 Selected, with silk netting cover and silk cord. Each.25c

No. 8R708 Extra fine, small medium; ladies' cup shaped silk sponges. Each..............................35c

No. 8R711 Superfine, large ladies' cup shaped sponges, specially selected forms and shapes. Each..50c

Bleach Mediterranean Sponges, for toilet and bath.

No. 8R714 Small. Price, each....................8c
No. 8R717 Medium. Price, each..............15c
No. 8R720 Large. Price, each..................25c
No. 8R723 Extra large bath sponge. Price, ea.40c

Unbleached Sheep's Wool Sponges. A choice grade of fine, soft sponges; strong and durable, for either bathing purposes or cleaning fine carriages.

No. 8R726 Medium. Price, each...................40c
No. 8R729 Large. Price, each....................60c

Cleaning Sponges. Suitable for cleaning buggies, wood work, walls, etc. A strong natural unbleached sponge.

No. 8R732 Small. Price, each....................20c
No. 8R735 Large. Price, each....................35c

Chamois Skin

We are headquarters for Chamois Skins; buy them in large quantities and sell them for less than a retail druggist or dealer can buy them for. Chamois skins are very useful and should be in every household. Chamois skins are used as follows: Ladies use them for toilet purposes, for cleaning glass, wood work of all kinds, carriages, silverware, or any metal, lining pockets and for chest protectors.

Our Very Fine Toilet Chamois, for applying powder, etc., to the face. Size, about 5x6 inches.

No. 8R738 Price each..............................5c

Style	A	B	C
Size, inches	9x6½	12x9	14x11
Price, each	5c	10c	16c
Style	D	E	F
Size, inches	20x16	26x23	28x32
Price, each	32c	52c	80c

Note—If a chamois about size 14x11 inches is wanted, order No. 8R738 Style C.

Nursery Rubber Sheeting.

White.	Width, 27-in.	36-in.	45-in.	54-in.
No. 8R741 Price, per yard	.40c	54c	72c	90c

Tan Rubber Sheeting, soft as silk, very light in weight, strong and absolutely waterproof. For hospital and nursery use, also for making bathing caps, diapers, etc.

No. 8R744 36 inches wide. Per yard..........70c

Rubber Tubing.

Smooth or corrugated white, for bulb and fountain syringes.

No. 8R747 Price, per foot........................5c

White, black or maroon rubber tubing for feeding bottles.

No. 8R750 Price, per foot........................4c

No. 8R751 Glass tubes for nursing bottle fittings. Price, per dozen..................................10c

RUBBER GOODS.

Syringes, Etc.

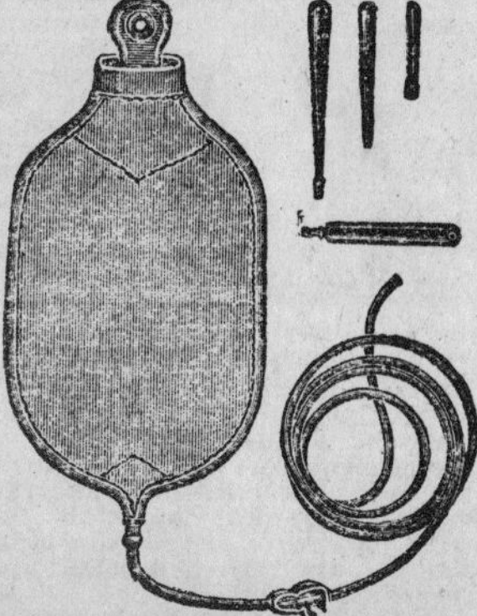

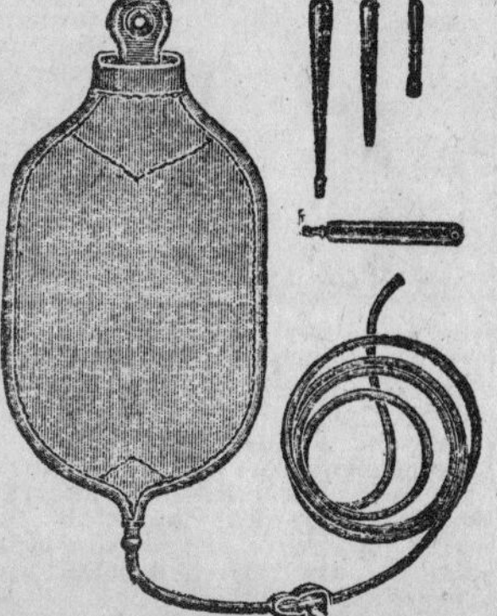

The S., R. & Co.'s Gem Fountain Syringe, made from good quality rubber, with hard rubber fittings, **four hard rubber pipes,** including large irrigating pipe, in a neat box, long rubber tubing with patent shut off.

No. 8R753 2 quarts, each..50c
No. 8R756 3 quarts, each..63c
No. 8R759 4 quarts, each..68c
Shipping weight, 18 ounces.

Reliable Fountain Syringe.

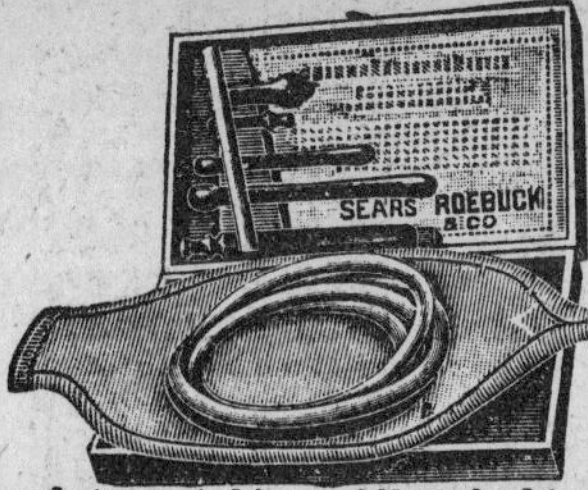

A Five Pipe Syringe, including the infant, vaginal, rectal, irrigator and nasal pipes and fine heavy rubber reinforced seam ribbed bag. Patent shut off and strong tubing. All packed in fine wooden box.

No. 8R762 2 quarts, each.........................$0.88
No. 8R765 3 quarts, each.........................97
No. 8R768 4 quarts, each.........................1.08

Shipping weight, 21 ounces.

Monarch Syringe.

A Combination Syringe and Water Bottle, including hard rubber connections and infant, vaginal, rectal, irrigator and nasal pipes and six feet of pure rubber tubing and water bottle of very superior grade, ribbed back rubber. Fitted with automatic shut off attachment. Packed in wooden box.

No. 8R771 2 quarts, each, complete.........$1.20
No. 8R774 3 quarts, each, complete...........1.30
No. 8R777 4 quarts, each, complete...........1.40

If by mail, postage extra, 20 cents.

Our Guaranteed Rapid Flow Perfection Fountain Syringe.

No. 8R780 Rapid Flow Fountain Syringe, with flushing size rubber tubing, which admits of a rapid flow of water; made of extra quality white rubber, **the simplest and best syringe made,** hard rubber infant, rectal, irrigator and vaginal screw pipes, packed in handsome platform box, at half drug store prices.

2 quarts, each........$0.95
3 quarts, each..........1.05
4 quarts, each..........1.15

Shipping weight, 25 ounces.

No. 8R783 S., R. & Co Acme Bulb Syringe. Put up in nice pasteboard box. Good quality rubber, two hard rubber pipes. Drug store price, 50 cents for same quality. Our price, each......25c

If by mail, postage extra, 5 cents.

Our 49-Cent Union Syringe.

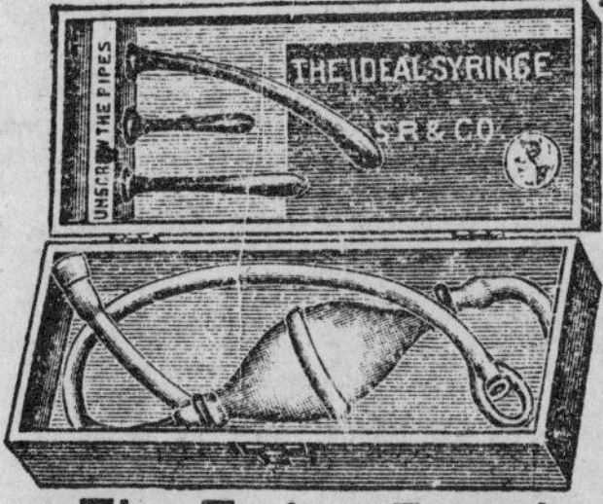

No. 8R786 Goodyear Union Syringe, with three hard rubber pipes, put up in a neat wooden box. Druggists ask $1.00 for this syringe. Our price, each..49c

If by mail, postage, extra, 10 cents.

The Tyrian Female Syringe for $1.00.

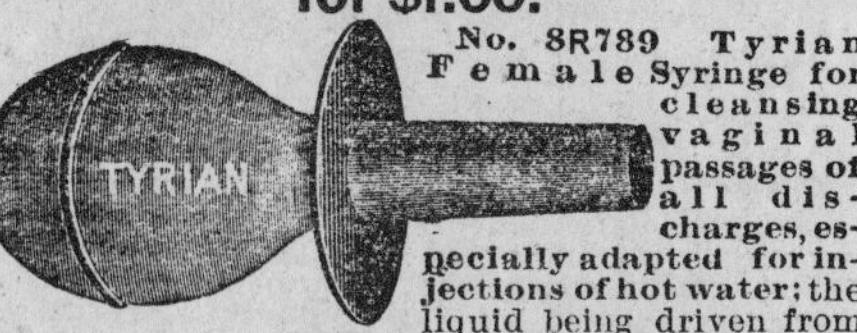

No. 8R789 Tyrian Female Syringe for cleansing vaginal passages of all discharges, especially adapted for injections of hot water; the liquid being driven from the syringe when the bulb is compressed and drawn back into it on relaxing the pressure, thus **giving an opportunity to thoroughly wash the diseased parts. Capacity, 8 ounces.** Made of one piece of soft rubber, with removable hard rubber shield. **Having no valves or connections, cannot get out of order.** Drug store price, $2.00. Our price, each.....$1.00

If by mail, postage extra, 13 cents.

No. 8R792 The S., R. & Co.'s Ladies' Perfe Syringe, the best female syringe. Constructed c the latest scientific principles—injection and su tion. Cleanses the vaginal passages thoroughly all discharges. Recommended by the medic profession as the safest and most efficient any syringe ever made. Especially adapted for i jections of hot water without soiling the clothin Made of one piece of fine soft rubber. Price, each. 9

If by mail, postage extra, 17 cents.

Dr. Tuller's Improved Vaginal Spray.

Patented Jan. 1st, 1901. This new injection and suction syringe is made entirely of rubber, no metal arts to corrode. The ball tip discharges **a revolving spray.** The new oval or elliptical shield prevents spilling. Dr. Tullar's syringe has the new **octagon bulb with a capacity of 11 ounces,** and is admitted to be the best invention of its class for **quick and thorough cleansing, also for medicated or hot injections.** This wonderful syringe is invaluable to every married woman.

No. 8R795 Price, each......$2.50

If by mail, postage extra, 20 cents.

The Ladies' Perfect Syringe.

Only perfect vaginal and recta syringe in the world. Injections ca be administered without leaking an soiling the clothing or necessitatin the use of a vessel. Can be use equally for rectal injections an vaginal irrigation. It will thor oughly cleanse by completely distend ing the parts, and drawing all dis charges out with the fluid into th bulb. Physicians and nurses will fin this syringe a great convenience, a with its use medicated solutions ca reach every minute part of the mucuou membrane better than can be done b applications through a speculum, an with much less trouble. It can be easily used by th patients themselves and cannot possibly get out o order. It is entirely made of hard and soft rubbe without valves or small openings of any kind to be come clogged or break. We guarantee it to be mor effective, more satisfactory and last longer tha any syringe on the market. Full instructions fo use with each syringe.

No. 8R798 Price, each, in box..............$1.7

If by mail, postage extra, 18 cents.

Hard Rubber Stem Syringe.

For Females.

Superior to other syringes of this class and a most perfect syringe for a far reaching vagina douche. Made with soft rubber bulb and hard rub ber stem. Has no valves. Cannot corrode or ge out of order. This is one of the most efficient syr inges for cleansing the vagina, and is highly recom mended by the best physicians to married ladies fo that purpose, and for the treatment of any loca disorder and female complaints.

No. 8R801 Price, each.................88

If by mail, postage extra, 10 cents.

Omega Syringe-Continuous Flow

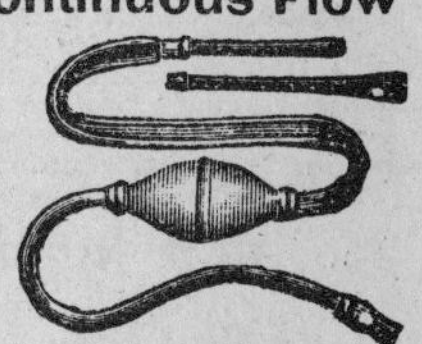

No. 8R804 Made of pure para rubber. Omega Syringe No. 5, continuous flow, with hard rubber vaginal and rectal pipes. The valves are **secured and cannot be lost. The continuous flow is the correct principle on which a syringe** should be made. Packed in neat maroon box. Price, each.....................50c

If by mail, postage extra, 10 cents.

No. 8R807 Omega Syringe No. 4, continuous flow. Hard rubber vaginal and rectal pipes, **valves secured and cannot be lost. Omega No. 4** has a flattened outlet tube which is made by a **specially invented process,** that produces the **continuous flow.** Packed in neat octagonal box. Each.....75c

If by mail, postage extra, 15 cents.

No. 8R810 Omega Syringe No 3, continuous flow. Has hard rubber vaginal, rectal and infant pipes, noiseless and non-corrosive sinker, patented screw joint socket, by which pipes are **quickly attached** without use of threads or washers. Packed in oval box. Price, each.........................$1.00

If by mail, postage extra, 10 cents.

Alpha Continuous Flowing Syringe.

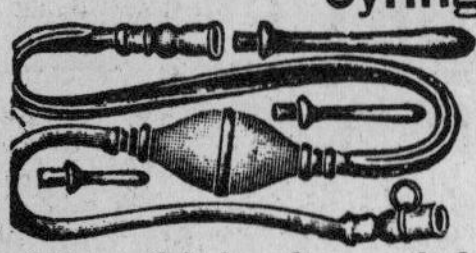

Made of best para rubber. All intermittent syringes inject more or less air, which is invariably drawn back into the tube while the bulb is expanding and refilling; this is often painful as well as dangerous. Not so with the Alpha Continuous Flowing Syringe.

No. 8R813 Alpha E Syringe, continuous flow, hard rubber vaginal, rectal and infant pipes, noiseless and non-corrosive sinker, valves cannot be lost. Packed in handsome cloth covered case with nickel plated clasp. Price, each.....$1.50

No. 8R816 Alpha D Syringe, continuous flow, fitted with extra large valve chambers, hard rubber vaginal, rectal, infant and nasal pipes and improved vaginal irrigating spray, noiseless and non-corrosive sinker. Packed in nice cloth covered case. Price, each.....$1.75

If by mail, postage extra, 15 cents.

Saratoga Ear and Ulcer Syringe.

No. 8R819 Eye, Ear, Ulcer and Abscess Syringe. Capacity, 1 ounce; injection pipe; is made of soft and flexible rubber. Will not injure or pain the inflamed parts. Price, each.....17c

If by mail, postage extra, 3 cents.

Hard Rubber Syringes.

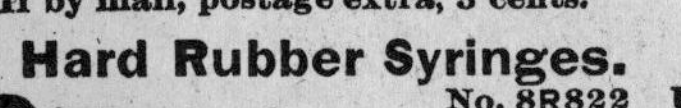

No. 8R822 Urethal or male Hard Rubber Syringe. Capacity, ½ ounce. Price.....14c

If by mail, postage extra, each 2 cents.

No. 8R825 Vaginal Hard Rubber Syringe. Capacity, 2 ounces. Price, each.....53c

If by mail, postage extra, each, 4 cents.

Excelsior Hot Water Bottles.

Every one warranted; special prices.

No. 8R828 2-qt. each.....60c
No. 8R831 3-qt. each.....65c
No. 8R834 4-qt. each.....70c

If by mail, postage extra, 2-qt., 14 cents; 3-qt., 16 cents, and 4-qt., 18 cents.

Flannel Covered Water Bottles.

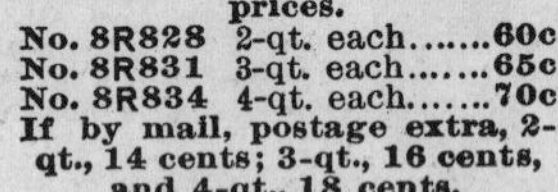

No. 8R837 Standard make best quality. Note our special prices.

2-qt. each.....$1.25
3-qt. each..... 1.30
4-qt. each..... 1.35

If by mail, postage extra, 17 cents.

Flannel Covered Face Bottles.

No. 8R840 Convenient for a great many uses. Holds ¼ pint. Price, each.....50c

If by mail, postage extra, 8 cents.

Invalid Air Cushions.

Goodyear Rubber Invalid Air Cushions. For use in the sick room for bed sores, etc. Is invaluable for invalids; soft, pliable and light. Weight, 18 oz.

	Diameter	Each
No. 8R843	12 inches	$1.25
No. 8R846	14 inches	1.35
No. 8R849	16 inches	1.50
No. 8R852	18 inches	1.65

Hospital Rubber Chair Cushions.

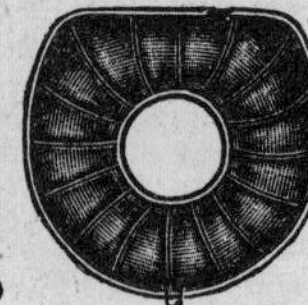

Strong and useful for persons engaged in sedentary occupations. Regular size 17½ inches in diameter. Opening in center of cushion, when inflated 6¼ inches. You will find these cushions of great comfort and conducive to your health and general well being. Weight, 30 ounces.

No. 8R855 Price, each...$3.60

Soft Rubber Bed Pans.

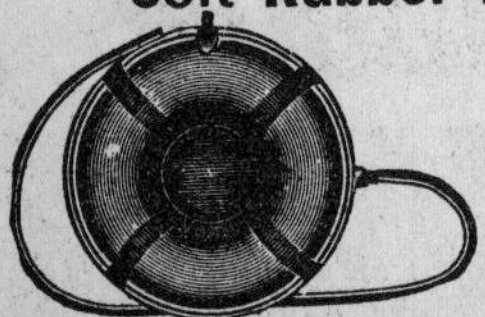

Round Bed Pans with outlet tube, soft rubber, substantial and convenient. Should be on hand in every well regulated household. Weight, 30 ozs.

No. 8R858 Price, each.....$2.15

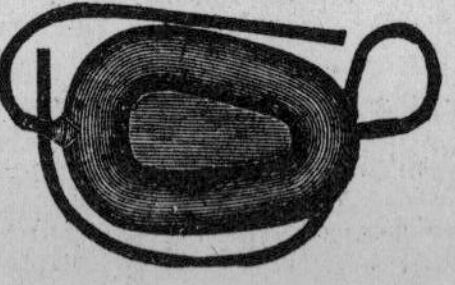

Oval Bed Pans, with outlet tube, soft rubber. The highest grade made. For ladies and men. A necessary article for the sick room. Weight, about 2 pounds.

No. 8R861 Price, each.....$2.90

Ice Caps.

Made of strong, impervious checked cloth on outside and heavy rubber coating on inside, with nickel screw cap. Very handy and convenient for ice applications on the head and other parts of the body.

No. 8R864 6-inch. Price, each.....$0.95
No. 8R867 9-inch. Price, each..... 1.20
No. 8R870 12-inch. Price, each..... 1.40

Stomach Tubes and Pumps.

No. 8R873 Fine Maroon Rubber Stomach Tubes, plain style. Price, each.....75c

No. 8R876 Very Fine Maroon Soft Rubber Stomach Tubes, with funnel ends. Each.....$1.00

No. 8R879 Fine Maroon Soft Rubber Stomach Tubes, funnel ends and bulb pump in center of tube. Price, each.....$1.25

Pure Gum Ice Bags.

For head, spine and throat applications. These ice bags are made of pure gum rubber and are the latest, most modern mode of applying ice to any portion of the human body in cases of fevers, accidents and general sickness. Should be kept in the house for emergency cases.

No. 8R882 Spinal Bag, 9½x3¼ inches. Price, each.....40c
No. 8R885 Spinal Bag, 11x3½ inches. Price, each.....50c
No. 8R888 Head Bag, 9½x6¼ inches. Price, each.....60c
No. 8R892 Head Bag, 11x6¼ inches. Price, each.....65c
No. 8R895 Ice Bags, for the throat. Size, 8 or 9 inches in length. Price, each.....$1.00
No. 8R898 10 or 11 inches in length. Each, 1.25

Catheters and Bougies.

No. 8R901 A very fine quality velvet eye soft rubber catheter, in all sizes, American scale, from No. 6 to No. 15. Price, each.....25c

No. 8R904 Imported Silk Linen Catheter, natural brown color, with easy oval eye, one end being funnel shape and the other solid, so that no aseptic matter can lodge. Sizes, 2 to 18, English scale. Price, each.....35c

No. 8R907 Imported Bougies, made of the same material as above, with no eye and with closed end. In sizes 3 to 18, English scale. Price, each.....25c

Rectal Tubes.

No. 8R910 Rectal Tubes, 20-inch, made of fine maroon rubber, in small, medium and large sizes. Price, each.....35c

Rubber Finger Cots and Tips.

No. 8R913 Heavy Black and Tan Rubber Finger Cots. Price, each.....3c

No. 8R916 Mizpah Antiseptic Finger Cots, made of pure rubber, very light in weight. Especially recommended for surgeons, chemists and photographers. Price, each.....4c

NOTE—Rubber goods ordered for personal use cannot be returned, for obvious reasons.

SOFT RUBBER URINAL BAGS.

For Boys and Men or Girls and Women.

For bed wetting and general incontinence of urine. For male and female children and adults. For day and night use.

Soft Rubber Urinal Bag, the most comfortable pattern made, of the best material, for male, day or night use. Weight, 8 ounces.

No. 8R943 Price.....$1.10
No. 8R946 Short, for boys..... 1.00

Soft Rubber Urinal Bags.

Soft Rubber Urinal Bag, most improved pattern, made of the very best material, for female use. Weight, 10 ounces.

No. 8R949 Price.....$1.10

No. 8R943 No. 8R949

Pure Gum Soft Rubber Bag.

Pure Gum Soft Rubber Bag, for male. Large size, convenient pattern. Weight, 6 ounces.

No. 8R952 Price.....95c

Urinal Bags.

No. 8R955 Soft Rubber Urinal Bag, improved French pattern; day use for females. Price, each...$1.85

Postage extra, each, 20c.

Soft Rubber Urinal Bag.

No. 8R958 Soft Rubber Urinal Bag, day and night use for male; improved French pattern, with waist belt ready to use without other attachments. Price, each.....$1.95

No. 8R955 No. 8R958

If by mail, postage extra, each, 20 cents.

Magic Flesh Builder and Cupper.

An entirely new and scientific invention. Has no equal as a developer. Makes it possible for every lady to possess a well rounded, plump, beautiful figure. Rebuilds shrunken tissues of the bust, neck, arms, and the only method which permanently removes wrinkles, and makes the sunken cheek smooth, full and developed. Operates same as the Wrinkle Remover, only more powerful.

No. 8R961 Price, each.....50c

If by mail, postage extra, 9 cents.

Seamless Para Gloves.

Seamless Para Gloves. By wearing them at night during sleep, you will obtain a hand as fair as an infant's, without the least injury. They will remove wrinkles, callouses, tan, sallowness, freckles and discolorations as if by magic. With care they will last for years. Made of the pure transparent rubber, same as face mask. State size when you order.

No. 8R964 Price, per pair, only.....$1.25

If by mail, postage extra, 6 cents.

Genuine Nonpareil Rubber Gloves.

Advertised and sold everywhere for $1.25.

Our price only 95 cents.

Nonpareil Gloves keep the hands soft and white and are unequalled for ladies' use in doing housework. They are strong, soft and pliable, and can be worn without the slightest inconvenience in doing work of the most delicate nature. Every pair fully guaranteed. Order a half size to one size larger than your kid glove number.

No. 8R967 Genuine Nonpareil Rubber Gloves. Price, per pair.....95c

If by mail, postage extra, 5 cents.

The Toilet Mask.

The Art of Beautifying the Complexion.

Every lady knows the value of a Mask made of transparent rubber, acid cured, for the removal of freckles, liver spots, and other facial blemishes. As a bleacher it cannot be excelled and will give any lady the fine, soft, velvety skin of a child. The great trouble has been that few have been able to afford these Masks, as they never have been sold for less than $5.00, and sometimes as high as $10.00. We have been fortunate enough to make terms with the manufacturers of these Masks which enables us to sell them for $2.00 each. This Mask is composed entirely of the purest natural material brought from the forests of Para and Guiana, scientifically treated and incorporated with healing agents, molded to the form of a Mask. It is safe, simple, cleanly and effective for beautifying purposes, and never injures the most delicate complexion. Usually sold for $5.00.

No. 8R971 Each complete Mask only.....$2.00

If by mail, postage extra, 2 cents.

Wrinkle Eradicator.

This convenient little article will remove wrinkles from around the eyes and nose and any part of the face. It invigorates the skin and keeps a perfect contour of the face.

No. 8R974 Our price only.....25c

If by mail, postage extra, 4 cents.

Rubber Gloves.

No. 8R977 Ladies' and Men's Short Rubber Gloves. Colors, tan or black. Sizes, 7, 8, 9. Per pair. 70c
Sizes 10 and 11. Per pair.....90c

No. 8R983 Ladies' and Men's Gauntlet Rubber Gloves. Black or tan. Sizes, 7, 8, 9. Price, per pair.....95c
Sizes, 10 and 11. Price, per pair.....$1.20

No. 8R985 Men's Heavy Rubber Mittens. Lined with sheeting. Black only. Per pair.....95c

If by mail, postage extra, 8 cents.

Always order a size larger in rubber gloves.

Goodyear Plant Sprinkler.

Plant Sprinkler for spraying plants and flowers without injury, for sprinkling clothing in the laundry, spraying carpets and clothing to prevent moths, spraying disinfectants in the sick room, etc. Capacity, 6 ounces.

No. 8R987 Price, each.....50c

If by mail, postage extra, 10 cents.

Toilet or Medicinal Atomizer.

Atomizer, for either Toilet or Medicinal Use. Hard rubber nozzle, rubber bulb of fine quality. Retailers ask as high as 75 cents for similar goods. Continuous spray.

No. 8R989 Price, each..38c

If by mail, postage extra, 10 cents.

Atomizer.

The most reliable and useful Atomizer in the world. Has three hard rubber tips. Can be used for spraying perfume, or disinfecting a sick room, or applying medicine to the throat or in the nose. It is made of the best materials, and with care will last a lifetime. Every household should have one. No better atomizer can be found in the market.

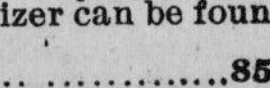

No. 8R991 Price.....85c

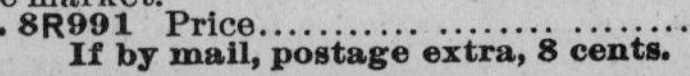

If by mail, postage extra, 8 cents.

Regular retail price, each..$1.95
OUR PRICE, EACH.....$0.73
OUR PRICE, PER DOZEN 7.20

For Removing Superfluous Hair

OUR FAMOUS PARISIAN DEPILATORY

For Removing Superfluous Hair

One bottle is usually sufficient for any case. Contains treatment that will cure.

AT 73c PER BOTTLE we offer our celebrated **PARISIAN DEPILATORY**, the only harmless and successful preparation on the market for removing unsightly, superfluous hair on the face, neck and arms. WE POSITIVELY GUARANTEE OUR PARISIAN DEPILATORY NOT TO HARM THE MOST SENSITIVE SKIN OR MAR THE MOST DELICATE COMPLEXION. Hair on the face, neck or arms, so embarrassing to ladies of refinement, can now be removed without danger or chance of failure. **The Parisian Depilatory instantly dissolves the hair wherever applied, removes it entirely and forever.**

THE GREATEST DRAWBACK TO PERFECT LOVELINESS in woman is a superfluous, unnatural growth of hair, where nature never intended it. The prettiest face is marred and disfigured by hair on the lips, cheeks or chin. By means of our **Parisian Depilatory** every vestige of hair can be removed, a perfect clean, smooth, soft, beautiful skin is assured.

NO UNPLEASANT EFFECTS. The Parisian Depilatory is not only perfectly harmless, but it has the additional effect of a fine cosmetic, softening the skin and improving the complexion. It leaves no burning sensation, it is entirely painless, easily applied; one application is usually sufficient for the most aggravated cases.

FAR SUPERIOR TO THE ELECTRIC NEEDLE. The electric needle will remove superfluous hair by destroying the roots, but it is a very dangerous operation. Serious results have often followed the use of the electric needle. **Parisian Depilatory is safe and sure. It cannot fail.** No matter what you have tried before or how stubborn the growth of hair is, **we guarantee our Parisian Depilatory will remove it entirely and effect a speedy and permanent cure.**

A WONDERFUL PREPARATION. Compounded in our own laboratory by a competent chemist. Every ounce is prepared under his personal supervision. The ingredients are the best and purest, carefully selected. **OUR SPECIAL PRICE of 73 cents per bottle is the lowest price ever heard of for a genuine Depilatory. Our 73 cent price covers only the actual cost of the materials and labor,** with our one small profit added.

DON'T PAY $1.00, $2.00 AND $3.00 for a so-called hair remover. Be careful about using the preparations of unknown concerns. Some of the hair removers, widely advertised, are very powerful, very corrosive; they remove the hair and often burn the skin or ruin the complexion forever. **You can use our Parisian Depilatory with perfect safety.** Leaves no marks, no ill effects, no one can tell that you are using a hair remover. No one will know the difference except in your improved appearance, the enhanced loveliness of the skin and complexion.

NO TOILET IS COMPLETE without the famous Parisian Depilatory. Ladies of refinement everywhere find the Parisian Depilatory an invaluable toilet requisite, a perfect and harmless hair remover. It removes the hair only where it is applied, does not interfere with the use of cosmetics, washes; has no effect whatever on the blood, complexion, health or hair, or any part of the person, except where it is applied. If you are bothered by superfluous hair, whether on face, neck or arms, if you want a perfectly smooth, clean, clear skin, **send for a bottle of our celebrated 73-cent Parisian Depilatory, the only absolutely harmless, unfailingly successful hair remover ever compounded.**

Our Celebrated Parisian Depilatory removes all superfluous hair and other imperfections, and leaves the skin soft, smooth and velvety.

No. 8R1095 Our price, per bottle........................(If by mail, postage and mailing tube extra, 7 cents)........................73 cents

THE PRINCESS BUST DEVELOPER AND BUST CREAM OR FOOD

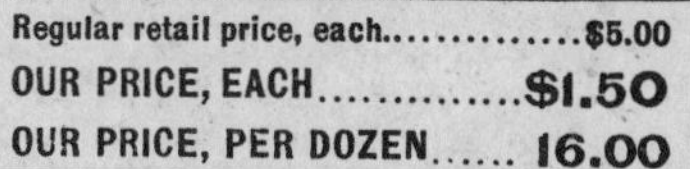

Regular retail price, each	$5.00
OUR PRICE, EACH	$1.50
OUR PRICE, PER DOZEN	16.00

SOLD UNDER A POSITIVE GUARANTEE TO ENLARGE ANY LADY'S BUST FROM 3 TO 5 INCHES. OUR SPECIAL INTRODUCTORY PRICE FOR DEVELOPER, BUST EXPANDER AND BUST FOOD, COMPLETE - - - - - - - - - - - $1.50

With every order for Princess Bust Developer and Bust Food, we furnish FREE one bottle of the GENUINE FLEUR DE LIS BUST EXPANDER and TISSUE BUILDER (retail price, 75 cents) without extra charge.

THE PRINCESS BUST DEVELOPER

IS A NEW SCIENTIFIC HELP TO NATURE.

COMBINED WITH THE USE OF THE BUST CREAM OR FOOD, FORMS A FULL FIRM WELL DEVELOPED BUST IN A FEW DAYS' USE.

It will build up and fill out all shrunken and undeveloped tissues, form a rounded, plump, perfectly developed bust, producing a beautiful figure.

THE PRINCESS BUST DEVELOPER AND CREAM FOOD is absolutely harmless, easy to use, perfectly safe and the only successful bust developer offered by any concern.

IF NATURE HAS NOT FAVORED YOU with that greatest charm, a symmetrically rounded bosom full and perfect, send for the **Princess Bust Developer** and you will be surprised, delighted and happy over the result of one week's use. No matter what you have tried before, no matter if you have used other so called Bust Developers, (paying $4.00, $5.00 or $6.00) without effect, our **Princess Developer will absolutely produce the desired result. We guarantee it, it has been proven by test and trial; and if you are not entirely satisfied with the result after giving it a fair trail, please return it to us and we will gladly refund your money.**

Unmailable on account of weight.

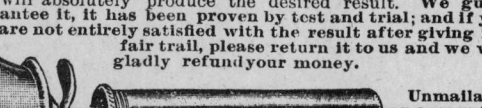

PRINCESS BUST DEVELOPER.
Comes in two sizes, 3½ and 5 inches in diameter. State size desired.

THE DEVELOPER is carefully made of nickel and aluminum, very finest finish throughout. Comes in two sizes, 3½ and 5 inches diameter. In ordering please state size desired. The developer gives the right exercise to the muscles of the bust, compels a free and normal circulation of the blood through the capillaries, glands and tissues of the flabby, undeveloped parts, these parts are soon restored to a healthy condition, they expand and fill out, become round, firm and beautiful.

THE BUST CREAM OR FOOD

IS APPLIED AS A MASSAGE.

It is a delightful cream preparation, put up by an eminent French chemist, and forms just the right food required for the starved skin and wasted tissues. The ingredients of the **Bust Food are mainly pure vegetable oils, perfectly harmless.** Combined in a way to form the finest nourishment for the bust glands. It is delicately perfumed and is

UNRIVALED FOR DEVELOPING THE BUST, ARMS AND NECK,

making a plump, full, rounded bosom, perfect neck and arms, a smooth skin, which before was scrawny, flat and flabby.

FULL DIRECTIONS ARE FURNISHED, SUCCESS IS ASSURED.

You need no longer regret that your form is not what you would like it to be. Ladies everywhere welcome the Princess Bust Developer and Cream Food as the greatest toilet requisite ever offered. We have letters from many of our lady customers, telling us the good results of the **Princess Developer**, how their busts enlarged from two to six inches, and expressing their gratitude for the big benefit derived.

BUST CREAM
OR FOOD
UNRIVALLED FOR
ENLARGEMENT OF THE BUST
SEARS, ROEBUCK & Co.
CHICAGO, ILL.
SOLE AGENTS.

THE PRINCESS BUST DEVELOPER AND FOOD is the only treatment that will actually, permanently develop and enlarge the bust, cause it to fill out to nature's full proportions, give that swelling, rounded, firm white bosom, that queenly bearing, so attractive to the opposite sex. Transforms a thin, awkward, unattractive girl or woman into an exquisitely formed, graceful, fascinating lady, positively without fail, absolutely without harm. Such a preparation has never before been offered. Don't fail to take advantage of it and order at once.

$1.50 is our Special Introductory Price for the PRINCESS DEVELOPER and BUST FOOD, Complete, the Lowest Price Ever Made on this Article.

DON'T PAY some unknown concern an extravagant price for a socalled bust developer. Be careful of the medicines and treatments offered by various irresponsible companies. **Send for the Princess Developer, complete with the Bust Food, at our special introductory price of $1.50, state whether you wish the 3½ or 5-inch developer, and if you are not entirely satisfied with the results, if your bust is not enlarged from 2 to 6 inches according to length of time used, without the slightest harm or inconvenience, return it, after giving it a trial, and we will refund your money. Don't put off ordering. Nowhere else can you buy a successful guaranteed bust developer for only $1.50. Order at once while we can produce these perfect goods at present cost.**

No. 8R1098 **Our Princess Bust Developer, Bust Expander and Bust Cream or Food.** Price, complete, including a bottle of Fleur de Lis Bust Expander, **$1.50**

OUR 60-CENT PRINCESS HAIR RESTORER.

No. 8R1101

Per Bottle, 60c.

A WONDERFUL NEW HAIR TONIC AND PRODUCER.

Restores the Natural Color, Preserves and Strengthens the Hair for Years, Promotes the Growth, Arrests Falling Hair, Feeds and Nourishes the Roots, Cures Dandruff and Scurf, and Allays all Scalp Irritations.

Regular Retail Price, per bottle, $1.00
Our Price, per bottle, ...60
Our Price, per dozen 6.00

Unmailable on account of weight.

The only absolutely effective, unfailingly successful, perfectly harmless, positively no-dye preparation on the market

that restores gray hair to its natural and youthful color, removes crusts, scales and dandruff, soothes irritating, itching surfaces, stimulates the hair follicles, supplies the roots with energy and nourishment, renders the hair beautifully soft, and makes the hair grow WHEN ALL ELSE FAILS.

EVERY SINGLE BOTTLE OF PRINCESS HAIR RESTORER is compounded especially in our own laboratory by our own skilled chemists, and according to the prescription of one who has made the hair and scalp, its diseases and cure, a life study.

PRINCESS HAIR RESTORER IS NOT AN EXPERIMENT, not an untried unknown, quack remedy, depending on enormous, glittering advertisements for sales, but it is a preparation of the very finest and most expensive ingredients that will positively cure any case of falling hair, stimulate the growth of new hair on bald heads, cure dandruff and other diseases of the scalp.

ARE YOU BALD?

IS YOUR HAIR THIN OR FALLING OUT?

DOES YOUR HAIR COME OUT EASILY AND GATHER ON THE COMB AND BRUSH WHEN YOU BRUSH IT?

DOES YOUR HEAD ITCH?

DO YOU HAVE DANDRUFF OR SCURF AND DO WHITE, DUST-LIKE PARTICLES SETTLE ON YOUR COAT COLLAR?

IS YOUR HAIR STIFF AND COARSE AND HARD TO BRUSH?

IS YOUR HAIR FADING OR HAS IT TURNED PREMATURELY GRAY?

IF YOUR HAIR SUFFERS in any one or more of these particulars, we would urge you by all means to order a bottle of **Princess Hair Restorer** as a trial, for speedy relief. Use it according to directions and you will be surprised and delighted at the wonderful results. **PRINCESS HAIR RESTORER NEVER FAILS.** It acts direct on the tiny roots of the hair, giving them required fresh nourishment, starts quick and energetic circulation in every hair cell, tones up the scalp, freshens the pores, stops falling and sickly hair, changes thin hair to a fine heavy growth, puts new life in dormant, sluggish hair cells on bald heads, producing in a short time an **absolutely new growth of hair. If your hair is fading or turning gray,** one bottle of Princess Hair Restorer will give it healthy life, renew its original color and restore it to youthful profusion and beauty.

USE IT ALWAYS IF YOU WANT A HEAD OF FINE, SILKY, GLOSSY HAIR, THE PRIDE OF EVERY WOMAM.

THE PRINCESS WORLD FAMED HAIR TONIC RESTORER SEARS, ROEBUCK AND CO. Cheapest Supply House on Earth WE SELL EVERYTHING 78-96 FULTON ST 73-87 DESPLAINES ST 13-31 WAYMAN ST. CHICAGO ILL.

Princess Hair Restorer Grows Hair Like This.

PRINCESS HAIR RESTORER IS GOOD FOR BOTH MEN AND WOMEN. Is equally effective on men's, women's and children's hair.

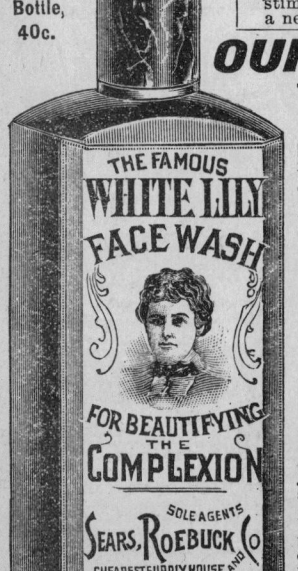

AS A CURE FOR DANDRUFF, as a tonic for thin and scanty hair, Princess Hair Restorer acts with quick and wonderful success. It removes crusts and scales, keeps the scalp clean and healthy, the roots at once respond to its vigorous action, dandruff is banished and a thick and healthy growth of hair is assured.

FOR A TOILET ARTICLE, as a fine hair dressing, no one who takes any pride in a nice head of hair can afford to be without a bottle always on the dresser. **Princess Hair Restorer** is delicately perfumed, and one light application imparts a delightful, refined fragrance. Neither oils, pomades, vaseline or other greases are required with our preparation.

DON'T SEND AWAY TO SOME UNKNOWN CONCERN for a so-called **Hair Grower,** that promise everything in their advertisement and do no good whatever, and may do a great deal of harm. **Don't send away to a cheap specialist and pay $1.00, $1.50 or $2.00 a bottle** for a worthless and perhaps injurious preparation. Don't be misled by catchy advertisements with baits of free trial sample bottle and fake examination offers—such people will draw you in, make you believe something awful is the matter and scare you into paying enormous prices for alleged remedies, when you can get the **genuine, tried, tested, proven and guaranteed Princess Hair Restorer at 60 cents a bottle,** the actual cost of the ingredients and labor of bottling, with our one small profit added.

No. 8R1104

Per Bottle, 40c.

PRINCESS HAIR RESTORER IS ABSOLUTELY HARMLESS—IT IS NOT A DYE. It will not injure the most delicate hair, it will not stain the daintiest head dress. Princess Hair Restorer works wonders with the hair. We get letters daily from people telling how much good it has done for them. It will do the same for you. You can sell a dozen bottles at a profit to yourself in your immediate neighborhood to people who see the good it has done and the wonderful results on your hair. **Order a bottle at 60 cents, which you can easily sell at $1.00 each,** and if you do not find it all and more than we claim for it, if you do not find it is just the hair tonic you want, stimulating the growth, cleansing the scalp, stopping hair from falling out, restoring natural color, curing dandruff or promoting a new growth of hair on a bald head, return it to us at once **AND WE WILL CHEERFULLY REFUND YOUR MONEY.**

OUR WHITE LILY FACE WASH.

40 CENTS PER BOTTLE.

Retail Price . . . $0.75
Our Price 40
Our Price per doz. 4.20

THE LADIES' FAVORITE TOILET PREPARATION.

An Invaluable Remedy for Pimples, Freckles, Sallowness, Roughness, Wrinkles, Tan, Blackheads and all Irritations and Imperfections of the Skin.

DIFFERENT FROM MOST COMPLEXION PREPARATIONS, our White Lily Face Wash contains not a particle of lead, silver, sulphur, arsenic, mercury or other poisonous mineral by which most complexion remedies, and particularly the advertised ones, produce a temporary smoothness and brilliancy of the skin. **White Lily Face Wash is clear and harmless as water,** contains no poison, no sediment, nothing to hurt the most tender and delicate skin. Its effect in quickly removing pimples, blackheads, freckles, roughness and tan is simply wonderful. **White Lily Face Wash smoothes out wrinkles and roughness,** all imperfections and irritations of the skin disappear, restores the delicate tint of girlhood and youth, leaving the skin soft and velvety. **Nothing is more attractive than a lovely complexion.**

DO YOU WANT TO BE BEAUTIFUL? Do you want a **spotless skin, a matchless complexion,** the envy and pride of everyone? **Send for a bottle of White Lily Face Wash,** use it according to directions and a perfect complexion will be the result. **We positively guarantee White Lily Face Wash** to permanently cure pimples, blackheads and other eruptions of the skin, to completely remove tan, freckles, blotches, sallowness, roughness, flabbiness, wrinkles and all other imperfections of the skin, face, neck, bust, arms and hands.

WHITE LILY FACE WASH has a wonderful sale. The market is full of injurious complexion preparations. If you intend to buy or to send away for some skin remedy, please send us a sample for analysis and report before you start to use it. It will cost you nothing, we will make no charge for the service, and as many, in fact, most of these preparations contain lead, arsenic, bismuth or mercury and are really dangerous in their effects, we may save you from some very serious skin disease. **Take no chances. Avoid all danger.** Use only a preparation that is absolutely harmless, one that you can depend on for a spotless skin, a positive beautifier that has been recommended by thousands of ladies.

THE FAMOUS WHITE LILY FACE WASH FOR BEAUTIFYING THE COMPLEXION SOLE AGENTS SEARS, ROEBUCK AND CO. CHEAPEST SUPPLY HOUSE ON EARTH CHICAGO ILL.

No. 8R1104

Recommended by Thousands of Beautiful Women.

USE ONLY THE GENUINE WHITE LILY FACE WASH, PREPARED AND SOLD BY US.

No. 8R1104 Regular retail price, per bottle, 75c; our price, per doz., $4.20; each............(If by mail, postage and tube extra, 15 cents.)............40c

Pomade Philacome.

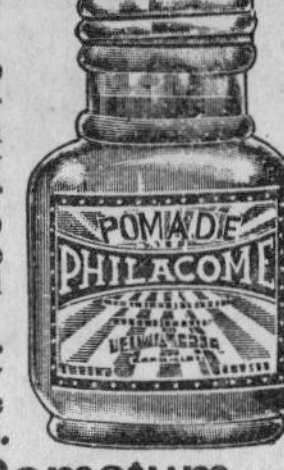

An exquisite dressing for the hair and mustache, nicely perfumed, and highest quality, in 2-ounce, large mouthed screw top bottle, very convenient for making application. This pomade is far superior to any other pomade usually retailing for 25 cents and even 50 cents per bottle.

No. 8R1162 Pomade Philacome. Our special price, 2-ounce screw top bottles, each..................16c
If by mail, postage extra, 5 cents.

Olive Wax Pomatum.

For fixing and laying the hair, whiskers and mustaches. Highly perfumed, each stick wrapped in tin foil.

No. 8R1165 Price, per stick.......7c
If by mail, postage extra, each, 1 cent.

French Cosmetique.

Wrapped in foil; black, pink or white. Retail price, 10 cents.

No. 8R1168 Price, per stick........5c
If by mail, postage extra, each, 1 cent.

Hair Curling Fluid.

This preparation will keep the hair in curl during the dampest or warmest weather; quite harmless to the hair; directions on each bottle.

No. 8R1171 Price, per bottle..15c
If by mail, postage and tube extra, per bottle, 16 cents.

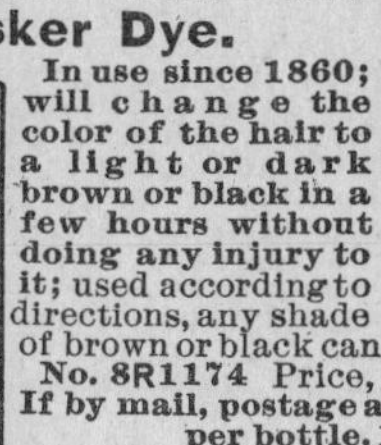

Old Reliable Hair and Whisker Dye.

In use since 1860; **will change the color of the hair to a light or dark brown or black in a few hours without doing any injury to** it; used according to directions, any shade of brown or black can be obtained.

No. 8R1174 Price, per bottle.38c
If by mail, postage and tube extra, per bottle, 16c.

Blondine.

The Famous Hair Bleach. This is a perfectly harmless preparation that will gradually turn the hair from any color to a beautiful blonde color. Any shade of color can be obtained, from light brown to golden by following the simple instructions which go with each bottle. We guarantee that no harm to the hair will result in using it, but rather it is cleansing and strengthening.

No. 8R1177 Price, small trial size bottle, each.................42c
Price, large bottle, each.......70c
If by mail, postage and tube extra, small, 16 cents; large, unmailable on acount of weight.

Shampoo Paste.

Removes dandruff, leaves the hair soft and keeps the scalp in a healthy condition; produces the finest foam, is the most economical shampoo and is unexcelled as a cleanser.

No. 8R1180 Price per small jar..........15c
Price, per large jar (50-cent size)..........................25c
If by mail, postage extra, each, small, 8 cents; large, unmailable on account of weight.

Petroleum Pomade Perfumed.

This is an excellent toilet article for chapped or rough skin, blotches, pimples. Also as a salve for sore lips. As a hair dressing it is much superior to the old style pomades and hair oils.

No. 8R1183 Price, per bottle..13c
If by mail, postage extra, per bottle, 8 cents.

Brilliantine.

An Imported French Hair Oil for making the hair soft and glossy. Gentlemen use it with advantage on the mustache to keep the hair in place and make it glossy.

No. 8R1186 Price, per bottle.....18c
If by mail, postage and tube extra, each, 15 cents.

Danderot.

The Great Scalp Cleaner and Tonic. Permanently cures dandruff, eczema, itching, hair falling out, humors, and all troubles of the scalp and hair. Will positively clear the scalp from dandruff and render it healthy, promoting the growth of the hair. It is recommended to ladies who desire long, glossy hair It keeps the hair soft and glossy; prevents baldness; makes the hair grow stronger.

No. 8R1189 Price, per bottle.. ....42c
Unmailable, on account weight.

Hair Elixir.

A beautiful dressing for the hair, making it soft and glossy; prevents it from splitting and falling out. Cures dandruff and makes the hair grow. **Our Hair Elixir is used and recommended by every professional hair dresser in large cities.** It is the only safe hair preserver known, and should be used especially for protecting and promoting a fine growth of hair.

No. 8R1192 Price, per bottle 45c
Unmailable on account of weight.

Eau De Quinine Hair Tonic.

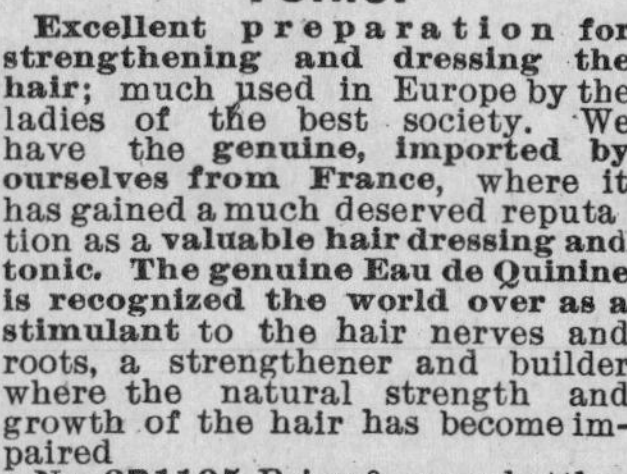

Excellent preparation for strengthening and dressing the hair; much used in Europe by the ladies of the best society. We have the **genuine, imported by ourselves from France,** where it has gained a much deserved reputation as a **valuable hair dressing and tonic. The genuine Eau de Quinine is recognized the world over as a stimulant** to the hair nerves and roots, a strengthener and builder where the natural strength and growth of the hair has become impaired

No. 8R1195 Price, 8-ounce bottles, 35c; 4-ounce bottles..............22c
If by mail, postage and tube extra, small, 16 cents; large, unmailable on account of weight.

TOOTH BRUSHES AND TOOTH PREPARATIONS.

Oriental Liquid Dentifrice.

The most perfect preparation for the teeth. Will keep them entirely **free from stains or discolorations.** It will effectually remove the tartar, hardens the gums and keeps the teeth as lovely as pearls, leaving a delicious after taste in the mouth for hours.

No. 8R1198 Per bottle..15c
If by mail, postage and tube extra, 12 cents

Pearl Tooth Powder.

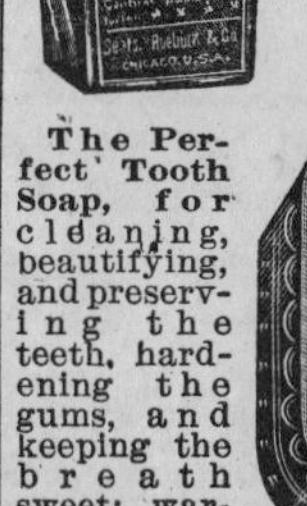

For the teeth. An excellent powder for cleansing, whitening and preserving the teeth. Will remove tartar and prevent decay. Contains nothing injurious. **Pearl Tooth Powder is today used in the homes of every up to date dentist,** and is highly recommended by the Dental Association as the best tooth powder. You could not get a better tooth powder at any price.

No. 8R1204 Price, per bottle..15c
If by mail, postage extra, each, 4 cents.

Sanitary Tooth Soap.

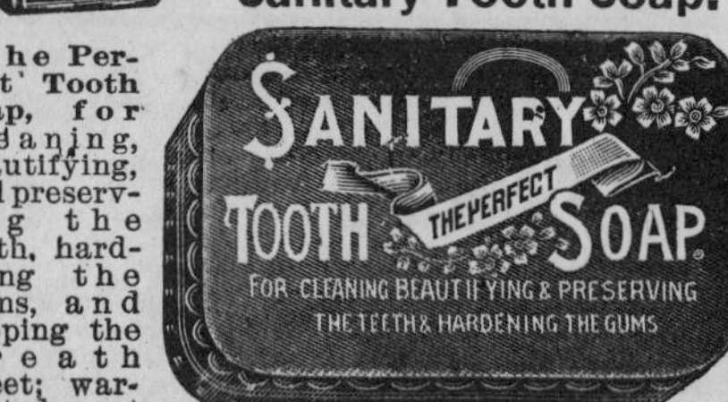

The Perfect Tooth Soap, for cleaning, beautifying, and preserving the teeth, hardening the gums, and keeping the breath sweet; warranted not injurious; in metallic box. Retail price, 25 cents.

No. 8R1207 Price, per box........................12c
If by mail, postage extra, 3 cents.

Dr. Lyon's Sanative Tooth Paste.

This well known tooth paste is without question the finest preparation furnished in metal tubes, and whitens, preserves and beautifies the teeth in the most satisfactory and effective manner. The metal tube style is a very convenient way of using a tooth preparation and is favored by many ladies and gentlemen who prefer it to tooth powders and tooth washes.

This splendid preparation is superior to those that always retail at 25 cents.

No. 8R1210 Dr. Lyon's Tooth Paste in tubes. Regular 25-cent size. Price, each......... .....17c

Toothache Wax.

For the cure of toothache. Easy to apply and gives almost instant relief. It is only necessary to break a small piece off and press it into the decayed part of the tooth.

No. 8R1211 Price, per vial.......................9c
If by mail, postage extra, each, 1 cent.

Tooth Brushes.

If by mail, postage on tooth brushes. extra, 2 cents.

No. 8R1213 A small White Bristle Tooth Brush, white handle. Price, each..................3c

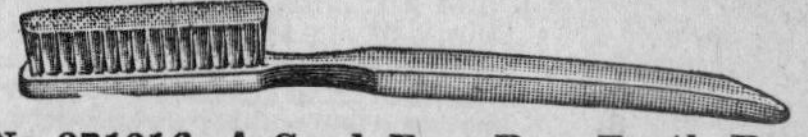

No. 8R1216 A Good Four-Row Tooth Brush, good bristles, nice white handle. Price, each......4c

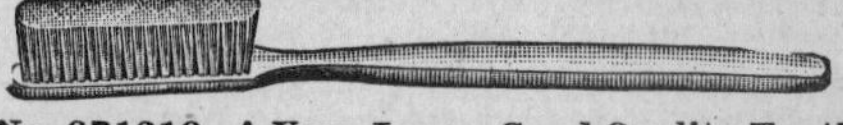

No. 8R1219 A Very Large, Good Quality Tooth Brush, pure white French bristles worth 20 cents, and usually sold at that price. Price, each............8c

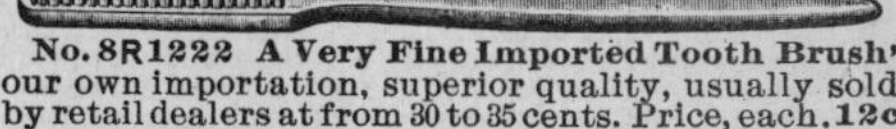

No. 8R1222 A Very Fine Imported Tooth Brush' our own importation, superior quality, usually sold by retail dealers at from 30 to 35 cents. Price, each..12c

No. 8R1225 This is one of the finest imported Tooth Brushes to be had, finest French imported bristles. Especially suitable for ladies.
Price, each..19c

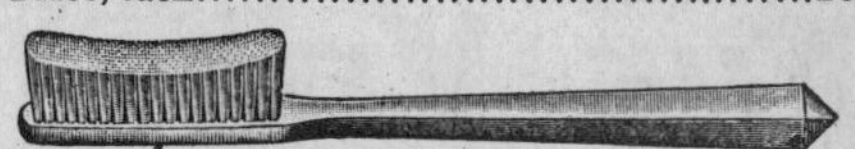

No. 8R1227 The highest grade of fine, imported French Tooth Brushes, four row, extra quality, new style, square handle.
Price, each...25c

No. 8R1228 Florence Dental Plate Tooth Brushes for cleaning artificial teeth. Each......24c

Nail Brushes.

No. 8R1231 Extra Fine Nail Brush, four rows of imported bristles, white bone handle; a brush that druggists and retail dealers usually ask 15 cents for.
Price, each.. 7c

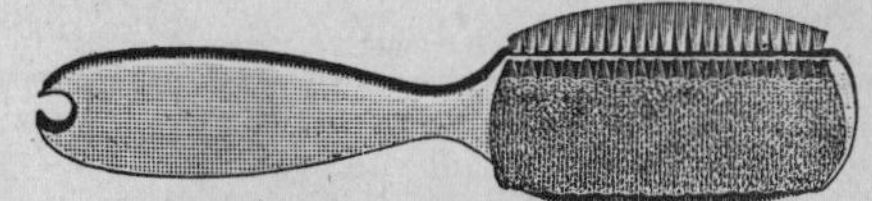

No. 8R1234 A very fine eight-row, Winged Nail Brush with nail cleaner and scourer; dealers ask 50 cents for brushes of this quality. Price, each..24c

Ear Cleaner.

Improved Ear Cleaner, spoon and ear sponge combined. A very useful and pretty little ivory toilet article.

No. 8R1237 Price, each. 10c
If by mail, postage extra, each, 1 cent.

SOLD UNDER OUR PERSONAL GUARANTEE

THE NEW IMPROVED RATIONAL BODY BRACE.

The Highest Grade, Most Perfect Woman's Brace for only $3.35. Guaranteed to be Not Only Equal, but Far Superior to Any Other Body Brace, Regardless of the Price at which they are Sold.

DO NOT PAY $8.00, $10.00 OR $12.00 for an inferior body brace when you can obtain from us the New Improved Rational Body Brace for only $3.35, guaranteed to render equal and better service than any other body brace, no matter what price you would be willing to pay for the same. You will never know what a Rational Body Brace means to a woman, as regards her comfort, general health and well-feeling, until you possess one of these genuine new improved Rational Body Braces, the greatest boon to weak, suffering womankind.

A WOMAN'S GENERAL HEALTH, strength, grace, erectness and beauty of form are regained and retained by wearing a properly adjusted Rational Body Brace. It will, in the most natural and always successful manner, cure the complaints of women. It will meet and remove the cause of weaknesses and organic displacements by applying its strengthening influence and natural support to parts of the body where it is most needed.

THE FRONT PAD and abdominal supporter are made of specially prepared scientifically and correctly tempered brass plates, which makes them pliable and strong. They quickly adjust themselves, and fit all figures. Every abdominal pad is leather covered and finely finished. The springs used in this brace are silver plated and welded, the recently discovered Bessemer process being employed for this purpose, which makes them practically indestructible. Four hard rubber pads form a joint attachment to these springs, arranged in a manner so as to make the hips the main part upon which the supporting power of the New Improved Rational Brace rests, thus relieving the weakened internal organs, muscles and nerves from all unnatural strain. The effect is an immediate feeling of relief to the wearer, followed by regular and natural functions of every organ of the body involved.

THE IMPROVED RATIONAL BODY BRACE is highly recommended by physicians for all persons suffering from general weakness, to persons whose shoulders droop and whose posture is neither natural nor correct. It is the proper and only comfortable brace for fat people. A large abdomen is often reduced a few inches per month as a result of relief afforded by the brace to the stretched and overloaded muscles.

IT IS THE ONLY APPLIANCE that should be used by women troubled with falling of the womb or other irregularities of the female organism, including unnatural discharges, painful, delayed or profuse menstruation; also for all affections of the bladder. For the removal of pains in the shoulder, backache, headache, pains in the chest and weakness of the lower limbs nothing will equal it.

THE IMPROVED RATIONAL BODY BRACE is an abdominal supporter and shoulder brace combined, constructed so as to form a natural support to every organ of the body, including the spine, ribs, lungs, heart, liver, bowels, womb; in fact every organ, bone and muscle of the human body. The supporting, strengthening and healing influence of the Rational Body Brace has never been approached by any other appliance. It assures to the wearer comfort, vigor, health, elasticity, ease, all of the utmost importance to women subject to physical changes, in all conditions and in every walk in life. The Improved Rational Body Brace is made of specially prepared material and is adjustable, thus always insuring a perfect fit. The upper portion of belt and shoulder pads consists of strong elastic webbing. The lower belt is non-elastic and as a result you will find in this appliance perfect support, yet absolute freedom for every movement of the body.

WHITE MATERIAL is used throughout, which can easily be laundered and kept clean and in a sanitary condition. Every part of the belt and straps is treated by a special process, so as to reduce absorption of perspiration to a minimum.

YOU CAN WEAR the Improved Rational Body Brace to suit your own convenience and as you may prefer, either under a corset, over vest, under closed drawers, over open drawers. The adjustable features of this brace makes it possible to wear the same appliance at all times; whether before or after confinement will make no difference.

WOMEN SHOULD NOT under any circumstances cease wearing the genuine newly improved Rational Body Brace before and after confinement. It will not only support them better than anything else, but will preserve their figure and, what is still more important, it may be the means of saving their life.

HOW TO ORDER. Take measure over vest and drawers; state size around body about two inches below tops of hip bones. Mention if extra large adjustment is desired, giving height and weight at the same time.

No. 8R1245 The Improved Rational Body Brace complete, only **$3.35**
If by mail, postage extra, 25 cents.

Every Rational Body Brace is Furnished by Us Under Our Personal Guarantee.

THE VENUS OR SANITARY PROTECTOR.

NOW ONLY 47c EACH! No woman who values comfort, cleanliness and health should be without it. The only practical protector. Perfect in fit. Safe in use.

THE ENORMOUS SALE of this grand protector has enabled us to manufacture it in such immensely large quantities, to reduce the cost of production to such an extent, that we are today in a position to offer this valuable appliance for the never heard of low price of 47 cents each.

THE VENUS PROTECTOR is made of a transparent India rubber sack which is very silky, soft and pliable and also very strong. This sack readily admits a napkin or any other soft substance like cheesecloth or cotton, and will hold it securely in the proper position. The belt is made of the very best lisle, non-elastic. The strap to which the sack is buckled is made of a superior grade of lisle elastic, which gives with the different movements of the body, thus keeping the protector always in the right place.

THE VENUS OR SANITARY PROTECTOR will save many times its cost in washing and bleaching. It is absolutely waterproof and thereby positively prevents soiling of the underwear. Each protector comes put up in a neatly finished box with full and explicit directions. With proper use will last a lifetime. After use each month all that is necessary is to clean it with a damp cloth or sponge. In ordering give waist measure.

POINTS OF EXCELLENCE in the Venus or Sanitary Protector. It is perfectly sanitary, comfortable, pliable and non-irritating; easily adjusted and readjusted, and indispensable to women walking, riding or traveling. Always clean and ready for use. Feels cool in summer and protects the wearer from cold in inclement weather. Retail price of the Venus or Sanitary Protector, $1.50 each.

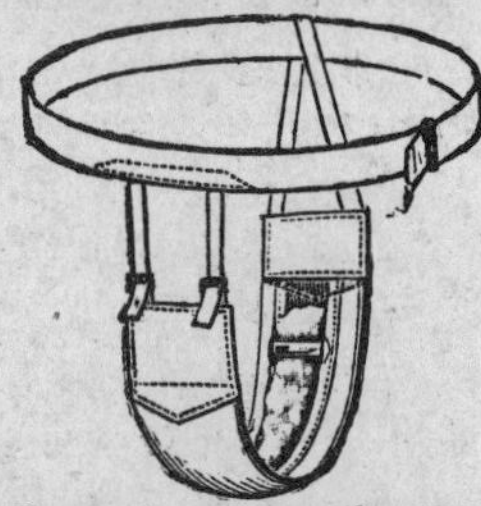

Engraving shows the napkin in place, ready for use.

No. 8R1250 Our special price, each...47c
If by mail, postage extra, each, 3 cents.

Absorbing Pads or Napkins for the protector, made of especially prepared muslin and medicated cotton.
No. 8R1252 Price, per dozen..............................25c
If by mail, postage extra, 6 cents.

A bottle of Sanitive Wash in concentrated form, sufficient for six months' supply, put up especially to be used in connection with the celebrated Venus or Sanitary Protector.
No. 8R1253 Sanitive Wash. Our special price, per bottle..............................20c
Unmailable on account of weight.

LADYLINE ANTISEPTIC SUPPOSITORIES.

THE NEVER FAILING LOCAL TREATMENT for the cure of inflammation, congestion and falling of the womb, antiversion, retroversion and prolapsus, dropsy of the womb, ulceration, polypus, tumor, leucorrhœa (whites), profuse, difficult and delayed menstruation, ovarian tumors, fibroid tumors, inflammation and congestion of the ovaries, and cancers in the early stages. The Ladyline Antiseptic Suppositories are soothing, healing, curing.

Retail Price, $1.50 to $2.00.

No. 8R1255 Our price, regular sized box, containing full month's treatment, only..................60c
Additional information and explicit instructions will be sent with each box.
If by mail, postage extra, 3 cents.

DEPARTMENT OF TRUSSES.

IMPORTANT REDUCTION IN TRUSS PRICES.

HAVING COMPLETED OUR NEW TRUSS FACTORY and employing the most expert operators in producing these appliances, we are today not only in a position to place at the disposal of our customers the finest grades, the most substantial made trusses, but in addition by installing many saving devices and the latest improved machinery for the manufacture of trusses, it has given us an opportunity to still further reduce our already very low prices on nearly every style of our trusses. **We can now sell our trusses at lower prices than others can manufacture them, ours being always superior in quality, finish and workmanship. Being made by expert truss operators, we can always guarantee a perfect fit and comfortable appliances.**

WE MAKE A SPECIALTY OF FITTING TRUSSES and are prepared to offer to our customers unusual advantages in these goods. We employ only expert and thoroughly competent truss manufacturers, and we guarantee to send to any of our customers a perfectly fitting truss that will give satisfaction. A most important point is that we will save you from one to two hundred per cent on any truss you purchase. **You take no risk in sending to us for a truss.** You can try on our trusses, and unless you are satisfied, both as regards quality, comfort in wearing it, and saving in money, you need not keep it.

ELASTIC BANDS Fine steel spring, covered either with silk, Russia leather or hard rubber, nickel plated trimmings, and soft, hard or water pads, every part the finest that can be procured, and workmanship unexcelled. We ask you to select which ever style in your judgment you deem most suitable for your case and give it a trial. We are confident concerning the result.

DON'T PAY YOUR DOCTOR A LARGE COMMISSION to procure for you a truss. We can fit you equally as well and save you many dollars.

DO NOT PAY YOUR DRUGGIST FROM $10.00 TO $25.00 FOR A TRUSS when for one-third the money we can furnish you a better one.

HOW TO ORDER State your height and weight, how long you have been ruptured, whether rupture is large or small, also state number of inches around the body on a line with the rupture, say whether rupture is on right or left side, or both. SELECT TRUSS WANTED BY NUMBER.

Fine Elastic Trusses.

For 98 cents we offer a Truss the equal of any Truss you can buy for $5.00.

OUR PRICES on trusses are based on the actual cost to produce with but our one small percentage of profit added, and we guarantee to save you fully one-half on any truss you order from us.

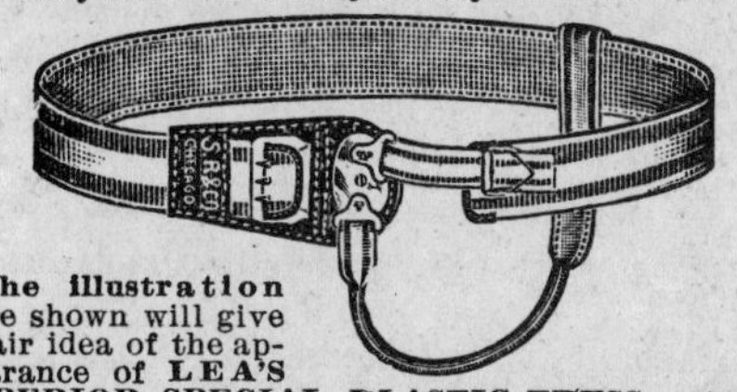

The illustration here shown will give a fair idea of the appearance of **LEA'S SUPERIOR SPECIAL ELASTIC TRUSS**, a truss whose superior qualities are acknowledged by the leading physicians and surgeons both in this country and abroad. **This truss has the highest grade belt, made of finest quality of heavy elastic**, the choicest elastic made. The belt possesses the additional feature that it can be taken off and lengthened or shortened as desired. It is fitted with **improved safety clutch fastenings**, complete with the **CELEBRATED WATER PAD**, acknowledged **the best pad in the world.** Some physicians of note claim for it that it will cure hernia when worn constantly. This truss is made for adults only, and can be had either **single or double, as desired.** The illustration shows the single truss. When ordering the single truss, customers must state whether it is wanted for **right or left side.**

No. 8R1300 Adults' size, single.............. $0.98
No. 8R1301 Adults' size, double.............. 1.75
If by mail, postage extra, 20 cents.

$2.45 Buys a $7.00 Truss.

Drug Stores and Specialty Truss Manufacturers would Charge you at least $7.00 for this kind of a Truss.

A Genuine Lever Elastic Truss, as shown in illustration, is **manufactured especially for us, and the genuine superiority of the truss is unquestioned.** We have yet to learn of one which has not given the very highest satisfaction; in fact, **customers who have used Our Lever Elastic Truss** would not use another of any description, no matter how expensively made. One very valuable feature of this truss is the fact that by means of the lever appliance **extra pressure may be obtained in cases of severe rupture.** There is no more comfortable Truss made. The belt is two inches wide, and is made of the very best of **heavy silk elastic webbing, with solid leather facings and brass trimmings.** This special high grade truss can be used either **single or double**, and will be sent with **two fine enamel finished pads.** Large size only.

No. 8R1307 Adults' size, with two pads..... $2.45
If by mail, postage extra, 20 cents.

A Jumbo Scrotal Truss for Only $2.15.

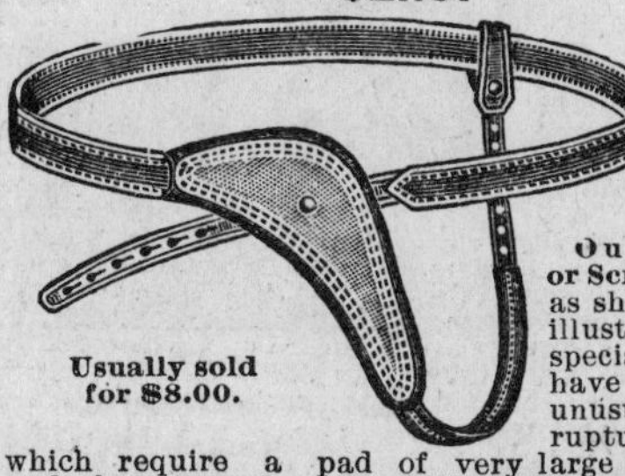

Usually sold for $8.00.

Our Jumbo or Scrotal Truss as shown in the illustration, is a special truss we have made for unusual cases of rupture, cases which require a pad of very large size. **The pad is covered with soft kid**, and is held firmly in place by means of an under strap as shown in illustration. **The belt is covered with Russia leather**, and is very easy and comfortable. **Such a truss will seldom or never sell at less than $8.00**, and we guarantee not only to save you money, but to give you the **best value you ever saw in a really high grade truss, one that will give perfect satisfaction or we will refund money.** Made only in adults' size, either **single or double.** When ordering the single truss, always say **whether for right or left side.**

No. 8R1310 Adults' size, single.............. $2.15
No. 8R1311 Adults' size, double 4.25
If by mail, postage extra, 20 cents.

45 Cents Buys a $2.50 Truss.

45c is the Lowest Price ever made on a Truss of this Style and Quality.

OUR TRUSSES are made by one of the best makers in America, such goods as you can get only from the most reliable establishments at fancy prices.

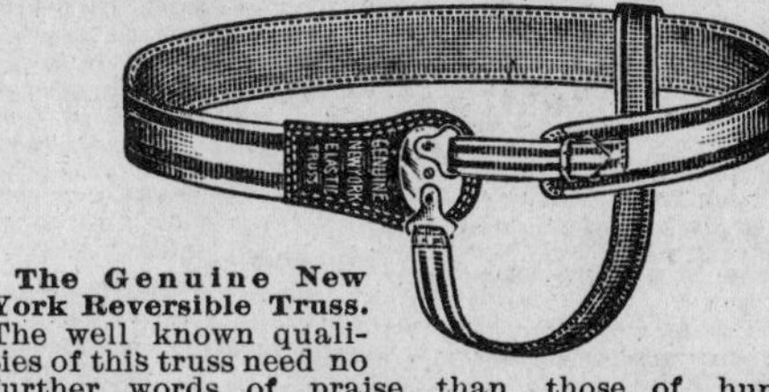

The Genuine New York Reversible Truss. The well known qualities of this truss need no further words of praise than those of hundreds who are today using it with the **greatest satisfaction and comfort.** The belt is 1¼ inches wide and is made of **extra heavy elastic web of the very best quality. Fitted with nickel fastenings, with solid fronts and fine enamel pad.** The illustration will give you some idea of the appearance of this **high grade truss.** As shown in the cut we furnish it in either **single or double, as needed.** The single truss is made for either right or left side, and in ordering **customers must be sure to state for which side. Remember, our New York Truss has the best improved safety clutch fastenings,** the most reliable fastenings made. Furnished in large size for adults or small size for children. **Compare our prices with any other trusses made of equal or inferior quality.**

No. 8R1314 Our N.Y. Truss for adults, single..45c
No. 8R1315 Our N.Y. Truss for adults, doub....98c
No. 8R1316 Our N. Y. Truss for children, single...44c
No. 8R1317 Our N. Y. Truss for children, double...96c
If by mail, postage extra, 20 cents.

SUPERIOR SPRING TRUSSES.

Improved Chase Reversible Truss, $1.32.

Would Cost You Twice as Much at Retail.

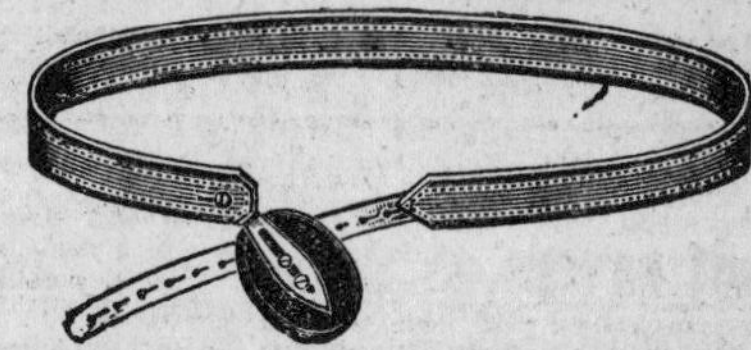

We endeavor to give you some idea of the appearance of our **High Grade Improved Chase Reversible Truss.** This truss is so constructed that it may be worn either right or left. **The extra strong spring steel belt is silk covered**, and is not only unusually lasting, but it is very easy and comfortable, yielding readily to the motion of the body. The joint neck permits the pad to be **adjusted readily as desired. Fine extension enamel pad.** Made large or small for adults or children. For adults it can be made either **single or double.**

No. 8R1322 Adults' size, single............ $1.32
No. 8R1323 Adults' size, double 2.05
No. 8R1324 Child's size, single............ 1.30
If by mail, postage extra, 20 cents.

Fine French Truss.

Extra Light Weight, Special Value.

Single.

The illustrations will give you a very good idea of the appearance and construction of our **fine French Trusses.** We show the single and double for adults, and single for children. This truss is positively the lightest weight made.

Double.

The belt proper is made of the very **best spring steel** covered with **best Russia leather.** The cushion pads are covered with fine soft kid. It is an easy fitting truss and usually gives satisfaction. The regular price of this truss in retail stores is **$5.00.** In ordering always be sure to give the measurement correctly and state what side the rupture is on.

No. 8R1330 Adults' size, single............ $1.85
No. 8R1331 Adults' size, double............ 3.70
No. 8R1332 Child's size, single............ 1.25
No. 8R1333 Child's size, double............ 2.70
If by mail, postage extra, 20 cents.

High Grade Improved French Truss.

A $6.00 Truss for $1.45.

Remember, We Make a Specialty of Fitting Trusses.

Our High Grade Improved French Truss is a special make, manufactured by us, and possesses many features that will commend themselves to the careful buyer. The belt is of the **very finest spring steel**, covered with leather, easy and comfortable. **The pad is adjustable**, and can be extended and placed exactly in the proper position. **Kid covered cushion pad, not reversible.** You can get a fair idea of the appearance of this **Special Improved French Truss** from the picture. The use of this truss by thousands of satisfied purchasers is sufficient guarantee of quality and service. **Any truss bought of us and not found entirely satisfactory**, may be returned to us **at our expense**, and we will cheerfully refund your money. Made only in large size for adults. In ordering single truss, always say whether for **right or left side.**

No. 8R1337 Our special price, single $1.45
No. 8R1338 Our special price, double 2.80
If by mail, postage extra, 20 cents.

Electric Battery Plasters.

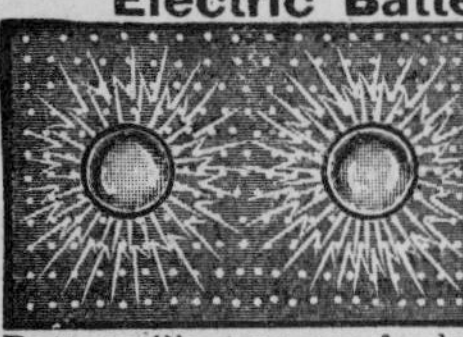

Actual electric current, not mere plates. Positive relief to women from the common and distressing backache incident to the sex at periods; also for rheumatic, kidney and muscular pains in back. These Battery Plasters are for local application only, and should be worn over the region of the pain. They will relieve all pains and weakness that can be reached by an external application of an electric current. If used according to instructions, the battery on this plaster will generate a strong galvanic current, which makes the plaster effective. Besides the tonic effect of the electric current, it stimulates the absorption of the medicament contained in the plaster.

No. 8R1580 Price, each **40c**

If by mail, postage extra, 3 cents.

Electric Insoles.

A boon to those troubled with poor circulation and cold feet. If the feet are kept warm the body will be less subject to the various complaints arising from colds. **These Electric Insoles** contain the pure polished metals arranged in such a manner that a mild pleasant current is produced along the soles of the feet, which stimulates the blood and keeps it circulating constantly. **They are worn with good results for cold feet, and to keep the feet dry.**

No. 8R1582 Price, per pair........................ **60c**

If by mail, postage extra, 10 cents.

Electric Ring for Rheumatism.

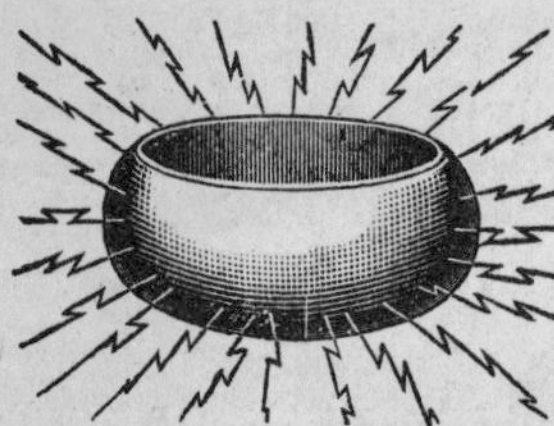

These are the first rings introduced into the United States, all others being imitations. Their popularity has caused many rings to be placed on sale that are without any curative properties.

No. 8R1585 Gray metal, polished. Price, each.. **50c**

No. 8R1588 Gray metal, gold plated on outside. Price each........................ **95c**

If by mail, postage extra, each, 2 cents.

GIVE CATALOGUE NUMBER IN FULL WHEN YOU WRITE YOUR ORDER.

Hypodermic Syringes.

Hypodermic Syringe, nickel plated, with two needles, two vials and extra wire, in neat morocco case.

No. 8R1591 Each.. **$1.00**

If by mail, postage extra, 8 cents.

Hypodermic Syringe, nickel plated, more complete instrument than above, with two needles, four vials, extra wire, etc., in morocco case.

No. 8R1594 Price, each........................ **$1.50**

If by mail, postage extra, 8 cents.

Hypodermic Syringe, best grade, four vials, two needles, extra wire, and washers, in closed end, aluminum pocket case.

No. 8R1597 Price, each........................ **$2.00**

If by mail, postage extra, 8 cents.

Needles reinforced for hypodermic syringes. Assorted sizes.

No. 8R1600 Price, each.......... **23c**

Needles, regular, for Hypodermic Syringes.

No. 8R1602 Each.......... **13c**

Hypodermic Syringe

With Glass Barrel. Protected by a metal cylinder, open both sides, with graduations on piston rod, finger rests same as cut, and cap on end to prevent wearing out of plunge. In fine nickel case with spring cover.

No. 8R1603 Each.... **$2.00**

Postage extra, 12 cents.

Veterinary Hypodermic Syringe and Aspirator.

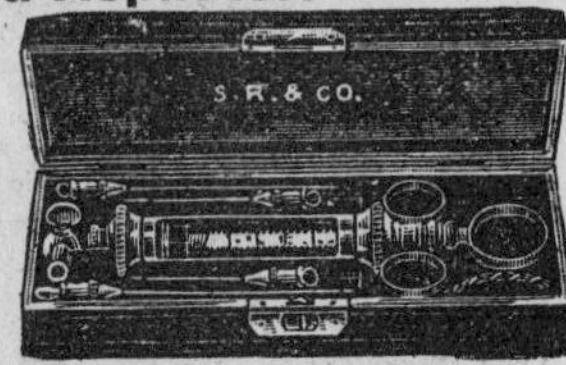

Veterinary Hypodermic Syringe and Aspirator, in pocket case, fitted with three finger rings, adjustable cock, three sizes of needles, trocar and canula.

No. 8R1606 Price, complete... **$2.50**

If by mail, postage extra, 16 cents.

Improved Antitoxin Syringe.

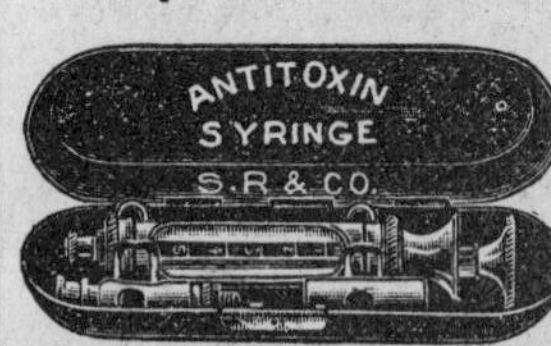

Improved Antitoxin Syringe. The syringe is carefully made according to the latest improvements, every part can be sterilized, the packing is of specially prepared rubber and will not wear out, the plunger is adjustable, is fitted with two needles and coupling.

No. 8R1609 Price........................ **$2.50**

If by mail, postage extra, 16 cents.

Brown's Hoof Ointment.

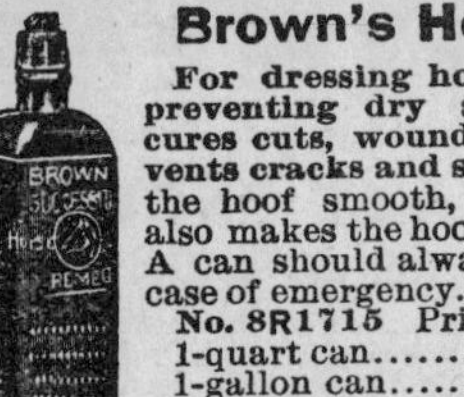

For dressing horses' feet, curing and preventing dry and contracted feet, cures cuts, wounds, sores, bruises, prevents cracks and shelly hoofs, and keeps the hoof smooth, tough and black. It also makes the hoof healthy and polished. A can should always be kept on hand in case of emergency. It saves doctors' bills.

No. 8R1715 Price, 1-pint can.. **$0.60**
1-quart can........................ **1.00**
1-gallon can........................ **3.50**
5-gallon can........................ **13.50**

Unmailable on account of weight.

Milk Oil Sheep Dip.

All sheep should be dipped. Why? Because it pays. In these free wool days undipped sheep won't pay. A good dip improves the wool, strengthens the sheep, prevents attacks of insects. Regular dipping with a good dip improves succeeding clips. Dipping pays if sheep are free from parasites, and when they are suffering from ticks or scab it pays doubly and more noticeably. Can a man, tortured with itch, thrive? No more can a sheep with the lightest touch of scab or if eaten by ticks. **Try our Milk Oil Sheep Dip. It never fails to cure scab or mange, and it is sure death to lice, ticks and fleas.** It is not poisonous. Directions for use on every can. One gallon makes 50 gallons of wash.

No. 8R1718 Price, per gallon........................ **$1.20**
5 gallons........................ **5.00**
10 gallons........................ **9.50**

Unmailable on account of weight.

We also Sell Cooper's Dip.

Which almost every sheep grower knows. The genuine, imported by ourselves.

No. 8R1721

Packet to make............	25 gal.	100 gal.	1,000 gal.
Price, per packet..........	**60c**	**$2.00**	**$16.00**

We will sell you any dip that is on the market and at the lowest possible prices.

Unmailable on account of weight.

Dog Medicines.

Milk Oil Mange Cure.

A reliable cure for mange on dogs. Will keep the skin free from all disease, and the hair soft and glossy. It is not poison and is pleasant to apply.

No. 8R1724 Per pint bottle..... **35c**
Price, per quart bottle............ **50c**

Unmailable on account of weight.

Improved Condition Powder.

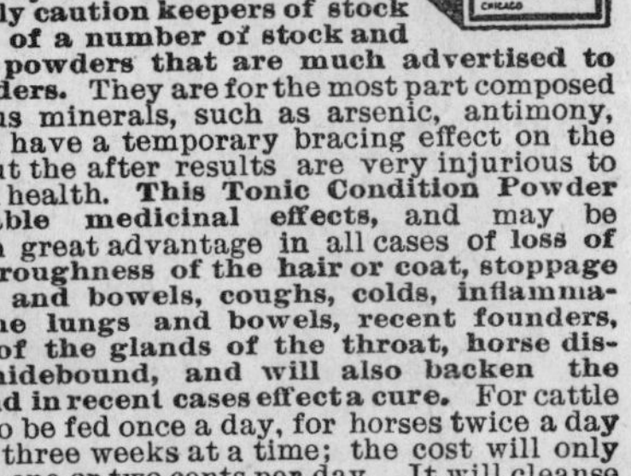

A Valuable Tonic Condition Powder carefully prepared by our veterinary surgeon from health giving, nutritious herbs, seeds, barks and roots. It therefore can be fed to the most delicate animal with perfect safety as a tonic. **We cannot too strongly caution keepers of stock to beware of a number of stock and condition powders that are much advertised to work wonders.** They are for the most part composed of injurious minerals, such as arsenic, antimony, etc., which have a temporary bracing effect on the animal, but the after results are very injurious to its general health. **This Tonic Condition Powder has valuable medicinal effects, and may be given with great advantage in all cases of loss of appetite, roughness of the hair or coat, stoppage of water and bowels, coughs, colds, inflammation of the lungs and bowels, recent founders, swellings of the glands of the throat, horse distemper, hidebound, and will also backen the heaves, and in recent cases effect a cure.** For cattle it ought to be fed once a day, for horses twice a day for two or three weeks at a time; the cost will only amount to one or two cents per day. It will cleanse and cool the blood, sweeten the stomach and bring the animal to a strong and healthy condition.

No. 8R1728 Put up in 1-pound packages... **$0.15**
Put up in 3-pound packages.... **.40**
Put up in 5-pound packages.... **.60**
Put up in 10-pound packages.... **1.00**
Put up in 25-pound packages.... **2.00**
Put up in 50-pound packages.... **3.50**
Put up in 100-pound packages.... **6.00**

VETERINARY DEPARTMENT

...AGRICULTURAL DEPARTMENT...

VETERINARY MEDICINES AND HEALTH FOODS FOR FARMERS AND RAISERS OF STOCK.

KEEP YOUR ANIMALS HEALTHY AND SAVE MONEY AND WORRY.

WE PRESENT TO OUR CUSTOMERS a most valuable and complete line of internal and external remedies and health foods for horses, cattle, sheep, hogs, poultry, dogs, and all domestic animals. These have been carefully selected by our Veterinary Surgeon, and we guarantee them to be the **best preparations of this kind ever offered to the farmer and raiser of stock.** You can thoroughly rely on what we say concerning each of them. **When your animals are sick and out of condition give these remedies a trial.** You will be surprised with the good results. Your animals will soon become well again and feel in better condition than ever. You will find enclosed with each package, **complete instructions how to use these remedies, and also valuable information how to treat sick animals.**

Veterinary Blister.

A Good Blister for Animals is a Rare and Valuable Article.

We have spent much time and made many experiments in preparing a **really practical and thoroughly reliable blister that can be applied easily,** and good results follow. We have submitted samples to the **best veterinary surgeons in the country and they have approved of it,** and are using it daily in their practice. It is unexcelled for **bone spavin, ring bone, splint, curb, bog spavin, blood spavin, thoroughpin, etc. Removes wind puffs, callouses, etc., from kicks and bruises, thickening of tendons, etc.** Full information how to use it and a description of bone spavin, etc., with each package.

No. 8R1700 Price, per box........................ **40c**

If by mail, postage extra, per box, 8 cents.

Veterinary Fever Remedy.

Give in all diseases that are accompanied by fever. Give early in lung fever, pneumonia, bronchitis, pleurisy, laryngitis, sore throat, distemper, cold, etc. **It is a positive cure, if given promptly, in an attack of laminitis, or founder,** and accompanied by hot poultices to the horse's feet, it will remove the congestion and **effect a permanent cure in a few hours.** In case of inflammation of the bowels, given with **Star Crescent Colic Cure,** and hot applications to the belly, gives relief to the patient and **cures the disease in a few hours.**

No. 3R1703 Price, per bottle **40c**

Unmailable on account of weight.

Veterinary Wire Cut Remedy.

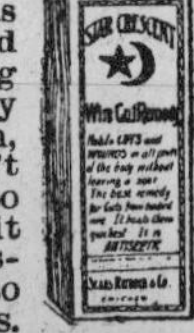

This is a remedy which should always be within reach. It is worth many times its cost when wanted.

It will heal cuts and wounds in all parts of the body without leaving a scar. **It is the best remedy for cuts from barbed wire; it heals them the quickest.** In using this remedy it is not necessary to sew any cuts; if you have a flap that hangs down, fasten it in place by a bandage, **but don't close the sore—give it a free chance to** discharge. By applying this remedy it will soon heal. **It is an antiseptic, destroying all germs and foul odors.** It also preserves the sores from flies and insects.

No. 8R1706 Price, per bottle........ **40c**

Unmailable on account of weight.

Veterinary Eye Water.

Apply to the eye three times a day by dropping three or four or several drops in the ball of the eye. If the eye is red or swollen on the inside of the lids, foment it several times a day with hot water, and keep the animal in a darkened and well ventilated stable. Feed on light and easily digested food, such as bran mash, carrots, etc.

No. 8R1730 Price, per bottle........................ **25c**

If by mail, postage and tube extra, 12 cents.

SEND 15 CENTS

for a year's subscription to our Money Saving Grocery Price List.

Homeopathic Remedies for Farm and Stable.

These remedies cure all diseases of horses, cows, dogs, sheep, poultry and other animals. Many a valuable animal has been saved by the timely use of these specifics. They are easy to give, quick to act, and harmless, always leave the animal in good condition. Full instructions to give the medicine and how to treat the case are inclosed with every bottle.

Single bottle, containing over 50 doses, usual price 50 cents.

No. 8R1769 Our price....................40c

The complete set packed in a neat box, forming a valuable medicine chest, only....................**$3.00**

No. 8R1772 For fevers, chills, congestion, etc.

No. 8R1775 For strangles, glanders, distemper, influenza, quinsy, nasal catarrh, sore throat, etc.

No. 8R1778 For bronchitis, coughs, pleuro-pneumonia, inflammation of lungs, etc.

No. 8R1781 For indigestion, constipation, ill condition, overfed, staggers.

No. 8R1784 For rheumatism, strains, spavin, lameness, etc.

No. 8R1787 For urinary and kidney difficulties, diseases of the bladder, difficult and painful urination, etc.

No. 8R1790 For worms, botts, grubbs, debility.

No. 8R1793 For colic, diarrhœa, dysentery, stomach ache.

No. 8R1796 For mange, grease and skin diseases.

Poultry Foods and Medicines.

We would recommend our customers to buy their poultry remedies only from a firm in whom they have confidence, and who guarantee every article they offer to be exactly as represented. We know our remedies will give satisfaction, they have been used by poultry raisers for years past with the best results. A well fed animal is one that pays. We recommend the following for keeping the fowls **healthy, great egg producers, and fatteners for the market. We will enclose with each order for any of our Poultry Foods, a small book called "POINTERS OR POINTS ON POULTRY RAISING," or will send one by mail to anyone who will send a one cent stamp to pay the postage.**

Brown's Lice Killer.

No disease known to the poultry fraternity can compare in its ravages to that wrought by the numerous family of insects known as "Chicken Lice." From the beginning to the end of the poultryman's career it is a continuous fight against vermin. **We here present to our customers a lice killer which we guarantee to eradicate thoroughly not only the mites and chiggers, but the body lice on fowls, by application to the roosts and nest boxes, this being the simplest** and best method of treating a large number of fowls. All that is necessary is to paint with our lice killer the roosts, roost supports, nest boxes and all cracks or crevices that form a lodging place for the vermin. It is easily applied and does the work thoroughly, killing not only the **lice but also the mites and eggs. For a scaly leg it is invaluable** to the poultryman, as fowls that roost on poles that are occasionally painted with our lice killer will never have a sign of that unsightly disease.

No. 8R1799 Price, 1-gallon cans, 75c; ½-gallon cans....................40c

Paris Green and London Purple.

In Liquid Form.

For spraying all kinds of fruit trees, vines and plants. Sure death to potato bugs, chinch bugs, curculio, canker and cotton worms, etc.

Prompt and pleasing results. Only one trial necessary to convince you. Are much better to handle than the powder and equally effectual when the directions are followed as given on each can. **Be sure and use the liquid and avoid the danger of getting poisoned.** It mingles freely when put with water and never settles. It being a liquid it discharges freely from the nozzle or sprinkler.

Liquid Paris Green.

For spraying all kinds of fruit trees, vines and plants. Is sure death to potato bugs, chinch bugs, curculio, canker worms, etc. One can is sufficientfor 180 gallons of water. Full instructions how to use it on every can.

No. 8R1802 Price, per can..........25c

Liquid London Purple.

For spraying all kinds of fruit trees, vines and plants. Is sure death to potato bugs, chinch bugs, curculio, canker worms, etc. Sufficient for 100 gallons of water. Directions how to use it to the best advantage.

No. 8R1804 Price, per can..........25c

Purple Jack.

Sure death to the worm that eats the head of the cabbage or the fruit of the tomato.

No. 8R1805 Price, per can....................25c

Kerosene Emulsion.

For spraying and washing fruit trees, vines, plants, field crops and domestic animals. Destroys plant lice, red spiders, scales, mealy bugs, lice on cattle and hogs, tick on sheep. One can is sufficient for 50 gallons.

No. 8R1808 Price, per can....................35c

Bordeaux Mixture.

Compounded from the old formula, but by an entirely new process. Prevents blight, rot, mildew and rust. Destroys all fungus growth on vegetation. One can is sufficient to dilute with 35 to 50 gallons of water.

No. 8R1811 Price, per can....................25c

Fleming's Lump Jaw Cure.

HOW IT CURES.—Fleming's Lump Jaw Cure is a liquid that is applied externally. It has remarkable penetrating qualities. Through the local absorbents and minor blood vessels it reaches and destroys every germ. When the germs are destroyed the tumor is dead, and nature proceeds to throw it off as it would any other foreign body. Some may judge that a remedy that will act as quickly as this is apt to be harmful, but instead of this it is absolutely beneficial. It protects the animal, for if a tumor were removed by ordinary methods there would be danger of blood poisoning, but **Fleming's Lump Jaw Cure is a powerful antiseptic and disinfectant.** It kills all poison, it stimulates a healthy growth of tissue, and a large tumor is often removed with not even a scar remaining. Many animals have been cured with our remedy; have passed the most rigid inspection and then been exported. Only one or two applications are usually required to cure when the disease first starts, and two or three applications are needed for cases moderately advanced.

No. 8R1814 Price, per bottle..........**$1.65**

If by mail, postage and tube extra, per bottle, 16c.

Black Leg Vaccine Outfit.

Complete and containing a mortar, pestle, funnel, graduate glass and filter paper to prepare the vaccine, also a fine hypodermic syringe, with needles, etc., to inject same. This outfit will answer all requirements for the use of the vaccine distributed by the government or any other vaccine in powder form. The syringe is graduated for doses, and is complete and furnished alone or with extra needles if desired. The outfit is put up in a neat polished hardwood case. Size, 7x6x4 inches. Weight, 4 pounds.

No. 8R1817 Complete vaccine outfit.......**$3.75**

No. 8R1820 Syringe only..........**2.50**

Pasteur's Black Leg Vaccine in Powder Form.

To be used in connection with the above outfit. Can be furnished in two kinds, No. 1 requiring only one application; No. 2, two applications. No. 1 is naturally the most convenient and most desirable, but No. 2, which consists of a double application vaccine, first lymph and second lymph, is the best and more generally used.

No. 8R1823 Pasteur Single Black Leg Vaccine, one application. Package sufficient for 10 head of cattle 9 months old and upwards, or 12 head less than 9 months old. Price, per package..........**$1.50**

No. 8R1826 Pasteur Double Black Leg Vaccine, two applications. Sufficient for 10 head 12 months old, or about 15 head between 6 and 12 months old. Price, per package..........**$2.00**

Black Leg Cord Vaccine.

This vaccine cord is ready for use and is administered in one application, requiring no syringe, only a needle being necessary. Complete instructions with each package.

No. 8R1829 Black Leg Cord Vaccine, sufficient for 10 head. Price, per package..........**$1.50**

No. 8R1832 Black Leg Cord Vaccine, sufficient for 20 head. Price, per package..........**$2.50**

No. 8R1835 Black Leg Cord Vaccine, sufficient for 50 head. Price, per package..........**$6.00**

The above prices include one black leg cord needle free of charge. Extra needles supplied at 25c each.

Veterinary Cough Powder.

A sure cure for all coughs, colds, distemper, laryngitis, pneumonia, pleurisy, etc. Full instructions for use with description of the symptoms of distemper on each package.

No. 8R1836 Price, per box..25c

If by mail, postage extra, 12 cents.

Gall Cure.

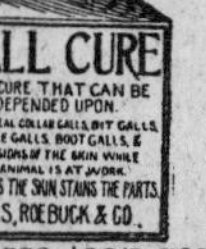

A gall cure that can be depended upon. It will heal collar galls, bit galls, saddle galls, boot galls, and abrasions of the skin, while the animal is at work. Toughens the skin, stains the parts and makes a galled horse look respectable. Quickest cure, most economical and humane treatment.

No. 8R1837 Price, per box....................25c

If by mail, postage extra, 4 cents.

GIVE CATALOGUE NUMBER IN FULL WHEN YOU WRITE YOUR ORDER

Veterinary Instruments.

In veterinary goods we illustrate only a few instruments that are commonly used by everyone owning a horse, but we are in a position to supply anything made in this line, and will quote prices on application.

Wolf Tooth Forceps, bayonet pattern. Length, 13 in. Nickel plated.

No. 8R1838 Price, each....................**$2.65**

Wolf Tooth Forceps, curved, nickel plated. Length, 9 inches.

No. 8R1841 Price, ea...**$2.25**

Small Molar Splinter Forceps, nickel plated. 13 inches.

No. 8R1844 Price, each....................**$2.70**

Straight Incisor Cutters.

No. 8R1847 Price....**$2 70**

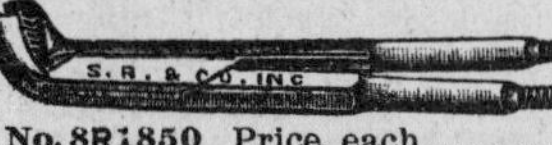

Molar Extracting Forceps. Handle extra.

No. 8R1850 Price, each....................**$5.50**

Open and Closed Molar Cutters. Handles extra. When ordering mention the kind wanted.

No. 8R1853 Price, each....................**$5.50**

Handles for cutters and extractors.

No. 8R1856 Price, per pair....................**$2.50**

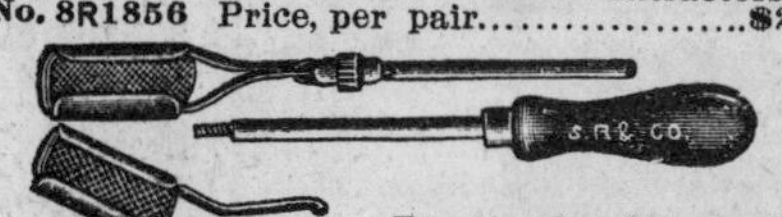

Dunn's Combined Float consists of one straight float for use on the upper and lower molars, and one angular float for use on the first molar teeth, no screws to rust and files cannot drop out.

No. 8R1859 Price, per set....................**$3.50**

Combination Horse Mouth Float.

Jointed, copper plated, fine nickel finish and adjustable. Consists of three pieces straight and angular with two separate files. Can be used for upper and lower molars, also for first molar teeth.

No. 8R1862 Price, per set....................**$2.15**

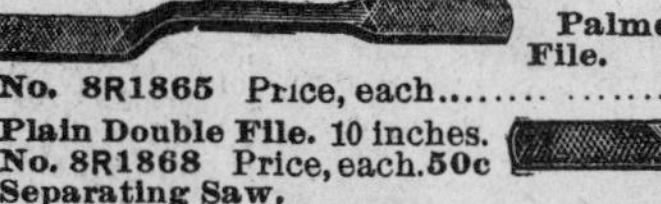

Palmer's Dental File.

No. 8R1865 Price, each....................**$1.00**

Plain Double File. 10 inches.

No. 8R1868 Price, each.**50c**

Separating Saw.

No. 8R1871 Price, each....................**$1.00**

Simmon's Pus Scoops.

No. 8R1874 Price, each.**$1.75**

Balling Iron. Weight, 1¼ lbs; plain.

No. 8R1877 Price, each..........**$0.75**

Nickel plated, 1.25

Castrating Knives.

No. 8R1880 Spring back. Each...**$1.00**

No. 8R1880

Ziegler's Castrating Knife.

No. 8R1883 Ea. **$1.50**

If by mail, postage extra, 4 cents.

Horse Flems. Brass handle.

No. 8R1886 Price, ea., one blade..........35c

Two blades..........50c

Three blades.......70c

If by mail, postage extra, 5 cents.

Spring Lancet.

No. 8R1889 Guarded. Price, each.....**$2.25**

No. 8R1889

If by mail, postage extra, 10 cents.

Seton Needles.

No. 8R1892 Plain, Price, 18-inch. **$1.00**; 12-inch, 90c; 6-inch....**50c**

Seton Needles, jointed.

No. 8R1895 Price, 12-inch, 1 joint..........**$1.50**

18-inch, 2 joints..........**2.00**

If by mail, postage extra, 15 cents.

Fetlock Shears.

No. 8R1898 Price....................**$1.00**

Braided Silk.

No. 8R1901 Four sizes on card; white. Price, per card....................**50c**

SPECIAL DEPARTMENT OF VAPOR BATH CABINETS.

OUR SPECIAL

$2.95 Peerless Vapor Bath Cabinet.

FOR ONLY $2.95 we offer this genuine Peerless Vapor Bath Cabinet as the only good and practical low priced bath cabinet made. We offer the $2.95 Peerless Vapor Bath Cabinet as the equal of cabinets you will find advertised in thousands of papers at $4.00 and $5.00.

THE ILLUSTRATION on the right will give you a good idea of the appearance of our $2.95 Vapor Bath Cabinet in use, but you must try it to appreciate the convenience of the cabinet and the excellent value we are offering. It is made of strong woven goods, impervious to the vapor, as it is rubber lined throughout. It is made of a square galvanized steel frame, regular four-wall room construction, and is not one of the cheap collapsible or crush cabinets which merely rest on the shoulders of the party using them.

WITH EVERY $2.95 VAPOR BATH CABINET we furnish a complete alcohol heater, and vaporizing pan as illustrated. With a small quantity of wood alcohol, which can be purchased at any drug store at a very small expense, to burn in the alcohol heater, and our $2.95 Bath Cabinet, you are in position to take any of the Turkish, Russian, vapor or medicated baths so highly recommended by physicians, and which cost $1.00 or $2.00 in regular bath houses.

WE FURNISH FULL DIRECTIONS and complete formulas how to prepare and take Turkish, Russian, hot air, steam or vapor baths, perfumed or medicated, in your own home with our $2.95 Cabinet, at a cost of less than 3 cents a bath.

THE IMPROVED Peerless Turkish and Vapor Bath Cabinet at $2.95 represents a four walled room, rubber lined, with galvanized steel wire frames, and it will fold into the smallest space of any square folding bath cabinet. The cover material is of the best rubber coated muslin. Size, 28x30½x42 inches. Weight, complete, 11½ pounds.

AS THE LOWEST PRICE HOME BATHING APPLIANCE, our $2.95 Peerless Bath Cabinet is without an equal. While we recommend the purchase of one of our higher priced cabinets, our Peerless is fully guaranteed in every respect, will give entire satisfaction, and is the lowest priced bath cabinet ever offered. Many people go to Hot Springs, Mineral Springs and other health resorts for the purpose of taking the bath.

OUR $2.95 CABINET brings these baths within the reach of the poorest person in the country. With this cabinet you can receive in your own room all the beneficial treatment offered at such health resorts or sanitariums at an expense that is almost nothing. There isn't a man, woman or child that vapor baths will not benefit. Everyone, whether in health or in disease, should use a vapor cabinet bath. It is a perfect and natural way of freeing the skin and tissues of the poisons that clog and injure the system and produce disease. $2.95 is by far the lowest price ever made on a high grade square folding bath cabinet. $2.95 is a price based on the actual producing cost of the cabinet, with the smallest margin of profit added. It is a price much lower than you can buy a good bath cabinet from any other concern, and with the well known benefits from vapor baths, everyone should avail himself of this price without delay.

No. 8R2800 Our Special Price..$2.95

OUR BROWN BATH CABINET No. 2, $5.25

The illustration shows the appearance of the Brown No. 1 and No. 2 Bath Cabinets closed in use.

OUR SPECIAL BROWN CABINET No. 2 is made of the very best material and made on the most scientific principles. It is a cabinet large enough to enable you to take a foot bath while you are taking a Turkish bath. It is made with a hinged door in the side, and while many other cabinets have a door, the whole side must be opened for entrance. The top of the Brown Cabinet No. 2 is in two pieces. The Brown top is a very great convenience in entering as well as in cooling off. The construction of our Brown Cabinet No. 2 is most substantial. The covering is of special cabinet material (rubber coating inside, checked drill outside), that never stretches, thoroughly vapor proof. The frame never weakens. Steel braces are so fitted to every corner that the cabinet when open is a solid and substantial room. In cooling off, both sides of the top may be unbuttoned and thrown back. The whole cabinet is so jointed and hinged it can be put away in the smallest possible space. When you have finished using the cabinet, simply loosen the braces, tip the frame and it folds up completely. Any child can open and close it in a second.

SPECIAL ADVANTAGES OF THE BROWN CABINET. You require no assistant—everything is so simple and convenient. You simply open the door, step in, close the door and you are immediately getting the full benefit of the high temperature. Temperature can be regulated at the will of the bather. Plenty of room in the cabinet to move about, sponge, towel and cool the body perfectly. A five-minute vapor bath in a Brown cabinet starts the millions of skin pores at work expelling the dirt, impurities and poisons from the system, does more good than six months of drug taking. No other cabinet is so simple to operate, to open and close, folds up into such small space; is more convenient, compact, strong, light, roomy, handsome, durable or gives such excellent satisfaction.

We furnish free with our BROWN CABINET No. 2 at $5.25, a supply of vapor preparations for four weekly medicated baths as follows:

A supply of vapor preparations for four weekly medicated baths for the treatment of muscular and chronic rheumatism, eczema, skin diseases, parasites, neuralgia, reducing inflammation.

A supply of vapor preparations for four weekly medicated vapor baths for the treatment of fevers, colds, nervousness, nervous diseases, nervous exhaustion, bronchial congestion, enlargement of the liver, general weakness, debility, bronchitis, pleurisy, inflammation of the air passages, urinary complaints, bronchial and laryngial troubles.

A supply of vapor preparations for four weekly medicated vapor baths for the treatment of influenza, la grippe, sleeplessness, nervousness, hysteria, nausea, spasms, vomiting.

A supply of vapor preparations for four weekly medicated vapor baths for the treatment of constipation, enlarged glands, gastric troubles, congestion of liver and kidneys, jaundice, dyspepsia, tonsilitis, quinsy, irregular menstruation, syphilis, chronic scrofula, profuse perspiration.

No. 8R2810 Our special price, complete with stove and vaporizer..$5.25

Our Highest Grade BROWN BATH CABINET No. 1, $7.95

FOR $7.95 we offer the highest grade bath cabinet of the celebrated Brown make as the very finest and highest grade bath cabinet made. There is no better bath cabinet construction possible.

THE FRAME of the Brown Bath Cabinet is made of the only wood that is serviceable. The wood is kiln dried in a very high degree of heat and especially treated. The frame is guaranteed to stand both dry heat and vapor heat without warping. The cover used on the Brown Cabinet is non-absorbent, germproof, antiseptic and odorless. This material is the result of years of experiment. It is not only perfect for the purpose, but practically lasts forever.

OUR $7.95 BATH CABINET is constructed with double walls of the best rubber coated material that can be made, everlasting and always new. This gives a black rubber coating inside and outside, with air space between. The top is of double faced material, rubber coated both sides and held firmly in place by snap buttons. The construction of our special $7.95 Cabinet is without doubt the best ever shown.

A COLD IS CURED IN ONE NIGHT. Any kind of a cough or cold, throat trouble, affected bronchial tubes, cold on the chest or lungs is effectually cured with one good hot vapor bath taken according to directions. For nervous diseases, nervous debility, nervous prostration, nervous exhaustion, sleeplessness, overworked men and women of all classes, the Brown Bath Cabinet treatment is a grand relief. The vapor both soothes the tired nerves, permits a more vigorous circulation of blood, thus restoring energy to the exhausted system.

No. 8R2815 Our special price..$7.95

FACE STEAMER FREE.

This illustration shows the appearance of the Brown No. 1 and No. 2 Bath Cabinets open.

WE FURNISH FREE with this, our best BROWN BATH CABINET, No. 1, at $7.95, the same supply of vapor preparations for the sixteen baths as given with the $5.25 Cabinet No. 2, and in addition, a complete internal treatment for one month to be used in connection with the bath, covering each of the following complaints:

Cold,
Fevers,
Cough,
Muscular and Chronic Rheumatism,
Influenza,
Grippe,
Muscular Pains and Soreness,
Neuralgia,
Tonsilitis,
General Weakness,
Debility,
Pleurisy and Inflammation of air passages,
General Tonic,
Quinsy,
Malarial Troubles,
Enlarged Spleen,
Constipation,
Dyspepsia,
Enlarged Glands,
Gastric Troubles,
Congestion of Liver and Kidneys,
Jaundice,
Biliousness,
Colic,
Nausea,
Spasms,
Vomiting,
Sick Headache,
Painful Menstruation,
Acute Neuralgia,
Pains in Back,
Nervousness,
Nervous Diseases,
Nervous Exhaustion,
Hysteria,
Sleeplessness,
Asthma,
Weakness,
Heart Troubles,
Dizziness,
Debility,
Palpitation of the Heart,
Swelling of Feet or Hands,
Eczema,
Skin Diseases,
Parasites,
Scrofula,
Stimulating Skin and Kidneys,
Syphilis,
Reducing Inflammation,
Gonorrhœa,
Gleet,
Kidney and Urinary Troubes.

VAPOR BATHS are great for blood and skin diseases. For the relief and cure of scrofula, eczema, salt rheum, hives, pimples, ulcers, boils, carbuncles, barbers' itch, oily skin, poor complexion or the hundred other evidences of bad blood and skin imperfections, vapor baths are simply wonderful. For rheumatism and neuralgia, chronic, acute or inflammatory, our vapor baths have been known to cure where everything else had failed to give relief.

AT OUR SPECIAL $7.95 PRICE we furnish this No. 1 Brown Cabinet complete with face steaming attachment, complete with alcohol stove and vaporizer and complete instructions and formulas how to prepare and take any kind of a Turkish or vapor bath.

Department of ELECTRIC BELTS.

SEND for our completely illustrated, confidential, free, electric belt catalogue with most complete descriptions of the different Heidelberg Electric Belts, the disorders for which they are recommended and testimonials from the cured. . . . .

TEN DAYS' WEARING TRIAL FREE. While we are compelled to ask cash with your order, we still allow you ten days' wearing trial free. Select the belt you want, give us the number of inches around body at waist, and we will send the belt to you by express. There will be nothing on the package to indicate its contents. You can take the belt home and wear it, give it a thorough trial, and if it does not give you the relief you expect, if you have any reason to believe that the belt will not effect a speedy and permanent cure, pack the belt back in the same plain box in which it came, return it to us within 10 days and we will return your money.

TEN DAYS' FREE TRIAL gives you every chance to see, examine and try the belt, and satisfy yourself that the Heidelberg Electric Belt will do more for you than any electric belt made. Will cure you by the wonderful aid of electricity where every other means have failed.

THE GENUINE HEIDELBERG Alternating Current Electric Belt is the only electric belt which has a positive current regulation; the only electric belt in which the current is always completely under the control of the wearer; the only electric belt where the current can be in an instant adjusted from the lightest to the heaviest gauge, where there is positively no danger of an unpleasant shock or too strong a current, even from our

GIANT POWER 80-GAUGE BELT

THE HEIDELBERG combines the good, new and up to date features of all other makes of electric belts, without their drawbacks, defects and discomforts, with exclusive and distinctive advantages not found in other makes. Positively wonderful in its quick cure of all nervous and organic disorders arising from any cause whatever. The nerve building, health giving, vigor restoring current penetrates and permeates every one of the affected parts; every nerve, tissue and fiber responds at once to its healing, vitalizing power.

HEALTH, STRENGTH, SUPERB MANLINESS, YOUTHFUL VIGOR IS THE RESULT . . . . .

OUR SPECIAL inside prices of $4.00, $6.00 $8.00, $12.00 and $18.00 are less than one-half the prices charged by others for inferior belts. Our special prices are made only to cover the cost to the manufacturer, who gives us the exclusive sale of the Heidelberg Belt in America, with but our one small percentage of profit added.

FROM THESE ILLUSTRATIONS and descriptions you can get a good idea of the style, make and effectiveness of the Heidelberg Electric Belts, and you can order a belt from these pages with every assurance of satisfaction; but if you should like to learn more in regard to them, if you want more extended descriptions and a fuller account of the disorders for which electric treatment is especially recommended, **send for our Free Electric Belt Catalogue.** We send free on request a handsomely illustrated booklet, describing all of the Heidelberg Electric Belts in detail, showing just how each part is made, a complete explanation of the nervous and muscular system, and describing the effect of the electric current on the diseases for which the belts are recommended. This confidential booklet will be mailed to anyone on application, and we urge everyone who is interested in the slightest manner, or who has taken drugs or other treatment without success, **to send for our Free Electric Belt Catalogue.**

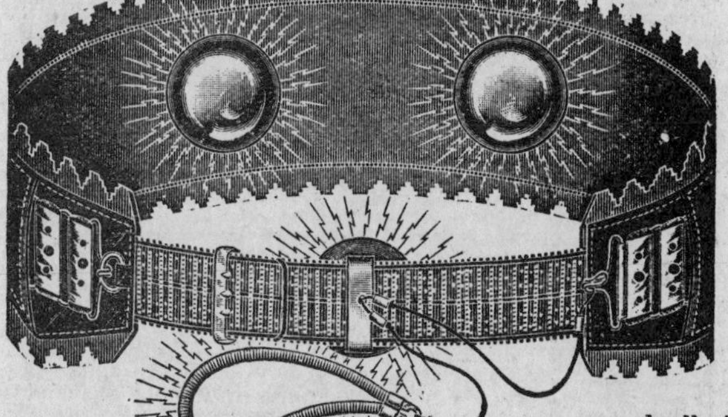

OUR $4.00 PRIMARY HEIDELBERG ELECTRIC BELT.

We furnish the Genuine Heidelberg Electric Belt in 20-Gauge Current for only $4.00.

THE 20-GAUGE CURRENT is just the right strength for the pains in the back, loins and groin, neuralgia, headache, indigestion, kidney complaints and such cases of nervous and sexual exhaustion not too severe or of long standing.

THE $4.00 HEIDELBERG ELECTRIC BELT is superior to the old style galvanic currents, or the intense shocks given by physicians' big electric machines, especially if the nerves are weak or easily upset. The $4.00 belt supplies a mild continuous current, charges every nerve and cell with the vitalizing current, keeps up a regular and vigorous action of all the organs of the body, gives a free and healthy action to all vital functions. Ten days' wear of our $4.00 belt will produce a marked change for the better, thirty days is sufficient to prove its wonderful merit beyond any question or doubt.

DESCRIPTION of our 20-gauge Heidelberg Electric Belt: **Selected materials throughout. Most careful construction in every detail.** Belt proper is made of heavy satin, interlined with light canvas, silk stitched to high finished leather and felt. The satin and canvas forms the outer part of the casing, the leather and felt the inner. **The battery lies between the canvas and the leather.** The fine soft finished felt lies next to the body. Extension straps are made of best selected elastic webbing. Ten cells, each of the celebrated Heidelberg triple construction, form the battery. A 20-gauge maximum current is produced. The battery is of the usual Heidelberg construction, the most concentrated and powerful alternating producing current, very quick in generating power, very lasting.

ALL CONNECTIONS are double soldered and reinforced. Wire connections are fine AA grade copper annealed wire covered with woven insulation, felted ends. Three large electrodes, each 2⅜ inches in diameter, afford the conducting surface and carry the current to parts desired. **The electrodes are movable, admit a ready adjustment.** They are made of a special composition metal, extremely sensitive to the slightest current, silver plated and highly polished.

THE SUSPENSORY is made of best spiral quadruple silver plated wires oval in shape. Has a flat inner surface; very comfortable. The suspensory carries the soothing current direct to the sensitive sexual organism. No medicine, no local treatment can compare in its strengthening effect on these parts with electricity. The Heidelberg Electric Belt saturates these nerves and cells with the vitalizing current. Every disorder and disease peculiar to these organs yields immediately. **Impotency, varicocele, emissions, losses, drains, from any cause, are some of the troubles cured by the $4.00 20-gauge current.** If, however, a stronger current is desired for such troubles in an aggravated form, we urge by all means our **Giant Power 80-gauge Belt at $18.00.**

OUR $4.00 HEIDELBERG ELECTRIC BELT comes complete with stomach attachment and spiral suspensory. The stomach attachment for indigestion, constipation and general debility of the stomach is invaluable. Promotes the digestive organs, tones up the liver and strengthens the assimilative power. Even that terrible disease, cancer of the stomach, has been known to be arrested, to yield to and be cured by the wearing of a genuine Heidelberg Electric Belt.

No. 8R3000 Our 20-gauge Current Belt, complete with stomach attachment and spiral suspensory. Our price........ $4.00
No. 8R3005 Our 30-gauge Current Belt, complete with stomach attachment and spiral suspensory. Our price........ 6.00
No. 8R3010 Our 40-gauge Electric Belt, complete with stomach attachment and spiral suspensory. Our price........ 8.00

OUR $12.00 HEIDELBERG BELT.

$12.00 IS OUR PRICE for this powerful 60-gauge genuine Heidelberg Belt. **Electric Belts equal to our $12.00 15-cell, 60-gauge current Heidelberg,** are being sold by widely advertised doctors at **$40.00 and upwards,** and yet all of these high priced Electric Belts lack the peculiar strengthening curative properties of the Heidelberg Alternating Current Belts. **The Heidelberg Belt seeks the weak, diseased parts at once.** It produces an invigorating current of magnetic and galvanic electricity, **wonderful cure for seminal or vital weakness, nervous debility or impotence, stops almost immediately the unnatural waste or loss of vitality.** The $12.00 Belt has just the power required for cases that are not too aggravated; will help any man or woman suffering from any organic disease no matter of how long standing.

OUR SPECIAL $12.00 HEIDELBERG BELT is one of the simplest Electric Belts made. Has no complicated parts to get out of order. It is easily adjusted, perfect in fit, **most comfortable Electric Belt made.** Self adjusting, no discomfort while worn, easily put on or off, perfectly sanitary; made of high grade materials throughout; will last forever. **Our $12.00 Belt is a result of years of scientific study and experiment,** it is a belt that combines the latest features, comfort and health giving points not to be found in any other make.

GOOD FOR EITHER SEX. Our $12.00 Belt can be worn (without the suspensory attachment), by women and is invaluable for all cases of female weakness. The electric current is a great strengthener, in most cases the only treatment required by women suffering from weakness peculiar to their sex. **Every member of the family can be benefited by the use of a Genuine Heidelberg Belt.** We have instances where one of our Heidelberg Belts has been worn successively by five or six members of one family, all of whom experienced good results. Remember, the belt need not be worn constantly; three or four hours' wear at a time is sufficient.

IF YOU HAVE ANY DOUBTS AS TO THE EFFICACY OF OUR HEIDELBERG ELECTRIC BELTS, let us send you our complete book describing them and explaining the electric treatment in detail. **Our Free Electric Belt Catalogue** contains numberless letters from people who have worn the Heidelberg Electric Belt and realized wonderful benefit from its use. Perhaps among these letters you will find a case similar to your own and may be induced to give the belt a trial, and thus secure the relief you have heretofore looked for in vain.

DON'T FAIL to send for our **FREE Electric Belt Catalogue.**

No. 8R3015 Our 60-gauge Electric Belt. Price........ **$12.00**

OUR

$18.00 Giant Power Heidelberg Electric Belt

Sent on 10 Days' Free Trial

FOR ONLY $18.00 WE OFFER THE GENUINE 80-GAUGE CURRENT HEIDELBERG ALTERNATING, SELF-REGULATING and ADJUSTING ELECTRIC BELT AS THE HIGHEST GRADE, VERY FINEST ELECTRIC BELT EVER MADE, AS THE ONLY SUCCESSFUL ELECTRIC BELT TREATMENT, as the most wonderful relief and cure of all chronic and nervous diseases, all diseases, disorders and weaknesses peculiar to men, NO MATTER FROM WHAT CAUSE OR HOW LONG STANDING.

$18.00 IS OUR LOW PRICE, **based on the actual cost to manufacture, for this highest grade electric belt,** a superior belt to those usually sold at $30.00 to $50.00. **Our $18.00 Giant Power Belt is the result of years of scientific study and experiment,** it is the very highest grade, a belt that has all the best features of other electric belts without their drawbacks, defects and discomforts, with exclusive and distinctive advantages not found in other makes. Positively wonderful in its quick cure of all nervous and organic disorders arising from any cause, whether natural weakness, excesses, indiscretions, etc. The nerve building, health giving, vigor restoring current penetrates and permeates the affected parts; every nerve, tissue and fiber responds at once to its healing, vitalizing power; health, strength, superb manliness, youthful vigor is the result.

OUR GIANT POWER **80-gauge Current Genuine Heidelberg Alternating Electric Belt at $18.00** will do you more good in one week than six months of doctoring. The Heidelberg Electric Belt for disorders of the nerves, stomach, liver and kidneys, for weakness, diseased or debilitated condition of the sexual organs from any cause whatever, is worth all the drugs and chemicals, pills, tablets, washes, injections and other remedies put together. Its strengthening, healing and vitalizing power is magical—never before equaled.

HAVE YOU DOCTORED? **Have you perhaps written to some quack, so called institute or self styled men's physician,** have you tried various so called remedies for your peculiar trouble without success, without getting any help, perhaps not even temporary relief. Perhaps you are discouraged; maybe hopeless. **Don't give up. Don't despair. You may yet be cured.** The Giant Power Heidelberg Electric Belt is just what you need. Just what you should wear. Send for our Giant Power 80-gauge Current Heidelberg Electric Belt at once, wear it according to directions. In a day you will feel a difference, in two days there will be a marked change for the better, in three days you will experience relief, in a week or two weeks your system will be filled with the grand health giving current, in a month **you will be a new man.**

OUR GIANT POWER 80-GAUGE HEIDELBERG ELECTRIC BELT AT $18.00

comes complete with the finest stomach attachment and most perfect, comfortable electric sack suspensory ever produced. The lower illustration shows the style of these attachments, but you must see and examine, wear them, to appreciate the comfort and convenience. The suspensory encircles the organ, carries the vitalizing, soothing current direct to these delicate nerves and fibers, strengthens and enlarges this part in a most wonderful manner. The sack suspensory forms part of the circuit. The electric current must traverse every one of the innumerable nerves and fibers. Every wearing brings the current in contact with the organ; every wearing means that part of the organ is traversed through and through with the strengthening, healing current; means a liveliness imparted, a vigor induced, a tone returned, a joy restored that thousands of dollars' worth of medicine and doctors' prescriptions would never give.

DON'T SUFFER IN SILENCE, **don't endure in secret.** $18.00 will buy our Giant Power 80-Gauge Current Genuine Heidelberg Electric Belt. $18.00 will enable you to face the world anew. $18.00 will bring to you health and strength, vigor, manliness and happiness, a bigger measure for your money, a greater bargain than you could ever possibly secure in any other purchase.

ARE YOU IN DOUBT? **Have you tried so called remedies without avail and fear to take advantage of this great offer?** Do you hesitate because some unreliable firm or doctor took advantage of you? With us you run no possible risk. **Let us send you one of our Genuine Giant Power 80-gauge Heidelberg Electric Belts under the liberal condition of our offer.** We will send you the belt, then after ten days' fair trial if you have any reason to be dissatisfied, if you are not greatly benefited, return the belt to us and we will refund your money.

HOW THE 80-GAUGE HEIDELBERG ELECTRIC BELT IS MADE. **Every $18.00 80-Gauge Electric Belt of the Heidelberg make is the very finest belt that can be manufactured,** made of the highest grade materials money will buy, put together by scientific, skilled mechanics, hand made and finished in every part. The casing for the battery of cells is made of an extra quality very fine selected satin, a grade prepared particularly for this purpose, absolutely non-conducting, lined with a genuine Brighton insulating flannel, and then a layer of close woven non-conducting duck, forming the very best and perfect insulating case possible.

THE BATTERY **In our $18.00 Giant Power Heidelberg Electric Belt we furnish the new and genuine Heidelberg battery,** consisting of triple cells, producing an 80-gauge current. The battery is made of a secret, highly excitable, metal alloy and composition of silver and copper, a combination producing the quickest, most powerful and lasting current. **No battery in any other make can compare in any respect to the Heidelberg.** One cell of a Heidelberg battery, with its distinctive triple construction and special composition, has more strength, produces more current, than two cells of the ordinary **electric belts usually advertised.**

ELECTRODES. **Four large and one extra large (five in all) electrodes secure a fine equal distribution of the current to the** proper organs and affected parts. The electrodes are large size, splendid conducting surface, extra full and finely silver plated. The four electrodes in back are 2 inches across, the front and largest electrode is 5 inches across. Wonderful in its treatment of diseases of the stomach, liver and kidneys. Carries the life giving electric fluid straight to the affected parts. The big current bearing electrodes can be adjusted for any position, any part, any organ, bringing it in the direct route of the current. **For a weak or deranged nervous system the electric treatment has splendid results.** It stops losses, repairs waste, gives tone to every tissue and muscle. The whole body feels the good effect. No words can describe the change in health, feeling, vitality, even character, from the result of wearing a **genuine Heidelberg Giant Power Electric Belt.**

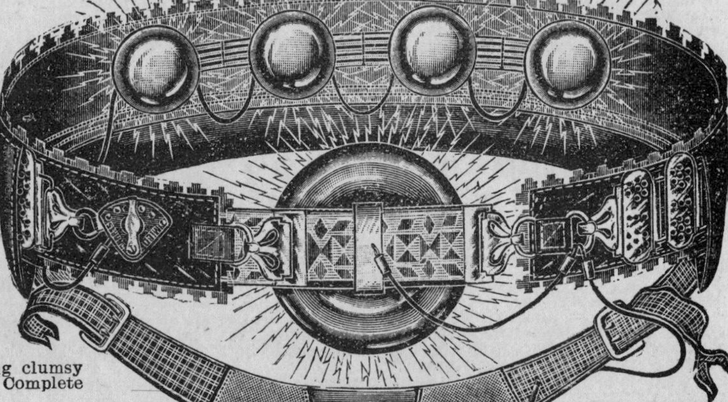

EVERY BELT IS PUT OUT UNDER OUR BINDING GUARANTEE

for more current, more power, more and quicker relief than any belt sold at three times the price. Simple, comfortable, efficient. Nothing clumsy about the belt, nothing uncomfortable. No one can tell if you wear it. Complete instructions for use and wear sent with every belt.

CURRENT REGULATOR. **Every 80-gauge Heidelberg Electric Belt is provided with our own special and perfect current regulator,** a feature imitated (but not successfully) by every electric belt maker in the country. By means of this regulator the current can be instantly adjusted to any strength desired without removing the belt from the body. You can make it mild, medium or strong, just as you like, just as your case requires. No possibility of your receiving an unpleasant shock, no chance to get a current too strong and irritate tender parts. Six different strengths, different degrees of current are possible. A simple movement of a tiny one-inch lever does it. You get just the strength, just the gauge of current required.

THE 80-GAUGE CURRENT **is marvelous, really magical in its power.** Will cure any case, no matter how obstinate, how long standing. Tones up the system, drives out disease, fortifies the body against cold, against sick attacks of any kind. Perfect in its relief and cure of the peculiar diseases of men. For those sexually weak or impotent or suffering from any trouble of the sexual organs the **Giant 80-gauge Belt affords relief when everything else has failed.** The stimulating alternating current forces a vigorous circulation of blood into the seminal glands, enlivening them into a healthy glow. They quickly respond to this infusion of energy, dormant nerves wake up and expand, general circulation is produced, youthful vigor displaces the tired out feeling, natural power returns. In most cases of sexual weakness the full power of this belt is required, but a cure is certain. The 80-gauge current absolutely doubles the sexual force and power.

No. 8R3020 OUR 80-GAUGE CURRENT BELT............$18.00

FOR QUICK RELIEF **for an ultimate speedy cure of all weaknesses, no matter from what cause, nothing can equal, nothing, whether drugs or chemicals, approaches the 80-gauge Heidelberg Alternating Current Electric Belt at $18.00.** The Heidelberg Electric Belt is the best, most reliable, most harmless yet powerful, most efficient and the cheapest cure possible. Don't let a specialist bleed you. Don't pay $25.00, $30.00 or $50.00 for an electric belt not one-half as good as the **Genuine 80-gauge Giant Power Alternating Current Heidelberg Electric Belt at $18.00. Send for one of our $18.00 belts immediately. Throw physic to the dogs. Strengthen and cure yourself at once.**

HARDWARE DEPARTMENT.

OUR HARDWARE DEPARTMENT is one of the strongest in our house. Retail dealers cannot compete with us as the prices we quote are the same as their cost, and in some cases even less.

WE GUARANTEE THE QUALITY of everything offered in this line. You will find every good and reliable maker of hardware represented on these pages, standard goods known everywhere, and we do not handle unreliable or trashy goods at any price.

IF YOU INTEND TO BUY HARDWARE of any kind, if you contemplate building a house, a barn, a granary, or other building, or if you intend to buy tools of any description, do not fail to go over these prices very carefully and compare them with what you would have to pay at home for equal goods. We are sure we can save you 25 per cent to 50 per cent on everything in this line.

FREIGHT RATES ARE LOW ON HARDWARE. Almost everything in hardware can go at third or fourth class rates, especially the heavier goods. Refer to our table of freight rates on pages 7 to 10, and you will see that the freight will amount to next to nothing as compared to the saving in price.

THIS DEPARTMENT has been greatly enlarged within the last few months, and by reason of its rapidly increasing trade this big outlet for goods gives us a still greater purchasing power, and we can show our customers a larger percentage of saving. We reserve the right to refuse orders from dealers.

THE PRICES on a few items quoted in this catalogue are subject to market changes. If there is any reduction in cost, we will give you the benefit; if any advance, we will charge you the difference. This, however, rarely occurs as we fully protect ourselves by contract, and when it does, we make the difference in cost to you the exact difference in cost to us. Our records show that we reduce our prices and refund the difference to our customers ten times where we are compelled to advance the price and charge them more one time.

CUTLERY DEPARTMENT.

TABLE CUTLERY. Our Table Cutlery is made by the most reliable and well known factories in this country. Our goods are the latest and best patterns possible to obtain. They are made of only the best steel, are fully warranted, and the workmanship cannot be excelled. We do not handle inferior grades known as seconds.

PRICE OF KNIVES ONLY. We will furnish KNIVES ONLY in any of the patterns quoted (except as noted). The price of one dozen knives only is 15 cents more than the price of the set of same style knives and forks. Six knives and six forks constitute a set. If by mail, 25 to 40 cents per set extra for postage. Note our reduced prices.

ALL ORDERS WILL BE FILLED AT PRICES PRINTED IN LATEST EDITION OF OUR CATALOGUE.

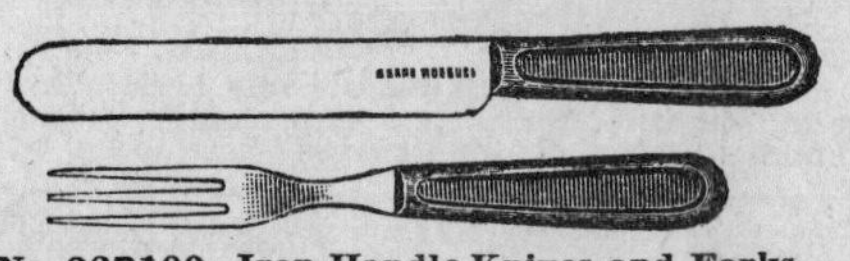

No. 28R100 Iron Handle Knives and Forks. Price, per set, 6 knives and 6 forks..........37c
No. 28R101 Iron Handle Knives only. Per doz. 49c

No. 28R112 Cocobolo Handle Knives and Forks, no bolster. Per set, 6 knives and 6 forks..........38c
No. 28R113 Cocobolo Handle Knives only. Price, per dozen..........50c

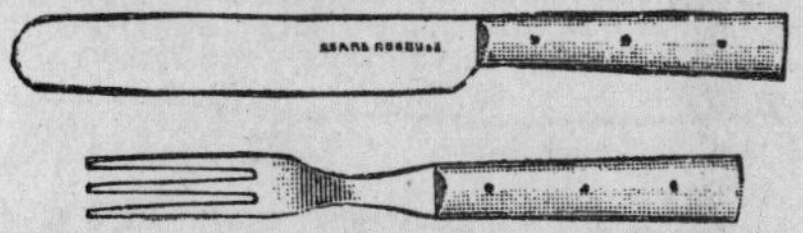

No. 28R114 White Bone Handle Knives and Forks, no bolster. Per set, 6 knives and 6 forks..68c
No. 28R115 White Bone Handle Knives only. Price, per dozen..........80c

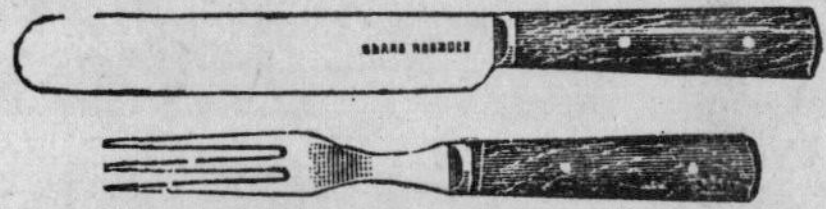

No. 28R125 Cocobolo Handle Knives and Forks, single bolster. Per set, 6 knives and 6 forks......60c
No. 28R126 Ebony Handle Knives and Forks, single bolster. Same pattern as No. 28R125. Price, per set, 6 knives and 6 forks..........72c

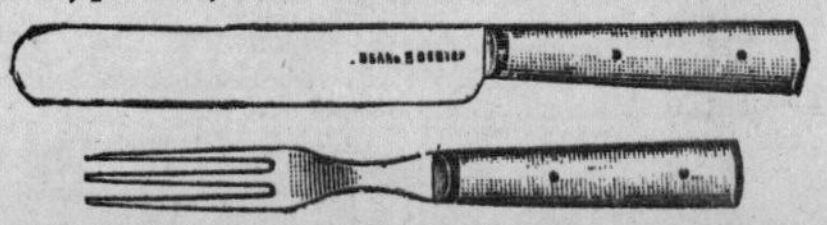

No. 28R127 White Bone Handle Knives and Forks, single bolster. Per set, 6 knives and 6 forks......88c

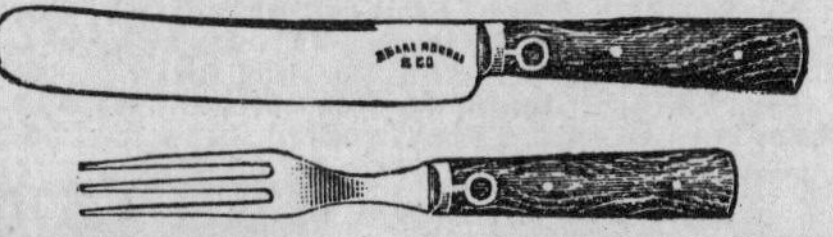

No. 28R134 Fancy Ring Pattern, Cocobolo Handle Knives and Forks, swaged scimiter blades. Price, per set, 6 knives and 6 forks..........88c
No. 28R135 Same as No. 28R134, with ebony handles. Per set, 6 knives and 6 forks..........$1.02

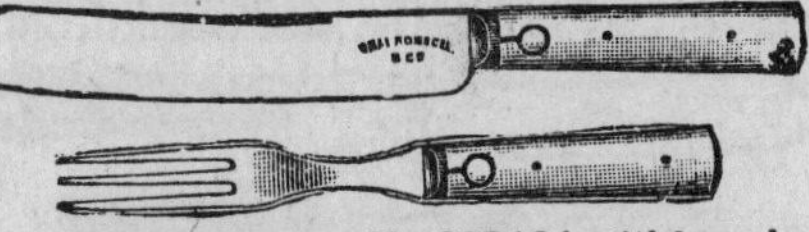

No. 28R136 Same as No. 28R134, with bone handles. Per set, 6 knives and 6 forks..........$1.23

No. 28R143 Fancy Shape Cocobolo Handle Knives and Forks, with one cross pattern bolster. Swaged scimiter blades. Taper point handle. Price, per set, 6 knives and 6 forks..........$1.00
No. 28R144 Same as No. 28R143, with ebony handles. Per set, 6 knives and 6 forks..........$1.24

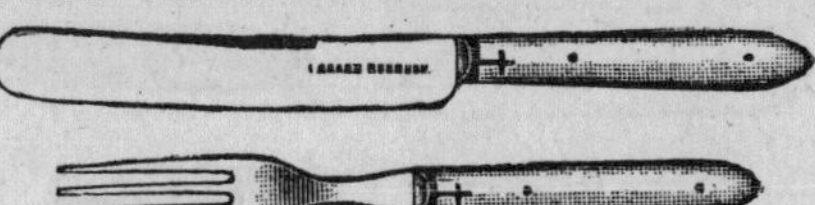

No. 28R145 Same as No. 28R143, with bone handles. Per set, 6 knives and 6 forks..........$1.65

No. 28R152 Double Bolstered Cocobolo Handle Knives and Forks. Per set, 6 knives and 6 forks. 71c
No. 28R153 Same as No. 28R152, with ebony handles. Per set, 6 knives and 6 forks..........82c

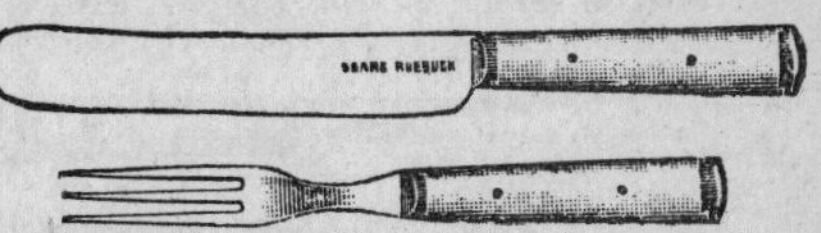

No. 28R154 Double Bolstered Bone Handle Knives and Forks. Per set, 6 knives and 6 forks. 98c

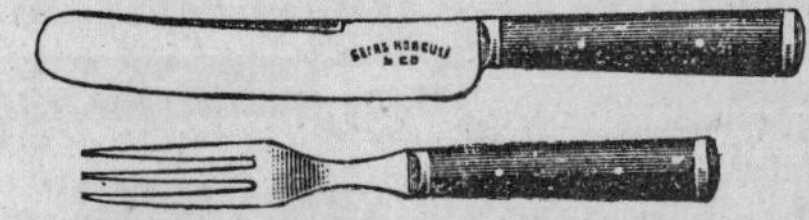

No. 28R161 Double Bolstered Knives and Forks, cocobolo handles, scimiter blades. Price, per set, 6 knives and 6 forks..........77c
No. 28R162 Same as No. 28R161, with ebony handles. Per set, 6 knives and 6 forks..........88c

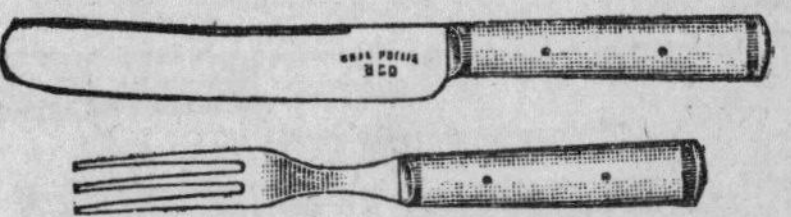

No. 28R163 Same as No. 28R161, with bone handles. Per set, 6 knives and 6 forks..........$1.05

No. 28R170 Double Ring Pattern Knives and Forks, cocobolo handles. Price, per set, 6 knives and 6 forks..........90c
No. 28R171 Same as No. 28R170, with ebony handles. Per set, 6 knives and 6 forks..........$1.04

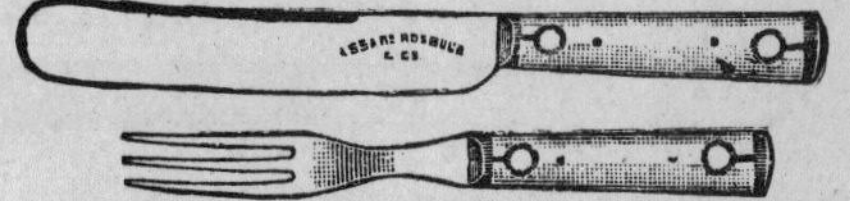

No. 28R172 Same as No. 28R170, with bone handles. Per set, 6 knives and 6 forks..........$1.35

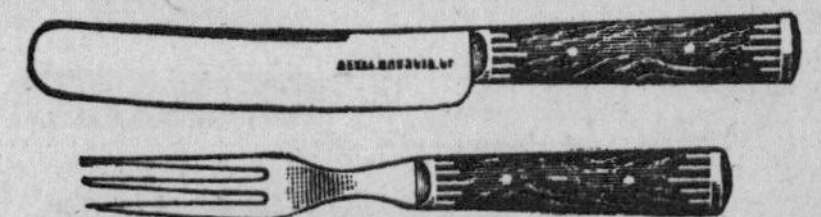

No. 28R179 German Style, Cocobolo Handle, Knives and Forks, swaged scimiter blades. Price, per set, 6 knives and 6 forks..........$1.05
No. 28R180 German Style Knives and Forks. Same as No. 28R179, with ebony handle. Price, per set, 6 knives and 6 forks..........$1.20

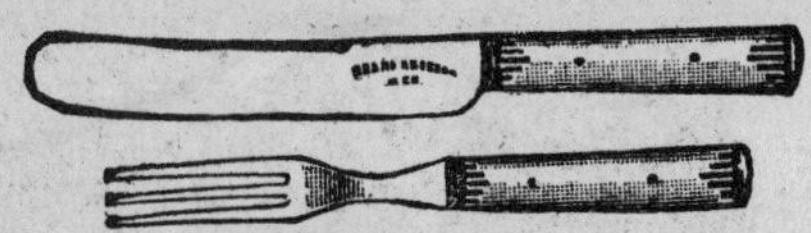

No. 28R181 German style, bone handle Knives and Forks, swaged scimiter blades.
Price, per set, 6 knives and 6 forks........$1.57

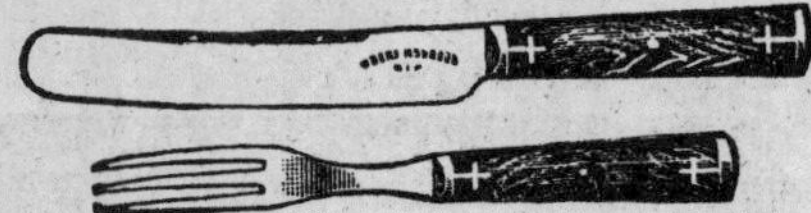

No. 28R188 Cross pattern, double bolstered, cocobolo handles, swaged scimiter blades, Knives and Forks. Price, per set, 6 knives and 6 forks, $1.05
No. 28R189 Same as No. 28R188, with ebony handles. Price, per set, 6 knives and 6 forks. $1.20

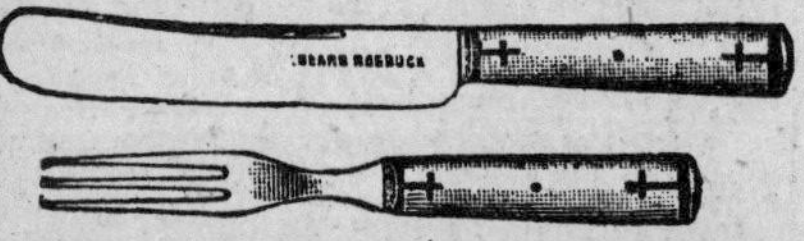

No. 28R190 Same as No. 28R188, with bone handles. Price, per set, 6 knives and 6 forks..$1.58

No. 28R197 English pattern, double cross, bolstered cocobolo handle, swaged scimiter blades, Knives and Forks.
Price, per set, 6 knives and 6 forks..........$1.15
No. 28R198 Same as No. 28R197, with ebony handles. Price, per set, 6 knives and 6 forks..$1.29

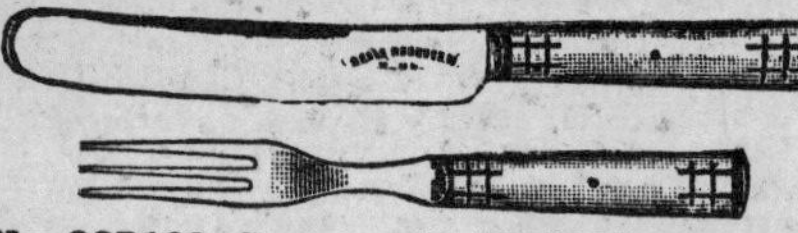

No. 28R199 Same as No. 28R197, with bone handles. Price, per set, 6 knives and 6 forks...$1.63

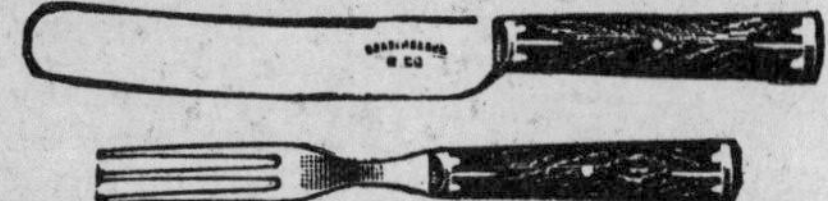

No. 28R206 Double bolster, swaged scimiter blades, cocobolo handle Knives and Forks.
Price, per set, 6 knives and 6 forks..........$1.06
No. 28R207 Same as No. 28R206, with ebony handles. Price, per set, 6 knives and 6 forks..$1.21

No. 28R208 Same as No. 28R206, with bone handles. Price, per set, 6 knives and 6 forks..$1.57

No. 28R215 French pattern bolster, cocobolo handle Knives and Forks, swaged scimiter blades.
Price, per set, 6 knives and 6 forks............$1.34
No. 28R216 Same as No. 28R215, with ebony handles. Price, per set, 6 knives and 6 forks..$1.48

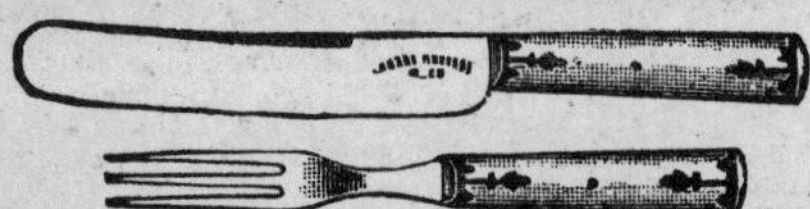

No. 28R217 French pattern bolster, bone handle Knives and Forks. Set, 6 knives and 6 forks..$1.85

No. 28R224 Our latest style cross pattern, cocobolo handles, swaged scimiter blades.
Price, per set, 6 knives and 6 forks...........$1.20
No. 28R225 Same as No. 28R224, with ebony handles. Price, per set, 6 knives and 6 forks..$1.40

No. 28R226 Same as No. 28R224, with bone handles. Price, per set, 6 knives and 6 forks..$1.75

No. 28R233 Swedish pattern bolster, cocobolo handles, swaged scimiter blades.
Price, per set, 6 knives and 6 forks...........$1.54
No. 28R234 Same as No. 28R233, with ebony handles. Price, per set, 6 knives and 6 forks..$1.66

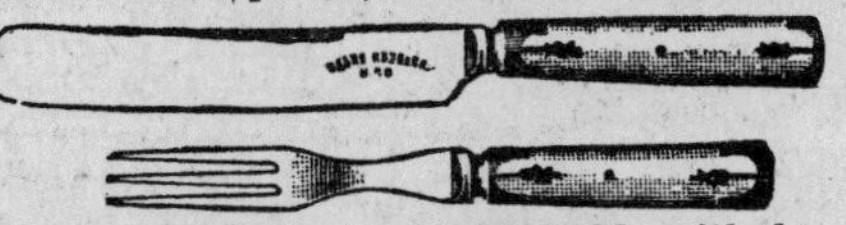

No. 28R235 Same as No. 28R233, with bone handles. Price, per set, 6 knives and 6 forks..$2.04

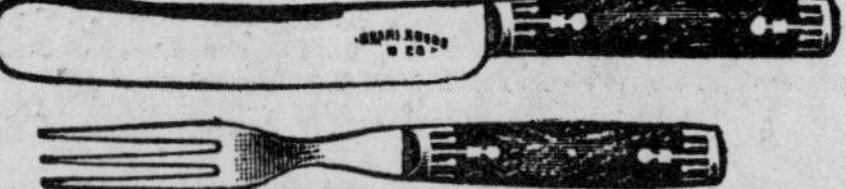

No. 28R242 Fancy double bolster, cocobolo handles, Knives and Forks, swaged scimiter blades, swell handles. Per set, 6 knives and 6 forks..$1.45
No. 28R243 Same as No. 28R242, with ebony handles. Per set, 6 knives and 6 forks... ....$1.59

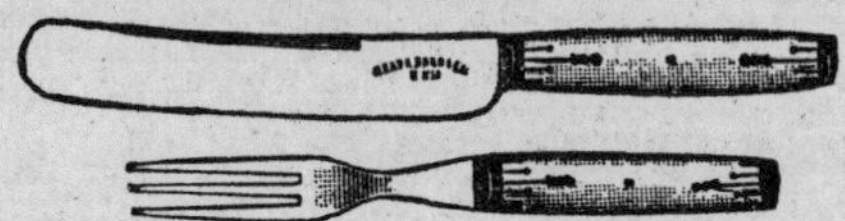

No. 28R244 Same as No. 28R242, with bone handles. Per set, 6 knives and 6 forks $1.96

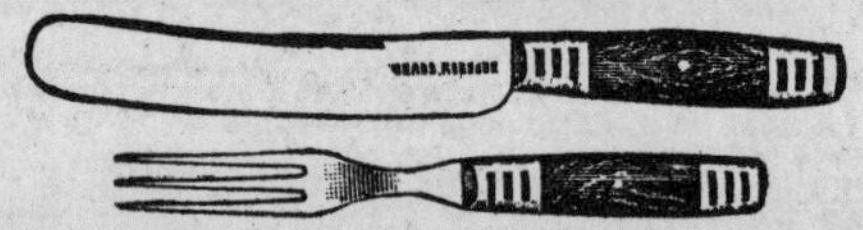

No. 28R251 Fancy double link bolster, swelled cocobolo handles, Knives and Forks, swaged scimiter blades. Per set, 6 knives and 6 forks.......$1.45
No. 28R252 Same as No. 28R251, with ebony handles. Per set, 6 knives and 6 forks........$1.59

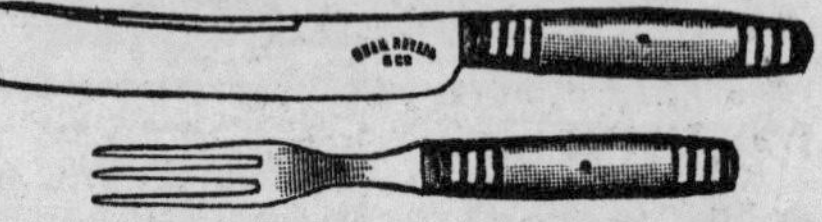

No. 28R253 Same as No. 28R251, with bone handles. Per set, 6 knives and 6 forks........$1.96

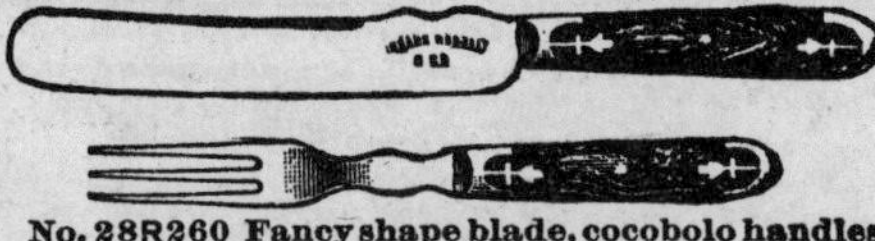

No. 28R260 Fancy shape blade, cocobolo handles, with fancy double bolster; swaged scimiter blades.
Price, per set, 6 knives and 6 forks...........$1.47
No. 28R261 Same as No. 28R260, with ebony handles. Per set, 6 knives and 6 forks........$1.60

No. 28R263 Same as No. 28R260, with bone handles. Per set, 6 knives and 6 forks.........$1.98

No. 28R265 Imitation stag handles, double bolster Knives and Forks, swaged scimiter blades.
Price, per set, 6 knives and 6 forks..........$1.32

No. 28R270 Hard rubber handles, medium blades. Per set, 6 knives and 6 forks.........$2.36
No. 28R271 Hard rubber handle, Dessert Knives and Forks. Per set, 6 knives and 6 forks. $2.03

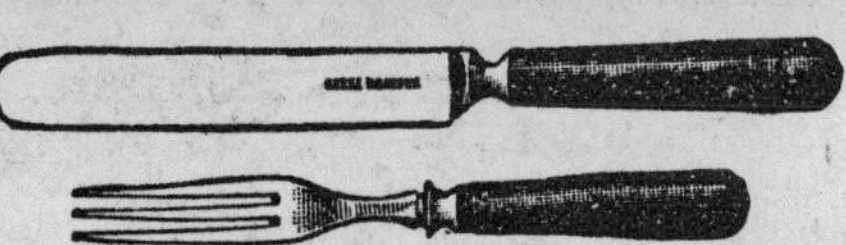

No. 28R272 Hard rubber handles, medium blades.
Per set, six knives and six forks...........$2.49
No. 28R273 Hard rubber handle, Dessert Knives and Forks. Per set, 6 knives and 6 forks......$2.15

No. 28R274 White celluloid handle medium Knives and Forks.
Price, per set, 6 knives and 6 forks............$2.50
No. 28R275 White celluloid handle medium knives only. More durable than ivory. Will not crack or change color. Ordinarily used with silver forks. Preferred to a plated knife because they can be sharpened. Price, per dozen.................$2.67

No. 28R283 Tinned steel knives and forks. Forged from steel, and are heavily coated with pure block tin to prevent rust. We do not break sets.
Price, per set 6 knives and 6 forks..............54c

No. 28R287 Tinned Steel Table Knives and Forks. Put up in cardboard case as illustrated. Handles of forks are same as knives. We do not break sets.
Price, per set, 6 knives and 6 forks...........98c

No. 28R293 Cocobolo swell handle knives and four-tined forks. Single bolster; swaged scimiter blade. Price, per set, 6 knives and 6 forks.....$1 28

No. 28R296 White bone swell handle knives and four-tined forks same as preceding, except the handle. Price, per set, 6 knives and 6 forks, $1.89

No. 28R299 White bone handle knives and four-tined forks. Double bolster; swaged scimiter blade. A handsome and durable article.
Price, per set, 6 knives and 6 forks............$1.75

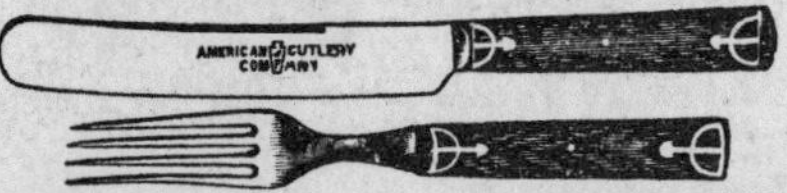

No. 28R304 Cocobolo handle knives and four-tined forks. Double fancy bolster; swaged scimiter blades. Price, per set, 6 knives and 6 forks....$1.48

No. 28R307 White bone handle knives and four-tined forks. Double fancy bolsters; swaged scimiter blades.
Price, per set, 6 knives and 6 forks............$2.00

No. 28R310 Cocobolo handle knives and four-tined forks. Double fancy bolsters; swaged scimiter blades. A very neat and attractive pattern.
Price, per set, 6 knives and 6 forks............$1.70

No. 28R314 White bone handle knives and four-tined forks. Double fancy bolster; swaged scimiter blades. Price, per set, 6 knives and 6 forks....$2.35

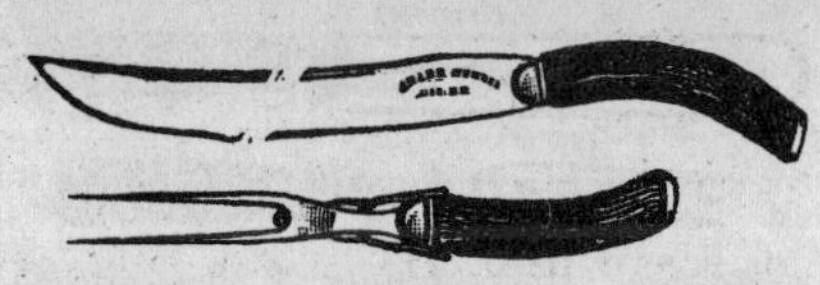

No. 28R412 Stag Handle Carvers. Fancy blade of fine quality steel with neat bolster and cap.
Per pair, one knife, 8-inch blade, and fork.....70c
No. 28R413 Same as above, with 9-inch blade.
Price, per pair, one knife and one fork..........78c
No. 28R414 Stag handle steels, to match....42c

Carvers of Extra Quality.

The following carvers are the very highest grade, equal to anything made in this country or Europe. They are finely finished and blades are warranted fine cutters.

NOTE REDUCED PRICES. Lower than such goods were ever sold. The reduction is in price only; quality and finish is better than ever before.

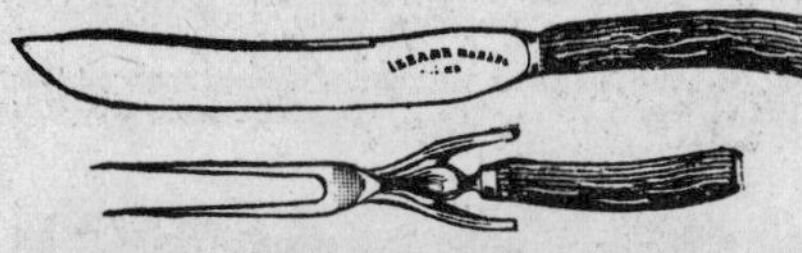

No. 28R415 Fancy Blade Stag Handle Carvers.
Per pair, one knife and one fork, 8-inch blade...$1.35
No. 28R416 9-inch blade.......................... 1.51
No. 28R417 Steels to match, each.. .... .52

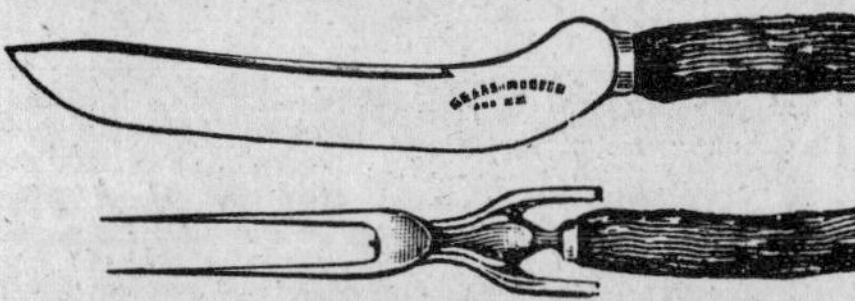

No. 28R418 Fancy Blade, Stag Handle Carvers.
Per pair, one knife and one fork, 8-inch blade, $1.41
No. 28R419 9-inch blade.......................... 1.69
No. 28R420 Steel to match, each........... .52

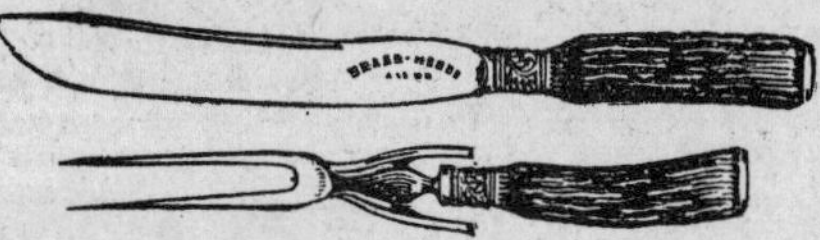

No. 28R440 Fancy Blade Stag Handle Carvers. Fancy silver plated bolster and cap.

Length of blade, inches..............	8	9
Per pair, one knife and one fork.....	$1.62	$1.92
Steel to match, each..........................		.71

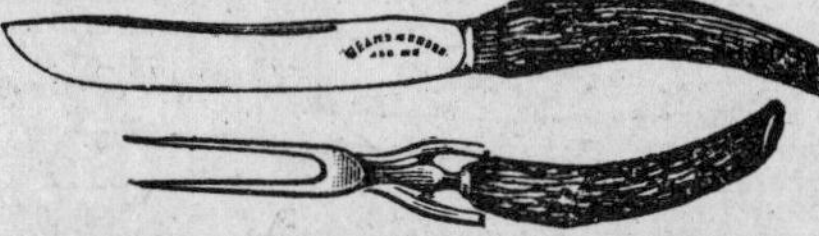

No. 28R443 Fancy Blade Stag Handle Carvers Fancy handle.

Length of blade, inches	8	9
Per pair, one knife and one fork.....	$1.78	$2.06
Steel to match, each...........................		.86

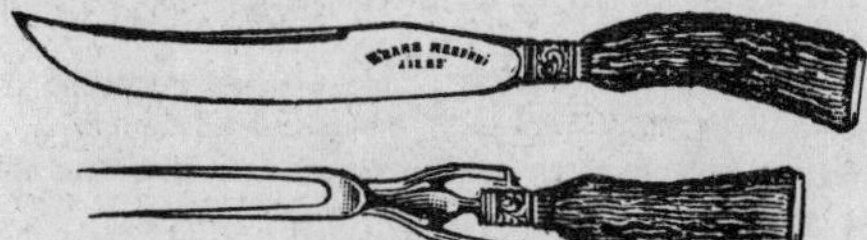

No. 28R446 Fancy Stag Handle Carvers. Fancy heavily silver plated bolster and ferrule.

Length of blade, inches.........	8	9
Per pair, one knife and one fork.......	$2.28	$2.57
Steel to match, each.............................		1.07

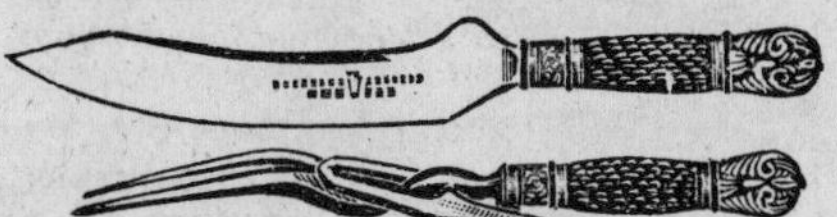

No. 28R450 Fancy Blade Stag Handle Carvers. Fancy silver plated bolsters.

Length of blade, inches..................	8	9
Per pair, one knife and one fork....	$2.15	$2.40
Steel to match...		1.00

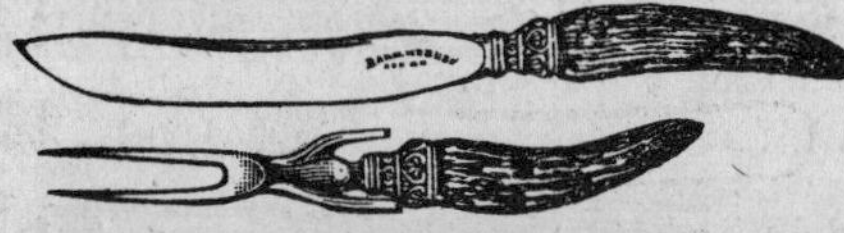

No. 28R460 Fancy Stag Handle Carvers. Fancy silver plated bolster.

Length of blade, inches..............	8	9
Per pair, one knife and one fork......	$2.50	$2.77
Steel to match, each................................		1.22

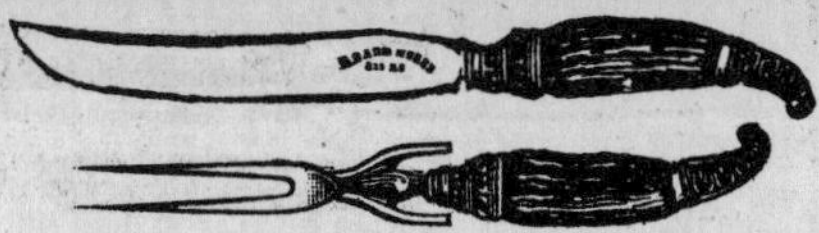

No. 28R463 Fancy Stag Handle Carvers. Fancy silver plated bolsters and tips. Best of steel blade, beautifully polished. **Quality is warranted.**

Length of blade, inches...............	8	9
Price, per pair, one knife and one fork,	$3.20	$3.47
Steel to match, each.............................		1.77

No. 28R466 White Celluloid Handle Carvers. Solid steel bolsters. Blade 8 inches long.
Price, per pair $1.60
Steel to match, each... .... .60

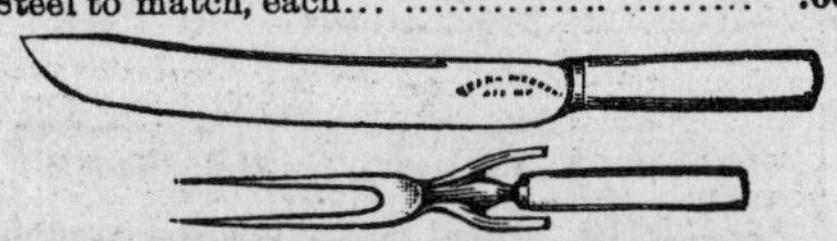

No. 28R469 Grained Celluloid Handle Carvers. Looks like ivory. Will wear better and will not crack. Fancy blade.

Length of blade, in.	8	9
Price, per pair........................	$1.71	$2.00
Steel to match, each..............................		.63

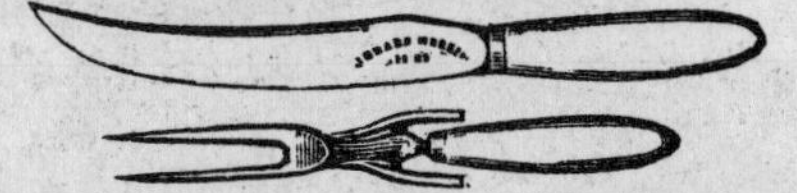

No. 28R472 Grained Celluloid Handled Carvers with difficulty distinguished from ivory, which it will outlast. Blades of best steel, finely finished. Pair consists of knife and fork.

Length of blade, inches..............	8	9
Price, per pair........................	$1.72	$2.00
Steel to match, each.............................		.63

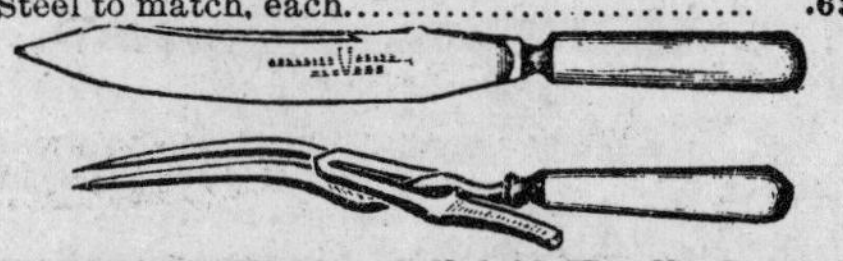

No. 28R473 Flaring Celluloid Handle Carvers. Swaged scimiter blade. Solid steel concaved bolster.

Length of blade, inches...........	8	9
Price, per pair............	$1.65	$1.90
Steel to match, each.......................		.60

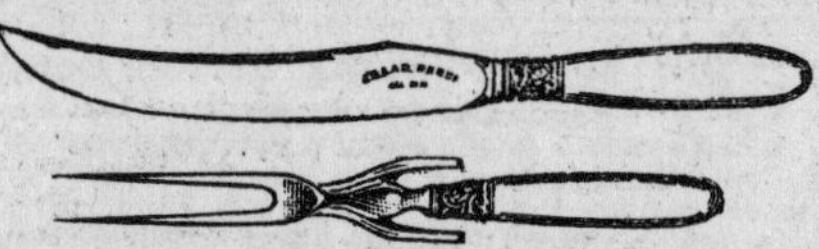

No. 28R475 Celluloid Handle Carvers, with silver plated bolster. A carver with best steel blade and every merit of beauty and finish. Pair consists of knife and fork.

Length of blade, in..	8	9
Price, per pair.......	$2.28	$2.57
Steel to match, each........................		.90

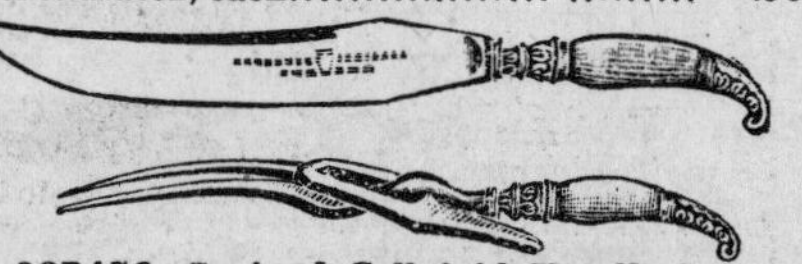

No. 28R476 Grained Celluloid Handle Carver. Swaged fancy blades, silver plated bolsters; handles look almost exactly like ivory and are more durable, Will not crack or stain.

Length of blade, inches.....	8	9
Per pair, one knife and one fork..	$4.80	$5.10
Steel to match, each........................		2.10

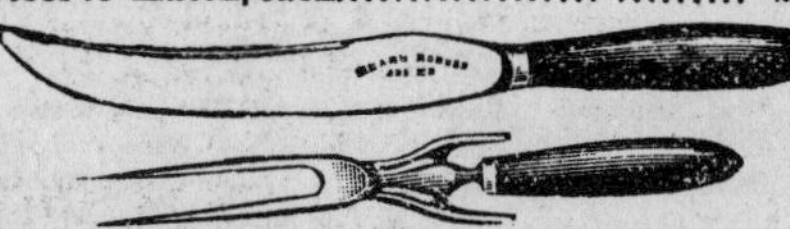

No. 28R478 Black Rubber Handle Carvers. Handles warranted not to split in hot water. Steel blades of the very best quality.

Length of blade, inches.............	8	9
Per pair, one knife and one fork..	$1.33	$1.60
Steel to match, each.............................		.53

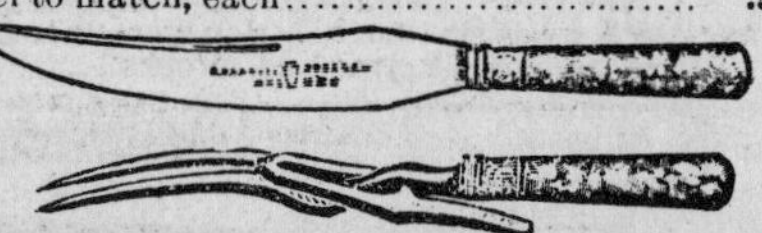

No. 28R482 Solid Pearl Handle, Fancy Blade Carvers, with sterling silver bolsters. They are handsomely finished and cutting qualities are guaranteed.

Length of blade, inches.....	8	9
Per pair, one knife and one fork...	$4.75	$5.00
Steel to match, each..................................		2.00

No. 28R500 Stag Handle Carving Knife, Fork and Steel. Fancy swaged blades, 8 inches long, nickel plated bolster. Put up complete in fancy case as illustrated. Price for complete set.....$1.44

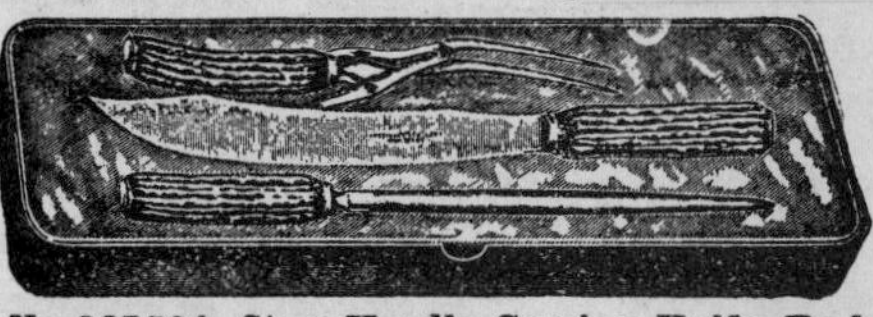

No. 28R504 Stag Handle Carving Knife, Fork and Steel. Fancy blade, 8 inches long, solid steel bolsters. Put up in fancy case.
Price for complete set.................................$2.33

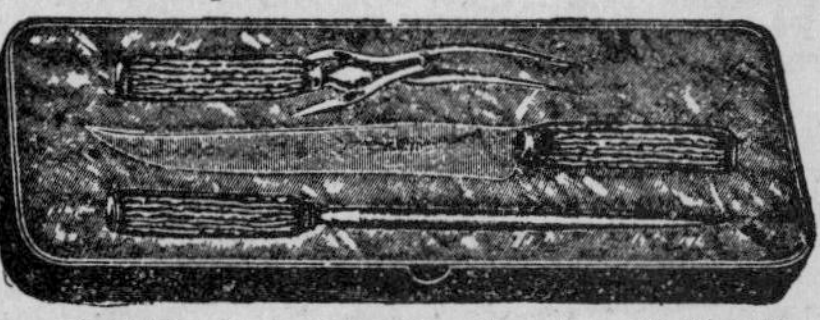

No. 28R508 Stag Handle Carving Knife, Fork and Steel. Fancy swaged blade, 8 inches long, solid steel bolster. Put up in fancy case.
Price for set, as illustrated....... ....$2.37

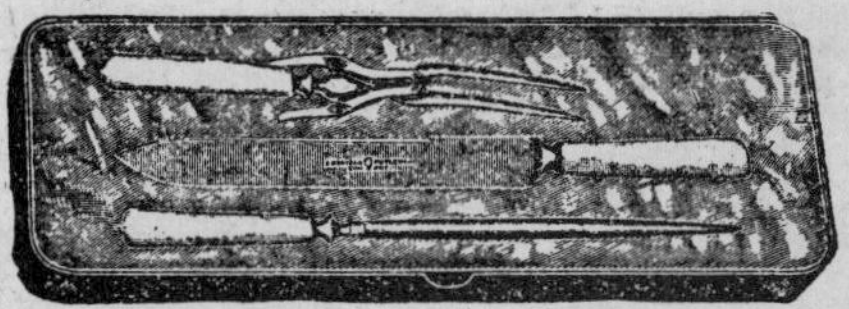

No. 28R510 White Celluloid Handle Carving Knife, Fork and Steel, put up in fancy case. Blade, 8 inches long, solid steel bolster. A neat set.
Price, complete as illustrated........................$2.75

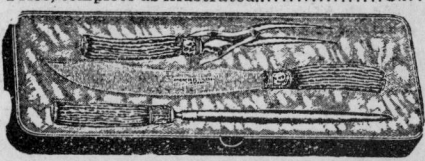

No. 28R512 Stag Handle Carving Set, consisting of knife, fork and steel put up in fancy case. Blade, 9 inches long, sterling silver ferrules. A set that is sure to please.
Price, complete as illustrated.......................$3.40

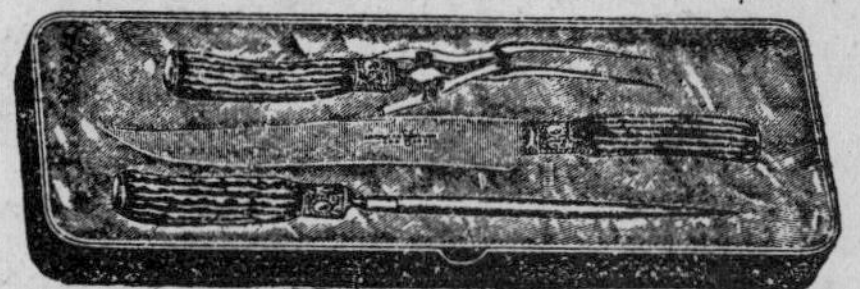

No. 28R514 Stag Handle Carving Knife, Fork and Steel, in fancy case. Fancy swaged blade, 9 inches long, sterling silver bolster. The shape of blade is very popular and the pattern throughout is neat and attractive.
Price, complete as illustrated.........................$3.45

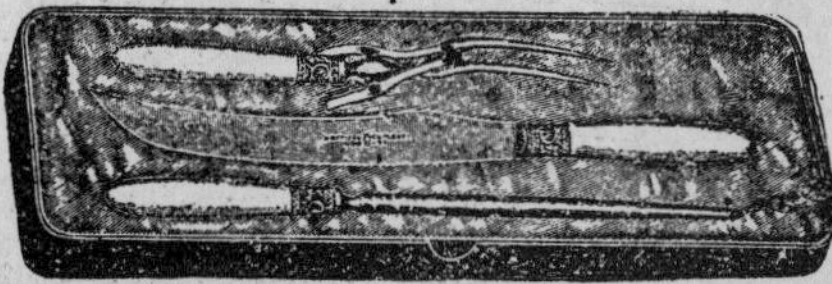

No. 28R518 Grained Celluloid Handle Carving Set, consisting of knife, fork and steel in fancy case. Fancy blade, 9 inches long. Silver plated bolsters. This handle is an imitation of ivory—looks just as nice—and is more durable; it will not crack or become stained with use.
Price, per set as illustrated.........................$3.73

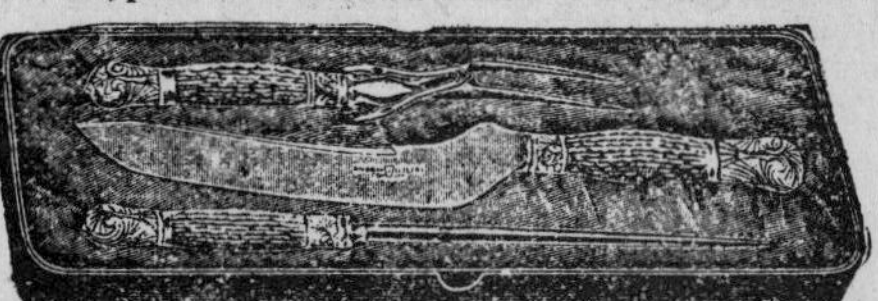

No. 28R519 Stag Handle Carving Knife, Fork and Steel, in fancy case. Fancy blade, 9 inches long. Silver plated bolsters. A favorite pattern having a very rich appearance.
Price, per set as illustrated...........................$3.85

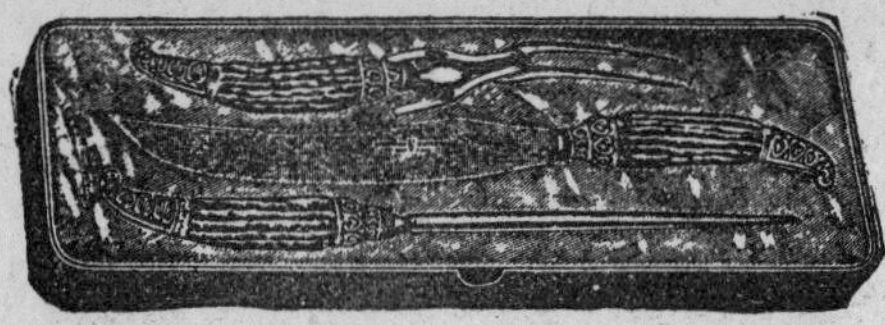

No. 28R523 Stag Handle Carving Knife, Fork and Steel in fancy case. Fancy blade, 9 inches long. Silver plated bolsters. A popular and handsome set with quality and workmanship fully guaranteed.
Price, per set, as illustrated..................$5.33

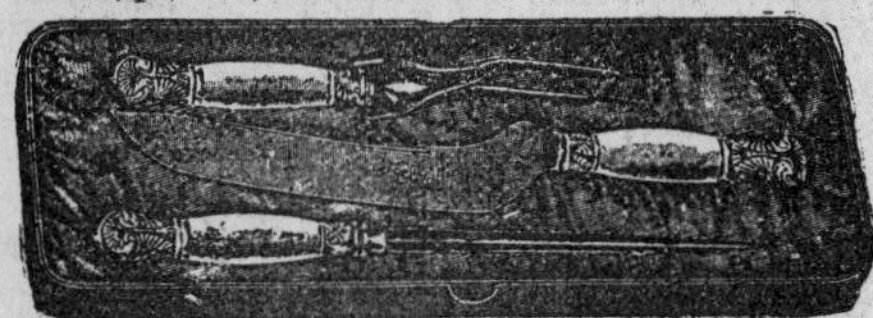

No. 28R526 Grained Celluloid Handle Carving Set, consisting of knife, fork and steel, in fancy case. Fancy blade, 9 inches long; silver plated bolsters. A very desirable set.
Price, complete, as illustrated................$5.88

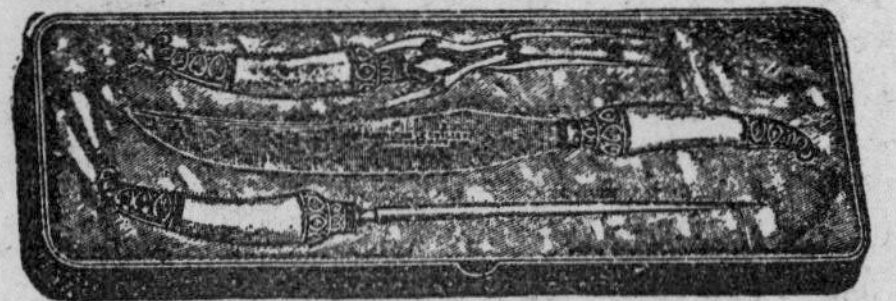

No. 28R529 Grained Celluloid Handle Carving Set, consisting of knife, fork and steel, in fancy case. Swaged fancy blade, 9 inches long; silver plated bolsters. Quality and workmanship beyond criticism. Price, complete, as illustrated.........$7.95

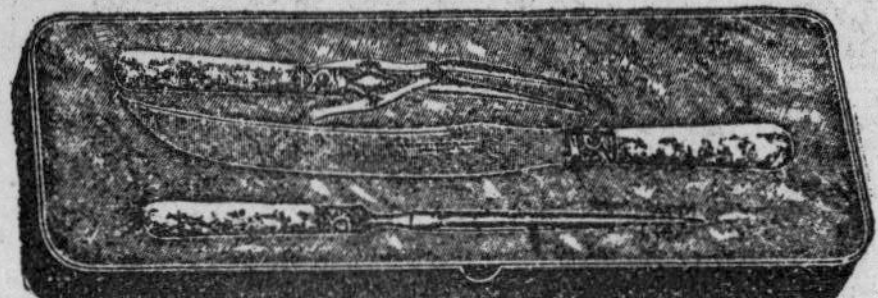

No. 28R532 Solid Pearl Handle Carving Knife, Fork and Steel, put up in fancy case. Blade 9 inches long; sterling silver bolsters. Great care is used in selecting the pearl for handles, and workmanship is carefully inspected. A handsome and practical gift. Price, per set, as illustrated....$7.98

BREAD KNIVES.

No. 28R562 Bread Knife, polished steel blade, 7½ inches long, firmly set in hardwood handle.
Price, each..12c

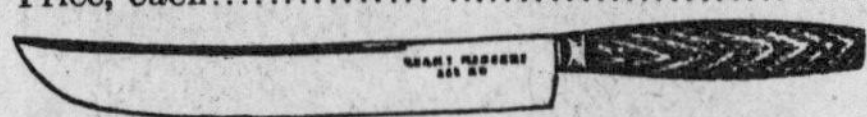

No. 28R565 Bread Knife, cocobolo handle, best steel blade, 8 inches long, finely finished. Each..24c

No. 28R566 Bread Knife, serrated edge, steel blade, black enameled wood handle. Blade, 7 inches long. Price, each......................................7c

No. 28R570 Bread Knife, serrated edge, steel blade 10 inches long, natural polished hardwood handle. Price, each..................................8c

No. 28R574 Bread Knife, highest grade steel blade, fancy shape, 10 inches long, with serrated edge; cocobolo solid handle, finely polished, patent nickel plated ferrule. A very fine article both for cutting qualities and looks. Price, each.........25c

No. 28R580 Saw Back Ham Slicer, with serrated edge, 8 inches long. Will slice bread hot or cold. The best thing on earth for cutting frosted cake. Cuts meat or bone. Easily sharpened with an ordinary steel. Natural polished hardwood handle.
Price, each..12c

Christy Pattern Knife Sets.

No. 28R583 The Genuine Christy Knife Sets. Every blade warranted to be made of the best cutlery steel. Bread, cake and paring knife.
Per set of three knives...........................50c

No. 28R586 Christy Pattern Knife Sets, made of the best cold rolled nickel steel. Will give satisfaction. Handles firmly swaged to the blade and will never come loose. Set consists of bread, cake and paring knife. Per set of three knives............16c

Kitchen Fork.

No. 28R587 Heavy Polished Steel Carving Fork. Made from one piece of steel. Indestructible. Whole length, 10 inches. Price, each..................10c

No. 28R588 Wood Handle Paring Knife. Blade of best steel. Each....................................5c

Paring Knives.

No. 28R589 Vegetable Parer. Takes off an even peel. Is easily sharpened and cleaned. Just the thing for Saratoga chips.
Price, each..6c

Kitchen Knives.

No. 28R594 Cocobolo Handle Kitchen Knife. Blade made of a superior quality of steel that will take a fine edge and hold it a long time without needing sharpening. Length of blade, 3⅞ inches.
Price, each..7c

No. 28R595 Cocobolo Handle Kitchen Knife. Lap bolster. Best cutlery steel blade. Length of blade, 3⅞ inches. Price, each..........................8c

No. 28R596 Cocobolo Handle Hand Fitting Kitchen Knife. The shape of the handle and the peculiar shape of the blade makes this the most popular kitchen knife. Ours are made from the best grade cutlery steel; honestly made and correctly tempered. Length of blade, 3¼ inches.
Price, each..9c

No. 28R597 Shoe Knife. Best steel blade, square point, brass ferrule, hardwood handle. An excellent kitchen knife. Each.................9c

No. 28R598 Beech Handle Fish Scaling Knife. Length of blade, 5 inches. For quickly removing all the scales, it is just the thing. Price, each.......25c

No. 28R599 Knife, Scissors and Skate Sharpener. A few seconds only is required to sharpen the kitchen knives or a pair of scissors. Screwed to a small block of wood of a suitable size for the hand, it makes a neat skate sharpener that will concave the skate runner.
Price, each..5c

If by mail, postage extra, each, 3 cents.

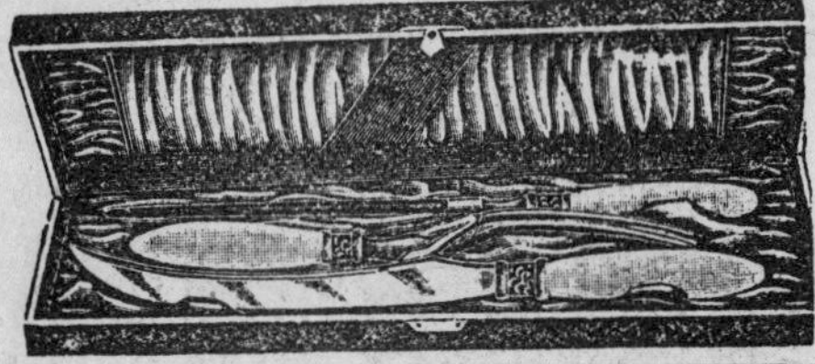

Our $4.07 Carving Set, in Satin Lined Case.

No. 28R533 Carving Set in richly finished satin lined leather covered case, consists of a finely finished 9-inch carving knife, fork and steel with grained celluloid handles and artistic ferrules. These look exactly like ivory.
Price, complete, as described above..........$4.07

No. 28R534 Empty Satin Lined Leather Covered Case, will fit any carving set we sell. Same as shown in illustration without the carvers.
Price, each..$2.10

SEARS, ROEBUCK & CO.'S BUTCHER KNIVES.

THE BEST MADE. Our guarantee is as follows: If any Butcher Knife, Skinning Knife or Sticking Knife purchased from us, on which our name is stamped, does not prove as good or better than any knife you ever had, return it to us and money will be cheerfully refunded without argument. Nearly the total value of these knives is in the blades.

THEY ARE INTENDED TO SELL ON THEIR QUALITY, NOT ON THEIR LOOKS.

Remember when comparing prices of these knives that the **blades are all hand forged**—not made by machinery.

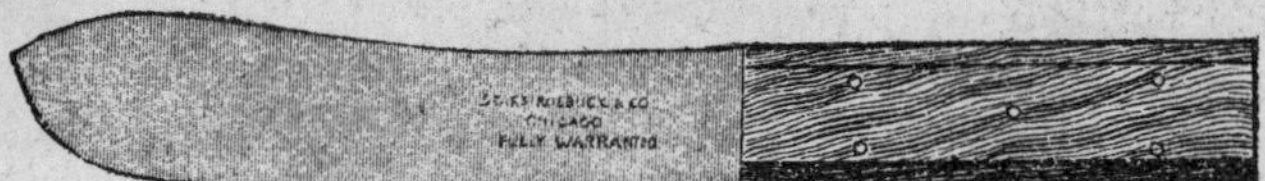

No. 28R600 Sears, Roebuck & Co.'s Butcher Knives. Beech handle. Blades **hand hammered** from best quality high grade steel. They are fully warranted. Read our guarantee above.

Length of blade	5-in.	5½-in.	6-in.	7-in.	8-in.	10-in.	12-in.
Price, each	12c	14c	15c	21c	27c	41c	58c

Sears, Roebuck & Co.'s Skinning Knives.

No. 28R601 Sears, Roebuck & Co.'s Skinning Knives. Beech handle. Blades **hand hammered** from best quality high grade steel. They are fully warranted. Read our guarantee.

Length of blade	5-in.	5½-in.	6-in.	6½-in.	7-in.
Price, each	12c	14c	15c	18c	21c

Sears, Roebuck & Co.'s Sticking Knives.

No. 28R602 Sears, Roebuck & Co.'s Sticking Knives. Beech handle, blades **hand hammered** from best quality high grade steel. They are fully warranted. Read our guarantee.

Length of blade	5-inch	5½-inch	6-inch	6½-inch
Price, each	12c	14c	15c	18c

No. 28R615 Cocobolo Handle Butcher Knife, 6-inch steel blade, cocobolo handle with bolster, three rivets in handle. Price, each..................................8c

No. 28R617 Double Bolster, Cocobolo Handle, Butcher Knife, 6-inch steel blade. Price, each......15c

No. 28R620 Single Bolster Butcher Knife, cocobolo handle, riveted, 6-inch steel blade.
Price, each.........24c

No. 28R622 Ebony Handle Clip Point Butcher Knife, made of best cutlery steel, stronger than the ordinary butcher knife. It is made the same pattern as a hunting knife for rough, heavy work.

Length of blade	6-inch	6½-inch	7-inch
Price, each	25c	28c	30c

No. 28R623 Prussian Pattern Butcher Knife. Handle fastened with saw screws; fits the hand perfectly. Made from the finest butcher knife steel and warranted to give satisfaction.

Length of blade, inches	6	7	8
Price, each	28c	30c	35c

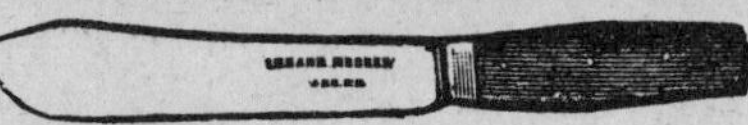

No. 28R625 Butcher Knife, cocobolo handle, single bolstered and strongly riveted, best steel blade.

Length of blade, in.	6	7	8	9	10	12	14
Price, each	19c	26c	32c	38c	47c	73c	$1.00

No. 28R635 French Cook's Knife, ebony handle, lap bolster, best steel blade. The best knife to buy for carving and general use in the kitchen. **Warranted.**

Length of blade, in.	6	8	10	12	14	16
Price, each	47c	58c	73c	78c	$1.00	$1.33

No. 28R646 Genuine Wilson's Butcher Knives, beechwood handles.

Length of blade, inches	5	5½	6	7	8	10
Price, each	17c	20c	23c	33c	43c	64c

Genuine Wilson Butcher Knives.

STAMPED I. WILSON.

Imitations of this Knife are frequently sold. If not stamped on blade I. WILSON they are counterfeits.

No. 28R647 Genuine Wilson's Sticking Knives, beechwood handles.

Length of blade, inches	5½	6	6½
Price, each	22c	24c	29c

No. 28R648 Genuine Wilson's Skinning Knives, beechwood handles.

Length of blade, inches	6	6½
Price, each	26c	28c

No. 28R649 Genuine Wilson's latest pattern, Boomerang Steak Knife, beech handle.

Length of blade, inches	10	11	12
Price, each	67c	85c	$1.00

No. 28R650 The Genuine Wilson's Butchers' Steel, cocoa handle, very best material and finish; the favorite with butchers in all parts of the world.

Length, inches	10	12	14
Price, each	75c	90c	$1.10

No. 28R651 The Genuine Wilson's Butchers' Steel. Stag handle, finest quality, best finish. Length, 12 inches. Price 90c

SEARS, ROEBUCK & CO.'S SHEARS AND SCISSORS.

WARRANTED AS GOOD OR BETTER THAN ANY OTHER, REGARDLESS OF PRICE.

OUR GUARANTEE If they are not in every way satisfactory they may be returned within 30 days, and money will be refunded or another pair sent to replace any not satisfactory. The shape of the blades makes them very stiff. **They have steel laid blades and are finished in a superior manner. The fitting of the joints is as near perfect** as the highest mechanical skill and careful inspection can make it. A drop of oil should be put on the joints of shears and scissors occasionally, and the blades should be kept free from dust and grit, which quickly causes the blades to become dull. **Don't use the shears to pull carpet tacks, draw corks, lift stove lids, etc., and then expect them to cut.** While we claim our shears are the **best on earth**, they cannot be used for such purposes and give good satisfaction. **Do not let the low prices at which we sell these shears lead you to think the quality is not of the very best.** These shears are not made by the "shear trust"--**our prices are not dictated by any combination,** and we give our customers the advantage of our large contract, with but our usual one small profit added. **If you want the best shears made, try the SEARS, ROEBUCK & CO. BRAND. Size of shears is the entire length.**

Sears, Roebuck & Co.'s Shears, Straight Trimmers.

No. 28R751 Sears, Roebuck & Co.'s Shears (Straight Trimmers). Japanned handles, steel laid blade. Will cut clear to the points and keep sharp longer than any other we know of. **Fully warranted, as explained in heading above.**

Whole length, inches	6	7	8	9	10
Length of cut	2¾	3¼	3⅞	4¼	5
Price, each	27c	32c	36c	43c	57c

No. 28R752 Sears, Roebuck & Co.'s Shears (Straight Trimmers). Full nickel plated, otherwise like those previously quoted. While the cutting qualities are the same in all shears of our brand, the nickel plated shear is most popular because it costs but very little more and looks much nicer.

Whole length, inches	6	7	8	9	10
Length of cut	2¾	3¼	3⅞	4¼	5
Price, each	30c	35c	40c	48c	63c

Sears, Roebuck & Co.'s Shears, Bent Trimmers.

No. 28R753 Sears, Roebuck & Co.'s Shears (Bent Trimmers). Japanned handles. For use on a table or board or for following a line the bent handle shear is most convenient. **Fully warranted.**

Whole length, inches	8	9	10
Length of cut	3⅞	4¼	5
Price, each	39c	50c	61c

No. 28R754 Sears, Roebuck & Co.'s Shears (Bent Trimmers). Full nickel plated, otherwise same as described under preceding number. Will cut clear to the points. Will cut more thickness of cloth, will keep sharp longer than other brands. **They are fully warranted.**

Whole length, inches	8	9	10
Length of cut	3⅞	4¼	5
Price, each	43c	55c	67c

No. 28R755 Sears, Roebuck & Co.'s Ladies' Scissors are made of special steel of superior quality, by the same workmen who have made our shears (which have attained wonderful popularity) and are tempered, fitted and inspected with the greatest care. They are fully guaranteed both in quality and finish. Like our shears **they are tempered by a patent process** and the temper of every one is just the same. Finely polished and full nickel plated. Every piece warranted.

Full length	3	3½	4	4½	5	6	7
Length of cut	1	1¼	1¾	2	2¼	2⅞	3½
Price, each	23c	25c	26c	27c	28c	30c	38c

No. 28R756 Sears, Roebuck & Co.'s Pocket Scissor. Made of the same special steel, with the same care and skill, by the same workmen who make all shears and scissors bearing our brands. They are full nickel plated and warranted.

Full length	4	4½	5
Length of cut	1¾	2	2¼
Price, each	27c	28c	29c

Sears, Roebuck & Co.'s Barber Shears.

Made on the most approved model; a shear that fits the hand perfectly and works easily and smoothly. The blades are laid with a special steel and tempered by a patent process. Every shear is highly finished and must pass a rigid inspection before leaving factory, and we fully guarantee every pair we send out to give perfect satisfaction. They are made for right hand only.

No. 28R758 Sears, Roebuck & Co.'s Barber Shears. Full nickel plated and polished; warranted.

Whole length, inches	7	7½	8	8½	9
Length of cut, inches	3	3¼	3½	3⅞	4½
Price, per pair	35c	38c	40c	43c	48c

No. 28R759 Sears, Roebuck & Co.'s Barber Shears, with enameled handles and full nickel plated blades; warranted.

Whole length, inches	7	7½	8	8½	9
Length of cut, inches	3	3¼	3½	3⅞	4½
Price, per pair	32c	35c	36c	40c	44c

Heinisch First Quality Shears.

SIZE OF SCISSORS AND SHEARS IS THE ENTIRE LENGTH.

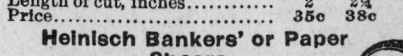

No. 28R760 Heinisch Straight Trimmers, japanned handles, finest laid steel blades. Fully warranted.

Size, inches	6	7	8	9	10
Price, each	36c	42c	48c	57c	75c

Heinisch Straight Trimmers.

No. 28R762 Heinisch Straight Trimmers, laid steel blades, full nickel plated, fully warranted.

Size, inches	6	6½	7	7½	8	8½	9
Price, each	45c	50c	55c	59c	60c	65c	72c

Left Hand Shears.

No. 28R763 Heinisch Left Hand Straight Trimmers, nickel plated. Size, 8½ inches. Price, each $1.00

Heinisch Bent Trimmers.

No. 28R764 Heinisch Bent Trimmers, japanned handles, finest quality. Laid steel blades. Fully warranted.

Size, inches	8	9	10	12
Price, each	51c	66c	84c	$1.00

R. Heinisch Tailors' Shears.

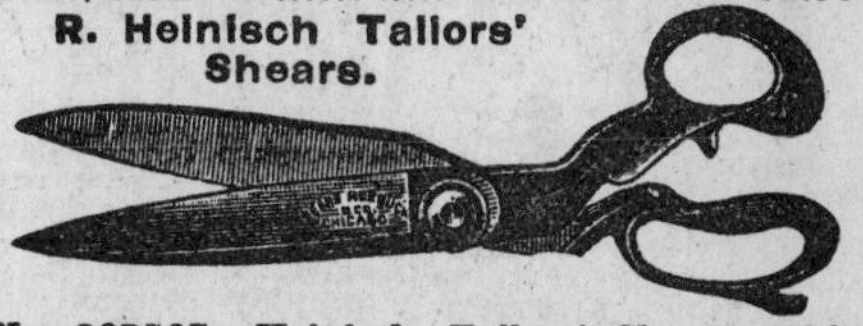

No. 28R767 Heinisch Tailors' Shears, with japanned handles. Recognized as the standard tailors' shears. Every pair warranted.

No.	Full Length	Length of Cut	Price, each
3	12 inches	6 inches	$2.45
3½	12¼ inches	6⅛ inches	2.80
4	12¾ inches	6¼ inches	3.50
4½	13 inches	6⅛ inches	4.20
5	13 inches	6½ inches	5.60
6	13¾ inches	6½ inches	6.30
7	14 inches	6⅞ inches	7.00
8	14¼ inches	7¼ inches	7.70
9	14¾ inches	7½ inches	8.40

Heinisch Special Tailors' Shears.

No. 28R768 Heinisch's Special Tailors' Shears **are used by carriage trimmers, upholsterers, carpet layers, etc., and by tailors as a trimming shears.** Made in one size only. Full length, 11¾ inches. Length of cut, 5¾ inches. Have black japanned handles. Fully warranted. Price, each....$1.90

No. 28R769 Heinisch's Tailors' Points, with black japanned handle. Every pair fully guaranteed.

Whole length, inches	5	5½	6
Length of cut, inches	2	2¼	2½
Price	35c	38c	40c

Heinisch Bankers' or Paper Shears.

No. 28R770 Heinisch's Bankers' or Paper Shears, with black japanned handles. Warranted.

Whole length, inches	12	14
Length of cut, inches	7	8½
Price	97c	$1.20

No. 28R775 Heinisch Barbers' Shears, japanned handles. Laid steel blades, warranted.

Size, inches	8	8½	9
Price, each	50c	53c	56c

No. 28R776 Heinisch Barbers' Shears. Finely polished and full nickel plated; laid steel blades. Every pair warranted.

Size, inches	8	8½	9
Price, each	70c	73c	76c

No. 28R777 Heinisch Left Hand Barbers' Shears. Japanned handles. Laid steel blades; only one size made; length, 9 inches. Price, each....75c

The following line of scissors, No. 28R780 to No. 28R790, are made in Europe and will give satisfaction to the user, but they are not warranted.

Embroidery Scissors.

No. 28R780 Fancy Embroidery Scissors, nickeled blades, gilt handles, best quality. Each......34c

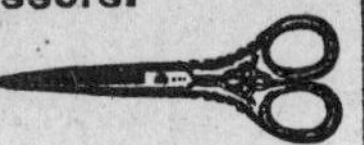

Size of scissors and shears is the entire length.

No. 28R781 Fancy Gilt Handle Scissors, nickel plated blades, superior quality and finish. Price, 5-inch, 36c; 6-inch....40c

Size of scissors and shears is the entire length.

No. 28R782 Buttonhole Scissors, with adjustable thumbscrew highly polished, fully warranted. Each......25c

Size of scissors and shears is the entire length.

Buttonhole Scissors.

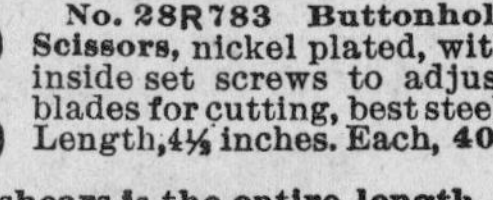

No. 28R783 Buttonhole Scissors, nickel plated, with inside set screws to adjust blades for cutting, best steel. Length, 4½ inches. Each, 40c

Size of scissors and shears is the entire length.

Pocket Scissors.

No. 28R784 Pocket Scissors, good steel, polished, 4 inches. Each......20c

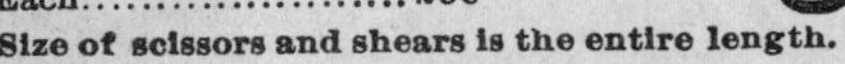

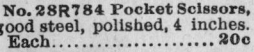

Size of scissors and shears is the entire length.

Folding Pocket Scissors.

No. 28R788 Folding Pocket Scissors, in case; nickel plated; length when open, 4 inches; length folded, 2¼ inches. Price, each......20c

Size of scissors and shears is the entire length.

Best Cast Steel Nickel Plated Nail Scissors for 45 Cents.

No. 28R789 Nail Scissors for trimming nails on both hands and feet. Best cast steel, highly tempered, nickel plated, 4 inches. Each......45c

Size of scissors and shears is the entire length.

Manicure Scissors.

No. 28R790 Manicure Scissors, made of best steel, highly tempered, nickel plated, curved ends. Each......60c

Size of scissors and shears is the entire length.

Our 25-Cent Corn Rasp.

No. 28R791 Corn Rasp, is made of high grade Black Diamond file steel, and will last a lifetime. Those whose nerves will not permit the use of a knife or razor, will find this just the thing. Length, 3⅞ inches; weight, 2 ounces. Price, each......25c

Tracing Wheels.

No. 28R792 Tracing Wheel, hardwood handle, blue steel wheel, teeth sharp and perfect. Price, each......4c

No. 28R793 Double Adjustable Tracing Wheel, with set screw, enameled handle. Price, each......9c

No. 28R794 Metal Handle Tracing Wheel, finely nickel plated and finished. Made reversible, so when not in use the wheel is entirely inclosed in handle. When lying in a work basket will not injure or become entangled with other articles. Price, each......9c

Pinking Iron.

No. 28R795 Pinking Iron, diamond tooth. ⅜, ½, ⅝, ¾, ⅞ or 1 inch. Price, each......5c

If by mail, postage extra, each, 3 cents.

Nail Clipper.

No. 28R799 Nail Clipper. The best thing ever invented for the purpose. Small and light to carry in the pocket. Made of fine steel, nickel plated. Price, each......20c

GIVE CATALOGUE NUMBER IN FULL WHEN YOU WRITE YOUR ORDER

NEW POCKET KNIVES DIRECT FROM OUR OWN FACTORY.

WE CALL YOUR ATTENTION **especially to this handsome new line of highest grade American made pocket and pen knives, our Sears, Roebuck & Co. brand.** They are made in our own factory in New York, where the cost of production is reduced to the actual cost of material and labor, all of which we give you the benefit of, adding only our one small percentage of profit. **You can buy a pocket or pen knife from us at just what it costs to make in our factory, with but our one small percentage of profit added;** less than dealers can buy in any quantity.

TO GIVE OUR CUSTOMERS a better pocket or pen knife than we have heretofore been able to buy; a pen knife made from the best selected material, made, fitted and finished by cutlery mechanics; a knife that we can send out under our binding guarantee; to give this kind of a knife at a very much lower price than ever before, we have been induced to start our own pocket cutlery factory.

THIS FACTORY **is located in the state of New York.** It is under the direct management of one of the largest and best cutlery makers in this country. We have employed a class of mechanics that insures the highest grade of work. We have succeeded in turning out a knife of better material, better finish, a more lasting article, and at a price, quality for quality, less than inferior knives have been costing us heretofore.

THERE IS NO ONE **that can begin to compete with us in price.** If you order a knife from us at 50 cents to $1.00, you will find it a better made, better finished and by far a better lasting knife than any knife you can buy elsewhere at 75 cents to $2.00.

These large, correct illustrations, reproduced from life in the exact size and shape, will give you a clear idea of their general appearance.

SEND US YOUR ORDER **for any one of these knives,** and if you do not find it perfectly satisfactory, if you are not convinced that you are buying it cheaper than your storekeeper at home can buy, you can return it to us at our expense, and we will return your money.

WE OFFER THIS SEASON **a special line of American pocket knives** that are made from the best material that can be obtained regardless of cost. All work is done by skilled mechanics, particular attention being paid to making a keen cutting knife that will carry a lasting edge.

THE BLADES ARE FORGED **from S. C. Wardlow's best English special blade steel,** the finest and the best that can be procured for knife blades. We even use Wardlow's steel for the springs, which costs nearly double the price at which ordinary spring steel can be bought, but which greatly improves the wearing qualities of the knife, and adds greatly to its durability. **Every blade, from the cheapest to the best which bears our brand, is hammered out by hand.** Instead of using iron for the lining of our cheaper knives, we pay more for steel because it makes a much stronger and better knife.

EVERY KNIFE BLADE IS TEMPERED **by the copper plate process,** by a man who has been doing this work for thirty years in the best cutlery factories in the world.

WE USE 18 PER CENT GERMAN SILVER **in our caps and bolsters** which makes a much stronger bolster, and looks and wears much better. In fact there is nothing better that can be used in the caps and bolster of a knife. There is no better method of manufacturing; there is no better method of tempering, and we have not yet seen any line of pocket knives in which so much care was used in grinding, finishing and fitting, and the chief point, the one above all others is, that our knives will cut; they will carry an edge; they will give better satisfaction in every way than any knife you have ever purchased, no matter where it was made.

WE HAVE SHAPES AND PATTERNS **that will no doubt be imitated by some unscrupulous manufacturers,** and we must caution purchasers to look for our name, which is stamped on the tang of the knife blade, if you wish to be sure of getting our quality knife. To secure our knives, our quality, our finish, they must bear our brand.

OUR POCKET KNIVES **are fully guaranteed in every way.** This means we guarantee the blades to be free from flaws, and guarantee them to be neither too hard nor too soft. This does not mean that we guarantee the knives not to break. If we were to do this, we would be obliged to temper them so soft they would be of no practical use for cutting. They are not intended to be used as mortising chisels, tack pullers, can openers, screwdrivers, crowbars, or any of the purposes by which pocket knives are frequently misused.

IF A RAZOR EDGE **is put on any of the blades that bear our brand, we will guarantee any of them to shave,** but a razor edge should never be put on a pocket knife. To get a proper edge on a pocket knife blade, the blade should be held at an angle of about 20 or 25 degrees, and drawn from shoulder to point on each side until a true edge is obtained. This makes a stiff, keen cutting edge, and enables us to furnish a much higher tempered knife blade than we would were the blade to be laid flat and brought down to a razor edge.

ALL POCKET KNIVES **should occasionally be oiled at the joint so the blade will not wear into the spring.** Vaseline makes a very good lubricant for this purpose.

ALL THE ILLUSTRATIONS SHOW EXACT SIZE AND SHAPE, being engraved direct from photograph. It is impossible, however, to show in a picture the beautiful finish, the fine workmanship and the high quality.

No. 28R830 Our Cheapest S., R. & Co.'s Pocket Knife. Has rosewood handle, steel lining, iron bolsters. The blade is not as heavy and strong as it should be for rough usage, but it makes an excellent jack knife for a boy, or for ordinary purposes. **The illustration shows exact size and shape of knife.** Price, each......(If by mail, postage extra, 4 cents)......23c

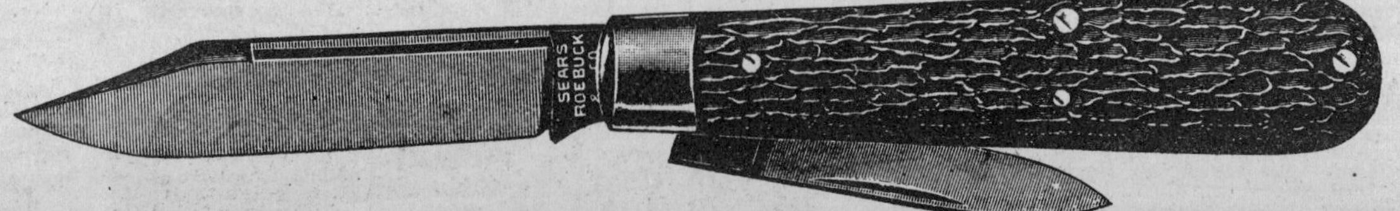

No. 28R833 Pocket Knife, stag handle, two blades, steel lining, iron bolsters. This is our cheapest, standard, full weight knife; is durable, and will give splendid satisfaction. The illustration shows exact size and shape of knife. Price, each......25c

If by mail, postage extra, 5 cents.

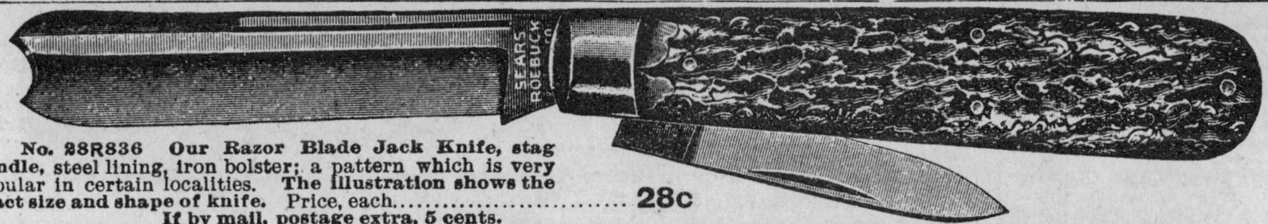

No. 28R836 Our Razor Blade Jack Knife, stag handle, steel lining, iron bolster; a pattern which is very popular in certain localities. **The illustration shows the exact size and shape of knife.** Price, each............................ **28c**
If by mail, postage extra, 5 cents.

No. 28R838 Our Stag Handle Chain Knife, two blades, steel lining, iron bolsters and cap, German silver shield, with chain of suitable length to fasten over button. This is a good, strong, serviceable knife, and one that you cannot lose. **The illustration shows exact size and shape of knife.** Price, each..................(**If by mail, postage extra, 6 cents**)................. **37c**

No. 28R840 A medium weight, finely finished knife, with white bone handle, brass lining, finished inside and out, German silver bolster and caps and shield. This shape and style of knife was at one time one of the most popular jack knives in the country, and is still a favorite with many. **The illustration shows exact size and shape of knife.** Price, each ....(**If by mail, postage extra, 5 cents**)........................ **44c**

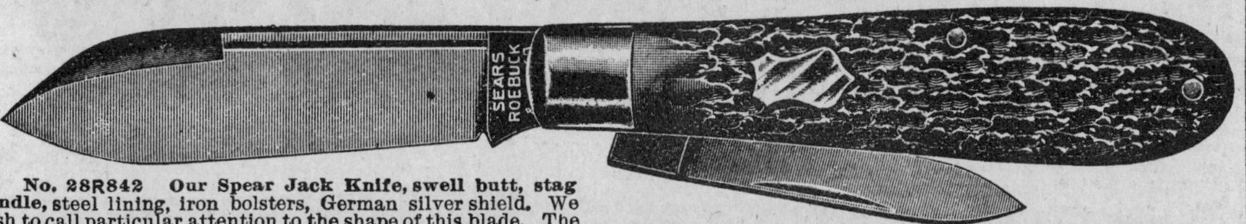

No. 28R842 Our Spear Jack Knife, swell butt, stag handle, steel lining, iron bolsters, German silver shield. We wish to call particular attention to the shape of this blade. The cutting edge is carried out well towards the point in a straight line and the knife is full where the greatest wear comes. Many manufacturers in finishing a knife, grind away half its life. This is one of the most popular pattern knives made, and is strong enough for any purpose. **The illustration shows exact size and shape of knife.** Price, each.............................. **45c**
If by mail, postage extra, 5 cents.

No. 28R845 Solid Worth Jack Knife. Is made to last and fitted and finished to please the most particular; stag handle, brass lining, finished inside and out, iron bolsters and caps, German silver shield. **The illustration shows exact size and shape of knife.** Price, each.............................(**If by mail, postage extra, 6 cents**)............ **47c**

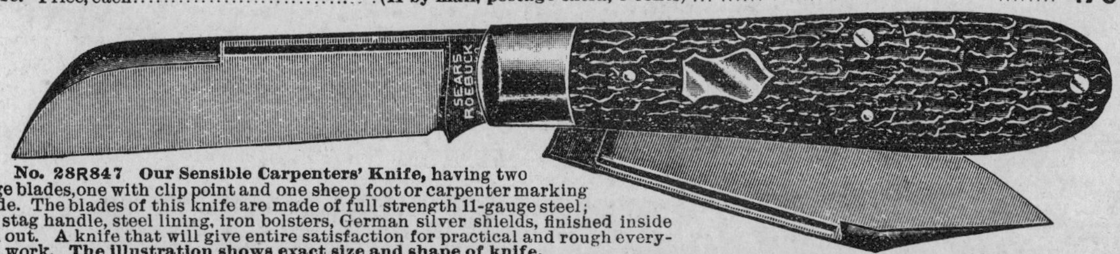

No. 28R847 Our Sensible Carpenters' Knife, having two large blades, one with clip point and one sheep foot or carpenter marking blade. The blades of this knife are made of full strength 11-gauge steel; has stag handle, steel lining, iron bolsters, German silver shields, finished inside and out. A knife that will give entire satisfaction for practical and rough everyday work. **The illustration shows exact size and shape of knife.**
Price, each...........(**If by mail, postage extra, 6 cents**)............ **48c**

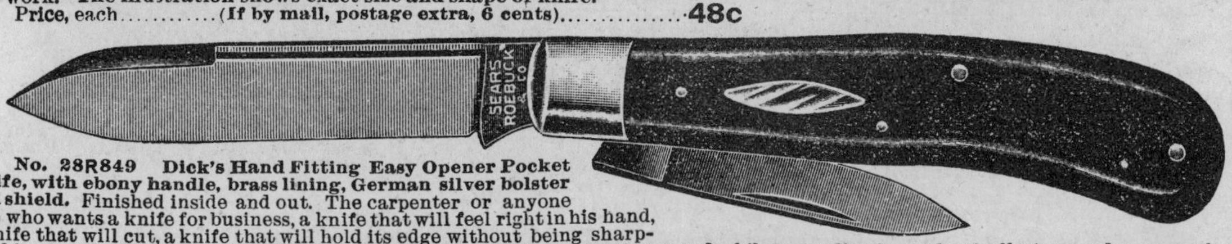

No. 28R849 Dick's Hand Fitting Easy Opener Pocket Knife, with ebony handle, brass lining, German silver bolster and shield. Finished inside and out. The carpenter or anyone else who wants a knife for business, a knife that will feel right in his hand, a knife that will cut, a knife that will hold its edge without being sharpened frequently, will buy this knife. This knife is a distinctly new pattern; and while every line is mechanically true and correct, the general shape of the knife being so different from anything heretofore shown may cause a doubt on account of its shape, but so confident are we of its popularity when once used we will guarantee to exchange any of these knives provided they have not been used, and pay the postage both ways, if not entirely satisfactory after you have held it in your hands once. **The illustration shows exact size and shape of knife.** Price, each........................(**If by mail, postage extra, 4 cents**)................ **45c**

No. 28R850 Another Dick's Easy Opener Pocket Knife, same as one previously described, with stag handle, German silver bolster caps and shield, brass lining. Finished inside and out. An attractive and serviceable knife that is sure to please. **The illustration shows exact size and shape of knife.** Price, each...(**If by mail, postage extra, 5c**)... **50c**

No. 28R854 Our Balloon Shaped Two-Blade Cocoa Handle Pocket Knife, German silver fancy bolster and shield, brass lining, finely finished inside and out. This shape is very popular and makes an attractive looking knife which lays nicely in the hand. **The illustration shows exact size and shape of knife.**
Price, each......... **49c**
If by mail, postage extra, 5 cents.

No. 28R881 Our Texas Stock Knife. A pattern of knife which is popular with stock raisers all over the world, has clip, sheep foot and spaying blades, stag handle, German silver bolsters and shield, brass lined, highly finished inside and out. This is our most popular cattle knife, and is made just as good as we know how to make them. **The illustration shows the exact size and shape of knife.**

Price, each..(If by mail, postage extra, 5 cents)..**90c**

No. 28R884 Our Sampson Pruning Knife. Blade made of 10-gauge steel. The shape of blade, method of grinding, etc., being according to the ideas of one of the best fruit growers in the country, a man who has used pruning knives for many years of his life, and who had this original made just exactly the way he wanted it regardless of expense. To make one knife in this way would cost at least $3.00, but by manufacturing them in large quantities we are able to offer you the best pruning knife that the best workmen in the United States can produce with the best material that can be found in the world at a price but very little more than is usually paid for ordinary goods. **The illustration shows exact size and shape of knife.**

Price, each..(If by mail, postage extra, 6 cents)..**42c**

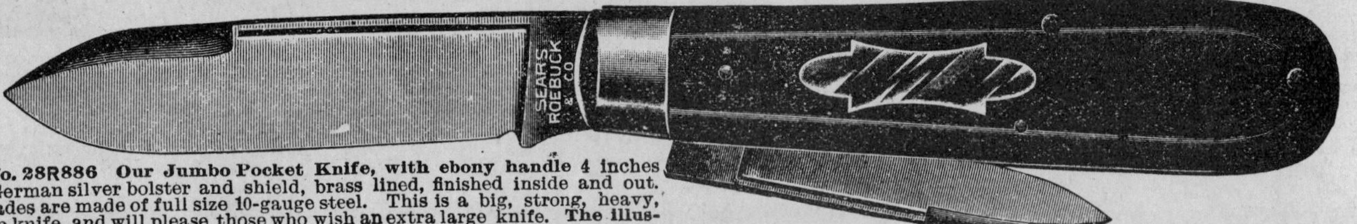

No. 28R886 Our Jumbo Pocket Knife, with ebony handle 4 inches long; German silver bolster and shield, brass lined, finished inside and out. The blades are made of full size 10-gauge steel. This is a big, strong, heavy, durable knife, and will please those who wish an extra large knife. **The illustration shows exact size and shape of knife.**

Price, each..(If by mail, postage extra, 6 cents)..**49c**

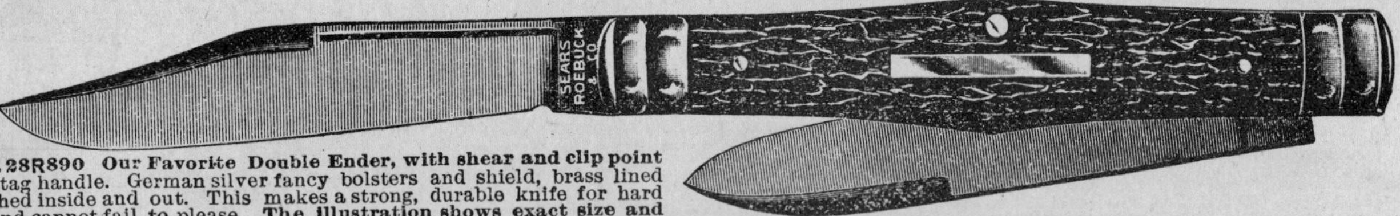

No. 28R890 Our Favorite Double Ender, with shear and clip point blades, stag handle. German silver fancy bolsters and shield, brass lined and finished inside and out. This makes a strong, durable knife for hard service and cannot fail to please. **The illustration shows exact size and shape of knife.** Price, each..(If by mail, postage extra, 5 cents)..**60c**

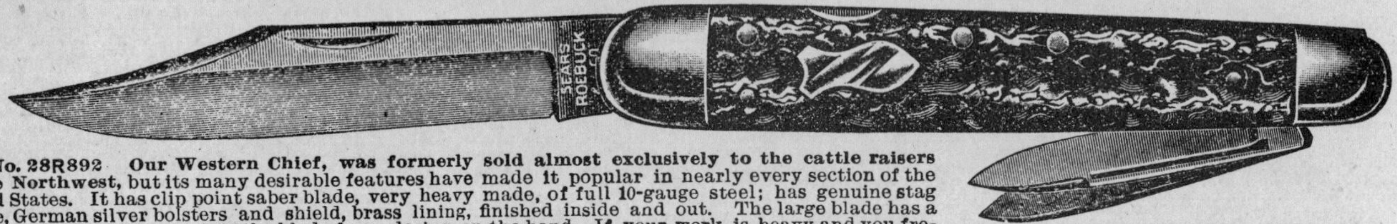

No. 28R892 Our Western Chief, was formerly sold almost exclusively to the cattle raisers of the Northwest, but its many desirable features have made it popular in nearly every section of the United States. It has clip point saber blade, very heavy made, of full 10-gauge steel; has genuine stag handle, German silver bolsters and shield, brass lining, finished inside and out. The large blade has a flush lock back, which prevents the blade from closing on the hand. If your work is heavy and you frequently break knives, we advise you to give this pattern of knife a trial, for it will certainly stand more abuse than any knife of its class which we know of. **The illustration shows exact size and shape of knife.** Price, each..**$1.05**

If by mail, postage extra, 6 cents.

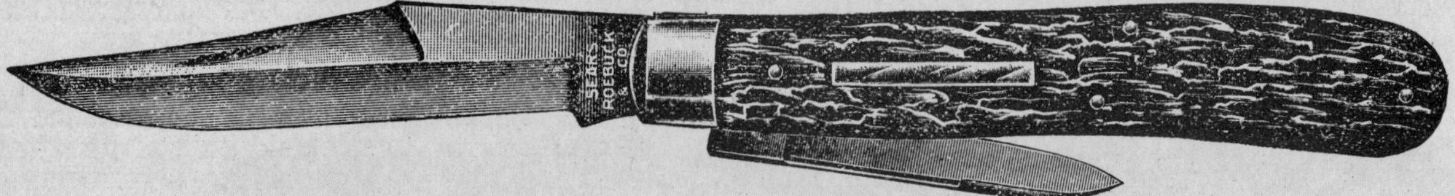

No. 28R895 Texas Tooth Pick, has stag handle, German silver bolsters and shield, brass lining, finely finished inside and out. Clip point saber blade. While the blade is long and slim the peculiar shape makes it very strong and durable as well as an excellent whittler. Every time we sell one of this pattern knife it brings us other orders from our customers and friends who see and admire it. **The illustration shows exact size and shape of knife.**

Price, each..(If by mail, postage extra, 6 cents)..**50c**

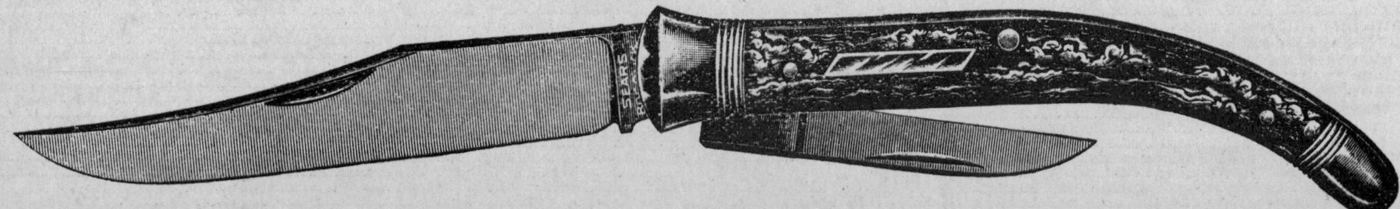

No. 28R896 Austrian Hunter. We have had a large sale for this pattern of knife, which we have imported from Austria, and while the quality of the knife was not first class the peculiar shape of the handle and blade have made it very popular; and believing there is a demand for a knife of this shape, made thoroughly honest in every way, of good cutting qualities and workmanship, better finished, we have reproduced the pattern in our line of American goods. It has a clip point blade as shown in illustration, stag handle, fancy iron bolster and caps, German silver shield, steel lining, finely finished inside and out. **The illustration shows exact size and shape of knife.** Price, each..(If by mail, postage extra, 6 cents)..**94c**

The following five patterns of pocket knives—the celebrated NON-XLL brand—are made in England. They are fully warranted.

No. 28R1072 A NON-XLL Knife of an improved **Barlow Pattern,** strong, durable, with blades of the best English steel and genuine stag handle. Has clip point on large blade and iron lining. Octagon bolster, highly polished blades. A fully warranted knife for little money. Length of handle, 3¼ inches; length with large blade open, 6 inches.
Price, each....30c

No. 28R1073 Another NON-XLL Improved Barlow Pattern Knife. Similar to the one above, but with the old fashioned razor blade. Genuine stag handle; fully warranted. Length of handle, 3⅜ inches, and with large blade open, 6 inches.
Price, each....30c

No. 28R1103 A NON-XLL Pocket Knife, with two large blades; one spaying blade and one spear blade; genuine stag handle, iron lined. Length of handle, 3⅝ inches; entire length with large blade open, 6⅝ inches. For cutting qualities this knife cannot be excelled. **Fully warranted.**
Price, each....50c

No. 28R1133 NON-XLL Pruning Knife, with Budding or Spaying Blade. Best English steel, fully warranted, genuine stag handle, iron lining and double bolster. Strong and well made. Length of handle, 4 inches; length, with large blade open, 6⅝ inches. Price, each....95c

No. 28R1135 The NON-XLL Sportsman Combination Knife. This pattern knife is usually sold in a quality that is very poor—this is a good one. A kit of tools in itself; has large and small blades, fleam, hoof pick, corkscrew, reamer, screwdriver, tweezers and toothpick. Made of the best English steel, with genuine stag handle, and fully warranted. Length of handle, 3⅝ inches; length with large blade open, 6½ inches. Price, each....$1.50

Genuine Joh. Engstrom Swedish Hunting Knife.

Blade can be removed, folded into its frame, and replaced in the handle. This knife is a popular woodworkers' tool, as well as a hunting knife. Has solid boxwood handle. **The blade is best of steel, and the maker's name is a guarantee of cutting qualities and temper.** We have this knife in three sizes.

No. 28R1310 Genuine Joh. Engstrom Swedish Hunting Knife, as described above. Length of handle, 2⅞ inches. Price, each....45c
No. 28R1311 Genuine Joh. Engstrom Swedish Hunting Knife, as described above. Length of handle, 3¼ inches. Price, each....59c
No. 28R1312 Genuine Joh. Engstrom Swedish Hunting Knife, as described above. Length of handle, 4⅜ inches. Price, each....64c

Sloyd or Swedish Carpenters' Bench Knife. Does not close. Intended for the tool chest or work bench. Used everywhere in manual training schools. Made from the finest quality of Swedish razor steel. They are very desirable for heavy work. The tang of the blade passes entirely through the handle.
No. 28R1315 Swedish Carpenters' Bench Knife. Length of blade, 2¼ inches. Price, each....25c
No. 28R1316 Swedish Carpenters' Bench Knife. Length of blade, 3¼ inches. Price, each....30c

Push Button Knives.

MADE IN AMERICA. **Pressure on the button opens the knife and locks the blades so it cannot close. The cutting qualities of these knives are first class and their convenience has made them very popular. But one hand is required to open or close these knives.**

No. 28R1320 Push Button Knife. One blade clip point, stag handle, single bolster, iron lined. Length of handle, 3⅞ inches; length with blade open, 6⅞ inches. Price, each....60c

No. 28R1324 Push Button Knife. One blade, clip point, stag handle, single bolster, iron lined. Length of handle, 4¾ inches; length with blade open, 8⅜ inches. Price, each....75c

No. 28R1326 Push Button Knife. Two blades, stag handle, brass lined. Length of handle, 3⅜ inches; length with large blade open, 5¼ inches.
Price, each....60c

No. 28R1328 This is a knife that is especially desirable for teamsters. Has cocoa handle, German silver bolster, tips and shields, brass lined. Length of handle, 3½ inches; length with the large blade open, 6¼ inches. Instead of having an ordinary small blade, this knife is furnished with a gouge shaped blade, which will bore a ⅛-inch hole through the traces or any part of the harness, and will bore equally well in wood. Price, each....54c

Rack Knives.

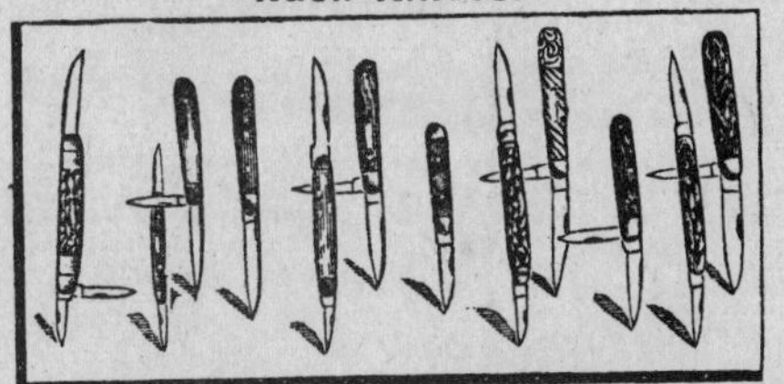

No. 28R1332 Assorted Knives. We have had many calls for cheap knives for knife racks, and above we show an assortment of 12 styles of knives suitable for this purpose. **We do not sell less than a dozen and do not break dozens.** They are as good or better than the class of goods usually sold for this purpose, but they are not good enough for our customers to use. Price, per dozen, all different (one of each pattern as shown in cut)....$1.25

Pen Knives.

The following four patterns of pen knives are of German make, not guaranteed. They are all right to sharpen pencils, cut finger nails, etc. The quality and finish is better than you will expect for the price.

No. 28R1500 Two-Blade, Pearl Handle Ladies' Knife, brass lined; a pretty knife. Price, each....16c

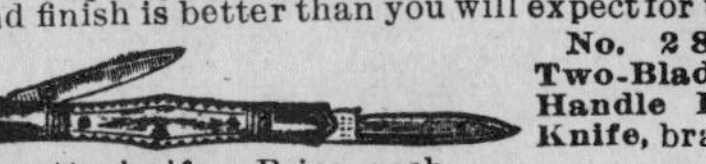

No. 28R1505 Two-Blade, Corrugated Pearl Handle Ladies' Knife, polished steel blades, and a beauty. Length, 2¾ inches. Price, each....25c

No. 28R1510 Two-Blade, Ladies' Knife, pearl handle, brass lined, finely finished and warranted. Length, 2¾ inches. Price, each....35c

No. 28R1550 Four-Blade, Ebony Handle Pen Knife, elongated shield, brass lined. Length, 3½ inches. A neat knife. Price, each....30c

Combination Pen Knife, $1.85.

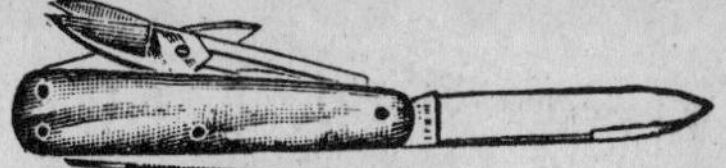

No. 28R1553 A Warranted Pearl Handle Combination Knife, has two blades, pair scissors and nail file, German silver lined, crocus polish. Made in the best possible manner and a most desirable pen knife. Length of handle, 2¼ inches; length with large blade open, 4⅛ inches. Price, each....$1.85

Knife Hones.

No. 28R1674 Pocket Knife Hone. A sharp grit natural stone on wood handle with razor strop, leather back. Hone is 4x1 inches, whole length about 6½ inches. Price, each....15c

No. 28R1676 Pocket Emery Hone. A fine emery knife hone in case. Price, each....10c

Knife Purses.

No. 28R1677 Knife Purse, will take almost any pen knife. When ordered with knife we send purse to fit knife. They are not large enough for jack knives. Price, each, without knife....8c

Shaving Sets.

THE CHEAPEST SET WE OFFER IS MADE OF GOOD GOODS.

There have been many shaving sets gotten up for sale in so-called racket stores or department stores. Quality is no consideration in such cases, the only point being to get up a set at the least possible price. The following sets will be found to be made up of **reliable goods that will give satisfaction in every case.**

No. 28R1995 Our Bon Ton Shaving Set consists of your choice of any razor quoted in our cutlery department, except our High Art Razor; 1 double swing barbers' razor strop, horsehide and linen with metallic end and swivel; 1 barbers' shaving brush, white bristles, with buffalo horn ferrule; 1 handsomely decorated shaving mug with partition; 1 cake of the **celebrated Yankee shaving soap (the genuine).** If you are well posted in qualities of these goods you must admit that **this set is the best that money can buy.**

Make your order for the above shaving set thus: "No. 28R1995, 1 shaving set with No....... razor," filling in the blank with the catalogue number of the razor you select.
Our price for entire outfit....$2.75

No. 28R1997 Our Acme Shaving Set consists of 1 Sears, Roebuck & Co.'s Acme razor, 1 double swing razor strop (canvas and horsehide with metal ends and swivel), 1 good shaving brush, 1 decorated shaving mug, 1 cake shaving soap. **Remember, the razor is fully warranted.**
Our price for the complete set....$1.75

No. 28R1998 Our Winner Shaving Set consists of 1 medium hollow ground razor (warranted), 1 horsehide swing strop, 1 decorated shaving mug, 1 cake shaving soap, 1 good shaving brush, **all good, reliable goods.** Our price for entire set....$1.25

No. 28R1999 Our Competition Shaving Set is offered in competition with those sets found in 99-cent stores, but it is far superior to such goods. It is our intention always to describe all articles exactly as they are, consequently we cannot recommend this set any more than to say it will be found better than you can possibly procure elsewhere at anything like this price. The razor is a good shaver and the strop, etc., will give satisfaction in use. It is wonderful value for the price. The set consists of 1 hollow ground razor, 1 swing strop, 1 shaving brush, 1 divided shaving mug, 1 cake shaving soap.
Our price for the entire set....95c

REMEMBER THAT SEARS, ROEBUCK & CO.'S RAZORS ARE THE BEST ON EARTH.

SEE OUR COMPLETE LINE OF RAZORS, LATHER BRUSHES, STROPS, MUGS, HAIR CLIPPERS, ETC., ...ON THE FOLLOWING PAGES....

Sears, Roebuck & Co.'s Razors

...OUR... High Art Razor...

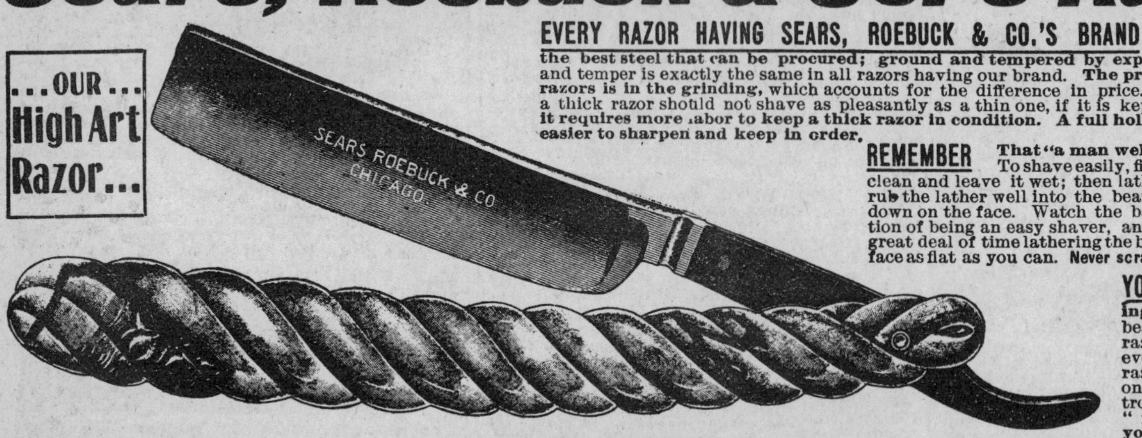

EVERY RAZOR HAVING SEARS, ROEBUCK & CO.'S BRAND is fully warranted. The blades are made from the best steel that can be procured; ground and tempered by experts. The quality of steel and temper is exactly the same in all razors having our brand. **The principal expense in making razors is in the grinding, which accounts for the difference in price.** There is no reason why a thick razor should not shave as pleasantly as a thin one, if it is kept in as good an edge, but it requires more labor to keep a thick razor in condition. **A full hollow ground razor is much easier to sharpen and keep in order.**

REMEMBER That "a man well lathered is half shaved." To shave easily, first wash your face perfectly clean and leave it wet; then lather it well with a brush and rub the lather well into the beard so that the lather gets down on the face. Watch the barber who has the reputation of being an easy shaver, and you will find he spends a great deal of time lathering the beard. Lay the blade on your face as flat as you can. **Never scrape your face, cut off the beard.**

YOUR BEARD should guide you in selecting a razor. A heavy, wiry beard requires a wide, heavy razor. A man who shaves every day can use a lighter razor than he who shaves but once a week. If you have had trouble in finding a razor to "fit your beard," we can fit you. A razor with ⅝-inch blade fits an ordinary beard. A razor with ½-inch blade fits the man with a light beard or one who shaves every day. It is also fine for shaving the second time over. A razor with a ¾-inch blade fits the coarse, heavy beard.

SEARS, ROEBUCK & CO.'S RAZORS ARE THE BEST ON EARTH. **NONE GENUINE UNLESS STAMPED ON TANG WITH OUR NAME. Beware of inferior razors which may look the same or have the same etchings on blade. Look for our name on the tang. These razors are fully warranted, but a razor must be returned to us in good condition, showing no signs of abuse, or we will not exchange it for another. Sears, Roebuck & Co.'s High Art Razor.** Ground on a 1½-inch stone by an expert grinder. Has black rubber tang with fancy imitation onyx handle. Made from the highest grade steel and in the best possible manner, regardless of cost. **Guaranteed to shave any beard or it may be returned and money will be refunded or a new razor given instead.**

No. 28R3000 Sears, Roebuck & Co.'s High Art Razor, with ½-inch blade. Price, each........**$2.45**

No. 28R3001 Sears, Roebuck & Co.'s High Art Razor, with ⅝-inch blade. Price, each........**$2.50**

No. 28R3002 Sears, Roebuck & Co.'s High Art Razor, with ¾-inch blade. Price, each........**$2.55**

No. 28R3006 Sears, Roebuck & Co.'s Barbers' Razor. Extra hollow ground, ½-inch blade. **Fully warranted.** Price, each..........................**$1.50**

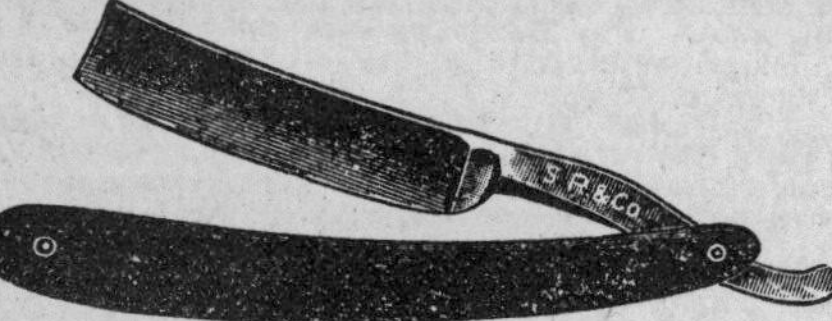

No. 28R3009 Sears, Roebuck & Co.'s Barbers' Razor. Extra hollow ground, ⅝-inch blade. **Fully warranted.** Price, each..........................**$1.50**

No. 28R3015 Sears, Roebuck & Co.'s Barbers' Razor. Extra hollow ground, ¾-inch blade. **Fully warranted.** Price, each..........................**$1.50**

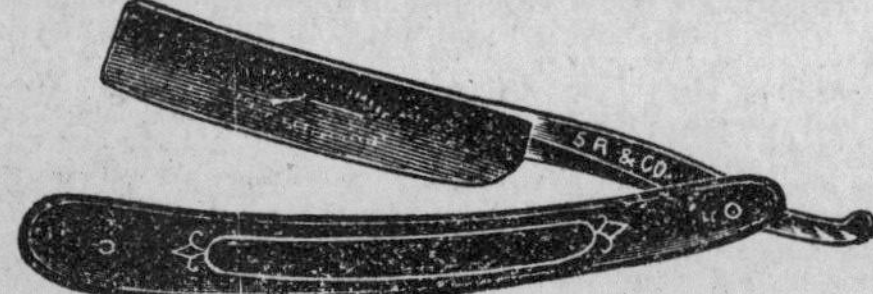

No. 28R3019 Sears, Roebuck & Co.'s Medium Hollow Ground Razor. Hollow point, ⅝-inch blade. Price, each..........................**58c**

No. 28R3024 The Original "Naval" Razor is an old, well known razor, with an established reputation, ⅝-inch blade. Price, each..........................**75c**

If Razors are Sent by Mail, Postage must be paid by you.

IT'S 10 CENTS FOR EACH RAZOR....

No. 28R3028 Sears, Roebuck & Co.'s Acme Razor. Full hollow ground, ⅝-inch blade. This razor will probably "fit" more beards than any razor we sell. **It is ground by experts and is suitable for barbers' use.** Razors that are not its equal are usually sold at $1.50. **To advertise our cutlery department we shall sell it for..........................98c**

No. 28R3030 Sears, Roebuck & Co.'s Prince Razor. Extra hollow ground, ⅝-inch blade; round point. **A very superior razor for private or barbers' use.** Price, each..........................**$1.35**

No. 28R3033 Sears, Roebuck & Co.'s Our Favorite Razor is a very thin, extra hollow ground razor for barbers' use. This razor requires careful handling to be kept in proper condition, but if properly stropped **will give excellent satisfaction in private use;** ⅝-inch blade. Price, each........**$1.45**

No. 28R3035 Sears, Roebuck & Co.'s Extra Hollow Ground Razor, with fancy grained celluloid handles for barbers' or private use; ⅝-inch blade. **A very handsome razor.** Price, each........**$1.60**

No. 28R3040 Sears, Roebuck & Co.'s Victor Razor. Hollow point, fancy celluloid handle; ⅝-in. blade. **A popular razor for private use.** Each,**$1.65**

No. 28R3044 Sears, Roebuck & Co.'s Clean Shave Razor is another finely ground fancy razor, suitable for either barbers' or private use. Has ⅝-inch blade. Fancy celluloid handle. Price, each..........................**$1.65**

No. 28R3048 Sears, Roebuck & Co.'s Fancy Celluloid Handle Razor. Best steel blade, hollow ground, finest finish, ⅝-in. blade. Price, each..**$1.75**

A $3.00 Razor for $2.00.

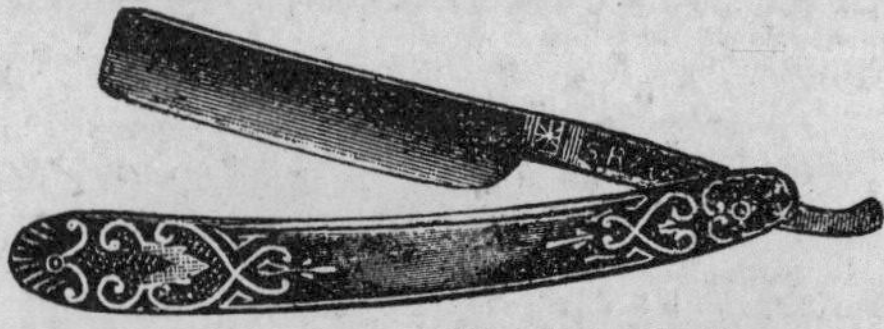

No. 28R3050 Sears, Roebuck & Co.'s Ivory Tang Razor is a very finely ground razor with ivory tang and fancy grained celluloid handle. Only an expert would know this was not a real ivory handle. It makes an elegant present and is a first class shaver. Price, each..........................**$2.00**

No. 28R3052 Fancy Celluloid Handle Razor. One of the best razors made for private or barbers' use. Full hollow ground, warranted best material, ⅝-inch blade. Price, each..........................**$2.00**

IMPORTED RAZORS.

The following Razors are selected from the lines of well known manufacturers and are guaranteed to be exactly as represented.

Jos. Allen & Sons, Celebrated NON-XLL Razors.

No. 28R3100 NON-XLL Razor, grained celluloid handle, imitation ivory; full hollow ground, square point, ⅝-inch blade, finely polished and etched; **is made by Jos. Allen & Sons,** one of the leading cutlery manufacturers of Sheffield, England, and is fully warranted. Price, each..........................**$1.25**

Non-XLL Razors.

No. 28R3102 NON-XLL Razor, fancy carved celluloid handle, ⅝-inch blade, with round point, full hollow ground, polished and etched. A razor which is warranted, and which cannot fail to give satisfaction. Price, each..............$1.25

Wostenholm Razors.

No. 28R3106 Wostenholm's New Pipe Razor, ½-inch blade, best quality hollow ground. A little gem and a dandy shaver; no better steel put in a razor. Every one likes it; warranted. Price, each... .98c

No. 28R3108 Original Pipe Razor, square point, medium hollow ground, black rubber handle, best steel mirror finish. Fully warranted. ⅝-inch blade. Price, each............$1.15

No. 28R3112 Full Hollow Ground Wostenholm Pipe Razor, black rubber handle, one of the best razors made. Fully warranted. ⅝-inch blade. Price, each..............................$1.50

Wade & Butcher's Razors.

No. 28R3115 Wade & Butcher's Hollow Point, medium hollow ground razor, rubber handle. Fully warranted and a superior cutter, ⅝-inch blade. Price, each..........................85c

No. 28R3121 Wade & Butcher's Special Razor. Full hollow ground. A superfine barbers' razor. Black rubber handle. Width of blade, ⅝-inch. Price, each.........$1.50

No. 28R3122 Wade & Butcher's Special Razor. Same as above, except blade is ¾-inch wide. Price, each..............................$1.50

H. Boker's Tree Brand Razors.

No. 28R3126 H. Boker's Tree Brand Razor, black rubber handle, hollow point, ⅝-inch blade, a finely made razor of serviceable quality. Warranted. Price, each..............................60c

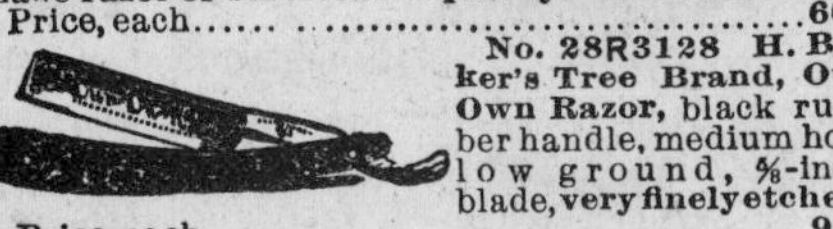

No. 28R3128 H. Boker's Tree Brand, Our Own Razor, black rubber handle, medium hollow ground, ⅝-inch blade, very finely etched. Price, each..............................95c

No. 28R3130 Tree Razor, black rubber handle, hollow point, medium hollow ground, ⅝-inch blade. Fully warranted. If properly used will require no honing in private use. Price, each..............................$1.40

No. 28R3135 Tree Razor, black rubber handle, square point, full hollow ground, ⅝-inch blade. Warranted best steel. A favorite razor with barbers. Price, each......$1.75

No. 28R3140 Tree Brand, Fancy Celluloid Handle Razor, finely ground, best ⅝-inch steel blade. Fully warranted. Price, each..............................$1.75

Swedish Razors.

No. 28R3145 Genuine John Engstrom Swedish Razor. A popular pattern, finely ground, warranted best ⅝-inch steel blade. Price, each..............98c

Joseph Rodgers & Son's Razors.

No. 28R3160 Joseph Rodgers & Sons' Medium Hollow Ground Razor, with ⅝-inch blade. Black rubber handle. Price, each..............................70c

No. 28R3162 Joseph Rodgers & Sons' Extra Hollow Ground Special Barbers' Razor, with square point. Black handle. Width of blade.. ½-inch ⅝-inch ¾-inch Price, each.......... $1.40 $1.50 $1.60

Shaving Mugs.

No. 28R3170 Carlsbad China Shaving Mug. Floral decorations. Gold line. Price, each..............................15c

No. 28R3172 Genuine Austrian China Shaving Mug. Floral decorations. Heavily gold stippled. Price, each..............................25c

No. 28R3173 German China Shaving Mug, with partition for soap. Floral decorations. Gold lined. Price, each..............................20c

No. 28R3175 Genuine Hapsburg China Shaving Mug, with partition for soap. Neat floral decorations heavily gold stippled on edges and handle. Price, each..............................50c

The Genuine Star Safety Razor.

No. 28R3190 Star Safety Razor. An invention which obviates all danger of cutting the face. It is especially adapted to old and young, and is indispensable to travelers, miners and persons camping out. Blades of best steel and full concave, which can be easily removed and placed in handle for stropping. Full nickel plated, packed in latest improved box. Price, each..............$1.42 **If by mail, postage extra, 5 cents.**

No. 28R3191 Extra Blades for Star Safety Razor. Price, each..............................98c

No. 28R3195 Stropping Machine for Star Safety Razor, without strop. A swing strop should be used with this machine. Price, each............$1.65

No. 28R3198 Prepared Canvas Strop for the Star Safety Razor. Price, each..............................39c

No. 28R3199 The Improved Diagonal Finish Leather Strop for the Star Safety Razor. Price, each..............................83c

Star Safety Razor Sets.

No. 28R3220 Star Safety Razor Combination Set consists of a Star Safety Razor, Stropping Machine and Diagonal Finish Leather Strop, all packed complete in imitation leather case. Just the thing for tourists' use. Price of complete set........$4.00

No. 28R3225 The Jewel Case. Put up in elegant satin lined morocco case, and contains one safety frame and one blade. Price..............$2.25

No. 28R3227 The Gem Case. Elegantly finished in morocco. Contains one safety frame with two blades, and is a gem in the full sense of the word. Price..............$3.30

No. 28R3229 The Traveling Case. Put up in elegant satin lined morocco case, and contains one safety frame with two perfectly adjusted blades of fine silver steel; box of finely perfumed shaving soap; holder for stropping and honing blades; shaving brush, comb and cosmetique; in fact, everything requisite for an easy, quick and luxurious shave. Price..............................$5.40

No. 28R3232 The Favorite Case. Contains one safety frame and seven blades—one blade for each day in the week. This case is especially adapted to the wants of those who find a razor works easier by frequent changing. It is a very elaborate and handsome affair, put up in morocco and lined with satin. Price..............................$9.00

Favorite Traveling Outfit.

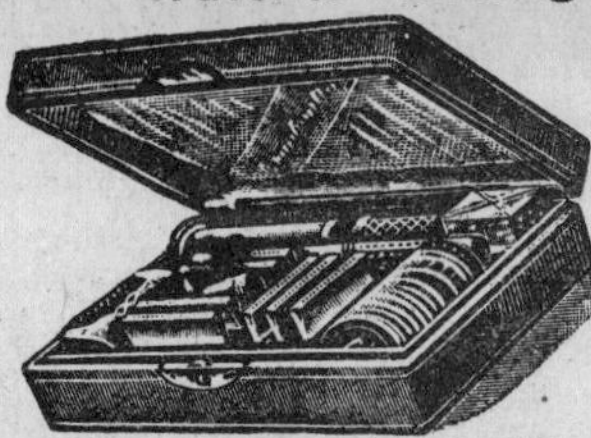

No. 28R3234 Favorite Traveling Case. To the long distance traveler, this case is invaluable. The case is a fine combination of both our Traveling and Favorite cases in one. The covering of case is of leather and the inside of satin. The interior contains one frame of Star Razor, seven blades, one candle, soap, comb, cosmetique and brush. With good care this case will last a lifetime. Price......$12.50

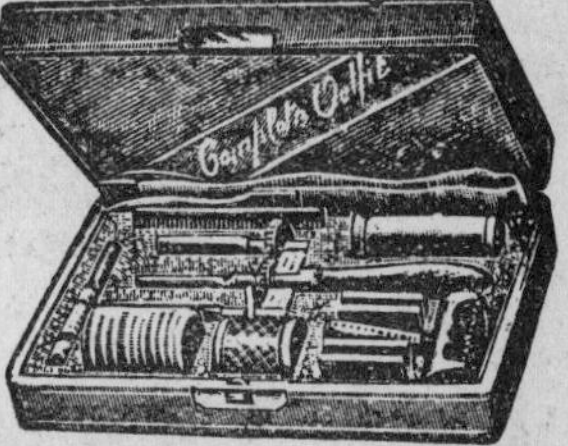

No. 28R3237 Complete Outfit. This handsome case, with its galaxy of everything necessary for shaving, is a perfect beauty. It holds four highly tempered blades of the first quality, one frame, one famous strop machine, strop, razor handle, soap, comb, cosmetique and brush. The interior of the case is doeskin and the covering of fancy leather. Price..............................$15.00

Razor Strops.

The best razor is no good without a first class strop.

No. 28R3250 Combination Four-Side Extension Razor Strop. A good strop for little money. Price, each..............................20c

No. 28R3253 Belt Two-Side Extension Razor Strop. A fair grade strop. Price, each..............................25c

No. 28R3256 Combination Four-Side Extension Razor Strop with cushion buff. A fine strop. Price, each..............................35c

No. 28R3260 Cushion Strop, Four-Side. This is a very superior strop of this old favorite style. Price, each..............................50c

No. 28R3262 Double Swing Razor Strop, black leather on one side, tubular cotton hose on the other; has swivel and black enameled wood handle. Width, 2 inches; entire length, 22½ inches. Price, each, 25c

No. 28R3265 Double Swing Razor Strop. Porpoise hide oil finished leather on one side and prepared tubular cotton hose on the other; has a swivel and fashioned handle. Width, 2 inches; entire length, 23 inches. Price, each..............35c

A Leader at 50 Cents.

No. 28R3267 Our 50-cent Leader. This strop is better value than we have ever before been able to offer at this price. This is a double swing strop. Special porpoise hide oil finished leather on one side and extra prepared webbing on the other. Has swivel and padded leather handles. Width, 2¼ inches; entire length, 24 inches. Price, each..............50c

No. 28R3270 Boar Skin, Double Swing, Razor Strop. Boar skin on one side, satin finished horsehide leather on the other; the boar skin and horsehide being cemented together. This has been a very popular seller with us, and we have had no complaints from it. **Has swivel, link and fashioned handle.** Width, 2 inches; entire length, 25 inches. Price, each..............................60c

No. 28R3272 Double Swing Strop, porpoise hide oil finished leather on one side and pure Irish linen hose, prepared and polished, on the other. **Nickel plated removable swivel, fashioned handle.** A fine strop for professional barbers. Width, 2¼ inches; entire length, 25 inches. Price, each............**75c**

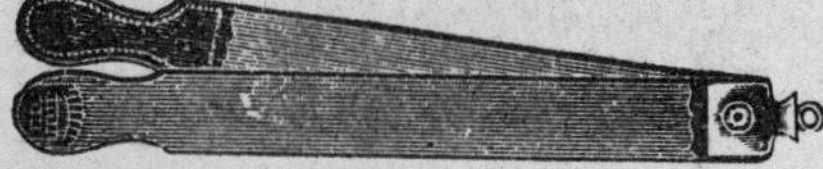

No. 28R3276 Double Swing Strop, very extra quality, satin finished genuine horsehide leather on one side and pure Irish linen hose, prepared and polished, on the other. **Removable nickel plated swivel, fashioned handle.** A superior strop, good and durable for any use. Width, 2¼ inches; entire length, 25 inches. Price, each......**$1.00**

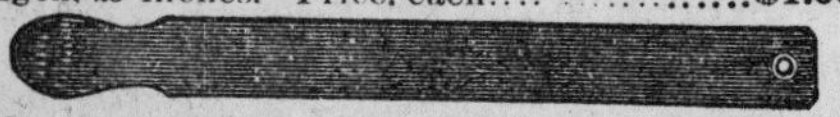

No. 28R3280 Single Swing Barbers' Strop, porpoise hide oil finished prepared leather. The strop that barbers buy. **Fashioned handle and eyelet.** Width, 2¼ inches; entire length, 24 inches. Price, each......**25c**

No. 28R3284 Single Swing Barbers' Strop. Pure Irish linen, prepared and polished especially for professional barbers' use. **Fashioned leather handle and eyelet.** Width, 2¼ inches; entire length, 24 inches. Price, each......**35c**

No. 28R3287 Extra Fine Selected Shell Horsehide Razor Strop. Single swing. Width, 2¼ inches; entire length, 24 inches. Used by first class barbers. Price, each......**75c**

Razor Strop Holder.

No. 28R3295 Razor Strop Holder with Swivel. Will hold two single swing strops. Width, 2 inches. Price, each, **10c**

Razor Hones.

No. 28R3300 A Very Good Belgian Razor Hone, that will give satisfaction in private use. We sell them for the same amount of money you must pay to have your razor honed once. Price...**25c**
If by mail, postage extra, 15 cents.

No. 28R3302 A Superfine Belgian Razor Hone, special selection for our trade. Each hone packed in neat cardboard case; every one perfect; suitable for private or barbers' use. Price, each.........**50c**
If by mail, postage extra, 25 cents.

No. 28R3305 Extra Superfine Belgian Razor Hones for professional use. Price, each.........**75c**
If by mail, postage extra, 25 cents.

No. 28R3306 Barbers' Special Belgian Hone, selected especially for the best barbers' trade. In quality it is the very best and in shape the most convenient for barbers' use. Each hone packed in strong paper box. Size, 5x2½ inches. Price, each.........**$1.75**
If by mail, postage extra, 25 cents.

No. 28R3307 Barbers' Special Belgian Hone, same as above, only smaller. Size, 4x2 inches. Price, each......**83c**
If by mail, postage extra, 18 cents.

Genuine Swaty Hones.

No. 28R3308 The Genuine Swaty Hones, small size, for private use. Price, each......**49c**
If by mail, postage extra, 15 cents.

No. 28R3312 The Genuine Swaty Hones, larger size, for barbers' use. Considered by many barbers the best. Sold by barbers' supply houses at $2.50. Our price.....(Postage extra, 25 cents)......**$1.10**

German Water Hones.

No. 28R3318 Dark Blue German Water Hones with "rubbers." Length, 7 inches. Price, each..**20c**

No. 28R3319 Barbers' Gem German Water Hones, especially selected for barbers' use. Size, 5x2½ inches. Put up in a strong paper box. Price, each......(Postage extra, 25 cents)......**50c**

Razor Strop Paste.

No. 28R3320 Razorine. For sharpening razors, spread lightly and evenly over strop. **Directions with each package.** Price, per cake......**11c**
If by mail, postage extra, 2 cents.

Shaving or Lather Brushes.

Weight of each brush, 3 ounces.

No. 28R3350 Black Enameled Handle Shaving Brush. White bristles. Length of bristles, 2 inches. Diameter of brush at handle, ⅝-inch. **A very good brush for the money.** Price, each......**5c**

No. 28R3354 Brown Enameled Handle Shaving Brush. White bristles; nickel plated metal ferrules. Length of bristles, 2 inches. Diameter of brush at ferrule, 1⅓-inch. **A well set, durable brush.** Each..**10c**

No. 28R3360 Brown Enameled Handle Shaving Brush. White bristles; wire bound. Length of bristles, 2⅛ inches. Diameter of brush at ferrule, ⅝-inch. **This is a large, well set, durable brush, and is exceedingly good value.** Price, each......**15c**

Patent Folding Handle Tourists' Shaving Brush.

No. 28R3362 White bristles, nickle ferrule. Length of bristles, 2 inches. Diameter of brush at ferrule, ⅝-inch. **Cut shows brush ready for shaving.** When not in use the ferrule can be unscrewed and placed in the hollow handle, making the package only 2½ inches long and ¾ inch in diameter. All metal parts are made from brass and are heavily nickel plated. Price, each......**18c**

No. 28R3365 Walnut Handle Shaving Brush. White bristles; with patent fasteners; twine bound. Length of bristles, 2⅛ inches. Diameter of brush at binding, ⅞ inch. **This is a very popular brush, and one that cannot fail to give satisfaction.** Price, each.....**15c**

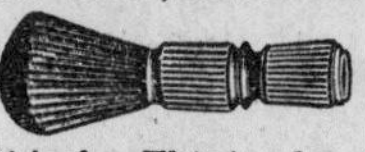

No. 28R3370 Beech Handle Shaving Brush. Imitation badger hair, with metal ferrule. The stock of this brush is the best black bristles, with a row of badger hair on outside, giving it the appearance of a genuine badger hair brush. Handle is a very good imitation of boxwood. **It is a very popular shape, and a brush that will give satisfaction in every way.** The bristles and hair are 2 inches long. Diameter of brush at ferrule, ¾ inch. Price, each......**22c**

No. 28R3372 Fancy Carved White Celluloid Shaving Brush. White bristles. Length of bristles, 2 inches. Diameter of brush at ferrule, ¾-inch. Bristles well set. Price, each......**25c**

No. 28R3373 Fancy Celluloid Handle Shaving Brush. Imitation badger hair. Length of hair, 2 inches. Diameter of brush at ferrule, ¾ inch. This is a brush that is frequently sold as a genuine badger hair brush, but a portion of the stock from which the brush is made is bristles. **It is a brush which has a fine appearance and will give excellent satisfaction in use.** Price, each......**43c**

No. 28R3378 Fancy Celluloid Handle Shaving Brush. Genuine badger hair. Fancy carved horn ferrule. Length of hair, 1¾ inches. Diameter of brush, ¾ inch. Every hair in this brush is guaranteed genuine badger hair. **It is well set and a brush that cannot fail to please.** Price, each......**75c**

No. 28R3380 Barbers' Shaving Brush, No. 1, or Standard Size. This is a popular professional barbers' brush, with boxwood handle. Rubber ferrule. Guaranteed never to shed bristles. The stock is 2¼ inches long. Diameter of brush at ferrule is ⅞ inch. Price, each......**24c**

No. 28R3381 Barbers' Shaving Brush. Size No. 3, boxwood handle, rubber ferrule. Length of bristles, 2⅝ inches. Diameter of brush at ferrule, 1 inch. Same style and quality as No. 28R3380 only larger. **Guaranteed never to shed bristles.** Price, each......**34c**

No. 28R3382 Barbers' Shaving Brush. Handle imitation boxwood. Ferrule imitation rubber. The stock is white bristles, 1⅞ inches long. Diameter of brush at ferrule, ¾ inch. A brush that looks almost as good as the brush described in catalogue under No. 28R3380 **and sold by some dealers for nearly the same price we ask for that, but it is not as good. It's cheap at our price.** Price, each......**8c**

No. 28R3400 Shaving Cabinet, complete with fancy celluloid handle warranted razor, extra hollow ground, double swing canvas and horsehide strop, cake of Williams' Yankee shaving soap, decorated shaving mug, large size well set lather brush. The front of cabinet is furnished with mirror 5¼x8¼ inches. The mirror and door may be adjusted to any angle. The bottom shelf can be pushed in out of the way when not in use. Price for shaving set, complete, with cabinet......**$4.00**
No. 28R3401 Price of cabinet only......**1.35**

Barbers' Hair Clippers.

For Human Hair only. For Horse and Dog Clippers, see Harness Department.

No. 28R3450 Barbers' Hair Clipper. A new improved pattern. The tension bolt is set forward as shown in illustration, making a better cutting clipper. The bottom plate is hollowed so only the points of teeth touch the scalp. Workmanship first class. A clipper that is a favorite with first class barbers. Price, each......**$1.45**

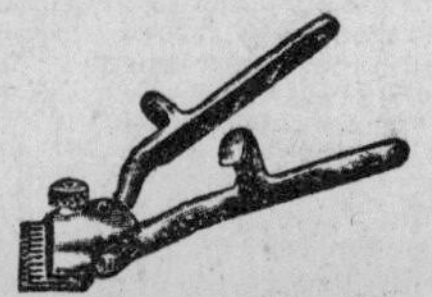

No. 28R3451 Springs for above Clipper, each .10

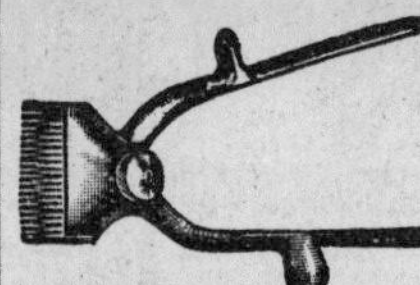

No. 28R3456 Hair Clipper, is full nickel plated. Has concealed spring, that is easily replaced if broken. This style clipper is very popular. Cuts hair one-eighth of an inch long. A full size, well made, good cutting barbers' hair clipper. Weight, 9 ounces. Price, each.....**63c**

Repairs for Above Clippers.

No. 28R3457	Springs, each	10c
No. 28R3458	Top plates, each	40c
No. 28R3459	Bottom plates, each	40c

SPECIAL NOTICE—When ordering repairs for clippers be sure to give us the NAME of the clipper and all marks that appear on it. We do not furnish springs or repairs for any clipper, except those that have been purchased from us. If clippers are sent by mail you must send us 15 cents extra to pay postage. If too much money is sent we will return balance.

No. 28R3464 Hair Clipper. Is also a full size, well made, good cutting barbers' hair clipper. **Full nickel plated.** The spring can be easily removed and **adjusted to a different tension,** if desired, which cannot be done with any other medium priced clipper. **The most satisfactory clipper for family use.** Cuts hair one-eighth of an inch long. Weight, 9 oz. Each, **58c**

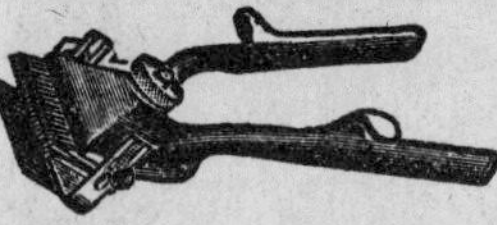

Repairs for Above Clippers.

No. 28R3465	Springs, each	12c
No. 28R3466	Top plates, each	40c
No. 28R3467	Bottom plates, each	40c

No. 28R3475 Adjustable Toilet Clipper. A very handy article for family use. Used to cut pompadour and in trimming whiskers. Has a metal comb, which may be slipped on and used to regulate the length of hair to be cut. The comb can be instantly taken off or put on, without removing screws. Will cut any length from ⅛ to ¾ inch. Price, complete, with comb......**$2.80**

Repairs for Adjustable Toilet Clippers.

No. 28R3476	Springs, each	$0.10
No. 28R3477	Top plates, each	.74
No. 28R3478	Bottom plates, each	1.23

No. 28R3485 Ball Bearing Hair Clipper, will cut hair equal to the best. Best of material. Made with the most expensive machinery by expert machinists. **Works easily and does not tire the hand.** Cuts hair one-eighth of an inch long. Price......**$1.37**

No. 28R3486 Springs for above Clipper, each, 10c

No. 28R3493 The Columbian Hair Clipper is a favorite with barbers and is so well and favorably known that we deem it is sufficient to say that we sell the genuine, full nickel plated. Cuts hair one-eighth of an inch long. Weight, 9 ounces. Price, each......**$1.13**

Repairs for Columbian Hair Clipper:

No. 28R3494	Springs, each	10c
No. 28R3495	Top plates, each	80c
No. 28R3496	Bottom plates, each	80c

Adjustable Combs.

No. 28R3512 Adjustable Comb, fits either No. 28R3464 or No. 28R3493 Clipper. It increases the length of cut one-sixteenth of an inch. Price, each......**23c**

• **No. 28R3513 Adjustable Comb,** same as above, to increase the length of cut three-sixteenths of an inch. Price, each......**25c**

No. 28R3520 The King Ball Bearing Hair Clipper is a strictly first class high grade clipper. Very popular with barbers who cater to first class trade. The tension bolt is set forward of the lever spring, almost directly over the teeth, which insures the best cutting results. The ball bearings reduce the friction to a minimum. Has diamond scored bottom plate (as shown in the small cut between the handles). Cuts hair one-eighth of an inch long. Weight, 10 ounces. Price, each.....**$1.90**

Repairs for above Clippers:

No. 28R3521	Springs, each	$0.10
No. 28R3522	Extra top plates, each	1.00
No. 28R3523	Extra bottom plates, each	1.50

No. 28R3524 Extra adjustable comb to increase the length of cut one-sixteenth of an inch. Each, **60c**

No. 28R3525 Extra adjustable comb to increase the length of cut three-sixteenths of an inch. Price, each......**60c**

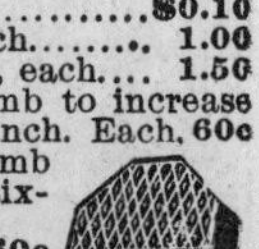

Brown & Sharp's Barbers' Clippers, Bressant Pattern.

No. 28R3540	0. B. & S., cuts 1/16-inch.	Each,	$2.40
No. 28R3541	1. B. & S., cuts ⅛-inch.	Each,	2.45
No. 28R3542	2. B. & S., cuts ¼-inch.	Each,	3.00
No. 28R3543	3. B. & S., cuts 5/16-inch.	Each,	3.50
No. 28R3544	Springs for above clipper.	Each,	.15

BARBERS' CHAIRS.

OUR BARBERS' CHAIRS are made by a factory which leads in the manufacture of Barbers' Chairs and Barbers' Furniture. After a thorough and critical examination we decided that while this line cost us considerable more money than others might be bought for, that there was more difference in real value than in price. Experienced first class barbers decided this chair had many features that were most desirable. A first class mechanic examined the construction and workmanship and pronounced it stronger, better made, better finished, simpler and less liable to get out of order than either of the other makes of chairs we compared with it. They are strictly up to date twentieth century goods.

OUR HYDRAULIC CHAIRS, as illustrated herewith, are raised and lowered by foot power to any desired height. No great exertion is required, no matter whether the customer is heavy or light. One of the greatest advantages in this chair is the simplicity of construction, there being no complicated parts which are not easily understood and which can easily get out of order.

THE HAND LEVER at the side of the chair controls the revolving and reclining movements and by placing it in different positions the chair can be reclined to any desired position.

A FOOT TREADLE is used to raise and lower the chair by hydraulic power. A few strokes of the treadle raises the chair to the desired height. To lower the chair, a step upon the treadle is all that is necessary, and the chair gradually and easily drops until the foot is removed from the treadle. Removing the foot automatically locks the chair, and no further locking or unlocking is necessary.

THE SPINDLE OR STEM of the chair is of liberal size, is smoothly bored and finished and fitted over a cylinder in the base, which has been turned with the same accuracy as a steam engine cylinder. All the moving parts are usually submerged in specially prepared oil and are therefore most thoroughly lubricated. It is self-evident that this arrangement insures very smooth and easy motions.

THESE CHAIRS are vastly superior to those requiring the use of the hand to raise and lower them, an investigation will prove this to your complete satisfaction.

THE WOODWORK of the chair is oak. Legs protected with brass mountings. All metallic parts are nickel plated.

No. 28R3600 Our Hydraulic Chair raises and lowers, revolves and reclines, upholstered in a good quality of mohair plush; colors, crimson, maroon, green or old gold. If color wanted is not stated in order we make our own selection. Solid brass feet, all metal parts heavily nickel plated. Price....$30.20

Weight, packed for shipment, about 225 pounds.

No. 28R3605 Hydraulic Chair upholstered in leather, any color. If color wanted is not stated in order we make our own selection. Solid brass feet, all metal parts heavily nickel plated.
Price....$30.70

Weight, packed for shipment, about 225 pounds.

No. 28R3645 **Mirror, may be used in combination with the dresser or shelf quoted on this page.** It has imitation walnut frame, beaded panels, varnish finish, engraved and gilded, with 17x30-inch German plate. Frame, 26 inches wide. Price, each....$4.80

No. 28R3650 Mirror, same as above, with 18x40-inch German plate. Price, each....$5.60

No. 28R3655 Mirror, with oak frame, carved and engraved panels, rubbed hard oil finish, with 17x30-inch bevel German plate.
Price, each....$7.20

No. 28R3660 Mirror, with oak frame, with 18x40-inch bevel German plate....$9.20

For other mirrors see index.

$19.44

OUR REVOLVING AND RECLINING BARBERS' CHAIR is first class in every way, but our price is very little more than is commonly asked for the old style r clining chair that does not revolve.

IT IS MADE OF OAK. Legs are protected with brass mountings. All metallic parts are strong and well finished. We offer this chair in two styles, the cheapest having all the metal parts japan finished, the higher priced ones being heavily nickel plated. One is just as serviceable as the other, the only difference is in appearence. There is an old saying "appearance goes a great ways," and we know of no business where appearances go further than in the barber shop. If a barber wishes to get and keep the best trade his shop must be attractive. Our chairs and furniture will make an attractive shop.

No. 28R3610 Our Revolving and Reclining Barbers' Chair, upholstered in mohair plush; colors, crimson, maroon, green or old gold. If color desired is not stated in order we make the selection. Complete as shown in illustration, except it has no scroll on the sides, being perfectly plain with metal parts japanned.
Price....$19.44

Weight, packed for shipment, about 210 pounds.

No. 28R3615 Same chair, with metal parts nickel plated. Price....$21.60

No. 28R3620 Same chair, upholstered in leather, any color, japanned trimmings.
Price, each....$23.04

No. 28R3625 Same chair as above, with metal parts nickel plated.
Price, each....$25.20

WE SHIP barbers' chairs and barbers' furniture direct from the factory in St. Louis, Mo. Sell for cash with order only, hence avoid the losses and expense that firms which sell on the installment plan must provide for. We are satisfied with one small profit, and give better goods than you can procure elsewhere at anything like our prices. At the prices printed we pack the goods with the utmost care and deliver them free on board cars at St. Louis, Mo., from which point the purchaser must pay freight charges. For other items in Barbers' Supplies, such as bay rum and other toilet articles, combs, brushes, etc., consult the index.

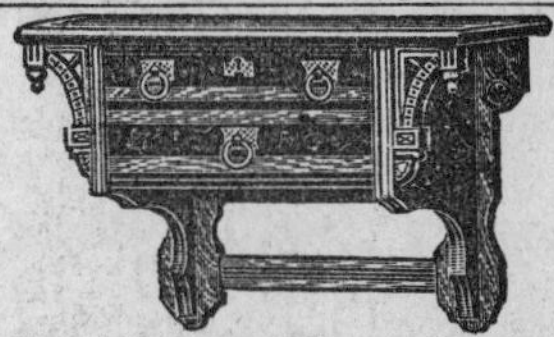

No. 28R3630 Mirror bracket, intended to be used in combination with the mirror shown opposite. Is made in black walnut, engraved, with gilt trimmings. Has two drawers. Top, 12x26 inches. Price, $3.00

No. 28R3635 Mirror bracket, same as above, made in oak..$3.00

No. 28R3640 Dressing Case, made of black walnut in French oil finish, brass trimmings. Spring hinges on drop doors, lock on drawers. Top, 24 in. wide. Price, with wood top, $7.20
Price, with Tennessee marble top....$8.40

OUR MIRROR DRESSING CASE is of a new and popular design, made of oak, veneered columns and raised panels, nicely carved and engraved. Size of glass, 18x40 inches and 24x30 inches. Solid brass trimmings, spring hinges on the drop doors and locks on the drawers. The height is 7 feet 2 inches. Length for three chairs, as illustrated, 15 feet. Add 52 inches for each additional chair. Furnished with Tennessee marble top.

No. 28R3665	Arranged for two chairs. Price	$ 82.80
No. 28R3670	Arranged for three chairs. Price	113.76
No. 28R3675	Arranged for four chairs. Price	144.72
No. 28R3680	Arranged for five chairs. Price	175.68

No. 28R3685 Dressing Case, made of black walnut, French oil finish. Spring hinges on drop doors, lock on drawers. Height, 3 feet 6 inches; size of top, 15x28 inches.

Price, with wood top....$ 9.60
Price, with Tennessee marble top....11.20

No. 28R3690 Dressing Case, same as above, made of oak.
Price, with wood top....$ 9.60
Price, with Tennessee marble top....11.20

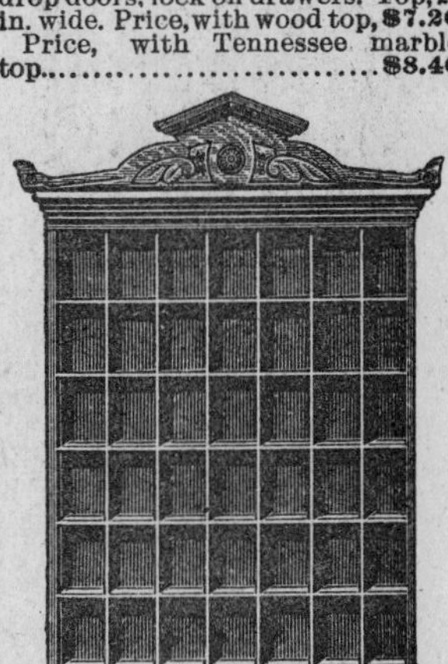

No. 28R3695 Cup Case, made of black walnut, carved and engraved, hard oil finish. May be put up on shelf brackets or used in combination with dressers shown on this page

Number of holes in case	25	42	72	99
Price, per case	$4.00	$7.20	$14.40	$18.40

No. 28R3700 Cup Case, same as above, made of oak.

Number of holes in case	25	42	72	99
Price, per case	$4.00	$7.20	$14.40	$18.40

MECHANICS' TOOLS.

THERE ARE NO BETTER TOOLS MADE than those we sell. We guarantee the quality of every one. Our constantly increasing trade in this line is proof of the values we furnish. A comparison will show that our prices are below any kind of competition.

CARPENTERS, BUILDERS, MECHANICS of all classes are especially requested to give this department their attention, note the money we can save them and SEND THEIR ORDERS TO US.

SAWS.

Sears, Roebuck & Co.'s Circular, Cross Cut, Rip, Hand, Panel and Buck Saws are warranted as follows: If these saws do not prove as good or better than any saws you ever had return them and money will be refunded.

Patent ground and tempered solid teeth of extra quality, superior workmanship. Circular saws must not be filed with a square corner in gullet. If so filed any saw will most likely crack. Our guarantee does not cover saws cracked from this cause, or if not kept in proper condition.

No. 35R101 Cut Off Saw. Sears, Roebuck & Co.'s warranted.

No. 35R102 Rip Saw. Sears, Roebuck & Co.'s warranted. **Read remarks following price list before making out your order.**

Diameter, Inches	Thickness, Gauge	Size of hole, Inches	Price, each	Diameter, Inches	Thickness, Gauge	Size of hole, Inches	Price, each
4	19	¾	$0.48	20	13	1 5/16	$ 4.08
5	19	¾	.58	22	12	1 5/16	4.80
6	18	¾	.68	24	11	1⅜	5.76
7	18	¾	.82	26	11	1⅜	6.72
8	18	⅞	.96	28	10	1½	7.68
9	17	⅞	1.20	30	10	1½	8.64
10	16	1	1.44	36	9	1⅝	12.24
11	16	1	1 68	40	9	2	15.75
12	15	1	1.80	44	8	2	22.50
14	15	1⅛	2.16	50	7	2	36.00
16	14	1⅛	2.64	54	7	2	45.00
18	13	1¼	3.36	60	6	2	65.25

If you want a saw in any way different from above list, do not give any catalogue number, and be sure to give full specifications. We aim to carry the above sizes up to 30 inches in stock at all times ready for prompt shipment, but can ship saws with odd size holes or made to order with but the usual delay. Any saw made to order will not be taken back or exchanged and order cannot be countermanded after having been placed in work. If saw is wanted with pin holes send a paper pattern giving exact location. Order blanks for ordering saws will be furnished on request.

Circular Saw Mandrels.

No. 35R125 Circular Saw Mandrels, with pulley on end, of the latest and most approved pattern. **Our Mandrels are made with pulley on right hand side when saw is running toward you with left hand thread, unless otherwise ordered.**

Diam. of Pulley, inches	Face of Pulley, inches	Diam. of Flange, inches	Length of Shaft, inches	Diam. of Shaft, inches	Size of hole in Saw, inches	Price of Mandrel, Complete
2½	3½	2½	16½	1 1/16	1	$ 3.85
3	4	3	19	1 3/16	1⅛	4.20
3½	4½	3½	21½	1 5/16	1¼	4.55
4	5	4	24	1 7/16	1 5/16	4.90
4½	5½	4½	26	1 7/16	1 5/16	5.25
5	6	5	28	1 7/16	1⅜	5.60
5½	6½	5½	30½	1 7/16	1⅜	7.54
6	7	6	32½	1 9/16	1½	9.80
7	8	6	37	1 11/16	1⅝	11.20
8	8	6	41	1 13/16	1⅝	15.25

CROSS CUT SAWS.

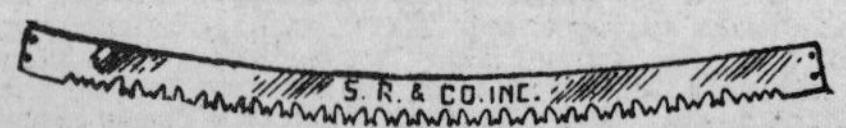

No. 35R200 Sears, Roebuck & Co.'s Two-Man, Narrow Cross Cut Saws. Warranted. Champion tooth, without handles.

5½-foot, weight, 3¾ pounds, price, each........**88c**
6 -foot, weight, 4 pounds, price, each........**96c**

Cross Cut Saws.

No. 35R208 Sears, Roebuck & Co.'s regular width, Champion Tooth, Two-Man Cross Cut Saws. Warranted. Without handles.

Length, feet	Weight, lbs.	Price, each	Length, feet	Weight, lbs.	Price, each
5	5¼	$1.40	6	6¾	$1.68
5½	6¼	1.54	6½	7	1.82

No. 35R212 Disston's Plain Tooth, No. 2, Two-Man Cross Cut Saws. Two gauges thinner on back than on teeth. Price quoted is without handles.

Length, feet	5½	6	7
Price, each	$1.76	$1.92	$2.24

No. 35R214 Disston's Champion Tooth Two-Man Cross Cut Saw. Two gauges thinner on back than on teeth. Price quoted is without handles.

Length, feet	5	5½	6	6½	7
Weight, pounds	6	7	8	8¾	9
Price, each	$1.50	$1.65	$1.80	$1.95	$2.10

No. 35R216 Disston's Great American Tooth Two-Man Cross Cut Saw. Four gauges thinner on back than on teeth and is well adapted for all kinds of timber. 14 gauge on tooth edge, 18 gauge on the back. Price quoted is without handles.

Length, feet	4½	5	5½	6
Price, each	$1.62	$1.80	$1.98	$2.16

No. 35R218 Disston's Diamond Tooth Two-Man Cross Cut Saw. Two gauges thinner on back than on teeth. Price quoted is without handles.

Length, feet	4½	5	5½	6
Price, each	$1.49	$1.65	$1.82	$1.98

No. 35R220 Toledo Blade Two-Man Cross Cut Saw. This saw is made from the best tough crucible steel and with much care. It is ground four gauges thinner on the back, toothed to end of saw. Aluminum steel is used in this saw and reports say they are giving the best of satisfaction wherever used. Price quoted is without handles.

Length, feet	5	5½	6	6½
Price, each	$2.65	$2.92	$3.18	$3.45

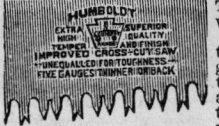

No. 35R222 Humboldt Two-Man Cross Cut Saw, without handles.

This saw is even gauge on teeth from end to end, and ground five gauges thinner throughout the entire back, and will retain its gauge as the saw wears narrow. The very best tough crucible steel is used in this saw, and each saw is set and sharpened ready for use. This saw is toothed to the ends of the saw for Pacific coast trade.

Length, feet	5	5½	6	6½	7
Price, each	$2.65	$2.92	$3.18	$3.45	$3.71

No. 35R228 Sears, Roebuck & Co.'s One-Man Cross Cut Saws. Champion tooth; supplementary handle. **Warranted.**

Length, feet	Weight, lbs.	Price, each	Length, feet	Weight, lbs.	Price, each
3	3¾	$0.96	4	5¼	$1.28
3½	4¼	1.12	4½	6¼	1.44

Saw Handles.

No. 35R250 Handle for One-Man Cross Cut Saw.
Price, each........................**15c**

No. 35R251 Supplementary Handle for One-Man Cross Cut Saw. Price, each.................**8c**

No. 35R254 Patent Loop Cross Cut Saw Handles.
Price, per pair **10c**

No. 35R255 Reversible Cross Cut Saw Handles.
Price, per pair..............**11c**

No. 35R254 No. 35R255

SAW TOOLS.

No. 35R265 With this saw tool the teeth can be brought to the same amount of set and in perfect condition to cut fast and easy. It insures absolute accuracy in set, side dressing, jointing and cutting down the rakers; can be used in the woods or shop. **Directions for use packed with each tool.** We consider this the best saw tool ever placed on the market.
Price of combination saw tool, complete......**$1.00**

Swages.

The Conqueror Swage has always given satisfaction and is indispensable to any sawyer who uses the spread set. Every one sold by us is warranted perfect and to give satisfaction.

No. 35R270 Conqueror Swage No. 1, for large circular saws. Price, each..........................**$2.30**

No. 35R271 Conqueror Swage No. 2, for small circular and mill saws. Price, each.................**$1.88**

No. 35R272 Conqueror Swage No. 3, for small circular saws. Price, each.......... ....**$1.50**

Cross Cut Saw Sets.

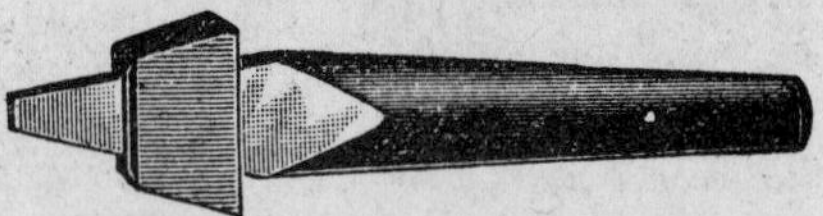

No. 35R275 The Whiting Pattern Saw Set for Cross Cut Saws only. Simple and effective and a favorite with lumbermen. Price, each............**40c**

Band Saws, Filed and Set.

No. 35R290 Band Saws. Not joined.
No. 35R291 Band Saws. Joined.

Width	Gauge	Price per foot, not Joined	Extra for Joining
¼-in.	21	5½c	20c
⅜-in.	21	6¼c	20c
½-in.	21	6¾c	20c
⅝-in.	21	7½c	25c
¾-in.	20	8½c	25c
⅞-in.	20	9c	25c
1 -in.	20	10¾c	30c
1⅛-in.	20	11¾c	30c
1¼-in.	19	13c	30c
1⅜-in.	19	14c	40c
1½-in.	19	15¼c	40c

No. 35R292 Silver Solder for Brazing Band Saws. We do not sell less than one ounce.
Price, per ounce **90c**

The Turner Brazing Outfit.

No. 35R296 For brazing band saws. Consists of 1 holder for clamping saws while being brazed, 1 Turner brazing lamp, 1 pound Turner brazing mixture. Repairing broken band saws is a very simple operation, quickly and inexpensively done when the Turner outfit is used. The holder for clamping saws may be placed in a vise or screwed to a bench. The Turner brazing lamp flame is a small, concentrated, pointed flame of intense heat which makes the braze in a few seconds. The directions sent with each outfit are full and complete, and the work is made so easy and simple by the Turner brazer that any employee can do it successfully. Saws up to 1½ or 2 inches are easily and quickly brazed in a permanent manner at almost no expense.

Complete outfit in a box.
Price, per outfit.................................**$9.25**

SEARS, ROEBUCK & CO.'S HAND SAWS.

A STRICTLY GUARANTEED SAW. NO BETTER MADE.

TRY SEARS, ROEBUCK & CO.'S SAWS AND YOU WILL USE NO OTHER.

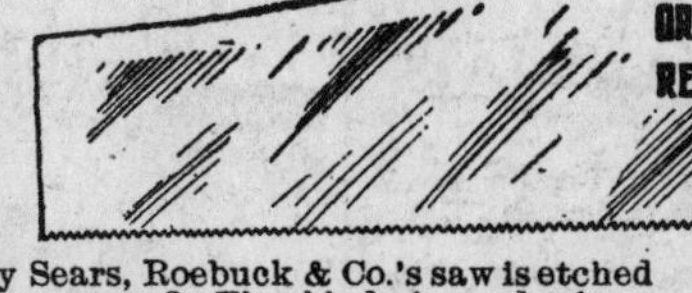

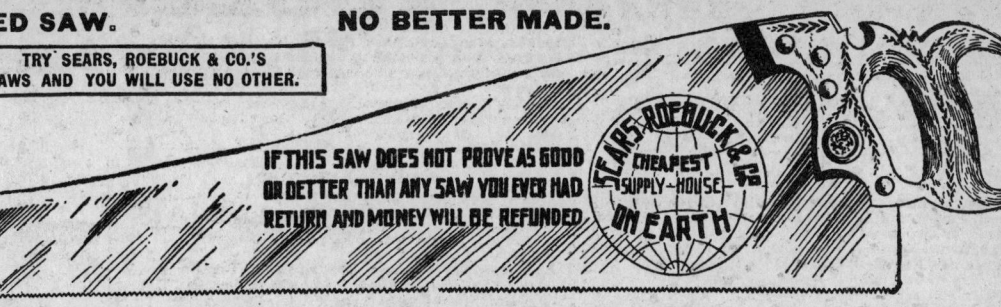

No. 35R330 This is the best saw made. We have it made especially for our trade by a manufacturer whose reputation for making first class goods is not excelled by anyone anywhere. We contract for immense quantities and **are able to sell to consumer at less than retail dealers can buy at wholesale.** Our selling price is not controlled by any combination or trust. We give our customers the same guarantee that we demanded and secured from the manufacturers, and that is **the best, fairest and most complete guarantee we could write.** The blade of every Sears, Roebuck & Co.'s saw is etched as shown in illustration. **Why pay more?** The blade is made from selected spring steel, patent ground and tempered, handle carved and polished, five improved screws, hand filed and set.

BE SURE TO STATE ...POINTS WANTED... WHEN ORDERING. | **IF NOT GIVEN, WE USE OUR JUDGMENT IN FILLING ORDER.**

PRICE LIST OF SEARS, ROEBUCK & CO.'S SAWS.

Length	Points to the inch	Price	Length	Points to the inch	Price
18-inch Panel	9, 10, 11 or 12	$0.90	30-inch Hand	6, 7 or 8	$1.50
20-inch Panel	9, 10, 11 or 12	1.00	24-inch Rip	5, 5½, 6 or 6½	1.18
22-inch Panel	9, 10, 11 or 12	1.10	26-inch Rip	5, 5½ or 6	1.28
24-inch Hand	7, 8, 9, 10, 11 or 12	1.15	28-inch Rip	4, 4½, 5, 5½ or 6	1.40
26-inch Hand	6, 7, 8, 9, 10, 11 or 12	1.25	30-inch Rip	4½ or 5	1.55
28-inch Hand	6, 7 or 8	1.37			

We cannot furnish these saws in points other than listed above.

Ice Saws.

No. 35R298 Hand Ice Saw, with iron handle.

Length, inches	24	26	28	30
Price, each	78c	85c	94c	$1.00

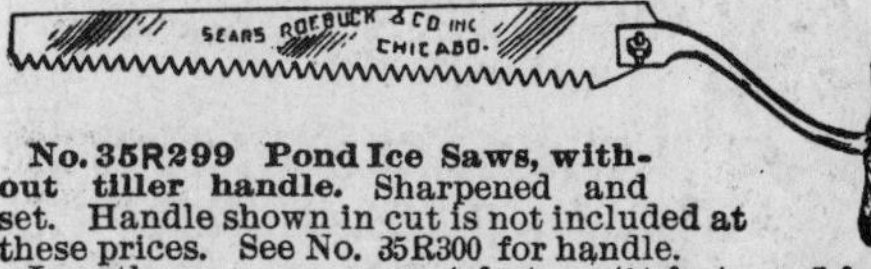

No. 35R299 Pond Ice Saws, without tiller handle. Sharpened and set. Handle shown in cut is not included at these prices. See No. 35R300 for handle.

Length	4 feet	4½ feet	5 feet
Price, each	$1.76	$1.98	$2.20

No. 35R300 Extra Tiller Handles, for Pond Ice Saws. Price, each 60c

No. 35R340 Sears, Roebuck & Co.'s Back Saw, apple handle, polished edges, blued back. Fully warranted.

Size, inches	10	12	14	16
Price, each	66c	80c	92c	$1.06

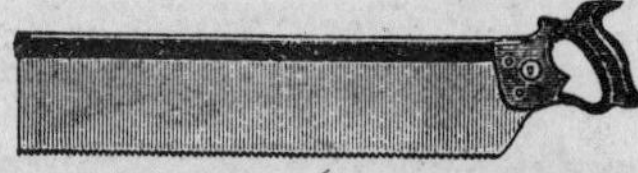

No. 35R344 Disston's Miter Box Back Saw, measuring 4 inches under the back. Length of saw is entire length of blade. The toothed edge being about 2 inches shorter.

Length, inches	22	24	28
Price, each	$1.75	$1.85	$2.00

No. 35R345 Disston's Miter Box Back Saw, measuring 5 inches under the back.

Length, inches	24	28
Price, each	$1.94	$2.33

No. 35R346 This Saw is not intended for mechanics' use, but for a household saw or for anyone who has but little use for a saw. **It is not warranted.** Length given is length of blade. Handle is not included in measurements. Beech handle, three brass screws, filed and set.

Length, inches	12	14	16	18	22	26
Price, each	20c	22c	25c	27c	30c	33c

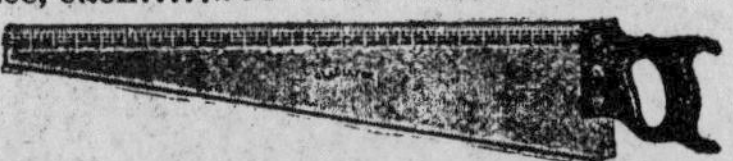

No. 35R348 This Saw, as shown in cut, is a combination of Hand Saw, square, rule and straight edge. It is not warranted, but is as good or better than any combination saw made. Beech handle, three brass screws, ruled back, filed and set. **Made one size only.** Length, 26 inches. Price, each....50c

No. 35R350 While this Saw is not warranted, it is a fair grade saw, and has given excellent satisfaction. Blade is cast steel, patent ground and tempered, walnut handle with steel plate on handle, three brass screws; filed and set.

Length, inches	18	22	26	28 Rip
Price, each	45c	50c	53c	65c

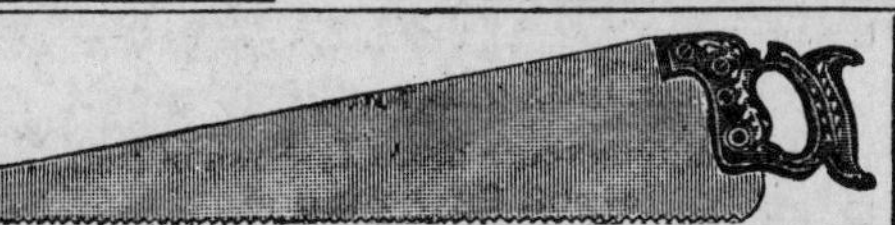

No. 35R353 Jenning's A 7½ Hand Panel and Rip Saws. This saw is on new old lines, 6 inches wide at butt, 1½ inches at point. A saw that has been worn down by constant use becomes invaluable to the owner, as it can be used for many purposes where a full width saw is unwieldy. They are made of the best refined spring steel, ground four gauges thin on back, full beveled filed and set, carved and full polished handle, four improved brass screws. The 18, 20, 22 and 24-inch sizes come in 9, 10, 11 and 12 points. The 26-inch size comes 6, 7, 8, 9, 10, 11 and 12 points. The 28-inch size comes 4½, 5, 5½ and 6 points to the inch. Every saw is warranted.

Length, in.	18	20	22	24	26	28 Rip.
Price, each	$1.08	$1.23	$1.33	$1.47	$1.54	$1.96

Henry Disston & Sons' Saws.

Below we show some of the leading numbers of this well known brand. We guarantee them to be the genuine Disston's Saws.

No. 35R360 Disston's No. 7 Panel, Hand and Rip Saws. Warranted.

16-inch panel,	9 to 12 points, each	$0.80
18-inch panel,	9 to 12 points, each	.90
20-inch panel,	8 to 12 points, each	1.00
22-inch panel,	8 to 12 points, each	1.13
24-inch hand,	8 to 12 points, each	1.18
26-inch hand,	6 to 12 points, each	1.32
28-inch rip,	4½ to 6 points, each	1.47

No. 35R363 Disston D-8, Panel, Hand, and Rip Saws. Skew back, apple handle, polished edge, five improved screws. Rip saws have graduated teeth and thumb hold in handle. **Warranted.**

16-inch panel,	9 to 12 points, each	$0.91
18-inch panel,	9 to 12 points, each	1.00
20-inch panel,	8 to 12 points, each	1.10
22-inch panel,	8 to 12 points, each	1.22
24-inch hand,	8 to 12 points, each	1.32
26-inch hand,	6 to 12 points, each	1.45
28-inch rip,	4½ to 6 points, each	1.56

No. 35R365 Disston & Sons' No. 12 Panel, Hand and Rip Saws. Same shape blade as No. 35R360. **Extra refined London spring steel;** selected and highly polished blade; apple handle, carved and polished; four improved brass screws. **Warranted.**

18-inch panel,	9 to 12 points, each	$1.25
20-inch panel,	8 to 12 points, each	1.38
22-inch panel,	8 to 12 points, each	1.50
24-inch hand,	8 to 12 points, each	1.63
26-inch hand,	6 to 12 points, each	1.84
28-inch rip,	5 to 6 points, each	2.00

Disston & Sons' No. 120 Panel, Hand and Rip Saws.

No. 35R370 Disston & Sons' No. 120 Panel, Hand and Rip Saws, extra London spring steel. Carved and polished, apple handle, skew back, five screws. They are made to run without set, and are so highly tempered that an attempt to set them would break the teeth. **Saws broken from this cause cannot be returned.** In order to file properly, a 6-inch safe back cant file, made expressly for this purpose, should be used. Cannot be used in green lumber. **Warranted.**

20-inch panel,	8 to 12 points, each	$1.65
22-inch panel,	8 to 12 points, each	1.86
24-inch hand,	8 to 12 points, each	2.00
26-inch hand,	6 to 12 points, each	2.20
28-inch rip,	5 to 6 points, each	2.25

No. 35R375 Disston & Sons' Gauge Saw, adapted to tenoning, shouldering, dovetailing, curving, cog cutting or any purpose where a definite depth of cut is required. **Same grade as Disston's No. 7 Saws.** Length of blade, 26 inches. Price, each......$1.65

No. 35R380 Disston & Sons' Compass Saws, with apple handle.

Length, inches	10	12	14	16
Price, each	27c	28c	30c	40c

No. 35R381 Standard Compass Saw. Beech handle

Length, inches	10	12	14
Price, each	11c	12c	13c

No. 35R385 Sears, Roebuck & Co.'s Keyhole Saw, with iron pad. This is a cheap and convenient combination of a keyhole saw, saw pad and screwdriver. Price, each.....14c

No. 35R386 Keyhole Saw Blades, can be used in above pad or in an ordinary file handle or chisel handle. Price, each..........8c

No. 35R395 Disston's Adjustable Compass Saws, carved and polished apple handle, with adjusting lever.

Length, inches	10	12	14
Price, each	32c	35c	38c

Nests of Saws.

No. 35R400 Sears, Roebuck & Co.'s Nest of Saws, consisting of 1 handle, 1 keyhole blade, 1 compass blade, 1 table or pruning blade; **all interchangeable in the handle.** Price,.......73c

Saw Handles.

No. 35R405 Hand Saw Handles, common beechwood, with varnished edges. Weight, 10 oz. Price, each...7c

No. 35R406 Panel Saw Handles common varnished edges. Price.....7c

No. 35R408 Handles for S., R. & Co.'s Saws.

To fit saw	28-in.	26-in.	22-in.	20-in.	18-in.
Price, each	30c	25c	23c	22c	20c

No. 35R410 Handles for Disston's No. 7 Saws.

To fit saws	Rip, 28-in.	Hand, 26, 24-in.	Panel, 22, 20-in.	Panel, 18, 16-in.
Price, each	20c	16c	14c	13c

No. 35R412 Handles for Disston's D-8 Saws.

To fit saws	Rip, 28-in.	Hand, 26, 24-in.	Panel, 22, 20-in.	Panel, 18, 16-in.
Price, each	30c	25c	23c	22c

No. 35R414 Handles for Disston's No. 12 Saws.

To fit saws	Rip, 28-in.	Hand, 26, 24-in.	Panel, 22, 20-in.
Price, each	50c	45c	43c

No. 35R416 Handles for Disston's No. 120 Saws.

To fit saws	Rip, 28-in.	Hand, 26, 24-in.	Panel, 22, 20-in.
Price, each	53c	48c	46c

No. 35R418 Compass Saw Handle, each......10c

Our $8.15 Foot Power Lathe.

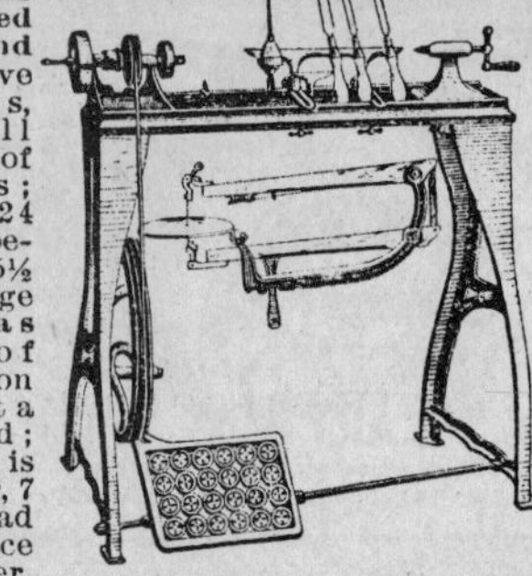

No. 35R520 This Lathe is provided with a long and short tool rest, five turning tools, wrench and drill points. Swing of lathe, 5 inches; length of bed, 24 inches; distance between center, 15½ inches. The large **drive wheel has two grooves** of varying depths on its face to give it a change of speed; the higher speed is 11 to 1; the lower, 7 to 1; the lathe head has a 2-inch face plate, a spur center, a screw center for turning cups and also a drill chuck to hold from 1/32 to ¼-inch round twist drills for drilling wood or iron. **The lathe is thoroughly built and highly finished,** the plain and polished parts being nickel plated. Weight, 56 pounds. Weight, boxed, ready to ship, 70 lbs. Price..............**$8.15**

No. 35R521 The same Lathe, with scroll saw attachments. Weight, boxed, ready to ship, 70 pounds. Price...**$9.80**

No. 35R522 Circular Saw Attachment for Goodell Lathe, complete with 3-inch saw. Price, each..**$1.00**

No. 35R523 Extra clamps to hold saw blades in saws, **Nos. 35R510-35R512 and Scroll Attachment to Goodell Lathe.** Sold in pairs only.

Price, per pair...**29c**

Lathe and Saw.

Intended for the use of boys and amateurs. Not a tool for the carpenter shop, as it is too light for heavy work.

The Companion Lathe is built on same castings as the Goodell, described under No. 35R520, but is not so highly finished. Neither do we furnish chuck with this lathe, or more than three turning tools. Thousands of them have been sold, and as far as we know none have failed to give satisfaction.

No. 35R524 Price of lathe only and tools, without scroll saw attachment..............**$5.88**

No. 35R525 Price of scroll saw attachment, each...............**$1.32**

Combined Foot and Power 20-Inch Band Saws.

No. 35R540 This machine is especially arranged for foot power as shown. It is provided with one heavy band wheel, gearing to increase the speed, and two treadles. The operator is enabled to attain a good speed and the heavy band wheel serves to carry past the dead point. There is furnished an extra lever which is to bolt on the left hand end of the foot treadle. This is applied when the aid of a second hand is required on heavy work.

Each machine is furnished with two saw blades and outfit for brazing broken saws. Weight, 350 pounds, 20-inch machine with gearing and foot treadles for one or two men, no pulleys...**$39.25**

20-inch machine with foot power attachments and pulleys for foot or belt power...... **42.35**

Extra saw blades, each.............................. **1.25**

At above prices we deliver free on board cars at our factory in Ohio.

Twenty-Inch Band Saw for Power.

No. 35R545 Dimensions—Height over all, 66 inches. Floor to center of pulleys, 28¾ inches. Floor to top of table, 40 inches. Table to upper saw guide when up, 7 inches. Saw to frame at back of table, 20 inches. Band wheels, 20 inches diameter. Floor space, 24x24 inches.

Band Wheels—Upper and lower wheels are turned perfectly true, balanced, and covered with endless rubber tires of best quality. Upper wheel can be adjusted in any direction while machine is running, to keep saw in proper alignment, and has also an up and down adjustment of several inches, to accommodate saws of different lengths.

Saw Blades—We furnish two saws with each machine—¼ and ⅜ No. 22 gauge, 10 feet 1 inch long, set and sharpened ready for use.

Pulleys—Tight and loose, 7 inches diameter for 3 inch belt provided with shifter and lever as shown; no counter shaft required.

Table—20x24 inches, made of narrow hardwood strips, glued together and held permanent with iron cleats underneath. The table can be tilted to any desired angle for **bevel sawing**—especially desirable for pattern work. **Shipping Weight**—300 pounds.

Speed—350 to 400 revolutions per minute.

Price, complete, delivered free on board cars at our factory in Ohio.......................................**$31.65**

Extra Saw Blades for above machine, each....**1.25**

Hand or Speed Lathes.

The illustration shows our 9-inch and 10-inch Hand or Speed Lathes, arranged with foot motion.

They are in all respects carefully and accurately built and finished in the best manner. They are furnished complete with steel spindles, gun metal boxes, heavy bearings, and proper adjustments for wear. With each lathe is furnished a face plate, pair of centers, hand rest, and either a foot motion or a countershaft, as may be desired. All these lathes have hollow spindle.

No. 35R550 Speed Lathe, with foot power.

No. 35R551 Speed Lathe, with countershaft instead of foot power.

When ordering be sure to give proper catalogue number to designate style wanted.

PRICES.

9-inch swing, 25 inches between centers......	**$24.95**
9-inch swing, 37 inches between centers........	**29.50**
10-inch swing, 28 inches between centers......	**33.90**
10-inch swing, 40 inches between centers......	**36.90**
10-inch swing, 52 inches between centers	**41.25**

At above prices we deliver the lathes free on board cars at our factory in Cincinnati, from which place the customer must pay the freight.

Lathe Tools for Metal Turning.

No. 35R552 A set of ten tools, suitable for any of our lathes, ground and tempered ready for use, consists of: 1st, left side tool; 2d, right side tool; 3d, diamond point; 4th, diamond point; 5th, cut-off tool; 6th, smoothing tool; 7th, thread tool; 8th, bent thread tool; 9th, inside tool; 10th, inside tool. If not ordered with lathe, give number of lathe they are wanted for, or state size of shank.

Price, per set, complete.................................**$3.60**

Set of Wood Turning Tools.

Suitable for Any Lathe.

No. 35R553 Consisting of two turning gouges, ⅜ and ½-inch; two turning chisels, ⅜ and ¾-inch; one cutting-off tool; one inside tool; one square graver; one pair 5-inch double calipers. Tools are all handled. Price, per set, complete..........**$3.40**

Nine-Inch Screw Cutting Lathe.

This illustration shows our 9-inch screw cutting lathe. The design, material and construction are of the highest grade and the tool is fully guaranteed. It has all the essential features of a high grade engine lathe of larger dimensions, and it is without doubt the best small foot lathe now on the market. For any work within its capacity it cannot be excelled. Head is detachable. Tail Stock sets over for taper turning. Carriage is gibbed both front and back. Rack and gears are cut from the solid metal. With each lathe is furnished a face plate, two pointed centers, wrenches as shown in illustration, gears to cut all standard threads from 3 to 40, and either a foot motion or a countershaft.

Dimensions.

Swings over bed	9 inches
Swings over carriage	6⅝ inches
Length of bed	40 inches
Takes between centers	25 inches
Front bearing	$1\frac{3}{16}$x1¾ inches long
Hole through spindle	½-inch

Has 3-speed cone for 1-inch belt. Weight, 325 lbs.

No. 35R555 Nine-inch Screw Cutting Lathe, as described above, with foot motion............**$53.90**

No. 35R556 Nine-inch Screw Cutting Lathe, with countershaft...**$54.10**

No. 35R557 With both foot motion and countershaft...**$59.20**

At above prices we deliver lathes free on board cars in Cincinnati from which point the purchaser must pay the freight.

Send for special descriptive circular, giving full description of our line of turning lathes and price list of changes and extras.

Special Tools to Fit Either 9 or 10-Inch Lathes.

No. 35R580	Cut No. 1—Blank Chuck.......	**$1.25**
No. 35R581	Cut No. 2—Drill Chuck.........	**1.25**
No. 35R582	Cut No. 3—3-Prong Chuck......	**1.25**
No. 35R583	Cut No. 4—Chuck Plate.........	**1.25**
No. 35R584	Cut No. 5—Screw Face Plate...	**1.25**

Special circular showing our complete line of lathes with prices of changes and extras sent free on request.

6 7 8 12 11 10 9

No. 35R585	Cut No. 6—Drill Pad...........	**$1.25**
No. 35R586	Cut No. 7—Spur Center.........	**1.50**
No. 35R587	Cut No. 8—Steel Drill Chuck, ⅜-inch hole.........	**1.50**
No. 35R588	Cut No. 9—Square Center......	**1.25**
No. 35R589	Cut No. 10—Cup Center.........	**1.25**
No. 35R590	Cut No. 11—Taper Plugs to fit Chucks............	**1.25**
No. 35R591	Cut No. 12—Crouch Center.....	**1.25**

Lathe Dogs.

No. 35R593 Patent Lathe Dogs, with steel screw. Lathe turned and finished.

No.	Opening, Inch	Price Each
1	⅜	12c
2	½	12c
3	¾	14c
4	1	15c
5	1¼	18c
6	1½	19c
7	1¾	20c
8	2	21c

Lathe Arbors.

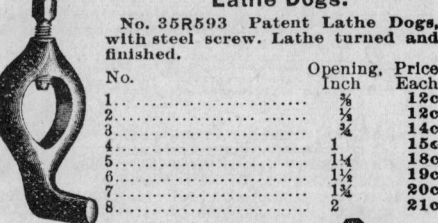

No. 35R630 Polished Steel, for holding small saws and emery wheels to be used in chuck of lathe.

Diameter inches......	¼	5/16	⅜	½	⅝	¾
Collars, open, inches.	⅝	1	1	1¼	1¼	1¼
Price, each...	45c	70c	78c	85c	$1.08	$1.20

Buck Saws.

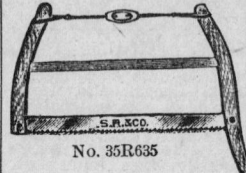

No. 35R635 Plain Frame Wood Saw, blade 30 inches, not warranted, complete with loop saw rod.

Price, each..........**35c**

No. 35R636 Braced Frame Wood Saw, maple frame, painted red, best tinned rod, 30-inch, **Sears, Roebuck & Co.'s** brand blade. **Warranted.** Each........**45c**

S.R.&CO.

No. 35R635

No. 35R637 Braced Frame Wood Saw, maple frame, painted red, best **tinned rod,** 30-inch, **Sears, Roebuck & Co.'s** brand blued blade. Warranted.

Price, each.........**46c**

S.R.&CO. INC

Nos. 35R636-35R376

No. 35R650 Loop Buck Saw Rods, will span from 19 to 22 inches. Weight, 10 ounces. Price, each....**5c**

No. 35R651 Best Tinned Loop Saw Rods, span from 19 to 22 inches. Heaviest saw rod made—threads will not strip. Price, each.......................**9c**

Ten-Inch Screw Cutting Lathe.

Illustration represents our new and improved 10-inch Screw Cutting Lathe, which has been designed to do accurate and substantial work with ease and rapidity. This, as well as our other lathes, is made of the very best material, while the workmanship and finish are of the highest grade. The **head stock** is detachable so as to admit of readjustment should the spindle become untrue. The **tail stock** has an adjustable side movement for taper turning. The **carriage** is gibbed to the bed both front and back, rendering it very stiff. It is detachable for hand work, and can be thrown into feed instantly for turning or screw cutting. The **bed** is thoroughly braced. The **gears** and **rack** are cut from solid metal. This lathe is provided with the **reverse movement** in head stock. With each lathe is furnished a face plate, two pointed centers, wrenches as shown in cut, gears to cut all standard threads from 3 to 40, and either a foot motion or countershaft. **Dimensions:** Swings over bed, 10 inches; swings over carriage, 7½ inches; length of bed, 48 inches; takes between centers, 28 inches; front bearing, $1\frac{5}{16}$-inches diameter by 2⅛ inches long; hole through spindle, $\frac{9}{16}$ inches.

Has 3-speed cone for 1¼-inch belt. Weight, 470 pounds.

No. 35R570 Ten-inch Screw Cutting Lathe with foot motion...............................**$79.90**

No. 35R571 Ten-inch Screw Cutting Lathe with countershaft..................................**79.95**

No. 35R572 With both foot motion and countershaft...**87.50**

No. 35R820 Sears, Roebuck & Co.'s Brand Half Round Smooth Files.

Size, inches..	3	4	6	8	10	12
Weight, oz...	2	2	4	7	12	20
Each.........	$0.10	$0.10	$0.12	$0.15	$0.17	$0.23
Per dozen....	1.13	1.14	1.34	1.70	2.00	2.72

No. 35R824 Sears, Roebuck & Co.'s Brand Half Rund Wood Rasps.

Sie, inch es..........	8	10	12	14
Weight, ounces....	6	11	18	28
Each	$0.17	$0.22	$0.30	$0.40
Per dozen..........	1.98	2.60	3.60	4.75

No. 35R826 Sears, Roebuck & Co.'s Brand Half Round Cabinet Rasp; same shape as wood rasps, but not so coarse cut.

Size, inches.....	6	8	10	12	14
Each...........	$0.17	$0.21	$0.29	$0.39	$0.49
Per dozen.......	1.98	2.51	3.43	4.47	5.81

No. 35R828 Sears, Roebuck & Co.'s BrandHalf Round Cabinet Files.

Size, inches.............	8	10	12
Each.....	$0.17	$0.23	$0.31
Per dozen..........	1.98	2.69	3.67

No. 35R830 Sears, Roebuck & Co.'s Knife Files.

Size, inches.............	4	5	6
Each.....................	$0.09	$0.10	$0.12
Per dozen..................	1.06	1.20	1.36

No. 35R832 Sears, Roebuck & Co.'s Brand Cant Saw Files.

Size, inches.........	5	6	8	10
Each.......	$0.08	$0.09	$0.11	$0.15
Per dozen...........	.93	1.06	1.26	1.71

No. 35R835 Sears, Roebuck & Co.'s Brand Pit Saw Files.

Size, inches............	5	6	8
Each	$0.09	$0.10	$0.12
Per dozen..................	1.03	1.14	1.40

No. 35R837 Sears, Roebuck & Co.'s Brand Band Saw Files.

Size, inches........	4	5	6	8
Each..............	$0.05	$0.06	$0.08	$0.11
Per dozen......	.57	.69	.92	1.32

FRONT VIEW

BACK VIEW

No. 35R840 H. Disston's Sons & Co.'s Brand Safe Back Cant Saw Files, especially adapted for Disston's No. 120 saw. Size, 6 inches.
Price, per dozen, $1.33; each....................12c

No. 35R841 H. Disston's Sons & Co.'s Brand Great American File. Especially adapted for Disston's great American tooth saw.

Size, inches..............	8	10
Each..............................	$0.15	$0.19
Per dozen............................	1.78	2.17

Needle Files.

No. 35R850 Needle Files, with Wire Handles; assorted, two each—flat, square, round, half round and oval; one each—three square and knife; sold only in above assortment. **We positively will not break packages.**
Price, per dozen, assorted as above...............70c

File Brushes.

No. 35R858 File Brush or Cleaner. Steel wire set in leather. **The most durable file brush in the market.** Price, each...............9c

File Handles.

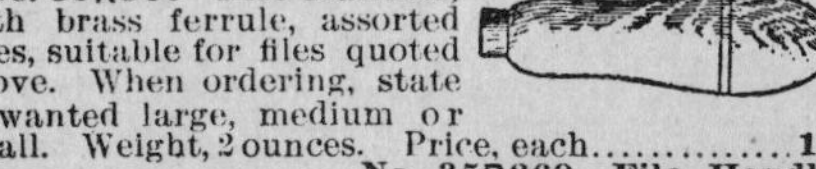

No. 35R860 File Handles, with brass ferrule, assorted sizes, suitable for files quoted above. When ordering, state if wanted large, medium or small. Weight, 2 ounces. Price, each...............1c

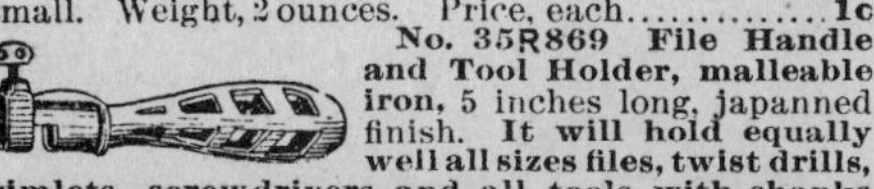

No. 35R869 File Handle and Tool Holder, malleable iron, 5 inches long, japanned finish. **It will hold equally well all sizes files, twist drills, gimlets, screwdrivers and all tools with shanks less than ⅜ of an inch square, round or flat.** Weight, 6 ounces. Price, each...............9c

EMERY WHEELS.

The Acme Emery Wheel is made especially for our trade by manufacturers who have established a most enviable reputation for making high grade, satisfactory wheels. The wheels made for us are exactly the same grade in every respect as those which they have made for years, and on which they have built up their business and reputation. The only way they differ is in the label. The manufacturers sell this wheel to the consumer at **nearly twice the price we charge** and would not furnish us with goods with their labels to sell at our prices. Our label instead of theirs don't detract a particle from the value of the wheels, but it makes the price lower.

DIRECTIONS FOR ORDERING.

Always state **diameter, thickness, size of arbor hole and shape of face, the kind of material to be ground, whether surface or edge grinding and fine or coarse work is required; whether the work is light or heavy; speed at which wheel is run.**

DIRECTIONS FOR USING.

Acme Emery Wheels will do the best work when run at a surface speed of one mile a minute, but for hardened tool grinding a slower speed is advisable. Before putting a wheel on the mandrel, tap it lightly with a hammer to ascertain that it is sound. If it rings it has not suffered from ill usage, and may be safely put to use.

All our wheels are thoroughly tested at a much higher strain than that to which they are subjected in use, and all are packed carefully. In transportation they may be broken, hence the necessity of testing immediately before running them.

Always use iron flanges on both sides of the wheel. The flanges ought to be about one-third of the diameter of the wheel or larger. Rubber or leather washers should be used, especially with thin wheels.

All emery machines should be provided with rests on which the article to be ground is held.

Wheels should run toward the operator, with the rests close to the face of the wheel. Very often wheels are broken by castings being caught between the wheels and rests by getting out of the workman's hands.

PRICE LIST OF EMERY WHEELS

No. 35R883 Flat Face Emery Wheels. **No. 35R884** Bevel Face Emery Wheels.
No. 35R885 Round Face Emery Wheels.

We cannot fill your order for Emery Wheels unless you give diameter, thickness and size of hole.

Diameter of Wheel	THICKNESS											
	¼	⅜	½	⅝	¾	1	1¼	1½	1¾	2	2¼	2½
2	$0.09	$0.11	$0.12	$0.13	$0.14	$0.15	$0.16	$ 0.17	$ 0.18	$ 0.19	$ 0.21	$ 0.22
2½	.10	.13	.16	.17	.18	.21	.23	.25	.27	.29	.32	.35
3	.12	.15	.18	.21	.23	.27	.30	.32	.35	.39	.40	.44
3½	.15	.19	.23	.25	.27	.32	.37	.42	.47	.51	.56	.62
4	.19	.23	.27	.29	.32	.39	.46	.53	.60	.65	.68	.78
4½	.22	.26	.31	.34	.37	.45	.51	.59	.66	.73	.81	.88
5	.24	.29	.35	.39	.43	.51	.63	.72	.83	.91	1.01	1.12
6	.34	.39	.42	.51	.60	.73	.89	1.03	1.20	1.35	1.51	1.66
7	.44	.50	.54	.65	.75	.95	1.18	1.35	1.44	1.63	1.95	2.05
8	.50	.57	.63	.75	.87	1.08	1.37	1.49	1.71	1.94	2.16	2.40
9	.60	.67	.75	.84	.92	1.18	1.48	1.74	2.00	2.25	2.52	2.78
10	.72	.82	.89	1.06	1.23	1.43	1.74	2.05	2.34	2.65	2.95	3.25
12	.84	.91	.96	1.20	1.36	1.67	2.05	2.41	2.87	3.15	3.53	3.93
14	....	....	1.40	1.65	1.90	2.39	2.89	3.39	3.88	4.38	4.88	5.37
16	....	....	....	....	2.44	3.09	3.75	4.37	5.02	5.63	6.30	6.93
18	....	....	....	....	2.98	3.82	4.67	5.52	6.36	7.20	8.05	8.90
20	....	....	....	....	...	4.56	5.57	6.59	7.58	8.60	9.62	10.64
22	....	....	....	....	....	5.63	6.98	8.32	9.67	10.98	12.35	13.70
24	....	....	....	....	....	6.53	8.10	9.65	11.25	12.80	14.40	15.98
26	....	....	....	....	....	....	9.65	11.49	13.28	15.08	16.88	18.68
30	....	....	....	....	....	....	...	13.70	16.20	18.70	21.15	23.63
36	....	....	....	....	....	....	....	21.35	24.92	28.35	31.85	35.00

Emery Wheel Stands.

No. 35R891 Emery Wheel Stand for power. Will run two 6-inch emery wheels, 1 inch thick, has ¾-inch steel spindle, ½ inch between flanges. Pulley 2 inches in diameter, 1⅜-inch face. Weight, 9 pounds.
Price, each...............$2.20
Price does not include wheels.

No. 35R892 Will run two wheels 10 inches in diameter and 1½ inches thick, has steel spindle 1 inch in diameter in bearings, ¾ inch between flanges. The bearings are 2 inches long and adjustable; mounted with brass oil cups. Pulleys 2¼ inches diameter, 1¾ inch face. **Two adjustable knuckle joint rests, as shown in cut.** Weight, 25 lbs.
Price, each...............$5.00

Our $7.20 Emery Wheel Stand.

No. 35R893 Emery Wheel Stand. Will run two wheels 12 inches in diameter and 2 inches thick, has steel spindles, 18 inches long and 1$\frac{1}{16}$-inch diameter in bearings, 1 inch between flanges. The bearings are 2¼ inches long and same style as engine lathe bearings, mounted with brass oil cups. Pulleys 3½ inches diameter, 2¼-inch face. Weight, 40 pounds. Price...............$7.20

Our $9.60 Emery Wheel Stand.

No. 35R894 Emery Wheel Stand. Will run two wheels 16 inches in diameter and 2½ inches thick, has steel spindles 1$\frac{3}{16}$-inch diameter in bearings, 1¼ inches between flanges. **The bearings** are 4 inches long and same style as engine lathe bearings, **mounted with brass oil cups.** Pulley 3¾ inches diameter, 2½-inch face. **These stands are provided with two rests which are knuckle jointed, and can be set at any desired angle.** Weight, 65 pounds.
Price...............$9.60

FREIGHT IS A SMALL ITEM. By referring to the introductory pages of this catalogue you can calculate what the freight will cost you.

Counter Shaft.

No. 35R911 Counter Shaft. The shaft is ⅞ inch in diameter; fast and loose pulleys 3¾ inches in diameter, 1¾-inch face; driving pulley 8 inches in diameter, 1¾-inch face, suitable for No. 35R891 grinder.
Price, each...............$2.67

No. 35R912 Counter Shaft. The shaft is 1 inch in diameter; fast and loose pulley 5 inches in diameter, 2¼-inch face; driving pulley 9½ inches in diameter, 2¼-inch face, suitable for No. 35R892 grinder. Price, each...$4.00

No. 35R913 Counter Shaft. The shaft is 1⅛ inch in diameter; fast and loose pulley 6 inches in diameter, 3-inch face; driving pulley 12 inches in diameter, 2¾-inch face, suitable for Nos. 35R893 and 35R894 grinder. Price, each...............$5.33

Polishing Heads.

No. 35R925 Polishing Head, height 6 inches, length of spindle 9 inches; taper left hand screw 2½ inches long. Drill chuck and collars on other end. Pulley 2 inches in diameter for cord or belt. Price, each...............75c

Unbleached Muslin Buffs.

No. 35R935 18 pieces in each section.

Diameter..................	6	8	10
Price, per section.......	7c	10c	14c

Polishing Material.

No. 35R940 Rouge. Price, per pound...............16c
No. 35R941 Crocus. Price, per pound...............10c
No. 35R942 Tripoli composition. Price, per lb. 7c
No. 35R943 Emery, exceptionally fine grade.

No. grains..................	24	36	60	flour
Price, per pound........	8c	8c	8c	5c

The above grains are most commonly used. No. 24 is coarse; No. 36 is medium; No. 60 is fine; flour is very fine. We can furnish any grain required. Special prices quoted on kegs or ton lots on request.

Emery Wheel Dresser.

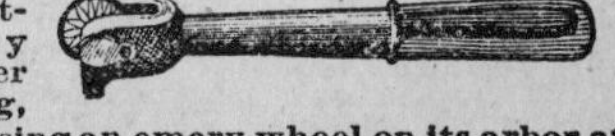

No. 35R947 The Huntington Pattern Emery Wheel Dresser for sharpening, trueing or dressing an emery wheel on its arbor at full speed. It leaves the wheel clean and sharp and in the best possible condition for cutting.
Price, each, with two sets of cutters...............43c
No. 35R948 Extra cutters. Will fit any dresser of this pattern—quality the best. Per set...............8c

Knife and Scissors Grinder.

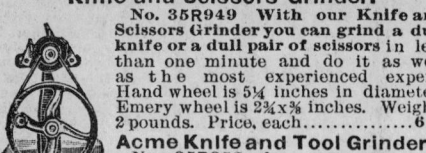

No. 35R949 With our Knife and Scissors Grinder you can grind a dull knife or a dull pair of scissors in less than one minute and do it as well as the most experienced expert. Hand wheel is 5¼ inches in diameter. Emery wheel is 2¾x⅜ inches. Weight, 2 pounds. Price, each..............67c

Acme Knife and Tool Grinder.

No. 35R952 Acme Knife and Tool Grinder can be clamped to a bench or shelf and is always ready to edge a dull knife or tool at the right time. It will grind a chisel, plane, or any tool to a perfect bevel and any bevel required. It will grind better and twice as quick as it can be done on a grindstone. Hand wheel is 10½ inches in diameter. Emery wheel is 4x¾ inches. Weight, 7 lbs. Price, each..............$1.87

Schofield's Geared Emery Wheel.

No. 35R953 Schofield's Steel Frame, Bi-Treadle Geared Emery Wheel. It will grind twice as fast as any other foot power grinder ever made, because the full weight and power of the operator is applied in doing the work. It is especially adapted for use in blacksmith shops and all repair shops, and for all kinds of tool grinding. All complete with 8x¾-inch emery stone. Weight, 35 pounds. Price, each..............$5.25

Emery Oil Stones.

No. 35R960 The lightning rapidity with which they sharpen a tool, without taking the temper from the steel, **is marvelous.** A keen edge may be obtained in **half the time** required by the use of **the quarried stone.** They are made with a **coarse and fine side,** thus combining **two stones in one,** the coarse side to be used for taking out nicks and for rapid cutting; the fine side for putting on a fine, keen edge.

Length	Width	Thickness	Price, each
7 13/16	1 13/16	15/16	23c
6¾	1 15/16	1	21c
6⅞	2 7/16	¾	22c
5⅞	1 15/16	9/16	15c
3⅞	⅞	⅜	9c
2 7/16	7/16	⅜	6c

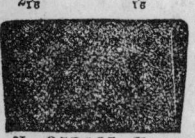

No. 35R963 Emery Gouge Slips, are 3 9/16 inches long, 2 inches wide, ½ inch thick on one edge and ¼ inch thick on the other. Price, each 9c

No. 35R965 Emery Axe Stone, is of a convenient size to carry in the pocket. One of these stones will take out a small nick in the edge of an axe very quickly. Made in two sizes. 2½x2½x⅜ inches, price, each....... 9c
2x2x⅝ inches, price, each.............. 6c

No. 35R972 Emery Razor Hone, is far superior to natural stone and at the same time **much lower in price.** Size, 6x2x⅛ inches. Price, each..............50c

No. 35R975 Emery Knife Sharpener; has nickel plated shield and hardwood handle. Emery 8 inches long; whole length (including handle), 12 inches. Weight, 6 ounces. Price, each.............. 6c

No. 35R976, Emery Knife Sharpener; emery 10 inches long; whole length (including handle), 14 inches. Weight, 8 ounces. Price, each..............9c

Oil Stones.

Sears, Roebuck & Co.'s QUICK CUT oil stone—the best oil stone on the market for general purposes. Guaranteed to give satisfaction. Fine grit, fast cutters. Use lard oil; if necessary, reduce with alcohol. If used with water only it surpasses the ordinary oil stone.

No. 35R980 Sears, Roebuck & Co.'s Quick Cut Oil Stone, mounted in a finely finished chestnut case.
3½x1¼, each....12c
6 x2 , each....21c
7 x2 , each....25c
8 x2 , each....27c

No. 35R981 Sears, Roebuck & Co.'s Quick Cut Oil Stones.
5x1¾x ¾, each, 8c
8x2 x ¾, each, 16c
8x2 x1⅛, each, 24c

No. 35R982 Pike's Lily White Oil Stone, is perfectly white, of uniform texture, free from foreign substances. It is the most satisfactory oil stone for carpenters' and general woodworkers' tools. It is a soft, free grit, quick cutting stone. Weight, about 1 pound. Price, each......45c

No. 35R983 Pike's Lily White Oil Stone, soft, free grit. Weight, about 1½ pounds. Price, each, 68c

No. 35R984 Pike's Lily White Oil Stone, medium hard, fine grit. Will stand under a tool of hard temper and give a very smooth edge. Weight, about 1 pound. Price, each..............45c

No. 35R985 Pike's Lily White Oil Stone, medium hard, fine grit. Weight, about 1½ pounds. Price, each..............68c

No. 35R992 Washita Oil Stones, mounted in mahogany case, best quality selected stones, **soft, even grain and will not glaze if used properly.** Size, 6x1⅞x1. Weight, 22 ounces. Price, each..............52c

No. 35R993 Washita Oil Stone, mounted in mahogany case, same as above, only larger; selected size 7x1⅞x1. Weight, 25 ounces. Price, each......57c

No. 35R998 Washita Oil Stone, without case, same quality as above, selected stones, weighing about 1 lb. Price, each..............27c

No. 35R999 Washita Oil Stone, without case, same quality as above, weighing about 1½ pounds. Price, each..............41c

No. 35R1005 Hindoostan Oil Stone, without case, weighing about 1 pound. Price, each..............10c

No. 35R1006 Hindoostan Oil Stone, without case, weighing about 1½ pounds. Price, each..............15c

No. 35R1012 Round Edge Washita Slips, same quality as our Washita Oil stones. From 3½ to 5 inches long. Price, each..............17c

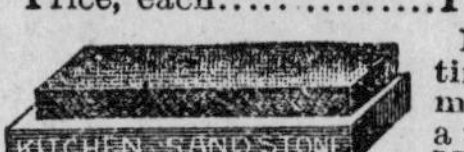

No. 35R1020 A fast cutting sand stone for shoemakers' use, table, kitchen and butcher knives. Mounted as shown in illustration. Length, 8 inches; width, 1½ inches. Weight, 1¼ pounds. Price, each..............8c

No. 35R1023 Soft Arkansas Oil Stone Wheels; are from ¼ to ½ inch thick and have from ¼ to ½ inch holes.

Diameter, inches	1½	2	2½	3
Price, each	$1.69	$2.25	$2.81	$3.38

Grindstones.

No. 35R1025 Kitchen Grindstone with water trough and frame, as illustrated, solid first quality stone. Will put a keen edge on all kinds of tools.

Diameter of stone, inches	6	8	10
Price, each	64c	85c	$1.00

Mounted Grindstone, complete; frame, foot power, crank and fixtures. It is taken apart for shipping, but it is quickly and easily set up. The usual thickness of stones is from 1¾ to 2½ inches. **Nothing but a select grade of first quality stone is used. We do not sell second quality stones.**

No. 35R1031 No. 1 stone. Weighs 100 to 110 pounds. Price, each..............$3.10

No. 35R1032 No. 2 stone. Weighs 70 to 80 pounds. Price, each..............$2.90

No. 35R1033 No. 3 stone. Weighs 40 to 50 pounds. Price, each..............$2.75

No. 35R1038 Unmounted grindstones of the best quality Huron grit, without frame or fixtures of any kind. Weight, from 40 to 200 pounds. Price, per pound..............1½c

Lathe Grindstones.

No. 35R1039 Lathe Grindstone, fine even grit, free from gravel or hard spots. Every one turned true; far better than an emery wheel for putting a cutting edge on tools.

Diameter, inches	6	8	10	12
Thickness, inches	1 to 1¼	1 to 1¾	1¼ to 1¾	1½ to 2
Price, each	50c	54c	62c	75c

No. 35R1040 Cast Iron Grindstone Fixtures. By using these fixtures stone is quickly centered and hung. **No danger of splitting stone** as is the case when a common shaft is used and held with wood wedges.

Weight, pounds	6	6	6½	8¼
Inches long	15	17	19	21
For pound stone	40	60	80	100
Price, each	23c	28c	30c	35c

No. 35R1041 Extra Heavy Grindstone Fixtures, with extra heavy broad faced turned anti-friction rollers, much stronger and better than fixtures quoted above.

Length of shaft, inches	19	21	24	28
Suitable for pounds stone	150	175	200	225
Price, per set	65c	70c	80c	90c

Foot Power Grindstone.

No. 35R1045 Foot Power Grindstone, extra select quality stone, 14x1¾ inches. The size and weight **give it great speed and capacity.** As the illustration shows, the stone is operated by a wooden pitman, which will prove **durable and satisfactory.** It weighs, boxed, 85 pounds. Price, each..............$3.68

Double Treadle Grindstone.

No. 35R1048 Double Treadle Grindstone, with wrought steel frame and seat. Weight of stone, 50 to 60 pounds. Price, complete..$3.60

No. 35R1049 Double Treadle Grindstone, with wrought steel frame (same as cut) and ball bearings. Price..............$3.85

No. 35R1052 Auto Ball Bearing Grindstone. The frame is extra heavy, made of seasoned hard wood, fitted with detachable fixtures, with ball bearings on the pitman rods as well as on the shaft. It has a comfortable saddle. The usual thickness of stones is from 1¾ to 2¼ inches. They are shipped "knocked down," but can be easily and quickly set up by any one.

Size stone, lbs	100 to 110	70 to 80	40 to 50
Price, each	$3.60	$3.35	$3.20

Merrill's Leveling Instrument.

Merrill's Leveling Instrument does all the work of a surveyor's transit at a small fraction of the cost. This apparatus transforms an ordinary spirit level into a perfect leveling instrument. It can be used for squaring and leveling buildings, platting grounds and determining grades, angles and elevations. It is also especially adapted for irrigation ditches, sewers and drains.

The leveling instrument is constructed principally of brass and is well finished to insure accuracy in its operations.

The tripod stand is very simple, being cast in one piece, with lugs for attaching the legs. It also has the adjusting screws and **the transit.** This latter is also cast in one piece and accurately finished in its working parts. In the lower end of the stem is a small hole for attaching a plumb. The periphery of the transit is graduated to the degrees of a circle for determining angles, squaring buildings, lots, etc.

The level sights, one of which is provided with fine cross wires and the other with a minute peephole, are carefully and accurately adjusted. Attached to the tripod stand is a pointer for registering the degrees. This has a knife edge which comes into close contact with the degree marks.

Illustration shows the instrument set up for use. A portion of the tripod stand is cut away to show the manner of adjustment.

No. 35R1055 A Complete Leveling Outfit, consisting of tripod stand, graduated transit, indicator, level sights, together with all necessary screws and instructions for adjusting and operating the instrument, securely packed.

Tripod legs and level are not included. If level is wanted please make a selection from our catalogue. Tripod legs can be made by the purchaser. Price, complete..............$5.88

No. 35R1056 Level Sights. Are accurate and reliable and can be quickly adjusted to fit any level. Price, per pair....49c

No. 35R1057 Targets. Are made of heavy sheet metal with a broad cleat on the back to retain a staff, and provided with a spring having sufficient tension to retain them at any desired height. The upper edge of the staple exactly coincides with the horizontal cross line on the face to facilitate reading the numbers on the staff. We do not furnish the staff. Price, each... 73c

Carpenters' Boxwood Rules—Continued.

No. 35R1184 Two-foot Rule. Square joints, edge plates, spaced 8ths, 10ths and 16ths, and drafting scale, four-fold, 1⅜ inches wide. Weight, 4 ounces. Price, each 15c

No. 35R1186 Two-Foot Rule. Square joints, full brassbound, spaced 8ths, 10ths, 12ths and 16ths, and drafting scale, four-fold, 1 inch wide. Price, each 25c

No. 35R1188 One-Foot Rule. Arch joints, edge plates, spaced 8ths and 16ths, four-fold, ⅝ inch wide. Price, each 10c

No. 35R1192 One-Foot Rule. Arch joints, full brass bound, spaced 8ths and 16ths, four-fold, ⅝ inch. Price, each 20c

No. 35R1193 Two-Foot Rule. Arch joints, outside edges brass bound, spaced 8ths, 10ths, 12ths and 16ths, and drafting scale, four-fold, 1 inch wide. Price, each....22c

No. 35R1196 Two-Foot Rule. Arch joints, full brass bound, spaced 8ths, 10ths, 12ths, 16ths, and drafting scale, four-fold, 1 inch wide. Price, each 25c

No. 35R1199 Two-Foot Rule. Arch joint, full brass bound, spaced 8ths, 10ths, 16ths, and drafting scale, four-fold, 1⅜ inches wide. Price, each 34c

No. 35R1200 Two-Foot Rule. Double arch joints, full brass bound, spaced 8ths, 10ths, 12ths and 16ths, drafting scale four-fold, 1⅜ inches wide. **The best boxwood rule made.** Price, each 40c

No. 35R1204 Three-Foot, Four-Fold Rule. Arch joint, middle plates, four-fold, 8ths and 16ths of inches. 1 inch wide. Price, each 14c

No. 35R1207 Carriage Makers' Four-Foot, Four-Fold Rule. Arch joint, bound, 8ths and 16ths of inches. 1½ inches wide. Price, each 80c

No. 35R1210 Pattern Makers' Shrinkage Rule, boxwood, 8ths and 16ths of inches, 24¼ inches, or shrinkage of ⅛ of an inch to the foot. Each....59c

No. 35R1214 One-Foot Caliper Rule. Arch joints, full brass bound, spaced 8ths, 10ths, 12ths and 16ths, four-fold; width, 1 inch. Price, each 35c

No. 35R1216 One-Foot Caliper Rule. Four-fold, arch joints, edge plates, spaced in 8ths, 10ths, 12ths and 16ths. One inch wide. Price, each 21c

No. 35R1218 6-inch Caliper Rule. Two-fold square joints, spaced 8ths, 10ths, 12ths and 16ths. Width, ⅝ inch. Each..12c

No. 35R1225 Two-Foot Architects' Rule. Arch joint, edge plates, spaced 8ths, 10ths, 12ths and 16ths with **inside beveled edges and architects' drafting scale**, four-fold, 1 inch wide. Price, each 26c

No. 35R1227 The Old Standard Slide Rule, two-foot, two-fold, arch joints bitted. Gunter's slide, spaced 8ths, 10ths and 16ths inch, 100th of a foot, drafting and octagonal scale. 1½ inches wide. Price, each 27c

No. 35R1229 Yard Stick, brass tips, polished. Price, each 12c

No. 35R1233 Stanley's Zig-Zag Rules. **These rules are made of flexible hardwood, with plated steel** joints and tips, each joint containing a stiff spring which holds the rule rigid when open. Much superior to the cheap imported rule of this style which is commonly sold.

Length, feet	2	3	4	5	6	8
Price, each	11c	17c	22c	28c	33c	44c

Stanley's Extension Rule.

No. 35R1236 Stanley's Extension Rule. For accurately measuring a curtain fixture, window seat, threshold, or any space between two fixed surfaces.

Feet	2 to 4	3 to 6	4 to 8	5 to 10
Price, each	44c	50c	55c	66c

No. 35R1239 Stanley's Gauging Rod is graduated in Wine Measure, up to 120 gallons, on one side, and in inches and parts of inches on the other side.

Directions.—To ascertain the capacity of a barrel insert the rod in the bung hole, in a slanting direction to the chine, note point on the rod which comes exactly in the middle of the bung hole, on a line with the under side of the stave; then reverse the process, running the point of the rod to the chine at the other end of the barrel; and if the bung hole is exactly in the middle of the barrel, the result will be the same as before, and the capacity of the barrel will be shown. If the measurements differ, add them together and divide by two, and you have the number of gallons the barrel will hold. Price, each 25c

No. 35R1240 Stanley's Wantage Rod has eight tables, or lines for barrels of 16, 23, 27, 32, 36, 42, 45 and 48 gallons.

Directions.—Having found the capacity of the barrel by use of the gauge rod, insert the wantage rod perpendicularly in the bung hole, holding it so that the brass lip points toward the head of the barrel; lower it slowly until the lip comes just under the inner side of the stave, then withdraw it, being careful not to let the rod go any further into the barrel; and the mark where the rod is wet, on the line which has the full capacity of the barrel at the top, shows the number of gallons that are wanting to fill it. Price, each 20c

Stanley's Ivory Rules.

No. 35R1248 Ivory Rule; 1 foot; four-fold; square joints; **German silver edge plates**, as shown in cut; spaced 8ths and 16ths of an inch; ⅝ inch wide. Price, each 81c

No. 35R1249 Ivory Rule; 1-foot; four-fold; round joints; middle plates; spaced 8ths and 16ths of an inch; ⅝ inch wide. Price, each 48c

No. 35R1254 Ivory Rule; 1-foot; four-fold; square joints; German silver edge plates; spaced 8ths, 10ths, 12ths and 16ths of an inch; ¾ inch wide. Price, each $1.09

No. 35R1255 Ivory Rule. Two-foot, four-fold, square joints, German silver edge plates, spaced 8ths, 10ths, 12ths and 16ths of an inch. Price, each $2.40

No. 35R1260 Ivory Caliper Rule, 6-inch, two-fold, german silver trimmings, **square joints**, spaced 8ths, 10ths, 12ths and 16ths of an inch, ⅝ inch wide. Price, each 65c

No. 35R1261 Ivory Caliper Rule. 6-inch, two-fold, square joints, **German silver bound**, spaced 8ths and 16ths of an inch, ⅞ inch wide. Price, each $1.15

No. 35R1265 Ivory Caliper Rule, 1-foot, four-fold, square joints, **German silver bound**, spaced 8ths and 16ths of an inch, ⅝ inch wide. Price, each $1.90

Rule Gauge.

No. 35R1275 Rule Gauge is substantially made of the best brass, then nickeled and polished. The cut shows gauge and the manner of applying it to a rule. It saves all wear on the fingers as well as danger from splinters. It is just the thing for **sign painters to space off their work with.** Fits rules 1 inch wide only. Price, each 15c

Steel Rules.

Very neat and convenient for light work. Made of spring steel, hardened, and will bend to a 3-inch circle. The corners and edges will not wear off, and the figures and divisions are always plain. **All these rules are ⅝ inch wide** and are graduated 16th of inches on both sides.

No. 35R1276 One-Foot Three-Fold, Steel Pocket Rule. Price, each 19c

No. 35R1278 Two-Foot, Six-Fold, Steel Pocket Rule. Price, each 35c

No. 35R1281 Three-Foot, Six-Fold, Steel Pocket Rule. Price, each 52c

No. 35R1283 Four-Foot, Eight-Fold Steel Pocket Rule. Price, each 68c

These Rules are ¾-inch wide.

No. 35R1286 Two-Foot, Two-Fold **Steel Rule**, spaced 16ths of inch on one side, 8ths on the other. Price, each 47c

No. 35R1288 Two-Foot, Two-Fold Steel Rule, spaced 16ths on one side, circumference inches on the other. The wheelwrights' rule. Price, each. 70c

Steel Rules—Continued.

These rules, like those previously quoted, are made of hardened steel. The corners and edges will not wear off, the figures and divisions are always plain. They are provided with a hole at one end for hanging up at the bench.

No. 35R1292 One-Foot Rule, width ¾-inch, spaced 8ths on one side, 16ths on the other. Marked on lower edge only. Price, each 20c

No. 35R1293 Two-Foot Rule, width ¾-inch, spaced 8ths on one side, 16ths on the other. Marked on lower edge only. Price, each 38c

No. 35R1296 One-Foot Rule, 1¼ inches wide, spaced 8ths on upper edge, 16ths on lower edge, both sides alike. Price, each 39c

No. 35R1297 Two-Foot Rule, 1¼ inches wide, spaced 8ths on upper edge, 16ths on lower edge, both sides alike. Price, each 70c

Hickory Log Rules.

These rules are made of the finest second growth hickory, the butt or first cut only being used. They are rived out and shaved down by hand, and no cross grained stock is used. The figures are burned on the wood. No amount of use in rain or snow will efface them. Made with either Doyle or Scribner scale, marked to scale from 8 to 20 feet, or 12 to 24 feet logs, every two feet.

In ordering, always state whether 8 to 20 or 12 to 24 is wanted. Also be sure that our catalogue number calls for the scale you want.

No. 35R1300 Square Head Log Rule. Figured 48 inches. Scribner's scale. Full length 4 feet 8 inches, to scale 8 to 20 feet. Price, each 72c

No. 35R1301 Square Head Log Rule. Scribner's scale. Figured 48 inches, to scale 12 to 24 feet. Price, each 72c

No. 35R1305 Square Head Log Rule. Figured 36 inches. Scribner's scale. Full length, 3½ feet, to scale 8 to 20 feet. Price, each 62c

No. 35R1306 Square Head Log Rule. Scribner's scale. Figured 36 inches, to scale 12 to 24 feet. Price, each 62c

No. 35R1308 Same as No. 35R1300, except has Doyle's scale. Price, each 72c

No. 35R1309 Same as No. 35R1301, except has Doyle's scale. Price, each 72c

No. 35R1310 Same as No. 35R1305, except has Doyle's scale. Price, each 62c

No. 35R1311 Same as No. 35R1306, except has Doyle's scale. Price, each 62c

Solid Hook Log Rule.

No. 35R1316 Solid Hook Log Rule. Figured 48 inches; entire length, 4 feet 8 inches, to scale 8 to 20 feet; Doyle's scale. Price, each 72c

No. 35R1317 Solid Hook Log Rule. Figured 48 inches, to scale 12 to 24 feet; Doyle's scale. Price, each 72c

No. 35R1318 Same as No. 35R1316 except made with Scribner's scale. Price, each....72c

No. 35R1319 Same as No. 35R1317, except has Scribner's scale. Price, each 72c

No. 35R1323 Walking Cane Log Rule, has Doyle's Revised Tables, and gives the number of feet of one inch square edged boards which can be sawed from a log of any size, from 12 to 36 inches in diameter and 12 to 22 feet long. The figures immediately under the head of the cane are for the lengths of logs in feet. Under these figures, on the same line at the mark nearest the diameter of the log will be found the number of feet the log will make. Price, each...45c

Hickory Board Rules.

No. 35R1326 Board Rule. Burnt figures, 3-tier, 3-foot board rule, patent socket steel head, a good, low priced, serviceable rule. Marked on one side to measure 12, 14, 16 on the other 8, 10, 18 feet. Price, each..67c

No. 35R1327 Board Rule, same as No. 35R1326, except it is marked on one side 12, 14, 16, the other 18, 20, 22 feet. Price, each 67c

N. B.—Full length of rules given above including 6-inch handle.

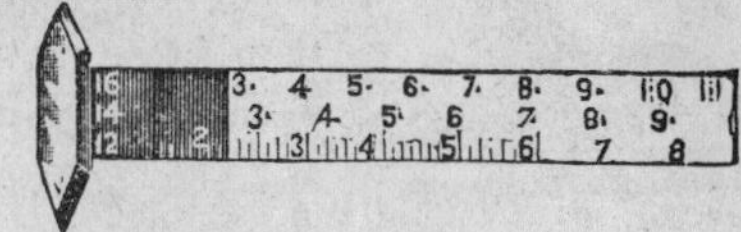

No. 35R1330 Board Rule, burnt figures. Made of the very best selected second growth white hickory. Has extra heavy brazed diamond heads, steel caps and brass shoulders, and every rule is inspected and tested before being shipped. It is the rule for regular yard work, and most commonly used. 3-tier, 3-foot board rule, marked on one side to measure 12, 14, 16 feet, on the other 8, 10, 18 feet. Price, each..88c

No. 35R1331 Same as No. 35R1330, except is marked on one side to measure 12, 14, 16 feet, on the other, 18, 20, 22 feet. Price, each 88c

S., R. & Co.'s Adjustable Planes.

CONTINUED.

No. 35R1975 Sears, Roebuck & Co.'s Adjustable Wood Bottom Fore Plane, No. 028. Length, 18 inches; cutter 2⅜ inches. Price, each.........90c

No. 35R1978 Sears, Roebuck & Co.'s Adjustable Wood Bottom Fore Plane, No. 029. Length, 20 inches; cutter, 2⅜ inches. Price, each..........91c

No. 35R1979 Sears, Roebuck & Co.'s Adjustable Wood Bottom Jointer Plane, No. 030. Length, 22 inches; cutter, 2⅜ inches. Price, each...........97c

No. 35R1983 Sears, Roebuck & Co.'s Adjustable Wood Bottom Jointer Plane, No. 031. Length, 24 inches; cutter, 2⅜ inches. Price, each.......... 98c

No. 35R1986 Sears, Roebuck & Co.'s Adjustable Wood Bottom Jointer Plane, No. 032. Length, 26 inches; cutter, 2⅝ inches. Price, each.........$1.05

No. 35R1989 Sears, Roebuck & Co.'s Adjustable Wood Bottom Jointer Plane, No. 033. Length, 28 inches; cutter, 2⅝ inches. Price, each.........$1.08

No. 35R1992 Sears, Roebuck & Co.'s Adjustable Wood Bottom Jointer Plane, No. 034. Length, 30 inches; cutter, 2⅝ inches. Price, each.........$1.14

Plane Irons for S., R. & Co.'s Adjustable Planes.

When ordering, state if double iron or single (cutting) iron is wanted, and give our number of plane for which iron is wanted.

No. 35R1995 Single or Cutting Irons for Sears, Roebuck & Co.'s Adjustable Planes.

Width	1¾	2	2⅛	2⅜	2⅝
Price, each	23c	24c	25c	30c	35c

No. 35R1996 Double Irons or Cutting Iron and Cap for Sears, Roebuck & Co.'s Adjustable Planes.

Width	1¾	2	2⅛	2⅜	2⅝
Price, each	37c	39c	40c	45c	52c

Sears, Roebuck & Co.'s Block Planes.

Sears, Roebuck & Co.'s Block Planes are well made for practical use. Great care is used to have the sides true, as well as the face. The cutters are made from a grade of steel that has been proven to be the best for this purpose. They are warranted to give satisfaction.

No. 35R2053 Sears, Roebuck & Co.'s Iron Block Plane, No. 0102; length, 5½ inches; 1¼-inch cutter. Weight, 14 ounces. Price, each..13c

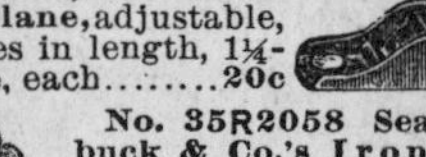

No. 35R2055 Sears, Roebuck & Co.'s Iron Block Plane, adjustable, No. 0103; 5½ inches in length, 1¼-inch cutter. Price, each.........20c

No. 35R2058 Sears, Roebuck & Co.'s Iron Block Plane, No. 0110; length, 7½ inches; 1⅜-inch cutter. Weight, 1 pound 14 ounces. Price, each...........................20c

No. 35R2061 Sears, Roebuck & Co.'s Iron Block Plane, adjustable, No. 0120; 7½ inches in length, 1⅜-inch cutter. Price, each........28c

No. 35R2064 Sears, Roebuck & Co.'s Iron Block Plane, No. 0130; double ender; length, 8 inches, 1⅜-inch cutter. By reversing the cutter and clamping wedge, as shown by dotted lines in cut, this plane can be made to plane close up into corners. Weight, 1 pound 14 ounces. Price, each...................26c

No. 35R2066 Sears, Roebuck & Co.'s Iron Block Plane, adjustable, No. 0220; 7½ inches in length; 1⅜-inch cutter. Price, each........29c

The following four Sears, Roebuck & Co.'s Block Planes have an adjustment to set edge of cutter square with face of plane, as well as adjustment to move cutter up and down; they are also provided with a convenient thumb hold.

No. 35R2075 Sears, Roebuck & Co.'s Block Plane, No. 09½; lateral and longitudinal adjustment; 6 inches in length; 1¾-inch cutter. Price, each.........49c

No. 35R2076 Sears, Roebuck & Co.'s Block Plane, No. 015; lateral and longitudinal adjustment, 7 inches in length, 1¾-inch cutter. Price, each...........................52c

No. 35R2081 Sears, Roebuck & Co.'s Low Angle Block Plane, No. 060; lateral and longitudinal adjustment, 6 inches in length, 1⅝-inch cutter. Each...50c

No. 35R2083 Sears, Roebuck & Co.'s Low Angle Block Plane, No. 065; lateral and longitudinal adjustment, 7 inches in length, 1¾-inch cutter. Price, each 58c

Stanley's Iron Block Planes.

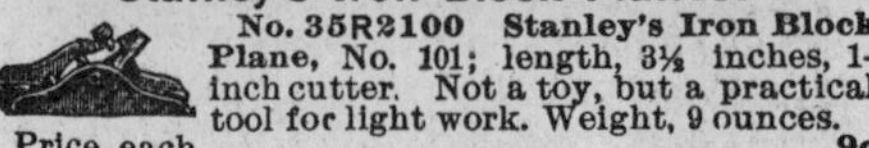

No. 35R2100 Stanley's Iron Block Plane, No. 101; length, 3½ inches, 1-inch cutter. Not a toy, but a practical tool for light work. Weight, 9 ounces. Price, each...........................9c

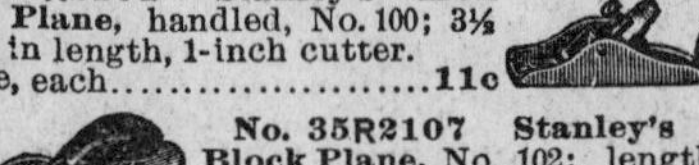

No. 35R2104 Stanley's Iron Block Plane, handled, No. 100; 3½ inches in length, 1-inch cutter. Price, each...........................11c

No. 35R2107 Stanley's Iron Block Plane, No. 102; length, 5½ inches, 1¼-inch cutter. Weight, 14 ounces. Price, each 18c

No. 35R2109 Stanley's Iron Block Plane, adjustable, No. 103; 5½ inches in length, 1¼-inch cutter. Price, each 26c

No. 35R2112 Stanley's Iron Block Plane, No. 110; length, 7½ inches; 1⅜-inch cutter. Weight, 1 pound, 14 ounces. Price, each...........................25c

No. 35R2113 Stanley's Iron Block Plane, adjustable, No. 120; 7½ inches in length, 1⅜-inch cutter. Price, each...............37c

No. 35R2116 Stanley's Iron Block Plane, No. 130; double ender; length, 8 in., 1⅜-inch cutter. By reversing the cutter and clamping wedge, as shown by dotted lines in cut, this plane can be made to plane close up into corners. Weight, 1 pound 14 ounces. Price, each...........................33c

No. 35R2120 Stanley's Iron Block Plane, adjustable, No. 220; 7½ inches in length, 1⅜-inch cutter. Price, each...............37c

Bailey's Block Planes with Stanley's Patent Throat Adjustment.

For opening or closing the throat of the plane, as coarse or fine work may require. By moving the eccentric plate to the right the throat can be closed. A single turn of the knob will fasten the plate and secure any desired width for the throat.

No. 35R2124 Bailey's Patent Iron Block Plane, No. 9½, length, 6 inches; 1¾-inch cutter. Adjustable cutter, adjustable throat. Weight, 1 lb. 10 oz. Price, each..66c

No. 35R2127 Same shape and adjustments as above, No. 15, 7 inches long, 1¾-inch cutter. Weight, 1 pound 14 ounces. Price, each 70c

No. 35R2132 Adjustable cutter, adjustable throat, rosewood handle. Length, 6 inches, No. 9¾, with 1¾-inch cutter. Price, each, 77c

No. 35R2135 Bailey's Block Plane, No. 15½. Same as above. Length, 7 inches, with 1¾-inch cutter. Price, each...........................81c

Bailey's Knuckle Joint Planes.

This plane has a knuckle joint in the cap, and placing the cap in position clamps the cutter securely in its seat. Has nickel plated trimmings and all adjustments same as above planes.

No. 35R2138 Bailey's Knuckle Joint Plane, No. 18, as above. Length, 6 inches, 1¾-inch cutter. Weight 1 pound 10 ounces. Price, each...........75c

No. 35R2140 Bailey's Knuckle Joint Plane, No. 19, as above. Length, 7 inches, 1¾-inch cutter. Weight, 1 pound 14 ounces. Price, each 80c

No. 35R2144 Stanley's Low Angle Block Plane, No. 60, 6 inches in length, 1⅜-inch cutter. Weight, 1½ pounds. Price, each...............66c

No. 35R2145 Stanley's Low Angle Block Plane, No. 65, 7 inches in length, 1⅜-inch cutter. Weight, 1¾ pounds. Price, each...........................75c

No. 35R2160 The Genuine Bailey Iron Cabinetmakers' Adjustable Block Plane, No. 9. Length, 10 inches; 2-inch cutter. Weight, 4½ pounds. **Designed for extra fine cabinet work, car finishers, musical instrument case makers, etc.** Price, each...............$2.63

No. 35R2161 Rabbet and Block Plane, No. 140, detachable side, 7 inches long, 1¾-in. cutter. **A detachable side will easily change this tool from a Block Plane to a Rabbet Plane, or vice versa. The cutter is set on askew.** Price...........84c

No. 35R2168 Carriage Makers' Rabbet Plane, No. 10½, 9 in. in length, 2⅛ in. cutter. Price, each...$1.63

No. 35R2169 Carriage Makers' Rabbet Plane, No. 10, 13 in. in length, 2⅛ in. cutter. Price, each...$1.97

No. 35R2172 Stanley's Adjustable Scraper Plane, length 9 inches; 3 inch cutter. Price.....$1.32

This tool is used for scraping and finishing veneers or cabinet work. It can be used equally well as a tooth plane, and will do excellent work in scraping off old paint and glue.

No. 35R2173 Cutters, for veneer scraping....15c

No. 35R2174 Cutters, for toothing, Nos. 22, 28, 32 (22, 28 or 32 teeth per inch)...........................18c

No. 35R2180 Stanley's Improved Scrub Plane, No. 40, has a single iron with the cutting edge rounded. It is particularly adapted for roughing down work before using other planes. Stock is 9½ inches long with 1¼-inch cutter. Price, each...........................68c

No. 35R2184 Stanley's Adjustable Circular Plane, with flexible steel face, which, by turning the knob on the front of the plane, can be **easily shaped to any required arc either concave or convex.** Weight, 3¾ pounds. Price, each...........................$1.70

No. 35R2188 Stanley's Adjustable Circular Plane with flexible steel face which can be made concave or convex by turning the screw which is attached to its center. **Nickel plated.** 1¾-inch cutter. Price, each..$2.59

No. 35R2190 Adjustable Chamfer Plane. The front section of this plane, to which cutter is attached, can be moved up and down. It can be firmly secured to the rear section, at any desired point, by means of a thumbscrew. Without the use of any other tool this plane will do perfect chamfer, or stop chamfer work of all ordinary widths. When the faces of both sections are even it can be used as an ordinary bench plane. Length, 9 inches; 1⅝-inch cutter. Weight, 3 pounds. Price, each...............$1.38

No. 35R2193 Beading attachment for above chamfer plane. For beading or molding a chamfer this additional attachment can be furnished, with six cutters, sharpened at both ends, including a large variety of ornamental forms. This attachment is not included with above plane. Price, for attachment...........................66c

No. 35R2195 Bull Nose Rabbet Plane, iron stock, 4 inches in length, 1-inch cutter. Price, each...........................20c

ABOUT FREIGHT AND EXPRESS

It is seldom necessary to write to us to ask what the freight or express will amount to. The weight of almost every item is given under the description. If you will refer to pages 7 to 10 you can get the rate of freight or express to a point near you in your state which will be almost, if not exactly, the same rate as to your nearest railroad station. From this you can calculate almost exactly what the freight or express will amount to on any shipment to your town, and you will find it will amount to next to nothing as compared to what you will save in price. By noting the weight and the express or freight rates you can tell almost exactly what the cost of transportation will be, and save the trouble and delay of writing us for this information.

Stanley's Adjustable Bull Nose Rabbet Plane.

No. 35R2198 Stanley's Adjustable Bull Nose Rabbet Plane, with adjustable throat, nickel plated, No. 90. This plane is designed for fine cabinet work where extreme accuracy is desired. The sides and bottom being square with each other, the plane will lie perfectly flat on either side, and can be used right or left. Rabbet plane, 4 inches in length, 1-inch cutter, each....................... **$1.32**

Side Rabbet Plane.

A convenient tool for side rabbeting and trimming dados, moldings and grooves of all sorts. A reversible nosepiece will give the tool a form by which it will work close up into corners when required. Side rabbet plane, 4 inches in length.

No. 35R2204 Right hand. Price............... **54c**
No. 35R2205 Left hand. Price................ **55c**

Stanley's Rabbet Plane.

Stanley's Improved Rabbet Plane. This plane will lie perfectly flat on either side, **and can be used with right or left hand equally well while planing into corners or up against perpendicular surfaces;** has spur which can be removed when not wanted. Length 8 inches; 1½-inch cutter. Weight 3½ pounds.

No. 35R2209 1½ inches wide, with spur, each. **75c**
No. 35R2210 1¼ inches wide, with spur, each. **74c**
No. 35R2211 1 inch wide, with spur, each. **73c**

Duplex Rabbet Plane.

Remove the arm to which the fence is secured and a Handled Rabbet Plane is had, and with two seats for the cutter, so that the tool can be used as a Bull Nose Rabbet if required. The arm to which the fence is secured can be screwed into either side of the stock, thus making a superior right or left hand filletster with adjustable spur and depth gauge.

No. 35R2215 Duplex Rabbet Plane and filletster as above. Length, 8½ inches; 1½-inch cutter. Weight, 3¼ pounds. Price, each................... **99c**

Tonguing and Grooving (Match) Plane.

This plane has two separate cutters at suitable distance apart. When the guide or fence is set, as shown in cut, both cutters work and a tongue can be made. **The fence is hung on a pivot** and can be swung around end for end. This movement covers one of the cutters, and also furnishes a guide for grooving an exact match for the tongue. **In working thicker than 1-inch stuff with No. 48 plane,** or ½-inch stuff with No. 49, place the extra wide cutter in right hand side of the plane. The tongue and the groove will be **equally removed from the center of the edges** on extra thick or thin boards, **and a perfect match will be made.**

No. 35R2218 Tonguing and Grooving Plane (commonly called Match Plane), as above, which will match board of any thickness from ¾ to 1¼ inches thick. Weight, 2¾ pounds. (No. 48.) Price, each.. **$1.68**

No. 35R2219 Tonguing and Grooving Plane, as above, which will match board any thickness from ⅜ to ¾ inch. Weight, 2¾ lbs. (No. 49.) Price, each.. **$1.69**

Stanley's Bull Nose Plow and Matching Plane.

Two interchangeable front parts go with this tool. The form shown above is that of a Bull Nose Plow; and the cutter will easily work up to, and into a ½-inch hole, or any larger size—as in sash fitting, stair work, etc. With the other front on, it takes the ordinary form of a plow, and is adapted to all regular uses. With each tool eight plow bits (⅛, 3/16, ¼, 5/16, ⅜, 7/16, ½, ⅝-inch), and a slitting blade are furnished; also a tonguing tool, ¼-inch.

No. 35R2223 Nickel plated, with ten tools, bits, etc. No. 143. Price, each....................... **$3.28**

No. 35R2224 Nickel plated, with ten tools and a filletster. No. 141. Price, each..................... **$4.59**

Stanley's Universal Plane.

Picture shows the plane adjusted for making moldings.

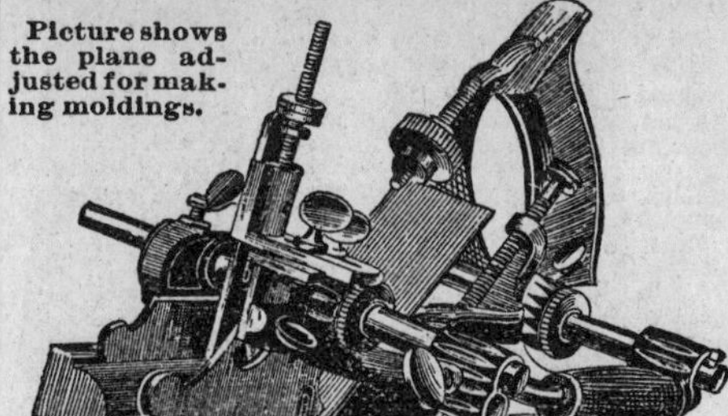

No. 35R2228 Stanley's Patent Universal Plane (No. 55), nickel plated, including molding plane, match sash, chamfer, beading, reeding, fluting, hollow, round plow, dado, rabbet, filletster and slitting plane, with 52 cutters, **packed in four separate cases, and the whole outfit packed in a neat wooden box.**

This tool, in the hands of an ordinary carpenter, can be used for all lines of work covered by a full assortment of so called fancy planes.

Price, complete................................... **$9.80**

Traut's Adjustable Dado, Plow, etc., No. 46.

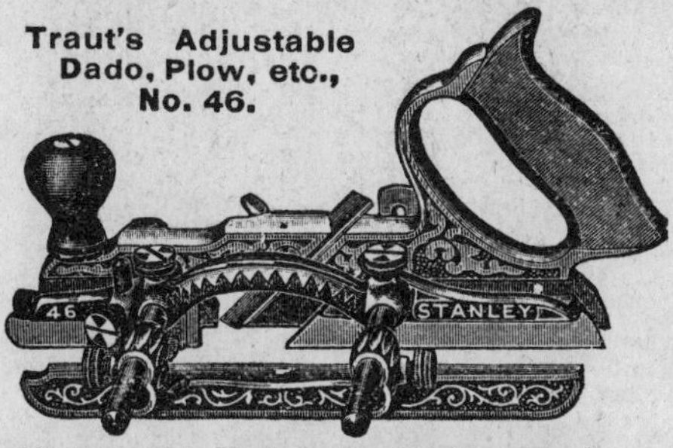

No. 35R2230 Made by the Stanley Rule & Level Co. This tool is accompanied by eight plow and dado bits (3/16, ¼, 5/16, ⅜, ½, ⅝, ⅞ and 1¼ inch), a filletster cutter, a slitting tool and a tonguing tool. All except the slitting blade are secured in the main stock on a skew.

Price, nickel plated, including eleven tools, plow bits, slitting and tonguing tools, etc., **$4.55**

No. 35R2232 Adjustable Dado, No. 47. This tool has the same stock and arms as shown above, but it can be used as a dado only.

Price, nickel plated, including bits (⅜, ½, ⅝, ⅞, 1¼ inch), and slitting tool (six tools).. **$2.63**

Stanley's Beading, Rabbet and Slitting Plane.

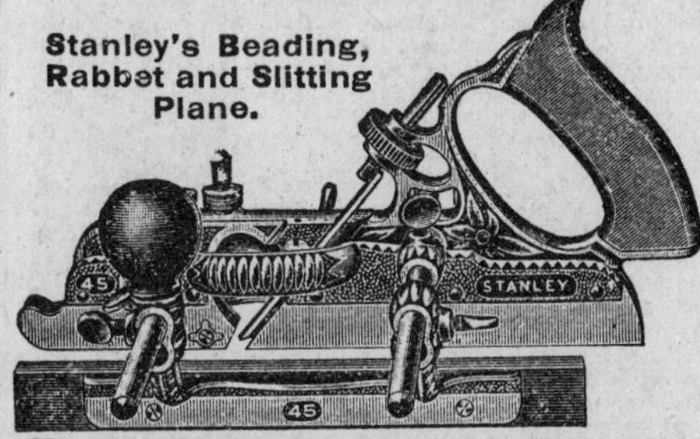

No. 35R2237 Stanley's Patent Adjustable Beading, Rabbet and Slitting Plane. (No. 45.) This in each of its several forms will do **first class work,** even in the hands of an **ordinary mechanic.** Directions for forming the different tools which can be made from this plane, accompany each plane, and are easily understood by any one of ordinary intelligence. This plane embraces (1) beading and center beading plane; (2) rabbet and filletster; (3) dado; (4) plow; (5) matching plane; (6) sash plane, (7) a superior slitting plane. Each plane has seven beading tools (⅛, 3/16, ¼, 5/16, ⅜, 7/16, and ½-inch) ten plow and dado bits (⅛, 3/16, ¼, 5/16, ⅜, 7/16, ½, ⅝, ¾, and ⅞-inch), a slitting blade, a tonguing tool, and a sash tool. Weight, 6¼ pounds.

Price, complete with tools, as above, each.... **$4.90**

Extras for No. 35R2237 Plane.

The following tools can be used with above plane, but are not included in above combination.

No. 35R2239 Hollows and Rounds for above plane.

Nos.	6	8	10	12
Cutter, width, inches......	½	⅝	¾	1
Works, circle, inches......	¾	1	1¼	1½
Price, per pair..........	95c	96c	97c	98c

Nosing Tools.

No. 35R2241 Nosing Tool, 1¼-inch. (Attach same as above.) Price, each.................................. **66c**

Reeding Cutters.

No. 35R2244 Size of Beads, either ⅛, 3/16 or ¼-inch, are same price. State size wanted when ordering.

To make beads............	2	3	4	5
Price, each..............	15c	22c	32c	40c

Siegley's Combination Plane.

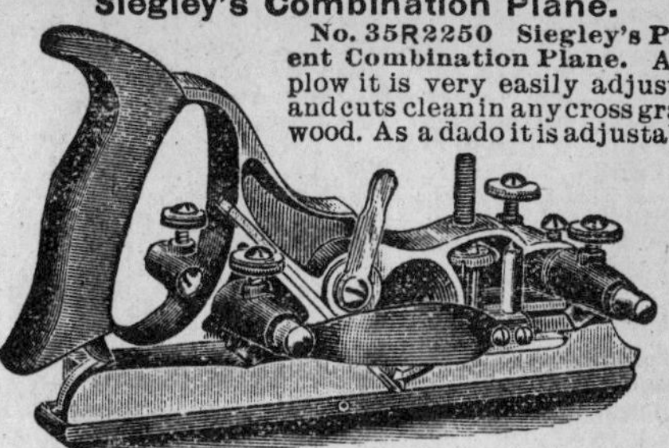

No. 35R2250 Siegley's Patent Combination Plane. As a plow it is very easily adjusted and cuts clean in any cross grain wood. As a dado it is adjustable from ⅜ of an inch to any width. The advance cutters are fastened by set screws holding the cutter firmly in slanting position. As a match plane it makes tongue and groove that exactly match. As a beading plane, it does the work of six of the old fashioned wood planes. The plane is nickel plated, making a handsome as well as a serviceable tool.

Price.. **$4.50**

Stanley's Floor Plane.

No. 35R2253 Stanley's Floor Plane. This tool will be found useful for planing floors, bowling alleys, skating rinks, decks of vessels, etc. The construction of the plane will enable the owner to do more work, with less outlay of strength, than can be done with any other tool. The weight of the plane is about 10 pounds, and the full length of the handle, 45 inches; 10½ inches in length, 2⅝-inch cutter. Price, ea., **$2.96**

Adjustable Beading Plane.

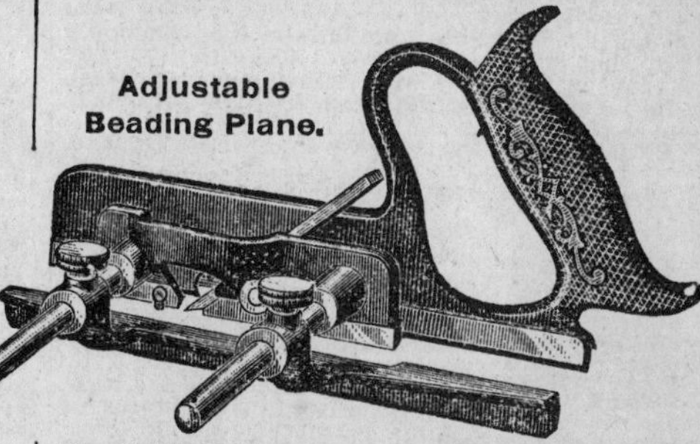

No. 35R2255 Patent Adjustable Beading Plane. This plane will do all the work for which fourteen common wood bead planes would be required. Has spur cutter for use when beading across the grain. **By adjustment of the fence** center beading can be done any distance up to 5 inches from the edge of a board. Price, complete, including seven bits, sizes ⅛, 3/16, ¼, 5/16, ⅜, 7/16, ½-inch. Price, each.......... **$2.75**

No. 35R2258 Core Box Plane. This plane is constructed so that the sides can be extended by additional sections, 2½ inches wide until **a diameter of 10 inches can be worked** if desired.

Price (with one pair of additional sections), for working semi-circles, up to 5 inches diameter, each.. **$2.63**

No. 35R2261 Extra Additional Sections, for working large diameters.

Price, per pair......... **66c**

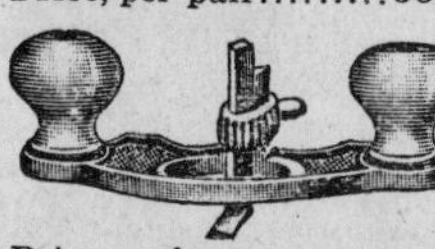

No. 35R2264 Stanley's Woodworkers Router Plane, with closed throat. Nickel plated stock, with steel bits (¼ and ½-inch).

Price, each.. **80c**

No. 35R2265 Stanley's Router will smooth the bottom of grooves, panels or all depressions below the general surface of any wood work, and will rapidly rout out mortises for sash, frame, pulleys, etc. The bits can also be clamped to the back side of the upright post and outside of the stock; in this position they will plane into corners which cannot be easily reached with any other tool; has iron stock nickel plated, and steel bits (¼ and ½-inch).

Price, complete...................................... **95c**

No. 35R2273 Single Handed Beader, for beading, reeding or fluting diagonal lines, etc. Nickel plated, with six steel cutters and one blank.

Price, each.......... **53c**

No. 35R2670 Sears, Roebuck & Co.'s Ship Carpenters' Adze, with spur head. Warranted.
Width of cut, inches..... 4¼ 4½
Price, each.. $1.12 $1.15

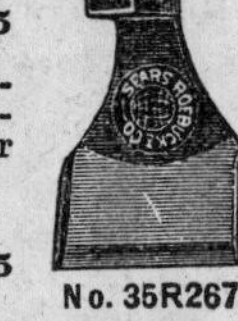

No. 35R2671 Sears, Roebuck & Co.'s Ship Carpenters' Adze, with lip and spur head. Warranted.
Width of cut, inches...... 4¼ 4½
Price, each .. $1.33 $1.35

No. 35R2670 No. 35R2671

No. 35R2674 Selected Quality Carpenters' Adze Handle, 34 inches long. Price, each.......17c

OUR NEW LINE OF WARRANTED AXES.

OUR LINE OF AXES this season is selected from the most popular patterns of the oldest and best known axe makers in the world. They are warranted against defects in material or workmanship. All have taper eye, which is larger on the outside. This binds the handle and prevents its getting loose. The cheapest axe we sell is made from just as good material as is used in our best axe, and it is made and tempered with the same care. The difference in our price represents the difference in cost of labor in making. While our Red Ridge will give satisfaction, our Hubbard's Hollow Ground Lippincott Brand will chop easier and is well worth every cent of the additional cost. Our prices represent the cost to manufacture, with only our one small percentage of profit added. **Lumbermen who use large quantities of axes are asked to compare our prices with the prices which they have been paying. While we make no discounts for quantity, and sell one axe just as low as a dozen, our price will be found lower than commonly asked when sold in dozen lots. We also give you the exact weights you want.** You can have a dozen all one weight if desired; you don't have to take them as packed assorted by the manufacturers.

REMEMBER. Every axe we sell is warranted.

Red Ridge, Michigan Pattern Axe.

No. 35R2677 Red Ridge, Michigan pattern axe. This axe is handsomely finished in red with polished bit. In its manufacture a full portion of the best quality crucible steel is used. Each axe is carefully tempered by hand, is hand hammered and carefully inspected in every process of manufacture. The special bevel in this axe enables it to enter and leave the timber with the least possible resistance. Aside from this valuable feature, it is larger than the ordinary axe of the same weight, which makes it well balanced. Weight, 3, 3½, 3¾, 4, 4½ and 5 pounds. Price 44c

Red Ridge, Michigan Pattern Double Bit Axe.

No. 35R2678 Red Ridge, Michigan Pattern Double Bit Axe. Is made in like manner and finish as above. Weight, 3½, 3¾, 4, 4½ and 5 pounds.
Price, each..............66c

Red Ridge, Single Bit Handled, Michigan Pattern Axe.

No. 35R2679 Red Ridge, Single Bit Handled, Michigan Pattern Axe. Same as described above, with a good hickory handle, correctly put in. Weight, not including handle, 3½, 4 and 4½ pounds. Price....56c

Hunt's Superior Axes. Yankee Pattern.

No. 35R2680 These are finished in black with polished bit. The first axe of this brand was manufactured from best refined tool steel in 1826 and the company has been most careful to maintain the high reputation it has always enjoyed. Each one is hand tempered and carefully inspected before leaving the factory. Weights are 3, 3½, 3¾, 4, 4½ and 5 pounds.
No. 35R2680 Price, each....58c

Hurd's Razor Blade Single Bit Dayton Pattern Axe.

No. 35R2682 Hand made, natural gas temper finish. This axe has been on the market and been recognized as one of the highest quality axes as far as quality and workmanship goes for many years. It is made with a taper eye, which prevents it getting loose on the handle. Each axe is hand tempered and closely examined before leaving the factory. Weights, 3, 3½, 3¾, 4, 4½ and 5 pounds.
No. 35R2682 Price, each..57c

Hurd's Razor Blade.

No. 35R2683 Hurd's Razor Blade Double Bit Wisconsin Pattern Axe; same hand made natural gas temper finish as single bit described previously. Weights, 3½, 3¾, 4, 4½, 5 and 5½ pounds.
No. 35R2683 Price, each.................. ....78c

The Jamestown Axe, Western Crown Pattern.

No. 35R2686 Full polished and etched with blue phantom bevel. It has been in the market a number of years and the verdict of the choppers is that it is correctly made. Each axe is hand hammered and tempered by hand. It is so made that it enters and leaves the wood freely and will not become stubbed after grinding. Weight, 3, 3½, 3¾, 4, 4½ and 5 pounds.
Price, each................54c

No. 35R2687 Jamestown Axe, double bit, Michigan pattern, quality and finish same as above. Weight, 3½, 3¾, 4, 4½, 5 and 5½ pounds.
Price......78c

Our Best Axe.

No. 35R2688 C.W. Hubbard's Patented Easy Chopping Hollow Ground Axe (Lippincott Brand, Dayton Pattern). Altogether a new innovation and promises to be the axe of the future, for the reason that from the peculiar construction of the bit **it is the easiest chopping axe in the world.** Look at the picture and notice that the axe is **hollow ground.** This feature enables it to enter and leave the wood with the least possible amount of resistance, and considerably less grinding is necessary to keep it in good condition than with the ordinary axe. The axe is finely polished and deeply etched, and is not only the best and easiest chopping, but the handsomest axe on the market today. All of our axes are made with a taper eye, which prevents them from becoming loose on the handle. Weights, 3, 3½, 3¾, 4, 4½ and 5 pounds. Warranted. Price, each...............70c

No. 35R2690 Niagara Boys' Handled Axe, made from best cast steel, handsomely finished in red with blue bevels. They are made with the same care and go through the same inspection as our men's axes. Weight, including handle, which is about 28 inches in length, is about 3¼ pounds.
Price, each......... .....42c

Hurd's Hunters' Hatchet.

No. 35R2693 Ideal black finish, made by the same skilled workmen who make our regular Hurd's axes. The handle is about 14 inches long. It is a convenient tool for household use as it takes the place of either axe, hatchet or hammer. It weighs only about 1½ pounds with handle. Price,......36c

GIVE CATALOGUE NUMBER IN FULL WHEN YOU WRITE YOUR ORDER

No. 35R2728 The Sager Special Chemical Process Axe. Sold by retail dealers everywhere at from $1.00 to $1.25. The axe is Michigan pattern, black finish, just as it comes from the hammer. Every one honed to a razor edge. As we shall hereafter sell another brand of axes, we desire to close out this brand and in order to dispose of them quickly, we have fitted them with a No. 1 hickory handle, and offer them all ready to use while they last for 59 cents. Specify weight desired, and we will fill order as near as we can. Also state what axe we shall send if these are all sold. Price, each..................59c

Axe Handles.

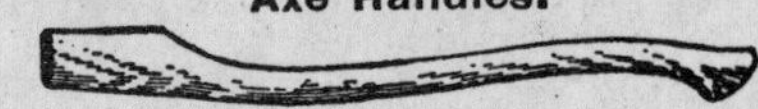

No. 35R2735 Common Quality Turned Axe Handle, 36 inches long. Price, each...............9c
No. 35R2738 Standard Quality Turned Axe Handle, 36 inches long. Price, each..............14c
No. 35R2740 Standard Quality Turned Boys' Axe Handle, 28 inches long. Price, each.............15c

No. 35R2745 Selected Quality Hand Shaved Axe Handle, 36 inches long. Price, each. 18c
No. 35R2747 Extra Selected Quality Hand Shaved Axe Handle, 36 inches long. The best handle we can find. Price, each...............23c

No. 35R2752 Extra Selected Quality Double Bit Axe Handles, 36 inches long, hand shaved. Excellent value. Price, each.......................20c

Axe Wedges.

No. 35R2755 So well known, description is not necessary. Weighs 5 ounces.
Price, each,.....................2c

No. 35R2759 Solid Cast Steel Wood Choppers' Wedges. Weight, 4 lbs.
Price, each..........15c
Weight, 5 lbs., each..19c

No. 35R2762 Truckee Pattern Wood Choppers' Wedge, extra tool steel, oil finished.

Weight.	4 lbs.	6 lbs.	8 lbs.
Price, each........	20c	30c	40c

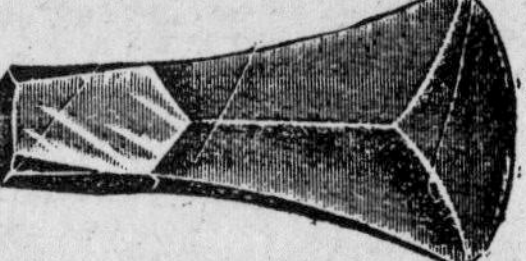

No. 35R2766 Oregon Pattern, Wood Choppers' Wedge, solid cast steel. Oil finished.
Weight, 4 lbs., 24c. 6 lbs., 36c; 8 lbs. 48c

No. 35R2769 Falling Wedge, solid cast steel, oil finished.

Weight.....	4 lbs.	6 lbs.	8 lbs.
Price, each,	36c	54c	72c

No. 35R2772 Saw Log Wedge; solid cast steel oil finished.
Weight, 1¼ lb., 15c; 2 lbs., 20c; 2½ lbs., 25c; 3 lbs....................30c

No. 35R2775 Wood Choppers' Maul, straight cut pattern, solid cast steel. Polished bit and poll, body painted blue.

Weight.........	5 lbs.	6 lbs.	7 lbs.	8 lbs.	10 lbs.
Price, each.....	38c	45c	53c	59c	74c

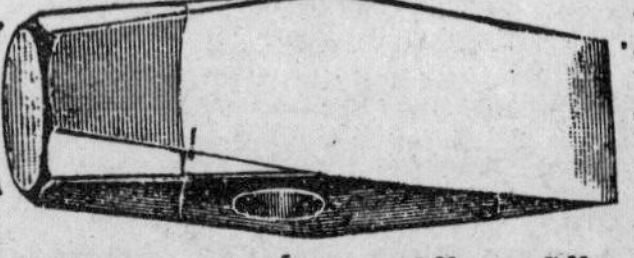

No. 35R2778 Wood Choppers' Maul. Oregon pattern, solid cast steel, oil finished, polished face. No better made.

Weight, pounds..	5	6	7	8	10
Price, each.......	38c	45c	53c	59c	74c

No. 35R2785 Wrought Iron Beetle Rings. Made of flat iron 1 inch wide, 1/16-inch thick.

Diameter, inches...	4½	5	6
Weight, pounds....	1¼	1½	1¾
Price, each.........	10c	12c	14c

Sears, Roebuck & Co.'s Nail Hammers.

A real good hammer gives satisfaction to the user. A poor hammer is about the meanest thing in the tool line. We sell the best hammers made and at prices that are right.

No. 35R2800 Sears, Roebuck & Co.'s Brand Nail Hammer. Octagon neck and poll. Made of the very best tool steel; finely polished and nickel plated. **OUR NAME etched on hammer. They are proportioned right; they hang right; claws are right shape to draw a nail without breaking the claw; temper is right.** Polished hickory handle. **Guaranteed. If not satisfactory return to us and money will be refunded.**

Size..........................	1	1½	2
Weight, without handle........	1¼ lb.	1 lb.	13 oz.
Price, each......................	59c	53c	50c

By the improved form of the groove this hammer will hold any size or shape of cut or wire nails. With it one can drive nails beyond ordinary reach.

No. 35R2803 Nail Holding Hammer, made from the best quality, crucible steel. Only one size and shape made. Weight, 1 lb. 3 oz., without handle. Price, each, with handle 73c

No. 35R2806 Wedge Plate Hammers are forged from the best cast steel; handles of the best second growth hickory. **The malleable wedge plate strengthens the handle and at the same time keeps the head from getting loose or coming off. We guarantee every hammer to be first class.** Weight of head, 1 pound; bell face. Each, **54c**

No. 35R2807 Same hammer, plain face. Each, 54c

David Maydole's Nail Hammers.

Maydole's Hammers are made from the very best of crucible cast steel. The claws and face are not tempered the same, but each to the proper temper for the work it is required to do. The eye is left soft, so it never splits or cracks at the eye. The handles are best second growth hickory (selected stock). Every hammer is fully guaranteed.

No. 35R2810 The Genuine David Maydole's Nail Hammers. Adze eye, plain face, polished hickory handles. Weights do not include handles.

No..........	1	1¼	2	3
Weight.....1¼ lbs.		1 lb.	13 oz.	7½ oz.
Price, each.	63c	58c	53c	48c

No. 35R2811 The Genuine David Maydole's Nail Hammers. Adze eye, bell face, polished; hickory handle. Weights do not include handles.

No.	11	11½	12	13
Weight....................	1 lb. 3 oz.	1 lb.	12 oz.	7 oz.
Price, each.............	64c	59c	54c	49c

Bell face hammers are rounded on the face. They do not slip from the head of the nail, and there are no sharp corners to mar the surface of the wood when nail is driven home.

Forged Steel Nail Hammers.

The following Hammers, No. 35R2815 and No. 35R2816, are forged from the best cast steel and are warranted against flaws and not to be soft. They are not so highly finished and polished as the higher priced goods, but for common use **they give excellent satisfaction.** Don't compare these hammers with cast iron goods like No. 35R2820. We tell you that cast iron hammers are no good and you will find them so. **We tell you that these hammers are all right and you will not be disappointed if you buy one.**

No. 35R2815 Adze Eye Plain Face Cast Steel Nail Hammer, warranted against flaws and not to be too soft.

Size	Weight	Each
1	1¼ lbs.	29c
1½	1 lb.	27c
2	13 oz.	25c

Weight of handle not included in stating weight.

No. 35R2816 Adze Eye, Bell Face, Cast Steel Nail Hammers. Warranted against flaws and not to be too soft.

Size............	11	11½	12
Weight...1¼ lbs.		1 lb.	13 oz.
Price.....	29c	27c	25c

Cast Iron Nail Hammers

No. 35R2820 Cast Iron Hammers are positively no good. We have a few of these hammers in stock, which we would rather keep than sell to our customers. **If you must have them, we will sell you a light one for 8 cents or a full size for 10 cents.** You will be sorry if you buy one. **Can't you afford to buy a first class hammer at our prices for them? See how cheap they are.**

Hammer Handles.

Selected Quality Nail Hammer Handles.

No. 35R2825 Adze Eye Nail Hammer Handles. Length, 14 inches.
Price, each..... ....4c

No. 35R2845 Nail Puller. Saves time, labor, cases and nails. No merchant, carpenter or plumber can afford to be without a nail puller. **It pays for itself.**
No. 1, weight 5 pounds, each..........49c

Mallets.

No. 35R2850 Square Hickory Mallets. Head is 6½x2¾x3¾ inches; mortised handle. Weight, about 1¾ pounds.
Price, each..............11c

No. 35R2853 Square Lignum Vitæ Mallets. Head is 6½x2¾x3¾ inches. Weight, 2¼ lbs. Price, each, 22c

Iron Bound Mallet.

No. 35R2856 Round Malleable Iron Mallet, with inserted hickory faces. Head is 5¾x3 inches. Weight, 3½ pounds.
Price, each... ....33c

Rawhide Bound Mallets.

No. 35R2860 Rawhide Bound Mallets. The most durable, finest finished and handsomest made. Positively will not split. The rawhide binding has all the desirable qualities and none of the objectionable features of iron ferrules, while the spring of the hide-facing cushions the blow and prevents jarring, greatly relieving the arm of the user.

2 -inch face, each...............32c
2½-inch face, each...............42c
3 -inch face, each...............45c

Vulcanized Fiber Head Mallet.

No. 35R2861 Thoroughly kiln-dried wood, body and handle. Handle screws in. The bands are of malleable iron, riveted to the body, and tapering on the inside to hold the fiber heads firmly in place. The fiber heads are sufficiently elastic to form a cushion, relieving the arm from the jarring occasioned by the force of the blow.

Diameter of face, inches..	2	2½	3	3½
Price, each...............	35c	40c	48c	64c

Chisels and Gouges.

CONDITIONS OF WARRANTY.

We warrant all chisels sold by us to be perfect when they leave the store, so far as the material and workmanship are concerned. If a tool proves too soft and bends on the edge or breaks in consequence of a flaw in the steel, and is returned to us within 30 days from date of purchase, a new tool will be given in exchange. If it shows abuse or is broken where the steel is sound, it will not be exchanged.

No. 35R2875 Tanged Firmer Chisels, solid cast steel, warranted, polished, with handle included.

Size,	¼	⅜	½	⅝	¾	⅞	1	1¼	1½	1¾	2
Each,	17c	18c	19c	20c	22c	23c	26c	34c	40c	49c	56c

No. 35R2876 Tanged Firmer Gouges, warranted solid cast steel, polished. Outside bevel, with handle included.

Size,	¼	⅜	½	⅝	¾	⅞	1	1¼	1½	1¾	2
Each,	17c	18c	19c	20c	21c	23c	28c	35c	43c	55c	65c

GIVE CATALOGUE NUMBER IN FULL WHEN YOU WRITE YOUR ORDER

SEARS, ROEBUCK & CO.'S HIGH GRADE WARRANTED CHISELS.

Socket Firmer Chisel.

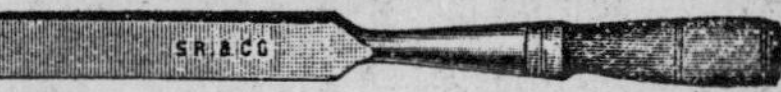

No. 35R2880 Socket Firmer Chisels, with leather tip handles. Blades are 6 inches long. For quality of material, finish and cutting qualities these chisels cannot be equaled at the price. **They are high grade, first class tools. Warranted.**

Size......		¼	⅜	½	⅝	¾
Price.....		19c	20c	22c	24c	26c
Size......	⅞	1	1¼	1½	1¾	2
Price.....	27c	29c	32c	34c	36c	39c

No. 35R2881 Socket Firmer Chisels, beveled edge, **leather tipped handles.** These are high grade tools, **made in the best manner of the best materials.** Bevel blade, 6 inches long. **Warranted.**

Size............	⅛	¼	⅜	½	⅝	¾	⅞
Price, each...	22c	23c	24c	26c	28c	30c	31c
Size.	1	1¼	1½	1¾	2		
Price, each...	33c	36c	38c	40c	43c		

Socket Framing Chisel.

No. 35R2887 Socket Framing Chisel; blade 8 inches long; high grade fine finish, with handles. Handles have iron ring on end **to prevent splitting. Warranted.**

Size, inches,	⅜	½	¾	1	1¼	1½	1¾	2
Price, each,	27c	28c	30c	36c	41c	45c	50c	54c

Socket Corner Chisel.

No. 35R2889 Socket Corner Chisel; extra cast steel, polished outside, with handle. Handle has iron ring on end to prevent splitting. Size given is width of each face.

Size, inches...............	¾	1	1¼
Price, each	64c	73c	82c

No. 35R2893 Socket Slick; extra cast steel, polished; with handle, as shown in illustration. Warranted.

Size, inches........	2½	3	3½	4
Price, each........	92c	$1.00	$1.19	$1.37

Chisel Grinder.

No. 35R2897 This is a new invention for holding chisels, plane irons, etc., while grinding them. When put in the holder and brought to the right bevel with the adjusting screw, **nothing is left to do but to bear it on the stone,** and it will grind all right without further care.
Price, each.............65c

Buck's Chisels.

Buck's Chisels and Gouges have attained a reputation for excellence of their fine cutting qualities known everywhere. When you get a tool stamped "Buck" you are getting the finest tempered, keenest cutting tool that can be bought. Three generations have made the work of forging, hardening and tempering edge tools a practical life study, and now have attained a standard that cannot be excelled. **All goods warranted against flaws and not to be too soft.** Do not condemn the cutting quality of any new tool until you have ground it more than once, as you will often find a perfect edge on the second if not on the first grinding.

No. 35R2900 Buck's Tanged Firmer Chisels, ground sharp and honed, with polished appletree handles. The 1-inch chisel blade is 5½ inches long from the bolster. Other sizes in proportion. **Warranted.**

Size, inches,	⅛	3/16	¼	5/16	⅜	½	⅝
Price, each,	20c	21c	22c	23c	24c	26c	29c
Size, inches,	¾	⅞	1	1¼	1½	1¾	2
Price, each,	31c	34c	36c	47c	56c	67c	78c

Buck's Tanged Firmer Gouges.

No. 35R2903 Buck's Tanged Firmer Gouges, beveled outside, ground sharp, with best quality applewood handles. The 1-inch blade is 5½ inches long from the bolster. **Other sizes in proportion. Warranted.**

Size, inches...	⅛	3/16	¼	5/16	⅜	½	⅝
Price, each...	26c	27c	28c	29c	30c	32c	34c
Size, inches...	¾	⅞	1	1¼	1½	1¾	2
Price, each...	37c	41c	43c	56c	67c	79c	93c

Screwdriver.

No. 35R3074 Screwdriver, beech handle, capped ferrule, round shank blades. Shank is diamond shape with wings (shown by dark line in illustration) and is forced in by heavy pressure, making it impossible to turn in the handle. The blades are forged from a special grade of tough steel and great care is taken to secure the proper temper.

Length of blade, inches...	2	3	4	5
Price, each.........	4c	5c	7c	8c
Length of blade, inches...	6	8	10	12
Price, each.........	9c	13c	15c	20c

Champion Screwdrivers.

No. 35R3077 The Genuine Champion. Made by Tower & Lyon. **We guarantee every blade not to turn, pull out or develop any imperfections in temper, quality or finish.** Handle is dyed rosewood and has a high glossy finish. Ferrule and blade polished.

Size of blade, inches...	3	4	5	6	8	10
Whole length, inches..	7½	9	11¼	12½	15	17
Price, each............	15c	20c	25c	27c	36c	45c

No. 35R3080 Champion Pattern Screwdriver, forged from a very tough grade of crucible cast steel. Not so finely finished or highly polished as No. 35R3077 screwdriver, but **quality is fully guaranteed.**

Size of blade..	3-in.	4-in.	5-in.	6-in.	8-in.	10-in.
Whole length.	7½	9	11¼	12½	15	17
Price, each...	10c	11c	14c	16c	20c	25c

No. 35R3083 Yankee Ratchet Screwdriver. Right and left hand, and rigid. The materials and workmanship are of superior quality in every detail. The drivers are strong, durable, handsomely finished. The friction in ratchet mechanism is so slight as to be hardly felt, the backward movement is as easy as in a good stem winder and just as noiseless. When a screw is screwed in it stays where put, and is not screwed out when handle is turned back. For right hand or to ratchet a screw in, push the slide to end of slot towards bit; for left hand or to ratchet a screw out, push the slide towards handle of driver. If slide is placed midway between ends of slot, the blade is held rigidly and the driver can be used as an ordinary screwdriver with fixed blade. Made in the following sizes:

Inches.......	4	5	6	8	10	12
Price, each..	33c	37c	42c	50c	60c	65c

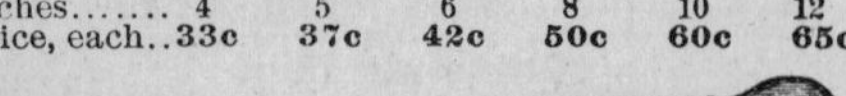

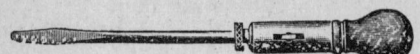

No. 35R3085 Yankee Ratchet Screwdriver, right and left hand and rigid, with finger turn on blade. **A light blade screwdriver for small screws in electric work, etc.** It has on its blade a knurled washer as shown in cut, and by means of this to turn the blade with a finger and the thumb. This permits the hand holding the handle to press steadily against the screw and prevent the screw from wobbling, while the thumb and finger can turn or ratchet the blade until screw is well started in its place, when it is driven home by the hand on the handle. In taking out a screw, it is started by turning blade by handle until loose, and then run out by thumb and finger operating knurled washer. In this way the work is accomplished much more easily and rapidly. The adjustment for right or left hand is same as in No. 35R3083. In all the sizes the blade is $\frac{3}{32}$ inch diameter, and handles are same, the only difference being in the length of the blades. The material and workmanship are of superior quality in every detail. Every tool is guaranteed. Made in the following sizes:

Inches..........	2	3	4	5
Price, each......	27c	32c	35c	38c

No. 35R3986 Yankee Ratchet Screwdriver No. 12 is made for the especial use of gunsmiths, electricians and other mechanics requiring a strong screwdriver with a short stub blade. It is right and left hand and rigid. Made in one size only. Blade, $\frac{5}{16}$ inch in diameter, 1⅓ inches long. Entire length of screwdriver, 5¾ inches. Price, each....42c

No. 35R3087 Yankee Pocket Magazine Screwdriver is made with four detachable blades of varying widths and thicknesses to suit different size screws. The blades are kept in magazine formed by handle. The tool is small and convenient to carry in the pocket, measuring when closed only 3 inches long and ⅝ inch in diameter and weighing only 2 ounces. It is made of steel, handsomely polished and nickel plated.
Price, each....................................45c

Yankee Spiral Ratchet Screwdriver.

Yankee Spiral Ratchet Screwdriver, right hand only and rigid. Is designed to push or ratchet screws into place, but not to take them out in that way. It is arranged to be used as a rigid driver by simply moving shifter to opposite end of slot. Three bits are furnished with each tool.

No. 35R3091 Size 1. Extreme length extended, including bit, 14 inches; length of push or stroke, 4 inches. Price, each..............................82c

No. 35R3092 Size 2. Extreme length extended, including bit, 17 inches; length of push or stroke, 5 inches. Price, each..............................94c

No. 35R3093 Size 3. Extreme length extended, including bit, 19 inches; length of push or stroke, 6 inches. Price, each..............................$1.05

Goodell's Automatic Screwdriver.

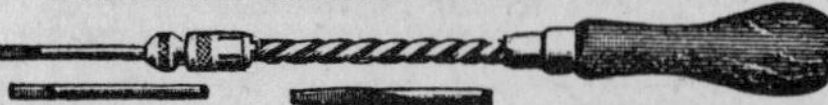

Goodell's Automatic Screwdriver can be used as a spiral ratchet or plain screwdriver.

No. 35R3096 Goodell's Spiral Screwdriver No. 1, stained cherry handle. Length closed, 7½ inches; open, 11½ inches, with three forged steel bits.
Price, each..............................88c

No. 35R3097 Goodell's Spiral Screwdriver No. 2, stained cherry handle. Length closed, 9 inches; length open, 13 inches, with three forged steel bits.
Price, each..............................$1.00

Reversible Automatic Screwdriver.

No. 35R3100 Goodell's Reversible Automatic Interchangeable Screwdriver No. 22. The simplest, most compact. The strongest and in every way the most practical tool for both driving and drawing screws automatically. It has two separate and distinct spirals, each working entirely independent of the other; each furnished with three blades. Weight, 14 ounces. Price, each..................$1.12

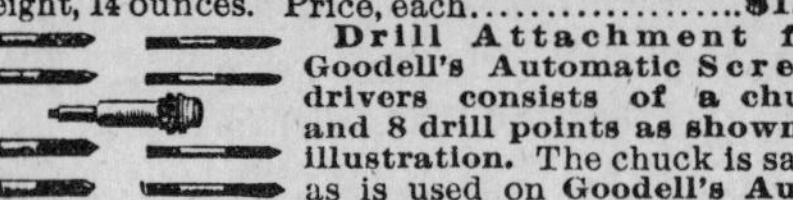

Drill Attachment for Goodell's Automatic Screwdrivers consists of a chuck and 8 drill points as shown in illustration. The chuck is same as is used on Goodell's Automatic Drill. The shank is steel milled to fit the socket of the screwdriver, for which it is intended. This attachment converts the automatic screwdriver into an automatic drill.

No. 35R3101 Drill Attachment, Size 1, fits Goodell's Automatic Screwdriver No. 1. Our catalogue No. 35R3096. Price, for attachment with eight drill points..............................49c

No. 35R3102 Drill Attachment, Size 2, fits Goodell's Automatic Screwdriver Nos. 2 and 22. Our catalogue Nos. 35R3097 and 35R3100.
Price, for attachment with eight drill points...50c

Our $1.14 Spiral Ratchet Screwdriver.

No. 35R3106 Yankee Spiral Ratchet Screwdriver, right and left hand, and rigid; can be used as a rigid screwdriver in any part of its length, as well as to push or ratchet screws in or out; convenient in size and of light weight, yet stronger in these vital points than any similar tool now made. Neither pawls nor ratchets can bend, break or get out of order. The friction in ratchet mechanism is so slight as to be hardly felt, the backward movement, like **our Yankee Ratchet Driver,** is as easy as in a good stem winder, and quite as noiseless. The nuts working in spiral are of brass and with the spiral grooves in rod are so designed that the wear has been reduced to a minimum. A long continued test in our factory shows that after driving fifty thousand screws with one tool there is no perceptible wear in the nuts. The chuck for holding the bits is simple in construction and positive in its hold on bits, and will outlast any other chuck made. **Three bits are included with each tool.** The extreme length of tool with bit in chuck is 13¼ inches when closed, and 19¼ inches when extended. Price, each..............................$1.14

No. 35R3107 Yankee Chuck with drill points, for use in No. 35R3106 Yankee Spiral Ratchet Screwdriver. Eight drill points, $\frac{1}{16}$-inch to $\frac{11}{64}$-inch inclusive, are furnished with each chuck. The chuck and eight drill points are put up in a small round wooden box.
Price, per set of 1 chuck and 8 drills............40c

No. 35R3112 Reid's Lightning Brace, size 2, with two screwdrivers, bits and one boring bit. Length, closed, 12¼ inches; length, extended, 21¼ inches. Weight, 12 ounces.
Price, each..............................$1.10

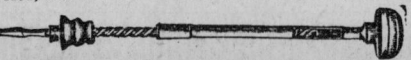

No. 35R3113 Reid's Lightning Brace, size 1, with one screwdriver bit. Length, closed, 15¼ inches, extended, 27 inches. Weight, 1 lb. 10 oz. Each..$1.35

Hand Drills.

No. 35R3120 Hand Drill, nickel plated, hollow head with hardwood screw cap; containing six drill points. Length, 10½ inches. Weight, 14 ounces.
Price, each..............................45c

No. 35R3121 Extra Drill Points for above hand drill. Price, per set of six..............................15c

No. 35R3125 Goodell's Hand Drill, made of malleable iron with steel spindle and rosewood head and handle. The handle is hollow and contains six drill points of various sizes. **The jaws are of forged steel and will hold perfectly drill shanks of any shape from $\frac{1}{32}$ to ⅛ inch in diameter.** Each..$1.10

No. 35R3126 Extra Drill Points for above stock.
Price, per set..............................40c

No. 35R3127 Millers Falls Hand Drill No. 1.
Malleable iron frame, steel spindle, hollow cocobolo handle, which contains eight fluted drill points, chuck is nickel plated and has three jaws, resting in solid sockets, and there are no springs to get out of place or out of order. They hold drills from 0 to $\frac{3}{16}$. An extra handle, as shown in cut, is furnished with this drill. Price, including 8 fluted drill points, $1.10

No. 35R3132 Extra drill points for above drill.
Price, per set..............................36c

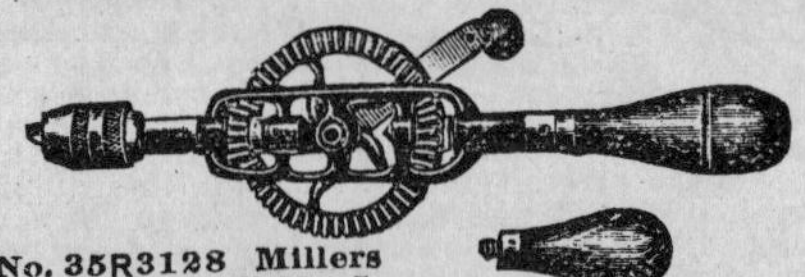

No. 35R3128 Millers Falls Hand Drill No. 5.
Malleable iron frame, steel spindle, hollow cocobolo handle which contains eight fluted drill points. Chuck is nickel plated and has three jaws resting in solid sockets, and there are no springs to get out of order. It is double geared, and is provided with a wide rim gear, to be grasped between thumb and fingers when the drill is used for delicate work. In this manner it can be run without liability of breaking points. Length over all, 11½ inches. Weight, 20 ounces. Price, including eight fluted drill points. $1.30

No. 35R3129 Extra Drill Points for above drill.
Price, per set of eight..............................37c

No. 35R3130 The handle is of hollow brass, nickel plated, used as a receptacle for the drill points, each contained in a separate numbered compartment. **Each drill is fitted with eight fluted drill points. The frame is of malleable iron, strong and light.** The large and small gears are both cut, and run smoothly without hitching. The steel chuck is a model one, with knurled nut, well finished, and three hardened steel jaws which will hold equally well the fluted drills in the handle, or any twist drill from $\frac{1}{4}$ down to No. 80. Price, each..............................$1.40

No. 35R3131 Extra Drill Points for above drill.
Price, per set of eight..............................37c

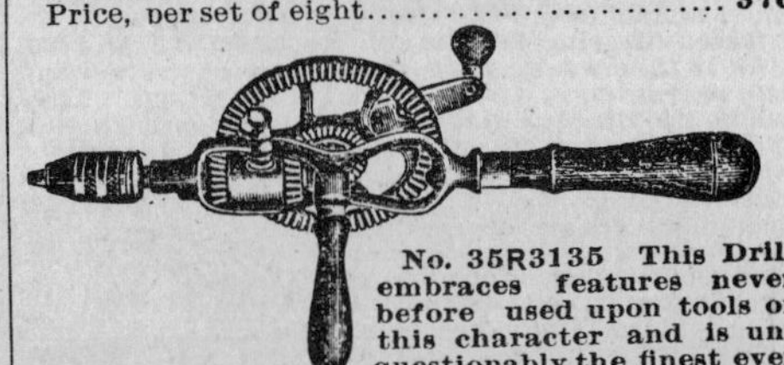

No. 35R3135 This Drill embraces features never before used upon tools of this character and is unquestionably the finest ever produced. It has double gears, two speeds, and a chuck, with capacity to ⅜-inch, as noted below. **Frame,** malleable iron, japanned. **Handle,** polished hardwood, screw cap. **Gears,** cut teeth. **Speeds,** it has two speeds, changed by turning the nut on the frame marked "F" and "S." **Chuck** three-jawed, capacity 0 to ⅜-inch, has knurled nut, nickel plated, well made and accurate. Spindle runs in a hardened steel cone bearing. No drill points are furnished with this tool. Price, each..............................$2.20

Barber Improved Ratchet Braces.

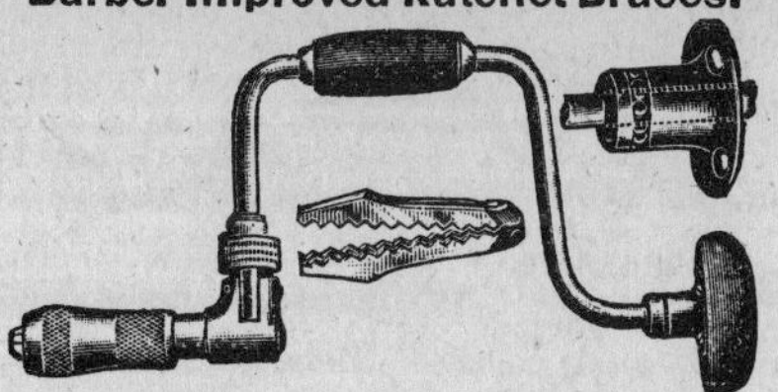

No. 35R3199 The Latest Improved Barber Ratchet Braces with alligator jaws and ball bearing head. Made by the Millers Falls Co. Jaws hold round or square shank drills or auger bits of all sizes. The sweep is made from steel. The jaws are forged from steel. The wood handle has brass rings inserted in each end so it cannot split off. The chuck has a hardened steel anti-friction washer between the two sockets, thus reducing the wear. The head has a bearing of steel balls, running on hardened steel plates, so no wear can take place, as the friction is reduced to the minimum. The brace is heavily nickel plated and warranted in every particular. They are made as nearly perfection as is possible in durability, quality of material and workmanship, and beauty of finish. The 10-inch sweep is best for general work. The 6-inch size is a favorite with electricians.

Sweep, inches	6	8	10	12	14
Price, each...	$1.14	$1.25	$1.35	$1.47	$1.58

Fray's Ratchet Bit Braces.

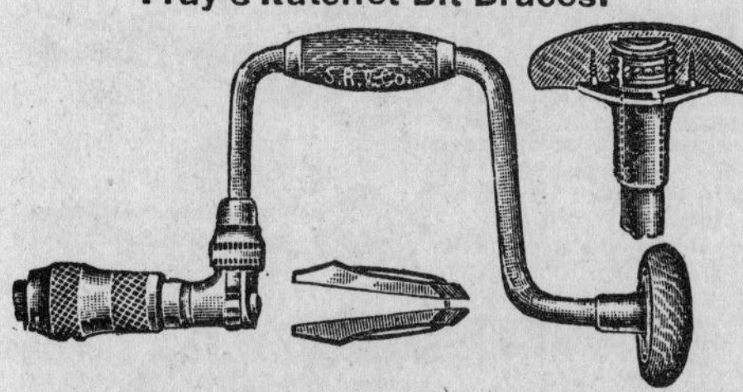

No. 35R3200 Fray's Ratchet Braces above illustrated are first class in every respect, and fully guaranteed. The sweep, pawls, jaws and ratchet are steel, handles and heads are cocobolo, all metal parts are nickel plated, and fully finished throughout. The peculiar features of these braces are the internal cam ring to operate the pawls, and the spring (of best music wire) attached to the jaws, **which give them perfect automatic action in operating when liberated by the unscrewing of the sleeve,** and in no way interferes with their fitting any shape bit or tool shank. **Head has ball bearings as shown in illustration.**

Sweep, inches......	8	10	12	14
Price, each........	$1.28	$1.39	$1.50	$1.64

REFER TO PAGES 7 TO 10 FOR FREIGHT AND EXPRESS RATES.

You can tell almost exactly what the freight or express will amount to on your goods without writing to us for this information.

Spofford Bit Braces.

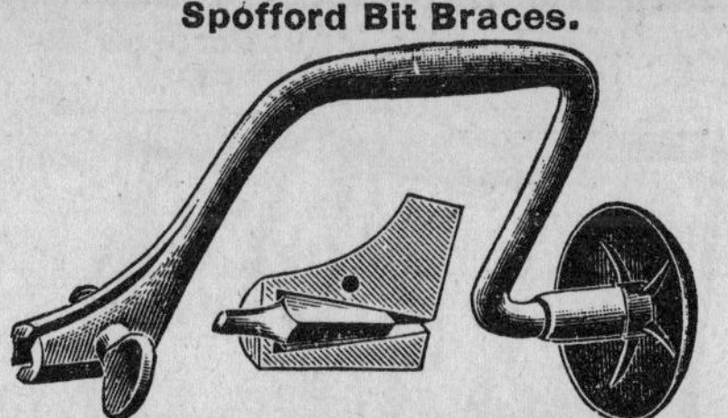

No. 35R3207 Spofford Bit Brace with metal head. This is positively the strongest as well as the most simple brace manufactured. It is furnished with a forged Bessemer steel thumbscrew, which will never strip or wear out. Will hold bits of any size and is made to stand wear and tear.

8-inch sweep, each, 69c 12-inch sweep, each, $0.90
10-inch sweep, each, 80c 14-inch sweep, each, 1.00

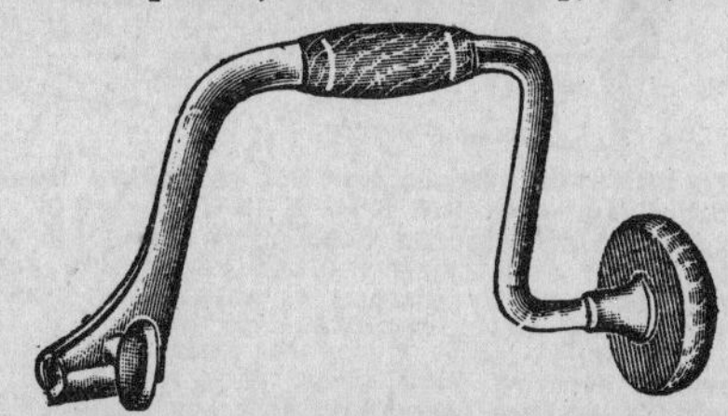

No. 35R3210 Spofford's Bit Brace has been in market for years, and there is no doubt it **will stand more rough usage and abuse than any other made.** Will hold all sizes auger bits, gimlet bits, or bit stock drills. Bits are quickly fastened in and **can't pull out. It's a great favorite with blacksmiths and carriage builders.** Solid steel, nickel plated, cocobolo head and handle, adjustable bit holder. **It's the only brace made as large as 17-inch sweep.**

Sweep, inches..	8	10	12	14	17
Price, each....	88c	99c	$1.10	$1.20	$1.26

Corner Braces.

No. 35R3215 Corner Brace. With this brace a hole can be bored in a corner in places where no other brace **can be used to advantage. It is a favorite with electricians, bell hangers, gas fitters, plumbers, cabinet makers, carpenters and other mechanics.** It is well made and finely finished. Steel rods, full nickel plated, with cocobolo head and handles. **Made in two sizes.**

Price, each, 8-inch sweep.......................$2.20
Price, each, 10-inch sweep.......................2.30

Drill and Ratchet Braces.

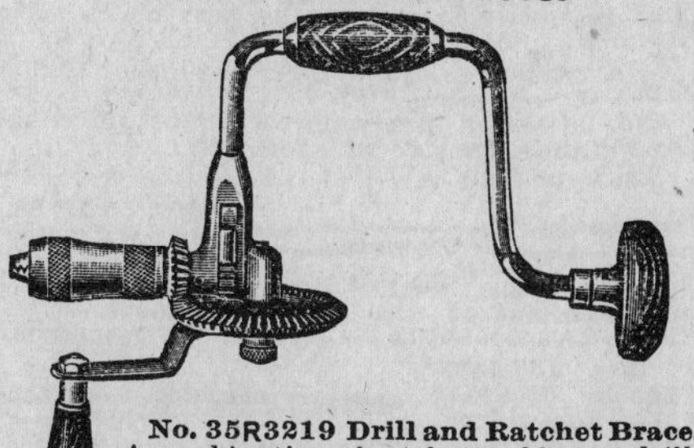

No. 35R3219 Drill and Ratchet Brace. A combination of ratchet and breast drill. Barber's 10-inch nickel plated steel sweep, **ball bearing head,** alligator jaws, made by the Millers Falls Co. The jaws are forged from steel, the wood handle has brass rings inserted in each end so it cannot split off. The chuck has a hardened steel anti-friction washer between the two sockets, thus reducing the wear. The head has a bearing of steel balls, running on hardened steel plates, so no wear can take place, as the friction is reduced to the minimum. The brace is heavily nickel plated and warranted in every particular. The drill gear is detachable and is easily and **quickly adjusted.** Jaws hold all kinds of bits and drills. Price, each..................$2.40

Angular Boring Machines.

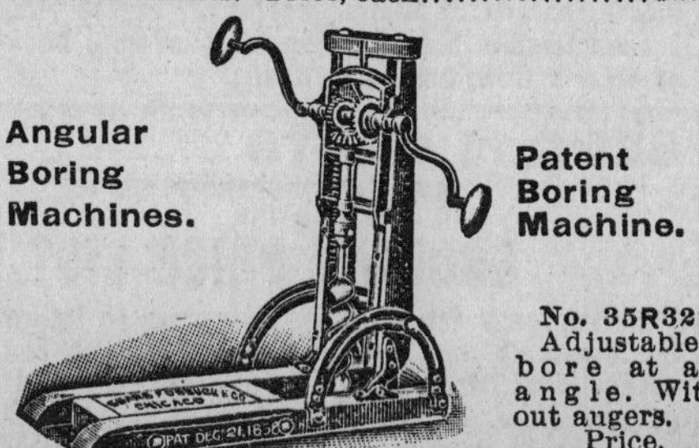

Patent Boring Machine.

No. 35R3225 Adjustable to bore at any angle. Without augers. Price, each......$2.80

GIVE CATALOGUE NUMBER IN FULL WHEN YOU WRITE YOUR ORDER.

The Boss Boring Machine.

The Boss is rapidly taking the place of all other boring machines on the market, having advantages known to all that commend it to carpenters and ship builders everywhere. Gear gives speed on one chuck equal to that of cranks, and on another chuck one and one-half times that of the cranks. All iron except the base. Adjustable to bore at any angle.

No. 35R3226 Price, without augers........................$4.00

Millers Falls Boring Machine

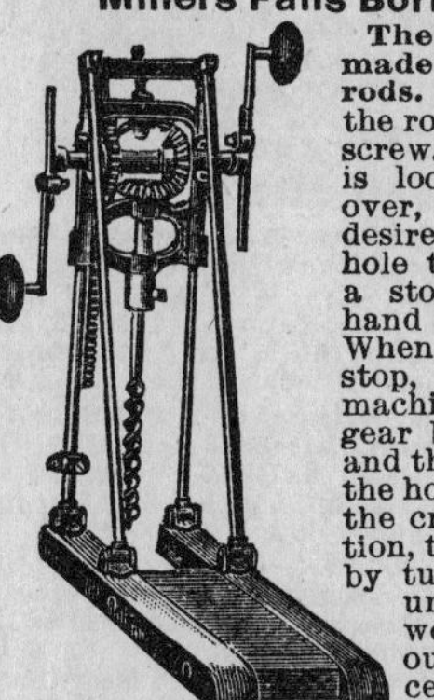

The frame and braces are made of ½-inch round steel rods. Braces are attached to the rods at the top by a set screw. When this set screw is loosened the frame falls over, so as to bore at any desired angle. The depth of hole to be bored is fixed by a stop, as seen on the left hand upright rod in the cut. When the frame strikes this stop, lift the latch and the machine throws itself into gear by the use of a spring, and the auger is lifted out of the hole by continuing to turn the crank in the same direction, then it is dropped down by turning the crank back until the auger strikes the wood, when it is thrown out of gear, and proceeds to bore the next hole. As seen in the cut, the machine has adjustable cranks which fully regulate its speed and power.

No. 35R3229 Price, without augers..........$6.45

Boring Machine Augers.

No. 35R3230 Extra Quality Augers for above or any other boring machine of standard make.

Size, inches....	¼	⅜	½	⅝	¾	⅞
Price, each.....	25c	25c	25c	25c	25c	25c
Size, inches....	1	1¼	1½	1¾	2	
Price, each.....	30c	35c	42c	50c	60c	

Bailey's Boring Machine Auger.

No. 35R3231 This Auger will bore with less friction, will bore smoother, will bore deeper without withdrawing than any auger we have ever seen. They are made of a high grade crucible steel, well finished and carefully inspected.

Size, inches.,	¾	⅞	1	1¼	1½	1¾	2
Price, each..	45c	48c	52c	58c	65c	71c	77c

Carpenters' Augers.

No. 35R3235 Extra Quality Carpenters' Auger. Handle not included at price given. Extra cast steel, **full polished; nut on end of shank.**

Size, inches....	¾	⅞	1	1¼	1½	1¾
Price, each....	20c	23c	25c	30c	38c	45c
Size, inches....	2	2¼	2½	2¾	3	
Price, each....	55c	$1.00	$1.25	$1.50	$1.75	

Auger Handles.

No. 35R3239 Will fit any size auger, and is quickly removed, so augers can be easily packed in tool chest. **Only one handle required for a full set of augers.** Weight, 1 pound. Price, each...17c

No. 35R3240 Common Auger Handles. When ordering state for what size auger the handle is wanted. Price, each..........3c

Pratt's Ratchet Auger Handle.

No. 35R3242 The chuck of this ratchet auger handle opens wide enough to take in auger shanks with the nuts on. It can be used like a common auger handle, or by putting on the ratchet it can be used with both handles, but without shifting the hands. In cramped places, one handle is taken off and placed at a right angle with the other. The wood on the detachable handle revolves. The metal part of the handle is polished and nickel plated. **It also answers the purpose of a ratchet drill.** Price, each.............................$1.75

Bit Sets in Boxes.

87c to $2.75 for sets of 6, 8 or 13 fine cast steel auger bits in neat polished wood boxes.

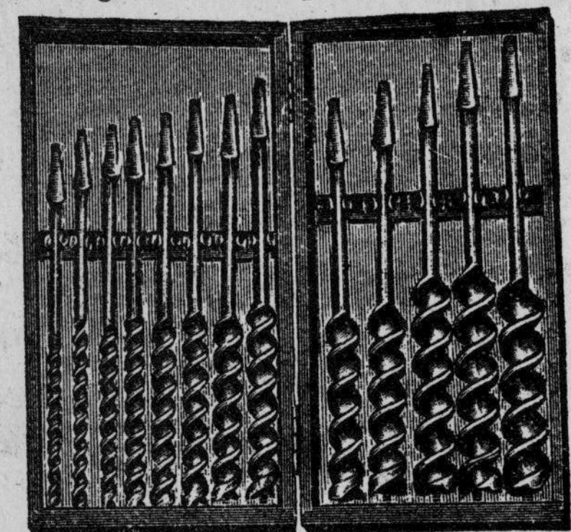

No. 35R3365 Set of Six Selected Extra Cast Steel, Common Pattern Auger Bits, with double spur and lip, nicely finished. Size, 1/4, 3/8, 1/2, 5/8, 3/4 and 1 inch. Put up in a finely finished, fancy hardwood box, as per illustration. Every bit is fully warranted. Weight, per set, 2 pounds. Price, per set........**87c**

No. 35R3368 Our Favorite Set of Eight Selected Extra Cast Steel Common Pattern Auger Bits with double spur and lip, nicely finished. **Warranted.** Size, 1/4, 5/16, 3/8, 1/2, 5/8, 3/4, 7/8 and 1 inch. Put up in a nicely finished fancy hardwood box. Weight, per set, 2 3/4 pounds. Price, per set **$1.12**

No. 35R3371 Our Acme Set of Eight Selected Extension Lip Auger Bits, warranted equal to the best bit made by anyone. Size, 1/4, 5/16, 3/8, 1/2, 5/8, 3/4, 7/8 and 1-inch. Put up in a finely finished fancy hardwood box. Weight, per set, 2 3/4 lbs. Per set....**$1.65**

No. 35R3374 Set of 13 Selected Extra Cast Steel Common Pattern Auger Bits, with double spur and lip, one each size from 1/4 to 1 inch, put up in a nicely polished fancy hardwood box. Weight, per set, 5 lbs. Price, per set..................................**$1.83**

No. 35R3377 Set of 13 Selected Extension Lip Auger Bits, one each size from 1/4 to 1 inch, put up in a nicely finished fancy hardwood box, guaranteed to be equal to the best bit made. Weight, per set, 5 lbs. Price, per set..**$2.75**

Bailey Bits in Sets.

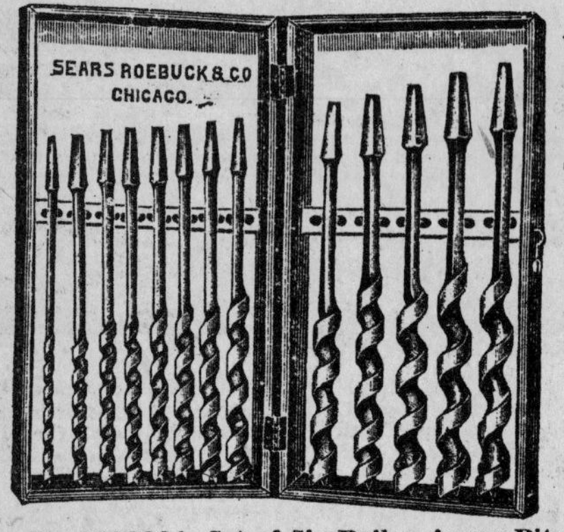

In Fancy Boxes, Nicely Varnished. (For description of bit see No. 35R3275.)

No. 35R3384 Set of Six Bailey Auger Bits, one each size, 1/4, 3/8, 1/2, 5/8, 3/4 and 1-inch, put up in same style box as shown in illustration. Per set....**$1.61**

No. 35R3387 Set of Nine Bailey Auger Bits, one each size, 1/4, 5/16, 3/8, 7/16, 1/2, 5/8, 3/4, 7/8 and 1-inch, put up in same style box as shown. Per set..........**$2.20**

No. 35R3390 Set of Thirteen Bailey Auger Bits, one each size, 1/4 to 1-inch, in box.............**$3.25**

No. 35R3399 C. E. Jennings & Co.'s Single Twist Extension Lip Auger Bits, as described under No. 35R3270, put up in a quartered oak bit box. One each size from 4/16 to 16/16, (13 bits). Per set...**$5.50**

MAKE UP A SHIPMENT OF 100 POUNDS TO GO BY FREIGHT.

If you will refer to the freight rates in the front of this book you can tell just what the goods will cost laid down at your station.

Brace and Bit Sets.

No. 35R3400 Brace and Bit Set. Ball bearing ratchet brace, nickel plated, 10-inch sweep, rosewood head and handle, **steel clad head**, hardened steel jaws; strictly first class, high grade goods; eight extra selected cast steel auger bits; common pattern, with double spur and lip. Sizes, 1/4, 5/16, 3/8, 1/2, 5/8, 3/4, 7/8 and 1-inch. **Every bit warranted. Three German Gimlet Bits**, sizes, 1/16, 1/8 and 3/16. All in a finely finished hardwood box. Price, complete, **$2.25**

No. 35R3403 Brace and Bit Set. We furnish our No. 35R3197 brace, with 10-inch sweep. Has ball bearing steel capped head. Rosewood head and handles; will hold round shank twist drills and all styles square shank bits. The finest finish possible. **Heavily nickel plated. Eight extension lip auger bits.** Sizes, 1/4, 5/16, 3/8, 1/2, 5/8, 3/4, 7/8 and 1 inch. **Every bit guaranteed equal to the best made. Three German gimlet bits**, sizes 1/16, 1/8 and 3/16 inch. One Clark's expansion bit, cutting any size hole from 7/8 to 3 inches. In a hardwood box. Price, set.....**$4.07**

No. 35R3404 Brace and Bit. Set same as above except the expansive bit is left out. Price, per set..**$3.09**

No. 35R3419 Screwdriver, to use in bit brace, is 5 1/2 inches long. **Forged from extra cast steel.** Not to be compared with cheap cast goods, of which there are too many in the market. W't, 5 oz. Each..**6c**

No. 35R3422 Square Reamer Bits. Forged from extra cast steel. Weight, 5 ounces. Price, each....**8c**

SEND 5 CENTS

FOR OUR CLOTH SAMPLE BOOK OF

MEN'S CUSTOM TAILORING.

For 5 cents (stamps accepted) we send a handsome sample book of men's custom tailoring goods, containing samples of a full line of materials for suits, pants, overcoats and ulsters, which we make to measure at the lowest prices, about one-half the prices charged by tailors generally. Please send 5 cents for this money saving cloth sample book of MEN'S CUSTOM TAILORING.

SEND 15 CENTS

FOR A YEAR'S SUBSCRIPTION TO OUR MONEY SAVING

GROCERY PRICE LIST.

Revised and issued every sixty days to follow the lowest Chicago prices on groceries. We can save you $1.00 to $5.00 on any ordinary sized grocery order, $10.00 to $50.00 a year on all the groceries you use. Don't fail to send 15 cents for this money saving GROCERY PRICE LIST.

Reamer Bits.

No. 35R3425 Octagon Reamer Bits. Forged from extra cast steel. Weight, 5 ounces. Price, each.**10c**

No. 35R3428 Flat Countersink Bit for metal. Forged from cast steel; polished. Weight, 5 oz. Each.. .**7c**

No. 35R3430 Rosehead Countersink Bit for metal or wood. Polished cast steel. Weight, 5 oz. Each..**7c**

No. 35R3433 Snail Head Countersink for wood. Polished cast steel. Weight, 5 ounces. Price, each..........**7c**

No. 35R3437 Countersink for wood, with gauge. Weight, 5 oz. Each....**16c**

Clark's Countersink.

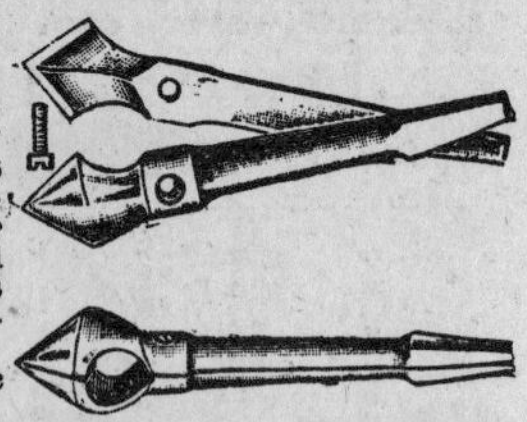

No. 35R3440 Clark's Countersink for wood. Without doubt the best countersink made for wood. **Can be opened for sharpening as shown in illustration.** Weight, 5 oz. Price, each.....**25c**

Metal Drills.

No. 35R3448

Metal Drills, forged cast steel, to fit a bit brace.

Size, inches....	3/16	1/4	5/16	3/8	7/16	1/2	9/16	5/8
Price, each,....	8c	9c	9c	9c	9c	11c	12c	13c

Twist Drills.

No. 35R3450 Twist Drills for bit brace.

Will drill metal or bore wood. The price is now so low everyone owning a bit brace should have a set of these drills. Keep point of drill well oiled when drilling metal.

Size,	1/16	3/32	1/8	5/32	3/16	7/32	1/4	9/32	5/16	11/32
Each,	5c	5c	6c	8c	9c	11c	12c	14c	16c	19c
Size,	3/8	13/32	7/16	15/32	1/2	5/8	3/4	7/8	1-inch.	
Each,	22c	24c	26c	29c	30c	48c	59c	70c	83c	

Patent Wood Brace Drills.

No. 35R3556 These drills are for wood only, but are not injured by accidental contact with nails, screws or other metal, and can be kept sharp by grinding.

Size, inches........	1/8	5/32	3/16	7/32	1/4	9/32	5/16	11/32
Each................	7c	8c	9c	11c	13c	15c	15c	17c
Size, inches........	3/8	13/32	7/16	15/32	1/2	5/8	3/4	
Each................	17c	19c	19c	21c	21c	25c	29c	

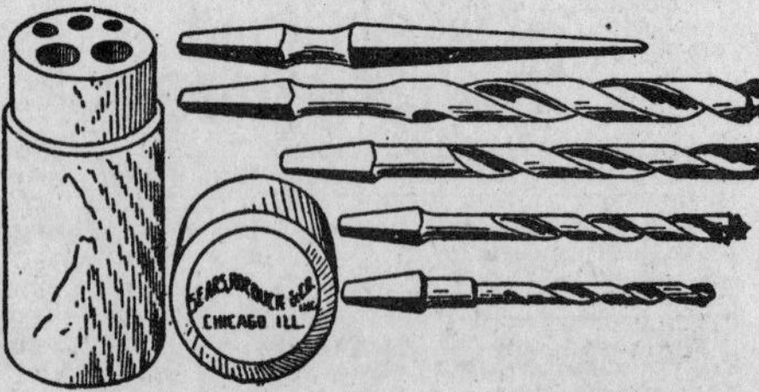

No. 35R3563 Five-piece set consists of four Bit Stock Twist Drills—one each size, 1/4, 5/16, 3/8 and 1/2-inch, and one extra quality square reamer bit. Put up in a round wood case, which serves as a permanent receptacle for the tools. Drills will bore either wood or iron. Price, for complete set with box **$1.00**

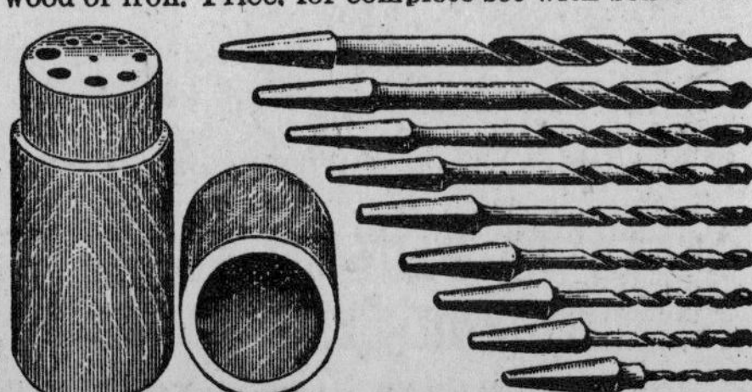

No. 35R3566 Set of 9 Bit Stock Drills, put up in a wood box similar to above (without reamer). Sizes are as follows: 1/16, 3/32, 1/8, 5/32, 3/16, 7/32, 1/4, 5/16 and 3/8 inches. Price, per set, complete.............**$1.10**

Pocket Set of Bit Stock Drills.

No. 35R3569 Pocket Set of Bit Stock Drills consists of 7 sizes of a superior quality of Bit Stock Drills as described under No. 35R3450. Put up in a case as shown, of a convenient size to be carried in the coat pocket. The case is a wood block covered with an imitation of morocco leather. Sizes, 4, 5, 6, 7, 8, 10 and 12 thirty-seconds. Weight of set, complete, 11 ounces. Per set....**95c**

No. 35R3570 Pocket Set of Syracuse Wood Bit Stock Drills, as described under No. 35R3556, put up in a case same as above and the same sizes.
Price, per set....................................**96c**

Straight Shank Drills.

No. 35R3572 Straight Shank Twist Drills cannot be used in the ordinary bit brace. They must be used in a chuck made for round shank drills. The shank and twist is the same size.

Diameter	Length	Price, per dozen	Price, each
1/16	2½	$0.38	$0.04
5/64	2⅝	.42	.04
3/32	2¾	.45	.04
7/64	2⅞	.49	.05
⅛	3	.54	.05
9/64	3⅛	.60	.05
5/32	3¼	.68	.06
11/64	3⅜	.75	.07
3/16	3½	.82	.07
13/64	3⅝	.90	.08
7/32	3¾	.98	.09
15/64	3⅞	1.08	.09
¼	4	1.17	.10
17/64	4⅛	1.27	.11
9/32	4¼	1.36	.12
19/64	4⅜	1.46	.13
5/16	4½	1.57	.14
21/64	4⅝	1.68	.14
11/32	4¾	1.80	.15
23/64	4⅞	1.90	.16
⅜	5	2.02	.17
25/64	5⅛	2.13	.18
13/32	5¼	2.25	.19
27/64	5⅜	2.40	.20
7/16	5½	2.55	.22
29/64	5⅝	2.70	.23
15/32	5¾	2.80	.24
31/64	5⅞	2.90	.25
½	6	3.00	.25

Round Shank Drills.

No. 35R3575 Twist Drill with round shank for drill presses. Will drill metal or bore wood. The shank of all sizes is ½ inch in diameter, 2½ in. long.

Sizes.....	⅛	5/32	3/16	7/32	¼	9/32	5/16	11/32
Each....	17c	18c	19c	21c	23c	24c	26c	27c
Sizes.....	⅜	13/32	7/16	15/32	½	17/32	9/16	19/32
Each.....	28c	29c	30c	31c	32c	33c	34c	37c
Sizes.....	⅝	21/32	11/16	23/32	¾	25/32	13/16	27/32
Each.....	39c	41c	43c	45c	47c	49c	50c	52c
Sizes.....	⅞	29/32	15/16	31/32	1 inch			
Each.....	54c	56c	60c	63c	67c			

Empty Tool Chests, at $5.40 to $6.86.

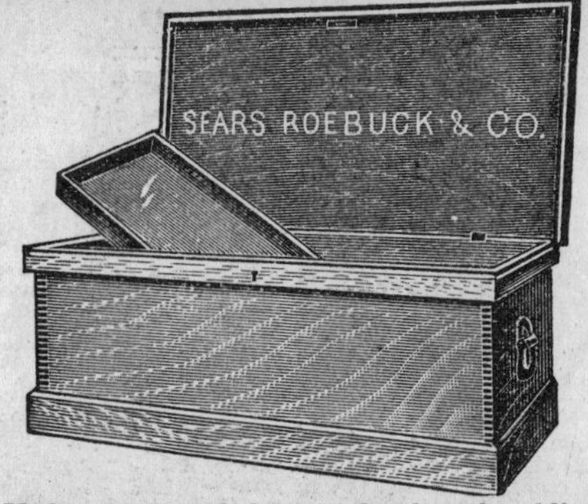

Made of selected chestnut, hardwood moldings, sliding tray, fitted with lock and key, and nicely varnished.

No. 35R3609 Empty Tool Chest, 28x15x14 inches (inside measurements), with two sliding trays, saw rack, etc. Price, each..........**$5.40**

No. 35R3611 Empty Tool Chest, 30½x15x14 inches (inside measurements), with two sliding trays, saw rack, etc. Price, each............**$6.12**

No. 35R3613 Empty Tool Chest, 32x18x16 inches (inside measurements), with two sliding trays, having saw racks to take in full length saws. Price, each..................................**$6.86**

Cabinet Makers' Bench.

No. 35R3620 Cabinet Makers' Bench. Every piece of wood used in this bench is maple, except handle of screw, which is hickory. Inferior goods have elm stand and basswood back top. The front top is made of pieces 2⅛ inches wide and 2¾ inches thick, glued together to prevent warping. The front top is 16 inches wide and back top (which is recessed) is 8 inches wide. Screws are 24 inches long and 2¼ inches in diameter over the thread. It is put together with bolts, making the best and strongest cabinet makers' bench on the market. Length 6½ feet, width 2 feet, height 34 inches. Weight, crated for shipment, 190 pounds. Price, each.............................**$8.55**

No. 35R3625 Steel Spring Bench Hook, suitable for above bench.
Price, each.............**30c**

No. 35R3660 Washer Cutter for Bit Brace. Extra fine steel knives, polished. Cuts any size washer with any size hole up to 5½ inches in diameter. Price, each........**34c**

Wrenches.

No. 35 R 3670 Pocket Screw Wrench, all iron, tinned. Whole length when closed 3¾ inches. Takes nut ⅝-inch. Weight, 7 ounces. Price, each.........................**7c**

No. 35R3673 Bicycle Wrench. Length, 5½ inches. Jaws open 1½ inches, forged steel, nickel plated. A good wrench for light work or family use. Weight, 5¼ ounces. Price, each.......................................**9c**

No. 35R3678 Solid Cast Steel Alligator Wrench. Length, 5¾ inches. Capacity, ¼ to ¾-inch; for holding or turning round or square bolts or nuts. Weight, 7 ounces. Price, each..**12c**

For other Alligator Wrenches, see Index.

Wrenches.

No. 35R3682 Always Ready Wrench, forged from steel of superior quality, oil tempered, nickel plated.

	1	2	2½	3
Holds nuts or pipe, inches..	¼-¾	¼-1¼	¼-1¾	¾-1¾
Price, each..................	18c	25c	38c	59c

No. 35R3686 Screw Wrench, wrought iron bar, head and screw. The 10-inch size is best for general purposes.

Size, inches,	6	8	10	12	15
Weight,	1 lb.	1 lb. 6 oz.	2 lbs.	2½ lbs.	3½ lbs.
Price, each.	20c	22c	27c	31c	53c

No. 35R3689 Genuine L. Coes' Improved Knife Handle Wrench. Made of the very best materials, thoroughly case hardened, and every wrench warranted.

Size Wrench,	6	8	10	12	15	18	21 inch.
Will open,.	⅞	1¼	1¾	2⅛	2⅝	3	4⅛ inch.
Price, each	41c	46c	55c	65c	$1.11	$1.39	$1.67

Pincers, Pliers and Nippers.

No. 35R3700 Carpenters' Pincers, with claw on handle, forged from superior steel, adapted for the work.

Size, inches...............	6	8	10	12
Price, each................	15c	20c	25c	30c

No. 35R3701 Sears, Roebuck & Co.'s Extra High Grade Special Carpenters' Pincers have a cutting edge and will cut small wire brads, etc. They are made from strong, tough steel, carefully finished and tempered. They are full polished all over. We believe no carpenter's pincer has before been made as good as carpenters would like to have them, and therefore we have made this just as good as we know how, regardless of cost. To this cost we have added only our one small profit. Length, 8 inches.
Price, each..**42c**

No. 35R3704 Flat Nose Pliers, box joint, wrought with steel face jaws. Made by Peck, Stow & Wilcox Co. A good, cheap plier. Weight, about 7 ounces.

Size, inches..................	4	5	6
Price, each..................	14c	15c	19c

No. 35R3705 Utica Drop Forge and Tool Co.'s Flat Nose Pliers are made from the best quality of tool steel and should not be confused with the cheap goods commonly sold. Temper and quality the best. Forged from tough tool steel.

Length, inches............	3	4	5	6	8
Price, each..................	19c	20c	23c	30c	49c

No. 35R3706 Round Nose Pliers, box joint. Wrought with steel face jaws. Made by Peck, Stow & Wilcox Co.

Size, inches..................	4	5	6
Price, each..................	14c	15c	19c

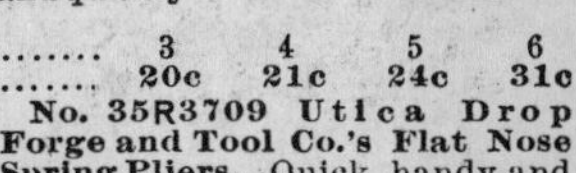

No. 35R3708 Utica Drop Forge and Tool Co.'s Round Nose Pliers. Forged from tool steel. Temper and quality the best.

Length, inches.........	3	4	5	6
Price, each..............	20c	21c	24c	31c

No. 35R3709 Utica Drop Forge and Tool Co.'s Flat Nose Spring Pliers. Quick, handy and always ready. Temper and quality the best. Forged from tool steel. Spring between the handles holds the jaws open always ready for use.

Length, inches..........	4	5	6	8
Price, each........... ...	24c	27c	36c	58c

No. 35R3711 Utica Drop Forge and Tool Co.'s Round Nose Spring Pliers. Forged from tool steel. Temper and quality the best. Jaws always open ready for use.

Length, inches..........	4	[illegible]	[illegible]
Price, each..............	25c	[illegible]	37c

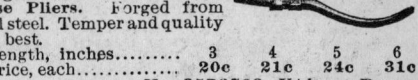

No. 35R3712 The Lodi Flat Nose Plier. A low priced, solid steel plier that is strong and serviceable. Nothing near as good has ever before been offered at twice the price we ask. They are light, but strong and stiff.

Size, inches.......................	4	5	6
Weight.............................	2 oz.	3 oz.	5 oz.
Price, each........................	5c	8c	10c

EMPTY TOOL CHESTS.

These chests are made of selected hard woods and are furnished with Yale pattern locks, nickel plated drawer pulls and cup handles. Each chest is provided with a brass elbow to hold up lid, and a device for locking all the drawers at once, automatically.

No. 35R3600 Machinist's Chest; contains a deep receptacle at the top and one drawer. The outside dimensions of these chests are as follows: 15½ inches long by 9½ inches wide by 9 inches high. The receptacle at the top measures inside, 12¾ inches long by 6¾ inches wide by 4 inches deep and drawer measure inside 11¾ inches by 5¾ inches by 2 1/16 inches. There is also a space under the drawer 1¼ inches deep. Made of chestnut with black walnut moldings.
Price, each **$3.43**

No. 35R3602 With two drawers. Outside dimensions, 20⅝ inches long by 13 inches wide by 9⅞ inches high. Inside dimensions are as follows: Receptacle under lid, 18x10¼x3⅛ inches; first drawer, 16⅞x9x1⅜ inches; second drawer, 16⅞x9x2⅝ inches; space under second drawer, 1 inch deep. With two drawers. Made of chestnut, with black walnut panels. Price, each..................................**$4.67**

No. 35R3604 With three drawers. Outside dimensions, 23½ inches long by 14½ inches wide by 12 inches high. Inside dimensions are as follows: Receptacle under lid, 21x11¾x3⅛ inches; first drawer, 20x10½x1 inches; second drawer, 20x10½x1⅛ inches; third drawer, 20x10½x2½ inches; space under bottom drawer, 1⅜ inches. With three drawers, made of chestnut, with black walnut panels.
Price, each **$5.88**

No. 35R3606 With three drawers. Outside dimensions, 29½ inches long by 14½ inches wide by 12 inches high. Inside dimensions are as follows: Receptacle under lid, 27x11⅝x3⅛ inches; first drawer, 25⅞x10½x1⅛ inches; second drawer, 25⅞x10½x1⅝ inches; third drawer, 25⅞x10½x2½ inches; space under bottom drawer, 1 inch deep. With three drawers, made of chestnut, with black walnut panels. Price, each....**$7.35**

The Fay Patent Outside and Inside Calipers.

No. 35R4750 represents a new Inside Transfer Caliper, with either solid or spring nut. The bow is stiff, **making the caliper reliable. After calipering inside a chambered cavity, by pressing the legs together they may be withdrawn, and as they spring back will show the exact size calipered.**

No. 35R4748 Outside.	Solid Nut	Spring Nut
2½-inch	$0.80	$0.92
3 -inch	.81	.93
4 -inch	.87	1.00
5 -inch	.88	1.02
6 -inch	1.08	1.20
No. 35R4750 Inside.	**Solid Nut**	**Spring Nut**
3-inch	$0.80	$0.92
4-inch	.87	1.00
5-inch	.88	1.02
6-inch	1.08	1.20

Starrett's Fay Patent Thread and Inside Calipers.

No. 35R4756 Thread Calipers.

Inch	Solid Nut	Spring Nut
3	$0.80	$0.92
4	.88	1.00
5	.89	1.02

No. 35R4758 Inside Calipers.

Inch	Solid Nut
4	.87c
5	.88c

Inside calipers are not made to receive the spring nut.

Starrett's Yankee Outside and Inside Calipers.

The Yankee Calipers and Dividers are not quite so heavy as those quoted in previous numbers and cost less. They are much liked, and, on account of the price, are preferred by many to the highest cost tools. **All sizes are supplied with either the solid or quick adjusting nut.**

No. 35R4766 Represents a new Yankee Inside Transfer Caliper with either spring or solid nut. The bow is stiff, making the caliper reliable. After calipering inside of chambered cavity, by springing in the legs they may be withdrawn, and, as they spring back, will show the exact size calipered.

No. 35R4768 Is outside caliper, having same features.

No. 35R4768 No. 35R4766

Price List of Outside and Inside Yankee Calipers.

	Solid Nut	Spring Nut
2½-inch, each	$0.52	$0.72
3 -inch, each	.56	.76
4 -inch, each	.60	.80
5 -inch, each	.64	.84
6 -inch, each	.68	.88
8 -inch, each	.80	1.00

Yankee Spring Dividers.

No. 35R4772	Solid Nut	Spring Nut
2½-inch, each	$0.52	$0.72
3 -inch, each	.56	.76
4 -inch, each	.60	.80
5 -inch, each	.64	.84
6 -inch, each	.68	.88
8 -inch, each	.87	1.08

Yankee Inside and Keyhole Calipers.

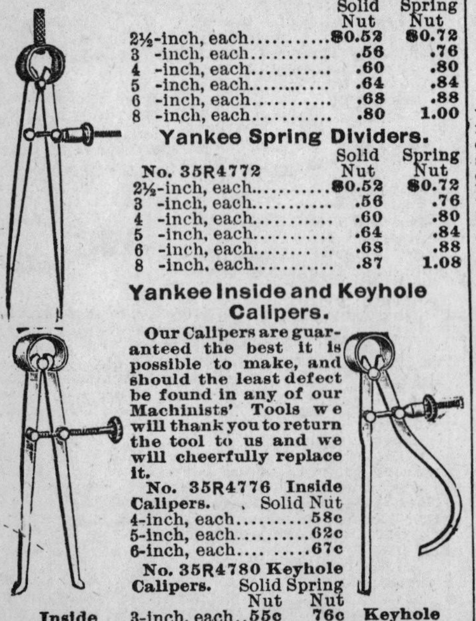

Our Calipers are guaranteed the best it is possible to make, and should the least defect be found in any of our Machinists' Tools we will thank you to return the tool to us and we will cheerfully replace it.

No. 35R4776 Inside Calipers.

	Solid Nut
4-inch, each	58c
5-inch, each	62c
6-inch, each	67c

No. 35R4780 Keyhole Calipers.

	Solid Nut	Spring Nut
3-inch, each	55c	76c
4-inch, each	59c	80c

Inside Caliper Keyhole Caliper

Starrett's Yankee Thread Calipers.

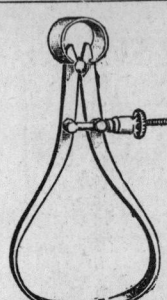

No. 35R4786

3-inch, with solid nut	52c
4-inch, with solid nut	56c
5-inch, with solid nut	60c
3-inch, with spring nut	71c
4-inch, with spring nut	75c
5-inch, with spring nut	78c

In ordering machinists' tools from us you not only get the best made, but save a large percentage of the price asked by dealers.

Starrett's Improved Extension Divider.

No. 35R4790 This is a well made, nicely finished divider, with auxiliary caliper legs, which, together with a common pencil, form convenient combinations. Our patent locking nut between the arms, against which a spiral spring acts, is a valuable feature. After the fine adjustment is made, the nut may be turned back, locking spring and arms firmly, thus remedying the weak point which renders the common wing divider only as stiff as the adjusting spring. **A full threaded nut on the stud,** through which the quadrant passes, is a more durable fastener than two or three threads tapped in the arm to hold the wing of the old style. **The head and arms of this tool are made from the best malleable iron, the rest of steel.** The points are hardened and warranted first class. The smallest size is 7 inches long; by adjustment of points becomes 9 inches, and will scribe a 22-inch circle; will caliper 11 inches outside and 13 inches inside. The second size is 9 inches, by adjustment of points becomes 12 inches, and will scribe a 30-inch circle, and caliper 14 inches outside and 16 inches inside.

7-inch, with divider legs only	$1.00
9-inch, with divider legs only	1.20
7-inch, complete	1.80
9-inch, complete	2.00

Ball Points.

No. 35R4796 For use with No. 35R4790 Dividers. This attachment consists of four balls, of 1⅛-inch, 1-inch, ¾-inch, and ½-inch diameter respectively, and a holder which fits divider leg. It is used to form a seat for the divider leg in describing circles around a hole.

Price, complete, four balls and holder............95c
Price, either ball or holder............20c

No. 35R4832 Machinists' Marking Awls. Twisted steel, one end bent, polished points. Price, each.......15c

No. 35R4836 Machinists' Marking Awl, polished and nickel plated. The chuck firmly holds an ordinary sewing needle which has the flexibility so much desired in a marking awl. The knob on end of handle may be unscrewed and extra needles kept in handle, which is hollow. The most minute circle may be marked with this awl.
Price, each............25c

Starrett's Improved Scriber.

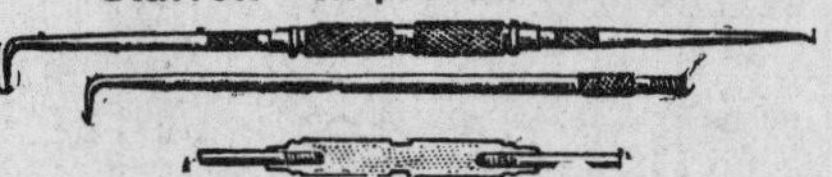

No. 35R4842 This Scriber is made for mechanics who want a better thing than has been heretofore obtained. These points are made of a fine grade of steel, nicely tempered. The knurled stock is of sufficient size to be easily held without cramping or turning in the fingers. The long bent point will be found a valuable auxiliary for reaching through holes, etc. Length, with short bent point, 9 inches; with long point, 12 inches. **All parts are interchangeable. The knurled sleeve is nickeled.**
Price, complete............40c

Starrett's Improved Adjustable Sleeve Scriber.

No. 35R4848 The Knurled Sleeve has hole clear through and a clamping device at each end, adapting it for slipping on or off different tools, securely holding them near to or away from the working point. The knurled sleeve is nickeled. **This scriber is made in two lengths,** 8 inches and 12 inches. Tool makers will find the small size more desirable for general use, and the larger one for heavier work. For pattern makers a knife scriber, made of a fine grade of steel, is supplied as an auxiliary.
Price, either size, without knife point............45c
Knife point, extra............15c
The 8-inch, being the more popular size, will be sent, unless otherwise ordered.

Ball Centering Tool.

No. 35R4865 Bell Centering Tool. A very useful little tool; a big saver of time; knurled and nicely polished. Diameter, 1¼ inches. Price, each......40c

Starrett's Nickel Plated Pocket Levels.

No. 35R4880	2½-inch	32c
No. 35R4882	3½-inch	40c

HARDWARE such as nearly all kinds of mechanical tools, light shelf and building hardware is accepted generally by railroad companies at second class freight rates, which generally average 40 to 50 cents per 100 pounds for 500 miles. By referring to pages 7 to 10 you can get the freight rate for 100 pounds to your nearest point, which is almost exactly the same as to your town, and you will see the freight will amount to next to nothing as compared to what you will save in price. Many heavy articles in hardware take still lower rates, such as third, fourth and fifth class.

Putty Knives.

No. 35R6511 Putty Knife with stiff blade, square point, cocobolo handle, lap bolster, strongly riveted. A superior tool. Weight, 4 ounces. Price, each............15c

No. 35R6513 Putty Knife with **spring blade,** square point, cocobolo handle, lap bolster. Strongly riveted. Weight, 4 ounces. Price, each..........15c

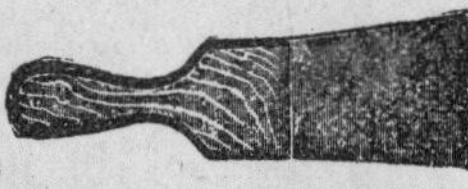

No. 35R6516 Putty Knife with **stiff blade,** bevel point, cocobolo handle, lap bolster. A high grade knife. Weight, 4 ounces. Price, each............18c

No. 35R6520 Putty Knife with **spring blade,** bevel point, cocobolo handle, lap bolster. Weight, 4 ounces.
Price, each............18c

Scraping Knife.

No. 35R6523 Scraping Knife. Best steel blade, cocobolo handle, lap bolster. Weight, 5 to 7 ounces each.

Width of blade, inches	2½	3	3½	4
Price, each	35c	42c	48c	54c

No. 35R6524 Wall Scraping Knife, stiff blade, 3-inch square point, beech handles. Shipping weight, 7 ounces. Each......12c

No. 35R6525 Spatulas or Painters' Pallette Knives, lap bolstered cocoa handles.

Length of blade, inches	4	6	8	10
Price, each	18c	23c	38c	63c

Patent Pending.

No. 35R6526 Perfection Knife Grip. The invention of a practical paper hanger strengthens the blade. Easy on hand, will cut eight thicknesses of paper or shade cloth easier than a knife without the grip will cut one. It is made of aluminum, can never wear out, get out of order or break. **Fits any knife.**
Price, each, without knife............25c

No. 35R6529 Paper Hangers' Square Point Butting Knife, same as illustrated in above cut, without grip, extra quality steel, wood handle. Shipping weight, 3 ounces. Price, each............20c

No. 35R6530 Paper Hangers' Round Point Butting Knife, best of steel, blade 3 inches long.
Price, each............20c

No. 35R6531 Paper Hangers' Straight Edge, walnut and maple, made of a number of pieces to prevent warping, 7 feet long. Shipping weight, 4 pounds. Price, each............$1.00

PAINTS, OILS AND VARNISHES.
WE SELL PAINTS OF ALL KINDS,
Everything in the line of Linseed Oil, Varnish, Stains, etc., at the lowest prices ever heard of.
See page 23 for prices on paint, or, if you prefer to see the color samples,
SEND 2 CENTS
FOR OUR HANDSOME COLOR SAMPLE BOOK OF EVERYTHING IN PAINTS WITH LOWEST PRICES.

Glass Cutters.

No. 35R6527 Revolving Steel Wheel Glass Cutter, metal handle polished and bronzed, extra quality cutting wheel. Price, each............4c

No. 35R6528 Revolving Steel Wheel Glass Cutter, bronzed, with knife sharpener, corkscrew and can opener combined.
Price, each............4c

No. 35R6532 A fine durable Glass Cutter, with putty knife on end.
Price, each............7c

No. 35R6533 Glass Cutter. Damascus Coal Carbon Disc Wheel Glass Cutter. The finest revolving wheel glass cutter made, rosewood handle, solid steel head. Price, each.........15c

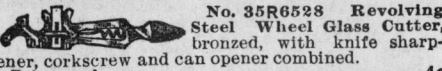

No. 35R6534 Goodell's Improved Glass Cutters with turret head. The cutters are carefully hardened and ground by special process. Polished and nickel plated frame; turret head, six cutter wheels, which can be instantly revolved to place. Nickel plated ferrule, rosewood finish handle.
Price, each............23c

Glaziers' Diamonds.

Our Glaziers' Diamonds are made of the best quality genuine diamonds. The mountings are made in the very best possible manner, highly finished and heavily nickel plated. We guarantee our diamonds to reset not less than four times and give good satisfaction, provided they are sent to us to reset. NEVER CUT TWICE IN THE SAME PLACE.

No. 35R6535 Ebony Handle Keyed Diamond, for single thick glass. Price, each..............$2.65

No. 35R6538 The Standard Ebony Handle Keyed Diamond, for single thick glass. A good diamond for ordinary use. Price, each $2.90

No. 35R6541 Cocoa Handle Keyed Diamond, for single thick glass. A very cheap diamond when quality is considered. Price, each..............$3.25

No. 35R6543 Superior Cocoa Handle Keyed Diamond. A very fine diamond for general use. Will cut double strength glass. Price, each...$4.35

No. 35R6546 Snakewood Handle Extra Superior Keyed Diamond. Cuts anything except plate glass. Price, each..............................$5.95

No. 35R6549 Superior Cocoa Handle Keyed Plate Glass Diamond. A very superior cutter for general use, and will cut plate glass. Each....$9.00

No. 35R6552 Snakewood Handle, Extra Superior Keyed Plate Glass Diamond. Cuts any kind of rough or polished plate glass. Glaziers who have learned that glass broken in cutting with a diamond too small for the work, soon amounts to more than the cost of the diamond, will have no hesitancy in selecting this one as being the cheapest in the end. **Dealers have always charged an exorbitant profit on this class of diamonds, selling them as high as $20.00.** By contracting for a large number and selling them at our usual one small profit, we are able to make the price.............................$10.95

Anyone can cut glass with this tool successfully. Genuine diamond, finished in the best manner and metal parts nickel plated. Hold the diamond, as shown in cut, against the ruler. Place it perpendicularly on the glass, so it rests on the diamond and guide wheel, the wheel towards you. Press on it gradually, until it makes a singing sound, not a harsh noise. Draw over the glass slowly and uniformly. **Never cut twice in the same place.**

No. 35R6555 Ebony handle. Will cut single strength glass. Price, each.........$2.95

No. 35R6556 Cocoa handle, Superior Diamond. A very fine diamond for general use, will cut double strength glass. Price, each.......................$4.35

No. 35R6557 Snakewood handle, extra Superior Diamond. Will cut anything excepting plate glass. Price, each..............................$5.95

BRUSHES.

IN OUR LINE OF BRUSHES listed below, we aim to quote such as are more commonly used.

THESE GOODS ARE ALL OF DURABLE QUALITY.

THE WAR IN CHINA has caused the price of brushes to advance. We bought a very large quantity and will not raise our prices until those goods contracted for are sold. When they are sold we will have to advance our prices, for **WE WILL NOT REDUCE THE QUALITY of the brushes we sell.**

Camel's Hair Brushes.

No. 35R6560 Camel Hair Lettering Pencils, rose bound, fine quality. Hair, 1 inch long.

Sizes	1	2	3	4	5	6	7	8
Price, each	2c	2c	3c	3c	3c	3c	4c	4c
Price, per dozen	16c	19c	21c	23c	25c	28c	34c	38c

No. 35R6563 Superfine Quality Camel Hair Lettering Pencils, red and green silk and silver binding. Hair, 1 inch long.

Sizes	1	2	3	4	5	6	7	8
Each	2c	3c	3c	4c	5c	5c	6c	7c
Price, per doz.	19c	22c	28c	34c	44c	50c	56c	63c

No. 35R6566 Camel Hair Striping Pencils. Rose bound, fine quality; hair, 2 inches long.

Size	1	2	3	4	5	6	7	8
Price, each	2c	3c	3c	3c	4c	4c	5c	6c
Price, per dozen	19c	22c	26c	31c	38c	44c	50c	56c

No. 35R6569 Camel Hair Striping Pencils. Red and green silk and silver binding, superfine quality; hair, 2½ inches long.

Size	1	2	3	4	5	6	7	8
Price, each	3c	3c	4c	5c	6c	7c	8c	9c
Price, per dozen	24c	30c	38c	48c	59c	69c	81c	91c

No. 35R6572 Camel Hair Swan Quill Pencils for lettering and striping.

Size, inches	⅛	¾	1	1¼
Price, each	5c	5c	6c	6c
Price, per dozen	41c	44c	50c	56c

Size, inches	1½	1¾	2	2¼
Price, each	6c	7c	7c	8c
Price, per dozen	63c	69c	75c	81c

OUR ONLY TERMS ARE CASH WITH ORDER.

We guarantee satisfaction or refund the money.

Camel Hair Brushes.

No. 35R6575 Camel Hair Flat or Sword Stripers, square ends, tin ferrules, without handle, for carriage work. Hair, 1½ to 2¼ inches long.

Size	1	2	3	4
Price, each	6c	7c	8c	9c
Price, per dozen	63c	75c	90c	98c

No. 35R6578 Camel Hair Dagger Stripers. Diagonal ends, copper wire bound, small cedar handles, for carriage work. Hair, 1¼ to 2¼ inches long.

Size	1	2	3	4
Price, each	11c	12c	13c	14c
Price, per dozen	$1.13	$1.35	$1.45	$1.50

No. 35R6581 Camel Hair Marking Brushes. Polished handles.

Size	1	2	3	4
Price, each	4c	4c	5c	5c
Price, per dozen	38c	40c	44c	50c

No. 35R6582 Camel Hair Lacquering Brushes. Polished handles, fine quality, round.

Size	1	2	3	4	5	6
Price, each	4c	4c	4c	5c	7c	9c
Price, per dozen	34c	38c	44c	56c	75c	94c

No. 35R6585 Camel Hair Lacquering Brushes. Polished handles, fine quality, flat.

Size	⅜	½	⅝	¾	⅞	1
Price, each	6c	7c	8c	10c	12c	15c
Price, per doz.	60c	72c	85c	$1.10	$1.32	$1.50

Mottling Brushes.

No. 35R6590 Pure Camel Hair Mottling Brushes or Spalters. Short cedar handles, fine quality.

Size, inches	1	1½	2	2½	3
Price, each	14c	21c	28c	38c	50c

No. 35R6593 Color Brush, same as No. 35R6590 brass bound, a thicker brush.

Size, inches	1	1½	2	2½	3
Price, each	19c	28c	38c	56c	75c

Blenders.

No. 35R6596 Round Badger Hair Blenders or Softeners for graining and oil painting, polished handles.

Size	1	2	3	4	5	6
Price, each	16c	19c	25c	34c	41c	47c
Size	7	8	9	10	11	12
Price, each	59c	66c	75c	94c	$1.13	$1.38

No. 35R6597 Flat Knotted Badger Hair Blenders, polished handles, set in bone.

Size, in.	2	2½	3	3½	4	4½	5	5½	6
Each	$0.63	.81	.94	1.13	1.25	1.38	1.50	1.75	1.88

Flowing Varnish Brushes.

No. 35R6599 Badger Hair Flowing Varnish Brushes, for fine varnishing, carriages, pianos, etc. Single thick. Chiseled.

Size, inches	1	1½	2	2½	3
Each	23c	34c	45c	56c	68c

No. 35R6603 Fitch Flowing Varnish Brushes, superfine quality, single thick.

Size, inches	1	1½	2	2½	3
Each	16c	23c	31c	39c	47c

Varnish Brushes.

No. 35R6607 Flat Varnish Brushes, black handles, tin ferrules.

Size, inches	1	1½	2	2½	3
Each	3c	5c	6c	8c	10c

No. 35R6610 Extra Flat Bristle Varnish Brushes, double thick, Chinese bristles, stained handles, tin ferrules.

Size, inches	1	1½	2	2½	3
Each	5c	7c	9c	11c	14c

No. 35R6614 Bristle Flowing Varnish Brushes, stained handles, with tin ferrules, black Chinese bristles, chiseled.

Size, inch	1	1½	2	2½	3
Each	6c	9c	13c	16c	22c

No. 35R6619 An extra fine, extra thick, soft elastic Chinese bristle flowing varnish brush. Something for the painter who does good work.

Size, inches	1	1½	2	2½	3
Each	13c	19c	25c	38c	50c

Davis Patent Wood Grainers.

No. 35R6624 The Davis Patent Wood Grainers, are composed of two rolls, 5½ inches in length and 1½ inches in diameter. The one which is corrugated can be used to imitate any known growth of wood. The other is used to reproduce growths of quartered oak. They are very easily handled, and require but very little practice to make one fully proficient in their use, and with proper care, such as all tools require, they will last for years, as there is nothing to get out of order. Plain, simple directions packed with each set. Weight, 15 ounces. Price, per pair..........$2.85

Steel Grainers.

No. 35R6625 Taylors' English Graining Combs. Best quality steel, in sets of 12 assorted, 1 to 4 inches, in tin compartment case. Price, per set..............$1.00

Marking Brushes.

No. 35R6630 Bristle Marking Brushes, round polished handles.

Size	1	2	3	4	5	6
Price, each	3c	3c	3c	3c	4c	4c
Price, per dozen	20c	22c	25c	26c	28c	31c

Sash Tools.

No. 35R6631 Ex. Ex. French Sash Tools. All fine white bristles, wire bound.

Size	1	2	3	4	5	6	7	8	9	10
Price, ea.	3c	4c	5c	6c	7c	8c	9c	$0.10	$0.12	$0.14
Per doz.	30c	37c	50c	60c	75c	90c	98c	1.05	1.28	1.50

No. 35R6634 Extra Quality Flat Bristle Artists' Brushes or Fitch Tools, white bristles, black handles, tin ferrules.

Size, inches	½	¾	1	1¼	1½
Price, each	5c	7c	$0.10	$0.14	$0.17
Per dozen	45c	75c	1.05	1.50	1.87

Paint Brushes.

Length Given is Length of Bristles Clear of Binding or Ferrule.

No. 35R6637 Round Paint Brushes, wire bound, white bristles outside, mixed center.

Size	1-0	2-0	3-0	4-0	5-0	6-0
Length, inches	3	3¼	3½	3¾	4	4¼
Price, each	22c	25c	28c	31c	38c	41c

No. 35R6640 Round Paint Brushes, wire bound. All best selected Russian bristles.

Size	1-0	2-0	3-0	4-0	5-0	6-0
Length, inches	3⅜	3⅞	4⅛	4⅜	4⅝	4⅞
Price, each	50c	63c	78c	$1.06	$1.31	$1.50

No. 35R6643 Oval Paint Brushes, all white Russia bristles. A brush that will do a good job and wear well.

Size	1-0	2-0	3-0	4-0	5-0	6-0
Length, inches	3⅜	3⅞	4⅛	4⅜	4⅝	4⅞
Price, each	53c	69c	81c	$1.13	$1.32	$1.50

Oval Varnish Brushes.

Length Given is Length of Bristles Clear of Binding or Ferrule.

No. 35R6647 Chiseled Oval Varnish Brushes, very elastic; best selected black Chinese bristles; nickel plated rings.

Size	1-0	2-0	3-0	4-0	5-0	6-0
Length, inches	2⅛	2⅜	3	3	3¼	3½
Price, each	30c	41c	47c	53c	63c	75c

Wall Brushes.

Length given is length of bristles clear of binding or ferrule.

No. 35R6650 Wall Brush. A good working brush, all Chinese bristles.

Width, inches	2½	3	3½	4	4½
Length	2	2⅛	2¼	2½	2⅞
Each	10c	14c	19c	25c	28c

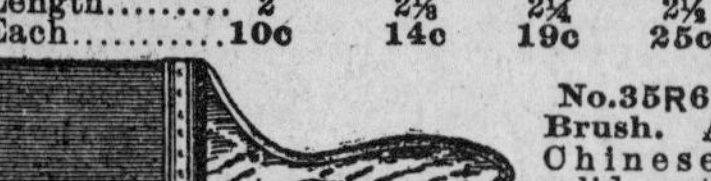

No. 35R6654 Wall Brush. All black Chinese bristles, solid center. This brush will do good work.

Size, inches	3	3¼	4	4½	5
Length, inches	2¾	3	3¼	3½	3⅞
Price, each	28c	38c	50c	63c	75c

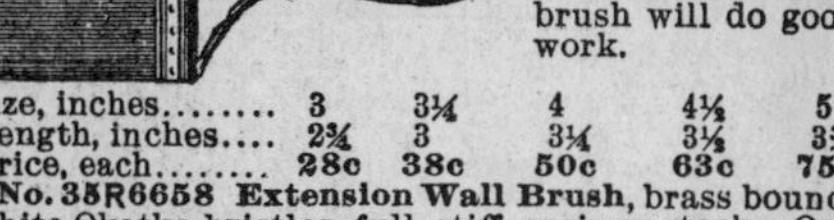

No. 35R6658 Extension Wall Brush, brass bound, white Okatka bristles, full, stiff, springy stock. Our standard brush for painters' use.

Size	6	7	8	9
Width, inches	3	3½	4	4½
Length, bristles	3⅞	4⅛	4⅜	4⅝
Price, each	59c	81c	$1.13	$1.50
Size	10	20	30	40
Width, inches	5	3½	4	4
Length, bristles	3⅞	4⅝	4⅝	4⅞
Price, each	$1.68	$0.94	$1.32	$1.50

Paint Brushes.

No. 35R6661 Stucco Paint Brushes. Full stock, no plug, very full and stiff, extra long, and very best selected white Russian bristles, leather bound. Used mostly by frescoers and for stucco work.

Sizes, inches	3½	4	4½	5
Length, inches	4⅛	4⅜	4⅝	4⅞
Price, each	$1.00	$1.25	$1.50	$1.75

Calcimine Brushes.

Length given is length of bristles clear of binding or ferrule.

No. 35R6668 Calcimine Brush for common work, white casing, with gray center.

Width, inches	6	7	8
Length	3½	3¾	4¼
Each	25c	31c	38c

No. 35R6672 Calcimine Brush. White bristles. Excellent quality.

Size, inches	6	7	8
Length	3⅜	3⅜	3⅞
Price, each	68c	81c	$1.00

No. 35R6675 Selected Russian White Bristles Calcimine Brushes, brass bound.

Size, inches, 7; length, 4⅝. Price, each....$1.69
Size, inches, 8; length, 4⅝. Price, each....2.06

No. 35R6680 New York Style Calcimine Brushes. Extra heavy, specially selected Russian bristles, finest workmanship, will last a lifetime. Size, inches, 7; length, 5⅝. Price, each..$3.00
Size, inches, 8; length, 5⅞. Price, each..3.38

Whitewash Brushes.

No. 35R6685 Whitewash Brush, white tampico stock (not a bristle in it). The stock is soft and white. Used for whitewashing fences, outbuildings, etc.

Width, inches	6	7	8
Length, inches	2¾	3	3
Price, each	9c	10c	13c

Whitewash Brushes—Continued.

No. 35R6688 Whitewash Brush, all American bristle, white outside. A fair quality brush for common work. Width, 7½ in.; length of bristle, 2⅝ in. Price, each....25c

No. 35R6692 Whitewash Brush, all white bristles; looks well and works well.

Width, inches	7	8	9
Length	2⅝	3	3¾
Price, each	31c	47c	63c

No. 35R6695 Extension Whitewash Brush, all white bristle, exceedingly good value at the price.

Width, inches, 8; length, inches, 3⅝. Each...$0.94
Width, inches, 9; length, inches, 3⅞. Each...1.13

No. 35R6699 Whitewash Brush, all white Russia bristles; extension style. A brush that's used by many calciminers and whitewashers.

Width, inches	8	8¼
Length, inches	4¼	4⅝
Price, each	$1.69	$2.07

Stucco Whitewash Brush.

No. 35R6704 Stucco Whitewash Brush. Wide and heavy for whitewashers' and plasterers' use. Made of the finest white Okatka bristles.

Width, inches	9	9	9
Length, inches	4⅝	5⅛	5⅝
Price, each	$2.62	$3.37	$4.50

Plasterers' Brushes.

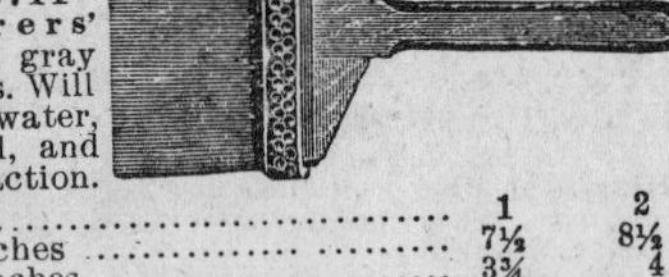

No. 35R6711 Plasterers' Brush. All gray stiff bristles. Will hold lots of water, wear well, and give satisfaction.

Size	1	2
Width, inches	7½	8¼
Length, inches	3¾	4
Price, each	$1.75	$2.25

Painters' Dusters.

No. 35R6720 Painters' Dusters. Gray bristle, black outside. Raised center.

Size	1	4
Length	4	4¾
Price, each	37c	50c

Paperhangers' Brushes.

No. 35R6724 Paperhangers' Brushes. Two rows stiff Chinese bristles, 2⅛ inches long.

Width, inches	10	12
Price, each	69c	94c

Brick Liners.

No. 35R6729 Brick Liners, white bristles.

Size, inches	2	2½	3
Price, each	6c	7c	8c

Roofing Brushes.

No. 35R3038 Roofing Brush. Mixed gray stock, 4 inches long.

Knots	2	3
Price, each	38c	56c

No. 35R3039 Roofing Brush of superior quality. Gray mixed center, cased with black Chinese bristles. A brush that will do lots of work.

Knots	2	3	4
Price, each	63c	94c	$1.19

Glue Brushes.

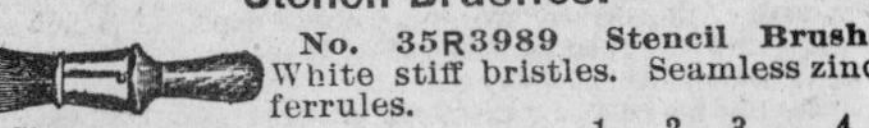

No. 35R6735 Glue Brushes. Made entirely of metal and bristle and will stand the constant shrinking and swelling that glu brushes are subjected to. Iron handle, brass ferrule and all white bristle.

Size	2	4	6
Length, inches	2¾	3	3¼
Price, each	22c	31c	47c

Stencil Brushes.

No. 35R3989 Stencil Brush. White stiff bristles. Seamless zinc ferrules.

Size	1	2	3	4
Price, each	5c	8c	10c	13c

GIVE CATALOGUE NUMBER IN FULL WHEN YOU WRITE YOUR ORDER

No. 35R6000 PRICE, $2.22.

OUR $2.22 EVERY DAY TOOL SET.

$2.22 FOR A SET of tools you could not buy in any market for less than $3.50. Tools that would retail in any hardware store at from $3.50 to $4.50. **OUR EVERY DAY SET** of tools for $2.22 is shown in the accompanying illustration, exact representation of the tools arranged on a board as engraved from a photograph. **EACH AND EVERY TOOL** in this set is a good practical tool, selected from our regular stock, suitable for all purposes, all kinds of job work and repairing. This is a serviceable household set and will save its cost in a short time. **IT IS A FINE PRESENT** for a boy and makes an excellent set of tools for a boy.

THIS SPECIAL SET AT $2.22 CONSISTS OF THE FOLLOWING STRICTLY STANDARD GRADE TOOLS.

1 Hand Saw—Blade 18-inches long.
1 Warranted Nail Hammer.
1 Bit Brace.
4 Double Cut Gimlet Bits, Assorted Sizes.
3 Warranted Cast Steel Double Spur Auger Bits; one each ⅜, ½ and ¾ inch.
1 Compass Saw, 14-inch, which can also be used as a Rip Saw.
1 Carpenter's Two-Foot, Four-Fold Boxwood Rule.
1 Screwdriver with Forged Steel Blade 5 inches long.
1 Monkey Wrench, length 8 inches.
1 Stanley's Block Plane, length 5½ inches.
1 Warranted Socket Firmer Chisel, ½-inch.
1 Combined Anvil and Vise, 1½-inch jaws, opens 1¾ inch, weight, 1¼ pounds.
1 Stanley's Rosewood Handle Try Square with 6-inch Blade.

TOTAL, 18 TOOLS, FOR ONLY $2.22.

Weight, packed for shipment, 15 pounds

OUR $5.28 WOOD BUTCHERS' SET.

DO YOUR OWN CARPENTER WORK and save five times the cost of this outfit by keeping your property in perfect order, saving time and carpenters' and wagon makers' bills. The tools included in this set are needed in every family. They are selected from our regular stock and are all STRICTLY HIGH GRADE TOOLS. We pack them in a neat wooden box with one tray, well made and nicely finished, with hinges and lock. The box is stained and varnished, and is large enough to hold other articles that you might wish to keep in your tool box. All the tools are not shown in the illustration.

READ THE DESCRIPTION AND REMEMBER that each and every tool is guaranteed exactly as represented, and if not found so can be returned and money will be refunded without argument. The set consists of the following tools: 1 SEARS, ROEBUCK & CO.'S SAW, 22 inches long, fully warranted. 1 TWO-FOOT RULE, 4-fold, 1-inch wide, made by The Stanley Rule & Level Co. 1 TRY SQUARE, with rosewood handle, brass lined, length of blade 6 inches, made by The Stanley Rule & Level Co. 1 COMBINATION PLIER AND WIRE CUTTER, 5½ inches long. 1 BIT BRACE, 10-inch sweep, like illustration. 4 AUGER BITS, 1 each size, ⅜, ½, ¾ and 1-inch. 5 GIMLET BITS, German Pattern, 1 each size $\frac{3}{16}$, ⅛, $\frac{3}{16}$, ¼, $\frac{5}{16}$. 1 SOLID STEEL NAIL HAMMER, warranted, weighs 1 pound. 1 DRAW KNIFE, 8-inch cut. 1 SPOKE SHAVE, with two cutters, one straight and the other convex. 2 SOCKET FIRMER CHISELS, 1 each, ½ and 1-inch. 1 SCREWDRIVER, 5-inch blade. 1 BEECH JACK PLANE, 16 inches long, 2¼-inch double iron, made by The Ohio Tool Co. 1 IRON BLOCK PLANE, 5¼ inches long, 1¼-inch cutter, made by The Stanley Rule & Level Co. 1 GOOD CARPENTERS' PENCIL.

WE FURNISH OUR WOOD BUTCHERS' SET WITH THIS NEAT BOX AS DESCRIBED FOR $5.28

No. 35R6045 Price, $5.28

Weight, packed for shipment, 40 pounds. See freight rates, pages 7 to 10.

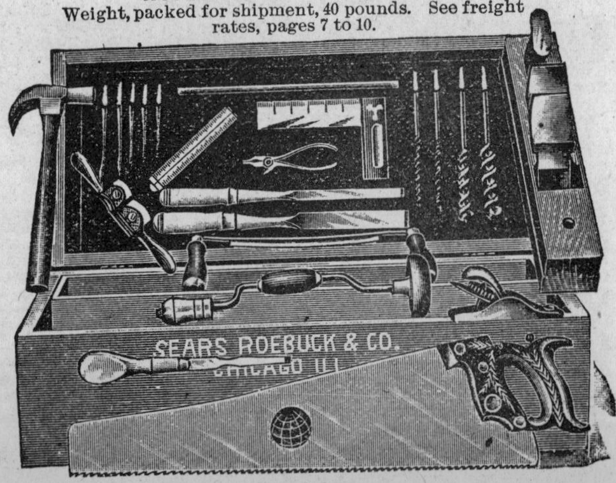

Our $9.95 "Artisan's Choice" Tool Set.

FOR $9.95 WE FURNISH THE TOOLS AS LISTED BELOW COMPLETE WITH TOOL CHEST AS ILLUSTRATED.

THE TOOLS ARE SELECTED from our regular stock, and quality of everything is guaranteed. Those who want first class, high grade tools, but who do not wish to invest as much money as our "Acme" or "Our Very Best" set costs will be pleased with this set. There is ample space in the chest to keep more tools, as you may add to the set from time to time.

DO NOT COMPARE THE QUALITY OF THESE TOOLS WITH THOSE COMMONLY SOLD IN CHESTS AT ABOUT THIS PRICE.

SO FAR AS WE KNOW we are the only firm putting up a tool set at this price and using high grade tools, tools that will satisfy any carpenter or mechanic; goods that will make friends and customers for us.

No. 35R6012 Our "Artisan's Choice" Tool Set consists of the following tools:

1 **Sears, Roebuck & Co.'s Hand Saw,** 24-inch.
1 **Sears, Roebuck & Co.'s Rip Saw,** 24-inch.
1 **Standard Compass Saw,** 12-inch.
1 **Sears, Roebuck & Co.'s Adjustable Jack Plane,** length, 15 inches, with 2-inch cutter.
1 **Sears, Roebuck & Co.'s Iron Block Plane.** Length, 7½ inches, with 1¾-inch cutter.
1 **Adze Eye Bell Face Nail Hammer.** Weight, 1 pound. Warranted.
3 **Sears, Roebuck & Co.'s Socket Firmer Chisels,** with leather top handles Sizes, ¼, ½ and 1-inch. Warranted.
1 **Ratchet Bit Brace,** 10-inch sweep.
5 **German Gimlet Bits.** Sizes, 1/16, ⅛, 3/16, ¼ and 5/16-inch.
5 **Best Cast Steel Double Spur and Lip Auger Bits.** Sizes, ⅜, ½, ⅝, ¾ and 1-inch.
1 **Countersink** for wood.
1 **Countersink** for metal.
1 **Reamer.**
1 **Boxwood Rule,** 2-ft., four-fold, square joints with drafting scale.
1 **Try Square,** 6-inch blade.
1 **Screwdriver,** 5-inch blade.
1 **Nail Set,** 3/32-point.
1 **Steel Shingling Hatchet,** 4-inch cut. Warranted.
1 **Drawing Knife,** 8-inch cut. Warranted.
1 **Mounted Oil Stone,** 6-inch.
1 **Steel Square,** No. 7, extra quality.
1 **Pair 6-inch Buttons Pliers.**
1 **Monkey Wrench,** 10-inch.
1 **Slim Taper File,** 6-inch.
1 **Universal Tool Handle.**

No. 35R6012 Price of the above tools packed in chest as illustrated and described.. **$9.95**

WEIGHT, PACKED FOR SHIPMENT, 75 POUNDS. **SEE FREIGHT RATES, PAGES 7 TO 10.**

OUR ACME CARPENTER CHEST OF TOOLS FOR $13.95.

EACH AND EVERY ARTICLE GUARANTEED TO BE EXACTLY AS DESCRIBED. EVERY TOOL GOOD ENOUGH FOR ANY CARPENTER OR MECHANIC.

$13.95 BUYS A $25.00 OUTFIT.

QUALITY. We cannot too strongly emphasize the fact that all these tools are strictly **FIRST CLASS HIGH GRADE GOODS.** To build up the enormous tool trade which we have established, it was necessary for us to furnish the best goods we could procure; and to hold and still further increase our tool trade, it is necessary that we continue to deal with our patrons as in the past.

READ CAREFULLY THE DESCRIPTION OF GOODS AND REMEMBER THAT EVERY ARTICLE IS GUARANTEED EXACTLY AS REPRESENTED.

No. 35R6030 ORDER BY NUMBER.

LIST AND DESCRIPTION OF TOOLS IN OUR ACME CHEST OF TOOLS:

SAWS. We furnish four saws:
1 **Rip Saw,** 28 inches long, with walnut handle, with steel plate on handle. It is a fair grade saw, but not warranted.
1 **Hand Saw, Sears, Roebuck & Co.'s,** 26 inches long, with carved handle, fully warranted.
1 **Panel Saw, Sears, Roebuck & Co.'s,** 18 inches long, with carved handle, fully warranted.
1 **Compass Saw,** length, 14 inches.

Every Sears, Roebuck & Co.'s saw is etched on blade: **"If this saw does not prove as good or better than any saw you ever had, return it to us and money will be refunded."**

PLANES. We furnish four planes, all made by **The Stanley Rule & Level Co.,** and no one makes better goods.
1 **Stanley Wood Smooth Plane.** Length, 8 in., with 1¾-in. cutter.
1 **Stanley Wood Jack Plane.** Length, 15 in., with 2⅛-in. cutter.
1 **Stanley Wood Fore Plane.** Length, 20 in., with 2⅜-in. cutter.
1 **Stanley Iron Block Plane.** Length, 5½ in., with 1¼-in. cutter.

Remember we guarantee that these Planes are genuine, made by The Stanley Rule & Level Co.

MISCELLANEOUS TOOLS. **Sears, Roebuck & Co.'s Improved Morrill's Saw Set.** Considered the best made.
Saw Clamp. To hold saws for filing. Jaws are 9½ inches long, adjustment is by a lever.
2 **Slim Taper Saw Files.** One 4½ inches long, and one 6 inches long.
1 **No. 7 Steel Square.** Guaranteed to be equal to any No. 7 square made by anyone. The body of square is 2 inches wide, 24 inches long. The tongue of square is 16 inches long, 1½ inches wide, marked on both sides, spaced to eighths.
1 **Carpenters' Pincers.** Best grade, length, 8 inches.
1 **Combination Wire Cutter and Pliers.** Length, 5½ inches.
1 **Knurled Cup Point Nail Set.**
1 **Spring Tube Punch,** for cutting holes in leather, etc.
100 **Slotted Rivets,** assorted lengths, in nice tin box.
1 **Iron Bench Screw.** Length, 13 inches, diameter, 1 inch.
4 **Iron Clamps.** Open, 2¼ inches.
1 **Beechwood Improved Marking Gauge. Made by The Stanley Rule & Level Co.** Will run a gauge line with accuracy, either straight or around curves of any degree, either concave or convex.
1 **Pair of Wing Dividers.** Length, 8 inches, polished cast steel, with adjusting screw.
1 **Chalk Line, Reel and Awl,** as shown in cut.
1 **Braided Cotton Chalk Line.** Medium size.
12 **Cakes of Carpenters' Chalk.** Assorted colors, red, white and blue, and 1 **Carpenters' Lead Pencil** of good quality.
1 **Plumb and Level, adjustable.** Made by **The Stanley Rule & Level Co.,** polished mahogany, arched top plates; two side views. Length, 28 inches.
1 **Try Square.** Brass lined with rosewood handle, square inside or outside. Length of blade from inside the handle, 6 inches. It is made by **The Stanley Rule & Level Co.**
1 **Sliding T Bevel,** with rosewood handle, brass tipped, 8-inch blade, flush adjusting screw so bevel can be used right or left hand, either side up. It is made by **The Stanley Rule & Level Co.**
1 **Boxwood Rule.** Made by **The Stanley Rule & Level Co.,** two-foot, four-fold, square joints, edge plates, spaced 8ths, 10ths, 12ths and 16ths, with drafting scale, 1 inch wide.
1 **Shingling Hatchet.** Weight, 1 pound 7 ounces, **warranted.**
1 **Nail Hammer.** Weight, 1 pound, **warranted.**
1 **Monkey Wrench.** Length, 10 inches.
1 **Draw Knife.** Length of cut, 8 inches.
1 **Spoke Shave,** with double cutter, one straight and one concave.
1 **Socket Framing Chisel.** Width, 1-inch, with ring on handle to prevent splitting.
3 **Socket Firmer Chisels.** 1 each, ¼, ½ and 1-inch chisels, **fully warranted.**
1 **Cold Chisel,** made by **The Vaughan & Bushnell Mfg. Co.,** of ½-inch octagon steel.
1 **Screwdriver,** with beech handle and 6-inch blade.
1 **Ratchet Bit Brace,** made of 7/16-inch cold drawn steel rod. Head and handle of hardwood, 10-in. sweep.
7 **Auger Bits.** 1 each size, ¼, 5/16, ⅜, ½, ⅝, ¾ and 1-in.
3 **German Pattern Gimlet Bits.** 1 each size, 1/16, ⅛ and 3/16-inch.

We pack the ACME set of Carpenters' Tools in a chest, with one tray, well made, stained and varnished, with hinges and lock. Weight, packed for shipment, 90 pounds. **SEE FREIGHT RATES, PAGES 7 TO 10.**

No. 35R6030 OUR PRICE FOR ALL THE ABOVE TOOLS PACKED IN THIS CHEST IS ONLY $13.95.

OUR VERY BEST TOOL CHEST.

FOR $22.95 WE FURNISH A STRICTLY HIGH GRADE SET OF MECHANICS' TOOLS,

THE EQUAL OF ANYTHING YOU CAN BUY ANYWHERE AT $35.00 TO $40.00.

IF YOU WERE TO GO INTO ANY RETAIL STORE IN THE COUNTRY AND PICK THESE TOOLS OUT SINGLY, YOU WOULD PAY DOUBLE THE PRICE, AND WOULD EVEN THEN BE UNABLE TO GET THE SAME HIGH GRADE GOODS. IN FACT, IT IS A CLASS OF GOODS YOU WILL FIND ONLY IN THE VERY BEST TOOL STORES IN LARGE CITIES, AND THERE ONLY AT VERY HIGH PRICES.

Mechanics in all branches and from every State in the Union have learned of the extraordinary values we are giving in the highest grades of mechanics' tools, and the result is we have established a business in this line second to none, and the call we have had for complete sets of high grade tools has induced us to get up this combination as the highest value ever offered by any house.

Hardware, such as nearly all kinds of mechanical tools, light shelf and building hardware, is accepted generally by railroad companies at second class freight rates, which generally average 40 to 50 cents per 100 pounds for 500 miles. By referring to pages 7 to 10 you can get the freight rate for 100 pounds to your nearest point, which is almost exactly the same as to your town, and you will see the freight will amount to next to nothing as compared to what you will save in price. Many heavy articles in hardware take still lower rates, such as third, fourth and fifth class.

No. 35R6060

$22.95

No. 35R6060

$22.95

No. 35R6060 Price, $22.95

We have endeavored, in the above illustration, to give you some idea of what this set consists. The engraving shown is drawn by our artist direct from a photograph. **Our Very Best Tool Set**, as the name implies, consists of the very best of everything—tools such as are used by the very best mechanics; tools you will take pleasure in working with; tools you will take pride in keeping in fine condition; tools that will give you satisfaction in every way. Space does not allow us to give a lengthy description of each article, but you will find more detailed description under articles where listed singly in our catalogue. Any man who is well informed as to grade and value of tools will admit that this set of tools is of the highest class and wonderful value for the money.

Our tool chest we pack this set of tools in is made with sliding tray; well and strongly made, finely finished, stained and varnished; has hinges and lock. Outside measurements of chest, 33¼ inches long, 17¾ inches wide, 9¼ inches deep. Read carefully the list and description of tools in this set. **Remember, we fully guarantee each and every tool to be perfect in material and workmanship. Consider the reputation of the brands; consider our reputation as dealers in fine high grade mechanics' tools**, and we are sure you will agree that the price we name for the complete outfit of tool chest is indeed wonderfully low.

Below is complete list of the different tools furnished in this our Special $22.95 Mechanics' Tool Set.

1 Sears, Roebuck & Co.'s Warranted Shingling Hatchet, all steel, full polished and etched, 3⅞-inch cut.
1 Sears, Roebuck & Co.'s Warranted Hammer, made of best tool steel, highly nickel plated. Has octagon poll and polished hickory handle. Size, 1½. Weight, 1 pound.
1 Adjustable Saw Clamp for filing and setting saws to clamp on bench or table. Can be instantly adjusted to any angle.
1 Sears, Roebuck & Co.'s Original Morrill's Pattern Saw Set, with improved anvil, will set hand, panel, rip, meat, buck or band saws.
1 Stanley's Combined Try and Miter Square, 7½-inch blade, brass lined rosewood handle and graduated steel blade.
1 Stanley's Sliding "T" Bevel, 10-inch blade, rosewood handle, brass tipped with flush adjusting screw and steel blade.
1 2-foot Rule, full brass bound, double arch joints, four fold with drafting scale, 1⅜ inch wide. The best boxwood rule made.
1 Stanley Improved Marking Gauge, made of beechwood with boxwood thumbscrew. Marked in inches.
1 Sears, Roebuck & Co.'s Quick Cut Oil Stone, Size, 7x2 inches. Mounted in finished chestnut case.
1 Awl and Tool Set with 10 forged steel awls and tools and hollow cocobolo handle which holds tools when not in use.
4 Warranted High Grade Socket Firmer Chisels, have bevel edge blades. 6 inches long and polished handles. One of each of the following sizes: ¼, ½, 1 and 1½-inch.
1 New Pattern Combined Plier and Wire Cutter, 6-inch. All steel. Tempered jaws and all nickel plated.
1 Pair Carpenters' Pincers. 8-inch. With claw on handle. Forged from superior steel.
1 Wrought Iron Bench Screw. 1 inch in diameter, with patent collar, double thread and wood handle.
1 Warranted Cast Steel Draw Knife. 10-inch razor blade.
1 Polished Cast Steel Wing Divider. 8-inch.
1 Warranted Tool Steel Machinists' Screwdriver. 6-inch blade. Round, corrugated, imitation rosewood handle.
1 Sears, Roebuck & Co.'s Warranted High Grade Rip Saw. 28-inch.
1 Sears, Roebuck & Co.'s Warranted High Grade Hand Saw. 26-inch.
1 Sears, Roebuck & Co.'s Warranted High Grade Panel Saw. 20-inch.
1 Nest of Saws, consisting of 1 Handle, 1 Key Hole Blade, 1 Compass Blade, 1 Pruning Blade. All interchangeable in the handle.
1 No. 3 Extra Quality Steel Square. Size of body, 24x2 inches; size of tongue, 16x1½ inches. Marked in sixteenths, twelfths and fourths, and also with Brace and Essex Board Measure.
1 Stanley Adjustable Plumb and Level, mahogany polished, Proved Glasses, Arched Top Plates, brass tipped, with two side views.
1 Genuine Bailey Adjustable Wood Smooth Plane, with handle. Length, 9 inches. 2-inch cutter.
1 Genuine Bailey Adjustable Wood Jack Plane. Length, 15 inches. 2⅛-inch cutter.
1 Genuine Bailey Adjustable Wood Jointer Plane. Length, 26 inches. 2⅝-inch cutter.
1 Genuine Bailey Adjustable Knuckle Joint Plane, with nickel plated trimmings. Length, 6 inches. 1¾-inch cutter.
1 10-inch Sweep, Ball Bearing Ratchet Brace. Has ball bearings, thus reducing friction to a minimum. Solid rosewood, steel lined head. Finely finished and heavily nickel plated.
10 Jennings' Pattern, Extension Lip, Double Spur, Tool Steel Auger Bits. All fully warranted. 1 of each of the following sizes: ¼, $\frac{5}{16}$, ⅜, $\frac{7}{16}$, ½, $\frac{9}{16}$, ⅝, ¾, ⅞, and 1 inch.
8 Cast Steel, German Pattern, Gimlet Bits. 1 of each of the following sizes: $\frac{1}{16}$, $\frac{3}{32}$, ⅛, $\frac{5}{32}$, $\frac{3}{16}$, $\frac{7}{32}$, ¼ and $\frac{5}{16}$ inch.
1 Sears, Roebuck & Co.'s Warranted Full Polished and etched, All Steel Broad Hatchet. 4½-inch cut.
2 Countersink Bits, forged from cast steel and polished. 1 each; flat head for metal and snail head for wood.
1 Screwdriver Bit, for use in bit brace, 5½ inches long, forged from cast steel.
1 Square Reamer Bit, for use in bit brace, forged from cast steel.
3 Knurled Cup Point Nail Sets. Assorted sizes.
1 Iron Handle Spoke Shave, with adjustable cap and 2⅛-inch steel cutter.
3 Sears, Roebuck & Co's Slim Taper Saw Files. 1 of each size; 4, 5 and 6-inch.
1 Monkey Wrench. 10-inch.
1 Nickel Plated Coping Saw, with 1 dozen extra blades.
1 Bench Stop, screw adjusting, with reversible cast steel head.
2 Sets 10-inch Hand Screw Clamps, made of seasoned hard wood.
1 Square Hickory Mallet, mortised handle. Head is 6½x2¾x3¾ inches.
6 Cakes Assorted Colors Carpenters' Chalk.
1 Beechwood Chalk Line Reel and Awl.
3 Hanks Braided Chalk Line.

Shipping weight, 100 pounds.

ALL THE ABOVE HIGH GRADE TOOLS ARE FIRST CLASS IN EVERY WAY. PACKED IN TOOL CHEST, AS DESCRIBED, FOR $22.95.

The index may list an occasional offering that cannot be found in the catalogue because of the necessary deletion of some pages, explained in the Publisher's Note, following the Introduction.

DEPARTMENT INDEX

TO THOSE WHO WISH TO REFER TO ANY ONE DEPARTMENT and not to any special item, we direct you to the following abridged department index; but if you are looking for any special item you will find it in the itemized index arranged alphabetically on these colored pages.

IF YOU FAIL TO FIND THE ITEM YOU ARE LOOKING FOR UNDER THE ITEMIZED INDEX, refer to the department and search carefully for the article you are looking for; otherwise you might overlook it, as we may have the exact same article indexed under a different number. In other words, if you should fail to find the item you are looking for in the itemized index, by referring to the department you are almost sure to find it, for there is scarcely an article imaginable that will not be found in the columns of this book.

INDEX

REMEMBER - - -

OUR ONLY TERMS ARE CASH WITH THE ORDER.

REMEMBER, ALSO, WE GUARANTEE SAFE DELIVERY OF GOODS and entire satisfaction or we will immediately return your money.

READ

OUR CASH WITH ORDER TERMS EXPLANATION,

On pages 1 and 2 of this catalogue.

READ WHAT OUR BANKERS SAY OF OUR RELIABILITY on pages 12 and 13.

CLOTH SAMPLE BOOK No. 52R.

SEND 5 CENTS FOR OUR HANDSOME BOOK OF CLOTH SAMPLES OF

Men's Custom Tailoring,

BOOK No. 52R,

showing a fair sized cloth sample of our entire line of foreign and domestic fabrics for men's suits, overcoats, etc. The book also contains fashion plates, fashion figures, tape measure, order blanks, rules for measurement, etc. An immense line of fine fabrics which we make to measure at prices ranging from $7.50 upwards. This booklet will be mailed to any address on receipt of 5 cents. If you are interested in men's fine custom tailoring at the very lowest prices, send 5 cents for our sample book No. 52R.

Merchants' Wall Paper Samples.

TO ACCOMMODATE MERCHANTS, PAINTERS, PAPER HANGERS, WE HAVE GOTTEN OUT A VERY LARGE BOOK, SHOWING SAMPLES 18 INCHES SQUARE OF EVERYTHING IN OUR LINE OF WALL PAPER, INCLUDING SIDE WALL, CEILING, AND BORDER.

IT IS ONE OF THE HANDSOMEST WALL PAPER SAMPLE BOOKS ISSUED,

and the prices are so low that any merchant, painter or paperhanger can make a big saving by making his selections from this big book. This big book of wall paper samples will be sent to any address on receipt of 25c

Men's Ready Made Clothing Sample Booklet No. 56R.

SEND 5 CENTS FOR OUR COMPLETE CLOTH SAMPLE BOOKLET OF READY MADE CLOTHING,

Showing samples of our entire line of MEN'S READY MADE SUITS, OVERCOATS, ETC.

THE BOOKLET INCLUDES TAPE MEASURE, FASHION FIGURES, SIMPLE RULES FOR SELF MEASUREMENT, ETC.

THE BOOKLET WILL BE SENT TO ANY ADDRESS ON RECEIPT OF 5 CENTS.

Men's Ready Made Clothing

..SAMPLE BOOKLET No. 56R..

SEND 5 CENTS FOR A COMPLETE CLOTH SAMPLE BOOKLET OF READY MADE CLOTHING SHOWING SAMPLES OF OUR ENTIRE LINE OF MEN'S READY MADE SUITS, OVERCOATS, ETC.

THE BOOKLET INCLUDES TAPE MEASURE, FASHION FIGURES, SIMPLE RULES FOR SELF MEASUREMENT, ETC., AND WILL BE SENT TO ANY ADDRESS ON RECEIPT OF 5 CENTS.

MERCHANTS'

WALL PAPER SAMPLES

To accommodate merchants, painters and paper hangers, we have gotten out a VERY LARGE BOOK, showing samples 18 inches square of everything in our line of wall paper, including side wall, ceiling and border.

IT IS ONE OF THE HANDSOMEST

WALL PAPER SAMPLE BOOKS ISSUED,

and the prices are so low that any merchant, painter or paper hanger can make a big saving by making his selections from this big book.

THIS BIG BOOK OF WALL PAPER SAMPLES will be sent to any address on receipt of **25 CENTS.**

MEN'S READY MADE
CLOTHING SAMPLE BOOKLET
No. 56R.

SEND 5 CENTS for our complete cloth sample booklet of ready made clothing, showing samples of our entire line of

MEN'S READY MADE SUITS, OVERCOATS, ETC.

THE BOOKLET INCLUDES TAPE MEASURE, FASHION FIGURES, SIMPLE RULES FOR SELF MEASUREMENT, ETC. ....

And will be sent to any address on receipt of 5 cts.

Our Paint Color Book.

SEND US 2 CENTS (stamps accepted) for our handsome sample book, containing samples of each color of our complete line of

...READY MIXED PAINTS FOR ALL PURPOSES...

EVERYTHING IN **PAINTERS' SUPPLIES.**

Information how to figure amount of paint required, and our money saving prices on paints, oils, brushes, etc.

THIS FINE PAINT SAMPLE BOOKLET WILL BE MAILED TO ANY ADDRESS ON RECEIPT OF 2 CENTS.

Subscribe for Ou Grocery Price List.

SEND US 15 CENTS for a year's subscription to our GROCERY PRICE LIST, revised and issued every 60 days, the most complete grocery price list published, illustrating and describing everything in

...STAPLE AND FANCY GROCERIES...

with prices below any kind of competition. We will send our grocery price list by mail every 60 days for one year postpaid on receipt of 15 cents.

Do not fail to send 15 cents for a year's paid subscription to our

GROCERY PRICE LIST.

WALL PAPER SAMPLE BOOKLET

We issue a handsome book of samples of

Wall Paper

showing a fair sized sample of every number in our line of new wall papers, all offered at prices that will admit of no competition,

PRICES NEVER BEFORE ATTEMPTED

This book of samples of wall paper will be mailed to any address on receipt of 2 cents. If you intend to do any papering, do not fail to

SEND 2 CENTS FOR OUR WALL PAPER SAMPLE BOOK.

Subscribe for Ou Grocery Price List.

SEND US 15 CENTS for a year's subscription to our GROCERY PRICE LIST, revised and issued every 60 days, the most complete grocery price list published, illustrating and describing everything in

...STAPLE AND FANCY GROCERIES...

with prices below any kind of competition. We will send our grocery price list by mail every 60 days for one year postpaid on receipt of 15 cents.

Do not fail to send 15 cents for a year's paid subscription to our

GROCERY PRICE LIST.

WALL PAPER SAMPLE BOOKLET

We issue a handsome book of samples of

Wall Paper

showing a fair sized sample of every number in our line of new wall papers, all offered at prices that will admit of no competition,

PRICES NEVER BEFORE ATTEMPTED

This book of samples of wall paper will be mailed to any address on receipt of 2 cents. If you intend to do any papering, do not fail to

SEND 2 CENTS FOR OUR WALL PAPER SAMPLE BOOK.

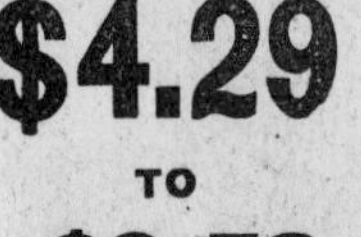

$4.29 TO $9.52

OUR GREAT STOVE LEADER.

AT $4.29 TO $9.52, ACCORDING TO SIZE AND SPECIFICATIONS, WE OFFER THIS,

OUR ACME OAK WITH ALL THE NEW IMPROVEMENTS.

Delivered on the cars at our foundry in Northern Ohio, as our greatest leader for 1902—a wonder of value, the greatest achievement in stove making of the season. From this large illustration, printed from an engraving of a photograph taken direct from the stove, you can form some idea of the extraordinary value we are offering in a high grade heater for this season, but the stove must be seen to be appreciated. You can scarcely imagine how it is possible to build a stove for the little money we are offering this to our customers.

A WONDER OF THE STOVE INDUSTRY

There is not a manufacturer of heating stoves in America that will not see our catalogue and be attracted by this most extraordinary offer, and the most astonishing thing will be how it is possible for anyone to make the stove for the money.

HOW WE CAN MAKE THE PRICE. Early in the Spring of 1901 the new patterns for this stove were gotten out by one of the largest stove manufacturers in the country. The patterns were submitted to us with all their improvements, as the **finest thing of the kind on the market,** and we were asked to figure on the entire product of the factory—the entire capacity of their heating stove department—and by buying all material at that time when raw material was low, and working during **spring and summer season when labor was cheap,** running factory to full capacity, we learned that it would be possible to reduce the actual cost of producing this stove to what to us and other stove makers **was a heretofore unheard of price,** and believing our one million customers everywhere would appreciate this bargain, and would take the entire lot of stoves off our hands during 1902, we closed this contract. **It was the largest contract ever placed in this country for one kind of a heating stove,** and hence, the lowest selling price ever known in this country for high grade heating stove.

OUR PRICE IS YOUR PRICE The $4.29 to $9.52 price we quote you is the actual cost to us on our season's contract basis, with but one small percentage of profit added. **Such value as was never known** and was never before offered by us or any other house. **Our $4.29 Acme Oak Heating Stove is the latest,** handsomest Oak pattern. It is mounted with 18-gauge smooth steel, heavy cast iron fire pot, has shaking and draw center grate for coal, has double circular wood grate which is so constructed that the fire can be kept under complete control. **Large ash pan, large feed doors.** Has highly polished, heavily nickel plated foot rails, large nickel plated name plate, nickel plated top ring, handsome nickel plated fancy urn. Nickel plated hinge pins and knobs, large swing top, cooking lid under swing top. Check drafts at collar and in feed door. **The Acme Oak is one of the handsomest heating stoves on the market.** It is nice enough for any home, and would ornament any parlor. **BURNS ANYTHING.** The Acme Oak is suitable for wood, hard coal, soft coal, coke or anything that can be burned in a stove.

THIS STOVE will be furnished at $4.29 to $9.52, in the different sizes as listed below. Height of stoves as given is from floor to base of urn. We can furnish the three larger sizes with self feeding magazines at 75 cents for No. 214, $1.00 for No. 216, and $1.25 for No. 218, extra.

CASH WITH ORDER PRICES OF ACME OAK HEATING STOVES. DELIVERED ON THE CARS AT OUR FOUNDRY IN NORTHERN OHIO.

Catalogue Number	Stove No.	Dia. of Fire Pot	Height Inches	Floor Space Inches	Size Pipe to fit Collar	Weight Pounds	Price with Wood Grate	Price with Coal Grate	Price with Both Grates
22R477	210	10	38	16 x16	5 in.	86	$4.29	$4.34	$4.56
22R478	212	12	40	18¼x18¼	6 in.	114	5.04	5.09	5.34
22R479	214	14	43	20¾x20¾	6 in.	146	6.19	6.24	6.65
22R480	216	16	44	22¾x22¾	6 in.	175	7.40	7.45	7.95
22R481	218	18	47	25 x25	7 in.	210	8.90	8.95	9.52

WE CAN ALWAYS FURNISH REPAIRS FOR ACMES.

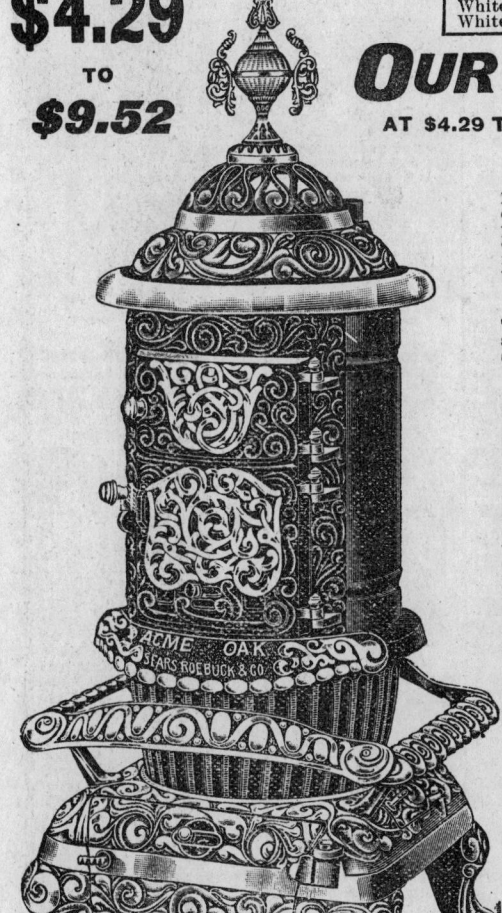

Builders' Hardware

THE GOODS WE LIST in this department are guaranteed for quality. They are made in proper proportions and are not only beautiful in design, but are correct from a mechanical standpoint. There is a big profit for your local hardware dealer on locks, door knobs, hinges, latches, sash fixtures, etc., and we sell all of these goods so close that no matter how little you wish to buy, we will save you enough to pay you for sending to Chicago for the goods.

THE FREIGHT RATES on hardware and building material are low and will amount to almost nothing compared to the saving in price.

IF YOU ARE GOING TO BUILD, make out a list, or have your carpenter or architect make it out for you, of all the goods you will require in this line. Refer to these goods in this catalogue for prices, or if you wish, send the list to us and we will quote you the price for each and every article, and for the entire bill delivered at your nearest railroad station. You will find that our prices will surprise you in the money you can save, and if you do not order your goods from us, we will compel your local dealer to sell you the cheapest bill of goods he ever sold, and in any case we will save you money.

DON'T BE PERSUADED to use a poor quality of hardware. Hardware in a building is a small item in the total cost, even if the very best is used. For example, the difference in cost between good locks and poor locks is so little that the owner would not consider it a saving to use poor locks if he were posted on the matter. Because the work is so easily concealed, poor locks are used to save a few cents. We furnish complete lines in the desirable finishes.

WE HAVE MADE THE DESCRIPTIONS SO EXPLICIT, giving sizes and prices, that the architect may specify that which pleases him, or which suits his particular work, with the assurance of getting just what is desired. Each design is first shown in the lock sets, and then the other trimmings are illustrated further on. Every article is guaranteed to be exactly as we represent it, and if not found so it may be returned and the money will be refunded.

WE SHOW SEVEN COMPLETE LINES. We show three complete lines of plain goods in all the popular finishes, and four complete lines of ornamental goods. We have everything that is desirable in these lines, and you will find this department most complete in every respect, and we can save you so much money on these goods that you cannot afford to buy them from your local dealer, whose cost in many cases is more than our price to you.

SAMPLES. We have made arrangements to furnish small samples which are made in the same finishes as our various lines of locks and trimmings, and which will show the exact appearance of any goods of the same finish. We will be pleased to send a set of these samples to anyone who is interested, on receipt of 5 cents (stamps accepted).

ORNAMENTAL GENUINE BRONZE LOCK SETS.

Antique Copper Finish Front Door Cylinder Locks.

No. 9R300 Front Door Cylinder Lock Set. Antique, copper sand finished trimmings as shown in cut. Matches lock sets Nos. 9R325 to 9R338. Size of lock, 4¾x3¾ inches; reversible for either right or left hand doors; easy spring. **Bronze metal cylinder, bronze metal front and strike, bronze metal bolts and thumb knob, three gold plated keys,** same as shown in cut. The same key operates both the night latch and the dead bolt. **2½-inch wrought bronze metal knob** for outside of door and **2¼-inch wrought bronze metal knob** for inside of door. Wrought bronze metal long escutcheon for outside of door, size, 2¾x10 inches. **A handsome, strong and secure lock.**
Price, per set, complete........................**$4.12**

No. 9R301 The above front door lock set with **vestibule latch to match,** and keys to pass. Size of latch, ¼x3⅛ inches. Reversible, easy spring. The cylinder, front, strike and bolt are **genuine bronze metal, antique copper sand blast finish.** Long escutcheon for outside of door. Size, 2¾x10 inches.
Price of lock set and vestibule set, complete...**$7.12**

Front Door Cylinder Locks.

No. 9R310 Front Door Cylinder Lock Set. Antique copper finish; lock, 4¾x3¾ inches; reversible, for either right or left hand door; easy spring. Cylinder, front, strike, bolts and thumb knob are genuine bronze metal; furnished with three gold plated keys like one shown in cut; solid wrought bronze metal door knobs; 2½-inch knob for outside of door and 2¼-inch for inside of door; long escutcheon for outside of door, 2⅛x8 inches, made of solid wrought bronze metal, antique copper finish. This lock set matches lock sets from Nos. 9R515 to 9R568.
Price, per set........................**$4.25**

No. 9R311 The above front door lock set, with vestibule latch to match and keys to pass; size, 4x3¼ inches; bronze metal cylinder, front, strike and bolts; 2¼-inch solid wrought bronze metal knobs; long wrought bronze metal escutcheon for outside of door, size, 2⅛x8 inches; all finished in antique copper.
Price of lock set and vestibule set, complete...**$7.37**

No. 9R312 Front Door Lock Set. Same as No. 9R310, except it is finished in plain bronze, highly polished. Will match any bronze finished hardware.
Price, per set........................**$4.12**

No. 9R313 Front Door and Vestibule Lock Set combined. Same as No. 9R311, except finished in plain bronze metal, highly polished.
Price, per set........................**$7.12**

IN ORDERING GOODS FROM THIS DEPARTMENT

Make your order large enough, if possible, to make a FREIGHT SHIPMENT OF 100 POUNDS in which way the transportation charges will amount to very little.

FOR OUR PATRONS who desire the best, we offer a line of Genuine Bronze Lock Sets and Trimmings from Nos. 9R325 to 9R345. The design is new and neat. The finish is very desirable for oak, birch, sycamore, or any of the natural finish hardwood trimmings.

For Butts, Bolts, Cupboard Catches and other trimmings to match this finish, plain sand finish goods are commonly used. See pages which follow lock sets.

Front Door Lock Sets.

No. 9R325 Genuine Bronze Front Door Lock Set. Lock is furnished with **antique copper, sand finish trimmings,** as shown in cut. Reversible, for right or left hand doors. Size, 4¾x3⅛ inches; one nickel plated steel key for lock bolt and two for night latch; cast bronze front and bolts; easy spring; **wrought bronze knobs,** 2¼ inches in diameter; ⁵⁄₁₆-inch swivel spindle; wrought bronze escutcheon for outside of door, size, 7⅛x2¼ inches. Packed, complete, with screws. All the **bronzed trimmings** are finished **antique copper, sand finish.** Per set, **$1.25**

No. 9R327 Genuine Bronze Front Door and Vestibule Door Set to match No. 9R325 Front Door Lock Set, with keys to pass. Latch is reversible, for right or left hand doors. Size of latch, 3¾x3¼ inches. Two nickel plated steel keys. **Cast bronze front and bolts;** easy spring; knobs 2¼ inches in diameter; ⁵⁄₁₆-inch swivel spindle. **Long escutcheon for outside of door is wrought bronze,** 7⅛x2¼ inches. **All bronze** trimmings finished **antique copper, sand finish.** Front door and vestibule locks. Packed, complete, with screws.
Price, per set........................**$2.38**

For Cylinder Front Door Lock Sets to match this line see No. 9R300.

Inside Lock Sets.

No. 9R332 Genuine Bronze Inside Lock Set. Lock reversible for right or left hand doors. Sizes, 3½x3¼. **Cast bronze front and bolts; wrought bronze knobs,** 2¼ inches in diameter. **Two wrought bronze long escutcheons,** 5¾x1⅞ inches. Packed complete with screws. All trimmings are finished **antique copper, sand finish.**
Price, per set........ **79c**

Sliding Door Lock Sets.

Small cut to the left shows astragal front.

No. 9R336 Genuine Bronze Sliding Door Lock Set for single door, flat fronts. Size of lock, 5¼x3¼ inches. Bronze fronts, bolt and pull. Two wrought bronze cup escutcheons, 6x2⅜ inches; length of key adjustable for doors from 1⅜ to 2 inches thick. All trimmings finished. Antique copper, sand finished. Packed complete, with screws.
Price, per set........................**$1.12**

No. 9R337 Genuine Bronze Sliding Door Lock Set for double doors, flat fronts. Same as No. 9R336, with 4 cup escutcheons and box strike. Price, per set. **$1.63**

No. 9R338 Genuine Bronze Sliding Door Lock Set for double doors, astragal front. Same as No. 9R337, except it has astragal or round front. Price, per set, **$1.93**

Push Buttons.

No. 9R342 Genuine Bronze Push Button for Electric Bells. Wrought bronze, 4x2⅜ inches. Finished antique copper, sand finish. Packed complete with screws. Price, each...........**23c**

Flush Sash Lifts.

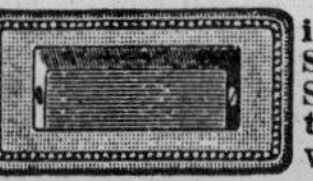

No. 9R345 Genuine Bronze Flush Sash Lifts. Wrought bronze. Size, 3x1¼ inches. **Finished antique copper, sand finish.** Packed with screws. Price, each......**5c**
Price, per dozen............**59c**

Plated Ornamental Lock Sets.

FOR THOSE DESIRING A CHEAPER LINE OF ORNAMENTAL GOODS in the antique copper, sand finish, we offer in the following numbers, from Nos. 9R373 to 9R392, **a very handsome design.** This differs from the preceding design in that it is **electro copper plated and sand finished on iron instead of on bronze.** Some dealers sell as sand finish, goods which are electro copper plated and **tumbled,** which produces a finish which, for **a short time,** looks exactly like sand finish. **Ours are guaranteed to be GENUINE SAND FINISH.** Note carefully the measurements of escutcheons. They are much larger than usually found on sets of similar description. This line is **OUR BEST SELLER.**

Front Door Lock Sets.

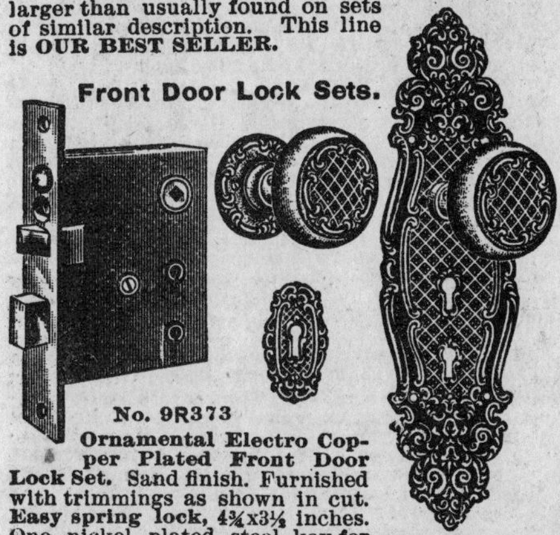

No. 9R373

Ornamental Electro Copper Plated Front Door Lock Set. Sand finish. Furnished with trimmings as shown in cut. **Easy spring lock,** 4¾x3½ inches. One nickel plated steel key for lock bolt and two for night latch. Knobs, 2¼ inches in diameter. **Long escutcheons** for outside of front door, 11x2¾ inches. Trimmings are **electro copper plated, sand finish.** Packed complete with screws.
Price, per set.......... ....94c

No. 9R375 Front Door and Vestibule Door Set to Match No. 9R373 front door latch set; latch, 3¾x3½ inches. **Two nickel plated steel keys;** knob 2¼ inches in diameter, long escutcheon, same design as above, 9x2¾ inches. Keys to pass. Trimmings are **electro copper plated, sand finish.** Packed complete with screws. Price, per set..........................$1.87

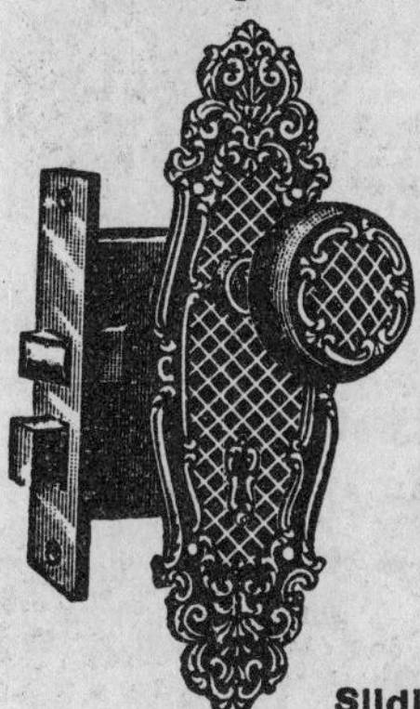

Inside Lock Sets.

No. 9R378 Ornamental Electro Bronze Plated Inside Lock Set. Lock 3½x3¼ inches, with nickel plated steel key, wrought front; knobs, 2¼ inches in diameter; two long escutcheons, 9x2¾ inches. All trimmings are heavily **electro bronze plated antique copper, sand finish.** Packed complete, with screws.
Price, per set.......45c

Sliding Door Lock Sets.

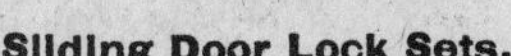

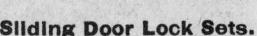

Small cut to the left shows the astragal front.

No. 9R383 Ornamental Electro Bronze Plated Sliding Door Lock Set. Flat front for single doors. Lock, 5¼x3¼ inches. Bronze bolt and pull. Brass key. Two cup escutcheons, 9x2¾ inches electro bronze plated, finished antique copper, sand finish. Packed, complete, with screws. Price, per set....94c

No. 9R384 Ornamental Electro Bronze Plated Sliding Door Lock Set. Flat front for double doors. Lock, 5¼x3¼ inches. Bronze bolt and pull. Brass key. Four cup escutcheons, 9x2¾ inches. **Electro bronze plated. Finished antique copper, sand finish.** Packed complete with screws. Price, per set....$1.34

No. 9R385 Sliding Door Lock Set. Same as No. 9R384, except it has astragal front.
Price, per set..$1.50

Flush Sash Lifts.

No. 9R390 Ornamental Electro Bronze Plated Flush Sash Lift. Finished antique, copper sand finish. Size, 3x1¼ inches.
Price, per doz., **35c**; each..**3c**

Hook Sash Lifts.

No. 9R391 Ornamental Electro Bronze Plated Hook Sash Lift. Finished antique, sand copper finish. Size, 2x1⅛ inches. Price, each.....**2c**
Per dozen...........................**24c**

Butts.

No. 9R392 Ornamental Electro Bronze Plated Door Butts. Finished antique copper, sand finish. Packed complete with screws.

Size,	3x3	3½x3½	4x4	4½x4½
Per pair,	18c	21c	25c	30c

For other trimmings to match this finish, see plain sand finish goods in pages following lock sets.

Genuine Bronze Ornamental Lock Sets and House Trimmings.

THESE ELEGANT SETS Nos. 9R423 to 9R441 are selected with great care, not only for the beauty of design, but because they are **made by one of the most favorably known manufacturers** in the world, a manufacturer who knows **no other than the very highest grade hardware** it is possible to produce.

YOU WILL OBSERVE that we **arrange these goods in such a manner that the inexperienced buyer will be able to select all the necessary** lock sets, sash lifts and **all trimmings of the same pattern with no difficulty whatever.**

IN BUYING YOUR BUILDERS' HARDWARE from us, you not only **get the best in every way** but the price represents **a saving of from 33⅓ to 50 per cent.**

Genuine Bronze Ornamental Lock Sets and House Trimmings.

These goods have Genuine Bronze Trimmings. We also show the same design in **Electro Bronze Plated** goods. The raised surfaces (shown by white line in cuts) **are polished.** The background is dark.

Front Door Lock Sets.

No. 9R423 Genuine Bronze Front Door Lock Set is furnished with trimmings as shown in cut, packed complete with screws. Lock is reversible for either right or left hand door. Size, 4¾x3½ inches, with **one nickel plated steel key** for lock bolt, and two for night latch. Has wrought bronze knobs, 2¼ inches in diameter. **The long escutcheon** for outside of door is wrought bronze. Size, 7x1⅞ inches. Price of lock set, complete..............**$1.04**

Inside Lock Sets.

No. 9R424 Genuine Bronze Inside Lock Set, is furnished with trimmings, as shown in cut. Size of lock, 3½x3¼ inches. Reversible for either right or left hand doors. Nickel plated steel key. **Wrought bronze front.** Bronze bolts. Wrought bronze knobs, 2¼ inches in diameter. Two **wrought bronze long escutcheons,** 5½x1⅝ inches. Packed complete, with screws. Price, per set..............................**63c**

Bronze Lock Set.

No. 9R425 Genuine Bronze Lock Set, is furnished with trimmings as shown in cut. Reversible lock, bronze bolts. Size, 3½x3¼ inches. **Nickel plated steel** key, wrought bronze front; jet knobs, 2¼ inches in diameter. **Two long escutcheons, wrought bronze;** size, 5½x1⅝ inches. Packed complete with screws.
Price, per set....**51c**

Sliding Door Lock Sets.

No. 9R430 Genuine Bronze Sliding Door Lock Set, for single door, flat fronts. Size of lock, 5¼x3¼ inches, brass key; has two wrought bronze cup escutcheons, 4x2⅛ inches. Packed complete, with screws. Price, per set..............................**94c**

No. 9R431 Genuine Bronze Sliding Door Lock Set, for double doors, with **bronze front bolt and pull.** Has four wrought bronze cup escutcheons, 4x2⅛ inches. Packed complete, with screws.
Price, per set..**$1.32**

No. 9R432 Same as No. 9R431, except has astragal or round fronts. Price, per set........**$1.62**

Push Buttons.

No. 9R435 Genuine Bronze Push Button for electric bells, with patent sliding electric contact. Diameter, 2¼ inches.
Price, each..............................**25c**

Flush Sash Lifts.

No. 9R440 Genuine Bronze Flush Sash Lift. Size, 3x1¼ inches. Packed, complete, with screws. Price, each.............**5c**
Per dozen.............................**50c**

Hook Sash Lifts.

No. 9R441 Genuine Bronze Hook Sash Lift. Size of plate, 1⅝x⅞ inches. Packed with screws.
Price, per dozen, **42c**; each....**4c**
For other trimmings to match these goods, see pages following lock sets.

Electro Bronze Plated Ornamental Lock Sets and House Trimmings.

Our Electro Bronze Plated Goods are heavy, well made goods. The background is dark. **The raised surfaces** (shown in illustration by white lines) **are polished and electro bronze plated.** The bronze is put on the iron just as silver is put on silver plated table knives and forks. These goods have been very popular. The design is one of the latest and best. The goods are durable and will give satisfaction.

Front Door Lock Sets.

No. 9R453 Electro Bronze Plated Front Door Lock Set, is furnished with knobs and escutcheons as shown—complete with screws. Lock is reversible for either right or left hand doors. Size, 4¾x3½ inches with one **nickel plated steel key** for lock bolt and two for night latch. **The long escutcheon** for outside of door is 7¼x1⅞ inches.
Price of lock set, complete.............................**84c**

Genuine Bronze Ball Tip Loose Pin Butts.

For China Closets, Cupboards, Etc.

No. 9R980 Genuine Wrought Bronze Ball Tip Butts, plain bronze finish, highly polished. Packed with screws.

Size, open	2½x1¾	3x2
Price, per pair	14c	22c

No. 9R983 Genuine Wrought Bronze Ball Tip Butts, antique copper finish, highly polished. Packed with screws.

Size open	2½x1¾	3x2
Price, per pair	18c	29c

No. 9R986 Genuine Wrought Bronze Ball Tip Butts, antique copper sand finish. Packed with screws.

Size, open	2½x1¾	3x2
Price, per pair	19c	30c

Steel Transom Butts.

No. 9R1000 Steel Transom Butts, fast joint electro copper plated, plain polished, bronze finish.

Size	2½x2½	3x3	3½x3½
Per pair	18c	20c	27c

No. 9R1004 Steel Transom Butts, fast joint electro copper plated, antique copper finish.

Size	2½x2½	3x3	3½x3½
Per pair	19c	24c	29c

No. 9R1009 Steel Transom Butts, fast joint, electro copper plated, antique copper, sand finish.

Size	2½x2½	3x3	3½x3½
Per pair	14c	19c	22c

Extension Flush Bolts.

No. 9R1052 Electro Copper Plated, Antique Copper, sand finish, extension flush bolt. Can be used equally well for either top or bottom of doors. This pattern matches any of our sand finish goods.

Sizes, inches	12	18	24
Price	47c	48c	49c

No. 9R1055 Electro Copper Plated, Antique Copper Finish, Extension Flush Bolt. To match any of our antique copper finish goods.

Sizes, inches	12	18	24
Price	44c	45c	46c

No. 9R1058 Genuine Bronze Metal, Highly Polished Extension Flush Bolt. To match any of our polished bronze finish goods.

Sizes, inches	12	18	24
Price	67c	68c	69c

Chain Door Fasts.

No. 9R1063 Electro Copper Plated, Antique Copper Finish Chain Door Fasts, with extra heavy chain. To match any antique copper finish goods. Size, 6 inch, Price, each, 25c

No. 9R1067 Electro Bronze Plated, Plain Polished Bronze Chain Door Fasts. Matches any plain polished bronze finish goods. Size, 6 inches. Price, each 24c

For other Chain Door Fasts, see Index.

Letter Box Plates.

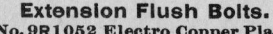

No. 9R1071 Electro Copper Plated, Antique Copper Finish Letter Box Plate, with both outside and inside plate. Size of outside plate is 7⅛x2¾ inches, with opening 4¾x1⅛ inches. Matches any antique copper finish goods. Price, complete 38c

No. 9R1075 Electro Bronze Plated, Plain Polished Bronze Finished Letter Box Plate, with both outside and inside plate. Size of outside plate, 7⅛x2¾ inches, with opening 4¾x1⅛ inches. Matches any plain polished bronze finish goods. Price, complete..35c

For other Letter Box Plates, see Index.

Push Plates.

No. 9R1083 Electro Copper Plated, Antique Copper, Sand Finish Push Plate. Size, 10½x2½ inches. Matches any sand finish goods. Price, each 33c

No. 9R1086 Electro Bronze Plated, Antique Copper Finish Push Plate. Size, 10½x2½ inches. Matches any antique copper finish goods. Price, each....32c

No. 9R1089 Genuine Bronze Metal, Plain Polished Finish Push Plate. Size, 10½x2½ inches. Matches any plain polished bronze finish goods. Price, each 43c

Door Bolts.

No. 9R1095 Electro Copper Plated, Antique Copper Finish Barrel Bolts. Wrought bolt. Bronze metal knob, matches any antique copper finish goods.

Size	3-in.	4-in.
Price, each	13c	14c

No. 9R1098 Electro Bronze Plated, Plain Polished Bronze Finish Barrel Bolts. Wrought bolt. Bronze metal knob. Matches any plain polished bronze finish goods.

Size	3-in.	4-in.
Price, each	11c	12c

For other Door Bolts, see Index.

Mortise Bolts.

No. 9R1102 Electro Copper Plated, Antique Copper Finish Mortise Bolts. Matches any antique copper finish goods. Price, each 10c

No. 9R1105 Genuine Bronze Metal, Highly Polished Mortise Bolts. Matches any plain polished bronze finish goods. Price, each 11c

For other Mortise Bolts, see Index.

Bar Sash Lifts.

No. 9R1109 Bar Sash Lifts, electro copper plated, antique copper finish. Size, 3⅜ inches. Price, per dozen, 85c; each....8c

No. 9R1112 Bar Sash Lifts, electro copper plated, plain polished bronze finish. Size, 3⅜ inches. Price, per dozen, 74c; each 7c

No. 9R1115 Genuine Bronze Bar Sash Lifts, antique copper finish. Size, 3⅜ inches. Price, per dozen, $1.46; each 13c

No. 9R1118 Genuine Bronze Bar Sash Lifts, plain polished bronze finish. Size, 3⅜ inches. Price, per dozen, $1.26; each 11c

Sash Fasts.

No. 9R1126 Electro Copper Plated Antique Copper, Sand Finish Sash Fasts. Matches any sand finish goods. Price, per dozen, 94c; each 8c

No. 9R1129 Electro Copper Plated Antique Copper Sash Fasts. Matches any antique copper finish goods. Price, per dozen, 88c; each. ..8c

No. 9R1132 Electro Bronze Plated Plain Polished Bronze Finish Sash Fasts. Matches any polished bronze finish goods. Price, per dozen, 87c; each 8c

For other Sash Locks see Index.

Sash Sockets.

No. 9R1143 Electro Copper Plated Antique Copper Finish Sash Sockets. Matches any antique copper finish goods.

Price, each 3c
Price, per dozen 30c

No. 9R1147 Electro Bronze Plated, Plain Polished, Bronze Finish, Sash Sockets. Matches any polished bronze finish goods. Price, per dozen, 25c; each 3c

Cupboard Catches.

No. 9R1160 Electro Copper Plated, Antique Copper Finish Cupboard Catch, wrought steel patent triangular bolt. Packed complete with screws. Matches any antique copper finish goods. Price, per dozen, 68c; each 6c

No. 9R1163 Electro Copper Plated, Polished Bronze Finished Cupboard Catch, wrought steel, patent triangular bolt. Packed complete with screws. Matches any polished bronze finish goods. Price, per dozen, 62c; each 6c

For other Cupboard Catches, see Index.

Window Catches.

No. 9R1174 Electro Copper Plated Antique Copper Finish, French Window Catch. Matches any antique copper finish goods. Packed complete with screws.

Price, each 8c
Price, per dozen 85c

No. 9R1177 Electro Bronze Plated, Polished Bronze Finish, French Window Catch. Matches any polished bronze finish goods. Packed complete with screws. Price, per dozen, 75c; each 7c

For other Window Catches, see Index.

Cupboard Turns.

No. 9R1183 Electro Copper Plated, Antique Copper Finish, Cupboard Turn. A new and beautiful design. Will match any antique copper finish goods.

Price, each $0.14
Per dozen 1.62

No. 9R1186 Genuine Bronze Metal Polished Bronze Finish Cupboard Turn. Same design as No. 9R1183. Will match any polished bronze finish goods. Price, per dozen, $2.37; each 20c

No. 9R1189 Electro Bronze Plated Polished Bronze Finish Cupboard Turns. Same design as No. 9R1183. Will match any polished bronze finish goods. Price, per dozen, $1.43; each 12c

Cupboard Turns as shown in this illustration will go on a stile 1 inch wide.

No. 9R1194 Electro Copper Plated, Antique Copper, Sand Finish, Cupboard Turn, with patent Diamond No Friction Bolt. T handle. Packed complete, with screws. Matches any antique copper sand finish goods. Price, per dozen, $1.82; each 16c

No. 9R1197 Electro Copper Plated, Antique Copper Finish, Cupboard Turn. Same style as No. 9R1194. Matches any antique copper finish goods. Price, per dozen, $1.75; each 15c

No. 9R1200 Electro Bronze Plated, Plain Polished, Bronze Finish Cupboard Turn. Same style as No. 9R1194. Matches any polished bronze finish goods. Price, per dozen, $1.55; each 13c

No. 9R1204 Genuine Bronze Metal, Polished, Bronze Finish Cupboard Turn. Same style as No. 9R1194. Matches any polished bronze finish goods. Price, per dozen, $2.36; each 20c

Transom Catches.

No. 9R1209 Transom Catch, plain electro bronze plated and polished. Size, 1⅞x1⅛ inches. Regular bevel latch for transoms opening in.

Price, each $0.14
Per dozen 1.58

No. 9R1212 Transom Catch, plain electro copper plated, antique copper finish. Size, 1⅞x1⅛ inches. Regular bevel latch for transoms opening in. Price, each $0.16
Per dozen 1.82

Drawer Pulls.

No. 9R1225 Electro Copper Plated, Antique Copper, Sand Finish Drawer Pull. Large; 3⅞ inches long. Will match any antique copper sand finish goods. Price, per dozen, 48c; each 4c

No. 9R1228 Drawer Pull. Same description as No. 9R1225, except it is medium sized; 3 inches long. Price, per dozen, 43c; each 4c

No. 9R1231 Electro Copper Plated, Antique Copper Finish Drawer Pull. Same design as No. 9R1225. Large; 3⅞ inches long. Will match any antique copper finish goods. Price, per dozen, 46c; each..4c

No. 9R1234 Drawer Pull. Same as No. 9R1231, except it is medium sized; 3 inches long. Price, per dozen, 41c; each 4c

No. 9R1237 Genuine Bronze Metal Polished, Bronze Finish Drawer Pull. Same design as No. 9R1225. Large; 3⅞ inches long. Will match any polished bronze finish goods. Price, per dozen, 64c; each 6c

No. 9R1240 Drawer Pull. Same as No. 9R1237 except it is medium; 3 inches long. Price, per dozen, 55c; each 5c

No. 9R1243 Electro Bronze Plated Polished, Bronze Finish Drawer Pull. Same design as No. 9R1225. Large; 3⅞ inches long. Will match any polished bronze finish goods. Price, per dozen, 43c; each 4c

No. 9R1246 Drawer Pull. Same as No. 9R1234, except it is medium; 3 inches long. Price, per dozen, 38c; each 4c

Hat and Coat Hooks.

No. 9R1260 Electro Copper Plated, Antique Copper Finish, Wrought Steel Hat and Coat Hooks. Medium; 3¼ inches. Will match any antique copper finish goods. Price, per dozen, 46c; each 4c

No. 9R1263 Genuine Wrought Bronze Metal, Polished Bronze Finish, Hat and Coat Hooks. Medium; 3¼ inches. Will match any polished bronze finish goods. Price, per dozen, $1.20; each 10c

No. 9R1266 Electro Bronze Plated, Polished, Bronze Finish Hat and Coat Hooks. Medium; 3¼ inches. Will match any polished bronze finish goods. Price, per dozen, 40c; each 4c

Ornamental House Trimmings.

In the following Nos., 9R1300 to 9R1368, we show a very standard line of trimmings. They will match lock sets Nos. 9R423 to 9R490.

Butts.

No. 9R1300 Ornamental Electro Bronze Plated Butts. Packed complete with screws.

Size, inches	3x3	3½x3½	4x4
Price, per pair	22c	24c	28c
Size, inches		4½x4½	5x5
Price, per pair		33c	38c

Chain Bolts.

No. 9R1303 Ornamental Electro Bronze Plated Chain Bolt. Size, 6 x 2⅛ inches. Packed complete with screws. Price, each 21c

Foot Bolts.

No. 9R1306 Ornamental Electro Bronze Plated Foot Bolt. Size, 6x2⅛ inches. Packed complete with screws. Price, each 21c

Flush Bolts.

No. 9R1309 Ornamental Electro Bronze Plated Flush Bolt. Size, 6x1 inch. Sunken thumbpiece. Packed complete with screws. Price, each 10c

No. 9R1312 Ornamental Electro Bronze Plated Flush Bolt. Size, 12x1 inch. Sunken thumbpiece. Packed complete with screws. Price, each 16c

Chain Door Fastener.

No. 9R1315 Ornamental Electro Bronze Plated Chain Door Fastener. Size, 1⅛x6 inches. Packed complete with screws. This allows the door to be opened a few inches and securely holds it there. A guard against tramps and other intruders. Price, each 25c

Letter Drop Plates.

No. 9R1318 Ornamental Electro Bronze Plated Letter Drop Plate. Size of plate, 2¼ x 7⅜ inches. Size of opening, 1⅛x4⅛ inches. Packed with screws. Price, each 18c

GIVE CATALOGUE NUMBER IN FULL WHEN YOU WRITE YOUR ORDER

The Eclipse Door Check.

Illustrated at bottom of previous page, showing both check and spring applied to door.

Is simple, durable, easy to apply, easy to keep in order—all points that tell. It successfully prevents doors from slamming. Can be applied to either the door or casing as desired. The check can be instantly varied for light or heavy draft. All parts are interchangeable so in case of accidental breakage any part may be replaced at small expense. Complete directions for putting up and adjusting are packed with each check.

No. 9R2034 Eclipse Door Check, Tuscan Bronze Finish. Prices are for check only, for spring see preceding page.

For ordinary doors, diameter of cylinder, 1¼ inches. Price, each............ $1.17

For wide doors, diameter of cylinder, 2 inches. Price, each............ $1.65

For very wide doors, diameter of cylinder, 2¼ inches. Price, each............ $2.32

Spring Hinges.

No. 9R2036 Hold Back Spring Hinges. Holds the door securely shut, and when opened past the center holds it open. These are full size, heavy goods. Weight, per pair, 1 lb.

Price, per pair, without screws.... 8c

Per dozen pairs............ 87c

Double Action Spring Hinges.

Double Action Spring Hinges for screen doors, to swing both ways; japanned iron.

No. 9R2039 For doors not more than 1⅛ inches thick. Per pair.. 18c

Patent No-Slam Screen Door Check.

No. 9R2045 An Automatic Check for Screen Doors. Can be applied to any screen door in connection with any door spring or spring hinge. It is a durable check and will not rack the door. Rubber ball, nickel plated trimmings. Price, each......... 19c

The Warner Screen Door Check.

No. 9R2047 To be used on doors having spring hinges or a door spring. Is adjustable and can be used for panel doors 1¼ inches thick or lighter, but intended principally for screen doors. It is easily put on, as there are no loose parts, and the directions for putting on are exceedingly simple and easily understood by anyone. Price, each............ 37c

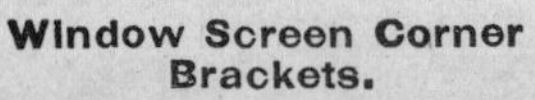

Window Screen Corner Brackets.

No. 9R2049 Tuscan bronzed, packed with screws, four brackets to a set.

Price, per set............ 6c

Per dozen sets............ 62c

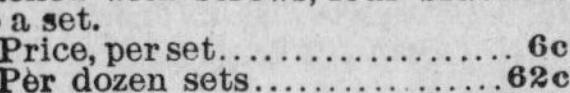

Door Screen Brackets.

No. 9R2050 Tuscan bronzed, with screws. Four large corner brackets and two center pieces to a set. Price, per set.......... $0.18

Dozen sets. 2.12

Screen Door Brace.

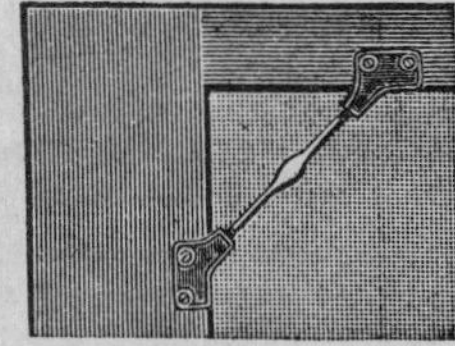

No. 9R2053 This Brace is intended for screen doors which have sagged so as to strike the door frame. The bolt has right and left screws at the ends, and by turning this bolt the door is readily brought back to its proper position and held there. Can be used on any screen door, and will prevent sagging, so that the door will swing freely and close tight. It can be adjusted at any time without the use of tools.

Price, each............ 5c

Warner Door Spring.

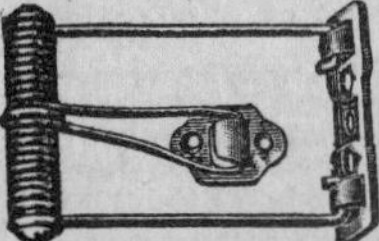

No. 9R2061 The old favorite from latest improved patterns and designs. Up to date in all points.

Price, each............ 6c

GIVE CATALOGUE NUMBER IN FULL

WHEN YOU WRITE YOUR ORDER.

Screen Door Springs.

No. 9R2065 Coiled Wire Door Spring, made of heavy steel spring wire, japanned, adjustable tension. Weight, 11 ounces.

Price, each......... 9c

The Torrey Door Spring.

No. 9R2066 Torrey Door Spring, is without doubt the best cheap door spring made. So well known, description is not necessary. Weight, 12 ounces.

Price, each............ 11c

No. 9R2066

Spiral Door Springs.

Spiral Door Spring, attached to door by two screw eyes. It consists of a closely coiled steel wire spring, made in four different sizes, of the best crucible steel wire with hooks at each end and screw eyes to be inserted in door and casing and bracket for off-set. If properly adjusted, nothing can be more effective.

No. 9R2071 For screen doors. Each.......... 3c

No. 9R2072 For ordinary inside door. Each.. 4c

No. 9R2073 For outside door. Each.......... 5c

No. 9R2074 For heavy outside door. Each.... 6c

Screen Door Catches.

No. 9R2080 Screen Door Catch, German bronzed iron with stop, for doors from ⅝ to 1⅜ inches thick. This is the style commonly used, and is **for inside of door opening out.** Packed complete with knobs and screws.

Price, each............ 11c

No. 9R2081 Screen Door Catch. Same as shown above, electro bronze plated.

Price, each............ 20c

Screen Door Catches.

No. 9R2082 Screen Door Catch. Electro bronze plated, for doors ⅝ to 1⅜ inches thick, **for inside of doors opening in.** This is not much used. Be sure to order the right catch.

Price, each............ 20c

No. 9R2083 Screen Door Catch, same as above, German bronzed.

Price, each............ 11c

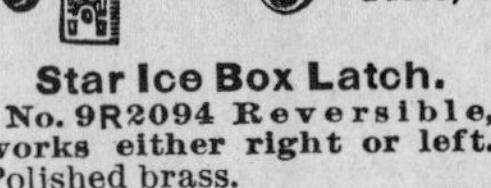

Star Ice Box Latch.

No. 9R2094 Reversible, works either right or left. Polished brass.

Price, each 54c

No. 9R2096 Star Ice Box Latch, solid brass, polished and nickel plated.

Price, each............ 60c

Thumb Latches.

No. 9R2100 Enameled Thumb Latch; very handsome. Weight, about 1 pound. Packed complete with screws. **Suitable for doors ⅞ to 1½ inches thick.**

Price, each 5c

Door Latches.

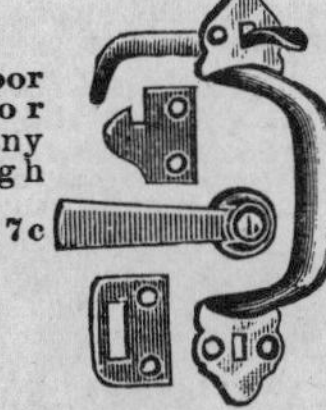

No. 9R2104 Japanned Door Latch, just the thing for barn doors hung on hinges, or any heavy door subject to rough usage.

Price, each... 7c

Japanned Store Door Latch.

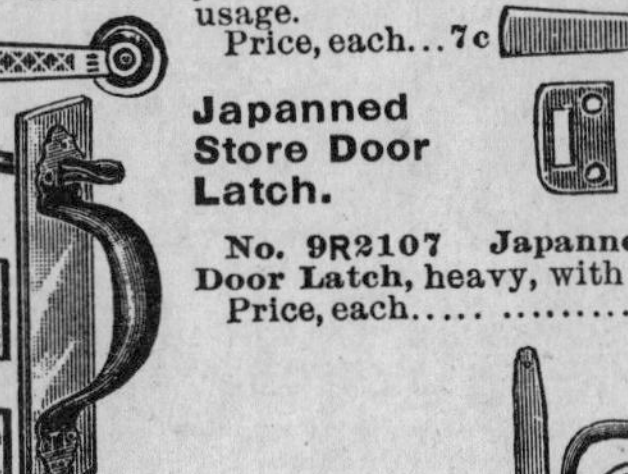

No. 9R2107 Japanned Store Door Latch, heavy, with plate.

Price, each............ 9c

Barn Door Latches.

No. 9R2110 Barn Door Latches. Japanned, extra heavy; with wrought latch.

Price, each............ 10c

ALUMINUM LETTERS AND FIGURES.

THERE IS NO METAL SO WELL ADAPTED FOR HOUSE NUMBERS AND SIGNS AS ALUMINUM. It does not rust, tarnish or corrode, but will always retain its bright silvery luster, and is not affected in any way by being exposed to the weather. Our letters and figures are made of heavy cast aluminum, of a pleasing pattern, with surface all polished and edges rounded, except the 2-inch numbers, which are flat, and are provided with prongs on back for the purpose of securing them onto wood. By the use of these letters and figures you can make durable, elegant looking signs at a less price than you could have an inferior sign made by a sign painter. **Postage on 2-inch, per dozen, 5 cents; 3-inch, per dozen, 7 cents.**

No. 9R2112 Cast Aluminum Letters, 3 inches high.

Price, each, any letter.......... 8c

No. 9R2113 Cast Aluminum Periods or Commas, for use with above. Price, each.............. 2c

No. 9R2114 Cast Aluminum Figures. 2 inches high. Flat.

Price, each, any figure.............. 5c

No 9R2115 Cast Aluminum Figures, 3 inches high. Oval.

Price, each, any figure.......... 7c

Iron and Brass House Numbers.

No. 9R2116 House Number, Flat, made of iron, polished and **nickel plated; 3 inches long;** provided with spurs, so no screws are necessary to fasten them on.

Price, each............ 3c

No. 9R2117 House Number, Oval, made of brass, handsomely designed, finely polished, and heavily **nickel plated; 3 inches long;** no screws required to fasten them on. Price, each............ 7c

Iron Storm Threshold.

No. 9R2120 No matter how exposed your doors may be or how severe the rain may beat against them, no rain will beat under them if you **use this iron storm threshold.** From 30 to 36 inches, inclusive, are cast in one piece; above 36 inches the sizes are made with a centerpiece, 30 inches in length and ends to make **any size desired.** Size given is width between jambs.

Size, inches	28	30	32	34	36	38	40
Price, each	55c	57c	58c	72c	90c	$1.00	$1.07

Weights range from 7 lbs. up, according to size. See Nos. 9R2475 to 9R2484 for weatherstrips.

Foot Scrapers.

No. 9R2125 Made from one piece best Bessemer steel. 6 inches wide, 3¾ inches high, edge dressed smooth so that it will remove mud or ice without cutting the shoe. Will not bend, and being made from steel instead of cast iron, cannot be broken by a sharp blow. Price, each...... 11c

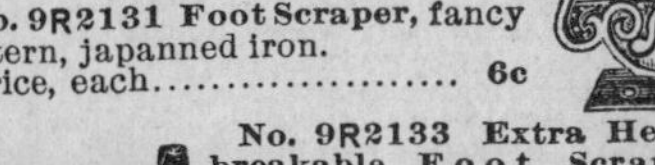

No. 9R2128 Iron, japanned, to screw on step. Weight, 10 ounces.

Price, each............ 4c

No. 9R2131 Foot Scraper, fancy pattern, japanned iron.

Price, each............ 6c

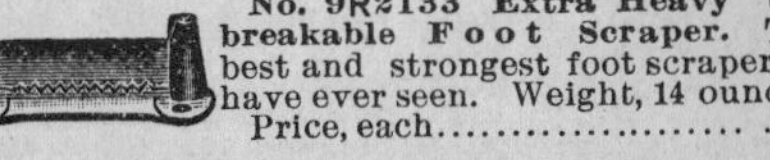

No. 9R2133 Extra Heavy Unbreakable Foot Scraper. The best and strongest foot scraper we have ever seen. Weight, 14 ounces.

Price, each............ 7c

Wrought Iron Door Bolts.

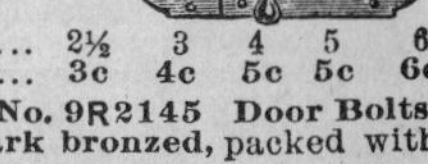

No. 9R2140 Wrought Iron Door Bolts. Japanned plate; brass knob; polished bolt.

Length of bolt, inches	2½	3	4	5	6
Price, each	3c	4c	5c	5c	6c

No. 9R2145 Door Bolts, dark bronzed, packed with screws.

3-inch, each............ 6c

4-inch, each............ 7c

5-inch, each............ 8c

No. 9R2146 Spring, square bolt; wrought iron; polished bolt; japanned plate.

Size, inches	3	4	5	6
Price, each	3c	4c	5c	6c

Neck Bolts.

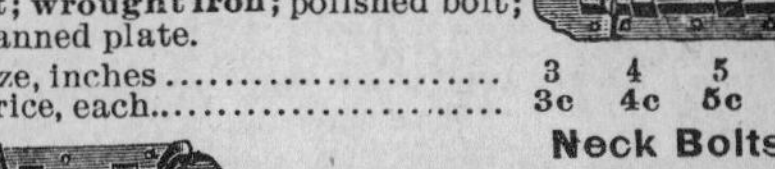

No. 9R2147 Neck bolts; wrought iron; polished bolt; japanned plate.

Size, inches	3	4	5	6
Price, each	3c	4c	5c	6c

Barn Door Bolts.

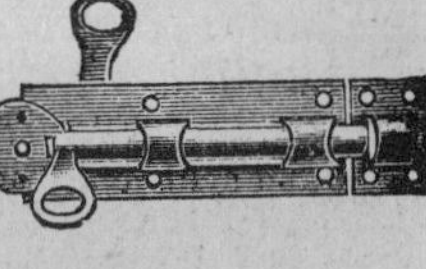

No. 9R2150 Barn Door Bolts, japanned, with heavy bolt. Length, 8 inches.

Price, each........ 17c

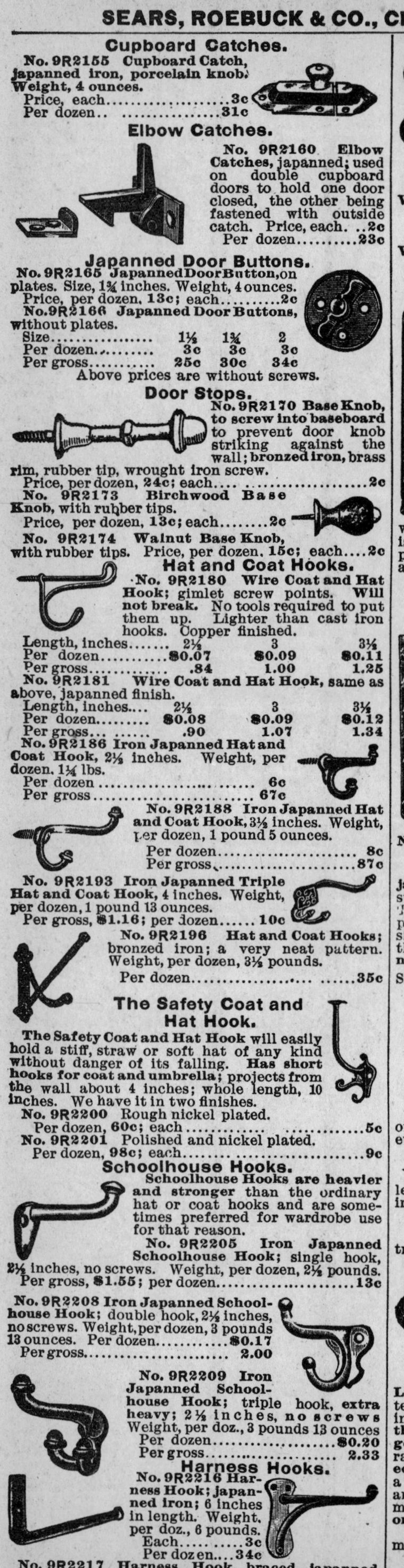

Cupboard Catches.

No. 9R2155 Cupboard Catch, japanned iron, porcelain knob. Weight, 4 ounces.
Price, each..........................3c
Per dozen.. ....31c

Elbow Catches.

No. 9R2160 Elbow Catches, japanned; used on double cupboard doors to hold one door closed, the other being fastened with outside catch. Price, each. ..2c
Per dozen..........23c

Japanned Door Buttons.

No. 9R2165 Japanned Door Button, on plates. Size, 1¾ inches. Weight, 4 ounces.
Price, per dozen, 13c; each..........2c

No. 9R2166 Japanned Door Buttons, without plates.

Size	1½	1¾	2
Per dozen	3c	3c	3c
Per gross	25c	30c	34c

Above prices are without screws.

Door Stops.

No. 9R2170 Base Knob, to screw into baseboard to prevent door knob striking against the wall; **bronzed iron, brass rim,** rubber tip, wrought iron screw.
Price, per dozen, 24c; each..........2c

No. 9R2173 Birchwood Base Knob, with rubber tips.
Price, per dozen, 13c; each........2c

No. 9R2174 Walnut Base Knob, with rubber tips. Price, per dozen, 15c; each....2c

Hat and Coat Hooks.

No. 9R2180 Wire Coat and Hat Hook; gimlet screw points. **Will not break.** No tools required to put them up. Lighter than cast iron hooks. Copper finished.

Length, inches	2½	3	3½
Per dozen	$0.07	$0.09	$0.11
Per gross	.84	1.00	1.25

No. 9R2181 Wire Coat and Hat Hook, same as above, japanned finish.

Length, inches	2½	3	3½
Per dozen	$0.08	$0.09	$0.12
Per gross	.90	1.07	1.34

No. 9R2186 Iron Japanned Hat and Coat Hook, 2½ inches. Weight, per dozen, 1¼ lbs.
Per dozen..........6c
Per gross..........67c

No. 9R2188 Iron Japanned Hat and Coat Hook, 3½ inches. Weight, per dozen, 1 pound 5 ounces.
Per dozen..........8c
Per gross..........87c

No. 9R2193 Iron Japanned Triple Hat and Coat Hook, 4 inches. Weight, per dozen, 1 pound 13 ounces.
Per gross, $1.16; per dozen......10c

No. 9R2196 Hat and Coat Hooks; bronzed iron; a very neat pattern. Weight, per dozen, 3½ pounds.
Per dozen..........35c

The Safety Coat and Hat Hook.

The Safety Coat and Hat Hook will easily hold a stiff, straw or soft hat of any kind without danger of its falling. **Has short hooks for coat and umbrella;** projects from the wall about 4 inches; whole length, 10 inches. We have it in two finishes.

No. 9R2200 Rough nickel plated.
Per dozen, 60c; each..........5c

No. 9R2201 Polished and nickel plated.
Per dozen, 98c; each..........9c

Schoolhouse Hooks.

Schoolhouse Hooks are heavier and stronger than the ordinary hat or coat hooks and are sometimes preferred for wardrobe use for that reason.

No. 9R2205 Iron Japanned Schoolhouse Hook; single hook, 2½ inches, no screws. Weight, per dozen, 2½ pounds.
Per gross, $1.55; per dozen..........13c

No. 9R2208 Iron Japanned Schoolhouse Hook; double hook, 2½ inches, no screws. Weight, per dozen, 3 pounds 13 ounces. Per dozen..........$0.17
Per gross..........2.00

No. 9R2209 Iron Japanned Schoolhouse Hook; triple hook, extra heavy; 2½ inches, no screws. Weight, per doz., 3 pounds 13 ounces
Per dozen..........$0.20
Per gross..........2.33

Harness Hooks.

No. 9R2216 Harness Hook; japanned iron; 6 inches in length. Weight, per doz., 6 pounds.
Each..........3c
Per dozen....34c

No. 9R2217 Harness Hook, braced, japanned iron, 8 inches long. Weight, per dozen, 10½ pounds.
Per dozen, 50c; each..........5c

Harness Hooks.

No. 9R2220 Harness Hooks; japanned, extra heavy.

Length, ins.	6	8	10½
Price, each..	5c	5c	17c
Per dozen...	49c	58c	$2.00

Wardrobe Hooks.

No. 9R2225 Coppered Wire Wardrobe Hook. Length, 2 inches.
Price, per dozen..........$0.13
Per gross..........1.45

No. 9R2226 Japanned Wire Wardrobe Hook. Length, 2¼ inches.
Price, per dozen..........$0.13
Per gross..........1.55

Folding Steel Shelf Bracket.

No. 9R2257 Folding Steel Shelf Bracket. As easy to operate as a table leaf. Locks automatically when lifted up, folds down against the wall entirely out of the way when not in use. **A boon to housekeepers for kitchen, pantry, dining room and sewing room shelves.** Takes the place of a small table. Just the thing for shelves in stores to display goods on. Indispensable in many places where a shelf is not in constant use, or where space is limited. Made for shelves 8 to 20 inches wide. A pair of any size will easily support 500 pounds. They are finished in beautiful black enamel.

Sizes, inches	8x8	12x12	16x16
Price, per pair	20c	30c	50c

Shelf Brackets.

No. 9R2260 Wire Shelf Brackets, japanned. Are stronger and lighter than cast iron brackets.

Size	4x5	5x7	6x8
Per pair..	3c	4c	6c
Size....	7x9	8x10	10x12
Per pair..	7c	8c	11c

No. 9R2260

No. 9R2262 Shelf Brackets. German bronzed, fancy design, same as cut.

Size	Per pair
4x 5	7c
5x 7	10c
6x 8	11c
8x10	17c
9x12	24c

No. 9R2262

No. 9R2263 Shelf Brackets; japanned; made of wrought steel and will never break. They are rapidly taking the place of the common cast iron shelf brackets, which are brittle and unreliable. **Price does not include screws.**

Size, inches	Price, per pair
3x4	3c
4x5	4c
5x7	6c
6x8	8c
7x9	9c
8x10	11c
10x12	15c
12x14	23c

Hand Rail Screws.

No. 9R2288 Hand Rail Screws, made of wrought iron, with two nuts. Diameter, 5/16-inch; length, 4½ inches.
Price, per dozen, 32c; each..........3c

No. 9R2289 Hand Rail Screw, made of wrought iron, with one nut and gimlet pointed screw. Diameter, 5/16-inch; length, 4 inches. Price, per dozen, 25c; each..........3c

Hand Rail Brackets.

No. 9R2290 Hand Rail Bracket, electro bronze plated, 3½ inches.
Price, each..........15c

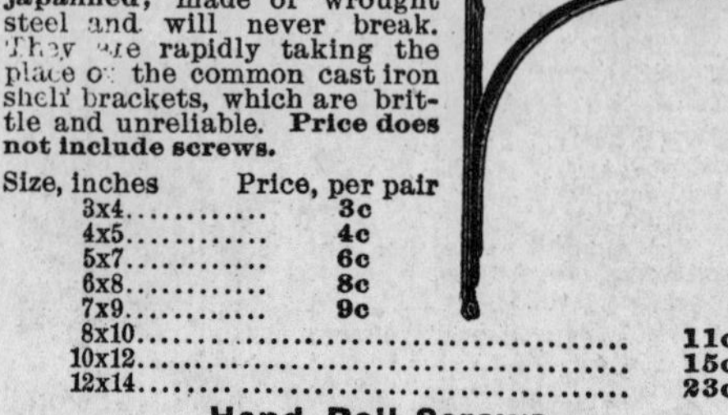

Sash Fasts.

No. 9R2300 Sash Lock; a neat pattern, enameled, iron finish. Price, each, 3c
Per dozen..........32c

Ives' Sash Locks.

Ives' Burglar Proof Sash Lock is pronounced by architects and builders to be the best in use. **When locked they draw the two sashes tightly together,** which prevents their rattling. **They cannot be opened from the outside** by putting a thin knife blade between sash and pushing the hook open, as is the case with common sash locks. **They are ornamental and easily put on.** Packed with screws.

No. 9R2325 Ives' Burglar Proof Sash Lock, medium size, Ogee tipped, ornamental iron.
Price, per dozen, 39c; each..........4c

No. 9R2328 Ives' Burglar Proof Sash Lock, medium size, ornamental iron; bronzed, with bronze metal knob. Price, per dozen, 68c; each..........6c

No. 9R2331 Ives' Burglar Proof Sash Locks. Large size, ornamental iron, bronzed bell tip.
Price, each..........4c
Per dozen..........48c

No. 9R2334 Ives' Burglar Proof Sash Lock. Large size, ornamental iron, bronzed, with bronze metal bell tip. Price, per dozen, 85c; each..........8c

No. 9R2337 Ives' Bell Tip Plain Sash Fasts. Medium size, electro bronze plated.
Price, each..........$0.12
Per dozen..........1.40

No. 9R2340 Ives' Bell Tip Plain Sash Fasts, medium size, genuine bronze metal, highly polished. Price, per dozen, $2.80; each..........23c

No. 9R2343 Ives' Bell Tip Plain Sash Fasts. Large size. Electro bronze plated.
Price, each...$0.21
Per dozen.... 2.45

No. 9R2346 Ives' Bell Tip Plain Sash Fasts. Large size. Electro copper plated, antique copper finish. Price, per dozen, $2.63; each..........22c

No. 9R2349 Ives' Bell Tip Plain Sash Fasts. Large size. Genuine bronze metal. Highly polished.
Price, per dozen, $3.92; each..........33c

The Signal Sash Lock.

This cut illustrates the simplest sash lock ever invented. It cannot be picked or tampered with, and is perfectly burglar proof.

The part to which the lever is attached fastens on upper sash and locks with certainty over the wide front plate. The lever is in plain sight when unlocked and there can be no mistake made in locking the sash. It lifts the upper sash to place and draws both sash together tight.

No. 9R2370 Signal Sash Lock, made of iron, copal bronzed; packed complete, with screws.
Price, per dozen, 36c; each..........3c

No. 9R2372 Signal Sash Lock, electro bronze plated, plain polished finish; packed complete, with screws.
Price, per dozen, 96c; each..........8c

No. 9R2374 Signal Sash Lock, electro bronze plated, antique copper finish; packed complete, with screws.
Price, per dozen, 96c; each..........8c

No. 9R2377 Signal Sash Lock, made of genuine bronze metal, plain polished finish; packed complete, with screws. Price, per dozen, $2.00; each, 17c

Window Springs.

No. 9R2390 Window Springs, screw socket. Self fastening iron case. Malleable iron bolt. Fits ¾-inch hole.
Per dozen..........20c

Window Screen Frame Spring Bolts.

No. 9R2395 Window Spring Bolt, for screen frames, japanned, tin case. Length of case, ⅞ inch, entire length, 3 inches. Per gross, $1.22; per doz., 11c

Window Spring Bolts.

No. 9R2397 Window Spring Bolts, japanned, silvered tip, tin case. Per gross, $1.18; per dozen, 10c

No. 9R2400 Window Spring Bolts, japanned tip, tin case. Weight, per doz., 14 oz. Price, per gross, 83c; per dozen..........7c

Stop Bead Screws and Washers.

For windows and doors. With beveled washers.

No. 9R2405 Blued Stop Bead Screws and Washers complete.
Per gross, 39c; per dozen..........4c

No. 9R2406 Antique Copper Plated (on iron) Stop Bead Screws and Washers complete.
Per gross, 54c; per dozen..........5c

No. 9R2407 Nickel plated (on iron) Stop Bead Screws and Washers complete.
Per gross, 70c; per dozen..........6c

No. 9R2408 Genuine Bronze Stop Bead Screws and Washers, plain bronze finish, complete.
Per gross, $1.10; per dozen..........10c

No. 9R2409 Genuine Bronze Stop Bead Screws and Washers, antique copper finish, complete.
Per gross, $1.27; per dozen..........11c

No. 9R2410 Genuine Bronze Stop Bead Screws and Washers, nickel plated, complete.
Per gross, $1.50; per dozen..........13c

Ives' Stop Adjuster.

In appearance it is neat and ornamental, **affording a quick and simple adjustment of the shrinkage or expansion of window stops,** doing away with unsightly weather strips and anti-rattler devices. To apply, use one-half inch bit.

No. 9R2411 Ives' Stop Adjuster, as described above. With screws. Plain polished bronze metal.
Price, per gross, $2.00; per dozen..........17c

No. 9R2414 Ives' Stop Adjuster, as described above. With screws. Nickel plated.
Price, per gross, $2.44; per dozen..........21c

No. 9R2417 Ives' Stop Adjuster, as described above. With screws. Antique copper.
Price, per gross, $2.44; per dozen..........21c

Sash Pulleys.

No. 9R2425 Common Iron Sash Pulley. 2-inch ground wheel. Per dozen............18c

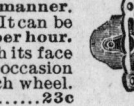

No. 9R2429 The Empire Pattern Sash Pulley. No screws required. All mortising done with an auger bit. No mortising or countersinking for face plate. Has ¼-inch steel axles. Ground 2-inch wheel. Per dozen.........23c

No.9R2430 The Common Sense Pattern Pulley. It is made in a first class manner. Mortise made with a 1-inch bit. It can be applied by hand at the **rate of 80 per hour.** It is firmly held by screws through its face plate, and easily removable when occasion requires. Plain face, polished 2-inch wheel. Price, per dozen..........................23c

Vanderbilt Sash Balances.

All Vanderbilt Balances are coppered inside as well as outside, therefore are not liable to rust.

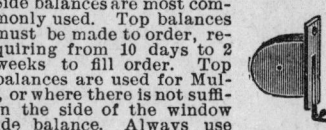

All balances are tested with great care and we fully warrant every one. **The above illustration shows the manner in which these balances are applied.** Directions are sent with each set. Prices below are for either side or top balances. Side balances are most commonly used. Top balances must be made to order, requiring from 10 days to 2 weeks to fill order. Top balances are used for Mullion windows, or where there is not sufficient room in the side of the window frame for side balance. Always use side balance when possible.

No. 9R2440 Vanderbilt Side Balances.
No. 9R2441 Vanderbilt Top Balances.

Per set of four balances, enough for two sashes.

Size No.	Weight of each sash, pounds	Height of sash, inches	Price per set
6	4 to 6	34	$0.80
8	6 to 8	34	.87
10	8 to 10	34	.90
12	10 to 12	44	1.04
14	12 to 14	44	1.18
16	14 to 16	44	1.25
18	16 to 18	48	1.35
20	18 to 20	48	1.45
22	20 to 22	48	1.52
24	22 to 24	48	1.62
26	24 to 26	50	1.72
28	26 to 28	50	1.82
30	28 to 30	50	1.86
32	30 to 32	50	1.92
34	32 to 34	50	1.99
36	34 to 36	50	2.06

We furnish any size balance up to 58 pounds. Prices quoted on application.

Sash Cord.

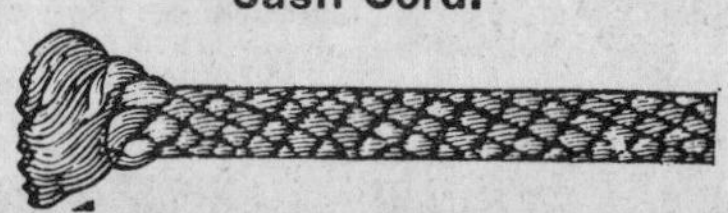

No. 9R2445 Silver Lake Braided Sash Cord, size, 8-32. Put up in bundles of 100 feet. Weight, about 2½ pounds to the bundle. Price, per bundle......70c

No. 9R2446 Standard Braided Cotton Sash Cord, not Silver Lake, but in our opinion **equal to it in every way.** Put up in bundles of 100 feet. Price, per bundle..........................52c

"American" Sash Chain.

While the first cost of chain is more than for cord, when the cost and annoyance of frequently replacing the cord is considered, it will be found to be nearly as cheap or cheaper.

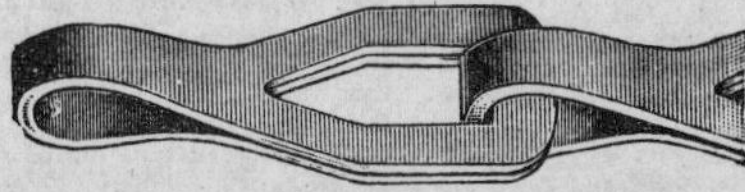

No. 9R2447 Polished Steel "American" Sash Chain. Capacity indicates the heaviest sash the chain should be used for.

Sizes	1	2
Capacity, pounds	130	80
Price, per foot	1¾c	1½c

No. 9R2448 Hercules Metal "American" Sash Chain. The most popular sash chain in the market. The kind used by the best architects and builders.

Sizes	1	2
Capacity, pounds	100	80
Price, per foot	3¾c	3c

No. 9R2449 Sash Weight Chain Fixtures. Consisting of fastening for sash and fastening for weight. Strong, durable and cheap. Set consists of attachments for one window of two sashes, or four weights. Price, per set.............8c

Transom Plates.

No. 9R2450 Sash Centers or Transom Plates, iron, japanned.

Length	1⅞	2⅞
Weight, per set, ounces	3	10
Price, per set of two	2c	4c
Per dozen sets	21c	40c

Set consists of two pairs of irons as shown in cut—four pieces in all.

Transom Lifters.

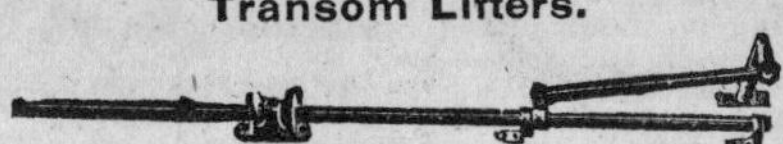

With this device transoms may be **lowered or raised at will with great ease and locked in** any position; no other fastenings required; when ordering, give size of transom and whether hinged at bottom, center or top. They are made from round iron rods, **bronzed and nicely finished.**

No. 9R2452 For transom hinged at top or hung in the middle.

Length	Diameter, ¼-inch Bronzed iron	Diameter, 5/16-inch Bronzed iron	Diameter, ⅜-inch Bronzed iron
3 feet. Each	12c	....	....
4 feet. Each	12c	27c	....
5 feet. Each	....	36c	41c
6 feet. Each	....	37c	51c
7 feet. Each	....	....	70c

No. 9R2453 To hang on bottom.

Length	Diameter		
4 feet.	5/16-inch.	Iron.	Each............36c
5 feet.	⅜-inch.	Iron.	Each............54c
6 feet.	⅜-inch	Iron.	Each............65c

WEATHER STRIPS.

It Is Economy to Use Weather Strips. The Cost Is Very Small and Can Be Saved in One Season on Fuel

to say nothing of the added comfort secured. Carpenters or any one without experience can make more than good day wages furnishing the strips and putting them up—and they can do it at a time when business is naturally dull. We ask those who buy in quantities to notice our very low prices.

We Sell Nothing but the Genuine Excelsior Weather Strip—The Best Made......

as we consider it is worth much more than the slight difference in cost over inferior goods. If less than four lengths are ordered, we must cut in short pieces to prevent breakage in shipping. Please specify to what lengths we shall cut. **Samples sent free on request.**

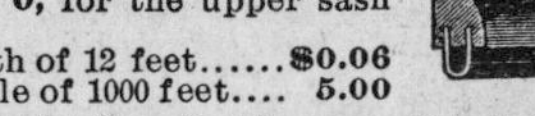

No.9R2475 The Excelsior Weather Strip, Size No. 0, for the upper sash of windows.
Price, per length of 12 feet......$0.06
Price, per bundle of 1000 feet.... 5.00

Weather Strips for Lower Sash.

No. 9R2476 The Excelsior Weather Strip, Size No. 1, for the lower sash of windows.
Price, per length of 12 feet.....$0.06
Price, per bundle of 1000 feet.. 5.00

Weather Strip for Doors.

No. 9R2477 The Excelsior Weather Strip, Size No. 1½, for sides and tops of doors.
Price, per length of 12 feet....$0.09
Price, per bundle of 1000 feet.. 6.88

No. 9R2478 The Excelsior Weather Strip, Size No. 2, for the center of windows.
Price, per length of 12 feet.......$0.09
Price, per bundle of 1000 feet........7.50

No. 9R2479 The Excelsior Weather Strip, Size No. 4, for bottom of light doors.
Price, per length of 12 feet..................12c
Price, per bundle of 1000 feet..........$10.00

No. 9R2480 The Excelsior Weather Strip, Size No. 7, for bottom of heavy doors.
Price, per length of 12 feet....$ 0.20
Price, per bundle of 1000 feet... 16.25

Patent Flexible Weather Strip.

No. 9R2481 Patent Rubber Flexible Weather Strip, Size No. 8, for the sides of windows. It is ⅝ inch wide. Put up in packages of 50 ft.
Price, per foot, any quantity.....1½c

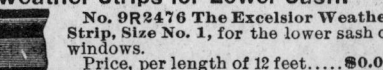

No. 9R2482 Patent Rubber Flexible Weather Strip, Size No. 9, for the sides of windows and doors. It is ½ inch wide. Put up in packages of 50 feet.
Price, per foot, any quantity..........2c

No. 9R2483 Patent Rubber Flexible Weather Strip, Size No. 10, for the sides and top of doors. It is ¾ inch wide. Put up in packages of 50 feet.
Price, per foot, any quantity.......2¼c

No. 9R2484 Patent Rubber Flexible Weather Strip. Size No. 11, for bottom of doors. It is 1-inch wide. Put up in packages of 50 feet.
Price, per foot, any quantity..........3c

Bosley's Rubber Threshold.

No. 9R2495 Bosley's Rubber Threshold. Constructed as shown in cut of two hardwood strips with pure rubber center piece properly fitted; this threshold will positively keep out snow, rain, cold and dust.

Length	3 ft.	3½ ft.	4 ft.	5 ft.	6 ft.
Each	64c	78c	88c	$1.18	$1.35

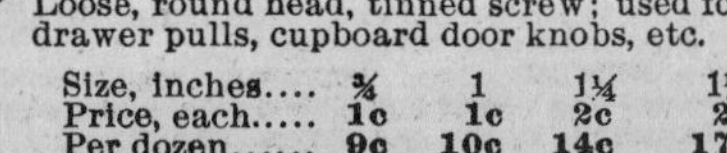

No. 9R2498 Porcelain Shutter Knobs. Loose, round head, tinned screw; used for drawer pulls, cupboard door knobs, etc.

Size, inches	¾	1	1¼	1½
Price, each	1c	1c	2c	2c
Per dozen	9c	10c	14c	17c

Drawer Pulls and Furniture Handles.

No. 9R2500 Flush Brass Drawer Pulls. Sizes given indicate width across plate.

Size, inches	1	1¼	1½
Weight, ounces	2	2	3
Price, each	5c	6c	8c
Per dozen	58c	72c	90

No. 9R2507 Tuscan Bronzed Drawer Pulls, 3½-inch. Packed complete with screws. Each weighs 4 ounces.
Price, each............2c
Per dozen.............15c

No. 9R2510 Fancy Stamped Furniture Handles. Gilt finish. Size of plate, 4x1¼ inches.
Price, each.................3c
Per dozen..................30c

No. 9R2512 Fancy Stamped Furniture Handles. Gilt finish. Size of plate, 4⅜x1⅝ inches.
Price, each....................4c
Per dozen.....................40c

No. 9R2515 Fancy Stamped Furniture Handles. Gilt finish. Size of plate, 5x2½ inches.
Price, each...........6c
Per dozen..........65c

No. 9R2518 Fancy Cast Furniture Handles. Gilt finish. Size of plate, 4¼x2¼ inches. Price, each 7c
Per dozen 75c

No. 9R2521 Fancy Cast Furniture Handles. Gilt finish. A new and handsome design. Size of plate, 4¼x2 inches.
Price, each..............$0.09
Per dozen................ 1.08

No. 9R2524 Fancy Cast Furniture Handles. Gilt finish. Size of plate, 4⅝x3¼ inches. A strong and handsome pull that is very popular.
Price, each............$0.14
Per dozen............ 1. 3

No. 9R2527 Drop Ring Pulls. Gilt finish, plate 1⅝ inch in diameter. The ring of this pull is iron, brass plated, making a strong, durable pull.
Price, per dozen, 35c; each....3c

No. 9R2530 Drop Ebony Pulls. Gilt finish plate; size of plate is 1⅝ inches in diameter; diameter of knob is 1¼ inches. Can be used on wood not thicker than 1¼ inches.
Price, per dozen, 39c; each......4c

No. 9R2532 Brass Knob Pulls. Diameter, 1-inch.
Price, each..... 6c
Per dozen........65c

No. 9R2533 Brass Knob Pulls. Diameter, 1¼ inches.
Price, per dozen, 87c; each.................8c

No. 9R2536 Fancy Cast Brass Knob Pulls. Diameter, 1½ inches.
Price, per doz., 78c; each....7c

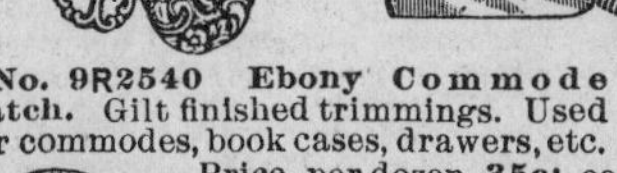

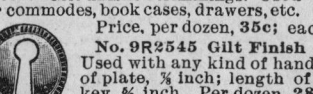

No. 9R2540 Ebony Commode Catch. Gilt finished trimmings. Used for commodes, book cases, drawers, etc.
Price, per dozen, 35c; each.........3c

No. 9R2545 Gilt Finish Escutcheon. Used with any kind of handle; diameter of plate, ⅞ inch; length of opening for key, ⅝ inch. Per dozen, 28c; each.. 3c

No. 9R2546 Fancy Stamped Escutcheon. Gilt finish. Used with any of our stamped handles. Size of plate, 1⅞x1⅛ inches; length of opening for key, ⅝ inch.
Per dozen, 16c; each...2c

No. 9R2548 Fancy Cast Escutcheon. Size, 2¼x1⅛ inches; length of opening for key, ⅝ inch. Used with any of our cast pulls or handles.
Price, each.........................3c
Per dozen..........................28c

No. 9R2550 Fancy Cast Escutcheon. Size, 2½x⅞ inches; opening for key, ⅝-inch. Price, each.......................3c
Per dozen.............................29c

Check Back Barn Door Hangers.

No. 9R2728 No screws or bolts furnished at the prices quoted. Diameter of wheel, inches 3 4 5 6
Price, per pair............18c 27 36c 45c

No. 9R2729 Double Flange Barn Door Rail to be used with above hangers, No. 9R2728; comes in pieces 2 feet long. No screws furnished at prices quoted.
Price, per foot..........2c

Barn Door Rollers.

No. 9R2733 Barn Door Steel Rollers to screw, wrought iron shank. Weight, 14 ozs. Price, each.......5c

No. 9R2735 Adjustable Steel Barn Door Stay Roller, does not turn from its proper position if correctly put on.
Price, each....8c

No. 9R2738 Barn Door Stay Rollers, adjustable to any thickness of door. Will always stay in the right position. The strongest adjustable stay in the market.
Price, each..........8c

No. 9R2742 Floor Stay Roller, for inside sliding barn doors. Heavy cast iron, japanned finish.
Price, each..........6c

No. 9R2746 Barn Door Pulls, extra heavy japanned. Weight, 10 ounces. Price, each..........3c

No. 9R2750 Yankee Door Catch for holding swing doors open. A very useful article for this purpose. Made of cast iron, japanned.
Price, each..........5c

Padlocks.

The Scandinavian Padlock is so well known it needs no description. Painted red. Two keys with each lock.
No. 9R2800 Size, 1⅝x2¼. Price, each....4c
If by mail, postage extra, each, 7 cents.
No. 9R2801 Size, 1⅝x2½. Price, each...5c
If by mail, postage extra, each, 11 cents.
No. 9R2802 Size, 1¾x3. Price, each..........6c
If by mail, postage extra, each, 15 cents.

No. 9R2805 Padlock. Case, cap and shackle made from hydro iron. All parts highly polished and quadruple nickel plated, making a cheap lock of exceptional brilliancy. Spring shackle, self locking, brass cylinder key guide, two flat steel keys each. Width, 2 inches. Each..10c

No. 9R2809 Case and cap formed of heavy steel, electro copper plated bright brass finish, steel shackle, keyhole guide of bronze metal, highly buffed; brass studs and rivet pins, tumblers, and two nickel plated steel keys. The action of the lock is spring opening and self locking. Width, 2 inches. Price, each..........12c

No. 9R2813 Solid Brass Padlocks, spring shackle, self locking, plain finish, complete with two flat steel keys. Size, 1⅜x2 inches. Price, each..........6c

Bronze Metal Padlocks.

No. 9R2816 Cast Bronze Metal Padlocks, self locking spring shackle. All inside work and springs are made of brass; extra quality and finish. Size, 1¼x2¼ inches; measurement includes shackle. Two flat steel keys. Price, each..........10c

No. 9R2819 Dust proof plunger, spring shackle, self locking, double locking bolts. Best padlock for the money ever sold. Size, which includes shackle, 1⅝x2⅝ in. Price, each.....19c

No. 9R2822 Spring shackle, self locking, all brass inside work, has 2 tumblers, etc. One of the most durable locks made; also **one of the most difficult locks to pick.** Complete with 2 keys. Size, 1⅞x2⅝ inches. Price, each...33c

No. 9R2823 Same Lock as above, with 9-inch tinned chain. Price, each..........37c

No. 9R2830 Spring shackle, self locking, spring drop over keyhole, rough finish; very heavy for **railroads, jails, warehouses, etc.** A strictly high grade lock and of the highest type of perfection in durability, workmanship and material. Nothing better made. Size, which includes shackle, 2⅝x3¼ inches. Two keys furnished with each lock.
Price, each..........58c

No. 9R2831 Same Lock as above with 10-inch japanned chain. Price, each..........64c

Solid Cast Gun Metal Extra Heavy Padlocks.

No. 9R2836 Extra strong shackle and locking bolts, bronze mechanism, dust proof plunger closing shackle opening, cylinder keyhole guide, spring shackle, self locking, two nickel plated flat steel keys. Width, 2 inches.
Price, each..........38c

No. 9R2837 Padlock, same as No. 9R2836. Width, 1⅝ inches. Price, each..........28c

No. 9R2838 Padlock, same as No. 9R2836. Width, 1⅛ inches. A strong and secure lock for cash boxes, etc. Price, each..........20c

No. 9R2845 Padlock, case, cap and shackle made from hydro iron. Locking mechanism and springs of bronze. This lock is exceptionally well made, highly polished and triple nickel plated. Spring shackle, self-locking brass cylinder key guide. Two flat, nickel plated steel keys. Width, 2¼ inches.
Price, each..........11c

No. 9R2848 Cast Gun Metal Four Lever Padlock. Phosphor bronze springs. Full independent levers operated with distinct key wards. Equal to any four-lever locks made. Two nickel plated steel keys. Width, 2 inches. Price, each..........24c

No. 9R2850 Six-Lever Padlocks are the finest, safest and most desirable padlock sold at a reasonable price. Cast bronze outside. Brass inside. Phosphor bronze springs, guaranteed not to rust or give out under the influence of any climate. **Two nickel plated flat steel keys** with each lock. Size, 2¼x2½ inches. Weight, 12 ounces.
Price, each..........33c

No. 9R2851 Same Lock as above, with tinned iron chain attached. Price, each..........40c

Long Shackle Six-Lever Padlocks.

Special Pattern Six-Lever Padlocks. Made of the same material as our No. 9R2850. **Has heavy elongated shackle.** Just the thing for gate or barn, as the long shackle will permit a chain or heavy staple being used. Size, 2¼x3 inches. **Complete with two flat steel keys.**
No. 9R2855 Price..........37c
No. 9R2856 Same Lock as above, with 9-inch tinned chain. Price, each..........45c

No. 9R2867 Wrought Iron Self Locking Padlocks. Size, 1⅞x2¼ inches.
Price, each..........4c

No. 9R2868 Wrought Iron Padlocks. Size, 2⅛x2⅞ in.
Price, each..........6c

No. 9R2869 Wrought Iron Brass Bushed Padlock, solid brass wheel, side ward, double chamber and double bitted keys. Extra fine finish. Size, 2⅝x3¼ in.
Price, each..........14c

Wrought Iron Padlocks, Brass Bushings.

No. 9R2870 Wrought Iron Padlocks, brass bushings, double chamber, one wheel ward revolving key pin, two double, bitted, flat steel keys, fine finish. Size, 2¼x3¾ inches.
Price, each..........16c

No. 9R2871 Wrought Iron Tumbler Chain Padlocks, with brass bushing on back, self locking, spring shackle with two flat double bitted steel keys, fine finish. Price, each..........20c

Small Padlocks.

No. 9R2872 Nickel Plated Brass Padlocks. Just the thing for small boxes, bags or dog collars. Width, 1 inch. Price, each......13c
No. 9R2873 Width, 1¼ inches. Price, each...14c
No. 9R2874 Width, 1½ inches. Price, each...15c

Drawer Locks.

No. 9R2900 Drawer Lock (may also be used for cupboard lock). Made of iron. Size, 2¼x1⅜ inches. Each.....5c

No. 9R2903 Drawer Lock. Made of iron. Size, 2x1¼ inches. Key pin, ⅝-inch from top of lock. **Three secure levers. Every key won't open this lock.** Price, each..........23c

Cupboard Locks.

No. 9R2908 Cupboard Lock. Bolt shoots right or left. Made of iron. Sizes, 3x1¾ inches. For doors not more than 1⅜ inches thick. Common key. Price, each..........4c

No. 9R2911 Cupboard Lock. Bolt shoots right or left. Made of iron. Size, 3x1¾ inches. For doors not more than 1⅜ inches thick. **Two secure levers.** Every key will not open this lock. Price, each..........23c

Chest Locks.

No. 9R2920 Brass Box Lock, for small boxes, cases, etc. Size, 1¼x¾ inches. Key pin, ⅛-inch from top of lock. Each.....5c

No. 9R2923 Brass Box Lock, like cut of No. 9R2920, Size, 1½x¾ inches. Key pin ⅜ inch from top of lock.
Price, each..........6c

No. 9R2926 Brass Box Lock, like cut of No. 9R2920 Size, 1⅜x1 inch. Key pin ⅛ inch from top of lock.
Price, each..........7c

No. 9R2929 Brass Chest Lock, double link. Size, 2x1¼ inches. Key pin ⅛ inch from top of lock.
Price, each..........16c

No. 9R2932 Brass Chest Lock, double link. Size, 2½x1⅛ inches. Key pin ¾ inch from top of lock.
Price, each..........18c

No. 9R2936 Spring Chest Lock. With double bitted key, size 4x3 inches, key pin 1¼ inches from top of lock, brass keyhole escutcheon.
Price, each..........42c

Brass Cylinder Locks.

Brass Cylinder Chest Lock. Size, 3x2 inches, 1⅛ inches from top of lock to center of keyhole, two flat steel keys, **four secure levers.**
No. 9R2940 For 1 -inch wood. Price, each...95c
No. 9R2941 For 1¼-inch wood. Price, each...96c
No. 9R2942 For 1½-inch wood. Price, each...97c

Secure Lever Locks.

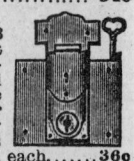

These locks cannot be picked except by a professional, and no key will unlock them unless it is like the original key. Each lock has two secure levers. We carry a full line of sizes. Note size carefully when ordering. Keys all different in a dozen.

No. 9R2950 Secure Lever Chest Lock. Double link, made of iron, size 1½x1⅛ inches, key pin ⅛ inch from top of lock. Price, each..........21c

No. 9R2951 Secure Lever Chest Lock. Double link, made of iron, size, 2x1¼ inches, key pin ⅝ inch from top of lock. Price, each..........22c

No. 9R2952 Secure Lever Chest Lock. Double link, made of iron, size, 2½x1¾ inches, key pin ¾ inch from top of lock. Price, each..........24c

No. 9R2953 Secure Lever Chest Lock. Double link, made of iron, size 3x2 inches, key pin ⅞ inch from top of lock. Price, each..........28c

No. 9R2954 Secure Lever Chest Lock. Double link, made of iron, size 3½x2¼ inches, key pin 1 inch from top of lock. Price, each..........31c

No. 9R2955 Secure Lever Chest Lock. Double link, made of iron, size 4x2⅝ inches, key pin 1¼ inches from top of lock. Price, each..........34c

Trunk Locks.

No. 9R2970 Trunk Lock. Size, 4x3 inches. Heavy iron, patent hasp. **A strong and durable lock,** well made and well finished. Each....12c

No. 9R2972 Excelsior Trunk Lock. Heavy wrought steel. Brass plated. Two keys. Price, each..........36c

COMBINATION LOCKS.

Strong, reliable, easily fitted. Not liable to get out of order. The chances of opening without previous knowledge of the combination do not exceed one in a million. Quickly unlocked. Directions for putting on and changing combination packed with each lock.

Combination Cupboard Locks.

No. 9R2975 Combination Cupboard Lock for use on lockers, closets, and cupboards in gymnasiums, etc. These combination locks soon earn their first cost by avoiding the expense and bother of replacing lost keys. As they are not worn by the action of a key, they are more durable. For either right or left hand doors. Size of lock case, 3x2¼ inches. Made of bronze and brass. The knobs and dial handsomely nickel plated. When ordering be sure to state what thickness of wood lock is to be used on.

Thickness of wood, inches....	⅞	1	1¼
Price, each..........	$1.20	$1.22	$1.25

Combination Drawer Locks.

No. 9R2977 Combination Drawer Lock. Size of lock case, 2x2¼ inches; drop, 1¼ inch; projects ¾ inch. Made of bronze and brass with the knob and dial handsomely nickel plated.

Thickness of wood, inches	Price, each
½	$1.08
¾	1.10
⅞	1.12

No. 9R2979 Combination Spring Lock for boxes or small chests. Size of lock case, 2x2¼ inches; drop, 1¼ inch. Made of bronze and brass with knob and dial handsomely nickel plated.

Thickness of wood, inches	Price, each
½	$1.50
¾	1.55
⅞	1.60

Combination Chest Locks.

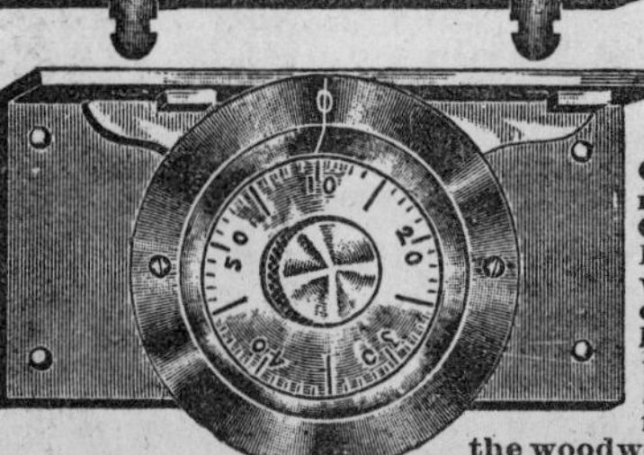

No. 9R2983 Combination Chest Lock, with flush dial to be let in so that the knob is flush with the woodwork. Made of brass with nickel plated dial. Packed complete with screws and directions. Size of lock case, 4x2¼ inches; drop, 1¾ inches.

Thickness of wood, in.	⅞	1	1¼	1½
Price, each..........	$1.98	$2.00	$2.03	$2.05

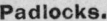

Roofing Tools.

The tools required for the proper application of our roofings and sidings are the fewest possible, and are now placed by us, as regards cost, within the reach of all.

Edging Tongs.

No. 9R3090 Edging Tongs; used in turning up the standing seam in roll cap roofing.
Price, each $1.50

Squeezing Tongs.

No. 9R3093 Squeezing Tongs; used in squeezing the seams on roll cap and pressed standing seam, or double cap roofing. Price, each, $1.50

Jointer.

No. 9R3095 Jointer or End Locker; used in making the end locks on V-crimp and pressed standing seam and other roofings.
Price, each 50c

Pressed Brick Siding.

No. 9R3096 Steel Pressed Brick Siding. A handsome, durable and fireproof siding at low cost. We furnish paint and nails. Weight per square, about 70 pounds.
Price, per square, painted, no allowance for lap $3.20
No. 9R3097 Price, per square, galvanized, $5.15

Beaded Sheets.

Our Beaded Steel Ceiling is made 25 inches to centers of outside bead, and any length to 10 feet. Beaded steel is used extensively for ceilings and sidings, and with a little care and ingenuity can be made very effective for ceiling work. In stock in 8-foot lengths.
No. 9R3120 Beaded Steel Sheets. 28-gauge. Weight, per square, about 69 lbs. We furnish complete with dry paint and nails.
Price, per square, no allowance for lap $3.25

Pressed Corrugated Iron.

Corrugated iron is used in very large quantities, and for varied purposes. One leading point should be carefully noted in comparing the different makes, and that is the distinction between pressed and rolled corrugated iron. The pressed being formed in dies and heavy presses, is always true in form; the rolled, as its name implies, is made on rolls, and cannot be true. The difference in the use of corrugated iron made by the two methods is, in the item for labor alone in laying it, from 20 to 25 per cent in favor of the pressed corrugated. We sell only the pressed corrugated.

Corrugated Iron, 28-gauge, with 2½-inch corrugations. Sheets are 26¼ inches wide. Allowing one corrugation for lap on each side, it leaves a covering surface 24 inches wide, which lays to advantage on rafters 24 inches, center to center. The end lap should be from 2 to 6 inches. Sheets are 5, 6, 7, 8, 9 and 10 feet long. We ship complete with dry paint and nails. If you send us a diagram as shown previously, we will send sheets that lay to best advantage. Painted, weighs 70 pounds per square. Galvanized, 85 pounds per square.
No. 9R3122 Price, per square, painted, no allowance for lap $3.00
No. 9R3123 Price, per square, galvanized, no allowance for lap $5.05

Corrugated Iron, 28-gauge, with 1¼-inch corrugations. Sheets same sizes as described above.
No. 9R3128 Painted both sides.
Price, per square, no allowance for lap $3.10
No. 9R3129 Galvanized, per square, no allowance for lap $5.15

Ridge Caps.

No. 9R3145 Ridge Cap. Makes a neat waterproof cap for the ridge of roofs. It is made in 8-foot lengths. We do not furnish cut lengths.

Diameter of roll, inches	1½	2	2½	3
Width of apron, inches	2	2½	3	3½
Price, per length, painted	32c	38c	45c	50c

No. 9R3146 Corrugated Ridge. Made in 2-foot lengths. We do not furnish cut lengths.
Price, per length, painted 22c

Lap Joint Eaves Trough.

No. 9R3150 Galvanized Lap Joint Eaves Trough. Made of 28-gauge steel, in 10-foot lengths. We do not furnish cut lengths.

Weight per length, pounds	5	5½	6	7	8
Size, inches	3½	4	4½	5	6
Price, per length	32c	36c	41c	48c	58c

Patent Slip Joint Eaves Trough.

No. 9R3151 Galvanized Slip Joint Eaves Trough. Made of 28-gauge steel. Made in 10-foot lengths. We do not furnish cut lengths. Size is taken inside of bead. Price includes one slip joint with each length of trough. Weighs about ½ pound per length more than lap joint.

Size, inches	3½	4	4½	5	6
Price, per length	34c	38c	43c	50c	60c

Galvanized Eaves Trough Corners.

No. 9R3153 Inside Corner, slip joint.
No. 9R3154 Inside Corner, lap joint.

Size	3½-inch	4-inch	5-inch	6-inch
Price, each	18c	21c	23c	26c

No. 9R3155 Outside Corner, slip joint.
No. 9R3156 Outside Corner, lap joint.

Size	3½-inch	4-inch	5-inch	6-inch
Price, each	18c	21c	23c	26c

Adjustable Outlets and End Cap.

The central cut in illustration above represents outlet in position, with end of trough closed with slip joint end cap. Outlet shown in small cut to the left is complete, and can be slipped on the trough at any point; the lip turned over the back edge of trough makes it perfectly secure and tight. Any one can put this on. No soldering needed.

No. 9R3160 Adjustable Outlet, shown in illustration by small cut on the left.

To fit eaves trough size	3½	4	4½	5	6
Price, each	23c	26c	29c	30c	35c

No. 9R3161 End Cap Slip Joint, shown in illustration by small cut on the right.

To fit eaves trough size	3½	4	4½	5	6
Price, each	6c	8c	9c	9c	10c

Eaves Trough Hangers.

No. 9R3170 Wire Eaves Trough Hanger.

Size	3½-in.	4-in.	4½-in.	5-in.	6-in.
Pr. doz	18c	23c	24c	25c	29c

No. 9R3172 Acme Eaves Trough Hangers, complete with rods and nut.

Size	3½-in.	4-in.	4½-in.	5-in.	6-in.
Per dozen	34c	35c	36c	38c	42c

No. 9R3173 Hanger Tongs and Wrench Combined. Price, each 50c

Corrugated Expanding Conductor.

Galvanized Corrugated Conductor is made in 10-foot lengths, without a cross seam. Will not burst when full of ice. No cut lengths furnished. Size of conductor suitable for eaves trough:

Size of eaves trough	3½	4	4½	5	6	7	8
Size of conductor	2	2	3	3	4	5	5

No. 9R3180 Round Corrugated Galvanized Conductor. Sizes, inches, 2 3 4 5 6
Price, per length... 40c 50c 68c 85c $1.00

GIVE CATALOGUE NUMBER IN FULL WHEN YOU WRITE YOUR ORDER

Elbows and Shoes.

Galvanized Flat Crimped Expanding.

When ordering, always specify by number the angle desired, as shown above.
No. 9R3181 Conductor Elbow, Angle No. 1.
No. 9R3182 Conductor Elbow, Angle No. 2.
No. 9R3183 Conductor Elbow, Angle No. 3.

Size, inches	2	3	4	5	6
Price, each	12c	15c	20c	25c	30c

No. 9R3184 Round Galvanized Corrugated Shoes.

Size, inches	2	3	4	5	6
Price, each	17c	21c	28c	34c	41c

Conductor Fastenings.

Tinned Conductor Hooks for round corrugated conductor.

Sizes, inches	2	3	4	5	6
No. 9R3185 For wood, per dozen	36c	47c	70c	86c	$1.08
No. 9R3186 For brick, per dozen	48c	72c	87c	$1.15	$1.35

Hooks for Conductors.

No. 9R3189 Tinned Conductor Hooks for corrugated round conductor.

Size, inches	2	3	4	5	6
For wood. Doz.	14c	29c	43c	59c	$1.13
For brick. Doz.	25c	40c	62c	87c	1.15

Conductor Strainers.

No. 9R3194 Galvanized Wire Conductor Strainers, placed in the outlet of eaves trough, prevents leaves, etc., from entering or stopping up the conductor. The size given designates the size outlet the strainer will fit.

Size, inches	2	3	4	5	6
Price, each	9c	11c	17c	20c	23c

Rain Water Cut Off.

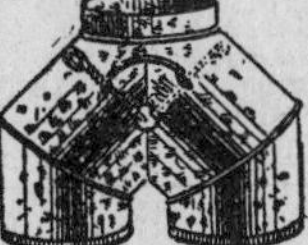

No. 9R3196 Galvanized Rain Water Cut Off; simple, durable and cheap.

Size	2-in.	3-in.	4-in.
Price, each	17c	20c	29c
Size	5-in.	6-in.	
Price, each	50c	60c	

Valley Tin.

No. 9R3198 Made of a good grade of tin plate in a continuous strip, locked and soldered. Full lengths are 50 feet long, but we can furnish any quantity.

	Per 50-ft. lengths	Per lineal foot
Width, 14 inches	$2.35	5½c
Width, 20 inches	3.35	7½c
Width, 28 inches	4.65	10½c

Tin Shingles or Flashings.

No. 9R3199 Made of a good grade of roofing tin and cut to exact sizes. Useful for repairing old roofs and in making a tight joint around chimneys, etc.

Size	Per 100	Each
5x 7 inches	$1.25	2c
7x10 inches	2.25	3c

OUR PRICES

ON METAL ROOFING, CONDUCTOR, EAVES TROUGH, ETC.

ARE SUBJECT TO MARKET CHANGES

PRICES ARE CORRECT at the time we go to press, but the market on this class of goods is in an unsettled condition. You can safely send us your orders at prices named, for if there should be a decline in the market we shall reduce our prices accordingly, and return the difference in cost to our customers.

OUR PRICES ARE ALWAYS RIGHT.

Our Customers are Always Safe in Dealing With Us.

MILL WORK. SASH, DOORS, BLINDS, AND MOLDINGS----

In this line we are prepared to save our patrons the unreasonable profit usually charged by the retail dealer. IT IS A COMMON PRACTICE with lumber dealers to sell Sash, Doors, etc., at a very small profit and get an exorbitant profit on the lumber. Look out for your local dealer on this scheme. On the other hand, they sometimes sell lumber at a small profit and make it up by an unreasonable profit on the Sash, Doors, etc.

HAVE A SEPARATE ESTIMATE MADE OF YOUR MILL WORK AND COMPARE WITH OUR PRICES. IT WILL PAY YOU TO DO SO.

OUR SPECIAL MILL WORK CATALOGUE IS REVISED EVERY TIME THE PRICES CHANGE, so our prices are always right at the bottom. You cannot afford to build a house without first consulting it, even if only to see that your local dealer does not overcharge you. **It is sent free on request.**

REMEMBER OUR GOODS ARE GUARANTEED to be strictly up to grade. We do not handle third quality doors. **Do not wait** until you need these goods before you send us your order. There is scarcely an order we receive but has some item that is irregular size or must be made, which causes **a delay of from five to ten days.** Some carpenters **cut a hole** and then order **a sash or door to fit it.** They should see **what size sash or door is regular** stock and cut the hole to fit the sash or door. This would enable us to **fill orders with more promptness,** and be more satisfactory to all parties concerned. All goods quoted by us in these lines are made of white pine, unless otherwise stated in descriptions.

FREIGHT RATES are very low on mill work. Do not let the matter of freight rates prevent you from sending your order to us. Get the rate from your station agent, or write to us for it. **Don't ask your local lumber dealer for freight rates.** Remember he is selfishly interested in the matter and his information may or may not be correct.

WE GUARANTEE SAFE DELIVERY and will REPLACE BROKEN GLASS on condition that consignee sends in paid expense bill, indorsed by freight agent, as to condition of doors or windows on arrival at destination, in order that we may put in claim against railroad company.

IN ORDER TO BE ABLE to continue to furnish sash, doors and mill work for some of the best houses that are being erected in the country, we must keep strictly up to date in designs, and therefore we offer this season an entirely new line of front doors. These doors were designed especially for us. They are new, and until our catalogue goes to press no doors of this pattern will have been sold. If you order one of these front doors from us you will have a door that is distinctly different from anything in your own vicinity; a door that is artistic. **They are securely crated for shipment. We furnish the doors ready for oil finish and they are always made after the order is received by us, so they will reach our customers perfectly clean.** Our carvings are wood, not a composition of sawdust and glue, such as are used in the cheap, inferior doors, which will soon crumble away. As these doors are made after the order is received you must allow from five to ten days for us to fill the order after it reaches us.

THE GLASS WE USE. By a process recently discovered, we produce design work of a most intricate and elaborate description at a very moderate cost. Notwithstanding the low cost, the work is not only as good but better than the most expensive work heretofore made, as it involves the delicate shades, perspective and halftone effects which have previously been considered impossible in this line of ornamentation. This glass must not be confounded with the ordinary sand blast work, as it is far more elaborate in general effects. This glass is used in our Floral and Woodland pattern doors. **Our combination geometric chipped glass is superior to anything that has ever been put on the market,** and the semi-obscurity, bright and general appropriateness of geometric chipped glazing are unexcelled. This glass is used in our Bon Ton doors.

WHEN SENDING US YOUR ORDER FOR DOORS AND SASH, DO NOT OVERLOOK OUR LINE OF BUILDERS' HARDWARE. We sell more builders' hardware to owners and builders, than any other concern on earth, and our prices will show you a saving of from 20 to 50 per cent from what you would have to pay were you to buy from your local dealer.

FANCY FRONT DOORS.

No. 9R3502 "Floral" Door, 1⅜ inches thick, solid molding, raised panels, glass capped top and bottom wood carvings. Glazed with first quality double strength glass, with neat flower design. For price see below.

No. 9R3503 "Floral" Door, 1¾ inches thick, otherwise same as above, For price see below.

No. 9R3506 "Woodland" Door, 1⅜ inches thick; solid molding, raised panels on both sides, glass capped top and bottom. Carved molding, door glazed with double strength glass, with tasty animal design. For price see below.

No. 9R3507 "Woodland" Door, 1¾ inches thick; otherwise same as above. For price see below.

No. 9R3510 "Bon Ton" Door, 1⅜ inches thick, solid moldings, raised panel pattern, panel hand carved, capped at bottom of glass, glazed with combination geometric chipped glass, glass center and colored cathedral, border light. For price see below.

No. 9R3511 "Bon Ton" Door, 1¾ inches thick, otherwise same as above. For price see below.

No. 9R3514 Our "Acme" Door, 1⅜ inches thick, solid molding, raised panels both sides, top panel hand carved. Capped top and bottom with heavy fancy hand carved wood ornament, glazed with leaded art glass, made up with a bevel plate glass center and venetian opalescent and cathedral glass. For price see below.

"Floral." "Woodland." "Bon Ton." "Acme." "Avenue." "Boulevard."

No. 9R3515 "Acme" Door, 1¾ inches thick, same as described above. For price see below.

No. 9R3518 "Avenue" Door, 1⅜ inches thick, solid molding, raised panels both sides, capped top and bottom, with side pillars and hand carved moldings, glazed with 1⅛-inch bevel polished plate glass. This is one of the handsomest doors ever made and is very rich. For price see below.

No. 9R3519 "Avenue" Door, 1¾ inches thick, same as described above. For price see below.

No. 9R3522 Our "Boulevard" Door, 1⅜ inches thick, flush artistic molded on one side, solid molded on the other. This door is glazed in 1⅛-inch bevel polished plate glass. This style of door is now used in the most expensively built houses in the country. It has a very rich appearance and is not gaudy. For price see below.

No. 9R3523 "Boulevard" Door, 1¾ inches thick. For price see below.

PRICE LIST OF FANCY FRONT DOORS.

Size	Thickness	Floral	Woodland	Bon Ton	Acme	Avenue	Boulevard
2 ft. 6 in. x 6 ft. 6 in.	1⅜	$4.15	$4.20	$5.05	$5.80	$5.85	$ 9.80
2 ft. 6 in. x 6 ft. 6 in.	1¾	5.45	5.50	6.35	7.10	7.15	11.10
2 ft. 8 in. x 6 ft. 8 in.	1⅜	4.40	4.45	5.25	6.00	6.50	12.15
2 ft. 8 in. x 6 ft. 8 in.	1¾	5.70	5.75	6.55	7.30	7.80	13.55
2 ft. 8 in. x 7 ft.	1⅜	5.00	5.05	5.85	6.40	7.15	13.20
2 ft. 8 in. x 7 ft.	1¾	6.30	6.35	7.15	7.70	8.45	14.50
2 ft. 10 in. x 6 ft. 10 in.	1⅜	4.95	5.00	5.75	6.20	7.40	14.05
2 ft. 10 in. x 6 ft. 10 in.	1¾	6.25	6.30	7.05	7.50	8.70	15.35
3 ft. x 7 ft.	1⅜	5.40	5.45	6.50	6.90	8.15	15.30
3 ft. x 7 ft.	1¾	6.70	6.75	7.80	8.20	9.45	16.60

Something New in the Cottage Oriel Windows.

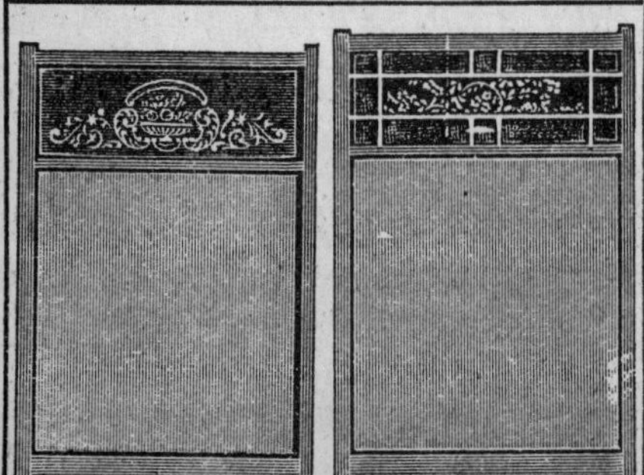

Kenwood Pattern. Glencoe Pattern.

THAT WE MAY GIVE OUR CUSTOMERS the very latest styles of goods that are strictly up to date, goods that are better than they can procure from local dealers, we have brought out these new cottage windows. They have been designed especially for us and can be obtained from no other source except they are counterfeits, and any other concern which will counterfeit our pattern, is likely to counterfeit the values and offer cheaper goods.

OUR KENWOOD PATTERN ORIEL WINDOW is made with plain double strength bottom light and double strength upper light with beautiful figure ornamentations. It is made either in one sash or as a check rail window, as you may desire.

No. 9R3428 Kenwood pattern window made in one sash.......................**For prices see list.**

No. 9R3429 Kenwood pattern window made in two check rail sash..................**For prices see list.**

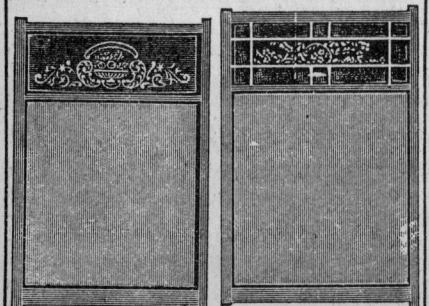

OUR GLENCOE PATTERN WINDOW is glazed with plain double strength glass in the bottom light, the top light is plain double strength center light with neat suitable design, with assorted border, lights made up of Ondoyant, Muranese Florentine, Alligator, Princess, Pyramidial, Iridescent and Arabesque arranged to harmonize. It is made either in one sash or in a check rail window, as may be desired.

No. 9R3430 Glencoe pattern window made in one sash. **For prices see list.**

No. 9R3431 Glencoe pattern window made in two check rail sash. **For prices see list.**

PRICE LIST OF COTTAGE WINDOWS.

Sizes of Opening	Sizes of Bottom Light	Sizes of Top Light	9R3428 Made in One Sash	9R3429 Made in Two Sash	9R3430 Made in One Sash	9R3431 Made in Two Sash
3 ft. 8 in. x 5 ft. 2 in.	40x42	40x14	$5.15	$5.20	$5.75	$5.80
3 ft. 10 in. x 5 ft. 6 in.	40x44	40x16	6.05	6.10	6.65	6.70
4 ft. x 5 ft. 6 in.	44x44	44x16	6.20	6.25	6.85	6.90
4 ft. 4 in. x 5 ft. 10 in.	48x46	48x18	7.50	7.55	7.20	7.25
4 ft. 4 in. x 6 ft. 2 in.	48x50	48x18	8.35	8.40	8.95	9.00
4 ft. 4 in. x 6 ft. 6 in.	48x54	48x18	9.05	9.10	9.65	9.70

Hog Ringers.

No. 9R4550 Hill's Pattern Hog Ringer. Price...6c

No. 9R4551 Hill's Pattern Hog Rings for above ringer; 100 rings in a box. Price, per dozen, 44c; per box............4c

No. 9R4552 Hill's Pattern Shoat Rings for above ringer; 100 rings in a box. Price, per doz., 44c; per box, 4c

No. 9R4553 Hill's Pattern Pig Rings for above ringer; 100 rings in a box. Price, per box..........4c Per dozen..........44c

No. 9R4554 Perfection Hog Ringer. Price, each..9c

No. 9R4555 Perfection Hog Rings, to be used with above ringer; 100 rings in a box. Price, per dozen boxes, 92c; per box............8c

Hill's Hog Holder.

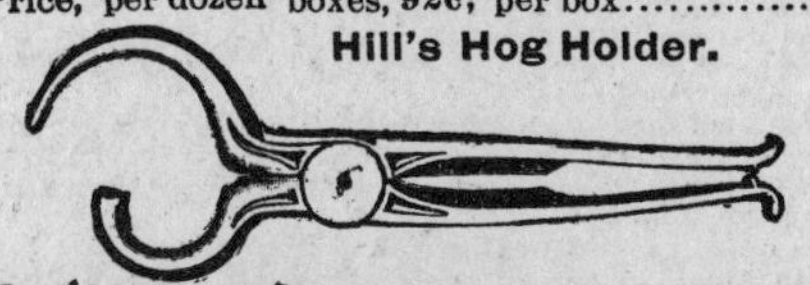

No. 9R4560 Hill's Hog Holder, for holding hogs when placing rings in nose. Price, each..........25c

Cattle Punch.

No. 9R4583 Cattle Marking Punch is made according to the idea of an experienced cattleman. It is made to do good work, and last. Length, 10 inches. Size of dies, 1 inch long by ⅜ to ⅝ inch wide, according to design. Only one die can be used with each punch, but by means of gauge any part of die can be cut from edge of ear. To cut full pattern from ear remove the gauge. Weight, 22 ounces. Price, each, your choice of any one of above dies..........$4.60

Stock Marking Punch.

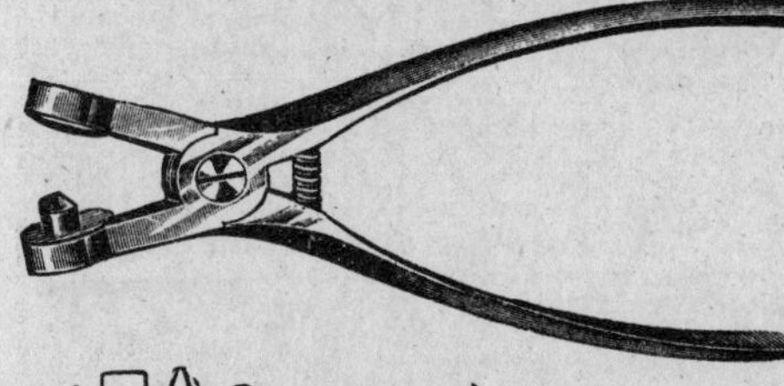

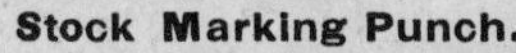

Nos. 1 2 3 4 5 6 7 8 9 10 11

No. 9R4586 Strong malleable iron handles, best steel cutting dies. Practical, strong and durable. The dies are from ¾ to ⅜-inch long; entire length of tool, 11¼ inches. The dies are hollow and cut, which is more humane than the use of solid dies which simply punch a hole through the ear. When ordering, state the number of the die you prefer. Weight, packed for mail or express, 1½ pounds. Price, each, your choice of any one of the above dies..........$1.75

Stock Marks.

No. 9R4600 Cast Iron Stock Marks, with raised letter—never wear out. Used with Perfection Ring and Ringer. Made only with any one single letter. Price, per dozen .... 5c Per 100..........38c

Brass Stock Marks.

Stock Mark to use with Perfection Ringer and Rings. Made of brass, about the size and thickness of a silver quarter dollar. The initial is stamped on mark with a steel stamp. State letter wanted when ordering. Ringer or rings are not included in prices quoted.

No. 9R4605 Stock Marks with any one letter or figure on one side. Price, per 100, 75c; per dozen..9c

No. 9R4606 Stock Marks with any two letters or figures on one side. Price, per 100, $1.25; per dozen.............15c

REFER TO HARNESS AND SADDLERY DEPARTMENT PAGES 382 TO 425 FOR THE BEST STOCK SADDLES AT THE LOWEST PRICES.

Stock Marks—Continued.

No. 9R4607 Stock Marks with any three letters or figures on one side. Price, per 100, $1.75; per dozen..........21c

No. 9R4608 Stock Marks, with consecutive numbers, on one side only—1-2-3-4-5—or any set of consecutive numbers not having more than three figures in the number. Price, per 100, $1.75; per doz., 21c

No. 9R4609 Stock Marks, with consecutive numbers on one side, any one letter or figure on the other. Price, per 100, $2.25; per dozen..........27c

No. 9R4610 Stock Marks, with consecutive numbers on one side, any two letters or figures on the other. Price, per 100, $2.75; per dozen..........33c

No. 9R4611 Stock Marks, with consecutive numbers on one side, any three letters or figures on the other. Price, per 100, $3.50; per dozen..........42c

Hog Tamer.

NEVER ROOT

No. 9R4615 Never Root Hog Tamer. Cuts across tip of nose with curve at each side and severing same in the middle, making two projections (above where two rings would be placed) heavy on the tips, their weight causing them to drop apart and heal quickly in that position; thus cutting only half as much as any other tamer, and leaving no loop to be torn off or hang over the nostrils. The tongs are made of good grade malleable iron; knife, of fine quality of steel, is T shaped and reversible, one edge for pigs and shoats, the other for large hogs—changed by removing the thumbscrew; holes in knife for thumbscrew are placed so as to make it self-adjusting to the gauges, on back of cutting plate, gauging the proper depth of cutting on various sizes of hogs. Weight, 15 ounces. Price, each..........60c

Hurd's Hog Tamer.

No. 9R4616 Hurd's Hog Tamer. Two different sizes of steel knives furnished with each tamer. Price, each 40c

Dehorning Tools.

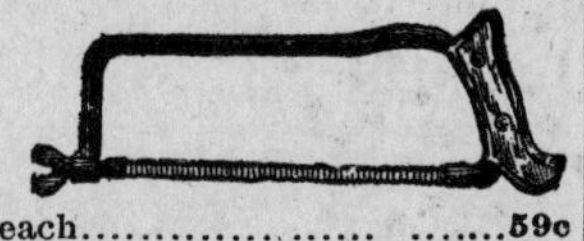

No. 9R4625 Dehorning Saw, with japanned malleable iron frame, beech handle, complete, with blade, 9½ inches long, ¼ inch wide. Price, each..........59c

No. 9R4626 Extra blades for this saw, each... 9c

Newton & McGee's Draw Cut Patent Dehorner.

With Latest Improvements. The frames are made of best malleable iron, and the blades of the best steel. Cuts perfectly smooth, heals quickly and causes the animal very little pain. They are fully guaranteed in every respect, and if any part should break from a flaw or defect, we will replace same without expense to the purchaser. They are made in three sizes.

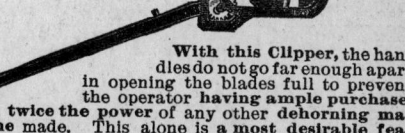

No. 9R4631 No. 1 Draw Cut Dehorner, is for calves only. Has a 2-inch opening. Length, 2 feet 3 inches. Weight, 4½ pounds. Price, each..........$2.90

No. 9R4632 No. 2 Draw Cut Dehorner, as described above, for young and medium aged cattle. Has a 3½-inch opening. Length, 3 feet 4 inches. Weight, 12 pounds. Price, each..........$5.25

No. 9R4633 No. 3 Draw Cut Dehorner, as described above, is for either young or old cattle. Has 4½-inch opening. Length, 3 feet 8 inches. Weight, 17 pounds. Price, each..........$5.70

Dr. H. W. Leavitt's Latest Dehorning Clipper.

With this Clipper, the handles do not go far enough apart in opening the blades full to prevent the operator having ample purchase, and twice the power of any other dehorning machine made. This alone is a most desirable feature, as this is power enough to clip any large horn with perfect ease to the operator. Will clip either small or large horns. Weight, 14 pounds.

No. 9R4638 Price, each..........$5.40

The Perfect Dehorner.

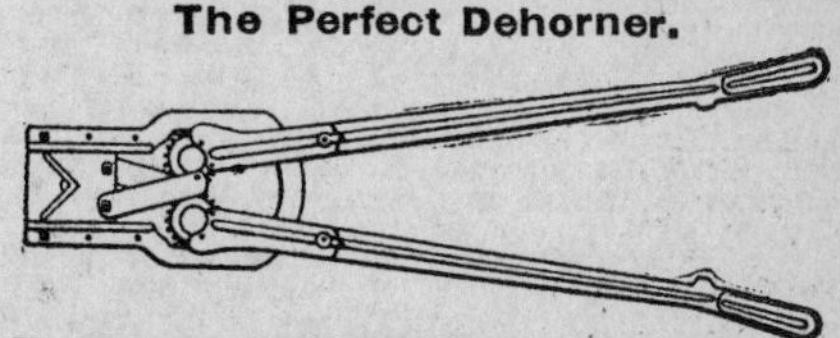

No. 9R4630 This Dehorner is offered to supply the demand for a simple, well made, strong dehorning tool at a low price. The main part of the instrument is made from wrought iron, the blades of tool steel, and it is practically unbreakable. The blades can be readily sharpened or replaced. The power obtained from the leverage is greater than in any other dehorner; it will cut instantly a horn of any size without crushing or twisting it. There are so few parts that we can sell these at a lower price than any dehorner made. Price, each..........$4.40

LEAVITT'S V SHAPE BLADE DEHORNING CLIPPER.

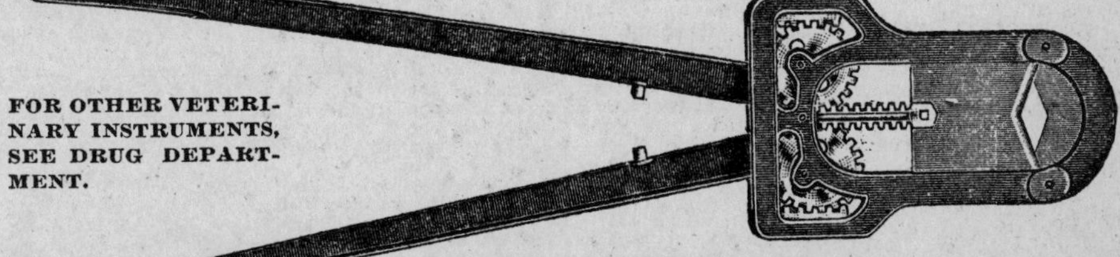

FOR OTHER VETERINARY INSTRUMENTS, SEE DRUG DEPARTMENT.

No. 9R4640 This illustration represents our V shape blade Dehorning Clipper, which cuts all around the horn as handles are closed. Knives cannot interlock, or cut into each other. Has double power and is guaranteed to be superior to any other dehorner made. This style dehorner is made in the large size (No. 3) only, but will clip any size horn from cattle of any age, smooth and clean.

In opening the blades, the handles do not go far enough apart to prevent the operator having ample purchase, and twice the power of any other dehorner made. This is a very desirable feature, as it has power enough to clip any large horn, with perfect ease to the operator.

ANOTHER IMPORTANT FEATURE.

It will be seen that in closing the clipper, the same power (the cogged handles) which drives the cogged plunger down on sliding blade, thus making a machine with two movable blades, with power from both sides of cogged handles. This clipper is made with only three bolts. One small bolt fastens cogged plunger to sliding knife, and acts as a stop for blade, making a 4-inch opening in large machine, which is large enough to admit any horn. The other two bolts fasten end blade.

WE CHALLENGE THE WORLD TO PRODUCE A CLIPPER WITH MERITS THAT EQUAL THE LEAVITT LATEST IMPROVED V SHAPE BLADE DEHORNING CLIPPER.

For we know that we have the best and most powerful Clipper on the market.

The material used in manufacturing this clipper is the best quality. The handles and U head frame are malleable, while the knives are of the best crescent steel; can be easily cleaned and do not tarnish, thus preventing all possibility of blood poisoning, often occurring from the use of inferior machines.

Every clipper is thoroughly tested before being sent out. Twisting or prying will cause the blades to break. We will not replace blades broken from this cause. Shipping weight, 14 pounds.

Price, each..........$5.25

No. 9R4641 Extra Sliding Knife for V blade Dehorner. Each.......... .40

No. 9R4642 Extra Stationary Knife for V blade Dehorner. Each.......... .40

No. 9R4643 Pair of Knives for V blade Dehorner. Per pair.......... .80

SEARS, ROEBUCK & CO.'S SHEEP SHEARS.

Our Sheep Shears are made of a high grade of cutlery steel, which is produced specially to meet the peculiar requirements of our goods. They are made with the best modern appliances and machinery, and our system of inspection is so thorough as to prevent any but perfect goods being sent out. **In finish and appearance,** as well as in quality and durability, our shears are superior to any other line on the market, either imported or domestic. **We guarantee every pair of shears to be perfect.** Each pair of sheep shears is examined and tested in wool before packing. **The blade of each shear is etched as follows:** "If this shear does not prove as good or better than any shear you ever had return it and money will be refunded." **Our prices are based on cost to manufacture** with only our one small profit added. We do not spend large sums to advertise the brand, we do not give away any to professional shearers to influence them to recommend our brands. We do make the best shear it is possible to produce and sell it at a price that cannot be named on shears which must bear a large advertising expense and the middleman profits.

No. 9R4652 Sears, Roebuck & Co.'s Great Western Sheep Shear. Double bow. Straight back and edge. **Full polished** blades. The shape and style used by professional shearers of the West. Don't let our low price cause you to doubt the quality of these shears. Our prices are as high as we think the best shear on earth should sell for—through our factory to consumer one profit plan. They are etched on blade as follows: "If this shear does not prove as good or better than any shear you ever had return it and money will be refunded."

Length of blade, inches	6	6½	7
Price, each	79c	82c	85c

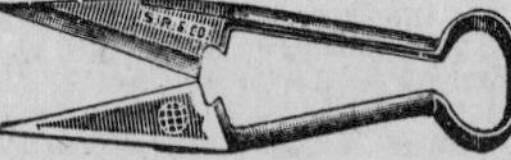

No. 9R4654 Sears, Roebuck & Co.'s Great Eastern Sheep Shear. Single bow. Bent handles. Full polished and swaged. The shape and style used in the Central and Eastern States. Same quality, workmanship and finish as described under preceding number.

Length of blade, inches	5¼	6	6¼
Price, each	79c	83c	86c

No. 9R4656 Sheep Shears, are made of the same high grade steel used in our S., R. & Co.'s Shears, but they are not so nicely finished nor so carefully inspected. They do not carry the same guarantee as those described above but they will do good work and are good enough for anyone who has only a small flock and does his own shearing. Bent handles. Half polished blades.

Length of blade, inches	5½	6
Price, each	52c	55c

For Sheep Shearing Machines, see Index.

No. 9R4659 The Celebrated Burgon & Ball's "B. B. A." Sheep Shears, double bow, straight swaged blades, polished; the kind that is used by professional sheep shearers.

Size, inches	6½	7
Price, each	$1.05	$1.10

Shepherds' Crooks.

No. 9R4660 Montana Shepherds' Crook. The best and strongest crook that has ever been placed on the market. Will hold the largest and strongest sheep. Pear shaped loop finished rounding on the inside so it can't injure the sheep. Owners of sheep appreciate the value of a crook with which they can catch and hold securely the sheep at first attempt. Thousands of these crooks are in use in the United States, and are giving perfect satisfaction. Price, each..... 73c

No. 9R4661 Bo-Peep Crook, same as Montana except is lighter. Price, each.......................65c

Cattle Leaders.

No. 9R4677 Malleable Iron Cattle Leaders, with brass spring; full size; regular goods, same as you pay double the price for or more. Price, each.......................5c

Bull Rings.

No. 9R4679 Copper Bull Rings, 2½ inches in diameter; polished, with screwdriver to fit. Price, each.....11c

No. 9R4683 Same as No. 9R4679, 3 inches in diameter. Price, each....14c

Bull Snaps.

No. 9R4687 Patent Bull Snap. Every one who handles a bull should have and always use this snap. You never know at what minute they will become vicious. **We furnish with snap three feet of chain,** with ring on end and three screw eyes. No wood handle furnished. Price, each.......................25c

Brass Ox Balls.

No. 9R4690 Brass Ox Balls, to put on the tips of the horns of vicious cattle. Octagon pattern. Medium size, ¾ inch. Price, each......3c
Large size, ⅞ inch. Price, each.............4c

Steel Ox Bow Pins.

No. 9R4691 Cast Steel Ox Bow Pins. Each....5c
NOTICE—The price on Bow Pins is for one only.

Cattle Tie Irons.

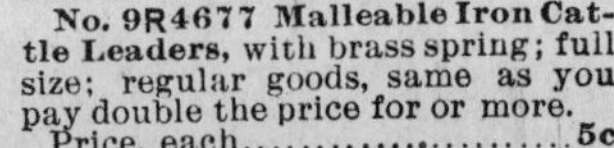

No. 9R4695 Cattle Tie Irons, tinned, with patent covered spring bolt snap. **Complete with thimble** for rope ⅝-inch or smaller. Weight, complete, 6 ounces.
Price, complete, per dozen, 60c; each.............6c

No. 9R4696 Thimble only; tinned; for rope ⅝-inch or smaller.
Price, per dozen, 33c; each..........3c

German Pattern Cow Ties.

No. 9R4697 Welded links, closed ring cow ties, with toggle.
Price, each............15c

No. 9R4698 Welded Links, Ohio Pattern Cow Ties, with two toggles. Price, each.................14c

Niagara Cow Ties.

The Niagara wire link is formed on the principal of a square knot. The greater the strain the tighter holds the knot, so that no force will pull its fastenings apart. Being made entirely by automatic machinery this chain can be turned out at a less cost than other patterns of chain and is therefore sold cheaper.

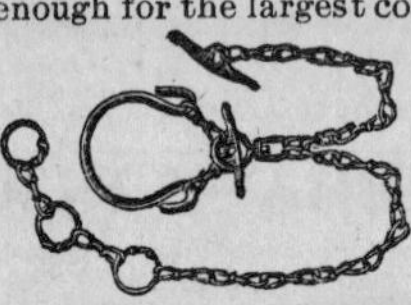

No. 9R4699 Niagara Wire Link Ohio Pattern Cow Ties, with toggle. Size, 2-0, suitable for ordinary size cows. This is the size and weight commonly sold.
Price, each.............12c

No. 9R4700 Niagara Wire Link Ohio Pattern Cow Ties, with toggle. Size, 4-0, large and strong for the largest cow. Price, each..................17c

No. 9R4701 Niagara Wire Link Closed Ring Cow Ties, with toggle. Size, 2-0. Large and strong enough for any ordinary size cow. The size that is commonly sold.
Price, each.............13c

No. 9R4702 Niagara Wire Link Closed Ring Cow Ties, with toggle. Size, 4-0. Large and strong enough for the largest cow. Price, each..............18c

No. 9R4703 Niagara Wire Link Open Ring Cow Ties, with toggle. Size, 2-0. Larger and strong enough for any ordinary size cow. The size that is commonly sold.
Price, each.............13c

No. 9R4704 Niagara Wire Link Open Ring Cow Ties with toggle. Size 4-0. Larger and strong enough for the largest cows.
Price, each..................18c

American Cow Ties.

The links of the American Cow Ties are stamped from a piece of steel, and chain is constructed entirely without welds, making the strongest and safest chain that can be produced. The flat chain is easier on stock.

No. 9R4707 The American Flat Link Ohio Pattern Cow Tie with two toggles. Size, 3-0. Larger and stronger than the size commonly sold.
Price, each...........17c

No. 9R4708 The American Flat Link Ohio Pattern Cow Tie with two toggles. Size, 5-0. The largest and strongest cow tie made. Will hold the biggest bull. Price, each.....................24c

No. 9R4709 The American Flat Link Closed Ring Cow Ties with toggle. Size, 3-0. Larger and stronger than the size commonly sold.
Price, each.............18c

No. 9R4710 The American Flat Link Closed Ring Cow Ties with toggle. Size, 5-0. The largest and strongest cow tie made. Will hold the biggest bull.
Price, each.....................26c

No. 9R4711 Open Ring American Link Cow Ties with toggle. Size, 3-0. Large and strong enough for the largest cow.
Price, each...........18c

No. 9R4712 Open Ring American Link Cow Ties with toggle. Size, 5-0. The largest and strongest cow tie made. Will tie the largest bull.
Price, each.....................26c

Combination Ohio Pattern Cow Ties.

No. 9R4713 Combination Ohio Pattern Cow Ties with two toggles. This tie has the American link to go around the neck and the Niagara wire link to fasten to stanchion or stall, thus giving the advantage of the flat link, which is easy on the neck at little more than the price of the regular chains. Size 2-0, large and strong enough for ordinary sized cows. The size that is commonly sold. Price, each.....13c

The accompanying illustration shows the Dominion or Short Cow Tie with stall fixtures. The cheapest, safest and most convenient tie for either cows or horses. This tie and fixture gives great freedom to the head and avoids the long chain which can entangle the animal's foot.

No. 9R4716 The Dominion Niagara Wire Link Cow Tie. Size 2-0 complete with stall fixtures. Large and strong enough for ordinary sized cows. Price, each................15c

No. 9R4717 The Dominion Niagara Wire Link Cow Ties. Size 4-0 complete with stall fixtures. Large and strong enough for the largest cows. Price, each.............................18c

No. 9R4718 The Dominion American Flat Link Cow Ties. Size 3-0 complete with stall fixtures. Larger and stronger than the size commonly sold.
Price, each.................................18c

No. 9R4719 The Dominion American Flat Link Cow Ties. Size 5-0 complete with stall fixtures. Large and strong enough for the biggest bull. The largest and strongest cow tie made. Price, each.24c

Hay Racks and Feed Boxes.

No. 9R4720 Cast Iron Corner Hay Rack. Weight, 29 lbs.
Price, each....................94c

No. 9R4723 Wrought Steel Corner Hay Rack; same shape as above but made of bent ½-inch steel rods. **State if to be placed on "off" or "near" side** of the horse. Price, each, $1.50

Cast Iron Feed Boxes.

No. 9R4725 Cast Iron Corner Feed Box; is 16 inches on each side; 10 inches deep. Weight, 28 pounds.
Price, each.......................87c

No. 9R4727 Slow Feed Corner Feed Box. It has seven small cells or pockets, from which the grain cannot be poked, and which absolutely prevent waste, and also prevent a greedy horse eating the grain too fast. Those who have tried it say: "It works complete." Each cell in the manger holds one pint. Weight, 25 pounds. Capacity, 15 quarts. Size, 17x17x6 inches deep. Price, each.............$1.50

Picket Pins and Chains.

No. 9R4735 Straight Fluted Malleable Iron Picket Pins, 15 inches long, with swivel. Weight, 1½ lbs.
Price, each..........7c

No. 9R4736 Spiral Wrought Iron Picket Pins. 14½ inches long, with swivel. Price, each...............14c

No. 9R4738 Picket Pin, stamped from steel, securing maximum strength with least amount of metal. Is equipped with steel swivel and ring, especially adapted for use with our tie-out or picket chains. Price, each..........9c

Eureka Wire Link Picket or Tie-out Chains are stronger, better and more durable than a rope. These chains have a stake ring 3¼ inches in diameter on one end, a steel swivel snap on the other, and a swivel in the center.

No. 9R4743 Eureka Wire Link Picket Chain, size 1. Light, but strong enough for a docile animal.

Length, feet	20	30	50
Price, each	39c	55c	88c

No. 9R4744 Eureka Wire Link Picket Chain, size 2. Heavy and strong enough for unruly animals.

Length, feet	20	30	50
Price, each	48c	68c	$1.05

Lariat Swivels.

No. 9R4747 Malleable Iron Lariat Swivels, 3 inches long. One eye ⅝ inch inside, the other ¾ inch inside.
Price, each.......................................3c
Per dozen.......................................25c

No. 9R4748 The American Wrought Steel Lariat Swivel, eyes ⅝ in. inside.
Price, per dozen, 40c; each..........4c

Tyler's Safety Weaner.

No. 9R4754 No sharp points in front to prick or gouge the cow. Perfectly safe and harmless. Is the only weaner having any side protection to prevent sucking sidewise, and is warranted to wean the most obstinate case without cruelty or injury. Does not go through the nose or swing loose to wear the nose or make it sore. Pat. Oct. 2, 1886.
No. 1, for small calves. Price, each.............16c
No. 2, for large calves. Price, each.............17c
No. 3, for yearlings. Price, each.............20c
No. 4, for two-year-olds and cows. Price, each..23c

Gopher Trap.

No. 9R4897 Out o' Sight. Gopher Trap. This is a perfect trap and better suited for the purpose intended than all other makes. We guarantee it to catch nineteen out of twenty gophers if set according to directions which accompany each trap.
Price, each................12c

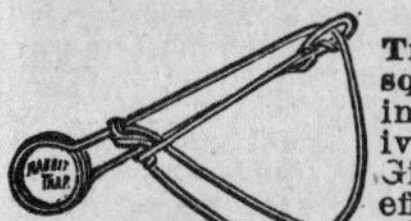

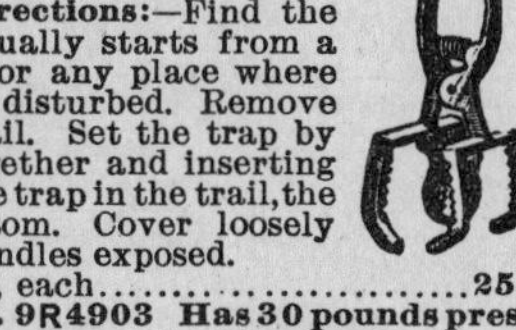

No. 9R4898 Stop Thief Trap, small size, for ground squirrels and all small burrowing animals. A light and effective trap made of spring steel. Give this trap a test and its effectiveness will astonish you.
Price, each................9c

No. 9R4899 Stop Thief Trap, large size, for rabbits, minks, skunks, etc. If properly set this trap is sure to catch. To successfully catch mink, select a place on the bank of a stream where mink tracks are seen and where there is but little room between the bank and the water. Make a hole in the bank 6 or 7 inches deep and a little smaller than the bow of the trap. Cut bait in small pieces and put in back end of the hole. Set trap over the hole so the trigger will be down. When set this way the animal will throw the trap with his body when it makes an effort to remove the bait. This insures catching around the neck or body, which kills at once and saves the skin and fur in good condition. Price, each......13c

The Bulldog Mole Trap is the simplest, most durable and effective on the market. Directions:—Find the main trail, which usually starts from a wood pile, a fence or any place where ground is not often disturbed. Remove dirt from top of trail. Set the trap by pressing handles together and inserting the tongue. Place the trap in the trail, the tongue touching bottom. Cover loosely with dirt, leaving handles exposed.
No. 9R4900 Price, each..........................25c

No. 9R4903 Has 30 pounds pressure when set. The spears are 5 inches long, made of hard steel, which are firmly set in a malleable plate. The plunger is made of hard steel, is firmly fastened in the center of the spear plate, and is supplied with a finger or hand hold at its upper end. It has a notch filed in for the trigger to catch it when set. It can be altered very easily so the trap will throw to suit the ground, as it should throw with less pressure in sand than clay or sod. The trigger and trip are simple and durable, they are automatic, set by gravity.
Price, each.........................48c

"Out o' Sight" Mole Trap.

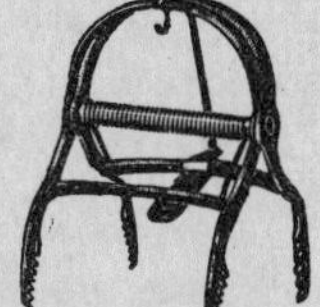

No. 9R4906 The latest improved mole trap—a new departure—having many advantages over all others. On account of its simplicity, not complicated or easy to get out of order, easily set without danger to yourself, and can be used in hot beds without interfering with the glass cover. This trap can be set without disturbing the runway, the pedal being so sensitive that it is impossible for the mole to pass under without throwing the trap. **The secret of mole catching is** the use of a good trap and to know their habits and established runways; full explanation of the habits, etc., furnished with each trap. **A practical field trial** has been given this trap with unequaled results. Made by practical trap makers of long experience and guaranteed to give satisfaction.
Price, each...............................53c

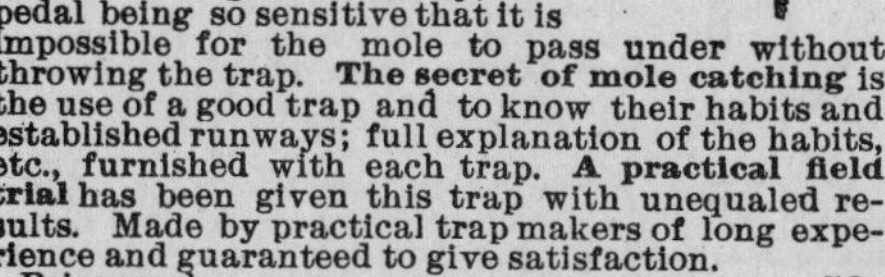

ICE SKATES.

We guarantee all our skates to be equal to the best goods made. SHIPMENT OF SKATES: The average weight of a pair of our skates is 35 ounces. They can be sent by mail to any part of the United States for 35c. The average express charges are from 25c to 45c to almost any part of the United States. Possibly **OUR CHEAPEST SKATES will not make a profitable shipment when ordered alone, but if ordered by freight to be packed with other goods the freight is comparatively nothing. Postage must be paid in advance.** We often receive orders like the following: "Send me one pair of skates, No. 9." We don't know if it's for a No. 9 child's shoe, a No. 9 man's shoe, or a 9-inch shoe. **WE WILL NOT ATTEMPT TO FILL ORDERS FOR SKATES UNLESS SIZE WANTED IS GIVEN IN INCHES. STATE LENGTH OF SHOE IN INCHES WHEN ORDERING. If ordered sent by mail, send us 35 cents more to pay postage.**

No. 9R4950 The runner of this skate is made of the very best cold rolled cast steel, which does not lose its edge readily. The toe and heel plates and all clamps are made of **the best quality of cold roll homogeneous steel.** The clamping mechanism has **been proved to be perfect.** Sizes from 8 to 12 inches.
Price, per pair..................................43c

No. 9R4951 This skate is same as No. 9R4950, except that all parts and runners are polished and nickel plated. Sizes, 8 to 12 inches. Per pair.. **65c**
When ordering skates give length of shoe in inches.

No. 9R4954 Hardened Skate. The steel used in this skate contains **a higher percentage of carbon,** and the runner is **carefully hardened and highly polished.** Toe and heel plates and clamps are made of **the best quality cold rolled open hearth steel.** Sizes, 8 to 12 inches. Price, per pair..............76c

No. 9R4955 Hardened Skate. Is the same material as No. 9R4954, but the edges of all plates and clamps are fine extra polish, the runner and all parts being **full nickel plated and polished.** Sizes, 8 to 12 inches. Price, per pair...................**$1.03**
When ordering skates give length of shoe in inches.

No. 9R4956 The runners are of welded iron and steel hardened, carefully tempered and highly polished. Sizes, 9 to 12 inches. Per pair......**$1.35**

No. 9R4957 Same as No. 9R4956, except all parts are fully polished and nickel plated. Per pair.**$1.80**
When ordering skates give length of shoe in inches.

No. 9R4959 Welded, hardened and tempered skate. This skate has the same construction as No. 9R4950 to No. 9R4957, but the material is of higher grade and it is **a more expensive skate to make.** The runner is made of the best iron and steel stock, **welded, hardened, tempered, nickel plated and highly polished.** The tops and all parts are **nickel plated** with polished edges. Sizes, 9 to 12 inches. Price, per pair.........................**$2.35**

No. 9R4961 This skate is same as No. 9R4959 except all parts are **full nickel plated and highly polished** on all surfaces. This is a strictly **high grade skate,** makes an elegant present. Sizes, 9 to 12 inches. Price, per pair..........................**$2.75**
When ordering skates give length of shoe in inches.

Racing Skates.

No. 9R4965 Full Racer. This celebrated speed skate is used and endorsed by the most noted fast skaters in the United States and Canada. It is of exceptional value for long distance or "straight away" skating. It embodies the latest and most up to date ideas in speed skate construction; tops are made of selected close grain beechwood, varnished, with highly nickel plated toe, heel and center plates. Runners are made of high grade cast steel, ⅛ inch thick and are bored, making the lightest possible skate; made with 14, 16 and 18-inch runners.
Price, per pair.................................**$2.47**

Donoghue Skates.

This skate is made under the personal supervision of Mr. Joseph F. Donoghue, world's champion skater, and is made of the highest grade of material, and by first class mechanics. Mahogany tops, hardened steel runners, nickel plated, russet harness leather straps, nickel tongue buckles. **This skate was designed by Mr. Donoghue, and has been** used for the past five years in **winning all his great races** and making his wonderful records, and his success is as much due to the perfection of these skates as to his own skill.

No. 9R4967 Made in three lengths, 14, 16 and 18 inches. Price, per pair..........................**$3.25**
When ordering skates give length of shoe in inches.

Speed Skates.

No. 9R4970 This New Speed Skate combines, in the shape and quality of its runners, all the points of excellence known to the champion speed skaters of the world. The shoe attachment is light and strong. Runners made from **cold rolled steel. All parts nickel plated** and buffed. Sizes, 10, 10½, 11, 11½ and 12 inches. Price, per pair...............**$2.05**

Antique Speed Skates.

No. 9R4973 This graceful and pleasing pattern has been recently introduced and is rapidly attaining popularity. The curve of the runners is such that they are adapted for speed and figure skating not requiring toe movements. They have been pronounced the easiest skate made. The shoe attachment is strong and secure, and saves the feet and legs the weariness occasioned by the use of straps in the wood top skates. **Runners are made of the best hand forged cold rolled steel,** and skate is heavily nickel plated and buffed. Sizes, 9½ to 12 inches. Price, per pair.............................**$2.10**
When ordering skates give length of shoe in inches.

Full Rocker Skate.

No. 9R4977 Full Rocker Skate. As we have had a large number of inquiries from our customers for the old fashioned rocker skate, we have had these skates manufactured for us by a first class skate maker, under the direct supervision of an old time skating enthusiast, and they are correct in every detail. Tops are made of selected beechwood and runners from best rolled steel. All runners are fastened to tops by a brass thimble, which prevents the woods from splitting. We furnish black straps ⅝x20 inches for heel and 1¾-inch broad toe straps with every pair. Sizes, 9¼ to 12 inches.
Price, per pair...**$1.10**

Ladies' Skates.

No. 9R4980 Ladies' Strap Skate. Runner is made of **cold rolled cast steel,** is highly polished with finely ground cutting edge. The foot and heel plates are made from the **best grade of cold rolled open hearth homogeneous steel.** The heel and toe straps are of the **best oak tanned russet grain leather,** tongue buckles and nickel plated heel bands. Sizes, 8 to 10½ inches. Price, per pair, **68c**

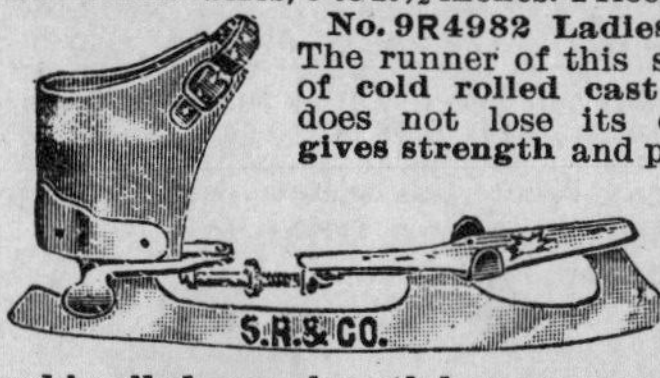

No. 9R4982 Ladies' Club Skate. The runner of this skate is made of **cold rolled cast steel,** which does not lose its edge readily, **gives strength** and permits a **high polish.** The foot and heel plates and all clamps are made of the **best grade cold rolled open hearth homogeneous steel.** Heel strap is the **best oak tanned russet grain leather,** with tongue buckles and nickel plated heel bands. Sizes, 8 to 10½ inches. Price, per pair..............**90c**

No. 9R4983 Ladies' Club Skate. Same as No. 9R4982, except that **all parts and runners are nickel plated and polished.** Sizes, 8 to 10½ inches.
Price, per pair...**$1.30**

No. 9R4985 Ladies' Skate. The runners are made from **welded iron and steel hardened.** Plate clamp and levers of **best quality cold rolled steel.** All parts polished and nickel plated. Sizes, 8½ to 10½ inches. Price, per pair.......**$2.38**
When ordering skates give length of shoe in inches.

$2.90 for Our Best Ladies' Skate.

No. 9R4987 Our Best Ladies' Skate. It has a **welded steel and iron runner perfectly tempered. All parts are full nickel plated and full polished on all surfaces** The heel straps have nickel plated tongue buckles and nickel plated heel bands. Sizes, 8½ to 10½ inches
Price, per pair..**$2.90**

Ankle Brace.

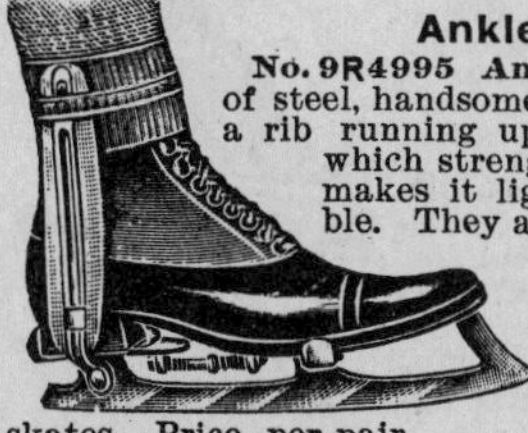

No. 9R4995 Ankle Brace. It is made of steel, handsomely nickel plated with a rib running up through the center which strengthens the brace and makes it light, strong and durable. They are trimmed with the best quality russet grain leather. Can be attached to any skate by a blacksmith. Price is for brace only without skates. Price, per pair...........................**63c**

Skate Sharpener.

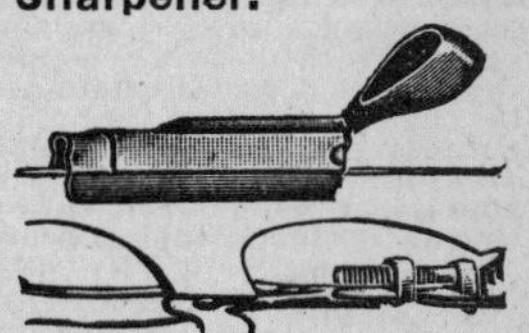

No. 9R4999 Skate Sharpener. This tool is scientific in construction and practical in use. It concaves a skate runner. Its adjustment to any skate is automatic. The only adjustment necessary for the operator to make is when the file is changed to a new side; then the tool opens like a jack knife and closes as easily. **Not a screw or a bolt is used in its construction. The files are cut on four sides**—two flat sides and two convex. It is nickel plated. Price, each..............................**12c**

Roller Skates.

No. 9R5010 This is a high grade skate, and may be used for sidewalk as well as for rink purposes. The adjustment is easily made. It is strong and durable and will hold the skate where it is put. The heel and toe plates are of the best steel, and will not break in use. The trucks are oscillating, and have rubber cushions. Have been in use for many years. The skate has grain leather heel and toe straps, and the heel band and buckles are nickel plated, and it has boxwood wheels. Only one size required. Price, per pair........**$1.75**

No. 9R5012 This is a high grade sidewalk skate, which is easily adjusted, and from experience has been proved to be the most desirable extension skate possible. The adjustment, while easily made, is strong and durable, and will hold the skate where it is put and gives no trouble. The heel and toe plates are of the best homogeneous open hearth steel, and will not break in use. The skate is full strapped, with nickel heel band and buckles. Price, per pair....**46c**

No. 9R5015 This Skate is one which is desirable for rink use. Has oscillating trucks, rubber cushions; the top is of beechwood, the wheels of boxwood, the straps of black pebbled leather and the heel band is nickel plated. We do not carry this skate in stock and cannot sell less quantity than one dozen. We deliver these skates free on board cars at factory in Massachusetts. Price, per dozen pairs....**$11.40**
When ordering, do not fail to state sizes wanted.

Enterprise Food Chopper.

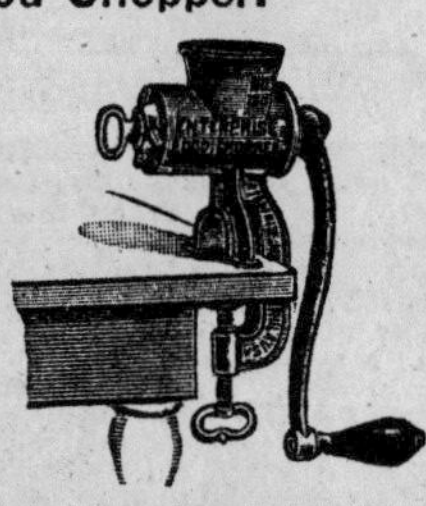

No. 9R5035 The Enterprise Food and Meat Chopper. Being made by the Enterprise Manufacturing Co., is an absolute guarantee that it is the best chopper made. **It will chop raw meat,** cooked meat, vegetables of all kinds, bread and crackers and will make peanut butter. **It will chop any kind of food any size you wish for any kind of dish.** Can be cleaned in a minute, is always ready and never gets out of order. Four knives, one each, fine, medium and coarse and nut butter cutter furnished with each machine. The bearing is of phosphor bronze, which reduces the friction, makes the machine easier to turn and will last much longer. Will chop two pounds of meat per minute. Weight, 4½ pounds. Price, each......**$1.00**

The Sterling Food Chopper.

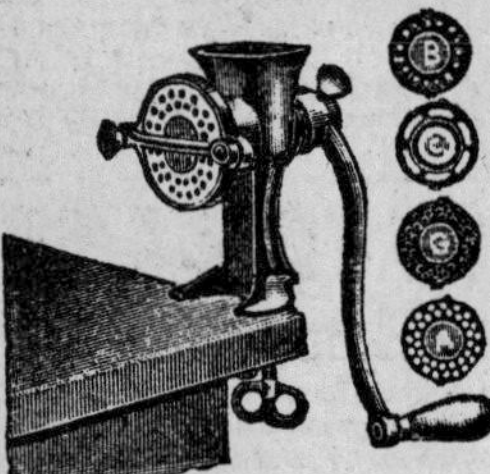

No. 9R5045 The Sterling Meat and Food Chopper will cut meat and any kind of food. Is self sharpening, easy to clean, quickly taken apart, strong and durable. It has a grating attachment not provided with other choppers, that will deliver horseradish and similar articles as well as a grater. Furnished with four cutting plates.
Price, each **$1.07**

No. 9R5050 A Meat Chopper That Chops, simple, durable, handy, cheap, easily cleaned, **can be taken apart** and put together again in less than one minute. **All parts are heavily tinned to prevent rusting.** Runs easily, cuts either meat or vegetables. **Cutters are self sharpening.** No family need be without a meat chopper.
Our price..**85c**

The Enterprise Food Choppers.

The Enterprise Choppers cut the meat as with a pair of scissors, and do not grind or tear it. It is impossible for any strings, sinews or gristle to pass through without being chopped. The small quantity of uncut meat remaining in the machine can be cut by running through some of the already cut meat a second time. **All parts are interchangeable and can be replaced at small cost. The cutting parts being steel, they are vastly superior to the cast iron ones of other makes of choppers.** By means of the stuffing attachment, which we furnish at a small additional cost, they make excellent sausage stuffers.

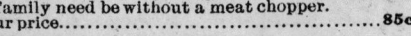

No. 9R5063 Genuine Enterprise Meat Choppers, small family size, with clamp (No. 5) chops 1½ pounds per minute. Weight, 4¾ pounds.
Price, each.............**$1.60**

Our $2.40 Meat Chopper.

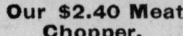

No. 9R5064 Family Size Enterprise Meat Chopper, with clamp (No. 10) chops 3 lbs. per minute. Weight, 8 lbs.
Price, each **$2.40**

Enterprise Meat Chopper for $2.00.

No. 9R5067 Family Size Enterprise Meat Chopper, with legs to screw on bench or table (No. 12) chops 3 pounds per minute.
Price, each......**$2.00**

No. 9R5068 Hotel Size Enterprise Meat Chopper, with legs to screw to table or bench. (No. 22) chops 4 pounds per minute. Weight, 12 pounds. Price, each........**$3.20**

No. 9R5070 Butchers' Size Enterprise Meat Chopper, with legs to screw on table or bench. (No. 32) chops 5 lbs. per minute. Weight, 18 lbs.
Price, each, **$4.80**

No. 9R5072 Butchers' Size Enterprise Meat Chopper, with fly wheel. (No. 232) chops 5 lbs. per minute. Weight complete, 38 pounds.
Price, each, **$7.60**

Stuffing Attachments for Enterprise Meat Chopper.

No. 9R5075 Stuffing Attachments for Enterprise Meat Chopper. After the meat has been chopped, remove the knife and plate, place the attachment against the cylinder, screw the ring up moderately tight, and the machine is ready for work. They are made of spun brass, nickel plated, and are very strong and durable. Made in two sizes of tube, viz: ¾ inch and 1¼ inches. When ordering, be sure to give number of chopper for which attachment is wanted.

Price, each, with ¾-inch tube. To fit chopper—

No. 5	No. 10	No. 12	No. 22	No. 32	No. 232
30c	35c	35c	45c	55c	55c

Price, each, with 1¼-inch tube. To fit chopper—

No. 5	No. 10	No. 12	No. 22	No. 32	No. 232
44c	54c	54c	67c	90c	90c

Extra Knives for Enterprise Meat Choppers.

No. 9R5076 Knives for Enterprise Meat Choppers.
Price: To fit chopper No. 5, 28c; No. 10, 30c; No. 12, 30c; No. 22, 50c; No. 32, 65c; No. 232..........................**65c**

Extra Plates for Enterprise Meat Choppers.

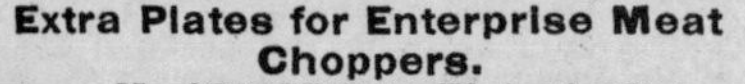

No. 9R5077 Extra Plates for Enterprise Meat Choppers. When ordering, be sure to give number of chopper for which the plate is wanted. The plate having $\frac{3}{16}$-inch holes is most commonly used, and is what is furnished with choppers.
With $\frac{3}{16}$, ¼, $\frac{5}{16}$ or ⅜-inch holes.
Price, each: To fit chopper No. 5, 30c; No. 10, 50c; No. 12, 50c; No. 22, 75c; No. 32, 90c; No. 232.....**90c**

Sausage Stuffer.

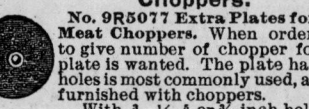

Lever Sausage Stuffer. Iron japanned. No. 0 for butchers' use; No. 1 for family use.
No. 9R5083 Size 0. Price, each..............**83c**
No. 9R5084 Size 1. Price, each..............**59c**

Enterprise Sausage Stuffer, Fruit and Lard Press.

Unexcelled for butchers' or farmers' use for stuffing sausages and pressing lard. For kitchen use there is nothing like it for pressing fruit for making jellies, wine, etc. Full directions for use are sent with each press.

No. 9R5090 Two-quart size, japanned, rack movement. Weight, 21 pounds.
Price, each **$2.35**

No. 9R5092 Four-quart size, japanned, screw movement Weight, 30 lbs.
Price, each, **$3.95**

No. 9R5094 Eight-quart size, japanned, screw movement. Weight, 44 pounds.
Price, each **$5.15**

Sensible Fruit and Lard Press.

A well made and handsome press for making jellies, wines, syrups, lard, etc. Made with special reference to strength, and guaranteed against breakage under any fair usage. A special advantage is the split nut in the yoke. It is not necessary to turn the hand wheel except when the fruit is actually under pressure, for the thread of the screw can be introduced into the nut and the nut closed, or taken from the nut if open, at any point in the length of the screw, so no turning is needed to run it up or down, making this the quickest acting press made. Can be taken apart in a moment for cleaning. All parts are interchangeable and can be replaced at a slight expense in case of breakage.
No. 9R5097 2-quart size. Price, each......**$1.38**
No. 9R5098 4-quart size. Price, each...... **2.34**
No. 9R5099 10-quart size. Price, each...... **3.67**

Fruit, Wine and Jelly Press.

No. 9R5112 Combination Fruit, Wine and Jelly Press. Can be used for many purposes, such as making wines, jellies and fruit butter from fruits, the entire substance being extracted in one operation. Weight, 12½ pounds.
Price, each...........**$2.65**

Enterprise Juice Extractor.

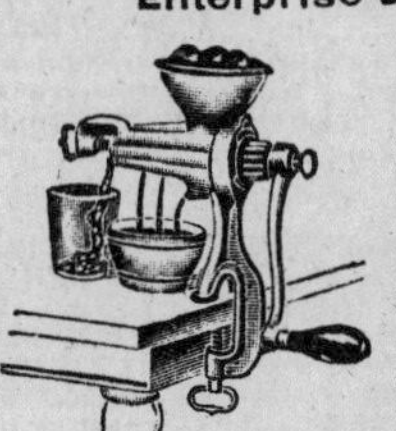

No. 9R5116 Enterprise Meat Juice Extractor No. 21, for the extraction of juice from meat, also answering for extracting seeds and juice from fruits. The machine being tinned, no metallic or inky flavor will be imparted to the material used. The dryness of pulp or refuse can be regulated by the thumbscrew at the outlet. Length, 9 inches; height, 12 inches. Weight, 7 pounds. Price, each..................**$2.00**

Wrought Steel Tinned Meat Hooks.

Our steel hooks will carry one-third more than iron hooks of same size.

No. 9R5125 Wrought Steel Tinned Meat Hooks, to drive.

Nos.	1	2	3	4	5	6
Size of steel	¼	¼	$\frac{5}{16}$	⅜	⅜	⅜
Price, per dozen	14c	15c	20c	26c	28c	40c

No. 9R5126 Wrought Steel Tinned Meat Hooks, to screw in.

Nos.	1	2	3	4	5	6
Size of steel	¼	¼	$\frac{5}{16}$	⅜	⅜	⅜
Price, per dozen	14c	15c	20c	26c	28c	40c

No. 9R5129 Wrought Steel Tinned Mutton Hooks, for 2-inch bar, made of $\frac{5}{16}$ square steel. Price, per dozen.....**37c**

No. 9R5132 Wrought Steel Tinned Beam Hooks, same shape as mutton hook, very heavy, for 2-inch bar, made of $\frac{7}{16}$ square steel. Weight, per dozen, 3 lbs. 15 oz.
Price, per dozen..................................**55c**

No. 9R5135 Wrought Steel Tinned Beam Hooks, with large round bend, very heavy, for 2-inch bar made of ½-inch steel. Weight, per dozen, 9¾ pounds.
Price, per dozen..................................**67c**

Cleavers.

No. 9R5150 Family Cleavers, cast steel blades forged and hardened. Is a very handy household article and should be in everyone's kitchen.
Price, each.......................................**25c**

Butchers' Choppers and Cleavers.

Extra cast steel, hickory handles.
No. 9R5160 7-inch cut, 1¼ lbs. Price, each, **58c**
No. 9R5161 8-inch cut, 1¾ lbs. Price, each, **68c**
No. 9R5162 Butchers' Cleavers, 9-inch cut. Weight, 3¼ pounds. Price, each........**75c**
No. 9R5163 Butchers' Cleavers, 10-inch cut. Weight, 4 pounds. Price, each..............**$1.12**
No. 9R5164 Butchers' Cleavers, 12-inch cut. Weight, 5 pounds. Price, each..............**$1.25**

Hog Scraper.

No. 9R5175 Hog Scraper. Will pay for itself the first time used. Wood handle with bolt extending through scraper. Made of No. 18 sheet steel. Price, each.........**18c**

No. 9R5176 Hog Scraper, made of No. 20 sheet iron.
Price, each.......................................**8c**

If you question the advisability of sending cash with your order, read page 1 and also the letters from our banks on page 12.

Painted Wire Cloth.

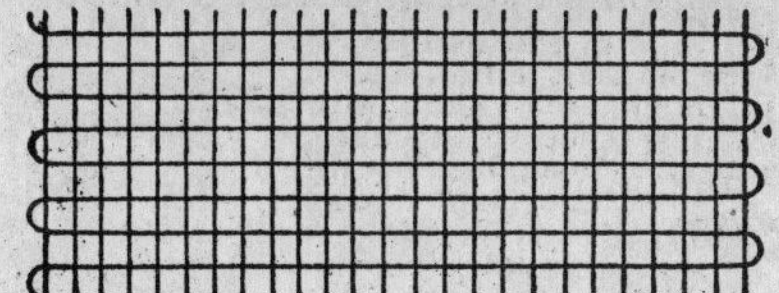

The illustration shows you the exact size of mesh. You can make your own screen doors and windows. Order just what wire cloth you require, but note the reduction in price when ordering in full rolls.

Best Acme Bessemer Steel Wire, painted black or green (double selvage), standard mesh.

No. 9R5640 Green Painted Wire Cloth.
No. 9R5641 Black Painted Wire Cloth.

Width	Per roll of 100 running feet	Per lineal foot	Width	Per roll of 100 running feet	Per lineal foot
24 in.	$2.40	3¼c	38 in.	$3.80	5 c
26 in.	2.60	3½c	40 in.	4.00	5¼c
28 in.	2.80	3¾c	42 in.	4.20	5½c
30 in.	3.00	4 c	44 in.	4.40	5¾c
32 in.	3.20	4¼c	46 in.	4.60	6 c
34 in.	3.40	4½c	48 in.	4.80	6¼c
36 in.	3.60	4¾c			

Wire Cloth Staples.

No. 9R5646 Wire Cloth Staples are much superior to common tacks. Two points enter the wood. **They lap over three wires,** hence hold the wire better, and not so many tacks required.
Price, per pound, 15c; per paper of 120 staples...2c

Window Screen Frames.

Has patent tongued corner irons, fitting into corresponding grooves in the frame, and insuring a perfect, square corner. **The side pieces are grooved to receive the guides** which attach to the window casing and are furnished with each set. **Size of sticks,** ⅝x1 inch, finished in black walnut stain. **Furnished with bead molding** to tack over edges of wire cloth. **We can furnish no other sizes than quoted below.**

No. 9R5650 To make frame 36x36 inches.
Price, each...17c
No. 9R5651 To make frame 42x42 inches.
Price, each...18c
No. 9R5652 To make frame 48x48 inches.
Price, each...20c

Window Screens.

No. 9R5658 Our Own Extension Window Screen has a perfect adjustment; **frames are finished in oil.** Wire cloth is the best to be obtained in the market. We claim for the screen **a perfect adjustment, stronger construction,** better material and smoother finish than can be found in any other. Made in the following sizes and no other size furnished.

Height	Width adjustable	Price each
18 inches	From 20 to 33 inches	17c
24 inches	From 24 to 37 inches	21c
30 inches	From 24 to 37 inches	26c

Screen Doors

are no longer considered a luxury, but one of the necessities of modern life. **The saving of damage to paint, paper, ceiling and furniture,** and the saving of labor for cleaning in one season will pay the first cost of screens for a home.

No. 9R5663 Four-Panel Screen Doors made from kiln dried pine with stiles 3 inches wide; natural wood finish, not covered with cheap paint to hide imperfections. The wire cloth—the best in the market—is painted and varnished. Cannot sag or stretch out. **Made only in the following sizes and no other sizes furnished.**

Thickness	Width	Height	Price, each
⅞ inch	2 ft. 6 in.	6 ft. 6 in.	60c
⅞ inch	2 ft. 8 in.	6 ft. 8 in.	61c
1⅛ inches	2 ft. 6 in.	6 ft. 6 in.	62c
1⅛ inches	2 ft. 8 in.	6 ft. 8 in.	63c
1⅛ inches	2 ft. 8 in.	7 ft. 0 in.	64c
1⅛ inches	2 ft. 10 in.	6 ft. 10 in.	65c
1⅛ inches	2 ft. 10 in.	7 ft. 0 in.	66c
1⅛ inches	3 ft. 10 in.	7 ft. 0 in.	67c

Fancy Screen Doors.

No. 9R5665 Fancy Screen Doors, made with flush moldings, from choice selected stock, thoroughly kiln dried; insuring a door that will not become loose at the joints; **covered with best black hard steel wire cloth,** stretched and securely fastened. Stiles 3 inches wide. **Finished natural color of the wood, with two coats of varnish.** Securely packed for shipment. Made in the following sizes, and no other sizes furnished. We have changed the pattern of this door this year, making it stronger and handsomer than the cut shows.

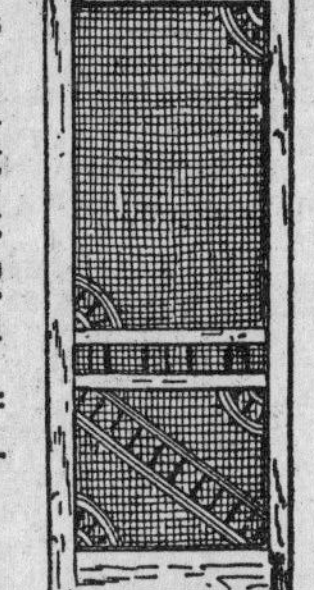

Thickness	Width	Height	Price
1⅛ in.	30 in.	78 in.	$1.16
1⅛ in.	32 in.	80 in.	1.17
1⅛ in.	34 in.	82 in.	1.18
1⅛ in.	36 in.	84 in.	1.19

No. 9R5670 Green Wire Screen Enamel. Ready for use and easily applied, does not clog meshes of screens, and one coat gives to old, rusty screens a rich, brilliant and lasting finish.
Price, ½-pint cans, each...15c
Price, 1-pint cans, each...30c

Galvanized Rigid Frame Door Mats.

No. 9R5706 These are the strongest, most durable and attractive ever manufactured. **Guaranteed to keep in perfect shape** under any usage. They are made of hard steel wire, galvanized.

Size	Each	Size	Each
16x24 in.	$0.70	30x48 in.	$1.86
18x30 in.	.87	36x48 in.	2.28
22x36 in.	1.23	36x60 in.	2.98
26x48 in.	1.68	36x72 in.	3.68

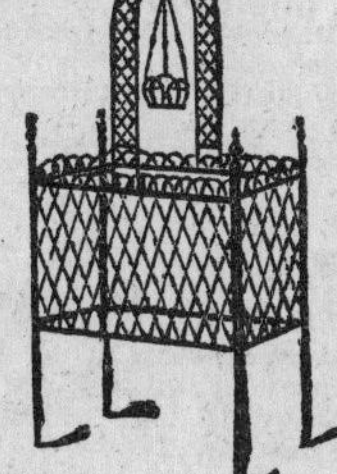

Grave Guard with Arch.

No. 9R5751 To protect and ornament a grave. Prevents small children from picking the flowers; keeps dogs, cats, etc., off of the grave. It is strongly made and nicely painted. Has angle steel frame fastened together with bolts. Is taken apart and securely crated for shipment, but can be easily and quickly put together by anyone. This makes freight charges less and insures the guard reaching destination in good condition.

Length, ft.	Width, in.	Height, in.	Price, each
4	21	24	$5.48
5	24	24	6.80
6	30	27	7.85
7	30	27	9.15

LAWN MOWERS.

OUR ACME HIGH GRADE LAWN MOWERS are guaranteed the best made. We invite a close comparison of our prices with those of any other house on strictly high grade machines.

In our New Sunrise Lawn Mower we claim to have the easiest running, best made and most complete medium priced lawn mower made. It is made from the best material and all parts are interchangeable. **The reel knife shaft** is made of solid steel, and runs in split phosphor bronze bushings. **It is fitted with large driving wheels, incased gearing, continuous spiral steel reel knives, accurately ground, adjustable handle, self acting and positive pawls,** steel handle braces, and a **bed knife made from the best lawn mower knife steel, which is finely ground and self sharpening.**

Wheels are 8¼ inches high. Reel revolves when turning corners either way, as there is a ratchet in each wheel. Makes very little noise. **This is a mower that was sold by retail dealers at from $4.00 to $5.00.** They have given such excellent satisfaction we have contracted for them this year, and by reason of our quantities purchased and our one small profit, we have reduced the price so that any one may own a good mower for a little money.

Nos	9R6022	9R6024	9R6026	9R6028
Size	12-inch	14-inch	16-inch	18-inch
Ship'g wgt., lbs.	38	40	42	45
Each	$2.25	$2.30	$2.35	$2.60

Our Acme Universal Catcher for $1.00.

This is a grass catcher that will fit any lawn mower made. Heavy canvas body, galvanized iron bottom. **The catcher is attached to the handle only** and is entirely independent of the mower proper. **Can be attached or taken off in an instant.** Can be used on any lawn mower made. Is guaranteed to give satisfaction in every case.

No. 9R6029 To fit 10, 12, 14 or 16-inch mower. $1.00
No. 9R6030 To fit 18 or 20-inch mower... 1.05
No. 9R6031 Grass Catcher, with wire frame, covered with striped awning duck, to fit mowers from 12 to 16 inches wide. Price, each...42c
No. 9R6032 Grass Catcher, to fit 16 to 20-inch mowers. Price, each...50c

OUR ACME LAWN MOWERS AT $3.40 TO $4.50.

HAVING FOUR CUTTING BLADES.

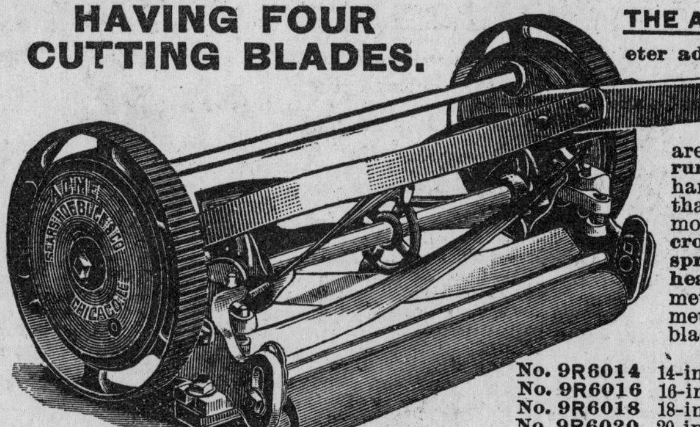

THE ACME MOWERS have the latest patent micrometer adjustment. This is our standard high grade Acme machine and greatly improved for this season. The drive wheels are open for 1 inch below the tread, though the working parts are completely enclosed. **It is the easiest running lawn mower made,** because the handle is so attached to the drive wheel that the power is applied to the center of motion. This mower has our **patent micrometer adjustment continuous cut, spring bed knife, noiseless ratchet, long heavy bearings** of phosphor bronze. Diameter of traction wheels, 9½ inches; diameter of reel, 6 inches, with four cutting blades. The 16-inch size is most popular.

No. 9R6014 14-inch mower. Weight, 47 lbs. Price. $3.40
No. 9R6016 16-inch mower. Weight, 49 lbs. Price. 3.70
No. 9R6018 18-inch mower. Weight, 51 lbs. Price. 4.15
No. 9R6020 20-inch mower. Weight, 57 lbs. Price. 4.50

ACME BALL BEARING LAWN MOWER.

Our Acme Ball Bearing Mower is of same design as our Acme, illustrated above. It is constructe on first class principles, adjustable throughout. Silent in operation. Cones and cups made of **solid con steel,** no pressed cups used. Ground perfect. **Best quality steel balls.** The cups, cones and balls ar dust proof, and made with as great a degree of perfection as the best bicycle. Wheels, 9½ inches high. Four-bladed revolving cutter. Cutter 6-inch diameter. Front bar, 6½ inches from the ground. Cuts close and does fine work. High wheels, easy running. Four cutting blades. **Spring bed knife, continuous cut.** The ball bearings will never need adjustment. **Guaranteed to give satisfaction or money refunded.** We offer our **Ball Bearing Mower** at the following prices.

Nos.	9R6035	9R6036	9R6037	9R6038
Sizes	14-inch	16-inch	18-inch	20-inch
Shipping weight, pounds	46	50	57	63
Price, each	$5.75	$6.00	$6.25	$6.75

OUR $6.95 PLATFORM SCALES.

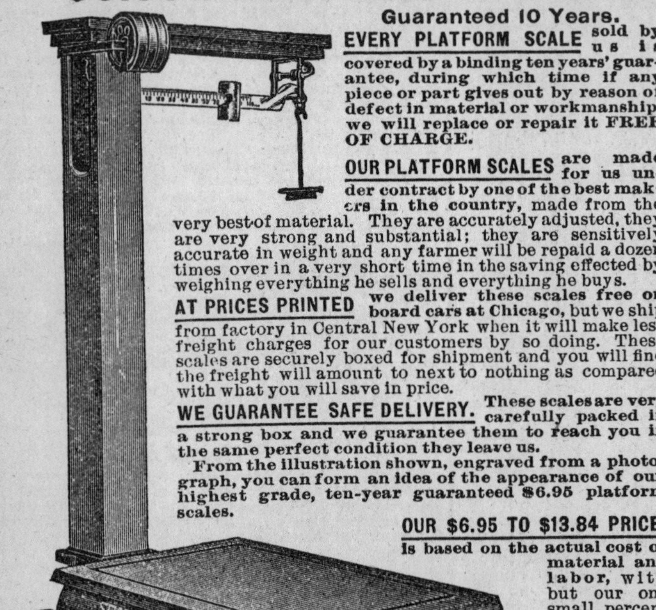

Guaranteed 10 Years.

EVERY PLATFORM SCALE sold by us is covered by a binding ten years' guarantee, during which time if any piece or part gives out by reason of defect in material or workmanship, we will replace or repair it FREE OF CHARGE.

OUR PLATFORM SCALES are made for us under contract by one of the best makers in the country, made from the very best of material. They are accurately adjusted, they are very strong and substantial; they are sensitively accurate in weight and any farmer will be repaid a dozen times over in a very short time in the saving effected by weighing everything he sells and everything he buys.

AT PRICES PRINTED we deliver these scales free on board cars at Chicago, but we ship from factory in Central New York when it will make less freight charges for our customers by so doing. These scales are securely boxed for shipment and you will find the freight will amount to next to nothing as compared with what you will save in price.

WE GUARANTEE SAFE DELIVERY. These scales are very carefully packed in a strong box and we guarantee them to reach you in the same perfect condition they leave us.

From the illustration shown, engraved from a photograph, you can form an idea of the appearance of our highest grade, ten-year guaranteed $6.95 platform scales.

OUR $6.95 TO $13.84 PRICE. is based on the actual cost of material and labor, with but our one small percentage of profit added, and is the lowest price ever named for the highest grade platform scales. We furnish these scales in capacity from 600 to 1,500 pounds at from $6.95 to $13.84 as quoted below. With our platform scales you can weigh every load of grain you sell before going to market, everything on the farm can be weighed, and it is not safe to do otherwise.

THESE SCALES are provided with the best steel pivots, carefully hardened and finished; have no check rods to bind or get out of place. The platform rests on adjustable chill bearings, which take the wear directly off the steel pivots, and the pivots remaining sharp, the scales act quick and sensitive. The scales are fitted with heavy, smoothly finished wheels, heavy wood center platform, sliding poise beam, sealed and tested.

EACH AND EVERY SIZE OF PLATFORM SCALE which we sell is made at the same factory and by the same skilled workmen, and it is just as much of an impossibility for a high class man to turn out crude, unfinished work, as it is for the ordinary common factory hand to turn out the high class of goods that are made by our expert mechanics.

Catalogue Number	Capacity	Beams Marked	Size of Platform	Shipping Weight	Price
9R5916	600 lbs.	50 lbs. by ⅛ lb.	17½x26¼ inches	150 lbs.	$ 6.95
9R5908	800 lbs.	50 lbs. by ⅛ lb.	18 x26¼ inches	160 lbs.	8.10
9R5910	1,000 lbs.	50 lbs. by ⅛ lb.	19 x26¼ inches	170 lbs.	9.58
9R5912	1,250 lbs.	100 lbs. by ⅛ lb.	19 x26¼ inches	235 lbs.	11.00
9R5915	1,500 lbs.	100 lbs. by ⅛ lb.	19 x27 inches	245 lbs.	13.84

We furnish the above grade of scales with bag rack as follows:

Catalogue No.	Capacity	Beams Marked	Size of Platform	Price
9R5916	600 pounds	50 lbs. by ⅛ lb.	17x25 inches	$ 8.45
9R5917	800 pounds	50 lbs. by ⅛ lb.	18x26 inches	9.60
9R5918	1,000 pounds	50 lbs. by ⅛ lb.	19x26 inches	11.58
9R5919	1,200 pounds	100 lbs. by ⅛ lb.	19x26 inches	12.50

OUR SPECIAL WAREHOUSE AND GROCERY PORTABLE PLATFORM SCALES.

We claim that no other manufacturer offers as good a weighing machine as this. Every particle of material that enters into the construction of these scales is the very best it is possible to procure, regardless of expense. The special mixtures of iron produce the strongest casting in the world. Selected material and the brains and labor of the best scale builders in the world, make these scales absolutely accurate in every way. **These platforms have adjustable chilled feet and hardened steel pivots.** In fact every ounce of steel that enters into the construction of these scales is carefully hardened. **While the scale quoted under preceding number is a strictly reliable scale guaranteed for ten years against defective material and workmanship and is guaranteed to weigh accurately,** this scale is still heavier and better. The capacity of the scale is rated by the amount it will weigh correctly and not by the weight the platform will sustain without breaking. For instance, a wagon scale that will weigh three tons correctly will not break under a load of four or five tons, but it would not give correct weight of over three tons and a heavier weight should not be put on the scales. Then again, as before stated, the scale is not rated by the weight it will sustain when carefully placed upon its platform. You take an ordinary 1200-pound scale and drop a bag of meal off your shoulder on the scale, and although the meal might not weigh more than 50 pounds, it would be very likely to break the scale. It would not be just for you to claim 50 pounds would break a 1200-pound scale. Boys and careless employees are likely to do just such things as this, and for that reason many prefer having a scale with a larger factor of safety than those quoted above, therefore we offer below a scale which is heavier and stronger and will stand more abuse (and by the way we do not guarantee any of our scales against abuse).

AT THE PRICES NAMED BELOW we deliver these scales free on board the cars at Chicago, from which point the customer must pay all the freight. To eastern and southeastern points we will ship from our factory in Central New York, as the freight would be less to them. The freight, however, amounts to but very little, and absolutely nothing when you compare our prices, with freight added, to the prices which you would be obliged to pay were you to procure the scales from any other source. Remember, these scales are guaranteed against any defect in material or workmanship for ten years.

Catalogue No.	Capacity	Beams Marked	Size of Platform	Price
9R5921	600 pounds	50 lbs. by ¼ lb.	16x24 inches	$11.50
9R5923	800 pounds	50 lbs. by ¼ lb.	17x24 inches	12.50
9R5924	1,000 pounds	50 lbs. by ¼ lb.	17x26 inches	14.00
9R5926	1,200 pounds	100 lbs. by ½ lb.	18x26 inches	15.75
9R5927	1,600 pounds	100 lbs. by ½ lb.	19x27 inches	17.50
9R5929	2,000 pounds	100 lbs. by ½ lb.	25x33 inches	20.00
9R5930	2,500 pounds	100 lbs. by ½ lb.	25x34 inches	22.50

Our Dairy Scale with Butter Salter Attachment.

No. 9R5938 Capacity, ½ ounce to 240 pounds. Same grade scale, same material and workmanship as described under our No. 9R5943. By using this scale the butter can be weighed and salted without figuring, avoids all guesswork, and makes every lot of butter the same. Beam marked 44 pounds by ¼ ounce. They are scaled carefully with the United States standard and are absolutely correct.
Price, each, complete..............$4.00

No. 9R5939 Extra High Grade Dairy Scale with Butter Salter attachment; capacity, ½-ounce to 250 pounds. All steel bearings, sensitive, accurate and durable. The mechanism is perfect. The castings are correct; pivots are the finest tool steel, case hardened. Beam marked 44 pounds by ¼ ounce. Price, each..............$6.00

Our $1.75 Platform Counter Scales.

FOR $1.75 WE OFFER THIS EXTRA LARGE 240-POUND PLATFORM COUNTER SCALE as the greatest value in scales ever offered by us or any other house; $1.75 barely covers the cost of material and labor, allowing us one small selling profit.

NOTWITHSTANDING the great advance in the cost of material and labor, we are still able to offer this 240-pound capacity platform scale at $1.75. We have a large stock on hand, and while they last they will be furnished at the low price, $1.75. These 240-pound, $1.75 heavy platform counter scales are made for us under contract by one of the best scale makers in America, made from the very best material, accurately adjusted and covered by a binding 10-years' guarantee.

OUR GUARANTEE. Every one of our 240-pound, $1.75 platform counter scales is covered by a 10 years' guarantee, during which time, if any piece or part gives out by reason of defect in material or workmanship we will replace or repair it free of charge.

THIS OUR SPECIAL $1.75 SCALE is an all purpose scale, and unless you have a larger scale or a full standard platform scale do not fail to take advantage of our special $1.75 price, for you will be repaid many times over during the year.

THESE SCALES WEIGH from ½ ounce to 240 pounds. They take the place in many ways of the regular platform scale. They have fine steel bearings, tin scoop, heavy brass beam. Weight, boxed for shipment, about 43 pounds. You will find the freight will amount to next to nothing, as compared with what you will save in price.

THERE ARE A NUMBER OF SCALES of from 200 to 250 pounds capacity being advertised at prices ranging very nearly the same as we offer this scale. We wish to say with reference to scales so advertised that this scale could be cheapened and offered for considerably less money, but if you want the best single beam platform scale we handle, our 10-year guaranteed scale, you will get no such platform scale elsewhere at anything like the price. Beam marked 44 pounds by ¼ ounce.

No. 9R5941 Our special price, each.............. ....$1.75

Our $2.85 Double Beam Platform Counter Scales.

FOR $2.85 we offer this high grade, 10-year guaranteed, double brass beam, counter scale as the equal of any counter scale made. $2.85 is a price based on the actual cost of material and labor, with but our one small percentage of profit added. A 240-pound platform counter scale for only $2.85.

These heavy double beam platform counter scales are made for us under contract by one of the best scale makers in this country. They are made from the best material that can be secured, and only the most skilled mechanics are employed. **They are carefully tested, accurately adjusted, and are covered by a binding guarantee.**

OUR 10-YEAR GUARANTEE. Every special $2.85, 240-Pound Platform Counter Scale is covered by a binding 10-year guarantee, during which time if any piece or part gives out by reason of defect in material or workmanship, we will replace or repair it free of charge. From the illustration engraved from a photograph, you can form some idea of the appearance of our special $2.85, 240-Pound Platform Counter Scale. If you do not wish to invest in a regular platform scale at $7.50 to $13.84, do not fail to order one of our counter scales. You will be repaid many times over for the $2.85 purchase price, in detecting errors, if not dishonesty, in the goods you buy and the produce you sell. These scales have a capacity of 240 pounds, they are extra large, extra strong and will serve almost any purpose. **Boxed for shipment, they weigh about 40 pounds.**

THESE SCALES are made with extra heavy brass beam, extra heavy tare beam. This is a great convenience and makes the scale one of the handiest in use. Every scale is tested before leaving the factory, and we guarantee them to be mechanically perfect. The beams are made of solid brass, full polished, accurately graduated. Beam marked 44 pounds by ¼ ounce.

AT $2.85 the scales come complete with double beam, scoop and extra weights, securely boxed, and we guarantee safe delivery.

No. 9R5942 Our special price........ ..$2.85

Our Extra Best Union Platform Grocers' Counter Scales.

No. 9R5943 Our Extra Best Union Platform Grocers' Counter Scales, with brass scoop and sliding poise. In this scale we have every essential feature in the highest priced scale sold; everything that is necessary to a first class weighing machine. By means of our taking practically the entire output of a factory, to sell them direct from factory to user, with one small profit added, we are able to offer you this extra best high grade grocers' scale, handsomely decorated and finished with heavy polished brass scoop, sliding poise, heavy solid brass beam, nickel plated. **We are able to make a price of only $5.00 on this scale.** This scale is suitable for fancy groceries, teas, coffees, etc., and our price is no more than you would pay for the scale, which we sell under No. 9R5941, if you bought it through the ordinary channels of trade. **It is guaranteed to weigh accurately on either corner of the platform or in the scoop. Capacity, ½ ounce to 244 pounds.** Finished in red enamel and gilt. Platform is 10½x13½ inches. Carefully packed in a wooden box for shipment. Beam marked 44 pounds by ⅛ ounces.
Price, each........ ....$5.00

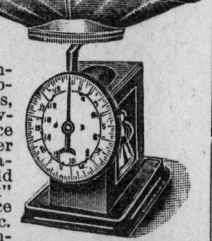

$5.00

American Family Scales.

No. 9R5959 Made of steel, with steel top, white enameled dial. Beautifully enameled and ornamented, Weighs 24 pounds by ounces. Occupies but little space, is light and easily moved. It can be regulated by turning the brass screw on top. Is always ready and is easily understood. It is a convenient scale to use and has no weights that can be lost. You can look this one in the face to prove its accuracy without looking for weights. Every scale examined before leaving the factory, and warranted correct. Price, each..............................92c

Our Gilt Edge Grocery Platform Counter Scales.

$9.85

No. 9R5944 Our Gilt Edge Grocery Platform Counter Scales, with heavy brass scoop, capacity 1 ounce to 250 pounds. Platform, 12x15 inches. Scales of the same pattern as this are sold by dealers at more than double our price. **This style of scale is very desirable for use in stores.** It combines extreme sensitiveness with accuracy and large capacity. The beam is on a level with the eye; the platform is large enough to hold a barrel of flour, and the scale is quick enough to weigh teas and spices. Instead of using a weight to balance the scoop, we use a poise which cannot get lost. **It has a heavy brass beam nickel plated and graduated on top sides.** The scale is handsomely decorated and securely packed for shipment. Capacity, 1 ounce to 250 pounds. Size of platform, 12x15 inches. Beam marked 60 pounds by ounces.
Price, each............$9.85

No. 9R5946 Butchers' Scale, marble slab; tested to weigh 32 pounds by ounces. Weight, carefully packed in box for shipment, 40 pounds. Price..................$7.50

No. 9R5947 Same as No. 9R5946; to weigh 64 pounds by 2 ounces. Weight, carefully packed in box for shipment, 40 pounds. Price....................$7.80

Agate Bearing Butcher Counter Scales.

No. 9R5948 Agate Bearing Butcher Counter Scales. Even balance, 10-inch double dial. Dial can be seen from both sides. Finely nickel plated sash, agate bearing, handsome black enameled base, and marble slab; weighs 30 pounds by ounces. This is the only spring balance on the market that has agate bearings, and is consequently very sensitive and accurate, and thoroughly reliable.
Price, each.... ....$10.67

No. 9R5948½ Same as No. 9R5948, only it weighs 15 pounds by ⅛ ounces, and is used in delicatessen stores, as well as meat markets. Price, each.$10.67

No. 9R5949 Butchers' and Grocers' Hanging Circular Spring Balances, aluminum dial, 6 inches in diameter, will not corrode or tarnish, black figures, white patent enameled pan, 11 inches in diameter, tinned iron bows and hooks. Weighs 24 pounds by ounces. Warranted sensitive and accurate. This is our leader.
Price, each......................$2.20

No. 9R5950 Circular Spring Balance for meat and fish markets. Weighs 30 pounds by ounces. Has 7-inch dial with glass sash, large figures. White enameled front, tin pan, tinned iron bows and swivel. Warranted accurate.
Price, each $3.40

No. 9R5951 Circular Spring Balance. The scale is for butchers' use exclusively. It weighs 30 pounds by ounces, has 7-inch dial with nickel plated glass sash, large figures, white enameled front, tinned iron bows, hooks and swivel, and has a fine porcelain pan. Sensitive and accurate; fully warranted. Each, $4.50

Market Balance.

No. 9R5952 Improved Market Balance. Extra large dial, diameter 8 inches and 10-inch sash, large, heavy figures, round, white patent enameled pan, nickel plated bows and German silver rings. Weighs 15 pounds by ⅛ ounces, and very desirable for butcher business. This is our highest grade scale. Warranted sensitive and accurate. Price, each..............$7.20

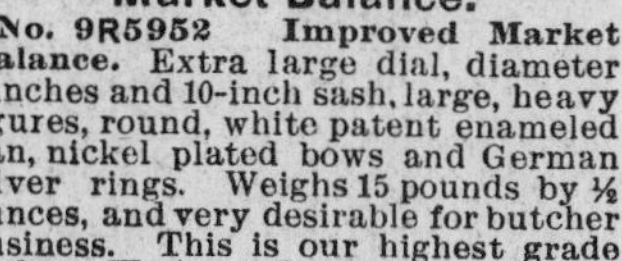

No. 9R5953 Same as No. 9R5952, only it weighs 30 pounds by the ounce.
Price, each.............................$7.22

No. 9R5954 Improved United States Market Balance. Extra large double dial, 8 inches in diameter with 10-inch sash. Dial can be seen from both sides. Large, heavy figures, nickel plated sash and bows, and German silver ring, round white patent enameled pan, warranted not to break. Weighs 30 pounds by ounces and used in all large markets. Sensitive and accurate. Price, each..........$10.80

No. 9R5955 Same as No. 9R5954, only it weighs 15 pounds by ⅛ ounces. Price, each...........$10.78

Our $1.65 Family Scales.

FOR $1.65 we offer this 25-pound family scale as the best scale of the kind on the market. This scale weighs from ¼ ounce up to 25 pounds. It is made for us under contract by one of the best makers. Every scale is guaranteed, and if it is not found perfect in every respect it can be returned to us at our expense, and your money will be refunded.

IT WILL PAY YOU TO BUY THIS SCALE and weigh your groceries and meat purchases, weigh the butter. Boxed for shipment, they weigh about 20 pounds. Beam marked 1½ pounds by ½ ounces.
No. 9R5956 Our special price, each.........$1.65

Our 68-Cent Family Scales.

No. 9R5957 Our 68-cent price should induce every family in the land to own a pair of these 4-pound scales. You may save the cost in one day's use. Even balance scales. Plain japanned. To weigh 4 pounds, with good tin scoop. Our price...............................68c

Our Household Scale for $1.12.

No. 9R5958 The Acme Household Scale. A handsome and reliable scale, weighs to 20 lbs. by ounces, has tin scoop, brass dial 5 inches in diameter. Guaranteed to be absolutely accurate at all weights, thoroughly tested before leaving the factory. The low price at which we are able to offer this scale will make it a favorite family and household scale. Will save "guesswork" in cooking, making mince meat, preserving fruit, etc. Will detect mistakes (intentional or otherwise), in weighing articles you buy. Every farmer and every family should by all means have one or more scales. Our prices place scales within the reach of everyone. Weight of scale, boxed for shipment, 7 pounds. Price, each. $1.12

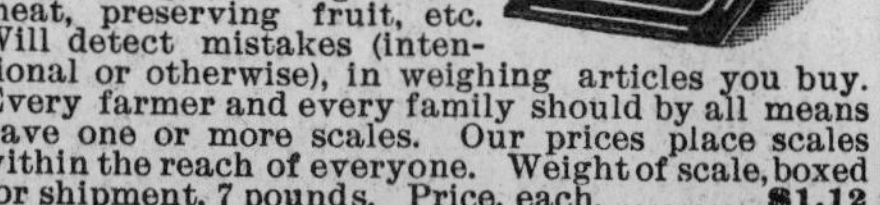

Spring Balances.

No. 9R5960 Spring Balance, to weigh 24 lbs. by ½ lbs. Shipping weight, 9 oz. Price, each.........6c

No. 9R5961 Spring Balance, to weigh 48 lbs. by pounds. Shipping weight, 12 oz. Price, each......13c

No. 9R5962 Spring Balance, with round tin dish; weighs 24 lbs. by ¼ pound. Shipping weight, 1¾ pounds. Price, each...........16c

No. 9R5963 Spring Balance, with round tin dish; weighs 50 lbs. by pounds. Shipping weight, 2½ pounds. Price, each.............24c

9R5960 9R5962

Finest Straight Spring Scale Made.

These scales are more compact, and have longer dials than other makes. While better in many ways than the old style, comparison will show that our prices are lower.

No.	Weight	Price
9R5972	50 pounds x ⅛ pound.	$0.36
9R5973	75 pounds x ¼ pound.	.88
9R5974	100 pounds x 1 pound.	1.05
9R5975	150 pounds x 1 pound.	1.30
9R5976	210 pounds x 2 pounds.	1.52

Ironclad Ice Scales.

No. 9R5979 The Famous Iron Clad Ice Balance, made entirely of malleable iron and cannot break. Compact and durable and not liable to get out of order. Fully guaranteed. Marked to 5 pound graduations.

Will weigh...........	200 pounds	300 pounds
Price, each...........	$2.40	$2.64

Professional Scale.

Every doctor should have one, No family should be without one. This is a very beautiful and accurate scale, beautifully finished in brass, nickel plated, and offered at about one-half retail price.
No. 9R5981 10-pound scale........30c
No. 9R5982 20-pound scale........40c

No. 9R5981

Steelyards.

No. 9R5985 Steelyards with steel bars, guaranteed to weigh absolutely correct. We could sell you cheaper steelyards that could not be depended on, for a very little less money, but we don't care to handle such goods. The 50-lb. size weighs by ¼ pounds, larger sizes by ½ pounds.

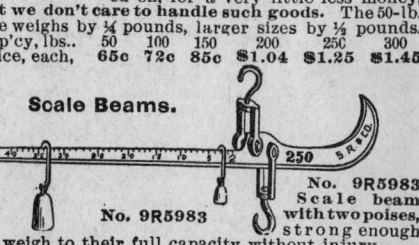

Cap'cy, lbs..	50	100	150	200	250	300
Price, each,	65c	72c	85c	$1.04	$1.25	$1.45

Scale Beams.

No. 9R5983 Scale beam with two poises, strong enough to weigh to their full capacity without injury.

No. 9R5983

Capacity, lbs.....	250	400	600	1,000	1,200
Price, complete...	$1.20	$1.84	$2.53	$4.21	$5.00

IF YOU WANT TO BUY

A SUIT, OVERCOAT, ULSTER OR A PAIR OF PANTS

Made to your exact measure at a price about one-half what tailors charge generally,

SEND 5 CENTS FOR OUR SAMPLE BOOK OF

MEN'S CUSTOM TAILORING.

SCHOOLHOUSE AND FACTORY BELLS AT $7.20 TO $22.50.

CHURCH BELLS AT $29.25 TO $112.50.

Bells for farm, schoolhouse, churches and elsewhere we will sell at prices based on the actual cost to manufacture, the cost of material and labor, with but our one small percentage of profit added. If you are in the market for a high grade, perfectly toned, guaranteed bell for schoolhouse, church, farm, or home, we are prepared to furnish you such a bell under our guarantee for quality and at a saving of from 25 to 50 per cent in price as against any price you can get from any dealer anywhere.

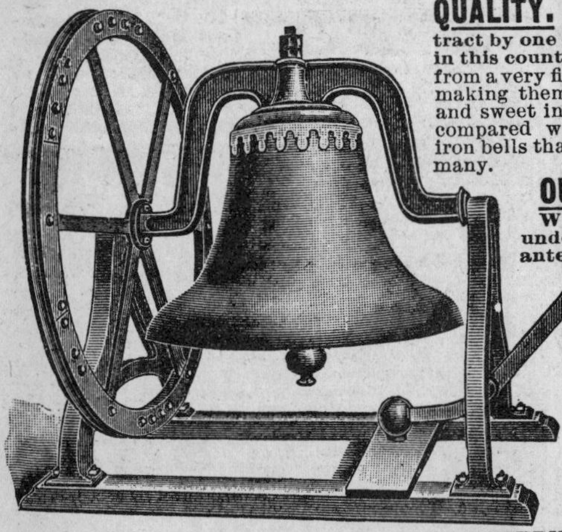

QUALITY. **Our bells are made for us under contract by one of the best makers in this country.** They are made from a very fine crystalline metal, making them loud, clear, round and sweet in tone and cannot be compared with the cheap cast iron bells that are advertised by many.

OUR GUARANTEE.

We put out every bell under our binding guarantee against breakage for five years, and if it is not perfectly satisfactory as to quality of tone, volume, finish, weight and durability; if it is not satisfactory in every way and if you do not find it lower in price than any bell you can buy elsewhere, you are at liberty to return it to us **AT OUR EXPENSE AND WE WILL RETURN YOUR MONEY.**

Church, Schoolhouse and Factory Bells.

No. 9R6050 These bells are CRYSTALLINE METAL and can be relied on under all circumstances and in all seasons. Nos. 20 to 28 are school or factory bells, and are not suitable for churches. Nos. 30 to 48, inclusive, are recommended for churches. Bells are numbered by the diameter in inches.

No.	Bells only, lbs.	Complete, lbs.	Price	No.	Bells only, lbs.	Complete, lbs.	Price
20	105	150	$ 7.20	36	550	800	$ 49.50
22	125	175	9.00	38	650	950	56.25
24	155	225	11.25	40	800	1,100	67.50
26	215	325	18.00	42	900	1,200	74.25
28	250	400	22.50	44	1,050	1,450	90.00
30	320	525	29.25	46	1,150	1,600	101.25
32	380	575	33.75	48	1,350	1,850	112.50
34	460	725	40.50				

The weights and prices above named are **for complete bells,** and include wood sills, iron wheel; and for Nos. 30, 32, 34, 36, 40, 44 and 48, tolling hammer without extra charge. **Tolling hammers** for Nos. 24, 26 and 28, when so ordered, **$3.00** each, extra. **The above prices are for bells delivered free on board cars at our factory in Southern Ohio.**

OUR BIG 83-CENT FARM BELL.

At 83c for 40 lbs., $1.17 for 50 lbs., $1.75 for 75 lbs., we offer this large, handsome crystalline metal farm bell as the greatest value ever offered in a bell of this kind.

This bell is hung on a heavy, strong and substantially built frame which bolts to a pole. The bell is full bronzed and at our special 83c to $1.75 price, according to weight, the bell comes complete with all mountings.

From the accompanying illustration, engraved from a photograph, you can get a general idea of the appearance of this our special 83c, $1.17 and $1.75 farm bell.

At our extremely low price, a price but a shade above the actual value of the raw material, there is no reason why any farm should be without one of our large farm bells. Erect a post, fasten this our 40, 50 or 75-lb. bell to the post and you will feel repaid for your purchase the first month. **No. 9R6055**

Size No. 1. Diameter at mouth, 15 inches. Weight with hangings, 40 pounds. Price...**83c**

Size No. 2. Diameter at mouth, 17 inches. Weight with hangings, 50 pounds. Price...**$1.17**

Size No. 3. Diameter at mouth, 19 inches. Weight complete with mountings, 75 pounds. Price...**$1.75**

Our Big $2.35 Farm Bell.

At $2.35 we offer this big 100-pound crystalline metal farm bell complete with all mountings as the equal of bells that sell at more than double the price.

Order this high grade bell and if you do not find it perfectly satisfactory and better than any bell you could get elsewhere at anything like the price, you can return it to us at our expense and we will return your money.

From the accompanying illustration, engraved from a photograph, you can form an idea of the appearance of this, our high grade, big $2.35 farm bell.

This bell is well finished, is extra fine tone, can be heard farther than any copper or tin bell of five times the cost, and far more durable.

At our $2.35 price the bell comes complete with all mountings, as illustrated above, ready for use.

No. 9R6056 Size No. 4. Diameter at mouth, 20 inches. Weight, with mountings, 100 pounds. Price...**$2.35**

WRITE FOR FREE CIRCULAR GIVING MORE COMPLETE DESCRIPTION OF OUR FARM, SCHOOLHOUSE AND CHURCH BELLS.

New Departure Door Bell.

It gives the electric ring. Made with either push button or turn plate, as described below. **No springs to get out of order.** It is simple and durable.

No. 9R6060 New Departure Cast Iron Rotary Turn Plate Door Bell. Electro copper plated, antique copper finish. Diameter of bell, 3 inches. Size of turn plate, 3¾ x 1¾ inches. **Very handsome design and wonderfully cheap.**

Price, each...**60c**

New Departure Rotary Door Bell.

No. 9R6063 New Departure Rotary Door Bell. Nickel plated bell, 3½ inches in diameter. **Wrought bronze metal turn plate,** finished antique copper. Size of turn plate, 2x4½ inches.

Price, complete...**98c**

No. 9R6066 New Departure Push Button Door Bell. **Nickel plated bell,** 3½ inches in diameter. **Wrought bronze metal push button case.** Antique copper finish. Size of case, 2x4⅛ inches. (Illustration shows push plate only.) Bell is same as No. 9R6063. Price, each.....**$1.05**

No. 9R6063

For Electric Bells, Burglar Alarms, See Index. No. 9R6066

Pull Down Lever Bell.

No. 9R6069 Bronze Plated Door Bell. Diameter of bell, 4 inches. **Pull down lever.** Packed complete with screws. Weight, 2 lbs. 2 oz.

Price, each, with pull.... **55c**

Bells are carried by railroad companies at a very low rate, third class, which usually averages 25 to 40 cents per 100 pounds for 500 miles. By referring to pages 7 to 10 you can get the third class rate per 100 pounds to a point nearest you, which is almost exactly the same as to your town, and you will see the freight will amount to next to nothing as compared to what you will save in price.

Sargent & Co.'s Patent Rotary Electric Ring Door Bells.

No. 9R6074 To turn, requires no winding. In the Rotary Electric Ring Bell we have the effect of the Electric Bell without any Electrical Appliance. The stroke is produced by rotating the bell turn, and it responds instantly with an electric ring sound to the slightest movement of the turn either way. The mechanism is compact and durable and may be depended upon every time. There are no springs to get out of order, there is no battery to replace, no winding required. Nickel plated bell metal bell, 3⅛ inches in diameter, with plain genuine bronze turn plate, polished bronze finish. Packed complete with screws.

Price, complete...**85c**

No. 9R6077 Door Bell, same as No. 9R6074, except the turn is antique copper finish.

Price, complete...**87c**

No. 9R6080 Door Bell, same as No. 9R6074, except the turn is like illustration at the right; finished antique copper sand finish.

Price, complete...**93c**

No. 9R6082 Door Bell, same as No. 9R6074, except the turn is like illustration at the left. Price, complete...**86c**

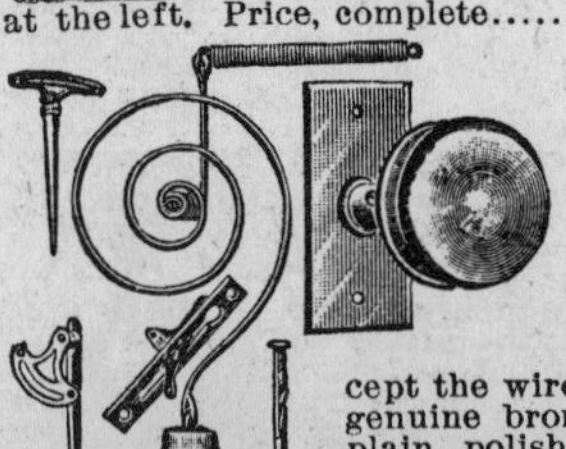

No. 9R6090 The Old Reliable House Bell on carriage; complete with attachments as illustrated; two side cranks and two end cranks (only one each shown). Nothing more needed except the wire. Bell metal bell, genuine bronze pull and plate, plain polished bronze finish.

Price, complete (except wire)...**83c**

No. 9R6091 Bell same as above, except pull and plate is ornamental design, genuine bronze. Will match lock sets Nos. 9R324 and 9R456. Price, complete (except wire).........**80c**

Alarm Door Bells.

No. 9R6097 Alarm Door Bells, double stroke, 4 inches, bronzed steel. To be fastened above the door so bell will ring when door is opened.

Price, each...**32c**

No. 9R6098 Alarm Door Bell, 4 inches, polished bell metal, nickel plated. Price, each...**71c**

Open Polished Bells.

No. 9R6100 Open Polished Bell Metal Bells may be used for a variety of purposes; make good sheepbells, a harness bell for milk wagons, drays, etc. **Genuine bell metal.** Full weight goods. Best shape for sound. Not made with extra flare to increase diameter of mouth.

Nos.	1	2	3	4	5	6
Diameter of mouth in ins.	2 3/16	2 7/16	2⅝	2⅞	3 5/16	3 9/16
Weight, each	3½	4	5½	6	9½	11
Price, each..	$0.07	$0.08	$0.10	$0.14	$0.18	$0.20
Per dozen....	.84	.90	1.18	1.60	2.13	2.39

Hand Bells.

No. 9R6112 Genuine Bell Metal. Full weight goods.

No.	Actual weight, ounces.	Diameter, inches.	Each
1	4	2¼	$0.10
3	7	2⅞	.16
5	13	3¾	.30
7	20	4⅞	.48
9	30	5⅜	.83
13	50	7	1.48
14	54	7¼	1.69

Tea Bells.

No. 9R6113 Tea Bell. All nickel plated and polished, 2¼-inch gong. Weight, 3 ounces.

Price, each...**15c**

Tea or Call Bell.

No. 9R6114 Tea or Call Bell. Highly nickel plated, 3⅛ inch gong. Fancy aluminum bronzed base. Pleasing tone. Weight, 11 ounces. Price, each...**30c**

Call Bell.

No. 9R6115 Call Bell. Large size, with 4⅝ inch nickel plated gong and bronzed base. A loud sounding bell suitable for school rooms, offices, etc. Weight, 17 ounces.

Price, each...**55c**

New Departure Tea Bells.

No. 9R6116 New Departure Tea or Call Bells; rings like an electric bell. Base, 3⅛ inches; gong, 2½ inches. Full nickel plated. Price, each..........95c

Rotary Tea Bells.

No. 9R6117 Rotary Tea Bell, all nickel plated. Has the electric ring. Base, 3¼ inches; gong, 2½ inches. Price, each..........60c

For SILVER BELLS, see Silverware Department. Refer to Index.

Trip Gong Bells.

No. 9R6125 Trip Gong Bells. Genuine bell metal.

3-in., weight 1 lb. 5 oz......	$0.44
4-in., weight 1½ lb........	.55
6-in., weight 2 lb. 13 oz....	.98
8-in., weight 6 lb..........	1.95
10-in., weight 9¾ lb........	3.50

Swiss Cow Bells.

These Swiss Cow Bells are made from Swiss bell metal. They are celebrated for their pure musical tone which can be heard a long distance and sounds entirely different from common bells.

Catalogue No.	Diameter at mouth	Weight	Widest strap that can be used	Price, each
9R6134	4 inches	1 lb.	1⅝-inch	$0.58
9R6135	5 inches	1¾ lbs.	2⅛-inch	.95
9R6136	6⅛ inches	3 lbs.	3 -inch	1.62

Cow Bells.

No. 9R6140 The Old Standard Cow Bell. Very loud tone and extra well made.

No.	0	2
Size of mouth	6 x4½	5⅛x3⅞
Height	6¼	5
Price, each	28c	19c
No.	3	5
Size of mouth	4½x3	3⅛x2⅝
Height	4¾	3¼
Price, each	15c	10c

Cow Bell Straps.

No. 10R2601 Fine Black Leather Cow Bell Straps, made with roller buckle and loop.

Width	Price, each	Width	Price, each
1 inch	20c	1¾ inches	33c
1¼ inches	25c	2 inches	45c
1½ inches	29c	3 inches	65c

Sheep Bells.

Sheep Bells, cast from bell metal. Complete with straps of suitable size.

No. 9R6141 Sheep Bell; height, 1⅝ inches; size of mouth, 1⅝x1⅞ inches, with strap. Price, each..........16c

No. 9R6142 Sheep Bell; height, 1⅞ inches; size of mouth, 1½x2 inches, with strap. Price, each..........19c

Measurements are for body of bell.

Turkey Bells.

No. 9R6146 Polished Bell Metal Turkey Bell. Diameter, 1¾ inches; enables the flock to be easily located, makes the foxes shy. Furnished complete with strap as shown. Weight, each, 3 ounces. Price, each..........10c

Sleigh Bells.

No. 9R6200 Dexter Body Strap with Chimes. 30 extra-tinned, genuine bell metal Dexter bells, riveted on high grade solid harness leather strap. These bells must not be compared with cast iron or stamped steel bells which are being largely sold this season. Price, per strap..$2.20

No. 9R6201 Dexter Body Strap with Chime, same as above but heavily nickel plated and polished on genuine bell metal. Price, per strap..........$2.90

No. 9R6204 Bodystrap consisting of thirty Nickel Plated, Pressed Steel Bells, diameter 1⅛ inch, securely fastened on 1-inch black harness leather straps. These bells are heavily copper plated before being nickeled, making a durable and handsome bell. Price, per strap..........$1.20

No. 9R6207 Body Strap consisting of 30 Nickel Plated Steel bells, 1¼-inch, otherwise same as above. Price, per strap..........$1.35

No. 9R6210 Body Strap; 24 No. 2 Tinned Rim Sleigh Bells, made of genuine bell metal, riveted on black harness leather strap. Price, per strap..$1.28

No. 9R6213 Body Strap; 30 No. 2 Tinned Rim Sleigh Bells, made of genuine bell metal, riveted on black harness leather strap. Price, per strap..$1.44

No. 9R6216 Body Strap; 30 No. 2 Extra Smooth Polished and Nickel Plated Rim Bells, made of genuine bell metal, riveted on black harness leather strap. Price, per strap..........$2.55

No. 9R6219 Body Strap; 36 No. 2 Extra Smooth, Polished and Nickel Plated Rim Bells, made of genuine bell metal, riveted on black harness leather strap. Price, per strap..........$2.77

No. 9R6222 Body Strap, consisting of 19 common tin cast, genuine bell metal, rim sleigh bells, riveted to black harness leather strap. Bells are assorted from No. 0 to No. 6, ranging in size from 1 inch to 1¾ inches in diameter. Price, per strap..........92c

No. 9R6223 Same as No. 9R6222, with 25 bells. Price, per strap..........$1.27

No. 9R6224 Same as No. 9R6222, with 31 bells. Price, per strap..........$1.37

No. 9R6228 Body Strap, consisting of 19 highly nickel plated genuine cast bell metal bells, No. 0 to 6; sizes assorted from 1 to 1¾ inches in diameter, riveted to black harness leather strap. These bells are heavily plated and will retain their brilliant finish for years. Price, per strap..........$1.73

No. 9R6229 Same as No. 9R6228, with 25 bells. Price, per strap..........$2.07

No. 9R6230 Same as No. 9R6228, with 31 bells. Price, per strap..........$2.36

No. 9R6235 Body Strap consisting of 19 Polished Rim Sleigh Bells made of genuine cast bell metal. Wire fastened on heavy russet harness leather lined with grain leather. Sizes, No. 2 to No. 6; 1¼ inch to 1¾ inch in diameter. Price, per strap..$1.20

No. 9R6237 Body Strap consisting of 19 round polished cast bell metal bells on leather strap, fastened same as above; assorted sizes, from No. 2 to No. 8 bells; diameter, 1¼ to 2⅛ inches. Per strap..$1.33

No. 9R6240 Body Strap consisting of 23 Round Polished Bells on leather strap, wire fastened same as above; assorted sizes, from No. 1 to No. 8; diameter, 1⅛ to 2⅛ inches. Price, per strap..........$1.55

No. 9R6243 Body Strap consisting of 23 Round Polished Bells on leather strap, wire fastened same as above; assorted sizes, from No. 5 to No. 13; diameter, 1⅝ to 2⅞ inches. Price, per strap..........$2.67

No. 9R6250 Neck Strap, consisting of 9 round polished, cast, genuine bell metal bells. Wire fastened on heavy russet harness leather, lined with grain leather; sizes assorted from No. 1 to No. 5. Diameter, from 1⅛ to 1⅝ inches. Price, per strap..........48c

No. 9R6251 Neck Strap, consisting of 15 round polished, cast, genuine bell metal bells. Same style as above; sizes, from No. 2 to No. 9; diameter, from 1¼ inches to 2¼ inches. Price, per strap....97c

Loose Bells.

No. 9R6260 Polished Loose Sleigh Bells, for the convenience of those who wish to make their own straps of bells. Made of genuine bell metal, natural finish.

We will furnish any quantity at dozen prices.

Numbers	1	2	3	4	5	6	7
Diameter, inches	1⅛	1¼	1⅜	1½	1⅝	1¾	1⅞
Price, per doz.	$0.20	$0.28	$0.38	$0.46	$0.54	$0.59	$0.73
Numbers	8	9	10	12	14	16	18
Diameter, inches	2⅛	2¼	2⅜	2⅝	3	3¼	3¾
Price, per doz.	$0.88	$0.98	$1.20	$1.74	$2.56	$4.10	$4.62

Loose Swedish Sleigh Bells.

No. 9R6265 Loose Swedish Sleigh Bells, made of genuine high grade cast bell metal, polished. These bells have a distinct tone, entirely different from the common sleigh bells, which makes them a great favorite in some localities.

Numbers	7	9	11	13	15
Diameter, inches	2	2¼	2½	2¾	3¼
Price, each	23c	26c	40c	47c	56c
Price, per dozen	$2.75	3.10	4.75	5.55	6.65

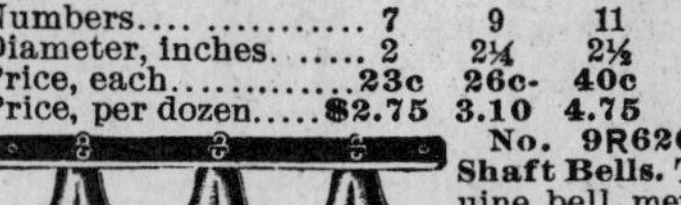

No. 9R6269 Open Shaft Bells. Tinned genuine bell metal on substantial leather straps; diameter, 2⅛ inches. The tongue is secured to an eye cast in the bell and cannot drop off. Set consists of 6 bells, 3 on each strap. Price, per set..........39c

No. 9R6272 Nickel Plated Steel Gong Shaft Chimes, heavily copper plated before being nickeled. While this bell lacks the rich tone of the genuine bell metal bells, it is a nice looking bell and is used extensively and cannot fail to give satisfaction for the price. Set consists of two straps with three bells on each. Per set..........36c

No. 9R6274 Nickel Plated Steel Gong Shaft Chimes, same as above but has beaded edge, which adds to the tone, appearance and strength of the bell. Set consists of two straps with 3 bells on each. Price, per set....40c

No. 9R6277 Nickel Plated Steel Gong Shaft Chimes beaded same as above. Set consists of two straps with four bells on each. Price, per set..........64c

No. 9R6280 Nickel Plated Guaranteed Wrought Steel Cup Chimes. Heavy electro copper plated before nickeling. This is our highest grade steel bell and has a well earned reputation for durability and clearness of tone. Set consists of two straps with four bells of graduated sizes on each. Price, per set..........85c

No. 9R6283 Genuine Cast Bell Metal Band Shaft Chimes, highly nickel plated and buffed. Notwithstanding our low price on this chime we guarantee that it is a solid cast metal bell of superior tone. Set consists of two straps with three bells on each strap. Per set....80c

No. 9R6285 Graduated Band Chime, made of wrought brass, heavily nickel plated and polished. Set consists of two straps with four bells on each. Price, per set..........$1.35

No. 9R6288 Mikado Chime, made of pure high grade cast bell metal, finely polished and nickel plated. A bell for which your local dealer would charge you $2.25 to $3.00. For finish, quality and tone this bell cannot be excelled at the price. Price, per set, consisting of two straps with four graduated bells on each..........$1.45

No. 9R6291 Nickel Plated Swiss Shaft Chimes. Made of pure cast Swiss bell metal; these bells are harmonized and have a beautiful tone. Three bells on metal strap, six bells to a set. Price, per set..........$1.12

No. 9R6294 Harmonized Swiss Shaft Chimes. Pure Swiss bell metal, highly nickel plated bells on japanned iron strap, 4 bells on a strap; 8 bells to set. Price, per set..........$1.44

No. 9R6297 Large Swiss Shaft Chimes, clear and musical in tone. Pure bell metal, tuned by experts. Intervals 1, 3, 5, 8; highly nickel plated bells on japanned iron strap. Eight bells to set. Price, per set..........$2.70

No. 9R6300 Beaded Gong Pole Chimes, nickel plated on genuine bell metal, finely polished. Set consists of five bells of graduated sizes mounted on japanned iron strap. Price, per single strap......90c

No. 9R6303 Harmonized Swiss Pole Chime, made of pure Swiss bell metal, highly nickel plated and mounted on japanned iron strap. Set consists of six bells of graduated sizes, harmonized by an expert. Price, per single strap..........$1.40

No. 9R6305 Swiss Pole Chime. Highest grade manufactured, of pure Swiss bell metal, beautifully polished and nickel plated. Set consists of nine harmonized bells of graduated sizes, and will please those who desire the best. Price, per single strap..$2.47

No. 9R6320 Russian Saddle Chime. Pure bell metal gong, fancy metal frame, all nicely nickel plated. Price, each..........95c

No. 9R6323 Russian Saddle Chimes. Three genuine bell metal gongs, mounted on a steel frame and all heavily nickel plated. Price, each.......$1.00

No. 9R6327 Russian Saddle Chime with double bell metal gong and fancy metal frame, all nicely nickel plated and polished. Price, each.... $1.45

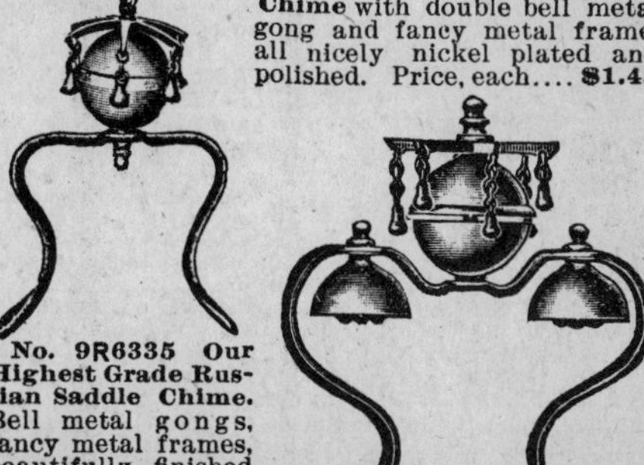

No. 9R6335 Our Highest Grade Russian Saddle Chime. Bell metal gongs, fancy metal frames, beautifully finished in best nickel plate. Price, each..$2.50

FIREPROOF SAFES

LARGE, MEDIUM AND SMALL FIREPROOF SAFES FOR BANKS . . . MERCHANTS, PUBLIC INSTITUTIONS, PRIVATE USE AND FOR HOME.

AT $6.25 AND UPWARDS, ACCORDING TO SIZE, we offer a line of the highest grade fireproof safes on the market, and we believe our uniformly low prices should attract the attention of every buyer who is interested in saving from **50 to 100 per cent in the purchasing of a safe.** We are at this writing in receipt of a letter of testimony from a party who purchased a **300-pound safe,** saying that it just went through a raging hot fire for 18 hours, and while it was the smallest safe (**the largest weighing 1500 pounds and upward**) that was in this fire, it was the only safe in which **the contents were in perfect condition,** and in which the combination worked perfectly **even after 16 or 18 hours red hot test.** This is but one sample of the hundreds of testimonials which speak for the satisfactory construction of our special high grade fireproof work.

CONSTRUCTION. **Our Fireproof Safes are constructed by forming outer and inner boxes of wrought steel, between** which the **concrete filling** is introduced in a semi-liquid state, permeating and reaching into every crevice, making the whole structure, when hardened, **a solid mass.** The filling soon becomes hard and dry as limestone rock, **and never corrodes the steel,** which is sufficiently thick to cause great strength in connection with the filling, and yet not thick enough to prove injurious as a conductor of heat. **The secret of its fireproof qualities is the chemical change that takes place upon being heated to a certain temperature,** which generates a vapor that fills all the pores in the concrete, thereby forming **a cool, moist wall entirely around the contents** during their subjection to the heat. **The outside steel box is formed of one continuous steel (not iron) plate,** forming top, sides and bottom. This box is securely attached to heavy front and back angle frames, forming in outline as nearly as possible one solid piece. The doors are stepped or flanged in the usual manner and secured by front and back bolts.

OUR LOCKS. **All our safes are secured and protected by the Yale Four-Tumbler Combination Lock.** This lock is absolutely non-pickable and consists of a series of tumblers so arranged as to be susceptible to one million combinations. The various changes in the combination can be made by a very simple process. Directions for operating the lock and changing the combination are furnished with each safe. This lock is so arranged that the door can be closed, bolts thrown, and the dial turned from five to ten numbers (practically **locking the safe**) without throwing the combination, which is of great importance, especially when wishing to leave the office a few moments and at the same time have the safe locked; on your return simply reverse the dial to the last number on which the combination is set and you can open the safe.

ABOUT THE FREIGHT. **Safes take the lowest rate of freight, or third class. They are shipped from the factory in Northern Indiana,** from which point the customer **must pay the freight,** but you will find the freight will amount to next to nothing as compared with what you will save in expense.

For example, third class freight will be for 200 miles, 15 to 20c per 100 pounds; 400 miles, 30c to 40c per 100 pounds; 700 miles, 40c to 50c per 100 pounds; 1000 miles, 60c to 75c per 100 pounds, from which you can calculate very closely what the freight will amount to.

MEASUREMENTS AND WEIGHTS. **All safes are measured from floor to top of safe, including wheels. The weight of a new fireproof safe can only be approximated.** In seasoning it will lose in weight from 50 to 150 pounds, depending upon its size. The weight has nothing whatever to do with the fireproof qualities. We make effort to reduce the weight of our safes on account of saving in freight rates to our customers.

Name painted on safe without extra charge when ordered.

We do not letter name on safe unless it is so ordered. Name should be carefully printed to avoid mistakes.

OUR $6.25 FIREPROOF SAFE.

No. 9R7100

FOR $6.25 WE OFFER OUR FAMILY FIREPROOF SAFE weighing 100 pounds, as a small house safe which should be in every home, as a safe place for holding all valuable papers, etc. While these safes are not positively burglar proof, they are proof against ordinary burglary and petty thieves, and absolutely safe against **any kind of fire.**

THIS SAFE AT $6.25 is intended for dwellings and home safe, and is equal to safes sold by other houses at $10.00 to $15.00.

THIS $6.25 SAFE IS ABSOLUTELY FIREPROOF. It is nicely finished throughout, has a deep fireproof door, latest burglar proof combination lock. It is 16¾ inches high outside, 10 inches inside, 10½ inches wide outside, 6½ inches inside, 13 inches deep outside, 8 inches inside. **Weighs 100 pounds. It is offered at $6.25 as the equal of any safe on the market sold by others at $10.00 to $15.00. This safe does not have T handle to operate the bolt and is not furnished with the four-tumbler Yale lock, which are on all other safes sold by us.**

No. 9R7100 Our price **$6.25**

OUR $12.25 FIREPROOF SAFE.

FOR $12.25 WE OFFER you a single door fireproof safe, the equal of anything you can buy elsewhere at $25.00. While the safe is intended more as a house safe, we have sold a great many to business men for offices, stores and other places where only a small safe is required as a protection to valuable papers, etc. **This safe is beautifully finished, rounded corners throughout, with the very best non-pickable combination lock, highly ornamented with** transfer decorations, painting, etc., and finished with your name handsomely lettered in gold, without extra charge. **This safe has a 5-flange door. Dimensions of safe:** Outside, 24x15x15 inches; inside, 12x8x9 inches; approximate weight, 225 pounds. **Arrangement of cabinet work:** One book space, 3½x12 inches; one sub-treasury with flat key lock, 4x5 inches; one dovetailed drawer, 3x4 inches; one pigeonhole, 3½x4 inches.

No. 9R7102

No. 9R7102 Our special price **$12.25**
No. 9R7103 Our special price, with inside door **13.50**

OUR $14.25 FIREPROOF SAFE.

AT $14.25 WE OFFER A REGULAR $35.00 SAFE. THIS IS A VERY POPULAR SIZE SAFE for home, small merchants, and the various places of business where a fireproof safe of limited capacity is required. **It is finished with round corners throughout,** handsomely ornamented with beautiful gold lines and hand painting, and we furnish it with your name in gold letters without extra charge. **It has a 5-flange door.**

No. 9R7104

DIMENSIONS OF SAFE: Outside measure, 25x17x16 inches; inside measure, 12½x9x10 inches; approximate weight, 300 pounds.

ARRANGEMENT OF CABINET WORK: One book space, 12¼ inches high, 5¼ inches wide, 9 inches deep; one sub-treasury, 6 inches high, 4¾ inches wide, 9 inches deep; one book space, 4 inches high, 4¾ inches wide, 9 inches deep; one drawer, 3 inches high, 4¾ inches wide, 9 inches deep.

No. 9R7104 Our special price **$14.25**
No. 9R7105 Our special price, with inner door **15.50**

Our $14.95 Safe has the same style cabinet work as our No. 9R7104, except it is larger. Outside dimensions, 27½x18¼x17 inches; inside dimensions, 13x10x10 inches; approximate weight, 400 pounds.

ARRANGEMENT OF CABINET WORK: One book space, 13 inches high, 5¼ inches wide, 9 inches deep; one sub-treasury, 6 inches high, 4¾ inches wide, 9 inches deep; one drawer, 3 inches high, 4¾ inches wide, 9 inches deep; one pigeonhole, 4 inches high, 4¾ inches wide, 9 inches deep.

No. 9R7106 Our special price **$14.95**
No. 9R7107 Our special price, with inner door **16.20**

Our $16.95 Fireproof Safe With Five-Flange Door.

THIS IS A STRICTLY HIGH GRADE FIREPROOF SAFE, one that retails everywhere at $45.00. It is designed **for homes, for merchants, for all classes of business men** who require a safe larger in dimensions, one with **more book room** than those previously illustrated. **This is a good sized safe for the country merchant.** Weighs **500 pounds.** Outside measure, **30x18¼x20 inches.** Inside measure, **15x10x12 inches.** Round corners, beautifully ornamented and decorated with handsome hand painted landscape views, etc. Furnished with **your name handsomely lettered in gold** when ordered.

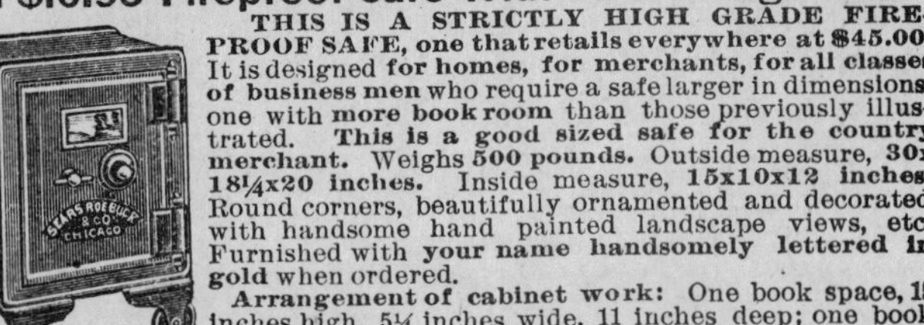

Arrangement of cabinet work: One book space, 15 inches high, 5¼ inches wide, 11 inches deep; one book space, 6 inches high, 4¾ inches wide, 11 inches deep; one sub-treasury, 6 inches high, 4¾ inches wide, 11 inches deep; one drawer, 3 inches high, 4¾ inches wide, 11 inches deep.

No. 9R7108 Our special price..$16.95
No. 9R7109 Our special price, with inner door **$18.20**

Our Business Man's Heavy Angled Safe with five-flange door. A safe that retails everywhere at about double our price. A practical size for merchants, lawyers, physicians, etc. Weight, 750 pounds. Outside measurements, height, 33 inches, width, 22¼ inches, depth, 23 inches; inside dimensions, height 18 inches, width 14 inches, depth, 14 inches. The safe is represented by illustration of our No. 9R7109. Safe and cabinet work is arranged the same.

Arrangement of cabinet work: One book space, 18 inches high, 9 inches wide, 13 inches deep; one sub-treasury, 6 inches high, 4¾ inches wide, 10 inches deep; one drawer, 3 inches high, 4¾ inches wide, 13 inches deep; two pigeonholes, 4¾ inches high, 4¾ inches wide, 13 inches deep.

No. 9R7110 Our special price **$20.90**
No. 9R7111 Our special price, with inner door **22.15**

Our $27.75 Fireproof Safe.

THIS IS A GOOD SIZED SAFE for all business purposes, weighs 1,050 pounds. Is offered at **$27.75** in competition with safes that sell everywhere at **$60.00.** Combination lock is capable of more than a thousand changes. **Made with chilled steel protector inner door (when ordered), solid 4-inch cement walls.** It is fitted with iron cash box, book and pigeonhole compartments, made with all the latest improvements known to safe making. **Dimensions, 39 in. high, 25¾ in. wide, 25 in. deep; approximate weight, 1,050 pounds.** Made with round corners throughout, beautifully ornamented and decorated, has handsome gold lines and hand painted landscapes, furnished with your own name handsomely lettered in gold free of charge, if so ordered. **From the illustration which shows our $27.75 Fireproof Safe open, you may see the internal arrangement of pigeonholes, etc.**

Arrangement of cabinet work: One book space, 19¼ inches high, 11 inches wide, 15 inches deep; one book space, 9½ inches high, 5½ inches wide, 15 inches deep; one sub-treasury, 6½ inches high, 5½ inches wide, 12 inches deep; two drawers, 3 inches high, 5½ inches wide, 15 inches deep; two pigeonholes, 3 inches high, 5½ inches wide, 15 inches deep. This safe is made with an inside door.

No. 9R7114 Our special price, each **$27.75**
No. 9R7115 Our special price, with inner door **$29.00**

Our $31.00 Business Man's Safe, with five-flange door, is made exactly like our No. 9R7114, except it is 3 inches deeper. Height, 39 inches, width, 25¾ inches, depth, 28 inches; approximate weight, 1,150 pounds.

Arrangement of cabinet work: One book space, 19¼ inches high, 11 inches wide, 18 inches deep; one book space, 9½ inches high, 5½ inches wide, 18 inches deep; one sub-treasury, 6½ inches high, 5½ inches wide, 12 inches deep; two drawers, 3 inches high, 5½ inches wide, 18 inches deep; two pigeonholes, 3 inches high, 5½ inches wide, 18 inches deep.

No. 9R7116 Our special price **$31.00**
No. 9R7117 Our special price, with inner door **32.25**

HOUSE FURNISHING HARDWARE DEPARTMENT.

IT IS OUR AIM to illustrate and describe in the following pages, a full and complete line of house furnishing hardware and culinary utensils such as is found only in the highest class hardware stores in large cities.

WE GIVE OUR CUSTOMERS THE BENEFIT of an assortment of all grades of goods, from the cheapest to the most expensive to select from, which has heretofore been enjoyed only by the comparatively few who chanced to reside in large cities, and in many lines we show a greater variety than is carried in stock by any one retail store even in the largest cities.

THERE IS NO MANUFACTURER of high grade kitchen utensils whose goods are not represented in our stock and we illustrate in our catalogue a great variety of labor saving devices, which tend to make the house work a pleasure instead of drudgery.

OUR LINE OF WASHING MACHINES is the most extensive in America and includes every pattern for which there is any demand. Our refrigerators are made by one of the largest and oldest makers in the country, are of the most approved pattern, and our Seroco porcelain enameled, steel lined refrigerator represents the most advanced ideas in sanitary refrigerator construction. In fact, there is not an article in this line, large or small of any merit, which you will not find listed in the following pages, and at prices which are fixed **20 to 60 per cent** lower than it would cost you at home.

WE DO NOT DEAL with middlemen or wholesale dealers; all our goods are bought direct from the manufacturers, and owing to the quantities of goods our enormous trade requires, we are their most desirable customers and buy lower than any wholesale dealer in the country. We sell these goods to you at but a small advance over manufacturers' cost, and at a lower price than the ordinary retail dealer can buy them from his wholesaler.

GREATEST VALUES EVER KNOWN IN WASHING MACHINES.

We Ask Your Orders for These Well Known and Highest Grade Machines Made, Because We Offer the Best and Can Save You Money.

INSTRUCTIONS FOR USING COMBINATION WASHERS. Fill machine from one-half to two-thirds full of hot strong soap suds, and put in six or seven sheets or the equivalent of these clothes for one washing. Work the machine from ten to twelve minutes, wring out and rinse through clear water, blue and hang on the line. Always keep nuts and bolts on machine tight. A wrench is provided with each machine for this purpose. All bearings should be kept slightly lubricated. Do not allow water to stand in machine. Dry out well after using and keep lid open.

HOW TO USE the Fulton American, Scott's Western, Desplaines American, Chicago American or Continental Washers. Soak your clothes the evening before washday, soaping the dirty spots well with good hard soap. When thoroughly soaked, pass them through wringer and place them in the machine. Do not put over six to eight shirts and about half-dozen towels or handkerchiefs in the machine, then fill the machine with hot, strong soap suds until the clothes are well covered, work the lever about ten minutes, wring, rinse and blue your clothes, and they are ready for the line. If accustomed to it, boil the clothes before rinsing; it is not absolutely necessary when good soap is used.

DIRECTIONS FOR USING the Quick and Easy and Sears Washers. Soak the clothes and soap the dirty parts well before washing. Put in the necessary amount of clothes to be washed and add a wash boiler full of hot soapy water, or enough to cover the clothes thoroughly. Operate the machine about ten minutes. Take off the dirty water and fill the machine with clear water. Operate the machine about two or three minutes and the clothes will be rinsed. When through washing, rinse the machine with cold water, hang up lower cylinder on the upper one. Allow the machine to stand open until thoroughly dry.

WE SHIP OUR No. 23R100 to No. 23R138 WASHING MACHINES from Ft. Wayne, Ind., and St. Louis, Mo., and our Nos. 23R140 and 23R143 from Richmond, Va., where we can save our customers any freight by doing so, otherwise we ship from Chicago.

Fulton American No. 1 Washer.

Illustration showing inside crate removed.

No. 23R100 This machine is our old standby improved, with our patent malleable iron enameled pinwheel. The crate inside is independent of the tub and can be removed after the washing is done. The machine is made out of white pine, painted and grained an ash color and finished in every respect first class. It will wash five shirts at a time clean, without the use of a washboard, and is fully warranted in every respect. Size, 23x11 inches. Weight, 54 pounds. Price, each............**$4.44**

The Chicago American Washer, No. 22.

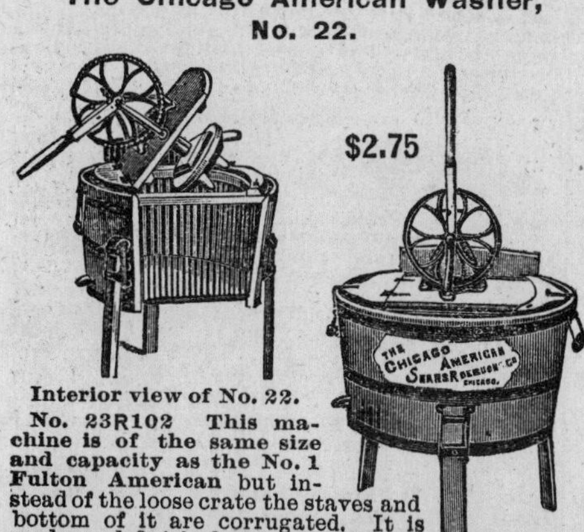

Interior view of No. 22.

No. 23R102 This machine is of the same size and capacity as the No. 1 Fulton American but instead of the loose crate the staves and bottom of it are corrugated. It is made and finished the same as the No. 1, and warranted to do good work. Parties wanting a cheaper machine will do well to try this before buying any other. Inside dimensions, 23x11 inches. Weight, 47 pounds.
Price, each............................**$2.75**

The Desplaines American Washer No. 5.

No. 23R104 This machine was gotten up at the special request of some of our customers. It is of the same make and finish as our No. 22 Chicago American. Staves and bottom are corrugated; in fact it is the No. 22 Chicago American reversed. Inside dimensions, 23x11 inches. Weight, 47 pounds.
Price, each.......**$2.72**

$2.72

The Sears Washer.

No. 23R110 This machine is made on the rubber principle, the same as used in the Quick and Easy but has two cylinders working in opposite directions at the same motion of the crank shaft, thus cleaning the clothes quicker and more thoroughly than the former machine. It will not tear the clothes and on account of the balance wheel, the machine will work so easy that a child can work it without being fatigued. We have found that the yellow cottonwood grown in the low lands of Arkansas and Mississippi is the best lumber for washing machines, and we have adopted the same in all the box machines. Well made, well painted and varnished, and all the iron parts coming in contact with the water are heavily tinned or galvanized. Weight, 93 pounds.
Price, each, wringer not included..............**$5.66**

The Acme Combination Washer.

This Machine is Warranted not to Leak.

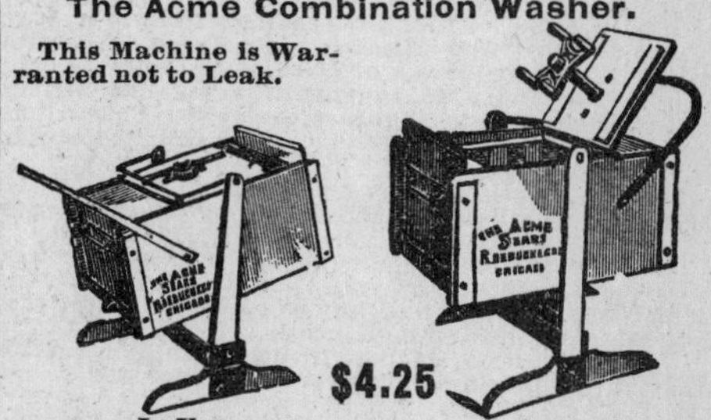

In Use Open

The latest and as we believe the best invention in Washing Machines yet made. This machine combines the reciprocal pinwheel motion with an oscillating movement of the whole suds box. The main advantage that we claim for this machine is that **it works fully one-third easier than any other machine** that operates with a pinwheel agitator, that it takes less water (only four pails), and that it is more simple in construction than any other machine now on the market. The machine when open, locks itself, so that a wringer can be attached on the wringer board without tilting it; a small key inserted in the gear will keep it from tilting when full, thereby preventing accidents of any kind. The machine is well made out of the best yellow cottonwood, finished in superior and excellent style, and we can recommend it and will warrant the same as **the best family washer** that we know of. A 30 days' guarantee goes with every machine sold.

No. 23R114 Family Size Acme Combination Washer No. 11. Size, 15½x25½x10½ inches. Weight, 67 pounds. Price, each............................**$4.25**

No. 23R116 Family Size Ball Bearing Acme Combination Washer No. 6. Weight, 73 pounds.
Price, each..............................**$4.90**

No. 23R118 Large Size Acme Combination Washer No. 12. Size, 17½x25½x12½ inches. Weight, 71 pounds. Price, each..............................**$5.00**

No. 23R120 Large Size Ball Bearing Acme Combination Washer No. 7. Weight, 77 pounds.
Price, each..............................**$5.65**

The Genuine Improved Scott's Western Washer.

The Standard family machine. The make up and finish of our **Scott's Western** will be the same as heretofore, and will not be excelled by any other make. **All of the bolts, washers, nuts, nails,** in fact all iron parts that come in contact with the clothing are **heavily tinned,** absolutely no danger of rust spots on the clothes. Fitted up with our patented round post, and **malleable iron enameled pinwheel,** the greatest invention of the age in washing machines. Made in two sizes—No. 2 and No. 3. The former is the family size.

No. 23R124 Scott's Western Washing Machine, size No. 2. Inside dimensions, 17¾x23½x10½ inches. Weight, 62 pounds. Price, each..............**$2.85**

No. 23R126 Scott's Western Washing Machine, size No. 3. Inside dimensions, 19½x25½x11½ inches. Weight, 65 pounds. Price, each..............**$3.10**

ABOUT FREIGHT AND EXPRESS. It is seldom necessary to write us to ask what the freight or express will amount to. The weight of almost every item is given under the description. If you will refer to pages 7 to 10 you can get the rate of freight or express to a point near you in your state which will be almost, if not exactly, the same rate as to your nearest railroad station. **From this you can calculate almost exactly what the freight or express will amount to on any shipment to your town and you will find it will amount to next to nothing as compared to what you will save in price. By noting the weight and the express or freight rates you can tell almost exactly what the cost of the transportation will be and save the trouble and delay of writing us for this information.**

The Seroco Ball Bearing Wringer.

No. 23R218 This Wringer has wheel top screws, steel adjustment spring, double gear cog wheels, tub clamps that will fasten to galvanized iron, fiber or wooden tubs. **The tub clamp is fastened to the wringer by a bolt,** which passes entirely through the wringer, making the strongest fastening known. **The ball bearings reduce the friction to a minimum** and materially lighten the hardest part of the wash day. There have been wringers placed on the market with roller bearings, and there have been wringers sold with ball bearings, which are to be adjusted and frequently get out of order. **The ball bearings in this wringer are so constructed that it is absolutely impossible for them to break or get out of order in any way. We wish to caution users against putting too much pressure against the rolls.** This wringer turns so easily that if you have been accustomed to using a wringer with ordinary bearings, you will think that this one is not wringing dry because it turns so easily. You should not put much pressure on the top screws for you will destroy the rolls. If you will simply put enough pressure on the rolls to wring the clothes dry you will find that this wringer will work better than any you can find in the market. The rolls are high grade, guaranteed for one year. Size, 10x1¾ inches. Price, each.........**$2.24**

Shipping weight, about 10 pounds.

The Genuine Curtis Five-Year Wringer.

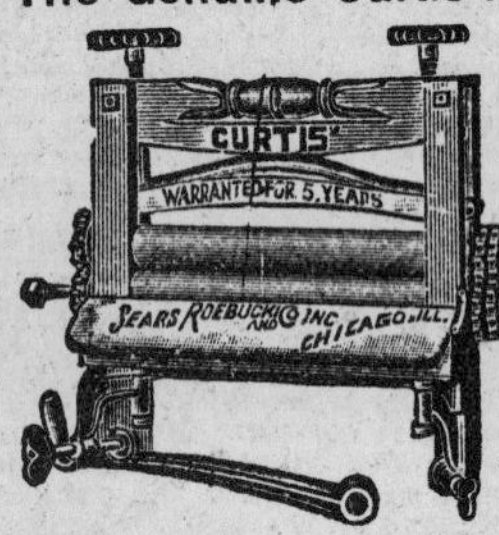

GUARANTEED 5 YEARS.

No. 23R223 The Genuine Curtis Guaranteed Wringer. Rolls guaranteed for five years by Sears, Roebuck & Co. Any roll proving defective within five years will be replaced free of charge. None genuine unless our name appears on the apron. **Beware of imitations.** This wringer has a steel spring which gives an even and elastic pressure, and an **improved guide board,** which spreads the clothes as they pass between the rolls, causing the rolls to wear more evenly and **lessening the wear on the clothing. You cannot buy a better wringer than this,** because better rolls are not made. We have contracted for the entire output of this wringer and must sell them. Our price, combined with **our guarantee,** should enable us to dispose of them quickly. Size of rolls, 10x1¾ (guaranteed for five years). Price, each...............**$3.25**

Hotel or Laundry Wringer for Stationary Tubs.

No. 23R230 Wringer for stationary tubs and large round tubs. Has reversible tub clamp arranged to swing to either side of wringer; clamps open 2 inches. This is the latest improved **Hotel Wringer,** having steel pressure spring. Rolls are strictly high grade —guaranteed for one year. Size of rolls, 12x2 inches. Price, each. **$4.65**

No. 23R232 The Hotel Wringer for stationary tubs only. Same as above, except is larger. Size of rolls, 14x2 inches. Price, each..**$5.94**

The Alpine Bench Wringer.

No. 23R234 The Alpine Bench Wringer. We have often heard said, "It's more work to hold the tubs than to turn the wringer." Use a Bench Wringer and you don't have to hold the tub. **The bench is strong and durable, large enough to accommodate two large tubs.** When not in use bench folds up, taking but little more room than an ordinary wringer and much less than the old fashioned wash bench. **The apron is reversible** so clothes can be put in from either side. **The wringer is well made. Rolls are guaranteed for one year.** Size of rolls, 10x1¾ inches. Price, each.........**$2.65**

Mangles.

Comparatively few people appreciate the value of a mangle; in fact, many have never heard of a mangle, but in Europe they are very extensively used and considered as indispensable as a wringer. **It is an established fact that clothes which have been mangled are more healthful than when finished by the hot iron,** for the reason that the meshes of the material are left open, whereas the hot iron closes them. **Articles mangled retain original whiteness and never spoil by scorching.**

N. B. They are not suitable for shirts and clothes with buttons.

No. 23R250 Household Mangle with Ball Bearings. Can be attached to any table. Size of wood rolls, 24x3¼ inches.
Price, each....**$5.55**

No. 23R252 Household Mangle same as above without ball bearings.
Price, each..**$5.00**

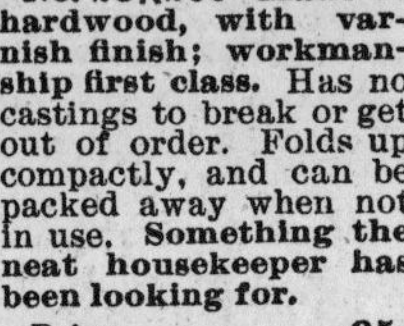

Universal Mangle.

No. 23R256 Universal Mangle for heavy work in laundries, hotels and institutions wherever a great deal of laundry work is done. Also suitable for large families. It is not suitable for shirts and clothes with buttons. Size of wood rolls, 24x4½ inches.
Price, each. **$13.30**

Folding Wash Bench.

No. 23R260 Made of hardwood, with varnish finish; workmanship first class. Has no castings to break or get out of order. Folds up compactly, and can be packed away when not in use. **Something the neat housekeeper has been looking for.**
Price..............**95c**

Sink or Window Cleaner.

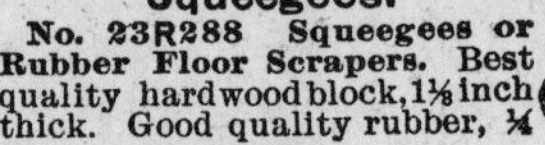

No. 23R282 Sink or Window Cleaner. A wood block and handle. A rubber strip inserted in wood block. Length of rubber, 5 inches.
Weight, each, 2 ounces. Price, each..............**4c**

No. 23R285 Peerless Window Cleaner. For cleaning and drying windows and floors; 12 inches wide. Each..........**20c**

Squeegees.

No. 23R288 Squeegees or Rubber Floor Scrapers. Best quality hardwood block, 1⅛ inch thick. Good quality rubber, ⅜ in. thick.

Length......	12-in.	14-in.	16-in.
Each.........	27c	30c	36c

No. 23R294 Squeegees or Rubber Floor Scrapers. Block, ⅜-inch thick. Pure rubber, $\frac{3}{16}$-inch thick.

Lengths..................	12-in.	14-in.	16-in.
Price, each.............	20c	23c	25c

Mop Handles.

No. 23R300 Mop Handle and Brush Holder Combined. A reliable article made from latest improved patterns, with free working and effective screw, hardwood handles.
Price, each.................**8c**

No. 23R303 Mop Head. Made of extra **heavy wire, with iron screw head,** thumbscrew to hold handle firm when screwed down upon rags.
Each.................**7c**

No. 23R315 Cotton Mops. 9 lbs. to the dozen. Price, per dozen, **$1.00**; each..................**9c**

No. 23R316 Cotton Mops. 12 lbs. to the dozen. Price, per dozen, **$1.25**; each..................**11c**

Self Wringing Mops.

No. 23R324 The Erie Self Wringing Mop. The mops made of cotton coils, large and full size. **The hands do not come in contact with the water, the mop being wrung at arm's length. The use of scalding water is another important advantage. The floor washes easier, cleaner and quicker,** and dries more readily.
Price, each.................**25c**

Mop Wringers.

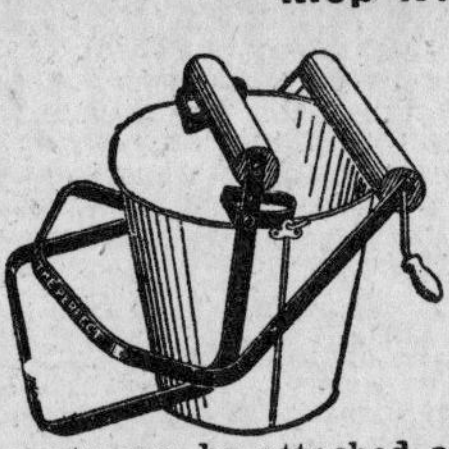

No. 23R328 Perfect Mop Wringer. Is made throughout (except rollers) of Bessemer steel, strong and effective, foot lever shafted to allow rollers to separate without use of springs while mop is being adjusted. Mop may be pulled through by standing with both feet on lever or wrung by turning crank. Entire arrangements can be attached and detached on any size pail. Boiling water can be used together with strong soap or lye solution, as it is not necessary for hands to come in contact with liquid. Weight, 8 pounds.
Price, each, without pail, **$1.20**

No. 23R330 Schmuck's Mop Wringers, manufactured of **wrought iron,** the rollers **made of hard maple,** chemically treated, and will fit any size pail. **Every wringer warranted.**
Price, for wringer with pail, each.....................**$1.90**

MRS. POTTS' SAD IRONS With Forged Stretcher Handle.

The only Potts' sads having forged stretcher handle. Admitted by all to be **the best sad iron made.** Set consists of one iron with rounded end, weight 4 pounds; two with regular ends, one weighs 5⅛ pounds and one 5⅝ pounds; one detachable wood handle with **forged stretcher.** This handle will not **break if you happen to drop it on the floor;** one iron stand.

No. 23R345 The original genuine Mrs. Pott's Sad Iron, in sets of three, with detachable wood handle, having forged stretcher as described above and iron stand, finely polished. Price, per set............**67c**

No. 23R346 Set of three genuine Mrs. Potts' Sads, as above, finely polished and nickel plated.
Price, per set..........................**73c**

No. 23R350 Extra handle with forged stretcher, **won't break, if you happen to drop it on the floor.**
Price, each..........................**15c**

No. 23R353 Extra handle with cast stretcher.
Price, each..........................**5c**

If by mail, postage extra, 10 cents.

No. 23R360 Mrs. Potts' Solid Sad Iron, nickel plated without handle. Handle No. 23R350 or 23R353 fits this iron.

Weight, lbs...	4	5	6	7	8	9	10
Price, each...	18c	23c	27c	32c	36c	41c	45c

No. 23R365 Family Outfit of Sad Irons; consists of one set of three of our No. 23R346 nickel plated sad irons, one nickel plated Chinese polishing iron with all round edges, weight, 3 pounds; one nickel plated double pointed girls' iron, weight, 1⅝ pounds. All above have detachable cold handles and two iron stands are included, making set complete in every detail for ironing of any kind. These are all the genuine original Mrs. Potts' sad irons; are better made, better finished and superior in every detail to imitations. Packed in a neat varnished box with end handles, making them attractive and convenient for the tidy housekeeper and a tasty and suitable present, always appreciable. Price, per set..........**$2.83**

Sad Irons.

No. 23R370 Cold Handle Sleeve or Flounce Iron. Nickel plated, 7 inches long, with detachable Potts pattern handle. Price, each..........................**55c**

No. 23R375 Common Pattern Sad Irons, with face finely polished. Weights given are not guaranteed exact. They are the manufacturers' weights (so-called) and are as near as it is possible to make them.

W'g't, lbs..	5	6	7	8	9
Price, ea..	18c	21c	25c	28c	32c

Sad Iron Stands.

No. 23R390 Sad Iron Stands bronzed iron. Price, each........**4c**

No. 23R393 Chinese Laundry Iron. Made with round heel and edges and adapted especially for laundry work. Nickel plated.

Size No.	1	2	3
Weight, lbs.	5¼	6¼	7
Each,	35c	45c	50c

Polishing Irons.

No. 23R397 Troy Polishing Irons, with perforated bottom, nicely polished. Weight, 4 lbs. Price, each, 28c

No. 23R399 Troy Polishing Iron, with smooth bottom, nickel plated. Weight, 4 pounds. Price, each...34c

No. 23R401 Troy Polishing Iron, with smooth bottom, polished. Weight, 4 pounds. Price, each..30c

Charcoal Irons.

No. 23R408 Family Charcoal Irons, with removable top, wood handle with tin shield, one flue. Weight, 6½ pounds. Price, each......................85c

Tailors' Goose.

No. 23R412 Tailors' Goose, with extra polished face.

Weight, lbs.,	12	14	16	18	20	22
Price, each,	48c	56c	64c	72c	80c	88c

No. 23R430 Asbestos Flat Iron Holder is a durable and desirable article for handling flat irons and hot dishes. Size, 5¾x5¾ inches. Weight, 2 ounces. Price, each...5c

Crown Hand Fluters.

No. 23R442 Crown Hand Fluter has a plate 5½ inches long and 3 inches wide, and a roll 1⅜ inches diameter. The plate rests on a japanned cast base. The heating iron is cast on the bottom of the plate. In order to heat the plate it is lifted off the base and placed on the stove, and when hot put back on the base. Both plate and roll are finely polished. The handle and yoke to hold roll is made in one piece of malleable iron. This handle also serves as a lifter, to handle plate in removing it to and from the base. All parts not polished are neatly japanned. Weight, 2¾ pounds. Price, each..65c

No. 23R444 Crown Hand Fluter has a plate 7 inches long and 3¼ inches wide and a roll 2⅜ inches diameter. Both roll and plate are finely polished and nickel plated. The plate is furnished with stops at each end, to prevent roll running off and tearing the goods. The plate is hinged to the base, and does not require to be lifted off and laid aside to remove heating iron. The heating irons are laid in a recess of the base, under plate. Two irons are furnished with each fluter and a lifter to handle them. The handle is of wood, and yoke holding roll of malleable iron. All parts not nickel plated are neatly japanned. Weight, 3¼ pounds. Price, each.................................$1.15

Crown Fluting Machine for $3.25.

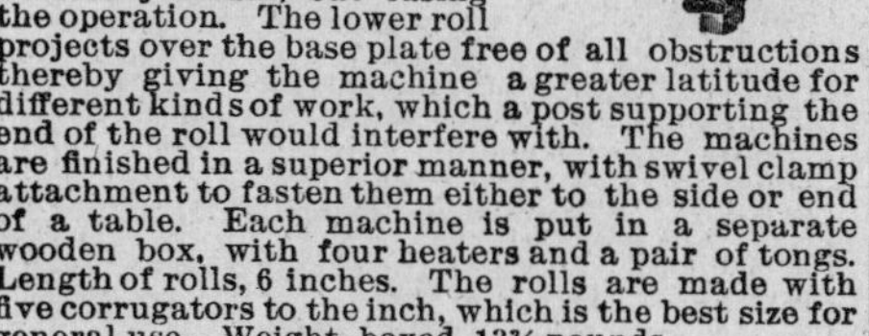

No. 23R446 Crown Fluting Machine has for many years past been the leading machine of its kind in the market. It is preeminently the best fluting machine made. The spring is so placed that the separating of the rolls for the putting in the work does not compress or affect it in the least, thus not only saving the spring unnecessary strain, but easing the operation. The lower roll projects over the base plate free of all obstructions thereby giving the machine a greater latitude for different kinds of work, which a post supporting the end of the roll would interfere with. The machines are finished in a superior manner, with swivel clamp attachment to fasten them either to the side or end of a table. Each machine is put in a separate wooden box, with four heaters and a pair of tongs. Length of rolls, 6 inches. The rolls are made with five corrugators to the inch, which is the best size for general use. Weight, boxed, 13¾ pounds. Price, each..$3.25

CARPET SWEEPERS.

Our line of Carpet Sweepers for quality, superior workmanship, efficiency in operation and elegance of finish, is unexcelled by any other line of Carpet Sweepers on the market. Only the very best materials enter into the construction of these carpet sweepers; oak, maple and sycamore of the choicest cuts are the woods used for making our sweeper cases. In selecting and finishing the lumber for the cases, special care is taken to secure the best grain effects possible; the finest furniture does not receive more careful attention in this respect. **Each and every sweeper box is hand rubbed and polished.**

THE WHEELS on each end of the sweeper are fitted with solid rubber tires, which make the sweeper practically noiseless when in use.

THE BRUSHES, the most important part of the sweeper, are made of very stiff bristles of the highest grade. The friction wheels are held in place by a spring against the rubber tired wheels, and when the sweeper is pushed over the floor or carpet, the wheels turning against the friction wheels, cause the brush to revolve very rapidly, throwing the dust or dirt from the floor into the dust pans; a dust pan being placed on each side of the brush. The dust pans can be dumped or cleaned out by pressing a small lever, which extends up through the sweeper case on either side. The brush, being enclosed in practically a dust proof case, prevents the dust from flying about the room and settling back on the floor and furniture; is much cleaner and does the work much more thoroughly than an ordinary broom, and is far more economical, as **our carpet sweepers will outlast many brooms and render far better and more satisfactory service.**

ALL OUR SWEEPERS, even the lowest priced one, are fitted with broom action. The brush is so placed in the sweeper case that by bearing on the handle, the pressure of the brush on the carpet or floor can be regulated in the same manner as with a broom, and with the same result, thus making it equally practical for bare floors or for carpets of the longest or shortest nap.

EACH SWEEPER CASE has a solid rubber band ⅛-inch thick and ⅜-inch wide, extending entirely around it horizontally, which prevents the scratching of the wood work or furniture when the sweeper is pushed against it.

No. 23R470 The Acme Carpet Sweeper is made according to our own specifications by the oldest maker of carpet sweepers in the world. It has every desirable feature known, and no expense has been spared to construct a sweeper that **will please our patrons.** Costs no more than four good brooms and will outwear several dozen. **Will follow a broom on any carpet and remove more dirt** and dust than the broom did, with very much less labor. **Does not wear out a carpet** as a broom does, and in this way saves its cost in a short time. This sweeper has perfect friction. **The dust pans are easily opened.** The case is handsomely polished, natural wood finished in natural or antique oak and mahogany. **Has broom action** reversible bail; rubber furniture protector. **Sold under our usual guarantee**—if not as good or better than any sweeper you ever had, return to us and money will be refunded. Weight, about 6 lbs. Price, each..$1.65

No. 23R473 Our Imperial Carpet Sweeper. The best known and most widely sold carpet sweeper in the world. **Contains the famous broom action,** and every other feature necessary in a first class sweeper. Made from the best selected cabinet woods in an assortment of attractive finishes. Full nickel plated trimming. Nickel plated on copper, which is the best method known and permits the highest possible finish and will not rust or tarnish. **Has rubber furniture protector encircling the case;** patent reversible bail spring, wheels outside the case; our everlasting pure bristle brush; pans operate independently by an easy pressure of the finger. Weight, 6 pounds. Price, each..$1.98

GIVE CATALOGUE NUMBER IN FULL WHEN YOU WRITE YOUR ORDER

No. 23R476 Our Elite Carpet Sweeper, the latest pattern, and differing in appearance from any other sweeper on the market. **A sweeper of the highest grade,** with one of the handsomest case designs. Only the choicest quarter sawed oak and sycamore is used, being finished in antique and golden oak, mahogany, natural sycamore, and our special finish, hand rubbed and polished; full nickel trimmings on copper, which is the best method known and permits the highest possible finish and will not rust or tarnish. **It contains our broom action, our reversible bail,** and our pure bristle everlasting brush, adapted to be easily removed from the sweeper. **Its spring dumping device** is convenient, opening one pan at a time. Length of case, 14 inches. **Its construction throughout** is as perfect as care and skill can make it. Each, $2.35

Lamp Chimney Cleaners.

No. 23R500 Wire Chimney Cleaner. Dish cloth holder, cork puller, etc. Each....5c

Pot Cleaners.

Pot Chain or wire ring Dish Cloth.

No. 23R506 Small size. Each..3c

No. 23R508 Large size. Each..4c

No. 23R510 The Sensible Pot Chain and Scraper is a new and useful article, each ring is double, which **makes it very durable.** The handle is malleable iron; the **blade is steel;** the handle and scraper are tinned. Weight, 4 ounces. Price, each..........................8c

Dish Mop.

No. 23R516 Wash your dishes without putting your hands into hot water. This dish mop is made of cotton and is securely fastened to handle. Length 12 inches. Weight, 4 ounces. Price, each..........6c

Can Openers.

No. 23R524 Star Can Opener, considered one of the best can openers made. Steel blade, malleable iron guide, **nickel plated, antique oak handle with brass ferrule.** A handsome and reliable article. Length, 6½ inches. Weight, 3 ounces. Price, each..........................6c

No. 23R528 Can Opener, steel blade, cast handle. Price, each..3c

No. 23R532 Can Opener. Will cut either round or square cans better than any can opener made, and it is impossible for anyone to cut themselves on account of the opener slipping. It will always cut up close to the outer edge of the tin. It is made of one piece of the best steel. It will not slip. It cannot get out of order. Price, each..5c

No. 23R535 Sprague Can Opener is without question the best can opener in the market. Price, each..5c

Mincing Knives.

No. 23R548 Eclipse Solid Steel Mincer. Handle and blade formed of one piece of bright steel. Indestructible. Always clean. No rivets to wear loose. No wooden handle to shrink swell, loosen, split or fill with rancid grease. Weight, 5 ounces. Price, each, 8c

No. 23R550 Gem Solid Steel Mincer. Same style as above **made of the best cutlery steel.** Weight, 7 ounces. Price, each..........................15c

No. 23R554 Gem Double Blade Solid Steel Mincer. Made of best cutlery steel. Retains a keen cutting edge. Will outlast a score of cheap mincers. The blades of the double mincer being connected by steel spring shanks, clogging is positively prevented. Weight, 10 ounces. Price, each..21c

No. 23R557 Double Mincing Knife. Polished steel blades; enameled handle. Weight, 8 ounces. Price, each, 5c

No. 23R560 Mincing Knife. Cast steel blade, **ground sharp;** solid malleable iron handle which can't split or get loose. **Blade and handle nickel plated to prevent rusting.** Each..9c

No. 23R590 Strawberry Huller. Nips the hull off of the berry without crushing the berry or staining the fingers. Will hull the ripest fruit and keep it in perfect shape intact for table use. Makes what is often a disagreeable task a pleasure and saves one half the time. Made of spring brass, heavily nickel plated and polished. Price, each..........................4c

Henis Fruit Presses.

No. 23R610 Henis Fruit and Vegetable Press and Strainer; can be used for a variety of purposes; is especially recommended for mashing potatoes. Potatoes, after being forced through the strainer have a delicious creamy taste that no other method of mashing will impart. Weight, 20 ounces. Price, each..........................19c

Potato and Food Slicer.

With grater attachment. Easy to operate. Easy to clean. Knives are of tempered steel, can be adjusted to cut different thicknesses. Will slice evenly and nicely. It is thoroughly tin coated, cuts rapidly, will not get out of order. Clamps to table. Remove slicer, substitute grater by loosening a single screw in handle.

No. 23R635 Potato and Food Slicer, with grater attachment Price, each........................$1.25

No. 23R637 Potato and Food Slicer, without grater attachment Price, each........................95c

Steak Pounders.

No. 23R645 The Star Steak Pounder, Ice Pick and Shave. Malleable iron, plain finish.
Price, each........................6c

No. 23R647 The Star Steak Pounder, Ice Pick and Shave. Full nickel plated.
Price, each........................9c

Fish Scalers.

No. 23R662 Fish Scaler, cast iron, japanned. Length, inches. Weight, 9 ounces. Price, each........................4c

No. 23R680 Revolving Grater, for grating horseradish, cocoanut, pumpkins, squash, lemons, crackers, cheese, etc. **The cylinder is 3 inches in diameter** and 3 inches long. No family should be without one. Weight, 1 pound, 10 ounces.
Price, each........................43c

No. 23R684 Revolving Grater, larger than No. 23R680; cylinder 6 inches in diameter, 5 inches in length. Weight, 7 pounds, 7 ounces.
Price, each........................$1.20

No. 23R686 Revolving Slicer for slicing apples, Saratoga potatoes, pumpkins, cucumbers and other vegetables. Weight, 1 pound, 13 ounces. Price, each........................42c

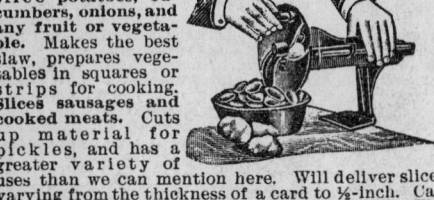

No. 23R690 The Sterling Slicer will slice potatoes, cucumbers, onions, and any fruit or vegetable. Makes the best slaw, prepares vegetables in squares or strips for cooking. **Slices sausages and cooked meats.** Cuts up material for pickles, and has a greater variety of uses than we can mention here. Will deliver slices varying from the thickness of a card to ½-inch. Can be used for making small quantities of kraut. The blade is of tempered cutlery steel, and is so protected that only by carelessness can the operator cut himself. Price, each........................$1.35

Enterprise Cherry Stoner

No. 23R710 The accompanying illustration shows the Enterprise Cherry Stoner, which is intended to stone cherries with rapidity. **It is adjusted by thumbscrews** to adapt it to the different size cherry stones. It is nicely tinned to prevent rust.
Price, each........................63c

Rollman Cherry Seeder.

No. 23R714 This Perfect Cherry Seeder does not crush the cherry or cause any loss of juice; a perfect machine for large, small or California cherries. The seed extracting knife drives the seed into one dish and actually throws the cherry into another. The marks of the knife can scarcely be seen on the seeded fruit. It seeds from 20 to 30 quarts per hour. No grinding; no mashing; no loss of juice. Heavily tinned to prevent rust. Price, each.....68c

No. 23R720 Enterprise Raisin and Grape Seeder is simple in construction, easily adjusted, does the work rapidly and effectually, seeding the raisins wet or dry, better work being obtained if wet. The ordinary washing given by every good housekeeper makes the raisins sufficiently wet. Will seed grapes for preserving and cooking purposes. The raisins should be sprinkled in the hopper as fast as the roller will grasp them. The best results will be obtained by feeding them one at a time. Will seed a pound in five minutes. Weight, 1¾ pounds.
Price, each........................67c

Apple Parer, Corer and Slicer.

No. 23R735 Little Star Parer, Corer, and Slicer, with push off. This is the only machine so constructed that parings and juice cannot fall upon it. The only parer in which the paring knife always faces the fruit when brought against it; will operate successfully on large or soft fruit. The fork and slicing knives are tinned so that the fruit will not turn black; has tinned screw, with thread brazed on; castings are heavy, and every machine is tested before leaving factory. In our opinion, this is the best family machine on the market. Price, each......39c

Rocking Table Apple Parer.

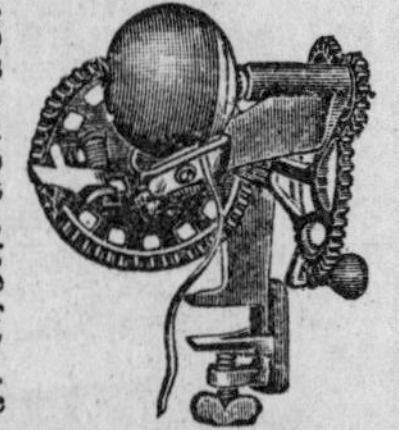

No. 23R738 Apple Parer, with push off. This machine is so arranged that parings and juice cannot fall upon it. It is provided with improved clamping device so that the table will not be jammed. It is stronger and more durable, has less gears and working parts, will pare closer to the fork, keep cleaner, do better work and more of it than any other machine on the market.
Price, each........................48c

Apple Parers.

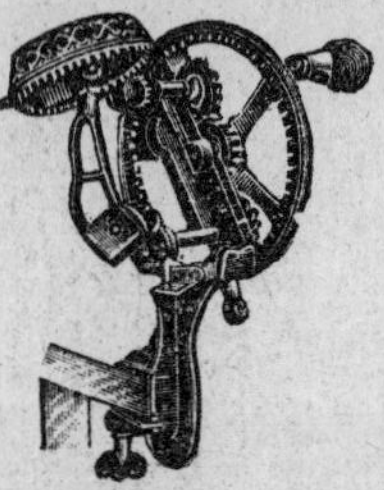

No. 23R742 This is the best known and most popular apple parer ever invented. Every machine works perfectly, all parts being accurately fitted and put together in the best possible manner. **Machine should be fastened to corner of table,** as shown in illustration. Parings fall clear of machine and table. Gearing cannot clog with parings. **Has curved knife** and all latest improvements.
Price, each........................63c

No. 23R744 Rotary Knife, Family Peach and Apple Parer. Strong, substantial, simple and complete, it does first class work and is not liable to get out of order. It takes off a very thin paring, saving a large amount of waste. It is the only machine that successfully pares peaches. Price, each.....98c

Pepper and Spice Mills.

No. 23R850 Pepper and Spice Mill. To be used as a pepper box on the table or in the kitchen. Buy whole pepper and spice and grind them as used. You will have pure and fresh spices. Height, 3 inches; diameter, 1¾ inches. Made entirely of metal, all handsomely nickel plated. Grinds coarse or fine as desired. With ordinary care will last twenty years. Weight, 9 ounces. Price, each..........20c

No. 23R852 Pepper and Spice Mill. Buy the pure unground pepper and spice, and grind it as you use it, thus preventing adulteration and retaining its full strength. This mill is made of walnut, highly polished, with nickeled top. Height, 4¼ inches; diameter 2 inches.
Price, each........................23c

No. 23R855 Pepper and Spice Mill. Made of polished maple, barrel shaped. Remember that the adulterations found in ground spice are frequently injurious to health. Height, 3⅛ inches; diameter, 2⅛ inches. Price, each....30c

COFFEE MILLS

Tin Canister Coffee Mill.

No. 23R875 Tin Canister Coffee Mill. Made with japanned tin, canister holding one pound of coffee and cup for catching and measuring the ground coffee. **The canister is practically air tight and by buying the coffee in the bean and grinding it just as you need it, you secure the full strength of the bean,** as it is well known that coffee rapidly loses its strength if allowed to stand after grinding.
Price, each.29c

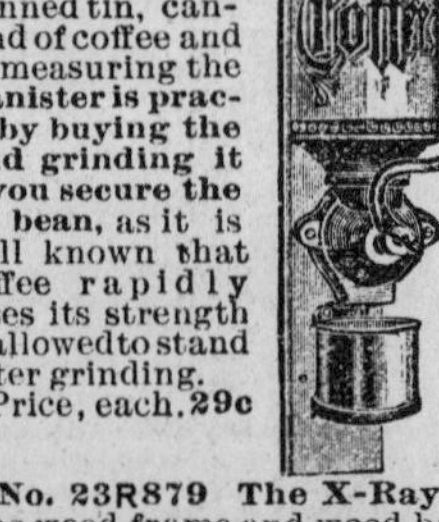

No. 23R879 The X-Ray Mill, has wood frame and wood hopper with glass front, so coffee is always in sight. A 1-pound wall mill of entirely new design. Easily regulated to grind fine or coarse, as desired. Turns easy. Grinds fast. The mill is well made, strong and durable, and is warranted to give satisfaction.
Price, each........................43c

Jewel Coffee Mill.

No. 23R882 Jewel Coffee Mill With heavy ornamental glass canister, capacity, one pound; graduated on side to show exact amount of coffee on hand. It is provided with our latest improved grinding burrs. Will grind fine or coarse or pulverize coffee if desired. The iron parts and receiving cup are finished in red enamel, and the Jewel is without exception the best and most attractive mill in the market. Each one packed in a wood box.
Price, each........................57c

Coffee Mill With Glass Hopper.

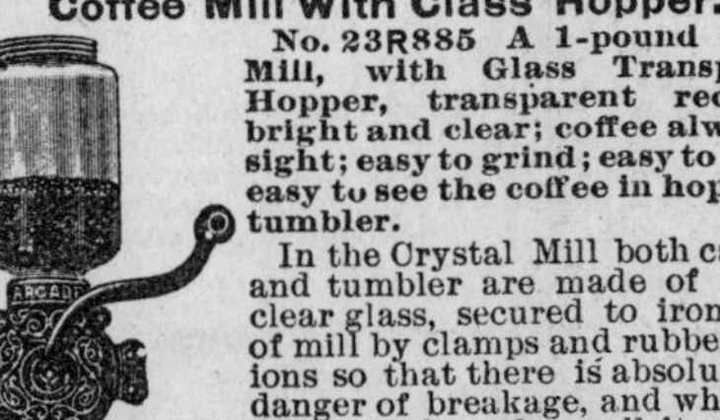

No. 23R885 A 1-pound Coffee Mill, with Glass Transparent Hopper, transparent receiver; bright and clear; coffee always in sight; easy to grind; easy to clean; easy to see the coffee in hopper or tumbler.

In the Crystal Mill both canister and tumbler are made of bright, clear glass, secured to iron frame of mill by clamps and rubber cushions so that there is absolutely no danger of breakage, and when mill is fastened to the wall it makes a handsome appearance, and you can always tell at a glance just how you are fixed for coffee. The capacity of the mill is ample for ordinary family use. Fully warranted.
Price, each........................73c

No. 23R892 New Home Coffee Mill. Wood top, iron cover and side handle. **This mill has large hopper capacity,** holding over a pound of coffee. It is constructed of the best material. **The box is made of hardwood,** highly polished and varnished and supplied with **our improved grinding burrs,** which are warranted to pulverize coffee if desired. Size, 6¾x6¾x8 inches.
Price, each 44c

No. 23R894 A Sunk Hopper Mill with hinged cover, hardwood box, with dovetailed corners, highly polished and covered with best copal varnish, nickel plated trimmings. **Very attractive. These mills have a** patent regulator and a grinding burr specially constructed so as to pulverize coffee when desired. Box 7x7x5½ inches. Price, each...48c

No. 23R896 A Large, Handsome, Sunk Hopper Mill, with an all iron top, hinged cover and hardwood box, with dovetailed corners, highly finished and covered with best copal varnish. These mills have **a patent regulator and grinding burr** specially constructed so as to pulverize coffee if desired. **A substantial mill of large capacity.** Box, 7x7x5¼ inches. Price, each........................42c

No. 23R901 A Sunk Hopper Mill, with hinged cover, hardwood top, with dovetailed corners, **highly polished** and covered with best copal varnish. **Gold bronze trimmings. These mills have a patent regulator** and a grinding burr specially constructed so as to pulverize coffee when desired. Size of box, 7x7x5¼ inches.
Price, each........................39c

No. 23R904 Raised Hopper Mill with hinged cover, hardwood box and dovetailed corners, highly polished and covered with best copal varnish, **bronzed irons, patent regulator** and improved grinder burr that will **thoroughly pulverize coffee** when desired. This mill has an ornamental top to the box, which makes it strong and durable. Price, 38c

Favorite Coffee Mill.

No. 23R907 Raised Covered Hopper Mill with hinged cover, hardwood box, dovetailed corners, highly polished and covered with best copal varnish, japanned iron, patent regulator and improved grinding burr that will thoroughly pulverize coffee when desired. Size of box, 6½x6½x4 inches.
Price, each... ....31c

A Raised Hopper Open Top Mill, hardwood box, dovetailed corners, highly polished and covered with best copal varnish, japanned iron, patent regulator and improved grinding burr.
No. 23R910 Size of box, 7x7x4½ inches. Each....29c
No. 23R912 Size of box, 6x6x3¾ inches. Each....24c

Our 18-Cent Coffee Mill.

No. 23R916 Coffee Mill, whitewood box, 6x6x3¾ inches, japanned iron.
Price, each..............18c

Our 20-Cent Side Coffee Mill.

No. 23R922 Side Mill, hardwood board, polished and varnished, iron japanned, medium size.
Price, each.........20c

National Coffee Mills.

Our line of National Coffee Mills is manufactured for us by one of the oldest and most reliable makers of this class of goods in the United States. In quality they are superior to any mills on the market, regardless of price. **They have all the latest improvements in mechanical construction,** are the most beautiful in design and most handsomely finished. They are fast grinders and easy runners. **We guarantee them to be strictly first class in material and in workmanship and in** grinding capacity equal to other makes of mills of corresponding sizes regardless of price. You will run no risk whatever in buying one of our National mills. You can inspect it and try it and if it is not in every way all we claim for it return it at our expense and we will refund all freight charges you have paid and return your money. **By comparing our prices you will find that these mills will cost you from 25 to 50 per cent less than any other make of mill of equal capacity.** We ship all sizes direct from our factory in Illinois, near Chicago, and as we do not have the expense of handling and hauling and no freight charges to pay we can and do sell them at but a small advance over the actual cost to manufacture. Don't buy too small a mill. A mill which is amply large enough for your requirements is much more satisfactory and will cost you less than a smaller size of other makes.

No. 23R945 The Little National Coffee Mill, for household use. Handsomely finished in red and gold. Fly wheels, 9¾ inches in diameter. Iron hopper holding ½ pound. Height, 11½ inches. Shipping weight, 20 pounds. Will grind ¼ pound per minute.
Price, each..........$2.40

No. 23R947 National Counter Mill, handsomely finished in red and gold. Fly wheels, 11¾ inches in diameter. Iron hopper holding 1 pound. Height, 18 inches. Shipping weight, 37 pounds. Will grind ⅓ pound per minute.
Price, each.......... ....$3.60

No. 23R948 National Counter Mill. Same as No. 23R947, but larger. Handsomely finished in red and gold. Has decorated iron hopper holding 1½ pounds of coffee. Height of mill, 21 inches. Fly wheels, 14½ inches in diameter. Will grind ½ pound of coffee per minute. Shipping weight, 59 pounds.
Price, each..$4.80

No. 23R950 National Coffee Mill. Beautifully finished in red and gold, with heavily nickel plated brass hopper holding 1¼ pounds of coffee. Height of mill, 22¾ inches; diameter of fly wheels, 11¾ inches. Will grind ⅓ pound of coffee per minute. Shipping weight, 34 pounds. Fully warranted. Price, each..............$5.40

No. 23R952 National Coffee Mill, same as No. 23R950, but larger. Vermilion and gold finish, with heavily nickel plated hopper holding 1¼ pounds of coffee. Height of mill, 24¾ inches; diameter of fly wheels, 14½ inches. Will grind ½ pound of coffee per minute. Shipping weight, 54 pounds. Fully warranted. Price, each.......$7.20

National Coffee Mills.

No. 23R954 National Coffee Mill. Handsomely finished in red and gold with decorated iron hopper holding 2 pounds of coffee. Is 24½ inches high; fly wheels are 16¾ inches in diameter. Will grind 1 pound of coffee per minute. Shipping weight, 72 pounds. Fully warranted.
Price, each...................$6.00

No. 23R956 National Coffee Mill. Same as No. 23R954, but larger. Red and gold finish, decorated iron hopper holding 2 pounds of coffee. Height, 28¾ inches; diameter of fly wheels, 19½ inches. Will grind 1½ pounds of coffee per minute. Can be regulated to grind coarse or fine while running. Shipping weight, 95 pounds. Fully warranted. Price, each..................$9.00

No. 23R958 National Coffee Mill. Finely finished in vermilion and gold with fancy nickel plated brass hopper holding 2¾ pounds of coffee. This mill is 27½ inches high, has 16¾-inch fly wheels. Grinds 1 pound of coffee per minute. Shipping weight, 65 pounds. Warranted.
Price, each............ $8.40

No. 23R960 National Coffee Mill, same as No. 23R958 but larger. Finished in vermilion and gold in the best possible manner; has nickel plated spun brass hopper holding 2¾ pounds of coffee. Height, 32 inches; diameter of fly wheels, 19½ inches. Can be regulated to grind coarse or fine while running. Grinds 1½ pounds of coffee per minute. Shipping weight, 85 pounds. Fully warranted.
Price, each..$10.80

No. 23R962 National Coffee Mill. Finished in red, black or wine color with gold striping, and decorated iron hopper. Capacity, 4½ pounds of coffee. This is the most popular counter mill for grocery stores, hotels, etc. Will grind 2 pounds of coffee per minute, and can be regulated to grind fine or coarse while running. Height, 39½ inches; diameter of fly wheels, 28 inches. Shipping weight, 188 pounds.
Price, each..$12.60

No. 23R964 National Coffee Mill. Same style as No. 23R962 mill, but with heavily nickel plated spun brass hopper. Balance of mill finished in red, black, or wine color with gold striping. Hopper holds 5 pounds and will grind 2 pounds of coffee per minute. Easily regulated to grind fine or coarse while running. Height, 37¼ inches; diameter of fly wheels, 28 inches. Shipping weight, 176 pounds.
Price, each..$13.80

National Floor Mills.

Special attention is called to the device used on our floor mills for fastening the grinders to shaft, and the removal of obstructions, such as stones and nails, found in all grades of coffee. The grinders are placed on the shaft in such a manner that should a nail or stone find its way into the mill the grinders would stop the moment the obstruction came in contact with the first tooth, while the shaft and wheels could revolve without injuring the mill. By turning the hand wheel regulator back the obstruction falls through into the coffee pan.

No. 23R966 National Floor Mill. This is the favorite floor mill for grocery stores. Finished in red, black, or wine color with gold striping and nicely decorated. Has nickel plated brass hopper holding 5 pounds of coffee. Will grind 2 pounds of coffee per minute. Easily regulated to grind fine or coarse while running. Height, 63½ inches; diameter of fly wheel, 28 inches. Shipping weight, 215 pounds. Fully warranted.
Price, each..$18.00

No. 23R968 National Floor Mill. Like No. 23R966, but larger. This is our finest mill, suitable for high class grocery and coffee stores. Beautifully finished in vermilion, black, or wine color, gold striped and decorated. Heavy nickel plated brass hopper. Has brass oil cups and fittings, and steel grinders 9½ inches in diameter. Hopper holds 8¾ pounds of coffee, will grind 2½ pounds per minute. Fly wheel, 34¼ inches in diameter. Height, 68½ inches. Shipping weight, 350 pounds. Fully warranted.
Price, each.......................................$27.00

REFER TO PAGES 7 to 10 FOR FREIGHT AND EXPRESS RATES.

You can tell almost exactly what the freight or express will amount to on your goods without writing to us for this information.

Corkscrews.

No. 23R1080 Folding Corkscrew, nicely polished. Weight, 2 ounces. Price, each..........5c

No. 23R1082 Pocket Corkscrew. Each in nickel case, case serving as handle, which is passed through ring in screw.
No. 23R1080 Weight, 2 oz. Price, each, 12c No. 23R1082

Bartenders' Corkscrews.

The screws are made of best quality steel, nickel plated. Polished applewood handles. Special shaped worm, which prevents drawing through the cork. **Every screw tested.**

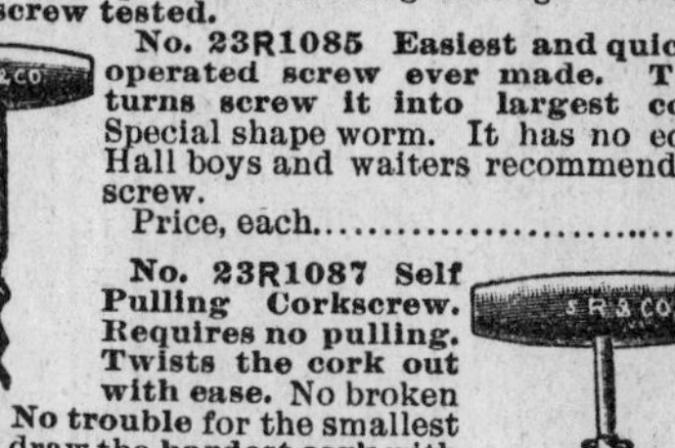

No. 23R1085 Easiest and quickest operated screw ever made. Three turns screw it into largest corks. Special shape worm. It has no equal. Hall boys and waiters recommend this screw.
Price, each..17c

No. 23R1087 Self Pulling Corkscrew. Requires no pulling. Twists the cork out with ease. No broken bottles. No trouble for the smallest child to draw the hardest cork with this screw. Price, each.........23c

No. 23R1090 Combination Folding Pocket Corkscrew and Wire Cutter. Made entirely of steel heavily nickel plated and does the work perfectly. By resting fulcrum on edge of bottle neck and using the handle as a lever the hardest cork can be extracted with ease. Takes up no more room than a pocket knife. Length, closed, 4¼ inches. Weight, 2 ounces. Price, each...........39c

Cork Pullers.

No. 23R1096 The No. 2 Modern Cork Puller. Can be attached to any upright surface, as an ice box, door frame, or wall. Is always ready for use at all times, does away with all annoyance in drawing corks; pulls any cork in one second. It is small and compact, it is never lost, and is a great ornament, being handsomely engraved and nickel plated. A short, upward movement of the handle causes the corkscrew or worm to rotate into the cork, and pushing the handle down extracts the cork from the bottle; same movement repeated causes the corkscrew to rotate out of the extracted cork which is automatically discharged from the machine. It requires but little power and operation is instantaneous.
Price, each..$1.37

No. 23R1098 No. 1 Modern Cork Puller, for use in saloons, restaurants, soda fountains, etc. This machine is clamped by a thumbscrew to a bar, counter or shelf. It is identical with the No. 23R1096 machine except in its method of attachment, and after a thorough test has proven a universal favorite with bartenders, etc. One motion of the handle extracts any cork and automatically discharges the extracted cork from the machine, or a cork can be drawn part way only, when desired. It is strong, simple and ornamental, being heavily nickel plated and engraved. Requires but little power and will draw any cork in one second.
Price, each..$1.55

Champion Cork Puller.

No. 23R1100 Champion Cork Puller, with improved bottle holding clamp. Neat, strong, compact and durable. Operation simple, effective and safe. For use in hotels, barrooms, clubs, restaurants, or wherever a stationary puller can be used. Has been thoroughly tested and is guaranteed to give perfect satisfaction. Weight, 6 pounds. Height above counter when set up, 5 inches. The frame is heavily nickel plated. The worm and other working parts are made of best grade of oil tempered steel and warranted to stand the work. Price, each........................$2.50

Daisy Cork Puller.

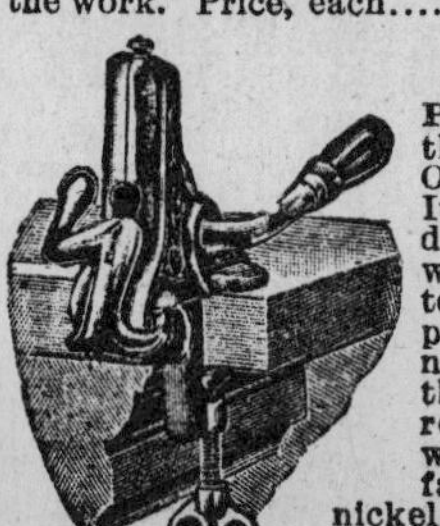

No. 23R1102 Daisy Cork Puller, with a perfect bottle holding attachment. Operation quick and sure. It is neat, compact and durable, and has not a single weak point. Has steel cutter fastened at one side of puller, and by turning the neck of the bottle against this cutter all wires are readily removed. Provided with clamp and screw for fastening. All polished and nickel plated. Weight, 8 pounds. Fully guaranteed. Each..$3.60.

OUR REFRIGERATOR DEPARTMENT.

FROM THIS ILLUSTRATION WE ENDEAVOR TO SHOW **the construction of our Michigan Refrigerator.** The illustration shows the circulation of the air, arrangement of shelves and drip cup in position. It will be noticed that **the air after passing over the ice falls directly under the provision chambers,** displacing the warmer and lighter air and forcing it up the flues on either end, where, by contact with the ice it is purified, cooled, and again falls, thus keeping up constant circulation.

PLEASE NOTE that we do not have any condensation on exposed metal plates, but carry the air directly to the ice, which is the greatest purifier known to modern science.

THESE REFRIGERATORS are constructed with an inside case of **odorless and tasteless lumber,** matched and clamped together with nails and glue, and fastened to hardwood cleats, making it a thoroughly air tight, strong cabinet in itself. The insulator used is charcoal sheathing, which is odorless and tasteless, and a perfect non-conductor.

THE OUTSIDE CASE OF OUR CHEAPEST LINE IS SOLID ASH, **the best lumber ever found for refrigerators; highly polished.** It is nailed and glued to the cleats which bind the inside case, thus making it one of the strongest and most durable refrigerators ever built.

The drip cup is shown in this cut closed. To empty it pull the rod, and it will throw it over All the wood in the provision chamber is covered with the metal, and there is no chance for it to become tainted or musty. Our refrigerators are paneled, top, sides, back and bottom, and finished as in no other makes.

OUR BINDING GUARANTEE.

WE GUARANTEE EVERY MICHIGAN REFRIGERATOR to be made of the very best material throughout, to be constructed on the latest improved and most scientific principles, to be found exactly as represented in every respect, and to give universal satisfaction; and if found otherwise than as stated we will refund any money sent us and pay **freight charges both ways.**

REFRIGERATORS are shipped from our factory in Southern Michigan. Refrigerators are accepted at second class freight rate by all railroad companies, which is usually from 40 to 50 cents per 100 pounds for 500 miles. By refering to pages 7 to 10 you can get the second class freight rate per 100 pounds to a point nearest you, which is almost exactly the same as to your town, and you will see the freight will amount to next to nothing as compared to what you will save in price.

Michigan Ash Refrigerators.

Michigan single door Refrigerator from $5.94 to $11.39

For general description and construction of refrigerator see heading. Understand, every refrigerator is **guaranteed to be exactly as represented, and if not found so may be returned at our expense and your money will be cheerfully refunded.**

It is manufactured of kiln dried ash lumber, beautifully finished antique, brass lock, fancy surface hinges, anti-friction casters.

All these refrigerators above $5.94 are fitted with two shelves and provision chambers.

No.	23R1000	23R1002	23R1004
Length, inches	24	27	30
Depth, inches	17	18	19
Height, inches	39	41	43
Ice capacity, lbs.	36	45	61
Shipp'g weight, lbs.	100	115	140
Price	$5.94	$7.84	$9.00

No. 23R1006 Same as No. 23R1002, with porcelain lined water cooler, and faucet to match trimmings; water cooler reduces ice capacity to 34 pounds. Price, each. ...**$9.73**

No. 23R1008 Same as No. 23R1004, with porcelain lined water cooler, and faucet to match trimmings; water cooler reduces ice capacity to 47 pounds. Price, each........................**$11.39**

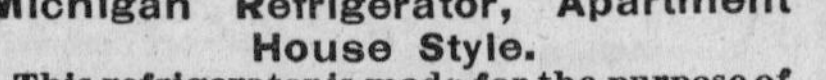

Inside Measurements of Refrigerators and Ice Boxes.

No.	Inside Measurements of Ice Space			Inside Measurements of Provision Space		
	Width	Height	Depth	Width	Height	Depth
23R1000	15½	9	11¼	16½	15	11¾
23R1002	18	9¾	12	20	16	12½
23R1004	20½	10¾	12¼	22½	17½	13
23R1006	12	9¾	12	20	16	12½
23R1008	14	10¾	12¼	22½	17½	13
23R1012	27	11	15	28¼	29¾	14½
23R1013	20	11	15	28¼	20¾	14½
23R1019	26	14	14¾	28½	19	15
23R1021	27	11½	16½	12½	21	18
23R1023	28	12	19	13½	22	20
23R1025	30¾	12½	20	14¾	22¾	21
23R1030	17	16½	13½	20½	22½	13
23R1033	19	11½	16	20	23	17
23R1040	21	14	14½	....	....	....
23R1041	26	15	15½	....	....	....
23R1042	27	17	16½	....	....	....
23R1043	29	18	19	....	....	....
23R1044	33	21	21	....	....	....

Michigan Refrigerator, Apartment House Style.

This refrigerator is made for the purpose of giving you a refrigerator of large capacity and still occupy small space in a room.

It is manufactured of the very best kiln dried ash lumber, beautifully finished antique, has solid brass locks, **finished surface hinges,** patent drip cup.

No. 23R1030 Length, 28 inches; depth, 19 inches; height, 55 inches; ice capacity, 65 pounds. Price...........................**$11.70**

Shipping weight, 170 pounds.

No. 23R1030

Michigan Refrigerator, Extra Large Size, Apartment House Style.

The refrigerator is of same style as one previously quoted, except that it is larger and has a special finish. It is very desirable for those wishing a refrigerator of large capacity and having limited space to put it.

No. 23R1033 Length, 31 inches; depth, 22 inches; height, 54 inches; ice capacity, 75 pounds; shipping weight, 212 pounds. Price **$14.00**

No. 23R1033

Our Michigan Double Door Refrigerator at $13.35 and $15.74.

This is a **very popular size Refrigerator. The ice chest is very large,** will hold artificial ice, and is the only first class refrigerator of this size made in which the chest will **take in artificial ice. It is manufactured from the very best selected kiln dried ash lumber, handsomely carved, trimmed and polished.**

No. 23R1012 Dimensions: Length, 36 inches; depth, 21 inches; height, 46 inches. **Ice capacity, 100 pounds.**

Price, each....................**$13.35**

Shipping weight, 229 pounds.

No. 23R1013 Same as No. 23R1012 with porcelain lined water cooler and faucet. **Ice capacity, 84 pounds.**

Price, each........................**$15.74**

Our Michigan Double Door Refrigerators,

With double doors in front of ice receptacle.

Made from the **very best selected kiln dried ash**; finished antique, highly polished, **beautifully carved.** It is trimmed with fancy **heavy bronze** trimmings throughout. The top is solid and makes a very useful sideboard, besides being a perfect refrigerator.

The upper doors are arranged so that the ice can be placed in the chamber without the inconvenience of raising the upper lid, and when the ice does not fill the large chamber, it serves as a place for storage around the ice. **The ice chamber of this refrigerator is made extra large. It is constructed with a view to giving the greatest amount of room possible.**

We do not hesitate to guarantee it in every respect, and **we are offering it at about one-half the price charged by retail dealers.**

No.	Length, inches	Depth, inches	Height, inches	Ice Capacity, pounds	Shipping weight	Price
23R1019	36	21	50	110	220 lbs.	$16.67
23R1021	40	24	52	170	290 lbs.	21.00
23R1023	42	27	54	190	310 lbs.	23.00
23R1025	45	28	56	220	367 lbs.	25.95

The smallest size in above list has no division in the Provision Chamber.

Our Michigan Hardwood Ice Chest at $4.95 to $9.44.

We offer the best made chest in the market at from $4.95 to $9.44 and we would invite you to compare these prices and quality with those of any other house, and if we cannot save you money and furnish you a much better chest we will not ask you to send us your order. Most ice chests are not made with walls constructed same as refrigerators and with same insulation. These are made in the same manner and with the same care as our highest priced refrigerators. We do not handle the cheap grade ice chest, for while it may look all right we know it won't satisfy our customers and we **must** furnish goods that will **satisfy** our customers when used.

Nos. 23R1040 to 23R1044

No.	Length, inches	Depth, inches	Height, inches	Shipping wt., pounds	Price
23R1040	29	20	25	85	$4.95
23R1041	32	21	26	93	5.76
23R1042	35	23	29	118	6.95
23R1043	37	25	31	130	7.96
23R1044	41	27	33	176	9.44

Refrigerator Pans.

No. 23R6828 Made of heavy galvanized iron with side handles. Will never rust.

Diameter, 12 inches; depth, 4½ inches. Price, each........................**20c**
Diameter, 14 inches; depth, 5 inches. Price, each........................**24c**
Diameter, 16 inches; depth, 5 inches. Price, each........................**30c**

THE SEROCO REFRIGERATOR.

OUR SEROCO REFRIGERATORS ARE NEW 1902 PATTERNS.

Made of solid quarter sawed white oak, antique finish, with 1-inch beveled panels on front and sides. All trimmings are heavy solid brass, nicely nickel plated. **The woodwork is rubbed finish,** as nice a finish as you will see on any sideboard, and make a beautiful piece of furniture for any dining room. Being solid tops, they can be used as a sideboard. The backs and bottoms of all these refrigerators are made in small panels to prevent warping and cracking. The provision chambers are lined with heavy, strong white porcelain enameled steel, making it sanitary, odorless, easily kept clean as a sheet of glass, and durable. It has every advantage of the tile lined refrigerators at much less cost, and it will not break, crack, chip off or come open in the joints. The ice receptacle is lined throughout with heavy metal, with extra strong ice rack. No wood exposed any where on the inside of these refrigerators, hence no odor from wood to taint the food. Fitted with self closing drip cup, removable ice rack, removable white porcelain enameled steel shelves for provision space, removable waste pipe, self retaining casters and swinging base board. This box is insulated with inside lining, inner wood wall, mineral felt insulation, an air space, charcoal sheathing and the outside wall, making practically six walls. **The doors of these refrigerators give more protection than any other refrigerators.** They are made extra thick and are insulated with charcoal sheathing, an air space and mineral felt. This gives perfect circulation of dry air at all times and will keep food a long time without danger of tainting or molding. To get the best results from any refrigerator, the ice receptacle should at all times be kept well supplied with ice. It gives better results and lessens the ice bill, for the more ice in the ice space, the slower it melts. Porcelain lined refrigerators are found only in a few of the first class retail stores of the cities and larger towns, and have heretofore been sold at about double our prices. At the prices printed we deliver the goods free on board the cars at our factory in Southern Michigan, from which point our customers must pay the freight. To some points the rate is less than it would be if shipped from Chicago, to many points it is exactly the same, and to a few points the extra freight charge would be no more then we would be obliged to add to the price if we printed the price shipped from Chicago.

We are getting out a new line of cheaper white enamel lined refrigerators made of ash. They are not ready as this catalogue goes to print, but a special catalogue will be sent free on request to those who wish a cheaper grade of enamel lined refrigerators. They will be ready about February 1st. They will be no cheaper than this line when actual value is considered, but will be lower in price than similar goods are sold by other dealers.

We cover these refrigerators with heavy paper and pack them securely in a strong crate to insure their reaching our customers in first class condition.

No. 23R1050 Our Seroco Apartment House Quarter Sawed Solid White Oak Refrigerator, with heavy, white porcelain lined provision chamber. Ice receptacle holds 125 pounds of ice, and a 100-pound piece will go in easily without any chipping, avoiding dirt and waste. It has heavy raised beveled panels on front and sides, and also is paneled on back and bottom, making it warp proof. It will never warp or crack. All the hinges and fastenings are made of solid brass heavily nickel plated. The ice compartment is lined throughout with strong, heavy metal nickel plated, leaving no wood exposed. This prevents all odor. The ice rack is made extra heavy and strong. The shelves in provision chamber, the ice rack and waste pipe are removable. Outside dimensions, 33 inches wide, 23 inches deep, 55 inches high. **Shipping weight, 300 pounds.**
Price, each.. .. ..**$27.50**

No. 23R1052 Our Seroco Apartment House Solid Quarter Sawed Oak White Porcelain Enameled Steel Lined Refrigerator, with three doors. Has all the desirable features found in all and any Seroco refrigerator. An advantage of having two doors in the provision space is that when the small door is opened it does not admit as much warm air as one large door would. The apartment style refrigerator is very desirable where rooms are small and floor space needs to be saved. 36 inches wide, 24 inches deep, 65 inches high. Ice capacity, 150 pounds. Shipping weight, 375 pounds. Price, each.......... **$36.30**

No. 23R1054 Our Seroco Solid Quarter Sawed Oak, White Porcelain Enameled, Steel Lined Refrigerator, with four doors and two separate provision chambers. The ice chamber will take a full cake of 200 pounds of artificial ice, and leave space to spare. This is one of the most desirable sizes for family use. Very roomy and economical on ice. Has all the good points found in an Seroco refrigerator. 43 inches wide, 27 inches deep, 56 inches high. Ice capacity, 425 pounds. Shipping weight, 310 pounds. Price, each. **$40.70**

No. 23R1056 Our Seroco Solid Quarter Sawed Oak, White Porcelain Enameled Steel Lined Refrigerator. This style refrigerator is designed for large families, boarding houses, hotels, restaurants and clubs. After having this illustration made we found the two small doors on left provision space were not as desirable as one large door and therefore we will make this refrigerator with four doors instead of five as shown in illustration. Outside measurements, 50 inches wide, 28 inches deep, 65 inches high. Ice capacity, 650 pounds. Shipping weight, 540 pounds.
Price, each..................**$53.90**

ICE CREAM FREEZERS.

SHEPARD'S LIGHTNING ICE CREAM FREEZERS. Lightning quadruple motion, automatic scraper, famous wheel dasher, combination hinge top gearing, completely covered. Compared with other freezers, we find: **THIS TUB IS CEDAR,** competitors use pine; has round electric welded wire hoop, galvanized, competitors' have flat hoops; can is full size and made from one size heavier tin than is used in other freezers. **Cast iron cover with drawn steel bottom,** competitors have sheet tin cover and bottom; **FREEZES AS QUICKLY AS ANY OTHER IN THE MARKET, WITH MUCH LESS EFFORT. All parts that come in contact with the cream heavily coated with pure block tin.** All other trimmings smoothly galvanized. **Uses 25 per cent less ice and salt than any other freezer.**

No. 23R1060

Size, quarts....	2	3	4	6	8	10	12	14		14	20
Price, each.....	$1.53	$1.66	$2.04	$2.67	$3.32	$4.47	$5.50	$6.43	With fly wheel,	$8.92	$12.34

No. 23R1062 The Blizzard Freezer has been made to fill a demand for low price goods and to give at the same time a freezer of superior quality in material and workmanship. It is single action, the can revolving, while the dasher is held in the crossbar or top plate. Its simple construction, fewer parts, less labor and material permit a lower price, and yet, at the same time, to use exactly the same pail and can as in our other freezers. The Blizzard Freezer is unquestionably the best freezer for the money ever put on the market. Pails of best Virginia white cedar, with electric welded wire hoops, guaranteed not to fall off.

Size...........	2-qt.	3-qt.	4-qt.	6-qt.	8-qt.	10-qt.	12-qt.	14-qt.
Price, each....	$1.38	$1.53	$1.79	$2.33	$2.92	$3.97	$4.81	$5.63

Little Corkscrew Pressure Valve.

No. 23R1120 This valve is used for keeping "beer and other liquids fresh and will do so for an almost indefinite time," by the aid of air, particularly for the purpose of keeping beer fresh in the keg for picnic parties, private clubs and boarding house keepers and farmers. It is a common occurrence for beer to get flat in half an hour after keg is tapped. By using the Little Corkscrew Pressure Valve your beer or other liquids are kept pure and fresh as long as you wish. **Directions:** Screw the valve into the cork in the keg to the top of the thread, which will bring the hole in small end of screw inside of keg. Then pump with a full stroke until you have the required pressure. Do not remove valve until keg is empty. Can be easily carried in pocket. Weighs only ½ pound. Price, each...**30c**

Ice Cream Disher.

No. 23R1070 Ice Cream Dishers. Have two revolving knives which cut the cream loose. By one-half turn of the button the cream slips out a smooth and perfect cone. Sizes designate the number of dishes to the quart.

Sizes......................	4s	5s	6s	8s	10s
Each......................	14c	13c	12c	11c	10c

Lemon Squeezers.

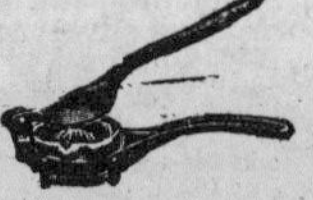

No. 23R1142 Lemon Squeezer, japanned, with heavy glass cup resting on rubber ring.
Price, each....................**18c**

No. 23R1144 Lemon Squeezer. Bowls are made of white porcelain; plunger from hardwood, and is detachable. The frame is of gray iron, japan finish; **the handsomest and most complete lemon squeezer** in the market. Price, each........**15c**

No. 23R1147 Malleable Iron Lemon Squeezer, fully tinned, strong and durable.
Price, each............ **8c**

Glass Lemon Squeezer.

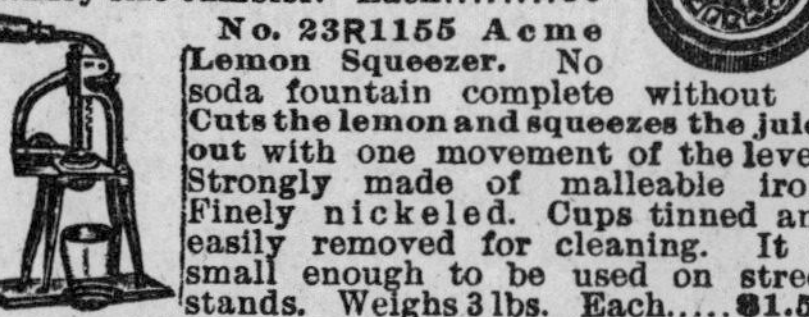

No. 23R1152 Glass Lemon Squeezer. The best made for private use; fits any ordinary size tumbler. Each........**5c**

No. 23R1155 Acme Lemon Squeezer. No soda fountain complete without it. **Cuts the lemon and squeezes the juice out with one movement of the lever.** Strongly made of malleable iron. Finely nickeled. Cups tinned and easily removed for cleaning. It is small enough to be used on street stands. Weighs 3 lbs. Each.....**$1.50**

The Modern Lemon Squeezer.

Always ready for use and easy to operate.

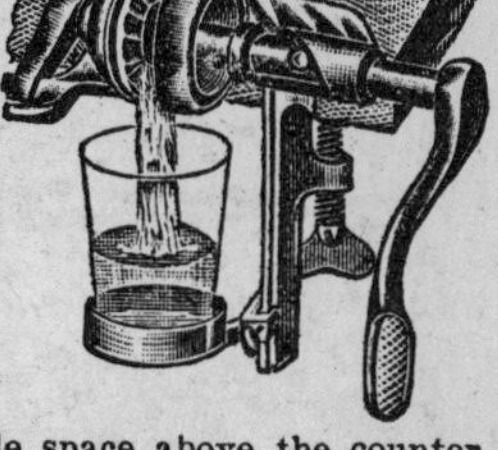

This machine is beautifully nickel plated and is the highest grade article of its kind yet produced. All parts that come in contact with the lemon are made of solid polished aluminum, insuring perfect sanitary cleanliness.

The machine is warranted perfect, being roller bearing, and a slight power applied to the handle will give 1200 pounds pressure against the lemon.

Occupies no valuable space above the counter, the handle hanging in the position shown above. It is simplicity itself, as there are no cogs or wheels to get out of order or clog up. It is absolutely the only squeezer that will not splash juice all over the operator.

No. 23R1153 Price, each........................**$2.00**

Semi-Circular Flower Stand.

No. 23R1660 With Trellis, 3 feet, 6 inches wide, 28 inches deep, 5 feet, 8 inches high, will hold from 18 to 24 pots. Weight, 21 lbs. Price, **$3.32**

No. 23R1661 Small semi-circular flower stand, same as above except that it has no trellis, 36 inches high. Weight, 15 lbs. Price.... **$2.60**

Semi-Circular Stand.

No. 23R1664 With Trellis, 6 feet, 8 inches high, 4 feet long, 32 inches deep. Weight, 30 pounds. Price, each.. **$4.75**

No. 23R1665 Stand same as above without trellis, 3 feet, 8 inches high. Weight, 24 pounds. Price, each....... **$4.04**

No. 23R1668 With Arch, three shelves 3 feet 3 inches long, 6 feet 6 inches high, 30 inches deep. Will hold from 24 to 30 pots. Weighs 25 pounds. **Price includes arch and basket.** Price, each.............. **$3.80**

No. 23R1669 Stand the same as above, **without arch or basket.** 42 inches high, shelves 3 feet 2 in. long. Weighs 20 lbs. Price, each...... **$3.09**

No. 23R1672 Pyramid Flower Stand with gothic arch and basket, 6 feet, 6 inches high, 4 feet wide and 22 inches deep. Will hold from 35 to 40 pots. Weighs 35 lbs. Price.. **$4.70**

No. 23R1673 Stand same as above without arch, 42 inches high. Weighs 29 lbs. Price, each... **$4.00**

Window Flower Pot Shelves.

Window Flower Pot Shelves are intended to be put on the outside of window frame sill or they may be used inside to set flower pots on. They are 7 inches wide with border 4½ inches high, finished in green and gold.

No. 23R1692 33 inches long. Each............ **47c**
No. 23R1694 36 inches long. Each............ **48c**
No. 23R1696 39 inches long. Each............ **49c**

Flower Pot Brackets.

No. 23R1730 Bronzed Iron, 5-inch arm, shelf 4 inches in diameter. Weight, 12 ounces. Price, each.................. **7c**

No. 23R1733 Dark antique bronzed iron, 2 shelves, 12-inch arm, one 5½-inch shelf and one 4-inch shelf. Weight, 25 ounces. Each.. ..**37c**

No. 23R1735 Flower Pot Brackets. Enameled; length of arm, 12 inches, diameter of dishes, one 5-inch and one 6-inch. Price, each........ **25c**

No. 23R1738 Flower Pot Bracket. Enameled; length of arms, 12 inches, diameter of dishes, two 5 inches and two 6 inches, complete as shown. Price...... **50c**

No. 23R1742 Flower Pot Bracket, iron, antique verde finish; **will hold 4 pots**; one 12-inch arm and two 6-inch; diameter of dishes, three 5-inch, and one 5½-inch. Weight, 5 lbs. Price.... **68c**

Tack Hammers.

No. 23R1760 Tack Hammer. Polished iron, hickory handle, claw in end of handle. Price, **4c**

Magnetic Tack Hammer.

No. 23R1762 The head of this hammer is magnetic, and it will pick up and hold tack for driving; hickory handle with steel claw. Price, each.......................... **8c**

No. 23R1765 Malleable Iron Tack Hammer. Tinned, upholsterers' pattern; hickory handle. Price, each........................ **10c**

Tack and Nail Pullers.

No. 23R1770 Forged Steel Tack Claws. Polished blade, riveted tang. The best we can buy. Price, each...................... **6c**

No. 23R1773 Tack Puller. Sure and quick; don't bend the tacks; ebonized handle; steel jaws. Price, each.... **5c**

Carpet Stretchers.

No. 23R1790 Common Carpet Stretcher. We do not furnish handle An old broom handle is just the thing and everybody has one. Price, each........................ **10c**

No. 23R1793 Carpet Stretcher, is light and durable, simple in construction and powerful, as it has a short fulcrum and good length of lever, which makes it easy to operate and is waranted not to injure the finest carpet. It holds the carpet in position after it is drawn to its proper place, thus giving the operator the free use of both hands with which to do the nailing. Price, **30c**

No. 23R1795 Carpet Stretcher, with tack hammer and claw. The drawbar is long enough to get enough bearing on carpet, so **there is no danger of tearing.** The takeup is automatic. Weight, 1 pound, 11 ounces. Price, each......... **49c**

No. 23R1805 The Hieronymus Furniture Joint or Chair Rung Fastener, for repairing any joint in hardwood. Will hold chair rungs better than glue or any other fastening. Only lower and upper rungs need the fastenings, as they are sufficient to hold all. **Will be found useful for many other purposes that will suggest themselves to the user.** Put up in packages containing 40 fasteners. Directions for use with each box, and any boy or woman can repair furniture with them. Cut shows full size. Price, per box containing 40 fasteners........... **4c**

Rat and Mouse Traps.

No. 23R1826 Rat Trap. This trap can always be **depended on to catch rats every time.** It kills them instantly without drawing blood, or otherwise scenting the trap. Weight, 1½ lbs. Price, each.................. **8c**

No. 23R1829 The American Rat Trap is a wonderfully effective rat catcher. Is used in the leading hotels, market houses, and public institutions. Many testimonials prove that they will catch rats up to their full capacity night after night, as long as the rats hold out. No. 3, or family size, is 17 inches long; capacity, 20 rats. Price, each.... **33c**

No. 23R1830 The American Rat Trap, No. 1 or hotel size; 21 inches long; capacity 50 rats. Price, each.................................. **$1.10**

No. 23R1832 The American Mouse Trap, same pattern as No. 23R1829 Rat Trap only smaller; length 7½ inches. Price, each.............................. **20c**

No. 23R1836 Rat Trap. This is an excellent trap, **thoroughly well made.** Size, 6x11 inches. Price, each...................... **25c**

No. 23R1840 Revolving Mouse Trap, made of heavy steel wire. Price, each.............. **12c**

No. 23R1842 This is the most **successful mouse catcher ever invented.** One mouse sets the trap for the next one that comes along; will hold several. Price, each......... **9c**

No. 23R1845 Choke Mouse Traps, round pattern, 5 holes. Price, each............. **6c**

No. 23R1850 Mouse Trap. As a sure mouse catcher it is **a sure thing. Mice can't touch the bait and live.** Price, each.................. **3c**

No. 23R1852 Rat Trap. Same style as No. 23R1850 mouse trap, except it is larger. When rats get too wise for other traps try this one. It fools them every time. Price, each............ **9c**

E-Z-Ketch Mouse and Rat Traps are the best that have ever been invented. They are made entirely of metal and consequently will not warp or get out of order like wood block traps. They can be easily washed and cleansed from all odors and impurities. Used with or without bait. When bait is used it is put beneath the trap and an animal is bound to spring the trap before touching the bait. They have the safest and easiest set and surest trigger. **E-Z to ketch, E-Z to bait, E-Z to clean.**

No. 23R1856 E-Z-Ketch Mouse Trap. Price, **4c**

No. 23R1857 E-Z-Ketch Rat Trap. Same pattern as mouse trap but larger. Price, each....... **10c**

Cotton Twine.

No. 23R1900 Cotton Twine. Size suitable for household or grocers' use. Six balls to the pound. Per ball.............................. **4c**

Manila Clothes Lines—Pure Stock.

	No. 23R1938	No. 23R1939	No. 23R1940
Length	50 feet	75 feet	100 feet
Each	12c	18c	24c

Cotton Clothes Lines.

	No. 23R1946	No. 23R1947	No. 23R1948
Length	60 feet	80 feet	100 feet
Each	11c	15c	17c

Braided Cotton Clothes Lines.

Braided Cotton Clothes Lines are used for many purposes, such as driving lines, awning ropes, sash cords, etc. They are practically waterproof, and **will not kink.** Will out last six common ones.

	No. 23R1950	No. 23R1951	No. 23R1952
Length	50 feet	75 feet	100 feet
Each	15c	23c	30c

Galvanized Wire Clothes Lines.

No. 23R1960 Wire Clothes Line, 100 feet long, made of six strands of No. 18 wire. Flexible, and will not rust. Price, each........................ **22c**

No. 23R1962 Wire Clothes Line, 100 feet long, made of six strands of No. 20 wire. Each......... **15c**

No. 23R1975 Clothes Line Pulleys, jointed on plate. Japanned. Price, each........................ **5c**

No. 23R1976 Galvanized. Price, each.............. **7c**

No. 23R1980 Clothes Line Hooks, japanned, heavy. Weight, 6 ounces. Price, each.............. **2c**

No. 23R1984 Line Cleats; length from tip to tip of horn, 2 inches; japanned. Price, per dozen, 15c; each............ **2c**

No. 23R1985 Galvanized; per dozen, 24c; each, **2c**

Clothes Line Reels.

No. 23R1992 Line Reel or Clothes Drier Casting. Has a socket which fastens over the top of a post. **The reel revolves on this socket** and is made for four bars. From 100 to 200 feet of line can be strung on bars (according to length of bars), and this can be hung full of clothes without moving basket or wading through deep snow in the winter. Price, each............. **43c**

Nut Crackers.

No. 23R2000 Nut Cracker, nickel plated. Length, 5 inches. Each......... **5c**

No. 23R2002 Old Dog Tray Nut Cracker, will crack any nut not larger than 1⅛ inch in diameter. The dog is 13¾ inches long from nose to tip of tail, stands 6¼ inches high. Weighs complete 4½ pounds. It is often used to set on the floor to hold doors open to desired position. Our price, each.................. **40c**

No. 23R2007 Lever Nut Crack. The kind that confectioners, bakers and dealers in nuts use. Cracks any kind of a nut. Mounted on wood base. Price, each.... **14c**

Broom Holders.

No. 23R2010 Broom Holder. A very simple and useful arrangement, which **always keeps broom in good shape.** Price, each.............................. **3c**

No. 23R2012 The Acme Broom Holder is much superior to any that we have ever seen. **It is handsomely nickel plated** and has hooks to hang the dust pan and brush on. Projects four inches from the wall. Weight, 5 oz. Fastens to wall with two screws. Price, each............................ **6c**

Towel Holder.

No. 23R2020 Towel Holder, nickel plated, can be screwed into the wall and securely holds towel. Price, each......... **8c**

Lamp Chimney Stoves.

No. 23R2025 Lamp Chimney Stove. Fits any ordinary crimped top lamp chimney. Water may be boiled in a few minutes. Price, each........................ **3c**

Alcohol Stove.

No. 23R2030 Alcohol Stove. No possibility of danger; base tightly packed with asbestos; cover extinguishes the flame; **nicely finished**; the whole neatly packed in box. An exceedingly useful article at all times. Price, each.............. **11c**

Collapsing Cups.

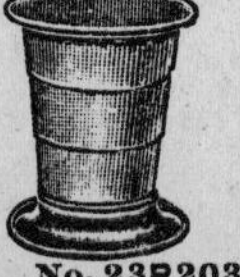

No. 23R2035 Collapsing Cup. Folds into a small space, and packed in neat box. Handy for bicyclers and travelers, and at picnics. Made of polished tin. Size extended, 2⅛x5⅝ inches. Weight, 1¼ ounces. Price, each................ **10c**

No. 23R2037 Collapsing Cup, small size, light and convenient. Made of polished tin, and packed in neat paper box. Size, extended, 2x2⅛ inches. Weight, 1 ounce. Price, each............... **6c**

DEPARTMENT OF COMBINATION OUTFITS AND HOUSE FURNISHINGS.

ABOUT THE QUALITY.

Different from many department and novelty stores who sell assortments of inferior goods, our assortments are all made up from regular stock merchandise of the highest grade, every article that goes into every combination we offer is strictly a high standard quality and so guaranteed, and if not found to be such in every instance you are at liberty to return goods to us and we will cheerfully refund your money. We are able to make this extraordinary offer on combination outfits by reason of buying up immense quantities of the different articles during the dull seasons, when the manufacturers have little to do and are willing to make very close prices; at the same time when it is quiet with us we can assemble the outfits, pack them, get them ready for shipment. As it costs no more to handle the complete outfit once ready for shipment than one single item in the lot, we can afford to figure our profit even lower than on a general line. All this you get the benefit of in our prices.

No. 23R3007 $4.25
No. 23R3008 4.93
No. 23R3009 5.47

ORDER BY NUMBER.

PEERLESS STEEL ENAMELED WARE OUTFITS.

We have made up a combination of Peerless Steel Enameled Ware in three different sizes which we are able to offer in the complete assortment as listed below at $4.25, $4.93 and $5.47, in competition with anything you can buy anywhere at double the price. This Peerless Enameled Steel Ware is the highest grade, strictly firsts, not seconds, made by the best makers in America. These outfits consist of the following articles:

1 Peerless Enameled Steel Tea Kettle.
1 Peerless Enameled Steel Coffee Pot.
1 Peerless Enameled Steel Tea Pot.
2 Peerless Enameled Steel Preserving Kettles.
1 Peerless Enameled Steel Saucepan.
2 Peerless Enameled Steel Pudding Pans.
1 Peerless Enameled Steel Wash Basin.
1 Peerless Enameled Steel Windsor Pattern Dipper.
4 Peerless Enameled Steel Pie Plates, 9 inches in diameter.
1 Peerless Enameled Steel Soap Dish to hang on the wall.
1 Peerless Enameled Steel Dish Pan.
1 Peerless Enameled Steel Soup Ladle.

No. 23R3007 Our Peerless Enameled Steel Outfit for No. 7 Stove. Weight, 45 pounds. Price, complete............$4.25
No. 23R3008 Our Peerless Enameled Steel Outfit for No. 8 Stove. Weight, 50 pounds. Price, complete..............$4.93
No. 23R3009 Our Peerless Enameled Steel Outfit for No. 9 Stove. Weight, 60 pounds. Price, complete...................$5.47

STOVE FURNISHING SETS.

MADE UP FROM FULL SIZE, FIRST QUALITY GOODS.

The first figure in stove size designates the size furniture that fits the stove
THUS... No. 8-18 stove takes No. 8 furniture.
No. 9-18 stove takes No. 9 furniture.

QUEEN ASSORTMENT.

1 Copper Bottom Tin Wash Boiler
1 Copper Bottom Tin Tea Kettle
1 Cast Iron Stove Kettle
1 Cast Iron Spider
1 Wrought Iron Fry Pan, 10 inches
1 4-pint Tin Tea Pot
1 5-quart Tin Coffee Pot
1 10-quart Retinned Dish Pan
2 Black Dripping Pans, 10x12 and 10x14 inches
1 Tin Bread Pan, 5⅝x10¾x3 inches
2 Com'n Square Bread Tins, 7¾x11¾x1½ in.
1 Revolv'g Flour Sifter
1 Box Grater
1 Biscuit Cutter
1 Dover Egg Beater
1 Dozen 3-inch Plain Patty Pans
½ Dozen 9-inch Tin Pie Plates
1 14-inch Tin Basting Spoon
1 Cake Turner
1 1-quart Tin Cup
1 Vegetable Fork
1 Tin Dipper
1 Flathandl'd Skimmer
1 Fire Shovel
1 Tin Wash Basin
1 Tube Cake Pan, 10-in.

No. 23R3017 Price, Queen assortment for No. 7 stove. Weight, 65 pounds...........$3.64
No. 23R3018 Price, Queen assortment for No. 8 stove. Weight, 70 pounds..........$3.85
No. 23R3019 Price, Queen assortment for No. 9 stove. Weight, 75 pounds..........$4.16

ACME ASSORTMENT.

1 Heavy IX-Tin Copper Bottom Wash Boiler
1 Iron Stove Kettle
1 Tin Cover to fit
1 Iron Tea Kettle
1 Iron Spider 1 Fry Pan
1 Stove Shovel
1 Nickel Plated Copper 5-pint Coffee Pot
1 Nickel Plated Copper 4-pint Tea Pot
1 Retinned Preserving Kettle
1 Cover to fit
1 Retinned Saucepan
1 Cover to fit
1 Basting Spoon
1 Tin Muffin Frame, 12 cups
½ Dozen Tin Pie Plates, 9-inch
1 Extra Heavy Retin'd Dish Pan, 14 quarts
1 1-Piece Tin Cup, 1 p't.
1 Galvanized Water Dipper, 2 quarts
1 Flathandl'd Skimmer
1 Vegetable Fork
2 Drip Pan, 10x12, 10x14
3 Tin Bread Pans
2 Tin Cake Pans
1 Dozen Assorted Patty Pans. 1 Rolling Pin
1 Cake Turner
1 Retinned Colander
1 Cake Cutter
1 Biscuit Cutter
1 Doughnut Cutter
1 Nutmeg Grater
1 Large Grater
1 Patent Flour Sifter
1 Dover Egg Beater
1 Covered Japanned Dust Pan
1 Butcher Knife
1 Paring Knife
1 Mincing Knife, double blades, 1 Bread Board
1 Wood Potato Masher
1 Oval Hardwood Chopping Tray
1 Steamer
1 Set Mrs. Potts' Sad Irons, consisting of Three Irons, Handle and Stand

No. 23R3027 Acme Assortment for No. 7 stove. Weight, 110 lbs. Price..........$7.00
No. 23R3028 Acme Assortment for No. 8 stove. Weight, 115 lbs. Price..........$7.31
No. 23R3029 Acme Assortment for No. 9 stove. Weight, 120 lbs. Price..........$7.77

OUR SPECIAL $1.30 HOUSEKEEPERS' OUTFIT OF TINWARE.

Every piece we show in this lot is strictly high grade, standard goods. There is not a piece in the whole outfit but what is in everyday use. If there happens to be one or more articles in this outfit you have no use for, do not hesitate to take advantage of the offer; you are getting a good portion of the outfit for nothing, and when you get the $1.30 price you can afford to pay $1.30 for this outfit if you give away one-third of the articles. The remainder will be very cheap at $1.30.

No. 23R3033 ORDER BY NUMBER.

Our $1.30 Set of Tinware consists of the following articles:

1 Heavily Retinned Dish Pan, 10-quart size
3 Retinned Pudding Pans, one each 1, 2 and 3 qt. size
1 Retinned Milk Pan, 4-quart size
1 Spout Strainer to attach to spout of Tea Pot
1 Wire Handle Bowl Strainer, diameter 5 inches, to strain soups, etc.
1 Retinned Wire Soap Bracket, to hang on the wall
1 Doughnut Cutter, diameter 3 inches
1 Biscuit Cutter, diameter 3 inches
1 Soap Saver. Uses up all the small pieces of soap
1 Wire Pot Chain. 1 Nutmeg Grater
1 Pieced Tin Cup, 1-pint size
1 Wood Handle Slotted Mixing Spoon
1 Tinned Steel Kitchen Fork, 3 prongs, 12½ inches long.
1 Apple Corer, size 3¼x6 inches
1 Wire Potato Masher, heavy retinned wire and hardwood handle
1 Dover Egg Beater, regular family size
1 Rubber Scraper, used for cleaning windows and also for cleaning sinks
1 Dredge Box, japanned, size 3x3½ inches
2 Tin Graters with enameled wood handles, 1 each size, 5½x13 and 3x6½ inches
1 Retinned Wire Broiler, size 9x6 inches
1 Heavy Asbestos Stove Mat, 9 inches in diameter with metal rim
1 Wood Handle Preserving Spoon. 1 Glass Cutter.

No. 23R3033 Our price for the entire outfit as listed above, weight 15 pounds..........$1.30

OUR $4.90, $5.43 AND $6.13 STOVE AND KITCHEN TINWARE OUTFIT.

EVERYTHING NEEDED IN THE KITCHEN or in the home. More tinware than you would be able to buy in any retail store at more than double the price. The goods we offer in this outfit are all strictly high standard grades. Full sizes and quality guaranteed. Outfit includes the following:

1 IX Tin Wash Boiler, with flat copper bottom
1 IX Tin Tea Kettle, with flat copper bottom
1 IX Tin Coffee Pot, with copper bowl bottom and enameled wood handle
1 IX Tin Tea Pot, with copper bowl bottom and enameled wood handle
1 Retinned Wash Basin
1 IX Tin Dipper, with heavy copper bottom
2 Heavily Retinned Preserving Kettles
1 Heavily Retinned Saucepan
2 Retinned Pudding Pans. 1 IC Tin Colander
1 Heavily Retinned Dish Pan
1 IC Tin Steamer, with rimmed cover
4 Tin Pie Plates, 9 inches in diameter
3 Tin Bread Pans. 1 Tin Oblong Pan
1 Deep Oblong Pan
1 Tin Measure, 1-quart size, graduated by one-half pints. 1 Tin Funnel
1 Tin Grater, with enameled wood handle
1 Retinned Soup Ladle, with enameled wood handle. 1 Tin Gravy Strainer
10 Assorted Cake, Cooky, Biscuit and Doughnut Cutters 1 Nutmeg Grater
1 Retinned Flat Handle Skimmer
1 Cake Turner, with enameled wood handle
12 Assorted Tin Patty Pans
1 Patent Rotary Flour Sifter
1 Covered Japanned Dust Pan
2 Retinned Threaded Basting Spoons
1 Tinned Kitchen Fork, 3 prong, length 12½ inches. 1 Dover Egg Beater
3 Assorted Tin Pot covers, to fit kettles and sauce pan. 1 Square Japanned Match Box
1 Polished Lipped Frying Pan, with always cool handle
2 Sheet Iron Dripping or Roasting Pans

No. 23R3037 Our Stove and Kitchen Tinware Set for No. 7 Stove. Weight, 55 pounds. Price, complete..........$4.90
No. 23R3038 Our Stove and Kitchen Tinware Set for No. 8 Stove. Weight, 60 pounds. Price, complete..........$5.43
No. 23R3039 Our Stove and Kitchen Tinware Set for No. 9 Stove. Weight, 70 pounds. Price, complete..........6.13

IRON FIRE DOGS.

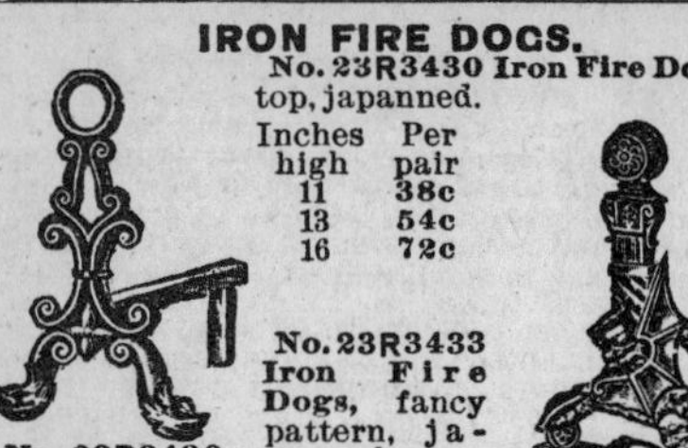

No. 23R3430 Iron Fire Dogs, ring top, japanned.

Inches high	Per pair
11	38c
13	54c
16	72c

No. 23R3433 Iron Fire Dogs, fancy pattern, japanned.

Inches high	14	16
Price, per pair	76c	95c

No. 23R3430 No. 23R3433

No. 23R3436 Cast Brass Andirons, urn pattern. A strong, heavy andiron, not to be compared with cheap goods with spun ornaments.

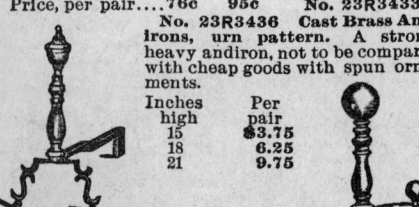

Inches high	Per pair
15	$3.75
18	6.25
21	9.75

No. 23R3436

No. 23R3437 Cast Brass Andirons, colonial pattern, circular; 16 inches high, with back heads.
Price, per pair..........$9.98

No. 23R3437

No. 23R3450 No. 23R3451

No. 23R3450 Open Coal Hods, japanned.
16-inch, weight, 2⅜ pounds. Price, each..........22c
17-inch, weight, 2½ pounds. Price, each..........25c
18-inch, weight, 2¾ pounds. Price, each..........28c

No. 23R3451 Open Coal Hods, galvanized.
16-inch, weight, 2¾ pounds. Price, each..........27c
17-inch, weight, 3 pounds. Price, each..........30c
18-inch, weight, 3½ pounds. Price, each..........33c

No. 23R3454 No. 23R3455

No. 23R3454 Funnel Coal Hods, japanned.
17-inch, weight, 2⅞ pounds. Price, each..........30c

No. 23R3455 Funnel Coal Hods, galvanized.
17-inch, weight, 3½ pounds. Price, each..........36c

Mosaic Stove Boards.

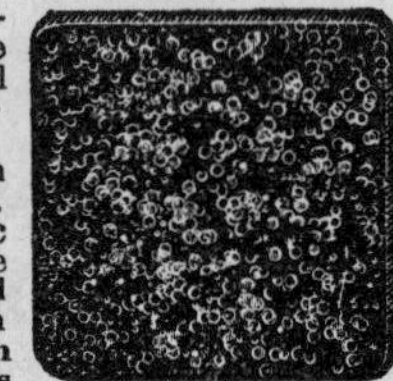

Made of sheet steel enameled under a temperature of 240 degrees of heat. Will not rust or fade. Not affected by heat from any stove. Can be scrubbed like oilcloth and will retain their colors. Made to represent mosaic tiling, which is a new feature in a stove board. **The metal is 20 per cent heavier than any other board and as much better as enameled ware is better than tinware.** They are lined with wood.

No.	Size	Weight, pounds	Price
23R3471	26x26	7⅜	54c
23R3472	26x32	9⅜	63c
23R3473	28x28	8¼	59c
23R3474	28x34	10	71c
23R3475	30x30	9¾	66c
23R3476	33x33	11⅝	76c
23R3477	30x38	12⅜	79c
23R3478	36x36	12¾	89c
23R3479	32x42	15⅝	94c

Stove Lining.

No. 23R3490 Asbestos Plastic Stove Lining, composed of asbestos and other fireproof materials; is easily applied with a trowel, and makes a durable and economical lining for cook stoves; **useful for repairing broken brick or iron lining.**
5-pound pails, each...25c 10-pound pails, each..45c

No. 23R3492 The Acme Stove Lining Cement for lining stoves, ranges, etc., and repairing old brick linings. It never sets until it is burned. If directions are closely followed it will not crack or crumble. The 12-pound package is enough to brick a stove. The 6-pound package will make a back. Full directions with each package so that no one can make a mistake.
Price per box, containing 6 pounds..........23c
Price per box, containing 12 pounds..........42c

BARREL COVER ASH SIFTER.

No. 23R3496 Barrel Cover Ash Sifter with cover, will fit a sugar barrel. Inside box measures 12x12 inches, outside box has cover; made of pine, stained; a good serviceable sifter at a low price. Weight, each, 8½ lbs. Price, each..28c

Brass Preserving Kettles.

No. 23R3510 **Will not hold quite as much as represented.**
1½ gallon, 10-inch. Price....$0.97
2 gallon, 11-inch. Price.... 1.16
3 gallon, 13-inch. Price.... 1.50
4 gallon, 14-inch. Price.... 1.93
5 gallon, 15-inch. Price.... 2.49
6 gallon, 16-inch. Price.... 2.87

Porcelain Lined Cast Preserving Kettles.

No. 23R3514

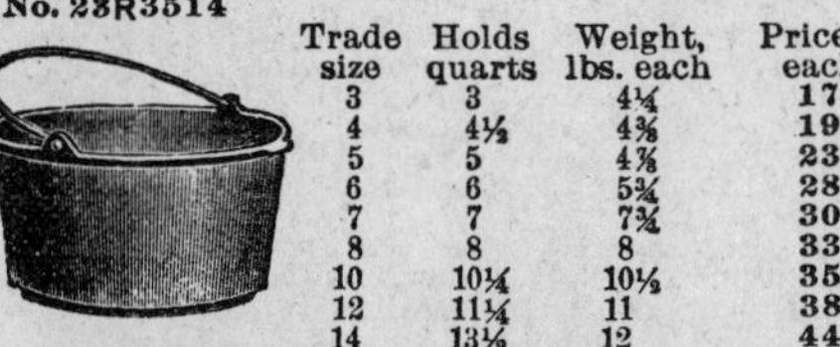

Trade size	Holds quarts	Weight, lbs. each	Price, each
3	3	4¼	17c
4	4½	4⅝	19c
5	5	4⅞	23c
6	6	5¾	28c
7	7	7¾	30c
8	8	8	33c
10	10¼	10½	35c
12	11¼	11	38c
14	13½	12	44c

Bake Oven.

No. 23R3518 Bake Oven, deep pattern, with bails and covers. These ovens are **designed for camp use;** can be set in center of wood fire without injury to contents; cover fits down snug, so that nothing can get inside.

No.	Diam. at top	Weight, lbs.	Price, each	No.	Diam. at top	Weight, lbs.	Price, each
3	10-inch	11	36c	1	12-inch	14	61c
2	11-inch	13	48c	0	14-inch	17	76c

No. 23R3521 Iron Tea Kettles, wood handle.
No. 7, weight, 8 pounds. Each.31c
No. 8, weight, 9 pounds. Each.34c
No. 9, weight, 11 pounds. Each.38c

No. 23R3522 Iron Stove Pots.

Size, inches	7	8	9
Weight, pounds	7¼	8¾	10½
Price, each	33c	38c	44c

Stove Kettles.

No. 23R3523 Iron Stove Kettle.

No.	7	8	9
Weight, lbs.	6¼	7⅞	11
Price, each	29c	31c	38c

Scotch Bowls.

No. 23R3524 Iron Scotch Bowl.

Diameter at top, inches	10	11	12
Weight, pounds	4¾	5¾	6
Price, each	20c	22c	27c

NOTE—Sometimes water in certain localities causes iron kettles to rust or discolor articles cooked in them. This can easily be prevented by using the kettle the first time for boiling salted meat; or, Mrs. Rorer recommends boiling suet and salt before using iron kettles.

Spiders.

No. 23R3525 Iron Spider.

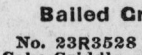

Size, inches	7	8	9	10
Weight, pounds	3¼	3¾	5¼	5½
Price, each	13c	16c	18c	22c

No. 23R3526 Iron Side Handle Griddle.

Size, inches	7	8	9
Weight, pounds	2¼	2⅛	3¼
Price, each	11c	12c	14c

Bailed Griddles.

No. 23R3528 Iron Round Cake Griddle, with bail.

Size, inches	12	14
Weight, pounds	6	7¼
Price, each	22c	29c

No. 23R3530 Long Griddles.

Size	7	8	9
Weight, pounds	5	5½	6½
Price, each	19c	23c	29c

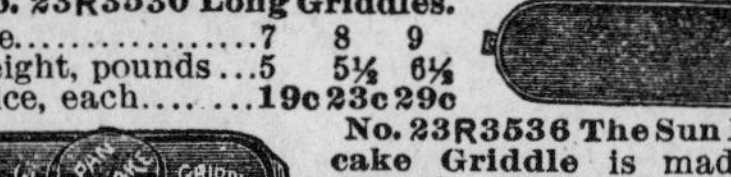

No. 23R3536 The Sun Pancake Griddle is made of wrought steel; is strong and durable, heats quickly and is lighter than any other griddle made. The batter is first poured into the little round hinged pans. When done on the first side the round pans are turned over with a fork into the long pan, and while the cakes are finishing, the round pans are refilled, and so on, thus baking at the actual rate of six cakes a minute. Weight, 1¾ pounds. Price, each..........29c

No. 23R3538 Iron Flat Iron Heaters. Will save one-half the time in heating irons. Deep pattern.

Size	7	8	9
Weight, pounds	5¼	6	7
Price, each	21c	25c	30c

Flat Iron Heaters.

No. 23R3540 Sad Iron Heater, for gas, gasoline or oil stoves, heats three irons at one time and will keep two rapid ironers supplied with hot irons. The heat coming in direct contact with the irons heats them much faster than can be done on heaters with closed sides. Price, each..........25c

Gem Pans.

No. 23R3542 Iron Gem Pan, deep; 11 cups. Weight, 5 pounds. Price, each..........17c

No. 23R3543 Iron Gem Pan, oval pattern. Weight, 3¼ pounds. 11 cups; shallow. Price, each...14c

IMPERIAL STOVE HOLLOW WARE.

IMPERIAL STOVE HOLLOW WARE IS MADE OF SMOOTH CAST GRAY IRON

heavily coated on the inside with pure white porcelain and on the outside with mottled blue and white enamel, all of which is united with the cast iron at an intense heat, thereby forming a perfect union of the two, which no subsequent heating can destroy. It is easy to clean, of pleasing appearance, and we warrant every piece to give satisfaction. The numbers given designate the size of stove the article is intended for.

Imperial Spider.

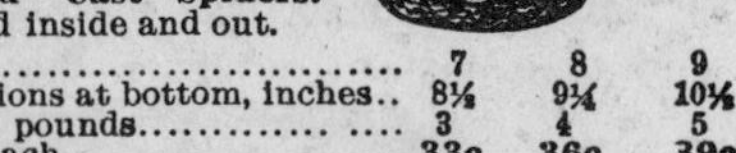

No. 23R3565 Imperial Enameled Cast Spiders. Enameled inside and out.

No.	7	8	9
Dimensions at bottom, inches	8⅛	9¼	10⅛
Weight, pounds	3	4	5
Price, each	33c	36c	39c

Imperial Kettle.

No. 23R3567 Imperial All Enameled Cast Kettle.

Number	7	8	9
Diameter at top in.	9½	10⅝	11⅛
Depth, inches	6½	7⅛	8
Weight, pounds	5⅜	7½	9
Price, each	60c	62c	63c

Imperial Stove Pots.

No. 23R3570 Imperial All Enameled Cast Stove Pots.

Number	7	8	9
Diameter at top, inches	9¼	10⅜	11⅛
Depth, inches	6⅜	7⅜	8⅛
Weight, pounds	6¼	8	11⅛
Price, each	66c	67c	69c

Imperial Tea Kettles.

No. 23R3574 Imperial All Enameled Cast Stove Tea Kettles.

No.	7	8	9
Capacity, qts.	5½	6½	9
Weight, lbs.	7¾	8½	11
Price, each	90c	96c	$1.05

New Idea Kettles.

No. 23R3577 New Idea Cast Iron Kettles. White porcelain lined and enameled on outside with mottled blue porcelain. Smooth as glass and as easy to clean as a china dish. An ideal kettle for preserving fruits, etc., as it is not affected by acids, does not stain and will not discolor anything cooked in it.

Capacity, qts.	3	4	6	8	10	12	14	16	20	24
Weight, lbs.	4	4¼	6⅛	7½	8⅜	11¼	12¼	15	17½	19¼
Price, each	32c	36c	44c	52c	56c	60c	70c	80c	$1.00	$1.20

Ham Boilers.

No. 23R3585 Ham Boiler. Made of cast iron and lined with white porcelain; also used by many as a wash boiler; will not rust or discolor the clothes and with ordinary care should last a lifetime. Size indicates the size stove it will fit.

No. 23R3585

Size	7	8	9
Length, inches	19	21½	24
Width, inches	9⅝	11¼	13
Weight, pounds	20	22½	31
Price, each	$1.20	$1.40	$1.58

Asbestos Stove Mat.

No. 23R3700 A household necessity. This mat is made of asbestos of superior quality, and is scorch proof as well as fireproof. Any cooking utensil used upon it becomes absolutely scorch proof. **Diameter, 9 inches.** Weight, each, 2 oz.
Price, each..........3c
Per dozen..........25c

Crown Asbestos Toaster.

No. 23R3702 Crown Asbestos Toasters consists of an asbestos disc covered with steel wire cloth, the lower surface being covered with sheet steel. Has a corrugated steel rim and always cool Alaska handle. For toasting bread, rusks or crackers on gas, gasoline or coal stove it is fine. Can also be used under cooking utensils to keep food from scorching or for any purpose for which the asbestos stove mats are used. Diameter, 8⅝ inches. Weight, 10 ounces. Price, each 9c

Waffle Irons.

No. 23R3712 Simple in construction, convenient to handle, easy to clean, none better made.

Size, No.	8	9
Weight, each, pounds	8¼	10
Price, each	70c	75c

No. 23R3714 Twin Waffle Iron for large family and boarding house use. This is the most up to date waffle iron made. Can be used on gas, gasoline or coal stove with equal facility, and without removing the pan from frame and by its use delicious waffles may be had without any more labor than is required to make common griddle cakes. Capacity six waffles, three in each pan. Has a hinge consisting of two half balls cast solid into pans, and can be instantly separated for cleaning. Weight, 10 pounds.
Price, each $1.12

Soapstone Griddles.

No. 23R3732 Round Soapstone Griddle, hooped, with handles. No grease required.

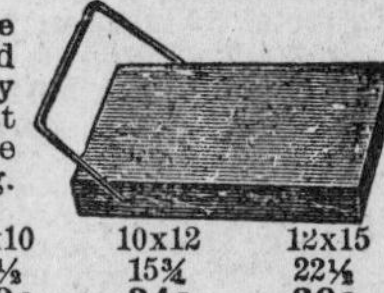

Diameter, in	10	12	14	16
Weight, lbs.	5½	6⅝	9½	13¾
Price, each	41c	59c	78c	88c

No. 23R3733 Oval Soapstone Griddles, hooped, with handles.

Size, inches	8x16	9x18	10x20	11x22
Weight, each, pounds	7¼	9¼	11¼	13⅛
Price, each	62c	72c	88c	$1.06

No. 23R3741 Soapstone Foot Warmer. Can be heated in oven or on top of an ordinary stove and will hold the heat a long time. Will keep the feet warm when sleighing. Much used for bed warming.

Size, inches	6x8	8x10	10x12	12x15
Weight, each, lbs.	5¼	9½	15¾	22½
Price	14c	19c	24c	29c

Lehman's Heater.

Lehman's Heater is a metallic case 7¼ inches wide, 3½ inches deep and from 14 to 20 inches long—used to keep the feet warm when riding. The heating material is a specially prepared coal, each piece 7¾ inches long, 2½ inches wide, and 1¼ inches thick. One-third of one of these pieces is sufficient for giving a steady, continuous heat for twelve hours in ordinarily cold weather. If only wanted for a short time, it can be extinguished with water and used again. **The Lehman Heater** is free from smoke or odor. No danger from fire. This is the genuine Lehman's Heater. Dangerous and worthless imitations are sold at less prices.

No. 23R3745 Lehman's Heater. Width, 7¼ inches, depth, 3½ inches; length, 14 inches. Weight, each, 4½ pounds. Price, each, without coal $2.35
No. 23R3746 Same as above, covered with Brussels Carpet 3.00
No. 23R3747 Lehman's Heater. Width, 7¼ inches; depth, 3½ inches; length, 20 inches. Weight, each, 6½ pounds. Price 3.60
No. 23R3748 Same as above, covered with Brussels Carpet 4.50
No. 23R3752 Lehman's Coal, in Boxes, containing 12 pieces. Weight, 8¾ lbs. Per box ... .64
No. 23R3753 Lehman's Coal, in Boxes, containing 100 pieces, suitable for liverymen, or owners of hacks, cabs, etc. Price, per box .. 5.40

Sugar Kettle.

No. 23R3775 Sugar or Wash Kettles, with bails, milled and painted. No. 8, 40-gallon kettle, is the largest cast iron kettle, with bail, made. Average weight of kettles is given below.

	Actual measure	Weight	Each
No. 1	8 gallons	25 pounds	$1.00
No. 2	10 gallons	30 pounds	1.25
No. 3	15 gallons	42 pounds	1.60
No. 4	18 gallons	48 pounds	2.00
No. 5	21½ gallons	52 pounds	2.25
No. 6	25 gallons	65 pounds	2.75
No. 7	30 gallons	85 pounds	3.10
No. 8	40 gallons	120 pounds	3.53

Copper Kettles.

	Size, gallons	Weight, about	Diam. on top inside	Deep, inches	Price, each
No. 23R3786	20	29 lbs.	22 in.	14½	$ 7.25
No. 23R3787	25	32 lbs.	23½ in.	15	8.00
No. 23R3788	30	39 lbs.	24½ in.	17½	9.75
No. 23R3789	36	46 lbs.	26 in.	19	11.50
No. 23R3790	40	48 lbs.	27 in.	19¼	12.00

Crown Steel Broiler.

No. 23R3808 Crown Self Basting Steel Broiler. A broiler that broils and bastes perfectly. The juices of the meat are retained by the corrugated bars, and the meat is being thoroughly basted on one side while the other is broiling. Turn the broiler frequently and you will get the best results. Can be used over coal, gas or gasoline fire and is strong and light. Diameter, 10½ inches. Weight, 1¼ pounds. Price, each 23c

The Morgan Broiler.

No. 23R3810 The Morgan Broilers. It is self basting, and instead of the gravy creating a suffocating smoke and disagreeable odor, it runs into the corrugations, is broiled into the meat, making an otherwise dry, tough steak tender and juicy. It makes no difference what kind of stove you use, gasoline, wood, coal, gas or oil, the Morgan Broiler is adapted to them all. Will not crack, warp or break; is easily cleaned, fits any stove; does not affect the draught nor deaden the fire. Weight, each, 2½ pounds. Price, each 35c

Dripping Pans.

No. 23R3815 Refined Smooth Steel Dripping Pans.

Size, in.	Weight, each, lbs.	Each	Size in.	Weight, each, lbs.	Each
7x10	¾	7c	10x14	1½	12c
7x14	1⅛	9c	11x16	1¾	13c
8x12	1	10c	12x17	2	14c
10x12	1¼	11c	14x17	2⅜	16c

Self-Basting Roasting Pans.

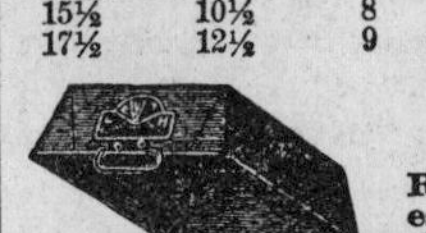

No. 23R3817 Self Basting Roasting Pan. This is an entirely new pan. The projections shown in cut collect the condensation from the steam and cause it to fall on the meat instead of running down the sides of the pan. It is made of smooth iron.

Length.	Width.	Height.	Price, each.
15⅝	10½	8	27c
17½	12½	9	36c

The Acme Roasting Pan.

No. 23R3820 The Acme Roasting Pan is the strongest and best roasting pan in the market. The bottom is strengthened by two ribs. Has a heavy rack which keeps the meat out of the gravy. It is made of a fine grade of smooth steel. **Try the pan for baking bread and you will never use anything else.** Notice the very low prices. They are sold by agents at more than twice our price.

No.	Width	Length	Height	Wt. lbs.	Price, Each
1	9	13	7½	3½	42c
2	10	15	7⅞	4	50c
3	11	16	8½	4½	58c
4	13	18	9½	6⅛	68c

Roasting Pans.

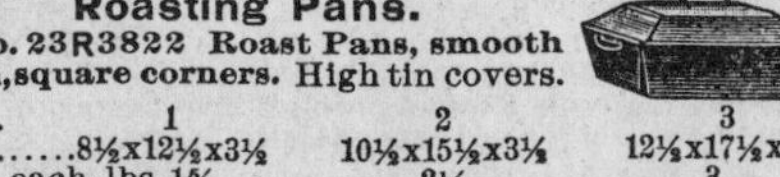

No. 23R3822 Roast Pans, smooth iron, square corners. High tin covers.

Nos.	1	2	3
Size	8½x12½x3½	10½x15½x3½	12½x17½x3½
Wt., each, lbs.	1⅝	2¼	3
Each	24c	32c	35c

Acme Frying Pans.

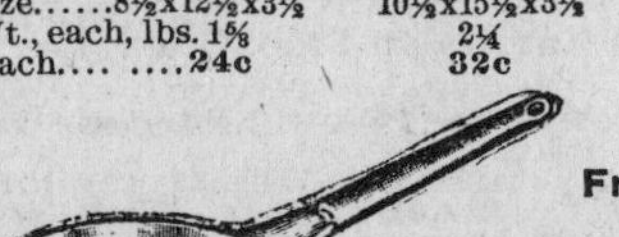

No. 23R3830 Stamped Seamless Lipped Frying Pans. Polished, with patent handle. Always cool.

Nos.	3	4	5	6
Diameter at top, inches	9⅞	10⅜	10⅞	11¾
Weight, each, pounds	1	1⅛	1⅛	1¾
Price, each	13c	15c	18c	20c

Omelette Pan.

No. 23R3834 Asbestos, Lined Steel, Omelette Pan. Consists of two distinct blued steel pans spun together, the bottom space between them containing a sheet of asbestos making it proof against burning and spreading the heat evenly over entire bottom. It is intended for making omelettes, frying eggs or light cooking of any kind. Has always cool Alaska handle. Diameter, 8¾ inches; depth, 1 inch; weight, 10 ounces. Price, each 12c

GIVE CATALOGUE NUMBER IN FULL WHEN YOU WRITE YOUR ORDER

Steam Cooker.

No. 23R3837 You can cook sauer kraut, onions, cabbage and pudding at the same time, without any one of them partaking of the odor or flavor of the other. It cooks well but never burns. It saves fuel, stove space, fits any stove, and saves one-quarter of the food which is lost when cooked the old way. Specially adapted for oil, gas and gasoline stoves, where space is limited. Well made from good heavy tin, with copper bottom on bottom vessel.

Vessels	4	4	4	5	5
Quarts, each	2	3	5	3	5
Diam., in.	7⅝	9	10¼	9	10¼
Price, each	$1.00	$1.15	$1.34	$1.45	$1.63

Tea Kettle Water Still.

No. 23R3853 Tea Kettle Water Still consists of two parts or vessels scientifically constructed for the purpose of condensing the steam generated in an ordinary tea kettle into pure distilled water. The spout of the condenser fits the spout of any tea kettle, and to operate simply put the required amount of water into the tea kettle, but do not fill above spout so as to prevent free passage of steam; then fill the upper vessel of the condenser with cold water and set inside the lower one, and set on a shelf or bracket close to stove. Steam is driven in from the tea kettle, circulates around the cool surface of the inner vessel is condensed or changed back to water—trickles down like dew and runs off at the small spout of the outer vessel, where it can be caught in bottles and set aside to cool for future use. There are 264 square inches of condensing surface, hence, distilled water is produced very rapidly. **It is absolutely pure, contains no disease germs, no lime or mineral matter and is as clear as crystal.** Typhoid fever is impossible where distilled water is used. It cures rheumatism and is a wonderful solvent and cleanser of the human system. The water is aerated and rendered palatable by introduction of air through tubes on each side of the vessel, and this air is sterilized by passing the hot steam over the air tubes within the vessel. The still is made from first quality XX charcoal tin, 10 inches in diameter, 13 inches high. Weight, packed for shipment, 13 pounds.
Price, each, without tea kettle $3.35

CAST ALUMINUM WARE.

Each utensil is cast solid in one piece leaving no seams or joints to leak. It is strong and stiff. It does not tarnish and can be kept bright by cleaning same as silverware. Each piece is thoroughly inspected and guaranteed perfect in every detail.

Cast Aluminum Tea Kettle.

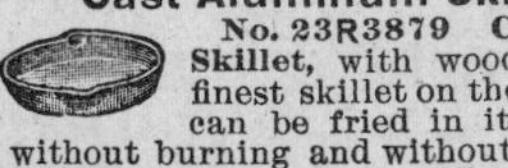

No. 23R3875 Cast Aluminum Tea Kettle. Cast solid in one piece with no seams or rivets. No plating to wear off.

Sizes	7	8	9
Weight, ea., lbs.	2½	2¾	3½
Price, each	$2.20	$2.31	$2.70

Cast Aluminum Kettle.

No. 23R3877 Cast Aluminum Kettle. Cast solid in one piece. For preserving, it has no equal. Fruit acids do not affect it. **It will not burn or stick.**

Quarts	2	4	6	8
Holds qts.	2	4	5¾	8
Wt., ea., lbs.	1	1½	2⅛	2⅝
Price, ea.	$1.50	$1.75	$1.87	$2.52

Cast Aluminum Skillet.

No. 23R3879 Cast Aluminum Skillet, with wood handle. The finest skillet on the market. Food can be fried in it to a delicious brown without burning and without sticking to the skillet.

Size	7	8	9
Weight, each, pounds	1⅛	1⅜	1¾
Price, each	$1.20	$1.30	$1.50

Cast Aluminum Griddles.

No. 23R3880 Cast Aluminum Griddles. Will not warp or crack. Made extra heavy to hold the heat. Cakes can be cooked on this griddle to a delicious brown, and will not burn or stick, **without using any grease.** It makes no smoke, and leaves the cake clean and delicate.

	With side handle		With bail	
Size	8	9	12	14
Weight, each, lbs.	1⅛	1¼	1⅝	2⅜
Each	$1.26	$1.50	$1.60	$2.06

HARDWARE OF NEARLY ALL KINDS

is accepted generally by railroad companies at second class freight rates, which generally average 40 to 50 cents per 100 pounds for 500 miles. By referring to pages 7 to 10 you can get the freight rate for 100 pounds to your nearest point, which is almost exactly the same as to your town, and you will see the freight will amount to next to nothing as compared to what you will save in price. Many heavy articles in hardware take still lower rates, such as third, fourth and fifth class.

Solid Steel Ware.

No. 23R3891 Solid Steel Seamless Taper Stove Kettles, are made from one piece of wrought steel. The bottom is much thicker than the sides. Tinned to prevent rusting. Flat bottom.

No. 7 Diameter, 8¼ inches; depth, 6 inches. Weight, 2⅞ pounds....63c

No. 8 Diameter, 10 inches; depth, 7 inches. Weight, 4 pounds........................$0.75

No. 9 Diameter, 11 inches; depth, 7¼ inches. Weight, 4⅜ pounds. Price, each............... .88

No. 10 Diameter, 12 inches; depth, 7 inches. Weight, 5 pounds Price, each.................. 1.00

Seamless Spiders.

No. 23R3893 Solid steel, solid handle. Pressed hot from No. 14 Stubbs' gauge steel and guaranteed not to warp; polished.

No.	Diameter at top, inches.	Diameter at bottom, inches.	Weight, ea., lbs.	Price, ea.
7	9¼	8	2	24c
8	10⅜	9	3	29c
9	11¼	10	4	34c
10	12⅜	11	4¼	40c
12	13½	12	5⅛	47c

Seamless Cake Griddles.

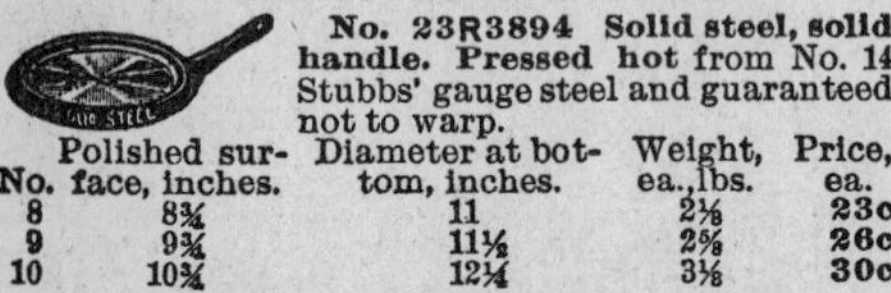

No. 23R3894 Solid steel, solid handle. Pressed hot from No. 14 Stubbs' gauge steel and guaranteed not to warp.

No.	Polished surface, inches.	Diameter at bottom, inches.	Weight, ea., lbs.	Price, ea.
8	8¾	11	2⅛	23c
9	9¾	11½	2⅝	26c
10	10¾	12¼	3⅛	30c

Seamless Bailed Griddles.

No. 23R3895 Solid Steel, Bailed, Seamless Griddles. Clean as glass. These solid steel cake griddles take the cake.

No.	Polished surface, inches	Diameter at bottom, inches	Weight, ea., lbs.	Price, ea.
12	11¾	13⅝	3¼	38c
14	12¾	14⅝	4¼	42c
16	13¾	15¼	5	47c

SOLID STEEL LAVA ENAMENED WARE.

Our Solid Steel Lava Enameled Ware is made of heavy steel, rolled especially for this purpose, and is covered with three coats of very hard and elastic enamel, the surface of which is as smooth as the most delicate of china. The inside or lining is a pure white porcelain, and the outside is white mottled with a delicate shade of brown.

FOR PURITY OF MATERIALS, DURABILITY AND EXCELLENCE OF WORKMANSHIP, THIS WARE IS WITHOUT AN EQUAL.

We guarantee every piece, and while it costs a trifle more than ordinary enameled ware, it will be found to be the cheapest in the end.

Solid Steel Lava Enameled Spiders.

No. 23R3896 Solid Steel Lava Enameled Spiders, made from one piece of 14-gauge steel, triple coated with enamel.

Number	7	8	9	10	12
Diameter at bottom, inches	8	9	10	11	12
Weight, pounds	3	4	5¼	5¼	6½
Price, each	36c	42c	50c	62c	73c

Solid Steel Lava Enameled Kettle.

No. 23R3897 Solid Steel Lava Enameled Taper Stove Kettle. Flat bottom. Made of 16-gauge steel. The heaviest enameled kettle made. Not affected by acids and unequaled for preserving fruits, etc.

Number	7	8	9	10
Diameter, inches	7¾	8¾	9¾	10¾
Depth, inches	6¼	6¾	7¼	7¾
Weight, pounds	4½	5	6	7
Price, each	69c	83c	97c	$1.11

Solid Steel Lava Enameled Tea Kettle.

No. 23R3898 Solid Steel Lava Enameled Tea Kettle. Latest pattern seamless body. Flat bottom. With ordinary care a tea kettle of this ware should outlast a dozen tin tea kettles.

Number	7	8	9
Capacity, quarts	5	7	8
Weight, pounds	3½	3¾	4
Price, each	93c	$1.13	$1.30

Solid Steel Lava Enameled Wash Basin.

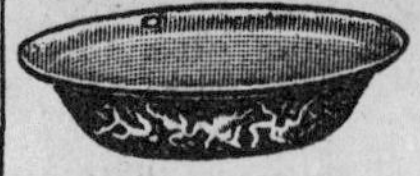

No. 23R3899 Solid Steel Lava Enameled Wash Basin. Durable and easy to clean.

Number	28	30	32
Diameter inches	11¼	12⅛	13
Weight, pounds	1⅛	1¾	2
Price, each	19c	23c	28c

Hot Water Urn.

No. 23R3900 Solid Steel, Lava Enameled Hot Water Urn, for saloons, barber shops and private families. Royal purple or blue outside, white inside, nickel plated faucets.

No. 7. Capacity, 7 quarts. Weight, 4⅞ lbs. Each, $1.68

No. 8. Capacity, 9 quarts. Weight, 5⅝ lbs. Each...$1.82

No. 9. Capacity, 13 quarts. Weight, 6⅛ pounds. Price, each......................................$1.96

Lava Enameled Filters.

No. 23R3912 They are as easily kept clean as a china dish, and unlike the common crock filters cannot be broken. Filtration in this filter is obtained by percolation through a porous natural stone by force of gravity. **No filth or putrid matter can possibly get below the surface.** The first few buckets of water filtered have a slight taste of the rock, but it is in no way injurious to health. Two or three times a week scrub off the top of the stone with a small broom or brush, and the filter is then ready for use again. Each vessel holds 3 gallons. Capacity, 8 gallons per day. Weight, 13⅝ pounds. Price, $2.67

PEERLESS ENAMELED STEEL WARE.

Our Peerless Enameled Steel Ware is formed from sheet steel, and after being put together is enameled inside and outside a gray color, handsomely mottled.

FOR CLEANLINESS, PURITY, DURABILITY AND BEAUTY, THIS WARE IS UNEXCELLED BY ANY OTHER GRAY ENAMELED STEEL GOODS ON THE MARKET.

It is entirely free from lead, arsenic and antimony, metals so often used in enamels of this appearance. We buy enameled ware from the makers and are satisfied with our usual small profit.

NO SECONDS OR IMPERFECT GOODS SOLD.

ABOUT SIZES.

All Tinware and Enameled Ware is usually listed by all manufacturers and dealers at what is known as trade measure. Some articles actually hold more than trade measure, most articles hold about the same, and a few articles do not hold the quantity indicated by trade measure. For the guidance of those who are not familiar with trade size, we also give actual capacity on each utensil. **When comparing our price with those of other dealers, remember that our goods are standard size, the same size as listed by all manufacturers and dealers as the same trade size.**

Peerless Enameled Steel Coffee Boiler.

No. 23R4000 Peerless Enameled Steel Flat Bottom Coffee Boiler, with retinned cover.

Size 6. Holds 6 quarts, weight 2¼ lbs., each, 71c
Size 8½. Holds 8 quarts, weight 2⅝ lbs., each, 78c
Size 11½. Holds 11 quarts, weight 3¼ lbs., each, 93c

Peerless Enameled Steel Teapots.

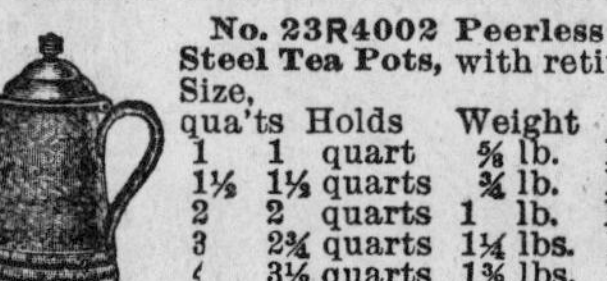

No. 23R4002 Peerless Enameled Steel Tea Pots, with retinned cover.

Size, qua'ts	Holds	Weight	Price
1	1 quart	⅝ lb.	Each....30c
1½	1½ quarts	¾ lb.	Each....34c
2	2 quarts	1 lb.	Each....39c
3	2¾ quarts	1¼ lbs.	Each....44c
4	3½ quarts	1⅜ lbs.	Each....49c
5	4 quarts	1½ lbs.	Each....56c

Peerless Enameled Steel Coffee Pots.

No. 23R4004 Peerless Enameled Steel Lipped Coffee Pots. Retinned covers. Actual capacity and weights same as tea pots of same size.

	Price
Size, 1 quart. Each	30c
Size, 1½ quarts. Each	34c
Size, 2 quarts. Each	39c
Size, 3 quarts, holds 2¾ quarts. Each	44c
Size, 4 quarts, holds 3½ quarts. Each	49c
Size, 5 quarts, holds 4 quarts. Each	56c

Peerless Enameled Steel Tea Steepers.

No. 23R4007 Peerless Enameled Steel Seamless Tea Steepers. Retinned covers.

Size, pts	Holds	Weight	Inches	Price
1½	1¼ pints	6 oz.	4⅜x3½	25c
2	2 pints	10 oz.	4⅞x4	27c

Enameled Steel Flat Bottom Tea Kettles.

No. 23R4009

Size, No.	qts	Holds	Dia. of bot.	Weight each	Price each
4	2	2 qts.	7¾	1⅜ lbs.	$0.49
5	3	2¾ qts.	8¼	1½ lbs.	.56
6	4	3½ qts.	9	1¾ lbs.	.64
7	5	4½ qts.	10	2¼ lbs.	.73
8	7	6 qts.	11	2½ lbs.	.86
9	8	7½ qts.	11¼	3 lbs.	1.03
10	11	9½ qts.	12	3⅛ lbs.	1.22

Peerless Enameled Steel Colanders.

No. 23R4011 Peerless Enameled Steel Family Colanders.

Inches	10x4	10½x4⅝	12x5⅛
Weight, lbs.	⅞	1	1⅛
Price, each	30c	37c	44c

Peerless Enameled Steel Wash Basins.

No. 23R4012 Peerless Enameled Steel Wash Basins, with patent rings.

No.	26	28	30	32
Inches	10⅝x2¾	11⅝x2⅞	12¼x3⅛	13x3⅜
Weight, each, lbs.	½	⅝	¾	⅞
Price, each	17c	20c	22c	27c

Peerless Enameled Steel Deep Dish Pans.

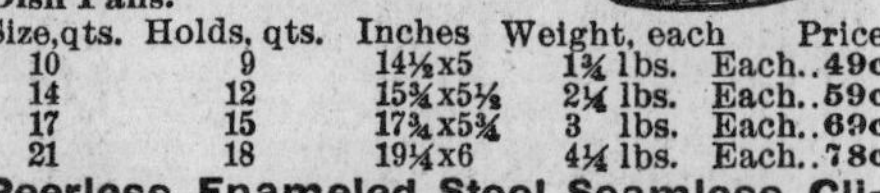

No. 23R4015 Peerless Enameled Steel Improved Deep Dish Pans.

Size, qts.	Holds, qts.	Inches	Weight, each	Price
10	9	14⅛x5	1¾ lbs.	Each..49c
14	12	15⅜x5¼	2¼ lbs.	Each..59c
17	15	17⅜x5¾	3 lbs.	Each..69c
21	18	19⅛x6	4¼ lbs.	Each..78c

Peerless Enameled Steel Seamless Climax Cook Pots.

Arranged with patent Climax bottom which prevents burning or scorching and affords protection to that portion of the vessel that in ordinary usage receives the most wear.

No. 23R4018 Peerless Enameled Steel Seamless Climax Cook Pot, with retinned cover. Sizes are actual capacity. 2 quarts, 6⅜x4 inches. Weight, 1¼ lbs. Price, each.......44c

3 quarts, 8x4⅛ inches. Weight, 1⅜ lbs. Price, each. 52c
5 quarts, 9x5 inches. Weight, 2⅛ lbs. Price, each. 59c
7 quarts, 9⅝x6 inches. Weight, 2¾ lbs. Price, each. 66c

Peerless Enameled Steel Climax Saucepans.

With patent Climax bottom same as above. Milk and cereals can be cooked in these vessels without danger of scorching or burning.

No. 23R4020 Peerless Enameled Steel Covered Seamless Climax Saucepans, with retinned cover. Sizes are actual capacity.

Quarts	2	3	5	7
Inches	6⅜x4	8x4⅛	9x5	9⅝x6
Weight, each, lbs.	1¼	1⅜	2⅛	2¾
Price, each	44c	52c	59c	66c

Peerless Enameled Steel Strong Lipped Saucepans.

No. 23R4021

Quarts	1	1½	2	2½	3
Holds qts.	⅞	1¼	1½	2⅛	2⅜
Inches	6x2⅛	6¼x3¼	7x3½	7⅜x3½	8⅛x3⅜
Weight, lbs.	⅝	½	⅝	¾	⅞
Price, each	14c	16c	19c	21c	25c

Quarts	4	5	6	7½
Holds, qts.	3¼	4¼	6	7
Inches	9x4	9⅝x4¼	11x5	11¼x5½
Weight, lbs.	1	1¼	1¾	2
Price, each	28c	32c	37c	44c

Peerless Enameled Steel Berlin Saucepans.

No. 23R4022 Peerless Enameled Steel Patent Covered Berlin Saucepans, with retinned covers. Sizes are actual capacity.

Quarts	2	3	5	7
Size, inches	6⅜x4¼	8x4⅞	8⅛x5⅝	9⅝x6⅛
Weight, each, pounds	1	1¼	1¾	2¼
Price, each	32c	39c	49c	59c

Peerless Enameled Steel Covered Seamless Berlin Kettles With Retinned Covers.

Sizes are actual capacity.

No. 23R4025

Quarts	2	3	5	7
Inches	6⅜x4¼	8x4⅞	8⅛x5⅝	9⅝x6⅛
Weight, each, pounds	1	1¼	1¾	2¼
Price, each	32c	39c	49c	59c

DON'T FAIL TO SPECIFY THE

Catalogue Number and Trade Size

WHEN ORDERING.

True Blue Enameled Ware.

No. 23R4441 True Blue Enameled Ware Pie Plates, full size.

Size, inches:	7x⅝	8x⅝	9x⅝	10x1	11x1
Prices, each	$0.12	$0.14	$0.18	$0.19	$0.23
Per dozen	1.33	1.64	1.95	2.26	2.67

No. 23R4442 True Blue Enameled Ware Extra Deep Pie Plates, full size.

Inches	9	10	11	12
Price, each	$0.18	$0.22	$0.26	$0.33
Per dozen	2.05	2.56	3.08	3.89

No. 23R4445 True Blue Enameled Ware Flat Bottom Dinner Plates, full size.

Inches	8	8½	9	10
Price, each	$0.15	$0.16	$0.19	$0.23
Per dozen	1.75	1.95	2.26	2.67

No. 23R4448 True Blue Enameled Ware Drinking Cups.

No.	8	9	10	11	12
Inches	3½x2¼	4x2½	4¼x2¾	4½x3	4¾x3¼
Price, each	$0.12	$0.13	$0.14	$0.16	$0.18
Per dozen	1.44	1.54	1.64	1.85	2.05

No. 23R4450 True Blue Enameled Ware Cups and Saucers. Cup is 4x2¼ inches, saucer is 5¾ inches. Cups, per dozen, $1.54; each, 13c; Saucers, per dozen, $1.22; each.....11c

No. 23R4452 True Blue Enameled Ware Soup Bowls.
Inches.....5¾x2⅜
Price, each.....$0.21
Per dozen.....2.46

No. 23R4455 True Blue Enameled Ware Seamless Water Pitchers.

No.	1	2	3	4
Quarts	1½	2	3	4
Holds, quarts	1	2	2½	3
Price, each	52c	62c	72c	93c

No. 23R4458 True Blue Enameled Ware Patent Seamless Milk or Rice Boilers, with enameled cover to fit both vessels.

No.	Quarts inside Boiler	Holds Quarts	Price, Each.
52	1	1⅛	$0.82
53	2	1⅞	1.06
54	3	3	1.37
56	4	4½	1.55

No. 23R4462 True Blue Enameled Ware Flaring Dippers, flat handles.

No	110	111	113
Inches	4¼x2	4½x2¼	5¼x2¼
Price, each,	18c	19c	24c

No. 23R4463 True Blue Enameled Ware Windsor Dippers, with round handles.

No.	410	412	414
Inches	5x2½	5½x3	6½x3¼
Price, ea.,	24c	28c	35c

No. 23R4464 True Blue Enameled Ware Patent Cocoa Shaped Dippers. Black enameled wood handles. No. 55, 1 pint. Actual capacity, ⅝-pint.
Price, each....35c

No. 23R4464

No. 23R4468 True Blue Enameled Ware Soup Ladles, threaded handles, No. 38, 3¼x1⅝ inches. Price, each.....14c

No. 23R4471 True Blue Enameled Ware Threaded Basting Spoons.

Inches	10	12	14	16	18	20
Price, ea.	10c	11c	12c	14c	16c	19c

No. 23R4474 True Blue Enameled Ware Deep Lipped Fry Pans.

No.	3	4	5	6
Inches	9¾x1¾	10x2	11¼x2	12x2
Bottom measure, inches	7½	8	9	10
Price, each	35c	41c	48c	55c

True Blue Enameled Ware.

No. 23R4477 True Blue Enameled Ware Wall Soap Dishes, with grates. No. 60, inches, 6½x4x1½. Each....21c

True Blue Enameled Ware Cuspidors.

No. 23R4480

No.	1	6
Inches	7x4	8x5½
Price, each	33c	62c

True Blue Enameled Ware Self-Righting Cuspidor.

No. 23R4481 No. 9—7⅝x4½ inches. Price, each. 63c

True Blue Enameled Ware Chambers.

No. 23R4485

No.	1	1½	2
Inches	7x4½	8½x4⅞	9¾x5½
Price, each,	41c	52c	62c

True Blue Enameled Ware Chamber Covers to Fit Chambers.

No. 23R4486

No.	01	01½	02
Price, each,	18c	21c	24c

PIECED TINWARE.

Measurements in inches are correct—size given in quarts is manufacturer's measure—vessels will not hold as many quarts as size given, except where we use the word HOLDS.

Notice.

Wash boilers are being constantly reduced in size. A No. 8 boiler is being sold that is not any larger than our No. 7. We shall maintain standard size. When comparing our prices with those of others, please compare sizes and weights also.

Tin Wash Boilers, IX.

No. 23R5000 Flat copper bottoms, full sizes. Drop handles.

Nos.	7	8	9
Inches	9½x18½	10⅜x20¼	11⅝x22½
Weight, lbs.	5	6	6½
Price, each,	75c	85c	98c

Copper Rim Wash Boilers, IX.

No. 23R5002 Copper rim, flat copper bottoms, full sizes. Drop handles.

Nos.	7	8	9
Inches	9½x18½	10⅜x20¼	11⅝x22½
Weight, lbs.	5½	6¼	6¾
Price, each,	96c	$1.06	$1.24

Acme Tin Wash Boiler, IXXX.

No. 23R5005 Full size, oval, IXXX, flat copper bottoms. The best tin wash boiler made, full sizes.

Nos.	7	8	9
Inches	9½x18½	10⅜x20¼	11⅝x22½
Weight, lbs.	7½	7¾	8
Price, each,	$1.19	$1.41	$1.73

Copper Wash Boilers.

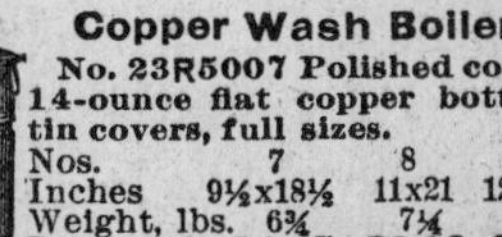

No. 23R5007 Polished copper, 14-ounce flat copper bottoms, tin covers, full sizes.

Nos.	7	8	9
Inches	9½x18½	11x21	12x22½
Weight, lbs.	6¾	7¼	8
Price, each,	$1.97	$2.16	$2.34

Acme Copper Wash Boilers.

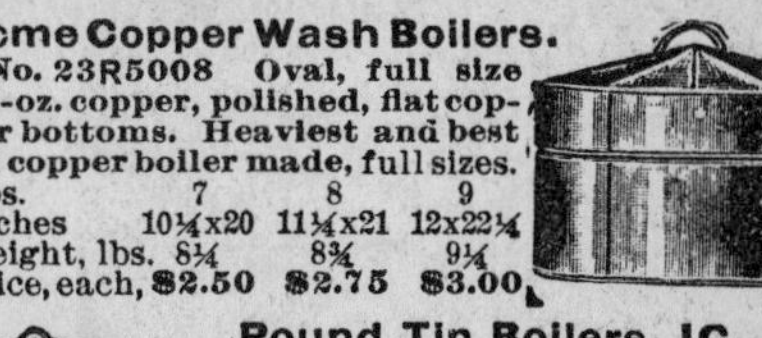

No. 23R5008 Oval, full size 16-oz. copper, polished, flat copper bottoms. Heaviest and best all copper boiler made, full sizes.

Nos.	7	8	9
Inches	10¼x20	11¼x21	12x22¼
Weight, lbs.	8¼	8¾	9¼
Price, each,	$2.50	$2.75	$3.00

Round Tin Boilers, IC.

No. 23R5020 Flat copper bottoms. No. 7, 8¼x5¾ inches. Weight, 1¼ pounds.
Price, each.....34c
No. 8, 9½x5¾ inches. Weight, 1½ pounds.
Price, each.....39c
No. 9, 10½x5¾ inches. Weight, 1⅝ lbs. Price, each, 42c

Tin Coffee Boilers, IX.

No. 23R5030 Flat copper bottoms.

Nos.	7	8	9
Holds qts.	5	7	8½
Inches	9x8½	9½x9	10½x9½
Wt., each, lb.	1	1⅜	1⅞
Price, each	36c	42c	50c

Tin Colanders, IC.

No. 23R5032 Eastern pattern.

Inches	10	12
Weight, each, pound	⅝	¾
Price, each,	9c	13c

GIVE CATALOGUE NUMBER IN FULL WHEN YOU WRITE YOUR ORDER

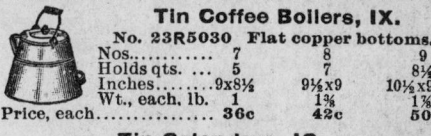

Cake Cutters, IC.

No. 23R5036 Star. Size, 3 inches. Weight, each, 2 ozs. Price, per dozen, 22c; each..2c

No. 23R5037 Heart. Size, 3 inches. Weight, each, 2 ounces. Price, per dozen, 22c; each.....2c

No. 23R5038 Animal. Assorted styles. Weight, each, 2 ounces. Price, per dozen, 33c; each...3c

Biscuit Cutters, IC.

No. 23R5044 Size, 3 inches. Weight, each, 2 ounces. Price, per dozen, 20c; each.....2c

Doughnut Cutters, IC.

No. 23R5046 Size, 3 inches. Weight, each, 2 ounces. Price, per dozen, 25c; each....3c

Cooky Cutters, IC.

No. 23R5047 Size, 3½ inches. Weight, each, 2 ounces. Price, per doz., 30c; each..3c

Card Party Cake Cutters.

For cakes resembling the different denominations of cards.

No. 23R5050 Hearts. Size, 2¾x3¾ inches.
Diamonds. Size, 2¾x2½ inches.
Clubs. Size, 2¾x3 inches.
Spades. Size, 2¾x3 inches.
Sold in sets of four cutters only.
Weight, per set, 8 ounces.
Price, per set.....10c

Apple Corers, IC.

No. 23R5055 Size, 3¼x6 inches. Weight, each, 2 ounces.
Price, each.....4c
Per dozen.....38c

Tea Steepers, IC.

No. 23R5059 Trade size, 1 quart. Holds 1 pint. Weight, 6 ounces.

Quarts	1
Inches	4¼x3¼
Price, each	7c

No. 23R5062 Straight Drinking Cups, IC.

Pints	½	1
Holds pints	⅛	⅞
Inches	3½x2	3¾x2¾
Weight each, ounces,	3	4
Price, each	2c	3c
Per dozen	19c	27c
Quarts	1	2
Holds quarts	⅞	⅞
Inches	4⅝x4½	5¾x4⅝
Weight each, ounces	6	8
Price, each	5c	7c
Per dozen	55c	73c

No. 23R5067 Embossed Tin Mug, basket pattern. At five feet away this mug cannot be distinguished from a silver plated mug. The tin is heavy and **double,** with strong tubed handle that will not come off. This mug is made on an entirely new principle, and is made to last. Holds ½ pint; weight, each, 6 ounces.
Price, each.....8c

Miners' Squib Cases, IC.

No. 23R5071 Round. 1⅛x7 inches. Weight, each, 2 ounces.
Price, per dozen., 44c; each.....4c

Miners' Lamp.

No. 23R5073 One Hook. Weight, each, 2 ounces.
Price, each.....8c
Per dozen.....85c

Miners' Canteens, IC.

No. 23R5079

Quarts	1	2
Holds quarts	1	1⅞
Inches	6¼	7¾
Weight each, ounces.	8	10
Price, each	9c	$0.12
Per dozen	98c	1.33

No. 23R5080 Miners' Candlestick. Forged steel. The most popular pattern.
Price, each.....30c

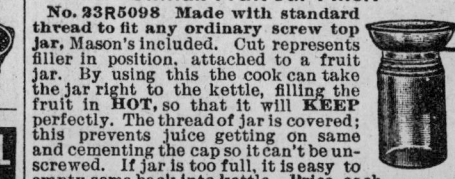

Water Dippers.

No. 23R5090
Tin Bottoms, IC.

Quarts	1	2
Holds quarts	¾	1⅛
Inches	5½x3	6⅛x3⅞
Weight each, oz.,	4	6
Price, each	6c	7c

No. 23R5092 Copper Bottoms, IX. Two quarts; holds 1⅛ quarts; weight, 8 ounces; size, 6⅛x3⅞ inches.
Price, each.....13c

Climax Fruit Jar Filler.

No. 23R5098 Made with standard thread to fit any ordinary screw top jar, Mason's included. Cut represents filler in position, attached to a fruit jar. By using this the cook can take the jar right to the kettle, filling the fruit in **HOT,** so that it will **KEEP** perfectly. The thread of jar is covered; this prevents juice getting on same and cementing the cap so it can't be unscrewed. If jar is too full, it is easy to empty some back into kettle. Price, each.....8c

Acme Tea Pots, IX.

No. 23R5270 Copper bowl bottoms, enameled wood handles, hinged one-piece covers.

Quarts	1½	2	3	4	5
Holds, qts.	1	1¾	2¼	3¼	4¼
Inches	5⅜	5⅝	6	6⅛	7
Weight, lbs.	⅝	¾	⅞	1⅛	1¼
Price, each	23c	26c	28c	31c	34c

Gem Tea Pots, IC.

No. 23R5272 Flat tin bottoms, tin handles.

Pints	2	3
Holds, pints	1¾	2¼
Inches	4⅝x5¼	5⅛x5¾
Weight, lbs	⅜	½
Price, each	11c	13c
Pints	4	5
Holds, pints	3	4
Inches	5½x6¼	5⅞x7
Weight, lbs	⅝	¾
Price, each	14c	15c

Tea Pot, XX Block Tin. Nickel Plated.

No. 23R5276 Satin finish inside, with copper bottoms.

Pints	3	4	5	6
Holds, pints	2¾	3⅜	4	5½
Price, each	36c	39c	42c	45c

Coffee Pot, XX Block Tin. Nickel Plated.

No. 23R5278 Satin finish inside, with copper bottoms.

Pints	3	4	5	6
Holds, pints	2¾	3⅜	4	5½
Price, each	36c	39c	42c	45c

All Copper, Nickel Plated Tea and Coffee Pots.

Made of full weight 14-ounce copper, heavily coated with pure block tin on the inside, and highly polished and heavily nickel plated on the outside.

Nickel Plated Copper Tea Pots.

No. 23R5280 Patent wood handle, always cool.

Pints	3	4	5	6
Holds	2¾	3⅜	4	5½
Weight, lbs.	¾	⅞	1	1¼
Price, each	50c	54c	60c	65c

Nickel Plated Coffee Pots.

No. 23R5282 Patent wood handle, always cool.

Pints	4	5	6	8
Holds	3⅜	4	5½	6½
Weight, lbs.	¾	⅞	1⅛	1¼
Price, each	54c	60c	65c	75c

Tea Pots—Copper, Nickel Plated.

No. 23R5288 Engraved, satin finish inside.

Pints	3	4	5
Holds pints	2¾	3⅜	4
Price, each	82c	86c	92c

Coffee Pots—Copper, Nickel Plated.

No. 23R5290 Engraved, satin finish inside.

Pints	3	4	5	6
Holds pts.	2¾	3⅜	4	5½
Each	82c	86c	92c	98c

Flaring Marking Pots, IC.

No. 23R5310 1 quart, holds ¾ quart, 6¼x4 inches. Weight, 5 ounces. Price, each 12c

Steamers, IC.

No. 23R5312 Rimmed covers.

Nos.	7	8	9
Inches	9½x5	10½x5	11¼x5½
Weight, lbs.	1⅛	1¼	1½
Price, each	19c	22c	25c

Deep Bread Pans, IC.

No. 23R5316

No.	Inches	Weight, each, oz.	Each	Per Doz.
1	9¾x5x3	6	6c	66c
2	10¼x6¼x3¼	8	7c	76c
3	12x6¼x3¼	10	8c	85c

Handled Bread Pans, IC.

No. 23R5318 Size, 14x9x2¼ inches. Weight, 15 ounces. Each $0.13
Per dozen 1.45

Square Pans, IC.

No. 23R5319 Common. Size, 7¾x11¾ x1⅜ inches. Weight, each, 6 ounces. Price, per dozen, 62c; each........6c

No. 23R5320 Deep. Size, 6¼x10¼x 2¼ inches. Weight, each, 7 ounces. Price, per dozen, 65c; each.......6c

Ideal Bread Pan.

The Ideal Bread Pan makes a crisp, moist and wholesome loaf a certainty. It bakes evenly through and through. There is no danger of burning, and no special care is required. The crust is smooth and even, and the loaf of beautiful shape. The bread is more nutritious, more tasty, and more digestible. There is no heavy crust.

No. 23R5324 Double Pan. Size, 13⅝x10 inches. Weight, each, 10 ounces. Price, each $0.22
Price, per dozen 2.53

No. 23R5326 Single Pan. Size, 13⅛x5 inches. Weight, each, 8 ounces. Price, each $0.10
Price, per dozen 1.08

Milk Strainers, IC.

No. 23R5332 With rims.

Inches	10	12
Weight, lbs.	½	¾
Price, each	9c	13c

Milk Strainers, IC.

No. 23R5333 Brass Strainer, with hoops. Size, 10 inches. Weight, 10 ounces. Price, each 12c

Retinned Wash Bowls, IC.

No. 23R5345 With eyelets.

Inches	10½	11½	13
Weight, each	8 ozs.	9 ozs.	10 ozs.
Price, each	8c	9c	11c

Family Colanders.

No. 23R5348 Retinned; 11½ inches. Weight, each, 10 ounces.
Price, each $0.15
Price, per dozen 1.75

Retinned Drinking Cups.

No. 23R5350

Inches	3⅞	4⅝	5
Weight, each, ozs.	2	3	4
Price, each	4c	5c	5c
Per dozen	38c	49c	56c

Retinned Water Dippers.

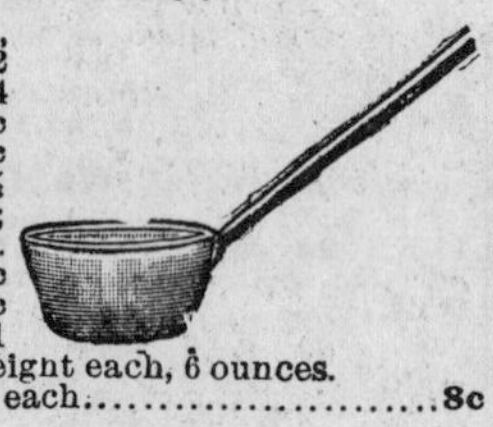

No. 23R5352 Size ½ qt., holds ⅜ quart; 4¼x2 inches; weight, each, 4 ounces. Price, each...6c
Price, per dozen....62c
Size, 1 quart, holds ⅝ quart, 5⅜x2⅝ inches; weight, each, 5 ounces. Price, each.......7c
Price, per dozen...73c
Size, 2 quarts, holds 1 quart, 5¾x2½ inches; weight each, 6 ounces. Price, per dozen, 85c; each........8c

Retinned Preserve Kettles.

No. 23R5359

Size Qts	Holds	Inches	Weight	Price Each
2½	2 qts.	7¾x3½	½ lb.	10c
3	2¾ qts.	8⅝x3⅞	⅝ lb.	12c
4	3½ qts.	9¼x4	¾ lb.	13c
5	4 qts.	9¾x4⅛	¾ lb.	15c
6	5 qts.	10½x4¼	⅞ lb.	17c
8	6¾ qts.	11¼x4¾	1 lb.	18c

Retinned Soup Ladles.

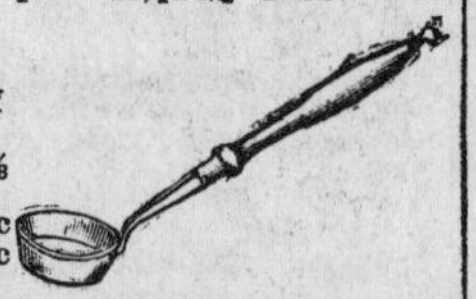

No. 23R5362 Wood handles.

Inches	3¾	4⅛
Weight, each, ozs.	3	4
Price, each	5c	6c
Per dozen	52c	61c

Retinned Solid Ladles.

No. 23R5365

Inches	3¾	3⅞	4¼
Weight, each, ozs.	4	5	6
Price, each	6c	6c	7c
Per dozen	61c	66c	73c

Retinned Pierced Ladles.

No. 23R5367

Inches	3¾	3⅞	4¼
Weight, ozs.	4	5	6
Price, each	6c	7c	7c
Per dozen	63c	73c	76c

Plain Scalloped Cake Pans.

No. 23R5375 Without tubes.

Inches	8	10
Weight, each, ounces	4	6
Price, each	4c	5c
Per dozen	44c	54c

Plain Scalloped Cake Pans.

No. 23R5377 With tubes.

Inches	8	10
Weight, each, ounces	4	6
Price, each	5c	6c
Per dozen	54c	66c

Retinned Round Cake Pans.

No. 23R5380 Shallow, with tubes.

Quarts	3	5
Holds quarts	2	3½
Inches	9⅝x2⅜	11⅜x2⅜
Weight, each, ozs.	6	10
Price, each	10c	13c

Retinned Round Cake Pans.

No. 23R5382 Deep, with tubes.

Quarts	3	6
Holds quarts	2½	4½
Inches	9¼x3½	11½x3½
Weight, each, ozs.	6	12
Price, each	11c	15c

Turk Head Cake Molds.

No. 23R5385 Retinned, with tubes.

Size, quarts	3	5
Holds quarts	1¾	3
Inches	8x3½	9½x4
Weight, each, ounces	8	12
Price, each	12c	17c

Retinned Angel Cake Pans, IC.

No. 23R5387 With tubes. Size, 9⅝x4 inches. Weight, each, 12 oz. Price, each 18c

No. 23R5396 Plain Muffin Pans.

Inches	7¼x14¼
Cups	8
Size of cups	3¼x1
Weight, each	½ lb.
Price, each	12c

Inches, 10¾x14¼; cups, 12; size of cups, 3¼x1. Weight, each, ¾ lb. Price.. ..17c

No. 23R5398 Corn Cake Pans, plain.

Inches	Cups	Size of Cups	Weight, each	Price
37¼x14¼	8	¼x1½	⅝ pound	13c
10¾x14¼	12	3¼x1½	⅞ pound	18c

Turk Head Pans.

No. 23R5400 Plain. Size, 7¼x14 inches; No. of cups, 8; size of cups, 3¼x1½ inches. Weight, each, ½ pound.
Price, each 13c
Size, 10¾x14¼ inches; number of cups, 12; size of cups, 3¼x1½ inches. Weight, ¾ pound. Each...18c

Retinned Sauce Pans.

No. 23R5402 Lipped.

Quarts	1	1½	2
Holds, quarts	¾	1	1½
Inches	5⅞x2⅝	6½x2¾	7x3¾
Weight, each, oz.	4	6	8
Price, each	7c	8c	10c

Inches	7¾x3½	8¼x3⅞	9¼x4	9¾x4⅛
Quarts	2½	3	4	5
Holds, quarts	1¾	2	3	4
Weight, each, oz.	10	12	13	14
Price, each	11c	13c	14c	16c

6 quarts (holds 5 quarts), weight, 16 ozs. Each...18c
8 quarts (holds 6 quarts), weight, 18 ozs. Each...20c

Retinned Dairy Pans, IC.

No. 23R5405

Quarts	4	5
Inches	10⅞x2½	11⅞x2⅝
Holds, quarts	2¾	3½
Weig't, each, oz	8	10
Each	9c	$0.10
Per dozen	98c	1.10

Quarts	6	8	10	12
Inches	12⅝x2¾	13¼x2⅞	14¾x3	15½x3¼
Holds, quarts	4¼	5½	6	7
Weight, each, oz.	11	12	13	14
Each	$0.12	$0.13	$0.15	$0.17
Per dozen	1.33	1.46	1.72	1.95

Retinned Pudding Pans, IC.

No. 23R5409

Quarts	1	2	3
Inches	7x2⅞	8¼x3	9¼x3⅛
Holds, quarts	1	1¾	2½
Weight, each, oz.	4	5	6
Price, each	6c	8c	9c
Per dozen	66c	87c	98c

Inches	10x3½	10¾x3⅝	11½x3½
Quarts	4	5	6
Holds, quarts	3¼	4	5
Weight, each, ounces	7	8	10
Price, each	10c	$0.12	$0.13
Per dozen	$1.10	1.35	1.48

Retinned Dish Pans, IX.

No. 23R5415

Qts.	Inch.	Holds, quarts	Wgt. each, lbs.	Price, each
10	14½x5⅛	9	1¼	25c
14	16¼x5½	12	1¾	30c
17	17¾x5⅝	15	2	36c
21	19½x6	18	2½	41c

Retinned Dish Pans, IXXX.

No. 23R5417 Extra heavy.

Quarts	10	14	17	21
Holds, quarts	9	12	15	18
Inches	14½	16¼	17¾	19½
Weight, each, pounds	1¾	2½	3	3¾
Price, each	36c	41c	46c	52c

Retinned Bread Raisers.

No. 23R5420 Sizes are actual capacity. Extra heavy.

Quarts	10	14	17	21
Inches	14½	16¼	17¾	19½
Weight, each, lbs.	2¼	2¾	3	4⅛
Each	49c	57c	68c	79c

Retinned Milk Strainers.

No. 23R5424 Feet fast.

Inches	10⅛	11
Weight, each, oz.	8	10½
Price, each	13c	15c

Plain Gravy Strainers.

No. 23R5429 Tin handles.
Inches.........4¾x2½
Weight, each, ounces..... 3
Price, each........ 4c

Pierced Milk Skimmers.

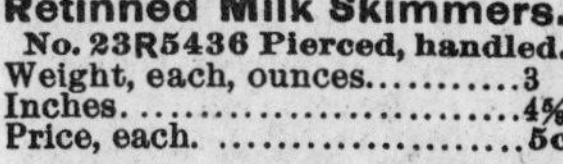

No. 23R5434 No handles.
Inches..........5¾x6½
Weight, each, ounces.......... 2
Price, each.......... 2c

Retinned Milk Skimmers.

No. 23R5436 Pierced, handled.
Weight, each, ounces..........3
Inches..........4⅝
Price, each..........5c

Retinned Flat Skimmers.

No. 23R5438 Fl handles.
4¾ inches Weight, each, 4 ounces. Each..........5c
5½ inches Weight, each, 6 ounces. Each..........7c

Cake Turners.

No. 23R5445 Enameled wood handles. 2⅞x3¾ inches. Weight, each, 2 ounces. Price, each..........3c

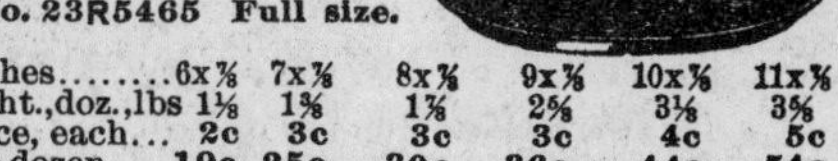

Retinned Covered Scoops.

No. 23R5450

Inches	6¾x4¾	9¾x6¾
Weight, each, ounces	5	8
Price, each	13c	21c

Shallow Pie Plates.

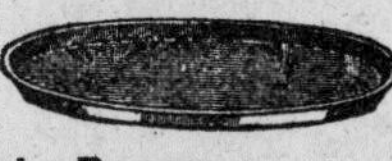

No. 23R5465 Full size.

Inches	6x⅞	7x⅞	8x⅞	9x⅞	10x⅞	11x⅞
Wght.,doz.,lbs	1⅛	1⅜	1⅞	2⅜	3⅛	3⅝
Price, each	2c	3c	3c	3c	4c	5c
Per dozen	19c	25c	30c	36c	44c	54c

Deep Pie Plates.

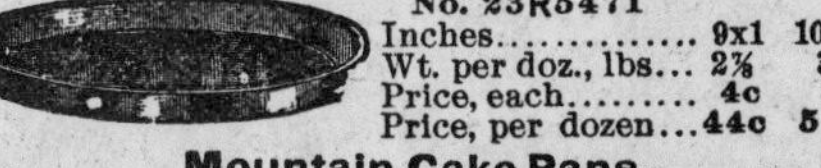

No. 23R5467

Inches	9x1¼	10x1¼
Wt. doz..lbs.	2½	3⅛
Price, each.	4c	5c
Per dozen	41c	49c

Shallow Jelly Cake Pans.

No. 23R5470

Inches	9x⅛	10x⅛
Wt. per doz., lbs	2¾	3¼
Price, each	4c	4c
Price, per dozen	38c	46c

Deep Jelly Cake Pans.

No. 23R5471

Inches	9x1	10x1
Wt. per doz., lbs	2⅞	3¾
Price, each	4c	5c
Price, per dozen	44c	52c

Mountain Cake Pans.

No. 23R5473

Inches	9x1⅝	10x1⅝
Wt. per doz., lbs.	3¼	4¼
Price, each	4c	5c
Price, per doz	46c	57c

Lettered Plates.

No. 23R5478 Size, 6 inches.
Weight per dozen, pounds... 1⅛
Price, each.......... 2c
Price, per dozen.......... 19c

Plain Round Patty Pans.

No. 23R5485

Inches	3	4
Weight per doz., oz	6	9
Price, per dozen	6c	10c

Star Patty Pans.

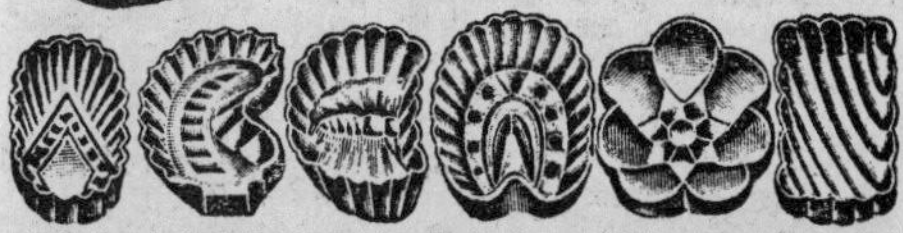

No. 23R5486 Size, 3 inches. Weight, per dozen, 6 ounces.
Price, per dozen..........8c

Scalloped Round Patty Pans.

No. 23R5488 Deep.

Inches	3	4
Weight, per doz., ounces	7	9
Price, per dozen	6c	10c

Heart Patty Pans.

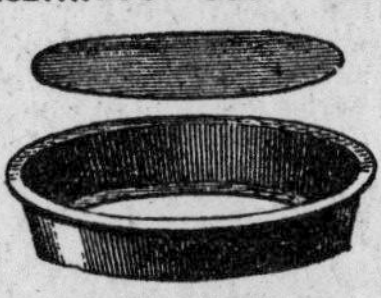

No. 23R5490 Size, 3 inches. Weight, per dozen, 6 ounces.
Price, per dozen..........8c

No. 23R5494 Set of 6 Assorted Tin Tart or Patty Pans. One of each pattern shown in cut; also used as individual jelly molds. We do not break sets. Weight, per set, 3 ounces.
Price, per set of 6 pans..........10c

Loose Bottom Pie Plate.

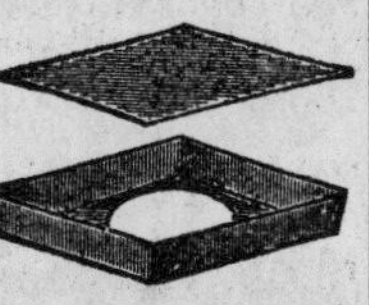

No. 23R5505 Loose Bottom Pie Plate, shallow, round, for layer cakes and pies.

Inches	8x1	9x1	10x1
Wt. doz. oz..	3⅓	4¼	5⅛
Price, each..	5c	5c	6c
Price, doz	49c	60c	65c

Loose Bottom Cake Pan.

No. 23R5507 Loose Bottom Cake Pan. Deep, round, for loaf cakes and bread. Size, 10¼x2⅞ inches. Weight, each, 7 ounces.
Price, each..........12c

Loose Bottom Tubed Cake Pan.

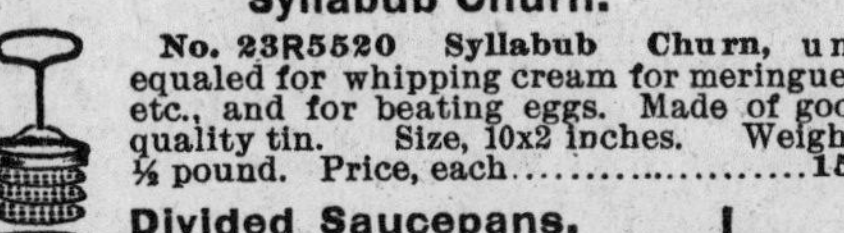

No. 23R5509 Loose Bottom Tubed Cake Pan. Round, with tube. Extra plain bottoms for angel food.
Size, inches..........9¼x2¾
Weight, each, ounces... 8
Price, each..........12c
Size, inches..........10¾x2⅞
Weight, each, ounces.. 10
Price, each..........16c

Loose Bottom Square Cake Pan.

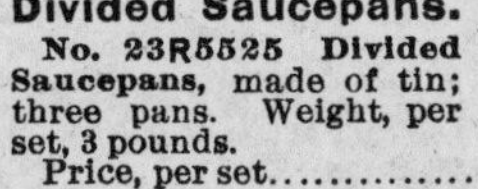

No. 23R5510 Loose Bottom Square Cake Pan.

Inches	8¾x8¾x1⅝	9x9x2⅝
Wt.each, oz.	10	12
Each	12c	16c

Loose Bottom Bread Pan.

No. 23R5512 Loose Bottom Oblong Bread or Cake Pan. Size, 5⅛x9⅝x2¼ inches.
Weight, each, ounces.... 10
Price, each..........12c
Size, 6⅛x10½x2¾ inches.
Weight, each, ounces.... 12
Price, each..........16c

Spring Cake Pans.

No. 23R5517 Spring Cake Pans. You need not spoil your cake in taking it out of the pan, as the side is hinged and is readily removed, leaving the cake standing on the flat bottom of pan. Made of good quality tin.

	Diameter	Depth	Weight	Price, each
Small size	7⅞ in.	2 in.	7 ozs.	23c
Medium size	8⅝ in.	2¼ in.	8 ozs.	27c
Large size	9⅛ in.	2½ in.	10 ozs.	29c

Syllabub Churn.

No. 23R5520 Syllabub Churn, unequaled for whipping cream for meringues, etc., and for beating eggs. Made of good quality tin. Size, 10x2 inches. Weight, ½ pound. Price, each..........15c

Divided Saucepans.

No. 23R5525 Divided Saucepans, made of tin; three pans. Weight, per set, 3 pounds.
Price, per set..........78c

Flour Sifters.

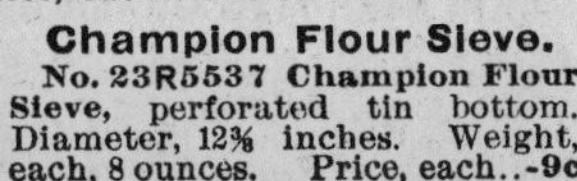

No. 23R5528 Flour Sifter. Has straight sides and flat bottom, thereby increasing the wire cloth surface, making it one of the quickest sifters made, and for this reason also can be used with one hand by shaking it like you would a sieve. For mixing baking powder with the flour it cannot be surpassed. Has a detachable and adjustable agitator. As a fruit strainer and washer there is nothing better on the market. Size of body, 3x6 inches.
Price, each..........10c

Rotary Flour Sifters.

No. 23R5530 Rotary Flour Sifter, also serves as a scoop. Full size, well made. Weight, each, 8 ounces.
Price, each.....10c

No. 23R5532 Rotary Flour Sifter. Weight, each, 8 ounces.
Price, each..........9c

Flour Sieve.

No. 23R5536 Tin Rim Sieve, plated wire bottom, 18 meshes to the inch, 12½ inches diameter, well put together; made of heavy tin. Weight, each, 6 ounces. Price, each..........13c

Champion Flour Sieve.

No. 23R5537 Champion Flour Sieve, perforated tin bottom. Diameter, 12⅝ inches. Weight, each, 8 ounces. Price, each..9c

Ringed Pot Covers, IC Tin.

No. 23R5545 Hemmed edges.

Inches	8½	9
Price, each	4c	4c
Inches	9½ 10	10½
Price, each	4c 5c	5c
Inches	11	11½
Price, each	5c	6c
Inches	12	12½
Price, each	6c	7c

Miners' Gold Pans.

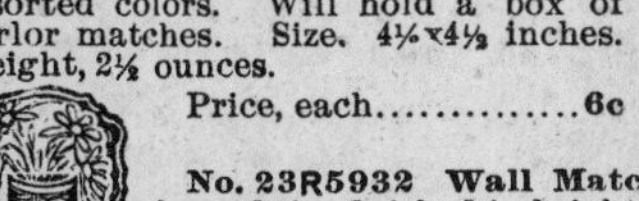

No. 23R5548 Miners' Gold Pan, smooth steel, polished, inside diameter, 16½ inches. Weight, 1⅞ pounds.
Price, each..........20c

DECORATED JAPANNED TINWARE.

Our Decorated Japanned Tinware is of European manufacture and is beautifully lithographed in bright colors and pleasing designs. Owing to the quantities in which we import it we are able to sell it at about the same price as the ordinary japanned tinware, which it far excels in attractiveness and beauty.

No. 23R5900 Decorated Japanned Oblong Tray. Made of heavy tin and finished in bright colors. Size, 15¾x12 inches. Weight, 14 ounces.
Price, each..........29c

No. 23R5904 Decorated Japanned Spice Box. Well made, with rounded corners and decorated in colors. Has six round inside boxes labeled for various spices. Size, 7x4¾x3¾ inches. Weight, 14 ounces. Price, each..........48c

No. 23R5912 Decorated Japanned Comb and Brush Case, embossed and finished in bright colors with mirror in center. Size, 10½x7¼ inches. Weight, 8 ounces.
Price, each..........25c

No. 23R5915 Decorated Japanned Comb Case, same as above but smaller and without mirror. Size, 8¾x3¼ inches. Weight, 2 ounces.
Price, each..........5c

Tea and Coffee Canisters.

Made of tin and decorated in fancy colors, with porcelain knob; well made and artistic.

No. 23R5921 Tea Canister, one-pound size. Weight, 5 ounces. Price, each....10c

No. 23R5922 Coffee Canister, one-pound size. Weight, 8 ounces.
Price, each..........10c

No. 23R5923 Tea Canister, two-pound size.
Price, each..........12c

No. 23R5924 Coffee Canister, two-pound size. Price, each..........12c

No. 23R5926 Pepper Shaker; fancy decorated tin, assorted colors. Size, 3¼x2 inches. Weight, 1 ounce. Price, each......5c

No. 23R5930 Decorated Tin Square Match Safe, embossed and finished in assorted colors. Will hold a box of parlor matches. Size, 4¼x4½ inches. Weight, 2½ ounces.
Price, each..........6c

No. 23R5932 Wall Match Safe, embossed tin, finished in bright colors with scratcher. Size, 7¾x4 inches. Weight, 1 ounce.
Price, each..........5c

No. 23R5935 Child's Decorated Tin Mug. Assorted designs, bright colors. Large size, 3x3⅜ inches. Weight, 2 ounces. Price, each...6c

No. 23R5937 Child's Decorated Tin Mug. Same as above, but smaller. Just the thing for the little ones. Size, 2¾x2½ inches. Weight, 1 ounce. Price, each..........4c

PLEASE DO NOT CUT, TEAR OR MUTILATE THIS CATALOGUE.

IF YOU WILL ORDER BY NUMBER, state clearly what is marked, there is no necessity for cutting out and returning any catalogue illustration or description.

PRESERVE THIS CATALOGUE CAREFULLY. IT IS YOUR GUIDE TO ECONOMICAL BUYING.

JAPANNED WARE.

Flour Boxes.

No. 23R6000 Hinged covers, decorated.

Pounds	25	50
Weight, each, pounds	2½	4
Inches	10x20	12x22
Price, each	54c	72c
Pounds		100
Weight, each, pounds		7
Inches		14½x28
Price, each		$1.02

Cream City Flour Bin and Sifter, IX.

No. 23R6002 Japanned and nicely ornamented. The sifter proper is protected from pressure by the flour in the bin by our **new shield** which enables the reels to work easily and smoothly, and obviates all grinding through of foreign substances. The flour is protected from coming in contact with the iron crank by an **angular tin sleeve, and a tin skirt** below the sifter prevents the flour from scattering all over the bottom of the bin, but instead directs it into the proper receptacle. The sifter rests on a strong ring, which extends all around the inside of the bin, holding it securely in place, and still allowing it to be easily removed for cleaning.

Pounds	25	50	100
Weight, crated, pounds	10½	16	21
Inches	10¼x23	13x27¼	15½x33¼
Price, each	$1.34	$1.67	$2.33

Square Bread Boxes.

No. 23R6005 Japanned.

Inches	9¼x9¼x13½
Weight, lbs.	2½
Price, each	46c
Inches	10¼x11½x15
Weight, lbs.	3
Price, each	54c
Inches	10⅜x12¼x17
Weight, lbs.	3¾
Price, each	63c

Round Sugar Boxes.

No. 23R6009

Inches	10x10	12x12
Weight, each, pounds	2	3
Price, each	42c	60c

Knife and Fork Boxes.

No. 23R6015 Open.

Inches	2¾x8¾x13¼
Weight, each, pounds	1¼
Price, each	30c

Folding Lunch Boxes.

No. 23R6019 Without flasks.

Nos.	1	2
Inches	7½x3¾x3¾	9x4x4
Weight, ea. oz.	10	11
Each	14c	17c

With flask. Weight, each, 1 pound, 9x4x4 ......41c

Round Spice Box.

No. 23R6025 Covered, round inside boxes. 7½ inches. Weight, each, 1¾ pounds. Price, each..42c

Box Graters.

No. 23R6029 2x5 inches. Weight, each, 2 ounces.
Price, each 2c

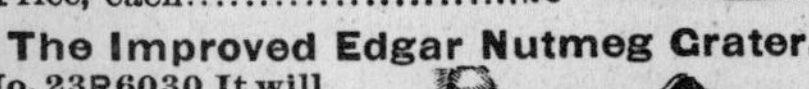

The Improved Edgar Nutmeg Grater.

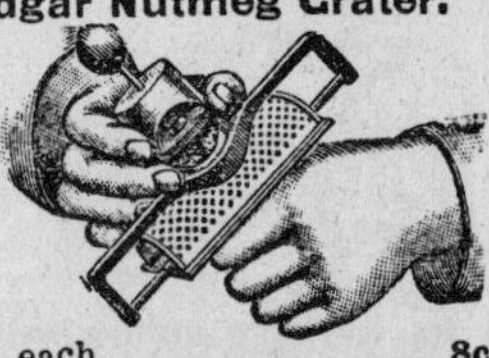

No. 23R6030 It will not clog, tear the fingers, nor drop the nutmeg. It grates the nutmeg very fine, distributes it evenly, and grates it all up, leaving no pieces. It is simple and durable. Weight, each, 4 oz.
Price, per dozen, 84c; each 8c

Dinner Horns.

No. 23R6035 With improved mouthpiece.

	Plain	Japanned
Inches	9	9
Weight, ounces	3	3
Price, each	4c	5c
Per dozen	42c	51c

Large Dinner Horns.

No. 23R6038 Japanned. Improved mouthpiece. 13¼ inches. Weight, 4 ounces.
Price, per dozen, 60c; each 5c

No. 23R6043 Comb Cases. Assorted colors, 2⅝x5½x7 inches. Weight, each, 4 oz.
Price, each 5c
Per dozen 54c

Dredge Boxes.

No. 23R6047 Size, 2¼x3½. Weight, each, 4 ounces.
Price, per dozen, 42c; each 4c

Pepper Boxes.

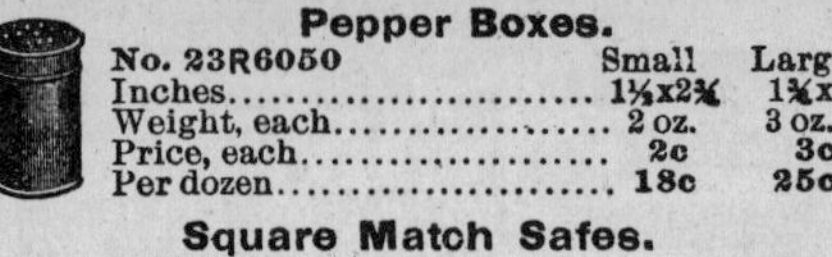

No. 23R6050

	Small	Large
Inches	1¼x2¾	1¾x3
Weight, each	2 oz.	3 oz.
Price, each	2c	3c
Per dozen	18c	25c

Square Match Safes.

No. 23R6052

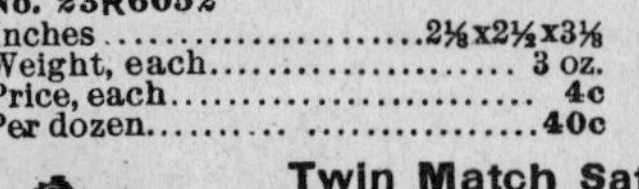

Inches	2½x2½x3⅛
Weight, each	3 oz.
Price, each	4c
Per dozen	40c

Twin Match Safes.

No. 23R6053 Assorted colors.

Inches	4½x5
Weight, each	3 oz.
Price, each	3c
Per dozen	36c

Match Box Holder and Safe.

No. 23R6055 Match Box Holder and Safe. Holds full box of 200 matches. Nicely finished. Weight, each, 4 ounces.
Price, each 8c

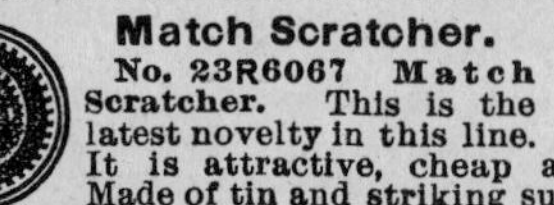

Match Scratcher.

No. 23R6067 Match Scratcher. This is the latest novelty in this line. It is attractive, cheap and durable. Made of tin and striking surface of best quality of emery cloth. Diameter, 5 inches. Weight, 1 ounce. Price, each 4c

Light Cash Boxes.

No. 23R6080 With lock.

Inches.	9½	10½	11½	13
Wgt., lbs.	1¼	1½	1¾	2½
Price, ea.	44c	49c	54c	63c

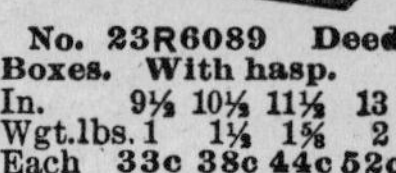

No. 23R6089 Deed Boxes. With hasp.

In.	9½	10½	11½	13
Wgt. lbs.	1	1¼	1⅝	2
Each	33c	38c	44c	52c

Combination Lock Cash or Treasure Boxes.

No. 23R6090 These boxes are made from very heavy stock, finished in black enamel, striped with rich gold bronze. The dial is large and legible. The owner can set a new combination as often as may be required without taking the lock to pieces. Trays are not furnished with boxes. For trays see following number. Extreme outside measures of all boxes are ⅜ to ½ inch larger than sizes below. Knobs project ⅝ inch beyond the ribs.

Length, inside	9 in.	10½ in.	12 in.	14 in.
Width	6 in.	7 in.	8 in.	10 in.
Depth	3¾ in.	4⅛ in.	5¼ in.	6¼ in.
Boxes, price, each	$2.74	$2.90	$3.13	$3.52

No. 23R6092 Inside Partitioned Trays, to fit inside our No. 23R6090 cash box.

Size, inches	9	10½	12	14
Price, each	39c	59c	63c	$1.17

Fire Proof Cash Box.

No. 23R6094 Fire Proof Cash Box. The fire proof walls of this box are sufficiently thick to make it absolutely fire proof in any residence. It is a perfectly safe receptacle for deeds, bonds, contracts, mortgages, notes, insurance policies, tax receipts, jewelry, etc. To test this box we had one subjected to an intense heat in a furnace. Not only was the iron heated red hot, but it reached a white heat, which is the point just before iron melts. The contents of box were not even marred. No fire could ever occur out in the open air to equal the intense heat to which this box was subjected. Furnished with a first class padlock with two keys. Dimensions: Outside—13 inches long, 9 inches wide, 6½ inches deep; inside—10 inches long, 6 inches wide, 3 inches deep. Approximate weight, 50 pounds. Price, each $3.95

Bill Head Boxes.

No. 23R6095

Parts	1	2	3
Inches	1⅛x9x6¾	2¼x9x9½	3¼x9x13
Weight	6 oz.	12 oz.	1⅜ lbs.
Each	22c	30c	41c

Postoffice Boxes.

No. 23R6097

Parts	Wt. ea. lbs.	Inches	Price, each
1	½	4½x4⅝x6	22c
2	⅞	4½x7⅝x6¼	30c
3	1	4½x1 x6¼	36c

Candlesticks.

No. 23R6105 Japanned Candlesticks. Weight, 2 ounces. Size, 5 inches.
Price, each 3c
Per dozen 35c

Cuspidors.

No. 23R6112 Cottage Cuspidors, gold band. Weight, 6 oz. Size, 3x7 inches.
Price, each 8c
Per dozen 85c

No. 23R6113 Cuspidors, decorated. Weight, each, 8 ounces. Size, 5½x7 inches.
Price, each $0.13
Per dozen 1.50

No 23R6116 Nickel Plated Cuspidors. Weight, each, 8 oz. Size, 5x7½ inches. Price, each 22c

No. 23R6119 Cast Iron Cuspidors. White enameled inside, outside painted, assorted colors, banded. Weight, 5¼ pounds. Size, 6x8 inches.
Price, each 45c

Spittoons.

No. 23R6125 Assorted colors. Weight, each, 10 ounces. Size, 2¼x8 inches.
Price, per dozen, $1.58; each ... 14c

Fancy Water Coolers.

No. 23R6130 Water Coolers, double wall, fitted with non-conducting material, galvanized iron reservoir, handsomely decorated in various colors, side handles, nickel plated faucets.

Gallons	2	3	4
Wt., each, crated	13	20	25
Each	$1.33	$1.67	$2.00

Gallons	6	8	10
Weight, each, crated, lbs.	30	45	55
Each	$2.33	$2.67	$3.33

Tea or Coffee Canisters.

Hinged Covers.

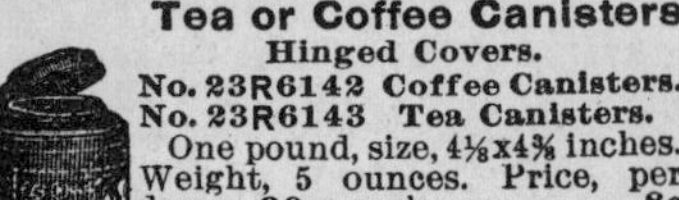

No. 23R6142 Coffee Canisters.
No. 23R6143 Tea Canisters.
One pound, size, 4⅛x4⅜ inches. Weight, 5 ounces. Price, per dozen, 90c; each 8c
Two pounds, size, 5⅝x6 inches. Weight, 8 ounces. Price, per dozen, $1.28; each 11c
Three pounds, size, 6¼x6⅜ inches. Weight, 12 ounces. Price, per dozen, $1.66; each 14c

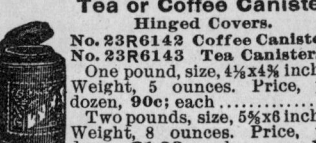

Slop Jars and Chamber Pails.

No. 23R6155 Bailed Slop Jars. Assorted colors, banded. Weight, 1¾ pounds. Size, 9¼x11 inches.
Price, each 27c

No. 23R6158 Chamber Pails. Assorted colors; nicely japanned, inside and out.

Quarts	10	12	14
Holds, qts.	9	11	13
Size	10¼x10¼	11x11¼	11¼x12¾
Weight, each, pounds	2	2¼	2¾
Price, each	27c	30c	36c

Challenge Odorless Commode and Slop Bucket Combined.

No. 23R6162 It is impossible for the foul air to escape, even when the lid is removed, as there is inside the lid a receptacle that holds a deodorizer, and which neutralizes all gases inside the commode. The disinfectant (2 tablespoonfuls of chloride of lime), needs only to be renewed once in two weeks at a small cost. It is indispensable in the sick room, especially in cases of contagious diseases and fevers. Does not have to be emptied until filled, no matter how long it stands. Cut shows construction. Made of heavy galvanized iron, and has no paint to hold stench or disease germs. Has removable seat, etc. It needs only to be seen to convince you of its wonderful merit. Holds 9 quarts. Weight, 6¾ pounds. Price, each $1.40

Dust Pans, IC.

No. 23R6175 Japanned, round tin handles. Weight, each, 6 ounces. Size, 9x13 inches.
Price, each 6c
Per dozen 71c

Covered Dust Pans, IC.

No. 23R6177 Japanned, round tin handles. Weight, each, 8 ounces. Size, 9x13 inches.
Price, each $0.09
Per dozen 1.05

Dust Pans with Brushes.

No. 23R6180 Assorted colors. Weight, 1 pound. Size, 10x12¾ inches.
Price, each 50c

Tea or Coffee Strainers.

Enameled Handle Strainer. With extra fine wire gauze. The best strainer made.
No. 23R6605 Small. Weight, each, 2 ounces. Price, each 5c
No. 23R6606 Medium. Weight, each, 2½ ounces. Price, each 6c
No. 23R6607 Large. Weight, each, 3 ounces. Price, each 8c

No. 23R6609 Tea and Coffee Strainer. Made of pure aluminum. Will not tarnish or corrode: light and easily cleaned; will just fit over an ordinary cup. Weight, 1 ounce. Price, each 12c

Spout Strainer.

No. 23R6610 To attach to spout of tea pot. Weight, 2 ounces. Price, each...2c

Tea or Coffee Balls. Tinned wire with hinge and catch. Put the tea or coffee in the ball and drop it into the pot and boil in the usual way. You will get the full strength of the tea or coffee without grounds or tea leaves, and a strainer is not necessary.
No. 23R6612 Small size, 1⅛x2⅛ inches. Weight, 1 ounce. Price, each 5c
No. 23R6614 Large size, 2⅜x3¼ inches. Weight, 1 ounce. Price, each 7c

Enameled Sink Strainer.

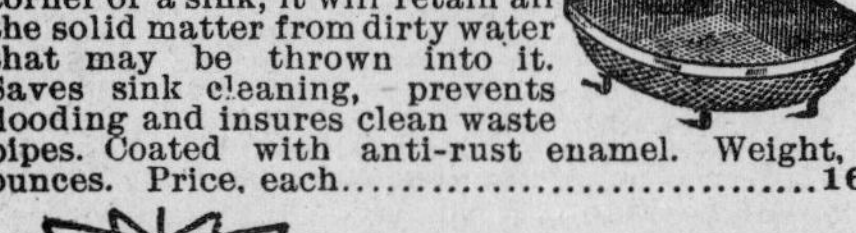

No. 23R6616 When placed in the corner of a sink, it will retain all the solid matter from dirty water that may be thrown into it. Saves sink cleaning, prevents flooding and insures clean waste pipes. Coated with anti-rust enamel. Weight, 8 ounces. Price, each 16c

No. 23R6621 Tea or Coffee Pot Stand, made of bright finish wire. Weight, 2 ounces. Price, each 4c

No. 23R6622 Tea or Coffee Pot Stand. Glazed semi-porcelain tile with neat blue pattern, set in plated wire frame. Size, 5¼ inches square. Weight, 8 ounces. Price, each 23c

Vegetable Strainer.

No. 23R6624 Wire Handled Vegetable Strainer. Weight, 3 ounces. Price, per dozen, 45c; each....5c

Wire Toasters.

No. 23R6627 Wire Toaster, wood handle. Weight, 5 ounces. Each....3c

Spoon Egg Beater.

No. 23R6630 Retinned. Weight, 2 ounces. Each...4c
Per dozen.....45c

Surprise Egg Beater.

No. 23R6632
Weight, 1 ounce.
Price, each 2c
Per dozen..........14c

Dover Egg Beaters.

No. 23R6633 Dover Egg Beater. Length, 9 inches. Weight, 5 ounces. Wheels and handle are Tuscan bronzed; beater and frame heavily tinned and retinned. The kind and size commonly sold for 10 to 15 cents. Price, each 5c
No. 23R6634 Dover Egg Beater. Length, 10¾ inches. Weight, 7 ounces. **ALL PARTS TINNED** and retinned to prevent rust. Easy to clean. Price, each 8c
No. 23R6636 Dover Egg Beater. Length, 12½ inches. Weight, 15 ounces. The hotel size; strong and durable; wheels and handle are Tuscan bronzed; beater and frame heavily tinned. Price, each...16c

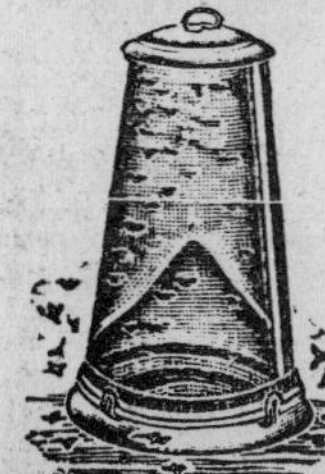

Champion Fly Trap.

No. 23R6643 Champion Fly Trap. Excels anything of the kind ever offered. **Over 3,000 sold last season.** This year it is still further perfected, better than ever. Weight, 7 ounces.
Price, each $0.11
Price, dozen 1.25

Wire Fly Killer.

No. 23R6647 Wire Fly Killer. Kills a fly on the wall without crushing it and picks it up without staining the wall or paper. The wire cuts the air, so the fly does not feel any fanning of the air and will not get away. Price, each 6c

Card Racks and Holders.

No. 23R6655 Folding Card Racks. These are very useful articles for holding cards, photos, etc. It admits of very handsome decoration with ribbons. Just the thing for amateur photographers. Made of twisted steel wire, brightly tinned. It folds up into a small package and cannot be injured in shipping.

Size, in.	11x17	14½x21	17x26	20½x30
Holds picture	28	45	66	91
Price, each	8c	10c	13c	16c

No. 23R6658 Single Card Holder, made of twisted steel wire, brightly tinned.

Length, inches	10	12	18	24
Price, each	5c	7c	9c	14c

No. 23R6660 Double Card Holder, made of twisted steel wire, brightly tinned.

Length, inches	10	12	18	24
Price, each	10c	15c	20c	25c

Umbrella Stands.

No. 23R6672 Round Umbrella Stand, artistic wrought iron work. This is by far the prettiest umbrella stand ever made for the money: finished in dead black, absolutely rust proof, electro brass plated pans. Height, 26 inches; diameter, 9 inches.
Price, each $1.25

No. 23R6674 Square Umbrella Stand. This is a somewhat more elaborate design than the round stand; is heavier in appearance, holds a few more umbrellas, being 9 inches square; finished in dead black, absolutely rust proof, electro brass plated pans. Height, 26 inches.
Price, each $1.87

OUR GALVANIZED WARE.

Is the highest grade made, non-destructible and by far cheaper in the end than tin or any lower priced ware. All galvanized after being made and will not leak.

No. 23R6800 Galvanized Wash Boilers.

No.	Size	Weight, each	Price, each
7	9½x18¼	5¼ lbs.	73c
8	10¾x20⅛	7¼ lbs.	78c
9	12 x22½	8 lbs.	89c

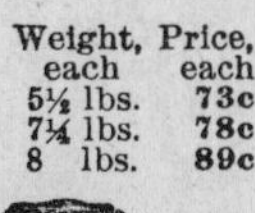

No. 23R6802 Galvanized Tea Kettle.

Number	7	8	9
Weight, each	1¾ lbs.	1⅞ lbs.	2¾ lbs
Price	36c	41c	46c

No. 23R6805 Galvanized Wash Bowls.

Size, inches	11½	13
Weight	⅞ lb.	1 lb.
Price, each	9c	12c

No. 23R6809 Galvanized Well Buckets.

Quarts	10	12	14
Holds, quarts	9	10½	12½
Size	9x11¼	9x12¼	9x13¾
Weight, pounds	2¼	2½	3¼
Price, each	25c	28c	31c

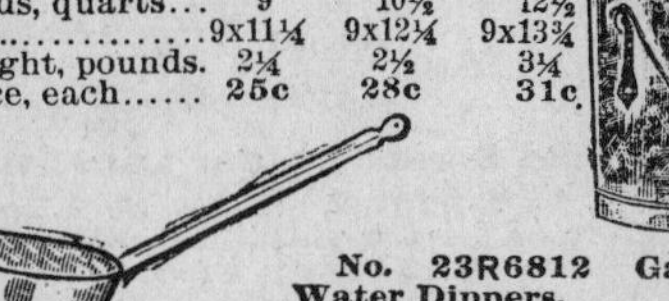

No. 23R6812 Galvanized Water Dippers.

Quarts	2	3
Holds, quarts	1¼	2½
Size	6½x3½	7¾x4¼
Weight, ounces	10	14
Price, each	10c	13c

Galvanized Bailed Slop Jar.

No. 23R6815 Size, 10 quarts (actual capacity). Weight, 2¼ pounds.
Price, each 31c

Galvanized Chamber Pails.

No. 23R6817 Worth a dozen cheap tin or wooden pails. 12 quarts. Holds 11¼ quarts. Weight, 2¼ pounds. Price, each 36c

Galvanized Water Pails.

No. 23R6820 Sizes are actual capacity.

Quarts	10	12	14
Weight, pounds	2	3	3½
Price, each	18c	20c	23c

Galvanized Stock Pails.

No. 23R6825 Worth a dozen cheap tin or wooden pails.

Quarts	16	20
Holds, quarts	15	19
Weight, pounds	3¼	3¾
Price, each	36c	46c

Galvanized Refrigerator Pans.

No. 23R6828

Inches	12	14	16
Weight, pounds	1¾	2¼	2¾
Price, each	20c	24c	30c

Galvanized Sprinklers.

No. 23R6833

Each	Holds	Weight	Price
6 qts.	5 qts.	1⅛ lbs.	30c
8 qts.	7½ qts.	2 lbs.	36c
10 qts.	10 qts.	2½ lbs.	41c
12 qts.	12 qts.	2¾ lbs.	46c
16 qts.	16 qts.	3¼ lbs.	57c

Galvanized Wash-Tubs.

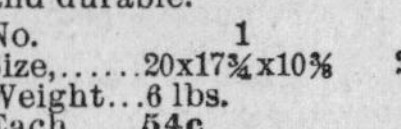

No. 23R6836 Heavy Galvanized Washtubs; no leaking, no hoops to fall off, strong and durable.

No.	1	2	3
Size	20x17¾x10⅝	22x17¼x10¾	24½x21⅜x10¾
Weight	6 lbs.	7 lbs.	9 lbs.
Each	54c	60c	68c

Wringer Attachments.

No. 23R6837 For clamping wringer on galvanized tub. A set consists of two devices like cut. Weight, 6 ounces.
Per set 6c

Galvanized Measures.

No. 23R6842 U. S. Standard. With iron bottoms.

Size	4 qts.	1 peck	½ bus.	1 bus.
Weighs	1 lb.	1⅝ lbs.	2⅝ lbs.	3½ lbs.
Each	16c	25c	33c	45c

Galvanized Steel Baskets.

Galvanized Steel Bushel Baskets are provided with extra heavy corrugated bottoms, thus insuring great strength.
No. 23R6844 ½-bushel graduated to ½, 1 and 1½ pecks, Weight, 3⅜ pounds. Each.....38c
No. 23R6845 1 bushel. Weight, 5½ pounds. Price, each 54c
No. 23R6846 1½-bushel. Weight, 7 pounds. Price, each 71c

Oil Cans.

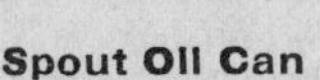

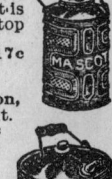

No. 23R6900 The body of this can is glass, protected by a jacket of tin. It is well made, and will not leak where top is attached. Weight, about 5¼ pounds.
Price, each 17c

Spout Oil Can.

No. 23R6902 Galvanized Iron, with lined screw on top and spout.
2 gals. Weight, 2 lbs. Each..29c
1 gal. Weight, 1¼ lbs. Each, 17c

Spout Oil Can

No. 23R6905 Galvanized Iron, Corrugated. A substantial and perfectly air tight can, for general use, for oil and gasoline.
3 gallons. Weight, 2¼ lbs. Each...39c
5 gallons. Weight, 3¾ lbs. Each...51c

...SEND 15 CENTS...

FOR A YEARS' SUBSCRIPTION TO OUR

MONEY SAVING GROCERY PRICE LIST,

revised and issued every sixty days to follow the lowest Chicago prices on groceries. We can save you $1.00 to $5.00 on any ordinary sized grocery order, $10.00 to $50.00 a year on all the groceries you use. Don't fail to send 15 cents for this money saving Grocery Price List.

Faucet Can.

No. 23R6907 The Faucet Can. The most desirable faucet can made. Corrugated galvanized iron; brass faucet, nickel plated.
3 gallons. Weight, 2½ lbs. Each..**49c**
5 gallons. Weight, 3¾ lbs. Each..**54c**

The Swinging Can.

No. 23R6910 Galvanized iron, corrugated, with spring valve spout. It is absolutely the most convenient can made, all the objectionable features in pump and faucet cans are overcome. The frame work is cut from **heavy steel** and is **separable from the can** when taken to the store. **Warranted to be satisfactory.** To fill the lamp, swing the can in position and **push the button.** Only one size, 5 gallons. Weight, 4¾ pounds. Price, each.......................**78c**

Pump Can.

No. 23R6912 Galvanized iron, corrugated, with tin top. Supplied with steady steam pumps which are removable from the can, will give satisfaction in every way. Only one size made, 5 gals. Weight, 4 pounds. Price, each..**72c**

Non-Overflowing Pump Can.

The pump is made with a double tube. The inner tube transfers the oil to the lamp, and the outer tube carries the overflow back into the can. **Adjustable spout** to fill the lamp from the top or side of the can. **The body and bottom** is made of the best galvanized iron, corrugated. Heavy tin top, with a hinge cover over the pump, which excludes dust, dirt and rain. **Every pump is warranted** to give satisfaction and will last as long as the can, as it is the most durable pump ever made.

No. 23R6914 Size, 3 gallons. Weight, 3½ pounds. Price, each.................................**78c**
No. 23R6915 Size, 5 gallons. Weight, 4¼ pounds. Price, each.................................**$1.08**
No. 23R6916 Size, 10 gallons. Weight, 7½ pounds. Price, each.................................**$1.50**

Copperized Steel Oilers.

No. 23R6950 The Celebrated W. & H. Seamless Copperized Steel Oilers are cheap, durable and elegant. They are heavily electro copper plated on the inside to prevent rust and to prevent the oil from becoming gritty. On the outside they perfectly resemble solid burnished copper. The 9-inch nozzles are bent, all others are straight. Have clock steel spring bottoms.

Diameter of bottom....	2¾	3⅜	3⅜	3⅜	3¾	4⅛	4⅛
Length of nozzle, inches	2½	3	5	9	3	3	9
Weight, each, ounces...	2	3	4	5	6	7	8
Price, each..........	**13c**	**16c**	**17c**	**19c**	**22c**	**27c**	**30c**

Zinc Oilers.

No. 23R6955 Zinc Oilers, spring bottom.

Size................	0	1	2	4	5
Weight, ounces...	1	2	2½	3	4
Price, each.........	**5c**	**6c**	**8c**	**10c**	**13c**

No. 0 is small, 2 inches across bottom and holds about ⅛ pint. No. 5 is 4¾ inches across bottom and holds about 1 pint. The others are graduated between. The weights vary from 4 to 7 ounces.

Automatic Oilers.

No. 23R6958 Automatic Zinc Oilers. This oiler cannot be tipped over like the ordinary zinc oiler. When accidentally overthrown it will immediately resume an upright position because of the rounding shape of sides and very heavy bottom; consequently no oil can be accidentally spilled from this oiler.

No....................	1	2	3
Holds, ounces.......	3	4	6
Weight, ounces......	5	6	7
Price, each...........	**22c**	**25c**	**28c**

Mowing Machine Oilers.

Mowing Machine Oilers. Tin; bent or straight spout, holds about ⅛ pint. Weight, 5 ounces.
No. 23R6975 Bent spout. Price, each.....**5c**
No. 23R6976 Straight spout. Price, each, **5c**

Copper Plated Mowing Machine Oilers.

No. 23R6983 Copper plated inside and outside. Made of one piece of steel, holds about ⅛ pint. Weight, each, 6 ounces. Price, each..............**17c**

Railroad Oilers.

No. 23R6990 Copperized Steel Railroad Oiler. Anti-rust; used by the leading railroads of the country. Heavily electro copper plated inside to prevent rusting. The outside perfectly resembles burnished copper. Called the one-pint oiler. Diameter, 3⅝ inches; height of body, 5 inches; 12-inch nozzle. Weight, 10 ounces. Price...**45c**

No. 23R6992 Copperized Steel Railroad Oiler. Called the one-quart oiler. Diameter, 4½ inches; height of body, 6 inches; 18-inch nozzle. Weight, 14 ounces. Price, **55c**

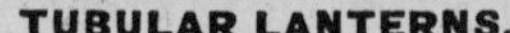

TUBULAR LANTERNS.

We illustrate all the latest designs and our Lanterns have the latest improvements. We show a larger variety to select from. They are safe and reliable. While our prices are lower than formerly, we still maintain our superior quality.

In selecting a lantern you should aim to secure the safest and best. Remember there are some makes of cheap lanterns that cause much annoyance as well as damage. The difference in price between our lanterns, the very best, and inferior makes is but a few cents.

Dietz Square Lift, or Star Tubular Lantern.

For Kerosene.

Our 47c Lantern has no equal for the money. Over 8,000 sold last year.

No. 23R7000 This is the old reliable Square Lift Lantern.

We have sold it for years, and it gives universal satisfaction. One of our most popular lanterns. The globe is raised by the thumb piece on top. No. 1 burner, ⅝-inch wick. No. 0 globe. Weight, about 1¾ pounds.
Price, each.....................**47c**

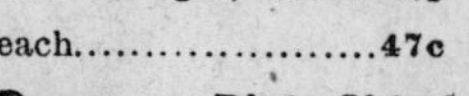

Dietz Side Lift or Victor Tubular Lantern.

For Kerosene.

No. 23R7002 This is the most popular lantern on the market today.

The crank at the side raises and lowers the globe and locks the burner in place when down. A late improvement on this lantern consists of a bend on the guard wire over which the crank moves, thus perfectly locking the globe frame and burner down. No. 1 burner, ⅝-inch wick. No. 0 globe. Weight, about 1¾ pounds.
Price, each..... ....**47c**

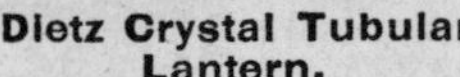

Dietz Crystal Tubular Lantern.

No. 23R7005 This is a strongly guarded tubular lantern with a glass fount instead of tin. This enables the user to see how much oil is in the fount, **and the fount will never leak.** Fitted with our improved side lift. While the fount on this lantern is strongly guarded and is not liable to breakage, still in case of accidentally breaking it can easily be removed and a new one put in. No. 1 burner, ⅝-inch wick, No. 0 globe. Weight, about 2½ pounds. Price, each.............**68c**

Dietz U. S. Brass and Nickel Plated Tubular Lantern.

No. 23R7007 This is the smallest tubular lantern we make. Made of brass, very handsome. For use around the house and for ladies' use it cannot be excelled. No. 0 burner, ⅜-inch wick, U. S. globe, Weight, 1¼ pounds.
Price, each.....................**63c**
No. 23R7008 Same as above, **nickel plated.** Price, each.....**95c**

Dietz No. 1B Side Lift Tubular Lantern.

For Kerosene.

No. 23R7012 This Lantern has the No. 2 burner, 1-inch wick, and should fill a want where a large amount of light is needed in a hand lantern. **The oil pot** holds 1½ pints of oil, and the lantern will burn nineteen hours without refilling. No. 2 burner, 1-inch wick. No. 0 globe. Weight, about 2 pounds.
Price, each.................**69c**

Ham's Cold Blast Tubular Lantern.

No. 23R7015 Cold Blast No. 2, Round Tube, Bottom Lift, Tin Tubular Lantern; No. 2 burner, 1-inch wick, No. 0 globe. Globe removable without taking off the guard. This lantern being made on the same principle as a street lamp, with **wind break,** makes it a superior lantern in its burning qualities. Very desirable for use in places where there are strong drafts of wind. It is **especially adapted for use in mills** and other places where there is considerable dust, **as the burner will not clog up.** The tubes are made from one piece, without elbow or joints. Gives a fine light. We have noticed when one of these lanterns goes to a town we get more orders from the same locality. Weight, 2¼ lbs. Each...**80c**

Dietz Junior Cold Blast Lantern.

No. 23R7016 Only 12 inches high and gives a light equal to many lanterns double its size. It can be filled, lighted, regulated and extinguished without removing the globe. It burns on the cold blast principle, taking most of its air supply from above the globe and will not blow out in the strongest wind. Our Junior Cold Blast possesses all the advantages of our regular No. 2 cold blast lantern, but in more compact form, and is unequaled where a light, handy lantern is required.
Price, each **65c**

Dietz Safety Tubular Mill Lantern.

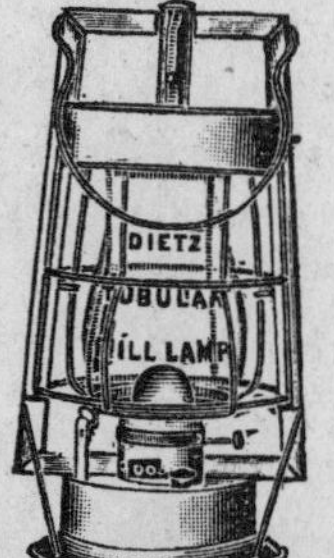

No. 23R7017 The burner is locked in place by two positive locks on globe frame, which work automatically. In addition to this a padlock may be used to secure the globe frame and the guard frame permanently, if desired.

The guard has our patent wind break, which prevents access to the flame over the top of the globe. It is extra strong, well made, and is locked in position by an automatic spring.

The base of the lantern is given extra strength, and is locked permanently to the frame by the use of our patent side braces, holding them firmly together, independent of solder, burns with a clear white flame, and the oil never heats. **The oil fount** holds 1¼ pints of oil, will burn 19 hours without refilling, with a solid drawn, retinned oil fount. **This lantern has been endorsed by insurance men wherever shown as the safest kerosene burning lantern made.** Improved burner. ⅝-inch wick. No. 0 globe. Weight, 2½ lbs. Each, **95c**

Dietz Square Lift Brass Tubular Fire Department Lantern.

For Kerosene.

No. 23R7020 This is a good, strong lantern, made of heavy polished brass and fitted with our patent wind break guard. Our Fire Department Lanterns have all our latest improvements. Are made extra heavy, with large double oil pots. Adopted by the American fire engine companies in the principal fire departments and insurance patrols in the United States. No. 1 burner. ⅝-inch wick. No. 0 globe. Weight, 3 pounds.
Price, each.............................**$2.20**

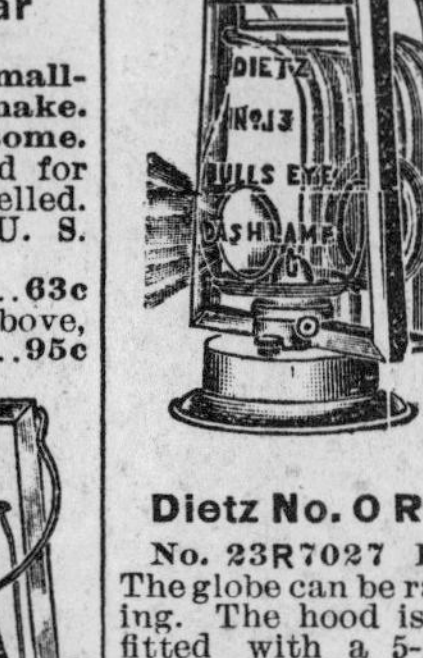

Dietz Buckeye or No. 13 Tubular Slide and Dash Lantern.

No. 23R7025 This is really a very handy combination; it serves as a hand lantern and a side or dash lamp. We furnish it japanned blue. The lamp can be fastened under the body of the vehicle by means of a holder. (See No. 23R7052.) We furnish this lamp with our new bull's-eye lens—a bull's eye attached to the perforated plate. It is superior in every way to the bull's-eye globe. No. 1 burner, ⅝-inch wick, No. 0 globe. Weight, about 2¼ lbs. Each......**70c**

Dietz No. 0 Reflector Tubular Lantern.

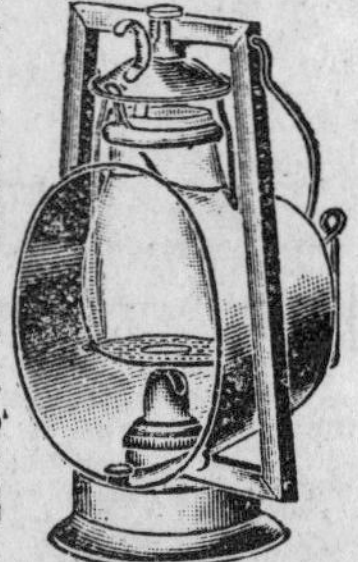

No. 23R7027 For Kerosene. The globe can be raised for lighting. The hood is 6 inches deep, fitted with a 5-inch silvered glass reflector and a spring fastening for dash. Can be used also as a hand lantern or wall lamp. It is a desirable lantern for night driving, and will throw a strong light over 100 feet. We have never heard of one of them blowing or jarring out. The lamp can be fastened under the body of vehicle, by means of our Warner holders. (See No. 23R7052.) No. 1 long cone burner, ⅝-inch wick, No. 0 globe. Weight, about 2¾ lbs.
Price, each.. ....**$1.15**

Cold Blast Dash Lamp.

No. 23R7030 Cold Blast Dash Lamp. No. 2 burner, 1-inch wick, No. 0 globe. This lamp is intended for use when a very powerful light is required. It will not blow out in the strongest wind, and does not flicker as much as a lantern without wind break. We furnish this lantern japanned blue. Weight, 2¾ pounds. Price, each..........**$1.00**

Gasoline and Oil Torches.

No. 23R7300 The Acme Gasoline Torches, for indoor or outdoor lighting; are not affected by wind, rain cold or heat. They produce a large, brilliant, white flame, equal in volume to ten gas jet flames. The reservoir holds nearly six quarts, and when filled will burn full flame for nine hours. Weight, 3¼ pounds.
Price, each........................**$1.00**

..Gasoline Torch.. No. 23R7300

Double Burner Torches.

No. 23R7302 Acme Gasoline Torch, with two burners, controlled by separate valves, so only one may be used if desired. The burners are 34 inches apart. Weight, 5¼ pounds.
Price, each........................**$2.25**

No. 23R7305 Gasoline Torch Burners, same as used on our Acme Gasoline Torch. Weight, 1¼ pounds.
Price, each, without pipe or tank..**85c**

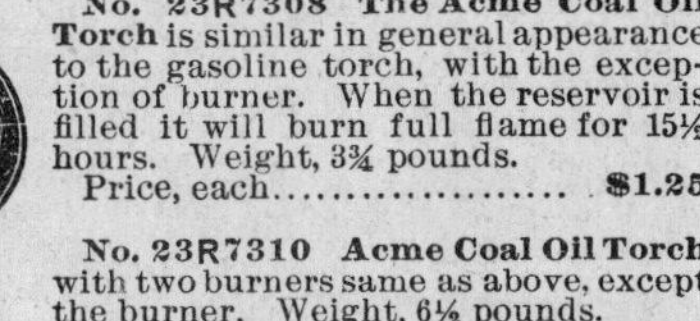

No. 23R7308 The Acme Coal Oil Torch is similar in general appearance to the gasoline torch, with the exception of burner. When the reservoir is filled it will burn full flame for 15½ hours. Weight, 3¾ pounds.
Price, each........................**$1.25**

No. 23R7310 Acme Coal Oil Torch with two burners same as above, except the burner. Weight, 6½ pounds.
Price, each........................**$2.65**

No. 23R7312 Coal Oil Torch Burners, same as used on our Acme Coal Oil Torch. Weight, 1¾ pounds.
Price, each, without pipe or tank........................**$1.10**

...Oil Torch... No. 23R7308

Our Acme Torches are the highest grade made. They are made to special specifications and are worth double the many cheaper makes.

WOODENWARE DEPARTMENT.

OUR CEDAR WOODENWARE is made for us under contract in Virginia by the best maker in America, and is the highest grade goods on the market.

Cedarware with Electric Welded Hoops, Galvanized.

No wood known to man will resist decay equal to Virginia white cedar.

The Electric Welded Hoops used on this ware are sunk in grooves, and are three to four times as strong as a flat hoop, and consequently do not stretch when the wood expands, as is the case with a flat hoop, and therefore do not fall off when the tub or pail dries out.

These hoops are too strong to break and can't fall off.

Cedar Tubs.

With Electric Welded Hoops.

Made from the best Virginia white cedar. These tubs have met with wonderful success among our many customers. They are **light, still very strong and durable,** and are painted with the best oils and paint. They are guaranteed never to fall down. **Those familiar with the lasting qualities of cedar shingles** and posts will appreciate the value of this material when used in tubs and pails. **We have four sizes.**

No. 23R8000

Size, No.	Diam. at Top	Diam. at Bottom	Depth	Holds gallons	Weight, pounds	Price, each
0	23⅝	21⅝	12⅜	21	16	95c
1	22⅝	19	11⅝	16	14	68c
2	20⅝	17⅝	10⅝	32	10	64c
3	18⅝	16⅝	9⅛	9½	8	50c

Sizes given above are inside measurements.

Cedar Water Pails.

With Galvanized Electric Welded Hoops.

These Pails have proven to be the greatest selling article we have ever put on the market. They are impervious to water; very light and strong, and in every way superior to any pail ever made. Made of the best Virginia cedar.

No. 23R8012 Two-Hoop Cedar Pail. Painted with the purest and best lead and oil on the outside. Diameter inside of top, 11¼ inches; diameter inside of bottom, 8⅞ inches; depth, inside, 8 inches; holds 2¾ gallons. Weight, 2½ pounds.
Price, per dozen, **$2.00**; each........................**17c**

No. 23R8013 Three-Hoop Cedar Pails. Painted with the purest and best lead and oil on the outside. Diameter inside of top, 11⅝ inches; diameter inside bottom, 9¼ inches; depth, 9⅝ inches; holds 3¾ gallons. Weight, 2¾ pounds.
Price, per dozen, **$2.26**; each........................**19c**

Cedar Water Pails—Continued.

No. 23R8014 Three-Hoop Cedar Pails. Made of the best selected Virginia white cedar, and finished in natural wood. **Nickel plated electric welded hoop,** smoothly finished; a very handsome pail. Diameter inside top, 11¼ inches; diameter inside bottom, 8⅞ inches; depth inside, 8 inches; holds 2¾ gallons. Weight, 3 pounds. Price, per dozen, **$2.80**; each, **24c**

Cedar Water Can or Sugar Bucket.

No. 23R8026 This is one of the most useful articles we sell. It has a handsome knob cover to lift off. Especially adapted for drinking water, as it keeps all dust and trash out. It is a well known fact **the oil of cedar is death to nearly all forms of insect life.** This property of the wood makes this bucket especially valuable to preserve anything from the attacks of ants and other insects. **Finished in natural wood,** with three flat brass hoops. We have them in three sizes.

Size	Diam., top	Diam., bottom	Depth	Holds, gallons	Weight, pounds	Price, each
1	9	11	8½	3	5	55c
2	8¼	10½	8	2½	4	48c
3	7⅛	9	7⅞	1½	3¼	38c

The measurements above are inside measure.

PAILS.

Standard Ware.

No. 23R8035 Two-hoop, pine. Weight, 3 pounds.
Price, each........................**13c**

No. 23R8036 Three-hoop, pine. Weight, 3¼ pounds.
Price, each........................**14c**

Stable Pails.

No. 23R8040 The J I C Oak Stable Pail has a strap ear runing down sides of bucket that laps under the staves at the bottom. Has flush bottom so if horse gets his foot in the pail, he cannot break the pail. **Considered by all horsemen the best stable pail made.** Weight, 8½ pounds.
Price, each........................**36c**

Well Buckets.

No. 23R8046 The King Oak Well Bucket is the largest, strongest and best shaped well bucket made. Has strap ear which laps under the staves at the bottom, as shown in cut. Weight, 8 pounds.
Price, as shown in cut, each......**40c**

No. 23R8047 The King Oak Well Bucket, same as above with swivel on bail. Weight, 8¾ pounds.
Price, each........................**45c**

For Well Wheels, Well Chains, etc., see Index.

Sugar Buckets.

With Wood Hoops.

No. 23R8060 Holds 10 pounds. Weight, 2⅝ pounds. Price, each, **30c**

No. 23R8061 Holds 25 pounds. Weight, 3⅞ pounds. Price, each, **35c**

No. 23R8062 Holds 50 pounds. Weight, 6¾ pounds. Price, each, **40c**

Tubs.

Standard Ware—Pine.

No. 23R8075 Extra large, 27 inches diameter at top. Weight, 15 pounds. Each, **85c**

No. 23R8076 No. 1 Pine. Diameter at top, 24½ inches. Weight, 13 pounds. Each, **60c**

No. 23R8077 No. 2 Pine. Diameter at top, 23½ inches. Weight, 9 pounds. Each, **50c**

No. 23R8078 No. 3 Pine. Diameter at top, 20 inches. Weight, 6½ pounds. Price, each........................**40c**

Washboards.

Our line of washboards is made for us by a manufacturer who has the reputation of making the best washboards on the market. They are of the strongest construction and finished in the best possible manner. **We carry a variety of sizes and the most popular patterns,** and have selected our boards **with the idea of giving our customers the best possible value for their money.**

No. 23R8085 The Brass King Washboard. The finest family size washboard manufactured. The rubbing surface is made of a sheet of hard spring brass; it will not corrode, crack or get out of shape; has the latest improved corrugated cable crimp and will do the washing with one half the labor required on ordinary boards. It is not necessary to rub hard, the board will do the work. Has protector top and open back braced by bent truss rods so that rubbing surface can never sag. We guarantee every Brass King washboard for five years and will replace any that give out within that time. Weight, 2½ pounds.
Price, each........................**45c**

Washboards—Continued.

No. 23R8087 Red Star Double Washboard. Standard family size, select quality; rubbing surface is an extra heavy solid zinc without wood backing. Has fancy crimp on one side and plain crimp on the other. Has hard maple legs braced by a steel rod passing through zinc and riveted on outside. Has protector top. A very strong and extra well finished board. Weight, 3¼ pounds. Price, each........**33c**

No. 23R8089 Regal Protector Washboard. An extra large board. Rubbing surface measures 12x13 inches. Has heavy single zinc surface with extra deep globe crimp, making it a very easy washer; hardwood frame; protector top; ventilated back. A first class board for large families and boarding houses. Weight, 3½ pounds.
Price, each........................**27c**

No. 23R8090 The Old Reliable Banner Globe Double Washboard. Standard family size; double zinc surface; globe crimp on one side and plain crimp on the other; hardwood frame and stationary protector top; strong and well made. One of the most popular washboards made. Weight, 2¾ pounds.
Price, each........................**25c**

No. 23R8092 Bijou Washboards. A novelty, with soap board and top made of heavy galvanized iron; standard family size; heavy, extra deep globe crimp zinc; saves hard rubbing; protector top; hardwood frame; ventilated back; very strong. Weight, 3½ pounds. Price, each........................**24c**

No. 23R8094 Saginaw Globe Washboard. Standard family size, single zinc rubbing surface with extra deep globe crimp. Solid hardwood frame with protector top, ventilated back. A first quality, well finished board. Weight, 3 pounds.
Price, each........................**22c**

No. 23R8096 Leader Washboard. Single zinc rubbing surface with globe crimp. Protector top. A strong and durable board at a small price. Weight, 2 pounds. Price, each........................**15c**

No. 23R8098 Langtry Washboards. Small size, and intended to be used in a pail for washing small articles; has globe crimp zinc rubbing surface. Size, 8¼x6¾ inches. Strongly made, the same as our larger boards and will stand rough usage. Weight, 1½ pounds. Price, each........................**12c**

Clothes Pins.

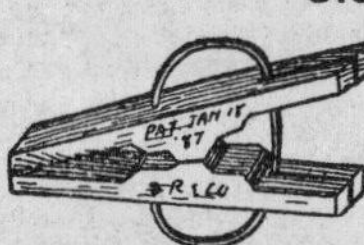

No. 23R8115 Hoyt's Spring Clothes Pins are made of white basswood and the spring is one continuous piece of galvanized spring wire. Simple and convenient and **the cheapest when durability is considered.** Weight, per gross, 3 pounds. Price, per dozen......**3c**
Per gross........................**25c**

No. 23R8117 U. S. Clothes Pins, patent spring, 12 dozen in box. Weight, per gross, 4¼ pounds.
Price, per gross, **65c**; per dozen........................**6c**

No. 23R8120 Clothes Pins, standard goods, full count. Weight, per gross, 3½ pounds. We do not sell less than one gross.
Price, per gross........................**15c**
Price, per box, containing 5 gross........**53c**

No. 23R8122 Metallic Spring Clothes Pin. Will never split or fall off in the severest storm or freeze to the clothes in the greatest frost. They are made of wire, heavily galvanized, so **that it is impossible for them to rust.** They have been tested in all sorts of weather and found to be all we claim. Weight, per dozen, 6 ounces.
Per gross, **76c**; per dozen...**7c**

Clothes Line Reel.

No. 23R8132 Clothes Line Reel, made of hardwood. Keeps the line clean. Prevents kinks. Has revolving handle. Weight, ½ pound. Each....**10c**

Chopping Bowls.

No. 23R8140 Chopping Bowls. Extra quality, with heavy rims, prevents checking.

Inches	13	15	17	19
Weight, each, lb.	1⅝	2⅝	3¼	4
Price, each	8c	11c	18c	27c
Per dozen	87c	$1.30	$2.16	$3.24

Oblong Chopping Tray.

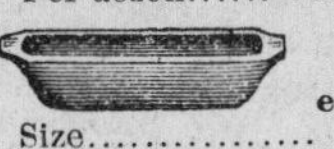

No. 23R8142 Hardwood Patent Oblong Chopping Trays.

Size	12 x 22	11 x 21	10½ x 19½
Weight, each, lbs.	3½	2½	2¼
Price, each	35c	25c	20c

Steak Mauls.

No. 23R8146 Steak Mauls. Weight, 8 ounces.
Price, each........................**5c**

Lemon Squeezers.

No. 23R8149 Hard wood Lemon Squeezers. Weight, ⅝ pound.
Price, each........................**6c**

Kraut Forks.

No. 23R8152 Kraut Forks. Weight, 3 ounces.
Price, each........................**5c**

Potato Mashers.

No. 23R8160 Potato Mashers, with driven handles. Weight, 6 oz. Price, each.........3c

No. 23R8161 Potato Mashers, made complete with handle, all from one piece of wood. Weight, each, 10 ounces. Price, each..........4c

Spoons.

No. 23R8165 Wood Kitchen Spoons, 14 inches long. Weight, each, 3 ounces. Price, each..........2c

Mustard Spoons.

No. 23R8166 Mustard Spoon. Made of boxwood, polished. Length, 4¾ inches. Weight, ¼ ounce. Price, each..........2c

No. 23R8167 Mustard Spoon. Selected white bone, round bowl. Length, 4¾ inches. Weight, ¼ ounce. Price, each..........5c

No. 23R8168 Mustard Spoon. Selected white bone, with large oval bowl. Length, 4¾ inches. Weight, ¼ ounce. Price, each..........5c

No. 23R8169 Salad Set, consisting of polished boxwood fork and spoon, 9¾ inches long. Weight, per pair, 1½ ounces. Price, per pair..........23c

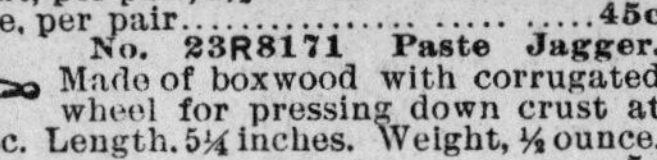

No. 23R8170 Imported Hand Carved Salad Set, like cut. Made of hardwood and well finished. Length, 10 inches. Weight, per pair, 1½ ounces. Price, per pair..........45c

No. 23R8171 Paste Jagger. Made of boxwood with corrugated wheel for pressing down crust at rim of pies, etc. Length, 5¼ inches. Weight, ½ ounce. Price, each..........5c

Rolling Pins.

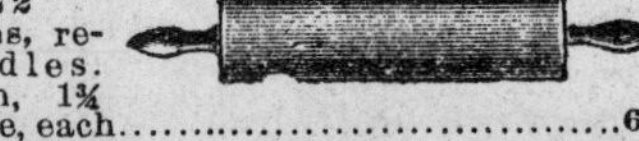

No. 23R8172 Rolling Pins, revolving handles. Weight, each, 1¾ pounds. Price, each..........6c

Fancy Cake Roller.

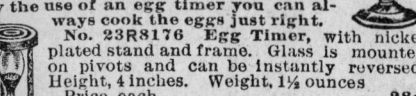

No. 23R8174 Fancy Cake Roller or Springerle Formen, made of hardwood with twelve assorted deeply hand carved designs. Twelve cakes made with one turn of the roller. Indispensable for fancy cooks and will last a lifetime. Weight, 1¼ pounds. Each..........75c

Egg Timers.

These handy little articles are rapidly becoming a necessity in well regulated kitchens. In operation they are similar to the old fashioned hour glass, the length of time required to cook the eggs being regulated by the time required for the sand to run from the upper to lower bulb. **By the use of an egg timer you can always cook the eggs just right.**

No. 23R8176 Egg Timer, with nickel plated stand and frame. Glass is mounted on pivots and can be instantly reversed. Height, 4 inches. Weight, 1½ ounces. Price, each..........28c

No. 23R8177 Egg Timer. Hour glass pattern with fancy wood frame. Height, 3 inches. Weight, 1 ounce. Price, each..........10c

Napkin Rings.

No. 23R8178 Napkin Rings, plain hardwood, in assorted designs, finely polished. Weight, each, 2 ounces. Price, each..........10c

No. 23R8179 Napkin Ring, solid seamless aluminum, satin finished with beaded edges. Looks like silver and will never tarnish. Weight, ½ ounce. Price, each..........11c

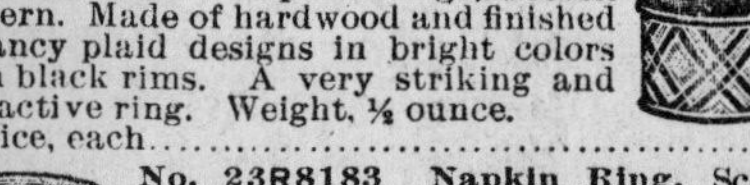

No. 23R8182 Napkin Rings, Scotch pattern. Made of hardwood and finished in fancy plaid designs in bright colors with black rims. A very striking and attractive ring. Weight, ¼ ounce. Price, each..........7c

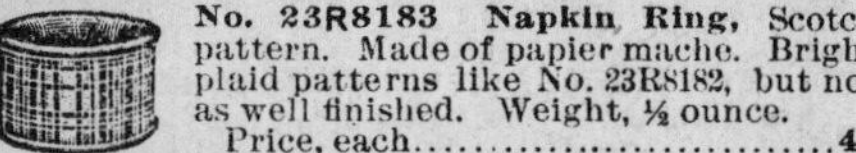

No. 23R8183 Napkin Ring, Scotch pattern. Made of papier mache. Bright plaid patterns like No. 23R8182, but not as well finished. Weight, ½ ounce. Price, each..........4c

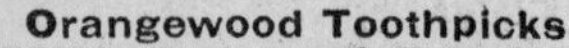

No. 23R8185 Napkin Ring, turned in one piece from selected white bone. 1⅜ inches in diameter. A small, neat ring. Weight, ½ ounce. Price, each..........10c

Orangewood Toothpicks.

No. 23R8190 Orangewood Toothpicks, imported from Portugal. Whittled out by hand to fine point on each end. The best toothpick made. Put up in bunches of 400 picks. Weight, per bunch, 3 ounces. Price, per bunch..........8c

Wood Toothpicks.

No. 23R8192 Hardwood Toothpicks, double points. Standard size box holding about 1,800 picks. 100 boxes in case. Weight, per box, 8 ounces. Price, per case, $2.05; per box..........3c

Hardwood Bread Board.

No. 23R8200 Hardwood Bread Board, hand carved and well finished. No family should be without one. Diameter, 11 inches. Weight, 1¼ pounds. Price, each..........23c

Bread or Pastry Boards.

No. 23R8203 Bread or Pastry Boards, made of poplar wood.

Size	Weight	Each	Size	Weight	Each
16x22	4¼ lbs.	20c	20x27	5¾ lbs.	25c
18x24	5¼ lbs.	22c	20x30	6½ lbs.	28c

No. 23R8207 Hardwood Meat Boards. Size, 12x16x⅞ inches. Price, each..........15c

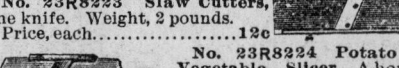

No. 23R8210 Knife Cleaner for cleaning and polishing steel knives and forks consists of a hardwood board 14x4 inches covered with a cleaning composition. So simple that no directions are required, simply rubbing the knife on the cleaner does the work. Weight, 10 ounces. Price, each..........11c

Fruit and Vegetable Slicer.

No. 23R8220 Fruit and Vegetable Slicer. For slicing apples, pears, bananas, potatoes, beets, carrots, cucumbers, turnips, radishes, etc. Makes dainty and attractive perforated flutings and Saratoga chips, also shoestrings, etc. No waste; anybody can use it. Cut above shows two perforated slices made with this slicer. Price, each..........15c

Slaw Cutters.

No. 23R8223 Slaw Cutters, one knife. Weight, 2 pounds. Price, each..........12c

No. 23R8224 Potato or Vegetable Slicer. A household convenience for making Saratoga chips, cutting slaw or slicing fruits or vegetables for pies, soups, etc. Made of hardwood with steel knife. Size, 10¾x3¼ inches. Weight, 4 ounces. Price, each..........10c

Adjustable Knife Kraut Cutters.

This cutter can be adjusted in less than a minute to cut coarse or fine as desired.

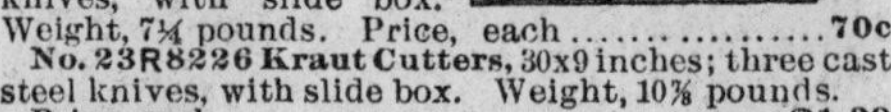

No. 23R8225 Kraut Cutters, 8x26 inches; three cast steel, adjustable knives, with slide box. Weight, 7¼ pounds. Price, each..........70c

No. 23R8226 Kraut Cutters, 30x9 inches; three cast steel knives, with slide box. Weight, 10⅞ pounds. Price, each..........$1.39

Spice Cabinets.

No. 23R8250 Spice Cabinet. Neatly constructed, an ornamental cabinet for holding and preserving spices. **Eight drawers marked for contents.** Very handsome for any use to which a cabinet can be put. Made of ash, oil finish. Size, 12x18 inches. Weight, 5¼ lbs. Each..........40c

No. 23R8252 Spice Cabinet. Polished hardwood and extra well finished. Has eight drawers with zinc labels for various kinds of spices. Size of cabinet, 9¼x17 inches. An extra nice cabinet. Weight, 3½ pounds. Price, each..........$1.15

Medicine Cabinet.

No. 23R8255 Medicine or Handy Cabinet, 12x16 inches, made of ash, nicely trimmed, for holding medicine bottles or anything that necessity or convenience may suggest. Every family should have one. Weight, 6 pounds. Each..........45c

Salt Box.

No. 23R8261 Salt Box, made of nice clear wood, is 4½x5 inches square and will hold two small bags of salt. Weight, each, 14 ounces. Each..........8c

Hardwood Salt Box.

No. 23R8263 Hardwood Salt Box. The front is made of alternating strips of dark and light wood, varnished and highly polished to bring out the beautiful grain of the wood. Has fancy metal plate, engraved with the word Salt. An artistic kitchen necessity. Will hold a small pack of salt. Is 10 inches high and 5¼ inches wide. Weight, each, 1 pound. Price, each..........17c

Knife and Fork Boxes.

No. 23R8270 Knife and Fork Box, with three compartments. Size of box, 14¼x9¾ inches. Made of hardwood, the outside being veneered with alternating strips of light and dark wood. It is well made and finely finished throughout and much superior to the ordinary box of this kind. Weight, 1¾ pounds. Price, each..........57c

Wooden Measures, Iron Bound.

No. 23R8290 ½ bushel, iron bound. Price, each..........19c

No. 23R8291 Peck. Ea., 17c

No. 23R8292 ½ peck. Ea., 13c

No. 23R8293 2 quarts. Ea., 12c

No. 23R8294 1 quart. Ea., 8c

No. 23R8295 Set of the above measures, one of each size. Weight, per set, 9¼ pounds. Price, per set..........70c

No. 23R8340 Patent Folding One-Bushel Crate, for fruit, vegetables, etc. Light, strong and durable, simple and easily folded, no nails, screws or tools required. Slats are made of selected hard maple with **corners all rounded to prevent bruising of contents.** Will outlast many baskets. Can be piled one upon another without damaging contents. Price, each..........20c

No. 23R8355 Towel Roller, white wood, plain. Size, 21x4 inches. Price, each..........6c

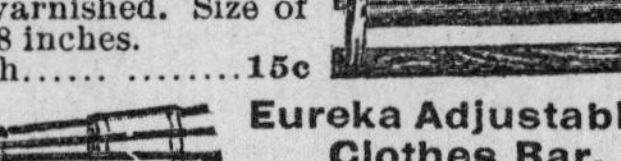

No. 23R8357 Towel Roller, hardwood, varnished. Size of roller, 1⅜x18 inches. Price, each..........15c

Eureka Adjustable Clothes Bar.

No. 23R8395 Eureka Adjustable Clothes Bar, intended to fasten to the wall. When not in use takes the space of an ordinary broom. The bars are 3 feet in length, with gilt tips; **a very convenient household article.** Weight, 4 pounds. Each..........30c

No. 23R8396 Same as No. 23R8395, with six bars, 2 feet long. Weight, 1½ pounds. Each..........15c

Clothes Bar.

Cheapest, Strongest and Best in the World.

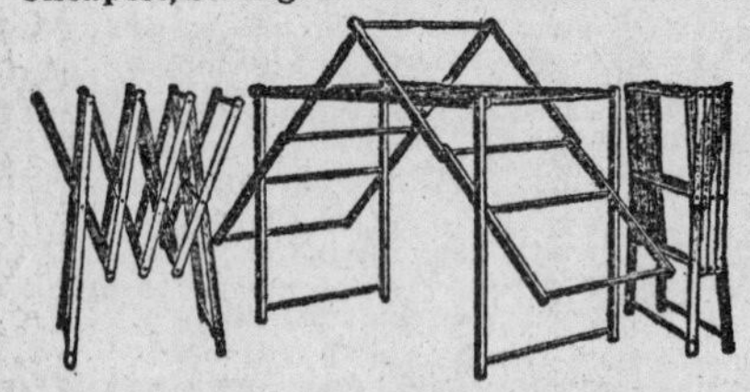

No. 23R8400 Folding Clothes Bar. Every bar is made of clear basswood. Rods, ⅜-inch, slats and legs, ⅞-inch in thickness and width. **Free of knots and nicely finished.** Width, 2 feet 4 inches; height, open, 4 feet 1 inch; length, open, 6 feet 6 inches; height, closed, 3 feet 3 inches; thickness, closed, 6 inches. Weight, 8 pounds. Price, each..........60c

Ironing Boards.

No. 23R8412 Ironing Boards, made of poplar wood.

Length, 4 feet.	Weight, 6 lbs.	Price, each, 28c
Length, 4½ feet.	Weight, 7 lbs.	Price, each, 35c
Length, 5 feet.	Weight, 7½ lbs.	Price, each, 41c
Length, 5½ feet.	Weight, 9 lbs.	Price, each, 45c
Length, 6 feet.	Weight, 11 lbs.	Price, each, 49c

Folding Ironing Boards.

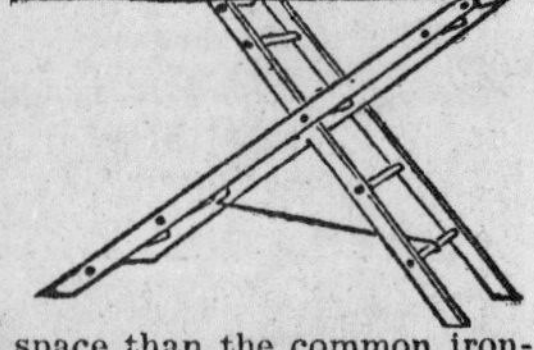

No. 23R8414 This convenient household article is in great favor wherever shown. It has basswood top. The legs are of hardwood, and the table may be easily and quickly adjusted to three different heights. When not in use occupies but little more space than the common ironing board. Weight, 14 pounds. Price, each..........45c

SEE PAGE ..20..

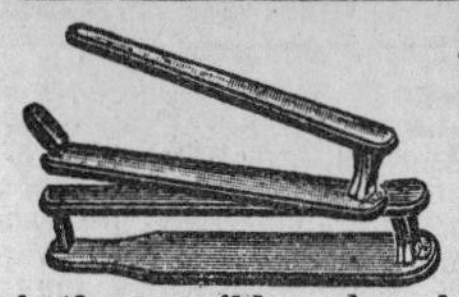

Bosom Board, Shirt Waist and Sleeve Ironing and Pressing Board.

The accompanying cut illustrates our shirt waist and sleeve ironing and pressing boards. They are both reversible and can both be opened to receive sleeve as shown in cut.

No. 23R8422 Double Sleeve Board, one side tapers from 3¾ to 2 inches and is suitable for sleeves of children's dresses. The other side tapers from 4¾ to 3¼ inches, and is suitable for sleeves of ladies' waists; strongly made and nicely finished. It is shown by top board in above cut. Length, 29 inches. Weight, 3¼ pounds. Price, each..............................25c

No. 23R8423 Combination Shirt Bosom and Sleeve Board, illustrated by the bottom board in above cut. The bosom board is just right for a shirt or shirt waist. The sleeve board tapers from 4¾ to 3¼ inches; length, 29 inches. Weight, 4½ pounds. Price, each..............................30c

Lap Cutting Boards.

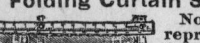

No. 23R8445 Lap Cutting Board, striped, oil finished and polished, with yard measure stamped on it. Size, 20x36 inches. Weight, 4½ lbs. Price, each..............60c

No. 23R8447 Lap Cutting Board. Same shape as No. 23R8445; made of white wood, plain. Size, 20x36 inches. Weight, 4 pounds. Price, each..............................47c

No. 23R8448 Folding Striped Lap Board. Hard oil finish; can be rolled up and put into small space and be put out of the way. It measures 20x36 inches and has a yard measure printed on the edge. Weight, 3½ pounds. Price, each..............................83c

Folding Curtain Stretcher.

No. 23R8462 This cut represents our new Adjustable Folding Stretcher, with a scale corresponding with pins, stamped on the entire stretcher. The side bars are connected by an edgewise inwardly folding, self-locking hinge, overlapping the rail joints, clamped together by a central clamping bolt.

With these new features this stretcher is unequaled for rigidity and simplicity.

The whole stretcher may be folded together without the removal of any of its parts. Weight, 8½ pounds. Price, each..............................75c

No. 23R8464 Folding Curtain Stretcher. Can be adjusted to fit any size curtain. Triple nickel plated pins, guaranteed not to rust. At the cost of laundering two pair of lace curtains, the housekeeper can secure one of these stretchers, and also obviate the customary laundry damage to curtains. Size, 6x12 feet. Weight, 9¾ pounds. Price, each......64c

Bottle Corker.

No. 23R8480 Bottle Corker, made of selected close grained hardwood and oil finished. Weight, 10 ounces. Price, each..........50c

Wood Faucets.

No. 23R8494 Wood Faucets, made of selected hard maple. Boiled in pure linseed oil and fully warranted.

No.	1	3	5	6
Length, inches	7	8½	10½	11½
Weight, ounces	5	6	8	10
Price, each	4c	6c	8c	9c

Step Ladders.

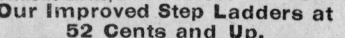

Has malleable iron brackets joining top to sides and legs, which prevent ladder from spreading. We claim it is the best finished and strongest cheap ladder put on the market.

No. 23R8520 Standard Step Ladder, with shelf.

No. 23R8521 Standard Step Ladder, without shelf.

Length, feet	3	4	5
Price, with shelf	25c	30c	40c
Price, without shelf	17c	22c	32c
Length, feet	6	8	10
Price, with shelf	45c	55c	70c
Price, without shelf	37c	47c	62c

Our Improved Step Ladders at 52 Cents and Up.

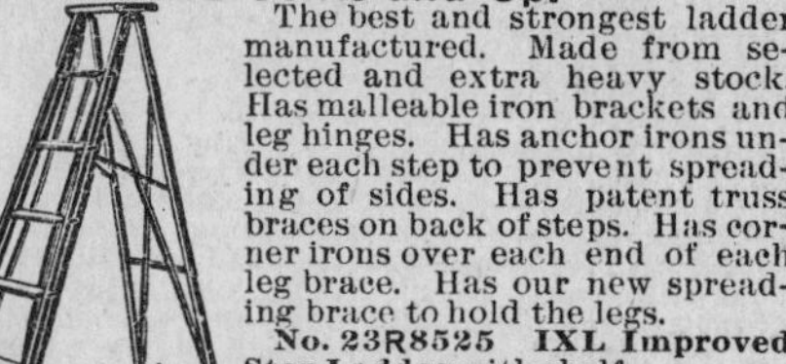

The best and strongest ladder manufactured. Made from selected and extra heavy stock. Has malleable iron brackets and leg hinges. Has anchor irons under each step to prevent spreading of sides. Has patent truss braces on back of steps. Has corner irons over each end of each leg brace. Has our new spreading brace to hold the legs.

No. 23R8525 IXL Improved Step Ladder with shelf.

No. 23R8526 IXL Improved Step Ladder without shelf.

Length, feet	3	4	5	6
Price, with shelf	61c	79c	97c	$1.14
Price, without shelf	52c	70c	88c	1.05
Length, feet		8	10	12
Price with shelf		$1.49	$1.84	$2.09
Price, without shelf		1.40	1.75	2.00

The Painters' Favorite.

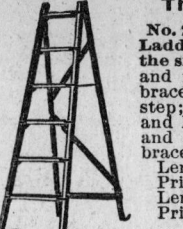

No. 23R8532 Strongest Painters' Ladder Made. Legs fold outside the sides. Has iron straps on sides and front of each step; has iron braces on sides and back of each step; has corner irons on braces and legs; has extra heavy stock and can be folded compactly; is braced at every point.

Length, feet	6	8	10
Price, each	$0.96	$1.28	$1.60
Length, feet	12	14	16
Price, each	$1.92	$2.24	$2.56

Hunter's Extension Step Ladder or Fruit Pickers' Ladder.

No. 23R8534 This is the most convenient ladder made and the only one that is practical. Is made extra strong and of select stock and is well braced with iron on front and rear. **Cannot be equaled for home or farm use.**

Extends from	Price, each
6 feet to 11 feet	$1.25
8 feet to 15 feet	1.70
10 feet to 19 feet	2.15
12 feet to 23 feet	2.60

Long Ladder.

No. 23R8538 Made from best of selected and seasoned lumber. Hickory rungs well fastened to sides; strong but light.

Length, feet	10	12	14	16
Price, each	$0.95	$1.14	$1.33	$1.52
Length, feet	18	20	22	24
Price, each	$1.71	$1.90	$2.09	$2.28

Extension Ladder.

No. 23R8542 Made from selected and seasoned Norway pine and hickory rungs. Our new double roller, single piece top iron is much stronger than two single rollers, and strengthens the ladder in its weakest place. Our hooks are also the best. **This is the best extension ladder manufactured.** We do not allow for lap. Made in two sections. Length, 20 to 60 feet.

Price, per foot..............................11c

If made in three sections, per foot..............................12c

Rope Extension Ladder.

No. 23R8544 Top section raised and lowered by rope and pulley attachment, easily handled. Has new roller, iron automatic locking hooks, and made same as our regular extension. We put our crank attachment for raising and lowering section on all these ladders, and crank and rope are furnished. Made only in two sections. Length, 20 to 60 feet. Price, per foot..............20c

Ball Top Seats.

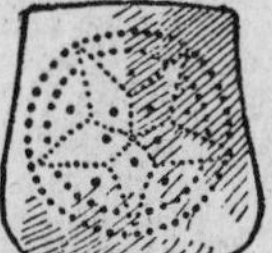

Cut shows shape of ball top seat. These chair seats are made from three pieces of birch veneer with grains crossing. Glued together under great pressure. **They cannot split.** Sizes given are measurements across the widest place.

No. 23R8570 Ball Top Chair Seats.
No. 23R8571 Square Chair Seats.

Size, inches	10	11	12	13	14	15
Weight, each, ounces	6	7	8	9	10	11
Price, each	3c	4c	5c	5c	5c	6c
Size, inches	16	17	18	20	22	24
Weight, each, ounces	12	14	18	20	30	34
Price, each	7c	8c	9c	10c	12c	14c

Chair Cane in Hanks.

No. 23R8578 Chair Cane. Extra selected all long in hanks of 1,000 feet. This is the highest grade chair cane on the market and while somewhat more expensive than the ordinary grades is the cheapest in the long run. We carry in stock fine, narrow medium, medium and common width. Always specify which is wanted.

Price, per hank..............................65c

No. 23R8579 Chair Cane. Extra No. 1 grade, not quite as good as the extra selected, but better than what is ordinarily furnished. In stock in fine, narrow medium, medium and common widths.

Price, per hank..............................55c

No. 23R8581 Binding Cane. Extra No. 1 grade, in hanks of 500 feet. Price, per hank..............55c

Oak Splint Corn Baskets.

No. 23R8602 This basket is stronger and can be used for more purposes around a farm than any other on the market; we carry it in a full line of sizes and shall be glad to have your order for any quantity you may desire.

Size, bushels	¾	1	1½
Weight, pounds	3	4	4¼
Price, each	40c	45c	60c
Size, bushels	2	3	4
Weight, pounds	5	6	8
Price, each	75c	95c	$1.30

Corn Baskets.

No. 23R8610 Corn Basket, patent stave, ½ bushel with handle. Weight, 2 pounds. Price, each..............13c

No. 23R8611 Corn Basket. Patent stave, 1 bushel. Weight, 3 pounds. Price, each..............16c

No. 23R8612 Corn Basket. Patent stave, 1½ bushels. Weight, 4 pounds. Price, each..............25c

No. 23R8613 Corn Basket. Patent stave, 2 bushels. Weight, 5 pounds. Price, each..............................30c

Clothes Baskets.

No. 23R8621 Clothes Basket. Willow, small. Weight, 3 pounds. Price, each..........45c

No. 23R8622 Clothes Basket. Willow, medium. Weight, 3½ pounds. Price, each..........53c

No. 23R8623 Clothes Basket. Willow, large. Price, each..........63c

No. 23R8640 Splasher Mats for protecting wall above wash stand. Made of waterproof sewed wood splints with assorted hand decorated centers. Size, 17¾x29¼ inches. Weight, each, 8 ounces. Price, per dozen, 85c; each..............8c

No. 23R8646 Table Mats made of Japanese matting assorted colors, with fancy plaited straw edges. These are light, neat and durable. Set consists of three mats, one each 6, 8 and 11 inches long. Weight, per set, 2 oz. Price, per set..............................15c

No. 23R8648 Table Mats. Made of alternating strips of light and dark hard wood, highly polished and securely glued to the cotton flannel back; can be rolled up into a small space. Set consists of three mats, lengths, 6¾, 8¼ and 10 inches. Weight, per set, 6 oz. Per set..20c

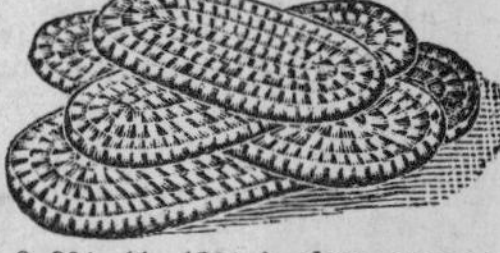

No. 23R8650 Fine Palm Leaf Table Mats, strong and neatly woven, for use under hot platters, etc. Prevents burning of table cloth and marring finish of table. Set consists of 4 oblong mats; length, 8, 9¾, 11, 12¾ inches, respectively. Sold in sets only. Weight, per set, 10 ounces. Price, per set of four, one of each size..............50c

No. 23R8655 Oiled Aprons, made of heavy double sheeting, thoroughly oiled with purest linseed oil. Prepared and treated so as to produce a waterproof coating that is durable and pliable and will not crack or peel, and is absolutely impervious to water. They are worn by butchers, fishermen, employes in packing houses, tanneries, laundries, creameries, etc. Are convenient to wear and cover entire body. Length, 41 to 45 inches. Width, 36 inches. Price, each..........72c

No. 23R8660 Our Best Oiled Apron, made of heavy ducking with drill lining, all thoroughly oiled with best quality linseed oil and perfectly waterproof. Has strap and buckle to fasten in back and shoulder straps with metal eyelets to fasten to. Double reinforced at all points where strength is required. An apron made to stand the hardest kind of wear and tear and give perfect satisfaction. Length, 52 inches. Width, 40 inches. Price, each..............................90c

FOR OTHER WORKING GARMENTS
PANTS, COATS OR OVERALLS,
REFER TO INDEX.

WE TREAT EVERYONE ALIKE.

WE HAVE NO SPECIAL PRICES FOR A FAVORED FEW . . . .

The man who buys a single article from us can buy as cheaply as the dealer who buys in dozen lots.

WE GIVE EVERYONE THE BENEFIT OF THE LOWEST POSSIBLE PRICES.

DEPARTMENT OF DAIRY SUPPLIES.

THE LARGE INCREASE IN OUR SALES IN DAIRY SUPPLIES INDICATES THAT OUR PRICES AND GOODS ARE RIGHT.

WE ARE IN A POSITION TO FURNISH ANYTHING that a dairyman may require at money saving prices. There are some items of which a careful description would require so much space that we have prepared special circulars, showing good, large illustrations, and giving explicit descriptions, which we will be pleased to mail on request.

SALT, BUTTER COLOR, ETC., **will be found in our grocery list.** Other goods used by dairymen will be found on other pages of our general catalogue. **We can furnish everything you want.**

MILK CANS. **In these days of close competition it is absolutely necessary for a dairyman to practice the most rigid economy in purchasing all the supplies that he uses. We believe the highest priced cans that we sell are the most economical.** In sections of the country where dairymen have been shipping milk the longest, you will find that they use the best cans they can buy, for they have found that while the expense at first is a little more, the life of the cans is enough longer to more than repay the extra cost. **The cans which we offer you this season are made by a manufacturer who has been making milk cans in the same factory which he now occupies for thirty-four years.** The cans are not only made from the best finished material, but are free from seams, rough soldering, and other imperfections. **The cans are not made by a trust,** as you can see by comparing our prices with the prices of dealers who handle goods made by a trust. There is no acid used in tinning, as every piece of steel used in the manufacture of these cans is tinned strictly **"Palm Oil Process."** The bodies of the best cans are riveted, the rivet heads being soldered on the inside smooth as glass.

SOME DEALERS **will tell you that the seamed bodies are better.** They say so because they can use a softer grade of steel, and labor costs much less when cans are made this way. If you have had any experience, you know that the body of a can should be stiff and hard to prevent denting. **Hard, stiff steel, such as used in our best grade cans,** cannot be double seamed. We double seam some of our cheaper cans, because it's cheaper to make them that way. The seamed bodies made of soft steel, will soon dent in use. **REMEMBER, the manufacturer of these cans belongs to no trust or combination.**

No. 23R9000 The Wisconsin Pattern Milk Can, seamless neck and cover, improved round handle, stamped seamless breast, heavy steel body, drawn steel bottom, strong heavy bottom hoop 2½ inches wide, breast hoop 1¼-inch angle steel, soldered top and bottom, breast is double seamed to the body, body is double seamed. Bottom is flanged and riveted to body and bottom hoop, all parts tinned and retinned before being put together. All inside seams heavily soldered with best solder and perfectly smooth, being known as loaded seams, leaving no crevices to collect sour milk or dirt. **They are easily cleaned. This style can is in use all over the United States for a wagon can for hauling milk or cream to creameries. We guarantee them to be actual capacity.**

Capacity, gallons	5	8	10
Average weight, pounds..	10	15	16½
Price, each	$1.40	$1.50	$1.60

No. 23R9003 The Iowa Pattern Railroad Stiff Steel Milk Shipping Can. This is the most popular of the many styles of cans and is used in every state in the Union. While medium priced, it is constructed to give great service; has seamless neck and cover with non-pull-off handle, improved round handles to prevent cut hands, stamped seamless breast with ⅝-inch half oval steel bumping band to protect can from getting jammed in. Heavy stiff steel body, will not dent, **riveted and soldered,** drawn steel bottom, heavy tinned steel bottom hoop 2½ inches wide; bottom is flanged and riveted through hoop and body. Realizing the hard usage to which these milk cans will be subjected, we use an extra amount of best pure solder, making them leak proof and durable. The seams are loaded by floating into them the best pure solder, making every part of the inside of the can as smooth as glass, leaving no little spaces or rough seams to collect sour milk. We have critically examined cans of this pattern from the leading can makers and have no hesitancy in claiming a better can of this pattern is not made. **Many of our customers tell us they have seen non so good. We guarantee actual capacity.**

Capacity, gallons.	5	8	10
Average weight, pounds	12½	17	18
Price, each	$1.50	$1.70	$1.80

No. 23R9006 The Elgin Pattern Railroad Stiff Steel Milk Shipping Can. Used largely in Illinois, Wisconsin and Iowa. Has seamless neck and cover with non-pull-off handle, improved round handle to prevent cut hands, stamped heavy steel breast with ⅝-inch half oval steel bumping band to prevent breast from being jammed in. Heavy stiff steel body (will not dent), riveted and soldered, drawn steel bottom, extra heavy, reversed bottom hoop, 1¾ inches wide, **riveted** through flange of bottom and body and projecting just far enough below body and bottom to protect both. **Before being put together every piece and part of this can is tinned and retinned and carefully inspected for defects,** thereby insuring a heavy coating of pure tin and an absolute preventative against rust. Besides using the best stock, great care is taken in construction. The seams are loaded by floating into them the best pure solder, so essential to the life of a good can. The inside of our cans are smooth as glass, having no shoulders or rough spots where milk can collect, and making them easy to clean. This can is stronger and better than its weight would indicate when compared with others (whose extra weight is largely made up of hoops), as the material in the body, breast and bottom is of extra heavy steel. While this can is stronger than those having outside hoops, the hoops are shorter and lighter owing to the improved construction. **We guarantee actual capacity.**

Capacity, gallons	5	8	10
Average weight, pounds...	11	18	21¾
Price, each	$1.55	$1.80	$2.00

No. 23R9010 The Chicago Pattern Railroad Stiff Steel Milk Shipping Can. Has seamless neck and cover with non-pull-off handle. Improved round handles to prevent cut hands. Stamped heavy steel breast with ⅝-inch half oval steel bumping band to prevent can from being jammed in. Heavy stiff steel body, will not dent, riveted and soldered. Extra heavy drawn steel bottom. Stiff beaded bottom hoop, having bead on which bottom rests, thereby preventing bottom being driven upwards. Rivets in bottom pass through beaded hoop flange on bottom and body, making them nearly as strong as if welded together. Like all the high grade cans sold by us, each and every part is tinned and retinned before being put together, which is a safeguard against rusting. Seams are loaded by floating into them the best pure solder, a very important feature in the construction of milk cans, and special care is taken to have every part of the inside of can as smooth as glass, leaving no shoulders, seams or rough places that will collect cream or milk. The breast, body, bottom etc., are same weight as our Elgin can. **This can is a favorite in Pennsylvania, Michigan, Illinois, Iowa and Wisconsin. We guarantee actual capacity.**

Capacity, gallons	5	8	10
Average weight, pounds	12	19	22
Price, each	$1.65	$1.95	$2.20

No. 23R9014 Burn Pattern Railroad Extra Stiff Steel Milk Shipping Can. Has seamless neck and cover with non-pull-off handle. Extra heavy stiff steel seamless breast. Improved round handles to prevent cut hands. Extra stiff heavy steel body, will not dent, riveted and soldered, extra heavy stiff steel drawn bottom, bottom rivets pass through flange of bottom, body of can and bottom hoop, making the strongest construction known. Breast hoop is 2¼ inches wide, is offset and riveted on ends, after which it is driven to place and soldered top and bottom. **A glance at this will convince you of its strength and how thoroughly it protects that part of the can where breast is soldered to the body.** Great care is used in inspecting every piece of material that enters into the construction of this can, and anything that shows the smallest imperfection is rejected. All parts are tinned and heavily retinned. All seams are loaded by floating into them the best pure solder. The entire inside of can is smooth as glass and easy to clean. **We guarantee full capacity.**

Capacity, gallons	8	10
Average weight, pounds	21½	24
Price, each	$1.95	$2.15

No. 23R9017 New York Pattern Railroad Extra Stiff Steel Milk Shipping Can. Has 7-inch seamless neck, extra heavy cover, will support a cake of ice without injury, and the cover is shaped so the cans can be piled two or three high. Has stamped steel breast with malleable drop handles, of the noiseless pattern; extra stiff heavy steel body riveted and soldered, the kind that will not dent; heavy drawn steel bottom; bottom hoop is 1¾ inches wide; bottom rivets pass through flange of bottom body and bottom hoop; breast hoop ⅝-inch half oval welded steel sweated on to breast to act as a bumper and prevent can from jamming in. An extra large quantity of best pure solder is floated into the seams, making the can unusually strong and the inside as smooth as glass; easily cleaned, with no shoulders, offsets, seams or rough places to collect sour milk or dirt. **This can is used in New York and by all the large condensing factories throughout the country. We guarantee full capacity.**

Capacity, gallons	5	8	10
Average weight, pounds	13	23	24
Price, each	$1.90	$2.15	$2.25

No. 23R9020 Binghamton, New York, Pattern Stiff Steel Railroad Milk Shipping Can. Seamless 6-inch neck, seamless stiff steel breast, malleable noiseless pattern drop handles. Stiff steel body, riveted and soldered. Drawn steel bottom. Bottom rivets pass through flange on bottom body of can and bottom hoop, **the strongest construction known.** Breast hoop is ⅝-inch half oval welded steel, sweated on to breast, protecting it from being jammed in. Bottom hoop 1¾ inches wide projects down just far enough to protect body and bottom and take all strain off the rivets. All parts are tinned and retinned before being put together, and are carefully inspected against defects. An extra amount of best pure solder is floated into the seams, enabling them to stand the rough usage to which they will be subjected. The cans are smooth as glass inside, having no shoulders, seams or rough places for milk to collect and sour. **This can is a favorite in Northern and Central New York, and we have no hesitancy in recommending it for hard usage. We guarantee full capacity.**

Capacity, gallons	5	8	10
Average weight, pounds	11½	17	18
Price, each	$1.80	$2.00	$2.10

No. 23R9023 Utica, New York, Pattern Steel Milk Can. Seamless 6-inch neck, seamless steel breast, malleable noiseless pattern drop handle, steel body grooved seams, double seamed to breast, drawn steel bottom. Breast hoop is 1¼-inch angle steel, welded, soldered top and bottom. Bottom hoop, 1¾ inches wide. Bottom rivets pass through flange of bottom, body and hoop. All seams are loaded. The inside of can is perfectly smooth. **While we do not recommend this as a shipping can to stand the hard usage to which they are subjected, we do say the material (except in weight) and workmanship are superior to many claimed to be suitable for this purpose. Our heavier cans are cheaper in the long run.**

Capacity, gallons	8	10
Average weight, pounds	16	17½
Price, each	$1.80	$1.90

No. 23R9026 The Cleveland Pattern Stiff Steel Railroad Milk Can. Deep, 7-inch seamless neck, extra heavy cover, will support a cake of ice without injury, and shaped so cans may be piled two or three high. Improved round handle, prevents cut hands, stamped, stiff steel breast with ⅝-inch half oval welded steel bumping band to protect cans from being jammed in, extra heavy stiff steel body, the kind that don't dent, riveted and soldered. Heavy drawn steel bottom, bottom hoop 1¾ inches wide, bottom rivets pass through flange of bottom body and bottom hoop, making the construction almost as strong as a solid weld. All parts are tinned and retinned and carefully inspected before being put together, all seams are loaded by floating into them the best pure solder, making the cans strong and the inside as smooth as glass, having no shoulder seams or rough places where milk can settle and sour. **This can is used by the largest shippers in Northern Ohio and we emphatically claim a better, stronger, more durable can is not made. We guarantee actual capacity.**

Capacity, gallons	5	8	10
Average weight, pounds..	13	21	23¾
Price, each	$1.90	$2.15	$2.35

No. 23R9029 St. Louis Pattern Extra Heavy Stiff Steel Railroad Milk Shipping Cans, 7-inch seamless neck, extra heavy cover (will support a cake of ice without injury); shaped so cans may be piled two or three high; malleable noiseless drop handles, extra strong seamless stamped steel breast with ⅝-inch half oval welded steel bumping band to protect can from being jammed in; extra heavy stiff steel body, the kind that don't dent, riveted and soldered; extra heavy drawn steel bottom; outside bottom hoop 1¾ inches wide, having a bead on the inside on which the bottom rests, thus preventing the bottom from being jammed upwards. Rivets pass through flange on bottom, body and bottom hoop, being the **strongest and most durable construction known to can makers.** Unusual care is taken in soldering this can, all seams are loaded by floating into them the best pure solder until seams are smooth as glass, leaving no shoulders or rough places where milk can collect and sour. All parts are tinned and retinned and most carefully inspected before being put together. **This can is used in Michigan, Missouri and California, and is one of the strongest and most durable cans made. We guarantee actual capacity.**

Capacity, gallons	5	8	10
Average weight, pounds..	12¾	21	24
Price, each	$1.90	$2.15	$2.35

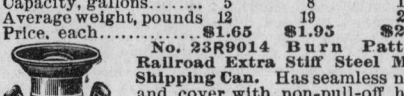

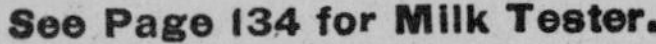
See Page 134 for Milk Tester.

Cheese Factory Milk Cans.

No. 23R9140 Factory Cans. Made of heavy steel, heavily coated with pure block tin. Has the improved handle and seamless floating cover.

Holds gal.,	15	20	30	40
Weight....	22	25	32	40
Each...	$2.65	2.95	3.45	4.25

Cheese Factory Milk Cans.

No. 23R9145 Has ventilated floating cover made from extra heavy charcoal tin. Body made from one piece Cookley K IXXXX best charcoal tin plate, double seamed and soldered. Bottom of extra heavy stiff steel plate flanged. Bottom hoop is 1¾ inches wide welded steel, having a bead on which bottom rests. Bottom rivets pass through flange on bottom, body and bottom hoop. Top and center hoops 2½ inch wide welded steel. Improved recessed malleable iron handle, fits snugly over the middle hoop and is riveted on both sides, so when these cans are riding together in a wagon the handles cannot punch holes in the body of can. All hoops are soldered top and bottom, top of body is rolled over outside of and down onto top hoop, and strongly soldered, leaving no raw edges. The bottom in this can will not sag from the weight of the milk, which is frequently a cause of complaint with light weight cans. All parts are tinned and retinned before being put together. Great care is taken in soldering these cans, realizing the strain to which they are subjected which requires plenty of solder to assure strength and no leaks. **Do not compare this can with some on the market made with a three piece body,** cast iron handles, light hoops and bottom. The weight of this can indicates plainly its actual value; although the price may seem high, when durability is considered, it's the cheapest can we or anyone else can offer. **We guarantee actual capacity.**

Capacity, gallons...	15	20	30	40	50
Average weight, lbs.	30	32	38¼	47¾	53
Price, each........	$3.60	$3.83	$4.30	$5.15	$6.00

No. 23R9146 Cheese Factory Can, same as previously described except **without center hoop.**

Capacity, gallons..	15	20	30	40	50
Price, each.........	$3.45	$3.68	$4.15	$5.00	$5.85

No. 23R9147 Cheese Factory Can, same as above with half round top, center hoop, and Whitney handles.

Capacity, gallons..	15	20	30	40	50
Price, each.........	$3.60	$3.83	$4.30	$5.15	$6.00

Factory Weigh Cans.

No. 23R9155 Factory Weigh Cans, made from the best IXXXX charcoal tin plate with sloping bottom and 3-inch Perfection faucet. Seams are very heavily loaded with the best pure solder. Securely crated for shipment.

Capacity, gals.,	40	60	80
Price each,	$6.50	$7.10	$8.30

Curd Scoops.

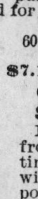

No. 23R9158 Curd Scoops, made from the best IXXXX charcoal tin plate strongly soldered and wired on edges. Weight, each 1½ pounds. Price, each............ 50c

Curd Pails.

No. 23R9159 Curd Pails, made from the best IXXXX charcoal tin plate, heavily soldered, double thick upper front edge. Weight, each 4 pounds.
Price, each..................... 90c

Factory Dipper.

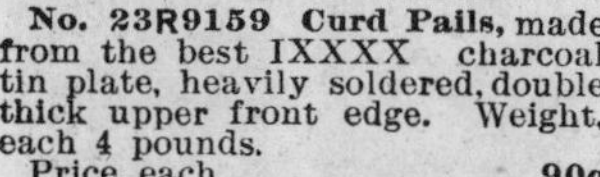

No. 23R9165 One Gallon Factory Dipper. Made of IXXXX charcoal tin, strongly soldered. Weight, each, 1½ pounds.
Price, each......................... 33c

Dairy Pails.

No. 23R9170 Heavy Dairy Pail, with drawn steel bottom, heavy steel bail with bail wood (not shown in illustration). Stock is tinned and retinned before being put together. Well soldered, smooth seams, strong and durable.

Actual capacity, qts.	12	14
Weight, each. lbs.....	3	3¼
Price, each..........	36c	38c

For other dairy pails, strainer pails, etc., see Index.

FOR DAIRY AND BUTTER SALTING SCALES SEE INDEX.

No. 23R9182 Separator Heating Vat. Made from heavy galvanized iron, lined with heavy IXXXX charcoal tin plate. Wired on edges and very heavily soldered. Has sloping bottom. Used for heating milk to the proper temperature before going to separator. It has steam connections. Crated for shipment.

Size, capacity............	1 separator	2 separators
Weight, pounds...	33	36
Price, each.............	$6.00	$7.00

The Sears Cream Separator.

After the most critical examination of all known separators, foreign and domestic, both as to construction and results obtained, we have selected the "Sears," which has proven itself by actual tests, to skim as close, run as easy and skim as much as any separator in use. It is easy to clean and so simply constructed that any one can run it. The bowl has but one cylinder; all the running parts are enclosed, removing all danger to the operator. You will not find any separator of same rated capacity (regardless of price) that will run easier, skim more, skim closer, make better butter, will skim hotter, will skim colder, or make more butter. **Our price, compared with others, may seem low, but remember, we guarantee it exactly as represented.** Complete and plain instructions sent with each machine. **At prices printed below, we deliver these separators free on board cars at our factory in Pennsylvania.**

No. 23R9186 Capacity, 250 pounds per hour.
Price, with stand, each............................ $48.75
Shipping weight, 174 pounds.

No. 23R9187 Capacity, 350 pounds per hour.
Price, with stand, each............................ $63.75
Shipping weight, 185 pounds.

No. 23R9188 Capacity, 500 pounds per hour.
Price, with stand, each............................ $75.00
Shipping weight, 214 pounds.

$4.00 extra for power attachment.

BY ACTUAL TESTS the above separators will skim 350, 450 and 600 pounds respectively. Descriptive circular sent free on request.

The Peerless Creamery.

No. 23R9192 The cabinet part of this creamery is made in refrigerator style, having a dead air space in the walls and lined with felt paper. The tanks are lined with best bloom galvanized iron, in which are placed the milk cans. These cans are placed in and near the front of tank, through openings in the lining of which two necks or sections of each can project. On one of these necks or sections is screwed the milk faucet for drawing off both the cream and the milk, and the other contains a glass through which may be seen the cream line when skimming. As the cans are placed at the front of the tank, they stand perpendicular, and the front of tank slopes from the top to the bottom, thus giving ample room in front of the cans for loose ice, and, if preferable, large blocks of ice can be put back of the cans. The water also circulates underneath, between and around the cans. The bottoms of the cans are rounding and slope from the back to the front. This causes the sediment in the milk to settle at the faucet and to be drawn off first with the milk when skimming. The cans can be removed, should it be necessary to take them out for repair or other purposes, by unscrewing the faucet and nut or bull's eye. The bottom of the water tank also slopes toward the front, thus allowing the settlings or dirt that may be in the ice to be washed out readily. If sufficient quantity of ice has been placed in the sink of the cabinet to reduce the milk in the cans to the required temperature, viz.: 45 degrees in the spring and summer, and 40 degrees late in the fall and winter, all cream can be raised in twelve hours or between milkings. By using running water at a temperature of 55 degrees, or by changing water of that temperature often enough to reduce the milk to the same temperature, all the cream can be obtained in twenty-four hours. In this manner of operating **The Peerless Creamery,** capacity for storing two milkings must be provided; in other words, order a creamery of double the capacity that you would were you intending to use ice. **Capacity of cans, 18 quarts each.**

We do not carry Nos. 6, 7 or 8 in stock and prices are (for these sizes) delivered free on board cars at Philadelphia. We also ship other sizes from factory if it makes less freight charges for customers.

No.	No. of cans	No. of cows	Height inches	Length inches	Width, inches	Weight pounds	Price
2	2	4 to 6	35	25	23	100	$19.44
3	3	7 to 9	35	34	23	125	23.76
4	4	10 to 12	35	41	23	160	28.80
5	6	13 to 18	35	61	23	220	37.44
6	8	19 to 24	35	77	23	280	43.98
7	10	25 to 30	35	80	23	320	50.25
8	12	31 to 36	35	96	23	440	52.95

The Star Barrel Churn.

This style of churn is old, tried and reliable, easy to operate and keep clean; it is absolutely impossible for this churn to leak, as the wear can be taken up as simply as one can turn a thumb nut. **The fasteners are attached to the outside of the churn,** and it will be seen from the cut that the bail and cover fastening is a compound leverage which **increases the pressure ten times more than any other** make of churn.

No. 23R9200 Five-gallon Barrel Churn, for 1 to 3 gallons of cream. Weight, 32 lbs.
Each $2.40

No. 23R9201 Nine-gallon Barrel Churn, for 1 to 5 gallons of cream. Weight, 46 pounds. Each.. $2.55

No. 23R9202 Fifteen-gallon Barrel Churn, for 1 to 7 gallons of cream. Weight, 50 lbs. Each... $2.70

No. 23R9203 Twenty-gallon Barrel Churn, for 2 to 9 gallons of cream. Weight, 67 lbs. Each... $3.00

No. 23R9204 Twenty-five-gallon Barrel Churn, for 2 to 12 gallons of cream. Weight, 77 pounds.
Each.. $3.60

No. 23R9205 Thirty-five-gallon Barrel Churn, for 3 to 16 gallons of cream. Weight, 95 pounds.
Each.. $4.80

The Sturges' Steel Churn.

No. 23R9212 The Original Genuine Sturges' Steel Churn, with all the latest 1901 improvements, stamped stiff steel cover with glass peep hole, which acts as a vent as well as enabling the operator to see how the churning is progressing without taking off the cover. Cork is ½-inch square, making it very durable and preventing leaks, and extends around the outside edge of cover. The bail adjustment is the quickest, safest and in every way the best. The mouth of this churn is full size of churn, leaving no projections or corners that are hard to clean. **There are no hoops to drop off, no seams to open up, no wood to take up sour milk.** The bottom is drawn steel flanged. There is a heavy steel hoop on the bottom, and bottom body and hoop are riveted and soldered together. The inside of can is perfectly smooth, having no rivet heads anywhere. The outside is handsomely decorated in colors. This can may be cleaned as easily as a glass dish, and its growing popularity is proof of its merit. **Frame is all steel and churns are securely crated for shipment.**

Actual capacity, gallons..........	9	15
Churns, gallons........	1 to 4	2 to 7
Average weight, crated, pounds..	56	70
Price, each..........	$5.00	$7.50

Curtis' Improved Square Box Churn.

No. 23R9215 Its compactness, durability and efficiency make it very desirable for a dairy of one cow or fifty. It is a great favorite and has been **improved in many respects,** until it is believed to be absolutely the most perfect box churn to be found anywhere. **The cover is of heavy tin** and securely fastened. The corners are **protected with iron caps** and are so constructed that when the buttermilk is drawn out and cleansed it will drain **perfectly dry.**

Holds, gallons......	7	10	12	20
Churns, gallons....	1 to 3	2 to 4	2 to 6	3 to 9
Weight, pounds....	32	35	37	45
Price..................	$3.50	$3.75	$3.95	$4.50
Holds, gallons......	26	40	60	80
Churns, gallons....	4 to 12	6 to 20	8 to 30	10 to 40
Weight, pounds....	60	125	200	250
Price..................	$5.50	$12.00	$17.25	$19.50

The **three largest sizes** are adapted to large dairies. They have a crank on one side, a long gudgeon for pulleys on the other; strong bands and rods running around the churn make them very substantial. **Tight and loose pulleys, $6.00 extra.**

Rectangular Churns.

No. 23R9216 The Rectangular Churn works the **easiest and quickest** of any churn on the market. At the **Dairy Fair,** held in Chicago, it **received the highest award,** a cash premium and diploma, in competition with the world. **Wisconsin butter won five medals** at the Centennial Exhibition at Philadelphia and four of these were **awarded to butter** made in the **Rectangular Churn.**

No.	Gals.	Weight	Price	No.	Gals.	Weight	Price
0	7	30	$3.50	3½	26	65	$5.50
1	10	33	3.75	4	40	130	7.00
2	12	35	3.95	5	60	200	10.40
3	20	55	4.50				

See page 134 for Milk Tester.

Union Churn.

You can make, gather, work and salt your butter without removing from the Union Churn, or without touching the butter with your hands. It churns with ease by the extra power and motion gained by gear wheels.

No. 23R9221 Union Churn, holding 5 gallons. Weight, 40 lbs. Each, **$3.25**

No. 23R9222 Union Churn, holding 7 gallons. Weight, 45 lbs. Each, **$3.75**

No. 23R9223 Union Churn, holding 10 gallons. Weight, 60 lbs. Each, **$4.35**

No. 23R9225 Union Churn, holding 12 gallons. Weight, 70 lbs. Each, **$6.00**

Improved Cedar Cylinder Churn.

$1.50 TO $2.25 for the Best Cedar Cylinder Churn made.

No. 23R9226 White Cedar Cylinder Churn. We use **a double dasher,** and the crank is locked to the churn with a clamp and thumbscrew, which **prevents leakage.** Lock cannot break. The top is large, and **dasher easily removed.** The hoops are **galvanized iron, and will not rust.** The best churn in use. Weights vary from 15 to 25 pounds.

Nos.	1	2	3	4
Will hold, gals.	2	4	7	10
Will churn, gals.	2	3	4	5
Price	$1.50	1.75	2.00	2.25

Dash Churn.

Common Dash Churns. A long handle goes through the cover at the top, with a dasher at the bottom which is worked up and down inside the churn. Weight, 6 to 12 pounds.

No. 23R9230 3-gallon dash churn. Price, each **53c**

No. 23R9231 4-gallon dash churn. Price, each **63c**

No. 23R9232 5-gallon dash churn. Price, each **75c**

No. 23R9233 6-gallon dash churn. Price, each **84c**

White Cedar Dash Churns.

No. 23R9234 White Cedar Dash Churn. The old way is considered by many the best, and we can safely recommend our cedar churns as the best dash churn made. Cedar is peculiarly adapted for milk and butter purposes.

Gallons	6	5	4
Sizes	22-inch	20-inch	18-inch
Weight	10¾	9½	6¾
Price, each	92c	72c	63c

Cottage Butter Worker.

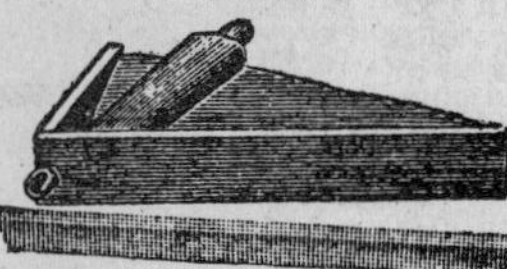

A convenient low priced worker that is placed upon a table when in use. The end is placed over the side of the table, and the drip falls into a vessel upon the floor.

No. 23R9240 For one or two cows. Each **$2.10**

No. 23R9241 For two or three cows. Each, **2.52**

No. 23R9242 For four or five cows. Each, **2.94**

Reid Butter Workers.

No. 23R9246 Size, 14x23 inches, to work **10 pounds of butter.** Shipping weight, 20 pounds. Each **$3.80**

No. 23R9247 Size, 17x27 inches, to work **20 pounds of butter.** Shipping weight, 25 pounds. Price, each **$4.43**

No. 23R9248 Size, 20x36 inches, to work **30 pounds of butter.** Price, each **$5.07**

No. 23R9249 Size, 23x36 inches, to work **50 pounds of butter.** Price, each **$6.33**

When it is to our customers' advantage to do so we ship from our factory in Pennsylvania.

Lever Butter Workers.

No. 23R9250 Its simplicity, saving of time, ease of operation and very low price commend it to every dairy. **No. 0 size,** 20 inches wide, works 15 pounds. Each **$3.43**

No. 23R9251 No. 1 size, 30 inches wide, works 25 pounds. Each **$4.07**

No. 23R9252 No. 2 size, 40 inches wide, works 35 pounds. Each **$4.75**

FOR DAIRYMEN'S OILED APRONS SEE No. 23R8655 ON PAGE 598.

Family Cheese Making Apparatus.

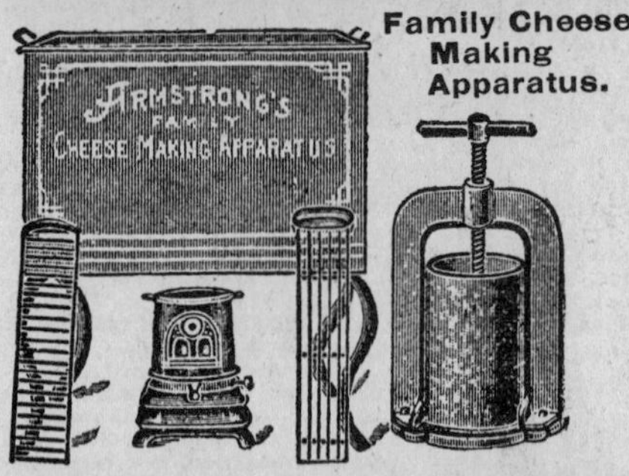

No. 23R9261 This is a very simple apparatus adapted to the wants of all **farmers or dairymen** who keep from 2 to 10 cows, or more. It will make from **2 to 10 pounds of cheese** each operation, according to the quantity of milk. It makes a perfect cheese each time, whether 2 pounds or 10 pounds.

The milk is heated by a coal oil lamp, which is easily kept under control. The heating vat is so constructed that the lamp gives all the heat that is necessary. The management of the heat is the secret of success in making good cheese. The entire apparatus is so light in weight that a lady can move it from one place to another with ease. **A lady can make cheese** in the kitchen or pantry, and carry on her household work at the same time. **With each machine we send simple and full instructions how to make cheese successfully.** Each apparatus is complete with heating vat, press, curd knives, lamp and thermometer, material, strong and well finished. **We also include sufficient rennet tablets, bandages and cheese color** to make a nice little batch of cheese. **Give catalogue number and state size.**

No.	Holding gals.	Weight, lbs.	Price
1	10	100	$12.25
2	20	155	19.60
3	30	160	24.50

Curtis' Babcock Farm Tester.

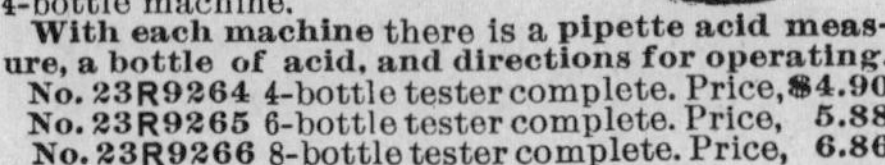

Every dairyman or farmer who keeps a half dozen cows ought to provide himself with one of these milk testers, if he cares the snap of his finger to know whether he has a cow in the herd that is worth keeping. **This tester is designed expressly for farm use,** and so low a price put on it that every man who owns two cows can have a 4-bottle machine.

With each machine there is a pipette acid measure, a bottle of acid, and directions for operating.

No. 23R9264 4-bottle tester complete. Price, **$4.90**

No. 23R9265 6-bottle tester complete. Price, **5.88**

No. 23R9266 8-bottle tester complete. Price, **6.86**

Babcock Milk Test.

With Roe's improved swinging heads.

No. 23R9267 Price, 4-bottle Tester, complete **$7.84**

No. 23R9268 Price, 8-bottle Tester, complete **$9.80**

No. 23R9269 Price, 12-bottle Tester, complete **$13.75**

No. 23R9270 Price, 24-bottle Tester **$20.60**

With each machine is included testing bottles, pipette acid measure and acid for 50 to 200 tests, according to size, and full directions for operating.

Fancy Square and Round Butter Molds.

Made from selected maple wood, and every one guaranteed perfect.

	Size of Mold		Weight of mold, lbs.	Ea.
No. 23R9300	2 lb.	**Fancy carving,** round.	1¼	16c
No. 23R9301	2 lb.	**Jersey cow,** round	1¼	28c
No. 23R9302	1 lb.	**Fancy carving,** round.	1	10c
No. 23R9303	1 lb.	**Jersey cow,** round	1	21c
No. 23R9304	½ lb.	**Fancy carving,** round.	¾	9c
No. 23R9305	½ lb.	**Jersey cow,** round	¾	18c
No. 23R9306	1 lb.	**Fancy carving,** square	1¼	18c
No. 23R9307	½ lb.	**Fancy carving,** square	1	16c

No. 23R9308 Individual Mold, fancy carving, round. Weight, each, 2 ounces. Price, each **4c**

No. 23R9309 Individual Mold, fancy carving, with any initial letter; round. Weight, each, 2 ounces. Price, each **5c**

No. 23R9310 Individual Mold, fancy carving; square. Weight, each, 2 ozs. Each **8c**

California Butter Molds.

No. 23R9315 This cut represents a very popular mold, and is used very extensively in all parts of the country. Size, 1 pound. Price, each **17c**

No. 23R9316 Size, 2 pounds. Price, each **18c**

No. 23R9317 Square California Butter Mold, one pound size. Weight, 1⅜ pounds. Price, each **17c**

No. 23R9318 Size, 2 pounds. Price, each **18c**

Butter Mold, New England Pattern.

These celebrated molds are made of selected white wood, and only brass hooks and screws are used throughout, so that there is **no possibility of rust** and consequent discoloration of the wood. The bottom is prevented from warping by **strong wooden cleats,** while the sides are grooved sufficiently deep to allow for swelling when in use, and are lock cornered together, thus securing the **utmost possible rigidity.** One great advantage of these molds over most other patterns on the market is that the **prints are released by a single motion and in perfect shape,** instead of being pushed forcibly through a form by a plunger, which injures the grain.

No. 23R9325 Price, half-pound size, **print 5 inches long, 2¼ inches wide, 1¼ inches deep.** Weight, ¾ pound. Price, each **62c**

No. 23R9326 One-pound size, **print 5 inches long, 4½ inches wide, 1¼ inches deep.** Weight, 1 lb. **77c**

No. 23R9327 Two-pound size, **print 10 inches long, 4½ inches wide, 1¼ inches deep.** Weight, 1½ pounds. Price, each **$1.00**

Butter Mold, Philadelphia Pattern.

No. 23R9330 Price, **half-pound size.** Weight, 1¼ lbs. Each **89c**

No. 23R9331 Price, **one-pound size.** Weight, 1¾ lbs. Each **98c**

No. 23R9332 Price, **two-pound size.** Weight, 3 lbs. Each **$1.45**

Lee's Shipping Box for Print Butter.

No. 23R9340 We offer the above as a low priced shipping box for large shippers; it is made strong and durable. Holds **48 1-lb. prints.** Price **$1.50**

No. 23R9341 Pearce Butter Mold, made expressly to fit Lee's and Curtis' shipping boxes. 1-lb. size. Weight, 1¼ lbs. Price, each **68c**

Curtis' Shipping Box for Print Butter.

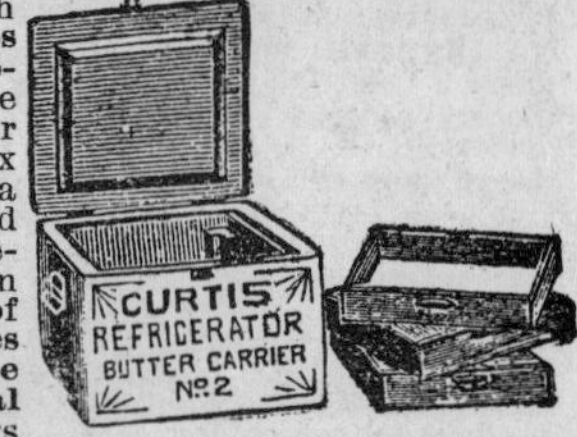

This shipping box is made with **two dead air spaces** around the box, doing away with the can of ice and water in center of the box that causes such a muss when tipped partly over by careless shippers, often injuring the sale of butter. **The boxes are made in the most substantial** manner, the trays being dovetailed together, and all inside work being of white wood, which is free from taint or smell. **Chest handles are put on the ends** for convenience in handling. **A shipping box will many times pay for itself** in three or four shippings.

No. 23R9346	**Capacity, 15 pounds.**	**Price... $3.19**
No. 23R9347	**Capacity, 20 pounds.**	**Price... 4.12**
No. 23R9348	**Capacity, 30 pounds.**	**Price... 4.90**
No. 23R9349	**Capacity, 45 pounds.**	**Price... 5.88**
No. 23R9350	**Capacity, 60 pounds.**	**Price... 6.60**
No. 23R9351	**Capacity, 80 pounds.**	**Price... 7.50**

Mrs. Bragg's Butter Fork.

No. 23R9359 A useful and convenient article to remove butter from the churn. In **general use throughout the country** in creamery and dairy, and considered almost indispensable. **Made of hard maple** and well finished. Length, 12 inches; width, 5 inches. Weight, 6 ounces. Price, each **9c**

Wooden Butter Spades and Ladles.

Weight, 4 ounces.

No. 23R9360 The Anderson Ladle. Each **7c**

No. 23R9362 The Acme Ladle. Each **4c**

No. 23R9363 Butter Spade. Each **4c**

Bradley Butter Boxes.

No. 23R9370 5 pounds, 12 in crate. Price, per crate **68c**

No. 23R9371 10 pounds, 6 in crate. Price, per crate **67c**

Bail Butter Boxes.

No. 23R9372 10-pound Bail Butter Boxes. Six boxes in a crate. Price, per crate **48c**

Ash Butter Tubs.

No. 23R9376 60 pounds, 5-hoop. Price, each **25c**

No. 23R9377 40 pounds, 4-hoop. Price, each **22c**

No. 23R9378 25 pounds, 4-hoop. Price, each **20c**

No. 23R9379 Butter Tub Tins, in packages, containing 1000. Weight, per package, 8 pounds. Price, per package **46c**

Sears, Roebuck & Co.
Blacksmith Tools
Every Farmer his own Blacksmith

BUY YOUR OWN TOOLS, DO YOUR OWN WORK, AND SAVE MONEY . . . . .

SHARPEN THE PLOWS, SHOE THE HORSES, SET THE LOOSE TIRES, MEND THE MACHINERY.

With an outfit selected from this list every farmer, ranchman and mechanic can be his own blacksmith. **NO DELAY FOR REPAIRS** in a busy season while the team and a man have gone to the blacksmith shop. Again, if you have an outfit you will improve rainy days to fix up things that are showing wear, and avoid costly, vexatious and dangerous breakages in a busy time. **OUR PRICES** quality considered, you will find by comparison are far below any competition. **FREIGHT IS VERY LOW** on this class of goods, and will add but very little to cost.

Riveting Hammers.

No. 24R100 The S., R. & Co.'s Brand Riveting Hammers, polished extra cast steel. Handles not included in weights.

No	0	1	2	3	5	7
Weight,	4 oz.	7 oz.	9 oz.	12 oz.	18 oz.	26 oz.
Price, each,	23c	25c	26c	27c	29c	35c

Riveting Hammer Handles.

No. 24R105 Riveting Hammer Handles. Length, 14 inches. Price, each.......3½c

Straight Pein Machinists' Hammers.

No. 24R109 High Grade Straight Pein Machinists' Hammer, half polished cast steel. Every hammer warranted. Select hickory handles. Weight does not include handle.

No.	00	0	1	2	3	4
Weight....	12 oz.	1 lb.	1 lb. 4 oz.	1 lb. 8 oz.	1 lb. 12 oz.	2 lb.
Price, each.	39c	41c	44c	48c	50c	55c

Cross Pein Machinists' Hammers.

No. 24R110 Machinists' Cross Pein Hammers. Made of high grade cast steel, fully warranted. Complete with select hickory handles.

No.	00	0	1	2	3	4
Weight...	12 oz.	1 lb.	1 lb. 4 oz.	1 lb. 8 oz.	1 lb. 12 oz.	2 lb.
Price, each	39c	41c	44c	48c	50c	55c

Farriers' Turning Hammers.

No. 24R115 Farriers' Turning Hammers, Chicago pattern, solid cast steel, with handles. Weights, without handles, 2, 2½ and 3 pounds.
Price, each, any weight........................85c

No. 24R117 Farriers' Turning Hammers, New York pattern. Weights, 2, 2½ and 3 pounds; weights do not include handle.
Price, each................................86c

Plow or Engineers' Hammers.

No. 24R120 Solid cast steel, finely polished; complete with handle.
Weight, 1 lb. 2 oz. No. 0. Price, each......38c
Weight, 2 lbs. No. 2. Price, each.........46c

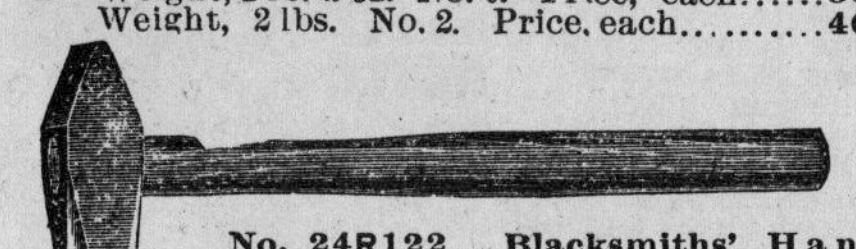

No. 24R122 Blacksmiths' Hand Hammer, extra fine steel; fully warranted; handles not included in weight.

No.	1	2	3	4
Weight........	2 lbs.	2 lbs. 10 ozs.	3 lbs.	3½ lbs.
Price, each...	43c	46c	48c	50c

Blacksmiths' Hand Hammer Handle.

No. 24R130 Blacksmiths' Hand Hammer Handles.
Length, 16-inch
Price, each..........5c
Length 18-inch. Price, each.....................6c

Machinists' Ball Pein Hammers.

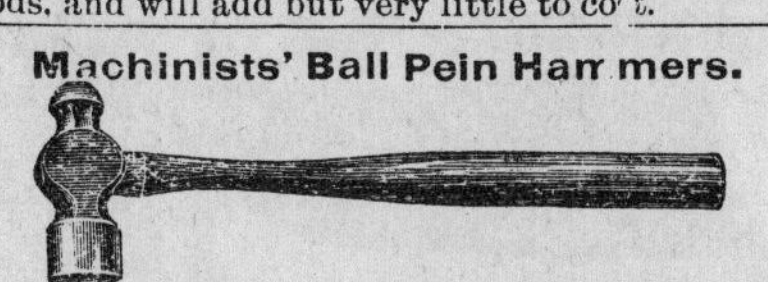

No. 24R132 The S., R. & Co.'s Brand Machinists' Ball Pein Hammers, half polished solid cast steel; hickory handle. Handles not included in weights.

No.......	00	0	1	2	3	4
Weight,	12 oz.	1 lb.	1¼ lbs.	1½ lbs.	1¾ lbs.	2 lbs.
Price, ea.,	37c	38c	39c	43c	45c	50c

Machinists' Hammer Handles.

No. 24R135 Machinists' Hammer Handles.
Length, 16-inch.
Price, each...... 6c
Length, 18-inch. Price, each.........................7c

Engineers' Ball Pein Hammers.

No. 24R139 The S., R. & Co.'s Brand Engineers' Hammer. Made with an extra heavy eye. The great fault with all engineers' or machinists' hammers is the breaking or splitting at the eye. We have here a hammer that we can warrant not to split and to be the finest balanced hammer made—just the thing where heavy work is to be done. Made of the finest English steel—comes full polished. Weight does not include handles.

No........	0	1	2	3	4
Weight.........	1 lb.	1¼ lb.	1½ lb.	1¾ lb.	2 lb.
Price, each..	47c	49c	52c	57c	60c

Heller Bros' Carriage Makers' Hammer.

No. 24R142 Genuine Heller Bros' Carriage Makers' Hammer. Made of the highest grade tool steel, tempered by a special process known only to the makers of Heller Bros.' goods. Nothing better made. Every hammer fully warranted. Weight (including handle), No. 9, 2¼ lbs. Price, each, 70c; No. 10, 2½ lbs. Price, each..........72c

Farriers' Hammers

No. 24R148 Farriers' Hammer; weight (not including handle), 10 oz., adze eye, cast steel, round pole, polished.
Price, each.....33c

Adze Eye Farriers' Hammer. Cincinnati Pattern.

No. 24R150 Solid Cast Steel Farriers' Hammer, full polished; guaranteed to be the best hammer sold by any one at the price. Weight, 14 to 18 oz. Handle not included in weight. Price, each..............................37c

Horseshoers' Driving Hammers.

No. 24R153 The Genuine Heller Bros.' Farriers' Hammers. Made of finest quality tool steel. Every hammer warranted. Weight, 11 to 20 oz. Each, 55c

Farriers' Driving Hammers.

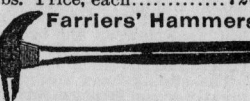

No. 24R156 The Genuine Heller Bros.—Heller Pattern Farriers' Hammer. Made of the best quality tool steel. Every hammer warranted. Weight, 13 to 20 oz. Handle not included in weight.
Price, each..65c

Scotch Farriers' Hammers.

No. 24R158, Round Face Farriers' Hammer. Made of solid steel. This hammer is acknowledged by all to be the best tool of its kind on the market. The rounding claw will draw a nail very easy and will do so without bending the same. Something you cannot do with any other make. Price, each.......................54c

Weight, 12 to 20 oz.

Blacksmiths' Ball Pein Hammers.

No. 24R160 The Genuine Heller Bros.' Ball Pein Hammers. Nothing better made. Every hammer fully warranted. Handle not included in weight.

Weight,	¾-lb.	1-lb.	1¼-lb.	1½-lb.
Price, each,	50c	52c	55c	58c

Blacksmiths' Fitting Hammers.

No. 24R162 Genuine Heller Bros.' Horseshoers' Fitting Hammers. Made of the best quality tool steel, finely finished. Every hammer warranted. Weight does not include handle. Weight, 2 to 3 pounds. Price, each.............$1.05

Horseshoers' Turning Hammers.

No. 24R165 Genuine Heller Bros.' Horseshoers' Turning or Cat's Head Hammer. Made of the best quality tool steel. Weight does not include handle.
Price, each.......................................$1.34
Weight, 2 to 3 pounds.

Electric Sharpening Hammers.

No. 24R168 Our Electric Horseshoers' Hammer has no equal for sharpening shoe. Pein is corrugated for drawing out the calks. Made of the best quality English steel; fully warranted. Price, each.................................$1.20

Weight, 2 to 3 pounds.

Heller Bros.' Rounding Hammers.

No. 24R171 Genuine Heller Bros.' Rounding Hammer. Made of the finest quality tool steel. Every hammer warranted. Weight does not include handle. Weight, 2 to 3 pounds. Price, each...........................$1.35

Cast Steel Blacksmiths' Sledges.

No. 24R174 Solid Cast Steel Blacksmiths' Sledges, without handles.

Size, lbs.	8	9	10	11	12	13	14	15	16	17
Each,	$0.48	.54	.60	.66	.72	.78	.84	.90	.96	1.02

No. 24R176 Handles for above, 36 inches long, shaved hickory.
Price, each.............................11½c

Horseshoers' Turning Sledges.

No. 24R177 Horseshoers' Turning Sledges. Made of the best cast steel, one solid piece, oil finished with polished faces. Weight, from 6 to 12 pounds. Price, per pound..8½c

Farriers' Pincers.

No. 24R178 Blacksmiths' Pincers, solid hammered cast steel, polished jaws. Length, 14 inches. Weight, 2 lbs. 10 oz. **Not for cutting nails.** Each...46c

High Grade Farriers' Pincers.

No. 24R180 Maud S High Grade Farriers' Pincers, made of the best tool steel, full polished. Something better than generally carried by the hardware trade.
Size, 14 inches. Weight, 2 lbs. 10 oz. Each....$1.05
Size, 16 inches. Weight, 3 lbs. Each. 1.32

Heller Bros'. Farriers' Pincers.

No. 24R181 Genuine Heller Bros. Farriers' Pincers. Finest tools on the market; nothing better made.
Size, 14 inches. Weight, 2½ lbs. Price, each..$1.35
Size, 16 inches. Weight, 3 lbs. Price, each.. 1.65

The Coolidge Wrench.

No. 24R353 A Patent Adjustable Bit Brace Wrench. Indispensable to every blacksmith, the necessity of every mechanic, meets the needs of every carpenter. The user of farming tools and wagons has long looked for it. Its operation is simplicity. A press of the thumb lug opens the jaws. It fits any bit brace, and handles all nuts and lag screws to 1 inch square. It will carry a nut without dropping it. It lets go by simply pulling away. It brings away the nut that has been unscrewed, and drops it by a press on the thumb lug. Weight, 1¼ pounds. Price, each............67c

Drop Forged Tire Measuring Wheel.

No. 24R355 This wheel is a drop forging, lathe turned, a perfect running wheel, firstclass. Weight, 1 pound. Price, each.........95c

Graduated Tire Measuring Wheel.

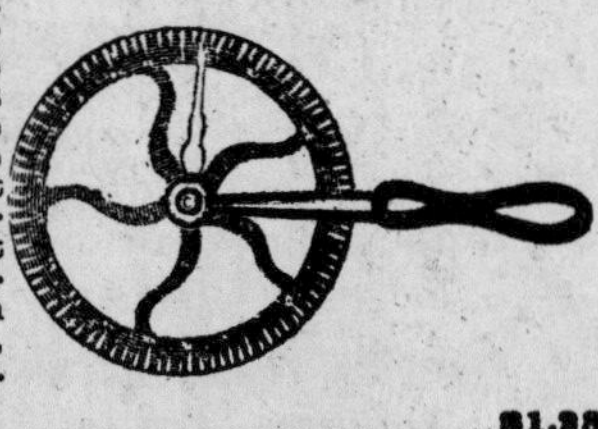

No. 24R356 Is a drop forging made so that the figures and lines are raised above the surface of the wheel and cannot be filled or defaced with rust or dirt. It is exactly 24 inches in circumference, with index hand. Weight, 1⅛ lbs. Price, each............$1.28

American Repair Machine.

No. 24R357 American Repair Machine, six tools in one, for farmers and mechanics, a mechanical wonder. It consists of **vise, drill, anvil, cut-off or hardie, pipe clamp and drill bit. Six tools** complete. The drill rod passes through the center of the screw, making a complete drill press. The ordinary square shank drill bits will fit this machine. No bits furnished at the following price. Weight, 30 pounds. Price, each............$2.85

The Gipsy Combination Anvil, Vise and Drilling Machine.

No. 24R359 The Gipsy combines four different tools: Anvil, straight vise, pipe vise, and drill press. Weighs complete, 45 lbs. It is put up for service and with proper **care will last a lifetime.** The anvil is 7 inches high, face is 8x3 inches; vise jaw 5½ inches wide and opens out 8 inches; length over all, 15 inches. The drill spindle is made for square shank drills. The spindle can be slipped out of its bearings and laid by when not using the drill. Price, each............$4.65

Hercules Combination Anvil and Vise.

In our Hercules Combination Anvil, Vise, Drill, etc., we have the only practical tool on the market. All the so called combinations are only toys and do not stand the wear and tear a tool of this kind is subjected to. This machine weighs 75 pounds. The drill has machine cut screw and takes any size square shank drill bits. The anvil is about 4 inches by 7½ inches with hardened face. Hardie is all steel and of good size. In the pipe vise which is under the anvil we have the only tool of its kind that will hold all sizes of pipe without crushing or becoming loose. The main frame is made of a steel bar which gives great strength as well as lightness. This part of the machine, by the way, is the weak part of all combination vises.

Having sold hundreds of combination vises, we are in a position to know the weak points in a machine of this kind and can say without fear of contradiction that this is the only **first class** combination vise on the market.

It is not a cheap machine, **as a tool of this weight (75 pounds) and construction cannot be manufactured as cheaply as the regular all cast iron vise.**

No ranchman, plumber or blacksmith should be without one.

Remember, this is the only practical combination tool sold by any one.

No. 24R360 Price, each............$9.50

Bench Vise.

Parallel Bench Vises for light work in metal or wood. "The Farmers' Vise."

No. 24R361 2¼-inch jaws; weight, 7½ pounds. Price, each........$0.90
No. 24R362 3-inch jaws; weight, 17½ pounds. Price, each........1.35
No. 24R363 4-inch jaws; weight, 38½ pounds. Price, each........2.30

Anvil and Vise.

The jaw is adjustable. By removing a pin, the inner jaw can be swung around so as to hold wedge or regular shape The anvil has a chilled, hardened and polished surface. This is the best anvil and vise of its kind.

No. 24R365 3½-in. jaw, 25 lbs. Price, each, $3.30
No. 24R366 4-in. jaw, 35 lbs. Price, each, 4.00
No. 24R367 4½-in. jaw, 40 lbs. Price, each, 4.80

No. 24R370 Anvil and Vise combined, with jaws for holding pipes. Has chilled face and jaws. Jaws are 3 inches wide; open 5 inches. Weight, 26 pounds. Price, each............96c

Sargent's Bench Vise.

The Sargent Bench Vise is one of the best known vises on the market and is not to be compared with common vises sold by other houses at cut prices. They are made of the best material, nicely finished, and guaranteed to be the best vise sold at the price or money refunded.

	Width of jaw	Open	Weight	Price ea.
No. 24R376	3⅛ in.	3½ in.	22½ lbs.	$ 3.15
No. 24R377	3⅝ in.	3½ in.	34 lbs.	4.00
No. 24R378	4⅛ in.	4½ in.	43 lbs.	4.40
No. 24R379	4⅝ in.	5½ in.	60 lbs.	5.75
No. 24R380	5⅝ in.	6 in.	80 lbs.	7.45

Seroco Rapid Transit Machinists' Vise.

We have at last discovered a Rapid Acting Vise which we are sure will meet with greater success than any vise on the market. Heretofore all so-called quick adjusting vises were worked with a lever that became loose in a very short time and it was impossible to secure a good grip on your work. In the **Seroco** we have corrected the mistake of other manufactures. This vise may be opened to its full extent or closed instantly and will always grip the work firmly. The double sliding bars leave a clear opening between the center of the jaws thus permitting long work to be placed between the center of the jaws insuring a firm and solid grip. **No other machinists' vise embraces** this simple and very important feature.

The sliding bars are made of steel which **adds** greatly to the strength and durability over cast bars as used on other makes. We claim for this vise: **Rapidity, durability, simplicity and strength.**

	Width of Jaw	Jaws Open	Weight	Price
No. 24R385	3 inches	4 inches	14 pounds	$ 3.45
No. 24R386	3½ inches	4½ inches	19 pounds	4.10
No. 24R387	4 inches	5 inches	28 pounds	5.00
No. 24R388	4½ inches	5½ inches	38 pounds	6.30
No. 24R389	5 inches	6½ inches	50 pounds	7.50
No. 24R390	6 inches	7½ inches	65 pounds	12.90

Machinists' Swivel Bottom Vise.

Same style and quality as No. 24R385, only with swivel base.

	Width of Jaw	Jaws Open	Weight	Price
No. 24R391	3 inches	4 inches	18 pounds	$4.40
No. 24R392	3½ inches	4½ inches	26 pounds	5.00
No. 24R393	4 inches	5 inches	38 pounds	6.00
No. 24R394	4½ inches	5½ inches	47 pounds	7.50
No. 24R395	5 inches	6½ inches	65 pounds	8.75
No. 24R396	6 inches	7½ inches	78 pounds	14.45

Parker's Bench Vise.

The Parker Vises are equal in strength to any bench vise on the market, and the steel faces are milled and fitted to the jaws, and can be renewed at a trifling cost.

No. 24R405 Length of jaws, 3¼ inches; weight, 23 pounds. Price, each............$3.90
No. 24R407 Length of jaws, 4⅛ inches weight, 41½ pounds. Price, each $6.20

Parker's Swivel Vise.

No. 24R410 Length of jaws, 2¼ inches; weight, 8½ pounds. Price, each......$2.60
No. 24R411 Length of jaws, 3¼ inches; weight 23 pounds. Price, each......$4.10

Parker's Patent Victor Vises.

This Vise has self adjusting back jaws, which automatically adapt themselves for holding wedge shaped pieces. The steel faces of these vises are milled and fitted to the jaws, and can be renewed at a trifling cost.

	Length of jaws	Weight	Price
No. 24R413	3¼ inches	25 lbs.	$5.10
No. 24R414	3⅝ inches	39 lbs.	5.50

Parker's Patent Swivel Victor Vises.

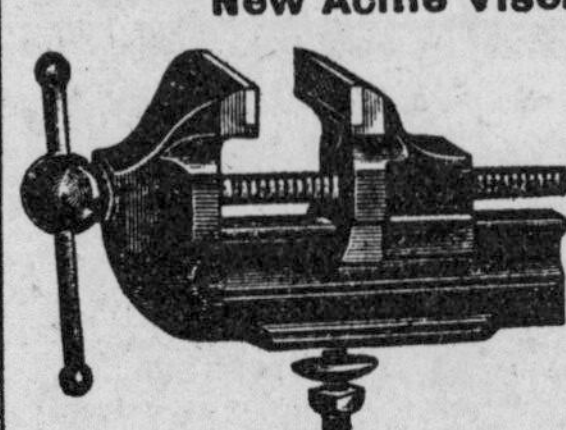

This Vise has swivel back jaw and swivel bottom.

No. 24R415 Length of jaws, 3¼ inches; weight, 30 pounds. Price, each..$5.60
No. 24R416 Length of jaws, 3⅝ inches; weight, 42 pounds. Price, each......$6.30

New Acme Vise.

To supply the growing demand for a strong, cheap, handy vise for common uses, we have added to our list the above implement, which we think is in every way suitable for the purpose. It is made of good material, with steel screw and welded steel jaws milled and cut, is strong, convenient, of ample weight and cheap. Head of swivel screw moves in groove running whole length of bottom plate, allowing operator to move vise out, in, or to any desired angle and fasten in position. The nut is made by a long, full thread cut in solid metal of back jaw. These vises are handsomely painted and polished, and are finished equal to any first class vise in the market.

No. 24R417 Jaws, 2¼ inches wide. Opens, 3 inches. Weight 8, pounds. Price............$1.20
No. 24R418 Jaws, 3¼ inches wide. Opens, 4 inches. Weight, 14 pounds. Price............$1.75
No. 24R419 Jaws, 4 inches wide. Opens, 6 inches. Weight, 28 pounds. Price............$2.75

New Shepard Vises.

The Shepard Vise is by far the best vise on the market for the money we ask for it. It has all the latest improvements, is strong and durable, nicely finished and for all ordinary work will answer the purpose of a high priced tool. This vise has steel sliding bars, screws, levers and jaws. The anvil is full polished.

	Width Jaw	Opens	Weight	Price, each
No. 24R422	2 in.	2 in.	2½ lbs.	$0.85
No. 24R423	2 in.	2 in.	4 lbs.	.95
No. 24R424	2½ in.	3 in.	11 lbs.	1.30
No. 24R425	3½ in.	4 in.	16 lbs.	1.75
No. 24R426	4 in.	6 in.	30 lbs.	2.60

GIVE CATALOGUE NUMBER IN FULL WHEN YOU WRITE YOUR ORDER

Acme Round Adjustable Split Die Screw Plates.

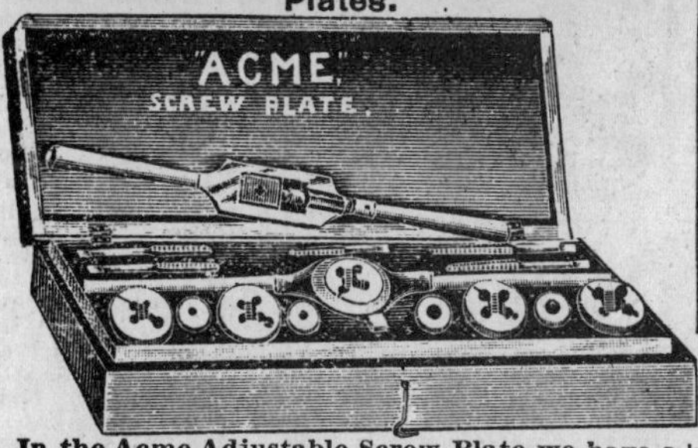

In the Acme Adjustable Screw Plate we have a plate that is second to none. It is a brand new plate made for our 1902 trade. We have taken the dozen or more plates now on the market and by using only the strong points of each have manufactured a plate which we think is by far the best shown by anyone. They are made of the very highest grade of steel fully guaranteed in every respect and more easily adjusted to sizes than any other plate made. They are furnished complete with adjustable top wrench put up in a strong hardwood case. The sizes given below are exact. Can furnish dies and taps 1/64-inch over size if so specified in your order.

No. 24R705 No. H Screw Plate, 14 inches long, 5 dies, 1½ inches in diameter, 5 guides and 5 taps with adjustable tap wrench, cutting ¼-inch, 20 threads; 5/16-inch, 18 threads; ⅜-inch, 16 threads; 7/16-inch, 14 threads; ½-inch, 12 threads. Per set..$6.45

No. 24R707 No. I-13 Screw Plate, 23 inches long, 7 dies 2 inches in diameter, 7 guides and 7 taps with adjustable tap wrench, cutting ¼-inch, 20 threads; 5/16-inch, 18 threads; ⅜-inch, 16 threads; 7/16-inch, 14 threads; ½-inch, 12 threads; ⅝-inch, 11 threads; ¾-inch, 10 threads. Price, per set..................$7.55

No. 24R710 No. J16 Screw Plate, 29 inches long, 9 dies 2¼ inches in diameter, 9 guides and 9 taps with adjustable tap wrench, cutting ¼-inch, 20 threads; 5/16-inch, 18 threads; ⅜-inch, 16 threads; 7/16-inch, 14 threads; ½-inch, 12 threads; ⅝-inch, 11 threads; ¾-inch, 10 threads; ⅞-inch, 9 threads, and 1-inch, 8 threads. Price, per set..............$14.00

No. 24R712 No. J18 Screw Plate, 29 inches long, 5 dies, 2¼ inches in diameter, 5 guides and 5 taps with adjustable tap wrench, cutting ½-inch, 12 threads; ⅝-inch, 11 thread; ¾-inch, 10 threads; ⅞-inch, 9 threads; 1-inch, 8 threads. Price, per set, $9.85

Lightning Screw Plates.

SET WITH 5 SIZES.
WITH TAP WRENCH.
1/8 5/32 3/16 7/32 1/4
ASSORTMENT O. STOCK 6 IN. LONG.

No.24R720 Lightning Screw Plate and Stock. Tap wrench and five size taps and guide, ⅛, 5/32, 3/16, 7/32, and ¼-inch. Stock, 6 inches long. V shaped thread sent unless otherwise ordered.

Price, complete, in wood case..........$3.70

Green River Screw Plates.

The Green River Screw Plate being one of the oldest and best known makes on the market it is hardly necessary for us to state that the quality both as to material and workmanship is up to the highest standard, **and its simplicity and durability with its modern price make it one of the best screw plates on the market.** It does the work at a single cut, **and is warranted not to strip the threads.** The dies are adjustable for wear, and to make bolts or nuts fit tightly or loosely as desired. **For close cutting up to a shoulder use the face side of die after starting the thread with the other side.**

No. 24R725 No. 1½, cuts from ¼ to ¾ inch; stock 22 inches long. 7 sizes; ¼, 5/16, ⅜, 7/16, ½, ⅝, ¾ inch taps; dies and guides complete in case.

Per set..................................$8.50

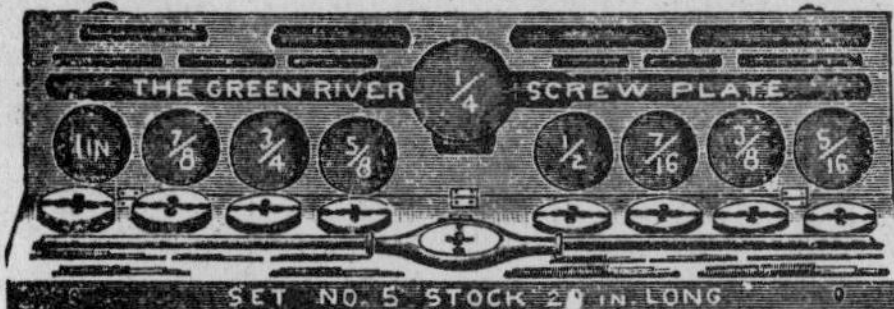

No. 24R727 The Green River Screw Plate, set No. 5, cuts from ¼ to 1 inch; stock 29 inches in length, 9 sizes; ¼, 5/16, ⅜, 7/16, ½, ⅝, ¾, ⅞ and 1-inch taps, dies and guides complete in case. Weight, 18 lbs.

Per set...................................$15.50

Other numbers of Green River Screw Plates quoted on request.

Lightning Screw Plates.

No. 24R730 This is one of the best screw plates made, has adjustable dies which can be taken up when worn. Cuts a fine thread at one cut. Is finely finished and fully warranted. Ask any machinist or blacksmith and they will tell you the **Lightning leads them all.** Sent 1/64 over size V shaped thread, unless otherwise ordered. Size O cuts from ¼ to 1 inch; stock is 29 inches long; cuts ¼, 5/16, ⅜, 7/16, ½, ⅝, ¾, ⅞ and 1 inch. Price, each............$16.85

Full Mounted Lightning Screw Plate.

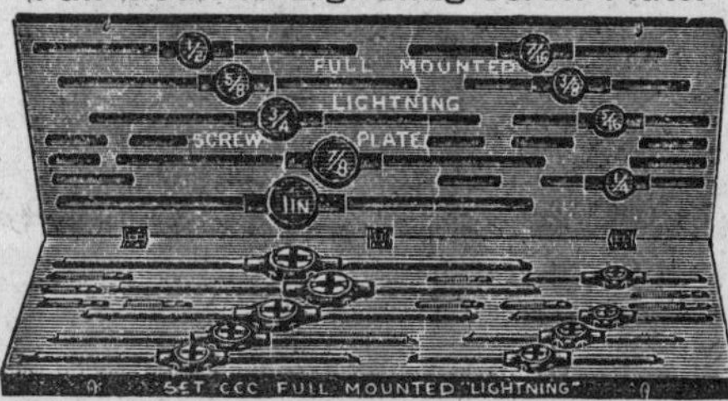

No. 24R732 The New Lightning Full Mounted Screw Plate. Same as our No. 24R730, with a stock for each die, which does away with changing dies every time you wish to cut a different size thread. Size CCC, 9 sizes, ¼, 5/16, ⅜, 7/16, ½, ⅝, ¾, ⅞ and 1-inch; complete with taps and dies of the above sizes, and a stock for each size. Comes put up in hardwood case.

Price, per set.......................................$17.15

Gunsmiths' Screw Plate.

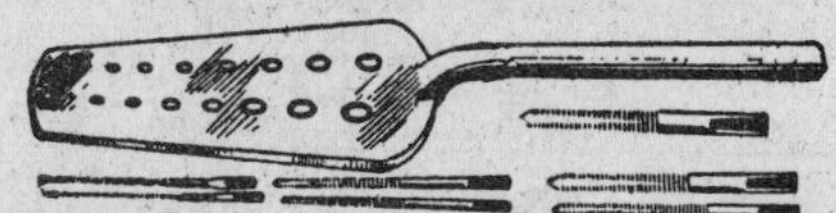

No. 24R739 Screw Plates, iron handles, will cut 14 different sizes from 3/32 to 5/16, intended for gunsmiths', jewelers' or model makers' use. Weight, 10 oz.

Price, each..90c

If by mail, postage extra, 10 cents.

Gunsmiths' Stocks and Dies.

At $1.65 to $2.20 we offer you our special Stocks and Dies in sets for gunsmiths, guaranteeing them the best gunsmith sets on the market. **Our $1.65, $1.85, $2.00 and $2.20** prices are based on actual cost to make with only our one small percentage of profit added.

Solid Steel Gunsmiths' and Jewelers' Screw Plates, nicely finished with separate dies.

No. 24R745 No. 5. Cuts from 2¼-32 to 5/32, 4 taps and 4 pair dies. Price......................................$1.65

No. 24R746 No. 6. Cuts from 3/32 to 5/32, 4 taps and 4 pair dies. Price......................................$1.85

No. 24R747 No. 7. Cuts from 3/32 to 7/32, 6 taps and 6 pair dies. Price......................................$2.00

No. 24R748 No. 8. Cuts from 5/32 to 12/32, 6 taps and 6 pair dies. Price......................................$2.20

Stoddard Tire Shrinker.

The Genuine Stoddard Tire Shrinker. This is one of the best known shrinkers on the market, and only the best materials are used in its construction. The clamp head, as shown in cut, prevents light tire from kinking—**a very serious drawback to most shrinkers.**

Made in two sizes only.

No. 24R755 No. 1 shrinks up to 2-inch tire. Weight, 100 lbs. Price, each........$5.00

No. 24R756 No. 2 shrinks up to 4-inch tire. Weight, 230 lbs. Price, each, $8.75

No. 24R757 No. 3 shrinks up to 4-inch tire, and has extra jaws for setting axle up to 1¾-inch. Weight, 110 lbs. Price, each..................$12.35

Little Giant Tire Upsetter.

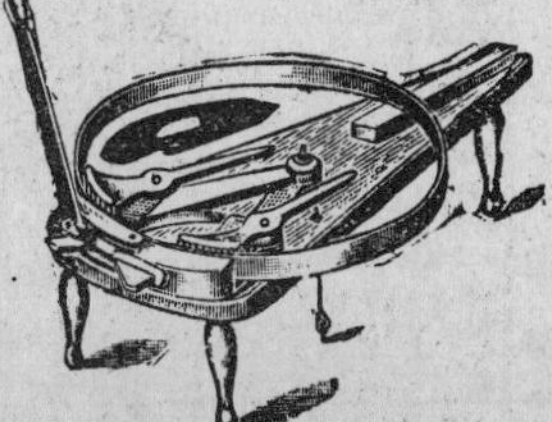

No. 24R762 No. 1 Little Giant will upset any size or diameter of tire, from the light buggy to the heavy tire, ½-inch thick to 2 inches wide. Weight, 100 lbs.

Price........$7.50

Little Giant Tire Upsetter, No. 2.

No. 24R764 No. 2 is heavier than No. 1, and lies on the floor; both jaws move. Will upset any tire, from a light buggy tire to a truck 4 inches wide, or bars of square or round iron up to 1¼ inches in diameter. Weight, 160 lbs. Price, each...................................$11.00

Mole Tire Shrinkers.

The operation of bringing down the lever grasps the tire and does the work; raising the lever opens it. By this means **it is not necessary to remove the tire** until it is upset as much as required. Can be successfully operated by one man. Sizes 2 and 3 furnished with anti-kink; size 1 without.

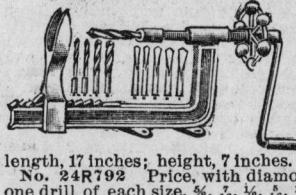

No. 24R770 Mole Tire Shrinker, size 1. Bed is 2¼ inches; weight, 120 lbs. Is adapted to general custom work. Price, each......$4.60

No. 24R773 Mole Tire Shrinker, size 2. Bed is 3 inches; weight, 195 lbs. Will do all but the heaviest work. Price, each..............................$5.70

No. 24R778 Mole Tire Shrinker, size 3. Bed is 4 inches; weight, 275 lbs. Will shrink all sizes, including heavy wagon and truck tires. Price, each, $6.90

Geared Tire Benders.

Geared Tire Benders, with rollers on steel shafts; made with iron base. A first class bender for little a money.

No. 24R784 Size No. 2, will bend tires up to and including 3½-inch tire. Price, each $3.75

No. 24R786 Size No. 2½, will bend tires up to and including 6-inch tire.

Price, each...$4.65

The Cincinnati Tire Bender.

No. 24R790 The Cincinnati Tire Bender, with rollers on steel shafts, is by far the best bender on the market. The double gearing makes it easy to operate; bends a perfect circle every time. Has patent adjustments for different thickness of tire. Length over all, 24 inches; diameter of rolls, 2¼ inches; length of rolls, 5 inches. Bends any size tire up to and including 5-inch. Price, each..........$5.90

Combination clamp and drill; the lowest priced good article of its kind on the market; has wrought iron screw feed, malleable frame, brass chuck, sliding clamps, weighs 6½ lbs. length, 17 inches; height, 7 inches.

No. 24R792 Price, with diamond pointed drills, one drill of each size, ⅝, 7/16, ½, 5/16, ⅛. Each....$1.70

No. 24R793 With Syracuse Twist Drills, furnished with one drill of the following sizes: ½, ⅜, 5/16, ¼, 3/16. Price, each.............................$2.30

No. 24R794 Extra drills for 24R792, per set..35c

No. 24R795 Extra drills for 24R793, per set..98c

Blacksmiths' Drills.

No. 24R800 The Old Standard Blacksmiths' Drill. Length, 29 inches; screw feed. **The hole in mandrel is square to hold drill points which the blacksmith must make.** We can not furnish drills to fit this machine. Weight, 29 lbs. Ea. $1.25

Bench Drill.

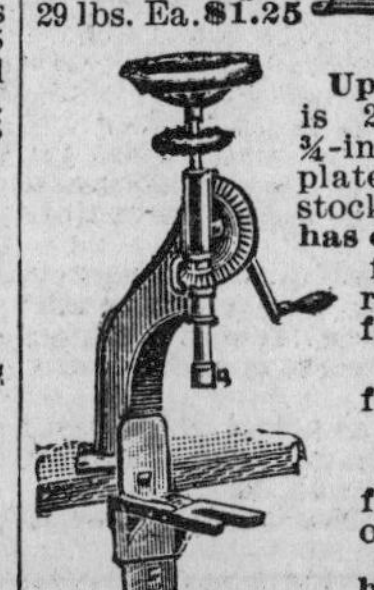

Upright Bench Drill. This drill is 26½ inches high, drills ⅛ to ¾-inch hole. Squares with bed plate; run of screw, 3½ inches; drill stock, 13/32 inch in diameter, **crank has extension for large drilling; is** fitted with chuck for square or round shank drills; has no self-feed attachment. Weight, 35 lbs.

No. 24R802 New Model Drill, for square shank drills only.

Special price, each........$4.00

No. 24R804 New Model Drill, for ½-inch round shank drills only. Special price, each..$4.00

Price does not include drill bits. **See Index for drill bits.**

The Universal Tool Grinder.

No. 24R955 This machine is adapted to do all kinds of grinding. It will do it with great rapidity and much better than the old time grindstone. You can grind anything on this machine from a razor to a plow point. It consists of the best make of vitrified emery wheel and can be used with or without water. It has a heavy frame and gearing and can easily attain a speed of 1500 revolutions a minute. It can be quickly adjusted to a bench and gives perfect satisfaction in every respect. The diameter of the wheel is 5 inches with a face of 1¼ inches. Price, each, **$2.15**

No. 24R956 Extra Stones for above Tool Grinder. In ordering state kind of work stone is wanted for. Size, 5x1¼x¾ inches.
Price, each....................................55c

Foot-Power Emery Wheel Grinding Machine.

Here is what every Blacksmith, Carpenter, Gunsmith, Marble or Granite Worker should have. It will pay for itself in one month in any shop. Always ready; can be moved about, as it is not fastened to the floor; occupies only 15x20 inches floor space; height 3½ feet. Will carry a wheel 4 to 10 inches in diameter. Diameter of mandrel, ¾-inch, downward thrust of pedals, 14 inches. It is made of the best material throughout, is light and durable, has been on the market for a number of years and has given universal satisfaction. In a blacksmith or gunsmith shop it will pay for itself in files alone in a very short time. Speed, 2000 revolutions per minute. Weight, 90 pounds. Comes complete with ¾x8-inch flat face emery wheel.

No. 24R960 Price, each....................**$10.25**
No. 24R961 Price, each, with buffing spindle....................**11.90**

Anvils.

No. 24R975 Cast Iron Anvils, with steel face. The face of this anvil is one solid piece of English tool steel, thoroughly welded to the body of the anvil by a patent process. The horn is covered with, and its extremity made entirely of cast steel. The face and horn are then accurately ground and tempered. We do not guarantee this anvil, but it will give satisfaction for light work.

No.	2	3	4	5
Weight, lbs.	20	30	40	50
Price	$2.15	$2.40	$2.75	$3.00
No.	6	7	8	9
Weight, lbs.	60	70	80	90
Price	$3.45	$3.65	$4.20	$4.70

Peter Wright's Anvils.

Wrought Iron with Steel Face.

No. 24R981 This well known anvil has stood the test for years, and is today the most popular anvil in the world. It is cheap enough for anybody and good enough for anyone. Don't buy an anvil too light for your work. A light anvil when struck a hard blow with a heavy hammer is sure to jump. **We carry a large stock,** but occasionally are not able to send exact weight ordered, but can always come within 5 pounds of the weight ordered. This anvil is sold by the pound, and price per pound varies with the size.

85 pounds to 500 pounds, per pound............9½c
71 pounds to 84 pounds, per pound............10½c
61 pounds to 70 pounds, per pound............11½c
51 pounds to 60 pounds, per pound............12 c
50 pounds and lighter, per pound............13 c

Peter Wright's Farriers' Anvil.

No. 24R982 Made of the best wrought iron with steel face, from ½-inch to ⅝-inch thick. When turning or fitting shoes, the entire length of horn is obtained by its being full width of the body at end of steel face. It has a suitable side horn for drawing toe clips, etc., and a thin steel heel for working small size shoes. Weight, 140 to 150 pounds.
Price, per pound....................12c

Pine Tar.

Carefully prepared from North Carolina pine. No horseshoer should be without it. Is cooling and healing and can be applied with oakum for diseased feet with excellent results.

No. 24R984

Gallon cans	½	1	2	3
Price, per can	26c	47c	80c	$1.10

LePage's Liquid Glue.

No. 24R985 LePage's Glue. Always ready for use.
Size, ⅛ gill. Price, each..........12c
Size, 1 gill. Price, each..........15c
Size, ½ pint. Price, each..........20c
Size, 1 pint. Price, each..........35c
Size, 1 quart Price, each..........60c

American Wrought Anvils.

HAVING SECURED THE EXCLUSIVE SALE of one of the best wrought anvils in the world, we have agreed to take the entire output, and in order to do so, we have reduced the price to where it will enable us to sell more anvils than any firm in the United States.

Only 7¼ Cents Per Pound.

THE TIME HAS PASSED WHEN WE MUST GO TO ENGLAND FOR OUR BEST ANVILS.

Having sold both the American and English anvils for a number of years, shipping them to every part of the United States, having been used by all kinds of mechanics, under all circumstances, we are in a position to know the merits of the different makes. In our American Wrought Anvil we have improved upon all foreign makes in shape, style and finish, until we now show the **finest high grade anvil** produced by anyone.

The body is made of the best quality wrought iron, with an extra heavy steel face welded to the body by an electric process, which makes it practically a solid steel anvil.

THE FACE is tempered by a special process, known only to the makers of this anvil, which warrants it against flaws, chipping, or being too soft. This, by the way, is the most difficult obstacle to overcome in anvil making. Hundreds of anvils, made of good material, are made useless by poor tempering, being either too hard or too soft.

THE FACE IS TRUED AND SHAPED BY A SPECIAL MACHINE so that every anvil is mechanically perfect; no hollow or uneven places. The horn is extra long with the Peter Wright shape, pattern and curve, nicely rounded. The hole for the **hardie is made true and straight,** so you experience no trouble by hardie or flatter sticking or not setting level. While these points seem small, the defects of nine-tenths of all anvils, both foreign and American make, now being sold, rest in the fact that these points are not looked after. **We cannot always furnish even weights; please allow five pounds either way.**

NOTICE—Never leave a hot piece of iron for any length of time on the face of an anvil, as this will surely draw the temper and thus make it soft. A great many anvils are ruined in this way.

No. 24R988 Weight, 80 pounds and up, per pound....................7¼c
Weight, 70 pounds to 80 pounds, per pound....................8¼c
Weight, 60 pounds to 70 pounds, per pound....................9¼c
Weight, 50 pounds to 59 pounds, per pound....................10¼c

DO YOUR OWN HORSESHOEING.

SAVE HORSESHOERS' BILLS, time and annoyance by owning one of our Horseshoers' Outfits. It takes very little experience to learn how to set and fit a horseshoe, and the time saved in going to town, or to a distant blacksmith shop and perhaps waiting three or four hours before being attended to, will pay for a set in one season's work. Nine times out of ten, when a shoe becomes loose or your horse needs to be shod, you are in the midst of harvesting or thrashing, when an hour lost means more than the price of an outfit. A stitch in time saves nine, and a nail in a shoe when it first shows signs of becoming loose will save the cost and time of resetting same.

ALL TOOLS AND MATERIAL in the following outfits are guaranteed to be exactly as represented or money refunded. They are all taken out of our regular stock, and not cheap sets made up for competition.

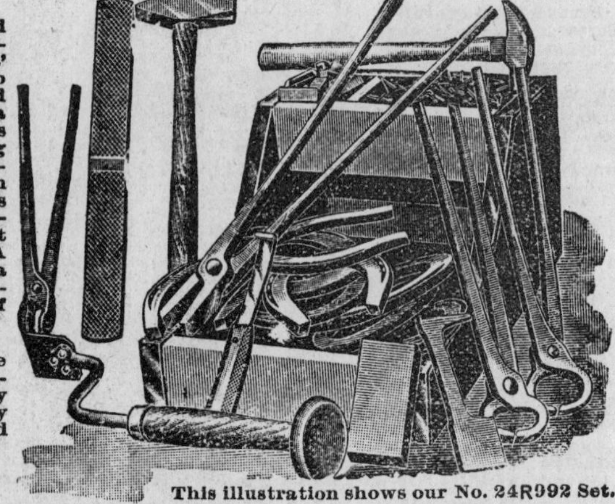

This illustration shows our No. 24R992 Set.

No. 24R990 HORSESHOERS' OUTFIT No. 1 FOR $2.65.

One Pair V. & B.'s Best Make Flat Lip Blacksmiths' Tongs. 20 inches long.
One S., R. & Co.'s Double Face Horse Rasp. 12 inches long. Nothing better made.
One Adze-Eye Farriers' Hammer. S., R. & Co.'s brand, full polished, best quality hickory handle. Weight, not including handle, 10 ounces.
One Celebrated Wostenholm IXL Farriers' Knife. Every knife fully warranted.
One Cast Steel Buffer.
One Pair of Farriers' Pincers. V. & B. make, solid hammered cast steel, polished jaws. Length, 14 inches.
One Pair Cutting Nippers. For cutting heads from horse nails, etc., made of best quality tool steel. Length, 14 inches.
Two Pounds Best Quality Horse Nails. Sizes, 7 and 8.
One Pound Toe Calks. Assorted sizes.

No. 24R990 Price, Complete Set....................$2.65

No. 24R992 HORSESHOERS' OUTFIT No. 2 FOR $4.75.

One Pair V. & B. Flat Lip Blacksmiths' Tongs. Drop forged from one solid piece, no welds. Weight, 2¼ pounds. Length, 20 inches.
One Pair V. & B. Solid Steel Horseshoers' Round Lip Tongs. Drop forged, nicely finished. Weight, 1 pound 5 ounces. Length, 12 inches.
One S., R. & Co.'s Brand Farriers' Hammer. *Adze Eye.* Round pole, full polished. Nothing better made. Weight (not including handle), 10 ounces.
One S., R. & Co.'s Brand Blacksmiths' Hand Hammer. Extra fine grade, fully warranted. Weight (hammer only without handle), 2 pounds 10 ounces.
One Pair V. & B. Farriers' Pincers. Solid hammered cast steel, polished jaws. Weight, 2 pounds 10 ounces. Length, 14 inches.
One pair V. & B. Cutting Nippers for cutting horse nails, etc., also for trimming horse's hoof. Made of solid steel, polished jaws. Length, 14 inches.
One V. & B. Horseshoers' Buffer for cutting off or driving out nails after having been driven in hoof. Made of solid tool steel.
One Keystone Farriers' Knife. Blade can be taken out and changed in case of a breakage. Far ahead of the old style knife.
One S., R. & Co.'s Double Face Horse Rasp. Nothing better sold by anyone. Length, 14 inches.
One Sargent's Buttress. Made of best grade cast steel, nicely finished.
One Clinch Block. A piece of cast steel used in clinching horse nails.
Three Sets Horseshoes. Best grade, any size, No. 2 to 6.
Two Pounds Ausable Horse Nails. Assorted 6, 7 and 8.
Three Pounds Toe Calks. Assorted sizes.
One Nail and Tool Box. Made of well seasoned whitewood.

No. 24R992 Price, Complete Set....................$4.75

OUR $14.25 OUTFIT OF BLACKSMITHS' TOOLS.

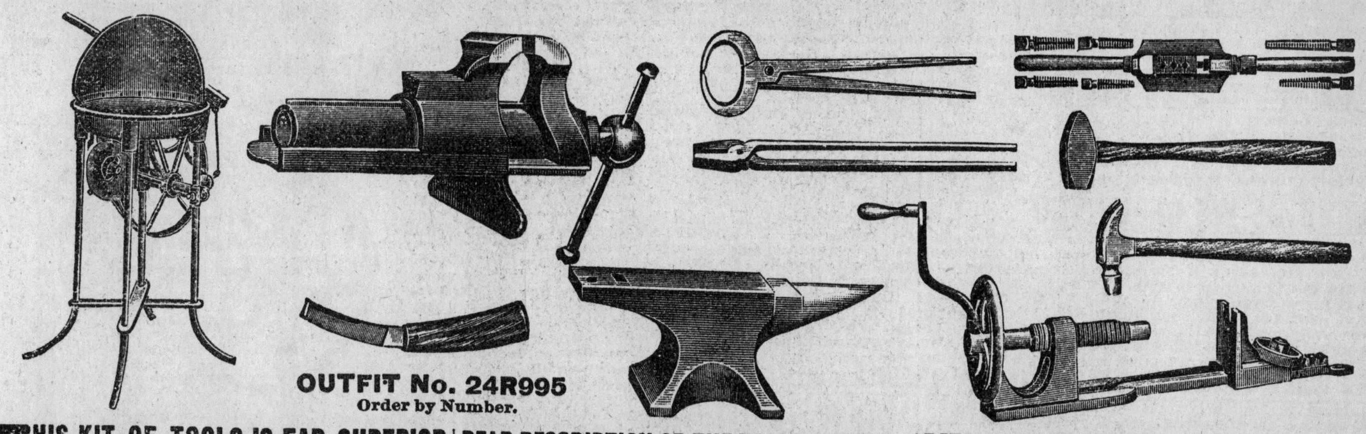

OUTFIT No. 24R995
Order by Number.

THIS KIT OF TOOLS IS FAR SUPERIOR TO THOSE USUALLY SOLD, ALL TOOLS being strictly First Quality Standard Tools, such as are used by mechanics. They are not of the class that are MERELY TO SELL. **THE PRICE is $14.25** At this price we deliver the outfit free on board cars at any freight depot in Chicago. You take no chances in sending cash in full with order, for we guarantee every article to be exactly as represented and if not found so the kit may be returned to us and

MONEY WILL BE CHEERFULLY REFUNDED WITHOUT ARGUMENT.

READ DESCRIPTION OF THE TOOLS. THE FORGE is a lever forge, built especially for farmers' use and light repairing. THE HEARTH is 18 inches in diameter. FAN, 6 inches in diameter. THE RATCHET is perfect and cannot get out of order. THE DRILL is a Standard horizontal drill, screw feed, and is furnished with chuck to take drills having square shank. THE ANVIL has a cast base with steel face and horn, same as our No. 24R975 anvils, and can be used the same as a solid wrought iron anvil. We guarantee the face of this anvil not to become detached from body of anvil; weight, 30 pounds. THE VISE is our Parallel Bench or Farmers' Vise; has steel face and screw finely finished. A good serviceable vise. Size, jaws, 3 inches; weight, 17½ pounds. THE STOCK AND DIES cut 5/8 to 3-16 right hand, 14, 18 and 22 threads to the inch, with 6 taps and 3 sets of dies. THE TONGS are dropped forged (no welds), length 20 inches. THE PINCERS are solid hammered cast steel, length, 14 inches. THE FARRIERS' KNIFE is the celebrated Wostenholm make. THE HAND HAMMER weighs 2 pounds (without handle), solid cast steel. THE FARRIERS' HAMMER weighs 10 ounces (without handle). All tools are strictly first class in material and workmanship. YOU WILL SAVE $14.25, the price of this outfit, in your own time and blacksmith bills. Shoe your horses, mend your machinery, your wagons. You can do any ordinary work. WORTH FIVE TIMES THE PRICE every year for keeping all your tools in perfect order.

No. 24R995 OUR PRICE OF $14.25 IS ASTONISHINGLY LOW

THE FARMERS' KIT OF BLACKSMITHS' TOOLS, $25.00.

FOR THE FARMER, STOCKMAN, PLANTER AND MECHANIC.

There have been many cheap kits of blacksmiths' tools sold, but never before has anyone offered a kit of standard, reliable tools. Read the description of each article.

THE FORGE. We furnish a lever forge having hearth 18 inches in diameter. It is furnished with 6-inch fan. The gear is the simplest, strongest and best ever put on a forge. Only a slight movement of the lever produces the strongest blast.

THE DRILL. We furnish a self feed post drill. Will drill to center of a 12-inch circle. Spindle is bored to take in drills having ½-inch round shank. In material and finish this drill is equal to any that is made.

No. 24R997 Our price for complete outfit, as above illustrated . . . **$25.00**

THE ANVIL. We furnish an anvil with steel face, accurately ground and tempered. Weight, 60 pounds. The face of this anvil is one solid piece of English tool steel, thoroughly welded to body of anvil by a patent process. The horn is covered with, and its extremity made entirely of cast steel.

ALL TOOLS furnished with this outfit are strictly first class, and are suitable for any small blacksmith's or farmer's use. You can compare this set with anything else in the market, for there's nothing offered like it.

THE VISE. We furnish a wrought iron solid box and screw blacksmith vise, with steel jaws, weighing 35 pounds.

THE SET OF STOCKS AND DIES. Cuts 5/8 to 3-16-inch right hand, 14, 18 and 22 threads to the inch, with six taps and three sets of dies. The hot cutter and cold cutter are 1⅜-inch cut. The hardie fits anvil. The tongs are 20 inches long. The pincers 14 inches long. The farrier's knife is the celebrated Wostenholm make. The hand hammer weighs 2 pounds without the handle. The farriers' hammer weighs 10 ounces without the handle. The buttress is 2-inch cut. The drills—We furnish 7 drills to fit drill; one each size, ¼, 5/16, ⅜, 7/16, ½, ⅝ and ⅝ inches.

OUR GUARANTEE covers every article in this set and if found defective in material or workmanship, it may be returned to us at our expense, and we will gladly replace it free of charge.

A BOOK ON HORSESHOEING.

A B C Guide to Sensible Horseshoeing.

No. 3R390 By D. Magner. Containing chapters on principles of shoeing, tips and thin shoes, simple method of curing any case, crack or fissure of toe; corns, causes and practical methods of curing; weak heels, their management; interfering, clicking or overreaching; stumbling; how to tell the age accurately; care of the teeth, treatment, etc. Contains colored plates and other illustrations. Size, 5⅜x7½ inches. Cloth.
Retail price, $1.50; our price. . .(If by mail, postage extra, 10c)........65c

The Modern Blacksmith.

Elementary rules for practical blacksmithing, rational horseshoeing and wagon making, with rules, tables and recipes useful to manufacturers, machinists, well drillers, engineers, liverymen, blacksmiths, wagon makers, horseshoers, farmers, amateurs, etc., by J. G. Holmstrom, practical blacksmith.
No. 3R394 Cloth, illustrated. Price........................68c
No. 3R396 Half morocco, illustrated. Price........................98c
If by mail, postage extra, 12 cents.

Special to Blacksmiths, Wagon Makers and Hardware Merchants, Dealers in Blacksmiths' and Wagon Makers' Tools, Materials and Supplies.

WE INVITE EVERY BLACKSMITH and wagon maker and every dealer who deals in their supplies to a careful comparison of our prices, description for description, quality for quality, with the prices they are now paying, with the lowest prices made for the same grade of goods by any jobber or manufacturer. We feel that at our prices we ought to have the trade of every blacksmith and wagon maker, either direct or through his dealer, for we know we can furnish the best goods in this line at lower prices than the dealer or the blacksmith or the wagon maker is now paying.

DEALERS, BLACKSMITHS AND WAGON MAKERS in every state and territory are sending us their orders for everything in this line. We have the trade of many of the most progressive in the best towns and cities in every state, and we feel that our prices should entitle us to the trade of every one. From the blacksmith or wagon maker, carriage or hardware dealer, we ask a trial order to convince you that we can serve you in this line as no other house can.

OUR LEADER FOR $5.95, EVERYTHING IN PORTABLE FORGES

WE BELIEVE WE ARE HEADQUARTERS for everything desirable in portable forges. We have made our contracts with several of the very largest and most reliable manufacturers in the country, concerns who are strictly headquarters for the manufacture of the highest grade portable forges on the market. **There are many cheap, inferior forges offered,** and even some of our competitors may attempt to meet or cut our prices, but when a forge is offered at within 10 or 20 per cent of the price we are able to name, **you can depend upon it you are not getting the same grade of work.**

WE GUARANTEE OUR FORGES to be exactly as represented, and if not found so, you can return them to us and we will cheerfully refund your money. **All our forges are made of the very best material,** are thoroughly well put together, and **guaranteed to give the best of service.** The prices we quote are for the forges carefully packed and delivered on board the cars in Chicago. You pay the freight, **but you will find the freight will amount to next to nothing as compared with what you will save in price.** There is perhaps no more necessary or economic machine on a farm than one of our **strictly high grade portable forges.** In one year it will save its cost ten times over in time, to say nothing of the saving in blacksmiths' bills.

AT $5.95 WE OFFER YOU a strictly high grade, fully guaranteed forge, which you could not duplicate elsewhere, in a wholesale way, at less than $10.00, and a forge that would retail at $12.00 or more. **This forge is especially designed for bridge, boiler and tank builders, miners, prospectors, elevated railroad builders, farmers, etc. We are able to get the price so low, $5.95,** that every farmer in selecting a forge should order this in preference to a cheaper one. The motion is a very simple device. It has a self acting ratchet; no springs or anything to get out of order. **It is made from the very best material.** The lever is connected with a segment of gears which speeds the driving wheel up to a very high speed. It requires a very slight movement of the lever to get the strongest blast. **This forge is supplied with a 9-inch fan, hearth is 21 inches in diameter.** Having but three legs, it stands very firmly on an uneven foundation, and is purposely made for the work we claim. **Height of forge, 30 inches; hearth, 21 inches in diameter; fan, 8 inches; weight, 80 pounds.** This is the largest forge we ever saw offered at anything like the price, and we would ask you to compare the size of hearth and fan with other forges at about the same price, and draw your own conclusions.

WE WANT TO SELL ANOTHER 5,000 OF THESE $5.95 FORGES during the coming year, and with the expectation that we will sell this number, we continue to make our price $5.95. By making our contract on this basis, we were able to get the price down to about the actual cost of material and labor. To this we have added only our one small percentage of profit, and as a result, **in buying a single forge from us at $5.95, you are practically buying on the basis of a contract for 5,000 forges.** This forge is accepted by the railroad companies at second class freight rate, and its weight is 80 pounds. By referring to the freight rates in the front of the book, you can calculate very closely what the freight will be, which you will find will amount to next to nothing, as compared with what you will save in price. **If you buy one of these forges from us at $5.95** you will be getting it for less than the average retail dealer pays for them at wholesale.

No. 24R1008 Price..........$5.95

No. 24R1008

Price $5.95

THE ACME FORGES.—PORTABLE LEVER TYPE.

The line of Acme Forges illustrated below will be found to contain those of suitable capacity for all classes of blacksmith work. A close examination of the several designs will clearly show that each individual machine is particularly adapted to the requirements for which it is recommended. A careful study of all the desirable features of a forge for a given service has been made and the greatest possible number embodied. In the construction of the Acme forges only the best materials and workmanship enter. The greatest accuracy is constantly insisted upon in the erection and assembling of the machines, which results in all parts being brought into the closest relation to each other. The most approved methods of securing them are employed. In consequence there is no gradual rattling loose or becoming wabbly after the machines are used for a time. All these deficiencies common to cheap forges will be found to be entirely avoided.

Attention is requested to the dust proof self-oiling bearings. The equal of these journals is not employed on any other forge on the market, and the use of them renders frequent oiling unnecessary. The hearths, coal boxes and water tanks will all be found of generous dimensions and of most convenient form. The tuyeres are of special design and thoroughly effective.

Remember when you buy a Forge from us, all sizes, weights, etc., will correspond with catalogue description. A great many houses stretch the sizes and weights by measuring the fan over all, and add to weight by weight of crate, etc. **We guarantee weights and sizes to be just as represented or money refunded.**

Our $4.95 Leader Forge.

No. 24R1009 Sears, Roebuck & Co.'s Portable Forge is especially built for farmers' and planters' use or for light repairing. Blacksmiths should buy a larger forge. This lever motion forge has pipe legs. Has 8-inch fan. Stands 30 inches high. Hearth is 18 inches in diameter. Will produce a welding heat on fine iron in five minutes. Compare weight, size of fan, etc., with any other make and you will see this is the cheapest forge for the size sold by any one. Weight, 65 pounds. Price, each.......**$4.95**

No. 24R1010 Lever Forge, same as above with half hood. Price, each..........................**$5.95**

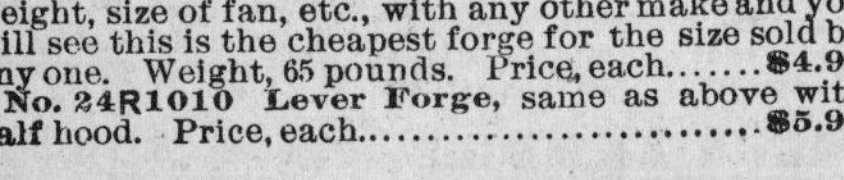

Our Acme No. 352 Forge.

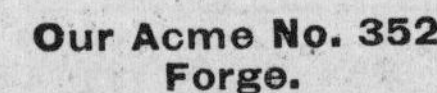

ONLY $11.20 FOR THIS SPLENDID FORGE.

No. 24R1012 This Forge is of the same high grade as our No. 24R1009 but with hood entirely closed. The large sliding door in front and smaller door in rear affords convenience in handling long bars. The escape of sparks, fumes and smoke is effectually prevented and this type of forge is particularly adapted to places where combustible material is lying about or where bright metal work is attacked by fumes from the fire. It is fitted with our patent ring oiling journal, used only on the Acme forges. Hearth, 22 inches; diameter fan, 10 inches; height, 33 inches. Weight, 90 pounds.

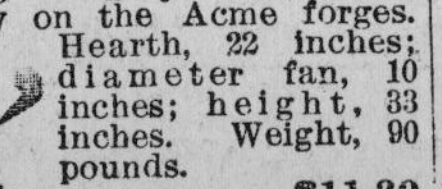

Price, each.................**$11.20**

Acme No. 300 Forge.

$10.90

No. 24R1014 Our No. 300 Acme is the largest high grade Forge for the money sold by any one. Owing to the increasing demands for a cheaper forge with an extra large fan and hearth, we have designed the above and a trial order will readily convince you we have the most durable, best finished and most perfect lever motion forge on the market. We have used the same quality of material as in our high priced forges, and have succeeded in outclassing them. It has our improved tuyere with **ball valves and oil ring journal bearings** used only on our Acme line of forges. It has a 12½-inch fan, 35x23-inch hearth, is 30 inches high and **weighs 120 pounds actual weight.** Will produce welding heat on 3-inch iron in five minutes. Price, each........**$10.90**

Acme No. 5 Forge.

No. 24R1016 This Forge is designed for general blacksmithing. Has a large roomy hearth and easy lever motion that gives a strong steady blast. Its durability and excellent service can be fully recommended. Note the size and weight of this forge. No. forge in the market will compare with it at the price. Size of hearth, 45x32 in. Has 14½-inch fan.

Height, 30 in. Weight, 300 lbs
Without water tank..**$12.00**
With water tank.....**13.00**

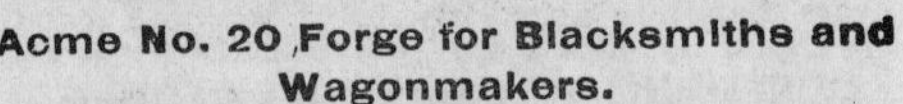

Acme No. 20 Forge for Blacksmiths and Wagonmakers.

No. 24R1018 This Forge has large, commodious hearth convenient for laying tools and work upon. A feature that will be fully appreciated by all smiths is the improved coal box with sloping bottom. **A 3-covered ball tuyere is used and a special pressure fan wheel** which gives strong and steady blast. An improved noiseless friction clutch is employed, and the forge is furnished with ring oiler journal bearings, which make frequent oilings unnecessary. A very substantial, easy running and durable forge **in** every respect. Fan, 16 inches; height, 30 inches; hearth, 32x45 inches. Weight, 350 pounds.

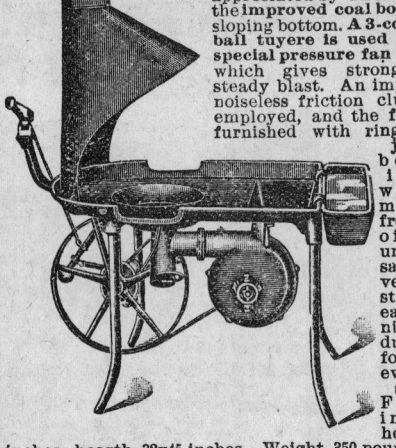

Price, with coal box or water tank **$16.50**
Price, with extra water tank as shown in cut **17.50**

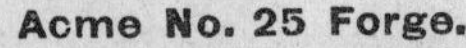

Acme No. 25 Forge.

OUR PRICE, $18.75, OFFERED IN COMPETITION WITH FORGES AT 25 PER CENT HIGHER PRICES.

No. 24R1020 This Forge is heavily and durably built. The proportions adapt it to general blacksmiths' use up to the heaviest kind of work. It is furnished with the latest type of ball tuyere iron with improved fire pot, combining center and side blast, which is able to stand continuous heavy work without burning out; an improved steel friction clutch is used. This is a high class forge in every detail. **It is furnished with our improved ring oiler journal bearings, which require less oiling than any type of journal made. These bearings are used exclusively on our forges.** Size hearth, 46x33 inches; fan, 16 inches. Weight, 300 pounds.

Price, with coal box..............................**$18.75**
Price, with coal box and water tank.........**19.75**

Acme No. 31 Forge.

$14.50

No. 24R1022 This Forge is the same design and dimensions as our No. 300, but with half hood for smoke removal which adapts it better for indoor use. For machine shops, stone cutters, railroad repair shops, mills, mines and general indoor work this forge will be found to be unsurpassed. The type of hood furnished insures as nearly perfect removal of smoke as can be effected in a forge of this type. No other of this class is so well adapted for surgical instrument factories, fine tool rooms or other uses where smoke and fumes are particularly objectionable. Perfectly noiseless in operation. Size, hearth, 35x23 inches; fan, 12½ inches; height, 30 inches. Weight, 130 pounds.

Price, with half hood as shown in cut........$14.50

Acme No. 15 Forge.

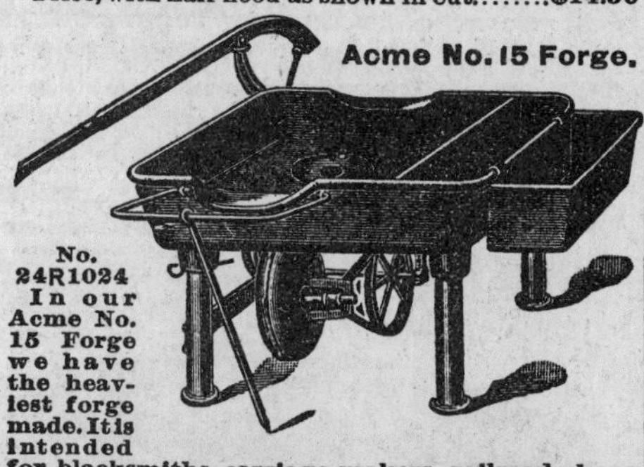

No. 24R1024 In our Acme No. 15 Forge we have the heaviest forge made. It is intended for blacksmiths, carriage makers, railroad shops and heavy forgings. It is the best built forge money will produce. The legs are short and extra heavy; stands 28 inches high; fire pan is **51x38 inches**, is supplied with the empire adjustable tuyere iron and cut off, which produces a powerful blast; also water and coal box. We furnish this forge without a hood, but can furnish a canopy to suspend over it if so desired at a small additional cost. **Actual weight, 500 pounds.** Price, each..........................$36.50

Price is f.o.b. factory in Central New York.

Acme Miners' and Prospectors' Portable Forge.

No. 24R1026 This Forge is the same as our large lever forge, but has shorter legs, making it more convenient for transportation. It is especially adapted for prospectors for carrying on mule back. It will heat iron 1¼ inches in diameter in five minutes and do heavier work if required. **The best miners' forge now on the market.** The case has sufficient room for a full line of blacksmith's tools. Size of hearth, 18 inches in diameter. Weight, 65 pounds.

Price, with case...$10.00

Cast Iron Swage Blocks.

Only 2¾ cents per pound.

Made of the best pig iron, used by blacksmiths in shaping iron in different designs.

No. 24R1028 No. 1. Size, 3⅝x10x14. Weight, about 110 pounds. Per pound..........................2¾c

No. 24R1029 No. 2. Size, 3⅞x11x15. Weight, about 135 pounds. Per pound..........................2¾c

No. 24R1030 No. 3. Size, 4¼x11x15. Weight, about 155 pounds. Per pound..........................2¾c

Cast Iron Leveling Blocks.

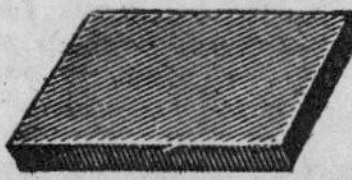

No. 24R1036 Especially intended for plow work. The blocks are made of **superior pig iron** and are accurately planed on one side. To ascertain the weight, figure 1 pound to 4 cubic inches. Come 1¼ to 3 inches thick by 14 to 24 inches wide and 18 to 30 inches long.

Price, per pound..........................2¾c

Blacksmiths' Cones or Mandrels.

Only 3 cents per pound.

No. 24R1040 Made of the best pig iron. No flaws.

Size	Height	Diam. at base	Diam. at top	Weight about	Price per lb.
1½	40 in.	10 in.	1 in.	105 lb.	3c
2	48 in.	12 in.	1 in.	120 lb.	3c
3	52 in.	14 in.	1 in.	160 lb.	3c
4	54 in.	16 in.	2 in.	240 lb.	3c

The above are estimated weights and may vary five pounds more or less. We charge for actual weight.

Horseshoers' Movable Foot Vise.

No. 24R1044 We have here the best foot vise for the money ever offered. It is made of wrought iron and steel, has reversible head block for sharpening shoes in winter. **The price we ask for it places it within the reach of a great many horseshoers who do not feel they can afford the more costly vise.** It stands 3 feet high, and weighs 60 pounds. Price, each, $6.40

Horseshoers' Foot Vise.

Guaranteed the best vise on the market.

New Green River Shoeing Vise and Bolt Header.

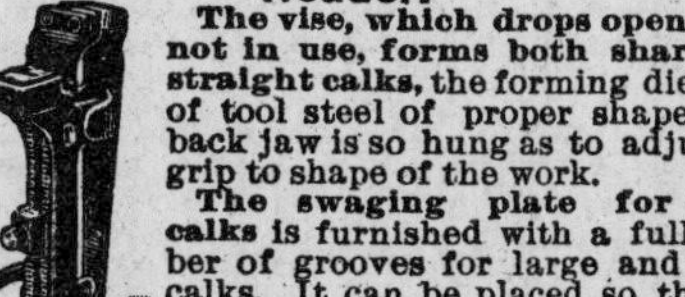

The vise, which drops open when not in use, forms both sharp and straight calks, the forming die being of tool steel of proper shape. The back jaw is so hung as to adjust the grip to shape of the work.

The swaging plate for sharp calks is furnished with a full number of grooves for large and small calks. It can be placed so that the grooves run either way as may be preferred.

The bolt heading dies are dropped into place or removed instantly without trouble. They are set firmly by driving a taper key which is always in place. Sizes, ¼, 5/16, ⅜, 7/16, ½, ⅝, ¾ inch. Any length up to 24 inches.

No. 24R1045 Price, complete for shoeing and bolt heading..........................$10.50

No. 24R1046 Price, for shoeing only (without bolt heading attachment)..........................$9.75

No. 24R1048 This is the most perfect tool of its kind yet produced. By a simple adjustment the grip of the jaws is adjusted to thick or thin shoes or iron, and by adjusting the stop **it can be made to lock itself or not, at pleasure, which is a feature that no other horseshoers' vise possesses.** The locking of the vise does away with an extra vise for filing shoes, and a slight touch of the toe under the foot lever releases it. **They are strongly made with steel jaws, one jaw being removable.** Height, 3 feet and 3 inches. Weight, 112 pounds. Face, 2 inches wide by 5¼ inches long. Complete with sharpening dies. Price, each..........$10.75

Blacksmiths' Aprons.

No. 24R1050 Sheepskin Aprons. Size, 26x34 inches. Price, each..........................$1.00

Horseshoers' Aprons.

No. 24R1052 Standard Split Leather Aprons, our own special brand. Size, 28 x38 inches. Each........$1.15

No. 24R1054 Pigskin Aprons. Size, 28x38 inches. Price, each..........$1.75

Mechanics' Aprons.

No. 24R1055 Made of a good quality of bed ticking, 30 inches wide, by 36 inches in length, with pockets and shoulder and waist straps. Stamped Sears, Roebuck & Co., Chicago, plainly on the front of each apron. The price without our name would be 45 cents each. Each......22c

The Jewel Spoke Tenoning Machine.

The Jewel Spoke Tenoning Machine, which is just being placed in the market, is intended as a substitute for the old-fashioned brace in cutting the tenon of a spoke. It is constructed upon simple mechanical lines and any of the leading hollow augers fit it. It cuts any size tenon quickly, accurately and easily. It absolutely avoids all the hard work necessary in cutting large spokes. It is so simple a ten-year-old boy can operate it. It is made of malleable iron and will last you a lifetime. We furnish this machine with out auger, any adjustable auger will fit it.

No. 24R1058 Price, each..........................$2.90

Peace's Spoke Tenoning Machine.

The Peace Machine has been used for the last ten years with general satisfaction. It is made in the most workmanlike manner, **all casting being malleable iron and the auger head made extra heavy. The knife starts on the blank of spokes and centers perfectly.** The auger is kept cutting by force of the spring. **Can be used on any size spoke or disc of wheel and is readily applied,** without removing from where spokes are driven. Cuts any size from ¼ to 1¼. Weight, 8 pounds.

No. 24R1060 Without felloe attachment....$8.00

No. 24R1061 Price, with felloe attachment.. 9.00

Dole & Deming's Spoke Tenon Machine.

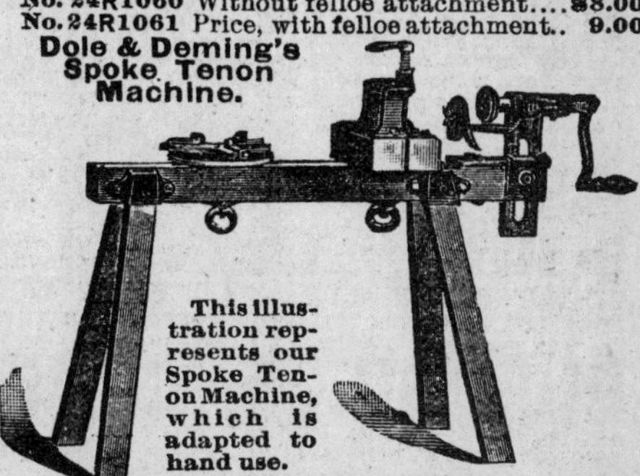

This illustration represents our Spoke Tenon Machine, which is adapted to hand use.

It is fitted with our Star Hollow Auger, and will cut tenons any size from 5/16 to 1 inch. The hub is held in a self centering chuck, which can be revolved to present the spokes to the hollow auger. The spokes are held firmly on the rest, and in line with the auger. Thus all the tenons are cut with the shoulders uniform in width and in the same plane. With a slight transformation it can be changed into a boring machine, for boring the felloes for the spokes, giving that accuracy in the work that can alone be attained by machinery. Above illustration shows the felloe boring attachment on the machine as shipped. Bit chucks with ½-inch round hole always furnished with the felloe boring attachment unless otherwise ordered. Prices, f. o. b. factory in Central Ohio.

No. 24R1067 Price, with felloe boring attachment..........................$19.00

No. 24R1068 Price, without felloe boring attachment..........................$15.00

Sears' Improved Blacksmithing Device.

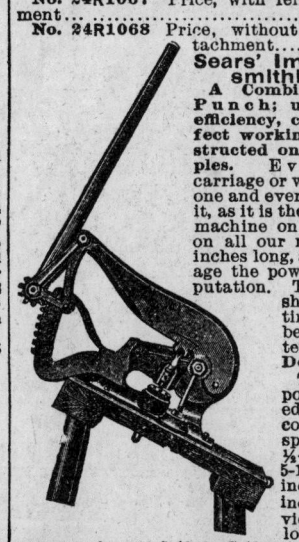

A Combined Shear and Punch; unequaled in efficiency, capacity and perfect working qualities; constructed on scientific principles. Every blacksmith, carriage or wagon maker needs one and every shop can afford it, as it is the cheapest and best machine on earth. The lever on all our machines is but 36 inches long, and with this leverage the power is beyond computation. The knives in the shears have two cutting edges which can be reversed and interchanged.

Description of No. 1.

This tool weighs 250 pounds and is mounted on a heavy stand, covering 1x5 feet floor space. It will punch a ½-inch hole through 5-16 inch iron, a ⅝-inch hole through ⅝-inch iron and is provided with the following sizes of punches, 3-16, ¼, 5-16, ⅜, 7-16, ½, and these punches are furnished with each machine. It will cut 3x½, 4x7/16, 5x⅜ inch cold iron and will cut plow steel and any size bolt or bar up to ¾ inch.

No. 24R1070 Price with all attachments, including six punches and revolving die..........$24.00

Prices on the following shears f. o. b. factory in Eastern Iowa.

Shear Only.

No. 24R1072 No. 2, weight, 225 pounds, will shear 3x½, 4x7/16, 5x⅜ cold iron, also plow steel, and will cut any size bolt or bar up to ¾-inch. Price, each $18.00

No. 24R1074 No. 3. This machine is especially designed for the country blacksmith and is the greatest labor saver on the market. It will shear 3x½, 4x7-16, 5x⅜ cold iron and will also cut plow steel. It will punch a ½-inch hole in 5-16 inch cold iron, a ⅝-inch hole through 7-16 inch cold iron, and will also punch soft plow lays, and is provided with the following sizes of punches: 3-16, ¼, 5-16, ⅜, 7-16, ½. It will cut any size bolt or bar up to ¾ inch. It has an attachment for welding on plow lays and any blacksmith after becoming accustomed to using it can put on from 6 to 8 lays a day, which you will readily see is a great labor saving. This attachment can be put on or taken off in one minute and when not in use can be taken off and the machine is then the same as our No. 1. The lever is but 36 inches long and machine is mounted on a heavy stand. It weighs 300 pounds. Price, with all attachments, including six punches and revolving die..........................$31.00

SEE NEXT PAGE FOR LARGER SIZES.

CARRIAGE HARDWARE AND SUPPLIES

IN CALLING YOUR ATTENTION to this complete department, we are confident that we can supply the great need of thousands of our customers who find it constantly necessary to replace various parts of their vehicles, but who have been paying exorbitant retail prices. We offer a line that has no equal in general excellence of material and finish. At the same time our contracts with manufacturers are so advantageous that we are in a position to make unusually low prices.

IN ORDERING BUGGY TOPS give measurements from center to center of holes in irons, as shown in cut; width from A to F, from B to E, from A to B, from C to D. State whether you want three or four bows, and give choice of color of lining.

IN ORDERING CUSHIONS give measurements from I to J on bottom of seat; from G to H, width of seat at bottom, and state if square or round corners are wanted.

IN ORDERING CUSHIONS WITH FALL give measurements of cushion as above, and also width of fall at the bottom and distance from bottom of seat to floor of buggy. Our buggy tops are shipped in light but strong crates, and are not liable to injury in transportation.

OUR TERMS are cash with the order. But if anything is not entirely satisfactory when received, return it to us and we will immediately return your money, including what you paid for transportation charges.

YOU WILL SAVE MONEY by buying your own needed repairs direct from us at manufacturers' lowest prices. Freight amounts to nothing compared with what you save in price. Nearly all these goods are taken at second class rate or lower.

OUR $6.25 COMPLETE BUGGY TOP.

No. 24R2500
FOR $6.25

We furnish this
BUGGY TOP
COMPLETE
with Full Length
SIDE AND...
BACK CURTAINS
with patent shifting rail which adjusts itself to any buggy. The latest style top in every way.

$6.25 IS A SPECIAL PRICE, based on the actual cost of material and labor, with but one small profit added.

MADE IN OUR OWN FACTORY.

WE BUILD THESE TOPS in our own factory here in Chicago; we build them in immense quantities. The bows, bow sockets, shifting rails, joints, prop nuts and finishings are contracted for direct from the largest manufacturers for cash. Our rubber drill, cloth linings and trimmings are contracted for in very large quantities, and it is by reason of the low price at which we have been able to buy the material and by reason of our manufacturing them in our own factory that we are able to name this extremely low price of $6.25.

No. 24R2500

FROM THE TWO ILLUSTRATIONS you can form an idea of the appearance of this, our special $6.25 Buggy Top. The one illustration shows the top; the other illustration shows one of the side curtains. We furnish a pair of side curtains and a full length back curtain.

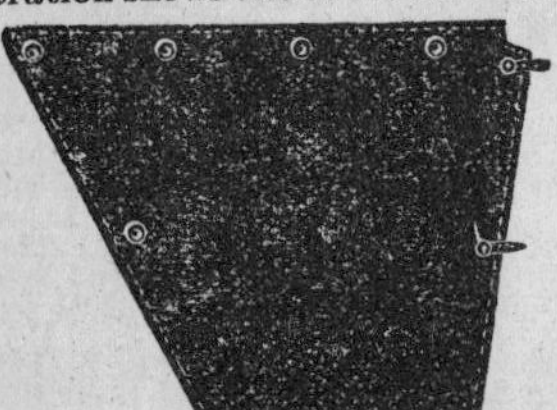

IN ORDERING BUGGY TOPS follow our rules for measurement as given above, and we can guarantee the top we furnish you will fit your buggy exactly.

THIS OUR $6.25 TOP IS MADE OF THOROUGHLY RELIABLE MATERIAL. The roof and the quarters are made of good quality extra heavy rubber drill, well padded; roof and back stays lined with No. 14 X cloth, and back stays stiffened with two thicknesses of buckram. Side and back curtains are made of good weight colored back drill. We use nothing but the highest grade tubular steel bow sockets of the latest pattern, full black enameled metal buckle loops, Thomas top props, patent concealed joints, japanned prop nuts, patent curtain fasteners, wrought iron rail with patent buttons, which make it adjustable to any buggy. Side and back curtains are full length, large glass fitted in back curtain, patent buttonholes used throughout.

OUR $5.75 DRILL TOP

AT $5.75 we furnish a Drill Top complete with side and back curtains. It is made of light black enameled drill, light material throughout, made to compete with the many cheap tops now being advertised, and while we do not guarantee it, for a very cheap top it will give good satisfaction.
No. 24R2502 Our special price........................$5.75
The Top weighs, crated for shipment, about 50 pounds, and you will find the freight will amount to next to nothing as compared with what you will save in price.

IN ORDERING BE SURE TO GIVE MEASURE AS PER DIAGRAM ABOVE. ...ALSO STATE WHETHER THREE OR FOUR-BOW TOP IS WANTED...

OUR SPECIAL

SILVER KING TOP, $8.25

FOR $8.25 we furnish this fine Buggy Top as described, a very showy top for a livery line and equal to tops usually sold at a much higher price.

No. 24R2504 This Top is made of the same material and with the same care as our No. 24R2505, but with silver trimmings throughout. Silver prop nuts, silver joints and fastenings on the back stays. The back stays and head linings are hand stitched, nicely corded with pinked edges. It makes a top that can be used on any buggy, especially where a stylish, up to date rig is wanted. Just the top for a livery or hack line, the silver trimmings showing off to fine advantage against the black panels of a buggy. Crated singly, weight, 50 pounds. Price, each, $8.25

No. 24R2505 Our No. 1 Buggy Top has either three or four bows as desired. This is a full 22-ounce rubber top with steel bow sockets, second growth top bows, wrought iron joints, japanned nuts, iron rivets. Thomas top props, concealed joints between two back bows. Top lined with heavy cloth, back stays lined, back curtain lined, rubber side curtains, indigo dyed back, glass in back curtains. Our special price for No. 1 Top, as above described, with quarter rail attached $7.45

No. 24R2506 Our No. 2, 28-Ounce, Buggy Top is in appearance just like No. 1 described above. However, our No. 2 has leather quarters and stay top, steel bow sockets, second growth top bows, wrought iron joints, japanned nuts, iron rivets, Thomas top props, top lined with all wool cloth, back stays lined, back curtain lined, rubber side curtains, front valance sewed on, indigo dyed No. 12 back, glass in back curtain. Three or four bows, as desired. Our special price, as described, with quarter rail attached, $11.25

Full Moroccoline Leather Top for $10.75

No. 24R2508 Our No. 5 Top is exactly same as our No. 4, except that it is covered with moroccoline leather. This is a perfect substitute for leather, it will not show scratches, is guaranteed not to crack or become soft. Moroccoline leather is embossed by the same process as real leather and will last fully as long as the genuine leather.
Price, each.......................................$10.75

Our Great Bargain Genuine Leather Top.

FOR $13.65 we furnish this GENUINE LEATHER TOP as the equal of leather tops that sell everywhere as high as $20.00.

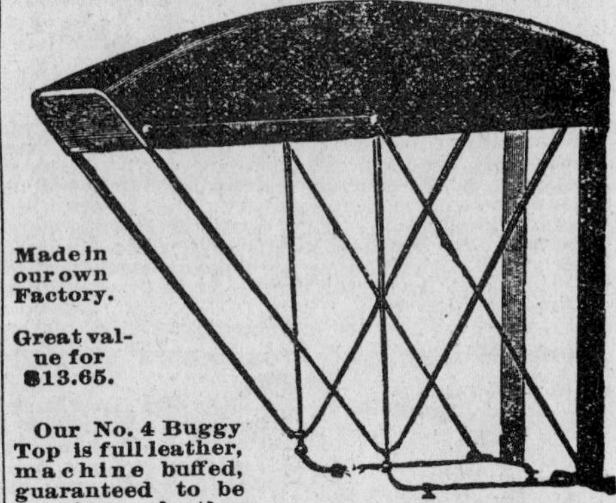

Made in our own Factory.

Great value for $13.65.

Our No. 4 Buggy Top is full leather, machine buffed, guaranteed to be genuine leather. This top is lined with all wool cloth, nicely corded, back stays lined and stiffened with two thicknesses of buckram, rubber side curtains with colored back; glass in back curtain. Steel bow sockets, second growth top bows, wrought iron joints, japanned nuts, iron rivets, Thomas top props, concealed joints between two back bows. Three or four bows, as desired.

No. 24R2510 Our special price on our No. 4 full leather top, with quarter rail attached......$13.65

EXTRAS.

No. 24R2512 Extra for our No. 2 rail welded to fit seat, with lazy back, wood, and attached to above top...$1.35

No. 24R2513 Extra for rubber side curtains. Per pair $2.20

Handy Top.

No. 24R2515 Our Handy Top is light, strong and durable, dispensing with half of the objectionable front bows; admits you to get in and out easily without any exertion whatever.
If this style top is wanted add 65 cents extra to price of any top shown in our catalogue.

A $20.00 Buggy Top for $11.35.

No. 24R2516 The accompanying illustration shows our No. 4 Buggy Top, complete with seat, in the white, full back, and cushion, with fall. **This top is made of 24-ounce rubber, with seat, wrought rail and joints.** Top and back stays lined with **all wool fast color cloth,** either blue or green, side and back curtains indigo dyed rubber, 12-ounce blue or green cloth on full back and cushion. These are either **biscuit or diamond tufted, and filled with selected moss.** Front and back valance nailed on. Black nuts and rivets. **Three or four steel socket bows, as desired.** Our special price on No. 4 top, complete, as described........................**$11.35**

No. 24R2518 Our No. 5 Buggy Top, complete, with full back and cushion, is made like shown in the picture of our No. 4; **28-ounce rubber drill and leather quarters and stay,** and is complete with seat, in the white, wrought rail and joints, three or four steel bows; top, back stays and back curtain **lined with all wool fast color cloth.** Rubber side curtains, 14-ounce blue or green cloth in full back and cushions. Weight, about 50 pounds. Front valance sewed on. Black nuts and iron rivets.
Our special price.............................**$16.00**

No. 24R2520 Our No. 6 Top is the finest buggy top made. It has machine buffed leather top and is complete with seat, in the white, cushion and full back. Wrought rail and joints. Lined throughout, except side curtains, with 10-ounce all wool fast color cloth. Rubber side curtains, **14-ounce blue or green cloth** on full back and cushion. The latter is tufted in **biscuit or diamond style,** and stuffed with moss. Black nuts and iron rivets. Valance sewed on. Style same as shown in picture of No. 4 buggy top. Three or four steel bows, as desired.
Our special price.............................**$20.00**

EXTRAS.

No. 24R2530 Extra rubber back curtains. Price, each..**$1.25**
No. 24R2532 Extra rubber back stays. Price, each.. **1.00**

Canopy Top Sun Shades.

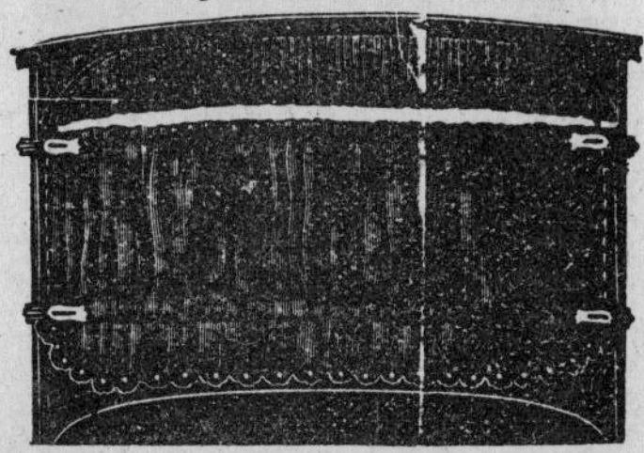

Canopy Top Sun Shades to use in connection with any canopy top, furnished complete ready for use. Length, 60 inches.

No. 24R2540 No. 6. Extra Heavy Silesia; color, dark blue. Price, each..............................**70c**
No. 24R2541 No. 3. Sateen; color, fast black **90c**
No. 24R2542 No. 1. Austra; color, fast black. Price, each.........................**$1.15**
No. 24R2543 No. 9. Glorioso Silk; color, dark blue or drab; nickel plated trimmings.......**$1.65**
No. 24R2544 No. 11. English Cloth; nickel plated trimmings, with silk fringe; color, dark blue. Price, each.................................**$2.35**

Canopy Tops.

In measuring for Canopy Top give exact distance from back of back seat to front end of body. Give exact width of seats from outside to outside on top. These canopy tops have drill roof X-cloth, head lining and fringe all around 7 inches deep. Weight, crated, about 70 pounds.

No. 24R2550 Our $7.30 Canopy Top is covered with black drill, lined with all wool X-cloth, and **ornamented with all wool fringe. Price for 5-foot length** or less top..............................**$7.30**
This price is without standards or curtains. See rule for giving measures in ordering **canopy tops above.**
For larger sizes over 5-foot, add extra **for each** additional foot,..............................**$1.35**

No. 24R2555 Complete set side and back curtains, indigo dyed rubber, for above tops.....**$4.00**

Extension Tops.

In measuring for extension tops for seats which require rails.
1. Give width of seats from out to out on top at A and C. 2. Give distance on top from B to C. 3. Give difference in height of seat bottoms, E to F. If seat has solid back as per cut, so state, and give length of same D to D.

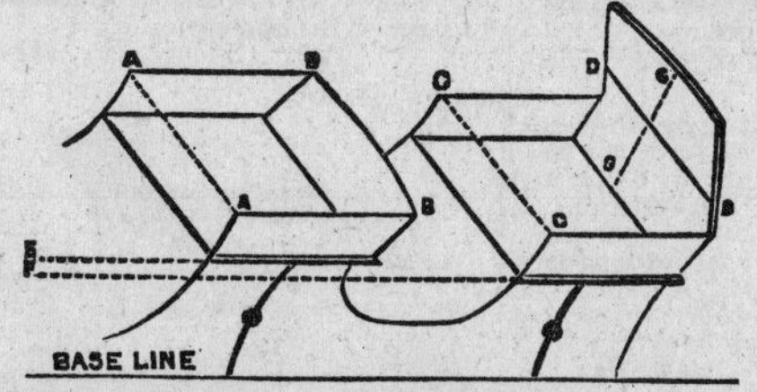

For seats that are ironed with stationary goose necks, prop rests and front eyes:
1. Give width from shoulder to shoulder of goose necks. 2. Give height of goose neck from seat bottom. 3. Give height of front eye from seat bottom. 4. Give height of prop rest from seat bottom. 5. Give difference in height of seat bottoms, E to F. 6. Give distance from A to B. 7. Give distance from C down to seat bottom. 8. Give upward curve of back panel.
Make a rough sketch of all ironed bodies and where the irons are situated, mark figures on same, plain. We cannot fill these orders without a definite knowledge of what is required.
All tops over 42 inches wide cost from **65c to $2.00** extra, in accordance with the extra width.

No. 24R2560 Our No. 7 Extension Top is a 4-bow, 22-ounce rubber top, lined throughout with all wool cloth, except side curtains, which are indigo dyed rubber. **Wrought iron joints,** japanned nuts and iron rivets. Front valance sewed on. No rail. Weight, crated, about 65 pounds. Our special price.............................**$11.70**

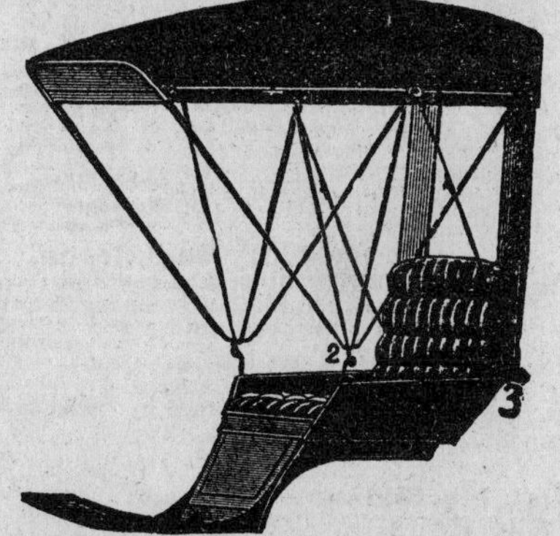

No. 24R2562 Our No. 8 Extension Top, just the same as our No. 7, described above, but has **leather quarter** and stay. Our special price. **$14.90**
No. 24R2564 Our No. 9 is a full leather Extension Top, otherwise just the same as No. 7, described above. Our special price.............**$22.65**

Phaeton Tops.

We can furnish Phaeton Tops of same material as Nos. 24R2504, 24R2505, 24R2506, 24R2508 and 24R2510 at same prices.

In measuring for Phaeton Tops, give nine measurements as below indicated, in order to insure a perfect fit and graceful outline.

1. From shoulder to shoulder of goose neck A to A, if seat is ironed, if not ironed, so state, and give measurement from out to out on top of seat at A A. 2. Length of back from out to out at B B. 3. From seat bottom F, up to a level line of goose neck centers, as shown by dotted line A to A, and down to F, or if seat is not ironed, to a level line on top of seat at that place. 4. From center of goose neck A to back side of seat back at point C. 5. From bottom of back stay at C, down to a level line of seat bottom or base line, as indicated by dotted line. 6. The upward curve of back panel from E, in center, down to dotted line. 7. The outward swell of back panel from D in center to dotted line. 8. From center of goose neck A back to center of prop. 9. From center of prop down to base line.
State whether back is straight or rounding.

Rolled Steel Canopy Top Standards.

No. 24R2570 Finished complete, as shown in cut. Made of ⅝-inch round steel; height, 36½ in. hind, 53 in. front. We can send these standards in halves if so desired. **Always sent as shown in cut unless otherwise ordered.** Price, per set of 2 front and 2 hind pieces.........**$1.50**

Steel Canopy Top Sockets.

No. 24R2572 Rolled Steel Canopy Top Socket to be used in connection with the above Canopy Top Standards.
Price, per set of four pieces.............................**20c**

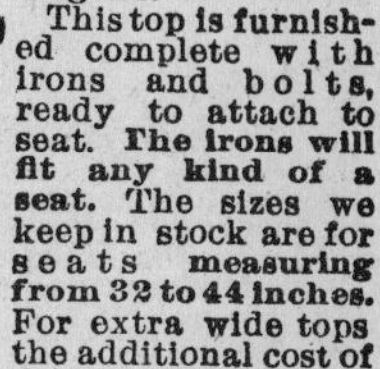

Wagon Sunshade Top.

Especially adapted for express and farm wagons.
This top is furnished complete with irons and bolts, ready to attach to seat. The irons will fit any kind of a seat. The sizes we keep in stock are for seats measuring from 32 to 44 inches. For extra wide tops the additional cost of making will be added. When ordering, **give width of seat** outside to outside on top of seat at back corner.

No. 24R2580 Covered with brown duck...**$2.45**
No. 24R2582 Covered with awning stripe. **2.85**

Our New 1902 Wagon Umbrella.

No. 24R2585 If you are looking for a bargain in wagon umbrellas, you will find it in our **$1.15 umbrella, which we send out as an advertisement.** **Only $1.15 for a $2.50 Umbrella.** It is a regular $2.50 article; is made with our new improved steel ribs and notches. Handle is white ash, of good size, oil finished, with patent foot socket and seat fixture. Is covered with fancy striped double faced duck, with removable cover, which can be taken off and repaired in case of an accident. The colors are red, white and orange. Each section having Sears, Roebuck & Co. painted on same, as shown in illustration. It is not a cheap affair, but an umbrella that sells for $2.50 without our name on same. Lettering is done in fast oil, guaranteed not to fade or run. Has six ribs, and a spread of 5 feet and 8 inches. Price, each..............................**$1.15**

Wagon Umbrellas With Fixture Sockets.

Compare our prices on these goods with those of other houses and see if we cannot save you 25 to 50 per cent on price. These umbrellas come with best quality heavy steel ribs and fixtures. Handles, 1¼-inch seasoned white ash, oiled and varnished. **Colors, blue, green or buff.** Heavy umbrella cloth muslin. **Be sure to state color wanted.**
The most complete fixtures yet produced. Made of the best malleable iron, light and strong, quickly applied, and holds the umbrella secure. We furnish all extras complete without extra charge.
No. 24R2587 36-inch, 8 ribs, with fixtures..$1.35
No. 24R2588 38-inch, 8 ribs, with fixtures.. 1.40
No. 24R2589 40-inch, 10 ribs, with fixtures. 1.70
No. 24R2590 40-inch, 10 ribs, double face duck, green inside, duck outside, with fixtures. **2.05**

$1.70 for the Best Wagon Umbrella Made.

This is the most popular umbrella on the market, **very latest and best. This umbrella has heavy duck covering,** in blue, brown or white. **Guaranteed strongest umbrella made,** 6 steel ribs, 1½-inch white ash handles, 5 feet 8-inch spread, cover removable. Price includes all fixtures complete.
No. 24R2592 This is the umbrella to buy, and our special price is below all others. Price...**$1.70**

Buggy Cushions and Falls and Full Backs

These goods are first class in all respects. We make strictly inside prices on these goods and can save you a large percentage on each purchase. The price of full back is just the same as that of the cushion with fall. **If you want both the full back and cushion with fall, the price will be just twice that of the cushion and fall alone. All these cushions are based on 34-inch length.** All larger sizes we charge 7 cents per inch extra. **In ordering cushions, give size of seat. Measure length and width on inside bottom of seat and do not include the flare.**
No. 24R2600 Black drill cushion with fall......70c
No. 24R2602 Black drill cushion without fall..65c
No. 24R2604 Rubber cushion with fall..........94c
No. 24R2606 Rubber cushion without fall.......80c
EXTRAS—We can furnish any of these cushions with springs for, extra..............................$0.75
Full backs with springs, extra............... 1.00

Full Backs.

This illustration shows the Full Back furnished with any of our cushions when wanted. If you wish a full back allow price of the cushion you order for same. For example, if No. 24R2600 cushion with full back to match is wanted, allow $1.40, or twice the price of cushion with fall.

No. 24R2607 Blue or green cloth cushion, plain top, with fall........$1.67

No. 24R2608 Blue or green cloth cushion, with fall, biscuit or diamond tufted, filled with moss. Price....$1.95

No. 24R2610 Fancy leather cushion and fall, plain top $2.75

No. 24R2612 Fancy leather cushion, without fall, plain top....................$2.50

No. 24R2613 Black leather cushion, with fall, plain top....................$2.95

No. 24R2614 Black leather cushion, without fall, plain top....................$2.50

No. 24R2615 Black split leather cushion, with fall, plain top....................$2.55

No. 24R2616 Black split leather cushion, without fall, plain top....................$2.00

No. 24R2617 Green or black artificial leather cushion, and fall....................$1.66

No. 24R2618 Same as No.24R2617, without fall $1.35

No. 24R2619 Brown corduroy cushion and fall, plain top....................$2.00

No. 24R2620 Brown corduroy cushion, without fall, plain top....................$1.75

No. 24R2622 Light colored, all wool, whipcord cushion with fall, tufted or plain top..........$1.85

No. 24R2624 Light colored, all wool, whipcord cushion without fall, tufted or plain top.......$1.75

..FULL BACKS AND CUSHIONS..

ALL STYLES SAME PRICE.

In ordering be sure to state style 1, 2, 3 or 4, as wanted.

Full Backs and Cushions, In sets, or cushion or full back only.

No. 24R2626 Made of 12-ounce blue or green cloth or whipcord.
Cushion with fall only............$2.40
Full back only. 2.40

Style 1

Seat cushion with fall, full back and arm rails, complete, as shown in illustration..$6.50

No. 24R2627 Made of deep buff leather.
Cushion and fall only..........$2.80
Full back only.......... 2.80

Style 2

Seat with arm rails, cushion with fall and full back complete, as shown in illustration....$7.35

No. 24R2628 Made of No. 1 machine buff leather.
Cushion and fall only..........$3.70
Full back only 3.70

Seat with arm rails, cushion, fall and full back, complete, as shown in illustration ...$9.15

Style 3

We show four patterns of seats which we furnish at same price.

In ordering be sure and give style wanted, No. 1, 2, 3 or 4. If you wish seat and outfit complete give width of seat across the bottom.

Order cushions and full backs the regular way, width across bottom.

Style 4

Toe Pads.

No. 24R2640 Patent Leather Toe Pads or Panel Protectors, placed on the side of the buggy, prevent the varnish from being scratched by the shoe while getting in or out of the buggy. The ornamental designs are embossed. They are an addition to the appearance of any buggy. 8 inches wide.
Per pair.......................................18c

Buggy Boots.

Buggy Boots are used to cover back of buggy box. Adds to appearance of vehicle and keeps out all dust, dirt, etc. Made complete ready to attach to buggy.

No. 24R2644 No. 1 made of enameled drill. Price.....75c

No. 24R2648 No. 2 made of enameled rubber. Price..$1.00

No. 24R2650 No. 3 made of leather. Price 2.00

In giving measurements give width No. 1 to No. 2, No. 2 to No. 3, No. 3 to No. 4, No. 4 to No. 5, No. 5 to No. 6.

Rubber Boot Straps.

This device is used for fastening buggy boots to buggy bodies. Fastenings are made of tinned wire; straps of pure gum (double thick).

No. 24R2653 Price, per pair 5c

Narrow Lazy Backs.

Complete, as shown in illustration.

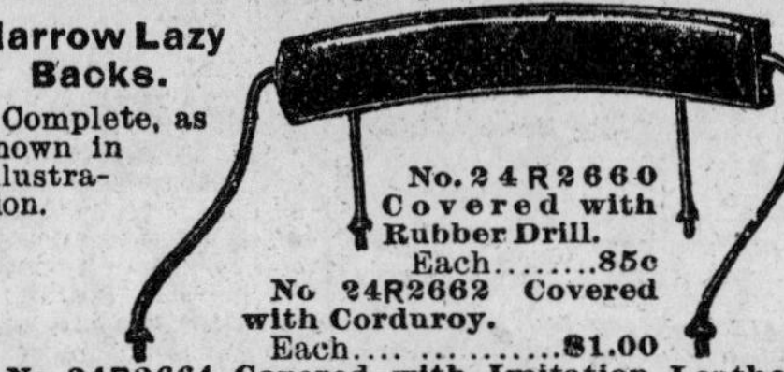

No. 24R2660 Covered with Rubber Drill. Each........85c

No. 24R2662 Covered with Corduroy. Each..........$1.00

No. 24R2664 Covered with Imitation Leather. Each..................................$1.15

Plain Full Lazy Backs.

Complete with irons; ready to attach to seat.

No. 24R2670 Covered with Drill. Each..$1.75

No. 24R2672 Covered with Brown Corduroy. Price, each..........$2.10

No. 24R26.. Covered with Black Leather. Price, each..........$2.75

Steel Cushion Springs.

Made of the best spring steel, carefully finished and tempered.

No. 24R2675 Pillow Spring size for lazy backs. Per dozen....12c

No. 24R2677 Cushion Spring size. Per dozen.............15c

Steel Lazy Back Irons.

No. 24R2680 Steel Lazy Back Irons, finished complete with hexagon nuts. Price, per set of four pieces.......15c

Steel Cushion Arm Rails.

No. 24R2682 Steel Cushion Arm Rails, furnished complete, as shown in illustration. Price, per pair. ... 22c

Adjustable Sliding Clip Rails.

Adjustable Sliding Clip Rails. Made of the best wrought iron, japanned. Complete, as shown in illustration.

No. 24R2688 Price, per set. 55c

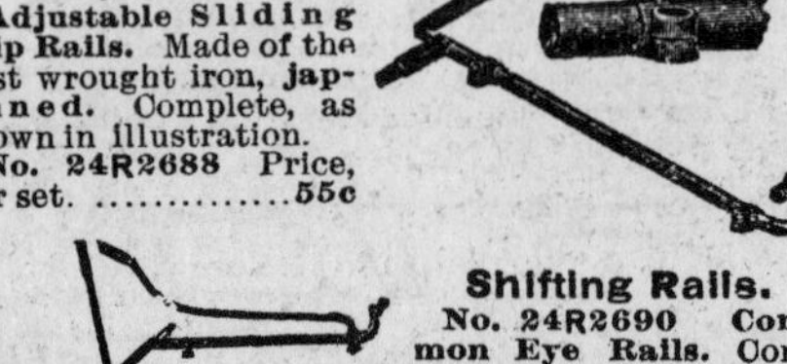

Shifting Rails.

No. 24R2690 Common Eye Rails. Complete in halves, japanned.
Price, per set......35c

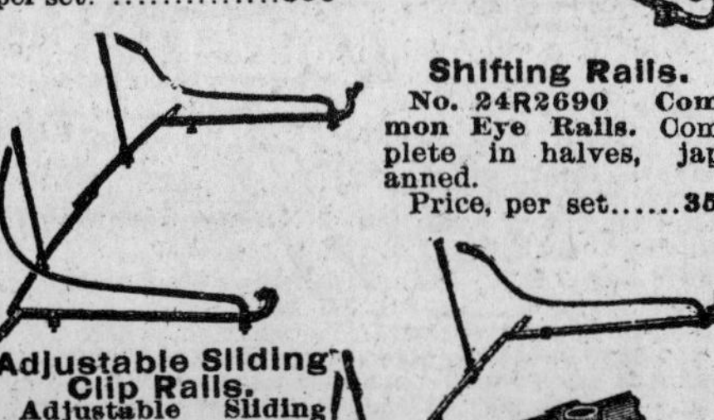

Adjustable Sliding Clip Rails.

Adjustable Sliding Clip Rails in Halves. Made of the best wrought iron, japanned. Complete, as shown in illustration.

No. 24R2692 Price, per set.....................40c

Top Props.

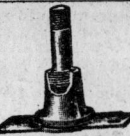

No. 24R2693 Thomas Malleable Top Props, complete as shown in illustration.
Price, per set..........................10c

Buggy Top Joints.

Buggy Top Joints, finished complete as shown in illustration, japanned, for 3 or 4 bows.

No. 24R2694 Price, per set, 55c

Concealed Joints.

Concealed Buggy Top Joints, furnished complete, as shown in illustration.

No. 24R2700 Price for 12-inch. Per pair......7c

No. 24R2701 Price for 14-inch. Per pair......9c

Crandal Pattern Steel Bow Sockets.

Crandal Pattern Three-Bow Tubular Steel Bow Sockets, japanned.

No. 24R2702 Price, per set..................................72c

Crandal Pattern Steel Bow Sockets.

Crandal Pattern Four-Bow Tubular Steel Bow Sockets, japanned.

No. 24R2703 Price, per set.....................................85c

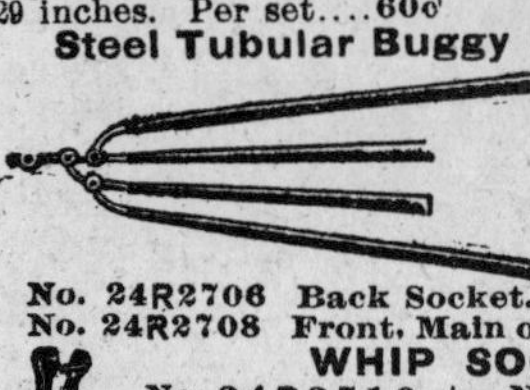

Steel Bow Sockets.

No. 24R2704 Steel Tubular Buggy Bow Sockets, japanned, 3-bow; length, 29 inches. Per set....60c

Steel Tubular Buggy Bow Sockets.

No. 24R2705 Steel Tubular Bow Sockets, 4-bow, japanned; length, 29 inches.
Price, per set, 75c

Single bow sockets.

No. 24R2706 Back Socket. Each..........25c

No. 24R2708 Front, Main or Off Set. Each, 20c

WHIP SOCKETS.

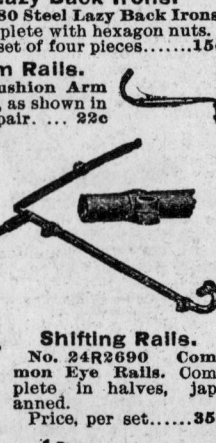

No. 24R2710 Skeleton Whip Sockets for leather dash. Each..5c

No. 24R2712 Metal Lever Whip Sockets, adjustable band fasteners riveted on. Length, 6½ inches, for leather dash. Price, each....8c

No. 24R2714 Iron Whip Socket and Rein Holder. Can be used on wood or leather dash with line spring. Price, each, 15c

No. 24R2716 Metal Whip Sockets, with flat spring. Can be attached to any dash. Price, each ..6c

No. 24R2718 Wood Top Whip Sockets, with rubber holder; holds whip securely and prevents rattling. Price, each..10c

No. 24R2720 Metal Bell Top Whip Socket with security band fasteners, nickel shell cap and bands. One of the neatest and best made sockets on the market. Price, each..16c

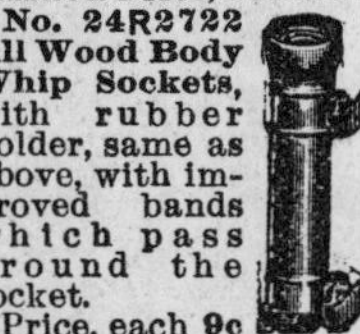

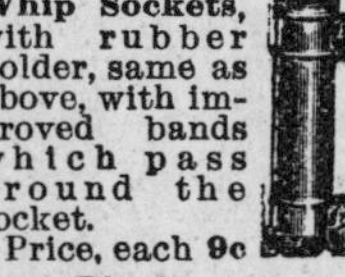

No. 24R2722 All Wood Body Whip Sockets, with rubber holder, same as above, with improved bands which pass around the socket. Price, each 9c

Black Enameled Cloth.

No. 24R2750 Leather Grain Muslin, 45 inches wide, white back. Price, per yard................17c

No. 24R2752 Leather Grain Drill, 50 inches wide, white back. Price, per yard.................25c

No. 24R2754 Glazed Drill (patent leather finish), 50 inches wide, white back. Price, per yard......25c

No. 24R2756 Enameled Duck, 50 inches wide, white back. Price, per yard.............................31c

No. 24R2758 Tan Back Drill (patent leather finish), 45 inches wide, tan back. Price, per yard, 33c

If any of the above cloths are wanted with green or blue back add 8 cents per yard to above prices.

Moroccoline Leather.

Moroccoline Leather is a perfect substitute for leather; it will not show scratches, it will not crack, does not become soft or sticky, and grease does not affect it. Moroccoline leather is embossed by the same process as genuine leather, will last fully as long, and costs only one-third as much as the genuine leather. Can furnish above in four different colors, as follows:

No. 24R2760 Black, 50 inches wide. Per yard, 87c

No. 24R2762 Green, 50 inches wide. Per yard, 87c

No. 24R2764 Dark Maroon, 50 inches wide. Price, per yard..................................87c

No. 24R2766 Tan, 50 inches wide. Per yard, 87c

Spring Buffers.

Buggy or Wagon Rubber Bumpers or Buffers, made of the best quality of rubber.

No. 24R3042 Size for 1¼-inch spring. Price, each...30c

No. 24R3044 Size for 1½-inch spring. Each, 45c

Carriage Lamps.

Latest Style Carriage Lamps. Made of the best material by one of the most reliable manufacturers in the United States. Every lamp carefully inspected before being sent out. Black japanned, with nickel trimmings. We furnish these lamps with either candle or kerosene burners. Size body, 4¼x3½ inches; oval flange, 5¼x4½ inches.

No. 24R3050 Price, candle burner, per pair..............$2.00

No. 24R3051 Price, kerosene burner, per pair..............$2.35

Fine Carriage or Surrey Lamps at $4.25 and $4.50.

Carriage or Surrey Lamps, with bevel edge glass, nickel plated trimmings. Size body, 4¾x3¾ inches.

No. 24R3055 Price, candle burner, per pair..............$4.25

No. 24R3056 Price, kerosene burner, per pair..............$4.50

The Kimball Carriage, Surrey or Brougham Lamps.

This is one of the finest lamps made; has bevel edge glass, with fancy side glass automatic candle raiser, full nickel trimmings; made of the best material and is good enough for any rig. In fact there is nothing better made. Size, fancy side glass, 5¼x4¼ inches; flange, 6¼x4⅞ in.

No. 24R3060 Price, candle burner, per pair..............$6.22

No. 24R3061 Price, kerosene burner, per pair..............$6.50

The "Garden City" Dash Lamp.

The "Garden City" Dash Lamps are made either to burn kerosene oil or candles and will stay lighted. Fill the oil reservoir and the lamp will burn from 16 to 18 hours, and stay lighted if the wick is trimmed before starting. Oil lamps are made with short French stems. Candle lamps will stay lighted, even if the bottom of the lamp is filled up to the top of the candle cap with tallow, as it does not interfere with the ventilation. Candle lamps will burn from four to five hours with one candle, and are made with long screw stems so that candles may be easily put into place without trouble. All candle lamps are made with long stems to make room for the spring, so that it will work perfectly. The lamp weighs less than 15 ounces, but is strong and well made. Has nickel head and stem, heavily plated, and black enamel body, red cut-glass jewels at side and rear. The front glass is a crystal and adds greatly to the general appearance of the lamp.

No. 24R3062 Garden City Dash Lamp, for oil, with japanned bracket; length, 10 inches. Each, $1.35

No. 24R3063 Garden City Dash Lamp, for candle, with japanned bracket; length, 11⅛ inches. Price, each..............$1.45

No. 24R3064 Garden City Dash Lamp Brackets, japanned only. Price, each..............35c

Automatic Carriage Lamp.

No. 24R3065 This lamp is built on simple and scientific principles. The Automatic Carriage Lamp is constructed to use granulated carbide. No wicks. No absorbents. No regulating valves. Burns when left alone. Cannot explode or blow up. Price, each..........$2.00

Carriage Lamp Candles.

Candles for the above lamps, best quality.

No. 24R3067 Size ⅞-in. diameter. Price, per dozen..............35c

No. 24R3068 Size 1 1/16-in. diameter. Price, per dozen..............50c

Climax Electric Carriage Lamp.

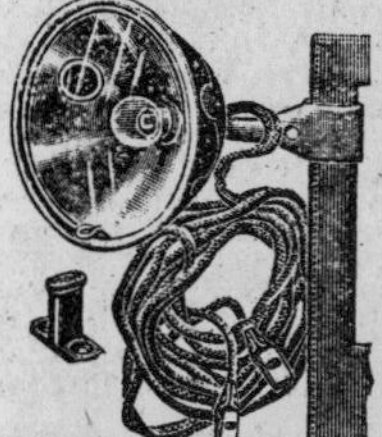

Climax Dry Battery Carriage Lamp. No oil, grease, dust, smoke, or jarring out. No changing batteries each night; will run 100 hours without recharging. Connect the wires and you have the most powerful light for carriage driving in the world; will throw a light 200 feet ahead of carriage. The bracket on this lamp can be placed on side or top of dash, on shaft, or under the carriage.

No. 24R3070 Price of lamp complete with one battery..............$6.95

New Batteries. Price, each..............3.75

New Electric Bulb. Price, each..............65

U. S. Odometer.

Above Reads 4652 8/10 Miles.

No. 24R3075 The U. S. Odometer registers the distance traveled by a horse. Everyone who has a horse and carriage will be interested in this instrument. Liverymen, physicians, speeders, etc., will find the Odometer of great practical value. Made for all sized wheels; sizes most used, 38, 40 and 42 inches. In ordering give height of front wheel. Price, each..............$2.10

If by mail, postage extra, 5 cents.

Buggy Aprons.

Patent Buggy Apron, made of waterproof cloth, extra heavy, adjustable to any width buggy dash. Weight, 2½ pounds. This apron is self adjustable and fills a long felt want. A band of impervious rubber goring is so made that the apron will adjust itself to any dash.

No. 24R3080 Buggy Apron, 20 to 26-inch dash. Price, each..............80c

No. 24R3082 Buggy Apron, medium, 22 to 28-inch dash. Price, each..............88c

No. 24R3084 Carriage Apron, heavy, 26 to 34-inch dash. Price, each..............$1.25

No. 24R3086 Phaeton Apron, extra heavy, 34 to 44-inch dash. Price, each..............$1.70

Eureka Buggy Shaft.

No. 24R3090 Made without mortise or tenon; having a malleable clamp box joint at intersection of cross bar and shaft, so recessed at either corner as to be drawn down with bolts, clamping the cross bar and shaft on top, bottom and both sides, forming a strong and rigid joint, maintaining the full strength of cross bar and shaft, to which is added the strength of the malleable clamp box, and obviates the looseness resulting from the shrinkage of the wooden parts. We guarantee the Eureka Shaft never to break at intersection of cross bar and shaft, as all others do. Comes in the white without paint or straps, but ironed complete. Size, 1⅜x2 inches. Price, per set..............$1.35

Buggy Evener and Singletree.

No. 24R3092 Buggy Evener and Singletree, finished, painted and ironed complete ready for use. Price, per set..............$1.00

Stay Straps.

No. 24R3094 Pole Stay Straps, same as used on carriage poles. Complete as shown in cut. Size, ⅞x52 inches. Price, per pair..............35c

Standard Buggy Shafts.

Made of select hickory well ironed throughout, cross bar mortised and fastened with T-plates, double reinforced shaft irons with extra heavy eye made of one solid piece of steel. No welds to break or become loose. The painted shafts have 17-inch leathers on ends, also on singletrees and holdbacks. Have 1-inch eye with 7/8-inch hole; width outside to outside, 44 inches, which is the standard width of all buggies.

Standard Buggy Shafts, ironed complete, either in the white or with paint, leather straps or trimmings.

No. 24R3096 Finished and ironed in the white, ready to paint, 1⅜x2 inches, which is buggy size. Price, per pair..............$1.05

No. 24R3098 Surrey size, 1½x2¼ inches. Price, per pair..............1.28

No. 24R3100 Painted black or red, ironed and trimmed complete, as shown in cut. Buggy size, 1⅜x2 inches. Price, per pair..............$1.75

No. 24R3102 Surrey size, 1½x2¼ inches. Price, per pair..............$1.95

Standard Buggy Shaft with Circle Bar.

Standard Buggy Shafts. Same as No. 23R3096 with extra circle, as shown in illustration, which gives greater strength and rigidness.

No. 24R3104 Size, 1⅜x2 inches, finished and ironed in the white, ready to paint. Price, each..............$1.45

No. 24R3105 Size, 1⅜x2 inches, painted black or red, ironed and trimmed complete. Price, each..............$2.15

Standard Carriage Poles.

Standard Carriage Poles, ironed and trimmed complete, either in white or painted black. High grade work at a price the ordinary manufacturer pays for the raw material. We use nothing but select hickory in all our poles; also wrought iron stays and tee plates well finished and ironed throughout. We furnish them complete with doubletree, singletree, neckyoke and stay straps.

No. 1, Buggy Pole, 1⅜x2 inches, with 1-inch eye, 7/8-inch hole, width of eyes outside to outside, 44 inches.

No. 24R3106 Price, complete in the white..............$2.35

No. 24R3107 Price, complete, painted..............2.75

No. 2 Surrey Pole, 1⅜x2¼ inches, with 1-inch eye, 7/8-inch hole, width of eyes outside to outside, 44 inches.

No. 24R3110 Price, complete in the white..$2.40

No. 24R3112 Price, complete, painted..............2.80

Standard Carriage Poles with Oval Iron Braces.

Special Standard Carriage Poles with oval iron braces. This pole is ironed with wrought top and bottom tees, hammer strap is welded solid to tee. Braces are neatly curved and all irons are polished. A first class job in every respect. Comes complete with doubletree, singletree and neckyoke.

No. 24R3113 Size 1⅜x2¼ inches, with 1-inch eye, in the white. Each, $3.00

No. 24R3114 Size 1⅜x2¼ inches, with 1-inch eye, painted black. Each..$3.50

Adjustable Carriage Pole.

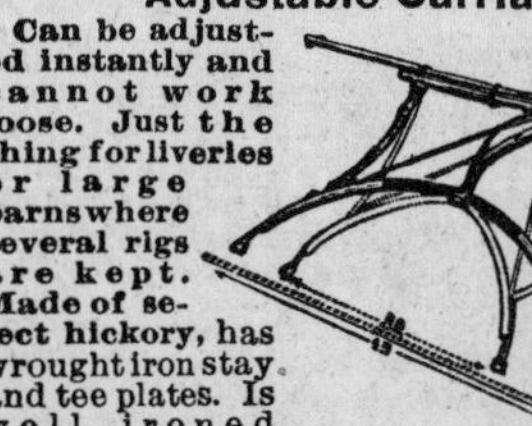

Can be adjusted instantly and cannot work loose. Just the thing for liveries or large barns where several rigs are kept. Made of select hickory, has wrought iron stay and tee plates. Is well ironed throughout, nicely finished, ready to attach to carriage. Furnished complete with doubletree, singletree, neckyoke and stay straps.

No. 1, Buggy Size, 1⅜x2 inches, with 1-inch eye.

No. 24R3115 Price, complete in the white..$3.50

No. 24R3116 Price, complete, painted..............4.00

No. 2, Surrey Size, 1⅜x2¼ inches, with 1-inch eye.

No. 24R3118 Price, complete in the white..$3.60

No. 24R3120 Price, complete, painted..............4.10

Anti-Rattlers.

No. 24R3122 The Dandy Shaft and Pole Coupling Anti-Rattlers. Made of steel, the head strengthened by a plate riveted on. To place in position, set the lower part in the coupling and drive them in. They will not break; the corrugation on the side prevents them from working out. Price, per pair..............5c

Anti-Rattler and Bolt Holders.

No. 24R3124 Anti-Rattler and Bolt Holders, made of Crescent patent cold rolled steel. It insures against the rattling of the shafts of any spring vehicle, is perfectly noiseless, will last as long as the buggy, and shafts can be taken off without trouble and replaced by a pole in a minute. Price, per pair..............7½c

Rubber Anti-Rattlers.

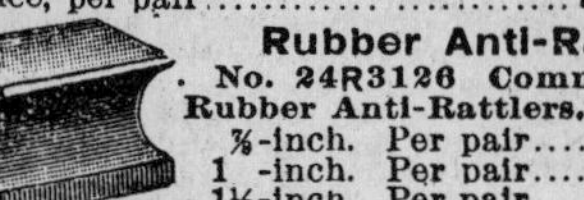

No. 24R3126 Common Pattern Rubber Anti-Rattlers.

⅝-inch. Per pair..............3c

1 -inch. Per pair..............8c

1⅛-inch. Per pair..............3½c

Wire Anti-Rattlers.

No. 24R3128 Wire Anti-Rattlers; made of steel wire; prevents rattling of the shafts. Price, per pair..............2c

GIVE CATALOGUE NUMBER IN FULL WHEN YOU WRITE YOUR ORDER

Stake Irons.

No. 24R3750 Malleable Iron Stake Irons for Express Wagons. Size for 1⅛ and 2¼ stake, 2½ inches deep, with ⅝-inch holes. Length over all, 7 inches. Price, each....18c

Bow Staples, (to rivet); state size and price.

	Size.	Weight, dozen.	Per dozen.
No. 24R3753	1½	17 ounces.	5c
No. 24R3754	1¾	20 ounces.	5½c
No. 24R3755	2	24 ounces.	6c

Wagon Bow Staples.

(To drive.) **State size wanted.**

No. 24R3759 Wagon Bow Staples, 1½, 1¾ and 2 inch. Weight per dozen, 15 ounces.
Price, per dozen....................7½c

No. 24R3765 Steel Wagon Stay Chains with twisted links. Size, ⅜-inch, length, 26 inches. Weight, 4 pounds per pair. Price, per pair..................22c

No. 24R3767 Steel Tongue or Pole Chains with twisted links. Size, ⅜ inch. Length, 33 inches. Weight, 6 pounds per pair.
Price, per pair..........................31c

Wagon Tongue Support.

No. 24R3770 Accompanying cut shows **our Common Sense Support for wagon tongues.** One of the greatest improvements of the age. One of these on your wagon will pay for itself many times over in the saving of horse flesh. You can **put it on any common wagon, and it can be adjusted to any desired height.** We consider it the most efficient **tongue support** made. Our special price......**$1.00**

Spiral Tongue Support.

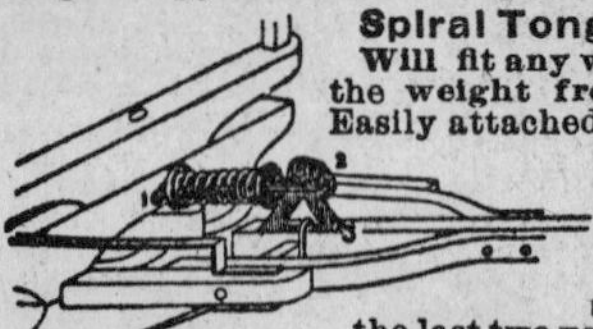

Will fit any wagon. Takes all the weight from horse's neck. Easily attached to wagon tongue. One of the most simple and durable supports on the market. We have sold thousands of them in the last two years and they have given universal satisfaction.

No. 24R3774 For light spring wagons.
Price, each..............................**$1.10**
No. 24R3775 For ordinary wagons. Price, each **1.30**
No. 24R3776 For heavy wagons. Price, each.. **1.45**

Ironed Neckyokes.

No. 24R3785 Neckyokes, 38-inch; hickory, ironed complete. Weight, 7¼ pounds; each.......34c
No. 24R3788 42-inch, each.............................42c
No. 24R3789 48x3-inch, each............................55c

Ironed Evener.

No. 24R3792 2x4x48 inches, wrought iron plates and malleable clevis, **complete,** as shown in cut, oiled. Price, each..........................40c

Coe's Patent Wagon Doubletree.

No. 24R3794 The Coe's Doubletree presents a new feature in wagon doubletrees. No lap links are needed in attaching singletrees. A 42-inch doubletree of this make is equal to 48-inch of other makes, because the singletree hitches on the extreme end. No clevis pins to wear away the wood or come unscrewed, or be stolen from the tree. It is as cheap as a common wagon doubletree and is stronger. The eye for our stay chains fastens around the tree and is not weakened by holes through it, as with the old style. Length, 42 inches. Weight, 9 pounds.
Price, each...48c

Plow Doubletree.

No. 24R3798 Select hickory, 36 inches long, 2¾ inches thick, with hook in center. Weight, about 8 pounds. Price, each..................................22c

Plow Double-tree Sets.

No. 24R3800 Made of select hickory, well ironed, a smooth, nice job, 36-inch evener, with singletree clevises, complete. Price, per set..........62c
Weight, about 15 pounds.

Plow Singletrees.

These are very fine **Singletrees,** made of selected woods, equipped with center clip hook and ferrule.

No. 24R3810 These Singletrees are not painted, but finished smooth and carefully oiled. Singletree, 26-inch, plow, **hickory, ironed.** Weight, 3¼ pounds.
Price, each.......................................11c
No. 24R3812 Plow Singletree, 30-inch, plow, **hickory, ironed.** Weight, 3¾ pounds. Each....13c

Wagon Singletrees.

Wagon Singletree, hickory, ironed, with ferrules and hooks. Weight, 6 pounds.
No. 24R3817 2¼x30 inches. Price, each.......19c
No. 24R3818 2½x36 inches. Price, each......26c
No. 24R3819 3x38 inches. Price, each.........40c

Strap End Singletrees.

No. 24R3822 Select Hickory, Strap End, Wagon Singletree; hook has ½ inch strap, well riveted on, and ⅝-inch hook. Size, 2⅝x36 inches. Weight, 6½ pounds. Price, each.........32c

Davis Safety Singletrees.

Wagon Singletree with Davis Patent Hooks. The only hook that will hold the tug under all conditions. Cannot become unhooked.
No. 24R3826 2¼x30 inches. Price, each.........19c
No. 24R3827 2½x36 inches. Price, each.........26c

The Celebrated Tubular Steel Doubletrees and Singletrees and Neckyokes.

These goods are past the experimental stage, having stood for the past five years the most severe and practical tests, and are at present used by hundreds of our customers with the best results. A trial will convince any practical person of their superiority over all similar articles made from wood. They weigh no more than wood of a good quality and will outwear a dozen of the latter. **In short, they are practically indestructible and will last a lifetime.**

Tubular Steel Plow Singletrees.

Northwestern Plow Singletree, painted with special iron paint which bakes to the singletree and remains permanent.

			Price
No. 24R3840	26-inch.	Weight, each, 4¼ lbs...	40c
No. 24R3842	28-inch.	Weight, each, 6 lbs....	43c
No. 24R3844	30-inch.	Weight, each, 7 lbs ...	49c

Tubular Steel Singletrees.

Tubular Steel Cultivator and Lead Bar Singletree with Hook in Center, painted with special iron paint baked on. **Cannot rust; will last forever.**

			Price
No. 24R3848	26-inch.	Weight, each, 5 pounds,	43c
No. 24R3850	28-inch.	Weight, each, 5½ lbs.....	45c
No. 24R3852	30-inch.	Weight, each, 7 pounds,	50c

Tubular Steel Wagon Two-Horse Singletrees.

Tubular Steel Two-Horse Wagon Singletrees with Ring in center, just the thing for heavy hauling. **Will haul the load of three wood singletrees.** Coated with a special iron paint baked on which remains permanent. **Will not rust.**
No. 24R3860 33-inch. Capacity, 2000 pounds. Weight, each, 9 pounds. Price, each...................70c
No. 24R3862 34-inch. Capacity, 2500 pounds. Weight, each, 10 pounds. Price, each..................85c
No. 24R3864 36-inch. Capacity, 4000 pounds. Weight, each, 12 pounds. Price, each...................95c

Tubular Steel Wagon Neckyoke.

No. 24R3868 Tubular Steel Wagon Neckyoke made of best grade Bessemer steel, coated with patent iron paint which prevents rusting. As light as wood and will outwear three common neckyokes. **Give this a trial and see if it is not the best neckyoke you ever used.** Weight, 12 pounds.
Price for 40-inch, each...............................98c

Tubular Steel Plow Doubletrees.

Tubular Steel Plow Doubletree in Sets Complete as shown in cut. Stronger and as light weight as wood; will last a lifetime. Furnished with hook in center and cockeye hooks pulling from back of singletree. Painted with a patent rust proof iron paint baked on, which we guarantee to remain permanent.
No. 24R3875 No. 0. Capacity 2000 lbs., doubletree 33 in. long, singletree 28 in. long. Price, per set. **$1.55**
No. 24R3876 No. 1. Capacity 3000 lbs., doubletree 36 in. long, singletree 30 in. long. Price, per set. **$1.80**

Tubular Steel Wagon Doubletree Sets.

Tubular Steel Wagon Doubletree Sets. Made of the same high grade of steel as the goods above. Just the thing for hauling grain, wood, etc., to market. In fact, in place where a breakdown means a day lost in going to town. You can't break them. Weight, No. 1, 35 pounds; weight, No. 2, 38 pounds.
No. 24R3880 No. 1. Capacity 2500 lbs., evener is 46 in. long, singletree 33 in. long. Price, per set. **$2.95**
No. 24R3882 No. 2. Capacity 4000 lbs., evener is 48 in. long, singletree 34 in. long. Price, per set. **$3.10**

Coe's Patent Tripletree.

No. 24R3890 In the Coes Patent Tripletree or Three-Horse Evener, we have the best thing of the kind now on the market. The bar is 40 inches long; eveners 30 inches, and singletrees 28 inches. Has self-locking end clips, etc. They are made extra strong and can be used for any kind of work on wagon or plow. Made of best grade hickory. Weight, 29 pounds. Price, per set.......................**$1.75**

Acme Three-Horse Evener.

Acme Three-Horse Evener is light, strong, neat and durable. A perfect three-horse equalizer; can be changed for two horses in one minute; is made of select hickory; the ends of all the eveners are riveted. Singletrees have twisted clip and full hooks. Size of woods used: Main evener, 1¾x3½x40 inches; small eveners, 1⅛x2¼x28 inches; singletrees, 26-inch.
No. 24R3894 Price, per set........................**$1.75**

Four-Horse Equalizer.

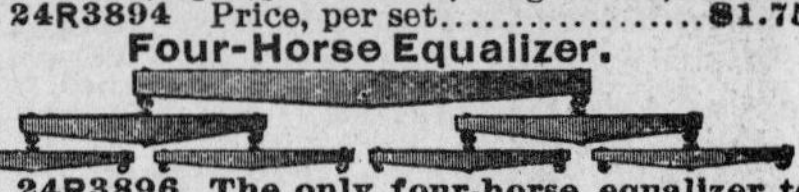

No. 24R3896 The only four-horse equalizer to use with or without a tongue. All parts are detachable. No side draft or combination lever. Pulls plow straight from center of beam, placing horse squarely in furrow, 34 inches or over from center of draft. Is right or left hand. Price, per set.... **$2.85**

Steel Buggy Axles.

S., R. & Co.'s half patent solid collar welded shoulder steel axles complete with boxing. We cannot furnish boxes only, nor axles without boxes. **A set of short bed axles** (commonly called axle stubs) consists of four axles with short bed, which are intended to be welded to old axles. **A set of long bed axles** consists of four axles with bed long enough to make axle complete by welding in the center. We sell one-half set at one-half the price of a full set, and one-quarter set at one-quarter the price of full set. We cannot weld axles or set boxes.

In ordering parts of sets be sure and state whether right or left hand is wanted.

No. 24R3900 Short bed. No. 24R3902 Long bed.

Size	Price, short bed	Price, long bed	Size	Price, short bed	Price, long bed
⅞x6½	$1.30	$1.65	1¼x7½	$2.09	$2.52
1 x6½	1.45	1.79	1⅜x7	2.84	3.50
1⅛x6½	1.69	2.07	1⅜x7½	2.85	3.55
1⅛x7	1.70	2.08	1½x8	3.75	4.40
1⅛x7½	1.71	2.09	1⅝x8	4.65	5.40
1¼x6½	2.07	2.50	1¾x9½	5.40	6.40
1¼x7	2.08	2.51			

We can furnish Fantail Axles same quality as above at 10 cents per set, extra.

Sarven Patent Wheels

WITH OR WITHOUT TIRES.

READ OUR PRICES FOR GENUINE SARVEN PATENT WHEELS, AND YOU WILL READILY SEE WE ARE THE LEADERS IN THE WHEEL BUSINESS.

WE do not hesitate to say our Standard Grade Wheels are the best wheel for the money, quality and workmanship considered, sold by anyone. The hubs are second growth elm, spokes and rims of second growth Ohio hickory. We receive a great number of letters from our customers asking how we can sell **standard grade** Sarven patent wheels, made of honest stock and of good workmanship at the low price quoted in our catalogue. This is easily answered when you stop to consider that we are the largest buyers of tired buggy wheels in the United States, having bought and sold twice as many wheels the past year as any other firm. That we buy for **spot cash** and by placing such large orders with one firm, they are able to manufacture wheels the year around.

A wheel factory generally runs about six months in the year, so you can readily see they are willing to make a great concession by reducing prices for this reason. It is much more profitable to keep running, if at a small loss, as the machinery becomes rusted, belting rots out and a general decay takes place the minute you shut down. As we stated above, all our wheels are made by a firm whose reputation for honest wheels is second to none in this country. Every wheel is carefully inspected before leaving the factory and if found imperfect in any way is rejected; the same care is taken when the wheels are received by us. They are made with the object of giving value received to the purchaser and are sold on their merits.

WE USE THE BEST GRADE ROUND EDGE STEEL TIRES, welded and set by machinery, which gives uniform dish to the wheels, and makes a better job in every way. They are bolted with the best grade tire bolts, between every spoke. The hubs have solid iron bands projecting over each end, which answers the purpose of a hub and sand band at the same time.

IF YOU HAVE A BUGGY OR CARRIAGE that is in fair shape with the exception of the wheels, which are usually worn out before the other parts, a set of our tired wheels—a set of axles and a coat of paint will give you a buggy that will last you several seasons at a very small outlay.

TAKE YOUR PENCIL AND DO A LITTLE FIGURING and see how easy we can save you 50 per cent on buggy wheels, and how cheaply you can make your old rig as good as new.

SARVEN PATENT WHEELS IN THE WHITE.

Without Tires. For Wheels With Tires, See Nos. 24R4416 to 24R4426.

GIVE HEIGHT OF WHEELS WANTED. **If no height is mentioned we use our judgment in filling orders. These prices are for a set of four wheels,** any height listed below. Half sets furnished at one-half the price of a set. **The hub length** is length of box which goes in the hub, rim band and hub or sand band not being measured.

WRITE US FOR PRICES ON HEAVIER SARVEN WHEELS, being careful to give size of spoke, length of hub, tread, depth of rim and height of wheels wanted. Thimble skeins cannot be used in Sarven Wheels. Steel axles must be used.

WHEELS IN THE WHITE WITHOUT TIRES.

Size of spoke, inches	1 1/16	1⅛	1¼	1⅜	1½	1¾	2⅛	2⅜
Length of hub, inches	6½	6½	7	7½	8	8½	10½	11
Width of tread, inches	⅞	1	1⅛	1¼	1½	1¾	2⅛	2⅜
Depth of rim, inches	1⅛	1¼	1⅜	1⅜	1¾	2¼	2½	3
No. 24R4400 Price, per set of 4 wheels, standard grade	$5.25	$5.35	$6.30	$7.25	$10.00			
No. 24R4402 Price, per set of 4 wheels, extra standard grade	6.75	6.80	7.65	9.00	11.50	$19.25	$25.00	
No. 24R4404 Price, per set of 4 wheels, special grade	8.65	8.80	9.65	11.00	13.50	21.25	28.00	$33.00

Diameter of above wheels, 3 feet 2 inches, 3 feet 4 inches, 3 feet 6 inches, 3 feet 8 inches, 3 feet 10 inches and 4 feet.

There should be 4 inches difference between front and hind wheels.

NEW BUGGY WHEELS WITH TIRES PUT ON CHEAPER THAN YOU CAN REPAIR YOUR OLD ONES.

SARVEN PATENT WHEELS, TIRED, BANDED. **It does not pay you to buy wheels without tires as the tires, bolts, washers, etc., bought at home at retail prices, will cost you as much as we ask for the wheels complete,** to say nothing of the labor of doing the work. It is no longer the custom to buy hubs, spokes, rims, etc., and make the wheels at the carriage shop, as the wheel factories do the work better, quicker and cheaper. **With our improved method of making wheels, welding tires by electricity, bolting and finishing by machinery,** we can do the work better than by hand, getting uniform dish and in every way more satisfactory. We use only selected forest stock thoroughly air seasoned; made mathematically and mechanically perfect, carefully finished and critically inspected before shipment. The tires are the best grade carriage steel, with round edges, are put on by hand and bolted between every spoke with Norway bolts.

IF OUR WHEELS **are not as we represent them to be, are found defective, are not of perfect workmanship, we will pay freight charges and drayage necessary to have them returned to us** and will replace them with a new set free of charge.

NO WHEELS **are warranted by us when the hubs in the size wheel you are ordering are so small in diameter** that cutting out the boxes leaves the spoke tenons less than ⅛-inch greater in length than the width of the spoke at shoulder.

IT IS A GREAT MISTAKE **to buy a wheel lighter than will correspond with your axles. We mention this fact as we have had cases where a customer would order a light ⅞-inch wheel** and cut the hub entirely away trying to fit 1¼-inch axles in same when he should have ordered a 1⅜-inch wheel.

Measure your axle and then compare the size with table below for size needed.

NOTICE: WE CANNOT PAINT WHEELS, FURNISH OR SET BOXES. PLEASE DO NOT ASK IT AS IT WILL ONLY DELAY ORDER.

SARVEN PATENT WHEELS WITH TIRES.

	Size of Spoke of Hub	Length of Hub where box goes in	Width of Rim	Size of Tire	Price per Set of 4 Wheels Stand'rd Grade	Price per Set of 4 Wheels Extra Grade	Weight per Set of 4 Wheels
No. 24R4416	1 1/16 in.	6½ in.	⅞ in.	3/16	$6.25	$7.00	90 lbs.
No. 24R4418	1⅛ in.	6½ in.	1 in.	¼	6.75	7.10	100 lbs.
No. 24R4420	1¼ in.	7 in.	1⅛ in.	5/16	8.00	8.00	125 lbs.
No. 24R4422	1⅜ in.	7½ in.	1¼ in.	⅜	9.30	9.80	160 lbs.
No. 24R4424	1½ in.	8 in.	1½ in.	½	15.00	21.00	240 lbs.
No. 24R4426	1¾ in.	9 in.	1¾ in.	⅝	28.00	35.00	375 lbs.

Diameter of above wheels, 3 ft. 2 in., 3 ft. 4 in., 3 ft. 6 in., 3 ft. 8 in., 3 ft. 10 in. and 4 ft.

Always allow 4 inches between size of front and hind wheels.

For example, 3 feet 4 inches and 3 feet 8 inches correspond; 3 feet 6 inches and 3 feet 10 inches; 3 feet 8 inches and 4 feet.

WE CARRY A LARGE STOCK OF THE ABOVE SIZES and can make prompt shipment. If no height is mentioned we send 3 feet 8 inches and 4 feet wheels. **In ordering wheels for repair work give length of box in your old wheel, which will be the length of hub required.** Two wheels sold at half the price of a set, one wheel at one-quarter the price of a set. **In ordering parts of sets be sure to give height.**

NOTICE.—As there seems to be more or less confusion existing as to the right size axles to use in the above wheels we give below the Standard Table of sizes. We have a great many orders for light wheels and say 1¼-inch axles, and the consequence is the hub is cut entirely out, putting the box in, leaving only ⅜ or ½-inch of spoke tenon and the result is the wheel soon goes to pieces, is condemned as **NO GOOD.** By following the table below you will avoid all this.

For No. 24R4416 Wheels use ⅞ x 6½ or 1 x 6½ Axles.
For No. 24R4418 Wheels use ⅞ x 6½ or 1 x 6½ Axles.
For No. 24R4420 Wheels use 1 x 7 or 1⅛ x 7 Axles.
For No. 24R4422 Wheels use 1⅛x7½ or 1¼x7½ Axles.
For No. 24R4424 Wheels use 1⅜x8 or 1½x8 Axles.
For No. 24R4426 Wheels use 1½x9 or 1⅝x9 Axles.

We carry in stock wheels 3 feet 2 inches, 3 feet 4 inches, 3 feet 6 inches, 3 feet 8 inches, 3 feet 10 inches and 4 feet, and can make prompt shipment. Prices on other sizes quoted upon application.

RUBBER TIRED BUGGY WHEELS,

Sarven Patent Buggy Wheels with Highest Grade Guaranteed Diamond Rubber Tires.

Owing to the increasing demand for Rubber Tired Wheels we have made arrangements with one of the largest manufacturers of rubber vehicle tires in the United States to furnish us 1000 sets of tires of the following sizes, and will now be able to sell you a high grade Sarven wheel with full metal bands complete with the **Best Rubber Tires** put on and bolted at a price that should secure your order if in need of a wheel of this kind. It is not necessary to mention that the Sarven patent wheel has no equal for wearing qualities, workmanship and finish. The tires are put on by machinery after first setting a steel channel tire on wheels, bolting same between every spoke, thus avoiding any chance of becoming loose from the rim. The rubber used is the **highest grade Para rubber** carefully vulcanized and is strictly first class. **Prices given below are for a high grade Sarven wheel in the white or oiled, with tires put on ready for use. For detail of sizes see steel tired sizes above.**

Number	Size of Spoke at Hub	Length of Hub where box goes	Price per set of 4 wheels
24R4435	1 1/16-inch	6 inches	$24.90
24R4436	1⅛-inch	6½ inches	27.90
24R4437	1¼-inch	7 inches	35.90
24R4438	1⅜-inch	7½ inches	36.95

Cast Bob Shoes.

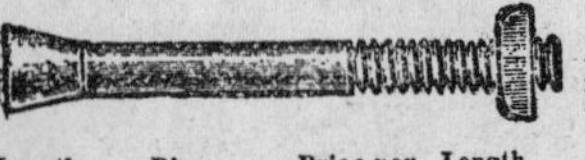

Cast Iron Bob Sleigh Shoes, interchangeable for right or left hand; 1⅛-inch tread, 2-inch on top and 1⅜-inch thick.

No. 24R4978

Length	Weight, per set of four	Per set
36 inches	74 pounds	$1.50
38 inches	79 pounds	1.60
40 inches	84 pounds	1.95
42 inches	89 pounds	2.00
44 inches	94 pounds	2.05
46 inches	99 pounds	2.10
48 inches	104 pounds	2.50

Sleigh Shoe Bolts.

No. 24R4980 Made of the best Norway iron.

Length, Inches	Diameter	Price per set of 16	Length, Inches	Diameter	Price per set of 16
4½	7/16 inch	30c	6½	7/16 inch	37c
5	7/16 inch	31c	7	7/16 inch	42c
5½	7/16 inch	33c	7½	7/16 inch	45c
6	7/16 inch	35c	8	7/16 inch	48c

Whalon's Patent Shifting Bar.

No. 24R4985 **The Latest and Best. This is the most practical adjustable bar ever invented.** It is easily and quickly adjusted to fit any sleigh, whether thills or pole, and can be shifted from center to side draft on sleigh without even unhitching the horse. These bars are made of best refined steel and Norway iron, and will last a lifetime. Fully warranted.
Price, each......**$1.60**

Light Spring Wagon Bobs.

No. 24R4988 The above Bobs are made mortiseless, that is, the knees are not mortised into the runners. We use a malleable T plate, which is riveted onto runners, which greatly strengthens same. Made of hardwood throughout. Furnished complete as shown in illustration with draw bar for center or side draft with shaft shackles and bolsters suited to any kind of a body. A first class bob in every respect; painted and varnished; color road cart, red or carmine shade. Size knees, runners and raves, 1¼x1⅜ inches; beams, 1¼x6 inches; hind bolsters oscillating; height of bolster from ground, 21 inches; length of runner, 3 feet 1 inch; width of track, 3 feet 1 inch. Price, per set......**$9.25**

Delivery and Pleasure Sleighs.

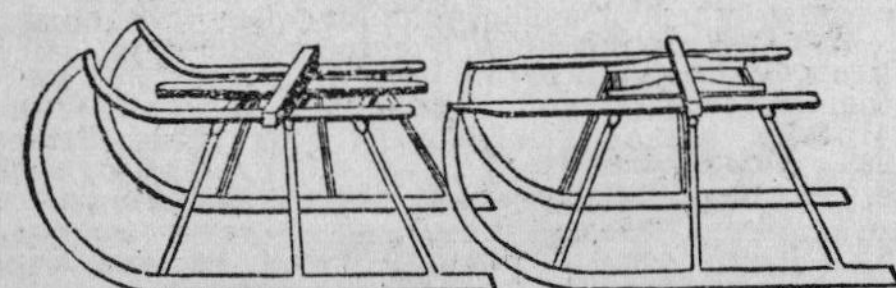

Our Patent Delivery and Pleasure Sleigh is without doubt the best sleigh for the purpose ever made. In it are combined lightness, strength and durability, and the simpleness of construction enables us to place it on the market at prices much below any other make of sleigh. Warranted to start and run easier and carry heavier loads with greater ease than any other sleigh on the market. During the past five years they have been distributed throughout every section of the country and the growing demand is the best evidence of their merit.

No. 24R4992 With 1-inch runner. Price...**$25.60**
No. 24R4994 With 1¼-inch runner. Price. **26.80**
No. 24R4996 With 1½-inch runner. Price. **27.85**

The above prices are for sleighs complete—ironed, painted and varnished. Cushions and shafts ready to hitch on as shown in illustration. If wanted with only one seat, deduct $2.50 from above prices. For pole in place of shafts, add $2.00 extra to above prices. For both shafts and pole, add $4.00 extra to above prices.

Bob Woods.

Finished Grocery Bob Woods, all made with three knees front and two hind, extra well finished, not ironed or painted, but ready for finishing.

No. 24R5000 1⅛x1⅛ tread. Per set......**$5.95**
No. 24R5002 1¼x1¾ tread. Per set......**6.85**

The Giant Patent Bob Runner.

$8.45 to $11.00 per Set.

This illustration represents a new style of fancy bob used as a hub runner, which we are now placing upon the market with great success. Constant complaint is made by those using the regular hub runner that they are not strong or durable, and cause much trouble in their constant calls for repairs. Our new patent hub runner combines all the requisites of a perfect runner. It is light in weight, strong and durable, and can be easily adjusted to any delivery wagon. The illustration represents the front bob of the set, the hind having a straight rave. No pole or shafts are used on these sleighs; the regular shafts or pole can be used, as the draft is direct from the wagon gear. **Made of best grade selected stock, ironed and furnished complete.**

No. 24R5010 1- inch runner. Per set.....**$8.45**
No. 24R5012 1⅛-inch runner. Per set..... **9.30**
No. 24R5013 1¼-inch runner. Per set.....**10.50**
No. 24R5014 1½-inch runner. Per set.....**11.00**

Pioneer Runner Attachments.

The Pioneer Runner is by far the best runner on the market, price and quality considered. They are made adjustable and can be changed instantly for narrow or wide track. Have steel boxes which cover the axle completely, thus protecting the arm of axle from snow and ice. Has four steel braces which, added to our patent clip, makes it one of the most rigid runners made. Runners and raves are made of the best grade selected stock. The oscillating device which clamps on to the axle is also adjustable and will fit square part of axle without wedging, which is a great drawback to most runners on the market. We use T plates instead of mortises, which strengthens the runner. Striped and painted ready for use.

	Size of axle to be used on	Weight, per set	Price, per set
No. 24R5016	⅞ or 1 -in.	35 lbs.	$5.30
No. 24R5018	1⅛ or 1¼-in.	55 lbs.	6.25
No. 24R5020	1⅜ or 1½-in.	75 lbs.	7.15
No. 24R5022	1⅝ or 1¾-in.	85 lbs.	8.90

Pioneer Runners for Two-Wheeled Rigs.

	Size of axle to be used on	Weight, per pair	Price, per pair
No. 24R5026	⅞-inch	30 lb.	$4.00
No. 24R5028	1-inch	30 lb.	4.00

Acme Sleigh Runners.

This is finely finished and the most desirable runner attachment yet out. It is easily attached, will fit on to almost any vehicle that runs on wheels, and it tracks with sleighs.

(Patented, April 21, 1896.)

When the runner is attached to a carriage **the end of the axle is protected by a box** made of two steel sheets pressed into the proper shape and **securely bolted together,** it being designed to **protect the axle further** by inserting cloth or leather between the sheets to prevent rubbing. **Holes are punched in the steel axle bearing,** so that the bolts fastening the bearings to the brace can be moved, and in this way the place of attaching the runner to the axle can be varied by six inches. **The rear runner is two inches higher** than forward, so that the body of the vehicle will be level.

	Size of axle to be used on	Weight, per set	Capacity	Price, per set
No. 24R5030	⅞ and 1 -in.	60 lbs.	1000 lbs.	$ 6.30
No. 24R5032	1⅛ and 1¼-in.	75 lbs.	2000 lbs.	8.25
No. 24R5034	1⅜ and 1½-in.	100 lbs.	3000 lbs.	10.50

The Mortiseless Bob Sled.

In our Mortiseless Bob we have the best all around sled on the market. It is very light and strong. The runners are solid bent second growth ash; shoes are cast, with grooved bottoms, which prevents slipping or sliding sideways. T plates are malleable iron, riveted and clinched, connecting the parts without mortise or tenon. They have great clearance, will run light, and are very strong. Bolsters 3 feet 2 inches between stakes. A first class sled in every particular. Prices are f. o. b. factory in Central Ohio. **Cast Shoes.**

	Horse	Knees	Size runner	Price
No. 24R5036	1 horse,	2-knee bob,	1⅜x2¼ in.,	$10.00
No. 24R5037	2 horse,	3-knee bob,	1⅜x2¼ in.,	11.25
No. 24R5038	2 horse,	3-knee bob,	2⅛x2¼ in.,	12.50

Special Bargains in Bob Sleds.

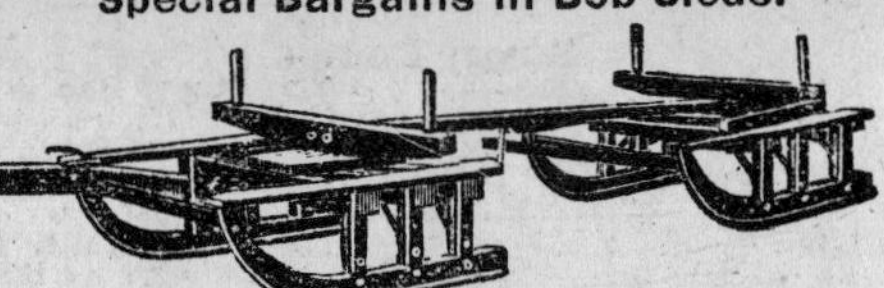

Cut Shows 6-knee Bob.

Where goods from this department are quoted f. o. b. factory, it is done to save the expense of freight, cartage and handling from Chicago. All the saving goes to the customer in the low prices we make. It enables us to quote a price direct from the factory that barely covers the cost of material and manufacturing with but our one small profit added, a price only made possible by reason of eliminating all the handling expense and shipping direct from factory.

We placed an order early in the season for the largest number of bobs ever sent out. By placing such an order we were able to procure the **best bob** for the money we have ever handled. While our knee bobs gave universal satisfaction last year, we expect to do still better this year by giving you a heavier and stronger sled, with knees mortised **top and bottom, (something no other firm furnishes)**; extra heavy chilled shoes, turned up behind; a great improvement on last year, as it enables the bob to be backed without catching in the uneven ground. This feature will be greatly appreciated by anyone hauling wood, etc., as you know it is impossible to use a sled of the old style in the woods or on swampy ground. We also furnish two reaches, one long and one short, which makes the bob run much steadier, and is easier to adjust to any length box or rack.

The raves are 6 inches wide by 48 inches long; runner, 1⅞ inches wide by 3 inches deep by 4 feet 8 inches long, with a 40-inch chilled shoe turned up behind.

Runners and raves are made of hickory elm, balance of bob oak and maple. They are well ironed and braced, and are made up in a workmanlike manner and are sent out with our guarantee to be made of sound material, free from all defects, and the **best bob you ever bought at the price, or money refunded.** Painted **four coats**, striped and varnished. They were made up this summer and are all ready for delivery. **No delays in shipping.** Weight, four-knee, about 400 pounds; six-knee, about 450 pounds. Prices quoted on the sleds are f. o. b. our factory in Southern Wisconsin.

Track 3 feet 2 inches **outside to outside of runner.**
No. 24R5040 Price, four-knee bob, per set. **$10.50**
No. 24R5042 Price, six-knee bob, per set.. **12.00**

Combination 4 and 6-Knee Bobs.

No. 24R5044 In order to accommodate our customers who wish a heavier bob in front or behind, we can furnish No. 24R5040 and No. 24R5042, with a 4-knee bob in front and a 6-knee bob behind, or 6 knees in front and 4 behind, just as you wish. **Be sure and state how you wish the combination made up, so as to avoid delays, etc.** Track, 3 feet 2 inches **outside to outside of runners.** Price, per set......**$13.75**

Special Bargains in Mandt Bob Sleds.

Our bob sleds are made by a concern which has a reputation in this line second to none. The manufacturers of these goods are recognized by all dealers as the makers of the **best bobs in the country**, and only the best are good enough for us to offer to our trade. We contracted for this line of goods for the reason that we learned by investigation that **nothing but the best of material entered into the construction of this work,** that this line of bobs was the best on the market, regardless of price.

These sleighs are all covered by the most binding two years' guarantee, during which time, if any piece or part gives out by reason of defect in material or workmanship, we will replace it free of charge. **With care they will last a natural lifetime.**

Our $13.25 Mandt Patent Steel Bob Sled.

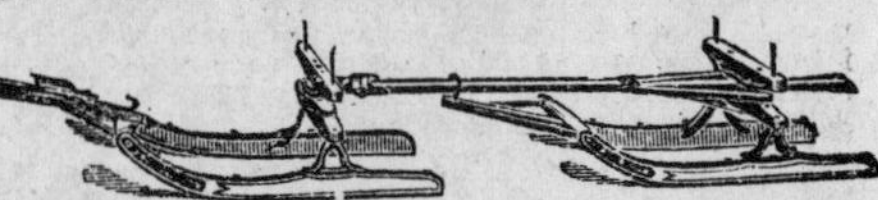

The Mandt Steel Knee Oscillating Bob is by all odds the lightest, strongest and most durable sled made. The knees are made of one solid piece of steel; all braces, plates, etc., are hand forged; beams, bolsters, reach and tongue are made of white oak; runner, of hickory elm. The size of runner is 2x4 in.x5 ft.; bolsters, 3⅛x4½; beams, 3½x4½; reach, 2x4. For use in the timber or on rough roads this sled has no equal, and at the price we ask for it you save a $5.00 bill on every set you buy. Price a sled of this description of your home merchant and see if we are not right. They are nicely painted, striped and varnished and are a first class sled in every respect. Track, 3 feet 2 inches outside to outside of runner. Our price is f. o. b. our factory in Southern Wisconsin.

No. 24R5048 Weight, 350 pounds. Price..**$13.25**

Buggy Bodies.

Piano Buggy Bodies in the white, not ironed or painted; 24 and 25 inches wide, and 48 or 50 and 52 inches long; panels, 8 inches deep. Weight, about 50 pounds. **Made of the best seasoned material.** The panels are well glued, clamped and screwed to frame, which make them stand the hard usage to which they are put. Dimensions given above are on bottom, outside to outside.

No. 24R5065 Finished and crated ready for shipment. Each.........................**$3.00**

Road Wagon Body.

No. 24R5067 Road Wagon Bodies. Material and workmanship the best money will produce, comes complete with seat as shown in cut; 24 inches wide, by 50 inches long. Price, each............**$2.75**

Corning Buggy Body.

No. 24R5068 The Corning Buggy Body is one of standard style. Next to the piano body it is the best selling body on the market. We use only thoroughly dry material. **Panels are clamped and screwed** to posts or frame and put up by first class mechanics. Sizes, 24 inches wide and 49 inches long. No paint or irons furnished. Finished in white, and crated, ready for shipment. Each............**$2.70**

Corning Stick Buggy Body.

No. 24R5072 Corning Stick Buggy or Road Wagon Body. Made the same as No. 24R5068. A first class body in every respect. Sizes, 24 inches wide by 49 inches long. **No irons or paint furnished.** Finished in the white and crated ready for shipment. Each..............................**$3.40**

Phaeton Bodies.

Phaeton Buggy Bodies. Made of well seasoned material, panels glued, clamped and screwed; hardwood throughout, nicely finished; size of body, 42x30 inches; seat, 33x18½ inches, back, 22½ inches; no irons or paint. Every body is hand made. Furnished in white only.

No. 24R5076 Price, each..... **$7.50**

Farmers' Surrey Bodies.

No. 24R5077 Farmers' Surrey Bodies, in the white. Made of the best material, finished ready for irons and paint. Size of body, 27 inches by 68 inches; comes complete with seats, as shown in cut. Price, each **$6.00**

Surrey Bodies.

No. 24R5078 Surrey Bodies, made of thoroughly dry material, full length rocker plate irons. Well clamped and screwed. A first class body in every respect. Size of body, 26 inches by 66 inches; seats, 26½x15 inches; hand made and well finished. Comes crated ready for shipment. Price, each......**$10.00**

Spring Wagon Bodies.

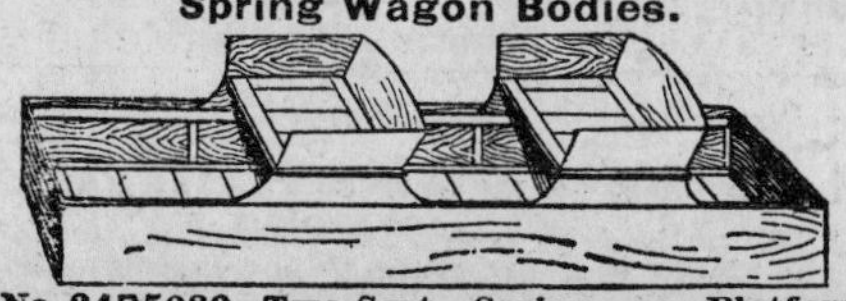

No. 24R5080 Two-Seat Spring or Platform Wagon Bodies. Made of well seasoned material; **all corners and panels clamped and screwed;** square corners, nicely finished; no irons or paint furnished; in the white only; size, 84x34 inches; complete, with two seats, as shown in cut. Price, each..**$5.70**

Brewster Buggy Gears with Self Oiling Axles.

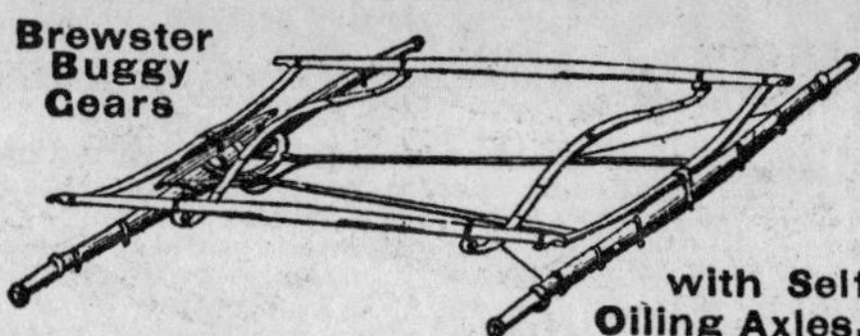

Brewster Buggy Gears, finished complete as shown in cut. They are very durable in construction, simple and not easily got out of order. **Furnished with 15/16-inch self oiling axles.** Brewster fifth wheel. Length, 55¼ inches between axle, for bodies, 20, 22, 23 or 25 inches wide. Track, 4 feet 4 inches, 4 feet 6 inches, 4 feet 8 inches or 5 feet. **Prices f. o. b. Factory.**

No. 24R5090 Weight, 125 lbs. Price, each.**$10.25**

End Spring Gear with Self Oiling Axles.

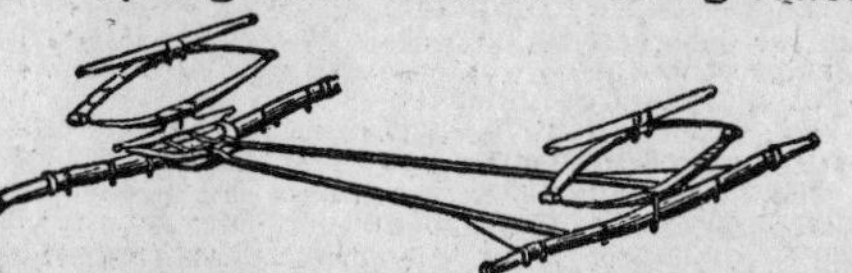

Elliptic Buggy Gears. Only the best material used in its construction. Button or rubber head. **Oil tempered springs.** Self oiling axles; Brewster fifth wheel; Norway bolts and clips. Finished complete as shown in cut. 1¼-inch spring; 15/16-inch axle; for bodies 22, 23 or 25 inches wide on bottom. Length, 56¾ inches or 59¾ inches between axles; 4 feet 4 inches, 4 feet 6 inches, 4 feet 8 inches or 5 feet track.

No. 24R5092 Weight, 125 lbs. Price, each..**$10.00**

Price is f. o. b. Factory.

Special Elliptic End Spring Gear.

No. 24R5094 Our Special End Spring Gear is precisely the same style as our No. 24R5092, only made of cheaper material. Has common 15/16-inch patent collar axles, common fifth wheel, etc. It is, however, the best gear for the money sold by anyone, and we list it to compete with the many so called cheap gears now on the market.

Price, complete as shown in cut... ....**$7.00**

Price is f. o. b. Factory.

Three-Spring Gears......

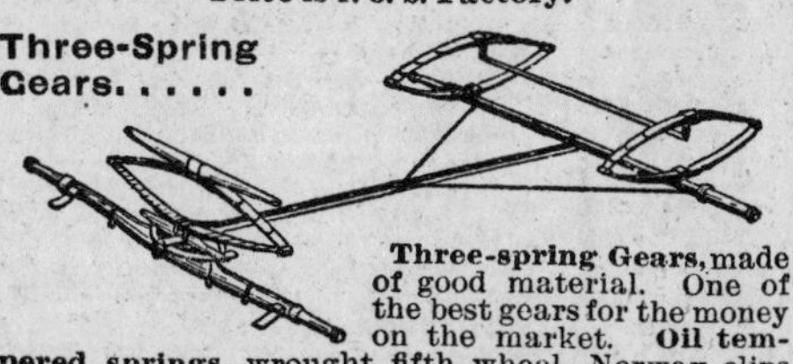

Three-spring Gears, made of good material. One of the best gears for the money on the market. **Oil tempered springs,** wrought fifth wheel, Norway clips and bolts throughout. Front spring 1½x7 leaf by 36 inches long; hind springs 1¼x4 leaf by 36 inches long. When desired we can furnish this gear for body to go on top of springs and spring bar so that a toeboard can be used. **Prices f. o. b. Factory.**

	Axle	Weight	Capacity	Price
No. 24R5096 No. 1	1-in.	150 lbs.	800 lbs.	**$11.85**
No. 24R5097 No. 2	1⅛-in.	150 lbs.	1,000 lbs.	**13.50**
No. 24R5098 No. 3	1¼-in.	175 lbs.	1,500 lbs.	**16.20**

F. & A. Business Gears.

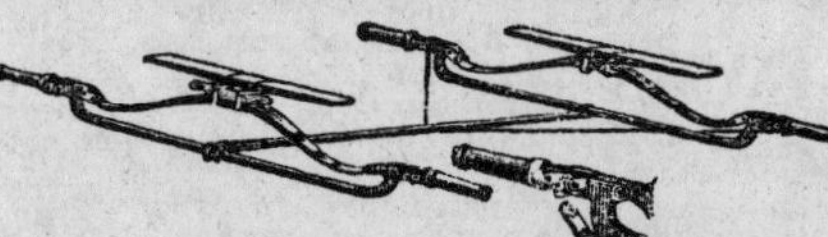

This Gear is made with our new improved cone hanger and spring loop, doing away with the wear on the bolt, and making them perfectly noiseless; made in two tracks only, 4 feet 8 inches and 5 feet. When ordering, give track and length and width of body.

	Axle	Weight	Capacity	Price
No. 24R5100 No. ½	⅞-in.	75 lbs.	450 to 600 lbs.	**$8.15**
No. 24R5102 No. 1	1-in.	100 lbs.	600 to 800 lbs.	**9.30**
No. 24R5104 No. 2	1⅛-in.	125 lbs.	1,000 lbs.	**10.35**

Prices f. o. b. Factory.

Improved Acme Duplex Gears.

Our Improved Acme Duplex Gear is unequaled for durability. By having a spring on each side of the axle we remove the objection experienced by having a single spring on rear or front of axle, as when going into a pitch hole it throws a strain on springs and couplings and works them loose, causing the wagon to rattle. By the use of our patent draw shackles, standard width pole and shaft are used. When ordering, give width of track and length and width of body to be used on same.

No.	Axle		Weight	Capacity	Price
24R5106	No.1	1-in.	125 lbs.	800 lbs.	**$ 9.90**
24R5107	No.2	1⅛-in.	125 lbs.	1,000 lbs.	**11.00**
24R5108	No.3	1¼-in.	135 lbs.	1,200 to 1,500 lbs.	**13.50**
24R5109	No.4	1⅜-in.	150 lbs.	1,700 to 1,800 lbs.	**16.70**
24R5110	No.5	1½-in.	175 lbs	2,200 to 2,500 lbs.	**21.90**

Prices f. o. b. Factory.

Fitch's Improved Combination Short Turn Duplex and Elliptic Gears.

We furnish this Gear complete, as shown in cut, ready to bolt body to gear. It hangs as low as our regular Duplex Gears and is adapted for delivery, express or pleasure wagon. When ordering, give track, width and length of body to be used on same.

		Axle, inches	Weight	Capacity, pounds	Price
No. 24R5112	No. 1	1	125 lbs.	800	**$13.00**
No. 24R5114	No. 2	1⅛	125 lbs.	1,000	**15.50**
No. 24R5116	No. 3	1¼	135 lbs.	1,200 to 1,500	**17.50**
No. 24R5118	No. 4	1⅜	150 lbs.	1,700 to 1,800	**21.00**
No. 24R5119	No. 5	1½	175 lbs.	2,200 to 2,500	**26.00**

Prices f. o. b. Factory.

Acme Improved Short Turn Gears.

After years of experimenting and study, the manufacturers of this gear now offer to the public one of the most perfect and durable Short Turn Duplex Gears on the market. The main object in short turn gears is that you can use a wider body and turn short. The body does not have any sliding motion, either front or back, where there would be any chance for it to rattle or make a noise. In the one-joint reach we use a cone shaped coupling, that can be tightened, taking up all wear and making it noiseless. In ordering, give track, width and length of body.

		Axle, inches	Weight	Capacity, pounds	Price
No. 24R5120	No. 1	1	125 lbs.	800	**$11.90**
No. 24R5121	No. 2	1⅛	125 lbs.	1,000	**13.70**
No. 24R5122	No. 3	1¼	135 lbs.	1,200 to 1,500	**15.25**
No. 24R5123	No. 4	1⅜	150 lbs.	1,700 to 1,800	**18.25**
No. 24R5124	No. 5	1½	175 lbs.	2,200 to 2,500	**23.00**

Prices f. o. b. Factory.

Acme Improved Combination Short Turn Duplex and Platform Gear.

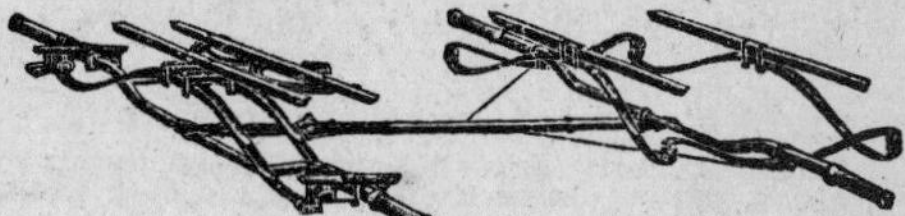

This is one of the most popular Gears we show; half platform and half duplex. Material and workmanship guaranteed to be the best.

		Axle	Capacity	Price
No. 24R5126	No. 1 has	1 x6½ in.	800 lbs..	**$13.65**
No. 24R5127	No. 2 has	1⅛x7 in.	1,000 lbs..	**14.80**
No. 24R5128	No. 3 has	1¼x7 in.	1,500 lbs..	**17.80**
No. 24R5129	No. 4 has	1⅜x7½ in.	1,800 lbs..	**22.00**
No. 24R5130	No. 5 has	1½x8 in.	2,200 lbs..	**27.00**

Prices f. o. b. Factory.

Double Elliptic Three-Spring Gears.

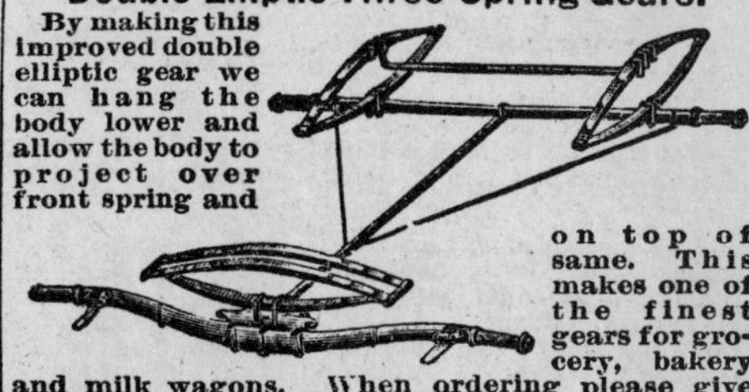

By making this improved double elliptic gear we can hang the body lower and allow the body to project over front spring and on top of same. This makes one of the finest gears for grocery, bakery and milk wagons. When ordering please give **track, length and width of box.**

No. 24R5131 No. 1 gear has 1-inch axle, capacity, 800 pounds. Weight, 150 lbs. Price........**$12.00**

No. 24R5132 No. 2 gear has 1⅛-inch axle, capacity, 1,000 pounds. Weight, 150 lbs. Price.....**$13.75**

No. 24R5134 No. 3 gear has 1¼-inch axle, capacity 1,500 pounds. Weight, 175 lbs. Price......**$16.75**

Prices f. o. b. Factory.

Double Elliptic End Spring Drop Axle Gear.

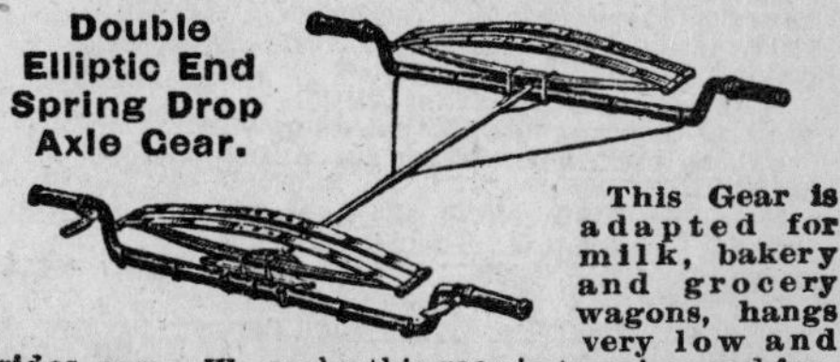

This Gear is adapted for milk, bakery and grocery wagons, hangs very low and rides easy. We make this gear in two sizes and furnish spring bars on both.

No. 24R5138 No. 1 gear has 1-inch axle, capacity, 800 pounds. Weight, 150 lbs. Price............**$12.25**

No. 24R5140 No. 2 gear has 1⅛-inch axle, capacity, 1,000 pounds. Weight, 150 lbs. Price.....**$14.25**

Prices f. o. b. Factory.

PUMP DEPARTMENT.

PROBABLY THERE IS NO OTHER LINE of goods that we sell on which we can save our customers more money than we can on pumps. We fit all our pumps, so anyone can set them in the well without any trouble. The only special tool required is a pipe tong. We sell a pipe tong for 59 cents, and everyone should have one. **IF IN DOUBT** write us, giving us this information: How deep is well? Is force pump or lift pump wanted? How much water is wanted per day? When water is to be drawn from a distance or forced to a distance, send a rough drawing showing position of pump, position of well, giving all angles and measurements. We will name our price on the best outfit.

Pitcher Spout Pumps.

This picture represents our Close Top Pitcher Spout Pump. These pumps are made in the very best manner and have the revolving bearer which by loosening the set screw allows handle to be placed on either side or back, in any position desired. **The cylinders of these pumps are bored true and polished.** They have trip valves, by which the water may be let out of the pump in the winter by raising the handle until it trips the lower valve. **They are fitted with connection for either lead or iron pipe. Pipe is not included in price.** (See No. 24R5710 for pipe.) We also make this pump with **Brass Lined Cylinder. It is a** well known fact that leather plungers operating in brass cylinders are almost indestructible. **We can fully recommend them where the best is wanted.**

	Iron	Brass lined
No. 24R5200 No. 1, 2½-inch cylinder for 1¼-inch pipe. Price, each........	$1.00	$2.30
No. 24R5202 No. 2, 3-inch cylinder for 1¼-inch pipe. Price, each.........	1.13	2.60
No. 24R5204 No. 3, 3½-inch cylinder for 1¼-inch pipe. Price, each.........	1.25	2.85
No. 24R5205 No. 4, 4-inch cylinder for 1½-inch pipe. Price, each..........	1.55	3.20

Pitcher Pumps.

Pitcher Pumps, with white enameled spout and cylinder, closed revolving top. Makes one of the neatest low price pumps on the market. Made same shape as our No. 24R5200 above.

No. 24R5206 No. 1, 2½-inch cylinder, for 1¼-inch pipe. Weight, 21½ pounds. Price, each..........$1.05
No. 24R5207 No. 2, 3-inch cylinder, for 1¼-inch pipe. Weight, 22½ pounds. Price, each..........$1.20
No. 24R5208 No. 3, 3½-inch cylinder for 1¼-inch, pipe. Weight, 23½ pounds. Price, each..........$1.30
No. 24R5209 No. 4, 4-inch cylinder, for 1½-inch pipe. Weight, 26½ pounds. Price, each..........$1.60

Acme Cistern Pumps.

In the Acme Cistern Pump we have the most up to date pump made. Extra finish, high grade, gray iron and brass, machine fitted. We have this pump in two styles, iron body and brass lined body. All are fitted for 1¼-inch lead or iron pipe and back outlet for 1-inch pipe, as per illustration.

No. 24R5214 3-inch iron body. Price, each..........$4.45
No. 24R5215 3-inch brass lined body. Price, each..........$5.00

Same pump without cock spout, but with common round spout and hose attachment.

No. 24R5221 3-inch iron body. Price, each, $3.20
No. 24R5222 3-inch brass lined body. Price, each.......................... 3.80

Iron and Brass Lined Force Pumps.

With Air Chamber, Revolving Bearer and Brass Piston Rod.

This is a staple pump for house use. It is usually placed on a kitchen sink or elevated platform, and used to force water up into a tank or reservoir to supply bathrooms and washbasins. **The air chamber is fitted with an outlet into which a draw cock may be screwed if desired. Hose may also be attached to the cock for sprinkling or fire purposes, in which case it is best to put a stop cock on the upward discharge. These pumps have brass valve seats, and are fitted for iron or lead pipe.**

Will not work satisfactorily in well or cistern over 25 feet deep.

Prices quoted below are for pump without cock at spout.

	Iron	Brass lined
No. 24R5225 No. 1, 2½-inch cylinder for 1-inch pipe. To fit ⅜-inch hose coupling. Price, each..........	$4.30	$6.50
No. 24R5226 No. 2, 2½-inch cylinder for 1-inch pipe. To fit ¾-inch hose coupling. Price, each..........	4.70	7.40
No. 24R5228 No. 4, 3-inch cylinder for 1¼-inch pipe. To fit 1-inch hose coupling. Price, each..........	5.70	8.70

If wanted with cock spout add **$1.00 to above prices.**

Iron and Brass Lined Force Pump.

This Pump is similar to our No. 24R5225 and the same description is applicable. It is only different in that it bolts to a plank and is designed to be fastened to the wall.

No. 1, 2¼-inch cylinder for 1-inch pipe. No. 2, 2¼-inch cylinder for 1-inch pipe. No. 4, 3-inch cylinder for 1¼-inch pipe. Complete as shown in cut.

No. 24R5232 No. 1, Iron, $5.35; Brass Lined, $7.50
No. 24R5233 No. 2, Iron, $5.70; Brass Lined, $7.40
No. 24R5235 No. 4, Iron, $6.70; Brass Lined, $8.70

We can fully recommend our brass lined pumps to be equal to an all brass one, and much cheaper. The cylinder is lined with a seamless drawn brass tube. The plunger, piston rod, stuffing nut, and all working parts are brass, and as leather plungers operating in brass cylinders are known to be almost indestructible, **parties wishing a first class pump will give them the unhesitating preference.**

House Force Pumps.

With Revolving Bearer and Brass Piston Rod.

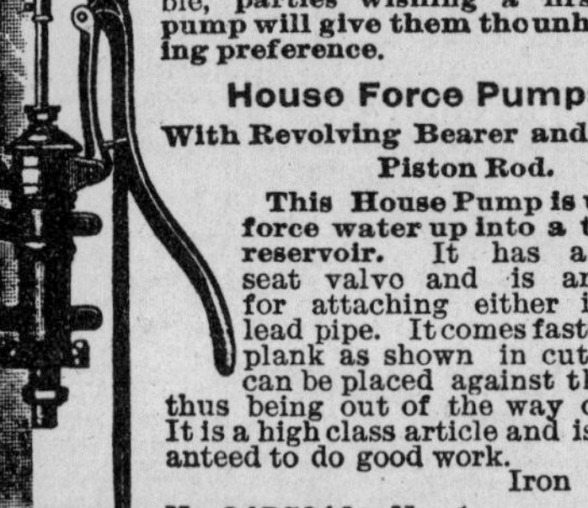

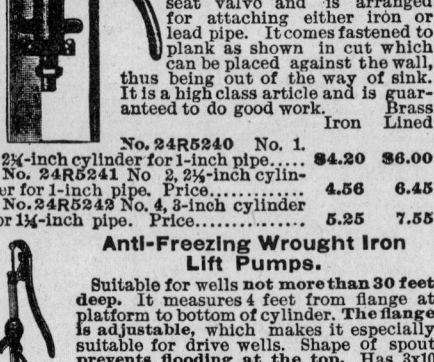

This House Pump is used to force water up into a tank or reservoir. It has a brass seat valve and is arranged for attaching either iron or lead pipe. It comes fastened to plank as shown in cut which can be placed against the wall, thus being out of the way of sink. It is a high class article and is guaranteed to do good work.

	Iron	Brass Lined
No. 24R5240 No. 1. 2¼-inch cylinder for 1-inch pipe.....	$4.20	$6.00
No. 24R5241 No 2, 2½-inch cylinder for 1-inch pipe. Price...........	4.56	6.45
No. 24R5242 No. 4, 3-inch cylinder for 1¼-inch pipe. Price...............	5.25	7.55

Anti-Freezing Wrought Iron Lift Pumps.

Suitable for wells not more than 30 feet deep. It measures 4 feet from flange at platform to bottom of cylinder. **The flange is adjustable, which makes it especially suitable for drive wells. Shape of spout prevents flooding at the top.** Has 3x10 iron cylinder of good quality, fitted for 1¼-inch iron pipe. If well is more than 20 feet deep, we recommend placing a foot valve on end of pipe at bottom of well.

No. 24R5250 Price for pump, as shown in cut..........................$3.35

NOTICE—This price does not include the pipe to reach from the bottom of the cylinder to the bottom of well. For pipe, see No. 24R5710.

Anti-Freezing Closed Top Lift Pumps.

Adapted for wells not more than 30 feet deep. Has revolving top, so handle may be placed on either side or at back of spout in any position desired. It measures four feet from platform to bottom of cylinder. The pipe connecting cylinder and pump screws into the pump at the spout, thus **leaving an air space around the the pipe above the platform, which is a preventive against freezing. The cylinder is of the best quality and is fitted for 1¼ inch pipe, unless otherwise ordered.** If well is more than 20 feet deep, we recommend placing a foot valve on end of pipe at bottom of the well. Pipe to reach from bottom of cylinder to bottom of well is not furnished at prices named below.

No. 24R5254 No. 2, 2½-inch cylinder. Price.........................$2.85
No. 24R5255 No. 3, 2¾-inch cylinder. Price.......................... 3.00
No. 24R5256 No. 4, 3-inch cylinder. Price, $3.10
No. 24R5257 No. 5, 3¼-inch cylinder. Price, 3.20
No. 24R5258 No. 6, 3½-inch cylinder. Price, 3.30

10-inch iron cylinders furnished with above pumps.

New Pattern Close Top Lift Pumps.

The bolts on cap and pitman are large, and will many times outwear the small ones in ordinary use. **The pipe is screwed into pump just below the spout, which prevents freezing in winter. Has revolving top, so handle may be placed in any desired position. Has swinging fulcrum. The cylinder is of the best quality, and fitted for 1¼ inch pipe.** It measures 4 feet from flange at platform to bottom of cylinder. **For wells not more than 25 or 30 feet deep,** order the pump as shown in cut, and enough pipe to reach from bottom of cylinder (4 feet from platform) to the bottom of well. **Extra pipe is not included with pump. For price of pipe, see No. 24R5710.**

No. 24R5264 No. 2, 2½-inch cylinder..$4.55
No. 24R5265 No. 3, 2¾-inch cylinder.. 4.60
No. 24R5266 No. 4, 3 -inch cylinder.. 4.70
No. 24R5267 No. 5, 3¼-inch cylinder.. 4.90
No. 24R5268 No. 6, 3½-inch cylinder.. 5.00

Above pump furnished with 10-inch iron cylinders. Brass cylinders furnished at an extra cost; see No. 24R5545 for difference in prices.

When this pump is ordered for a well more than 25 or 30 feet deep, the cylinder should be placed within 10 feet of the bottom of well. When so ordered, it takes more pump rod and pump rod couplings, and requires extra labor, for which we make an extra charge of 5 cents per foot for each foot the cylinder is put down. This charge is to be added to cost of pump and pipe complete.

NOTICE—The cost of pipe is not included in above extra charge. We give below a sample order for pump and pipe complete to reach 74 feet from platform with cylinder put down 65 feet.

No. 24R5266	1 pump, No. 4..........................	$ 4.70
No. 24R5710	70 feet black iron pipe 1¼ inch, at 8½ cents..........	5.95
	To putting cylinder down 65 feet, at 5 cents.	3.25
		$13.90

Heavy Lift Pump with Windmill Head.

Adapted for wells not more than 80 feet deep. May also be used for hand use. Pipe screws into standard at the spout. Has revolving top and swinging fulcrum. **All parts are strong and durable. We can fully recommend it as a first class pump.** Measures 4 feet from platform to bottom of cylinder. **For wells not more than 25 or 30 feet deep, order pump as shown in cut and enough 1¼-inch iron pipe to reach from bottom of cylinder (4 feet below platform) to bottom of well.** Price of pipe is not included in price of pump. Average weight, 80 pounds. **For price of pipe, see No. 24R5710.**

No. 24R5274 No. 2, 2½-inch cylinder.$3.60
No. 24R5275 No. 3, 2¾-inch cylinder 3.65
No. 24R5276 No. 4, 3 -inch cylinder. 3.70
No. 24R5277 No. 5. 3¼-inch cylinder. 3.80
No. 24R5278 No. 6, 3½-inch cylinder. 3.90

Above pump furnished with 10-inch iron cylinders; brass body cylinders furnished at an extra cost of difference in price of cylinders. See No. 24R5545 for prices on brass body cylinders. When this pump is ordered for wells more than 25 or 30 feet deep, cylinder should be placed within 10 feet of the bottom of the well, **for which we make an extra charge in addition to cost of pump and pipe,** same as explained under No. 24R5268.

Extra Heavy Lift Pump.

For Stockyards and Heavy Work.

This cut represents our Heavy Set Length Lift Pump, adapted for stockyards and wells where large quantities of water are required. It measures 4 feet from flange at platform to bottom of cylinder. **The set lengths are screwed in the pumps at the spout to prevent freezing in winter. The stocks are made very heavy and strong, and the cylinders are large and capable of throwing large quantities of water. We fully recommend it where a large amount of water is desired.** Average weight, 88 pounds.

No. 24R5285 3½-inch cylinder, fitted for 1½-inch pipe. Price..............**$3.75**
No. 24R5286 4-inch cylinder, fitted for 1½-inch pipe. Price....................**$3.85**

Above pumps are fitted with 10-inch iron cylinders; for brass body cylinders, see No. 24R5545. Can furnish brass body cylinders for difference in prices.

Price of pipe is not included in above prices. For pipe, see No. 24R5710.

FREIGHT IS A SMALL ITEM

By noting the weight in the description of the goods and referring to the introductory pages of this catalogue you can calculate what the freight will cost you, and in every case you will find it will amount to next to nothing compared to the saving in price.

Our $20.00 Acme Potato Bug Sprinkler.

It applies the poison upon two rows at once, and will cover 12 to 15 acres per day. Any boy that can drive a horse can perform more easily the same amount of work it heretofore required 12 men to perform in the same time. You have complete control over the quantity of water you wish to throw; opening or closing the valve with the lever. The wheels run on tubular axles and can be shifted to any width of rows desired, 2 to 3 feet. Weight, 450 pounds.

No. 24R5517 Price....... $20.00

Improved Spray and Force Pump.

Improved Spray and Force Pump. It is beyond question the most perfect and effective hand apparatus ever invented for throwing water. It supplies a universal want, for every family needs some kind of a Force Sprinkler and Pump. In variety of service, simplicity of construction and ease of operation, it has no equal. Is always ready for use, not liable to get out of order, and so light and convenient that it can be used easily and effectively by any one. Made of heavy, bright tin coated with Egyptian lacquer.

No. 24R5518 Price, each.....75c

Spraying Pump.

The construction of the pump requires the pressure on the handle to be all done on the down stroke, the pressure on the cylinder acting as a cushion, and partly forcing the handle up again, thus making it very easy of operation, requiring no foot rest or other device to steady it. The hose can be detached at the top of pump and a nozzle attached in its place, either for spraying, sprinkling, or throwing a solid stream. It is also arranged so that a small stream is discharged with great force from the bottom of the pump into the bucket or barrel, serving to thoroughly agitate the mixture at all times when the pump is in use. For washing buggies, windows, etc., it is very useful. It can also be used for whitewashing trees, barns, outhouses, etc., and for extinguishing fires.

No. 24R5520 Price, each.........$2.00
Weight, about 5 pounds.

Acme Portable Cast Force Pump.

Our Acme Portable Cast Force Pump is one of the most effective hand pumps on the market. Is made extra strong; nicely finished. Is adapted for spraying trees, washing windows and wagons, sprinkling lawns, etc. Furnished complete with hose and connections, brass nozzle and sprinkler.

No. 24R5523 Price, each........$3.95

Acme Fire Extinguisher.

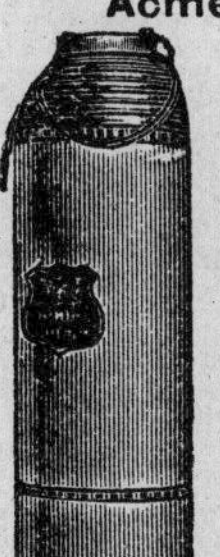

A device that every store, factory and residence should be equipped with. Absolute protection against loss by fire can now be assured to property owners at a small cost. The Acme Chemical Fire Extinguisher is the simplest and most powerful machine made. It is made of heavy copper securely riveted and soldered and highly polished. Holds three gallons and throws a stream 40 feet when in action. The solution used contains no acids to destroy fabrics, etc., although it is the most powerful fire extinguisher solution known. Solution for re-charging can be obtained from any druggist for 15 cents. Full directions sent with each machine. Weight when ready for use, 12 pounds.

No 24R5525 Price, each........................$5.00

Pump Cylinders.

By means of the cylinder water is raised and unless the cylinder is well made no good results can be obtained. A good cylinder must be bored true and plunger must fit accurately. Valves must be simple and durable. The cost of repairing a cylinder is usually more than its first cost, so it pays to get the best. Our cylinders are the best that skilled workmen can produce and our prices as low as equally well made goods can be sold for. Cylinders 10 inches long have 6-inch stroke and can be used in wells up to 35 feet deep. Cylinders 12 inches long have 6-inch stroke and can be used in wells up to 75 feet deep. Cylinders 14 inches long have 8-inch stroke and can be used in wells up to 150 feet deep. Cylinders 16 inches long have 10-inch stroke and can be used in wells up to 200 feet deep. Cylinders 2 inches in diameter are fitted for 1-inch pipe. Cylinders 3½ inches in diameter are fitted for 1½-inch pipe. Cylinders 4 inches in diameter are fitted for 2-inch pipe. All others fitted for 1¼-inch pipe.

No.	Diam. inch.	10 in. long	12 in. long	14 in. long	16 in. long	18 in. long
24R5528	2	$0.75	$1.10	$1.20	$1.20	$1.35
24R5529	2¼	.80	1.18	1.25	1.30	1.45
24R5530	2½	.90	1.20	1.30	1.40	1.50
24R5531	2¾	.98	1.30	1.40	1.50	1.60
24R5532	3	1.00	1.38	1.53	1.60	1.75
24R5533	3¼	1.25	1.50	1.75	1.95	2.05
24R5534	3½	1.40	1.80	2.00	2.25	2.50
24R5535	4	1.75	2.30	2.60	2.90	3.20

Brass Body Cylinders.

Brass Body Cylinders are practically as good as the solid brass, and much cheaper. The barrel is made of a seamless brass tube, and workmanship, stroke and capacity are all same as iron cylinders. 10 and 12-inch cylinders have 6-inch stroke, 14-inch cylinder has 8-inch stroke and 16-inch cylinder has 10-inch stroke.

No.	Diam. inches	10 in. long	12 in. long	14 in. long	16 in. long	18 in. long
24R5545	2	$2.13	$2.28	$2.43	$2.57	$2.70
24R5546	2¼	2.20	2.35	2.56	2.78	3.00
24R5547	2½	2.28	2.43	2.64	2.92	3.20
24R5548	2¾	2.43	2.57	2.78	3.04	3.36
24R5549	3	2.56	2.71	2.92	3.20	3.50
24R5550	3¼	2.78	2.82	3.14	3.42	3.70
24R5551	3½	3.00	3.21	3.49	3.85	4.20
24R5552	4	3.70	4.05	4.48	5.00	5.50

Artesian Well Brass Cylinders.

This cut represents our all brass cylinder to be used in artesian wells. The shell being made of heavy seamless brass tubing, fitted with hard brass or bronze ball valves and which are supplied with best cupped oak tanned leathers. This cylinder may be placed in open wells and in drilled wells where the pipe or casing is long enough to take the cylinder attachments. They are adapted to work in the deepest wells.

NOTICE—The plunger and lower valves may be removed through the connecting pipe, which is larger in diameter than the bore of the cylinder, thus making it convenient when repairs are necessary.

No.	Length of Cylinder	Stroke	Inside Diameter	Fitted for Pipe	Price, each
24R5560	36-inch	16-inch	1⅜-in.	1½ inch	$ 7.50
24R5561	33-inch	16-inch	1¾-in.	2 inch	9.50
24R5562	43-inch	24-inch	2¼-in.	2½ inch	15.00
24R5563	45-inch	24-inch	2¾-in.	3 inch	18.00
24R5564	49-inch	24-inch	3¼-in.	3½ inch	25.00
24R5565	51-inch	24-inch	3¾-in.	4 inch	36.00
24R5566	59-inch	30-inch	4¼-in.	4½ inch	46.00

Ball Valve Pump Cylinders.

In our Ball Valve Cylinder we have the best deep well cylinder made. In putting down a 75 to 300-foot well, it is very essential that you have a cylinder that will work well at all times and last a lifetime. Pulling up a pump of this kind costs money. This cylinder is fitted with a four-leather plunger and brass bronze ball valve, which will raise a greater amount of water and last longer than any cylinder on the market. Furnished with either inside or outside caps. Be sure and state kind wanted.

No.	Size, Inches	Fitted Pipe, Inches	Stroke, Inches	Iron	Brass Lined
24R5570	2 x16	1¼	8	$2.75	$3.68
24R5571	2¼x16	1¼	8	3.05	4.05
24R5572	2½x16	1¼	8	3.40	4.40
24R5573	2 x18	1¼	10	2.95	4.06
24R5574	2¼x18	1¼	10	3.20	4.45
24R5575	2½x18	1¼	10	3.57	4.80
24R5576	2¾x18	1¼	8	4.50	5.50
24R5577	3 x18	1¼	8	5.75	7.15
24R5578	2 x20	1¼	12	3.10	4.43
24R5579	2¼x20	1¼	12	3.40	4.82
24R5580	2½x20	1¼	12	3.75	4.95
24R5581	2¾x20	1¼	10	4.50	6.05
24R5582	3 x20	1¼	10	5.95	8.10

Irrigation Cylinders.

This is an extra large cylinder used for pumping large quantities of water or for irrigating. Can be used in any depth well, and by hand or windmill power. By using a stuffing box or a common tee, you have a pump that will answer for irrigating purposes, at very small cost. Has brass plunger cage, brass plunger poppet, two valve leathers, brass seat valve inseat cap; furnished with either inside or outside caps.

No.	Inside Diam., in.	L'gth, in.	Stroke, in.	Fitted for Pipe, in.	Brass, Price each
24R5584	5	18	12	3	$11.35
24R5585	6	18	12	3½	17.25
24R5586	8	18	12	5	32.00
24R5587	5	20	14	3	12.90
24R5588	6	20	14	3½	18.65
24R5589	8	20	14	5	36.00

Will be furnished with flange for spiral steel pipe same size as cylinder, if so ordered, in place of regular flange, for which no extra charge will be made.

Tubular Well Cylinders.

Used in deep tubular wells, or in wells where water has given out, and you wish to drive pipe further down. It slips inside the pipe and can be set at any desired distance; can be removed for repairing by simply disconnecting handle of pump and drawing cylinder out. No pump tools required. The body is made of seamless drawn brass tubing, with brass valves. Stroke, 12 inches. Not made smaller than 2 inches.

No. 24R5592 Size, 2-in. Each.......$2.20
No. 24R5593 Size, 2½-in. Each....... 3.35
No. 24R5594 Size, 3-in. Each........ 5.00

Seating Tool for Above Cylinder.

No. 24R5600 2 -in. cylinder. Each.....20c
No. 24R5602 2½-in. cylinder. Each.....25c
No. 24R5603 3 -in. cylinder. Each.....35c

Tubular Well Ball Valves.

Tubular Well Ball Valves. Extra heavy; well finished inside and out. One of the best made valves on the market. Set consists of one check and one plunger valve as shown in cut.

No. 24R5604 2-inch. Price, per set..........................$1.00
No. 24R5605 2½-inch. Price, per set..........................$2.30
No. 24R5606 3-inch. Price, per set..........................$3.00

Tubular Well Poppet Valves.

Extra Heavy Tubular Well Poppet Valves. Two leathers; nicely finished; furnished complete as shown in cut. Set consists of one each, check and plunger valve.

No. 24R5608 Size, 2-inch. Price, per set..........................95c
No. 24R5609 Size, 2½-inch. Price, per set..........................$2.20
No. 24R5610 Size, 3-inch. Price, per set..........................$2.90

Little Patent Automatic Pipe Holder.

Little Patent Automatic Pipe Holder, simple, strong and quick acting. Has adjustable set screw for different size pipe. Dog and catch are made of best grade steel. Every machine made of the best quality of material.

No. 24R5611 No. 1, holds pipe 1, 1¼ and 1½ inches. Price, each..........................$2.50

Little Giant Pipe Holder.

Something new in pipe holders. Will hold either 1, 1¼ or 1½-inch pipe. Dog has corrugated chilled surface; pipe cannot slip. Well made, nicely finished. A practical tool.

No. 24R5612 Price, each..................$2.80

Acme Pipe Puller.

This Puller is made in different sizes to fit pipe from 1 inch to 4 inches in diameter. Dies have threads that will not crush pipe or allow same to slip. Is large enough for the coupling of pipe to pass through. This puller is used in connection with jack screws which are placed under each lug or ear. For prices on jack screws see No. 24R1355, page 619. For pulling pipe this tool has no equal. Prices given below are for puller and one set of dies only. Be sure and state size wanted. Four or five different sizes can be used in the same holder, however.

No. 24R5613

No. 2 Puller with one Set of Dies either ¾, 1, 1¼, 1½ or 2-inch. Price, each..........................$1.45
No. 3 Puller with one Set of Dies either 2, 2½ or 3-inch. Price, each..........................$2.65
No. 4 Puller with one Set of Dies either 3½ or 4-inch. Price, each..........................$4.50
No. 6 Puller with one Set of Dies either 4, 4½ 5 or 6-inch. Price, each..........................$6.35

Price of Extra Dies.

Extra dies for No. 2 holder. ¾-in. 1-in. 1¼-in. 1½-in. 2-in.
Price, each.......... 55c 50c 45c 30c 30c
Extra dies for No. 3 holder, 2-in. 2½-in. 3-in.
Price, each.......... 48c 45c 45c
Extra dies for No. 4 holder, 3½-in. 4-in.
Price, each.......... $1.20 $1.05
Extra dies for No. 6 stock. 4-in. 4½-in. 5-in. 6-in.
Price, each.......... $1.80 $1.75 $1.65 $1.35

Pipe Lowering Machine.

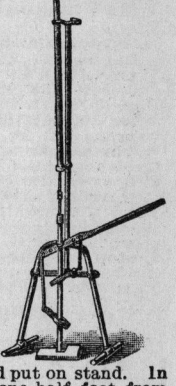

The accompanying illustration represents the grappler holding the pipe for putting in the well or taking out. To raise the pipe it only requires to operate the lever, as you would a pump handle, which raises the pipe at the rate of ten feet per minute. To lower the pipe in the well, take hold of the lever with the right hand, and left hand hold of the lower grapple, raise lever slightly and grapple at the same time, slide grapple up the pipe while lever descends until you reach the upper grapple, then reverse the operation, and raise the upper grapple while the lower one descends with the pipe. To put on stand, let the pipe down until 2 feet is above the platform, then put on extra grappler (not shown in the illustration) and let it rest on platform, take lifter away and put on stand. In taking out pump, raise stand one-half foot from platform, put on grappler and take off stand, then put on lifter. For putting in and taking out deep well pumps this machine has no equal. Should be owned by every pump man or anyone having deep wells to attend to.

No. 24R5614 Price, complete..................$7.35

Nipples.

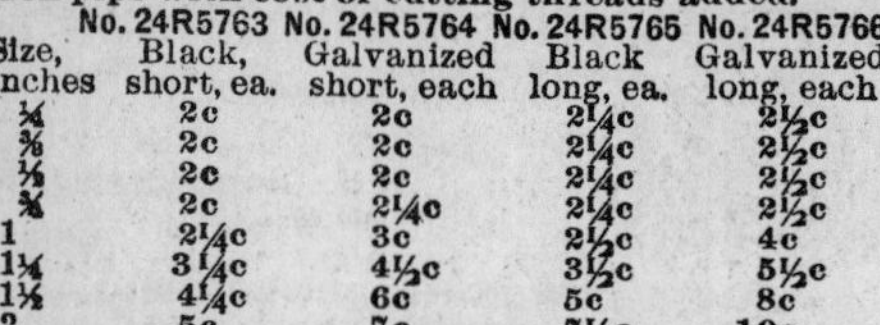

State length wanted.
All nipples 6 inches long and over will be charged at price per foot of iron pipe with cost of cutting threads added.

	No. 24R5763	No. 24R5764	No. 24R5765	No. 24R5766
Size, inches	Black, short, ea.	Galvanized short, each	Black long, ea.	Galvanized long, each
¼	2c	2c	2¼c	2½c
⅜	2c	2c	2¼c	2½c
½	2c	2c	2¼c	2½c
¾	2c	2¼c	2¼c	2½c
1	2¼c	3c	2½c	4c
1¼	3¼c	4½c	3½c	5½c
1½	4¼c	6c	5c	8c
2	5c	7c	7½c	10c

Malleable Return Bends, Open Pattern.

No. 24R5769 Black.

Pipe, in...	½	¾	1	1¼	1½	2
Black, ea..	5c	8c	13c	18c	26c	32c

Clark's Pipe Hangers.

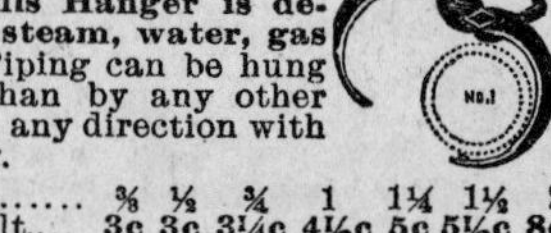

No. 24R5772 This Hanger is designed for use on steam, water, gas and soil piping. Piping can be hung closer to ceiling than by any other hanger. Swings in any direction with expansion of piping.

Size of pipe..............	⅜	½	¾	1	1¼	1½	2
Hanger, without bolt.....	3c	3c	3¼c	4½c	5c	5½c	8c

Cast Iron Pipe Flanges.

No. 24R5780 These Flanges are used for making pipe railings and where steel or wood tanks are tapped for pipe connections these flanges will make a much tighter connection and will last twice as long as the common lock nut, ordinarily used for this purpose.

Size of pipe, inches	Diam. of flange, inches	Price, each	Size of pipe, inches	Diam. of flange, inches	Price, each
⅜x	3	3½c	1¼	4½	7c
½x	3½	4½c	1¼	5	8½c
¾x	3½	5c	1½x	4½	7½c
¾	4	6c	1½	5	8¾c
¾	5	8c	2x	5½	10c
1x	4	6¼c	2	6	11c
1	5	8¼c	2	6½	13c
1¼x	4	6½c	2	7	18c

Flanges marked with an x are drilled for screws. Balance have no screw holes.

We can furnish above flanges in such sizes only on which we quote prices in above list.

Flange Unions.

No. 24R5782 Cast Iron Flange Unions are used in place of common unions where a tight connection is wanted especially on heavy work.

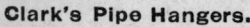

Size inches	Diameter of flange, inches	No. of bolts in each	Price each, black	Price each, galv.
½	3	3	11c	$0.22
¾	3⅛	3	13c	.25
1	3⅝	3	15c	.28
1¼	4⅛	4	18c	.34
1½	4⅛	4	22c	.42
2	5¼	4	27c	.55
2½	6⅛	4	37c	.68
3	6¾	4	41c	.83
3½	7½	4	49c	1.00
4	8⅜	5	57c	1.15

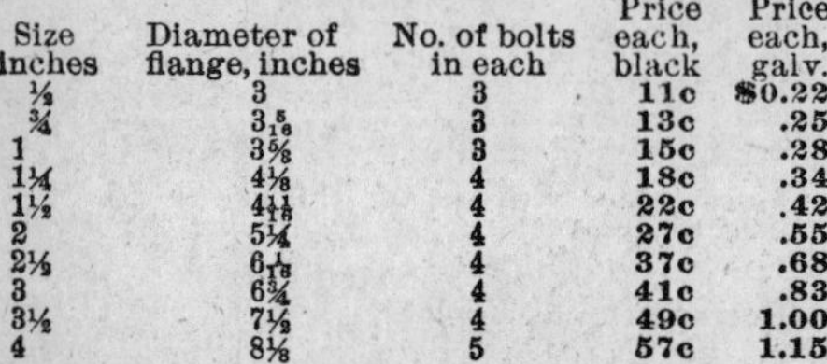

Straightway Wedge Gate Valves.

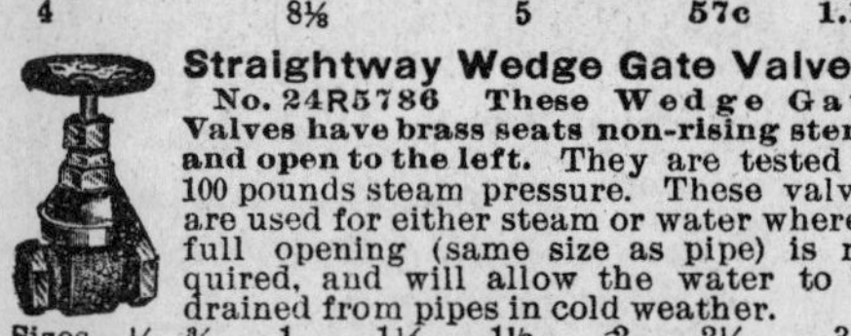

No. 24R5786 These Wedge Gate Valves have brass seats non-rising stems and open to the left. They are tested to 100 pounds steam pressure. These valves are used for either steam or water where a full opening (same size as pipe) is required, and will allow the water to be drained from pipes in cold weather.

Sizes,	½	¾	1	1¼	1½	2	2½	3
Each	74c	99c	$1.26	$1.84	$2.40	$3.50	$6.00	$8.30

Brass Straightway Double Gate Valves.

No. 24R5788 These Standard Double Disc Gate Valves have brass seats and rising stem, tested to 100 pounds steam pressure. In the construction of these valves the bearing of the wedge being central it acts uniformly on all parts of the disc, consequently it will force the disc to the seats and have an equal bearing on all parts. These valves are used either for steam or water where a full opening (same size of pipe), is required and will allow the water to be drained from pipes in cold weather.

Sizes,	½	¾	1	1¼	1½	2	2½	3
Each,	47c	64c	92c	$1.28	$1.83	$2.74	$5.00	$7.00

Standard Hose Valves.

No. 24R5810 Hose Valves with iron handle, loose swivel and leather discs. This is our quick opening hose valve. Opens and closes with half turn. The construction of this valve is such that the full area of water in the pipe can be obtained at once, which is an important item in a fire hose valve. Made of solid brass, finely finished. Guaranteed to be the best valve of its kind made.

Size, inches..	1	1¼	1½	2	2½
Price, each.....	$1.15	$1.35	$1.75	$2.70	$3.20

Radiator Valves.

No. 24R5812 Quick Opening Radiator Valves, for hot water or steam. Made of solid brass, finely finished. Hot water valve is furnished with by-pass. Insures continuous circulation, thereby preventing freezing, and is also furnished with union, as shown in cut. Both have full openings, wood wheels and brass discs.

For Hot Water.

Size, inches.....	¾	1	1¼	1½	2
Price, each	$0.85	$0.95	$1.25	$1.85	$2.75

No. 24R5814 For Steam.

Size, inches	¾	1	1¼	1½	2
Price, each...	$1.00	$1.20	$1.65	$2.20	$3.60

Standard Butterfly Valves.

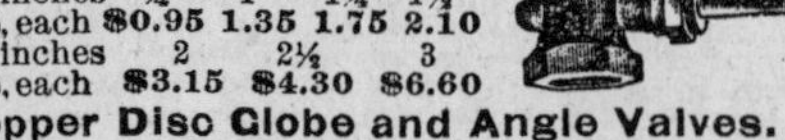

No. 24R5820 All Brass Butterfly Valves—nothing better made.

Size, inches	¾	1	1¼	1½
Price, each	$0.95	1.35	1.75	2.10
Size, inches	2	2½	3	
Price, each	$3.15	$4.30	$6.60	

Copper Disc Globe and Angle Valves.

This valve is fitted with copper disc and is a decided improvement over any other kind of removable disc on the market. The copper disc is unlike any other soft metal; it expands and contracts in exact ratio with the body of the valve, **thus insuring a tight joint at all times.** These valves can be furnished with composition discs at same price. When valves are wanted for water they will be furnished with soft disc.

No. 24R5824 Globe Valve.
No. 24R5825 Angle Valve.

When ordering be sure and state which style is wanted, Globe or Angle.

Size, inches	Price, each	Size, inches	Price, each
¼	$0.47	1¼	$1.70
⅜	.52	1½	2.30
½	.68	2	3.40
¾	.94	2½	6.80
1	1.15	3	9.00

Brass Globe Valves.

No. 24R5826

For pipe, inch...	¼	⅜	½	¾
Price, each......	24c	27c	34c	43c
For pipe, inch...	1	1¼	1½	2
Price, each......	59c	84c	$1.15	$1.50

Brass Angle Valves.

No. 24R5828

For pipe, inch..	¼	⅜	½	¾
Price, each.....	26c	28c	35c	44c
For pipe, inch....	1	1¼	1½	2
Price, each. ...	60c	85c	$1.16	$1.75

Brass Cross Valves.

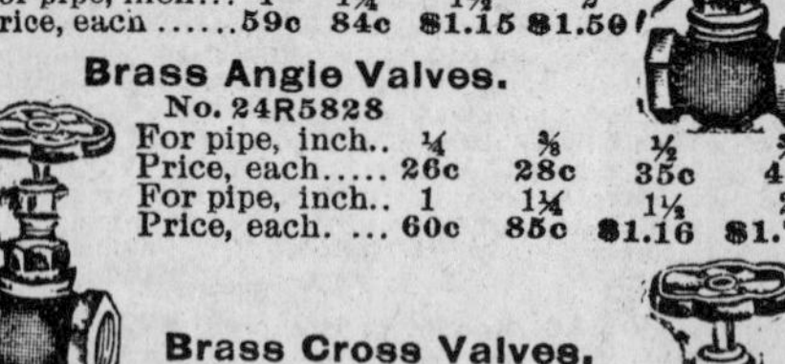

No. 24R5830

For pipe, in.	¼	⅜	½	¾
Price, each..	40c	42c	48c	80c
For pipe, in.	1	1¼	1½	2
Price, each..	80c	$1.05	$1.50	$2.50

Horizontal Check Valves.

No. 24R5832

For pipe in..	¼	⅜	½	¾
Price, each..	23c	24c	31c	39c
For pipe in.	1	1¼	1½	2
Price, each.	54c	77c	$1.09	$1.65

Brass Three-way Cocks.

No. 24R5834

For pipe, in.	½	¾	1	1¼
Price, each..	$0.83	$0.98	$1.23	$1.90
For pipe, in.	1½	2	2½	3
Price, each..	2.45	3.60	6.00	8.40

Steam Cocks.

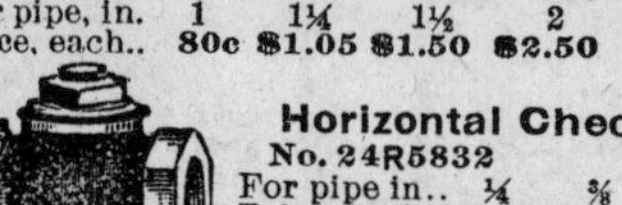

No. 24R5836 Brass Flat Head Steam Cocks, best quality.

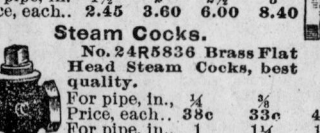

For pipe, in.,	¼	⅜	½	¾
Price, each..	38c	33c	42c	56c
For pipe, in.,	1	1¼	1½	2
Price, each..	$0.78	$1.23	$1.60	$2.40
For pipe, in.......			2½	3
Price, each........			$4.75	$7.40

Vertical Check Valves.

No. 24R5838 Brass Vertical Check Valves, best quality.

For pipe, inch.	¼	⅜	½	¾
Price, each	25c	27c	35c	43c
For pipe, inch.	1	1¼	1½	2
Price, each....	63c	90c	$1.24	$1.85

Swing Check Valve.

No. 24R5840 Brass Swing Check Valve.

Size, in.	½	¾	1	1¼	1½	2
Price,	66c	82c	$1.05	$1.27	$1.65	$2.25

Jenkins Bros.' Globe Valves.

No. 24R5850 Nothing better made in the way of a brass valve than Jenkins Bros.' Will last longer and give better satisfaction than any other make. All **brass goods bearing the Jenkins brand are fully warranted.**

Size, inches...	⅛	¼	⅜	½	¾
Each..........	47c	48c	54c	70c	95c
Size, inches.....	1	1¼	1½	2	
Each..........	$1.22	$1.73	$2.40	$3.80	

Jenkins Bros.' Angle Valves.

No. 24R5852

Size, inches.....	⅛	¼	⅜	½	¾
Each............	46c	47c	55c	70c	92c
Size, inches.....	1	1¼	1½	2	
Each............	$1.22	$1.75	$2.40	$3.82	

Jenkins Bros.' Cross Valves.

No. 24R5854

Size, inches...	⅜	½	¾	1
Price, each....	$0.90	$0.98	$1.10	$1.42
Size, inches....	1¼	1½	2	
Price, each....	$2.08	$2.80	$4.10	

Jenkins Bros.' Angle Check Valves.

No. 24R5856

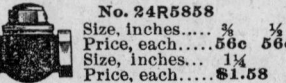

Size, inches......	⅜	½	¾	1
Price, each......	55c	62c	89c	$1.19
Size, inches......	1¼	1½	2	
Price, each......	$1.67	$1.98	$2.57	

Jenkins Bros.' Horizontal Check Valves

No. 24R5858

Size, inches.....	⅜	½	¾	1
Price, each....	56c	56c	83c	$1.10
Size, inches....	1¼	1½	2	
Price, each.....	$1.58	$2.03	$2.16	

Jenkins Bros.' Vertical Check Valves.

No. 24R5860

Size, inches......	⅜	½	¾	1
Price, each.......	56c	56c	82c	$1.13
Size, inches	1¼	1½	2	
Price, each.......	$1.55	$2.15	$3.25	

Water Pipe Stops.

No. 24R5870 Brass Rough Stop, lever handle, screwed for iron pipe.

Size, inches.....	½	¾	1
Price, plain, each.	35c	49c	74c
Size, inches.....	1¼	1½	2
Price, plain, each.	$1.12	1.55	2.70

Check and Waste.

No. 24R5872 All Brass Check and Waste, Lever Handle, screwed for iron pipe.

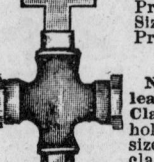

Size, in.	½	¾	1	1¼	1½
Each..	32c	45c	65c	$1.00	$1.45

Rough Brass Stop T Handle.

No. 24R5874 Rough Brass Stop T Handle screwed for iron pipe.

Size, inches..	½	¾	1
Price, each ..	28c	40c	60c
Size, inches..	1¼	1½	2
Price, each..	94c	$1.31	$2.23

Hydrant Clamp.

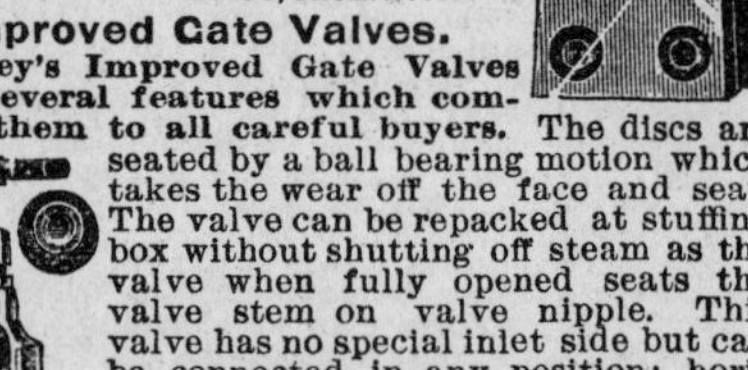

No. 24R5880 Malleable Iron Hydrant Clamp, with square hole; always give size hydrant cock clamp is to fit.

Price, each........6c

Improved Gate Valves.

Harvey's Improved Gate Valves have several features which commend them to all careful buyers. The discs are seated by a ball bearing motion which takes the wear off the face and seat. The valve can be repacked at stuffing box without shutting off steam as the valve when fully opened seats the valve stem on valve nipple. This valve has no special inlet side but can be connected in any position; horizontally, vertically or otherwise. Either side to the pressure. All parts are interchangeable and can be supplied on short notice.

No. 24R5882 Notice—All Brass.

Size.....	½	¾	1	1¼	1½	2	2½	3
Price, each.	43c	56c	80c	$1.25	$1.60	$2.40	$4.35	$6.00

Handy Gate Valves.

This is one of the most practical gates on the market, when open the passage is unobstructed; can be easily operated by a rod or rope from a distance. Can be used for pressure not to exceed 75 pounds.

No. 24R5886 Brass body.

Pipe size, inches..	½	¾	1	1¼	1½	2
Price, each.......	70c	80c	$1.10	$1.50	$2.15	$3.30

No. 24R5887 Iron body, brass mounted.

Pipe size, inches..	2	2½	3	3½	4
Price, each.......	$2.90	$5.00	$6.25	$7.50	$9.00

Hydrant Cocks.

No. 24R5890 Brass Hydrant Cocks, for iron pipe connections. T handle.

Size, inches.....	¾	1	1¼
Price, each......	63c	$1.06	$1.72

The Pickering Governor.

No. 24R6400 This Governor, by its accurate regulation and good workmanship, will commend itself wherever used. We guarantee to regulate accurately any style or size of engine and under all circumstances. For durability in all its parts, simplicity of construction, and economy in fuel, it cannot be excelled. Having no joints, its action is direct, thereby insuring great sensitiveness.

Size of Governor or diameter of steam pipe	½	¾	1	1¼	1½
Extreme height	14	14	18	19	25
Speed of Governor	500	500	450	450	420
Diam. pully on Gnr.	1½	1½	2	2	2½
Dia Cyl 300 ft. P Spd.		4	5	6	7
Dia Cyl 400 ft. P Spd.		3	4	5	6
Dia Cyl 500 ft. P Spd.			3½	4½	5
Dia Cyl 600 ft. P Spd				4	4½
Price, each	$9.90	$11.00	$12.50	$15.25	$17.50

Size of Governor or diameter of steam pipe	2	2¼	2½	3
Extreme height	26	30	31½	35
Speed of Governor	420	380	380	320
Diam. pully on Gnr.	2½	3	3	4
Dia Cyl 300 ft. P Spd.	9	10	12	14
Dia Cyl 400 ft. P Spd.	8	9	10	12
Dia Cyl 500 ft. P Spd.	7	8	9	10
Dia Cyl 600 ft. P Spd.	6	7	8	9
Price, each	$19.75	$23.00	$27.00	$33.00

Water Gauges.

No. 24R6402 With brass body, iron wheels and two guards to protect the glass tube. Prices are for gauges complete, as shown in cut.

Size	Rough	Finished
Pipe ⅜, Glass ½x10, each	78c	$1.10
Pipe ½, Glass ⅝x12, each	80c	1.25
Pipe ½, Glass ⅝x12, with four guards, finished body		1.55

Genuine Scotch Glass Tubes.

For Water Gauges.

No. 24R6406 These gauge glasses are imported by us direct, size labeled on end of each, and we warrant them equal to any. Lengths not regular, charged price of next longer tubes of same diameter.

Length		½	⅝	¾
10 inches	Price, each	5c	5c	6c
11 inches	Price, each	6c	6c	6c
12 inches	Price, each	7c	7c	7c
13 inches	Price, each	7c	7c	8c
14 inches	Price, each	7c	7c	8c
15 inches	Price, each	8c	8c	9c
16 inches	Price, each	8c	8c	10c

No. 24R6410 Patent Water Gauge Glass Cutter. Made of the best material. Cutters made of the finest imported steel, has spring and hand clamp not used on the common make. Nothing better made. Price, each $1.65

Babbitt Metal

No. 24R6450 The best low priced Babbitt Metal sold by any one. Used largely on mowers, farm machinery, pulleys, etc. No. 4, per pound 6½c

No. 24R6452 No. 3 Babbitt Metal. This grade is suitable for separators, horse powers; per lb... 9c

No. 24R6454 No. 1 Babbitt Metal. This grade metal is used for same purposes as the above metal, No. 24R6452, but a better grade. Price, per pound. 12c

No. 24R6456 No. 1 Lubricant Grade Babbitt Metal. This is a special grade of copper mixed metal used on high speed engines or on any piece of machinery where speed and durability are required. Price, per pound 20c

Magnolia Babbitt Metal.

No. 24R6460 The Magnolia brand of Babbitt Metal is one of the most popular brands now on the market. It has been widely advertised and has made a reputation second to none. Comes in bars of about 3½ pounds. Price, per pound 25c

Plumbers' Solder.

No. 24R6462 High Grade Plumbers' Solder, half and half. Comes in bars of about 1⅛ pounds each. We do not sell less than a bar. Price, per pound 18c

Pig Lead.

No. 24R6464 Genuine Pig Lead. Comes in pigs of about 80 pounds each. Price, per pound 5¾c

Block Tin.

No. 24R6466 Pure Block Tin. Comes in pigs of about 100 pounds; can also furnish bar tin in 1½-pound bars.

Price, bar tin, per pound 40c
Price, block tin, per pound 39c

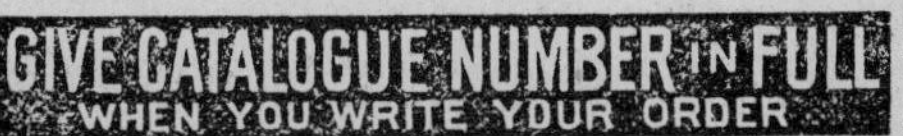

Crucibles.

No. 24R6470 Plumbago or Graphite Crucibles.

	Height	Diameter	Price, Each
No. 1	3¼-inch.	2⅝-inch.	$0.30
No. 2	4 -inch.	2⅞-inch.	.40
No. 3	4½-inch.	3½-inch.	.48
No. 4	5 -inch.	4 -inch.	.55
No. 5	5½-inch.	4⅛-inch.	.62
No. 6	5¾-inch.	4¼-inch.	.70
No. 8	6¾-inch.	5¼-inch.	.80
No. 10	7⅝-inch.	6 -inch.	1.00

Valve or Float.

No. 24R6475 This Valve and Float is used to regulate the supply of water in a watering trough. The Float is attached to the end of the lever, and as the water rises in the trough it shuts the valve. This Valve is positive in opening or closing under high or low pressure. No chance of friction or of sticking in position. It will resist almost any pressure, as the pitman connecting fulcrum and valve, comes in a straight line with thrust of pressure when valve is closed. **It has brass valve seat. By changing position of lever it will either open or close when used either on bottom or side of tank, or when two levers are used it can be used to open or close. Base is large, so that no lock nut is needed inside of the tank.**

Size, inches	¾	1	1¼	1½	2	2½
Price, each	75c	80c	90c	$1.75	$2.65	$4.50

Copper Tank Float.

No. 24R6478 To be used in connection with No. 24R6475 Valve. When fastened to lever will open and shut automatically. Size, 9½x2¾ inches.
Price, each 78c

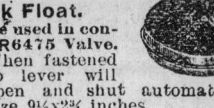

Our Little Giant Dumb Waiter.

No. 24R6480 In Our Little Giant Dumb Waiter or Elevator we have the only perfect working waiter on the market. It is made on scientific principles after years of study. Is easy to operate; does not get out of repair easily, and can be operated by a child. Only the best material is used in its construction. Just the thing for cafes, dinning rooms, apartment buildings, saloons, stores, factories, etc. Car, 24 inches wide, 20 inches deep, 28 inches high. **Made with or without movable shelves.**

Price is for complete waiter ready to put in.
Price, 1 story travel $43.00
Price, 2 story travel 47.00
Price, 3 story travel 54.00

PLUMBING GOODS AND SUPPLIES.

As space will not permit of listing a full line of these goods, we quote only such articles as are most commonly used in the country, but would state we can furnish anything you may wish in this line—Closets, Bath Tubs, Lavatories, Basins, Lead Pipe and Fittings, Soil Pipe, etc., and can guarantee to save you 75 per cent on same. We would be pleased to figure on outfits. If you are building, or contemplate doing so, send us your plans, giving exact measurements of all rooms, height of each floor and total height from roof to ground, also show exact location of tub, closet, lavatory, etc. State whether you have city water pressure or will get your water supply from a storage tank. If from tank, state where located, and, if possible, send specifications, showing how you would like your pipes, etc., laid out. State style and grade of plumbing wanted, and we will make you a net price which will include everything complete, and with the instructions we send any ordinary gasfitter or plumber can put them in.

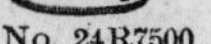

No. 24R7500

Enameled Iron Hopper Closets.

No. 24R7500 Enameled Iron Straight Hopper, self raising seat, complete as shown in cut, no waste or supply pipes or tank furnished at the price. Price, each.... $6.00

Frost Proof Closets.

Our Frost Proof Closets have frost proof brass valves, for outside and exposed places. The valve is below frost line, and is connected with hopper by a heavy chain, fastened to seat; when seat is depressed the valve is opened and hopper is flushed, when seat is relieved the supply is shut off and waste pipe opened allowing the water which is in pipe to drain direct into trap, therefore valve and pipe are at all times free from water. **We furnish above complete with cast iron hopper, enameled inside, self-raising seat, frost proof valve, 5 feet length of pipe, cast iron P trap, complete with chain and lever.** For cold or exposed places this outfit is the best on the market, water is always below frost line, it is easily connected, is substantially constructed and avoids rotting away of wooden supports as all water wastes direct into sewer.

No. 24R7503 Price, complete $10.75

No. 24R7504

Low Tank Wash Down Siphon Combination Closet.

No. 24R7504 Simple flushing valves. No float; nothing to get out of order. Gives a strong powerful flush, and a large positive refill. Bowls to rough in at 12 inches or 17 inches. Everything complete to properly set up closet. In ash, light or dark cherry plain oak, finished antique or plain varnish.

Price, with plain bowl $15.50
Add for embossed bowl 1.00

Hopper Closets.

No. 24R7506 Hopper Closets complete, as shown in cut, includes tall flushing rim hopper, single discharge siphon tank, seat and cover, nickel plated iron tank and seat brackets, flush and supply pipes, pull and chain, pipe holders with buffer and bolts.

Price, complete with oval hopper $13.25

No. 24R7506

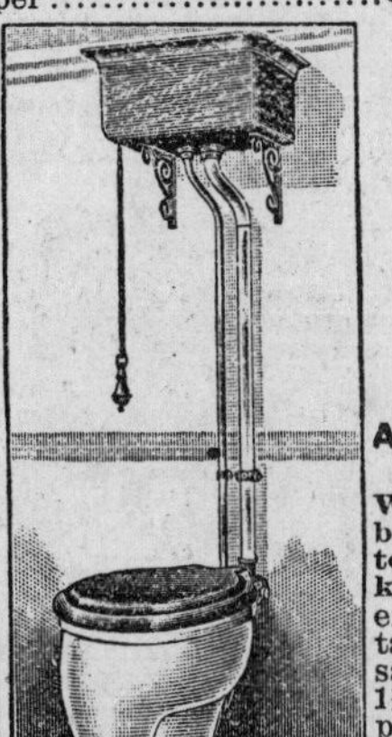

No. 24R7510

Acme Water Closets.

No. 24R7510 Our Acme Water Closet is by far the best finished and most up to date closet on the market. It has a round cornered natural oak siphon tank with double ¼-inch sawed oak attached seat, 1¼-inch nickel plated flush pipe and ½-inch nickel plated supply pipe, with No. 3 front wash-out with plain bowl. The bowl roughs at 8¾ inches from final finish of wall to center of the bend. The chain and pull and all fixtures are nickel plated. Tank is copper lined, has patent float cut off with chain and pull to flush closet. It is made of the very best materials throughout and the workmanship and finish are perfect. Furnished complete, ready for use, no fitting or extras required. Price, each $13.50

No. 24R7512 Closet, same as No. 24R7510 only without supply and waste pipes. Price...... $11.50

Siphon Jet Water Closets.

No. 24R7514 Water Closets complete, as shown in cut. Tank is copper lined. Outside made of quarter sawed oak; has siphon jet; embossed bowl; 1¼-inch nickel plated flush pipe; ½-inch nickel plated supply pipe. Bowl roughs in at 12 inches from final finish of wall to center of the bend. Has double oak seat attached to bowl; chain and pull nickel plated. Furnished complete with chain, pull, striker and floor bolts. **A very neat and substantial closet at a moderate price.**

Price, each $19.75

No. 24R7516 Closet, same as No. 24R7514, but without supply and waste pipes. Price, each $17.75

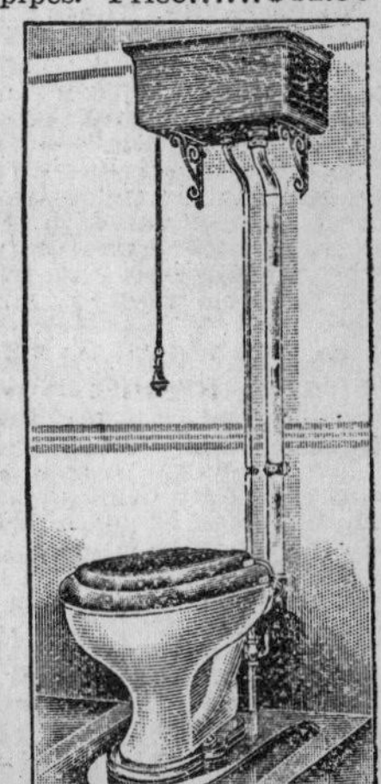

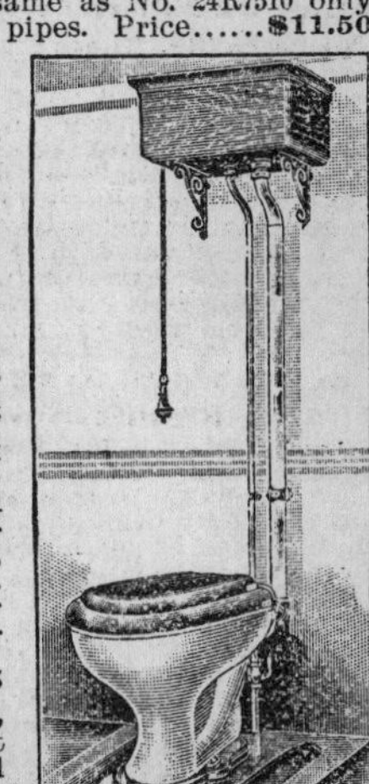

$6.75 Stationary Bath Tub.

This Tub is made of steel, is very strong and durable. Just the tub to make comfortable the home of those in moderate circumstances. No farm house is complete without the luxury of one of our bath tubs. This all steel bath tub is made of No. 20 galvanized sheet steel, coated inside with insoluble white enamel, the joints are supported by iron mountings, which terminate in four ornamental feet, the top is capped with polished oak rim, 3 inches wide, 1⅛ inches thick, the whole outside polished in a nile green tint, relieved with gold bronze. It is furnished with an overflow, as shown in cut, and patent connected waste, which is nickel plated fitting. **The 5½ foot size is the most satisfactory.**

No. 24R7520 Size, 4½ ft. Weight, 87 lbs. Price, $6.75
No. 24R7521 Size, 5 ft. Weight, 92 lbs. Price, 7.00
No. 24R7522 Size, 5½ ft. Weight, 96 lbs. Price, 7.25
No. 24R7523 Size, 6 ft. Weight, 105 lbs. Price, 9.00

Steel Clad Nickel Plated Bath Tub.

This Tub is made of steel with a lining of heavy white metal. Heavily nickel plated. Makes the neatest tub on the market. Easy to keep clean. Will last a lifetime. It is 28 inches wide, 17½ inches deep, 23½ inches from floor to top of rim, furnished with nickel plated waste and overflow, with heavy oak rim.

			Price
No. 24R7525	Length, 4½ ft.	Weight, 90 lbs..	$ 9.25
No. 24R7527	Length, 5½ ft.	Weight, 100 lbs..	10.60
No. 24R7528	Length, 6 ft.	Weight, 108 lbs..	11.50

Roll Rim Enameled Iron Baths.

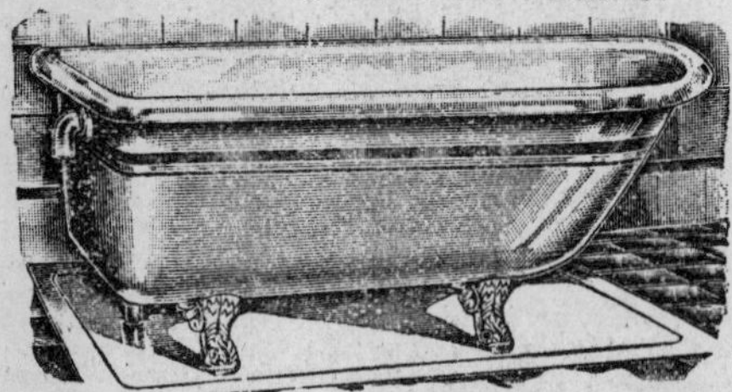

No. 24R7535 Best Grade Enameled Bath Tub, extra heavy weight enameling put on by a patent process, which we guarantee not to flake or peel off. We furnish the tub with 2¼-inch wide enameled roll rim; nickel plated overflow and waste plug with strainer; height on legs, 27 inches; width over all, 29 inches; depth inside, 20 inches. Average weight, 300 pounds.

Size tub...........	4½ ft.	5 ft.	5½ ft.
Length over rim..	4 ft. 9 in.	5 ft. 3 in.	5 ft. 9 in.
Length over all...	4 ft. 10 in.	5 ft. 4 in.	5 ft. 10 in.
Price, each.......	$18.50	$20.50	$21.70

White Enameled Bath Tub Complete.

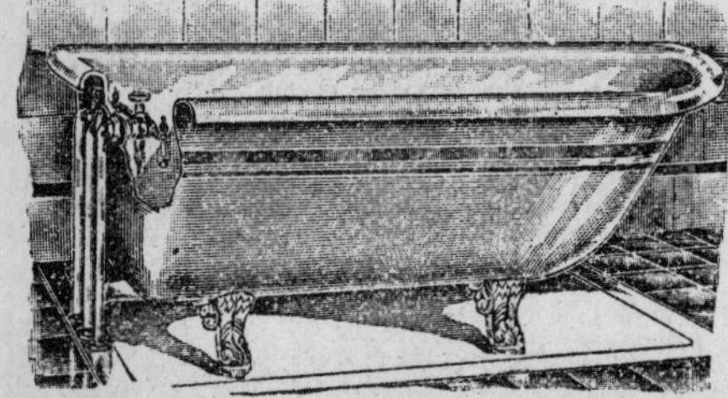

Roll Rim White Enameled Bath Tub, complete with No. 4½ Fuller Combination Cock. Has patent overflow, nickel plated plug and chain, ½-inch nickel plated supply pipe and outside nickel plated waste pipes; stands 27 inches high, 29 inches wide over all and 20 inches deep. This is one of the best tubs on the market. Everything about it is new and up to date. We guarantee the enameling not to crack or peel off. A first class tub in every respect. Good enough for any residence. Manufactured by one of the largest makers of plumbing goods in the United States and guaranteed to be perfect in every respect. Price includes everything complete, ready for use. Average weight, 300 pounds.

No. 24R7536 Size, 4½ feet. Price, each...$24.00
No. 24R7537 Size, 5 feet. Price, each... 24.50
No. 24R7538 Size, 5½ feet. Price, each... 28.00

Acme Folding Bath Tubs with Instantaneous Heater Combined.

In the Acme Folding we have the only first class low priced tub sold by anyone. The tubs are made of heavy galvanized steel, also white metal nickel plated. The galvanized tub is enameled inside, which is baked on by the same process as a bicycle frame is treated, and is warranted not to crack or peel off; while the white metal tub is made of a special grade of white metal or composition, which wears better than copper, this in turn is heavily nickel plated. We furnish these tubs with gasoline, artificial or natural gas instantaneous heaters, and guarantee either style to give perfect satisfaction. When closed it occupies a space 2⅛x2⅛x5 feet 8 inches, and the folding device is the simplest and strongest used on any tub. Just the thing for your summer home or where you have only a limited amount of space.

No. 24R7539 **Lined with galvanized steel, solid oak rim,** iron heater, two burners, enameled inside, baked on. Price, f. o. b. factory..............$22.00

No. 24R7540 **Lined with white metal nickel plated, solid oak,** iron heater, two burners, enameled outside, baked on. Price, f. o. b. factory......$25.00

No. 24R7541 **Lined with white metal nickel plated, solid oak rim, nickel plated heater,** two burners, enameled outside, baked on.
Price, f. o. b. factory.........................$27.50

When ordering, be sure to state whether you want to use gasoline, artificial or natural gas.

Oval Foot Tubs.

3X Extra Heavy Tin Foot Tubs, strong and well made, heavy handles, double seamed, etc. Furnished in assorted colors.

No. 24R7542 17x13¾ inches, each..............35c
No. 24R7543 18x14¾ inches, each..............42c
No. 24R7544 20x16⅛ inches, each..............45c

Infants' Bath Tubs.

Heavy 4X Tin Infants' Bath Tubs, well made, double seamed, strong rim and handles. Nicely japanned.

No. 24R7546 27 inches, each.................$0.85
No. 24R7547 30 inches, each....................95
No. 24R7548 33 inches, each..................1.20
No. 24R7549 36 inches, each..................1.40
No. 24R7550 42 inches, each..................1.75

Plunge Bath Tubs.

Extra Heavy Tin Plunge Bath Tubs, double seamed, heavy roll at top, extra wood bottom, waste pipe at end of tub. Nothing better made in a tin tub.

No. 24R7552 4 feet, each......................$5.00
5 feet, each......................5.50
6 feet, each......................6.50

Sitz Bath Tubs.

No. 24R7553 Sitz Bath Tubs, made of heavy 3X tin, heavy base and rim, nicely japanned and finished.

Inches.....	17x22x36	18¾x24x37
Price, each	$3.30	$4.00

Combination Bath Tub.

No. 24R7554 Combination Sitz Bath Tub, made of 3X tin, made extra strong, nicely japanned and finished. Nothing better made in a tin tub. Size, 19x34x36 inches.
Price, each.......................$3.85

Hat Shaped Bath Tub.

No. 24R7555 Hat Shaped Sitz Bath Tub, made of heavy 3X tin, japanned and varnished outside; has heavy base and legs. Size, 12¾x40 inches. Price, each.........................$4.10

Bath Tubs are accepted by most railroad companies as 2nd class freight, usually at from 40 cents to 50 cents per 100 pounds for 500 miles.

BY REFERRING TO PAGES 7 TO 10 you can get the 2nd class freight per 100 pounds to a point nearest you, which is almost exactly the same as to your town, and you will see it amounts to next to nothing as compared with the saving you will make in price.

Sanitary House Commodes.

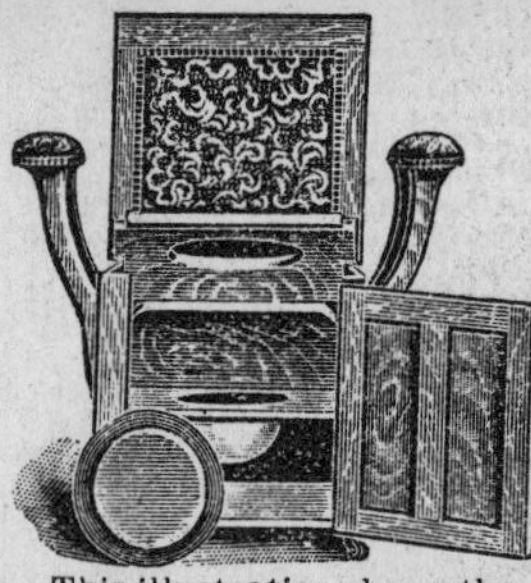

This illustration shows the upholstered commode open.

The Sanitary House Closet is a complete and satisfactory substitute for the porcelain water closet used in cities where sewer connections can be had.

The advantages of our House Closet over the stationary porcelain closet are that it can be moved into any room or up to the side of the bed for the sick, and with the noiseless, odorless receptacle cover, no germs can possibly affect the air. The price at which it is sold brings it within the reach of every family. You will consider it an indispensable necessity in your household in less than a month. It has been carefully designed with reference to its use, and is manufactured from the best material. It is made of hard wood throughout, and is well finished. Should be in every home.

This illustration shows the upholstered commode closed.

No. 24R7558 **Plain Closet.** Price...........$3.65
No. 24R7559 **Upholstered Closet.** Price.. 4.00

Safety Portable Automatic Closets.

This Closet is constructed of the best quality oak lumber, antique finish, the lumber being thoroughly kiln dried. All metal parts are brass with a heavy nickel plated finish. The receptacle for the excreta is all porcelain with a nickel plated brass handle, and is light and easy to carry. By merely raising the cover and seat-part of the closet, the pail or receptacle can be lifted out and the contents emptied at your convenience. The pail is very light, being 12 inches long, 9½ inches wide and 7½ inches deep. All other parts are also made as light as possible consistent with quality and durability, and the entire closet weighs only fifty pounds, crated and ready for shipment. **For the sick room it is a blessing, as even with a bathroom with closet on the same floor it is for the invalid a long distance to go even if only in the next room. For country residences, where lack of water connections prevent the use of regular closets, this portable closet is especially desired.**

No. 24R7560 Price, each......................$7.60

Open Plumbing Lavatories.

Italian marble slab, 20x24 inches, 1¼-inch thick, 8-inch back, 14-inch round patent overflow basin, nickel plated metal plug with rubber stopper, nickel plated S trap; No. 1 Fuller basin cocks, chain and stays, and nickel plated brackets.

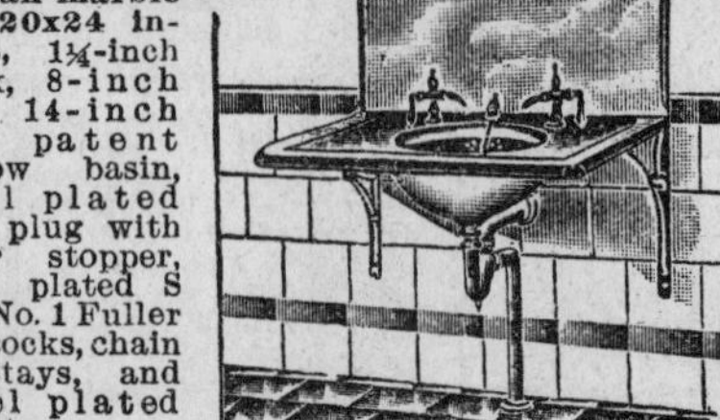

No. 24R7565 Price, as described $10.50

Open Plumbing Lavatory, furnished complete, as shown in cut. Back and bottom slabs are made of Italian and Tennessee pink marble, highly polished. Back slab is 8 inches high; bottom slab 20x24 inches, with 14-inch earthenware patent overflow bowl; nickel plated No. 1 basin cocks; nickel plated brackets, with nickel plated supply pipe and air chamber; plug and chain nickel plated. We guarantee all parts to be made of the best materials and workmanship to be perfect. Being all nickel plated, it does not require the care to keep it clean. Will not rust or corrode. We furnish everything complete, ready for use.

No. 24R7567 **Tennessee marble.** Each...$13.10
No. 24R7568 **Italian marble.** Each...... 13.25

Roll Rim Enameled Lavatories.

Roll Rim Enameled Lavatories are cast in one piece, have large improved patent overflow, ornamental exterior and are supplied with painted iron brackets, chain and waste plug coupling with rubber stopper. Length of back, 21 inches; size of bowl, 12x15 inches.

No. 24R7570 Price, **$6.25**

Roll Rim Enameled Corner Lavatories.

Enameled Iron Corner Lavatory, same as our No. 24R7570, only to use in a corner. Length of sides, 16 inches; size of bowl, 12x15 inches. They are furnished without brackets.

No. 24R7572 Price, **$6.00**

Sanitary Roll Rim Iron Wash Stands.

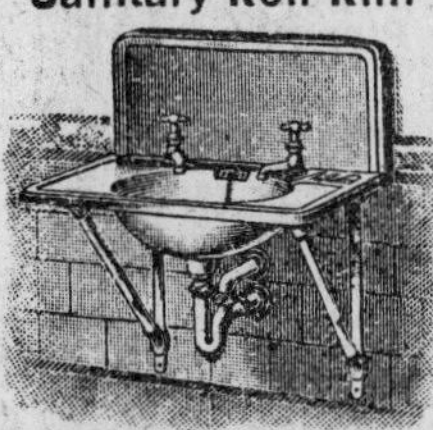

No. 24R7574 Roll Rim White Enameled Iron Lavatories; have the appearance of marble. All parts are accessible and carefully fitted together. All exposed surfaces are enameled or bronzed, making it a substantial and perfectly sanitary plumbing fixture, easily kept clean and bright. Wash Stand complete as shown, includes: 18x24-inch countersunk roll rim slab with soap tray and 12x15-inch oval, patent overflow basin, all cast in one piece; 10½-inch high roll rim back; full length nickel plated brackets; compression basin cocks; overflow strainer, chain and waste plug coupling with rubber stopper, all nickel plated.

Price, each..**$14.00**
Price, with nickel plated supply pipes..... 15.50

Roll Rim Iron Wash Stands.

No. 24R7576 Roll Rim White Enameled Iron Lavatories to place in corner of room. For description, sizes, etc., see No. 24R7574 above. In ordering be sure and state which corner of room stand is to be placed, right or left hand.

Price, each...**$15.00**
If wanted with nickel plated supply pipe, add $1.50 to the above price.

Enameled Iron Sectional Lavatories.

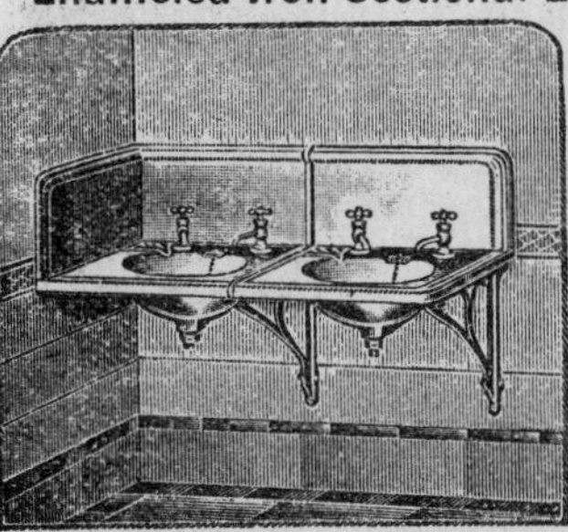

Enameled Iron Sectional Lavatories are especially adapted for hotel, restaurant and school house use. Size of each section, 18x24 inches. Height of back, 10½ inches. Length over all, 48 inches. Size of bowl, 12x15 inches. Furnished complete with four nickel plated compression basin cocks and two brackets, overflow, plug and chain.

In ordering, state whether right or left hand end is wanted.

No. 24R7578 Price, complete..............**$19.50**

Enameled Roll Rim Kitchen Sinks.

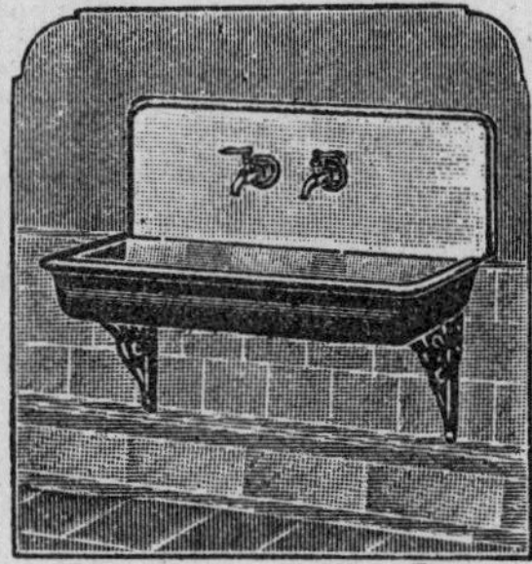

Enameled (Porcelain) Roll Rim Kitchen Sinks, with 12-inch back. Made of steel or cast iron, white enameled inside, painted blue outside. Makes one of the neatest, cleanest sinks ever put on the market. Furnished complete with faucets and brackets.

No. 24R7580	Steel Price, complete	Cast Iron Price, complete
Size, 18x30 inches	$6.95	$10.15
Size, 18x36 inches	7.80	11.00
Size, 20x36 inches	8.15	11.75
Size, 20x40 inches	8.85	12.65

REFER TO PAGES 7 TO 10 FOR FREIGHT AND EXPRESS RATES. You can tell almost exactly what the freight or express will amount to on your goods without writing to us for this information.

Enameled Roll Rim Sinks for Corner.

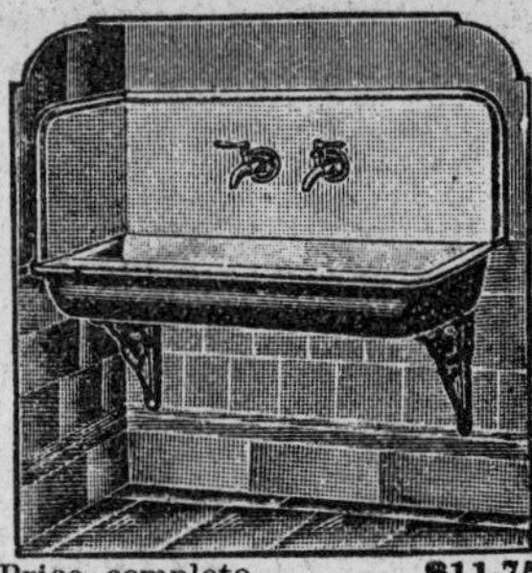

Cast Enameled Roll Rim Sinks for corner of room, with 12-inch back and sides, white enameled inside, painted blue outside. Made of high grade cast iron, free from all defects. Furnished complete with faucets and brackets.

No. 24R7582	
Size, 18x30 inches.	Price, complete..........$11.75
Size, 18x36 inches.	Price, complete.......... 12.70
Size, 20x36 inches.	Price, complete.......... 13.45
Size, 20x40 inches.	Price, complete.......... 14.40

Cast Enameled Kitchen Sinks.

No. 24R7584 Cast Enameled Roll Rim Kitchen Sinks, with 15-inch back, with air chamber, painted iron legs and brackets, drain board and nickel plated Fuller bibbs. A high grade sink, everything first class.

Size of Sink	With 24-inch Oak Drain Board. Price, complete	With 24-inch Enameled Drain Board. Price, complete
18x30 inches	$20.00	$22.50
18x36 inches	22.00	....
20x36 inches	22.40	25.00
20x40 inches	24.00	....

Acme Stoneware Kitchen Sinks.

No. 24R7586 Our Acme Stoneware Sinks have 16-inch high backs, patent metallic rims, brass strainer and waste connection; mosaic drain board, two Fuller faucets, two 18 to 24-inch extension legs (painted), and galvanized hanging soap cup. Guaranteed against leakage for ten years.

Size of sink	Size of drain board	Total length	Price
18x30x8 inches	18x20	50 inches	$11.25
20x36x8 inches	20x20	56 inches	12.40
20x45x8 inches	20x24	64 inches	13.40

Can furnish above sinks with brass rims in place of metallic rims for $2.25 in addition to price of any of above sizes.

GRANITINE LAUNDRY TUBS.

Granitine Combination Kitchen Sink and Laundry Tubs.

No. 24R7590 With high back, soap cup, strainer and painted iron legs. In ordering please state the height of back wanted. Backs higher than 16 inches will be charged extra. We do not furnish faucets unless specially ordered, but 16-inch backs, and faucet holes in the backs, will be sent unless otherwise ordered. All measurements are outside.

Length, feet	4	4½	5
Width, feet	2	2	2
Depth, inches	16	16	16
Price, 16-inch back	$11.00	$11.75	$12.25

Two Compartment Granitine Laundry Tubs.

With High Back and Soap Cup.

No. 24R7592 In ordering, please state the height of back wanted. We do not furnish faucets unless specially ordered. Tubs have zinc rims and 16-inch backs, and faucet holes in the high backs, will be sent unless otherwise ordered. All measurements are outside.

Length, feet	4	4½	5
Width, feet	2	2	2
Depth, inches	16	16	16
Price, 16-inch back	$10.00	$10.75	$11.25

Cast Sinks.

No. 24R7600 Cast Iron Sinks. Made of high grade gray iron, painted or white enameled inside, flat rims. Fitted for 1¼-inch lead pipe.

Size	Painted	White Enameled Inside, Painted Outside
Size, 16x24 in...	$0.82	$2.15
Size, 18x30 in...	1.10	2.45
Size, 18x36 in...	1.35	3.15
Size, 20x36 in...	1.60	3.45
Size 20x40 in...	1.85	3.85

Cast Slop Sinks.

No. 24R7604 Extra Heavy Cast Iron Slop Sinks.

Size, 16x16x10 inches. Price, each..............**$1.25**
Size, 14x20x12 inches. Price, each.............. 1.65

Cast Iron Corner Sinks.

No. 24R7606 Cast Iron Corner Sinks.

No. 1. Size, 20-inch sides, 28-inch front by 6 inches deep. Price, 90c
No. 2. Size, 22-inch sides, 31-inch front by 6½ inches deep. Price, each..........**$1.00**

Steel Sinks.

Wrought Steel Kitchen Sinks. These sinks are made from one plate of steel and superior to cast iron sinks in every particular, being lighter, stronger and more durable; are fitted for 1¼-inch lead or 1½-inch iron pipe, and come painted or galvanized in the following sizes:

No. 24R7608 Painted.

Size	Weight, lbs.	Each	Size	Weight, lbs.	Each
16x24x6	13	$1.40	20x30x6	21¾	$1.87
18x30x6	15¼	1.65	20x36x6	23	2.20
18x36x6	18½	2.00	20x40x6	25½	2.56

No. 24R7609 Galvanized.

Size	Weight, lbs.	Each	Size	Weight, lbs.	Each
16x24x6	13	$1.63	20x30x6	21¾	$2.20
18x30x6	15¼	2.00	20x36x6	23	2.56
18x36x6	18½	2.34	20x40x6	25½	2.92

Seamless Wrought Steel Sinks with Turned Edges. This sink is adapted for exposed or open plumbing and has improved brass strainer couplings. They are made of one piece of steel, are finely finished and one of the strongest sinks made. Cannot crack or rust out. Fitted for 1¼-inch lead pipe or 1½-inch iron pipe. Furnished in three finishes and sizes as follows:

No. 24R7613 Painted.

Size	Weight, lbs.	Each	Size	Weight, lbs.	Each
16x24x6	13	$1.43	20x30x6	22½	$1.90
18x30x6	15¼	1.68	20x36x6	23	2.25
18x36x6	18½	2.08	20x40x6	25½	2.60

No. 24R7614 Galvanized.

Size	Weight, lbs.	Each	Size	Weight, lbs.	Each
16x24x6	13½	$1.68	20x30x6	21¾	$2.25
18x30x6	18¾	2.00	20x36x6	28	2.60
18x36x6	24½	2.39	20x40x6	30	3.00

No. 24R7616 White Enameled Sinks, nicely finished; outside color blue.

Size	Weight, lbs.	Each	Size	Weight, lbs.	Each
16x24x6	14	$3.02	20x30x6	22½	$3.96
18x30x6	19¼	3.61	20x36x6	29	4.45
18x36x6	25	4.10	20x40x6	31	4.91

Seamless Wrought Steel Sink Backs.

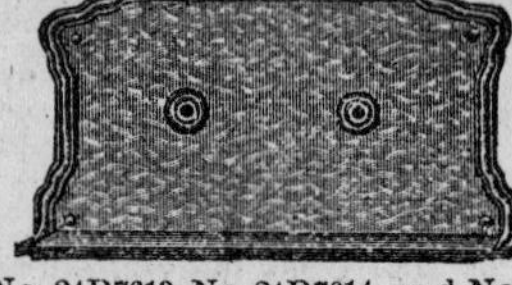

No. 24R7618 Seamless Wrought Steel Sink Backs, to be used in connection with our steel sinks. These backs **can be used only** on No. 24R7613, No. 24R7614, and No. 24R7616, or in other words on a turned edge sink.

Width, inches	24	30	36
Painted. Price, each	$0.62	$0.75	$0.94
Galvanized. Price, each	.85	.97	1.17
White enamel. Price, each	1.40	1.63	2.00

Adjustable Sink Brackets

Malleable Iron Adjustable Sink Brackets. Will fit all sizes of sinks that we carry. Made to be fastened to wall. Very neat in appearance.

No. 24R7620 Painted. Price, per pair......27c
No. 24R7621 Galvanized. Price, per pair..45c

Cast Iron Sink Legs.

No. 24R7623 Cast Iron Sink Legs, for kitchen sinks. Finished ready for use. Price, each..........40c

Sink Leg Bolts.

No. 24R7625 Screw Head Bolts, for sink legs. Made of steel. Price, each..........1c

Wash Basins.

No. 24R7635 Wash Basins, crystal enameled; common overflow; diameter, 14 in.; complete with stopper; fitted for either lead or iron pipe. Price, each, $1.65

Enameled Wash Basins.

Cast Iron Enameled Wash Basins. Made of the best grade gray iron. Made extra heavy; will last a lifetime. Common or patent overflow. Complete with stopper; fitted for either lead or iron pipe. Diameter, 14 inches.

No. 24R7637 Price, common overflow, each..........$2.00
No 24R7638 Price, patent overflow, each.... 2.10

Earthenware Basins.

Patent Overflow White Earthenware Basins for Metal or Rubber Plugs, smooth standard goods. Size, 14 inches in diameter.

No. 24R7640 Price, each, for metal plug..........70c
No. 24R7641 Price, each, for rubber plug..........90c

Oval Earthenware Basins.

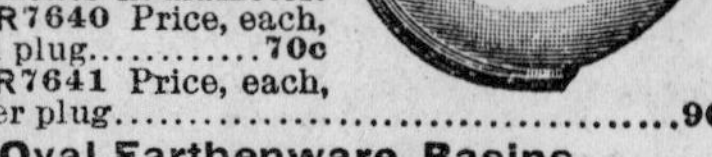

White Earthenware Oval Basins With Patent Overflow. Oval in shape. Size, 14x17 inches, for rubber or metal plugs.

No. 24R7643 Price, each, for rubber plugs..........$2.00
No. 24R7644 Price each, for metal plugs.... 1.80

Above prices on basins do not include plugs. For price on plugs see No. 24R7674.

Marble Slabs for Above Basins.

Best Grade White Marble Slabs, to be used in connection with above basin, finely finished for 14-inch bowl, round or oval, 20x24 inches, complete ready for use. Size, bottom slab, 20x24 inches.

No. 24R7648 Price, with 8-inch back, each. $4.50
No. 24R7649 Price, with 10-inch back, each. 4.75
No. 24R7650 Price, with 12-inch back, each 5.00

Same size and style as above. Made of Tennessee marble.

No. 24R7655 Price, with 8-inch back, each, $3.30
No. 24R7656 Price, with 10-inch back, each, 3.60
No. 24R7657 Price, with 12-inch back, each, 3.72

Marble Slabs for Corner.

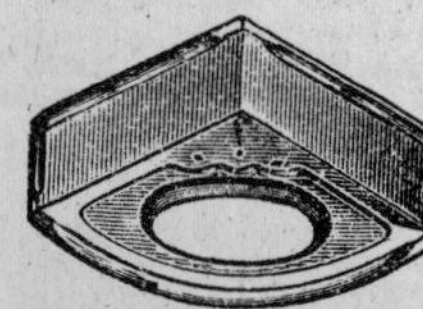

White Marble Slabs for Corner Basin, finished and polished complete, ready for use. Price includes two backs for corner. Size, square part, 20 inches.

No. 24R7659 Price, with 8-inch, back..........$4.60
No. 24R7660 Price, with 10-inch back..........$5.10
No. 24R7661 Price, with 12-inch back...... $5.50

Same size and style as above. Made of Tennessee marble.

No. 24R7665 Price, with 8-inch back, each, $3.45
No. 24R7666 Price, with 10-inch back, each, 3.85
No. 24R7667 Price, with 12-inch back, each, 4.15

Basin Clamps.

Basin Clamps, for use in connecting earthenware bowls and marble slab. Set consists of four for round and three for oval.

No. 24R7669 Price, per set....12c

Brackets for Basin Slabs.

No. 24R7671 Steel Brackets, nickel plated, suitable for Nos. 24R7648 and 24R7659 basin slabs. Size, 16x18 inches. Price, per pair, 60c

Metal Plugs with Rubber Stoppers.

No. 24R7672 Patent Overflow Basin Plugs with rubber stoppers; made of solid brass, nickel plated, to fit above basins. Each, 35c

Rubber Plugs.

No. 24R7674 Rubber Plugs, to fit our No. 24R7641 and No. 24R7643 basins. Price, each..........15c

Safety Chain.

No. 24R7676 Brass or Nickel Plated Safety Chain, to be used on plugs, stoppers, closet pulls, etc.

Size	00	0
Price, per yard, brass	5c	6c
Price, per yard, nickel	7c	8c

Urinals.

No. 24R7680 Iron Corner Urinal, enameled. Size, 9-inch, fitted for lead pipe. Price, each. 90c

No. 24R7682 Iron Half Circle Urinal, enameled. Size, 12-inch; fitted for lead pipe. Each...$1.00

Earthenware Urinals.

Flat Back Earthenware Urinals. Furnished without connections as shown in cut.

No. 24R7685 Size, 12x14 inches. Price, each..........$3.20
No. 24R7686 Size, 13x15 inches. Price, each..........$3.90

Philadelphia Pattern Hopper Closets.

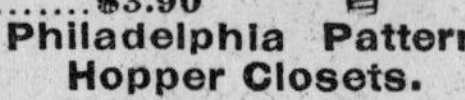

Enameled Iron Philadelphia Hoppers are enameled inside and painted outside. Must be connected with lead pipe direct to water pressure. Can be used with our No. 24R7720 seat. This makes a very cheap and neat outfit for use in basements or outside places.

No. 24R7690 Price, for Hopper only.......... $1.25

Washout Bowl.

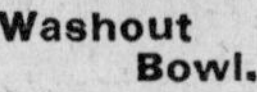

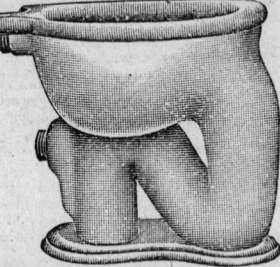

With Seat Attachment.

Plain Earthenware Washout Closet, complete with seat attachment, spud and vent coupling; first quality.

No. 24R7692 Each...$4.50

Combination Hopper and Trap.

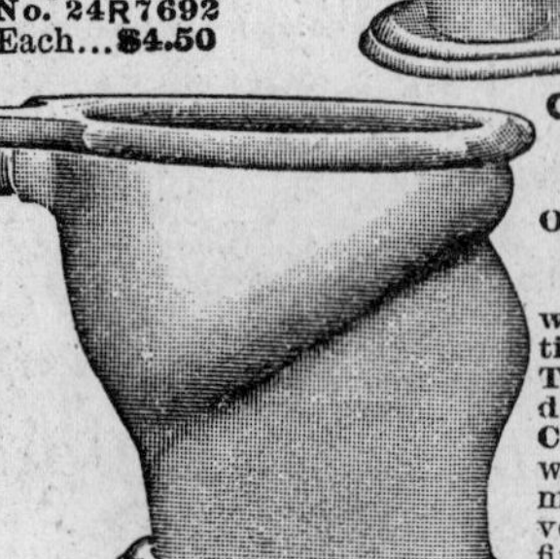

Or Wash-Down Siphon.

Plain Earthenware Combination Hopper and Trap, or Washdown Siphon Closet, complete with seat attachment, spud and vent coupling; first quality.

No. 24R7694 Price, each..$4.95

Siphon Jet Bowls.

Plain Earthenware Siphon Jet Closet Bowls, with seat attachments and spuds; first quality.

No. 24R7696 Each..$10.50

Lavatory Supply Pipes.

Extra Heavy Plain Wall Lavatory Supply Pipes, ⅜-inch, with slip joints and complete with wall flanges; brass, nickel plated.

No. 24R7699 Price, per pair.$1.25

Lavatory Supply Pipes.

Extra Heavy Plain Lavatory Supply Pipes, ⅜-inch, with slip joints and air chamber; brass, nickel plated. Complete with flanges.

No. 24R7700 Price, per pair. $2.45

Lavatory Traps.

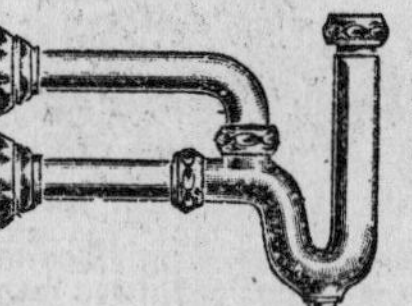

Extra Heavy Lavatory S Traps, 1¼-inch, vented. Complete with pipe to floor and vent to wall and flanges; made of brass, nickel plated.

No. 24R7702 Price, each.. ....$1.80

Lavatory Supply Pipes.

Extra Heavy Plain Wall Lavatory Supply Pipes, ⅜-inch, with slip joints and air chamber; complete with wall flanges; nickel plated.

No. 24R7704 Price, per pair.....$2.50

Lavatory Traps.

Extra Heavy 1¼-inch P Lavatory Trap, vented, with waste and vent to wall, complete with flanges.

No. 24R7706 Price, each..........$1.70

Bath Supply Pipes.

Extra Heavy Plain Straight Bath Supply Pipes, ½-inch, complete with flanges. Made of brass, nickel plated.

No. 24R7708 Price, per pair.....$1.10

Bath Supply Pipes.

Extra Heavy Plain Offset Supply Pipes, ½ inch, complete with flanges. Made of brass, nickel plated.

No. 24R7710 Size ½ inch, 45-degree offset. Price, per pair..........$1.40
Size, ½ inch, 90-degree offset. Price, per pair..........$1.45

Connected Bath Waste and Overflow.

No. 24R7714 Extra Heavy Nickel Plated Brass Connected Bath Waste and Overflow, with elbow top, complete with flanges.

Size, 1⅜ inches. Price, each.....$1.65
Size, 1½ inches. Price, each..... 1.75

Closet Seat with Cover.

No. 24R7720 Closet Seat with cover, furnished complete, well finished, etc. Furnished in oak, natural or antique, or light cherry. Each, $1.35

High Tanks.

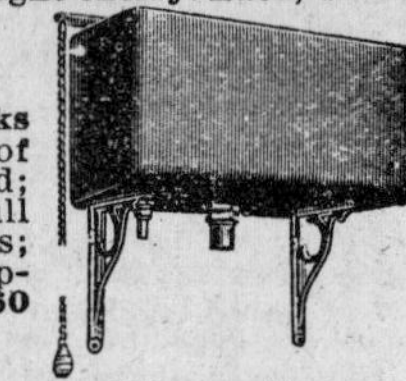

No. 24R7724 High Tanks for water closets. Made of solid oak, highly finished; complete with brackets, pull and chain; holds 5½ gallons; is lined with heavy sheet copper. Price, each..........$3.60

"Chicago" Instantaneous Water Heater.

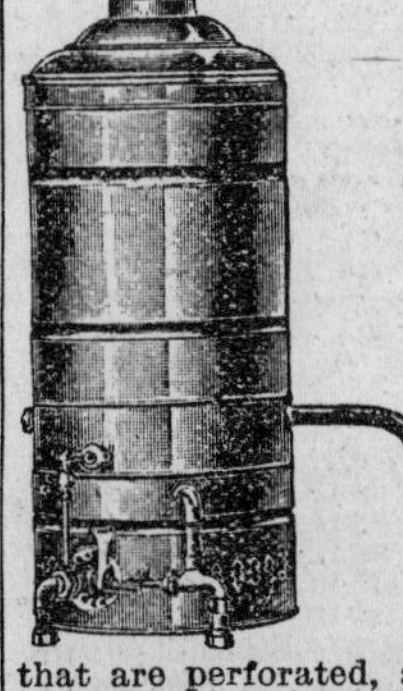

Recommended for the bath only. This Heater will heat two gallons of water a minute, raising the temperature of the water from fifty degrees to one hundred degrees, consuming but one and one-fourth cubic feet of gas a minute. This result is attained by allowing the ascending hot products of combustion of the gas to mingle with the downward flowing water, thereby extracting all the heat from the gas; there is no waste heat, as the products of combustion leave the heater cold. The interior parts consist of a series of upward and downward flaring pans that are perforated, and through which the heat ascends; they are stamped from solid sheets of copper and can be removed and replaced in a few moments. There is but one ounce of solder used in the entire construction of the heater, thereby decreasing the possibilities of leaks or requiring repairs. Dimensions: diameter, 12 inches; height, 28 inches. Shipping weight, 60 pounds.

No. 24R7735 Nickel plated. Each........$19.00

Water Heaters continued on following page.

Rival Water Heater.

This cut shows Heater attached to hot air furnace.

Rival Water Heater is a convenient and almost indespensable auxilary to a hot air furnace. It is placed just above the fire pot of the furnace and can be used to heat the water for kitchen, laundry and bathrooms or to supply hot water radiators in from one to ten rooms. It can be applied to any kind of furnace. **The advantage of this device,** when properly used, is that without consuming more coal it extracts more heat from the coal that is burned and at the same time conveying heat to room located at a considerable horizontal distance from the furnace. where it is almost impossible to get hot air to go.

The heater is made in semi-circular sections and can be used either single or double. If used single the heater is placed in the back of the furnace, close to the fire, the base facing the door. If double, the upper section is placed at right angles to the lower and comes level with the top of the furnace door, so that in neither case is there any obstruction to feeding. In operation the fire strikes the heater and is then thrown against the sides of the furnace, increasing the power of the furnace. This heater can be installed by any practical plumber and gives general satisfaction. The rating of the various sizes is given on the list, and 50 square feet of radiation may be taken as sufficient heat for an ordinary sized room, or a 30-gallon tank of water for domestic purposes. The diameter of each heater is also given so that intending purchasers may determine whether to use a large single heater or a small double one, according to the size of the furnace. In selecting a heater figure the net capacity about ten per cent less than rating to allow for piping. Two collars, with set screws, go with each single or double heater, but no pipe or nipples. Openings may be bushed for smaller pipe. We ship double heaters in two parts.

Single Heater.

Double Heater.

No. 24R7738

No.	Size Semi-circle Inches	Capacity Sq. Feet Direct Radiation	Size Pipe	Price
1	6 x 10	50	1¼	$ 3.15
2	10 x 16	110	2	5.00
3	11 x 18	130	2	5.65
4	11½ x 20	165	2½	6.90
5	13 x 22	195	2½	7.80
6	15 x 23	250	3	9.50
7	17 x 28	375	3	15.75

No. 24R7740

No.	Diameter Double Semi-circle Inches	Capacity Sq. Feet Direct Radiation	Size Pipe	Price
8	10	80	1¼	$ 6.25
9	16	185	2	10.00
10	18	225	2	11.25
11	20	285	2½	13.50
12	22	340	2½	15.60
13	25	435	3	20.00
14	28	700	3	30.00

Range Boilers.

RANGE BOILERS ARE USED only where there is a water supply furnished with constant pressure through pipes—which can only be obtained in towns and ties having water works.

Galvanized Steel Range Boilers, tested to 160 pounds pressure. We furnish our boilers complete with stands, inside tubes and brass couplings for lead pipe.

	Gal.	Height	W'ght	Price, each
No. 24R7745	30	60 in.	72 lbs.	$ 8.25
No. 24R7746	35	60 in.	76 lbs.	9.50
No. 24R7747	40	60 in.	85 lbs.	10.60
No. 24R7748	52	60 in.	120 lbs.	16.80
No. 24R7749	60	60 in.	150 lbs.	18.75

If any of above boilers are wanted without stand, deduct 60 cents from above prices.

SEND 5 CENTS FOR SAMPLES OF
MEN'S TAILOR MADE CLOTHING
AT LOWEST PRICES.

ACME TRIUMPH WATER HEATERS.

The Acme Triumph Water Heater is peculiarly adapted to meet the requirements for domestic use and to supply hot water for commercial purposes, as well as to heat residences, stores, etc. It is conveniently run and is constructed on practical and scientific principles, while it brings the cost of running an independent water heater down to a minimum. It is not only simple and easily cared for, but operates on the same principle as the waterback in a range and is just as safe as one. **The Acme Triumph Heaters** make it possible for every well regulated household to become supplied with an ideal hot water system. Our small sized heaters are far more convenient to handle than others, especially as each one has a fire door in the side and can be supplied with a coal magazine. Owners of apartment buildings find all of our sizes fuel savers and always to be depended on for providing tenants with an ample supply of hot water. The adoption of **our larger sizes for heating residences** is the result of their quick action in heat radiation, fuel economy, reliability and convenience. **Acme Triumph Water Heaters are used to heat water for domestic purposes** in residences, hotels, apartment houses and office buildings; in barber shops, baptistries, and wherever hot water is desired. They are also used for heating residences, offices, stores, greenhouses, conservatories, poultry houses, etc. In barber shops the heater is often utilized to heat water for the baths, in addition to that needed for shaving and shampooing. The number of tubs which can be supplied with hot water by the various sizes is shown in the following table. All sizes, whether furnished with a plain or magazine hood, have a fire door at the side. **The ash box is provided with a good shaking and dumping grate.** The upper ring is tapped for connecting the flow or supply pipes and the lower ring for the return pipes. These heaters are made tight at 200 pounds cold water pressure. The tubes are screwed into the lower ring and both screwed and packed by lock nuts at the upper ring. **All parts are made interchangeable.**

Catalogue No. 24R7755	No. 0	No. 0½	No. 1	No. 2	No. 3	No. 4	No. 5	No. 6
Price with plain hood, each	$19.00	$22.50	$30.00	$37.50	$55.00	$70.00	$100.00	$120.00
Price with magazine hood, each	21.00	24.00	34.00	41.00	63.00	78.00	110.00	126.00
Diameter, inches	12	12	14	16	21	21	30	30
Height over all, inches	31	35	48	48	55	68	70	70
Heating capacity of tanks, gals.	90	120	150	180	350	500	750	950
*Heating capacity for radiators, square feet	75	100	120	150	300	425	650	800
†No. of outlets and size, inches	2-1	2-1	2-1¼	2-1¼	2-1½	3-2	2-3	2-3
†No. of inlets and size, inches	2-1	2-1	2-1¼	2-1¼	2-1½	3-2	2-3	2-3
Approximate weight, pounds	160	175	320	395	795	895	1425	1550
Size of smoke stack suitable, in.	5	5	6	6	7	7	10	10
Number of bath tubs	1	2	3-4	5-6	8-10	14	18	24

* Direct surface, including or with flow and return pipes covered. † Unless otherwise ordered.
The fixtures comprise an ash box, grate, grate rest and shaker.

Acme Direct Steam or Water Radiators.

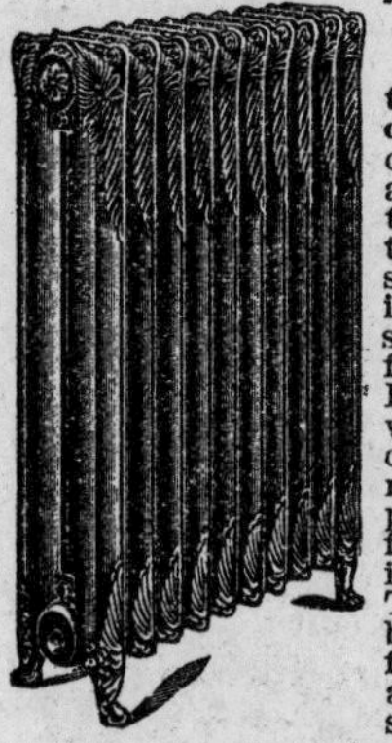

Our Acme Radiators are the latest thing in radiator design and construction; occupies less floor space for amount of heating surface than any other. Guaranteed to contain full area of heating surface claimed. The openings are large and unobstructed, no angles to check free and perfect circulation. If a connection at top of a hot water radiator is desired, it can readily be made by simply removing the ornamental plug. This is an important feature, as it is often called for in certain systems of piping. The castings are made of the best gray iron and are of uniform thickness. They are adapted to high or low pressure.

Number of Sections	Length Inches	Heating Surface—Square Feet. 45 Inches High, 5¼ square feet per section	37 Inches High, 4¼ square feet per section	31 Inches High, 3½ square feet per section	25 Inches High, 2¾ square feet per section	20 Inches High, 2¼ square feet per section
5	11 9/16	26¼	21¼	17½	13¾	11¼
6	13⅞	31½	25½	21	16½	13½
7	16 3/16	36¾	29¾	24½	19¼	15¾
8	18½	42	34	28	22	18
9	20 13/16	47¼	38¼	31½	24¾	20¼
10	23⅛	52½	42½	35	27½	22½
11	25 7/16	57¾	46¾	38½	30¼	24¾
12	27¾	63	51	42	33	27
13	30⅛	68¼	55¼	45½	35¾	29¼
14	32⅜	73½	59½	49	38½	31½
15	34 11/16	78¾	63¾	52½	41¼	33¾

Width of section 7½ inches. To ascertain the cost of a radiator multiply the number of square feet in the radiator you wish by the cost per square foot. For example, a 10-section radiator 37 inches high contains 42 square feet, at 22½ cents, will cost **$9.45**

No. 24R7760

Height	45-in.	37-in.	31-in.	25-in.	20-in.
Price per square foot,	22c	22½c	23½c	26c	29c

BATH ROOM SPECIALTIES.

Made of solid brass, nickel plated, will last forever. Nothing better made.

Match Box.

No. 24R7800 Solid Brass Match Box. Nickel plated.
Price, each........................72c

Cigar Rest.

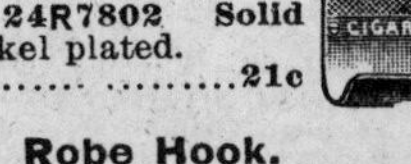

No. 24R7802 Solid Brass Cigar Rest. Nickel plated.
Price, each........................21c

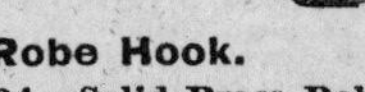

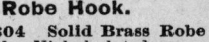

Robe Hook.

No. 24R7804 Solid Brass Robe or Clothes Hook. Nickel plated.
Price, each........................11c

Towel or Wash Rag Holder.

No. 24R7806 Brass Towel or Wash Rag Holder. Nickel plated.
Price, each........................6c

Hook for Razor Strop.

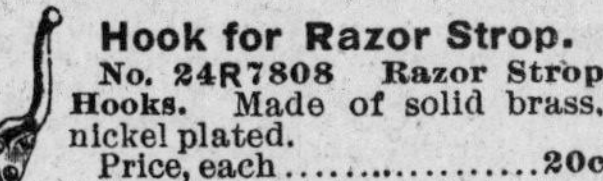

No. 24R7808 Razor Strop Hooks. Made of solid brass, nickel plated.
Price, each........................20c

Coat and Hat Hooks.

No. 24R7810 Coat and Hat Hooks. Made of brass, nickel plated. 6 inches high. Highly finished. Price, each........................20c

Coat and Hat Hooks.

No. 24R7812 Coat and Hat Hooks. Made of brass, nickel plated, highly finished, 7¾ inches high. Price, each........................40c

Robe Hooks.

No. 24R7814 Robe Hooks. Solid brass, nickel plated, highly finished.
Price, each........................32c

Tumbler Holders.

No. 24R7815 Solid Brass Tumbler Holders. Nickel plated.
Price, each........................48c

No. 24R7816 Solid Brass, Nickel Plated Tumbler Holders, to be fastened to the wall. Extra fine. Price is for holder only; no tumbler furnished.
Price, each........................85c

Combination Holders.

No. 24R7817 Combination Tumblers and Tooth Brush Holders. Made of brass, nickel plated, highly polished, heavy goods. Nothing better made.
Price, each........................$1.50

Tooth Brush Holders.

No. 24R7818 Solid Brass Tooth Brush Holders. Nickel plated. Holds six brushes.
Price, each........................50c

Soap Dish.

No. 24R7820 Solid Brass Soap Dish. Nickel plated.
Price, each........................24c

Solid Brass Soap Cups.

No. 24R7822 Shell Pattern Solid Brass Nickel Plated Soap Cups, to be fastened to the wall. **Finest finish, extra fine goods.** Size, 4x3 inches.
Price, each........................75c

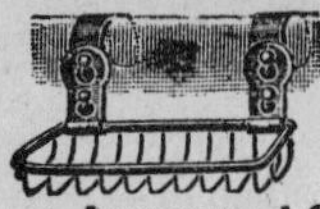

Improved Soap Holder.

No. 24R7824 Solid Brass Improved Soap Holder. Has detachable bands; can be used either on tub or wall. **Nickel plated.** Price, each..........48c

Improved Sponge and Soap Dish.

No. 24R7826 Solid Brass Improved Sponge Holder, with detachable soap dish. Soap dish can be placed on either end of holder. Bands that go over side of tub can be detached, when holder can be placed against side of wall if so desired. **Nickel plated.**
Price, each..........72c

Soap Cups.

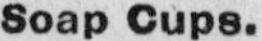

No. 24R7828 Soap Cups for the rim of the bath, solid brass, nickel plated, finely finished. Hanging rods can be adjusted so as to fit any tub. Size, 6x3½ inches.
Price, each..........80c

Sponge Holders.

No. 24R7830 Solid Brass Sponge Holders. Nickel plated. 7½ inches in diameter.
Price, each..........89c

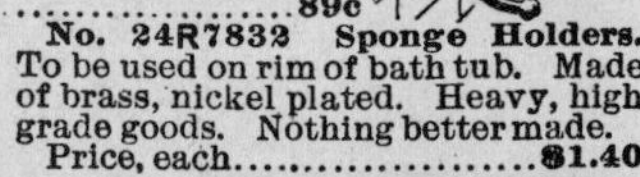

No. 24R7832 Sponge Holders. To be used on rim of bath tub. Made of brass, nickel plated. Heavy, high grade goods. Nothing better made.
Price, each..........$1.40

Sponge and Soap Holders.

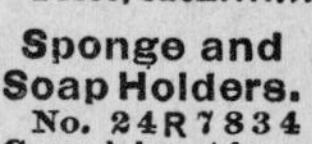

No. 24R7834 Combination Sponge and Soap Holders. To be used on rim of bath tub. Heavy, high grade goods. Sponge basket is 6¼ inches long, 5¾ inches wide, and 3 inches deep. Soap holder is 5½ inches long and 3 inches wide.
Price, each..........$1.75

Towel Racks.

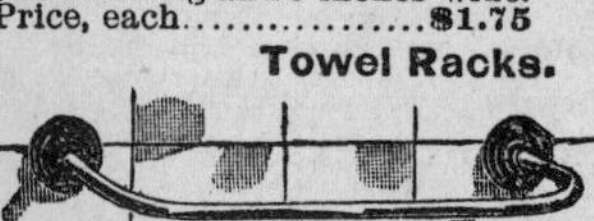

Nickel Plated Towel Racks. Strong and durable; finely finished bar is ⅝ inch in diameter; projects 2¼ inches from wall.

No. 24R7836 Length, 15 inches. Price, each..34c
No. 24R7837 Length, 18 inches. Price, each..37c
No. 24R7838 Length, 24 inches. Price, each..46c

No. 24R7840 Extra Heavy Towel Rack. Made of brass, nickel plated. Diameter of bar, ⅝ inch; width from wall, 3 inches. Size, 15 inches. Price, each..........60c
Size, 18 inches. Price, each..........70c
Size, 24 inches. Price, each..........85c

Folding Towel Racks.

No. 24R7842 Three Arm Nickel Plated Towel Racks, will not rust or corrode, nice enough for any bath room. Diameter of bars, ¼ inch; length, 12 inches.
Price, each..........60c

Roller Towel Racks.

No. 24R7844 Roller Towel Racks. Brackets are solid brass, nickel plated; roller is made of an extra heavy brass tube, nickel plated. Diameter of bar, 1 inch; width of bracket, 2¼ inches; length of roller, 18 inches.
Price, each..........$1.15

Toilet Paper Holders.

No. 24R7846 Solid Brass, Nickel Plated Toilet Paper Holder. Nicely finished, nice enough for any bath room. Will take roll 5 inches wide by 4 inches diameter.
Price, each..........25c

Paper Holders.

No. 24R7847 Solid Brass Toilet Paper Holder. Nickel plated, takes standard size paper.
Price, each..........36c

Paper Holders.

No. 24R7848 Solid Brass Toilet Paper Holders. Nickel plated, takes standard size paper.
Price, each..........72c

Paper Holders.

No. 24R7850 Solid Brass Toilet Paper Holder. Extra heavy, nothing better made, nickel plated, takes standard size paper.
Price, each..........$1.35

Bath Spray.

No. 24R7855 Nickel Plated Bath Spray, with 5 feet of rubber tubing to attach to faucet; rose is made of brass, nickel plated.
Price, each..........79c

Bath Seat.

No. 24R7857 Here is just what you want to make the bath room complete—a bath tub seat. Seat is made of oak, is 18x6 inches, with rounded corners. The supporting rods are ⁵⁄₁₆-inch brass, nickel plated. Rods are hinged under the seat, so they are adjustable to tubs of different widths. The ends of the rods are covered with rubber, so as not to mar the finish of tub rim. All parts of the best material and finest finish. **Nothing better made.**
Price, each..........$1.10

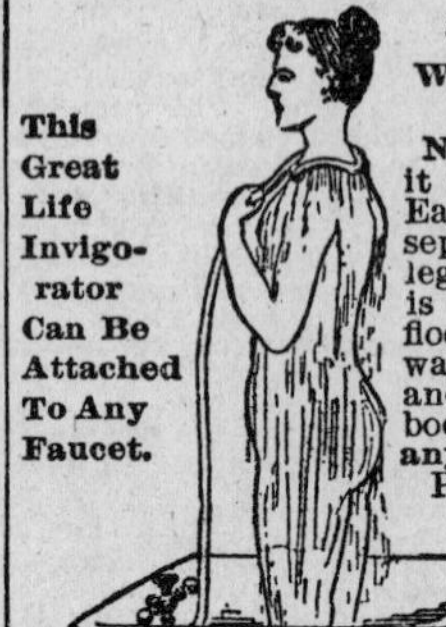

This Great Life Invigorator Can Be Attached To Any Faucet.

Shower Bath Yoke.

With 6 feet of hose, $1.20. Highly Nickel Plated.

No. 24R7859 A lady can use it without wetting her head. Each limb can be showered separately placing the arm or leg through the yoke. There is no splashing of walls or floor, as the sprays or jets of water are directed inwardly and flow over all parts of the body. **It can be attached to any faucet.**
Price, each..........$1.20

Cline's Portable Shower Bath.

No. 24R7862 A desirable necessity is to be found in Cline's Portable Shower Bath. No home is complete without a bath. As many homes are not provided with a tub, this little portable bath is constructed to fill the long felt want, for a small cost and no trouble. A full, invigorating, life giving bath, such as your physician prescribes; always ready.
Price, each..........$3.00

Acme Shower Baths.

No. 24R7865 Acme Shower Bath, pipe and all fixtures, made of heavy brass, nickel plated, complete with inlet air valve. Height, 7¼ feet. Distance from wall to center of shower, 18 inches. Diameter of shower, 8 inches. Diameter of curtain ring, 25 inches. **Nickel plated shower, with inlet air valve, supply pipe and valves only.**
Price..........$17.00

No. 24R7866 Nickel Plated Shower, with inlet air valve, complete with ring and rubber curtain, as shown in cut.
Price..........$31.00

Basin Cocks.

No. 24R7870 Compression Basin Cocks, T handle. Made of brass, finely finished and polished.
Price, each..........62c

Fuller Basin Cock.

No. 24R7872 High Grade Fuller Basin Cocks, furnished complete, nickel plated. Price, each..........87c

Combination Bath Cocks.

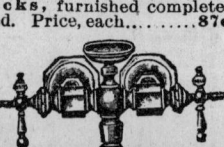

No. 24R7874 Cast Brass, Combination Hot and Cold Bath Cocks. Nickel plated, complete, ready for use. Nothing better made.
Price, each..........$2.10

Compression Plain Bibbs.

No. 24R7876 Compression Plain Bibbs, for lead pipe. Made of brass, finished and polished complete.
Size, inches.. ½ ¾ 1
Price, each..37c 52c $1.00

Compression Hose Bibbs.

No. 24R7878 Compression Hose Bibbs, for lead pipe. Made of brass, finely finished, complete.
Size, inches.... ½ ¾ 1
Price, each..... 43c 72c $1.10

Compression Plain Bibbs, with Flange.

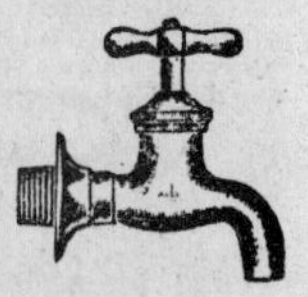

No. 24R7880 Plain Compression Bibbs, with flange, screwed for iron pipe. Made of brass, finely finished.
Size, inches..... ½ ¾ 1
Price, each......35c 55c 98c

Compression Hose Bibbs with Flange.

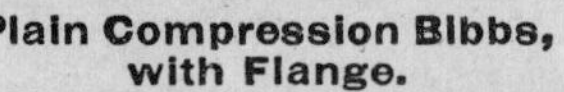

No. 24R7882 Compression Hose Bibbs, with flange, screwed for iron pipe. Made of brass, finely finished.
Size, inches..... ½ ¾ 1
Price, each......45c 59c $1.00

Plain Compression Bibbs, with Flange.

No. 24R7884 Plain Compression Bibbs, with flange, for lead pipe connection. Made of brass, highly finished.
Size, inches... ½ ¾ 1
Price, each..... 40c 60c $1.50

Compression Hose Bibbs, with Flange.

No. 24R7886 Compression Hose Bibbs, with flange, for lead pipe connection. Made of brass, highly finished
Size, inches....... ½ ¾ 1
Price, each........50c 65c $1.00

Fuller Bibbs, Plain, with Flange.

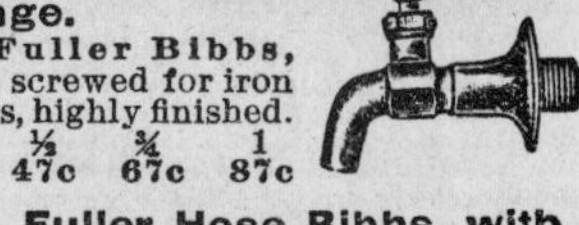

No. 24R7888 Fuller Bibbs, plain, with flange, screwed for iron pipe. Made of brass, highly finished.
Size, inches..... ½ ¾ 1
Price, each 47c 67c 87c

Fuller Hose Bibbs, with Flange.

No. 24R7890 Fuller Hose Bibbs, with flange, screwed for iron pipe. Made of brass, highly finished.
Size, inches..... ½ ¾ 1
Price, each...... 52c 72c 92c

Fuller Bibbs, Plain, with Flange.

No. 24R7892 Fuller Bibbs, plain, with flange, for lead pipe connection. Made of brass, highly polished.
Size, inches..... ½ ¾ 1
Price, each...... 50c 71c 91c

Fuller Hose Bibbs, with Flange.

No. 24R7894 Fuller Hose Bibbs, with flange, for lead pipe connection. Made of brass, highly finished.
Size, inches..... ½ ¾ 1
Price, each...... 56c 76c 96c

Fuller Bibbs, Plain.

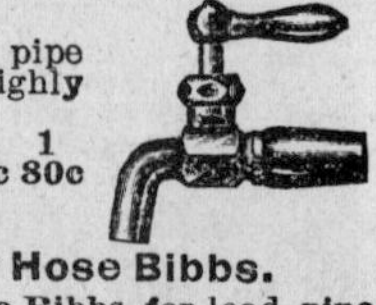

Plain Fuller Bibbs for lead pipe connection. Made of brass, highly polished.
No. 24R7896 Size, in. ½ ¾ 1
Price, each..........46c 66c 80c

Fuller Hose Bibbs.

Fuller Hose Bibbs for lead pipe connections. Made of brass, highly polished.
No. 24R7898 Size, in. ½ ¾ 1
Price, each..........51c 72c 90c

Bibbs.

No. 24R7900 Fuller Pattern Plain Bibbs, for iron pipe, finished brass.
Size, inches. ½ ¾ 1
Price, each..45c 65c 85c

No. 24R7902 Fuller Pattern Hose Bibbs, for iron pipe, finished brass.
Size, inches. ½ ¾ 1
Price, each..50c 70c 90c

Pipe Hooks.

Pipe Hooks for Soil Pipe.
No. 24R8080 Size 2-in. Each..3½c
No. 24R8081 Size 4-in. Each..5c

Pipe Rests.

No. 24R8083 Pipe Rests for Soil Pipe. Standard grade.
Size, 2 inches......Price, each 15c
Size, 4 inches......Price, each 25c

Cast S Traps.

Cast S Traps for soil pipe. Plain. Size, 4 inches.
No. 24R8085 Price, each, standard..........56c
No. 24R8086 Price, each, extra heavy..........90c

Cast Half S Traps.

Cast Half S Traps, for soil pipe. Size, 4 inches.
No. 24R8087 Price, each, standard..........55c
No. 24R8088 Price, each, extra heavy..........91c

Lead Traps.

No. 24R8090 4-Inch Lead Traps for closet connections. Full S style. Price, each..........$1.50
No. 24R8091 Lead Trap for closet connection. Half S style. Price, each..........$1.20

Tee Branch.

No. 24R8092 Cast Tee Branch for soil pipe.
Price each, 2-inch, standard, 20c; extra heavy, 27c
Price each, 4-inch, standard, 45c; extra heavy, 57c

Y Branch.

No. 24R8094 Cast Y Branch for soil pipe.

	Standard	Extra heavy
Price each, 2x2 inches..	20c	31c
Price, each, 4x2 inches..	43c	55c
Price each, 4x4 inches..	48c	61c

Sanitary Cross.

No. 24R8096 Cast Sanitary Cross, for soil pipe.

	Standard	Extra heavy
Price, each, 2x2 in...	35c	45c
Price, each, 4x4 in...	57c	72c

Off Set.

No. 24R8098 Cast Off Set, for soil pipe.

	Standard	Extra heavy
2-in. with 4-in. offset. Price,	16c	31c
2-in. with 6-in. offset. Price,	20c	34c
2-in. with 12-in. offset. Price,	29c	43c
4-in. with 4-in. offset. Price,	33c	47c
4-in. with 6-in. offset. Price,	39c	54c
4-in. with 12-in. offset. Price,	54c	72c

Quarter Bend with Heel Outlet.

No. 24R8100 Cast Quarter Bend, with heel outlet, for soil pipe.

	Standard	Extra heavy
Price, 2-in. with 2-in. heel outlet,	30c	33c
Price, 4-in. with 2-in. heel outlet.	45c	55c
Price, 4-in. with 4-in. heel outlet.	54c	65c

Service or Stop Cock Boxes.

No. 24R8105 Made of cast iron, japanned. Size, 3-inches in diameter, extends from 34 inches to 58 inches. Price, each..........$1.20

Cast Cesspools.

Cast Iron Cesspools, with belltrap, to be used in connection with soil pipe.
No. 24R8110 Size, 6x6-inch. Price, each..........30c
No. 24R8111 Size, 9x9-inch. Price, each...38c
No. 24R8112 Size, 13x13-inch. Price, each..........60c

Street Washers.

No. 24R8115 All parts which water comes in contact with are at the bottom, hence free from frost. Valves can be pulled out at top, thus avoiding digging up for repairs.

Size..........	¾ in.	¾ in.	1 in.	1 in.
To set in ground	3 ft.	4 ft.	3 ft.	4 ft.
Price, each.....	$2.90	$3.20	$3.40	$3.80

READ CAREFULLY the introductory pages of this catalogue. Note our CASH WITH ORDER TERMS and SATISFACTION GUARANTEE.

Pipe Hydrants.

No. 24R8117 When a cheap but serviceable hydrant is desired, we recommend our pipe hydrant. It attaches to the underground pipe below freezing point and is furnished with a brass shut-off valve. The drip from which drains the hydrant as soon as it is turned off, and prevents injury from frost.

	¾-inch	1-inch	1¼-inch
4 feet long	$1.55	$1.85	$2.85
5 feet long	1.60	1.92	3.00
6 feet long	1.65	2.00	3.20

Hydrants.

No. 24R8119 All parts of hydrant which water comes in contact with are at bottom out of the way of frost. It is anti-freezing. The waste operates perfectly, emptying the water from the rising pipe when the valve is closed and closing the waste when the valve is open. Valve can be pulled out at top when in need of repairs, thus avoiding the necessity of digging it up.

Size..........	¾ in.	¾ in.	1 in.	1 in.
To set in ground...	3 ft.	4 ft.	3 ft.	4 ft.
Price, each.........	$3.30	$3.60	$4.50	$4.80

Ventilating Grates.

No. 24R8125 Cast Iron Ventilating Grates.

Diameter	Price, each
Size, 7 inches..........	16c
Size, 10 inches..........	24c
Size, 12 inches..........	35c

Plumbers' Tools.

Solder Pots.

No. 24R8127 Solder Pots. Extra heavy.
Size 5. Price, each..........$0.38
Size 6. Price, each.......... .55
Size 8. Price, each.......... .85
Size 9. Price, each.......... 1.00

Gasoline Fire Pots.

No. 24R8130 Acme, fixed pump, two detachable shields for holding melting pot, complete with cast iron melting pot. Price, each..........$3.00

Plumbers' or Melting Ladles.

No. 24R8140 Steel bowl with wrought iron handle.
Size across bowl, 3 inches. Price, each..........12c
Size across bowl, 4 inches. Price, each..........15c
Size across bowl, 5 inches. Price, each..........20c

Pipe Bender.

A coil spring used in bending pipe. No kink in your pipes when you use this bender.
No. 24R8146 Size, 1¼ inches. Price, each.....60c
No. 24R8147 Size, 1½ inches. Price, each.....65c

Boxwood Dresser.

No. 24R8200 Plumbers' Boxwood Dressers. Price, each..........55c

Oval Shave Hook.

No. 24R8201 Plumbers' Oval Shave Hooks. Steel blade. Price, each..........16c

Turning Pins.

No. 24R8202 Plumbers' Turning Pin.
No. 1. Price....14c No. 3. Price....16c
No. 2. Price....15c

Rasps.

No. 24R8203 Plumbers' Rasps. First quality.
Size, 10-inch. Price, each..........30c
Size, 12-inch. Price, each..........33c
Size, 14-inch. Price, each..........45c

Bending Pins.

No. 24R8204 Plumbers' Bending Pins. Price, each..12c

Spring Yarning Irons.

No. 24R8205 Plumbers' Yarning Irons. Price, each..........28c

Calking Chisels.

No 24R8206 Plumbers' Right or Left Hand Calking Chisels. Price, each..........18c
No. 24R8207 Plumbers' Calking Chisel. Made of high grade steel. Price, each..........17c

Tap Borers.

No. 24R8208 Plumbers' Tap Borers. Made of high grade English steel. Price, each..........17c

Wing Dividers.

No. 24R8210 Wing Calipers or Dividers, with adjustable spring and screw. Polished cast steel; 6 inches long. Weight, 6 ounces. Price, each..........16c

Improved Firm Joint Calipers.

No. 24R8212 New Improved Outside Firm Joint Calipers. Made of high grade steel; finely finished.
Size, 4 inches. Price, each..........7c
Size, 8 inches. Price, each..........12c

Tape Measures.

Brass bound case, folding handle, with ½-inch oiled cotton tape,
No. 24R8214 To measure 25 feet. Price, each 18c
No. 24R8215 To measure 50 feet. Price, each 24c
No. 24R8216 To measure 66 feet. Price, each 29c
No. 24R8217 To measure 100 feet. Price, each 43c

Compass Saws.

No. 24R8220 Disston & Sons' Compass Saws, with apple handle.

Length, inches...	10	12	14	16
Price, each.......	27c	28c	30c	40c

No. 24R8222 Standard Compass Saw, beech handle

Length, inches..........	10	12	14
Price, each..........	11c	12c	13c

Tanged Firmer Gouges.

No. 24R8226 Tanged Firmer Gouges, warranted, solid cast steel, polished. Outside bevel, with handles included.

Size.	¼	⅜	½	⅝	¾	⅞	1	1¼	1½	1¾	2
Each.	17c	18c	19c	20c	21c	23c	28c	35c	43c	55c	65c

Two-foot Rules.

No. 24R8228 Two-foot Rule. Round joint, middle plates, spaced 8ths and 16ths, four-fold, 1 inch wide, weight, 3 ounces. Price, each..........7c
No. 24R8230 Two-foot Rule. Square joints, full brass bound, spaced 8ths, 10ths, 12ths and 16ths, and drafting scale, four-fold, 1 inch wide. Each 25c

Grease Boxes.

No. 24R8232 Handy Grease, Rosin and Flour Boxes combined. Price, each..........75c

Wiping Cloths.

No. 24R8234 Plumbers' Wiping Cloths. Neat and compact, made of the very best ticking. Price, each..........5c

Alcohol Lamps.

Gas Fitters' Alcohol Lamps, Made in both tin and brass, finely finished.
No. 24R8236 Tin. Price, each..36c
No. 24R8237 Brass. Price, each..75c

Plumbers' Toolbag

No. 24R8238 Plumbers' Toolbags. Made of the very best Brussels carpet.
Plain. Price, each..........$2.25
Leather sides and bottom. Price, each..........$3.00

Plumbers' Prepared Soil.

No. 24R8240 Plumbers' Prepared Soil. Best Grade.
Size, 1-pint cans. Price, each 27c
Size, 1-quart cans. Price, each.....46c

Cement for Steamfitters.

No. 24R8242 Steamfitters' Cement. It is impossible to do good work and make airtight joints without a cement of some kind. We have here a cement that has been used by one of the largest firms in the United States for over twenty years, with the most satisfactory results. Put up in 1-pound cans. Price, per can. 18c

Spun Oakum.

No. 24R8248 Best Grade Spun Oakum, for calking iron pipe, soil pipe and fittings. Price, per pound..........4c

Acme Pipe and Sink Cleaner.

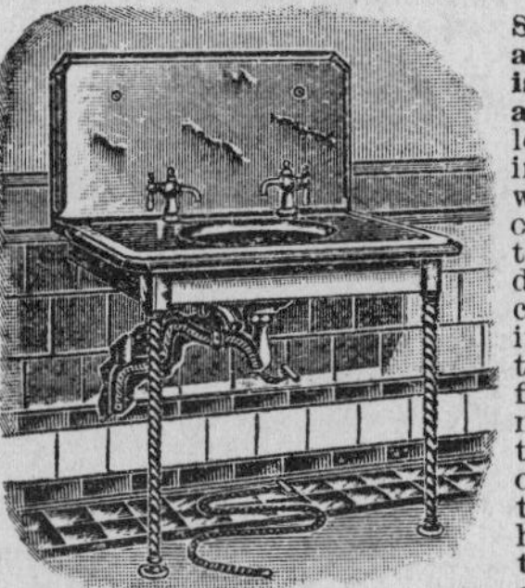

Acme Pipe and Sink Cleaner fits all drain pipes. It is made of steel and brass; is 6 feet long and ⅝ of an inch in diameter, with a handle at one end, a drill at the other. It can be disconnected in the center by unscrewing it. You can use the first section first, then if it does not reach, take off the handle, screw on the other section, then the handle and turn to the right. If the obstruction is in the closet, take off the first section, put on a corkscrew shaped hook that we send you, which will catch into any paper or rag that may be found in the closet and remove them. The above illustration shows the cleaner in operation.
No. 24R8255 Price, each..........70c

Handy Force Pump.

No. 24R8257 The Handy Force Pump is used for forcing stoppages and cleaning waste pipes, basins, closets and sinks, wash bowls, bath tubs, etc. No plumber, janitor, hotel, restaurant or residence should be without one. One stoppage of your pipes will pay for it. Thousands of them sold with the best results. It is made with a heavy rubber cup on the end of a 3-foot wood handle having a valve and air passage. Price, each............95c

Roofing Tin.

No. 24R8260 No. 1C Roofing Tin, high grade, lead finish, not porches, etc., smooth, even finish; cut to exact sizes, retinned, used mostly for flashings, covering roofs.

Size, inches	14x20	20x28
Number of sheets in box	112	112
Weight, per box, pounds	110	220
Price, per sheet	$0.06	$0.11
Price, per box	6.00	11.75

No. 24R8262 No. 1X Roofing Tin, same quality as our 1C, but much heavier; has more coating than any roofing tin on the market.

Size, inches	14x20	20x28
Number of sheets in box	112	112
Weight, per box, pounds	136	272
Price, per sheet	$0.07	$0.12
Price, per box	7.25	14.00

Lead Pipe.

No. 24R8264 Lead Pipe. Price subject to change without notice.

		Per foot
Lead pipe, ½ in. in diam., 1 lb. to foot		7c
Lead pipe, ¾ in. in diam., 2 lbs. to foot		14c
Lead pipe, 1 in. in diam., 2½ lbs. to foot		18c
Lead pipe, 1¼ in. in diam., 3 lbs. to foot		21c
Lead pipe, 1½ in. in diam., 4 lbs. to foot		28c
Lead pipe, 2 in. in diam., 5 lbs. to foot		35c

Extra Strong Lead Pipe.

No. 24R8266

Lead pipe, ⅛-in. diam., 1¾ lbs. to ft.	Per foot	13c
Lead pipe, ⅝-in. diam., 2½ lbs. to ft.	Per foot	18c
Lead pipe, ¾-in. diam., 3 lbs. to ft.	Per foot	21c
Lead pipe, 1-in. diam., 4 lbs. to ft.	Per foot	28c

Sheet Lead, Zinc and Copper.

No. 24R8268 Sheet Lead. In ordering give thickness wanted. Price, per pound............7½c

No. 24R8270 Best Grade Sheet Zinc. Cannot sell less than half sheet. 26-gauge, No. 9, 36 inches wide by 84 inches long. Weight, about 14 pounds.
Price, per sheet............$1.20
Price, per half sheet............ .65

No. 24R8272 Soft Sheet Copper. Not polished or tinned.

	Size of Sheet	Weight of Sheet	Price, per Sheet
14 oz.	14x48 in.	4 lbs. 5 oz.	$1.20

If you wish sheets tinned one side add 15c per sheet. We do not sell less than half sheet. Prices on other sizes and kinds of Copper quoted upon application.

Black Sheet Iron.

No. 24R8274 Size of sheet, 30x96 inches.

No.	Weight per Sheet	Price, per Whole Sheet
24	17 lbs.	93c
26	14 lbs.	75c
27	13 lbs.	70c

We cannot sell less than one full sheet.

Galvanized Sheet Iron.

No. 24R8276 Size of sheet, 28x96 inches.

No.	Weight per Sheet	Price, per Sheet
24	24 lbs.	$1.35
26	18 lbs.	1.20
27	16½ lbs.	1.00

SHEET TIN.

High Grade Bright Charcoal and Roofing Tin, guaranteed to be full size and free from defects. Prices subject to change without notice, but always furnished at lowest market price.

Charcoal Plates.

No. 24R8280 1C Bright, used for making all kinds of tinware, etc.

Size, inches	14x20	20x28
Number of sheets in a box	112	112
Weight, per box, pounds	108	216
Price, per sheet	$0.07	$0.14
Price, per box	7.50	14.50

No. 24R8282 1X Bright, a much heavier grade than the 1C above.

Size, inches	14x20	20x28
Number of sheets in a box	112	112
Weight, per box, pounds	135	270
Price, per sheet	$0.08	$0.16
Price, per box	8.25	16.20

No. 24R8284 No. 2X. Bright Sheet Tin, still heavier grade of tin than the 1X grade.

Size, inches	14x20	20x28
Number of sheets in a box	112	112
Weight, per box, pounds	157	314
Price, per sheet	$0.09¼	$0.18
Price, per box	9.75	19.00

No. 24R8286 No. 3X. Bright Sheet Tin, an extra grade used for milk cans, vats, etc.

Size, inches	14x20	20x28
Number of sheets in a box	112	112
Weight, per box, pounds	178	356
Price, per sheet	$ 0.10	$0.20
Price, per box	10.75	21.00

ELECTRICAL SUPPLIES.

As space will not permit our listing a full line of Electrical Supplies, we only show such articles as are required for wiring and lighting a residence, store, or factory, but would state we are in a position to furnish anything you may need in this line, and will be pleased to quote prices, know ing we can save you 33⅓ per cent on these goods. **See pages 661 and 662 for Electric Fixtures.**

Baby Knife Switches, 15 Amperes.

No. 24R8350 Electric Baby Knife Switches. Single throw, 15 amperes, single pole. Well made, finely finished.
Price, each............25c

Baby Knife Switches, 25 Amperes.

No. 24R8353 Electric Baby Knife Switches. Single throw, 25 amperes, double pole. Well made, finely finished.
Price, each............35c

Knife Switches, 35 Amperes, Fused.

No. 24R8354 Double Pole Slate Baby Knife Switches, 35 amperes. Double pole, single throw for fuse. Well made, finely finished.
Price, each............95c

Knife Switches, 35 Amperes, Three Pole.

No. 24R8355 Three-Pole Knife Switches, 35 amperes. Slate base, single throw, triple pole. Well made, finely finished.
Price, each............$1.10

Annunciator Wire.

No. 24R8356 High Grade Annunciator Wire. Double wound, No. 18.
Price, per pound............35c

Weatherproof Wire.

No. 24R8357 Triple Braid Weatherproof Wire.
No. 8, Price, per pound 25c
No. 10, Price, per pound 26c
No. 14, Price, per pound 30c

Lamp Cord.

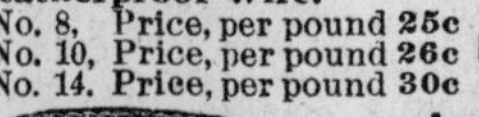

No. 24R8358 No. 18 Lamp Cord. Price, per yard............5c

Galvanized Steel Wire Strand.

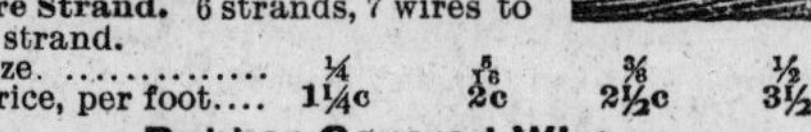

No. 24R8359 Galvanized Steel Wire Strand. 6 strands, 7 wires to the strand.

Size	¼	⅜	⅜	½
Price, per foot	1¼c	2c	2½c	3½c

Rubber Covered Wire.

No. 24R8360 Solid Conductor Rubber Covered Wire. 500 volts, braided outside. A high grade wire. Guaranteed.
Size No. 14, black core. Price, per foot............10½c
Size No. 12, black core. Price, per foot............15½c
Size No. 10, black core. Price, per foot............21 c

Circular Loom.

No. 24R8362 Circular Loom, a flexible conduit for interior wiring.
Size, ¼-inch inside diameter.
Price, per foot............5¼c
Size, ½-inch inside diameter.
Price, per foot............7c
Size, ¾-inch inside diameter. Price, per foot..10½c

Tape.

No. 24R8364 Grade A Tape, will not vulcanize with heat nor crack or harden and become defective by exposure and use. A first class tape in every respect. Sizes, ⅓, ¾, 1, 1½ inches wide.
Price, per pound............40c

Paiste Single Pole Switches.

No. 24R8366 Paiste Single Pole Switches. Metal top, 5 amperes, first quality. Price, each............21c

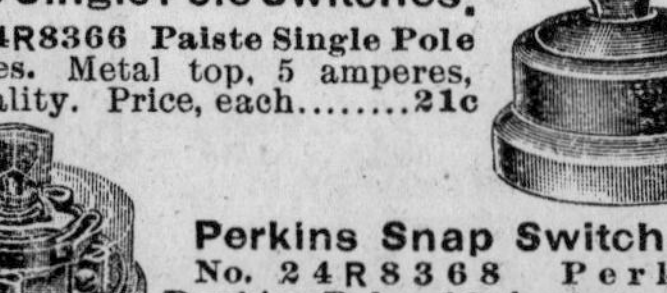

Perkins Snap Switches.

No. 24R8368 Perkins Double Pole 10-Ampere Snap Switches. Nickel plated cover.
Price, each............58c

GIVE CATALOGUE NUMBER IN FULL WHEN YOU WRITE YOUR ORDER

Edison Key Sockets.

No. 24R8370 Edison Key Sockets, fiber lined, polished.
Price, each............22c
Similar sockets in T. H. & Westinghouse base at same price.

Edison Keyless Sockets.

No. 24R8372 Edison Keyless Sockets, ⅛-inch pipe, plain.
Price, each............20c
Similar sockets in T. H. & Westinghouse base at same price.

Hard Rubber Weather Proof Sockets.

No. 24R8374 Edison Hard Rubber Weather Proof Sockets, for outside use.
Price, each............40c

Edison Key Wall Sockets.

No. 24R8376 Edison Key Wall Sockets, fiber lined.
Price, each............28c

Attachment Plugs.

No. 24R8378 Attaching Plugs for standard lamp sockets. Porcelain.
Price each............15c

Cord Adjusters.

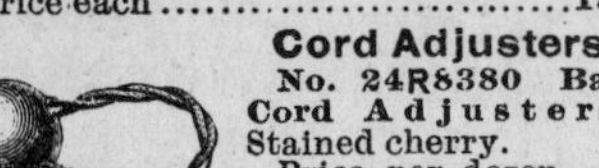

No. 24R8380 Ball Cord Adjusters. Stained cherry.
Price, per dozen............10c

Perfection Desk or Music Rack Clamp.

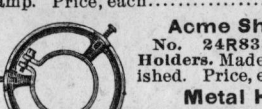

No. 24R8382 Perfection Desk or Music Rack Clamps. Made of brass, finely finished. Complete with socket, clamp, half metal shade and lamp. Price, each............$1.00

Acme Shade Holder.

No. 24R8384 Acme Shade Holders. Made of brass, finely finished. Price, each............6c

Metal Half Shades.

No. 24R8386 Metal Half Shades. Japanned. Green outside, white enameled inside.
Price, each............23c

Cutler-Hammer Starting Boxes.

No. 24R8388 Motor Starting Boxes with magnetic release. Absolutely fireproof. Impossible to leave the resistance in circuit and burn out the box. Simple, durable and reliable. Endorsed by the Board of Fire Underwriters. When ordering give horse power, voltage and make of motor.
For ¼-horse power 125 volt motor. Price............$4.00
For ½-horse power 125 volt motor. Price............5.30

Porcelain Shades.

No. 24R8390 High Grade Green and White Porcelain Shades. Cone shape.
Size, 7-inch. Price, each 30c
Size, 10-inch. Price, each 50c

Tin Shades.

No. 24R8392 Tin Shade, same as above, green outside and enameled inside.
Size, 7 inches. Price, each............10c
Size, 10 inches. Price, each............14c

Self-Tying Ceiling Button.

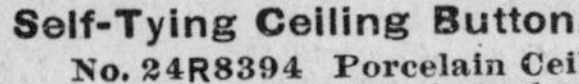

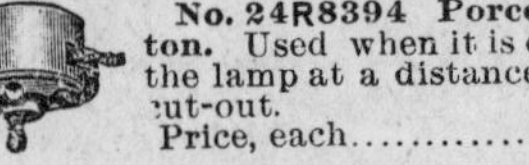

No. 24R8394 Porcelain Ceiling Button. Used when it is desired to suspend the lamp at a distance from the rosette cut-out.
Price, each............3½c

Edison Link Fuse Cut-Outs on Porcelain Bases.

No. 24R8396 Three-Wire Main Line Cut-Out. Capacity, 30 amperes.
Price, each............65c

Edison Plug Cut-Outs on Porcelain Base.

No. 24R8398 Three-Wire Double Three-Wire Branch, Six-Plug Edison Cut-Out.
Price, each............78c

Edison Fuse Plugs.

No. 24R8400 For use with plug cut-outs on porcelain bases. 3, 6, 10, 12, 15, 20, 25, 30 amperes capacity. In ordering, please state capacity wanted.
Price, each, any size............5½c

Porcelain Main Cut-Outs.

No. 24R8402 These Cut-Outs are provided with hole in side as shown. This gives perfect ventilation in case of fuse blowing. A special feature of our cut-outs is, they can be used for concealed work as well as cleat.
Price, each, 15 amperes..............15c
Price, each, 25 amperes..............25c
Price, each, 50 amperes..............55c

Fuse Links.

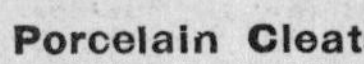

No. 24R8404 Three-Ampere Fuse Links, for Edison main or branch blocks; 35, 40, 45, 50, 60, 75, 90, and 100-ampere slots, 1½-inch centers.
Price, each..............2¼c

Porcelain Cleats.

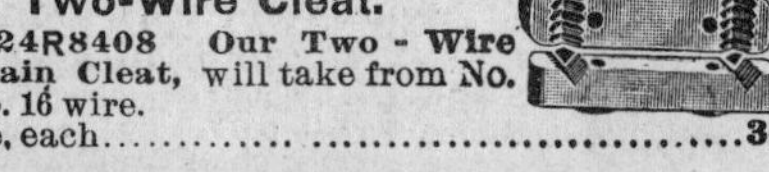

No. 24R8406 Our One-Wire Porcelain Cleat, will take from No. 8 to No. 16 wire.
Price, each..............2½c

Two-Wire Cleat.

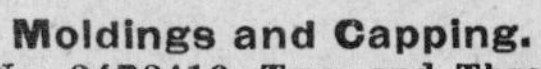

No. 24R8408 Our Two-Wire Porcelain Cleat, will take from No. 8 to No. 16 wire.
Price, each..............3c

Moldings and Capping.

No. 24R8410 Two and Three-Wire Molding and Capping for No. 8, 10 and 14 wire. For two wires, price, per 100 feet, unfinished, 60c; finished......80c
For three wires, price, per 100 feet, unfinished, 90c; finished..............$1.30

Clay and Porcelain Tubes.

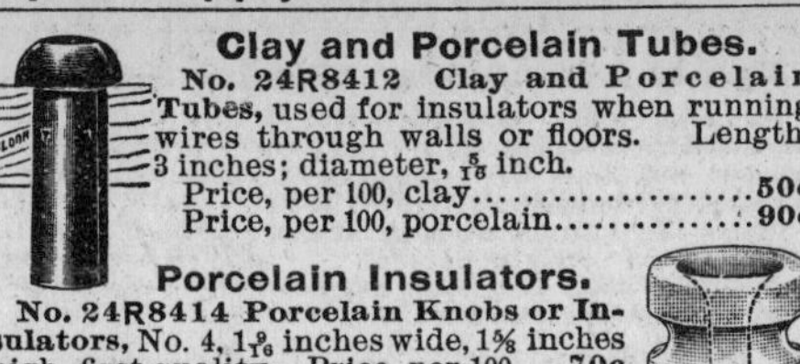

No. 24R8412 Clay and Porcelain Tubes, used for insulators when running wires through walls or floors. Length, 3 inches; diameter, $\frac{5}{16}$ inch.
Price, per 100, clay..............50c
Price, per 100, porcelain..............90c

Porcelain Insulators.

No. 24R8414 Porcelain Knobs or Insulators, No. 4, $1\frac{5}{16}$ inches wide, 1⅜ inches high, first quality. Price, per 100....70c

No. 24R8416 Porcelain Insulators, No. $5\frac{1}{16}$ inches wide, 1¾ inches high; first quality. Price, per 100..............55c

Glass Insulators.

No. 24R8417 Glass Insulators, first quality. Deep groove. Price, per 100..............50c

Oak Brackets.

No. 24R8419 Western Union Standard Oak Brackets. No. 1 timber, hand painted two coats. Price, per 100..$1.60

Oak Pins.

No. 24R8421 Western Union Standard. Second growth split timber, painted two coats.
Price, per 100..............$1.15

Lamp Guards.

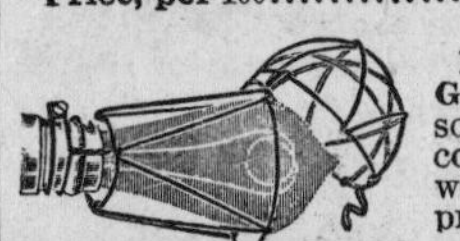

No. 24R8426 Wire Lamp Guards. Easily clamped to socket, keeps the lamp from coming in contact with woodwork or merchandise, prevents breakage, etc.
Price, each..............5c

Vestibule Gas Fixtures.

No. 24R8565

No. 24R8565 Vestibule or Hall Gas Fixtures. Made of drawn brass tubing, gilt finished. Comes complete as shown in cut with glass, etc. Length over all, 36 inches.
Price, each..............$2.65

Newel Gas Fixtures.

No. 24R8568

No. 24R8568 Newel Gas Fixtures made from drawn brass. Top plain, bottom rope finish, furnished complete as shown in cut. Price includes globe. Height, 20 inches.
Price, each..............$2.00

Niagara Portable Gas Lamp.

No. 24R8576 The Niagara Portable Gas Lamp is intended to be attached to a gas jet to be used on a table or stand as a drop light. Finely finished; new improved burner; gives a better light and burns less gas than the old style. Furnished complete, as shown in cut.
Price, each..............$2.65

GAS FIXTURES AND SUPPLIES.

Space will not permit our showing our complete line of these goods, but would state, however, that we can furnish anything you may want in the way of gas and electric fixtures, and know we can save you 50 per cent on same. The goods are manufactured by a reliable firm, made of the best material by skilled workmen and every article carefully inspected before leaving the factory. Compare our prices with those of other firms and see if what we say in regard to saving you 50 per cent is not correct.

Gilt Finish Gas Fixtures.

Three-Light Gas Fixtures, gilt finish, rope pattern. A very neat fixture; well made; finely finished; complete, ready for use. Length, 36 in. Spread, 27 in.

No. 24R8500

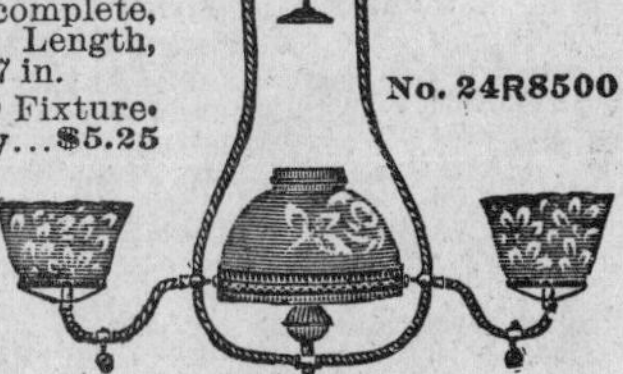

No. 24R8500 Fixture. Price, each, only...$5.25
No. 24R8501 Fixture with 10-inch decorated dome. Price, each, $6.25

Two to Four-Light Gas Fixtures.

Made of the best drawn brass tubes. Finely finished. Length, 36 inches; spread, 18 inches. Furnished complete as shown in cut.
No. 24R8505 Two-light, complete with two globes..........$3.00
No. 24R8506 Three-light, complete with three globes..........$4.00
No. 24R8507 Four-light, complete with four globes..........$5.00

No. 24R8506

Plain Gilt Gas Fixtures.

No. 24R8510

Gilt Finish Gas Fixtures. Made of the best material throughout, finely finished. Comes complete, ready to put up. Length, 36 inches; spread, 18 inches. Prices include globes, as shown in cut. Cut shows three-light fixture.
No. 24R8509 Two-light, complete with 2 globe. $1.95
No. 24R8510 Three-light, complete with 3 globes $2.55
No. 24R8511 Four-light, complete with 4 globes $3.25

Fancy Brass Gas Fixtures.

No. 24R8517

Fancy Gilt Finish Gas Fixtures. Made of best material, finely finished. Furnished complete, ready for use.

No.		Price, complete
24R8516	Two-light	$3.50
24R8517	Three-light	4.50
24R8518	Four-light	5.75

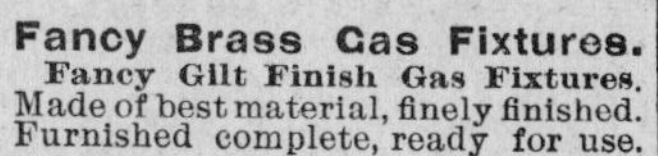

Fancy Candle Gas Fixtures.

No. 24R8525

Made of the best material, gilt finish. Furnished with imitation opal candles. This is an extra fine fixture, nice enough for any residence. They are finely finished. Nothing better made at the price. Length, 36 inches; spread, 14 inches.

No.		Price, complete.
24R8525	Two-light	$5.90
24R8526	Three-light	7.35
24R8527	Four-light	8.75

Gilt Finish Gas Fixtures.

No. 24R8532

Gilt Finish Gas Fixtures, complete as shown in cut.

No.	Length	Price, each
24R8532	30 inches	40c
24R8534	36 inches	48c

Fancy Single Burner Gas Fixture.

No. 24R8538

No. 24R8538 Fancy Single Burner Gas Fixture, plain gilt finish, furnished complete with globe as shown in cut. Length, 36 inches. Price, each. $1.25

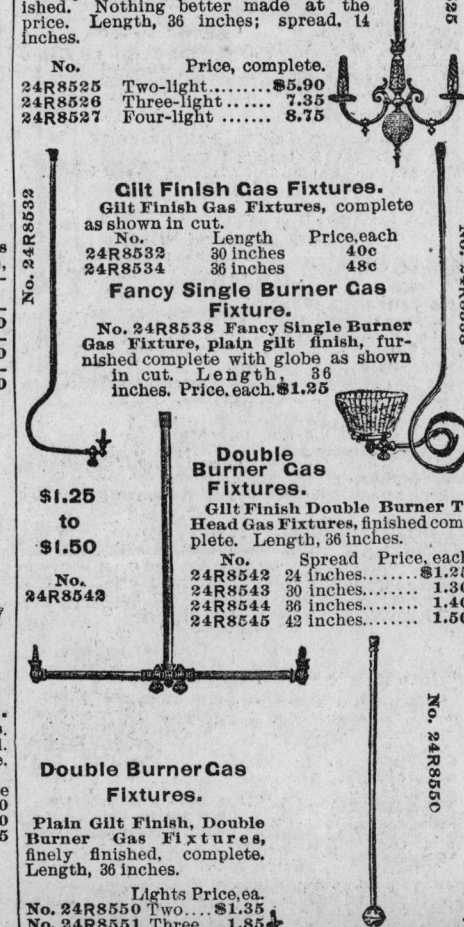

Double Burner Gas Fixtures.

$1.25 to $1.50

No. 24R8542

Gilt Finish Double Burner T-Head Gas Fixtures, finished complete. Length, 36 inches.

No.	Spread	Price, each
24R8542	24 inches	$1.25
24R8543	30 inches	1.30
24R8544	36 inches	1.40
24R8545	42 inches	1.50

Double Burner Gas Fixtures.

No. 24R8550

Plain Gilt Finish, Double Burner Gas Fixtures, finely finished, complete. Length, 36 inches.

	Lights	Price, ea.
No. 24R8550	Two	$1.35
No. 24R8551	Three	1.85
No. 24R8552	Four	2.40

Electric Fixtures.

NOTICE—In ordering electric fixtures be sure of kind of electric socket wanted. Your electric light man will give you the kind.

Fancy Electric Bracket.

No. 24R8580 One Light Bell Bracket, all brass, wired complete with socket, shade and holder. A very neat, low priced fixture.
Price, each..............$1.35

Electric Swing Bracket.

Swing, all brass bracket, wired complete with shade, socket and holder.
No. 24R8582 Price, each, one swing..............$1.75
No. 24R8584 Price, each, two swing..............2.25

Electric Swing Bracket.

No. 24R8586 Fancy All Brass One-Light Bracket, wired complete, shade, socket and holder.
Price, each..............$2.30

Electric Chandeliers.

All Brass Electric Chandeliers, rich gilt finish, wired complete, with shade holders and sockets. Length over all, 36 inches. If wanted longer than 36 inches, add 25 cents per foot.
No. 24R8590 Price, each, two lights..............$3.60
No. 24R8591 Price, each, three lights..............5.30
No. 24R8592 Price, each, four lights..............7.00

All Brass Electric Chandeliers, rich gilt finish, wired complete, with shade, holder and sockets. Length, 36 inches over all. If wanted longer than 36 inches, add 25 cents per foot.
No. 24R8595 Price, each, two lights.....$4.30
No. 24R8596 Price, each, three lights.... 6.00
No. 24R8597 Price, each, four lights. 7.65

Electric Chandeliers.

All Brass Electric Chandeliers. Rich gilt finish; wired complete; with shade holder and socket. Length, over all, 36 inches. **If wanted longer than 36 inches, add 25 cents per foot, extra.**
No. 24R8600 Price, two lights..............$5.25
No. 24R8601 Price, three lights..............$7.35
No. 24R8602 Price, four lights..............$9.35

Electric Pendant.

No. 24R8604 Two-Light All Brass Electric Pendant. Rich gilt finish; wired complete, with sockets, shade and holder.
Price, each..............$ 3.85

Fancy Electroliers.

Fancy All Brass Electroliers. Rich gilt finish, complete with shade, socket and holders. Length over all, 36 inches. **If wanted longer than 36 inches, add 25 cents per foot extra.**

		Each
No. 24R8610	2 lights.	$7.00
No. 24R8611	3 lights.	9.00
No. 24R8612	4 lights.	11.00

NOTICE—In ordering electric fixtures be sure to give kind of sockets wanted. Ask your electric light man for this information.

Electric Hall Lantern.

No. 24R8616 All Brass Lantern. Rich gilt finish, wired, complete, with shade, holder and socket. Length over all, 36 inches. **If wanted over 36 inches long, add 25 cents per foot extra.**
Price, each $3.65

Electric Pendant.

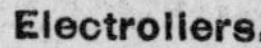

24R8618

No. 24R8618 One Light All Brass Electric Fixture, rich gilt finish, wired complete with shade, socket and holder. Length, 36 inches over all. If wanted over 36 inches, add 25 cents per foot extra. Price, each..........$1.45

Fancy Electric Pendant.

No. 24R8620 Fancy All Brass Electric Pendant, rich gilt finish, complete with shade, socket and holder. Length, over all, 36 inches. **If wanted longer than 36 inches, add 25 cents per foot extra.** Price, each..........$2.30

24R8620

Electroliers.

No. 24R8622 All Brass Electroliers, rich gilt finish, wired complete with shade, holder and socket. Length, over all, 36 inches. **If wanted over 36 inches long, add 25 cents per foot extra.**

Price, two lights..........$5.50
Price, three lights.... 7.50
Price, four lights..... 9.75

No. 24R8622

Electric Table Lamp.

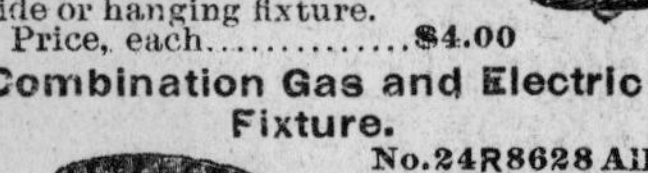

No. 24R8626 All Brass Table Lamp, rich gilt finish, wired complete with shade holder and socket, with 8 feet of wire and plug ready to attach to any side or hanging fixture.
Price, each..........$4.00

Combination Gas and Electric Fixture.

No. 24R8628 All Brass Gas and Electric Bracket. Rich gilt finish, wired complete with shade, holder and socket. Extends 8 inches from wall. Price, each..... $2.30

Combination Gas and Electric Chandelier.

No. 24R8630 All Brass Combination Gas and Electric Pendant. Rich gilt finish, wired complete with shade, holder and sockets. Length over all, 36 inches.
Price, each...... ....$3.00
If wanted over 36 inches long, add 25 cents per foot.

Combination Gas and Electric Chandeliers.

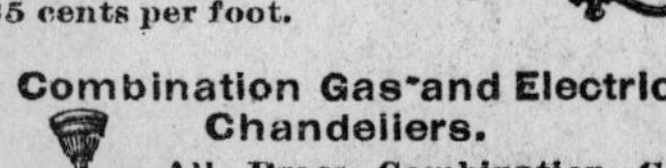

All Brass Combination Gas and Electric Chandeliers. Rich gilt finish, wired, complete with shade, holder and sockets. Length over all, 36 inches. If wanted over 36 inches long, add 25 cents per foot extra.
No. 24R8633 Price, two gas and two electric burners, complete $5.60
No. 24R8634 Price, three gas and three electric burners, complete..........$8.00
No. 24R8635 Price, four gas and four electric burners, complete..........$10.35

Combination Gas and Electric Fixtures.

All Brass Gas and Electric Newel Fixture. Rich gilt finish, wired complete with sockets, shades and holders. Height, 30 inches. If wanted over 30 inches high, add 25 cents per foot.
No. 24R8639 Price, one gas and two electric burners, as per cut..........$8.00
No. 24R8640 Price, one electric light only......... 4.65
No. 24R8641 Price, two electric lights only........ 6.75
No. 24R8642 Price, three electric lights only.. 8.00

Chandelier Hooks.

No. 24R8688 Malleable Iron Chandelier Hooks.
Size, ⅜-inch. Price, each..........7c
Size, ½-inch. Price, each..........8c

Gas Drop Elbows.

No. 24R8690 Malleable Iron Gas Drop Elbows; well finished.
Size, ⅛x¼ inch. Price, each....6c
Size, ⅜x¼ inch. Price, each....7c
Size, ⅜x⅜ inch. Price, each....7c
Size, ½x½ inch. Price, each....8c
Size, ¾x½ inch. Price, each...15c
Size, ¾x¾ inch. Price, each...15c

Drop Tees.

No. 24R8692 Malleable Iron Drop Tees; furnished complete.
Size, ⅜x⅜x¼ inch. Price, each 6c
Size, ⅜x⅜x⅜ inch. Price, each 6c
Size, ½x⅜x⅜ inch. Price, each 6c
Size, ½x½x⅜ inch. Price, each 8c
Size, ½x½x½ inch. Price, each 8c
Size, ¾x½x⅜ inch. Price, each...15c
Size, ¾x⅜x⅜ inch. Price, each...15c
Size, ¾x¾x⅜ inch. Price, each...15c

Wall Plates.

No. 24R8694 Malleable Iron Wall Plates.
Size, ⅜ inch. Price, each..........8c

Drop Light Sockets.

No. 24R8700 Brass Drop Light Sockets, finished complete.
Price, each..........8c

Stork Neck.

No. 24R8702

No. 24R8702 Stork Neck for Drop Light, gilt finish, complete. Price, each........ .10c

Cigar Lighters.

No. 24R8704 Brass, Gilt Finish Cigar Lighters, finely finished, complete with stand for counter.
Price, complete as shown in cut, each..........$3.15
Price, lighter only...... 1.15
Price, 2-foot hose only, per foot..........7c

Gas Lighters.

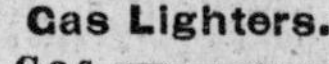

No. 24R8706 Gas Lighter. Hardwood handle, silver finish metal parts.
Price, each..........20c
No. 24R8708 Wax Tapers for above, 30 tapers in a box. Price, per box..........11c

Gas Stove Tubing.

No. 24R8715 Caldwell's Flexible Patent End Gas Stove Tubing. Inner tubing made of pure rubber, outside covering is made of braided mohair; will not crack or break. Comes in 4, 5, 6, 8 and 10-foot pieces.
Price, per foot..........4c
No. 24R8717 Portable or Drop Light Tubing. Pure India rubber inner tube with braided mohair covering. Comes complete with metal ends to connect to gas jet and lamp. Furnished in 6, 8 and 10-foot pieces only. Price, per foot..........4½c

Gas Brackets.

C Bend Gas Brackets, gilt finished.
No. 24R8720 Stiff. Price, each......30c
No. 24R8722 Swing. Price, each......40c

Gilt Finish Gas Brackets, finished complete.
No. 24R8724 1-swing. Price, each........45c
No. 24R8726 2-swing. Price, each..........50c
No. 24R8728 3-swing. Price, each..........70c

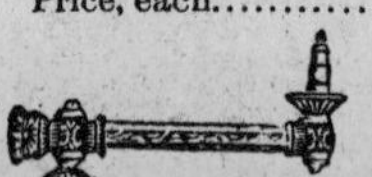

No. 24R8732 Gilt Finish Stiff Gas Brackets. Finished complete. Length, 6 inches.
Price, each..........25c

Gas Brackets.

Polished Brass Gas Brackets, finished complete.
No. 24R8733 Stiff tube. Price, each....40c
No. 24R8734 Swing tube. Price, each....60c

Polished Brass Gas Brackets. Square tube, finished complete.
No. 24R8736 Stiff tube. Price each..........35c
No. 24R8738 Swing tube. Price, each..........50c

No. 24R8742 Two-Light Pendant Cocks. Made of the best material, nicely finished.
Size, ⅜x¼ in. Price, ea..24c
Size, ⅜x⅛ in. Price, ea..25c
Size, ¼x⅛ in. Price, ea..26c

Straight Cocks.

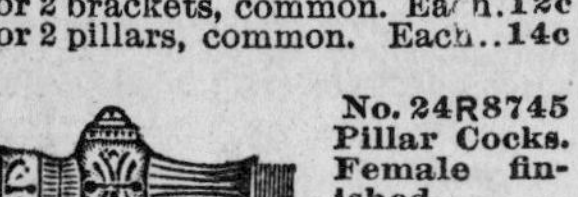

No. 24R8743 Straight Cocks, for gas fixtures, finished.
Size, ⅜x⅜-inch. Price, each....14c
Size, ⅜x¼-inch. Price, each. ..13c
Size, ⅜x⅛-inch. Price, each....12c
Size, ¼x¼-inch. Price, each....12c

No. 24R8744 Double Bodies Gas Fixtures.
For 2 brackets, common. Each.12c
For 2 pillars, common. Each..14c

No. 24R8745 Pillar Cocks. Female finished.
Size, ⅛-inch iron to burner. Price, each..........11c
Size, ¼-inch iron to burner. Price, each..........12c
Size, ⅜-inch iron to burner. Price, each..........13c
Size, ½-inch iron to burner. Price, each..........15c

Long L Burner Cocks.

No. 24R8747 Long L Burner Cocks for gas fixtures, finished. Length, 4½ inches.
Size, ¼-inch iron to burner. Price, each..........13c
Size, ⅜-inch iron to burner. Price, each......15c

Hose Pendant Cocks.

No. 24R8749 Hose Pendant Cocks for gas fixtures. Female finished.
Size, ⅛-inch iron to hose end. Price, each..........12c
Size, ¼-inch iron to hose end. Price, each..........13c
Size, ⅜-inch iron to hose end. Price, each..........14c
Size, ½-inch iron to hose end. Price, each..........16c

Stiff Joints.

No. 24R8752 Stiff Joints for gas fixtures; finished.
Size, ⅜x⅛-inch. Price, each..........5c
Size, ⅜x¼-inch. Price, each..........6c
Size, ⅜x⅜-inch. Price, each..........7c

Connecting Balls.

No. 24R8753 Connecting Balls for gas fixtures; finished.
Size, ⅜x⅜ inch. Price, each..........5c
Size, ½x½ inch. Price, each..........6c

Lengthening Piece.

No. 24R8754 Lengthening Piece for gas fixtures; finished.
Size, ⅜ to 1⅜ inch. Price, each..........7c

Straight Nozzles.

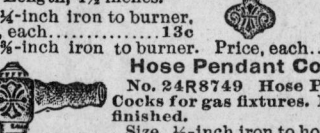

No. 24R8755 Straight Nozzles for gas fixtures; finished.
Size, ⅛-inch iron to burner. Price, each..3c
Size, ¼-inch iron to burner. Price, each..5c
Size, ⅜-inch iron to burner. Price, each..7c

Side Nozzles.

No. 24R8756 Side Nozzles for gas fixtures; finished.
Size, ⅛-inch iron to burner. Price, ea., 3c
Size, ¼-inch iron to burner. Price, ea., 5c
Size, ⅜-inch iron to burner. Price, ea., 7c

L Pendant Cocks.

No. 24R8757 L Pendant Cocks for gas fixtures; finished.
Size, ¼x⅛-inch. Price, each..14c
Size, ¼x¼-inch. Price, each..15c
Size, ⅜x⅛-inch. Price, each..16c
Size, ⅜x¼-inch. Price, each..17c

L Burner Cocks.

No. 24R8759 L Burner Cocks for gas fixtures; finished.
Size, ⅛-inch iron to burner. Price, each..........12c
Size, ¼-inch iron to burner. Price, each..........14c
Size, ⅜-inch iron to burner. Price, each..........16c
Size, ½-inch iron to burner. Price, each..........18c

Lava Tips.

No. 24R8762 Lava Tips for gas burners; regular standard size.
Price, per gross.. $1.65; per doz..16c

Brass Pillars.

No. 24R8764 Brass Pillars for gas burners, made of sheet brass; finished.
Price, per gross, $1.00; per dozen.........9c

By Passes.

No. 24R8766 By Passes for gas burners; made of brass; finely finished.
Price, each..................20c

Gem Self-Lighting Burner.

No. 24R8768 Made of brass; finely finished; wi'' fit any ordinary burner cock.
Price, each..............................35c

Tripods.

No. 24R8770 Tripods for gas burners; made of best grade brass wire. Size, 10-inch.
Price, each..........................12c

No. 24R8772 Brass Globe Holders for gas fixtures.
Size, 4-inch. Price, each 6c
Size, 5-inch. Price, each.....7c

Star Acetylene Gas Burner.

No. 24R8774 Gives a perfect, clear light, non-carbonizing, all lava.
Made in 1/8, 1/4, 1/3, 3/4 and 1-foot sizes.
Price, each... ....27c

Hahn's Improved Acetylene Gas Burners.

This is what is called a Twin Burner, having two outlets, which are so constructed as to mix the air with the gas, making a much brighter and steadier light.
No. 24R8776 Price, each...18c

Complete Safety Gas Lights.

No. 24R8780 This light consists of brass burner, mantles, patent safety chimney, either plain or corrugated, opal shade and improved glass draft attachment. Will cut your gas bill one-half. Fits any gas fixture. Price, each..... ....50c

Acme No. 10 Incandescent Gas Light.

No. 24R8782 There is no other gas light in existence as popular as our Acme No. 10. They are used by the thousands all over the United States. As a light producer and saver it has no equal. It is impossible to force more gas through it than is burned. Fits any fixture. We use only the best grade mantle. We furnish these burners for artificial or natural gas. In ordering be sure and state which is wanted.
Price, each, complete.........................45c

Safety Gas Lights.

Triumph Safety Gas Lights, complete with chimney, mantle, etc. Fits any gas fixture.
No. 24R8784 Price, each... ....30c

Gas and Gasoline Mantles.

We handle only the best grades of mantles and warrant them to give a bright, clear light. They come securely packed one in a box with full directions on each box how to place and adjust on lamp.

No. 24R8790 No. 1. Standard Grade Mantles, 60-candle power.
Price, each.......................9c

No. 24R8792 No. 3. XXX Grade Mantles, 80-candle power.
Price, each.......................11c

No. 24R8794 No. 5. Extra Grade Mantles, 100-candle power.
Price, each.......................18c

No. 24R8795 No. 6. Heavy weave, especially for high pressure gasoline lamps; 5 inches long; nothing better made.
Price, each..................................20c

Double Weave Mantle with Wire and Cap.

No. 24R8796 Extra Quality Double Weave Mantle with wire and cap, ready to put on burner. No adjusting or fitting.
Price, each.................................16c

Triple Weave Mantle.

No. 24R8797 Our Triple Weave Double Wire Mantle attached to cap is by far the longest lived mantle we sell. Cannot break by handling. Wire will not kink or drop over sideways. Will last longer than any mantle on the market.
Price, each......................20c

No. 24R8798 Genuine Welsbach-Yusea, extra double strength, 100-candle power, platinum tied, with nickel support combined with burner cap and gauze. Price, each.... ....45c

Argand Gas Burner.

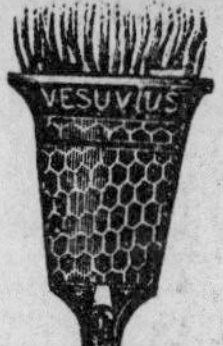

No. 24R8880 This is the most reliable gas burner on the market. No experiment; will last a lifetime. Nothing to break or burn out; fits any gas fixture. Complete with chimney. Price, each....39c

Mica Chimney.

No. 24R8882 Mica Chimney—cannot break, will last forever. Length, 7 inches. Fits our Nos. 24R8782 or 24R8880 burners. Price, each..................7c

New Idea Gas Lamp Chimney.

No. 24R8884 New Idea Gas Lamp Chimney, made extra heavy. Gives fine light, latest thing out, made of patent process flint glass.
Price, each......................................8c

Opal Smoke Shades.

Opal Smoke Shades to hang over gas fixtures. Complete, ready for use.
No. 24R8887 Size, 6-inch. Price, each.......................................14c
No. 24R8888 Size, 7-inch. Price, each.........15c
No. 24R8889 Size, 8-inch. Price, each........18c

Mica Smoke Shades.

Mica Smoke Bells, last forever; cannot crack.
No. 24R8892 Size, 3½ inches. Price each......5c
No. 24R8893 Size, 6 inches. Price, each 8c

Mica Canopies.

No. 24R8894 Mica Canopies mounted on twisted wires. Will not sag, always stays in position. Will fit any globe.
Price, each.......................5c

Incandescent Lamps.

No. 24R8896 These Lamps are produced by the foremost maker in the United States, and the highest skilled labor only is employed. Every lamp tested three hours before leaving the factory. The vacuum is the highest known in lamp manufacture, and the filaments will not sag in the bulb. Best lamps made for factory use, or where there is any vibration. Pure celluloid filaments; careful glass work; candle power maintained; no short lived lamps. We furnish these lamps with either Edison or T-H base; be sure and state which kind wanted. Price, each 30c
8, 10 or 16-candle power, 110-voltage.

Gas Globes.

No. 24R8899 Fine Fancy White Acid Cut Gas Globes. Every one perfect and free from flaws and defects. For 4-inch holder. Price, each...........18c

No. 24R8901 Ribbed Pattern Gas Globes. White acid figures, a very pretty design, for 4-inch holder.
Price, each........................23c

No. 24R8903 Flint Opalescent Gas Globes. A very nice design. Good enough for any gas fixture. For 4-inch holder. Price, each............. 37c

Pure Lead Glass Chimney.

No. 24R8905 Pure Lead Glass Chimneys, high grade. Size, 1⅛x7 inches, will fit our No. 24R8880 or 24R8882 burners. Price, each..................5c

Combination Cylinder Chimney.

No. 24R8907 Pure Lead Glass Combination Cylinder Chimney. Price includes asbestos washers.
Price, each..7c

Globes.

No. 24R8909 Pure Lead Glass Sand Blast Globes, or Plain Opal Globes.
Price, each, lead glass, sand blast,..8c
Price, each, opal.......................8½c

Opal Shades.

No. 24R8911 Best Quality Opal Shades, fluted pattern, 8 inches in diameter. Price, each............8c

Opal or Green Dome Shades.

No. 24R8913 Opal or Green Dome Shades, best quality, 10 inches in diameter. Price, each, opal...... ......15c
Price, each, green.. .... 75c

Acme Gas Stove.

No. 24R8914 Acme Gas Stove. Will boil a quart of water in three minutes. Simply slip over the gas jet and light. Made of malleable iron and tin with wire gauze. Will fit any ordinary gas burner. No screwing or fitting required. Price, each.......... .....10c

Acme Gas Plate.

No. 24R8915 Single Burner Gas Plate, black iron. Sizes, 6½x6½x3¼ inches.
Price, each.........25c

Sunshine Gas Stove.

No. 24R8916 Sunshine Gas Stove. A high grade stove. Material and workmanship the best. Will last a lifetime.

	Black finish	Nickel plated
One burner, each.........	$0.55	$0.65
Two burners, each.......	1.05	1.40

Liberty Gas Stove.

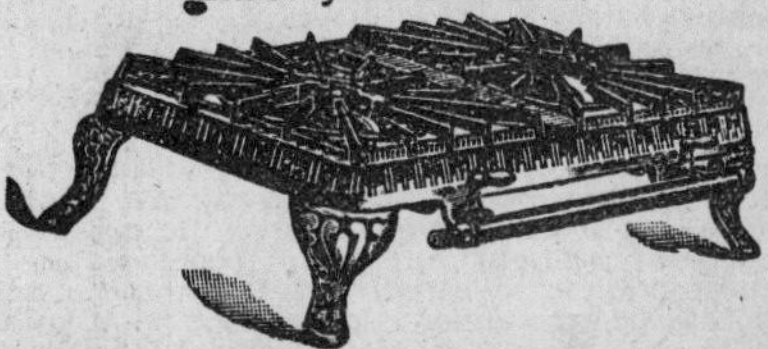

No. 24R8917 Liberty Gas Plates or Stoves. Made of best quality gray iron. One of the best stoves on the market. Furnished complete as shown in cut.

	Black finish	Nickel plated
One burner, each.........	$0.80	$0.95
Two burners, each.........	1.40	1.65
Three burners, each... .	2.15	2.40

The New Doyle Air-Burner Gas Stove.

No. 24R8918 The New Doyle Air-Burner Gas Stove is constructed on entirely different lines from any other stove on the market. This principle is adapted to all kinds of stoves, ranges, furnaces and boilers using coal, wood, oil or gas, and involves the admission of heated oxygen at a point where it is thoroughly mixed with the gases from the fuel, causing a secondary combustion to take place in the upper construction of the stoves, creating an intense heat, without smoke or soot, showing a saving in fuel of over 50 per cent. This stove, burning 10 to 12 feet of gas per hour, will heat a room 12x12 with 10-foot ceiling, in zero weather. It stands 30 inches high and weighs 40 pounds. Price, each..$7.20

The Acme Electric Fan.

The Acme Fan is of an entirely new design adapted to meet the requirements of the practical, careful and exacting buyer. One of the best features of the fan is its arrangement of bearings. It will be seen from the illustrations that the two journals are carried in a one-piece ring which maintains them in rigid relation and permits of no disarrangement of initial alignment, no matter how carelessly handled. A second unique feature is found in its adaptability for use either for desk or wall service. It is a desk fan and a wall bracket fan combined. A simple wrist movement combined with a lateral one, adjusts the blast to any required direction either as a desk or wall fixture. The blades and guard are highly polished and lacquered, and the brush holder and other parts are simple, strong and durable. The workmanship throughout is of a high order. No fan on the market can equal it. The standard finish is black enamel, but all enamels and several plated and polished finishes can be furnished if ordered in season. The fans are designed for 110-volt and 220-volt circuits and with three speeds, viz: 800, 1200 and 1600 revolutions per minute. Be sure and state which is wanted. Diameter of fan, 12 inches.

This illustration shows fan when placed on desk or table.

This illustration shows fan when placed against wall or post.

No. 24R8919 Price, each......................$10.25

Cotton Garden Hose.

The increased demand for light, durable, strong and absolutely reliable hose, suitable for gardens, lawns and other places for sprinkling has induced us to place on the market our New Process Rubber Lined Cotton Hose. The fabric is made from especially selected long fiber cotton and is perfect in construction. The rubber lining is of the very best quality, and by our process of manufacture we are enabled to produce a hose which cannot fail to give the very best results. **Put up in lengths of 50 feet with brass couplings. We do not sell less than full lengths of 50 feet. No extra charge for couplings.**

No. 24R8980 ¾-inch standard quality.
Price, per foot....................................9c

No. 24R8981 ¾-inch extra standard quality.
Price, per foot....................................10½c

Steam Hose.

No. 24R8982 Strictly Standard Made Steam Hose. This brand of hose needs no special introduction having been on the market for years and has given universal satisfaction. For ordinary steam pressure it may be depended on to answer every requirement.

Inside Diameter	Ply	Pressure, Pounds	Price, per ft.	Inside Diameter	Ply	Pressure, Pounds	Price per ft.
½ inch	3	40	18c	1½ inch	4	26.7	$0.50
¾ inch	4	53.3	28c	1½ inch	6	53.3	.80
1 inch	4	40	34c	2 inch	6	40	1.00
1¼ inch	4	32	45c				

Cotton Mill Hose.

No. 24R8984 Our Seamless Rubber Lined Cotton Mill Hose is adapted for hand engines, factories, warehouses, hotels, steamboats, public institutions, and wherever a light, durable and reliable hose for fire protection is required. It is full weight, made in the most careful manner, every section being mildew-proofed, and guaranteed to stand water pressure of 250 pounds. **Sold only in 25 or 50-foot pieces. We cannot sell less. Seamless, rubber lined.**

Diameter, inches...........	1½	2	2½	3
Price, per foot..............	22c	25c	35c	40c

Mill Hose Couplings.

No. 24R8986 For use on rubber and cotton fire hose. Same style as No. 24R8998.

Size, inches..............	1½	2	2½	3
Price, per pair...........	45c	70c	$1.60	$2.60

Hose Pipes or Nozzles.

No. 24R8988 Hose Nozzles made of brass, finely finished, to be used in connection with our No. 24R8984 fire hose.

Size, inches..............................	1½	2	2½
Length, inches............................	12	12	15
With screw tips. Price, each....	$1.35	$1.75	$3.25
With cock or cut off. Price, each,	2.15	3.00	6.00

Hudson Garden Hose Mender.

The simplest and most complete hose mending outfit made. Any one can use it. Set consists of 1 pair japanned pliers, 6 brass tubes, and 20 brass bands. Full directions sent with each box.

No. 24R8990 For ¾-inch hose.
Price, per set...32c

No. 24R8991 For 1-inch hose.
Price, per set...50c

EXTRAS:

No. 24R8992 Hose bands for ¾-in. hose, per doz. 8c
Hose bands for 1-inch hose; per dozen....................9c
Brass tubes for ¾-inch hose; per dozen...............30c
Iron tubes for 1-inch hose; per dozen.....................35c
Pliers, each...12c

Hose Splicers.

No. 24R8995 Metal Hose Menders. Where hose is broken or worn, the defective place may be cut out and the two ends joined together with the splicer.

Size, inches..................	½	¾	1
Price, each..................	2½c	3½c	4½c

Hose Nipples.

No. 24R8996 Brass Hose Nipples, to be used in connecting hose to iron pipe.

Size, inches..............	½	¾	1
Price, each..............	14c	15c	20c

All Brass Hose Couplings.

No. 24R8997 All Brass Hose Couplings. The lightest and easiest working coupling made. Size, ¾ inch.
Price, per pair...8c

Hose Couplings.

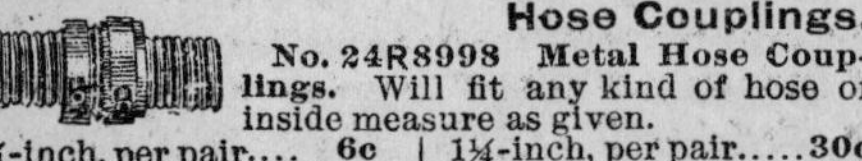

No. 24R8998 Metal Hose Couplings. Will fit any kind of hose of inside measure as given.

¾-inch, per pair.... 6c | 1¼-inch, per pair.....30c
1-inch, per pair.....12c | 1½-inch, per pair.....42c

Instantaneous Hose Coupler.

No. 24R8999 Instantaneous Hose Coupler. Guaranteed water tight. Simple and strong. Cannot get out of order. Comes complete as shown in cut.

Size, inches..........................	¾	1
Price, each..........................	15c	35c

Sure Grip Hose Clamps.

No. 24R9000 Made of wrought steel, which is guaranteed to be stronger and lighter and more pliable than any other cast clamp.
Size, ¾ inch. Price, each........... 3c
Size, 1 inch. Price, each.............4½

Rubber Tubing.

No. 24R9005 Pure Rubber Tubing, is used for siphoning liquors out of vats or barrels; for nursery bottles, syringes, and numerous other purposes. **It will not stand much pressure.** Made in two grades. Thin wall is $\frac{1}{16}$-inch thick. Thick wall is $\frac{3}{32}$-inch thick.

Diam. inch	Thin wall, per foot	Thick wall, per foot	Diam. inch	Thin wall, per foot	Thick wall, per foot
⅛	3c	3½c	⅜	8 c	9c
$\frac{3}{16}$	3c	4½c	½	8½c	10c
¼	5c	6 c	⅝	9 c	11c
$\frac{5}{16}$	6c	7 c	¾	10 c	13c

Gem Hose Nozzles.

No. 24R9007 The Improved Gem Hose Nozzle, by far the **best** combination nozzle made, throws a spray or solid stream.
For ¾-inch hose. Price..24c

Hose Nozzles.

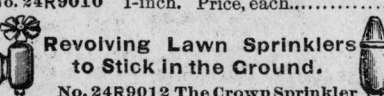

This Nozzle can be regulated to throw either a solid stream or a spray by simply turning the cock.

No. 24R9009 ¾-inch. Price, each.............34c
No. 24R9010 1-inch. Price, each.............59c

Revolving Lawn Sprinklers to Stick in the Ground.

No. 24R9012 The Crown Sprinkler will spray water perfectly for 10 to 20 feet each way. Made of brass, nickel plated, fits ¾-inch hose only.
Price, each...................................23c

No. 24R9014 The Little Wonder Lawn Sprinkler is one of the best sellers we have. It is strong, durable, and does the work. Each...9c

No. 24R9012 No. 24R9014

Adjustable Lawn Sprinklers.

No. 24R9016 The only adjustable sprinklers on the market. A turn of the screw does it. You can throw any size spray from a fine mist to large drops. Made of cast iron, japanned, with nickel plated brass screws. Cheapest sprinkler made. Size for ¾-inch hose.
Price, each..20c

The Maid of the Mist.

No. 24R9018 The Maid of the Mist is also an adjustable sprinkler, and very ornamental. It is made with a nickel plated bronze top and screw, and cast iron base japanned in colors. The top of this sprinkler can be taken off and used as a spray nozzle on the hose. Size for ¾-inch hose.
Price, each...65c

Fan Lawn Sprinkler.

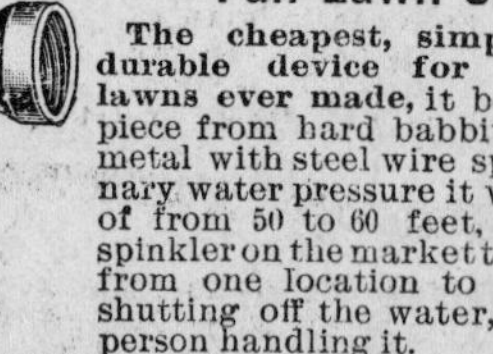

The cheapest, simplest and most durable device for sprinkling lawns ever made, it being cast in one piece from hard babbitt or composition metal with steel wire spike. With ordinary water pressure it will cover a space of from 50 to 60 feet, and is the only spinkler on the market that can be moved from one location to another without shutting off the water, or wetting the person handling it.

No. 24R9020 For ¾-inch hose. Price, each..17c
No. 24R9021 For 1-inch hose. Price, each..45c

Turbine Lawn Sprinklers.

No. 24R9023 ¾-inch aluminum bronzed, nickel plated head, adjustable to any angle. The Turbine is one of the most meritorious lawn sprinklers made. It can be used in water that is full of sand. The Turbine may be adjusted over the jet or at either side of it, thus giving a full circle or a half circle on either side. In addition to this, the top of the sprinkler may be unscrewed and attached directly to the end of the hose, and used in this way in connection with a hose holder.
Price, each...$1.05

Crescent Lawn Sprinkler.

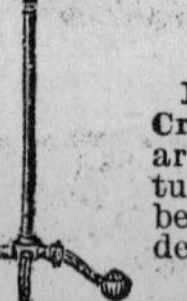

No. 24R9025 This cut shows our **Crescent Lawn Sprinkler.** It has four arms which revolve when the water is turned on. Stands 24 inches high. Can be moved from place to place without detaching.

Price, each.......................................$1.75

Hose Reels.

No. 24R9028 Hose Reel, strong and well made of hardwood, iron wheels. No hose included. Price, each....50c

Acme Hose Reel.

No. 24R9028

No. 24R9029 This Reel has been on the market for several seasons, and has proved to be a winner. It is made of hard wood throughout, painted vermilion, striped and varnished. The drum has cast iron heads or rims, with hardwood slats and does not put kinks or short bends in the hose when reeling it on. It has pawl and racket attachment and hose holder. Wheels are 6 inches in diameter. A first class reel in every respect.
Price, each...$1.40

Wirt's Patent Tubular All Steel Hose Reels.

No. 24R9030 The most complete garden reel made. Tubular frame, steel wire "holds," corrugated iron drum, 5½ inches in diameter; wheels, 7 inches in diameter. Hose cannot mildew on this reel owing to corrugated drum. Handsomely finished in vermilion and green. Four reels form natural crate. Weight, 10 pounds.
Price, each.....................$1.35

Tubular All Steel Hose Reel

No. 24R9031 This style reel is the most popular style now on the market. It is self winding; made throughout of steel; no wood to rot out; will last a lifetime; cannot break or give out. Height of reel, 21 inches. Capacity, 100 feet ¾-inch hose. Weight, 17 pounds.
Price, No. 10, each...$2.35

Hargraves Climbers.

Tree or Telegraph Pole Climbers 14 to 18 inches in Length.

No. 24R9034 Eastern Pattern

No. 24R9035 Western Pattern

Appreciating the fact that the life of linemen depends upon the quality and temper of these climbers, we have taken every pains in not only making the best finished article, but using nothing but the best material and workmanship in the construction of these goods.
Each pattern made in one piece.

No straps furnished at prices given below.

Western Pattern. Price, per pair.................$1.70
Eastern Pattern. Price, per pair.................2.00
Set of Four Straps. Price, per set...............1.00

Splicing Clamps.

No. 24R9037 These Clamps are made of especially prepared steel, well tempered and finished, **round hole; nothing better made. Full polished.** Price, each.................$1.50

No. 24R9038 Oval Hole Splicing Clamps, same as No. 24R9037, except shape of hole; full polished. Price, each..$1.50

Round and Square Flax Packings.

No. 24R9040 Round and Square Flax Packing. We are selling an excellent grade of American packing, using the best quality of Flax and Friction, with particular attention to **having it cut perfectly true.** A perfect packing for steam or water.

Diameter, inches	¼	⅜	½	⅝	¾	⅞	1
Weight, 12 ft. lbs.	½	1	1½	2½	3¾	5	6¼
High grade per lb.	22c	22c	22c	22c	22c	22c	22c

Manure Fork Handles.

No. 24R9149 Selected Quality Manure Fork Handle, with Malleable D. Price, each.......20c

Shovel and Spade Handles.

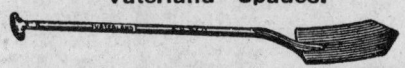

No. 24R9150 Selected Quality Shovel Handle, with wood D. Price, each.........18c

No. 24R9151 Selected Quality Spade Handle, with wood D. Price, each.........................20c

No. 24R9152 Selected Quality Long Shovel Handle. Price, each.........................11c

No. 24R9153 Selected Quality Long Spade Handle. Price, each.........................12c

Scoop Shovels.

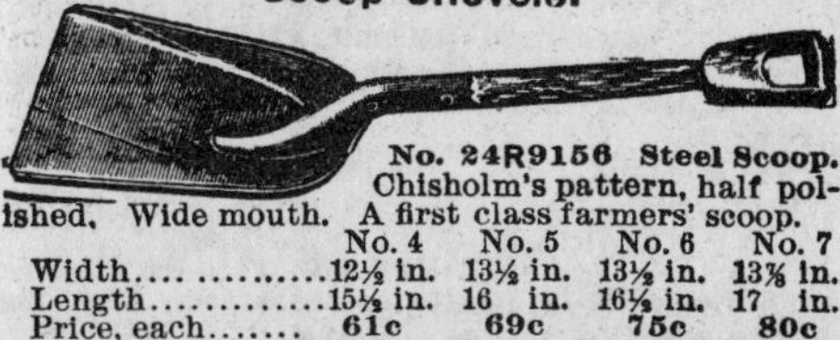

No. 24R9156 Steel Scoop. Chisholm's pattern, half polished. Wide mouth. A first class farmers' scoop.

	No. 4	No. 5	No. 6	No. 7
Width....	12½ in.	13⅛ in.	13⅛ in.	13⅞ in.
Length....	15½ in.	16 in.	16½ in.	17 in.
Price, each.......	61c	69c	75c	80c

No. 24R9160 Genuine Ames Patent Scoops. Made of extra grade cast steel. Full polished.

	No 3.	No. 4	No. 5	No. 6
Width of blade..	11½ in.	12 in.	12¼ in.	12½ in.
Price, each......	$1.20	$1.25	$1.30	$1.35

Furnace Scoops.

No. 24R6961 All Steel Furnace Scoops, D handle, narrow mouth. Length of blade, 14 inches; width at point, 9¼ inches. Made in one size only. Each..70c

Scoop Shovel Handles.

No. 24R9162 A1—Best Quality Scoop Shovel Handles. Price, each.........................14c

"Vaterland" Spades.

No. 24R9163 "Vaterland" Spades. Made of the highest grade steel, full polished. The cutting edges being angular, no steps are required, which allows the blade to scour from end to end. You can do more work with this spade than any tool made. We use extra all white hickory handles. Every spade fully warranted. Try one. Each.........95c

Wood Snow Shovels.

No. 24R9166 Wood Snow Shovels. Made of thoroughly seasoned lumber, pointed with No. 20 gauge steel formed to a cutting point and riveted over the edge of the blade. Blade is made of one piece of wood, 14 inches wide. A good shovel for the money. Size, 14x18 inches. Price, each.........20c

Steel Snow Shovels.

No. 24R9168 Steel Snow Shovels. With hollow or sunk back. Made of one solid piece of specially adapted steel. Light, strong and durable; will outwear a dozen wood shovels. Also makes a good furnace or barn shovel. Only select quality of handles used.
Price, with long handle.........................40c

Wire Potato Scoop.

No. 24R9170 Wire Potato Scoop. Size, 13¾x16 inches.
Price, each.........................$1.35

The Potato and Beet Scoop Fork.

No. 24R9173 This Fork is unequaled for handling corn, potatoes, onions, etc. Made of one solid piece of cast steel. Will screen dirt from vegetables; handle corn without sticking in the cobs; pitch fine manure better than any fork or shovel made. Made in three sizes as follows:
Eight tines, 11 inches wide and 14 inches long.
Price, each.........................$1.10
Ten tines, 14 inches wide and 15 inches long.
Price, each......................... 1.30
Twelve tines, 18 inches wide and 16 inches long. Price, each......................... 1.50

Drain Spades.

Drain Spade, solid steel, plain back, D handle, round point, blade tapers from 5½ inches at the step to 4½ inches at the point.
No. 24R9175 Length, 18 inches. Each.....$1.00
No. 24R9176 Length, 20 inches. Each 1.05

Post Spades.

No. 24R9179 Post Spade, solid steel square point, D handle, plain back. Size, 6½x18 inches. Each..95c
No. 24R9180 Same as No. 24R9179, 6½x20 inches. Price, each.........................$1.00

Round Point Tiling Spades.

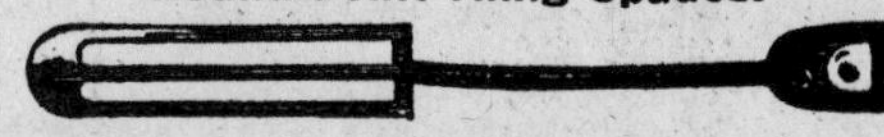

The well known and popular Boss Tiling Spade, made only in the following sizes:
No. 24R9183 Size, 4½x18, round point. Each..$1.45
No. 24R9184 Size, 4½x20, round point. Each... 1.50

Square Point Tiling Spades.

No. 24R9186 Size, 6½x18, square point. Ea. $1.55
No. 24R9187 Size, 6½x20, square point. Ea. 1.60

Drain Cleaners.

This Drain Tool is an improvement over any drain tool on the market. It is very strong and intended to last a long time. The parts are made of the best malleable iron, and the blade of shovel steel. The handle can be placed at any angle by raising the spring. When the spring is in position the blade is locked tightly and will not move or have a side motion.
No. 24R9190 Size, 4x16 inches. Price, each...61c
No. 24R9191 Size, 5x16 inches. Price, each...65c
No. 24R9192 Size, 6x16 inches. Price, each...68c

Spading Forks.

No. 24R9198 D Handle, Capped Ferrule, Spading Fork, four flat steel tines. Price, each......40c

No. 24R9199 D Handle, Strap Ferrule, Spading Fork, four steel tines. The strongest and best spading fork made. Price, each.........................44c

Coke Forks.

Coke Forks. Made of best cast steel, strapped ferrule, D handle.
No. 24R9205 Price, each, 10-tooth.........$1.00
No. 24R9206 Price, each, 12-tooth......... 1.20
No. 24R9207 Price, each, 14-tooth......... 1.40

Manure and Potato Hooks.

No. 24R9212 Manure Hooks, four tines, plain ferrule, made from one piece of best crucible steel. Price, each.............30c

Potato Hooks.

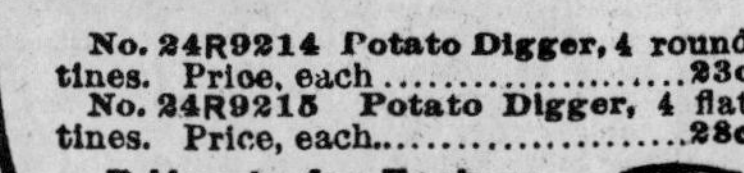

No. 24R9214 Potato Digger, 4 round tines. Price, each.........................23c
No. 24R9215 Potato Digger, 4 flat tines. Price, each.........................28c

D Heads for Fork or Shovel Handles.

No. 24R9217 Malleable D for fork or shovel handles.
Price, each 7c

The Acme Wooden Fork.

No. 24R9218 The Acme Wooden Fork is made of one piece of Indiana hickory, finished by hand. Just the thing around horses or cattle, being made of wood will not injure the animals. Also makes an excellent fork for field use. Price, each.........40c

The Wolverine Barley and "Headed Grain" Fork.

No. 24R9219 Thoroughly tried and found perfect. Unequaled for handling grain of all kinds, straw, flax, clover, etc. Made of hardwood throughout. The widest, lightest and strongest fork made.
Price, four-tine, each.........................45c
Price, six-tine, each.........................55c

Hay Forks.

This cut shows the Plain Ferrule.

Straight Handle, Plain Capped Ferrule Hay Forks, three oval tines, standard size and length; selected handles.

Length of handle, ft.,	No. 24R9220	No. 24R9221	No. 24R9222	No. 24R9223	No. 24R9224
	4	4½	5	5½	6
Price, each,	21c	22c	23c	24c	25c

Straight Handle, Capped and Strapped Ferrule Hay Forks, three oval tines, standard size and length; selected handles.

Length of handle, ft.,	No. 24R9226	No. 24R9227	No. 24R9228	No. 24R9229	No. 24R9230
	4	4½	5	5½	6
Price, each,	26c	27c	28c	29c	32c

Hay Forks.

This cut shows the Strapped Ferrule.

Bent Handle, Plain Capped Ferrule Hay Forks, three oval tines, standard size and length; selected handles.

Length of handle, ft.	No. 24R9232	No. 24R9233	No. 24R9234	No. 24R9235	No. 24R9236
	4	4½	5	5½	6
Price, each,	23c	24c	24c	27c	29c

Bent Handle, Capped and Strapped Ferrule Hay Forks, three oval tines, standard size and length; selected handles.

Length of handle, ft.	No. 24R9238	No. 24R9239	No. 24R9240	No. 24R9241	No. 24R9242
	4	4½	5	5½	6
Price, each,	26c	27c	28c	30c	32c

Four-Tine Hay Forks.

This cut shows Strapped Handle.

Bent Handle Capped and Plain Ferrule, four oval tines. Selected handles.

Catalogue No.	24R9244	24R9245	24R9246
Length of handles, feet....	4½	5	5½
Price each.	32c	33c	35c

Bent Handle, Capped and Strapped Ferrule, four oval tines. Selected handles.

Catalogue No.	24R9248	24R9249	24R9250
Length of handles, feet....	4½	5	5½
Price, each.	35c	36c	38c

Fork Handles.

No. 24R9256 Selected Quality Straight Hay Fork Handles. Length...... 4 ft. 4½ ft. 5 ft. 6 ft.
Price, each............ 6c 6c 7c 9c

No. 24R9257 Selected Quality Bent Hay Fork Handles. Length...... 4 ft. 4½ ft. 5 ft. 6 ft.
Price, each............ 7½c 7½c 8½c 11c

No. 24R9258 Selected Quality Bent Manure Fork Handles. Length .... 4 ft. 4½ ft.
Price, each.........................10c 11c

Manure Forks.

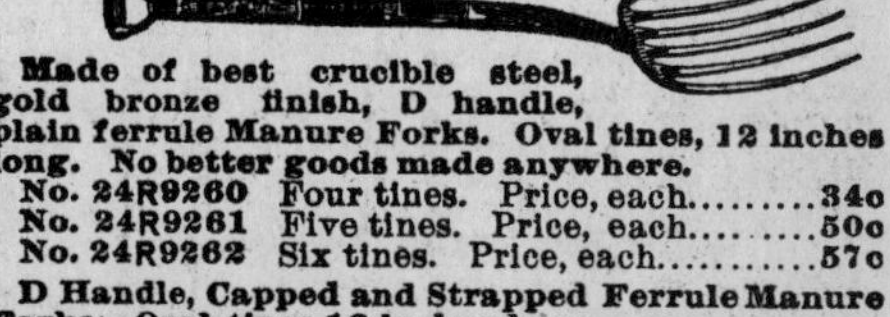

Made of best crucible steel, gold bronze finish, D handle, plain ferrule Manure Forks. Oval tines, 12 inches long. No better goods made anywhere.
No. 24R9260 Four tines. Price, each.........34c
No. 24R9261 Five tines. Price, each.........50c
No. 24R9262 Six tines. Price, each.........57c

D Handle, Capped and Strapped Ferrule Manure Forks. Oval tines 12 inches long.
No. 24R9265 Four tines. Price, each.........37c
No. 24R9266 Five tines. Price, each.........53c
No. 24R9267 Six tines. Price, each 60c

Pruning Shears.

No. 24R9358 Henry Pattern Pruning Shears, well made and finished, high grade steel blades, warranted, volute springs. Price, each..........27c

No. 24R9359 California Pattern Pruning Shears, made of the best material, polished steel blades, volute springs. Price, each..........34c

No. 24R9360 Extra High Grade Pruning Shears; 9-inch, full nickel plated. Finest shear made. Price, each..........50c

Cronk's Pruning Shears.

No. 24R9361 A trial will convince anyone that these shears will do the work easier and better than any shears on the market that cost twice or three times as much. They are solid steel and fully warranted. Are equal to the best, and nearly as cheap as the cheapest. When blades are worn down file away the stop and it will allow blades to pass same as when they were new.
Price, each..........32c

Our 65-Cent Pruning Shears.

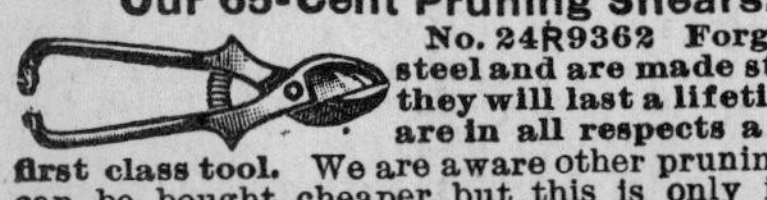

No. 24R9362 Forged solid steel and are made strong so they will last a lifetime and are in all respects a strictly first class tool. We are aware other pruning shears can be bought cheaper, but this is only intended when a good shear is needed. All vineyard men claim they cut much easier than any other shears they ever used. We guarantee them to be superior to any shears that cost double the money.
Price, each..........65c

Buckeye Pruning Shears.

No. 24R9363 Buckeye Pattern Pruning Shears, ash handle, 22 inches long, 2-inch cast steel cutter. Price, each..........50c

Cronk's Hedge Shears.

No. 24R9365 Made of the best material with shear cut, which makes them the easiest cutting shear on the market. Blades are English tool steel, handles 26 inches long, made of hardwood, nicely finished. We list them in two grades **light and extra heavy. Light grade, price, each..70c**
No. 24R9366 Extra heavy grade, price, each, 85c

Patent Fruit Gatherer.

The Acme Patent Fruit Gatherer, as the name implies, is a device for gathering fruit. It will pick apples, pears, plums and similar fruit from otherwise inaccessible places without bruise or injury of any kind. It is the simplest, lightest, strongest and most efficient device for this purpose on the market. **It will be observed that the Acme Fruit Gatherer is remarkably simple in construction, consisting simply of two semi-circular jaws which open and shut like scissors, by means of which the fruit is severed from the branch, and a netting tubing fastened to the jaws which receives the fruit, and without bruise or injury guides it to the ground,** hand or any receptacle in which the operator may desire to collect it. The fruit, being received in the tubing as rapidly as it is picked, may be gathered continuously without stopping to empty, as is necessary with other appliances of this nature, thus saving time. When properly handled it will not jar the branch and cause the other fruit thereon to fall, an objectionable feature of other fruit gatherers on the market, destroying more than they gather. **No branches will be broken as when climbing after the fruit.**
No. 24R9367 Price, each..........75c

Acme Telegraph Tree Pruner.

No. 24R9368 This improvement was originally designed for the use of telephone and telegraph men in keeping the wires free from overhanging branches of trees. Our regular Acme Pruner has long been a favorite with them, but the long pole has been somewhat unhandy on account of their limited means for transporting their tools. It has many features which should commend it to the favor of the fruit grower or nurseryman; it is, in fact, a modified form of the Acme Pruner, and while it is not recommended as a substitute for that implement, it works well, and is very strong and durable. The blade can be taken out to be sharpened; there is a steel coiled spring for throwing out the blade; the socket has a thread on the inside, and can thus be easily screwed on to a pole of any length. Price, each..........60c
Extra blades, each..........20c
Extra springs, each..........15c

The Waters Tree Pruner.

The Waters Tree Pruner, with latest improvements, is considered by fruit growers and gardeners the best in the market. Although the cutting blade is very thin, it being supported on both sides by the hook, makes it strong and durable. It will cut off the largest bough the hook will admit, and also clip the smallest twig. **No ladders are required, as pruning can be done while standing on the ground.**

No. 24R9369 Extra Knives for above pruners, each..........10c

No. 24R9370

Length, feet,	4	6	8	10	12
Weight, lbs.	2¼	3	3½	4	4½
Price, each,	33c	35c	42c	43c	56c

Spring Pruning Knife and Brush Hook.

No. 24R9371 It consists of a hollow iron shank having integral extensions, which guide and support the blade. Within the shank is a strong compression spring having squared ends and made of the best crucible steel, tempered in oil. A malleable iron pin which is riveted to blade passes through spring and is provided with a nut and washer, by which means the blade can be adjusted to give back "easy" or "hard," as desired. For cutting out blackberries, raspberries, etc., it has no equal. It will prune anything from a currant bush to an apple tree. Price, each..........57c

Hedge Shears.

No. 24R9373 Hedge Shears, notched blades, hardwood handles.

Size..........	8	9	10	12
Each..........	$1.00	$1.20	$1.35	$2.00

Pruning Hook and Saw.

No. 24R9374 Disston's Pruning Hook and Saw, can be used either with or without saw, as the saw is easily and quickly taken off. The pole is not furnished. Price, each..........$1.10

Hedge Knives.

No. 24R9375 Hedge Knives, made of the best English steel. Has strong ferrule, with rivet through ferrule and shank. **Length of blade, 18 inches;** finely finished.
Price, each..........65c

No. 24R9376 Hand Hammered Blade. Best hickory handled shank strongly fastened to handle with rivet through steel ferrule; blade ground and polished. **A high grade knife; nothing better made.**
Price, each..........70c

Molders' Tools.

In the following molders' tools we have only listed such tools as are in daily use, but can furnish any style or shape you may desire. They are made of the best material money will buy, by a firm that make more molders' tools than any one firm in the world. Every tool is warranted and can be returned at our expense if found defective.

Square Trowel.

No. 24R9378 Molders' Square Trowel. Highly finished. Nothing better made.

Length, inches..........	5	5½	6	6½
Width, 1¼ in. Price, each..	44c	48c	52c	....
Width, 1½ in. Price, each..	52c	55c	60c	68c
Width, 1¾ in. Price, each..	60c	64c	68c	76c

No. 1 Finishing Trowels.

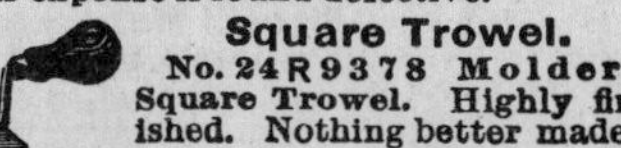

No. 24R9379 No. 1 Finishing Molders' Trowels, highly finished, A1 tools. Nothing better made.

Length, inches..........	5	5½	6	6½
Width, 1¼ in. Price, each..	44c	48c	52c	....
Width, 1½ in. Price, each..	53c	55c	60c	68c
Width, 1¾ in. Price, each..	....	64c	68c	76c

Molders' No. 2 Stove Tools.

No. 24R9380 Molders' High Grade No. 2 Stove Tools. Nothing better made.
Width, ⅝-inch. Price, each..27c
Width, ¾-inch. Price, each..32c

Molders' Stove Tools.

No. 24R9381 Molders' Stove Tools. Nos. 3 and 4. Small cut shows No. 3; large cut, No. 4.
No. 3, width, ⅝-in. Price, each.21c
No. 3, width, ¾-in. Price, each.32c
No. 4, width, ¾-inch. Price, each..........36c

Molders' Bench Lifters.

No. 24R9382 Molders' Fig. 12 No. 1 Bench Lifter. Nothing better made. Width, ⅜-inch. Price, each..........32c
Width, ½-inch. Price, each..........36c
Width, ⅝-inch. Price, each..........40c

Molders' Bench Lifters.

No. 24R9383 Molders' Fig. 14 Bent Bench Lifters. Nothing better made.

Width, inch..........	⅜	½	⅝	¾
Price, each..........	32c	36c	40c	44c

Molders' Bench Lifters.

No. 25R9384 Molders' Fig. 15 Yankee Bench Lifters. Nothing better made.

Width, inch..........	½	⅝	¾
Price, each..........	36c	40c	44c

Molders' Heart, Leaf and Square Tools.

Molders' Heart, Leaf and Square Tools. Fig. 22, heart and leaf, is shown in cut at top. Fig. 23, heart and square, is shown in cut at bottom. **Nothing better made.**

No. 24R9385 Fig. 22. Size, inches..	1	1¼	1½
Price, each..........	36c	44c	52c
No. 24R9386 Fig. 23. Size, inches..	1	1¼	1½
Price, each..........	36c	44c	52c

Molders' Taper and Square Tools.

No. 24R9387 Molders' Taper and Square Tools. Nothing better made.

Fig. 24, No. 1......	¾	1	1¼
Price, each........	36c	40c	48c

Molders' Slick and Square Spoons.

No. 24R9388 Molders' Slick and Square Spoons. Nothing better made. Fig. 27. Width, 1½ inches.
Price, each..........48c

Molders' Slick and Oval Spoons.

No. 24R9389 Molders' Slick and Oval Spoons. Nothing better made.

Fig. 29. Width,	1	1¼	1½
Price, each......	40c	48c	56c

Molders' Double Squares.

No. 24R9390 Molders' Double Squares. Nothing better made.
Fig. 37, size, ½-inch. Price, each..........36c
Fig. 37, size, ⅝-inch. Price, each..........40c
Fig. 37, size, ¾-inch. Price, each..........44c
Fig. 37, size, 1-inch. Price, each..........52c

Molders' Flange Lifters.

No. 24R9392 Molders' Flange Lifters. Nothing better made.

Fig. 42. Length, inches...	8	10	12	14
Fig. 42, size, ¼-in. Price, each,	24c	28c	32c	36c
Fig. 42, size, ⅜-in. Price, each,	28c	32c	36c	40c
Fig. 42, size, ½-in. Price, each,	....	36c	40c	44c
Fig. 42, size, ¾-in. Price, each,	....	....	....	52c

Fig. 42. Length, inches.......	16	18	20
Fig. 42, size, ¼-in. Price, each,	40c	....	....
Fig. 42, size, ⅜-in. Price, each,	44c	48c	....
Fig. 42, size, ½-in. Price, eech,	48c	52c	55c
Fig. 42, size, ¾-in. Price, each,	55c	60c	64c

Boiler Maker's Beading Tool.

No. 24R9395 Boiler Maker's Beading Tool. Made of high grade English steel. Price, each...45c

Mill Picks.

No. 24R9399 Mill Picks, made of special tool steel. Tempered by a secret process which insures an even temper; well finished ready for use. Weight, 1½ to 3 pounds each. Price, per pound..........33c

Sandstone Crandle.

Sandstone Crandles used for surfacing stone. Teeth are adjustable, and can be taken out and sharpened; furnished complete with handle.
No. 24R9400 Price, each, 10-tooth crandle..........$3.25

Stone Sledges.

No. 24R9402 Solid Cast Steel Stone Sledges.

Weight, lbs.	8	9	10	11	12	13	14	15	16
Price, each.	50c	59c	65c	71c	78c	84c	90c	97c	$1 04

GIVE CATALOGUE NUMBER IN FULL WHEN YOU WRITE YOUR ORDER

Post Mauls.

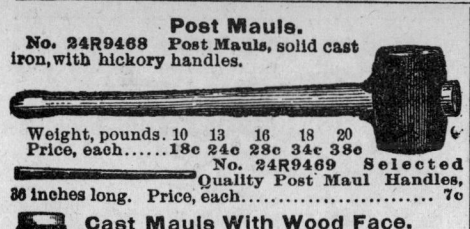

No. 24R9468 Post Mauls, solid cast iron, with hickory handles.

Weight, pounds	10	13	16	18	20
Price, each	18c	24c	28c	34c	38c

No. 24R9469 Selected Quality Post Maul Handles, 36 inches long. Price, each........................... 7c

Cast Mauls With Wood Face.

No. 24R9470 Cast Post Mauls, with wood face and wood handles.

Weight, pounds	10	14	16
Price, each	35c	40c	45c

Wood Mauls With Iron Rings.

No. 24R9472 Made of the best second growth, butt end and grub hickory. Furnished complete with hickory handles.

Size	3½x7	4x7	5x8	6x8	7x9	7x10	8x10
Price	87c	$1.00	$1.20	$1.30	$1.43	$1.65	$1.80

Railroad Picks.

No. 24R9474 Adze Eye, Cast Steel, Axe Finish Railroad Picks. Weights, 5 to 6 pounds.
Price, each........................... 37c

Railroad Pick Handles.

No. 24R9476 Selected Quality Railroad Pick Handles, 36 inches long. Price, each.................. 8c
Railroad pick handles are also used for mattocks.

Drifting Picks.

No. 24R9480 Drifting Picks, adze eye, oil finish.

No.	1	2	3	4
Weight, pounds	3	4	4½	5
Price, each	35c	39c	43c	47c

No. 24R9481 Selected Quality Drifting Pick Handles, 34 inches long, for above picks.
Price, each........................... 12c

Common Eye Coal Picks.

No. 24R9483 Made of best refined iron with steel points, ground and oil finished.

Weight	2 lbs.	2½ lbs.	3 lbs.	3½ lbs.	4 lbs.	4½ lbs.	5 lbs.
Each	30c	33c	35c	37c	39c	41c	43c

Adze Eye Coal Picks.

No. 24R9485 Adze Eye Coal Picks, made of refined iron with steel points, ground and oil finished.

Weight	2 lbs.	2½ lbs.	3 lbs.	3½ lbs.	4 lbs.	4½ lbs.	5 lbs.
Each	36c	39c	42c	44c	46c	50c	52c

Coal Pick Handles.

No. 24R9486 Select Hickory Coal Pick Handles, 34 inches long. Price, each........................ 8c

Miners' Short Ear Cutting Picks.

No. 24R9489 High Grade Short Ear Miners' Cutting Picks. The best shaped miners' pick sold by any one. Made by one of the largest concerns devoted to mining tools only in the United States. Every tool guaranteed. Weight, 2, 2¼ and 2½ pounds.
Price, each, any weight........................ 40c

Miners' Short Ear Mining Picks.

Miners' Short Ear Mining Picks. Made by one of the largest makers of mining tools in the United States. Material, shape and finish first class. Every tool guaranteed. Weights, 2, 2¼, and 2½ pounds.
No. 24R9490 Price, each, any weight......... 41c

Miners' Cast Steel Coal Wedges.

Cast Steel Coal Wedges. Regular pattern, suitable for most all coal mined in the United States. Every wedge warranted. Weights, 1½ to 5 pounds.
No. 24R9491 Price, per pound.................. 8½c

The New Acme Coal Miners' Post Drill.

No. 24R9493 Our New Improved Coal Miners' Post Drill is by far the best, simplest and lightest running machine on the market. It is the result of years of experimenting by practical miners. We warrant the machine in every particular. The thread box is made of high grade alloy which will outlast a dozen of the usual thread boxings made of malleable iron. We can furnish either square or feather edge augers. Price, shipped direct from factory in Southern Illinois, complete with side and end gear........................... $11.00

Star Miners' Lamp.

No. 24R9496 Star Miners' Lamp. Made of XXX tin; well made; nicely finished. Price, each................ 10c

Star Drivers' Lamp.

No. 24R9498 Star Drivers' Lamp. Well made and nicely finished. The best drivers' lamp on the market.
Price, each. 14c

Coal Miners' Caps.

No. 24R9500 Miners' Caps. Well made. Best lamp attachment used by anyone. No. 1 brown duck, as shown in illustration. Sizes, 6¾ to 7¼.
Price, each........................ 20c

Stone Picks.

No. 24R9503 Solid Cast Steel Stone Picks. High grade steel, with polished points. Weights, 5 lbs., 5½ lbs., 6 lbs., 6½ lbs., 7 lbs., 8 lbs. Price, per pound........................ 10c

Poll Picks.

No. 24R9505 Solid Cast Steel Poll Picks. Adze edge; ground and finished in oil.

Size	1	2	3	4	5	6
Weight	3½ lbs.	4 lbs.	4½ lbs.	5 lbs.	6 lbs.	7 lbs.
Price, each	59c	63c	66c	72c	80c	83c

Pick Mattocks.

No. 24R9507 Pick Mattock is a pick on one side and a mattock on the other, as shown in cut. Adze eye, extra tool steel, ax finish.
Price, each........................ 60c
No. 24R9508 Handle for above. Each...... 10c

Mattocks.

No. 24R9510 Mattock. Long cutter, cast steel, adze eye, axe finish. Weight, 5 to 6 pounds.
Price, each........................ 43c
No. 24R9511 Mattock. Short cutter, same as above. Weight, 4½ pounds. Price, each...... 41c
No. 24R9512 Handles for above. Hickory, 36 inches long. Price, each.................. 8c

Grub Hoes.

No. 24R9514 Grub Hoes, adze eye, cast steel, axe finish, blade is about 4 inches wide.
Price, each, 3 lbs..... 32c Price, each, 2½ lbs.. 31c

No. 24R9515 Selected Quality Grub Hoe Handles, 36 inches long. Price, each.............. 12c

Hazel Hoes.

No. 24R9517 Hazel Hoes. Size about 6-inch cut, 10 inches long, and weighs about 3 pounds. Adze eye, cast steel, axe finish. Price, each............ 48c
No. 24R9518 Handles for above.
Price, each........................ 13c

Planters' Eye Hoes.

Solid Forged Steel Planters' Hoes, without handles. Made of refined cast steel. Half polished blade. Prices are for blade only, without handles.

	No. 24R9520	No. 24R9521	No. 24R9522
Size	7 inches	7½ inches	8 inches
Price, each	27c	29c	37c

Planters' Hoe Handles.

No. 24R9524 Selected Quality Planters' Hoe Handles. Length, 5½ feet. Price, each.......... 10c

German Hoes.

Solid Eye Cast Steel German Hoes, with handles. Made of the best material, with select hickory handles. Blades full polished.

	No. 24R9526	24R9527	24R9528
Width of blade	6 inches	6½ inches	7 inches
Price, each	50c	58c	65c

Sluice Forks.

Long Handle Sluice Forks, with strapped and sapped ferrules. Made of the best imported tool steel. Nicely finished. Select A1 handles. Nothing better made.

	No. 24R9530	No. 24R9531
	8-tine	10-tine
Price, each	$1.00	$1.20

Plain Fork Ferrules.

Plain Wrought Fork Ferrules. Full polished.
No. 24R9535 Hay Fork size, per doz., 35c; each 3c
No. 24R9536 Manure Fork size, doz., 40c; each 4c
No. 24R9537 Spading Fork size, doz., 40c; each 4c

Strapped Fork Ferrules.

Strapped Wrought Fork Ferrules. Full polished.
No. 24R9538 Hay Fork size. Each................ 8c
No. 24R9539 Manure Fork size. Each.......... 9c
No. 24R9540 Spading Fork size. Each.......... 9c

Bush Hooks.

No. 24R9543 Bush Hooks, cast steel, extra quality, handled. Each......... 47c

Grain Sickles.

No. 24R9545 Grass Hook or Smooth Edge Sickle, good quality cast steel, medium size. Price, each............ 19c
No. 24R9546 The Old Fashioned Grain Sickle, with rough edge, **made from extra quality cast steel.** Price, each, large, 33c; medium, 25c; small........................ 17c

Scythe Grass Hook.

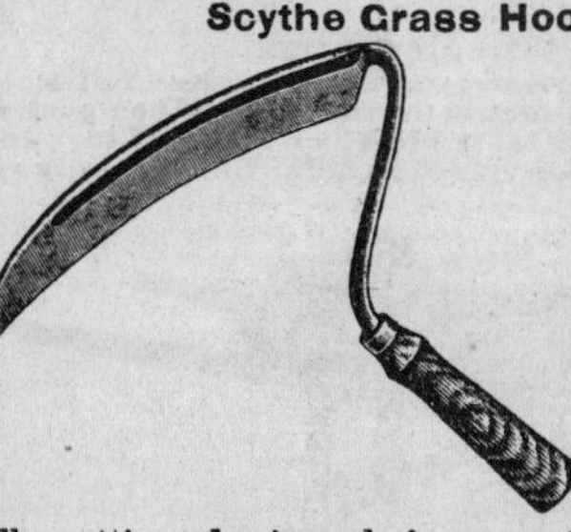

No. 24R9548 Borden's Grass Hook and Lawn Trimmer. It is made from three pieces of steel, welded together and drawn out in rods in suitable lengths to make a complete hook, including handle. The cutting edge is made from crucible steel, overlaid with soft steel, which protects the thin edge steel in center of blade. The handle is so arranged as to protect the hand from coming in contact with the ground. There is no hook on the market that has created such a demand in so short a time.
Price, each........................ 33c

Common Cant Hooks.

No. 24R9550 Common Cant Hooks, made of high grade steel with hardwood hand turned handle. A first class hook in every respect.

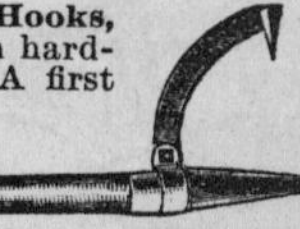

Size of Stock	Style of Hook	Price, each
2¾ inches.	No. 1 chisel point.	$1.35

Cant Hook Handles.

No. 24R9551 Extra Cant Hook Handles. Same as used in our No. 24R9550 Cant Hooks. First quality
Price, each.............. 30c.

Lug Hooks or Timber Grapples.

No. 24R9552 Lug Hooks or Timber Grapples, made of the best grade tool steel, hickory handles, common or duck bill. Price, each.. $1.75

Warehouse Trucks.

Warehouse Truck (like cut). Hardwood, well ironed, neatly finished. Axles turned and wheels bored. Steel nose, side straps, axles and legs. We guarantee this the best truck on the market, and, quality considered, 20 per cent cheaper in price than any other.

	Lgth. handles	Width	Weight	Price
No. 24R9682	3 feet 11 in.	19 in.	44 lbs.	$2.60
No. 24R9683	4 feet 4 in.	20 in.	56 lbs.	3.30
No. 24R9684	4 feet 8 in.	22 in.	77 lbs.	5.00

Daisy Truck.

No. 24R9690 Daisy Truck, with steam bent handles. Length of handle, 46 inches; width at nose, 12 inches; at upper cross-bar, 17½ inches. Weight, 30 pounds.

Price, each $1.35

The Phœnix Barrel Truck.

No. 24R9692 This Truck is nicely made, strong and durable, and is necessary in every store, warehouse or factory. It is adapted to any size barrel, keg or box. The handiest truck ever made for carrying garbage barrels and ash cans, as by simply setting the nose of the truck against the barrel and dropping the handle hook over the chine, the barrel is loaded on the truck without being touched by the hands. Price, each..........................$1.35

Handy Barrel Truck and Stand.

No. 24R9694 Malleable Iron Handy Barrel Truck and Stand. Handiest truck ever invented. It answers the purpose of a truck and stand at the same time. Indispensable for sugar, salt, pork, vinegar, etc. Can be used as warehouse truck for boxes. It has a positive action and will always run in a straight line.

No store or warehouse should be without six or more of the trucks.

Price, each 85c

Wheelbarrows.

This Wheelbarrow is well made. Has full sized tray; wheel, 16 inches in diameter. When packed for shipment wheel is bolted on inside of tray and legs are folded on side of handle. Can be easily set up by anyone.

No. 24R9700 Half Bolted Railroad Wheelbarrow, with wood wheel. Price, each..........$1.25
No. 24R9701 Half Bolted Railroad Wheelbarrow, with steel wheel. Price, each..........$1.35

Acme Steel Tray Wheelbarrow.

No. 24R9704 The handles and frame of these barrows are made of the best selected hardwood. Trays are of heavy sheet steel with edges turned over. Just the thing for canal, firemen, etc. Tray is made of No. 16 sheet steel with No. 1 steel wheels.

Price, each..........................$2.35

Lawn Wheelbarrow.

No. 24R9706 This is the handsomest and best lawn wheelbarrow made. They are fitted with steel wheels, 16 inches in diameter. These wheels are constructed on the latest improved model of the bicycle. Size of front, 12 inches by 19 inches; sides 12 inches by 28 inches; bottom, 21 inches by 27 inches. Weight, 40 pounds.

Our special price for this wheelbarrow.......$2.35

Boys' Barrow.

No. 24R9709 To meet the growing demand for a small, well made barrow, we have placed this barrow on the market. No poor material is used in its construction. It is well made throughout; nicely painted and striped. The legs are braced diagonally across, and have an iron brace around the bottom of the leg, making it very strong and neat in appearance. Put together entirely with bolts, and easily set up. Size of bed, wheel end, 14 inches; handle end, 17 inches; length, 22 inches; depth, 9½ inches; wheel, 17 inches in diameter; $\frac{5}{16}$-inch spokes; tire, ⅞x$\frac{3}{16}$-inch; axle, ⅝-inch. Weight, 20 pounds.

Price, each......................................$2.00

Mortar Wheelbarrow.

Tight box for wheeling mortar. Top iron banded, iron braced and well bolted. Size, of box at top, 27 inches wide at wheel; 30 inches long. Size of box at bottom, 19 inches wide, 20 inches long. Box 14 inches deep at wheel, 9 inches deep at handles. Frame is made of selected hardwood, full bolted. Weight, 40 pounds.

No. 24R9712 Price, wood wheel, each.......$2.25
No. 24R9713 Price, steel wheel, each....... 2.30

Clipper Garden Wheelbarrow.

No. 24R9715 Clipper Garden Wheelbarrow is strong, well made. Frame is made of selected hardwood. Mortised joints. Legs are one solid piece of wood which adds greatly to their strength and beauty. Nicely painted and striped. The best garden barrow made at any price. With 20-inch steel wheel.

Price, each..................................$2.60

Bent Handle Stone Barrow.

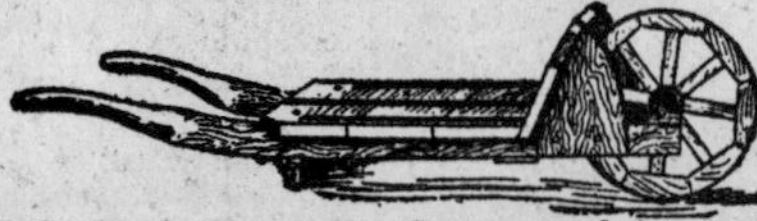

Made for heavy work. Bottom and front of 1½-inch hardwood, dressed and well seasoned. Barrows painted brown. Size of bottom, 28 inches wide, 27 inches long and 11 inches high in front. Handles, 2x3 inches, dressed, made of oak, rock elm or hickory.

No. 24R9718 Price, wood wheel, each........$2.85
No. 24R9719 Price, steel wheel, each.. .... 3.10

Heavy Steel Tray Barrow For $4.00.

No. 24R9723 The tray is made of one piece of No. 16 steel of the same thickness throughout. The edges of the trays are flanged and turned over a $\frac{5}{16}$-inch steel rod. This rod prevents the tray from breaking at the edge and makes it very much stronger. As the steel of the tray is of uniform thickness, there are no thin corners to give out after using a short time. These barrows are made to dump forward and are so constructed that at the dumping point they will not run back on the operator. They are well bolted and braced and made of the best material and painted. The wheels revolve on a heavy bolt which also passes through the handles and so materially strengthens the barrow.

Price, each...$4.00

Solid Pressed Steel Tray Barrow.

Coal and coke barrow, with one-piece tubular steel frame extending around in front of the wheel. Frame strongly braced and well ironed. The tray is made of best quality of steel, with wired edge. They will carry from 400 to 450 pounds of coal or five bushels of coke. Fitted with our extra heavy No. 4 wheel, 17 inches in diameter, tire 2¼x$\frac{5}{16}$-inch, nine $\frac{5}{16}$-inch spokes, ¾-inch axle.

No. 24R9726 Gauge of steel in tray, 15; length of tray on top, 41¼ inches; width of tray on top, 33 inches; depth at wheel, 12 inches; capacity, 6 cubic feet. Weight, 95 pounds. Price, each...........$7.00

No. 24R9727 Gauge of steel in tray, 13; length of tray on top, 41¼ inches; width of tray on top, 33 inches; depth at wheel, 12 inches; capacity, 6 cubic feet. Weight, 110 pounds. Price, each..........$8.00

Boss Charcoal Peanut Roasters.

The Boss Peanut and Coffee Roaster is the only successful roaster on the market. The material used in their construction is the finest grade smooth rolled sheet steel for the roasters, and XX bright tin and 16-ounce cold rolled copper for the warmers. Peanuts roasted in the Boss Roaster retain that delicate flavor which is essential to the good peanut, and which is only obtained through perfect roasting.

Prices are f. o. b. factory.		With Tin Warmer	With Copper Warmer
No. 24R9740	Size, 1 peck....	$10.15	$15.00
No. 24R9741	Size, ½ bushel.	12.25	17.50
No. 24R9742	Size, 1 bushel..	16.30	21.60

When ordering be sure and state size wanted; also tin or copper warmer.

Boss Gasoline Peanut Roasters.

Our Gasoline Roaster is made of the same material as the Charcoal Burner; has our new improved burners which makes it the most complete machine sold by anyone. No smoke, dust or ashes. So simple a boy can operate them. The fire can be started in a half minute. No more soggy or burnt peanuts, as these machines have steam heaters. 10 cents per day will roast and keep your peanuts or coffee warm and increase your trade 100 per cent.

When ordering, be sure and mention size wanted; also tin or copper warmer.

Prices are f. o. b. factory.		With Tin Warmer	With Copper Warmer
No. 24R9746	Size, 1 peck.....	$13.50	$17.50
No. 24R9747	Size, ½ bushel..	16.85	20.50
No. 24R9748	Size, 1 bushel..	23.00	24.30

No. 6 Boss Peanut Roaster.

No. 6 Gasoline Roaster is the same style and shape as No. 24R9746, with a cone shape glass dome or show case. Dome can be filled with peanuts, which makes a much more attractive display. Made in copper only. Prices are f. o. b. factory. Copper Warmer.

No. 24R9750 Size, 1 peck......................$18.50
No. 24R9751 Size, ½ bushel.................. 22.00
No. 24R9752 Size, 1 bushel.................. 26.00

READ WHAT OUR BANKERS SAY ON PAGE 12.

Agricultural Implement Department.

WE ARE HEADQUARTERS FOR EVERYTHING IN THE LINE OF IMPROVED AND UP TO DATE AGRICULTURAL IMPLEMENTS. OUR LINE IS COMPLETE, AND THE QUALITY AND WORKMANSHIP OF THE IMPLEMENTS WE HANDLE ARE FIRST CLASS IN EVERY RESPECT.

OUR IMPLEMENTS are made for us under special contracts and in very large quantities, by several of the largest and most reliable manufacturers in the country, concerns who have devoted their life's work to the manufacture of this class of goods, and who by their long experience, unexcelled facilities and special knowledge, are enabled to turn out the highest grade of work that can be produced, and at less cost than inferior goods can be produced by most other makers.

Prices on all Agricultural Implements are full cash with order. No discount.

OUR PRICES are based on the actual cost of material and labor, with but our one small percentage of profit added. We dispense with the long line of expenses which are incidental to the ordinary method of selling goods, and through the medium of our extensive contracts the cost of producing our goods is reduced to the lowest possible figure. This, in connection with the fact that we are satisfied with a very small margin of profit, depending on a large volume of business for final results, enables us to make the astonishingly low prices at which we sell our implements.

ALL AGRICULTURAL IMPLEMENTS which we sell are guaranteed to be made of good materials and in a workmanlike manner, and are warranted to do good work when correctly adjusted and properly operated. Any defect in material or workmanship appearing within one year, will be made good, by our furnishing free, new parts to take the place of the defective parts. If our implements are not found to be perfectly satisfactory write us immediately after receiving the goods, stating wherein they are not satisfactory, and if we cannot make adjustment to your satisfaction, we will give you instructions about returning the goods and will refund your money or send you other goods, as you may desire, and we will also pay the transportation charges.

OWING TO THE FACT that we can frequently save money for our customers and furnish them goods at lower prices by shipping from the factory, many of our implements are shipped direct from the factory. This however is done only when we can save you money by so doing, and we will ship from our main store whenever we believe it would be best to do so.

WE GUARANTEE the safe delivery of every implement which we ship and will furnish free, transportation prepaid, any part either broken or lost in transit, only requiring the purchaser to examine the goods when received, cause the agent of the transportation company to note shortage or breakage on the receipt for the freight charges you pay, and send the receipt to us when reporting the circumstances.

REPAIRS

For all Implements which we sell can and will be furnished promptly and at very low prices.

WE KEEP A CAREFUL RECORD of all Implements sold by us, and will be glad to give prompt reply to all letters asking for prices of repairs. In writing about repairs or in ordering repairs, be sure to give a careful description of the part wanted and the letters, figures or marks which are on the original piece, or, if there are no marks on the old piece, tell us what numbers appear on other prominent parts of the machine.

Always give name, size and kind of machine for which repair is wanted.

WEIGHTS given are as nearly correct as it is possible to give, but are not guaranteed, because on heavy goods the weights may vary either way owing to the variation in the weight of the materials without detriment to the goods.

ABOUT THE FREIGHT. Most agricultural implements are accepted at second class freight rate by nearly all railroad companies, which is usually from 40 to50 cents per 100 pounds for 500 miles. By referring to the pages in the front part of the catalogue devoted to freight classification and freight rates, you can easily determine about what the freight would be on any implement. On goods shipped direct from the factory, from points near Chicago, or in northern Illinois, or in southeastern Wisconsin, or in northern Indiana, unless the destination is very close to the shipping point, the rates are practically the same as from Chicago.

KENWOOD ALL STEEL WALKING PLOWS.

OUR KENWOOD ALL-STEEL WALKING PLOWS are absolutely as perfect as plows can be made. The design, shape and general construction is the same exactly as is universally commended and adopted by the leading plow manufacturers; in fact these plows are made for us under special contract, by one of the very best makers in this country, and are in every way identical with their regular goods. **They will scour in any soil and are especially adapted to the prairie land and black soil of the Central and Western States, and will do perfect work in trashy, loose land.**

THEY ARE LIGHT, STRONG AND DURABLE,

light running and easily handled, and guaranteed equal to any plow made, and better than many plows which are sold at much higher prices. The moldboards, shares and landsides are all made of the very best quality of soft center plow steel, and all are extra carefully hardened. The moldboards and shares are double shinned and the landside plates are medium high.

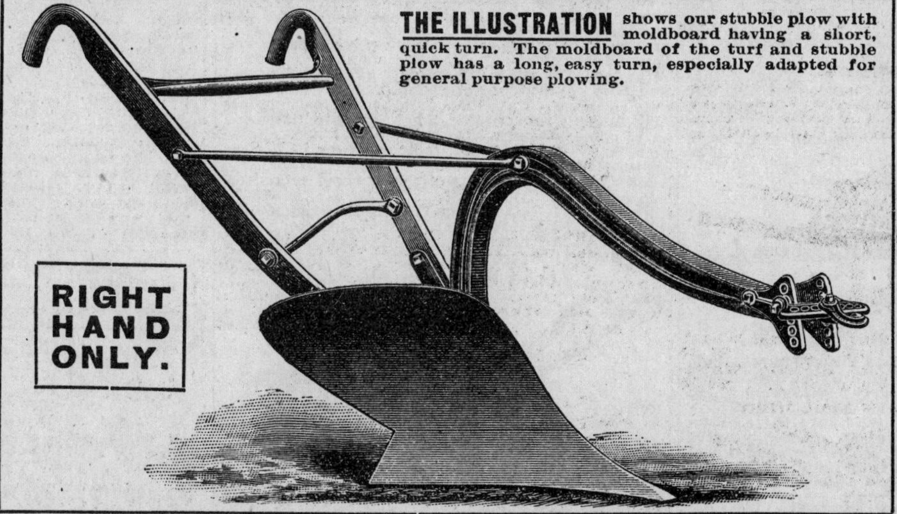

THE ILLUSTRATION shows our stubble plow with moldboard having a short, quick turn. The moldboard of the turf and stubble plow has a long, easy turn, especially adapted for general purpose plowing.

SHIPPED DIRECT FROM FACTORY IN NORTHERN ILLINOIS.

THESE PLOWS ARE STRONGLY PUT TOGETHER and firmly braced in the most approved manner. The handles are well braced, secured by iron straps at the bottom and set wide apart at the bottom, thus preventing clods from filling in between the handles. **Wood beams are southern oak,** well arched and made extra heavy directly over and forward of the standard. **Steel beams are double flanged,** thus making them light and very strong; they are highly arched so as to give ample clearance. **Each plow is**

FURNISHED WITH A BROAD ADJUSTABLE CLEVIS,

so that plow can be set to the required depth and used with any number of horses. **Any style coulter, wheel or jointer can be used, but are furnished only at extra price.** Made in right hand only, either wood or steel beam, and either stubble shape or turf and stubble shape. Guaranteed to be made of first class materials and in a workmanlike manner; well painted and nicely finished, and perfectly fitted for the work they are intended to do.

STUBBLE SHAPE PLOWS.

No.	Size	Weight	Price
WOOD BEAM.			
No. 73R69	Size 12-inch.	Weight, 93 pounds.	$ 8.50
No. 73R70	Size, 14-inch.	Weight, 98 pounds.	9.75
No. 73R71	Size 16-inch.	Weight, 105 pounds.	11.10
STEEL BEAM.			
No. 73R73	Size, 12-inch.	Weight, 95 pounds.	$ 8.55
No. 73R74	Size, 14-inch.	Weight, 100 pounds.	9.80
No. 73R75	Size, 16-inch.	Weight, 108 pounds.	11.15
Extra Steel Shares for Above Plows.			
No. 32R77	Size, 12-inch.	Weight, 11 pounds.	$ 1.90
No. 32R78	Size, 14-inch.	Weight, 13 pounds.	2.25
No. 32R79	Size, 16-inch.	Weight, 15 pounds.	2.55

TURF AND STUBBLE SHAPE OR GENERAL PURPOSE PLOWS.

No.	Size	Weight	Price
WOOD BEAM.			
No. 73R85	Size, 12-inch.	Weight, 97 pounds.	$ 8.95
No. 73R86	Size, 14-inch.	Weight, 102 pounds.	10.25
No. 73R87	Size, 16-inch.	Weight, 109 pounds.	11.45
STEEL BEAM.			
No. 73R89	Size, 12-inch.	Weight, 99 pounds.	$ 9.00
No. 73R90	Size, 14-inch.	Weight, 104 pounds.	10.30
No. 73R91	Size, 16-inch.	Weight, 111 pounds.	11.50
Eqtra Steel Shares for Above Plows.			
No. 32R93	Size, 12-inch.	Weight, 14 pounds.	$1.95
No. 32R94	Size, 14-inch.	Weight, 16 pounds.	2.30
No. 32R95	Size, 16-inch.	Weight, 18 pounds.	2.60

EXTRAS FOR STUBBLE, AND TURF AND STUBBLE PLOWS.

No. 32R125	**Fin Cutter.** Weight, 4 pounds.	$0.65
No. 32R126	**Reversible Coulter,** for wood beam. Weight, 6½ pounds	.81
No. 32R127	**Reversible Coulter,** for steel beam. Weight, 6½ pounds	1.01
No. 32R128	**Rolling Coulter,** for wood beam. Weight, 15 pounds	1.63
No. 32R129	**Rolling Coulter,** for steel beam. Weight, 15 pounds	$1.64
No. 32R132	**Gauge Wheel,** for wood beam. Weight, 13 pounds	.67
No. 32R133	**Gauge Wheel,** for steel beam. Weight, 13 pounds	.69

NOTE—You must specify for which plow extras are wanted.

All Steel, Wood Beam Pony Plows.

Extra Share furnished with each Plow.

Our light wood beam and steel beam all steel plows are guaranteed to do good service in the work they are intended for. They are fitted with steel moldboard, steel landside and steel share, and are very durable and guaranteed against breakage when caused by manifest defect in workmanship or material. They have steel standard cap, sloping landside and adjustable slip heel. The one-horse plows are especially adapted for cotton and corn land and for gardening purposes. The two-horse plows are suitable for stubble and light sod plowing.

No. 32R155 One-Horse Steel Plow, 7-inch cut. Weight, 38 pounds. Price.......................**$2.03**

No. 32R156 One-Horse Plow, 8-inch cut. Weight, 43 pounds. Price.......................**$2.39**

No. 32R157 One-Horse or Light Two-Horse Plow, 9-inch cut. Weight, 47 pounds. Price...**$2.63**

No. 32R158 Two-Horse Plow, 10-inch cut. Weight, 63 pounds. Price.......................**$3.77**

No. 32R159 Two-Horse Plow, 11-inch cut. Weight, 69 pounds. Price....**$4.36**

All Steel, Steel Beam Pony Plows.

Extra Share furnished with each Plow.

No. 32R165 One-Horse Steel Plow, 7-inch cut. Weight, 60 pounds. Price.......................**$2.93**

No. 32R166 One-Horse Plow, 8-inch cut. Weight, 65 pounds. Price.......................**$3.32**

No. 32R167 One-Horse or Light Two-Horse Plow, 9-inch cut. Weight, 70 pounds. Price...**$3.71**

No. 32R168 Two-Horse Plow, 10-inch cut. Weight, 87 pounds. Price.......................**$4.68**

No. 32R169 Two-Horse Plow, 11-inch cut. Weight, 92 pounds. Price.......................**$5.20**

Extra Shares for Pony Plows.

No. 32R170 For 7-inch plow..........**22c**
No. 32R171 For 8-inch plow..........**29c**
No. 32R172 For 9-inch plow..........**35c**
No. 32R173 For 10-inch plow..........**42c**
No. 32R174 For 11-inch plow..........**51c**

Gauge Wheels and Fin Cutters, for Pony Plows.

No. 32R160 Gauge Wheel, complete. State whether for wood or steel beam. Price..........**52c**

No. 32R161 Fin Cutter, for 7-inch, 8-inch and 9-inch plows. Price..........**23c**

No. 32R162 Fin Cutter, for 10-inch and 11-inch plows. Price..........**31c**

Full Chilled Plows.

Sears, Roebuck & Co.'s Full Chilled Plows. Made on the same lines as the original Oliver Plows. These are general purpose plows and can be used anywhere that a chilled plow will work. As a sand soil plow they have no equal. **We always ship these plows right hand, unless otherwise ordered. Extra share furnished with each plow. Shipped direct from factory in Northern Indiana.**

No.		Turns furrow, inches	Depth of furrow	Weight, lbs.	Price
32R175	A Right hand only	8	4½	50	$3.83
32R176	B Right hand only	10	5	65	4.98
32R177	10 Right hand only	11	5½	70	5.63
32R178	13 Right or left.....	11	6	85	6.37
32R179	19 Right or left.....	12	6½	100	6.75
32R180	20 Right or left.....	14	7	112	7.13
32R181	E1 Right or left.....	14	7	120	7.48
32R182	40 Right or left.....	16	9	125	7.52
32R183	Price of jointer, extra..............				1.56
32R184	Lead wheel, extra....................				.81

NOTE—Jointer and lead wheel cannot be used on No. 32R175 or No. 32R176.

Prices of Repairs for Chilled Plows.

Be sure and state whether plow repairs are wanted to turn furrow to the right or to the left.

No.		Standard	Mold B'd.	Landside	Shares Plain
32R195	A Right.........	$1.01	$1.02	38c	22c
32R196	B Right.........	1.22	1.36	55c	23c
32R197	10 Right.........	1.56	1.57	59c	31c
32R198	13 Right or left.	1.75	1.76	63c	32c
32R199	19 Right or left.	1.77	1.95	81c	35c
32R200	20 Right or left.	1.78	2.14	82c	36c
32R201	E1 Right or left.	1.96	2.33	83c	37c
32R202	40 Right or left.	1.97	2.34	84c	38c
32R203	Jointer points............				18c

Hazel Brush Plows.

A light, strong and very serviceable all around wood beam plow. Has heavy iron strap under beam, extra heavy landside bar and strong joint on slip share. Share is made of strong, tough, good wearing solid steel. Moldboard is extra hardened soft center steel; turf and stubble shape and double shinned. **Easy to handle, and will stand the wear and tear of very heavy work.** Price is without cutter, gauge shoe or gauge wheel. **Shipped direct from factory in Northern Illinois.**

No. 32R204 11-in. cut. Weight, 80 lbs. Price, **$7.80**
No. 32R205 12-in. cut. Weight, 83 lbs. Price, **8.30**
No. 32R206 13-in. cut. Weight, 87 lbs. Price, **8.70**
No. 32R207 14-in. cut. Weight, 90 lbs. Price, **9.10**
No. 32R208 Reversible Cutter. Price...... **.81**
No. 32R209 Gauge Shoe for above. Price.. **.35**
No. 32R210 Gauge Wheel for above. Price. **.68**
No. 32R211 Extra Share for 11-inch plow.. **1.94**
No. 32R212 Extra Share for 12-inch plow.. **1.96**
No. 32R213 Extra Share for 13-inch plow.. **2.27**
No. 32R214 Extra Share for 14-inch plow.. **2.28**

Steel Beam Brush Plows.

We have here a DOUBLE STEEL BEAM PLOW THAT IS A WORLD BEATER when you have rough and rooty land to break up.

It is very strong, the beam being **double**, that is, made of two steel beams placed side by side. This makes a beam much more rigid than a solid piece of steel, also lighter. **It has an extra high curve,** which allows brush, etc., to pass through—cannot foul or choke up. **It also makes an excellent plow for road work;** in fact, is a first class, all around plow, where strength and durability are required. **The braces and handles are extra heavy.** In short, we have here a plow that will outlast any wood beam plow made. It does not weigh as much as some of the clumsy plows sold by other firms, and is warranted to give perfect satisfaction, or money refunded. **We show the plow rigged with wheel and foot coulter,** but furnish the wheel and coulter only as extras. Has steel moldboards, cast points and landside, and cuts 13 inches. Price includes one extra point. Weight, without wheel or coulter, 130 pounds. **Shipped direct from factory in Southeastern Wisconsin.**

No. 32R215 13-inch cut, without wheel or coulter. Price....................................**$8.75**
No. 32R217 Extra Gauge Wheels. Price.each **.70**
No. 32R218 Foot Coulters and Clasps. Each **1.40**
No. 32R219 Knife Coulters and Clasps. Each **.92**
No. 32R220 Extra Points. Each.......... **.33**

Acme Vineyard Plows.

Our Old Reliable One-Horse Combination Plow is the best plow made for nurseries, orchards, vineyards, and all one-horse work. The beam is adjustable so the horse can walk in the furrow or on the land. The handles can be shifted to right or left, which enables the plowman to walk away from the row of trees or shrubs. The shape of moldboard makes the plow light draft and also cleans out the furrow in loose soil. Will turn a furrow 8 inches to 12 inches wide and 3 inches to 8 inches deep. Made with chilled landside and point, and with either steel or chilled moldboard. Furnished with one extra point. **As a vineyard plow it is the finest made.** Weight, 80 pounds. **Shipped direct from factory in Western Michigan.** Price is for plow, without wheel or coulter.

No. 32R224 Price, with steel moldboard.. **$6.45**
No. 32R225 Price, with chilled moldboard.. **5.05**
No. 32R226 Gauge Wheel, each.............. **.74**
No. 32R227 Coulters, each.............. **1.08**
No. 32R228 Extra points, each.............. **.29**

Refer to Pages 7 to 10 For Freight Rates.

Acme Prairie Breaking Plows.

Our Prairie Breaker combines many desirable qualities. Its construction is light and strong; the beam is adjustable; the shape is as near perfection as can be made; it turns a flat furrow with great ease and without breaking the sod; it is made with solid bar share, which is far superior to those formerly used on breakers. Shares are made to duplicate on all breakers. The many desirable qualities of this plow cannot help but bring it into great favor. **Shipped direct from factory in Northern Illinois.**

No. 32R249 Size, 12 inches; weight, 100 pounds; complete with rolling coulter, gauge wheel and extra share. Price.......................**$9.85**

No. 32R250 Size, 14 inches; weight, 125 pounds; complete with rolling coulter, gauge wheel and extra share. Price.......................**$10.75**

No. 32R251 Size, 16 inches; weight, 140 pounds; complete with rolling coulter, gauge wheel and extra share. Price.......................**$12.00**

No. 32R252 Extra 12-inch share. Price..... **1.63**
No. 32R253 Extra 14-inch share. Price..... **1.95**
No. 32R254 Extra 16-inch share. Price..... **2.28**

Railroad and Township Plows.

These plows cut narrow and deep furrows and are of light draft. Strong beams, handles and standards, and all well braced. Points put on with heavy bolts, and easily taken off and replaced. Moldboards, landsides and points interchangable. Beams are heavily ironed top and bottom, and are complete with wrought iron clevis with two strong rings on end. Moldboard and shares are double shinned and are made of the best quality of plow steel. The steel cutters are reversible and very strong. Handles are strapped on both sides with heavy iron. Made right hand only. **Shipped direct from factory in Southwestern Ohio.**

No. 32R257 Township Size. Weight, 130 pounds. Price.......................**$15.30**

No. 32R258 For 2 to 4 horses. Weight, 150 pounds. Price.......................**$18.95**

No. 32R259 For 4 to 6 horses, Weight, 200 pounds. Price.......................**$19.80**

No. 32R260 For 6 to 8 horses. Weight, 300 pounds. Price.......................**$25.20**

No. 32R261 Extra share for Township size. Weight, 20 pounds. Price,..................**$2.50**

No. 32R262 Extra share for 2 to 4-horse size. Weight, 25 pounds. Price..................**$3.19**

No. 32R263 Extra share for 4 to 6-horse size. Weight, 30 pounds. Price..................**$3.83**

No. 32R264 Extra share for 6 to 8-horse size. Weight, 35 pounds. Price..................**$4.47**

Star Gauge Wheels.

Our Star Gauge Wheels can be set so as to always run straight with the plow, whether the plow is used with two or more horses, and so as not to run the plow in or out of land. All parts are made of malleable iron, combining lightness and strength. The post has a loose spindle and the wheel a loose bushing, both of which, when worn out, can be replaced at very small cost, saving the expense of new wheel or post. **Will fit all makes of plows,** either wood or steel beam. Weight, 9 pounds.

No. 32R392 Gauge Wheel complete. Price....**92c**

Star Jointers.

Our Star Jointers are the best and most convenient jointers made. They are supplied with a perfect and genuine reversible steel point, having three distinct or separate wearing points, giving as much wear as three separate points such as are used on other style jointers. Perfect adjustable features allow of these jointers being set as may be desired. All parts interchangeable. Moldboard and point made of the best quality wrought steel, forged out under a drop hammer. We carry right hand only. Will fit all makes of plows, either wood or steel beam. The hanging cutter attachment, shown in connection with our King Rolling Coulters, can be used in place of the jointer, if desired, bolting direct to the jointer seat. Weight, 13 pounds.

No. 32R396 Jointer complete. Price......**$1.42**
No. 32R397 Extra steel points. Each....... **.32**
No. 32R398 Extra chilled points. Each.... **.14**

King Rolling Coulters.

For ease of adjustment, simplicity and durability, these coulters are the best in the world. They are well braced above the arms and cannot break at that point as is the case with many other makes of coulters. The shifting only requires the loosening of one bolt for up, down or side shift. The arms are held on by a bolt above them. The hub has a new device for taking up the wear and will outwear the blade. These coulters will fit all makes of plows, either wood or steel beam. To the left of the cut we show our hanging cutter attachment, which may be used in place of the coulter, bolting to the same seat, and which will be found very desirable in some soils. This attachment is furnished only at extra price shown below. Weight of coulters, about 16 pounds each. Weight of cutter attachment, about 4 pounds.

No. 32R400 King 12-inch Coulter. Price.....$1.55
No. 32R401 King 13-inch Coulter. Price..... 1.69
No. 32R402 King 14-inch Coulter. Price..... 1.75
No. 32R403 Hanging Cutter Attachment. Price........ 1.05

Star Rolling Coulters.

Our Star Coulter can be attached to any make of plow, either right or left hand, wood or steel beam. Adjustable to run deep or shallow as well as to right or left, in the simplest manner possible, without releasing clamp on beam. No wedges used or holes to bore in beam. Has conical chilled hubs. "'Tis simply perfection." Prices low, best quality. This is the coulter that is receiving so much praise from both dealers and farmers. Weight, about 15 pounds.

No. 32R407 Star 12-inch Coulter. Price....$1.90
No. 32R408 Star 13-inch Coulter. Price.... 2.00
No. 32R409 Star 14-inch Coulter. Price.... 2.10

Tongueless Sulky Plow.

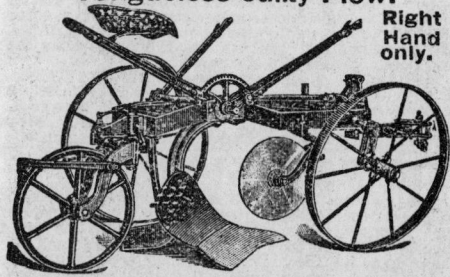

Right Hand only.

This Sulky Plow is a combination of strength and simplicity. It is built expressly for hard service; has direct beam hitch. Its three wheels are set at correct positions, so as to bring the weight true and on each alike. The front furrow wheel and the rear furrow wheel are locked square in line. They are operated with one foot trip, so that in turning they will both break from the direct line in which they are held and castor with the turn. The beam is very high in the throat, preventing clogging. The moldboard, landside and share are made of the best quality of soft center plow steel. The moldboard and share are double shinned and are tempered extra hard. Furnished complete with one set of tripletrees, one weed hook, one oil can, one wrench and a rolling coulter, or will furnish with jointer in place of rolling coulter if so ordered. The loose lever principle employed in this plow allows it to ride over stone without jarring the frame or operator, and obviating the danger of breakage, also insuring an even furrow bottom and a regular depth by allowing the frame to pass independently over rough and uneven places. This lever can be locked if desired. **In ordering, state whether you want stubble bottom or turf and stubble bottom.** Weight, about 510 pounds. Can be furnished with pole if so ordered. **Shipped direct from factory, which is near Chicago.**

No. 32R412 12-inch Sulky Plow. Price..$32.40
No. 32R413 14-inch Sulky Plow. Price.. 32.45
No. 32R414 16-inch Sulky Plow. Price.. 32.50
No. 32R415 12-inch Steel Share. Price.. 2.27
No. 32R416 14-inch Steel Share. Price.. 2.56
No. 32R417 16-inch Steel Share. Price.. 2.87

Wing Shovel Plow.

This is an admirable plow for hilling potatoes, etc. It is a single shovel plow with **adjustable steel wings**, which can be let out to any desired angle by means of punched spread rods. It is sometimes convenient to work these plows with but one wing, which can readily be done, or the two wings can be worked simultaneously at different angles. Weight, 35 pounds.

No. 32R420 Wing Shovel Plow. Price....$1.95

Acme Walking Gang Plow.

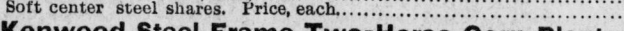

RIGHT HAND ONLY.

In the Acme Walking Gang Plow we have the best plow ever offered for anything like what we ask for it. It is a well made, practical plow, warranted to do good work. We claim this plow will skin sod from 1½ to 3 inches deep. **Will plow corn land** or oat stubble from 2 to 7 inches deep. Will cut and turn under all June grass on summer fallow, and do better work than any other plow on the market. Will prepare wheat and oat stubble for winter wheat in less than half the time required by a single plow or cultivator. While this plow will do good work in most parts of the country, we do not recommend it as a prairie breaker or on corn land where the stalks have not been cut. **Compare the price with a single plow** and you will see you are getting **three** plows for less than the price of two. Has three 9-inch plows, cutting 27 inches. Gangs with chilled shares are furnished with one extra set of shares. Weight, 300 pounds. **Shipped direct from factory in Western Michigan.**

No. 32R422 With chilled moldboard, landside and chilled shares. Price............$16.25
No. 32R423 With soft center steel moldboard, chilled landside and chilled shares. Price.. 18.00
No. 32R424 With soft center steel moldboard, chilled landside and cast steel shares. Price.. 18.90
No. 32R425 With soft center steel moldboard, landside and shares. Price........ 23.40
No. 32R426 Chilled shares. Price, each........ .24
No. 32R427 Cast steel shares. Price, each........ 1.08
No. 32R428 Soft center steel shares. Price, each........ 1.43

Kenwood Steel Frame Two-Horse Corn Planter.

Constructed entirely of steel and wrought iron, malleable and charcoal iron castings, and will outwear any other two-horse corn planter made. It is a full hill combination planter. Can be used either as a hand drop drill planter, or a check rower planter by only changing the plates. The drill is adjusted to different positions by changing the chain on different size sprocket wheels on the axle without changing plates; it will drop regularly one grain every 12, 16 or 20 inches apart. The frame is coupled close, giving the driver full and easy control. The forcing lever is attached to the two hounds which are placed at an equal distance from the runners, so that both runners are forced into the soil at equal depth. The drop is simple and sure. The succeeding hills drop down separate channels and are held at the heel of the runner for prompt deposit when check rower is operated. **Combination hand and foot lever is furnished** so that the planter can be rigidly set to the desired depth, or can be run flexible and under easy control of the driver's feet, allowing him the full use of his hands for taking care of team. The check rower is one of few parts, not complicated. One side always at rest. Stroke positive every time button passes through fork. Forks are made of soft center steel, carefully hardened, and are wide enough apart to prevent kinks in wire from making a stroke. Has automatic winding reel for laying out the wire and for rewinding when field is complete. The wire can be released by the driver pulling a cord without leaving seat. The wire is of the finest quality, and with ordinary care will last many years. Standard width, adjustable for 3-foot 6-inch and 3-foot 8-inch. Price includes three sets of hill plates and three sets of drill plates. Does not include eveners or neckyoke. Furnished regularly with concave wheels, but will furnish with flat wheels at same price, if so ordered. Open wheels will be furnished at 75 cents extra. **Shipped direct from factory in Southwestern Ohio.**

No. 32R500 **Corn Planter without check rower.** Weight, 400 pounds. Price........$21.60
No. 32R501 **Corn Planter with check rower,** automatic reel and 80 rods of wire, complete. Weight, 500 pounds........$29.70
No. 32R502 **Corn Planter with fertilizer attachment,** but without check rower. Weight, 450 pounds. Price........$33.60
No. 32R503 **Corn Planter with fertilizer attachment, check rower,** automatic reel and 80 rods of wire, complete. Weight, 550 pounds. Price........$40.90
No. 32R504 Extra check rower wire, per rod........ .05
No. 32R505 Extra plates, per pair........ .42
No. 32R506 Clod Fenders and Covering Hoes. Price, per set........ 2.55

Kenwood Steel Frame One-Horse Corn Drill, Cotton Planter and Fertilizer Distributor.

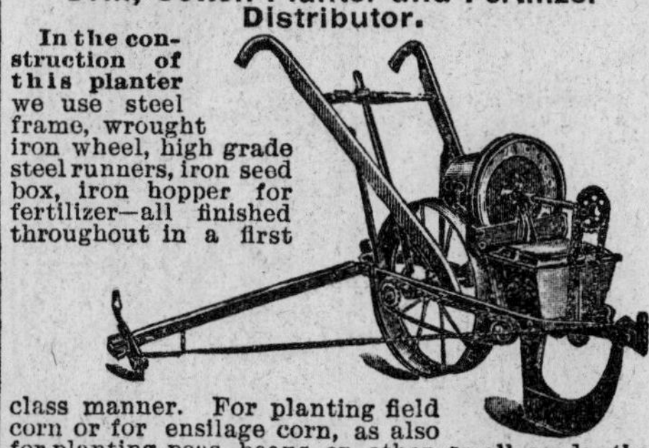

In the construction of this planter we use steel frame, wrought iron wheel, high grade steel runners, iron seed box, iron hopper for fertilizer—all finished throughout in a first class manner. For planting field corn or for ensilage corn, as also for planting peas, beans or other small seeds, the Kenwood is unequaled. It drops 12, 15, 18 and up to 24 inches apart, the distance being governed by number of holes in seed plates. The lever for throwing in and out of gear is near the operator; it can be changed without stopping horse. All wearing parts are large and true; there is no complicated machinery about the machine. Price includes three regular plates and one blank plate, also the marker, but does not include whiffletree or marker rope. Extra plates can be furnished to drop from 2 inches to 4 feet apart, and thick plates to drop more than one kernel at a time. Can also furnish extra plates to plant broom corn, pop corn, beans, peas, beet seed, sorghum, millet, etc.

The Fertilizer Distributor is simple and positive, no delicate gears to get out of order; there are no slides or wheels to gum or clog. Fertilizer attachment is a drill drop, not a hill drop. Must be ordered with the drill as it cannot be attached except at factory. It is the most simple and perfect planter made. Shipped direct from factory in Southwestern Ohio.

No. 32R508 **Corn Drill only.** Weight, 100 pounds. Price........$8.75
No. 32R509 **Corn Drill with fertilizer attachment.** Weight, 125 pounds. Price........$11.00
No. 32R510 Extra plates. Price, each........ .24

We can furnish this drill with our pick feed cotton planting attachment, if ordered with the drill. Cannot be attached except at factory.

No. 32R511 Pick Feed Cotton Planting Attachment. Price........$2.80

Our $4.35 Cotton Planter.

This is a perfect, reliable and very desirable cotton planter, and one which has had a tremendous sale in the great cotton belt of the south. It is made of first class materials throughout, has a large hopper, a splendid agitator and a perfect feed regulating device. Center shovel is strong and cannot break. Driving wheel is made of wood, 16 inches in diameter, 3 inches thick and beveled to run in the trench made by the shovel. The coverer is supported by steel springs, which allows it to adjust itself to the condition of the ground and relieves the hands of all jarring. **This machine is also a first class fertilizer distributor as well as a cotton planter,** requiring no extra parts, and by adding the corn planting attachment it makes a splendid corn drill, dropping the kernels about 24 inches apart. Shipped direct from factory in Southwestern Ohio.

No. 32R512 **Cotton Planter only.** Weight, 65 pounds. Price........$4.35
No. 32R513 Corn Planting Attachment extra. Weight, 5 pounds. Price........80c

We can always furnish repairs for our implements at any time at the lowest prices. See notice on first page of this department.

Our Kenwood Steel Frame Disc Harrow.

In the manufacture of the Kenwood Disc Harrow, extreme care is exercised to the end that no inferior piece of material is made use of. Every part and piece is carefully examined and tested to see that the proper strength is contained in the material used, and every purchaser of a Kenwood Disc Harrow may feel assured that the machine is first class in every particular and is carefully made, from start to finish. The frame is made of $1\frac{1}{2}$x$1\frac{1}{2}$x$\frac{3}{16}$-inch angle steel pieces, having strength to withstand any test that the harrow may be put to. The axles are made of 1-inch square steel, every one being thoroughly tested before being placed in the machine. The discs have square holes to accommodate the axle, as also do the spools, so they all together form a solid piece, making it impossible for the discs to become loose on the axle. **The boxings are made on correct principles and are arranged to make the machine the lightest draft possible.** They are made in three parts, easy to adjust, and dust and dirt cannot accumulate in them. There is no wear on the boxings at the end, because we allow the gangs to come together at an angle, with all pressure against the buffer washers; no pressure on the boxings. There is no draft from the frame; the draft is entirely from the axles, four draft rods being attached directly in front of the boxings.

Eveners and whiffletrees are furnished free with all machines. Unlesss otherwise ordered harrows with 8, 10 or 12 discs will be furnished with 2-horse hitch, harrows with 14 discs will have 3-horse hitch, and harrows with 16 discs will have 4-horse hitch, but we will furnish either 3 or 4-horse hitch with any size, if so ordered. Price is for harrow complete as described, and with single lever. **Shipped direct from factory in Southwestern Ohio.**

No.	Discs		Width of Cut	Weight	Price
	No.	Diam.			
73R685...	8	16-inch	$4\frac{1}{2}$-feet	315 lbs.	$14.35
73R686...	10	16-inch	$5\frac{1}{2}$-feet	340 lbs.	15.55
73R687...	12	16-inch	$6\frac{1}{2}$-feet	370 lbs.	16.75
73R688...	14	16-inch	$7\frac{1}{2}$-feet	395 lbs.	17.95
73R689...	16	16-inch	$8\frac{1}{2}$-feet	445 lbs.	19.15
73R690...	10	18-inch	$5\frac{1}{2}$-feet	375 lbs.	18.00
73R691...	12	18-inch	$6\frac{1}{2}$-feet	405 lbs.	19.20
73R692...	14	18-inch	$7\frac{1}{2}$-feet	440 lbs.	20.40
73R693...	16	18-inch	$8\frac{1}{2}$-feet	495 lbs.	21.60
73R694...	10	20-inch	$5\frac{1}{2}$-feet	400 lbs.	19.25
73R695...	12	20-inch	$6\frac{1}{2}$-feet	435 lbs.	20.45
73R696...	14	20-inch	$7\frac{1}{2}$-feet	465 lbs.	21.65
73R697...	16	20-inch	$8\frac{1}{2}$-feet	530 lbs.	22.85

For Double Lever Harrow add 75 cents.

Our Improved Disc Harrow with Seeder Attachment.

This Improved Disc Harrow with seeder attachment has the same features as is found in drills, except that the seed is scattered broadcast in front of the blades where it is covered. **It has a perfect force feed, which is a very essential feature; it is driven from both sections, and the drive chain is always in line; the driver sits where he can see at all times whether the seeds are discharged properly;** it has a perfect index, showing the quantity sown to the acre; has a covering hoe in the center, back of and between the center discs; **it is nicely and substantially put up in every way. The harrow is our regular Kenwood Steel Frame Disc Harrow.**

Please note that the seeder can be taken off and the disc used as a separate machine, giving you two perfect machines in one, or that one-half of seeder can be removed and the other half used. Shipped direct from factory in Southwestern Ohio.

No. 32R700 Disc Harrow Seeder, with 12 16-inch discs. Weight, 550 pounds. Price............**$31.50**

No. 32R703 Disc Harrow Seeder, with 12 18-inch discs. Weight, 595 pounds. Price............**$33.90**

No. 32R706 Disc Harrow Seeder, with 12 20-inch discs. Weight, 635 pounds. Price............**$35.15**

Mower and Reaper Sections.

We are prepared to furnish the very best quality of mower and reaper sections, as listed below, put up in boxes of 20 sections, including 40 rivets for same, a few of the rivets being long for use under the knife head. These sections are of standard make, and are perfect in every respect. We do not furnish sections other than those we list, nor do we break boxes or furnish rivets separately. Price is for box of 20 sections, including rivets. When ordering, give catalogue number and full description, and send paper pattern of old section, showing size of section and location of rivet holes.

No. 32R715 Smooth Mower Sections, as below. Price, per box of 20 sections, with rivets............**70c**

- Buckeye, 3x$3\frac{3}{8}$, low punch, used from 1879 to 1894.
- Buckeye, 3x$3\frac{3}{8}$, high punch, used 1895 and since.
- Buckeye (Adriance), 3x$3\frac{3}{16}$, used on all mowers 1883 and since.
- Champion, 3x$3\frac{3}{16}$, used on draw cut mowers 1899 and since.
- Champion, 3x$3\frac{5}{16}$, used on new mower or Haymaker.
- Champion, 3x$3\frac{9}{16}$, used on mower 1893 to 1899.
- Deering, 3x$3\frac{1}{4}$, used on all mowers since 1889.
- Empire, 3x$3\frac{3}{8}$, used on all mowers.
- Standard or Emerson, 3x$3\frac{1}{8}$, used on all mowers.
- Red, White and Blue, 3x$3\frac{1}{8}$, used on all mowers.
- Knowlton, 3x$3\frac{5}{16}$, used on all mowers.
- McCormick, 3x$3\frac{3}{16}$, used on all mowers since 1888.
- Milwaukee, 3x$3\frac{1}{8}$, used on all mowers.
- Osborne, 3x3, low punch, used on all mowers prior to 1893.
- Osborne, 3x3, high punch, used on all mowers since 1894.
- Plano, 3x$3\frac{1}{8}$, used on all mowers since 1887.
- Wood, 3x$3\frac{1}{8}$, used on all enclosed gear and tubular 1900 mowers.
- Wood, 3x$2\frac{5}{8}$, used on all tubular mowers prior to 1899.
- Ann Arbor Advance, $2\frac{1}{2}$x$3\frac{1}{4}$, used since 1882.

No. 32R720 Serrated Reaper Sections, as below. Price, per box of 20 sections, with rivets............**72c**

- Buckeye, 3x$2\frac{1}{2}$, used on all frameless binders.
- Champion, 3x$2\frac{5}{8}$ (notched), used on all binders since 1882.
- Deering, $3\frac{1}{8}$x$2\frac{1}{8}$, used on all improved steel binders.
- Deering, $3\frac{1}{8}$x$2\frac{5}{16}$, used on all Pony binders.
- Milwaukee, $3\frac{1}{8}$x$2\frac{5}{16}$, used on all binders since 1890.
- Minneapolis, $3\frac{1}{8}$x$2\frac{7}{16}$, used on all binders since 1883.
- McCormick, 3x$2\frac{1}{8}$, used on all binders since 1879.
- Osborne, 3x$2\frac{1}{4}$, used on all binders since 1878.
- Plano, 3x$2\frac{3}{16}$, used on all binders since 1884.

The Farmers' Delight Disc Sharpener.

A simple and practical device for sharpening and polishing disc harrows and disc cultivators. Any disc harrow can be sharpened and polished without taking discs apart. It is made entirely of steel, and the only one manufactured using an emery block to polish and put a razor edge on the disc. The knife is made of very best tool steel, and can be sharpened on any grindstone.

No. 32R725 Disc Sharpener. Price.......**$1.25**

No. 32R726 Extra cutter knives. Price, each **22c**

Our Boss Sickle Grinder.

This implement comprises a first class grindstone with sickle grinder attachment, and as either is worth double its cost. The cost of it is a trifle more than the ordinary grindstone and it will answer for all purposes. **The stone is accurately centered, hung true, and does perfect work.** The diameter of the stone is 18 inches; it is $2\frac{3}{4}$ inches thick and the complete outfit weighs 112 pounds.

No. 32R728 Boss Sickle Grinder. Price............**$3.63**

Kenwood Disc Sharpener.

Greatly improved for this season. Back geared, most powerful machine of the kind made, saves its cost in sharpening one or two machines. For sharpening disc harrows and cultivators. A bonanza for blacksmiths, a money maker for the dealer. Will sharpen discs from 12 to 20 inches diameter. Our perfect centering device will center accurately any disc. Most convenient and practical disc sharpener made. There is no chattering or jumping of the cutter. One cutter will sharpen one dozen sets of discs. Has our improved roller carrier for the disc. The double gear makes the disc revolve slowly, and gives twice the power of other machines. We can furnish a pully 10x$2\frac{1}{2}$ inches so that the sharpener can be run by power.

No. 32R731 Kenwood Disc Sharpener. Weight, 40 pounds. Price............**$2.55**

No. 32R732 Pulley for power. Weight, 10 pounds. Price............**84c**

No. 32R733 Extra cutter knives. Price, each, **23c**

OUR $5.49 KENWOOD ENDGATE BROADCAST SEEDER.

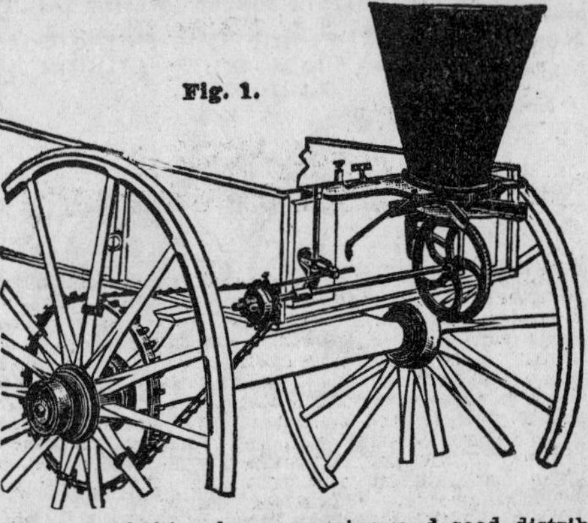

Fig. 1.

This seeder is so well known that it scarcely needs a description. It will be found in the store of nearly every implement dealer, and the dealer would charge you from $8.00 to $10.00 for the machine. We have made a large contract for these seeders and now offer them to our customers at a small advance over what we pay for them, simply adding our one small percentage of profit to the actual factory cost. Our selling price is lower than the dealer must pay for this seeder and our customers get the benefit of our buying in large quantities.

Figure 1 shows the seeder as it appears when attached to the end of the wagon and ready for use. The large sprocket wheel attaches to the left hind wheel of the wagon, being secured by two spoke clips and two hook bolts, which we furnish. The driving chain is No. 34 link belting, 10 feet long, running onto a sprocket wheel which is fitted with a spring clutch, so that in starting there is no sudden jar or strain on the gearing.

Figure 2 is a rear view of the seeder, showing plainly the arrangement of the main shaft, spring clutch, small sprocket wheel, shifting lever, gearing and seed distributor.

Figure 3 is a top view of the seeder with hopper removed, showing the cut-off slides, the stirring pin and shaft cap, the seed openings and the lever which adjusts the size of these openings. The feeding device of this machine consists of two steel plates, each having two square holes the full size of the feed opening punched in them.

Fig. 3.

Fig. 2.

These plates are connected by links, which cause the plates to move in opposite directions. They are actuated by a single lever which moves in a graduated segment, as shown in the top view of the sower. Moving the lever in one direction closes the openings through which the seed is discharged on the distributor, and moving it in the other direction opens them. Directions, which are attached to the sower, indicate at what point to set the lever in order to sow any desired quantity of seed per acre. This machine will sow 100 acres of wheat per day, with team traveling at the rate of two and one-half miles per hour. Other kinds of grain or seed at the proportionate rates. It will sow perfectly any kind of grain or seeds when they are properly cleaned and at any desired amount per acre. It will also sow fertilizers, salt, lime, ashes, etc.

THE WIDTH OF CAST IS AS FOLLOWS:

Wheat............	from 36 to 40 feet wide	Clover............	from 14 to 16 feet wide
Barley, rye and rice............	from 30 to 34 feet wide	Hungarian and millet............	from 12 to 14 feet wide
Oats............	from 28 to 32 feet wide	Timothy............	from 12 to 14 feet wide
Flax............	from 20 to 24 feet wide	Plaster, salt, etc............	from 16 to 20 feet wide

The end board and the main shaft of the Kenwood Endgate Broadcast Seeder are each made long enough so that the machine can be used on either a wide or narrow track wagon, or a wide or narrow bed. **In other words, the Kenwood is universally adapted for all wagons,** and for all classes of broadcast sowing. Price is for the seeder delivered free on board cars at the factory in Southeastern Wisconsin.

No. 73R800 Endgate Seeder, complete. Weight, 100 pounds. Price............**$5.49**

Hand Grass Seed Strippers.

King's Kentucky Blue Grass Strippers. Just the thing for gathering grass seed. The blades are made of English steel, strong and durable; will last a lifetime. Twenty bushels of seed can be gathered in a day with one of these machines. No farmer should be without one.

Weight, 4 pounds.

No. 32R1050 Seed Stripper. Price........................**$1.30**

The Little Giant Steel Bow Broadcast Hand Seed Sower.

With this seeder, when properly used, you can distribute wheat 56 feet to a round, flax seed 36 feet, clover seed 36 feet, timothy 27 feet, oats 36 feet. It will also sow rye, barley, millet, hungarian corn or any grain or seed that can be sown broadcast. This seeder has a light centrifugal wheel at bottom, 11 inches in diameter, that is revolved rapidly in opposite directions by means of a bow, scattering the seed with great velocity. Weight, 3 lbs.

No. 32R1055 Bow Seed Sower. Price........**98c**

Acme Seed Sower.

The Acme comprises a solid malleable iron frame to which the few parts are attached, making it therefore absolutely impossible to get out of order from ordinary usage. The distributer is superior to all others and not used on any other machine. A great feature of this machine is that the crank can be used either on the right or left side, therefore enabling either a right or left handed operator to use it with ease. It will sow wheat, rye, oats, barley, rice, flax, millet, turnip seed, clover and all kinds of grasses, in fact, all seeds sown broadcast. Also fertilizer, ashes, salt, etc. It will sow wheat or rye 50 feet at a round; buckwheat, 45 feet; flax, clover, timothy and millet, 30 to 36 feet; grass seeds, from 15 to 30 feet. Other seeds, etc., owing to their nature and condition. Full directions with each machine. Weight, 3½ pounds.

No. 32R1056 Acme Seed Sower. Price........**83c**

Little Giant Geared Hand Seeder.

This is one of the best known, as well as best made hand seeders in the market. Has a pressed tin distributing wheel, and lathe centered gears held rigid by a malleable iron frame, not found in any other sower; will sow timothy, clover, oats, barley, buckwheat, etc., in fact, **any kind of seed that can be broadcasted.** Will sow 60 acres of wheat or 65 acres of clover seed in a day of ten hours. Weight, 4 pounds.

No. 32R1057 Geared Seeder. Price.......**$1.29**

The Granger Seeder.

The Granger Broadcast Hand Seeder, for sowing all kinds of grain and grass seeds, sows on an average of six acres per hour at a common walking gait. The bag and hopper will hold about 22 quarts.

Weight, 5½ pounds.

No. 32R1058 Granger Seeder. Price........**$1.90**

Our Wheelbarrow Grass Seeder.

Our New Kenwood Wheelbarrow Grass Seeder is made for sowing all kinds of clover and grass seed, alfalfa, hungarian, millet, flax, etc., and is put up by experienced workmen out of good material. It has a light iron wheel with a wide tire, a light, strong frame and will sow all these seeds evenly and accurately, either mixed or separate, in any quantity required per acre. When winds prevail this style of seeder is a great success; they can be used by any man or boy and will sow 25 to 50 acres per day. They sow absolutely perfect and our new seeder has many improvements over anything else in the market. We pack these securely for long shipments. Weight, packed for shipment, 50 pounds. Shipped direct from factory in Southern Michigan.

No. 32R1065 12-foot Wheelbarrow Seeder. Price........................**$5.00**
No. 32R1066 14-foot Wheelbarrow Seeder. Price........................**$5.32**
No. 32R1067 16-foot Wheelbarrow Seeder. Price........................**$5.64**

Star Corn Shock Compresser.

One man can do the work of two with our Star Corn Shock Compresser. No farmer can afford to be without one. You simply place the supporting hook in shock as shown in cut. Pass the binding twine through the loop in the supporting hook. Take the end of rope with ring on and also the end of twine and walk around the shock. Place the ring on small hook at end of compresser. Then pull on the loose end of the rope until the shock is drawn as tight as you wish. Then by drawing the rope away from the shock the compresser will grip the rope and hold it, while you tie the twine. To remove compresser draw the rope toward the shock and the grip will loosen. It can then be easily removed to the next shock. Weight, 2¼ pounds.

No. 32R1080 Corn Shock Compresser. Price, **66c**

Acme Patent Corn Binder.

Strongest and best tie made for corn, grain and bags. The rope will last from three to five years. The hook will last a lifetime. All complete and ready for use, and is by far the cheapest and best. Cheaper than straw. Put up in packages of 100 ties. We cannot sell less than 100.

No. 32R1082 Corn Binders. Price, per 100..**70c**

Potato Planters.

With these planters potatoes can be planted better and cheaper than by any other method. Simple, strong, durable and easy to operate. At one operation the holes are made, seed dropped and covered. Plants uniformly any depth desired. The seed is always deposited in moist earth, which will therefore give sure and quick growth.

When planted with these planters the crop can be tilled so as to keep the surface of the ground level, which is an advantage in dry seasons. It is impossible to pick up the seed with this planter. Plants three acres a day. The receptacles of both planters are made on the same principle, but the tube planter conveys the seed to the receptacle so there is no stooping or lifting the planter to the hand.

No. 32R1090 Stick Planter. Weight, 3 pounds. Price........................**63c**
No. 32R1091 Tube Planter. Weight, 4¾ pounds. Price........................**91c**

Segment Corn and Bean Planter.

This is a perfect one-hand corn and bean planter. It is extremely accurate. The slide is a segment of a circle having its center where the jaws are pivoted together—in other words, the pivots on which the jaws open and shut are the hub of a wheel of which the slide is a part of the rim—so there is no friction nor lost motion. The seed box and hopper are galvanized iron, the brush is genuine Chinese bristles, and the working parts are pressed or stamped out of sheet steel, which makes them light, strong and accurate. All parts are interchangeable. Weight, 4¼ pounds.

No. 32R1092 Segment Planter. Price.......**90c**

Masters' Rapid Plant Setter.

The only hand mechanical plant setter on the market; is built on scientific principles throughout. Its conical jaws are made of heavy sheet steel, and the main body or water reservoir and plant tube of heavy tinned plate. The water valve is of brass with rubber packing. The valve rod and trip spring are of steel wire; thumb button and other fittings are also of brass. The machine is well put together with rivets and solder, and will last for years. **No stooping when using it. All kinds of plants, such as cabbage, tobacco, tomato, cauliflower, strawberries, sweet potato, sugar beets, etc., are set, watered and covered at one operation.** The roots are deposited below the surface where the ground is cool and damp. You never have to wait for a shower; plants may be safely set out when large enough regardless of weather—no matter how dry and dusty the ground may be. **Every farmer and truck grower should have one.** Use **liquid fertilizer** to set with if possible. This will insure a quick start and a strong growth. Printed instructions for making and using home made liquid fertilizer at no cost but your own work to prepare it, sent free with each plant setter; also full directions how to operate, goes out with every machine. Weight, when empty, 4½ pounds.

No. 32R1095 Plant Setter. Price.........**$3.25**

Triumph Corn Planter.

Triumph Hand Corn Planters are adapted to all sorts of soil, never clog, and the operator can **see the corn deposited** in the ground. They are the most durable planter on the market, all working parts being malleable iron and the blades steel. Can be used on sod or plowed ground. Weight, 4½ pounds.

No. 32R1097 Triumph Planter. Price.......**56c**
No. 32R1098 Triumph Planter with pumpkin seed attachment. Price........................**76c**

The Eclipse Hand Corn Planter.

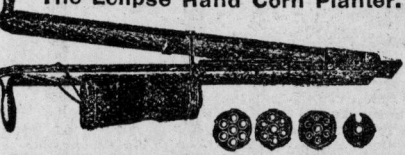

The Eclipse Corn Planter has given unequaled satisfaction during several seasons. It eclipses all others, has a positive feed and four changes of discs. It is extremely simple and works much easier than other styles. Weight, 8 pounds.

No. 32R1100 Eclipse Planter. Price.........**67c**

Harvester Canvas Tighteners.

As a harvester canvas tightener, this device has no equal. The prongs of the hook engage with the buckle, the end of the lever is put through one of the holes in the strap, and it is then a very easy matter to draw the canvas tight and buckle it. Will be found convenient for many other purposes. Weight, 5 ounces.

No. 32R1145 Canvas Tightener. Price......**16c**

Kenwood Anti-Jolt Seat Spring.

This Seat Spring consists of an iron frame which bolts to the seat standard of the machine to which the seat spring is attached, this frame having a slotted hole so that proper adjustment can be made. Another frame, to which the seat attaches, is suspended above by eight strong coil springs. The whole is constructed as lightly as is consistent with ample strength. **Can be applied to all kinds of farm machinery, wagons, carts, etc.** Will fit any seat, and will be found a very desirable article, adding comfort to the operation of the machine. Weight, 10 pounds.

No. 32R1147 Seat Spring. Price...........**$1.69**

The Sears, Roebuck & Co.'s Iron Mower.

Perfect floating and rocking bar, cutter bar carried on wheels, no weight on horses' neck, perfect tilting device, perfect foot lever and lifting spring, wonderful strength.

We spare no expense that is necessary to make our Iron Mower the best. Long experience, careful study and expensive experimenting, we believe, justify us in saying that we know what is necessary to make **a strictly first class mowing machine.** This we manufacture, and do not make or offer for sale a low grade mower.

The frame is cast in one piece, with the bearings for the shafting cast on it and made heavy enough to secure the requisite strength and stiffness to fully guard against breakages.

The gears are the fewest in number possible, and are completely covered, so that at all times they are protected from dust and dirt, and will never wear out if the bearings are properly oiled.

The pitman is attached to the knife by a ball and socket, so that all wear can be taken up. The cutter bar is **"all right"** and provision for taking up all wear of the knives is made. **Steel guard plates are used,** which can be ground without being removed from the guards. The pitman lines up with the knives. The weight of cutter bar is carried on wheels. The foot lever works very easily. No side draft. **We make but one size, 4½-foot cut.** Price includes one extra sickle. Weighs 750 pounds. **Shipped direct from factory in Southern Michigan.**

No. 32R1150 Iron Mower. Price........**$33.50**

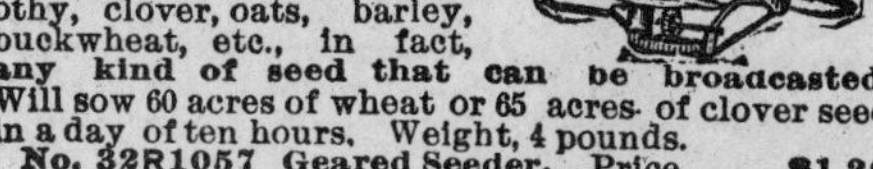

Our $11.90 Kenwood Hand Dump Hay Rake.

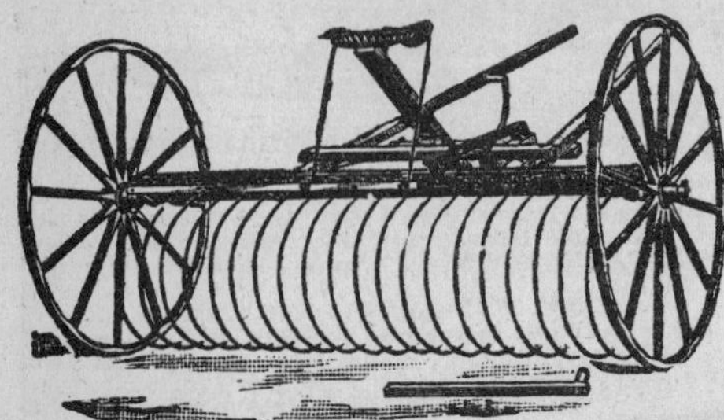

Our Kenwood is a strictly high grade hay rake, the equal of rakes that retail at double the price. This is a good substantial rake, extra strong, 20-tooth, 8-foot, made with steel wheels. The wheels are attached by malleable iron holders, the teeth are fastened by a separate bolt, constructed and shaped so as to glide under the hay. The teeth raise high when dumping and drop the entire quantity of hay gathered. Any child, old enough to drive, can operate it. **The rake is made by one of the best makers in this country. Made of the highest grade malleable iron,** seasoned hardwood and steel, highest grade wrought spindles, easily adjusted for any variety of crop or service. The shafts are hinged so that the draft of the horse assists in discharging the hay; no effort required to move the lock lever. Price includes singletree. **Shipped direct from factory in Southwestern Ohio.**

No. 32R1160 8-foot, 20-tooth rake. Weight, 270 pounds. Price............................**$11.90**

Combined Hand and Foot Dump Hay Rakes.

Similar to our Kenwood Hand Dump Rakes, but with teeth coiled at base and arranged so that teeth can be depressed and held firmly down to a position which will rake effectually matted and tangled grass. All with steel wheels. 8-foot rake is with shafts only; 10-foot and 12-foot rakes with combination pole and shafts. Price includes singletree. **Shipped direct from factory in Southwestern Ohio.**

No. 32R1161 8-foot, 20-tooth rake. Weight, 280 pounds. Price,..................................**$14.65**

No. 32R1162 10-foot, 25-tooth rake. Weight, 315 pounds. Price,..................................**$15.85**

No. 32R1163 12-foot, 30-tooth rake. Weight, 340 pounds. Price,..................................**$17.75**

Acme Umbrella Holder.

Every farmer should have our Acme Umbrella Holder; can be attached to any mower, harvester, land roller, etc. One hot day in the field will more than pay for it. Price given below is for holder only. Weight, 2 pounds.

No. 32R1164 Umbrella Holder. Price, 38c

Easy Self Dump Hay Rakes.

These Rakes are models of simplicity and neatness, though light and strong, and the most durable rake on the market, and we claim, the most perfect rake to work, the easiest to ride, the lightest draft and the simplest to operate. **Our patent sled runner tooth,** which prevents the rake from scratching or taking up grass roots, is connected to the rake head by metal tooth sections, carrying 5 and 6 teeth each and the same can be put on or taken out one section at a time. **The rake dumps from both wheels,** each ratchet being encased, which prevents the wheel from winding with hay; is noiseless in operation and drops back without the least jar. **The dumping device is engaged by pressing the foot on the lever;** the rake in operation, is entirely under the control of the operator by our improved foot treadle when raking rough or uneven ground. **The cleaners or strippers** are each oscillating independent of each other, and hold the hay from rolling when the rake is filling; prevents the same from sliding into the wheels. **Our seat is one of great comfort,** arranged upon an easy steel spring, adjustable to accommodate either a small boy or a man, and arranged at a point of balance which prevents weight upon the horse's back. Furnished with combination pole and shafts. **Shipped direct from factory to user.**

No. 32R1165 20-tooth, steel wheel rake, 8 feet. Weight, 350 pounds. Price..............................**$17.15**

No. 32R1167 25-tooth, steel wheel rake, 10 feet. Weight, 385 pounds. Price..............................**$18.80**

Revolving Hay Rake.

This Rake is simple in construction, strong and durable. Made from the best material that can be procured. **Always under the control of the driver.** It is held down firmly by the cross piece on the two center teeth. When ready to dump, raise the handle and it dumps easily. When dumped, there is a steel spring on either side to catch and hold it in place. For the money asked, we claim it to be the best rake made. Head is 9 feet long, and has 14 hickory teeth. **Weight, 65 pounds. Shipped direct from factory in Southwestern Indiana.**

No. 32R1170 Rake, with round teeth. Price.**$3.00**

No. 32R1171 Rake, with square teeth. Price. **3.32**

Acme Hay Tedders.

The tedder forks are made of the **very best quality crucible spring steel on our peculiar pattern, and** the shape and sweep of the forks are just right to do perfect work. **The convenient shifting device has two levers,** one for raising and lowering frame, the other for throwing in and out of gear, which can be used easily without dismounting. Six-fork machine furnished with combination pole and shafts, **for one** or two horses. Eight-fork machine, with pole **only,** for two horses. Weight, 450 pounds. **Shipped direct from factory in Southern Michigan.**

No. 32R1175 6-fork tedder, 8 feet. Price, **$22.30**

No. 32R1176 8-fork tedder, 10 feet. Price, **24.55**

Our $31.20 Kenwood Hay Loader.

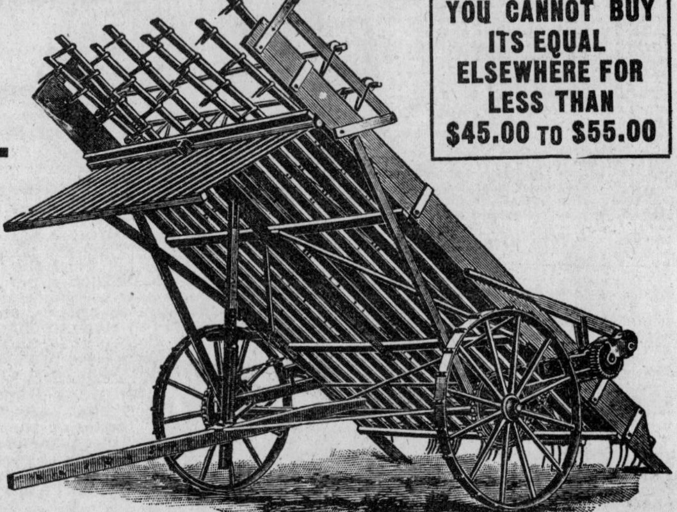

YOU CANNOT BUY ITS EQUAL ELSEWHERE FOR LESS THAN $45.00 TO $55.00

FOR $31.20 WE OFFER THIS HAY LOADER with the assurance that its possession **will place its owner in the best position for taking care of his hay crop in the most economical manner. We furnish you this loader for $31.20, a price much lower than these loaders can be purchased for even by the wholesale trade.** We have a special contract for a very large number of these loaders, and have been fortunate in purchasing them at a figure which enables us to save our customers a large amount of money.

THESE LOADERS embody all the essential principles necessary to make them the most practical machine on the market. They have been built and sold under the manufacturer's name for several years, and have been proven to be equal to any loader made in this country. **Special care is used in the construction of these machines to have every** part made strong and durable, and suitable for the special work which each part has to do. The great advantage of a hay loader over loading by hand, is the quickness with which the hay can be gathered, which feature is at all times appreciated, but which is especially good in showery weather.

THESE LOADERS will take from the swath all kinds of hay. Though we do not recommend them for work in swampy land for the loading of heavy marsh hay, and while the loaders will do very nice work under anything like reasonable circumstances, it is of course understood by every farmer that where the hay is very fine and light, it might sometimes be found necessary to rake the hay into light windrows. We say light windrows, because no loader will do good work in loading from heavy windrows.

THE LOADER IS OPERATED WITH A CRANK SHAFT, driven direct from the sprocket wheels attached to the wheels of the loader by malleable iron detachable link belting. Attached to the crank shaft are fork or rake arms at the lower end of which rakes, each with six tines, are attached. Along the under side of each of the arms there are small carrying forks, which carry the hay to the top of the loader, from which it is delivered to the wagon. **Levers** are attached to each end of the crank shaft for raising and lowering the rake or fork arms so they may be operated at any desired height. **The wheels are** of wood with an iron hub, and are fitted with steel tires having projections which engage with the ground and assure a positive motion.

THESE ARE THE SIMPLEST and lightest running of the many hay loaders now on the market, easy to set up and easy to operate. They are made of good material, and are guaranteed to give good results when properly set up and operated. **Remember our price is much lower than the same style of machine can be purchased for by the dealer, all of which saving is in favor of our customers. Shipped direct from factory in Southeastern Wisconsin.**

No. 32R1180 Hay Loader. Weight, 800 pounds. Price.......**$31.20**

KENWOOD STEEL WINDMILLS AND ANGLE STEEL TOWERS

A Wonderful Record.

No line of Steel Windmills and Angle Steel Towers ever before became so well and favorably known, in so short a time, as the Kenwood Steel Windmills and Towers, which we have introduced and sold to our customers. For several years we sold them, in a small way, under the name "Acme," and finding that they were goods which could not be excelled and which we could unhesitatingly guarantee in every respect, we adopted the name "KENWOOD," issued the most complete Windmill Catalogue ever published, advertised them extensively and brought them prominently before the consumer. We felt perfectly safe in doing this, as our previous experience had proven the excellence of the goods.

THE RESULTS HAVE BEEN MARVELOUS.

From a few orders a week, our sales have increased until we now contract for the entire and exclusive sale of the output of the factory, which is next to the largest windmill factory in the United States, the home of the steel windmill.

KENWOOD STEEL WINDMILLS AND TOWERS

ARE NOW KNOWN throughout the entire United States, and are everywhere recognized and acknowledged to be the standard of excellence in windmill and tower design and construction, and

THE VERY BEST GOODS THAT MONEY CAN BUY.

OUR PRICES ARE EXCEEDINGLY LOW.

Contracting, as we do, for the entire output of the factory, and giving the factory so much business that they are constantly increasing their capacity, and consequently placing them in a position where they can purchase material much below the regular market value, and manufacture the goods at the very lowest shop cost, we are able to obtain these windmills and towers at a very little over the actual cost of the material and labor necessary to produce them. Our prices are based on the actual cost of manufacturing the goods and with but our one small percentage of profit added. All the selling expenses of traveling salesmen, wholesale houses, retail dealers, solicitors, collectors, bad debts, long-time interest, handling, double storage, etc., are eliminated.

Our Price is a Simple Proposition

IT IS A

SPOT CASH PRICE

A material and labor factory cost with our profit added, and our profit is small.

THIS ENABLES US TO SELL

Our No. 32R1202, Painted 8-Foot Steel Pumping Windmills, for........$15.05
or Our No. 32R1210, Galvanized 8-Foot Steel Pumping Windmills for...$16.65

Prices which cannot be duplicated by anyone on windmills equal in quality to the KENWOOD WINDMILLS. Considering the present cost of material and labor, these prices are much lower than were ever before offered. Prices on other sizes of Kenwood Windmills, and on Towers and Windmill Attachments will be found to be equally low.

NONE BETTER MADE AND FEW AS GOOD.

SHIPMENTS OF ALL WINDMILLS, Towers and Windmill Attachments, except where we specify otherwise, are made direct from the factory in Southeastern Wisconsin, from which place you must pay the freight. In ordering be careful to state whether the mill is to go on wood or steel tower or wood mast, and if for wood mast, give size of mast. When mills are to go on wood tower or wood mast, proper fittings are furnished without extra charge, but if for steel tower, unless the tower is ordered with the mill, no tower cap is furnished except at extra price.

OUR BINDING GUARANTEE. TO SATISFY OUR CUSTOMERS that our windmills and towers are as good as we represent them to be and that our statements are made in absolute good faith, we furnish OUR BINDING GUARANTEE with every windmill and tower, of which the following is an exact copy:

THIS ILLUSTRATION shows a KENWOOD PUMPING WINDMILL, mounted on a 40-foot KENWOOD STEEL TOWER, connected to a pump, with a stock watering tank close to the base of the tower. A splendid outfit for stock watering purposes.

OUR WINDMILLS are built of steel practically indestructible; built to require little care, and with little care last forever; built with a view of giving the greatest amount of power for equal velocity of wind, and we believe the Kenwood Windmill will pump more water in a lighter wind than any other windmill made.

Certificate No.________________

CERTIFICATE OF GUARANTY.

THIS IS TO CERTIFY, that the Kenwood Steel Windmill and Angle Steel Tower, sold under invoice number which corresponds with number of this Certificate, is warranted to be perfect in material and manufacture, and to be perfect in operation, if correctly put up and properly managed.

IT IS FURTHER GUARANTEED, that the Kenwood Steel Windmill, when properly erected and cared for, will endure as hard service and do as much work as any windmill made; and that the Kenwood Steel Tower, when erected according to our directions, will safely support in all winds (except cyclones and tornadoes), the size of windmill for which the tower is designed, and that the tower will not buckle or blow down unless the anchorage gives way. Any defects in material or workmanship will be made good to the purchaser, within one year from date of this certificate, by our furnishing without charge, corresponding new parts free on board cars.

SEARS ROEBUCK AND CO.

Dated, Chicago, Ill.,________________

THE KENWOOD Steel Pumping and Steel Power Windmills and Towers are MADE EXCLUSIVELY FOR US UNDER A SPECIAL CONTRACT, by one of the best windmill makers in this country. They are built from the very best of material throughout, on the very latest lines, embodying every good feature in windmill building, as adopted by the very best makers. Nothing but the very best of material enters into their construction. There is nothing in a Kenwood to get out of order, simple to care for, needs less care than almost any other windmill. Heavy enough in every part to be very strong and durable and not so heavy as to be hard to manage and hard to run; strengthened in many points where other mills are weak, lightened in several points where other mills are heavy and hard to manage; in other words a perfect windmill, containing all the good points of all windmills, with the defects of none.

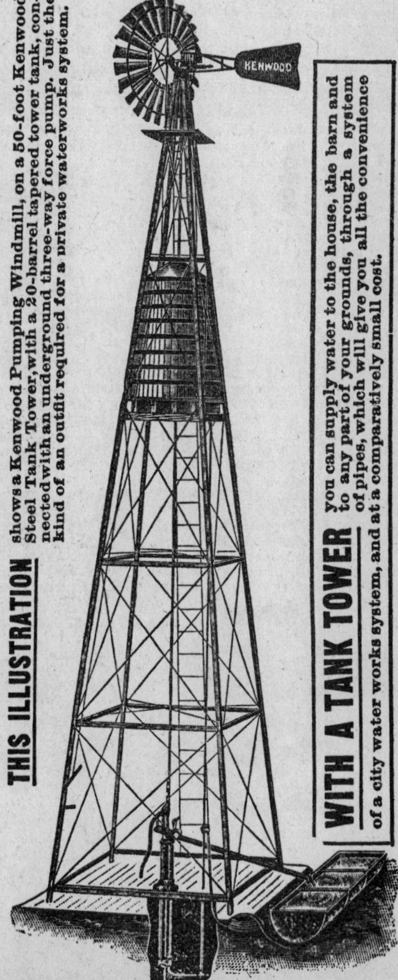

THIS ILLUSTRATION shows a Kenwood Pumping Windmill, on a 50-foot Kenwood Steel Tank Tower, with a 20-barrel tapered tower tank, connected with an underground three-way force pump. Just the kind of an outfit required for a private waterworks system.

WITH A TANK TOWER you can supply water to the house, the barn and to any part of your grounds, through a system of pipes, which will give you all the convenience of a city water works system, and at a comparatively small cost.

FOR PRICES SEE PAGES 693 TO 695.

THE CONSTRUCTION OF THE KENWOOD WINDMILLS IS PERFECT.

THE WIND WHEELS are made up in six sections, supported by angle steel arms which are strongly bolted to a large center casting and substantially braced by six front braces. The outer circles of all wheels and the inner circles of 12-foot, 14-foot and 16-foot wheels are angle steel, while the inner circles of the smaller wheels are flat steel turned edgewise, giving great strength and rigidity where most required.

THE SAILS are sheet steel, heavy enough so that we are not compelled to bead them to obtain the necessary strength, and as the brackets to which they are riveted are secured to the back of the sails, the face or front of the sail offers no resistance to the full effectiveness of the wind. The width, angle and curvature of the sails are such as, by exhaustive experiments, have been proven to be the most desirable and efficient under average conditions.

ALL SHAFT BEARINGS **are babbited with high grade Babbit metal, and every bearing is provided with a suitable oiling device.** A good grade of oil should be used on shaft bearings, but heavy grease should be used on gears and sliding surfaces.

THE VANE **is smooth sheet steel, fishtail in form,** beaded around the edge and firmly riveted to a heavy steel backbone, all being thoroughly braced and secured to the vane hinge, which is attached to the head of the mill in such a manner and position as to compensate for the tendency of the wind and motion of the wheel to turn the mill out of the proper angle, thus utilizing the full power of the wind until the required velocity is attained. The strongest, handsomest and best vane used on any windmill.

THE SPRING GOVERNOR **as applied to our Kenwood Windmills is a simple and effective governing device, and makes** a perfect windmill regulator, which, by its action on the vane, holds the wheel at the proper angle to develop only the required velocity for its work in heavy winds, and causes it to face the lighter winds and obtain their full force and effect. **Our spring governors are adjustable,** and our 12-foot, 14-foot and 16-foot windmills are fitted with an auxiliary lever and weight governor, which is also adjustable. Kenwood Windmills are supplied with an effectual brake, which is applied as the mill is pulled out and which absolutely holds the wheel still when the wheel is locked out of the wind.

KENWOOD STEEL PUMPING WINDMILLS ARE BACK GEARED.

Back geared windmills develop more power and give better results under average conditions than it is possible to obtain from direct stroke mills. Our pumping mills are geared back 1 to 2½, that is, the pump rod makes one stroke each way while the wind wheel revolves two and one-half times. **An additional advantage is gained through the rocker arm mechanism which actuates the pump rod, the travel of the pump rod being slower on the up stroke than on the down stroke, thus utilizing the full power of the wheel on the up or lifting stroke.** The rocker-arm is so constructed that the pitman, which connects with the pump rod, moves in a perpendicular line; therefore, there is no side strain or loss of power through useless friction. **The stroke of our 8-foot, 9-foot and 10-foot pumping mills is** 4½ inches, 6 inches and 8 inches; of the 12-foot mill, 6 inches, 9 inches and 12 inches. All pumping mills are set on medium stroke, unless otherwise ordered.

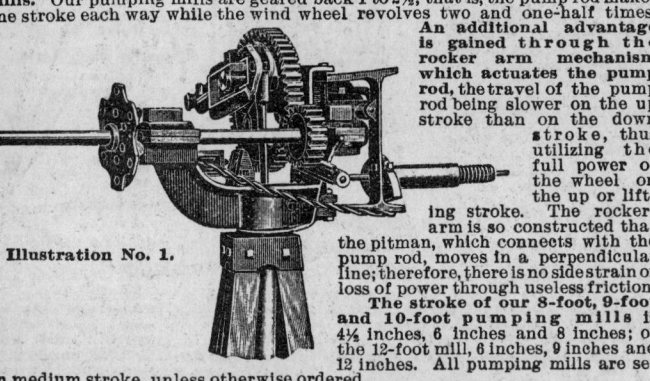

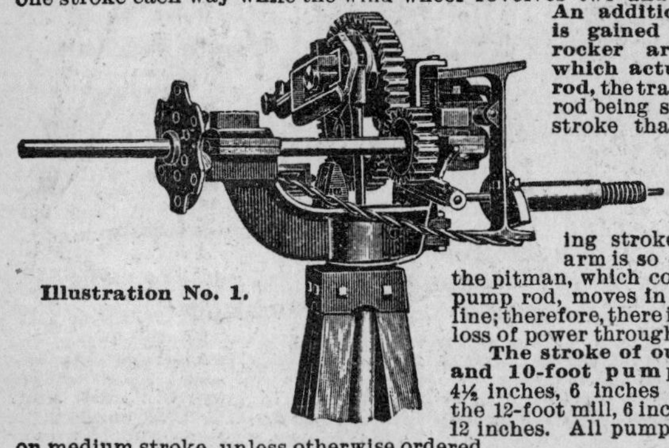

Illustration No. 1.

The illustrations Nos. 1, 2 and 3, on this page, show the engine head of the 8-foot, 9-foot and 10-foot Kenwood Pumping Windmills. The illustrations Nos. 4, 5 and 6 are of the engine head of the 12-foot Kenwood Pumping Windmills. These illustrations are taken in three different positions, so as to show different positions of the mechanism.

The illustrations Nos. 1 and 4 are views taken at the right of the mill and in front of the wheel, and they show the main shaft, the wheel spider attached to same, the spur pinion keyed to the shaft, and the great distance between the main shaft bearings; this being one of the important features of the Kenwood Windmills, both pumping and power.

Where most other windmills support the wheel by one long bearing entirely in front of the turntable, the Kenwood Windmills are supplied with two bearings, one in front and one back of the turntable. It requires no argument to prove that this is the proper manner of supporting windmill wheels. It divides the wear on the shaft, furnishes proper support for the wheel and causes the windmill to balance properly and turn easily; hence, the Kenwood Windmills respond readily to light winds. In the illustrations Nos. 1 and 4 the rocker arm which actuates the pump rod is shown at its extreme height and ready for the return or downward stroke. These pictures also show the manner of connecting the pull-out chain, and also the manner in which the brake shoe, which is attached to the vane hinge, operates the brake lever. The brake lever, as will be seen, projects under the main shaft and back of the spur pinion, and is supplied with a roller to overcome friction. The brake wedge, when the vane and wheel are pulled into parallel lines, slides under the roller of the brake lever and raises the lever, causing the brake shoe to grip firmly on the inner surface of the main gear. As the brake wedge is adjustable, any desired tension can be put upon the brake shoe and the Kenwood Windmills will stand absolutely still whenever the wheel is pulled out of the wind.

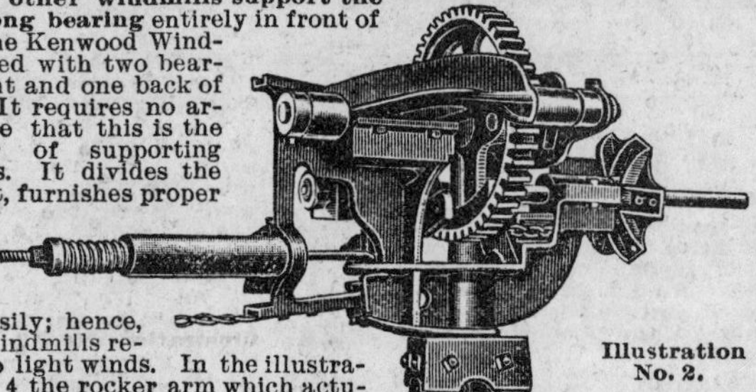

Illustration No. 2.

The illustrations Nos. 2 and 5 are views taken at a point back of the wheel and to right of the vane. They particularly show the bracket box which supports the main gear, and to which the rocker arm is hinged; also the inner end of the brake lever with the brake shoe attached, and the manner in which the brake shoe engages with the inner surface of the main gear.

The illustrations Nos. 3 and 6 are views taken from a point in front of the mill and to the left of the wheel. They show the rocker arm at the lowest point of its movement and indicate the position of this arm at the beginning of the up stroke of the pump rod. The rocker arm, as will be seen, is actuated by the wrist pin, which passes through the sliding brass box and is secured firmly in one of the stroke holes of the main gear.

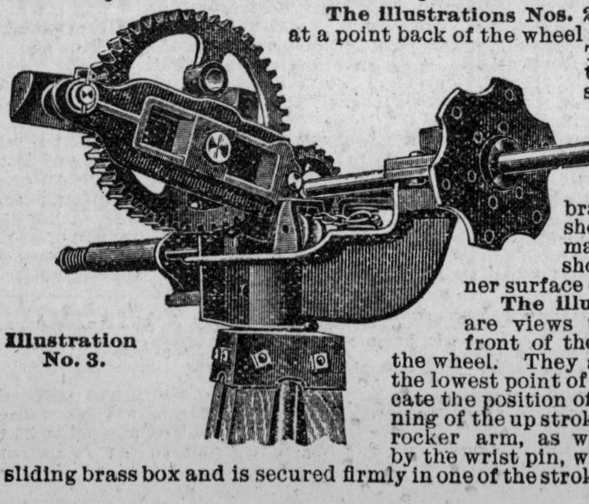

Illustration No. 3.

When the pump rod is on the upward stroke the wrist pin and sliding brass box are toward the end of the center opening of the rocker arm. This rocker arm being hinged on a fulcrum pin, it will be readily seen that the leverage at this particular point is very long and consequently that the free end of the rocker arm travels slowly during the entire up stroke of the pump rod. As the main gear revolves and the sliding brass box is carried toward the hinged end of the rocker arm, the leverage becomes shorter and the movement of the end of the rocker arm much faster on the down stroke than on the up stroke. **Illustration No. 2 gives a very clear idea of the horizontal governor spring,** spring rod and adjusting nut as used on 8, 9 and 10-foot windmills.

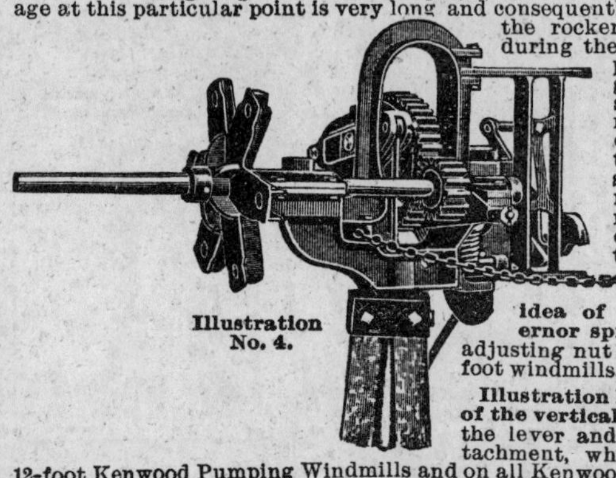

Illustration No. 4.

Illustration No. 5 shows a portion of the vertical governor spring and the lever and weight governor attachment, which are used on the 12-foot Kenwood Pumping Windmills and on all Kenwood Power Windmills.

The main shaft in 8-foot and 9-foot Kenwood Pumping Windmills is 1⅛ inches diameter, in 10-foot pumping windmills it is 1¼ inches diameter, and in 12-foot pumping windmills it is 1½ inches in diameter—much heavier and stronger than in other makes of pumping windmills.

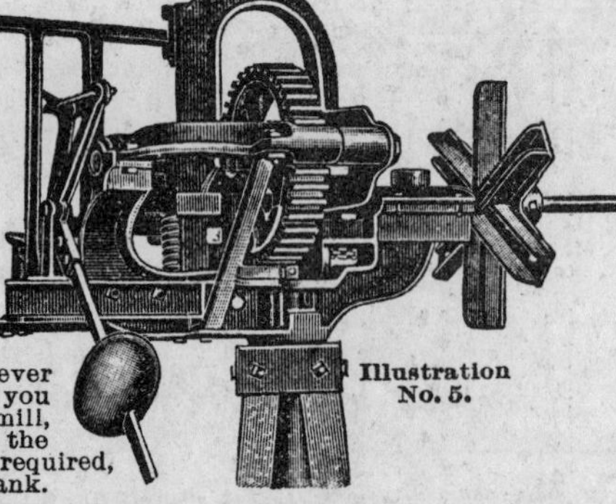

Illustration No. 5.

PUMPING WINDMILL OUTFITS.

A Pumping Windmill Outfit consists of a windmill alone to go on a wood tower, or a windmill and whatever height of steel tower you may require, or a windmill, a steel tank tower of the height which may be required, and a tapered tower tank.

How Kenwood Pumping Windmills Can be Used.

The windmill and tower may be set directly over the well, so that the pump will be in the center of the tower, or the tower can be set close to a spring or other water supply, a well hole dug in the center of the tower, the pump set so as to be operated direct by the windmill, and the water drawn by suction from the spring or other water supply, provided the water supply is not more than twenty feet below the pump cylinder. Of course the success of this plan will depend very much upon the distance from the pump to the water supply, and it must be distinctly understood that all piping must be connected with air tight joints.

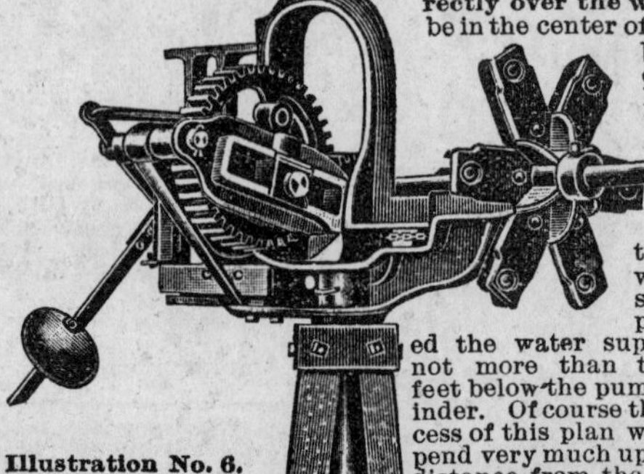

Illustration No. 6.

Where it is not possible to set the tower and windmill over the well, and the distance is great between the windmill and the water supply, it is always best to place the pump directly over the water supply, and to operate it by means of quadrant levers, one lever being connected to the pump rod of the windmill and the other to the pump, and the two levers being connected by wires.

The Kenwood Pumping Windmill may also be utilized for grinding small grain. This work can be accomplished by using our Boss Windmill Grinder, which will be found illustrated and priced in another part of this catalogue.

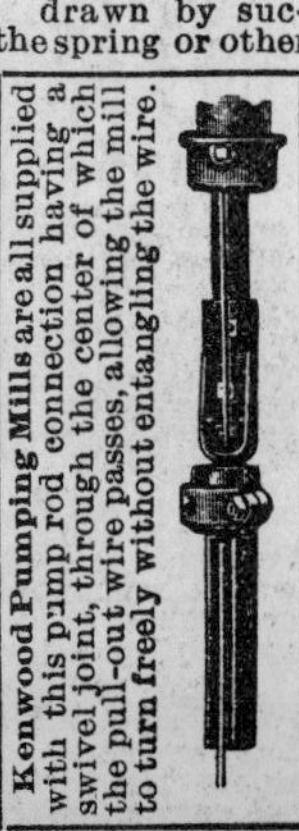

Kenwood Pumping Mills are all supplied with this pump rod connection having a swivel joint, through the center of which the pull-out wire passes, allowing the mill to turn freely without entangling the wire.

FOR PRICES, SEE PAGES 693 TO 695.

KENWOOD FOUR-POST ANGLE STEEL TOWERS.

The Kenwood Steel Windmill Towers are absolutely the best, strongest and most substantial towers which can be made. By this, we do not mean that in every case they are heavier than some other towers, but we do mean that the towers are in every way heavy enough to support the windmills for which they are designed, and still leave a large percentage of extra strength for safety. Further than this, they are the best braced towers which can be made.

Every section of the tower is independently braced by round steel braces, which are not reduced in size either by threads or in any other way. These braces are tightened by a specially designed clamp, by means of which an equal tension is put upon every pair of braces. There are eight of these braces for every ten feet of tower. In addition to this, the Kenwood Steel Towers are braced diagonally across the tower, from corner post to corner post, a style of bracing not employed in the manufacture of other windmill towers, but one of the special features of the Kenwood Towers, and a feature which adds great strength and rigidity to the tower.

Kenwood Towers Do Not Blow Down.

In all the time in which the Kenwood Steel Tower has been used (and that is for many years), the manufacturers have only had one tower reported to them as having been blown down. That tower was blown down by the heaviest wind storm this country ever knew, a storm which wrecked the City of Galveston, and which would be expected to wreck any building or piece of machinery which was in its path.

The corner posts of the Kenwood Towers are made of the best quality of angle steel, with a large fillet or round corner where the two legs of the angle meet on the inner side. These steel posts in size are large enough to be abundantly strong, and from the top of the tower down they are increased in size in every 20-foot section, thus increasing the strength as the tower broadens, where increased strength is most needed. **The Kenwood Towers are strongly braced with angle steel cross girts running from corner post to corner post, on every side, at frequent intervals,** these cross girts being made heavier and stronger for each section toward the base of the tower, and a set of these cross girts is furnished for the extreme base of the tower, near where the corner posts are secured to the anchor posts.

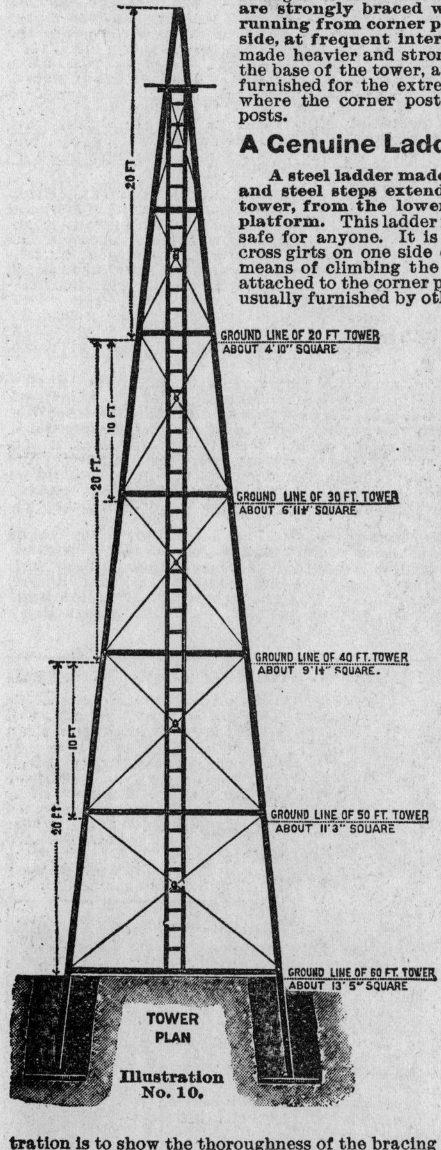

A Genuine Ladder. Safe to Climb.

A steel ladder made of heavy angle steel sides and steel steps extends the entire height of the tower, from the lower set of cross girts to the platform. This ladder is easy to climb and perfectly safe for anyone. It is bolted to the center of the cross girts on one side of the tower, a much better means of climbing the tower than on the pot hooks attached to the corner posts of the tower, as they are usually furnished by other tower manufacturers.

By referring to the table of prices and weights, you will find that we manufacture different sizes and weights of towers for the different sizes and kinds of windmills. Ordinary towers for pumping windmills and for power windmills are supplied with very heavy angle steel anchor posts, to the bottom of which there is riveted malleable iron anchor plates, which are provided with bolt holes for the purpose of securing to the foundation planks. Tank towers, or towers which are made to support tanks, instead of being supplied with anchor posts are provided with heavy cast iron foot plates, which bolt to the bottom of the tower corner posts, and heavy foundation rods, which are made long enough to pass through the brick or stone foundation, which should be built to support this style of tower, and by means of which the foundation plates are securely bolted to the masonry piers.

20 FT.
GROUND LINE OF 20 FT. TOWER ABOUT 4' 10" SQUARE
10 FT.
20 FT.
GROUND LINE OF 30 FT. TOWER ABOUT 6' 11" SQUARE
GROUND LINE OF 40 FT. TOWER ABOUT 9' 1" SQUARE.
10 FT.
20 FT.
GROUND LINE OF 50 FT. TOWER ABOUT 11' 3" SQUARE
GROUND LINE OF 60 FT. TOWER ABOUT 13' 5" SQUARE
TOWER PLAN

Illustration No. 10.

Strongest Construction Possible.

Illustration No. 10 is a plan of the Kenwood Steel Tower, showing the general form of construction and giving the principal measurements. **Illustration No. 11 shows the lower 10 feet of a 30-foot Kenwood Four-Post Angle Steel Tower.** The special purpose of this illustration is to show the thoroughness of the bracing employed in our towers. As will be seen, the corner posts are bolted together at a point just below the cross girts. A set of cross girts is provided for every 10-foot section, the last set being close to the ground and just above the anchor post joints.

Each 10-foot section of the tower is thoroughly braced by four sets of round steel brace rods, which brace rods are not reduced in size in any way, but have an eye turned at each end of them. These brace rods run from the upper cross girt joint diagonally across the side of the tower to the joint of the next lower cross girt.

The two rods on each side of the tower cross each other at a point near the center of the section. Here they are clamped together by specially devised clamps, by means of which the brace rods can be tightened so as to make the tower absolutely rigid and firm. In every case, however, each rod of each pair bears the same tension as is placed on its mate, so that it is impossible to get an uneven tension on any pair of the rods. In addition to this style of bracing, which is superior to the braces ordinarily used, we employ another style of bracing seldom found in towers of other makes. In other words, we run diagonal cross rods from corner post to corner post, by means of which the tower is squared up, making it as strong and rigid as it would be were it a solid steel box.

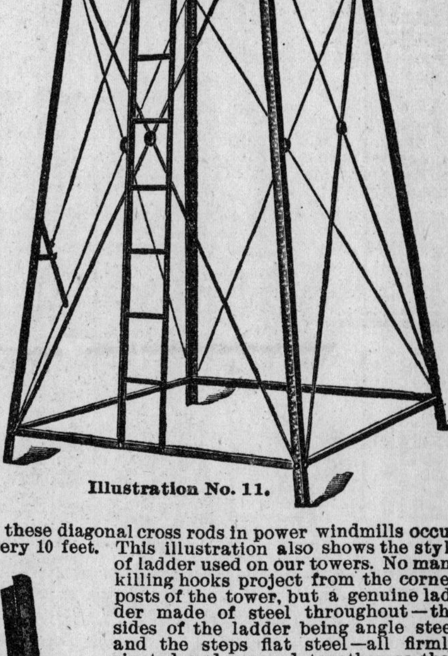

Illustration No. 11.

In towers for pumping windmills these diagonal cross rods radiate from the pump rod guide in the center of the tower and they are placed one set in every 10-foot section. In towers for power windmills the diagonal cross rods radiate from the center boxing, which is provided for the vertical shafting. As bearings are supplied for this vertical shafting at points about 6¼ feet apart, these diagonal cross rods in power windmills occur every 6¼ feet instead of every 10 feet. This illustration also shows the style of ladder used on our towers. No man-killing hooks project from the corner posts of the tower, but a genuine ladder made of steel throughout—the sides of the ladder being angle steel and the steps flat steel—all firmly riveted and secured together so that the ladder is perfectly safe for any one to climb. Attached to the left post of the tower we show the pull-out lever, which is always furnished by us when windmills and towers are ordered together.

Illustration No. 12.

In illustration No. 12 we show a section of one corner of the tower, illustrating the manner of bolting the corner posts together, bolting the cross girts and brace rods to the corner posts, and the manner in which the diagonal cross rods are secured to the corner of the tower. As will be seen, the lower posts, being wider than the upper posts, lap outside the upper posts, keeping the inner edges of the posts even and in line with each other.

We call particular attention to the small illustration, No. 13. It shows plainly the manner in which our tower brace rods are clamped together where they cross, and shows that the brace rod running from the upper left hand corner to the lower right hand corner must cross the other brace rod outside of it. When these clamps are put upon the brace rods and bolted together they can be tapped lightly with a hammer until the rods are drawn perfectly tight, then the clamp bolts can be screwed up so that it will be impossible for the clamps to move out of position.

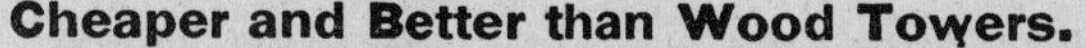

Illustration No. 13.

Cheaper and Better than Wood Towers.

Steel towers are far more substantial than either wood towers or masts, and when erected they present a much handsomer appearance. We are sincere when we advise our customers to purchase a steel tower when they purchase a windmill. Steel towers cost but little, if any, more than wood towers, and if you buy a Kenwood Steel Tower you obtain one which is perfect in design, substantial and abundantly strong in all parts.

If you are putting up a power windmill outfit and erect the windmill on a steel tower, you can build a house either within or around the base of the tower, and arrange your machinery within and about it to suit your convenience. The tower can be erected close to your barn, so that line shafting can be run into the barn, and all arrangements for transmitting power, either to machinery or pump, can be made more conveniently than would be the case if the windmill was erected over the barn. **At our one small profit prices, you can ill afford to erect your windmill on anything but a Kenwood Steel Tower.**

WE ADVISE OUR CUSTOMERS IN ORDERING A WINDMILL TO INCLUDE WITH THEIR ORDER AN ORDER FOR A STEEL TOWER TO MATCH.

While our windmills are adapted for and thousands of them are erected on wood towers, our price for steel towers is a price that barely covers the cost of material and labor, and makes the first cost to you for a steel tower but a little more than a wood tower; in the end the steel tower is by far the cheaper.

FOR PRICES SEE PAGES 693 TO 695.

USEFUL INFORMATION PERTAINING TO WINDMILLS.

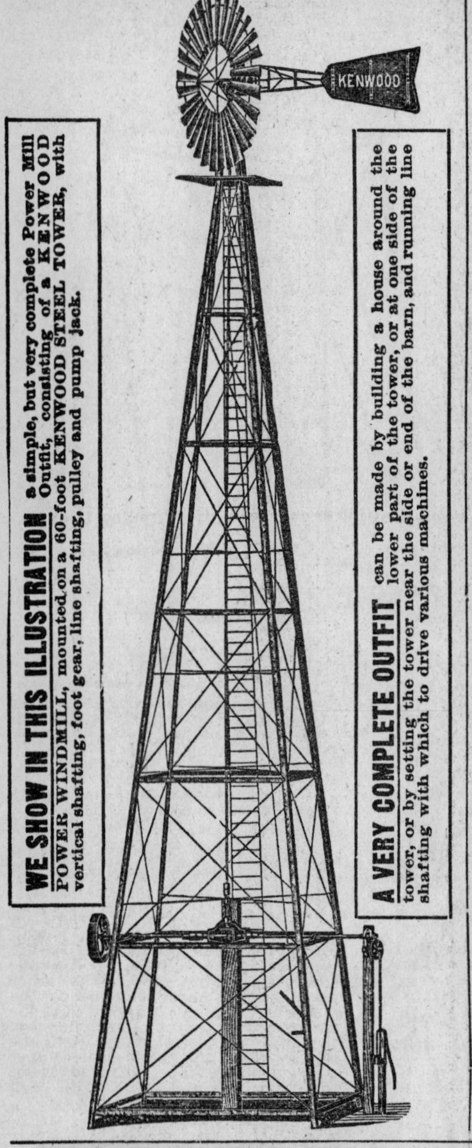

KENWOOD
WE SHOW IN THIS ILLUSTRATION a simple, but very complete Power Mill Outfit, consisting of a KENWOOD POWER WINDMILL, mounted on a 60-foot KENWOOD STEEL TOWER, with vertical shafting, foot gear, line shafting, pulley and pump jack.
A VERY COMPLETE OUTFIT can be made by building a house around the lower part of the tower, or at one side of the tower, or by setting the tower near the side or end of the barn, and running line shafting with which to drive various machines.

Diameter of Wheel, Size of Cylinder and Size of Suction Pipe, Which We Recommend for a Given Depth of Well or Elevation of Water.

Diameter of Windmill Wheel	10 Feet Elevation of Water				25 Feet Elevation of Water				50 Feet Elevation of Water				75 Feet Elevation of Water				100 Feet Elevation of Water			
	Length of Stroke	Diameter of Cylinder	Size of Suction Pipe	Gallons Per Hour	Length of Stroke	Diameter of Cylinder	Size of Suction Pipe	Gallons Per Hour	Length of Stroke	Diameter of Cylinder	Size of Suction Pipe	Gallons Per Hour	Length of Stroke	Diameter of Cylinder	Size of Suction Pipe	Gallons Per Hour	Length of Stroke	Diameter of Cylinder	Size of Suction Pipe	Gallons Per Hour
Ft.	In.	In.	In.		In.	In.	In.		In.	In.	In.		In.	In.	In.		In.	In.	In.	
8	....	....	....	....	**8**	**3½**	**1½**	**800**	**8**	**3**	**1¼**	**586**	**8**	**2½**	**1¼**	408	8	2¼	1¼	330
8	**6**	**5**	**3**	**1224**	6	4	2	784	6	3¼	1¼	518	6	2¾	1¼	371	**6**	**2½**	**1¼**	**306**
8	....	....	....	....	....	....	....	....	4½	3½	1¼	450	4½	3	1¼	330	4½	2¾	1¼	278
9	....	....	....	....	**8**	**4**	**2**	**1045**	8	3¼	1¼	690	8	2¾	1¼	495	**8**	**2½**	**1¼**	**408**
9	**6**	**6**	**3½**	**1763**	....	....	....	....	**6**	**3½**	**1½**	**600**	**6**	**3**	**1¼**	**440**	6	2¾	1¼	371
9	....	....	....	....	4½	5	3	918	4½	4	2	588	4½	3¼	1¼	389	4½	3	1¼	330
10	**8**	**6**	**3½**	**2418**	....	....	....	....	**8**	**3½**	**1½**	**800**	**8**	**3**	**1¼**	**586**	8	2¾	1¼	495
10	....	....	....	....	**6**	**5**	**3**	**1224**	6	4	2	784	6	3¼	1¼	518	**6**	**3**	**1¼**	**440**
10	....	....	....	....	4½	6	3½	1322	....	....	....	....	4½	3½	1½	450	4½	3¼	1¼	389
12	**12**	**8**	**5**	**7268**	12	5	3	2448	**12**	**4**	**2**	**1568**	12	3½	1	1200	12	3	1¼	880
12	....	....	....	....	**9**	**6**	**3½**	**2644**	....	....	....	....	**9**	**4**	**2**	**1176**	**9**	**3½**	**1½**	**900**
12	....	....	....	....	....	....	....	....	6	5	3	1224	....	....	....	....	6	4	2	784

Diameter of Windmill Wheel	125 Feet Elevation of Water				150 Feet Elevation of Water				200 Feet Elevation of Water				250 Feet Elevation of Water				300 Feet Elevation of Water			
	Length of Stroke	Diameter of Cylinder	Size of Suction Pipe	Gallons Per Hour	Length of Stroke	Diameter of Cylinder	Size of Suction Pipe	Gallons Per Hour	Length of Stroke	Diameter of Cylinder	Size of Suction Pipe	Gallons Per Hour	Length of Stroke	Diameter of Cylinder	Size of Suction Pipe	Gallons Per Hour	Length of Stroke	Diameter of Cylinder	Size of Suction Pipe	Gallons Per Hour
Ft.	In.	In.	In.		In.	In.	In.		In.	In.	In.		In.	In.	In.		In.	In.	In.	
8	**8**	**2**	**1¼**	**261**	....	....	....	....	....	....	....	....	....	....	....	....	....	....	....	....
8	6	2¼	1¼	248	**6**	**2**	**1¼**	**196**	....	....	....	....	....	....	....	....	....	....	....	....
8	4½	2½	1¼	230	4½	2¼	1¼	186	**4½**	**2**	**1¼**	**147**	....	....	....	....	....	....	....	....
9	8	2¼	1¼	330	**8**	**2**	**1¼**	**261**	....	....	....	....	....	....	....	....	....	....	....	....
9	**6**	**2½**	**1¼**	**306**	6	2¼	1¼	248	**6**	**2**	**1¼**	**196**	....	....	....	....	....	....	....	....
9	4½	2¾	1¼	278	4½	2½	1¼	230	4½	2¼	1¼	186	**4½**	**2**	**1¼**	**147**	....	....	....	....
10	**8**	**2½**	**1¼**	**408**	8	2¼	1¼	330	**8**	**2**	**1¼**	**261**	....	....	....	....	....	....	....	....
10	6	2¾	1¼	371	**6**	**2½**	**1¼**	**306**	6	2¼	1¼	248	**6**	**2**	**1¼**	**19**	....	....	....	....
10	4½	3	1¼	330	4½	2¾	1¼	278	4½	2½	1¼	230	4½	2¼	1¼	186	**4½**	**2**	**1¼**	**147**
12	12	2¾	1¼	741	**12**	**2½**	**1¼**	**612**	12	2¼	1¼	496	12	2	1¼	392	....	....	....	....
12	**9**	**3**	**1¼**	**660**	9	2¾	1¼	556	**9**	**2½**	**1¼**	**459**	9	2¼	1¼	372	**9**	**2**	**1¼**	**294**
12	6	3¼	1¼	518	6	3	1¼	440	6	2¾	1¼	371	**6**	**2½**	**1¼**	**306**	6	2¼	1¼	248

In the above table we show the approximate amount of water elevated per hour by different sizes of windmills using different sizes of cylinders and at various strokes. This table is based upon the average amount of water the different windmills will lift with average winds to operate them when windmills and pumps are properly set and connected. In other words, it is estimated that, taken the year around, the windmill will elevate the amount of water shown in table on an average of eight hours per day. Capacity of pumping windmills will vary under different conditions, but whatever variations there may be, we guarantee that the Kenwood Windmill will pump as much water under the same conditions as any windmill of corresponding size and that they will operate in much lighter winds than most other windmills.

The heavy faced figures in the table show the size of cylinder, size of suction pipe and the length of stroke which we recommend for use in connection with the various windmills at stated elevations. For elevating water over 100 feet the work is too heavy and the strain too great for ordinary cylinders and small pipe. Deep well cylinders should be used for greater depth and in such cases whenever possible you should use pipe larger than the cylinder.

For general work do not select a cylinder larger than those recommended for 50-foot elevation. Cylinders larger than 4 inches cannot be used with ordinary pumps. 5-inch, 6-inch and 8-inch cylinders are used for irrigation purposes or in shallow wells only, and require special piping and fittings above the cylinders.

It has been found by experience that it requires, on an average, a wind of a velocity of four to five miles per hour to drive a steel windmill, and that the windmill will run, on an average, eight hours per day. The average velocity of wind in the United States is sixteen miles per hour for eight hours per day. From this it is quite evident that a windmill is a profitable investment, because when a good windmill is properly erected it becomes a faithful and reliable servant, **upon which you can depend for an average of eight hours of steady work for every day in the year, requiring no feed, no fuel, and but very little oil and attention.**

Table of Wind Velocity and Pressure.

Velocity of Wind: Miles per Hour	Velocity of Wind: Feet per Second	Pressure: In Lbs. per Sq. Ft.	Force of Wind	Velocity of Wind: Miles per Hour	Velocity of Wind: Feet per Second	Pressure: In Lbs. per Sq. Ft.	Force of Wind
1	1.47	.005	Hardly perceptible.	30	44.01	4.429	High wind.
2	2.93	.020	Just perceptible.	35	51.34	6.027	
3	4.40	.044		40	58.68	7.873	Very high storm.
4	5.87	.079	Gentle, pleasant wind.	45	66.01	9.963	
5	7.33	.123		50	73.35	12.300	
10	14.67	.492	Pleasant, brisk gale.	60	88.02	17.715	Great storm.
15	22.00	1.107		70			A hurricane that blows down trees, buildings, etc.
20	29.34	1.968	Very brisk.	80	117.36	31.490	
25	36.67	3.075					

Weight of Water In One Foot Length of Pipe.

Size	Lbs.	Size	Lbs.	Size	Lbs.	Size	Lbs.
½-in.	.086	1½-in.	.774	3 -in.	3.087	4½-in.	6.966
1 -in.	.343	2 -in.	1.372	3½-in.	4.214	5 -in.	8.575
1¼-in.	.537	2½-in.	2.159	4 -in.	5.488	6 -in.	12.348

Amount of Water Discharged by One Inch of Pump Stroke.

Diam. cylinder, inches..	2	2¼	2½	2¾	3	3¼	3½	4	5	6	8
Gallons, per stroke......	.0136	.0172	.0212	.0257	.0306	.0359	.0416	.0544	.0850	.1224	.2176

To ascertain the capacity of a pump with any diameter of cylinder given in above table, multiply the gallons per stroke, as given in the table, by the length of pump stroke, and the result thus obtained by the number of pump strokes per minute. This result multiplied by sixty will give the capacity in gallons per hour.

The capacity of single and double acting pumps is precisely the same, the difference being that the single acting pump discharges all the water on the up stroke of the pump rod, while the double acting pump discharges half on the up stroke and half on the down stroke of the pump rod.

IN THIS ILLUSTRATION

we show the Kenwood Power Windmill as it appears when mounted on a wood mast over the barn, showing the manner of bracing the mast with our steel guy rods and how various machines may be driven by the power developed by the windmill.

FOR PRICES SEE PAGES 693 TO 695.

Kenwood One-Horse Sweep Power.

A good, strong external geared One-Horse Sweep Power, speeded at 25 revolutions to one round of the horse, or at about 75 revolutions per minute. Frame is made of heavy, well seasoned hardwood, firmly put together with bolts and rods, and is strongly braced. Furnished complete with one short and one long tumbling rod, (about 20 feet in all), one slip knuckle, two safety knuckles, two rod rests, one sweep and one lead pole. Shaft is squared for 1-inch coupling. Weight, 500 pounds. Shipped direct from factory in Southeastern Wisconsin.

No. 32R1810 One-Horse Sweep Power. Price....................**$17.45**

Acme Two-Horse Sweep Power.

□ **Every ounce of power is applied directly to the tumbling rod,** there being **absolutely no loss by cramp** in any direction, having no center bearings; all **shafts are steel** and all boxes babbited.

Traverse rollers hold the master wheel in place of slides. Each power has a right and left motion; coupling on one side the tumbling rod turns toward the horses; and on the other side with the horses. **They are from new plans and patterns** and have been fully tested in all parts of the country on all kinds of work. We offer the best powers made and will so guarantee. Each power is **furnished complete with two sweeps,** two sweep rods, two tumbling rods, three couplings, rod block, platform and a coil spring draft hitch for each sweep. Shafts are squared for 1-inch coupling. Weight, 700 pounds; high speed, 32 revolutions; low speed 10 revolutions to one round of the horses. **Shipped direct from factory to user.**

No. 32R1812 Two-Horse Sweep Power. Price....................**$19.25**

Acme Four, Six and Eight-Horse Sweep Powers.

Our Four, Six and Eight-Horse Powers are practically the same as our two-horse power, only made **much heavier** and are stronger in every way. Shafts are squared for 1⅛-inch couplings. They are furnished complete, as described above. The four-horse power is furnished with two sweeps and two lead poles for two teams, **high** speed 51 revolutions, low speed 10⅕ revolutions to one round of the horses. If wanted with four sweeps, price will be same as for six-horse power. **Shipped direct from factory to user.**

No. 32R1813 **Four-Horse Power.** Weight, 1000 pounds. Price....**$27.40**

No. 32R1814 **Six-Horse Power,** furnished with four sweeps and speeded same as four-horse power. Weight, 1100 pounds. Price....................**$32.40**

No. 32R1815 **Eight-Horse Power,** furnished with four sweeps. High speed 65 revolutions, low speed 12⅕ revolutions to one round of the horses. Weight, 1400 pounds. Price....................**$43.15**

Safety Couplings.

All parts are duplicates, so that a broken piece is easily replaced. **It will not heat; it will not cut; it has no pin to wear out;** it greatly reduces the **friction; guaranteed to outwear any other coupling.** Carried in stock to fit 1, 1⅛ or 1¼ squared shaft. Weight, 12 pounds.

No. 32R1816 Safety Coupling, 1-inch square. Price..........**68c**
No. 32R1817 Safety Coupling, 1⅛-inch square. Price..........**70c**
No. 32R1818 Safety Coupling, 1¼-inch square. Price..........**72c**

Slip Couplings or Knuckles.

Made to take the place of safety couplings and to run either right or left hand. Will allow machinery to continue in motion after the horse power has stopped. Weight, about 18 pounds.

No. 32R1819 Slip Coupling, 1-inch square. Price..........**$1.26**
No. 32R1820 Slip Coupling, 1⅛-inch square. Price.......... **1.28**
No. 32R1821 Slip Coupling, 1¼-inch square. Price.......... **1.30**

Our Overhead One-Horse Power.

This style of horse power is very convenient and popular, because, owing to its construction, it has many advantages not found in down powers. It is especially adapted for use in a barn where several horses are kept, or in small livery stables. The power can be bolted to the timbers above the driveway and machines can be set on the floor either above or below the power. When not in use the center post can be lifted from its socket and put out of the way, leaving the floor clear for other purposes. Then when power is to be used again all that is necessary is to set the post in place, hitch the horse to the sweep and go ahead. The center post which we furnish is made of 6-inch by 6-inch timber and is 12 feet long. It is amply strong and can be cut to any desired length. The 1⅛-inch driving shaft, to which the pulley is attached, is regularly made so that the measurement from center of master wheel to center of pulley face is 3 feet 3 inches, but additional shafting can be coupled to this shaft so as to change position of pulley or allow the use of other pulleys. The driving pulley is 18 inches in diameter with 3-inch face and makes 37⅕ revolutions to one round of the horse, or about 135 revolutions per minute. Additional shafting or change in size of pulley is extra. Length of sweep from center of post to eye-bolt is 7 feet 6 inches. For driving small feed cutters, corn shellers, feed grinders, wood saws, etc., this power cannot be excelled. Weight, 450 pounds. Shipped direct from factory in Southeastern Wisconsin.

No. 32R1823 **Overhead Horse Power.** Price....................**$18.45**
No. 32R1824 **Extra Line Shaft,** per foot.............. **.32**

Acme Tread Horse Powers.

Our Acme Tread Horse Powers are especially designed for farm and shop use. They are adapted to run various farm machines, wood saws, etc., and for operating light machinery in blacksmith or jobbing shops. These powers are built in the best possible manner out of first class materials. The treads are of best seasoned maple. Power can be set at any desired pitch so as to develop more or less power as needed. We make these powers in two sizes, either of which can be mounted on two wheel trucks so that they can be easily moved about. **The speed is right for feed grinders, fodder cutters, wood saws, etc.** All of these powers are furnished complete with a governor, which regulates the speed perfectly, and with brake for stopping the machine. Trucks are extra, but will be furnished at prices quoted below. **Shipped direct from factory in Southeastern Wisconsin.**

No. 32R1825 **One-Horse Double Geared Tread Power,** with speed regulator. Weight, 1600 pounds. Price....................**$62.00**

No. 32R1826 **Two-Horse Double Geared Tread Power,** with speed regulator. Weight, 2800 pounds. Price....................**$78.30**

No. 32R1829 **Two-Wheel Trucks,** complete with pole for above powers. Weight, 350 pounds. Price....................**$15.90**

Our $9.35 Little Wonder Grinding Mill.

This little mill fully warrants the name by which it is known. It is compact, occupying a very small amount of floor space; weighs but 90 pounds, and is fitted with 5½-inch burrs of the most approved design, an extra set of burrs being furnished with the mill. The driving pulley is 7 inches in diameter, with 4-inch face and should make from 700 to 1300 revolutions per minute. Capacity of grinder, at these speeds, is from 8 to 15 bushels of mixed feed per hour. The burrs are arranged so that they cannot run together when hopper is empty and consequently they will last much longer than burrs used in ordinary mills. Shipped direct from factory in Northern Illinois.

No. 32R1858 **Little Wonder Grinding Mill.** Price....................**$9.35**
No. 32R1859 Extra burrs, per pair; weight, 4 pounds. Price........ **.70**

Acme Windmill Feed Grinder.

The illustration shows this mill with the pulley attachment, and the smaller illustration shows the sprocket wheel attachment. The sprocket grinder was gotten up especially for windmills and is adapted to 12 to 16 feet geared wheels. The sprocket wheels are 6 and 10 inches in diameter, fitted for No. 52 link chain belting. We can also furnish the driving sprocket with spring clutch complete for line shaft on windmill which taken together makes a complete outfit at a very reasonable price. **Capacity, 8 to 15 bushels per hour according to the velocity of the wind and size of wheel used.** In ordering this kind of a mill be sure to give the diameter of the line shaft if driving sprocket and spring clutch are wanted.

The pulley grinder is similar in all respects to the sprocket grinder, as described above, only it is furnished with a 6-inch pulley with a 6-inch face. Furnished with three sets of 6-inch right hand burrs. Weight, 125 pounds. **Shipped direct from factory in Eastern Minnesota.**

No. 32R1860 **Acme Windmill Feed Grinder.** Price....................**$13.45**
No. 32R1861 Price of extra burrs, per pair.................... **1.00**
No. 32R1862 Price for 6 and 10-inch double driving sprocket with spring clutch complete, for line shaft of windmill.................... **1.95**

State whether grinder is wanted with pulley or with sprocket wheel.

Our New Improved Acme Sweep Grinder.

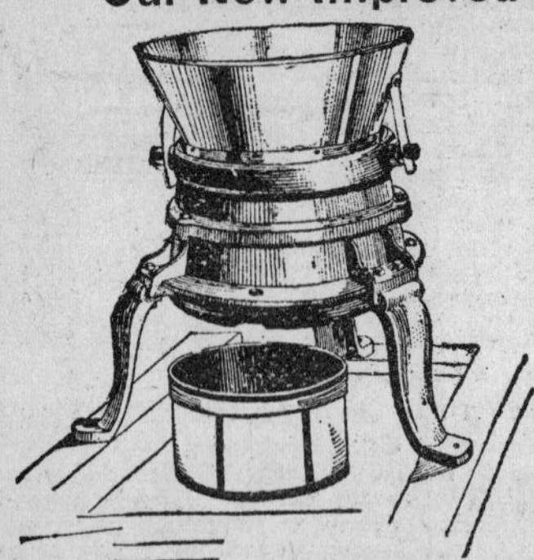

This is one of the best grinders on the market. Grinds ear corn, new or dry, shelled corn alone or mixed with other grain for chopped feed, oats, etc., and is so arranged that the interior parts of the mill revolve with the revolutions of the team. **The power is applied directly to the grinding parts, thereby making the draft very light. Our grinder rings, or burrs, have a peculiar dress** by means of which the broken pieces of cob and whole grains are **gradually reduced to the fineness desired,** so that we produce a better quality of feed with less work to the team. It is provided with breakers or crowders which force the grain into the burrs. This mill will grind 10 to 15 bushels of shelled corn per hour; corn on ear, 6 to 10 bushels per hour; is warranted not to choke on new or old corn, damp or dry. Capacity is based on medium grinding of dry corn. Regularly furnished with coarse burrs. Fine burrs are required for grinding oats or other small grains. Price is complete with sweep. A perfect sweep mill of large capacity. **Shipped direct from factory in Southwestern Ohio.**

No. 32R1944 **No. 1 Acme Sweep Grinder,** has 284 square inches of grinding surface. Weight, 400 pounds. Price........ **$15.35**

No. 32R1945 Extra grinding rings for No. 1 mill. Per pair........ 3.45

No. 32R1946 No. 2 Acme Sweep Grinder, has 369 square inches of grinding surface. Weight, 500 pounds. Price........ 17.45

No. 32R1947 Extra grinding rings for No. 2 mill. Per pair........ 4.35

NOTE—When ordering extra grinding rings, state whether you want fine or coarse rings. Coarse rings will be sent unless otherwise specified.

Big Four Ball Bearing Corn and Cob Mill.

The best built and most powerful mill which can be made. Every part of this grinder is strong and substantial, and its perfect work commends it to all who desire a mill of large capacity. It will grind ear corn, either dry or damp, and any kind of small grain, and **has a capacity of from 15 to 30 bushels per hour,** depending upon the number of horses used. Furnished with a double lever so that two or four horses can be used. Always furnished with coarse burrs unless otherwise ordered. Fine burrs are required for grinding oats or other small grains. Grinding surface, 404 square inches. For better illustration we show the grinder in parts, with hopper and sweeps removed. Price is complete with sweep. Weight, 1,250 pounds. **Shipped direct from factory in Southwestern Ohio.**

No. 32R1952 **Big Four Mill.** Price........ **$34.40**

No. 32R1953 Extra grinding rings. Price, per pair........ 6.25

NOTE—When ordering extra grinding rings, state whether you want fine or coarse rings. Coarse rings will be sent unless otherwise specified.

Kenwood Triple Geared Feed Mill.

To supply the demand for something better than the regular style of sweep grinder, we offer a new and up to date geared mill, so geared as to greatly increase the grinding capacity with the same amount of power applied. The grinding rings revolve in opposite directions at a ratio of more than three to one, that is, one revolution of the sweep revolves the inside ring more than three times in one direction while the outside ring makes one revolution in the opposite direction. The rings are about 17 inches diameter, with a width of 3½ inches, giving large grinding surface. The inside ring is made with sharp and quite prominent corrugations, so shaped as to make a force feed and shearing cut. Only one set of burrs are required for grinding coarse or fine feed, as these burrs are fitted with a regulating disc for grinding small grain. The disc should be removed when grinding ear corn. Price is complete with sweep. Weight, 550 pounds. **Shipped direct from factory in Northern Illinois.**

No. 32R1954 **Triple Geared Feed Mill.** Price........ **$19.20**

No. 32R1955 Outside grinding ring. Price........ 1.40

No. 32R1956 Inside grinding ring. Price........ 1.35

Model Pea Huller.

In our Model Pea Huller we have without doubt the most complete and perfect machine, for hulling (or shelling) and separating all kinds of field peas. We guarantee the machine to hull and clean 10 to 15 bushels per hour, by hand, and 25 to 30 bushels per hour if power is used. It is very compact; the size being 18⅛ inches wide, 48⅛ inches high, 53 inches long and weighs 375 pounds. From experience we feel safe in recommending our Huller, for farms raising 50 to 1,000 bushels of peas. For cleaning corn, wheat or oats, this machine is also valuable. It will clean dust and trash from the grain at the rate of 250 to 350 bushels per day. It does not grade the grain, however, and should be used as cleaner only. Seed peas are always in great demand, and with one of our hullers you can add $500.00 to your bank account each season. **Full directions sent with each machine.** This machine is not intended to hull peas with vines attached. **Shipped from factory in Southern Tennessee.**

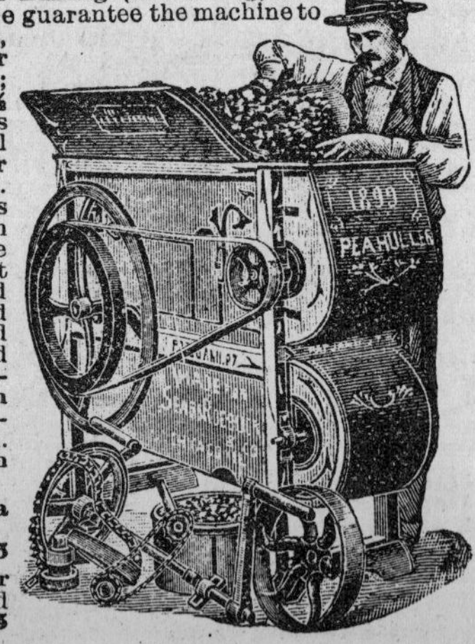

No. 32R1975 **No. 1 Hand Power Pea Huller,** with two 18-inch cranks. Price........ **$21.65**

No. 32R1976 **No. 1 Hand or Power Pea Huller,** with 14-inch pulley and two 18-inch cranks. Price........ **$23.65**

Our $7.98 Ajax Fanning Mill.

This mill has a very short and quick shake or movement to the shoe, and double the screening surface of the ordinary mill. The short shake is obtained by an eccentric located upon the fan shaft between the shaker rod plate and the shaft box. The arm projecting from this eccentric extends into the shake rod guide, and all lost motion is taken up by a spring on this arm. This short shake is a very important feature in the cleaning of fine seeds. There are two spouts attached to the shoe, one being the grader spout and the other being so arranged that all the grain or seeds which pass over the lower screen may be delivered at the side of the mill opposite the crank side. A groove above the lower screen is so arranged that another screen may be put in the shoe and all seeds which pass over this screen will be discharged under the fan drum, thus making one more separation than can be made by other makes of fanning mills. **The regular outfit furnished with this mill is called a Grain Outfit,** and consists of one wheat or rye hurdle, with zinc top and wire middle and bottom sieves; one corn or oats sieve; one barley or bean sieve; one wheat grader; two wheat or barley screens, and one cheat or cockle board. Additional sieves and screens for separating cheat and cockle, cleaning clover, timothy, flax, etc., are extra. These mills are always shipped knocked down as shown in cut, unless otherwise ordered, thereby saving one-half in freight. Weight, 120 pounds. **Shipped direct from factory in Southeastern Wisconsin.**

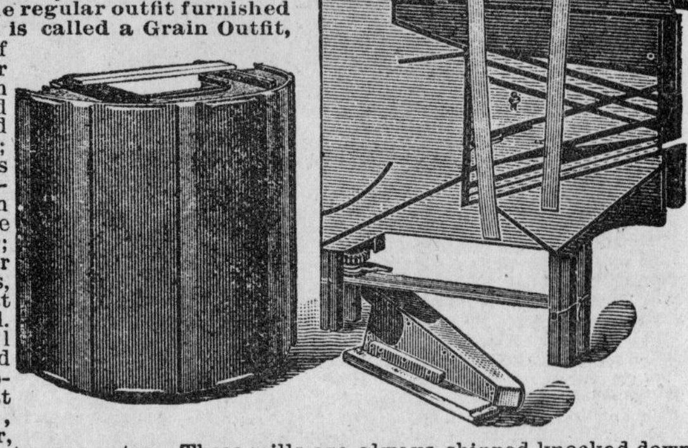

No. 32R2000 **Ajax Fanning Mill.** Price........ **$7.98**

No. 32R2001 **Extra Wire Sieves or Screens.** Price, each........ .37

No. 32R2002 **Extra Wire Flax Sieve and Screen.** Per set........ .71

No. 32R2003 **Extra Wire Clover Sieve and Screen.** Per set........ .72

No. 32R2004 **Extra Wire Timothy Sieve and Screen.** Per set........ .73

No. 32R2005 **Extra Wire Hungarian or Millet Sieve and Screen.** Price, per set........ .74

No. 32R2006 **Extra Hurdles.** Each........ 1.63

No. 32R2007 **Extra Blinds.** Price, per set........ .22

Kenwood Warehouse Fanning Mill.

This mill has two shoes which move in opposite directions. The upper shoe carries the sieves which separate the straws and coarse materials from the grain or seeds being cleaned. The lower shoe extends the entire depth of the mill and carries the screens which separate the dirt, fine seeds, etc. As is well known, the most important part of seed cleaning is done by the lower screens; therefore, as this mill has three or four times the screening surface found in other mills of corresponding size, it will be readily understood that it is by far the best mill. Perfect grading is accomplished by means of the combination of screens and discharge spouts in lower shoe. **Both shoes rest on roller bearings,** making the movement smooth and even. The shaking device is very substantial and is so arranged that it can be graduated to meet all requirements, from a long shake for chaffing grains, to a very short and quick shake such as is necessary for the perfect cleaning of fine seeds. **The regular outfit furnished with this mill is called a grain outfit,** and consists of one wheat or rye hurdle, with zinc top and wire middle and bottom sieves; one corn or oats sieve; one barley or bean sieve; three wheat or barley screens; one pair of fan blinds, and one cheat or cockle board. **Additional sieves and screens** will be furnished at prices shown below. Always shipped set up unless otherwise ordered. If "knocked down" an extra charge of $1.50 will be made. The mill is 39 inches wide, sieves 20 inches deep, screen shoe 48 inches deep. Has 6x3-inch tight and loose pulleys. Capacity of mill 150 to 300 bushels of wheat per hour. Weight, 325 pounds. **Shipped direct from factory in Southeastern Wisconsin.**

No. 32R2030 **Warehouse Fanning Mill.** Price........ **$20.40**

No. 32R2031 Extra wire sieves. Price, each........ .69

No. 32R2032 Extra wire screens. Price, each........ .82

No. 32R2033 Flax outfit, 1 sieve and 2 screens. Price........ 2.30

No. 32R2034 Clover outfit, 1 sieve and 2 screens. Price........ 2.31

No. 32R2035 Timothy outfit, 1 sieve and 2 screens. Price........ 2.32

No. 32R2036 Hungarian or millet outfit, 1 sieve and 2 screens. Price 2.33

No. 32R2037 Extra hurdles. Price, each........ 2.60

No. 32R2038 Blinds. Price, per pair........ .27

Acme Outdoor Hot Air Brooders.

These Brooders can be used either outdoor or indoor, and are equally desirable in either place. They are warmed by top heat exclusively, the hot air tank being located in the rear half of the brooder. Only the best of materials are used in the construction of these brooders and we unhesitatingly guarantee them to be perfect and satisfactory in every

way. Furnished complete with metal bowl lamp, thermometer, runway and all attachments. The 200-chick size is a double machine, heated by one lamp. **Shipped direct from factory in Western Illinois.**

	Capacity	Weight	Price
No. 32R2584	50 chicks	56 pounds	**$ 4.73**
No. 32R2585	100 chicks	94 pounds	**6.65**
No. 32R2586	200 chicks	168 pounds	**11.70**

Acme Outdoor Hot Water Brooder.

Exactly the same as our Acme Outdoor Hot Air Brooder, except that heat is supplied by hot water contained in a copper tank. Furnished complete with metal bowl lamp, thermometer, runway and all attachments. **Shipped direct from factory in Western Illinois.**

	Capacity	Weight	Price
No. 32R2591	200 chicks	178 pounds	**$13.95**

Acme Indoor Hot Air Incubator, Brooder and Yard Combined.

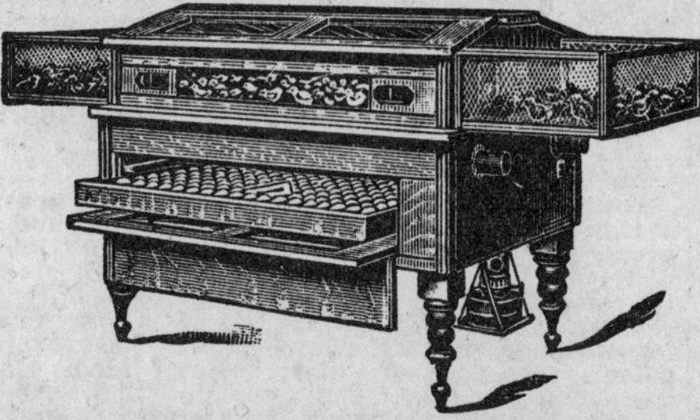

The usefulness and economy of the Incubator and Brooder combined is too well known to need extensive explanation. The surplus heat which escapes from the incubator is utilized in heating the brooder. The incubator part of our combined incubator and brooder is the same style and description as our high grade Improved Acme Incubator, heated, fitted and furnished in the same manner and supplied with the same extras. The brooder is built on top of the incubator, and the yards at the ends of the brooder. The 50-egg or chick size has one yard only, the other sizes a yard at each end. The 300 and 400-egg or chick sizes are double machines and are fitted with two lamps. For special description of the heating apparatus, see description of our Improved Acme Hot Air Incubators. Shipped direct from factory in Western Illinois.

	Capacity	Weight	Price
No. 32R2600	50 eggs or chicks	80 lbs.	**$13.85**
No. 32R2601	100 eggs or chicks	190 lbs.	**22.10**
No. 32R2603	200 eggs or chicks	270 lbs.	**29.90**
No. 32R2604	300 eggs or chicks	370 lbs.	**38.50**
No. 32R2605	400 eggs or chicks	470 lbs.	**46.15**

Acme Indoor Hot Water Incubator, Brooder and Yard Combined.

These machines are exactly like the Acme Indoor Hot Air Incubator, Brooder and Yard combined, and are fitted and furnished in the same manner, except that the incubator is the same as the Improved Acme Hot Water Incubator, to which we refer you for special description. Shipped direct from factory in Western Illinois.

	Capacity	Weight	Price
No. 32R2606	50 eggs or chicks	85 lbs.	**$16.80**
No. 32R2607	100 eggs or chicks	200 lbs.	**27.40**
No. 32R2608	150 eggs or chicks	240 lbs.	**29.95**
No. 32R2609	200 eggs or chicks	285 lbs.	**34.20**
No. 32R2610	300 eggs or chicks	410 lbs.	**46.20**
No. 32R2611	400 eggs or chicks	500 lbs.	**54.60**

Acme Sectional Double Loop Indoor Hot Water Brooders.

For extensive breeders these are the most economical brooders on the market. The heating system is perfect, the materials used are the best which can be obtained, and only experienced and careful workmen are employed in making these brooders. Made in six sizes, from 3 feet to 18 feet long. Two lamps furnished with each size, one at each end of the four smaller sizes and two in the center of the two largest sizes. The hot water pipes of the smaller sizes extend toward the center from each heater, but in the larger sizes the pipes extend both ways from the center, and in these the heat can be shut off from one end of the brooder when not in use. The lamp bodies are metal, the water boilers and the reservoir above them are made of cold rolled copper, and the piping is such as is used by steamfitters. Furnished complete with thermometer, runways and all attachments. **Shipped direct from factory in Western Illinois.**

	Length	Capacity	Weight	Price
No. 32R2612	3 feet	125 chicks	65 lbs.	**$10.30**
No. 32R2613	6 feet	250 chicks	100 lbs.	**12.75**
No. 32R2614	9 feet	375 chicks	160 lbs.	**15.45**
No. 32R2615	12 feet	500 chicks	210 lbs.	**18.00**
No. 32R2616	15 feet	625 chicks	260 lbs.	**20.20**
No. 32R2617	18 feet	750 chicks	310 lbs.	**22.70**

Our Acme Egg Cabinets.

Every poultry raiser should have one or more of these cabinets in which to preserve eggs for hatching purposes. They are supplied with patent turning trays, so that all the eggs in one tray are turned with one movement. The device will be appreciated because it is well known that eggs for hatching should be turned every twenty-four hours, otherwise the yolk will adhere to the shell and the eggs will not hatch. **Shipped direct from factory in Western Illinois.**

	Capacity	Weight	Price
No. 32R2618	100 eggs	20 pounds	**$2.93**
No. 32R2619	200 eggs	34 pounds	**3.42**
No. 32R2620	300 eggs	50 pounds	**3.92**
No. 32R2621	400 eggs	65 pounds	**4.90**

Farmer's Favorite Brood Coops.

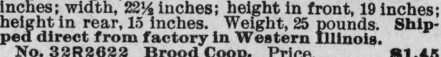

A practical and convenient nursery for young chicks. A perfect safeguard through the night against cats, minks, weasles, rats, etc. Both the front and the back of these coops are furnished with doors that are easily and securely fastened, but which do not interfere with the perfect ventilation of the coop. Length, 2 feet, 7 inches; width, 22½ inches; height in front, 19 inches; height in rear, 15 inches. Weight, 25 pounds. **Shipped direct from factory in Western Illinois.**

No. 32R2622 Brood Coop. Price..........**$1.45**

Metallic Poultry Feed Troughs.

When a large number of fowls are raised there is a great waste of soft feed when fed in the ordinary way. These feed troughs prevent such waste. They are made of japanned iron with coppered wire guards, and at the price we offer them will save their cost in a month's time. Length, 18 inches; width, 8½ inches. Weight, 4 pounds.

No. 32R2623 Feed Trough. Price...........**92c**

Galvanized Poultry Drinking Fountains.

A Fountain which can be easily cleaned and which will not burst open should the water be allowed to freeze in it, unless it is entirely full and frozen solid. The interior can be scalded and water will be fresh and clean at all times and nearly as cool as it would be in an earthen vessel. **Made entirely of galvanized iron.**

No. 32R2624 Fountain. Capacity, 2 quarts. Weight, 1½ pounds. Price..............................**33c**

No. 32R2625 Fountain. Capacity, 1 gallon. Weight, 2½ pounds. Price..............................**42c**

No. 32R2626 Fountain. Capacity, 2 gallons. Weight, 4 pounds. Price..............................**57c**

Adjustable Egg Carrier.

A convenient, light and durable crate, which will carry any number of eggs up to 12 dozen. It consists of a wood case fitted with standard egg fillers and is equipped with an adjustable cover and a combination lifter and fastener. The lid can be dropped and secured at any desired point, holding the eggs secure and safe from breakage.

No. 32R2627 Egg Carrier. Weight, 6¾ lbs. Price...**29c**

Genuine Humpty Dumpty Folding Egg Crate.

Will hold twelve dozen eggs complete with fillers. Avoids broken eggs, prevents mistakes in counting, folds up flat for shipping or carrying when there are no eggs in it. Strongly made with hard maple slats. Weight, 5½ pounds.

No. 32R2628 Egg Crate. Price..............................**23c**

Metallic Hen's Nests.

These nests are made from steel wire, japanned. They are clean, afford no place for vermin and are recommended by poultry raisers everywhere. Can be fastened to the wall with two screws.

No. 32R2629 Hen's Nest. Weight, 5 ounces. Price..................**5c**

Folding Egg Tester.

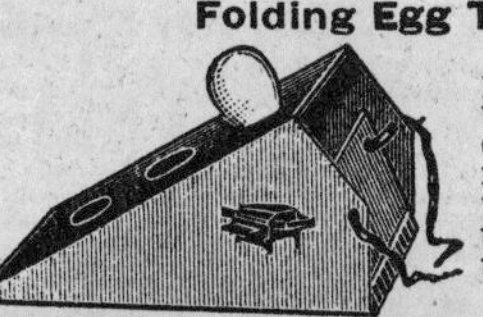

This is a very simple and inexpensive tester, but perfect in every respect. It is made of pasteboard with holes to receive the eggs and a mirror to reflect the light. Weight, 3 ounces.

No. 32R2630 Egg Tester. Price..............**11c**

Metallic Egg Testers.

Consisting of a metal bowl lamp, a metallic chimney with mica window and a testing tube which fits onto the chimney over the mica window. The eggs are placed over the end of the testing tube, between the eye and the light. Made with either galvanized or copper bowl lamp. Chimney will fit ordinary lamp burners.

No. 32R2631 Egg Tester, with galvanized bowl lamp. Weight, 16 ounces. Price...**91c**

No. 32R2632 Egg Tester, with copper bowl lamp. Weight, 18 ounces. Price..**$1.19**

No. 32R2633 Chimney and testing tube only. Weight, 6 ounces. Price..............................**29c**

Spring Lever Poultry Punch.

If you wish to keep a record of your chickens of the different breeds, hatches, strains, etc., there is no better way than by using our spring lever punch. It makes a clean cut, will not tear the web, and its operation is not obstructed by the hands of the operator. Weight, 2 ounces.

No. 32R2634 Poultry Punch. Price........**27c**

Poultry Fountain and Hen House Warmer.

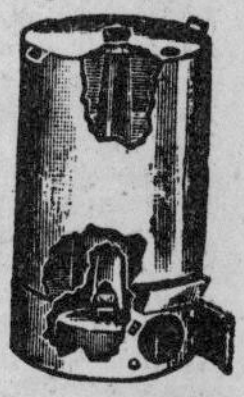

The Acme Poultry Fountain and Hen House Warmer holds about 10 gallons of water and is so constructed as to supply the poultry with water just as fast and no faster than they drink it. The cups out of which they drink fill automatically. **The heat from the lamp, and radiation from the water always keep your hen house comfortable. Water always clean and fresh, and poultry never without drink.** Weight crated, 20 pounds.

No. 32R2635 Poultry Fountain. Price....**$3.35**

Poultry Fountain, Warmer and Feeder.

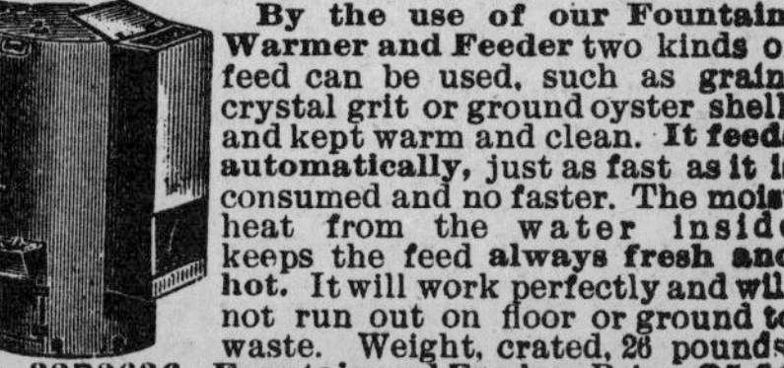

By the use of our Fountain, Warmer and Feeder two kinds of feed can be used, such as grain, crystal grit or ground oyster shell, and kept warm and clean. **It feeds automatically,** just as fast as it is consumed and no faster. **The moist heat from the water inside keeps the feed always fresh and hot.** It will work perfectly and will not run out on floor or ground to waste. Weight, crated, 26 pounds.

No. 32R2636 Fountain and Feeder. Price...**$5.00**

OUR $24.45 KENWOOD HAND HAY PRESS.

THIS IS ONE OF THE GREATEST MONEY MAKING AND MONEY SAVING DEVICES ever invented in the way of an agricultural implement. No farm can be considered complete without it. No matter how much or how little baling is done with a power press, there is always a certain amount of hay, straw, etc., which will go to waste unless there be some means of saving it. **Our Kenwood Hand Hay Press provides this means. It is cheap, it is compact, it is powerful, and above all it is practical.** With it two men, or one man and a boy can bale from two to four tons per day, turning out perfect bales of a uniform size, weighing from 90 to 110 pounds per bale, depending upon the condition of the hay.

WITH THIS PRESS you can not only bale hay and straw, but corn husks, flax, tow, hops, cotton, waste paper, or any other material which can be put up in bales. All of this work can be done at odd times, during stormy days, or when there is nothing else requiring attention. This press is made of the very best quality of hardwood lumber, is strongly braced throughout, has malleable iron hinges and corner irons, and is put together with bolts, making the press exceedingly substantial. It is 3 feet wide by 5 feet long on the base, 11 feet 4 inches high when plunger is at its highest point, 6 feet 10 inches high when plunger is down. The lever which operates the plunger is 8 feet long, and through the compound principle which is applied between this lever and the plunger, a weight of 100 pounds on the end of the lever gives a pressure of about 10 tons on the plunger, compressing the hay perfectly. Press can be operated freely in a space of about 6 by 14 feet. Height from floor to bottom of charging chamber is 3 feet 9 inches; charging chamber is 17 inches by 21 inches. Hay is placed in the press when plunger is at its highest point, the plunger is released by a foot lever and allowed to fall upon the loose hay, then the operator compresses the hay by means of the lever. The plunger is raised by a rope which runs over a sheave and attaches to the lever, one movement of the lever raising the plunger to its full height.

THE BALING CHAMBER is 17 inches by 21 inches by 3 feet 6 inches, and the four sides are corrugated or grooved, effectually preventing the hay from springing back when the plunger is raised for a new charge. The bottom of the charging chamber is hinged and can be raised so as to force all loose ends under the plunger, and the bale is as compact and smooth as can be made with a power press.

The front door and one side are held in place by a lock lever. When bale is completed this lever is released, the front door opened wide and the side door swung away from the bale. The bale ties are put through grooves at the top and bottom from the back and tied in front. Plunger is then raised, bale removed and door closed and locked, ready for another bale. Use 10 feet No. 15 Single Loop Bale Ties. **No more useful machine can be placed on the farm, and at our price no farmer can afford to be without a Kenwood Hand Hay Press. Will pay for itself in six to eight days' work. Shipped direct from factory in Southern Michigan.**

No. 32R2945 **Hay Press.** Weight, 425 pounds. Price..........**$24.45**

No. 32R2946 **Bale Ties for above.** Weight, 35 lbs. Price, per bundle **$1.35**

Acme No. 1 Full Circle Hay Press.

In our Acme No. 1 Full Circle Press we have a press that will do more and better work than any horse power press on the market. This press has been on the market for the past five years, and during that time has made a record for itself that cannot be beaten. It is made largely of steel, and all castings are very heavy and made in such a way that breakage is almost impossible. The plunger is 4 inches thick, 10 inches wide and 16 feet long, and works forward on a 36-inch stroke. Size of bale, 14x18 inches and 36 inches long, which weighs as near 100 pounds as possible. Plunger makes two strokes to one round of horses. We furnish our patent lifting Jack with each press without extra charge, which enables you to lower the press in position for use with ease. Weight, 2,600 pounds. **Shipped direct from factory in Eastern Minnesota.**

No. 32R2950 No. 1 Hay Press. Price...**$144.00**

Our New Acme No. 2 Patent Full Circle Hay Press.

The Acme No. 2 Single Stroke Press. With this machine we are introducing some entirely new ideas of the application of power to **horse hay presses.** For efficiency, simplicity and durability, it stands without an equal. We challenge anybody to produce a machine that will press as much hay with as little horse power as this one will. It is the simplest press imaginable. Nothing about it that is likely to break. Only ten castings on it. Its simplicity **makes it an ideal farmers' press, and its low price puts it within the reach of all.** The power leverage is about 1 to 132; more than **twice** what other presses use. We use only a 10-foot sweep and one horse. If the bales do not run too heavy, one horse will work our press all day, just as easily as he will draw his load on a wagon. **It is strictly a two-horse press operated easily with one horse.** It gets its great capacity as a one-horse press from the idea of a short sweep; the horse makes nearly double the number of revolutions per minute that are made on the ordinary two-horse press. Then its large feed opening enables it to take large forks of hay. **Four men, a boy to drive and one horse constitutes the crew. On the road the power is carried on top of the baler. It is easily loaded and unloaded by two men and one horse.** Bale chamber 17x21 inches opening and the plunger has a 39-inch stroke. Weight, 3,800 pounds. **Shipped direct from factory in Southern Michigan.**

No. 32R2960 No. 2 Hay Press. Price...**$182.25**

SEND 15 CENTS FOR A YEARS' SUBSCRIPTION TO OUR MONEY SAVING **GROCERY PRICE LIST.**

Acme No. 3 Power Hay Press.

In our Acme No. 3 Hay Press, we have the most complete, easiest running and simplest press we have ever handled. It is not a complication of cogwheels, levers, etc., but has fewer parts than any power press on the market. It requires 8 to 10-horse power to run it to its full capacity; size of bale, 14x18 inches, to weigh from 100 to 110 pounds; capacity, 1 bale per minute. We can also furnish the press for horse power when so desired, which consists of countershaft and attachment for tumbling rod. Weight of press complete, 4,500 pounds. **Shipped direct from factory in Eastern Minnesota.**

No. 32R2970 No. 3 Hay Press, complete for steam power. Price....................**$180.30**

No. 32R2971 No. 3 Hay Press, complete for horse power. Price....................**$195.00**

Genuine Smith Tree and Stump Pullers.

No. 2 Smith Stump Puller.

Each No. 2 machine is supplied with a 6-foot anchor loop, a 50-foot pull rope with hook and coupling attached, a drum lock to hold what is pulled, and a stop for the sweep to hold it from revolving back. This size machine is strong enough for two horses on a 12-foot sweep. We ship the machine complete, except poles, as poles can be cut in the timber where machine is to be used, saving freight from factory. We do not use a rope longer than 50 feet in one piece; each rope is prepared to couple to another rope; our coupler weighs only 6 pounds, is as strong as the rope and couples as easy as hooking a chain. To do away with slack rope we drop off a piece. As all the rope is not all the time in use, there is less rope to handle and consequently less wear on the rope. **Price includes everything described above. Weight, 275 pounds. Shipped direct from factory in Southeastern Minnesota.**

No. 32R3030 No. 2 Stump Puller. Price..**$24.00**

No. 3 Smith Stump Puller.

The description of No. 3 is the same as that given of No. 2, except in the amount of rope, and in the weight, strength and capacity of the machine itself. This machine is supplied with our new 25-foot anchor rope, anchoring to a tree, or close to a stump, or far enough from a tree or stump to operate between the anchor stump and the stump being pulled, without having to cut a tree or stump down to allow the sweep to pass over. This machine is also supplied with a 50-foot pull rope with hook and coupling attached. This machine is strong enough for two horses on a 14-foot sweep; the drum winds 80 feet of rope. Shipping weight, 400 pounds. **Shipped direct from factory in Southeastern Minnesota.**

No. 32R3031 No. 3 Stump Puller. Price..**$33.60**

No. 4 Smith Stump Puller.

This machine comes under the same general description as Nos. 2 and 3. Each machine is supplied with a 25-foot anchor rope, a 75-foot pull rope with hook and coupling attached (this rope is our special tempered best steel stump puller rope), a drum lock to hold what is pulled, a stop on the sweep to hold it from going back, a throw-off to ungear sweep from drum, to let off rope, or to allow team to cross pull rope with loose tugs, or to allow sweep to swing part way back to make the pull without crossing the rope. We ship the machine complete except poles, as poles can be cut in the timber where the machine is to be used and bolted on, saving freight; we send bolts. Each part of this machine is strong enough for two horses on a 16-foot sweep. It pulls trees and stumps from 1-inch to 5 feet in diameter; it pulls trees faster than ten men can cut the same trees down; it pulls 300 stumps in a day; it clears two acres in a day; it saves the labor of ten men; it will never wear out and cannot be broken when our instructions are followed. Shipping weight, 500 pounds. **Shipped direct from factory in Southeastern Minnesota.**

No. 32R3032 No. 4 Stump Puller. Price..**$38.70**

No. 11 Smith Stump Puller.

This machine is extra strong and very heavy. It is made especially for pulling large pine, and is giving perfect satisfaction in the various timber districts where it is in general use. This puller is fitted complete with 25-foot anchor rope, 75 feet of pull rope with hooks and couplings attached. Warranted for two horses on a 20-foot sweep. We do not furnish poles, as they can be cut where machine is to be used, thus saving freight. Weight, complete as described, 900 pounds. **Shipped direct from factory in Southeastern Minnesota.**

No. 32R3033 No. 11 Stump Puller. Price..**$55.40**

NOTE—We do not guarantee stump puller rope against breakage, because while we furnish the **best rope which can be made, there is no steel rope which will not break if it is bent around a short turn or allowed to kink.** ¾-inch special steel stump puller rope, with hemp center, furnished with above stump pullers.

Attachments and Extras for Smith Stump Pullers.

No. 32R3040 **¾-inch Special Steel Stump Puller Rope,** sold only in 25 or 50-foot lengths. Price, per foot, couplings and hooks not included..........**$0.25**

No. 32R3041 **Couplers for above rope.** Price, each....................**$1.05**

No. 32R3042 **Patent Multiplying Pulley,** complete with hitch rope. Price..........**$7.50**

No. 32R3043 **Patent Snatch Block.** Price, 14.10

No. 32R3044 **Combination Pulley Blocks,** to increase power four times. Price..........**$11.00**

No. 32R3045 **Double Hitches.** Price...... 5.00

No. 32R3046 **Patent Pulley Blocks,** to double power. Price....................**$9.35**

No. 32R3047 **Patent Rope Shortener.** Price, 5.05

No. 32R3048 **Patent Low Stump and Root Hook.** Price....................**$9.85**

No. 32R3049 **Double Pointed Steel Root Hook.** Price....................**$5.10**

No. 32R3050 **Patent Rope Hook.** Price... 1.65

No. 32R3051 **Patent 25-foot Anchor Rope.** Price....................**$8.95**

No. 32R3052 **Patent 9-foot Anchor Rope.** Price....................**$4.95**

No. 32R3053 **Patent 6-foot Anchor Rope.** Price....................**$4.20**

NOTE—When ordering stump puller rope remember to order one coupler and one patent rope hook for each piece of rope.

Acme Tilting Table Pole Saw Frame.

This cut represents our Acme Pole Saw. The name suggests the purpose for which this saw is intended, and to meet the demand for such a machine **we have spared no pains in making every part first class.** The shafts are 1½-inch steel, running in babbitted boxes. **Notice the balance wheel shaft** runs clear across the frame in heavy boxes at each end, pulley 5-inch diameter and 6-inch face. **The saw works equally well on cordwood and is just the thing for every farmer.** Arbor fitted for blade with 1⅜-inch hole. All fully guaranteed. Price does not include saw blade. We always ship right hand frame unless left hand frame is ordered. Weight, 350 pounds. **Shipped direct from factory, which is near Chicago.**

No. 32R3812 Saw Frame, with 95-pound balance wheel. Price..**$17.00**

No. 32R3813 Saw Frame, with 125-pound balance wheel. Price..**$17.75**

Acme Tilting Table Wood Saw Frame.

The frame is of hardwood, strongly mortised, the joints fastened by iron bolts at both top and bottom. The shaft of saw or mandrel is steel. The boxes or bearings are extra long to insure steadiness. The feed frame holds long or short timber with equal facility. Has 1½-inch steel shaft; arbor is fitted for saw with 1⅜-inch hole. Price does not include saw blade. We always ship right hand frame unless left hand frame is ordered. Weight, 275 pounds. **Shipped direct from factory, which is near Chicago.**

No. 32R3820 Saw Frame, with 95-pound balance wheel. Price..**$14.00**

No. 32R3821 Saw Frame, with 125-pound balance wheel. Price..**$14.75**

No. 32R3822 Extension Parts for attaching table outside of saw, so that long poles may be sawed. Price..**$1.30**

Saw Frame Irons.

No. 32R3832 Complete set of irons for sliding table wood saw frame, consisting of 1 saw arbor with collars, 1 pair of boxes, 1 pulley 5 inches in diameter by 6-inch face, 1 95-pound balance wheel, 1 set of standard track with rollers, and 1 set of table irons. Weight, 184 pounds. Price........................**$10.30**

No. 32R3833 Complete set of irons for tilting table pole saw frame, consisting of 1 saw arbor with collars, 1 pair of boxes, 1 pulley 5 inches in diameter by 6-inch face, 1 95-pound balance wheel, 1 intermediate pulley with stud and bracket, 1 countershaft with pulley and boxes, 1 set of table irons and 1 saw guard. Weight, 268 pounds. Price.....**$12.50**

No. 32R3834 Complete set of irons for tilting table wood saw frame, consisting of 1 saw arbor with collars, 1 pair of boxes, 1 pulley 5 inches in diameter by 6-inch face, 1 95-pound balance wheel, 1 set of table irons and 1 saw guard. Weight, 192 pounds. Price..**$9.50**

For 125-pound balance wheel in place of 95-pound wheel, add..**75c**

NOTE—Our saw arbors are about 4 feet 2 inches long. We are not prepared to furnish other than regular irons as described above. Shipped direct from factory, which is near Chicago.

Sears, Roebuck & Co.'s Circular Cut-Off Saws.

Patent ground and tempered solid teeth of extra quality, superior workmanship. Circular saws must not be filed with a square corner in gullet. If so filed any saw will most likely crack. Our guarantee does not cover saws cracked from this cause, or if not kept in proper condition. Price does not include filing or setting.

No. 35R132

Diam.	Thickness, Gauge	Size of Hole	Price each
20 inches	13	1⅜ inches	$4.08
22 inches	12	1⅜ inches	4.80
24 inches	11	1⅜ inches	5.76
26 inches	11	1⅜ inches	6.72
28 inches	10	1⅜ inches	7.68
30 inches	10	1⅜ inches	8.64

Size of hole given above is special, for our wood and pole saw frames which require saws with 1⅜-inch hole. In ordering saws remember to state size of hole, as well as diameter of saw wanted.

One Man Sawing Machine.

This machine is sold at a low price and is an efficient and easy running implement; furnished with the very best grade Champion tooth saw; has all the advantages of any hand power cross cut saw made; the uncomfortable bent position when sawing in the usual way is overcome and **a natural upright position secured,** enabling the full force and weight of the body to be thrown on the saw. Intended for sawing logs after trees are down. Weight, 44 pounds.

No. 32R3850 Sawing Machine, with one 5-foot saw. Price..**$6.40**

No. 32R3851 Extra Saw Blades. Each... **2.45**

Mosher Bag Holder.

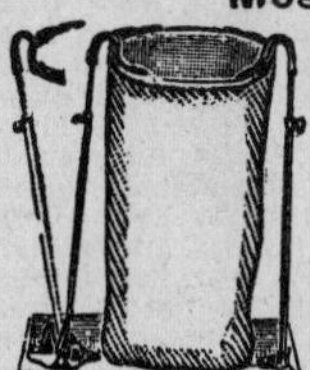

This is the only holder adapted to all sizes of bags, from a 48-pound flour sack to a 6-bushel gunny sack. One man can take off and put on 15 to 20 bags per minute. **Does not tear the bag. Has malleable jaws, with wrought iron pipe standards and steel spring. Weight, 20 pounds.**

No. 32R3875 Bag Holder. Price..**$2.60**

Perfection Sack Holder.

The Perfection Sack Holder has no equal, because: It is the only sack holder that fits any length of sack. It will not injure sack. A sack filled by using the Perfection Sack Holder needs no refilling; others do. It will hold sack without hem. It requires little space and can be used in almost any place. With ordinary care it will last a lifetime.

No. 32R3877 Sack Holder. Price..**$1.20**

Our Perfect Bag Holder.

The only bag holder made which does not require a special frame to support it and which is convenient to carry from place to place. It does not require two men to fill a bag with grain. One man can do it all with this holder. All that is necessary is to hang the bag holder on the side of the bin or crib, or on the end of the wagon box if you are out in the field or on a frame, as shown in cut, place the grain bag on the holder and shovel the grain in. It holds bag perfectly, and the mouth wide open. There is nothing about this holder to lacerate the hands or tear the bag. It is made entirely of wrought iron, and will last a lifetime. **The small cut at the bottom shows the bag holder complete.** Weight, 2¼ pounds.

No. 32R3878 Perfect Bag Holder. Price....**70c**

The Merrimac Hand Carts.

Having received numerous calls for a hand cart made of better material, finished better, of lighter construction, we have added the Merrimac Carts to our line. They are, without doubt, the strongest, lightest and easiest running cart made. The Merrimac Hand Cart is thoroughly painted and varnished. The body is made of wood and is well ironed. It is strong, durable, neat and light. Fine, oil tempered springs and the best metallic wheel made. **The leg being V shaped** and pivoted at its two extremities to the body forms an effective handle brace, hooked by turning the handle roll. **The wheels are lower than the top of box** to carry trunks and boxes, or anything of large size, with the horn on top of front posts to hold the same from sliding off. **Our claims for the Merrimac Hand Cart:** Extreme lightness; our carts weighing only about one-third of an ordinary hand cart. A boy of ten years is able to take 250 pounds in these carts. Size inside body, 39x20¼ inches; wheels, 26 inches high; carrying capacity, 250 pounds. Weight, 62 pounds.

No. 32R3880 Two-Wheel Merrimac Cart. Price..**$6.00**

Merrimac Three-Wheel Hand Cart.

For description of this cart see No. 32R3880. In construction and size it is the same with the addition of a third wheel in front. Size inside body, 39x20¼ inches; depth 9½ inches; wheels, 26 inches high; carrying capacity, 250 pounds. Weight, 68 pounds.

No. 32R3882 Three-Wheel Merrimac Cart. Price..**$6.40**

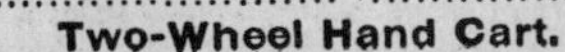

Two-Wheel Hand Cart.

This is a very useful cart on the farm. Has 36-inch steel wheels, box is 24x36 inches in size, 10 inches deep. Has drop end gate, bent handles, iron foot rest, iron hubs, is well painted and striped. Weight, 85 pounds.

No. 32R3884 Two-Wheel Hand Cart. Price....**$4.50**

Three-Wheel Hand Cart.

Same style and size as our No. 32R3884 except that it has a third wheel in front which assists in crossing gutters, etc. This style cart is used largely throughout the South. For size, etc., see No. 32R3884.

No. 32R3886 Three-Wheel Hand Cart. Price..**$5.00**

ACME COMBINED POLE SAW FRAME AND JACK.

This outfit is especially adapted for use with a sweep horse power, so that the power may be attached direct to the jack. It is made with tilting table saw frame, as shown in cut, or with sliding table saw frame. The advantages are: First, you have an 8-foot foundation for your sawing machine; but one setting of the saw frame is all that is required.

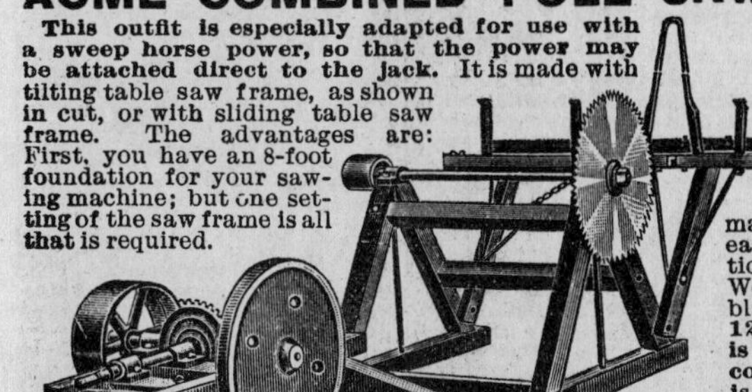

The only staking down that is required is a couple of iron stakes, or drag teeth, driven in the center holes in each side of the frame base to keep the frame from working endwise, the saw frame and jack being spliced with slotted irons which form a belt tightener between the belt and the saw frame, and a hinge by which the jack may be folded up against the saw, so it may be easily moved from place to place. For description see our Acme Tilting and Sliding Table Wood Saw Frames. Price does not include saw blade. Average weight, 625 pounds. **Requires 12 feet of 6-inch 4-ply rubber belting, which is extra. Jack shaft is squared for 1⅛-inch coupling. Shipped direct from factory, which is near Chicago.**

No. 32R3824 Combined Tilting Table Pole Saw Frame and Jack with 95-pound balance wheel. Price.....**$20.50**

No. 32R3825 Combined Tilting Table Pole Saw Frame and Jack with 125-pound balance wheel. Price........................**$21.25**

No. 32R3826 Combined Sliding Table Pole Saw Frame and Jack with 95-pound balance wheel. Price..**$21.50**

No. 32R3827 Combined Sliding Table Pole Saw Frame and Jack with 125-lb. balance wheel. Price.. **22.25**

Our Steel Frame Barrel Cart.

This Cart is made entirely of steel, no wood being used in its construction. Wheels are 36 inches high. The frame, wheels, and all are made of the very best Bessemer steel, all made extra strong and will stand any kind of usage. We do not furnish the barrel, but only the frame, wheels, and irons to attach to barrel. It will fit any kind of a kerosene, molasses, or vinegar barrel. Barrel bolts to the two side bars and axle irons with three bolts on each side. Weight, 55 pounds.

No. 32R3887 Steel Frame Barrel Cart. Price...... **$3.25**

Our $2.95 Wood Frame Barrel Cart.

We furnish the cart only, which can be attached to any barrel. **Very useful for gardening and feeding purposes.** Large flanges to fit barrel. Is secured to barrel by two bolts on each side and one through cross bar. Please note that we do not furnish the barrel, but any good molasses or kerosene barrel will answer. Has 36-inch steel wheels. Weight, 65 pounds.

No. 32R3888 Wood Frame Barrel Cart. Price...... **$2.95**

General Utility Cart.

Almost indispensable on any farm. The illustrations show this combination barrel and general utility cart used as a handcart with box; the dotted lines in the illustration showing the manner in which the box can be dumped, also as a barrel cart with the box removed, which can be done in an instant, also the cart with wire reel attachment, for paying out or winding up fence wire. The attachment to barrel and the attachment for the automatic dumping of the box are also shown in one of the illustrations. **The barrel irons have good strong gudgeons and bolt to each side of the barrel.** The cart will pick up the barrel or box in a moment. **One cart answers for any number of barrels required.** Wheels are 36 inches high. Box is 4 feet long, 2 feet, 6 inches wide, 6 inches deep. Please note that we do not furnish the barrel, but any kerosene, molasses or vinegar barrel will answer. Weight, 100 pounds.

No. 32R3889 General Utility Cart, with box and one pair of barrel irons. Price...... **$5.05**
No. 32R3890 General Utility Cart, without box, but with one pair of barrel irons. Price...... **$3.90**
No. 32R3891 Price of box extra... 1.50
No. 32R3892 Price of box irons, per pair... .45
No. 32R3893 Price of barrel irons, per pair. .46
No. 32R3894 Price of axle irons, per pair... .47
No. 32R3895 Price of wire reel attachment 1.49
No. 32R3896 Steel wheels for carts, 36 inches in diameter, 1¼-inch tire, 4¾-inch hub for ⅞-inch axle. Price, per pair...... **$1.90**

The Acme Shoveling Board for $1.35.

No loose parts to be detached or to be lost. The rods do not extend below the box to catch or get bent. It is not attached to the box, **making it more substantial.** It can be thrown on top of the box without detaching. **Very useful in dumping grain or shelled corn, or on hog or sheep racks.** Weight, 45 pounds.

No. 32R3925 Shoveling Board. Price..... **$1.35**

SEE PAGES 7 TO 10 FOR FREIGHT RATES.

Acme Combination Grain, Hay and Stock Rack.

The Acme Combination Grain, Hay and Stock Rack is the only practical combination rack built. Warranted to carry 4,500 pounds. A rear end stock gate and a rear hay standard are furnished with each rack. The box sides are made 3 feet 2 inches wide by 12 inches deep. Made in 14 and 16-foot lengths; furnished complete as shown in cut. **Shipped direct from factory in Central Michigan.** Weight, about 400 pounds.

No. 32R3930 14-foot Rack. Price...... **$12.25**
No. 32R3931 16-foot Rack. Price....... **12.95**

The Acme Automatic Stock Waterer.

Operated by a simple float, which is connected to a rust proof valve that can be easily taken out, but is thoroughly protected by our latest improved partition. Our pan and nipple being cast solid, there is no possibility of leak, no leather joint to become rotten and fall out. **This is a great improvement** over others now in the market. We have claims which thoroughly cover this invention. Many hogs die from disease which originates in filthy water or filthy wood troughs. Bad water is full of cholera germs, so get an Acme Watering Trough and have clean, pure water for your stock at all times. Partitions and lid are cast together, so trough can be easily cleaned without taking apart. Our Acme Troughs will supply many head of hogs, sheep, calves, etc., for they cannot waste the water. One trough may be used to supply two pens. Each end of trough holds about one gallon of water. Weight, 13 pounds.

No. 32R3935 Stock Waterer. Price........ **$1.10**

Acme No. 2 Stock Waterer.

The latest and most up to date waterer on the market. Operated by a metal ball float connected to a rust proof valve closing on a rubber valve seat. It is entirely automatic. As soon as the pan fills up to near the top the float shuts the water off and no more can run out until the stock come to drink. The float chamber is inside of the barrel or tank and is out of the way of all mud and trash. It is impossible for mud to gather under the float. **One trough may be used to supply two pens** and will furnish water for 150 to 200 head of hogs, calves, chickens, etc., for they cannot waste the water. **Our No. 2 is quickly attached to a barrel or stock tank** by boring a 2-inch auger hole, placing the stem of float chamber through it and tightening the cap over the end of stem with two bolts. Weight, 11 pounds.

No. 32R3937 No. 2 Stock Waterer. Price, **$1.15**

Acme No. 4 Stock Waterer.

For horses, dairy barns, etc. Has double drinking compartments, also improved eccentric valve which prevents leakage, etc. Can be attached to city water pressure for private barns, etc. Those who are using this system of watering, claim that their cows give more milk during the cold weather because they have water where they can sip it a little at a time. **Some state that the increase is 25 per cent.** At this rate the pans would pay for themselves in a very short time. Pans are easily connected by running a pipe along the floor from supply tank and connecting each pan with a short piece of pipe. Each pan waters two cows. For private stables and livery barns, we make the pan fitted with an eccentric valve which will operate up to 80 pound pressure, any heavier pressure merely holds the valve shut. For street watering in small towns where there is no sewer system and where saving of water is an object, these waterers are a great convenience. Weight, 30 pounds.

No. 32R3939 No. 4 Stock Waterer, tapped for 1-inch pipe. Price...... **$2.65**
No. 32R3940 No. 4 Stock Waterer, tapped for ¾-inch pipe and fitted with eccentric valve to work up to 80-pound city pressure. Price........ **$3.90**

Our Round Cast Iron Pig Trough.

In each trough there are eight compartments; eight large hogs can eat at one time. Different kinds of feed can be fed at the same time, the bowls preventing them mixing. **Hogs cannot upset the trough and waste their feed,** nor is there any leaking. Made of cast iron, they will not break; in fact are indestructible. Height, 24 inches; width, 32 inches. Weight, 120 pounds.

No. 32R3942 Round Pig Trough. Price.. **$4.85**

Our Half Round Cast Iron Pig Trough.

This Trough is made with four compartments, and is intended to be placed beside a fence or building, allowing four hogs to eat at one time. Height, 24 inches; width across back, 32 inches. Weight, 100 pounds.

No. 32R3943 Half Round Pig Trough. Price...... **$3.95**

Our All Steel Road Scrapers.

Made from heavy plates of steel specially hardened and stamped from one sheet without joints, seam or rivet. **It is superior to any other drag scraper on the market.** The bowl being made of **thicker and harder steel** enables it to scour where all other scrapers fail, and, owing to the sharp, rounded nose, will enter the ground more readily than any other scraper. **Bowls are steel, perfect working, handles are best hardwood. Will guarantee this scraper in every particular.** Is made in three sizes, without runners and with narrow double runners, and in two sizes with broad single runners. No. 3 carries 3½ cubic feet; No. 2 carries 5 cubic feet, and No. 1 carries 7 cubic feet. No. 3 weighs 80 pounds; No. 2 weighs 90 pounds; No. 1 weighs 100 pounds. **Shipped direct from factory in Southwestern Ohio.**

No. 32R3957 No. 3 Scraper, without runners. Price...... **$3.45**
No. 32R3958 No. 2 Scraper, without runners. Price...... **3.78**
No. 32R3959 No. 1 Scraper, without runners. Price...... **4.10**
No. 32R3960 No. 3 Scraper, with double runners. Price...... **3.70**
No. 32R3961 No. 2 Scraper, with double runners. Price...... **4.05**
No. 32R3962 No. 1 Scraper, with double runners. Price...... **4.35**
No. 32R3964 No. 2 Scraper, with broad single runner. Price...... **4.40**
No. 32R3965 No. 1 Scraper, with broad single runner. Price...... **4.68**

Doan Ditchers.

The Doan Ditcher is a great favorite among contractors and road makers for cleaning out and filling ditches and leveling roads and uneven places. It is made of well seasoned hardwood, and has a bit made of special steel, 48 inches long, 7 inches wide and ¾-inch thick, being about 2 inches wider than most makers furnish. The ditchers are well ironed and bolted, and the hounds are made of 1¾x¾-inch steel, with ⅝-inch cable chain. We guarantee these ditchers fully. Weight, 75 pounds. **Shipped direct from factory in Central Michigan.**

No. 32R3975 Doan Ditcher. Price........ **$4.45**

Tongue Scraper, Leveler and Ditcher.

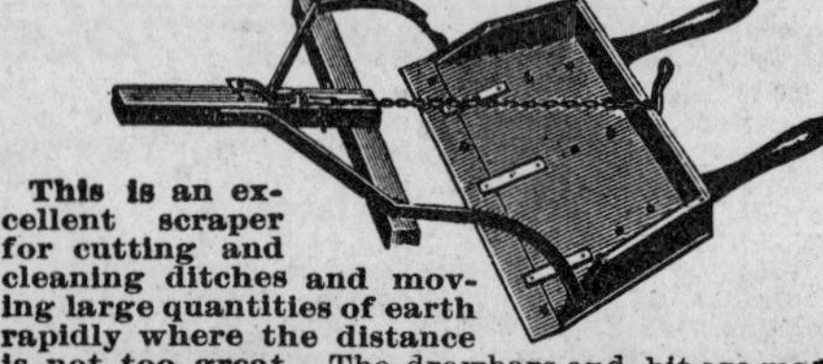

This is an excellent scraper for cutting and cleaning ditches and moving large quantities of earth rapidly where the distance is not too great. The drawbars and bit are made of the best quality of steel. It is well ironed and bolted and made of well seasoned oak lumber. The driver can fill and dump it with ease. **Large size,** width, 48 inches. Weight, 135 pounds. **Shipped direct from factory in Southwestern Ohio.**

No. 32R3980 Tongue Scraper. Price...... **$5.00**

Sewing Machine Headquarters

WE FEEL THAT WE ARE JUSTLY ENTITLED to the distinction of being headquarters for sewing machines, for even our competitors will have to admit that we are the largest dealers in sewing machines in America.

WE SELL MANY TIMES AS MANY SEWING MACHINES as all other catalogue or mail order houses combined; more than the combined capacity of four of the leading sewing machine factories with a daily output of over 500 sewing machines, our sales averaging for a nine-hour day one sewing machine per minute. We have been able to effect savings in the cost of manufacturing the many different parts that go into a sewing machine. We have been able to make many improvements, bringing our machines up to the highest standard of quality, and on our one small percentage profit plan, offer them direct to our customers at prices that baffle any attempt to compete with us.

EVERY SEWING MACHINE MANUFACTURER and dealer knows that in the past five years we have done more to improve and compel others in competing with us to improve the quality of their machines, and have done more to compel others to sell their machines at lower prices than all the sewing machine makers and dealers combined have done in all the past years.

OUR SEWING MACHINES are to be found in every town and community in the United States. The MINNESOTA, HOWARD, BURDICK, NEW QUEEN, EDGEMERE and SEROCO sewing machines will be found in every neighborhood, in every town and community, in every city in the Union, and so it hardly seems necessary for us to explain to you the many essential points in which our finest machine, how the Minnesota is the superior of any other sewing machine made regardless of price, how our Howard machine can only be compared with the highest priced machine sold by exclusive agents, and how our Burdick, New Queen, Edgemere and Seroco machines are superior to sewing machines widely advertised by many who only make a feeble attempt to compete with us; how the machines we sell in five-drawer drop cabinet style at $8.95, $10.45, $11.95 and $12.85 are really worth two of the machines that are now being sold by a number of merchants who retail them at $15.00 to $25.00.

ASK YOUR NEIGHBORS ABOUT OUR SEWING MACHINES, for the best proof of quality is the actual test. There are some of our sewing machines in your town, in your neighborhood. Possibly a friend, a relative, maybe your next door neighbor, has one of our machines. If not, and you will write us, we will give you the names of a number of people in your immediate vicinity who are using our machines, purchased from us. Look at their machines, ask them how they like them, how they compare with other machines they know of or have used. Ask them how much they feel they have saved by buying their sewing machine from us. All we ask is that you make this little investigation before buying a sewing machine from your dealer at home or ordering one elsewhere. We have read in catalogues, circulars and newspaper advertisements glowing descriptions and wonderful claims for sewing machines of a grade that we would not care to handle, and so we are anxious to leave the matter of ordering the sewing machine to the result of a little investigation on your part among people in your neighborhood who are using our machines.

OUR SEWING MACHINE ORDERS come largely from people who know the machines. They have learned all about them from friends or neighbors who have used them. They have found from the experience of their friends or neighbors that our machines in quality of material, mechanical construction, durability and finish, are not to be compared with cheap grades of machines with which the market is flooded. They appreciate our success in raising the quality and reducing the cost to the very minimum, and naming prices direct to our customers that barely cover the cost of material and labor with but our one small percentage of profit added.

ABOUT THE MINNESOTA SEWING MACHINE. While all our sewing machines, from the lowest priced, the $8.95 five-drawer drop head Seroco, to the very best, are good, sterling quality and will give entire satisfaction, we feel and honestly believe that our highest grade machine, the Minnesota, is the finest, the best sewing machine on the market regardless of price, and we believe, if there is one in your immediate neighborhood (and there surely is more than one), the people who own them believe as we do and would have no other, and so before you decide on the kind of a machine to buy or where to buy it, we urge you to first see and examine a Minnesota, and ask the party who owns and has used it what they think of it. If you do not know just where to see one, just what neighbor of yours has one, write us and we will give you the names of people in your neighborhood who own a Minnesota sewing machine.

A facsimile of our 20-year Guarantee.

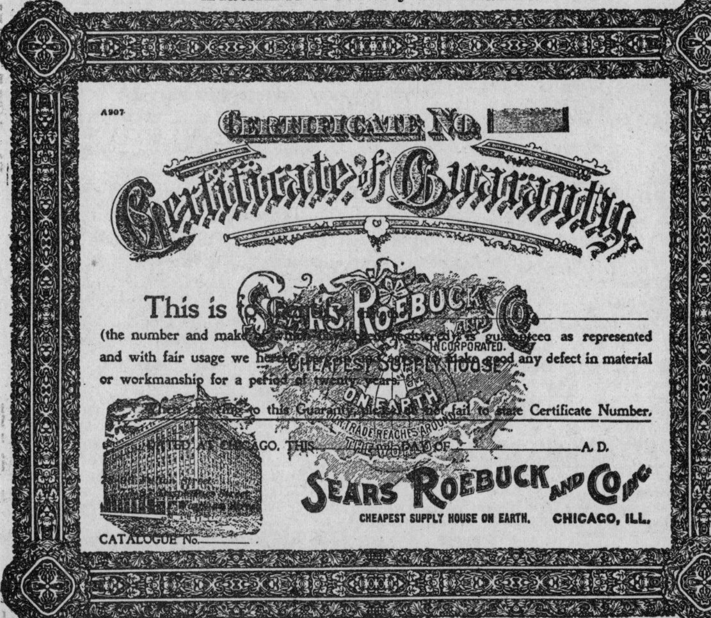

Certificate No.

Certificate of Guaranty

This is Sears, Roebuck and Co. Incorporated. Cheapest Supply House on Earth.

(the number and make ... guaranteed as represented and with fair usage we ... any defect in material or workmanship for a period of twenty years.

... to this Guaranty ... fail to state Certificate Number.

Dated at Chicago, this ... day of ... A.D.

Sears Roebuck and Co. Inc.

Cheapest Supply House on Earth. Chicago, Ill.

Catalogue No.

WE WOULD MUCH PREFER to leave the question of quality, durability, price, general satisfaction, etc., to the judgment of people not interested in our business, who have had a chance to try our machines, and whom we are sure will be pleased to honestly advise you. We know that other houses may make the same claims that we make. We would especially urge that you make a little investigation yourself to see if they have a right to make the claims that we make, if they can really furnish you a sewing machine of our quality at our price. So if you do not feel like ordering direct from our catalogue, we would be only too glad to leave the matter of advising you entirely in the hands of disinterested people in your own neighborhood who know all about it.

Our Terms of Shipment.

THREE MONTHS' FREE TRIAL OFFER: To relieve you of any possible risk, to avoid any chance of misunderstanding or disappointment, to give you the privilege of making any change you wish, we will send you any sewing machine in our line, with the understanding and agreement that if at any time within three months you become dissatisfied with your purchase for any reason whatever, without a word of explanation on your part, you can return the sewing machine to us at our expense of freight charges both ways and WE WILL IMMEDIATELY RETURN YOUR MONEY.

OUR SEWING MACHINES ARE PUT OUT UNDER A 20 YEARS' WRITTEN BINDING GUARANTEE, as explained below, under a three months' free trial offer, by which we bargain and agree to return your money at any time the machine is returned to us and pay the freight charges both ways.

WE REQUIRE THE FULL AMOUNT OF CASH TO ACCOMPANY ALL ORDERS. We do this in the interest of economy, of lower prices, for by reducing the clerical expense of handling C. O. D. shipments we make a saving and thereby name lower prices, and we also save you the charge that the express companies always make for the return of C. O. D. money to us, which is from 25 to 50 cents. While we ask everyone to send the full amount of cash with their orders, your order and money is accepted, of course, with the understanding that if the machine is not perfectly satisfactory it can be returned to us at our expense and your money will be immediately returned to you. We ask for cash in full with orders only in the interest of our customers, the buyers, to save them the extra express charges of 25 to 50 cents and the saving we make in clerical expense, which is deducted from our selling price. We feel that our reputation already established in every community for fair and honorable dealing, our financial standing at home and elsewhere, the bank references we print on pages 11 and 12, all tend to make everyone feel perfectly secure in sending their money to us, just as much so as if they were putting it into the strongest bank in the country, for we return money just as cheerfully as we receive it, and we do not want you to keep anything you buy from us, if it is not entirely satisfactory to you.

REPAIRS OR SUPPLIES for machines listed in this catalogue, such as needles, bobbins, shuttles, attachments, etc., may be secured from us at any time at lowest possible prices. As we carry a complete stock of all parts used in the construction or operation of our machines, we can fill orders for supplies promptly and without delay. The supplies furnished by us for our machines are the genuine parts, manufactured by the makers of the machines. Under the terms of our contract with the manufacturers we can furnish repairs for our machines at any time in the future. An order for repairs placed with us ten or fifteen years from date will be filled as promptly and as accurately as an order placed today. See page 741 for price on sewing machine supplies.

OUR THREE MONTHS' TRIAL AGREEMENT CONTRACT AND BINDING 20-YEAR GUARANTEE ACCOMPANIES EACH MACHINE.

A facsimile of our Three Months' Trial Agreement.

MEMORANDUM OF AGREEMENT.

This is to Certify That this machine, No......., is sold by us with the understanding and agreement that if it does not prove entirely satisfactory in every respect to the purchaser, it CAN BE RETURNED AT ANY TIME WITHIN THREE MONTHS FROM DATE,............ ....190.., and the full amount paid for the machine, including freight charges, will be cheerfully refunded to the purchaser.

References by special permission: [SIGNED]

National City Bank, German Exchange Bank, } New York.
Metropolitan National Bank, Corn Exchange Bank, } Chicago.

SEARS ROEBUCK AND CO

THE FREIGHT CHARGES will be but a small item; in fact, will amount to next to nothing as compared to what you will save in price, by sending your order to us. The freight charges will average 40 cents for 200 miles, 60 cents for 400 miles, and $1.25 for 1000 miles; greater or lesser distances in proportion.

IN SENDING YOUR ORDER TO US CONSIDER THESE POINTS:

A first class, high grade sewing machine at manufacturers' prices.
Our binding guarantee.
NO RISK, MONEY IN FULL REFUNDED IF NOT SATISFACTORY.
Small amount pays the freight charges.

We hope to receive your order, and assure you it will command our most prompt and careful attention. In sending your order to us, please be sure to give the catalogue number, name and price of the sewing machine on the order blank.

DO NOT HESITATE TO ORDER A MACHINE.
IT WILL BE SHIPPED ENTIRELY AT OUR RISK.

AS TO OUR RELIABILITY. We are incorporated under the laws of the State of Illinois, with a cash capital and surplus of over Two Million Dollars. We refer, by special permission, to the National City Bank or German Exchange Bank of New York, to the Metropolitan National Bank or Corn Exchange National Bank of Chicago, or to any railroad company, express company or resident of Chicago, and we would advise you before ordering elsewhere to write any friend you may have in Chicago to come to our store and see and examine our sewing machines, and then examine the machines offered by any other house in this city, and if they don't write you that you can get a much finer machine from us for less money than you can buy elsewhere, we will not expect your order.

$10.45 Buys Our New Queen Sewing Machine

FOR ONLY $10.45

WE ARE ABLE TO OFFER OUR 20-YEAR GUARANTEED, 5-DRAWER, DROP HEAD CABINET, NEW QUEEN SEWING MACHINE, THE LOWEST PRICE ON A HIGH GRADE SEWING MACHINE EVER ATTEMPTED.

FOR ONLY $10.45

$10.45

THE MACHINE WEIGHS, crated for shipment, 120 pounds, and the freight charges will amount to nothing compared to what you will save in price.

IF YOUR HOME DEALER or agent is trying to sell you a sewing machine at $25.00 to $50.00, or if you have been offered a sewing machine by any catalogue or mail order house at any price approaching our special $10.45 price for the NEW QUEEN SEWING MACHINE, we urge that before you place your order elsewhere, you see and examine one of our New Queen Sewing Machines, now being used in your neighborhood. There are a number of these machines in your own vicinity, possibly some of your friends or relatives are using a New Queen. If not, and you do not know of one or more who have the New Queen machine, write us and we will give you the names of people in your own neighborhood who have bought from us and are now using the New Queen, this special $10.45 drop cabinet sewing machine. So, unless you order direct from our catalogue, before buying from any other house, please let us give you the names of people you know who are using this machine. They are among your own neighbors. They will tell you how much better it is than any of the many cheap machines on the market. They will tell you how very satisfactory it is and how much money they saved by buying from us.

WE ARE SELLING SUCH A HIGH GRADE OF SEWING MACHINES and at prices so much lower than other houses, and our sewing machines are giving such general satisfaction, and they are now so well known in every community (on an average over 200 of our machines being used in every community in the United States), that no one need send to us for a sewing machine until they have seen and examined our machines in their own neighborhood and learned from the people who are using them whether we can give them better value for their money than they can possibly get elsewhere.

SELLING MORE MACHINES than all other mail order houses combined, more machines than four of the largest factories in this country, our machines have been wonderfully improved in quality, greatly reduced in cost, and by doing away with all advertising expense, getting 50 cents for our big catalogue, getting cash in full with orders for all sewing machines, we reduced our expense of handling to the very minimum and give you the benefit in the lowest price ever quoted for a strictly high grade machine, and all we ask of you before ordering is that you ask the people in your neighborhood who own our machine, if from their own experience they have not gotten from us a better machine than they could possibly get elsewhere at the price.

THE NEW QUEEN HEAD is one of the best high arm heads made. It has all the latest improvements, all the up to date points. Positive four-motion feed, self threading, vibrating shuttle, automatic bobbin winder, adjustable bearings, patent tension liberator, improved nickel plated loose wheel, adjustable presser foot, improved shuttle carrier, patent needle bar, patent dress guard, patent belt controller. The head is handsomely decorated and ornamented, full nickel plated face plate, black enameled base, handsome colored transfer ornamentations, beautiful nickel trimmings throughout.

$10.45

No. 26R15

ORDER BY NUMBER.

THIS ILLUSTRATION shows our special $10.45 New Queen Sewing Machine, open, head raised and leaf extended ready for use.

CABINET. THE NEW QUEEN CABINET is a very handsome 5-drawer, drop head cabinet, the newest style, made of selected oak, beautifully finished and highly polished. Comes with four side drawers and one center drawer, the latest 1902 model skeleton frame, carved, paneled, embossed and decorated and beautifully finished throughout. The cabinet is furnished with nickel drawer pulls, rests on four casters, has a Saxton adjustable treadle, one of the best full enameled iron stands made.

FINISH. This machine is given an extra fine finish throughout. Heavy nickel plated face plate, nickel plated balance wheel, fine full finished enameling, fancy color decoration and ornamentation.

IT HAS BEEN CUSTOMARY with all dealers to furnish a complete set of attachments with every machine, ADDING THE COST OF THESE ATTACHMENTS TO THE PRICE OF THE MACHINE, whether the customer requires them or not. We have found, from our past experience, that but a small per cent of our customers have use for all of the attachments; in fact, a great many of our customers do not require any. We, therefore, decided to offer this machine at

THE LOW PRICE OF $10.45,

giving you the privilege of procuring such attachments as you desire at cost price. If you require any or all of the extra attachments, remit us sufficient to cover price of such attachments.

HIGH ARM

The $10.45 New Queen has one of the HIGHEST ARMS OF ANY SEWING MACHINE MADE, giving ample room for the handling of large and bulky material.

THE ABOVE ILLUSTRATION gives you an idea of the appearance of our Special $10.45 5-drawer, Drop Head Cabinet, New Queen Sewing Machine closed, to be used as a writing desk, center table or stand. The head drops completely from sight, table folds up, and being of highly polished and finished antique oak, forms a beautiful piece of furniture.

WE FURNISH FREE WITH THE MACHINE: 1 Oil Can, filled with oil; 6 Bobbins (1 in machine, 5 extra), 2 Screwdrivers, 1 Package Needles, 1 Cloth Guide and Screw, 1 Quilter Guide.

BELOW WE QUOTE SPECIAL PRICES ON ATTACHMENTS, WHICH ARE EXTRA:

1 Thread Cutter, 1 Braider Foot, 1 Binder, 1 Set of Hemmers	25c
1 Tucker	15c
1 Ruffler	30c
COMPLETE SET, including 1 Thread Cutter, 1 Braider Foot, 1 Binder, 1 Set of Hemmers, 1 Tucker, 1 Ruffler, packed in velvet lined box	70c

THE INSTRUCTION BOOK, which we furnish with this machine, shows how to use all the above mentioned attachments, and if you desire to order a full set or any part of a set, we ask you to be sure and mention exactly what you desire.

ALL ATTACHMENTS ARE GUARANTEED FIRST CLASS in every respect, made of best quality steel, beautifully nickel plated and finished, and guaranteed to fit the machine and work perfectly. NEEDLES, BOBBINS, SHUTTLES and all necessary supplies for this machine can be secured from us at any time without delay. See page 741 for prices on sewing machine supplies.

No. 26R15 NEW QUEEN, 5-DRAWER DROP HEAD MACHINE... - $10.45

(Without Attachments.)

OUR DROP LEAF AND BOX COVER BURDICK SEWING MACHINES

...THE MECHANICAL CONSTRUCTION OF OUR BURDICK MACHINES IS FULLY DESCRIBED ON PAGE 725...

REMEMBER, IF YOU HAVE ANY DOUBT AS TO THE QUALITY OF OUR SEWING MACHINES, if there is any doubt in your mind as to our machines being better than any other sewing machine advertised by any other house at much higher prices, there are quite a number of these machines in your own neighborhood. We have sold these machines to people in your immediate vicinity. You can see them there, examine them, and get an opinion from people who have used them, people who will not hesitate to tell you that no other house sells a sewing machine that will compare with ours at anything like the price. You should also bear in mind that repairs and supplies can always be had from us for any of our machines for the years to come, and at a MUCH LOWER COST TO YOU THAN OTHERS FURNISH SUPPLIES OR REPAIRS.

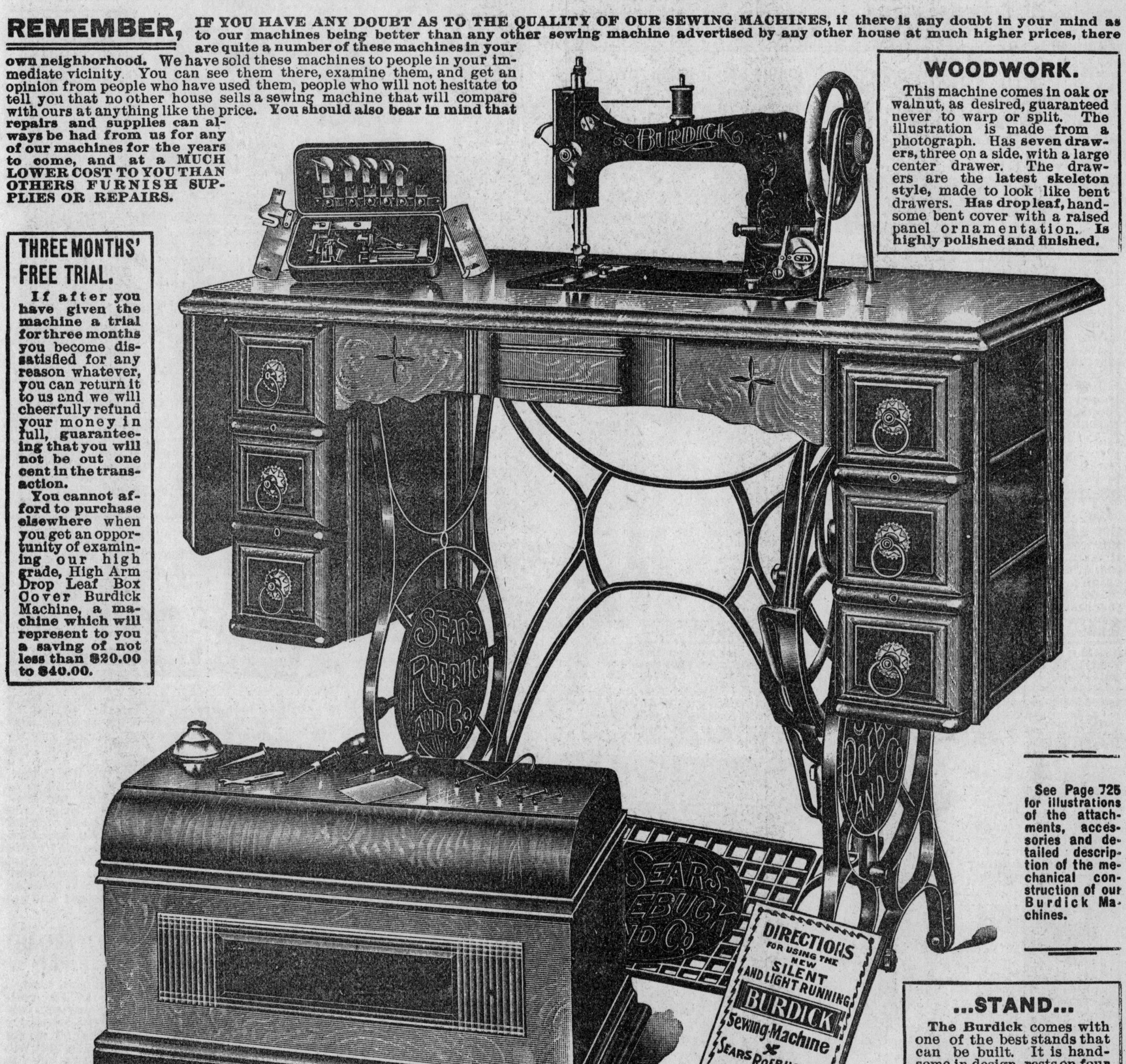

WOODWORK.

This machine comes in oak or walnut, as desired, guaranteed never to warp or split. The illustration is made from a photograph. Has seven drawers, three on a side, with a large center drawer. The drawers are the latest skeleton style, made to look like bent drawers. Has drop leaf, handsome bent cover with a raised panel ornamentation. Is highly polished and finished.

THREE MONTHS' FREE TRIAL.

If after you have given the machine a trial for three months you become dissatisfied for any reason whatever, you can return it to us and we will cheerfully refund your money in full, guaranteeing that you will not be out one cent in the transaction.

You cannot afford to purchase elsewhere when you get an opportunity of examining our high grade, High Arm Drop Leaf Box Cover Burdick Machine, a machine which will represent to you a saving of not less than $20.00 to $40.00.

See Page 725 for illustrations of the attachments, accessories and detailed description of the mechanical construction of our Burdick Machines.

...STAND...

The Burdick comes with one of the best stands that can be built. It is handsome in design, rests on four casters, treadle is hung on adjustable anti-friction hardened steel centers, producing an absolutely light and easy running stand.

No. 26R28 3 Drawers (without attachments)................ **$12.35**
No. 26R30 5 Drawers (without attachments)................ **12.80**
No. 26R32 7 Drawers (without attachments)................ **13.20**

These prices are quoted on the machines placed free on board the cars at our factory, Dayton, Ohio. At 75 cents extra we furnish a complete set of foot attachments in handsome velvet lined metal box.

ATTACHMENTS.

One Ruffler	One Tucker	One Shirring Plate
One Under Braider	One Binder	One Short Foot

Set Hemmers, different widths up to ⅝ inch.

NEEDLES, BOBBINS, SHUTTLES, ATTACHMENTS or other parts of this machine can be duplicated by us at any time without delay. We carry a full stock of supplies for practically every machine now in use in the United States.

NOTE OUR REMARKABLY LOW PRICES FOR PARTS QUOTED ON PAGE 741.

The head on this machine is the same as is used on our Burdick Drop Head Machine, fully described on page 727. A complete set of accessories and instruction book are furnished with this machine.

ACCESSORIES.

One Oil Can	One Screwdriver	One Cloth Guide
One Package Needles	One Quilter	Six Bobbins

DO NOT COMPARE THIS MACHINE with the cheap machines on the market offered by other dealers. See and examine it and you will quickly recognize its superior quality. You can save $20.00 to $40.00 by buying this machine.

THIS TELLS JUST WHAT FREIGHT YOU WILL HAVE TO PAY:

A sewing machine weighs, crated for shipment, 125 pounds. The railroad companies carry sewing machines at first class freight rate. On pages 7 to 10 you will find the first class freight rate for 100 pounds to a point nearest your town. The freight will be almost, is not exactly the same to your town, so you can tell almost to a penny what the freight will amount to. As a rule the freight on a sewing machine averages about 60 to 75 cents for 500 miles, 80 cents to $1.25 for 1000 miles.

OUR SPECIAL $12.85 DROP HEAD BURDICK SEWING MACHINE

With every Drop Head Cabinet Burdick Sewing Machine we issue a written binding 20 years' guarantee, by the terms and conditions of which, if any piece or part gives out by reason of defect in material or workmanship, we will replace or repair it free of charge.

THREE MONTHS' TRIAL.

If after you have given the machine a trial for three months you become dissatisfied for any reason whatever, you can return it to us and we will cheerfully refund your money in full, guaranteeing that you will not be out one cent in the transaction.

You cannot afford to purchase elsewhere when you get an opportunity of examining our high grade, high arm, drop head Burdick machine; a machine which will represent to you a saving of not less than $20.00 to $40.00.

Our Three Months' Trial Contract Accompanies This Machine.

From this illustration you can form some idea of the appearance of our special $12.85 five-drawer drop head cabinet Sewing Machine when open for use. This illustration shows the machine with head raised and set in place for work, with the cover extended as a sewing machine table. There is no handsomer sewing machine cabinet made, no better device for the protection of a sewing machine head.

$12.85

No. 26R35
Order by Number.

NEEDLES, BOBBINS, SHUTTLES AND ATTACHMENTS

are the parts of a sewing machine which are subject to the greatest wear. In order to supply our customers promptly, we carry a full stock of the above mentioned parts as well as all other parts used in the construction or operation of our machines. By our contract with the manufacturers we will be able to furnish you with repairs at any time in the future, and an order for repairs placed with us fifteen years from date would be filled as promptly as an order placed today. See page 741 for prices on Sewing Machine Supplies.

The Burdick Drop Desk Cabinet Sewing Machine weighs 120 pounds, and the freight will average about 75 cents for each 500 miles; greater or lesser distances in proportion.

THE BURDICK HEAD.

The Burdick Sewing Machine Head is a strictly high grade sewing machine head, made for us under contract by one of the very best makers in the country, made from strictly high grade material by skilled mechanics. It has a large high arm head, handsomely decorated and ornamented, and excepting our Minnesota, we guarantee it the equal of any sewing machine head on the market. This illustration will give you some idea of the appearance of our special $12.85 five-drawer drop head cabinet Burdick when closed, with head dropped beneath the cabinet, and in this shape the machine can be used as a writing desk, center table or stand, and being made of quarter sawed oak, finished antique, highly polished, decorated and ornamented, makes a very handsome and useful piece of furniture.

$12.85

No. 26R35
ORDER BY NUMBER.

$12.85

A SEWING MACHINE, WRITING DESK, CENTER TABLE or BOOK STAND IN ONE.

HOW WE MAKE THE PRICE $12.85

OUR $12.85 PRICE

Is based on the actual cost of material and labor with but our one small percentage of profit added. In order to sell this machine at $12.85 we must buy the sewing machine heads, the cabinet work, the stand work, the attachments and accessories in immense quantities for cash, to which we add our one small percentage of profit.

For Complete Description of the Mechanical Construction, Accessories and Attachments,
See Page, 729.

BY GETTING 50 CENTS

for our large catalogue, deducting the advertising expense from our selling prices, as the largest dealers in sewing machines in the world, having greatly improved the quality and reduced the cost, getting cash in full with all orders, thus saving clerical expense, we furnish such sewing machines as can be had from no other house at anything approaching our price, and we refer you to the hundreds of thousands of buyers who are now using our machines. There are some in your own neighborhood. If you do not know where they are, write us and we will give you their names and you can see and examine our machines and get the opinions of the owners.

THIS TELLS JUST WHAT FREIGHT YOU WILL HAVE TO PAY.

A sewing machine weighs, crated for shipment, 125 pounds. The railroad companies carry sewing machines at first class freight rate. On pages 7 to 10 you will find the first class freight rate for 100 pounds to a point nearest your town. The freight will be almost, if not exactly the same to your town, so you can tell almost to a penny what the freight will amount to. As a rule the freight on a sewing machine averages about 60 to 75 cents for 500 miles, 80 cents to $1.25 for 1000 miles.

While our customers invariably send cash in full with their order, as these are our only terms, we send with every machine a

THREE MONTHS' FREE TRIAL CERTIFICATE

by the conditions of which, if they become dissatisfied with the machine at any time within three months, they can return it to us and we will immediately return their money.

AT 75 CENTS we furnish a full set of the latest improved foot attachments, packed in a handsome velvet lined metal box, fully described on page 725.

No. 26R35	5-Drawer Drop Head Burdick, without attachments......	$12.85
No. 26R37	7-Drawer Drop Head Burdick, without attachments.....	13.35

Our factory is located at Dayton, Ohio, and we will place your machine free on board the cars at that point.

$16.15 buys the BURDICK Full Cabinet MACHINE...

FOR $16.15 We offer this FULL SOLID OAK CABINET BURDICK MACHINE as the equal of machines that retail at two to four times the price.

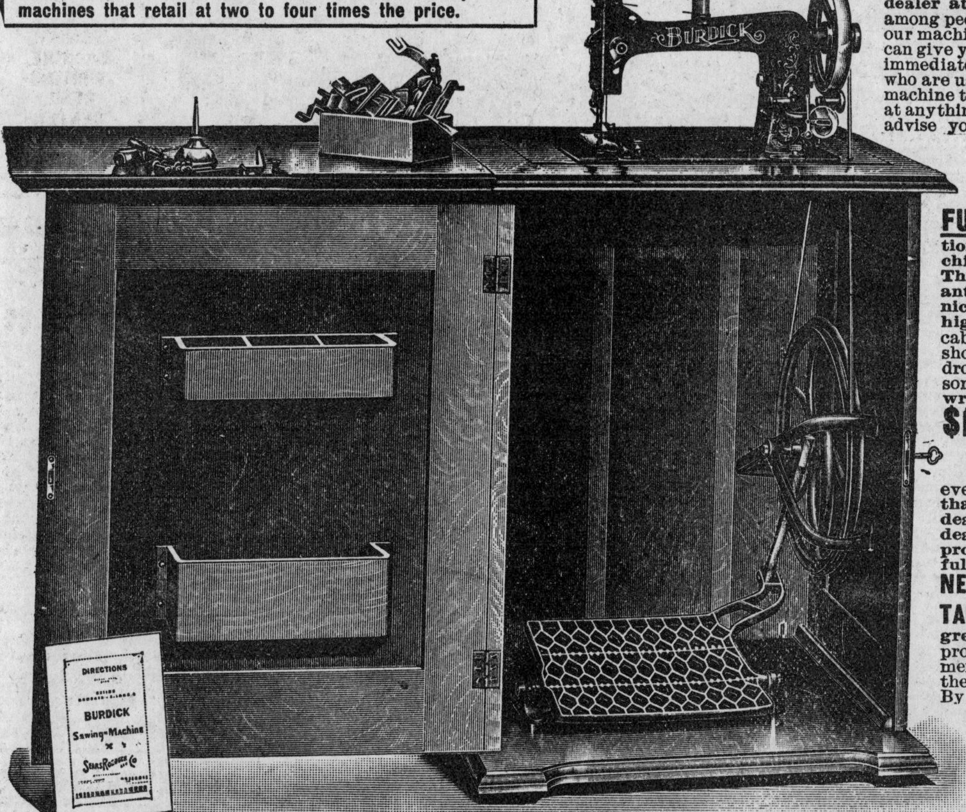

No. 26R38 Open.

BEFORE ORDERING A SEWING MACHINE from any other house, or before buying from your dealer at home, if you would make a little inquiry among people in your own neighborhood who are using our machines (if you do not know where to find them we can give you the names of a number of people in your immediate neighborhood who have them), these people who are using our machines would tell you there is no machine that will begin to compare with our machines at anything approaching the price we quote. They will advise you by all means to send your order to us. **To get your order for one of our sewing machines it is only necessary for you to make a little inquiry of people in your neighborhood, who are now using our machines.**

FULL DESK CABINET. As will be seen from the two illustrations, this our high grade $16.15 Burdick Machine is furnished with a full desk cabinet. The cabinet is made of solid oak finished in antique, made of heavy built up moldings, nicely ornamented, handsomely carved and highly polished. The one illustration shows the cabinet open ready for use, the other illustration shows the cabinet closed. The head of machine dropped from sight, and closed, it makes a handsome piece of furniture to be used as a **stand, writing desk or table.**

$16.15 is a price based on the actual cost of material and labor, with but our one small percentage of profit added. $16.15 is a lower price than was ever made for this grade of machine with full desk cabinet, even in carload lots to dealers. $16.15 is a price that will save you all the profit your retail dealer would make, all the profit the wholesale dealer would make, and a good part of the profit the manufacturer would make on any full cabinet machine he would offer you.

NEEDLES, BOBBINS, SHUTTLES AND ATTACHMENTS are the parts of a sewing machine which are subject to the greatest wear. In order to supply our customers promptly, we carry a full stock of the above mentioned parts as well as all other parts used in the construction or operation of our machines. By our contract with manufacturers, we will be able to furnish repairs for our machines at any time in the future. See page 741 for prices on sewing machine supplies.

IF EVERYONE WHO KNOWS US and knows our machines don't tell you that we will furnish you a better machine for less money than anyone else will furnish you, we will not expect your order.

THE BURDICK HEAD AND ATTACHMENTS

are fully described on other pages in this catalogue. By referring to other pages in this catalogue you will find the Burdick head and attachments fully described in all the different parts, and from the description of the head and attachments found elsewhere, and from the illustrations shown hereon of our full sewing machine cabinet, we trust you will be able to form some idea of the value we are offering in our $16.15 machine.

At $16.15 We offer this machine under our **BINDING 20-YEAR GUARANTEE**

We send it out with the understanding that you can return it at any time within three months if you are not perfectly satisfied with it, all at our expense, all money paid us to be immediately refunded.

...THIS TELLS JUST WHAT... FREIGHT YOU WILL HAVE TO PAY A sewing machine weighs crated for shipment, 125 pounds. The railroad companies carry sewing machines at first class freight rate. On pages 7 to 10 you will find the first class freight rate for 100 pounds to a point nearest your town. The freight will be almost, if not exactly the same to your town, so you can tell almost to a penny what the freight will amount to. As a rule the freight on a sewing machine averages about 60 to 75 cents for 500 miles; 80 cents to $1.25 for 1000 miles.

ARE YOU ACQUAINTED WITH THE BURDICK MACHINE?

If you are not acquainted with the Burdick Sewing Machine, if you do not know of one in your immediate neighborhood, write us and we will give you the names and addresses of people in your own locality who own these machines which they have bought from us. You can go and see them, examine the machines, talk with the parties who own them and take their advice about ordering from us. If they advise you to order a Burdick Sewing Machine, then consider the most extraordinary value we are giving in the HIGH GRADE BURDICK with handsome, highly polished, solid oak, full sewing machine cabinet at.................... **$16.15**

DON'T ORDER A SEWING MACHINE ELSEWHERE......

DON'T BUY A MACHINE FROM YOUR LOCAL DEALER AT HOME

until you have seen, examined and compared our machine with the machine offered by the other party, and if our machine is not better finished, lighter running, better in every way and lower in price than the best offer you can get from anyone else, when compared side by side,

Return Our Machine at Our Expense, and We Will Immediately Return Your Money.

No. 26R38 Full cabinet (without attachments)..........$16.15
Complete set of attachments (See page 730)................ .75
$16.15 is our price for this machine free on board the cars at our factory, Dayton, Ohio.

No. 26R38 Closed.

CLOSED, IT MAKES A BEAUTIFUL DESK, TABLE OR STAND.

OUR HIGH GRADE MINNESOTA $23.20

No. 26R70

ORDER BY NUMBER.

WITH AUTOMATIC... DROP DESK CABINET $23.20

Finest Sewing Machine Cabinet made. Highly polished panels faced with Italian veneering. Runs on rollers. Can be used as a writing desk. Handsomely ornamented and a pretty piece of furniture for every home.

THE HEAD, MECHANISM, ATTACHMENTS AND ACCESSORIES OF THIS MACHINE ARE THE SAME AS WE FURNISH WITH ALL OF OUR

HIGH GRADE MINNESOTA MACHINES.

For illustrations and complete description of the head, mechanical construction, attachments, etc., etc., see pages 734 and 735.

While our customers invariably send cash in full with their order, as these are our only terms, we send with every machine a THREE MONTHS' free trial certificate, by the conditions of which if they become dissatisfied with the machine at any time within three months, they can return it to us and we will immediately return their money.

ILLUSTRATION SHOWING CABINET OPEN.

ILLUSTRATION SHOWING HOW CABINET OPENS.

FOR BEAUTY OF DESIGN AND FINISH THIS CABINET IS NOT TO BE EQUALED

TO FURNISH THE BEST CABINET MADE and outdo others we have had made for our **Minnesota a special automatic drop desk cabinet,** which we furnish in either solid antique oak or black walnut as desired. As the **oak cabinet is the most popular,** we always send the cabinet in antique oak unless walnut is specified in the order. **No cabinet will compare with it.** When closed it has the appearance of **a beautiful writing desk** and can be used as such. It has a green cloth covered top and makes a nice, **attractive piece of furniture for any drawing room.** When so desired we can furnish the top solid without cloth cover. **By a practical and patented device** when you lift and turn the top over to the left, the sewing machine head will rise to the surface of the table **ready for sewing.** The machine head moves up and down and as it is counterbalanced it requires but little or no exertion to put it in place. In the upper part of the **two doors pockets are built,** and inside the case, as shown in the illustration, are two drawers with nickel plated ring pulls, **for attachments and accessories. Each cabinet is provided** with a lock and the two front doors as well as the cover can be securely locked. **The cabinet is highly polished, beautifully veneered, carved, ornamented and decorated.**

THIS MACHINE IS OUR LEADER. We are able to furnish you a regular **$75.00 sewing machine for $23.20,** and at our price there is no such value to be had elsewhere in sewing machines. Anyone in need of a sewing machine will naturally reason like this: A sewing machine as good as the Minnesota with even the cheapest kind of a cabinet would cost from the average retail dealer or agent at least $45.00, and at once take advantage of the opportunity offered to secure this regular $75.00 machine for $23.20, with the very best cabinet made, with a saving of $22.00 over the price they would be compelled to pay for a machine equal to the Minnesota, with the cheapest kind of a cabinet.

NEEDLES, BOBBINS, SHUTTLES, ATTACHMENTS and all other parts used in the construction and operation of this machine may be secured from us at any time. **Our prices on supplies are consistent with the low prices of our machines. See page 741 for list of supplies and prices.**

YOU ASSUME NO RISK of any nature whatsoever in sending cash with your order, as we are a reliable and responsible concern, and ready to make good at all times any promise, and with every machine send our **BINDING GUARANTEE FOR 20 YEARS.** If the machine, after examination and a thorough trial, is not found as represented in our catalogue and equal to any machine on the market, you can return it to us at our expense and your money in full will be cheerfully and promptly refunded, and we will pay the freight.

THERE ARE MANY SUPERIOR FEATURES which can only be appreciated after the machine is seen, and the more an operator uses it the better he likes it. **It has extra table room,** as you will observe from the illustration showing the machine open ready for use. It has a **large balance wheel, runs noiselessly** and with about half the necessary power required for ordinary machines.

The freight charges amount to very little (comparatively nothing), considering the amount we are able to save you on the purchase price. We are anxious to have one of these machines in every home, knowing that it would be one of the best advertisements we could have in any neighborhood. So sure are we that every customer will be so well pleased that we may expect many flattering recommendations to their friends and neighbors, which will result in our securing increased patronage in every section where we ship one of these machines.

You cannot afford to purchase elsewhere before you have seen and tried this machine if you would like to save from $25.00 to $45.00. You assume no risk whatever, when you purchase from us, as we give you a 20-year written binding guarantee.

THIS TELLS JUST WHAT FREIGHT YOU WILL HAVE TO PAY:

A sewing machine weighs, crated for shipment, 150 pounds. The railroad companies carry sewing machines at first class freight rate. On pages 7 to 10 you will find the first class freight rate for 100 pounds to a point nearest your town. The freight will be almost, if not exactly, the same to your town, so you can tell almost to a penny what the freight will amount to.

No. 26R70 Automatic drop desk oak cabinet, with cloth or solid top, as desired. Our special price, without attachments, free on board the cars at our factory, Dayton, Ohio...... **$23.20**

Full Set of Attachments, as Illustrated on Page 735, 75 Cents.

ILLUSTRATION SHOWING CABINET CLOSED.

FURNITURE

OF EVERY KIND AT LOWER PRICES THAN EVER.

OUR FURNITURE DEPARTMENT for this year has been entirely revised, new and better lines of goods have been introduced, and ALL PUT ON A PRICE BASIS THAT WILL MAKE OUR LEADERSHIP UNQUESTIONED.

OUR FACILITIES FOR SUPPLYING OUR CUSTOMERS with the best grades of furniture manufactured at the lowest possible prices were never as good as they are this season. Our manufacturing connections are such that in most lines our customers can buy from us for less money than retail dealers must pay for equal qualities.

WE INVITE A CAREFUL COMPARISON of our very handsome and complete lines of parlor suites, bedroom suites, iron beds, chairs, dining room furniture, etc., with those of other houses, AND ESPECIALLY OUR PRICES AS AGAINST THEIRS.

REMEMBER, CASH IN FULL MUST BE SENT WITH ALL ORDERS.

WE ASK CASH IN FULL WITH THE ORDER for your interest as well as ours, as fully explained on page 1 of this catalogue. All of our furniture is covered by OUR BINDING GUARANTEE, and your order is accepted by us with the understanding that the goods will please you in every way or you can return them at our expense of transportation charges both ways and we will return your money.

OUR DINING ROOM AND KITCHEN CHAIRS are strictly high grade, made for us under contract by the best maker in America. Order these chairs from us and you will find for quality of wood, strength, style and finish, you cannot equal them elsewhere at within 50 per cent of our price.

SPECIAL LEADERS IN DINING ROOM AND KITCHEN CHAIRS.

Our 45-Cent Chair.

No. 1R3 The Wood Seat Chair shown in the illustration is especially well constructed and neatly striped. This is a kitchen chair that can seldom be obtained at retail at 65 cents. Our special price is made with a view of proving our ability to render better value than any other house in existence. This chair is made with four spindles, bow back, fancy ornamental stripes. It is made of hardwood and finished in golden oak.
Our special price, each........ ....45c

63 Cents Buys this Handsome $1.00 Dining Chair.

No. 1R9 At the above price we are offering a diner which for solid construction, handsome design and style will compare favorably with chairs offered by many dealers at even double our price. Made of select stock, carefully seasoned. It is durable, put up by one of the best manufacturers, and is very choice. The workmanship is that which only skilled wood workers can produce. This chair is well finished and the handsome carving adds greatly to its appearance. Fancy spindles in back, solid wood seat and strong, well braced legs. Golden oak finish. Our special price, each.....63c

OUR 95-CENT LEADER.

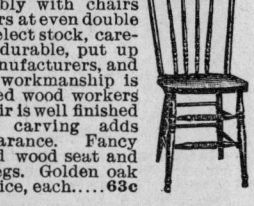

THIS HANDSOME NEW 1902 DESIGN is one of our most serviceable and comfortable dining room chairs. It is solid, yet rich and handsome in appearance; has a large, comfortable back, flat steam bent slats, upper back panel richly carved, has a full shaped seat; in fact, it is offered as the greatest chair value ever offered by us or any other house.
No. 1R11 Our price, each.....95c

Our $1.10 Leader.

No. 1R12 For $1.10 we offer this unusually rich and attractive Dining Room Chair, with beautifully carved back, exactly as illustrated, as the equal of chairs that will sell in regular furniture stores at $2.00 and $2.25. $1.10 is a price figured on the actual cost of material and labor with but our one small percentage of profit added. This chair is made especially broad and roomy. Has full braced arms, full shaped seat; it is strong and durable as a chair can be made, and with ordinary usage will last a lifetime.
No. 1R12 Our special price, each............$1.10

New Pattern High Back Wood Seat Chair.

No. 1R13 This is a new pattern of High back Wood Seat Chair. The design is one of the handsomest of the many we are showing this season. Made of best quality of rock elm, thoroughly seasoned; high back posts and spindles are of graceful design; the top is large and handsomely carved; it has a comfortable seat and is secure; the legs are well braced by nine stretchers of pleasing design. The finish is gloss and is better than most of the so called polish finishes. Price, each......$1.15

Our 99-Cent Cane Seat Wonder.

No. 1R15 This our 99-Cent New Design Cane Seat Dining Room Chair, we offer in competition with and equal to chairs that will be offered everywhere by furniture dealers at prices varying from $1.50 to $2.50. This handsome dining room chair is made from solid oak and beautifully finished golden. It has a hand woven cane seat and brace arm. The back is beautifully turned and carved, as illustrated, producing an ornamental finish. It is made by one of the finest furniture manufacturers in the country whose name is a guarantee for material. Our special price.. .....99c

Our $1.25 Diner.

No. 1R19 This is an unusually attractive cane seat chair; with the latest style hand carved heavy back panel, supported by full braced and fancy turned posts and spindles. Full cane seat, making it a special bargain at the price we quote. One of the newest and best patterns, and made in best selected rock elm. Finished golden.
Price, each ..$1.25

No. 1R27 An Unusually Rich and Attractive Dining Room Chair, beautiful quarter sawed oak in back panels, and broad and roomy full braced arms, and full, fine woven cane seat. As strong and durable as a chair can be made and will last a lifetime. Cannot be duplicated for $2.00. Our price, each................................$1.47

At $1.60 an Extraordinary Chair Value.

No. 1R33 The handsomest chair ever shown for the money. You have never seen its equal. This is no mistake. We guarantee to furnish you a chair exactly like the one we represent. It is fine enough to adorn the best of homes. Cannot fail to suit the most fastidious. Note the excellent features: Rich hand carvings on back panels, full braced arms, fancy turned spindles. apron front; made of selected rock elm with handsome golden oak finish with full fine woven cane seat. A chair that cannot fail to impress everyone, owing to its beauty and many excellent features.
No. 1R33 Price, each..............................$1.60

Cane or Leather Seat Dining Room Chairs.

A chair that is finely made, comfortable, fashionable and durable, made of very finest quality of golden oak, quarter sawed. Has a fine piano polish, richly carved back, and the best hand made cane seat, full boxed. French legs, plain, substantial and elegant.
No. 1R37 Price, each..... $2.35
No. 1R38 Leather Seat.
Price, each.................. 2.95

Our $1.50 University Chair.

No. 1R200 This Chair is thoroughly well made from very fine selected oak. The back and arms are extra well braced by means of iron rods passing through the seat. The chair is decidedly comfortable, and after being once used is considered an absolute necessity. Wood seat, perfectly finished.
Our special price $1.50

Wonderful Value at $1.75.

PRICE THIS GRADE AT ANY RETAIL FURNITURE STORE

No. 1R202 A Roomy and Comfortable High Back Chair, a steam bent braced arm and nicely carved back panel; has wood seat, and is strongly made and well finished, of the best rock elm, finished golden.
Price, each, $1.75

Invalids' Chair.

No. 1R206 This Highly Finished Invalids' Chair has high back and arms with box under the seat which opens from the back, and is large enough for any chamber. This is a very convenient piece of furniture for any sick room, and no family should be without one. Our special price...$3.40

Office Chairs, Screw and Spring Base.

No. 1R208 Office Chair. Is very comfortable, thoroughly well made and handsome in appearance. The back posts are well bolted to seat. Cane seat is hand woven, and the spring may be adjusted to any degree of tension desired, while the chair may be raised or lowered by means of the screw in steel plate. This chair is made of the very finest rock elm and finished golden oak.
Our special price, each......$3.25

Our $4.45 Office Chair.

No. 1R212 A Large, Comfortable, High Back Office Chair. Carved top and front; made of best selected quarter sawed oak, finished golden; has the best patented screw and spring base, and is strong, durable and comfortable.
Price, each..............$4.45

$5.20 Buys a $6.75 Office Chair.

This chair would retail at $6.75 to $8.25. We save you $1.50 to $3.00.

No. 1R214 A Large, Comfortable and Roomy High Back Office Chair. Carved top and front, bent slats in back, made of best selected rock elm, finished golden; has the best patented screw and spring base, and is strong and durable. Price. $5.20

Our Desk Stools.

No. 1R223 The Desk Stool which we illustrate is substantially made, strongly braced, handsome golden oak finished, and has an excellent appearance. It is made of very fine rock elm, kiln dried. It is an excellent stool for the money and cannot be secured for less than 50 per cent above our price.

No. 1R224	18 inches high, wood seat. Price.	$0.50
No. 1R225	18 inches high, cane seat. Price.	.70
No. 1R226	24 inches high, wood seat. Price.	.65
No. 1R227	24 inches high, cane seat. Price.	.90
No. 1R228	33 inches high, wood seat. Price.	.90
No. 1R229	33 inches high, cane seat. Price.	1.10

90-Cent Nursery Chair.

No. 1R250 This Chair is really a household necessity, and no family with children should be without one. It is made up of the best rock elm, handsomely decorated, has full back with three spindles. It is strongly constructed, and finished either in regular or antique oak or red.
Our special price, each..............90c

No. 1R256 Same as No. 1R250, with table in front, as shown in illustration. Our special price... $1.10

Our $1.15 Child's Rocker.

No. 1R262 Child's Rocker. The comfortable back is beautifully carved and has an elegant appearance. The arms are securely attached to back and seat. Seat is wood, legs are strong and well braced the rockers are securely attached to them. We make this rocker of the very best kiln dried elm and finish it in antique oak.
Our special price, each.............$1.15

Our $1.10 High Chair.

No. 1R275 You will see from the illustration that it is strongly built and very handy. This chair is made of the best rock elm, kiln dried and thoroughly seasoned, adjustable table, which swings over child's head so that the child can be placed in the chair before adjusting the table. The chair is finished either in red or antique, as may be desired.
Our special price, each........$1.10

Latest Style Child's High Chair.

Our Latest Style Child's High Chair, here illustrated, is made with either wood or cane seat. It has large drop table and is made of thoroughly seasoned golden oak, highly finished, making it one of the best grades on the market. The back panel and posts are deeply and elegantly carved.

No. 1R277 Wood Seat. Our special price..............................$1.69
No. 1R278 Cane Seat. Our special price..............................$1.90

Combination High Chair and Carriage, $2.45.

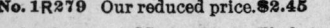

A Combination High Chair and Carriage that is perfect and never gets out of order. Easily changed from a stationary high chair, which will not roll, to a low go-cart, making a very useful piece of furniture. This chair has wide carved back panel and has dark golden oak finish. We have greatly reduced the price, which will cause this chair to be a great favorite the coming season.

No. 1R279 Our reduced price.$2.45

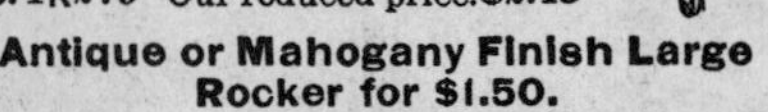

Antique or Mahogany Finish Large Rocker for $1.50.

No one will believe it possible to produce such a Rocker for $1.50. One of the most extraordinary bargains ever offered at the price. We save you at least 50 per cent of what many a local dealer would charge you. Made of finest selected rock elm, carefully seasoned, and constructed by the most expert cabinet makers. This rocker will prove an ornament anywhere. The heavily carved panel back is handsome in design, while the neat turned spindles add greatly to the appearance of the chair. The bent arms are braced with iron rods. While the rocker is graceful in outline, it is very strongly made and will last a lifetime. We finish it in either antique or mahogany, as desired. In ordering be sure to state which finish you want.

No. 1R306 Our price, antique finish.........$1.50
No. 1R307 Our price, mahogany finish.........1.55

Ladies' Sewing Rockers.

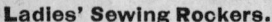

Exceptional value. A beautifully carved Rocker, with fancy shaped top, fancy turned posts and spindles. Made of rock elm, finished golden oak. A very well made, serviceable chair. Retails regularly at $2.50.

No. 1R308 With wood seat. Our special price............$1.40
No. 1R310 Same chair as No. 1R308, excepting it has cane seat. Our special price............$1.55

Beautifully Carved Cobbler Seat Rocker, in Antique or Mahogany Finish.

In this handsome and especially well made Cobbler Seat Rocker, we are offering a rare bargain. This rocker is made of selected rock elm, with high carved back of handsome design, fancy turned spindles, easy and comfortable cobbler seat of embossed leather. Extra large, with bent arms. Securely braced with iron rods. A most ornamental and durable addition to parlor or library. Made either in antique or mahogany finish. In ordering be sure to say which finish you want.

No. 1R313 Our price, antique finish.........$1.75
No. 1R314 Our price, mahogany finish.......1.80

Elegant Rocker for $2.25.

A Rocker that in appearance is one of the most striking and handsome we are showing this season. Has high back, richly carved panels, steam bent braced arms, and full shaped seat. Is unusually well made; rock elm, and finished in golden elm or imitation mahogany.

No. 1R318 Price, each, golden elm..............................$2.25
No. 1R319 Our price, mahogany finished..............................$2.30

Our Special $2.50 Rocker.

No. 1R320 A beautiful high back fully carved Rocker, with full cobbler leather seat. Made of the best selected oak, finished golden; broad and roomy and very comfortable. Also made in mahogany finish.

Price..............................$2.50

The Farmer's Friend.

You can scarcely believe it possible to secure such a large, roomy rocker as shown in this illustration, for the extremely low price quoted. It is hand carved and polished and has heavy steam bent arm posts and slat spindles; it is well braced in every way and has dark golden oak finish. The large seat and high shaped back makes this chair very comfortable and desirable.

No. 1R321 Our special price, wood seat..............................$2.95
No. 1R322 Our special price, cane seat..............................3.40
No. 1R323 Our special price, genuine leather seat..............................$4.35

One of Our Big Bargains for $3.15.

The manufacturer put it into our power to sell this high grade rocker, such as you can get at no other place at anything like the price. Made of the finest quality of golden oak or mahogany. Highly hand polished, has elaborately hand carved back and fancy turned spindles, the latest fancy colored embossed leather seat, well braced and fancy turned arms, and with ordinary care is guaranteed to last a lifetime.

No. 1R339 Price, each, golden oak..............................$3.15
No. 1R340 Price, each, mahogany finish....$3.20

Our $3.45 Golden Oak Rocker.

No. 1R346 A beautiful rocker of the latest pattern. Large and comfortable, with high paneled back richly carved. Made of the best seasoned and selected quarter sawed golden oak, elegantly finished, making a rocker that will be an ornament to any room.

Our special price......$3.45

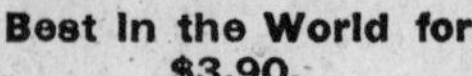

Best in the World for $3.90.

This is one of those handsome pieces that make the home beautiful. It is large and comfortable, elegantly carved back and panel front and of unusually attractive design. Frame is made of selected quartered golden oak or birch with mahogany finish; has full upholstered seat and back, covered in three-toned velours.

No. 1R349 Price, each, oak..............................$3.90
No. 1R350 Price, each, mahogany finish..............$3.95

Veneered Fancy Rockers.

Made in quarter sawed golden oak or veneered imitation mahogany, as desired. An artistic, fancy rocker, new, novel and very comfortable; full shaped seat, strongly braced, elegant in appearance and will give service and comfort.

No. 1R412 Price, in quarter sawed golden oak, each...$2.93
No. 1R413 Price, in imitation mahogany, each.....$2.98

Our $4.60 Veneered Rocker.

Another of those beautiful veneer Rockers of superb design; finished golden oak, quarter sawed or imitation mahogany. The panels are richly carved and spindles are of fancy turnings. It is very pretty, and will adorn any parlor.

No. 1R414 Price, each, oak..............................$4.60
No. 1R415 Price, each, mahogany finish..............$4.65

$5.40 Buys This Handsome Veneered Rocker.

Imitation mahogany and quartered golden oak, veneered seat and back, polished. One of our most handsome and attractive up to date rockers, very roomy and comfortable, neatly carved, has pretty curved seat, neat carvings on panel, is very strong and durable.

No. 1R420 Price, quarter sawed golden oak..$5.40
No. 1R421 Price, imitation mahogany......5.45

A FEW SPECIAL BARGAINS
....IN....
Reed and Rattan Rockers and Chairs.

No. 1R450 A very neat and pretty Rocker. Made of the best imported reeds; full braced and supported arms; panel front, medium high back. Perfect in construction and finish.

Price..............................$2.25

A Fine Lawn Rocker for $2.35.

Ask your local dealer for a price on the new Randall Rocker and learn how much money you will save by ordering from us.

No. 1R452 The illustration will give you some idea of the appearance, comfort and durability of our Veranda Rocker with reed seat and back. This rocker is just as strong and just as comfortable as the all reed or rattan rockers, which are sold by retail dealers at from $6.00 to $9.00. It is thoroughly well constructed, the frame being of fine kiln dried wood, and the entire chair being finished in shellac or cherry. A very necessary article of furniture for the summer months, and a rocker that will be found just as comfortable and just as desirable for house use. Our special price, each.............$2.35

Our Special $2.55 Reed Rocker is a Wonder of Value.

No. 1R454 A very pretty and comfortable Ladies' Reed Rocker, made of the best materials in a very attractive design; has a high fancy back, well supported with braced arms, and is an attractive and useful piece of furniture. In shellac or natural finish.

Price..............................$2.55

Worth $7.00. Our Price, $3.95.

No. 1R455 A superb comfort Rocker of the finest materials, honestly constructed for service as well as for appearance. Made in combination of plain and colored reeds and is an attractive and desirable addition to the home furnishings.

Price..............................$3.95

$4.40 Buys a $6.50 Reed Rocker.

No. 1R460 A large, comfortable Rocker, made of best selected reeds, interwoven with fancy colors, full roll arm, graceful outlines and very roomy, and guaranteed for years of comfort and service. Price..............$4.40

A Handsome New Design.

No. 1R464 This Beautiful Rocker is made of selected quarter sawed oak, finished antique and the finest selected reeds. The seat and back are upholstered in the finest silk plush, tufted, and it is a rich and elegant adornment to the home.

Price..............................$5.00

Our New Reception Chair, Very Stylish and Only $6.25.

No. 1R474 Artistic Reception Chair, unusually graceful and pretty, yet very comfortable; well made of the finest of reeds, and very strong; fit to adorn any parlor. In shellac finish.

Price, each.......$6.25

WHEN ORDERING

CHAIRS

we advise our customers to make up an order of at least 100 pounds weight, thereby reducing the average cost of transportation, as all railroad companies quote a special 100-pound rate. See pages 7 to 10.

Our $1.35 Kitchen Table.

No. 1R500 Kitchen Table. Is made of oak with basswood top and oak legs, has large roomy drawer. It is strongly constructed and has bolt leg fasteners. It can be taken apart for shipping, thus saving very largely on freight. This table is a household necessity and no kitchen is complete without it. Nicely finished. Weighs about 40 pounds. **Size of top, 27x42 inches.** Price, each............... **$1.35**

Solid Oak Extension Table for $3.25.

No. 1R504 This is the cheapest solid oak extension table (quality considered) ever offered by us. Compare it with tables sold by other dealers at from $4.00 to $5.00. Size is 33x42 inches and full length 5 feet. It has iron bolt leg construction, making the table exceptionally strong and durable. Shipping weight, about 90 pounds.
Our special price............................ **$3.25**

Our $2.70 Breakfast Table.

No. 1R508 This is one of the most desirable and necessary articles of furniture, and one that is convenient for breakfast use or for general kitchen use. This is not an extension table, but the leaves at either side may be dropped so that the table will take up little space when not in use. It is made of **solid oak with antique finish.** The size of top is 29 inches wide by 52 inches long. The table can be taken apart and shipped knocked down, thus saving freight charges. Shipping weight, about 90 pounds. Our special price, each............... **$2.70**

Our Great Bargain for $3.75.

No. 1R512 Extension Table. Is exceptionally massive, especially well constructed of **solid oak.** The legs are made with the bolt fastenings and are furnished complete with a set of casters. The size of the top is 33x42 inches when closed. Compare the size and quality of our tables with those offered by other dealers, and you will readily recognize that our prices are unusually low. Shipping weight, 100 lbs.
Our special price, 6-foot table................ **$3.75**
Our special price, 8-foot table................ **4.55**

Our Solid Oak, Round Top Extension Table at $3.90.

No. 1R516 Table is made of solid oak throughout, substantially built and exceptionally well finished. The legs are fastened with iron bolts at the corners as shown in the illustration, making the construction unusually strong and the table perfectly firm and solid. The dimensions of the top are 42x42 inches and it comes in 6 and 8-foot lengths. Complete with casters. Shipping weight about 100 pounds.
Our special price, 6-foot table................ **$3.90**
Our special price, 8-foot table................ **4.95**

No. 1R520 The Old Fashioned Round Drop Leaf Table, which we show in the illustration, is an old time favorite and never goes out of date; nor does it lose any of its desirable features. **It is made of solid oak,** with an oval top, the size of which is 42x52 inches. Can be taken apart and shipped knocked down, thus saving very largely in the freight rate. It comes in three sizes at the following prices. Complete with casters. Weight, about 100 pounds.
Price, 6-foot table........................ **$4.45**
Price, 8-foot table........................ **5.35**
Price, 10-foot table........................ **6.25**

Our $4.75 Solid Oak Extension Table.

NOT ASH.

No. 1R524 This table is made of the best selected and thoroughly seasoned oak. Size of top, 42x42 inches when closed. The legs are iron bolted, and in every way the table is substantial and well finished. Complete with casters. Weight, packed, about 160 pounds.
Price, 6-foot table........................ **$4.75**
Price, 8-foot table........................ **5.65**
Price, 10-foot table........................ **6.55**
Price, 12-foot table........................ **7.45**

No. 1R528 This Extension Table is one of the greatest bargains we have ever offered in an extension table. Made of solid oak, has six legs 3 inches in diameter, joined with handsomely carved stretcher, adding not alone to the appearance, but to its solidity as well. The top is 42x42 inches when closed. Complete with casters. Shipping weight, about 170 pounds.
Price, 6-foot table........................ **$4.95**
Price, 8-foot table........................ **5.85**
Price, 10-foot table........................ **6.70**
Price, 12-foot table........................ **7.60**

No. 1R532 This Extension Table is made of solid oak; golden finish. The top measures 42x42 inches when closed. As shown in the illustration it has six massive, fancy turned legs, the end ones being joined by a handsomely carved stretcher, which adds greatly both to the appearance and strength of the table. Complete with casters. Shipping weight, about 165 pounds.
Price, 6-foot table........................ **$5.25**
Price, 8-foot table........................ **6.15**
Price, 10-foot table........................ **7.05**
Price, 12-foot table........................ **8.95**

No. 1R535 This Extension Table has claw feet, six massive legs, the outside legs being joined by handsomely carved stretchers, which add greatly to the strength of the table as well as the appearance. The top of the table measures 42x42 inches when closed. Compare this table with other tables of the same style, and you will readily recognize the exceptional value we are offering. Shipping weight, about 175 pounds.
Price, 6-foot table........................ **$5.85**
Price, 8-foot table........................ **6.85**
Price, 10-foot table........................ **7.75**
Price, 12-foot table........................ **8.75**

No. 1R540 This Table is made from carefully selected extra heavy golden oak, exceptionally well finished. Has five large 5-inch hand turned and fluted legs; has a very large heavy top 42x42 inches in size. It is a table you must see, examine and compare with others to appreciate its real worth. Complete with casters. Weight, packed for shipment, 175 pounds.
Price, 6-foot table........................ **$6.90**
Price, 8-foot table........................ **7.85**
Price, 10-foot table........................ **8.80**
Price, 12-foot table........................ **9.75**

No. 1R544 This Table is made of solid oak. It has five handsomely turned 5-inch legs. Top measures 42x42 inches when closed. This table is finished in antique. Complete with casters. Shipping weight, about 175 pounds.
Price, 6-foot table........................ **$ 7.80**
Price, 8-foot table........................ **8.75**
Price, 10-foot table........................ **9.70**
Price, 12-foot table........................ **10.65**

No. 1R548 Solid Oak Pillar Table, one of the newest designs for 1902. The top measures 42 inches in diameter, and is rubbed finish. This style of table generally sells at a very much higher price than we ask, but we offer it at our one small percentage of profit. Complete with casters. Shipping weight, about 150 pounds.
Price, 6-foot table........................ **$ 8.70**
Price, 8-foot table........................ **9.75**
Price, 10-foot table........................ **10.65**
Price, 12-foot table........................ **11.60**

No. 1R552 This Table is made of solid oak. Top measures 42 inches in diameter. The legs measure 6 inches in diameter and are handsomely turned and fluted, as shown in the illustration. This table is one of the most substantial extension tables it is possible to procure, and will be sure to please the most exacting customer. Shipping weight, about 195 pounds.

Price, 6-foot table............................$ 9.95
Price, 8-foot table............................10.90
Price, 10-foot table............................11.85
Price, 12-foot table............................12.80

No. 1R556 This Round Top Pillar Extension Table is one of the latest designs for 1902, and will compare favorably with Pillar tables which are offered by other dealers at double the price we quote. **This table is made of solid oak.** The top measures 42 inches in diameter, and is rubbed finish. Shipping weight, 165 pounds

Price, 6-foot table............................$10.35
Price, 8-foot table............................11.25
Price, 10-foot table............................12.15
Price, 12-foot table............................13.10

No. 1R560 The illustration shows our prettiest design, a Pillar Round Top Extension Table. It is made of solid oak, beautifully finished. The top of the table measures 46 inches in diameter, and is beautifully ornamented with beaded molding, while the legs are handsomely carved and ornamented, making it one of the most attractive tables which we can furnish. Shipping weight, about 175 pounds.

Price, 6-foot table............................$12.45
Price, 8-foot table............................13.35
Price, 10-foot table............................14.25
Price, 12-foot table............................15.20

No. 1R564 This table is mounted on five massive 5-inch beautifully turned and highly finished carved legs. The rim of top is in a new, rich, attractive, heavily carved rococo design. The table is made of the finest selected, seasoned golden oak, beautifully finished, highly polished top. The top is 46x46 inches in size. Legs are fitted with improved casters. It has all the latest improvements, the finish and the appearance of tables that sell at two to three times the price. Weight, crated for shipment, about 190 pounds.

Price, 8-foot table............................$12.95
Price, 10-foot table............................14.50
Price, 12-foot table............................16.85

No. 1R568 For massiveness and solidity there is nothing to equal this most beautifully and elaborately designed table. This is one of the handsomest of our line; has five large, massive legs with the richest and most elaborate tracing and carving and is very strong. Made of the best quality solid golden oak. The top is 46x46 inches when closed. Fitted with improved ball bearing casters. Weight, packed for shipment, 210 pounds.

Price, 8-foot table............................$13.95
Price, 10-foot table............................14.90
Price, 12-foot table............................15.85

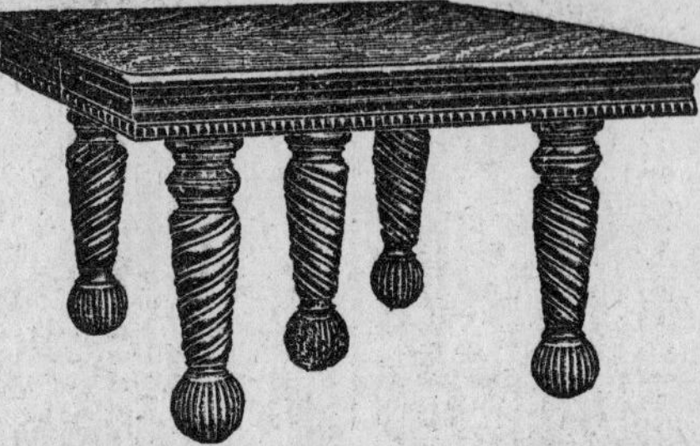

No. 1R572 This Table is made from carefully selected extra heavy quarter sawed golden oak, rubbed and polished to a piano finish. Has five massive hand turned and beaded legs; fancy trimmings on all four sides; has a very large heavy top, 45x45 inches in size. Legs are fitted with improved ball bearing casters. This is one of the handsomest tables shown this season, regardless of price. It is a table you must see, examine and compare with others to appreciate its real worth. Shipping weight, 225 pounds.

Price, 8-foot table............................$13.95
Price, 10-foot table............................15.50
Price, 12-foot table............................17.10

Our $14.60 Extension Table.

No. 1R576 Order this table and if you do not find it one of the richest, handsomest and altogether best tables in your section, and about one-half the price charged by others, you can return it at our expense and we will return your money. This is such a table as you will find only in the finest city retail stores. It is made of elegantly finished quarter sawed oak, highly polished. Top is 45x45 inches. Has very heavy, massively finished 7½-inch legs fitted with the very latest improved ball bearing casters. This table comes either square as illustrated, or with round top as desired. In ordering, be sure to state whether you wish square or round top. Shipping weight, 225 pounds.

Price, 8-foot table............................$14.60
Price, 10-foot table............................15.70
Price, 12-foot table............................17.80

No. 1R578 Same table as above, with 48x48-inch top, round or square, as desired, extra $2.00.

THREE SPECIAL BARGAINS IN CHINA CLOSETS.

Our $10.95 China Closet.

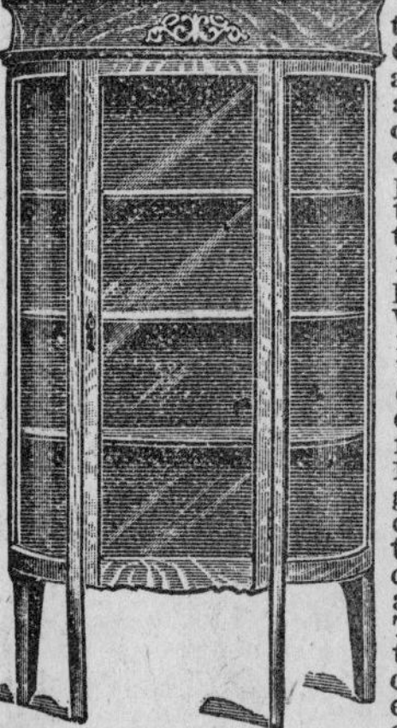

At $10.95 we offer this handsome China Closet on the basis of actual cost of material and labor with but our one small percentage of profit added. Shipped direct from our factory at Rockford, Ill., thereby saving all intermediate profits and expense of handling, all of which enables us to make the low price which we quote. This closet is made of solid quarter sawed oak, is 5 feet 5 inches high, 2 feet 11 inches wide. Has bent glass ends, a handsomely carved and decorated top panel, is excellently constructed throughout and beautifully finished. This is without exception the best china closet for the money ever put on the market, and the exceptional value we are offering can only be recognized and appreciated after you have had an opportunity of examining one of these closets. We guarantee satisfaction or we will refund your money in full. Every closet is carefully crated to insure safe delivery. Shipping weight, 150 pounds.

No. 1R701 Our special price............................$10.95

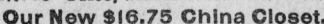

This is one of the handsomest china closets of the season shown by any makers. Entirely new for this season, up to date in every particular. From the illustration you can get some little idea of the handsome effect worked out in this $11.85 closet. It is made of carefully selected quarter sawed oak, beautifully finished. Stands 69 inches high and 40 inches wide. Made with the latest 1902 bent glass sides, extra heavy glass doors. 6x16 inches imported French bevel mirror, extra quality. Finished back; shelves are grooved and adjustable. Has all the up to date features of the highest priced china closet made. **Is a china closet nice enough to occupy a place in any dining room in the land.** Weight, 175 pounds.

No. 1R704 Price, without mirror............................$11.85
No. 1R705 Price, with mirror............................12.95

Our New $16.75 China Closet.

No. 1R710 At $16.75 we offer this China Closet in competition with closets that sell everywhere at double the price. Order this closet at $16.75, and if you do not find it equal to any china closet you can get from your dealer at home for $30.00, you can return it at our expense and we will cheerfully refund your money. From the illustration engraved by our artist from a photograph you can form but a faint idea of the beautiful effect that is worked out in this 1902 design. **This is an extremely handsome piece of furniture.** This closet is made from carefully selected quarter sawed oak, given a piano polish finish. It is fitted with an 8x20 imported French bevel plate mirror. It is richly carved, decorated and ornamented. Has latest bent glass ends, heavy glass door; is 74 inches high and 42 inches wide. Finished with handsome canopy top, ornamental shelves. Very latest effects for this season. **At our special $16.75 price** we furnish complete with casters packed in burlap and delivered on board the cars.

Weight, packed, about 190 pounds.
Our special price............................$16.75

OUR KITCHEN CABINETS.

KITCHEN CABINETS ARE AN INVENTION FOR ASSISTING THE HOUSEKEEPER. **We know of nothing that is more satisfactory or convenient for household use than a Kitchen Cabinet.** It represents the course of progress in ideas in kitchen furniture, and is constructed with a view of saving the housewife many weary steps. In our line of kitchen cabinets we illustrate and describe what would be considered the most serviceable articles of this description at from $3.50 for our cheapest cabinet without top to for $8.45 our finest cabinet with handsome cupboard top, as illustrated below.

THESE CABINETS **are made for us by two of the best manufacturers of Kitchen Cabinets in the United States,** and our prices are based on the actual factory cost with but our usual one small percentage of profit added, and if you were to compare our cabinets with those offered by other dealers which are the same in appearance and may be valued at the same or even lower price, the superior quality of our cabinets will be readily recognized. The $3.50 cabinet we offer with a view of showing what can be produced in this line of furniture at a low price, representing an article of excellent value for the price, but not to be compared in quality, construction or material with our better cabinets, though in appearance the cabinets offered by other dealers may be the same as ours.

BEFORE PLACING YOUR ORDER ELSEWHERE, **we advise you to order one of our cabinets, and if not found all and even more than we** represent it and the greatest value ever offered, same can be returned to us at our expense and your money will be refunded in full.

ABOUT THE FREIGHT. **Our cheapest Kitchen Cabinets are shipped from Chicago,** but our higher grade cabinets, with and without tops, are all shipped direct from our factory in Central Indiana, and all are most carefully crated and packed to insure safe delivery. They are so constructed that the lower portions of the legs are removed and placed inside of the cabinet for convenience of packing and can be readily put together. This adds to the safe handling of cabinets in transit and insures a much lower rate of freight.

$3.50 Kitchen Cabinet.

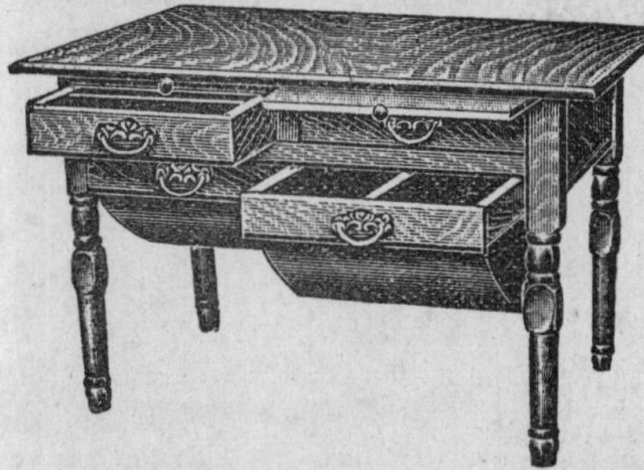

No. 1R750 This cabinet is made of hardwood and has basswood top, 27x48 inches in size. It contains two flour bins, two drawers with compartments for cutlery, etc., and two slides. The cabinet is well constructed and will prove a very serviceable article. This cabinet should be compared with cabinets offered by other dealers at from $4.50 to $6.00. Shipping weight, 100 pounds.
Our special price............................**$3.50**

Our High Grade Acme Kitchen Cabinets.

No. 1R754 The cabinet in this illustration represents our high grade Acme Cabinet, the best cabinet without top in the market, regardless of price. The top is made of selected white wood, 28 inches wide, and 48 inches long. The frame throughout is made of the best grade, selected kiln dried hardwood, beautifully finished. It contains a flour bin which holds 60 pounds of flour, two meal or sugar bins, one bread board and meat board and two large drawers, one of which is partitioned off for spices.

SWINGING BINS. The most unique feature of this cabinet is the construction of the bins, they are poised on the lower cross bar so that they swing forward, causing them to open and shut without a particle of friction and in this respect are far superior to any cabinet on the market in which the drawers either drop or slide on a rail which requires considerable muscular effort to operate, while the bin in our table as shown in the illustration can be tipped forward with but the slightest effort.

MOUSE AND DUST PROOF. The bottoms are made of wood, which keeps the flour perfectly dry, and when the bins are closed they are perfectly mouse and dust proof. They can be easily lifted out and cleaned, which is not the case with most cabinets of other manufacture. Shipping weight, 100 pounds. Our special price.............**$4.95**

SEND US 15 CENTS

for a years' subscription to our

MONEY SAVING GROCERY PRICE LIST,

revised and issued every 60 days.

YOU CAN SAVE 15 TO 30 PER CENT **by buying your groceries of us. Don't fail to send 15 cents for a years' subscription.**

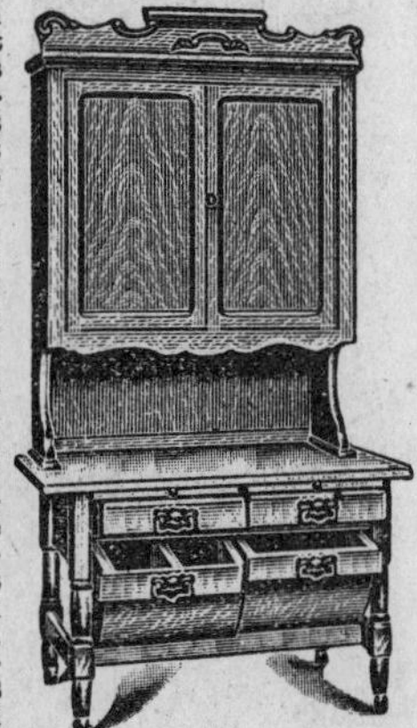

No. 1R758 Kitchen Cabinet. This Cabinet is exactly the same as our No. 1R754, containing all the excellent features of that cabinet and in addition thereto a handsome top, as illustrated. With the top complete the cabinet is 7 feet high, 4 feet long and 28 inches wide. The cupboard is subdivided into compartments which can be used for various articles required in the kitchen, and makes the cabinet a very valuable piece of furniture, especially where people want to economize in space and cannot have a kitchen safe and table in the same room. This cabinet is guaranteed absolutely first class in every respect and should not be compared with cheaper cabinets offered by other dealers. Shipping weight, 160 pounds.
Our special price.................................**$7.45**

WHEN YOU ORDER A KITCHEN CABINET
refer to our
GROCERY DEPARTMENT
and order a Supply of Groceries at the same time.

Our Finest Kitchen Cabinet for $8.45.

No. 1R760 Kitchen Cabinet. Same description applies as to No. 1R754, excepting that it has a top. The top is unique in so far that it is compact and yet very roomy. It is provided with a cupboard 18½ inches long, 8½ inches high and 11 inches deep. This cupboard is designed to hold baking powder, soda, large salt and pepper boxes used in the kitchen, condiments and seasonings of various kinds, in fact all the articles which are used in preparing food. It is also provided with a separate compartment for the rolling pin, though this will hold much more. It contains in addition four drawers which are quite deep. These are intended to hold strings, corks and miscellaneous articles necessary to the housewife. There is a large separate shelf for the soap box so that it may be out of the way from the table proper. There is a row of brass hooks to be used for the egg beater, butcher knife, large kitchen spoons, etc. In addition to all this is a generous shelf on top running the full width of the cabinet, on which are usually placed cans of coffee, tea and other articles.

The cabinet complete with base and top really leaves nothing to be desired in the preparation of eatables. The height of the top above the table is 32 inches. The height of the cabinet complete is 5 feet, 2 inches. The length of the table top is 4 feet. The length of the cabinet top is 43½ inches. The depth of the table top is 28 inches and the outside depth of the cabinet top is 13 inches. Shipping weight, 150 pounds.
Our special price.................................**$8.45**

Our $8.10 Kitchen Cabinet.

No. 1R762 Kitchen Cabinet. This cabinet is exactly the same as our No. 1R754, with the exception that it has a very handsome top, which is 40 inches high, 39 inches wide and 13 inches deep, making the cabinet complete 6 feet 10 inches high, 48 inches long and 28 inches wide. As shown in the illustration this cabinet has glass doors instead of panels or individual compartments. The arrangement of the top is as convenient as can be made for the convenience of the housewife. There is a large separate shelf for the soap dish and a row of brass hooks which can be used for egg beater, kitchen spoons, etc. This cabinet is not alone a very useful article, but a very ornamental piece of furniture for any kitchen. Shipping weight, 170 pounds. Our special price..................**$8.10**

Our $5.75 Solid Golden Oak 1902 Cupboard.

No. 1R780 This Handsome New Style Oak Cupboard is the very latest design for 1902, the latest style crockery or china closet. Made for us under contract by one of the best makers of high grade furniture. **It is made from the finest selected genuine golden oak,** highly polished, beautifully carved and decorated. It stands 7 feet high, 3 feet 4 inches wide, 14 inches deep. It is fitted with double thick heavy glass doors, two drawers with brass pulls. The lower cupboard is made with heavy double doors, fitted with lock and key. The inside of the upper and lower cupboards have adjustable shelves. Full finished inside and out. **Shipped direct from our factory in Northeastern Indiana.** Shipping weight, 140 pounds. Price, each..........**$5.75**

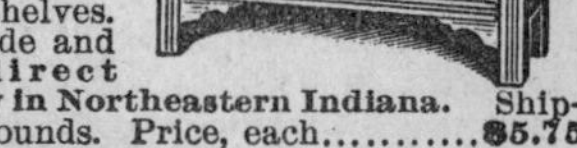

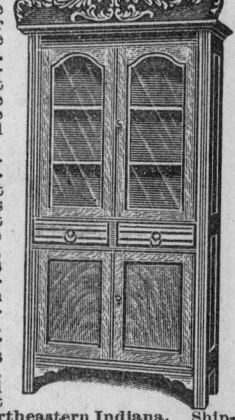

A $12.00 Kitchen Cupboard for $5.95.

No. 1R784 An Attractive and Handsome Kitchen Cupboard of solid golden oak, very large and roomy. Is 6 feet 11 inches high, 40 inches wide and 18 inches deep; has two drawers and shelves in top and cupboard. Panels, drawers and top beautifully carved. A very sensible and useful piece of furniture. Weight, 140 pounds. **Shipped direct from our factory in Northeastern Indiana.**

PRICE, EACH

$5.95

Extra Large Handsomely Carved Cupboard for $6.20.

No. 1R788 This most handsome and roomy cupboard is made of selected oak, finely finished; has two drawers, large cupboard and shelves; is 6 feet 11 inches high, 43 inches wide and 20 inches deep. Panels, drawers and top richly carved. When once used it is hard to keep house without one. Weight, 140 pounds. **Shipped direct from our factory in Northeastern Indiana.**

PRICE, EACH

$6.20

Our $10.95 Leader.

No. 1R1030 Order this sideboard at $10.95, and if you do not find it equal to any sideboard offered by other dealers at from $13.50 to $25.00, you can return it at our expense, and we will cheerfully refund your money in full. This sideboard is made of solid oak, golden finish, is 21 inches wide and 42 inches high, has handsome 12x20-inch bevel plate mirror, two top serpentine swell drawers and one large straight front drawer. One of the upper drawers is lined for silver. As shown in the illustration, the entire sideboard is handsomely decorated with carvings and fancy brass knobs, handles and locks. Complete with set of casters and delivered on board cars in Chicago. Shipping weight, 175 pounds.
Our special price........................$10 95

Our Special $12.95 Sideboard.

No. 1R1032 For **$12.95 we offer this handsome new 1902 Oak Sideboard as the equal of sideboards that sell everywhere at $15.00 to $18.00.** From the illustration, engraved by our artist from a photograph, you can get some idea of this handsome 1902 oak sideboard. **Our $12.95 price is based** on the actual cost of material and labor, with but our one small margin of profit added. It is lower than dealers can buy in carload lots. This board is made of carefully selected golden oak, 46 inches long and 21 inches wide, has 17x30-inch bevel plate mirror, two full serpentine shaped top drawers and one straight drawer. One upper drawer is lined for silver. In the finish it is handsomely carved and decorated, beautiful trimmings throughout. **At our special $12.95 price it comes carefully packed in burlap, complete with casters.** Shipping weight, 115 pounds.
Our special price..........................$12.95

$13.65 Buys This Beauty.

No. 1R1034 **One of the best sideboards ever offered** that has such good features for so low a price. Made of golden oak; is 46 inches long and 21 inches wide. Both the upper drawers are full swell and serpentine shaped, has a pattern French bevel mirror, size 17x30 inches. **Is very prettily carved and well made** and finished; upper drawer lined for silver, and has neat, pretty brass trimmings. Weight, about 175 pounds.
Price........$13.65

No. 1R1036 **This Beautiful Canopy Cabinet Top Sideboard is finished with rich carving,** and is polished like a piano. The mirror is 18x30 inches, of the finest bevel French plate. Has two bracketed shelves for ornaments. Has two upper drawers, one of which is lined for silver, and a large linen drawer and two cupboards. Top is 23x46 inches and made of the finest golden quarter sawed oak, and fitted with best handles and casters. One that will be appreciated for its many attractive features. Shipped direct from our factory near Grand Rapids, Mich. Customer pays the freight from the factory. Shipping weight, 175 pounds.
Price..... ....$15.90

$16.95 for this Handsomely Carved Sideboard.

No. 1R1038 Made of **the best golden oak,** with a graceful serpentine shaped top, 48 inches long and 24 inches wide; two upper swell front drawers, one lined for silver, and a large linen drawer; **is handsomely and boldly carved and** has a shaped bevel French plate mirror 16x28 inches; a real bargain. Shipped direct from our factory near Grand Rapids, Mich. Customer pays the freight from the factory. Shipping weight, 175 pounds.
Price, each.....$16.95

$17.90 Buys a Regular $30.00 Sideboard.

These sideboards are shipped direct from our factory near Grand Rapids, Mich., from which point the customer pays the freight.

No. 1R1040 **This small illustration will give you but a faint idea of the general appearance** of this rich heavy, elaborately carved and finished sideboard. **This massive sideboard is made from the best material that can be secured;** carefully selected golden oak, quarter sawed; given a high piano polish finish; is fitted with a fine imported bevel French plate mirror, 16x28 inches; has the latest rich serpentine top; drawers are 48 inches long, 25 inches wide; small upper drawers; the entire front and legs are richly carved by hand. **No attempt at describing this massive piece of furniture will do it justice. Shipping weight, 195 pounds.**
Price..$17.90

No. 1R1042 **A roomy, elegant Sideboard, in the finest of quarter sawed golden oak.** Heavy, rich carvings, finely polished; has two upper drawers, full swell, one lined for silver, and large lower drawer for linens, also two roomy cupboards. Top is 48x24 inches, with pattern 18x40-inch bevel French plate mirror; trimmings and casters the best, and is a sideboard fit to adorn any well furnished home. Shipped direct from our factory near Grand Rapids, Mich. Customer pays the freight from the factory. Shipping weight, 200 pounds.
Price..... ....$21.85

One of the Most Elegant of Our Many Up to Date Sideboards.

Shipped direct from our factory near Grand Rapids, Mich., customer pays freight from factory.

No. 1R1044 **This is an extremely handsome and attractive Sideboard.** Very large and roomy; elegant carvings on top and base and an up to date design; made of the finest selected quarter sawed golden oak with the best finish; upper drawer lined for silver; shaped top, 25x60 inches; pattern bevel plate mirror, 18x40 inches; the best ever shown for the money and cannot fail to please where elegance combined with quality is desired. Shipping weight, 225 pounds. Price..$31.60

COMBINATION SIDEBOARDS AND GLASS CLOSETS.

In listing the four handsome Combination Buffets and Glass Closets illustrated below, we are supplying an article for which there has been an increasing demand. As heretofore, in all lines of furniture which we quote in our catalogue, we consider the most important points of interest to our customers, superior quality of material, honest workmanship, beauty of design and finish and all at money saving prices.

In order to enable us to quote our usual low prices, we have based our prices in every case on the actual factory cost, adding only our usual one small percentage of profit shipping direct from the factory at Rockford, Ill., thereby saving any intermediate expenses which would otherwise accrue and have to be added to the cost of the goods. Every sideboard is packed and crated to insure safe delivery.

No. 1R1050 This Handsome Combination Sideboard was designed especially for us as an inexpensive case but which embodies all the features for service of the highest priced cases. It is 69 inches high, 49 inches wide, is made of quarter sawed oak, beautifully carved and ornamented and highly finished throughout. The mirror is 14x20 inches, and is the latest pattern French bevel plate. As shown in the illustration, the buffet part of the case has two roomy drawers and a large cupboard. The glass closet at the left has a glass door and glass ends, making the sideboard a very handsome as well as useful piece of furniture. Shipping weight, 175 pounds.
No. 1R1050 Our special price $19.85

No. 1R1052 This Combination Sideboard is somewhat more ornamental than our No. 1R1050, having a semi-canopy top with handsome pillar support. The case is 68 inches high, 50 inches wide, and has a 16x22-inch mirror and double swell drawers. The case is made of quarter sawed oak, highly polished and beautifully carved and finished throughout. Trimmed with fancy cast brass handles and locks, and supplied with a full set of ball bearing casters. Shipping weight, 185 pounds.
No. 1R1052 Our special price..............$23.45

No. 1R1056 The case is made of **quarter sawed oak** throughout, magnificently carved and highly polished. Unlike most sideboards, this has a large top drawer and two smaller ones which can be used for cutlery, besides two roomy cupboards. Case is 70 inches high, and 55 inches wide. The mirror is one of the latest shaped French bevel plate, measuring 20x22 inches. The door of the glass closet is bent glass and the closet has glass at each side. The entire case is trimmed throughout with handsome brass handles, hinges and locks, and is supplied with a set of ball bearing casters. Shipping weight, 225 pounds.
No. 1R1056 Our special price..............$29.85

Parlor Stands and Tables.

No. 1R1208 This Handsome Table is made of the best oak, finished antique and piano polished. Size of top, 24x24 inches; has good lower shelf and fancy turned legs; is absolutely first class in construction and finish. Weight, 25 pounds. Price..............$1.15

No. 1R1209 Same as above, with glass ball and brass feet. Price..............$1.50

No. 1R1214 This Handsome Table is made of the best oak, finished golden, also imitation mahogany; beautifully carved rim on top. Size of top, 24x24 inches; has good lower shelf and fancy turned legs; is absolutely first class in construction and finish. Weight, 30 pounds. Price..............$1.75

No. 1R1215 Mahogany finish. Price.$1.80

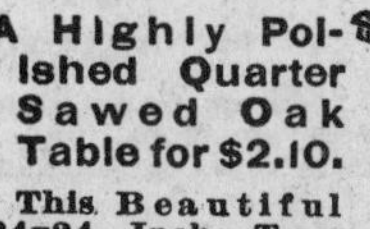

A beautiful pattern of table; exquisite in design and striking in appearance; pretty, neat carving on the rim; has turned legs and large fancy shaped lower shelf. One of our very best and newest creations. Made in quarter sawed oak finished golden and imitation mahogany, and the construction and finish cannot be improved. Size of top, 24x24 inches. Shipping weight, 30 pounds.

No. 1R1218 In oak. Price, each..........$1.90
No. 1R1219 In imitation mahogany. Each.1.95

A Highly Polished Quarter Sawed Oak Table for $2.10.

This Beautiful 24x24-Inch Top Parlor Table is made in select quartered oak, finished golden or in imitation mahogany finish; has a tapered fluted leg and exquisitely shaped shelf, highly polished throughout. Weight, 30 pounds.

No. 1R1220 Quarter sawed oak. Price....$2.10
No. 1R1221 Imitation mahogany. Price. 2.15

No. 1R1222 We believe this Table is one of the most attractive that we shall show this season. The top rim is richly carved in a most artistic manner and is 24x24 inches square. Lower shelf is roomy and fastened to rope turned heavy legs. Has heavy glass balls and claw feet; a real gem. Made in quarter sawed oak, finished golden, also mahogany finish. Highly polished.

Price..............$2.85
No. 1R1223 Same, without brass feet. Price, each..............$2.45

Be sure and state finish desired.

This is a very graceful and pretty table, regular $5.00 value. Designed for parlor or sitting room; has handsomely shaped top. Has French shaped legs and large fancy shaped lower shelf, making a convenient place to put books or ornaments; is made in solid quarter sawed oak or imitation mahogany, highly polished, and is constructed and finished in the best manner possible. Shipping weight, about 30 pounds.

No. 1R1226 Quarter sawed oak. Price, each,$3.60
No. 1R1227 Imitation mahogany. Each...... 3.65

One of our richest Parlor Tables, made of the finest quarter sawed oak or birch, with a rich mahogany finish. Highly polished. Artistic top, with beautifully carved ornaments underneath, fancy shaped lower shelf. Fine rope turned legs. Very massive and heavy glass balls and brass claw feet. Size of top, 24x24 inches, and is a beautiful parlor addition. Shipping weight, 35 pounds.

No. 1R1236 Oak. Our special price..........$3.80
No. 1R1237 Same table as No. 1R1236, mahogany finish. Price..........$3.85

$3.70 is the Price in Polished Oak.

No. 1R1238 This is a neat and pretty Parlor Table, of excellent design. Has pretty shaped top, rim and legs, lower shelf with fancy carved brackets. Size of top, 22x30 inches, and made of polished oak, finished antique. Price...$3.70

Handsome, rich, heavy and stylish is this, one of our best productions. Artistic shaped top, richly carved, 27x27 inches square. Lower shelf very roomy and fastened to rope turned legs. Heavy glass balls and brass claw feet. A beautiful table, made in the finest of oak, quarter sawed, golden finish. Also furnished in a rich, dark mahogany finish. Highly polished. Shipping weight about 60 pounds.

No. 1R1240 Oak. Price..........$4.85
No. 1R1241 Mahogany finish. Price.......... 4.90

No. 1R1242 A genuine mahogany French Marquetry inlaid table; has a heavy 2-inch molding. Legs are beautifully carved, making, we believe, a strong and durable table for the parlor. Has a roomy lower shelf for books. Top, 24x24 inches, piano polished. The carving on the legs is dull finish. Shipping weight, 30 pounds. Our special price..........$5.95

One of the most artistic and refined designs in our line. Made of quarter sawed golden oak or genuine mahogany. Handsomely carved and highly polished. Has a large 24x24-inch shaped top with fancy shelf and graceful legs. Weight, 50 pounds.

No. 1R1244 Our price in oak.....$6.70
No. 1R1245 Price, mahogany 6.75

No. 1R1246 This handsome carved leg table is one of the best values in our line. Made of select quartered oak, finished golden; highly polished; size of top, 28x28 inches; has a heavy top, a large lower shelf with extra large turned legs and glass ball brass claw feet, exceedingly ornamental, well made and very large. Just the thing for a fine parlor or sitting room. A good size for a lamp and books. This is a high grade table at a bargain. Weight, 55 pounds. Price..............$8.90

No. 1R1248 Parlor Table, well made of the finest genuine mahogany, beautifully hand carved and polished. Top is 30 inches in diameter. Has carved legs, with glass ball claw feet; shaped lower shelf and heavy shaped rim under top. A very artistic design. Weight, about 60 pounds. Price, mahogany only...$8.95

Massive Library Table for $5.90.

A good, roomy Library or Reading Table, made of solid oak or birch finished mahogany; highly polished throughout. Size of top, 24x36 inches, with a roomy drawer fitted with cast brass handles and a large lower shelf. Plain, neat and attractive, and a useful household adjunct. Shipping weight, about 50 pounds.

No. 1R1250 Price, in oak..........$5.90
No. 1R1251 Price, mahogany finish.......... 5.95

Our $7.45 Library Table.

No. 1R1252 Library Table, made of golden oak, or birch finished in a beautiful shade of mahogany; has heavy twisted legs with large shelf and one drawer, fitted with best cast brass handle. Size of top, 26x46 inches; a high grade table at a very low figure; stock is select and handsome; a good sensible style. Weight, about 65 pounds. Price, $7.45

$9.85 for this Massive Table.

No. 1R1254 A heavy, massive Table, suitable alike for the library or sitting room. Made in quartered oak. Top, 26x46 inches. Very roomy drawer, heavy cast brass handles and large shelf, suitable for books and papers. Heavy, massive, square legs. A good, sensible, everyday table. Shipping weight, 65 pounds. Price..........$9.85

Onyx Top Brass Table for $3.70.

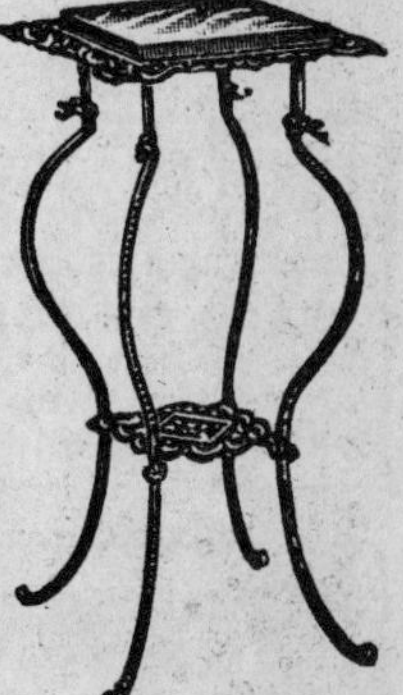

No. 1R1275 Lacquered brass, of a rich and very attractive pattern, with the celebrated onyx top; table is 30 inches high; top, 13¼ inches square, and onyx is 8 inches square; is unusually graceful in its outlines, and for the effect produced, is the cheapest stand ever offered. Price..........$3.70

Combination Sewing Cabinet and Work Table.

Our Ladies' Combination Sewing Cabinet and Work Table, so compact and useful as to be practically indispensable to the housewife. Height, 27 inches; top, 20x44 inches. Made in solid oak throughout. Drawers, 11x15 inches inside; are fitted with good locks, has a yard measure on top, and occupies a floor space of only 19x20 inches when closed; is castered and finished in golden oak. Shipped from our factory in Central Michigan. Shipping weight, 60 pounds.

No. 1R1295 Price..............$5.89

BOOKCASES

AT $5.60, $6.95, $8.20, $8.95 AND $13.90 **we offer a line of handsome quarter sawed oak bookcases in very rich new 1902 designs, as the equal of bookcases that dealers generally sell at double the price.** We are headquarters on these cases. We take the output of one of the largest makers of bookcases; our prices are based on the actual cost of material and labor, with but our one small percentage of profit added. If you order a bookcase from us and you do not find it perfectly satisfactory, **the greatest value ever shown**, the equal of bookcases that your dealer at home asks double the price for, **you can return the case to us at our expense and we will refund your money.**

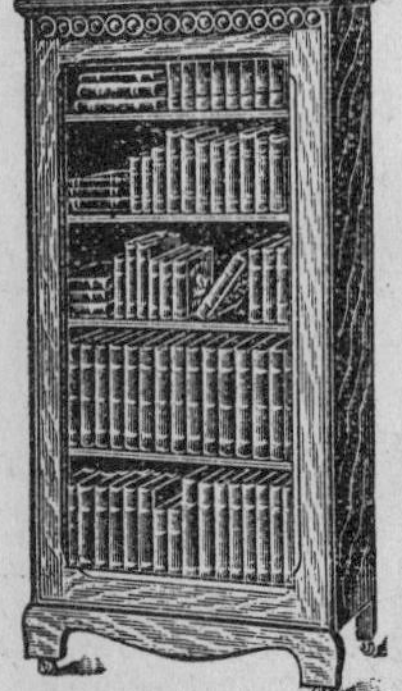

$5.60 for This $10.00 Bookcase.

No. 1R1300 Neat, Attractive, Roomy Bookcase. Upper panel carved. Height, 52 inches; width, 24 inches; depth, 12 inches. Made of ash, finished in imitation quarter sawed golden oak or birch imitation mahogany; adjustable shelves, glass door. Takes up very little room space. Weight, crated, 75 pounds.
Price, oak finish..... **$5.60**
Price, mahogany finish...................... **5.65**

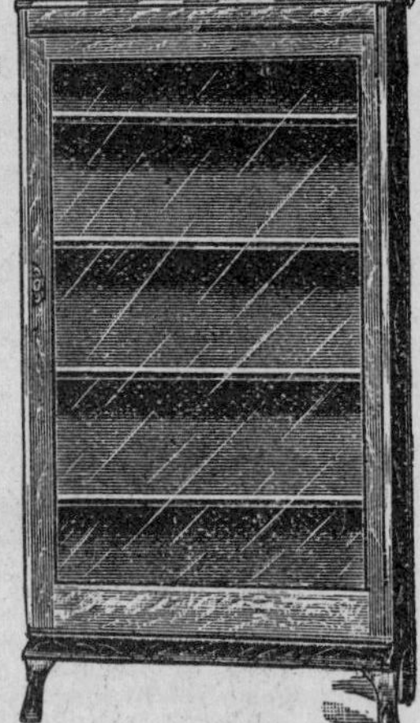

Our $6.95 Oak Bookcase.

Retails everywhere at $10.00.

No. 1R1301 Bookcase, 57 inches high and 32 inches wide, is made of quartered golden oak, with handsome finish. The door is of double thick glass, the shelves are adjustable, the back is of solid oak and well finished inside. This is the cheapest bookcase made for the money. Shipping weight, 90 pounds.
Price......... **$6.95**

Our $8.20 and $8.95 Solid Oak Bookcase.

From the small illustration by our artist from a photograph, you can get some idea of this handsome case. It is made of carefully selected, quarter sawed golden oak finish or imitation mahogany as desired. This handsomely carved and trimmed case has high piano finish, is made with durable shelves and nice back; handsome top ornamentation; extra heavy glass in doors. Is 65 inches high and 37 inches wide. **At our special $8.20 price we furnish it complete with handsome pattern, bevel French plate mirror,** 6x16 inches. **In ordering be sure to state whether you wish quarter sawed oak or imitation mahogany.** Shipping weight, 115 pounds.
No. 1R1302 Price, without mirror.......... **$8.20**
No. 1R1304 Price, with mirror complete... **8.95**

Our $6.95 Oak Bookcase.

No. 1R1305 This Handsome Oak Bookcase is the very latest style for 1902, made for us under contract by one of the best makers of high grade cases. **It is made from the very finest, carefully selected golden oak,** beautifully carved and ornamented. It stands 6 feet high, 3 feet 4 inches wide, 14 inches deep; has four strong, adjustable shelves, big double doors fitted with double thick glass, with lock and key. Has two drawers at bottom, fitted with brass pulls, full finished inside and out; can also be used as a china closet and cupboard. **Shipped direct from our factory in Northeastern Indiana. Price, each.. $6.95**
Weight, packed for shipment, 140 pounds.

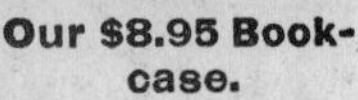

Our $8.95 Bookcase.

No. 1R1306 Bookcase is 5 feet 9 inches high and 38 inches wide, and made of quarter sawed oak, and very neatly finished in golden oak; the shelves are adjustable and the doors are of extra double thick glass. This case has finest inside finish, the casters are ball bearing. While the illustration will give you a fair idea of the appearance of this handsome case, it must be seen to be fully appreciated.
Shipping weight 130 pounds. Price. **$8.95**

No. 1R1310 At $13.90 we offer this large, massive, extra heavy quarter sawed golden oak Bookcase, in the new 1902 pillar design, as the equal of bookcases that sell everywhere at about double the price. Our small illustration will give you but a faint idea of the richness, the beauty, the high finish, the extra value offered in this rich three-door bookcase. **This is a very heavy, richly finished bookcase;** every bookcase made from carefully selected quarter sawed golden oak, with a high piano polish finish. Has three doors, as illustrated; doors are fitted with double thick glass; adjustable shelves; the bookcase is large and roomy; it is 61 inches wide and 57 inches high. Weight, complete, 175 pounds.
Price.......................... .... **$13.90**

Our Only Terms are Cash With Order.

WHY WE ASK CASH with all orders, and why you are perfectly safe in sending cash with your order, is fully explained on the first page of our large catalogue.

ALWAYS REMEMBER we accept your money and your order with the distinct understanding that the goods shall prove perfectly satisfactory to you in every way or we will cheerfully refund your money, including transportation charges.

YOUR MONEY IS AS SAFE WITH US AS WITH ANY BANK IN THE COUNTRY.

GIVE CATALOGUE NUMBER IN FULL WHEN YOU WRITE YOUR ORDER

OUR CELEBRATED BAUCH EXPANSION BOOKCASE.

EQUAL to the BEST in QUALITY, and CHEAPER than the lowest in PRICE.

THE EXTENSION BOOKCASE is the latest patent device in the library furniture line and a most valuable acquisition to any home.

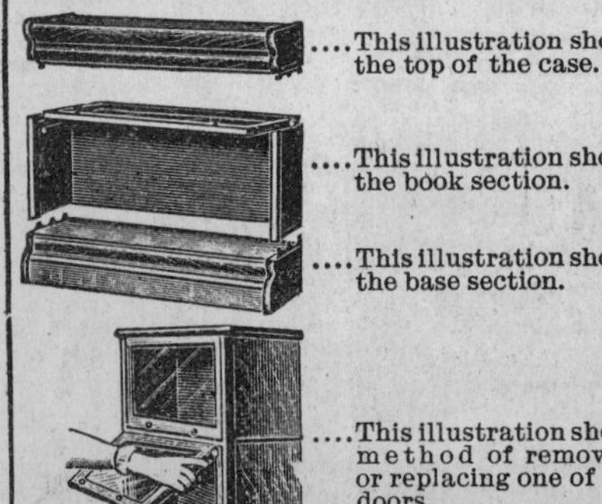

....This illustration shows the top of the case.

....This illustration shows the book section.

....This illustration shows the base section.

....This illustration shows method of removing or replacing one of the doors.

THESE BOOKCASES are so constructed that they can be adapted to the smallest library of books and can be increased to accommodate any number of books which will not exceed 13¼ inches in height.

WE FURNISH the Bauch Extension Bookcase in quarter sawed golden oak or genuine mahogany veneered finish, made of the very best grade of material, hand rubbed and polished. The top has a very handsome veneered roll as shown in the illustration. The material used in the construction of these cases is of the best quality, thoroughly seasoned and dried, which is essential in the construction of any article of furniture.

THIS BOOKCASE is so constructed that it can be shipped knocked down, which makes possible a great saving in freight. It is exceptionally strong in construction, having in the top part a very deep groove and on the lower part a tongue, which fits into the groove in top section, holding it very strong and making it as firm as if it were made of one piece. The case can be easily put together and can be increased horizontally or vertically as may be required. We furnish them with or without drawers as illustrated. One special feature found only in our cases is the ease with which the glass door can be removed or replaced if necessary. The doors slide on roller bearings and operate very easily. They can be opened or closed without any effort. In this respect, they are far superior to the old fashioned bookcase doors, as any one section can be opened independent of another. The dimensions of the case do not vary excepting in the height to allow for the different sized books. The cases can be had in three different heights, 9¼, 11¼ and 13¼ inches.

Our prices are nearly the same whether furnished in quarter sawed oak or genuine mahogany, veneered. When ordering be sure to state finish desired.

Outside Measurements	Width, Inches	Depth, Inches	Height, Inches	Price Quartered G'ldenOak	Price Veneered Mahogany
Base Section..........	34½	12½	8	$1.50	$1.55
Top Section (regular).....	34½	12½	8	1.65	1.70
Two Drawer Section.......	34½	12½	12	2.90	2.95
Book Section, with door...	34½	10½	9¼	2.50	2.55
Book Section, with door...	34½	10½	11¼	2.70	2.75
Book Section, with door...	34½	10½	13¼	2.95	3.00

The illustration below shows the complete case, comprising top, four book sections, drawer sections and base.

This bookcase can be furnished complete with four 9¼ inch book sections in quartered oak for $14.55. In veneered mahogany for $14.85.

OUR LINE OF COMBINATION BOOKCASES AND WRITING DESKS.

IN THESE HANDSOME ARTICLES OF FURNITURE we show a quality of goods that will be found only in the best furniture stores in large cities, and there at nearly double the prices we are able to name. There is nothing more desirable for the home, nothing that adorns the room to a greater extent than a fine combination bookcase and writing desk. These bookcases are made for us under contract, all in one factory by one of the best makers of this specialty furniture in the country, and our prices are based on factory cost, with but our one small percentage of profit added.

IF YOU WANT TO APPRECIATE THE EXTRAORDINARY VALUES we are offering in these high grade cases, you must compare our prices with those asked by others for furniture of equal quality. We acknowledge no competition in this line, for in most cases our prices are less than retail furniture dealers pay when they buy such grades.

OUR GUARANTEE. If you order one of these fine bookcases and desks, and after received do not find it entirely satisfactory in every way, you are at liberty to return it to us at our expense of transportation charges both ways, and we will immediately return your money

THE FREIGHT IS A SMALL ITEM. By noting the weight under each description, and referring to pages 7 to 10, you can calculate just what the freight will amount to, without writing to us for this information. In every case you will find it will be next to nothing as compared to the saving in price.

Our Special $7.90 Bookcase and Desk.

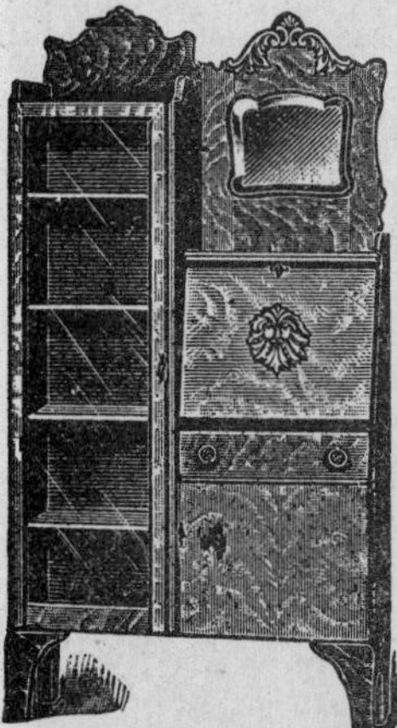

No. 1R1312 This Handsome Combination Bookcase and Desk is made of quarter sawed golden oak, excellently made and finished. It is 66 inches high and 35 inches wide and is fitted with a 10x12-inch handsomely shaped, French pattern plate mirror. The inside of desk is provided with pigeonholes for envelopes, writing paper and other stationery, and the lid drops into position forming a writing table. Below this is a roomy cupboard with a door having the appearance of a drawer and cupboard together, making the case a very handsome as well as useful piece of furniture. All compartments are fitted with locks and keys, trimmings of table and door are all of solid brass. The case is fitted complete with casters and we guarantee it to reach you in perfect condition. There is no dealer who is offering a case which will equal ours in quality at anywhere near our price. Shipping weight, 150 pounds.
Shipped direct from factory at Rockford, Ill.
Our special price, oak only....................**$7.90**

Only $9.45. Match It If You Can Elsewhere for Less Than $14.00.

No. 1R1315 Combination Bookcase and Desk made of quarter sawed golden oak, highly polished, beautifully carved, as shown in the illustration. This case is 68 inches high, 44 inches wide and has a beautifully shaped French pattern bevel plate mirror, 12x12 inches in size. The writing desk is provided with compartments for envelopes, writing paper and other stationery, and the lower part is a roomy cupboard. The left part of the case is arranged with adjustable shelves for books. The glass door is double thick, the trimmings are all of solid brass and the case is fitted with casters. Shipping weight, 125 pounds. Shipped direct from factory at Rockford, Ill. This case retails regularly at from $12.00 to $15.00.
Our special price, in oak only....................**$9.45**

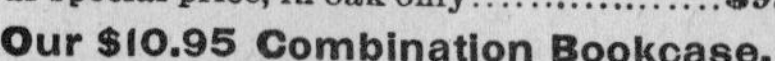

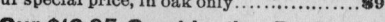

Our $10.95 Combination Bookcase.

Combination Bookcase, made of quarter sawed golden oak; has an oval French pattern bevel plate mirror, 10x14 inches. The inside of desk is very neatly pigeonholed and has a large, roomy drawer; also a cupboard door with a shelf inside. The shelves are adjustable; the back is either a solid oak or birch, neatly paneled, and the case is well finished inside; the size of the case is 6 feet 2 inches high and 3 feet 4 inches wide; **the glass door is double thick;** the trimmings, or drawer pulls, are of brass; best quality casters. Weight, 145 pounds.
No. 1R1316 Price, in oak, each..**$10.95**

Our Leader, at $11.45.

Combination Case is 69 inches high, 39 inches wide, is made of quarter sawed oak throughout, beautifully carved and highly polished. The handsomely shaped French bevel plate mirror is 12x12 inches in size. The case is trimmed with best quality brass handles, hinges and locks, and mounted on ball bearing casters. Carefully packed and crated and shipped direct from our factory at Rockford, Ill. Shipping weight, 140 pounds.

No. 1R1317 Our special price **$11.45**

Combination Bookcase, 6 feet 3 inches high, 3 feet 5 inches wide, with a French pattern bevel plate mirror, 10x14 inches; the carving is hand made, **the door is of double thick glass,** the inside is pigeonholed and has a drawer. There is one large, roomy drawer and cupboaad below the desk lid. This case is made of solid golden oak, quarter sawed, with a very fine finish. Also made in curly birch, finished in imitation mahogany; **the back is either solid oak or birch,** and well finished inside; drawer pulls are of brass; **each drawer and door has lock and key;** the shelves are adjustable. Casters come with this bookcase. Shipping weight, 155 pounds.
No. 1R1318 Price, in oak....................**$11.60**
No. 1R1319 Price, in imitation mahogany. **11.65**

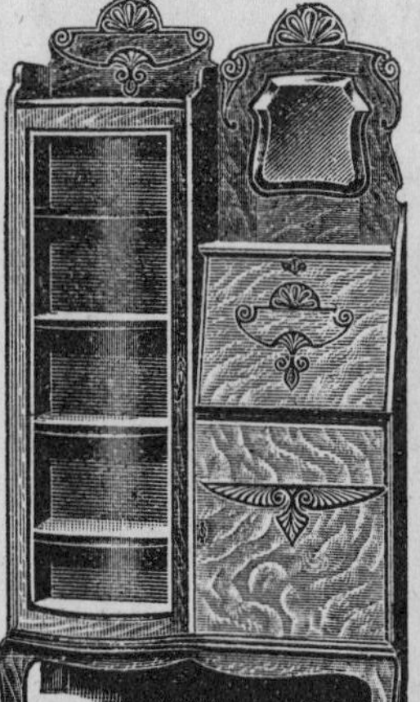

No. 1R1320 This Handsome Combination Bookcase and Writing Desk is 5 feet 8 inches high and 3 feet 2 inches wide, is made of solid quarter sawed oak, beautifully carved and highly polished throughout. The handsomely shaped French bevel plate mirror measures 12x12 inches; the door of the bookcase is bent glass, usually found only in the very highest priced cases. The interior of the desk is provided with compartments for envelopes, writing paper and other stationery, while the lower part of the writing desk forms a handsome cupboard. The desk is trimmed with best quality brass trimmings and supplied with ball bearing casters. We ship these cases direct from our factory at Rockford, Ill., basing our price on the actual factory cost with but our one small percentage of profit added. Every case is carefully crated to insure safe delivery. Shipping weight, 150 pounds.
Our special price.......................... ..**$11.95**

Combination Case and Writing Desk, $12.70.

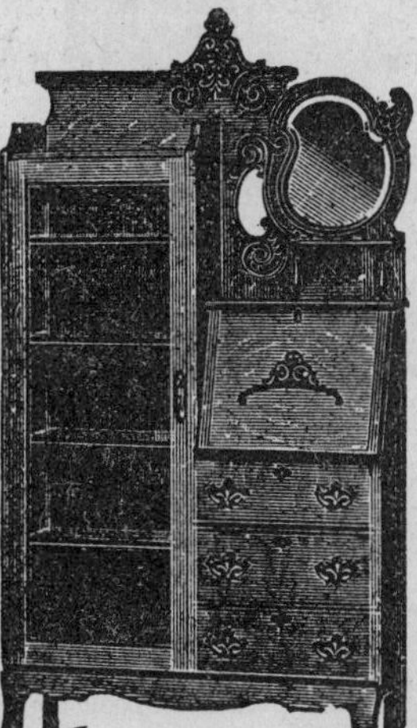

No. 1R1321 This Handsome Combination Bookcase is made of the finest quarter sawed golden oak and is very attractive in design; is richly carved; has shaped bevel mirror, 12x14 inches; has three roomy drawers and has four adjustable shelves; large writing lid; interior of desk nicely arranged for stationery; full double glass front; is 74 inches high and 41 inches wide; complete with locks, best trimmings, and casters, etc. Weight, 165 pounds.
Price, each, **$12.70**

No. 1R1324 This Handsome High Grade Combination Bookcase and Writing Desk is one of the latest 1902 styles, especially designed for us by one of the best manufacturers of this class of goods in the United States. This case is 70 inches high, 39 inches wide and is made of the best quality quarter sawed oak throughout; beautifully carved and decorated and highly polished. As shown in the illustration, there is a cupboard over the writing desk with a handsome French bevel plate 10x16-inch mirror in the door. Just below the writing desk is a drawer with swell front. The door of the bookcase has bent glass, which is generally used only on the highest priced cases. The entire case is beautifully trimmed with best quality brass cast trimmings and furnished complete with a set of ball bearing casters. Carefully packed and crated and shipped direct from our factory at Rockford, Ill. Shipping weight, 160 pounds. Our special price....................**$14.60**

Our $13.95 Combination Bookcase.

No. 1R1333 Combination Bookcase. 6 feet high, 3 feet 4 inches wide, with a French pattern bevel mirror, 16x18 inches; the carving is hand made, the glass in the door is of extra double thickness; the inside of desk is pigeonholed and has a drawer in center; there are three large drawers below the desk and each drawer has lock and key. This bookcase is made of solid oak and is finished in golden oak. The shelves are adjustable, the drawer pulls are solid cast brass. The back of case is solid oak and paneled inside; the inside is well finished, the casters are ball bearing. Shipping weight, 200 pounds.
Price, each.......................................**$13.95**

Handsomely Carved Combination Bookcase and Writing Desk.

No. 1R1325 Combination Bookcase and Writing Desk. Made of the finest quarter sawed golden oak and polished like a piano. The carving on this case is extra fine. Height, 6 feet 3 inches; width, 59 inches. Has a beautiful 14x12-inch French bevel mirror, three large swell drawers fitted with locks and cast brass handles. **The doors contain the best of glass. The desk is partitioned with pigeonholes and drawers,** and all shelves in bookcase are adjustable. Has cabinet and shelf over each book compartment. Weight, 200 pounds.
Price, only......................................**$21.95**

A $50.00 Combination Bookcase for $26.95.

No. 1R1327 The best type of the cabinetmakers' art. A piece of furniture that is perfect in workmanship and material. One of the finest combination bookcases ever shown. Bold, rich carvings, and elegantly made of the finest quarter sawed oak; is very roomy and useful; has large plate glass mirror in back, 18x18 inches; **three roomy drawers, two large book compartments.** The interior of the desk is well arranged for paper and other articles necessary for literary work. It is 5 feet 6 inches wide and 6 feet 2 inches high. Will beautify any parlor or library. Shipping weight, 240 pounds.
Price..**$26.95**

LADIES' WRITING DESKS.

No Such Desk at Retail for Less Than $8.00.

No. 1R1402 A Dainty and Artistic Writing Desk in the finest quarter sawed oak, finely made and finished, richly carved writing lid, roomy lower drawer; is 26 inches wide and has French shaped legs. A real beauty for a very low price. Weight, 50 pounds.
Price, wood back..**$4.40**
Price, mirror back, **4.95**

Our $5.00 Desk.

No. 1R1404 A Neat and Attractive Writing Desk of the finest quarter sawed oak. Neat, pretty carvings. Interior arranged for papers, stationery, etc. Is 27 inches wide. Weight, 50 pounds.
Price.............**$5.00**

$5.25 Buys This Beautiful and Dainty Desk.

No. 1R1406 A Very Dainty and Pretty Ladies' Writing Desk, made of golden oak. Has the French leg, is very neatly carved, has good large drawer and **interior nicely divided for stationery.** A useful and ornamental addition to a home. Is 51 inches high and 24 inches wide. Weight, 50 pounds.
Price, in oak....**$5.25**

A Rare Bargain at $5.75.

No. 1R1410 This is a very pretty Ladies' House Desk, made of golden oak, is very neatly carved, has lower drawer and **interior of desk nicely divided for papers, books and stationery.** An attractive household article. Is 51 inches high and 24 inches wide. Shipping weight, 50 pounds.
Price, each......**$5.75**

Ladies' Desk for $6.25.

No. 1R1416 A Very Pretty Ladies' House Desk, made of quarter sawed oak, highly polished, handsomely carved. Interior of desk is nicely divided for paper, books and stationery; a very attractive and useful article for the home; is 32 inches wide and very roomy. Shipping weight, 50 pounds.
Price.............**$6.25**

Our $9.45 Ladies' Writing Desk.

Ladies' Desk; 4 feet 10 inches high, 29 inches wide; with 8x14-inch French bevel plate mirror. This desk is **made of solid oak,** partly quarter sawed. Also made in birch, and is finished in a high gloss finish, either in antique oak or imitation mahogany. **The inside is pigeonholed, and has one drawer in center,** also two large drawers and upper shelf. The hand carving is beautiful, and the trimmings are of brass. Casters are ball bearing. Shipping weight, 100 pounds.
No. 1R1420 Price, in oak..........**$9.45**
No. 1R1422 Price, each, in mahogany finish..........**$9.75**

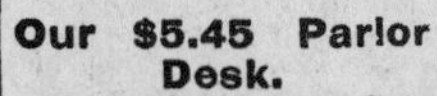

Only $3.85 for this Handsome Drop Leaf Desk.

An ornament to a home. A convenience that will be invaluable.

No. 1R1428 This Beautiful Little Desk is made of golden oak, polished; has a large drop leaf and inside is nicely partitioned with pigeonholes and drawer; top is ornamented with shelf; has shelf also in lower part for books and a brass rod with rings for curtain, well made and beautifully finished. Weight, 60 pounds.
Price, each........**$3.85**

Our $5.45 Parlor Desk.

Made in our own factory. Prices based on actual factory cost.

No. 1R1430 Parlor Desk, neat design, well made of select golden oak, prettily hand carved and highly hand polished. Has large drop leaf fitted with lock, and inside is nicely partitioned with pigeonholes. The lower part can be used for books, and has a brass rod for curtain; also has a good French bevel mirror and a large shelf in upper part. Height, 5 feet; width, 2 feet 6 inches. Weight, about 70 pounds.
Price, only......**$5.45**

Our $5.95 Parlor Desk.

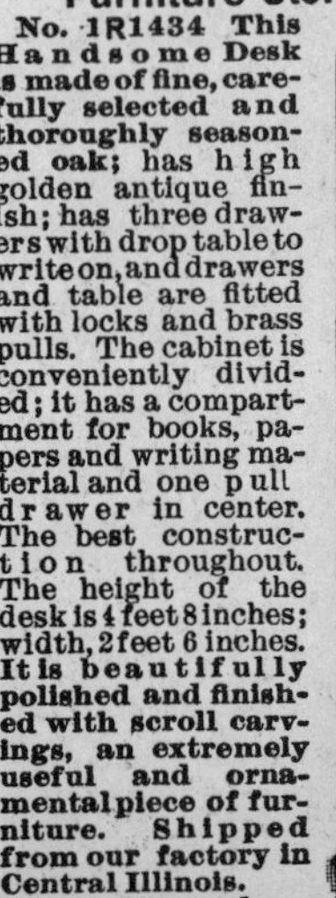

No. 1R1432 Parlor Desk. A graceful and good, sensible design. Made of select golden oak stock. Width, 30 inches; height, 63 inches. Inside is nicely partitioned with pigeonholes. Has a large drop leaf and a shelf in lower part which can be used for books; also a brass rod and rings for curtain. **The top is ornamented with two shelves and a good French bevel mirror.** Weight, 90 pounds. **Shipped from factory in Western Michigan.**
Price, in quartered oak............**$5.95**

$6.20 Buys this Handsome Desk that Furniture Stores Ask $10.00 For.

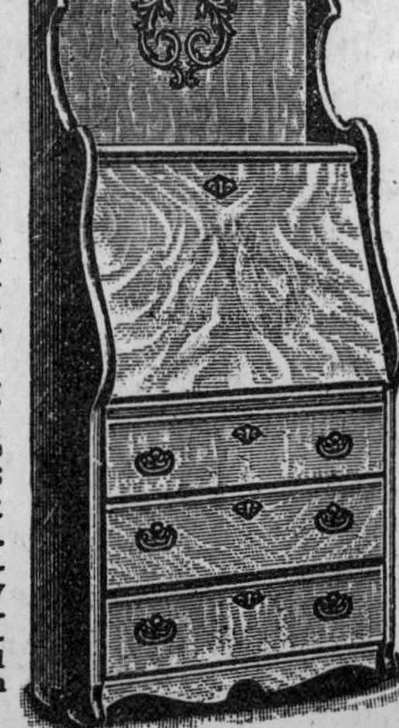

No. 1R1434 This Handsome Desk is made of fine, carefully selected and thoroughly seasoned oak; has high golden antique finish; has three drawers with drop table to write on, and drawers and table are fitted with locks and brass pulls. The cabinet is conveniently divided; it has a compartment for books, papers and writing material and one pull drawer in center. The best construction throughout. The height of the desk is 4 feet 8 inches; width, 2 feet 6 inches. **It is beautifully polished and finished with scroll carvings, an extremely useful and ornamental piece of furniture. Shipped from our factory in Central Illinois.** Weight, 80 pounds.
Our price.................................**$6.20**

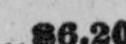

WONDERFUL VALUES IN OFFICE DESKS.

IN OUR LINE OF OFFICE DESKS we show the most serviceable styles, manufactured expressly for us by two of the largest makers of office desks, whose factories are located in the greatest hardwood lumber section in the United States, making it possible to turn out a superior quality of desk at an extremely low price. Only the best quality of thoroughly kiln dried lumber, oils, varnish, hardware and glue are used in the construction of the desks, which makes it possible for us to guarantee every desk. Compare carefully the size, description and price of our desks with those offered by other dealers and you will quickly recognize the saving it is possible for you to make by placing your order with us. We do not believe that our desks can be duplicated elsewhere at within $3.00 to $5.00 of the price we quote. **Every desk is carefully packed and shipped direct from the factory in Southern Indiana or Southern Michigan,** which alone enables us to quote such extremely low prices. But we reserve the privilege of shipping from Chicago when convenient.

MOST ALL RAILROAD COMPANIES **takes Desks at first class freight rates.** By referring to pages 7 to 10, you can get the first class rate to the town nearest to you, which is almost, if not exactly, the same as to your town. With this rate per 100 pounds and the weight as given under each desk, you can tell almost exactly what the freight will amount to. It will amount to nothing compared to what you will save in price.

A Solid Oak, Flat Top Desk for $8.95.

This Desk is made of solid oak, is 54 inches long, 30 inches wide and 30 inches high. It measures 24 inches between the pedestals and has four drawers on the left side and one drawer on the right side over the cupboard, which is arranged for books and papers. The top of the desk is made up of built up wood, insuring it against warping or splitting. This desk is undoubtedly one of the greatest values in flat top desks ever offered by any dealer. Shipping weight, 150 pounds.

No. 1R1442 Our special price................**$8.95**

No. 1R1444 Same Desk as No. 1R1442, excepting that it is only 48 inches long instead of 54 inches. Our special price................................**$8.45**

Our $9.25 Flat Top Office Desk.

No. 1R1450 This Flat Top Office Desk is made of solid oak, beautifully finished, heavy paneled sides and back, imitation leather top. Size, 4 feet 2 inches by 30 inches. Has four drawers, fitted with lock and key, heavy piano legs, well made and finished throughout. Weight, 150 pounds. Price, each..**$9.25**

A Roll Top Curtain Desk for $10.45.

No. 1R1452 This Desk is without doubt the lowest priced curtain desk ever offered by any dealer. This desk is 44 inches long, 45 inches high and 30 inches wide. As shown in the illustration, it has three drawers on the left side and a roomy cupboard on the right side for books. The desk top and all panels are made of three-ply built up stock. The drawers are all dovetailed and the entire desk is built in a thoroughly substantial manner and excellently finished. Must be seen to be appreciated. Shipping weight, about 180 pounds.

Our special price..................................**$10.45**

OUR GREAT BARGAIN OFFICE DESK

This High Grade Roll Top Desk for $11.95.

No. 1R1456 This Desk is without doubt the greatest value ever offered in a roll top curtain desk. In fact, it is a desk not found for sale by other dealers, being made expressly for us. The illustration is a reproduction of a photograph of the desk, which gives but a fair idea of the exceptional value which it represents. **It is all oak,** 48 inches long, 30 inches wide and 46 inches high; has five drawers, four on the left side, and one on the right side over a roomy cupboard, partitioned off for papers and books. This desk has a very roomy cupboard at the side which is not usually put in desks of this style. In all of the details this desk is the same as the very highest grade desks made, having extension slides, the regulation size pigeonholes and drawers and two small corner drawers, besides racks for pencils, pens, etc. The desk has full finished back and is finished and polished all around. Has flexible dustproof curtain and excellent quality automatic spring lock, and is mounted on extra heavy, patent chilled, ball bearing casters. If you are contemplating purchasing a desk, you should not think of ordering elsewhere. Shipping weight, about 200 pounds.

Our special price..................................**$11.95**

Our Special $12.75 Roll Top Desk.

No. 1R1460 This desk is 4 feet 2 inches long, 2 feet 6 inches wide, 3 feet 8 inches high. **It is made of carefully selected oak,** beautifully finished in golden antique; full finished back. **The ends are built with three panels, while most all other desks of this grade have only two panels.** Extension slides, quarter sawed sycamore pigeonhole cases; combination lock on drawers; spring lock with duplicate keys on curtain; four drawers on left side; lower partition for books; book closet on right hand side; drawers, pencil rests and card racks in interior. Desk is highly polished; has a beautiful finish; dust proof curtain. **At our special $12.75 price, the desk** comes complete on rollers carefully packed in burlap and delivered on board the cars at our factory in Southern Michigan. Weight, 200 pounds.

Our special price..................................**$12.75**

A Bargain at $18.45.

No. 1R1463 High Curtain Office Desk, 4 feet long, 2 feet 6 inches wide, 4 feet 1 inch high; dust and knife proof curtain. Oak, finished antique; extension slides, finished back, quarter sawed sycamore pigeonhole case, six wood pigeonhole filing boxes. Combination lock on drawers, spring lock with duplicate keys on curtain. Three drawers on left side, the lower partitioned for books; book closet on right hand side. Also furnished with closed panel back to order. Weight, 230 pounds. Price............**$18.45**

Great Value at $18.65.

No. 1R1465 Our High Curtain Office Desk, 4 feet 2 inches long, 2 feet 6 inches wide, 4 feet 1 inch high; dust and knife proof curtain. Oak, finished antique; extension slides, finished back, quarter sawed sycamore pigeonhole case. Combination lock on drawers, spring lock with duplicate keys on curtain. Three drawers on each side. Deep bottom drawers partitioned for books. Large center drawer. Three drawers, pen rests and card racks in interior. Also furnished with closed panel back to order. Weight, 235 pounds. Price......................**$18.65**

No. 1R1466 Same style of desk as 1R1465, only **5 feet long** instead of 4 feet 2 inches.

Our special price..................................**$18.95**

Our $19.95 High Grade Curtain Desk.

High Curtain Office Desk, 4 feet 6 inches long, 2 feet 6 inches wide, 4 feet 1 inch high; well made, of solid oak and polished. Has lap joint, dust and knife proof curtain, a solid oak writing bed. Oak, finished antique; extension slides, finished back, quarter sawed sycamore pigeonhole case. Combination lock on drawers, spring lock with duplicate keys on curtain; three drawers on each side, deep bottom drawers partitioned for books; two drawers, pen rests and card racks in interior; also with closed panel back to order. Weight, 185 pounds.

No. 1R1467 Price, 4-foot..................**$19.95**

No. 1R1468 Price, 5-foot.................. **21.45**

Big Values in Bedroom Suites.

WITH OUR LINE OF BEDROOM SUITES enlarged, greatly improved, brought right up to date to include the very newest styles for this season, and at greatly reduced prices, we are prepared to save you so much money we feel you cannot afford to buy a bedroom suite elsewhere.

THE WONDERFUL GROWTH of our furniture department has made it possible for us to make much larger contracts with the manufacturers than ever before, thus reducing the cost to us and enabling us to make lower prices to you. By a careful comparison of our prices with those of any other house or with your dealer at home, we know, quality for quality, we can save you from $5.00 to $50.00 on a bedroom suite, and can give you newer and more stylish patterns than you would likely be able to get from your local furniture dealers.

HOW WE ARE ABLE TO MAKE THE PRICES SO LOW, and how it is possible for us to reduce our prices on bedroom suites below any previous quotations. OUR BEDROOM SUITES ARE MADE FOR US UNDER CONTRACT by three of the best manufacturers in this country—one Michigan manufacturer, one Indiana manufacturer and one Wisconsin manufacturer, and our output has increased to such an extent that we are able to contract in each case for a very large part of the output of the factory, and these factories desiring to run at full capacity the year around, are willing to take our contract at next to cost, the cost of material and labor, as it facilitates the working of their factory and enables them to run every working day at full capacity and thus reduce the cost, not only on the suites they make for us, but on the suites they sell to other people. As a result, we own our bedroom suites this season, including all the newest designs, at about the cost of the material and labor, and our price to you is but our one small percentage of profit above the actual cost.

WE HAVE FIGURED THE COST ON EVERY SUITE, first, on the basis of the number of feet of oak, ash or other lumber. We have then figured the cost of the mill work, of the hand carving, and the cost of assembling and finishing, the net cost of the hardware, the cost of the plate glass in Europe with freight and duty added, and on this basis of calculation we own our bedroom suites and on this basis we offer them to you with but our one small percentage of profit added, which means a saving on any suite you buy from us of from $5.00 to $50.00, according to the suite you select.

TO APPRECIATE THE VALUE WE ARE GIVING IN BEDROOM SUITES you must see, examine and compare our suites with those offered by others at within 20 to 40 per cent of our prices. Unfortunately, you cannot by illustration and description compare satisfactorily for the real value, but if you will take any suite that we advertise and place it alongside of any suite offered by any other house at anything approaching our price, you will at once see that with our facilities we are furnishing a much higher grade of goods at a much lower price than you can possibly buy elsewhere.

ABOUT FACTORY SHIPMENTS. To reduce our selling price to you to the lowest possible point, you will note on a number of suites we have reserved the right to ship either from our store in Chicago, or direct from the factory where made, either in Wisconsin, Indiana or Michigan. **This means a big saving to you,** for where we ship from the factory direct there is nothing added for freight, handling or storage in Chicago, and as a result you can buy one bedroom suite from us for less than dealers can buy in carload lots, in fact, as before stated, you cannot appreciate the values we are giving in this line until you have seen and compared them with other goods.

QUALITY OF MATERIAL AND CONSTRUCTION. Our suites, from the cheapest to the best, are all thoroughly well made, all from carefully selected material, extra well finished. We use nothing but the highest grade of thoroughly seasoned lumber. You will find every piece stronger, better fitting, better finished, more lasting and more satisfactory than is turned out from the average factory.

OUR PLATE GLASS IS ALL HIGH GRADE BEVEL GLASS. We use none of the cheap domestic plate. Our suites are all fully equipped, all castered, all full finished, every piece guaranteed.

OUR TERMS OF SHIPMENT. While we require the full amount of cash to accompany all orders, we accept your order with the understanding and agreement that the suite will reach you in perfect order and be found perfectly satisfactory, otherwise, you can return it to us at our expense of freight charges both ways and we will immediately return your money.

HOW WE PACK FOR SHIPMENT. Every suite is carefully packed for shipment to insure its reaching you in the same perfect condition it leaves our store or the factory. It is well packed in heavy paper, excelsior and burlap. It rarely ever happens that a suite is delivered with even the slightest scratch or mar.

ABOUT FREIGHT CHARGES. The freight charges on a bedroom suite will amount to next to nothing as compared to what you will save in price. The beds are accepted by the railroad companies at second class freight rate. The dressers and commodes at first class freight rate. The weight of each is given under each description and by referring to pages 7 to 10 you can ascertain the first and second class rate for 100 pounds to a point near you in your state. The freight will be nearly, if not exactly the same to your town. In this way you can calculate almost to a penny what the freight will amount to, and you will find it will amount to next to nothing as compared to what you will save in price. **FOR EXAMPLE:** From many points within 400 to 600 miles of Chicago, the freight on an average three-piece bedroom suite will amount to $1.00 to $1.75, whereas the saving will be from $5.00 to $50.00, depending on the suite selected and the price asked by your dealer at home.

UNDERSTAND, you take no risk in sending us your order and your money, for we accept it with the understanding that if the bedroom suite does not reach you in perfect condition and is not in every way satisfactory and a much better suite than you can possibly buy elsewhere for the money, you are at liberty to return it to us at our expense of freight charges both ways and we will immediately return your money.

Our Cheapest Bedroom Suite.

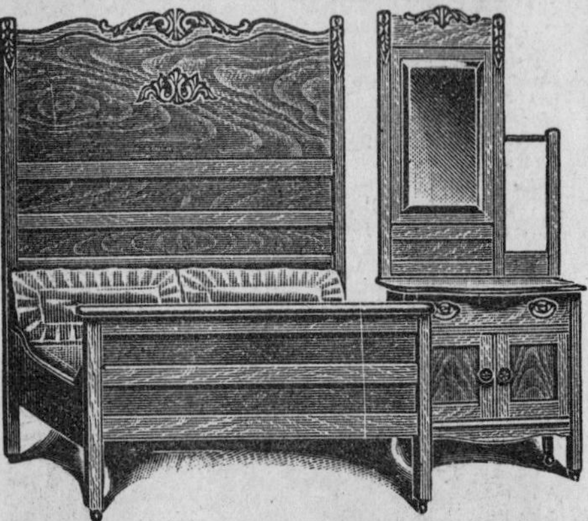

We show in the accompanying illustration a chamber suite of two pieces, suitable for hotels or for bedrooms that are too small for the larger size three-piece suites. This suite is **made of the best selected seasoned hard wood,** is thoroughly well put together and is finished golden. Is 6 feet high with 4-foot 2-inch slats. Top of headboard is fancy pattern shaped and decorated with heavy molding, giving it a very neat appearance. **The combination washstand and dresser** is 30x18 inches, of a style which matches the bed perfectly. The top is handsomely carved. The dresser is fitted with large, roomy drawer and large compartment below. The mirror is of excellent imported German plate glass and is 14x24 inches in size.

No. 1R1615	Weight, about 90 pounds.	Price of bed	$2.75
No. 1R1616	Weight, about 75 pounds.	Price of dresser	6.20
No. 1R1617		Price of complete suite	$8.95

Our Leader for $11.45, Former Price, $12.75.

At $11.45 We Are Far Below any Attempted Competition.

No. 1R1618 In this hardwood suite we offer more value for the money than was ever offered before in the line of bedroom furniture. We illustrate the bed, dresser and washstand; suite consists of three pieces. **Bed—the bed is 6 feet long, and has 4-foot 2-inch slats.** The head of the bed is 6 feet high, is handsomely decorated with heavy molding. Bed sides are thoroughly substantial and the construction of the bed is such as will give great service. **Dresser—the square dresser is very handsome and has beautifully carved top with large square German plate bevel mirror, 20x24 inches in size.** Fitted with four very large, roomy drawers, having cast brass handles. The suite throughout is finished very handsomely in golden. **Commode—the commode or washstand has drawer and cupboard, with splasher back.**

Our special price for three-piece suite, complete........ **$11.45**
Shipping weight, 225 pounds.

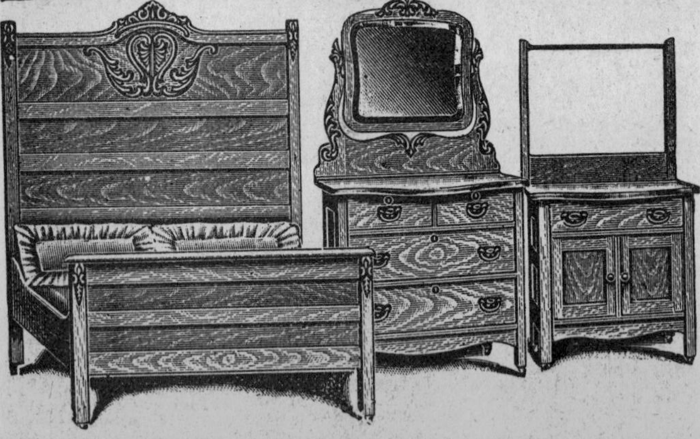

Great Value at $13.95.

In this handsome northern hardwood suite we offer more value for the money than was ever offered before in the line of bedroom furniture. Suite consists of three pieces, finished a beautiful golden oak. **Bed—the bed is 6 feet high and has 4-foot 5-inch slats.** The head of bed is handsomely decorated with heavy molding. Bed sides are thoroughly substantial and the construction of the bed is such as will give great service. **Dresser—the square dresser, 38 inches wide, with two upper drawers, is very handsome and has beautifully carved top with large shaped French plate mirror, 20x24 inches in size.** Fitted with very large, roomy drawers having cast brass handles. The suite throughout is finished very handsomely. **Commode—the commode or washstand has one drawer and cupboard, with splasher back.**

No. 1R1622	Weight, about 100 pounds.	Price of bed	$2.85
No. 1R1623	Weight, about 100 pounds.	Price of dresser	8.35
No. 1R1624	Weight, about 35 pounds.	Price of commode	2.75
No. 1R1625		Price of complete suite	$13.95

Most all railroad companies take bedroom suites at first class freight rates. By referring to pages 7 to 10, you can get the first class rate to the town nearest to you, which is almost, if not exactly the same as to your town.

With this rate per 100 pounds and the weight as given under each suite you can tell almost exactly what the freight will amount to. It will amount to nothing compared to what you will save in price.

Reduced from $17.40 to $14.90.

Bedroom Suite, made of the best selected northern hardwood, finished golden. We can recommend it as being good, substantial, well finished and honestly constructed. This bedroom suite consists of bed, dresser and commode, and is one of the best values shown this season. The bed is nicely carved, and is 6 feet high and 4 feet 6 inches wide; sides are thoroughly substantial. The construction of the bed is such as will give you years of good, honest service. The dresser is handsome; is fitted with extra quality bevel mirror, 22x28 inches; top and sides of mirror frame are artistically carved; dresser top is double and 42 inches in size; drawers are very large and roomy. Commode has 30-inch swell shaped front top, top drawer, two small drawers, and large cupboard.

No. 1R1630 Weight, 100 pounds. Price of bed........ $2.95
No. 1R1631 Weight, 100 pounds. Price of dresser........ 8.70
No. 1R1632 Weight, 40 pounds. Price of commode........ 3.25
No. 1R1633 Price of complete suite........ $14.90

Great Value at $15.50.

This suite represents one of the greatest bargains we have ever been able to offer in the shape of a three-piece suite with cheval dresser. We embody in this suite the latest ideas of the best designers and manufacturers of bedroom furniture. The dresser and commode have the double swell top drawers, which together with the handsome carved decorations and brass ornaments make the suite especially attractive. We can furnish the suite in golden oak finish or imitation mahogany as desired. Every piece is supplied with ball bearing casters. The bedstead is 6 feet 6 inches in height, and has 4 feet 6-inch slats. The dresser measures 20x44 inches, and has a fine French bevel plate mirror 16x26 inches in size. The size of the top of the washstand is 17x33 inches, and is constructed to correspond with the bed and dresser.

We ship this suite direct from our factory in Northern Indiana, but reserve the privilege of forwarding same from our store when convenient.

No. 1R1634 Weight, 100 pounds. Price of bed........ $3.75
No. 1R1635 Weight, 100 pounds. Price of dresser........ 8.35
No. 1R1636 Weight, 50 pounds. Price of commode........ 3.40
No. 1R1637 Price of complete suite........ $15.50

Most all railroad companies take bedroom suites at first class freight rates. By referring to pages 7 to 10 you can get the first class rate to the town nearest you, which is almost if not exactly the same as to your town. With this rate per 100 pounds and the weight as given under each suite you can tell almost exactly what the freight will amount to. It will amount to nothing compared to what you will save in price.

Solid Oak Bedroom Suite for $15.75.

It is not possible in an illustration to show the genuine value of this bedroom suite. It seems scarcely possible to furnish a strictly first class bedroom suite, made of solid golden oak, at $15.75. It is handsome in design, beautifully finished and decorated with tasteful carvings. The dresser and commode are fitted with best quality brass trimmings and all three pieces are fitted with ball bearing casters. The bed is full size, being 6 feet 4 inches high and 4 feet 6 inches wide. The dresser is 44 inches long and 20 inches wide, has double top and French bevel plate 28x22-inch mirror, handsome double, swell top drawers, besides two full size, roomy straight front drawers. The washstand measures 34x18 inches, has a full swell top drawer to match the dresser, two lower drawers and a large roomy cupboard. We ship this suite direct from our factory in Northern Indiana, but reserve the privilege of shipping from our store when convenient.

No. 1R1642 Weight, 120 pounds. Price of bed........ $3.55
No. 1R1643 Weight, 125 pounds. Price of dresser........ 8.95
No. 1R1644 Weight, 60 pounds. Price of commode........ 3.25
No. 1R1645 Price of complete suite........ $15.75

One of Our Handsomest and Latest Design Bedroom Suites for $16.95.

For only $16.95 we offer this very handsome, beautifully carved, elegantly finished three-piece Bedroom Suite, as one of the very best values in our entire stock. This suite should not be compared with suites offered by other dealers at anywhere near our price, as it is equal in quality and finish to suites that retail regularly at $28.00 to $35.00. It is made of solid oak, handsomely carved and decorated, as shown in the illustration. The trimmings are best quality brass, and each piece is fitted with ball bearing casters. The bed is full size, and measures 6 feet 4 inches in height and 4 feet 6 inches in width. The dresser measures 20x44 inches, and has double deck top, double swell top drawers and two large, roomy straight front drawers. The handsomely shaped mirror is French bevel plate, 22x28 inches. The commode is 18x34 inches, has splasher back and swell drawer to match the dresser, besides two lower drawers and a roomy cupboard. We ship this suite direct from our factory in Northern Indiana, but reserve the privilege of shipping from our store when convenient.

No. 1R1658 Weight, 120 pounds. Price of bed........ $4.15
No. 1R1659 Weight, 125 pounds. Price of dresser........ 9.45
No. 1R1660 Weight, 60 pounds. Price of commode........ 3.35
No. 1R1661 Price of complete suite........ $16.95

This High Grade Oak Suite With Cheval Dresser, at $18.75.

A WONDER OF VALUE. SUCH A SUITE AS FURNITURE STORES GENERALLY PRICE AT $24.00 TO $28.00.

This suite consists of three pieces, as shown in the illustration, having a cheval dresser instead of the regular style generally offered by other dealers. All three pieces are made of the choicest golden oak, the wood being carefully selected and kiln dried. The design is one of the latest for 1902, the dresser and commode having full swell top drawer, and all three pieces being elaborately carved and handsomely finished. The bed is full size, being 6 feet 4 inches high and 4 feet 6 inches wide. The dresser measures 20x44 inches, has French bevel plate mirror, 18x40 inches, and a very roomy cupboard, as shown in the illustration. The commode measures 18x34 inches and matches the dresser perfectly. Each piece of the suite is fitted with ball bearing casters. We ship direct from our factory in Northern Indiana, but reserve the privilege of shipping from our store when convenient.

No. 1R1650 Weight, 120 pounds. Price of bed........ $ 4.35
No. 1R1651 Weight, 125 pounds. Price of dresser........ 10.95
No. 1R1652 Weight, 60 pounds. Price of commode........ 3.45
No. 1R1653 Price of complete suite........ $18.75

$1.95 for a Regular $2.75 Bed.

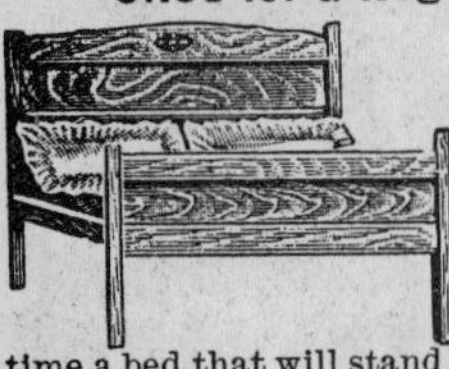

At $1.95 we offer a bed which your retail dealer would ask at least $2.75 for; in fact, we think many dealers would ask $3.00 to $4.00 for such a bed. The bed which we illustrate is offered to meet the demand for something very low priced and at the same time a bed that will stand usage and is thoroughly well constructed of excellent material. This bedstead is made of the best elm, is well finished in antique, is put together substantially and carefully by the best workmen, and will give ample service. It is 3 feet 4 inches high. Shipping weight, 75 pounds.

No. 1R1750 Price, 3-foot slats $1.95
No. 1R1751 Price, 3-foot 6-inch slats 1.95
No. 1R1752 Price, 4-foot 2-inch slats 1.95

$2.25 Buys a Regular $3.50 Bed.

At $2.25 we offer a bed which dealers sell from $3.00 to $5.00. The bed shown in illustration is very strongly constructed and substantial and is very much lower than others retail such values for; it is made of the best selected rock elm, finished in antique and is thoroughly seasoned; it is very neat in appearance, being nicely carved and finished. Shipping weight, 75 pounds.

No. 1R1754 Price, 3-foot 6-inch slats $2.25
No. 1R1755 Price, 4-foot 2-inch slats 2.25

Handsomely Finished Bed for $2.65.

No. 1R1757 This Bed is made of solid elm, finished antique. The head is decorated with fancy hand carving; the top panels on both head and footboard are handsomely finished and fitted; it is very solidly constructed and will last a lifetime. It is 4 feet 6 inches high. We furnish it in 3-foot 6-inch and 4-foot 2-inch. Shipping weight, 75 pounds.

Price, each $2.65

DEPARTMENT OF FOLDING BEDS.

Our Folding Beds are made by one of the largest and most reliable manufacturers in the country, makers of the highest grade goods. **They are all made from thoroughly seasoned material, and for workmanship, durability and general finish cannot be excelled.**

Our Special $7.95 Mantel Bed.

No. 1R1759 This illustration, engraved from a photograph, shows the bed with open front. It is made for curtain. The head and footboards are alike, thus affording a choice of ends for the head. **These beds are all shipped knocked down.** They go in a small space and **take a low freight rate.** Size, inside, open, 48x72 inches; closed, height, 53 inches; length, 81 inches; depth, 21 inches. These beds are **made of thoroughly seasoned hardwood, finished antique.** Shipping weight, 75 pounds.

Price, each $7.95

A Leader at $9.75.

Solid elm, finished in golden oak. Woven wire mattress with two-row spiral springs support. Size, closed, 54 inches high, 55 inches wide, 20 inches deep. Size, open, outside, 55x75 inches; inside, 48x72 inches. Mattress to fit should be 3 feet 10 inches by 6 feet with a 2½-inch box and, to be flexible enough, should be made of moss, cotton or hair. Also made in three-quarter size (inside measure, 42x72 inches), and single size (inside measure, 38x72 inches). Shipping weight (full size), 170 pounds.

No. 1R1761 Price, with wood back .... $ 9.75
No. 1R1762 Price, with mirror back 10.95

Our $10.25 Folding Bed.

Oak front, built up oak panels, finished in golden oak. Woven wire mattress with two-row spiral springs support. Size, closed, 54 inches high, 55 inches wide, 20 inches deep. Size, open, outside, 55x75 in.; inside, 48x72 in. Mattress to fit should be 3 feet 10 inches by 6 feet with a 2½-inch box, and to be flexible enough, should be made of moss, hair or cotton. Also made in three-quarter size (inside measure, 42x72 inches), and single size (inside measure, 38x72 inches). Shipping weight (full size), 193 pounds.

No. 1R1766 Price, plain back $10.25
No. 1R1767 Price, with mirror back 11.95

We Challenge Competition on This Bed at $12.45.

No. 1R1768 Oak, golden finish. Built up veneered oak panels, carved. Woven wire mattress with three-row spiral springs support. Size, closed, 58 inches high, 55 inches wide, 20 inches deep. Size, open, outside, 55x75 inches; inside, 48x72 inches. Mattress to fit should be 3 feet 10 inches by 6 feet, with a 2½-inch box, and to be flexible enough, should be made of moss, cotton or hair. Also made in three-quarter size (inside measure, 42x72 inches), and single size (inside measure, 38 x72 inches). Shipping weight (full size), 200 pounds.

Price, each $12.45

$14.95 Buys This Solid Oak Richly Carved Folding Bed.

No. 1R1769 Oak, golden finish. Built up veneered oak panels. Woven wire mattress, with three-row spiral springs support. Size, closed, 58 inches high, 55 inches wide, 20 inches deep. Size, open, outside, 55x75 inches; inside, 48x72 inches. Mattress to fit should be 3 feet 10 inches by 6 feet, with a 2½-inch box, and to be flexible enough, should be made of moss, cotton or hair. Also made in three-quarter size (inside measure, 42x72 inches), and single size (inside measure, 38x72 inches). Shipping weight (full size), 206 pounds.

Price, each $14.95

$19.45. Ornamental as Well as Useful.

No. 1R1772 Golden oak, gloss finish, richly carved. Has 18x40-inch German bevel plate mirror. Self adjusting and locking metal swing legs. Fitted with fine woven wire spring. Will not tip the back. Size, closed, 78 inches high, 57 inches wide, 24 inches deep. Size, open, outside, 57x80 inches; inside, 50x74 inches. Mattress to fit should be 4x6 feet, with a 3-inch box. Shipping weight, 279 pounds.

Price $19.45

No. 1R1773 Same bed as No. 1R1772, but with handsome carved decorated panel instead of mirror.

Our special price $17.95

Our $1.45 Washstand.

No. 1R1900 This Washstand, as illustrated herewith, is made from thoroughly seasoned elm and ashwood mixed, highly finished in antique; has one drawer and lower shelf. Top, 16x23 inches. Weight, 35 pounds.

Price, each .. $1.45

Our $3.30 Commode.

No. 1R1908 This Commode is made of thoroughly seasoned hardwood, finished antique. It has one drawer and cabinet. Size of top, 17x30 inches. Drawer is fitted with fancy metal pulls. Weight, 50 pounds.

Price, each $3.30

No. 1R1909 Same Commode as No. 1R1908, except it is made of oak.

Our special price $3.50

White Enamel Commode for $4.35.

No. 1R1910 This is a beautiful hardwood white enamel Commode, considered very stylish and especially well adapted for use with iron beds. Has a beautifully shaped double top, 33 inches long, with serpentine swell double top drawer. The commode is fitted with best quality brass trimmings and casters. Shipping weight, about 65 pounds. Our price $4.35

No. 1R1911 Same Commode as No. 1R1910 finished golden oak $3.95

No. 1R1912 Same Commode as No. 1R1910, in mahogany finish $3.90

Elegant Toilet Washstand for $5.45.

No. 1R1914 This Toilet Washstand is especially adapted for small bedrooms and hotels. Made of best selected and well seasoned rock elm; finished antique oak and furnished with large, roomy drawer and large compartment below the drawer. **The mirror is** excellent German plate glass **and is 12x20 inches in size.** **Shipping weight, 70 pounds.**

Price $5.45

$7.95 Toilet Washstand.

No. 1R1916 This Toilet Washstand is likewise adapted for small bedrooms and hotels. Made of best selected and well seasoned rock elm; finished in golden oak and furnished with one large, roomy drawer and large compartment below the drawer. Swell front. The mirror is excellent French bevel plate glass and is 14x24 inches in size; size of top, 18x36 inches. Shipping weight, 70 pounds.

Price, each $7.95

A Solid Oak Chiffonier for $3.75.

No. 1R1920 This is the best cheap chiffonier on the market. Made of solid oak, and nicely finished. Has five large drawers, all fitted with locks and keys. Width, 30 inches; depth, 17 inches. We guarantee all drawers to work smoothly. Good value and sure to please you. Can be returned at our expense if not as represented. Weight, 100 pounds.

Price, only $3.75

Our $4.95 Chiffonier.

No. 1R1922 A Neat Chiffonier of solid golden oak, highly polished; has five drawers and cupboard or hat box; has 17x30-inch serpentine shaped top; is very neatly trimmed, and a very sensible and useful piece of furniture. Weight, 100 pounds. Price, each.$4.95

Our $6.45 Chiffonier.

No. 1R1924 This is another new design which we are selling at a very low price. Made of **solid oak,** carved and nicely finished; top 17x30 inches. Has a good 11x17-inch mirror. The drawers are all very large and roomy, and are fitted with locks and keys. All chiffoniers are fitted with casters and all the cabinet work is extra good. Weight, 125 pounds.

Price, only..........$6.45

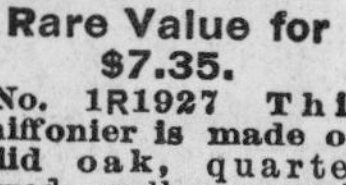

Rare Value for $7.35.

No. 1R1927 This Chiffonier is made of solid oak, quarter sawed, well seasoned; wood selected from the very best of lumber and the finish is the best gloss golden oak. Size is 4 feet 10 inches high, and 19x31-inch top, double deck. This chiffonier has three large and two small drawers, with a cabinet. The trimmings or drawer pulls are of the best solid brass castings; each drawer is fitted with a lock and key. Shipping weight, 100 pounds.

Price, in oak.....$7.35

Our $7.85 Chiffonier.

No. 1R1929 A Chiffonier that is useful and ornamental; has five large drawers for storage; is made of selected golden oak, well constructed and finished; has 11x17-inch bevel French mirror and serpentine shaped top, 17x30 inches, and neat, pretty trimmings. **This is one of the best values in chiffoniers which we offer this season.** Shipping weight, about 125 pounds.

Price, each...........$7.85

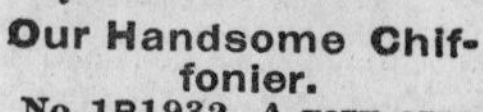

Our Handsome Chiffonier.

No. 1R1932 A very ornamental and useful pattern; made of selected antique oak; has three large and two small drawers and one hat box; has a shaped bevel French mirror, 11x17 inches; has a shaped top, 17x32 inches, and is well trimmed and finished. Shipping weight, about 125 pounds.

Price, each $8.15

Our $8.95 Bargain.

No. 1R1935 A very ornamental and useful pattern; made of selected golden oak; has three large and two small drawers and one hat box; drawers and hat box full swell; has a shaped top, 22x36 inches, and is well trimmed and finished. Shipping weight, about 135 pounds.

Price, each.......$8.95

No. 1R1936 Chiffonier is made of solid oak, partly quarter sawed and thoroughly seasoned. Size, 5 feet 10 inches high; top, 19x31 inches. Has French pattern bevel plate mirror, 12x20 inches; is finished in a fine antique oak polish. The top drawer is swell front; it also has a very neat and useful cabinet; every drawer has a lock and key. The trimmings or drawer pulls are of solid brass. Shipping weight, 100 pounds.

Price, in oak.....$10.85

A Very Handsome Chiffonier, to go with brass or iron beds. All hand polished and neatly carved. Has shaped serpentine front, cast brass handles, French legs and large 20x20 French bevel mirror. Shaped double top, 20x34 inches. Weight, 140 pounds. Shipped from our factory near Grand Rapids, Mich. Customer pays the freight from factory.

No. 1R1951 Price, genuine mahogany..........$13.50

No. 1R1952 Price, golden oak......................$13.50

Our $8.75 and $10.95 Dressing Tables.

Shipped from the Factory, near Grand Rapids, Mich. Customer pays freight from factory.

No. 1R2050 A very dainty and ornamental piece for the bedroom. Made to go with golden oak, bird's-eye maple and solid mahogany suites and iron beds; cabinet work, finish and stock are of the very highest grade. **This pretty little dressing table is made of quartered golden oak.** All handsomely polished and hand carved. Has a large 16x20-inch French bevel mirror, and a drawer swell shape with cast brass handles.

Weight, 60 lbs. Price, any wood. $8.75

$8.75

$10.95

No. 1R2052 Dressing Table, all beautifully hand polished. Has shaped swell front and dainty French legs, two drawers with cast brass handle, a large 16x20-inch pattern French bevel mirror. Size of top, 18x32 inches. Weight, 60 pounds.

Price, in solid mahogany, golden oak or bird's-eye maple, each..........$10.95

We list below a few special single dressers, but call attention to the fact that we can furnish any dresser shown in our large and handsome line of bedroom suites at remarkably low prices. No handsomer designs or better values ever shown by anyone at double our prices.

Dressers can be shipped at first class freight rate, which adds but little to the cost and still makes the price much lower than the same quality of dresser can be purchased for of your local dealer.

No. 1R2141 This is a beautiful hardwood dresser, finished golden oak, considered very stylish and adapted for use with iron beds. Size of top is 38 inches, and has a mirror 18x20 inches. Has two upper drawers and two roomy lower drawers trimmed with nice brass handles. Shipping weight, about 120 pounds.

Price.............$6.80

No. 1R2143 Same as above, made of solid oak, with 20x24 bevel plate mirror. Price..........$7.95

$7.95 for This $12.00 Dresser.

No. 1R2145 This Dresser is made of thoroughly seasoned elm in antique oak finish. Is fitted with a shaped French bevel plate mirror, 20x24 inches; has serpentine shaped dresser top. Size, 21x38 inches. Drawers are fitted with locks and keys, fancy pulls and casters, and is a very neat and pretty article. Shipping weight, about 120 pounds.

Price, in oak finish, $7.95

Beautiful White Enameled Dresser for $9.95.

No. 1R2150 This is a beautiful hardwood White Enameled Dresser, considered very stylish and adapted for use with iron beds. Has handsomely shaped double top, 21x42 inches, and has a bevel mirror 20x24 inches. Has two upper full swell drawers and two roomy lower drawers trimmed with nice brass handles. Shipped from factory in Central Michigan. Customer pays freight from factory. Shipping weight, about 150 pounds.

Price..........$9.95

No. 1R2151 Same Dresser as No. 1R2150, but golden oak finish. Our special price, $9.35

No. 1R2152 Same Dresser as No. 1R2150, but mahogany finish. Our special price $9.30

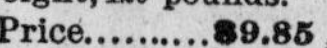

Our $9.85 Dresser.

No. 1R2158 Very Neat and Attractive Dresser; one of the best designs, shaped top, 21x44 inches; is fitted with a **heavy German bevel plate mirror, 24x30 inches,** and is very neatly carved; has two upper drawers on dresser; drawer pulls and other **trimmings are of very best brass castings,** and each drawer has lock and key. Casters come with this dresser. Weight, 120 pounds.

Price..........$9.85

No Better Value Offered, $11.95.

No. 1R2164 This Beautiful Dresser is made of solid selected golden oak, and is one of the most attractive odd dressers we are showing among our new patterns. It is highly polished, beautifully carved and ornamented; it is fitted with a 24x30-inch unique shaped French bevel plate mirror, has serpentine shaped top, 44 inches, and has full swell front upper drawers; comes complete with handsome trimmings and best casters. Weight, 120 pounds. Price..........$11.95

IRON BEDS.

REDUCED PRICES IN EVERYTHING IN IRON AND BRASS BEDS FOR THIS SEASON.

IN IRON AND BRASS BEDS we are recognized headquarters for we are offering for this season prices lower than ever before, lower prices than are made by the largest wholesale dealers in this line.

NEW STYLES FOR THIS SEASON. We call your attention to our line of iron and brass trimmed and brass beds as new styles for this season, the very latest designs, most of them specially designed for our trade. The most showy, strongest and altogether the best line of iron, brass trimmed and brass beds on the market and at prices much lower than are offered by any other house.

WE ESPECIALLY RECOMMEND OUR IRON BEDS. Select an iron bed, springs and mattress, and dresser and commode, and you have a thoroughly up to date sanitary three-piece bedroom suite. You have the same suite that nine-tenths of the city buyers are now selecting when furnishing the bedrooms of their houses, and you have the opportunity through our special price offers of buying the goods at a much lower price than the same goods can possibly be bought for elsewhere.

IRON BEDS are especially recommended for their cleanliness. They will not rust. Physicians recommend them above any other bed. No other bed should be used in the sick room. They are used altogether in hospitals and leading sanitariums. They are always bright, always clean, always airy. They are not destructible. They will never wear out.

ABOUT THE QUALITY. We guarantee for our iron beds a better finish, a better enamel and more strength than in any other line of iron beds made. Our beds enameled in white carry the finest quality of enamel baked in four coats. Highly polished and finished. They are extra well braced throughout and every bed is put out under our binding guarantee.

Our $2.45 Iron Bed.

No. 1R2406 At $2.45, reduced from last year's price, we offer this our lowest priced Iron Bed, as the quality of beds that sell everywhere at double the price. This reduced price is made possible by reason of our controlling the output of the factory. This special $2.45 bed is straight foot, pillars are ⅝-inch, top and bottom rods ⅝-inch, other rods ⅜-inch; gilt chills. Height of bed, 51½ inches; height of foot, 45 inches. Comes in four widths, 3 feet, 3 feet 6 inches, 4 feet, and 4 feet 6 inches. **In ordering be sure and state the width wanted.** Comes complete with casters. Guaranteed the greatest value ever shown. Weight, packed for shipment, 50 pounds. Our special price........................**$2.45**

A Substantial Iron Bed for $2.85.

No. 1R2410 This Iron Bed has strong iron 1$\frac{1}{16}$-inch posts, while the cross rod and fillings are made of ⅜-inch and $\frac{5}{16}$-inch material. The posts are surmounted by very fancy brass vases. We furnish this bed, with ball bearing casters, either 3 feet, 3 feet 6 inches, 4 feet, or 4 feet 6 inches wide. This bed, being finished in white enamel, presents a very elegant appearance and is very substantial in every respect. Height of head, 48 inches; height of foot, 42 inches. Weight, packed for shipment, about 55 pounds.
Our special price **$2.85**

A $6.00 Iron Bed for $3.40.

No. 1R2411 This Iron Bed which we are offering at **$3.40** is fully $1.50 less than a bed of this quality is sold for by any other house. **It is finished in baked white enamel,** has 1⅛-inch posts and ⅜-inch fillers; it has brass cast vases and mounts, and is made in the following sizes: 3 feet 6 inches, 4 feet, 4 feet 6 inches. Height of head, 54 inches; height of foot, 44 inches. Weight, 66 pounds.
Our special price..................................**$3.40**

REFER TO PAGES 7 TO 10 FOR FREIGHT RATES.

Our $3.95 Value.

No. 1R2412 This is an impressive looking bed, standing 58 inches high; is made of selected materials, and finished in the best white baked enamel. Posts, 1$\frac{1}{16}$-inch; fillers, $\frac{5}{16}$-inch and ⅜-inch. Has brass caps and vases, and full foot end. The construction and details are so perfect as to render it **practically indestructible.** This bed is made 4 feet 6 inches in width. **We are selling it at an astonishingly low price.** Weight, about 75 pounds. Price, each..**$3.95**

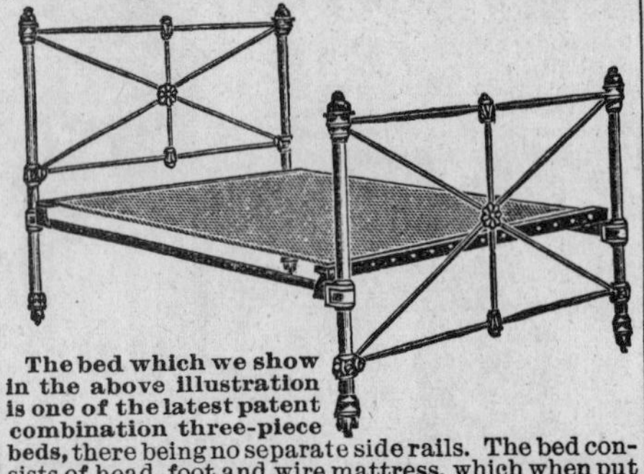

The bed which we show in the above illustration is one of the latest patent combination three-piece beds, there being no separate side rails. The bed consists of head, foot and wire mattress, which when put together, are exactly the same as regulation iron beds, but can be furnished at much less money than the iron bed with separate wire mattress, on account of the saving of the side rails. **The beds are baked white enamel, made very strong, and are as durable as any other iron bed made.** The posts are made of 1$\frac{1}{16}$-inch iron and are mounted with brass caps. The filling rods are ⅜ and $\frac{5}{16}$-inch, and are designed with a view of adding to the strength of the bed. Shipping weight, about 100 pounds.

No. 1R2414 3 feet 6 inches. Price..........**$4.15**
No. 1R2415 4 feet 6 inches. Price..........**4.25**

No. 1R2416 This Attractive Iron Bed, of exceptionally neat design, is finished in baked white enamel, which is guaranteed to stand. It has 1$\frac{1}{16}$-inch posts and ⅜-inch fillers; has cast brass knobs and vases, and full foot end. Height of head, 63 inches; height of foot, 51 inches. Made in the following widths: 3 feet 6 inches, and 4 feet 6 inches. Weight, 76 pounds. Price, each.......... **$4.25**

No. 1R2418 This is one of our newest designs, unusually neat and handsome. The head is 55 inches high, has 1$\frac{1}{16}$-inch posts with ⅜ and $\frac{5}{16}$-inch fillings and ⅝-inch top pillar. The bed is finished in baked white enamel, ornamented with brass rosettes and brass tips at end of scrolls. Made in full size, 4 feet 6 inches, only. Shipping weight, 80 pounds.
Our special price..**$4.45**

No 1R2424 The pillars are of iron and 1$\frac{1}{16}$ inches in diameter. The filling is $\frac{5}{16}$ and ⅜ inch in diameter. **The rods are surmounted by fancy brass vases,** adding elegance to an already handsome bed. The height of the head is 60 inches. **We furnish this bed in two sizes, 3 feet 6 inches, or 4 feet 6 inches wide,** as may be desired. In all cases the bed is 6 feet long. It is finished with the **best white enamel,** in several coats. Shipping weight, 84 pounds. Each..**$4.50**

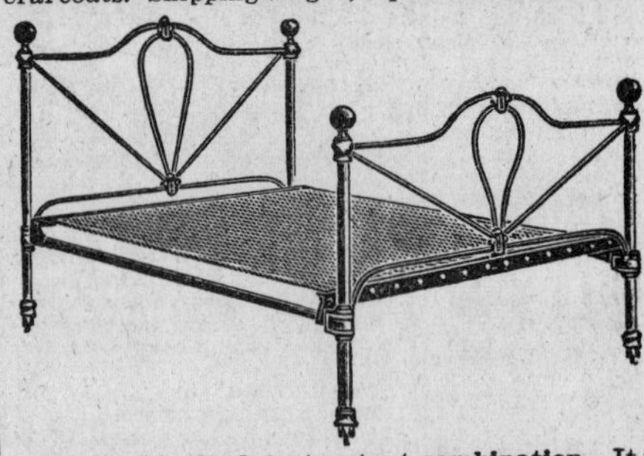

This Bed is the latest patent combination. It is composed of three parts only, the head, the foot and wire mattress, and has no side rails. The saving of the side rails makes the price of the bed much lower than one of the same grade with separate mattress, and furthermore makes it possible to pack and ship the bed at less expense. **This is as strong and durable as any iron bed made.** The posts are 1$\frac{1}{16}$-inch iron mounted with ¼-inch brass vases. The filling rods are ⅜ and $\frac{5}{16}$-inch. This is one of the greatest bargains in iron beds which we list. Shipping weight, 100 pounds.

No. 1R2426 Price, 3-foot 6-inch bed........ **$4.60**
No. 1R2427 Price, 4-foot 6-inch bed........ **4.70**

Our $4.75 Brass Trimmed Iron Bed.

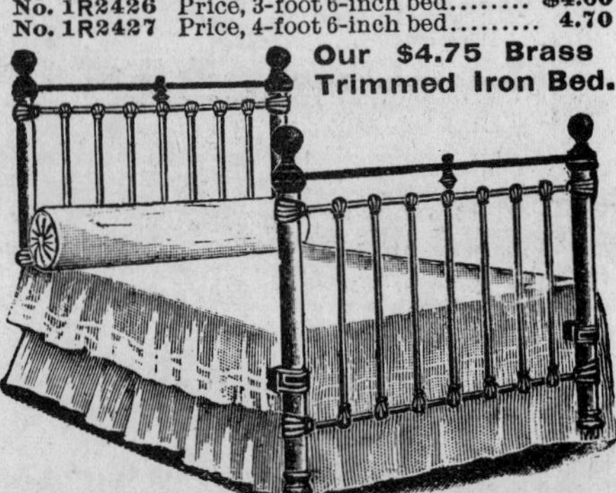

No. 1R2428 One of our most popular patterns. Made of the best malleable iron. Baked white enamel finish and superior construction; 1$\frac{1}{16}$-inch pillars, and has ½-inch **brass top rail on both head and foot.** Height of head, 58 inches; height of foot, 42 inches. Has brass spindles and top mounts, and four rich cast brass vases. This is a design of which purchasers never tire and **gives universal satisfaction.** Is made in the following sizes: 3 feet, 3 feet 6 inches, 4 feet, 4 feet 6 inches. Shipping weight, 90 pounds. Sold at the very low price of.......**$4.75**

Only $4.95.

No. 1R2430 This Iron Bed is constructed differently than the average iron bed, as it has the curved top rail instead of posts and vases, making it specially strong; as shown in the illustration, it is of handsome design and is sure to please. The head is 65 inches high; the posts are 1 1/16 inches with 5/8-inch top bent pillar. 5/8 and 5/16-inch filling. Baked white enamel finish, decorated with brass rosettes and tips. Made in full size only, 4 feet 6 inches. Shipping weight, about 90 pounds.
Our special price..$4.95

No. 1R2434 This is an impressive looking bed, standing 57 inches at the head and 45 inches at the foot, is made of malleable iron, and finished in the best baked white enamel. Posts, 1 1/16-inch; fillers, 5/16-inch and 5/8-inch. Has brass caps, vases, and rosettes and full extension foot end. The construction and details are so perfect as to render it practically indestructible. This bed weighs about 85 pounds and is made in the following widths: 3 feet 6 inches, and 4 feet 6 inches. We are selling it at an astonishingly low price. Price, each..........$5.10

Our Combination Three-Piece Bed.

This bed is one of the latest patent combination beds, comprised of head, foot and wire springs only without separate side rails. This bed is so constructed that the wire spring forms the side rails and on account of this the price will be found much lower than our regular iron bed of same grade with wire spring. This bed is exceptionally strong, having 1 1/8-inch posts and surmounted by handsome brass vases, and has brass top rails. We furnish it only in baked white enamel finish. Compare this bed with beds sold by other dealers, and you will readily recognize the saving you will make by ordering from us. Shipping weight, about 165 pounds.
No. 1R2436 Price, 3-foot 6-inch bed........ $5.30
No. 1R2437 Price, 4-foot 6-inch bed......... 5.45

Our $5.90 Bed.

No. 1R2444 This Bed is made of the best selected iron, is 72 inches high, all rods, cross pieces, pillars, etc., being of the very best material. The pillars are 1 1/16 inches in diameter, the spindles, cross rods, ornamental iron work being 5/16 inch in diameter. The pillars are surmounted by handsome brass knobs and has brass tips and rosettes.

The design is new and ornamental, while the extended foot rail adds to its already handsome appearance. We furnish this bed 4 feet 6 inches wide by 6 feet long and finished in handsome white enamel of the very best quality. Weight, packed for shipment, 110 pounds. Our special price............$5.90

No. 1R2452 Customers contemplating the purchase of an iron bed will find this pattern unusually attractive, being very graceful in its lines. It is made of malleable iron, handsomely finished in white enamel and perfectly constructed. Has 1/4-inch pillars, 5/8-inch and 5/16-inch filling and brass vases and caps. Height of head, 56 inches; height of foot, 45 inches. Made in the following width: 4 feet 6 inches. Weight, about 91 pounds.
Price, each..$6.75

Our $7.75 Massive, Heavy Bed.

No. 1R2454 A handsome, massive, heavy bed, fit to adorn any perfectly furnished sleeping room, the pattern being beautiful and up to date, unusually well made and finished. Has continuous 1 1/16-inch pillars, heavy fillings, 7/16-inch top rails. Made in 4 feet 6 inches only. Height of head, 63 inches, and of foot, 46 1/2 inches. Weight, 128 pounds.
Price, each..$7.75

No. 1R2458 A universally attractive design. This bed is 59 inches high and 4 feet 6 inches wide; has 1 1/4-inch posts surmounted with 1 1/2-inch vases. The fillings are 5/8 x 5/16 inch with full 5/8-inch brass top rails and full brass top mounts. The bed contains ten brass rosettes and all the scrolls are tipped with brass caps. The bed also has best quality ball bearing lignum casters. Shipping weight, 125 pounds.
Our special price...............................$7.95

No. 1R2462 This is another novelty in a high grade, up to date heavy iron bed. Made of selected material, trimmed and ornamented with heavy white enameled chills on head and foot. This is the richest and neatest design ever produced for the money in a heavy bed. Size of posts, 1 1/4 inches; fillings, 1/2 and 5/8 inch; height at head, 73 inches. We also furnish this bed in black, maroon, blue or pink, if desired, and regularly furnished in the white enamel. The bed is handsome enough for any home, and we recommend it as highly as any bed made. Complete with full set of ball bearing casters. Size, 4 1/2x6 1/2 feet. Weight, 150 pounds.
Price..$8.25

Our $8.95 Leader.

No. 1R2466 This Bed is 65 inches high and 4 feet 6 inches wide. The posts are made of 1 1/16-inch iron and the fillings 1/2 and 5/8-inch. The four brass scrolls and ten brass rosettes add greatly to the appearance of the bed and make it very attractive. The iron scrolls are all brass tipped. The bed is finished in baked white enamel. The bed is provided with best quality ball bearing lignum casters. Shipping weight, 125 pounds.
Our special price.......................................$8.95

$9.85 Buys This Massive Bed.

No. 1R2470 This Massive Iron Bed is without doubt one of the handsomest shown in our catalogue. In point of quality it is equal to beds offered by other dealers at from $12.00 to $16.00. It is 68 inches high, has 1 1/16-inch posts, 1 1/16-inch top rail and 5/8-inch filling. The chills are exceptionally massive, of pretty design and are all decorated with gold, giving the bed an elegant, at the same time a modest appearance. We furnish it in full size only, 4 feet 6 inches wide, but in any color desired; white, pink, blue, maroon, black or dark green. Every bed is fitted with a set of best quality lignum ball bearing casters. Shipping weight, 175 pounds.
Our special price, any color.......................$9.85
Be sure to state color desired.

Our Finest Iron Bed for $10.45.

No. 1R2474 This Bed is the best and highest priced iron bed we list, and is exactly the same grade as other dealers sell at $15.00 to $20.00. It is 65 inches high, has heavy 1 1/16-inch pillars with 1 1/4-inch fancy shaped top pillar and 5/8 and 5/8-inch filling. The chills are of unusually handsome design, and are all decorated with gold, which in contrast with the beautiful enamel finish put on the bed, makes it as attractive as any iron bed ever made. We can furnish the bed in any color of enamel desired: White, black, pink, blue, maroon or olive. Full size only, 4 feet 6 inches, fitted with set of best quality lignum ball bearing casters. Shipping weight, 165 pounds.
Our special price, any color.......................$10.45
Be sure to state color desired.

IRON BEDS ARE TAKEN BY nearly all railroad companies at second class rate, which usually averages from 40 to 50 cents per hundred pounds for 500 miles. **By referring to pages 7 to 10 you can get the second class freight rates per 100 pounds to your nearest town.** It will be almost exactly the same as to your town, and you can figure just what the freight will be on any iron bed to your place. It will be next to nothing compared to what you will save in price.

STEEL MANTLE FOLDING BED.

This illustration shows bed open.

This illustration shows bed when closed.

We show above our all metal folding bed which is made with a fine woven wire fabric supported with fifteen of the best tempered coil springs, making it impossible for the fabric to sag. It has a brass curtain rod with brass rings ready to attach the curtains so that lower portion may be covered in the day time. The top of the bed is stationary and so arranged that when bed is opened it forms head piece. The foot piece folds under the top of the bed and in that position holds the mattress in place when bed is closed. There are no weights of any kind used in the bed so it is impossible for it to close up when sleeping in same, at the same time it is so made that a child can operate it. Height, when closed, 50 inches; depth, 24 inches; length, open, 6 feet, 2 inches. Finished in bronze colors. Shipping weight, 125 pounds.

No. 1R2477 Our special price, 3-foot bed........ $6.45
No. 1R2478 Our special price, 3-foot, 6-inch bed........ 6.75
No. 1R2479 Our special price, 4-foot bed........ 7.45

Neat and Attractive Brass Bed.

$14.90

No. 1R2482 **Bow Foot, Full Brass Bedstead,** of neat and attractive design, made of the finest brass tubing, lacquered and polished. **We can guarantee the finish with proper care to last indefinitely.** Has 1-inch pillars, 2-inch vases; top and bottom rails, ⅝-inch; height of bed at head 61 inches, at foot 40 inches. **The bed is low in price, but for quality absolutely beyond criticism.** Made in the following widths: 3 feet, 3 feet 6 inches, 4 feet and 4 feet 6 inches. Weight, full size, crated, 175 pounds.
Our special price, each........ $14.90

A Superb Brass Bed for

$19.95

No. 1R2486 **A Superb Brass Bed,** made of the finest materials and guaranteed to wear and hold its finish for a lifetime. The pillars are 1-inch, vases 2-inch, top and bottom rails, ⅝-inch; head is 56 inches high and the footboard, which is swell, is 40 inches high. An unusually fine bed for little money. Furnished 3 feet, 3 feet 6 inches, 4 feet and 4 feet 6 inches width. Weight, full size, packed, 190 pounds. Price, each........ $19.95

Our $1.35 Cot.

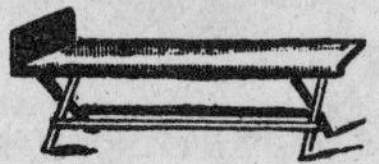

No. 1R2662 **This Cot is made of the very best quality of canvas.** The frame is of seasoned hard maple, and **is very strong and substantially built.** 29 inches wide. Shipping weight, about 35 pounds. Price.. $1.35

Universal Woven Wire Cot for $1.39.

This Cot has a seasoned hard maple frame, well braced with a fine fabric of woven wire.
No. 1R2667 Size, 2 feet 6 inches wide by 6 feet 2 inches long. Each..... $1.39
No. 1R2668 Size, 3 feet wide by 6 feet 2 inches long. Shipping weight, about 35 pounds. Price, each.. $1.50

Our $2.15 Woven Wire Folding Bed.

This Cot is very strong. The frame is made from the best seasoned hard maple, springs of the **best quality woven wire.**
No. 1R2670 Size, 2 feet 6 inches wide by 6 feet long. Price, each....... $2.15
No. 1R2671 Size, 3 feet wide by 6 feet long. Weight, about 35 pounds. Price........ $2.35

Folding Steel Cot, for $3.45.

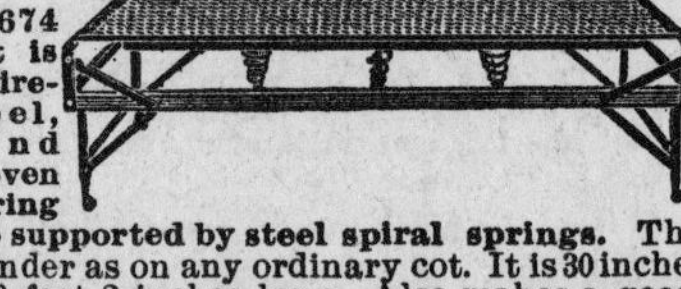

No. 1R2674 **This Cot is made entirely of steel, braced, and has a woven wire spring edged top supported by steel spiral springs.** The legs fold under as on any ordinary cot. It is 30 inches wide and 6 feet 2 inches long. Also makes a good, soft, comfortable couch with a pillow and an oriental covering thrown over it. **One of the best values in our stock,** and anyone desiring a good, solid, well made article at a very low price, will not be disappointed in this. Shipping weight, about 75 pounds.
Price, without drapery........ $3.45

No. 1R2676 **A Good, Strong Cradle, made of hardwood, antique finish;** a full slatted bottom; strong, substantial and sensible; made for service. We have made an exceptionally low price. Size, 24x44 inches. Weight, 30 pounds. Price... $1.40

Our $1.50 Hardwood Cradle.

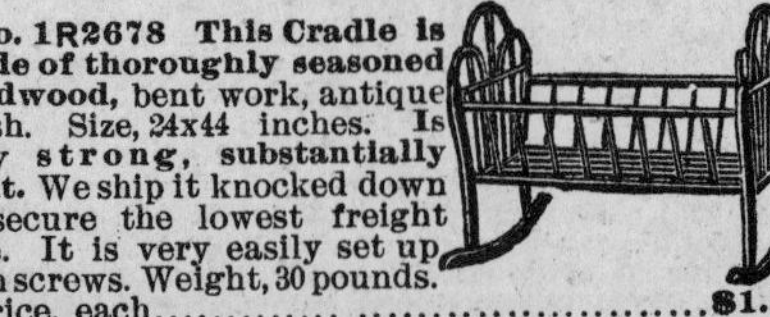

No. 1R2678 **This Cradle is made of thoroughly seasoned hardwood, bent work,** antique finish. Size, 24x44 inches. **Is very strong, substantially built.** We ship it knocked down to secure the lowest freight rate. It is very easily set up with screws. Weight, 30 pounds.
Price, each........ $1.50

IRON BEDS are taken by nearly all railroad companies at second class rate, which usually averages from 40 to 50 cents per 100 pounds for 500 miles. By referring to pages 7 to 10 you can get the second class freight rate per 100 pounds to your nearest town. It will be almost exactly the same as to your town, and you can figure just what the freight will be on any iron bed to your place.

IT WILL BE NEXT TO NOTHING COMPARED TO WHAT YOU WILL SAVE IN PRICE.

Our Special $1.60 Cradle.

No. 1R2680 **This is a very handsome, substantial cradle, furnished complete with woven wire mattress.** The frame is made of thoroughly seasoned hardwood, finished in antique or imitation mahogany, as desired. It is well constructed and fully guaranteed. Comes in size 24x44 inches. Shipping weight, about 30 pounds.
Our price, each........ $1.60

Our $2.00 Swing Cradle,

No. 1R2692 **This Cradle,** as illustrated above, is made **of thoroughly seasoned hardwood, bent frame.** Finished antique. Size, 24x44 inches. Shipped knocked down. Weight, 30 pounds.
Price, each........ $2.00

Our $2.70 Patent Swing Cradle.

No. 1R2694 **This is the latest Patent Swing Cradle.** It is made of solid maple, finished antique. Comes complete with woven wire mattress. **Rocks perfectly level and is mounted on casters.** We ship this cradle knocked down so as to take the lowest freight rate and you will find the freight will amount to next to nothing as compared with what you will save in price. Weight, 35 pounds.
Price, each........ $2.70
No. 1R2695 **Same Cradle** as No. 1R2694, only **made of solid oak.** Our special price........ $2.95

Our $1.55 Child's Folding Crib.

With woven wire mattress. Size, 30x54 inches. Finished in maple, natural, or mahogany, as desired. Has the new adjustable brace, and **is one of the strongest and most durable child's beds made.** Weight, about 25 pounds.
No. 1R2696 Price........ $1.55
No. 1R2697 **The same Crib;** size, 36x60 inches. Our price........ $1.90

Child's $2.15 Folding Top Crib.

This Crib is fitted with our new adjustable brace, which gives it a rigid leg when raised, and being mounted on casters can be readily moved about without falling down. **It is a very simple arrangement,** there being no hook or spring catches to unfasten. It folds upon the inside of the crib, so that it may be rolled under an ordinary bedstead without removing the bedding from the crib. Very substantially made. Where an extra high side is wanted, this makes the **neatest, best, and most practical side on the market.** Finished in natural maple or imitation mahogany, as desired. Shipping weight, about 30 pounds.
No. 1R2698 Size, 30x54 inches, with folding top. Price........ $2.15
No. 1R2699 Size, 30x60 inches, with folding top. Price........ $2.40

CHILDREN'S FOLDING BEDS, ETC.

A Good, Well Made Child's Iron Bed, neat and attractive in appearance, comes furnished with a first class woven wire spring. Bed posts are ⅜-inch in diameter, has pretty knobs and the iron scroll work adds to its fine appearance; has deep sides, is made of the best materials, is 2 feet 6 inches wide and 4 feet 6 inches long. Can also be furnished 3 feet wide and 5 feet long. Shipping weight, 80 pounds.
No. 1R2700 Price, for 4-foot 6-inch bed.... $5.35
No. 1R2701 Price, for 5-foot bed........ 5.60

Extra Well Made Child's Folding Bed, $4.50.

This Beautiful Folding Bed is made 30x60 inches in size, is furnished with a fine woven wire mattress. Is made to fold up with all the bedding left in bed. **Finished in natural maple or imitation mahogany.** Weight, about 75 pounds.
No. 1R2706 Price, each, size 30x60........ $4.50
No. 1R2707 Same as above, size 40x60 inches 5.40

$6.75 for this $10.00 Child's Folding Bed.

This Folding Bed is fitted **with a fine woven wire mattress and folds up with all bedding left in bed.** Finished in antique or imitation mahogany, **as desired.** Weight, about 85 pounds.
No. 1R2709 Price, 30x60-inch bed........ $6.75
No. 1R2710 Price, 40x60 inch bed........ $7.30

SPRINGS, MATTRESSES, PILLOWS, FEATHERS, ETC.

We render every assistance towards comfort by quoting the best goods made at the lowest possible prices. Any old standbys which have been found most satisfactory in every respect we continue to catalogue. **New devices in the way of mattresses, springs,** etc., which are worth considering, are quoted below.

In ordering wire mattresses or hair mattresses, in fact any kind of a mattress, be sure to state the size of bed for which the mattress is intended.

SPRINGS FOR IRON OR WOODEN BEDS.

We will make our springs any size desired, or to fit any size of bed. Be sure to give size of slat when ordering, also state if springs are for an iron or wood bed, as the springs for iron beds are made with extended sides. Give sizes plainly. If you want 4 feet wide by 6 feet long, give it thus: 4-0x6-0, and never 4x6. Our woven wire mattresses measure 1 inch less in width and 1½ inch less in length than marked.

Our Patent Bed Slat for Iron or Brass Beds.

No. 1R2700 We call your attention to our Patent Bed Slat. **This slat** is adjustable and used to support steel **spiral** springs on iron or brass bedsteads. They are very strong and durable and can be adjusted to any size bed. Shipping weight, 35 pounds.

Price, per set, which includes four slats...... **$1.45**

Slats are not required for woven wire springs that are framed, as they come with extended sides.

Our Special $1.10 Woven Wire Springs.

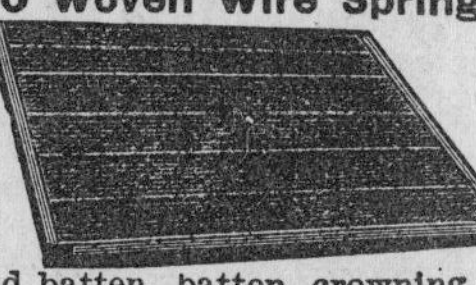

No. 1R2755 This Woven Wire Spring is the regular standard spring. Frame made of thoroughly seasoned hard maple, thick batten, perfectly tight joints between end rail and batten, batten crowning as shown, giving great strength. No putty used. **It is a good clean spring, and is the best low priced bed made.** All our woven wire springs have patent end fastenings for the fabric, making it impossible for any of the wires to become loosened by any strain that will ever be put upon them. Shipping weight, 35 pounds. Price, each.......... **$1.10**

$1.59 Buys a $2.25 Woven Wire Spring.

No. 1R2759 This Woven Wire Spring, illustrated above, is made of the very best material throughout. Has a double end bar so that the fabric can be stretched to any desired tension, which is the only positive and practical extension made. Made with this double end bar and with a high grade wire, this spring will last a lifetime. Aside from the double end bar, it is constructed the same as our spring No. 1R2755. Shipping weight, 40 pounds.

Our special price........................... **$1.59**

$1.80 Buys a $3.50 Woven Wire Spring.

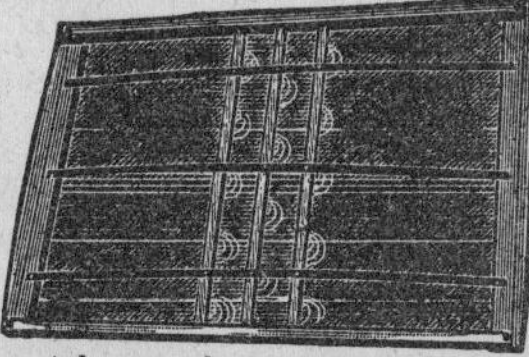

No. 1R2768 This Spring is made with the support of three rows of steel spring slats, the slats supported by three substantial iron straps running from head to foot of spring. Slats are free at end and support is very rigid and substantial. We do not know what we can say that will express the general excellence of this spring better than the picture itself. One can readily see that **the principle of construction is perfect for comfort.** The material used in the woven wire fabric and frame is the best. Shipping weight, 40 pounds.

Our special price........................... **$1.80**

Our $3.15 Woven Wire Spring.

No. 1R2786 This Special Woven Wire Spring is supported by spiral springs having the following valuable features: In place of the ordinary cross slats it has a band iron support, each two pieces being yoked together, as shown in illustration, **this construction preventing any lateral motion.** Each pair of supports is connected with the pair at the opposite end of the spring by a screw thread swivel joint. The springs are fastened directly to the band iron supports at the bottom, and the fabric at top cannot by any possibility get out of place unless intentionally removed. There are no hooks, links, connections or any other small material to break or get loose and rattle. By the use of this construction **a much deeper spring can be used** than in any ordinarily supported spring, hence **a very much greater degree of elasticity** is imparted to the supporting surface. The tightening swivels are turned with perfect ease, no wrench or tools of any kind being required. To change the tension no removal of any portion of the bedding is necessary, the swivels being underneath and easily accessible from either side. The picture shows the bottom of the spring to exhibit its construction. Shipping weight, 45 pounds.

Our special price.......................... **$3.15**

No. 1R2805 Iron Frame Spring. This spring is made with extended sides for iron or brass beds. Frame is made of angle steel ends and sides, with an extra fine grade of woven wire fabric, and supported by 24 steel spiral springs. We will guarantee this spring not to sag; clean and will wear forever. Weight, 55 lbs.

Price, each.................................. **$2.90**

No. 1R2806 Iron Frame Spring, same as No. 1R2805, without support. Is covered with a fine weave fabric and makes a very durable spring. Weight, 45 pounds. Price, each.................. **$2.45**

Our $3.45 Metallic Woven Wire Spring.

No. 1R2809 This Spring is the same as No. 1R2808, with the exception that **it has steel supporter attached to the frame,** with six **helical springs.** Like our No. 1R2808 it is especially designed for iron and brass beds and comes in the following widths: 3 feet, 3 feet 6 inches, 4 feet and 4 feet 6 inches. All springs 6 feet long. Shipping weight, about 60 pounds.

Our special price.......................... **$3.45**

Our $2.75 Metallic Frame Woven Wire Spring.

No. 1R2810 Iron Frame Spring, same as No. 1R2809, without support. Is covered with a fine weave fabric, strong and durable.

Our special price.......................... **$2.75**

Look at Our $1.80 Spiral Springs.

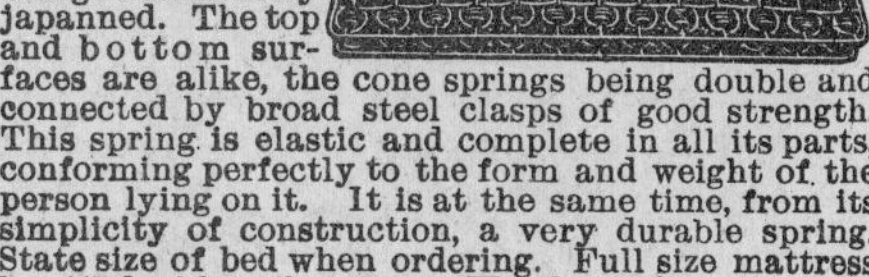

No. 1R2814 Our $1.80 Spiral Springs. This spring is thoroughly well made, the all steel coil being handsomely japanned. The top and bottom surfaces are alike, the cone springs being double and connected by broad steel clasps of good strength. This spring is elastic and complete in all its parts, conforming perfectly to the form and weight of the person lying on it. It is at the same time, from its simplicity of construction, a very durable spring. State size of bed when ordering. Full size mattress has 117 double coil springs. Weight, 25 pounds.

Our special price.......................... **$1.80**

Genuine Smith Spring for $2.95.

Smith's Genuine No. 27 Bed Spring, which we quote at the special price of **$2.95,** looks like No. 1R2814. **The Smith spring** is made of the finest No. 12 steel wire, and has 117 springs tempered to perfection and finely japanned. Each spring is composed of **a double reverse coil,** made on a principle which is unique and perfect, producing a specially strong, durable and comfortable spring. **Be sure to state size of bed when ordering.** Weight, 47 pounds.

No. 1R2815 Price, each.......................... **$2.95**

No. 1R2816 Exactly the same as No. 1R2815 but is made to fold in center. Our special price...... **$3.40**

A Novelty in a Spring for Iron Beds. No Slats Required.

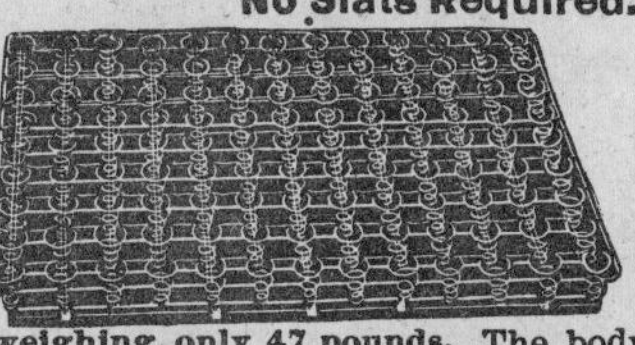

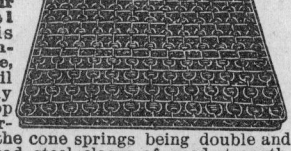

No. 1R2822 The special features of this spring are a rigid base of unusual strength and extreme lightness in weight, weighing only 47 pounds. The body of the bed is composed of 117 highly tempered spiral springs, one attached to the other and forming an all over spring edge. Noiseless, comfortable and a mighty durable bed. The rigid base makes it impossible for the bed to get out of shape. The springs so placed make the bed soft and pliable, **and the combination of the iron bottom and all wire top makes the most perfect spring bed ever placed on the market,** no slats being required for iron beds, and only three for wood beds. We can also furnish this spring for wood beds. (In ordering be sure and state for which you wish to use same.) Give size wanted. Price, each... **$3.95**

Upholstered Box Spring Mattresses.

For brass, iron and wood bedsteads. They are the only ideal spring mattresses for metal bedsteads. They contain 72 of the finest tempered spiral steel springs, and have the celebrated twin springs on edges, holding the structure perfectly in shape. The cut represents the mattress for metal beds, having a rabbet edge, the extended edges resting upon the side and end rails, thus entirely doing away with bed slats. The width of upholstered springs for metal bedsteads is always the same as the out measure of the rails, 4-6, 4-0, 3-6, 3-0, and the regular length is 6-4. The corners are cut out for a bow foot bed at one end; for a straight foot the corners are round. Springs for a wood bed are regular 1-inch space all around. If the bedstead measures 4-6x6-4, the regular size of spring should be 4-4x6-2. Weight, about 75 pounds.

No. 1R2829 Price, tow top.......................... **8.30**
No. 1R2830 Price, moss top.......................... **9.60**
No. 1R2831 Price, hair top.......................... **$10.00**

Great Values in Mattresses.

As will be seen from the following quotations, we show a great variety of mattresses in all the different makes; and as before explained, we have endeavored to include only thoroughly **first class goods, such as we can recommend and guarantee.** We have based our **selling** price on the actual cost to manufacture, with **only our** one small percentage of profit added, and **if you will compare** the prices with those of any other house you will see **they mean a great saving to you.** Our customers should take advantage of the following special prices in making up their orders for furniture or other merchandise. The addition of one or two mattresses will add very little to the freight charges, and will make a great difference in the cost to you.

We guarantee every mattress we offer to be full weight, to be exactly as represented, and of the highest standard quality, and if not found so you are at liberty to return them at our expense and we will cheerfully refund your money.

This line includes the cheap and medium grades, embracing such staple goods as **Combination Excelsior, Wool or Cotton Tops. We no longer offer what is known as all wool or No. 2 Cotton Mattresses, as they have been found unsatisfactory and unsanitary.** We recommend the combination mattress as the very best medium priced mattress, and you will note that our prices are extremely low. **The prices quoted below are for any size bed. Be sure to state size of bed for which mattress is required.**

No. 1R2850 An All Excelsior Mattress, a good honest, serviceable article. Price.................. **$1.50**

No. 1R2851 An Excelsior Mattress with best white cotton top, bound tick. Price.............. **$2.00**

No. 1R2852 An All Husk Mattress, good selected materials, perfectly pure. Price................. **$2.35**

No. 1R2857 Our Excelsior Mattress with best cotton top and bottom, bound tick. Our price.. **$2.40**

No. 1R2859 An All Husk Mattress, with cotton top and bottom, good quality, bound tick. Price.. **$2.70**

No. 1R2860 The Best Pure Maryland Husk Mattress with cotton top, bound tick. Price... **$3.75**

No. 1R2867 Our Special Combination Mattress. Made of elastic felt, with a body of sea moss and excelsior. Can be used either side, is covered with fine satin finished tick, full bound, has 6-inch border, finished imperial edges, with round corners. The finest value ever offered. Our special price.......... **$3.95**

No. 1R2868 Our $4.10 Sanitary Sea Moss Mattress. This mattress is made from sanitary sea moss. Cotton top, bound tick, and two rows of tufts on edges. Price.................................. **$4.10**

No. 1R2869 Our $4.85 Moss Mattress. This mattress is made of extra No. 2 double ginned moss. Cotton top, sides and bottom. Bound tick, two rows of tufts on edges. Price.. **$4.85**

No. 1R2876 Our $5.95 Cotton Mattress. This mattress is made of our selected super white cotton. Bound tick, two rows of tufts on edges. Price.. **$5.95**

No. 1R2880 Our Finest Moss Mattress for $6.50. This mattress is made of XXXX double ginned moss. Bound tick, two rows of tufts on edges. Price.. **$6.50**

When made in two parts 35 cents extra.

A $15.00 Felt Mattress for $7.95.

A GREAT REDUCTION IN THE PRICE OF OUR GENUINE ELASTIC FELT MATTRESS.

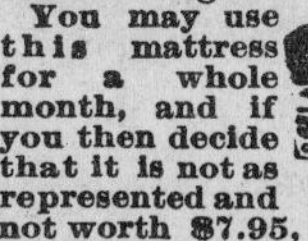

No. 1R2882 All the ease of the highest priced hair mattress. The cleanest mattress in the world. No other mattress will wear so long. You may use this mattress for a whole month, and if you then decide that it is not as represented and not worth $7.95, send it back to us and we will cheerfully refund your money.

WHAT IS FELT? Felt is made of light fibrous material, thoroughly cleaned and purified and bleached to perfect whiteness. This material is wonderfully elastic and is laid in sheets, as shown in the illustration. These layers are forced down by hand and closed in the tick and by the very nature of the fiber cannot get out of shape, become hard in spots, as is the case with all other mattresses.

THE FELT MATTRESS does not absorb moisture, is not affected by changes of atmosphere, and is hence perfectly dry at all times. Warranted against being infested by vermin, a wonderful advantage possessed by no other material. The tick can be taken off and washed very readily. From the fact that this mattress never loses its shape and never becomes lumpy, it does not require repicking or restuffing. Be sure to state exact size of mattress wanted.

No. 1R2882 Our special price, each.......... **$7.95**

OUR MATTRESSES ARE ALL FULL WEIGHT, PACKED IN BURLAP AND GUARANTEED . . . .

NEW, PURE AND SANITARY.

Always be sure to mention size of bed for which mattress is required.

A Magnificent Hall Rack That Will Compare with Those Sold at Retail for $25.00.

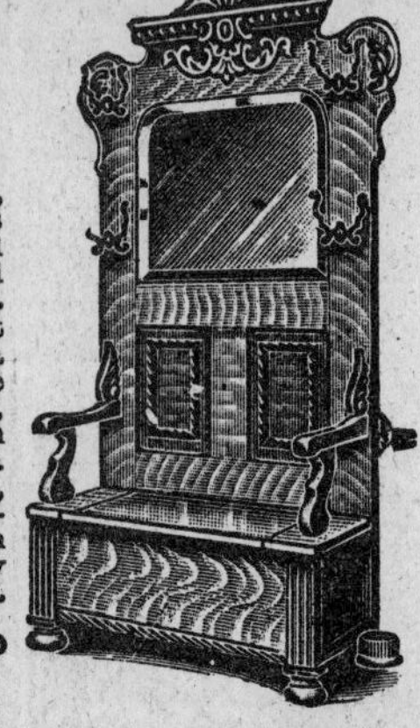

No. 1R3230 Hall Tree, rich and handsome. Is made of quarter sawed golden oak, hand carved and highly polished. Has large double hat hooks, an umbrella holder and a lid to large hall seat. Has a large, beautiful 30x24-inch French bevel mirror. Height, 86 inches; width, 52 inches. **A very massive and elegant design and retails for nearly double our price.** Weight, 180 pounds.
Price, each.....$17.90

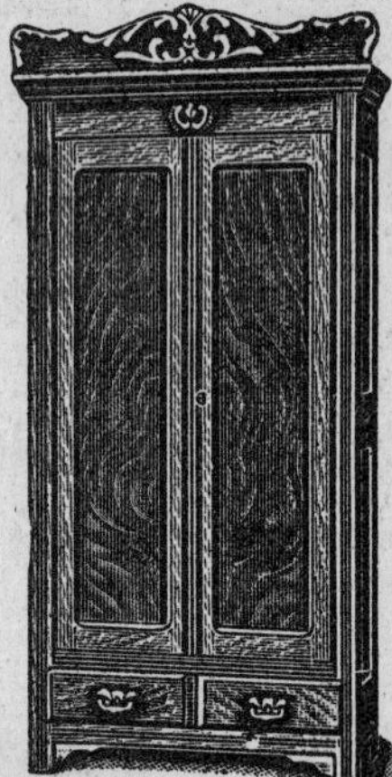

$19.75 Buys a $27.00 Hall Tree.

A New, Rich Design.

No. 1R3236 A Handsome Showy Piece of Hall Decoration, of elegant design and made of the best quarter sawed golden oak, **has heavy rich carving** and a very large bevel plate French mirror, size, 18x40 inches; is 3 feet 4 inches wide, and 7 feet 1 inch high; is highly polished and constructed beyond criticism. Weight, ready for shipment, 170 pounds.

Price, each, $19.75

A NEW LINE OF FINE WARDROBES

Shipped direct from our factory in Central Indiana. Can be shipped either set up or knocked down.

Wardrobe Made of Solid Oak for $6.60.

No. 1R3242 This Wardrobe is made of solid golden oak thoroughly seasoned and finished; height, 7 feet 6 inches; width, 3 feet 3 inches; depth, 1 foot 4 inches. Two doors and two drawers. **This is by far the cheapest and best wardrobe on the market,** when you take into consideration the quality of material used in its construction and its good workmanship. **Will last a lifetime.** Weight, 140 pounds.

Price, each, $6.60

No. 1R3244 Same Wardrobe as No. 1R3242 shown above, but larger size. Dimensions are 7 feet 6 inches high, 3 feet 9 inches wide and 16 inches deep. Shipping weight, 160 pounds.
Our special price..............................$7.62

Special Value for $7.25.

Retail Furniture Stores ask $10.00 to $12.00.

No. 1R3248 This Wardrobe is constructed of the best selected oak and is unusually well made and finished, and richly carved. Is 7 feet 6 inches high, 39 inches wide and 16 inches deep; has two large doors, finely carved, and two large drawers, and is fitted with hooks and shelves. Weight, 140 pounds.

Price, each, $7.25

No. 1R3250 Same Wardrobe as No. 1R3248 shown above, but larger in size. It is 7 feet 6 inches high, 3 feet 9 inches wide and 17 inches deep. Shipping weight, 160 pounds.
Our special price..............................$8.20

A $15.00 Wardrobe for $7.85.

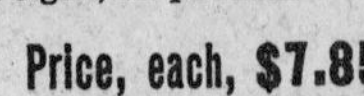

No. 1R3260 One of our very best values in wardrobes; made of selected golden oak; is beyond criticism in construction and finish; no better can be had; has rich, heavy, attractive carvings; is 7 feet 6 inches high, 3 feet 3 inches wide and is 16 inches deep, making it very roomy; has two large paneled doors and two large roomy drawers, fitted with shelf and hooks. A useful and ornamental house furnishing. Can be shipped knocked down or set up. Weight, 140 pounds.

Price, each, $7.85

No. 1R3262 Same Wardrobe as No. 1R3260 shown above, but is larger. Height, 7 feet 6 inches, width, 3 feet 9 inches. Weight, 160 pounds.
Price, each.......................................$8.90

A 75-Cent Engraving Complete With Frame.

A picture sold by dealers at $1.50, and by agents as high as $2.00. This beautiful engraving of horses heads is a fine copy of a famous painting, and is most handsomely framed in a circular ebonized frame, so exact an imitation of ebony that one can scarcely detect the difference between it and the genuine. The frame is ornamented, a gilt pearl inside border, and with a tasty gilt monogram of horseshoe, whip and spur. In offering this striking picture and frame for 75 cents we consider it a rare bargain, one that our customers will not overlook. Diameter of picture, 10 inches; diameter of frame, 16 inches.
No. 1R3506 Price, complete....................75c

Yards of Flowers and Fruits.

Outside size, 11x37. Glass, 8x34

No. 1R3542 Studies in flowers and fruits in colors. Framed in 1½-inch gilt frames with metal gilt corner ornaments. Pictures and frames complete. Can furnish the following studies: **Roses, as shown above, tulips, wild roses, violets, pansies, apples and grapes, cherries, roses and snowballs, roses and lilacs, wild violets.** Price, each..........$1.00

Our $1.25 Colored Photograph Pictures.

No. 1R3546 For $1.25 we furnish this handsome colored photograph as shown in illustration, complete with a heavy richly ornamented frame. This picture is 28x32 inches in size, a rich colored photograph, the same kind of a picture as retails in the art stores in this city, without the frame, glass or mounting, as high as $4.00. This is one of the handsomest colored photograph subjects that we have seen, and mounted with a deep mat and heavy richly carved frame, it makes a very handsome picture. This picture is in size, 20x24 inches, frame, 28x32 inches. Frame is a 4-inch richly ornamented gold frame, mounted with deep mat and heavy glass. Our special price..$1.25

$1.25 Our Special Price for This Our Handsomest Colored Photograph.

No. 1R3576 $1.25 is a special price made possible by reason of buying these pictures, frames and mountings in very large quantities for cash, and adding but our one small percentage of profit.

This handsome colored photograph picture alone, without frame or mounting, would retail at city art stores at $4.00 and upwards. It is a subject that must be seen to be appreciated. **This handsome colored photograph is mounted under glass in a heavy 4-inch carved frame, finished in hard ivory enamel, beautifully tinted on the edges with blue, and tipped in gilt.**
Our special price.... ....$1.25

Our $1.85 Colored Artograph Picture.

No. 1R3578 For $1.85 we furnish this handsome colored artograph picture, outside measurement 30x44 inches, size of picture 20x34 inches.

Complete with heavy frame and glass, the equal of pictures that sell in the finest art stores in cities at greatly advanced prices.

The Artograph process produces the very finest effect and you will appreciate this when you have received the picture. This picture is mounted on a heavy 5-inch frame finished in hard ivory enamel, with center and inside molding beautifully tinted in a rich green and gold. Our special price....$1.85

Our Special $1.95 Water Color Picture.

No. 1R3580 For $1.95 we offer this magnificent picture, a facsimile of a genuine water color, a very large picture. Outside measurement is 30x40 inches, inside measure 20x30 inches. In offering this handsome picture complete with frame and glass at the extremely low price of $1.95, we have endeavored to give our customers most extraordinary value.

DESCRIPTION—This magnificent facsimile water color picture is 20x30 inches in size, inside measurement.

FRAME—This picture has a superb 5-inch frame, finished a rich sea green and gold, handsomely carved and ornamented. Size of frame, outside measure, 30x40 inches. It is mounted complete, with deep matting and heavy, clear glass.
Our special price..............................$1.95

Wall Pockets.

No. 1R3610 Handsome Wall Pocket. Outside measurement 15x18 inches; finished in light blue enamel and copper tips and fitted with fine landscape study in colors under glass. Price, each, ...55c

No. 1R3618 A Large, Ornamental Wall Pocket. Size, outside, 17x24 inches; finished in cream enamel, with olive green shade on the side and edge, and gilt tops, and fitted with a landscape oleograph. Price, each.........60c

No. 1R3620 This Beautiful Wall Pocket looks like illustration No. 1R3618, is 18x21 inches outside, enameled white and shaded; finished with gilt tips; front is fitted with a handsome study in colors. Price..65c

Our 75-Cent Mahogany Wall Pocket.

No. 1R3632 New Mahogany Finish Wall Pocket, showing the grain of the wood. The outer frame is of 2-inch molding, with four heavy brass corner pieces; inner frame is of 1-inch molding with pastel facsimile under glass. Outside size, about 15x18 inches.
Price........................75c

Fancy Ornamented Wall Pocket for 85 Cents.

No. 1R3638 An attractive and useful house ornament is this Wall Pocket. It is 16 x 20 inches outside measure; the wood is oak finish with ornaments in steel bronze; front is fitted with a handsome study in colors.
Price, each..............85c

A Fine Plate Mirror for 35 Cents.

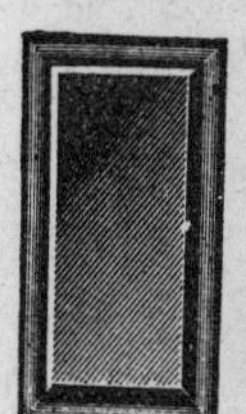

No. 1R3750 Dealers make very large profits on this class of goods. They are compelled to from the fact that they sell at such high prices that their sales are comparatively small, hence they make up for their small sales by large profits. **This mirror is made with heavy handsome solid oak frame, beautifully** polished, and very finely fitted by the best workmen. We fit the mirror with the best French glass made, in the following sizes, at the prices named below:

Size of frame	Size of plate	Weight	French Plain	French Bevel
1¼-inch	7x 9 inches	....	$0.35	$0.55
1¼-inch	8x10 inches	....	.40	.60
1¼-inch	9x12 inches	4 pounds	.45	.90
1¼-inch	10x14 inches	....	.60	1.00
1¼-inch	10x17 inches	....	.90	1.15
2¼-inch	12x20 inches	10 pounds	1.05	1.75
2¼-inch	13x22 inches	....	1.25	1.80
2¼-inch	14x24 inches	15 pounds	1.35	2.20
2¼-inch	15x26 inches	....	1.95	2.75
2¼-inch	16x28 inches	20 pounds	2.15	3.00
2¼-inch	17x30 inches	....	2.90	3.35
2¼-inch	18x36 inches	22 pounds	3.10	4.25
2¼-inch	18x40 inches	30 pounds	3.60	4.75

Elegant Framed French Plate Mirrors at 35 Cents Up. Composition Frame.

No. 1R3756 Finished in imitation oak, walnut or green. Fitted with French plate.

Size of Plate	
7 x9 inches	$0.35
8x10 inches	.45
9x12 inches	.60
10x14 inches	.75
10x17 inches	.90
12x20 inches	1.25

Plain and Bevel French Plate Mirrors in Brass Ornamented Frames at from 40 Cents to $1.95.

No. 1R3762 Handsome Parlor Mirror, frame 1½ inches wide, with four handsome brass ornaments in the corners. Made in quarter sawed oak, antique finish or rich, dark mahogany finish; neat lines, and is one of our best low priced patterns.

Plain French Plate.		Bevel French Plate	
7x 9 inches	$0.40	7x 9 inches	$0.60
8x10 inches	.45	8x10 inches	.70
9x12 inches	.65	9x12 inches	.90
10x14 inches	.75	10x14 inches	1.00
10x17 inches	.90	10x17 inches	1.15
12x20 inches	1.25	12x20 inches	1.55
13x22 inches	1.50	13x22 inches	1.80
14x24 inches	1.65	14x24 inches	1.95

Our 50-Cent Mirror.

No. 1R3768 This Mirror has a solid oak frame, is nicely finished and beautifully polished. Is fitted with French bevel plate mirror.

Size of plate	Bevel	Plain
10x10 inches	$0.75	$0.50
12x12 inches	1.00	.75
14x14 inches	1.42	1.08
16x16 inches	1.80	1.35

Triplicate Toilet Mirror.

No. 1R3780 Made of 1¼-inch or 1-inch oak, finished in golden oak. Highly polished or Flemish oak, finished backs, fancy nickel plated hinges, when closed overlapping each other. Fitted with French plate. **The only thing for ladies' toilet or gentlemen's shaving mirror.**

Size of plate		French plain	French bevel
9x12 inches	Price	$2.70	$3.60
10x14 inches	Price	3.25	3.95

Fancy Pier Mirror, Florentine Design.

No. 1R3786 Fancy Pier Mirror, for parlor, made of heavy 4-inch molding, finely ornamented in Florentine design, carved and finished in gold with shaded ornaments. Rich and ornamental. Frame 4 inches wide, finished in gold, cut out openings, fitted with French bevel plate.
Size, 16x20 inches. Price. $3.00
Size, 14x24 inches. Price.. 3.40
Size, 18x40 inches. Price.. 4.85

No. 1R3792 Made of select 4-inch oak, finished in golden, very highly polished, or Flemish oak with large cast brass ornamental corners. Fitted with French plate, plain or bevel.

Size of Plate	Plain	Bevel
17x30 inches	$3.75	$4.30
18x32 inches	4.40	4.75
18x36 inches	4.75	4.95
18x40 inches	4.95	5.45

Special Value Pier Mirror for $4.30.

A mirror that would sell at retail for $7.50.

No. 1R3798 This handsome Mirror has a 6-inch frame finished in green and gold or white and gold with heavy raised ornamental stem and lining; both sides of stem are **finished fine green bronze or white enamel.** Size of plate, 18x40 inches.
Price, plain French plate mirror....................$4.30
Price, bevel French plate mirror....................$4.90

Something Exceptionally Fine for $5.55.

No. 1R3806 This is a strikingly beautiful Mirror. Has a handsome heavy 6¼-inch frame, made of the finest materials, finished with back and stem **heavily ornamented gilt, artistic cut openings** on back, with gold burnishes on corners; inside is a wide burnished lining; next to same an ornamental gilt lining. Size of plate, 18x40 inches.
Price, French plate mirror..$5.55
Price, French bevel mirror...5.85

$5.75 Buys This $7.50 Pier Mirror.

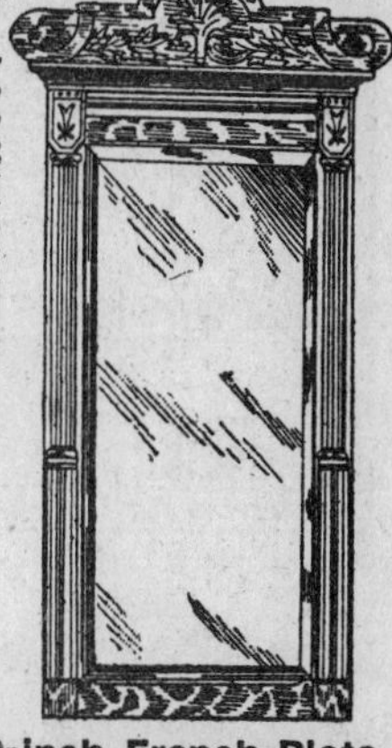

Very best quality, very latest design.

No. 1R3810 This Mirror has a very heavy, solid golden oak frame, or imitation mahogany, with heavy top carving of rich pattern, and fluted columns on frame and is very attractive and ornamental. Size of plate is 18x40 inches.

Price, in imported German plate mirror....$5.75

Price, in imported German bevel mirror...$5.95

18x40-inch French Plate Mirror for $5.70.

No. 1R3816 Mirror. Frame is 7 inches wide, finished in pearl green and tinted with gold; gold burnishes on the heavy ornamented corners. A beautiful parlor decoration, fitted with the best imported French plate, 18x40 inches.
Price, plain mirror..................................$5.70
Price, bevel mirror..................................6.05

Our Special $7.95 French Pier Mirror.

No. 1R3822 There is perhaps nothing that adds more to the elegant appearance of a room than a handsome and stylish pier mirror, such as we show in the illustration. **It is very heavy and massive in appearance,** and, at the same time, elegant in outline and rich in ornamentation. The height of the frame is 90 inches, width 28 inches. The frame made of the **best solid oak, with very handsome finish** and fitted with a shelf below the mirror. The mirror itself is made of the very best French plate glass imported to this country, and is 18 inches wide by 40 inches high. It is consequently very large in size. We pack these mirrors very carefully and they are sure to reach you in the very best condition and give you the highest satisfaction.

Our special price, with plain French plate.$7.95
Our special price with finest imported French bevel plate..$8.75

No. 1R3826 Pier Mirror. Strikingly rich and elegant. Made of select oak, finished in golden oak or curly birch in mahogany finish. Handsome hand carved top, turned pillars. 90 inches high, 28 inches wide. Fitted with French plate, 18x40 inches.
Price, French plain..................................$10.00
Price, French bevel..................................10.45

No. 1R3832 Pier Mirror, made of select oak, finished in golden oak, carved top and molding; width, 30 inches; height, 93 inches. Fitted with French plate, 20x60 inches.
Price, French plain $13.60
Price, French bevel..................................15.35

No. 1R3838 Pier Mirror, made of select oak, finished in golden oak or curly birch in mahogany finish. Highly polished, raised hand carving and rope pillars. Outside measurements—width, 30 inches; height, 93 inches. Fitted with French plate and 4-inch French bevel circle on top of mirror. Size of plate, 20x60 inches.
Price, French plain..................................$17.75
Price, French bevel..................................19.95

NEW DESIGNS IN HIGH GRADE COUCHES.

AT CUT PRICES, prices lower than ever before named by us or any other house, prices made possible by building these couches in our own factory in Chicago, or in a factory that is controlled by us, a factory located near the railroad tracks in the outer edge of Chicago, equipped with every modern machinery for the manufacturing of frames, for the sewing, tufting, upholstering and making of couches, we are able to offer for this year an entirely new line of couches in all the very latest effects, in all the latest designs of frames and shapes, offer all the new materials at prices heretofore unknown, prices that barely cover the cost of material and labor, with but our one small percentage of profit added.

BY OUR WONDERFULLY LOW PRICES we have built up the largest couch business in this country; we have become recognized by the furniture trade everywhere as headquarters for everything in couches, as makers of the lowest prices, leaders in prices with which no other maker or dealer will attempt to compete.

THE COVERING MATERIALS, the velours, leather, plushes and other covering materials are bought direct from the mills in carload lots, the frames are made in the factory by the use of automatic machinery and all this is done to reduce the cost to the very minimum, and to the first cost we add our one small percentage of profit, making you prices, quality considered against which no other house will attempt to compete, prices about one-half the price charged by dealers generally.

SPECIAL TO FURNITURE DEALERS: To the furniture dealer who appreciates high grade goods, and who is ever on the alert for values, for lower prices than any other manufacturer can make, we ask your attention especially, as well as the attention of our two millions of customers, to this line of new couches under our guarantee of quality, under guarantee of prices, the lowest prices ever attempted, lower prices than are made by any other house anywhere.

All our couches made with the patent naper tufting buttons which will not pull out and canvas over the springs, making them practically indestructible.

THE FREIGHT will amount to very little as compared to what you save in price. Couches weigh from 75 to 100 pounds. Railroad companies carry them at one and one-half times first class rate. By referring to pages 7 to 10 you can get the rate to your nearest point, which is about the same as it will be to your town, and thus tell exactly what the freight will amount to.

OUR SPECIAL $3.95 COUCH.

AT $3.95 we offer this couch greatly reduced in price from last season and materially improved in quality and style, brought right up to date in its new design as illustrated. While we recommend a better couch and urge you to select one of our higher grades, yet for $3.95 we guarantee this couch far superior to anything ever attempted at anything like the price.

$3.95

From the illustration, engraved by our artist from a photograph, you can form some idea of the wonderful value we are offering in this couch at the extremely low price of $3.95. This couch is made on a new hardwood frame. The frame is well braced, has full spring seat and is upholstered in three-tone velours cloth. Do not compare this upholstering with any of the cheap one or two-tone velours on the market with which so many of the cheap couches on the market are covered. It is ornamented with tasseled fringe. The couch is 27 inches wide by 72 inches long, and while we recommend you to buy one of our finer couches, either our special big $7.45 couch or even a higher grade, if you want a couch at a lower price we guarantee this the best value ever shown in a couch at anything approaching our $3.95 price. Weight, 75 pounds.

No. 1R5000 Price.......................................$3.95

OUR NEW MATTRESS TUFTED $4.90 COUCH.

FOR $4.90 we offer this couch reduced more than $1.00 in price and improved in quality for this season, the handsomest couch on the market at anything approaching the price. This illustration gives you an idea of the general appearance and style of the couch, but you must see it to appreciate it. It is good full size, 27 inches wide by 74 inches long, extra well upholstered throughout. We use nothing but select tempered steel springs, and it is upholstered with full spring edges. We use in the upholstering an extra quality of three-toned velours cloth in handsome new pattern effects, in the very latest shades, a cloth that will outwear three of the cheaper couches upholstered in cheap one and two-toned goods. The couch comes nicely shaped, nicely tufted as illustrated, deep fringed trimming.

$4.90

AT OUR SPECIAL $4.90 PRICE we furnish it complete, burlaped, castered and delivered on board the cars in Chicago. Weight, 75 pounds.

No. 1R5004 Our special price, upholstered in three-tone velours cloth.......................................$4.90

OUR NEW FANCY GLENHAM COUCH, $5.95.

$5.95

REDUCED FROM $8.00. A difference in price of $2.05 and greatly improved for this season. Our $2.05 reduction in price is made possible by reason of our improved facilities for manufacturing. Understand, you own these couches direct from our factory on the basis of the cost of the material and labor, with but our one small percentage of profit added. This illustration will give you some idea of the appearance of this handsome couch. It is full size, 72x27 inches, frame is of hardwood throughout and is finished in oak or imitation mahogany. The frame work shown is nicely carved as illustrated in picture, with heavy claw legs. This couch contains a full set of the best oil tempered steel springs drawn from high carbon cold rolled steel, 24 springs in all. Spring edge with a steel edge wire, and the springs are all securely tied, insuring the best service. The couch is nicely tufted as shown in illustration and well constructed throughout, covered in the best quality high colored imported velours. Heavy duck canvas over the springs. State color and finish desired and we will guarantee to please you. Shipping weight, 85 pounds.

No. 1R5006 Our special price.......................................$5.95

OUR NEW $6.25 DEEP TUFTED COUCH.

$6.25

AT $6.25 AND $6.95, according to covering, we offer this handsome new design in a full shaped, heavy biscuit button tufted, full fringed couch, in competition with couches that sell generally at about double the price. Understand, our special $6.25 and $6.95 prices are prices that barely cover the cost of material and labor, with but our one small percentage of profit added, prices at which you own the couches for less money than your dealer can buy in quantities. The illustration will give you some idea of the handsome effect worked out in this new pattern at $6.25 and $6.95. This is one of our most attractive couches among our many patterns for this season. It is extra deep tufted, is extra large, being 30 inches wide and 75 inches long. We use only the best tempered steel springs; couch is made with full spring edges; the frames are extra strong. We use the celebrated naper tufting button, which is guaranteed not to pull off and greatly increases the wearing qualities of the couch. The three-tone velours cloth we use is extra high grade and comes in all the very latest pattern effects and handsome colorings. We can furnish you almost any color effect wanted. The couches are trimmed all around with deep wool fringe, handsome cord and tassels. Couches weigh about 75 to 90 pounds. Nearly all railroad companies carry them at one and one-half times first class freight rates. By referring to pages 7 to 10 you can get the first class rate to your nearest point, which is about, if not exactly, the same as to your town, and thus tell almost exactly what the freight will amount to. It will amount to next to nothing compared with what you will save in price.

No. 1R5012 Our special price, upholstered in three-tone velours.......................................$6.25

No. 1R5013 Our special price, upholstered in French Gobelin tapestry.......................................6.95

SPECIAL VALUES IN LEATHER COUCHES

WE DIRECT YOUR ATTENTION especially to our line of high grade leather and imitation leather couches in the very latest designs for this season, couches from one of the best makers in this country, and at prices heretofore unknown.

OUR LEATHER COUCHES are made for us under contract by one of the best makers of leather couches in this country. We take the large part of the output of the factory, and the cost to us is based on the actual cost of the material and labor with but a small manufacturers' profit added, thus enabling us to offer an extra high grade of leather couch work at prices lower than ever before quoted.

THE GRADE OF LEATHER COUCHES we offer is such as can be compared only with the couches that are carried by the best furniture dealers in the cities and there offered at about double the prices.

IN THE MANUFACTURE of our leather couches special attention is paid to the quality of leather covering made. We use only strong, well finished hardwood frames. We use the highest grade of tempered steel springs, and while our prices are below any kind of competition, our couches should not be compared with any of the many cheap grades on the market, where poor grade of split leather, inferior frames and cheaply made work is offered.

EVERY COUCH IS SENT OUT UNDER OUR BINDING GUARANTEE. We guarantee it to reach you in the same perfect condition it leaves us, and to prove entirely satisfactory to you, otherwise you can return it to us at our expense of freight charges both ways and we will immediately return your money. The leather couches weigh, crated for shipment, from 100 to 125 pounds, and you will find the freight will amount to nothing as compared with what you will save in price.

If you really want a first class couch, one that there is practically no wear out to, we especially recommend that you select the leather covered couch.

$13.45

THIS HANDSOME COUCH ONLY $13.45 covered with a special grade of imitation leather, and for $18.90, covered in genuine leather, we furnish this handsome couch as illustrated, the equal of couches that retail generally at nearly double the price.

THIS COUCH is made with a very handsome hardwood frame of the latest rococo design as illustrated, with large claw feet; the frame is finished in golden oak or imitation mahogany. It comes upholstered either in genuine leather or best imitation leather as desired, trimmed with leather and gimp, and is stuffed with the highest grade of southern moss. Only the best steel springs are used; has full spring seat, spring head and spring edges. The couch is 78 inches long, 27 inches wide, and weighs 100 pounds, and we are sure at our special $18.90 price there is no genuine leather couch made that will approach it either in style, finish or durability.

No. 1R5119 Price, upholstered in best imitation leather.............$13.45
No. 1R5120 Price, upholstered in genuine leather.............18.90

$14.25

THIS COUCH IS MADE on a large, heavy hardwood frame, elegantly finished with extra heavy, beautifully shaped and carved legs. The frame is finished in golden oak or imitation mahogany as desired. • The spring construction is the highest grade made, no twine being used in tying the springs. It has the best steel wire bottom, and the bottom is left open to plain view, giving perfect ventilation. Heavy duck canvas over the springs; extra quality of hair filling, both sides of the couch are finished alike, so that the couch can be used in any room. Full button tufted with deep diamond tufts, full spring edges. It is 78 inches long, 30 inches wide, and weighs 110 pounds.

OUR SPECIAL PRICE of $14.25 and $20.50 barely covers the cost of material and labor with but our one small percentage of profit added. If you order this couch from us and are not perfectly satisfied with it when received, and do not consider it equal to couches that sell generally at for $10.00 to $15.06 more money, return it to us at our expense, and we will immediately return your money.

No. 1R5121 Price, upholstered in imitation leather.............$14.25
No. 1R5122 Price, upholstered in genuine leather.............$20.50

$14.95

FOR $14.95 upholstered in the best grade of imitation leather, or for $21.60 upholstered in high grade, full finished genuine machine buffed leather, we offer you this handsome, new, richly finished couch, as the equal of couches that sell generally for almost double the money. This couch is mounted on one of the handsomest and heaviest hardwood couch frames made, an entirely new pattern, beautifully shaped, handsomely carved and decorated as shown in the illustration, with extra heavy claw feet. It is an extra large, deep tufted couch, small deep diamond tufts, full spring top, head and edges. The spring construction is of the highest grade, no twine being used in tying the springs. They are covered complete with extra heavy duck canvas, and filled with extra high grade of hair throughout.

OUR SPECIAL $21.60 PRICE for this couch upholstered in extra high grade genuine machine buffed leather, with frame of oak or mahogany finish as desired, barely covers the cost of labor and material with but our one small percentage of profit added.

Couches weigh about 75 to 125 pounds. Nearly all railroad companies carry them at one and one-half times first class freight rates. By referring to pages 7 to 10 you can get the first class rate to your nearest point which is about, if not exactly the same as to your town, and thus tell almost exactly what the freight will amount to. It will amount to next to nothing as compared to what you will save in price. Shipping weight, 110 lbs.

No. 1R5125 Price, upholstered in imitation leather.............$14.95
No. 1R5126 Price, upholstered in genuine leather.............21.60

$26.50 BUYS OUR HIGHEST GRADE EXTRA LARGE GENUINE MACHINE BUFFED LEATHER COVER STUFFED COUCH.

$19.95

AT $26.50 upholstered in genuine leather, $19.95 upholstered in the highest grade imitation leather, we offer this our highest grade couch in an entirely new style for this season, as one of the handsomest couches on the market, the equal of any couch you can buy from your dealers at home at about double the price. If you will send us your order and money we will send the couch to you, guaranteeing it to reach you in perfect condition, and if not found in every way satisfactory, you can return it to us at our expense of freight charges both ways and we will immediately return your money.

THIS HANDSOME, BIG OVERSTUFFED COUCH is covered in an extra high grade, full finished machine buffed leather, one of the largest couches made, being 80 inches long and 30 inches wide. The frame is made of selected hardwood throughout with very heavy carved legs. We furnish the frame either in golden oak or imitation mahogany as desired. The upholstering is done in the best possible manner. We use the neat, small deep diamond tufts, hand tufted throughout; the highest grade of steel tufting buttons are used. As will be seen from the illustration, it is leather finished on the sides. Nothing handsomer has been produced in a leather couch. It has the best possible steel construction, finished without any tying of twine. The springs are covered underneath with a heavy duck canvas. Only a selected grade of hair is used in the upholstering. It is a couch that must be seen, examined and compared with other couches that sell at about double the price, to appreciate the value given.

Shipping weight, 110 pounds.
No. 1R5127 Price, upholstered in imitation leather, $19.95
No. 1R5128 Price, upholstered in genuine leather... 26.50

BED LOUNGES.

OUR NEW LINE OF BED LOUNGES OR COMBINATION COUCHES IS THE VERY LATEST STYLE FOR THIS SEASON.

THEY ARE FROM ONE OF THE BEST MAKERS IN THIS COUNTRY . . . . They are made for us under contract and at our special prices barely cover cost of material and labor with but our one small percentage of profit added.

AS A GUARANTEE THAT WE CAN FURNISH YOU A BED LOUNGE OR COMBINATION BED COUCH for very much less money than you can get elsewhere, if you send us your order and money we will send you the lounge or couch by freight, with the understanding that if not found entirely satisfactory when received it can be returned to us at our expense of freight charges both ways and we will return your money.

THE BED LOUNGE OR BED COUCH IS ONE OF THE MOST CONVENIENT PIECES OF FURNITURE you can have in your home. Closed, it makes a handsome piece of furniture, a beautiful lounge or couch. Open, you have a large roomy, comfortable, full spring bed. In small houses or where room is limited and where it is desirable at times to make a bed up in a living room or parlor, this bed lounge or bed couch serves to make the room both a living room and a sleeping room. During the day you have a handsome, comfortable piece of furniture, a lounge or couch. At night you have a large, full width, full spring bed.

WE ASK THAT YOU DO NOT CLASS OUR BED LOUNGES OR COUCHES with any of the many cheap lines on the market. Our couches are made with extra heavy, strong, reinforced and handsomely finished hardwood frames. Only

HIGH GRADE COIL SPRINGS

are used, with extra quality of covering. The factory employs only skilled mechanics and as a result we turn out a line of combination bed lounges and couches at prices below any kind of competition, and such couches as can be found only in the best retail stores.

AT OUR SPECIAL PRICES, PRICES THAT BARELY COVER THE COST OF MATERIAL AND LABOR, with but our one small percentage of profit added, we deliver these couches, carefully packed and wrapped in burlap, on board cars at the factory in a suburb of Chicago, about twenty miles from the city, from which point you must pay the freight.

OUR $7.45 BED LOUNGE.

$7.45

AT $7.45 upholstered in a special high grade of colored velours cloth, we offer this combination lounge and full size bed in an entirely new style for this season. It is an extra large lounge, mounted on a heavy handsomely finished hardwood frame, the equal of bed lounges that retail generally at double the price. **This lounge is 72 inches long by 46 inches wide when open. Closed it is 23 inches wide by 73 inches long. The frame is extra heavy, made of selected hardwood. We will furnish it in golden oak or imitation mahogany as desired.** It has extra quality of woven wire springs, and the bed is supported by steel coiled springs on both sides and center of bed, making a very soft and comfortable bed. It has a good quality of cotton top mattress, good ticking. This couch weighs, crated for shipment, about 150 pounds. It is carried by railroad companies at 1½-times first class rate. The freight will average for 500 miles about $1.25. **For exact freight rate to your place see pages 7 to 10.** The freight to the point nearest you is almost exactly the same as to your town.

No. 1R5133 Price for lounge, upholstered in good quality colored velours cloth.......... $7.45
No. 1R5134 Price for lounge, upholstered in imported French Gobelin tapestry.......... 7.85
No. 1R5135 Price for lounge, upholstered in extra quality of crushed plush.......... 8.45

OUR $7.75 OVERSTUFFED COMBINATION LOUNGE AND BED.

$7.75

THIS IS A HANDSOME, extra large combination lounge **and full sized bed in the very latest style for this season. The bed closed, is 24 inches wide by 72 inches long. Open, it is 46 inches wide by 72 inches long.** It is mounted on a very strong, beautifully finished, handsomely carved and decorated hardwood frame, upholstered in the very latest style. Has a handsomely finished carved and decorated back and will be furnished in golden oak or imitation mahogany as desired. It is made with a woven wire spring bed, supported by steel coiled springs on both sides and center. Has good quality of cotton top mattress, good ticking, and our special $7.75 price barely covers the cost of material and labor with but our one small percentage of profit added. **Crated for shipment, it weighs 150 pounds,** and is accepted by nearly all railroad companies at 1½-times first class freight rate. By referring to pages 7 to 10 you can get the rate for 100 pounds to a point nearest your town, which will be almost exactly the same as to your town.

No. 1R5136 Price for lounge, upholstered in extra quality colored velours cloth, new pattern.......... $7.75
No. 1R5137 Price for lounge, upholstered in extra quality French Gobelin tapestry.......... 8.25
No. 1R5138 Price for lounge, upholstered in crushed plush.......... 8.75

OUR HANDSOME $7.90 COMBINATION LOUNGE AND FULL SIZED FULL SPRING BED.

$7.90

THIS IS AN EXTRA LARGE, beautifully finished combination bed and lounge, mounted on heavy hardwood frame. The frame is beautifully decorated and handsomely finished, and can be furnished in golden oak or imitation mahogany finish as desired. The lounge is extra large, 27 inches long by 46 inches wide when open. We use a good quality of cotton top mattress on the bed, made of extra quality ticking. It contains a woven wire spring, supported by coiled springs on the side and center of bed. Our price of $7.90 barely covers the cost of material and labor, with but our one small percentage of profit added. The lounge weighs, crated for shipment, 150 pounds, and is accepted by railroad companies generally at 1½-times first class rate. **The freight rate to the point nearest your town,** as shown on pages 7 to 10, is almost, if not exactly the same as the rate to your town and you will see the freight will amount to next to nothing as compared to what you will save in the price.

No. 1R5141 Price for lounge, upholstered in extra quality colored velours cloth of latest pattern.......... $7.90
No. 1R5142 Price for lounge, upholstered in French Gobelin tapestry, beautifully colored, handsome design.. 8.40
No. 1R5143 Price for lounge, upholstered in extra quality of crushed plush.......... 8.90

OUR BIG, HEAVY, FULL UPHOLSTERED HANDSOME ROCOCO DESIGN

COMBINATION FULL SIZED BED AND HANDSOME LOUNGE FOR $8.95

$8.95

AT $8.95 TO $10.90, according to grade of covering, we will furnish this as one of the handsomest combination lounges and beds we make. This lounge is mounted on a very handsome, extra heavy, beautifully finished, nicely carved and decorated hardwood frame, which comes in either **solid golden oak or imitation mahogany as desired.** Full spring throughout, beautifully finished, upholstered side and upholstered back, and the new rococo design back is handsomely shaped with a beautiful hardwood frame. We use only the very best grade of coiled steel springs, solid spring edges, extra cotton top mattress, good ticking. **Our special price barely covers the cost of material and labor with but our one small percentage of profit added.** The lounge weighs, packed for shipment, about 150 pounds, and is accepted by the railroad companies generally at one and one-half times first class freight rate. On pages 7 to 10 you will find the freight rate per 100 pounds to a point nearest your town, which is about the same as to your station, and you can tell almost to a penny what the freight will amount to, and you will find it will amount to next to nothing as compared to what you will save in price.

No. 1R5144 Price for lounge, upholstered in high grade velours cloth, in latest designs and colors.......... **$8.95**
No. 1R5145 Price for lounge, upholstered in French Goblin tapestry, beautiful coloring and latest design..... **9.75**
No. 1R5146 Price for lounge, upholstered in crushed plush, extra quality.. **10.90**

Our Roman Divan Couch.

THIS BEAUTIFUL DIVAN COUCH is one of the most attractive, and at the same time serviceable pieces of furniture ever manufactured. It is so constructed that both ends can be adjusted to any angle, making a beautiful and comfortable couch as well as sofa. The divan couch is illustrated showing it both open and closed, with and without back. The couch without back is reversible and can be used either side facing the front. **The frame is hardwood, finished in golden oak or imitation mahogany. The couch without back measures 40 inches between the arms when the ends are raised, and 90 inches long when they are down; is 30 inches wide, has 8 rows deep tufts put in with the celebrated Naper tufting button, which cannot pull out.** It contains 38 of the best steel springs drawn from a special high carbon clock spring, steel wire. It is upholstered in the highest style of the art; a heavy duck canvas is used over the springs and the filling is of fine tow covered with cotton. The attachment is very simple and is operated as follows: To place either head straight, raise to the highest point and a little beyond that and the head will drop down level. It can be easily raised to any one of five different positions according to the angle desired. There are no strings to pull and the attachment is automatic. There is not a prettier piece of furniture in existence today, notwithstanding it has so many combinations. It answers as a divan, sofa, Davenport and adjustable bed couch, and is equally comfortable in any position.

THE LATEST INVENTION ...IN... Upholstered Furniture.

This illustration shows ends in upright position forming a regular divan.

This illustration shows ends in proper position to form a regular couch.

WE CAN FURNISH this Divan Couch in velours, imported French Gobelin tapestry or crushed plush, at our special prices, prices that barely cover the cost of material and labor with but our one small percentage of profit added. We deliver these couches carefully packed and wrapped in burlap, on board cars at our factory within twenty miles of Chicago, from which point you must pay the freight, and which will be but a small item compared to the great value which we are offering you.

THE COUCHES weigh, crated for shipment, about 150 pounds, and are accepted by nearly all railroad companies at one and one-half times first class freight rate. By referring to pages 7 to 10 you can get the rate for 100 pounds, which will enable you to readily estimate what the freight charges will be to your nearest railroad station.

No. 1R5147 Price for Divan Couch without back, upholstered in high color, good quality velours cloth.. **$11.75**
No. 1R5148 Price for Divan Couch without back, upholstered in imported French Gobelin tapestry.. **12.45**
No. 1R5149 Price for Divan Couch without back, upholstered in best quality crushed plush.. **13.75**

This illustration shows couch with back forming a regular Davenport.

DIVAN COUCH WITH HIGH BACK.

THE DIVAN COUCHES with high back are in every respect as described above, but are not reversible the same as the couches without back, as they can only be used with one side to the front, but which is oftentimes more desirable.

No. 1R5152 Price for Divan Couch with back, upholstered with high colored velours cloth...... **$13.45**
No. 1R5153 Price for Divan Couch with high back, upholstered in imported French Gobelin tapestry.. **14.25**
No. 1R5154 Price for Divan Couch with back, upholstered in best quality crushed plush........ **15.50**

This illustration shows the couch with back, one end down and one at medium slope.

Our Special $7.97 Parlor Cabinet.

No. 1R5350 For $7.97 we offer this handsome new design in a beautifully finished Parlor Cabinet as the equal of anything you can buy anywhere at $12.00 to $15.00. This is the very latest production for this season, one of the handsomest cabinets made. **No parlor is properly furnished if it does not include one of our new and handsome cabinets.** The illustration will give you some idea of the beautiful effect worked out in this new cabinet. It is made of selected birch, given the highest mahogany finish, beautifully polished. Stands 54 inches high, is 27 inches wide. It is handsomely ornamented with two mirrors, one shaped double plate French mirror, 8x20 inches; one bevel shaped French mirror, 10x16 inches. **This handsome cabinet will compare favorably with cabinets that are being sold in this city in the most fashionable furniture stores at two or three times the price.** It is a class of goods you will find only in the most fashionable stores and there at fancy prices.

Our special price........................$7.97

Shipping weight, about 80 pounds.

Parlor Cabinet, $10.62.

No. 1R5355 This Handsome and Attractive Parlor Cabinet, made of the finest birch with a rich mahogany finish, with pretty ornamental shelves and two bevel plate French mirrors one 26x7 and one 16x12 inches, is 60 inches high and 32 inches wide, is graceful in outline and a welcome and beautiful addition to a parlor.

Price, each.....$10.62

...pping weight, about 80 pounds.

Music Cabinet.

No. 1R5360 Music Cabinet. Made of birch finished mahogany; select stock, all beautifully polished. Height, 38 inches; width, 18 inches; depth, 13 inches; has inside shelves. **Very stylish and artistic design.** Weight, 60 pounds. **A high grade article in every respect.**

Price, each..........$3.70

Our $4.35 Music Cabinet.

No. 1R5364 A Handsome Music Cabinet. Mahogany finish on select birch or golden oak, all beautifully hand polished. Has a door, and inside is nicely arranged with shelves for sheet music. Height, 38 inches; width, 18 inches. Weight, 60 pounds. **The stock is prettier than solid mahogany. Very ornamental.**

Price, each..........$4.35

No. 1R5368 Music Cabinet, veneered mahogany; also has French legs and carved panel, an exceedingly artistic and handsome ornament for the parlor. Height, 39 inches; width, 20 inches. Has a door with lock, and inside is nicely arranged with shelves for sheet music, also has upper drawer and lower shelf, highly polished. A beauty and a bargain at our price. Weight, 72 pounds.

Price, only.........$10.95

Fancy Chairs.

Upholstered Chair.

No 1R5450 This Handsome Chair is best known as the Napoleon Design, thoroughly well put together and very substantial. The size of the seat, which is upholstered in various grades of material, is 18 inches square. This article will be an ornament to any home, and is a most desirable purchase. We pack the chair very carefully for shipment. Weight, 25 lbs.

Price, upholstered in silk tapestry..........$2.72
Price, upholstered in brocatelle.............. 3.47
Price, upholstered in silk damask............ 3.72

Fancy Chair for $3.60.

No. 1R5455 A dainty, odd chair, with neat, graceful lines, made of curly birch, finished a rich mahogany color; back is finely carved and is handsomely covered in silk tapestry, damask or brocatelle. **A beautiful parlor decoration.**

Price, upholstered in velours..............$3.60
Price, upholstered in brocatelle 3.95
Price, upholstered in silk damask............$4.20

Shipping weight, about 25 pounds.

Special Value for $3.90.

No. 1R5459 Corner and Reception Chair. This illustration represents one of the handsomest corner reception chairs shown this season. The frame is of striking and original design, made of solid, thoroughly seasoned birch; finished dark mahogany; hand polished. It has a well made upholstered spring seat, making it an ornamental as well as a useful addition to the furnishing of any parlor. Weight, about 25 pounds.

Price, upholstered in B velours..............$3.90
Price, upholstered in brocatelle.............. 4.50
Price, upholstered in silk damask.............. 4.70

Roman Chair for $4.95.

No. 1R5468 Finished in imitation mahogany only. High back and arms, as illustrated in cut. Spring seat, upholstered in beautiful velours, silk tapestry, silk brocatelle or silk damask. Has beautiful marquetry transfer ornaments in the back, and is elegantly finished. It makes a very handsome parlor chair.

Price, upholstered in velours..............$4.95
Price, upholstered in mercerized tapestry...... 5.25
Price, upholstered in brocatelle..............$5.75
Price, upholstered in silk damask.............. 5.95

Shipping weight, about 25 pounds.

A $10.00 Roman Chair for $5.90.

No. 1R5472 A dainty, odd Roman Chair, having graceful, neat lines; at the same time, is a very comfortable chair; back is richly carved and has dainty light open work; is made of 5-ply selected birch and has artistic inlaid center piece; front is also richly carved, and has shaped spindles under the arms; is very strongly made and is finished a rich dark mahogany color; seat is handsomely biscuit tufted; is 33 inches high and 26 inches wide. Weight, about 25 lbs.

Price, upholstered in velours..............$5.90
Price, upholstered in silk tapestry.......... 6.75
Price, upholstered in silk damask.......... 6.95

Our Special $4.10 Ornamental Rocker.

No. 1R5474 At $4.10 to $5.20, according to upholstering, we offer this handsome new Rocker for this season as one of the most stylish rockers on the market, the equal of anything you can buy elsewhere at double the price. This rocker is a very ornamental piece of furniture, built on such lines as to afford not only the greatest amount of strength, but also give unusual beauty. Has large spring seat, well upholstered. The frame is of solid birch, finished in dark mahogany, given the highest possible finish; it is beautifully shaped, carved and decorated. Our special prices are as follows:

Upholstered in fine imported velours..........$4.10
Upholstered in fine imported silk tapestry... 4.20
Upholstered in fine imported silk brocatelle.. 4.95
Upholstered in fine imported silk damask.... 5.20

Shipping weight, about 25 pounds.

High Back Reception Chair

No. 1R5476 This beautiful little chair can be furnished in imitation mahogany only. It is a spring seat, nicely upholstered in fancy velours, brocatelle or silk damask. The back, as you will see by the illustration, is beautifully scrolled, sawed and carved and nicely finished. The chair is very neat in appearance, and cannot be excelled for the price as a parlor or reception chair. Weight, about 25 pounds.

Price, upholstered in velours..........................$3.95
Price, upholstered in mercerized tapestry.... 4.45
Price, upholstered in brocatelle.............. 4.95
Price, upholstered in silk damask.............. 5.45

Handsome $4.10 Rocker.

No. 1R5482 A new design, very ornamental. Built on such lines as to afford not only the **greatest amount of strength, but also giving unusual beauty. It has a large spring seat,** well upholstered. The frame is of solid birch, finished in dark mahogany. Shipping weight, 35 pounds.

Price, upholstered in B corduroy or velours.$4.10
Price, upholstered in G brocatelle............$4.45

$8.00 Upholstered Chair for $4.90.

No. 1R5492 This illustration represents our Students' Sleepy Hollow Chair. It is shaped so as to afford solid comfort; nicely tufted. It is an ideal reading chair. The frame is made of solid oak, finished antique.

Price, upholstered in A cotton tapestry.....$4.90
Price, upholstered in B corduroy velours...$5.30
Price, upholstered in D crushed plush.......$7.60
Price, upholstered in E silk tapestry......... 7.65

Also furnished as a Rocker for 75 cents extra.

Student Rocker.

No. 1R5522 This Handsome Rocker has a massive golden oak frame. Hand polish finish. Spring edges, spring seat and spring back. The chair is extra large and the back is high enough so that the tufted top, shown on chair, forms a head rest. Tufted front and top with the best tow and cotton top filling. Furnished in velours, French Gobelin tapestry, crushed plush, brocatelle and leather. **When made in leather the top is not tufted.** Shipping weight, 40 pounds.

Price, upholstered in velours..................$8.95
Price, upholstered in French Gobelin tapestry..........$ 9.54
Price, upholstered in crushed plush........ 9.75
Price, upholstered in imitation leather...... 9.95
Price, upholstered in genuine leather........ 12.25

Our $8.75 Library Rocker.

No. 1R5524 This illustration represents one of the latest and best designs of library rockers. The frame is of massive construction, so proportioned as to afford the greatest amount of comfort. It is beautifully upholstered, with a deep spring seat and spring back and top roll. This rocker may be had in golden oak. **We are offering this rocker at extraordinary low prices.** Weight, 75 pounds.

Price, upholstered in three-tone velours...$ 8.75
Price, upholstered in silk tapestry........... 9.50
Price, upholstered in best leather.......... 11.40

Our Home Comfort Rocker.

No. 1R5526 Massive frame, oak or mahogany finish, spring seat and back, well made of the best tempered steel springs and the best materials, roomy, durable and comfortable for parlor, library or living room. Weight, 90 pounds.

Price, upholstered in velours..........................$9.45
Price, upholstered in silk tapestry..........................$ 9.85
Price, upholstered in best leather............ 11.95

Magnificent Rocker for $10.98.

No. 1R5528 This is a Rocker that is without a doubt elegant enough for the best appointed home. We offer it at a price which brings it within the reach of all. Made of the finest quarter sawed golden oak, has beautiful carved feet, artistic design, fancy turned arm posts, broad shaped comfortable arms and upholstered with the finest materials, has full spring seat and back, and is unusually roomy and comfortable. Weight, 75 pounds.

Price, upholstered in three-tone velours....$10.98
Price, upholstered in silk tapestry.......... 11.90
Price, upholstered in Howell's best leather. 13.97

No. 1R5532 Arm Chair, same as above.

Price, upholstered in three-tone velours... $ 9.98
Price, upholstered in silk tapestry.......... 11.40
Price, upholstered in Howell's best leather. 13.35

A Marvel of Value at $17.95.

No. 1R5548 The acme of comfort is obtained in this large and comfortable easy chair or rocker; made of the best materials, such as tempered steel springs, hair and best leather covering. We are satisfied that this chair will be welcomed by those desiring an honest, well made and comfortable chair or rocker. Weight, 100 pounds.

Price, upholstered in 3-tone velours....$17.95
Price, upholstered in silk tapestry..........$19.90
Price, upholstered in genuine leather....... 25.98

Our $5.40 Divan.

No. 1R5556 Selected birch, finished a rich dark mahogany with piano polish, full spring seat and edge, back being trimmed with tufted border. **Size, 34 inches long, 22 inches wide, 38 inches high. Weight, 45 pounds.**

Price, upholstered in three-tone velours.....$5.40
Price, upholstered in silk tapestry............ 5.70
Price, upholstered in brocatelle............... 6.30
Price, upholstered in silk damask.............. 6.70

Be sure to state kind of upholstering you desire.

All Overstuffed Parlor Divan.

No. 1R5558 Divan, full spring seat, containing the best high carbon steel springs. It is large and roomy, measuring 40 inches wide, with deep overskirt wool fringe, brass ornaments and trimmings as shown in cut. Weight, 60 pounds.

Price, upholstered in velours...................$5.65
Price, upholstered in French Gobelin tapestry 5.95
Price, upholstered in mercerized tapestry... 6.45
Price, upholstered in brocatelle............... 7.95
Price, upholstered in damask.................. 8.45

Be sure to state style of upholstering desired.

Special Value Divan at $6.95 to $8.95.

No. 1R5560 Richly designed back, beautifully scrolled and inlaid with colored woods, gracefully shaped. Front arm reinforced with shaped spindles, made of selected birch, with a rich mahogany finish; made in the best manner, of the very best materials and all of the features are the latest; 40 inches long and 33 inches high. Weight, 45 pounds.

Price, upholstered in velours.....................$6.95
Price, upholstered in silk tapestry............ 7.75
Price, upholstered in silk brocatelle.......... 8.25
Price, upholstered in silk damask............. 8.95

All Overstuffed Divan.

No. 1R5562 Divan frame is of hardwood. Spring seat and spring edges, tufted front with a heavy ruffle all around back. The front is of the best tow and cotton top and contains a full set of high carbon, steel wire springs. With a deep overskirt wool fringe. This is no cheap shoddy stuff, but is high class in workmanship, design and material. Weight, 75 pounds.

Price, upholstered in velours...................$7.25
Price, upholstered in French Gobelin tapestry 7.65
Price, upholstered in mercerized tapestry.... 7.95
Price, upholstered in brocatelle............... 9.45
Price, upholstered in silk damask............. 9.95

When ordering be sure to state which kind of upholstering you desire.

Our Very Latest Morris Reclining Easy Chair, $4.25.

The back is adjustable; to four positions and has the very latest and most substantial adjustable attachment in use and is easily adjusted. The frame is substantially built and is large and roomy and can be furnished in golden oak or imitation mahogany, with reversible cushions and the best wood wool filling which makes the most substantial and lasting filling for Morris chair cushions. The frame is nicely carved and finished, as shown in cut. This style represents an exceptionally good value and the design is of the very latest, just gotten out for 1902. The shipping weight of the chair is 50 pounds and is shipped with back detached insuring the lowest freight rates. No household is complete without one of these comfortable chairs. They will wear a lifetime as the cushions can be reversed when worn on one side. Size between the arms, 21 inches. The length of the back cushion is 30 inches which forms the regular large size Morris chair. Upholstered in the best grade high colored velours.

No. 1R5570 Our special price...................$4.25

Our $4.95 Morris Easy Reclining Chair.

This new design of Morris easy reclining chair has been mounted on an especially handsome frame of extra weight, with specially made cushions of extra weight and quality, to supply the demand of those who wish something even finer than our special $4.25 Morris Chair. **We offer it at $4.95,** just enough to cover the cost of manufacturing, with but our one small percentage of profit added. **It is the equal of chairs that sell everywhere at more than double the price.** From this large illustration you can get some idea of the rich appearance produced in this chair. The frame is of very heavy solid oak or curly birch, finished in golden oak or imitation mahogany as desired; one of the largest, heaviest, strongest and handsomest Morris chair frames made. The cushions are reversible, they are made extra heavy and are filled with the most substantial filling, and the covering is of an extra quality of the very latest effect high colored velours and both sides of cushions are alike. The back is adjustable, can be adjusted to any position. Shipping weight, 50 pounds.

No. 1R5574 Price, upholstered in high colored velours.....................................$4.95

An Excellent Morris Chair for $5.45.

We offer this new style Morris chair as the greatest value ever shown in a Morris chair; the equal of chairs that sell everywhere at double the price and more. We feel we are furnishing in this, the greatest value ever shown in this kind of a chair, a chair you must see, examine and compare with chairs that others sell at double the price, to appreciate the value. This illustration will give you some idea of the appearance of this new, handsome 1902 Morris Chair, a chair made with reversible seat and back cushion; cushion can be removed; has the very latest adjustable reclining back, which can be adjusted for any position. This chair is made of the finest especially selected solid golden oak; extra heavy, elaborately carved front panel and legs; handsomely turned spindles; reversible loose cushions, upholstered in the highest style of the art in fine imported three-tone velours, the most comfortable and easy chair made. Shipping weight, 50 pounds.

No. 1R5576 Price, in high colored velours. $5.45

Our $6.45 High Grade Morris Chair.

This our special high grade Morris chair is of an extra massive frame, which is put together in the most substantial manner. The wood is of a selected quarter sawed oak or birch, finished in either golden oak or mahogany. This chair you will find is one of the greatest values ever shown in a Morris chair. The finish is an extra high hand polish. This illustration will give you some idea of the appearance of this handsome 1902 Morris chair. This chair is made by a factory that makes nothing but high grade furniture and through a large contract we have made we are able to offer this chair at such a low price and cannot be bought elsewhere for twice the amount. The cushions are reversible, both sides alike, and can be removed if desired. The filling is of the very best quality and covering is of the very latest effect in high colored velours. The back is adjustable to any angle and we especially recommend this chair as a most comfortable and substantial piece of furniture. The chair is securely packed and the weight complete ready for shipment is 60 pounds.

No. 1R5578 Our special price, upholstered in high colored velours...............................$6.45

Department of Upholstered Furniture.

THIS DEPARTMENT has been greatly enlarged and improved, and following the very latest styles in upholstery, in frame work, covering and making, we present this new line of goods at prices based on the actual cost to produce, the cost of material and labor, with but our one small percentage of profit added, prices from which practically all advertising expense has been deducted, all made possible by getting paid in advance 50 cents each for our large catalogues, and as a result you can buy from us anything in upholstered furniture, couches, chairs or parlor suites, at such prices as can be had from no other house, greater value than any dealer can obtain, even if bought in car load lots.

OUR GUARANTEE AND REFUND OFFER. We will accept your order and money with the understanding that when you receive the goods, if they do not reach you in the same perfect condition they leave us, or if for any reason whatever you are not satisfied with your purchase, you are not convinced you have received from us such value as you could not possibly get elsewhere, you can return the goods to us at our expense of freight charges both ways and we will return your money.

OUR UPHOLSTERED FURNITURE is made for us under contract by one of the best makers. Only the most skilled mechanics are employed. We have followed the very latest styles, to give our customers the same style and grade of goods that are handled by the most fashionable city retail furniture dealers, where they are usually sold at fancy prices.

IN THE FRAME WORK, the coverings, the springs, the canvas and stuffing, we use a higher grade of goods, a better class of material than is used by the average maker of upholstery, and you will find an upholstered couch, chair, divan, or other piece you may buy of us will have a distinctiveness in style, workmanship and finish not found in the ordinary grade of goods. You will find our goods more lasting, more satisfactory, and at least one-third lower in price than anything furnished by others that will approach our goods in general appearance and style.

ABOUT THE FREIGHT. Most railroad companies accept upholstered furniture at one and one-half times first class freight rates. By referring to pages 7 to 10 you can get the first class freight rate for 100 pounds to a point near you. The rate to your place would be almost, if not exactly, the same, and as the weight is given under each description, you can calculate almost exactly what the freight will amount to on any piece or suite to your town. You will find it will amount to next to nothing as compared to what you will save in price.

UNDERSTAND, if we cannot furnish you anything you wish in upholstered furniture at a much lower price than you can possibly buy it elsewhere, we do not wish you to keep the goods. If you order a couch, chair or suite from us and after you receive it you do not find it is of far greater value than you can get elsewhere, very much cheaper than you can buy from any house that furnishes catalogues free, or for 5, 10 or 15 cents in postage, you can return the goods to us and we will immediately return your money together with any freight charges paid.

EVERY PARLOR SUITE IS MADE UP SPECIAL, and we therefore require from seven to ten days after the order is received before we can make shipment.

IN ORDERING, BE SURE TO STATE STYLE OF UPHOLSTERING AND IF SINGLE PIECE OR COMPLETE SUITE IS WANTED.

Our New $9.95 Three-Piece Parlor Suite.

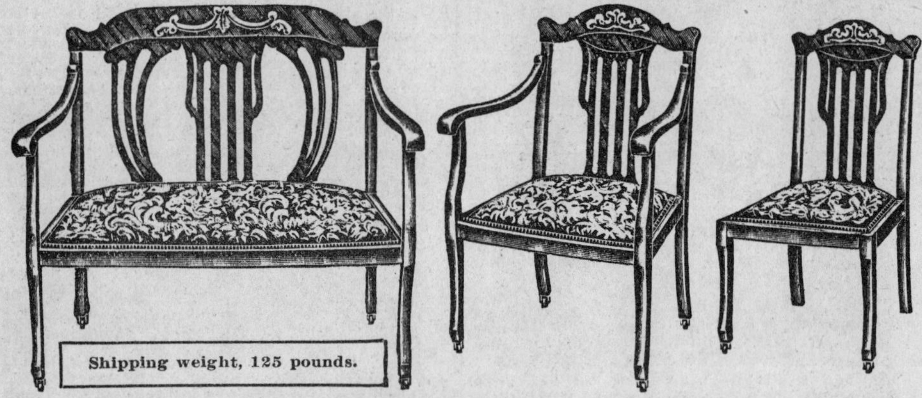

Shipping weight, 125 pounds.

AT $9.95 TO $11.95, according to covering, we offer this new design in a handsome three-piece parlor suite, consisting of....

DIVAN, ARM CHAIR AND PARLOR CHAIR,

in one of the newest, tastiest, neatest and altogether handsomest effects for this season. In offering this suite at

$9.95 TO $11.95

we assure our customers that they are buying these goods at less than dealers can buy in any quantity. They come from our own factory in this city, and you own them at just what they cost to build, the cost of material and labor, with but our one small percentage of profit added.

OUR NEW THREE-PIECE PARLOR SUITES, consisting of divan, arm chair and parlor chair, the pattern is very neat and attractive, is handsomely ornamented, is made of the finest birch with a rich mahogany finish. Spring seats, containing full set of high carbon steel springs supported by steel wire.

PRICES FOR COMPLETE SUITE OF THREE PIECES.

No. 1R6002	Upholstered n High Colored Velours	$ 9.95
No. 1R6004	Upholstered in Crushed Plush	10.40
No. 1R6006	Upholstered in Mercerized Tapestry	10.55
No. 1R6008	Upholstered in Silk Brocatelle	11.40
No. 1R6010	Upholstered in Silk Damask	11.95

PRICES FOR SINGLE PIECES.

	Colored Velours	Crushed Plush	Mercerized Tapestry	Silk Brocatelle	Silk Damask
Divan	$4.65	$4.90	$4.95	$5.55	$5.75
Arm Chair	2.95	3.10	3.15	3.30	3.45
Reception Chair	2.35	2.40	2.45	2.55	2.75

$12.40 Buys an $18.00 Three-Piece Parlor Suite.

THE DESIGN of this beautiful Three-Piece Parlor Suite is the latest for this season, and one of the handsomest that has been produced by any manufacturer. It is after the style of the very expensive $75.00 or $100.00 three-piece suites sold by the most exclusive retail stores in large cities, and will ordinarily be taken for a suite which will retail at $50.00.

WE MAKE this suite of the best selected birch, and being finished in handsome mahogany finish, it is extremely elegant in appearance. The mahogany finish and birch is preferred by many to genuine mahogany, and of course the difference in cost to make is very much less. The illustrations will give you some idea of the handsome hand carving and beautiful decorations.

The arm posts are graceful in design, and the entire suite is made by experienced workmen, who use great care to add strength to the various pieces without detracting from the beauty of the design. Each piece has the best steel springs, with upholstery in a variety of styles, which you may select to your entire satisfaction.

WE UPHOLSTER THIS SUITE in a variety of popular colors, and will have each suite covered with the same colored upholstering or each piece of a harmonizing color, as you may desire. We would advise your leaving the selection of colors to our designer, who will follow your tastes to your entire satisfaction. Each piece comes complete with a full set of the best casters. All parlor suites are carefully inspected before they leave the house, and we undertake to avoid any possible dissatisfaction by seeing that in no way shall there be any defect or imperfection in any single piece.

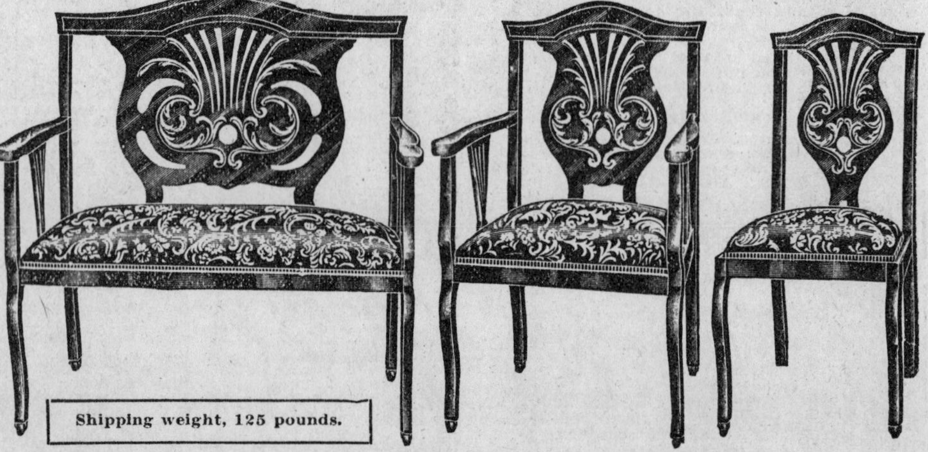

Shipping weight, 125 pounds.

PRICES FOR COMPLETE SUITE OF THREE PIECES.

No. 1R6020	Upholstered in High Colored Velours	$12.40
No. 1R6022	Upholstered in Crushed Plush	13.20
No. 1R6024	Upholstered in Mercerized Tapestry	13.35
No. 1R6026	Upholstered in Silk Brocatelle	14.25
No. 1R6028	Upholstered in Silk Damask	14.65

PRICES FOR SINGLE PIECES.

	Colored Velours	Crushed Plush	Mercerized Tapestry	Silk Brocatelle	Silk Damask
Divan	$6.10	$6.40	$6.45	$7.05	$7.25
Arm Chair	3.85	4.10	4.15	4.35	4.45
Reception Chair	2.45	2.70	2.75	2.85	2.95

OUR SPECIAL HIGH BACK AND HIGH ARM ROMAN DESIGN 3-PIECE SUITE.

All suites are carefully packed so as to insure safe delivery and to avoid any possible damages in transit. The suite is carefully inspected by a special inspector before it is packed up for shipment. Weight, 125 pounds.

THIS HANDSOME SUITE is made of the best selected kiln dried birch, finished in a handsome mahogany finish. The varnish is not merely laid on but is rubbed and polished and shows up the same as you will find on the highest grade pianos. The high back and high arm effect of the sofa and arm chair will only be found in the highest class of fancy furniture. The wood work in the backs is beautifully hand carved and scrolled. The arm supports and front posts are graceful and neat in appearance. **The strength and wearing qualities have all been maintained in this suite.** Each piece has a full set of steel springs, drawn from a high carbon wire and are supported by steel corrugated wires, which is the only substantial method in use today. The filling is of the very best quality and the upholstering is in the varieties and coloring such as you may choose according to the prices offered below. In ordering please state the choice of coloring, but we would advise you to leave the harmonizing to our specialist at such work as he is most certain to please you.

PRICES FOR COMPLETE SUITE OF THREE PIECES:

No. 1R6040	Upholstered in High Colored Velours	$16.45
No. 1R6042	Upholstered in Crushed Plush	17.10
No. 1R6044	Upholstered in Mercerized Tapestry	17.25
No. 1R6046	Upholstered in Silk Brocatelle	18.95
No. 1R6048	Upholstered in Silk Damask	19.35

PRICES FOR SINGLE PIECES:

	Colored Velours	Crushed Plush	Mercerized Tapestry	Silk Brocatelle	Silk Damask
Sofa	$8.15	$8.45	$8.50	$9.45	$9.60
Arm Chair	5.15	5.35	5.40	5.95	6.10
Reception Chair	3.15	3.30	3.35	3.55	3.65

OUR $17.55 GENUINE TURKISH THREE-PIECE PARLOR SUITE.

THIS ELEGANT THREE-PIECE TURKISH PARLOR SUITE consists of one tete-a-tete, one gents' easy chair, and one parlor or reception chairs, three pieces, and all these pieces are made in extra large size, with extra high backs and large comfortable seats, and are the very latest designs. The upholstering or covering of this suite is the latest design or pattern of imported goods; each piece is covered with a different color; the suite is beautifully upholstered with tufted plush bands on upper backs, and trimmed with a heavy worsted fringe. The suite is made with the best springs and spring edges, and every piece is made with spring back. This is, without doubt, one of the best parlor suites put on the market at the price we ask, and will be an ornament to any home.

YOU WOULD GET NOTHING FINER if you were to go to the best store in the city and pay double the price.

PRICES FOR COMPLETE SUITE OF THREE PIECES, SOFA, ARM CHAIR AND RECEPTION CHAIR:

No. 1R6060	Upholstered in High Colored Velours	$17.55
No. 1R6062	Upholstered in French Gobelin Tapestry	18.60
No. 1R6064	Upholstered in Crushed Plush	19.70
No. 1R6066	Upholstered in Mercerized Tapestry	20.10
No. 1R6068	Upholstered in Silk Brocatelle	22.25
No. 1R6070	Upholstered in Silk Damask	23.65

PRICES FOR SINGLE PIECES:

	Colored Velours	French Gobelin Tapestry	Crushed Plush	Mercerized Tapestry	Silk Brocatelle	Silk Damask
Sofa	$8.40	$8.85	$9.25	$9.45	$10.60	$10.95
Arm Chair	5.40	5.80	6.30	6.40	7.25	7.85
Rocker	6.15	6.45	6.95	7.10	8.10	8.40
Reception Chair	3.75	3.95	4.15	4.25	4.70	4.85

OUR NEW SPECIAL $12.45 FIVE-PIECE FRAMED UPHOLSTERED PARLOR SUITE.

THIS FIVE-PIECE SUITE consists of one large sofa, one large rocker, one large easy chair and two parlor chairs. The illustration shows the sofa, the rocker, the easy chair and one of the two parlor chairs.

THIS SUITE is made on new improved frames for this season, extra strong, hardwood frames, finished in imitation mahogany which wears fully as good as genuine mahogany wood. Each piece is upholstered in a different coloring, five different shades to harmonize perfectly. Each piece has spring seat, the springs being made of the best tempered steel. The finish is unusually high for a suite at so low a price.

PRICES FOR COMPLETE SUITE OF FIVE PIECES:

No. 1R6080	Upholstered in High Colored Velours	$12.45
No. 1R6082	Upholstered in French Gobelin Tapestry	13.70
No. 1R6084	Upholstered in Crushed Plush	14.20
No. 1R6086	Upholstered in Mercerized Tapestry	14.40
No. 1R6088	Upholstered in Silk Brocatelle	15.75
No. 1R6090	Upholstered in Silk Damask	16.80

PRICES FOR SINGLE PIECES:

	Colored Velours	French Gobelin Tapestry	Crushed Plush	Mercerized Tapestry	Silk Brocatelle	Silk Damask
Sofa	$3.95	$4.25	$4.45	$4.50	$4.95	$5.30
Arm Chair	2.20	2.45	2.45	2.55	2.85	2.95
Rocker	3.20	3.45	3.65	3.65	3.75	3.95
Reception Chair	1.55	1.75	1.80	1.85	2.10	2.30

SHIPPED DIRECT FROM OUR FACTORY, NEAR CHICAGO, FROM WHICH POINT THE CUSTOMER PAYS THE FREIGHT.

OUR $14.95 5-PIECE UPHOLSTERED PARLOR SUITE.

AT $14.95 we offer this parlor suite as the greatest value ever furnished in this line.

HOW WE CAN MAKE THIS HERETOFORE UNHEARD OF PRICE of $14.95 is fully explained under the heading of new designs in High Grade Couches. It is made in the one factory that makes nothing but these suites and our upholstered couches. Our $14.95 price is below the lowest wholesale price, much lower than dealers can buy in the largest quantities.

BELOW WE QUOTE PRICES ON **SINGLE PIECES,** making it possible to order a **THREE-PIECE, FOUR-PIECE OR SIX-PIECE SUITE.**

$14.95

THESE SUITES are made on the very latest style hardwood frames. They are made extra strong, extra well braced throughout. Springs are the genuine Eagleton highest grade tempered steel springs. The suite is upholstered in the highest style of the art. We use the genuine Welton three-tone velours upholstering cloth and imported French Gobelin tapestry in the very latest style patterns and colorings, at least three different shades in each suite, all harmonizing perfectly. Each piece is fully overstuffed, handsomely decorated and finished, with deep fringe, fancy binding, and decorated with a handsome rococo brass gimp ornamentation.

PRICES FOR COMPLETE SUITE OF FIVE PIECES:

No. 1R6094 Upholstered in High Colored Velours.........$14.95
No. 1R6096 Upholstered in French Gobelin Tapestry..... 16.40

PRICES FOR SINGLE PIECES:

	Colored Velours	French Gobelin Tapestry
Sofa	$4.75	$5.25
Arm Chair	3.00	3.25
Rocker	3.65	3.90
Reception Chair	1.75	1.95

THIS SUITE CONSISTS OF THE FOLLOWING FIVE HANDSOME PIECES: One large sofa, 36 inches high, 23 inches wide and 52 inches long; one large rocker, 33 inches high and 28 inches wide; one large easy chair, 34 inches high, 28 inches wide; and two large parlor chairs, each 31 inches high and 20 inches wide. Weight, packed for shipment, 200 pounds.

THIS BEAUTIFUL 5-PIECE $30.00 PARLOR SUITE FOR $15.45

OUR PRICE OF $15.45 on this suite represents little or nothing beyond the actual cost of material and labor in the making of this suite, with but a small profit added. In offering this suite to our customers at $15.45 we have cut off the profits of the middlemen and in shipping direct from the factory, give you the benefit of direct factory prices. We put you in a position to buy direct from the factory, in the same position that the dealer is in who buys from the jobbers before selling to you. The saving of these various profits is for your benefit.

THE FRAME is made of the very best hardwood, handsomely decorated with hand carvings, beautifully finished and polished, and in every point of appearance attention has been given that no detail shall be overlooked whereby the suite shall be less finished and artistic than it should be.

EACH PIECE of this beautiful parlor suite has spring edge and the seats are fitted with the very best steel springs, supported by steel corrugated wires in place of webbing which sags and tears so easily and leaves the springs down. The bottom is open to plain view and ventilation. The quality of the springs has been looked to, insuring lasting quality. In buying many of the cheap suites sold by retail dealers, the outside appearance will very frequently catch the eye and the entire making of the suite has been handled with a view to giving everything to appearance and little of anything to durability. In every detail of construction, in every piece and part that enters into this beautiful parlor suite great care has been exercised that nothing but the best materials, best wood, best upholstering, best springs, etc., shall be used.

$15.45

IN THE MAKING ...OF... UPHOLSTERED FURNITURE

two classes of workmen are employed, those who work on cheap, shoddy furniture and those who work on the higher grade goods, and it is this latter class of workmen who have been employed on this special parlor suite. This insures to you not only a handsome appearance but durability, both of which features are essential in SECURING PARLOR FURNITURE OF WHICH YOU WILL BE PROUD.

—)●(—

THIS FIVE-PIECE SET . . .

consists of a large sofa, 48 inches long; one large rocker, 24 inches wide; one large easy chair, 24 inches wide; and two large parlor chairs. The extreme height of the sofa is 38 inches. Weight, packed for shipment, 175 pounds.

SAMPLES.

If you want samples send 5 cents and we will send you samples of three-tone velours, crushed plush, silk tapestry, brocatelle or silk damask. In sending for samples, be sure to state just what you want.

...$15.45 TO $21.45...

IT IS BEAUTIFUL IN DESIGN, a style that is exceedingly popular in large cities and found in the best retail stores. Neither time nor money has been spared in elaborating on the pattern to make it tasty and desirable in every respect.

ABOUT THE FREIGHT. THIS SUITE weighs, when packed for shipment, about 175 pounds. The freight will be very little when compared with what we save you on the price of the suite.

...UPHOLSTERING...

We upholster this suite with the materials as stated below. The upholstering is done by the highest class mechanics that can be employed and the stylish appearance of the suite is the result of not only a special quality of upholstering material, but of the expertness of the workmen employed.

PRICES FOR COMPLETE SUITE OF FIVE PIECES:

No. 1R6149 Upholstered in Colored Velours $15.45
No. 1R6150 Upholstered in French Gobelin Tapestry 17.55
No. 1R6152 Upholstered in Crushed Plush..... 18.40
No. 1R6154 Upholstered in Mercerized Tapestry 18.75
No. 1R6156 Upholstered in Silk Brocatelle..... 20.25
No. 1R6158 Upholstered in Silk Damask....... 21.45

PRICES FOR SINGLE PIECES:

	Colored Velours	French Gobelin Tapestry	Crushed Plush	Mercerized Tapestry	Silk Brocatelle	Silk Damask
Sofa	$4.95	$5.45	$5.70	$5.80	$6.45	$6.95
Arm Chair	2.85	3.15	3.45	3.50	3.85	3.95
Rocker	3.75	4.25	4.35	4.45	4.75	4.95
Reception Chair	1.95	2.35	2.45	2.50	2.60	2.80

OUR $19.70 SWELL SUITE.

IN OFFERING THIS HANDSOME FIVE-PIECE SUITE TO YOU AT $19.70 we believe that no such value has ever been offered before by us or any concern. The frames are substantially made of the **best selected birch with fine mahogany finish.** The mahogany finish on birch is very popular. **It gives the same general effect as genuine mahogany,** and is very much less expensive; at the same time the material is lasting and durable, and you have the same strength as you would have in genuine mahogany furniture. **The beautiful carving on the back** of each piece is very decorative in effect and adds greatly to the desirability of the furniture. **Each piece has extra soft spring seat** and spring edge supported with steel corrugated wires in place where all others use the troublesome webbing which sags and tears and the springs go down. This steel bottom prevents all this trouble: we use heavy duck cloth over springs. Bottom is left open to air and ventilation and leaves no chance for moths. Price upholstered in the various grades quoted below. The back panels are of artistic design and the upper bands are tufted in silk plush, making a very effective finish. **The suite consists of a large sofa, 48 inches wide; large rocker, 24 inches wide; large easy chair, 24 inches wide; two large parlor chairs, 19½ inches wide, one only being illustrated.**

PRICES FOR SINGLE PIECES:

	Colored Velours	French Gobelin Tapestry	Crushed Plush	Mercerized Tapestry	Silk Brocatelle	Silk Damask
Sofa	$6.45	$6.75	$6.95	$7.00	$7.85	$8.25
Arm Chair	3.55	3.75	3.95	4.10	4.35	4.65
Rocker	4.60	4.85	4.95	5.10	5.40	5.75
Reception Chair	2.55	2.75	2.90	3.00	3.25	3.45

PRICES FOR COMPLETE SUITE OF FIVE PIECES:

No. 1R6170 Upholstered in High Colored Velours **$19.70**

No. 1R6172 Upholstered in French Gobelin Tapestry ... **$20.85**

No. 1R6174 Upholstered in Crushed Plush **$21.70**

No. 1R6176 Upholstered in Mercerized Tapestry **$22.20**

No. 1R6178 Upholstered in Silk Brocatelle **$24.10**

No. 1R6180 Upholstered in Silk Damask **$25.55**

The weight of the suite when packed ready for shipment is about 180 pounds.

We pack the suite with care and use every pains that the goods may reach you in perfect condition.

OUR BIG FIVE-PIECE $20.75 LEADER.

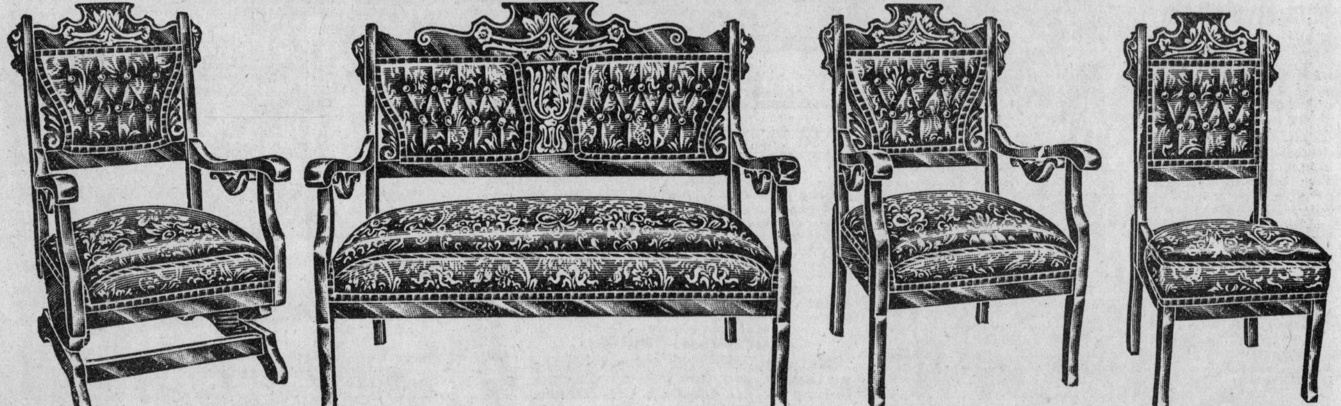

THE FRAMES ARE MADE in solid birch imitation mahogany. The frames are beautifully carved, decorated and ornamented, all the wood is thoroughly seasoned, carefully fitted, glued, screwed, braced and plugged. The illustrations will give you some idea of the ornamentation. They are very highly polished and finished, and are equal to anything you can buy anywhere regardless of price.

THIS FIVE-PIECE SUITE consists of one large sofa, one large rocker, one large arm chair, and two reception chairs, only one being shown in the illustration. We exercise great care in packing these pieces so as to insure safe delivery. The entire suite packed for shipment weighs 175 pounds. The small amount of freight which you have to pay on this will be no comparison to the saving on the price.

PRICES FOR COMPLETE SUITE OF FIVE PIECES:

No. 1R6202	Upholstered in High Colored Velours	$20.75
No. 1R6204	Upholstered in French Gobelin Tapestry	21.70
No. 1R6206	Upholstered in Crushed Plush	22.60
No. 1R6208	Upholstered in Mercerized Tapestry	23.05
No. 1R6210	Upholstered in Silk Brocatelle	25.10
No, 1R6212	Upholstered in Silk Damask	25.90

UPHOLSTERING. **These special suites are upholstered in the best possible manner.** We furnish them upholstered in different materials at the prices quoted. In the upholstering nothing but the very best grades of springs are used, including full spring seats and edges the springs being supported by a steel corrugated wire, in place of webbing, which is generally used by other parties, and which so easily gives way and leaves down the whole seat of the chair. We use a heavy duck canvas over the springs in place of burlap, which is so commonly used, and which is very undesirable on account of its poor wearing qualities. The bottom of each piece is left open to air and ventilation. The inner construction of the suite can be plainly seen from the bottom.

THE BACKS **of this suite are diamond tufted, as shown in the illustration.** This can only be found in the highest grade furniture such as this suite represents.

PRICES FOR SINGLE PIECES:

	Colored Velours	French Gobelin Tapestry	Crushed Plush	Mercerized Tapestry	Silk Brocatelle	Silk Damask
Sofa	$6.95	$7.20	$7.45	$7.60	$8.45	$8.70
Arm Chair	3.75	3.95	3.95	4.05	4.40	4.45
Rocker	4.95	5.20	5.40	5.40	5.85	5.95
Reception Chair	2.55	2.70	2.90	3.00	3.20	3.40

OUR CROCKERY AND GLASSWARE DEPARTMENT.

WE SHOW ON THIS AND THE FOLLOWING PAGES such an assortment of strictly high grade ware as will seldom be found in any retail stores, except in large cities, a grade of goods that is made by potteries of world wide reputation, potteries celebrated for making only the best.

WE ARE ONLY TOO ANXIOUS to have these goods compared with anything that you can buy at retail, or from any other concern. We are satisfied we can save you 50 per cent in your crockery purchases. Such sets as we sell for $4.98, $5.98, $6.89, $7.75 and other prices, are positively equal to sets that often sell at retail at twice the price; they are the very latest and most attractive designs on the market, none of the old fashioned patterns and styles of decoration such as dealers have been accustomed to carrying in their stores for years.

IN BUYING ONE OF THESE DINNER SETS FROM US you obtain them at the bare cost of material and labor, with but our one small profit added; you buy them from us under our binding guarantee that they shall be found as represented or we will cheerfully refund your money.

WE PACK EACH SET VERY CAREFULLY in barrels or crates and we seldom if ever hear of any breakage.

DISHES ARE CARRIED BY NEARLY ALL RAILROAD companies at second class rate and the 100-piece set weighs, barreled, about 100 pounds. The second class rate averages from 40 to 50 cents per 100 pounds for 500 miles. By referring to pages 7 to 10 you can get the second class freight rate to the point nearest you, which will be almost exactly the same as to your town, and thus you can figure very close to what your freight will amount to. It will amount to nothing as compared to what you will save in price.

OUR $4.98 100-PIECE, AMERICAN MADE, SEMI-VITREOUS CHINA DINNER SET.

THIS SET is the highest grade genuine semi-vitreous china; as hard as flint; goods that will stand an unusual amount of hard service. Pure white in color, and guaranteed not to craze. Very latest shape, as shown in illustration, making a set in white suitable for any house. From the accompanying illustration you can form some idea of the appearance of this beautiful 100-PIECE WHITE SEMI-VITREOUS CHINA DINNER SET, but you must see it to appreciate the value we are offering. We believe it the handsomest shaped white dinner set in the market.

THIS 100-PIECE SET CONSISTS OF THE FOLLOWING PIECES:

12 Soup Plates
12 Plates, 5-inch
12 Plates, 7-inch
12 Coffee Cups
12 Saucers
12 Individual Butters
12 Fruit Plates, 3-inch
1 Platter, 8-inch
1 Platter, 12-inch
1 Baker, 7-inch
1 Baker, 8-inch
1 Covered Dish, 8-inch, (2 pieces)
1 Pickle Dish
1 Sauce Boat
1 Covered Butter Dish (3 pieces)
1 Sugar Bowl (2 pieces)
1 Extra Bowl
1 Large Pitcher
1 Medium Pitcher.

Packed in barrels and shipped direct from the pottery in Eastern Ohio, from which point customer pays freight.

No. 2R301 Our special price, 100-piece set complete.......... **$4.98**

$5.98 FOR A 100-PIECE WAVERLY SEMI-PORCELAIN DINNER SET.

Shipped from our pottery in Ohio.

FOR $5.98 WE OFFER THIS HANDSOMELY DECORATED 100-PIECE DINNER SET IN THE VERY LATEST STYLE PATTERN DECORATION, AND AS THE EQUAL OF SETS THAT RETAIL AT MORE THAN DOUBLE THE PRICE.

FOR A HANDSOME MEDIUM PRICE 100-PIECE SET, order this, our special $5.98 set. If you do not find it fully up to your expectation and entirely satisfactory return it to us at our expense and we will cheerfully refund your money.

AT $5.98 we furnish this set just as illustrated in the accompanying picture. It is carefully packed for shipment in a barrel and delivered on board the cars at the pottery in Ohio, and the entire set weighs about 80 pounds. The freight will range from 30 to 75 cents for the first 500 miles, and no difference how far away you live, our prices are so very low that the freight will be a very small item when compared with what we save you in price.

DESCRIPTION OF OUR $5.98 100-PIECE DINNER SET.

This set comes beautifully decorated in green, blue or brown in a handsome design as illustrated. This 100-piece set consists of the following pieces:

12 Tea Cups with handles
12 Tea Saucers
12 Dinner Plates
12 Breakfast Plates
12 Tea or Pie Plates
12 Sauce Plates
12 Butter Plates
1 Medium Platter
1 Large Platter
1 Open Vegetable Dish
2 Covered Vegetable Dishes (4 pieces)
1 Sugar Bowl (2 pieces)
1 Cream Pitcher
1 Pickle Dish
1 Slop Bowl
1 Covered Butter Dish (3 pieces)
1 Sauce Boat
100 pieces in all.

REMEMBER, WE GUARANTEE OUR DINNER SETS NOT TO CRAZE.

We guarantee that, quality considered, size and assortment, you will be able to find no such price elsewhere, and we will be only too glad to have you compare our prices with any other prices you will be able to get, and we feel sure that measuring quality with quality, style with style and price with price, you cannot do otherwise than favor us with your order.

No. 2R304 Waverly 100-Piece Dinner Set, our special price.. **$5.98**

OUR HOLBEIN 56-PIECE DINNER SET FOR $4.55.

WE ARE OFFERING FOR $4.55 a 56-piece set identically the same pattern and the style of decoration as shown in the illustration of the 100-piece dinner set above. This 56-piece set is identical in every respect with the 100-piece set, except that the assortment is smaller. The decoration is either blue, green or brown, as you may desire, and, like our 100-piece dinner set, the pieces are warranted not to craze. The 56-piece dinner set consists of the following assortment:

6 Tea Cups
6 Tea Saucers
6 Plates, 7-inch
6 Plates, 6-inch
6 Plates, 5-inch
6 Fruit Saucers, 4-inch
6 Individual Butters
1 Platter, 8-inch
1 Platter, 10-inch
1 Open Vegetable Dish, 7-inch
1 Covered Vegetable Dish, 8-inch (2 pieces)
1 Cream Pitcher
1 Sauce Boat
1 Pickle Dish
1 Covered Butter Dish (3 pieces)
1 Slop Bowl
1 Covered Sugar Bowl (2 pieces)
56 pieces in all.

No. 2R305 Our Holbein 56-Piece Dinner Set, Our special price.......... **$4.55**

PREMIER DINNER SET.

$6.89

MADE BY WOOD & SONS, ENGLAND.

THIS SET IS A GOOD QUALITY OF ENGLISH SEMI-PORCELAIN WARE. The decoration is printed under the glaze, and consists of a handsome border design. If you want a good serviceable dinner set at a low price this set will surely suit you. We can furnish this set in any of the following colors: Dark blue, green or brown. When ordering kindly specify color you desire.

SET CONSISTS OF 100 PIECES, AS FOLLOWS:

12 Dinner Plates
12 Breakfast Plates
12 Tea Plates
12 Sauce Plates
12 Individual Butter Plates
12 Tea Cups
12 Tea Saucers
1 Open Vegetable Dish
2 Covered Vegetable Dishes (4-pieces)
1 Platter, 10-inch
1 Platter, 12-inch
1 Sugar Bowl (2 pieces)
1 Cream Pitcher
1 Pickle Dish
1 Bowl
1 Covered Butter Dish (3 pieces)
1 Sauce Boat

Complete 100-piece set, packed in barrel; shipping weight, 80 pounds.

No. 2R308 Our special price.. **$6.89**

ADELPHI DINNER SET.

$7.75

MANUFACTURED BY W. H. GRINDLEY & CO., TUNSTALL, ENGLAND.

THIS SET IS A PURE WHITE WITH A BRILLIANT GLAZE. Every piece modeled in beautiful outlines. The ware is embossed with a dainty scroll design, which has heretofore been the distinguishing feature of Haviland china. To better realize this wonderfu' bargain, we quote the price of Haviland plain white dinner set of the same number of pieces as our Adelphi set, the price of which would be $19.82.

THIS SET CONSISTS OF 100 PIECES, AS FOLLOWS:

12 Dinner Plates
12 Breakfast Plates
12 Tea Plates
12 Sauce Plates
12 Individual Butter Plates
12 Tea Cups
12 Tea Saucers
1 Platter, 10-inch
1 Covered Vegetable Dish (2 pieces)
1 Oval Open Vegetable Dish
1 Round Open Vegetable Dish
1 Covered Sugar Bowl (2 pieces)
1 Platter, 12-inch
1 Sauce Boat
1 Pickle Dish
1 Slop Bowl
1 Covered Butter Dish (3 pieces)
1 Quart Size Pitcher
1 Cream Pitcher

Complete 100-piece set, packed in barrel; shipping weight, 100 pounds.

No. 2R312 Our special price.. **$7.75**

In addition to the regular set quoted above, we can furnish the following pieces:

Coffee Cups and Saucers. Per dozen.........$1.46 | Soup Plates, regular deep shape. Per dozen....94c | Soup Plates, new coupe shape. Per dozen......99c

OUR GLENMORE ROSE DINNER SET FOR $8.45.

$8.45

THE GLENMORE DINNER SET as illustrated is the best quality American made china, made by a pottery known for its unusually high quality of goods. The decorations of our Glenmore set are not the usual printed or colored decorations shown by other dealers, but are put on by the decalcomanie process, being a much truer and finer reproduction of the flowers than the ordinary print. The colors are beautiful rose and green floral design, and all handles, knobs and covers are beautifully traced with gold, which together with the floral decorations give this set a very beautiful appearance. The decorations are so put on that with ordinary wear they will last a lifetime. Guaranteed not to craze.

THIS 100-PIECE DINNER SET COMES IN THE FOLLOWING ASSORTMENT:

12 Dinner Plates
12 Breakfast Plates
12 Tea Plates
12 Sauce Plates
12 Individual Butter Plates
12 Tea Cups
12 Tea Saucers
1 Platter, 10-inch
1 Platter, 12-inch
1 Covered Vegetable Dish (2 pieces)
1 Oval Open Vegetable Dish
1 Round Open Vegetable Dish
1 Covered Sugar Bowl (2 pieces)
1 Sauce Boat
1 Pickle Dish
1 Slop Bowl
1 Covered Butter Dish (3 pieces)
1 Quart Size Pitcher
1 Cream Pitcher

Complete 100-piece set packed in a barrel and shipped direct from the pottery in Western Pennsylvania. Shipping weight, about 90 pounds.

No. 2R314 Our special price.. **$8.45**

In addition to the regular set quoted above, we furnish the following pieces:

Coffee Cups and Saucers. Per dozen.........$1.38 | Soup Plates, regular deep shape. Per dozen..$1.23 | Soup Plates, new coupe shape. Per dozen.......99c

OUR $7.90 DAVIDSON TAYLOR & CO.'S 100-PIECE SEMI-PORCELAIN DINNER SET.

THIS NEW DESIGN from the Davidson, Taylor & Co.'s potteries will be considered a bargain at even double our direct from pottery price, $7.90. It means that you are securing a strictly high class, hand finished dinner set of 100 pieces at the bare cost to manufacture at the pottery, with but our one small profit added; it means a saving to you of fully 50 per cent of what your local dealer would charge. The illustration will give you some idea of the handsome appearance of the set with delicate decoration, but you can only form an accurate opinion of its high standard of excellence by a personal examination.

WE ASK YOU TO COMPARE our special direct from the pottery price, $7.90, with any price you can obtain on any set of similar value. We feel sure that after such comparison you will be all the more inclined to favor us with your order. The genuine Davidson, Taylor & Co.'s ware is celebrated for its lightness of weight, purity of color, its handsome finish and durability and we guarantee it not to craze.

DECORATION. Handsome free hand finished, filled in color decoration, which we furnish in combination of green, blue and pink, is a new, dainty, beautiful floral design, beautifully executed and full fired. Ask your dealer for his price on such a 100-piece dinner set, compare our prices with his, or any other prices, and we will certainly expect your order. Shipped from pottery in Ohio.

Our $7.90 100-piece dinner set consists of the following pieces:

12 Tea Cups with handles	1 Medium Platter	1 Pickle Dish
12 Tea Saucers	1 Large Platter	1 Slop Bowl
12 Dinner Plates	1 Open Vegetable Dish	1 Covered Butter Dish (3 pieces)
12 Breakfast Plates	2 Covered Vegetable Dishes (4 pieces)	1 Sauce Boat
12 Tea or Pie Plates	1 Sugar Bowl (2 pieces)	**100 pieces in all.**
12 Sauce Plates	1 Cream Pitcher	
12 Butter Plates		

No. 2R318 Our special price, 100-Piece Dinner Set, complete. **$7.90**

OUR $8.35 NEWTON, WAYLAND & CO.'S 100-PIECE VERUS CHINA DINNER SET.

Shipped from the Pottery in Ohio. Shipping weight, 80 pounds.

CONTRACTING FOR THESE HIGH GRADE DINNER SETS with some of the largest potteries in carload lots at inside cash prices, and adding thereto but our one small margin of profit, the delivery of these goods to the consumer at a saving of 50 per cent is easily understood.

IN CONTRACTING FOR A LARGE SUPPLY OF THESE NEWTON, WAYLAND & CO.'S CHINA DINNER SETS we have done so after thoroughly satisfying ourselves that this is a set that we not only can guarantee, but one which we can recommend with every confidence of its giving satisfaction and delight to the purchaser.

AS STATED ABOVE, this 100-piece Dinner Set at $8.35 is made by Newton, Wayland & Co., makers of the celebrated non-crazing, light verus china, a handsome, clear, glossy, highly finished white ware. The Wayland shape is entirely new for this season is one of the handsomest shaped sets we have seen. Beautiful covered dishes, pitchers and cups, and daintily shaped plates and platters. The gold finished and colored decorations of this set are the free hand finished colored floral decorations in combination of pink, blue and green flowers. The dishes have gold trimmed edges, the handles being gold tipped and all pieces being traced with gold lines.

AN ILLUSTRATION AND DESCRIPTION can very faintly, and very meagerly, represent to a customer the actual merits and handsome appearance of any high class dinner set such as we describe herein.

THIS $8.35 100-PIECE DINNER SET CONSISTS OF THE FOLLOWING PIECES:

12 Tea Cups with Handles	12 Butter Plates	1 Sugar Bowl (2 pieces)
12 Tea Saucers	1 Medium Platter	1 Cream Pitcher
12 Dinner Plates	1 Large Platter	1 Pickle Dish
12 Breakfast Plates	1 Open Vegetable Dish	1 Slop Bowl
12 Tea or Pie Plates	2 Covered Vegetable Dishes (4 pieces)	1 Covered Butter Dish (3 pieces)
12 Sauce Plates		1 Sauce Boat

No. 2R320 Wayland Pattern 100-piece Dinner Set. Our price, complete.... .... **$8.35**

A GENUINE BELMONT 100-PIECE DINNER SET FOR $8.58.

Shipped from the pottery in Southern Ohio.

AT $8.58 we offer one of our very finest dinner sets, a sample of the very finest ware we handle. Our Belmont 100-Piece Dinner Set is far better value than you will ever find in anything but the highest class retail stores of large cities, a grade of goods which is seldom or never carried in the smaller stores, even though you are asked double the price for other sets.

THIS GENUINE BELMONT DINNER SET is the very finest three fired, extremely light ware, extra white, water smoothed, glazed verus porcelain. From the illustration you can form some idea at least of the extremely handsome shape, one of the handsomest shapes shown on the market by any potter. It is new style in every respect, and the remarkably exquisite shape makes it a dinner set by itself, one without a peer. This Belmont Dinner Set is made by a pottery noted for the unusual superior quality of its goods; dinner ware that is unrivaled by any manufacturer, a dinner set that any one would be proud to own. The beautiful hand finished, colored decoration, in delicate pink, white and yellow flowers and green foliage decoration, free hand filled, is the latest and most delicate finish and decoration shown on any dinner set we have ever had the pleasure of handling. You must see this set to appreciate it, for no illustration or no description could possibly do it half justice.

THE COMPOSITION OF THIS 100-PIECE DINNER SET IS AS FOLLOWS:

12 Tea Cups with Handles	1 Open Vegetable Dish
12 Tea Saucers	2 Covered Vegetable Dishes (4 pieces)
12 Dinner Plates	1 Sugar Bowl (2 pieces)
12 Breakfast Plates	1 Cream Pitcher
12 Tea or Pie Plates	1 Pickle Dish
12 Sauce Plates	1 Slop Bowl
12 Butter Plates	1 Covered Butter Dish (3 pieces)
1 Medium Platter	1 Sauce Boat
1 Large Platter	

REMEMBER THAT WE DO NOT BREAK DINNER SETS. Our price of $8.58 is for the entire set, as above illustrated and described. No single pieces or portions of sets will be sold under any consideration.

No. 2R322 Genuine Belmont 100-Piece Dinner Set. Our special price.....**$8.58**

$11.28 "WOODLAND" DINNER SET. MADE BY ALFRED MEAKIN, TUNSTALL, ENGLAND.

THE WOODLAND DINNER SET is the latest and best production of this celebrated potter. The ware is light in weight and elegantly finished with an embossed design. The decoration is a beautiful "Decalcomanie" design, consisting of sprays of violets and green leaves in natural colorings on a silvery gray background. The decoration is so finely executed that it is impossible for an ordinary critic to distinguish this set from a Haviland china set costing three times as much; and while this set combines all the beauty and elegance of fine French china it has the advantage of being very much stronger. Gold trimmings enliven the decorations and add much to its beauty.

SET CONSISTS OF 100 PIECES, AS FOLLOWS:

12 Dinner Plates
12 Breakfast Plates
12 Sauce Plates
12 Tea Plates
12 Tea Cups
12 Tea Saucers
12 Individual Butter Plates
1 Platter, 10-inch
1 Platter, 12-inch
1 Covered Vegetable Dish (2 pieces)
1 Oval open Vegetable Dish
1 Round open Vegetable Dish
1 Covered Sugar Bowl (2 pieces)
1 Covered Butter Dish (3 pieces)
1 Slop Bowl
1 Sauce Boat
1 Pickle Dish
1 Quart Pitcher
1 Cream Pitcher

No. 2R348 Complete 100-piece set, packed in a barrel; shipping weight, 80 pounds. Our special price........ **$11.28**

In addition to the regular set quoted above we can furnish the following pieces:

Coffee Cups and Saucers. Per dozen......$2.09 Soup Plates, regular deep shape. Per dozen $1.43 Soup Plates, new coupe shape. Per dozen....$1.90

$11.45 THE SUPERB DINNER SET. MADE BY UPPER HANLEY POTTERY CO., ENGLAND.

THE WARE IS AS HARD AS FLINT, the glaze is warranted never to craze. The decoration is a continuous border design, printed under the glaze, in the new shade of soft edges so popular in china decorations. The decoration is illuminated with heavy gold tracings, all of the petals of the flowers being outlined with gold and the green of all pieces finished with a heavy gold line, in addition the handles of the large pieces, and all embossed parts are gold traced. The rich green underglaze decoration, the elaborate gold tracing, the elegant shape and rich finish of these goods combine in making one of the handsomest designs ever offered in wares of moderate price.

SET CONSISTS OF 100 PIECES, AS FOLLOWS:

12 Dinner Plates
12 Breakfast Plates
12 Tea Plates
12 Sauce Plates
12 Individual Butter Plates
12 Tea Cups
12 Tea Saucers
1 Platter, 10-inch
1 Platter, 12-inch
1 Covered Vegetable Dish (2 pieces)
1 Oval Open Vegetable Dish
1 Round Open Vegetable Dish
1 Covered Sugar Bowl (2 pieces)
1 Covered Butter Dish (3 pieces)
1 Quart Size Pitcher
1 Sauce Boat
1 Pickle Dish
1 Slop Bowl
1 Cream Pitcher

No. 2R350 Complete 100-piece set, packed in barrel; shipping weight, 80 pounds. Our special price........ **$11.45**

$11.75 PRINCESS DINNER SET. MADE BY W. H. GRINDLEY & CO., TUNSTALL, ENGLAND

THIS SET IS ONE OF THE VERY BEST TRANSFER DESIGNS EVER MADE. The ware is the celebrated Grindley English semi-porcelain fully warranted never to craze. The shape is a plain oval, a new and very artistic shape. The decoration is a fine example of transfer work and consists of sprays of pink roses with green leaves on a delicate blue background, which makes an exceedingly handsome effect. Every piece heavily gilded with gold tracing. This set is very rich, the plain shape, elegant decoration and elaborate tracings combine in making a set that would be hard to tell from the best makes of French china, and the cost is about one-fifth, while this set is much stronger than any china set you can purchase.

SET CONSISTS OF 100 PIECES, AS FOLLOWS:

12 Dinner Plates
12 Breakfast Plates
12 Tea Plates
12 Individual Butter Plates
12 Sauce Plates
12 Tea Cups
12 Tea Saucers
1 Platter, 10-inch
1 Platter, 12-inch
1 Covered Vegetable Dish (2 pieces)
1 Oval Open Vegetable Dish
1 Round Open Vegetable Dish
1 Covered Sugar Bowl (2 pieces)
1 Covered Butter Dish (3 pieces)
1 Quart Size Pitcher
1 Sauce Boat
1 Pickle Dish
1 Slop Bowl
1 Cream Pitcher

No. 2R354 Complete 100 piece set, packed in barrel, shipping weight, 80 pounds. Our special price........ **$11.75**

OUR $19.95 HAVILAND FRENCH CHINA 100-PIECE DINNER SET.

FOR $19.95 we offer this handsome decorated 100-piece dinner set of genuine French china, made in Limoges, France, by that celebrated, world wide known maker, Theodore Haviland, maker of the celebrated unmatchable Haviland China.

AT $19.95 we are selling a complete 100-piece Haviland Dinner Set, at about one-half the price charged by others. This is one of our newest, most stylish and best 100-piece Haviland dinner sets, made by this noted maker, new for this season, and at a price no dealer, no importer will attempt to compete with.

$19.95

No. 2R376

ORDER BY NUMBER.

THE 100 PIECES COMPRISING THE FULL HAVILAND DINNER SET ARE AS FOLLOWS:

12 Coupe Soup Plates
12 Plates, 8½-inch
12 Plates, 6½-inch
12 Cups
12 Saucers
12 Individual Butters
12 Fruit Plates
1 Platter, 12-inch
1 Platter, 14-inch
1 Baker
1 Round Covered Dish (2 pieces)
1 Oval Covered Dish (2 pieces)
1 Pickle Dish
1 Covered Butter Dish (3 pieces)
1 Sauce Boat (2 pieces)
1 Sugar Bowl (2 pieces)
1 Cream Pitcher

The weight of this 100-piece Haviland Dinner Set when carefully packed in a barrel is about 100 pounds, and the freight will amount to a very small item when compared with the saving.

No. 2R376 Our special price........ **$19.95**

SPECIAL FOR HOTELS, RESTAURANTS, BOARDING HOUSES, ETC.

NOTE OUR SPECIAL PRICES FOR BIG HOTEL TRADE. PRICES BELOW POTTERY JOBBING LIST.

GENUINE STONEWARE WHITE CHINA.

OUR ONLY OPEN STOCK GOODS are the plain white stoneware china shown in the accompanying illustration and quoted below. These are the most durable earthenware made, warranted not to craze, handsome in design and rare value. For hotels this ware is without equal. We have sold thousands of dollars worth of this china to scores of hotels throughout the country and have yet to hear a complaint from any one of them. Our prices are based on the lowest possible cost of production with the smallest possible margin of profit added, and in buying these goods from us you obtain them on the same or a lower basis of price than your local dealer himself can buy them at.

WE WILL MAKE UP ANY ASSORTMENT from the open stock quotations given below, but must decline all orders for open stock amounting to less than $5.00; that is, you can make up your order for $5.00 worth of plates alone if you wish, or the minimum amount of the purchase may include cups and saucers, plates, platters, pitchers or anything you may desire. It is to be understood, of course, that the amount of the purchase can be more than $5.00. A great many hotels purchase a complete outfit of this china amounting to from $50.00 to $75.00. **We pack every assortment very carefully in a cask or barrel and ship by freight from our pottery in Eastern Ohio, from which point the customer pays the freight.**

No. 2R385

Tea Cups and Saucers, per dozen	67c	**Platters**, 16-inch, each	50c
Coffee Cups and Saucers, per dozen	66c	**Bakers**, 3-inch, each	6c
Plates, 8-inch, Dinner, per dozen	63c	**Bakers**, 7-inch, each	10c
Plates, 7-inch, Breakfast, per dozen	57c	**Bakers**, 8-inch, each	12c
Plates, 6-inch, Tea, per dozen	45c	**Bakers**, 9-inch, each	13c
Plates, 5-inch, Pie, per dozen	34c	**Scallops**, 6-inch, each	8c
Plates, 7-inch, Soup, per dozen	57c	**Scallops**, 7-inch, each	10c
Fruit Saucers, 4-inch, per dozen	50c	**Scallops**, 8-inch, each	14c
Individual Butters, per dozen	17c	**Scallops**, 9-inch, each	18c
Oyster Bowls, per dozen	72c	**Oyster Tureen**, each	55c
Tea Pot, each	25c	**Sauce Tureen**, each	28c
Sugar Bowl, each	20c	**Sauce Boat**, each	14c
Cream Pitcher, each	8c	**Oval Covered Dish**, each	40c
Bread Plates, each	10c	**Round Covered Dish**, each	40c
Bowls, 1 pint, each	6c	**Covered Butter Dish**, each	30c
Bowls, 1 quart, each	9c	**Pickle Dish**, each	10c
Platters, 4-inch, each	5c	**Pitcher**, 6½-pint, each	33c
Platters, 8-inch, each	9c	**Pitcher**, 5-pint, each	20c
Platters, 10-inch, each	16c	**Pitcher**, 1-quart, each	10c
Platters, 12-inch, each	20c	**Pitcher**, 1-pint, each	8c
Platters, 14-inch, each	32c		

Remember that we do not Accept Orders for Open Stock Graniteware where the Order Amounts to Less than $5.00.

FINEST QUALITY AMERICAN TOILET SETS.

SHIPPED FROM OUR POTTERIES IN EASTERN OHIO AND SOUTHERN INDIANA.

$2.20

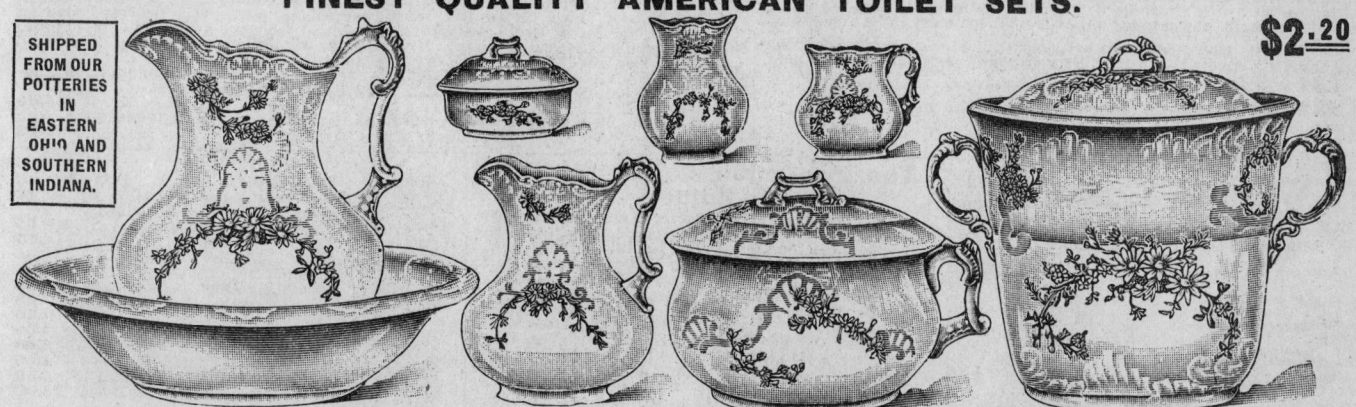

The Ardmore Toilet Set.

THIS SET is made of the finest quality of American semi-porcelain ware. The shape is considered by experts to be the best ever made in toilet ware. The decoration is elegantly printed in delicate shades of brown or blue. We carry this set in two assortments, as follows: **Be sure to specify which color you prefer.** Packed in barrels. Shipping weight, about 80 pounds.

No. 2R392 **10-Piece Toilet Set,** consisting of wash bowl and pitcher, covered chamber, covered soap dish, hot water pitcher, brush vase and mug. Price........ **$2.20**

No. 2R394 **12-Piece Toilet Set.** Same assortment as 10-piece set, with large slop jar and cover. Price........ **$3.90**

The Glenwood Toilet Set.

OUR GLENWOOD TOILET SET is the same shape as the Ardmore, illustrated above, but differently decorated. **Very best quality of American semi-porcelain ware. All pieces extra large size and handsomely modeled. The decoration is a work of art and consists of a beautiful hand painted spray of flowers in a delicate shade of violet, pink and yellow colorings with green sprays.** The decoration is further enhanced by gold trimmings on every piece. Packed in barrels. Shipping weight, about 80 pounds. We can furnish this set in either of the following assortments:

No. 2R396 **10-Piece Toilet Set,** consisting of wash bowl and pitcher, covered chamber, covered soap dish, hot water pitcher, brush vase and mug. Price........ **$2.90**

No. 2R398 **12-Piece Toilet Set.** Same assortment as 10-piece set, with large slop jar and cover added. Price........ **$4.39**

OUR NEWPORT TOILET SET AT $3.75.

OUR NEWPORT TOILET SET is one of the very latest and handsomest patterns put on the market, beautifully decorated with yellow and pink chrysanthemum blossoms and foliage as shown in the illustration, in addition to which every piece is heavily decorated with gold. The gold decorations are not simply lines and tracings as are usually put on toilet sets, but a heavy deep stippled effect which gives the toilet set a most luxurious appearance. We consider this set one of the handsomest we have ever been able to furnish, and being made by one of the most reliable potteries in America, we can guarantee it to be strictly high grade.

Each set is carefully packed complete in a barrel to insure safe delivery and shipped direct from the pottery in Western West Virginia.

No. 2R402 10-Piece Toilet Set, consisting of wash bowl, pitcher, covered chamber (2 pieces), covered soap dish (3 pieces), hot water pitcher, brush vase and mug.

Our special price.......... **$3.75**

No. 2R404 12-Piece Toilet Set, same assortment as the 10-piece toilet set No. 2R402, with a large slop jar and cover added, as illustrated.

Our special price.......... **$5.45**

OUR KOSMO TOILET SET.

THE FINEST TOILET SET WE FURNISH. NOTHING BETTER MADE.

THE LATEST PRODUCTION OF THE POTTERS' ART. A tapering tankard effect that is very shapely, modeled and carved with great skill. A perfectly clear white semi-porcelain body, with gracefully curved embossed lines, which are exquisitely traced in rich, yellow gold. This white and gold design will harmonize with any color decoration in bedrooms. Every set is carefully packed in a barrel and shipped direct from the pottery in Eastern Ohio.

No. 2R406 10-Piece Toilet Set, consisting of wash bowl and pitcher, covered chamber, covered soap dish, hot water pitcher, brush vase and mug.

Price.......... $3.95

No. 2R408 12-Piece Toilet Set. Same assortment as 10-piece set, with large slop jar and cover, as illustrated.

Price.......... $5.95

ANOTHER NOVELTY IN THE KOSMO TOILET SHAPE. The top of this set is tinted a dark olive green, gently blending toward the center to a soft salmon color, and finally receding to the same rich green at the bottom, matching the top tint. The effect of this handsome and striking combination of perfect coloring is made more attractive by the rich, full gold tracing on all embossed lines, giving it a most luxurious appearance. We have made a special effort to avoid everything gaudy, and feel this combination will appeal to the most refined taste. Every set is carefully packed in a barrel and shipped direct from the factory in Eastern Ohio.

No. 2R410 10-Piece Toilet Set, consisting of wash bowl and pitcher, covered chamber, covered soap dish, hot water pitcher, brush vase and mug.

Price.......... $5.50

No. 2R412 12-Piece Toilet Set. Same assortment as 10-piece set, with large slop jar and cover added. Price.......... $7.98

Easily cleaned, accessible for ice. Economical, sanitary, convenient.

The Perfection Separable Water Bottle.

The Perfection Water Bottle is acknowledged the world over to be the most perfect container for water, milk, iced tea, coffee, lemonade, wines, etc., that has ever been produced. Being separable, it can be locked and unlocked. When locked, it excludes dust and all foreign matter, and when unlocked and the parts separated, it is easily cleaned and readily receives ice and anything else that is desirable to place in the bowl of the container. This container combines all the good points of both water pitcher and water bottle and is free from the ordinary disadvantages of the water bottle. In case of breakage of any part, it can be replaced, as all the parts are interchangeable; that is, the neck can be bought for an old bowl, or a bowl can be bought for an old neck, which prolongs the life and use of the container, and reduces the cost. All things considered, "perfection" is the only word that fully expresses the economy and sanitary features of this bottle. Years of experiment have produced machinery that enables us to put the price within the reach of everyone.

No. 2R603 Price, only.......... 50c

STONEWARE.

No. 2R605 Milk Pans, white glaze, thoroughly vitrified, most healthful and nonabsorbent article made for cooking milk or cereals of any kind, oatmeal, cracked wheat, etc., or baking puddings. Will neither discolor or change the flavor of food cooked in it, in any manner; can be easily cleaned. Made in six sizes.

¼-gallon, each.......... 5c	¾-gallon, each.......... 7½c	1½-gallon, each.......... 14c
½-gallon, each.......... 6c	1-gallon, each.......... 9c	2-gallon, each.......... 18c

Stone Jars.

No. 2R610 Stone Jars in all sizes from ⅛ of a gallon up to 40 gallons. Bristol white glaze.

Each, ⅛-gallon	$0.05
Each, ¼-gallon	.05
Each, ½-gallon	.06
Each, 1-gallon	.10
Each, 2-gallon	.18
Each, 3-gallon	.28
Each, 4-gallon	.40

Each, 5-gallon	$0.50	Each, 15-gallon	2.00
Each, 8-gallon	.60	Each, 20-gallon	3.00
Each, 8-gallon	.80	Each, 25-gallon	4.00
Each, 10-gallon	1.10	Each, 30-gallon	4.50
Each, 12-gallon	1.40	Each, 40-gallon	10.00

Covers of Jars.

Each, 1 to 3 gallons, inclusive	8c
Each, 4 to 6 gallons, inclusive	10c
Each, 8-10-12 gallons	20c
Each, 15-20 gallons	35c
Each, 25-30 gallons	60c
Each, 40 gallons	75c

Bean Pots.

No. 2R615 Genuine Boston Bean Pots, for baking beans; in four sizes; walnut brown glaze.

1-quart, with cover, each.. 9c
2-quart, with cover, each.. 12c
4-quart, with cover, each.. 15c
8-quart, with cover, each.. 25c

Stoneware Jugs.

No. 2R620 Jugs in all sizes from ¼ of a gallon to 5 gallons, white glaze, best quality stoneware and full measure.

¼-gallon	6c
½-gallon	8c
1-gallon	12c
2-gallon	25c
3-gallon	35c
4-gallon	45c
5-gallon	55c

Also 5-gallon jugs for cider and other beverages with faucet hole.

Stoneware Water Coolers.

No. 2R625 Stoneware Water Coolers. Fitted with nickel or wood faucets and covers very high bristol glaze. Healthiest and best, always clean, makes a fine appearing package, can be used for colored or uncolored beverages of any kind. Medicinal, hard, soft or well waters; positively acid proof.

Metal Faucets.

2 gallons, complete	$0.80
4 gallons, complete	1.00
5 gallons, complete	1.20
6 gallons, complete	1.35
8 gallons, complete	1.60
10 gallons, complete	2.00

Wood Faucets.

2 gallons, complete	$0.40
4 gallons, complete	.60
5 gallons, complete	.70
6 gallons, complete	.90
8 gallons, complete	1.25
10 gallons, complete	1.50

Water Filters.

No. 2R630 The Success Stoneware Filter, made in two sizes. The family size has two 4-gallon jars, the upper one holding the filtering block and the lower one being the water cooler. The hotel size has two 10-gallon jars, with three filtering blocks in the bottom of the upper jar and the lower jar holding ten gallons of filtered water. The filtering blocks are 4 inches in diameter and height, hollowed out on the inside, and turned out of natural Tripoli stone, the best filtering material known. These blocks fit on metal tubes running through and fastened to the bottom of top jar, can be filled off the drip tube, cleaned and replaced, in two minutes, and with no trouble. The water passes from the upper jar through the walls of the filtering block, and thus through the drip tube into the lower jar. **This is by far the cheapest water filter ever manufactured, and a complete success. Thousands are in use.** Water filtered by this filter has been analyzed and approved by the State University of Ohio and other bacteriological colleges throughout the country.

Price, each, family size	$3.79
Price, each, hotel size	8.49

No. 2R635 Butter Churns with covers and best white maple wood dashers, white glaze, in seven sizes:

2-gallon, each	$0.40
3-gallon, each	.50
4-gallon, each	.65
5-gallon, each	.75
6-gallon, each	.90
8-gallon, each	1.15
10-gallon, each	1.50

No. 2R640 Fancy Pipkins, Cream or Syrup Pitchers; can also be used for cooking purposes; with covers and stoneware handles; upper half and inside white glaze, lower half cherry brown glaze. Four sizes.

1-pint, each	10c
2-pint, each	15c
3-pint, each	20c
4-pint, each	25c

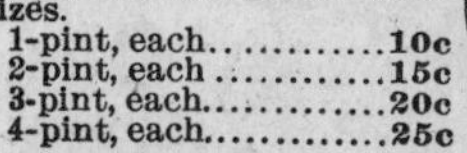

No. 2R645 Chicken Fountains. By using these fountains young chickens cannot drown. The water is always pure and clean, as chickens cannot get into the same; they are money savers by saving young chickens from death and preserving the health of the old ones. Can be easily and thoroughly cleaned. Three sizes.

½-gallon, each	30c
1-gallon, each	40c
2-gallon, each	50c

Send 15 Cents for a Years' Subscription to our

MONEY-SAVING

GROCERY PRICE LIST.

33-PIECE GLASS SET FOR $1.45.

No. 2R650 Handsome imitation cut glass design. This is a good practical outfit, as we have included a larger quantity of the pieces that are used every day.

SET CONSISTS OF 33 PIECES AS FOLLOWS:

- 12 Water Tumblers
- 12 Sauce or Berry Dishes
- 1 Large Berry Bowl
- 1 Large ½-gallon Pitcher
- 1 Pickle Dish
- 1 Spoon Holder
- 1 Sugar Bowl
- 1 Butter Dish
- 1 Cream Pitcher

No. 2R650 Price, Complete Outfit........ **$1.45**

OUR $1.75 40-PIECE GLASS OUTFIT.

No. 2R655 Imitation cut glass design. The pattern is the newest produced this year and exceedingly beautiful. We feel confident that you never heard of such a wonderful assortment of glassware for so little money.

SET CONSISTS OF 40 PIECES AS FOLLOWS:

- 6 Water Tumblers
- 6 Goblets
- 6 Salt and Pepper Shakers
- 12 Berry Saucers
- 1 Large Berry Bowl
- 1 Large ½-gallon Water Pitcher
- 1 Butter Dish
- 1 Sugar Bowl
- 1 Cream Pitcher
- 1 Spoon Holder
- 1 Pickle Dish
- 1 Tall Celery Glass

No. 2R655 Price, Complete Outfit........ **$1.75**

GENERAL DESCRIPTION OF OUR BRILLIANT GLASSWARE SET.

This set is made of the very finest quality of crystal pressed glass, the bull's-eye design bringing out all the fire and brilliancy which is so characteristic of genuine cut glass; in fact, those who are not experts in glassware would readily believe that it is the real cut glass. Every piece is elegantly finished and of good practical size.

THIS SET CONSISTS OF 39 PIECES, AS FOLLOWS:

- 1 Spoon Holder
- 1 Cream Pitcher
- 12 Berry Saucers
- 1 Celery Tray
- 1 Vinegar Bottle
- 1 Butter Dish (2 pieces)
- 1 Sugar Bowl (2 pieces)
- 1 8-inch Berry or Salad Dish
- 12 Water Tumblers
- 1 Half-Gallon Pitcher
- 1 Silver Plated Pepper Shaker
- 1 Silver Plated Salt Shaker
- 1 Large Footed Fruit Bowl
- 1 Molasses Pitcher
- 1 Toothpick Holder

WE PACK THIS COMPLETE SET very carefully and it is sure to be carried safely and reach you in perfect condition. We guarantee this handsome imitation cut glass set to be exactly as represented, or we will cheerfully refund your money.

We do not Break Glass Sets. The Set is Sold Complete as described above.

No. 2R685 Our Brilliant Imitation Cut Glass Set of 39 Pieces.
Our special price........ **$2.98**

THE CHOICEST GLASSWARE OF TWO FACTORIES

An Assortment of Glassware for $1.90 | WHO EVER HEARD OF THE PRICE? | Lower Than Dealers Can Buy.

A GREAT CUT IN GLASSWARE.

No. 2R675

Order by number.

$1.90

The price of Glassware has been wonderfully reduced. We are on the bottom. We have two outfits at prices never before heard of.

No. 2R675 This complete outfit for $1.90. No charge for package; we pack and deliver at depot free of charge a complete outfit, consisting of the following 36 pieces; 6 tumblers, 6 goblets, 12 4-inch berry saucers, 1 8-inch berry dish, 1 sugar bowl, 1 butter dish, 1 spoon holder, 1 cream pitcher, 1 ½-gallon water pitcher, 1 celery dish, 1 pickle dish, 1 tall open fruit bowl and 1 cake stand. The complete outfit for..........$1.90

Freight will be very little. 25 cents will take a package 500 miles; 50 cents will pay the freight to most any point. Send $1.90 and the outfit will be sent to you at once.

Weight, packed for shipment, 40 pounds.

Decorate your table with one of our sets of glassware and you will surely say: "Never before were such goods sold for so little money."

We pack our glassware in boxes, employing only skilled packers, and we have yet to hear of a shipment being damaged under ordinary circumstances.

OUR $2.75 GLASSWARE OUTFIT.—39 ELEGANT PIECES.

JUST LIKE CUT GLASS AT ABOUT 7 CENTS APIECE.

WE MAKE IT A POINT to carry a line that is just as handsome and stylish as the market affords.

Many a rich man's table is decorated with glassware no handsomer than this pattern.

Would retail at $10.00 and upward. OUR SPECIAL CUT PRICE is $2.75. No charge for packing or delivering to depot. We do that free. An expert only could tell it from a $100 glass outfit.

This elegant 39-piece set must be seen to be appreciated. It is an exact reproduction of the celebrated English "Prism" cut glass and is finished so that it requires an expert to detect the difference. The large pitcher, in particular, is a very handsome piece of glass, and, if it were genuine cut, would alone be worth $20.00, but the glass manufacturers have so improved that we are able to sell this assortment at a fraction of the cost of a single item of the genuine cut glass, and very few could possibly tell the difference. Your neighbors will pronounce it genuine cut glass. These goods are very heavy, beautifully finished, and each piece is a work of art. This outfit consists of 1 butter dish, 1 sugar bowl, 1 spoon holder, 1 cream pitcher, 12 berry saucers, 1 8-inch berry or salad dish, 12 water tumblers, 1 ½-gallon pitcher, 1 celery tray, 1 silver plated salt shaker, 1 silver plated pepper shaker, 1 large footed fruit bowl, 1 molasses pitcher, 1 vinegar bottle, 1 toothpick holder. Every one who sees this set will want one.

No. 2R680 Order by number.

Weight, packed for shipment, 40 pounds.

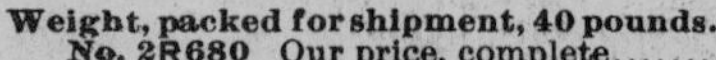

No. 2R680 Our price, complete.......... **$2.75**

Our $1.95 Lamp.

No. 2R700 Reading Lamp. Nickel plated, 10-inch dome shade. The very best lamp made for use as a reading lamp. Always clean, largest quantity of light, best burner made; this lamp has no equal for actual utility. Shipping weight, 25 pounds Price, each....$1.95

No. 2R702 C. Lamp. This is one of the most staple lamps in the market. Is very strong and substantial, and will last a lifetime. You need no chimney with this lamp, the shade and the illuminator taking the place of chimney, and thus saving you from the breakage of chimneys. Shipping weight, 20 pounds.
Price, each.............................98c

Perfection Student Lamp.

No. 2R708 Perfection Student Lamp. This lamp has been used for so many years that a description of it is unnecessary. It is, without a doubt, the peer of all study lamps. Perfectly safe and reliable. Lamp can be adjusted to any height. Shipping weight, 25 pounds.
Nickel plated, plain white shades.................................$3.45
Nickel plated, green shades.... 3.75

Night Lamps.

No. 2R712 Brass Night Lamp. 7¾ inches high, complete Gem burner, chimney and wick.
Price, each......................20c

No. 2R716 Glass Night Lamp. This is the most practical night lamp made. The lamp is fitted with a revolving reflector and a bracket which enables you to hang lamp on wall. Height, 7¾ inches. Price, complete..................28c

2R716 2R712

Wall Lamp.

No. 2R720 This Very Useful Lamp jumped into popularity at once because of its great utility and low price. It has removable glass fount and reflector, No. 2 Sun burner and chimney. Is made to hang on a wall or rest on a table and reflector can be taken off if desired. Shipping weight, 8 pounds.
Price, each.............................38c

Bracket Lamps.

No. 2R722 Too well known to need further introduction. The Kitchen Bracket Lamp still keeps in popular favor. The lamp is finished in French bronze, has glass fount, No. 2 Sun burner and 7-inch silvered glass reflector and No 2 Sun chimney. Shipping weight, 15 pounds. Price, each..............75c

No. 2R724 The Most Popular Kitchen and Hall Lamp ever made, and our style is the strongest and best finished on the market. We complete it with No 2 glass fount having outside filler, No. 2 Sun burner and chimney and 8-inch silvered glass reflector. Shipping weight, 15 pounds. Price, each.......90c

Glass Stand Lamps.

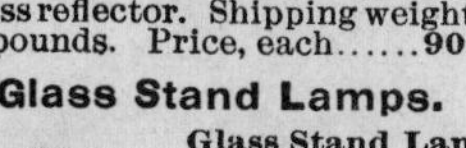

Glass Stand Lamps, priced with Sun burners, wicks and chimneys. In this grade we show only the heavy plain style having sunk top to catch oil. Shipping weight, 10 pounds.

No. 2R730 Height, 9½ inches. No. 1 burner. Price, each.......................35c

No. 2R732 Height, 10½ inches. No. 2 burner. Price, each.......................45c

Glass Stand Lamps, shrunk-on collars; no plaster, collars cannot work loose, and lamps are stronger and heavier than the ordinary grade. Priced with Sun burners, wicks and chimneys. Shipping weight, 10 pounds.

No. 2R734 Height, 10½ inches. No. 2 burner. Price, each......................55c

No. 2R735 Height, 11 inches. No. 2 burner. Price, each......................60c

Glass Hand Lamp.

No. 2R738 Footed Glass Hand Lamp. Just the thing for bedrooms and to carry around the house, into closets, etc. Shipping weight, 8 pounds.
Price with No. 1 Sun burner, wick and chimney. Each.....28c

Footed Hand Lamp.

No. 2R742 "Shrunk-on" collar; no plaster. A lamp to last must be made well. On this style the collars are pressed on by machinery and cannot work loose. The lamps are heavier and less liable to break. Price includes No. 1 Sun burner, wick and chimney. Shipping weight, 18 pounds. Price, each..35c

Center Draft Bracket Lamp.

No. 2R750 Where a strong light is needed, we recommend this lamp. Bracket is made of cast iron and is finished in French bronze. The lamp fount is the celebrated Royal and is fitted with burner giving a light equal to 75 candle-power. **Fount is made of brass, highly polished, and will hold enough oil to burn 8 hours.** The reflector is 10 inches in diameter and is made of silvered glass, and is so arranged that it can be adjusted to throw the light wherever needed. This is the most powerful light giver made. Shipping weight, 25 pounds.
Price, complete..................................$2.98

HANGING LAMPS.

Our Leader at $1.98

No. 2R780 Ball Weight Extension Hanging Lamp, 14 inches plain white dome shade. No. 2 Sun burner and chimney. **Frame is gold lacquered finish,** equal in every respect to lamps your dealer will ask $3.00 for. Our special price....$1.98

No. 2R782 Same lamp as above with automatic spring extension. Length, closed, 25 inches; extended, 60 inches.
Shipping weight, 25 pounds.
Price, complete..........$2.48

No. 2R780

Our $2.95 Library Lamp.

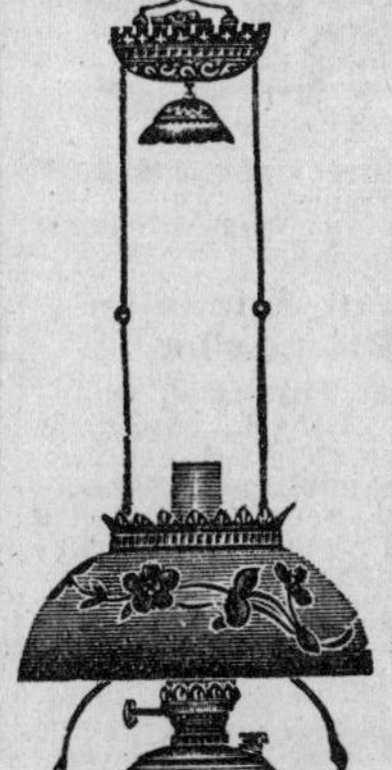

No. 2R784 Library Lamp. Has extra heavy frame, handsomely decorated shade and fount to match, automatic spring extension. Length, closed, 25 inches; extended, 61 inches. Extra large No. 3 burner. Handsomely decorated shade and oil fount to match. The spring extension makes lamp suitable for a high or low ceiling. Each lamp packed complete in a barrel to insure safe delivery. Shipping weight, 45 pounds.
Price, complete........$2.95

$3.75 Buys This Library Lamp.

No. 2R784

No. 2R788 Library Lamp, automatic spring extension. Length, closed, 25 inches; extended, 61 inches. Plain white 14-inch dome shade. No. 2 Climax burner. **Frame is finished in rich gold.** Thirty cut glass pendants suspended from shade band. Each lamp packed complete in a barrel to insure safe delivery.
Price, complete. $3.75

No. 2R790 Same lamp as above trimmed with handsomely decorated dome shade and fount. Shipping weight, 50 pounds.
Price, complete..$4.24

No. 2R788

MAKE UP AN ORDER of 100 pounds in weight. **REFER TO OUR COMPLETE GROCERY DEPARTMENT** pages 14 to 23, and include some goods in this line, SUGAR, COFFEE, TEA, ETC.

Handsomely Decorated Library Lamps.

No. 2R792 Library Lamp, automatic spring extension. Length, closed, 25 inches; extended, 61 inches. The shade and fount are elegantly **decorated with a handsome flower design** on tinted background. **Extra heavy gold lacquered frame.** No. 2 Climax burner. Shade band is trimmed with thirty elegant cut glass pendants. Each lamp carefully packed, complete in a barrel to insure safe delivery. Shipping weight, 50 pounds.
Price, complete..$4.90

No. 2R792

Our $5.95 Library Lamp.

No. 2R796 Library Lamp, automatic spring extension. Length, closed, 25 inches; extended, 61 inches. The burner is the **celebrated No. 2 Royal center draft, 75-candle power.** Oil fount is removable for purposes of cleaning and filling. Elegant **decorated shade and fount,** genuine hand painted flower design in natural colors on tinted background. **Frame is made of brass finished in rich gold.** Shade band trimmed with thirty genuine cut glass pendants. Each lamp carefully packed complete in a barrel to insure safe delivery. Shipping weight, 50 pounds.
Price, complete....$5.95

No. 2R796

A $12.00 Hanging Lamp for $6.85.

No. 2R800 Library Lamp, same general description as No. 2R796, with this exception: **Extra heavy cast frame gold lacquered finish, and an exceptionally fine hand painted shade and fount.** The decorations are chrysanthemums in natural and lifelike colors on a delicately tinted background. Packed complete in a barrel to insure safe delivery. Shipping weight, 50 pounds.
Price, complete..$6.85

No. 2R8 00

No. 2R804 Parlor Extension Lamp fitted with No. 2 Royal center draft fount, 75-candle power, removable for purpose of filling. **Automatic sp'ng extension.** Length closed, 25 inches; extended, 61 inches. **Can be used in room with either high or low ceiling.** Easy to keep clean as lamp has no prisms. **Metal work rich gold lacquer.** Vase and globe are decorated to match. **Genuine hand painted floral designs** on a rich background of either red, blue or brown.

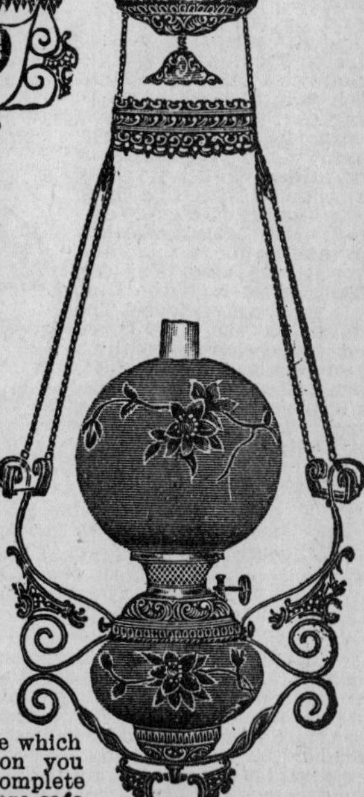

In ordering state which color of decoration you desire. Packed complete in a barrel to insure safe delivery. Shipping weight, 50 pounds. Price, complete..........................$6.98

Zenith Hall Lamp.

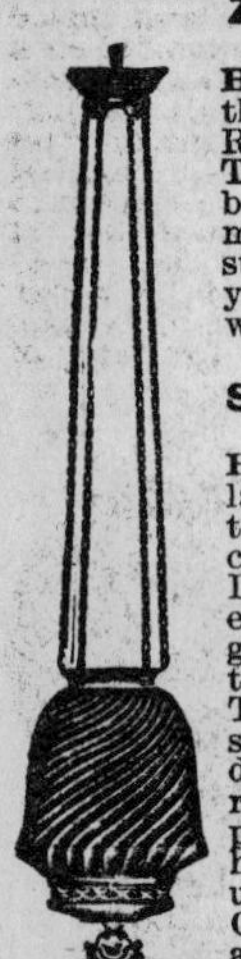

No. 2R816 Zenith Hall Lamp. Just the thing for a small hall. Ruby, opal or pink globe. This is the cheapest and best hall lamp in the market. In ordering state which color globe you prefer. Shipping weight, 25 pounds.
Price............ $1.49

Square Hall Lamp.

No. 2R819 Square Hall Lamp. This is a larger and better lamp than the Zenith and costs very little more. In two colors, crystal etched or ruby etched glass as desired. Be sure to state color desired. This hall lamp is handsome enough for any dwelling. It is an exact reproduction of the high priced gas lamp that has always been so popular. Length, 36 inches. Complete with burner and chimney. Shipping weight, 25 pounds.

No. 2R816 Our price........$2.49 No. 2R819

Store Lamps.

No. 2R825 Store Lamp. The best and cheapest in the market. For large areas and where good light is required only the best lamps should be procured. We keep them and guarantee every lamp we sell to give perfect satisfaction. The Juno gives a steady and white light. Just the thing to throw light on a window display. Complete as illustrated, 15-inch tin shade, suitable for store or window lights, 65-candle power. Shipping weight, 40 lbs.
Price, brass finish, $2.00
Price, nickel finish, 2.25

No. 2R830 Same lamp as No. 2R825 only trimmed with 10-inch white porcelain dome shade which makes a much neater lamp without much greater cost. Shipping weight, 50 pounds.
Price, brass finish............................$2.45
Price, nickel finish............................2.75

The Juno Mammoth Store and Hall Lamps.

No. 2R834 Juno Mammoth Store and Hall Lamp, 400-candle power. The strongest and best finished lamp on the market. The wick movement is perfect and so simple that a child can rewick the lamp. Patent lock ring to hold fount in ring obviates all danger of fount jarring out of frame. Fount taken out from below for filling. You are taking no chances with this lamp as we guarantee every one to give perfect satisfaction, or we will replace them and pay all expenses. The lock ring used to hold the Juno is a great convenience. The fount can easily be taken out from below for refilling. Complete, as illustrated, 14-inch plain dome shade, suitable for churches, halls, stores, etc. Each lamp is carefully packed in a barrel to insure safe delivery. Shipping weight, 40 pounds.
Price, complete, brass finish..................$3.69
Price, complete, nickel finish..................4.25

No. 2R836 Same lamp as above only it is trimmed with a 20-inch tin shade, making a cheaper and more suitable lamp for saw mills, factories, etc.
Price, complete, brass finish..................$3.25
Price, complete, nickel finish..................3.50

No. 2R838 Same lamp as above, trimmed with 14-inch white dome shade and fitted with an automatic spring extension so it can be lowered for cleaning or lighting without the use of step ladder or chairs. Length of lamp, closed, 42 inches; fully extended, 78 inches. Money cannot buy a finer constructed lamp. This makes an ideal lamp for churches, halls and fine stores. Very handsome in appearance. Shipping weight, 50 pounds.
Price, complete, brass finish..................$5.98
Price, complete, nickel finish..................6.75

Our $7.15 Chandelier

Chandelier, with patent automatic extension for raising and lowering. A handsome chandelier at a price that puts it within the reach of all. This beautiful parlor fixture, **useful as well as ornamental,** is finished in **rich gold bronze,** and completed with **etched globes of a very popular shape.** The burner is of a new design that can **be lighted and trimmed without removing the globe or chimney,** thus avoiding the possibility of breakage in handling them. We furnish this fixture in the following sizes: Shipping weight, 50 to 75 pounds.

No. 2R867 **Two-light,** complete.................$ 7.15
No. 2R868 **Three-light,** complete, as shown 9.10
No. 2R869 **Four-light,** complete..................11.70

Polished Bronze Chandelier.

Chandelier. Polished Bronze, rich gold finish. The metal ball in center of chandelier is finished in rich enamel, either ruby or green. Length of chandelier, 36 inches; has patent extension, which extends 21 inches, making length of chandelier fully opened 57 in. The globes are crystal glass finished with a handsome etched design. The burners can be lighted and trimmed without removing globes or chimney. We can furnish this chandelier in either three or four-light.

No. 2R872 Price, complete, three lights...$11.95
Shipping weight, 60 pounds.
No. 2R874 Price, complete, four lights..... 13.60
Shipping weight, 90 pounds.

Patent Extension Chandelier.

Patent Extension Chandelier. Length, closed, 36 inches; extended, 57 inches. This chandelier is elegantly finished in rich gold, has colored metal center; trimmed with unique burners, which can be trimmed and lighted without removing chimney or globes. Trimmed with fine etched crystal globes. Shipping weight of three-light chandeliers, about 75 pounds; the four light, 90 pounds.

No. 2R878 Price, complete, three lights...$13.65
No. 2R879 Price, complete, four lights.... 16.25

Church or Hall Chandelier. Same chandelier as above, except burners. This fixture is trimmed with the celebrated B. & H. No. 1 center draft burners, each light 50-candle power.

No. 2R882 Price, complete, three lights...$16.35
No. 2R883 Price, complete, four lights.... 18.85

Our 98c Banquet Lamp.

No. 2R890 We have reduced the price of this beautiful banquet lamp from $1.55 to 98 cents, bringing the price within the reach of all, so that there is no reason why any family should not have a banquet lamp to help decorate their home. This lamp is 21 inches high, and has a tinted globe and bowl, shading from white to green, with beautiful floral decorations, as illustrated. It is furnished with a No. 2 brass burner and rests upon a cast brass base. When securely packed in a box this lamp will weigh about 25 pounds, and we hope that you will include one of these lamps in your next order which is to go forward by freight, thus reducing the charges to a minimum.
Our special price............98c

Our Very Finest Lamp for $6.95.

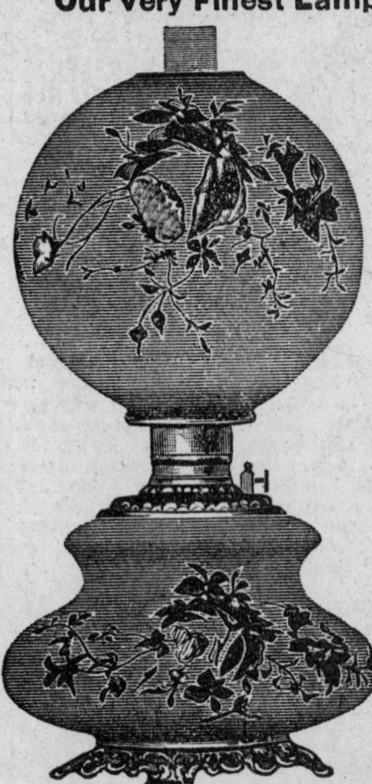

No. 2R900 For $6.95 we offer you one of the largest, handsomest, and best banquet lamps made, a lamp equal to those that retail at double our price. It stands 25 inches high, has a 12-inch globe and 13-inch bowl, resting on a gold plated stand. Both globe and bowl are delicately tinted and the decoration consists of natural color flowers, put on the globe before the last firing by free hand work so that it will not fade or rub off. The fount is removable and made of bright pressed brass. The lamp is equipped with the best large No. 2 Royal 100-candle power center draft burner. This lamp is so large and handsome that no illustration can do it justice. It is securely packed in a barrel and weighs 40 pounds.
Our special price.......................................$6.95

Our $5.90 Cerise Banquet Lamp.

No. 2R902 This is the celebrated Cottage Cerise Lamp, which is only manufactured by one factory in the United States. Both globe and bowl are of the one dark red shade with the velvet finish, making a very soft light at night. This cerise color is not on the outside of the globe or bowl, but is in the glass itself, giving a much better light than those which are tinted on the outside of glass and hand decorated. It is an ornament to any parlor either day or night. It is 25 inches high with a 12-inch globe and 14-inch bowl. It has a No. 2 Royal center draft burner and removable brass oil fount. Packed securely in a barrel, weighing 40 pounds.
Our special price.......................................$5.90

Our Big $5.65 Vase Banquet Lamp.

No. 2R904 This handsome lamp is nearly the same pattern as No. 2R900, but slightly smaller in size and different decoration. It has the popular tinted globe and bowl with the distinct free hand decoration, making it an ornament to any home. It has the cast brass gold plated base, and a brass oil fount with No. 2 center draft burner. It stands 24 inches high, with a 10½-inch globe and 12½-inch bowl. The burners of all our center draft lamps are easily taken apart and cleaned so that you will experience no trouble along this line. Our $5.65 price means a saving of fully 50 per cent on this particular lamp. Securely packed in a barrel weighing 40 pounds.
Our special price.......................................$5.65

No. 2R906 This Lamp is the largest high grade lamp ever offered for the extremely low price which we quote. It is handsomely tinted and beautifully decorated with natural color floral decorations, as shown in the illustration. It is larger, handsomer and better than you would be likely to find in your own town. and the equal of lamps that retail in cities at double our price. It has the center draft No. 2 Royal burner with a wick attachment, as illustrated, on each of our lamps, which causes the entire wick to be raised at once, making a very even light. This lamp stands 30 inches high and has a 10½-inch globe, and bowl is 8 inches wide and 16½ inches deep, resting upon a cast brass gold plated base. The brass oil fount is removable. and the regular size as the other lamps, holding about three pints of oil, so that it does not make the lamp too heavy, but yet giving the lamp sufficient oil so that it will burn for several evenings. Each one of our lamps come securely packed in a barrel and will weigh about 40 pounds, so that they can be shipped by freight with other goods safely. Our price...**$3.75**

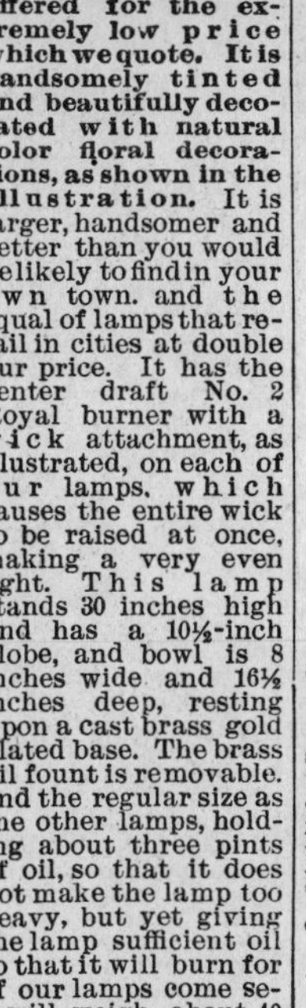

No. 2R916

Our $1.50 Banquet Lamp.

No. 2R916 One of the handsomest lamps shown this season, latest and handsomest design decoration. Stands 21 inches high, 9½-inch globe, 8-inch bowl, decorated exactly as shown in illustration and **the most wonderful value ever offered at $1.50.**

Our special price....**$1.50**

Our $1.85 Vase Banquet Lamp.

No. 2R918 This Handsome Vase Lamp, an entirely new and handsome design, is offered at $1.85 in competition with lamps that sell at double the price. It is 17 inches high, has 9-inch globe, 10-inch bowl. It is beautifully colored and hand decorated as illustrated.

Our special price.............................**$1.85**

No. 2R918

No. 2R922 This Large and Beautiful Banquet Lamp is 21½ inches high and is blue and white shaded and tinted globe and bowl, mounted on a heavy cast brass base, as illustrated. It is of the latest pattern and has beautiful free hand decorations in natural floral designs. It is fitted with a No. 2 brass burner of the best make which can be easily cleaned and kept in order. This lamp is a special bargain at our extremely low price of $1.15. Weight, packed, 25 pounds

Price.....**$1.15**

No. 2R924 This Large Beautiful Lamp, illustrated, has dark and light shaded brown bowl decorated as illustrated. It is 21¼ inches high, and has a large globe. It is the very cheapest lamp ever offered with the removable brass fount and No. 2 Royal center draft burner. It comes carefully packed in a box, weighing 30 pounds.

Our special price......**$1.58**

No. 2R908 No. 2R910

Our $2.10 Lamp.

No. 2R908 This Handsome Banquet Lamp is 23 inches high, has 9-inch globe, removable oil fount, fitted with the celebrated No. 2 Royal centerdraft burner of 75 candle power. Beautifully colored and free hand painted, as illustrated. Our special price.**$2.10**

Our $3.15 Banquet Lamp.

No. 2R910 This Lamp is 36 inches high, has 10-inch globe and 9-inch bowl, center draft, removable fount, handsomely decorated in beautiful free hand colorings, **gold plated base and mountings.**

Our special price........**$3.15**

Our $1.95 Banquet Lamp

No. 2R912 This Lamp is 25 inches high, has 9-inch globe, removable oil fount, No. 3 Climax burner, neat hand flower decoration on pink background. **Wonderful value at $1.95.**

Our special price....... **$1.95**

No. 2R912

No. 2R914

Our $1.25 Leader.

No. 2R914 For $1.25 we offer in this a lamp that retails at double the price. It is 19½ inches high, has 8-inch globe, 7½-inch bowl, stands on a beautiful metal base. It is handsomely tinted and ornamented. Special price..**$1.25**

SUNBURST GASOLINE INCANDESCENT LAMPS.

The Cheapest and Most Brilliant Light on Earth—Absolutely Safe and Reliable.

A new departure in the construction and principle of the generator and gasoline fount. The Sunburst is superior to all other lamps because there are no needle valves to clog up; no stuffing boxes to leak; no asbestos packing, requiring constant renewal; no dismantling in order to clean; no complicated mechanism to get out of order. So simple that any child can easily understand and operate it.

1st.—It requires very little time to start the generator. 2d.—The method of filtering the gasoline before it reaches the generator reduces the possibility of clogging to a minimum. 3d.—Our system of packing the tube with corundum, thus minutely subdividing the gasoline before it is delivered into the Bunsen burner, insures a steady and even light. It will not flicker or flash; in fact the candle power does not vary one iota from one hour to the other. 4th.—Our Bunsen burner is so constituted that it automatically regulates the amount of gasoline and air, and hence a perfect combustion is at all times maintained. 5th.—The simplicity of the burner is such that it cannot get out of order. 6th.—By simply removing one screw the entire interior of the gasoline passage is exposed, for the purpose of cleaning, when required. This feature is possessed by no other generator manufactured.

One gallon of gasoline burns sixty hours. No smoke. No odor. Absolutely safe. The most economical light in use. Fully approved by the Fire Insurance Underwriters.

Fancy Two-Burner Gasoline Fixture.

No. 2R950 Fancy Two-Burner Gasoline Fixture. Made of brass throughout, spun brass tank, etc., a lamp nice enough for any residence, finely finished, heavy mantle and glassware. Price, complete, as shown in cut.....**$7.00**

One-Burner Fancy Gasoline Fixture.

No. 2R956 One-Burner All Brass Gasoline Fixture. Spun brass tank, extra heavy tubing, fancy scroll bracket, large opal shade, heavy mantle and glassware. One of the handsomest lamps made.

Price, complete as shown in illustration............**$4.25**

Students' Gasoline Lamp.

No. 2R962 All brass, Nickel Plated Gasoline Students' Lamp; removable tank; burner and lamp can be raised or lowered. Extra heavy base, which prevents lamp from upsetting. A very handsome lamp, nice enough for any library. Easily moved from place to place. Price, complete, as shown in cut............ ....**$3.98**

Automatic Lamp Extension.

No. 2R966 Ornamental Hanging Lamp Extension. Should be used on all gasoline lamps where ceiling is high. **Allows the lamp to be lowered when refilling, etc. Not necessary to remove lamp from hook.** Can also be used on all kinds of hanging lamps, gasoline or kerosene.

Price, each...................................**$1.15**

The Vapor Lamp.

The construction of Vapor Lamps is thoroughly first class in every respect. They are made entirely of heavy brass (18-gauge fount), oxidized copper finish, lacquered, and present a very handsome appearance. Each lamp is carefully tested and examined before shipment to make sure that it is perfect. **The lamp is not in any way complicated;** there is nothing to get out of order and it is easy to operate. **This lamp differs from our regular gasoline lamp inasmuch as we use air pressure instead of gravity pressure.** By the air pressure system we give five times the candle power to be obtained from an ordinary lamp. **For stores, barber shops, halls, skating rinks and billiard rooms it has no equal.** Two lamps will light a large size store and hall, as each lamp gives 500-candle power.

No. 2R970 The complete lamp includes the burner, deflector, lighting cup, alcohol can, chimney, fluted shade, mantle and holder, air pump and wrench. Price, each............ ......**$8.00**

Little Wonder Lamp.

No. 2R974 The chief advantage of our Little Wonder is that it has none of the objectionable features of other forms of lighting. With 5 cents worth of gasoline it will produce a light throughout the night superior to any electric arc. No breeze or draft of air is strong enough to blow it out or affect its steadiness in any way. Specially adapted for public places. It is the newest of our gasoline vapor lamps to be pronounced absolutely safe. **No kind of glassware is needed in connection with The Little Wonder light.** Fragile globes can be dispensed with and there is absolutely no neecssity for shades, reflectors or any other glass. When we say **The Little Wonder** can be used without shade or glassware of any kind we do not wish to convey the impression that a globe cannot be used if so desired. **The Little Wonder lamp is handsomely nickel plated and beautifully finished. It is a high air pressure lamp, 500-candle power light.** Simple in construction and easy to operate. The cost of running expense is less than kerosene and will not exceed ½-cent per hour. With every lamp we furnish free an air pump, wrench, alcohol can, two mantles, one metal shade and funnel; all carefully packed. Shipping weight, 8 pounds.

No. 2R974 Our special price, complete..................................**$9.80**

No. 2R975 Little Wonder Lamp. Same as described above, with traparent globe.

Price..**$10.30**

For extra mantles refer to Nos. 24R8790 and 24R8798, inclusive.

...SPECIAL... DEPARTMENT OF BABY CARRIAGES, GO CARTS AND INVALID CHAIRS.

OUR LINE IS COMPLETE, our styles the latest and our prices represent a saving to you over the prices usually asked of at least thirty per cent.

EVERY UPHOLSTERED GO-CART, SLEEPER AND CARRIAGE IS MADE UP SPECIAL and we therefore require from three to five days time after the order is received by us before we can make shipment.

SPECIAL FINISH. Any carriage, except oak, can be finished in cherry, antique, XVIth century or empire, without extra charge.

Colors in Which Upholstering is Furnished.

In Ordering Do not Fail to State Color Wanted.

Glenmore Cloth—Sapphire, cardinal, olive, golden brown, myrtle.

Turkish Cloth—Sapphire, cardinal, olive, golden brown, myrtle.

Armure Tapestry—Sapphire, cardinal, olive, golden brown, myrtle.

Velours—Sapphire, cardinal, myrtle, golden brown, olive, nile, pomegranate, steel.

Mercerized Damask—Sapphire, cardinal, myrtle, golden brown, olive, nile, pomegranate, steel.

Iridescent Corduroy—Sapphire, cardinal, myrtle, golden brown, tan.

Extra Quality Velours—Sapphire, cardinal, olive, golden brown, myrtle, nile, pomegranate, steel.

Brocatelle—Sapphire, cardinal, olive, golden brown, myrtle, nile, pomegranate, steel.

Imported Corduroy—Tan, myrtle, sapphire, golden brown.

Silk Plush—Sapphire, cardinal, olive, golden brown, myrtle, nile, pomegranate, turquoise, cerise.

Silk Damask—Sapphire, cardinal, olive, golden brown, myrtle, nile, pomegranate, turquoise, cerise.

Fine English Broadcloth—Tan, myrtle.

Extra Quality Silk Plush—Sapphire, cardinal, olive, golden brown, myrtle, nile, pomegranate, turquoise, cerise.

Extra Quality Silk Damask—Sapphire, cardinal, olive, golden brown, myrtle, nile, pomegranate, turquoise, cerise.

Lace Covers for Baby Carriages and Sleeper Carts.

No. 25R1 Figured Lappet Cloth, with ruffle edge. Price, each.....45c

No. 25R2 Fine White India Lawn, with double plaited ruffle. Price, each.....67c

These are lace covers only, not parasols.

No. 25R3 Plain White Net, with double ruffle of same, trimmed with fancy braid. Price, each, $1.12

No. 25R4 Plain White Net, with three point d'esprit net ruffles, trimmed with fancy braid. Price, each.....$1.35

These are lace covers only, not parassol.

No. 25R5 Plain White Net, with two deep ruffles of same, trimmed with silk ribbon. Each.....$1.58

No. 25R6 Point d'Esprit Net, with four deep ruffles of same, trimmed with wide Valenciennes lace. Price, each.....$2.20

These are lace covers only, not parasols.

No. 25R7 Fine Plain White Net, with seven ruffles of same, all edges trimmed with Valenciennes lace. Price, each.....$2.65

These are lace covers only, not parasols.

PARASOLS.

No. 25R10 Silesia, scalloped edge. Price.....39c
No. 25R11 Sateen, lace edge. Price, each.....73c
No. 25R12 Sateen, ruffle edge. Price, each.....74c
No. 25R13 Sateen, with fancy ruffle. Price.....98c
No. 25R14 Sateen, with two deep ruffles. Each, 99c
No. 25R15 Silk Satin, lined, ruffle edge. Ea., $1.62
No. 25R16 Sateen, with point d'esprit net cover, silk satin ruffle, Valenciennes lace edge. Price, $1.63
No. 25R17 Silk Satin, lined, lace edge with satin heading. Price, each.....$1.64
No. 25R18 Silk Satin, lined, with narrow draped ruffle, straight ruffle at bottom. Price, each...$2.23
No. 25R19 Silk Satin, lined, with deep draped ruffle. Price, each.....$2.24
No. 25R20 Fine Quality Silk Satin, lined, flounced ruffle with puffing. Price, each.....$2.73
No. 25R21 Fine Quality Silk Satin, lined, with deep cascaded ruffle. Price, each.....$2.74
No. 25R22 Fine Quality Silk Satin, lined, with three flounced ruffles and puffing. Price, each..$3.23

Prices for Parts.

No. 25R23 Axles, tinned. Price, each.....19c
No. 25R24 Braces, tinned. Price, each.....6c
No. 25R25 Brakes, tinned. Price, each.....18c
No. 25R27 Carriage Straps, good quality. Ea., 12c
No. 25R29 Handles Complete, finished. Per set, 50c
No. 25R30 Axle Nuts. Price, each.....5c
No. 25R31 Parasol Rods, tinned. Price, each...18c
No. 25R32 Parasol Rod Top Balls, nickeled. Ea., 5c
No. 25R33 Patent Rod Clamps. Price, each...21c
No. 25R34 Patent Rod Clamp Thumbscrew. Price, each.....10c
No. 25R35 Front Springs, for carriage, tinned. Price, each.....18c
No. 25R36 Back Springs, for carriage, tinned. Price, each.....15c

Plain Tire Steel Wheels, Tinned.

No. 25R41 10-inch. Price, each.....34c
No. 25R42 14-inch. Price, each.....45c
No. 25R43 20-inch. Price, each.....54c
No. 25R44 22-inch. Price, each.....69c

Rubber Tire Steel Wheels, Tinned.

No. 25R45 10-inch. Price, each.....59c
No. 25R46 14-inch. Price, each.....84c
No. 25R47 20-inch. Price, each.....89c
No. 25R48 22-inch. Price, each.....$1.10

Go-carts from Nos. 25R102 to 25R124, inclusive, do not have reclining backs, and cannot be used as sleeper carts. Go-Carts from Nos. 25R183 to 25R125, inclusive, are made with adjustable reclining backs, and can be used as sleeping coaches.

GO-CARTS. Our $2.28 Go-Carts.

This cart is extra strong, made from a good grade of wood, with reed body, nicely finished; fancy embossed bottom; heavy tin plated steel wheels, wood step.

No. 25R102 Without upholstering or parasol. Special price..$2.28

No. 25R103 Upholstered with removable denim cushion in seat and back. Price..$2.78

No. 25R104 Upholstered with removable denim cushions in seat and back. Has silesia parasol, with scalloped edge. Complete with fixtures. Our special price.....$3.68

Extra for rubber tired wheels, 50 cents.

Our $2.79 Go-Cart.

This cart has a good body, trimmed with hand woven reed arm rest and back, well finished. Has handsome embossed seat, heavy Bessemer steel wheels, steel springs and wood step.

No. 25R109 Without upholstering or parasol. Special price.....$2.79

No. 25R110 Upholstered with removable denim cushions in seat and back. Price..$3.29

No. 25R111 Upholstered with removable denim cushion in seat and back, and has parasol made of silesia, with scalloped edge. Complete with fixtures. Our special price.....$4.19

Extra for rubber tired wheels, 50 cents.

Our $3.48 Go-Cart.

This cart is made of the best reeds and is very roomy, strong and durable, is shellaced and varnished. Has cane seat, low step, best quality steel wheels, fitted with patent automatic brake; is perfect in every respect.

No. 25R116 Without upholstering or parasol. Our special price, each....$3.48

No. 25R117 Upholstered with removable Glenmore cloth cushions in seat and back. Our special price, each.....$3.98

No. 25R118 Upholstered with removable Glenmore cloth cushions in seat and back, and has parasol made of sateen with ruffle edge. Complete with fixtures. Our special price.....$5.23

Extra for rubber tired wheels, 50 cents.

The body of this Go-Cart is made of the best quality of reeds, with heavy full roll running across the back and arms as shown in the illustration. Closely woven cane seat, handsomely ornamented dash, steel running gear, patent automatic brake. This is one of the latest designs for 1902, and is a very handsome cart.

No. 25R119 Without upholstering or parasol. Price, $4.77

No. 25R120 Upholstered with removable iridescent corduroy cushions in seat and back. Our special price.....$5.25

No. 25R121 Upholstered with removable iridescent corduroy cushions in seat and back, has fine quality sateen parasol with two deep ruffles and fixtures. Our special price.....$6.98

Rubber tired wheels, 50 cents extra.

Our Finest Go-Cart. Latest 1902 Design.

The body is made of the best imported reeds closely woven. Has high back, full cane seat, steel running gear and broad, low step; fitted with patent automatic foot brake.

No. 25R122 Without upholstering or parasol. Our price..$5.98

No. 25R123 Upholstered with removable iridescent corduroy cushions in seat and back. Price...$6.89

No. 25R124 Upholstered with removable iridescent corduroy in seat and back; sateen parasol with fancy ruffles and fixtures. Price, each.....$8.35

Rubber tired wheels, 50 cents extra.

SLEEPER CARTS.

These carts are made so that the back will fall back to a reclining position for the baby to sleep; at the same time the dash front is automatically raised as the back is reclined. When the baby falls asleep the back is dropped and the child is at once in an easy reclining sleeping position. The back and dash can be operated independently or simultaneously as desired.

Has tinned steel running gear, with brake. Extra large and roomy, has broad, closely woven cane seat, back and step; has an adjustable device to recline the back so as to make a sleeping cart, at the same time the foot is automatically raised as the back is lowered.

No. 25R125 Without upholstering or parasol. Our special price, $4.19

No. 25R126 With removable Glenmore cloth cushions in seat, back and dash. Our price...$4.90

No. 25R127 With cushions in seat, back and dash, and sateen parasol with ruffled edge and fixtures. Our special price.....$5.95

No. 25R128 With removable denim cushions in seat, back, dash and sides; and with parasol of sateen with ruffle edge and fixtures. Price....$6.45

Extra for rubber tired wheels, 50 cents.

Our $4.78 Sleeper Cart.

Made of the best imported Manila reeds. Has elegant design of reed work on sides and an extra high back. Hand woven cane seat and cane back. Patent automatic foot brake, patent device for adjusting back, the foot being raised automatically as the back is lowered.

No. 25R130 Without upholstering or parasol. Our price.....$4.78

No. 25R131 Upholstered with removable Glenmore cloth cushions in seat, back and dash. Our special price.....$5.60

No. 25R132 Upholstered with removable cushions in seat, back and dash and with parasol of sateen, with ruffle edge and fixtures. Price, $6.80

No. 25R133 Upholstered with denim cushions in seat, back, dash and sides, and with parasol of sateen with ruffle edge and fixtures. Price...$7.40

Extra for rubber tired wheels, 50 cents.

Our $5.22 Sleeper Cart.

Made of the finest imported reeds, with the best full plated steel running gear, patent automatic brake. It has the patent device for lowering and adjusting the back, the foot being raised automatically when the back is lowered; has hand woven cane seat and back.

No. 25R135 Without upholstering or parasol. Our special price.....$5.22

No. 25R136 Upholstered with removable armure tapestry cloth cushions in back, seat and dash. Our special price.....$6.20

No. 25R137 Same as No. 25R136 and with sateen parasol with ruffle edge and fixtures. Our special price.....$7.65

No. 25R138 Upholstered with removable armure tapestry cushions in back, seat, dash and sides, and with sateen parasol, with ruffle edge and fixtures. Our special price.....$8.40

Extra for rubber tired wheels, 50 cents.

Our $6.17 Go-Cart Sleeper.

The body of this cart is handsomely worked into an elaborate design with closely woven reeds; cane seat and back; it is full finished, shellacked and varnished; highest grade full plated steel running gear; adjustable back which raises the foot automatically; Kinley automatic brake.

No. 25R140 Without upholstering or parasol. Our price...$6.17

No. 25R141 Upholstered with four-color velours, removable cushions in seat, back and dash. Our price..$7.85

No. 25R142 Same as No. 25R141 and complete with sateen parasol with fancy ruffles and fixtures. Our special price....$9.25

No. 25R143 Upholstered with removable velours cushions in seat, back, dash and sides, sateen parasol with fancy ruffles and fixtures. Each, $9.98

Extra for rubber tired wheels, 50 cents.

Our Jewel Oak Go-Cart Sleeper for $6.98.

This sleeper is made of the best selected quarter sawed golden oak, highly polished. It has a fine close woven cane seat.

No. 25R145 Without upholstering or parasol. Each, $6.98

No. 25R146 Upholstered with removable iridescent corduroy seat, back and dash, no parasol. Price.....$8.80

No. 25R147 Upholstered with removable iridescent corduroy seat, back and dash, sateen parasol with fancy ruffles and fixtures. Price (Extra for rubber tired wheels, 50c), $9.20

A Bargain for $7.22.

A rich, attractive, and durable Go-Cart Sleeper, with closely woven sides and large French rolls running to the foot. It has cane seat, high cane back and roomy foot, making it very attractive and desirable. Has highest grade full plated steel running gear, patent automatic foot brake and adjustable back and foot.

No. 25R150 Without upholstering or parasol. Price.....$7.22

No. 25R151 Upholstered removable iridescent corduroy cushions seat, back and dash. Price, each............$8.80

No. 25R152 Upholstered removable iridescent corduroy cushions, seat, back and dash, sateen parasol with fancy ruffles and fixtures. Each, $10.20

No. 25R153 Upholstered removable iridescent corduroy cushions, seat, back, dash and sides, sateen parasol with fancy ruffles and fixtures. Each, $10.95

Extra for rubber tired wheels, 50 cents.

The material that enters into its construction is of the best quality and guaranteed to give the very best of satisfaction. The body is made of closely woven, imported reeds shaped into beautiful figures, making a very pretty as well as useful cart. It has cane seat and back, full steel running gear with automatic brake. It has high back and low, roomy step. Back and step can be adjusted in position automatically.

No. 25R155 Without upholstering or parasol. Each, $7.56

No. 25R156 Upholstered with removable iridescent corduroy cushion, seat, back and dash..$8.56

No. 25R157 Upholstered with removable iridescent corduroy cushion, seat, back and dash, handsome sateen parasol with fancy ruffle and fixtures. Our special price......................$9.16

No. 25R158 Upholstered with removable iridescent corduroy cushions, seat, back, dash and sides, has handsome sateen parasol with fancy ruffles and fixtures. Our special price..........$10.16

Extra for rubber tired wheels, 50 cents.

An original and novel design in a Sleeper Cart, made with imported reeds woven into an artistic pattern. Has highest grade full plated steel running gear, patent automatic foot brake; broad, roomy low step patent device for adjusting the back, which raises the foot automatically as the back is lowered.

No. 25R160 Without upholstering or parasol. Ea., $7.85

No. 25R161 Upholstered with removable two-color velours cushions in seat, back and dash. Price..$8.85

No. 25R162 Upholstered with velours cushions, seat, back and dash and with parasol of sateen with fancy ruffles and fixtures. Our special price.................$9.35

No. 25R163 Upholstered with velours cushions, seat, back, dash and sides, sateen parasol with fancy ruffles and fixtures. Our special price........$10.35

Extra for rubber tired wheels, 50 cents.

The reed body is a beautiful pattern made of the very best selected Manila reeds, durable and stylish in appearance. It has a high back and a low, roomy step.

No. 25R165 Without upholstering or parasol. Price, $8.75

No. 25R166 Upholstered removable velours cushions, seat, back and dash. Price, each..$9.98

No. 25R167 Upholstered removable velours cushions, seat, back and dash, sateen parasol with fancy ruffles and fixtures. Price, $10.48

No. 25R168 Upholstered velours cushions seat, back, dash and sides, sateen parasol with fancy ruffles and fixtures. Our price..$11.48

Extra for rubber tired wheels, 50 cents.

This is an elegant, large and roomy cart, made of the very finest imported reeds, closely woven cane seat and back, full finished, shellaced and varnished. Has the highest grade full tin plated steel running gear, patent foot brake, patent device for raising and lowering the back, which also raises and lowers the step, working automatically.

No. 25R170 Without upholstering or parasol. Price....$9.52

No. 25R171 Upholstered with removable two-color extra quality velours cushions in seat, back and dash. Our special price.........................$10.70

No. 25R172 Upholstered with removable extra quality velours cushions seat back and dash; with parasol of silk satin, lined, with fancy ruffles and fixtures. Our special price...................$12.98

No. 25R173 Upholstered with removable extra quality velours seat, back, dash and sides, silk satin parasol, lined, ruffle edge and fixtures. Each. $14.23

Extra for rubber tired wheels, 50 cents.

This cart has reed body of very handsome design. Every piece of material which is used is of the best quality and is made up by only the most expert workmen. It has full cane seat with high back, broad and roomy step, full steel running gear with steel wheels, patent foot brake and patent device for raising and lowering the back and step.

No. 25R175 Without upholstering or parasol. Price.. ..$11.98

No. 25R176 Upholstered with removable extra quality velours cushions, back and dash. Our special price, $13.23

No. 25R177 Upholstered with removable extra quality velours cushions, seat, back and dash; with handsome silk satin lined parasol, with ruffled edge and fixtures. Our special price... ....$15.38

No. 25R178 Same as No. 25R177, but has sides upholstered also. Our special price.........$16.63

Extra for rubber tired wheels, 50 cents.

Our Very Finest Sleeper Cart for $13.35

The body is all made of closely woven imported reed and is large and roomy; has a high and comfortable back and a closely woven cane seat. Has high grade, tin plated, steel running gear and patent foot brake. The back and step can be raised or lowered automatically.

No. 25R180 Without upholstering or parasol. Price......$13.35

No. 25R181 Upholstered in removable imported iridescent corduroy cushions, seat, back and dash. Price $14.60

No. 25R182 Upholstered in removable iridescent corduroy cushions, seat, back and dash with handsome silk satin lined parasol with ruffled edge and fixtures. Our special price.. ......$16.75

No. 25R183 Same as No. 25R182, but has sides upholstered also. Our special price.........$17.95

Extra for rubber tired wheels, 50 cents.

Our $3.65 Baby Carriage.

No. 25R221 It is made of good material throughout. Heavy maple frame; body is mitered, glued and fitted at corners, well finished. The gear, including the wheels, axles, springs and brake are of Bessemer steel, nicely plated. It is upholstered in a nice shade of Glenmore cloth, a good substantial material. It has a cane embossed finished bottom, one piece long bent handle with solid brace irons. The parasol is detachable, made of a good quality of silesia, fancy scalloped edge, as illustrated. Our special price.........$3.65

Extra for rubber tired wheels, 65 cents.

Our $4.40 Baby Carriage.

No. 25R226 The frame is made of seasoned maple, mitered, glued, screwed and plugged at joints. The upholstering is an extra quality Turkish cloth. It comes upholstered in various colors as described on page 804. Highest grade Walker gear, full plated and best quality steel axles, springs, Kinley automatic brake. Parasol is silesia, scalloped edge. Our special price....$4.40

Extra for rubber tired wheels, 65 cents.

Our $4.89 Carriage.

No. 25R232 This is a new style carriage. Frame is made of seasoned maple; body from a good quality of rattan, woven in a substantial manner, upholstered in Glenmore cloth which we furnish in vacolors as described on page 804. The gear is the celebrated Walker Bessemer steel gear, heavily plated and finished, fitted with the Kinley automatic brake. Parasol, as illustrated, made of good quality silesia with fancy scalloped edges as illustrated. Our price.........$4.89

No. 25R233 Upholstered in Glenmore cloth and plush. Has handsome sateen parasol with ruffle edge and fixtures. Our special price...............$5.46

Extra for rubber tired wheels, 65 cents.

Our $16.66 Baby Carriage.

Our $16.66 Baby Carriage is made expressly for us by one of the most expert designers of baby carriages, and embodies the most beautiful woven reed work which it is possible to produce. The body is large and roomy and exceptionally well made; has a high back crowned with beautiful woven reed effects and has full closely woven cane bottom. The gear is of best quality full plated steel construction with steel wheels and automatic brake. The upholstering is of the very best quality throughout. In fact, every part and piece that enters into the construction of this carriage, together with the workmanship, is of the very best grade and is sure to give unqualified satisfaction.

No. 25R322 Upholstered in removable silk damask and silk plush with fine quality silk satin lining in the back. The parasol is silk satin, lined throughout, with deep cascaded ruffle and all fixtures. Our special price....................$16.66

No. 25R323 Upholstered throughout with removable silk plush, otherwise same as No. 25R322. Our special price....................$17.11

Extra for rubber tired wheels, 65 cents.

A Regular $25.00 Carriage for $17.56.

For $17.56 we offer this carriage as one of the finest which we manufacture, of unusually attractive design and one of the prettiest carriages on the market. The reed work is most artistic, and from the illustration one can hardly judge of the real beauty of this carriage. The body is made of the best quality imported reeds; has an unusually high beautifully shaped back with very ornamental sides and large closely woven reed dash. The upholstering is of the very best quality, and in every detail this carriage is strictly high grade. The gear is of the very best quality, full plated, steel construction thoroughly braced throughout, making it strong and durable. It has steel wheels with automatic brake.

No. 25R324 The upholstering is all removable and is of the best quality silk damask and silk plush, having back lining of fine quality silk satin. The parasol is made of fine quality silk satin, lined throughout, and has flounce ruffle with puffing and all fixtures. Our special price....................$17.56

No. 25R325 Upholstered in silk plush throughout. Otherwise same as No. 25R324. Our special price....................$18.95

Rubber tired wheels, 65 cents extra.

A Strictly High Grade Baby Carriage.

With one exception this is the very best carriage which we furnish. In fact, it is nearly equal to our highest grade in every respect, with the exception of the slight difference in the cost of the woven work in the body. It is of the very latest design, being highly artistic and at the same time of most serviceable construction. The body is unusually large and roomy; has a high back with beautiful French roll at the top and full French roll at the sides, with dash to correspond. It has full steel running gear of the very best construction, steel wheels and automatic brake, full plated throughout. The upholstering is of the very best quality; in fact, there is nothing better made.

No. 25R328 Upholstered in removable silk damask and silk plush with fine quality silk satin lining in the back. The parasol is fine quality silk satin, lined throughout, with flounced ruffle with puffing and complete with all fixtures. Our special price....................$19.43

No. 25R329 Upholstered in removable silk plush. Otherwise same as No. 25R328. Our special price....................$19.98

Rubber tired wheels, 65 cents extra.

Our Very Finest Carriage.

This carriage is made of the very best material that money can buy. It is upholstered in an extra quality silk damask, tufted in diamonds with fancy pipes, silk cords and tassels, fine quality silk satin back lining. The body is made of closely woven reeds, full shellaced and finished; fine hand woven cane bottom. **Parasol is very attractive, a new design of fine quality silk satin, lined, with three** flounced ruffles and puffing.

No. 25R340 Our special price, each.......$20.43

No. 25R341 Upholstered in extra quality of silk plush, otherwise the same as above..........$20.88

Extra for rubber tired wheels, 65 cents.

Twin Carriage, $11.58.

For $11.58 we furnish this Twin Carriage as the equal of carriages that will retail at far more than our price. The body is made extra large and roomy, extra strong throughout. Strong, maple frame, mitered, screwed, glued and plugged at joints. Pattern woven cane bottom. Fine imported reed work, hand woven, nicely finished and heavily shellaced. The upholstering is of the best grade. Best Walker gear, extra heavy Bessemer steel wheels, axles, springs and Kinley automatic brake.

No. 25R344 Upholstered in Glenmore cloth with plush rolls, sateen parasols with ruffle edge..$11.58

No. 25R345 Upholstered in armure tapestry with silk plush rolls, silk satin parasols, lined, ruffle edge....................$13.35

Extra for rubber tires, 65 cents.

ALL GO-CARTS, SLEEPERS AND CARRIAGES are made special, and we therefore require 3 to 5 days after order is received before we can make shipment.

WHEN ORDERING a Go-Cart, Sleeper or Carriage be sure to state color of upholstering desired. For a list of all different colors which we can furnish, see introductory description on page 804.

INVALIDS' CHAIRS.

This comfortable Invalids' Chair is a substantial wheel chair, and at $10.75 is wonderful value.

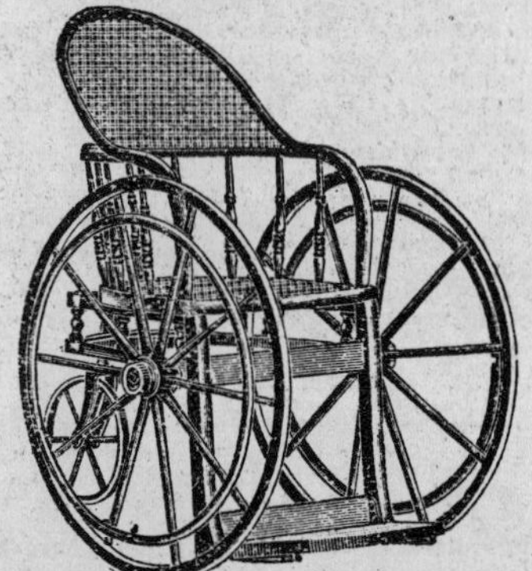

No. 25R800 The chair shown above is a good, strong, serviceable chair built for comfort and durability. It is light and can be easily handled and makes a splendid indoor chair. The dimensions of this chair are as follows: Width of seat, 18 inches; height of back, 20 inches; distance from seat to foot rest, 17 inches; front wheels, 28 inches; back wheel, 12 inches.

Price of this chair with wood or steel wheels..	$10.75
Hand rims, extra	.75
Push handles, extra	.75
Rubber tired wheels, extra	7.60
Ball bearing rubber tired wheels, extra....	11.40
Leather cushion for seat, extra...	2.20

Our $13.75 Invalids' Wheel Chair is the Equal of Those Selling as High as $25.00.

No. 25R804 In designing this chair for the use of invalids everything for their comfort has been considered. It is light, strong and durable, yet so constructed as to afford the greatest comfort without sacrificing any of the necessary strength. **The frame work is of oak and fitted with open cane,** which is cool and elastic and practically never wears out. The dimensions are such as to be large enough for a person weighing 250 pounds, and we make larger sizes to order. The back is of sufficient size to rest the head and shoulders and the arm rests are such as to comfortably rest the forearm without danger of the hands coming in contact with the wheels. **The reclining attachment is very simple; in fact, it is practically automatic and there is nothing to get out of order.** The foot rest swings out of the way, making it an easy chair to get in and out of. A chair of equal merits has never before been offered for so low a price. The dimensions of this chair are as follows: The back, 29 inches high; the seat, 19x17 inches; front wheels, 28 inches; back wheel, 12 inches; distance from seat to the foot rest is 17 inches. This chair will go through any ordinary doorway.

Price of this chair with steel or wood wheels	$13.75
Hand rims on wheels, extra..	.75
Push handles on back, extra	.75
Rubber tired wheels, extra	7.60
Ball bearing rubber tired wheels, extra....	11.40
Damask cushions for back, seat and leg rests, extra	7.70

Our $21.75 Rattan Invalids' Chair.

THIS INVALIDS' CHAIR is sold by specialty dealers in these goods at almost double our price. We ask only our one small percentage of profit above the actual manufacturing cost.

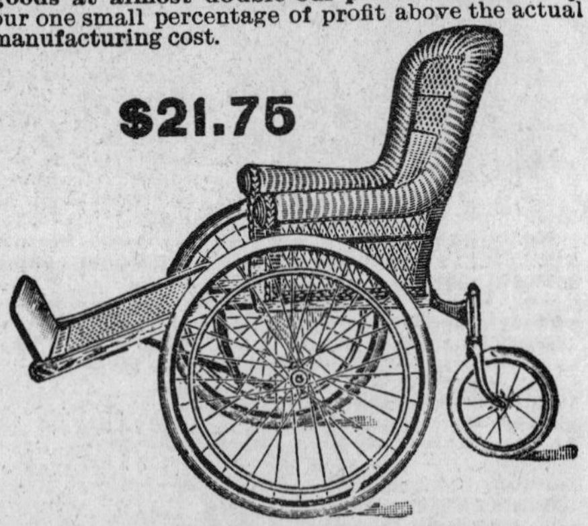

No. 25R808 The above chair is one intended for indoor as well as outdoor use. The body is made of rattan wicker work, so shaped as to afford the greatest amount of comfort. The leg rests which form so essential a part of invalids' chairs, is especially designed on this chair to give the greatest amount of comfort and at the same time the adjustment is very easy and such that it will not get out of order. The leg rests are made to extend automatically several inches when they are raised on a level with the seat. **This chair can be propelled by the occupant by using the hand rims which are attached to the wheels, and as the back caster wheel turns in any direction, the chair is easily guided and requires no effort to propel it from place to place.** The dimensions of this chair are as follows: The back is 28 inches high, the seat is 18x17½ inches, the distance from the seat to the footboard when down is 17 inches.

The price of this chair with steel or wood wheels is	$21.75
Hand rims on wheels, extra	.75
Rubber tired wheels extra	7.60
Ball bearing rubber tired wheels, extra....	11.40
Push handles, extra	.75
Pneumatic tires, extra	3.80
Leather cushion for seat, extra	2.20

MEMORIAL DEPARTMENT.

THE WORLD'S BEST ROYAL BLUE VERMONT MARBLE. IT IS EVERYWHERE CONCEDED TO BE THE FINEST IN THE WORLD. It is of rich, unfading color, and superior to the other blue marbles on the market which lose their color on exposure to the weather. A FINE, CLOSE GRAINED MARBLE.

OUR SUPERIOR FINISHING. We do not use oxalic acid, and we employ only skilled artisans. We do not have our work done by the piece, but only employ day labor, thus securing the best possible fineness in finish.

WE OFFER YOU the handsome Marble Markers shown on this page at half the prices you can buy them from your nearest marble dealer. Our low prices are cash with the order, delivered on the cars at our mills and quarry in Vermont.

SEND US ANY LETTERING YOU MAY DESIRE CARVED IN THE MARBLE and we will charge you but 6 cents per letter for ordinary sunk inscription letters, as shown in name and date lines; 2½ cents each for sunk verse letters, and on larger tombstones where raised letters are required we will charge you but 18 cents per letter for 2x⅛-inch letters raised in panel. If it is not exactly as represented and the lettering handsomely engraved according to your instructions, you can return it to us and we will refund the money.

FOR OTHER DESIGNS AT LOWEST PRICES WRITE FOR OUR NEW SPECIAL MONUMENT CATALOGUE.

UNHEARD OF VALUE AT $15.15 AND UPWARDS.

—LETTERS.—

Ordinary Sunk Inscription, name and dates..6c per letter
Sunk Verse ....2½c per letter
2x⅛-inch Raised in Panel...................18c per letter

LIKE EVERY ONE of our higher grade tombstones, this monument is made in the same famous quarry, and, by reason of having been made there, you are guaranteed a quality which you might not expect anywhere else.

The measurements of the smaller size of this tombstone are as follows: Bottom base, 1 foot 4 inches, by 1 foot 4 inches, by 8 inches. Base, 1 foot, by 1 foot, by 6 inches. Shaft, 2 feet 6 inches, by 8 inches, by 8 inches. Height over all, 3 feet 8 inches. This tombstone is made in the following variety of colors, cash with order, delivered on the cars at our Vermont quarry:

No. 22R1755 Dark vein marble, 455 lbs....$15.15
No. 22R1756 Florence No. 2, 455 lbs........ 15.20
No. 22R1757 Dark mottled marble, 455 lbs. 16.10
No. 22R1758 Extra dark vein marble, 455 pounds........ 16.15
No. 22R1759 Average Florence marble, 455 pounds........ 16.20
No. 22R1760 Extra dark mottled marble, 455 pounds........ 17.05
No. 22R1761 Florence No. 1, 455 lbs........ 17.10

A LARGER SIZE AT $23.85 TO $26.70.

The next largest size of this handsome monument is as follows: Bottom base, 1 foot 6 inches, by 1 foot 6 inches, by 10 inches. Base, 1 foot 2 inches, by 1 foot 2 inches, by 8 inches. Shaft, 2 feet 10 inches, by 10 inches, by 10 inches. Height over all, 4 feet 4 inches. Our special prices on this size are as follows:

No. 22R1762 Dark vein marble, 800 lbs....$23.85
No. 22R1763 Florence No. 2, 800 lbs........ 23.90
No. 22R1764 Dark mottled marble, 800 lbs. 25.40
No. 22R1765 Extra dark vein marble, 800 pounds........ 25.45
No. 22R1766 Average Florence marble, 800 pounds........ 25.50
No. 22R1767 Extra dark mottled marble, 800 pounds........ 26.65
No. 22R1768 Florence No. 1, 800 pounds... 26.70

OUR HANDSOME $5.10 MARKER.

No. 22R1400 OUR $5.10 price includes the Marker and Base complete, but without any lettering as appears in the illustration, and the price is based on the actual cost of cutting the work out of the quarry with but our one small percentage of profit added. **This stone is handsomely polished, and as shown in the illustration, it is trimmed with tracing and beveling.** Height, with base, 1 foot 6 inches; size of base, 16x8x6 inches; marker, 12x12x4 inches.

No. 22R1400 Price, cash with order, delivered on the cars at our quarry. 125 pounds........$5.10

For sunk name and date letters **6 cents each**; for sunk verse letters, **2½ cents each.**

OUR RICH $7.00 MARKER.

No. 22R1412 THIS $7.00 Marker is the same size and of the same rich unfading Royal Blue Marble as our fine $6.99 marker, but of a different style of carving, tracing and shape. It is furnished complete with the base, delivered on the cars at our Vermont quarry. Height with base, 1 foot 8 inches; size of base, 18x8x6 inches; size of marker, 14x14x4 inches.

No. 22R1412 Price, cash with order, 151 lbs..$7.00

For sunk name and date letters, **6 cents each**; for sunk verse letters, **2½ cents each.**

OUR FINE $6.99 MARKER.

No. 22R1408 AT $6.99 we furnish this Marker, made of the same beautiful Royal Blue Vermont Marble as our $5.10 marker shown above, but a larger size, being 20 inches high and 18 inches wide at the base. It is thicker, heavier, and of different style, shape and carving. It is furnished complete with the base, delivered on the cars at our quarry in Vermont. Height with base, 1 foot 8 inches; size of base, 18x8x6 inches; size of marker, 14x14x4 inches.

No. 22R1408 Price, cash with order, 151 lbs..$6.99

For sunk name and date letters, **6 cents each**; for sunk verse letters, **2½ cents each.**

OUR SUPERIOR $7.65 TOMBSTONE.

No. 22R1416 AT $7.65 we offer this Royal Blue Marble Marker, made of the same rich, unfading Vermont marble as all the others, but measuring 24 inches high and 18 inches wide at base. Delivered on the cars at our Vermont quarry. Height with base, 2 feet; size of base, 18x8x8 inches; size of marker, 16x14x4 inches.

No. 22R1416 Price, cash with order, 206 lbs..$7.65

For sunk name and date letters, **6 cents each**; for sunk verse letters, **2½ cents each.**

ALL MARBLE WORK is carefully boxed and delivered on the cars at our quarry in Vermont, and guaranteed to reach you in perfect order or we will replace it free of charge. Where we quote prices delivered on the cars at quarry it is done to save the expense of freight, cartage and handling into and out of our store in Chicago, and all the saving goes to the customer in the low prices we make, prices only made possible by eliminating all the handling expenses.

ABOUT THE FREIGHT. The weight of each tombstone is given. The average rates of freight east of the Mississippi River on them is 25 to 50 cents per hundred pounds, and south of the Ohio River from 50 cents to $1.00 per hundred pounds; west of the Mississippi River, east of the Rocky Mountains, from $1.00 to $1.50 per hundred pounds, greater or lesser distances in proportion; so you will find the freight will amount to next to nothing as compared with what you will save in price.

DEPARTMENT OF STOVES

We call attention to our complete Department of Strictly High Grade Cast Iron Stoves, Ranges and Heaters, Steel Ranges, Air Tight Heaters, Gasoline and Oil Stoves at prices lower than we have ever named before, prices much lower than you will find quoted by any other concern.

OUR NEW LINES FOR THIS SEASON include the new Improved Mississippi Valley line for soft coal or wood, shipped from our new foundry on the upper Mississippi River, for the convenience of our trade west, northwest and southwest of Chicago. The very latest thing in cast iron stoves, made from patterns that are new for this season, and offered at about half the price charged by retail dealers. Our line for this season also includes a number of cook stoves from entirely new patterns, stoves molded from patterns that were made under contract for us, embracing the good qualities of all strictly high grade stoves, with the defects of none.

OUR STEEL RANGE LINE IS OFFERED TO YOU AS THE HIGHEST GRADE WORK ON THE MARKET.

RANGES COMBINING THE GOOD QUALITIES OF ALL OTHER STEEL RANGES WITH THE DEFECTS OF NONE, and the price is based on the actual cost of material and labor, with but our one small percentage of profit added. Prices so low you can save from 25 to 50 per cent by placing your order in our hands.

HOW WE MAKE THE PRICES SO LOW. We are able to name a price on any stove we show direct to the user, which is considerably less than dealers can buy same grade of stoves in larger quantities. This is made possible by reason of our contracting with several of the best makers in the country for the entire product of their foundry, having the goods made up during the dull summer and early fall season, figuring the cost on a basis of the raw material, the labor, etc., and charging but one small percentage of profit, which results in our being able to deliver stoves to your door at prices, quality considered, heretofore unknown.

OUR BINDING GUARANTEE GOES WITH EVERY STOVE certifying that the stove is perfect in manufacture, perfect in operation, and unequaled by any other stove or range of its class for convenience, completeness, durability, economy in the consumption of fuel, and in the practical results that may be obtained by its use. That it is perfectly adapted to the fuel, and for the purpose for which it is made. That any defects in material or workmanship will be made good to purchaser without charge.

WHAT THE FREIGHT AMOUNTS TO. The freight charges you will have to pay on any stove or range will amount to next to nothing, as compared with what you will save in price. All stoves are accepted by railroad companies at third class freight rate, and by referring to freight classification in front of book, you will see just what the third class freight rate is to different points in every state in the Union, and under the description of every stove we give the weight of the different size stoves, and in this way you can calculate very closely what freight will amount to to your place. For example, you will find third class rates from Chicago to Alabama is from 75 cents to $1.03 per hundred pounds, and if a stove weighs 200 pounds, the freight rate from Chicago to Alabama will be from $1.50 to $2.06. To all points in Canada, third class freight rate is 55 cents, and the freight on stove weighing 200 pounds would be $1.10. To a point in Indiana the freight on a stove weighing 200 pounds, you will observe, will be from 40 to 50 cents; to Iowa, 58 to 90 cents; to Maine, $1.10 to $1.28. A 200-pound stove to any point in Massachusetts, $1.10. To a far distant point, like New Mexico, the freight on a stove weighing 200 pounds would be from $2.74 to $4.14. From this you can calculate, almost to a penny, what the freight rate will be to your place, and you will see it will add next to nothing to the cost, as compared with what you would be compelled to pay your local dealer.

OUR ACME LINE OF STOVES AND RANGES embody more distinct and original features of merit than are to be found in all other makes combined, and every Acme Stove is made of materials of the highest quality, fashioned by expert mechanics.

OUR GUARANTEE AGAINST BREAKAGE. So confident are we of the quality of the goods we offer and that they will invariably reach you in the same perfect condition they leave us, that we make this most liberal offer: Should any stove arrive badly damaged—such as any piece or part broken—you can pay the freight bill, have the agent note the condition of the stove on the freight bill, showing what part or parts are broken and then send the freight bill to us and we will immediately send you, free of charge, new castings to replace broken ones.

OUR ONLY TERMS ARE CASH IN FULL WITH THE ORDER. We have discontinued making C. O. D. shipments solely in the interest of lower prices and less expense to our customers, as fully explained in the introductory pages of our catalogue. A C.O.D. shipment means that the customer must pay an extra charge to the express company for returning the money to us; it also means extra clerical work for us, extra expense, all of which must be figured in when adjusting our selling prices, and to save this expense and to make possible lower prices than ever before, we now ask cash in full with all orders.

REMEMBER we only ask you to send cash in full with your order so that we may give you the benefit of the lowest price it is possible to make, so that you need not pay anything extra in the price for an expense from which you derive no benefit and which adds nothing to the intrinsic value of the stove or other merchandise. Understand, we not only save the expense in the clerical work that is necessary on C. O. D. shipments but you save the extra cost of 25 to 50 cents express charges on return of the money to us, which is necessary on C. O. D. shipments.

WE GUARANTEE the stove to reach you in perfect condition, guarantee it to satisfy you in every way, guarantee to give you such value as you could not possibly get elsewhere, and if we fail in any one of these conditions you can return the stove to us at our expense of freight charges both ways and we will immediately return your money.

READ OUR DESCRIPTIONS CAREFULLY. In comparing our prices with those of other concerns, note carefully the size, the height and the weight. Many concerns quote stove prices that look attractive, but if you examine carefully the measurements and the weight you will find that the goods are skimped somewhere. Remember also that our stoves are exactly as described in every detail, and when we say a stove weighs 420 pounds we do not mean that it weighs 415 pounds or 410 pounds.

IF YOU ARE IN THE MARKET for stoves of any kind, a stove, range, heater, anything in this department, you cannot afford to send your order elsewhere. We can save you so much money in this department, give you such high grade goods at such low prices, such satisfactory service in every way, that purely in your own interest you must send your order to us.

All stoves and ranges will be shipped from our factories to save you freight and secure prompt delivery to you.

CHEAP FREIGHT WEST. If you live west, northwest or southwest of Chicago, give careful attention to our celebrated Mississippi Valley line of stoves and ranges, shown on pages 815 to 818, which we ship from our new foundry on the upper Mississippi. This foundry has been added to our enormous stove business to supply our Western friends at less freight than from elsewhere and to secure more prompt delivery to them of these fine goods.

CHEAP FREIGHT EAST. If you live east of Chicago, give careful attention to our old reliable Ohio line, which we ship from our foundry in Central Ohio, giving everybody east and southeast of Chicago the benefit of less freight and more prompt delivery than if shipped from Chicago.

WE RECOGNIZE NO COMPETITION ON STOVES. Operating as we do, taking the entire product of several of the best and largest foundries in this country, that work under the most economical conditions, with the latest type of automatic labor saving machinery, with no selling expenses, such as traveling men, advertising, clerical help, etc., incident to stoves sold in the regular way to dealers, buying the raw material to the best advantage in the largest quantities, with absolutely the minimum of handling expense, we can make prices on the highest grades of stoves that include absolutely nothing but one small percentage of profit above the actual manufacturing cost.

STOVE REPAIRS.

PLEASE NOTICE. WE CAN ALWAYS FURNISH REPAIRS FOR ACMES. In ordering repairs for stoves, it is very important to give your purchase invoice number or the most complete and explicit information possible. By strictly adhering to the following rules, a great deal of annoyance, expense and delay may be averted.

1st. State whether stove is for coal only, for wood only, or a combined wood and coal burning construction.

2d. If cook stove or range, say if square top, or with reservoir.

3d. The back of a stove is at the pipe collar. Stand facing the hearth on a cook stove or facing the oven door of a range.

4th. Give full number. In many instances the same size of cooking holes are placed on different stove bodies, viz., 7-18, 8-18, 8-20, 9-20, etc., and the single No. 7, 8 or 9 in this case would be no indication of the correct size of the stove.

5th. Be particular to furnish all dates, if any, shown on stove.

6th. When legs are desired, say if stove is supplied with legs only or on leg base.

7th. Give name and number of stove in full.

OUR ACME STEEL RANGES AT $15.35 TO $24.85, CASH WITH THE ORDER,

DELIVERED ON THE CARS AT OUR FOUNDRY IN CENTRAL OHIO.

THE ACME REGAL STEEL RANGES ARE THE LATEST DESIGNS, improved in all points of construction, far surpassing any we have ever made before, and are thoroughly up to date 1902 patterns. NOTHING IN THE MARKET CAN COMPARE WITH THEM FOR BEAUTY, ELEGANCE AND EFFICIENCY IN OPERATION.

BEGINNING AT $15.35 for a genuine steel range, 6-hole size with 16-inch oven, to $24.85 for an extra large range with porcelain lined reservoir, high closet and 20-inch oven, we offer such values in strictly high grade thoroughly guaranteed steel ranges as was never before shown by us or any other house. We not only issue with every Steel Range a written binding guarantee, but so confident are we of our ability to furnish you almost double the value you can get elsewhere, we will refund you the price if you report it unsatisfactory any time within 30 days.

HOW ACME STEEL RANGES ARE MADE. The Acme Steel Range is made of sheet steel which is two gauges thicker than that commonly used in steel ranges, and, to the best of our knowledge, the steel in these ranges is one gauge heavier than in any steel range manufactured by any other concern in America. Don't compare these Steel Ranges with any wrought iron ranges on the market which resemble the Acme Steel Range only in appearance.

ACME STEEL RANGES have the very best cast stove plate tops, covers, centers and fire box. Don't let anybody deceive you that any range has steel top, covers and centers. The best top to stand fire is made of cast stove plate, and all so-called steel tops are malleable castings and will not last as long as ours.

OVEN PLATES. The oven plates in the Acme Steel Ranges are wrought steel and held immovably in place by surrounding wrought steel construction. The liability of its being warped or broken from unequal expansion is therefore entirely obviated. The oven bottom is well braced and bolted, and cannot warp. The oven is also ventilated, which adds greatly to the baking and roasting qualities.

GUARANTEED ASBESTOS LINED. These ranges are lined throughout with asbestos, a fireproof material and a non-conductor. Prevents heat from radiating into room and effectually retains it in the range, insuring more comfort and more pleasantness in the kitchen and prevents the japan from being burned off the outside. It also concentrates the heat in the oven, thus economizing fuel and making the oven a quick baker.

REMOVABLE DUPLEX GRATE. With every Acme Steel Range we furnish a heavy duplex grate for either hard or soft coal or wood, so arranged that it can be changed to a wood grate instantly. The duplex grate can be drawn out of front of range without disturbing the fire linings. When an Acme Steel Range is used for wood only we furnish an extension fire box, which allows a longer stick of wood to be used in the stove; so in ordering range, do not fail to state whether it is for wood or coal or both wood and coal.

OUR RANGES are offered as the best money can buy and at prices based on the actual cost of material and labor, with but our one small percentage of profit added.

BEAR IN MIND that these prices are too low to include any cooking utensils or stove pipe. If you desire any stove furniture it must be shipped direct from our stock in Chicago, while these ranges are sent from our foundry in Central Ohio. This makes two shipments, one from our foundry and one from our store. For this reason we especially urge you to make your order for cooking utensils large enough to be profitable to you, remembering that 50 to 100 pounds will, as a rule, go by freight from Chicago for as low a freight charge as 10 pounds.

DELIVERED ON CARS AT OUR FOUNDRY IN CENTRAL OHIO.

At $15.35 to $24.85

According to size, as listed below, we furnish our ACME REGAL, highest grade six-hole steel range on the market in competition with any range you can buy elsewhere at 50 per cent more money. We furnish the Acme Regal steel range, guaranteeing it to be made of heavier sheet steel than any other stove; guaranteeing it to be asbestos lined, thus insuring you economy of fuel; guaranteeing the nickel plating to be of the highest grade; guaranteeing the stove to possess all the good qualities of every strictly high grade steel range, with the defects of none.

THIS RANGE IS HIGHLY NICKEL PLATED THROUGHOUT. **Nickel bands on front edges of top of stove, nickeled oven door frame, nickel panel on oven door;** nickel clean out door, fire door, and nickel ash door, all highly finished, polished and nickeled, and we believe the handsomest range on the market. **THE OVEN OPENING** is the same size as the oven bottom, thus allowing as large a baking pan to enter as the oven will receive.

THE MAIN TOP, COVERS AND CENTERS are made of the very finest cast stove plate, from the purest pig iron, and not to be confused with malleable top ranges, sometimes called "steel," to deceive.

THIS STOVE IS HIGHLY ENAMELED with the very best quality locomotive black, has highest grade removable **Duplex grate,** for either coal or wood, or both. **We guarantee it to bake quicker, consume less fuel,** give better service, and that you will find it the handsomest range on the market, regardless of price.

OUR ACME REGAL RANGES have been manufactured with a view to furnish our customers the handsomest, most economical, most durable, and in every way the highest grade range possible to produce, and with a view of giving them the benefit of the reduced cost to manufacture where large quantities are turned out on a spot cash basis, and on this basis we quote our prices of **$15.35** to **$24.85** on the sizes listed. If you don't find, when you get the range, that you have saved from $10.00 to $15.00 in price, you are at liberty to return range to us and we will cheerfully refund the money.

WE FURNISH THIS Six-Hole Acme Regal Range at **$15.35** to **$24.85** in the sizes and dimensions listed. Prices do not include pipe or cooking utensils. See pages 580 to 593. Delivered on cars at our foundry in Central Ohio.

WE SHOW YOU this stove with a high closet and reservoir in a large illustration on the next page to give you a better idea of its appearance, and to show you it is the handsomest, best and greatest value ever before offered by us or any other house. **This is the popular style, the greatest value and our special leader;** highly nickel plated and ornamented throughout, as previously described, with nickel plated bands, shields, doors, trimmings, etc. Highly burnished and polished. Contains every good feature of every high grade range made, with the defects of none. Heavier steel plate, better lining better interlining, better construction, better trimming, more economical and far more handsome than any other range on the market.

Measurements Without Reservoir. Nos. 22R11 to 22R30

Range No.	Size of Lids	Size of Oven, inches	Size of Main Top, inches	Size of End Shelf, inches	Height to Main Top, inches	Length of Fire Box for Wood, Inches	Size of Pipe to Fit Collar, Inches
8-17	No. 8	16x19x14	33½x28	7½x21½	29¾	24	7
8-19	No. 8	18x19x14	35½x28	7½x21½	29¾	24	7
8-21	No. 8	20x21x14	37½x30	7½x21½	29¾	26	7
9-19	No. 9	18x21x14	36½x30	7½x21½	29¾	26	7
9-21	No. 9	20x21x14	37½x30	7½x21½	29¾	26	7

Measurements With Reservoir. Nos. 22R32 to 22R50

Range No.	Size of Lids	Size of Oven, inches	Size of Top and Reservoir, inches	Height to Main Top, inches	Length of Fire Box for Wood	Size of Pipe to Fit Collar
8-17	No. 8	16x19x14	46 x28	29¾	24 in.	7 in.
8-19	No. 8	18x19x14	47 x28	29¾	24 in.	7 in.
8-21	No. 8	20x21x14	49½x30	29¾	26 in.	7 in.
9-19	No. 9	18x21x14	47½x30	29¾	26 in.	7 in.
9-21	No. 9	20x21x14	49½x30	29¾	26 in.	7 in.

Acme Regal Steel Range.

SQUARE AND BACK GUARD.

FOR COAL OR WOOD.

Catalogue Number	Number	Size of Oven, inches	Shipping Weight	Price
22R11	8-17	16x19x14	291	$15.35
22R13	8-19	18x19x14	302	16.85
22R14	8-21	20x21x14	322	18.85
22R15	9-19	18x21x14	320	16.90
22R16	9-21	20x21x14	322	18.90

Shipped from our factory in Central Ohio.

These prices do not include any pipe or cooking utensils. **See pages 580 to 593.**

For complete description and measurements, see above.

Acme Regal Steel Range.

SQUARE WITH HIGH SHELF.

FOR COAL OR WOOD.

Catalogue Number	Number	Size of Oven, inches	Shipping Weight	Price
22R18	8-17	16x19x14	327	$17.05
22R20	8-19	18x19x14	338	18.55
22R21	8-21	20x21x14	358	20.55
22R22	9-19	18x21x14	357	18.58
22R23	9-21	20x21x14	359	20.60

Shipped from our factory in Central Ohio.

These prices do not include any pipe or cooking utensils. **See pages 580 to 593.**

For complete description and measurements, see first column on this page.

Acme Regal Steel Range.

SQUARE WITH HIGH CLOSET.

FOR COAL OR WOOD.

Catalogue Number	Number	Size of Oven, inches	Shipping Weight	Price
22R25	8-17	16x19x14	340	$18.65
22R27	8-19	18x19x14	351	20.15
22R28	8-21	20x21x14	372	22.15
22R29	9-19	18x21x14	371	20.20
22R30	9-21	20x21x14	373	22.20

Shipped from our factory in Central Ohio.

These prices do not include any pipe or cooking utensils. **See pages 580 to 593.**

For complete description and measurements, see first column on this page.

Water Front for Acme Regal Range, each, $3.00

Water fronts are used only where there is a water supply furnished with constant pressure through pipes—which can only be obtained in towns and cities having water works.

Acme Regal Steel Range.

WITH PORCELAIN LINED RESERVOIR AND BACK GUARD.

FOR COAL OR WOOD.

Catalogue Number	Number	Size of Oven, inches	Shipping Weight	Price
22R32	8-17	16x19x14	345	$18.00
22R34	8-19	18x19x14	350	19.50
22R35	8-21	20x21x14	380	21.50
22R36	9-19	18x21x14	370	19.55
22R37	9-21	20x21x14	380	21.55

Shipped from our factory in Central Ohio.

These prices do not include any pipe or cooking utensils. **See pages 580 to 593.**

For complete description and measurements, see first column on this page.

See large illustration on next page for prices with High Closet added.

Acme Regal Steel Range.

WITH HIGH SHELF AND PORCELAIN LINED RESERVOIR.

FOR COAL OR WOOD.

Catalogue Number	Number	Size of Oven, inches	Shipping Weight	Price
22R39	8-17	16x19x14	381	$19.70
22R41	8-19	18x19x14	386	22.19
22R42	8-21	20x21x14	416	24.20
22R43	9-19	18x21x14	407	22.25
22R44	9-21	20x21x14	417	24.25

Shipped from our factory in Central Ohio.

These prices do not include any pipe or cooking utensils. **See pages 580 to 593.**

For complete description and measurements, see first column on this page.

See large illustration on next page for prices with High Closet added.

OUR BINDING GUARANTEE. With every Steel Range we sell we issue a written binding guarantee, by the terms and conditions of which if any piece or part gives out by reason of defect in material or workmanship, we will replace it free of charge. Further, that it is strictly high grade, exactly as represented, and shall prove perfectly satisfactory, or we will refund all money paid us.

OUR ACME REGAL STEEL RANGE AT $21.30 TO $24.85.

DELIVERED ON CARS AT OUR FOUNDRY IN CENTRAL OHIO.

FOR COAL OR WOOD

This Acme Regal 6-hole, high closet reservoir steel range, at $15.35 to $24.85, according to size, is our

SPECIAL LEADER

We show you this stove with

A LARGE ILLUSTRATION

to give you a better idea of its appearance, and to show you it is the handsomest, best and greatest value ever before offered by us or any other house.

THIS IS THE POPULAR STYLE

THE GREATEST VALUE AND OUR SPECIAL LEADER; highly nickel plated and ornamented throughout, as previously described, with nickel plated bands, shields, doors, trimmings, etc. Highly burnished and polished. Contains every good feature of every

HIGH GRADE RANGE

made, with the defects of none. Heavier steel plate, better lining, better interlining, better construction, better trimming, more economical and far more handsome than any other range on the market.

THE MAIN TOP, COVERS, and centers, are made of the very finest cast stove plate, from the purest pig iron and not to be confused with malleable top ranges sometimes called "steel" to deceive.

OUR NEW 1902 DESIGN

Of these Ranges will be called

THE ACME REGAL.

CASH WITH THE ORDER.

PRICES DO NOT INCLUDE PIPE OR COOKING UTENSILS. SEE PAGES 580 TO 593.

We Recommend this Size and Style—This Special $21.30 to $24.85 Model—Above All Others.

WE FURNISH THIS RANGE in the different sizes mentioned at prices named delivered on cars at our foundry in Central Ohio. For complete description see first column on preceding page.

Price List of the ACME REGAL 6-HOLE STEEL RANGE with Porcelain Lined Reservoir and High Closet.

Catalogue Number	Range No.	Size of Lids	Size of Oven, Inches	Size of Main Top, Inches	Height to Main Top, Inches	Length of Fire Box for Wood	Size of Pipe to Fit Collar	Shipping Weight	PRICE
22R45	8-17	No. 8	16x19x14	46x28	29¾	24 in.	7 in.	394	$21.30
22R47	8-19	No. 8	18x19x14	47x28	29¾	24 in.	7 in.	399	22.80
22R48	8-21	No. 8	20x21x14	49½x30	29¾	26 in.	7 in.	430	24.80
22R49	9-19	No. 9	18x21x14	47½x30	29¾	26 in.	7 in.	421	22.85
22R50	9-21	No. 9	20x21x14	49½x30	29¾	26 in.	7 in.	431	24.85

Acme Western Coal Range.

WITH RESERVOIR AND HIGH SHELF.

FOR COAL OR WOOD.

Prices are cash with order, delivered on cars at our Mississippi Valley foundry. Prices do not include pipe or cooking utensils. See pages 580-593.

Catalogue Number	Stove Number	Size of Oven, inches	Weight, pounds	Price
22R186	8-20	18x18x12	420	$18.20
22R187	8-22	20x20x12½	465	20.35
22R188	9-22	20x20x12½	465	20.40

If desired without reservoir but with end shelf, deduct $2.50 from any size. If the high shelf is not desired, deduct $1.50 from any size.

This is the exact same range as the Acme Woodland quoted below as a wood burner. The same handsome rococo pattern, the same nickel plated trimmings throughout, the same highly finished ornamentations and decorations, the equal of any range on the market regardless of price.

OUR ACME WESTERN HIGH SHELF COAL AND WOOD RANGE, with large porcelain lined reservoir. This high shelf is ornamented with two highly polished nickel plated tea shelves, as illustrated.

DIMENSIONS.

Range Number	Size of Lids	Size of Top, Measuring Reservoir, inches	Fire Box when used for Wood, inches	Height to Main Top, inches
8-20	No. 8	46½x29	21½	29¾
8-22	No. 8	48½x30	23½	30
9-22	No. 9	48½x30	23½	30

Acme Woodland Wood Range.

WITH RESERVOIR AND HIGH SHELF.

FOR WOOD ONLY.

Prices are cash with the order, delivered on the cars at our foundry on the upper Mississippi River, and do not include pipe or cooking utensils. See pages 580 to 593.

Catalogue Number	Range Number	Size of Oven, inches	Weight, pounds	Price
22R195	8-20	18x18x12	405	$17.35
22R196	8-22	20x20x12½	450	19.00
22R197	9-22	20x20x12½	450	19.05

If desired without reservoir but with end shelf, deduct $2.50 from any size. If the high shelf is not desired, deduct $1.50 from any size.

IT IS EXACTLY THE SAME as the Acme Western, above illustrated, except that it does not burn coal. This is a wood burning range and is especially recommended to those who wish to burn wood, and as a better range to buy than a combination coal and wood burner.

DIMENSIONS.

Range Number	Size of Lid	Fire Box	Pipe Collar	Height to Main Top, inches	Top, Measuring Reservoir
8-20	No. 8	21½	7	29¾	45x29
3-22	No. 8	23½	7	30	47x30
9-22	No. 9	23½	7	30	47x30

OUR WORLD RENOWNED

OHIO LINE

OF COOK STOVES, RANGES AND HEATERS,

WHICH WE SHIP DIRECT FROM OUR FOUNDRY IN CENTRAL OHIO. THIS LINE OF CAST IRON STOVES IS ENTIRELY NEW FOR THE SEASON OF 1902.

IF YOU LIVE SOUTH OR EAST OF CHICAGO

make your selection from this our Old Reliable Ohio line of Acme stoves and ranges, taking advantage of the saving in freight and saving in time on the railroad. If you live south or east of Chicago, the freight will be less than from Chicago. If you live west or north of Chicago the freight will be about 30 cents per 100 pounds more than from Chicago. **The reason we can make the price so low:** We leave out the freight to Chicago, and leave out the cost of hauling and handling into and out of our store, making our price direct from foundry to consumer, barely covering the cost of material and labor with but our one small percentage of profit added. A price only made possible by eliminating all the handling expenses and shipping direct from the foundry. **Remember, if you require any cooking utensils or stove pipe they go direct from our store in Chicago, making two shipments, so make your order for stove furniture large enough to be a profitable shipment for you. Bear in mind 50 to 100 pounds will, as a rule, go by freight from Chicago at as low freight charges as 10 pounds.**

FOR 1902 **Our last year's models have been improved in many respects and entirely new models have been added, until we believe we show without any exception, the handsomest line of high grade 1902 cook stoves, ranges and heaters that will be shown by any dealer in America. We show a line of 348 stoves, ranges and heaters.**

PRICES **do not include stove pipe or cooking utensils. See pages 580 to 593.**

OUR ILLUSTRATIONS **have been engraved by our artists from photographs** taken direct from the stoves, with a view of assisting you in placing your order, and that **you may know exactly what you will get. But if you are at all undecided** as to the size of the stove wanted, from our description, you can, by measuring any part of your old stove and comparing with the dimensions given in our descriptions tell just how the stove you will get from us will compare in size with the one you now have.

WHEN YOU CONSIDER **the different styles and sizes our line of stoves embraces,** over 348 in number, were you to visit our place and were we to show you but one stove of a kind in the different styles and sizes as quoted in this catalogue, you would look at 348 stoves to see our entire line. **In this we give you an advantage against which no house has ever attempted to compete. Your local dealer at the very best can show you but a very small fraction of the variety from which you can select in this book,** We not only give you the advantage and prices on the very latest 1902 styles, but give you a selection embracing **348** distinct stoves.

OUR WARRANTY. **With every stove we issue a binding guarantee, by the terms and conditions of which, if any part or parts give out by reason of defect in workmanship or material, we will replace it free of charge.**

OUR GUARANTEE AGAINST BREAKAGE.

So confident are we of the quality of the goods we offer, and that they will invariably reach you in the same perfect condition they leave us, that we make this most liberal offer: Should any stove arrive badly damaged—such as any piece or part broken—you can pay the freight bill, have the agent note the condition of the stove on the freight bill, showing what part or parts are broken and then send the freight bill to us and we will immediately send you, free of charge, new castings to replace the broken ones.

STOVE REPAIRS.

PLEASE NOTICE. **We can always furnish repairs for Acmes. In ordering repairs for stoves, it is very important to give your purchase Invoice Number or the most complete and explicit information possible. By strictly adhering to the FOLLOWING RULES a great deal of annoyance, expense and delay may be averted:**

1st. State whether stove is for coal only, for wood only, or a combined wood and coal burning construction.

2d. If cook stove or range, say if square top, or with reservoir.

3d. The back of a stove is at the pipe collar. Stand facing the hearth on a cook stove or facing the oven door of a range.

4th. Give full number. In many instances the same size of cooking holes are placed on different stove bodies, viz., 7-18, 8-18, 8-20, 9-20, etc., and the single No. 7, 8 or 9 in this case would be no indication of the correct size of the stove.

5th. Be particular to furnish all dates, if any, shown on stove.

6th. When legs are desired, say if stove is supplied with legs only or on leg base.

7th. Give name and number of stove in full.

Acme Wonder Wood Cook.

WITHOUT RESERVOIR.

FOR WOOD ONLY.

Prices are cash with the order, delivered on the cars at our foundry in Central Ohio, and do not include any pipe or cooking utensils. See pages 580 to 593.

Catalogue Number	Stove Number	Size of Oven, inches	Weight, pounds	Price
22R200	7-16	15 x12½x10	148	$5.14
22R201	7-18	16½x14½x11	183	6.02
22R202	8-18	16½x14½x11	183	6.07
22R203	8-20	17½x16½x12	222	7.13
22R204	9-20	17½x16½x12	222	7.18

OUR ACME WONDER COOK STOVE **without reservoir, for burning wood only. This wood burning cook stove without reservoir, offered at $5.14 to $7.18 according to size, as listed, is the equal of** stoves that retail generally at $10.00 to $17.00. In construction it is strictly first class, has outside oven shelf, heavy covers, kicker for opening oven door and nickel plated knobs. Each stove is furnished with a lifter, and rake for cleaning ashes from under the oven.

Our Acme Wonder has every modern improvement known to stove making; it possesses all the good points of all first class stoves, with the defects of none.

DIMENSIONS.

Stove No.	Size of Lids	Size of Top	Height, inches	Pipe Collar, inches	Fire Box, inches
7-16	No. 7	21½x24½	24½	6	20
7-18	No. 7	24 x26¼	26	6	22
8-18	No. 8	24 x26¼	26	6	22
8-20	No. 8	25½x28¾	27	6	24
9-20	No. 9	25½x28¾	27	6	24

Acme Wonder Wood Cook.

WITH PORCELAIN LINED RESERVOIR.

FOR WOOD ONLY.

Prices are cash with the order, delivered on the cars at our Central Ohio foundry, and do not include pipe or cooking utensils. See pages 580 to 593.

Catalogue Number	Stove Number	Size of Oven, inches	Weight, pounds	Price
22R205	7-18	16½x14½x11	238	$ 8.95
22R206	8-18	16½x14½x11	238	9.00
22R207	8-20	17½x16½x12	280	10.05
22R208	9-20	17½x16½x12	280	10.10

OUR ACME WONDER COOK STOVE **with reservoir, for burning wood only. For a low price wood burning reservoir stove our Acme Wonder is without an equal. The Acme Wonder for 1902 has been greatly improved.** The patterns have been refinished; it will be better made than ever before, and we guarantee it equal to stoves that will sell everywhere at 33⅓ to 50 per cent more money. We furnish this our Acme Wonder cooking stove at $8.95 to $10.10 in any of the sizes as listed above with porcelain lined reservoir.

DIMENSIONS.

Stove Number	Size of Lids	Top, Including Reservoir	Height inches	Pipe Collar, inches	Fire Box, in.
7-18	No. 7	24 x36¼	26	6	22
8-18	No. 8	24 x36¼	26	6	22
8-20	No. 8	25½x38¾	27	6	24
9-20	No. 9	25½x38¾	27	6	24

Acme Queen Coal Cook.
WITHOUT RESERVOIR.

FOR COAL OR WOOD.

Prices are cash with the order, delivered on the cars at our foundry in Central Ohio, and do not include any pipe or cooking utensils. See pages 580 to 593.

Catalogue Number	Stove Number	Size of Oven, inches	Weight, pounds	Price
22R326	7-14	13¾x13 x 9	172	$5.55
22R327	7-16	16 x14½x10	202	6.85
22R328	8-16	16 x14½x10	202	6.90
22R329	8-18	18 x17 x11	244	8.20
22R330	9-18	18 x17 x11	244	8.25

Oven measurements do not include the swell of oven door.

Our Acme Queen is a coal burning stove, but is suitable for hard coal, soft coal or wood. We furnish with every stove an extra grate for wood, and you can use it for wood or for coal.

It has very large flues, cut tops, heavy cut centers supported by post, heavy covers, heavy linings with very heavy sectional fire back, large bailed ash pan, slide hearth plate, outside oven shelf, pouch feed, oven door kicker, nickel plated panel on oven door, nickel plated name plate on front door, nickel plated door knobs and tin lined oven door.

When ashes are removed from under oven they are scraped into the hearth, avoiding all possibility of spilling the ashes on the floor when cleaning stove.

Each stove is furnished with a lifter, shaker and scraper for removing the ashes from under the oven.

If you do not burn coal at all make your selection from the Acme Leader, Catalogue Nos. 22R209 to 22R213. DIMENSIONS.

Stove No.	Size of Lids	Top, not measuring Shelf	Size of Shelf	Height	Pipe Collar	Fire Box
7-14	No. 7	20½x27½	20½x7	24	6	15
7-16	No. 7	22 x29½	22 x7	26½	6	16½
8-16	No. 8	22 x29½	22 x7	26½	6	16½
8-18	No. 8	24 x33	24 x7	28½	7	18
9-18	No. 9	24 x33	24 x7	28½	7	18

Acme Queen Coal Cook.
WITH PORCELAIN LINED RESERVOIR.

FOR COAL OR WOOD.

Prices are cash with the order, delivered on the cars at our Central Ohio foundry, and do not include any pipe or cooking utensils. See pages 580 to 593

Catalogue Number	Stove Number	Size of Oven inches	Weight, pounds	Price
22R331	7-16	16x14½x10	255	$ 9.48
22R332	8-16	16x14½x10	255	9.53
22R333	8-18	18x17 x11	300	10.60
22R334	9-18	18x17 x11	300	10.65

Oven measurements do not include swell of oven door. If you do not use coal at all, make your selection from the Acme Leader, Catalogue Nos. 22R214 to 22R217. Always state which fuel you desire to use.

At $9.48 to $10.65 delivered on the cars at our foundry in Central Ohio. This is the exact same stove as the Acme Queen previously illustrated under No. 22R326, at $5.55 to $8.25, with the addition of the large porcelain lined reservoir as shown in illustration. DIMENSIONS.

Stove No.	Size of Lids	Top, including Reservoir	Height	Pipe Collar	Fire Box
7-16	No. 7	22x40	26½	6	16½
8-16	No. 8	22x40	26½	6	16½
8-18	No. 8	24x44	28½	7	18
9-18	No. 9	24x44	28½	7	18

Acme Royal Coal Cook.
WITHOUT RESERVOIR.

FOR COAL OR WOOD.

Prices are cash with the order, delivered on the cars at our Central Ohio foundry, and do not include any pipe or cooking utensils. See pages 580 to 593.

Catalogue Number	Stove No.	Size of Oven, inches	Weight, pounds	Price
22R343	7-18	17½x14½x11	305	$10.53
22R344	8-18	17½x14½x11	305	10.58
22R345	7-20	19½x16½x12	333	12.00
22R346	8-20	19½x16½x12	333	12.05
22R347	9-20	19½x16½x12	335	12.10
22R348	8-22	21½x18½x12½	374	14.08
22R349	9-22	21½x18½x12½	375	14.13

Oven measurements do not include swell of oven door.

If you do not use coal at all, order the Wood Burning Royal, from Nos. 22R230 to 22R236. Always state what fuel you desire to burn.

This Acme Royal Cook Stove is designed as a combination stove for hard coal, soft coal, coke, wood, or anything that can be burned in a stove. For further description see the stove below, where it is shown with a reservoir. **DIMENSIONS.**

Stove No.	Size of Lids	Top, not measuring End Shelf	Size of End Shelf	Fire Box	Pipe Collar	Hg't
7-18	No. 7	22x31	8x22	17x8x8	7	28
8-18	No. 8	22x31	8x22	17x8x8	7	28
7-20	No. 7	23x33	9x23	19x9x9	7	30
8-20	No. 8	23x33	9x23	19x9x9	7	30
9-20	No. 9	23x33	9x23	19x9x9	7	30
8-22	No. 8	25x35	9x25	21x9x9	7	31
9-22	No. 9	25x35	9x25	21x9x9	7	31

Acme Royal Coal Cook.
WITH PORCELAIN LINED RESERVOIR.

FOR COAL OR WOOD.

Prices are cash with the order, delivered on the cars at our foundry in Central Ohio, and do not include any pipe or cooking utensils. See pages 580 to 593.

Catalogue Number	Stove Number	Size of Oven, inches	Weight, pounds	Price
22R350	7-18	17½x14½x11	350	$12.04
22R351	8-18	17½x14½x11	350	12.09
22R352	7-20	19½x16½x12	395	14.04
22R353	8-20	19½x16½x12	395	14.09
22R354	9-20	19½x16½x12	396	14.14
22R355	8-22	21½x18½x12½	443	16.67
22R356	9-22	21½x18½x12½	445	16.72

Oven measurements do not include swell of oven door.

If you do not use coal at all, order the wood burning Royal, from Catalogue Nos. 22R237 to 22R243.

This is the exact same stove as the ACME ROYAL previously illustrated and described as Nos. 22R343 to 22R349, with the addition of the large porcelain lined reservoir. It has the same handsome rococo pattern, same large square oven door, same large oven, highly nickel plated trimmings throughout, beautifully ornamented and decorated, has large end shelf, large nickel plated oven shelf, large nickel plated panel on oven door, handsome nickel name plate, most expensive nickel "Alaska always cold door knobs" throughout. For an all coal stove, for a combination stove for all kinds of fuel, this is the best cook stove on the market regardless of price. **DIMENSIONS.**

Stove No.	Size of Lids	Top including Reservoir	Fire Box	Pipe Collar	Height
7-18	No. 7	22x42	17x8x8	7	28
8-18	No. 8	22x42	17x8x8	7	28
7-20	No. 7	23x45	19x9x9	7	30
8-20	No. 8	23x45	19x9x9	7	30
9-20	No. 9	23x45	19x9x9	7	30
8-22	No. 8	25x46	21x9x9	7	31
9-22	No. 9	25x46	21x9x9	7	31

Acme Peerless Coal Cook.
WITH PORCELAIN LINED RESERVOIR.

FOR COAL OR WOOD.

Prices are cash with the order, delivered on the cars at our Central Ohio foundry, and do not include any pipe or cooking utensils. See pages 580 to 593.

Catalogue Number	Stove Number	Size of Oven inches	Weight, pounds	Price
22R360	7-18	18x18x12	310	$12.80
22R361	8-18	18x18x12	310	12.85
22R362	8-20	20x20x12½	355	14.65
22R363	9-20	20x20x12½	355	14.70

Oven measurements do not include the swell of oven door.

If desired without reservoir, but with end shelf, deduct $2.00 from any size.

If you do not use coal at all, order the Acme Harvest from Catalogue Nos. 22R254 to 22R257. It is the same stove for wood only.

THE ACME PEERLESS has very large flues, cut top with heavy cut centers, supported by post, heavy covers, heavy linings, with very heavy sectional fire back. Large bailed ash pan, slide hearth plate, outside oven shelf, oven door kicker, ornamented base, nickeled name plate on front door, nickel plated panels on oven door, nickel plated door knobs, tin lined oven door, swing feed.

Stove No.	Size of Lids	Top, including Reservoir	Height	Pipe Collar	Fire Box
7-18	No. 7	38 x 25	31	7	20
8-18	No. 8	38 x 25	31	7	20
8-20	No. 8	39½ x 26	31½	7	21½
9-20	No. 9	40½ x 26	31½	7	21½

Acme Duchess Coal Range.
WITH RESERVOIR AND HIGH SHELF.

FOUR-HOLE RANGE. FOR COAL OR WOOD.

Prices are cash with order, delivered on cars at our Central Ohio foundry, and do not include any pipe or cooking utensils. See pages 580 to 593.

Catalogue Number	Stove Number	Size of Oven inches	Weight pounds	Price
22R368	8-18	18 x 18 x 12	356	$14.20
22R369	8-20	20 x 20 x 12½	390	16.15
22R370	9-20	20 x 20 x 12½	390	16.30

Oven measurements do not include the swell of oven door.

If desired without Reservoir, but with End Shelf, deduct $2.25 from any size. Water front to fit any size, price $2.50 extra. If the High Shelf is not desired, deduct $1.00 from any size.

THE ACME DUCHESS has the same general description as the Acme Peerless shown above, but with a high shelf and handsome nickel plated tea shelves, as illustrated.

If you do not use coal at all, order the Acme Empress from catalogue No. 22R263 to No. 22R265 It is the same range for wood only.

Range No.	Size of Lids	Top, including Reservoir	Height	Pipe Collar	Fire Box
8-18	8	38 x 26	31	7	20
8-20	8	39½ x 27	31½	7	21½
9-20	9	40½ x 27	31½	7	21½

EIGHT WONDERFUL STOVE VALUES

THESE EIGHT MOST EXTRAORDINARY STOVE VALUES ARE SHOWN IN LARGE ILLUSTRATIONS AND PRINTED ON COLORED PAPER, INSERTED IN OUR CATALOGUE FOR THE REASON THAT THERE ARE ONLY A LIMITED NUMBER TO BE SOLD AT THE PRICE, AND WHEN THOSE WE HAVE ON HAND ARE DISPOSED OF, NO MORE CAN BE HAD AT THE SPECIAL PRICES HERE QUOTED.

IN SEVERAL INSTANCES WE ARE OFFERING THESE STOVES AT BUT LITTLE MORE THAN THE ACTUAL VALUE OF THE IRON.

This would be a most extraordinary opportunity for stove dealers to lay in a supply of high grade stoves, for at the price we offer them YOU CAN SAVE ONE-HALF, as against any price you can get from any stove jobber or manufacturer.

From the illustration engraved from a photograph, you can form some idea of the appearance of this our big IDEAL ACME KING high shelf Range, but you must see it to appreciate what it really is.

$13.95

BUYS THIS BIG 475-POUND, HIGH SHELF, COMBINATION WOOD AND COAL, SQUARE OVEN, RESERVOIR RANGE.

AT

$13.95

YOU ARE GETTING THIS STOVE AT LESS THAN 3 CENTS PER POUND, AND YET IT IS ONE OF THE STRONGEST, HANDSOMEST AND THE BEST LARGE, RESERVOIR RANGE MADE. IT IS THE EQUAL OF RANGES THAT SELL GENERALLY AT $30.00 TO $40.00.

UNDERSTAND, THESE EIGHT STOVES ARE ALL STRICTLY HIGH GRADE, ALL UP TO DATE IN STYLE.

Every stove is covered by a **Binding Guarantee,** and we guarantee it to reach you in the same perfect condition it leaves the foundry, and if any part is broken in transit we will replace or repair it free of charge. Further, we will

ALWAYS KEEP A COMPLETE STOCK OF CASTINGS

of all the different parts of all these stoves, so that in the years to come, if you need to replace any part of any one of these stoves, we can furnish you the castings you want at a very low price.

UNDERSTAND, all orders must be accompanied by the full amount of cash; but if you send us your order for one of these stoves and it is not perfectly satisfactory when received,

IF YOU ARE NOT CONVINCED IT IS A MOST EXTRAORDINARY STOVE BARGAIN,

you can return it to us at our expense and we will

IMMEDIATELY RETURN YOU YOUR MONEY.

THIS IS A 6-HOLE RANGE, 8-18 SIZE, 18x18 INCHES; 9-20 SIZE, 20x20 INCHES OVEN RANGE; FOR HARD COAL, SOFT COAL OR WOOD (BURNS ANYTHING). A VERY HANDSOME NEW DESIGN, WITH NEW, LARGE SQUARE OVEN DOOR.

THIS RANGE is made with extra high cast pipe ornamented shelf, as illustrated, made with extra large enameled reservoir with japanned cover, large flues under reservoir, allowing heat to pass directly under reservoir—no flame touching sides—thus heating water very rapidly. Range is made with extended fire chamber for wood, and we furnish either a genuine duplex grate for coal and wood or a special wood grate for wood only, as desired. Made with cut top, heavy lids and centers, sectional back wall, heavy ribbed top oven plate.

THERE IS NO RANGE MADE THAT WILL CONSUME LESS FUEL OR BAKE BETTER.

IT IS HANDSOMELY FINISHED and decorated, has large, square, nickel plated ornamentations on oven door, reservoir extension, stove doors and pipe section; fancy nickel plated teapot holders, nickel towel rod, hand burnished edges.

THE IDEAL ACME KING RANGE

stands on a handsomely ornamented base, as illustrated, and is in every way

AS COMPLETE AND PERFECT A RANGE AS IT IS POSSIBLE TO BUILD.

	No. 8-18	No. 9-20
Full length of range from hearth to reservoir top	54¼ inches	56⅛ inches
Length of main top, including reservoir	45⅛ inches	47⅛ inches
Width of main top	28 inches	29 inches
Length of fire box, for wood only	22 inches	25 inches
Length of fire box, for coal only	16 inches	18 inches
Length of coal fire box changed to wood	22 inches	24 inches

No. 96R1130 Our special price for the Ideal Acme King Range complete. Size 8-18, Weight 475 pounds **$13.95**

No. 96R1132 Our special price for the Ideal Acme King Range complete, Size 9-20, Weight 555 pounds **$16.75**

$9.54 Buys the NEW MODEL COAL AND WOOD PRINCESS RESERVOIR COOK STOVE.

AT $9.54 in the smallest size and $10.98 in the popular 8-18 size (a big reduction from all previous quotations), we will dispose of our surplus stock of high grade Princess cook stoves. When our surplus stock is disposed of no more of these stoves can be had at the price. We would, therefore, advise you to place your order at once.

UNDERSTAND, we guarantee the stove to reach you in perfect condition and please you or we will immediately return your money, and in the years to come you can always get castings from us for repairs and at a very low cost to you.

THIS STOVE is made in our own foundry in Northern Ohio from the best material that can be procured. From the illustration, engraved from a photograph, you can form some idea of the appearance of this handsome reservoir cook stove.

THE ACME PRINCESS burns hard coal, soft coal, coke, wood or anything for fuel. It is made with very large flues, cut tops, heavy cut centers supported by post, heavy covers, heavy linings with very heavy sectional fire back; large bailed ash pan, slide hearth plate, nickeled outside oven shelf, pouch feed, oven door kicker, nickel plated panel on oven door, nickel plated door knobs, heavy tin lined oven door. When ashes are removed from under oven they are scraped into the hearth, avoiding all possibility of spilling ashes on the floor when cleaning the stove.

THE ACME PRINCESS is furnished with a lifter, shaker and scraper for removing the ashes from under the oven. It is fitted with a large porcelain lined reservoir, as shown in the illustration, and is furnished on a large handsome rococo pattern base. It has every up to date feature of every high grade reservoir cook stove, every improvement up to 1902, and is one of the best reservoir cook stoves on the market.

Until our surplus stock is disposed of we will furnish the Acme Princess in the following sizes at the special cut prices named:

PRICE LIST OF ACME PRINCESS WITH PORCELAIN LINED RESERVOIR.

Catalogue Number	Size	Size of Lids	Size of Oven, Inches	Size of Top Including Reservoir, Inches	Height, Inches	Pipe to Fit Collar, Inches	Length of Fire Box, Inches	Weight, Pounds	Price
96R1138	7-16	No. 7	16x14⅛x10	22x40	26⅛	6	16½	265	$ 9.54
96R1140	8-16	No. 8	16x14⅛x10	22x40	26⅛	6	16½	265	9.59
96R1142	8-18	No. 8	18x17 x11	24x44	28⅛	7	18	310	10.98
96R1144	9-18	No. 9	18x17 x11	24x44	28⅛	7	18	310	11.05

Our big ACME FOREST RESERVOIR WOOD BURNING COOK STOVE,

REDUCED TO $15.67.

HAVING PATTERNS and molding flasks to make the Acme Forest stoves in very large quantities, we find ourselves somewhat overstocked, and to dispose of the overstock at once, we are offering this big wood burning cook stove, either with or without reservoir, at about 3 cents per pound, only $15.67 for the big reservoir stove, a price heretofore unknown.

From the illustration, engraved by our artist from a photograph, you can get some idea of the appearance of this handsome, extra large, heavy wood burning cook stove. We furnish it either with reservoir, as illustrated, or without, as desired, at the following prices:

No. 96R1146 Price, No. 8, with reservoir......**$15.67**
No. 96R1150 Price, No. 8, without reservoir..**11.76**

These big stoves are made for wood exclusively. They will take wood 27 inches long. The Acme Forest is made from special patterns; has an extra large fire box, very large oven, giving you an extra heavy, handsome, durable stove.

OUR ACME FOREST has a very large oven, large fire box, cut main top, cut long center, lined short centers, heavy covers, tin lined oven door, side top shelf, outside oven door shelf, large nickel plated panels on oven door, nickel name plate on front door. Nickel plated towel rod, nickel knobs and hinge pins. Oven rack is 13½ inches wide and is 9¼ inches above the bottom of the oven.

IF YOU LIVE IN A TIMBER COUNTRY and burn wood and want a large, substantial, economical stove, a stove that will last for twenty years, one covered by our binding guarantee, we would recommend our Acme Forest Cook Stove as the greatest value ever offered.

To close out an overstock we offer the Acme Forest Wood Burning Cook Stove at the following special prices:

PRICE LIST OF ACME FOREST COOK STOVE, WITH PORCELAIN LINED RESERVOIR AS SHOWN.

Catalogue Number	Size	Size of Lids	Size of Oven, Inches	Size of Top Including Reservoir, Inches	Size of Pipe to Fit Collar, Inches	Length of Fire Box, Inches	Height, Inches	Weight, Pounds	Price
96R1146	8-22	No. 8	20x22x14	28x42	7	27	31½	460	$15.67
96R1148	9-22	No. 9	20x22x14	28x42	7	27	31½	460	15.72

PRICE LIST OF ACME FOREST COOK STOVE, WITHOUT RESERVOIR.

Catalogue Number	Size	Size of Lids	Size of Oven, Inches	Size of Top not Including Shelf, Inches	Size of Shelf, Inches	Size of Pipe to Fit Collar, Inches	Length of Fire Box, Inches	Height, Inches	Weight, Pounds	Price
96R1150	8-22	No. 8	20x22x14	28x32	7½x28	7	27	31½	368	$11.76
96R1152	9-22	No. 9	20x22x14	28x32	7½x28	7	27	31½	368	11.80

REMEMBER, that we do not include the flare of oven door in giving measurements of oven, as is customary with stove dealers. Including flare of oven door the size of oven in above stove is 23x22x14 inches.

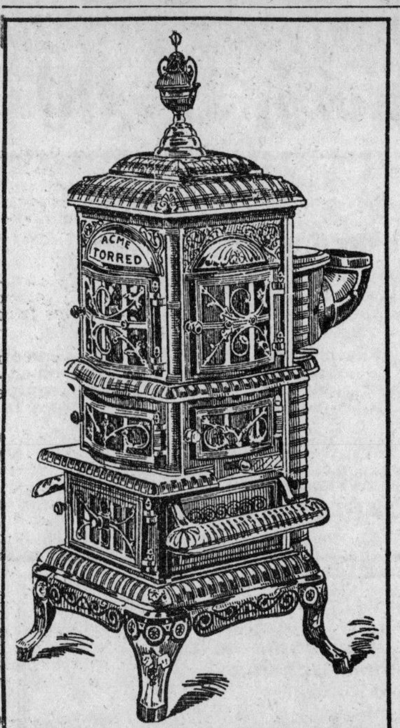

OUR $7.10 ACME TORRID Base Burning Parlor Heater.

AT $7.10, $8.08 AND $9.03, ACCORDING TO SIZE AS SHOWN BELOW, WE FURNISH THIS ACME TORRID SELF FEED BASE BURNING HEATER, COMPLETE WITH MAGAZINE AND FULL RETURN FLUE, THE EQUAL OF ANY BASE BURNING SELF FEEDING HARD COAL HEATER OF LIKE SIZES, YOU CAN BUY ANYWHERE AT DOUBLE THE PRICE.

THIS IS A NEAT PARLOR, BASE BURNER STOVE, new and attractive pattern, highly and tastefully ornamented; has draw center grate, large ash pan, cast elbow, mica in front and side doors; lined swing top with fancy urn.

THIS STOVE BURNS HARD COAL ONLY.

UNDERSTAND, AT THE PRICE WE FURNISH YOU THE STOVE COMPLETE, delivered on board cars at the foundry, from which place you must pay the freight, but the freight will amount to next to nothing as compared to what you will save in price. We guarantee the stove to reach you in the exact same perfect condition it leaves the foundry and if anything should be broken in transit, it will be repaired or replaced by us FREE OF COST TO YOU. If the stove is not perfectly satisfactory when received, you can return it to us at our expense of freight charges both ways, and we will immediately return your money.

We wish to further state that we will at all times have repairs for this stove, which we will furnish at foundry cost.

CASH WITH ORDER PRICES, DELIVERED ON THE CARS AT OUR FOUNDRY IN CENTRAL OHIO.

Catalogue Number	Size	Diameter of Fire Pot	Height	Floor Space	Size of Pipe to Fit Collar	Weight, Pounds	Price
96R1162	10	10	35½	17½x17½	5 inches	143	$7.10
96R1164	11	11	37½	18¼x18¼	5 inches	162	8.08
96R1166	12	12	38½	19¼x19¼	5 inches	186	9.03

Our Handsome Acme Comfort Parlor Heater

FOR $5.48, $6.46 AND $7.44 ACCORDING TO THE SIZE AS SHOWN BELOW.

THIS HANDSOME PARLOR HEATER is intended to burn either soft or hard coal, and at our price of $5.48, $6.46 and $7.44 is offered at about one-half the price the same grade of stove can be had elsewhere.

THIS IS AN ENTIRELY NEW DESIGN in a handsome direct draft, square heater. We have never seen its equal at anything like the price. It has center draw grate, large ash pan, mica in doors on three sides, swing top, nickel plated foot rails, nickel plated hinge pins and knobs. In fact the illustration does not do this stove justice for it is one of the handsomest stoves on the market. New design, very highly ornamented and decorated, and we guarantee it to produce more heat for the same amount of coal than any other heater on the market.

AT OUR SPECIAL PRICES we furnish the stove delivered on board cars at foundry in Central Ohio, from which point you must pay the freight, but you will find the freight will amount to next to nothing as compared to what you will save in price.

WE GUARANTEE the stove to reach you in the same perfect condition it leaves the foundry, and if anything is broken or defective, we will repair or replace it for you free of charge, and if the stove is not satisfactory, you can return it to us at our expense of freight charges both ways, and we will return your money.

Bear in mind, we can at all times furnish repairs and at the factory cost.

CASH WITH ORDER PRICES, DELIVERED ON THE CARS AT OUR FOUNDRY IN CENTRAL OHIO.

Catalogue Number	Size	Diameter of Fire Pot	Height, Inches	Floor Space	Pipe. Collar	Weight, Pounds	Price
96R1168	10	10	35½	17½x17½	5 inches	107	$5.48
96R1170	11	11	37½	18¼x18¼	5 inches	122	6.46
96R1172	12	12	38½	19¼x19¼	5 inches	135	7.44

The ornament is not included in measuring height.

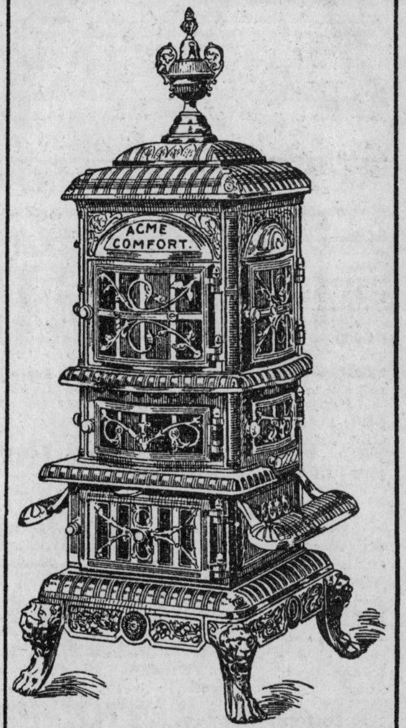

WE ALSO PROVIDE the smallest size of the Acme Comfort ready for a natural gas burner to be put in. The fire pot is reduced to 8 inches in diameter, and any of the round burners used in the natural gas districts can be put in it and it instantly becomes one of the best natural gas heaters in the market, showing the flame through the mica illumination.

ACME COMFORT FOR NATURAL GAS.

Catalogue Number	Stove No.	Diam. of Fire Pot	Height In.	Floor Space	Pipe, Collar	Weight	Price
96R1174	110	8 in.	35½	17½x17½	5 in.	107	$5.50

Our $2.98 Acme Oakling Heater.

No. 96R1176

To increase the sale of this stove and enable our factory to run to the full capacity of the patterns and flasks we have for the making of these stoves, we have reduced the price to $2.98, and we feel that we are offering in our ACME OAKLING, the equal of any stove you can buy elsewhere at $5.00.

THIS IS A COAL BURNING STOVE, A VERY POWERFUL HEATER AND A NICE LOOKING STOVE.

It has a swing top and fancy urn; dumping grate; cast iron fire pot, sheet steel body, nickel plated foot rails, made in one size only. Diameter of fire pot, 11 inches; height, not including ornament, 40 inches. Floor space, outside to outside of legs, 16x17 inches. Weight, 56 pounds. Takes 6-inch stove pipe.

IF YOU WILL SEND US YOUR ORDER FOR THIS STOVE WITH $2.98, we will send the stove to you with the understanding and agreement THAT IF IT IS NOT PERFECTLY SATISFACTORY WHEN RECEIVED, AND BY FAR THE GREATEST STOVE VALUE EVER SEEN

YOU CAN RETURN IT TO US AND WE WILL IMMEDIATELY RETURN YOUR MONEY.

MAGIC NATURAL GAS HEATER No. 19, $5.00

WITHOUT THE BURNER.

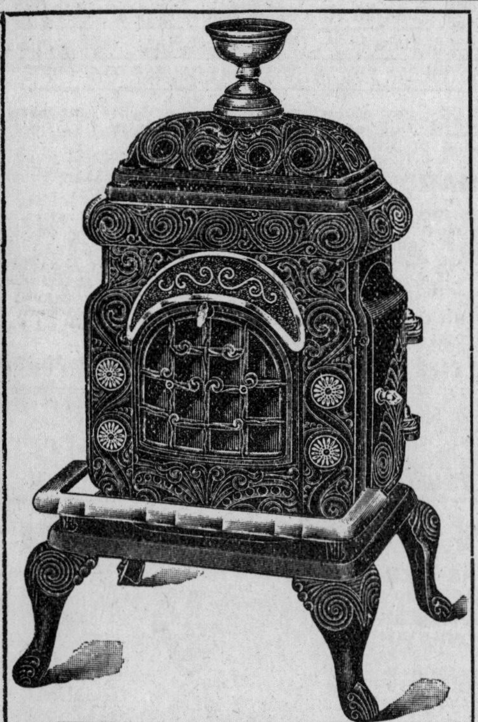

Cash with the order delivered on the cars at our Central Ohio Foundry.

WE OFFER this elegant mica illuminated natural gas heater at $5.00 as one of the best in the market. We do not add the price of the burner, on account of the regulations of the various Natural Gas companys requiring different sized holes drilled in the burners, according to the supply or pressure of the gas in different districts; but this stove is arranged so

YOU CAN APPLY ANY OF THE BURNERS SOLD BY YOUR LOCAL GAS COMPANY.

THIS ELEGANT STOVE... is furnished with a spun brass nickeled urn with bowl for holding water to moisten the air in the room. The dome cover swings aside exposing two cooking holes.

The crescent panel over the mica front is nickeled. The mica illumination shows the bright and cheerful fire. There are four ornamental tile rosettes, two on each side of the front.

THE FOOT RAIL IS NICKELED AND HANDSOMELY POLISHED.

No. 96R1182 STOVE No. 19, FOR NATURAL GAS. Price, without burner.................................... **$5.00**

THE STOVE IS PREPARED TO APPLY ANY BURNER SOLD BY ANY NATURAL GAS CO.

MAGIC NATURAL GAS HEATER No. 15, $3.75

WITHOUT THE BURNER.

Cash with the Order, Delivered on the Cars at Our Central Ohio Foundry.

THIS HANDSOME NATURAL GAS STOVE

HAS ALL THE FEATURES OF THE No. 19 SHOWN ABOVE, BUT IS NOT SO LARGE.

IT ALSO HAS a nickeled spun brass water urn, swing dome top, two cooking holes on main top, nickeled panel over mica front, illuminated mica front which can be removed at will as shown, six tile rosettes on the front and a highly polished nickeled foot rail.

No. 96R1184 STOVE No. 15, FOR NATURAL GAS. Price, without burner.................................... **$3.75**

THE REASON WE OFFER THESE NATURAL GAS STOVES WITHOUT THE BURNERS IS BECAUSE OF THE RESTRICTIONS PUT ON THE SIZE OF THE DRILLED HOLES IN THE BURNERS, ARE DIFFERENT IN THE VARIOUS NATURAL GAS DISTRICTS.

THE ILLUMINATED FRONT CAN BE REMOVED AT THE PLEASURE OF THE USER.

OUR $14.95 WORLD BEATER, PRICE SMASHER AND THE ENEMY OF TRUSTS

THE ACME AMERICAN RANGE.

WITH PORCELAIN LINED RESERVOIR AND HIGH SHELF.

FOR HARD COAL, SOFT COAL, WOOD OR ANYTHING USED FOR FUEL.

$14.95 Buys the No. 8-18

CASH WITH THE ORDER.

DELIVERED ON BOARD THE CARS AT OUR FOUNDRY IN CENTRAL OHIO.

State whether you wish to burn **WOOD ONLY, COAL ONLY, OR BOTH COAL AND WOOD,** and we will send you this new big 1902 model ACME AMERICAN 415-pound Range by freight on receipt of $14.95, and if not found perfectly satisfactory, exactly as represented, the handsomest range you ever saw, and the equal of any range you can buy elsewhere at $30.00 to $40.00, we will refund your money.

$14.95

THIS RANGE WEIGHS 415 POUNDS and the freight will average for 500 miles, $1.50 to $2.00; greater or lesser distances in proportion.

THIS RANGE is made in our own foundry by skilled mechanics, from the best material money can buy, is the handsomest, most ornamental, best baking and burning and most economical big square oven, high shelf range made.

WE ISSUE A BINDING GUARANTEE

Guarantee the stove to reach you in the same perfect condition it leaves our foundry.

MONEY CAN'T MAKE BETTER. Operating our own foundry we furnish better materials, heavier castings, heavier nickel finishings, better connections and fittings than any other foundry produces. From our own factory we save you the manufacturer's, wholesaler's and retailer's profit, and give you a better range than you can buy elsewhere. Our special $14.95 price is based on the actual cost of material and labor, with but our one small profit added.

THIS BIG CAST IRON RANGE is made from the very finest Camden stove pig iron. Latest 1902 rococo molding, large square tin lined oven door, large deep porcelain lined reservoir, handsome rococo base, large high rococo shelf, heavy nickel trimmings throughout, nickel oven door panel, nickel shelf, nickel draft door, nickel tea shelf, pins, hinges, knobs, handles, etc. Duplex grate, cut tops and centers, large flues, bailed ash pan, slide hearth plate.

WE CAN ALWAYS FURNISH REPAIRS FOR ACME STOVES AND RANGES.

Prices are Cash with the Order. Delivered on the cars at our Central Ohio foundry.

Catl'g No.	Size	Size of Lids	Size of Oven	Size of Top Measuring Reservoir	Size of Fire Box when used for wood	Height to Main Top	Weight	Price
22R375	8-18	No. 8	17½x16x11½	42x25	17x8x8	28 in.	415 lbs.	$14.95

If desired without reservoir, but with end shelf, deduct $2.00.

If high shelf is not wanted, deduct $2.00.

Oven measurements **DO NOT** include swell of oven door, and **DO NOT** include pipe or cooking utensils. See pages 580 to 593.

If you do not burn coal at all, make your order read **WOOD ONLY**, and get the exclusively **WOOD FIRE BOX** which will measure 22x9x9, but will **NOT** burn coal at all.

ACME BRILLIANT BASE BURNER.

DOUBLE HEATER.

FOR ANTHRACITE COAL OR CRUSH COKE.

$19.30 to $26.15 delivered on the cars at our foundry in Pennsylvania.

THIS HARD COAL HEATER for 1902 is the finest the world produces, a dream of an artist in design, trimming, finishing. In its construction throughout the highest of high grade base burners. The equal of any base burning hard coal heater made by any maker regardless of price.

NICKEL FINISH. We believe we put more nickel on the Acme Brilliant Base Burner than is used on any base burning heater made. The nickel finish includes a large handsomely ornamented spun brass nickel urn—we believe the handsomest nickel plated urn that is used on any base burner made; heavy, nickel plated swing top of the very latest design, full nickel dome head of a new design, heavily nickeled corner wings, heavily nickeled hearth plate, heavily nickeled ash door panel, heavily nickeled foot rails, heavily nickeled name plate and the stove stands on a full heavy nickel plated frame with nickel plated legs. The nickel plating is done by the very best process (the XXX triple plated brand), highly polished.

It is made with a double heating flue to which a pipe can be attached for heating an upper room or increasing the heat in the lower room; **it is made with the very latest Johnson self feeding magazine;** handsomely finished double swing mica doors on the front of the two larger sizes and a single swing mica door on the front of the No. 22. All sizes have swing mica doors on the sides. Heavy, large, non-destructible fire pot; latest Akron Duplex grate, with shaking ring; **large ash pan; Osgood's patent full base heating flues, tea kettle attachment and cast elbow at back. We guarantee satisfaction.**

$19.30 TO $26.15

ONLY by comparison of our goods and prices can you fully appreciate the money we can save you . . . .

These prices are cash with the order. Delivered on the cars at our foundry in Pennsylvania.

Catalogue Number	Stove Number	Fire Pot	Floor to Urn Base	Floor Space	Size Pipe Collar	Weight, pounds	Price
22R460	22	12	48½	21½x21	6 in.	284	$19.30
22R461	24	14	50½	24 x24	6 in.	320	22.85
22R462	26	16	53½	26¼x26¼	6 in.	375	26.15

For prices on pipe and zinc boards, see pages 581 and 582.

DELIVERY GUARANTEE. **At the prices quoted we furnish these goods delivered on board the cars at our foundry in Pennsylvania, and we guarantee the stove to reach you in the same perfect condition it leaves us, and if any piece or part is broken on arrival we will replace it free of any charge to you.**

ABOUT THE FREIGHT. Stoves take a low freight rate (third class) and the freight will average for 100 pounds for 500 miles about 80 cents, greater or lesser distances in proportion, so you will find the freight will amount to next to nothing as compared with what you will save in price.

ACME RADIANT BASE BURNER.

FOR ANTHRACITE COAL OR CRUSH COKE.

OUR SPECIAL $10.90 TO $17.50 PRICES **are made possible by reason of having contracted with the manufacturer for his entire output of**

BASE BURNING HEATERS

and shipped direct from the foundry in Pennsylvania, leaving out of the price all of the expenses of handling into and out of our store in Chicago.

DELIVERY GUARANTEE. **Every stove is shipped carefully crated, and we guarantee it to reach you in the same perfect condition it leaves us, and if any part is broken we will replace it free of any cost to you.**

THIS NEW MODEL base burning heater embodies all the new up to date features; every improvement excepting the double heating flue found in our Acme Brilliant, is combined in the Acme Radiant. It is supplied with **the latest self feeding magazine,** handsomely finished swing mica doors on three sides, extra heavy fire pot, has the best Eclipse Duplex grate with shaking ring, large ash pan, large base heating flue, tea kettle attachment at back, cast elbow.

TRIMMINGS. **The Acme Radiant** is beautifully trimmed and finished. Has a very large handsome spun brass nickel urn; nickeled swing top, full nickeled dome head, full nickeled corner columns, full nickeled heavy name plate, nickeled foot rails, nickeled ash door panel, full nickeled legs and nickeled rococo frame base.

$10.90 TO $17.50

EVERY penny we can save by buying low, cutting off advertising expense, getting paid for catalogues and samples, we give to our customers in the way of lower prices.

These prices are cash with the order. Delivered on the cars at our foundry in Pennsylvania.

Catalogue Number	Stove Number	Size of Fire Pot, inches	Floor to Base of Urn inches	Floor Space inches	Size Pipe Collar	Weight, lbs.	Price
22R463	114	9	38	16½x18½	5 in.	164	$10.90
22R464	115	10½	40	17¾x20¼	5 in.	192	12.65
22R465	116	12	42	19 x21	5 in.	221	14.45
22R466	117	14	45	21½x24½	5 in.	270	17.50

For prices on pipe and zinc boards, see pages 581 and 582.

ACME CARBON DOUBLE HEATER.

FOR SOFT COAL OR HARD COAL.

ALL CAST IRON. DOUBLE CASED. IS AS NEAR AIR TIGHT AS AN ALL CAST STOVE CAN BE MADE. ENTIRELY NEW DESIGN. IS A DOOR FEED AND DOES NOT HAVE ANY SELF FEEDING MAGAZINE. HAS BALL BEARING DRAW CENTER GRATE.

THE ACME CARBON **DOUBLE HEATER has hot air opening as shown in the illustration, to which a 6-inch pipe can be attached to heat an upper room, or is covered with a nickeled open cap to let the heat out into the lower room, as desired.** The draft supply is regulated by an eccentric cam or wheel, enabling the user to give it any amount of draft, or cut it off air tight, as desired. The outer casing is artistically carved open fretwork and can be removed when necessary, without getting a mechanic. All doors and joints are fitted absolutely air tight. Supplied with a cast elbow for smoke collar.

STOVES ARE CARRIED by railroad companies at a low rate (third class), which usually averages from 25 to 40 cents per 100 pounds for 500 miles. On pages 7 to 10 you can get the third class freight rate from Chicago to a point nearest you which is almost exactly the same as to your town. You will find the freight will amount to next to nothing on a stove compared to what you will save in price.

$8.65 TO $15.75

OUR stoves will be found in every neighborhood. Your neighbors can recommend them to you . . . .

OUR new design for 1902 will be ready for the fall trade and will be sent on all orders after the stock of this design is exhausted.

Delivered on the cars at our foundry at $8.65 to $15.75 for cash with the order.

Catalogue Number	Fire Pot	Height, without Urn	Pipe Collar	Floor Space	Weight, pounds	Price
22R467	10-in.	40½ in.	6	20 x20	166	$ 8.65
22R468	12-in.	43 in.	6	21½x21½	204	10.85
22R469	14-in.	46 in.	6	24 x24	255	13.40
22R470	16-in.	49 in.	6	26 x26	310	15.75

SPECIAL FEATURES. **Spun brass nickeled urn. Nickeled swing top. Nickeled main top. Nickeled front panels. Nickeled "always cold" door handle. Check register in fire door. Nickeled draft supply. Nickeled shaker. Deep ash pan. Nickeled foot rails. Nickeled legs.**

WHERE WE QUOTE PRICES **delivered on the cars at factory it is done to save the expense of freight, cartage and handling into and out of our store in Chicago and all the saving goes to the customer in the low prices we make.** It enables us to quote you a price direct from the factory that barely covers the cost of material and manufacturing with but our one small percentage of profit added. A price only made possible by eliminating all the handling expenses. If you live east of Indiana the freight will be less than from Chicago. If you live in Indiana the freight will be about the same as from Chicago. If you live west of Chicago the freight will be only 40 to 50 cents per 100 pounds more than from Chicago, but you save it all in the low prices we quote.

WE CAN ALWAYS FURNISH REPAIRS FOR ACME STOVES AND RANGES. . . . . . .

ACME SEROCO

HOT BLAST AIR TIGHT SHEET STEEL HEATER FOR HARD OR SOFT COAL.

AT $7.50 TO $10.95, according to size, delivered on the cars at our foundry in Northern Illinois. **This is without exception the most economical and most serviceable** hot blast draft air tight sheet steel coal burner made. **Made to burn hard coal, soft coal or coke,** and, as will be seen from skeleton description, it possesses all the very latest improvements. **This hot blast heater consumes 85 per cent of the smoke.** A very powerful and quick acting heater. **It is handsomely ornamented with nickel plated foot rails, nickel top band,** and has patent double cover on top. **Manufacturers claim that 1¼ tons ordinary grade soft coal** will last as long and give as much heat as one ton of the very best hard coal, and that it will hold fire of soft coal over night.

From this illustration you can form an idea of the appearance of this handsome new model air tight hot blast heater.

$7.50
TO
$10.95
IF YOU HESITATE TO SEND FULL CASH WITH YOUR ORDER, ASK YOUR NEIGHBORS ABOUT US AND READ WHAT OUR BANKERS SAY ON PAGES 12 and 13.
ACME SEROCO

Cash with order prices, delivered on the cars at our foundry in Northern Illinois.

Catalogue Number	Stove No.	Diameter	Height, Floor to Urn Base	Shipping weight	Price
22R472	145	12 in.	39½ in.	110 lbs.	$ 7.50
22R473	165	14 in.	41¾ in.	120 lbs.	8.45
22R474	185	16 in.	45 in.	162 lbs.	9.55
22R475	215	19 in.	45¾ in.	198 lbs.	10.95

Skeleton illustration showing inner construction of our Acme Seroco Coal Air Tight Hot Blast Sheet Steel Heater, for burning hard or soft coal.

OUR ONLY TERMS ARE CASH WITH THE ORDER.

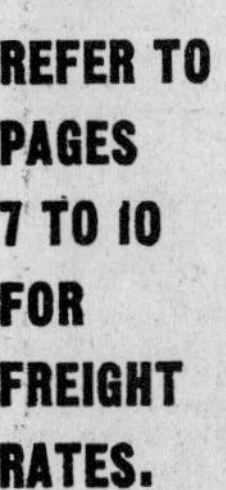

REFER TO PAGES 7 TO 10 FOR FREIGHT RATES.

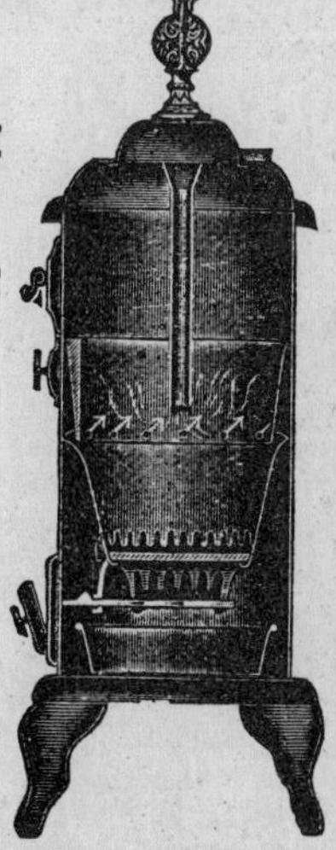

THESE LOW PRICES ARE POSSIBLE BY REASON OF OUR GETTING 50 CENTS FOR EVERY ONE OF OUR BIG CATALOGUES. IN THIS WAY ALL ADVERTISING EXPENSE HAS BEEN DEDUCTED FROM OUR SELLING PRICES. WITH OTHER HOUSES THE FREE CATALOGUE AND FREE SAMPLE EXPENSE IS ADDED TO THE SELLING PRICES.

THE TOP of the stove lifts up for feeding in the fuel. The dome swing top swings conveniently aside so the top of stove can be used for heating a kettle when desired. Has powerful central down draft smoke consumer. Mica front feed door. Handsome design and finish. A better stove for the money than ever before put on the market. **Has ornamented cast top and cast bottom.** It has a nickeled ring around the top of the stove and two air inlets. Is furnished with the **draw center shaking grate.** Heavy cast fire pot, cast lining above fire pot and 20-gauge steel lining above that. Has polished stee body. Patent double cover on top

ACME OAK

At $4.29 to $9.52.

DELIVERED ON THE CARS AT OUR FOUNDRY IN CENTRAL OHIO.

A WONDER OF THE STOVE INDUSTRY.

There is not a manufacturer of heating stoves in America that will not see our catalogue and be attracted by this most extraordinary offer, and the most astonishing thing will be how it is possible for anyone to make the stove for the money.

Retail dealers everywhere are glad to buy these stoves even in quantities at our special $4.29 price. Anything extraordinary that we secure, our customers get the benefit.

OUR PRICE IS YOUR PRICE.

The $4.29 to $9.52 price we quote you is the actual cost to us on our season's contract basis, with but one small percentage of profit added. **Such value as was never known** and never before offered by us or any other house.

$4.29
TO
$9.52
STOVE DEALERS AND OTHERS WILL FIND IT PROFITABLE TO BUY THEIR STOVES FROM US TO SELL THEM AGAIN.

Cash with order prices, delivered on the cars at our foundry in Central Ohio.

Catalogue Number	Stove Number	Diameter of Fire Pot	Height, inches	Floor Space, inches	Size Pipe to Fit Collar	Weight, pounds	Price, with Wood Grate	Price, with Coal Grate	Price, with Both Grates
22R477	210	10	38	16 x16	5-inch	86	$4.29	$4.34	$4.56
22R478	212	12	40	18½x18½	6-inch	114	5.04	5.09	5.94
22R479	214	14	43	20¾x20¾	6-inch	145	6.19	6.24	6.65
22R480	216	16	44	22¾x22¾	6-inch	175	7.40	7.45	7.95
22R481	218	18	47	25 x25	7-inch	210	8.90	8.95	9.52

Height of stoves as given is from floor to base of urn. We can furnish the three larger sizes with self feeding magazines, for anthracite coal only, for 75 cents for No. 214, $1.00 for No. 216, and $1.25 for No. 218, EXTRA.

OUR $4.29 **Acme Oak Heating Stove is the latest, handsomest oak pattern. It is mounted with smooth steel, heavy cast iron fire pot, has shaking and draw center grate for coal,** has double circular wood grate which is so constructed that the fire can be kept under complete control. Large ash pan, large feed doors. Has highly polished heavily nickel plated foot rails, large nickel plated name plate, nickel plated top ring, handsome nickel plated fancy urn. Nickel plated hinge pins and knobs, large swing top, cooking lid under swing top. Check drafts at collar and in feed door. The Acme Oak is one of the handsomest heating stoves on the market. It is nice enough for any home, and would ornament any parlor.

BURNS ANYTHING. **The Acme Oak is suitable for wood, hard coal, soft coal, coke,** or anything that can be burned in a stove.

DON'T PAY RETAIL PRICES **for your heating stoves this season.** Price commonly charged by retail dealers is $1.00 for each inch in diameter, or $14.00 for 214, $16.00 for 216, $18.00 for 218. You would pay your retail dealer almost **double the price** we ask for the stove. You pay him $1.00 for each inch in diameter.

WE CAN ALWAYS FURNISH REPAIRS FOR ACMES.

WHERE WE QUOTE PRICES **delivered on the cars at foundry, it is done to save the expense of freight, cartage, and handling into and out of our store in Chicago,** and all the saving goes to the customer in the low prices we make. It enables us to quote you a price direct from the foundry that barely covers the cost of material and manufacturing, with but our one small percentage of profit added. A price only made possible by eliminating all the handling expenses.

THE IRON AGE

FOR COAL ONLY.

MADE IN SEVEN SIZES, **from $2.70 to $11.95, according to size, delivered on the cars at our western foundry on the Upper Mississippi River.**

Has large ash pit, cast foot rails, annular draft ring admitting the draft equally all around the shaking grate, opening and closing automatically as you shake the grate. The top is so constructed that an extension sheet iron drum can be attached at any time.

Cash with order prices, delivered on the cars at our Mississippi Valley foundry.

Catalogue Number	Stove Number	Diam. of Fire Pot	Height, inches	Size Pipe	Weight, pounds	Price
22R486	9	10 in.	33	5½	67	$ 2.70
22R487	10	11 in.	36	5½	85	3.20
22R488	11	13 in.	37½	5½	105	3.65
22R489	12	13½ in.	40½	6	130	4.40
22R490	14	16 in.	44½	6	172	5.75
22R491	16	18 in.	50	7	225	7.25
22R492	22	21 in.	55	7	407	11.95

THE ACME GIANT.

BURNS COAL ONLY.

MADE IN FOUR SIZES, **from $4.59 to $11.25,** delivered on the cars at our foundry in Central Ohio. This is a large, heavy cannon stove of extra heating power. Adapted for schools, churches, halls, stores, shops, or any place where a heavy stove is required. Has swing feed door, large ash pit, cast foot rails, draw center and shaking grate, nickel plated knobs, extra heavy fire pot. The top is so arranged that drum can be attached at any time.

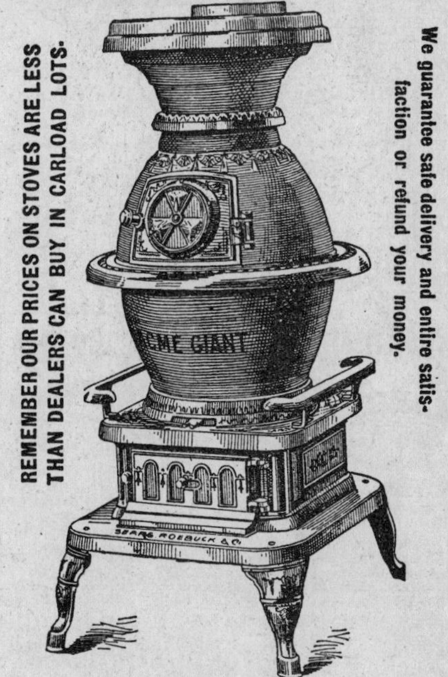

REMEMBER OUR PRICES ON STOVES ARE LESS THAN DEALERS CAN BUY IN CARLOAD LOTS.
ACME GIANT
SEARS ROEBUCK & CO.
We guarantee safe delivery and entire satisfaction or refund your money.

Cash with order prices, delivered on the cars at our Central Ohio foundry.

Catalogue Number	Stove Number	Diam. of Fire Pot	Height, inches	Floor Space, inches	Weight, pounds	Price
22R493	13	13 in.	40	18 x 20	117	$ 4.59
22R494	15	15 in.	45½	20½x 23½	155	6.32
22R495	17	17 in.	47	22 x 25½	206	8.45
22R496	20	20 in.	56	25 x 28	272	11.25

THE ACME RED JACKET CANNON.

AT $1.65 TO $2.75.

THIS IS A CHEAP HEATING STOVE FOR BURNING COAL ONLY.

THE ACME CANNON has swing ash pit door, register in feed door, shaking and dumping grate. Made only in four sizes. You can form some idea of our prices and for how little money we are furnishing high grade stoves, when you compare the weight of the stove with the price, about 4 cents per pound. **Our prices are money saving prices.**

Cash with order prices, delivered on the cars either at our Central Ohio or our Mississippi Valley foundry.

Catalogue Number	Size	Diameter of Fire Pot	Height, inches	Size of Pipe to Fit Collar	Weight, pounds	Price
22R497	6	9 inches	23½	5 inches	40	$1.65
22R498	7	10 inches	27½	5 inches	46	2.05
22R499	8	11 inches	29½	6 inches	55	2.30
22R500	9	12 inches	32	6 inches	66	2.75

THE ACME JACK-PET LAUNDRY.

AT $2.44 TO $2.73.

FOR COAL.

This is a neat and desirable stove for laundry use. Has dumping grate, two covers, large front feed and takes a large boiler. It is made in three sizes. All take 6-inch stove pipe. Having succeeded in reducing our selling prices to $2.44 to $2.73 for this Acme Jack-Pet laundry stove, about 4 cents per pound, and guarantee the stove equal to any made regardless of cost, we believe you will agree no other firm makes such prices.

Cash with order prices, delivered on the cars either at our Central Ohio or our Mississippi Valley foundry.

Catalogue Number	Size	Size of Covers	Diameter of Fire Pot	Height, inches	Weight, pounds	Price
22R502	7	7 inches	11 inches	22½	64	$2.44
22R503	88	8 inches	11 inches	22½	64	2.49
22R504	8	8 inches	12½ inches	23½	76	2.73

THE ACME PRIDE-HERO, $2.90.

FOR COAL.

This is an entirely new and novel stove for the laundry. Will hold eight sad irons around the fire pot and will take a large boiler on the top at the same time. The irons lay close to the fire and heat very quickly. Has two 8-inch covers, large pouch feed and dumping grate. Made in one size only. Top surface, 20x14 inches. Collar takes 6-inch stove pipe. Diameter of fire pot, 12½ inches. Weight, 90 pounds.

No. 22R505 No. 8. Cash with order price, **$2.90**

Delivered on the cars either at our Central Ohio or our Mississippi Valley foundry.

Remember, the freight rate on stoves is very low. The cost of transportation on a stove need not be considered when you consider what we save for you in price. No one can compete with us in stoves.

ELK LAUNDRY.—FOUR HOLES.

FOR COAL.

SOMETHING NEW. **Our four-hole Elk laundry stove at $3.75, delivered on the cars at our Mississippi Valley foundry; has dumping grate, four cooking holes and with our Acme Drum Oven at $1.50 extra would make a complete cooking stove.** Weight, 95 pounds.

No. 22R506 Price, No. 8, cash with order....**$3.75**

ACME CHAMPION BOXWOOD.

FOR BURNING WOOD.

AT $2.00 TO $5.85 **This is a handsome and well made box heating stove. Every plate is constructed to avoid cracking. Has swing hearth, swing top, and large feed door.** The sizes indicate the length wood that the stove will take. Size 18 has one 6-inch cover. Size 22 has one 7-inch cover. Size 25 has two 7-inch covers. Sizes 28 and 30 have two 8-inch covers and short center. Sizes 34 and 36 have two 9-inch covers and short center in swing top.

Cash with order prices, delivered on the cars either at our Central Ohio or our Mississippi Valley foundry. The size indicates the length of wood.

Catalogue Number	Size	Height inches	Size Pipe to Fit Collar	Weight, pounds	Price
22R507	18	19½	5 inches	51	$2.00
22R508	22	21½	6 inches	60	2.70
22R509	25	23	6 inches	92	3.40
22R510	28	26	6 inches	112	4.00
22R511	30	26	6 inches	115	4.15
22R512	34	29½	6 inches	159	5.70
22R513	36	29½	6 inches	165	5.85

ACME DRUM OVEN, $1.50.

ATTACH TO ANY 6-INCH STOVE PIPE.

No. 22R515 Oven, 18x14½ inches. Price...**$1.50**

Quick baker, and saves the waste of heat passing up the pipe.

ACME COTTAGE HEATER.

FOR COAL OR WOOD.

AT $3.80 TO $6.60 **according to size and as illustrated, is a first class cottage stove for burning coal or wood.** It has a heavy cast iron body, shaking and dumping grate for coal and swing fenders for wood. This stove is trimmed with a fancy highly polished **nickel plated** foot rail flush with hearth, handsome **nickel plated** panel on upper front door. Made with large open fancy swing top, and is fitted with a large back extension shelf; made with two covers and short center in top; end shelf; **nickel plated urn, nickel plated knobs and hinges.**

For those burning wood only, this stove can be fitted with an oven for baking. The extra cost will be $1.00 on any size. Access to the oven would be through the large upper front door.

Cash with order prices, delivered on the cars at our foundry in Central Ohio

Catalogue Number	Stove No.	Length of Fire Box	Height, inches	Floor Space, inches	Weight, pounds	Price for Wood	Price for Coal	Price, Coal and Wood
22R521	21	19	35	16x22	100	$3.80	$4.30	$4.50
22R523	23	21	37	18x24	120	4.60	5.20	5.40
22R525	25	23	39	20x26	145	5.55	6.35	6.60

Ornament is not included in measuring heights. All sizes take 6-inch stove pipe.

ACME MAGIC TODD HEATER.

BURNS WOOD ONLY.

THE BODY **is made of smooth steel. It has nickeled urn on the swing top, with a cooking hole beneath. Has nickeled ornaments at each end of top, nickeled name plate, nickeled foot rail, knobs and hinge pins. Drop smoke plate inside of fire door.**

Cash with order prices delivered on the cars at our foundry in Central Ohio.

Catalogue Number	Stove Number	Length of Fire Box, inches	Size of door opening, inches	Height, inches	Floor Space, inches	Size of pipe to fit Collar, inches	Weight, pounds	Price
22R526	26	24	9x16	28	19x20	6	130	$5.45
22R528	28	26	9x16	28	19x22	6	140	6.15
22R530	30	28	11x18	30	20x26	6	175	7.15
22R532	32	30	11x18	30	20x28	6	185	7.85

SHEET STEEL AIR-TIGHT HEATING STOVES, $1.10 AND UPWARD.

DELIVERED ON THE CARS AT OUR FOUNDRY IN NORTHERN ILLINOIS.

OUR LINE OF SHEET STEEL AIR-TIGHT HEATERS includes the very best selection from the best makers in the country, and does not include any of the inferior makes on the market. We sold over ten thousand air-tight sheet steel heaters last season, and all the time we were far behind on our orders, and, as the indications point to a much larger trade this season, we have made very extensive preparations to not only be able to fill our orders promptly, but with such a line of air-tight heaters as will not be offered by any other house, and at prices so low that our customers can order from us, pay the freight, which will add next to nothing to the cost, and own the best air-tight heater that can be made, at about half the price charged by retail dealers.

OUR HOT AIR-TIGHT HEATER.

FOR WOOD.

It is the cheapest steel air-tight handled by us or any other house. While it is small, it is good and suitable for small rooms. It is a direct draft stove, taking in the draft at the ash opening. Has oval sheet body 18 inches long.

Catalogue Number	Stove Number	Body	Shipping Weight	Price
22R533	18	18x15x15	22 pounds	$1.10

The following direct draft air-tights are constructed exactly the same as the Dot, excepting they have a screw draft register in the ash opening, while the Dot has only slide register to let in the draft below. The sizes quoted below will give you heat enough for various sized rooms up to the largest family rooms. All of these are offered **without foot rails. Cash with the order.**

Catalogue Number	Stove Number	Body	Shipping Weight	Price
22R534	180	18x15x15	26 pounds	$1.39
22R535	200	20x17x20	34 pounds	1.80
22R536	240	24x17x24	36 pounds	2.25
22R537	300	29x17x24	44 pounds	3.10

$1.99 AND UPWARD.

THIS ILLUSTRATION shows our better grade, with hot blast down draft. A better stove than those quoted above, for the following reasons: **The hot blast draft heats the air before it reaches the fuel, thus producing perfect combustion.** The cover to ash opening is locked securely, to prevent blowing off. It is honestly constructed of good material, with heavy lining, and **cannot fail to give satisfaction.** The body is made of 26-gauge smooth steel, the lining is 20-gauge. Has fine nickel urn and screw draft. **It will burn chunks, knots, chips, straw, cobs, hay, or trash,** or anything used for fuel, except coal. The pipe should be provided with a damper. Put two or three inches of ashes in bottom of stove before building fire, and always leave about this quantity when cleaning the stove. Will keep fire over night. In setting up this stove, put the crimped end of stove pipe down. **The feed opening is 10½ to 12½ inches in diameter; the ash opening is 6½ inches in diameter; all sizes take 6-inch stove pipe.** It has a check draft in the stove top, neat ornament on cover of fuel opening; screw draft adjuster in ash cover.

Cash with the order, delivered on the cars at our foundry in Northern Illinois.

Price List of the Acme Air-Tight Smooth Steel Heater without Foot Rails.

Catalogue Number	No.	Length, inches	Width, inches	Height of Body	Size of Feed Opening	Size of Ash Opening	Shipping Weight	Price, Smooth Steel
22R538	20	20	16½	20 in.	10½ in.	6½ in.	37 lbs.	$1.99
22R539	24	24	17	24 in.	12½ in.	6½ in.	41 lbs.	2.25
22R540	30	29	17	24 in.	12½ in.	6½ in.	46 lbs.	2.65

Price List of the Acme Air-Tight Polished Steel Heater without Foot Rails.

Catalogue Number	No.	Length, inches	Width, inches	Height of Body	Size of Feed Opening	Size of Ash Opening	Shipping Weight	Price, Polished Steel
22R541	120	20	16½	20 in.	10½ in.	6½ in.	38 lbs.	$2.40
22R542	124	24	17	24 in.	12½ in.	6½ in.	42 lbs.	2.70
22R543	130	29	17	24 in.	12½ in.	6½ in.	48 lbs.	3.38

Price List of the Acme Air-Tight Smooth Steel Heater with Foot Rails.

Catalogue Number	No.	Length, inches	Width, inches	Height of Body	Size of Feed Opening	Size of Ash Opening	Shipping Weight, pounds	Price, Smooth Steel
22R544	205	20	16½	20 in.	10½ in.	6½ in.	41	$2.45
22R545	245	24	17	24 in.	12½ in.	6½ in.	45	2.80
22R546	305	29	17	24 in.	12½ in.	6¼ in.	50	3.30

Price List of the Acme Air-Tight Polished Steel Heater with Foot Rails.

Catalogue Number	No.	Length, inches	Width, inches	Height of Body	Size of Feed Opening	Size of Ash Opening	Shipping Weight, pounds	Price, Polished Steel
22R547	1205	20	16½	20 in.	10½ in.	6½ in.	42	$2.85
22R548	1245	24	17	24 in.	12½ in.	6½ in.	46	3.25
22R549	1305	29	17	24 in.	12½ in.	6½ in.	52	4.10

All of the above air-tights are for wood and will not burn coal at all.

OUR $5.65 AND $6.75 ACME AIR-TIGHT.

FOR WOOD ONLY.

This illustration shows our Acme Air-Tight Heating Stove with hot blast draft and hot air circulating system. This stove burns everything (excepting coal) that is used for fuel. The feed opening is 10¼ inches in diameter. The ash opening is 6⅛ inches in diameter. Height of stove, 45 inches. Height of body, 26 inches. Size of pipe to fit collar is 6 inches.

Cash with order prices of the Acme Air-Tight polished steel Heating Stove, with hot blast draft and hot air circulating system, delivered on the cars at our foundry in Northern Illinois.

Catalogue Number	Number	Length, inches	Width, inches	Shipping Weight, pounds	Price
22R550	26	26	17	110	$5.65
22R551	32	32	18	140	6.75

No. 22R550 $5.65 and $6.75

OUR $5.40 AND $6.15 ACME COAL AIR-TIGHT SHEET STEEL HEATER.

FOR HARD OR SOFT COAL.

No. 22R555 $5.40

From this illustration you can form an idea of the appearance of this handsome new model air-tight hot blast heater.

It is handsomely ornamented with nickel plated foot rails, nickel plated hot blast dampers, screw adjustment, **highly ornamented with nickel plated ornaments, double cover on top.**

This is one of the latest and most modern stoves on the market. The body is made of smooth steel, has cast ornamented top, cast fire pot, cast lining extending up as far as draft inlet with 20-gauge steel lining above that. Furnished with the popular **"draw center" shaking grate, and ash pan.** These stoves are claimed without any contradiction to consume 85 per cent of the smoke. All sizes use 6-inch stove pipe.

Cash with order prices delivered on the cars at our Northern Illinois foundry.

Catalogue Number	No.	Body	Total Height	Fire Pot	Weight Crated	Price
22R555	155	14x29	43 in.	12 in.	95 lbs.	$5.40
22R556	175	16x31	45 in.	14 in.	110 lbs.	6.15

OUR $7.75 ACME AIR-TIGHT SHEET STEEL HEATER

COAL BURNING.

This is without exception the highest grade, most economical, best finished and most serviceable hot blast draft air-tight sheet iron coal burner made. Made to burn hard coal, soft coal or coke, and possesses all the very latest improvements —everything that can make it the very best stove of the kind on the market. **This hot air heater consumes 85 per cent of the smoke.** Most economical stove made; it is a very powerful and quick acting heater. **Has ornamented cast top, cast corrugated bottom, double jacket.** It has a nickeled rim around the top of the stove and two air inlets. Is furnished with the **draw center shaking grate and ash pan.** Heavy cast fire pot, cast lining above fire pot to air inlet and 20-gauge steel lining above that. Has polished steel body. Patent double cover on top.

Cash with order prices, delivered on the cars at our foundry in Northern Illinois.

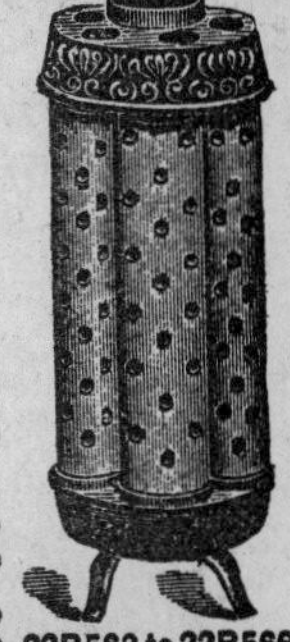
No. 22R557 $7.75 to $10.90

Catalogue Number	No.	Body	Total Height	Fire Pot	Weight Crated	Price
22R557	17	16x31	45 in.	14 in.	140 lbs.	$ 7.75
22R558	19	18x33	47 in.	16 in.	168 lbs.	9.00
22R559	22	21x37	51 in.	19 in.	210 lbs.	10.90

THE NEW ERA RADIATOR.

It stops the heat on its way to the chimney and makes it do double duty. You can place a **New Era Radiator** on the stove pipe in the same room with the stove. It will actually save from one-quarter to one-half the fuel. Actual tests have proved it time and time again.

SQUARE STYLE.

This style is only adapted for floors above the stove. They are very handsome in design, and are bought by many who would not otherwise run a stove pipe through their house.

Cannot be used with soft coal.

No. 22R560 For 6-inch stove pipe. Body made of Woods' Refined Iron. Cast iron top and base; nickel plated feet. Size of base, 17½x13¾ inches; height, with legs, 37 inches. Weight, crated, 60 pounds. Price, each........................ $4.40

No. 22R561 Same as above, except the body is made of Woods' patent planished iron. Price, each........................ $5.05

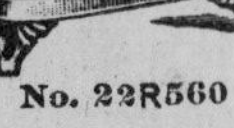
No. 22R560

CYLINDRICAL STYLE.

To meet the demand for a cheaper Radiator, this style is added. It is smaller but very efficient either on the back of a stove or to heat small upper rooms.

Cannot be used with soft coal.

No. 22R562 For 6-inch stove pipe. Made of Woods' Refined Iron. Diameter, 10 inches; height, 28 inches. Weight, crated, 24 pounds. Price, each........................ $2.05

No. 22R562

The Original Round Style.

....HARD OR SOFT COAL....

This style has been successfully sold for many years. They are adapted either for the back of a stove or an upper room or hall.

Furnished with inner tubes for hard coal and without inner tubes for soft coal, for 6-inch stove pipe. Made from Woods' refined iron (sheet steel), with cast iron ends. They are polished, ready to set up, before they leave the factory. Diameter, 12¼ inches; height, with legs, 38 inches. Weight, crated, 50 pounds.

No. 22R563 For soft coal. $4.10
No. 22R564 For hard coal 4.20

Same as above, except it is made of Woods' patent planished iron.

No. 22R565 For hard coal. $4.80
No. 22R566 For soft coal.. 4.70

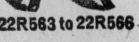

22R563 to 22R566

OIL HEATING STOVES.

OIL HEATING STOVES are a great convenience for heating rooms where there is no chimney. They are perfectly safe, no more danger than with an ordinary lamp. If the wick needs trimming, don't cut it, simply rub the crust off with a cloth or brush. Use only the best grade of kerosene or coal oil. Don't spill any oil on the tank when filling, it might cause an odor. Our wick raising device is so constructed that it grips the wick on both sides and raises it evenly, and it is impossible for it to bind. Anyone can put in a new wick in a minute. This is a very important feature in an oil stove.

GUARANTEE. All our Oil Heaters are carefully inspected before shipment and are warranted to do all we claim. Directions for the care and operation accompany each stove. If after these directions have been followed any stove is found faulty or defective the same can be returned to us and money will be refunded without an argument.

Acme Beauty.

Real heat makers. The entire stove is made of sheet steel. The burner is made of brass. Our new wick raising device raises the wick evenly and does not get out of order. They are fine in appearance and as good as they look. Prices are cash with the order.

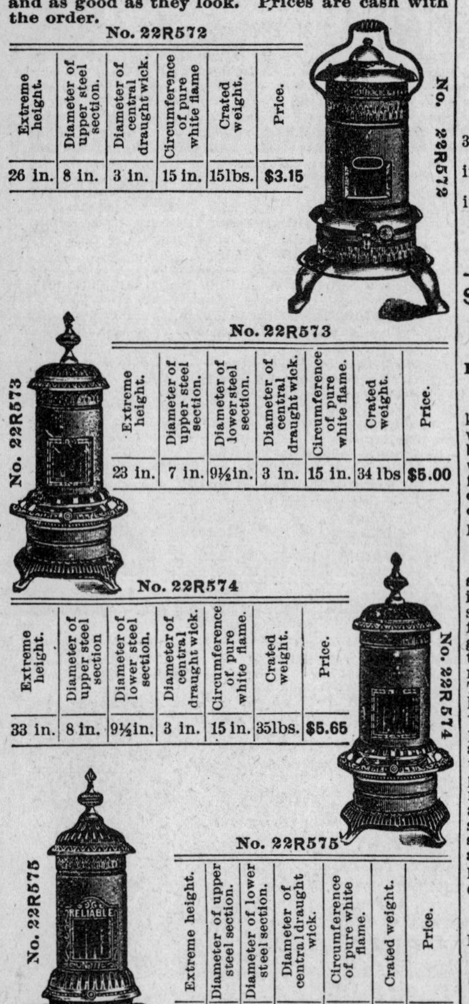

No. 22R572

Extreme height.	Diameter of upper steel section.	Diameter of central draught wick.	Circumference of pure white flame	Crated weight.	Price.
26 in.	8 in.	3 in.	15 in.	15 lbs.	$3.15

No. 22R572

No. 22R573

Extreme height.	Diameter of upper steel section.	Diameter of lower steel section.	Diameter of central draught wick.	Circumference of pure white flame.	Crated weight.	Price.
23 in.	7 in.	9½ in.	3 in.	15 in.	34 lbs	$5.00

No. 22R573

No. 22R574

Extreme height.	Diameter of upper steel section	Diameter of lower steel section.	Diameter of central draught wick.	Circumference of pure white flame.	Crated weight.	Price.
33 in.	8 in.	9½ in.	3 in.	15 in.	35 lbs.	$5.65

No. 22R574

No. 22R575

Extreme height.	Diameter of upper steel section.	Diameter of lower steel section.	Diameter of central draught wick.	Circumference of pure white flame.	Crated weight.	Price.
40 in.	8 in.	10 in.	3 in.	15 in.	50 lbs.	$6.90

No. 22R575

No. 22R576 Wicks for any of the above Oil Heaters. Price, each............ 9c

We cannot furnish wicks for stoves not sold by us.

Our 35-Cent Lamp Stove.

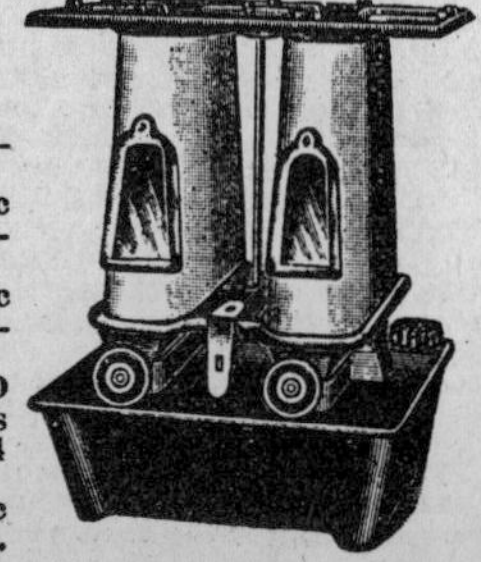

No. 22R577 One-Burner Lamp Stove. Price, each...... ...35c

No. 22R578 Two-Burner Lamp Stove. Price, each.........70c

No. 22R579 Three-Burner Lamp Stove. Price, each.......$1.00

No. 22R580 Wicks for above stoves, 4 inches wide. Price, each...........3c

Cash with order prices.

OIL COOKING STOVES.

Reliance Oil Stoves.

The Reliance is a well made stove in every particular, and is the cheapest well made stove on the market.

No. 22R581 No. 102¼, Single. Has two burners 3¼ inches wide. Price, 64c

No. 22R582 No. 102½, Single. Has two 4-inch burners. Price........88c

No. 22R583 No. 103, Single. Has three 4-inch burners. Price.......................$1.13

Cash with order prices.

No. 22R584 No. 102¼, Double. Has four burners 3¼ inches wide. Price..............................$1.33

No. 22R585 No. 102½, Double. Has four burners 4 inches wide. Price..............................$1.84

No. 22R586 No. 103, Double. Has six burners 4 inches wide. Price..............................$2.33

No. 22R587 3-inch wicks. Price, each..........2c

No. 22R588 4-inch wicks. Price, each..........3c

No. 22R589 3½-inch wicks. Price, each.......3c

Cash with order prices.

$4.55 Buys Our High Grade Acme Wickless Blue Flame Kerosene Oil Stove.

Delivered on the cars at our factory in Northern Illinois.

THIS STOVE WILL BURN KEROSENE. With kerosene it has the great advantage that it is a wickless stove. No wick is required, and we believe that we stand in no fear of contradiction when we say that it is the only successful blue flame wickless stove made. It is easily and quickly lighted, has powerful burners and is durable, convenient and most economical.

DESCRIPTION OF OUR CELEBRATED ACME WICKLESS BLUE FLAME OIL STOVE.

Frame made of extra quality sheet and band steel with middle brace. The supply tank containing the oil is removable, and can be taken off the stove without removing troublesome bolts or screws for the purpose of filling the reservoir with oil or gasoline. If these stoves are set anywhere near level, the lighter cannot be flooded, because the oil cannot rise any higher than the level in the lower reservoir. The flame will, therefore, always remain the same height, no matter how wide open you have the supply valve, but you can reduce it to a simmering flame by partially closing the valve. You light the stove exactly as you would light a lamp, and when combustion is started the flame becomes a blue flame of perfect combustion. The stove is so simple that really no directions are required. We, however, attach a card of simple instructions to each stove. We make special ovens for use on these stoves, and these ovens are the most perfect made and warranted to bake satisfactorily. See next page for sizes and prices on ovens.

CASH WITH ORDER PRICES OF OUR ACME WICKLESS BLUE FLAME CABINET OIL STOVE, SHORT LEG.

Delivered on cars at our Northern Illinois factory.

No. 22R590

No. 22R590 No. 42, two-burner. Size of top, 22x15 inches; height, 14 inches. Price...........$4.55 Weight, crated, 40 pounds.

No. 22R591 No. 43, three-burner. Size of top, 33x15 inches; height, 14 inches. Price..............................$5.95 Weight, crated, 50 pounds.

The steel burner shells on our Acme Wickless Stove give the largest and hottest blue flame of any oil stove on the market

PRICES OF OUR HIGH FRAME ACME WICKLESS BLUE FLAME CABINET OIL STOVE.

No. 22R592

No. 22R592 High Stove, No. 422. Two burners. Size of top, 22x15 inches; height, 24 inches. Price...........$6.00 Weight, crated, 50 pounds.

No. 22R593 High Stove, No. 433. Three burners. Size of top, 33x15 inches; height, 24 inches. Price...........$7.70 Weight, crated, 55 pounds.

No. 22R594 Step Stove, No. 425. Two burners on top and one burner on step. Size of top, 22x15 inches; size of step, 11½x15 inches; height to top of stove, 24 inches. Weight, crated, 60 pounds. Price, $9.10

See next page for price of our special drop door ovens.

Remember that the steel burner shells on all of our Acme Wickless Stoves give the largest and hottest blue flame of any oil stove made.

GASOLINE STOVES.

If everybody used the Sears, Roebuck & Co.'s Acme Gasoline Stoves or if all other stoves were as honestly made there would be no such thing as a gasoline stove explosion. Don't use cheap gasoline. Cheap gasoline clogs the burners and is more dangerous than gunpowder or dynamite. Our stove uses less gasoline than any other and it costs less to run it with 74 degrees deodorized gasoline than others with the cheap, dangerous, unsatisfactory low degree gasoline.

We can furnish repairs for the Acme Gasoline Stoves, but never have any calls for repairs. This indicates that the stoves are durable.

Acme Process Gasoline Stoves.

All stoves are strongly and substantially built, beautifully finished and elegantly designed.

Hot air and vaporizing tubes are connected with removable cast iron elbows, easily taken apart, so that the vaporizers can be taken out and cleaned. Vaporizers are made of perforated brass and of the latest scientific construction. Burner Drums are of the best sheet brass, and have cast iron tops and bottoms. Cone seats are made of cast iron. Cone seats have large iron flanges so as to protect the drums from heat, grease and dirt, which have always caused burner drums to either burn or rust off at the top. This improvement makes all hot air conductors indestructible. A great improvement and one worthy of your consideration. Burners are fastened together with two bolts, easily taken apart. Tanks for 1902 will be simple, perfect and a proven success. Needle points on valves are made of German silver wire, they will never rust or corrode, and will always insure a steady drip. Tanks are so constructed that they cannot be removed for filling until all valves have been closed. Acme Process stoves will run perfectly in cold weather.

THE ACME STEP PROCESS CABINET RANGE.

$21.65 cash with order for this $35.00 Cabinet Range.

No. 22R595 The Acme Step Process Cabinet Range (No. 30). This range is not only of great cooking capacity but is the most artistic patterned and finest finished range on the market this season. It is the highest of all high grades. A stove that retails for $35.00. Three burners on top, one burner on step and one extra large burner under oven. Size of main top, 35x25 inches; size of step top, 15x21 inches. Size of end shelf, 7x21 inches. Height of range, 36 inches. Weight, crated, 252 pounds. Price, cash with order......................$21.65

No. 22R596 No. 28 (without step). Weight, 224 pounds. Price..$19.00

Our $17.00 Acme Process Cabinet Range.

No. 22R597 Acme Process Cabinet Range (No. 24) is very desirable for small families, or where floor space is limited. It is very compact. Extra large burner under the oven. Very handsome, and warranted to be a perfect baker. Two burners on top. One extra large burner under the oven. Size of main top, 27x25 inches. Size of end shelf, 7x21. Height of range, 36 inches. Weight, crated, 192 pounds. Price each, cash with order.$17.00

DEPARTMENT OF COLORED DRESS GOODS.

OUR NEW POLICY of getting 50 cents for each large catalogue, receiving payment in advance for all samples of dress goods furnished, thus practically doing away with all advertising expense, and our present policy of requiring the full amount of cash to accompany all orders, greatly reducing our clerical expense, makes it possible, with our immense buying power, to show in this, our Dress Goods Department, a line of all the newest novelties as well as the most staple dress goods, in colored, fancy and black, in domestics, and in silks, values that will astonish and please everyone who sends for samples from this department, or who takes advantage of any of the hundreds of extraordinary price values quoted herein.

TO GIVE YOU FAR MORE VALUE for your money than you can possibly get elsewhere, with a view to furnishing you dress goods at even lower prices than dealers can buy in case lots, prices that will mean a saving to you of from one-quarter to one-half, as against any price that other houses can name, solely in your own interest, with the one object in view, namely, to give you much more for your money than you can possibly get elsewhere, we have inaugurated our new policy of getting pay for all catalogues, all samples, and deducting all advertising expense from our selling prices, making our terms of cash in full with the order in the interest of greater economy, all done to give you the greatest possible value for your dollar.

YOU CANNOT APPRECIATE THE VALUES we are giving in this department from any illustration or description contained herein. By comparing our catalogue with catalogues published by any other house, or by attempting to compare the samples with any others of your storekeepers at home or any house abroad, or our illustrations and descriptions, you can scarcely appreciate the amount of money we can save you, how much you will gain by sending to us your order for needed dress, skirt, waist pattern or other goods.

TO UNDERSTAND FULLY how much we can give you for your money, how great an advantage our new policy gives us over all competitors, how much you can save on every yard of dress goods by sending your order to us, either write to us for such samples as you want, under our terms of 1 cent for samples of each number, and compare the samples with those furnished by any other house, or better still, select the goods wanted from our catalogue illustrations and descriptions, send us your order and your money with the understanding that if the goods are not perfectly satisfactory when received, and when compared with the same or similar goods furnished by your storekeeper at home, or by any dealer anywhere, if you do not find ours, quality for quality, very much lower in price, you can return the goods to us at our expense of express or freight charges both ways and we will immediately return your money. **You would know you could not afford to buy one yard of dress goods, silks or domestics,** not one yard of anything in the dress goods line from your storekeeper at home or from any dealer anywhere if you could first examine and compare our prices with those of other houses. We therefore urge that before ordering dress goods or silks of any kind for any purpose, you either get samples from us, or send us your order selected from our catalogue, with the understanding that your money is to be immediately returned to you, if we do not please you and save you money.

OUR LINE OF COLORED DRESS GOODS as well as all staple black goods, silks, domestics, etc., includes the very latest styles for this season. We are direct importers, buying these goods direct from the makers, both at home and abroad. We place with them the largest contracts that are placed by any buyers in this country, and we own the goods on the basis of the actual cost to produce with but one small profit added and without adding anything for advertising expense, and with the most economic system of handling we are able to name prices against which there can be no competition.

ECONOMY IN ORDERING. In ordering dress goods we always urge that our customers order two or more dress, waist, or skirt patterns at a time. If you only need one dress pattern try and get a friend or neighbor to join you and make up an order for two or more dress patterns, for in this way it will reduce the express charges on the goods you will order to next to nothing, the express charges for 15 or 20 yards being very little more than for from 5 to 10 yards. **The express charges, however, you will find, even on a single dress, skirt or waist pattern, will amount to next to nothing as compared to what you will save in price.**

OUR GUARANTEE AND REFUND OFFER. You can select any goods from this catalogue, send us your order with your money, with the understanding and agreement on our part that if the goods are not found perfectly satisfactory when received, and you are not convinced that you are saving money by ordering from us, you can return the goods to us at our expense, and we will immediately return your money.

WHY SAMPLES ARE NOT NECESSARY. While we will furnish samples of any numbers wanted on our regular terms, as explained on this page, we always recommend that our customers make their selections from the illustrations and descriptions and do not delay to write for samples. If you will state the goods wanted by catalogue number, give us an idea of color and pattern wanted, also state complexion and color of hair of the party for whom the dress goods is wanted, we will always assist you by giving you the services of our professional or expert dress goods men, and see that you get the very best values possible to furnish, we, of course, guaranteeing that the color, pattern and all will be satisfactory or we will immediately return your money. By making your selections from the catalogue illustrations or descriptions, without first writing for samples, an expert in the department will select for you the very best thing in our house as to color, pattern, style, etc., in accordance with your wants, and such as will be most becoming to your complexion.

DRESS GOODS SAMPLES FURNISHED AT ONE CENT PER NUMBER.

To those who wish to see samples of dress goods before ordering, we will from our sampling department furnish you samples of anything in our dress goods line, including fancy, colored, black or other dress goods, silks, etc., at 1 cent per catalogue number. By this means we will furnish you a sample of all the shades and patterns represented by any one catalogue number, for 1 cent. In the one number there may be from one to two dozen different shades or patterns and the 1 cent you send for that number will entitle you to as many samples as there may be shades or patterns under that number, so, in writing for dress goods samples, be sure to state the catalogue number of samples wanted, enclose 1 cent for each number, and all the samples under each number will be sent to you by return mail, postpaid.

UNDERSTAND, YOU MAY ASK FOR SAMPLES of a certain black goods and only one sample will be furnished on that number. You may call for another number in colored goods, and we may have as many as one dozen different shades in this number, and a sample of each one, representing our entire line under that number, will be sent you for the 1 cent. Most houses furnish samples of dress goods free for the asking, send out from 25 to 100 samples, and as such houses are known to furnish samples free, we know from our own experience, that thousands of applications for free samples are received from people who have no thought of buying, but simply write for samples out of curiosity, many of the applications coming from children, and in this way the free sampling expense is enormous and must be added to the selling price of the goods, so when you buy a dress pattern from any house that furnishes samples free for the asking, you can be sure, in addition to the real value of the goods you pay for, you are paying for a good many sets of samples that have been distributed free among people who never order.

IF YOU DO NOT feel like selecting the goods you want from the catalogue illustrations and descriptions, **sending us your order with the understanding that the goods must be perfectly satisfactory or your money will be returned;** if you want to see samples first, be sure to state what samples are wanted, by number, enclosing 1 cent for each catalogue number, and the samples will be sent you by mail, postpaid. After you have received the samples and selected the goods wanted, you can send us your order with the understanding than if you are not convinced, when you receive the goods, that at our price you have saved more than ten times the money sent for samples, as against any price you can get from any other house, **we will cheerfully refund the money paid us for samples.**

Our 12-Cent Persian Wool Mixture.

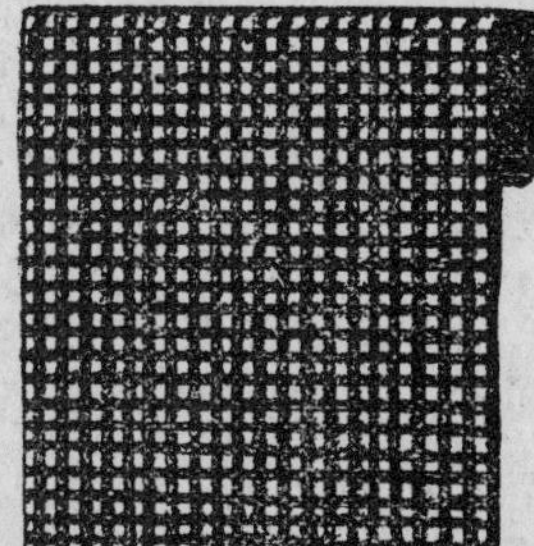

At our special 12-cent price this is one of the most serviceable dress materials in our line. We took the output of one of the best mills on this number. These goods make up very neat and stylish in children's, misses' and ladies' costumes, and are in fact the equal of what your storekeeper would ask double the price for. **They come in handsome new Persian mixtures, neat checks,** and in colors of tan, medium blue, brown, green and purple. Let us help you make a selection of a 10-yard dress pattern for **$1.20** and the value will surprise you. Width, 33 inches.

No. 14R6 Price, per yard.......................12c

Samples of this number furnished for 1 cent, including sample of every shade carried in the number.

Our New 32-Cent Mercerized Suiting.

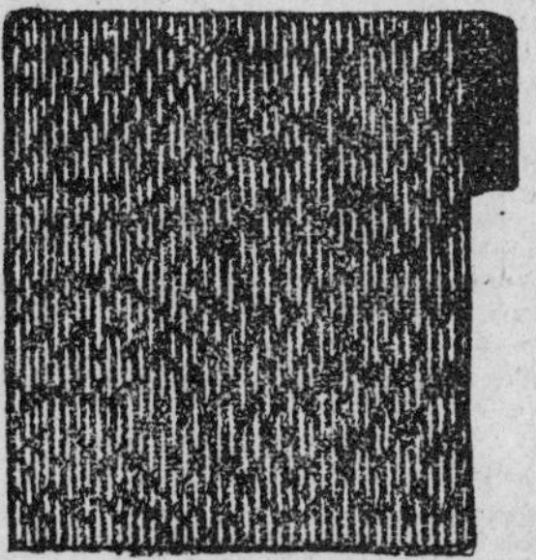

This is a new effect for this season fresh from one of the best New England mills. An immense purchase makes our 32-cent price possible. This is a decided novelty, good medium weight. Comes in a combination of colors, blue and black, mixed red and black, red and green, gray and blue, and also red and navy. 36 inches wide; eight yards makes a liberal dress pattern. **There is nothing at the price more stylish for a ladies', misses', or child's suit.** Select this number and give us an idea of color wanted.

No. 14R12 Our special price, per yard..........32c

Samples of this number furnished for 1 cent, including sample of every shade carried in the number.

Our 39-Cent Imported Illuminated English Novelty Changeable Mohair Granite Dress Goods.

In a variety of color mixtures, we offer at 39 cents per yard for a 37-inch width this handsome new effect in a wool changeable English novelty dress goods fabric as one of our leaders. At 39 cents this is a big leader with us this season, is a special leader for the reason that we closed out the looms to get the price. We took what was left from the mills at a special cut price to close out the entire stock of this number, and as a result we can offer you the goods at 39 cents per yard under our guarantee that it is considerably lower in price than dealers can buy through regular wholesale houses in any quantity. **At 39 cents per yard we are offering you this fabric at one-half the price at which it will sell generally.** These goods come in handsome mixtures in illuminated or changeable color effects in all the different combinations as described. It makes up into very handsome combination suits and skirts suitable for women, misses and children of all ages, and all complexions. **Send us your order for a dress pattern of 7 yards, enclose $2.73, give us an idea of color desired,** state your complexion, allow an expert to assist you in selecting the most desirable shade for your complexion from our stock. It comes in the following illuminated changeable color combinations: Red and blue, green and brown, cerise and green, new blue and brown, petunia and olive. Don't write for samples. We guarantee to give you better satisfaction in assisting you to select without samples than when endeavoring to select from small samples. Width, 37 in.

No. 14R15 Price, per yard.......................**$0.39**

Price for full 7-yard dress pattern............**2.73**

Samples of this number furnished for 1c, including sample of every shade carried in the number.

Our New 19-Cent 40-inch Fancy Pierola Dress Goods.

At 19 cents for this new 40-inch fabric we are underselling the biggest jobbers. This is a new and stylish novelty, medium weight, and will give thorough satisfaction. **Comes in a nobby line of combinations of blue and black, red and black, green and black, brown and black, tan and black, garnet and black, violet and black, purple and black, gray and black,** all the very latest effects for this season. It is a fabric that will make up handsomely in a skirt or full dress for any lady. State color combination wanted, or better still state your complexion and color of hair and let us assist you in the selection. These goods are 40 inches wide, and a 7-yard pattern, costing **$1.33** will make an ample dress pattern.

No. 14R10 Our cut price, per yard.......................19c

Samples of this number furnished for 1 cent, including sample of every shade carried in the number.

OUR RECORD BREAKING COMBINATION SALE OF HIGH COST, HIGH CLASS,

36-INCH DRESS GOODS.

AT 25 CENTS PER YARD WE OFFER THE FOLLOWING SEVEN STUPENDOUS BARGAINS.

EACH OF THESE BEAUTIFUL NEW STYLE wool, silk and wool, and also mercerized silk, crepon and bourette effects, as described in the following seven illustrations and descriptions. These goods are better than anything that has ever been offered by any retailer or jobber, or even by a manufacturer, at less than 50 cents per yard. We have bought them in tremendous quantities, and in order to effect a quick sale of the same we have named a price of 25 cents per yard. The same goods we sold last summer up to 45 cents per yard as one of the biggest bargains we had ever shown. They sold rapidly, in fact, went like wildfire, and we were encouraged to accept the entire residue stock of one of the biggest mills in this country. We have decided to make one price for the entire lot. HAVE YOUR CHOICE. They are all 25 cents per yard. Send us one cent for samples of either of the following seven numbers that go in this great reduction sale.

READ OUR 5 CENT PAPER PATTERN OFFER ON PAGE 858.

Our New 25-Cent Fancy Mercerized Silk and Wool Novelty Dress Goods.

25 CENTS PER YARD.

7-YARD DRESS PATTERN, $1.75

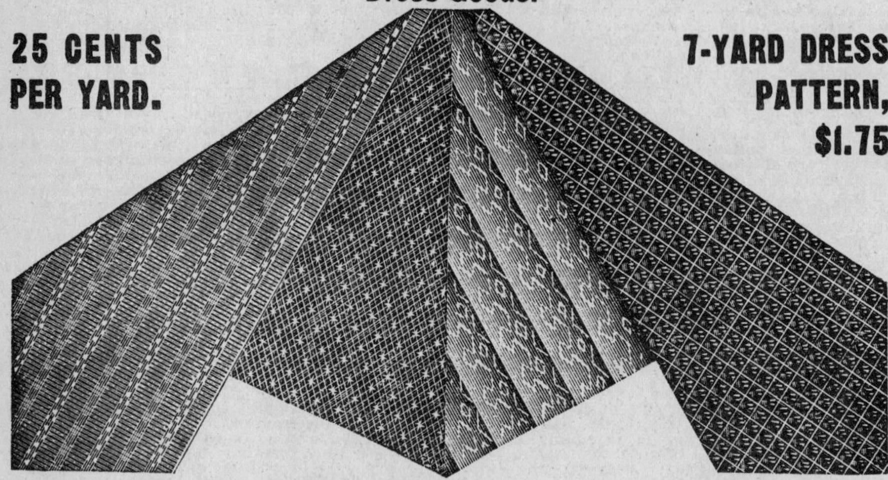

From the accompanying combination illustration we have endeavored to give you some idea of the different effects worked out in this our new line of novelties in mercerized silk and wool dress goods. When these goods were first shown by the mills they were offered to the largest jobbers of the country at 43½ cents, and at this price the leading jobbing houses of the country have been supplied. To this they must add their profit for selling to retail dealers, and the retail dealer adds a handsome profit to his already high cost. Our buyer on the ground made the mill an offer for all the goods remaining unsold and his offer was accepted; therefore we are able to close out the entire lot, adding our one percentage of profit, nothing for free samples or catalogues, and name you a price of 25 cents for this handsome 36-inch wool and silk mixed novelty goods; offer them to you at about one-half the price at which they will retail everywhere this season. For all kinds of dress garments for women, misses and children these new effects are most desirable; entirely new, rich in effect, handsome in every way and at one-half the price you can buy elsewhere. They come in checks, stripes and solid colored grounds and contrasting colors to relieve the stripe and check. They also come in matelasse effects. The color combinations will be found to be green and white, blue and white, black and white, pink and white, lavender or blue and black, black and gold, green and black, black and red, black and blue, brown and white, solid Jacquard brown, solid Jacquard black, solid Jacquard blue, solid Jacquard red, solid Jacquard purple, solid Jacquard green and other stylish colors and handsome combinations of colorings. We have an immense line of colorings and patterns, suitable for all possible purposes. Don't write for samples, but state color combination wanted; state your complexion and leave the selection to one of our professional dress goods men and he will select the handsomest thing we have in an assortment of over 150 combinations, the very handsomest thing we have, and if it is not entirely satisfactory to you when received, return it and we will immediately return your money. We urge you to order from this description and leave it to us to assist you in making your selection rather than send for samples, as the line is too big to show you a sample of each design of these handsome goods, and we are confident we can make a selection that will in every way please you. Width, 36 inches.

No. 14R16 For 7-yard dress pattern, $1.75. Reduction sale price, per yard 25c

Samples of this number furnished for 1 cent, including sample of every shade and pattern carried in the number.

25-Cent Hit and Miss Parisian Novelty.

For 25 cents we offer this new handsome hit-and-miss stripe effect in Parisian dress goods; new for this season; the equal of anything your storekeeper would furnish you at 40 to 50 cents. We secured ten cases of these goods in connection with another purchase. We got them at the very closest price, which makes possible our special 25 cent offer. These goods are 36 inches wide; seven yards make a dress pattern and at $1.75 for the dress pattern you save from $1.00 to $2.00 in cost. **It is not necessary to delay to write for samples.** If left somewhat to our judgment in selection of colors we give you the services of an expert and guarantee to please you. These goods are medium weight and they are suitable for suits for all ages. They come in a variety of colors of blue and black, tan and black, red and black, green and black, brown and black, also gray and black.

No. 14R17 Our special reduced price, per yard. 25c

Samples of this number furnished for 1 cent, including sample of every shade carried in the number.

Our 25-Cent, 36-Inch English Pure Worsted Suiting, Checks and Mixtures.

A beautiful piece of goods—your home dealer would ask you at least 50 cents a yard. Don't wait to write for samples.

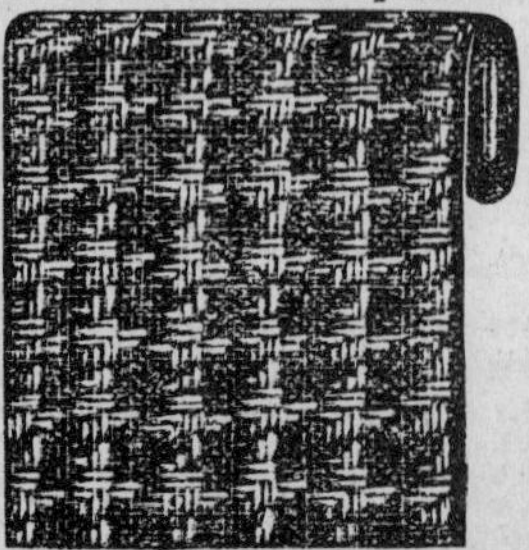

These are the swellest styles that come from the west of England. Goods that imitate materials that sell at from 75 to $1.50 per yard. These beautiful mixtures of shades of gray, also shades of brown, are the genuine Bannockburn styles. Soft blending shades, with mixtures of blue, also red, and other softening shades with gray and brown. Seven yards makes a large dress pattern. They are suitable for ladies, misses and children. If you do not say it is one of the best bargains that you have ever seen, that the price is less than your home dealer, return the goods to us at our expense, and we will immediately refund your money.

No. 14R19 Width, 36 inches. Price, per yard, 25c

Samples of this number furnished for 1 cent, including sample of every shade carried in the number.

Our 25-Cent Lizard Effect Novelty.

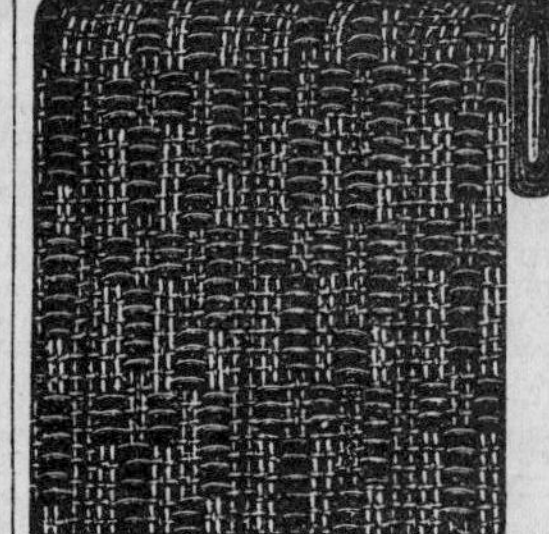

36-inch Changeable Suiting Cloth reduced 14 cents in price.

Order a 7-yard dress pattern at $1.75, and if you do not pay it is equal to anything you can buy from your store-keeper at home at double the price, you can return it to us at our expense and we will return your money. **Too much cannot be said in favor of this handsome new 36-inch suiting at the 25-cent price.** The illustration cannot do justice to the goods, but if you will give us an idea of the complexion with which you wish the goods to harmonize, **we will guarantee to more than please you in it. This is a good weight, heavy silk surface, worsted effect,** has a two-toned effect produced by a random colored pin shot over a black background. It really has all the appearance of fine imported $1.00 goods. It comes in handsome combination of red and navy, mixed green and black, black and gold and purple and black; also brown and black. It is 36 inches wide, and the greatest value ever shown by any house in a two-toned novelty goods.

No. 14R46 Our special reduced price, per yard, 25c

Samples of this number furnished for 1 cent, including sample of every shade carried in the number.

25 Cents for our Checked Dundee Reversible Suiting Cloth.

At 25 cents per yard, 36 inches wide, $1.75 for full suit of 7 yards, we offer this new fancy check, closely woven, heavy weight goods, as one of the very handsomest things shown this season and at about one-half the price charged by storekeepers generally. **This is a firm weave;** the pattern is of a very small pinhead check effect relieved by ¼-inch plaid effected by cross lines of contrasting colors. This is a fabric that will be **very popular in the best city dry goods stores this year, where it will be sold to fashionable trade at 50 to 75 cents. This fabric is especially adapted to tailor made garments,** equally suitable for children's or misses' suits, or ladies' trimmed dresses. Comes in a variety of beautiful colors, including tan, drab and brown mixed; turquoise blue, black and white, and tan, blue and green mixed; also Empire green and granite mixed. **We urge our customers not to wait to receive samples. Give us a** little privilege in the selection of colors; **leave it just a little to our taste, and you will get the very best thing possible,** if you will make your selection from the illustrations and descriptions.

No. 14R49 Our special reduced price, per yard, 25c

Samples of this number furnished for 1 cent, including sample of every shade carried in the number.

Our New 25-Cent Silk Mixed Bannockburn Dress Goods.

At 25 cents per yard, or $1.75 for a 7-yard pattern of this 36-inch goods, we believe we are offering in this new handsome, broken plaid effect the value that will mean a saving to you of 50 per cent. We believe in the dress pattern at $1.75 you will save from $1.00 to $2.00. This is a new broken plaid, formed by small broken ⅛-inch plaid relieved by ¼-inch dotted hair lines of contrasting color in silk. For one of the handsomest new silk mixed plaids on the market, a fabric that will make up very rich in a dress for old or young; a fabric, which in the different colors, a selection can be made to harmonize with any other goods used in combination. Becoming to any complexion. **These goods come in gray, white and orange; black, gray and red; gray, blue and red; steel blue and gray, and white and black mixtures.** In selecting colors we always advise to send first and second choice, but we urge our customers especially to let us have some privilege in the selection. Goods are 36 inches wide.

No. 14R53 Our special reduced price, per yard, 25c

Samples of this number furnished for 1 cent, including sample of every shade carried in the number.

Our 39-Cent, 36-Inch New Persian Mottled Novelty Suiting Cloth.

At 39 cents per yard, $2.73 for the full 7-yard dress pattern of 36-inch goods, we offer this handsome new Persian Mottled Effect Dress Goods in a good weight; for all around wear is the equal of anything you can buy elsewhere at from $1.00 to $2.00 more for the dress. **This is one of the latest effects in new novelty goods;** a new product from one of the best mills in this country. The pattern is made up of very narrow invisible mottled check, stripe effect, giving a richness seldom found in this class of goods at anything like the price. It comes in a beautiful assortment of colors, including peacock blue, gold and brown mixed, purple, tan and gold mixed. **We also have a very small supply of a few other rich mixtures, and if you will** state your complexion or give us an idea of the color wanted and allow us to make the selection we will agree to please you, even more than you could possibly be suited if your selection was made from samples. Width, 36 inches.

No. 14R61 Price, per yard.....................**39c**

Samples of this number furnished for 1c, including sample of every shade carried in the number.

Our $1.50 Dress Goods Offer.

For $1.50 we furnish a full dress pattern of seven yards of this genuine imported French two-toned Jacquard Dress Suiting, a new 1902 French mercerized fabric, a regular $3.00 value, **22 cents per single yard, $1.50** for a full seven-yard dress pattern. **We bought an immense quantity of this number in various colorings as below described.** We bought them under the market at a forced sale at less than cost to manufacture, and while our sales have been enormous we still have a big stock on hand, and with a view of giving our customers the further opportunity to avail themselves of this sale, we are confining it to our catalogue with the hope that we will be able to fill all orders during the life of this catalogue, the next twelve months. They are right from the fashion centers of France, and we offer them in full dress patterns of seven yards at **$1.50** or in any quantity at 22 cents per yard, 50 per cent less than dealers can buy in hundred piece lots. These goods are good weight, suitable for dresses for young or old and for all seasons. They are firmly woven, guaranteed for service, woven with a handsome crepon effect, such fabrics as are shown generally in fashionable retail stores. **Colorings: All the very latest shades and combinations.** They include black and blue, black and cardinal, rose and tan, green and black, turquoise and black; tan, green and red combinations, heliotrope and tan, gray and white, rose and white, dark brown and tan. **Don't wait to write for samples.** Give us an idea of coloring wanted, what you wish to use the goods for, an idea as to complexion, and we will give you the service of an expert and make for you such a selection as you could not select from any line of samples. Nearly all our customers leave the selection to us and we invariably please them.

No. 14R63 Width, 40 inches; price, per yard, **$0.22**
Full dress pattern of 7 yards................. **1.50**

Samples of this number furnished for 1c, including sample of every shade carried in the number.

63-Cent Imported Wool Novelty Oxford.

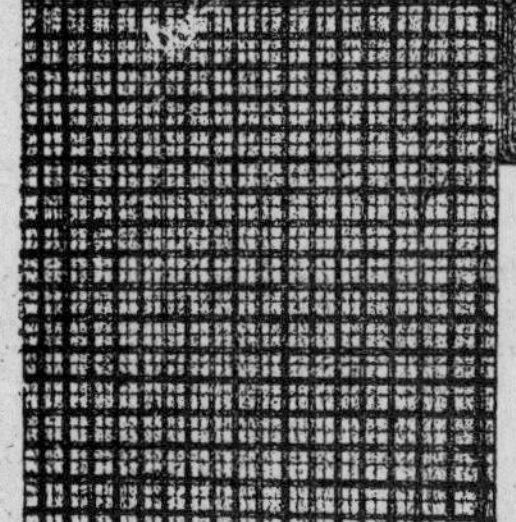

At 63 cents per yard for 43-inch goods, $4.40 for the full 7-yard dress pattern, of this 43-inch goods, we offer this new, handsome, high grade, imported silk and wool mixed novelty dress goods. This is one of the handsomest fabrics of the season; reversible; it has a good weight; has a very small check in invisible plaid effect. **Comes in a handsome combination of colors,** including black, heliotrope and white mixed, tan, black and white, navy and white, black and white, also brown and white. **This is a very suitable novelty goods,** makes up very handsome in a full dress, skirt or waist; suitable for all ages, and at **our special 63-cent or $4.40 suit price,** saves you from $2.00 to $4.00 on a suit. Width, 43 inches.

No. 14R65 Our special price, per yard.... ....**63c**

Samples of this number furnished for 1c, including sample of every shade carried in the number.

Our 69-Cent Imported Silk Mixed Matelasse Novelty Suiting Cloth.

A heavy 46-inch width fancy, imported silk mixed dress goods, such as retails generally at $1.00 to $1.25 a yard. Entirely new for this season from a famous French manufacturer, a very beautiful effect in a rough, silk finished, raised fancy crepon effect weave. A 6-yard dress pattern at our special price of 69 cents per yard, or $4.14, would guarantee a saving in value to you of from $3.00 to $3.50 and a new effect such as you would not find outside of the most fashionable city retail stores. **69 cents is a price made possible by reason of a very large purchase,** the eliminating of all free sample and catalogue expense, the adding of only our one small percentage of profit. **Order on our satisfaction guaranteed plan,** state color and quantity wanted, enclose our price and if you are not in every way pleased, return the goods at our expense and we will return your money. **There is nothing woven that is richer in a fine, full dress pattern** (six yards a full pattern). It is especially suitable for ladies' full tailor made costumes, and has a weight to make it suitable for a skirt with jacket. It comes in a variety of handsome color combinations, including black and heliotrope, mixed green, brown and black; red and black, gold and black, also blue and black. Width, 46 inches.

No. 14R67 Price, per yard.........................**69c**

Samples of this number furnished for 1 cent, including sample of every shade carried in the number.

Our Wonderful 5-Cent Worsted Plaid.

This is a soft, beautiful, serge twilled, worsted plaid. We bought over five thousand pieces from the manufacturer at a ridiculous price, thus being enabled to quote them to sell at 5 cents per yard. These goods come in a variety of beautiful colorings, green, brown, red, blue, yellow, tan, etc., and medium and large outlined plaid effects. They average about 50 yards to the piece, and we sell them oftener in pieces than we do in smaller lengths. **You cannot fail to appreciate the great value offered in this, our great plaid leader.** They include various size plaid designs and colorings, and are the proper thing for children's, misses' or ladies' wear. They have the appearance of a wool material, and cost the price of an ordinary calico. Width, 22 inches.

No. 14R69 Price, per yard.........................**$0.05**
Full piece of 50 yards......................... **2.50**

Samples of this number furnished for 1 cent, including sample of every shade carried in the number.

Our 49-Cent Shepherd Check.

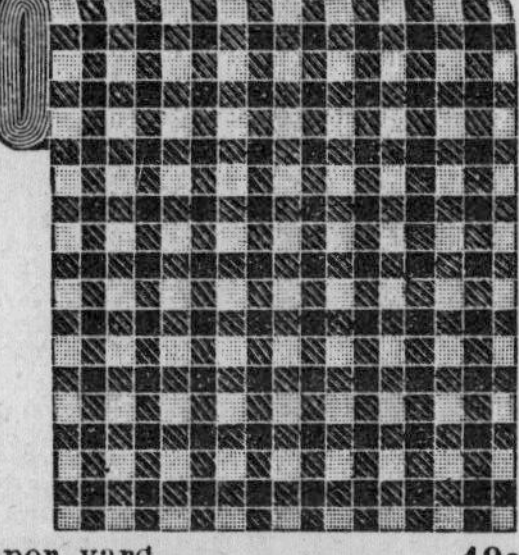

This is a fine, all wool Shepherd Check fabric, checks of black and white and blue and white. The checks are about ⅛, ¼ and ⅜-inch square, the goods are extra good weight, woven expressly for us under contract and offered at 49 cents in competition with fabrics that sell at 75 cents and upwards. Width, 38 inches.

No. 14R71 Price, per yard.........................**49c**

Samples of this number furnished for 1 cent, including sample of every shade carried in the number.

Our 8½-Cent Novelty Dress Plaid.

Fresh from the looms; correct in style and design.

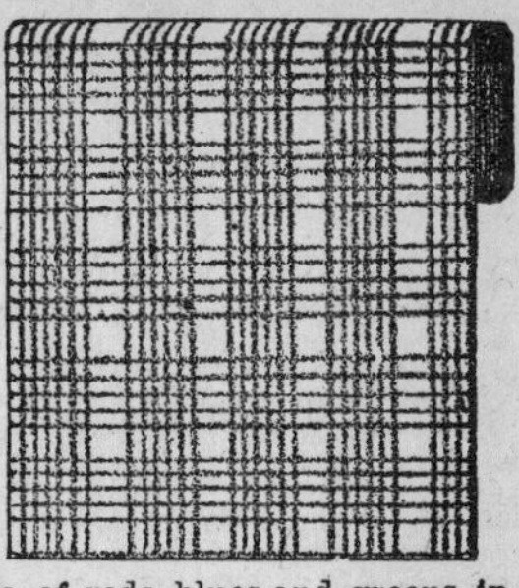

This is a new plaid for this season. We bought an immense quantity of these goods direct from the mill in order to make **this extraordinary price offer of 8½ cents per yard.** They are goods that are especially suitable for children's wear. They come in all the very latest effects for this season, and include combinations of reds, blues and greens, interwoven with contrasting shades. These plaids will retail everywhere this season at from 12 to 15 cents per yard. **We know that our special 8½-cent price** is so much below market that you will be astonished at the value you will receive. These goods come 28 inches wide and at **our special 8½-cent price,** while we will fill any order no matter how small, we make the price expecting a liberal percentage of the orders to be in full piece lots of about 50 yards, and if we do not get a fair percentage of full piece orders, the cost of cutting up the goods will more than absorb our profit. Width, 28 inches.

No. 14R73 Price, per yard.........................**8½c**

Samples of this number furnished for 1 cent, including sample of every shade carried in the number.

Our 10-Cent Scotch Plaid.

Nothing Prettier for Children's Dresses.

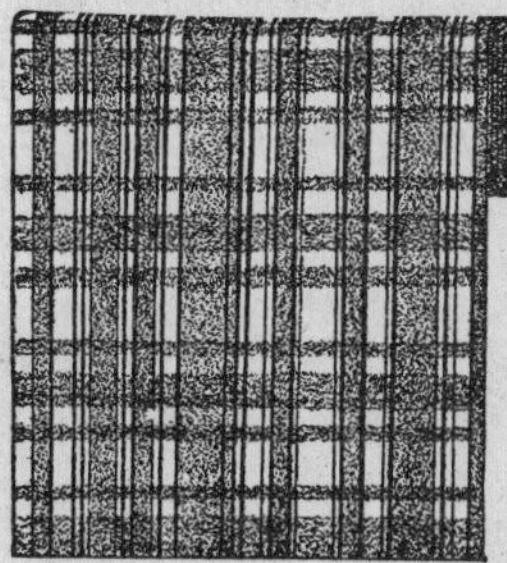

This new 10-cent Scotch Plaid is offered in competition with anything you can buy from your storekeeper at home at 15 to 18 cents. It is a goods we have imported in immense quantities in order to make this astonishingly low price. It is a heavier and better cloth than our 8½-cent plaid, hence we recommend it. **It comes in all the latest effects—serge** grounds and mummie weaves, and comes in a beautiful array of colorings and combinations. **Give us an idea of the color you want,** leave it to our judgment to select, and we will give you the best value in Scotch plaids that ever went out of any house. **The goods are especially suitable for children's garments.** We get many orders for full piece lots of about 50 yards, and if it were not so we could not afford to cut these goods up in any lengths at our astonishingly low price of 10 cents. Width, 28 inches.

No. 14R75 Price, per yard.........................**10c**

Samples of this number furnished for 1 cent, including sample of every shade carried in the number.

Our 24-Cent Fancy Imported Scotch Plaid.

Your home dealer pays more than 24 cents for this grade of goods.

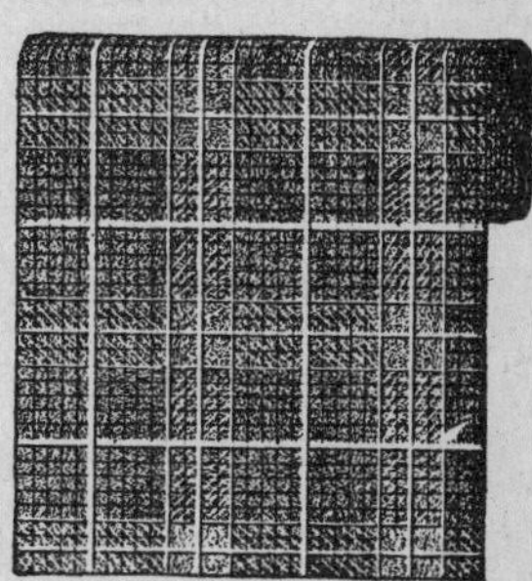

This is one of the handsomest good weight, imported Scotch plaids shown this season. It is extraordinary value at the price. **Our 24-cent price is made possible by reason of an unusually large contract.** This is a serge weave, wool and mercerized silk mixture. Makes up very handsome for ladies' waists and children's dresses. The figure is about a ¾-inch plaid, and further outlined by a plaid of about 1¼ inches. **These goods are made extra serviceable** and woven with a view of resembling a fabric worth double the price. Comes in handsome color combinations of gold, green, navy and white. **Give us an idea of the coloring wanted;** we will send these goods to you with the understanding that if they are not in every way satisfactory, you can return them to us at our expense and we will return your money. Width, 34 inches.

No. 14R77 Price, per yard.........................**24c**

Samples of this number furnished for 1 cent, including sample of every shade carried in the number.

GIVE CATALOGUE NUMBER IN FULL WHEN YOU WRITE YOUR ORDER

24-Cent French Pure Wool Jersey Flannel.

This All Pure Wool Jersey French Flannel at 24 cents, is equal to goods that sell everywhere at 35 to 45 cents a yard. It is especially desirable for ladies' waists, suits and house dresses; goods that are very popular and come in a beautiful line of colorings, such as tan, cardinal, wine, rose, cerise, nile, white, cream, lavender, brown, light blue, pink, violet, heliotrope, myrtle, old rose and black. Width, 28 inches.

No. 14R121 Price, per yard, reduced to.......**24c**

Samples of this number furnished for 1 cent, including sample of every shade carried in the number.

Imported All Wool French Flannel.

This is the very choicest material for shirt waists or ladies' house wrappers. It has a neat twill and is made of the very finest wool. We are direct importers of this popular fabric, and our immense purchase has made it possible for us to name a price that is less than any wholesale dealer or jobber owns them at, **and the quality is such as can be found in high class city stores** and then at 65 to 75 cents per yard. Width, 29 inches.

No. 14R123 Our special price, per yard........**39c**

Samples of this number furnished for 1 cent, including sample of every shade carried in the number.

Our 47-Cent All Wool Albatross Cloth.

This Very Fine, All Wool, Imported Albatross Cloth is the equal of fabrics that sell everywhere at 75 cents and upward. It is a soft, handsome fabric, having a beautiful crape effect; is one of the most stylish fabrics for graduating or wedding dresses; also desirable for evening costumes in light pink, light blue, old rose, ox blood, cream, white, heliotrope, violet, lavender, green, nile green, silver gray, tan, cardinal and black. **Send us your order direct from the catalogue, give us a little privilege in selecting just the shade to harmonize with your complexion, and we will surprise you in value.** Width, 38 inches.

No. 14R125 Price, per yard....................**47c**

Samples of this number furnished for 1 cent, including sample of every shade carried in the number.

Our New 98-Cent Fine Imported All Silk and Wool Lansdowne Silk Sublime.

For a very handsome material for wedding, reception and evening costumes, there is nothing within 75 cents per yard of the price that will approach these new fabrics. This is a line of very fine Lansdownes that we have just imported from a celebrated French maker. We got them in at a saving of about 20 per cent over last year's price on inferior goods. We have no hesitation in saying that **no retailers, however large, can attempt to meet our 98-cent price.** These goods are 40 inches wide, they come in all the latest shades, including cream, white, rose, corn, nile, pink, gray, tan, heliotrope, porcelain, blue and cardinal, also black. **This fine, all pure silk and wool goods must be seen to be appreciated; but if you will give us an idea of the color wanted, your complexion and color of hair, we will select a suitable shade and send you just what you want at a saving of about one-half in price.** Width, 40 inches.

No. 14R127 Price, per yard.................**98c**

Samples of this number furnished for 1 cent, including sample of every shade carried in the number.

OUR NEW DEPARTMENT OF IMPORTED FANCY WOOL AND SILK AND WOOL FRENCH WAISTING MATERIALS.

These beautiful waisting fabrics have jumped into universal popularity this season and the style will be more in demand this spring than ever. We have picked out three of the handsomest and most stylish designs in the newest and most up to date colorings and will establish three popular prices.

Our first stunning bargain in swell all wool batiste white silk stripe waisting at 59 cents per yard, is one of the very prettiest designs obtainable. The illustration will give you an idea of this pretty effect. The solid strip of color is about ⅝-inch wide and the white fancy silk stripe ¼-inch wide. The pretty colors in which this waisting comes are royal blue, reseda (or moss green), heliotrope, pink, tan, cardinal, cadet, black and solid cream. All the colors quoted with the exception of the cream are solid relieved by the quarter inch fancy white stripe. In the black and white it is particularly effective. **This we consider our leading number in this popular waisting fabric, and the price of 59 cents which we make is about one half of what will be charged by the ordinary storekeeper.** We have evidence that these goods in inferior designs are being sold in large city stores at 85 cents and $1.00. Get your neighbors to club with you in making your selection and thus save on express charges, send our price, and if the goods are not entirely satisfactory, if they are not as pretty as our description would lead you to expect them to be, if in any way you are not satisfied with your purchase, return the goods to us and we will immediately refund your money.

No. 14R129 Width, 28 inches. Price, per yard. **59c**

Samples of this number furnished for 1 cent, including sample of every shade carried in the number.

Our 63-Cent Handsome Silk Striped, All Wool Waisting Cloth.

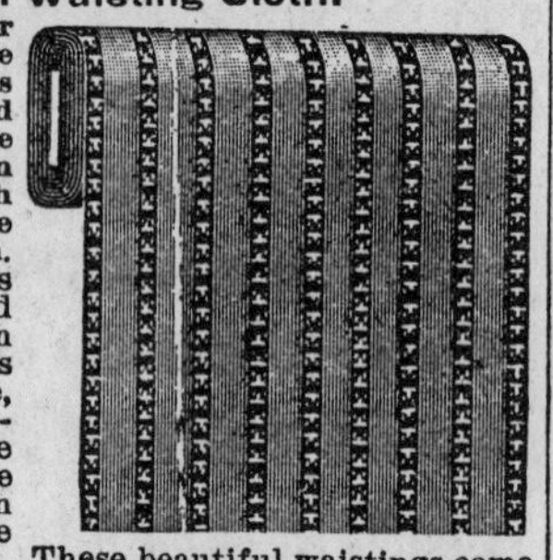

This is another of our remarkable values, the style is entirely new and exclusive. These goods will be worn by the most stylish dressers of the coming season. They are goods equal to those sold in the metropolitan or large city stores at double our price, and are not obtainable elsewhere. We have the exclusive right to this design and control the manufacture of it. These beautiful waistings come in some of the most beautiful tints and colorings, among which are porcelain or cadet blue with fancy black stripe relieved by white, as shown in the illustration. The stripes on each of the colors which we quote are the same width, and in all cases are black and white. The center, which is about ⅝-inch wide, is of the colors which we quote, that is, black, gray, turquoise, rose, light blue, heliotrope, tan, moss green, cerise, violet, medium light blue, rose, cardinal, navy blue, and rich maroon. The beautiful effect of this black and white fancy stripe on these colors has to be seen to be appreciated.

No. 14R131 Width, 28 inches. Price, per yard. **63c**

Samples of this number furnished for 1 cent, including sample of every shade carried in the number.

The Acme of Stylish Waistings Is Reached in Our Beautiful 89-Cent English Cable Cord on a Fancy Viola Batiste Solid Colored Ground Work.

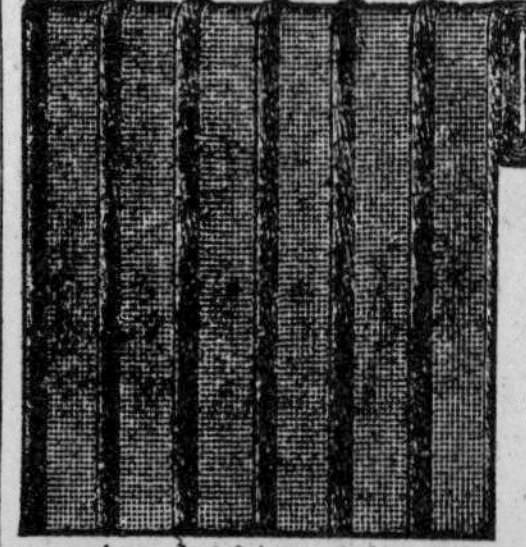

The accompanying illustration gives you an idea of the pretty spiral cord effect in this beautiful English cable cord waisting. This is an entirely new design, and comes in solid colors only. It is something that cannot be bought from the ordinary retailer. It is practically controlled by us. The colors are cream, reseda (or moss green), cadet blue, rich cardinal, rose, tan, royal blue, and black.

No. 14R133 Width, 28 inches. Price, per yard, **89c**

Samples of this number furnished for 1 cent, including sample of every shade carried in the number.

Our Swellest and Most Exclusively New Production in All Wool 44-Inch Viola Crepe at 98 Cents Per Yard.

This has the silky finish of a crepe de chine that would sell in high class city stores at $2.50 to $3.50 per yard. The weave and the finish are so distinctly beautiful as to make a description almost impossible. You have to see the goods to appreciate them. The swell costumes made of this exquisite material are to be seen in first class suit departments **at prices ranging anywhere from $75.00 to $125.00.** (We recommend for the lining of this handsome material our No. 14R3048, 27-inch extra heavy, colored taffeta silk.) The colors are French gray, light blue, pink, cream, turquoise, nile green, old rose, heliotrope, violet, tan, medium tobacco brown, new blue, rich cardinal, light yellow, and also black. **Send us your order for one or more dresses of this handsome material, including our price, and if the goods are not everything as expected and more, if they are not even better than our powers of description to picture them to you,** return them to us at our expense and we will immediately refund your money. Width, 44 inches.

No. 14R135 Price, per yard...................**98c**

Samples of this number furnished for 1 cent, including sample of every shade carried in the number.

Our 89-Cent Imported Melrose Suiting.

These 42-inch goods are from one of the famous French looms. We bought a large quantity of this cloth in order to secure a price. We own these goods below today's market and **our special 89-cent price barely covers the cost to us,** with but our one small percentage of profit added. These goods would retail in the best stores at $1.25 to $1.50 a yard. **There is nothing handsomer, nothing newer, nothing more stylish for a ladies' dress.** They are fine, pure Australian wool and the weave is one of the handsomest shown this season. **Order a 6-yard dress pattern of these goods at our special $5.34 price, give us an idea of the coloring wanted and let us help you in selecting the shade,** and we will send it to you with the understanding that if you do not find you have saved from $2.00 to $4.00 in price, you can return the goods to us and we will cheerfully return your money. **These goods come in all the latest shades,** including gray, tan, rose, new blue, cardinal, garnet, ultramarine blue, medium brown, navy, myrtle, also in black. Width, 42 inches.

No. 14R137 Price, per yard...................**89c**

Samples of this number furnished for 1 cent, including sample of every shade carried in the number.

OUR LATEST INNOVATION IN COLORED DRESS WEAVES.

44-Inch Sharkskin at 98 Cents Per Yard.

An entirely new fabric. This handsome, imported French fabric has somewhat the appearance of an armure, but different from an armure. The weave resembles little ⅛-inch irregular squares with a little pebble surface that resembles the skin of a shark. **This has sprung into great popularity for the coming season. In fact it is indorsed by the very best costume makers and by ladies of fashion. We highly recommend it to people of exclusive tastes that wish something out of the common.** This fabric we can thoroughly recommend as being one of the best values that we could possibly offer. We placed our order for such a quantity that we got the price at the lowest, even lower than any jobber, importer or commission house, as our European buyer placed his order with one of the largest manufacturers in France at a price down to the very closest cost of material and workmanship. The few high class retailers who will handle these goods in this country will look for a very fancy profit on the same. We will carry out our old policy of the cost to us with a very small margin of profit added. We will sell you for 98 cents per yard this beautiful fabric and we are certain we will save you from 50 to 75 cents per yard. The handsome colorings in which we present this sharkskin cloth are gray, tan, old rose, reseda, moss green, cardinal, wine, myrtle, brown, royal blue, navy blue and also black.

No. 14R139 Width, 44 inches. Price, per yard. **98c**

Samples of this number furnished for 1 cent, including sample of every shade carried in the number.

Black Dress Goods Department.

Our Black Dress Goods Department never was so strong as at the present time. We never before had such a great variety of new, staple and desirable Black Dress Goods. Never before have we been able to give such extraordinary values.

WHY WE CAN UNDERSELL ANY OTHER HOUSE on black dress goods. We have made a special feature of the black goods department. We have in charge of our black dress goods one of the most able buyers and expert judges in this country. With his knowledge of the mills, the markets, the fabrics, the intrinsic value of the goods on which he is bidding, we have put special effort on this line; we have singled out our black goods department and advertised it widely in the newspapers, magazines and other journals until we have created a trade that gives us a buying power on black goods not approached by any other house. We have developed an outlet that makes it possible for us to go to a mill and take their entire output of certain styles. We have an output that enables us, whenever there is a big sale of foreign goods, to name a price on the entire lot. We have, in fact, attained a position that makes it possible for us to, in a great measure, dictate the price, and it is by giving our customers the benefit of all these advantages, asking but our one small percentage of profit above the actual cost to us in any quantity, that we have been able to cut our prices down to where they are so attractive, that if you once order a dress, skirt or waist pattern from our black goods department, we are sure of your future orders and the orders of your friends and neighbors.

WHY IT IS NOT NECESSARY TO SEND FOR SAMPLES. While we are glad to furnish s on our regular terms, those who make their selections from the rampand descriptions and rely on our judgment to give them the very best value in our house, are also satisfied, better satisfied, in fact, when they give us some little license in helping them to select, than when they themselves select from samples; for, from a small sample, say two inches square, it is impossible for you to judge the patterns and real value as well as if you were in our store selecting the goods from a piece. This we do, and give you the judgment of a professional black dress goods man, when you send us your order direct from the catalogue; and, furthermore, if you order a dress pattern, and we have an odd piece of better goods, if there is any way we can possibly give you anything, even more than we advertise, you are sure to get it. Select anything from our black dress goods department, send us your order. You take no risk in doing so, for if the goods are not found perfectly satisfactory in every way, you can return them to us at our expense and we will return your money.

DRESS GOODS SAMPLES. As previously explained, we will send dress goods samples upon receipt of 1 cent for each catalogue number you want samples of. We do not ask you to remit this amount simply in order to cover the cost of samples, for it does not do this, but to protect us against the thousands who ask for samples out of mere curiosity with no idea of buying, thus incurring for us an expense which we, like all other houses which furnish samples free, must add to the price of the goods. This season we are determined that nothing shall be added to the goods but our one small percentage of profit. We make this request only to protect you, not us; to give you the benefit of the lowest possible price. We believe our customers and all other intelligent readers will appreciate our motive in their behalf.

OUR FINE IMPORTED ALL WOOL BLACK SERGE DEPARTMENT.

IN DIRECTING YOUR ATTENTION to our line of fine imported all wool black serges at prices ranging from 22 cents per yard upwards, we wish to say that we are willing to accept your order for any one of these imported serges with the understanding that if the goods are not perfectly satisfactory when received and you do not find them in price from 25 to 50 per cent lower than you can buy the same grade of serge elsewhere, you can return the goods to us at our expense and we will return your money.

WE ARE RECOGNIZED HEADQUARTERS on fine imported all wool black serge fabrics. We buy the goods ourselves direct from the foreign looms.

WE BUY THEM IN QUANTITIES that give us the lowest possible first cost; they are landed here in the most economic way and nothing is added for wasted free cloth sampling or free cataloguing, our one small percentage of profit only is added to our cost and as a result, at from 39 cents upwards as listed we can furnish you a grade of fine imported all wool black serges such as no retail dealer in this country can buy even in dozen piece lots. There is no such thing as matching our imported black serges at anything approaching our selling price.

DON'T WAIT TO WRITE FOR SAMPLES. Understand we sell to you under a guarantee to satisfy. When you get the goods if you are not more than satisfied with anything you buy, do not find it all and more than we claim for it, much greater value than you can buy elsewhere, you can return the goods at our expense and we will immediately return your money.

Our 69-Cent Imported Black English Storm Serge Dress Goods.

We ask 69 cents for our very finest Imported English Worsted. This is a black, closely woven, wear resisting, thoroughly shrunken serge fabric, such as you will find only in the most fashionable stores. If you order a dress pattern from this number you will get such value and service as you could not possibly get elsewhere. We put out every piece under our binding guarantee, and every piece is guaranteed to us by the mills as all strictly pure wool, thoroughly shrunken, carefully woven and of most extraordinary value. Width, 45 inches.

No. 14R828 Price, per yard.......................69c

Sample of this number furnished for 1 cent.

Our 22-Cent Black English Serge.

For 22 cents per yard of 40-inch width, we offer this imported black English serge as the equal of serges that sell everywhere at 25 to 35 cents. While this is not a high grade serge, it is the best serge fabric ever shown at a 22-cent price. It is a good, strong weave, will give excellent wear and we guarantee satisfaction. We have cut up thousands of pieces of these goods with universal satisfaction to the buyers. Width, 40 inches.

No. 14R801 Price, per yard.................... 22c

Sample of this number furnished for 1 cent.

Our 39-Cent Imported All Wool 36-Inch Black French Serge.

At 39 cents per yard for this 36-inch width goods we offer this good weight fine all pure Australian wool Etamene weave French serge as the greatest serge value ever offered by us or any other house. The stability of this fabric needs no mention for all kinds of women's, children's and misses' wearing apparel, for all seasons and almost all occasions. It is always staple, never gets old, and for wearing quality there is nothing woven of the same weight that will give better service. We are constantly cutting up hundreds of pieces of these goods. We are the largest distributors for these mills in this country, all of which combine to make possible the prices we make, which cannot be made by any other house. If you want a fast black all wool serge from one of the best French looms, for a dress skirt, or other garment, do not hesitate to send your order for this 39-cent serge under our guarantee to satisfy, our guarantee that it is unmatchable, our guarantee that no such value is being attempted by any other house. Width, 36 inches.

No. 14R805 Price, per yard.......................39c

Sample of this number furnished for 1 cent.

Black French Serge, waterproof finish. This is first class cloth and will hold its color, it is strictly pure wool. Width, 46 inches.

No. 14R808 Price, per yard.....................48c

Black French Serge, all fine wool. This is a splendid wearing cloth and we will guarantee it will give entire satisfaction. Equal to any 75c to $1.00 serge sold by the retailers. Has a high lustrous black and will not spot. Color is absolutely fast. Width, 46 inches.

No. 14R813 Price, per yard.....................54c

Black French Serge, fine waterproof finish, made of purest wool, same on both sides; this cloth we can strongly recommend for wear and durability. Width, 46 inches.

No. 14R816 Price, per yard.....................64c

Black Worsted Serge, strictly first quality wool. This cloth has a rich, medium twill, and will outclass anything for wear and appearance. Width, 46 inches.

No. 14R820 Price, per yard.....................79c

Black Storm Serges and Cheviots.

Black Storm Serge, strictly all wool and wiry, good, serviceable and desirable. Width, 38 inches.

No. 14R822 Price, per yard..39c

Black Storm Serge, absolutely the best wearing article to be had; dustproof and will last for years. Width, 38 inches. Our special number.

No. 14R824 Price, per yard..49c

Black Camel Hair Cheviot, soft fleece and will not wear rough, very stylish for skirts or suits; guaranteed unmatchable at less than $1.25 per yard. Width, 45 inches.

No. 14R826 Our special price, per yard......89c

Samples of any one of the above catalogue numbers furnished for 1 cent.

Our 98-Cent Imported Black English Whipcord Serge.

Reduced from $1.19. We give you a saving of 21 cents per yard on these goods, with a guarantee that we are at least 35 cents below the lowest jobbing market. Send us your order for a suit from this English Whipcord Serge, and if you do not find that you have saved from $3.00 to $5.00 on your suit, we will take the goods back and return your money. This imported black Whipcord Serge is from one of the best English mills. It is one of the old reliable, can't-be-worn-out kind. Has a handsome raised diagonal twill, goods that make up very elegant in a tailor made suit; especially desirable for special skirts; has a rich, fast color, very lustrous surface; is one of the greatest values in black goods we have ever been able to offer. Width, 48 inches.

No. 14R830 Price, per yard.................... 98c

Sample of this number furnished for 1 cent.

READ OUR EXTRAORDINARY **PAPER PATTERN OFFER** ON PAGE 858.

OUR 59-CENT STORM SERGE.

For 59 cents per yard we offer a 45-inch imported English Black Storm Serge Cloth, a goods that sells everywhere at 90 cents to $1.00 a yard; the most serviceable, best wearing fabric on the market, a goods that will last for years. Our 59-cent price is made possible by reason of having made a very large contract with one of the best English mills, and our special 59-cent price is based on the actual cost to us under our season's contract, with but one small percentage of profit added. Order a skirt or dress pattern from this number, and we will send it to you with the understanding that if it is not perfectly satisfactory, if you are not convinced you have saved from $2.00 to $3.00 on a dress pattern, you can return the goods to us at our expense and we will return your money. Width, 45 inches.

No. 14R832 Price, per yard.......................................59c

Sample of this number furnished for 1 cent.

Our 46-Inch Black Satin Soleil, at $1.09.

This is one of the richest new French weaves for this season. It has a bayadere raised rich smooth cord effect across the width of the goods, and its surface has a very rich, lustrous satin finish. These goods are very reliable as to color, and for wearing qualities there is nothing in the way of all wool dress goods that can compare with them. A dress of this handsome material can be made of six yards. The price of $6.54 is a saving to our customers of from $2.00 to $5.00 on one of these dresses. The goods, if you buy them in the regular way in high toned city stores (and they are not obtainable anywhere else), would cost from $1.75 to $2.50 per yard. Width, 46 inches.

No. 14R892 Price, per yard..........................$1.09
Sample of this number furnished for 1 cent.

French Imported Black Sebastopol Suiting.

This new and beautiful French weave is coming into great popularity. Ladies that wish something in a black dress, having a very pretty and fine weave, just a little different from cashmeres and Henriettas, that are so fashionable, at the same time somewhat of a novelty. This beautiful weave has the effect of parallel lines, on a very fine silk finish wool surface, lines one-eighth of an inch in width. It has a little more weight than the ordinary Henriettas; has double warp, and is strictly all wool. Ladies of refined taste cannot fail to appreciate this handsome new French black Sebastopol cloth. The illustration will give you a faint idea of the style of this handsome fabric. Width, 42 inches.

No. 14R896 Price, per yard......................98c
Sample of this number furnished for 1 cent.

Black 48-Inch Gloria Silk at 69 Cents per Yard.

This is a very handsome one-half silk fabric, the warp being all silk and the filling of a very fine quality of mercerized lisle thread. These goods make up very nicely in waists, ladies' skirts, and are also used for entire costumes. This goods has a very beautiful shade of medium black, known as the lustrous, blooming black goods. The color is thoroughly reliable and the goods sell ordinarily in retail stores for $1.00 per yard. We make a specialty of this pretty number and it is one of the best values that we give. Width, 48 inches.

No. 14R898 Price, per yard..........................69c
Sample of this number furnished for 1 cent.

Pure Wool 50-Inch English Black Pebble Cheviot, at 89 Cents.

Six yards makes a full dress pattern, and if you will send us $5.34 for full suit pattern of this heavy weight English goods and do not say you have saved from $3.00 to $6.00 on your purchase you can return the goods to us at our expense of charges both ways and we will immediately return your money. Don't wait to write for samples in ordering this number. We guarantee the goods to please you or we will immediately return your money in every case. This is a heavy weight fabric woven in England by one of the best cheviot makers in England, made of pure selected Australian wool, is fast black, has a rich heavy raised pebble surface effect on heavy cheviot ground. Our 89 cent price is based on the actual cost to produce, with but our one small percentage of profit added, nothing added for wasted free samples or catalogues. It is lower than dealers can buy in quantities, is equal to anything you can buy from your storekeeper at from $1.50 to $2.00 per yard, a fabric that ordinarily commands a fancy price. By the time it reaches the retail dealer he has to pay $1.00 per yard for it, sometimes $1.25, and he has to place it with his high priced stock, and usually sells it at $1.50 to $2.00 per yard. Our special factory to consumer price is only 89 cents. Width, 50 inches.

No. 14R900 Price, per yard...........................$0.89
Price for 6-yard dress pattern..............................5.34
Sample of this number furnished for 1 cent.

Our 48-Inch Heavy Black English All Wool Natte Suiting.

This is a very pretty weave of fine imported English suiting. It is in appearance like the French Mistral weave that sells from $3.00 to $4.00 per yard. This goods has an appearance of considerable weight and still is not heavy. Is suited for all seasons of the year, and is a decided novelty in black goods. This low price of 98 cents per yard is made on the basis of the actual cost to import; no handling by any outside parties—wholesaler, jobber or retailer. We do our own importing. Also, on account of the fact that the free catalogues and free sampling have been eliminated from our business, all of the profits that accrue go direct to our customers in the way of a saving on price. Send for 6-yard dress pattern of this beautiful black suiting, $5.88, or 98 cents per yard, for as many yards as you require, and if the goods are not all that we describe, and more, return them to us at our expense and we will immediately refund your money. Width, 48 inches.

No. 14R902 Price, per yard..............................98c
Samples of this number furnished for 1 cent.

REFER TO PAGE 858.

5 Cents for the Best Paper Patterns. Include One with Dress Goods Order.

Our Newest Black Goods Novelty at 98 Cents Per Yard.

50-inch London Twine Cloth at 98 cents per yard. This handsome black goods resembles a very fine quality of iron frame silk grenadine. It is made of pure, all wool worsted of a very silky, lustrous finish and medium weight. This is a goods that will be appreciated by lovers of the very choicest and newest productions in black goods. This is used very much over a silk foundation and it shows the silk through as it is a small weave, about a sixteenth of an inch mesh. We are sure that it will be one of the most popular things in our black dress goods stock the coming spring and summer of 1902. The goods are 50 inches wide, and it takes but about five or six yards to make an entire costume. The goods are a very brilliant, perfect black, and we know they cannot fail to please ladies of taste for fine black dress goods. Be sure and order one or more of these dresses. If when received you do not find them to be all and more than we have claimed for them, better goods than you can buy at anywhere from $1.50 to $2.25 per yard at any other house, return them to us and we will immediately refund your money. This beautiful 50-inch London twine cloth we have also in a beautiful shade of navy blue. Width, 50 inches.

No. 14R906 Price, per yard......................98c
Samples of this number furnished for 1 cent, including sample of every shade carried in the number.

SPECIAL EXTRAORDINARY BLACK GOODS OFFERING.

48-Inch Extra Fine French Suiting Venetian, $1.75.

We offer this our finest black dress or costume cloth as one of the richest, dressiest, and most luxurious all wool, satin finish suitings to be found anywhere. These goods are not obtainable at any price except in highest toned exclusive city stores, and then at a price of from $2.50 to $3.50 per yard. We submit this as one of our biggest bargains in our entire black dress goods department. It comes in black only. Order a dress from description and we guarantee that you will pronounce it the biggest value that you ever saw in black dress goods, a value that will create business for us with all your neighbors. Should you order from description and not be thoroughly satisfied that what we have said abour this is not more than true, that the value you get is something phenomenal, if not in every respect entirely satisfactory; return it to us at our expense and your money will be cheerfully refunded.

No. 14R908 Width, 48 inches. Price, per yard, $1.75
Sample of this number furnished for 1 cent.

Our 98-Cent 45-Inch Fine Imported Black All Wool Worsted Satin Effect Armure English Dress Fabric.

At 98 cents we offer this exclusive number from one of the best English looms, a fabric that can only be had from us and two or three other fashionable city retailers in this country, a newer, richer, handsomer silk finished, fast black, all wool dress goods than you can get in any ordinary dry goods store, a pattern that will give you a dress or other garment not to be matched by anyone in your neighborhood, at the same time in quality the equal of anything you can buy from your dealer at home at $1.50 to $2.00 a yard.

This is a good heavy weight, fast black, woven from all pure selected Australian wool, giving a rich ribbed silk surface effect. The pattern is an invisible black silk armure weave, the very latest for this season.

Send us your order, enclose our price, don't wait to write for samples, for we guarantee to satisfy or immediately return your money. If you do not find that you have saved from $3.00 to $5.00 on a dress pattern, and have something richer, handsomer, newer, more stylish, and altogether more satisfactory than you can possibly get elsewhere; if you do not find that you have received in this dress pattern something that warrants your having it made up in the best possible style, by the best lady or gentleman tailor in your neighborhood, you can return it to us at our expense, and we will immediately return your money.

Our 98-cent price barely covers the cost to produce, with but our one small percentage of profit added. It is less than old style goods of the same grade are being sold at wholesale. It is, in fact, a revelation in style and price making, and we guarantee it or send your money back.

Our old customers do not write for samples. They accept our descriptions and illustrations and our guarantee, and we always give them the best value, the handsomest things we have in our house.

No. 14R904 Width, 45 inches. Price, per yard..............................98c
Sample of this number furnished for 1 cent.

GETTING 50 CENTS

FOR EVERY ONE OF OUR BIG CATALOGUES

Getting paid for all samples, is one reason why we can make these astonishingly low prices in every department. We do not have the big expense for free samples and free catalogues that all other mail order houses have, and which expense must be and is added to the selling price of every article.

WHEN YOU BUY GOODS OF US

you are not compelled to pay a share of the cost of thousands of catalogues and samples sent to people who never buy. The prices that we ask cover simply the first cost of the goods with but our one small percentage of profit added, nothing included for free catalogues, free samples, the expenses other houses have. We ask 50 cents for our large catalogue and pay for all samples that we may name lower prices than you can find in any other catalogue.

BLACK GOODS SPECIALTIES

39-Cent Black French Novelty Suiting.

This is a genuine imported, all pure wool, French novelty suiting; a very popular fabric and one that we can recommend for quality. It is a good medium weight, and a grade that will be found in the best retail dry goods stores, in large cities. **We can furnish it in a variety of designs, all new and up to date.** Width, 42 inches.

No. 14R918 Price, per yard.......................... 39c

Sample of this number furnished for 1 cent.

Our 76-Cent New Camel's Hair Suiting.

Reduced from 89 cents to 76 cents, a saving of 13 cents, by reason of an extraordinary contract placed this year. **This is one of the handsomest things in black goods for this season.** It is a kind of an invisible or honeycomb effect, made of pure Australian wool, comes from one of the best English mills; very handsome in a suit or skirt. **Guaranteed long fast black,** pure wool, and we are confident we are 50 cents below the retail market. Width, 46 inches.

No. 14R920 Price, per yard.......................76c

Sample of this number furnished for 1 cent.

Our 24-Cent Fancy Black Dress Goods.

This is an extra fine, Jacquard effect, fast black dress goods. Comes in the latest small and medium designs; a goods that is guaranteed to give satisfaction in every way. It is one of the leaders in our black goods department, and at our special 24-cent price is a wonder of value. These goods are **suitable for year around wear,** and will make up nicely into almost any kind of a dress. Width, 42 inches.

No. 14R922 Price, per yard....................24c

Sample of this number furnished for 1 cent

Our 79-Cent Imported Novelty Epingeline.

Reduced from 98 cents to 85 cents and now offered at the astonishingly low price of 79 cents. The saving we have made with the English maker we give to you, and we guarantee our price below anything offered by anyone else, wholesaler or retailer. **This is a fine, all wool English fabric, with a fine velours cord running horizontally across the cloth.** Width, 44 inches.

No. 14R924 Price, per yard..........................79c

Sample of this number furnished for 1 cent.

Our 69-Cent Heavy Weight Black Mohair Crepon.

These goods are 42 inches wide, extra heavy weight, firmly woven, a hard silky surface, raised satin, crepon design on corded velours background. It is a solid fast black imported brilliant French goods, extra fine value; a goods that will give extraordinary wear and make up into an exceedingly handsome costume. For a crepon of as good a quality as this, retail dealers charge about double our special price. If you do not find it extraordinary value, return the goods to us and we will refund your money. Width, 42 inches.

No. 14R926 Price, per yard.................. 69c

Sample of this number furnished for 1 cent.

Our 79c Black English Mohair Crepon.

79 cents is a reduction in price, first from $1.25 and then from $1.10. We changed mills on these goods, we made a contract, we believe the lowest ever secured on this grade of English Mohair, away below the lowest jobbing market, and we give you the benefit of our purchase. **These goods should not be classed with the poor grades of crepon, of which there are so many on the market.** It is a fabric that has a heavy blistered raised pattern, a value that cannot be approached by any other house, goods that will make up very handsome in a skirt or suit. Width, 42 inches.

No. 14R928 Price, per yard.....................79c

Sample of this number furnished for 1 cent.

Our $1.24 Extra Heavy, High Grade, Imported Black Silk and Wool French Crepon.

Reduced from $1.70 a yard. A saving of 46 cents per yard. We are today 46 cents per yard below the jobbing price. You cannot imagine the value we can give you in this $1.24 goods. You must see it to appreciate it. We urge you to send us your order for a dress pattern, with the understanding that if you do not save from $5.00 upwards in your purchase, we will immediately return your money. **This black silk and wool mixed crepon is a handsome serpentine effect, very dainty design.** This is a decided novelty in black goods, very much admired by good dressers. These goods look very rich in an entire suit and will make a very handsome skirt. Width, 42 inches.

No. 14R930 Price, per yard...............$1.24

Sample of this number furnished for 1 cent.

Our $1.48 Imported French Black Silk and Wool Crepon.

Reduced from $2.25; a reduction of 77 cents. We changed mills on these goods in order to effect a saving in price. We did it under a guarantee for quality, and we are pleased to announce that from this mill they came out better than ever before. We have control of the output and at $1.48 this fabric can be had only from us. **The designs are entirely new for this season, they come in a handsome assortment, have a very heavy embossed or blistered effect.** If you want a very rich dress, something nicer than you can get from your storekeeper at home, we urge you to let us send you a dress pattern from this fabric, with the understanding that **if it isn't perfectly satisfactory, if you do not feel that you have saved at least $5.00 in price, you can return the goods to us at our expense and we will return your money.** Width, 42 inches.

No. 14R932 Price, per yard...............$1.48

Sample of this number furnished for 1 cent.

Our 39-Cent Black Figured Mohair.

Reduced from 50 cents. A saving of 11 cents effected by our contract with a different mill. This is a beautiful cloth, goods that will hold its color. There is no better wearing fabric. It will make up elegantly in skirts or entire suits. Is a goods that makes up very dressy. **It is a cloth you must see and examine to appreciate its value.** If you will send us your order for a suit pattern from these goods, we will send it to you with the understanding that if it isn't all and more than we claim we will refund your money. Width, 38 inches.

No. 14R936 Price, per yard.............. 39c

Sample of this number furnished for 1 cent.

HOW WE MAKE OUR PRICES SO LOW.

Buying from Foreign and American mills at prices lower than most jobbers. We have no large expense of expensive samples to add to the cost. We sell with but our one small profit added to manufacturer's cost.

PLUSHES.

We do not sample Plushes.

Our Sir Titus Salt Famous London Dyed Seal Plushes.

We carry a line of this fine imported goods, the highest grade seal plush goods on the market. There is nothing that will compare with them for ladies' seal plush capes, jackets or coats, and our prices are on the basis of importing the goods, bought direct from the English makers. **These goods are a perfect imitation of the genuine Alaska seal fur.** The dye is just as durable, and a coat or jacket made from this fabric gives you a **garment having the appearance of a $200.00 seal garment.**

Our $1.98 Seal Plush Cloaking.

This $1.98 Seal Plush is of extraordinary value. We name a price direct from the maker. You will find this superior to anything you would be likely to get from your storekeeper at home. We offer these goods with the understanding that if they are not perfectly satisfactory, you can return them to us at our expense and we will return your money. Width, 52 inches.

No. 14R1156 Price, per yard..............$1.98

Our $2.50 Seal Plush Fabric.

This is a perfect imitation of a seal that would cost you a fabulous amount of money and is a real London dye. The price of these goods in an ordinary retail way is double the price that we quote. Width, 52 inches.

No. 14R1160 Price, per yard................$2.50

Our $3.50 Imported Seal Plush.

This is the acme of elegance in a London Dye Seal Plush. These goods are sold in the best retail stores (no better quality) at $6.00. Width, 52 inches.

No. 14R1164 Price, per yard $3.50

LINING DEPARTMENT.

Be sure to order your dress linings from us, as you will save money on every item; we buy them in such large quantities that it enables us to quote them at rock bottom prices. **We only handle the most reliable brands.**

We do not sample Linings.

Dress Linings in Sets.

Lining Set, put up in black, drab, slate and brown, contains 6 yards kid finished cambric, 2 yards corset jean or waist lining and 1 yard wigan for stiffening.

No. 14R1600 Price, per set.....................39c

Lining Set, put up in black, drab, slate or brown, contains 6 yards good kid finish cambric, 2 yards silk finished percaline waist lining, and 1½ yards best imported linen canvas for skirt stiffening.

No. 14R1604 Price, per set............ ..... 65c

Our 95-Cent Lining Set.

Lining Set, put up in black, drab or brown, contains 5 yards of 36-inch taffeta skirt lining, 2 yards fancy silesia waist lining, and 1½ yards of best French canvas.

No. 14R1608

Price, per set......95c

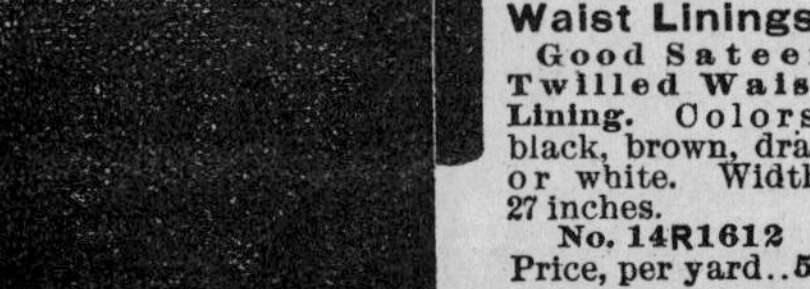

Waist Linings.

Good Sateen Twilled Waist Lining. Colors, black, brown, drab or white. Width, 27 inches.

No. 14R1612

Price, per yard..5c

Best Sateen Twilled Waist Lining. Colors, black, brown, drab or white. Width, 27 inches

No. 14R1616

Price, per yard..7c

Silesias.

We do not sample Silesias.

Good Quality Silesia. Comes in black and all staple colors. Width, 36 inches.

No. 14R1620

Price, per yard. ...8c

Columbia Silesias. Very strong and firm. Comes in black and all staple colors. Width, 36 inches.

No. 14R1624

Price, per yard...10c

Roman Silesias. Extra fine twill. Comes in black and all staple colors. Width, 36 inches.

No. 14R1628 Price, per yard.................12½c

Fancy Silesias. Comes in stripes and figures, both light and dark colors. Width, 36 inches.

No. 14R1632 Price, per yard.....................14c

Fancy Silesias. Black one side, figured the other. This is a splendid quality and has a satin finish. Width, 36 inches.

No. 14R1636 Price, per yard...................15c

Percalines.

We do not sample Percalines.

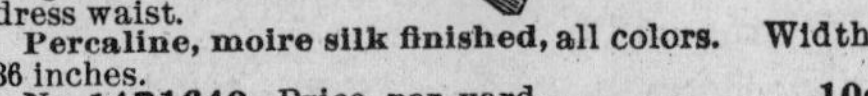

A soft waist lining, now much used. While light in weight, it is firm and does not stretch, and is preferred to any other lining by ladies who have their dresses tightly fitted. Owing to its light, silky texture it does not make bulky seams or enlarge the size of the dress waist.

Percaline, moire silk finished, all colors. Width, 36 inches.

No. 14R1640 Price, per yard.....................10c

Our 12-Cent Kid Finished Percaline.

This Percaline is 36 inches wide, comes in all colors and black, and at **12 cents is a big leader with us.** Width, 36 inches.

No. 14R1644 Price, per yard......................12c

Our 15-Cent Percaline.

This is an extra quality of percaline, a goods that retails generally at 20 to 25 cents a yard. It is light, but firm, and insures a perfect fit in making a waist. All colors and black. Width, 36 inches.

No. 14R1648 Price, per yard.......................15c

Kid Finished 64x64 Cloth Skirt Linings.

Best Soft Kid Finished Cambric. Colors, slate, drab, gray, light, medium, or dark brown; black, tan, myrtle, navy or wine; all shades. 25 inches wide.

No. 14R1652

Price, per yard 3½c

Fast Black Cambric, warranted perfectly fast dye. 25 inches wide.

No. 14R1656 Price, per yard......................5c

Paper Cambric, double fold, in black, brown, drab or slate. 36 inches wide.

No. 14R1658 Price, per yard.........................7c

Taffeta Skirt Linings.

Taffeta Skirt Lining; not the poor grade, but a good quality lining. Comes in black, brown and slate. Width, 36 inches.

No. 14R1660 Price, per yard......................7c

Taffeta Skirt Lining, extra fine quality, the proper thing for the better class of dress goods. Comes in fast black, and all colors. Width, 36 inches.

No. 14R1664 Price, per yard........................10c

Nearsilk for Dress Linings.

Nearsilk, not silk but resembling silk. Well known goods. It is used for lining the very highest grade of dresses. Nothing richer, has the appearance of all silk goods. We can furnish it in all colors. Width, 36 inches.

No. 14R1668 Price, per yard........................20c

Our 12-Cent, 36-Inch, Carlisle Satin Stripe, Silk Finished Taffeta Skirt Lining.

These goods are used for lining the highest grade dresses. Has a very broad satin stripe on a black taffeta ground, comes in solid black only, and is one of the most fashionable things for dress skirt lining, a goods that sells in regular lining stores at not less than 20 cents a yard. Width, 36 inches.

No. 14R1672 Price, per yard.......................12c

Our 18-Cent New Mercerized Colored Heavy Silk Skirtings.

These goods are 32 inches wide and come in several beautiful colorings as well as black. This is absolutely as perfect as the heaviest and best silk shown in the market and will wear better. Comes in cardinal, plum, navy, cerise, rose and black. Width, 32 inches.

No. 14R1674 Price, per yard........................18c

36-Inch Mercerized or Spun Glass Rustling Skirt Lining.

This is one of the most popular and newest materials for lining ladies' skirts. It resembles silk, is mellow and crisp, and has a very beautiful, silky finish, medium weight, and comes in black, brown, drab, tan, cerise, violet, myrtle, cardinal, yellow, nile green, lavender, slate and gray. This is a very nice and serviceable lining for medium cost dresses. Width, 36 inches.

No. 14R1675 Price, per yard..........................12½c

LININGS FOR STIFFENING.

For bottoms of dresses, collars, cuffs and tailors' use. We carry a big stock of linings for stiffening, a better variety than can be found in any of the smaller stores throughout the country, a stock as complete as it is possible to make it.

We do not sample these goods.

Wigan.

Wigan, black, gray or white, similar to crinoline, but stiffer, with less body than canvas.

No. 14R1676 Width, 33 inches. Price, per yard..6c

Grass Cloth.

Grass Cloth, a very light weight, wiry stiffening, much used for skirts and interlinings. Colors, gray, brown, black, white or natural tan.

No. 14R1680 Width, 36 inches. Price, per yard.7c

Elastic Canvas.

Elastic Canvas, good quality, the proper thing for bottoms of skirts. Comes in black, brown, drab, white or gray. Width, 27 inches.

No. 14R1684 Price, per yard.......................7c

Shrunken Linen Finished Duck.

This is one of the most serviceable facings shown for stiffening the bottom of dress skirts. This being thoroughly shrunk, makes the dress skirt hold its shape. These goods are sold at from 15 to 20 cents in ordinary lining stores. Comes in black, gray and brown. Width, 27 inches.

No. 14R1688 Price, per yard................. 12c

26-Inch All Linen Canvas Duck.

This is absolutely all pure Irish linen, is heavy and stiff. It is one of the best and most popular linen canvases on the market. It insures a perfect shape to the dress skirt, and will give excellent wear.

No. 14R1692 Width, 26 inches. Price, per yard..12c

Linen Canvas.

Linen Canvas. French elastic, the best lining for bottoms of dresses; it retains its stiffness longer than any other lining; no dress can set well without it. Colors, white, natural linen, brown, gray or black. Medium grade. Width, 26 inches.

No. 14R1696 Price, per yard......................14c

Our 18-Cent French Linen Elastic Canvas.

This is absolutely the best linen facing canvas in the market, goods sold by some of the metropolitan city stores as high as 35 cents per yard. We buy these goods in hundred case lots, and the price which we name is slightly within a very small margin of what the goods cost in the largest quantities. Width, 27 inches.

No. 14R1700 Price, per yard.........................18c

Herringbone and French Hair Cloths.

The very best material for a permanent stiffening for the better grades of silk or wool dress skirts. We keep only the best and in 24-inch width.

No. 14R1701 **24-inch Herringbone Hair Cloth,** in black, white or gray. Price, per yard................39c

No. 14R1702 **24-inch French Hair Cloth,** in black, gray or white. Price, per yard..............45c

Crinoline.

Crinoline; black, brown, slate or white; extra heavy. Width, 33 inches.

No. 14R1704 Price, per yard........................ 8c

Buckram.

Buckram, similar to wigan; put up in rolls. In black or white only. Width, 24 inches.

No. 14R1708 Price, per yard..........................10c

Collar Canvas.

This is an addition to our lining stock that we sell in rolls of ten yards, and is something that is always needed by dressmakers; in fact, it is useful in any house where people make their own dresses, or in making the new styles of stock collars. **We will sell you a piece of ten yards for 95 cents.** It is a medium stiff and a very good canvas, such as you pay ordinarily in a lining store or lining department in an ordinary retail store 20 cents a yard for. We will not cut this in quantities of less than ten yard. Width, 23 inches.

No. 14R1710 Price, per 10-yard piece 95c

Black Moreen Skirting.

27-inch Wool Moreen Heavy Black Skirtings are the most durable materials made for petticoats or underskirts. They are of extra weight, and lustrous silky black. These handsome skirtings sell in the large retail stores in New York and Chicago at 65 cents and 75 cents.

No. 14R1712 Width, 27 inches. Price, per yard..43c

New Roman Stripe Taffeta Skirt Lining.

These stylish Roman stripe linings come in a variety of variegated handsome colored stripes, combined with black. This material is also used extensively for petticoats. It is very durable, and in pretty Persian, Roman and Ottoman effects, nothing more dressy can be imaginable. Width, 36 inches.

No. 14R1714 Price, per yard.......................15c

..Our Mammoth Silk Department..

Only those who have patronized this department, only such of our customers as have ordered silks from our house, and have had a chance to see, examine and compare our goods with those offered by their storekeepers at home and other catalogue houses, can appreciate the values we are giving in this department.

BY ABOLISHING OUR ADVERTISING EXPENSE, getting 50 cents for our big catalogue and receiving cash in advance for silk and dress goods samples furnished, by getting the full amount of cash with all orders, thus reducing our clerical expenses, deducting all this expense that other houses must add to their selling price, by giving you the benefit of this saving and then by figuring our profits on silks on the exact same basis as we figure our profits on the most staple commodities in our store, namely, one small percentage of profit above the actual cost to produce, as one of the largest buyers of silks in this country, every silk price quotation is a wonder of value and so much lower in price than other houses for the same quality of goods that you must see, examine and compare the silks we offer with those offered by other houses to appreciate the values we are giving.

BY BREAKING AWAY FROM THE LONG ESTABLISHED CUSTOM of the dry good trade, by which fancy profits have been asked for everything in silks, placing these goods on our one small profit basis, giving our customers the benefit of all advertising and unnecessary expenses, thus making still lower prices, this department has grown until we are today one of the largest handlers of foreign and domestic silks in this country.

WE BUY OUR SILKS DIRECT from the largest foreign and domestic makers, we buy them in quantities that secure for us the very lowest prices, and to the cost to us is added only our one small percentage of profit.

OUR GUARANTEE AND MONEY REFUND OFFER.

SELECT ANY SILK FROM THIS CATALOGUE, ordering by number and description, and we will send the silk to you by mail or express, as directed, and if, when received, it is not found perfectly satisfactory, if you are not convinced that you have saved from one-quarter to one-half in price, if you do not feel that you have received such value for your money as you could not possibly get elsewhere, you can return the goods to us at our expense of express charges both ways and we will immediately return your money.

...ABOUT EXPRESS AND POSTAGE CHARGES...

THE TRANSPORTATION CHARGES ON SILKS are very light, and this cost will be next to nothing as compared to what you will save in price. Silks can be sent by mail, postpaid, at an expense ranging from 3 to 4 cents per yard, according to the weight of the goods. 10 to 35 cents will pay the postage on any waist, skirt or suit pattern.

AS A MATTER OF ECONOMY we especially recommend that you order two or more waist, skirt or suit patterns, even if you have to get a neighbor to join with you, for two patterns can be sent by express to almost any point for about the same cost as one, and by dividing the express charges between you, you reduce the express charges on the goods you want to only a few cents.

SAMPLES FURNISHED AT 1 CENT PER NUMBER.

WHILE WE ALWAYS ADVISE OUR CUSTOMERS to make up their order from the catalogue illustrations and descriptions, and without waiting to first write for samples, send your order and your money to us, always with the understanding that if the goods are not perfectly satisfactory, you can return them to us at our expense and we will immediately return your money, we will, however, furnish samples of any of our silks or any kind of dress goods at 1 cent per catalogue number. Simply state the samples wanted by catalogue number, enclose 1 cent for each number selected and the samples will be sent you by return mail, postpaid.

BY 1 CENT PER NUMBER we mean all the samples furnished under that number. For example: Under one number there may be as many as a dozen or more shades or patterns, in which case you will for the 1 cent receive the entire line of samples, of colorings and patterns of that number. On the other hand, it may be a plain goods and there is only one shade and pattern, in which case there will be only one sample sent. You will, however, in each case get for the 1 cent sent us everything we have in our stock quoted under that number.

THE ADVANTAGE IN ORDERING DIRECT FROM THE CATALOGUE.

IF YOU WILL STATE THE GOODS WANTED, by catalogue number, give us an idea of the color and pattern wanted, state what you wish to use the goods for, and your complexion and color of hair, we will give you free the services of a professional silk man who will select for you the very best thing in our stock becoming your complexion for the purpose wanted. We really feel we can do better by you if you order direct from the catalogue, and we recommend that you do not delay to first write for samples, for understand, you take no risk, for we will immediately return your money if you are not perfectly satisfied.

MOST HOUSES furnish samples of silk and other fabrics free for the asking, and from experience in the past we know it is very expensive, for hundreds of thousands of samples in this way are sent to people who have no thought of buying, and all this enormous expense is added to the selling price of the goods. We save all this by getting paid for all samples, and when you order a dress pattern from us you do not pay for 25 to 100 sets of samples that have been sent out to people who never buy.

EVERYTHING IN OUR HOUSE is done solely in the interest of our customers, our aim being to give the greatest possible value for the money and still leave us one uniform, small percentage of profit.

IF YOU HAVE ANY USE for anything in silks, you cannot afford to order elsewhere until you have seen and examined samples of our goods, and compared them with goods offered by other houses and learned how much you can save by buying from us.

Our 19-Inch, 29-Cent, Handsome Jacquard Silk.

This comes in a very neat, handsome pattern; one of the biggest values that we show. Equal in effect and wearing qualities to a silk that costs 75 cents per yard. It has a silk face and the design is copied from one of the finest imported silks. **Strong and reliable, suitable for waists, whole suits and trimmings.** The colors are pink and light green, tan and turquoise, rose and turquoise, olive and cardinal, navy and cardinal, rose and gold, black and empire green, purple and black, black and medium navy blue, heliotrope and white, also cardinal and black. This is a silk that would cost 50 cents per yard if bought ordinarily in a retail store, a silk that is confined to us by one of the largest manufacturers, a silk that, at this price, cannot be matched by anybody. It is not all silk but it answers all the purposes of silk. It has a very rich silk face. Width, 19 inches.

No. 14R2000 Price, per yard..................29c

Samples of this number furnished for 1 cent, including sample of every shade carried in the number.

Our Brocaded Heavy Marie Antoinette Silks.

The illustration gives you an idea of the pretty pattern of these swell satin brocaded silks. To appreciate the quality of this silk it has to be seen in the piece. It makes up beautifully in suits, waists and for trimmings. We have secured the entire control of this beautiful line of brocades. They have the appearance of the rich French damasse satin brocaded silks that sell at from $1.25 to $2.50 per yard. This goods comes in handsome combinations in heliotrope and gold, rose and nile green, light blue and pink, navy and cardinal, empire green and cardinal, black and apple green, black and new blue, black and purple, and black and cardinal. Order any number of yards of this handsome damasse Marie Antoinette Silk, and if not fully satisfactory, even better than you can buy of your home dealer at double the money, we will cheerfully refund your money. Width, 19 inches.

No. 14R2004 Price, per yard..................39c

Samples of this number furnished for 1 cent, including sample of every shade carried in the number.

Our Handsome Brocaded Changeable Parmacelle Silks at 33c Per Yard.

It has the appearance and general effect of silks that sell for three times the price that we ask for it. It has a good weight, and the designs are remarkably pretty. The combinations of colorings are the very newest and up to date for the season of 1902. The goods are not strictly all silk but the silk is manipulated with a lisle thread mercerized to a brightness that is equal to silk. In fact, the face is all silk. This goods is really in effect a dollar silk. These handsome combinations of colors are rose and nile, turquoise and pink, cardinal and olive, navy and maroon, heliotrope and maize, black and empire green, black and purple, black and Nazarine blue, also white and navy. We thoroughly recommend these silks for service, and at this price they are wonderful value. Order any number of yards for any purpose for which the richest brocaded silks can be used, and if not thoroughly satisfied you may return them to us at our expense, and we will immediately refund your money.

No. 14R2010 Width, 19 inches. Price, per yd. 33c

Samples of this number furnished for 1c, including sample of every shade carried in the number

Our Famous 39-Cent Dimanche Granite Silks.

This is a very beautiful striped silk, comes in handsome colorings, silk that has the weight and effect of goods that cost twice the money that we charge for this silk. Will give unbounded satisfaction and positively will wear as well as silks that cost four times as much. The illustration will give you a faint idea of the beautiful pattern effects in which this silk comes. Stripes are fashionable and this beautiful striped granite silk is the very choicest silk creation that has been produced this season. The colors are rose, pink, turquoise, heliotrope, navy, green, yellow, purple, red and also black and white. These goods are fully 19 inches wide. They are the handsomest silks that are shown for the spring of 1902.

No. 14R2008 Width, 19 inches. Price, per yard.................39c

Samples of this number furnished for 1 cent, including sample of every shade carried in the number.

Our 29-Cent 18-Inch Silk Foulards.

This is an up to date, 20th century silk, one of the handsomest shown. It is 18 inches wide. The colors are navy, new blue, also black. Comes in pretty designs, such as geometrical figures, also hairlines, stripes and polka-dots. This silk will certainly be one of the leading fashions for the coming season. Width, 18 in.

No. 14R2012 Our special price, per yard......29c

Samples of this number furnished for 1c, including sample of every shade carried in the number

45-Cent Kai Kai Wash Silk.

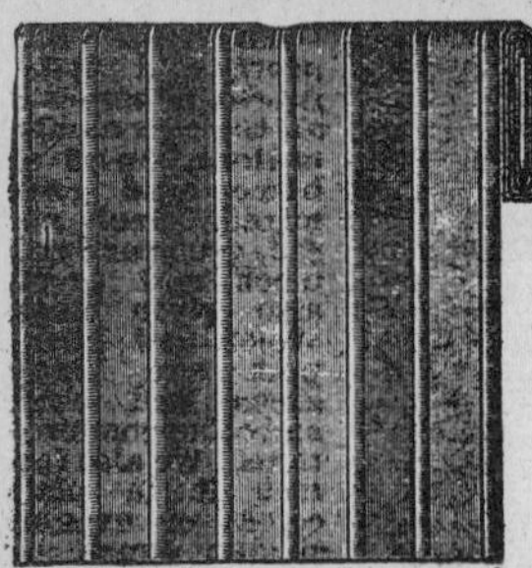

Our extra heavy 18-inch, pure silk Kai Kai Japanese Cords. This is the latest, heaviest and most up to date Japanese corded washable silk to be found on the market. We have imported these silks direct from Japan. We have bought them at a price that makes it possible for us to sell them to our customers throughout the world at a price lower than they can be bought for in the largest quantities from jobbers, brokers or retailers. These are absolutely pure silk Japanese Kai Kai cords. They are goods that will give splendid wear, wash without fading, silk that has the appearance of goods that are selling in large city stores at 75 cents and $1.00. These silks come in a variety of beautiful shades, colorings and effects. They come in stripes, checks and plaids. They come in medium and light colors. They are the most appropriate silks for shirt waists and for dainty, swell costumes. The color combinations include shades of violet, pink, green, purple, cerise, cadet, primrose, lavender, porcelain, nile, gray and other rich combinations with white. Send us your order for this extra heavy, fancy Kai Kai Japanese wash silk, accompanied by the price, and if not found entirely satisfactory in every respect, return it to us and your money will be cheerfully refunded. Width, 18 inches.

No. 14R2064 Price, per yard..................45c

Samples of this number furnished for 1 cent, including sample of every shade and pattern carried in the number.

Our 19-Inch Extra Heavy Japanese Corded Jacquard Habutai Wash Silks

These are the richest and handsomest wash silks imported. The illustration gives you a faint idea of the designs in which they come. These silks are the very height of style. They are goods finer than have ever before been brought from Japan. They are goods that are equal in every way to silks that sell at $1.00 to $1.25 in French and domestic American silks. They are silks of which we have exclusive sale and we have imported them from Japan direct ourselves. It is impossible to thoroughly describe the handsome designs and colors in which we are showing these silks; you must see them in the piece to thoroughly appreciate them. They come in colors: Pink, salmon, rose, heliotrope, violet, lavender, nile green, cardinal, yellow, straw, maize or ange, purple, light blue, turquoise, and cerise, also black. Every piece and every yard we guarantee perfect in every respect. The silk is bright and clear and the colorings are exquisite. All of the patterns come with jacquard effect stripes and the black alone comes solid color, corded, and the other patterns described are relieved by white corded stripes. Do not fail to order one of these our richest wash silks. Nobody in your neighborhood will have anything nearly so rich. They are goods that will be thoroughly appreciated, goods that will give satisfaction and goods that will thoroughly advertise our silk department as the department of all departments, where bargains in up to date silks can be had. Order a waist, a suit, or any number of yards, and if not found thoroughly satisfactory, return to us at once and we will refund your money. Width, 19 inches.

No. 14R2068 Price, per yard..................59c

Samples of this number furnished for 1 cent, including sample of every shade and pattern carried in the number.

GIVE CATALOGUE NUMBER IN FULL WHEN YOU WRITE YOUR ORDER

OUR BIG $1.09 SEASON LEADER.

At $1.09 per yard we are offering these goods at less than the largest wholesale dealers can buy the same grade of corded silk in any quantity. No illustration or description will give you an idea of the beautiful effect and the fine quality shown in this, our $1.09 line. Don't wait to write for samples when ordering. No set of small samples would give you any idea of the value. Simply enclose our price with your order, give us an idea of the coloring wanted, state your complexion, what garment you wish to make, and leave it somewhat to the judgment of an expert silk man to give you the finest thing in our line to match your complexion. This handsome pompadour taffeta colored silk is one of the most popular corded silks on the market. It comes in all the very latest shades as described, entirely new, strictly up to date, a 20th century goods in pure silk taffeta, with wide cords on a variety of beautiful tinted grounds in delicate shades, also striped with a ¾-inch swivel floral effect. It will make a beautiful, dressy waist. It is especially elegant for fancy waists, also suitable for costumes; in fact, the black goods, with their beautiful colored floral effects, will make you a complete costume such as others in your neighborhood will not own. These goods come 20 inches in width, and in a big variety of new shades, including cream, white, blonde blue, shell pink, corn, violet and also black, reseda, porcelain, new blue and bright cardinal; also black with contrasting beautiful floral designs, red on white; violet and green on white; shades of rose, cardinal and green and blonde blue; shades of green, cerise, pink and cardinal on shell pink; cardinal, rose and green on yellow; violet and green on white; and violet, red and empire green on reseda. Empire green and cerise on porcelain; cerise, fuchsia and green on new blue; bright olive, pink and rose on bright cardinal; cerise, pink and green on black; green and violet shaded to purple on black. Too much cannot be said in favor of these handsome corded silks.

No. 14R2072 Width, 20 inches. Price, per yard..................$1.09

Samples of this number furnished for 1 cent, including sample of every shade carried in the number.

A 63-CENT SPIRAL CORD WONDER.

AT 63 CENTS PER YARD of 19-inch width, we offer this new genuine La Dorris spiral cord, heavy weight, all pure imported French taffeta silk, in all the latest shades as one of the handsomest silks on the market for waists, suits, etc.

HOW WE CAN MAKE THE PRICE 63 CENTS. We are the largest handlers of this grade of fine imported French silks in the market, and at 63 cents per yard, or $2.52 for a 4-yard waist pattern, we have created a demand, which has come to us largely by duplicate orders, that has made it possible to take the entire output from this noted French maker. Furnishing an extra heavy all pure silk in a handsome spiral cord effect, as illustrated, in the most perfect imitation of the hand corded silks that sell generally at $3.00 per yard and upwards, so closely resembling the $3.00 goods that really only experts can tell the difference, our sale on this handsome spiral cord silk has become enormous, and today we offer you the goods in any quantity at 63 cents per yard, while dealers cannot buy silk approaching this in quality, style and effect (even in dozen-piece lots) at anything like the 63-cent price we quote to you. Send us your order, enclose our price and 1½ cents per yard extra if you wish us to ship by mail postpaid, and if you are not perfectly satisfied and you do not say it is one of the latest things and by far the greatest value you have ever seen, you can return it to us at our expense and we will return your money.

Silk waist when made up from our 63-cent La Dorris corded taffeta silk.

THIS TAFFETA SILK COMES in cream, white, blonde blue, turquoise blue, shell pink, rose pink, red, old rose, cerise, cardinal, scarlet, brown, lilac, lavender, heliotrope, yellow, nile green, reseda, purple, navy, gray, national blue and black. In ordering be sure to state shade wanted.

IT'S NOT NECESSARY TO SEND FOR SAMPLES. We guarantee the quality and we guarantee to please you. Simply state the shade wanted, the number of yards, enclose the price and 1½ cents per yard extra if to be sent by mail postpaid, and if it is not all and more than we claim for it, you can return it to us at our expense and we will return your money.

No. 14R2076 Width, 19 inches. Price, per yard..................63c

Samples of this number furnished for 1 cent, including sample of every shade carried in the number.

OUR 69-CENT PLISSE TUCKED TAFFETA SILK.

FOR 69 CENTS PER YARD, of 19-inch width, we furnish this handsome, new, rich, tucked taffeta silk in the different shades as described, a big, new leader, the equal of silks that are retailed everywhere at $1.25 to $1.50 a yard.

UNDER OUR NEW POLICY, with no expense for wasted samples or catalogues, the price we ask barely covers the cost to manufacture, with but our one small profit added, less than dealers can buy in any quantity.

69 CENTS PER YARD, a 4-yard waist pattern for $2.76, a 14-yard costume pattern for $9.66.

SEND US YOUR ORDER for a waist or costume pattern, enclose our price, we will send you the goods with the understanding that if they are not perfectly satisfactory and far greater value than you could get elsewhere, you can return them to us at our expense and we will return your money.

ENTIRELY NEW FOR THIS SEASON, a rich, handsome, silk tucked taffeta, such as you will find only in the most fashionable city retail stores and there at about double our price; a good, heavy, extra durable silk, especially desirable for a handsome waist and especially rich in a full gown or combination costume of waist and skirt. It comes in rose, rose pink, shell pink, blonde blue, sky blue, lavender, heliotrope, white and cream. This is a silk you must see to appreciate the quality in its new, rich effect. It has ½-inch crinkled stripes bound both sides with two rows of corded silk lines, these alternating with ⅛-inch plain and ¼-inch crinkled, and then with narrow raised silk ribbed lines.

THIS SILK SENT by mail postpaid on receipt of price and 1½ cents per yard extra for postage.

Illustration of this handsome tucked taffeta silk made up in a waist.

No. 14R2080 Width, 19 inches. Price, per yard..................69c

Samples of this number furnished for 1 cent, including sample of every shade carried in the number.

OUR 49-CENT FINE IMPORTED TAFFETA SILK.

FOR 49 CENTS PER YARD we offer you this taffeta silk as a regular $1.00 value. 49 cents per yard is less than cost to manufacture and much lower than dealers can buy in any quantity. A large New York silk house was compelled to raise money, and asked us for a spot cash offer on 3,500 pieces of this fine silk. We made them a ridiculously low offer; but, to our surprise, it was promptly accepted, to get immediate money. To give our customers the advantage of our purchase we add but our one small percentage of profit and make the heretofore unheard of price of 49 cents for this regular $1.00 silk.

SEND US YOUR ORDER, enclose our price and 1½ cents per yard, extra, if you wish us to send by mail postpaid, and we will send you this silk with the understanding that if it is not perfectly satisfactory, all and more than we claim for it, the equal of anything you can buy from your storekeeper at home at $1.00 or more per yard, you can return it to us at our expense, and we will return your money. We have on hand over 1,200 pieces, and, confining the sale to the orders that come from our catalogue, hope to be able to supply our customers in any quantity they want until the next catalogue (No. 112) is issued.

This illustration gives you an idea of our 49-cent silk made up in a waist. Of course, you can make it up any style.

WITH OUR IMMENSE BUYING POWER and with the eliminating of the expense of free samples and free catalogues, our price offerings are so startling that they can only be understood when seen, examined and compared with the goods offered by others.

THIS IS A GENUINE GUINET ET CIE fine, all pure silk, rustling taffeta, one of the very best silks made, positively the very latest style, and more in demand than any other silk manufactured today; a good weight, 19 inches wide; makes up very stylish in a handsome silk waist or silk suit, and is especially desirable as a foundation, to be covered with laces that are so popular. These silks come in a big variety of beautiful colors, including everything for the street, evening and receptions—pink, coral, blue, turquoise, maize, straw, lavender, heliotrope, purple, cardinal, scarlet, wine, steel, silver, gray, brown, tan, ecru, nile, empire, olive and myrtle green, old rose, cerise, American beauty, reseda, national blue, light and dark navy, white, cream and black.

DON'T WAIT TO WRITE FOR SAMPLES. It is a useless delay and expense. We guarantee to please you in shade or quality, or return your money. Order four yards for a waist pattern, ten yards for a skirt pattern, or fourteen yards for a dress pattern; enclose our price and 1½ cents per yard extra, if you wish the goods sent by mail postpaid, state shade wanted, and, if you do not receive the greatest value ever shown in your section, we will immediately return your money. Where one dress pattern of this goods goes, dozens soon follow. These silk values are extremely contagious — when seen, they spread. They are unmatchable; no chance for dissatisfaction. Nothing like it was ever before attempted.

No. 14R2084 Width, 19 inches. Price, per yard........49c

Samples of this number furnished for 1 cent, including sample of every shade carried in the number.

Plain Surah Silks.

We have discontinued the low numbers in Surah Silk, as experience has taught us that they do not give satisfaction. We have decided to handle only the perfect and better grade of Surah Silks.

Send 1 cent for samples of any single number.

Surah Silk, all silk, not the low grade so much on the market. We can furnish it in any color, both light and dark. Width, 19 inches.

No. 14R2086 Price, per yard, 35c

Plain Surah Silk. Extra fine quality, all colors, with a very close weave, all pure silk. Width, 19 inches.

No. 14R2088 Price, per yard..50c

Plain China and Japanese Pure Silk. Washable Habutai Silks.

Send 1 cent for samples of any single number.

Plain China Silk. We can furnish any and every color. Dark and medium, also evening and opera shades. Width, 19 inches.

No. 14R2090 Price, per yard........25c

Plain Japanese Habutai Silk. Every thread silk. We can furnish all colors. Dark, medium, evening tints and high opera shades. Width, 21 inches.

No. 14R2092 Price, per yard........32c

Plain Japanese Habutai Silk, extra fine quality, all colors. Dark, medium, evening and high opera shades. Width, 24 inches.

No. 14R2096 Price, per yard........35c

Plain Japanese Silk. All colors. Dark, medium and high colors, also evening tints. Same as above, but 27 inches wide.

No. 14R3000 Price, per yard........48c

Cream White Habutai Silks.

This is a very light, soft, natural finished silk, and is very durable and strong. Is very much in demand for fine underwear, dresses, waists, etc. Washes beautifully.

No. 14R3004 20-inch. Price, per yard........29c

Pure Silk White Japanese Habutai.

No. 14R3008 24-inch. Price, per yard........39c

No. 14R3012 27-inch. Price, per yard........43c

Samples of any one catalogue number furnished for one cent, including sample of every shade carried in the number.

Duchesse Parisian Novelty Silk, 98c.

Our most popular all Silk Satin Duchesse Railroad Cord Parisian Novelty. This exquisite fancy all silk fabric is suitable for entire costumes, for waists, or to be used in combination with other rich silks or wool materials. It is 20 inches wide. The black is in proportion just as it shows here and the lighter effects are in cerise, violet, brown, new blue, purple; also lavender. Width, 20 inches.

No. 14R3016 Price, per yard........98c

Samples of this number furnished for 1 cent, including sample of every shade carried in the number.

Plaid Silks.

Plaid Silks are particularly stylish this season for ladies' and misses' waists, suits and for combination with wool materials, also for trimmings. We have the very swellest new up to date styles in a bewildering line of pretty color combinations. They are our own importations and are the very heaviest all silk taffetas with luxurious handsome outlining stripes, forming block plaids and broken plaids. We show these handsome all silk plaids in only two qualities on which we have pounded down the prices to 59 cents and 75 cents. They are values for 75 cents and $1.00. The colors are combinations: Cerise and green, red and green, turquoise and green, brown and blue, blue and red, pink, white and green, black and white, red and white, black and cardinal, blue and white, green and white, in fact almost any coloring that would be becoming to all ages, styles and complexions. We have these qualities also in black and white and blue and white, small, medium and large shepherd checks.

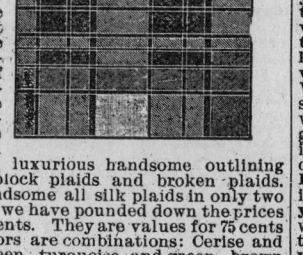

No. 14R3020 Width, 19 inches. Price, per yard. 59c

No. 14R3024 Width, 20 inches. Price, per yard. 75c

Samples of this number furnished for 1 cent, including sample of every shade carried in the number.

OUR SPECIAL SILK DEPARTMENT

Of Evening Shades or Light Colors in Plain and Figured Silks.

IN THESE HANDSOME evening or light shades we have an immense assortment, a great aggregation of heretofore unheard of values in novelties, the latest productions from the best makers. We have demoralized the prices.

Evening Shades and Staple Colors in Figured Silks.

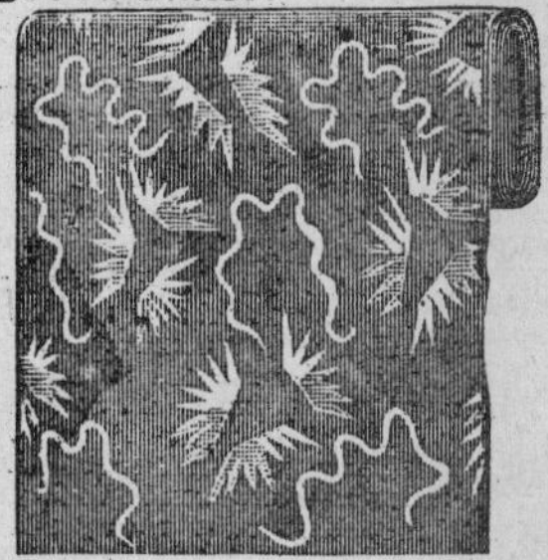

Brocaded Silk, solid colors, the figure the same color as ground work. A very pretty silk, and most suitable for evening waists and dresses; can furnish it in cardinal, U. S. military red, empire green, nile, cadet, old rose, pink, rose pink, light blue, yellow, garnet, navy, new blue, cerise, violet, lavender, heliotrope, porcelain, cream or white. Width, 19 inches.

No. 14R3028 Price, per yard........37c

Samples of this number furnished for 1 cent, including sample of every shade carried in the number.

Our New 63-Cent Cream or White Brocaded Satin.

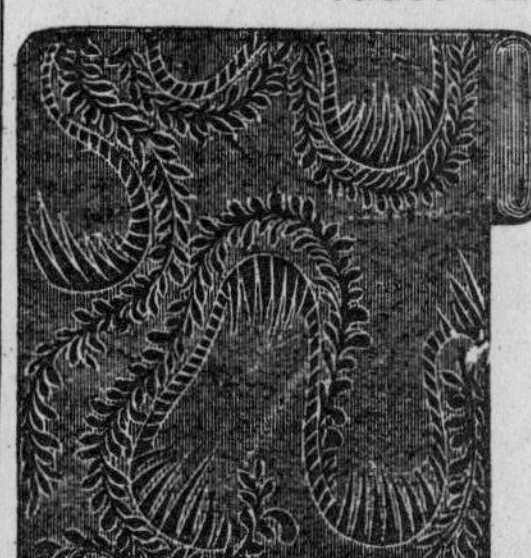

This new silk has a very fine silk luster and comes in very handsome patterns. It is entirely new for this season. It is a special pattern for party and wedding costumes. It comes in very handsome designs, in delicate shades of cream or white, also light pink, light blue, lavender, violet, cardinal, rose, turquoise, fuchsia and yellow brocade satin. Send us your order for a dress pattern, and if you do not find it most extraordinary value, a very rich effect for the money, we will immediately return your money. In ordering, mention whether small, medium or large design is wanted. Width, 19 inches.

No. 14R3032 Price, per yard........63c

Samples of this number furnished for 1 cent, including sample of every shade and pattern carried in the number.

Brocaded Damasse Satins in White, Cream and Opera Shades, All Pure Silk, Rich and Heavy.

For only 98 cents we offer this new handsome evening silk, one of the richest patterns shown, as the equal of silks that are sold generally at nearly 50 per cent more money. It comes in the newest shades and will make up most beautifully.

At 98 cents per yard we consider this one of the best values in our entire silk department. These goods are worth at least 30 cents more per yard than the goods we were compelled to ask 98 cents for last season. We bought a big line of these handsome evening silks at a very low price, which makes possible this wonderful value offering. This is a 20-inch goods, good weight, all pure silk, rich luster finish. Comes in white or cream, pink, light blue, lavender and other fashionable shades. **It is a heavy brocaded Duchesse satin.** The illustration will give you some idea of the pattern effect, but **you must send us your order, give us an idea of the pattern and shade wanted, whether large or small design, let us make the selection for you, with the understanding that you can return the goods to us if they are not in every way satisfactory. No samples will do these goods justice.** You must leave the selection somewhat to us. We will make it our business to please you and save you money. Width, 20 inches.

No. 14R3036 Price, per yard........98c

Samples of this number furnished for 1 cent, including sample of every shade carried in the number.

GIVE CATALOGUE NUMBER IN FULL WHEN YOU WRITE YOUR ORDER

OUR MAMMOTH Black Silk Department.

NO ILLUSTRATIONS OR DESCRIPTIONS, no attempt to compare our catalogue with other catalogues, nothing but seeing the samples, or better still, seeing the goods themselves, will enable you to appreciate how much more value we can give you in black silks than you can get from any other house

PUTTING OUR ENTIRE LINE OF SILKS on the same basis of profit as the most staple goods in our house, charging 50 cents for our big catalogue and receiving payment in advance for all samples, thus deducting all advertising expense from our selling prices, reducing our cost of handling by getting cash in full with all orders, we offer from this, our Black Silk Goods Department, values not even approached by any other house. We can furnish you a waist, skirt or suit pattern at a lower price per yard than dealers can buy the same grade of goods in dozen piece lots.

OUR GUARANTEE AND REFUND OFFER

TO CONVINCE YOU that we have no competition in this line, and that you can buy from us at lower prices than you can buy elsewhere, we only ask that you either send for samples to compare or send us your order with the understanding and agreement that if the goods, when received, are not perfectly satisfactory, and much greater value for your money than you could possibly get from any other house, you can return them to us at our expense of express charges both ways and we will immediately return your money.

MOST HOUSES FURNISH SAMPLES of silks free for the asking, and they send out thousands of samples to people who never buy, and for every single sample that brings an order, dozens of samples are cut up that never bring orders. We, too, could furnish samples free for the asking if we, like others, would add 10 to 20 per cent to the selling price of the goods.

IF YOU WANT SAMPLES of silk we will furnish them at 1 cent per catalogue number. When you order we will save you from 10 to 100 times the cost of the samples we furnish you. By 1 cent per catalogue number we mean that we will furnish you samples of our entire line under that number. There may be one or one dozen samples, depending on the number of patterns and colorings in the number.

WHILE WE CHEERFULLY FURNISH SAMPLES at 1 cent per number, we recommend that you make up your order from the catalogue illustrations and descriptions without delaying to get samples. You take no risk, for we will send you the goods with the understanding that if they are not perfectly satisfactory when received, you can return them to us at our expense and we will immediately return your money.

SILKS CAN BE SENT BY MAIL, postpaid, at an expense of 3 to 4 cents per yard, depending on the weight. By express two waist, skirt or dress patterns can be sent for about the same cost as one. We therefore urge that you make your order as large as possible, even by getting your friends to join with you, in this way reducing the transportation charges to next to nothing.

BLACK CHINESE AND JAPANESE SILKS.

Black China Silk. Good quality, 18 inches wide.
No. 14R3120 Price, per yard........25c

Black Japanese Washable Silk. All silk. Width, 21 inches.
No. 14R3124 Price, per yard........29c

Black Japanese Washable Silk. Strictly fast black, 24 inches wide.
No. 14R3128 Price, per yard........35c

Black Japanese Washable Silk. All silk, extra good quality, 27 inches wide.
No. 14R3132 Price, per yard........42c

Our 59-Cent Black Japanese Silk.

This is a fine all silk goods, extra good quality. 27 inches wide, indelible color, thoroughly washable, and at 59 cents it is a value we guarantee. Width, 27 inches.
No. 14R3136 Price, per yard........59c

Black Surah Silk, good quality, not the poor grade, but a good, substantial silk. Width, 19 inches.
No. 14R3140 Price, per yard........33c

Black Surah Silk, extra heavy all silk, and splendid value for the price. Width, 20 inches.
No. 14R3144 Price, per yard........48c

Samples of any number furnished for 1 cent.

Black Taffeta Dress Silks.

Every number quoted in this line guaranteed unbreakable.

Black Taffeta Silk. All pure silks, no better value for the money. Width, 19 inches.
No. 14R3148 Price, per yard........49c

Sample of this number furnished for 1 cent.

Our Extraordinary, Special, 19-Inch Black Extra Heavy Quality of Guaranteed Pure Silk Rustling Taffeta.

This extraordinary number is entirely new for this season. It is a number which we are satisfied will be very popular. This is a price based upon a very large purchase that we have just consummated. We have about fifteen hundred pieces of this extremely perfect, all pure silk 19-inch taffeta, and have decided to sell it for 59 cents per yard. This quality will compare favorably with goods found in ordinary retail stores at anywhere from 75 to 89 cents per yard. It is heavy; it is of a crisp yet mellow finish; it is a quality that is absolutely trustworthy. Send us your order for a waist, skirt or entire dress pattern and if it does not prove entirely satisfactory, better really than you would expect from our description, return it to us and we will immediately refund your money.

No. 14R3152 Width, 19 inches. Price, per yard, 59c

Sample of this number furnished for 1 cent.

OUR UNTEARABLE GUARANTEED EXTRA HEAVY WEIGHT BLACK TAFFETA DRESS SILKS AT 69, 79 AND 98 CENTS.

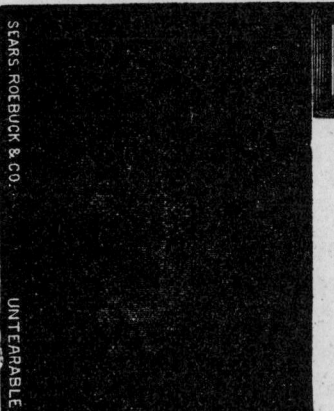

AT 69 CENTS, 79 CENTS AND 98 CENTS PER YARD, according to width, for 21, 24 and 27-inch goods, we call your attention to this extra fine extra heavy imported French black taffeta silk as the equal of taffeta silks that sell everywhere at almost double our price.

WE KNOW THAT OUR CUSTOMERS, who want a good substantial wear resisting heavy black taffeta silk dress or skirt, want nothing but a serviceable, reliable goods, they want a taffeta silk that is untearable. We know that people generally hesitate about buying a taffeta silk dress pattern for the reason there are so many unreliable taffeta silks made, goods that do not give satisfaction, and that merchants cannot and will not guarantee for quality, but to overcome this we placed our contract with one of the best makers in Lyons, France.

OUR CONTRACT CALLED FOR AN EXTRA HEAVY WEIGHT, beautifully finished, all pure, fast black taffeta silk that the manufacturer would guarantee to us in every way as to quality, guarantee it to be untearable, and the contract further stated that every yard of these goods should have woven in the selvage the words, "Sears, Roebuck & Co.'s Untearable." Our contract called for the highest grade of taffeta silk that this famous maker could produce, a quality of goods that we could send out under our binding guarantee covering every detail as to quality, wear and general satisfaction, so to the thousands who would appreciate a beautiful dress or skirt made from the finest quality of fast black taffeta silk, they might order from us with every assurance and with our positive guarantee that they would get such a silk as they would find only in the most fashionable city retail stores, a silk not to be found in the ordinary dry goods store, a grade of goods that is produced only by this one maker in Lyons, France, the only taffeta silk that we have ever dared to put out under our positive guarantee as to quality, a guarantee woven into the selvage of every yard that goes out of our house.

IT IS VALUES LIKE THESE THAT HAVE MADE OUR HOUSE FAMOUS,

that have built up the biggest mail order dry goods trade in the country. It is our aim that every piece of goods that goes out of this department shall be an advertisement for us, A BIG ADVERTISEMENT, an advertisement far better than anything we might say in the newspapers or even in our catalogue.

WE WANT YOU TO RECOMMEND US TO YOUR FRIENDS AND NEIGHBORS.

We want their trade too, and we know that when we send you this untearable, guaranteed, extra heavy weight black taffeta silk at 69, 79 or 98 cents per yard, according to width, we have given you a value that will surprise and delight you, that will cause you to say a good word in our favor whenever the occasion arises, and that will be a better argument, A STRONGER PLEA FOR YOUR FUTURE ORDERS THAN ANYTHING WE COULD DO.

OUR SPECIAL 69-CENT, 79-CENT AND 98-CENT PRICE is based on the actual cost to produce. The goods are worth more money. We are selling these goods on the same one small percentage of profit margin as we sell our most staple domestics, above the actual cost, under our big contract with the manufacturer. You must order a dress or skirt pattern to appreciate the body, weight, luster and mellow finish of this beautiful fast black French fabric.

FOR A RICH DRESS, for all ages and all seasons, for the most staple fabric that can be made up in women's garments, there is hardly a thing woven that approaches this famous Lyons heavy black taffeta goods.

SEND US YOUR ORDER FOR A SUIT, WAIST OR SKIRT PATTERN. DON'T WAIT TO WRITE FOR SAMPLES. ENCLOSE OUR PRICE.

UNDERSTAND, we give you our guarantee that it will please you, and if for any reason you are not satisfied you can return it at our expense and we will immediately refund your money.

WE ARE ANXIOUS FOR THE FIRST ORDER IN EVERY TOWN on this most extraordinary number, anxious for the good it will do us as an advertisement. We know where one dress pattern of this number goes in a community other orders will soon follow. If you have a dress properly made from this black silk you will have the handsomest black silk costume in your neighborhood, no one will be able to approach it.

REMEMBER FOR 5 CENTS YOU CAN GET A FINE PAPER PATTERN THAT WILL ENABLE YOU TO MAKE UP THE GOODS. SEE PAGE 858.

No. 14R3156 Width, 21 inches. Price, per yard........69c
No. 14R3160 Width, 24 inches. Price, per yard........79c
No. 14R3164 Width, 27 inches. Price, per yard........98c

Sample of this number furnished for 1 cent.

$1.50 Buys the Very Finest 44-Inch All Pure Silk Black Grenadine that we Have in Our Store.

A Grenadine equal to goods which you will be charged a large price for by people in moderately large cities and not obtainable in the smaller stores. In fact, the goods that we have are exclusive with us. They cannot be bought at any price except in a few large importing retail houses in New York and Chicago. We import these goods direct. We own them at the very lowest possible price to produce. We have not put on a fancy price, but have put on a profit the same as on all our fancy and staple dress goods, a price that covers the cost and a very small margin added for profit. These goods come in beaded effects, genuine satin stripes and also jetted cross stripes, also in floral designs and fishnet patterns. This is the kind of silk grenadine that silk houses make their money on by charging you anywhere from $2.00 to $3.00 per yard for, and it is the kind of silk grenadine that goes into the most elegant costumes turned out by most exclusive suit houses. If you order a dress or more of this goods in any of our various designs and they do not prove to be all and even more than we claim for them, if they are not the greatest value that you have ever seen, if they do not equal anything that you have ever seen offered at from $2.50 to $3.00 per yard, return them to us and we will immediately refund your money. Width, 44 inches.

No. 14R3344 Price, per yard........ $1.50
Samples of this number furnished for 1 cent.

OUR 55-CENT BLACK BROCADED GROSGRAIN SILK LEADER.

AT 55 CENTS PER YARD, $2.20 for a 4-yard waist pattern, $5.50 for a 10-yard skirt pattern or $7.70 for a 14-yard suit pattern, this French Grosgrain Brocaded Silk has through the press been offered by us to over thirty million people, and our sales have grown to where today we control the market on this particular brand of heavy weight pure French black brocaded silk. The small illustration, engraved from a photograph, will give you but a faint idea of the handsome pattern effect, of which we have a big variety of new large, medium and small designs. No illustration will give you any idea of the beautiful finish, body, or the real merit in this rich, heavy, all pure silk French fabric.

SEND YOUR ORDER, enclose the price and 1½ cents per yard extra if to be sent by mail postpaid. Don't wait to write for samples for we guarantee satisfaction. We will send the silk to you with the understanding that if it is not perfectly satisfactory, all and more than we claim for it, you can return it to us at our expense and we will return your money.

BY SELLING FOR 55 CENTS PER YARD an imported black French Grosgrain Brocaded Silk, the equal of black brocades that retail in the best city stores at $1.25 to $1.50 a yard, our sales on these goods have been enormous and one order means almost immediate duplicate orders from every friend and neighbor of the buyer. There is nothing more staple; it is a goods that is suitable for all seasons and all ages and as good ten years from today as today. It is a fine, rich, pure black French silk. The floral and geometrical designs are new, rich effects for waists, skirts, capes and suits. The goods are most staple.

AT 55 CENTS PER YARD through us you get these goods direct from France from one of the most noted French makers. You get a value that is puzzling the silk industry of the country.

CONTROLLING THE OUTPUT, no expense for wasted free samples or free catalogues, our prices preclude any kind of comparison. Don't wait for samples. Order under our guarantee to please. Width, 19 inches.

No. 14R3348 Price, per yard........ 55c
Samples of this number furnished for 1 cent.

DEPARTMENT OF BLACK AND COLORED VELVETS AND VELVETEENS.

IN EVERYTHING IN VELVETS AND VELVETEENS we are recognized headquarters. Importing these goods direct from the best known manufacturers abroad, we put our prices on the basis of our one small percentage of profit above the actual cost to import, above the cost to make on the other side, duty and transportation charges added. The result is, you can buy these goods from us in any quantity for as little, if not less, than your storekeeper at home can buy in any quantity.

WE HAVE ENDEAVORED to make our Dress Goods Department in every branch, in every detail, the strongest in the land; and on the basis of more and better value for your money than you can possibly get elsewhere, we earnestly call your attention to our following special values in velvets and velveteens:

Black Velveteens.

18-inch close pile silk finish Velveteen.
No. 14R3350
Price, per yard, 25c

Our Specialty. The Velveteen we recommend, 22 inches wide, a good quality cloth, of good heavy weight. We have bought a large manufacturer's entire output of this quality, and can offer a much superior article than usual at the price. People wishing a high grade velveteen at the usual price of cheap, shoddy goods, should be very particular to order this number. The quantity is large, but we expect a big run on this number, so we would suggest that orders be sent in early. Usual price of this velveteen, 75 cents per yard.

No. 14R3352 Special price, per yard........ 45c

24 inches wide, a perfect copy of a Lyons silk velvet with deep rich shade of black. This superior quality of velveteen is equal in color and rich luster to anything sold in ordinary retail stores at $1.50 to $2.00 per yard. Suited for jackets, waists or entire costumes.

No. 14R3356 Price, per yard........ 75c
Samples of this number furnished for 1 cent, including sample of every shade carried in the number.

Colored Velveteens.

Colored Velveteen, 18 inches wide, comes in brown, navy, cardinal and green only.
No. 14R3358
Price, per yard, 25c

Colored Velveteen, 22 inches wide, comes in brown, navy, cardinal, green, yellow, tan, gray, olive, myrtle, sky blue, royal blue, slate, peacock and gobelin blue, old rose, sapphire blue, purple, cerise, violet, cornflower, pink, lavender, cream and white.

No. 14R3359 Price, per yard........ 45c

Colored Silk Finish Velveteen. One of the best qualities made. It is a perfect copy of a Lyons silk imported velvet. Is suited for ladies' costumes, jackets or waists—also for boys' and misses' suits. We can furnish this in all shades, both light and dark. Width, 24 inches.

No. 14R3360 Price, per yard........ 75c
Samples of this number furnished for 1 cent, including sample of every shade carried in the number.

GIVE CATALOGUE NUMBER IN FULL WHEN YOU WRITE YOUR ORDER

Black Croize Silk Lyons Velvets.

Black Croize Silk Velvets, 18 inches wide. A pure silk face perfect black.
No. 14R3364
Price, per yard. 75c

Black Croize Silk Velvets, our leader, 18 inches wide. Our special quality.
No. 14R3368
Price, per yard. 98c

Black Croize Silk Velvets. A fine finished, close pile velvet, as good as your retailer would sell you for $2.00. Width, 18½ inches.

No. 14R3372 Price, per yard........ $1.25
Sample of this number furnished for 1 cent, including samples of every shade carried in the number.

Colored Croize Silk Velvets.

WE MATCH EVERY SHADE.

A Choice Quality Silk Faced Croize Back Velvet, durable and fine. 18 inches wide, comes in all colors. Dark, medium and evening, also high opera shades.
No. 14R3376
Price, per yard, 65c

French Silk Velvet, with Croize back, a pure silk pile and guaranteed to be sold by us at a saving of 50 to 75 per cent to our customers. We can furnish this grade in over one hundred shades, dark, medium, light opera and evening shades. Suitable for entire costumes, jackets, waists or trimmings. Width, 19 inches.

No. 14R3380 Price, per yard........ 75c
Samples of this number furnished for 1 cent, including sample of every shade carried in the number.

Lyons Colored Croize Silk Velvets.

All Colors. Quality Guaranteed.

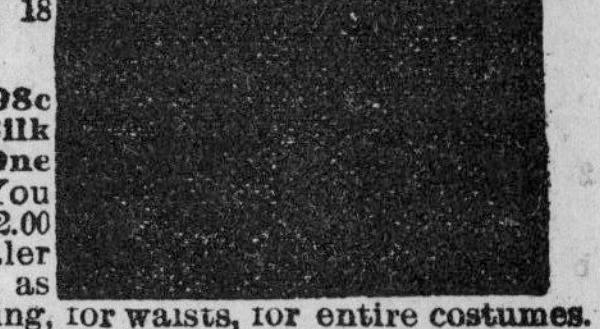

This is our most popular seller; comes in all colors. For trimming, for suits, waists or for millinery purposes. Dark, medium and evening colors, also high opera shades. 18 inches wide.
No. 14R3384
Price, per yard. 98c

Lyons Colored Silk Croize Velvets. One of the finest. You pay as high as $2.00 to your local dealer for velvet not as good. For trimming, for waists, for entire costumes. Comes in every choice color—dark, medium, also evening tints. 19 inches wide.

No. 14R3388 Price, per yard........ $1.25
Samples of this number furnished for 1 cent, including sample of every shade carried in the number.

OUR BIG

PAPER PATTERN SALE

WHAT thousands of our dress goods customers have asked for, now the opportunity is given. On page 858 we quote a complete variety of the best reliable paper patterns at only 5 cents each, the kind that sell everywhere at 15 to 25 cents. When you order dress goods, select a paper pattern and include it in your order. You can then make up the goods yourself as well as an expert dressmaker. We show the latest styles, our patterns are reliable and every lady patronizing this department should not fail to take advantage of.

OUR BIG 5-CENT PAPER PATTERN OFFER

BIG SALE OF PAPER PATTERNS.

WE HAVE RECEIVED SO MANY REQUESTS from our customers who order dress goods, silks and wash goods, for a pattern with which they could make up the goods, we have decided to place paper patterns on sale as an accommodation to the patrons of this department.

WITHOUT ANY IDEA OF PROFIT on the patterns described on this page, we present these paper patterns and would suggest that when you order dress goods you include the pattern desired with your order.

5 CENTS is our price for any one of these patterns. They are such patterns as retail everywhere at 15 to 25 cents each. They are the latest styles for every season. These paper patterns are absolutely correct. They are made by the best maker of paper patterns in this country. They are strictly reliable, the same patterns that are used by the best dressmakers, and we absolutely guarantee the correctness of any paper pattern we furnish. We guarantee if the directions are properly followed that the waist, skirt or dress, whatever the garment, will be a success and will be perfect fitting. Of course we cannot guarantee the accuracy or skill of the one who cuts or makes up the goods.

UNDERSTAND, we quote these paper patterns at the low price of 5 cents each, merely as an accommodation to our customers. There is not a cent of profit in it for us. We do not expect the patterns to be ordered alone, for, as stated in the introductory pages of this catalogue, we do not accept orders for less than 50 cents; but when you are making up an order for dress goods or goods for a waist, skirt or full costume, we recommend that you note these paper patterns carefully and include one with your order.

FULL AND COMPLETE INSTRUCTIONS accompany every paper pattern. All patterns are furnished in sizes, waists, 32 to 42 inches bust measure; skirt patterns in sizes 22 to 34 inches, waist measure. **In ordering, be sure to give size desired and number of pattern.** We can only furnish the patterns in these sizes and only those patterns as described on this page, which are the leading styles.

Ladies' Street Jacket or Coat.

No. 14R5000 This coat is in six sizes, from 32 to 42 inches bust measure, and will require for making in the medium size, 2⅝ yards of 42-inch material or 2¼ yards of 54-inch material.
Price, each............5c

Ladies' Shirt Waist.

No. 14R5004 This shirt waist of severe simplicity is adapted to the various styles of plain, fancy or corded silks, also to several styles of wash silks as illustrated and described in the silk section of our catalogue. It also is suitable to be used for shirt waists made of any of our extensive assortment and styles of goods as illustrated and described in our wash goods department. In our stylish dress goods department will be found many styles in Henriettas, French flannels and many of the popular fancy silks and stylish waistings for which this pattern is adapted. It comes in sizes 32 to 42 inches bust measure. The 36-inch size requires 3½ yards of 27-inch or 1⅞ yards of 42-inch material. Price, each 5c

Ladies' Waist.

No. 14R5008 Closing at the back and having a fitted lining. This comes in six sizes, 32 to 42 inches bust measure. As pictured, the waist is made of cream silk crepon, and the collar, cuffs and girdle are made of stitched velvet. Soft, pliable materials in silk or wool will make up prettily after this pattern and it is also adapted for higher grades of silk mixtures in the numerous designs that may be found in our dress goods and wash goods departments. Size 36 requires 2 yards of 42-inch material, with ½ yard of velvet for trimming.
Price, each............5c

Ladies' Shirt Waist.

No. 14R5012 Sizes 32 to 42 inches bust measure. This is one of the newest models of the ever popular shirt waists. The back is perfectly plain. The tucks at the top of each front terminate at yoke depth and the fullness at the waist is gathered. The edge of the right front finishes with a narrow box plait. A smart stock collar adjusted over a collar band finishes the neck. The sleeves consist of full upper portions, lengthened by bell-shaped cuffs. This handsome pattern for a shirt waist is adapted for all suitable fabrics, such as French flannels, velvet, fancy or plain silks, satin duchesse, also many rich silks which we show. Size 36 of this design will require 3¼ yards of 27-inch material, with ⅜ yard of velvet for trimming. Price, each............5c

Ladies' Shirt Waist Costume.

No. 14R5016 This stylish yet simple gown, as illustrated in this number, is adapted for home or street wear. The smooth fitting waist and fitted collar are adapted to any fancy treatment, such as edged with lace, gimp or any other appropriate material. The vest is attached to the right front and hooks on the left front. At the neck is a close fitting stock, topped with a dainty little flare collar of embroidery. The sailor collar forms a stylish and becoming accessory. The sleeves are cut in one piece and gathered at the wrists into narrow bands. The skirt is five-gored, the fullness at the back being arranged in an underfolded plait. The deep circular flounce gives the desired flare at the foot, where the skirt measures in the round length 3½ yards. This pattern is cut from 32 to 40 inches bust measure. Size 36 requires 11⅛ yards of 27-inch material, ⅜ yard of any selected material for vest and stock. This design is adapted for most of the many beautiful styles of wash silks, corded or printed silks and it is also very nice for flannels, cashmeres and Henriettas and the many goods that are described in our dress goods, silks and fine wash goods departments.
Price, each............5c

Ladies' Yoke Wrapper.

No. 14R5020 To be made with or without bertha. This pattern, as represented, is an ideal home gown. The noticeable feature is the pretty bertha collar, the use of which is optional. The one-piece sleeve is finished with a narrow cuff. All light weight woolen and wash fabrics will lend themselves readily to the mode. Also foulards, various styles of cheviots, fine printed muslins, swisses, etc., as illustrated and described in our dress goods, silk and fine wash goods departments. This pattern comes in six sizes, from 32 to 44 inches bust measure. Size 36 requires 8 yards of 32-inch material, ½ yard of velvet for bertha.
Price, each............5c

Little Girls' Dress.

No. 14R5024 This certainly is a pretty style for a miss of from 6 to 12 years of age. This pretty little frock, as represented, is of cashmere with velvet trimming. Velvet or tucked silk is suitable for trimming. The waist is cut with a fitted lining, upon which the plastron of tucked taffeta is placed. Gathers regulate the fullness at the waist line, which droops ever so little in front. There is a very pretty bertha collar made of any preferred material, such as fancy velvet or silk. The neck is finished with a plain collar band. The one piece skirt is gathered at the back, and attached at the waist. Size 8 requires 1¾ yards of 42-inch material, ⅝ yards of tucked silk and ¾ yards of velvet. Price, each..........5c

Misses' Shirt Waist Costume.

No. 14R5028 This handsome design for a costume for a miss from 12 to 16 years of age is one of the handsomest designs shown this season. This handsome design is adapted for all classes of silk and also the various lines of fine wash goods. The sleeves are fitted with one seam and have strap cuffs. The five-gored skirt is finished with a circular flounce that gives a decided flare at the bottom. (The use of this flounce is optional.) The pattern is cut from 12 to 16 years. Size 14 requires 8¼ yards of 27-inch material, ⅜ of a yard of tucked silk or other trimming for vest and ⅛ yard of satin velvet, or any other selected material for collar.
Price, each.................5c

Ladies' Seven-Gored Flare Skirt.

No. 14R5032 This up to date skirt comes in sizes waist measure 22 to 32 inches. This is a practical design for a skirt cut from material of any width, including cloths, woolens, silks, cheviots and also wash goods. The original model is of black taffeta, simply made, without garniture of any kind. The medium size measures at the bottom or lower edge 4½ yards. The skirt may be trimmed in any preferred way. Size 26 requires 5¾ yards of 42-inch material. There is no doubt but what this would make up one of the handsomest skirts shown for the spring, summer and autumn, 1902. In our many lines of dress goods, silks and fine wash goods as described and illustrated in the various departments, can be found handsome materials for this up to date skirt. Price, each...............5c

Ladies' Five-Gored Flare Skirt.

No. 14R5036 This five-gored skirt is an excellent model for the economical dressmaker. It may be cut from any goods of moderate width. The upper portion fits snugly and each gore is sprung below the knee, forming the fashionable flare which measures 4 yards in the medium size. This handsome pattern is adapted to all kinds of home spun, broadcloths, cheviots, Henriettas, and in the various silks and silk mixtures; also can be used for the various styles of fancy silks and can be trimmed to suit the taste of the wearer; also made without trimming, or decoration of any kind. The original is made of broadcloth without decorations, and hangs gracefully, with a very slight train at the back. Comes in sizes 22 to 32 inches waist measure. Size 26 requires 5¼ yards of 42-inch material. Price, each..................5c

Ladies' Five-Gored Skirts.

No. 14R5040 To be made with one, two or three graduated circular flounces, the back to be laid in an under folded box plait or gathered. This is the very acme of fashion for the season of 1902. This is the latest five-gored skirt, supplemented by three circular flounces, one, two or three of which may be used. Two views of the back of the skirt are given, one with the fullness gathered. This handsome skirt is adapted for materials such as satin brocades, satin duchesse, fancy printed silks, corded silks, various printed summer silks and taffetas. Also in the grenadines, fancy nets, mistrals, English twine cloths, etc., found in our fancy dress goods department and it is also very handsome made of muslins which will be found illustrated and described in our fine wash goods department. See our tempting prices on fine grenadines, which are very stylish made up in this pattern. This pattern comes in sizes 22 to 30 inches waist measure. To make size 24, with three flounces, requires 16¼ yards of 21-inch material, or 8 yards of 42 inch material. This is adapted for trimming of various kinds, as will be found in our silk department and also in our trimming department.
Price, each..............................5c

Domestic Department.

DETERMINED TO UNDERSELL all kinds of competition, determined that our prices shall be lower than any retailer, wholesaler, or other dealer on this most staple line of bleached and unbleached sheetings, carpet warps, waddings, canvas, ducks, drills, tickings, denims, shirtings, cotton battings, and especially on that great staple for the farmer, grain bags, we have made such an offer in this department as will place us in a position not to be reached by any other dealer in this country.

OUR GUARANTEE OFFER. Select any needed goods from this department, send your order to us, and if the goods do not prove all we claim for them; if you are not convinced you are getting such value as you could not get elsewhere, if everyone who sees the goods you purchase does not admit we are below the lowest market of today, you can return the goods to us at our expense and we will return your money.

WE DO NOT SAMPLE DOMESTICS.

REMEMBER, you have the assistance of an expert in this department in filling your order. You will find the goods perfectly satisfactory or we will return your money.

Heav, Unbleached Muslins.

36-inch, unbleached muslin, manufactured specially for us. This is a record-breaking bargain, and our leader.
No. 36R2 36 inches wide. Price, per yard.............4c

Unbleached, Heavy Muslin. A splendid quality, with fine texture, full 36 inches wide.
No. 36R3 Price, per yard, 4¾c

Unbleached, Extra Strong and Heavy Cotton Cloth, full standard muslin of a reliable brand. 36 inches wide.
No. 36R7 Price, per yard, 5¾c

Unbleached, Extra Heavy Muslin. Strong and uniform. Manufactured expressly for us.
No. 36R8 Per yard....6¾c

Muslins, Fine Unbleached.

Unbleached Cotton, the good reliable kind, with a nice soft round thread. This number we specially recommend to housekeepers; it washes easily, and will bleach out nice and white. 36 inches wide.
No. 36R15 Price, per yard.........................5½c

Unbleached Sheeting, special value. Perfect fine weave. Width, 40 inches.
No. 36R16 Price, per yard.........................7c

Unbleached Sheeting. Fine, close woven; will bleach easily. 40 inches wide.
No. 36R17 Price, per yard.........................7½c

Unbleached, Wide Sheetings.

The following list is based on the actual cost of the raw cotton and to manufacture with a very small percentage of profit added. The quality of this line of sheetings is the best that can be produced.

Unbleached Sheeting. Width, 42 inches.
No. 36R24 Price, per yard....8¾c

Unbleached Sheeting. Width, 45 inches.
No. 36R26 Price, per yard....9¾c

Unbleached Sheeting. Width, 54 inches.
No. 36R30 Price, per yard..12¾c

Unbleached Sheeting. Width, 68 inches.
No. 36R34 Price, per yard..14¾c

Unbleached Sheeting. Width, 80 inches.
No. 36R38 Price, per yard.................16¾c

Unbleached Sheeting. Width, 88 inches.
No. 36R42 Price, per yard.................19½c

Unbleached Sheeting. Width, 96 inches.
No. 36R46 Price, per yard.................23½c

Unbleached Wide Sheetings.

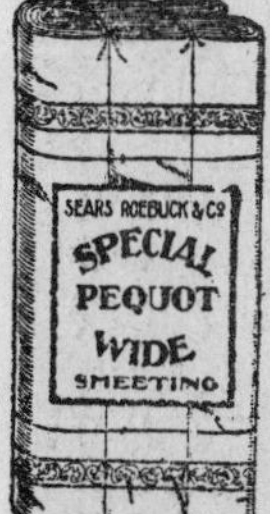

The following list is on one of the very best unbleached sheetings manufactured, and the prices quoted are below the lowest wholesale or jobbing prices.

No. 36R50 **Unbleached Sheeting.** Width, 45 inches. Per yard.....11½c
No. 36R54 **Unbleached Sheeting.** Width, 54 inches. Per yard.....14½c
No. 36R58 **Unbleached Sheeting.** Width, 68 inches. Per yard.....19½c
No. 36R62 **Unbleached Sheeting.** Width, 80 inches. Per yard.....21½c
No. 36R68 **Unbleached Sheeting.** Width, 88 inches. Per yard.....23½c

SEND CASH IN FULL WITH ALL ORDERS.

Bleached Muslin.

Bleached Muslin, special value. 36 inches wide.
No. 36R79 Price, per yard..4¾c

Bleached Muslin, extra quality, will give splendid wear. Width, 36 inches.
No. 36R83 Price, per yard..5¾c

Bleached Muslin, full standard, a splendid wearing cotton and nothing better made for the price. 36 inches wide.
No. 36R87 Price, per yard..6¾c

Bleached Muslin, a nice, soft, even finish, full bleached and will wear like iron. This is a good, reliable quality. 36 inches wide.
No. 36R91 Price, per yard..7½c

The Fern Muslin, fully bleached and is manufactured from fine long staple cotton, counting 196 threads to the inch, and is especially adapted for ladies' and children's fine garments, and warranted perfect in manufacture and finish. 36 inches wide.
No. 36R95 Price, per yard.....................10c

Wide Sheetings, Bleached.

Bleached Sheeting, good quality. Width, 42 inches.
No. 36R105 Price, per yard.........................9¾c
Bleached Sheeting, good quality. Width, 45 inches.
No. 36R109 Price, per yard.........................11¾c
Bleached Sheeting, good quality. Width, 50 inches.
No. 36R114 Price, per yard.........................13¾c
Bleached Sheeting, good quality. Width, 54 inches.
No. 36R119 Price, per yard.........................14¾c
Bleached Sheeting, good quality. Width, 68 inches.
No. 36R124 Price, per yard.........................16¾c
Bleached Sheeting, good quality. Width, 80 inches.
No. 36R129 Price, per yard.........................19½c
Bleached Sheeting, good quality. Width, 88 inches.
No. 36R133 Price, per yard.........................22¾c
Bleached Sheeting, good quality. Width 96 inches.
No. 36R137 Price, per yard.........................24½c

Best Qualities.

Bleached Sheeting, best quality. Width, 42 inches.
No. 36R145 Price, per yard.........................11¾c
Bleached Sheeting, best quality. Width, 45 inches.
No. 36R149 Price, per yard.........................13¾c
Bleached Sheeting, best quality. Width, 50 inches.
No. 36R153 Price, per yard.........................15½c
Bleached Sheeting, best quality. Width, 54 inches.
No. 36R157 Price, per yard.........................17½c
Bleached Sheeting, best quality. Width, 60 inches.
No. 36R161 Price, per yard.........................20¾c
Bleached Sheeting, best quality. Width, 68 inches.
No. 36R165 Price, per yard.........................22¾c
Bleached Sheeting, best quality. Width, 80 inches.
No. 36R169 Price, per yard.........................25½c
Bleached Sheeting, best quality. Width, 88 inches.
No. 36R173 Price, per yard.........................27½c

Half Bleached Muslin and Pillow Case Cottons.

36 Inches Wide, Soft, Even Finish, Half Bleached Fine Muslin.
No. 36R177 Price, per yard.........................7½c

45-Inch Half Bleached Pillow Case Cotton. A perfect cotton.
No. 36R181 Price, per yard.........................11c

50-Inch Half Bleached Pillow Case Cotton. Our special make.
No. 36R185 Price, per yard.........................12c

Wide Sheetings, Half Bleached.

Half Bleached Sheeting, same quality as bleached. A good, substantial and well made cotton. Width, 68 inches.
No. 36R189 Price, per yard.........................17c

Half Bleached Sheeting, same quality as bleached. A good, substantial and well made cotton. Width, 80 inches.
No. 36R193 Price, per yard.........................19c

Half Bleached Sheeting. A good, substantial and well made cotton. Width, 88 inches.
No. 36R197 Price, per yard.........................21½c

Twilled Bleached Sheeting.

Twilled Cotton Bleached, especially adapted for nightgowns; a nice, soft, even texture, and well made in every respect. 36 inches wide.
No. 36R205 Price, per yard.........................10½c

Twilled Bleached Sheeting, fully bleached, nothing better manufactured for wear. Width, 81 inches.
No. 36R209 Price, per yard.........................23½c

Twilled Bleached Sheeting, same quality as above. Width, 90 inches.
No. 36R213 Price, per yard.........................27½c

Sign Painters' Muslin.

This muslin is in great demand by painters, sign writers, etc. It has a stiff finish, comes pure white, 36 inches wide, is of standard quality, and our price is the lowest price at which this material was ever offered. It is a price paid for hundreds of cases by jobbers and large handlers of cotton goods. It is a brand made for us only, from the fact that we have it made in one of our mills which we control the output of, and we give it to our customers at the exact cost of production with a very small profit added. Width, 36 inches.
No. 36R215 Price, per yard.........................5¼c

36-Inch Extra Fine White Cambric Muslins.

White Sweet Violets Superior Cambric. Splendid value for the money. 36 inches wide.
No. 36R217 Price, per yard.........................8c

Berkley White Cambric, good standard quality. 36 inches wide.
No. 36R222 Price, per yard.........................10c

Jones' White Cambric, the old reliable. 36 inches wide.
No. 36R226 Price, per yard.........................14c

GIVE CATALOGUE NUMBER IN FULL WHEN YOU WRITE YOUR ORDER

Cheese, Butter and Dairy Cloth.

Unbleached Cheese Cloth. 36 inches wide.
No. 36R237 Price, per yard. 2½c

Unbleached Cheese Cloth. 36 inches wide.
No. 36R241 Price, per yard..3½c

Bleached Butter Cloth. 36 inches wide.
No. 36R245 Price, per yard..3½c

Colored Cheese Cloth. 25 inches wide. Comes in yellow, orange, cardinal, violet, navy, rose, lavender, nile green, pink, pale blue and white.
No. 36R249 Price, per yard..4c

Colored Cheese Cloth. 36 inches wide. Comes in yellow, violet, cardinal, orange, lavender, pink, pale blue, nile and white.
No. 36R253 Price, per yard..6c

Sea Island Cotton Batiste.

A beautiful, sheer material 36 inches wide used largely for draperies and quiltings, also used for ladies' and misses' suitings. It has the appearance of a fine nun's veiling. It comes in white, cream, light blue, pink, heliotrope, yellow, lavender and also black. This is a very fine, soft finished sea island cotton material, and is a marvel of cheapness.
No. 36R255 Width, 36 inches. Price, per yard, 7½c

DEPARTMENT OF READY MADE SHEETS AND PILLOW CASES.

We manufacture our own sheets and pillow cases and therefore are enabled to sell the ready made goods at a price impossible by any other house; the cost of the material and the small cost of making on account of the tremendous quantities that we dispose of, and to this add our one small margin of profit. **We offer our special brands, "Leader," "Champion" and "Superior," as the best values ever offered in sheets and pillow cases.** We control large mills which manufacture almost entirely for us the different grades of manufactured cotton goods, and one of our largest mills is continually weaving and turning out for us the various grades of narrow and wide sheetings, both bleached and unbleached. The goods selected for these our special brands of sheets are the very best that we can have turned out. We guarantee them perfect in every respect and the biggest values ever offered.

Ready Hemmed "Leader" Special Bleached Sheets.

No. 36R256 Price, each
Size, 63x90 inches.........................42c
Size, 72x90 inches.........................47c
Size, 81x90 inches.........................51c
Size, 90x90 inches.........................57c

Ready Made Extra Fine and Heavy Hemmed Bleached "Champion" Sheets.

No. 36R257 Price, each
Size, 63x90 inches.........................52c
Size, 72x90 inches.........................57c
Size, 81x90 inches.........................62c
Size, 90x90 inches.........................73c

Ready Made Bleached Hemmed "Superior" Sheets.

These sheets are made of extra heavy bleached muslin, and are uniform and perfect in weave.

Size, inches	63x90	72x90	81x90	90x90
No. 36R258 Price, each	56c	62c	65c	76c

Ready Made Hemmed Unbleached Sheets.

In unbleached sheets we have but one extraordinary, special number, our "Leader," same muslin as No. 36R256, only not bleached.

Size, inches	63x90	72x90	81x90	90x90
No. 36R261 Price, each	36½c	44c	49c	52c

Ready Made Pillow Cases.

Ready Made Pillow Cases, made in three strong numbers, quality the same grade as "Leader," "Champion" and "Superior" sheets. We do not sell pillow cases unbleached. All of our pillow cases are thoroughly grass bleached and strictly reliable for weave, finish and wear.

"Leader" Bleached Pillow Cases.
No. 36R262 Size, 20¼x34 inches. Price, each.........................12c
No. 36R263 Size, 22x34 inches. Price, each.........................13c
No. 36R265 **"Champion" Bleached Pillow Cases.** Size, 20¼x34 inches. Price, each.........................14c
No. 36R266 Size, 22x34 inches. Price, each.........................16c
No. 36R267 **"Superior" Bleached Pillow Cases.** Size, 20¼x34 inches. Price, each.........................16c
No. 36R268 Size, 22x34 inches. Price, each...17c

Extra Quality Hemstitched Bleached Sheets and Pillow Cases.

These sheets have a double hemstitch, and are of a very fine and heavy texture.

No. 36R269 Bleached Hemstitched Sheets. Size, 81x90 inches. Price, each.........63c

No. 36R270 Bleached Hemstitched Pillow Cases. Size, 22x34 inches. Price, each....21c

No. 36R277 Unbleached Drilling, used for boat sails, pockets, etc.; extra heavy. Width, 29 inches.
Price, per yard...........6c

No. 36R281 Unbleached Drilling. Width, 29 inches. Weight, about 7 ounces to the yard. Price, per yard.........8c

Bed Ticking.

These goods are made in blue and white in various width stripes.

Bed Ticking. 30 inches wide.
No. 36R285 Per yard.....5½c

Bed Ticking. 31 inches wide.
No. 36R289 Per yard.....8½c

Bed Ticking. 32 inches wide.
No. 36R293 Per yard.....12c

Bed Ticking, extra fine quality, with a firm close weave. Width, 32 inches.
No. 36R297 Per yard.....14c

Bed Ticking. 36 inches wide.
No. 36R301 Per yard.....17c

Bed Ticking. Extra heavy sateen finish S. R. & Co.'s special. Width, 60 inches.
No. 36R305 Per yard....29c

German Turkey Red Linen Ticking. Warranted to hold feathers and will hold its color. It is oil boiled turkey red, sateen finished, medium weight. Width, 33 inches.
No. 36R309 Price, per yard...................21c

Blue Denims.

Blue Denim, strong and durable, **fast colors.** 28 inches wide.
No. 36R313 Price, per yard.....................9½c

Blue Denim, extra heavy, one of the best qualities made. Width, 28 inches.
No. 36R316 Price, per yard.....................11c

Blue Denim, extra heavy twill and **will wear like iron.** Width, 28 inches.
No. 36R320 Price, per yard.....................12½c

Brown Denims.

Brown Denim, good quality and close weave. Width, 28 inches.
No. 36R324 Price, per yard.....................9½c

Brown Denim, good, strong, reliable grade, good weight. Width, 28 inches.
No. 36R328 Price, per yard.....................11c

Brown Denim, extra quality, strong and heavy. Width, 28 inches.
No. 36R332 Price, per yard.....................12½c

Awning Ticking.

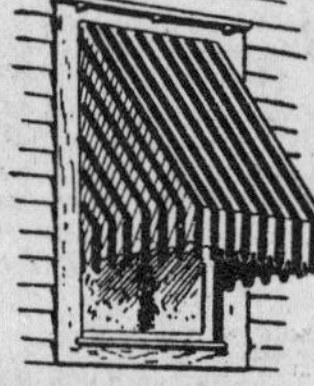

Awning Ticking, twilled and satin finished, comes in **drab and red and drab and blue, wide stripes,** fast colors. Width, 32 inches.
No. 36R336 Price, per yard...........12c

Awning Ticking, same width and colors as above but much **heavier and better quality.**
No. 36R340 Price, per yard...........15c

Ivanhoe Cheviot Shirting.

Ivanhoe Cheviot Shirting. A strong, serviceable shirting, specially adapted for men's shirts, children's dresses, aprons, etc., strictly fast colors, comes in a variety of checks and plaids, also stripes, blues, brown, reds, greens, also combinations of black. Width, 26 inches.
No. 36R345 Price, per yard.....................6c

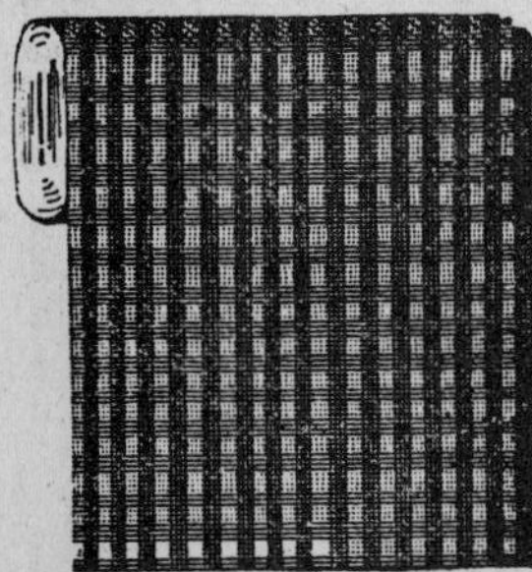

Cheviot Shirting, strong and heavy, comes in stripes and checks of **blue and white and blue and red, fast colors.** Width, 29 inches.
No. 36R349 Price, per yard...7c

Cheviot Shirting, medium weight; comes in a pretty **assortment of stripes and checks;** a good reliable cloth, strictly fast colors. Width, 29 inches.
No. 36R353 Price, per yard.....................9c

Fine Cheviots for Fancy Shirts, Madras and other weaves. Comes in a pretty assortment of styles, both light and dark. **The proper thing for summer wear;** fast colors. Comes in pretty checks and stripes. Width, 31 inches.
No. 36R357 Price, per yard.....................12c

Bull Hide Shirting.

Bull Hide Shirting, strong and heavy and will wear like iron. Black and white stripe or figured. Width, 29 inches.
No. 36R361 Price, per yard...........9c

Bull Hide Shirting, same as above, but comes in blue and white striped or figured.
Width, 29 inches.
No. 36R365 Price, per yard.....................10c

Fleeceback Shirting.

Fleeceback Shirting, splendid wearing goods, the proper thing for everyday use, strong and serviceable, comes in neat dark colorings. Is sure to please. Width, 29 inches.
No. 36R369 Price, per yard.....................11c

Mosquito Netting.

Mosquito Netting, sold by the piece only. Colors, pink, yellow, emerald green, blue, red, white and black. Width, 58 inches.
No. 36R374 Full piece of about 8 yards for....38c

Cotton Wadding.

Cotton Wadding, slate color only, good cotton, nicely glazed. Size, about 32x36 inches.
No. 36R378 Price, per sheet.....................2c

Cotton Wadding, white, nicely finished, clean and white. Size, about 30x36 inches.
No. 36R379 Price, per sheet.....................2½c

Tinted Wadding.
For Fancy Work.

Fancy French Tinted Wadding, in sheets. Colors, light blue, pink, nile, yellow. Size, about 28x36 inches.
No. 36R385 Price, per sheet.....................3c

Wool Sheet Wadding. Sheets of fine Australian wool. Size, 18x36 inches. Brown or white. Makes a light and soft filling for comforters; does not become lumpy; has the feeling of a down filling.
No. 36R386 Price, per sheet.....................17c

Cotton Batting.

Almost all dealers have their batts put up today with but 12 ounces, or three-fourths of a pound to the roll, which makes comparisons of prices by the roll obviously unfair, unless weight is taken into consideration.

All our rolls of Cotton Batting weigh 16 ounces—1 pound each, except the first number which weighs full 14 ounces. Our batts are patent folded, and are not simply a wad of cotton to be repicked and put into the quilt in bunches; each batt is nicely papered, is folded, and will open up all the same thickness. 36 inches wide and 7 feet long. Cotton batting is put up 50 pounds to the bale.

Cotton Batting, fair quality.
No. 36R400 Price, per roll, 14 oz. to a roll, each...8c

Cotton Batting, good quality, nice and clean and good value for the money.
No. 36R401 Price, per roll, each...........10c

Cotton Batting, nice clean fine rolls, 16 ounces.
No. 36R402 Price, each.....................12½c

Cotton Batting, one of the finest qualities made, pure white and clean.
No. 36R403 Price, per roll...........15c

Snow White Antiseptic Cotton Batting, 16-ounce rolls, used for medical purposes.
No. 36R404 Price, per roll...........17c

Carpet Warp.

Our warp is carefully made of the best cotton, hard and evenly twisted, of uniform size and long reel; 4-ply No. 8¼ yarn, 90-in. reel; five pounds will make 25 yards of yard wide carpet. We do not sell less than five pounds of white or any one color. **White Warp** (sold in five-pound bundles only) net weight.
No. 36R412 Price, per pound...........16½c

Colored Cotton Warp (sold in five pound-bundles only) net weight.
No. 36R416 Price, per pound...........18½c

Colored Carpet Warp comes in brown, orange, red, green, black, medium blue, yellow and slate; one color in each bundle.

Carpet Warp on Spools.

These Spools are ready for the Warper. They save the weaver tedious hand winding. Put up in 5-pound boxes. 10¼-pound spools. Exclusive selling agents in Chicago.
No. 36R420 Price, colored, per pound.......20c
No. 36R425 Price, white...........17½c

Grain Bags.

We especially recommend our Sears, Roebuck & Co. special 16-ounce, two-bushel bag. It is equally as good as bags that are on the market at 20 and 25 cents. This bag is especially made for us in immense lots, and to advertise our cotton goods department we add but a very small percentage of profit to the actual cost.
No. 36R426 Price, each..15c
No. 36R429 Stark A Bags. Price, each...........16½c
No. 36R430 American A Bags. Price, each.......14½c

White Duck or Canvas.

No. 36R441 Extra Heavy Duck, used for tents, awnings, stack covers, harvester aprons, etc.

Width	Weight per Square Yard about 20 oz. Price per yard	Weight per Square Yard about 18 oz. Price per yard	Weight per Square Yard about 15 oz. Price per yard	Weight per Square Yard about 13 oz. Price per yard
28 inch.	$0.26	$0.25	$0.20	$0.19
30 inch.	.28	.26	.22	.20
34 inch.	.31	.29	.25	.23
36 inch.	.34	.30	.26	.25
38 inch.	.36	.32	.28	.26
40 inch.	.38	.34	.30	.27
44 inch.	.42	.38	.33	.30
48 inch.	.45	.41	.35	.32
52 inch.	.48	.44	.38	.35
56 inch.	.53	.48	.40	.38
60 inch.	.56	.51	.44	.41
66 inch.	.63	.55	.48	.45
72 inch.	.68	.61	.51	.48
84 inch.	.81	.75	.64	.65
96 inch.	1.06	.95	.81	.75
120 inch	1.36	1.21	1.02	.94

White Duck or Canvas, 8 oz. weight; width, 29 ins.
No. 36R444 Price, per yard.....................9½c

White Duck or Canvas, 10 oz. weight, 30 inches wide.
No. 36R448 Price, per yard.....................12½c

THE NATIONAL FLAG.
Made of All Wool Bunting.

	L'gth ft.	Each		L'gth ft.	Each
No. 36R452	5	$1.25	No. 36R457	12	$4.50
No. 36R453	6	1.50	No. 36R458	14	5.50
No. 36R454	7	2.00	No. 36R459	16	7.00
No. 36R455	8	2.35	No. 36R460	18	8.50
No. 36R456	10	3.50	No. 36R461	20	9.75

We cannot guarantee prices on flags, as they are subject to change. We will give market value the day the order is received.

National Decorating Bunting.

No. 36R465 Print Cloth, similar to bunting, printed in red, white and blue stripes, with stars. 21 inches wide.
Price, per yard.....................4½c

No. 36R466 Tri-Color Bunting. Width, 25 inches. Striped with wide bands of red, white and blue plain, no stars.
Price, per yard.....................4¾c

No. 36R467 27-inch Serpentine Crinkled French Cotton Crape; a stylish suiting suitable for ball dresses, stage and evening wear; comes in all opera shades such as pink, cardinal, nile, yellow, violet, cerise, blue, lavender, etc. Very rich for decorative purposes. Price, per yard.....................12½c

No. 36R468 Muslin Flags, mounted on sticks.

Muslin Flags.

Size....2 x3 inches.	Price, per gross........	$0.17
Size....2½x4 inches.	Price, per gross........	.22
Size....4 x6 inches.	Price, per gross........	.35
Size....4½x7 inches.	Price, per gross........	.48
Size....6 x9½ inches.	Price, per gross........	.88
Size....8 x14 inches.	Price, per gross........	1.70

Table Oilcloths.

No. 36R472 No. 36R476

Best Quality Table Oilcloths. Marble oil cloth. 45 inches wide.
No. 36R472 Price, per yard.....................16c

Best Quality Table Oilcloth. Oak and fancy patterns. 45 inches wide.
No. 36R476 Price, per yard.....................15c

Shelf Oilcloth, white or fancy wood patterns. 12 ins. wide. Scalloped edges, printed with pretty lace effects.
No. 36R478 Price, per piece of twelve yards...60c

Black Pebbled Enameled Oilcloth. Width, 45 ins.
No. 36R480 Price, per yard.....................22c

Black Enameled Oilcloth. Width, 43 inches.
No. 36R482 Price, per yard.....................27c

Linen Goods Department

WE ARE MAKING THIS ONE OF THE STRONGEST DEPARTMENTS IN OUR HOUSE.

We have secured the services of one of the best linen goods men in the country—a man whose education in the linen goods business started with his work in the mills in Scotland and Ireland and who has been identified with the linen goods business as manufacturer, jobber and handler generally for the last twenty years. In acquiring the services of this man we have made buying connections with the best makers of linen in Ireland, Scotland and Germany, as well as this country.

WE HAVE MADE SOME OF THE LARGEST CONTRACTS for this season that have ever been placed with foreign or domestic mills. We have made these contracts in order to get the very lowest possible price, and to insure our being at all times able to fill orders promptly and exactly in accordance with our illustrations and descriptions, and always at the very lowest market price; **always for as little, if not less, money than your storekeeper can buy in any quantity.**

ON TOWELING OF ALL KINDS we are absolutely headquarters. We own these goods at but a shade above the cost of manufacture, and we are making an effort to establish the largest trade of foreign and domestic toweling in this country, and to do this we have narrowed down our margin to but a shade above the actual cost of handling. If you are in need of any toweling in any of the different grades, foreign or domestic goods, and will make your selection from this year's catalogue, you will get such value as never before went out of this or any other house. In ordering merchandise do not overlook this department. **Be sure to include the needed toweling or other linens and you will be surprised at the money we will save you.**

IN TABLE CLOTHS our purchases have been exceedingly large, and on our foreign and domestic table linen, covers, napkins, table sets, etc., we are offering astonishing values. We have greatly increased our line to include all the very latest productions for this season; all the new fancy and staple things, and our prices are made to practically compel the orders to come our way. **If you buy anything in table linen, you will be sure to pay from 25 to 50 per cent more in price.** Not satisfied with the business we have done heretofore in this department of linen goods, we have taken it up for this season on a most extensive scale. We have compared the values we are now offering with those offered by other houses, and we know they are below the lowest. **We know we are giving better value for your money than can be offered by any other house.**

UNDERSTAND, everything from our Linen Goods Department goes out under our binding guarantee. If you order anything that is not perfectly satisfactory in every way, if you have any reason to be dissatisfied, you can return the goods to us at our expense, and we will immediately return your money.

Our 15-Cent Turkey Red Damask.

Turkey Red Table Damask, fast colors, pretty patterns. Width, 52 inches.

No. 36R494 Price, per yard.......15c

Our Finest Turkey Red Damask at 39 Cents a Yard.

For an exceptional value in Turkey red, we recommend our 39-cent goods. The colors are oil boiled and strictly fast, and the beautiful satin finish stamps the damask as the best. We furnish this Turkey red in handsome floral and dice patterns, two of the designs being shown in the illustrations. You have your choice of pattern. **Be sure to state which you want when you order.** Full 58 inches wide.

No. 36R510 Our special price, per yard.... ....39c

Our 21-Cent Turkey Red Table Damask.

At 21 cents a yard we are offering this damask, which is a real oil boiled Turkey red, a quality that is well recognized by all progressive dealers, who aim to keep the best. The colors are strictly fast, and the value we give in these goods is exceptional. Such Turkey red will seldom be bought elsewhere at less than 30 cents a yard, and as much as 35 cents is often asked. It is full 58 inches wide. We show in the illustrations both the **floral and dice patterns. In ordering, be sure to state which pattern is wanted.** You have your choice.

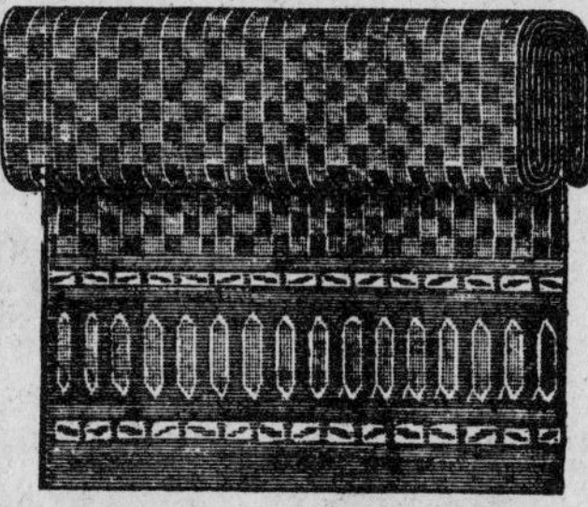

No. 36R498 Our special price, per yard..... ....21c

62-Inch Bleached All Linen Table Damask at 49 Cents.

This is one of our leading numbers in table damask, and is one of the best values we are offering in this department. The ordinary storekeeper would charge you from 65 to 75 cents per yard, and the city stores consider it a leader at from 55 to 65 cents. Full 62 inches wide; warranted all pure linen. Grand variety of choice patterns.

No. 36R522 Price, per yard.....................49c

Our 29-Cent Turkey Red Damask.

Extra Fine Quality Turkey Red Damask, fine satin finish, very close weave, comes in pretty floral and dice designs; the colors are strictly fast. This is one of the best qualities made. Width, 58 inches.

No. 36R502 Price, per yard.....................29c

Bleached Table Damask, 26 Cents.

Bleached Union Table Damask, in a great variety of handsome designs. An exceptional value. Width, 58 inches.

No. 36R514 Price, per yard.......26c

Our 69-Cent Table Damask.

Bleached Table Damask. Guaranteed purest of linen, of exceptional quality, beautiful satin finish with neat floral designs and borders to match. Width, 70 inches.

No. 36R526 Price, per yard......69c

Rare Value in Colored Table Damask at 35 Cents Per Yard.

Very Fine Quality Table Damask, green and red combination. **Colors guaranteed fast.** Comes in rich floral and dice patterns. Width, 58 inches.

No. 36R506 Price, per yard......35c

Our 43-Cent Bleached Linen Table Damask.

Bleached Linen Table Damask, strong and durable; splendid value for the money. Comes in assorted pretty designs. Width, 58 inches.

No. 36R518 Price, per yard...... 43c

Satin Finished Pure Linen Damask at 79c

Imported Satin Finished Pure Linen Bleached Table Damask. This is an excellent quality and cannot be surpassed for the price; it comes in beautiful raised patterns and must be seen to be appreciated. Width, 70 inches.

No. 36R530 Price, per yard.....................79c

Our $2.50 napkins, size 24x24 inches, match the above number of damask.

Our Handsome $6.48 Table Set.

$6.48 is our low price for this Pure Linen Table Set, one of the best values ever offered.

White Hemstitched Table Set. Pure white, strictly high grade set and pure linen. Nothing more appropriate as a present than one of these beautiful Table Sets. Size, 66x102 inches, and one dozen napkins, size, 19x19 inches, to match.
No. 36R644 Price, per set............$6.48

NAPKINS.

We do not sell less than ½ dozen napkins, but the price for ½-dozen lots is at dozen rates.

Bleached Union Damask Napkins, not the poor kind, but a good, heavy napkin for the price. Size, 14½ x 14½ inches.
No. 36R648 Price, per dozen............59c

Bleached Linen Napkins.

Superior Quality Bleached Linen Napkins. Handsome floral patterns in new designs. Extra quality. Especially good wearing. Size, 17x17 inches.
No. 36R652 Price, per dozen............75c

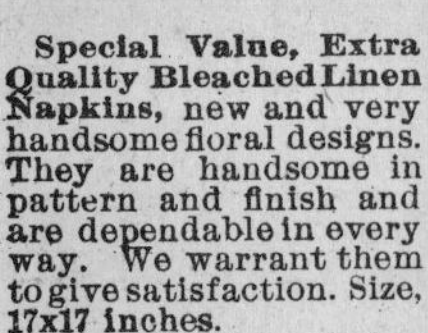

Special Value, Extra Quality Bleached Linen Napkins, new and very handsome floral designs. They are handsome in pattern and finish and are dependable in every way. We warrant them to give satisfaction. Size, 17x17 inches.
No. 36R656 Price, per dozen............98c

Silver Bleached Imported Napkins.

Extra Fine Silver Bleached All Linen Imported Napkins, with charming floral designs, good heavy weight, close woven and extra fine finish. Size, 19½x19½ inches.
No. 36R660 Price, per dozen..........$1.25

Best Irish Linen Napkins.

This is one of our leading numbers. It is good generous size, and is made of the very best Irish linen, has a very fine finish. Comes in beautiful floral and geometrical designs with handsome border. Size, 20x20 inches.
No. 36R664 Price, per dozen..............$1.50

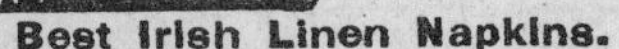

Bleached Pure White Damask.

For $2.00 per dozen we offer this napkin as the equal of those in regular dry goods stores at 40 per cent higher prices.

Excellent Quality Pure Bleached Linen Napkins, pretty floral designs, German manufacture. This napkin is good enough for a palace. Size, 22x22 inches.
No. 36R668 Price, per dozen............$2.00

Real German Bleached Satin Finished Napkins, heavy weight and closely woven. All pure linen and thoroughly dependable; handsome floral patterns, one of our specially clever values. Will match our No. 36R530 Table Linen. Size, 22x22 inches.
No. 36R672 Price, per dozen..............$2.50

Our Fine $3.00 Satin Finish Napkins.

Extra High Grade Imported Satin Finish Linen Napkins. Elegant quality and will wear for years. Size, 24x24 inches.
No. 36R676 Price, per dozen...............$3.00

Very Finest Grade of Imported German Linen Napkins. Nothing finer made. Silver bleached. This napkin will last for years. Comes in pretty floral designs. Size, 24x24 inches.
No. 36R680 Price, per dozen..............$3.88
The above napkin will match our $1.19 Table Damask.

Fringed Napkins.

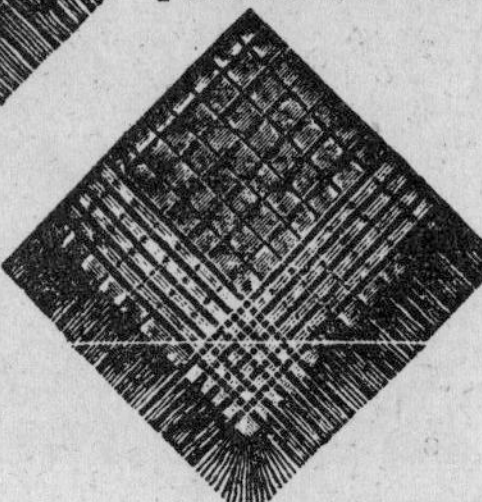

Fringed Bleached Napkins, all linen. Pink and blue checked patterns. Size, 12x12 inches.
No. 36R684 Price, per dozen.. ......30c

Fringed Bleached Napkins, all linen. Red or blue checked patterns. Size, 15x15.
No. 36R690 Price, per dozen.........39c
If by mail, postage extra, 9 cents.

Fringed Bleached Napkins, all linen. Very fine quality, with a fine satin finish, plain centers with colored borders. Size, 16x16 inches.
No. 36R694 Price, per dozen.........75c

Extra Fine Quality Fringed Bleached Napkins, all linen. Fine select stock. Be sure and order some of these, as they are extra good value. Comes in plain white only. Size, 16x16 in.
No. 36R698 Price, per dozen.........79c

Doylies.

Pure White Fringed Damask Doylies, 7-inch, round. These are an exceptional value and we sell millions of them every season. Size, 7 inches in diameter.
No. 36R702 Price, per dozen..............39c

Pure White Fringed Round Doylies. Pure linen. Size, 9 inches.
No. 36R706 Price, each......7c

Pure White Fringed Round Damask Doylies. This is a special good value. Size, 12 inches.
No. 36R710 Price, each..............10c

Fringed White Oval All Pure Linen 9x12-inch Doylies.
No. 36R714 Price, each..............8c

Pure White Linen Doylies.

Fringed White All Pure Scotch Linen Oval Damask Doylies. Size, 12x15 inches.
No. 36R718 Our special price, each..............10c

Pure White Fringed All Pure Linen Oval Doylies. Come in a very pretty variety of designs. Size, 14x18 inches.
No. 36R722 Price, each..............15c

Pure White Linen Scotch Damask Oval Doylies. This is one of our best bargains in our linen department. Size, 16x20 inches.
No. 36R726 Price, each..............18c

Pure White Tied Fringed 16x16-inch Damask Doylies. Come in a variety of pretty designs.
No. 36R730 Price, each..............12½c

Pure White All Linen Open Work Tied Fringed Doylies. Size, 16x16 inches.
No. 36R732 Price, each..............17c

Tray Cloths.

Pure White Damask Hemstitched Tray Cloths. Size, 18x27 inches. Come in special designs.
No. 36R734 Each, 29c

Hemstitched Pure White All Linen Tray Cloths. Size, 20x30 inches.
No. 36R736 Our special price, each......39c

Table Scarfs.

Fringed, Colored Center, White Border Table Scarfs. These are strictly all pure linen and make a very pretty sideboard or table scarf. Size, 16x50 inches. These come in pink, red, blue and salmon centers with very pretty white border.
No. 36R738 Price, each..............18c

Fringed with Colored Center, All Linen Table Scarfs. Size, 16x70 inches. Come in very handsome designs; pink, red, blue and salmon centers with handsome white border.
No. 36R740 Price, each..............22c

Pure White Linen Damask Table Scarfs.

All Pure Linen Pure White Hemstitched Damask Table Scarfs. These are the most beautiful table scarfs shown in any linen department. They are our own special designs and we guarantee that the price which we quote is at least 25 per cent less than you could buy from your home dealer. Come in very pretty designs.
No. 36R742 Size, 18x45 inches, 69c; size, 18x54 inches, 79c; size, 18x72 inches..............93c

All Pure Linen White Hemstitched Damask Table Scarfs with pretty open work in special designs. These are a very fine quality of Richardson's best Irish linen. We have our own special designs in these beautiful open work hemstitched damask scarfs.
No. 36R744 Size, 18x54 inches. Price..............$1.29
Size, 18x72 inches..............1.69

Pure White Hemstitched Table Squares.

These are special designs manufactured expressly for us by one of the best Dundee, Scotland, linen manufacturers.
No. 36R748 **Pure White Damask Hemstitched Table Squares.** Price, each, 15-inch, 20c; 18-inch, 30c; 24-inch, 45c; 32-inch, 59c; 36-inch, $1.25; 45-inch, $1.69; 54-inch..............$2.25

Bleached Turkish Embroidered Scarfs.

These Beautiful Veney Scarfs make a pretty and serviceable decoration for chairs, stands, bureaus and couches. They are made of looped thread, like Turkish towels. They come in tinted ground, such as pink, blue, nile and yellow, and also white, with pretty contrasting printings in floral effects. They are very serviceable, and will wash. Size, 18x60 inches, including fringe.
No. 36R749 Price.........19c

Same as above. Size, 14x32 inches.
No. 36R751 Price..............15c

Bleached Turkish Terry Cloth or Toweling, 18-inch, used extensively for hand towels, roller towels, bath robes, bath mittens, bureau cloths, children's mittens, also for stand and bureau covers. Width, 18 inches.
No. 36R754 Price, per yard..............12½c

Bleached Terry Cloth, 20 inches wide, extra heavy.
No. 36R756 Price, per yard..............20c

Loom Damask Towels.

Loom Damask Fringed Half Bleached Linen Towels. Nothing like them ever sold for the money. A world beater. Size, 14x27 in.
No. 36R908 Price, per dozen 65c
Shipping weight, 18 ounces.

All Linen Half Bleached Damask Fringed Towels, with fancy center and colored border. These towels are exceptionally strong and serviceable. Size, 14½x32 inches.
No. 36R910 Each, 9c
Weight, per doz., 28 ozs.

Loom Damask Fringed Towel. Comes in beautiful assortment of center patterns and colored borders. **Extra heavy quality.** Size, 18x36 inches.
No. 36R914 Each, 12c
Shipping weight, per doz., 36 ounces.

Our 15-Cent Bleached All Linen Damask Towels.

Good Quality Bleached All Linen Damask Towels. Fancy border with open work on each end. **Long knotted fringe.** Very handsome figured centers in new designs. Size, 17x37 inches.
No. 36R918 Each......15c
Postage extra, each, 4 cents.

Bleached Fringed Damask Towels.

Extra Large Bleached Fringed German Damask Towel, with beautiful fancy center and colored border. Size, 19½x44 inches.
No. 36R922 Price, each........................21c

Bleached Satin Damask Towels.

Bleached Satin Damask Towels. All linen with heavy knotted fringe and hand tied open work at each end. **Beautiful floral figured center and handsome colored borders.** Size, 20x42 inches.
No. 36R926 Price....25c

Very Fine Quality Satin Damask Linen Towels.

Very Fine Quality Bleached Satin Damask All Linen Towels. Very heavy knotted fringe. Comes in plain white only. Size, 20½x43½ inches.
No. 36R930
Price, each. 25c

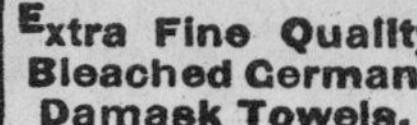

Extra Fine Quality Bleached German Damask Towels.

Heavy knotted fringe; has a beautiful satin finish, all pure linen. They are very large and can be used as commode or bureau covers, or chair scarfs; you cannot afford to be without some of these, as they are worth a great deal more than the price we charge for them. Come in assorted colored borders and also plain white. **Note the size, 22x46 inches.**
No. 36R934 Each..27c

Fine Quality Satin Damask Towels.

Made of Pure German Linen. Beautiful Quality Satin Damask Towel, all pure white, and made of pure German linen. It comes in pretty pattern as per cut, has an extra heavy knotted fringe, and must be seen to be appreciated. Size, 22x47½ inches.
No. 36R944 Price, each.............. ....37c

Our Highest Grade Satin Damask Towels.

Extra Superfine Quality Bleached Satin Damask Towels, purest double warp linen. Comes in plain white only; no colored borders. It has a perfectly plain center, with a beautiful floral border between two rows of high grade open work; it also has an elegant hemstitch; can also be used as a bureau or chair scarf. This is positively one the best qualities made, and will last for years. Size, 22½x53 inches.
No. 36R952 Price, each.....................72c

Linen Satin Damask Towels.

Extra Fine All Linen Satin Damask Towels, with two rows of open work on each end, **beautiful pearl pattern center,** all white, and heavy, knotted fringe. Excellent value. Size, 22x41 inches.
No. 36R940 Price, each.....................42c

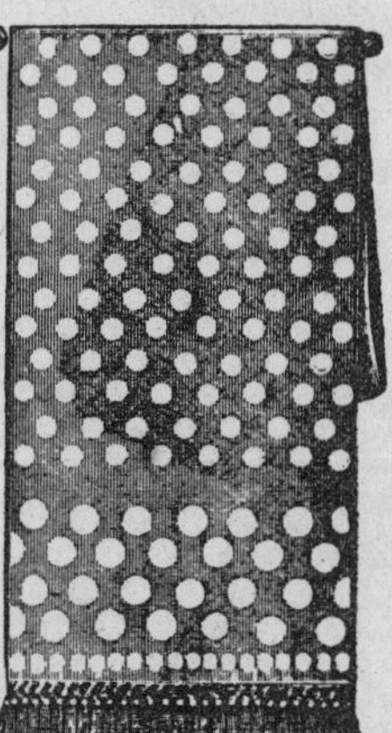

Double Warp Satin Damask Towels.

Extra High Grade Satin Damask Double Warp, Pure Linen German Towels, come in white only. This is a beautiful towel, and is one of the best qualities manufactured; it has long knotted fringe and will last for years. Comes in floral and geometrical designs. Size, 22x48½ inches.
No. 36R948 Price, each 49c
If by mail, postage extra, each, 5 cents.

TURKISH TOWELS.

Our 5 and 8-Cent Turkish Towels.

Genuine Turkish Towels, cream color; good heavy weight and specially good value. Size, 16x30 inches.
No. 36R954 Price, each.............................5c
Shipping weight, 30 ounces per dozen.

Genuine Turkish Towels; cream or unbleached; extra heavy weight. Size, 19x42 inches. Specially good value.
No. 36R956 Price, each..............................8c
Shipping weight, 3 pounds per dozen.

No. 36R956

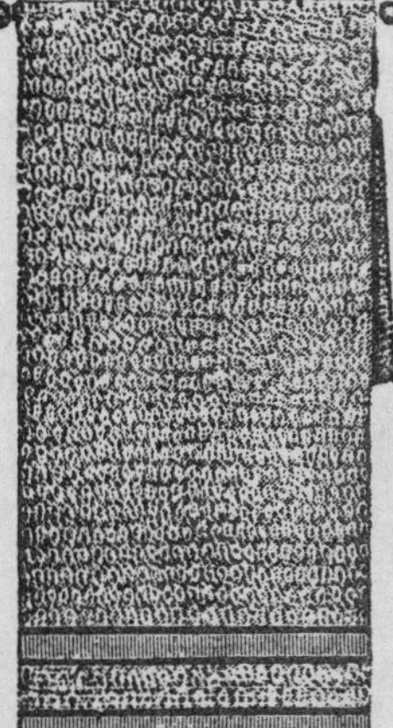

No. 36R964

Special Value at 12 Cents.

This is an exceptionally fine towel, extra heavy, large sized unbleached Turkish towel. Your local dealer asks at least 20 cents for a towel of this quality. **Handsomely made towel with red border.** Full size, 21x51 inches.
No. 36R960 Special price, each..........12c
If by mail, postage extra, each, 6 cents.

Unbleached Turkish Towels, extra heavy weight, soft and firm. Size, 23x53 inches.
No. 36R964 Price, each...............17c
If by mail, postage extra, each, 8 cents.

No. 36R970 Unbleached Turkish Towels, extra heavy and large; one of the finest qualities made. Long nap. Size, 26x54 inches. Price, each........25c
If by mail, postage extra, each, 14 cents.

Bleached Turkish Towels.

Bleached Turkish Towels, nice and soft, snow white and splendid value for the money. Size, 16x35 inches. **Shipping weight, 32 ounces per dozen.**
No. 36R974 Price, each.........................8c

Beautiful Quality, Snow White Turkish Towels, with a long soft nap. Size, 20½x45 inches.
No. 36R980 Price, 12c
Shipping weight, 50 ounces per dozen.

Extra Heavy, Snow White Turkish Towels, Size, 21x48 inches.
No. 36R984 Each, 16c
If by mail, postage extra, each, 7 cents.

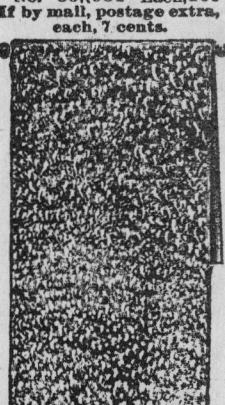

Beautiful Quality Turkish Towels, snow white, a splendid towel for the money. Size, 22x48½ inches.
No. 36R990 Each, 25c
If by mail, postage extra, each, 10 cents.

Bleached Turkish Towels, one of the finest grades made. Size, 25x52 inches.
No. 36R993 Price, 28c
If by mail, postage extra, 12 cents.

Turkish Face Cloths.

No. 36R998 Unbleached Turkish Face Cloths. Will not sell less than one dozen. Size, 8x9½ inches. Per dozen. 15c
If by mail, postage extra, 5 cents.

No. 36R1002 Unbleached Turkish Face Cloths. Will not sell less than one dozen. Per dozen....25c
If by mail, postage extra, 8 cents.

No. 36R1006 Bleached Turkish Face Cloths, extra fine quality, full size. Price, per dozen....35c
If by mail, postage extra, 8 cents.

No. 36R1010 Bleached Turkish Face Cloths, one of the finest and heaviest qualities made; full size. Price, per dozen...45c
If by mail, postage extra, 12 cents.

MARSEILLES, CROCHET, HONEYCOMB AND FANCY COLORED

BED SPREADS.

WITH AND WITHOUT FRINGE

Our stock in this line is of the best and prices are the lowest.

No. 36R1020 White Honeycomb or Crochet Bed Spreads. Full size, 70x75 inches. Good value. Weight, 26 ounces. Price, each.......................... **49c**

No. 36R1022 White Honeycomb Bed Spreads. Handsome Marseilles patterns. Hemmed ready for use. Size, 75x82 inches. Weight, 36 oz. Each..... **73c**

No. 36R1024 Extra Heavy White Honeycomb Bed Spreads. Made from double twisted yarns—very large size. Beautiful patterns. Hemmed ready for use. Weight, 3 pounds. Price, each.......................... **95c**

No. 36R1026 Fine Fancy Colored Honeycomb Bed Spreads. With heavy knotted fringe. Made in brown, red or blue. Absolutely fast colors. Reversible and can be used on either side. Full size. Weight, 3 lbs. Price, each...... **$1.15**

No. 36R1028 Fine White Honeycomb Bed Spreads. Full double bed size. Handsome Marseilles patterns. Hemmed and all ready for use. Weight, 3½ pounds. Price, each.......................... **$1.19**

No. 36R1030 Colored Mitcheline Bed Spreads, something similar to a Marseilles, but not so heavy. This is a very pretty spread and will wear and hold its color to the last. It has a pretty border to match center. Comes in blue and white and pink and white. Extra large. 12-4 size. Weight, 3¾ pounds. Price, each.......................... **$1.29**

No. 36R1032 Fine Marseilles Bed Spreads, with beautiful raised patterns. Large full size. Handsome and serviceable. Weight, 3¾ lbs. Price, each, **$1.75**

No. 36R1034 Extra Quality White Marseilles Bed Spreads. Diamond center surrounded with artistic floral designs. Very rich in appearance. Extra heavy and very durable. Full double bed size. Weight, 4¼ lbs. Price, each..... **$2.50**

No. 36R1036 Extra High Grade White Marseilles Bed Spreads. Particularly desirable on account of their fine weave and rich designs. Floral and scroll patterns with satin effect finish. Extra large, full size. Weight, 5 pounds. Price, each.......................... **$3.65**

No. 36R1038 Extra Superfine Quality White Marseilles Bed Spreads With heavy and rich border, in beautiful raised floral patterns; this is one of the finest qualities imported. Extra large size. Weight, 5½ pounds. Price, each... **$5.00**

No. 36R1040 White Fringed Honeycomb Bed Spreads. Fringed spreads are very popular, and are getting to be very much used; this number is splendid value for the money; **heavy knotted fringe.** Full size. Weight, 2¼ pounds. Price, each.......................... **90c**

No. 36R1042 White Fringed Bed Spreads, Marseilles pattern, heavy knotted fringe. Extra large size, and no better value to be had. Price, each.. **$1.39**

WONDERFUL WHITE GOODS VALUE.

WE SHOW WONDERFUL WHITE GOODS VALUES. **In calling your attention to this, our special White Goods Department, a sub-department in our general department of wash dress goods, linens, etc.; wonderful, because we do not hesitate to say, without fear of contradiction, that this season we are giving values heretofore unknown in white goods.**

THE GENTLEMAN IN CHARGE OF THIS DEPARTMENT, **who has given his life's experience in the handling of white goods and linens,** and whose services we have secured from one of the largest white goods dealers in this country, said to us when we told him that our selling prices on white goods should be the one small profit above the actual cost, and that every advantage he had secured in buying must go to our customers and not to us, even though his purchases had been particularly well made by reason of his skill in detecting values and his instructions to buy in large quantities, that this was an entirely new departure for him, and that it was customary with all wholesalers of white goods to get liberal profits, and on many of the higher priced goods to get fancy profits. **We told him—new departure that it may be—it was our fixed policy that our customers must own our goods at just what they cost us, with but our one uniformly small percentage of profit added.**

WE CALL YOUR ATTENTION **to our big line of White Goods, carefully selected and purchased under contract from the largest makers of these goods;** our new line of white Victoria Lawns, India Linens, White Organdies, India Mull, Swiss Mull, Dotted Swiss, Pique, Linens, Nainsooks, new plain, fancy and colored Dimities, all the very latest and handsomest lace effects. **We invite your attention to these new goods purchased for this season as described and quoted in this department,** with the promise that if you will send us your order you will get such value as you could not possibly get elsewhere; that you can buy in the smallest quantity from us from this department for even less than your storekeeper at home can buy in any quantity.

OUR GUARANTEE OFFER. **Select any goods from this, our White Goods Department.** If you want a handsome summer costume, a waist or other garment from which these new and handsome white goods productions can be made, send us your order, and if the goods when received are not perfectly satisfactory, **if they are not much greater value than you could possibly get elsewhere,** if you are not convinced that we are saving you all the profit your storekeeper at home would make, and more, **return the goods to us at our expense of express charges both ways, and we will immediately return your money.**

White India Linons.

White India Linon. Nice and fine, and splendid value for the money.
No. 36R1076 Price, per yard........ 7c

White India Linon. Very fair quality, 30 inches wide.
No. 36R1077 Price, per yard........ 9c

White India Linon. Extra fine quality; 32 inches wide.
No. 36R1078 Price, per yard........ 14c

Fine Quality India Linon, nice texture. This is one of our popular numbers.
No. 36R1079 Price, per yard........ 19c

Extra Quality White India Linon. Very fine grade; 33 inches wide.
No. 36R1080 Price, per yard........ 22c

White India Linon. Positively the finest quality made; 33 inches wide.
No. 36R1081 Price, per yard........ 29c

White Victoria Lawns.

White Victoria Lawn. Very choice quality, 26 inches wide.
No. 36R1082 Price, per yard........ 8c

White Victoria Lawn. Good quality, clean, fine texture. Width, 32 inches.
No. 36R1083 Price, per yard........ 10c

White Victoria Lawn. Fine clean quality, made from long, staple yarns. This is a very popular number. Width, 32 inches.
No. 36R1084 Price, per yard........ 12½c

White Victoria Lawn. Extra fine quality, smooth weave, clean and free from dressing. Width, 32 inches.
No. 36R1085 Price, per yard........ 15c

White Victoria Lawn. Manufactured and finished expressly for us. Clean, fine texture; very perfect goods. These goods we buy in very large quantities from the manufacturers. We are direct importers, consequently you pay no profits to jobbers or retailers. This quality, if purchased from an ordinary city or country retailer, would be sold for from 30 to 35 cents per yard. Width, 32 inches.
No. 36R1086 Price, per yard........ 20c

Special Value in White Victoria Lawn at 25 Cents.

White Victoria Lawn. This is an exceptional value and one of the finest qualities of white Victoria lawn procurable, such as is handled by high class city stores, and then at double the price we charge you. It is used extensively for ladies' fine underwear and for children's dresses. Width, 40 inches.
No. 36R1087 Price, per yard........ 25c

Black Victoria Lawn.

Plain Black Victoria Lawn. A fine finish, perfect weave, warranted fast color, 29 inches wide.
No. 36R1088
Price, per yard, 12½c

Plain Black Lawn. Extra fine even finish. Guaranteed fast black. Width, 30 inches.
No. 36R1089
Price, per yard.. 16c

Plain Black Lawn. Good fast black; one of the finest qualities made. Width, 30 in.
No. 36R1094 Price, per yard........ 25c

Persian Lawns.

These soft, fleecy, beautiful, white goods are really the finest and most beautiful in texture of anything shown in white goods. They are goods that are used by ladies of extremely good taste and ladies who appreciate something of the very finest for purposes such as for fine lingere, for children's dresses and for ladies' fine evening and reception dresses. They really outshine silks in their soft and beautiful texture. **All the numbers we quote you will find to be of extremely good value, values which you cannot find in any store,** in fact, these are qualities which cannot be found except in the very finest city retail establishments and then at fancy prices.

White Persian Lawns. Our White Persian Lawns are the very choicest imported. Nothing finer or more sheer could be found. These justly popular white goods are finer, more sheer, and also more popular than the India linens, for people wanting thin white goods. They are adapted for graduation dresses, also reception gowns. At 20 cents we furnish a beautiful 32-inch white Persian lawn. This is a quality that retails everywhere at from 25 cents to 35 cents.
No. 36R1090 Price, per yard........ 20c

White Persian Lawn, 32 inches wide, beautiful silky finish, warranted to give splendid satisfaction and wear.
No. 36R1091 Price, per yard........ 25c

White Persian Lawn, 32 inches wide, one of the handsomest qualities we carry and one of our most popular selling numbers.
No. 36R1092 Price, per yard........ 30c

Fine White Persian Lawn at 35 Cents.

White Persian Lawn, one of the handsomest Persian lawns imported, beautifully finished. This is the quality of white Persian lawns to be found only in high class stores and invariably sells at from 50 cents up. Width, 32 inches.
No. 36R1093 Price, per yard........ 35c

Black India Linon.

Positively fast black and will not crock or fade by exposure to the sun. This fabric is generally called India linen, which is misleading, as it is made of select sea island cotton, very fine and sheer, with a smooth, silky finish; **is very popular and durable. Extra good values guaranteed in each number.** Width, 32¼ inches.

Fine Quality India Linon, positive fast black.
No. 36R1095
Price, per yard, 12½c

Extra Fine Quality India Linon, positive fast black.
No. 36R1096
Price, per yard.. 20c

Black India Linon. Extra fine quality. Nothing better made. Fast black. Width, 30 inches.
No. 36R1097
Price, per yard.. 30c

WHEN YOU MAKE UP YOUR ORDER FOR

DRESS GOODS

NOTE OUR WONDERFUL 5 CENT PAPER PATTERN OFFER ON PAGE 858.

White French Organdies.

We are direct importers of these beautiful dress goods that are so popular for wedding, graduating and reception gowns. Never were these goods so popular as they are for this season. We have added some very special numbers to the lines which we originally carried. **Being direct importers, we are able to make you a great saving on this particular line of goods.**

Very Sheer and Fine White French 68-Inch Organdie for 39 cents. Such a quality as the ordinary retailer sells at from 50 to 75 cents per yard. Full 68-inch goods.
No. 36R1100 Our special price, per yard........ 39c

White Organdie, good quality, fine and sheer and extra good value for the money. Width, 68 inches.
No. 36R1102 Price, per yard.... 50c

White Organdie, a beautiful sheer fabric and one of the finest of imported goods. Width, 68 inches.
No. 36R1104 Price, per yard........ 75c

Our Very Best Pure White French Organdie.

Very Best Imported French Organdie Goods that sell in regular way by your home dealer and also in the metropolitan stores at not less than $1.25 and some at $1.75 per yard. We will save you anywhere from 50 to 75 cents per yard on every yard purchased from us of this beautiful and fashionable French White Dress Organdie. Full 68 inches wide.
No. 36R1106 Our special price........ 98c

Checked and Striped Nainsooks.

This is not the cheap goods such as handled by country stores for twice our price, but it is a firm, well made imported nainsook. Comes in an endless variety of neat checks and stripes. **All pure white.**

White Check and Stripe Nainsook. Width, 25 inches.

No. 36R1108 Our special price, per yard........ 5c

White Check and Stripe Nainsook, much better quality than above. Width, 25 inches.
No. 36R1110 Price, per yard........ 6c

White Check and Stripe Nainsook, very pretty for children's use. Width, 25 inches.
No. 36R1112 Price, per yard........ 10c

Extra Quality Checked and Striped Nainsooks.

Extra Quality Check and Stripe Nainsook, with a beautiful finish. Width, 25 inches.
No. 36R1114 Price, per yard........ 15c

Extra Quality Check and Stripe Nainsook, one of the best made. Width, 25 inches.
No. 36R1116 Price, per yard........ 25c

Satin Stripe Nainsooks.

Satin Stripe Nainsook, very neat and dressy. Width, 25 inches.
No. 36R1118 Price, per yard........ 7½c

Extra Fine Quality Satin Stripe Nainsook. Width, 25 inches.
No. 36R1120 Price, per yard........ 12½c

Superfine Quality of Satin Nainsook, in neat check, curb check, herringbone and hairline stripes.
No. 36R1124 Price, per yard........ 15c

White Lace Stripe Lawn.

White Lace Stripe Lawn; comes in small and medium stripes. This will be a rapid seller; splendid value. Width, 28 inches.
No. 36R1128 Price, per yard........ 10½c

White Cross Barred Dimity.

This handsome white fabric is made on a lawn texture, with dainty cross lines, and comes 28 inches wide. Is always desirable and popular for children's dresses, gimps and aprons, and is very serviceable. **Comes in a variety of small and medium checks,** in even and also broken effects.
No. 36R1130
Per yard........ 12½c

DEPARTMENT OF WASH DRESS GOODS

THIS, OUR WASH DRESS GOODS DEPARTMENT has been completely reorganized for this season, our lines have been greatly enlarged, we have made exceedingly large contracts with foreign and domestic mills, and by the most economic handling, with but our one small percentage of profit added, we can safely say that you can buy one yard or one piece from us for as little, if not less, than your storekeeper at home can buy in hundred-piece lots.

THE GOODS WE SHOW are the very latest for this season, new patterns and new styles that are being turned out for the first time; a class of goods, the larger part of which you will find only in the most fashionable city retail stores, and there at almost double our price.

WE KNOW WE CAN FURNISH YOU SUCH VALUE and such new styles as you cannot get elsewhere; we know you will be so well pleased with any waist or dress pattern that you would order from us, that you would be sure to favor us with your future orders, and influence your friends and neighbors to send their orders to us.

AT FROM 5 TO 19 CENTS PER YARD we offer you your choice of twelve special numbers in fine imported French, English and Scotch summer dress fabrics, the equal of anything you can buy elsewhere at 50 to 100 per cent more money. These twelve numbers are offered in competition with goods that will be sold by representative dealers everywhere at about double the price.

THE GREATEST VALUES IN ENTIRELY NEW, UP TO DATE, HIGH CLASS SUMMER FABRICS THAT EVER WENT OUT OF THIS OR ANY OTHER HOUSE

OUR SPECIAL OFFER. DO NOT WAIT FOR SAMPLES. (If you want samples first send 1 cent for each catalogue number.) Select the goods you will want for a dress or shirt waist pattern. Give us an idea of the color and pattern wanted. We will send them to you with the understanding that if they are not perfectly satisfactory, and the greatest value ever shown in your section at anything like the price, if they are not new, handsome, and up to date, matchable only by the very newest effects as shown in the choicest city stores at about double our price, you can return the goods to us at our expense, and we will return your money. You must see and examine these goods, compare them with the goods offered by other storekeepers, to appreciate the value we are giving.

Our 5-Cent Fancy Printed Scotch Corded Dimity.

No. 36R1350 This is an especially nice imported Scotch goods for ladies', misses' and children's summer dresses. It is 25 inches wide, thoroughly fast color; goods you cannot buy elsewhere at less than 10 cents. Comes in a great variety of colorings on white ground. Also a big line of Jardiniere printings on dark and high colored grounds; also tints. **Give us an idea of the coloring wanted and we will guarantee to please you.** Width, 25 inches.

Price, per yard........................5c

Our 15-Cent Imported Extra Fine French 32-Inch Sheer Organdie.

No. 36R1355 This is a very stylish goods for summer dresses—used by the most fashionable trade. Goods that sells regularly at 25 to 35 cents. It is a quality good enough to be used over silk. Comes in a multitude of beautiful large, medium and small patterns on white grounds. Also on dark, staple and tinted grounds. **Give us an idea of the coloring wanted and we will guarantee to please you in this handsome new French goods.** Width, 32 inches.

Price, per yard........................15c

Our 12½-Cent Anderson Imported Scotch Gingham.

No. 36R1360 This is a fancy plaid imported dress goods. Extra quality. Soft silk finish. Thoroughly fast colors, and goods that retail at 25 to 35 cents. Highest grade gingham, imported. Comes in large, medium and small plaids in a big variety of colorings. **Give us an idea of the size of plaid and coloring wanted and we will guarantee to please you.** Width, 32 inches.

Price, per yard........................12½c

Our Fancy 12-Cent, 32-Inch Sheer Printed Lawn.

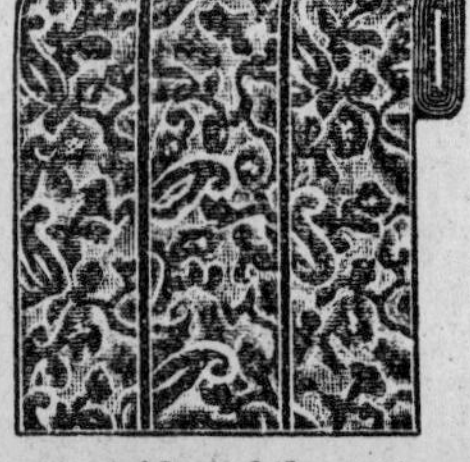

No. 36R1365 A regular 20-cent goods, entirely new for this season, and one of the handsomest things of the kind in the market. It is 32 inches wide, comes in a great variety of patterns and colorings on white grounds, tinted grounds and printings of suitable shades. This is a Victoria lawn, and the cloth itself is worth 25 cents more than the price we charge for it; printed in beautiful designs. **Give us an idea of the pattern and coloring wanted, and we will guarantee to please you.** Width, 32 inches.

Price, per yard........................12c

Samples of any catalogue number on this page sent for 1 cent, including sample of every shade and pattern carried in the number.

Our New 15-Cent Corded Printed Pique.

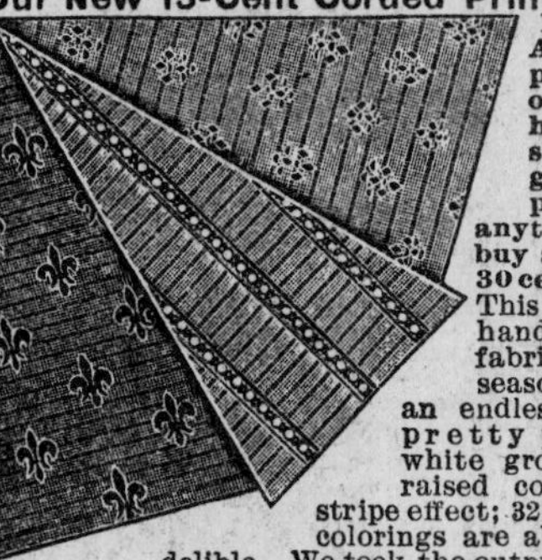

No. 36R1370 At 15 cents per yard we offer this new handsome summer goods in competition with anything you can buy anywhere at 30 cents per yard. This is one of the handsomest wash fabrics shown this season. Comes in an endless variety of pretty printings on white grounds; has a raised corded rolled stripe effect; 32 inches wide; colorings are absolutely indelible. We took the output of the mill on this goods and name you a price much less than jobbers can buy in case lots. **This is one of our biggest values for spring and summer.** Order a dress pattern from this particular piece, **give us an idea of the coloring and pattern, and if you do not say it is equal to anything you can buy elsewhere for double the price, we will return your money.** Width, 32 inches. Price, per yard........................15c

Our 10-Cent Fancy Imported Printed Percale.

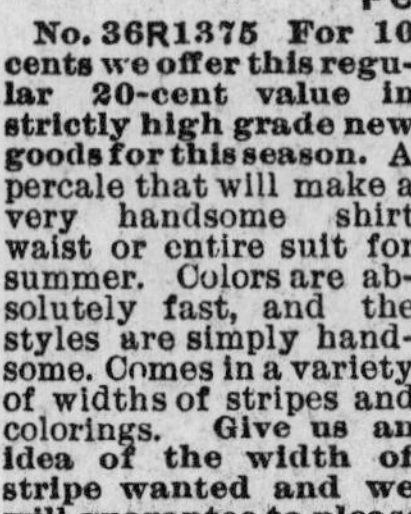

No. 36R1375 For 10 cents we offer this regular 20-cent value in strictly high grade new goods for this season. A percale that will make a very handsome shirt waist or entire suit for summer. Colors are absolutely fast, and the styles are simply handsome. Comes in a variety of widths of stripes and colorings. **Give us an idea of the width of stripe wanted and we will guarantee to please you.** Width, 32 inches.

Price, per yard........................10c

Our 11-Cent 36-Inch Printed Dress Percale.

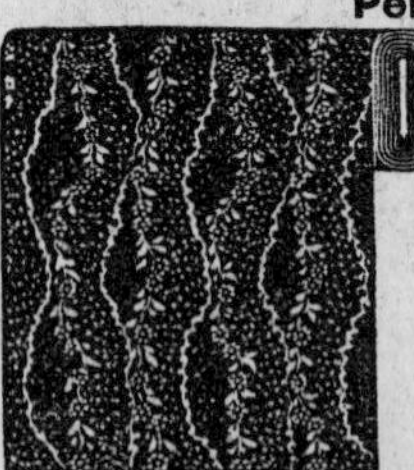

No. 36R1379 From the illustration you can get some idea of the appearance or pattern of these goods. They are entirely new for this season. It is a regular 20-cent value. They are made of combed sea island cotton, and in appearance are a marvel of beauty. These goods come in stripes, also in geometrical, small, medium and large scroll designs. We can furnish these goods in every known coloring, in dark, medium and staple. **Give us an idea of the color and pattern wanted and we will agree to please you.** Width, 36 inches.

Price, per yard........................11c

Our New 15-Cent Imported Extra Fine French Penang.

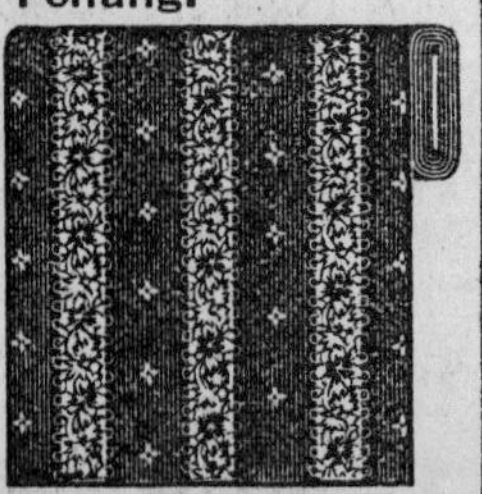

No. 36R1384 At 15 cents we offer this goods, entirely new for this season, in competition with anything you can buy at 25 to 35 cents. This is one of the handsomest things in the French Penang that will be shown this season. It is 34 inches wide; has a beautiful silk finish surface, an extra fine piece of goods. Will make a beautiful waist or suit. Comes in a pretty line of fashionable colorings and we guarantee that it will not fade. **Give us an idea of color and design wanted, whether you wish scroll or stripe, and if you are not more than pleased with the goods you can return them to us at our expense and we will return your money.** Width, 34 inches. Price, per yard..15c

Our 10-Cent Imported French Lace Striped Lawn.

No. 36R1388 For a very beautiful imported French goods for a summer waist or dress you will find this equal to the imported goods that cost five times the price. If you order these goods and you do not say they are equal to anything you can buy from your storekeeper at home at double the price, we will return your money. **This is one of the handsomest French summer goods that has been shown this season.** It is a sheer material, has very latest effect stripes, and a beautiful print over all. Makes up very beautifully over a contrasting color and would make a handsome suit if trimmed with lace. **Give us an idea of the color and pattern wanted and we will guarantee to send you such goods as were never seen in your section at anything like the price.** Width, 32 in. Per yard, **10c**

Our New Fancy Imported 9-Cent Corded Lawn.

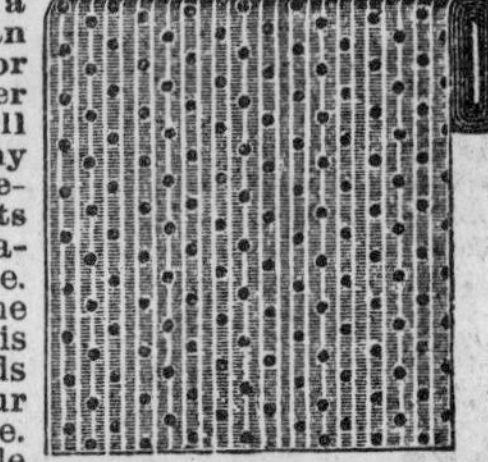

No. 36R1395 For a handsome lawn in an entirely new effect for this season for summer waist or dress, you will find this equal to any thing you can buy elsewhere at 20 to 25 cents per yard. The illustration does not do it justice. It has a very handsome raised cord effect. It is the same class of goods that is being sold in your city at double our price. It is a value we are able to offer by reason of controlling a big part of the output of the mill. These goods are 28 inches, come in a variety of dainty prints, blue, pink, violet, etc., on white ground. **Give us an idea of the color and pattern wanted and we will guarantee to please you.** Width, 28 inches. Price, per yard.............9c

Our 19-Cent Imported Fancy Scotch Printed Lawn.

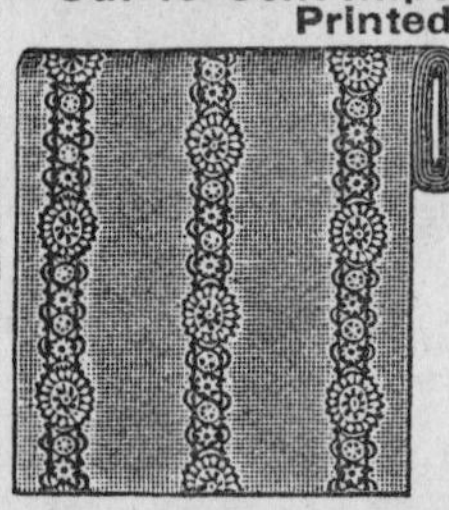

No. 36R1400 For 19 cents we offer this fine imported Scotch lawn in the very latest effect for this season. It is 32 inches wide, and is the equal of lawns that will sell everywhere this season at 35 to 50 cents. This is one of the handsomest Scotch lawns on the market. Will make up very nice in a waist or dress. **Is entirely new for this season. Has a** handsome dimity cord, and comes in the most beautiful variety of prints, of one, two and up to seven-tone printings. This is one of the highest grade imported dimities that it is possible to buy at any price, and the colors are guaranteed absolutely fast. Not a poor design in the lot. All prints are on white and colored backgrounds. **Give us an idea of the colorings or prints wanted and we will guarantee to please you.** Width, 32 inches.

Price, per yard........................19c

Our New Fancy 14-Cent Imported Scotch Gingham.

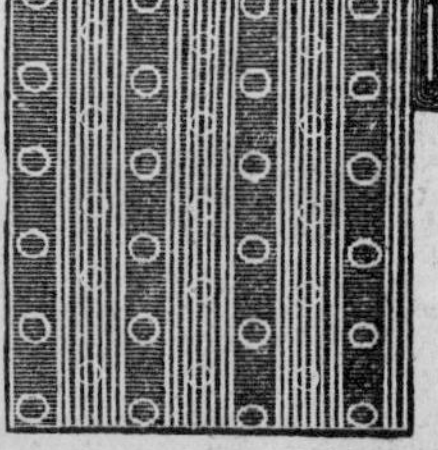

No. 36R1405 These goods are 31 inches wide, extra quality, imported Scotch gingham. Entirely new for this season, from one of the best Scotch mills. Offered at our special 14-cent price, in competition with anything of the same class that you can buy elsewhere at 25 cents. Especially desirable for ladies' shirt waists, or for entire outing suits. **High grade, up to date, 20th century style goods.** Comes in stripes, plaids and large and small effects. Colorings are pink, blue, violet, lavender, cardinal; also contrasting colors in green. **Give us an idea of the color and pattern wanted, and if we do not send you such value as you cannot get elsewhere at less than 50 per cent of the price, we will return your money.** Width, 32 inches. Price, per yard........................14c

BARGAINS IN STAPLE PRINTS.

Our Big 5-Cent Print Offer.

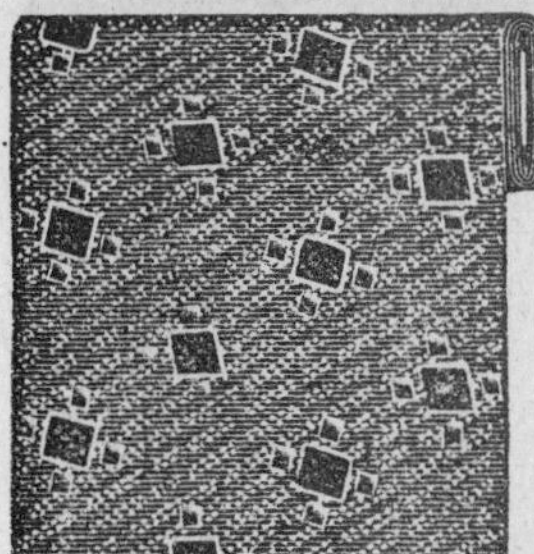

No. 36R1546 This is an extraordinary print value, a quality that sells in dry goods stores at 7 and 8 cents. Medium and Dark Staple Prints. Comes in biscuit brown and chocolate fancies, heliotrope, purple, bright red, garnet, etc.; good durable cloth, 26 inches wide.

Price, per yard, 5c

Comforter or Robe Prints at 5½ Cents.

No. 36R1550 Large Scroll Oriental Comforter Prints. Bright colors, comes in palm leaf, floral and cashmere designs on red, orange, blue, brown or heliotrope grounds. Width, 26 inches.

Per yard....5½c

Our 6-Cent Robe Prints.

No. 36R1554 Bright Robe Prints. Goods that are usually retailed at 8 and 9 cents. Fast colors, handsome patterns. In cardinal, brown, yellow, garnet, blue, wine, black or purple grounds, with bright contrasting, free scroll and floral patterns. Width, 26 inches.

Price, per yard, 6c

Fast Color Robe Prints at 7 Cents.

No. 36R1558 Oil Boiled Robe Prints. Absolutely fast colors. Comes in bright red, cardinal, garnet, purple, violet, yellow, green, rose or black ground, with a large pattern free scroll or floral in contrasting bright colors; very durable, and will surely give satisfaction. Width, 26 inches.

Price, per yard, 7c

Indigo Blue Dress Prints.

No. 36R1562 Full Standard Genuine Old Indigo Blue Dress Prints. Comes in stripes, polkadots and also floral and scroll designs, white on indigo blue. Width, 25 inches.

Price, per yard, 5c

Excellent Value at 6 Cents.

For only 6 cents we offer this Indigo Print as the equal of blue prints that retail everywhere at 8 and 9 cents a yard.

No. 36R1566 Best Heavy Dutch Indigo Blue Dress Prints. Large assortment of printings in white, small, medium and large flowers, stripes, dots, etc. Width, 25 inches.

Price, per yard..6c

Our 8-Cent 29-inch German Indigo Blue Dress Prints.

New Designs, similar to illustration.

No. 36R1570 29-Inch Heavy German Indigo Blue Dress Prints. Strong, heavy cloth, indigo blue grounds with dots, sprays, stripes and floral designs in white. Never before offered under 10 cents. Width, 29 inches.

Price, per yard, 8c

Extra Heavy 32-inch Dutch Prints at 10 Cents.

No. 36R1574 Extra Heavy Strong Dutch Indigo Blue Print. Very serviceable and the very best quality. Your retailer sells this print at 12½ cents. Comes in dots, figures and stripes, white on dark indigo blue.

Width, 32 inches.

Price, per yard, 10c

Satin Foulard Dress Prints.

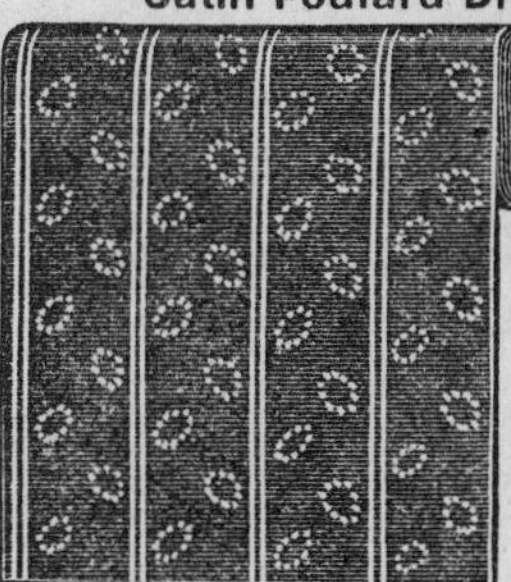

No. 36R1575 This is a very popular cloth for waists, dresses and wrappers. We offer it in a big variety of styles and colorings and very choice designs. The colors are both light and dark, also medium, dots and figures, and also floral designs. The grounds are heliotrope, navy, cardinal, plum, also lavender. Width, 30 inches.

Price, per yard..........10c

Turkey Red Prints at 5c.

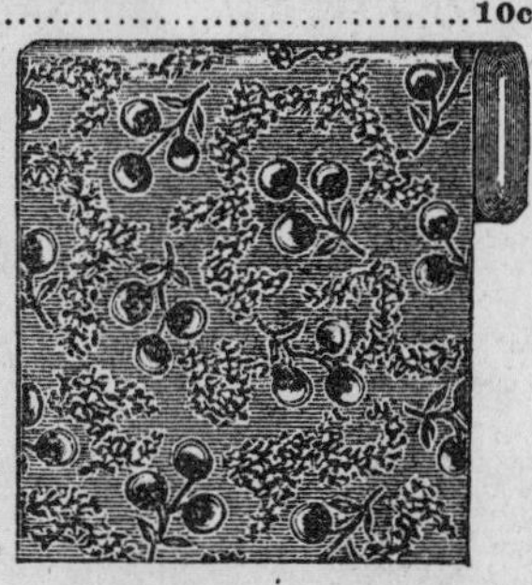

No. 36R1576 The Very Best Oil Boiled Turkey Red Prints. A fine cloth, guaranteed color; comes with either white or black printings in new and pretty patterns, polkadots, small, medium and large; even stripes, checks, plaids and neat figures.

Width. 25 inches.

Price, per yard, 5c

Great Values in Turkey Red Prints at 5 and 10 Cents.

No. 36R1578 Plain Oil Boiled 26-Inch Turkey Red Prints. Color is thoroughly fast.

Width, 26 inches.

Price, per yard, 5c

No. 36R1582 31-Inch Extra Quality Turkey Red Print, solid color. This is absolutely fast oil boiled color and the best quality made.

Width, 31 inches.

Price, per yard, 10c

No. 36R1586 Solid Colored Dress Prints. Very heaviest and best cloth, colors are fast and perfect; colors are cardinal, brown, green, black, navy, yellow and new blue. Width, 25 inches. Per yard.....6c

Make up a freight shipment of 100 pounds; it wont cost much more for transportation than a small express package. If you can't use any other goods, refer to our grocery department, pages 14 to 23. You can always use groceries. Include these with your order and make up a freight shipment.

Our 5-Cent Mourning Prints.

No. 36R1590 Silver Gray and Fast Black and White Prints, in neat patterns, medium or large size floral designs, scrolls or stripes. All new designs bought for this season.

Width, 25 inches.

Price, per yard, 5 Cents.

Mourning Prints at 5½ Cents a Yard.

No. 36R1594 Very Best Quality of Mourning Prints, comes in jasper mixture, silver gray, also black and white, in choice, carefully selected styles, many of them exclusive with us. These prints are very swell, and are worn by ladies or misses, are neat, and will wash without fading. Width, 25 inches.

Price, per yard, 5½c

Garibaldi Prints at 5½ Cents.

No. 36R1600 This is one of our prettiest and most serviceable prints. Comes with black ground, with red stripes, dots and neat figures. Width, 25 inches.

Price, per yard, 5½ Cents.

Cadet Blue Fancy Figured Dress Prints.

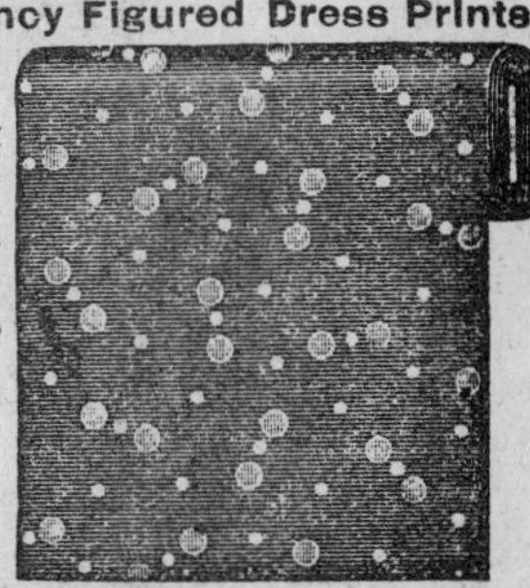

No. 36R1604 A pretty blue gray with white printings in choice figures, dots, stripes and floral designs, decidedly new and stylish. Width, 25 inches.

Price, per yard, 5½ Cents.

Cardinal Dress Prints.

No. 36R1608 A very choice soft cambric finished Print. A rich shade of red ground with pretty white printings, dots, stripes, sprays and floral designs, Width 25 inches.

Price, per yard, 5 Cents.

German Red Check and Plaid Prints.

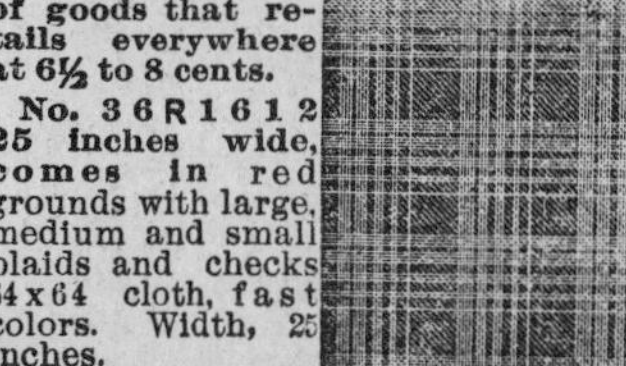

This is a quality of goods that retails everywhere at 6½ to 8 cents.

No. 36R1612 25 inches wide, comes in red grounds with large, medium and small plaids and checks 64x64 cloth, fast colors. Width, 25 inches.

Price, per yard, 5½ Cents.

White Silk Warp Flannels.

No. 36R1742 White Silk Warp Flannel, with a very fine wool filling; non-shrinkable. Width, 32 inches.

Price, per yard........... .83c

54-Inch Old Reliable Mackinaw Flannels.

No. 36R1744 A great life preserver for lumbermen, miners, cattlemen, and others exposed in cold climates; also used for ladies' skirts; all pure wool. Weight, 17 ounces. This is the best flannel of this class on the market. Comes in navy blue or scarlet. Width, 54 inches. Price, per yard.......85c

Fancy Wool Eiderdown.

No. 36R1746 This is one of the most beautiful materials for dressing sacks, wrappers, tea gowns, children's cloaks, etc., and the quality is very fine. Comes in choice soft tone shades in blue, pink, rose, tan, cardinal or cream grounds, etc., with effective contrasting colored stripes and figures. Width, 27 inches.

Price, per yard.....31c

Plain Wool Eiderdown.

No. 36R1750 A specially fine quality, comes in cream, tan, pink, light blue, cardinal and gray. Most retailers sell this quality at 50 cents.

Width, 26 inches.

Price, per yard.....33c

Daisy Cloth.

No. 36R1752 32-Inch Daisy Cloth, a very beautiful plain fleeced close nap flannel. Comes only in cream, pink and blue. Very pretty shades, suitable for dressing sacks, tea gowns, children's dresses and for nightdresses.

Width, 32 inches.

Our special low price, per yard..................10c

White Table Felt or Silence Cloth.

No. 36R1754 50-Inch Table Felt. Heavy, a good quality. Comes in white only.

Price, per yard.................................35c

SILK EMBROIDERED WHITE FLANNELS.

This is a department that is always of interest to ladies in search of beautiful flannels for infants' wear. We have made an entire change in the designs and qualities, and also in the prices that we submit this season. Every pattern is a gem and the price is much less than is asked for inferior goods by other houses. **All of our flannels are specially selected and of exceedingly perfect texture, pure, clean, white, and the embroidery is firmly done with a superior quality of silk.** They are thoroughly washable, are uniformly 36 inches wide, and are finished with a 2-inch folded edge. The goods are correctly illustrated, the descriptions are accurate and the goods guaranteed to be exactly as represented.

Our 36-Inch Wide Cream Wool Flannel, with a beautiful heavy hemstitch 1 inch wide, with silk embroidery. This is a very nice quality of flannel and the design is entirely new for this season. Width of flannel, 36 inches; width of embroidery, 1 inch.

No. 36R1758 Price, per yard 49c

All Wool Cream Baby Flannels, Embroidered.

Our All Wool Cream Baby Flannel, with a handsome 1½-inch scalloped, pure white embroidery. The illustration gives a faint idea of the beauty of this handsome embroidery. The edge is very heavily finished, and we consider this number one of the best flannels in our catalogue. Width of flannel, 36 inches; width of embroidery, 1½ inches.

No. 36R1762 Price, per yard.....................49c

Our 36-Inch Fine Cream All Wool Flannel, has a beautiful design of hemstitch, with heavy leaf effect of silk washable embroidery. This is a very nice quality of all wool flannel, and the illustration will show what a very beautiful design we have selected for this very reasonable price. Width, 36 inches; width of silk embroidery, 1¾ inches.

No. 36R1766 Price, per yard.......................52c

The above illustration shows a handsome design in our all pure wool cream flannel. Especially adapted for children's long skirts and ladies' fine under garments. We have been very careful and were particular in selecting something entirely new in design. The cut does not do justice to the heavy wide embroidery, which looks very narrow as seen in the picture, but we assure you the embroidery is very heavy and 2 inches wide. Width of flannel, 36 inches; width of embroidery, 2 inches.

No. 36R1770 Price, per yard...................59c

This is a remarkably pretty design of embroidery, worked upon a very nice, fine, all wool cream baby flannel. Too much cannot be said about the beauty of this embroidery, as it is a new design and something that any lady will be proud of. It is impossible for us with this small illustration to do justice to the heavy and perfect work. The embroidery is extra heavy and the scallops are very firmly embroidered. Width of flannel, 36 inches; width of embroidery, 2 inches.

No. 36R1774 Price, per yard.......................69c

Our Hemstitched Embroidered All Wool Cream Baby Flannel. This is one of the nicest styles that we show in embroidery insertion effect. The illustration will give you a faint idea of the beauty of this embroidered flannel, which is one of our prettiest numbers and the price is very low. We have contracted for 1,000 pieces of the above embroidery flannel, and at the popular price at which we are enabled to sell it, there is no doubt but that the demand will clear out our stock in a very short time. **Our price, which is the price of the flannel direct from the manufacturer,** the embroidery done by an embroiderer, who takes the contract for a tremendous quantity, and with our one small profit added it goes to you for **73 cents,** which is a saving of at least 12 cents a yard, and you rarely buy it for less than $1.00, which would be a saving of 17 cents. Width of flannel, 36 inches; width of embroidery, 1¾ inches.

No. 36R1778 Price, per yard.......................73c

Our 89-Cent Embroidery Flannel.

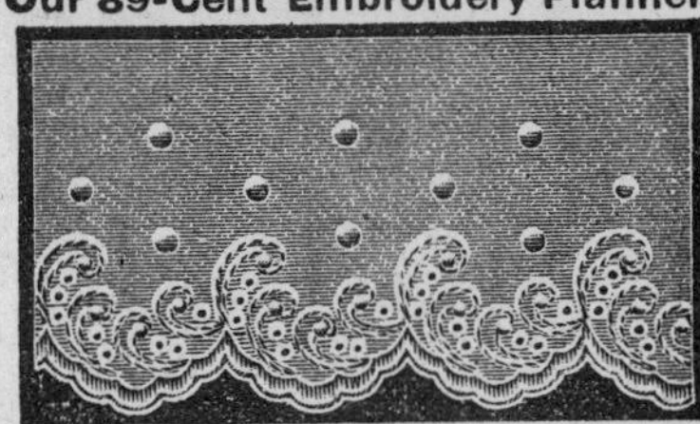

This Flannel is equal to the goods we sold durin previous seasons at $1.19 per yard. At 89 cents w have lowered the price, and it has been made possi ble by contracting with the manufacturers of the flannel and with the embroidery companies, and getting the very lowest prices for the largest quantities. A very fine quality of white all wool flannel. It is very firm and perfectly edged. Width of flannel, 36 inches; width of embroidery, 2⅛ inches.

No. 36R1782 Price, per yard........ ....89c

This 36-Inch All Wool Embroidered Cream Flannel is one of the prettiest designs it has been our pleasure to select for this new line of embroidery flannels for our new catalogue. The accompanying cut gives you a faint idea of the heavy, wide embroidery as it will appear when you see the goods. The actual width of embroidery is 4 inches, and the quality of flannel is one of the very best you can buy anywhere. In fact, at retail the flannel alone, not embroidered, from a retail store would cost at least $1.00 per yard this width. Width of flannel, 36 inches; width of embroidery, 4 inches.

No. 36R1784 Price, per yard.....................98c

This pretty design of embroidery on our best 36-inch cream all wool flannel will prove one of the handsomest designs, and indeed will be a surprise for style and quality at this small price. This flannel, if it were bought in ordinary or fancy goods departments, would cost anywhere from $1.50 to $1.75 per yard. Nothing is to be seen anywhere like it in scalloped flannels, the scalloped edge of firm and compact profusion of perfect embroidery. The floral design, as above, is simply perfect. Width of embroidery, 2¼ inches; width of flannel, 36 inches.

No. 36R1786 Price, per yard.............. $1.19

The above illustration is a correct picture of the widest and handsomest embroidered cream, all wool flannel we are showing this season. This handsome design is 5½ inches in width and has a massive strong embroidery. Like the above outline, the flannel upon which this is embroidered is one of the handsomest imported, equal to a flannel that costs twice the amount which we ask for it. This goods was bought in large lots and the embroidery is done under special contract. Width of flannel, 36 inches; width of embroidery, 5½ inches.

No. 36R1788 Price, per yard.................. $1.39

BLANKET VALUES.

OUR BLANKET DEPARTMENT is one of the largest divisions in our Dry Goods Department, and for several seasons we have been recognized headquarters in this line. As direct agents for several of the largest mills, we are placed on a price basis not enjoyed by any of the ordinary wholesale houses. We are in a position where we can and do give to our customers who order in any quantity better values and lower prices than your storekeeper at home can get from the wholesale houses in any quantity. Our blankets, of which we show an extensive line, are made for us by the best makers in this country. We own them on the basis of the actual cost of material and labor, to which we add but our one small percentage of profit.

WE HAVE SOLD THOUSANDS OF CASES the past few seasons. They have gone into almost every town in the United States. If you have not patronized our Blanket Department surely some of your neighbors have, and we refer you to them as to the values we have given. If they tell you that they have gotten from us such values in blankets as they could not get elsewhere, such blankets as was never shown in their section at anything like the price, and that we are furnishing much better goods for the money than you can get from any other house, we will naturally expect you to send us your order. There is nothing more staple with us, nothing on which greater economy is studied in order to make a price than on this staple article, blankets. It is one of the granulated sugar calculations of our house.

DON'T PAY RETAIL PRICES FOR THESE GOODS. Blankets are sold by storekeepers generally at exceptionally large profits above an already high cost to the retailer. We save you the retailer's profit and part of the profit he pays to the wholesale house.

OUR BLANKET DEPARTMENT is one of the year around bee hives of our house. It is a class of goods that is always in season. In scarlet bed blankets we show a variety of the very latest productions, with handsome borders, at prices that will astonish you when you see them. In extra heavy scarlet Klondike or Indian blankets we are putting out values heretofore unknown.

IN THE REGULATION U. S. ARMY BLANKETS we believe we show the best blanket of the kind ever turned out of any mill, and our price to you is figured on the cost of the wool, the weaving, the making and our one small percentage of profit added. In gray bed blankets, also white blankets as illustrated and described below, we show the special value numbers as selected from our entire line, values unapproachable by any house; and from a good grade white cotton blanket to our selected all Saxony wool blanket, one of the finest blankets on the market, we guarantee such values as go out of no other house. Our blankets ranging from $5.00 per pair upwards are made for us by the best maker in this country. It is a class of goods you will find only in the very best stores and there at about double our prices.

OUR FINEST BLANKETS come from the wool centers of Oregon, where the finest, heaviest, softest, best wearing and altogether the highest grade blankets are produced. You can only appreciate the values we are giving in this department by seeing, examining and comparing the blankets we furnish with those furnished by others at higher prices.

OUR NEW HEAVY $4.39 BLANKET LEADER.

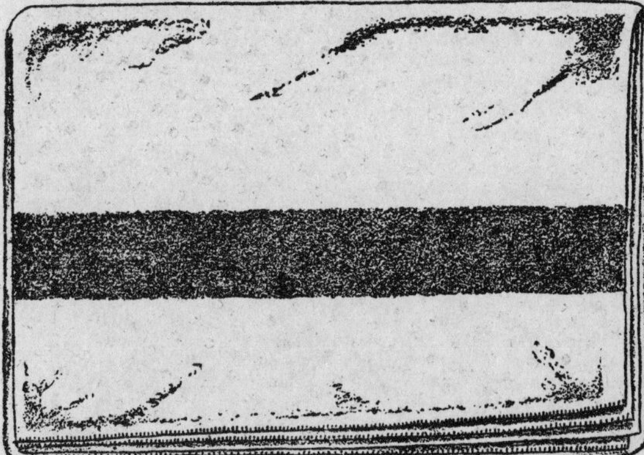

At $4.39 per pair we offer this heavy, 7-pound all wool Cyclone Blanket as our biggest leader for 1902, a regular $7.50 value. At $4.39 per pair we feel confident we are offering in this, our extra heavy, full 7-pound, all wool Cyclone Blanket, the greatest blanket value that ever went out of this or any other house. Our $4.39 price is made possible by reason of our taking the output of the mill on this one number. It is a blanket that has heretofore wholesaled at $5.50 to $6.00, and retailed generally at $7.50 to $8.00. We furnish these blankets in pure white with dark blue border. They are extra heavy, soft and fleecy, made from all pure selected wool, made by one of the best blanket makers in this country, in a big western mill. It is only by taking the entire output of the mill, reducing the cost of material and labor and by adding but one small percentage of profit that we can offer this most extraordinary value in this genuine all wool 7-pound Cyclone Blanket at $4.39 per pair. Send us $4.39 for a pair of these blankets, and if you do not find them the greatest value ever shown in a heavy, 7-pound all wool blanket, you can return them to us at our expense, and we will immediately return your money. Size, 62x80 inches.

No. 37R67 Our special price, per pair........ $4.39

KLONDIKE BLANKETS.

Extra Heavy Scarlet Klondike or Indian Blankets.

Extra Heavy Scarlet Klondike or Indian Blankets, made of good quality wool with a black border. There is none better made in this grade; it is very soft and warm. Weight, 7 pounds. Size, 68x76 inches.

No. 37R2 Price, per pair........ $4.98

Klondike or Camping Wool Blankets. Comes in blue gray, 7 pounds weight. Full 10-4 size. Colored border. A splendid blanket for wear and comfort.

No. 37R3 Price, per pair........ $3.95

Klondike or Camping Blankets. Extra good quality wool, color, blue gray, with black border. Weight, 10 pounds. Is absolutely non-shrinkable, double weave with an extra strong warp, also double warp selvedge, which makes it non-tearable; requires no special care in washing. Size, 62x82 inches.

No. 37R5 Price, per pair........ $6.50

Scarlet Bed Blankets, $2.98, $3.90 and $4.98.

Scarlet Bed Blankets, pure medicated dye, fine stock border. Weight, 4 pounds. Strictly all wool. Full 10-4 size.

No. 37R6 Price, per pair........ $2.98

Scarlet Bed Blankets, all pure California wool, medicated dye, colored border. Weight, 5 pounds. Full 11-4 size. A splendid blanket.

No. 37R8 Price, per pair........ $3.90

Scarlet Bed Blankets, extra fine California wool, pure medicated dye, thoroughly shrunk, colored border, mohair bound. Weight, 5 pound. Full 11-4 size, or 72x84 inches.

No. 37R9 Price, per pair........ $4.98

Our $7.25 Scarlet Bed Blankets.

Scarlet Bed Blankets, extra fine grade California wool, thoroughly shrunk and reliable; this blanket must be seen to be appreciated; mohair bound. Weight, 6 pounds. 11-4 size, or 72x84. Colored border.

No. 37R10 Price, per pair........ $7.25

$12.00 Blankets for $8.75.

Scarlet Bed Blankets, extra superfine, pure medicated dye; very finest grade California wool; deep mohair binding; thoroughly shrunk; colored border. Extra large 11-4 size, 72x84 inches. Weight, 6 pounds.

No. 37R13 Price, per pair........ $8.75

Our Finest 7-Pound Pure Fleece Wool Blankets at $9.98 Per Pair.

Scarlet Bed Blankets. Fine quality, pure fine fleece wool, handsomely bound. Size, 76x88 inches, Weight, 7 pounds.

No. 37R16 Price, per pair........ $9.98

REGULATION U. S. ARMY BLANKETS.

Regulation U. S. Army Blankets. Weight, 10 pounds. Color, silver gray, with wide black border. This is one of the finest blankets made of this class and will wear for years. Size, 62x82 inches.

No. 37R56 Price, per pair........ $7.25

Jack Frost Blankets.

This Celebrated Wool Blanket has been our very best advertisement in previous seasons. Comes in tan, gray or sanitary color only. It positively cannot be beat for warmth and service. Full extra large size and very heavy.

No. 37R65 Our special price, per pair...... $3.00

WHITE OR GRAY BED BLANKETS.

48 CENTS TO $12.50 PER PAIR.

No. 37R69 **Good Grade Cotton Blanket**, with fancy colored border, 10-4 or regular size. Come in white and gray. Per pair....... 48c

No. 37R71 **White or Gray Blankets**, with fancy colored borders, heavy fleece, 11-4 or full size. Price, per pair........ 70c

No. 37R73 **Blankets**, extra heavy and well napped; splendid value for the money. Come in gray or white. Fancy colored borders. Full 11-4 size. Price, per pair........ 95c

No. 37R75 **White Blankets**, excellent value; fancy colored borders; good reliable goods. Extra heavy fleece; full 11-4 size. Weight, 4 pounds. Price, per pair........ $1.35

No. 37R76 **Extra Large Size Gray Blankets.** Wool filled. The best value ever offered in a medium grade blanket. Size, 11-4. Weight, 6 pounds. Colored borders. Price, per pair........ $1.68

No. 37R77 **White Blankets**, part wool filled; fancy colored borders. Extra large 11-4 size; splendid values. Weight, 5 pounds. Price, per pair........ $1.75

No. 37R78 **Excellent Grade Large Size Gray Blankets**, wood filled, a good quality mixed blanket and reliable, colored borders, 11-4 size. Weight, 5½ pounds. Price, per pair........ $2.35

No. 37R79 **White Blankets**, all wool filled; extra good value. This blanket will wear better and give far better satisfaction than a cheap all wool blanket. Full size, 11-4. Fancy colored borders. Weight, 5 pounds. Price, per pair........ $2.75

No. 37R81 **Blankets.** Strictly all pure wool. This blanket is splendid value for the money and one we can strongly recommend. Comes in white and gray. Fancy colored borders and fully 4 pounds weight. Full 10-4 size. Price, per pair........ $2.98

No. 37R83 **Blankets.** Strictly all wool. This is an extra good blanket and will give thorough satisfaction. Comes in white or gray. Fancy colored borders. Weight, fully 5 pounds. Full 11-4 size. Price, per pair........ $3.95

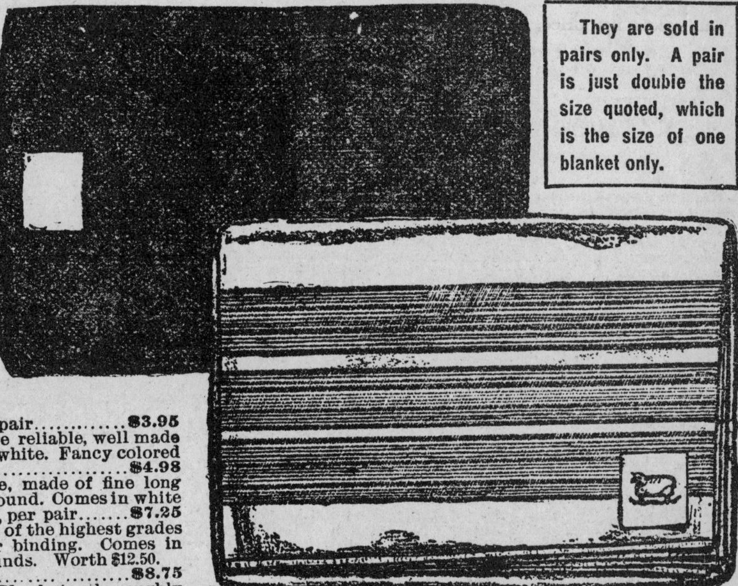

They are sold in pairs only. A pair is just double the size quoted, which is the size of one blanket only.

No. 37R85 **Blankets.** Extra fine California lambs' wool. These are reliable, well made goods and worth a good deal more than we charge. Come in gray or white. Fancy colored borders. Full 11-4 size. Weight, 5½ pounds. Price, per pair........ $4.98

No. 37R87 **Extra Fine California Bed Blankets**, very fine texture, made of fine long staple wool, thoroughly shrunk, with fancy colored borders, and mohair bound. Comes in white or gray. Weight, 6 pounds. Extra large, 11-4 size, or 72x84 inches. Price, per pair........ $7.25

No. 37R89 **Extra Superfine California Bed Blankets.** This is one of the highest grades made, thoroughly shrunk and reliable, fancy borders and deep mohair binding. Comes in white or gray. Extra large, 11-4 size, or 72x84 inches. Weight, about 6 pounds. Worth $12.50. Price, per pair........ $8.75

No. 37R91 **Beautiful Quality Highest Grade Lambs' Wool Bed Blankets**, thoroughly shrunk. This excellent quality blanket must be seen to be appreciated; beautifully finished, fancy colored borders. Comes in white or gray. Extra large size, or 72x84 inches. Price, per pair........ $9.95

No. 37R93 **This Blanket is made of the finest quality of selected Saxony wool**, with deep luxurious fleece, and is of an extraordinary size (76x88 inches). Nothing finer shown anywhere. Comes in white only. Has a silk binding and handsome colored borders. Price, per pair........ $12.50

No. 37R95 **Crib Blankets.** Fine white wool filled; mohair bound and fancy colored borders. Size, 30x40 inches. Price, per pair........ 80c

No. 37R97 **White Crib Blankets.** Extra fine California wool filled; a very fine quality and well worth $2.25 per pair. Fancy colored borders. Size, 30x40 inches. A bargain.

Our special price, per pair........ $1.49

QUILTED BED COMFORTS

37R129-$1.25

37R131--$1.75

37R135 $1.80

37R133--$1.98

37R121--47c

37R125--85c

37R137--$2.75

37R127--$1.00

COMFORTERS.

WE ARE POSITIVE WE CAN SAVE YOU MONEY ON COMFORTERS. BE SURE AND INCLUDE THEM IN YOUR ORDER FOR FALL AND WINTER SUPPLIES.

No. 37R121 Quilted Bed Comforters, covered with dark fancy figured print. Single bed size.
Price, each........................47c

No. 37R123 Quilted Bed Comforters, covered with dark and light fancy figured print. Full size.
Price, each........................69c

No. 37R125 Reversible Bed Comforters, covered on both sides with fancy robe print. Full size.
Price, each........................85c

No. 37R127 Quilted Chintz Covered Bed Comforters, figured turkey red on one side and plain on the other, fast colors. Full size.
Price, each........................$1.00

Special Value at $1.25.

No. 37R129 Quilted Comforters, the standard grade, the good reliable kind. Covered with handsome figured print of medium colors and plain colored lining. Full size.
Price, each........................$1.25

No. 37R131 Handsome and Reliable Comforters. Covered with fancy figured sateen and plain color lining. Full size. We can strongly recommend this number, it is soft and well made.
Price, each........................$1.75

No. 37R133 Good Reliable Comforters, fancy figured sateen and plain colored lining. Comes in medium colors. Extra good value. Full size.
Price, each........................$1.98

No. 37R135 Hand Made Summer Weight Tufted Comforters, covered with handsome figured silkoline, principally light colors. Full size.
Price, each........................$1.80

$2.75 Buys a $4.00 Comforter.

No. 37R137 Figured Sateen Bed Comforters, the satisfactory kind, with good quality plain sateen lining, rich colorings and guaranteed fast. They are sure to please you. Full size.
Price, each........................$2.75

No. 37R139 Handsome Elderdown Bed Comforters. Filled with pure down. Plain on one side, fancy floral designs on the other. Warranted fast colors. Regular bed size.
Price, each........................$4.25

No. 37R141 Elderdown Bed Comforters. Extra fine quality, well filled with pure down. Light or dark colors. Soft and downy. One of the finest comforts that money can buy.
Price, each........................$5.25

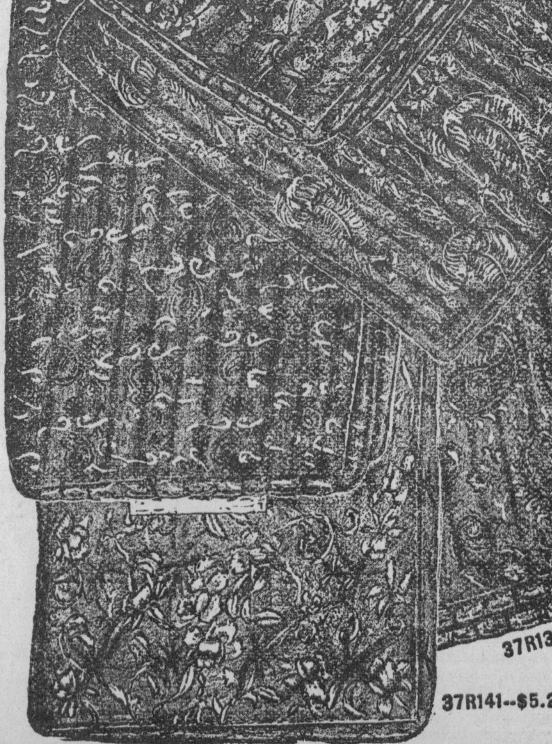

DEPARTMENT OF LACE CURTAINS.

OUR LACE CURTAIN DEPARTMENT has grown to where our sales are enormously large, we being one of the largest distributers of lace curtains in this country, and by reason of our position, from time to time we have been able to make contracts and so control the production and the cost of production, as to be able to get out new and exclusive designs, and improve the quality generally to that extent that we are today recognized headquarters as the makers of low prices on the highest grades of foreign and domestic lace curtains. You can buy a low, medium or high grade lace curtain from us, one pair at a time, for less money than your storekeeper at home can buy in quantities.

OUR LACE CURTAINS are made for us under contract by the best foreign and domestic makers. We place our contract for an entire season in two directions, taking the entire output of the mills, and we therefore take pleasure in calling your attention to the line of lace curtains we show, extending to you this unqualified guaranteed offer. Select any pair of lace curtains from our line, enclose our price, and we will send them to you with the understanding and agreement that if they are not perfectly satisfactory when received, if you do not feel that you have saved about one half in price by sending your order to us, you can return the curtains to us at our expense of freight or express charges both ways, and we will immediately return your money.

IN THIS OUR ENLARGED LACE CURTAIN DEPARTMENT we show a handsome line of Nottingham, Renaissance, Irish Point, Swiss, French embroidered and Brussels net lace curtains, in especially new designs for this season, many of them exclusive patterns, curtains that can be had only from us.

IN DIRECTING YOUR ATTENTION to our big new line of foreign and domestic curtains we especially urge that you do not compare them with any of the cheap, trashy stuff that find their way into country stores in country towns. The curtains we show are made by manufacturers whose product goes almost exclusively to the representative city retail stores, and it is only in city retail stores that you can select lace curtains that will compare in style and quality with what we offer, and there you will be compelled to pay about double our price.

IF YOU INTEND BUYING LACE CURTAINS we are extremely anxious to receive your order, if only for a sample pair; anxious to send you even one pair of curtains, that you may see how much more style is shown in our line than anything you can buy from your dealer at home; anxious to show you how much money we can save you. We know if we receive your order for one pair of lace curtains as a sample we shall be sure to receive a further order, and you will be so well pleased with the curtains we send you, you will advise your friends to send their orders to us.

EVERY LACE CURTAIN WE SHOW THIS SEASON is entirely new, fresh, direct from the mills, on our season's contract. We have no old stock. If you order from us you will get the very latest class of goods that is going out to the most fashionable city retail stores. They are extra new numbers and you will get the curtains at prices based on the actual cost to produce, the cost of material and labor at the mill, with but our one small percentage of profit added. UNDERSTAND, we do not break pairs of curtains, and we do not send samples, but every curtain is sent out under our binding guarantee as to quality, and our guarantee that it will please you, and if you are not perfectly satisfied, you can return them to us at our expense and we will return your money.

Irish Point Lace Curtains at $2.98.

Irish Point Lace Curtains, come in cream or white, exactly like illustration, not the poor grade so much on the market; a very soft, close net, with very artistic designs; overlocked edges. No better value to be had for the money. Length, 3 yards; width, 45 inches.
No. 37R150 Price, per pair.................. **$2.98**
If by mail, postage extra, 12 cents.

$3.98 Beautiful Irish Point Lace Curtains

If you do not say that these curtains are splendid value at our importers' price, return them to us and we will refund money.

Irish Point Lace Curtains, have a beautiful worked border and pretty scroll center. This is undoubtedly an elegant curtain for the price, exactly as illustrated, and we expect this number to be a very rapid seller. We can furnish it in cream or white, mention which you desire. Length 3½ yards; width, 50 inches.
No. 37R152 Price, per pair.................. **$3.98**
If by mail, postage extra, 16 cents.

Special Value in Irish Point Lace Curtains for $5.25 per Pair.

Irish Point Lace Curtains. Beautiful high grade goods, well finished. The border is exceedingly rich, showing an abundance of high art work on a very fine quality of netting; the center is relieved with a neat spray with an occasional figure of openwork, comes in white or cream. Length, 3½ yards; width, 50 inches. **(If by mail, postage extra, 22 cents.)**
No. 37R154 Price, per pair.................. **$5.25**

Very High Grade Irish Point Lace.

High Grade Irish Point Curtains. Strictly high art work as per cut shown. This curtain must be seen to be appreciated. Beautiful and well made goods, such curtains can only be procured from first class stores, and this number is bound to be a winner. Comes in white only. Length, 3½ yards; width, 50 in.
No. 37R156 Price, per pair.................. **$7.50**
If by mail, postage extra, 27 cents.

Genuine Imported White Brussels Net Lace Curtains.

Genuine High Grade Brussels Curtains, not the imitation, but our own direct importation. The designs are delicate and exquisite, as per illustration; this curtain will be a big advertisement for us, as it is fit for a mansion. Comes in white only. Length, 3½ yards; width, 50 inches. **(Postage, extra, 10c.)**
No. 37R158 Price, per pair.................. **$6.75**

Our $7.19 Brussels Lace Curtains.

The handsome curtain shown in the above illustration is our highest grade Brussels curtain, one that is sure to be a great advertisement for us wherever it goes. We are large importers of fine curtains, and this is by far one of the best values we have ever handled. It is made by one of the largest factories in St. Gall, Switzerland, the **home of Brussels lace curtain making.** The design is entirely new for this season, and, as you can see by the cut, is delicate and pleasing to the eye. It comes in white only, and is 50 inches wide and 3½ yards long. We do not break pairs of lace curtains. **Our prices are always by the pair,** and these prices are always so low that we are only too glad to have you compare them, quality for quality, with any other prices you can get elsewhere.
No. 37R160 Our special price, per pair **$7.19**
If by mail, postage extra, 12 cents.

Our Newest Nottingham Lace Curtain Novelty.

The accompanying illustration will give you an idea of this, the handsomest curtain that it has been our pleasure to present to our multitude of customers all over the world. We are the exclusive handlers of this beautiful new style of lace curtains. The size is 3¼ yards long by 60 inches wide. It is one solid piece of lace, the lambrequin effect as shown in the cut for the top. This curtain has the effect of curtains that sell for $3.50 to $5.00. It comes in white, also cream. Length 3¼ yards; width 60 inches. **(Postage, extra, 16 cents.)**
No. 37R161 Price, each.................. **$1.25**

Our Taped and Hemstitched Mull Ruffled Curtains.

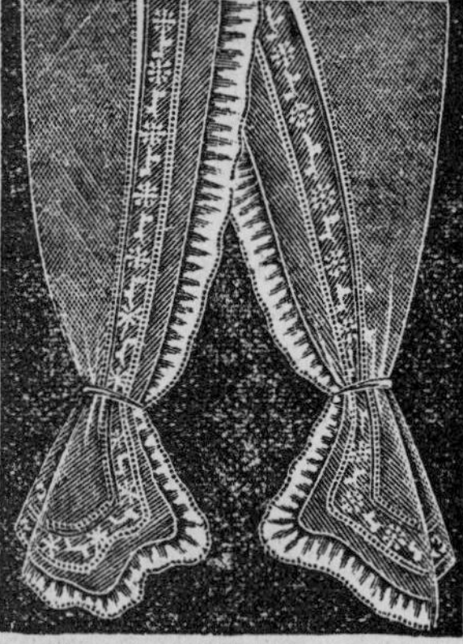

This is a beautiful new, stylish, dainty muslin curtain; is most perfectly made and most durable of any curtain in our collection. The illustration will show you the beauty of this curtain, and is a correct illustration. Size is 3 yards long and 40 inches wide. Suitable for bed rooms, dining rooms, etc.

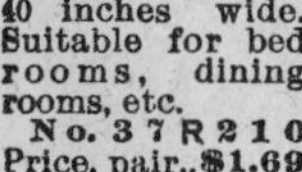

No. 37R210
Price, pair..$1.69

Our $1.75 Ruffled Curtain Wonder.

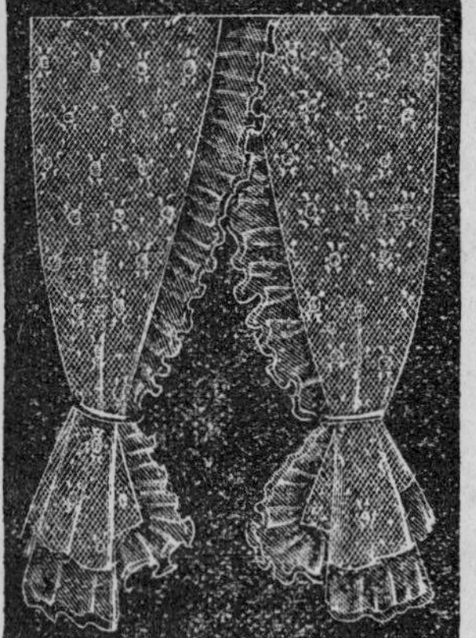

For $1.75 we give you one of the handsomest curtains imaginable. Comes in a sheer beautiful mull, with a medallion figure through center, as per illustration. Taped ruffles, and is in every way one of the most durable and sightly ruffles to be found anywhere. Our price of $1.75 is whittled down to the very lowest cost of material and for making, with nothing but our one small margin of profit added. This curtain at $1.75 is equal in price and for wearing qualities to curtains that sell in ordinary dry goods and furniture stores at from $3.00 to $3.50. Size, 3 yards long by 45 inches wide.

No. 37R212 Price, per pair.... ....$1.75

Our $1.60 Fish Net Ruffled Curtain Bargain.

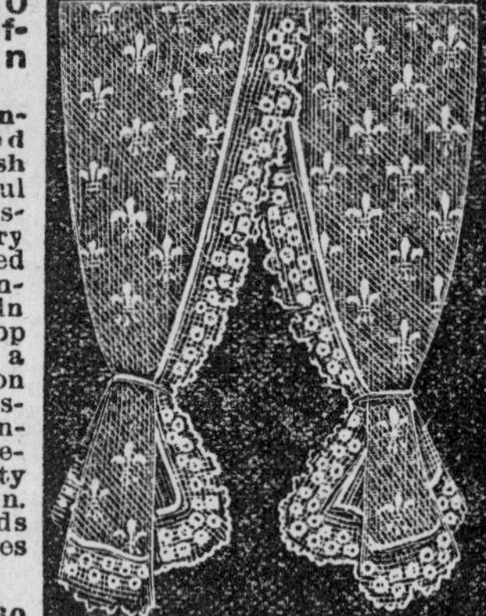

This is a genuine imported Swiss loop fish net, a beautiful design like illustration, the very choicest ruffled curtains obtainable. Comes in strong white loop fish net, with a pretty medallion design like illustration. You cannot fail to appreciate the beauty of this curtain. Size is 3 yards long and 42 inches wide.

No. 37R213
Per pair....$1.60

Our $1.19 Fish Net Lace Curtain, a Curtain that will Seldom Retail at Less Than $2.00.

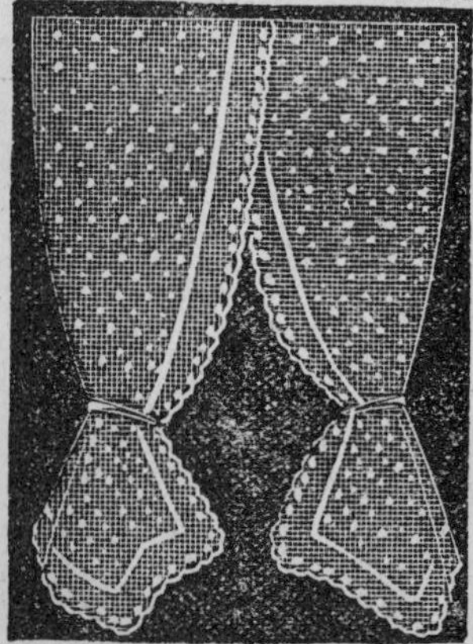

Our $1.19 special extraordinary bargain is a pure white pretty design of fish net lace with a deep ruffled edge, like illustration. Our $1.19 price is phenomenal, as it merely covers the cost of the material. It is bought direct from the manufacturers in large quantities, the price of making, and our one small percentage of profit added. This curtain is equal to any that is shown by the ordinary upholstery and lace curtain departments at double our price. This curtain is 3 yards long and 40 inches wide, strong and durable, and at the same time a very dainty, chic pattern; will launder perfectly.

No. 37R214 Price, per pair.................$1.19

Our $1.49 Fish Net Lace Ruffled Curtain.

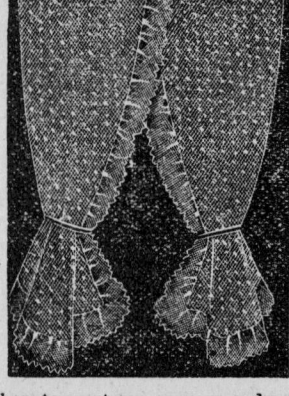

This is another of our special bargains in this pretty style of curtain that is so very popular this season. The size is 3 yards long by 45 inches wide. The design, as per illustration, is very pretty. It launders beautifully. The color is pure white. Our price of $1.49 is remarkable. Order one or more pair of these curtains, or in fact any of the curtains quoted in our line of ruffled curtains, and if description, size and quality does not answer our description, return them to us at our expense and we will refund your money. This $1.49 curtain is used extensively by hotels for their dining rooms, or in fact for all purposes for which a curtain is used.

No. 37R216 Price, per pair..........................$1.49

Our $1.59 White Torchon Lace Trimmed Brussels Net Ruffled Curtain.

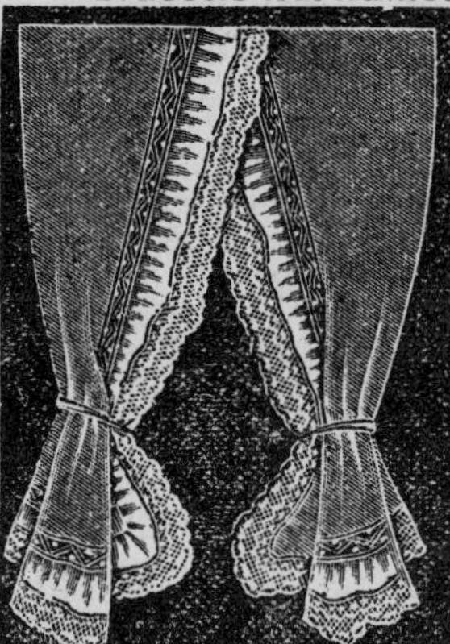

This is a novelty and one of the newest and prettiest designs in our unmatchable line of ruffled curtains. Come in a beautiful quality of white Brussels net, with a white ruffle, torchon lace insertion 2 inches wide, and an edge 2 inches wide to match, like illustration. This beautiful curtain is 3 yards long and 44 inches wide.

No. 37R220
Price, per pair, ...$1.59
Postage, 10c.

Our $1.98 Brussels Net Ruffled Curtain.

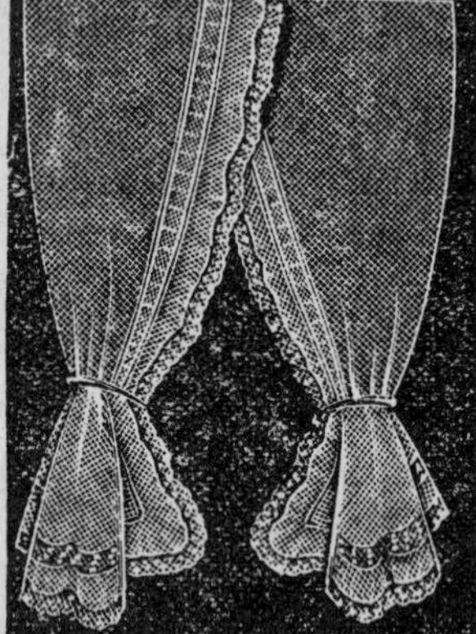

Comes with a very deep ruffle, with an insertion of Valenciennes lace, with edging to match, as shown by the illustration. This is a very pretty design of ruffled Brussels net curtain. It is made very durable; will wash nicely. Size, 3 yards long by 40 inches wide. Our price of $1.98 is based on the very smallest price of cost of material and making, and our one small percentage of profit added.

No. 37R222
Per pair....$1.98

Our $2.50 50-inch Wide Brussels Net Ruffled Curtain.

This Curtain is made like illustration. Two rows of Honiton insertion, with taped edge on ruffle, and with imitation of hand drawn work, making a finish to the ruffle; and also Honiton lace edge on ruffle to match insertion. Our price of $2.50 is at least $1.00 less than the same quality of ruffled lace curtains was ever sold at by any dealer.

No. 37R224
Size, 50 inches wide and 3 yards long. Price, per pair........$2.50

Our $2.95 Brussels Net Ruffled Curtain.

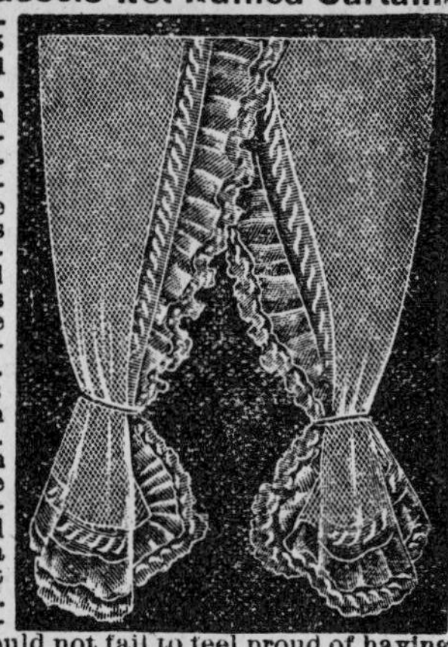

This is a handsome curtain, 45 inches wide and 3 yards long. It has a 4½-inch wide heavy torchon lace insertion, with a corresponding edge to match. It is strong and durable, stylish and washable, and is in all the acme of beauty in a ruffled curtain. These curtains are a new design for this season. Goods are shown by no other house outside of metropolitan cities, and they are in only a few of the most exclusive houses. The most fastidious housewife could not fail to feel proud of having one or more pairs of this beautiful torchon trimmed Brussels ruffled curtains in the best rooms of her house. The torchon lace used in the making of this curtain, also the net, are special importations; the design of lace is exclusive, and new for this season.

No. 37R226 Size, 45 inches wide and 3 yards long.
Price, per pair.......................................$2.95

Our $3.25 Medallion Brussels Net Ruffled Lace Curtains.

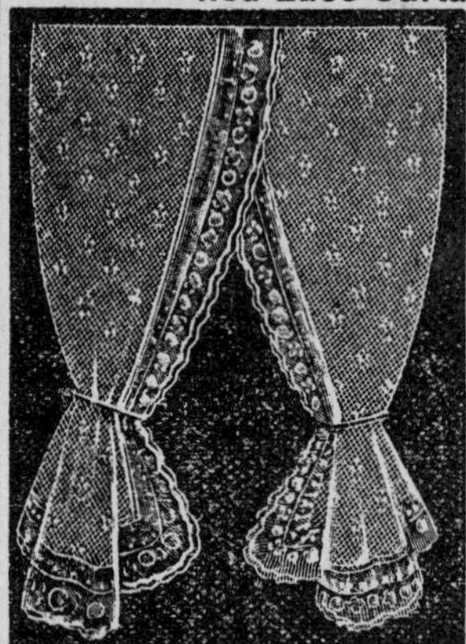

The lace is of a very fine, dainty quality, at the same time strong, with a handsome medallion design at intervals over the surface. It has a deep 3-inch Valenciennes lace for ruffle, with a pretty taped finished edge inside of ruffle. This curtain will launder beautifully. It has the effect of a real imported French Brussels net curtain, that would ordinarily sell at $12.00 to $15.00 a pair. It is 42 inches wide, and 3 yards long. The thread of which this curtain is made is of the finest sea island cotton, and is wear resisting, washable and stylish. The curtain is a gem, and is suited for the best rooms in the best house in the land.

No. 37R228 Price, per pair. **(Postage, 14c)**. $3.25

Handsome Fish Net Curtain Material at 12½ Cents per Yard.

Loop White Fish Net, for curtains, etc. A pretty and durable strong twisted netting. Comes in cream, also white. 36 inches wide.

No. 37R250 Price, per yard........12½c

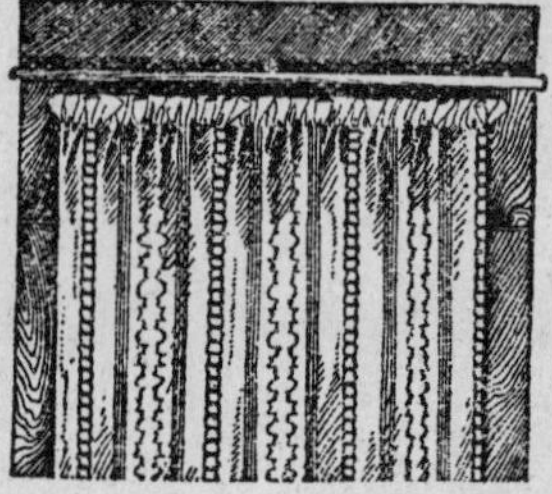

Fine Embroidered Mull Curtain Material at 10 Cents per Yard.

36-Inch Pure White Embroidered and Hemstitch Mull. A pretty sheer dainty curtain material like cut. This is a genuine bargain.

No. 37R252 Per yard.............10c

22 Cents per Yard, Fleur de Lis Loop Fish Net.

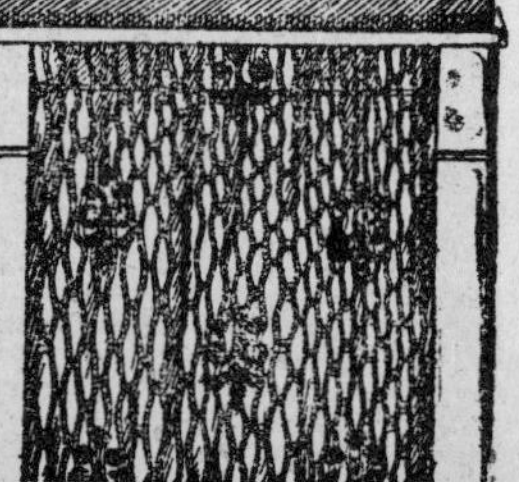

This is a rare pretty pattern of strong Loop Fish Net. Comes in cream, also white. Width, 50 inches. Style like cut.

No. 37R254 Per yard...........22c

If by mail, postage extra, on lace curtains, about 18 cents per pair.

WONDERFUL VALUES IN CHENILLE, TAPESTRY AND ORIENTAL CURTAINS.

OUR VALUES as shown in this special department are most extraordinary. The goods are entirely new for this season, we own them direct from one of the largest mills in this country. These special draperies are made for us under contract by a mill of which we control the output, and our prices are based on the actual cost of material and labor, with but our one small percentage of profit added, less than dealers can buy in any quantity.

IN ORDERING carpets, rugs, wall paper or other furnishings or decorations, do not fail to include the necessary draperies—chenille, tapestry or oriental curtains.

YOU WILL BE SURPRISED at the money we can save you, surprised at the beautiful new designs and new effects we can furnish you. When you see and compare the goods sold by others you will also be surprised at the great saving in price.

EVERY CURTAIN IS GUARANTEED as to quality, style and price. If you order one or more curtains from us, and you do not find them all and even more than we claim for them, and such value as you could not possibly get elsewhere, you can return the goods to us at our expense of freight or express charges both ways and we will immediately return your money.

OUR NEW $1.98 CHENILLE CURTAINS.

No. 37R750 At $1.98 per pair, we offer this new, handsome design as the equal of chenille curtains that sell everywhere at about double the price. From the illustration you can get some idea of the appearance of these handsome new curtains, a good quality of chenille, not the poor grade; heavy chenille tassels with dado border. Come in colors, olive, terra cotta, cardinal, tan or blue. Width, 36 inches each; length, 3 yards. Our special $1.98 price barely covers the cost of material and labor, with but our one small percentage of profit added.

No. 37R750

Price, per pair.........$1.98

Our Heavy, Rich $4.95 Chenille Curtains.

No. 37R762 For $4.95 per pair we offer this extra heavy, richly decorated, new design, in 46-inch width, 3 yards long, as the equal of anything in new 1902 chenille curtains you can buy at $7.00 to $10.00 per pair. This illustration will give you but a faint idea of the beautiful effect worked out in this new design. These are our very finest chenille curtains, the finest chenille curtain turned out by the manufacturer. There is positively nothing better. In this curtain is worked out a heavy, rich, 27-inch fancy border, trimmed with heavy tassel fringe. Come in colors, terra cotta, slate, bronze, peacock, olive, garnet or cardinal. They are 46 inches wide and 3 yards long. Understand, we are willing to send these curtains to you with our guarantee that you will find them perfectly satisfactory, handsomer, richer and altogether better than anything you could get from your dealer at home at greatly advanced prices.

No. 37R762 Price, per pair, $4.95

Our New $2.87 Chenille Curtains.

No. 37R754 For $2.87 per pair we offer these large, handsome, richly finished, new 1902 style Chenille Curtains as the equal of curtains that sell everywhere at $4.00 to $5.00 per pair. Our special $2.87 price is made possible by reason of buying these goods direct from the mill in large quantities, buying them at factory cost, and our special $2.87 price barely covers this cost, with but our one small percentage of profit added. The illustration will give you some idea of the appearance of these curtains, but you must see them to appreciate the real value we are giving. Understand, you can order a pair of these curtains with the understanding that if they are not all and even more than we claim for them, you can return them to us at our expense and we will cheerfully return your money. These chenille curtains are extra quality, have very rich borders, long tassels; one of the handsomest effects shown this season. They come in beautiful colorings, olive, terra cotta, cardinal, tan or blue. Give us an idea of the coloring wanted, let us know what other colors the curtains are to harmonize with. These curtains come 42 inches wide and 3 yards long.

No. 37R754 Price, per pair, $2.87

A RARE TAPESTRY CURTAIN VALUE AT $1.49.

Comes in a big line of colors, including peacock, cardinal, garnet, medium navy, olive, terra cotta, tan, empire green, in pretty combinations. This handsome tapestry curtain is our leading number and a value the greatest ever offered. You would pay $2.00 to $2.50 for a curtain with less style in ordinary stores, and under the most favorable circumstances it would be cheap at $1.75. Pattern like illustration. Size, 3 yards long, 34 inches wide.

No. 38R763

Price, per pair.........$1.49

Our $3.98 Extra Heavy New Chenille Curtains.

No. 37R758 At $3.98 per pair we offer these extra heavy, extra large, 46-inch wide, Chenille Curtains as one of the handsomest things shown this season; a new design expressly for us, from one of the best mills in this country, a pair of chenille curtains such as would retail at $6.00 to $8.00. From the illustration, engraved from a photograph, you can get some idea of these curtains, but you must see them, examine them and compare them with curtains sold at double the price to appreciate their real value. Understand, these curtains are the very latest in style for this season, from one of the best mills in the country; rich, new border effect; very heavy, long tassels. They come in a variety of beautiful colorings, including olive, terra cotta, cardinal, tan and blue. Give us an idea of the coloring wanted, the colors they are to harmonize with, and we will send the curtains to you with our guarantee that they will please you or we will return your money. Width, each, 46 inches; length, 3 yards.

No. 37R758 Price, per pair. $3.98

Our New $1.87 Tapestry Curtains.

No. 37R766 At $1.87 we offer these new Tapestry or Satin Damask Curtains, an entirely new design for this season and from one of the largest makers of tapestry curtains. We feel confident that after you have seen and examined them you will agree with us they are such value as was never before offered by any house. From the above illustration, engraved by our artist direct from a photograph, you can form some idea of the handsome pattern effect in these curtains, but you must really see them to appreciate their value. They come in a variety of handsome combinations of colorings. The predominating colors are olive, terra cotta or cardinal with other pretty colors to combine. They have a deep heavy fringe; are 36 inches wide and 3 yards long. If you wish a really handsome thing in a satin damask, fringed curtain, in an entirely new, rich design for this season, at a very low price, we guarantee that you will find in these curtains such value as you could not possibly get elsewhere.

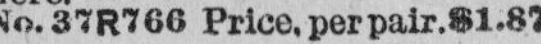

No. 37R766 Price, per pair. $1.87

OUR NEW $4.25 HIGH GRADE OTTOMAN CURTAINS OR PORTIERES.

At $4.25 per pair we offer these large rich portieres direct from the best maker in this country. The price barely covers the cost of material and labor, with but our one small percentage of profit added. These curtains must be seen, examined and compared with other curtains to appreciate the beauty and value we are giving. They come in red and tan, red and green, blue and tan, terra cotta and tan, tobacco brown and tan, olive green and tan, emerald green and tan, emerald green and red. They are 50 inches wide, 3¼ yards long.

No. 37R784

PRICE, PER PAIR **$4.25**

OUR GREATEST AND BEST EXTRA HEAVY MERCERIZED SILK LUXURIOUS PORTIERES $6.48

This is a material lustrous and fine, also heavy and with all the richness of a $25.00 all silk portiere. A drapery suited for the homes of millionaires. Pretty in design (like cut) and the color combinations are superb. They are rich shades of cardinal, old rose, olive, tobacco brown, empire green, dark peacock blue and terra cotta. Size, 50 inches wide, 3 yards long.

No. 37R788

PRICE, PER PAIR **$6.48**

OUR NEW ENLARGED DRAPERY DEPARTMENT.

THIS, OUR SPECIAL DEPARTMENT OF DRAPERIES, a department devoted exclusively to the handling of all the very latest, most fashionable, up to date fabrics of foreign and domestic weaves for all decorating purposes, is in point of values given, heretofore unheard of price offerings, new and attractive styles, exclusive designs in foreign and domestic goods, not to be equaled by any other line shown in this country. From the small illustrations and descriptions you can form but little idea of the extraordinary values, the handsome new effects we are offering in this, our department of draperies.

OUR GUARANTEE OFFER. Select any number from the illustration and description, send us your order, enclose our price, and we will send the goods to you with the understanding that if they are not perfectly satisfactory, exactly as represented, and such value as you could not get elsewhere; if you don't find them more stylish and more up to date, if you don't see that they have a distinctiveness and exclusive style not to be had outside of the most fashionable city retail stores; if you do not feel that you can so decorate your room or your home as to give it an artistic effect that your neighbor cannot effect with the goods she buys from your home merchant, and above all, if you do not feel that you have saved about one-half in price, you can return the goods to us at our expense of charges both ways and we will immediately return your money.

THE NUMBERS SUBMITTED are new for this season, right up to date. Among them are designs exclusively our own. You will find for beautifying and decorating your home, your room, or the hundred and one purposes for which these new. artistic numbers can be used, there is nothing shown that will compare with this line.

HOW WE MAKE THE PRICES SO VERY LOW. These goods are made for us under contract by the very best makers. We buy them in immense quantities for cash, thus reducing the first cost to the very minimum, and adding but our one small percentage of profit, we offer these goods for even less than dealers can buy in any quantity.

UNDERSTAND, we cannot furnish samples. These goods are never sampled, but your order will be shipped under our guarantee that the goods will please you or your money will be immediately returned to you. In ordering carpets, curtains, in ordering wall paper, furniture or other merchandise, don't overlook this our special drapery department. Your order for furniture, carpet, rugs or wall paper will not be complete without including the needed draperies from this, our new enlarged and price reduced department. **There is not a number in the line that will not please you, no value that will not surprise you.**

OUR NEW HANDSOME 36-INCH BAGDAG DRAPERIES

FOR 15 CENTS PER YARD.

These are the genuine Bagdad colors. They are imported goods.

THEY ARE GOODS THAT SELL EVERYWHERE AT 25 AND AS HIGH AS 35 CENTS PER YARD.

We have bought a tremendous lot of these imported genuine Bagdad materials at about 50 cents on the dollar, and as long as they last, which we think will be about the term of this catalogue, which is twelve months, we will be able to supply these beautiful draperies in any quantity. They are swell patterns, and the accompanying illustration gives you a faint idea of the patterns. They have a beautiful combination of colorings and are handsomely worked out in Oriental fabrics, in which yellows, Indian reds and soft tan blues, also green, have prominence. The colorings that prevail in these beautiful Bagdad draperies are navies, reds, greens, olives, cadet blue, porcelain, tans, yellows and nile green. Width, 36 inches.

No. 37R849 Price, per yard......**15c**

Fancy Oriental Cretonne Drapery at 12½ Cents a Yard.

No. 37R858 Fancy Oriental Cretonne. An entirely new fabric and is sure to be a rapid seller. Medium weight. Proper thing for furniture covering, hangings, etc. Comes in light blue, rose, cream and pink grounds with pretty colorings to harmonize. Width, 36 inches. Price, per yard............12½c

No. 37R862 Figured Sateen Drapery. A very rich cloth. It is a splendid quality sateen. Pink, rose, red, blue, olive, yellow and nile green grounds with pretty colorings to harmonize. Width, 36 inches. Very rich for sofa pillows.

Price, per yd., 15 Cents.

Handsome English Cretonne at 6½ Cents a Yard.

No. 37R866 English Cretonne or Drapery. Proper thing for furniture covering or hangings. It is a good strong cloth with a twill. Comes in black, navy, cream, red or green grounds, with pretty contrasting figures. Width, 25 inches. Price, per yard, 6½c

Our 13-Cent English Cretonne.

No. 37R870 English Cretonne resembling above but much higher grade of goods. This number comes in dark rich colorings, also light grounds, such as rose, nile green, terra cotta, and light blue, with pretty contrasting colors. Width, 30 inches.

Price, per yd., 13 Cents.

Tinsel Drapery.

No. 37R850 Tinsel Drapery. A very pretty thing for draperies of all kinds. Comes in cardinal, terra cotta, blue and olive backgrounds, with other pretty colorings to harmonize. Width, 27 inches.

Price, per yard, 8 Cents.

Silkoline.

No. 37R854 Handsome Figured Silkoline. Not the poor grade so much on the market, but a good quality cloth. Comes in blue, pink, yellow, nile, terra cotta and red grounds, with pretty contrasting figures. Width, 36 inches.

Price, per yard, 10 Cents.

Denims for Drapery or Fancy Work.

No. 37R874 Fancy Denim, the proper thing for draperies or fancy work. Comes in very rich colorings, good quality cloth. Colors are nile green, terra cotta, olive or blue grounds, with contrasting figures. Width, 34 inches.

Price, per yd., 12 1-2 Cents.

Extra Quality Heavy Printed Upholstery Velours at 49 ents Per Yard.

PRICE, PER YARD,
49 CENTS
Width, 29 inches

This is a quality of fine and heavy velours resembling a close pile plush, handsomely printed in designs like the accompanying illustration. A quality that sells at from 75 cents to $1.25 per yard in the majority of upholstery departments, and not to be found except in the best houses at any price. Colors are crimson, medium brown, olive and empire green. Width, 29 inches.

No. 37R922 Price, per yard.................. 49c

Our 98-Cent 25-Inch Imported Silk Drapery and Upholstery Plush.

For 98 cents we furnish this beautiful heavy weight silk plush in solid colors of all the beautiful colorings as described, as the equal of any 25-inch silk plush you can buy elsewhere at $1.50 to $2.00 per yard. We own these goods at the mill cost, to which we add only our one small percentage of profit. It is the biggest seller in our entire line for handsome silk plush upholstery and decorative purposes. It is made expressly for decorating fine homes, especially used for upholstery and decorating cozy nooks, Oriental rooms, also for lambrequins, curtains, etc. It comes in the following plain, rich colors: Cardinal, garnet, gold, turquoise, national blue, olive and tabac brown. Don't write for samples; simply give us an idea of the color, enclose our price and we will send the goods to you with the understanding that if they are not all and more than we claim for them, and better value than you can buy elsewhere, you can return them to us at our expense and we will immediately return your money. Width, 25 inches.

No. 37R923 Price, per yard.......................98c

Crushed Upholstery Plush.

No. 37R924 Crushed Upholstery Plush. There is nothing more durable for furniture covering. Extra heavy. Colors in gold, olive, bronze, terra cotta or cardinal. Width, 24 inches. Price, per yard......98c

Felt for Table, Drapery, Etc.

No. 37R925 Felt, good quality, suitable for tables, draperies and fancy work. Comes in all colors. Width, 72 inches. Price, per yard.....$1.19

Chenille and Tapestry Table Covers.

If by mail, postage extra, on Nos. 37R950, 37R970—8 cents; on Nos. 37R956, 37R972—18 cents; Nos. 37R959, 37R974—22 cents; Nos. 37R976, 37R990—34 cents; Nos. 37R978, 37R992—38 cents.

No. 37R950

No. 37R950 Chenille Table or Stand Covers, pretty patterns. Size, including fringe, 34x34 inches. Price, each. 35c

No. 37R953 A Very Pretty Chenille Table Cover. Comes in very rich colorings, good quality. Size. 54x54 inches, including fringe. Price, each 70c If by mail, postage extra, 14c

No. 37R956 Extra Heavy Chenille Table Cover. Comes in dark rich colorings. Size, 54x54 inches, including fringe. Price, each.................................. 89c

No. 37R959 Very Finest Quality Chenille Table Cover. Looks rich and will wear for years. Very heavy fringe. Size, 54x54 inches, including fringe. Price, each..$1.00

No. 37R962 Extra Large and Heavy Chenille Table Covers. Full size. Suitable for parlor or sitting room table; nothing larger in this class of goods; comes in a very heavy fringe and beautiful quality chenille. Price, each.......................$2.25

Fine Tapestry Table Covers at 43 Cents and Up.

No. 37R970 Tapestry Stand or Table Cover. Comes in pretty design; predominating colors, nile, olive, terra cotta or red. Size, 36x36 inches. Price, each. 43c

No. 37R972 Tapestry Table Cover. Comes in rich colorings, beautiful designs. The predominating colors are light or dark blue, light or dark green, red, rose, brown, tan or peacock. Size, including fringe, 54x54 inches. Price, each......79c

No. 37R974 Tapestry Table Covers. Extra fine quality. Beautiful rich colorings, which are green and red combination and red and tan combination. Size, 54x54 inches, including fringe. Price, each. 98c

No. 37R976 Tapestry Table Covers. Beautiful quality and colorings. The predominating colors are red, green, olive or blue, with other pretty colors to harmonize. Size, 58x58 inches. Price, each...$1.45

No. 37R978 Tapestry Table Cover, extra large, 72x72 inches, suitable for center or dining room tables, comes in solid colors with pretty designs, same color as ground work, a splendid cover for the money. Comes in red, green, olive or brown. Price, each.....$1.49

$2.50 Ottoman Table Cover for $1.69.

No. 37R990 Extra High Grade Ottoman Table Cover, very rich, and will give splendid wear; comes in pretty contrasting designs in peacock, green or cardinal grounds. Size, 58x58 inches. Price, each, $1.69

No. 37R992 Beautiful Fancy Tapestry Table Cover, comes in very large full size, intended for large center tables; it is almost two yards square; it is certainly a beauty and we expect it to be a very rapid seller. Come in red mixed, blue mixed and also green mixed; has a beautiful heavy fringe; is reversible and can be used on both sides. Price, each...........................$2.75

ROPE PORTIERES.

Rope Portieres look very rich and nobby; they are handsome and ornamental drapings, and they do not darken the doorways.

Fine Rope Portieres for $1.39.

No. 37R1000 Rope Portieres, like cut, ⅜-inch cord, interwoven with tinsel; can be adjusted to fit any doorway up to 6 feet wide; length of portiere, 7½ feet; the pretty combinations are red and green mixed, golden brown and olive and also empire green and rose mixed.

PRICE, EACH, $1.39

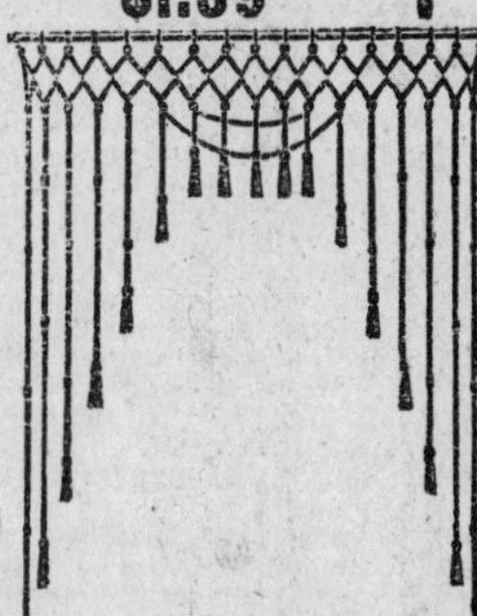

Our $2.25 Rope Portiere.

No. 37R1004 Rope Portieres, like illustration; same colorings and quality as above, but much heavier and richer; this is extra good value for the money.

PRICE, EACH, $2.25

$2.49 Rope Portiere.

No. 37R1008 Rope Portieres, made of ⅜-inch solid cord in different colors combined, such as red and green combinations, empire green and rose, peacock blue and tan, olive and pink and also light and dark green and red mixed, exactly like cut. Will fit any doorway. Excellent value.

PRICE, EACH, $2.49

$3.98 Rope Portiere.

No. 37R1012 Rope Portieres. The reliable, up to date kind. "OUR GREAT LEADER," and can't be beat. Will fit any doorway; a beautiful and rich portiere, and will be very much admired. Must be seen to be appreciated. Same combination of colors as No. 37R1008, but an exquisite heavy cord.

PRICE, EACH, $3.98

$4.59 Rope Portiere.

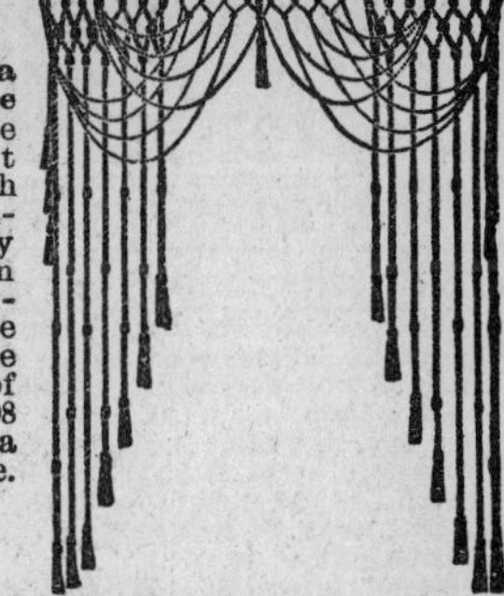

No. 37R1016 Extra High Grade Rope Portiere. One of the finest and highest grades produced; rich enough for a mansion. Is made of 3-ply ¾-inch combination cord, extra heavy, exactly like cut. We can furnish it in the same combination of colors as Nos. 37R1008 and 37R1012. This is a most elaborate drape.

PRICE, EACH, $4.59

Fancy Ottoman Couch Covers, A Rare Bargain for $1.98.

No. 37R1020 Fancy Ottoman Couch Covers. A very fine grade of tapestry, has a small neat twill, and the designs are simply exquisite; beautiful Oriental fancy stripes, as per cut. The combination of colors are gobelin, gold, laurel green, cardinal and tan, all combined, which makes it a very rich cover, and will harmonize with surroundings. Has pretty tassel fringe and is reversible. Width, 50 inches; length, 3 yards. Price, each.......................$1.98

Our $3.25 Oriental Tapestry Couch Cover, Usual Retail Price, $4.00 to $5.00.

No. 37R1024 We have added to the Upholstery Department a beautiful Oriental Tapestry Couch Cover. This is one of the handsomest designs ever shown in Oriental tapestry. Comes in rich colorings, with gold, black and blue; garnet, green and gold; empire green, tan and gold. This beautiful couch cover is 50 inches wide inside of fringe. Fringed all around, and is altogether one of the handsomest couch covers to be found anywhere. A cover that would sell ordinarily in carpet stores and upholstery departments in a retail way at from $4.00 to $5.00. Our special price for this beautiful couch cover.......... ....$3.25

ABOUT FREIGHT AND EXPRESS

It is seldom necessary to write us to ask what the freight or express will amount to. The weight of almost every item is given under the description.

BY REFERRING TO PAGES 7 TO 10

you can get the rate of freight and express to a point near you in your state, which will be almost, if not exactly, the same rate as to your nearest railroad station. From this you can calculate almost exactly what the freight or express will amount to on any shipment to your town, and you will find it will amount to next to nothing as compared to what you will save in price.

CARPET AND RUG DEPARTMENT.

FOR BIG VALUES in Carpets, Rugs, Linoleums, Oil Cloths, Mattings, etc.; for unapproachable prices on everything that goes to make up one of the largest exclusive Carpet Departments in the country, we call your attention especially to the illustrations, descriptions and the cut price quotations we are offering in this department this season.

WE CUT, MATCH AND SEW ANY CARPET WHEN SIZE OF ROOM OR DIMENSIONS ARE GIVEN. FOR 36-INCH CARPET, 3 CENTS PER YARD FOR 27-INCH CARPET, 5 CENTS PER YARD

OUR CARPET DEPARTMENT has been widely advertised by our customers by reason of the splendid values we have been furnishing first with one special leader, then another, until the sale of several of the numbers illustrated has consumed the entire capacity of the mill running on such special numbers, and by this enormous outlet, by going to a mill with a capacity on one line of goods of say ten pieces per day, and thus inducing them, under contract, to increase their output to twenty pieces per day, thus reducing the cost of manufacture, we have been able to shade the cost to us. every penny of which has gone to our customers in the way of a lower price, and in return for this we get increased sales, increased volume.

FROM THE COLORED ILLUSTRATIONS, which have been engraved and reproduced by the late color process from photographs taken direct from the carpets, you can get a very clear idea of the handsome patterns we are furnishing, although the carpet must really be seen to be appreciated, for these color illustrations are reproductions. They are reduced from a yard square, therefore, the handsome pattern effect is very much diminished. Want of space, and with a disposition to economize, with a view to squeezing every price possibility, we only show a portion of our carpets in color illustrations.

FROM THE BLACK ILLUSTRATIONS, however, you can get a very good idea of the carpets as to pattern and style, and if you will select any carpet, linoleum, oilcloth or rug from the illustrations and descriptions, and will send your order to us, we will send you the carpet with the understanding that if it is not perfectly satisfactory in every way, you are at liberty to return it to us at our expense of freight charges both ways and we will immediately return your money.

NEW STYLES. In our Carpet Department for this season we have endeavored to show the very latest styles for this seasons the same class of goods that will be found in the best city stores. New designs, as carefully selected, represent the very best productions for this year, and if you order a carpet from us, you will get a newer, nicer and handsomer design, more up to date in pattern, coloring and make than you would be likely to get in any ordinary market.

A COMPLETE SET of large samples of our carpets, including every number in our line, will be furnished on receipt of $1.00, and the $1.00 will be returned to you when the samples are returned to us, express prepaid.

YOU WILL NOT FIND IT NECESSARY to send for samples before ordering, for the color illustrations will give you a very good idea of the pattern and color effect, and we have endeavored in our descriptions to be so plain that you could order the carpet direct from our catalogue from the illustrations and descriptions almost as intelligently as you could order from large samples of the carpet, with almost the same satisfaction as if you were in our store selecting the carpets from our stock.

WHILE WE DO NOT RECOMMEND that you delay to first write for samples—we especially urge that you make your selection from our catalogue, from the descriptions and illustrations, always with the understanding that if the carpet is not perfectly satisfactory when received, you can return it to us at our expense, and we will immediately refund your money.

OUR COMPLETE LINE OF SAMPLES comprises from 25 to 40 samples. The ingrain and granite carpet samples are furnished in size about 18x9 inches, and the Brussels and velvet carpets, 27x9 inches, size large enough to give you a very good idea of the pattern, color effect and quality and one of the most complete lines of carpets shown by any house or maker.

THIS BIG LINE OF SAMPLES will be sent to any address on receipt of $1.00, the $1.00 to be returned to you on the following conditions:—We send this line of samples to you by express, and if the samples are returned to us by express prepaid, we will immediately refund your $1.00. Understand, you are under no obligation to return the samples to us. If you keep them to make any use of them we, of course, will reserve the right to retain the $1.00 you send us to partly reimburse us for the cost of the samples sent you.

WHILE WE ISSUE THE BIGGEST SET OF CARPET SAMPLES that is furnished by any mail order house, they are gotten out very nicely, they are good size, there is one sample of every number in our line, and with these samples you can tell just exactly what you are getting, the same as if you were in our store selecting the carpet from stock, and we would be pleased to send you the complete set on receipt of $1.00. We wish to repeat that we recommend that you do not wait to write for samples, but select the carpet wanted from the illustrations and descriptions and send us your order, with the understanding and agreement that if the carpet is not perfectly satisfactory when received, you can return it at our expense of freight charges both ways, and we will immediately return your money.

Our 12-Cent Hemp Carpet.

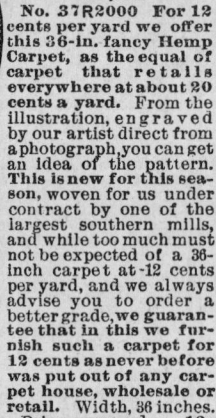

No. 37R2000 For 12 cents per yard we offer this 36-in. fancy Hemp Carpet, as the equal of carpet that retails everywhere at about 20 cents a yard. From the illustration, engraved by our artist direct from a photograph, you can get an idea of the pattern. **This is new for this season,** woven for us under contract by one of the largest southern mills, and while too much must not be expected of a 36-inch carpet at 12 cents per yard, and we always advise you to order a better grade, we guarantee that in this we furnish such a carpet for 12 cents as never before was put out of any carpet house, wholesale or retail. Width, 36 inches. Price, per yard.....12c

Our Special 19-Cent Hemp Carpet.

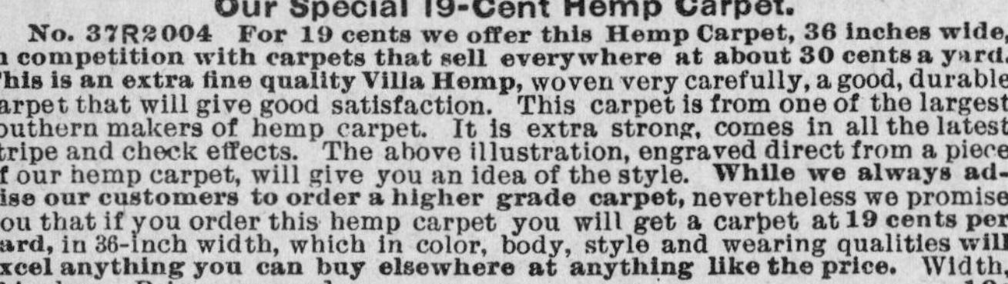

No. 37R2004 For 19 cents we offer this Hemp Carpet, 36 inches wide, in competition with carpets that sell everywhere at about 30 cents a yard. This is an extra fine quality Villa Hemp, woven very carefully, a good, durable carpet that will give good satisfaction. This carpet is from one of the largest southern makers of hemp carpet. It is extra strong, comes in all the latest stripe and check effects. The above illustration, engraved direct from a piece of our hemp carpet, will give you an idea of the style. **While we always advise our customers to order a higher grade carpet, nevertheless we promise you that if you order this hemp carpet you will get a carpet at 19 cents per yard,** in 36-inch width, **which in color, body, style and wearing qualities will excel anything you can buy elsewhere at anything like the price.** Width, 36 inches. Price, per yard.......................................19c

25 Cents Buys Our Best Hemp Carpet.

No. 37R2008 For 25 cents per yard we offer this 36-inch extra super quality IXL Hemp Carpet, from one of the best southern mills. **Our 25-cent price** is made possible by reason of taking the output of this mill, a mill located where it can turn out better carpet for less money than any other mill in the country. **This is one of the best hemp carpets made.** You must see it, examine it and compare it with other hemp carpets to appreciate the value we are giving. **It is a good, heavy, firm hemp in a fancy stripe weave.** The above illustration, engraved by our artist from a photograph, will give you an idea of the average pattern effect of this carpet. **If you want an A1 hemp carpet we advise you by all means to order this, our highest grade.** It is a carpet the equal of carpets that are retailed generally at 35 to 50 cents. **Send us your order,** give us an idea of the stripe pattern wanted, let us know what room or rooms the carpet is to be used for, and if we do not send you a hemp carpet **such as you never saw before at anything like the price,** you can return it to us at our expense and we will cheerfully return your money. Width. 36 inches. Price, per yard.......................................25c

Our Finest Rag Carpet, 34 Cents.

No. 37R2011 For 34 cents we offer this, our very best quality, extra heavy rag carpet, as the equal of carpet that sells everywhere at 50 cents and upwards. This rag carpet, like our cheaper 27-cent carpet, we own under contract, bought from the same mill. It is extra heavy and extra strong, comes in a very handsome rag pattern. There is no better rag carpet of the kind made. **The colorings are beautiful and we can guarantee the carpet for wear.** Let us know the size of the room you wish to cover, **give us an idea of the colorings wanted,** and we will send you a carpet with a guarantee that it will be all and more than you expect or we will return your money. Width, 36 inches. Price, per yard.......................................34c

Our 27-Cent Rag Carpet.

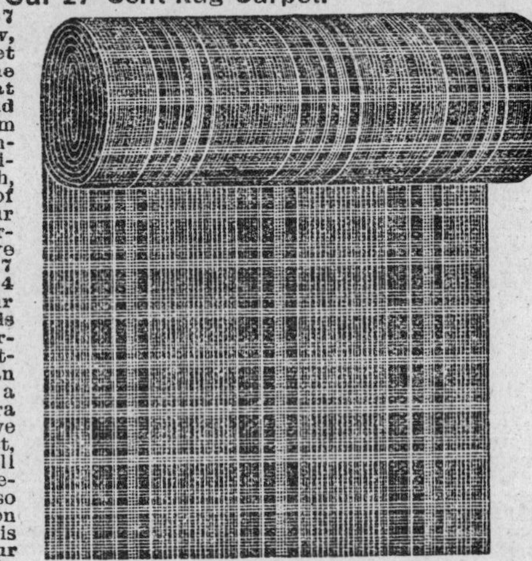

No. 37R2012 For 27 cents we offer this new, handsome Rag Carpet as a special value, the equal of carpet that you have no doubt paid 40 to 50 cents for. From this illustration, engraved by our artist direct from a photograph, you can get some idea of the appearance of our new, high grade rag carpets, of which we have two numbers, one at 27 cents and one at 34 cents per yard. **Our special 27-cent price is below the lowest market today.** We contracted for this carpet with an eastern mill that had a very large stock of extra fine material on hand, we closed our contract, which protects us for all the carpet we will require for this season, so throughout the season we can furnish you this rag carpet, under our guarantee for quality, at a much lower price than it will probably ever again be sold. **This is a splendid quality of rag carpet at the price;** is a pretty pattern, will give thorough satisfaction, comes 36 inches wide, and is a carpet you must see, examine and compare with other carpets to appreciate its value and its exceptionally rich colorings. **Give us an idea of the room you wish to carpet, order this, our special 27-cent rag carpet,** and if you do not say that it is such value as you have never seen before, return it to us at our expense and we will return your money. Width, 36 inches. Price, per yard.............27c

Special Extraordinary Sale of Extra Heavy Three-Ply All Wool Ingrain Carpet, at 79 Cents Per Yard.

This is one of the highest grades of three-ply carpets manufactured, is strictly all pure Australian wool. Nothing better shown in all wool, three-ply ingrain carpets at any price. The accompanying illustration will give you an idea of the design and the colorings will be found superb. The colors are dark, red predominating, with bright olive, tan and terra cotta forming the smaller designs. The large scroll is composed of the light olive stem outlined and bordered with dark cream. The effect of these combinations of color is something very much above the ordinary. **It is a carpet that will give extraordinary wear and can be turned, as it has a very beautiful combination of colors on either side and is perfectly finished.** We recommend this carpet as equal to carpets retailed at $1.39 to $1.50 per yard in exclusive carpet houses, jobbing houses and department stores. **No. 37R2016** Price, per yard.......................................79c

58 Cents Buys This Heavy Weight Ingrain Carpet.

58 cents per yard buys this heavy weight reversible all wool extra super ingrain carpet, in one of the richest dark red backgrounds, and newest rich floral designs shown this season. For color illustrations showing the coloring and pattern effect, see colored plate on page 893.

For 58 cents per yard we offer this new, handsome, rich dark red background all wool ingrain carpet, a reversible, extra super ingrain carpet from one of the best makers in America, as the equal of carpets that sell everywhere at 75 cents and upwards.

This is a new, handsome, rich design, as taken from one of the richest and most expensive carpets on the market this year. It has all the style, all the color, all the new pattern effect of a carpet that costs many times the price we ask, is in style such a carpet as you could not get excepting from the most fashionable city carpet stores, and in quality is equal to carpets that sell at 25 cents to 40 cents more per yard.

This 58-cent all wool two-ply extra super reversible ingrain carpet has all the weight, all the strength, all the wearing qualities and far more style than most of the three-ply ingrains on the market. For a handsome, red mixed carpet for parlor or other room, it will give you every satisfaction. We have established a reputation as the largest dealers in high grade carpets in America, selling direct to the consumer. We cut up thousands of yards every day.

This handsome 58-cent new number comes in dark, deep rich red, with brown, and the tan floral effect is produced by a combination of scarlet, white, light tan and crimson. Width, 36 inches.

No. 37R1872 Price, per yard......58c

For 3 cents per yard extra, we will cut, match, make and sew this carpet to fit any size room for which you will furnish measurements.

58 Cents per Yard Buys This Extra Quality All Wool Ingrain Carpet,

in one of the richest, handsomest and newest olive green effects, a new design, and a rich coloring such as you can get only in the most expensive carpets in fashionable city retail stores. For illustration, showing coloring and pattern effect, as reproduced by the latest color photographic process, see page 893.

At 58 cents we have brought out in this carpet a reproduction of one of the richest and most expensive carpets shown this season. We have duplicated in coloring and in pattern, in surface effect, everything that is shown in the most fashionable, new designs in the most expensive carpets, as offered by the most fashionable city retail carpet dealers. This one of those rich, new, green backgrounds on which is a handsome checkered and floral leaflet design, and you must see, examine and compare this carpet with other and more common carpets to appreciate the value we are offering.

This carpet has a handsome, rich, green background with leaf effect brought out in very light tan and yellow, the general effect being very pretty, soft and harmonious. Width, 36 inches.

No. 37R1877 Price, per yard......58c

At 58 Cents We Offer This Carpet as the Equal of What is Usually Sold at 75 Cents to $1.00.

For 3 cents per yard extra, we will cut, match, make and sew this carpet to fit any sized room for which you will furnish measurements.

58 cents per yard buys this handsome, new, rich, red background carpet in a handsome, heavy floral design, entirely new for this season. A good weight, wear resisting all wool ingrain carpet, which we offer at 58 cents in competition with the more common styles of ingrain carpet that retails generally at from 75 cents to $1.00 a yard. For color illustration showing the colorings and pattern effect as reproduced from a yard and a half length, by the late photographic color process, see page 893. 58 cents is our special price, a price based on the actual cost of material and labor with but our one small percentage of profit added. This our special 58-cent two-ply ingrain carpet has a rich, dark red background with a large scroll and floral design effect, covering the entire surface and worked out in the following beautiful, harmonious colors: light blue, yellow, crimson, all blending into a tan effect so very fashionable this season. Width, 36 inches.

No. 37R1882 Price, per yard......58c

For 3 cents a yard extra, we will cut, match, make and sew this carpet to fit any room for which you will furnish measurements.

58 Cents for This All Wool Ingrain Carpet.

58 cents per yard buys this our new design in green, with a handsome good weight, all wool ingrain carpet, the equal of carpets that sell generally at 75 cents and upwards.

For colored illustration, showing the colorings and pattern, as reduced from a 1½-yard length by the late photographic color process of which the colors are reproduced in their natural shades, see page 893.

58 cents a yard for this new, handsome, green background, all wool ingrain means a saving to you of from 25 to 40 cents per yard. For example: If you need 25 yards of this carpet to cover your room, you will save from $5.00 to $10.00 by sending your order to us, and you will get in this our special 58-cent ingrain carpet a newer and handsomer design than you can get from your dealer at home, as it is a new design for this season direct from the mills, one that has never been shown before, a design copied after one of this season's richest patterns. This carpet is made for us under contract by one of the best carpet makers in America. Under our contract we own the carpet at the cost of material and labor, to which we add our one small percentage of profit, and as a result you can buy it from us at less than dealers can buy in any quantity. This carpet has a rich dark green background, design of fancy medallion, maple leaf and ferns, brought out in white, golden red, blue and bright emerald green. For a carpet for the parlor, library, bedroom or other room you will find this the most desirable carpet you can possibly get at the price. Width, 36 inches.

No. 37R1887 Price, per yard......58c

For 3 cents per yard extra we will cut, match and sew this carpet to fit any sized room for which you will furnish measurements.

48 Cents is Our Wonderfully Low Price.

48 cents per yard buys this new design in a handsome, heavy weight, reversible two-ply, wear resisting, wool filled cotton chain ingrain carpet, one of the richest, dark red backgrounds, with new large tan scroll effects, one of the handsomest numbers shown this season, a carpet the equal of those that sell generally at 60 to 75 cents per yard. For colored illustration, showing the color and design as reproduced from a yard and a half length, by the latest photographic color process, see page 893.

At 48 cents per yard we offer this handsome, heavy weight, wool filled cotton chain ingrain carpet, one of the greatest values in our carpet department, entirely new for this season. This carpet has a rich, dark red background, very large scroll designs, covering nearly the entire surface, worked out in tan and yellow, giving the carpet a rich tan and red effect. Our special 48-cent price barely covers the cost of material and labor, with but our one small percentage of profit added. It is less than dealers can buy in any quantity. Understand, we will accept your order with the understanding, if the carpet is not entirely satisfactory in every way, you can return it to us and we will return your money.

No. 37R1892 Width, 36 inches. Price, per yard......48c

For 3 cents extra per yard we will cut, match, make and sew this carpet for any sized room.

This Beautiful Pattern Only 48 Cents.

At 48 cents we offer this handsome, heavy weight, reversible two-ply wool filled cotton chain, heavy weight wear resisting ingrain carpet in a rich green background, with one of the handsomest new scroll and floral designs shown this season, the equal of carpets that sell generally at 60 cents to 70 cents per yard. For colored illustration, showing the coloring and pattern reproduced from yard and half length, by the latest color photographic process, see page 893. At 48 cents per yard for this heavy weight, reversible two-ply wool filled cotton chain ingrain carpet, will mean a saving to you of 15 to 25 cents on every yard, from $2.50 to $5.00 saving on the carpeting of any ordinary room. 48 cents barely covers the cost of material and labor with but our one small percentage of profit added, less than dealers can buy in carload lots, the lowest price ever made on this grade of ingrain carpet. We take the entire output of the mills. One loom runs for us on the one number the year around, which alone makes possible this extremely low price.

This new design, heavy weight, reversible, two-ply wool filled cotton chain ingrain carpet comes in a rich, deep, empire green background, with large scroll covering the entire face, with handsome floral and large leaf worked out in the following beautiful color combination: black, crimson, white and yellow, making a general tan and empire green effect. This carpet is suitable for all rooms, for parlor, library, hall, bedroom, etc. Width, 36 inches.

No. 37R1894 Price, per yard......48c

CHURCH CARPETS.

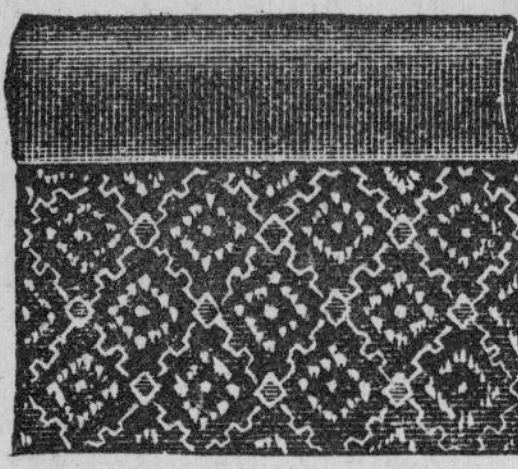

66 cents per yard buys this rich, handsome, new, dark empire green, genuine 9-wire tapestry Brussels carpet, a carpet the equal of carpets that sell generally at 85 cents to $1.00 per yard. **For color illustration as reproduced from a yard and half length by the latest photographic color process, showing the** coloring and the pattern, see page 891. **At 66 cents per yard, a price that barely covers the cost of material and labor,** a lower price than dealers can buy in any quantity, we offer this genuine 9-wire, closely woven, wear resisting, heavy weight tapestry Brussels carpet in one of the richest dark empire green shades in a small handsome pattern, entirely new for this season, one of the richest and handsomest tapestry Brussels carpets woven in this country. **For 5 cents extra per yard we will cut, match and sew this carpet to fit any room desired.** Width, 27 inches.

No. 37R1925 Our special price, per yard......**66c**

For 66 cents we offer this handsome, heavy weight, wear resisting, 9-wire Brussels carpet in this rich, new, modest, small design, our own exclusive pattern, entirely new for this season, a carpet the equal in quality, superior in design and color, to carpets that retail at 85 cents to $1.00 per yard. For color illustration, see page 891. **At 66 cents per yard for 27-inch width, for a handsome small pattern carpet in a beautiful color combination, a carpet especially suitable for churches, lodges, large rooms, etc.,** also equally adapted for home use, parlors, bedrooms, or other rooms. **For 5 cents per yard we will match, cut and sew this carpet, if size of room and dimensions are given.** Width, 27 inches.

No. 37R1929 Our special price, per yard......**66c**

At 66 cents per yard we offer this new, handsome, rich, dark red background tapestry Brussels carpet, with a new small figure, as the equal of carpets that sell everywhere at 85 cents to $1.00 a yard. **For colored illustration,** showing the colorings and new pattern, as reproduced from a yard and half length, by the photographic process, see page 891. **This is a genuine 9-wire wear resisting, heavy weight tapestry Brussels pattern in a new, rich, small, modest design, the latest thing** for this season. **This carpet has a rich, deep red background,** with small design decorations in which is mixed yellow, turquoise, bright olive, cherry, black and cerise. **This pattern is especially desirable for carpeting churches, halls, lodges;** makes a rich floor covering for a large hotel parlor or dining room, is suitable for public school rooms, bed rooms, halls or stairways. **At 5 cents extra per yard, we will cut, match and sew this carpet to fit any room desired.** Width, 27 inches.

No. 37R1933 Price, per yard.......................**66c**

Our Big, New, Dark Red 58-Cent Leader.

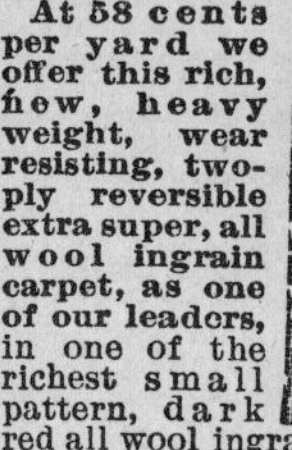

At 58 cents per yard we offer this rich, new, heavy weight, wear resisting, two-ply reversible extra super, all wool ingrain carpet, as one of our leaders, in one of the richest small pattern, dark red all wool ingrain carpets woven.

For color illustration of this handsome pattern, showing the extraordinary effect that is brought out in this our wonder number at 58 cents per yard, reproduced from a yard and a half length by the late photographic color process, see page 892.

At 3 cents extra per yard, if you so desire, we will cut, match, and sew this carpet to fit any room. Width, 36 inches.

No. 37R1937 Price, per yard.......................**58c**

This special 58-cent heavy weight two-ply reversible ingrain carpet is an entirely new pattern for this season, with a small figured green background, relieved with small figures of light tan and green mixed. For color illustration, showing colorings and pattern, reproduced from a yard and a half length, by the new photographic color process, see page 892. **This carpet is suitable for all purposes where a modest green background with a small figured effect is wanted. At 3 cents per yard extra we will cut and make this carpet to fit any sized room for which you will furnish measurements.** Width, 36 inches.

No. 37R1938 Price, per yard.....................**58c**

Our New Heavy Weight Special 58-Cent Two-Ply Wool Ingrain Carpet.

For color illustration showing colors and pattern reproduced by the late color photographic process, see page 892.

This is one of the heaviest, strongest, best wearing reversible ingrain carpets on the market. The pattern is entirely new for this season, has a rich deep red background with small design decoration, in which is mixed ecru and tan. This pattern is especially desirable for churches, halls, lodges, etc. It also makes a rich floor covering for large hotel parlors or dining rooms; also is suitable for bedrooms and living rooms. It is, in fact, an all purpose heavy weight reversible ingrain carpet, a new number for this season.

For 3 cents per yard extra we will cut and sew this carpet to fit any room according to your measurements. Width, 36 inches.

No. 37R1939 Price, per yard.....................**58c**

FLOOR OILCLOTHS AND LINOLEUMS.

Our 23-Cent Fancy Floor Oilcloths.

For illustration showing the exact colorings see page 894. At 23 cents per yard for one-yard width to 46 cents per yard for two-yard width we offer this rich, handsome pattern of heavy weight, extra strong floor oilcloth. This is one of the greatest values ever shown. It is very low in price but the quality will prove to be extraordinary. It is one the greatest values ever shown by any house. This oilcloth is made for us under contract by one of the best makers in this country. The color effects, pattern and material that are used in its construction are closely inspected by our buyer for this department. We have reduced the price to the actual cost of the labor and material and to this we add but our one small percentage of profit. If it is not entirely satisfactory, a greater value than you could get elsewhere for double the money, you have the privilege of returning it and your money will be refunded.

Width, yards	1	1½	2
No. 37R1941 Price, per yard	**23c**	**35c**	**46c**

Our New Imported 26-Cent Extra Quality Floor Oilcloth.

At 26 cents for one yard wide, or 52 cents for two yards wide. For color illustration showing the extra pattern and colorings as reproduced by the late photographic color process, see page 894. This is a very extra quality heavy floor oilcloth which we offer at 26 cents and 52 cents, according to width. We have reproduced some of the most expensive floor oilcloths—cloths that sell at double the price at which we offer this oilcloth, and we have affected in this our 26-cent oil cloth all the weight, the pattern and the lustrous color and surface effect that you will get in the highest priced goods.

Width, yards	1	1½	2
No. 37R1942 Price, per yard	**26c**	**39c**	**52c**

At 34 to 85 cents we offer you our highest grade, heaviest, best and most wear resisting floor oilcloth. This beautiful pattern has an extra lustrous finish and is equal to the finest imported oilcloth that sells at double the price, a better oilcloth than you can get at your dealer's at home. A cloth that is equal to those which sell at double our prices. For illustration from the new photographic color process showing the exact colorings and pattern, see page 894. We do not furnish samples of floor linoleums and oilcloths, but will fill your order and if not perfectly satisfied when received you may return it and we will refund your money.

Width, yards	1	1¼	1½	2	2¼
No. 37R1943 Per yard	**34c**	**43c**	**51c**	**68c**	**85c**

At 95 cents for two yards wide and $2.35 for four yards wide, the only two widths in which this handsome, extra heavy linoleum is made, we offer this linoleum as the equal of any English linoleums that sell at double the price. This linoleum is made for us on a contract by the best maker in America, and we guarantee that for weight, color and depth of lustrous surface effect and finish that this is the superior to the productions in this pattern by the English manufacturers that sell at double the money. These goods should not be compared with cheap American goods as they have not the attractive pattern nor have they the lasting surface effected in this our extra grade of linoleum. **For illustration showing the exact colorings and the pattern in which this linoleum comes see page 894.**

Widths, yards	2	4
No. 37R1945 Price, per yard	**95c**	**$2.35**

At 95 cents for 2 yards width of this, our genuine Rostrand Linoleum. At 95 cents, $1.20 and $2.35, according to the width, 2, 2½ and 4 yards, we offer this, our genuine Rostrand linoleum, as a perfect reproduction of the genuine English linoleum that sells everywhere for more than double the price. **For color illustration showing the exact effect and pattern as reproduced by the late photographic process see page 894. At 95 cents to $2.35,** according to the width, the price is based on the lowest possible cost of production with but our one small percentage of profit added. We guarantee this to be equal, for wearing qualities, etc., to the English productions which sell at double the price.

Width, yards	2	2½	4
No. 36R1946 Price, per yard	**$0.95**	**$1.20**	**$2.35**

At 95c, $1.20 and $2.35 for widths of 2, 2½ and 4 yards, we offer this new, extra heavy linoleum as the equal of any English linoleums that sell at double the price. We secured in this high grade linoleum the genuine English, heavy surface effect; and they should not be compared with the cheap American goods that have not the attractive pattern and lasting surface. **See page 894 for color plate showing the exact pattern and color combinations** effected in this handsome high grade linoleum.

Width, yards	2	2½	4
No. 37R1947 Price, per yard	**$0.95**	**$1.20**	**$2.35**

Our New Extra Heavy Quality Linoleum.

In 2 and 4-yard widths, a linoleum heavier and better than anything that we have ever shown before. This linoleum is made by us under special contract, the material and pattern dictated and furnished by our expert linoleum buyer. The price has been cut to the very lowest from the fact of our immense outlet for this class of goods. **See page 894 for illustration showing the exact colors and pattern, reproduced** by the late photographic color process.

Width, yards	2	4
No. 37R1948 Price, per yard	**$1.35**	**$2.70**

Two Special Values in Heavy Weight Linoleums.

The accompanying illustration shows the pattern of another of our extra heavy, new linoleums, goods that are equal to the goods produced by the best foreign makers and which we sell at less than half the price that we would be compelled to charge you if we dealt in foreign goods. **See page 894 for illustration showing the exact colorings and pattern effects of this one of our handsomest and most reliable linoleums.**

This is a splendid, heavy weight, wear resisting linoleum, a good quality, a grade of goods that retails everywhere at nearly double our price.

No. 37R1949 Width, yards.. 2 4
Price, per yard.................$1.25 $2.70

The accompanying illustration gives you an idea of the beautiful pattern of another style of our extra heavy new linoleums. See page 894 for illustration in colors, showing the exact combination of colorings and the design of this one of our very best, in fact the very best linoleum procurable, linoleum with weight and wear resisting qualities and depth of surface material that you will find in the most expensive imported goods, and at one-half the price that we would be obliged to charge you if we were **importers of English linoleums.** The three last described qualities of linoleums are **made under our linoleum buyer's instructions,** as regards colorings, designs and weight, and we absolutely guarantee these goods for wear.

No. 37R1951 Width, yards.. 2 4
Price, per yard..................$1.25 $2.70

Our Heavy Floral 25-Cent Granite Carpet.

For 25 cents per yard for this full 36-inch width carpet, we offer this new, handsome, heavy weight, wear resisting, new floral design granite carpet in the very latest style, produced in the richest, heavy, new 1902 color effects, including rich green background with red and tan floral effects, a rich red background with tan and green floral effects; also a dark wine background with brown and rose effects. In ordering be sure to state whether you wish the red, green or dark wine background. **The small illustration, engraved by our artist from a photograph, will give you but a little idea of the beautiful coloring effect,** the handsome new floral design, the up to date style worked out in this rich, heavy weight, wear resisting, genuine granite carpet, which we are offering this season at the astonishingly low price of 25 cents per yard. The design is entirely new for this season, the colors are extra rich, beautifully blended, perfect harmony is effected and every color is absolutely fast color. **At 25 cents per yard for 36-inch width you have in this, our new 1902 Granite Carpet,** a carpet which, for wear, style, lasting colors, for all ordinary purposes, is the equal of carpets that sell everywhere at double the price and more. **The past season we have cut up thousands of yards of granite carpet made by this same mill.** The carpets have been shipped to almost every town in the United States. They have been used for parlors, bedrooms, halls, used for public halls, lodge rooms, hotels, etc., etc. They have proven extremely popular among the better class of hotels where large quantities have been bought for the carpeting of halls, parlors and reception rooms. They have been pronounced by everyone the greatest value ever shown in a heavy weight carpet at anything like the price. **This, our new number at 25 cents per yard, is a big improvement over the granite carpet we have been running the past season.** The manager of our carpet department has taken the matter up with the mill with a view of producing a heavier, finer, handsomer, and in every way a better granite carpet with new designs and new color effects for this season, and in getting out this granite carpet we have patterned and colored it after one of the most expensive Wilton velvet carpets so as to give you in this carpet at a very low price a carpet having all the style effect of a very much more expensive carpet.

HOW WE MAKE THE PRICE 25 CENTS. **This carpet is manufactured for us under contract in North Carolina where labor and material is very cheap,** made by a manufacturer whose mill is run by water power, where everything combines to the making from selected sea island cotton an extra heavy carpet, giving it all the appearance of a heavy wool carpet and still at the very minimum of cost, and to carry out our contract the most rapid carpet making machinery has been employed, machinery where we can now run three yards of carpet at the expense it formerly took to make one. By taking the output of this mill, reducing the cost to us to the cost of labor and material, the cheapest point in the United States, we can by adding our one small percentage of profit, offer you in this, our special new 1902 Granite Carpet a carpet the equal of anything that dealers can buy in quantities at 30 to 35 cents a yard, the equal of carpet that sells generally at about double our price. **No illustration or description will give you an idea of the values we are giving, and we do not furnish samples of carpets;** but if you will order by number, state the number of yards wanted or the size of the room or rooms you wish to cover, state whether you wish red, green or dark wine background, send your order to us enclosing our price, we will send the carpet to you with the understanding that if you do not find it such value as you could not possibly get elsewhere at anything like the price, if it isn't a surprise to everyone who sees it, you can return it to us at our expense and we will immediately return your money. **Understand, we do not furnish samples of any carpets,** but we guarantee them to please you in every way or we will immediately return your money. Remember this carpet is full 36 inches wide, entirely new for this season and **guaranteed the greatest value ever shown by any house.** Width, 36 inches.

No. 37R2021 Special price, per yard - 25c

Our Special 29-Cent Ingrain Carpet.

For 29 cents per yard we offer this 36-inch extra heavy wool and cotton mixed Ingrain as an entirely new number for this season, made by one of the best mills in this country, a mill which heretofore has not made carpet to retail at less than 50 cents a yard. **We have prevailed upon this mill to turn out for us a carpet that would have the appearance of carpet worth double the price,** and yet be a good, substantial carpet that we could put out under a binding guarantee for quality, something that would be accepted as very exceptional value at our special factory to consumer price. From the illustration, engraved by our artist, you can form some idea of the beautiful design effected in this carpet at 29 cents. However, it must be seen to be appreciated. **This carpet comes in a variety of beautiful colorings, including combinations of empire green and tan; garnet, tan and green, tan and cardinal. Send us your order,** we guarantee the goods to please you, and if you don't find it such a carpet as was never before shown at anything like the price, you can return it to us at our expense and we will return your money. Width, 36 inches.

No. 37R2024 Price, per yard - - - 29c

OUR NEW 1902 31-CENT INGRAIN LEADER.

THIS SPECIAL 31-CENT heavy weight 36-inch width Ingrain Carpet is entirely new for 1902; has the very latest colorings, including red background with tan and tobacco floral combination effect; also green background with tan and red floral effect. In ordering be sure to state whether you wish red or green background. **We feel confident we are offering at 31 cents per yard in this, our heavy union wool and cotton mixed ingrain carpet, the greatest value ever shown by any house in an up to date, new, wear resisting ingrain carpet.**

From the small illustration you can get but a faint idea of the beautiful coloring and handsome design worked out in this new number. It is the very latest effect for 1902, designed by one of the best carpet designers, copied after one of the most expensive Wilton carpets. It is a large maple leaf and rose design, the colors blending handsomely, and for a carpet for parlor, library, hall and bedroom, for a general purpose, wear resisting, richly colored carpet at a very low price, a price little more than one-half that charged by dealers generally, we especially recommend this, our new 31-cent leader.

HOW WE MAKE THE PRICE 31 CENTS. **As this carpet has never been sold to dealers in any quantity as low as 31 cents,** we feel that we should explain that our special 31 cent price is made possible by reason of our taking the entire output of an eastern mill. Under our contract this carpet is put on twelve looms where it is run the year around, and by keeping the carpet constantly on the same looms without any change, and by buying the materials in very large quantities for cash, the cost of manufacture is reduced to the very minimum; and to the actual cost to produce, the cost of material and labor, is added our one small percentage of profit; hence you can buy this heavy weight, union wool and cotton mixed, new design, rich, fast color ingrain carpet, in 36-inch width, at the heretofore unheard of price of 31 cents per yard.

REVERSIBLE. **This carpet is reversible. It can be worn on one side and then turned to the other, giving you almost double wear. Don't write for samples. We guarantee every carpet to give satisfaction** or we will immediately return your money. State the color wanted, state the number of yards wanted, enclose our price, and we will send you the carpet with the understanding that if it is not perfectly satisfactory, one of the handsomest ingrain carpets you have ever seen, the greatest value ever shown in your section, you can return it to us at our expense and we will immediately return your money. Width, 36 inches.

No. 37R2025 Price, per yard - - 31c

Carpet Linings.

No. 37R2041 Felt Carpet Lining, or paper in rolls of 50 yards. Weight, about 31 pounds. Price, per roll..........45c

No. 37R2042 Sewed Carpet Lining, filled with jute; 36 inches wide. Keeps the floor nice and warm and protects the carpet. Price, per yard........$0.02
Full bale of 200 yards..........3.90

No. 37R2043 Carpet Bindings, cotton carpet binding, 1 inch wide; 12-yard rolls, assorted colors. Price, per roll..........11c

...IN THE PRICES WE MAKE ON CARPETS...

as well as other goods, all catalogue and sampling expense has been deducted. We get paid for all catalogues and sample books, and for this reason

CAN SELL CHEAPER THAN OTHER HOUSES CAN.

Our New 35-Cent Fancy Ingrain Leader.

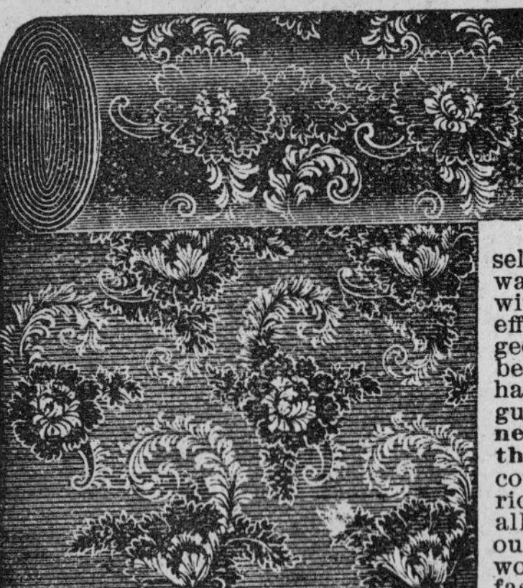

At 35 cents per yard, for full 36-inch width, we offer this new, heavy weight, one-half wool Ingrain Carpet in your choice of colors, in one of the newest, handsomest and most stylish 1902 patterns shown by any carpet maker. At 35 cents per yard we guarantee this carpet the equal of carpets that sell everywhere at 50 cents and upwards. Comes in green background with tan and brown scroll and floral effect; also in red background with geen and tan scroll and floral effect, beautifully blended, the colorings harmonizing perfectly. All colorings guaranteed to be fast. **This is a special new 1902 prize pattern from one of the biggest carpet makers in this country**, as copied by us from their richest and highest priced, three-ply, all wool ingrain. We feel we have put out in this, our special 35-cent, one-half wool, heavy ingrain carpet, all the new fast coloring effects, all the beautiful pattern designs, that you would get in the richest and most expensive three-ply, all-wool ingrain carpet made. **For a rich carpet for a parlor, a library, bedrooms, halls, or other rooms, you will find this carpet will give you every satisfaction.** It is one of the best wearing one half wool ingrains we have. **Our special 35-cent price is made possible by reason of our enormous output.** We are recognized as one of the largest buyers of carpeting in America. We take the output of several of the largest carpet mills in the country. We have revolutionized price making in this entire line by revolutionizing the method of selling goods. **If you will state the color wanted, the number of yards, and enclose our price, we will send any carpet to you with the understanding that if it isn't perfectly satisfactory**, all we claim for it, and far greater value than you could get elsewhere, you can return it to us at our expense, and we will immediately return your money. **We have no competition in the carpet line.** We are giving such values as never before went out of any house. You must see the carpeting we furnish to appreciate what we are doing. **This small illustration, engraved from the carpet**, will give you but a little idea of the beautiful design worked out in this, our special 35-cent number, but we guarantee it will more than please you. Width 36 inches.

No. 37R2029 Price, per yard..35c

Our Big 33-Cent Ingrain Leader.

No. 37R2031 For 33 cents **a yard we have advertised this carpet far and wide in the magazines, journals and other periodicals, as a carpet the equal of carpets that sell everywhere at nearly double the price.** Thousands of pieces of this special 33-cent two-ply ingrain have been cut up at our 33-cent price and have been shipped to almost every town in the United States. **From almost every order that goes out of our house we get duplicate orders.** We get letters saying that no such values were ever before seen, letters asking if we can fill additional orders at the price, letters asking us if we have not made a mistake in sending a bigger value. From the above illustration, engraved by our artist from a photograph, you can get some idea of the appearance of this handsome 33-cent carpet. **This is a high grade, wool mixed, new 1902 pattern ingrain carpet**, 36 inches wide. Comes in either a green background with tan scroll or a red ground with a tan scroll, as desired. This carpet is made for us under contract by one of the best carpet makers in America. **It is made extra strong and serviceable**, every yard is guaranteed and **our special 33-cent price** is based on the actual cost of material and labor, with but our one small percentage of profit added. **Send us your order for this carpet with the understanding that if when received it is not found perfectly satisfactory**, all and more than you expect, you can return it to us at our expense of freight charges both ways and we will return your money. Width, 36 inches.

No. 37R2031 Price, per yard..33c

A 60-Cent Wool Filled Ingrain Carpet for 45 Cents.

No. 37R2036 For 45 cents **we offer this Handsome New Wool Filled Ingrain Carpet as the equal of carpets that sell everywhere at greatly advanced prices.** This carpet must be seen, examined and compared with other carpets to appreciate the value we are giving. **It is the best quality manufactured in a wool filled carpet and we cannot recommend it too strongly.** The designs are the very newest for this season and the color combinations are simply beautiful. They come in dark red and tan mixed shades. **This is a special, high grade, closely woven, two-ply, wool filled ingrain carpet** that we put out under our binding guarantee, a carpet that will give extra service, such a carpet as you could not get elsewhere at anything like the price, a style that you will find only in the carpet stores of large cities. Width 36 inches.

No. 37R2036 Our price, per yard..45c

WONDERFUL STAIR CARPET VALUES.

With a determination that our values even in stair carpets shall be in keeping with our most extraordinary values in regular carpeting, we offer you the following four special numbers as selected from two of the best mills in this country, at a price that is practically mill price, a price that any ordinary wholesale dealer would today be compelled to pay the mill to buy.

Our 11-Cent Hemp Stair Carpet.

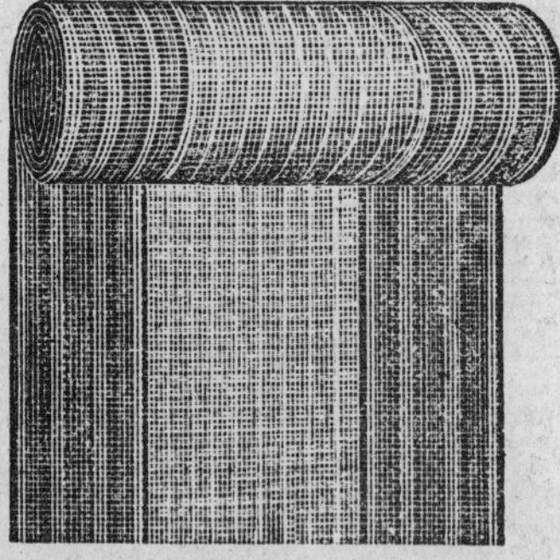

No. 37R2050 For 11 cents per yard we offer this 18-inch Hemp Stair Carpet as our leader for this season. From the illustration, engraved by our artist from a photograph, you can form some idea of the stripe pattern effect of this carpet, but, unfortunately, we cannot show you the colorings. This carpet comes with a tan mixed center and red border. **While we always advise that in selecting a carpet you take one of our better number of high priced carpets**, and get something especially new and handsome, yet at the price, **11 cents per yard**, this 18-inch stair carpet cannot be duplicated in any market in this country. **Do not wait to write for samples.** Send us your order; we will send the carpet to you under our guarantee for quality and satisfaction, and **if the carpet does not please you, you are at liberty to return it to us at our expense and we will immediately return your money.** Width, 18 inches.

No. 37R2050 Price, per yard..11c

Our Special 19-Cent Granite Carpet.

No. 37R2060 For 19 cents per yard, 22½-inch width, **we offer this New 1902 Granite Stair Carpet as the equal of carpet that sells everywhere at much higher prices.** From the illustration, engraved by our artist from a photograph, you can get some idea of the appearance, **the new 1902 design shown in this handsome 19-cent granite stair carpet.** This is a granite carpet that has a handsomer pattern and will give better wear than any ingrain carpet at anything like the price. **It comes in a rich assortment of colorings**, both red and tan and green and tan. **In ordering be sure to state color wanted.** Understand, every carpet is put out under our binding guarantee as to quality, we guarantee it to please you in every way, and if it does not, you can return it to us at our expense, and we will return your money. Width, 22½ inches.

No. 37R2060 Price, per yard..19c

Extra Heavy Ingrain Stair Carpet for 39 Cents.

No. 37R2064 For 39 cents **we offer this Handsome, Extra Heavy Ingrain Stair Carpet in 22½-inch width, as the finest stair carpet we handle.** A number entirely new for this season, from one of the best mills in this country, and if you order this carpet and do not find it equal to anything you can buy from your storekeeper at home at 60 cents per yard, we will cheerfully return your money. From the illustration, engraved by our artist from a photograph, **you can get some idea of the new 1902 pattern effect.** It comes in a beautiful combination of colorings. **Give us an idea of the coloring wanted and we will guarantee to please you.** Width, 22½ inches.

No. 37R2064 Price, per yard.....39c

Our New 1902 73-Cent Tapestry Brussels Stair Carpet.

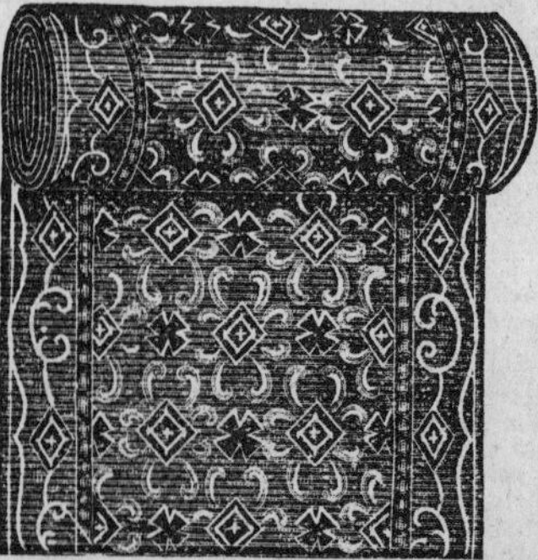

At 73 cents per yard we offer this brand new, up to date, rich, highly colored, 10-wire, heavy, wear resisting Tapestry Brussels Stair Carpet in 27-inch width as one of the richest, handsomest and biggest value stair carpets we have ever offered. **At 73 cents per yard** we are offering this rich, new, 1902 Tapestry Brussels Carpet as our biggest stair carpet leader. It is a genuine 10-wire, heavy weight tapestry Brussels stair carpet, in 27-inch width, made by the celebrated Dobson Carpet Mills, makers of the finest tapestry Brussels on the market. **The illustration will give you but a little idea of the rich, handsome pattern worked out in this**, our new Brussels stair carpet. It comes in rich combinations of cardinal, empire green, with white and wood colors. It is a simple design suited to go with any carpet. It is also used extensively instead of rugs in hallways. The colors are richly blended to a beautiful dark border. **We do not furnish samples of carpets**, and the illustration will give you but a faint idea of what we furnish in this, our special 73-cent leader; but if you will send us your order, enclose our price, we will guarantee the carpet to please you and to be the equal of carpets that sell everywhere at greatly advanced prices. **If you do not find it so you can return it to us at our expense and we will immediately return your money.** Width, 27 inches.

No. 37R2065 Price, per yard..73c

BIG FLOOR RUGS OR ART SQUARES.

THESE RUGS, COMMONLY KNOWN AS ART SQUARES, are furnished in the various sizes as quoted below, for the purpose of covering the floor of an entire room. For example: If your room is 8½ to 9 feet by 10 to 11½ feet, our smallest size rug, or art square, size, 7½x9 feet, will cover the floor and leave you from one foot to eighteen inches floor margin, or border. **These large bordered floor rugs, or art squares, are very popular used as rugs in place of carpets.** They are simply laid without lining or tacks as a carpet, and can be easily rolled up, removed, cleaned and replaced. **In cities, especially, it is fast becoming the custom to use these large bordered rugs, or art squares, in preference to the laying permanently of carpets.**

IF YOU WISH ONE OR MORE **large border trimmed rugs, if you are looking for something of this kind for your rooms in place of carpets, select the art squares, or bordered rugs, from the following illustrations and descriptions, send your order to us.** We will send the rugs to you with the understanding that if they are not perfectly satisfactory in every way, the equal of anything you can buy elsewhere at greatly advanced prices, you can return them to us at our expense and we will return your money.

NEW STYLES FOR THIS SEASON. **Our large bordered rugs are the very latest effects for 1902.** They come to us from one of the largest rug makers in America, a factory whose entire plant is devoted to the turning out of new and special up to date designs in these large square border trimmed rugs.

HEAVY INGRAIN RUGS AT $1.83 TO $3.59.

At $1.83 to $3.59, according to size (sizes ranging from 6 feet by 9 feet to 9 feet by 12 feet), **we offer these new rugs for this season at $1.83 to $3.59 in competition with rugs that sell everywhere at almost double the price.** From this illustration, which has been engraved by our artist from a photograph, you can get an idea of the general pattern effect of these new style, large bordered room rugs. **You will observe they are made with regular granite centers with handsome wide granite borders, with colored floral decorations to harmonize perfectly with the center, and each end of the rug is fringed. This very small illustration of a corner of the rug,** greatly reduced in size in order to print in this catalogue, gives you but a faint idea of the rug. When you see it you will be pleased with it, and if not, you can return it to us at our expense and we will return your money. **These, our Granite Rugs, are extra strong and heavy,** will give excellent wear, and our prices barely cover the cost of material and labor, with but our one small percentage of profit added.

No. 37R2400	Special Granite Rug.	Size, 6 x 9 feet	$1.83
No. 37R2401	Special Granite Rug.	Size, 7½x 9 feet	2.29
No. 37R2402	Special Granite Rug.	Size, 9 x 9 feet	2.49
No. 37R2403	Special Granite Rug.	Size, 9 x10½ feet	3.24
No. 37R2404	Special Granite Rug.	Size, 9 x12 feet	3.59

OUR FINEST BRUSSELS RUG, $13.50.

No. 37R2412 For $13.50 we offer this extra heavy 9x12-foot Brussels Rug or Art Square. A large border trimmed rug for a large room, a rug that would fit a room 10x12, 10x13 or 11x15; most any ordinary large room which a rug 9x12 feet will fit, with a suitable border of from 1 to 3 feet on either side. **This is one of the handsomest Brussels rugs shown this season,** an entirely new design, gotten out expressly for us, and our $13.50 price barely covers the cost of material and labor, with but our one small percentage of profit added. From the illustration, engraved by our artist from a photograph, you can form some idea of **the appearance of this handsome Brussels rug which we furnish at $13.50.** It is made from genuine high grade Brussels carpet, strictly high grade standard goods, the border beautifully harmonizing with the center. **The predominating colors are greens, blues, wines, tan and corn, intermixed with pretty contrasting colors.** Give us an idea of the colors wanted, and we will send you this rug with the understanding that, if it does not prove all and more than you expect, **if you do not find it the equal of rugs your dealer at home would furnish at $20.00,** you can return it to us at our expense of freight charges both ways and we will return your money.

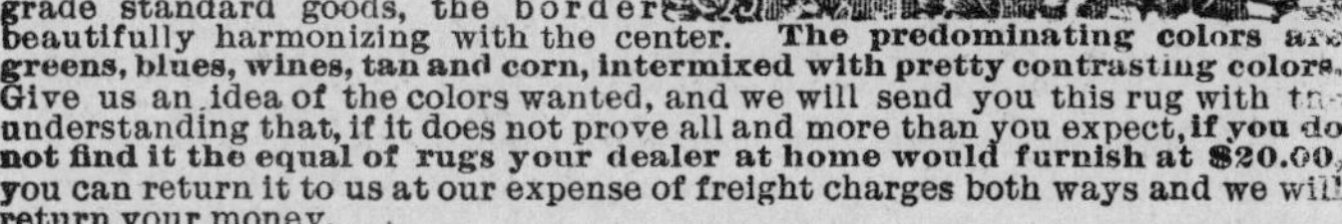

No. 37R2412 Special price for rug, 9x12 feet........ $13.50

Our Best All Wool Extra Large Border Trimmed Floor Rugs or Art Squares at $4.35 to $11.60, According to Size.

For $4.35 for a rug 7½x9 feet to $11.60 for a rug 12x15 feet in size, we offer these extra heavy, handsome heavy bordered all wool rugs, entirely new effects for this season, as the greatest value shown by any house. From the illustration, engraved by our artist from a photograph, showing a small corner of the rug with border trimmed effect, and the fringe effect which is at both ends of the rug, you can form some idea of the appearance of these handsome art squares or large bordered rugs. **They come in a variety of beautiful colorings.** The border harmonizes in pattern and color with the center of square. They are made from strictly high grade wool. They come in green, tan and red with other bright colors to harmonize. **Give us an idea of the coloring and pattern wanted and we will guarantee to please you.**

Our special prices on these handsome all wool art squares or rugs are as follows:

No. 37R2420	Special price for rug,	7½x 9 feet	$ 4.35
No. 37R2421	Special price for rug,	9 x 9 feet	5.22
No. 37R2422	Special price for rug,	9 x10½ feet	6.09
No. 37R2423	Special price for rug,	9 x12 feet	6.96
No. 37R2424	Special price for rug,	9 x13½ feet	7.83
No. 37R2425	Special price for rug,	12 x12 feet	9.25
No. 37R2426	Special price for rug,	12 x15 feet	11.60

OILCLOTH RUGS.

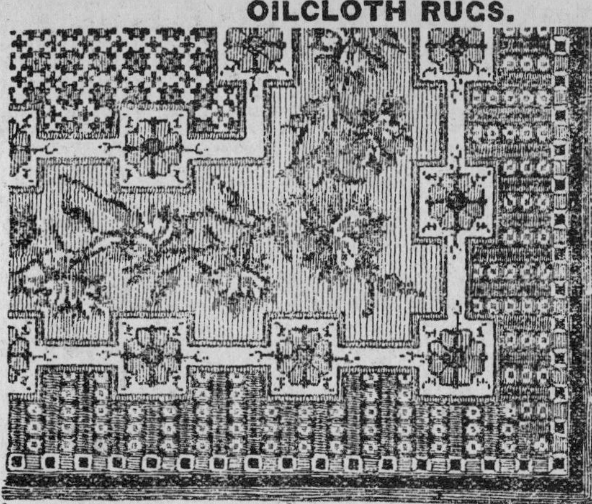

Our very latest Oilcloth Rugs or Stove Squares, good quality oilcloth. Comes in a pretty tan ground, with red predominating, like illustration.

No. 37R2450 1½ yds. square.
Price, **69c**

No. 37R2451 2 yards square.
Price, **$1.09**

Wonderful Matting Values.

In plain and fancy Japanese and Chinese Mattings, now so very popular and largely used in place of carpeting for halls, bedrooms, porches, dining rooms, summer cottages, summer hotels, clubs, public halls, etc., etc., extremely popular the year around, in place of carpeting, everywhere in warm climates and in the warmer months in colder climates, now very fashionable in house furnishing and decorating everywhere. We are headquarters for everything in this line.

We import these goods direct from China and Japan, and we own them at the lowest possible cost to import. There is no jobber, no wholesaler, however large, that owns Oriental matting from China and Japan at a lower cost than we, and to the net cost to us landed in Chicago under the most favorable ocean freight rate arrangement, we add our one small percentage of profit, and, as a result, you can get the finest Chinese and Japanese matting from us, at lower prices than your dealer can buy in quantity, at about one-half the price your storekeeper at home would charge you.

All matting comes in 36-inch widths, 1 yard wide; also, regularly in 40-yard pieces, or 40 yards to a roll. We especially urge that in ordering matting, so far as possible, you order in full pieces, full rolls of 40 yards. While we will, to accommodate our customers, cut rolls to any length, our extremely low prices are fixed on the basis of full rolls, and unless a very large percentage of our sales can be made in roll lots, we will sustain a loss in this department, for our very small margin will not admit of our selling any considerable portion of these goods in less than roll lots.

A full roll of 40 yards is always desirable. There are dozens of ways you can use it. If you have a few yards left over it will come handy in a dozen ways for recarpeting and recovering in the time to come.

At 15 to 29 cents per yard we furnish these fancy imported Japanese mattings, the equal of mattings that sell generally at almost double the price. **At 15 cents per yard of full 36-inch width, we furnish a fancy matting** in the new 1902 design, in a beautiful Oriental coloring, the equal of matting that sells everywhere at 25 cents; and our 29-cent matting is a new number of our own importation, one of the heaviest, richest and most expensive mattings that has ever been shown, rich enough for any room, used largely for covering drawing rooms, parlors, etc., in some of the summer homes of millionaires.

No. 37R2500 Fancy Matting, very good quality and pretty, 36 inches wide. Colors, medium. Price, per yard........ 15c

No. 37R2502 Fancy Check or Plain Straw Color Matting, very fine quality for price and durable. Price, per yard........ 20c

No. 37R2504 The Japanese Straw Matting; nothing its equal. This matting is pure cotton warp, very durable; medium colors. **Extra good value.** Price, per yard.. 22c

No. 37R2510 This number of Matting is the very latest importation from Japan, a pretty fancy Japanese, pure cotton warp. Comes in the following colors: blue, green and red ground, with other pretty contrasting colors. Our special price, per yard........ 25c

No. 37R2520 The Jointless. A very handsome matting. It wears as well as any matting you would pay double the amount for. Comes in checks and fancy colors, light or dark. Price, per yard........ 23c

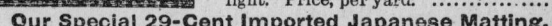

No. 37R2522 Extra Heavy China Matting, very heavy and the best quality manufactured for the money. Weighs 90 pounds to the roll. We may not be able to purchase this line at present prices, as the duties **on all grades have advanced, but we have at present on hand a large stock.** This grade comes in check and fancy colors, dark and light. Price, per yard........ 28c

Our Special 29-Cent Imported Japanese Matting.

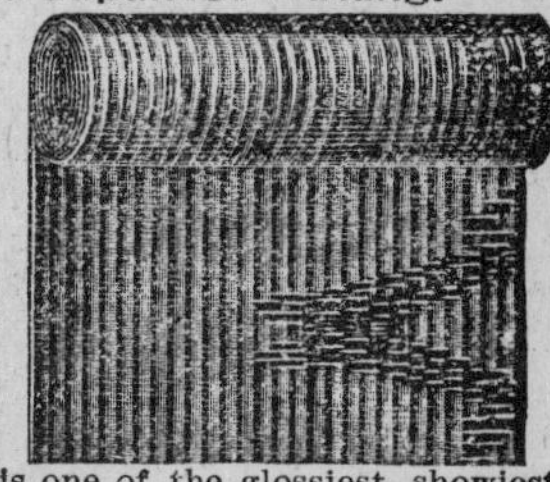

At 29 cents per yard we furnish this extra fine imported Oriental Japanese matting in 36-inch width. Comes regularly in pieces of 40 yards, but we will cut this number in any length wanted. It is one of the heaviest, richest and handsomest imported Japanese mattings on the market; a matting that is being used largely for decorating the most expensive summer homes. **We have sold this matting to some of the most prominent families in the country for decorating their seashore and lake residences. It is a rich Japanese yellow and Oriental green stripe effect alternating;** has a very handsome Oriental design at intervals, bringing out a rich, handsome Oriental Japanese effect. It is one of the glossiest, showiest strongest, heaviest, best wearing and altogether the richest Oriental matting on the market. **State the number of yards wanted, enclose our price, we will send this our richest Japanese Oriental matting to you with the understanding that if it is not perfectly satisfactory and the greatest value you have ever seen,** you can return it to us at our expense and we will return your money.

No. 37R2528 Width, 36 inches. Price, per yard........ 29c

Our matting weighs from 60 to 90 pounds to the roll, and the freight will amount to next to nothing as compared to what you will save in price.

OUR PRICES IN WINDOW SHADES.

IN ORDERING WINDOW SHADES an allowance of about 6 inches must be made from lengths quoted. Shades quoted size 3x6 feet are cut 6 feet long before they are mounted. The hemming and mounting take up about 6 inches. The 6-foot mounted shade will, therefore, measure but 5½ feet; the 7-foot shades will measure about 6½ feet. All of our shades are mounted and ready to hang; we do not sell them any other way.

THREE FEET WIDE is the regular stock size of window shades. Any shades narrower than three feet or wider than three feet will have to be made to order expressly, therefore costing more in proportion. We require cash in full for special made shades.

IMPORTANT NOTICE. THE LENGTHS QUOTED ON WINDOW SHADES ARE MANUFACTURERS' MEASUREMENTS.

OUR GUARANTEE FOR QUALITY. These goods come to us direct from two of the largest makers in this country. Every piece in this department is guaranteed to us by the manufacturer as to quality of material, workmanship and finish, and the same guarantee goes to you from us.

PRICES QUOTED include brackets and slats. Shade pulls, cords, etc., are extra and can be selected from our quotations in another column.

LETTERING. The price for lettering window shades with gold letters is 33 cents per running foot. Shade cloth 48 inches and wider is made of a heavy fabric and will not always exactly match colors in narrower and cheaper cloth.

Plain Opaque Window Shades.

No. 37R2800 Plain Water Color Opaque Window Shades. Mounted on patent spring rollers. Made plain without fringe or dado. Colors: Light olive, pea green, terra cotta, dark green, ecru or light buff, olive and robin's egg blue. Always state color desired. Size, 3x6 feet (manufacturers' measurement). Price, each.....25c

No. 37R2803 Plain Water Color Opaque Window Shades, same as above, but cut down less than 3 feet wide. Price, each.....30c

No. 37R2806 Plain Opaque Shades, same quality and colors as above. Size, 3x7 feet (manufacturers' measurement). Price, each.....30c

No. 37R2809 Same as No. 37R2806, **cut down, less than 3 feet wide.** Price, each.....35c

No. 37R2812 Plain Water Color Opaque Window Shades. Same exact quality as above. Size, 3x8 feet. Price, each.....35c

Fringed Window Shades.

No. 37R2818 Fringed Water Colored Opaque Window Shades, with very handsome 3¼-inch fringe at bottom. **Mounted on patent spring rollers.** Colors: Light olive, pea green, terra cotta, robin's egg blue, dark green, olive, ecru or light buff. Size, 3x6 feet (manufacturers' measurement). Price, each.....35c

No. 37R2820 Fringed Water Color Opaque Window Shades, same quality as above, but cut down to less than 3 feet wide. Price, each.....40c

No. 37R2823 Fringed Water Color Opaque Window Shades. Same quality as No. 37R2818, but 7 feet long. Price, each.....40c

No. 37R2826 Fringed Water Color Opaque Window Shades. Same as No. 37R2823, but cut down to less than 3 feet wide. Price, each.....45c

No. 37R2829 Fringed Opaque Window Shades. Same as No. 37R2823, but size 3x8 feet. Price, each, **50c**

All Window Shades from Nos. 37R2800 to 37R2829 inclusive are not made wider than 3 feet.

Best Quality Window Shades.

No. 37R2830 Plain Opaque Shades. Made from very best grade oil opaque, and mounted on patent spring rollers. Plain, without fringe or dado. Colors: White, light olive, dark green, light buff, terra cotta, olive, pea green and robin's egg blue. Size, 3x6 feet. Price, each.....40c

No. 37R2833 Plain Opaque Shades, same as above, cut down to less than 3 feet wide. Price.....50c

No. 37R2836 Plain Opaque Shades, same quality as No. 37R2830, but 3x7 feet. Price, each.....45c

No. 37R2839 Same as No. 37R2836, but cut down to less than 3 feet wide. Price, each.....55c

No. 37R2842 Plain Opaque Shades, same quality as No. 37R2830, but 3x8 feet. Price, each.....50c

Following are prices on the above shades made to order in the following widths and 6 feet long:

No. 37R2845 Over 36 inches wide up to 42 inches wide. Price, each.....$1.05
Over 42 inches wide up to 45 inches wide. Each, 1.11
Over 45 inches wide up to 48 inches wide. Each, 1.21
Over 48 inches wide up to 54 inches wide. Each, 1.47
Over 54 inches wide up to 63 inches wide. Each, 1.79

Above sizes in 7 and 8 feet long, at 10 cents each extra for the 7-foot and 20 cents extra for 8-foot.

Fringed Oil Opaque.

No. 37R2850 Fringed Oil Opaque Window Shades, made from best quality oil opaque cloth, same fringe as illustrated in our cheaper shades. Colors are white, light buff, light olive, dark green, terra cotta, olive, pea green, robin's egg blue. Size, 3x6 feet. Price, each.....50c

Fringed Oil Opaque Shades.

No. 37R2860 Fringed Oil Opaque Window Shades, made from best quality oil opaque cloth, same fringe as in No. 37R2818 shades. Colors are white, light olive, dark green, light buff, terra cotta, olive, pea green, and robin's egg blue. Size, 3x7 feet. Each. **55c**

No. 37R2862 Same as No. 37R2860, but cut down to less than 3 feet wide. Price, each.....65c

No. 37R2864 Fringed shades, No. 37R2860, made to order in the following widths and 7 feet long:
Over 36 in. wide up to 42 in. wide, price, each... $1.30
Over 42 in. wide up to 45 in. wide, price, each... 1.40
Over 45 in. wide up to 48 in. wide, price, each... 1.60
Over 48 in. wide up to 54 in. wide, price, each... 1.85
Over 54 in. wide up to 63 in. wide, price, each... 2.25

Above sizes in 8 feet long at 10 cents each extra.

No. 37R2866 Fringed Oil Opaque Window Shades, same as No. 37R2860, but 8 feet long. Price, each...60c

Lace Trimmed Window Shades.

GENUINE HAND MADE.

No. 37R2875 Lace Trimmed Window Shades, made from very best quality oil opaque shade cloth, **mounted on patent spring rollers.** Beautiful lace edging on bottom, 4¼ inches deep. Colors: White, light olive, dark green, light buff, terra cotta, olive, pea green. Size, 3x6 feet (manufacturers' measurement). Price, each.....55c

No. 37R2877 Lace Trimmed Window Shades, same as No. 37R2875, but cut down to less than 3 feet wide. Price, each.....65c

No. 37R2879 Lace Trimmed Window Shades, same as No. 37R2875, but 7 feet long. Price, each.....60c

No. 37R2881 Same exactly as No. 37R2879, but cut down to less than 3 feet wide. Price, each.....70c

No. 37R2883 Lace Trimmed Window Shades. Same quality as preceding numbers, but size 3x8 feet. Price, each.....70c

Following are same quality as No. 37R2883, made to order in the following widths and 6 feet long:

No. 37R2885 Over 36 inches wide up to 42 inches wide inclusive. Each.....$1.45
Over 42 inches wide up to 45 inches wide. Each 1.55
Over 45 inches wide up to 48 inches wide. Each 1.75
Over 48 inches wide up to 54 inches wide. Each 2.05
Over 54 inches wide up to 63 inches wide. Each 2.45

We can furnish the above sizes in shades 7 and 8 feet long, at 10 cents each extra for the 7-foot and 20 cents each extra for the 8-foot.

Lace and Insertion Window Shades

GENUINE HAND MADE.

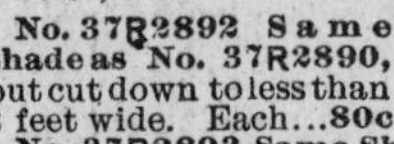

No. 37R2890 Best Quality Oil Opaque Window Shades with lace and insertion as per cut. One of the richest things to be had in shades; looks very rich. We can furnish them in the following colors, light olive, buff, cream, dark olive, pea green. Size, 3x6. Price, each.....70c

No. 37R2892 Same shade as No. 37R2890, but cut down to less than 3 feet wide. Each...80c

No. 37R2893 Same Shade as above, but size 3x7. Price, each.....75c

No. 37R2894 Same as above, cut down to less than 3 feet wide. Price, each.....85c

No. 37R2896 Lace and Insertion Shades, same quality as No. 37R2890, but size 3x8 feet. Price, each.....85c

No. 37R2898 Same Shade as No. 37R2896, cut down to less than 3 feet wide. Price, each.....95c

Following are prices on Best Oil Opaque Window Shades with lace and insertion, same quality as preceding numbers, made to order in the following widths and 6 feet long.

No. 37R2905 Price, each
Over 36 inches wide, up to 42 inches wide.....$1.75
Over 42 inches wide, up to 45 inches wide..... 1.90
Over 45 inches wide, up to 48 inches wide..... 2.15
Over 48 inches wide, up to 54 inches wide..... 2.50
Over 54 inches wide, up to 63 inches wide..... 2.95

We can furnish the above sizes in shades 7 and 8 feet long, at 10 cents each extra for the 7-foot and 20 cents each extra for the 8-foot.

The Sans Gene Perfection Window Shade Adjuster.

No. 37R2906 The most simple and useful invention of the age. With this adjuster attached to your window shade you can shade any part of your window, either the bottom or the middle, without shading the balance of it. It is particularly adapted for bath rooms, bed rooms and toilet rooms. With the Perfection Window Shade Adjuster you can shade the lower part of your window so that the interior of the room is hidden from view from the outside, while the upper part of the window may be open to admit light, air, etc. **Can be adjusted to any shade in five minutes; can't get out of order; will last a lifetime.** Is so cheap that you can afford to have it on every window. Price, each.....14c

Shade Fringe.

No. 37R2907 Extra Fine Quality Shade Fringe, fancy knotted heading. Heavy and handsome. Width, 3¼ inches. Same pattern as used on shades No. 37R2818 (see illustration). All staple colors. Price, per yard.....7c

Shade Lace.

No. 37R2908 Very Handsome Shade Lace, same pattern and quality as used on No. 37R2875 shades, as per illustrations; all staple colors; new pattern. Width, 3¼ inches. Price, per yard.....15c

Shade Pulls.

No. 37R2909 Ring Shade Pulls. Handsome silver and copper finish. Price, each.....5c
Shipping weight, 1 ounce each.

Spiral Bar Shade Pulls.

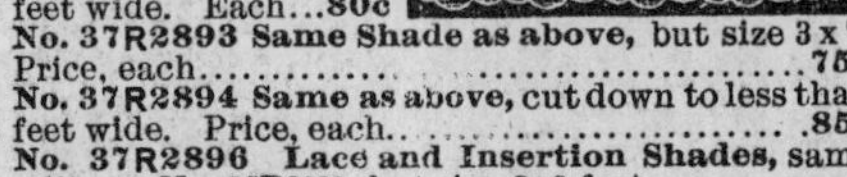

37R2930

No. 37R2930 Spiral Bar Shade Pulls with drop chains. Handsomely finished in silver effect. Price, each.....5c

No. 37R2931 Spiral Bar Shade Pulls. Same as above, with copper or gilt finish. Price, each.....5c

SPECIAL SIZE MADE TO ORDER SHADES.

FOR STORES, OFFICES AND RESIDENCES. The following shades we make to order from the very best quality hand made oil painted opaque shade cloth. It usually requires about four days to have special size shades made to order. We require the full amount of cash with the order in every instance.

COLORS.—Special size shades are made only in the following colors: Dark green, olive, terra cotta, Spanish olive, stone, pea green and light buff or ecru.

State whether width you desire is width of cloth or roller measure. Roller measure means from end to end of tips. We quote the width of cloth when complete.

Lettering.

Price for lettering window shades with Shaded Gilt Lettering is 33 cents per running foot, EXTRA. Shade cloth, 48 inches and wider, is made of **heavier fabric and will not always exactly match colors of smaller shades.**

If the exact size you wish is not given in the following schedule, the next larger size will be charged, but the shade will be cut the exact size you order.

No. 37R2920 Order by number, size and price.

Finished Length in feet.	WIDTH OF SHADES IN INCHES.											
	38 in.	42 in.	45 in.	48 in.	54 in.	63 in.	72 in.	81 in.	90 in.	100 in.	106 in.	120 in.
4 ft.	$0.56	$0.85	$0.91	$0.99	$1.13	$1.45	$1.86	$2.25	$2.61	$3.00	$3.19	$ 6.50
5 ft.	.64	.95	.99	1.12	1.31	1.62	2.07	2.49	2.90	3.34	3.58	7.27
6 ft.	.70	1.05	1.11	1.21	1.47	1.79	2.28	2.73	3.19	3.68	3.97	8.05
7 ft.	.79	1.14	1.21	1.38	1.64	1.96	2.49	3.00	3.47	4.03	4.37	8.83
8 ft.	.85	1.27	1.34	1.50	1.78	2.17	2.69	3.22	3.77	4.37	4.76	9.65
9 ft.	.94	1.45	1.55	1.72	2.07	2.44	3.08	3.62	4.28	4.96	5.40	10.65
10 ft.	1.12	1.56	1.66	1.85	2.23	2.62	3.26	3.90	4.57	5.30	5.79	11.40
11 ft.	1.21	1.67	1.77	1.97	2.38	2.81	3.47	4.14	4.86	7.06	7.60	12.21
12 ft.	1.27	1.86	1.96	2.21	2.65	3.11	3.84	4.53	5.36	7.65	8.23	13.20
13 ft.	1.63	2.07	2.20	2.38	3.10	3.43	4.19	4.77	5.65	7.99	8.63	14.02
14 ft.	1.70	2.18	2.31	2.51	3.26	3.60	4.40	5.03	5.93	8.34	8.98	14.78
15 ft.	1.86	2.35	2.50	2.80	3.55	3.92	4.76	5.44	6.46	8.91	9.65	15.81

Vestibule Rods for Sash Curtains.

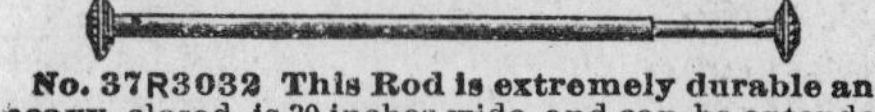

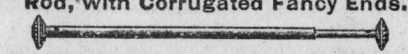

No. 37R3030 Telescope Vestibule Rods. Made with brackets complete; can be adjusted inside or outside the rods; are made of two brass tubes, one sliding inside of the other, and will extend 24 to 44 inches. ⅜-inch rod. Price, each 10c

Our Heavy Brass Telescope or Extension Rod, with Corrugated Fancy Ends.

No. 37R3032 This Rod is extremely durable and heavy, closed is 30 inches wide and can be extended to 54 inches. It comes with bracket complete. Price, each....................12c

No. 37R3034 Telescope Vestibule Rods. With pretty corrugated ball ends, as per cut; a very fancy rod, complete with screws. Will extend 28 to 54 inches. Price, each....................18c

Stair Pads.

No. 37R3038 Stair Pads, 22½ and 27 inches long. Price, per dozen....................$1.20

Curtain Poles.

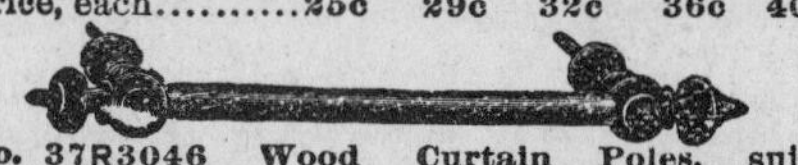

No. 37R3042 Wood Trimmed Curtain Poles, 1⅜-inch, finished in California walnut, mahogany, oak and ebony. Price includes two turned wooden ends, two brackets for ends and sufficient quantity of rings for pole. **Don't fail to mention kind of finish wanted.**

Length	5 ft.	6 ft.	7 ft.	8 ft.	9 ft.
Price, each	25c	29c	32c	36c	40c

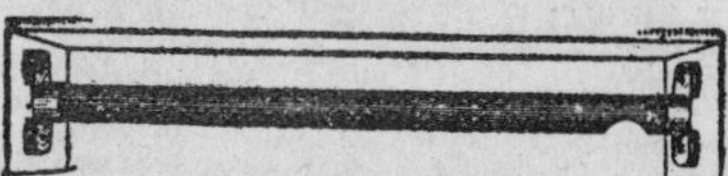

No. 37R3046 Wood Curtain Poles, suitable for bedrooms or sash curtains, ¾-inch, finished antique oak only. Price includes brackets and ends. No rings included. Length, 4 feet. Price........12c
Length, 5 feet. Price....................15c

No. 37R3050 Brass Trimmed Curtain Poles, 1⅜-inch poles, finished in oak, mahogany, walnut and ebony, complete with two brass ends, two brass brackets and sufficient quantity of rings for pole.

Length	5 ft.	6 ft.	7 ft.	8 ft.	9 ft.
Price, each	19c	23c	26c	29c	32c

Curtain Poles and Sockets.

No. 37R3054 Curtain Pole and Bracket or Socket, complete. As per cut, a brass socket with 1⅜-inch pole, no screws or nails required. It fits on inside on casing and has rubber ends. Cut pole ¾ inch shorter than space between opening and attach brackets. Complete with poles.

Length	5 ft.	6 ft.	7 ft.	8 ft.	9 ft.
Price, each	22c	26c	29c	33c	36c

White Enameled Poles.

No. 37R3058 White Enameled Corrugated Cottage Curtain Pole. With fancy corrugated ball ends and also fancy rosette screws, as per cut. This is the prettiest rod in the market and is sure to please. ¾-inch rod, 4 feet only. Complete with fixtures. Our special price, each....................15c

Brass Stair Rods.

No. 37R3070 Brass Stair Rods. Price, 24-inch, per dozen..........85c
26-inch, per dozen..95c; 30-inch, per dozen.....$1.15

Wood Stair Rods.

No. 37R3074 Wood Stair Rods, acorn tip, finely finished. Come in antique oak only, in 26 and 30 inches long, with screws. Our price, each........4c

Brass Tassel Hooks.

No. 37R3078 Nicely Polished. Price, each..........5c

Picture Molding Hooks.

No. 37R3082 Brass Plate Picture Hooks. Price, per dozen..........4c

Picture Molding Hooks.

No. 37R3084 This is the solid Brass Molding Hook. Our price, each........2c

Rug Fasteners.

No. 37R3086 The New Patent Rug Fastener. Just the article to keep rugs and art squares fastened to the floor. Price, per dozen..........40c

Curtain Loops, Etc.

37R3100

No. 37R3100 A White Cotton Curtain Loop, cord and tassels. Price, per pair..........8c

No. 37R3102 Curtain Loops, cord and tassels, to be used with tapestry curtains. Per pair..15c

No. 37R3104 Heavy Chenille Curtain Loops, cord and tassels. Price, per pair..........19c

No. 37R3106

No. 37R3106 Brass Curtain Chain, a good strong chain usually sold for very much more money. Per pair..........7c

No. 37R3108 Spiral Curtain Chains, pretty, strong and durable. Per pair.. 14c

Rug Fringes.

No. 37R3120 Wool Rug Fringe, with gimp heading 3 inches deep; tan, olive or red combinations, also plain colors. Price, per yard..........6c

No. 37R3122 Knotted Rug Fringe, 4 inches wide, tan, olive or red, plain or combination. Price, per yard..........10c

Furniture Fringes.

No. 37R3126 Cotton Furniture Fringe, heavy and durable. Comes in all combinations of colors to match furniture covering. A very pretty fringe for the money. Full width, 7 inches. Price, per yard..........10c

Worsted Furniture Fringe.

No. 37R3134 Comes in a very fancy heading and deep fringe, full width in combination of colors to match all furniture coverings. Full width, 7 inches. Price, per yard........15c

Our 20-Cent Heavy Furniture Fringe.

No. 37R3136 Extra High Grade Worsted Furniture Fringe, has beautiful heavy strands and tassels, with fancy deep heading on a good quality of fringe. We can furnish any combination of colors to match furniture coverings. Full width, 7 inches. Price, per yard..........20c

Hassocks and Foot Rests.

Child's Hassocks.

9x9 inches, 4 inches high. This serviceable and pretty little tapestry Brussels covered hassock, solidly made, is an ornament as well as a practical piece of furniture for any home.

No. 37R3180 Price, each...19c

No. 37R3200 Our Popular, Low Priced Hassock is 12 inches in diameter and 5½ inches high, covered with fine tapestry Brussels carpet. **Don't fail to order one of these comfortable and beautiful hassocks.** Our special price, each......39c

No. 37R3201 Same, covered with velvet or moquette carpet. Price, each....59c

The illustration represents the choicest and most stylish original shape hassock in our collection. Size, 12x14 inches, 6 inches high. Covered with a good quality of Brussels carpet.

No. 37R3205 Price....49c

This illustration is exactly as the stool herein described will look. It is made from a true photograph. It has wood frame with steel wire legs. It is an ornament for any house, covered with velvet. Size, 10x14 inches, 9 inches high.

No. 37R3209 Price....................75c

The Star Hassock.

A very strong and ornamental Hassock. Size, 13x13 inches, 6 inches high. Velvet covered in pretty designs.

No. 37R3211 Price, each..63c

No. 37R3216 Our Beautiful 12x12-inch Hassock, 6½ inches high; covered in most beautiful designs in fine durable tapestry carpet. This will make a very pretty ornament in any sitting room or parlor. Price, each..........63c

No 37R3217 Same, covered with velvet carpet. Price, each....................69c

The illustration gives a good idea of the handsome style of this durable and ornamental hassock. It is covered with a superior quality of Wilton velvet carpet. Size, 12x12 inches, 6½ inches high.

No. 37R3221 Price, each..75c

No. 37R3234 Our Octagon Ottoman Foot Rest. Comes 11x13 inches and 9¼ inches high. **This is a very beautiful home decoration.** It is something that should be in every parlor or sitting room. Covered with best tapestry carpet. Price, each, 63c

In ordering furniture, carpets, portieres or anything in these parallel lines, **don't omit one of these beautiful ottomans.**

No. 37R3235 Covered with moquette or velvet carpet. Price, each....................75c

Special, Extraordinary.

This Extra Large Velvet Hassock. We are the originators of this grand Oriental sumptuous hassock. The design is exclusive with us. Size, 15x15 inches, 9 inches high.

No. 37R3241 Price..85c

Our Great Bargain in Hassock and Slipper Box Combined.

No. 37R3251 This is strongly made and covered with the best tapestry or velvet carpet. Size, 9¾x17½ inches, and is 7 inches high. This is one of the most convenient, ornamental and comfortable foot rests that can be furnished.

The price makes it within the reach of all. This is certainly a great bargain and should be in every home. Don't fail to order one of these beautiful combination hassocks. Our special price, each, covered with Brussels carpet....................89c

No. 37R3256 Covered with velvet carpet....98c

Our Parlor Stools or Foot Rests.

(Can also be used for children's low seats.)

No. 37R3260 These stools have wood frames, malleable iron legs, finished in gold bronze. They will certainly make an ornament for any house. They are covered with velvet carpet only, and the price is simply phenomenal, considering the value which we give you in one of these serviceable and convenient stools or foot rests. Size, 11x11 inches, 7 inches high.

No. 37R3260 Price, each....................59c

Our Commode, for Use in Bedrooms.

This is one of the most useful articles that could be in any house. Convenient for children or for sickness. **These commodes are made of fine imitation oak, with a beautiful top covered with fine Brussels carpet.** Size, 15½ inches high and 14½ inches square. These commodes are something that should certainly be in every well regulated house. The convenience for one week would overcome the expense.

No. 37R3264 Price, each....................$1.98

No. 37R3265 Price, each, with pan..........2.48

----- OUR BIG -----
WALL PAPER DEPARTMENT.

WITH A VIEW of placing our customers in a position where they can buy wall paper in the very latest styles at the very lowest prices, where they can buy the best paper in all the very latest colorings and designs, new for the season, direct from the factory at manufacturers' prices, prices that barely cover the cost of material and labor, with but our one small percentage of profit added, we have been attracted by several concerns that have grown large in the exclusive wall paper business, selling wall paper direct to wall paper hangers and to the consumer. We have known that their methods of handling were expensive and they must necessarily get an abnormal profit, they must add to the cost of making and printing wall paper an excessive profit. We have therefore studied the wall paper question very carefully, we have investigated the possible sources of supply, the methods employed by exclusive wall paper handlers and others in the buying and selling of wall paper, and we have found, as we expected, that wall paper is indeed generally sold at very large profits. With these facts before us we started out with a view of arranging for a source of supply, where the goods could be purchased in the very best qualities, in the very latest and handsomest effects at the very minimum of cost, where all unnecessary running expenses were eliminated, and adding our one small percentage of profit to this cost we call your attention to and offer you herein a line of wall papers in the very latest effects, the same styles and qualities as you will find in the best exclusive wall paper houses in this and other large cities, **and yet we offer these goods at about one half the price charged by the retailer generally.**

DIRECT FROM THE MILL. **In buying wall paper from us you practically buy it direct from the mill.** We have made our arrangements for supply with a big wall paper manufacturer in this city. Taking our contract he has arranged his contract for materials, colors, etc., to accommodate our order. He has increased his facilities, and by materially increasing his output by reason of our order, he figures that he can reduce the cost of manufacture, giving him an advantage on the goods he sells to the regular wholesale trade, and for this reason can afford to turn the paper over to us, what we require, at factory cost. **We give you the benefit of this arrangement. We only ask you one small profit above the actual cost to us.**

OUR GUARANTEE. **We guarantee the wall paper we advertise and sell to be exactly as represented and to prove perfectly satisfactory,** and if you order any wall paper from us, and you do not find it all and even more than you expect, and such value as you could not possibly get elsewhere, you can return it to us at our expense of freight charges both ways and we will return your money.

ABOUT THE WALL PAPER TRUST. **A greater part of the wall paper manufactured in this country today is controlled by a combination who endeavor to fix prices that are out of reason.** We wish to say that the mill that supplies us is not in the trust. There is no combination, no arrangement, no calculation for more profit than enough to pay for the making and our one small profit added.

SAMPLES. **We issue a book of wall paper samples, a book containing all our leaders, all the new novelties, all the most desirable things in our line of wall papers.** These samples are good size, from which you can select your paper just the same as if you were in our store selecting the paper from stock. **This book of samples will be mailed, postage prepaid, upon receipt of 2 cents.** If you wish to receive a full line of samples of our best numbers in wall paper for this season, send a 2-cent stamp for sample book and the book will be sent to you by return mail, together with complete instructions on paper hanging, etc. You will be surprised at the values represented in the samples contained in this book.

OUR BIG WALL PAPER BOOK FOR DEALERS, AGENTS, CANVASSERS, PAPER HANGERS, PAINTERS, CONTRACTORS, ETC. **For the benefit of people who deal in wall paper, for paper hangers, contractors, etc.,** and also for such of our customers as wish an extra large line of big samples from which to make their selections, we issue this very large book of wall paper samples, a book 18 inches square and about 1¼ inches thick, containing an immense line of the most staple and fancy wall papers, in all the new designs, all fully described and priced on each sample. **As this book is a very large and expensive book to get up, one that is made especially to interest careful, close buying dealers, paper hangers,** contractors, etc., we require all applications for this big dealers' wall paper book to be accompanied by 25 cents. We ask 25 cents from each applicant as an evidence of good faith and to help pay for the cost of the book.

TO PAPER HANGERS. **If you are a paper hanger you cannot afford to be without this big sample book.** It shows the handsomest line of wall papers for this season and at prices much lower than you are now paying. With this big book of samples you can make closer prices on your work and bigger profits to yourself, for you will find our prices much lower than the prices you are now paying. **This big book is issued especially in the interest of wall paper hangers.**

TO WALL PAPER DEALERS. **If you are a dealer in wall paper you cannot afford to be without our dealers' big book,** for the line of samples cannot be equaled by any line you are now carrying. You will find our prices so much lower than the prices you are now paying that you can control the sale of wall paper in your section and still make more profit than you are now making.

TO AGENTS AND CANVASSERS. **If you are now soliciting orders for wall paper in your section, do not fail to send 25 cents for this dealers' big book.** You will find the line handsomer and better than the line you are showing and the prices are very much lower. From our big book you can no doubt sell wall paper at what your paper now costs you and still make a handsome profit.

TO CONTRACTORS, RENTAL AGENTS, PAINTERS AND OTHERS who buy **wall paper in quantities we especially urge that** you send 25 cents for the dealers' big book. You will be surprised at the prices and at the big line we show. You will find that at our prices you can afford to re-paper rooms that otherwise would not be papered. You will find the expense of re-papering will be very different from what it would be at the price you are now paying.

SPECIALLY TO OUR CUSTOMERS, **those who wish wall paper to redecorate rooms in their own homes. If you simply wish to buy paper enough to re-paper one, two or three rooms in your own home,** and wish to make a selection from our entire line, one of the biggest assortments of wall paper shown by any maker of new patterns and designs for this season, and at prices very much lower than any other house can furnish, instead of sending 2 cents for the small sample book, send us 25 cents for this our big dealers' book.

THIS BIG BOOK **closed measures 18x18 inches, 1½ feet square. Each sample is 18 inches square.** The book weighs about five pounds, is one of the largest and handsomest and most complete books of wall paper samples published. The book contains an immense line of all the very latest designs in handsome colorings for this season; large samples of wall, border and ceiling papers for all purposes, for homes, bedrooms, dining rooms, halls, kitchens, etc., for public buildings, churches, schools, halls, etc. Everything very complete and at prices heretofore unknown, prices much lower than ever before, prices less than dealers can buy elsewhere in any quantity.

BEFORE ORDERING **wall paper elsewhere, if you wish the big line, with large samples 18 inches square, one of the biggest books published, send 25 cents for the dealers' book.**

WHY WE RECOMMEND YOU TO SEND 25 CENTS **for the dealers' big sample book. In the small book it is impossible to give an idea of the handsome designs and pattern effects,** especially of the larger patterns, nor does the small book contain samples of borders or ceilings; whereas if you send 25 cents for the dealers' big book, a book that contains samples 18x18 inches square, you can see the entire pattern, all the colorings and blendings, and the big book also contains samples of the borders and ceilings to match the side wall paper.

IF YOU WANT TO KNOW **just exactly the design, just the size of the pattern, all the colorings, etc.,** if you wish to know just what kind of border and ceiling paper will be furnished to match the wall paper, we recommend by all means that you send 25 cents for the big book.

TO REDUCE THE COST **of our 25-cent dealers' wall paper book to next to nothing,** we advise getting your neighbors interested, one, two or even four or five, thus reducing the cost of the book to each one of you to but a few cents, 5 to 10 cents, and you will find you will save the cost of the book many times over on your first order for wall paper; besides you will have the satisfaction of selecting from one of the largest books published, from an immense line of samples including samples of border and ceiling as well as side wall paper, samples 18 inches square, from which you can see just what the pattern and colorings are.

SAMPLES NOT NECESSARY IN ORDERING. **Our wall paper department is in charge of an experienced wall paper man, an expert in the selecting of harmonizing shades and designs,** and without sending for samples, if you will select the paper wanted from the following illustrations and descriptions, and will tell us for what kind of rooms the paper is wanted, give us an idea of color and pattern, let us know the color of the carpet, furniture or other decorations of the room, we will give you the service of an expert designer and wall paper maker in selecting the most harmonizing wall paper for your wants. **He will give you the best values in our house, and you will, we are sure, be better pleased with his selection than if you yourself were selecting it from samples.** All our old customers who have bought wall paper from us almost invariably leave the selecting of harmonizing shades and colorings to the expert in this department, and they tell us they get much better effects, and better satisfaction than when they themselves make the selection from samples.

RULES FOR MEASURING A ROOM. **Measure the length and breadth of the room, then multiply by two; multiply the result by the height of the room in feet.** To allow for doors and windows, multiply the height of each by the width; add same together and deduct from amount. Then divide by 60. The result is the number of double rolls required for side walls. **This rule makes all necessary allowance for waste and matching.**

Example: Room 15 feet long, 12 feet wide, 9 feet high. One window, 6x4 feet; one door, 7x4 feet; one window, 3½x4 feet.

15 plus 12x2=54x9=486
66
60)420
Double rolls.. 7

1 window 6x4=24
1 door 7x4=28
1 window 3½x4=14
66

The number of rolls required for ceiling is ascertained the same way, dividing the number of square feet by 60.

Example: Room 15 feet long, 12 feet wide.

15x12=180
60)180
Double rolls.... 3

Wall paper weighs about 1¼ pounds per double roll. Always state what room paper is for. We do not trim wall paper because the edges being exposed, if damaged in transit, would render perfect matching impossible.

Our prices, unless otherwise stated, are always for double rolls. Wall paper, unless otherwise specified, is sold only by the double roll. All papers have borders and ceilings to match.

This Wall Paper only 2 Cents Per Roll.

At 2 cents per single roll or 4 cents per double roll we offer this handsome wall paper in new designs for this season, the equal of wall paper that sells at more than double the price; a big improvement over our last year's widely advertised 2½-cent paper, a reduction in price of ½ cent per single roll, and improved in quality, a handsomer and better pattern than ever before. **You should see the samples of the wall, border and ceiling paper of this number to appreciate the value we are giving,** and we therefore urge that you send 25 cents for the dealers' big book and get these big 18-inch square samples.

From this illustration, showing the side wall paper, the border and ceiling paper, you can get at least some idea of the effect brought out in this our cheapest paper, our special 2-cent leader. **While you can order direct from the catalogue illustrations and descriptions** with every assurance that the paper will be in every way satisfactory, we especially recommend that you send for our book of samples, either sending 2 cents for the sample book or 25 cents for the dealers' big book which gives samples of border, ceiling and wall paper, and shows you all the colors and pattern effect. **To those who do not wish to wait to send for samples** will say this is a nine-ounce paper, with a light cream ground, with handsome scroll and fretwork in terra cotta, with beautiful spray and bouquet effect in nile green, brought out with nice mica and bronze effects. **This paper has a 9-inch border** and a ceiling in very neat scroll effect in garnet and turquoise blue on a light cream background. If you order from the catalogue without waiting for samples, we guarantee the paper to please you or we will return your money.

We furnish this our specially advertised wall paper at the following special prices:

No. 37R3300 Price for side wall and ceiling paper, per single roll........2c
No. 37R3302 Price for side wall and ceiling paper, double roll..........4c
No. 37R3304 Price for 9-inch border to match, per single yard..........1c

Our Special 9-Cent Wall Paper.

The Price is Small But The Value is Surprisingly Good, You Would Ordinarily Pay For Such A Paper 15 to 18 Cents.

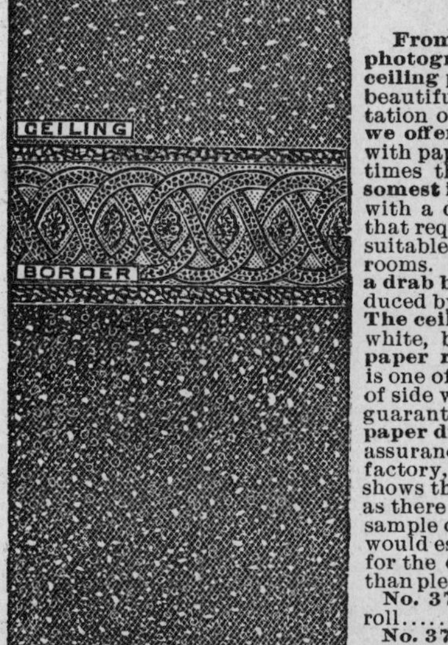

From this illustration, engraved from a photograph, showing the wall, border and ceiling paper, you can get some idea of the beautiful effect brought out in this fine, imitation of granite wall paper. **It is a paper we offer at 9 cents per roll** in competition with paper that sells generally at two to four times the price. **This is one of the handsomest imitations of granite made,** a paper with a drab background, well covered, one that requires no matching, and is especially suitable for kitchens, dining rooms and bedrooms. **The border is 9 inches wide with a drab background,** with granite effect produced by small designs in dark red and olive. **The ceiling is tan background,** dotted with white, bright olive green and black. **This paper requires no matching in hanging,** is one of the latest styles and a combination of side wall, border and ceiling, which we can guarantee to please. **You can order this paper direct from the catalogue,** with every assurance that it will be found entirely satisfactory, and our small 2-cent sample book shows this paper up as well as the large book, as there is no large pattern, but to get a large sample of side wall, border and ceiling we would especially urge that you send 25 cents for the dealers' big book. You will be more than pleased with the line shown in this book.

No. 37R3306 Price for side wall, double roll..9c
No. 37R3308 Price for ceiling to match, double roll..9c
No. 37R3310 Price for 9-inch border, per single yard..1½c

Our New 9-Cent Green Tile Wall Paper.

At Our 9 Cent Price, Dealers Can Buy From Us And Sell at A Nice Profit.

The illustration showing the wall, border and ceiling paper will give you some idea of the handsome effect brought out in this, our new 9-cent paper. This is an entirely new design for this season, a beautiful tile pattern, in medium green ground with maroon outline and dark green filler. This paper is especially desirable for halls, bath rooms, also for bedrooms, in fact, a good all purpose wall paper. **Our special price of 9 cents per double roll** is about one-half to one-third the price asked by others. The small sample book will give you a fair idea of this paper, but in order to show the pattern clearly we give you a sample of both side wall, border and ceiling, and we advise, in sending for samples, that you send 25 cents for the dealers' big book. You can, however, order direct from the catalogue with every assurance that the paper will give perfect satisfaction, and if not, that you can return it to us and we will return your money.

No. 37R3312 Price for side wall, double roll..9c
No. 37R3314 Price for ceiling, per double roll..9c
No. 37R3316 Price for 9-inch border, per single yard..1½c

Our 9-Cent Popular Home Paper.

For a rich, yet modest paper for the home, an all purpose paper for living rooms, etc., kitchen, dining room, library, parlors, bedrooms, halls, for an all purpose paper, in a neat new shade and new design, we offer this handsome paper, made on a French gray ground, at 9 cents per double roll, in competition with paper that sells generally for 25 cents and upwards. **This paper is made on a dark French gray background with beautiful festoons of daisies** in a delicate shade of old rose, with green foliage. It has a 9-inch border to match, with very light nile green ground, with festoons of daisies and green foliage, the same as in the side wall. The colors are very nicely blended and graduated from a dark shade of French gray to a light nile green at the top. The ceiling has background in a very light shade of nile green with clusters of daisies in a delicate shade of pink and white with green sprays. **Our 2-cent small sample book gives you a very good idea of the side wall paper,** although it will not show the whole pattern effect. The dealers' big 25-cent book will give you a large sample of side wall, ceiling and border, but you can order direct from the catalogue without first writing for a sample, with every assurance that the paper will please you in every way or we will immediately return your money.

No. 37R3318 Price for side wall, per double roll..9c
No. 37R3319 Price for ceiling, per double roll..9c
No. 37R3320 Price for 9-inch border, per single yard..1½c

Our New 8-Cent Turquoise Blue Combination Paper.

Entirely New For This Season And A Handsome Design.

From the illustration showing the side wall, border and ceiling paper you can get some idea of the pattern effect brought out in this new design. The paper is extra good weight. The colorings are the very best and the paper is offered at from one-half to one-third the price charged by dealers generally. **It is a very rich turquoise blue combination, suitable especially for halls, dining rooms, bedrooms, small stores, etc.,** and is brought out in a dark choke effect with light blue and silver scrolls. The border is 9 inches in width, blending harmoniously in colors with the side wall, while the ceiling is a handsome contrast in a much lighter shade with nile green background and very handsome silver and dark blue scroll effects. **The small 2-cent sample book will give you a good idea of the side wall paper,** although the dealers' big 25-cent book will be necessary to get a large sample of the side wall, ceiling and border. **Many of our customers, however, order direct from our catalogue,** knowing that they will get just what they want, or we will immediately return their money.

No. 37R3322 Price for side wall, per double roll..8c
No. 37R3324 Price for ceiling, per double roll..8c
No. 37R3326 Price for 9-inch border, per single yard..

Our 9-Cent Marie Antoinette Paper for Parlors.

For a handsome, new stripe effect, in a rich paper, at a low price, for parlors, bedrooms, libraries, halls, in fact, for an all purpose paper we especially recommend this new number. This is a Marie Antoinette stripe on a drab background. The flowers are treated in different shades of purple, producing a very dainty effect.

The great value of a striped pattern is to change the appearance of a room having a low ceiling, making it appear much higher. This is a very rich, dainty paper, and must be seen in the sample to be appreciated. The border is a handsome 9-inch border, the colors blending perfectly with the side wall from a very light shade of cream to a soft drab, beautifully decorated with purple and green floral and striped effect. The ceiling is a very light cream background with neat leaves of green and purple rosebud effects.

From the 2-cent sample book you can tell exactly what the side wall paper will be; or you can order direct from the catalogue, with our guarantee that the paper will please you; or, from the dealers' big book, you can get a good idea of the side wall, ceiling and border.

No. 37R3328 Price for side wall paper, per double roll.....9c

No. 37R3330 Price for ceiling, per double roll.....9c

No. 37R3332 Price for 9-inch border, per single yard.....1½c

Our 9-Cent Glimmer Terra Cotta.

At 9 cents per double roll we offer this handsome new number, a heavy weight paper, a rich terra cotta background brought out with beautiful new shades of red and green finished in two handsome shades of glimmer silver and nile green. **This paper is especially suitable for halls, dining rooms, bedrooms, churches, public rooms, etc.** It has a very rich border in which the colors are handsomely blended. The ceiling has a background of very rich warm salmon shade, with very pretty designs in dark red and green. **The illustration gives you an idea of the general appearance of the side wall, border and ceiling effect,** and from the small 2-cent sample book you can get a fair idea of the paper, but to see the whole design of the side wall, border and ceiling you should have our big 25-cent dealers' book. **Many of our customers order without first sending for samples,** for they understand they get such values as they could not possibly get elsewhere, and we guarantee the paper to please or we will immediately return your money.

No. 37R3334 Price for side wall, per double roll.....9c

No. 37R3336 Price for ceiling, per double roll.....9c

No. 37R3338 Price for 9-inch border, per single yard.....1½c

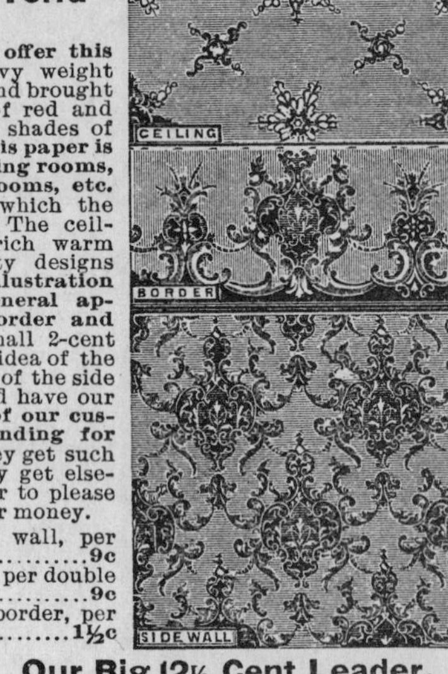

Our Big 12½ Cent Leader.

At 12½ cents per double roll for side wall and ceiling paper, and 2 cents per single yard for 18-inch border, we offer this as one of the biggest leaders in our line, one of the handsomest papers shown this season, a paper the equal of anything you can buy from your dealers at home at 30 to 50 cents per roll. **This is a paper that must be seen to be appreciated,** and unfortunately the small 2-cent sample book will not do it justice. To see the rich pattern effect, the harmonizing colorings and design worked out in the big 18-inch border and the ceiling, you must have our dealers' big 25-cent book. You will surely save from 20 to 30 cents on every roll of this paper you buy from us. **Our special price of 12½ cents per double roll barely covers the cost to manufacture** with but one small percentage of profit added. It is the lowest price ever made on this grade of paper. The illustration showing the side wall, border and ceiling will give you but a slight idea of the pattern or value of this paper. **This is a conventional design, on a very striking, rich Jacqueminot rose red colored background,** with an under print of a corresponding shade of rose red. A very striking feature of this paper is the black and green scroll. The border is 18 inches wide. It is the same colors as the side wall, and gradually turns at the top to a very delicate straw shade, blending perfectly with the ceiling paper, which has a soft straw ground with very large outlined medallion scroll effect, the flower worked out in white, pink and green.

This is an all purpose paper, suitable for parlors, libraries, dining rooms, halls, public buildings of all kinds. It is one of the richest, handsomest, newest and best things in our line and one of our biggest leaders for this season.

No. 37R3340 Price for side wall, per double roll.....12½c

No. 37R3342 Price for ceiling paper, per double roll.....12½c

No. 37R3344 Price for 18-inch border, per single yard.....2c

Our New Special 7-Cent Gilt Paper.

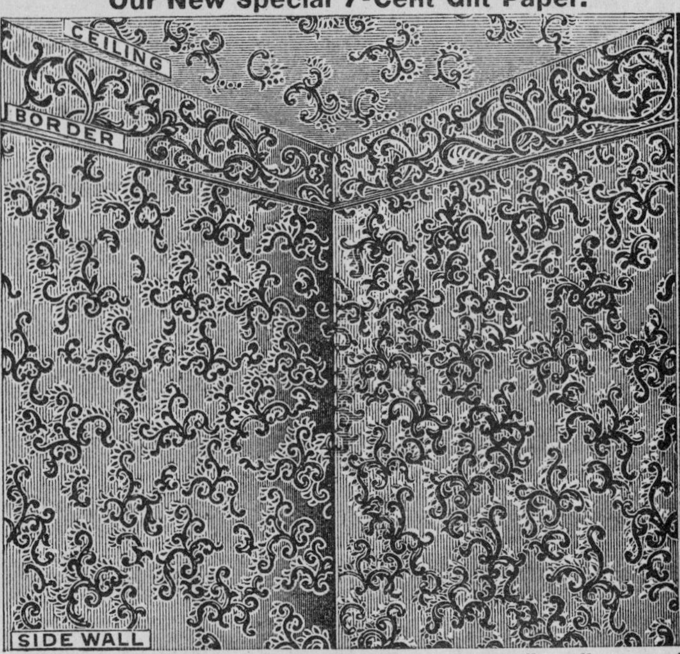

At 7 cents per double roll we offer this handsome gilt wall paper. A beautiful new pattern for this season in a cream ground with a beautiful scroll effect in two shades of green, with gold outline, as the equal of wall paper that sells everywhere at 15 cents to 25 cents a double roll.

This, our special number, is entirely new for this season. It has a soft cream background with beautiful scrolls in two shades of green, with gold outline. The 9-inch border to match is made in a similar design, though larger. The ceiling is a lighter tint, with much more delicate scroll work; the whole effecting a handsome combination, making a paper especially suitable for light parlors or bedrooms, also suitable for libraries, dining rooms, etc. It is also especially recommended for hotels; it is, in fact, an all purpose gilt paper and offered at a price heretofore unknown.

No. 37R3346 Price for side wall paper, per double roll.....7c

No. 37R3348 Price for ceiling paper, per double roll.....7c

No. 37R3350 Price for 9-inch border, per single yard.....1½c

Our Special 11-Cent Embossed Paper.

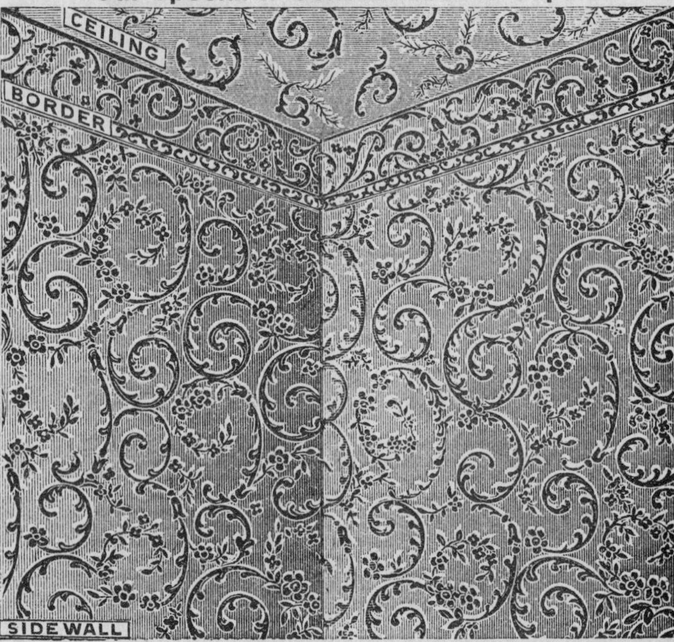

For 11 cents per double roll we offer this rich, embossed paper in an entirely new design for this season, in competition with wall paper which sells for from 25 cents to 50 cents per double roll. **Our special price of 11 cents for double roll** barely covers the cost for material and labor, with but our one small percentage of profit added. **Understand, you can order direct from the catalogue descriptions,** with our guarantee that the paper will please you or your money will be immediately returned to you, or on receipt of 2 cents, we will send you our small sample book, showing samples of the side wall paper, or, on receipt of 25 cents we will send you the big dealers' book showing samples of this and our complete line of side wall, ceiling and borders. This is one of the handsomest new light shades for this season. It is an embossed paper made with a light green background, a beautiful scroll pattern printed with gold, silver and patent green bronzes. **The ceiling paper is in a lighter** shade with a very light green background, harmonizing perfectly with the wall and border. **This handsome embossed gold, silver and bronze finished paper is especially suitable for parlors,** libraries and bedrooms. It is, in fact, a handsome, delicate, all purpose paper, suitable for almost any room in the home.

No. 37R3352 Price for side wall, per double roll.....11c

No. 37R3354 Price for ceiling paper, per double roll.....11c

No. 37R3356 Price for 9-inch border, per single yard.....2c

22 Cents Buys a Regular 50-Cent Paper.

For 22 cents per double roll we offer this as one of the richest, heaviest, gold bronze finished papers on the market, a paper rich enough and good enough to decorate any room, such paper as will only be found in the most fashionable city stores, a paper that is often furnished by paper hangers at prices ranging as high as 75 cents to $1.00 per double roll. **Our special price of 22 cents for double roll** barely covers the cost of material and labor, with but our one small percentage of profit added. **Don't fail to send 25 cents for the dealers' big book** if you think you will be interested in this, one of the richest wall papers made. The pattern is such that it can only be appreciated by seeing a large sample in the dealers' big book, both a large sample of the heavy 18-inch border and the ceiling. No description we could offer would do this paper justice. It is a paper that must be seen, examined and compared with paper that sells at from two to three times the price we ask to appreciate the value we are giving.

From the illustration we have endeavored to give you just a little idea of the style of this paper as shown in the side wall, border and ceiling. It is positively one of the richest, handsomest and neatest things for this season, such a paper as you could not get from your dealers at home. The side wall is a rich conventional design, drawn on a rich heavy maroon background. It has a velvet brown center, brought out by lighter shades of red, surrounded by a pleasing combination of different colored bronzes. The border is 18 inches wide, the heavy maroon blending softly into rich pink at the top. The entire border is decorated after the same style as the wall paper in heavy colored bronzes, the border matching the rich reddish cream ceiling paper, which is decorated with handsome bronze scroll work and gold bronze and green floral effects. **This is a very rich all purpose paper.** It is one of the richest papers for libraries, drawing rooms, halls, dining rooms, public buildings of all kinds, and is particularly adapted to lodge rooms, etc.; there is nothing that will be more suitable. **If you do not wish to wait to write for the big dealers' 25-cent book send us your order taken direct from the catalogue** and we will guarantee the paper to please you or we will immediately return your money.

No. 37R3358 Price for side wall, per double roll........................22c
No. 37R3360 Price for ceiling, per double roll........................22c
No. 37R3362 Price for 18-inch border, per single yard........................3½c

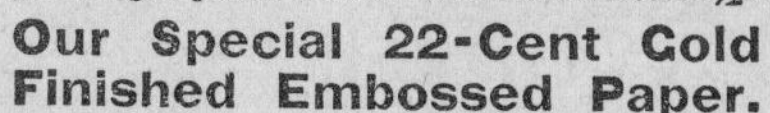

Our Special 22-Cent Gold Finished Embossed Paper.

This design is entirely new for this season, one of the richest shown by any wall paper maker. Our 22-cent price is about one-third the price charged by dealers generally. This is a paper that sells everywhere for from 50 cents to 75 cents per double roll. Nothing but a large sample will give you an idea of the colorings and pattern effect worked out in this new number. **If you send us 25 cents for our dealers' big book, you will get a large sample of the wall paper,** the 18-inch border and the ceiling from which to make a selection. Or you can send your order direct from the catalogue with the understanding that if the paper is not perfectly satisfactory, much greater value than you could get elsewhere, you can return it at our expense and we will immediately return your money. The illustration gives you an idea of the beautiful pattern effect as worked out in the side wall, border and ceiling. This is a new and handsome embossed floral paper on a delicate cream ground. The combination of rich colors and bronze used in the new rococo scroll adds greatly to the pleasing effect. **For a rich paper for a parlor there is nothing nicer made.** It is also suitable for libraries, dining rooms, halls and other rooms, and especially recommended as a very rich gold bronze, floral embossed paper for parlors.

No. 37R3364 Price for side wall, per double roll........................22c
No. 37R3366 Price for ceiling paper, per double roll........................22c
No. 37R3368 Price for 18-inch border, per single yard........................4c

Our 22-Cent Leader.

The illustration will give you some idea of the harmonizing pattern effect worked out in the wall, 18-inch border and ceiling. This paper is a French gray ground with a new green stripe effect. It has a massive rococo scroll surrounding an empire green wreath. It is finished in the same designs as the wall paper, the colorings running from a rich empire green to a soft tan, the whole handsomely finished in gold. The ceiling paper is a rich tan ground with beautiful green, gold and floral scroll and wreath designs. **This paper is especially recommended for large rooms,** such as churches, lodges, halls and other public places. It is adapted for rooms in hotels, etc.

No. 37R3370 Price for side wall, per double roll........................22c
No. 37R3372 Price for ceiling, per double roll........................22c
No. 37R3374 Price for 18-inch border, per single yard........................4c

Our 20-Cent Embossed Bronzed Paper.

At 20 cents per double roll we offer this rich, heavy, embossed bronze paper, in an entirely new design for this season as the equal of paper that sells generally at 50 cents to 60 cents per double roll. The sample in the small 2-cent book will give you an idea of the coloring and quality, but to get the pattern and all the design in the side wall, ceiling and heavy 18-inch border you should send 25 cents for the dealers' big book. Or, you can order direct from the catalogue description with our guarantee that the paper will please you and be found better than you can buy elsewhere at double the price, or we will immediately return your money.

In the illustration we simply give you a slight idea of the new, harmonizing pattern effect worked out in the side wall, border and ceiling. The paper must be seen, examined and compared with paper that sells at double the price to appreciate the value we offer.

This is a rich, embossed paper, treated in three shades of bronze with a moss green choke on an apple green ground. It is one of the richest colorings and handsomest designs in a new green shade that is shown this season. The border matches perfectly the side walls and ceiling, is also in three shades of bronze with moss green and apple green ground, the heavy green blending into a delicate light green. The ceiling is a beautiful light green, richly embossed, relieved by a handsome medallion of green, white and gold. This paper is suitable for parlors, halls, libraries, in fact any room where a very rich embossed gold finish paper is wanted.

No. 37R3382 Side wall, per double roll..**20c**
No. 37R3384 Ceiling, per double roll...**20c**
No. 37R3386 18-inch border, single yard **4c**

Our Rich 22-Cent Tapestry Leader.

At 22 cents per double roll we offer a tapestry wall paper the equal of papers that sell generally at 50 cents to 75 cents per double roll. This is one of the richest numbers in our line, a paper you must see, examine and compare with other papers to appreciate the value we offer. A small sample, such as is furnished in **our 2-cent booklet,** will give you but a slight idea of its appearance. To get the full pattern and samples of the border and ceiling as well, **you should send 25 cents for the dealers' big book, or order direct from the catalogue** under our guarantee that the paper will prove entirely satisfactory or your money will be immediately returned to you.

In this illustration we have endeavored to give you some idea of the style of this paper, both the wall, border and ceiling, and nothing but the big samples will show you the real value we furnish. This is a new tapestry design on a pure Vernon green background, the rich combination of maroon and old gold colors in the set figures produces a striking effect. **The surrounding scroll is silver and green bronze,** affording a harmonious contrast. **This is one of the papers that is being offered by the most fashionable city dealers,** and such a paper as you will not find in country towns. The heavy 18-inch border is decorated similar to the wall paper, with very large free hand gold and silver scroll effects, the colors running from a dark Vernon green to a soft shade of light nile. The ceiling is a rich light nile green, relieved by **beautiful red, gold and silver scroll effects.**

No. 37R3388 Price for side wall, per double roll........................22c
No. 37R3390 Ceiling, per double roll..**22c**
No. 37R3392 Price for 18-inch border per single yard........................4c

TOYS AND GAMES.

Baby Swings.

No. 29R2 Baby Swing; has hardwood seat, 11 inches square, upholstered in cretonne; intended to be hung in a doorway; furnished with cotton rope and two hooks to hang it on; has no springs.
Price, each....................37c
Shipping weight, 3 pounds.

Jumper Springs.

No. 29R4 Springs for Baby Swings; made of heavy steel spring wire, 15 inches long. By adding a pair of these springs to above swing you have a baby jumper. Many people buy these springs and make their own jumper. Springs come in pairs. **Shipping weight, 2 pounds.** Price for springs only, per pair, 39c

Baby Jumpers.

This Jumper combines in one article a baby swing, reclining chair, crib and jumper; strong and large enough for a child six years old; child cannot fall out. Should the baby fall asleep while in the chair it can be adjusted to a crib without disturbing the child. **It is light and simple, yet substantial and perfect.**

No. 29R8 Baby Jumper, complete, with springs and cotton rope and hooks, with veneer seat and back, not upholstered. **Shipping** weight, 12 lbs. Price, each..$1.23

No. 29R12 Baby Jumper, complete, with springs, rope and hooks, upholstered in cretonne, like cut. **Shipping weight, 12 pounds.** Price, each....$1.75

Baby Jumper and Swing Combined.

No. 29R15 The stand is made on the best mechanical principles; will support a tested weight of 150 pounds. The only baby jumper that has a perfect reclining chair and foot rest and is adjustable. You can make a chair, cradle or crib by a single movement. All material used in the construction of the stand and chair is the best selected hard wood. Can be folded up when not in use and laid to one side. **You would not take three times the price and be without after having used same.** Shipping weight, 30 pounds. Price, each....................$3.29

Tothill's Baby Tender.

No. 29R17 Made on the principle of a reclining chair, is strong and durable, adjusted to any position from chair to crib in a minute by locked ratchet. Child can be placed upright or reclining; has an easy, soothing, swinging motion which all the children like—so does mother and nurse; simple and substantial. Price, each...$1.85
Shipping weight, 20 pounds.

Shoo Fly Rockers.

No. 29R43 Shoo Fly, 18x36 inches; painted and dappled; has painted hardwood seat, bent rocker and hair tail.
Price, each..........58c
Shipping wgt., 10 lbs.

No. 29R45 Shoo Fly. 21x38, same as No. 29R43, but is upholstered in cretonne. **Shipping weight, 12 pounds.** Price...75c

No. 29R47 Shoo Fly, 24x40 inches, neatly painted and dappled; has box in front to hold child's toys, and is upholstered in cretonne; hair tail, bent rockers. **Shipping weight, 13 pounds.** Price.........$1.08

Swinging Shoo Fly Rockers.

No. 29R49 Swinging Shoo Fly, easy to operate, no danger of child falling out; nicely upholstered in cretonne and painted dapple gray.
Price, each........$1.65
Shipping weight, 20 pounds.

Patent Swing Horses.

No. 29R51 Swing Horse, 19 inches high from floor to saddle, nicely trimmed, has hair mane and tail.
This horse requires very little strength to operate, and for that reason is a decided improvement over the old style rocking horse. Each........$1.75
Shipping weight, 24 pounds.

No. 29R53 Swing Horse, 21 inches high, from floor to saddle, otherwise same as No. 29R51.
Shipping weight, 23½ pounds. Each......$2.50

No. 29R55 Swing Horse, 22 inches high from floor to saddle, trimmed in a superior manner.
Shipping weight, 28 pounds. Each.........$2.95

Galloping Horse.

No. 29R57 A Galloping Horse, nicely painted and ornamented stand, English saddle with enameled cloth; enamel cloth saddle flaps, trimmed with fancy color wool fringe, hair main and tail, stirrups and martingales with reins, heavy breast plating, 6x6-inch block, 32 inches high from floor to head. **Shipping weight, 40 pounds.** Price, $3.25

BOYS' WAGONS.

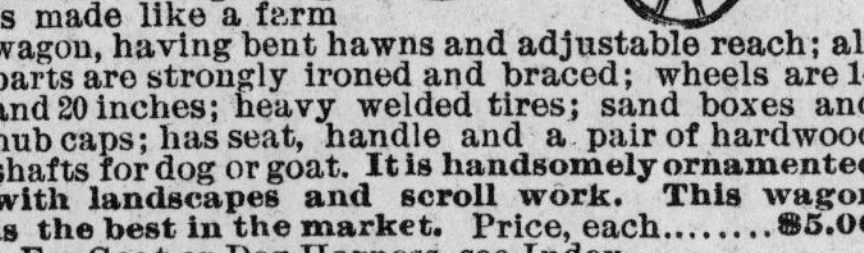

No. 29R58 Iron axles; body, 14x28 inches; wheels, 12 and 16 inches. Hardwood paneled body, landscape painting, scrolled and varnished, hub caps, high seat and dashboard. Iron braced, heavy iron axles in iron thimble skein, oval tires welded and shrunk on. Same as cut. Price, each.........$1.95
Shipping weight, 28 pounds.

Boys' Farm Wagon.

No. 29R62 Boys' Farm Wagon, with pole and shafts. Body, 18x36 inches, with hardwood frame. The sides and ends can be taken off, leaving bed with stakes. The gearing is made like a farm wagon, having bent hawns and adjustable reach; all parts are strongly ironed and braced; wheels are 14 and 20 inches; heavy welded tires; sand boxes and hub caps; has seat, handle and a pair of hardwood shafts for dog or goat. **It is handsomely ornamented with landscapes and scroll work. This wagon is the best in the market.** Price, each........$5.00

For Goat or Dog Harness, see Index.

Shipping weight, 54 pounds.

Boys' Express Wagons.

Boys' Steel Wagons. The best and strongest steel wagon made; finely painted and ornamented, steel box, malleable iron gear, tinned steel wheels.

No. 29R64 Body, 13x26-inch; wheels, 10 and 14-inch. **Shipping weight, 18 pounds.** Each....$1.20
No. 29R68 Body, 14x28-inch; wheels, 12 and 16-inch. **Shipping weight, 18 pounds.** Each....$1.30
No. 29R72 Body, 15x30-inch; wheels, 14 and 18-inch. **Shipping weight, 20 pounds.** Each....$1.50

The Eclipse Tricycle Wagon.

The Tricycle Wagon, the latest and best liked wagon made. The Eclipse is the lightest running and best made on the market. The body and back of seat are made of sheet steel, gear is of malleable iron, and wheels of tinned steel. The propelling arrangement is made of wrought iron, and is operated on the same principle as a tricycle. The lock corner handle can be used either to pull or steer the wagon. The seat and seat boards are hinged and can be folded down, thereby making a perfectly flush bottom. Body, 14x34 inches. Wheels, 12 and 18 inches. **Shipping weight, 20 pounds.**
No. 29R73 Price, each.........................$2.99

Child's Buggy.

No. 29R76 Made of the best seasoned wood, nicely painted, body 13x26 inches, with steel wheels 12 and 16 inches in diameter, iron axles, iron tongue draw and 5th wheel. Has hub caps, seat and whip with whip in socket. **These buggies are being more universally used and are a very convenient form for giving the child a ride instead of the baby buggy.**
Price, each $1.98
Shipping weight, 28 pounds.

The Penny Saver.

No. 29R147 A perfect registering bank; no key, no combination. Each time a cent is dropped into the bank the bell rings and the register indicates. Opens automatically at each 50 cents. The total always in sight. **They are attractive and interesting to children.** The mechanism is made of steel, and will not break or get out of order. **It is highly interesting to children, and for this reason will encourage them to save. Shipping weight, 5 pounds.** Price, each..........85c

New Registering Self Accounting Bank.

No. 29R149 Registers pennies, nickels, dimes, quarters and half dollars. Not only registers the amount but adds up the total as each coin is deposited. This bank is pronounced the finest work of mechanism ever invented. The bank is made of steel, handsomely lithographed. Order at once. Size, 6½x6x4½ inches. **Shipping weight, 1½ pounds.**
Price, each............87c

The Bear Bank.

No. 29R151 You place a coin in proper position on the barrel of the rifle, press the lever, and the rifle shoots the coin into the bear. Finished in fancy colors. Size, 10¼x7¾x3¼ inches.
Price, each.... .85c
Shipping weight, 6 pounds.

The Little Gem Dime Savings Bank.

No. 29R155 Locks itself and registers the amount deposited. Opens automatically when $5.00 in dimes have been deposited without use of force; nickel plated, and can be carried conveniently in your vest pocket.
Price, each 6c
If by mail, postage extra, each, 2 cents.

No. 29R157 Made same as above to hold and register 50 pennies. This gives the little ones an opportunity to save their spare pennies. Price, each..8c
If by mail, postage extra, 4 cents.

The Ready Change Holder.

No. 29R159 A most convenient form of carrying or saving change. A place for pennies, nickels, dimes and quarters. Nickel plated.
Price, each...............7c
If by mail, postage extra, 3 cents.

Remember the Maine.

Shipping weight, 64 ozs.

No. 29R161 The Battleship Bank. Handsomely nickel plated and enameled in colors. Puzzle combination lock. A handsome mantel ornament; large, strong and durable. Length, 10½ inches. Price...85c

No. 29R173 Perfect working toy range, nickel plated and polished edges; furnished with skillet, stewpot, lifter and length of pipe. Length, 8 inches; width, 5⅛ inches; height, 5 inches. A model range and sold by many at 75 cents.
Price, each....50c
Shipping weight, 4½ pounds.

No. 29R175 This is an ideal range, and for style, elegance and goodness is hard to beat; finished in nickel; furnished with skillet, pot, shovel, lifter, and length of pipe; in the back is a hot water receptacle. A perfect model toy stove. Length, 10 inches; width, 6½ inches; height, 6 inches. Price.........90c
Shipping weight, 7 pounds.

The Laughing Camera.

No. 29R176 The Laughing Camera. A whole passing show. Furnishes more amusement than you would get in a circus. Your friends grotesquely photographed. Stout people look thin and thin people look stout. By getting a focus on passing pedestrians, horses, cars, etc., the most ludicrous pictures are witnessed. **The passerby takes on the swinging stride of a grand-daddy-longlegs, horses look like giraffes.**
Price, each.......................................13c
If by mail, postage extra, 5 cents.

Triumph Toy Sewing Machine.

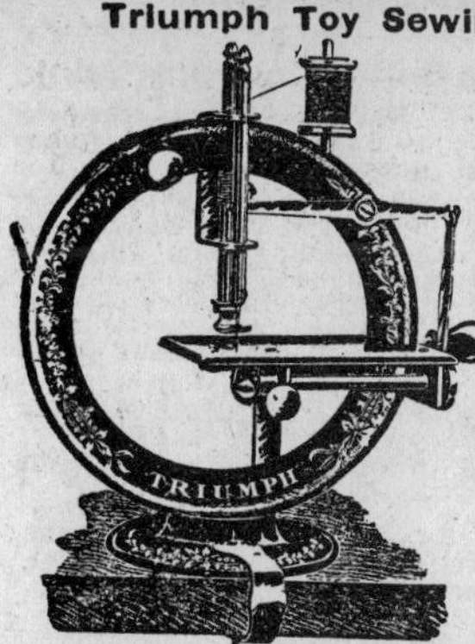

No. 29R177 A first class machine that will sew perfectly. It has the latest patent feed motion, a perfect stitch regulator, uses the Wilcox & Gibbs self setting needle which has a short blade and long shank and is not easily broken. On account of the simple devices embodied in its construction it runs lighter and quieter than any machine made. **It is fastened to the table with a clamp furnished with each machine. Elegantly enameled and finished in flower designs. Suitable for the little miss, for the nursery maid, for all kinds of plain family sewing and is adapted largely for kindergarten use.** Each machine is packed in a separate box with an extra needle and clamp, thoroughly tested and adjusted, and is sent out with a sample of sewing done on it, showing it leaves the factory in perfect working order. Height, 7½ inches; width, 6½ inches. Price, each..........$1.25

Shipping weight, 23 ounces.

The Prismatic Top.

No. 29R199 A fascinating and interesting toy, will amuse by the hour. This scientific toy is an entirely new thing in tops; will spin for 10 or 12 minutes. When it is in motion, you drop one of the paper discs over the spindle, it will settle down on the face of the top. You touch the revolving disc with the color of paint you desire and immediately beautiful circular rims of color spring into existence. The most exquisite combinations are possible. Top is made of metal, perfectly balanced with Bessemer steel spindle case, hardened point. Box of prismatic water colors, camel's hair brush, 25 paper discs. Comes packed complete in cardboard box. Price, each..........................22c

Extra box of colors, 5c; extra paper discs, per hundred......(Shipping weight, 10 ounces).......5c

Steam Toy Engines are not designed for practical use, such as running a machine, etc. They are for instruction and amusement, and will operate toy engine attachments and burn alcohol.

The Weeden Horizontal Engine No. 21.

No. 29R299 The Weeden Horizontal Engine No. 21. This engine has a highly polished brass boiler, firmly fastened upon substantial base. Finished in colors. The whistle and safety valve are locked on top of boiler, and are made steam tight by means of small rubber washers. If broken these parts can be easily removed and new ones put on. The engine is provided with an extra large balance wheel and nickeled cylinder, running easily and rapidly, and presenting a very fine appearance. **Every engine thoroughly tested and warranted.** Packed securely in wooden locked corner box, with full directions. Base, 4x6 inches; height, 7½ inches. Burns alcohol. Price, each....95c

Shipping weight, 36 ounces.

Weeden's Horizontal Engine No. 7.

No. 29R301 Weeden's Horizontal Engine No. 7. This engine has a highly polished brass boiler and Russia iron fire box and base. The frame and working parts are also of Russia iron and strongly put together. Every part is finely finished and altogether it is a very substantial and attractive engine. Base, 4½x5¾ inches. Length of boiler, 4¾ inches. **Thoroughly tested and packed in wooden box.** Burns alcohol. Price, each..(If by mail, postage extra, 32c)..$1.35

The Weeden Horizontal Engine No. 14.

No. 29R302 Has large, highly polished brass boiler, trimmed with steam dome whistle and safety valve, and connected to steam chest on cylinder by polished brass pipe. The frame case is malleable iron, to which boiler and engine are firmly attached. The cylinder, steam chest and slide rest are cast in one piece and cannot get out of order. **Runs rapidly and easily, and is one of the most satisfactory and popular steam toys.** Every engine thoroughly tested and packed in wooden box. Burns alcohol. Price, each..$2.25

Shipping weight, 5 pounds.

The Weeden Double Engine No. 18.

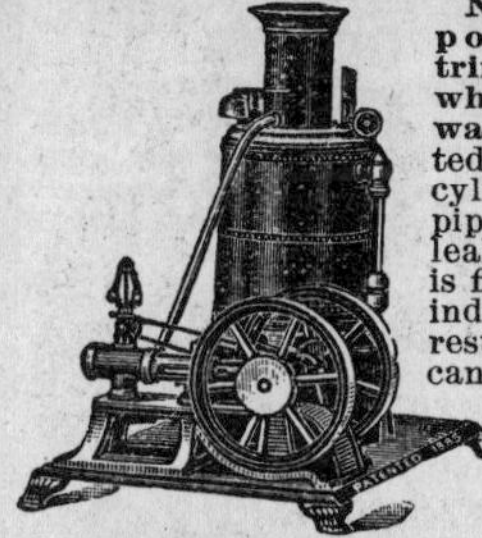

No. 29R303 Has large polished brass boiler, trimmed with steam dome whistle, safety valve and water gauge. It is connected to the steam chest on cylinder by brass steam pipe. The frame is best malleable iron, to which engine is firmly attached. The cylinder, steam chest and slide rest are cast in one piece and cannot get out of order. The slide eccentric and connecting rod are all cut from heavy sheet brass and fastened securely together. **Runs rapidly and easily.** Each engine thoroughly tested and warranted. Packed securely in wooden box, with full directions. Burns alcohol. Price, each.............................$3.50

Unmailable on account of weight.

Shipping weight, 7 pounds.

Mechanical Warship.

No. 29R331 Running in a circle. Two detachable masts, with pennants, davits and a lifeboat on each side, four cannons protected by shields. This is a very interesting toy.

Price, each.... ......44c

Shipping weight, 20 ounces.

Mechanical Automobile.

No. 29R335 Mechanical Automobile, open shape, with engineer. When wound up will run similar to the figure 8. Highly colored, with imitation rubber tires; will amuse and instruct the children.

Price, each..........17c

Shipping weight, 8 ozs.

The Balky Mule.

No. 29R341 The Balky Mule. The most realistic toy of its kind ever produced; a perfect miniature donkey cart and its driver, which moves forward about three feet, stops and apparently at the command of the driver, who pulls the reins just at the right time, the donkey kicks and starts backward; it automatically repeats the movement several times. Is wound with key. Price, each.....29c

Shipping weight, 10 ounces.

The Canary Bird Whistle.

No. 29R343 The Canary Bird Whistle. Made of metal. All the pretty notes of the canary can be imitated. Lots of fun for boys and girls. Price, each.................4c

If by mail, postage extra, 3 cents.

Toy China Tea Sets.

No. 29R377 Toy China Tea Set, consists of cups, saucers, teapot, sugar bowl and creamer, about 16 pieces, small 25-cent value packed in paper box. Per set 15c

Shipping weight, 10 ounces.

No. 29R379 Toy China Tea Set, consisting of decorated plates, cups, saucers, tea pot, creamer, sugar bowl, about 23 pieces. Price, per set................25c

Shipping weight, 20 ounces.

No. 29R381 Toy China Tea Set, consisting of about 17 pieces, decorated plates, cups, saucers, tea pot, creamer and sugar bowl. Larger size, and very interesting for a child. Splendid 75-cent value.

Price, per set....... ....50c

Shipping weight, 48 ounces.

No. 29R383 Toy China Tea Set, consisting of about 25 pieces, finely decorated plates, cups, saucers, tea pot, creamer and sugar bowl. Large size and extra value. Price, per set.............................75c

Shipping weight, 56 ounces.

No. 29R385 Toy China Tea Set, consisting of about 25 pieces, decorated cups, saucers, plates, tea pot, creamer and sugar bowl. Our larger size set, and suitable for misses up to 14 or 15 years of age. **Unmailable on account of weight.**

Price, per set..................................$1.00

Shipping weight, 7 pounds.

No. 29R387 Toy China Tea Set. This, our finest set, consists of 23 pieces finely decorated cups, saucers, plates, teapot, creamer, sugar bowl, etc., larger cups and saucers, and suitable for young misses for an afternoon tea. Equal to any $2.00 value.

Price, per set..................................$1.40

Shipping weight, 9 pounds.

Britannia Tea Sets.

No. 29R391 Britannia tea set, consisting of about 15 pieces, silver finished teapot, sugar bowl, sugar tongs, creamer, plates, cups, etc. Put up in neat pasteboard box. Set..10c

Shipping weight, 7 ounces.

No. 29R393 Britannia tea set, consisting of about 23 pieces, silver finished, assortment same as above, but a little larger size. Per set............20c

Shipping weight, 15 ounces.

No. 29R395 Britannia tea set, silver finished, about 24 pieces, and still larger than above.

Price, per set.......................... ......43c

Shipping weight, 28 ounces.

No. 29R397 Britannia tea set, consisting of about 24 pieces, silver finished dishes, very handsome filigree design and practical size, assortment about same as above, and the largest size we carry.

Price, per set..75c

Shipping weight, 40 ounces.

Snip Snaps.

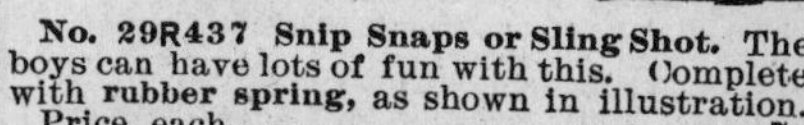

No. 29R437 Snip Snaps or Sling Shot. The boys can have lots of fun with this. Complete with rubber spring, as shown in illustration.

Price, each..7c

If by mail, postage extra, each, 3 cents.

No. 29R439 Extra Rubbers for the above sling shot. Each.... ....4c

Slate Surface Blackboards.

Our Blackboards are without question the very best on the market, having a perfect slate surface, and chalk need not necessarily be used—a common slate pencil will work to perfection. Double faced, and can be used on the other side. Each part is provided with a receptacle for holding the chalk or slate pencil. The frames are nicely molded, and the joints are perfect.

No. 29R461 Size, 17x18 inches. Price, each....25c

Shipping weight, 32 ounces.

No. 29R463 Size, 22x24 inches. Price, each.....50c

Shipping weight, 64 ounces.

No. 29R465 Is extra quality and finish, and is adapted to school use. Has handsome frame of hardwood, varnished, and has extra large swinging tray for chalk extending across the entire bottom, adjusted to be used for either side of the blackboard. Size, 28x29 inches. Price, each.....................70c

Unmailable, on account of weight; 10 pounds.

No. 29R469 Panorama Blackboard, made of ash handsomely finished in the antique. The Blackboard is reversible—that is, it revolves so that either or both sides can be used. The blackboard is fitted with a panorama arrangement at the top, which revolves, showing different views as copy, including alphabet, musical scale, historical picture views, etc. The blackboard has the best slate surface, on which a slate pencil or chalk may be used. Height, 40 inches; width, 25 inches. Size of blackboard is 15x21¾ inches. **The best ever shown at the money.** Price, each..$1.00

Shipping weight, 10 pounds.

The Majestic Doll.

The highest grade and finest doll ever produced. The body is the human shape, made of an indestructible composition flesh colored material, ball joints, moving eyes, hips, shoulders, elbows and wrists; also moving head and moving eyes, with eyelashes, open mouth, showing teeth; the very finest quality sewed wig made of human hair; has extra quality shoes and stockings; comes dressed in a fine lace and ribbon trimmed chemise. The eyes are tied with strings to back of head to prevent breaking when shipped. Comes in three sizes, as follows:

No. 29R651 Majestic Doll, as described above. Length, 18 inches. Price, each....$1.85

Shipping weight, 4½ pounds.

No. 29R653 Majestic Doll, as described above. Length, 23½ inches. Price, each $2.95

Shipping weight, 5½ pounds.

No. 29R655 Majestic Doll, as described above. Length, 25½ inches. This doll usually retails at $7.50. Price, each..(Shipping weight, 8 pounds)...$4.25

WHEN YOU MAKE UP

AN ORDER FOR TOYS,

TRY TO INCLUDE OTHER GOODS SUFFICIENT FOR A 100-POUND FREIGHT SHIPMENT AND THUS

SAVE ON THE EXPRESS CHARGES.

OUR FINEST KID BODY DOLLS.

They have double riveted patent joint hip and knees, fine American beauty bisque head, flowing curls, moving eyes and fitted with shoes and stockings. Will sit up or can be adjusted in different positions. The best quality kid and as pretty and perfect a doll as you could wish for. Come in following sizes:

No. 29R657 Kid Body Doll, riveted joints, etc., as described above. Length, 14½ inches. Price, each.........50c
Shipping weight, 1 pound.

No. 29R659 Kid Body Doll, riveted joints, etc., as described above. Length, 17 inches. Price, each.........68c
Shipping weight, 1¼ pounds.

No. 29R661 Kid Body Doll, riveted joints, etc., as described above. Length, 18½ inches. Price, each.........95c
Shipping weight, 1¾ pounds.

No. 29R663 Kid Body Doll, riveted joints, etc., as described above. Length, 21 inches. Price, each.........$1.25
Shipping weight, 2 pounds.

No. 29R665 Kid Body Doll, riveted joints, etc., as described above. Length, 23¼ inches. **Shipping weight, 2¾ pounds.** Price, each.........$1.67

No. 29R667 Kid Body Doll, riveted joints, etc., as described above. Length, 26 inches. **Shipping weight, 4 pounds.** Price, each.........$2.45

Best Kid Body Dolls.

No. 29R671 Kid Body Doll, straight body, bisque head, with pasted wig. Length, 11¼ inches. Is as good a doll as is usually sold for 25 cents. Each..15c
Shipping weight, 14 ounces.

No. 29R675 Kid Doll, double jointed body, bisque head with flowing curls, steady eyes. Length, 13 inches. Best doll ever sold at the price. **Shipping weight, 1¾ pounds.** Price, each..25c

No. 29R679 Kid Doll, double jointed and fat body, bisque head, flowing curls and steady eyes. Length, 16 inches. Splendid value. **Shipping weight, 2 pounds.** Price, each....50c

No. 29R681 Kid Doll, double jointed and fat body, bisque head, flowing curls and steady eyes. Length, 18½ inches. Regular $1.00 value. **Shipping weight, 3 pounds.** Price, each.. 70c

No. 29R683 Kid Doll, double jointed body, bisque head, sewed curls, steady eyes. Length, 21 inches. The greatest value for the price. **Shipping weight, 6 pounds.** Price, each....95c

Kid Body Dolls with Moving Eyes.

No. 29R685 Kid Body Dolls, double jointed body, bisque head, flowing curls and moving eyes. Length, 15 inches. **Shipping weight, 3 pounds.** Each....50c

No. 29R689 Kid Body Dolls, double jointed body, bisque head, with sewed curls and moving eyes. Length, 16½ inches. Price, each.........75c
Shipping weight, 6 pounds.

No. 29R691 A Kid Body Doll, double jointed body, bisque head with a full wig, moving eyes. Length, 20 inches. Price, each.........$1.00
Shipping weight, 6 pounds.

No. 29R693 Kid Body Doll, double jointed body, bisque head, with full wig and moving eyes. Length, 21 inches. Price, each.........$1.25

No. 29R695 Kid Doll with cork body, double jointed, bisque head and full flowing wig, moving eyes. This high grade kid doll we offer at a very special price. Length, 22 inches. Price, each..$1.50

No. 29R697 Kid Doll with cork body, heavier body than above, double jointed, bisque head, with full flowing wig and moving eyes. This is a very large and handsome doll, 23 inches long. Price, each.........$1.95

Dressed Dolls.

Exceptionally pretty; stylishly dressed; better values for less money than you ever bought them for before.

No. 29R715 Dressed Doll, Bisque head and flowing hair, steady eyes, jointed body, pretty costume. Length, 12 inches. **Shipping weight, 28 ounces.** Price.........25c

No. 29R719 Dressed Doll, jointed body, steady eyes, bisque head, flowing hair. Length, 14 inches. Pretty costume and hat. Excellent value. **Shipping weight, 36 ounces.** Price.........50c

No. 29R721 Stylishly Dressed Doll, similar to above, but larger body, steady eye and prettier costume, regular $1.00 value. 16 inches long. **Shipping weight, 42 oz.** Price.........75c

No. 29R723 Handsomely Dressed Doll, bisque head, flowing curls, jointed body and moving eyes, new and pretty costumes. Length, 18 inches. Best value ever offered at the price. **Shipping weight, 42 ounces.** Price.........95c

No. 29R725 Handsomely Dressed Doll, bisque head, flowing curls, jointed body and moving eyes. A very tastefully gotten up costume, and the highest grade doll that we sell. Length, 20 inches. **Shipping weight, 54 ounces.** Price.........$1.50

DRESSED SAILOR DOLLS.

Sailor Girl Dolls.

No. 29R735 Sailor Girl Doll, bisque head, flowing hair, solid eyes, dressed to represent a girl in sailor costume. A very pretty doll. Length, 13 inches. Price, each.........50c
Shipping weight, 20 ounces.

No. 29R737 Sailor Girl Doll, similar to above. Length, 11 inches and smaller body. Price, each.........25c
Shipping weight, 15 ounces.

Sailor Boy Dolls.

No. 29R739 Sailor Boy Doll, dressed to represent a boy in sailor costume, companion doll to sailor girl. Length, 13 inches. Price, each.........50c
Shipping weight, 20 ounces.

No. 29R741 Sailor Boy Doll, similar to above. Length, 11 inches. Price, each.........25c
Shipping weight, 15 ounces.

No. 29R743 Infants in long white dresses. Dress and hood embroidered and lace trimmed. Bisque heads with curls, stationary eyes. Something new and pretty. Length, without dress, 8½ inches. Price, each.........25c
Shipping weight, 13 ounces.

Rag Dolls—The American Maid.

Indestructible Dolls, something like our grandmother used to make for the baby; serviceable, well designed and planned in every respect. In three sizes.

No. 29R747 American Maid Rag Doll. 11½ inches high. Price.......25c

No. 29R749 American Maid Rag Doll. 16 inches high. Price.........50c

No. 29R751 American Maid Rag Doll. 17½ inches high. Price..70c

No. 29R765 Fine Kid Doll Bodies, extra quality kid full stout bodies, shoes and stockings. We are able to quote much lower prices than ever before made.

Style	Length, inches	Inches across shoulders	Shipping weight, oz.	Price, each
1	10	2¾	12	20c
2	13	3¼	15	30c
3	14	3½	20	40c
4	15¾	3¾	26	50c
5	17¼	4	34	65c
6	19¼	4½	45	80c

Pink Silesia Doll Bodies.

No. 29R769 Made of good quality silesia with leather arms. This body will give excellent wear and is very satisfactory. Comes in the following sizes:

Length, inches	Inches across shoulders	Shipping weight, oz.	Price, each
10½	2¼	8	10c
14	3½	14	17c
17½	4	20	23c
20¼	5	30	29c
22½	5½	36	38c

Minerva Indestructible Metal Doll Heads.

No. 29R781 These Doll Heads are imported from Germany, they combine the durability of sheet metal and the beauty of bisque, are light in weight, washable, and will not chip; will stand any reasonable wear. Small children cannot injure them, larger ones love them for their unequaled beauty. The eyes are clear and tender, head flexible at the bust, and fitted with sewing holes, making it easy to adjust and fasten them to body. Come in sizes as follows:

Style	Height, inches	Inches across shoulders	Shipping weight, ounces	Price, each
2	3⅜	2¾	5	25c
3	3¾	3	6	30c
4	4⅜	3⅜	8	35c
5	4½	3⅝	9	45c
6	5	4	10	55c
7	6¼	4½	12	75c
8	6¾	5½	14	90c

Nos. 7 and 8 have open mouths and showing teeth.

The Minerva Indestructible Doll Head.

No. 29R785 The Minerva Indestructible Doll Head with moving glass eyes, open lips showing teeth, and very fine sewed curly wig. The Minerva heads made of the best flexible sheet brass can be given to the smallest child with perfect safety, as the metal is covered with a pure, wholesome paint which is manufactured especially for the purpose. Come in sizes as follows:

Style	Height, inches	Inches across shoulders	Shipping weight, ozs.	Price, each
1	4	3	9	$0.50
3	4¾	3¼	12	.75
5	5¾	4⅜	14	1.25
7	6⅝	4⅞	16	1.50

Bisque Doll Heads, Stationary Eyes.

No. 29R789 First Quality Bisque Doll Heads, the faces are especially beautiful, showing teeth, have stationary eyes, curly flowing wigs, either blondes or brunettes, and full model bust. Sizes:

Style	Height, inches	Inches across shoulders	Shipping weight	Price, each
1	3¾	3	10 oz.	$0.10
3	4	3¼	12 oz.	.15
5	4¾	3¾	18 oz.	.20
7	5	4¼	22 oz.	.25
9	6	5	25 oz.	.38
11	6¾	5¾	28 oz.	.60
13	7	6	30 oz.	.97
15	7½	6½	35 oz.	1.50

As the heads increase in height and width, other proportions increase materially.

Bisque Doll Heads, Moving Eyes.

No. 29R791 Same as No. 29R789, but with moving eyes.

Style	Height inches	Inches across shoulders	Shipping weight	Price, each
2	3¾	3	10 oz.	$0.15
4	4	3¼	12 oz.	.20
6	4¾	3¾	18 oz.	.25
8	5	4¼	22 oz.	.30
10	6	5	25 oz.	.45
12	6¾	5¾	28 oz.	.70
14	7	6	30 oz.	1.20
16	7½	6½	36 oz.	1.65

Musical Gray Rubber Dolls, Plain.

No. 29R815 Something the children can't break and excellent values. Large bodies.

Size 10, length 7 inches. Each, $0.25
Size 20, length 9 inches. Each, .50
Size 30, length 10¼ inches. Each, .75
Size 40, length 11¾ inches. Each, 1.00

The size of body increases proportionately to the length.

If by mail, postage extra, 4c, 6c, 8c and 10c.

Musical Gray Rubber Dolls.

No. 29R819 With knitted worsted dress and hat. Very desirable doll for small children. The length measurement includes the knitted hat.

Size 01, length 8 inches. Each...25c
Size 02, length 10½ inches. Each...50c
Size 03, length 11½ inches. Each...70c
Size 04, length 12½ inches. Each...95c

If by mail, postage extra, 4c, 6c, 8c

Kite Flying Has Become a Craze.

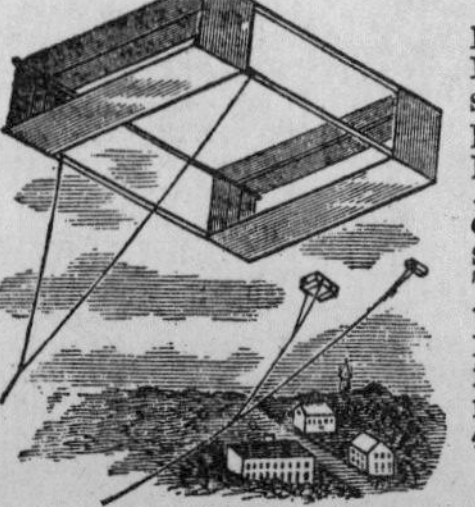

No. 29R995 Horsman's Box Kite. The Naval Blue Hill Box Kite. A sensible and practical pastime for boys, and it pleases the men also. A team of two or more can be sent up and will support heavy weights. They are built on scientific principles. Size 30x14x14 inches. It is folded in a small roll and can be mailed. Shipping weight, 46 ounces. Price, each.........17c

Kites Continued on Next Page.

KITES.—Continued.

No. 29R997 Blue Hill Box Kite No. 50. This kite has more square inches of surface than the original $1.00 kites first placed upon the market in 1897. Kites of this kind have attained a height of two miles. Anybody can fly the Blue Hill box kite which goes straight up from the hand like a bird will fly in a moderate breeze and yet no wind short of a gale is too strong for it. Size, 30x20x10 inches; width of bands 7¼ inches. Shipping weight, 48 ounces. Price, each........60c

No. 29R999 Horsman's Blue Hill Box Kite No. 100. This is an improved style and has proved a grand success. Similar to the above No. 50 Blue Hill kite but larger. Size, 36x24x10 inches; width of bands, 11½ inches. It does not dive but flies like a bird. Shipping weight, 48 ounces. Price, each.......**$1.00**

The Eddy Kite for $1.65.

No. 29R1000 The Eddy Kite. The Tailless Kite has won not only a national but a world wide reputation. **The Eddy Kite will fly in a very moderate wind,** and because of its exceedingly light pull is especially suitable for small boys. The Eddy Kite folds compactly into a cloth bag like a fishing rod and is very little larger. Size, 6 feet in height when opened out. Price, each...(Not mailable).....**$1.65**

No. 29R1001 Horsman's Blue Hill Kite No. 1. A scientific marvel, a recent and most remarkable achievement in the kite craft. Is constructed to **faithfully represent a full rigged racing sloop,** with jib and mainsail and globe topsail set. The sails are so ingeniously constructed in catching the wind they drive the ship upwards. The kite has great buoyancy and sails on the wind as if riding the waves. Will rise in a very moderate breeze. A very fascinating kite for young and old. Stands 4 feet high. Any child can fly it. Shipping weight, 64 oz. Price, each........**$1.75**

No. 29R1003 No. X Fine Flax Kite Line, 300 feet on a spool, for naval kites. Shipping weight, 4 ounces. Price, per spool........9c

No. 29R1005 No. 11 Flax Kite Line suitable for flying No. 50 and No. 100 box kites and No. 1. Shipped in ¼-pound balls. Length, 400 feet. Shipping weight, 9 ounces. Price, per ball........20c

No. 29R1007 No. 12 Flax Kite Line suitable for flying No. 50 and No. 100 box kites and No. 1. Shipped in ½-pound balls. Length, 800 feet. Shipping weight, 10 ounces. Price, per ball........38c

No. 29R1009 No. 24 Flax Kite Line suitable for flying No. 100 box kites in a very strong wind. ½-pound balls, length, 400 feet. Shipping weight, 10 ounces. Price, per ball........50c

No. 29R1011 No. 18 Flax Kite Line, ½-pound balls, 600 feet to fly No. 100 box kites. Ship kite and Eddy kite. Price, per ball........46c

Shipping weight, 13 ounces.

Latest Novelty, Croaking Frog.

No. 29R1017 By pressing the little rubber bulb, the frog is made to hop and at the same time produce a croaking sound, which is a very correct imitation of the real frog. Bound to be a source of great amusement to the children and grown folks as well. Each....25c

If by mail, postage extra, 6 cents.

Rattle and Whistle.

No. 29R1027 Rattle and Whistle, for the baby. Price, each........3c

Shipping weight, 4 ounces.

The Rattle Pacifier for 9 Cents.

No. 29R1029 The Rattle Pacifier, the best rattle, teething ring and plaything ever invented for the babies. It has rubber nipple, bone shields, teething ring and bells. **Made good and strong.** Price, each.....9c

If by mail, postage extra, each, 5 cents.

Celluloid Rattle.

No. 29R1033 Celluloid Rattles (with whistle), 6 inches long, come in very pretty assorted colors. Each........23c

If by mail, postage extra, each, 5 cents.

Celluloid Teething Ring.

No. 29R1037 Celluloid Teething Ring, pure white. Far superior to rubber. Price, each........8c

If by mail, postage extra, 2 cents.

No. 29R1041 Rubber Teething Rings, best white rubber. Price, each........3c

If by mail, postage extra, each, 1 cent.

Papier Mache Return Ball.

No. 29R1047 Papier Mache Return Ball, unbreakable, with long rubber string and ring on end. Is hollow, has rattle inside, and the outside of ball is decorated with a picture of the world, with the continents and oceans in different colors. The Equator is represented by a gold band. Size, 3 inches in diameter. Price, each........4c

If by mail, postage extra, 3 cents.

Hollow Rubber Bat Balls.

No. 29R1051 White Rubber Bat Balls. (Hollow.)

Size	10	20	30	40
Diameter in inches	1⅝	1⅞	2¼	2½
Weight, ounces	2	3	3	4
Each	3c	5c	8c	8c

No. 29R1053 White Inflated Rubber Balls.

Size	105	115	130	145	165
Diameter in inches	1⅝	1⅞	2½	3	4
Each	4c	5c	8c	12c	21c

THE SEROCO REVERSIBLE GAME BOARD.

51 Games and Revolving Game Board Stand.

The Complete Outfit, Board and Stand, for $1.95

The Seroco Reversible Game Board is the only board with circles to shoot from; fifty-one games may be played. Made of the very best hard ash wood with three-ply veneer. The board is 28½ inches square, the circles and checker board stenciled on in green and red bronze which is very artistic. The illustration shows both sides of the board. Some of the games that can be played on the board are Pyramid, Chicago, Continuous, Bottle and Pin Pool, Billiards, Three Ring, Carrom Game, Checkers, Backgammon, Crokinole, etc. With each board is furnished 29 beautifully polished hardwood rings, two nicely turned and polished cues, one set ten pins with movable back, billiard attachment and numbered rings. No expense has been spared to make this board the very best. The game can be played by from two to eight persons.

The Game Board Stand for Seroco Board, is a firm support for the board at the proper height for players to sit on chairs. **It revolves, making it convenient.** Made of hard wood and varnished, rubber tips on bottom. Folds up in a small, compact package. Regular value of stand is 50 cents.

No. 29R1723 The Seroco Game Board and the Revolving Stand........$1.95
Shipping weight, board and stand, 17 lbs.

No. 29R1724 Revolving Game Board Stand, same as above for Seroco, Carrom or Crokinole Boards, Price, each........25c

Shipping weight, 30 ounces.

No. 29R1725 Complete set extra discs, ten pins and numbers for the Seroco Game Board. Price, per set........(Shipping weight, 6 ounces)........25c

Crokinole Boards.

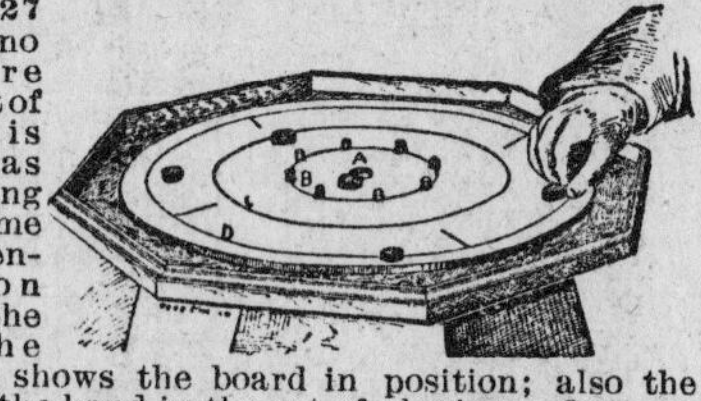

No. 29R1727 There is no game where the element of chance is smaller, as the winning of the game depends entirely upon the skill of the player. The illustration shows the board in position; also the position of the hand in the act of playing. Octagon shape, 32 inches across; made of polished ash. Price........88c

Shipping weight, 15 pounds.

Extra Crokinole Discs, per set........20c

No. 29R1729 Felt Lined Crokinole board, made of oak, highly polished. Price........**$1.57**

Shipping weight, 18 pounds.

No. 29R1731 Folding Chess or Checkerboard, lithographed in red and black and covered with imported morocco paper. Squares, 1 inch. Size of board, 14x14 inches. Price, each........10c

Shipping weight, 10 ounces.

No. 29R1733 Folding Chess or Checkerboard, with extra lithographed surface and varnished squares in 1⅝-inch in red and black with gold lines. Border 1½-inch wide, white and red and black and gold. Covered with best imported morocco paper. Size of board, 16x16 inches. Price, each...(Shipping weight, 1¼ pounds)...20c

No. 29R1735 Folding Chess or Checkerboard. This high grade checkerboard has black and red squares 1½ inches, with gold lines ⅛ inch wide. The border is 2 inches wide in red, black and gold; covered with fine black embossed paper. Our best board. Size, 18x18 inches. Price, each........30c

Shipping weight, 1½ pounds.

No. 29R1739 Folding Backgammon Board, same style as above, squares 1½ inches, lined off with gold and varnished, with fancy illuminated paper. Fitted with complete set of checkers and two dice cups. (No dice.) Size of board, 15x15 inches. Price........20c

Shipping weight, 1¼ pounds.

No. 29R1741 Folding Backgammon Board in book form, squares 1½ inches, finished in durable embossed imitation leather. Fitted with dice cups (no dice) and complete set of checkers in separate box. Size of board, 15x15 inches. Price.....(Shipping weight, 1½ pounds.).....45c

No. 29R1743 Backgammon Board. This is a very high grade board, made of imported material called keratol, similar to leather. Finished in high colors. Size, 15x15 inches. Price, each........75c

Shipping weight, 2 pounds.

Spanish-American Chess Men.

No. 29R1745 Spanish-American Chess Men. 32 pieces in the set, finished in black and yellow. Put up in nice pasteboard box. Usually retail at 50 cents. Price, per set...30c

Shipping weight, 10 ounces.

No. 29R1747 Chess Men. Good size. French pattern, made of hardwood, finished in black and white, 32 pieces in a set. Put up in nice wood box with sliding cover. Price, per set........50c

Shipping weight, 15 ounces.

Checkers.

No. 29R1749 Star Checkers. Made of hardwood in natural and black. 1¼ inches in diameter, 30 pieces in set. Price, per set........5c

Shipping weight, 6 ounces.

Interlocking Checkers.

No. 29R1751 Interlocking Checkers. Consisting of 30 pieces of enameled hard wood, diameter 1¼ inches. With the old style checker men you must hold both men to move a king, with these the rings interlock, and they may be moved as one man. Per set.....10c

Shipping weight, 10 ounces.

No. 29R1753 The King Embossed Checkers. 30 pieces of hard polished wood, 1¼ inches in diameter, packed in highly polished wood box, sliding covers. Price, per set........20c

Shipping weight, 12 ounces.

One-Inch Crown Checkers.

No. 29R1755 Enameled Crown Checkers. Consists of 30 pieces highly enameled, 1-inch diameter, packed in strong paper boxes. Price, per set....15c

Shipping weight, 10 ounces.

Dominoes.

No. 29R1757 The Stellar Hardwood Dominoes, ⅜x1⅛ inches, made of white wood with printed star dots. Set of 28 pieces in box. Price, per set....5c

Shipping weight, 5 ounces.

No. 29R1759 Quarter Arabesque Domino, with round corners, made of selected hard maple, 28 pieces. Size, ⅞x1⅝ inches. Put up in paper boxes with special engraved label. Price, per set........10c

Shipping weight, 7 ounces.

No. 29R1761 Double 9 Ebon Dominoes, consisting of 55 pieces. This is an entirely new set and we do not think a double nine domino has ever been offered at the price. In heavy paper boxes. Price, per set..22c

Shipping weight, 9 ounces.

Nubian Dominoes.

No. 29R1763 Arabesque Nubian Dominoes, consisting of 28 pieces with a new and fancy design. The goodness and cheapness of this beautiful domino will more than satisfy you. In strong paper box with special engraved and varnished label. Price, per set........35c

Shipping weight, 9 ounces.

No. 29R1765 The Magna Domino. Set of 28 pieces, 2⅛x1⅛ inches, packed in very heavy paper box. As you will notice by the dimensions this domino is of unusual size. Each piece perfect and durable. Price, per set........50c

Shipping weight, 15 ounces.

No. 29R1767 Crown Domino. Consisting of 28 pieces with fancy crown design on top. This is a special good number and put up in strong paper boxes with handsome lithographed label. Price, each........25c

Shipping weight, 12 ounces.

No. 29R1769 Double 9 Domino. Consisting of 55 pieces the same as the regular black domino, with the addition of 7's, 8's and 9's; more persons can play and the game has greater possibilities. Put up in frame boxes with labels glossed. Price, per set........75c

Shipping weight, 23 ounces.

Lotto.

No. 29R1771 Wood frame box, size, 4½x7½ inches, with sleeve and lift cover, 24 cards, 90 wood discs, numbered, with inside box containing glasses and counters. Covered with fine lithograph labels. Price, each........25c

Shipping weight, 20 ounces.

No. 29R1773 Lotto, better grade than above, wood frame box, with sleeve and hinge cover, 24 large cards, 90 wood discs, numbered, pack 50 cards, counters of different colors in inside box, also separate inside box of glasses. A large, elegant set. Price........50c

Shipping weight, 2 pounds.

Ouija, or Egyptian Luck Board.

No. 29R1775 Without a doubt the most remarkable and interesting and mystifying production of the age. Its operations are always interesting and sometimes invaluable; answering, as it does, questions concerning the past, present and future. Full directions for operating the Ouija board accompany each board. Packed each one in a pasteboard box. **Cannot be sent by mail.** Price, each...**$1.00**

Shipping weight, 3 pounds.

Planchette.

No. 29R1777 The Planchette Board is made of fine polished heart shaped board, about 7 inches long, has brass casters, with fine hardwood wheels and a substantial pencil holder and pencil, each packed in a closed paper box with full directions for operating.
Price, each 40c
Shipping weight, 8 ounces.

Hart's Second Quality Squeezers, No. 35.

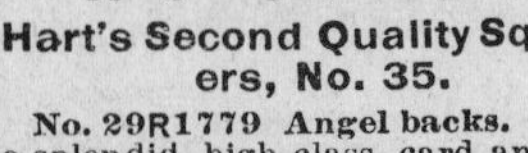

No. 29R1779 Angel backs. This is a splendid high class card and thoroughly known.
Price, per pack 18c
Shipping weight, per pack, 4 ounces.

Waterproof Playing Cards.

No. 29R1781 Tally-Ho, Waterproof Finish, No. 9, half linen, round cornered, double index, extra enameled; large variety of handsomely designed backs in different tints and colors; **the best enameled card at the price in the market. Washable.**
Price, per pack 15c
If by mail, postage extra, per pack, 5c.

The Mascot No. 69 Playing Cards.

No. 29R1785 A Highly Finished Enameled Card, made in a large assortment of fancy backs in colors and very popular and durable.
Price, per pack 19c
Shipping weight, per pack, 4 ounces.

Climax Cards for 24 Cents.

No. 29R1787 Climax, No. 14, enameled, round cornered, linen cards, double indexed, beautifully designed backs in tints and colors.
Price, per pack 24c
If by mail, postage extra, per pack, 5 cents.

No. 29R1789 Empire No. 97, round corners, double indexed, assorted backs. Price, per pack 17c
If by mail, postage extra, per pack, 5 cents.

No. 29R1791 Flag Back, waterproof, half linen stock; an old favorite. It has the American flag stamped on back in colored inks.
Price, per pack 18c
If by mail, postage extra, per pack, 5 cents.

No. 29R1793 Bicycle No. 808, superior ivory enameled finish, a variety of appropriate backs, used largely by professional and other card players throughout the world. Weight, 4 ounces.
Price, per pack 15c

Steamboat Waterproof Cards.

No. 29R1795 Steamboat Waterproof Cards, round corners, double index, made in plaid blue star, green star, Spanish wave and calico backs. Weight, packed, 4 ounces. Price, per pack 7c
If by mail, postage extra, per pack, 5 cents.

American Whist League.

No. 29R1803 American Whist League Waterproof. Extra enameled, half linen stock. The best enamel card made. Weight, 4 ounces.
Price, per pack 20c
If by mail, postage extra, per pack, 5 cents.

Spanish Monte Cards.

No. 29R1805 Barcelona, No. 49, Spanish Monte Cards, 48 cards in pack, assortment of backs and colors. Weight, packed, 3 ounces. Price, per pack 32c
If by mail, postage extra, per pack, 5 cents.

Tournament Whist No. 2.

No. 29R1807 Tournament Whist, No. 2. Size, 2½x3½ inches, made especially for regular and duplicate whist, enameled, round corners, double indexed, assortment of fancy backs and colors. Weight, packed, 4 ounces. Price, per pack 22c
If by mail, postage extra, per pack, 5 cents.

Seal Grain Leather Card Case.

No. 29R1809 Very convenient for traveling, as well as for the house. Full deck of fine gilt edged cards, with case.
Price, for case and cards ..50c
If by mail, postage extra, 6 cents.

Poker Chips.

These Poker Chips are made by one of the largest manufacturers in the United States and are guaranteed for quality, durability and finish. The designs are handsomely engraved. Can only furnish in colors and assortments as specified.

No. 29R1817 Composition Poker Chips. Ivory finish, warranted not to chip or warp. 1½ inches in diameter, put up 100 in a box, assorted as follows: 50 white, 25 red and 25 blue, or solid colors.
Price, per box of 100 ....23c
Shipping weight, 32 ounces.

Engraved Poker Chips.

No. 29R1821 Texas Steer engraved design on composition. Ivory finish, warranted not to chip or warp. 1½ inches in diameter. Put up 100 in a box, assorted as follows: 50 white, 25 red and 25 blue. Price, per box of 100 ....52c
Shipping weight, 30 ounces.

No. 29R1823 The Lily. Engraved design on composition. Ivory finish. 1½ inches in diameter. Put up 100 in a box, assorted as follows: 50 white, 25 red and 25 blue. Price, per box of 100 ....52c
Shipping weight, 30 ounces.

No. 29R1825 The Doghead Poker Chip. Engraved design on composition ivory. 1½ inches in diameter. **This is one of the best poker chips in the market for practical use.** Packed 100 in a box, assorted as follows; 50 white, 25 red and 25 blue. Price, per box of 100..43c
Shipping weight, 30 ounces.

Our Special Design Poker Chips.

No. 29R1841 Special S., R. & Co. design engraved poker chip. This is a very neat and elegant design. Size, 1½ inches in diameter. Assorted 100 in box as follows: 50 white 25 blue and 25 red.
Price, per box of 100 ....53c
Shipping weight, 30 ounces.

Fine Poker Chips at 52 Cents a Hundred.

No. 29R1845 The American Eagle. A beautiful engraved design on composition ivory, warranted not to chip or warp. 1½ inches in diameter. Put up 100 in a box, assorted as follows: 50 white, 25 red and 25 blue, or solid colors.
Price, per box of 100 ....52c
Shipping weight, 30 ounces.

Composition Ivory Poker Chips.

No. 29R1849 Lotus Poker Chips. Engraved design on composition ivory, warranted not to chip or warp. Packed 100 in a box, assorted as follows: 50 white, 25 red and 25 blue.
Price, per box of 100 ....52c
Shipping weight, 30 ounces.

Inlaid Unbreakable Poker Chips.

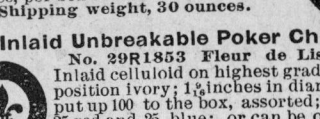

No. 29R1853 Fleur de Lis design. Inlaid celluloid on highest grade of composition ivory; 1⅛ inches in diameter and put up 100 to the box, assorted; 50 white 25 red and 25 blue; or can be ordered in the solid colors, 100 to box; red, white, blue, yellow, pink or brown. Absolutely perfect in every respect, warranted to stack perfectly, and used a great deal by professionals.
Price, per box of 100 ....$2.29
Shipping weight, 34 ounces.

Dice.

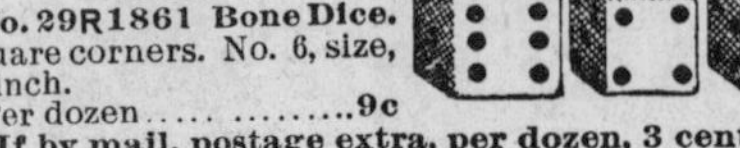

No. 29R1861 Bone Dice. Square corners. No. 6, size, ½-inch.
Per dozen 9c
If by mail, postage extra, per dozen, 3 cents.

Bone Dice at 15 to 36 Cents a Dozen.

No. 29R1865 Bone Dice. Square corners. No. 8, size, ⁷⁄₁₆-inch. Per dozen 15c
If by mail, postage extra, per dozen, 6 cents.

No. 29R1869 Bone Dice. Round corners. No. 9, size, ⅝-inch. Per dozen 22c
If by mail, postage extra, per dozen, 6 cents.

No. 29R1873 Bone Dice. Square corners. No. 10, large size. Per dozen 36c
If by mail, postage extra, per dozen, 6 cents.

Celluloid Dice.

No. 29R1877 Celluloid Dice, cream color, with colored spots, ⅝-inch. Per set (five dice to set)...31c
If by mail, postage extra, per set of five, 3 cents.

Celluloid Poker Dice.

No. 29R1881 Representing Ace, King, Queen, Jack, Ten and Nine spots. Fine ivory finished celluloid, perfect goods. Set of five pieces in box.
Price, per set 43c
If by mail, postage extra, per set, 4 cents.

Transparent Celluloid Dice.

No. 29R1885 Made of pure transparent celluloid. Are clear as glass; colors green, magenta or saffron. Put up five in a box. Size, ⅝-inch.
Price, per set (five dice to a set) 48c
If by mail, postage extra, per set, 3 cents.

Blank Dice.

No. 29R1891 Blank Bone Dice, no spots on either side. Size, ⅝-inch.
Price, per dozen 29c
If by mail, postage extra, per dozen, 6 cents.

Vegetable Ivory Dice.

No. 29R1893 This is the latest style in dice, is made of the pure ivory nut. Are absolutely perfect. Size, ⅔-inch.
Per set (five in a set)..26c
If by mail, postage extra, per set, 3 cents.

Dice Cups.

No. 29R1897 Sole Leather Dice Cup, 2 inches in diameter, 3 inches deep. Natural color.
Each 12c
If by mail, postage extra, each, 4 cents.

No. 29R1901 Sole Leather Dice Cup, extra heavy, 2⅛ inches in diameter, 3¼ inches deep. Tan color. Each 22c
If by mail, postage extra, each, 5 cents.

LeCount's Patent Cribbage Board.

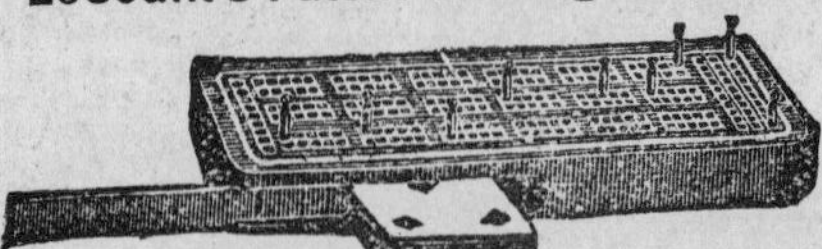

No. 29R1909 Polished Metal Nickel Plate, with three double rows drilled holes, to score for three or six persons; face of polished black walnut with compartment for one pack of cards and another compartment containing nine steel cribbage pegs. Size, 2⅞x10½ inches. Price, each 35c
Shipping weight, 20 ounces.

VEILINGS.

Latest up to date novelties in veilings. We sell only the best grades, at prices much less than you would pay for inferior goods elsewhere.

If by mail allow 2 cents per yard for postage; if you send too much we will refund balance.

Plain Tuxedo Silk Veiling.

No. 18R2 Plain Tuxedo Silk Veiling, as per illustration on figure. 18 inches wide. Black only.
Price, per yard 8c

No. 18R6 Plain Tuxedo Silk Veiling, double mesh, fancy weave. 18 inches wide. Colors, black or cream.
Price, per yard 16c

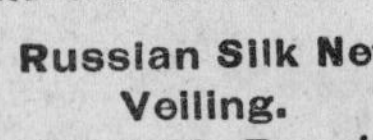

Russian Silk Net Veiling.

No. 18R8 Russian Silk Net Veiling, late Parisian design, 18 inches wide. Colors, black or cream. Per yard 19c

Plain Tuxedo Silk Veiling.

No. 18R10 Plain Tuxedo Silk Veiling, with chenille dot. 18 inches wide. Colors, black or cream.
Price, per yard 8c

Russian Silk Net Veiling.

No. 18R18 Russian Net Silk Veiling, with chenille dots. 18 inches wide. Rich and dressy. Comes in black or cream.
Price, per yard 19c

No. 18R20 Fancy Russian Silk Net Veiling, with large chenille dots. 18 inches wide. For a nobby and durable veil we recommend this. Comes in black or cream.
Price, per yard 23c

Silk Tuxedo Veiling.

No. 18R22 Silk Tuxedo Veiling, with three small chenille dots, as illustrated. A new dressy veiling. Colors, black or cream. Width, 18 inches.
Price, per yard 20c

Dotted Silk Grenadine Veiling.

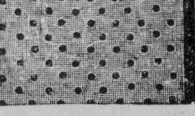

No. 18R24 Dotted Silk Grenadine Veiling. Stylish and rich; the net is very fine with medium size chenille dots and a pretty satin border. 18 inches wide. Colors, black or cream.
Price, per yard 24c

Our 16-Cent Silk Veiling.

No. 18R28 A 14-inch, plain Sewing Silk Veiling, with border of three narrow, satin stripes, as per illustration. **A very popular veiling.** Colors, come in black, cream, navy, brown or cardinal.
Price, per yard........................16c

Our 22-Cent Silk Veiling.

No. 18R32 The very best quality of Sewing Silk Veiling, 19 inches wide, neat ½-inch satin stripe border. This veiling is used the year around and always gives entire satisfaction. This quality usually retails at 40 cents. Colors same as above No. 18R28.
Our price, per yard...............22c

17-Inch Plain Brussels Net.

No. 18R36 Brussels Veiling. Very rich and dressy veiling, **one of the prettiest plain veilings worn** and very extensively used. **Very durable.** Comes in black only.
Special price, per yard........19c

Chiffon Veiling.

CHIFFON VEILINGS, especially those with the large chenille dots, are exceptionally good and stylish.

No. 18R40 Plain Silk Chiffon Veiling, soft and rich, especially desirable for a plain veil, with fast edge borders. Width, 14 inches. Comes in black navy and cream. Price, per yard........................22c

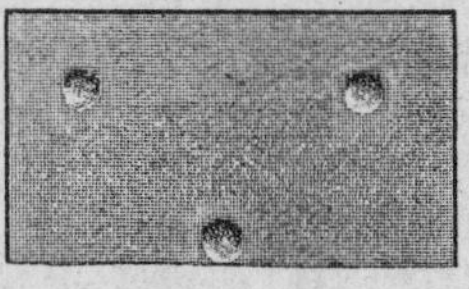

No. 18R41 Silk Chiffon Veiling. An excellent quality chiffon, with large silk chenille dots. We can furnish this veiling in the following combinations of colors: Black with black dots, black with white dots, white with white dots, white with black dots, navy blue with white dots, and brown with white dots. This veiling usually retails at 35 cents per yard. Width, 18 inches.
Price, per yard........................22c

No. 18R42 Finest Quality Silk Chiffon Veiling, with large silk chenille dots. A soft lustrous mesh. Comes in plain white mesh with white dots, white mesh with black dots, all black mesh with white dots. Width, 18 inches. Price, per yard..........48c

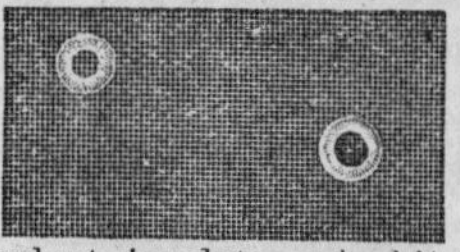

No. 18R43 Silk Chiffon Veiling, with the new velvet ring dot. This is an extremely stylish and popular veiling. Comes in plain black with white velvet ring dots, black with black velvet ring dots, and white with black velvet dots. Width 18 inches. Price, per yard.................30c

Wool-Barege Veiling.

No. 18R44 Fine Imported All Wool Barege Veiling. 23 inches wide. Comes in black, navy, brown or gray. Usually retailed at 35 cents.
Price, per yard........................25c

White Silk Illusion.

No. 18R48 White Silk Illusion, 72 inches wide, for bridal veils. Price, per yard...................59c

No. 18R52 72-inch White Silk Illusion or Bridal Veiling, finer quality; well worth $1.50.
Special price, per yard........................87c

Black Silk Brussels Net.

No. 18R56 Black Silk Brussels Net, plain, 27 inches wide. Price, per yard........................19c

No. 18R60 Black Silk Brussels Net, plain, 27 inches wide. Finer quality. Price, per yard.....29c

No. 18R64 Black Silk Brussels Net, plain, finer quality than above. Width, 27 inches.
Price, per yard........................36c

Wash Blondes.

No. 18R68 White Cotton Wash Blonde Net, 27 inches wide. Price, per yard...................13c

No. 18R72 White Cotton Wash Blonde Net, much finer mesh than above. Width, 27 inches.
Price, per yard........................21c

Mourning Veils.

No. 18R80 Mourning Veils of Nuns' Veiling, with border. Size, 36x45 inches. Each............98c

No. 18R84 Mourning Veil of finer quality of Nun's Veiling, with border; very elegant and fine. Size, 40x60 inches. Each........................$1.98

Black Nuns' Veiling.

No. 18R88 Nuns' Veiling, with border, for mourning veils, 40 inches wide. Price, per yard........64c

No. 18R92 Nuns' Veiling, with border, for mourning veils, 42 inches wide, finer quality.
Price, per yard........................83c

No. 18R96 Nuns' Veiling, with border for mourning veils, 42 inches wide, very fine in texture.
Price, per yard........................$1.39

Black English Crape.

No. 18R100 Black English Crape, for veiling and trimming. 27 inches wide. Price, per yard......60c

No. 18R104 Black English Crape, 36 inches wide, finer quality. Price, per yard....................$1.35

Mousseline de Soie, 42 Cents per Yard.

No. 18R108 Plain Silk Mousseline de Soie. A gauze like trimming, thin as chiffon, but a stiffer finish, for millinery purposes and waist trimmings. Colors, light blue, pink, nile green, cerise, new shades of old rose and heliotrope, white, cream and black. 42 inches wide. This is a very fine quality. Price, per yard........................42c

Silk Chiffon, 41 Cents per Yard.

No. 18R112 A very popular trimming, made similar to the mousseline de soie, but has the soft finish and showing more the silk luster, often preferred by many. Colors, light blue, pink, lilac, white, cream or black. 42 inches wide. 75-cent value. Price, per yard........................41c

No. 18R124 Liberty Silk, a soft trimming similar to the chiffon but a trifle heavier, and having a very bright and lustrous finish. Width, 42 inches. Colors, black, white or cream. 75 cents is the regular retail price. Price, per yard....................47c

LACE DEPARTMENT.

We have made extraordinary efforts in our LACE DEPARTMENT to have every desirable style of lace represented in our catalogue. Our buyers having made special importations in immense quantities, enables us to name prices far below what the retail merchant buys them for.

SEND CASH IN FULL, ADDING POSTAGE, WHEN YOU DESIRE LACES SENT BY MAIL. If you send too much money, we refund balance. **We do not send samples of laces.** Our illustrations and descriptions are accurate. If not just as represented, and worth a great deal more than we quote, you may return your purchase and we will cheerfully refund money.

On account of the extremely low prices we quote we do not sell less than a full dozen yards, unless we so state in description. By comparison you will find you pay no more for the full dozen yards than you would buy a few yards for elsewhere. Wouldn't you rather have a full dozen for the same price or less than a few yards would cost?

American or Pillow Lace.

No. 18R140 American or Pillow Lace, especially used for pillow cases and other trimmings. Comes in four widths. **We do not sell less than 12-yard pieces.**

Width, inches	2½	2⅞	3⅞	4¾
Price, 12 yards	17c	22c	32c	38c

If by mail, postage extra, per 12 yards, 4 cents.

American or Pillow Lace.

No. 18R144 American or Pillow Lace, a very extra and fine quality, used for pillow cases and other trimmings. Comes in three widths. **We do not sell less than 12-yard pieces.**

Width, inches	2	3⅛	4½	5¼
Price, 12 yards	25c	42c	51c	63c

If by mail, postage extra, per 12 yards, 4 cents.

No. 18R146 Everlasting Trimming. This well known and desirable lace is largely used and makes a very pretty trimming for aprons, wrappers, underwear, ginghams and children's dresses. Very durable.

Width, inches	⅝	1	1¼
Price, per dozen yards	15c	19c	24c

No. 18R148 Machine Made Torchon Lace, used for muslin underwear, children's dresses, etc. We quote unusually low prices. Sold only in 12-yard pieces.

Width inches	⅜	½	¾	1
Per doz. yds	3c	5c	7c	9c
Width, inches	1⅜	1¾	3	
Per doz. yds	14c	18c	29c	

Sevilla Torchon Lace

No. 18R152 Sevilla Torchon Lace. A new and decidedly pretty pattern, a very serviceable lace, used for undergarments, aprons and wash dresses. **We sell this lace by the dozen yards only,** at less than wholesale prices.

Width, inches	Price, per dozen yards
⅛	10c
1	19c
1⅝	30c
2⅝	56c
3¾	73c

Sevilla Torchon Insertion.

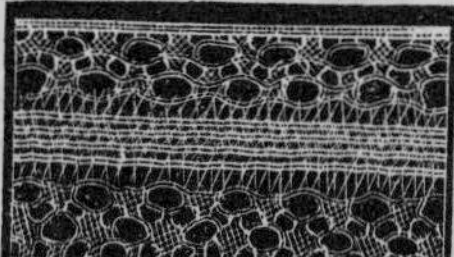

No. 18R156 Sevilla Torchon Insertion to match the above lace. Width, 1⅜ inches.
Price, per doz. yds..28c

No. 18R158 Fine English Nottingham Torchon Lace. A new and pretty design. Very desirable for trimming underwear, dresses, sacques, etc. Comes in three widths.

Width, in	1½	2¼	3¼
Per doz. yds.	28c	42c	54c

No. 18R160 English Nottingham Torchon Insertion, to match above laces. Width, 1¼ inches.
Price, per dozen yards........................29c

No. 18R162 Fine Nottingham Torchon Lace, with pearled edge. A new and excellent design; durable and washable. Comes in four widths.

Width, inches	1	1⅝
Per doz. yards	21c	36c
Width, inches	2½	3⅝
Per doz. yards	49c	72c

No. 18R166 Fine Nottingham Torchon Insertion, to match above laces. Width, 1¼ inches.
Price, per doz. yds. 27c

English Torchon Lace.

No. 18R170 Fine English Nottingham Torchon Lace. Made of very fine cotton thread; the exact imitation of the hand made torchon. Will wash and wear just as well. A very dainty pattern. Excellent for trimming undergarments, aprons, and all wash fabrics. Sold only by the dozen yards, and comes in five widths.

Width, inches	1¼	1⅞	2½	2¾	3¾
Price, per dozen yards	32c	45c	57c	63c	81c

No. 18R174 Fine English Nottingham Torchon Lace Insertion, Cluny pattern, to match above lace. Width, 1¼ inches.
Price, per dozen yards........................32c

No. 18R178 Fine Woven Thread Nottingham Torchon Lace. Very fine thread. This is a very dainty, delicate design and makes an extremely pretty trimming for children's dresses and fine muslin undergarments. Comes in four widths.

Width, inches	¾	1⅛	2	2½
Price, per dozen yards	25c	38c	57c	69c

No. 18R182 Very Fine Thread Nottingham Torchon Insertion, to match above lace. Width, 1⅛ inches. Price, per dozen yards........................39c

No. 18R186 Fine Nottingham Drawn Work Torchon, with beading for drawing No. 1 ribbon through. A very delicate and pretty pattern which we highly recommend, costing you one-half what same quality is sold for elsewhere. Comes in three widths.

Width, inches	¾	1⅛	2
Price, per dozen yards	31c	42c	63c

No. 18R190 Nottingham Drawn Work Insertion, with beading for drawing No. 1 ribbon through, to match above laces. Width, 1 inch.
Price, per dozen yards........................37c

No. 18R194 Real Linen Hand Made Torchon Lace from the best manufacturer in Germany, runs smooth and even and a very pretty design. Comes in four widths.

Width, inches	⅝	1¼	2⅜	3½
Price, per yard	4c	7c	11c	17c

No. 18R198 Real Linen Hand Made Torchon Insertion, to match above hand made lace. We can furnish this in two widths.
Price, per yard. Width, 1-inch, 6c; 1⅜-inch, 8c.

No. 18R202 Platte Valenciennes Lace. Tulip pattern; a very dainty trimming for infants' wear, undergarments, etc. Comes in four widths.

Width, inches	1⅛	2	3½	4½
Per doz. yards	21c	38c	57c	69c

No. 18R206 Platte Valenciennes Lace Insertion, to match above lace Width, 1⅜ inches.
Price, per dozen yards........................25c

GIVE CATALOGUE NUMBER IN FULL WHEN YOU WRITE YOUR ORDER

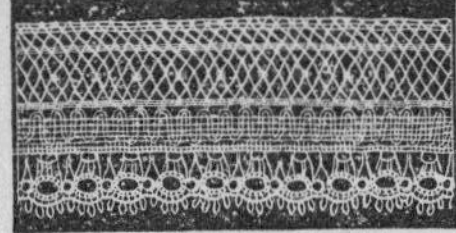

No. 18R410 White French Valenciennes Lace, a ribbon effect, a new and pretty pattern, comes in three widths.

Width, inches	½	¾	1
Price, per dozen yards	21c	28c	34c

No. 18R414 White French Valenciennes Lace Insertion, ribbon effect, to match above lace. Width, ⅝-inch. Price, per dozen yards.........22c

No. 18R418 White Valenciennes Mecklin Lace, as per illustration, a very fine thread and a delicate design, comes in three widths.

Width, inches	⅝	⅞	1⅛
Price, per dozen yards	25c	32c	39c

No. 18R422 White Valenciennes Lace Insertion, to match above lace. Width, ¾ inch. Price, per dozen yards.........31c

Black Valenciennes Laces.

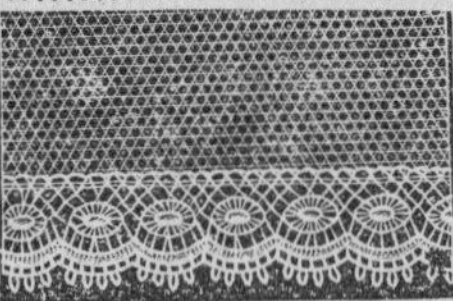

No. 18R426 Black French Valenciennes Lace, strictly fast dye, comes in three widths.

Width, inches	⅝	¾	1¼
Price, per dozen yards	16c	22c	33c

No. 18R430 Black French Valenciennes Lace Insertion, to match above lace. Width, ¾ inch. Price, per dozen yards.........23c

No. 18R434 Black French Valenciennes Lace, a very fine thread, gooseneck pattern, a very desirable trimming, comes in three widths.

Width, inches	½	¾	1
Price, per dozen yards	18c	30c	38c

No. 18R438 Black French Valenciennes Lace Insertion, to match above lace. Width, ¾ inch. Price, per dozen yards.........31c

No. 18R442 White Bobonet Footing, with Valenciennes lace edge, used exclusively for lace handkerchiefs and muslin wear. Comes in two widths.

Width, inches	⅞	1⅝
Price, per yard	4c	7c

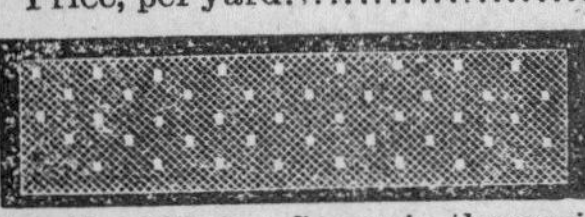

No. 18R446 White Bobonet Point d'Esprit Footing, with Honiton Valenciennes edge. Comes in two widths.

Width, inches	1	1⅝
Price, per yard	5c	8c

No. 18R452 Plain White Bobonet Footing, used for lace handkerchiefs, etc. Comes in two widths.

Width, inches	1	1⅝
Price, per yard	2c	3c

No. 18R456 Plain White Bobonet Footing. A very fine, close mesh, suitable for very fine work. Comes in three widths.

Width, inches	1	1½	2
Price, per yard	3c	4c	6c

No. 18R460 Point d'Esprit Bobonet Footing. A fine, close net; very pretty and desirable for handkerchiefs. Comes in three widths.

Width, inches	⅞	1⅜	1¾
Price, per yard	4c	5c	6c

No. 18R464 Fine White Valenciennes Beading. Very neat and dainty pattern, used largely in connection with laces and embroideries. Width, ½ inch. Price, per dozen yards...11c

No. 18R468 Black Valenciennes Beading. Same as above illustration, only black. Price, per dozen yards.........12c

No. 18R472 Fine White Beading. This is a much finer and daintier pattern than the above, and the best quality that we handle. Width, ½ inch. Price, per dozen yards.........18c

No. 18R476 Black Valenciennes Beading. The finer quality, same as above illustration, only black. Price, per dozen yards.........19c

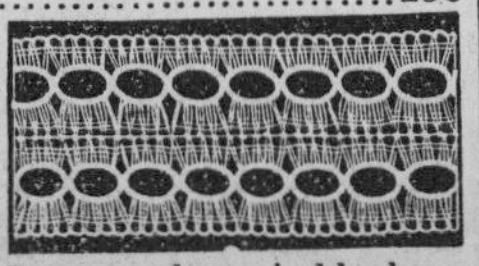

No. 18R480 2-Row Fine White Beading. These beadings are very much in demand and extensively used. Width, 1 inch. Our special price, per dozen yards......24c

No. 18R484 2-Row Valenciennes Beading. Same as above, in black. Price, per dozen yards.........25c

No. 18R488 White Nottingham Lace Allover. For yokes, dresses, etc. Width, 18 inches. Price, per yard.....21c

No. 18R489 Butter Color Nottingham Lace Allover. Same pattern as above. Width, 18 inches. Price, per yard.........21c

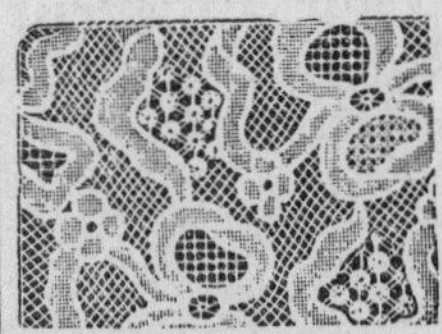

No. 18R491 English Nottingham White Lace Allover. Torchon effect. A new and effective pattern. Width, 18 inches. Price, per yard.....24c

No. 18R492 Nottingham Lace Allover. A very dainty bow knot design, a lacy, stylish allover. We quote a very low price on it. Can be ordered in white or butter color. Width, 18 inches. Price, per yard.....33c

No. 18R493 Valenciennes and Embroidery Effect White Lace Allover. Pretty bow knot design, a very excellent and stylish pattern. Width, 18 inches. Price, per yard.....37c

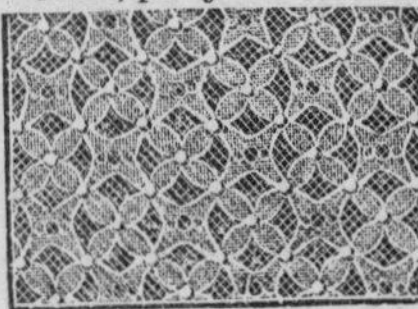

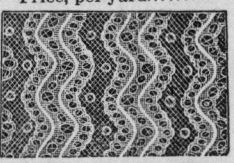

No. 18R495 White Allover. Valenciennes Renaissance effect. Our own special design. Width, 18 inches. Price, per yard.......42c

No. 18R496 White Lace Allover. Serpentine galoon effect, as per illustration. This is a very striking and pretty design. Width, 18 inches. Price, per yard.....44c

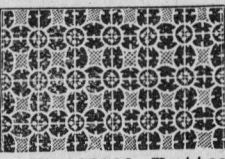

No. 18R497 White Allover Cluny Torchon effect, very neat and dainty. Width, 18 inches. Price, per yard... 50c

No. 18R499 Butter Color Plauen Venisse Lace Allover. This is a very desirable and effective design. Width, 18 inches. Price, per yard.....62c

No. 18R500 Butter Color Plauen Venisse Lace Allover. Same class of goods as above but much finer and closer workmanship. See illustration. Width, 18 inches. Price, per yard.....93c

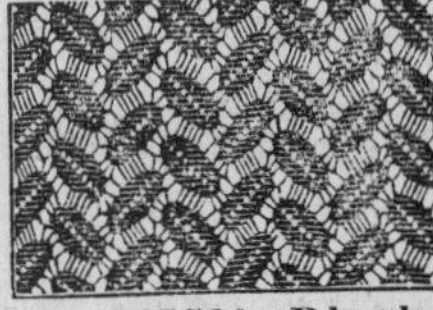

No. 18R501 Black Lace Allover. A pretty pattern and splendid value. Width, 18 inches. Price, per yard.....23c

No. 18R503 Black Lace All over. Duchesse effect. Durable and stylish. Width, 18 inches. Price, per yard 31c

No. 18R504 Black Silk Chantilly Lace Allover. In galoon striped, large and effective design. Width, 18 inches. Price, per yard.. 59c

No. 18R505 Black French Silk Chantilly Lace Allover. Bow knot design, ribbon effect. A dainty and handsome pattern. Width, 18 inches. Price, per yard 76c

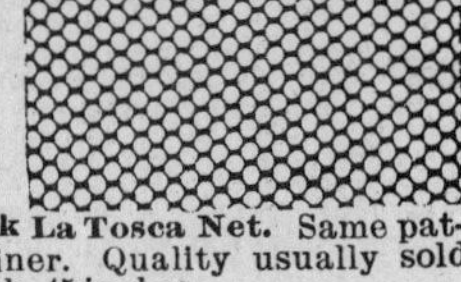

No. 18R506 Black Russian La Tosca Net. Sometimes known as the fish net allover. Used for waists and to cover entire skirts. Width, 45 inches. Price, per yard.....48c

No. 18R507 Black Silk La Tosca Net. Same pattern as above but much finer. Quality usually sold elsewhere for $1.25. Width, 45 inches. Special price, per yard.........75c

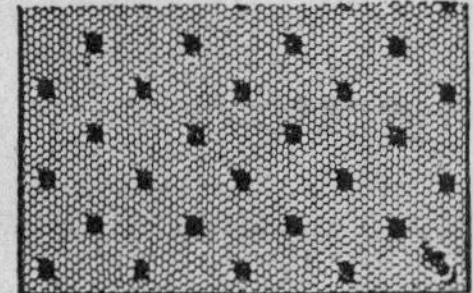

No. 18R508 Black Silk Point d'Esprit Lace Allover. The very newest for making Jabots, lace boas, for waist fronts and lace dresses. Width, 42 inches. Price, per yard .78c

No. 18R509 Black French Lace Allover. An all silk net with large flower design. Used for waists, dresses, etc. Width, 42 inches. Price, per yard.....92c

EMBROIDERIES.

New and beautiful designs in Swiss and Nainsook and Cambric edgings with insertions to match. Also a complete line of embroidery All-Overs. While the illustrations give a very correct idea of the design, they will hardly give you the correct idea of the extremely good values that we offer you at the prices listed. We quote the entire width of embroidery, the design of which will be in proportion to the entire width. **We do not send samples of embroideries, as you can judge from the patterns what the goods are.** You run no risk in sending us your order. If you do not get better values than you can possibly obtain elsewhere and at least 20 to 25 per cent cheaper than you can buy them from your home dealer, you need not keep them. **We cheerfully exchange or refund money whenever you are not satisfied.**

If you order embroideries sent by mail, allow about 1 cent per yard extra for postage; if you send too much we will refund balance.

No. 18R520 White Cambric Edging, small, neat design. Width, 1 inch. Price, per yard..3c

No. 18R524 White Cambric Edging. Splendid value. Width 1¼ inches. Per yard.........4c

No. 18R528 White Cambric Edging. New scroll design. Width, 2¼ inches. Price, per yard......6c

No. 18R532 White Cambric Embroidery Edging. New pattern. Width, 2¾ inches. Price, per yard......7c

No. 18R534 White Cambric Embroidery Edging. Pretty open work design. Width, 2½ inches. Per yard......8c

No. 18R538 White Cambric Embroidery. A clear, pretty pattern. Width, 3 inches. Price, per yard......9c

No. 18R542 White Cambric Embroidery. Nice work on good cloth. Width, 3⅜ inches. Price, per yard 10c

No. 18R546 White Cambric Embroidery. A clear, open work pattern. Looks much better in piece than in illustration. Width, 4⅛ inches. Per yard.....10c

No. 18R550 White Cambric Embroidery. An entirely new idea, and very dainty. Width, 3¼ inches. Price, per yard.....12c

No. 18R558 White Cambric Embroidery. Our own exclusive pattern. Very handsome. Width, 6¼ inches.
Price, per yard.....16c

No. 18R566 White Cambric Embroidery. Bowknot design. An elegant and effective design. Width, 6 inches.
Price, per yard.....18c

No. 18R574 White Cambric Embroidery. A large, clear pattern. Especially suitable for muslin wear and dresses. Width, 8¼ inches.
Price, per yard.....24c

No. 18R586 White Cambric Embroidery. Special leaf design. A beautiful open work pattern. Entire width, 8½ inches.
Price, per yard....31c

No. 18R590 White Cambric Embroidery. Skirting width. This is a very elaborate and striking design. Our own special importation. Width, 12 inches.
Price, per yard.....39c

No. 18R554 White Cambric Embroidery. An exclusive design. Width, 5¼ inches.
Price, per yard.....13c

No. 18R562 White Cambric Embroidery. This is an excellent and striking pattern. Width, 5½ inches.
Price, per yard.....17c

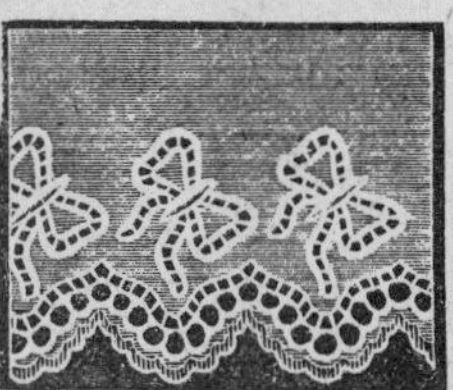

No. 18R570 White Cambric Embroidery. This is an elaborate and pretty pattern. Good quality work on good quality muslin. Width, 6 inches.
Price, per yard.....20c

No. 18R578 White Cambric Embroidery. An elegant and striking design. Sold at a very low price. Width, 8½ inches.
Price, per yard....29c

No. 18R589 White Cambric Embroidery. Skirting width. A large, elaborate design. Width of work, 5¼ inches; entire width of cloth, 12 inches.
Price, per yard.....27c

No. 18R598 White Nainsook Edging. Neat and pretty. Width, 1½ inches.
Price, per yard......5c

No. 18R606 White Nainsook Embroidery. Special pattern. Width, 3½ inches.
Price, per yard.....11c

No. 18R614 White Nainsook Embroidery. Special scroll pattern, which looks very pretty in the piece. Width, 4¼ inches.
Price, per yard.... 15c

No. 18R622 White Nainsook Embroidery. Bow knot design, blind embroidery work, which will wear and give excellent satisfaction. Width, 7 inches.
Price, per yard.....23c

No. 18R628 White Swiss Embroidery Edging. Good work, in nice cloth. Width, 1½ inches.
Price, per yard......5c

No. 18R636 White Swiss Embroidery. Fine quality open work, on good cloth. Width, 4¼ inches.
Price, per yard.....10c

No. 18R644 White Swiss Embroidery. This is our own exclusive design. Very elaborate and pretty. Width, 6¾ inches.
Price, per yard.....16c

No. 18R594 White Nainsook Embroidery Edging. Width, 1¼ inches.
Price, per yard......3c

No. 18R602 White Nainsook Embroidery. A special value. Width, 2¾ inches.
Price, per yard 8c

No. 18R610 White Nainsook Embroidery. Exceptionally neat. Width, 3¾ inches.
Price, per yard.....12c

No. 18R618 White Nainsook Embroidery. This exquisite pattern is exclusively our own, on very fine cloth. Width, 4¾ inches.
Price, per yard.....17c

No. 18R626 White Swiss Embroidery Edging. Width, 1 inch.
Price, per yard....2½c

No. 18R632 White Swiss Embroidery. A neat, delicate pattern. Width, 3¾ inches.
Price, per yard......8c

No. 18R640 White Swiss Embroidery. A fine, delicate pattern. Width, 6½ inches.
Price, per yard.....12c

No. 18R648 Colored Cambric Embroidery. The colors are embroidered on white cambric and we can furnish them in the following colors: Navy blue work on white cloth, red on white, and pink on white Width, 1½ inches. Price, per yard.............5c

No. 18R650 White Cambric with Colored Embroidery Work. This is a very neat and dainty pattern. We can furnish in the following combinations: Navy blue embroidered on white cambric, red embroidered on white, and pink embroidered on white. Width, 3 inches.
Price, per yard.........9c

No. 18R654 Matched Nainsook Sets. This is a very delicate and exquisite design, especially desirable for infants' wear and fine muslin garments. Comes in three widths with insertion to match.

Width, inches	1⅜	2¼	2⅞
Price, per yard	8c	11c	14c

No. 18R658 White Nainsook Insertion. Same design and to match above set. Width, 1⅜ inches.
Price, per yard... .10c

No. 18R662 Special Matched Set Fine Nainsook Embroidery, with a very delicate and exquisite bow knot design. You will be particularly well pleased with this set. Comes in three widths with insertion to match.

Width, inches	4	5¾	6⅞
Price, per yard	17c	25c	34c

No. 18R666 White Nainsook Insertion. Bow knot design to match above set. Width, 2½ inches.
Price, per yard....14c

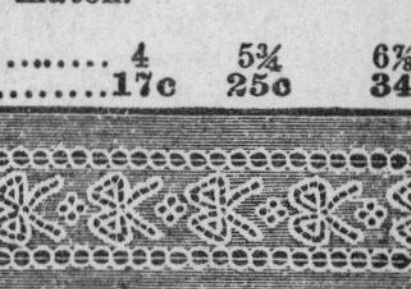

No. 18R670 White Cambric Insertion Width, 1⅜ inches.
Price, per yard..... 4c

No. 18R674 White Cambric Insertion. A very desirable pattern. Width,1¾ inches.
Price, per yard.......6c

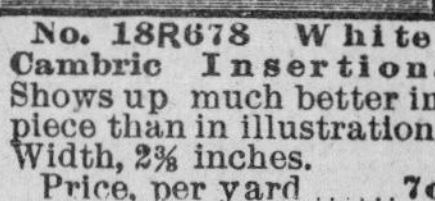

No. 18R678 White Cambric Insertion. Shows up much better in piece than in illustration. Width, 2⅜ inches.
Price, per yard......7c

No. 18R682 White Cambric Insertion. This elaborate design is worked on a fine cloth and is exceptional value. Width, 2¼ inches.
Price, per yard.... 10c

No. 18R686 White Cambric Insertion. This is a very dainty and delicate design. Width, 2 inches.
Price, per yard....13c

No. 18R690 White Nainsook Insertion. A small, neat pattern. Width, 1 inch.
Price, per yard.............4c

No. 18R694 White Nainsook Insertion. A delicate and pretty embroidery. Width, 1¼ inches.

Price, per yard.............6c

No. 18R698 White Nainsook Insertion. Fancy scroll design with beading effect. Width, 1¾ inches. Per yard. 9c

No. 18R702 White Nainsook Insertion. An exceptionally pretty pattern. Width, 1¾ inches. Per yard....10c

No. 18R706 White Nainsook Insertion. One of the prettiest designs. Width, 2 inches.
Price, per yard.....12c

No. 18R710 White Swiss Insertion. Width, ⅝-inch. Per yard....4c

No. 18R714 White Swiss Insertion. Width, 1¼ inches. Our special price, per yard........6c

All Silk Taffeta Plaid Ribbon No. 7.

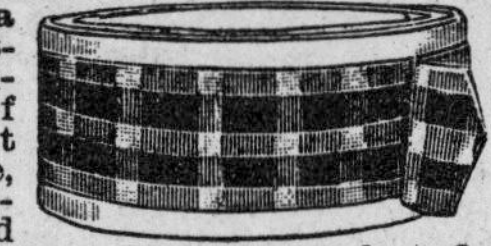

No. 18R894 This is a very new and pretty pattern, with elegant contrasting combination of colors, such as pink, light blue, canary, turquoise, lilac, cardinal predominating, also black and white plaid. **Mention color.** Price, per yard.....6c

Fancy Silk Striped Ribbon.

No. 18R898 Corded effect with brocaded flowers, as per illustration. We imported an immense quantity of this ribbon, which enables us to offer it at an extremely low price. **Width, 3 inches.** Colors, pink and white, light blue and white, yellow and white, cardinal and white, lilac and white, turquoise and white. 20c value.
Price, per yard..........11c

Fancy All Silk Taffeta Ribbon with Fancy Woven Stripes.

No. 18R900 A line of black alternating with white, very pretty combinations and stylish trimmings for all purposes. You will find this a very desirable style. Width, 2⅞ inches. Can be ordered in all colors.
Price, per yard...... ....13c

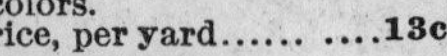

All Silk Taffeta Plaid Ribbon.

No. 18R904 Very new and delicate combinations of colors. Very stylish for sashes, neck and millinery purposes; excellent combinations of colors. State what color you wish to predominate; can furnish all colors. **Width, 3½ inches.** 32c value.
Price, per yard..........19c

All Silk Fancy Plaid Ribbon.

Our Finest Quality of Taffeta Plaid Ribbon.

No. 18R908 Used for all kinds of trimming purposes, such as bows, loops, belts, etc., in all the principal combinations of colors, such as pink, cardinal, light blue, lilac, yellow, etc., predominating. Please state which color you wish to predominate. You will be more than pleased with this ribbon. **Width, 4½ inches.** Value 45c. Price, per yard..............29c

All Silk Fancy Striped Ribbon.

No. 18R911 Stripped effects will be among the most popular ribbons this season. This is a very handsome design and can be ordered in the following combinations of colors: Pink and white, light blue and white, cardinal and white, lilac and white, yellow and white, etc. A delicate and dainty pattern usually retailed at 25 cents. **Width, 3¼ inches.**
Price, per yard..........17c

All Silk Fancy Striped Taffeta Ribbon.

No. 18R913 With polka dot edges as per illustration. The center, which has a corded effect, is all white, while the edges can be ordered in pink, light blue, cardinal, lilac, yellow or all white. The polka dot effects continue to be among the best sellers among fancy ribbons. This is a very desirable and effective pattern. **Width, 4¼ inches.**
Price, per yard..........30c

Fancy Black and White Striped All Silk Taffeta Ribbon.

No. 18R915 This is a particularly stylish pattern, very desirable for all trimming purposes. **Width, 4⅛ inches.**
Price, per yard.........28c

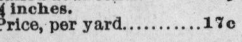

TUCKINGS.

Below we show an excellent list of the different quality tuckings in cambric, nainsook and swiss. Tuckings are very much in demand for shirt waists, yokes, etc. We promise you much better values than you can possibly obtain elsewhere.

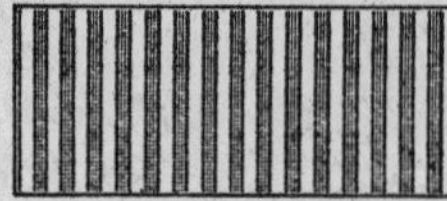

No. 18R919 White Cambric Tucking, with 53 tucks. Width, 22 inches.
Price, per yard....35c
If by mail, postage extra, per yard, 2 cents.

No. 18R921 White Cambric Tucking, finer quality than above, with close, fine tucks. Width, 19 inches.
Price, per yard..........49c
If by mail, postage extra, per yard, 2 cents.

No. 18R923 Fine White Nainsook Tucking, contains 72 tucks. Width, 24 inches. Price, per yard.65c
If by mail, postage extra, per yard, 2 cents.

No. 18R925 Fine Nainsook Tucking, very fine quality; contains 109 small, dainty tucks. Width, 23 inches. Price, per yard..........78c
If by mail, postage extra, per yard, 2 cents.

No. 18R927 White Swiss Tucking, on a fine quality cloth; contains 137 tucks. Width, 24 inches.
Price, per yard..........80c
If by mail, postage extra, per yard, 2 cents.

No. 18R929 Black Swiss Tucking, on fine black swiss; a fine sheer cloth; contains 94 1/16-inch tucks. Width, 23 inches. Price, per yard..........82c
If by mail, postage extra, per yard, 2 cents.

No. 18R931 White Cambric Tucking, with very fine cluster tucks, 7 close tucks to the cluster. A very fine quality of cloth. Width, 20 inches.
Price, per yard. 62c
If by mail, postage extra, per yard, 2 cents.

No. 18R933 White Nainsook Cluster Tucking, on very fine cloth, containing 145 fine tucks, 5 small tucks to the cluster. Width, 27 inches.
Price, per yard..........90c
If by mail, postage extra, per yard, 2 cents.

No. 18R935 Tucked Liberty Silk, for fronts and yokes. 19 inches wide, 72 tucks. Colors, black and white.
Price, per yard..$2.40

No. 18R937 Tucked Mousseline de Soie. Same style as above. 21 inches wide, 54 tucks. Colors, black and white. Price, per yard..........$1.35

No. 18R939 Japanese Silk Shirring or Fronting, with 40 neatly spaced tucks; a very desirable trimming for yokes, dress fronts and neckwear. 19 inches wide. Colors, black and white. This is measured stretched. Price, per yard..........$1.29

A COMPLETE ASSORTMENT OF FANS.

Original designs. Attractive patterns.

No. 18R951 Folding Black Fan, a very convenient form. Sticks are black leatherette covered. All black only.
Price, each.. .... 9c
If by mail, postage extra, 2 cents.

No. 18R953 Folding or Pocket Fan, with highly polished nickel frame and fancy gilded decorated top. Usually retailed at 25 cents.
Price, each.........19c
If by mail, postage extra, 4 cents.

Japanese Silk and Hand Painted Folding Fans.

No. 18R955 Decorated Japanese Folding Fan, in tinted colors on good parchment. Enameled sticks.
Each 5c
If by mail, postage extra, 2 cents.

No. 18R957 Fancy Paper Chromo Fan, with spangles and fancy decorated painting enameled sticks. 25-cent value.
Price, each. 12c
If by mail, postage extra, 2 cents.

No. 18R959 Ladies' Plain Black Fan, made of Japanese silk, plain black polished sticks. Regular 50-cent fan. Each....24c
If by mail, postage extra, 3 cents.

No. 18R961 This is a Silk Marcelaine, plain black fan, with daintily carved ebony sticks, picot edged top and bottom. The best black fan on the market.
Price, each..........50c
If by mail, postage extra, 3 cents.

No. 18R963 This Spangled Gauze Fan has black lace edge top, carved ebony sticks, picot edged bottom. A very dainty and beautiful fan, our own exclusive style, rich and beautiful looking. Black only.
Price, each..........59c
If by mail, postage extra, 3 cents.

No. 18R965 White China Silk Fan, with white lace top. The fan is prettily decorated with spangles and appliqued braid, fancy decorated sticks. Exceptional value. Price, each..........49c
If by mail, postage extra, 3 cents.

No. 18R967 Dainty China Silk Fan, with silver pressed gallery sticks, little bows of silk cover entire top of fan, as per illustration, with gold spangles on the body of fan. Copy of very high priced Parisian novelty. Pretty for evening wear. Can be ordered in black or white.
Price, each..........78c
If by mail, postage extra, 3 cents.

No. 18R969 Fine Silk Marcelaine Fan, with lace trimmed top and bottom, hand-painted decorations and spangled. An extremely dainty and desirable style. Silver pressed, decorated sticks. Can be ordered in black or white.
Price, each..........80c
If by mail, postage extra, 3 cents.

No. 18R971 Fine Silk Marcelaine Fan, with dainty white hand-painting silver lines decorating same. Fine silk lace top and white carved bone sticks, imitation of ivory.
Price, each..........88c
If by mail, postage extra, 3 cents.

No. 18R973 Fine China Silk, pretty luminous shaded hand decorations with silver lines, painted top and bottom, white enameled sticks.
Price, each........25c
If by mail, postage extra, 3 cents.

No. 18R975 Fancy Leaf Fan. Our own special importation. Each leaf has fancy decorations of tinsel, a decided novelty; everybody will admire it. Colors, rose pink, light blue or white. Price, each..........26c
If by mail, postage extra, 3 cents.

FANS CONTINUED ON NEXT PAGE.

FANS—Continued from Preceding Page.

No. 18R977 Black and White Combination China Silk Fan. Hand decorations as per illustration. An extreme novelty and very elegant. Carved ebony sticks with picot edged top and bottom.
Price, each......47c
If by mail, postage extra, 3 cents.

No. 18R979 A Black and White Creation, White China Silk, with black silk lace top and black spangles. The decorations are hand painted, black and white flowers, and carved ebony sticks. Picot edged bottom. This is a very high class and dainty fan.
Price, each......83c
If by mail, postage extra, 3 cents.

No. 18R981 High Grade Silk Marcelaine Lace Fan, dainty white hand painted and spangled decorations, elegant carved spangled bone sticks, very artistic and stylish fan, worth $2.00, white only.
Price, each......$1.20
If by mail, postage extra, 4 cents.

A $2.50 Quality for $1.42.

No. 18R983 Very High Grade Silk Marcelaine Fan, with gold pressed sticks, silk lace top and fancy scallop of crepe lisse, fastened with a fine tinsel braid. This is a decidedly high class and artistic fan. Can be ordered in black or white.
Price, each......$1.42
If by mail, postage extra, 4 cents.

Splendid Values in Feather Fans.

No. 18R985 Ladies' Medium Small Pretty Feather Fan, spangled; embossed sticks to match. Color, cream, pink and blue. Each, 23c
If by mail, postage extra, 3 cents.

No. 18R987 Ladies' Very Elegant Coque Feather Fan, the feathers having a very soft downy effect. A very beautiful fan, white embossed sticks to match. Colors, cream, black, pink or blue.
Price, each......47c
If by mail, postage extra, 5 cents.

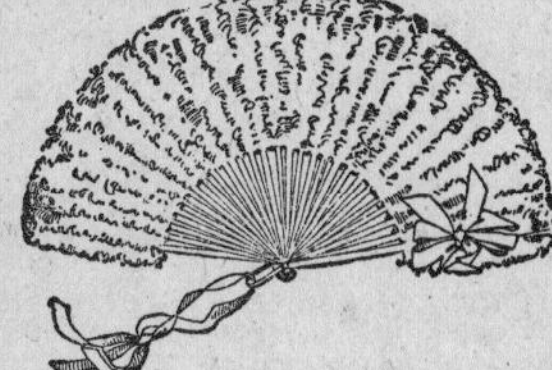

No. 18R989 Genuine Ostrich Feather Fan, new size, made of fine quality ostrich stock, white enameled sticks; you will find this a rare bargain at the special price we quote. Colors, cream or black.
Price, each....83c
If by mail, postage extra, 5 cents.

LADIES' NECKWEAR.

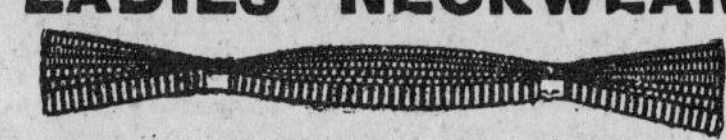

No. 18R991 Satin Club Ties for Ladies; colors, black, cardinal, navy, cream, pink or blue. Each..9c
If by mail, postage extra, each, 3 cents.

No. 18R993 Plain China Silk Club Ties for Ladies. Same colors as above. Price, three for 25c; each, 10c
If by mail, postage extra, each, 3 cents.

No. 18R995 Ladies' Reversible Bat Wing Silk Tie. Colors, black, white, navy, cardinal or royal blue.
Price, each......19c
If by mail, postage extra, 2 cents.

No. 18R997 Ladies' All Silk Reversible Four in Hand Tie. Colors, black, white, cardinal, royal blue or navy. Ea., 23c
If by mail, postage extra, 2 cents.

No. 18R999 The newest style Satin Crushed Stock Collar, gathered in graceful folds, like illustration. Colors, black, white, navy, cardinal, light blue or pink. Price, each....18c
If by mail, postage extra, 3 cents.

No. 18R1001 Ladies' rich, dressy Velvet Stock Collar, same style as above. Colors, black, white, navy, cardinal, light blue or pink. Price, each...18c
If by mail, postage extra, 3 cents.

No. 18R1003 Fancy Stock Collar, made of liberty silk, puffed and shirred. A very dressy, stylish stock at a very small price, considering value. Colors, cerise, light blue, pink, cream, white, cardinal or black. Price, each....23c
If by mail, postage extra, 4 cents.

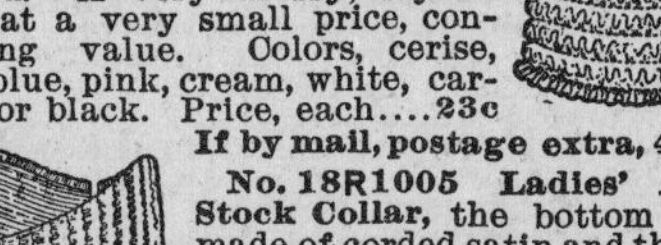

No. 18R1005 Ladies' Fancy Stock Collar, the bottom part is made of corded satin and the upper part of tucked shirred white Nainsook. A new and pretty style. Colors, pink, blue, cardinal or cream. Price, each......22c
If by mail, postage extra, 4 cents.

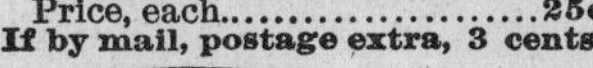

No. 18R1007 Ladies' new Turnover Silk Stock Collar, with hemstitched edges and attached bow of contrasting color, a very neat appearing collar. Colors, black, white, cream, pink, light blue or cardinal.
Price, each......25c
If by mail, postage extra, 3 cents.

No. 18R1009 Ladies' Heavy China Silk Stock Collar, with five rows of stitching. Large butterfly shape bow. Edged with pretty design of Venisse lace. Colors, cream, pink, light or cardinal. Price, each 49c
By mail, postage extra, 4c.

Liberty Silk Stock Collar and Bow.

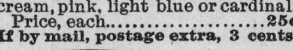

No. 18R1011 Ladies' Fancy Stock Collar and Large Bow, made of fine liberty silk. The collar and bow are trimmed with a fine narrow, juby ruche, as per illustration. A very tasty and pretty collar. Colors, pink, blue, cream or black,
Price, each......73c
If by mail, postage extra, 8 cents.

Combination Collar and Tie.

No. 18R1013 Made of a fine quality of white lawn with fancy shirred and tucked lawn tabs on collar, bound with colored lawn. Long flowing lawn ends bound with colored lawn. Colors of binding, pink, white or blue. To be tied as shown in cut.
Price, each......24c
If by mail, postage extra, 2 cents.

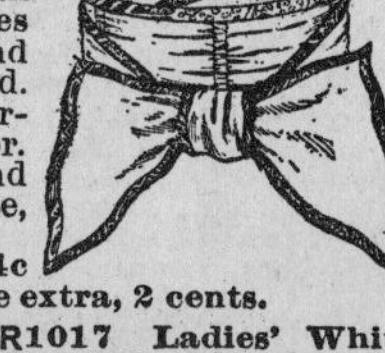

No. 18R1015 Japanese Silk Tie, 54 inches long, 5 inches wide at ends. Neckband neatly shirred and tucked. Entire edge bound with Persian silk of contrasting color. Wound once around neck and tied in bow. Colors, white, pink, blue or black.
Price, each......44c
If by mail, postage extra, 2 cents.

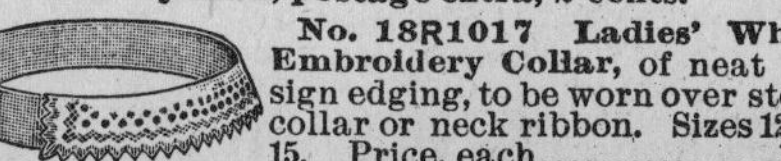

No. 18R1017 Ladies' White Embroidery Collar, of neat design edging, to be worn over stock collar or neck ribbon. Sizes 12 to 15. Price, each......10c
If by mail, postage extra, 2 cents.

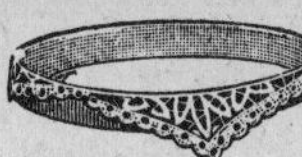

No. 18R1019 Ladies' White Embroidery Turnover Collar finer quality than No. 18R1017 trimmed ends in neat triangular design. Sizes 12 to 15.
Price, each...(If by mail, postage extra, 2c)...12c

No. 18R1021 Ladies' Wash Blonde Lace Tie, ends trimmed with double row of shirred ruche, new and dainty.
Price, each......25c
If by mail, postage extra, 2 cents.

No. 18R1023 Ladies' White Blonde Lace Tie, with double row of Valenciennes lace insertion, full length and width.
Price, each......45c
If by mail, postage extra, 2 cents.

No. 18R1025 Ladies' Liberty Silk Tie, with wide ruffle edge, 66 inches long by 6 inches wide, with two neat rows of Nottingham lace insertion, as shown in cut. Colors: cream, light blue or pink, with insertion of white lace, black with black lace insertion or black with white lace insertion. A very showy and stylish tie.
Price, each......50c
If by mail, postage extra, 3 cents.

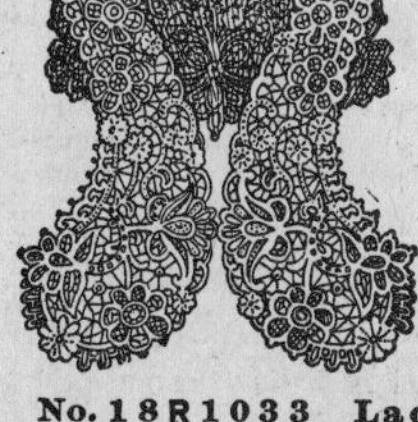

No. 18R1027 Ladies' Liberty Silk Flowing End Tie, with double ruffle edge, dainty silk lace ends, 66 inches long by 6½ inches wide. Colors: cream, light blue or pink with white lace edging, black with black lace edging or black with white lace edging, an exceptionally pretty style. Price, each......97c
If by mail, postage extra, 3 cents.

No. 18R1029 Ladies' Fine Silk Ties, with fine plaited ends and very dressy. Colors, cream, pink, blue or black. Length, 74 inches; width, 7½ inches.
Price, each..(If by mail, postage extra, 2c)....70c

No. 18R1031 Ladies' Very Fine Ecru Colored Bolero or Revere Collar, made of pretty design Plauen Venisse lace, with square sailor back collar. New effect and very popular.
Price, each......$1.23
If by mail, postage extra, 6 cents.

No. 18R1033 Ladies' Black Liberty Silk Neck Ruff, with two ruffles on collar, wide plaited flowing ends, a very pretty and desirable collarette. Colors, black or cream.
Price, each......$1.47
If by mail, postage extra, 6 cents.

No. 18R1035 The newest creation in neck ruff, made of black liberty silk, with long flowing plaited ends, two rows of neat shirring as shown in cut, double ruffled collar with edge ruffle plaited. A handsome collarette. Elegant and dressy. Colors, black and cream.
Our special price, each..$1.99
If by mail, postage extra, 6 cents.

For Ostrich Feather Boas see Millinery Department.

Ruchings.

No. 18R1037 Silk Crepe Lisse Ruching, double plaited top. Width, 1¼ inches. Colors, white, cream or black.
Price, per yard......10c
If by mail, postage extra, per yard, 2 cents.

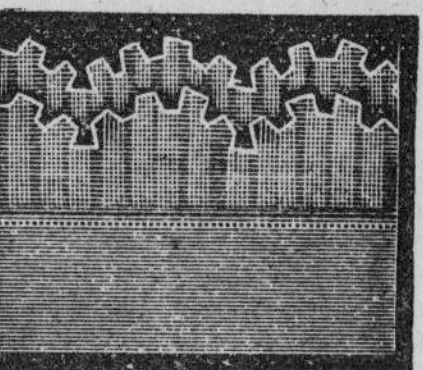

No. 18R1045 Silk Crepe Lisse Ruching, double box plaited style, a very handsome and effective ruching. Width, 1⅜ inches. Colors, black, white or cream. Per yard......25c
If by mail, postage extra, per yard, 2 cents.

Celluloid Collars.

No. 18R1047 Ladies' Celluloid Perforated Collar, to be worn under neck ribbon. With it you can arrange any ribbon to give the effect of a costly stock collar. Perfect in shape and bound with silk ribbon under chin to prevent the irritation that is produced by other stiff collars. Protects the ribbon from perspiration and saves laundry bills. Sizes, 12 to 15 and comes in two widths, 1¾ and 2½ inches. **Be sure to give size and width when ordering.** Price, each..(Postage extra, 2 cents)..10c

Ladies' Best Linen Collars.

No. 18R1049 Ladies' 4-ply Linen Collars, front 2½ inches, back 2 inches. Sizes, 12½ to 15. Price..........10c

No. 18R1051 Ladies' 4-ply Linen Collar, front 2 inches, back 1¾ inches. Sizes, 12½ to 15. Price..........10c

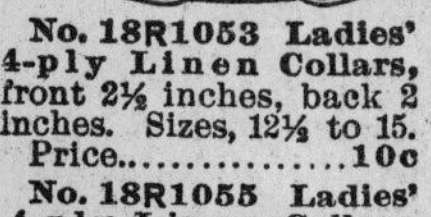

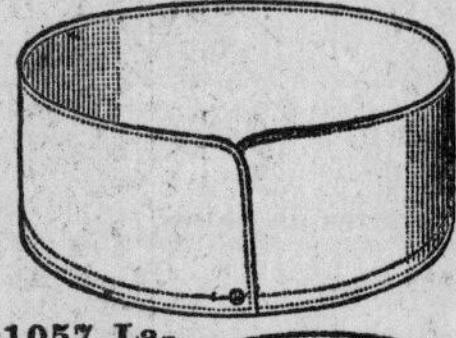

No. 18R1053 Ladies' 4-ply Linen Collars, front 2½ inches, back 2 inches. Sizes, 12½ to 15. Price..........10c

No. 18R1055 Ladies' 4-ply Linen Collars, front 2½ inches, back 1⅞ inches. Sizes, 12½ to 15. Price..........10c

No. 18R1057 Ladies' 4-ply Linen Collars, front 2¼ inches, back 2 inches. Sizes, 12½ to 15. Price..........10c

No. 18R1061 Ladies' 4-ply Linen Collars, front 2¼ inches, back 1¾ inches. Sizes, 12½ to 15 collars. Price...(Postage extra, 3 cents)...10c

No. 18R1057 No. 18R1061

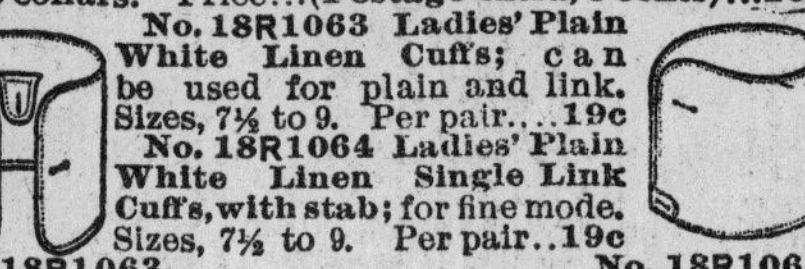

No. 18R1063 Ladies' Plain White Linen Cuffs; can be used for plain and link. Sizes, 7½ to 9. Per pair....19c

No. 18R1064 Ladies' Plain White Linen Single Link Cuffs, with stab; for fine mode. Sizes, 7½ to 9. Per pair..19c

No. 18R1063 Width 2½ inches. No. 18R1064 Width, 3½ inches.

If by mail, postage extra, per pair, 3 cents.

Collar Forms.

No. 18R1065 The Perfection Collar Form, new straight effect, shaped to conform with neck; suitable for adjusting latest style neckwear; made of special grade buckram cloth lined and bound. Sizes, 13, 14 and 15. Price..........8c

Gauze Covered Wire Frame.

No. 18R1067 This collar is made of gauze covered over a wire frame work, which makes a very light collar, at the same time a strong one. It is self adjustable, being fastened by a patent hooking device. Used as a support for ribbon collars, etc. Price, each..........12c

Skeleton Wire Frames.

No. 18R1068 Fastened with new patent hooking device in the back, strong and durable, very cool for summer wear, allowing perfect ventilation for lace or chiffon collars and are used as a support for ribbon collars. Price, each..........11c

If by mail, postage extra, each, 3 cents.

WOMEN'S FANCY WORK.

We present a most complete line of newest fancy work and materials.

No. 18R1069 Stamped Doilies and Center Pieces, on good quality union linen cloth, to be worked with wash embroidery silks. Pretty assorted floral designs, namely: Strawberry, carnations, double rose, wild rose, violets, forget-me-nots.

Size, in. square...	5	9	12	14	18	22	24
Price, each.........	3c	4c	5c	10c	15c	18c	22c

Postage extra, each, 2c to 5c.

Fine Linen Center Pieces.

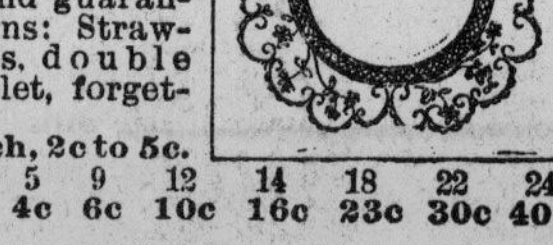

No. 18R1073 Stamped Linen Doilies and Center Pieces, pretty floral designs, splendid values and guaranteed linen. Designs: Strawberries, carnations, double rose, wild rose, violet, forget-me-nots, etc.

Postage extra, each, 2c to 5c.

Size, in. square..	5	9	12	14	18	22	24
Price, each......	4c	6c	10c	16c	23c	30c	40c

Battenberg Edge Center Pieces.

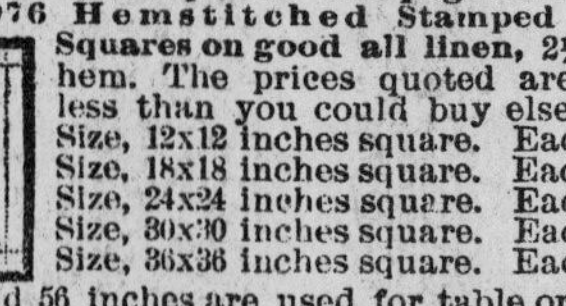

No. 18R1075 Battenberg Edge Stamped Linen Center Pieces, representing the very latest in stamped raw edge linen, the above is stamped on a very fine No. 9 art embroidery linen in a large variety of patterns, in the following sizes:

Size, in. sq.	9	12	14
Price, each	5c	9c	14c
Size, in. sq.	18	22	24
Price, each	19c	27c	36c

If by mail, postage extra, each, 2 to 5 cents.

Complete line of Embroidery Silks to work above pieces at lowest prices. **See page 947.**

No. 18R1076 Hemstitched Stamped Linen Squares on good all linen, 2½-inch hem. The prices quoted are much less than you could buy elsewhere.

Size, 12x12 inches square. Each, 18c
Size, 18x18 inches square. Each, 25c
Size, 24x24 inches square. Each, 39c
Size, 30x30 inches square. Each, 55c
Size, 36x36 inches square. Each, 75c

Sizes, 30 and 56 inches are used for table or stand covers.

If by mail, postage extra, each, 5 cents.

No. 18R1077 Hemstitched Linen Dresser Scarf, 2½-inch hem, very pretty stamped designs, and a scarf of extraordinary value. Size, 18x54 inches. Price, each..........50c

If by mail, postage extra, each, 5 cents.

Hemstitched Linen Dresser Scarf.

No. 18R1095 Hemstitched Linen Dresser Scarf, a high grade linen, fancy drawn work corners, new and pretty stamped designs. Size, 18x54 inches. Price, each..........75c

If by mail, postage extra, each, 4 cents.

No. 18R1097 Fringed Cotton Dresser Scarf, stamped in neat designs. A good scarf for little money. Size, 16x50 inches. Price, each..........12c

If by mail, postage extra, each, 4 cents.

No. 18R1099 Hemstitched Stamped Linen Squares, fancy drawn open work border, stamped in pretty designs.

Size, 12x12 inches square. Each, 18c
Size, 18x18 inches square. Each, 25c
Size, 24x24 inches square. Each, 35c
Size, 30x30 inches square. Each, 50c
Size, 36x36 inches square. Each, 70c

If by mail, postage extra, each, 3 cents.

No. 18R1100 Stamped Linen Hemstitched Squares, on very fine quality all linen with fancy drawn open work corners, pretty designs, our very highest grade.

Sizes, inches square,	12	18	24	30	36
Price, each............	25c	35c	50c	65c	80c

If by mail, postage extra, 5 cents.

No. 18R1101 Stamped Linen Hemstitched Tray Cloth, on good quality linen, stamped in pretty designs. Size, 18x27 inches. Price, each..........25c

No. 18R1103 Stamped Linen Hemstitched Tray Cloth, on fine linen, with fancy drawn open work corners. Size, 18x27 inches. Price, each..........50c

If by mail, postage extra, each, 3 cents.

Splashers.

No. 18R1105 Stamped Splashers, on white cotton duck cloth, fringed on three sides. Size, 18x27 inches. Each..........10c

If by mail, postage extra, each, 3 cents.

Stamped Momie Linen Splasher.

No. 18R1107 Stamped Momie Linen Splasher, with fancy open work and tied fringe; choice stamped designs. Size, 18x27 inches. Price, each..........25c

If by mail, postage extra, each, 3 cents.

Stamped Table Covers.

No. 18R1108 Handsome Table Covers. 33 inches square, linen fringed all around, stamped and tinted in beautiful colors, center to be worked with silks or linen floss. Material, white cotton cloth. Each..........25c

If by mail, postage extra, 10 cents.

Stamped Shoe Pocket.

No. 18R1113 Brown Linen Shoe Bag. Stamped, two pockets, with brass eyelets to hang up. Size, 10x16 inches. Assorted patterns. Price, each..........10c

If by mail, postage extra, 4 cents.

Photo Frame, Stamped.

No. 18R1117 Cabinet Size Photo Frame. Stamped on white art linen, the prettiest picture frame imaginable. Usually retailed at 10 cents. Price, each..........5c

If by mail, postage extra, 1 cent.

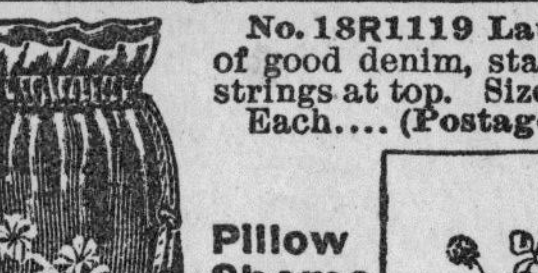

No. 18R1119 Laundry Bags. Made of good denim, stamped; good draw strings at top. Size, 16¾x31 inches. Each.... (Postage, 6 cents)....53c

Pillow Shams Stamped.

No. 18R1121 Good Quality Muslin Shams. Stamped in assorted designs. A very desirable sham. Size, 30x30. Per pair. 15c

If by mail, postage extra, 5 cents.

Pillow Shams, Stamped.

No. 18R1123 Made on good muslin, one sham stamped "I Slept and Dreamed that Life Was Beauty," and the other sham stamped "I Woke and Found that Life Was Duty." Size, 30x30. Price, per pair......20c

If by mail, postage extra, 5 cents.

No. 18R1125 White Muslin Pillow Shams. Embroidered in fast color red embroidery cotton. Size, 30x30. Peacock pattern. Price, per pair, 25c

No. 18R1127 White Muslin Pillow Sham. Same quality as above pattern, in fast color red embroidery cotton. **"Good Night"** worked on one sham and **"Good Morning"** on the other. Price, per pair......25c

If by mail, postage extra, 5 cents.

Hemstitched, spachtel and ruffled shams, **see page 927.**

No. 18R1133 The Chicago Pillow Sham Holder. The most simple and best holder on the market, can be instantly clamped to any size metal or wooden bed without screws or tools of any kind. The clamps are padded and cannot mar the finest finish or enamel. **Shipping weight, 20 oz. Price, each...50c**

Burlap Rug Patterns.

The cut gives an illustration of one of the rug patterns, showing the manner of placing it on frame for working. Take four slats similar to bed slats, making a frame; stretch pattern over frame; then after hemming pattern proceed to work same by following the lines with the various colors designated.

Ottoman Burlap Patterns.

For material for working burlap patterns, see zephyrs, page 948.

No. 18R1135 Pattern 40. Pretty flower design burlap rug pattern. Size, 23x41 inches. Price, each.......(Postage extra, 5 cents)........22c

No. 18R1137 Pattern 9. Ottoman. Large rose leaves and buds with nice border. Size, 18x20 inches. Price, each......(Postage extra, 3 cents)........11c

No. 18R1139 Pattern 8. Ottoman. Floral center of roses, pansy and bell flower, octagon border; very pretty. Size, 20x20 inches. Price, each........11c

If by mail, postage extra, 3 cents.

No. 18R1143 Pattern 6. Ottoman. Cat's head in center, octagon border in two colors; neat design. Size, 20x20 inches. Price, each..........11c

If by mail, postage extra, 3 cents.

No. 18R1153 Pattern 19. ½x1 yard. A spaniel dog lying on a box, very clearly printed in moss and brown colors in center. A branch, with roses, leaves and buds, at each end, and a plain border. **Each, 25c**

If by mail, postage extra, 7 cents.

No. 18R1154 Pattern 93. ⅔x1⅛ yards. A nice floral center, consisting of red and moss roses, leaves, buds, lilies, etc., beautifully arranged, with a plain scroll surrounding the center, and three autumn leaves in each corner, and a plain border. Price, each......(Postage extra, 7 cents)........35c

No. 18R1155 Pattern 22. ¾x1½ yards. A very pretty scroll border, with a stag standing near a lake of water, very pretty landscape scenery, etc., in the center. A very nice sofa rug. **Price, each, 50c**

If by mail, postage extra, 7 cents.

Rags worked into the proper patterns with the improved rug machine produce very rich and handsome rugs and ottomans, having a tapestry effect which gives no suggestion of the cheapness of the material.

No. 18R1156 The Novelty Rug Machine. For working rugs, ottomans, chair covers, cushions and the above burlap patterns. Price, each..........30c

If by mail, postage extra, 5 cents.

No. 18R1157 Fine Rug Machine Needles. For working on plush, satin, etc. Price, each..........3c

Stamping Pattern Outfits.

Stamp your own linen. Stamping patterns perforated, new and desirable patterns. Our outfits contain the following articles:

No. 18R1159 The Quinette Stamping Outfit. Consists of 26 full sized, new and pretty stamping patterns, one complete alphabet, one box black and one box blue stamping powder with each set. Price, per outfit...25c
If by mail, postage extra, 8 cents.

No. 18R1160 The Seroco Stamping Outfit. Consists of 75 full sized patterns for stamping any and all kinds of linens and sofa pillows, **one complete alphabet,** and one box black and one box blue stamping powder with each set. Price, per outfit.50c
If by mail, postage extra, 8 cents.

No. 18R1161 Stamping Powder. Put up in boxes. Colors, blue or black. Price, per box..................5c
If by mail, postage extra, 3 cents.

Tatting Shuttle.

No. 18R1162 White Bone Tatting Shuttle. Highly polished. Price, each.....4c

No. 18R1163 Rubber Tatting Shuttles. Hard rubber, highly polished. Price, each..................12c
If by mail, postage extra, 2 cents.

Needle Emeries.

No. 18R1164 Strawberry Needle Emeries. Should be in every lady's workbasket. Price, each..................4c
If by mail, postage extra, 2 cents.

Initial Letters.

No. 18R1165 Initial Letters. Worked in fast color turkey red, for marking shirts, underwear, handkerchiefs, etc., put up 36 on a card. Any letter. Price, per card of 36..5c
If by mail, postage extra, each, 1 cent.

Ornaments for Fancy Work.

No. 18R1167 Silk Chenille Balls for fancy work, about ¾ inch in diameter, can be used for **finishing all kinds of fancy work.** Colors, white, pink, rose, blue, green, red or yellow. Price, per dozen..... 8c
If by mail, postage extra, per dozen, 2 cents.

Silk Tassels.

No. 18R1168 Silk Tassels, about 2½ inches long, made in almost every color, good silk loops, can be used for all kinds of fancy work. Per doz...6c
If by mail, postage extra, per dozen, 2 cents.

No. 18R1169 Silk Tassels, about 2½ inches long, very full and heavy, comes in all colors, for fancy work.
Price, per dozen......25c
If by mail, postage extra, per dozen, 2 cents.

Silk Tassel Fringe.

No. 18R1170 Silk Tassel Fringe, comes in nearly all colors, heading of silk ¼ inch wide, tassels nearly 2 inches long, for fancy work. This fringe is worth 15 cents per yard. Price, per yard.........10c
If by mail, postage extra, per yard, 1 cent.

Fringes.

For window shades, curtains, stand covers and all kinds of fancy work. Always mention predominating color wanted, or if practical send a sample.

No. 18R1171 Ball Fringe, cotton; comes in red, olive, white, cream, pink and white, and blue and white. Full width, 1½ inches. Price, per yard..............3c
If by mail, postage extra, per dozen yards, 5 cents.

Furniture Gimp.

No. 18R1172 Furniture Gimp, silk mixed, ½ inch wide, in all staple colors. Price, per yard..........2c
If by mail, postage extra, per dozen yards, 4 cents.

No. 18R1173 Furniture Gimp, extra quality silk mixed, ½ inch wide in all staple colors. Per yard..3c
If by mail, postage extra, per dozen yards, 4 cents.

No. 18R1174 Imitation Fruit and Vegetable in natural tints. Suitable for fancy work, such as lambrequins, curtains, etc. Assortment as follows: Apple, pear, plum, banana and carrot. In ordering state which kind you desire. Price, each..........................5c
If by mail, postage extra, each, 4 cents.

Crepe Paper.

No. 18R1175 Crepe Paper. This paper comes on rolls 20 inches wide; about 10 feet in each roll. Crepe paper is used for making **lamp shades, dolls, photograph frames, fancy boxes, etc.** Comes in the following colors: Light amber, dark amber, apple, moss, grass, nile and sea green; light blush pink, dark blush pink, pale and dark coral, celestial blue, heliotrope, violet, virgin white, apricot, ruby red, canary or black. Price, per roll.........................8c
If by mail, postage extra, 6 cents.

Dennison's Imported Tissue Paper.

No. 18R1176 This paper is used for making artificial flowers, doll dresses, for all kinds of decorations and fancy work. Size of sheet, 20x30 inches.

All colors excepting red. Price, per sheet......1c
Red tissue paper. Price, per sheet..............2c

Colors of Plain Tissue Paper.

No.	Color	No.	Color
G. B.	White	017	Olive Green
B. 1.	Pearl	9b	Olive Green, m'd'm d'k
30	Blue, light	9c	Olive Green, dark
31	Blue, medium	8a	Blue Green
35	Blue, dark	15x	Grass Green
T4	Apricot	63	Lavender, light
70x	Brown, light	120	Lavender, m'd'm light
72	Brown, medium	123	Purple, medium
72a	Brown, dark	124	Purple, medium dark
90x	Cream	68a	Purple, dark
20a	Yellow, light	126b	Purple, dark
20	Yellow, medium light	81	Salmon, light
21	Yellow, medium	86	Salmon, medium
22	Yellow, medium	87x	Salmon, dark
22c	Yellow, dark	48	Pink, light
98	Orange, light	48½	Pink, medium light
94	Orange, medium light	48x	Pink, medium
96	Orange, medium	40	Pink, medium
96x	Orange, medium dark	41x	Pink, medium dark
95a	Orange, medium dark	45	Pink, dark
95c	Orange, dark	55	Red, light
95d	Orange, darker	55a	Red, medium
111	Black	55b	Red, dark
0	Green, light	53c	Red, dark
12	Green, medium	155	Red, very dark

If by mail, postage extra, per dozen, 4 cents.

Our 4-Cent Shelf Paper.

No. 18R1177 Shelf Paper. Made of very high grade, smooth finished, heavy book paper. Pinked and embossed in pieces 12 inches wide and 10 yards long. Colors, white, blue, pink, yellow or green.
Price, per 10-yard piece....4c
If by mail, postage extra, per piece, 7 cents.

Paper Napkins.

No. 18R1178 Paper Napkins, printed in two colors (new patterns). On finest white silk tissue paper, guaranteed fast colors, assorted, 10 patterns to a thousand. We do not sell less than 100 of a pattern. Size, 14x14 inches. Price, per 100..................8c
If by mail, postage extra, 7 cents.

Lamp Shade Frames.

No. 18R1179 Wire Frames for making lamp shades. 14 to 18 inches across. Price, each...............12c
Shipping weight, 28 ounces.

No. 18R1180 Asbestos Collars, to be placed inside of shade to prevent it taking fire. Price, each..............................5c
If by mail, postage extra, 5 cents.

"Art and Decoration in Crepe and Tissue Paper."

No. 18R1181 "Art and Decoration in Crepe and Tissue Paper." Tells how to make all kinds of tissue paper work. **It contains samples of all the colors of tissue papers; 144 pages.**
Price, each...5c
If by mail, postage extra, 4 cents.

No. 18R1182 Spooled Wire for Tissue Paper Work. Green and white. Covered or plain tinned wire. Price, per spool..................................4c
If by mail, postage extra, 3 cents.

No. 18R1183 Thomas' Snowflake Paste for tissue paper work. Price, per bottle........................7c

Rubber Flower Stem Tubing.

No. 18R1184 Rubber Tubing for Flower Stems.
Price, per yard.........3c
If by mail, postage extra, per dozen yards, 2 cents.

Combination Tinsel Cord.

No. 18R1185 Combination Silk Chenille and Tinsel Cord for fancy work. Colors, red, yellow, pink, light blue, old gold, lavender, black or white. Price, per yard..........................5c
If by mail, postage extra, per dozen yards, 2 cents.

Sofa Cushion Cords.

No. 18R1186 Sofa Cushion Cord, used around sofa cushions. Comes in all combinations of colors to match material used for pillow top. Colors same as No. 18R1187.
Price, per yard.......................................5c
If by mail, postage extra, per dozen yards, 2 cents.

Silk Sofa Cushion Cord.

No. 18R1187 This is a heavy silk twist cord, extensively used for binding around pillow cushions. Can be ordered in the following combination of colors: black and yellow; green and pink; navy blue, brown and tan; green, tan and cardinal; light blue and yellow; navy blue and orange; black and cardinal. We can also furnish them in the following plain colors: pink, light blue, light green, yellow, cardinal or royal blue. Price, per yard....9c
If by mail, postage extra, per dozen yards, 2 cents.

No. 18R1188 The Duchess Embroidery Hoop. Does not require winding. The felt cushion on the inner hoop, gives the proper tension to **hold tightly** a light or heavy fabric. Made of selected light colored wood, true in circle and will never warp or get out of shape. Size, 4, 5, 6, 7 or 8 inches. Price, set of four hoops, 42c; each.......13c
If by mail, postage extra, 2 cents.

Wood Embroidery Hoops.

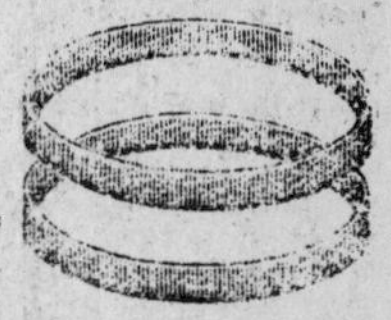

No. 18R1189 Wood Embroidery Hoops. Made of selected wood and will not warp. Size, 4, 5, 6, 7 or 8 inches.
Price, per pair.........5c
If by mail, postage extra, 3 cents.

Handkerchief Centers.

Fine Linen—Two Sizes.

No. 18R1190 Fine Quality Handkerchief Centers. Made from very fine linen cloth, with hemstitched borders. They are used for centers, around which lace can be sewed, also suitable for art centers and fancy work. Made in sizes as below.
Size, 6 inches square, ⅛-inch hem. Each...........10c
Size, 9 inches square, ¼-inch hem. Each 14c
If by mail, postage extra, each, 1 ce

Battenberg Patterns.

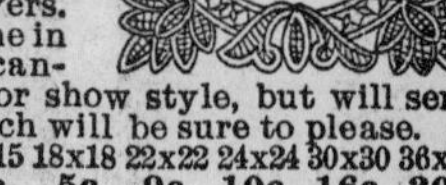

No. 18R1191 Stamped on a good quality of pink silesia, showing the stitches and giving the amount of braid and number of rings to be used on each pattern. We can furnish all sizes of squares, also for tray cloths, dresser scarfs, handkerchiefs, collars and revers. Battenberg patterns come in assorted designs. We cannot furnish description or show style, but will send you desirable styles which will be sure to please.

Size, inches,	9x9	12x12	15x15	18x18	22x22	24x24	30x30	36x36
Price, each,	2c	3c	4c	5c	9c	10c	16c	20c

Size, inches,	Handk'f Pat.	20x54	Collars and Revere Patterns.
Price, each,	6c	20c	10c

Battenberg Rings.

No. 18R1192 Black Silk Battenberg Rings, for Battenberg work. Illustration shows actual size.

Size, No.	1	2	3
Price, per dozen	6c	8c	10c

If by mail, postage extra, 2 cents.

Battenberg Rings.

No. 1. No. 2. No. 3. No. 4. No. 5.

No. 18R1193 Battenberg Rings, for making Battenberg work, the illustrations showing actual sizes.

Size, No.	1	2	3	4	5
Price, per dozen,	2c	2c	3c	3c	4c

If by mail, postage extra, 2 cents.

No. 18R1194 Ecru Battenberg Rings, for Battenberg work. Sizes as above.

Size, No.	1	2	3	4
Price, per dozen	3c	3c	4c	4c

If by mail, postage extra, 2 cents.

Battenberg Lace Braid.

No. 18R1195 Linen Battenberg Lace Braid, No. 8, exact size of illustration. Colors, white or ecru, Price, per dozen yards....(If by mail, postage extra, 2 cents)....10c

No. 18R1196 Linen Battenberg Lace Braid, No. 6, same as above, but a size smaller. Size of illustration. Colors, white or ecru. Price, per dozen yards..........................8c
If by mail, postage extra, per dozen yards, 2 cents.

No. 18R1197 Linen Battenberg Lace Braid, No. 5, size of illustration. Colors, white or ecru. Price, per dozen yards.....................7c

No. 18R1198 Black Silk Battenberg Lace Braid, exact size of illustration.
Price, per dozen yards..............................31c

No. 18R1199 Black Silk Battenberg Lace Braid, exact size of illustration.
Price, per dozen yards..............................36c

No. 18R1200 Black Silk Battenberg Lace Braid, exact size of illustration.
Price, per dozen yards............42c

No. 18R1201 Ecru Colored Battenberg Braid. Suitable for boleros and yokes, exact size of illustration. Price, per dozen yards............23c

Honiton Point Lace Braid.

No. 18R1202 Honiton Point Lace Braid, very fine. We do not sell less than 1 dozen yards. Price, per dozen yards......19c
If by mail, postage extra, per dozen yards, 2 cents.

No. 18R1203 Honiton Point Lace Braid. We do not sell less than 1 dozen yards. Per dozen yards......9c

No. 18R1204 White Point Lace, Purling Braid, exact size of illustration. We do not sell less than 1 dozen yards.
Price, per dozen yards............10c

No. 18R1205 Black Silk Point Lace Purling Braid. Same design and size as No. 18R1204. We do not sell less than 1 dozen yards.
Price, per dozen yards............17c

No. 18R1207 Honiton Point Lace Braid, exact size of illustration. We do not sell less than 1 dozen yards. Price, per dozen yards............28c

No. 18R1208 Honiton Point Lace Braid, exact size of illustration. We do not sell less than 1 dozen yards.
Price, per dozen yards............30c

No. 18R1211 White Honiton Point Lace Braid. Exact size and design of illustration. We do not sell less than 1 dozen yards. Price, per dozen yards............27c

No. 18R1213 White Honiton Point Lace Braid. Exact size and design of illustration. We do not sell less than 1 dozen yards. Price, per dozen yards............29c

No. 18R1215 Honiton Point Lace Braid, same size as illustration.
Price, per yard......3c

No. 18R1217 Imported Fancy Purling Lace Braid, exact size of illustration. Price, per dozen yards............20c

No. 18R1219 Imported Fancy Purling Lace Braid, for Battenberg work, exact size of illustration Price, per dozen yards............25c

No. 18R1221 Imported Purling Lace Braid, for Battenberg work, exact size of illustration. Price, per dozen yards............30c

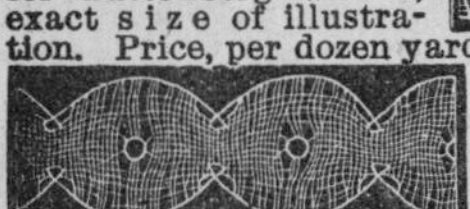

No. 18R1223 Imported Duchess Lace Braid, exact size of illustration.
Price, per yard......5c

No. 18R1225 Imported Black Duchess Lace Braid. Same design and size as No. 18R1223. Per yard 8c

No. 18R1227 Honiton Point Lace Braid.
Price, per yard...5c

No. 18R1229 Honiton Point Lace Braid.
Price, per yard..4c

No. 18R1231 Honiton Point Lace Braid.
Price, per yard..7c

No. 18R1233 Honiton Point Lace Braid, exact size of illustration.
Price, per yard............6c

Lace Thread For Lace Making.

No. 18R1235 The red mill French Lace Thread known as the Au-Moulin-Rouge, for Battenberg and Honiton lace work; comes in white in the following sizes: 50, 80, 100, 150, 250, 300, 500, 600, 800, 1000. Per ball, 4c

No. 18R1236 Cream Lace Thread, same as No. 18R1235. Comes in the following sizes: 50, 100, 200, 300, 500, 800, 1000. Price, per ball............4c

No. 18R1237 Arabian or new dark ecru colored Lace Thread. Comes in sizes as follows: 50, 80, 100 200. Price, per ball............4c

Linen Battenberg Lace Thread.

No. 18R1239 Ideal Divisible Linen Battenberg Lace Thread. Six fold. One or more threads can be used, according to the thickness of the lace thread required. White only.
Price, per skein............5c

Silk Embroidery Floss; for complete assortment see threads.

Pansy Design.

No. 18R1241 Stamped Sofa Cushion Cover, on a pretty fancy weave cloth, ribbon and pansy design. Front and back.

Price, each, 22 Cents.

No. 18R1242 Same design as above on ecru colored art ticking with olive colored back of same material. Front and back. Price, each............37c

"Daisies Won't Tell."

No. 18R1243 Stamped Sofa Cushion Cover, on ecru basket weave cloth, the design, "Daisies Won't Tell," to be worked in silk. This cover has had an immense sale and is very attractive. Front and back.
Price, each....22c

No. 18R1244 Same design as above on ecru colored art ticking with olive colored back of same material. Front and back. Price, each,............37c

Carnation Design Cushion Cover.

No. 18R1245 With new and elaborate carnation design on ecru colored art ticking with olive colored back of same material.

Price, each 37 Cents.

No. 18R1246 Same design as above on a pretty fancy weave cloth. Front and back. Price, each. 22c

Stamped Sofa Cushion Cover.

No. 18R1247 On a new fancy weave cloth which is very dainty and pretty. Design, "Only a Breath of Violets," with clusters of violets. Front and back piece. Price, each...22c

No. 18R1249 Same design as above on ecru colored art ticking with olive green colored back of same material.
Price, each............37c

Poppy Design Cushion Cover.

No. 18R1251 On ecru colored art ticking, large handsome poppy design. This makes a handsome cushion. Front and back.
Price, each............37c

No. 18R1252 Same design as above on a pretty fancy weave cloth. Front and back.
Price, each............22c

American Beauty Cushion Cover.

No. 18R1253 On ecru colored art ticking. Design, large American Beauty roses with foliage. A very excellent design. Front and back.
Price, each............37c

No. 18R1255 Same design as above on a pretty fancy weave cloth. Front and back.
Price, each. 22c

Satin Sofa Cushion Cover.

No. 18R1256 Hand painted on heavy white satin, very highly colored tints, fast color, ready to be used. We can furnish these satin covers hand painted on cream satin in large American Beauty roses or large poppy designs. Size, 22x22 inches.
Price, each............67c

Indian Head Design.

No. 18R1257 Lithographed Sofa Cushion Cover, something new. The design is on drill, lithographed in high tinted colors; is not to be worked.

Price, each.....**25c**

Carmencita Design.

No. 18R1260 Lithographed Sofa Cushion Cover. Latest and most popular design, "Carmencita." Lithographed in high tinted colors, all ready for use; not to be worked.

Price, each, 25 Cents.

Lilies Design.

No. 18R1263 Stamped Sofa Cushion Cover on fine quality ticking with olive green colored back. Design "Lilies." Front and back.

Price, each, 37 Cents.

No. 18R1265 The hit of the season. "Just Because She Made Dem Goo Goo Eyes," as sung by frogdom; illustrated in natural tints. Made on best quality ecru ticking with olive green colored back. Front and back.
Price, each....**37c**

Spachtel Shams, Scarfs, Tidies and Doylies.

The designs which we offer this season in Spachtel or Irish point work are the newest, daintiest and most exclusive anyone could possibly buy. Our goods are all imported, made by expert European operators and professional designers; tamboured on best quality lawn; will wash and wear splendidly, and are much superior to the domestic article. At the extremely low prices we quote and the extensive assortment we show, we anticipate a very large business in this line. Note carefully the strongly bound edges, chic designs and low prices. All shams can be ordered single or in pairs just as desired.

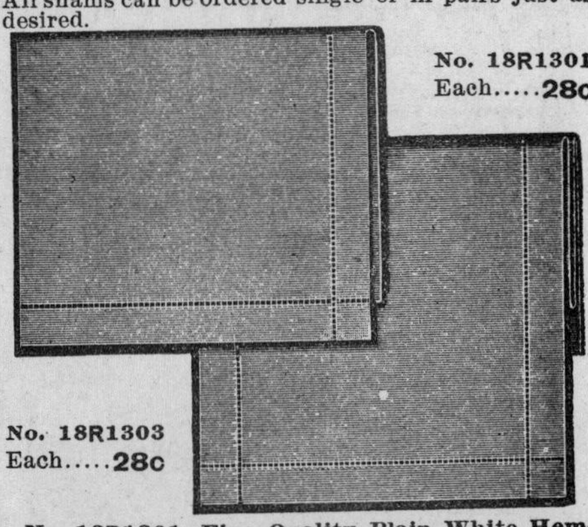

No. 18R1301 Each.....28c

No. 18R1303 Each.....28c

No. 18R1301 Fine Quality Plain White Hemstitched French Lawn Pillow Sham or Cover. Width of hem, 2 inches. Size, 32x32 inches.
Price, each............28c
If by mail, postage extra, 4 cents.

No. 18R1303 Fine Quality Plain White Hemstitched French Lawn Scarf, to match above sham. Can be ordered separately. Width of hem, 2 inches. Size, 20x54 inches. Price, each............28c
If by mail, postage extra, 4 cents.

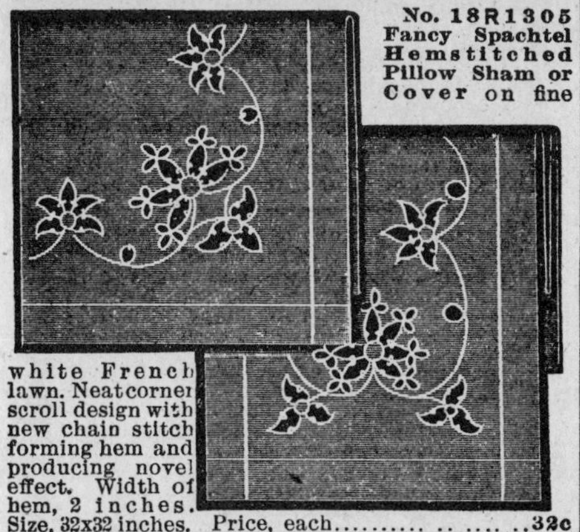

No. 18R1305 Fancy Spachtel Hemstitched Pillow Sham or Cover on fine white French lawn. Neat corner scroll design with new chain stitch forming hem and producing novel effect. Width of hem, 2 inches. Size, 32x32 inches. Price, each..........32c
If by mail, postage extra, 4 cents.

No. 18R1307 Fancy Spachtel Hemstitched Scarf. Same quality lawn and same design as above. Size, 20x54 inches. Price, each..........32c
If by mail, postage extra, 4 cents.

No. 18R1309 Spachtel or Irish Point Sham or Table Cover. Made of fine white French lawn neatly embroidered on edges and center as shown in illustration. Size, 32x32 inches. Price, each..33c
If by mail, postage extra, 4 cents.

No. 18R1311 Spachtel or Irish Point Scarf, to match above sham. Can be ordered separately. Size, 19x54 inches Price, each..........33c
If by mail, postage extra, 4 cents.

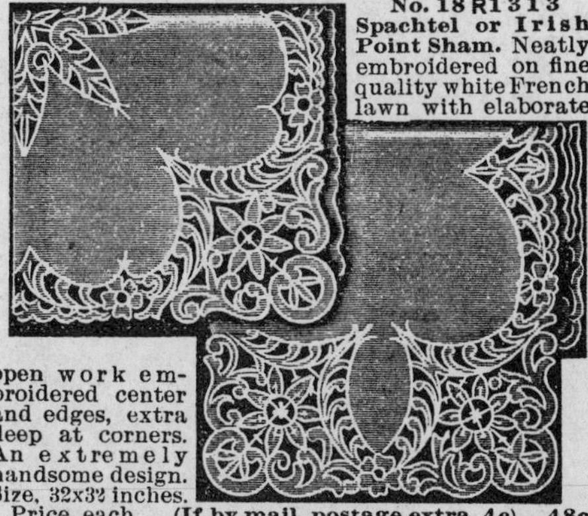

No. 18R1313 Spachtel or Irish Point Sham. Neatly embroidered on fine quality white French lawn with elaborate open work embroidered center and edges, extra deep at corners. An extremely handsome design. Size, 32x32 inches.
Price, each....(If by mail, postage extra, 4c)....48c

No. 18R1315 Spachtel or Irish Point Scarf, to match above sham. Can be ordered separately. Size, 18x54 in. Price, each......48c
Postage extra, 4c.

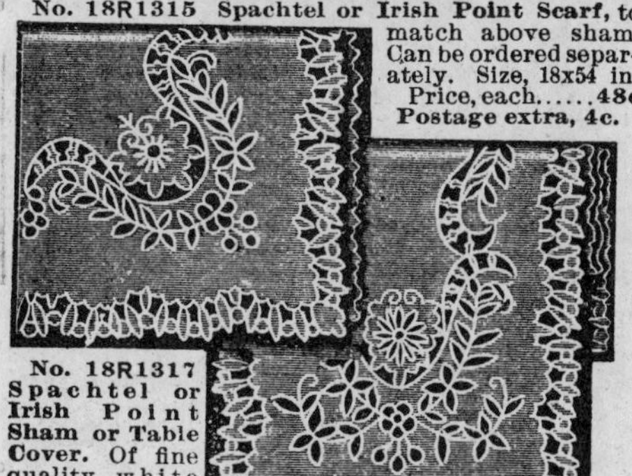

No. 18R1317 Spachtel or Irish Point Sham or Table Cover. Of fine quality white French lawn with very neat scalloped edge and handsome open work waved design around a plain center, giving it a rich effect. Size, 32x32 inches.
Each...(If by mail, postage extra, 5 cents)....62c

No. 18R1319 Spachtel or Irish Point Scarf, to match above sham; same quality and design. Can be ordered separately. Size, 18x54 inches.
Each....(If by mail, postage extra, 5 cents)....62c

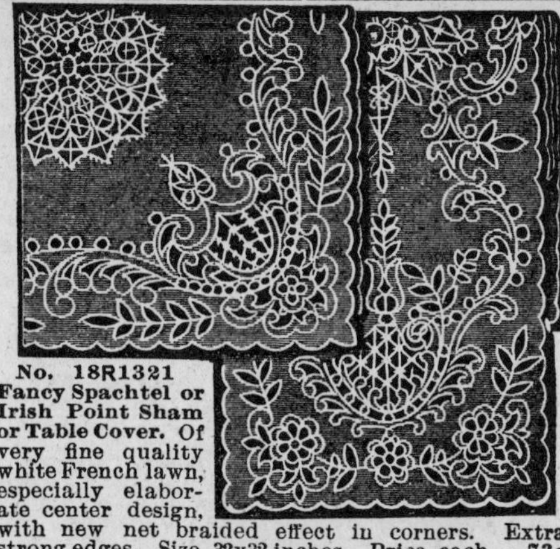

No. 18R1321 Fancy Spachtel or Irish Point Sham or Table Cover. Of very fine quality white French lawn, especially elaborate center design, with new net braided effect in corners. Extra strong edges. Size, 32x32 inches. Price, each....73c
If by mail, postage extra, 5 cents.

No. 18R1323 Fancy Spachtel or Irish Point Scarf, to match above sham. Same design and quality. Size, 20x54 in. Ea..73c
Postage extra, 5c.

No. 18R1325 Spachtel or Irish Point Sham or Table Cover. Neatly embroidered on extra quality white French lawn, open work edges with new heavy stitched corded floral design on corners and center. This design is entirely new and very effective. Size, 32x32 inches.
Price, each ....(If by mail, postage extra, 5c)..99c

No. 18R1327 Spachtel or Irish Point Scarf, to match above sham. Same quality lawn and design. Size, 20x54 inches. Price, each..........99c
If by mail, postage extra, 5 cents.

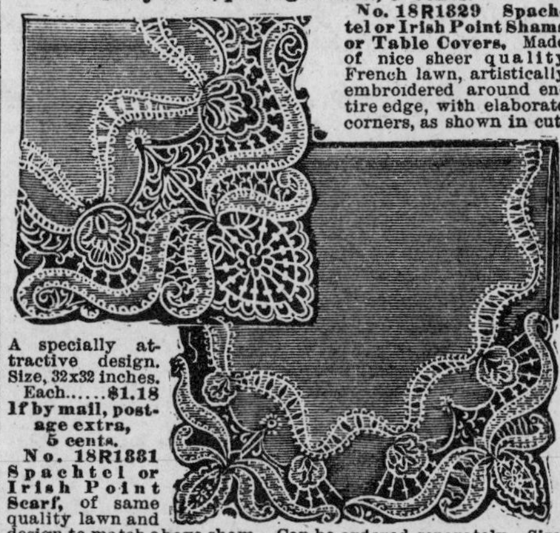

No. 18R1329 Spachtel or Irish Point Shams or Table Covers. Made of nice sheer quality French lawn, artistically embroidered around entire edge, with elaborate corners, as shown in cut. A specially attractive design. Size, 32x32 inches. Each......$1.18
If by mail, postage extra, 5 cents.

No. 18R1331 Spachtel or Irish Point Scarf, of same quality lawn and design to match above sham. Can be ordered separately. Size, 20x54 inches. Each..........$1.18
If by mail, postage extra, 5 cents.

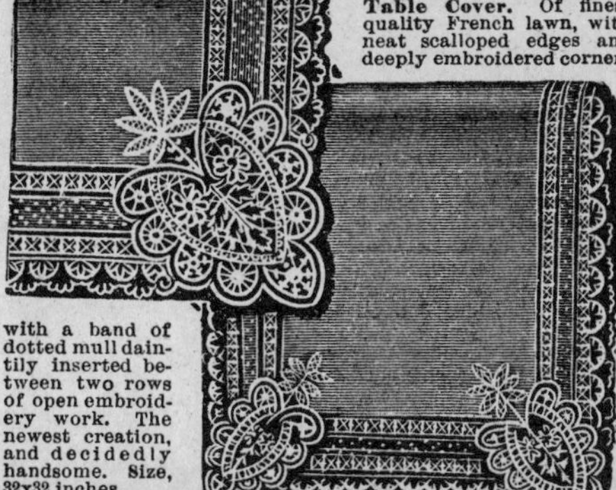

No. 18R1333 Spachtel or Irish Point Shams or Table Cover. Of finest quality French lawn, with neat scalloped edges and deeply embroidered corners with a band of dotted mull daintily inserted between two rows of open embroidery work. The newest creation, and decidedly handsome. Size, 32x32 inches.
Each.....$1.39
If by mail, postage extra, 5 cents.

No. 18R1335 Spachtel or Irish Point Scarf, of same quality lawn and design as above sham. Can be ordered separately. Size, 20x54 inches. Each..(If by mail, postage extra, 5c.).$1.39

New Empire Ruffled Sham, 49 Cents.

New Empire Ruffled Scarf, 49 Cents.

No. 18R1337 Ruffled Shams. Made of a fine quality of white French lawn, new empire work in very pretty design. Nice wide ruffle. A decided novelty in shams. Size, 32x32 inches.
Price, each..........49c
If by mail, postage extra, 5 cents.

No. 18R1339 Ruffled Scarf. Made of the same quality of lawn as the above shams and designed to match same. Size, 18x54 inches. Price, each.....49c
If by mail, postage extra, 5 cents.

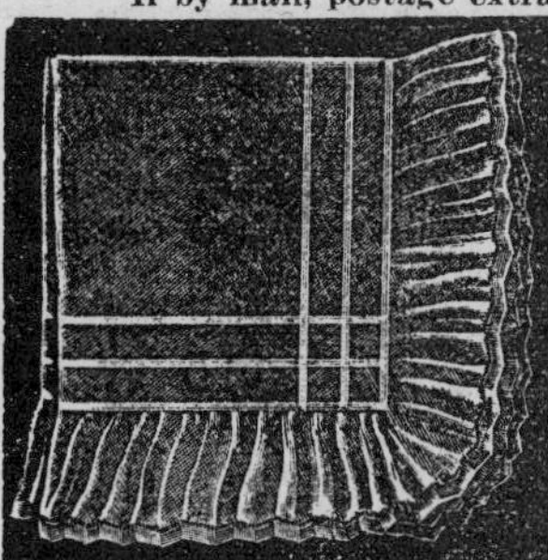

No. 18R1340 White Lawn Pillow Shams, with fancy white hemstitched ruffle and fancy braid design on inside of square. This makes a very elaborate sham. Will wash and wear well. Size, 32x32 inches.
Per pair....92c
If by mail, postage extra, 5 cents.

No. 18R1342 White Lawn Pillow Shams. On the inner square of sham is a fancy design with English torchon insertion and the entire edge or ruffle is made of the same Nottingham torchon lace and insertion. This is a very elegant and rich sham. Will wash well and is very durable. Size, 32x32 inches,
Per pair..$2.24
If by mail, postage extra, 5 cents.

French Lawn Doilies.

No. 18R1344 White French Lawn Spachtel Doilies. Strongly bound edges, handsome open work pattern, square design. Four sizes, as follows:

Size, inches..	9	12
Price, each ..	8c	15c
Size, inches..	16	20
Price, each..	21c	28c

If by mail, postage extra, 3 cents.

White Lawn Doilies and Tidies, at 4 Cents to 22 Cents.

No. 18R1346 White French Lawn Spachtel Doilies and Tidies. Very pretty open work embroidered pattern, round design, as shown in illustration. Comes in five sizes, as follows:

Size, in...	7	9	12
Price, ea.	4c	8c	12c
Size, inches.	16	20	
Price, each.	18c	22c	

If by mail, postage extra, 3 cents.

All Lace Doily, 19 Cents.

No. 18R1348 Beautiful Hand Made All Lace Renaissance Square Doily. Same as illustration.
Size, 8x8 inches.
Price, each..........19c
If by mail, postage extra, 3 cents.

Our 34-Cent Tidy.

No. 18R1350 Hand Made All Lace Renaissance Tidy. Most popular style of fancy work. Handsome square design as shown in cut. Size, 12x12 inches.
Price, each.........34c
If by mail, postage extra, 3 cents.

Fine Lace Tidy for 88 Cents.

No. 18R1352 Extremely Handsome, Hand Made All Lace Renaissance Square Tidy. With heavy embroidered Battenberg ring and fleur de lis center pattern, as illustrated. Size, 18x18 inches.
Price, each.........88c
If by mail, postage extra, 3 cents.

Our $1.47 Lace Square.

No. 18R1354 Exquisitely Designed, Hand Made All Lace Renaissance Square. With heavy embroidered Battenberg rings, tastefully arranged in each corner and unique center design, as shown in cut. Size, 20x20 inches.
Price, each...$1.47
If by mail, postage extra, 3 cents.

Our 28-Cent Hand Made Lace Doily.

No. 18R1356 Hand Made Linen Renaissance Lace Doily, with all linen center. square design as shown in cut. Size, 8x8 inches. Price, each.....28c
If by mail, postage extra, 3 cents.

Hand Made All Linen Dollies, Tidies and Scarfs.

Our 43-Cent Doily.

No. 18R1358 Hand Made Linen Dolly, with Renaissance lace edge and all linen center. A pretty and tasty design. Size, 10x10 inches.
Price, each.....43c
If by mail, postage extra, 3 cents.

89-Cents Buys This Beautiful Tidy.

No.18R1360 Hand Made Renaissance Lace Edge Linen Center Tidy. With Battenberg rings neatly arranged in each corner, as cut. Size, 20x20 inches.
Price, each.........89c
If by mail, postage extra, each, 3 cents.

Handmade Renaissance, $1.50

No. 18R1362 Very Fine Quality Hand Made Renaissance Lace Edge Linen Center Tidy. A very pretty and exclusive design and extra value. Size, 20 x 20 inches.
Price, each..$1.50
If by mail, postage extra, each, 3 cents.

This is a Beauty, $2.38

No. 18R1364 Renaissance Scarf. Made of all linen center and beautifully arranged Battenberg lace edge. A handsome design. Size, 18x54 inches.
Price, each.....$2.38
If by mail, postage extra, 4 cents.

One of the Finest, $3.49.

No. 18R1365 Renaissance Scarf. With all linen center and elaborate Battenberg lace edge pattern. Our best quality and artistically designed. Size, 20x54 inches.
Price, each.. $3.49
If by mail, postage extra, 4 cents.

An Exquisite Design, $2.48

No. 18R1366 All Lace Hand Made Renaissance Scarf. The latest in fancy work. Handsome and exquisite design. Made entirely of lace thread and Battenberg braid. Size, 18x54 inches.
Price, each.... $2.48
If by mail, postage extra, 4 cents.

Our All Lace Hand Made Scarf for $3.88.

No. 18R1368 All Lace Hand Made Renaissance Scarf. Elaborately designed and well made with Battenberg rings neatly grouped in corners as shown in cut. Size, 18x54 inches.
Price, each.....$3.88
If by mail, postage extra, 4 cents.

UMBRELLAS AND PARASOLS.

LATEST DESIGNS, HIGHEST QUALITY MATERIAL USED, BEST WORKMANSHIP. UMBRELLAS CANNOT BE SENT BY MAIL ON ACCOUNT OF LENGTH. Weight of umbrella from 1 to 1¾ pounds.

No. 18R1800 Fast Black English Twilled Cotton Carolo Umbrella. Natural Congo loop or hook handle. Size, 26 inches.
Price.........49c

No.18R1804 Fast Black English Twilled Carolo Umbrella. Paragon frame, steel rod, with natural Congo hook loop or tied handle, like cut. Size, 26 inches.
Price.........69c

No. 18R1808 Fast Black Gloria Silk Umbrella; 7-rib, paragon frame, steel rod and natural Congo loop or tied handle. Regular $1.25 umbrella. Size, 26 inches.
Price.........98c

18R1808

Ladies' Twilled Silk Umbrellas.

We recommend for quality and wear.

No. 18R1812 The Otto Miller Gloria Twilled Silk Umbrella. Paragon frame, steel rod and black carved rubber handle. Same quality umbrella usually retailed at $1.75. Size, 26 inches.
Price.........$1.10

No. 18R1816 Ladies' Twilled Silk Umbrella, with furze wood, sterling silver trimmed hook handle; steel rod, paragon frame; also sterling silver swedge at end of handle. Size, 26 inches.
Price, each.........$1.20

Ladies' Silk Umbrella for $1.25.

No. 18R1820 Ladies' Twilled Silk Umbrella, with straight white pearl handle, sterling silver band and swedge on handle; steel rod, best paragon frame. **Makes a very nobby little umbrella.** Size, 26 inches.
Special price, each.........$1.25

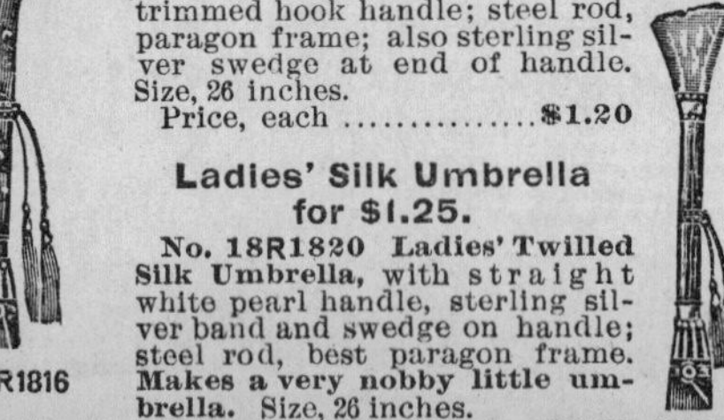

18R1816 18R1820

Best Quality Silk Umbrella, $2.25.

18R1824

No. 18R1824 Ladies' Best Quality Twilled Silk Umbrella, with small neat buckhorn hook handle, sterling silver mounted; also sterling silver bands and swedges, steel rod, paragon frame, silk case and tassels. **A very swell umbrella, and guaranteed for wear.** Size, 26 inches.
Price, each.........$2.25

No. 18R1828 Ladies' High Grade Quality Twilled Silk Umbrella, with silk case and tassels to match. Straight handle with ivory shoulder and sterling silver top and swedge; large space on top of handle for name or monogram, steel rod, paragon frame, a fine, tight roll umbrella. Size, 26 inches.
Price, each.........$2.30

No. 18R1832 Ladies' Superfine Quality Guaranteed Twilled Silk Umbrella, with silk case and tassels to match, steel rod, paragon frame, a very elegant design, straight princess handle made of weichsel wood and having sterling silver trimmings. Size, 26 inches.
Price, each.........$2.75

18R1832 18R1828

Our $1.50 Ladies' Umbrella.

No. 18R1836 Ladies' Tight Roll Fine Taffeta Silk Umbrella, with Congo wood hook and loop handle, steel rod, paragon frame, case and tassels to match. Extra value. Size, 26 inches.
Price, each.........$1.50

No. 18R1840 Ladies' Tight Roll Taffeta Silk Umbrella, with silk case and tassels to match, steel rod, best paragon frame, finely selected box wood hook handle with heavy sterling silver trimmings. Very nobby. Size, 26 inches.
Price, each.........$2.15

18R1840 18R1836

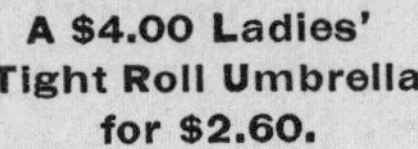

A $4.00 Ladies' Tight Roll Umbrella for $2.60.

No. 18R1844 Ladies' Tight Roll Taffeta Silk Umbrella, with tape edge, steel rod, paragon frame, silk case and tassels to match. Elegant pearl hook handle with sterling silver mountings. A very neat and stylish design; good quality. Size, 26 inches. Price..$2.60

18R1844

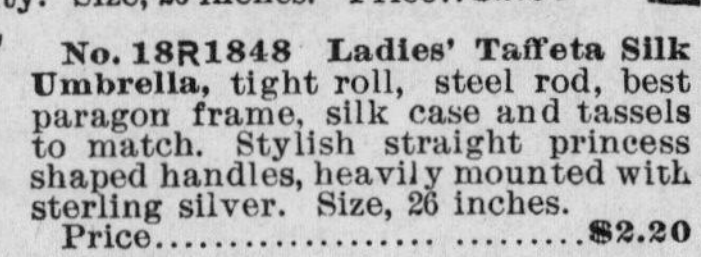

No. 18R1848 Ladies' Taffeta Silk Umbrella, tight roll, steel rod, best paragon frame, silk case and tassels to match. Stylish straight princess shaped handles, heavily mounted with sterling silver. Size, 26 inches.
Price.........$2.20

No. 18R1852 Ladies' Best Quality Tight Roll Taffeta Silk Umbrella, with silk case and tassels, steel rod, paragon frame, heavily mounted with sterling silver and pearl handle in straight princess shape. **The best quality and finest made and very stylish design.** Size, 26 inches. Price.........$3.25

18R1848 18R1852

No. 18R1856 Ladies' Colored Silk Umbrella, with silk case and tassel to match. Congo loop handle. A very tight roll umbrella, steel rod and paragon frame. Colors, navy blue and cardinal. Size, 26 inches.
Price, each.........$1.60

18R1856

Special Design High Grade Handle Colored Silk Umbrella.

No. 18R1860 Ladies' Best Quality All Silk Colored Serge Umbrella, with silk case and tassels to match, steel rod, paragon frame, handsome design, straight pearl handle with sterling silver band and swedge. Colors, garnet, brown, navy blue and dark green. Size, 26 inches.
Price, each.........$3.25

No. 18R1864 Ladies' Colored Silk Umbrella, with fancy colored border. Fine quality all silk serge, case and tassels to match, steel rod, paragon frame, princess shape furze wood handle, with pretty sterling silver mountings. Colors, garnet, brown, navy blue, and also in black. Size, 26 inches. Price, each.........$3.95

18R1864

No. 18R1868 Men's Mercerized Silk Umbrella, with steel rod, paragon frame, case and tassels to match, Prince of Wales Congo wood hook handle, sterling silver trimmed. We highly recommend this umbrella for looks and durability. Comes in three sizes.

Size, inches	26	28	30
Price, each	$1.00	$1.10	$1.20

18R1868

Men's Twilled Silk Umbrella.

No. 18R1872 Men's Twilled Silk Umbrella, good wearing quality with steel rod, paragon frame and Prince of Wales hook handle in selected Congo wood.

Size, inches.. 26 28
Price, each.. $1.00 $1.10

18R1872

Best Quality Twilled Silk Umbrella.

No. 18R1876 Men's Best Quality Twilled Silk Umbrella, Prince of Wales Congo wood hook handle, steel rod, paragon frame and a close, tight roll, with sterling silver mountings and swedge, silk case and tassels.

Size, inches.......... 26 28
Price, each.......... $1.95 $2.15

18R1876

No. 18R1880 Men's Fine Taffeta Silk Tight Roll Umbrella, with steel rod, paragon frame, silk case and tassels, Prince of Wales shaped Congo wood hook handle, excellent value.

Size, inches.. 26 28
Price, each.. $1.50 $1.75

18R1880

No. 18R1884 Men's Taffeta Silk Umbrella, tight roll, steel rod, paragon frame; fine, large weichsel wood hook handle with heavy sterling silver mountings, silk case and tassels.

Size, inches 26 28
Each...... $2.25 $2.50

18R1884

No. 18R1888 Men's Taffeta Silk Umbrella. Silk case and tassels, tight roll, steel rod, paragon frame; large, French horn hook handle with sterling silver band and swedge. A very popular and stylish umbrella. Good wearing quality.

Size, inches.. 26 28
Price, each, $2.40 $2.60

18R1888

Men's Fine Taffeta Silk Umbrellas.

No. 18R1892 Men's Fine Taffeta Silk Umbrella, with tape edge, silk case and tassels, steel rod, paragon frame, finely selected furze wood hook handle with sterling silver mountings. A very desirable umbrella and good value.

Size, inches.......... 26 28
Price, each.......... $2.75 $2.95

18R1892

PARASOLS FOR CHILDREN.

Rich, dainty and low priced.

No. 18R1920 Child's Fancy Colored Parasol, with pinked edge, natural wood handle. Size, 12 inches. Comes in cardinal, light blue, pink or white.
Price, each.......... 18c
If by mail, postage extra, 16 cents.

No. 18R1922 Child's Fancy Colored Mercerized Silk Parasol, with pinked edge corded effect, a very neat and pretty style. Natural wool handle. Can be ordered in white, light blue, pink or cardinal.
Size, 10 inches. Each.......... 38c
Size, 12 inches. Each.......... 44c
If by mail, postage extra, 18 cents.

No. 18R1926 Child's Fancy Colored Parasol, with two full ruffles, pinked edges, neat bamboo handle. Colors, white, pink, light blue, cardinal or navy.
Size, 12 inches. Price, each.......... 58c
Size, 14 inches. Price, each.......... 65c
If by mail, postage extra, 18 cents.

No. 18R1930 This is our better grade Child's Fancy Colored India Silk Coaching Style Parasol, with stitched edges, with nice silk puff at top to match body of parasol; a dainty affair. Comes in white, pink, light blue, cardinal or navy.

Size, inches	14	16	18
Price, each	75c	87c	99c

If by mail, postage extra, 20 cents.

LADIES' PARASOLS.

Black Coaching Parasol, $1.20.

No. 18R1934 Ladies' Black Gloria Silk Stitched Edge Coaching Parasol, with puff at top and fancy black carved wood handle; a very excellent and desirable style. Price, each.......... $1.20
If by mail, postage extra, 20 cents.

No. 18R1938 Ladies' White India Silk Parasol, good quality silk, coaching style, straight edge, fancy bamboo handle; regular $1.50 value.
Our special price, each.......... 99c
If by mail, postage extra, 20 cents.

White India Silk Parasol, with Ruffle, $1.25.

No. 18R1942 Ladies' White India Silk Parasol, good quality silk, with one large ruffle, pinked edge, puff at top, fancy bamboo handle; special value.
Price, each.......... $1.25
If by mail, postage extra, 20 cents.

Ladies' Silk Parasols.

No. 18R1946 Ladies' Black Gloria Silk Parasol with four rows of hemstitching on top and bottom, has full silk puff at top, fancy black carved sticks. This makes a very stylish and desirable parasol, rich and neat, worth $2.50. Price, each, $1.80
If by mail, postage extra, 25c

18R1946

No. 18R1950 Ladies' India Silk Parasol, good quality silk with two large ruffles of fine sewing silk veiling, with satin stripe around edge of ruffles, full puff at top, fancy Congo wood handle. Either in loops or ties. This is a very desirable and dressy parasol, can be ordered either in black or white.
Price, each.......... $2.40
If by mail, postage extra, 25 cents.

No. 18R1954 This very stylish and elegant India Silk Parasol has two wide ruffles of silk chiffon, with large chiffon puff on top, a very fluffy and pretty parasol, handsome stick and handle to correspond. This parasol can be had in black or white. Price.......... $2.75
If by mail, postage extra, 25 cents.

18R1950

Men's Canes.

18R1958 18R1962 18R1966 18R1978

No. 18R1958 Loaded Cane, steel rod, spun cloth cover, with knob on top. A very nice cane. Each, 10c

No. 18R1962 Genuine Hickory Cane, crook handle, highly finished in shellac, dark color, very serviceable, and an excellent support for an elderly man. Medium size. Price, each.......... 25c

No. 18R1966 Natural Congo Crook Cane, medium size, steel ferrule tip. An excellent article. Each, 30c

No. 18R1970 Genuine Congo Crook Cane, natural color, nickel ferrule tip, ornamented with sterling silver end. A very stylish cane, universally used.
Price, each.......... 50c

No. 18R1974 Fine Natural Congo Cane, with fancy horn handle, stylish metal band around crook, steel ferrule tip. A very dressy cane.
Price, each.......... 85c

No. 18R1978 Fine Imported Congo Crook Cane, steel ferruled tip, with elaborate design, sterling silver ornament on crook. A cane used by the best dressers, and worth a great deal more than we ask.
Price, each.......... $1.25

DRESS TRIMMINGS AND BRAIDS

We offer you a very choice selection of up to date fashionable trimmings. Our buyer has devoted a long time to selecting just the right things. You get the price advantage of 25 to 50 per cent, the result of our immense purchases and our close margin way of selling.

No. 18R2050 All Silk Yoke or Dress Front, made of silk president and tubular braid, with chiffon, and edged with Renaissance lace. The latest in trimmings. Very swell and nobby.
Price, each.......... 85c
If by mail, postage extra, 10 cents.

Very Fine White Pearl Front for $1.00.

No. 18R2070 White Pearl Front. This effective bead garniture is very showy, rich, and attractive, and a handsome trimming for light costumes, and especially adapted for evening wear. **A great deal handsomer than it looks in the above illustration.** Would be very cheap for $2.00, and we know that you will be more than pleased with it. Price...... $1.00
If by mail, postage extra, 22 cents.

Frog Loops for Cloaks and Suits.

No. 18R2074 Finest Quality Strictly Fast Black Pure Mohair Frog Loops. Same style as illustration.
Price, each..... 25c

No. 18R2078 Finest Quality Fast Black Pure Silk Frog Loops. Same style as above. Each.......... 35c

No. 18R2080 Silk and Satin Cord, fancy gimp trimming. Exact size of illustration. Price, per yard.......... 4c
If by mail, postage extra, per yard, 2 cents.

Dress Trimmings.

No. 18R2084 Black Silk Fancy Cord Trimming, as per illustration. A new pattern. Width ½ inch. Price, per yard.......... 6c
If by mail, postage extra, per yard, 2 cents.

No. 18R2088 Fancy Black Silk Cord Trimming. A very elegant, stylish and dainty dress trimming. Width, 1 inch
Price, per yard.......... 11c
If by mail, postage extra, per yard, 2 cents.

No. 18R2092 Silk Trimming, made of president braid and a narrow tubular braid; an exceedingly pretty combination and a very distinctive pattern. Width, 1⅛ inches. Price, per yard.. 21c
If by mail, postage extra, per yard, 2 cents.

No. 18R2096 Black Silk Applique Trimming. Silk braid over chiffon leaves a very rich and effective trimming. Width, 1⅛ inches.
Price, per yard.......... 24c

Large Leaf Pattern Silk Chiffon Appliqued

No. 18R2100 Stunning Black Applique Trimming. Fine silk braid on silk chiffon; very dainty and effective for waists and skirts. Width, 2¼ inches. Worth 75 cents. Our price, per yard. 44c

Silk Trimming at 5 Cents a Yard.

No. 18R2104 Fancy Silk Braid Trimming, a very neat and entirely new design. Colors, cream, gray, tan, brown, cardinal, navy blue and black. Width, ¼ inch.
Price, per yard.......... 5c
If by mail, postage extra, per yard, 2 cents.

No. 18R2108 Fancy Silk Braid Dress Trimming. New fancy shell pattern; an exceedingly pretty and stylish design. Colors, cream and black. Width, ½ inch. Price, per yard.......... 10c

Gold and Colored Mixed Trimmings.

No. 18R2112 A Pretty Tinsel Mixed Narrow Band Trimming. The illustration shows the exact size. Colors of center can be ordered as follows: White, black, navy, brown and cardinal.
Price, per yard.......... 4c

No. 18R2116 Silk and Tinsel Mixed Trimming. This is an exceedingly lustrous and pretty trimming. Colors, black, cream, light blue, pink, cardinal and castor. Good 10-cent value. Per yard.... 5c

No. 18R2120 Black and Gold Tinsel Band Trimming. Width, ¾ inch. A decidedly pretty and stylish trimming. Per yard... 10c

No. 18R2121 Fancy Novelty Silk Braid Trimming. A very dainty and stylish pattern. Width, ¾ inch. Can be ordered in plain black, cream, or black and white combination, which is now very popular. Price, per yard.......... 10c
If by mail, postage extra, per yard, 2 cents.

Appliqued Fancy Silk Chiffon Trimming.

No. 18R2122 Appliqued fancy scroll design, a very handsome and effective trimming quite heavily appliqued. Colors, black and white. Width, 1 inch.
Price, per yard.......... 17c

No. 18R2123 Combination Chiffon and Silk Applique Trimming. A new fabric, pretty, neat and effective design. Width, 1 inch. Colors, black and white. Price, per yard.....................21c

No. 18R2125 Fancy Chiffon and Silk Applique in neat floral design, heavily embossed with silk, giving a massive and rich effect. Will be worn extensively by good dressers. Width, 2 inches. Colors, black and white. Price, per yard.....29c

No. 18R2128 Black Silk Taffeta Applique Trimming. A very pretty and stylish trimming. Width, 1⅛ inches. Price, per yard.....................15c

No. 18R2132 Black Silk Taffeta Applique Trimming. A very rich and effective trimming. Width 2¼ inches. Price, per yard....39c

No. 18R2136 White Bead Trimming, as per illustration. Width, ⅝ inch. Price, per yard.....................8c
If by mail, postage extra, per yard, 2 cents.

No. 18R2140 White Bead Trimming with pearl centers, as per illustration. Width, ¾ inch.

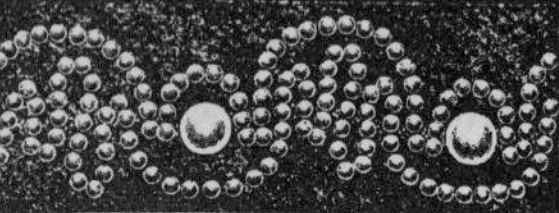

Price, per yard.....................15c
If by mail, postage extra, per yard, 2 cents.

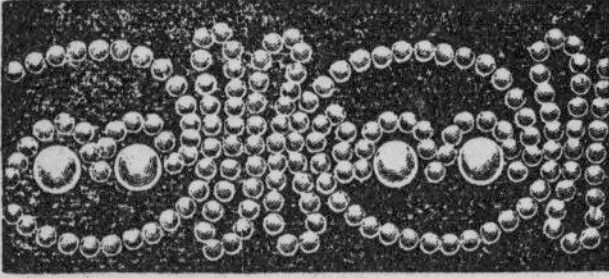

No. 18R2144 White Bead Trimming with pearl centers. A pretty and elaborate design. Width, 1 inch. Price, per yard.....................22c
If by mail, postage extra, per yard, 2 cents.

No. 18R2148 Black Jet Bead Trimming, exact size of illustration. Price, per yard.....................5c
If by mail, postage extra, 2 cents.

Black Bright Bead Trimming.

No. 18R2152 Black Bright Bead Trimming. A very neat and tasty design. Width, ⅝ inch. Price, per yard.....7c

No. 18R2156 Black Jet Bead Trimming, a very desirable pattern. Width, ⅛ inch. Price, per yard.....................7c

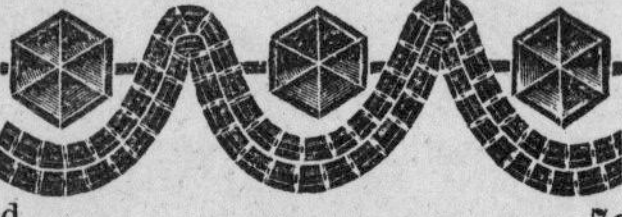

No. 18R2158 Black Jet Bead Trimming, as per illustration. Width, ⅝ inch. Per yard...5c
If by mail, postage extra, 2 cents.

No. 18R2160 Black Jet Bead Trimming. A new design. Width, 1 inch. Per yard..8c
If by mail, postage extra, 2 cents.

No. 18R2164 Black Jet Bead Trimming, a very dainty and elaborate design. Width, 1⅛ inches. Price, per yard....15c
If by mail, postage extra, per yard, 2c.

No. 18R2168 Black Jet Bead Trimming. This is an elegant and pretty pattern. Width, 1½ inches. Price, per yard.........18c
If by mail, postage extra, per yard, 2 cents.

No. 18R2172 Jet Spangled One-Row Band Trimming. Exact width of illustration, $\frac{5}{16}$ inch. Price, per yard.....................5c

No. 18R2176 Jet Spangled Two-Row Band Trimming. Width, ⅝ inch. Price, per yard.....................10c
If by mail, postage extra, per yard, 2 cents.

No. 18R2180 Black Spangle and Jet Bead Trimming, a neat and pretty effect, exact size of illustration. Price, per yard.....................8c
If by mail, postage extra, per yard, 2 cents.

No. 18R2181 Fine Spangle and Jet Bead Trimming, wave effect. Width, ¾ inch. Price, per yard.....................10c
If by mail, postage extra, per yard, 2 cents.

No. 18R2183 Black Spangle and Jet Bead Trimming, wave or serpentine effect, larger spangles. Width, 1 inch.

Price, per yard.....................14c
If by mail, postage extra, per yard, 2 cents.

No. 18R2185 Black Spangle and Jet Bead Trimming, our own exclusive pattern, rich and elegant. Width, 1¼ inches. Price, per yard.....................22c
If by mail, postage extra, per yard, 2 cents.

No. 18R2187 Black Spangle and Jet Bead Trimming, worked on a lace net, very stylish and handsome. Width, ¾ inch. Price, per yard......41c
If by mail, postage extra, per yard, 2 cents.

No. 18R2189 Black Spangle and Jet Bead Trimming, applique, on fine silk chiffon net. A very delicate and dainty pattern. A very stylish trimming. Width, 1 inch. Price, per yard.....................42c
If by mail, postage extra, per yard, 2 cents.

Black Silk Ruffling.

No. 18R2191 Black Dainty Silk Ruffling for trimming dresses, skirts, etc., as per illustration. Width, 2¾ inches. Price, per yard....35c
If by mail, postage extra, per yard, 2 cents.

No. 18R2192 Large Juby Ruching, made of satin ribbon, width, 1¼ inch, for trimming skirts and waists. Can be ordered in black or white. Price, per yard.....................19c
If by mail, postage extra, per yard, 2 cents.

No. 18R2195 Silk Juby Trimming, in black or cream. Width, ⅝ inch. Price, per yard..8c
If by mail, postage extra, per yard, 2 cents.

Spangled All Over Net.

No. 18R2210 Spangled All Over Net. On fine silk net, a very dainty and stylish flower pattern, suitable for fronts and yokings. One-half yard is sufficient to make a back and front yoke. Width, 27 inches. Price, per yard..........$1.95
If by mail, postage extra, per yard, 10 cents.

No. 18R2214 Silk Lacing Cord, black and colors. Silk lacing cord in black and all colors. Price, per yard.....................2½c
If by mail, postage extra, per yard, 2 cents.

Silk Cable Cord.

No. 18R2218 Silk Cable Cord. Can be used for cushions and furniture trimmings. Comes in black and colors, size of illustration. Price, per yard.....................5c
If by mail, postage extra, per yard, 2 cents.

Cream or Black Hercules Braid.

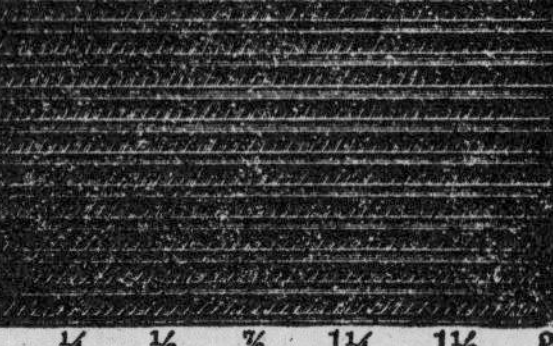

No. 18R2234 Mohair Hercules Braid. Comes in black or cream color.

Width, inches	¼	½	⅞	1¼	1½	2
Price, per yard	1c	2c	3c	4c	5c	7c

Black Diamond Braid.

No. 18R2238 Black Diamond Braid, basket weave hercules, always a stylish and rich trimming, also extensively used for skirt binding.

Lines	4	6	10	14	24
Width, inches	⅛	⅛	¾	1⅛	2
Price, per yard	2c	3c	6c	8c	10c

Black Silk Hercules, Pearl Edges.

No. 18R2242 A very stylish and lasting trimming.

Width, inches	¼	⅝	¾	1
Price, per yard	3c	7c	9c	10c

Plain and Fancy Silk Hercules Braids.

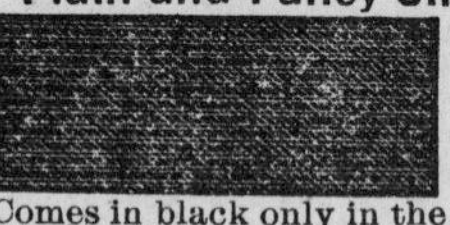

No. 18R2243 Fine Quality Silk Hercules Braid. Very fine ribbed, to be used for dress and cloak trimming, also desirable for coat binding. Comes in black only in the following widths:

Lines	4	8	12	14	16
Width, inches	$\frac{3}{16}$	$\frac{5}{16}$	⅝	¾	1
Price, per yard	2c	4c	6c	8c	10c

No. 18R2244 Fancy Silk Braid Trimming, new dumb bell design. A very desirable dress or jacket trimming, the different widths are used together or single. Black only, in three widths.

Width, inches	⅝	¾	1
Price, per yard	6c	9c	14c

Novelty Satin Braid.

No. 18R2245 Fancy Corded Satin Braid Trimming. This popular trimming is used in single or the combination of widths together for stylish dresses or jackets. Comes in black, three widths as follows:

Width, inches	$\frac{5}{16}$	⅝	¾
Price, per yard	8c	10c	12c

Wash Braids.

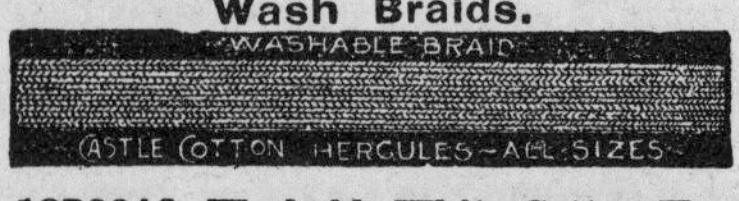

No. 18R2246 Washable White Cotton Hercules Braid, makes a very neat, stylish and durable trimming, white only.

Width, inches	⅛	¼	½	¾	1⅛
Price, per yard	½c	1c	2c	4c	5c

No. 18R2248 White Cotton Soutache (washable), to be used on waists and wash dresses. Extensively worn. Comes in three widths. Exact size of illustration. This is the better grade soutache.

Width, inches	⅛	⅛	$\frac{3}{16}$
Price, per dozen yards	6c	8c	10c

No. 18R2250 Mohair Soutache Braid, for trimming, black and staple colors. Price, per dozen yards.....................8c

No. 18R2254 Silk Soutache Braid, extra quality in black and colors. Price, per yard.....................1½c

Genuine Alligator Purse.

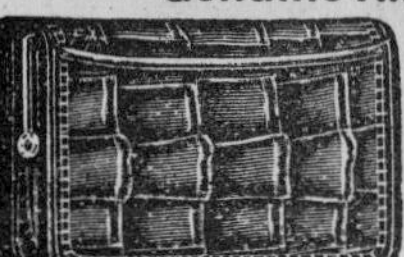

No. 18R2591 Genuine Alligator Purse, leather facing, with block bottom, gusseted, has three regular, one tuck and coin pocket in nickel spring catch frame, also one handkerchief pocket on back. Size, 3 x 4½ inches. Excellent style and great value. Price, each.....49c
If by mail, postage extra, 4 cents.

Paragon Handkerchief Books.

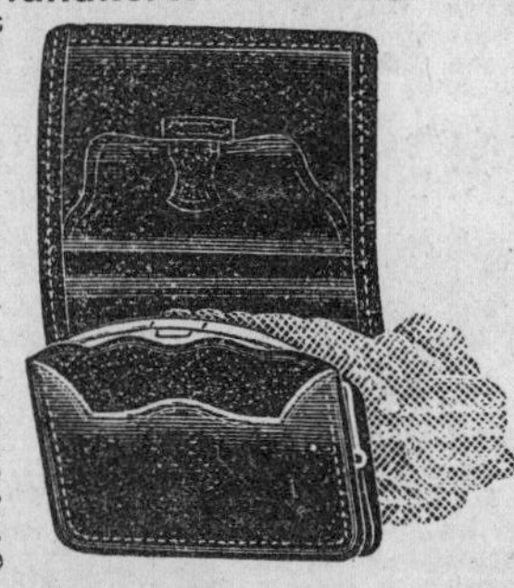

A very convenient book for carrying a handkerchief without risk of losing or soiling same. It has all the features of a regularly made book, and its special construction admits of carrying a handkerchief without increasing its bulk. All made with gusseted block bottom and made with slotted frame, preventing tearing down of pockets. Comes in three qualities.

No. 18R2593 Paragon Handkerchief Book. Leather, imitation seal, imitation seal and leather facings, two regular, one fancy card, one tuck, handkerchief and coin pocket in oval, wide mouth frame. Size, 3¼x4½ inches. Price, each.....46c

No. 18R2595 Paragon Handkerchief Pocketbook. Made of good quality seal grain leather, with calf and seal grain leather facings, one fancy card, one tuck, handkerchief and coin pocket, fine nickel frame. Size, 3¼x4½ inches. Price, each..........72c
If by mail, postage extra, 4 cents.

No. 18R2599 Genuine Seal Paragon Handkerchief Book. Seal and calf facing. This is made similar to above Paragon books, made of finest seal leather, and best workmanship. Size, 3¼x4½ inches. Price, each..........93c
If by mail, postage extra, 4 cents.

Ladies' Fine Seal Leather Block Bottom Pocketbook.

No. 18R2614 With chamois lined coin pocket, snap frame, faced throughout with seal leather and block bottom. Size, 3x4¾ inches. Usual $1.00 pocketbook.
Price, each..........78c
If by mail, postage extra, 5 cents.

Genuine Seal Ladies' Pocketbook.

No. 18R2615 Our highest grade book, with all the good points a good pocketbook should have. Genuine seal and calf facing, round bottom, three regular, one fancy card, one tuck and one coin pocket, in fine nickel spring catch frame. Size, 3½x4½ inches.
Price, each.........$1.62
If by mail, postage extra, 4 cents.

Ladies' Black Seal Purse, only 20 Cents.

No. 18R2617 Ladies' Black Seal Combination Purse. With fancy metal corners; regular card pocket and one leather faced pocket with flap and tuck; coin pocket with snap frame. Size, 3x4⅛ inches. Splendid value.
Price, each..........20c
If by mail, postage extra, each, 4 cents.

No. 18R2619 Cape goat leather, an extremely handsome pocket book, in black, brown or tan, cape goat and leather facings; three regular, one fancy card, one tuck and coin pocket, in nickel spring catch frame, mounted with open work embossed gilt rim. Size, 3¼x4½ inches. Colors, black, brown and tan. Price, each..........46c
If by mail, postage extra, each 4 cents.

No. 18R2620 Initials. Sterling silver, plain type, 1½ inches high, have the fastenings and are easily put on. For purses, etc. Each..........21c
If by mail, postage extra, 2 cents.

Ladies' Fine Walrus Pocketbook.

No. 18R2621 This Stylish Pocketbook has three regular, one fancy card, one tuck and coin pocket, in nickel spring catch frame. Mounted with genuine sterling silver corners. Colors, gray or black. Size, 2¾x4¾ inches. Price, each..........56c
If by mail, postage extra, each, 4 cents.

Ladies' Genuine Seal Leather Pocketbook.

No. 18R2623 With highly polished genuine calf facings. This high grade purse has three regular, one fancy card, one tuck and coin pocket, in best nickel spring catch frame. Stitched and gusseted, mounted with very handsome sterling silver corners. This is a very high grade pocketbook and sold for double the price we ask for it. Black only. Size, 3⅛x4⅝ inches.
Each. **(If by mail, postage extra, each, 4c)**..$1.17

Genuine Texas Steer High Grade Fancy Pocketbook.

No. 18R2627 Black and colors. Genuine steer and calf facings, block bottom, gusseted, three regular, one fancy card, one tuck and coin pocket in nickel spring catch frame, mounted with l'art Nouveaux oxidized sterling silver trimming. Size, 3¼x4½ inches. Colors, stone gray, brown or black. Each.....$1.88
If by mail, postage extra, 6 cents.

Our 96-Cent Ladies' Pocketbook.

No. 18R2631 Mexican Hand Carved Leather Ladies' Pocketbook. Assorted designs, leather facing, three regular, one tuck and coin pocket, in nickel spring catch frame. The Mexican hand carved books have an immense sale; a very nobby book. Size, 3x4½ inches.
Each... **(If by mail, postage extra, 5 cents)**...96c

Genuine Alligator Ladies' Pocketbook.

No. 18R2633 Genuine Hornback Alligator Ladies' Pocketbook. Fine calf facing block bottom, gusseted, three regular, one tuck and coin pocket in fine nickel spring catch frame. Size, 3x4½ inches. This fine horned alligator book is very popular, pretty and stylish, and sold by us at a very low price.
Each.. **(If by mail, postage extra, 6 cents)**..$3.19

Ladies' Cut Steel Beaded Bags.

They have become more and more stylish. Every lady wants one.

No. 18R2637 Beaded Bag. Genuine hand made, cut steel beaded bag, with steel bead fringe, chamois back and handsome silver plated frame, chain and hook, chamois lined and inside pocket. Very stylish; all the go. Size, 4x4½ inches. Price, each....$3.29
If by mail, postage extra, 10 cents.

No. 18R2639 Hand Made Beaded Cut Steel Bag. Same style as above but larger. Size, 5x4½ in.
Price, each..........$4.95
If by mail, postage extra, 12 cents.

Ladies' Fine Beaded Chatelaine Purse.

No. 18R2643 Made of steel beads and looped fringe all around, chamois lined, chain and belt hook. A very handsome bag at a very low price. Size, 4⅛x6¼ inches. Price, each..........$1.50
If by mail, postage extra, 10 cents.

Ladies' Steel Bead Chatelaine Purse.

No. 18R2645 Mounted handsomely with fine nickel frame, chain and belt hook attachment, beaded loop fringe all around, chamois lined. This purse is usually retailed at $1.50. Size, 4x4¾ inches. Price, each..........$1.00
If by mail, postage extra, 8 cents.

Novelty Metal Chatelaine Bags.

No. 18R2647 Made of fancy links of white metal, silver finish, with chain belt hook. A very stylish purse. Size, 2⅛x3¼ inches.
Price, each..........49c
If by mail, postage extra, 5 cents.

Ladies' Fancy Metal Chatelaine Purse in Nickel or Silvered.

No. 18R2649 The design is a reproduction of the high priced all silver purse. Chain and belt hook to match. This is a very dainty and elegant purse. Size, 3x5 inches. Price, each..........75c
If by mail, postage extra, 6 cents.

Ladies' Genuine Alligator Chatelaine Purse.

No. 18R2651 With fancy metal frame, ball catch, chain and attachment for belt. Size, 4½x4¾ inches. Price, each..........$1.25
If by mail, postage extra, 10 cents.

Chatelaine Bags.

No. 18R2653 Seal Grain Leather Bag. One leather lined pocket, gilt riveted ball catch frame, gilt chain with attachment for belt. Size, 3x3½ inches. A very convenient and pretty bag.
Price, each..........23c
If by mail, postage extra, 6 cents.

Ladies' Chatelaine Bag.

No. 18R2655 Ladies' Seal Grain Leather Chatelaine Bag. With nickel riveted frame, the front of frame covered with leather, patent nickeled catch fastener, leather straps and belt hook. Size, 6x6½ inches.
Price, each..........46c

No. 18R2657 Ladies' Chatelaine Bag, similar shape to above, made of finest real seal, leather lined, best frame. A substantial wearing as well as elegant bag. Black only.
Price, each..........$1.00
If by mail, postage extra, each, 8 cents.

Black Leather Chatelaine Bag.

No. 18R2691 Black Leather Chatelaine Bag. Imitation walrus, riveted frame with leather front, spring catch, one regular and one outside handkerchief pocket; wide bottom and sides. Size, 5¾x6¼ inches. This is an exceptionally fine, stylish book and exceptional value.
Price, each..........95c
If by mail, postage extra, 8 cents.

Special Value for 43 Cents.

No. 18R2698 Ladies' Shopping Bag. Of seal grain leatherette, bound with gimp cord all around; two small outside pockets, one with nickeled catch, sateen top with drawing strings, 2 leather handles. Size, 6¾x10 inches.
Price, each...43c
Shipping weight, 14 ounces.

Seal Grain Leather Shopping Bag.

No. 18R2702 Ladies' Shopping Bag. Made of seal grain leather, bound all around with silk gimp cord, one large and two small outside pockets, with oxidized catch, good quality sateen top with draw strings, two leather handles. Size, 10¼ inches deep by 14¼ inches wide.
Price, each..........75c
Shipping weight, 20 oz.

Our $1.12 Opera Shopping Bag.

No. 18R2703 Opera Shopping Bag. Made of black moire silk, round extension frame with filigree top, fancy gilt tops. Silk cord handles. We recommend this number. Size, 8¾x9 inches.
Price, each............$1.12
If by mail, postage extra, 7 cents.

Quaker Purse.

No. 18R2705 Genuine Pigskin. 2 pockets. Size, 2¼x2½ inches. Its peculiar shape and formation admit of handling the coin without danger of losing its contents. Price, each...39c
If by mail, postage extra, 3 cents.

SPECIAL VALUES IN MEN'S POCKETBOOKS AND CARD CASES.

All the novelties as well as staples in this line. Note our prices carefully. A pocketbook or card case makes an acceptable present.

Men's Coin Purse and Bill Fold.

No. 18R2707 Coin Purse and Bill Fold. A handy book for gents, with a compartment for silver and bills; made of best New Zealand calf. Size, closed, 3x3½ inches.
Price, each.....................46c
If by mail, postage extra, 3 cents.

No. 18R2709 Bill Fold. Made of seal grain leather, faced with calf grain, has flap strap and patent button fastener. Size, 2¾x3½ inches when closed.
Price, each.........19c
If by mail, postage extra, each, 3 cents.

Men's Patent Box Flap Book.

No. 18R2711 Seal leather, with five regular pockets and four smaller pockets, bound and stitched. A very convenient purse for men. Size, 2¾x4 in.
Price, each.......46c
If by mail, postage extra, each, 4 cents.

Seal Grain Leather Card Cases.

No. 18R2713 Card Case of Seal Grain Leather. One ticket and two regular pockets, one with flap and tuck strap. Size, 3x4½ inches. Each........21c

No. 18R2715 Card Case of Seal Leather in black only. Size, 2¾x4½ inches. Inside finished in smooth calf and seal, one ticket and two regular pockets, one with flap and tuck strap; also place for stamps. Price, each, 47c
If by mail, postage extra, each, 4 cents.

Men's Heavy Sheep Strap Pocketbooks.

No. 18R2717 Fine calf finish three pockets and bill fold, with flap and tuck strap. Stitched all around. Size, 2¾x4¾ inches.
Price, each.... ....19c
If by mail, postage extra, each, 4 cents.

No. 18R2719 Men's Extra Selected Quality Sheep Strap Book. English calf finish, four regular pockets and stamp pocket, bill fold with flap and tuck strap; warranted all leather throughout; heavily stitched all around. Size, 2¾x4¾ inches. Each.......36c
If by mail, postage extra, each, 3 cents.

English Calfskin Pocketbook.

No. 18R2721 Highly polished finish and faced with kid; four regular and three small pockets. Bill fold, with flap and tuck strap. Size, 2¾x4¾ inches.
Price, each...........52c
If by mail, postage extra, each, 3 cents.

Seal Leather Strap Pocketbook.

No. 18R2723 Four regular pockets, bill fold, with flap and tuck strap, leather faced. Regular $1.00 pocketbook. Size, 2¾x4¾ inches.
Price, each...... ......69c
If by mail, postage extra, each, 3 cents.

Grain Leather Pocketbook.

No. 18R2725 Five large pockets and three small inner pockets. A pliable and serviceable purse. Size, 2¾x4 inches. Price, each........44c
If by mail, postage extra, each, 3 cents.

No. 18R2729 Fine Morocco Grain Leather Billbook. Four large full size pockets, also card and ticket pocket; kid faced and canvas lined. Size, 3½x8 inches. Price, each........ ....36c
If by mail, postage extra, each, 5 cents.

No. 18R2731 Fine Morocco Finish Leather Billbook. Size, 3¾x6¾ in. Three large and two small pockets, kid faced and finely finished. **An excellent book for carrying letters and papers.**
Each........50c
If by mail, postage extra, each, 5 cents.

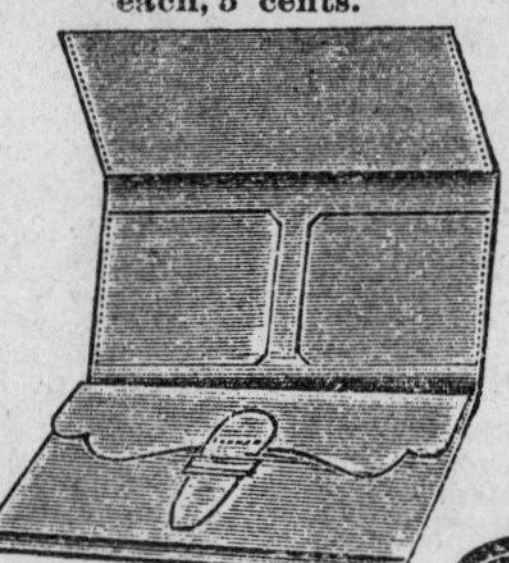

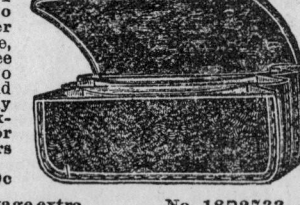

No. 18R2733 Gentlemen's Billbook. Made of fine quality, smooth calf, yellow finish leather. Stitched throughout. Has two regular pockets and two bill folds, one side of which is secured by flap and tuck. Size, 3¾x8 inches. **One of the most durable and best books made.**
Price, each....55c
If by mail, postage extra, each, 6 cents.

No. 18R2735 The Secret Pocket Billbooks. Kid faced and canvas lined; fine morocco grained leather, three large, two small, and one secret burglar proof pocket; finely made and finished throughout. Size, 3¼x8 inches. Price, each..50c
If by mail, postage extra, each, 5 cents.

$1.50 Value for 89 Cents.

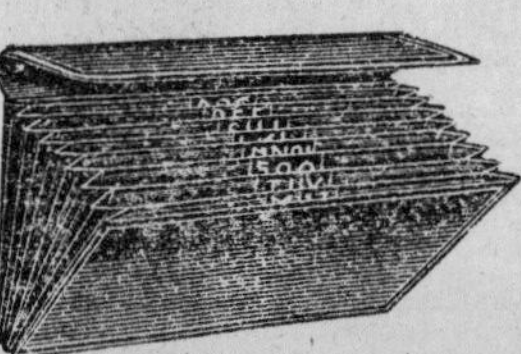

No. 18R2737 Extra Fine Morocco Grain Leather Billbook. Eight large pockets alphabetically indexed, also seven smaller pockets for bills and currency; leather faced and canvas lined. **Specially adapted for collectors and as a deposit for notes and bills.** Large size, 4¼x10 inches. Price, each...........89c
If by mail, postage extra, each, 12 cents.

Ladies' Belts.

No. 18R2789 Ladies' Double Faced Patent Leather Scoop Back Belt. New fancy point shaped in back, trimmed with six small gilt buttons; black enameled harness buckle; a pretty belt. Sizes, 22 to 30 inches. Price, each...........15c
If by mail, postage extra, 4 cents.

No. 18R2792 Ladies' Shaped Patent Leather Belt. Stitched on both sides, with ooze leather back, giving it three-fold strength as well as fine finish. Nickel harness buckle. Sizes, 22 to 30 inches.
Price, each...................................25c
If by mail, postage extra, 4 cents.

No. 18R2796 Ladies' Fancy Cable Ribbed All Silk Elastic Belt. With fancy dip buckle in gilt or oxidized, with turquoise setting. Black only. Price, each...............................47c
If by mail, postage extra, 3 cents.

No. 18R2798 Ladies' Black Silk Belts. Good quality 2-inch silk belting, with entirely new design buckles. Sizes, 22 to 36 inches. Price, each.................30c
If by mail, postage extra, 4 cents.

Genuine Calfskin Belt.

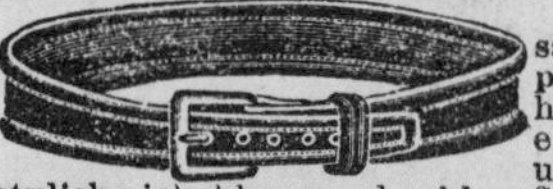

No. 18R2800 Dull satin finish. A soft, pliable leather belt, hand turned, cord edge. Guaranteed unbreakable. A very stylish nickel harness buckle. Sizes, 22 to 30 inches. Black only. Price, each...............................46c
If by mail, postage extra, 4 cents.

The Arabella Velvet Belt.

No. 18R2804 Rich appearing. Trimmed in back with twenty cut steel studs, mercerized lining and pretty nickel harness buckle. A very stylish, dainty belt. Width, 1⅞ inches. Sizes, 22 to 30 inches. Price, each........50c
If by mail, postage extra, 4 cents.

Mercerized Tucked Belts.

No. 18R2808 With fancy dip buckles in either gold or oxidized. Width in back, 2⅞ inches. A pretty and shapely belt, Black only. Sizes, 22 to 32 inches. Price, each...........................25c
If by mail, postage extra, 4 cents.

Tucked Satin Belt.

No. 18R2812 Made of good quality satin with a pretty dip shaped stone set buckle. Settings may be had in amethyst or turquoise. Width in back, 2⅞ inches. A very dressy, form fitting belt. Black only. Sizes, 22 to 30 inches. Price, each..........47c
If by mail, postage extra, 4 cents.

Shaped Taffeta Silk Belt.

No. 18R2816 Three and one-half inches wide, with fancy dip front ornamented buckle. The back is boned with featherbone, fits snugly to the figure in graceful folds and is exceedingly pretty. Black only. Sizes, 22 to 30 inches.
Price, each...................................49c
If by mail, postage extra, 4 cents.

Fancy Brocaded All Silk Ribbon Belts.

No. 18R2820 Drapes and sets closely to the waist, with large heavy silk porthole fastenings for buckles in front. This is a very stylish and attractive belt. Width of ribbon, 3½ inches. Sizes, 22 to 30 inches. Price, each........50c
If by mail, postage extra, 4 cents.

Ladies' Vassar Back or Neck Comb.

No. 18R3006 Vassar Back or Neck Comb, with the turn over flap to hold the stray locks, highly polished imitation tortoise shell. Width, 3¾ inches. Regular 20-cent value. Price, each.............10c
If by mail, postage extra, each, 2 cents.

No. 18R3010 Vassar Back Comb, with the turn over flap which catches the stray locks and holds them fast; imitation tortoise shell, very highly polished and round finished teeth. Width, 4⅛ inches. Each....25c
If by mail, postage extra, each, 3 cents.

No. 18R3014 Vassar Back or Neck Comb. Highly polished, exact imitation of the real tortoise, with the turn over flap to hold stray locks; flap is ornamented with nineteen brilliant rhinestone settings, finished round teeth. A very superior and stylish ornament. Price, each...... ....44c
If by mail, postage extra, each, 3 cents.

No. 18R3018 Fancy Vassar Back or Neck Comb. Highly polished, imitation of the real tortoise shell, with the flap for holding stray locks; flap is ornamented with five large baroque pearls which look just as well as the genuine. A very elegant comb. Width, 4¾ inches. Price, each... ....42c
If by mail, postage extra, each, 3 cents.

LADIES' JEWELED POMPADOUR COMBS.

Turquoise Setting.

No. 18R3021 Ladies' Jeweled Pompadour Comb. Imitation tortoise shell, handsomely mounted with twenty-eight turquoise in gilt setting. The latest, most stylish and aristocratically designed comb on the market.
Price, each.......................................29c
If by mail, postage extra, each, 5 cents.

Pearl Setting.

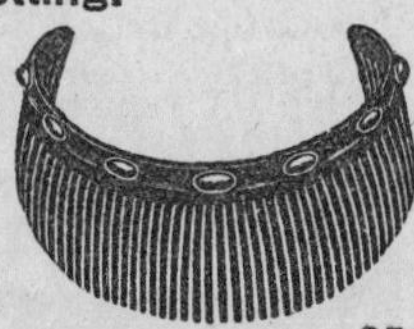

No. 18R3022 Pearl Jeweled Pompadour Comb. Imitation of the tortoise shell, highly polished, ornamented with seven baroque pearls, set in gold rim mountings, which are extremely stylish. The comb is a regular 50-cent value.
Our special price...... ....25c
If by mail, postage extra, each, 5 cents.

Rhinestone Setting.

No. 18R3024 Ladies' Jeweled Pompadour Comb. Imitation tortoise shell, set with forty-two brilliant rhinestones, very closely set, durable as well as handsome. This same quality comb is retailed at 50c. Very high grade. Price, each..25c
If by mail, postage extra, each, 5 cents.

No. 18R3026 Ladies' Jeweled Pompadour Comb. Similar to No. 18R3024, but a heavier comb. Imitation tortoise shell and very closely set with forty-two fine quality brilliant rhinestones.
Price, each.......................................38c
If by mail, postage extra, each, 5 cents.

Imitation Tortoise Shell.

No. 18R3028 Celluloid Pompadour Comb. Imitation tortoise shell, used to produce a puffy pompadour effect, and is inserted with the teeth of comb to the front, or to the back. Price, each, 15c
If by mail, postage extra, each, 5 cents.

No. 18R3030 Celluloid Pompadour Comb, same style as above but much heavier and longer teeth.
Price, each.......................................22c
If by mail, postage extra, each, 5 cents.

Ladies' Hair Lock Retainers.

No. 18R3032 Gold Plated Hair Lock Retainers. Round shaped, 1⅛x1⅛ inches. Sold elsewhere at 10 cents.
Price, each.......................5c

No. 18R3038 Gold Plated Hair Lock Retainers. High grade burnished and lacquered, and will not tarnish. The 25-cent quality at the jewelers'.
Price, each.......................................10c

No. 18R3039 Imitation Tortoise Shell Hair Lock Retainer. On long curved shape two inches long, mounted with gilt knobs, arranged as shown in cut. Price, each..............10c
If by mail, postage extra, 2 cents.

New Hair Barrettes.

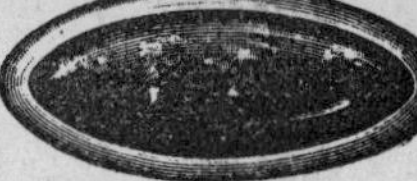

No. 18R3042 Hair Lock Retainer for back of head. Something new and elegant. The center is a large turquoise setting with rim of highly polished imitation tortoise shell. This will be admired by everybody. Length, 1½ inches.
Price, each.......................................15c
If by mail, postage extra, each, 2 cents.

Hair Lock Retainer.

No. 18R3044 Same as above, with large turquoise setting and imitation tortoise shell rim. Length, 2 inches. Price, each..................20c
If by mail, postage extra, each, 2 cents.

Child's Celluloid Round Combs.

No. 18R3046 Is a Child's Celluloid Round Comb. Comes in imitation tortoise shell. A regular 15-cent comb.
Price, each.......................6c
If by mail, postage extra, each, 4 cents.

Children's Good Quality Round Combs.

No. 18R3048 Beautiful Unbreakable Circular Rubber Comb, like cut. One dozen round combs in a box. Weight, about 10 ounces. Price, each......6c
If by mail, postage extra, each, 4 cents.

Curling Irons.

Prices we quote on Curling Irons should be quite an item to you. We have all kinds, all sizes; save you just one-half on regular purchase prices.

No. 18R3052 Is made of polished steel; polished wood handle, medium size for general use. 7½ inches long. Price, each.............3c
If by mail, postage extra, each, 4 cents.

Mustache Curlers.

No. 18R3056 Duke Mustache Curler. Polished steel, nickel plated, antique oak handles. Length, 6 inches. Price, each..........................3c
If by mail, postage extra, each, 4 cents.

Tourist Folding Curling Iron.

No. 18R3060 The Tourist Folding Curling Iron, Made of polished steel, oak handles. Can be placed in such a position that iron can be heated over lamp chimney without holding iron.
Price, each.......................................5c
Shipping weight, 4 ounces.

No. 18R3064 Little Princess Medium Size Curler. Same style as the Duke above. Length, 7¾ inches. Price, each.............................4c
If by mail, postage extra, each, 4 cents.

Curling Iron.

No. 18R3072 Thelma Curling Iron. Made of fine polished steel, handsomely nickel plated, polished rosewood handles. A very fine curler. Length, 8½ inches.
Shipping weight, 4 ounces. Price, each..........7c

Waving Iron.

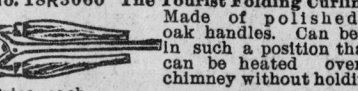

No. 18R3076 5-Prong Waving Iron, for waving the hair, made of good quality metal.
Price, each.......................................11c
If by mail, postage extra, each, 9 cents.

COMBS.

No. 18R4008 Horn Dressing Combs, 7 inches long. Nickel plated backs. Price, each....................6c
If by mail, postage extra, each, 4 cents.

No. 18R4009 Hard Rubber Dressing Comb. Neatly curved back, coarse and fine teeth. Length, 7 inches. Price, each..4c
If by mail, postage extra, 4 cents.

No. 18R4010 Strong, Hard Rubber Dressing Comb. Heavy square back, rounded teeth, coarse and fine. Length, 8 inches, Price, each..10c
If by mail, postage extra, 4 cents.

No. 18R4011 Hard Rubber Dressing Comb. With fancy carved back; coarse and fine teeth. Length, 8 inches. Usually retailed at 25 cents. Price, each.......................................14c
If by mail, postage extra, 4 cents.

COMBS—Continued.

No. 18R4013 Fancy Rope Back Hard Rubber Dressing Comb. Well finished, coarse and fine teeth. Length, 8 inches. A 30-cent comb.
Price, each.......................................19c
If by mail, postage extra, 4 cents.

No. 18R4015 Hard Rubber Dressing Comb. Same size and design as No. 18R4013, but all coarse teeth; extra heavy and well rounded. Length, 8 inches. Price, each.........................19c
If by mail, postage extra, 4 cents.

No. 18R4017 Very Substantial Hard Rubber Dressing Comb. Heavy curved kangaroo shaped back, well finished coarse and fine teeth; will not irritate the scalp; exceptional value.
Price, each... ....24c
If by mail, postage extra, 4 cents.

No. 18R4019 Extra Heavy Square Back Hard Rubber Dressing Comb. Hand sawed, round finished, coarse and fine teeth; will not injure the hair. Length, 9 inches. Usually retailed for 50 cents.
Price, each.......................................33c
If by mail, postage extra, 4 cents.

No. 18R4021 Extra Heavy Square Back Hard Rubber Dressing Comb. All coarse teeth; especially adapted for long, heavy hair; makes hair dressing a pleasure. Length, 9 inches. Price, each.........................33c
If by mail, postage extra, 4 cents.

No. 18R4023 Hard Rubber Dressing Comb. With handle, giving extra purchase on comb; all coarse teeth, just the thing for heavy and thick hair. Price, each............................30c
If by mail, postage extra, 4 cents

No. 18R4025 Superior Quality Hard Rubber Barbers' Comb. Coarse and fine teeth. Length, 6½ inches. Price, each.......................................5c
If by mail, postage extra, 4 cents.

No. 18R4027 Extra Super Quality Hard Rubber Barbers' Comb. With graduated coarse and fine teeth. A genteel comb for gentlemen. Length, 7¼ inches. Price, each...10c
If by mail, postage extra, 4 cents.

Tortoise Shell Barbers' Comb.

No. 18R4029 This Pretty Imitation Tortoise Shell Celluloid Barbers' Comb (gentleman's comb), 7 inches long, is really worth 25 cents. Price, each........10c
If by mail, postage extra, each, 4 cents.

Rubber Fine Combs.

No. 18R4031 Hard Rubber Fine Tooth Comb. Fine teeth on both sides, as shown in cut. Size, 3x1⅝ inches. Price, each...............4c
If by mail, postage extra, 4 cents.

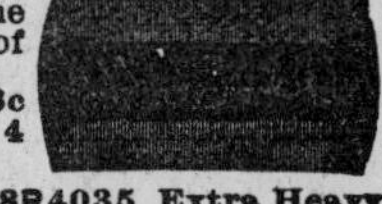

No. 18R4033 Hard Rubber Fine Comb. With curved fine teeth to conform to shape of head. Size, 4x2 inches.
Price, each.....................8c
If by mail, postage extra, 4 cents.

No. 18R4035 Extra Heavy Hard Rubber Fine Tooth Comb. Curved teeth, very durable and substantial comb. Size, 4⅛x2½ inches.
Price, each...............24c
If by mail, postage extra, 4 cents.

Our 25-Cent Ladies' Ebonite Dressing Comb.

No. 18R4071 The Handsome Ebonite Dressing Comb shown in above illustration is decorated with handsome sterling silver trimmings, as shown. The length of the comb is 6¾ inches, is excellent quality, such a comb as seldom retails less than 40 to 50 cents.
Our special price, each 25c
If by mail, postage extra, 4 cents.

Our 25-Cent Gents' Ebonite Dressing Comb.

No. 18R4075 This illustration shows Gents' Ebonite Dressing Comb. It is sterling silver trimmed, is 7 inches long, and is a very neat and desirable present.
Our special price, each.......................................25c
If by mail, postage extra, 3 cents.

Celluloid Combs.

Nothing is nicer than combs made of celluloid; pretty to look at and they are serviceable, too. Our prices are away below the retailers' cost.

No. 18R4084 A 7-inch White Celluloid Dressing Comb. Regular retail price, 25 cents. Each...9c

No. 18R4088 The same Comb as described above, in amber. Retailers ask 25 to 30 cents. Each. ...9c

If by mail, postage extra, each, 2 cents.

Celluloid Amber Dressing Comb for 12c.

No. 18R4092 A Beautiful 7½-Inch Beaded Back Celluloid Amber Dressing Comb. Coarse and fine teeth. Druggists ask as high as 35 cents for these combs. Price, each. .(If by mail, postage extra, 2c)...12c

White Celluloid Dressing Comb.

No. 18R4096 A Very Handsome 7½-inch Rope Back White Celluloid Dressing Comb. Good heavy weight. This comb is easily worth 40 cents. Price, each...19c

If by mail, postage extra, each, 2 cents.

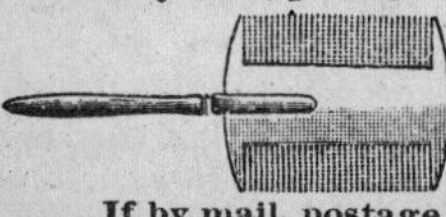

No. 18R4100 Infants' Celluloid Fine Combs. With handle. Full length 4½ inches. Colors, white, shell, or amber. Price, each...6c

If by mail, postage extra, each, 2 cents.

No. 18R4104 Infants' White Ivory Fine Combs. With handle, same as above. Full length, 4¼ inches. Price, each.. .(If by mail, postage extra, 2c)...9c

Best Aluminum Combs.

No. 18R4108 Aluminum Barber Combs. Coarse and fine teeth. 7 inches long. The best thing for the hair. Price, each...6c

If by mail, postage extra, each, 2 cents.

Ladies' Aluminum Combs.

No. 18R4116 Aluminum Dressing Comb. Coarse and fine teeth. Length, 7½ inches; width, 1½ inches. Regular 25-cent comb. Price, each...9c

If by mail, postage extra, each, 2 cents.

Ladies' Toilet Comb.

No. 18R4120 Ladies' Toilet Comb. With handle, satin finish aluminum, nicely engraved, 8 inches long and 1⅝ inches wide. All coarse teeth. Price, each....(If by mail, postage extra, 3c)...23c

Gents' Dressing Combs.

No. 18R4124 Gents' Dressing Comb. Satin finish aluminum fancy engraved. Coarse and fine teeth. Length, 7½ inches; width, 1 inch. Price, each....12c

If by mail, postage extra, each, 2 cents.

No. 18R4128 Aluminum Dressing Comb. With fancy engraved back. Length, 7⅛ inches; width, 1⅜ inches. Especially filed and finished teeth. Usually retailed at 50 cents. Price, each...15c

If by mail, postage extra, each, 2 cents.

No. 18R4131 Exceptionally Neat and Substantial Hard Rubber Pocket Comb. Coarse and fine teeth, in neat leatheroid case, 4 inches long. Price, each....(If by mail, postage extra, 4c)....5c

No. 18R4135 Extra Heavy Square Back Hard Rubber Pocket Comb. Coarse and fine teeth in leatheroid case; a very convenient article. Length, 4½ inches. Price, each...(If by mail, postage extra, 4c)...10c

Aluminum Pocket Combs.

No. 18R4140 Aluminum Pocket Comb. Fine and coarse teeth. 5 inches long. Straight backed. Durable and will not tarnish. Each..(If by mail, postage extra, ea., 2c).4c

Celluloid Pocket Combs.

No. 18R4144 Celluloid Pocket Comb in case, 3½ inches long. Regular retail price, 20 cents. Each....(If by mail, postage extra, each, 2c)....8c

ALL of our Wood Back Hair Brushes

From the cheapest number up, are made of one solid piece of wood. (Solid Back Hair Brushes.) Most hair brushes are made of two pieces of wood glued together, which, when wet, warp and come apart. **A Solid Back Hair Brush will outwear three ordinary hair brushes.** We sell our solid back hair brushes at less than the price usually asked for ordinary goods. **Remember that a solid back hair brush will last two or three times as long as an ordinary brush.** Hair brushes weigh from 6 to 8 ounces. Postage on hair brushes about 6 to 8 cents.

Fine Imported Infants' Hair Brushes.

No. 18R4148 Imported Fine White Goat Infants' Hair Brush; also suitable for ladies' toilet powder. Each...22c

If by mail, postage extra, each, 3 cents.

Our 7-Cent Hair Brush.

No. 18R4152 Is a Seven-Row Hair Brush, made of mixed stock — a brush that usually retails for 15 cents. Price, each 7c

If by mail, postage extra, each, 4 cents.

A 25-Cent Brush for 12 Cents.

No. 18R4156 A Medium Sized Round Back Hair Brush. Black Russian bristles; would be considered good value at 25 cents. Price, each..12c

If by mail, postage extra, each, 4 cents.

Special Value for 21 Cents.

No. 18R4164 A Good, Durable, 13-row Hair Brush, with a dark center bristle, large size, oval back of solid boxwood, **particularly adapted for family use.** This brush never retails for less than 50 cents. Price, each...21c

If by mail, postage extra, each, 10 cents.

Russian Bristle Hair Brushes.

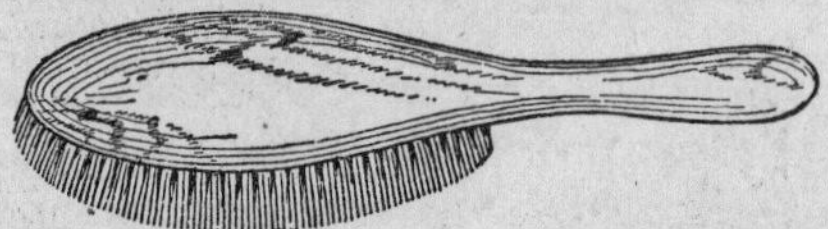

No. 18R4168 This Handsome Brush is made of nine rows of white Russian bristle, oval back, nicely polished, solid back. Price, each...35c

If by mail, postage extra, each, 7 cents.

No. 18R4172 This is a handsome 11-row fine dark Russian bristle, solid back, oval shape, mahogany wood, highly polished. Good 75-cent value. Price, each...47c

If by mail, postage extra, each, 7 cents.

Wire Hair Brushes.

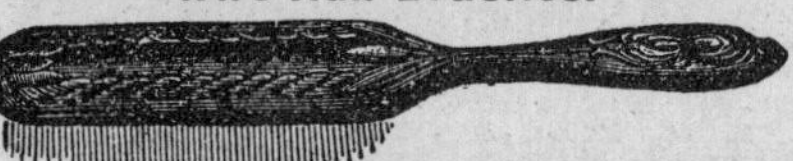

No. 18R4176 Small Size Metallic Wire Hair Brush; polished wood backs. Price, each....... . 7c

If by mail, postage extra, each, 5 cents.

No. 18R4180 10-Row Metallic Wire Hair Brush, straight or twist handles, nicely polished and decorated backs. Price, each...17c

If by mail, postage extra, each, 7 cents.

Florence Rubber Back Hair Brush.

No. 18R4184 The Florence Rubber Back Black Bristle Hair Brush. Easy to clean, nice to use. Value, 40 cents. Our price, each...18c

If by mail, postage extra, each, 8 cents.

Square Shaped Florence Hair Brush.

No. 18R4186 The back is made of a black composition with fancy embossed design; has 11 rows of medium length fine white best penetrating Russian bristles. A very substantial and durable brush. Size, 8¾x2⅜ inches. Price, each...41c

If by mail, postage extra, each, 9 cents.

This is a Genuine Siberian Bristle Brush, with a single bristle substituted for the ordinary tuft, the bristle being set in an **elastic air-cushioned base.** This construction enables it to penetrate the most luxuriant growth of hair without effort. It also prevents the possibility of injuring the hair or scalp. It will effectively remove dandruff without irritating the scalp. **It is clean, light and durable.**

No. 18R4192 Medium size, oak wood back.....69c

No. 18R4196 Large size, oak wood back.......88c

If by mail, postage extra, 3 cents.

Keep Clean Hair Brush.

No. 18R4198 This is a Large Sized Oval Shaped Black Ivory Finished Hair Brush, with fifteen rows of medium sized black pure bristles; the bristles being set in pure aluminum, which is waterproof and very easy to keep clean. This is the best brush made and cannot become foul by absorbing the water, oil and dirt like an ordinary brush. Size, 9¾x3¼ inches. Price, each...46c

If by mail, postage extra, each, 8 cents.

Beauty Brush for the Complexion.

No. 18R4200 It is especially constructed for improving the complexion. It removes **all roughness and dead cuticle, smoothing out the wrinkles, rendering the skin soft, pliant, and tinted with a healthy glow.** It is made of rubber—round, flexible, flattened end, tiny teeth taking the place of bristles. Removes wrinkles like magic. For physical development it is recommended by the highest in the profession for improving the circulation, exercising the muscles, and promoting a healthy action of the skin. Price, each...38c

If by mail, postage extra, each, 2 cents.

Flesh and Bath Brushes.

No. 18R4204 A Seven-Row Bath Brush, straight handle, white and black bristles, made of one solid piece of wood. Cannot split or warp when wet. Price, each......18c

If by mail, postage extra, each, 10 cents.

No. 18R4212 A very fine Six-Row Russian Bristle Bath Brush. Black and white bristles. Length of brush, 19 inches. Made of one solid piece of wood. Price, each....37c

If by mail, postage extra, each, 10 cents.

No. 18R4216 An Excellent Flesh Brush. 5½ inches long, with strap. Can be used dry or in the bath. Price, each...19c

If by mail, postage extra, each, 7c.

Bath Brush With Detachable Handle.

No. 18R4220 A Nine-Row All Bristle Bath Brush, with detachable handle; length of brush with handle attached, 16 inches. This brush has a strap, and when handle is detached, can be used dry as a friction brush. Price, each...74c

If by mail, postage extra, each, 15 cents.

Hand Brushes.

No. 18R4228 A Nicely Finished Six-Row Hand Brush, oval back, nicely polished. Price, each...5c

If by mail, postage extra, each, 3 cents.

SEE PAGE 21 FOR FINE

Toilet Soaps

AT LOWEST PRICES.

Cloth and Clothes Brushes.

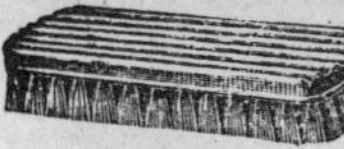

No. 18R4232 A Good Six-Row Cloth or Clothes Brush, black and white, solid fluted back, mixed stock, 8x2½ inches. Good value at 15 cents. Price, each.....9c
If by mail, postage extra, each, 7 cents.

No. 18R4236 A Very Fine Cloth Brush, made of black and white Russian bristles, nicely polished red wood backs. Price, each.....19c
If by mail, postage extra, each, 10 cents.

A 75-Cent Brush for 34 Cents.

No. 18R4240 This is an actual 75-cent brush, made of extra long pure gray bristles, solid rosewood, fancy curved back, a very serviceable brush. Price, each.....34c
If by mail, postage extra, each, 8 cents.

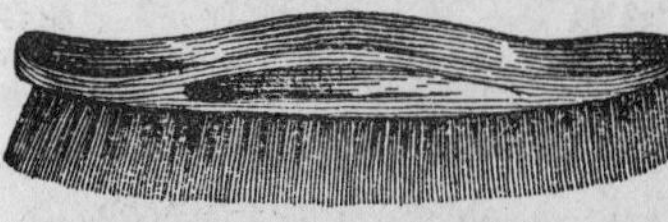

No. 18R4244 A Regular $1.00 Cloth Brush, made of very fine black Russian bristles, fancy curved rosewood back one solid piece, nicely polished. Size, 8½x2 inches. Price, each...39c
If by mail, postage extra, each, 8 cents.

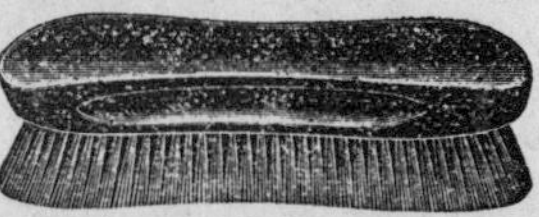

No. 18R4246 Cloth Brush, fancy shape back of one solid piece highly polished rosewood, mahogany finish, with long white pure Russian bristles, closely set. A brush retailed for $1.25; splendid value. Price, each.....68c
If by mail, postage extra, each, 7 cents.

Our Highest Grade Genuine Ebony Toilet Articles.

No. 18R4247 Genuine African Ebony Hair Brush, best quality of imported bristle, handsome sterling silver mounting, colonial design. Price, each.....94c
If by mail, postage extra, each, 7 cents.

No. 18R4249 Real Ebony Hair Brush, smaller size than above, with solid sterling silver mountings, finest quality imported bristle. A brush retailed at your jeweler's for $1.25. Our special price, each..64c
If by mail, postage extra, each, 7 cents.

No. 18R4251 Real Ebony Hair Brush; our highest grade brush; an 11-row finest long Russian bristle, particularly adapted for ladies' use, with large solid sterling silver mounting. Good $1.50 value. Price, each.....99c
If by mail, postage extra, each, 7 cents.

No. 18R4253 Genuine Ebony Military Brush, eleven rows fine white imported bristle, handsome sterling silver mountings; a brush that will give service and last a lifetime. The price has always been more than the average buyer wished to pay. Our price puts them within reach of all. Price, each.....72c
If by mail, postage extra, each, 6 cents.

No. 18R4255 Real Ebony Finest Quality Military Hair Brush; grooved back, an eleven-row fine Russian bristle, handsome sterling silver mounting. For real goodness can't be excelled. Price, each $1.09
If by mail, postage extra, each, 6 cents.

No. 18R4256 Finest Ebony Cloth Brush, for ladies or gentlemen, handsome sterling silver mounted, fine imported white bristle, regular $1.50 value. Price, each.....94c
If by mail, postage extra, each, 7 cents.

No. 18R4257 Real Ebony Velvet Brush, with long white imported bristle, for hats and fine cloth, a beautiful present for either ladies or gentlemen, genuine sterling silver mounted. Special value. Price, each.....77c
If by mail, postage extra, each, 7 cents.

Special Values in Fine Comb and Brush Sets.

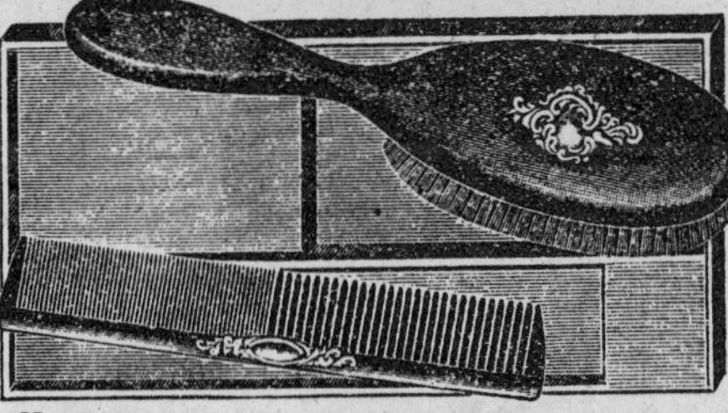

No. 18R4261 This Handsome Ebony Brush and Comb Set is trimmed with sterling silver mountings. The brush is of real ebony, and the comb is ebonized imitation of the real. Strictly high grade, and put up in a nice neat box. Worth double our price. Price, per set complete.....88c
Shipping weight, 12 ounces.

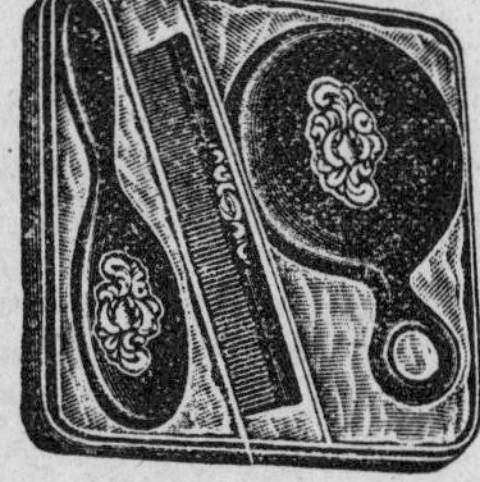

No. 18R4263 This Elegant Toilet Set consists of hair brush, ring hand mirror and comb, all handsomely mounted with sterling silver mountings, as shown in illustration. The brush and mirror are the ebonized wood in imitation of the real ebony. This set complete at the price we offer is a wonderful bargain. Nicely put up in white enameled paper box. Price, per set complete.....$1.68
Shipping weight, 35 ounces.

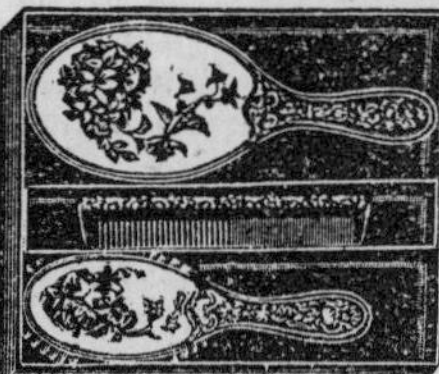

No. 18R4267 This Beautiful Toilet Set consists of mirror, brush and comb, all silver finished; handsome hand decorated porcelain backs, with metal embossed mountings. The mirror has a heavy beveled plate glass, the brush is a fine 11-row bristle, and the comb is a 7-inch shell. Price, per set, complete..(Shipping weight, 50 ounces)...$1.98

Traveling Sets.

No. 18R4268 Consisting of genuine ebony hair brush, nail and tooth brush, with imitation ebony comb, all put up in a fine seal grained leather case, with sterling silver mountings on same. Price, per set, complete....99c
Shipping weight, 16 ounces.

Our $1.79 Value.

No. 18R4269 Traveling Set, consisting of celluloid hair brush, tooth brush and comb and nickel soap box. All put up in a handsome seal grained leather case, with mirror on the case. Price, per set, complete.....$1.79
Shipping weight, 18 ounces.

Our $2.99 Traveling Set.

No. 18R4272 Genuine Black Seal Grained Leather Traveling Case. Lined with tan color seal grained leather. Containing one pair of high grade quality, genuine ebony solid back military brushes; mounted with sterling silver name plates. Good quality bristles in brushes. Case fastens with glove snap fastener. Regular $5.00 value. Price, per set, $2.99
Shipping weight, 20 ounces.

No. 18R4276 Fine Ebonized Hand Mirror, looks just as nice as real ebony, with fine beveled edge mirror, 5-inch glass, heavy sterling silver nameplate on back. This would be considered good value at $1.00. Our price, each.....56c
Shipping weight, 18 oz.

No. 18R4277 Genuine Ebony Hand Mirror. Ring shaped, same as above. Very heavy French plate mirror, with beveled edges. Heavily mounted with sterling silver on back. Regular retail price, $2.25. Our price, each.....$1.59
Shipping weight, 30 ounces.

Fine Toilet Mirrors at Small Cost.

No. 18R4278 Beautiful Toilet Mirrors. Square or round design. Made of carefully selected woods—oak, sycamore cherry, mahogany or maple, finished to a high piano polish, fitted with finest beveled French plate mirrors, either oval or square design. Made to stand on dresser or to hang up. Very desirable for a shaving mirror. This quality of mirrors never before sold for less than $2.50. Size, 5½x7½ inches. Price, each.....93c
Shipping weight, 26 ounces.

Florence Hand Mirrors.

No. 18R4290 A Fine Rubber Back Hand Mirror, back length of glass and handle combined, 10 inches; good, clear glass. Price, each.....18c
Shipping weight, 14 ounces.

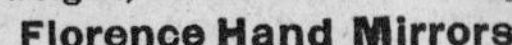

No. 18R4294 A Beautiful Beveled Glass Rubber Back Hand Mirror, black. Length, 9 inches. This is a regular 50-cent mirror. Price, each...21c
Shipping weight, 14 ounces.

No. 18R4295 Embossed Calf Leather Toilet Case, with French plate beveled mirror. The case contains shell pocket comb, nail, ear and tooth picks, lined with moire grosgrain silk with silk leaflet between glass and toilet articles. Size, 4x2⅜ inches. Price...42c
If by mail, postage extra, each, 4 cents.

Pocket Toilet Case.

No. 18R4298 Pocket Toilet Case, vest pocket size. (Cut shows it open.) Contains beveled mirror, celluloid comb and nail pick, case handsomely covered with Russia leather; valuable companion. Price, each.....16c
If by mail, postage extra, each, 5 cents.

Comb and Case.

No. 18R4302 Pocket Toilet Case. Highly polished horn comb; length, 5 inches. Put up in neat case with small mirror, as per illustration. Price (If by mail, postage extra, each, 2 cents) 4c

Celluloid Soap Boxes.

No. 18R4303 Celluloid Soap Boxes, white. Sizes, 3¼x2¼ inches. Price, each.....23c

No. 18R4304 Same as above, in amber and colors. Retailers get 50 cents for these boxes. Each.....34c
If by mail, postage extra, each, 6 cents.

No. 18R4305 Black Ebonized Celluloid Soap Box, with heavy sterling silver name plate to match the ebony sets and brushes. Price, each.....63c
If by mail, postage extra, 4 cents.

Perfume Atomizers.

No. 18R4313 Perfume Atomizer. New special shape; hand decorations. Thoroughly tested rubber bulb, with gold mounting. Shipping weight, 16 ounces. Price, each.....25c

No. 18R4315 Perfume Atomizer. Neat hand decorations. Thoroughly tested bulb, covered with silk net. The bottle rests on gilt stand. This usually retails at 75 cents. Shipping weight, 18 ounces. Our special price.....50c

No. 18R4316 This Pretty Perfume Atomizer is an entirely new and original design. The decorations are unique and handsome. Gold top and thoroughly tested rubber bulb, covered with silk net. $1.25 value. Shipping weight, 25 ounces. Price, each...78c

No. 18R4317 This is our highest grade Perfume Atomizer. Real cut glass, with handsome hand decorations in white and gold. The bottle rests on a gilt stand. Thoroughly tested bulb, covered with silk net. Shipping weight, 22 ounces. Price, each....98c

WE SELL MORE HAIR GOODS THAN ANY FIVE HOUSES IN THE COUNTRY.

WE IMPORT our hair from Europe in large quantities. It is bought for cash and we make up our switches, wigs, bangs, waves, etc., in the best manner possible, naming a price to you based on the actual cost to produce with but our one small percentage of profit added. **The enormous profit that has heretofore been charged by other concerns has made it impossible for many to own a nice switch,** but on our basis of one small profit above the actual cost to produce in quantities, a price which comes within the reach of all, we have established a trade in this line which excels in volume the business of any other five houses in America combined. **We guarantee every switch and every article of hair goods from this department.** If you buy a hair switch or any other article of hair goods and you do not find it exactly as represented and perfectly satisfactory in every way **you can return it to us within thirty days at our expense and we will cheerfully refund your money.**

HOW TO ORDER. **Enclose the necessary amount with your order, with five cents extra added to pay postage. Send us a good sized sample of hair cut as close to the roots as possible so** we can give you a perfect match. We will then send you the switch you select by mail, postage prepaid. **We will guarantee it to match perfectly and to be in every way satisfactory or we will immediately refund your money.** All our switches are made in three braids with the exception of the two-ounce twenty-inch which we price at 50 cents. This switch has a long stem, the balance quoted all having short stems. We would recommend that you order one of our short stem switches, **which costs but a trifle more and is more satisfactory.**

WE DO NOT GUARANTEE HAIR SWITCHES AGAINST FADING.

You will know from your own experience that even the hair on the head will change color. Any good hair switch will fade in time, and the length of time a switch holds its color depends largely on the care it receives. If with this understanding you do not feel like keeping the switch, **you are at liberty to return it to us and we will refund your money,** provided the switch is returned to us within thirty days from date of purchase.

N. B.—No grease or oil should be used on a switch. If your switch should begin to turn in color, we would suggest that you wash same in cold tea, which is very beneficial and darkens the color. As all switches are made special to order, you must allow from five to eight days to fill your order, but we often ship them within three days. **Be sure and send a good sized sample and allow five cents extra for postage.**

NOTE OUR FOLLOWING SPECIAL PRICES:

No. 18R4370 Prices for ordinary shades of hair switches:

Weight	Length	Price, each
Weight, 2 ounces	length, 20 inches	$0.50
Weight, 2 ounces	length, 20 inches	.75
Weight, 2 ounces	length, 22 inches	1.00
Weight, 3 ounces	length, 22 inches	1.19
Weight, 3 ounces	length, 24 inches	1.59
Weight, 3½ ounces	length, 26 inches	2.39
Weight, 4 ounces	length, 28 inches	3.65

The above 50-cent switch is long stem. All other switches are short stem. We advise you to buy the short stem switch and especially those quoted at $1 00 and upwards.

No. 18R4374 Gray Mixed, Red or Blonde Hair Switches are extra in price. They are made of a fine quality of hair, short stem, and finest workmanship. Prices as follows:

Weight	Length	Price, each
Weight, 2 ounces	length, 18 inches	$1.40
Weight, 2¼ ounces	length, 22 inches	2.25
Weight, 3 ounces	length, 23 inches	2.90
Weight, 3 ounces	length, 25 inches	4.25
Weight, 3½ ounces	length, 27 inches	6.95

PRICES FOR ALL WHITE OR NEARLY ALL WHITE HAIR SWITCHES.

No. 18R4375

Weight	Length	Price, each
Weight, 2 ounces	length, 20 inches	$2.10
Weight, 2¼ ounces	length, 22 inches	3.35
Weight, 3 ounces	length, 23 inches	4.25
Weight, 3 ounces	length, 25 inches	5.75
Weight, 3½ ounces	length, 27 inches	8.75

PRICES FOR NATURAL WAVY SWITCHES.

No. 18R4377 Best quality French hair, made on short stems.

Weight	Length	Price, each
Weight, 1½ ounces	length, 20 inches	$2.25
Weight, 2 ounces	length, 22 inches	4.25
Weight, 2½ ounces	length, 24 inches	5.65
Weight, 2¾ ounces	length, 26 inches	6.75

Gray and blonde shades will cost 50 per cent more than the above prices.

WAVES, BANGS AND WIGS.

All Wigs, Toupees, Waves, etc., being made to order, we ask three to four days' time in filling your order, and we require cash in full with order as on all other merchandise, guaranteeing satisfaction or refund of money.

BE SURE AND SEND A GOOD SIZED SAMPLE OF HAIR.

No. 18R4378 Melba Bang. Made of the best quality naturally curly hair, with vegetable lace parting, most suitable for youthful faces and a very popular style of hair dressing. Each $1.50
Gray and blonde hair, each 2.50
If by mail, postage extra, each, 5 cents.

Parisian Bang.

No. 18R4382 Parisian Bang. Ladies who do not require large, heavy front, will find this a little gem; light and fluffy, ventilated foundation.
Price, each..... $1.35
Gray and blonde hair, each $2.00
If by mail, postage extra, each, 5 cents.

Alice Wave.

No. 18R4386 Alice Wave, invisible hair lace; foundation natural, curly hair; 3-inch part, 12 inches from side to side. Price, each.......... $3.25
Gray and blonde hair. Price, each 4.50
If by mail, postage extra, each, 6 cents.

The Pompadour.

No. 18R4390 The Pompadour. This style, unlike the old style pompadour, is very light in weight. The soft wavy hair is combed over one's own hair in which small rolls of crape hair are placed to produce a puffy effect on sides and top.
Price, each.......... $3.50
Gray and blonde hair, each 5.00
If by mail, postage extra, each, 6 cents.

The Patent Pompadour.

No. 18R4394 The Patent Pompadour for simplicity, elegance and style is far superior to anything ever shown. It slips right on, is as dainty as a feminine heart could desire; it produces the fluffy fullness now so much in vogue and possesses none of the disagreeable qualities of the ordinary roll or pad. It is made on twisted wire, of the best long, curly hair and weighs only half an ounce. Can be worn with just the ends concealed under the lady's own hair, or may be used in place of the rolls and the wavy ends coiled in with the natural hair. **Send sample of hair.** Price, each.......... $1.50
If by mail, postage extra, each, 6 cents.

The Eugenia Wave.

No. 18R4398 The Eugenia Wave. This is a new and very becoming wave for middle aged and elderly ladies, made of the best quality natural curly French hair; easily dressed and cared for; 3½-inch parting.
Price, each... $4.00
Gray and blonde hair, each..... $6.00
If by mail, postage extra, each, 8 cents.

Ladies' Wigs—Short Hair.

Send measurement of head.

These wigs are all made of fine selected hair on ventilated open mesh foundation. Absolutely perfect in fit, having that graceful and natural appearance.

Short Curly Wig.

No. 18R4402 Ladies' Curly Dress Wig, made of natural short hair, with or without part, mounted on fine open mesh cotton foundation.
Each.... $10.00
Gray or blonde hair, each, $15.00
If by mail, postage extra, each, 14 cents.

No. 18R4406 Ladies' Wig. Same as above but mounted on silk foundation. Price, each.... $12.00
Gray or blonde hair, each.......... 18.00
If by mail, postage extra, each, 8 cents.

Ladies' Wigs—Long Hair.

Can be arranged in many different ways.

No. 18R4410 Made of the best selected hair on silk foundation, 18-inch hair.
Price, each $15.00
If by mail, postage extra, each, 10 cents.

No. 18R4414 Made same as above on silk foundation, 24-inch hair.
Price, each......... $18.00
If by mail, postage extra, each, 10 cents.

The above prices are for ordinary shades hair. Red, Blonde and Gray Hair cost 50 per cent more, which please add when you send order. Be sure and send sample of hair. Send measurement of head.

Men's Toupees

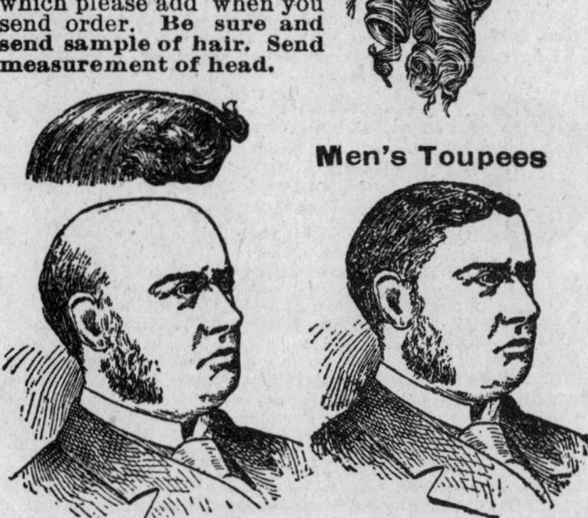

To measure for a Toupee or top piece, cut a piece of paper the exact size and shape of the bald spot, mark the crown and parting, enclose a lock of hair, and state if hair is to be straight or curly.

No. 18R4418 Men's Toupee, weft foundation.
Price, each. (If by mail, postage extra, 8c).. $5.50

No. 18R4422 Men's Toupee, ventilated foundation. Price, each.......... $10.00
If by mail, postage extra, each, 8 cents.

Red, Blonde and Gray Hair cost extra. Allow one-half more than above prices.

Remember, we guarantee a perfect fit and match if you follow instructions, or your money back.

How to Measure a Wig.

State style of wig, kind of parting, whether for right or left side; price and description as per list; to insure a good fit mention number of inches. Send sample of hair. Inches.

No. 1 Circumference of head.... ..
No. 2 Forehead to nape of neck. ..
No. 3 Ear to ear, across forehead ..
No. 4 Ear to ear, over top...... ..
No. 5 Temple to temple, round back.......... ..

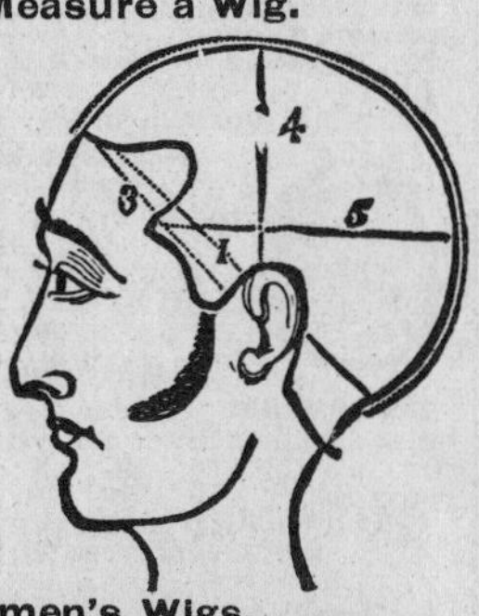

Gentlemen's Wigs.

Gentlemen's Wigs are made of the finest selected hair. We guarantee our work the highest grade, and they cannot be distinguished from the natural growth. **If by mail, postage extra, each, 8 cents.**

No. 18R4426 Men's Full Wigs. Weft with crown, cotton foundation. Price, each.......... $8.00

No. 18R4430 Men's Full Wigs. Gauze or silk parting. Price, each.......... $12.00

No. 18R4434 Men's Wigs. Ventilated with hair net parting. Price, each. $21.00

Red, Blonde and Gray Hair cost extra; allow one-half more than above prices.

Street Wigs for Colored People.

No. 18R4438 Street Dress Wig for Colored Women, made of human hair, bang with parting in front, the hair in back is 18 inches long, and done up high in back with a knot. Send measurements as shown in illustration in rules for measurement on this page. Price, each.......... $5.50
If by mail, postage extra, 8 cents.

No. 18R4442 Street Dress Wigs for Colored Men, made of human hair with parting on side. Send measurement as per instructions. Price, each, $4.50
If by mail, postage extra, 8 cents.

Theatrical Wigs and Beards of Every Description.

Full Beards.

No. 18R4446 Mustache on wire spring, common. Each...... 10c

No. 18R4450 Mustache, ventilated.
Price, each.......... 20c

No. 18R4454 Goatees.
Price, each.......... 10c

No. 18R4458 Whiskers, side. Each...... 75c

The above come in dark and medium shades only.
If by mail, postage extra, each, 3 cents.

No. 18R4462 Full Beard on wire. Each..... 68c
No. 18R4466 Full Beard, ventilated.
Price, each.......... $1.75
If by mail, postage extra, each, 3 cents.

Minstrel and Character Wigs.

No. 18R4470 Minstrel or Plain Black Negro Wigs.
Price, each.......... 49c

Court Wigs, Hair Nets, Imperial Hair Regenerator, Grease Paints, Etc.

No. 18R4474 Imperial Hair Regenerator, restores gray hair to the color of youth, regenerates bleached hair, gives it new life and vigor, and makes it any color desired; makes it beautiful, natural and healthy. Comes in seven shades: Black, dark or medium brown, chestnut, light chestnut, gold blonde, ash blonde. **Absolutely harmless.**
Price, per bottle.......... $1.35
Liquids cannot be mailed.

No. 18R4478 Court Wigs. Made up in first class style. Price, each, $3.25
If by mail, postage extra, each, 6c.

No. 18R4482 Fright Wigs.
Price, each.......... $3.50
If by mail, postage extra, each, 6c.

No. 18R4486 Invisible Hair Nets, made of the best quality of best silk netting, all colors. Price, each...... 7c
If by mail, postage extra, each, 2c.

No. 18R4490 Silk Hair Nets, medium size netting, all colors. Each... 7c
If by mail, postage extra, each, 2c.

No. 18R4494 Pencils for the Eyebrows, brown or black. Each...... 20c
If by mail, postage extra, each, 3c.

No. 18R4498 Blue Pencil for the veins.
Price, each.......... 20c
If by mail, postage extra, each, 3 cents.

No. 18R4502 Theater Rouge, in cakes on porcelain tablets, in paper boxes. Price, per box...... 20c
If by mail, postage extra, each, 3 cents.

No. 18R4506 Fard Indien, a preparation for shading the eyelashes artistically, making the eyes appear larger. Colors, light brown, dark brown and black.
Price, per box.......... 50c
If by mail, postage extra, each, 5 cents.

No. 18R4510 Rusma Depilatory Powder for the removal of superfluous hair from the lips, cheek, chin, arm, etc. Price.. 95c
If by mail, postage extra, each, 5 cents.

No. 18R4514 Toupee Paste, which is used to keep Toupee in place; heat and apply. Price, per stick.......... 42c
If by mail, postage extra, each, 5 cents.

No. 18R4518 Grease Paint, for make up purposes. Eight colors in a box. Price, per box.......... 70c
If by mail, postage extra, each, 5 cents.

No. 18R4522 Burnt Cork, in glass jars.
Price, per jar.......... 25c
If by mail, postage extra, each, 5 cents.

The Braided Wire Hair Rolls.

Made of the finest tempered wire, covered with knitted lace to match any shade of hair.

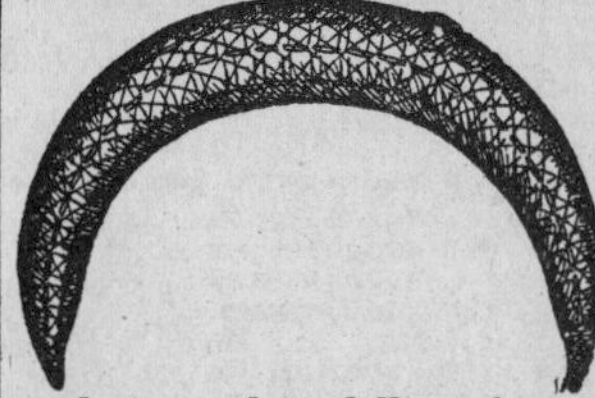

FOR THE LATEST STYLES OF HAIR DRESSING.

These rolls are most desirable for the pretty pompadour effects now so much in vogue. The only sanitary rolls made to produce fullness in any part of the hair. Can't become musty or damp from perspiration or injure the hair as do the rolls made of hair. No obstruction to hair pins. Comfortable, cool, cleanly and delightful.

No. 18R4526 4, 6 and 8-inch lengths. Each... 10c
No. 18R4530 12 and 15-inch lengths. Each... 15c
If by mail, postage extra, each, 4 cents.

BUTTON DEPARTMENT.

Pearl Buttons at Import Prices. Button Scale.

Accompanying cut shows actual size of buttons. The prices quoted per dozen are the lowest. No reductions for the gross.

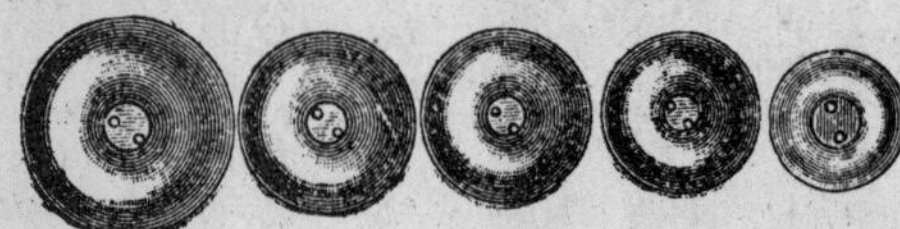

24-line 22-line 20-line 18-line 16-line

No. 18R4550 Half Fine White Pearl Buttons, 2 holes, good stock.

Size, line	16	18	20	22	24
Price, per dozen	2½c	3c	4c	4c	5c

If by mail, postage extra, per dozen, 2 cents.

No. 18R4554 Superfine Clear White Pearl Buttons.

Size, line	16	18	20	22	24
Price, per dozen	3c	4c	5c	5c	6c

If by mail, postage extra, per dozen, 2 cents.

No. 18R4558 Smoked Pearl Dress Buttons.

Size, line	16	18	20	22	24
Price, per dozen	4c	5c	5c	6c	6c

If by mail, postage extra, per dozen, 2 cents.

Ball Pearl Trimming Buttons.

No. 18R4559 The Small Ball Pearl Buttons are very much in demand for trimming. Superior quality fresh water or domestic pearl buttons, one-half ball size, two holes. Special prices as follows:

Size, lines	12	14	16
Price, per dozen	5c	6c	7c

No. 18R4560 High Grade Ball Pearl Button, imported mother of pearl, full one-half ball button with two holes, same as above. A very stylish and excellent button for trimming fine garments.

Size, lines	12	14	16
Price, per dozen	9c	10c	11c

No. 18R4561 Smoked Pearl Ball Buttons, with two holes; very stylish for white waists and other trimmings.

Size, lines	12	14	16
Price, per dozen	10c	11c	12c

No. 18R4563 Oriental Cat's Eye Ball Button with self shank, imported fine mother of pearl. This is a very handsome and dressy button.

Sizes	12	14	16
Price, per dozen	11c	13c	15c

No. 18R4564 Fine grade, full one-half ball plain white pearl trimming button with self shank. This is a good quality at a low price.

Size	12	14	16
Price, per dozen	8c	9c	10c

Choice of Any Design.

No. 18R4565 Pearl Shirt Button. Good clear quality (domestic). Choice of the three styles. Mention style wanted. Size, 16 line. Exact size of illustration. Price, per dozen.......7c

2 3 4

No. 18R4566 Pearl Shirt Buttons. The imported clear mother of pearl. Same three styles as above. Size, 16 line. Price, per dozen.......10c

No. 18R4567 Finest real mother of pearl. Size, 12 line, the small size shirt button. Size of illustration. Choice of the three styles. Price, per dozen.......8c

Pearl Buttons for Cloaks, Jackets and Dresses.

No. 18R4568 Large Pearl Buttons, used for street costumes and jackets. **Heavy clear imported pearl.**

Size in diameter. Inches	⅝	1⅛	1⅜	1½
Per doz.	18c	65c	80c	$1.10

If by mail, postage extra, per dozen, 3 cents.

No. 18R4569 Fancy Carved Fine Pearl Buttons, four holes, for jackets, cloaks and dresses; between a smoked and white color. Four sizes.

Size in diameter	⅝	1	1⅛	1¼
Per dozen	15c	30c	55c	75c

If by mail, postage extra, per doz., 3c.

No. 18R4574 Fancy Colored Agate Buttons. 22 lines. For gingham or cheap worsted dresses. Come one gross in box. Colors, slate, navy, pink, cream. Price, per dozen.......2c
If by mail, postage extra, per doz. 2c

Colored Vegetable Ivory Dress Button.

No. 18R4578 Plain Vegetable Ivory Buttons. 22 lines, with self shank and studded. Colors, white, pink, blue, cardinal, navy, myrtle, brown and black. Price, per dozen.......5c
If by mail, postage extra, per dozen, 2 cents.

Fancy Gilt Metal Buttons.

No. 18R4582 Fancy Gilt Metal Button, half ball shape, with self shanks. These will be extensively used. Illustrations show exact size of lines, 8, 10 and 12.

8-line 10-line 12-line

Size, lines	8	10	12	14
Price, per dozen	3c	4c	4c	5c

If by mail, postage extra, per dozen, 2 cents.

No. 18R4586 Flat Gilt Buttons, with self shank, dull fancy finish and bright edge on rim. The popular button.

Size, lines	10	12	14	16	18	20	22	24
Per doz.	2½c	3c	3½c	4c	4½c	5c	5½c	6c

If by mail, postage extra, per doz., 2c.

18 line

No. 18R4590 Fine Silk Diagonal Covered Buttons, for dress trimmings, etc., with self shank. Black only.

Size line	12	14	16	18	20
Price, per doz.	3c	4c	5c	6c	7c

If by mail, postage extra, per dozen, 2 cents.

No. 18R4594 Fine Covered Diagonal Mohair Buttons. Black only.

Size	Vest	Coat	Overcoat
Per dozen	6c	8c	10c

No. 18R4598 Fine Silk Covered Diagonal Buttons. Black only.

Size	Vest	Coat	Overcoat
Per dozen	7c	10c	15c

If by mail, postage extra, 2 cents.

Black Horn Buttons.

No. 18R4602 Black Horn Vest Buttons, highly polished. Price, per dozen.......4c
No. 18R4606 Black Horn Coat Buttons, same style as above. Price, per dozen.......6c
No. 18R4610 Black Horn Overcoat Buttons, same style as above. Price, per dozen.......10c
If by mail, postage extra, per dozen, 3 cents.

Officers' and G. A. R. Buttons.

No. 18R4614 Officers' Plated Brass Buttons.
Vest, per dozen.......13c
Coat, per dozen.......19c

No. 18R4618 G. A. R. Oval Top Republic Buttons.
Vest size, dozen..10c
Coat size, dozen..15c

Postage extra, per dozen, 3 cents.

No. 18R4622 Police Gold Plated Buttons.

Line	24 Vest Size	30 Coat Size
Price, per dozen	18c	35c

Anchor Brass Buttons.

No. 18R4626 Anchor Brass Buttons. Vest size, per dozen.......8c
Coat size, per dozen.......10c
Overcoat size, per dozen.......12c
If by mail, postage extra, per dozen, 3 cents.

Agate Buttons.

No. 18R4630 White Agate Buttons. See button scale for sizes.

Size	16	20	24	28	30
Per gross	4c	7c	9c	10c	11c

If by mail, postage extra, per dozen, 2 cents.

No. 18R4634 Fancy White Agate Buttons.

Size	16	20	24	28
Per gross	5c	9c	11c	15c

If by mail, postage extra, per dozen, 2 cents.

Hand Snap Buttons.

By the use of these buttons the traveling man, the farmer, the laborer, the mechanic, the growing boy and his father, of any profession, can instantly replace his missing buttons.

No. 18R4642 Black, Gold or Silvered Metal Snap Fly Buttons, one dozen in box. Per box.......4c

No. 18R4648 Black, Gold or Silvered Metal Snap Suspender Buttons, one dozen in box. Per box...5c

No. 18R4650 Automatic Bachelor Buttons. No needle required to put them on, and the only reliable button that can be taken off and used again. The most perfect and simple button. **Once used, always used.** The suspender size only. Price, per dozen, 7c
If by mail, postage extra, per dozen, 2 cents.

No. 18R4654 Washburne Bachelor Buttons. This button is so neat in appearance and fills such a universal want that it hardly needs recommendation; can be adjusted instantly and removed just as quickly. Comes in blued steel or nickel. Price, each.......4c
If by mail, postage extra, per dozen, 2 cents.

No. 18R4658 Washburne Drawer Supporter. Fastens same as button. Comes in blued steel or nickel. The neatest and best drawer supporter ever invented. Worn once always worn. Price, each...5c
If by mail, postage extra, per dozen, 2 cents.

Pants Buttons.

No. 18R4662 Black Metal Buttons, small or fly size. Price, per gross.......5c
No. 18R4666 Black Metal Buttons, suspender size. Price, per gross.......7c
No. 18R4670 Brass Fly Buttons, best quality. Price, per gross.......8c
No. 18R4674 Brass Suspender Buttons, best quality. Price, per gross.......9c
No. 18R4678 Universal Bone Pants Buttons. Black or white; used extensively for underwear, etc. Put up one gross in box. Sold only by gross. Price, per gross, suspender size, 25c; fly size..20c
If by mail, postage extra, per gross, 5 cents.
Pants buttons are put up in one gross boxes. We do not sell less than one box.

Collar Buttons.

No. 18R4682 Bone Collar Buttons; good size; come one dozen on a card. **We do not sell less than a card.** Price, per dozen.......3c
No. 18R4686 Pearl Collar Buttons, medium size; nice clear pearl. Price, each.......5c
No. 18R4690 Pearl Collar Button, good size, better quality pearl than above. Price, each.......8c
No. 18R4694 Washburne Scarf Fastener. This is without doubt the best scarf fastener ever made and the most convenient to adjust. It is easily removed and has no prongs or projections; can also be used in various other ways. Price, each.......2c
If by mail, postage extra, each, 1 cent.

Ladies' and Children's Hose Supporters.

Easy Catch Hose Supporter. This fastener has rubber covered post, which prevents hose from tearing. Made from good quality lisle elastic, pin tops and slide center. We retail this at about half what you would pay elsewhere for this grade of goods.

No. 18R4700 Child's Double Strap Stocking Supporters. Price, per pair.......5c
No. 18R4704 Misses' Double Strap Hose Supporters. Price, per pair.......7c
No. 18R4708 Young Ladies' Double Strap Hose Supporters. Price, per pair.......8c
If by mail, postage extra, per pair, 3 cents.
No. 18R4712 Ladies' Double Strap Hose Supporters. Price, per pair.......9c
If by mail, postage extra, per pair, 3 cents.

Flexo Grasp Hose Supporters. With special rubber button fasteners, guaranteed not to tear the hose. Made of the very finest English lisle elastic, pin top, with slide center for adjustment. Each pair warranted by the manufacturer. We particularly recommend this high grade of goods. There are none better made.

No. 18R4716 Child's Double Strap Hose Supporter, as described above. Price, per pair.......11c
No. 18R4720 Misses' Double Strap Hose Supporters, as described above. Price, per pair.......12c
No. 18R4724 Young Ladies' Double Strap Hose Supporters, as described above. Price, per pair..14c
No. 18R4728 Ladies' Double Strap Hose Supporters, as described above. Price, per pair.......16c
If by mail, postage extra, per pair, 3 cents.

Braces and Hose Supporters.

Made of good Lisle Elastic Webbing.

No. 18R4732 Ladies' Shoulder Braces, with hose supporters; black or white. Price, per pair.......16c
No. 18R4736 Misses' Shoulder Braces, with hose supporters; black or white. Price, per pair.......13c
No. 18R4740 Children's Shoulder Braces, with hose supporters; black or white. Price, per pair.......12c
If by mail, postage extra, per pair, 4 cents.

Ladies' Safety Belt and Hose Supporters.

No. 18R4744 Ladies' Combination Safety Belt and Hose Supporters. Belt made of good sateen and good lisle side elastics. Colors, black and white. Sizes, 22 to 36. Give waist measure. Price, each.......20c
If by mail, postage extra, each, 3 cents.

We recommend our Sanitary Napkin No. 18R4752 at 3 cents each to be used with the above Combination Belt. Ladies who have used them once will never be without them.

Ladies' Safety Belts.

No. 18R4748 Ladies' Safety Belts, made of sateen, rubber band across hips. Easy and convenient. Sizes, 22 to 36. Ask for one inch larger than your exact measure. Color, white only. Sizes every other inch; give waist measure. Price, each.......14c

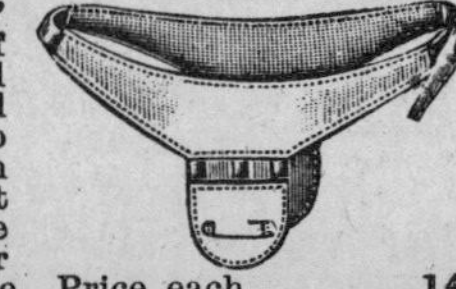

If by mail, postage extra, each, 2 cents.

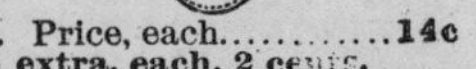

Serviettes.

No. 18R4752 Serviette Sanitary Cloth. These serviettes are made of the finest absorbent cotton, with a layer of absolutely impervious material, which insures cleanliness. Absolutely antiseptic, ready for instant use. These serviettes possess from three to four times the absorbent qualities of the best toweling. Recommended by the medical profession as indispensable in every lady's wardrobe. Medium and large sizes. Price, each....................3c
If by mail, postage extra, per dozen, 8 cents.

Ladies' Belt Hose Supporters.

No. 18R4760 Ladies' Satin Belt Hose Supporters, with fancy frilled side elastics. By using immense quantities we are enabled to offer at the price this very desirable supporter, really a good value for 50 cents. Colors, cardinal, pink, light blue, yellow or black. **Give waist measure.** Price, per pair, 24c
If by mail, postage extra, 3 cents.

Ladies' Silk Satin Belt Hose Supporters.

No. 18R4761 Ladies' Good Quality Satin Belt Hose Supporters. Silk elastic sides, a regular 50-cent quality, same style as above. Colors, red pink, blue, yellow or black. **Give waist measure.** Price, per pair....................17c
If by mail, postage extra, per pair, 3 cents.

Fine Satin Belt Hose Supporter for 47 Cents.

No. 18R4762 Ladies' Belt Hose Supporters, having the straight front effect; made of fine satin belting and extra wide. Fine quality fancy frilled elastic. Has the rubber button catch. Colors, black, light blue, pink or yellow. Always give waist measure.
Price, per pair....................47c
If by mail, postage extra, 3 cents.

24-Cent Belt Hose Supporter.

No. 18R4766 Ladies' Belt Hose Supporters. This style gives the desired straight front effect, without any strain upon the body. Made of a very fine mercerized cloth for belt and parts, with fine heavy lisle side elastics. Pretty buckle in center and rubber button catch. Can be ordered in black, light blue, pink or yellow. Always give waist measure. Price, per pair..............24c
If by mail, postage extra, 3 cents.

No. 18R4767 New "Regal" Abdominal Supporter, with mercerized non-elastic waist bands, made of elegant elastic, neat buckles and rubber buttons. This supporter is becoming immensely popular and highly recommended by all who have worn them. Colors, black, pink, light blue or yellow.
Price, per pair 50c
If by mail, postage extra, 5 cents.

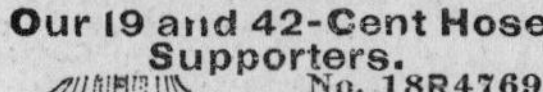

Our 19 and 42-Cent Hose Supporters.

No. 18R4769 Hooks on bottom of corset, giving the body a graceful appearance. The pair is made of satin, with slide in center for adjustment. Good quality silk overshot frilled elastic, with the rubber button catch. Colors, black, light blue, pink, red or yellow.
Price, per pair....................19c

No. 18R4773 The Marlowe Hose Supporters, same as above, but finer grade of satin. An all silk fancy frilled elastic; very beautiful design, and having the flexo grasp button fasteners. Each pair put up neatly in a box. Colors, black, light blue, pink, red, or yellow. Price, per pair....................42c
If by mail, postage extra, per pair, 3 cents.

Fancy Frilled Side Garters, 16 Cents per Pair.

No. 18R4777 Fancy Frilled Side Garters. Made of good quality silk over shot elastic. Nickel buckle in center, and pin top. Rubber button catch. Colors, black, pink, light blue or cardinal.
Price, per pair....................16c
If by mail, postage extra, 3 cents.

No. 18R4781 Fancy Frilled Side Garters. Made of high grade imported fancy frilled silk elastic. Very attractive buckle in center with flexo grasp fasteners. Colors, black, red, light blue, heliotrope or yellow.
Price, per pair......41c
If by mail, postage extra, 3 cents.

No. 18R4785 Fancy Frilled Side Garters. Our best quality. Made of fine imported all silk frilled elastic. Special fancy pattern. Gold filigree buckle in center, and gold pin top, with slide in center. Flexo grasp fasteners. Colors, black, light blue, cardinal, pink, heliotrope or yellow.
Price, per pair. ...(Postage extra, 3 cents.).....59c

Wire Sleeve Supporters.

No. 18R4812 Patent Duplex Ventilated Men's Arm Bands; fine nickeled steel wire, one pair in a box.
Price, per pair....................7c
If by mail, postage extra, per pair, 3 cents.

Children's Combination Belt and Supporter.

No. 18R4816 Children's Combination Belt and Supporter for Boys and Girls. The handiest, safest and most convenient waist and hose supporters on the market. Made of good sateen and lisle elastic sides. Sizes are from 2 to 12 years. **Be sure and give age.** Comes in white only.
Price, each..............19c
If by mail, postage extra, 4 cents.

The Nazareth Waist.

No. 18R4820 The Nazareth Waist for Boys and Girls. Made of elastic knit fabric, giving wear and comfort; strapped with tape to catch the strains the youngsters are apt to give. The Nazareth waist comes in sizes from 2 to 12 years. Be sure and give age.
Price, each..............19c
If by mail, postage extra, 5 cents.

Ladies' Elastic Garters.

No. 18R4825 Fancy Round Garters. Roman striped frilled elastic. Neat attractive buckle and two-color ribbon bow. Each pair in a neat box. Colors, black, red, light blue, or pink.
Price, per pair....................9c
If by mail, postage extra, per pair, 5 cents.

No. 18R4829 Fancy Round Garters. Of pretty mercerized tufted frilled elastic. Nice enameled motto buckle, such as "Hands off" and silk ribbon bows. Each pair in a box. Colors, black, red, light blue, or pink.
Price, per pair....................18c
If by mail, postage extra, per pair, 5 cents.

No. 18R4833 Fancy Round Garters. Mercerized frilled elastic. New design, with fancy nickel buckle and silk ribbon bows. Each pair of garters has a lucky rabbit's foot. Each pair put up in a neat box. All colors. Price, per pair..21c
If by mail, postage extra, per pair, 4 cents.

No. 18R4837 Fancy Round Garters. Made of extra wide fancy frilled elastic. Handsome nickel buckle, with silk ribbon bows. On each pair of garters is a small thermometer. Each pair put up in neat box. Colors, black, light blue, pink or cardinal. Price, per pair....................22c
If by mail, postage extra, per pair, 5 cents.

No. 18R4839 Ladies' Garters, made of fancy frilled elastic, nickeled buckles, large silk bows and neat leather purse with snap button. Comes in all colors.
An Old Tradition:
"A leathern purse about the knee suspended,
Shall to its wearer prove a fairy charm;
Her troubles, she will find, will soon be ended,
'Twill guard her well and keep her safe from harm."
Price, per pair....................24c
If by mail, postage extra, per pair, 5 cents.

Ladies' Fancy Round Garters.

No. 18R4841 Fancy Round Garter, made of fine quality of silk frilled elastic. Beautiful sunflower buckle enameled, and with large red stone setting in center. Finished with fine silk ribbon bows; very pretty design. Each pair in a box. Colors, black, pink, light blue, cardinal or yellow.
Price, per pair.....(Postage extra, 5 cents.)....42c

No. 18R4843 Fancy Round Garter, made of extra wide very fine quality of silk elastic. Extra fine filigree gold buckle, with very large silk ribbon bows. The buckles have fine jeweled settings. Each pair in a nice box. Colors, black, light blue, pink, cardinal or yellow. Price, per pair....................99c
If by mail, postage extra, per pair, 5 cents.

No. 18R4845 Fancy Round Garter, made of the highest grade of silk frilled elastic. Fine silk ribbon bow, and genuine sterling silver buckles. Each pair put up in a fancy box. Colors, black, light blue, pink, cardinal, or yellow.
Price, per pair....................$1.24
If by mail, postage extra, 5 cents.

Plain Lisle Elastic.

No. 18R4847 Black or White Lisle Loom Garter Elastic, good quality.
Price, per yard, ½-inch wide...3c
Price, per yard, ¾-inch wide...4c
If by mail, postage extra, per yard, 1 cent.

Hat Elastic.

No. 18R4849 Round Hat Elastic Cord, black or white.
Price, per yard..............1c
If by mail, postage extra, per dozen yards, 2 cents.

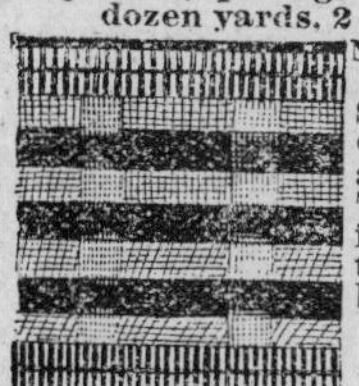

No. 18R4851 Plaid and Staple Fancy Garter Web, a great variety of patterns. This is a good, reliable quality, and the price cheaper than trashy goods are sold at by retail merchants.
Price, per yard..........2½c
If by mail, postage extra, per yard, 1 cent.

No. 18R4853 Fancy Frilled Elastic. Our own special design. As good as the usual 10-cent quality. Colors, black, white, blue, pink, cardinal and yellow. Price, per yard......4c
If by mail, postage extra, per yard, 1 cent.

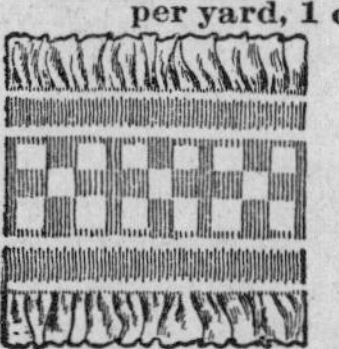

No. 18R4855 Fancy Frilled Silk Overshot Elastic. Pretty design, strong and durable. Colors are black, light blue, cardinal, heliotrope and pink.
Price, per yard..............7c
If by mail, postage extra, per yard, 1 cent.

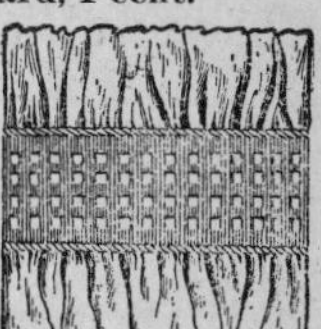

No. 18R4857 Fancy Frilled Silk Elastic, very high grade. 1⅝-inch width. This elastic is as good as the usual 20 and 25-cent qualities elsewhere. Colors, black, light blue, pink, cardinal, yellow or heliotrope.
Price, per yard..........14c
If by mail, postage extra, per yard, 1 cent.

No. 18R4859 Heavy Ribbed All Silk Elastic. The highest grade quality, 1 inch wide. Colors, black, pink, yellow, light blue, cardinal or violet.
Price, per yard 18c
If by mail, postage extra, per yard, 1 cent.

Improved Breast Suppor for Low or High Bust.

No. 18R4864 Made of strong, light material called Tampico fiber. By its use the weight of the breast is removed from the dress waist to the shoulders, giving coolness and comfort in warm weather, **producing a perfect shaped bust and free and easy movement of the body.** By its use all deficiency of development is supplied. They are just as essential for a slender person as for a stout one, and meet a long felt want for every woman and girl from the age of sixteen. **When ordering be sure and send the bust measure.** Sizes, 32 to 45.
Price, each....(Postage extra each, 5 cents.)......74c

Fairy Bust Forms.

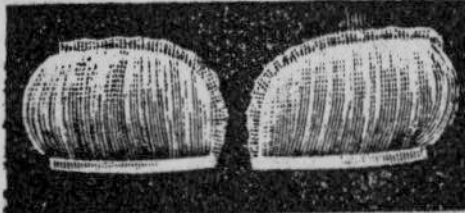

No. 18R4865 Fairy Bust Form. The lightest, most attractive bust form on the market; thoroughly hygienic, is adjusted to corset, conforms with every movement of the body, gives figure a graceful form. Made of fine quality lawn, edged with Valenciennes lace. Weight, only 2 ounces. Colors, black, white or drab. Price, each....................25c

If by mail, postage extra, 4 cents.

No. 18R4867 Fairy Bust Form. Same style as above, made of fine quality Japanese silk, edged with silk Prussian binding. The only bust form that can be worn with evening dress. Weight, 2 ounces. Colors, black, white, pink or blue. Price, each....................50c

If by mail, postage extra, 4 cents.

The Hygeia Bust Forms.

No. 18R4868 The Hygeia Bust Forms, made of the finest tempered braided wire. Oval in shape. Adjustable. Light as a feather. Comfortable and non-heating. They cannot injure the health nor retard development. Covered with fine lawn, and in such a way that the forms can be removed and the covering washed. A great improvement over any other form on the market. Covered in black if desired. Price....................44c

If by mail, postage extra, 5 cents.

The Parisienne Wire Bustle.

No. 18R4876 The Parisienne Woven Wire Bustle, made of highly tempered, black enameled, woven wire. The best shape, which it will always retain. Price, each.........19c

If by mail, postage extra, 5 cents.

Parisienne Hip Pad and Bustle.

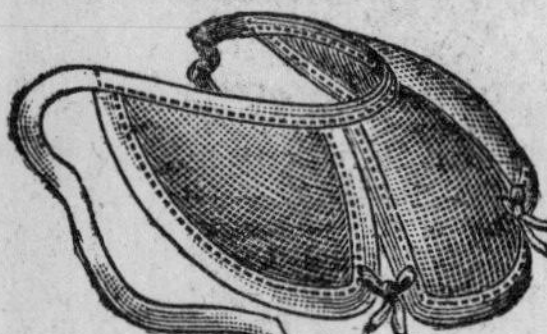

No. 18R4880 The Parisienne Hip Pad and Bustle, made of best tempered, black enameled, woven wire with hip pads of padded cloth. Perfect in shape, and light in weight. Very durable. Price, each...40c

If by mail, postage extra, each, 10 cents.

The Duchess Hip Pad and Bustle.

No. 18R4884 The Duchess Woven Wire Hip Pad and Bustle, made of best woven white wire, correct shape, very light and durable, and equal to any sold elsewhere for 75 cents or $1.00. Price, each...39c

If by mail, postage extra, 11 cents.

The Lenox Glove Fitting Hip Bustle.

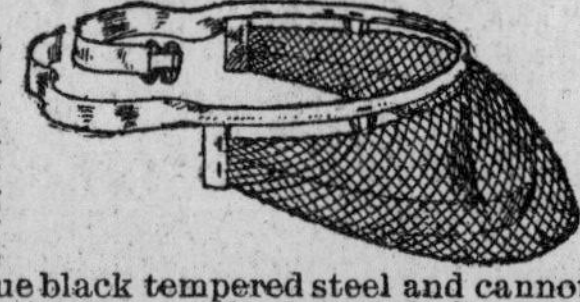

No. 18R4886 It rounds out the figure and produces the effect desired in prevailing fashions, extending over the hips very lightly and gracefully. Made of blue black tempered steel and cannot get out of shape, neither can it be detected. Suitable for rainy day skirts. Price, each....................37c

If by mail, postage extra, 10 cents.

CORSETS.

WE PRESENT TO OUR FRIENDS AND CUSTOMERS A REVISED ASSORTMENT OF CORSET SHAPES. The models and styles illustrated and described were selected to suit every taste, to fit every form, and the prices we name enable you to buy a high grade corset for less than you can get elsewhere.

WE SELL ONLY SUCH CORSETS AS WE CAN GUARANTEE AND RECOMMEND. They have been tested and tried by thousands of our customers, **AND THEY BUY THEM AGAIN.**

BE SURE AND GIVE YOUR WAIST MEASURE and observe the following rules in taking your measure: If you measure with corset on, deduct 2 to 2½ inches from waist sizes as shown on tape; this allows for spread of lacing in back. For example, if waist measure is 23 inches over corset, order size 21. If you take actual body measure, without corset or underclothing, you should deduct 3 or 4 inches, depending on how tight you lace. For example, if your waist measure is 25 inches without corset or underclothing, your size would be 21 or 22.

Allow 15 cents extra if you want a corset sent by mail.

Our Special Four-Hook Corset, 50 Cents.

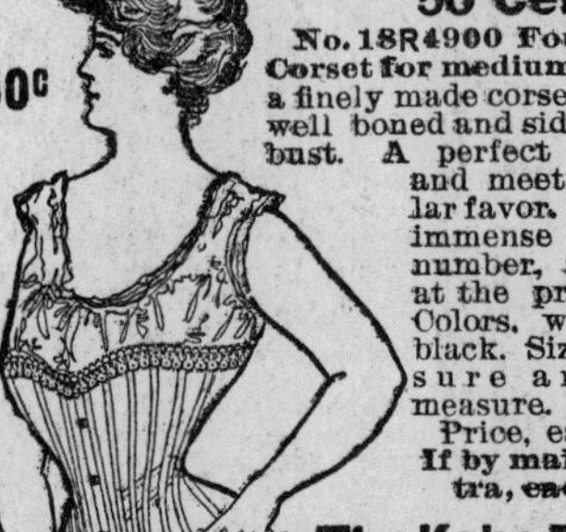

50c

No. 18R4900 Four-Hook Short Corset for medium form. This is a finely made corset of fine jeans, well boned and side steels, boned bust. A perfect fitting corset and meeting with popular favor. We predict an immense sale on this number, and especially at the price we quote. Colors, white, drab or black. Sizes, 18 to 30. Be sure and give waist measure. Price, each.........50c

If by mail, postage extra, each, 15 cents.

The Kabo Five-Hook Corset for the Average Figure, at 90 Cents.

90c

No. 18R4902 Long waist, medium form, five-hook. This is a corset made of fine French coutil strips of French sateen with silk edging. Molded on a perfect French model; stayed with double girdles at the waist lines. The bones and steels are made with a protecting covering for the ends, which prevents cutting through. A perfect fitting garment that will give entire satisfaction. **Equal to the $1.50 kind elsewhere.** Made in white, drab and black. Be sure to give waist measure.

Sizes, 18 to 30. Price, $0.90
Sizes, 31 to 36. Price, 1.15

If by mail, postage extra, each, 15 cents.

High Class Four-Hook Corset, 73 Cents.

$1.00 VALUE 73c

No. 18R4904 Our new four-hook, 13-inch Front Steel Corset, for medium figure; the new medium length waist and medium low bust. Made of very fine quality sateen lined with French coutil, handsome lace trimming both top and bottom with baby ribbon drawn through lace. The best quality and most stylish fitting corset to be had, and the equal of any $1.00 corset today on the market. Colors, black, drab or white. Sizes, 18 to 30. Be sure to give waist measure. Price, each..73c

If by mail, postage extra, each, 15 cents.

Bias Gored, Straight Front, Perfect Fitting, Erect Form, 50 Cents.

50c

No. 18R4906 A new, popular, bias gored, straight front corset, with set in gored busts. The latest low bust effect. Made of good imported coutil with extra heavy 10-inch front steel. This is equal to many of the regular $1.00 straight front corsets sold elsewhere. Colors, white or drab. Sizes, 18 to 30. Always give waist measure. Price, each.........50c

If by mail, postage extra, each, 15 cents.

Medium Figure, Erect Form, Full Gored, Straight Front, French Modeled Corset, 82 Cents.

82c

No. 18R4908 A full gored, straight front, French modeled corset, adapted to the slight and medium figures, affording freedom to the respiratory organs, possessing exceptional fitting qualities for figures that possess fine outlines of form, embodying perfect workmanship. Materials, drab and white coutil and black sateen. Equal to the $1.25 kind. Sizes, 18 to 30. Always give waist measure. Price, each....................82c

If by mail, postage extra, each, 15 cents.

Kabo Straight Front, No Brass Eyelets, 88 Cents.

88c

No. 18R4910 Ladies' Straight Front Corset, made of the best quality of corset jeans and boned with Kabo, with the looped lacer—no brass eyelets. Lace trimmed top and bottom. The straight front corset gives the military figure and the desired fullness at back and over hips. The Kabo straight front has all the good points. We are placing this corset on sale, value equal to the regular $1.50 style as sold elsewhere. Colors, black, white or drab. Sizes, 18 to 30. Be sure and give waist measure. Price, each....................88c

If by mail, postage extra, each, 15 cents.

Flexibone, French Model Military Figure, Suitable for the Average Shape, $1.33.

$1.33

No. 18R4912 A Bias Cut Full Gored Corset, in which are combined the qualities of perfect workmanship, durability and graceful shape. This garment is designed to mold the figure into graceful and well proportioned outlines, at the same time allowing the greatest freedom to the muscles. Has low bust, long skirt, with tabs for hose supporters. Made in fine coutil, drab and white, and in black sateen. Trimmed with handsome lace and ribbon. Sizes, 18 to 30. Be sure and give waist measure. Price, each..$1.33

If by mail, postage extra, each, 15 cents.

The Sahlin Perfect Form and Corset Combined, for Grace and Comfort.

Be sure and give measurements for the Sahlin Perfect Form and Corset Combined as follows:

Bust Measure Comes in Sizes: Inches	Around Waist Comes in Sizes: Inches
30	18-20-22
32	20-22-24
34	20-22-24-26
36	22-24-26-28
38	24-26-28-30
40	26-28-30-32

Sizes different from above must be made to order and cost 50 cents extra.

No. 18R4914 Sahlin Perfect Form and Corset Combined. Retains all the good and avoids the evil of ordinary corsets. Nothing is lost in style or shape. The bust will not cave in and, therefore, padding and interlining is avoided. The effect as here shown is an exact reproduction of a perfect form obtained only by wearing the Sahlin. No corset is necessary, as it is a corset and form combined, approved and endorsed by physicians and health reformers. Made of good quality corset coutil, white or drab. Give bust and waist measure. Sizes, 18 to 30.
Price, each..92c

No. 18R4915 Sahlin Perfect Form and Corset Combined. Same as above, made of fancy summer netting, white only. Give bust and waist measure. Sizes, 18 to 30. Price, each..92c
If by mail, postage extra, 18 cents.

Her Ladyship Corset cannot break over the hips.

79c

No. 18R4916 HerLadyship Corset is guaranteed not to break over the hips. These corsets are made of superior quality coutil, stripped with satin, handsomely silk flossed and heavy double silk edge, boned throughout with finest tempered capped end steels, with ten extra quality flexible side steels, five on each side, making this corset absolutely unbreakable and at the same time elastic to every motion of the body. Colors, black, drab or white. Sizes, 18 to 30. We offer this corset at a specially reduced price. Always give bust and waist measure. Price, each........................79c
If by mail, postage extra, 15 cents.

The Flexibone Molded Corset for the straight, correct figure. Made for durability.

$1.35

No. 18R4918 Medium Straight Front Corset, especially adapted for stout figures. If you have never worn **Flexibone,** you have never realized corset comfort, corset economy or corset possibilities. The **Straight Front Flexibone** embodies all the features embraced in the so-called self reducing corsets and is unencumbered by bands, straps, etc. They are ideal in shape and are made to **hold** and **mold** the figure to a degree you may never have experienced in any other corset. Made of best corset jeans. Finished with a substantial silk embroidered edge. Flexibone boned throughout and provided with the most substantial **hand set ball eyelets** that are found on no other make of corset. Besides, the manufacturer's guarantee is attached to every corset, which **insures full value** for your investment, protecting you against imperfections of workmanship or material. Colors, drab, black or white. Sizes, 18 to 30. Always give waist measure. Price, each..............................$1.35
If by mail, postage extra, 18 cents.

The New Kabo Hipless Corset with Elastic Sides, 95 Cents.

95c

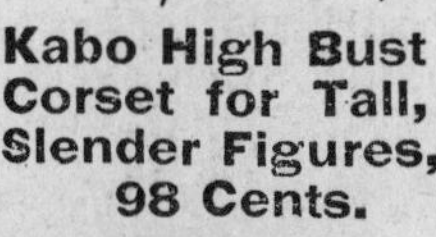

No. 18R4920 Kabo Hipless Corset, medium waist, full form, made of French sateen, single strip, full boned, cut out over hip, with elastic sides. Matchless for athletic purposes and comfort. No brass eyelets. Colors, white, drab or black. Sizes, 18 to 30.
Each......95c
Extra sizes, 31 to 36, 25 cents extra.
Each....$1.20
If by mail, postage extra, 15 cents.

Kabo High Bust Corset for Tall, Slender Figures, 98 Cents.

98c

No. 18R4922 Kabo high bust, extreme long waist, dress form; 6-hook, shaped shoulder straps, sateen covered strips embroidered edge. Suitable for tall, slender figures. No brass eyelets. Colors, white drab or black. Sizes, 18 to 30. Give waist measure.
Price, each.....98c
If by mail, postage extra, 15 cents.

Kabo Abdominal Corsets, Highly Recommended by Everybody, $1.50

$1.50

No. 18R4924 Kabo Abdominal Corset, medium waist, extension front, very heavy boning, made long below the waist, giving ample abdominal support. Elastic self conforming gores on side, sateen covered strips and improved side lacings. No brass eyelets. Colors, drab or black. Sizes, 19 to 30. Give waist measure.
Each.....$1.50
Extra sizes, 31 to 36, 25 cents extra.
Each.....$1.75
If by mail, postage extra, 15 cents.

The Jackson Favorite Waist is the Best Corset Waist in Every Way. 85 Cents.

85c

No. 18R4926 The Jackson Waist combines in the highest degree the embodiment of an elegant waist and corset combination. Its stays are ample, outlining a most graceful poise of figure, at the same time easy and comfortable; it is also adaptable as a negligee by the removal of side steels, which can be removed at will. Made of good sateen, in black or drab. Sizes, 18 to 30. Always give waist measure.
Price, each...85c
Extra sizes, 31 to 36. Each.....$1.15
If by mail, postage extra, 15 cents.

A Most Satisfying, Comfortable and Durable Nursing Corset. 75 Cents.

75c

No. 18R4928 S., R. & Co.'s Nursing Corset, five-hook reinforced clasp. Made of good corset jeans, entirely new principle, as it is easily adjusted, with patent snap button, and will permit use of nipple without the slightest inconvenience. Very pliable over sensitive parts; a boon to mothers. Boned bust, strong jeans girdle, two side steels. Color, drab only. Sizes, 18 to 30. Always give waist measure.
Price, each...75c
If by mail, postage extra, 15 cents.

The Kabo Nursing Corset. None Better Made. 95 Cents.

95c

No. 18R4930 Kabo Nursing Corset, five-hook, long waist, medium form. Constructed on scientific principles, improved snap glove fastener opening, well corded front and bust, English sateen single side strip. A corset that is sure to give entire satisfaction. No brass eyelets. Colors, black, white or drab. Sizes, 18 to 30. Always give the waist measure.
Price, each.. ...95c
If by mail, postage extra, 15 cents.

Our 25-Cent Summer Corset.

25c

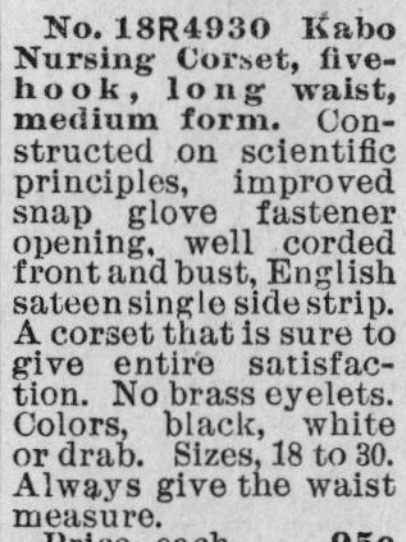

No. 18R4932 Single Bonestrip Summer Corset. Good quality of net and exceptional value for the low price we quote. Sizes, 18 to 30. Color, white. Always give waist measure.
Price, each...25c
If by mail, postage extra, 12 cents.

Our Five-Hook Summer Corset. Good Net, Best Value.

39c

No. 18R4934 Summer Corset, medium short waist, made of fine ventilating netting, satin covered, single strips with two reinforced side steels and reinforced 12-inch front steel; six bones or strips through waist line, which add strength and durability and also prevent stretching. A corset adapted and designed to fit the average figure. Sizes 18 to 30. Color, white. Always give waist measure.
Price, each......39c
If by mail, postage extra, 15 cents.

WE SHOW ALL THE LEADING STYLES IN

CORSETS

AND OUR PRICES MEAN A BIG SAVING.

Straight Front Fancy Summer Net Corset, 42 Cents.

42c

No. 18R4936 Our special straight front Ventilating Summer Corset, made of strong, durable, fancy summer netting, single boned strips with two sateen covered side steels and an extra heavy 10-inch, 4-hook front steel; a splendid wearing and satisfactory corset. This corset is made with heavy bones running entirely through the corset from front to back which prevents stretching or pulling out; has a medium low bust which is especially designed for the average full figure; pretty wide lace trimming at top adds style. Sizes 18 to 30. Always give waist measure. Price, each........42c
If by mail, postage extra, 15 cents.

Our Four-Hook Short Summer Corset.

50c

No. 18R4938 A very popular form fitting corset; made of fine strong netting, sateen girdle and strips, reinforced clasps and corded bust, finished with fine quality lace at top and bottom. We guarantee it equal to any corset sold for 75 cents. Sizes 18 to 30. Always give waist measure. Price, each...50c
If by mail, postage extra, 15 cents.

Straight Front Summer Net Corset, with Extension Tabs for Supporters.

48c

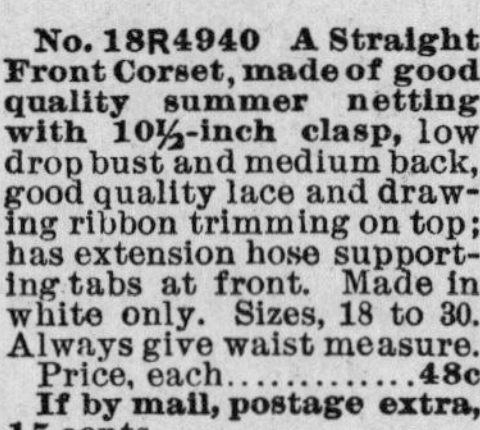

No. 18R4940 A Straight Front Corset, made of good quality summer netting with $10\frac{1}{2}$-inch clasp, low drop bust and medium back, good quality lace and drawing ribbon trimming on top; has extension hose supporting tabs at front. Made in white only. Sizes, 18 to 30. Always give waist measure. Price, each............48c
If by mail, postage extra, 15 cents.

Popular 49-Cent Batiste Girdle Corset.

49c

No. 18R4942 Ladies' Four-Hook Short Girdle Corsets, made of fine quality batiste. These girdles are exceedingly popular and extensively worn. We offer this corset as regular 75-cent value. Color, white only. Sizes, 18 to 30. Always give waist measure. Price, each.......49c
If by mail, postage extra, 15 cents.

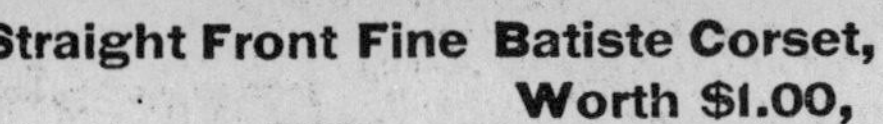

Straight Front Fine Batiste Corset, Worth $1.00, at Only 50 Cents.

50c

No. 18R4944 Full Bias Gored Batiste Corset, Straight front, military erect figure, has 2 side steels and 4 bone strips with extra heavy front 10-inch steel boned underneath, making a perfectly smooth surface. This is a medium waist with low bust adapted for a wide range of figures. Handsomely trimmed with pretty lace at top. White only. Sizes, 18 to 30. Always give waist measure.
Price, each.......50c
If by mail, postage extra, 15 cents.

Four-Hook Short Batiste Corset in Pink, Light Blue or White, 50 Cents.

50c

No. 18R4946 Our Special Model Fancy Girdle Corset, made of fine quality batiste, reinforced with six girdles, which makes the corset doubly strong; has $10\frac{1}{2}$-inch front steel of great pliability. Pretty lace and drawing ribbon trimming at top. A corset for the medium figure that will give entire satisfaction to the wearer. We can furnish this corset in white, pink and blue. Be sure and mention color. A very desirable style. Sizes, 18 to 30. Always give waist measure.
Price, each....................................50c
If by mail, postage extra, each, 15 cents.

48c

Five-Hook Batiste Corset, Medium Figure, 48 Cents.

No. 18R4950 Five-Hook White Batiste Corset. A splendid summer corset as well as for all seasons. A fine form fitting shape made in the best manner possible. Well boned and with girdles. Equal to the ordinary $1.00 value. Sizes, 18 to 30. Always give waist measure.
Price, each.... 48c
If by mail, postage extra, each, 15 cents.

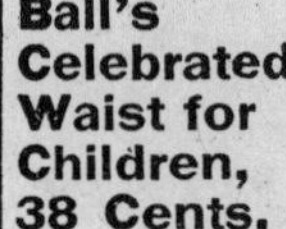

Ball's Celebrated Waist for Children, 38 Cents.

No. 18R4952 Dr. Ball's Child's Corset Waist will train your child's figure while young. The Dr. Ball's Waist is easy, comfortable and perfect fitting, patent tape fastened buttons and taped buttonholes. White or drab. Sizes, 18 to 28. Always give waist measure.
Price, each..38c
If by mail, postage extra, 10 cents.

38c

Misses' Strip Corset 40 Cents.

40c

No. 18R4954 Misses' Strip Corset, made of good quality corset jeans. This corset has a decidedly advantageous feature, being soft and pliable, which makes it most healthful for growing children. Colors, drab or white. Sizes, 18 to 26. Always give waist measure.
Price, each..40c
If by mail, postage extra, 12 cents.

The Coronet Jackson Waists for Misses are the Best, 55 Cts.

55c

No. 18R4956 Coronet Misses' Waist. We supply a long felt and needed want by the ambitious miss just blooming into womanhood, when her figure begins to take on the matronly form which this garment so beautifully displays; made of sateen, white or drab. Sizes, 18 to 28. Always give waist measure.
Price, each..55c
If by mail, postage extra, 12 cents.

OUR ONLY TERMS ARE CASH WITH THE ORDER
as fully explained on pages 1 and 2 of our big catalogue. We guarantee entire satisfaction or refund your money.

Dr. Ball's Elastic Corsets for Growing Girls, 75 Cents.

75c

No. 18R4958 Dr. Ball's Perfect Fitting Misses' Corset, an ideal corset for growing girls, shaped on scientific principles, made of fine, heavy drill, laced and elastic gored hook, shoulder straps and clasp front, lace edging. A perfect corset. White or drab. Sizes, 18 to 26. Always give waist measure.
Price, each..75c
If by mail, postage extra, 12 cents.

OUR

Corset Department

has shown a wonderful grow thin the last two years. By selling only the best models, correct form fitting corsets at prices never approached, we have built up a trade among our lady customers that is very flattering.

IF YOU HAVE NEVER BOUGHT A CORSET OF US, PLEASE

LET US TRY TO PLEASE YOU ON YOUR NEXT ORDER. . . .

THIMBLES, NEEDLES, THREAD, SEWING SUPPLIES, ETC.

Thimbles.

No. 18R4960 Aluminum Thimbles, light and durable, come one dozen in a box. Price, per dozen..8c

No. 18R4962 Fancy Gilt Thimbles, with band of coloring around; facsimile of real gold.
Price, each........................3c

No. 18R4964 German Silver Thimbles, all sizes.
Price, each........................3c

If by mail, postage extra, per doz., 5 cts.

No. 18R4966 Real Silver Plated Thimbles, ornamented with small gilt heart, as shown in illustration.
Price, each..............................4c

If by mail, postage extra, each, 2 cents.

The Harper's Helix Needles.

No. 18R4968 The Harper's Helix Needles, made in Redditch, England. The oldest, most reliable and best quality needle manufactured. All sizes, sharps and betweens. **Be sure to give size wanted.** Per paper.....2c

No. 18R4970 Self Threading Needle, perfectly polished, best tempered steel; threads itself by simply passing the thread over the eye of the needle; comes in all sizes; ten needles to paper. Price, per paper..........4c

Darning Needles.

No. 18R4972 Cloth Stuck. Put up ten to the paper, assorted sizes. Price, per paper..2c

Knitting Needle Sets.

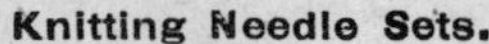

No. 18R4974 Put up five to the set, in round cabinet wood case. **Sizes ten to sixteen.** Size ten is coarsest, size sixteen is finest. Per set of five......3c

Crochet Hook Set.

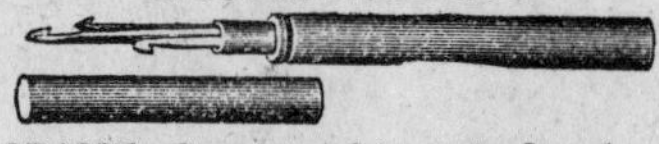

No. 18R4976 Consists of two steel and one bone crochet hook, put in round cabinet case.
Price, each, for set of three......................4c

A Magic Darner.

Mends Your Hosiery in a Hurry.

No. 18R4978 The Magic Darner is a machine recently invented and patented for mending hosiery, silk, wool or cotton, all kinds of underwear, napkins, table linens and, in fact, everything in the household that needs darning. One does not have to be an expert needle worker to mend lace curtains and other fine fabrics, the Magic Darner does it for you and saves you nineteen-twentieths of your time. You can take twenty stitches on the machine while you take one in the old way. Well worth $2.50. Price, each..............................16c

If by mail, postage extra, each, 5 cents.

Needle Cases.

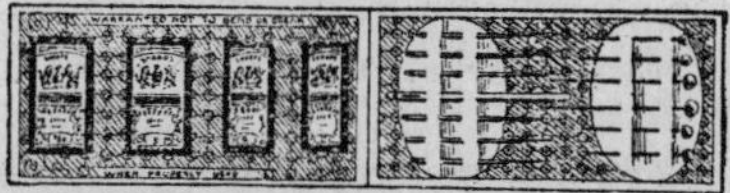

No. 18R4980 Our Needle Case contains four papers of needles, also other needles and pins. **These cases are usually retailed for 10 cents.**
Price, each.......................................2c

If by mail, postage extra, each, 2 cents.

No. 18R4982 The Chicago Combination Needle Case contains four papers of needles and a large variety of needles and pins. Size, 4½x7 inches when closed, three-fold. Price, each..........................9c

If by mail, postage extra, 3 cents.

Tape Measures.

No. 18R4984 TapeMeasure, printed on both sides, double-stitched (60 inches long), fine, heavy cloth, metal tip. **This grade of tape lines is suitable for tailors' or dressmakers' use.** Price, each...............2c

If by mail, postage extra, 2 cents.

No. 18R4986 Tailors' or Dressmakers' Tape Measures, fine cloth, figured on both sides; a very durable and satisfactory tape.
Price, each..5c

No. 18R4988 Nickeled Spring, 3-foot tape measure. Buying them as we do in immense quantities enables us to make the price we do. Each...7c

If by mail, postage extra, 2 cents.

No. 18R4990 Nickeled Spring Tape, 5-foot length; good tape and catch spring; won't get out of order, a handy article around the house.
Each.... 17c

If by mail, postage extra, 3 cents.

Victoria Plaiting Machine.

A Victoria Plaiting Machine and a hot iron is all you need.

No. 18R4992 Victoria Plaiting Machine, used by all leading dressmakers and milliners to make all kinds of trimmings. Two gauges go with each machine. No lady should be without one. Size of plaiter, 7⅛x14 inches; makes plaits 7 inches wide.
Price, each..............17c

Weight, when packed for shipment, 20 ounces.
For postage rate see page 4.

Egg Darner.

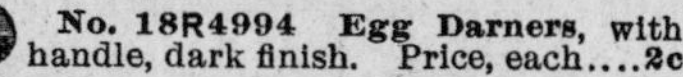

No. 18R4994 Egg Darners, with handle, dark finish. Price, each....2c

Magic Eradicator to Remove Grease Spot.

No. 18R4996 At last we can offer a perfectly reliable eradicator which will remove grease, oil, tar, pitch and paint from woolen goods, silks, carpets, clothes and hats. For cleaning kid gloves, applied with a flannel **its equal never known. Will not harm the goods.** You ought to order them by the gross and sell to your neighbors at the regular retail price for 25 cents. **You can make from $2.00 to $5.00 a day.**
Price, per box..9c

If by mail, postage extra, per box, 8 cents.

Adamantine Pins.

No. 18R4998 Pins are put up one dozen papers to the package. Adamantine pins, per package:

2 large,	3 medium,	4 small,
15c	13c	12c

Shipping weight, 16 ounces.

Brass Pins.

No. 18R5000 Brass Pins. 300 to each paper, 12 papers in each package. Per package:

2 large,	3 medium,	4 small.
31c	28c	25c

Shipping weight, 18 ounces.

No. 18R5002 The Sandow Best English Brass Pin, polished solid heads and needle points. **Contains 400 assorted pins.** Sizes, 2, 3 and 4. Put up in handsome gilt edged papers. 2 papers for 5c

If by mail, postage extra, per paper, 1 cent.

A Special Bargain in Pin Books.

No. 18R5004 Pin Books, 8 rows of 30 pins each, 240 pins. One row of black; all ne plus ultra high grade brass pins. Three sizes in book. Price, per book.........3c

If by mail, postage extra, 1 cent.

No. 18R5006 Black Pins, bright round jet heads. Per box of 50..2c

If by mail, postage extra, 1 cent.

No. 18R5008 Jet Black Mourning Pins, solid heads, assorted sizes; 200 in box.
Price, per box.......................................3c

If by mail, postage extra, 2 cents.

Fancy, Black and Colored Headed Pins.

No. 18R5010 Fancy Chromo Pins. Card contains 25 jet head black pins and 25 small fancy head black pins.
Price, per card.............................3c

If by mail, postage extra, 2 cents.

No. 18R5012 Cube of Black Headed Pins, put up as per illustration, containing about 56 assorted pins.
Price, each......................................3c

If by mail, postage extra, 2 cents.

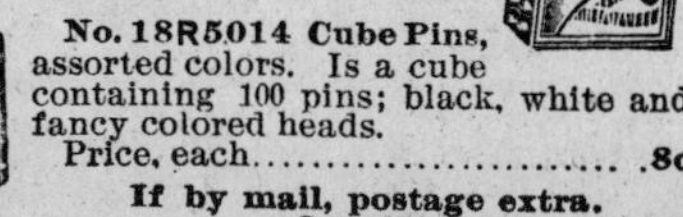

No. 18R5014 Cube Pins, assorted colors. Is a cube containing 100 pins; black, white and fancy colored heads.
Price, each..........................8c

If by mail, postage extra. 3 cents.

Hat and Shawl Pins.

No. 18R5016 Hat and Shawl Pins. Hat pins, with black heads, 5 or 6 inches long.
Price, per dozen..2c

No. 18R5018 Hat Pins, white heads, 5 inches long.
Price, per dozen..4c

No. 18R5020 Shawl or Belt Pins, large black heads, 2 inches long.
Price, per dozen..2c

If by mail, postage extra, 2 cents.

Fancy Shaped Jet Hat Pins.

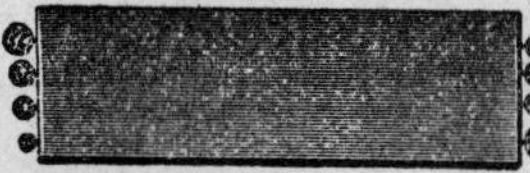

No. 18R5022 Put up on fancy cabinets, assorted sized heads. Eight to the cabinet.
Price, per cabinet.................................5c

If by mail, postage extra, 2 cents.

Safety Pin Book.

The Sensible Safety Pins are the cheapest and best nickeled safety pin and the most practical, having the double sided shield.

No. 18R5024 Sensible Safety Pin Book, contains two dozen small, medium and large assorted sensible nickeled safety pins.
Price, per book..6c

If by mail, postage extra, 3 cents.

Sensible Safety Pin.

Highly Polished, Nickel Plated.

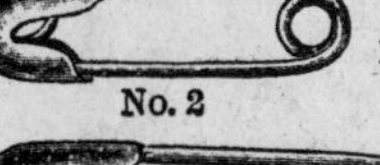

No. 2

Good Safety Pins for little money.

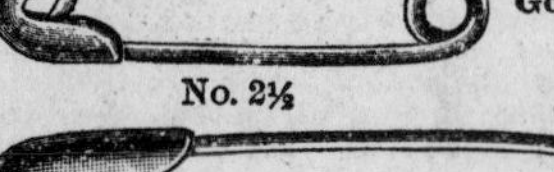

No. 2½

Illustrations Show Exact Size : : :

No. 3

No. 18R5026 Safety Pins.	No. 2	No. 2½	No. 3
Price, per dozen...	1c	2c	3c

If by mail, postage extra, per dozen, 2 cents.

No. 18R5028 Large Safety Blanket Pins, 4 inches long; the most substantial and practical pin made.
Price, six for 16c; each..................................3c

If by mail, postage extra, each, 2 cents.

Corset Clasps.

No. 18R5032 Corset Clasps, reinforced, double steel; covered with corset jeans; five hooks. Black, white or drab. Price, per pair.......................?c

If by mail, postage extra, per pair, 3 cents.

No. 18R5036 Four-Hook Corset Clasp, covered with a good quality of corset jeans, reinforced double steel. Black, white or drab.
Price, per pair..4c

If by mail, postage extra, per pair, 3 cents.

No. 18R5040 Fine French Sateen Covered Corset Steels, in black, white or drab, five hooks.
Price, per pair..6c

If by mail, postage extra, per pair, 3 cents.

No. 18R5044 Four-Hook French Sateen Covered Corset Steels, fine tempered steel. Colors black, white or drab.
Price, per pair..6c

If by mail, postage extra, per pair, 3 cents.

PAT. NO. 487411.
PAT. NO. 576,056.
Neverbreak
TRADE MARK.

Corset Laces.

No. 18R5048 The Neverbreak Corset Lace. Best lace made, will last as long as the corset, round cord 2½ yards long, white or black. Price, each. .2c

No. 18R5052 The Neverbreak Corset Lace. Same as above, white or black, 3 yards long.
Price, each..2c

No. 18R5056 Round Cotton Corset Laces, short, white or black. Price, per dozen..........................5c

No. 18R5060 Round Cotton Corset Laces, long, white or black. Price, per dozen..........................6c

No. 18R5064 Cotton Elastic Corset Laces. Length, 2½ yards; black or white. Price, per dozen.......18c

If by mail, postage extra, per dozen, 4 cents.

For complete assortment of shoe laces see Shoe Department

Key Chains.

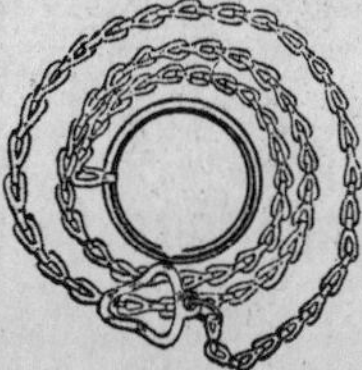

No. 18R5068 Steel Key Ring and Loop End. Extra well made and highly polished.
Price, each..........................4c

No. 18R5072 Aluminum Key Chain, light, strong and durable. Each..................6c

If by mail, postage extra, each, 2 cents.

Nickeled Tweezers.

No. 18R5080 Highly Polished Nickeled Tweezers. ear pick and hand cut nail file; regular 15-cent article. Price, each..........5c

If by mail, postage extra, 2 cents.

Coat Collar Spring.

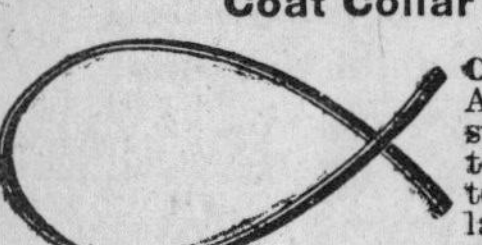

No. 18R5084 Patent Coat Collar Spring. Adjustable coat collar spring, made of best oil tempered steel, formed to fit the coat under collar, retaining the shape and keeping coat lapels in place. Price, each..........3c

If by mail, postage extra, each, 4 cents.

Pants and Vest Buckles.

No. 18R5088 Duplex Pants Buckles, self adjustable. Four strand for vests and pants. Price, each..........5c

No. 18R5092 Duplex Pants Buckles, 6 springs. Price, each..........6c

If by mail, postage extra, each, 1c; per doz., 9 cents.

Plain Buckles.

No. 18R5096 Black or White Pants Buckles. Price, per gross..........14c

If by mail, postage extra, per gross, 13 cents.

Pants Stretcher and Hanger.

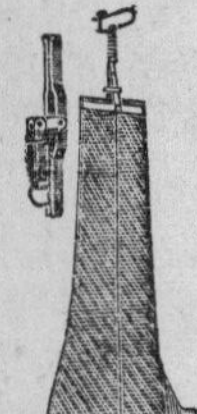

No. 18R5100 The Set Well Trousers Stretcher and Pants Hanger. Makes wrinkled clothes smooth, cures baggy knees and keeps your trousers in shape. Made of best steel, heavily nickel plated. The best hanger on the market today. Each......(Postage extra, 4c)......14c

Witchkloth.

No. 18R5104 Witchkloth, a specially prepared cloth for keeping all tableware, gold, silver, nickel, copper, plated ware, glass, etc., bright, clean and free from corrosions. It will not injure the most delicate surface; takes the place of all powders, polishes, liquids, and also chamois skins, and at less than one-fourth of the cost. Full directions how to use with each cloth. Size, 12x7 inches. Price, each..........10c

No. 18R5108 Witchkloth, for cleaning all kinds of metal ware and glass, same as above. Size, 25x14 inches. Price, each..(Postage extra, each, 2c)..19c

Devereaux Family System of Dressmaking

No. 18R5112 New improved French system of dressmaking, self taught in a few hours in your own home. For cutting ladies' and misses' and children's garments; is based on actual measure. Indorsed by professional cutters who have found it quicker, more simple and accurate than any system heretofore devised. Full set of instructions and life size diagram with each system, and **it is so simple that even a child can learn to use it without personal instruction.** Cuts all styles and sizes of garments. The Devereaux Tailor System has always sold for $10.00, which for the knowledge is well worth it. We have contracted, however, with the makers of same for several thousand, and shall offer them at a greatly reduced price. If they do not prove all we claim for them we will cheerfully refund your money. Tracing wheel and tape line with each set. A splendid article for canvassers, who can readily sell them at $6.00 to $10.00. Price, each..........**$1.79**

If by mail, postage extra, 30 cents.

Skirt Bindings of All Kinds.

No. 18R5116 Bias Velveteen Skirt Binding by the yard. The most economical way to buy it; order any quantity you need; 2 inches wide; black, and all colors. Price, per yard..........3c

No. 18R5120 Corduroy Velveteen Skirt Binding. Made of best double warp velveteen; cheapest kind to get. It costs a little more but lasts as long as the dress. All colors. Price, per yard..........4c

Brush Braid.

No. 18R5124 S., R. & Co.'s Brush Braid and Skirt Protector. We guarantee this braid all wool, is heavier than other makes and the best at any price. Colors, black, brown, myrtle, navy, royal blue, tan, cardinal, wine or drab. Price, per yard..........4c

Waterproof Bias Velveteen Skirt Binding.

Recommended by Dressmakers everywhere.

No. 18R5128 Waterproof Bias Velveteen Skirt Binding, protected by brush edge, the most serviceable and sightly binding ever produced; cut curved to fit the skirt; the brush edge is invisible and will not wear the most delicate shoes. Colors, black, navy, brown, myrtle, drab, cardinal or tan. Price, per yard..........5c

No. 18R5132 Velvet Top Brush Edge Skirt Binding. The velvet top for finish and elegance and brush edge for wear; the best and most popular binding. Colors, black, navy, brown, myrtle or drab. Price, per yard..........8c

Waterproof Dress Facing.

No. 18R5136 Waterproof Dress Facing. For elegance and durability it excels all others; will outwear the dress. Cut on the bias, which gives it the natural, graceful curve to conform with curve on the skirt. Colors, black, brown, navy, drab, tan, myrtle or cardinal. Price, per yard..........4c

Skirt Braid.

No. 18R5140 Star Skirt Braid. Unexcelled for durability. Width, ½-inch; 3 yards in a roll. All staple colors. Warranted fast color. Price, per roll..........4c

If by mail, postage extra, each, 2 cents.

Cotton Tape, Black and White.

No. 18R5144 Cotton Tape, in black or white. Comes 3 yards to the piece.

No.	4	6	8	10	12	16
Width, inches	3/16	⅜	½	⅝	11/16	¾
Price, per roll	1c	1c	1½c	1½c	2c	2c

No. 18R5148 Extra Super White Cotton Tape. Comes about 3½ to 4 yards to the roll. Comes in white and black only.

Width, inches	¼	⅜	½	⅝	¾
Price, per roll	2c	2c	3c	3c	4c

REFER TO PAGE 858

if you want a

PAPER PATTERN FOR 5 CENTS

that will enable you to make up your own dress.

Ladies' Ventilated Dress and Corset Protector.

No. 18R5152 Tades' Ventilated Dress and Corset Protector. Does away with the inconvenience of sewing in and taking out dress shields. A complete garment to be worn under the corset, protecting that garment as well as the waist from perspiration. May be easily removed and washed, being adjustable. One pair of protectors will take the place of a dozen pairs of the regular dress shields. Order by sizes as follows:

No. 3 can be adjusted for bust measures 28 to 33.
No. 4 can be adjusted for bust measures 34 to 39.
No. 5 can be adjusted for bust measures 40 to 46.
Price, per pair..........78c

If by mail, postage extra, 5 cents.

Ladies' Dress Shields.

No. 18R5156 Stockinet Dress Shields. Good shields for a little money.

Size	1 Small	2 Medium	3 Large
Price, per pair.	4c	5c	6c

Kleinert's Dress Shields.

No. 18R5160 Kleinert's Seamless Stockinet Dress Shields. Every pair warranted. Kleinert pays for the dress if it is ruined by perspiration while his shields are used in it, and Kleinert is responsible for what he says.

Size, No.	2	3	4
Price per pair,	13c	15c	17c

The Gem Dress Shield.

No. 18R5164 The Gem Pure Rubber Dress Shield. Kleinert pays for the dress if it is ruined by perspiration if his shields are used in it.

Size, No.	2	3	4
Price, per pair,	12c	14c	16c

Featherweight Dress Shield.

No. 18R5168 Featherweight Fine Nainsook Dress Shield.

Size, No.	2	3	4
Price, per pair,	12c	13c	15c

Alpha Dress Shields.

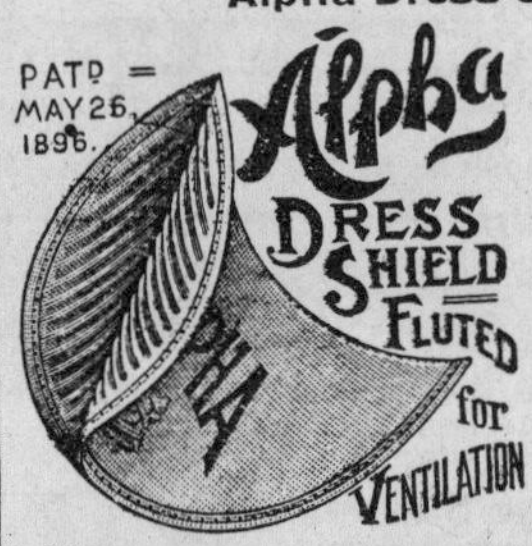

No. 18R5172 The Alpha Ventilating Dress Shields, light but substantial, pure Para rubber, absolutely odorless, can be washed and retain their fluted shape. Every lady wonders how she stood the old style, thick, plaster-like, odor creating shields when she has used the Alpha.

Sizes	2	3	4
Price, per pair	14c	16c	19c

Hooks and Eyes.

No. 18R5176 Swan Bill Hooks and Eyes. Straight shank, black or white. Nos. 3 and 4. Two dozen on a card. Price, per card..........1c

No. 18R5180 Hump Hooks and Eyes. Made of brass, japanned or silvered. Strong and durable and a hook and eye that we guarantee to our trade. Put up two dozen on a card. Sizes, Nos. 3 and 4. Price, per card of two dozen..........2c

If by mail, postage extra, per card, 2 cents.

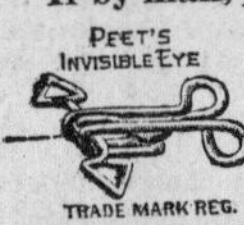

No. 18R5184 Peet's Invisible Eye. Making a flat seam and prevents gaping; indispensable to every dress to take the place of the silk loops, which have always been a source of great annoyance by their continual breaking. Used and endorsed by all leading dressmakers. Black or white. Price, for package of two dozen hooks and two dozen eyes..........8c

If by mail, postage extra, per card, 2 cents.

The Famous DeLong Hook and Eye.

"See That Hump?"

No. 18R5188 Oscar A. DeLong's Perfect Hooks and Eyes. The best grade of hooks and eyes on the market. Perfect hump, and recommended by all dress makers. Japanned or silvered on brass. Nos. 2, 3 and 4. Two dozen on a card. Price, per card..........6c

If by mail, postage extra, per card, 2 cents.

S., R. & Co.'s Special Hook and Eye.

No. 18R5192 The S., R. & Co.'s Special Hook and Eye (with a perfect hump). Made of best brass wire, highly finished, silvered or japanned; the best hook and eye made. Sizes, 3 and 4; two dozen on a card. Price, per card..........3c

If by mail, postage extra, per card, 2 cents.

"Featherbone."

No. 18R5193 "Featherbone" Piping Bone, made from quills, cotton covered, used for distending skirt ruffles, etc. Colors, black or drab. Price, per yard........................2½c

No. 18R5194 Twill Covered "Featherbone." The standard grade herringbone pattern, made from quills. A light, pliable elastic bone, for use in dresses, waists and corsets. Used by the best dressmakers in preference to whalebone. Colors, black, white or drab. Price, per yard........7c

No. 18R5195 "Featherbone." Grosgrain silk ribbon covered, for finest dresses, waists, etc. Colors, black, white, slate, pink or blue.
Price, per yard........................15c

Twin Dress Stays.

No. 18R5196 Made of two fine twin spring steels in a two-pocket woven webbing. Colors, cardinal, pink, blue, brown, drab, white or black.
Per set, (9 in set)...4c
If by mail, postage extra, 2 cents.

No. 18R5200 The Victoria Dress Stay. Aluminized roll steel, soft metallic tip, also double thickness sateen, protecting the satin finish sateen covering from the metal. Warranted not to puncture. Put up in sets of 9 stays, all colors. Per set, 6c
If by mail, postage extra, per set, 2 cents.

The Perfection Dress Stay.

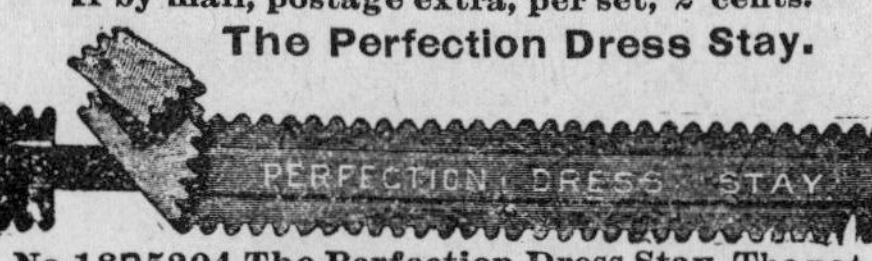

No. 18R5204 The Perfection Dress Stay. The patent triple silica tip, aluminized, watch spring steel, covered with fine satin finish sateen, gutta percha lined. Warranted not to puncture. Put up in sets of nine. All colors. Price, per set........8c
If by mail, postage extra, 2 cents.

The Ever Ready Dress Stay.

No. 18R5208 The Ever Ready Dress Stay. The best covered dress stay made. Endorsed by the leading dressmakers. Best tempered steel and rubber lined, covered with silk finish sateen. Guaranteed not to rust or work through. Colors, cardinal, pink, blue, lavender, slate, brown, black or white.
Price, per set (nine in set)........9c
If by mail, postage extra, 2 cents.

Dress Bone Casing.

No. 18R5212 Whalebone Casing, (6-yard pieces). Black, white and drab. Price, per piece........6c
If by mail, postage extra, 2 cents.

Seam Binding.

No. 18R5214 Silk Taffeta Seam Binding. Black, white, cardinal, blue, navy, yellow, pink, etc.
Price, per piece of nine yards........9c
If by mail, postage extra, 2 cents.

Ever Ready Mending Tissue.

No. 18R5220 The Ever Ready Mending Tissue. Mends perfectly rips or tears in gloves, clothing and fabric of all kinds, takes less time and accomplishes the purpose better than sewing. Size, 36 inches long by 2½ inches wide. Price, per sheet........4c
If by mail, postage extra, 2 cents.

Invisible Sew-on Fastener.

No. 18R5224 This Invisible Sew-on-Fastener. Used instead of hooks and eyes, and especially adapted for fastening skirts, shirt waists, etc.; no chance to catch or tear. Silvered or japanned. Price, per dozen........7c
If by mail, postage extra, 2 cents.

Not-a-Stitch Skirt Supporter.

No. 18R5228 This Supporter is scientifically constructed, of the best material, with finely nickeled parts and improved point, protected buckles and the only perfectly satisfactory skirt supporter made. Requires no sewing, easily operated, gives a perfect fit; with it the skirt cannot sag. Made in black, drab or white. Attachments for two skirts with each pair. Price........19c

No. 18R5232 The Ladies' Ideal Skirt and Waist Supporter with attachments for three skirts, made of German silver and will not rust or soil the finest fabric, holds skirt together without the use of hooks and eyes. This supporter is desirable for basques as well as shirt waists, will support the heaviest skirt and will carry the weight from the shoulders instead of on the waist line. Set complete with attachments for three skirts. Price........10c

The Dip Front Waist Holder and Skirt Supporter.

No. 18R5233 The dip front effect as shown in the illustration can be obtained with any skirt and waist. Combined perfect skirt supporter at back of waist with attachments giving dip effect at front. Can be worn with or without corsets, reversible on belt, giving long or short dip. The belt is adjustable to any waist size.

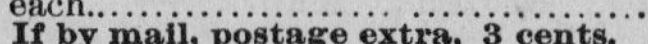

Price, each........20c
If by mail, postage extra, 3 cents.

Sewing Silk and Twist.

Corticelli Silk is warranted full size and full length. Black spool silks are marked OO, O, A, B, C and D. No. OO is the finest. No. O is next coarser, etc. Colored spool silks come in letter A only.

Corticelli Sewing Silk.

No. 18R5244 Corticelli Sewing Silk, 50-yard spools, black, white and all colors.
Per spool........4c

No. 18R5248 Corticelli Sewing Silk, 100-yard spools, black, white and all colors.
Price, per spool..8c

No. 18R5252 Corticelli Buttonhole Twist, 10-yard spools, black, white and all colors. Price, per spool, 1½c

The Corticelli Embroidery and Wash Silks are far superior in finish, smoothness and delicate shading to any silk on the market. Needleworkers find real satisfaction in every way by the use of the Corticelli wash silks.

Corticelli Embroidery Silk on Spools.

No. 18R5256 Corticelli Embroidery Silk, on spools, 3 yards, size, EE, all colors. Price, per dozen only...8c
If by mail, postage extra, per 100, 14 cents.

Corticelli Etching Silk.

No. 18R5260 Corticelli Etching Silk, size 500, positively a fast dye silk, medium size for outlining work and etching, 10 yards to the skein.
Price, per dozen skeins........30c

No. 18R5264 Corticelli Twisted Embroidery Silk. Size, EE. This size is the regular wash embroidery silk; fast color, pure dye, 10 yards in skein.
Price, per dozen skeins........30c

Corticelli Rope Embroidery Silk.

No. 18R5268 Corticelli Rope Embroidery Silk. Washing colors. A coarse silk, for bold designs either in outline or solid embroidery on heavy material, when rapid work is desired. Per dozen skeins........30c

Corticelli Filo Floss.

No. 18R5272 Corticelli Filo Floss. This is a fine size, slack twist, wash silk and is used for embroidery purposes of all kinds, but is especially desirable for embroidering on stamped linens, center pieces, doylies, etc. Comes in black, white and over 360 colors. Price, per dozen skeins........30c

No. 18R5273 Corticelli Persian Floss. A silk of two strands, loosely twisted and of high lustre. It is now very popular for finishing the edges of doilies and center pieces. Persian floss is made in colors, 880 to 887. **See color card No. 18R5284.**

No. 18R5274 Corticelli Roman Floss, somewhat coarser than Persian Floss and intended for embroidering larger designs on heavier material. Curtains, counterpanes and cushions are worked with this silk; made only in shades given in color card No. 18R5284.

Corticelli Waste Embroidery.

No. 18R5276 Corticelli Waste Embroidery Silk; assorted colors, odds and ends. Just the thing for fancy work. One ounce in package.
Price, per package........30c

No. 18R5280 Corticelli Knitting or Crochet Silk. In black, white and colors. Made of highest grade selected raw silk. We can furnish in two sizes: No. 300, which contains 150 yards to the ½-ounce ball, is used mostly and is a rather coarse thread. No. 500 which contains 250 yards to the ½-ounce ball is finer and is used for knitting mittens, stockings and other articles that require washing. Comes in black only. Price, per ball........35c
If by mail, postage extra, 2 cents.

No. 18R5281 Corticelli Purse Twist, for working new bead chatelaine bags and belts, ⅛ ounce on spool. Price, per spool........40c

Holder for Embroidery Silks.

No. 18R5282 This very clever invention for holding embroidery silks will save you five-fold the cost by saving your silks and loss of time and irritation. This is an eight leaf book and holds fifty-six skeins of silk. You can select one single thread at a time without tangling balance. Saves every thread where before you wasted half, and keeps them clean and fresh with all the colors arranged in plain view. Bound in an artistic cover. Every lady should have one. Price, each........28c
If by mail, postage extra, 4 cents.

Interesting to all Needle Workers.

No. 18R5284 It is very difficult for people using wash silk to order the exact shade they want by mail unless they send a sample. To overcome this we have arranged to have a number of color cards made showing over 350 shades of Corticelli wash embroidery silks, (each shade has a number); by selecting the shade you want and sending us the number, **you are sure to get just what you want.** We have also issued **"a flower book"** describing 70 flowers and how to embroider them.
Price, the two books for........5c
If by mail, postage extra, 3 cents.

The William Clark Spool Cotton, which we think is the best, strongest and smoothest thread made, will hereafter be known and sold as

The American Thread Co.'s Best Spool Cotton.

No. 18R5288 Double Spun, Best Six-Cord Machine Thread, never kinks or snarls in hand sewing and is perfection itself on any kind of a sewing machine. It will stand 100 per cent more friction (wearing longer) in proportion, than any other thread of equal grade; it is without an equal for stitching buttonholes, and sewing on buttons, often outlasting the fabric itself. **We highly recommend The American Thread Co.'s Best spool cotton.** Black and white in Nos. 8 to 100; and colors in Nos. 40, 50. Price, per spool........3¾c
If by mail, postage extra, per dozen, 10 cents.

Spool Cotton.

No. 18R5292 The New York Mills Basting Cotton (200 yards on each spool), a very superior cotton; the retail merchant gets 24 to 36 cents per dozen for these goods. Nos. 30 to 60 only, black or white, no colors. Our special price, per dozen........14c
Shipping weight, per dozen, 12 ounces.

The J. O. King Machine Thread.

No. 18R5296 The J. O. King Machine Spool Thread; nice and smooth, will run on any machine. Full length, 200 yards on each spool. Made from the best of selected cotton yarns, black and white, all numbers; colors in No. 50 only. **Retail merchants ask 4 cents per spool for thread that in many cases is not as good.** Price, per spool........1¾c
Shipping weight, 12 ounces.

No. 18R5300 Giant Thread. 100-yard spools, stronger than linen, smoother than silk, for all kinds of heavy sewing. **Nothing better for sewing carpets, buttons, etc., made.** Black, white and staple colors. Price, per spool........4c
Shipping weight, per dozen, 2 pounds.

Spool Linen.

No. 18R5304 Marshall's Linen Thread (100-yard spools, black only). Coarse and fine numbers.
Price, per spool........2½c

No. 18R5308 Barbour's (200-yard spools) Best Linen Thread. Numbers run from No. 25 (coarse) to No. 100 (fine), black, white, drab and whitish brown.
Price, per spool........7c

No. 18R5312 Carpet Thread, black, brown, green, red, drab, slates and staple colors.
Price, per ¼ pound (10 skeins)........17c

Silcoton.

To replace Crochet Cotton.

No. 18R5316 Silcoton. The latest article for crocheting and embroidering. Is a cotton thread with a soft twist and a silk finish, and so closely does it resemble the crochet silk that it is difficult to distinguish from the genuine, while the cost is no more than for the ordinary crochet cotton. Comes in plain and shaded colors, as follows:

Plain Colors—Nile green, moss green, olive green, light or medium yellow, scarlet, crimson, light blue, medium blue, pink, lilac, white, cream, black.

Shaded Colors—White, blue and pink; white, yellow and pink; white and yellow; white, green and pink; white and moss green; white and pink; white and blue; white and lilac; white and nile green.
Price, per spool........3c
If by mail, postage extra, per spool, 1 cent.

H. B. Embroidery Cotton.

H. B. Embroidery Cotton on spools; plain, solid colors, turkey red, black and white; three colors only. Nos. 8, 10, 12, 14, 16, 18, 20, 22, 24.
Will Not Crock or Wash Out.

No. 18R5320 Turkey Red H.B. Embroidery Cotton.
Price, per ball........1½c

No. 18R5324 Solid black H.B. Embroidery Cotton. Price, per ball........1½c

TRADE MARK.

No. 18R5326 Plain White H. B. Embroidery Cotton. Price, per ball........1½c
Shipping weight, per dozen, 5 ounces.

No. 18R5328 Navy Blue H. B. Embroidery Cotton. The best cotton made. Per ball........1½c

Knitting and Darning Cotton.

No. 18R5332 Crown White Knitting Cotton. Best quality, 4-thread, put up 10 balls to the pound and 2 pounds to the box. Any number, 6 to 24. Per ball........3½

No. 18R5336 Navy Blue Knitting Cotton. Same Quality as above, numbers 8 to 16. Per ball........3½c

No. 18R5340 Blue and White Mixed Knitting Cotton. Same quality as above. Nos. 8 to 16.
Per ball........3½c

Darning Cotton.

No. 18R5344 Best Fast Black Darning Cotton. Diagonally wound, 50 yards on a spool. Absolutely fast color; will stand washing and boiling. Also comes in brown, tan and gray. Price, per spool........1½c
If by mail, postage extra, 2 cents.

No. 18R5348 Darning Cotton, on cards. Colors, black, white, brown and tan. Per dozen only........7c

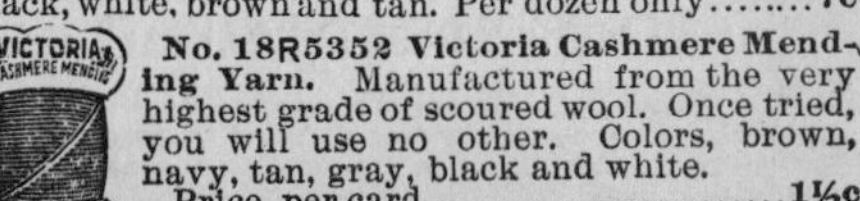

No. 18R5352 Victoria Cashmere Mending Yarn. Manufactured from the very highest grade of scoured wool. Once tried, you will use no other. Colors, brown, navy, tan, gray, black and white.
Price, per card........1½c
If by mail, postage extra, per dozen, 6c.

HIGHEST GRADE KNITTING YARNS.

It is a pleasure to sell GOOD GOODS. They prove more than satisfactory to the purchaser, who in turn buys again and recommends the house he trades with. Our Knitting Yarns are trade makers. They run smoother, wear longer and go farther to the pound than any other yarn.

SEND US YOUR ORDER FOR ANY OF OUR HIGH GRADE YARNS,

and if you do not find them even beyond your expectations, return them to us at our expense and we will refund money cheerfully.

Woolen Knitting Yarn.

No. 18R5370 Woolen Knitting Yarn, long wool; comes in solid colors only. Cardinal, navy blue, seal brown, black or white. Sixteen skeins to pound. Price, per pound 65c

German Yarns.

No. 18R5374 German Knitting Worsted Yarn, four skeins to the pound. Comes in the following colors: Cardinal, scarlet, medium and navy blue, purple, medium and seal brown, sheep's gray, black mixed, black or white.
Price, all colors, per pound....72c

No. 18R5378 Royal German Knitting Yarn, finest quality, four skeins to the pound; colors same as No. 18R5374. For a good satisfactory yarn buy the Royal, which contains a long wool filling and we guarantee every hank sold.
Price, all colors, per pound....86c

No. 18R5382 Fleisher's German Knitting Worsted Yarn, four skeins to the pound. Colors same as No. 18R5374. Fleisher's yarn needs no recommendation. It is too well known.
Price, all colors, per pound....92c

Saxony Wool Yarn

No. 18R5386 Saxony Wool Yarn. Imported. Made of the finest Australian wool; 20 skeins to the pound. Colors, scarlet, cardinal, wine, pink, light, medium or navy blue, medium or seal brown, black or white.
Price, black, white and colors, per pound....$1.09

No. 18R5390 Spanish Knitting Worsted Yarn. Imported, eight skeins to the pound. Colors, cardinal, navy blue, seal brown, black or white.
Price, black, white and colors, per pound....96c

Shetland Floss.

No. 18R5394 Shetland Floss, fine grade, twelve skeins to the pound, manufacturer's weight. Colors, light blue, medium blue, pink, lemon, lilac, cardinal, dove, black or white. Price, per skein, all colors...7c

No. 18R5398 Shetland Wool Yarn, twelve skeins to the pound. Colors, black or white only.
Price, per skein....8c

No. 18R5402 Coral Yarn. Imported, twelve skeins to the pound. Colors, cardinal, light blue, pink, yellow, garnet, peacock blue, black or white.
Price, black, white and colors, per pound....$1.44

No. 18R5406 Fairy Floss or Crinkled Yarn. Used for fancy knitting, eight skeins to the pound. Colors, black or white only. Price, per pound....99c

No. 18R5410 Germantown Wool Yarn, Imported, sixteen skeins to the pound. Colors, scarlet, cardinal, wine, light, medium or navy blue, seal brown, yellow, green, purple, drab, black or white.
Price, black, white and colors, per pound....$1.12

No. 18R5414 Angora Wool, best quality imported yarn. Colors, black, white and gray; 64 balls to the pound. Price, per ball 12c

Imported Ice Wool.

No. 18R5418 Ice Wool. Imported. Put up in 1/16-pound boxes, eight balls to the box. Colors, black, or white only. Price, per box (8 balls)....9c

No. 18R5422 Ice Wool. Imported. 1-ounce balls, put up eight balls to the box. Colors, black or white only. Price, per ball....10c

Zephyr Worsteds.

No. 18R5426 Zephyr Worsted. Imported. Berlin zephyr, 4-ply, called single. Colors, scarlet, cardinal, pink, wine, garnet, light, medium and navy blue, nile, medium and dark green, brown, tan, olive, orange, canary, gray, purple, black or white. Forty laps to the pound. Price, per lap....4c

No. 18R5430 Zephyr Worsted. Imported. Berlin zephyr, 2-ply, called split zephyr. Colors, same as No. 18R5426. Forty laps to the pound.
Price, per lap....4c

SEND A 2-CENT STAMP for our Wall Paper Sample Book. On receipt of 2 cents we will send a complete sample book of wall paper at lower prices than you can buy elsewhere.

GETTING 50 CENTS FOR OUR LARGE CATALOGUE GETTING PAY FOR OUR SAMPLES,

helps make these low prices possible. We do not add the expense of thousands of catalogues and samples to our selling prices, and make people who buy pay for thousands of catalogues and samples sent to people who do not buy. Other houses do this: we don't. As a result, our prices are lower than any other house.

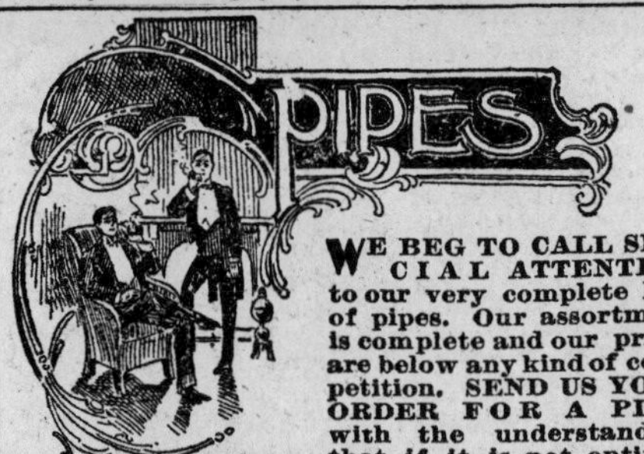

WE BEG TO CALL SPECIAL ATTENTION to our very complete line of pipes. Our assortment is complete and our prices are below any kind of competition. SEND US YOUR ORDER FOR A PIPE, with the understanding that if it is not entirely satisfactory in every way, by far better value than you could get elsewhere, you are at liberty to return it to us at our expense and we will immediately return your money.

Our 4-Cent Apple Wood Pipe.

No. 18R5450 Polished Apple Wood Pipe, with silver ferrule and rubber stem, 2¼ inches long. This is a well known 10-cent article.
Our price, each....4c
If by mail, postage extra, each, 2 cents.

Selected Corn Cob Pipe.

No. 18R5454 Fine Selected Corn Cob Pipes, extra large size bowl, finely polished, reed stems, a regular 10-cent article. Price, each...2c
If by mail, postage extra, each, 2 cents.

The Rough Rider.

No. 18R5458 Fine wood pipe, bulldog shape, rubber bit and silvered band. The Rough Rider is an excellent smoker.
Price, each....9c
If by mail, postage extra, each, 3 cents.

Elegant Brier Pipe for 14 Cents.

No. 18R5462 Very Elegant Brier Pipe, a medium size, 5½ inches long with polished hard rubber stem and nickel band. Price, each....14c
If by mail, postage extra, each, 3 cents.

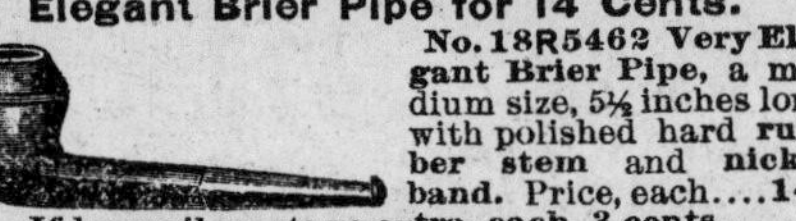

Our 19-Cent Chip Meerschaum.

No. 18R5466 Chip Meerschaum Pipe, medium size, handsomely nickel mounted. Chinese amber mouthpiece, good sized bowl. Price, each....19c
If by mail, postage extra, each, 3 cents.

22 Cents for a Self Cleaner.

No. 18R5470 Genuine French Brier English Bulldog Pipe. Handsome Vienna amber mouthpiece. Length, 5¼ inches, long self cleaner, handsome nickel band, finely made and finished.
Price, each....22c
If by mail, postage extra, each, 3 cents.

The New Ring Pipe.

For a Cool Smoke, and Preventing the Nicotine from Passing to the Mouth.

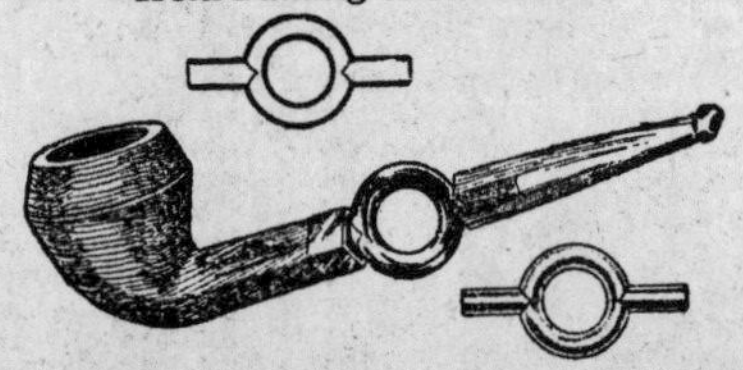

No. 18R5474 Genuine Brier Bowl, with imitation amber mouthpiece, and having the latest invention ring attachment. Tobacco in pipe is always kept dry, insuring a sweet, cool smoke. Easily cleaned. A boon for smokers. Price, each....38c
If by mail, postage extra, each, 5 cents.

No. 18R5478 New Ring Pipe with attachment, same as above, genuine brier bulldog pipe with genuine amber mouthpiece. A pipe you would pay the tobacconist $1.25 for without attachment.
Price, each....89c
If by mail, postage extra, each, 5 cents.

No. 18R5482 The New Ring Attachment which can be fitted to any pipe. Price, each....19c
If by mail, postage extra, each, 2 cents.

Students' Bulldog Pipe.

No. 18R5486 Students Favorite, dark colored, French Brier, English bulldog shape, handsome Chinese amber bit 2½ inches long, square nickel ferrule. Full size, very handsomely finished. Price, each.... 16c
If by mail, postage extra, each, 4 cents.

Dublin Shape.

No. 18R5490 French Brier Pipe, straight stem, Dublin shape bowl, 2-inch imitation amber mouthpiece. For a good smoke in a good pipe, buy this.
Price, each....19c
If by mail, postage extra, each, 5 cents.

Handsome Brier Pipe, Bulldog Shape.

No. 18R5494 Fine Brier Pipe, bulldog shape, with Chinese amber shove bit, plain nickel band, a very handsome pipe which we recommend very highly. Price, each....21c
If by mail, postage extra, each, 4 cents.

French Brier, 25 Cents.

No. 18R5498 For a long, cool smoke, we recommend this French Brier Pipe, made of highly stained dark polished French brier, with long, slender stem, Amberite mouthpiece and bulldog shaped bowl. Total length of pipe, 6 inches. Price, each....25c
If by mail, postage extra, each, 4 cents.

Bulldog Brier Pipe.

No. 18R5502 Bulldog Brier Pipe, with heavy curved Chinese amber shove bit, heavy nickel band on stem, a popular pipe usually sold at 50c.
Price, each....33c
If by mail, postage extra, each, 4 cents.

Bent Brier, 27 Cents.

No. 18R5510 Large Size Bent Brier Pipe, with rubber stem; fine covered nickel top; for a fine, lasting smoke this pipe can not be excelled.
Special price each. 27c
If by mail, postage extra, each, 3 cents.

Straight French Brier.

No. 18R5514 Straight French Brier Pipe, highly polished bowl, round stem, has a 2½-inch Chinese amber mouthpiece or stem, and a pipe that we can highly recommend. Price, each....36c
If by mail, postage extra, each, 5 cents.

Our 35-Cent Leader.

No. 18R5518 French Brier Pipe, highly polished dark brier, heavy bulldog pattern bowl, has 3½-inch horn mouthpiece with fancy nickel band; total length of pipe, 6¼ inches; a substantial and sightly pipe. Price....35c
If by mail, postage extra, each, 5 cents.

An Old Favorite.

No. 18R5522 Handsomely Carved Brier Bowl, cherry stem, 3 inches long, and rubber mouthpiece, entire length of pipe 7 inches. A pipe that is easily cleaned and kept in order and always gives satisfaction.
Our price, each. ...33c
If by mail, postage. extra, each, 6 cents

Fancy Brier Pipes.

Easily Cleaned.

No. 18R5526 The Always Clean Brier Bowl, long rubber stem, nicotine absorber, handsomely decorated cover; a pipe that can be taken apart in four pieces, and usually retails for $1.00.
Our price, each....34c
If by mail, postage extra, each, 7 cents.

The Yale Student.

No. 18R5530 Yale Student Pipe, is a heavy brier pipe with bent Chinese amber bit, heavy Bull Bitch shape. A fit companion for the millionaire, but at a price within reach of all. Price, each....39c
If by mail, postage extra, each, 4 cents.

27 Cents Buys a 50-Cent Pipe.

No. 18R5534 This splendid smoker is a French brier, bulldog shape bowl, with amberoid mouthpiece; the stem between bowl and mouthpiece is genuine Weichsel wood, and will not burn your tongue; worth 75 cents in the regular pipe stores.
Price, each..............27c
If by mail, postage extra, 5 cents.

French Brier Pipe for 39 Cents.

No. 18R5538 Handsome French Brier Pipe, straight bulldog shape, with clear Chinese amber stem and decorated band and bowl, **latest design. We highly recommend this pipe.**
Price, each..............39c

The Distiller Pipe, 44 Cents.

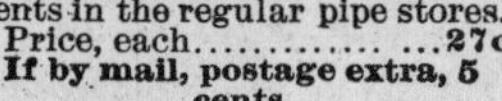

No. 18R5542 The Distiller Pipe. Greatest success of the century. Brier bowl with hard rubber stem. **Between bowl and stem is a glass tube which takes up the nicotine and saliva.** Draw out the mouthpiece and let out the nicotine; stem is easily replaced.
Price, each..............44c

German Porcelain Pipes.

No. 18R5546 German Porcelain Pipe, handsomely decorated; just the thing for a good old-fashioned smoke. This is an exceptionally fine and handsome German Porcelain Pipe. Made with very fine long stem, fitted with flexible top and **extra fine hard rubber mouthpiece. Long, genuine porcelain bowl artistically and handsomely decorated.** The bowl can readily be taken apart for cleaning, thus insuring **a clean, cool smoke.**
Price, each..............79c
If by mail, postage extra, 28 cents.

No. 18R5546

69 Cents for this Chip Meerschaum Pipe.

No. 18R5550 Large Sized Fine Vienna chip Meerschaum Pipe, large egg shaped bowl and handsome cherry stem with silk cord and tassel and Chinese amber mouthpiece. **An exceptionally handsome article.**

No. 18R5550 Price, each..............69c
If by mail, postage extra, 6 cents.

Turkish Water Pipe.

No. 18R5554 A genuine Turkish Water pipe; the bowl is made of fine colored glass, prettily decorated, and has a long flexible stem, with small amber mouthpiece connected to pipe. In the center of head is a thin glass tube through which the smoke passes. **The cup which holds the tobacco is made of Vienna Meerschaum,** which can be replaced, if desired, by the Vienna Meerschaum cigar holder, which comes with the set. Entire height of same is about 10 inches.
Price, each..............$1.94
Shipping weight, 1 pound.

No. 18R5558 Turkish Water Pipe, same as above, but having two flexible stems from which two persons can smoke at the same time. **The bowl is more elaborately decorated** than the above, and a little larger. Entire height about 10½ inches.
Price, each. (Shipping weight, 1 pound)... $2.75

Pipes in Leather Covered Cases.

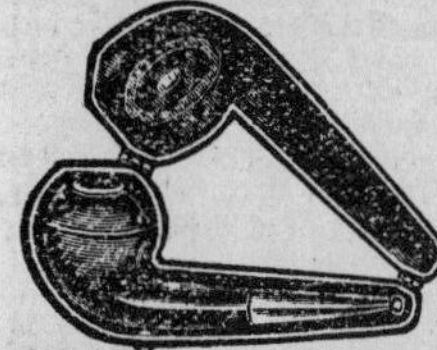

No. 18R5562 Genuine French Brier Pipe, English bulldog shape. Length, 5 inches. **Handsome Vienna amber** mouthpiece. Each one of these pipes is put up in a handsome leather covered case, with silk and velvet lining.
Price, each..............73c
If by mail, postage extra, each, 5 cents.

GIVE CATALOGUE NUMBER IN FULL WHEN YOU WRITE YOUR ORDER

79 Cents for a Rosewood Pipe.

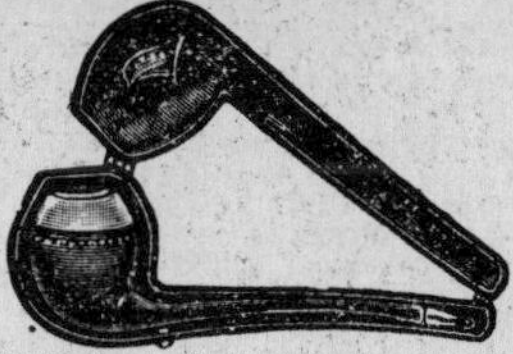

No. 18R5566 This is certainly one of the very handsomest pipes made. It is made from highly polished rosewood with removable set in bowl of **genuine meerschaum,** which can be unscrewed and easily cleaned. **Genuine Chinese amber mouthpiece;** length, 5½ inches. Put up in handsome leather covered, satin lined case.
Price, each..............79c
If by mail, postage extra, 4 cents.

Most Stores get $1.50 for this Grade.

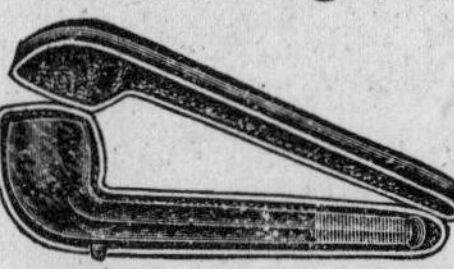

No. 18R5567 Flat Stem French Brier Pipe, with 1½-inch genuine amber mouthpiece. Has a medium small size bowl and is a very desirable shape. Pipe is very highly polished. Total length of pipe, 5½ inches. Inlaid in fine leather velvet lined case. A very desirable style.
Price, each..............92c
If by mail, postage extra, 4 cents.

A Handsome Shape, $1.75.

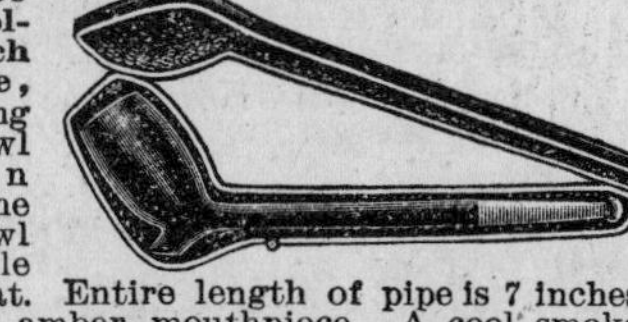

No. 18R5569 Highly Polished, French Brier Pipe, with slanting egg shape bowl and knob on bottom. The stem near bowl is round, while at end it is flat. Entire length of pipe is 7 inches, with 1¾-inch amber mouthpiece. A cool smoke, and a particularly desirable style.
Price, each..............$1.75
If by mail, postage extra, 5 cents.

Bull Dog Style, $1.47.

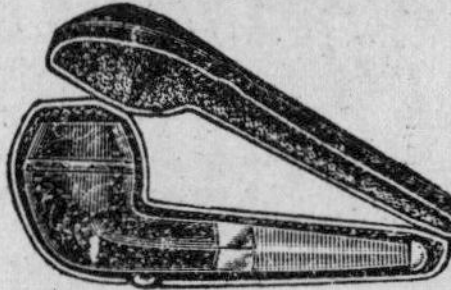

No. 18R5571 French Brier Pipe, bulldog shape, wih 2¼-inch genuine amber mouthpiece and trimmed with a sterling silver band between stem and pipe. Entire length of pipe, 5¼ inches. Large size, highly polished bowl. Inlaid in fine leather plush lined case.
Price, each..............$1.47
If by mail, postage extra, 5 cents.

A Beauty for a Present.

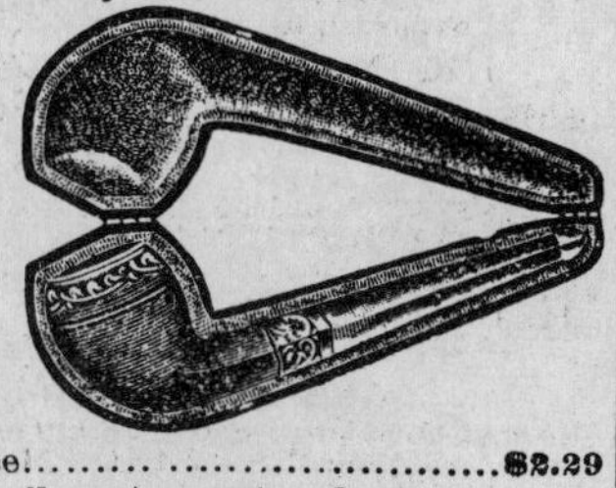

No. 18R5573 Fine French Brier Pipe, bulldog shape, with genuine amber mouthpiece, 3 inches long, highly polished bowl, with band of chased gold, also on stem, in elegant plush lined leather case. $3.75 value. Our price..............$2.29
If by mail, postage extra, 6 cents.

This $5.00 Pipe for $3.25.

No. 18R5575 Finest Quality French Brier Pipe, with heavy, wide, 3½-inch genuine amber mouthpiece. The bowl is ornamented with a heavy 14-karat gold band, and a heavy 14-karat gold band also connects the amber mouthpiece with the brier bowl. Total length of pipe, 6½ inches. Inlaid in an elegant plush lined chamois covered case. There are no finer goods made; real $5.00 value.
Price, each..............$3.25
If by mail, postage extra, 6 cents.

Fancy Egg Shape.

No. 18R5579 This is a fancy, egg shape, French Brier Pipe, with a round stem and ½-inch gold band and 4-inch amber mouthpiece. Entire length of pipe is 11 inches, making a delightful, cool smoke; inlaid in fine chamois, plush lined case. Price, each..............$2.88
If by mail, postage, extra, 6 cents.

Finest Quality French Brier Pipe.

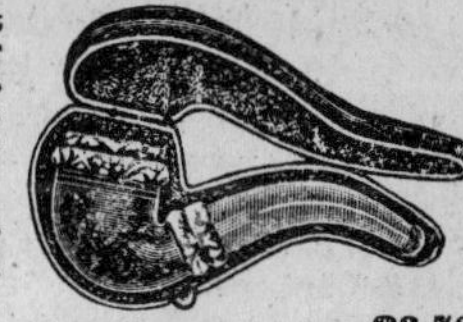

No. 18R5581 Finest Quality French Brier Pipe, Bull bitch shape. This handsome pipe has a thick curved genuine amber stem, heavily mounted in real gold, such a pipe as you never expect to pay less than $7.50 for elsewhere.
Price, each..............$3.72
If by mail, postage extra, each, 6 cents.

A Novelty Ball Shape Pipe, $1.85.

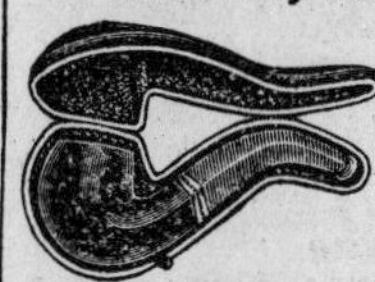

No. 18R5583 Fine French Brier Pipe, ball shape. Highly polished bowl, with curved, square, genuine amber stem and trimmed with small, gold band. Inlaid in leather lined case. A very desirable small pipe.
Price, each..............$1.85
If by mail, postage extra, 5 cents.

Special Value at $2.75.

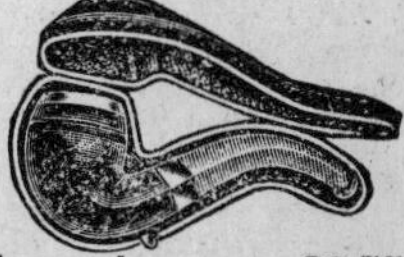

No. 18R5585 Highly Polished, Fine French Brier Pipe, bulldog shape, with curved 2½-inch genuine amber square stem; trimmed with gold band at top of the stem between the stem and bowl. A very handsome pipe. Inlaid in leather plush lined case. Price, each..............$2.75
If by mail, postage extra, 5 cents.

Handy Set Pipe, 87 Cents.

No. 18R5586 Well Shaped Brier Pipe, with clear bent Chinese amber stem, inlaid in plush lined pocket case. **A real bargain.** Price, each..............87c
If by mail, postage extra, 4 cents.

No. 18R5587 Fine French Brier Pipe, with a well shaped, large size, egg bowl; trimmed with curved sterling silver band and 2¾-inch genuine amber curved shove bit. Pipe inlaid in chamois, plush lined pocket case.
Price, each..............$1.89
If by mail, postage extra, 4 cents.

No. 18R5589 A well shaped genuine French Brier Pipe. Highly polished, with handsome chased gold bands on stem and top of bowl; genuine amber curved shove bit, 2¾ inches in length. Pipe is inlaid in handsome chamois, plush lined pocket case.
Price, each..............$2.95
If by mail, postage extra, 5 cents.

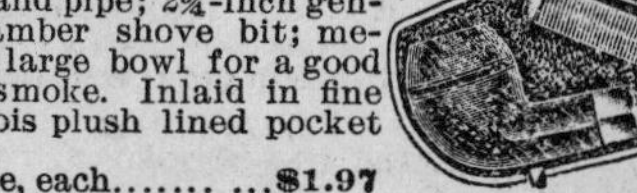

No. 18R5591 Square Stem, French Brier Bowl, very highly polished, heavy sterling silver band between stem and pipe; 2¾-inch genuine amber shove bit; medium large bowl for a good long smoke. Inlaid in fine chamois plush lined pocket case.
Price, each..............$1.97
If by mail, postage extra, 4 cents.

Smoker's Companion.

No. 18R5594 Smoker's Companion, consisting of two pipes, one straight French brier, bulldog shape, with 2-inch genuine amber mouthpiece, solid gold band, and one bent egg shape, highly polished French brier pipe with curved 2-inch genuine amber mouthpiece, solid gold band around stem, both pipes inlaid in a e iful chamois covered and silk plush lined case.
Price, per set..............$2.98
If by mail, postage extra, 6 cents.

FINE MEERSCHAUM PIPES.

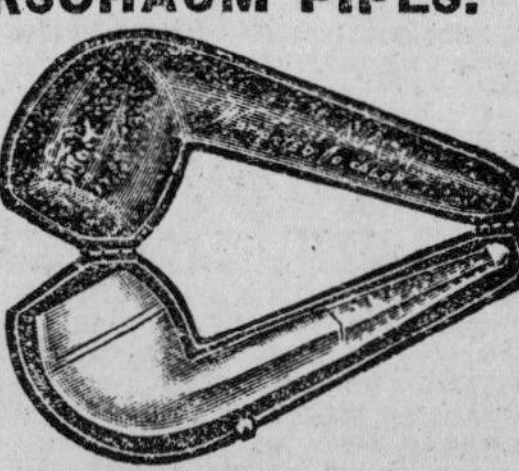

No. 18R5597 Chip Meerschaum Pipe, bulldog shape bowl, best English amber mouthpiece. We warrant this pipe to color; with satin lined leather covered case. **Do not unscrew stem from bowl.**
Price, each...97c
If by mail, postage extra, 5 cents.

Genuine Meerschaum Bowls.

No. 18R5599 Genuine Meerschaum Bowl, finest quality, egg shape. This style of meerschaum colors quickest, and the only quality and shape that will not break if you drop it; comes in fine chamois lined case; the finest grade of meerschaum on the market, in four sizes, as follows:
No. 5 bowl, each..$3.29 No. 7 bowl, each...$4.49
No. 6 bowl, each.. 3.82 No. 8 bowl, each... 5.21
If by mail, postage extra, each, 4 cents.

No. 18R5601 Genuine Weichsel Stem with real amber mouthpiece. Length, 6 inches. This stem is used in connection with the above meerschaum bowls.
Price, each..52c
If by mail, postage extra, 2 cents.

Our Fine Meerschaum Pipe, with Case, for $2.84.

No.18R5603 An Extra Fine Genuine Meerschaum Pipe, 5½ inches long, with fine 3-inch amber mouthpiece. Put up in handsome silk plush lined leather covered case. Unexcelled as a smoker.
Price, each........$2.84
If by mail, postage extra, 5 cents.

Genuine Block Meerschaum and Genuine Amber Stem.

No. 18R5605 Genuine Block Meerschaum Pipe, handsomely carved bowl, assorted designs, such as lions, dogs, deer, etc., amber mouthpiece, 2½ inches long, in a satin lined case. **Having received a large number of these pipes under particularly favorable circumstances we are able to offer unusual inducements.** Price, each..........................$2.73
If by mail, postage extra, 6 cents.

Our $4.95 Meerschaum Pipe.

No. 18R5607 Genuine Meerschaum Pipe, straight bulldog shape with 3-inch genuine amber mouthpiece, heavy chased gold band on stem and bowl inlaid in finest plush lined chamois covered case. No better pipe at any price. Price, each.................$4.95
If by mail, postage extra, each, 6 cents.

Our $4.25 First Quality Meerschaum Pipe.

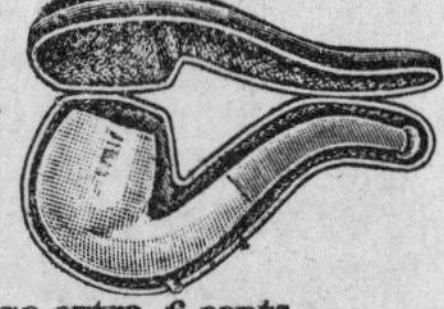

No. 18R5609 First Quality Fine Meerschaum Pipe, with band around stem; 3½-inch genuine amber mouthpiece. Has a medium sized egg shape bowl. Pipe inlaid in chamois covered leather case.
Price, each........$4.25
If by mail, postage extra, 6 cents.

Gold Mounted Meerschaum Pipe, $5.48.

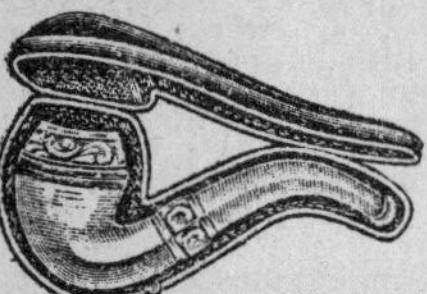

No. 18R5611 Square Stem, Curved Meerschaum Pipe. A very high grade quality pipe, with 3-inch square, genuine amber mouthpiece. Pipe is handsomely mounted with gold bands on top of bowl and around stem of pipe. Inlaid in fine chamois plush lined case. Price, each....................$5.48
If by mail, postage extra, 6 cents.

Combination Pipe and Cigar Holder.

No. 18R5613 Combination Pipe and Cigar Holder, fine meerschaum bowl with heavy gold band on stem and fine meerschaum cigar holder with heavy silver band, 2½-inch genuine amber, inserted mouthpiece which can be used on both pipe and cigar holder, making a very handsome combination set, the whole inlaid in beautiful plush lined leather covered pocket case.
Price, each..............$3.18
If by mail, postage extra, 6 cents.

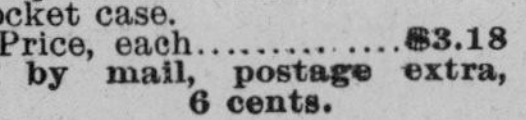

Our $4.19 Meerschaum Pipe.

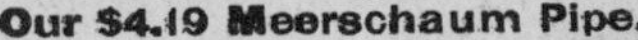

No. 18R5615 A Genuine Meerschaum, well shaped bowl, with curved genuine amber shove bit mouthpiece. The part of the bowl where amber mouthpiece sets in is mounted with fine gold band. Inlaid in chamois covered plush lined pocket case.
Price, each..........................$4.19
If by mail, postage extra, 4 cents.

SMOKERS' SUNDRIES.

No. 18R5617 Carved Brier Cigar Holder, with horn mouthpiece. Price, each...........13c
No. 18R5619 Brier Cigar Holder, horn mouthpiece. Price, each...........................9c
Shipping weight, 3 ounces.

Twisted Rubber Cigar Holder.

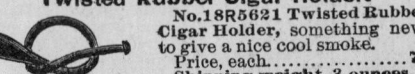

No.18R5621 Twisted Rubber Cigar Holder, something new, to give a nice cool smoke.
Price, each....................7c
Shipping weight, 3 ounces.

Solid Amber Cigar Holder.

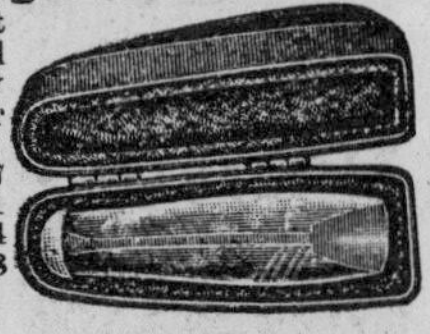

No. 18R5623 Finest quality, in chamois covered and plush lined case, a very fine article. Come in four sizes as follows:
1½-inch length, each..$0.97
2 -inch length, each.. 1.11
2½-inch length, each.. 1.34
3 -inch length, each.. 1.58
If by mail, postage extra, 2 cents.

Genuine Meerschaum Cigar Holders.

No. 18R5625 Genuine Meerschaum Cigar Holder, with amber mouthpiece. Comes in leather case.
Price, each..........................38c
If by mail, postage extra, 3 cents.

No.18R5627 Genuine Meerschaum Cigar Holder, fancy carved, with real amber bit, each in leather case. **Order by number.**
Price, each............57c
If by mail, postage extra, 3 cents.

No.18R5629 Genuine Meerschaum Cigar Holder, similar to above, but finer, with fine amber mouthpiece. The meerschaum has carved designs such as horse, dog, deer, etc., inlaid in fine leather case, satin and plush lined. Length, 3¼ inches.
Price, each..89c
If by mail, postage extra, 3 cents.

No.18R5631 Genuine Meerschaum Cigar Holder, elegantly carved designs similar to above, but much finer goods, real amber mouthpiece. Total length of holder, 3½ inches. In finest plush lined case.
Our special price, each.............................$1.62
If by mail, postage extra, 3 cents.

French Brier Cigar Holder.

No. 18R5633 French Brier Cigar Holder, with 1¼-inch genuine amber mouthpiece, ornamented with handsome design, gold trimmings. Total length of holder, 2½ inches. This is an extremely rich and handsome holder. Price, each...........................$2.65
If by mail, postage extra, 3 cents.

Rubber Mouthpieces.

No. 18R5635 2-inch straight rubber mouthpiece.
Price, each...2c
No. 18R5637 2½-inch curved rubber mouthpiece.
Price, each...4c
No. 18R5639 2-inch square rubber mouthpiece.
Price, each...4c
No. 18R5641 2½-inch rubber mouthpiece, with nickel ferrule. Price, each............................9c
If by mail, postage extra, 2 cents.

Our 13-Cent Weichsel Pipe Stem.

No. 18R5643 6½-inch Weichsel Pipe Stem, with curved mouthpiece. Price, each..........................13c
No. 18R5645 7-inch Cherry Pipe Stem, with curved mouthpiece. Price, each..........................9c
If by mail, postage extra, 3 cents.

Coin or Tobacco Pouch.

No. 18R5647 Prussian or Maltsters' Pouch. An excellent pouch for tobacco or coin. An inside pocket for gold. This pouch is manufactured from one solid piece of leather.
Price, each.......................12c
If by mail, postage extra, 3 cents.

Self Closing Rubber Pouch.

No. 18R5649 Raleigh Velvet Rubber Tobacco Pouch. Self closing, tan color. Diameter, 3⅜ inches. Keeps tobacco moist, clean and sweet. Each........19c
If by mail, postage extra, 3 cents.

CIGAR CASES.

No. 18R5718 Real Leather Cigar Case, telescope style; is soft in the pocket, and heavy enough to protect cigars. Price........21c
If by mail, postage extra, 5 cents.

Our 44-Cent Leather Cigar Case.

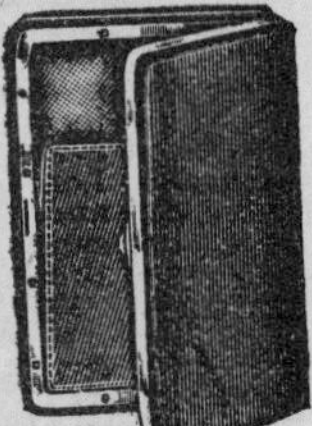

No. 18R5722 Fine Leather Cigar Case, plain style, has strong steel frame, highly polished. A very excellent case, which we offer at a special price. Each..44c
If by mail, postage extra, 6 cents.

Our 76 Cent Cigar Case

No. 18R5726 Fine Embossed Leather Cigar Case, with extra strong steel frame and lock, fancy silk embroidered inside. Suitable as a birthday or holiday gift.
Price........76c
If by mail, postage extra, 6 cents.

Our Finest Leather Cigar Case for $1.64.

No. 18R5730 Genuine Calfskin Leather Cigar Case, very highly polished, with riveted steel frame and lock. A very high grade, and our best cigar case, usually retailed in the regular cigar stores at from $2.50 to $3.00. Price, each...........$1.64
If by mail, postage extra, 6 cents.

Genuine Seal Grain Cowhide Leather Cigar Case.

No.18R5731 Leather lined, stitched and well made throughout, with handsome sterling silver name plate mounting. The most convenient and durable cigar case made. Price, each....$1.00
If by mail, postage extra, 5 cents.

Smokers' Stand, 98 Cents.

No. 18R5733 Smokers' Stand, hardwood base, ebony finish, resting on three ball feet, clover shape, holds brass polished cups for cigars, matches and removable tray for ashes, cigar cutter. A suitable present for a gentleman. Size, 7¼x8½x3½ inches.
Price, each............98c
Shipping weight, 2 pounds.

Nickeled Match Safe.

No. 18R5735 Nickeled Match Safe, smooth surface with stamped design, opens with a good spring.
Price, each..........................4c
If by mail, postage extra, 2 cents.

Plain Nickel Finished Match Safe

No. 18R5737 A Plain Nickel Finished Metal Match Safe, splendid value at the price. Price, each..........................9c
If by mail, postage extra, 2 cents.

Flask Shaped Safe.

No.18R5739 A Novelty Match Safe, shaped like a flask, nickel finish, neat and durable. Price, each.....................18c
If by mail, postage extra, 2 cents.

Combination Match Safe and Cigar Cutter.

No. 18R5741 Combination Match Safe and Cigar Cutter. These have been used and highly recommended by thousands. Nickel finish, leather covering, metal top and bottom. Convenient and durable. Price, each..................20c
If by mail, postage extra, 2 cents.

Silver Finished Metal Safes.

No. 18R5743 Silver Finished, handsomely Embossed Match Safe, new and striking design. Price, each..............23c
If by mail, postage extra, 2 cents.

No. 18R5745 This pretty match safe is made of German silver, with handsome embossed design of bright silver finish. Very neat and tasty design. Price, each..................46c
If by mail, postage extra, 2 cents.

LATEST DESIGNS IN STYLISH TRIMMED HATS.

AT 99 CENTS, $2.35, $3.25 AND UPWARDS.

WE SUBMIT ON THESE FOUR PAGES, the very newest effects in fashionable trimmed hats made especially for us from original designs, the same styles as will be shown by fashionable city milliners in large cities; styles that it will be impossible for you to secure in the stores in smaller towns, such goods as can be had only from the big millinery emporiums in metropolitan cities and there at two to three times our prices. These illustrations are made by artists direct from the hats, but it is impossible in a plain black and white drawing to give you a fair idea of the full beauty of these new hat creations. We ask you to read the descriptions carefully, note the illustrations and send us your order with the understanding that if the hat, when received, is not all and more than we claim for it, perfectly satisfactory, you are at liberty to return it to us at our expense and we will immediately return your money.

Wonderful Value.

99c

No. 39R101 Is a black dress shape fancy straw, slightly raised on the left. Very tastefully trimmed in the front with six large muslin roses and shaded foliage. Trimmed high to the right is a large rosette consisting of silk finished pink mull in half wheel effect, same extending all around the crown and falling over the back and caught on bandeau with loops of the same material. A very stylish young or middle aged ladies' hat. Shape can be ordered only in black or white, trimmings in any color desired, but looks very handsome as described. Price, each....... ....99c

$1.50

No. 39R103 Chipped shape, made of fancy lace braid, trimmed on the left side with a garland of roses, draped with silk Chantilly lace. Entirely around upper part of brim is a drapery of silk mull overlaid with imported thread straw braid. This drapery forms into a fold effect caught in the back with a handsome design fancy buckle. Velvet bandeau is draped with all silk satin and grosgrain ribbon. Can be ordered in black, brown, navy, castor and cream white. Price, each.................$1.50

Popular Short Back Sailor.

$2.35

No. 39R105 This is a very stylish dress hat, short back sailor, a very pretty new style fancy straw braid, trimmed very wide all round crown with a full drapery of cream taffeta silk and point de Paris lace of butter color. Directly in front is a large cluster of pretty carnations with foliage partly hidden between the folds of drapery. The under brim is covered with small folds of silk mull. This is a very pretty, jaunty and stylish hat. Can be ordered in black, white, pearl, castor or maize.

Price, each...............................$2.35

$1.95

No. 39R107 This is a hand made fancy straw braid dress hat, drooping slightly to front and back. The wire frame is covered with an imported hand made straw braid, trimmed fully to the left with artistically designed rosettes draped in plume effect. The entire crown is covered with an imported tinted foliage and buds. The facing is neat drawn work of narrow folds of pink silk finished mull, and the bandeau is covered with nicely made loops of the same material. An exceedingly becoming and effectively designed hat. Can be ordered in all colors,

Price, each.................. ....$1.95

$1.98

No. 39R109 This is one of our very stylish hats for young ladies. A hand made, natural colored straw braid, covered on a wire frame, trimmed fully in the front and all around the crown with wired loops of fine quality Japanese silk in three contrasting colors, white, pink and maize. The facing is made of narrow folds of maize colored mull, and the black velvetta bandeau is covered with three full size pink muslin roses. This is an exceedingly pretty hat for a young lady, richly and tastily designed, and at the price we offer is exceptionally good value. It can be ordered in any color desired. Price, each $1.98

Jaunty Turban.

$2.25

No. 39R111 Jaunty Large Black Turban, slightly raised on the left side. The turban made on a silk wire frame covered with silk finished black mull and overlaid with a very richly designed straw braid the braid being laid in folds all around the crown. The crown is made of a firm fancy edge black straw, very effectively and tastily trimmed on the left with a large drapery of black taffeta silk, same falling over the brim and caught on the bandeau. A large cluster of pink hyacinth flowers, interwoven with rose buds and foliage, completes the trimming of this very latest designed, handsome hand made turban. Black velvetta covered bandeau with puffs of silk taffeta over same. Can be ordered in black, white, pink or light blue, with trimmings to match. Price, each............ $2.25

$2.47 Buys this Swell Gainsborough.

$2.47

No. 39R113 Is a black lace mohair dress shape. A decided Gainsborough effect, trimmed low in the prevailing fashion. The entire hat is trimmed with a fine quality of Japanese silk, a combination of white and pink gathered and draped in breast effect, wired in folds that will insure its not losing its effect. The trimming consists of large, full blown pink poppies with large, tinted foliage. The velvette bandeau is covered with a fullness of Japanese silk, pink and white, drawn in graceful knots and bows. We can highly recommend this very stylish dress hat as one of the most becoming hats that will suit almost any taste. The shape is black only. The trimmings can be ordered in any combinations of colors desired.

Price, each.........$2.47

A Beautiful Design at $2.35.

$2.35

No. 39R115 A black, hand made dress shape, made on a wire frame, slightly raised on both sides and drooping front and back. The entire hat is covered with an imported straw braid of a very fine design. The trimming, fully in the front, consists of four large American beauty roses, in pink, with shaded foliage. Artistically made folds draped all around the crown of fine quality black Japanese silk. The entire under brim is covered with folds of black silk finished mull and the bandeau is trimmed with pretty foliage, which completes the trimmings of this very becoming hat. It can be ordered trimmed in white, pink or maize.

Price, each... ....$2.35

Mushroom Brim Effect, $2.45.

$2.45

No. 39R117 Ladies' dress shape. It is a handsome trimmed hat for the money. It has a mushroom brim effect, which droops gracefully over face in a very fetching manner. It is made of imported satin and lace braid in row and row, the edge being bound with narrow fancy braid and silk cable wire; trimmed with a large Alsatian bow of stitched black liberty satin. The same being caught in front with buckle of handsome design. A large cluster of pink American beauty roses is posed on left side of hat over which is draped black Chantilly lace in a very pretty manner. The lace is caught in front by a buckle and is draped over either side of hat and caught in the back with fancy ornaments. The end of lace forms the veil effect. The bandeau is draped with black liberty satin, which is caught with a genuine rhinestone ornament. Hat comes in black only. Trimming any color desired. Price, each, $2.45

Our $2.55 Dress Hat.

$2.55

No. 39R119 Hand Made Dress Hat, on silk wire frame, full shape, wide effect. This brim is covered with a combination of gray straw lace over mull. The trimming consists of a stylish drapery of pink silk finished full, intertwined with gray lace straw braid all around the brim, thereby making an attractive and very pretty combination. Around the crown, trimmed highly, are three full folds, in one-half wheel rosette effect, of gray silk finished mull. Tastily arranged between the folds, and entirely around front, is a large spray of six half blown pink muslin roses with heavy foliage and buds, velvette bandeau covered with four roses and foliage, completes the trimming of this prettily designed hat. Especially desirable for middle aged ladies. Can also be ordered in black and tan. Price, each..........$2.55

Very Becoming Style, $1.75.

$1.75

No. 39R121 This is a Castor Colored hand made straw dress shape, drooping slightly to front and back. Trimmed high to the left with fine artistically made rosettes of castor colored silk, finished mull edged with fine imported straw braid. The same combination extending on the right side in lower effect. Four large American beauty pink roses with generous foliage and buds directly over the brim. The facing is made of narrow folds of castor colored silk finished mull and a large bandeau covered with two American beauty pink roses and foliage completes the trimming of this very beautiful and becoming young ladies' hat. Can be ordered trimmed in all colors. Price, each..........$1.75

$1.95 Mourning Hat.

$1.95

No. 39R123 Our Special Mourning Hat. An extremely dressy shape and is draped with fine quality stylish cloth. Trimmed on both sides with a fine quality of crepe du chine in plume effect, edged with a pretty silk braid, giving it a decidedly fine appearance. Trimmed high in front and a little to the left, with three silk and satin roses of fine quality with black jet centers. Over velvet bandeau is a full puff of crepe du chine, which is met by the draping from around the crown. This is a very desirable hat. Price, each $1.95

$2.85 Chiffon Novelty.

$2.85

No. 39R125—An all tucked handmade chiffon dress hat, with the exception of the crown. The crown is covered with a black richly patterned lace straw braid. The trimming in the front and slightly to the left consists of wired loops of heavy China silk in a combination of pink and white, very full loops. The same is draped in folds extending around the crown and falling in loose ends over back of brim. Three large imported pink muslin roses over black velvette bandeau completes the trimming. A very dainty and at the same time a very stunning style. Can be ordered in any color. Price, each..........$2.85

An Exclusive Style With Us.

$2.69

No. 39R127 The above illustration represents a young or medium aged ladies' short back sailor with rolled edge 1½ inches high, made of imported fancy lace braid. The edge is garnished with fancy chain braid. Trimming consists of draperies of black taffeta silk very full entirely around upper part of brim, a profusion of Ragged Robin or bluettes flowers in wreath effect, which covers the entire left side of hat. On the left side of brim is a drapery of handsome, heavy Oriental braid caught with a band of velvet ribbon and three genuine cut steel cabochons. Lace and ribbon finish in the veil effect in back, the lace drooping over the hair and on to bandeau, which is garnished with a handsome bunch of crushed roses. This hat comes in black, white, navy or brown. An exceptionally pretty hat. Price, each..........$2.69

The Swell Sheperdess Effect.

$2.50

No. 39R129 The above illustration represents a ladies' hat which comes in black, brown, navy, castor or white. It is a rich combination of satin and lace braid. Shape is one of the newest of the season, being the newest Shepherdess effect with curved brim. The brim is draped with a coil of imported fancy black straw braid over light blue silk finished mull. The same being caught in the front with a fancy rhinestone buckle. On the left side front is a large bunch of imported foliage. The bandeau is garnished with three crushed roses and large bow of all silk satin and grosgrain ribbon. Price..........$2.50

A Very Stunning Style.

$3.25

No. 39R131 This is a large dress shape, made of fancy chip straw crown. Horsehair brim edged with fancy imported straw braid. It is one of the newest shapes, very stylish and dressy for spring and summer wear. It has a drooping brim in the mushroom effect, trimmed with a garland of pink silk moss, buds and foliage. Extending entirely around either side of hat and caught in the center by a genuine cut steel buckle is a handsome silk drapery of black maline with white dots, draped in the new wave effect over the flowers and caught in the back in veil effect; the same being edged with a handsome design of narrow silk lace. The velvet bandeau on the left side is garnished with a bow of all silk satin and grosgrain ribbon. This hat comes in black and white. A very stunning style. Price, each....$3.25

$1.15 Fancy Turban.

$1.15

No. 39R133 Black straw turban, a pretty lace and satin straw braid. The trimming in front and slightly to the left consists of a large rosette in full folds of silk finished black mull from which protrudes in a pretty way two handsome curled black quills. Around brim is a fold of fine thread hair braid; the same is continued in a full drapery around crown and extended under and to the velvette covered bandeau, all of which is caught by a cluster of violets. Directly in front of brim is a large handsome gilt buckle. The hat comes in black only, but the trimming of mull can be ordered in white, pink, gray or tan. Price, each..........$1.15

Another Pretty Turban.

$1.75

No. 39R135 In this illustration we show a very becoming turban, made of silk finished hand tucked black mull, drawn in graceful folds over a silk wire frame with hand made imported straw braid crown. The trimming slightly to the left consists of three large crushed muslin tea colored roses with rose buds and foliage extending to the front and around the crown of the hat. Slightly higher to the front are tucked folds of silk finished black mull, which gives the turban the full effect so much desired. Directly over the left side, falling over the brim and extending to the bandeau, are artistically made rosettes of the silk finished black mull. This is a very pretty and stylish turban and a very distinctive style. Can be ordered trimmed in pink, light blue, white or black with trimmings to match. Price, each..........$1.75

New Turban Style.

$2.35

No. 39R137 Gainsborough turban. Hand made on a wire frame, covered and draped with handsome imported straw braid. The brim is covered and draped with two folds of this imported braid while the crown, a semi-tam effect, is made of the same material. The trimming fully to the left is comprised of four large elegant pink crushed muslin roses with full foliage in tinted shades interspersed in the background of roses, with a large drape plume effect in full folds of black silk finished mull. The entire facing under brim is made of narrow gathered folds of pink silk taffeta draped tastily and effectively. The velvette bandeau is covered with a full puff of black silk finished mull and large pink crushed muslin rose. Can be ordered trimmed in any color. The pink and black effect is stylish and popular, and we recommend this combination of colors, but can change if desired.

Price, each......$2.35

Stylish Dress Turban.

$3.25

No. 39R139 This is a large, stylish dress turban, made on a silk wire frame. The entire brim is covered with narrow plaits of white silk tucked chiffon, while the Tam crown is made of a very fine white imported straw braid, trimmed plainly but stylishly and tastefully, on the left, with loops of white tucked silk chiffon — a very fine lustrous Louisine silk chiffon—which form a large, full rosette. A fold of black velvette all around the crown, the same falling over the brim and caught on the bandeau with two handsome steel buckles, completes the trimming of this beautiful hat, which for style and elegance cannot be equaled. It can be ordered trimmed in any color. Price, each....$3.25

Roll Brim Effect.

$3.40

No. 39R141 It is made on a wide frame, draped with a handsome design of imported black all over straw. The drapery and trimming consist of black silk taffeta edged with narrow black silk lace, which is caught in the front of crown by handsome genuine cut steel buckles and draped in a very fetching manner on either side, in a veil effect in the back. On the left side is a handsome cluster of imported pink silk poppies which reach entirely over the hat from back to front. The velvet bandeau is garnished with a bunch of imported French foliage, frosted effect. Comes in black and cream colors only. Price, each.... $3.40

New Box Turban.

$3.25

No. 39R143 One of the newest effects in box turbans. Made on wireframe, covered and draped with imported horsehair braid. The crown is formed of fancy braid caught in the center with a rosette in the button effect. Between the crown and brim is a handsome drapery of all silk taffeta which is draped entirely around the hat and forms with combination of braid a handsome knot effect on left side of the front. The same material is draped over on bandeau, which is caught with three handsome silk rosettes. Entirely around the outer part of brim is draped an imported lace veil, over which is caught a band of velvet ribbon and four genuine cut steel cabochons. Comes in black only, with lace in cream or white effect. Price, each.........$3.25

Childs' Dress Hat.

90c

No. 39R145 A very pretty hat for children, suitable for a miss from four to eight years of age. A white fancy rough straw with a row of pink straw inserted around the rim. Trimmed to the front in large full puffs or rosettes of pink silk finished mull with bound edges. Between the folds of rosettes are interspersed lilies of the valley with foliage. Underneath the front of the brim and a little to the side, is a hand made bandeau covered with lilies of the valley and foliage. Can be ordered trimmed in light blue, pink, cardinal or white. Price, each........90c

Misses' Dress Hat.

$2.25

No. 39R147 Leghorn dress hat for young ladies, gracefully bent into a very becoming shape. The trimming consists of a heavy drapery of a fine quality maize colored silk chiffon, drawn in full folds around the entire brim of the hat and gathered over same under and about the bandeau with full bows of white all silk satin faced ribbon. The bandeau is covered with black velvette. The entire trimming is in pretty contrast and harmony. Large clusters of tea colored wild flowers with contrasting centers complete the trimming of this elegant and tastefully designed hat. The hat comes in the natural leghorn only. Can be ordered trimmed in any color desired. Price, each...............$2.25

One of the Finest Creations of the Millinery Art
OUR $3.35 DRESS HAT.

A style that small millinery dealers may attempt to copy, but all will lack the grace, the style, the general exclusive effect that can be found only in our original design.

AT $3.35 WE OFFER IT AS THE EQUAL OF $5.00 HATS SOLD GENERALLY.

$3.35

No. 39R151 **A beautiful creation in black and white. A most striking and richly designed dress hat. This is a hand made dress hat on a silk wire frame. The crown is made of imported satin straw braid of a very rich design.** The trimming of full breast effect on either side, consists of large generous drapes or folds of narrow tucked black and white silk chiffon which extends entirely around brim and is caught by an elegant steel buckle over a full gathering of velvette which extends over the brim and is caught on the bandeau in a large bow, the same running around the crown and caught in back with a small sized steel buckle. The entire hat is a very modish and attractive design, rich and elegant and a model to be admired. If you paid three or four times the price we ask you could not get better value from the ordinary milliner. The black and white trimming, as described, we highly recommend, but can be ordered trimmed in any combination desired. Price, each.........................$3.35

BUY THIS SWELL HAT

AND WEAR A HAT BETTER, FINER, MORE STYLISH AND EXCLUSIVE THAN ANY ONE IN YOUR TOWN.

$4.50 IS OUR PRICE FOR THIS BEAUTIFUL PICTURE HAT—a price that is the despair of attempted competition and the joy of our lady customers.

$4.50

No. 39R153 **A large, dashing, picture hat, with a decided flare on left side, Gainsborough effect. This is a hand made shape on a silk wire frame, being one of our prettiest creations.** The entire hat, the brim as well as the crown, is covered with a plaque of imported satin straw braid, which is held on frame by a large fussy bow of all silk taffeta in loose effect, and which is met at ends by a twist of black silk velvet running around the crown. The trimming on side consists of six good quality black ostrich tips, which fall over top, under brim and well over the hair. The velvette bandeau is covered with three imported crushed muslin pink roses. The entire under brim is draped and gathered in graceful folds of narrow tucked silk chiffon, the whole forming a most striking, dressy and becoming appearance. Our most richly designed hat, patterned after the most popular Parisian design, which can only be produced by the most expensive city milliners, and this stunning hat should readily retail for $15.00. The straw plaque and ostrich feathers come in black only, but the tucked chiffon trimming on brim and the taffeta bow, as well as the roses, can be ordered in any color desired. We recommend the trimming in the combination of pink and black as described. Price, each............$4.50

For Girls 5 to 10 Years Old.

$1.18

No. 39R154 A very elegantly designed misses' white leghorn hat with fancy straw edge. This is an imported Italian leghorn flat, with fancy new designed crown, trimmed in the front, and slightly to the left are large, elaborate puffs of canary colored silk finished mull and wired loops of silk, satin faced ribbon, wired so as to hold them in place, and the ribbon is caught under the crown and to the bandeau. Tastily arranged in the folds of mull are sprays of full blown light blue lilies of the valley with foliage. A very pretty and effective hat for misses from five to ten years of age. Can be ordered trimmed in light blue, pink, cardinal or white. Price, each.......................$1.18

Genuine Parisian Style.

$5.75

No. 39R155 Elegant Parisian Gainsborough effect dress hat with semi-tam crown. A very elegant hat for stylish dressers. The entire wire frame is covered with white silk mull and overlaid with a black spangled net. The black and white combination of trimming is very stylish and much desired this season. The semi-tam crown is covered with an exceptionally pretty imported spangled crown. Over the brim and beneath the crown is a fold of black silk velvet, same extending to the back in a large bow and falling over the brim where it is caught on the bandeau. A large black Amazon real ostrich plume of very fine quality and six black satin roses complete the trimming of this richly millinered hat. Well worth $10.00. Can be ordered trimmed as described only. Price, each..................$5.75

$2.95

A New Shepherdess Style.

$2.15

No. 39R157 Hand made dress shape, drooping slightly front and back, shepherdess effect, made on a wire frame. The crown is covered with imported black straw braid, while the entire brim is draped with black lace straw netting, same being caught with straps of black velvetta ribbon bands extending entirely over and under the brim. The trimming fully to the left consists of large wired loops of black Chantilly lace and twelve large, double, full sized, pink poppies. The bandeau is covered with black velvetta puffs. This is indeed a becoming and stylishly designed hat, is very tasty and effective. Can be ordered in any color. Price, each.................................$2.15

A Fine Summer Leghorn.

$3.35

No. 39R159 Is one of the handsomest and most beautiful designs in a summer leghorn we have ever put before our trade. This hat is an imported Italian leghorn flat. The brim is caught up in a very pretty manner in back in a heart shape, also is caught up over the bandeau high on the left side. The trimming consists of a profusion of imported silk poppies (cerise color), and foliage, and covers the entire front and side of the hat. Caught on the left side of bandeau is a handsome design in an imported bobbinet wash veil. On the edge of hat is a handsome rhinestone cabochon with loops of black velvet ribbon extending to bandeau where same is caught with another cabochon of the same design. Loops of the velvet ribbon hang over the left side of bandeau on to hair. The lace veil is draped in a very becoming manner and is one of the latest up to date ideas in summer millinery. No one would be disappointed when seeing this hat. Hat comes in white only. Price...................................$3.35

Real Italian Leghorn.

No. 39R156 This is a very handsome and beautiful design dress hat for ladies. An imported Italian Leghorn straw on which the brim is caught and bent in a very pretty manner in a large flare effect. On the left side the trimming consists of a profusion of graceful folds of a very fine quality of pink and white Japanese silk drawn in loose folds and caught at a point in the back with a very handsome cut steel buckle. Directly under the left and over the black velvetta bandeau are two very large silk and velvet crushed roses with foliage, also a large stylish knot of the same quality Japanese silk. This effective hat as trimmed is a beautiful harmony of colors. The design can only be found in the very high class millinery establishments, which adds greatly to the cost. This is a splendid $6.00 value. The pink and white trimming is very pretty, but it can be ordered in any combination desired. Price, each..................................$2.95

Our $1.39 Bonnet.

$1.39

No. 39R161 A hand made, medium shaped bonnet covered with fancy straw braid, designed on a silk wire frame, trimmed very full in front. The trimming consists of large loops of all silk taffeta with fancy imported spangled aigrettes and natural colored satin lilacs, which makes a very pretty trimming of contrasting colors. Silk Chantilly lace directly over the crown and between the loops of taffeta gives it the desired fullness. The lace is drawn to either side of the bonnet and caught at the ends with bows of all silk satin ribbon, which are also used for the ties. Can be ordered in black only, with trimmings as described. Price, each.....................$1.39

Special Value in Mourning Bonnets for $2.25.

$2.25

No. 39R163 Close Fitting Bonnet of fine mourning goods, laid in tiny folds on edge of bonnet; mourning veil with border, draped in prevailing style. This close fitting mourning bonnet is the proper style, it is neat and tasty, just the kind that is now shown by milliners in metropolitan cities. Such a bonnet is sold by the larger milliners as a special bargain at $4.00. Price, each..........$2.25

A BEAUTIFUL STYLE FOR

MIDDLE AGED AND ELDERLY LADIES,

A QUALITY REGULAR MILLINERS GET $4.00 TO $5.00 FOR. . . . . .

Our $1.95 Bonnet.

$1.95

No. 39R165 A richly designed hand made bonnet made on a silk wire frame and covered with an imported hair straw lace braid. The trimming in front consists of a profusion of artistically made rosettes of a fine quality of silk mousseline de soie. Directly in the center of the rosette is a cluster of pretty violets with foliage and a large spray of imported aigrettes with fancy spangles. Long ties of all silk satin faced ribbon completes the trimming of this very tasty and becoming bonnet suitable for middle aged and elderly ladies. Black only. Price, each.....................$1.95

Marlowe, 25 Cents.

No. 39R167 Ladies' Canton Sailor Hat, very stylish for this season; trimmed with large ribbon band and bow. Colors, white and black. Big value. Price, each..25c

Cataract, 69 Cents.

No. 39R169 Ladies' Sailor Hat, split straw braid crown and Milan rim; same shape as above; trimmed with band and bow of faille ribbon. Colors, white and black. Price, each..69c

Speedway, $1.20.

No. 39R171 This is the best quality trimmed sailor; same shape as above, and of best quality fine split straw braid. Regular $2.00 value. Price, each..$1.20

Wabash, 75 Cents.

Rough Satin Jap Straws Are Very Popular.

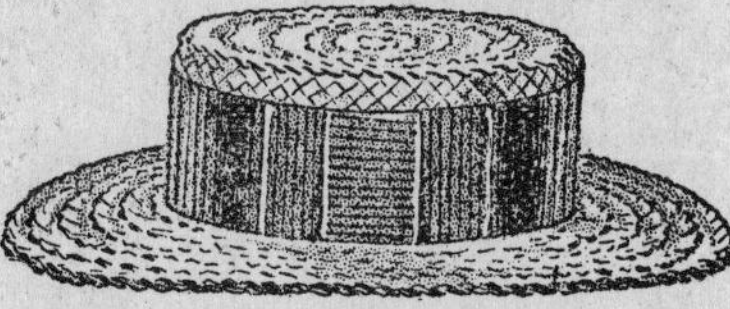

No. 39R173 Ladies' Trimmed Sailor in an entirely new design of white satin Jap braid with combination Milan straw, with band and bow of satin and grosgrain ribbon. Regular $1.25 value. Price, each..75c

Ramsey, $1.25.

No. 39R175 Ladies' Trimmed Sailor Hat, made of very fine quality white satin Jap braid, light and stylish which is very popular trimmed with band and bow of grosgrain ribbon. Color, white only. Price, each..$1.25

Madrid, 68 Cents.

No. 39R177 This is a very jaunty and stylish ready to wear hat for young ladies and misses, made of fine quality satin Jap braid with a band of blue all silk faille ribbon. Colors, white, pearl and maize. Price, each..68c

Midway, $1.00.

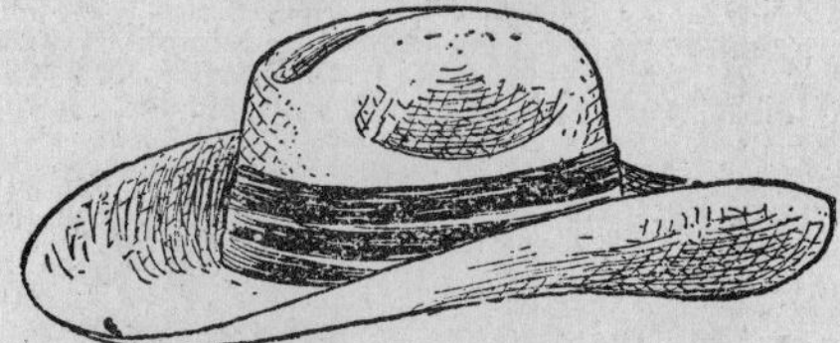

No. 39R179 Ladies' Ready to Wear Hat. Very striking style. This is a very fine quality in the Panama straw with turned up rim, trimmed around the crown with full fold of sateen, making a very stylish hat; in natural color only. Price, each..$1.00

Lazarre, 99 Cents.

No. 39R181 Ladies' Ready to Wear Stylish Hat, made of fine white satin Jap braid, trimmed very full, with a drapery of fancy striped fine quality China silk. Large sash and streamers in veil shape effect from back. Pretty and stylish. Colors, white, pearl and tan. Price, each..99c

The Holland, 59 Cents.

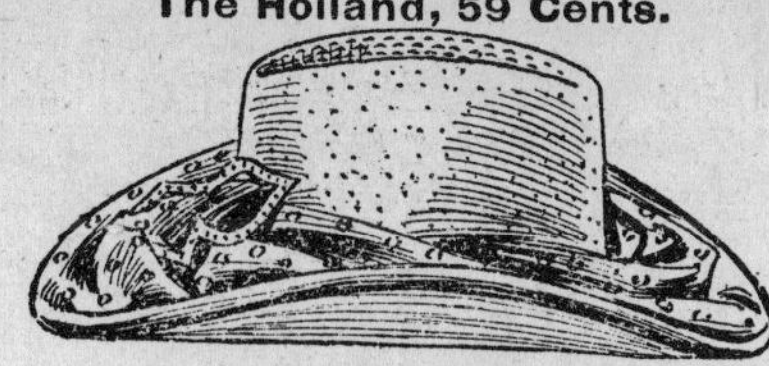

No. 39R183 Ladies' Ready to Wear Walking Hat, made of textile Panama, imitation of the real Panama straw. Draped full around the crown with a fold of fancy figured navy blue with white ring dot sateen and caught with a handsome buckle in front. Sold at the exclusive millinery stores for $1.00. Price, each..59c

The Estelle, 67 Cents.

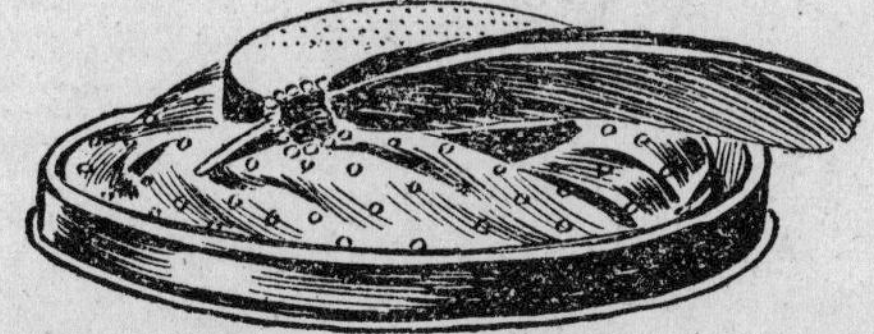

No. 39R185 Ready to Wear Hat, for young ladies and misses, made of our new textile Panama braid, very jaunty, trimmed all round crown with a full drapery of figured sateen and two folds of velvetta round the top and round the edge of rim. A long feather quill is caught at left side with a pretty buckle. Can be ordered trimmed in navy or combination cloth of green, tan and red. Price, each..67c

The Walton, 65 Cents.

No. 39R187 Ready to Wear Hat, for young ladies' and misses, made of the new textile Panama and trimmed with a fold of black velvetta, and trimmed high in front with a large bow of fancy figured Persian cloth and caught with a very handsome buckle. This is partially the old style short back sailor. Comes in natural color only. Price, each..65c

Oriental.

$1.10

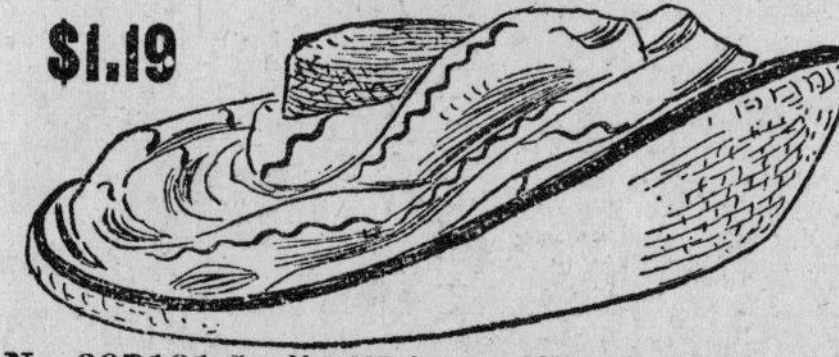

No. 39R189 A Jaunty Ready to Wear Hat, for young ladies. Made of satin Jap braid with full folds of Oriental design, sateen and grass cloth around crown; same made in large puffs over bandeau. Can be ordered in white, maize or pearl. Price, each..$1.10

Modena.

$1.19

No. 39R191 Ladies' Trimmed Ready to Wear Hat, made of Cuba braid, natural color, with velvet band at edge, with graceful folds around brim consisting of new and pretty striped grass cloth. Comes in natural color only. Price, each..$1.19

Sevilla.

$1.15

No. 39R193 Ladies' Stylish Ready to Wear Hat. A very pretty and becoming shape for the average person. Trimmed very full with a large fold of good quality China silk around the brim, and directly in front are three large rosettes made of straw braid and silk; a very becoming pattern. Can be ordered in white, black, navy or pearl. Price, each....$1.15

Lubin. **$1.39**

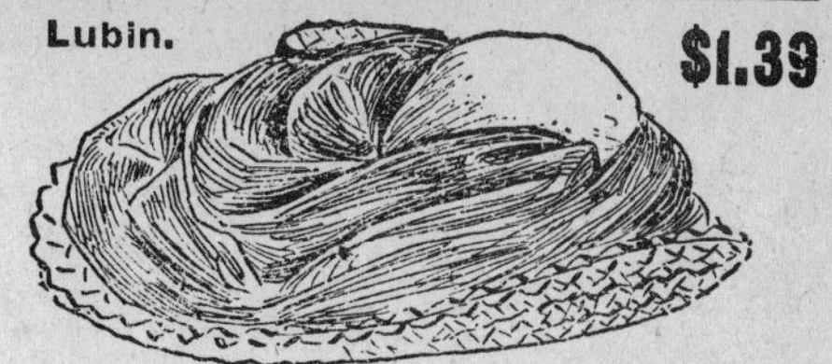

No. 39R195 Stylish Ready to Wear Hat for ladies, made of very fine quality satin Jap braid, and trimmed with a wide fold of fine China silk with feather breast. Can be ordered trimmed in white, black, pearl or navy. Regular $2.00 style. Price, each..$1.39

Retta. **96c**

No. 39R197 A Pretty Ready to Wear Hat, for misses, made of white satin Jap. braid, trimmed in a very stylish manner in a two-tone effect with a fancy faille fold of blue and white made into a large rosette in front and draped around the crown and falling in sash effect in the back. The trimming can be ordered in light blue and white, pink and white or castor and white, which are very pretty contrasting colors and very stylish and dressy. Price, each..96c

York. **74c**

No. 39R199 Stylish Ready to Wear Hat, for young ladies, made of fine satin Jap straw trimmed with a full drapery of fancy corded trimming extending around the crown and a large butterfly bow which is caught with a pretty steel buckle. Trimming can be ordered in white, pink, and light blue. Price, each..74c

Gillette. **87c**

No. 39R201 Ready to wear hat for young ladies. A very pretty striking pattern made of that light white satin Japanese braid and trimmed with full drapery of a fancy cloth. Can be ordered trimmed in cardinal, blue or brown. Price, each.....87c

Golf Girl. **80c**

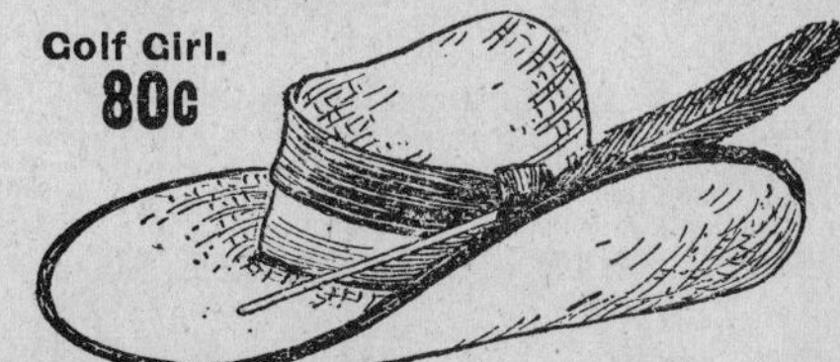

No. 39R203 Ready to wear hat for young ladies. A very jaunty and stylish design made of fancy mixed Cuba braid, natural ecru color. The edges of brim are bound with a fold of green velvette, while round the crown are folds of green velvette and red sateen with a large quill caught through at the left side. Contrast of colors, green and red, are very taking and becoming. This hat should be seen to be appreciated. Price, each....80c

Saratoga. **42c**

No. 39R205 Ladies' Untrimmed Dress Hat, nice, fancy, rough braid, short back sailor effect, with rolling brim at left side. Colors, black, castor, pearl or navy. Price, each..42c

Savoy.

47c

No. 39R207 **Ladies' stylish, dress shape, fine quality of satin Jap braid, light and substantial.** Satin braid will be very popular this season. Colors, black, maize, white or pearl.
Price, each..47c

Dresden.

46c

No. 39R209 **Ladies' stylish dress hat, large shape and large crown,** fine quality hair braid with fancy braid edge. Comes in black only.
Price, each..46c

Dunston.

50c

No. 39R211 **Ladies' Dress Hat, made of Cuba straw.** This is a new braid in the natural color very light and stylish. We recommend this as a very excellent style. Price, each........................50c

Fairfax.

50c

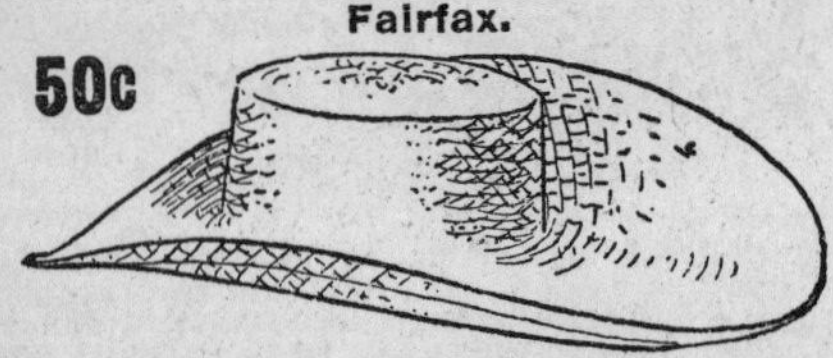

No. 39R213 **Ladies' Dress Hat with narrow rim slightly drooping at back and front,** is made of Cuba braid in the natural color; is very pretty and nobby. Price, each........................50c

Portland.

75c

No. 39R215 **Ladies' Dress Shape Hat,** made of very fine quality fancy straw braid and exceedingly dressy and stylish. Colors, black, pearl, tan or white. Price, each........................75c

Raleigh.

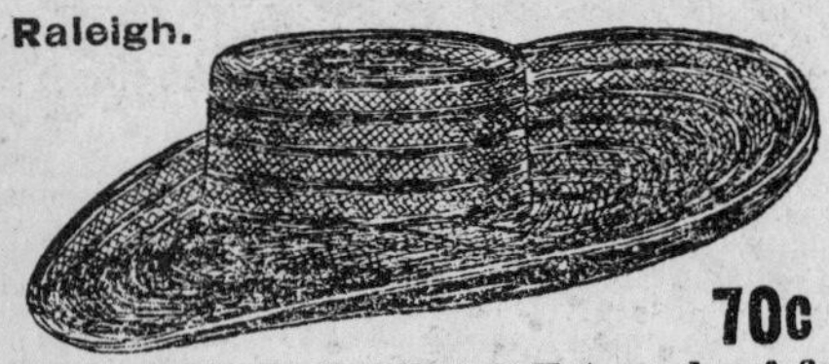

70c

No. 39R217 **Ladies' Dress Hat, made of fine hair braid.** A very pretty and light hat on the head, and splendid design. Colors, black and white.
Price, each..70c

Astoria.

75c

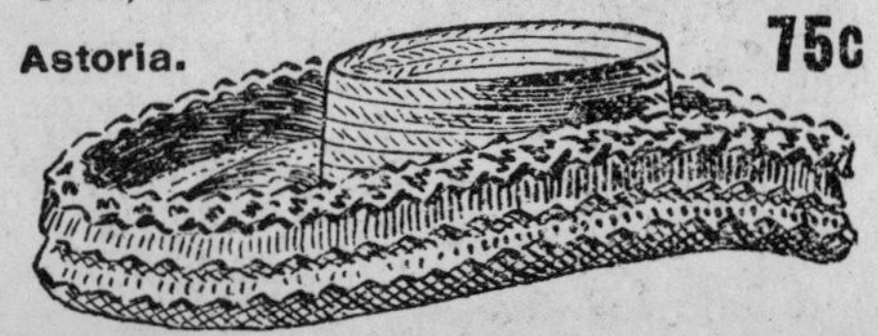

No. 39R219 **Ladies' Dress Hat, very new and light grade quality, fancy braid.** One of the most popular styles. Colors, black, white, pearl or castor.
Price, each..75c

Orient.

75c

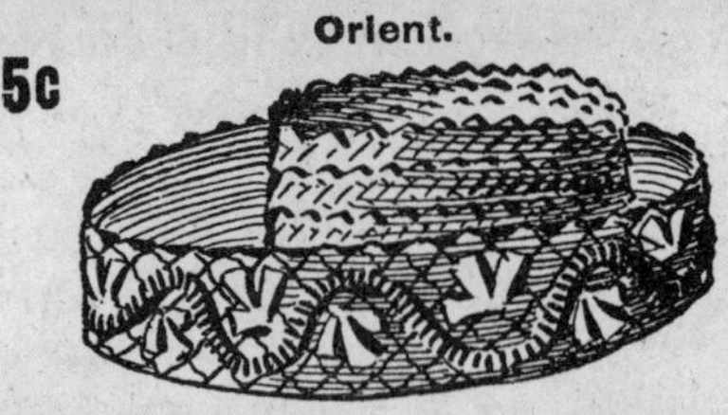

No. 39R221 **This is a very swell design, large turban** made of very high grade straw braid with fancy raised straw braid around the brim. Color, black only.
Price, each..75c

Florian.

No. 39R223 **Ladies' Turban, new large shape hat** that is being worn so much. Made of very fine quality straw braid, rich and nobby design. Colors, black, white, pearl or castor. Price, each........72c

Arlene.

25c

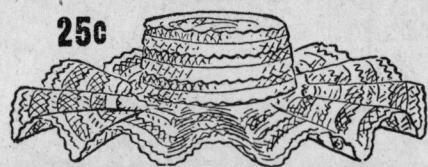

No. 39R225 **Child's Fancy Shape Hat,** of lace and pearl braid. Colors, white, cardinal or brown.
Price, each..25c

Ladies' and Misses' Leghorn Hats.

No. 39R227 **Good Quality Imported Leghorn Hat.** We only sell the best grade leghorn. Can be ordered for ladies, misses or children. White only.
Price, each..50c

No. 39R228 **Our Best Quality Leghorn Hat,** very closely woven, regular $1.50 quality. Can be ordered for ladies, misses or children. White only.
Price, each..38c

No. 39R229 **White Leghorn Hat, for children only,** with fancy straw braid edge. A very pretty hat for children. White only. Price, each......23c

Dandy.

24c

No. 39R230 **Pretty Sailor Hat for Little Boys or Girls.** Trimmed with satin ribbon and made of canton braid. Colors, white, navy, cardinal and brown.
Price, each..24c

Child's Fancy Straw Hat.

No. 39R231 **A Fancy Straw Hat for Children.** Trimmed around the crown with a full ruffle of mull designed in a very pretty manner. Colors, pink, light blue and white. Price, each....................25c

Trimmed Leghorn Hat for Misses.

67c

No. 39R233 **Misses' Leghorn Hat.** Tastily trimmed with mull in pretty folds around the crown, edged with fine satin straw braid, loops of same straw braid between folds of mull; trimmed in front with large rosette of mull and straw braid. Hat is white and any color trimming can be ordered by you either in white, light blue, pink or cardinal.
Price, each..67c

Special Trimmed Leghorn for Misses.

74c

No. 39R235 **White Leghorn Hat for Little Miss,** with fancy edge rim, trimmed with a very full fold of mull and edged with a dainty Valenciennes lace; around brim, in the center of mull, is a row of No. 1 baby satin ribbon; trimmed high in the front, a little to the left, with a large bow of mull and two large crushed muslin roses. A very pretty and stylish hat, and can be ordered trimmed in white, light blue or pink. Price, each..............................74c

Ladies' and Misses' Sunbonnets.

No. 39R237 **Ladies' Sunbonnet,** shirred all around face, with cape, made of a good quality of percale. The hood nicely laundered and stitched with three rows of white embroidery. Colors, navy blue, light blue, pink or cardinal. Usual price, 35 cents.
Price, each..22c

No. 39R239 **Misses' Sunbonnet,** shirred all around face, with cape and full hood, made exactly the same as above. Colors, navy blue, light blue, pink and cardinal.
Price, each..19c

FLOWERS.

No. 39R241 **Double Muslin Violets with Foliage;** light and dark, natural shades, three dozen in a bunch.
Price, per bunch..........4c

No. 39R243 **Large Bunch of Wood Violets with Foliage;** a full, elegant trimming. 50-cent value.
Price, per bunch...19c

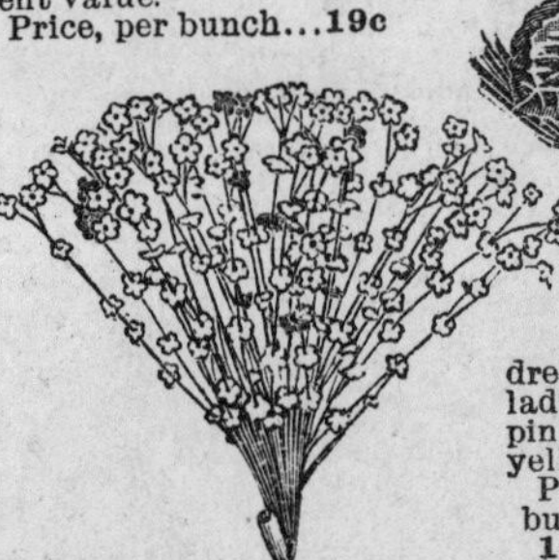

No. 39R245 **Full Spray Velvet Forget-Me-Nots,** pretty trimming for bonnets, children's hats and ladies' wear. Colors, pink, blue, white and yellow.
Per bunch
19c

No. 39R247 **Pretty Spray of Daisies,** with grass foliage, large brown center, contrasting colors. This will be a very stylish trimming this season.
Price, per bunch....................18c

Silk Bluettes, 42 Cents per Bunch.

No. 39R249 Silk Bluettes, six large flowers and buds. A very pretty and stylish trimming for this season which will be extensively used.
Price, per bunch............42c

Pretty Bunch of Lilies of the Valley, 25 Cents.

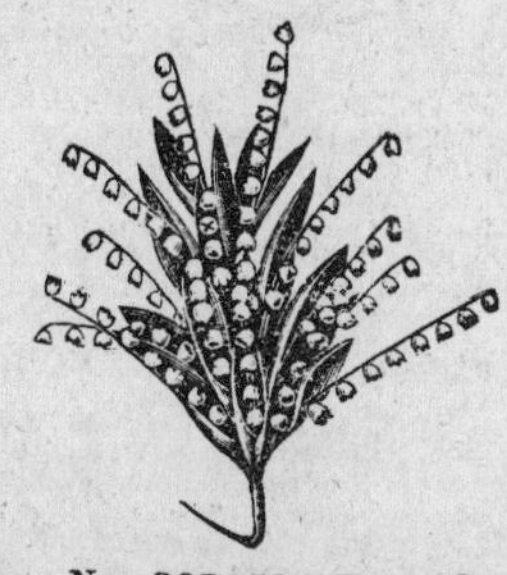

No. 39R251 This pretty bunch of Lilies of the Valley we quote much less than regular price.
Price, per bunch, 25c

No. 39R253 Very fine quality all silk Poppy with contrasting centers, twelve poppies in a bunch; this quality retails for 75 cents. Colors, red, pink and yellow.
Price, per bunch.......50c

No. 39R255 A large and elegant Chrysanthemum, an exceedingly showy and stylish trimming and very desirable. Colors, white, pink and yellow.
Price, each..................33c

Silk Rosebuds, Only 44 Cents.

No. 39R257 Dainty bunch of silk Rose Buds, medium large size, one bunch will make an elaborate trimming; rubber stems, very pretty and dainty trimming. Colors, pink, cardinal and white. Twelve buds to the bunch.
Price, per bunch.......44c

Silk and Velvet Roses.

No. 39R259 Silk and Velvet Rose, three to the bunch, a rich and pretty trimming. Exceptional value, which retails for from 25 to 35 cents. Colors, pink, white, cardinal, heliotrope and yellow.
Price, per bunch.........15c

No. 39R261 All silk or satin black crushed Roses, rubber stems, very fine quality. Colors, pink, white, cardinal, heliotrope or yellow. Bunch, 35c

Crushed Muslin Roses.

No. 39R263 Crushed Muslin Roses, three roses to the bunch; natural centers, rubber stems. Colors, cardinal, white, yellow, heliotrope.
Price, per bunch 11c

No. 39R265 Crushed Muslin Roses, with natural centers, larger size than above, of a finer quality of muslin, rubber stems. A very elegant flower. Colors, cardinal, pink, heliotrope, white and yellow. Regular 50-cent value.
Price, per bunch..19c

No. 39R267 Crushed Muslin Roses, three to the bunch, our very best and highest grade muslin rose. Those who are accustomed to fine millinery will appreciate quality. Colors, white, pink and jack.
Price, per bunch.......................42c

No. 39R269 Extra large Silk and Velvet Roses, two roses to the bunch, exceptionally pretty and dainty, with very full centers. Colors, jack, pink, white, tea and old rose.
Price, per bunch...37c

American Beauties, 17 Cents per Bunch.

No. 39R271 Large bunch of Full Blown American Beauty Roses, with full rose foliage, rubber stems. Colors, pink, jack and white.
Price, per bunch...........17c

No. 39R273 A very full and large bunch of fine quality American Beauty Roses with long rubber stems and very fine foliage and buds. These roses are made of a very fine quality of muslin, and are flowers that retails at large millinery stores at $1.25. Colors, jack, pink and white.
Price, per bunch.......................................73c
If by mail, postage extra, 4 cents.

No. 39R275 Crushed Muslin and Velvet Roses. Twelve large and very full muslin and velvet roses with rubber stems. Very fine quality flower used for very full trimming. Colors, jack, white and yellow.
Price, per bunch...............75c
If by mail, postage extra, 4 cents.

Geranium Foliage, 10 Cents per Bunch.

No. 39R277 A large bunch of Geranium foliage, green, with autumn tinted shade, worth 25 cents per bunch.
Price, per bunch.....10c
If by mail, postage extra, 4 cents.

No. 39R279 Three spray bunch of Rose Buds and Foliage; an excellent full trimming for very little price. Price, per bunch..................12c

No. 39R281 Violet Foliage and Violets. A very large and full bunch; would be good value at 40 cents. Price, per bunch..19c

No. 39R283 An exceptionally attractive and large bunch trimming of foliage with berries. A very stylish and popular trimming of dark tinted green autumn shade. Price, per bunch...........38c

Pretty Wreath of Velvet Forget-Me-Nots, 18 Cents.

No. 39R285 A pretty Wreath of Velvet Forget-me-nots with green foliage, a dainty trimming. Colors, cardinal, blue, pink or white.
Price, each.............................18c

Bluettes.

No. 39R287 A Wreath of Large Bluettes, a very elegant trimming, used for ladies' as well as children's hats.
Price, per bunch 27c

Extra Quality Bridal Wreath, 85 Cents.

No. 39R289 Bridal Wreath, extra quality; well made wax orange blossoms, including brooch and bouquet, rubber stemming; if you pay $3.00 elsewhere you get no better.
Price, $1.65

No. 39R291 Bridal Wreath with brooch and bouquet made of wax orange blossoms. Why pay extravagant prices elsewhere? Price, each, 85c

No. 39R293 Elegant Straight Quills, imitation of the fine eagle quills; look and wear just as well, very popular and dressy. Length about 12 to 14 inches. Black or white. Price, each..........................6c

No. 39R295 Pretty, broad quills, nice large size, special selected stock. Square cut top, as per illustration. Colors, black or white.
Price, each...4c

Angel Wings.

No. 39R297 Angel Wings. This is a padded wing that always retails at 50 cents. Colors, black, white, brown or navy. Price, per pair..........16c

No. 39R299 Angel Wings, same shape as above. Larger size; better quality. Colors, black or white. Price, per pair......... 33c

Stylish Aigrettes.

No. 39R301 Sweeping Paradise Aigrettes, long full feathers, six stems. A very handsome ornament. Colors, black or white.
Price, each.......50c

No. 39R303 Handsome Jetted Black Ostrich Aigrette, a full, rich trimming for hats. Black only.
Price, each...........................22c

Black Parrots, 45 Cents.

No. 39R305 Fine Selected Quality Black Parrots, rich, glossy and full length.
Price. 45c

No. 39R307 Black Feather Breast, which will be especially good on turbans as well as on hats. Splendid value. Black and white. Price, each.................................25c

No. 39R309 Pretty Feather Breasts, much larger and fuller than above. Breasts this season we highly recommend as a fashionable trimming, and this number is exceptional value. Colors, black, white and brown. Price, each..............................48c

No. 39R311 Fancy Black Jetted Coque Feather, a stylish and showy trimming at a very low price. A trifle less perhaps than your home dealer pays for them at wholesale.
Price, each.......................13c

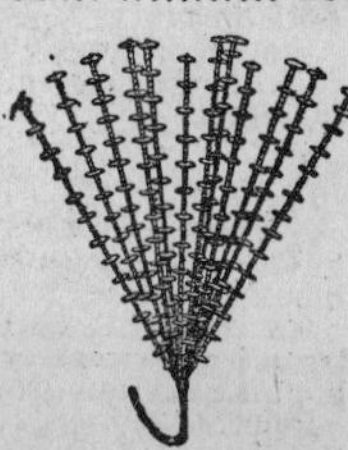

Jetted Aigrettes.

No. 39R313 Jetted Aigrette to be used in connection with other trimming, and very good on bonnets.
Price, each...............10c

GREAT SALE OF REAL OSTRICH FEATHER PLUMES AND TIPS.

Fine Demi-Plumes, 33 Cents and Upward

ALL OUR... **TIPS AND PLUMES** are made of THE HARD, GLOSSY OSTRICH STOCK

We do not handle the poor, fluffy goods.

No. 39R315 Our special 9-inch Demi-Plume, made from real ostrich feathers. Excellent quality and warranted to give perfect satisfaction Black only. Price, each....33c

No. 39R317 A very full 10-inch Demi-Plume, made from extra quality real ostrich feathers. Fine fiber and handsome curl. Very rich and glossy in appearance. Colors, black, cream or white. Always state color desired. Price, each............ 49c

No. 39R319 Real Ostrich Feather Demi-Plumes, 11 inches long, very heavy and plump, with fine soft curl. Exceptionally handsome. Fine fiber and glossy finish. Colors, black, cream or white. Always state color desired. Price, each..................................75c

No. 39R321 Real Ostrich Demi-Plumes. These are the next grade better than above. Fine selected stock. Length, 12 inches. Black, white or cream. Good $1.25 value. Price, each..87c

No. 39R323 Fine Ostrich Demi-Plume, 13-inch. Made of fine selected stock, hard finish, long and glossy fibers. Colors, black, cream or white. Price, each..$1.10

No. 39R325 Finest Quality Real Ostrich Feather Demi-Plume, 14 inches long, full and heavy, with exceptionally fine curl, glossy and beautiful. In fact, these are the richest and finest appearing plumes we have ever imported. Colors, black, cream or white. Price, each..$1.33

No. 39R327 Our Highest Grade and Best Quality Genuine Ostrich Feather Demi-Plume, made of glossy, hard fiber, ostrich stock, a rich, glossy black, fine curl, very handsome and plump, length full 15 inches. Colors, black, cream or white. Price, each..$1.62

Fine Ostrich Tips.

No. 39R329 Handsome Bunch of Real Ostrich Feather Tips, made of good quality ostrich, very handsome bunch at the price. We can furnish these tips in black only. Price, per bunch of three..............32c

No. 39R331 This Exceptionally Fine Quality Bunch Real Ostrich Feather Tips consists of three tips heavy stock select ostrich. We offer these tips at a special price, a price that you could not possibly duplicate for nearly twice what we ask. Colors, black, white or cream. Price, per bunch of three..........................59c

No. 39R333 This Elegant Bunch of Real Ostrich Tips, three in the bunch, is made of good, hard, glossy ostrich stock. The tips are made for our special use and are unexcelled for beauty and richness. Colors, black, cream or white. Price, per bunch of three..........................90c

No. 39R335 This Extra Fine Bunch of Rich, Full and Glossy Ostrich Feather Tips consists of three tips and has an exceptionally fine curl and full appearance. We specially recommend this number and you could not duplicate same elsewhere for less than $2.50. Colors, black, cream or white. Price, per bunch of three..........................$1.50

Amazon or Flat Plumes.

No. 39R337 Fine First Quality Real Ostrich Amazon Plumes. Extensively used, especially for the Gainsborough effects. Length, 14 inches. Colors, black, white or cream. Price, each..............$1.50

No. 39R339 Amazon Real Ostrich Plumes. Finer and larger than above. Length, 15 inches. Colors, black, white or cream. Price, each....$1.95

No. 39R341 Amazon Real Ostrich Plumes. Rich, glossy stock, long fibers. Length, 16 inches. Colors, black, white or cream. Price, each.... ......$2.29

GIVE CATALOGUE NUMBER IN FULL WHEN YOU WRITE YOUR ORDER

Spangled Jet Crown.

No. 39R345 Spangled Jet Crown, generously and closely spangled, a rich hat crown. Size, 12½x12½ inches. Regular 75-cent value. Price, each..............39c

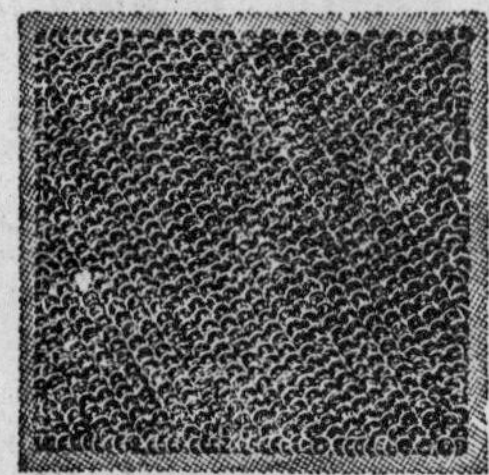

No. 39R349 Fancy Jeweled Spiral Hat Pin, with large center stone, surrounded by five oblong stones to match. Settings come in turquoise, ruby or emerald. Price, each.......5c If by mail, postage extra, 2 extra,

No. 39R351 Fancy Hat Pin. Made of pretty enameled metal, with large setting on top in garnet, turquoise or emerald. Price, each......10c

No. 39R353 Fancy Hat Pin. Made of twisted gilt with four small rhinestones and large setting on top of bright ruby, amethyst or emerald; regular 50-cent value. Price, each..........................25c

Spangled Jet Crown, 25 Cents.

No. 39R343 Spangled Jet Crown. Very popular this season. Size, 9x9 inches. Price, each....25c

Handsome Jet Crown for 58 Cents.

No. 39R347 Spangled Jet Crown. Solid work; closely spangled, very handsome and elaborate. Size, 12 x 12 inches. Price, each....58c

Brilliant Rhinestone Buckles.

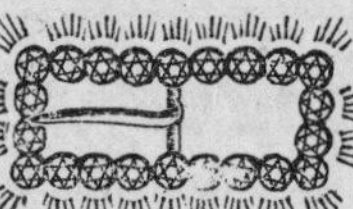

No. 39R355 Square shaped design. Size, ⅞x2 inches. Price, each..............10c **If by mail, postage extra, 2 cents.**

No. 39R357 Square shaped design, same as above, but larger. Size, 3½x1¼ inches. Price, each..15c **If by mail, postage extra, 2 cents.**

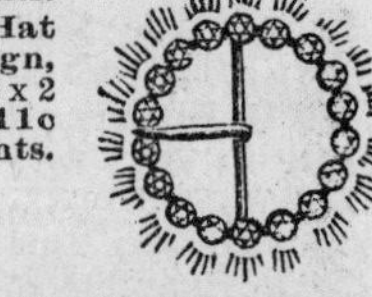

No. 39R359 An Excellent Hat [buc]kle, round, circular design, a very pretty shape. Size, 2 x 2 inches. Price, each...........11c **If by mail, postage extra, 2 cents.**

No. 39R361 Desirable size, new fancy shape. Size, 4⅓x2¼ inches. Price, each, 17c **If by mail, postage extra, 2 cents.**

Cut Steel Ornamental Buckles.

No. 39R363 New and pretty design. Size, 3⅓x2 inches. Price, each.....15c **If by mail, postage extra, 2 cents.**

No. 39R365 Very stylish design. Size, 3½x2¼ inches. Price, each.............25c **If by mail, postage extra, 2 cents.**

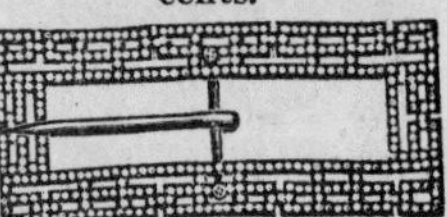

No. 39R367 For hat trimming or dresses. Square design. Size, 4½x 1¾ inches. Price....28c **If by mail, postage extra, 2 cents.**

Fancy Jet Trimming Buckle.

No. 39R369 With four large button shaped jet effects on either end. Diamond shaped. Size, 2⅝x4 inches. Price....25c **If by mail, postage extra, 2 cents.**

No. 39R371 Pretty Rhinestone Set Cabochon, round shape, a very handsome hat ornament. Size, 1⅛ inches. Price, each..............12c **If by mail, postage extra, 2 cents.**

No. 39R373 This Elegant Cut Steel Cabochon, is a very rich ornament for hat trimming. Size, 1⅝x1⅝ inches. Regular 25-cent value. Price, each..............11c **If by mail, postage extra, 2 cents.**

Black and White Mixed Coque Boas.

No. 39R375 Coque Feather Boas, a lovely combination black tipped with white ostrich, very stylish. Length, 50 inches. Price, each..................88c **If by mail, postage extra, 6 cents.**

No. 39R377 Fine quality Coque Feather Boas, very soft and downy, pointed feathers. Length, 50 inches. Can be ordered in black or white. Price, each..............$1.10 **If by mail, postage extra, 7 cents.**

Ostrich Neck Boas.

No. 39R379 Finest Real Ostrich Feather Boas. Rich, glossy black; only the fullest, finest stock. Very dressy and stylish. We quote them in three different lengths, as follows: Price, 27-inch, $3.95; 36-inch, $5.87; 54-inch, $8.98

No. 39R381 Fine Imported Palm Plants, extensively used for ornamenting parlors and halls. These plants are naturally prepared and very lasting. They come packed flat, without the pots. Sizes and prices are as follows:

Height, inches	Branches	Shipping Weight	Price Each
42	4	6 pounds	70c
42	5	8 pounds	95c

No. 39R383 Imported Artificial Rose Sprays. Large full blown American Beauty roses, with nine leaves, to be used in vases or pots for your center table and mantels. Look as pretty as the natural roses and will last indefinitely. Several of these roses make a large and handsome showing. Colors, pink, white cream jack, yellow and tea. Shipping weight each, 5 ounces; half dozen, 18 ounces. Price, each, without pot..........................45c

DEPARTMENT OF MEN'S AND WOMEN'S FURNISHING GOODS.

IN ORDERING GOODS from this department we especially urge that you use the utmost care in giving us proper measurements. In shirts, underwear, hats, gloves, in fact everything which requires a size, be sure that you state the size wanted in your order; otherwise it will be necessary to hold your order until we can hear from you. This means not only an expense to us, but a loss of time and a great deal of annoyance to yourself. With proper care on your part in making out your order, all this annoyance may be obviated.

OUR FURNISHING GOODS DEPARTMENT was never more complete than it is this season; never before have we been able to offer more attractive, stylish and low priced lines of everything included in this department. In ordering from us you are assured of not only buying the goods at the lowest possible prices, but you have the advantage of a selection equal to the very largest exclusive furnishing goods stores in metropolitan cities, a much finer and more varied assortment than is carried by the average dealer, and you may feel assured that whatever you find illustrated and described on these pages is correct in style.

WE RECOMMEND that wherever possible you combine your order for shirts, hosiery, underwear and other furnishing goods with such other supplies as you may need, or club together with your neighbors so as to make up a freight order. In this case the cost of transportation by freight on a supply of furnishing goods will be little or nothing compared with what we save you.

NOTE OUR PRICES. Every item in this department is a splendid value. The saving offered over the usual store prices varies from 20 to 50 per cent. Nearly all of our 75-cent items retail at $1.00, our $1.00 articles will cost you elsewhere $1.25 to $1.50. With no expense for free catalogues, free samples, etc., pricing our goods on the basis of actual manufacturing cost with but our one small percentage of profit added, we name prices on the best grade of furnishing goods that make competition for us simply out of the question.

UNLAUNDERED WHITE SHIRTS.

Always state size in your order.

No. 16R50 Men's Unlaundered Shirts, made of good muslin, double back and front, linen bosom and continuous facings. **Long bosom, open back style only.** Sizes, 14, 14½, 15, 15½, 16, 16½, 17 neckband. **What size do you wear?**
Price, per dozen, $4.20; each....................35c
If by mail, postage extra, each, 11 cents.

No. 16R54 Men's Unlaundered Shirts, made of New York Mills muslin, double back and front, continuous facings and gussets throughout, linen set in bosom. The best value possible at our low price. **Long bosom, open back style.** Sizes, 14, 14½, 15, 15½, 16, 16½, 17, 17½, 18 neckband. **What size do you wear?**
Price, per dozen, $5.40; six for $2.70; three for $1.35; each....................45c
If by mail, postage extra, each, 12 cents.

No. 16R58 Men's Fine Unlaundered Shirts, made from New York Mills muslin, with fine set in linen bosom, double front and back. A most exceptional quality. **Short bosom, open back only.** Sizes, 14, 14½, 15, 15½, 16, 16½, 17, 17½, 18 neckband. **What size do you wear?** Price, each....................45c
If by mail, postage extra, each, 14 cents.

No. 16R62 Men's Extra Quality Unlaundered White Shirts, made of the best heavy muslin, which insures durability, 2100 linen bosom. Reinforced at every vital point with gussets or facings. Double front and back. A strictly high grade shirt. Open back only. Sizes, 14, 14½, 15, 15½, 16, 16½, 17, 17½, 18 neckband.
Price, per dozen, $9.00; each....................75c
If by mail, postage extra, each, 14 cents.

Boys' Unlaundered White Shirts.

No. 16R66 Boys' Unlaundered White Shirts, made of New York Mills muslin, double front and back, linen bosom. Sizes, 12½, 13, 13½, 14 neckband.
Price, per dozen, $5.04; each....................42c
If by mail, postage extra, each, 10 cents.

LAUNDERED WHITE SHIRTS.

SPECIAL NOTICE—All our white shirts are made with split neckband in back. This prevents the collar button from coming in contact with neck, causing irritation. **Always state size of neckband. Men's sizes are 14, 14½, 15, 15½, 16, 16½ and 17. Extra sizes are 17½, 18, 18½, 19, 19½ and 20. Do not forget postage when ordering by mail.**

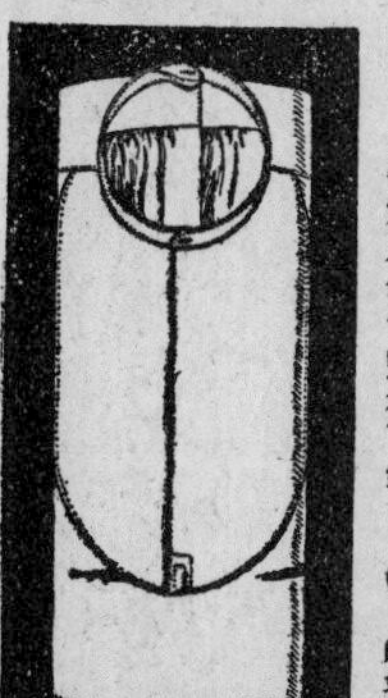
No. 16R84

A First Class Shirt for 60 Cents.

No. 16R80 Short bosom; special. Made of selected muslin, very strong and durable, with 4-ply linen bosom and bands. Neck protector in back (keeps collar button from coming in contact with neck). Made with short bosom. Sizes: 14, 14½, 15, 15½, 16, 16½, 17, 17½, 18; open back only.
Price, six for $3.60; three for $1.80; each....................60c
If by mail, postage extra, each, 14 cents.

Our Leader at 70 Cents.

No. 16R84 Short Bosom Shirt; **open front and back, faultless in fit; handsome in finish.** Made from the finest Fruit of the Loom muslin, with 2100 all linen four-ply bosom and band. Open front and back. Reinforced wherever a shirt should be. Absolutely perfect in every detail and fit. Neck protector in back; keeps collar button from coming in contact with neck. Retail price, $1.00. Sizes, 14, 14½, 15, 15½, 16, 16½, 17, 17½, 18. Always state size wanted.
Price, per dozen, $8.40; three for $2.10; each..70c
If by mail, postage extra, each, 14 cents.

$1.00 Shirt for 80 Cents.

No. 16R88 Men's Fine Laundered White Shirt, made in the short bosom style, open front and back. Made from fine Wamsutta muslin, with fine linen bosoms, split neckband, double stitched, flat felled seams, large full body. Equal to the best shirt retailing at $1.00, and superior to most of them. A strictly high grade, perfect fitting shirt. Sleeve lengths, 30 to 35 inches. Sizes, neckband, 14, 14½, 15, 15½, 16, 16½, 17, 17½, 18 inches.
Price, six for $4.80; three for $2.40; each..... 80c
If by mail, postage extra, each, 15 cents.

Long Bosom Shirts.

No. 16R92 Our 40-Cent Long Bosom Shirt. Men's laundered white dress shirt. The best that can be produced at this low price. Open back style only. Sizes, 14, 14½, 15, 15½, 16, 16½, 17.
Price, each....................$0.40
Price, per dozen....... 4.80
If by mail, postage extra, each, 13 cents.

Our Long Bosom Shirts at 60 Cents.

No. 16R96 Men's Laundered Dress Shirts; full length fine linen bosom, good weight muslin, gussets, facings full size, reinforced front and back, made with split neckband, which protects neck from collar button. **Open back only.** Sizes, 14, 14½, 15, 15½, 16, 16½, 17, 17½, 18 neckband. **What size do you wear?**
Price, half dozen, $3.60; each....................60c
If by mail, postage extra, each, 15 cents.

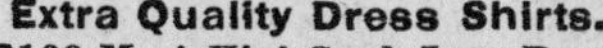

Extra Quality Dress Shirts.

No. 16R100 Men's High Grade Long Bosom Laundered White Dress Shirts. As perfect fitting as any, and large full sized body. Continuous facings. We warrant every shirt to be perfect and faultless in construction and fit. **Long bosom, open front and back.** Better than most shirts selling at $1.00. Sizes, 14, 14½, 15, 15½, 16, 16½, 17, 17½, 18 neckband. Sleeve lengths, 31 to 34 inches. Three for $2.40; each..80c
If by mail, postage extra, each, 15 cents.

No. 16R104 Men's High Grade Long Bosom Laundered White Dress Shirts; same as above but open back only. Sleeve lengths from 31 to 34 inches. Sizes, 14, 14½, 15, 15½, 16, 16½, 17, 17½, 18.
Price, six for $4.80; three for $2.40; each.....80c
If by mail, postage extra, each, 15 cents.

Men's Coat Shirt. 90 Cents.

No. 16R106 Men's Fine White Shirts; made in coat shirt style, opening all the way down the front, and is put on and off the same as a coat. Strictly high grade; perfect fitting in every particular. Made with medium length bosom; a comfortable and satisfactory shirt. Sizes, 14, 14½, 15, 15½, 16, 16½, 17, 17½.
Price, each....................90c
If by mail, postage extra, 15 cents.

Men's Full Dress Shirts, $1.00.

No. 16R108 Men's Finest White Laundered Shirts. Made from fine New York Mills muslin, 2000 linen bosom. Barred buttonholes, eyelets; made with bosom full dress size. Open front and back. This is one of our especially good numbers in shirts, and will equal many retailing at $1.50. **Made from strictly high grade muslin,** and fine linen bosom, double stitched, flat felled seams and continuous facings throughout. Sizes, 14, 14½, 15, 15½, 16, 16½, 17, 17½, 18; sleeve lengths, 30 to 35 inches. Each...$1.00

MacHurdie Full Dress Shirts.

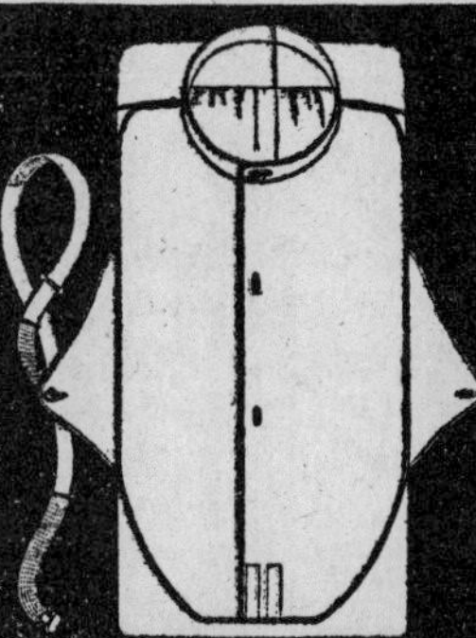

No. 16R112 The MacHurdie Dress Shirt is the most perfect shirt made to wear with full dress. The illustration shows the small insertions on each side to which is buttoned the elastic tape which passes around the back. In the center of tape is a sliding buckle. In this manner the bulging out over the vest and consequent discomfort is overcome. **Superior muslin and fine linen bosom.** Sizes, 14, 14½, 15, 15½, 16, 16½, 17, 17½. Sleeve lengths, 31 to 34 inches. Price, three for $4.05; each........$1.35
If by mail, postage extra, each, 17 cents.

No. 16R114 The MacHurdie Full Dress Shirt, same style as above, but with **cuffs attached.** Sizes, 14, 14½, 15, 15½, 16, 16½, 17, 17½. Price, each.....$1.85
If by mail, postage extra, each, 17 cents.

Fat Men's Laundered Dress Shirts.

No. 16R118 Fat Men's Special White Shirt. Fat men usually experience much difficulty in getting a shirt the right shape, large in the arms, armholes, across shoulders and around body. This shirt will fit nineteen out of twenty fat men every time; is strictly high grade, with gussets and continuous facings throughout. **Medium long bosom, open back only.** Sizes, 15, 15½, 16, 16½, 17, 17½, 18, 18½, 19, 19½, 20 neckband.
Price, six for $7.20; three for $3.60; each..$1.20
If by mail, postage extra, each, 16 cents.

Men's Fancy Embroidered Bosom Dress Shirts.

No. 16R122 Men's Fancy Embroidered Bosom White Dress Shirts. Strictly high grade New York Mills muslin, gussets and facings throughout, with vine like embroidery on bosom as shown in illustration. **Open back and front.** Sizes, 14, 14½, 15, 15½, 16, 16½, 17, 17½.
Price, each....................$0.85
Three for.................... 2.55
If by mail, postage extra, each, 15 cents.

No. 16R122

No. 16R126 Men's Fine Plaited Bosom Shirts; made in strictly high grade manner and perfect fitting. Long bosom with either wide or narrow plaits. A thoroughly well made dress shirt, staple and suitable all the year round. **Open back and front.** Sizes, 14, 14½, 15, 15½, 16, 16½, 17, 17½. **What size do you wear?** Price, each......$0.85
Three for.................... 2.55
If by mail, postage extra, each, 15 cents.

No. 16R134 Men's Percale All Colored Dress Shirts. Medium long bosom, open back only. Made of good quality percale that will wear well and give satisfactory service. In a large variety of stripes and fancy effects. One pair of cuffs to match. Sizes, 14, 14½, 15, 15½, 16, 16½, 17 only. **What size do you wear?**
Price, each..........$0.50
Three for.......... 1.50
If by mail, postage extra, each, 15 cents.

DON'T FAIL TO GIVE SIZE

Men's Laundered Colored Shirts, 70 Cents.

No. 16R138 Men's Fancy Laundered Shirts; made with stiff bosom, medium length; made from fine percale of a quality equal to that used in shirts retailing regularly at $1.00. **A strictly first class shirt; full size body. One pair link cuffs** to match. These are strictly good shirts that will fit and wear well. Our line comprises a large variety of stripes and fancy effects in blue, pink, purple, lavender, etc. We can please you in quality and color selection. Sizes, 14, 14½, 15, 15½, 16, 16½, 17 neckband.
Price, each....................$0.70
Three for.................... 2.10
Six for.................... 4.20
If by mail, postage extra, each, 15 cents.

FANCY BOSOM DRESS SHIRTS.

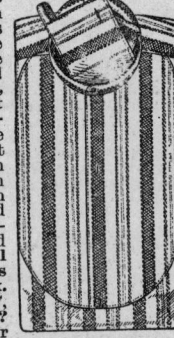

If by mail, postage extra, each, 13 cents.

No. 16R143 Men's Fine Dress Shirts; made with medium length bosoms, with pair of link cuffs; **Garner's fine percale**; gusset facings with patent splice at back buttonhole to prevent collar button from rubbing the neck. We have these goods in blue and white, pink and white, red and white and black and white stripes. Give color you prefer and you will be pleased with our selection. Open front and back. Sizes, 14, 14½, 15, 15½, 16, 16½, 17, 17½ and 18. **What size do you wear?** Price for three, **$2.70**; each..**90c**

Men's All Colored Dress Shirts, 85c.

No. 16R150 Men's Fine Dress Shirts; made medium length bosom, with one pair of link cuffs to match. A strictly high grade shirt; made from Garner's fine percale, which is the standard of the world in quality. **Gussets, facings, with patent splice at back buttonhole** to prevent collar button from rubbing the neck. We have the most select designs offered this season in blues, pinks, red and green stripes, in combinations, such as blue and white, pink and white, etc. Give color preference and you will be pleased with our selection. **The usual retail value of such shirts is $1.25. Open front and back.** Sizes, 14, 14½, 15, 15½, 16, 16½, 17, 17½, 18. **What size do you wear?** Price, six for **$5.10**; three for **$2.55**; each..................**85c**

If by mail, postage extra, each, 13 cents.

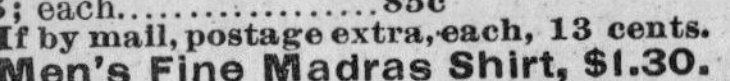

Men's Fine Madras Shirt, $1.30.

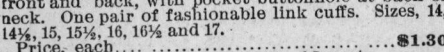

No. 16R152 Men's Fine Madras Shirts, made with medium length bosom, the comfortable kind. A strictly high grade shirt in every respect that will meet the demands of exacting dressers. We guarantee every shirt perfect fitting. There is no improvement known to the shirtmaker's art that is not to be found in this shirt. We cannot recommend a shirt of this kind too highly for wear, appearance, comfort and fast color. The colors are mainly in blue, pink and oxblood backgrounds overshot in contrasting colors in a large variety of stripes and figured effects. Shirts of this quality are invariably cheap in the end, and as all our patterns in these goods are up to date and new you will make no mistake in ordering this number. State color preference. Made open front and back, with pocket buttonhole at back of neck. One pair of fashionable link cuffs. Sizes, 14, 14½, 15, 15½, 16, 16½ and 17.
Price, each..........**$1.30**

If by mail, postage extra, 13 cents.

Men's Colored Shirts with Detachable Collars and Cuffs.

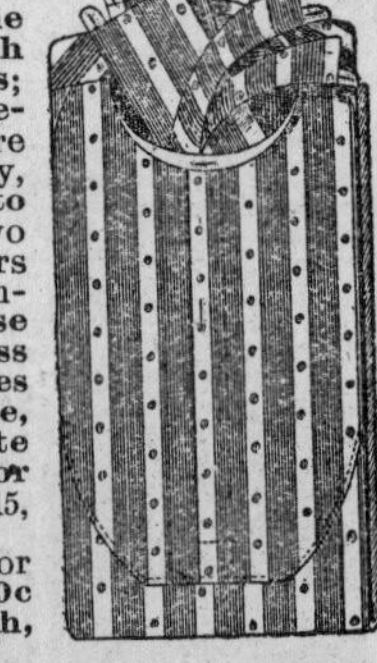

No. 16R160 Men's Fine French Percale Shirts, with detachable collars and cuffs; fast colors; open back; medium length bosom. They are made large and full sized body, and we guarantee them to give perfect satisfaction. Two detachable lay down collars and one pair of cuffs are included with each shirt. These goods do not retail for less than $1.00 each. Neat stripes and checks, such as blue, brown and pink on white background; also in scroll or all over effects. Sizes, 14½, 15, 15½, 16, 16½, 17.
Price, six for **$4.80**; three for **$2.40**; each..............**80c**

If by mail, postage extra, each, 15 cents.

Our Special Plaited Shirt for 90 Cents.

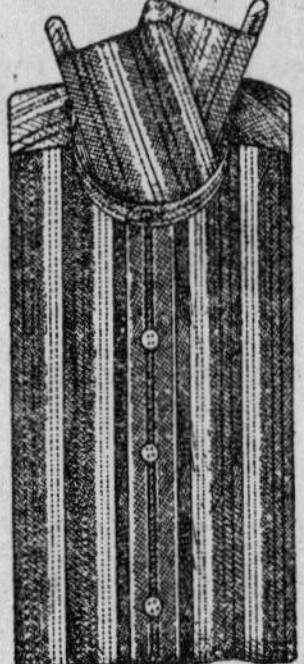

No. 16R176 Under this number we offer a fine quality of Madras shirt, equal to many that retail at $1.25 and are high grade manufacture in every respect, with one pair of cuffs to match, large full sized bodies with every improvement known to the shirtmaker's art. Made like a fine plain negligee shirt with the single exception that on each side of the bosom the stripes are gathered in such a manner as to be out of the ordinary, giving an effect that will be appreciated immediately by good dressers. We recommend this shirt very highly. Remember that when you buy high grade shirts from us you pay no fancy profits and if any shirt is not found exactly as represented and satisfactory in every respect it can be returned and we will immediately refund your money. The chief colors are blue and white, oxblood and white, also in **plain colors**, blue or oxblood, or fancy raised striped Madras in small figured designs. You will make no mistake in ordering three or more in a shirt of this kind, allowing us to assort them. We feel sure that our selection would meet your approval. Sizes, 14, 14½, 15, 15½, 16, 16½ and 17. Price, each..**90c**

If by mail, postage extra, 15 cents.

The Coolest Plaited Shirt, $1.00.

No. 16R178 Under this number we furnish something new, practical and desirable in negligee, semi-dress shirts. As may be seen in the illustration, the bosom proper is made of a mesh cloth, which is completely covered by the plaits, of which there are four on a side. This shirt is made of a new corded Madras cloth, which has a raised white stripe throughout and is printed in fast colors in small figured designs after the manner of the illustration. The background is white and the figures are in black, making one of the nobbiest black and white shirts shown this season. The pearl buttons are a very dark color and in harmony with the general appearance of the shirt. Made open front only, pocket neckband in the back, one pair of link cuffs. We cannot recommend a shirt of this kind too highly as it is of stylish design with points of practical merit We should be pleased to receive your order for on or more of this number. Sizes, 14, 14½, 15, 15½, 16, 16½ and 17. Price, each..........................**$1.00**

If by mail, postage extra, 16 cents.

Men's High Grade White Body Plaited Shirt

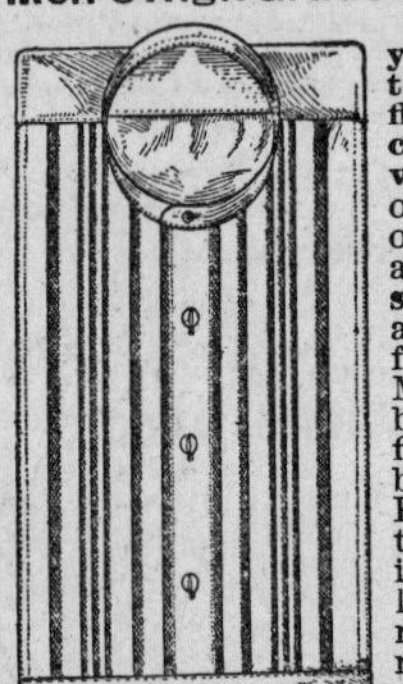

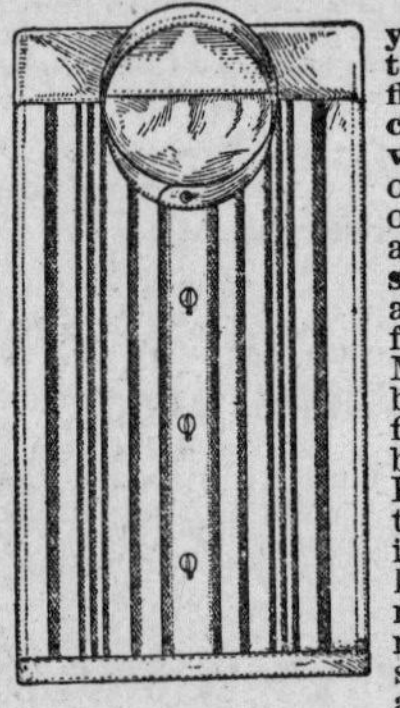

No. 16R180 We would call your attention in particular to this Shirt. Made with a flexible bosom, with a narrow colored plait inserted on a very fine cambric. The colors of the plaits are blue and oxblood, and when applied in a skillful manner as in this shirt, has a genteel, fresh, cool appearance that is seldom found in any negligee shirt. Made open front, full length bosom, and closed with three fine white pearl buttons. To be worn with white cuffs. Pocket neckband to prevent the collar button from bearing against the neck. Our illustration will show you the manner in which the shirt is made, and there is not a better style of shirt to be found in any store. Remember, this is a strictly high grade shirt, guaranteed to fit. State color preference. Sizes, 14, 14½, 15, 15½, 16, 16½ and 17.
Price, each..................................**$1.00**

If by mail, postage extra, each, 16 cents.

Our Special Leader, Plaited Shirt, $1.00.

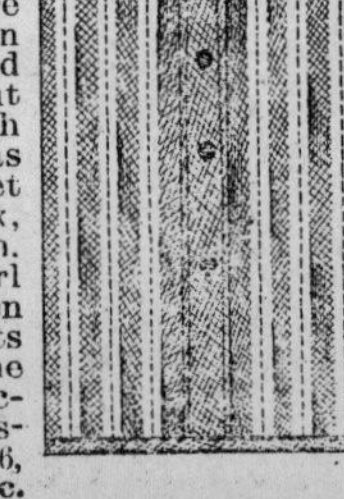

No. 16R184 Again we offer a new style plaited shirt of attractive and original design, a shirt that is to be found only in the leading furnishing stores in the country and then at almost prohibitive price. All shirts under this number are made of fine Madras cloth in solid blue or dark oxblood, and the bosom has no stiffness but has three white plaits on each side stitched down the center as shown in illustration. Pocket buttonhole in the back of neck, one pair of link cuffs to match, trimmed in three dark pearl buttons down the front. Open front only. The white plaits stitched onto the bosom in the manner shown are very effective and will please good dressers. Sizes, 14, 14½, 15, 15½, 16, 16½ and 17. **Postage extra, 16c.**
Price, each **$1.00**

All White Plaited Shirts.

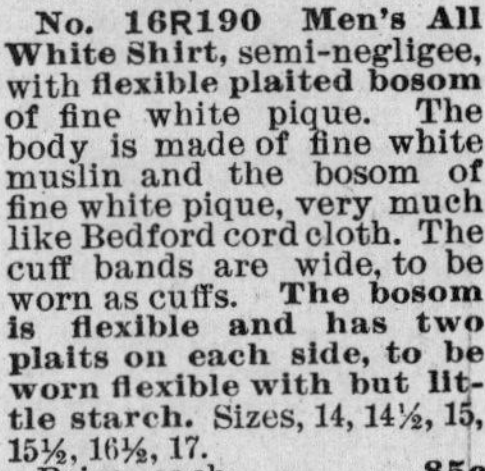

No. 16R190 Men's All White Shirt, semi-negligee, with **flexible plaited bosom** of fine white pique. The body is made of fine white muslin and the bosom of fine white pique, very much like Bedford cord cloth. The cuff bands are wide, to be worn as cuffs. **The bosom is flexible and has two plaits on each side, to be worn flexible with but little starch.** Sizes, 14, 14½, 15, 15½, 16½, 17.
Price, each..............**85c**

If by mail, postage extra, each, 16 cents.

Our New Novelty Summer Shirt.

No. 16R191 We offer herewith one of the newest shirts for this season, made as shown in the illustration with fancy striped percale body and fancy inserted open work bosom of a new French cloth, the special feature of which is a slightly open work design alternating with three rows of raised corded effects in a contrasting color. For instance, the corded effects are in either blue, red or black and the background is white. They are made open front only and close with three fine pearl buttons; one pair of linked cuffs. A novelty that will win much favor this season because new and at the same time a very comfortable, pleasing shirt. Sizes, 14, 14½, 15, 15½, 16, 16½ and 17.
Price, each.....................**80c**

If by mail, postage extra, each, 16 cents.

Men's Fine Quality Percale Shirts.

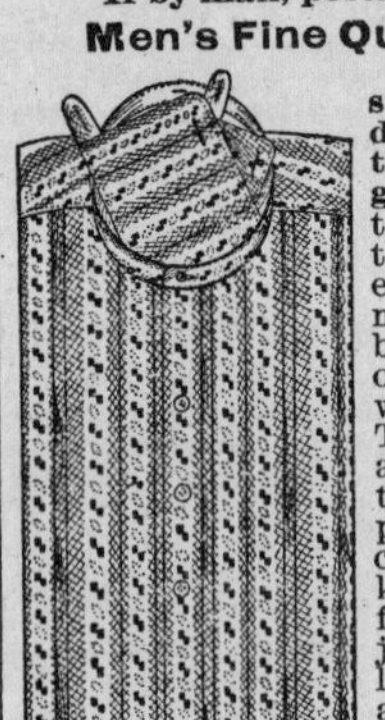

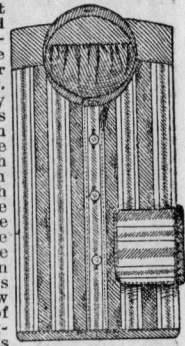

No. 16R193 In new and striking designs out of the ordinary in this kind of goods, at the same time not in any degree loud. We illustrate one of the patterns in which we have this shirt, and as may be observed from the illustration it is made with a large, flexible bosom with two double plaits on each side and closes in front with three fine pearl buttons. The shirt is open in front only and made with one pair of cuffs to match. The regular retail price of this shirt is $1.00. Because of our large output of this kind of goods we are able to offer them to our customers at just about the price they cost local dealers. The predominating colors are blue, pink and oxblood, and if you will name your choice of color in your order we shall be pleased to make careful selection. Sizes, 14, 14½, 15, 15½, 16, 16½ and 17. Price, each..............................**75c**

If by mail, postage extra, 17 cents.

Our Plaited Shirts for 50 Cents.

No. 16R195 50 cents is not very much to pay for a good shirt, but we believe that under this number we offer the very best shirt that has ever been shown for this money. The body is of good quality Madras cloth, full size, and is made up in the style shown in the illustration, with two wide plaits of contrasting cloth stitched on each side and down the center of the bosom, which is not stiff, closed with three pearl buttons, and the cuffs are attached, of the new negligee pattern and are made of the same material as the plaits on the bosom. You will say this is the best shirt you ever saw for **50 cents.** The bodies of the shirts are blue and oxblood, both colors popular this season. Sizes, 14, 14½, 15, 15½, 16, 16½ and 17. Price, six shirts for **$3.00**; three for **$1.50**; each...**50c**

If by mail, postage extra, each, 12 cents.

Men's All White Silk Front Shirts, 75 Cents.

No. 16R240 Men's All White Fine Muslin Body Shirts with silk bosom of white, either plain or in small white raised overshot effects. Retail value, $1.00. Sizes, 14, 14½, 15, 15½, 16, 16½, 17. Price, each, 75c

If by mail, postage extra, each, 12 cents.

Men's Colored Negligee Shirts.

Collars and Cuffs Attached.

No. 16R250 Men's Good Quality Laundered Percale Shirts with attached collars and cuffs. An excellent shirt for our low price. A large variety of stripes and plaids, etc. Sizes, 14½, 15, 15½, 16, 16½, 17.

What size do you wear?

Price, each $0.40
Three for 1.20
Six for 2.40

If by mail, postage extra, each, 12 cents.

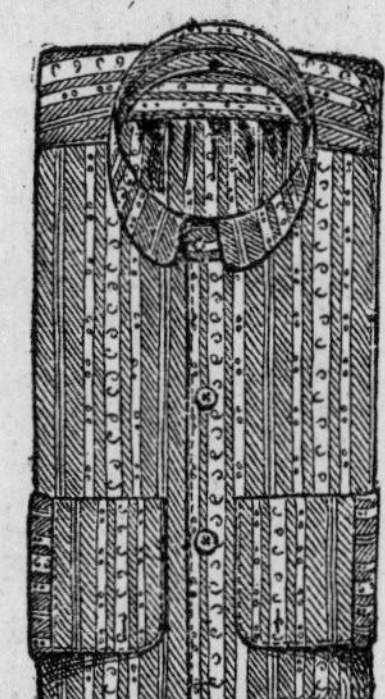

Men's Fine Percale Shirts, 60 Cents.

No. 16R254 Men's Fine Quality French Percale Shirts; laundered, with attached collar and cuffs. A shirt that will always give good wear and satisfaction. Full size, with gussets, facings and pearl buttons. New stripes and plaids. Sizes, 14½, 15, 15½, 16, 16½, 17, 17½.

Price, each $0.60
Three for 1.80
Six for 3.60

If by mail, postage extra, each, 14 cents.

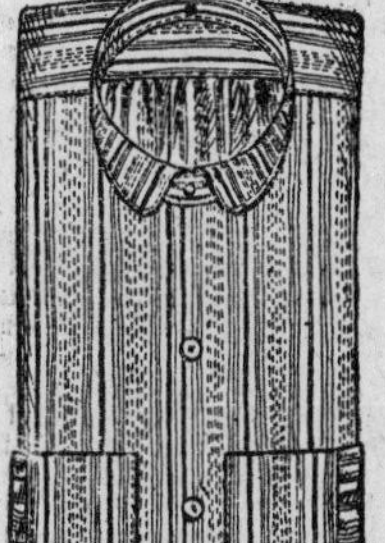

Our Special Value, 85 Cents.

No. 16R258 Men's Fine Laundered Madras Negligee Shirts; made from the fine imported woven Madras. They are extremely durable and the colors are absolutely fast. Collar is finely shaped, designed to fit the neck properly and cuffs are attached. Made in stripes and plaids, in which the predominating colors are white, blue and heliotrope, lavender and red. Sizes, 14½, 15, 15½, 16, 16½, 17, 17½.

Our price, each $0.85
Three for 2.55
Six for 5.10

If by mail, postage extra, each, 15 cents.

Our Special Soft Shirts.

With Button Down Collars, not Starched.

The Special Soft Shirt is called such because the collar is always in its place, being held so by concealed buttons under the collar on each side. This prevents it from slipping up around the neck, to an uncomfortable position, at the same time adding much to the appearance.

No. 16R270 Our New Negligee or Soft Shirt. Made large and full size, of fine, good weight Madras cloth, colors woven in. The patterns in this shirt are especially pleasing, made in stripes and plaids, with string ties to match. Pearl buttons, pocket on the side and yoke back. Don't forget, this shirt has the new button down stay in its place collar. Sizes, 14½, 15, 15½, 16, 16½, 17.

Price, each $0.68
Three for 2.04
Six for 4.08

If by mail, postage extra, each, 14 cents.

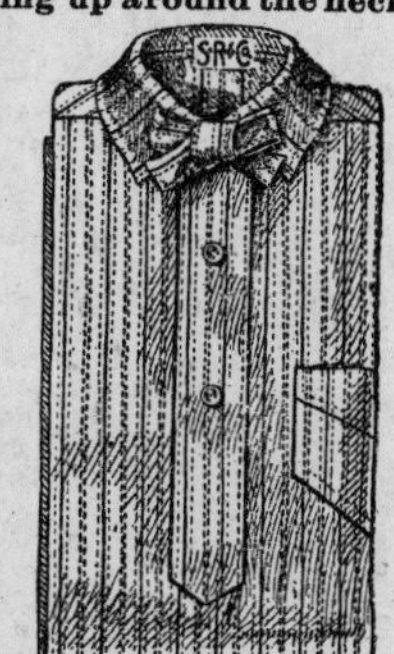

Our Special Value at 80 Cents.

No. 16R274 Men's Fine Light Weight Madras Shirts. Made in the best manner possible. Our new button down collar; necktie to match, which can be tied either in a knot or bow. One pocket, and cut large in the body. The color designs in these are pleasing to those desiring quiet effects. Made in stripes, blue, pink and black, etc. Sizes, 14½, 15, 15½, 16, 16½, 17.

Price, each $0.80
Three for 2.40
Six for 4.80
Per dozen 9.60

If by mail, postage extra, each, 10 cents.

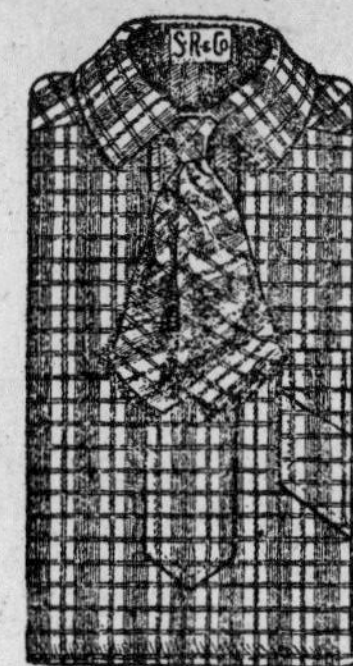

Our Great $1.00 Leader.

No. 16R278 Men's Fine Cheviot or Heavy Madras Cloth. Made with yoke back, large full body, new button down collar, and tie to match that can be tied either in a knot or bow. One pocket on left side. Beautiful plaids and checks, in which blue and white or pink and white are the predominating colors. An ideal, all around outing shirt. Sizes, 14½, 15, 15½, 16, 16½, 17.

Price, each $1.00
Three for 3.00
Six for 6.00
Per dozen 12.00

If by mail, postage extra, each, 14 cents.

Oxford Cloth Shirts for $1.50.

No. 16R292 Men's Fine Heavy Weight Oxford Cloth Shirts. The most durable of all cotton shirts made. Yoke back, large full body stitched with silk; an incomparable value and will outwear two or three ordinary shirts. Two pockets and tie of same fabric, which can be tied in a knot or bow. A most beautifully woven cloth, alternating in various colors over a light background, blue, green, pink stripes and plaids, etc. Sizes, 14½, 15, 15½, 16, 16½, 17. Regular retail price, $2.50.

Price, each $1.50
Three for 4.50
Six for 9.00

If by mail, postage extra, each, 12 cents.

Fine French Flannel Shirts for $1.90.

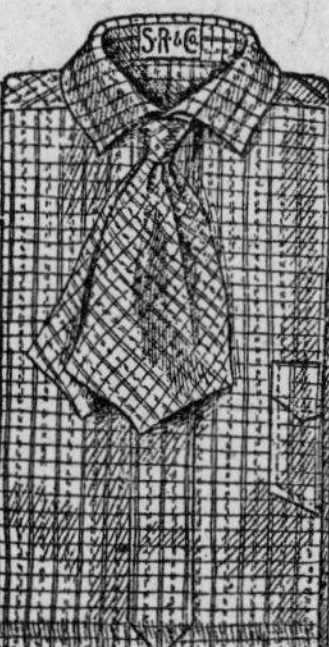

No. 16R296 Men's Fine Light Weight French Flannel Shirts. The cloth consists of about ⅝ wool to ⅜ fine cotton, and is shrunk before being made up, but should be carefully washed. This combination makes a most pleasing garment, as all the colors composing the pattern stand out in strong relief. Attractive quiet plaid and stripe effects in alternating colors of blue, black and brown. Two rows of silk stitching around the collar, and double silk stitching throughout the entire shirt. The tie to match is full length, and can be tied either in a knot or bow. The buttonholes are hand made and worked in silk; has pearl buttons in front, and two pockets. Sizes, 14½, 15, 15½, 16, 16½, 17.

Price, six for $11.40; three for $5.70; each $1.90

If by mail, postage extra, each, 10 cents.

Fine Silk Shirts for $2.90.

No. 16R300 Men's Fine Silk Shirts. Made with button down collar and tie to match. Made from cloth about 75 per cent pure silk, and has all the appearance of a pure silk shirt and will wear better. The finest workmanship, stitched with silk, and has every improvement known to the trade. The usual retail price, $5.00. A large variety of new and stylish patterns of modest and delicate colorings. Sizes, 14, 14½, 15, 15½, 16, 16½, 17.

Price, each $ 2.90
Three for 8.70
Six for 17.40

If by mail, postage extra, each, 10 cents.

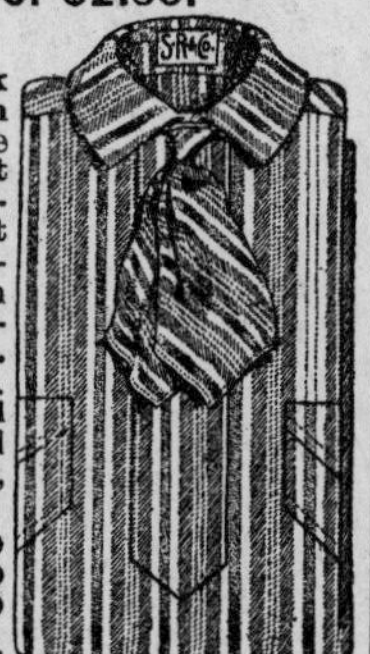

MEN'S EXTRA SIZE SHIRTS.

Fat Men's French Flannel Shirts.

Sizes, 17½, 18, 18½ and 19.

No. 16R310 Men's Fine French Flannel Shirts, extra size, light weight in light colors. French flannel is a very light weight and has sufficient cotton interwoven which modifies shrinkage in washing. A very fine twilled, soft cloth. Made with yoke back, felled seams, continuous facings and gussets. A strictly high grade shirt with tie to match of same material. One of our special values. Light weight, light stripes and plaids, hair line effects. Sizes, 17½, 18, 18½, 19.

Price, six for $12.00; three for $6.00; each, $2.00

If by mail, postage extra, each, 12 cents.

Men's Extra Size Negligee Shirts.

No. 16R314 Men's Extra Size Laundered Negligee Shirt, made from very fine French percale, fast colors. The assortment of patterns consists of modest designs in plaids and stripes; open front, collar and cuffs attached and large breast pocket. Extra well made. Sizes, 17½, 18, 18½, 19 only.

Price, six for $5.70; three for $2.85; each 95c

If by mail, postage extra, each, 18 cents.

Extra Size Working Shirts.

No. 16R318 Men's Extra Size Black and White Stripe Twilled Cotton Overshirts, made in extra size and very large bodies. Sizes, 17½, 18, 18½, 19.

Price, per dozen, $6.60; six for $3.30; three for $1.65; each 55c

If by mail, postage extra, each, 16 cents.

Extra Size Velours Cloth Shirts.

No. 16R328 Men's Extra Size Velours Cloth Cotton Shirts, made in dark colors in plaids and stripes. A soft surface cotton twill that will wear and wash well. Extra size bodies, yoke back, felled seams. Sizes, 17½, 18, 18½, 19.

Price, per dozen, $9.00; six for $4.50; three for $2.25; each 75c

If by mail, postage extra, each, 20 cents.

Extra Size Wool Cassimere Shirts.

No. 16R332 Men's Extra Size Fine Wool Cassimere Overshirts, in medium colors. Very large extra size body and yoke back, pearl buttons, a first class shirt with non-shrinking neckband. Sizes, 17½, 18, 18½, 19. Price, per dozen, $18.00; six for $9.00; three for $4.50; each $1.50

If by mail, postage extra, each, 23 cents.

Men's Extra Size Blue Flannel Shirts.

No. 16R336 Men's Extra Size Blue Flannel Shirts, made of fine quality Imperial flannel with sufficient mixture of cotton to avoid shrinkage. Yoke back, pearl buttons, lined neckband, extra large full sized bodies. Non-shrinking neckband. Sizes, 17½, 18, 18½, 19. Price, per dozen, $18.00; six for $9.00; three for $4.50; each $1.50

If by mail, postage extra, each, 25 cents.

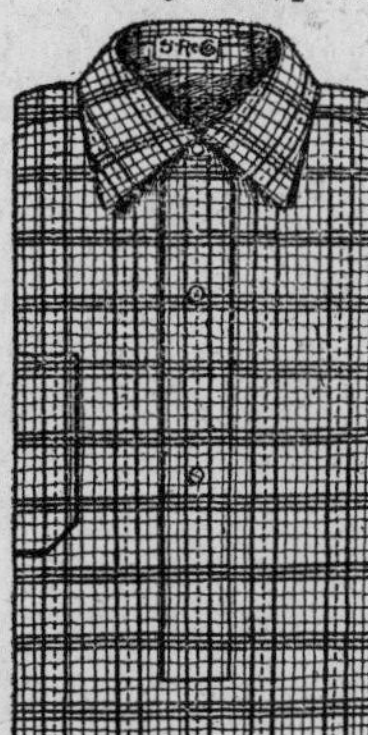

Men's Soft or Negligee Shirts.

Not starched. Sizes, 14½ to 17.

No. 16R340 This line of overshirts we have had made up for us in great quantities. They are made from Madras cloth, the colors and patterns are woven through and through (not printed). Cut full 36 inches long and never retail for less than 50 cents. Made with yoke back, felled seams, shaped shoulders and extension neckband. We have them in neat plaids, checks, stripes, assorted patterns and colors. Sizes, 14½, 15, 15½, 16, 16½, 17, only.

Price, each $0.45
Three for 1.35
Six for 2.70
Per dozen 5.40

If by mail, postage extra, each, 12 cents.

Men's Good Quality French Percale Shirts.

No. 16R344 Men's Good Quality French Percale, fast colors, in light colored stripes, plaids, etc. An excellent value in a soft shirt that will wash and wear well. Yoke back, pearl buttons, shaped shoulders, felled seams, gussets and full 36 inches long. Can be worn collars and cuffs starched. Sizes, 14½, 15, 15½, 16, 16½, 17.

Price, each $0.40
Three for 1.20
Six for 2.40
Per dozen 4.80

If by mail, postage extra, each, 12 cents.

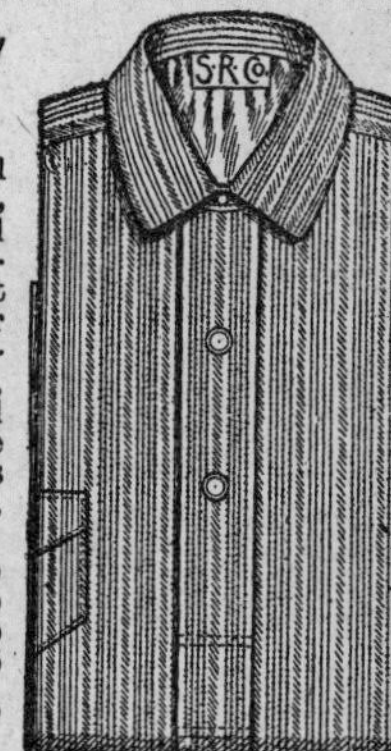

DON'T FAIL TO GIVE SIZE

Men's Sateen Shirts, 41 Cents.

No. 16R348 Men's Fine Sateen Soft Shirts. An excellent quality equal to many shirts at a much higher price. A large variety of stripes and plaids, light colors. Shaped shoulders, felled seams, extension neckband and 36 inches long. What size do you wear? Sizes, 14½, 15, 15½, 16, 16½, 17.

Price, each $0.41
Three for 1.23
Six for 2.46

If by mail, postage extra, each, 12 cents.

Fine Blue Flannel Shirts, $1.25.

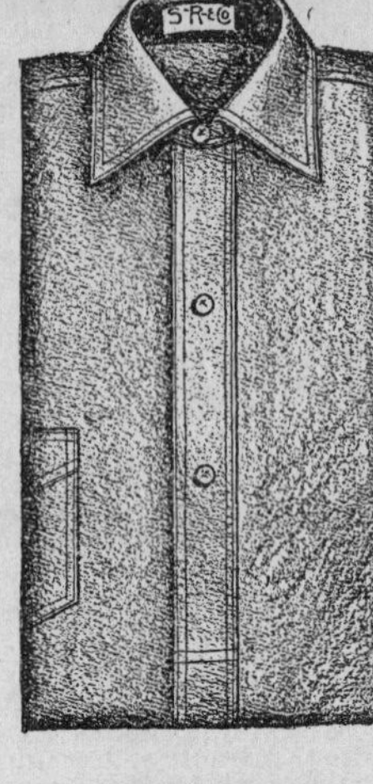

No. 16R536 Men's Fine Blue Flannel Winter Overshirts, made from fine blue flannel with a mixture of cotton sufficient to prevent shrinkage. Shaped shoulders, yoke back, pearl buttons, **extension non-shrinking neckband, gussets and faced sleeves. Full sized body, 36 inches long. A special value.** Regular retail value, $1.65. Sizes, 14½, 15, 15½, 16, 16½, 17.

Price, each.....$ 1.25
Three for....... 3.75
Six for.......... 7.50
Per dozen....... 15.00

If by mail, postage extra, each, 23 cents.

California Blue Flannel Shirts, $1.70.

No. 16R540 Men's Genuine California Blue Flannel Shirts. All from pure wool. **The California flannels are the best all wool flannels made.** They are smooth and even in surface and **absolutely fast in colors.** Made single breasted, yoke back, shaped shoulders, felled seams, faced sleeves, gussets, non-shrinking neckband, extension band, collar buttons down on each side and pearl buttons. A better shirt is not made. Retail price, $2.25. **Large body, 36 inches long.** Size, 14½, 15, 15½, 16, 16½, 17.

Price, each..$ 1.70
Three for... 5.10
Six for..... 10.20
Per dozen,.. 20.40

If by mail, postage extra, each, 19 cents.

Men's Double Breasted Blue Flannel Shirts, $1.00.

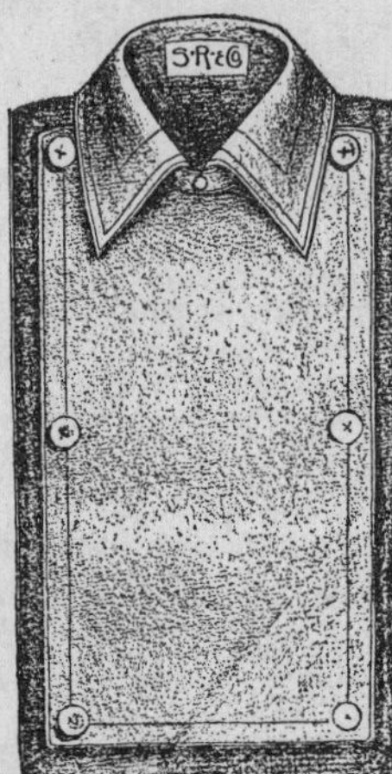

No. 16R544 Men's Double Breasted Full Winter Weight Blue Flannel Overshirts, made from good quality twilled union flannel. Large pearl buttons, non-shrinking band, yoke back, full size and length. The best value obtainable at this low price. Sizes, 14½, 15, 15½, 16, 16½ 17. **What size do you wear?**

Price, each.....$ 1.00
Three for....... 3.00
Six for. 6.00
Per dozen....... 12.00

If by mail, postage extra, each, 22 cents.

Our Special Value for $1.35.

No. 16R548 Men's Fine Double Breasted Blue Flannel Shirts, made from fine blue flannel with a sufficient mixture of cotton to prevent shrinkage, which also adds to its durability. Yoke back, pearl buttons, full size body, 36 inches long. You would pay your local merchant $1.75 for a shirt and not get one as good in workmanship or cloth. A special value at our low price. Sizes, 14½, 15, 15½, 16, 16½, 17.

Price, each.......$ 1.35
Three for......... 4.05
Six for........... 8.10
Per dozen......... 16.20

If by mail, postage extra, each, 23 cents.

Our Special Value Men's California Flannel Double Breasted Shirts at $2.00.

Cut shows folded in half.

No. 16R552 Men's Genuine California Twilled Blue Flannel. All pure wool California flannels are better than all others, **having smooth, even surface and better color.** Made yoke back, coat sleeves, large pearl buttons, **non-shrinking neckband.** Full size body, 36 inches long. You will pay $2.50 to $3.00 for this grade in your home town. Sizes, 14½, 15, 15½, 16, 16½ and 17. Per dozen, **$24.00;** six for **$12.00;** three for **$6.00;** each, **$2.00**

If by mail, postage extra, each, 24 cents.

Firemen's Shirts, $3.00.

No. 16R556 Firemen's Heavy Weight Twilled California Blue Flannel Shirts, made up in regulation firemen's style. **Double breasted, with white pearl buttons,** extra long pointed collar and double back, deep cuffs trimmed with pearl buttons, warranted first quality in every respect. **All wool and cut full size.** Sizes, 14½, 15, 15½, 16, 16½, 17. Positively unexcelled for wear and service. Retail value, $4.00.

Price, each...$ 3.00
Per dozen...... 36.00

If by mail, postage extra, each, 26 cents.

MEN'S NIGHTSHIRTS.

SPECIAL NOTE—Men's Nightshirts are not made in half sizes.

No. 16R600 Men's Plain White Bleached Muslin Nightshirts. Cut full large throughout. Double yoke back. **Large collar and cuffs.** Sizes, 14, 15, 16, 17, 18.

Price, each.............$0.45
Three for............... 1.35

If by mail, postage extra, each, 14 cents.

No. 16R604 Men's Fancy Front Nightshirts. Made from superior quality white muslin. Tastefully embroidered on collar and down the front in **beautiful contrasting colors.** Double yoke back. Full size and length. Sizes, 14, 15, 16, 17, 18.

Price, each.................$0.45
Three for.................. 1.35

If by mail, postage extra, each, 14 cents.

No. 16R608 Men's Embroidered Nightshirts. Fine Utica mills muslin. Yoke back and patent facings. New improved stitching. Cut full, large and very **richly embroidered** in contrasting colors on collar, front and cuffs. **Breast pocket embroidered to match.** Sizes, 14, 15, 16, 17, 18. Price, three for **$2.04;** each, **68c**

If by mail, postage extra, each, 14 cents.

Very Fine Muslin Nightshirts, 85 Cents.

No. 16R612 Men's Superfine Nightshirts. Made of finest Utica mills muslin with full yoke back. **Finest white pearl buttons** and patent facings. Cut full length and extra well made throughout. Front, collar and cuffs all handsomely **trimmed with insertion and richly embroidered in silk of contrasting shades,** cardinal, baby blue, rose, pink, opal, lavender, etc. Sizes, 14, 15, 16, 17, 18.

Price, each.....................$0.85
Three for....................... 2.55

If by mail, postage extra, each, 14 cents.

No. 16R614 Men's Extra Long Plain White Nightshirts, made of finest Utica mills muslin. Extra large body, 60 inches long, yoke back, pearl buttons, patent facings. Sizes, 15, 16, 17, 18, 19.

Price, three for **$2.85;** each....**95c**

If by mail, postage extra, each, 18 cents.

Men's French Flannelette Nightshirts.

No. 16R620 Men's Good Quality Flannelette or Domet Nightshirts. Full size body and well made; fancy plaids and stripes. **The soft, smooth cloth is particularly pleasant for sleeping garments.** Sizes, 14, 15, 16, 17, 18.

Price, each..................$0.45
Three for.................... 1.35

If by mail, postage extra, each, 16 cents.

No. 16R624 Men's Extra Fine French Flannelette Cloth Nightshirts. Try them once and you will never wear any other kind. **They are made in the best manner possible. Cut full length and have yoke back, white pearl buttons,** handkerchief pocket, large roll collar and double stitched seams. Soft and fine in texture. Made in light colors, neat combination stripes or checks. Sizes, 14, 15, 16, 17, 18, 19. **Healthful, durable and warm.**

Price, six for **$4.08;** three for **$2.04;** each....**68c**

If by mail, postage extra, each, 18 cents.

Extra Heavy Flannelette.

No. 16R628 Men's Flannel Nightshirts. Made of high grade extra heavy Domet flannel, cut 56 inches long, yoke back, white pearl buttons, handkerchief pocket and double stitched seams. They are soft and fluffy like swansdown, solid colors and stripes: light blue, pink or cream white. Sizes, 15, 16, 17, 18, 19, 20.

Price, three for **$2.85;** each..**95c**

Postage extra, each, 19 cents.

Extra Long Flannelette Nightshirts.

No. 16R632 Men's Extra Long Flannelette Nightshirts, of same quality as No. 16R628, but 60 inches in length. **Just the thing for cold weather.** A special comfort for tall men. Sizes, 15, 16, 17, 18, 19, 20.

Price, three for **$3.00;** each.**$1.00**

Postage extra, each, 20 cents.

Boys' Muslin Nightshirt.

No. 16R636 Boys' Muslin Nightshirts. Boys' good quality muslin nightshirts; full size and length. Sizes, 12, 13, 14.

Price, each....................42c

Postage extra, each, 10 cents.

Boys' Flannelette Nightshirt.

No. 16R640 Owing to the well merited popularity of Domet cloth nightshirts, we have had made for us a special value for boys or youths. Made of fine quality cloth in pretty plaids and stripes; longer than the regular shirt. **Healthful and durable.** Sizes, 12, 13, 14.

Price, each.................45c

Postage extra, each, 14 cents.

Men's Pajamas.

Men's Fine Pajamas. A very desirable two-piece sleeping or lounging suit, preferred by many men to the regular night robe. Just the thing for traveling, as their appearance admits of greater freedom than the usual kind of night shirts. Sizes to fit 34 to 44 breast; give breast measure in order.

No. 16R644 Men's Fine Cheviot Cloth Pajamas in fancy stripes and plaids, etc. Give chest measure.

Price, per suit.........**$1.50**

No. 16R648 Men's Fine Madras Cloth Pajamas, (colors woven into fabric) in elegant new plaids and stripes. Blue, pink, lavender, etc. Give chest measure. Regular $3.00 suit. Our price..........**$2.25**

Bath Robes.

No. 16R652 Fine Terry Cloth Bath Robe with Hood, in fancy fast color design. A useful garment, now very popular. Full length and size. Usual retail price, $5.00; our price.......**$3.00**

Lounging Robes.

No. 16R656 Men's Fine All Wool Blanket Cloth Lounging Robe, similar in style to the above, except that instead of hood it has a shapely coat collar. Comfortable as a house garment and particularly useful in traveling, being much more convenient than steamer shawls. Give preference for color and we will not disappoint you. For size give breast measure. Price.............**$7.50**

Boys' White Dress Shirts.

Sizes, 12, 12½, 13, 13½ and 14.

SPECIAL NOTE—For large youths requiring size 14 neck, order men's size 14. Allow 10 cents postage when ordering boys' shirts by mail.

No. 16R660 Boy's Fine Laundered White Dress Shirts. All linen bosom; superior quality muslin. Guaranteed to give good service. Sizes, 12, 12½, 13, 13½, 14. Price, each........................40c

No. 16R664 An Extra Fine Quality Boys' Laundered White Shirt, made from specially selected muslin with all linen bosom. Thoroughly well made and reinforced. Fine dress finish; open back. Sizes, 12, 12½, 13, 13½, 14. Price, each.................65c

BOYS' FANCY DRESS SHIRTS.

Boys' All Colored Percale Shirts.

No. 16R670 Boys' or Youths' All Colored Percale Shirts, with medium bosom, laundered, open back only; made of good quality percale, in large variety of stripes, plaids, blue, pink, red, etc. Sizes, 12, 12½, 13, 13½, 14. **What size do you wear?**

Price, each....................43c

If by mail, postage extra, each, 10 cents.

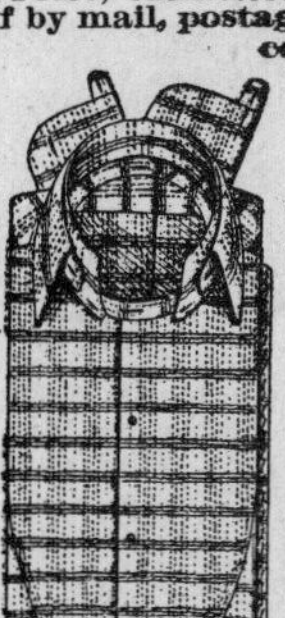

DON'T FAIL TO GIVE SIZE

Boys' Fine Dress Shirts.

No. 16R674 Boys' Fine French Percale Dress Shirts, made with two collars, one turn down and one standing, and one pair of cuffs to match. The patterns are the latest stripes and plaids in a large variety of effects, such as pink, blue, red, etc. A common sense shirt for a boy. Sizes, 12, 12½, 13, 13½, 14. Price, each.........$0.65

Three for.........1.95

If by mail, postage extra, each, 12 cents.

Boys' New Negligee Shirt, Plaited Front.

No. 16R675 A new novelty in shirts for boys that is sure to please, made just like the shirt his father wears, two pleats on each side of the bosom, closes in front with three pearl buttons, new style negligee band cuffs. To be worn with white collars, and will be found a stylish and pleasing shirt that may be laundered at home. The body is solid color, oxblood, pink or blue. Sizes, 12, 12½, 13, 13½ and 14 only.

Price, each..............$0.45

Three for.............1.35

If by mail, postage extra, each, 12 cents.

Boys' Negligee Shirts.

No. 16R678 Made of French percale, with two collars and one pair of cuffs to match. A sensible shirt which will give enduring satisfaction. The designs are in plaids and stripes on solid background, such as blue, pink, brown, etc. All pretty combinations. Never retails for less than 50 cents. **Do not forget size.** Sizes, 12, 12½, 13, 13½, 14.

Price, each..................$0.45

Six for..................2.70

If by mail, postage extra, each, 10 cents.

Boy's Laundered Negligee Shirts.

No. 16R682 Boys' Laundered Negligee Shirts. Made from fancy colored French percale, open front with attached turn down collar and cuffs. New and fashionable stripes, figures, plaids and pin checks; white ground with colorings of black, red, pink, blue, etc. Sizes, 12½, 13, 13½, 14. Fine dressy finish. Retail price is never less than 50 cents. Always mention size worn.

Price, each...................40c

If by mail, postage extra, each, 10 cents.

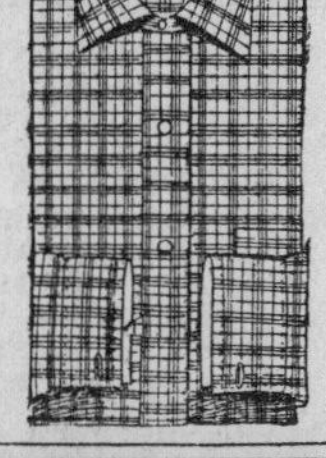

BOYS' OVERSHIRTS.

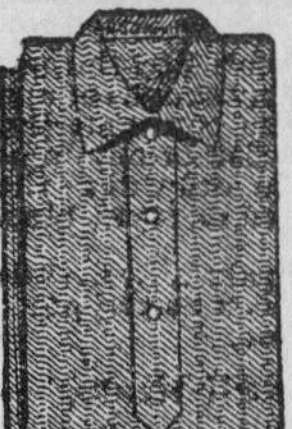

No. 16R700 Boys' Fancy Striped Cotton Overshirts. Assorted patterns, medium and light colors, very good values. Sizes, 12, 12½, 13, 13½, 14 only. Price, six for $1.38; each..........................23c

If by mail, postage extra, each, 7c.

No. 16R702 Boys' Fancy Striped Flannelette Overshirts. Soft and fine, will wash and wear well, **extra well made,** assorted light and medium colors, good weight; suitable for all seasons. Sizes, 12, 12½, 13, 13½, 14.

Price, six for $2.34; each....39c

If by mail, postage extra, each, 7c.

Boys' Black Sateen Overshirts, 40 Cents.

No. 16R706 Boys' Fast Black Sateen Overshirts. Finely made and finished, yoke back and breast pocket; **reliable in every way.** Sizes, 12, 12½, 13, 13½, 14. Price, each......$0.40

Six for..................2.40

If by mail, postage extra, each, 6 cents.

Good Value at 39 Cents.

No. 16R710 Boys' Black and White Twilled Cotton Overshirts, made in first class manner, double back and front, as in illustration. A good, strong working shirt. Sizes, 12½, 13, 13½, 14. Price, each......$0.39

Six for..................2.34

If by mail, postage extra, 10c.

No. 16R712 Boy's Plain Blue Woven Chambray Overshirts. One of the best fast color cloths that will stand repeated washing and hard wear; made in the same manner as No. 16R710. Sizes, 12½, 13, 13½, 14.

Price, each..............$0.39

Six for..................2.34

If by mail, postage extra, 10c.

WHAT SIZE DO YOU WEAR? Be sure and state size in your order.

BOYS' WINTER SHIRTS.

Boys' Fine Cotton Cassimere Shirts.

No. 16R714 Boys' Fine Cotton Cassimere Shirts, strong, good weight, well made and durable. Large variety of plaids and stripes, medium and dark colors. Sizes, 12½, 13, 13½, 14. **Don't forget size.**

Price, each..........................40c

If by mail, postage extra, each, 12 cents.

No. 16R718 Boys' Heavy Winter Weight Union Wool Cassimere Shirts. Medium and dark colors. Pearl buttons, extension neckband, felled seams and full size; assorted stripes, checks and mixtures; gray and brown predominating colors. **Finely finished neckband and breast pocket.** Sizes, 12½, 13, 13½, 14.

Price, each....................68c

If by mail, postage extra, each, 10 cents.

No. 16R722 Boys' Blue Flannel Overshirts, made of heavy union flannel, extension neckband, one pocket, pearl buttons, felled seams, yoke back and full size. A thoroughly good flannel shirt that will give entire satisfaction. Sizes, 12½, 13, 13½, 14.

Each....68c

If by mail, postage extra, each, 15 cents.

No. 16R726 Boys' Blue Flannel Overshirts, made with **double back and front,** extension neckband, pearl buttons, felled seams and full size; a warm, heavy shirt, 80 per cent wool; dependable; one that will wash and wear well. Sizes, 12½, 13, 13½, 14.

What size do you wear?

Each....80c

If by mail, postage extra, each, 16 cents.

Boys' Jersey Shirts, 40 Cents.

No. 16R730 Boys' Heavy Cotton Jersey Knit Overshirts, in dark colors, made with cord front only. A good warm winter overshirt. Sizes, 12½, 13, 13½, 14.

Price, each..............................40c

If by mail, postage extra, each, 17 cents.

HOSIERY DEPARTMENT.

OURS IS A PROGRESSIVE HOSIERY DEPARTMENT.

WE HAVE almost every kind of hosiery for men, women and children. This department has more than doubled in the past year and the growth is due to the careful attention to quality and our customers' orders. As in our other departments we purchase direct from the manufacturer doing away with excessive profits and offering them at the lowest possible price. We can save money for you if you buy your hosiery from us. When we say a hose is **all wool** we mean **all wool.** If merino, we mean wool and cotton mixed.

POSTAGE.—When ordering shipped by mail do not fail to include postage.

DON'T FAIL TO GIVE SIZE

Do not forget the importance of giving correct size that you may have a comfortable and proper fit.

How to Order Sizes Correctly.

Scale of Sizes.

Shoe	5-5½	6-6½	7-7½
Hose	9	9½	10
Shoe	8-8½	9-9½	10-10½-11
Hose	10½	11	11½

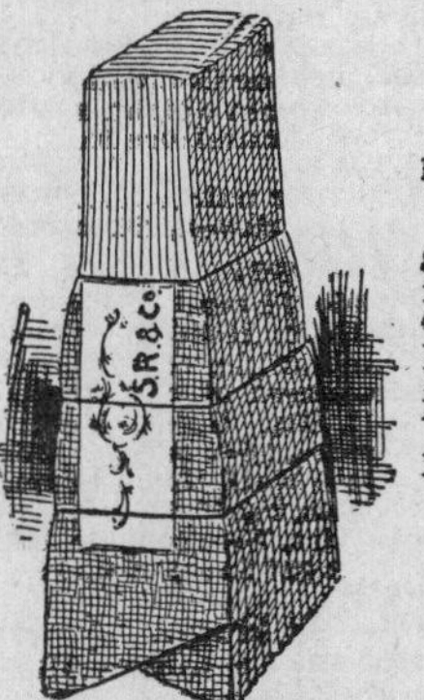

ROCKFORD SOCKS.

Made by the Nelson Knitting Co.

No. 16R2000 Men's Full Seamless Knit Half Hose in assorted gray mixtures. Good weight; suitable for wear all the year round. Extra good value. Weight, 1½ pounds to the dozen.

Price, per dozen..........55c

If by mail, postage extra, per dozen, 32 cents.

DON'T FAIL TO GIVE SIZE

Rockford Socks, 7 Cents.

The Nelson Knitting Co.'s Seamless Rockford Socks.

No. 16R2004 The Nelson Knitting Co.'s Seamless Rockford Socks. Blue or brown mixed. **Heavy double heel and toe, and fine finished ribbed tops.** Weight, 2¾ pounds to dozen. Every pair warranted.

Price, per pair.........7c

Per dozen pairs.........84c

No. 16R2004

Boys' Rockford Socks.

No. 16R2006 Boys' Heavy Cotton Rockford Socks. Blue mixed. Good socks for all year round wear. For boys and youths from 10 to 15 years of age.

Price, per dozen.......................65c

How to Order Sizes Correctly.

Scale of Sizes.

Shoe	5-5½	6-6½	7-7½
Hose	9	9½	10
Shoe	8-8½	9-9½	10-10½-11
Hose	10½	11	11½

MEN'S COTTON HALF HOSE.

DON'T FAIL TO GIVE SIZE

Clouded Cotton Half Hose.

No. 16R2008 Men's Fine Full Seamless Half Hose, in new and handsome brown and olive mixtures, also neat gray mixture; extra fine quality, with finely finished foot and elastic ribbed tops. **The equal of any 20-cent half hose in the market.** Weight, about 17 ounces to dozen.

Sizes, 9½, 10, 10½, 11, 11½.

Price, per pair.........$0.12

Per dozen pairs.........1.44

If by mail, postage extra, per pair, 2 cents; per dozen, 22 cents.

No. 16R2008

Men's Half Black Hose.

DON'T FAIL TO GIVE SIZE

No. 16R2012 Men's Fine Egyptian Combed Yarn Half Hose, seamless, made with black leg and natural ecru foot. Durable and easy on the feet. Our low price on this hose represents the cost to your local merchant. Elastic ribbed tops. Sizes, 9½, 10, 10½, 11, 11½.

Price, per pair..........$0.12

Per dozen pairs.........1.44

If by mail, postage extra, per pair, 2c; per dozen, 22c.

Men's British Half Hose at 12 Cents Per Pair.

No. 16R2016 Men's Genuine Cream Brown British Seamless Socks. Fine elastic ribbed tops, double heels and toes; knit to wear long and well and guaranteed to do so. Weight, 17 ounces to dozen. Sizes, 9½, 10, 10½, 11, 11½.
Price, per dozen pairs, $1.44; per pair.........12c
If by mail, postage extra, per pair, 2 cents; per dozen, 20 cents.

Men's Genuine British Half Hose, 23 Cents.

No. 16R2020 Our Great 40-Gauge Genuine British Socks. Medium weight; full seamless, with elastic ribbed tops and spliced heels and toes; ecru or cream brown color; strong and dependable. Sizes, 9½, 10, 10½, 11, 11½.
Price, per dozen pairs, $2.76; per pair..........23c
If by mail, postage extra, per pair, 2 cents; per dozen, 22 cents.

The Shawknit Half Hose.

Shawknit hosiery is noted for its wearing qualities in particular. They are made seamless on patented machines, insuring a correct shape. Shawknit is stamped on every pair.

No. 16R2026 Men's Plain Black or Clouded Gray Shawknit Cotton Half Hose, medium weight, about 18 ounces to the dozen. State color and size in your order. Sizes, 9½ 10, 10½, 11, 11½.
Price, per dozen pairs, $2.40; per pair.........20c
If by mail, postage extra, per dozen, 21 cents.

Men's Lisle Hose.

No. 16R2040 Genuine Lisle Thread Hose, 25 cents. Men's Pure Lisle Half Hose, of finest gauge, full fashioned foot and ankle, very elastic tops. An excellent hose, possessed of real worth and merit. Sizes, 9½ 10, 10½, 11, 11½. Color, black.
Price, per doz., $3.00; three pairs, 75c; per pair, 25c

No. 16R2044 Men's Pure Lisle Half Hose. Same as above, in brown and tan. Sizes, 9½, 10, 10½, 11, 11½.
Price, per doz., $3.00; three pairs, 75c; per pair, 25c

SPECIAL NOTE.—Do not forget to state size for Hosiery.

Men's Fine Silk Half Hose.

No. 16R2048 Men's Pure Silk Seamless Half Hose, extra quality imported stock; absolutely fast black and stainless. Sizes, 9½, 10, 10½, 11.
Price, three pairs for $3.00; per pair........$1.00

Fast Black Half Hose.

Every pair warranted fast color.

No. 16R2060 Men's Fast Black Cotton Half Hose. Full seamless, medium heavy weight. Fine elastic ribbed tops. Sizes, 9½, 10, 10½, 11. Extra good value.
Price, per dozen pairs, 84c; per pair...............7c
If by mail, postage extra, per pair, 2 cents; per dozen, 22 cents.

Men's Half Hose, 10 Cents.

No. 16R2064 Men's Fine Gauge, Absolutely Fast Black, Seamless Cotton Socks. Knit from fine combed Egyptian cotton, double heels and toes. Very soft and comfortable on the feet. Strong and full of good wearing qualities. Sizes, 9½, 10, 10½, 11, 11½. Price, per dozen pairs, $1.20; per pair......10c
If by mail, postage extra, per pair, 2 cents; per dozen, 22 cents.

Men's Extra Heavy Half Hose, 10 Cents.

No. 16R2066 Men's Heavy Strong Durable Cotton Half Hose, made from fine domestic cotton, seamless knitted, close ribbed tops, and extraordinary value at our low price; retailing everywhere at 15c per pair. One dozen pairs weigh about 2 pounds. Black only. Sizes, 9½, 10, 10½, 11, 11½.
Price, per dozen pairs, $1.20; per pair..........10c
If by mail, postage extra, per pair, 3 cents; per dozen, 34c.

DON'T FAIL TO GIVE SIZE

OUR GREAT LEADER.

Fast Black Genuine Maco Half Hose, 15 Cents.

No. 16R2068 Men's Extra Quality, Fast Black, Genuine Maco Cotton Half Hose, with three-ply heels and toes and fine elastic ribbed tops. Strictly high grade in every respect. Regular retail value, 20 to 25 cents. Sizes, 9½, 10, 10½, 11, 11½. Plain, fast black. Price, per dozen pairs, $1.80; per pair, 15c
If by mail, postage extra, per pair, 2 cents; per dozen pairs, 20 cents.

Our Special Value at 23 Cents.

No. 16R2072 Men's Extra Fine, Real Two Thread Maco Egyptian Cotton Socks. Plain black, with double heels, toes and spliced soles. Long elastic ribbed tops. Absolutely fast color. Strictly fine and high grade. If you want something extra fine, one of the best fine gauge cotton socks made, order this number and the value will please you. Sizes, 9, 9½, 10, 10½, 11, 11½.
Price, per pair.........$0.23
Per dozen pairs......... 2.76
If by mail, postage extra, per pair, 2 cents; per dozen pairs, 22 cents.

Men's Fine Mercerized Silk Half Hose, 20 Cents.

No. 16R2074 Men's Fine Mercerized Silk Half Hose, made from fine cotton yarn, treated by the new Mercer process, which gives it the appearance of and feels like silk. It retains this quality permanently, wears well and will give entire satisfaction, light weight, seamless, elastic ribbed tops and will fit the foot perfectly. Colors, black, tan, red or royal blue. Sizes, 9½, 10, 10½, 11.
Price, per dozen pairs, $2.40; per pair..........20c
If by mail, postage extra, per pair, 2 cents; per dozen pairs, 22 cents.

Men's Fancy Polka Dot Half Hose, 12 Cents.

DON'T FAIL TO GIVE SIZE

No. 16R2078 Men's Fine Cotton Half Hose, seamless, with close knit elastic ribbed tops. A thoroughly good hose that will give entire satisfaction. Made from fine cotton yarn, with colored polka dots, such as red, gold and white, etc., polka dots as shown in illustration. Color, black. Be sure to give color in order. If not stated we will assort them. Sizes, 9½, 10, 10½, 11.
Price, per pair..........$0.12
Per dozen pairs......... 1.44
If by mail, postage extra, per pair, 2 cents; per dozen pairs, 22 cents.

Lace Half Hose, 12 Cents.

No. 16R2084 Men's Half Hose in lace effect from heels up. Made of good quality cotton yarn, close fitting top and seamless feet. Something new this season. Retail price, 15 cents. Colors, black, blue, red or slate. State color and size in your order. Sizes, 9½, 10, 10½ and 11.
Price, per pair...........$0.12
Per dozen pairs.......... 1.44
If by mail, postage extra, per pair, 2 cents; per dozen pairs, 22 cents.

DON'T FAIL TO GIVE SIZE

Men's Fancy Half Hose at 13 Cents Per Pair.

No. 16R2085 Men's Fine Cotton Half Hose, made with close knit tops, seamless. They are made with a fancy scroll design extracted effects, as shown in illustration. A new novelty, the retail price of which is 20 cents per pair. This is not simply a fancy hose, but will prove a satisfactory hose for wear. Colors, black, blue or red, extracted in fancy contrasting designs, such as blue, red and gold, etc. Sizes, 9½, 10, 10½, 11. Where more than one pair is ordered, we assort colors.
Price, per pair..........$0.13
Per dozen pairs......... 1.56
If by mail, postage extra, per pair, 2 cents; per dozen pairs, 22 cents.

Our Extra Quality Lace, Half Hose, 21 Cents.

No. 16R2087 Men's Half Hose, knitted from fine, smooth Egyptian cotton yarn, seamless feet, perfect fitting and closely ribbed tops. A most astonishing value, superior to most qualities sold retail at 25 cents per pair. We want you to order this special value. Remember you save 48 cents per dozen on the retail price and get a better article. Solid colors, black, red or blue. Sizes, 9½ 10, 10½ and 11.
Price, per pair...........$0.21
Per half dozen pairs.... 1.26
If by mail, postage extra, per pair, 2 cents; per dozen pairs, 22 cents.

Our New Fancy Half Hose, Per Pair, 22 Cents.

No. 16R2088 Our illustration is a fair representation of one of the designs we furnish in this new half hose. They are strictly up to date and command fancy prices at retail. Made from fine Egyptian mercerized silk, the background is blue or red. The figures are in contrasting colors called extracted. All colors fast. The increased popularity of fancy hosiery is due largely to new processes, making colors fast. The lack of this has prevented many from buying. State color and size in your order. Sizes, 9½, 10, 10½ and 11.
Price, per pair..........$0.22
Per half dozen pairs.............. 1.32
If by mail, postage extra, per pair, 2 cents; per dozen pairs, 22 cents.

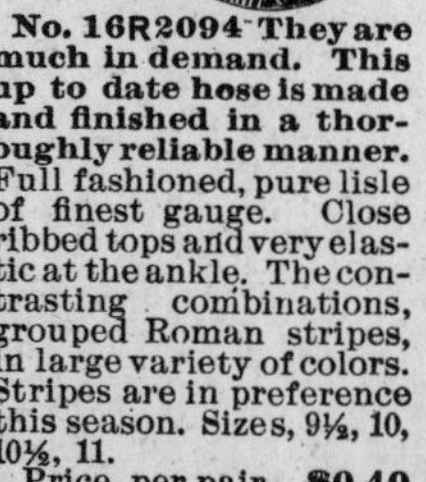

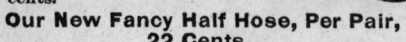

Fancy Imported Half Hose.

Very popular and more generally worn than ever before.

No. 16R2090 Men's Fancy Half Hose, fashioned and shaped to fit the foot perfectly. Made of fine Egyptian yarn and will give good service; elastic tops and fast colors. A first class article that will give good satisfaction. Assorted colors. Sizes, 9½, 10, 10½, 11.
Price, per pair.....$0.23
Per box, 6 pairs... 1.38
If by mail, postage extra, per half dozen pairs, 18 cents.

Our 40-Cent Fine Fancy Half Hose.

No. 16R2094 They are much in demand. This up to date hose is made and finished in a thoroughly reliable manner. Full fashioned, pure lisle of finest gauge. Close ribbed tops and very elastic at the ankle. The contrasting combinations, grouped Roman stripes, in large variety of colors. Stripes are in preference this season. Sizes, 9½, 10, 10½, 11.
Price, per pair...$0.40
Box of six pairs., 2.40
Postage extra, per pair, 2 cents; per dozen pairs, 22 cents.

Men's New Silk Stripe Half Hose.

No. 16R2102 We illustrate herewith Men's New Style Silk Stripe Fine Black Lisle Hose. This is a new effect, embroidered directly on the surface of the hose after it has been dyed and knit and stands out in strong relief. The colors embroidered are white, blue, light blue, dark blue, red and other shades. All subdued and no extreme effects. Sizes, 9½, 10, 10½, 11.
Price, per pair.......................$0.43
Per box of six pairs....... 2.58
If by mail, postage extra, for half dozen pairs, 16 cents.

Men's Silk Clocked Half Hose, 40 Cents.

No. 16R2106 Men's Fine Maco Egyptian Yarn Hose, double soles and heels, very fine gauge, embroidered with silk clock up the sides as shown in illustration. This is a superfine quality hose that invariably meets the approval of well dressed men. Regular retail price, per pair, 50 cents. Sizes, 9½, 10, 10½, 11.
Price, per pair............$0.40
Per box of six pairs...... 2.40
If by mail, postage extra, for half dozen pairs, 16 cents.

Men's Fine Novia Silk Plaited Half Hose.

No. 16R2110 Men's Fine Novia Silk Plaited Half Hose in solid black, very fine gauge, light weight with white tipped heels and toes. This hose feels and looks like silk, but wears better than pure silk. A very handsome, genteel light weight hose, never fails to give entire satisfaction and will meet the demands of men of exacting taste. Sizes, 9, 9½, 10, 10½, 11.
Price, per pair..............$0.43
Per box of six pairs...... 2.58
If by mail, postage extra, for half dozen pairs, 16 cents.

Black Hose with White Feet.

No. 16R2114 Men's Medium Weight Fast Black Cotton Half Hose, with white heels and toes and white soles, double heels and toes, and fine ribbed elastic tops; made from extra fine real Maco cotton; our own importation. Sizes, 9, 9½, 10, 10½, 11, 11½. Per pair......$0.22
Per dozen pairs........ 2.64
Postage extra, six pairs, 16c.
Always state size wanted when ordering hosiery. Your order will then be filled promptly and correctly.

Men's Lisle Half Hose, 43 Cents.

No. 16R2118 Men's Super Quality Extra Fine Gauge Half Hose. Made from fine black lisle thread, with fine double combed Egyptian cotton foot in its natural ecru color. This is an extra good hose for wear, wearing much better than a plain all black lisle. Egyptian lisle is a fine cotton yarn, hard twisted. Fine, closely knit tops. Sizes, 9, 9½, 10, 10½, 11.
Price, per box of six pairs, $2.58; per pair.......43c
If by mail, postage extra, six pairs, 16 cents.

Men's Tan Half Hose.

No. 16R2122 Men's Fine Tan Colored Cotton Half Hose. Full seamless, with **spliced heels and toes** and long elastic ribbed tops. Extra good value. Sizes, 9½, 10, 10½, 11.

Price, per dozen pairs, 84c; per pair.........7c

If by mail, postage extra, per pair, 2 cents; one dozen pairs, 22 cents.

Men's Tan Hose, 10 Cents.

No. 16R2126 Fine Gauge Seamless Cotton Half Hose. Knit from fine combed Egyptian yarn. Made with **double heels and toes.** Soft and fine and very easy on the feet. Plain tans and browns. Sizes, 9½, 10, 10½, 11, 11½.

Price, per dozen pairs, **$1.20;** per pair.........**10c**

If by mail, postage extra, per pair, 2 cents; one dozen pairs, 22 cents.

Men's Tan Hose, 15 Cents.

No. 16R2128 Men's Fine Domestic Tan Colored Real Maco Half Hose. Medium weight, with **double heels and toes** and elastic rib tops. **High grade and fine gauge.** Sizes, 9½, 10, 10½, 11, 11½. Retail value, 25 cents.

Price, per dozen pairs, **$1.80;** per pair.........**15c**

If by mail, postage extra, per pair, 2 cents; one dozen pairs, 20 cents.

Men's Tan Hose, 23 Cents.

No. 16R2132 Men's Plain Extra High Grade Genuine Maco Cotton Half Hose. Handsome shades of tan and brown. **Fine soft finish combed yarn, with double heels and toes and long elastic ribbed tops, full seamless and fast color.** Finely shaped foot and the most perfect fitting half hose made. Sizes, 9, 9½, 10, 10½, 11, 11½. Price, per dozen pairs, **$2.76;** three pairs for **69c;** per pair.........**23c**

If by mail, postage extra, per pair, 2 cents; one dozen pairs, 22 cents.

MEN'S FALL AND WINTER HALF HOSE.

We have all kinds of Men's Hosiery and each represents a particular selection and the pick of them all. Never before have we offered such values in hosiery. Many prices are reduced and on others the quality is better than for any previous season. What size hose do you wear?

Shoe	5½-6	6½-7	7½-8	8½-9	9½-10	10½-11
Hose	9½	10	10½	11	11½	

Always state the size hose in your order.

Men's Cotton Fleece Half Hose, 25 Cts.

No.16R2138 Men's Fine Black Cotton Half Hose, made from combed Egyptian cotton, good weight, about 1¾ pounds to the dozen pairs. Perfectly fashioned and shaped to fit the foot, a soft fleece is brushed up making them soft and smooth to the foot. The fleecing is permanent and will not wash off. Strictly fine gauge and high grade. Regular retail price, 35 cents. Black, only. Sizes, 9½, 10, 10½, 11, 11½.

Price, per half dozen pairs, **$1.50;** per pair.....**25c**

If by mail, postage extra, per pair, 3 cents; one dozen pairs, 30 cents.

Medium Winter Weight Half Hose for 12 Cents.

No. 16R2140 Men's Soft Finished, Wool Mixed, Merino Socks. Full seamless, with elastic ribbed tops, medium weight and perfect fitting. Natural gray color. These socks are soft and warm and are unexcelled at our low price. Sizes, 9½, 10, 10½, 11.

Price, per dozen pairs, **$1.44;** per pair.........**12c**

Men's Natural Wool Foot Half Hose, 20 Cents.

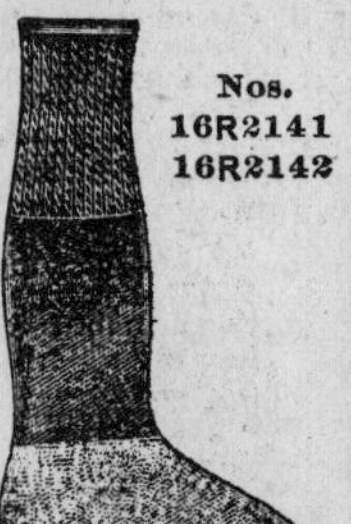

No. 16R2141 Men's Good Quality Woolen Half Hose, regular winter weight, made with natural gray wool foot and black woolen leg. An easy hose to darn and will wear better than an all black half hose of equal value. Knit seamless and will fit foot perfectly. Retail price, 25 cents. Sizes, 9½, 10, 10½, 11, 11½.

Nos. 16R2141 16R2142

Price, per half dozen pairs, **$1.20;** per pair.........**20c**

If by mail, postage extra, per pair, 3 cents; one dozen pairs, 30 cents.

Men's Worsted Half Hose, Natural Gray Foot, 38 Cents.

No. 16R2142 Men's Fine Quality Black Worsted Half Hose, knit with natural gray worsted foot. This is a practical sock that will not fail to please and give entire satisfaction. They are easy to darn and will wear better than hose with black feet. One of the finest products from domestic hosiery manufacturers, and retails for 50 cents per pair. Our price is the same as your merchant pays for like quality. A fine, genteel sock that invariably gives entire satisfaction. Sizes, 9½, 10, 10½, 11, 11½.

Price, per half dozen pairs.....**$2.28;** per pair, **38c**

If by mail, postage extra, 3 cents; one dozen pairs, 28 cents.

Medium Weight Merino Socks.

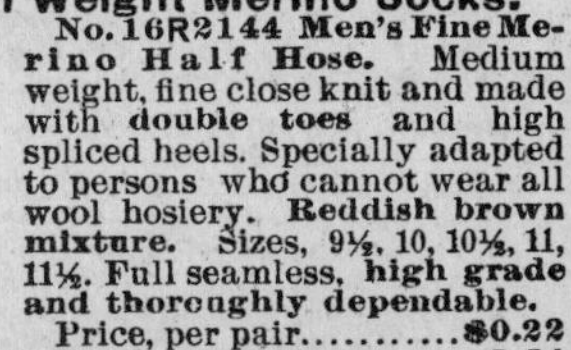

No. 16R2144 Men's Fine Merino Half Hose. Medium weight, fine close knit and made with **double toes** and high spliced heels. Specially adapted to persons who cannot wear all wool hosiery. **Reddish brown mixture.** Sizes, 9½, 10, 10½, 11, 11½. Full seamless, **high grade and thoroughly dependable.**

Price, per pair.........**$0.22**
Per dozen pairs.........**2.64**

If by mail, postage extra, per pair, 3 cents; one dozen pairs, 30 cents.

Medium Weight Worsted Socks, 20 Cts.

DONT FAIL TO
GIVE
SIZE

Weight, 24 ounces to the dozen.

No. 16R2148 Men's Fast Black Medium Weight Seamless Wool Worsted Half Hose; spliced heels and toes and long elastic ribbed tops. **Fine soft finish** and very easy on the feet. **Warranted fast color.** Sizes, 9½, 10, 10½, 11, 11½. Retail price, 25 to 35 cents.

Price, per pair.........**$0.20**
Per dozen pairs.........**2.40**

No. 16R2152 Men's Fine Wool Worsted Half Hose, same as above, in handsome tan and brown shades. Sizes, 9½, 10, 10½, 11, 11½. Per pair....**$0.20**
Per dozen pairs.........**2.40**

No. 16R2156 Men's Fine Wool Worsted Half Hose, same as above; natural gray. Sizes, 9½, 10, 10½, 11, 11½. Price, per dozen pairs, **$2.40;** per pair..**20c**

Our Great Leader, 25 Cents.

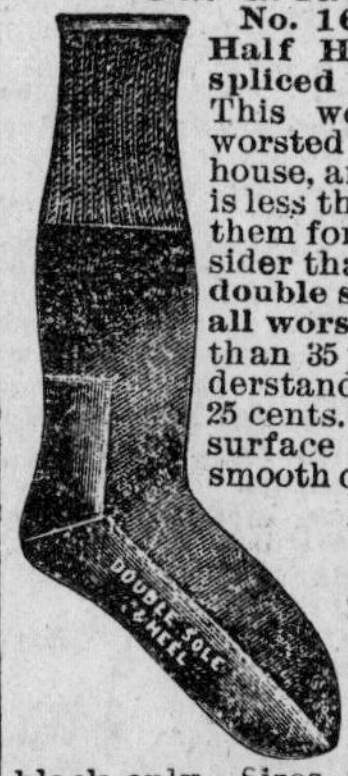

No. 16R2157 Men's All Worsted Half Hose, with double soles, high spliced heels and toes. Black only. This wonderful value in men's fine worsted half hose is unmatched by any house, and the price you pay us for them is less than your home merchant can buy them for in quantities. If you will consider that a **high spliced double heel, double sole and spliced toe half hose in all worsted** has never before sold for less than 35 to 50 cents per pair, you can understand what a bargain you will get for 25 cents. A worsted hose has not the loose surface of a woolen hose, but a fine, smooth close surface that will resist wear. If you want the most that can be bought for 25 cents a pair in men's fine half hose, order this one. If you do not consider it the best value you have ever seen and better than you could buy at home for 35 to 50 cents per pair, we will refund amount paid and transportation charges. Color, black only. Sizes, 9½, 10, 10½, 11, 11½. State size in your order. Per half dozen pairs, **$1.50;** per pair.**25c**

Postage extra, per pair, 3c; one dozen pairs, 34c.

Men's Worsted Half Hose, 37 Cents.

No. 16R2160 Fine gauge, soft and full of comfort and durability, medium heavy weight, with double heels and toes and elastic ribbed tops. **Regular 50-cent quality.** Colors, black, or natural gray. Sizes, 9½, 10, 10½, 11 and 11½.

Price, per pair.........**$0.37**
Three pairs.........**1.11**
Per dozen pairs.........**4.44**

Fine Heavy Worsted Hose, 42 Cents.

No. 16R2164 Men's Heavy Weight All Wool Worsted Socks. Fine and soft and **will not irritate the feet.** Made with **double heels and toes** and elastic ribbed tops. **These are the very best worsted socks ever sold at our low price.** We know they will please you. Made in plain black or natural gray, and every pair perfect in manufacture. Sizes, 9½, 10, 10½, 11 and 11½. Per dozen pairs, **$5.04;** three pairs for **$1.26;** per pair.........**42c**

Postage extra, per pair, 3c; one dozen pairs, 30c.

Men's Fine Silk and Worsted Half Hose, 39 Cents.

No. 16R2166 Men's Fine Half Hose, knit from fine worsted and silk, about half and half, a select quality in which the silk prevents shrinkage and at the same time makes the hose pleasant to the wearer who has sensitive feet and is annoyed by all wool or worsted socks. We would like you to try this genteel quality, which will be found warm and durable. Three colors, blue, dark brown and natural gray. Sizes, 9½, 10, 10½, 11 and 11½. State color and size in your order. Regular retail price, 50 cents.

Price, per pair.........**$0.39**
Per half dozen pairs..**2.34**

If by mail, postage extra, per pair, 3 cents; one dozen pairs, 30 cents.

Men's Fancy Woolen Half Hose, 40 Cents.

DONT FAIL TO
GIVE
SIZE

No. 16R2168 Men's Fine All Wool Worsted Fancy Woolen Socks, with fancy figures, one of which is shown in the illustration. These strictly high grade seamless half hose, which never retail for less than 50 cents per pair, are something new in woolen socks for gentlemen. The fancy hose is here to stay and we feel sure that our selections will please. Colors, blue, red or black background. Sizes, 9½, 10, 10½, 11.

Price, per pair.........**$0.40**
Per half dozen pairs, assorted.........**2.40**

If by mail, postage extra, per pair, 3 cents; per half dozen pairs, 15 cents.

Men's Fancy Woolen Half Hose, 23 Cents.

No. 16R2169 Men's All Wool Half Hose, in good quality embroidered in silk as shown in illustration. A very strong value at our low price. Color, black only; embroidered in blue or white silk. Sizes, 9½, 10, 10½, 11. Price, per pair.**$0.23**
Per half dozen pairs, assorted.........**1.38**

If by mail, postage extra, per pair, 4 cents; per half dozen pairs, 20 cents.

HEAVY WOOL HALF HOSE.

Not the extremely heavy kind, but heavier than cashmere and worsted. Average about 1½ to [illegible] **pounds in weight to the dozen. Do not forget size. Every pair of hose we handle we guarantee to be exactly as represented and described.**

How to Order Correct Size in Men's Socks

Shoe.........	6-6½	7-7½	8-8½	9-9½	10-10½-1
Half Hose..	9½	10	10½	11	11½

Men's Camel Hair Socks at 18 Cents.

No. 16R2170 Men's Camel Hair Merino Socks. The desirable weight for a warm winter hose. Made with long elastic ribbed tops and seamless. Good honest socks that will give excellent satisfaction. Weight, 30 ounces to the dozen. Sizes, 9½, 10, 10½, 11.

Price, per dozen pairs, **$2.16;** box of six pairs, **$1.08;** per pair.........**18c**

If by mail, postage extra, per pair, 3 cents; per dozen pairs, 34 cents.

18 Cents for Good Wool Socks.

No. 16R2176 Men's Heavy Domestic Wool Socks. Fine and soft, exceptionally warm and comfortable. **Three-fourths pure, clean wool, the most excellent value ever offered for the price.** Retail price, 25c per pair. **Full seamless** with elastic ribbed tops. Colors, natural sanitary gray or black. Sizes, 9½, 10, 10½, 11, 11½.

Price, per pair.........**$0.18**
Per box of one-half dozen ..**1.08**
Per dozen pairs.........**2.16**

If by mail, postage extra, per pair, 3c; per doz., 30c.

25 Cents for Fine Domestic wool Socks.

Healthful, Comfortable and Dependable.

No. 16R2180 Men's Fine Domestic All Wool Socks. Full seamless, with long elastic ribbed tops. Made from **pure, clean wool.** They are heavy, soft and very fine. Retail value, 35 cents. Made by a manufacturer with world wide reputation. We have them in two colors, plain black, and natural gray. Weight, 30 ounces to dozen. Sizes, 9½, 10, 10½, 11, 11½. **Special value.**

Price, per pair.........**$0.25**
Per box of one-half dozen **1.50**
Per dozen pairs.........**3.00**

If by mail, postage extra, per dozen, 34 cents.

FARMERS' OR LUMBERMEN'S HEAVY WOOL SOCKS.

They are made extra heavy and are particularly adapted to the use of lumbermen, farmers, teamsters, trappers, hunters, railroad men, and all others who follow outdoor pursuits in cold climates or extreme weather. Usually put up in bundles of one-half dozen pairs. We sell one pair as cheaply as we do one dozen.

Warm Woolen Socks, 11 Cents.

No. 16R2183 Men's Warm Woolen Socks, light brown in color; weight about 2¼ pounds to the dozen pairs; a good sock at a very low price, and retails at 15c per pair. Put up one-half dozen pairs to bundle.

Price, per half dozen pairs, 66c; per pair.........**11c**

If by mail, postage extra, per one-half dozen pairs, 18 cents.

Farmers' Blue Wool Socks, 14 Cents.

No. 16R2184 Farmers' Warm Woolen Socks, dark blue mixed color. Made from clean wool, and the same qualities your local merchant cannot sell you for less than 20 cents a pair. Seamless knitted.

Price, six pairs, **84c;** per pair.........**14c**

If by mail, postage extra, per pair, 4 cents; per dozen pairs, 40 cents.

Good Wool Socks at 18 Cents Per Pair.

No. 16R2186 Men's Extra Heavy Full Seamless Wool Mixed Socks, soft, warm and durable. Made with elastic ribbed tops. We have them in blue or natural gray mixtures. **They are full of real old fashioned goodness,** and will give better service than any hose on the market for the price. Regular retail price, 25 cents. Weight, per dozen, 2¾ pounds.

Price, per pair.........**$0.1**[illegible]
Per dozen pairs.........**2.1**[illegible]

If by mail, postage extra, per pair, 5 cents, per dozen pairs, 54 cents.

A Leader, 25 Cents.

No. 16R2190 Farmers' or Lumbermen's Wool Brown, Blue, Gray Mixed or Red Seamless Socks. Known everywhere for their good wearing properties. Under this number we furnish a value which we feel sure cannot be excelled by any other house. The wholesale price to your home merchant is $3.00 per dozen, and you buy them from us at this price. Weight, 4 pounds to dozen. **Extra strong and dependable.**

DON'T FAIL TO GIVE SIZE

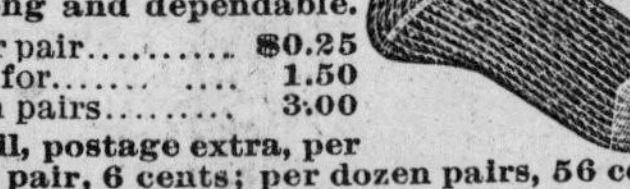

Price, per pair........ $0.25
Six pairs for........ 1.50
Per dozen pairs........ 3.00

If by mail, postage extra, per pair, 6 cents; per dozen pairs, 56 cents.

SHAKER RIBBED SOCKS.

No. 16R2192 At 17 cents per pair we offer these All Wool Shaker Socks that will cost you 25 cents per pair retail at home. We want your order for these excellent heavy woolen socks, because we can sell them cheaper than other stores. You can save 8 cents on every pair, and if you need one-half dozen pairs you can save 48 cents, or 96 cents to the dozen. **You cannot afford to pay extravagant profits,** and we want your order because we sell good socks cheaper than you can buy elsewhere. Weight, 3 pounds to the dozen.

Price, per pair........... $0.17
Per half dozen pairs..... 1.02
Per dozen pairs.......... 2.04

If by mail, postage extra, per pair, 5 cents.

Our 25-Cent Shaker Ribbed Socks.

No. 16R2194 Lumbermen's Extra Heavy All Wool Ribbed Shaker Socks, 25 cents. Made with long heavy ribbed legs. **Full of everlasting goodness and excellent wearing qualities.** Colors, scarlet, white, white and gray mixed. Weight, 3 pounds to dozen. Six pairs for $1.50; per pair..25c

If by mail, postage extra, per pair, 6 cents; per dozen pair, 56 cents.

U. S. A. Socks, 27 Cents.

No. 16R2196 These are the genuine regulation army wool sock. Long ribbed legs, full size, made from very fine domestic wool. Absolutely pure fine wool with no cotton mixture. They are warm and heavy, to be worn with boots or heavy shoes. Strictly government standard and one of the best wearing socks manufactured. One color, buckskin brown only. Weight, 3 pounds to the dozen.

Price, per pair.......... $0.27
Per half dozen pairs.... 1.62

If by mail, postage extra, per pair, 5 cents; per dozen pair, 56 cents.

Our Special Value for 35c.

No. 16R2200 Men's Shaker Socks, knitted with long ribbed legs from fine clean wool, with shaped heels and toes. This sock is as good as the average quality sold for 50 cents a pair. Heavy soft and warm, and we warrant every pair to be entirely satisfactory. Weight, 3 pounds to the dozen. Colors, gray or blue.

Price, per pair.................. $0.35
Six pairs for.................... 2.10
Per dozen pairs.................. 4.20

If by mail, postage extra, per pair, 5c.

DON'T FAIL TO GIVE SIZE

Our Special Leader Extra Heavy All Wool Socks, 36 Cents.

No. 16R2204 Lumbermen's Extra Heavy and Thick Strictly All Wool Socks. Full seamless with long heavy closely knit ribbed legs, as shown in illustration, shaped to fit leg, ribbed legs, and mixed heels and toes. Colors, dark gray, blue mixed, white or scarlet. **Unexcelled for wear.** Retail value, 50 cents per pair. Weight, 3¾ pounds to dozen.

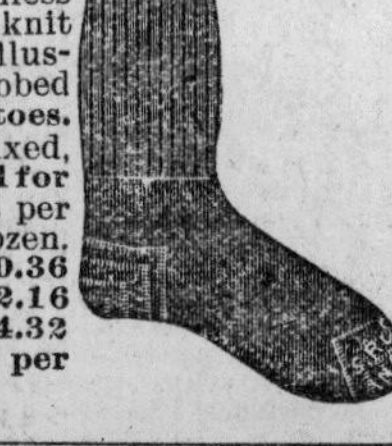

Price, per pair........... $0.36
Six pairs for............ 2.16
Per dozen pairs.......... 4.32

If by mail, postage extra, per pair, 5 cents.

GIVE CATALOGUE NUMBER IN FULL WHEN YOU WRITE YOUR ORDER

EXTRA HEAVY AND DURABLE PLAIN SOCKS, 40 CENTS.

No. 16R2206 Men's Extra Heavy Fine All Wool Plain Socks. Made of fine all wool yarn, closely and firmly knitted with ribbed and shaped heels and toes. Entirely free from shoddy—all clean wool and every pair warranted to give entire satisfaction. This quality never retails for less than 50 to 60 cents a pair, and our price is 20 per cent cheaper than you can buy at home. If you can use one dozen pairs you save $1.20 if you buy them from us. Weight to the dozen, 5 pounds. Colors, Oxford gray or navy blue.

Price, per pair.......... $0.40
Per half dozen pairs..... 2.40

If by mail, postage extra, per pair, 7c.

Extra Heavy Fancy Knit Lumbermen's Socks.

No. 16R2208 Lumbermen's or Farmers' Extra Heavy and Durable All Wool Close Knit Socks, fancy stripes, as in illustration. Weight, 4¾ pounds to the dozen. A favorite in the Northwest. Colors, red, figured or white and gray figured. Retail value, 50 cents.

Price, per pair........... $0.40
Per dozen pairs........... 4.80

40 Cents for German Socks.

The Heaviest Made to Wear Inside of Boots.

No. 16R2214 Men's Very Best Quality Hand Knit German Socks. Strictly all pure wool. **These socks are heavy, thick and strong, and are guaranteed to outwear any other kind of socks made.** They are full seamless with extra heavy long ribbed tops. **Unexcelled anywhere on earth for wearing qualities.** Soft, warm and comfortable. **Every pair warranted.** Dark fancy mixed colors or white. Weight, 6 pounds to dozen. Retail value, 50 cents.

Price, per pair.................. $0.40
Three pairs for..... $1.20
Per dozen pairs...... 4.80

Sportsmen's Hunting Stockings.

No. 16R2220 Sportsmen's Extra Heavy Long Ribbed Cotton Stockings, with double spliced heels and toes. Largely used by **hunters, fishermen, trappers, skaters and sportsmen in general.** These stockings are made full length and reach above the knee. Plain black. All sizes from 9 to 11½. **They are extra strong and durable and unexcelled for hard service.**

Price, per dozen pairs, $3.00; per pair.............25c

Boys' or Youths' Heavy Wool Socks, 15c.

No. 16R2224 Boys' Heavy Blue Mixed All Wool Socks. Full seamless, with elastic tops. Made especially for large boys or youths.

Price, per dozen pairs, $1.80; per pair..........15c

If by mail, postage extra, per pair, 4c.

Men's Garters.

No. 16R2230 Men's Elastic Web Garters, made in neat fancy striped patterns. Assorted colors. See adjoining illustration for style.

Price, per pair........................8c
Per dozen pairs........................96c

No. 16R2234 Men's Fine Silk Web Garters, made same style as adjoining illustration. Put up one pair in a box. Very fine, black, white, old gold, blue, etc. 20-cent quality.

Price, per pair.... $0.15
Per dozen pairs... 1.80

The Paris Garter, 22 Cents.

No. 16R2238 Men's Fine Half Hose Supporter, made with silk elastic, nickel trimmings. **A very comfortable garter** that holds the hose firmly, but will not tear. See illustration. One pair in box. Colors, black, white, gold, blue, etc.

Price, per pair....... $0.22
Per dozen pairs...... 2.64

If by mail, postage extra, 3 cents.

LADIES' HOSIERY.

SPECIAL NOTICE—In ordering Ladies' Hose, please refer to the following scale of sizes:

SCALE OF SIZES.

No. 1	Ladies' Shoe takes about 8 -inch hose.
No. 2	Ladies' Shoe takes about 8½-inch hose.
No. 3 and 4	Ladies' Shoe takes about 9 -inch hose.
No. 5 and 6	Ladies' Shoe takes about 9½-inch hose.
No. 7	Ladies' Shoe takes about 10 -inch hose.

If by mail, postage extra, per dozen pairs, 22 to 34 cents, on ladies' hose.

We sell all kinds of ladies' hosiery but cannot recommend or warrant the cheap grades. Hosiery at 5 cents will not wear well. Better qualities will be found cheapest in the long run.

Always give correct size in order. Always include sufficient postage when ordering hosiery shipped by mail.

LADIES' BLACK HOSIERY.

Ladies' Fast Black Cotton Hose.

No. 16R2300 Ladies' Fast Black Cotton Hose.

Price, per pair.... ....5c
Per dozen pairs.......................60c

A Satisfactory Stocking at 9 Cents.

No. 16R2304 Genuine Lawrence Mills Fast Black Cotton Hose. Made full size and length. Medium weight. **Strong and reliable.**

Price, per pair.............. $0.09
Per dozen pairs............. 1.08

A Good Stocking for 12 Cents

No. 16R2308 Ladies' Fast Black Cotton Hose. Made heavier weight and finer than the above. **Very durable and sure to satisfy. Double soles and heels.** Sizes, 8½, 9, 9½, 10.

Price, per pair................ $0.12
Per dozen pairs............... 1.44

A Satisfactory Hose, 15 Cts.

No. 16R2312 Full Seamless Hose. Warranted absolutely fast black and stainless. Soft, smooth finish, with elastic hemmed tops, double heels and double toes. **20-cent quality** when bought at retail. Sizes, 8½, 9, 9½, 10.

Price, per dozen pairs, $1.80; per pair..............15c

Ladies' Fine Ribbed Hose, 20 Cents.

No. 16R2316 Ladies' Fine Ribbed Leg Hose. Medium weight, seamless fast black, and closely knit plain foot. Sizes, 8½, 9, 9½, 10. Retail value, 25 cents. Price, per dozen pairs, $2.40; per pair...20c

Our Famous 25-Cent Black Hose.

Unequaled Anywhere.

No. 16R2320 Extra Fine Silky Finished Real Maco Cotton Hose. Plain black, with three-thread heels and toes; made from **extra selected combed yarn,** full seamless, finely shaped full fashioned hose. **Guaranteed absolutely fast black and stainless.** Nothing better ever sold for less than 35 cents retail. Weight, 2 pounds to the dozen. Sizes, 8½, 9, 9½, 10.

Price, per dozen pairs, $3.00; per pair..........25c

Ladies' Silk Hose, 25 Cents.

No. 16R2324 Ladies' Mercerized Silk Hose. Mercerized silk is fine Egyptian cotton, treated by the Mercer process, which gives the yarn the appearance of silk. It feels like silk and retains this surface permanently, a superior grade that will wear well. Perfect fitting, double heels and soles. Black only. Sizes, 8½, 9, 9½, 10.

Price, per dozen, $3.00; per pair.....................25c

Our Extra Fine 33-Cent Hose.

No. 16R2328 Ladies' Fine Fast Black Maco Cotton Hose. Very fine gauge and very soft and smooth, full fashioned and full regular made seamless, high spliced heels, double soles and perfectly shaped foot. A most exceptional value. Sizes, 8½, 9, 9½, 10.

Per dozen pairs, $3.96; three pairs, 99c; per pair 33c

50-Cent Ladies' Fine Black Hose, 39 Cts.

No. 16R2332 Ladies' Fast Black Hose. Plain black, full seamless, with high spliced heels and toes and double soles. Knit from finest imported Maco cotton. Extra fine gauge, medium light weight. 1¾ pounds to the dozen; soft as silk and absolutely fast color and stainless. Sizes, 8½, 9, 9½, 10. **The dependable kind.**

Price, per dozen pairs, $4.68; per pair..........39c

Ladies' Opera Length Hose

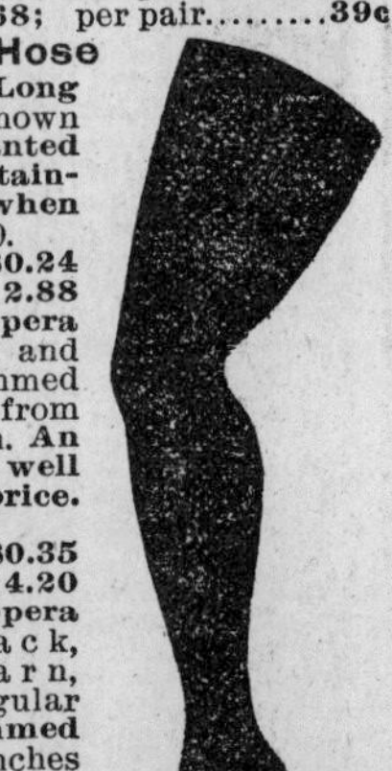

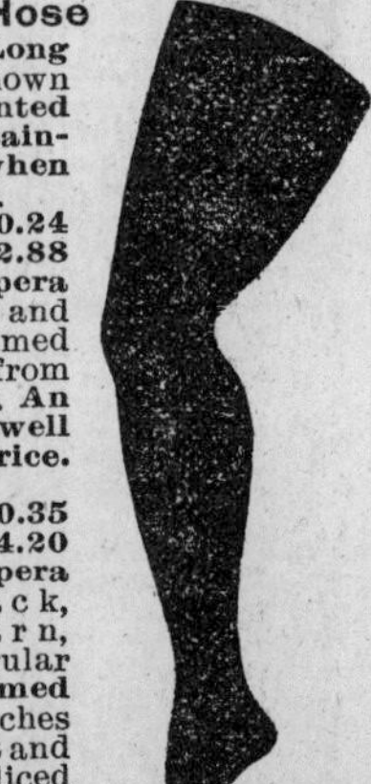

No. 16R2336 Ladies' Extra Long or Opera Length Hose, as shown in the illustration. **Warranted absolutely fast black and stainless. Always mention size when ordering.** Sizes, 8½, 9, 9½, 10.

Price, per pair.... .... $0.24
Per dozen pairs........... 2.88

No. 16R2340 Ladies' Opera Length Hose, fast black and full fashioned, elastic hemmed tops. 33 inches leg. Made from finest selected Egyptian yarn. **An extremely shapely hose, well made. Special value at this price.** Sizes, 8½, 9, 9½, 10.

Price, per pair $0.35
Per dozen pairs............ 4.20

No. 16R2344 Ladies' Opera Length Hose; fast black, made of finest Maco yarn, full fashioned and full regular made; **extra elastic hemmed tops;** the leg is full 34 inches long; very finely finished foot and handsomely shaped, high spliced heel and French finished toe; an **exceedingly handsome stocking.** Sizes, 8½, 9, 9½, 10.

Price, per dozen pairs, $5.40; per pair..........45c

Ladies' Out Size Hose.

Made with Extra Wide Legs.

For ladies' winter weight out size hose, see No. 16R2502.

No. 16R2348 Ladies' Seamless Out Size Hose, made with extra wide legs. **Fast black,** heavy cotton, with double heels and toes. Weight, 2 pounds to the dozen. Sizes, 8½, 9, 9½, 10.
Per pair......$0.18
Per dozen.... 2.16

Ladies' Out Size or Extra Wide Leg Hosiery.

No. 16R2352 Ladies' Fast Black, Out Size Cotton Hose, made with extra wide legs and **tops, spliced heels and double soles.** Sizes, 8½, 9, 9½, 10. Price, per six pairs, $1.50; per pair........25c

Ladies' Out Size Hose, 40 Cents.

No. 16R2360 Ladies' Out Size Hose, fast black, genuine Hermsdorf dye, good weight, **made of very fine selected Maco cotton,** which is **very soft** and will be appreciated by fleshy patrons. **Full regular** made, with extra finished foot, high **spliced heel,** French finished toe. Sizes, 8½, 9, 9½, 10.
Price, per dozen, pairs, $4.80; per pair.......40c

Unbleached Out Size Hose.

No. 16R2364 Ladies' Unbleached Balbriggan Hose, with extra large wide legs and tops. Full regular made. High spliced heel and French finished toe; ecru color. Sizes, 8½, 9, 9½, 10.
Price, per dozen pairs, $4.20; per pair..... ....35c
If by mail, postage extra, per pair, 4c; per doz. 45c.

Plain Black Lisle Hosiery.

No. 16R2368 Ladies' Plain Black Lisle Imported Hose, made from fine lisle thread. Fine fashioned and perfectly shaped, spliced heels and soles. Lisle hose are cool but not durable, a cotton hose at the same price will wear much better. **Do not forget size.** Sizes, 8½, 9, 9½, 10.
Price, per dozen pairs, $3.00; per pair.........25c
Postage extra, per pair, 3c; per dozen, 24c.

No. 16R2372 Ladies' Plain Black Lisle Imported Hose, finer quality than the above, very light weight, full fashioned, spliced heel and double soles. Sizes, 8½, 9, 9½, 10.
Price, per pair.....................$0.42
Three pairs for..................... 1.26
Per dozen pairs..................... 5.04

Black Lisle Hose.

With Balbriggan Heels, Toes and Soles.

No. 16R2376 Extra Quality Good Weight Lisle Hose, absolutely fast black and warranted stainless. Full seamless with double heels and toes; the heels, toes and soles are white, as shown in illustration. **This is an extra fine gauge hose and one of the most durable ever made;** they are soft and easy on the feet, **warranted to give lasting satisfaction in looks and wear;** trustworthy, dependable and comfortable stockings. Sizes, 8½, 9, 9½, 10.
Price, per dozen pairs, $5.04; three pairs for $1.26; per pair...............42c
If by mail, postage extra, per pair, 4 cents; per dozen, 45 cents.

Ladies' Silk Hose.

No. 16R2380 High Grade Novia Silk Hose. Full seamless, perfect fitting, spliced heels and toes, **absolutely fast black,** very fine and soft, and easy on the feet. Sizes, 8½, 9, 9½, 10. Price, per pair.........98c

No. 16R2382 Ladies' All Silk Hose, high class stock, full seamless and perfect fitting, spliced heels and toes, **warranted absolutely fast black,** one of our specially good values. Sizes, 8½, 9, 9½, 10.
Price, per pair.....................$1.48

No. 16R2384 Ladies' Fine Silk Hose, made of the finest and purest silk ever produced. Made same style as above. **Warranted fast black and stainless.** Extra fine gauge and the softest and smoothest ladies' hose ever made. Sizes, 8½, 9, 9½, 10.
Price, per pair.....................$2.47
If by mail, postage extra, per pair, 4c; per doz., 45c

Ladies' Plain Tan Colored Hose.

Suitable Weight for All Year Round.

No. 16R2390 Ladies' Plain Tan Colored Cotton Hose. Good weight and full seamless with spliced heels and toes. Elastic hemmed tops. Assorted light and dark shades of tan. Sizes, 8½, 9, 9½, 10.
Price, per dozen pairs, $1.44; per pair..........12c

No. 16R2394 Fine Tan Colored Hose. Extra high spliced heels and toes and double soles, medium weight and full seamless; **guaranteed absolutely fast color and thoroughly dependable.** Sizes, 8½, 9, 9½, 10. Price, per dozen, $1.80; three pairs for 45c; per pair.....................15c

No. 16R2396 Extra 40-Gauge Tan Colored Hose, 35-cent quality, **real two-thread Maco cotton,** extra high spliced heel, double sole. French finished toe, full regular made, very elastic hemmed top. Sizes, 8½, 9, 9½, 10. Price, per dozen pairs, $3.00; one-half dozen for $1.50; per pair...............25c

No. 16R2400 Ladies' Tan Cotton Hose. Made of the finest Maco yarn, silk finish; full regular made and fashioned; extra shaped leg and foot; spliced heels and toes. **This is really a beautiful stocking.** Sizes, 8½, 9, 9½, 10.
Price, per dozen pairs, $4.20; six pairs.......$2.10
Per pair.....................................35

Ladies' Stockings, with Ecru Cotton Foot, 15 Cents.

No. 16R2402 Ladies' Seamless Plain Cotton Hose, fast black legs, made with all ecru foot, as shown in illustration; an excellent hose, wearing better than all black, and easy to darn. These stockings are knitted fine gauge, and retail at 25 cents a pair. Color, black. Sizes, 8½, 9, 9½, 10.
Price, per pair.....................$0.15
Price, per dozen pairs.............. 1.80
If by mail, postage extra, per pair, 3c; per dozen pairs, 30c.
If you fail to give size, we cannot fill your order.

Ecru Feet Split Sole Cotton Hose, 22c.

No. 16R2404 Fast Black Hose, with cream colored unbleached heels, toes and soles; spliced heels and toes; made from **extra selected real Maco cotton,** soft, smooth and **very strong and durable.** Absolutely fast black and stainless. Can be used with slippers, as the white sole will not show above the top. Sizes, 8½, 9, 9½, 10. Price, **per pair**..........$0.22
Per dozen pairs..................... 2.64

Ladies' Fancy Hosiery.

No. 16R2408 Fancy Richelieu Ribbed Boot Top Hose, seamless, with black boot and fancy tops, in dainty combinations of baby blue, pink, red and lilac. Very pretty at such a low price. Sizes, 9, 9½, 10.
Price, per pair.....................$0.14
Per dozen pairs..................... 1.68
If by mail, postage extra, per pair, 3c; per dozen, 30c.

Ladies' Fancy Polka Dot Hosiery, 12 Cents.

No. 16R2412 Ladies' Fancy Polka Dot Hose in fine cotton, seamless, fast colors. This is the quality that usually retails at 20 cents per pair, and are a **special value at our low price.** Colors, **black,** with red, blue or white polka dots, **tan and red,** white polka dots only. Sizes, 8½, 9, 9½, 10. Price, per pair.....$0.12
Per dozen pairs..................... 1.44
If by mail, postage extra, per pair, 3 cents; per dozen, 30 cents.

Ladies' Fancy Hose, 12 Cents

No. 16R2413 Our illustration gives a fair representation of this new design in ladies' hose, knitted from clean cotton yarn. Fast colors; an astonishing value at our low price. You would be asked 18 or 20 cents a pair at your local store. Colors, black, blue, red and slate. State color and size in your order. Sizes, 8½, 9, 9½ and 10. Price, per pair.........$0.12
Per dozen pairs..................... 1.44
If by mail, postage extra, per pair, 3c; per dozen, 30c.

All Striped Hose, 29c.

No. 16R2416 Ladies' Fine Fashioned Fancy Egyptian Cotton Hose, made in a large variety of fancy stripes, in a great variety of colors. Fancy hose are now very popular. A special value unmatched at our price. Sizes, 8½, 9, 9½, 10.
Price, per pair.....................$0.29
Per box of six pairs, assorted, 1.84

Ladies' New Fancy Hose, 21c.

Retail Price, 25 Cents.

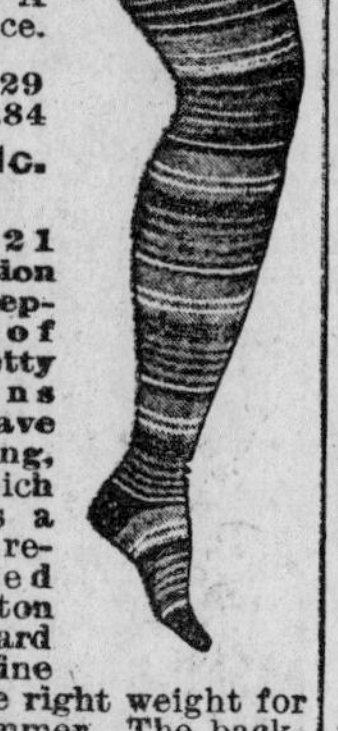

No. 16R2421 Our illustration gives a fair representation of one of the pretty new designs which we have in this stocking, a design which commands a fancy price at retail. Knitted from fine cotton yarn, standard weight and fine gauge, just the right weight for spring and summer. The background colors are blue, red and white. The figures are in contrast, as illustrated. You will make no mistake in ordering this number. State color and size in your order. Sizes, 8½, 9, 9½ and 10. Per pair.........$0.21
Price, per half dozen pairs.......... 1.26
If by mail, postage extra, per pair, 3 cents; per dozen pairs, 30 cents.

Ladies' Lace Hose, 12 Cents.

No. 16R2424 Ladies' Good Quality Seamless Lace Hose, of fine cotton, and an exceptional value at this low price. Colors, black, navy or cadet blue. Sizes, 8½, 9, 9½, 10.
Price, per pair.....................$0.12
Per dozen pairs..................... 1.44

Our New Lace Hose, 20 Cents Per Pair.

No. 16R2429 Ladies' New Style Lace Hose. Made in fancy knitted lace effect all the way down front of leg to the toe. A stocking that looks particularly well worn with low shoes. Knitted from fine quality yarn, and have **perfect fitting seamless feet.** Few stores sell this quality for 25 cents and most of them would ask you more. You can save at least 5 cents a pair, 60 cents per dozen if you buy them from us. Colors, **black,** red and blue. State color and size in order. Sizes, 8½, 9, 9½ and 10. Price, per pair...........$0.20
Per half dozen pairs................ 1.20
If by mail, postage extra, per pair, 3c; per dozen pairs, 30c.

Imported Richelieu Ribbed Lace Effect Lisle Hose, 40c.

No. 16R2436 A perfect hose in every respect. Strictly high grade; our idea of what a par excellence hose should be. Warranted absolutely stainless. They are full fashioned and have extra spliced heels. White tipped heels and toes. Imported by us and guaranteed to be all that we claim for them—and more. Colors, black, brown or tan. Sizes, 8½, 9, 9½, 10.
Price, per pair.....................$0.40
Per dozen pairs..................... 4.80

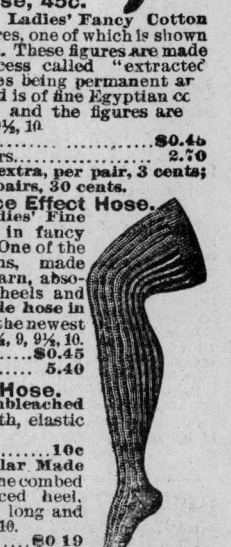

DON'T FAIL TO GIVE SIZE

Fancy Boot Hose, 45c.

No. 16R2441 Ladies' New Design Fancy Hose. Knit from fine Egyptian cotton, full fashioned and shaped to fit leg perfectly. Made with **fancy boot with different color fancy tops with a little white at the top of boot effect.** The boot or lower half of hose is **in colors** such as red, gray, blue, etc. **A very** handsome and exact copy of the **pattern** put in hosiery retailing at $1.00 to $2.00 per pair. Sizes, 8½, 9, 9½, 10.
Price, per pair.....................$0.45
Price, per half dozen pairs........ 2.70
If by mail, postage extra, per pair, 3 cents; per dozen pairs, 30 cents.

Silk Embroidered Hose, 45c.

No. 16R2442 Ladies' Fine Black Cotton Hose, full fashioned and elastic knitted; made with fancy silk embroidery, which work is done by hand. The illustration gives a fair representation, the hose being folded so as to show the front. The embroidery comes in lavender, blue, white, old rose, etc. We always assort them when several pairs are ordered unless otherwise stated. Sizes, 8½, 9, 9½, 10.
Price, per pair.....................$0.45
Per half-dozen pairs................ 2.70
If by mail, postage extra, per pair, 3 cents; per dozen pairs, 30 cents.

New Design Fancy Hose, 45c.

No. 16R2443 Ladies' Fancy Cotton Hose, in new figures, one of which is shown in the illustration. **These figures are made by a new process called "extracted color,"** the figures being permanent ar clear. The yarn used is of fine Egyptian cc ton dyed fast black and the figures are white. Sizes, 8½, 9, 9½, 10
Price, per pair.....................$0.45
Per half-dozen pairs................ 2.70
If by mail, postage extra, per pair, 3 cents; per dozen pairs, 30 cents.

Ladies' Fine Lace Effect Hose.

No. 16R2444 Ladies' Fine Lace Front Hose, in fancy open work designs. One of the newest importations, made from fine cotton yarn, absolutely fast black. Spliced heels and soles. **A strictly high grade hose in every respect.** If you want the newest order this number. Sizes, 8½, 9, 9½, 10.
Price, per pair.....................$0.45
Per dozen pairs..................... 5.40

Ladies' Balbri gan Hose.

No. 16R2450 Ladies' Unbleached Balbriggan Hose, full length, elastic top, full seamless foot.
Price, per pair.....................10c

No. 16R2454 Full Regular Made Balbriggan Hose, made of fine combed Egyptian yarn; high spliced heel, double toe and sole, extra long and elastic top. Sizes, 8½, 9, 9½, 10.
Price, per pair.....................$0 19
Per dozen pairs..................... 2.28

Ladies' White Cotton Hose.

No. 16R2458 Ladies' Extra Quality Plain White Cotton Hose. Fine gauge, full seamless, soft and smooth. Sizes, 8½, 9, 9½, 10. Price, per pair......23c

Ladies' Oxford Mixed Hose, 9 Cents.

True Merit in These Goods.

No. 16R2460 Ladies' Extra Quality Dark Oxford Gray Mixed Seamless Cotton Hose. Fine gauge and good medium weight for all the year round wear. Made by the famous Nelson Knitting Mills. We sell tons of them every year and have never had a single complaint in regard to them. They are soft and close knit, very strong and durable.

Price, per dozen pairs, **$1.08**; per pair............9c

If by mail, postage extra, per doz., 45c; per pair, 4c

LADIES' WINTER WEIGHT HOSIERY.

POSTAGE on Ladies' Winter Weight Hose will be 4 cents per pair and 40 cents per dozen, extra. Always include enough money for postage when ordering goods to be sent separately by mail.

SPECIAL NOTICE—In ordering Ladies' Hose, please refer to the following scale of sizes:

SCALE OF SIZES.

No. 1 ladies' shoe takes about 8 -inch hose.
No. 2 ladies' shoe takes about 8½-inch hose.
No. 3 and 4 ladies' shoe takes about 9 -inch hose.
No. 5 and 6 ladies' shoe takes about 9½-inch hose.
No. 7 ladies' shoe takes about 10 -inch hose.

If by mail, postage extra, 22 to 34 cents per dozen on ladies' hose.

Ladies' Fleece Lined Cotton Hose.

Plain leg, not ribbed.

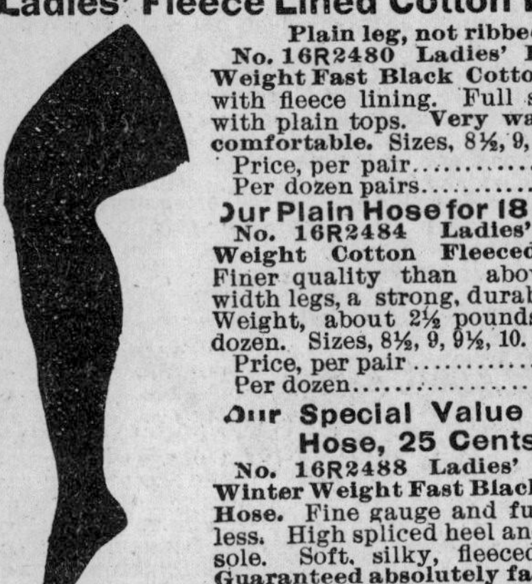

No. 16R2480 Ladies' Heavy Weight Fast Black Cotton Hose, with fleece lining. Full seamless with plain tops. **Very warm and comfortable.** Sizes, 8½, 9, 9½, 10.

Price, per pair.............**$0.12**
Per dozen pairs............ **1.44**

Our Plain Hose for 18 Cents.

No. 16R2484 Ladies' Full Weight Cotton Fleeced Hose. Finer quality than above, full width legs, a strong, durable hose. Weight, about 2½ pounds to the dozen. Sizes, 8½, 9, 9½, 10.

Price, per pair..............**$0.18**
Per dozen..................... **2.16**

Our Special Value Plain Hose, 25 Cents.

No. 16R2488 Ladies' Heavy Winter Weight Fast Black Cotton Hose. Fine gauge and full seamless. High spliced heel and double sole. Soft, silky, fleeced lining. **Guaranteed absolutely fast black and stainless.** There is no better hose sold at this price. You will be more than pleased with the quality. Sizes, 8½, 9, 9½, 10.

Price, per pair..............**$0.25**
Per dozen pairs............. **3.00**

Ladies' Fleeced Ribbed Hose, 20 Cents.

No. 16R2490 Ladies' Good Weight Ribbed Cotton Hose; shaped to fit the leg, properly made, very fine quality Egyptian cotton, with heavy durable foot. There is a soft fleecing on the inside of this hose, brushed up by a special machine, making it soft and non-irritating; absolutely fast black. Regular retail price, 25 cents. Sizes, 8½, 9, 9½, 10.

Price, per pair...............**$0.20**
Per half dozen pairs......... **1.20**

If by mail, postage extra, per pair, 4 cents; per dozen pairs, 36 cents.

SPECIAL NOTE—Do not forget to give size when ordering hosiery

Our 35-Cent Leader.

Plain legs, not ribbed.

No. 16R2494 Ladies' Finest Quality Heavy Weight Imported Cotton Hose. Fine, soft, silky fleece lining. Full fashioned seamless. **Fine gauge and warranted absolutely fast black and stainless.** Elastic tops and high spliced heels and double soles. **Thoroughly dependable in every way.** You cannot buy a better hose for 50 cents for warmth or wear. Weight about 3 pounds to the dozen. Sizes, 8½, 9, 9½, 10. Price, per dozen pairs, **$4.20**; per pair....**35c**

Ladies' Extra Heavy Cotton Hose.

Not Fleeced.

No. 16R2498 Ladies' Extra Heavy Black Hose. Made of fine Egyptian cotton and stainless. This is the heaviest full fashioned seamless cotton hose made for ladies and weighs about 3 pounds to dozen. Soft, smooth yarn more durable than any other. Will outwear two pair of ordinary hose. High spliced heels and double soles. A standard in value that cannot be surpassed. Regular retail price, 35 cents per pair. Sizes, 8½, 9, 9½, 10.

Price, per dozen pairs, **$3.00**; per pair.........**25c**

Out Size Fleeced Lined Hose.

No. 16R2502 Ladies' Winter Weight Fleece Lined Hose, out size, extra wide legs and tops. Egyptian cotton, absolutely fast black, with non-irritating fleeced lining, soft, warm and pleasant to the skin. A quality equal to any 35-cent hose at retail. Sizes, 8½, 9, 9½, 10. Price, per dozen pairs, **$3.00**; six pairs, **$1.50**; per pair.......................**25c**

If by mail, postage extra, per dozen, 40 cents.

LADIES' WOOL HOSIERY.

No. 16R2510 Ladies' Warranted Fast Black Wool Hose, plain, not ribbed, with fine merino heels and toes. Full seamless. This is positively the best value we have ever offered in wool hosiery. There are many grades of cheap hosiery, but this one you obtain from us at the wholesale price. Sizes, 9, 9½, 10.

Price, per dozen pairs, **$2.16**; six pairs, **$1.08**; per pair.......................**18c**

No. 16R2514 Ladies' Good Quality Ribbed Leg Wool Hose, fast black. An excellent hose at our low price that will give good service, and is equal to most hosiery sold at 25 cents retail. Sizes, 9, 9½, 10.

Price, per dozen pairs, **$2.16**; six pairs, **$1.08**; per pair.......................**18c**

If by mail, postage extra, per dozen, 40 cents; per pair, 4 cents.

THREE WONDERFUL VALUES AT 25 CENTS A PAIR.

EVERY PAIR WORTH 35 CENTS AT RETAIL. Do not confuse our values at 25 cents with those sold at retail. We sell the regular 25-cent qualities for 18 cents a pair. If you can match these values at home return goods and we will refund money and transportation charges.

Ladies' Fine All Wool Cashmere Hose, 25 Cents.

No. 16R2522 Under this number, which is another of our special qualities at 25 cents a pair, we furnish ladies' plain hose, made from fine wool cashmere yarn; full fashioned seamless, that will fit the leg perfectly. Again we call your attention to the fact that these qualities should not be confused with those sold by local merchants at 25 cents per pair. The quality furnished by us is equal to any he can buy at $3.00 per dozen, and you therefore pay us no more than he pays for the same quality, and for which he would be obliged to charge 35 cents a pair. Our three numbers of ladies' woolen hosiery at 25 cents a pair cannot be excelled, and we guarantee every pair to give entire satisfaction. This is a good winter weight, not extremely heavy, to be worn with any regular dress shoe. Double spliced heels and toes. Black only. Sizes, 8½, 9, 9½ 10.

Price, per pair..............**$0.25**
Per six pairs........ .... **1.50**

If by mail, postage extra, per pair, 4 cents; per dozen pairs, 42 cents

25 Cents for Ladies' 35-Cent Ribbed Wool Hose.

No. 16R2526 Ladies' Fast Black All Wool Ribbed Hose. Finely made and finished. **They are full of excellent wearing qualities, and will undoubtedly give long and lasting service to the wearer.** Made from specially prepared yarns, are full length and perfect fitting. **There is real economy in purchasing hosiery of this sort.** Spliced heels and toes. Regular 35-cent value at retail. **Note our special price on these stockings.** Sizes, 8½, 9, 9½, 10.

Price, per pair...............**$0.25**
Six for......................... **1.50**
Per dozen pairs................ **3.00**

If by mail, postage extra, per pair, 4 cents; per dozen, 40 cents.

Ladies' All Wool Heavy Ribbed Hose, 25 Cents.

No. 16R2527 Under this number we furnish one of the very best, strongest, warm, durable woolen hose manufactured, and our price of 25 cents represents the cost ($3.00 per dozen) to your local merchant. Do not confuse qualities such as we offer under this number, with anything sold at 25 cents retail, for we sell the regular 25-cent kind for 18 cents, and this quality is sold regular at 35 cents per pair. We want your order for this quality if you need a warm, good winter weight hose. They are made with spliced heels and toes, elastic and perfect fitting. A fine, clean domestic wool. We warrant every pair to give entire satisfaction. These goods are slightly heavier than No. 16R2526, but are not too heavy to be worn with any regular style shoe. Color, black only. Sizes, 8½, 9, 9½, 10.

Price, per pair...**$0.25**
Per half dozen pairs.......................... **1.50**

If by mail, postage extra, per pair, 4 cents; per dozen pairs, 44 cents.

Ladies' All Wool Oxford Gray or Blue Mixed Hose, 20 Cents.

No. 16R2530 Ladies' All Wool Fine Gauge Dark Oxford Gray or Blue Mixed Hose, with merino heels and toes. Plain knitted, medium weight. Full seamless and very soft, as well as **warm and comfortable.** Retail price, 25 cents. **We make a specialty of these stockings. They are of the wear well sort and have never failed to give satisfaction.** Medium heavy weight, shaped and perfect fitting.

Price, per pair.......................**$0.20**
Six pairs for.......................... **1.20**
Per dozen pairs....................... **2.40**

If by mail, postage extra, per pair, 4 cents; per dozen pairs, 40 cents.

Ladies' Northwest Stockings, 40 Cents.

No. 16R2536 Ladies' Extra Heavy and Thick All Wool Ribbed Hose. Blue mixed only. A veritable Northwest stocking. Heaviest weight ladies' wool hose made. Extra strong and durable. If you want the warmest stocking made for women order this number. Never retails for less than 50 cents per pair. Colors, black, blue or very dark Oxford mixed. Sizes, 9, 9½, 10. Price, per dozen pairs, **$4.80**; six pairs, **2.40**; per pair.......................**40c**

Heavy Ribbed Woolen Stockings, 25 Cents.

Blue Mixed, Oxford Mixed.

No. 16R2537 Under this number we furnish one of the best values ever offered in Ladies' Woolen Hose; that would cost your local merchant exactly the same price which you pay us for them. A heavy, fine, clean wool stocking, with long, heavy ribbed leg. Closely knitted, firm woolen foot, with spliced heel and toe. Heavy weight, but not so heavy but that they can be worn with a regular style shoe. If you want an extremely warm, heavy woolen stocking, we cannot recommend this number too highly. Colors, blue mixture or dark Oxford mixture. State color and size in order. Sizes, 9, 9½, 10.

Price, per half dozen pairs, **$1.50**; per pair....**25c**

If by mail, postage extra, per pair, 5 cents; per one-half dozen pairs, 25 cents.

OUR THREE SPECIAL VALUES FOR 35 CENTS.

We sell 50-cent woolen hose for 35 cents per pair, and warrant every pair to give entire satisfaction, and to be regular 50-cent values at retail.

Ladies' Worsted Hosiery, 35 Cents.

No. 16R2540 Ladies' All Wool Worsted Black Hose. Fine gauge, full seamless, with spliced heels and toes. Perfect fitting, fashioned and finely shaped. **Guaranteed absolutely fast black and stainless.** Comfortable as it is possible to make stockings. Our special value under this number retails throughout this country at 50 cents per pair, and you will recognize that this is not an empty boast, if you order the goods. Worsted hosiery is more durable than cashmere, and seldom irritates, having a smooth, wear resisting surface. Sizes, 8½, 9, 9½, 10.

Price, per pair...............**$0.35**
Six pairs for.................. **2.10**
Per dozen pairs.............. **4.20**

If by mail, postage extra, per pair, 4 cents; per dozen pairs, 40 cents.

DON'T FAIL TO MENTION SIZE WANTED.

Ladies' Medium Weight 35-Cent Leader Worsted Stocking, Ribbed Legs.

No. 16R2541 Again we offer another of our special 50c qualities at 35 cents per pair. This stocking is not so heavy as the one quoted on next page, but has the weight of a good, durable, fine cotton stocking; all fine, pure wool worsted; closely ribbed legs, seamless, perfect fitting, made with spliced heels and toes. Nowhere can you purchase such quality as we offer under this number, and if not equal to anything you can buy at home at 50 cents per pair, return and we will refund your money, together with transportation charges. We want you to purchase good hosiery, which is the cheapest in the long run, and therefore offer values most extraordinary, on our small profit plan. Color, black only. Sizes, 8½, 9, 9½, 10.

Price, per pair...............**$0.35**
Per half dozen pairs...... .... **2.10**

If by mail, postage extra, per pair, 4 cents; per dozen pairs, 40 cents.

BOYS' HOSIERY.

Boys' Merino Stockings.

No. 16R2670 Boys' Extra Heavy Merino Hose, with long ribbed legs. An excellent school stocking and will give good service. **Warranted fast black.** Always state size when you order. **Sizes, 7 to 10.**

Sizes	7	7½	8	8½
Price, per pair	$0.16	$0.17	$0.18	$0.19
Price, per ½ dozen	.96	1.02	1.08	1.14
Sizes	9	9½	10	
Price, per pair	$0.20	$0.21	$0.22	
Price, per ½ dozen	1.20	1.26	1.32	

If by mail, postage extra, per pair, 4 cents.

Boys' Heavy Winter Stockings.

17 to 25 cents per pair.

No. 16R2672 Boys' Heavy Warm Woolen Stockings, fast black, long ribbed legs and shaped heels and toes. Made from clean wool and we warrant them to be an especial value at our low price. A reliable, well made stocking. Always state size in your order.

Sizes,	6	6½	7	7½	8	8½	9	9½	10
Pair.	$0.17	0.18	0.19	0.20	0.21	0.22	0.23	0.24	0.25
½ doz.	1.02	1.08	1.14	1.20	1.26	1.32	1.38	1.44	1.50

If by mail, postage extra, per pair, 4 cents.

Our Hercules Wool Stockings for Boys.

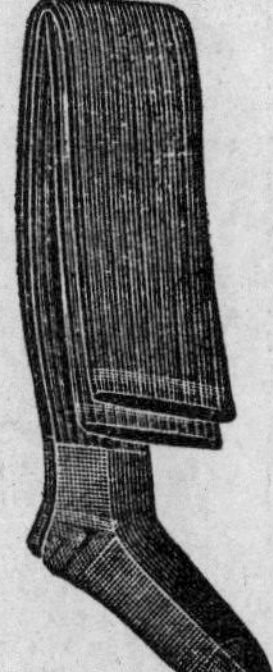

Will outwear any hose you have bought for your boy.

No.16R2674 Boys' Extra Heavy and Durable All Wool Hose with long heavy ribbed legs; made with shaped heels and toes, full seamless feet. These hose are manufactured especially for us and are of a superior quality for wear. It is unlikely that your local merchant handles such goods, as he would have to pay more than our selling price for them. They wear longer and give better satisfaction than any other. Black only.

Sizes	6	6½	7	7½	8
Price, per pair	$0.23	$0.24	$0.25	$0.26	$0.27
Per half dozen	1.38	1.44	1.50	1.56	1.62
Sizes		8½	9	9½	10
Price, per pair		$0.28	$0.29	$0.30	$0.31
Per half dozen pairs		1.68	1.74	1.80	1.86

If by mail, postage extra, per pair, 4 cents.

Boys' Oxford Rough Rider Stockings, Ribbed Legs.

Warm, strong, durable.

No. 16R2676 Boys' Oxford Stockings, made from clean domestic wool. Long full weight ribbed legs, shaped heel and toe. Oxford gray stockings are almost black, have but a small mixture of light wool, which is preferred by many to black. A good strong stocking suitable for boys or girls. Special value at our low price. Sizes, 6 to 9½.

Sizes	6	6½	7	7½	8	8½	9	9½
Per pair	$0.15	$0.16	$0.17	$0.18	$0.19	$0.20	$0.21	$0.22
Half dozen,	.90	.96	1.02	1.08	1.14	1.20	1.26	1.32

If by mail, postage extra, per pair, 4 cents.

Children's Wool Hosiery. 18 to 24 Cents.

Ribbed Legs.

No. 16R2682 Children's Good Quality Woolen Hose. Long ribbed legs, shaped heels and toes. A good low priced stocking that will wear well. Medium winter weight. Sizes, 5½ to 8½ only.

Sizes	5½	6	6½	7	7½	8	8½
Price, per pair	$0.18	.19	.20	.21	.22	.23	.24
Per half dozen	1.08	1.14	1.20	1.26	1.32	1.38	1.44

Children's Fine Worsted Ribbed Hose.

No. 16R2684 Misses' and Children's Extra Fine All Wool Fast Black Imported Worsted Ribbed Hose. Stockings of this quality have a fine, smooth surface and seldom irritate, but invariably prove durable. Fine close ribbed with merino heels and toes.

Sizes	5½	6	6½	7	7½	8	8½
Price, per pair	$0.23	.25	.27	.28	.30	.32	.34
Per half dozen	1.38	1.50	1.62	1.68	1.80	1.92	2.04

If by mail, postage extra, per pair, 4 cents.

Children's Cashmere Hose.

No. 16R2690 Boys' or Misses' Extra Fine Quality Ribbed Imported Cashmere Hose; strictly all pure wool of the finest quality. Soft, smooth and comfortable, perfect in fit, finish and workmanship. Fashioned and seamless, with double spliced heels and toes. Handsome shape. Absolutely fast black.

Sizes	5½	6	6½	7	7½	8	8½
Price, per pair	$0.40	.42	.44	.46	.48	.50	.52
Per ½ dozen	2.40	2.52	2.64	2.76	2.88	3.00	3.12

If by mail, postage extra, per pair, 3 cents.

Do Not Fail to Send 5 Cents

FOR OUR LARGE AND COMPLETE SAMPLE BOOKLET OF

BOYS' AND CHILDREN'S CLOTHING

at the lowest prices possible to name on goods that are guaranteed to please. Then order Clothing and Hose and other things all at once.

DON'T FORGET TO GIVE SIZES.

Misses' and Children's Plain Wool Hose.

(Not Ribbed.)

No. 16R2694 Misses' and Children's Plain Black Wool Hose, with merino heels and toes. Made from clean domestic wool and will not fail to be satisfactory. Full seamless, soft, warm and comfortable, and **very durable.**

Sizes	5½	6	6½	7
Per pair.	$0.16	$0.17	$0.18	$0.19
Per ½ doz.	.96	1.02	1.08	1.14
Sizes	7½	8	8½	
Per pair	$0.20	$0.21	$0.22	
Per ½ dozen	1.20	1.26	1.32	

If by mail, postage extra, pair, 3c

Misses' and Children's Plain Black Cashmere Hose.

No. 16R2698 Misses' and Children's Extra Quality Plain Black Fast Colored Cashmere Hose. We want you to order good hosiery, as you will find dependable qualities of this kind cheap in the long run. Full seamless, double knee, double heel and toe, **regular 35-cent value.**

Sizes	5½	6	6½	7
Price, per pair	$0.22	$0.23	$0.24	$0.25
Per half dozen	1.32	1.38	1.44	1.50
Sizes		7½	8	8½
Price, per pair		$0.26	$0.27	$0.28
Per half dozen		1.56	1.62	1.68

If by mail, postage extra, per pair, 3 cents; per dozen pairs, 33 cents.

Extra Quality Children's Cashmere Hose.

No. 16R2700 Misses' and Children's Extra Fine Imported Fast Black Cashmere Hose. Knitted from fine Australian wool, which is the best known wool. These hose are very elastic, soft and warm. Strictly high grade in every particular. High spliced heels, double soles. Superior quality.

Sizes	5	5½	6	6½
Price, per pair	$0.28	$0.30	$0.32	$0.34
Per half dozen	1.68	1.80	1.92	2.04
Sizes	7	7½	8	8½
Price, per pair	$0.36	$0.38	$0.40	$0.42
Per half dozen	2.16	2.28	2.40	2.52

If by mail, postage extra, per pair, 3 cents.

INFANTS' HOSE.

Sizes, 4, 4½, 5 and 5½.

No. 16R2710 Infants' Ribbed Fast Black Cotton Hose. Fine soft finish, close knit and full seamless. Per pair............9c
Per half dozen pairs............54c

No. 16R2714 Infants' Fine Ribbed Hose, made of fine yarn with fashioned feet. One of our strongest values. Colors, black, sky blue, pink, blue, tan, red and white. Sizes, 4, 4½, 5, 5½.
Price, per pair............12c
Per half dozen pairs............72c
Postage, per pair, 1 cent.

Infant's Silk Hosiery at 19 Cents Per Pair.

No. 16R2720 Infants' Fine Mercerized Silk Hose, fine ribbed legs, perfectly shaped foot. The mercerized process is that of making a fine Egyptian cotton yarn feel like silk; looks like silk and will wear better. The retail price of this stocking is 25 cents. You buy them from us at the same price that your local dealer will be obliged to pay for them. An especially fine number made in the following colors: Black, blue, white and red. State color and size when ordering. Sizes, 4½, 5, 5½, 6.
Price, per half dozen pairs, $1 14; per pair....19c
If by mail, postage extra, per pair, 2 cents; per dozen pairs, 18 cents.

Infants' Silk Tipped Hose.

No.16R2722 Infants' Extra Selected Fine Egyptian Yarn Cotton Hose, very fine elastic ribbed legs. Full seamless, **with pure silk heels and toes.** Made from the finest imported Maco yarn. Black or tan. Sizes, 4, 4½, 5, 5½.
Price, per half dozen pairs, $1.32; per pair.. .22c
If by mail, postage extra, per pair, 2 cents; per dozen pair, 18 cents.

Infants' Lace Effect Stockings.

No. 16R2728 Infants' Fine Cotton Stockings, in new style; drop stitch lace effect; made of smooth, soft, clean yarn; warranted to give entire satisfaction; perfectly shaped foot and leg. Retail price 15 to 20 cents. Color, black, white, red, pink, sky blue. Sizes, 4, 4½, 5, 5½, 6.
Price, per pair............12c
Per half dozen pairs............72c
If by mail, postage extra, per pair, 2 cents, per dozen pairs, 18 cents.

INFANTS' ALL WOOL RIBBED HOSE.

Sizes, 4, 4½, 5, 5½.

No. 16R2730 Infants Cashmere Hose, all wool ribbed, an excellent value. Colors, black cardinal pink, light blue or white.
Price, per doz., $1.44; six pairs, 72c; per pair. 12c
If by mail, postage extra, per pair, 2 cents; per dozen pairs, 18 cents.

Infants' Worsted Hose, 15 Cents.

No. 16R2740 Infants' Fine Worsted Ribbed Hose, with fine smooth worsted feet and merino tipped heels and toes. A special value at our low price. Black only. Sizes, 4, 4½, 5, 5½.
Price, per half dozen, 90; per pair............15c
If by mail, postage extra, per pair 2 cents.

Our Extra Quality Ribbed Hose, 23 Cents.

No. 16R2744 Infants' Superfine Cashmere Hose, made of pure Australian yarn of choice quality, with silk heels and toes; strictly high grade. Fine elastic knitted; easily put on or off. Colors, black, white, pink, red and blue. Be sure to state color and size in order. Sizes, 4, 4½, 5, 5½.
Price, per half dozen, $1.38; per pair............23c
If by mail, postage extra, per pair, 2 cents.

Infants' Red Woolen Hose.

No. 16R2746 Infants' Fine All Wool Worsted Stockings, made in bright scarlet or red color. Bright colors are very much in demand for infants' wear, and this one we believe to be the most dependable hose that can be sold at 25 cents. Fine elastic knitted. Closely ribbed legs, finely shaped feet. Sizes, 4½, 5, 5½, 6.
Price, per pair............$0.25
Per half dozen pairs............1.50
If by mail, postage extra, per pair, 2 cents; per dozen pairs, 20 cents.

Infants' Socks.

Sizes, 4, 4½, 5, 5½.

No.16R2754 Infants' Fine Cotton Socks, seamless, with fancy knit legs. Colors, white, light blue and pink only. Price, per half dozen, 90c; per pair..15c
If by mail, postage extra, per pair, 2 cents.

Our 25-Cent Infants' Socks.

No.16R2760 Infants' Mercerized Silk Socks, full fashioned foot and close ribbed tops; very fine. Colors, black, white, pink and light blue.
Price, per pair............$0.25
Per half dozen pairs............1.50
If by mail, postage extra, per pair, 2 cents.

Racine Feet.

No More Darning.

Racine feet are popular throughout the country, because they save labor and time. When stocking feet are worn out and the legs are still good, the sewing on of new feet makes practically a new stocking, which might otherwise have been thrown away. Mothers will appreciate this saving of time and money by sewing new feet on children's stockings. To attach the feet, turn leg of stocking inside out. Insert the foot inside the leg right side out, allowing the edges to meet, when they can be easily stitched on a machine or by hand, taking a seam about one-eighth of an inch wide. Children's sizes, 5, 5½, 6, 6½, 7, 7½, 8, 8½, 9, 9½, 10; ladies' sizes, 8, 8½, 9, 9½, 10; men's sizes, 9½, 10, 10½, 11.

No. 16R2764 Racine Feet, in fast black. Sizes, 5 to 11. Price, per dozen pairs, $1.08; per pair.... ..9c

No. 16R2765 Racine Feet, ecru color. Sizes, 5 to 11. Price, per dozen pairs, $1.08; per pair 9c

If by mail, postage extra, per pair, 1 cent.

BICYCLE OR GOLF HOSE.

No.16R2780

No. 16R2780 Men's Fine Ribbed Leg Woolen Bicycle Hose, footless (see cut) roll down tops. Will give good satisfaction. Colors, black, navy, maroon and green.
Price, per dozen, $5.40; per pair, 45c

No. 16R2782 Men's Fine Ribbed Leg All Wool Hose. A strong, durable article that will give lasting service. Roll down tops, shaped to fit leg perfectly. Made with fancy plaid tops. Plain color legs, Navy blue, black, brown, maroon and green. Per pair. 70c

No. 16R2782

If by mail, postage extra, per pair, 5 cents.

Fine Worsted Bicycle Hose.

No. 16R2784 Men's Fine Quality Worsted Bicycle Hose, made with fancy artistic Scotch designed tops, roll down, shaped legs, with drop stitch and footless. You seldom find a more genteel hose among the highest priced hose. Fitting the leg perfectly, they are very neat and dressy. Colors, brown, navy and black
Price, per pair............$1.00

If by mail postage extra, per pair 5 cents.

...OUR UNDERWEAR DEPARTMENT...

It is no exaggeration to say that our Underwear Department is complete in every detail, in the sense that we present to our customers only those articles in underwear which we know will give satisfaction.

Our line consists of more than 250 kinds, which cover the whole range of the different weights and qualities suitable for persons in any climate, and also those kinds frequently required or recommended by your physician for a particular purpose. Light weight for summer, medium weight for spring and fall, regular winter weight and the extra heavy kinds for those whose occupation subjects them to much exposure.

OUR PRICES. **Each and every price as stated in our Underwear Department represents a special value.** We do not offer one garment at cost, or less than cost, simply to attract your order and then overcharge you on other goods, but the sole aim and purpose in this department is to give the best value obtainable at the lowest price in each and every kind, and in this we believe we have excelled all our competitors. **We can save you from 25 to 40 per cent on this kind of goods,** as we purchase direct from the manufacturer and transfer direct to you with but the one small profit over the cost to produce.

WE WANT YOUR ORDER **because we can sell you good underwear the cheapest. Our stock is selected from thousands of different kinds and qualities,** by men of wide experience with this kind of merchandise, who exhaust every effort to obtain the honestly made underwear. We therefore have described each kind accurately, because we know how they are made, and what they are made of; and we warrant each to be exactly as represented, and if not will refund your money.

HOW TO ORDER UNDERWEAR. **Men's underwear, give breast and waist measure; women's underwear, give bust and waist measure; children's underwear, give bust and waist measure. Sizes are given in each quotation. Do not forget size or measurements. POSTAGE: Always include postage when ordering shipped by mail.**

MEN'S SUMMER UNDERWEAR.

Shirt Sizes: 34, 36, 38, 40, 42 and 44, chest measurement. Drawers sizes: 30, 32, 34, 36, 38, 40 and 42, waist measurement. Always mention size shirt and drawers when ordering underwear.

Blue Balbriggan Underwear, 20 Cents.

No. 16R5020 Men's Plain Blue Balbriggan Undershirt of fine cotton, summer weight. Ribbed cuffs and collarette neck. Retail value, 25 to 35 cents. Sizes, 34 to 42 breast measure. Price, each.....**$0.20**
Per dozen..... 2.40

No. 16R5021 Men's Plain Blue Drawers, to match above shirts. Sizes, waist measure 30 to 40 inches. Price, per dozen, **$2.40**; per pair........**20c**
If by mail, postage extra, each, 9 cents.

Men's Plain Balbriggan Underwear, 22c.

No. 16R5024 Men's Summer Weight Unbleached Balbriggan Undershirts. Fancy stitch collarette neck, ribbed cuffs and taped front. Sizes, 34 to 42 breast measure. Price, per dozen, **$2.64**; each..**22c**

No. 16R5025 Drawers to match above, made with double seat. Sizes, 30 to 40 waist measure.
Price, per dozen, **$2.64**; per pair..............**22c**
If by mail, postage extra, each, 9 cents.

Men's Plain Balbriggan Underwear, 33c.

No. 16R5028 Men's Fine Gauge French Balbriggan Undershirts. Fancy collarette neck, pearl buttons, and ribbed, close fitting cuffs; **fine soft silk finish; worth 45 cents at retail.** Ecru color only. Sizes, 34 to 44 breast measure only.
Price, per dozen, **$3.96**; each..............**33c**

No. 16R5029 Drawers to match above. Made with fine sateen band and pearl buttons. Sizes, 30 to 42 waist measure. Price, per pair..........**$0.33**
Per dozen..... 3.96
Three full suits of the above underwear..... 1.98
If by mail, postage extra, each, 9 cents.

Men's Honeycomb Knit Underwear, 40c.

Shirt and Drawers.

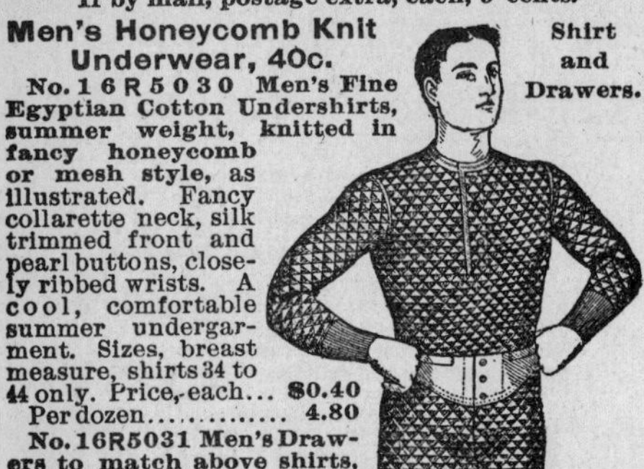

No. 16R5030 Men's Fine Egyptian Cotton Undershirts, summer weight, knitted in fancy honeycomb or mesh style, as illustrated. Fancy collarette neck, silk trimmed front and pearl buttons, closely ribbed wrists. A cool, comfortable summer undergarment. Sizes, breast measure, shirts 34 to 44 only. Price, each... **$0.40**
Per dozen..... 4.80

No. 16R5031 Men's Drawers to match above shirts, made with sateen band, pearl buttons, elastic covered never rip seams. Sizes, waist measure, 30 to 42. Price, per doz., **$4.80**; per pair..**40c**
Postage extra, each, 10 cents.

Men's Combed Egyptian Balbriggan Underwear, 40 Cents.

Our Special Leader.

No. 16R5034 Men's Extra Quality Fine French Balbriggan Undershirts. A very fine light weight summer under garment, with soft smooth surface. Fancy collarette neck and fine pearl buttons, Perfect fitting ribbed cuffs. A strictly high grade, first class under garment, equal to the best made retailing at 50 cents. Made from fine combed Egyptian yarn, and both shirts and drawers are stitched with the **Union special** covered elastic seam that will not rip or irritate. Plain ecru color only. Sizes, 34 to 44 breast measure. Per dozen, **$4.80**; each..**40c**

No. 16R5035 Men's Fine French Balbriggan Drawers to match above shirts. Made with sateen waistband. Three pearl buttons. Perfect fitting ankles. Drawer supporter and **double seat.** Sizes, 30 to 42 waist measure. Price, per pair........**$0.40**
Per dozen..... 4.80
By mail postage extra, each, 9c.

QUALITY. **Good underwear is healthful. Healthful underwear for winter must be made of clean wool,** and for this reason we recommend the better grades, as they are cheapest in the long run. Varying prices distinguish the qualities as produced by the manufacturer, but each is the best of its class. Our values in summer underwear excel all others, as you buy from us at practically the same money as your local merchant pays for like quality.

Men's Summer Balbriggan Underwear.

Medium Weight.

No. 16R5036 Men's Fine Balbriggan Undershirts, flat knitted from superior quality combed Egyptian cotton yarn. This garment is slightly heavier than No. 16R5034-5 and is usually called a "full weight" summer underwear, as distinguished from No. 16R5034, which is the light weight. This particular number is very durable and usually is sold for about 75 cents at retail. Perfect fitting, ribbed cuffs, pearl buttons and silk trimmed. Sizes, breast measure, 34 to 44. Price, each. **$0.50**
Per dozen..... 6.00

No. 16R5037 Men's Fine Balbriggan Drawers to match above shirts, sateen band, pearl buttons, patent never rip covered seams. Sizes, waist, measure, 30 to 42. Price, per doz., **$6.00** per pair, **50c**;
If by mail, postage extra, each, 12 cents.

Bon Bon French Balbriggans.

No. 16R5038 Men's High Grade Genuine French Balbriggan Undershirts, of the famous Bon Bon brand. Shaped shoulders, tailor cut. For more than forty years these shirts have been recognized as the best manufactured, Pearl buttons, ribbed elastic cuffs, ecru color. **Light weight underwear of very fine texture.** Sizes, 34 to 44 breast measure.
Price, per dozen, **$9.00**; each..............**75c**

No. 16R5039 Real French Balbriggan Drawers, to match above; suspender tapes and fine pearl buttons. Handsomely made and shaped. Sizes, 30 to 42 waist measure. Price, per doz., **$9.00**; per pair, **75c**
Three full suits of the above underwear, shirts and drawers, Price..............**$4.50**
If by mail, postage extra, 10 cents per garment.

Underwear for Fat Men.

No. 16R5044 Men's Extra Size French Balbriggan Undershirts. Fine gauge, soft silky finish, made from finest Egyptian yarn. Fancy collarette neck, pearl buttons and ribbed cuffs. **Full size and large.** Sizes, 44 to 52 chest measure. Retail value, $1.00. Ecru color.
Price, each.............**$0.79**
Per dozen..... 9.48

No. 16R5045 Men's Extra Size French Balbriggan Drawers to match above. Sizes, 44 to 52 waist measure.
Price, per pair.............**$0.79**
Per dozen..... 9.48
If by mail, postage extra, each, 10 cents.

Black Balbriggan Underwear.

No. 16R5050 Men's Fine Black Balbriggan Undershirts, trimmed with satin hemmed neck, pearl buttons, long sleeves, ribbed cuffs and hemmed tails. Color, absolutely fast black. Sizes, 34 to 44 breast measure. Price, per doz., **$5.16**; each....**43c**

No. 16R5051 Men's Fine Black Balbriggan Drawers to match above shirts, trimmed with pearl buttons, suspender tape, stitched throughout with the Union special covered seam, closely ribbed cuffs, Sizes, waist measure, 30 to 42 inches.
Price, per dozen, **$5.16**; per pair..............**43c**
If by mail, postage extra, per garment, 9 cents.

Genuine Bon Bon French Lisle Underwear, 90 Cents.

No. 16R5054 Men's Fine Lisle Thread Underwear of the famous Bon Bon French manufacture. A very light weight quality, made with French collarette neck, trimmed with fine pearl buttons, shaped shoulders, long sleeves, closely ribbed cuffs, hemmed tail. This is a superior quality. Lisle thread is very light and cool, but is not as durable as balbriggan, Color, ecru only. Sizes, breast measure, 34 to 44 inches. Price, each..............**90c**

No. 16R5055 Men's Fine Lisle Thread Drawers to match above undershirt, trimmed with drawer tape, fine pearl buttons, sateen waistband, closely ribbed cuffs and reinforced crotch, French adjustable back at waist. Sizes, waist measure, 30 to 42 inches. Price, per pair..............**90c**
If by mail, postage extra, per garment, 8 cents.

Men's Novia Mercerized Silk Underwear.

No. 16R5058 Men's Superfine Silk Undershirt, made by the Mercer process, in regular Novia silk color. Trimmed with French collarette neck, silk facing, pearl buttons, closely ribbed fine knit cuffs and hemmed tail. This is the same kind of goods as is frequently called silkine, American silk, etc. Wears superior to regular silk and washes better and costs but half the price of pure silk and will give much better satisfaction in every particular. We strongly recommend goods of this character for their general merit. Sizes, breast measure, 34 to 44 inches.
Price, each..............**95c**

No. 16R5059 Men's Fine Novia Silk Drawers to match above undershirt, trimmed with very heavy sateen band, suspender straps, four pearl buttons on front, closely ribbed anklets, stitched throughout with the Union special sewing machine covered seam, will not rip or irritate. Sizes, waist measure, 30 to 42 inches. Price, per pair..............**95c**
If by mail, postage extra, each, 10 cents.

Our Special Leader in Fine Underwear, 95 Cents.

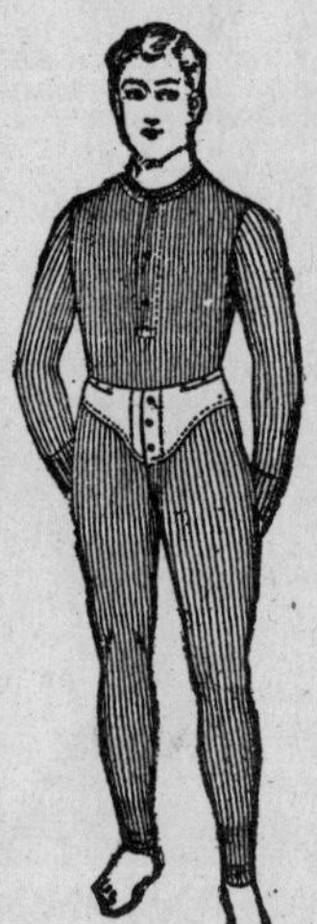

No. 16R5066 Men's Fine Plain Knitted Undershirts, made of the new yarn called American silk or mercerized silk, which is a very fine Egyptian cotton yarn treated by a special process, which gives the appearance of and many of the properties of silk. It will wear better than a silk garment, is always soft and smooth, and we guarantee every garment to be entirely satisfactory in every particular. Shirts are trimmed with collarette neck, silk front and pearl buttons, closely ribbed wrists and fine ribbed tail closely knitted onto the shirt, with no harsh seams anywhere. You have a choice of colors as follows: Fawn, light blue or pink. Be sure to state the color in your order. Both shirt and drawers are stitched throughout with Union special sewing machine. Stretchy seams which are stronger and more elastic than the seams of a regular made full fashioned undergarment. Will not rip or irritate. Sizes, breast measure, 34 to 44. Price, each..............**95c**

No. 16R5067 Men's Fine Mercerized Silk Drawers, to match above undershirts, made from same cloth, stitched throughout with the Union special sewing machine. Stretchy seams, fine sateen waistband, suspender tapes and pearl buttons. Sizes, waist measure, 30 to 42.
Price, per pair..............**$0.95**
For two full suits..... 3.80
If by mail, postage extra, each, 12 cents.

MEN'S FANCY UNDERWEAR.

Men's Striped Balbriggan Underwear, 41 Cents.

No. 16R5078 Men's Fine Fancy Balbriggan Undershirts, knit from fine Egyptian cotton, made in a very narrow ⅛-inch alternating white and blue stripe. A very pretty garment that never fails to give satisfaction. Fast color. Trimmed with collarette neck and pearl buttons. **Perfect fitting ribbed cuffs.** Never retails for less than 50 to 65 cents. Stitched throughout with never-rip seams. Sizes, 34 to 44 breast measure.
Price, each..............**41c**

No. 16R5079 Men's Fancy Balbriggan Drawers to match above shirts, made with satin waistband. Pearl buttons. Stitched throughout with never-rip covered elastic seams. Drawer supporter. Waist measure, 30 to 42. Price, per pair..........**41c**
If by mail, postage extra, each, 9 cents.

Men's Fancy Striped Balbriggan Underwear, 65 Cents.

No. 16R5084 Men's Fine Fancy Striped Balbriggan Undershirt of a novelty design, in which a black stripe predominates alternating with white in a wide broken stripe effect. Trimmed with pearl buttons and sateen neck and front. Stitched throughout with never-rip seams and strictly high grade. Usually retails at $1.00 each. **Our price is extremely low for this kind and quality.** Sizes, 34 to 44 breast measure.
Price, each..............**65c**

No. 16R5085 Men's Fine Fancy Striped Balbriggan Drawers to match above shirts, in waist measures 30 to 42.
Price, per pair..............**65c**
If by mail, postage extra, each, 9 cents.

DON'T FORGET TO STATE SIZE

WHEN YOU ORDER.

MEN'S JERSEY RIBBED SUMMER UNDERWEAR

Ecru Color.

No. 16R5090 Fine Derby Ribbed Balbriggan Shirts. Made from fine, soft finished, combed cotton yarn, pearl buttons, French collarette neck. Ecru or dark cream color. Sizes, 34 to 44 chest. **Always mention size wanted.** Per dozen, $3.96; each..33c

No. 16R5091 Derby Ribbed Balbriggan Drawers, to match above. Sizes, 30 to 42 waist.
Price, per dozen, $3.96; per pair..........33c
If by mail, postage extra, each, 9 cents.

Men's Ribbed Silk Striped Underwear, 41 Cents.

No. 16R5096 Men's Fine Jersey Ribbed Summer Weight Balbriggan Shirts, made with collarette neck. Satin trimmed front with pearl buttons. A very pretty novelty, sure to please and give entire satisfaction in wearing. Silk trimmed cuffs. Color, ecru with hair-line blue silk stripe. Retail value, 65c. Sizes, 34 to 44 breast measure.
Price, each..........41c

No. 16R5097 Men's Ribbed Silk Striped Drawers to match above shirts. Made with sateen waistband, drawer supporters, three pearl buttons and never rip elastic seams throughout. Sizes, 30 to 42 waist measure.
Price, per pair..........41c
If by mail, postage extra, 9 cents.

Men's Ecru Jersey Ribbed Underwear, 40 Cents.

No. 16R5102 Men's Jersey Ribbed Undershirts made from fine Egyptian cotton in plain balbriggan or ecru color. These are strictly finely finished goods that will not fail to please wearer and give lasting service. Stitched with Union special sewing machine covered elastic seams that will never rip or tear. Retails from 50 to 65 cents. Sizes, 34 to 44 breast measure. Price, each..........$0.40
Per dozen.......... 4.80

No. 16R5103 Men's Jersey Ribbed Drawers to match above shirts, trimmed with pearl buttons, sateen waistband and stitched with never tear seams. Sizes, waist measure, 30 to 42 inches. Per pair..$0.40
Per dozen.......... 4.80
If by mail, postage extra, each, 9 cents.

Men's Blue Ribbed Underwear, 42 Cents.

No. 16R5106 Men's Fancy Ribbed Balbriggan Undershirts. Handsome shade of cadet blue with fancy collarette neck, pearl buttons, taped front and ribbed cuffs, soft, silky finish, fast color, light weight and very durable. **Beautiful and trustworthy garments.** Sizes, chest 34 to 44 only.
Price, per dozen, $5.04; each..........42c

No. 16R5107 Cadet Blue Fancy Ribbed Drawers to match above, extra well made and finished. Sizes, waist 30 to 42 only. Per doz., $5.04; per pair..$0.42
Three full suits of the above underwear..... 2.52

FISH NET SHIRTS.

Fish net garments are made in shirts only.

No. 16R5110 Men's Fish Net Undershirts. Sateen front, short sleeves, soft finished. Sizes, 34 to 44. Ecru color.
Price, each......$0.23
Per dozen........ 2.76
If by mail, postage extra, 6 cents.

No. 16R5112 Men's Extra Quality Fish Net Undershirts. Cream color, with fine white covered buttons and front. **Short sleeves. The coolest undershirts made.** Sizes, 34 to 44. Price, per doz., $4.80; each.40c
If by mail, postage extra, 6 cents.

Silk Fish Net Undershirts.

No. 16R5114 Men's Fine Imported Fish Net Mercerized Silk Undershirt. This is a new style, fine net undershirt, trimmed with silk front and pearl buttons. Half sleeves. If you want the best of this kind of goods, something very soft, fine and smooth, order this garment. Shirts only, no drawers to match. We suggest wearing with this shirt, elastic seam jean drawers. Color, cream white only. Sizes, 34 to 44 breast measure.
Price, each..........90c
If by mail, postage extra, each, 7 cents.

Men's Jean Drawers, Stretchy Seam, 45c.

No. 16R5116 Men's Fine Jean Drawers, made with stretchy seams down each side of the leg, giving easy motion and greater comfort. The seams are of wide elastic ribbed balbriggan on the sides of the legs and in back, are self-adjusting, easy and comfortable. Ribbed anklets. Sizes, 30 to 44 waist measure and 30 to 34 inseam. Price, per pair..45c
If by mail, postage extra, per pair, 11 cents.

MEN'S UNION SUITS.

The greatly increased demand for men's union suits is due to their merit as a practical garment. Nearly every man has suffered from time to time the annoying tendency, particularly in warm weather, of his undershirt to roll up his back and the inclination of the drawers to slip to an uncomfortable position. This is all overcome by the simple, common sense garment called the union or combination suit. Those sold by us are based on scientific proportions and we guarantee a fit, except in cases of men who are of extreme proportions, far out of the ordinary.

Try our union suits and you will be surprised and pleased at the value furnished. They fit like the skin. You pay but the wholesale price.

Measurements for Size.

Always state height and weight in addition to the breast measure when ordering union suits.

80 Cents for $1.00 Union Suits.

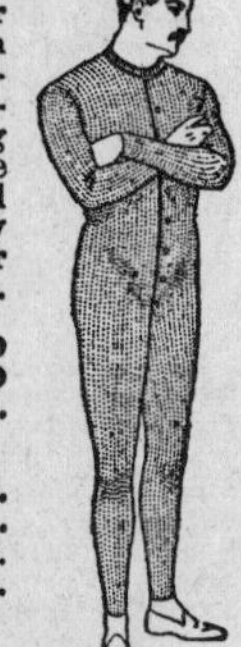

No. 16R5120 Men's Summer Weight Ribbed Egyptian Cotton Union Suits. This garment is carefully proportioned on scientific principles and will be found perfect fitting in every particular. They are made with fine pearl buttons, silk tipped cuffs and silk finished all the way down the front. A special value at our low price. Colors, sky blue or ecru. Sizes, 34 to 44 breast measure.
Price, each.......... $0.80
Per dozen.......... 9.60
If by mail, postage extra, 15 cents.

Men's Extra Sizes.

No. 16R5122 Men's Extra Sizes. Same as above. Ecru color only. Sizes, 46, 48, 50 and 52 breast measure.
Price, each..........$1.00
If by mail, postage extra, 19 cents.

DON'T FAIL TO GIVE SIZE

Men's Fine Lisle Union Suits, $1.40.

No. 16R5124 Men's Fine Lisle Thread Union Suits, ecru color, summer weight. Fine quality; high grade in every particular. Silk trimmed around neck; pearl buttons; perfect buttonholes; silk tipped cuffs and stitched throughout with Union special sewing machine never rip elastic covered seams. Retail value, $2.00. **A strictly high grade first class garment, one that is sure to prove satisfactory in every particular.** Sizes, 34 to 44 only. Price, per suit....$1.40
If by mail, postage extra, 12 cents.

Men's Summer Weight Worsted Union Suits.

No. 16R5128 Men's High Grade Extra Quality Medium Summer Weight All Worsted Ribbed Union Suits. Silk trimmed neck; fine pearl buttons; hand finished; Union special sewing machine covered seams throughout; silk tipped cuffs. A fine all worsted union suit that cannot fail to please and give entire satisfaction. The convenience and comfort of union suits has passed the experimental stage. Retail value, $3.00. We recommend them as the most satisfactory of all kinds of underwear for men. Color, light shade of natural gray. Sizes, 34 to 44 breast measure. Price, each..$2.35
If by mail, postage extra, 18 cents.

Men's Silk Union Suits, $1.75.

Fine Ribbed.

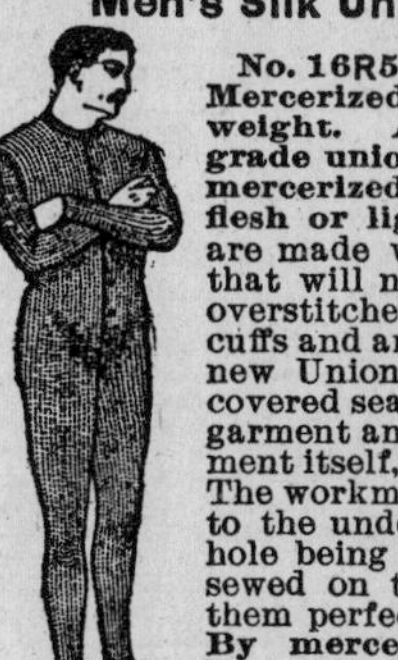

No. 16R5131 Men's Fine Ribbed Mercerized Silk Union Suits, summer weight. A superior quality, high grade union suit knitted from fine mercerized silk yarns in two colors, flesh or light blue. These garments are made with a perfect fitting neck that will not lose its shape and silk overstitched all around edging on cuffs and ankles. Stitching is of the new Union special sewing machine, covered seam that stretches with the garment and is stronger than the garment itself, will never rip or irritate. The workmanship is the finest known to the underwear trade, each buttonhole being properly finished, buttons sewed on to stay, and we guarantee them perfect fitting in every respect. **By mercerized silk we mean fine Egyptian cotton treated by the new Mercer process, by which the yarn is made to look like and feel like silk, retaining this surface permanently and will wear better than a regular cotton undergarment.** You will not find this undergarment retailed for less than $2.50 and most stores will charge three dollars. Our low prices are made possible only by buying these goods direct from the mill for cash. Order this number and you will surely be pleased. **Sizes, 34 to 44 breast measure. State your height, weight and breast measure and color when you order.**
Price, each..........$1.75
If by mail, postage extra, each, 18 cents.

MEN'S MEDIUM WEIGHT UNDERWEAR.

Summer Merino Underwear, 40 Cents.

No. 16R5150 Men's Medium Weight Natural Gray Mixed Summer Merino Undershirts. Soft wool finish, silk taped and trimmed neck and front, and ribbed cuffs. A good spring or fall underwear but preferred by many for summer wear. Retail value, 50 cents. **Fine pearl buttons.** Sizes, 34 to 44.
Price, per dozen, $4.80; each..........40c

No. 16R5151 Men's Gray Mixed Drawers to match above. Sizes, 30 to 42 waist measure.
Price, per pair..........$0.40
Three full suits for.......... 2.40
Per dozen.......... 4.80

Men's Medium Weight Underwear, 69 Cents.

No. 16R5154 Men's Fine Quality Natural Gray Wool Undershirts, light weight, soft and smooth. **Finely finished throughout,** pearl buttons, ribbed cuffs, etc.; non-irritating and non-shrinkable. Sizes, 34 to 44. **65 per cent wool.** A spring or fall weight.
Price, per dozen, $8.28; each..........69c

No. 16R5155 Men's Natural Gray Drawers, to match No. 16R5154. Sizes, 30 to 42.
Price, per dozen, $8.28; per pair..........69c
If by mail, postage extra, each, 11 cents.

Men's Medium Weight Underwear, 90 Cents.

No. 16R5160 Men's Fine Super or Medium Weight Underwear, natural gray in color, about 90 per cent pure wool. This is a soft, fine garment, made partly of Australian wool, suitable for all the year around wear. Trimmed with pearl buttons, closely ribbed cuffs and stitched throughout with the Union special sewing machine covered seam. **We strongly recommend goods of this character because of their great merit, and they never fail to give satisfaction. Color, natural gray only.** Sizes, 34 to 46 breast measure. Price, each..........90c

No. 16R5161 Men's Fine Natural Wool Drawers, to match above undershirt, trimmed with pearl buttons and suspender tapes, stitched throughout with the Union special sewing machine covered seams, that will not rip or tear. Sizes, 30 to 44 waist measure. Price, per pair..........90c
If by mail, postage extra, each garment, 11 cents.

Men's Brown Merino Underwear.

No. 16R5164 Men's Brown Merino Undershirts, made by the famous Norfolk, New Brunswick, mills. This garment contains about 60 per cent of wool and 40 per cent cotton, and is a non-shrinking medium or superweight undergarment, suitable to wear all the year around. They are made in the best manner known to the trade, carefully proportioned, closely ribbed cuffs and ribbed tail. Color, light mixed brown only. Sizes, 34 to 46 breast measure.
Price, each..........90c

No. 16R5165 Men's Fine Merino Drawers, to match above undershirts, trimmed with three pearl buttons, suspender straps, and stitched throughout with the Union sewing machine never rip covered seams. Sizes, 30 to 44 waist measure.
Price, per pair..........90c
If by mail, postage extra, each garment, 11 cents.

Our Special S., R. & Co. Medium Weight.

No. 16R5170 S., R. & Co. Finest Grade Medium Weight Health Undershirts, flat knit, fine soft surface. Made from pure Australian lamb's wool. These are the kind your physician would recommend particularly to those whose physical condition makes it imperative that fine pure woolen underwear should be worn. They are stitched throughout with the Union special sewing machine covered elastic seam. Natural sanitary gray color. Sizes, 34 to 50 breast measure.
Price, per dozen, $16.80; each..........$1.40

No. 16R5171 Medium Weight Sanitary Drawers to match above. Stitched with never rip or tear seams. Sizes, 30 to 48 waist measure.
Price, per dozen, $16.80; per pair..........$1.40
Two full suits for.......... 5.60
If by mail, postage extra, each, 11 cents.

Extra Quality Medium Weight Underwear.

No. 16R5174 Men's Extra Quality Medium Weight Natural Gray Underwear, made by the Norfolk, New Brunswick, Knitting Mills, whose reputation for honestly made goods is excelled by none. About 75 per cent wool, non-shrinking, in medium weight flat garment, not ribbed. A very high grade that never fails to give entire satisfaction. Sizes, 34 to 50 breast measure.
Price, each..........$1.90

No. 16R5175 Men's Fine Drawers, to match above shirts. Sizes, 30 to 50 waist measure.
Price, per pair..........$1.90
If by mail, postage extra, each, 12 cents.

Our Special S., R. & Co. Summer Weight Worsted Underwear.

No. 16R5178 S., R. & Co. Special Light Weight Natural Gray Sanitary Worsted Undershirts, flat knit, fine, soft, silky finish, handsomely made and trimmed, pearl button front, ribbed cuffs and high grade finish throughout. Light weight, no heavier than light weight French balbriggan. The lightest weight summer woolen underwear made for men. Retail price, $1.50. Sizes, 34 to 44 breast measure.
Price, each..........$1.00

No. 16R5179 S., R. & Co. Sanitary Drawers, to match above. Handsomely made and finished. Sizes, 30 to 42 waist measure. Price, per pair..........$1.00
Two full suits of the above underwear for... 4.00
If by mail, postage extra, each, 8 cents.

LADIES' SUMMER UNION SUITS.

Ladies' Cotton Union Suits.

For sizes: Bust, 30 to 40.

No. 16R5200 Ladies' White Cotton Union Suits, made like cut, in short sleeve, knee length. Sizes, 3, 4 and 5. 32 to 40 bust.
Price, each..............**$0.22**
Per dozen..............**2.64**

No. 16R5204 Ladies' New Lisle Finish Ribbed Summer Union Suits, square neck, sleeveless, silk finish neck and armholes, silk tape all around neck and armholes, and closed front. Knee length and form fitting waist. Color, white. Always give size. Sizes, 3, 4 and 5. Price, per suit.........**$0.40**
Per dozen..............**4.80**
If by mail, postage extra, per suit, 6 cents.

Ladies' Lace Trimmed Summer Union Suits.

No. 16R5205 Ladies' New Style Summer Union Suits, light weight, Jersey ribbed, silk trimmed around neck with silk tape, silk tape trimmed around armholes. Fancy lace trimmed bottoms, as shown in illustration. A new style, comfortable undergarment, that is meeting popular favor everywhere. Regular retail price, 50 cents. Our low price of 40 cents is made possible by buying these goods direct from the manufacturer, and at the same time we are able to give you a better garment than is sold at retail at 50 cents. White only. Sizes, 4, 5 and 6.
Price, each..................**$0.40**
Per dozen..................**4.80**
If by mail, postage extra, each, 12 cents.

Ladies' Fine Cotton Ribbed Union Suit.

No. 16R5208 Ladies' New Style Jersey Ribbed Union Suit, Button Across Bust. Perfect form fitting. This style commends itself over the straight across the bust style, as it is much more comfortable and perfect fitting. See illustration. Crocheted all around the neck and front. Knee length, with short wing sleeves. White only. Sizes, 3, 4, 5 and 6 to fit busts 30 to 40. Price, each..........**45c**
If by mail, postage extra, 9 cents.

Ladies' Union Suit, Long Sleeves, Knee Length.

No. 16R5212 Ladies' Fine Jersey Ribbed Union Suit. Made to button across bust in the manner shown in illustration. Same quality as above, but made with long sleeves. Knee length legs. Color, ecru. Sizes, 3, 4, 5 and 6 to fit busts 30 to 40.
Price, each..........................**45c**
If by mail, postage extra, 9 cents.

Ladies' Fine Lisle Union Suits, 75 Cents.

Button down front.

No. 16R5216 The Jersey Ribbed Union Suit. Pure white fine lisle thread. One of the best union suits we have ever offered, and no detail is spared to make this one of the finest. Curved silk crocheted neck, white silk ribbon, shaped form fitting waist and short wing sleeves. This suit opens all the way down front, and is easily put on and off, finished down front with fine white pearl buttons and fancy silk crochet edge. Comfortable as can be made. Sizes, 3, 4 and 5; knee length. Each.....**$0.75**
Price, per dozen...................**9.00**
If by mail, postage extra, 9 cents.

DON'T FAIL TO GIVE SIZE.

Ladies' Summer Union Suits, 80 Cents.

Busts, 32 to 40—Long Sleeves.

No. 16R5220 Ladies' Fine Ribbed Medium Summer Weight Egyptian Cotton Union Suits; long sleeves and ankle length, open down the front. **Fine white pearl buttons,** shaped waist, silk taped neck, crocheted silk edge around neck and down the front. A medium weight summer garment. **Always give size.** Sizes, 3, 4, 5 and 6.
Price, per suit..................**$0.80**
Per dozen..................**9.60**
If by mail, postage extra, per suit, 10 cents.

LADIES' SUMMER VESTS.

SIZES 3, 4 and 5. Size 3 is for 32-inch bust; Size 4 is for 34 and 36-inch bust; size 5 is for 38 and 40-inch bust. Allow 5 to 10 cents extra for postage per garment. For extra size vests, see Nos. 16R5306 and 16R5307.

NOTE—Do not fail to allow postage when ordering goods shipped by mail.

Ladies' Vests, 5 Cents.

No. 16R5246 Ladies' Sleeveless Ribbed Summer Vests, ecru or cream color, elastic. Sizes, 3, 4 and 5.
Price, per dozen, 60c; each..................5c

LADIES' SLEEVELESS VESTS.

No. 16R5250 Ladies' Fancy Ribbed Fine Cotton Vests, made with crocheted neck and armholes. Low round neck, with tape. In white only. Sizes, 4, 5 and 6 for busts, 30 to 38 inches.
Price, per dozen, **$1.20**; each.**10c**
If by mail, postage extra, 4 cents.

Ladies' Sleeveless Vests, 12 Cts.

No. 16R5251 Ladies' Sleeveless Vests, made from good quality cotton yarns, fancy trimmed neck and arm bands, fancy lace effect knitted throughout. Special value at our low price. White only. Sizes, 4, 5 and 6. Busts, 30 to 38 inches.
Price, each..............**12c**
If by mail, postage extra, each, 5 cents.

Ladies' Sleeveless Vests, 14 Cents.

No. 16R5255 Ladies' Sleeveless Vests, fancy lace trimmed arm bands and lace inserted front and back. A very pretty summer vest at an exceedingly low price. Color, white only. Sizes, 4, 5 and 6. Busts, 30 to 38 inches.
Price, each.........................**14c**
If by mail, postage extra, each, 5 cents.

Ladies' Sleeveless Vests, 17 Cents.

No. 6R5260 Ladies' Fine Swiss Ribbed Egyptian Cotton Vests, knit from fine, soft combed yarn, sleeveless, with silk trimmed neck and silk tape. Never retails for less than 25 cents. Color, white only. Sizes, 4, 5 and 6 for busts 30 to 38 inches.
Price, per dozen, **$2.04**; each, **17c**
If by mail, postage extra, 5 cents.

Ladies' Lace Trimmed Vests, 22 Cents.

No. 16R5264 Ladies' Fancy Lace Front and Back Vests, sleeveless. Swiss ribbed, made of fine Egyptian cotton. New and pretty design for this season, at about the price which your merchant pays for such goods. Retail value, 30 cents. Color, white only. Sizes, 4, 5 and 6; for busts 30 to 38.
Price, each....................**$0.22**
Per dozen....................**2.64**
If by mail, postage extra, 5 cents.

Lace Front Ladies' Vests, 21 Cents.

No. 16R5268 Ladies' Lisle Lace Vests. Ladies' new pattern fancy Lace Knit Lisle Ribbed Vest, summer weight, sleeveless. Fancy trimmed neck and armholes, with silk tape inserted. White only. A special value. Sizes, 4, 5 and 6; for busts 30 to 38 inches. Price, each......**$0.21**
Per dozen......................**2.52**
If by mail, postage extra, 5 cents.

DON'T FAIL TO GIVE SIZE

Ladies' Silk Vests, 22 Cents.

No. 16R5274 Ladies' Mercerized Silk Vests. Sleeveless. Fine mercerized silk vests with silk crotcheted neck and armholes and silk tape. Sizes, 4, 5 and 6, to fit busts 30 to 38. White only. This is special value at our low price.
Price, each....................**$0.22**
Per dozen....................**2.64**
If by mail, postage extra, 5 cents.

Ladies' Sleeveless Vests, 23 Cents.

Our Special Value.

No. 16R5278 Ladies' Fine Ribbed Vests, knit from fine combed Egyptian cotton yarn. Sleeveless. V neck, with silk tape inserted. Perfect form fitting. Especially strong value at our low price. Color, cream white.
Price, each....................**$0.23**
Per dozen....................**2.76**
If by mail, postage extra, 6 cents.

LADIES' SUMMER VESTS.

Wing Sleeve Vests, 12 Cts.

¼ Sleeves.

No. 16R5282 Ladies' Fine Jersey Ribbed Summer Vests. New fancy ribbed Egyptian cotton, with square fancy crocheted neck and short wing sleeves. Color, ecru. Sizes, 3, 4 and 5. These are very desirable garments and usually retail for 25 cents. Our price is different. Price, each........**$0.12**
Per dozen....................**1.44**
Postage extra, each, 5 cents.

Ladies' Wing Sleeve Vest, 15 Cents Each.

¼ Sleeves.

No. 16R5284 Ladies' Good Quality Wing Sleeve Vest, knit from fine Egyptian cotton yarn, with short wing sleeves, as shown in the illustration. Swiss ribbed, silk trimmed neck. Made in white only. Sizes, 4, 5 and 6.
Price, each..............**$0.15**
Per dozen..............**1.80**
If by mail, postage extra, each, 4 cents.

Ladies' Lisle Summer Vests, Wing Sleeves, Lace Trimmed, 22 Cents.

¼ Sleeves.

No. 16R5286 This is one of our specially good things in ladies' fine vests, silk crocheted trimmed neck with ribbon and a fancy lace front as shown in the illustration. These garments are all exceptional value and much better than usually sold at 25 cents retail. **All white only, perfect form fitting, thoroughly satisfactory vest.** Sizes, 4, 5 and 6.
Price, each..........................**$0.22**
Per dozen..........................**2.64**
If by mail, postage extra, each, 4 cents.

Ladies' Fine Silk Vests.

No. 16R5291 Made of the new American, or mercerized, silk, a fabric that is stronger than pure silk, has a perfect luster, feels like and wears like silk, but will be more durable. Fancy silk trimmed neck and armholes. This is an astonishing value, that will outwear two ordinary silk vests. If you desire something especially new and fine, order this number. Colors, white, pink or blue. Sizes, 4, 5 and 6. Price, each............**$0.40**
Per dozen............**4.80**
If by mail, postage extra, each, 5 cents.

Genuine Silk Vests, Sleeveless, 59 Cents.

No. 16R5293 Ladies' Fine Genuine Silk Vests, made with fancy lace trimming around neck and armholes. This trimming is of such a nature and quality that it will wash and wear well. Fine silk tape inserted around the armholes and about the neck. The garment is knitted, Swiss ribbed. We can recommend this number in fine, soft silk for its merit and wearing properties; a vest that frequently retails at 75 cents to $1.00, and is sold at our low price because we buy them direct from the manufacturer. This number will please you. Colors, white, black, sky blue or lavender. Sizes, 4, 5 and 6; bust, 32 to 40.
Price, each...(Postage extra, each, 5 cents)..**59c**

Ladies' Extra Size Summer Vests.

No. 16R5302 Ladies' Extra Size Ribbed Vests, low neck, sleeveless, with crocheted neck and silk tape. Busts 40, 42, 44. This is the regular 25-cent quality. Price, each..............................**17c**
If by mail, postage extra, 5 cents.

Ladies' Extra Size Vests, 25 Cents.

No. 16R5306 Busts 42, 44 and 46. Ladies' Extra Large Size Ribbed Summer Vests. Knit of fine combed Egyptian cotton yarn, sleeveless, crocheted neck, with silk tape. Sizes, 7, 8 and 9 for busts 42, 44 and 46. Price, each..........................**25c**

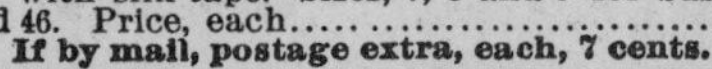
If by mail, postage extra, each, 7 cents.

Ladies' Extra Size Vests.
¼ Sleeves.

No. 16R5307 Ladies' Extra Size Fine Cotton Ribbed Summer Vest. In fine combed Egyptian cotton yarns, crocheted neck, short wing sleeves; same quality as No. 16R5306, and similar in style to illustration No 16R5286. Color, cream white. Bust, 42, 44 and 46. Sizes, 7, 8 and 9.
Price, per dozen, $3.00; each....................25c
If by mail, postage extra, each, 7 cents.

Ladies' Extra Size Drawers.
Sizes, 7, 8 and 9.

No. 16R5308 Ladies' Summer Ribbed Drawers, made in extra size. Same style and quality as above. Sizes, 7, 8 and 9. To match vests No. 16R5306. See also No. 16R5338. Price, per pair..................29c
If by mail, postage extra, each, 6 cents.

Ladies' Plain White Gauze Vests, Short Sleeves.

No. 16R5310 Ladies' Summer Gauze Vests, flat knit. Trimmed around neck and front with silk tape, and three pearl buttons. Sizes, 28, 30, 32, 34, 36, 38, 40 bust measure. (We do not handle ladies' drawers to match this vest.) This is the quality that usually retails at 50 cents. White, only.
Price, per dozen, $4.20; each....................35c
If by mail, postage extra, 5 cents.

Ladies' Long Sleeve Summer Vests, Suitable to Wear in All Seasons.

No. 16R5314 Ladies' Fine Combed Egyptian Cotton Vests, with high necks and long sleeves, shaped waist, crocheted neck with silk tape inserted. Fine pearl buttons. Sizes, 4, 5 and 6 to fit busts 30 to 40 inches. Color, cream white. This is a special value, usually retails at 35 cents.
Price, each..............$0.24
Per dozen.................2.88
If by mail, postage extra, 6 cents.

Ladies' Ribbed Vests.
SHORT SLEEVES.

No. 16R5320 Ladies' Fine Egyptian Cotton Vest, shaped to fit the form. Same quality as above, but with short sleeves. Silk crocheted neck with silk tape inserted. Pearl buttons. Color, cream white. Sizes, 4, 5 and 6 to fit busts 30 to 40.
Price, per dozen, $2.76; each....................22c
If by mail, postage extra, each, 6 cents.

Ladies' Silk Vests, 50 Cents.
LONG SLEEVES.

No. 16R5324 Ladies' Fine Mercerized Silk Vest, made with long sleeves, shaped waist. Fancy silk trimmed neck and close knit wrists. A very desirable light weight ribbed vest that will wear and wash better than lisle thread. Color, white only. Sizes, 4, 5, 6; for busts 30 to 40 inches. Price, each..50c
If by mail, postage extra, each, 6 cents.

LADIES' SUMMER RIBBED DRAWERS.

No. 16R5330 Ladies' Fine Jersey Ribbed Form Fitting Egyptian Cotton Drawers, knee length. Open back. Draw string and shaped waist. Sizes, 4, 5 and 6.
Price, per pair..................23c
If by mail, postage extra, 6 cents.

Ladies' Drawers, Lace Trimmed.

Lace Trimmed Drawers, 23 Cents.

No. 16R5338 Ladies' Jersey Ribbed Egyptian Cotton Drawers. Knee length. Trimmed with lace, as shown in illustration. Preferred by many to the close knit ends. These are extremely popular goods, being cool and comfortable for summer wear. Sizes, 4, 5, 6, 7, 8 and 9. White only. Per pair... 23c
If by mail, postage extra, each, 6 cents.

38 Cents for 50-Cent Lace Trimmed Drawers.

No. 16R5340 Ladies' Lace Trimmed Drawers, extra quality, made of fine Egyptian cotton yarn with wide fancy lace bottoms, of durable quality. Retails everywhere at 50 cents. White only. Sizes, 4, 5 and 6. Per pair, 38c
If by mail, postage extra, each, 6 cents.

Ladies' Ribbed Summer Merino Underwear.
Suitable for All-Year-Around Wear.

Long Sleeve Vests.

No. 16R5350 Ladies' Fine Ribbed Merino Wool Underwear. Half wool; medium light weight; fine ribbed; shaped waist and long sleeves; silk crocheted neck; pearl buttons. Cream white color only. Sizes, 3, 4, 5 and 6, to fit busts 30 to 40 inches. Price, each.........45c

Short Sleeve Vests.

No. 16R5351 Ladies' Short Sleeve Vest of the same kind and quality as the above, with short wing sleeves. Cream white only. Sizes, 3, 4, 5 and 6, to fit busts 30 to 40
Price, each...................45c
If by mail, postage extra, each, 8 cents.

Ankle Length Drawers.

No. 16R5352 Ladies' Fine Drawers to match above vest. Ankle length. Sizes, 3, 4, 5 and 6. (Order drawers same size as vest required.)
Price, per pair..........................45c
If by mail, postage extra, each, 7 cents.

Ladies' Ribbed Worsted Summer Underwear.
Suitable for All-Year Wear.

No. 16R5358 Ladies' Fine Cream White Worsted Ribbed Undervest, made with shaped waist, crocheted neck, with silk tape inserted. Pearl buttons. This is a medium weight ribbed vest, suitable for all year around wear, and preferred by many women to the heavier or extreme light weight. **A strictly first class high grade garment, with long sleeves.** Sizes, 3, 4, 5 and 6, suitable for busts 30 to 40 inches.
Price, each..................88c
No. 16R5359 Ladies' Fine Ribbed Cream White Worsted Drawers to match above undervests; ankle length. Sizes, 3, 4, 5 and 6. Price, each...........88c
If by mail, postage extra, per garment, 8 cents.

Ladies' Light Weight Worsted Underwear.

No. 16R5366 Ladies' Fine Plain Light Weight Worsted Vests, high neck and long sleeves. The lightest weight worsted underwear knit for ladies' wear, and is positively equal to most goods of this kind selling at retail for $1.50. Natural gray color, soft and very fine; 80 per cent wool. Weight, 4½ to 6 ounces, according to size. Sizes, 28 to 44.
Price, each..............................$1.00
No. 16R5367 Ladies' Fine Light Weight Wool Drawers, ankle length, to match above. Sizes, 28 to 44.
Price, per pair..............................$1.00
If by mail, postage extra, each, 6 cents.

GIRLS' AND MISSES' UNDERWEAR.
Ages, 2 to 14 years. Sizes are by length.

No. 16R5400 Girls' and Misses' Fine Cotton Vest, made Derby ribbed with shaped waist, sleeveless; crochet around neck and arm holes. A perfect fitting misses' or children's vest at a very low price. Sizes are by length. Sizes, 15, 18, 21, 24, 27 and 30 inches. Color, ecru. Be sure to give age or size in ordering.
Price, each......................10c
If by mail, postage extra, 3 cents.

Girls' and Misses' Fine Ribbed White Vests.
Ages, 2 to 14 years.

No. 16R5404 Girls' and Misses' Summer Vests, ribbed; made with short sleeves and crocheted neck. Closed in front with two pearl buttons. Sizes are by length.

Size........	15	18	21	24	27	30
Price, each,	12c	14c	16c	18c	20c	22c

Allow 5 cents extra per garment for postage.

Girls' and Misses' Summer Vests and Pants.
Ages, 2 to 14 years.

No. 16R5410 Children's Long Sleeve Fine Ribbed Summer Weight Cotton Vest, made with long sleeves, crocheted neck and front, two pearl buttons. Made in accurate sizes. **Sizes are by length.** Color, white, only.

Size....................	15	18	21	24	27	30
Price, each............	12c	14c	16c	18c	20c	22c

No. 16R5411 Children's Fine Ribbed Knee Pants. Open at sides; to match above vest. Order the same size pants as vests, as the pants are made in sizes to match those of the vests.

Size........	15	18	21	24	27	30
Price, each.....	12c	14c	16c	18c	20c	22c

Allow 5 cents extra per garment for postage.

Children's Gauze Undervests, Short Sleeves.
Sizes, 16 to 34 bust measure.

No. 16R5416 Children's Gauze Undervests. High neck and short sleeves. **Silk bound neck and front,** and hemmed tail, made from fine cotton, and will prove good wearing underwear. These are most excellent garments, and will give good satisfaction. **Sizes, 16 to 34 inches bust measure. Always give size when ordering.**

Infants' Sizes.

Size....	16	18	20	22
Price....	8c	10c	12c	14c

Boys' or Misses' Sizes.

Size....	24	26	28	30	32	34
Price....	16c	18c	20c	22c	24c	26c

If by mail, postage extra, each, 4 cents.

Children's Gauze Undervests, Long Sleeves.

No. 16R5417 Children's Fine White Gauze Summer Vests or Shirts, same as No. 16R5416, but made high neck and long sleeves.

Infants' Sizes.

Size........	16	18	20	22
Price........	9c	11c	13c	15c

Boys' or Misses' Sizes.

Size........	24	26	28	30	32	34
Price........	17c	19c	21c	23c	25c	27c

If by mail, postage extra, each, 4 cents.

Boys' or Youths' Balbriggan Underwear, 23 Cents.
Sizes, 24 to 34.

No. 16R5420 Boys' Balbriggan Summer Undershirts. Ecru color, well made and trimmed, elastic ribbed cuffs, French collarette neck. Sizes, 24 to 34 inches chest. Price, per dozen, $2.76; each.....23c
No. 16R5421 Boys' Ankle Length Drawers to match above shirts. Sizes, 24 to 34 waist.
Price, per dozen, $2.76; each....................23c
If by mail, postage extra, each, 3 cents.

50c Boys' Balbriggan Underwear, 38c.
Sizes, 22 to 34.

No. 16R5425 Boys' Fine Egyptian Cotton Balbriggan Undershirts, flat knit. This is a superior quality of fine cotton that will be appreciated for its fineness. Made high neck, long sleeves, and retails for 50 cents. Ecru color. Sizes, 22 to 34 breast measure.
Price, each....................38c
No. 16R5426 Boys' Fine Balbriggan Knickerbocker Knee Length Drawers (to wear with knee pants), nicely trimmed to match above shirts. Sizes, 22 to 30 waist. Price, per pair..................38c
No. 16R5427 Boys' Fine Balbriggan Ankle Length or Long Drawers to match above shirts. Sizes, 24 to 34 waist measure. Price, per pair.....38c
If by mail, postage extra, each, 4 cents.

Children's Medium Weight Underwear.

No. 16R5430 Children's Fine White Soft Medium Weight Undershirts. Flat knit, from fine soft white cotton and are usually called "merino." Nicely taped front and ribbed cuffs. Non-shrinkable and **warranted to give good service.** Suitable for nearly any climate or all-year-around wear.

Size......	16	18	20	22	24	26	28	30	32	34
Each.....	12c	15c	18c	21c	24c	27c	30c	33c	36c	39c

No. 16R5431 Children's White Soft Pantalets (open at side) to match above.

Size....	16	18	20	22	24	26	28	30	32	34
Each..	12c	15c	18c	21c	24c	27c	30c	33c	36c	39c

If by mail, postage extra, each, 4 cents.

WINTER UNDERWEAR DEPARTMENT.

It is important that we have the correct sizes when you order underwear. The sizes are stated in each quotation. The safe and sure way is to state both your breast and waist measure and we can then give your order prompt and accurate attention.

MEN'S FORM FITTING UNION SUITS.

SIZES: Give breast measure over vest close up under arms, and your height and weight.

A rational garment for men. Try our Union Suits for ease and comfort and you will wonder why you did not wear them before. Our Men's Union or Combination Suits fit. They are carefully and scientifically proportioned. We offer for your consideration only those suits that will fit, and we warrant them to be satisfactory in every particular.

80 Cents for $1.00 Men's Winter Weight Cotton Union Suits.

No. 16R6000 Men's Silver Gray Heavy Cotton Union Suits. Slightly fleeced on the inside, making them very soft and pleasant to the skin. Button down front. A special value at this low price. Finished neck and pearl buttons. Sizes, 34, 36, 38, 40, 42, 44. State breast, height and weight in your order.
Price, per dozen, $9.60; per suit.........................80c
No. 16R6001 Men's Fine Union Suits, knitted from fine cotton yarn, same quality as the above, but in ecru color. Sizes, breast 34, 36, 38, 40, 42, 44. State height, weight and breast measure in order.
Price, each..............$0.80
Per dozen..................9.60

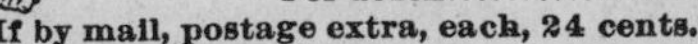

If by mail, postage extra, each, 24 cents.

Men's Heavy Egyptian Cotton Suits, $1.20.

No. 16R6003 Men's Fine Combed Egyptian Cotton Ribbed Union Suit. Many men prefer a fine non-irritating cotton suit to wool. This one will meet the most exacting requirements. Buttons down front and is trimmed with fine pearl buttons sewed on to stay, closely ribbed cuffs. If you want the best cotton suit you will get it under this number. Stitched throughout with special covered seams. Ecru color only. Sizes, 34, 36, 38, 40, 42, 44, breast. State height, weight and breast measure in order.

Price, each............**$ 1.20**
Per dozen............**14.40**

If you fail to give size we cannot fill your order.

If by mail, postage extra, each, 24 cents.

DON'T FAIL TO GIVE SIZE

GENUINE WORSTED SUITS, $2.00.

Sears, Roebuck & Co.'s Special.

No. 16R6006 Men's Fine Genuine Wool Worsted Suit in natural gray color. Our special value at this low price cannot be matched by any other house. We are confident that we have the best value ever offered and equal to suits sold by others for $3.00. They are warm ribbed suits, made from fine wool worsted 65 per cent, and fine cotton knitted between. Steam shrunk and cleaned; non-shrinking, if reasonable care is used in washing, and thoroughly reliable. Regular winter weight. Buttons sewed on to stay, and buttonholes carefully made. If you have not worn the combination or union suit, we recommend them to you. More comfortable than any other underclothing—as comfortable as your skin. Sizes, to fit breast measures 34, 36, 38, 40, 42, 44 inches. **State breast measure, height and weight in your order.**

Price, each............**$ 2.00**
Per half dozen........**12.00**

If by mail, postage extra, each, 24 cents.

Our Leader at $2.50.

No. 16R6009 Men's Fine Natural Gray Ribbed Sanitary Union Suits. Made from Australian lamb's wool. There is a slight mixture of cotton in this yarn which prevents extreme shrinkage and adds much to its wearing properties. **We want your order for this quality.** You could spend $3.50 per suit at retail and get no better. Don't forget height and weight in order. Non-irritating and comfortable. Strictly first class in every particular. Buttons down the front. Sizes, chest, 34, 36, 38, 40, 42, 44 inches. Give height, weight and breast measure in order.

Price, per suit.......... .....**$2.50**

If by mail, postage extra, 24 cents.

Men's Silk and Worsted Union Suit, $3.00.

No. 16R6012 Men's Fine Wool Worsted and Silk Union Suits. We offer this special fine quality at the price your merchant at home pays for them. These suits are full winter weight, about 75 per cent fine worsted yarn and 25 per cent silk, steam shrunk, silk finished buttonholes, pearl buttons, sewed on to stay, close fitting at wrists and ankles. The retail price is from $4.00 to $5.00, and we warrant every suit to give entire satisfaction. **Color, light blue.** Sizes, 34, 36, 38, 40, 42, 44 inches. **State height, weight and breast measure in your order.**

Price, each............**$3.00**

If by mail, postage extra, each, 24 cents.

Men's Special Extra Heavy Union Suit, $3.75.

No. 16R6014 Men's Fine All Pure Wool Worsted Extra Heavy and Durable Union Suit. This suit is made especially for us and is a quality much in demand in the Northern States. The average weight is 1¾ pounds. They are knitted from natural gray all wool worsted yarn of finest quality, fine pearl buttons sewed on to stay and carefully worked silk buttonholes. Not a single detail is overlooked to make this suit perfect. All union suits sold by us are stitched with the Union special sewing machine double covered elastic seam, which is stronger than the garment itself. Our price is as low as possible for this kind of goods, which is the best we can buy. Sizes, 34, 36, 38, 40, 42, 44 inches, breast measure. **State your height, weight and breast measure in your order.**

Price, each........ .....**$3.75**

If by mail, postage extra, each, 30 cents.

Dr. Wright's Health Union Suits, $1.75.

Flat Knit.

No. 16R6016 Dr. Wright's Health Combination or Union Suits, made flat knitted and cut to fit. The outer surface is of cotton and the inside surface of fine Australian wool, fleeced. The wool alone comes in contact with the skin. They are non-shrinking and heavier than the regular style suits. Silk bound and pearl buttons down front. Retail at $2.50. Sizes, 34, 36, 38, 40, 42, 44 inches breast measure. **State height, weight and breast measure in your order.**

Price, each..........**$ 1.75**
Price, one-half dozen **10.50**

If by mail, postage extra, each, 28 cents.

If you fail to give size we cannot fill your order for underwear.

DON'T FAIL TO GIVE SIZE

MEN'S WINTER UNDERWEAR.

IN ORDERING UNDERWEAR remember that regular sizes are as follows: **Shirt sizes, 34, 36, 38, 40, 42 and 44 inches chest measure. Drawers sizes, 30, 32, 34, 36, 38, 40 and 42 inches waist measure. ALWAYS GIVE CHEST AND WAIST MEASUREMENTS. Some of our customers state in their order (for illustration), "two suits, size 38." We do not know if this is waist or breast measure. Always state breast and waist measure, thereby avoiding mistakes and delay. Always include enough for postage when ordering underwear sent by mail.**

38 Cents for 50-Cent Men's Natural Gray Underwear.

No. 16R6030 Men's Heavy Winter Weight Natural Gray Wool Mixed Undershirts, well made and finished. Pearl buttons, ribbed cuffs and tail. Sizes, 34, 36, 38, 40, 42, 44 inches breast measure.

Price, per dozen, **$4.56**; each....................**38c**

No. 16R6031 Men's Heavy Winter Weight Drawers to match above. Sizes, 30, 32, 34, 36, 38, 40, 42 inches waist measure.

Price, per dozen, **$4.56**; per pair....................**38c**

Three full suits of the above underwear, shirts and drawers..**$2.28**

If by mail, postage extra, each, 17 cents.

Men's Camel's Hair Underwear, 38 Cents.

No. 16R6040 Men's Camel's Hair Color Undershirts, merino or part wool. Pearl buttons, ribbed cuffs and tail. Better than most underwear sold for 50 cents. Sizes, 34, 36, 38, 40, 42, 44 inches breast measure.

Price, per dozen, **$4.56**; each.......................**38c**

No. 16R6041 Men's Camel's Hair Drawers to match above shirts. Sizes, 30, 32, 34, 36, 38, 40, 42 inches waist measure.

Price, per dozen, **$4.56**; each.......................**38c**

Three full suits of the above underwear, shirts and drawers..**$2.28**

If by mail, postage extra, 17 cents.

DON'T FAIL TO GIVE SIZE

Men's Double Breasted Undershirts, 42 Cents.

No. 16R6050 Men's Natural Gray Winter Undershirts. Wool mixed, called merino. Double breasted, double back from shoulder down, about 14 inches long. Ribbed cuffs and pearl buttons. Sizes, 34, 36, 38, 40, 42, 44 inches breast measure.

Each........**$0.42**
Per dozen.. **5.04**

No. 16R6051 Men's Natural Gray Merino Drawers to match above. Sizes, 30, 32, 34, 36, 38, 40, 42 inches waist measure.

Each........**$0.38**
Per dozen.. **4.56**

If by mail, postage extra, 18 cents.

ALWAYS GIVE SIZE WHEN YOU ORDER.

Closed Front, Open Shoulder, Double Breasted Undershirts for 45 Cents.

No. 16R6052 Men's Warm Merino Fleeced Cotton Undershirts. Closely knitted, made with patent opening neck which unbuttons on each side of neck, leaving a liberal opening to take on or off. In this manner the double breast and back afford full protection, excluding the cold. Color, natural gray. Sizes, 34, 36, 38, 40, 42, 44 inches breast measure.

Price, each.. **$0.45**
Per dozen..... **5.40**

No. 16R6053 Men's Warm Merino Fleeced Cotton Drawers. Double stitched throughout, trimmed with three pearl buttons. Sizes, 30, 32, 34, 36, 38, 40, 42 inches waist measure.

Price, per dozen, **$4.80**; each..... ....**40c**

If by mail, postage extra, each, 18 cents.

MEN'S FLEECE LINED UNDERWEAR.

No. 16R6060 Men's Heavy Weight Camel's Hair Color Fleece Lined Cotton Undershirts. Handsomely made and trimmed, fine pearl buttons. Finished neck, taped front and double elastic ribbed cuffs. **Best fitting fleece lined garment ever offered at such a low price.** If you want good, cheap underwear do not pass this one. Sizes, 34, 36, 38, 40, 42, 44 inches breast measure.

Price, per dozen, **$4.56**; each....................**38c**

No. 16R6061 Men's Heavy Fleece Lined Drawers to match above. Extra well made throughout. Sizes, 30, 32, 34, 36, 38, 40, 42 inches waist measure.

Price, per dozen, **$4.56**; per pair................**38c**

Three full suits of the above underwear, shirts and drawers...(**Postage extra, each, 18 cents**).....**$2.28**

Heavy Wool Fleece Lined Underwear.

DON'T FAIL TO GIVE SIZE

No. 16R6070 Extra Special Men's Fine Heavy Light Blue Mixed Flat Knitted Undershirts, with heavy all wool fleece lining. The outside surface is of cotton, which prevents shrinkage. The fleecing is all wool. In this way the wool only comes in contact with the skin. We sold more than 3,000 dozen of this quality last season. Silk trimmed front, collarette neck, pearl buttons, and double knit ribbed cuffs. Double stitched and covered seams. We will send a small samples of this underwear upon receipt of 2 cents in stamps. Sizes, 34, 36, 38, 40, 42, 44, 46 inches breast measure.

Price, per dozen, **$5.04**; each..................**$0.42**

No. 16R6071 Men's Drawers to match above. All wool fleece lining. Sizes, 30, 32, 34, 36, 38, 40, 42, 44 inches waist measure.

Price, per dozen, **$5.04**; per pair.............**$0.42**
Two full suits, shirts and drawers............ **1.68**

State breast and waist measure.

If by mail, postage extra, each, 18 cents.

Dr. Wright's Australian Wool Underwear, $1.35.

DONT FAIL TO GIVE SIZE

No. 16R6310 Dr. Wright's Famous Underwear in extra fine quality. Not quite so heavy as No. 16R6300; made with a fine soft Australian wool fleecing, and a fine smooth close knit outer surface, silk taped neck, and pearl buttons and Union special covered seams throughout, and close ribbed cuffs. **This is a superior quality of the Dr. Wright's manufacture,** and usually retails at $2.00 each. We especially recommend this quality to persons with a sensitive skin, and as they are non-shrinking they invariably prove satisfactory. Natural mottled gray color. We will send small sample of this underwear upon receipt of 2 cents in stamps. Sizes, 34, 36, 38, 40, 42, 44 breast measure.

Price, per dozen, **$16.20**; each.............**$1.35**

No. 16R6311 Dr. Wright's Fine Wool Drawers to match shirt No. 16R6310, trimmed with pearl buttons, suspender tapes, close ribbed cuffs and never rip seams throughout. Sizes, 30, 32, 34, 36, 38, 40, 42 waist measure.

Price, per dozen, **$16.20**; each.............**$1.35**
Two full suits of the above underwear 5.40
If by mail, postage extra, each 18 cents.

Dr. Wright's Blue Underwear, Australian Fleeced, $1.40.

No. 16R6320 Dr. Wright's Fine Fleeced Wool Underwear, made in light blue color. A very durable garment with Australian wool fleecing. Trimmed around neck with silk, silk facing, pearl buttons, and close ribbed cuffs. **This is a very beautiful finished garment,** containing all the healthful properties of the garment quoted above, the only difference being this is light blue in color, and slightly heavier. The usual retail price is $2.00, and our price represents about the cost to your local merchant. We will send small sample of this underwear upon receipt of 2 cents in stamps. Sizes, 34, 36, 38, 40, 42, 44 breast measure.

Price, per dozen, **$16.80**; each.............**$1.40**

No. 16R6321 Dr. Wright's Fleece Lined Drawers, to match shirt No. 16R6320, trimmed with pearl buttons, suspender tapes, never rip seams throughout. Sizes, 30, 32, 34, 36, 38, 40, 42 waist measure.

Price, per dozen, **$16.80**; each.............**$1.40**
Two full suits of the above underwear 5.60
If by mail, postage extra, each, 18 cents.

Men's Silk Fleeced Underwear 80c

No. 16R6330 Men's Silk Fleeced Undershirts, made with silk trimmed neck and front, close fitting ribbed cuffs. **This is a special value,** made with silk fleecing that is very soft and non-irritating to the skin. It is durable and at our price will be found a most superior value. Made in light blue color only. Stitched throughout with special covered seams. Sizes, 34, 36, 38, 40, 42, 44 breast measure. Per dozen, **$9.60**; each.............**80c**

No. 16R6331 Men's Silk Fleeced Drawers, never-rip seams throughout to match shirt No. 16R6330. Sizes, 30, 32, 34, 36, 38, 40, 42 waist measure.

Price, per dozen, **$9.60**; each.............**$0.80**
Two full suits of the above underwear......... 3.20
If by mail, postage extra, each, 19 cents.

INCLUDE YOUR UNDERWEAR

WITH OTHER GOODS, AND MAKE A FREIGHT SHIPMENT IF YOU CAN,

AND SAVE EVEN MORE MONEY.

IF YOU FAIL TO GIVE SIZE WE CANNOT FILL YOUR ORDER.

EXTRA HEAVY WINTER UNDERWEAR.

THE UNDERWEAR quoted under this head is intended for rough wear and usage, for men exposed to the weather, and is designed for durability rather than fineness, and we recommend them in particular for the use of lumbermen, farmers, miners, surveyors, prospectors, etc.

SPECIAL NOTICE—Give two measurements, breast and waist.

No. 16R6340 Lumbermen's Heavy, Thick, Natural Gray Wool Undershirts, ribbed, trimmed with silk around neck, and pearl buttons, woolly surface, heavy, thick and warm. For the price this is the best heavy garment that can be offered, but we would recommend the higher grade immediately following as the cheapest in the long run. Weight, about 16 ounces. Sizes, breast measure, 36, 38, 40, 42, 44 inches. Price, per dozen, **$4.68**; each, **39c**

If by mail, postage extra, each, 19 cents.

No. 16R6341 Lumbermen's Heavy Wool Mixed Drawers, to match above shirt. Sizes, waist measure, 32, 34, 36, 38, 40, 42 inches.

Price, per dozen, **$4.68**; each........**39c**
If by mail, postage extra, each, 19 cents.

Our 75-Cent Lumbermen's Underwear.

No. 16R6350 Lumbermen's or Farmers' Extra Heavy Natural Gray Wool Undershirts, heavy, thick, soft surface, silk taped front and pearl buttons. These garments are unexcelled for their warmth and durability, and persons living in a very severe climate or requiring a very warm garment will find this quality invariably satisfactory. Our price represents about the cost to your local merchant. Average weight, 17 ounces. Three-fourths wool. Sizes, breast measure, 36, 38, 40, 42, 44, 46 inches.

Price, per dozen, **$9.00**; each.............**75c**
If by mail, postage extra, each, 20 cents.

No. 16R6351 Farmers' or Lumbermen's Extra Heavy Natural Gray Ribbed Wool Drawers, to match above shirt. Sizes, waist measure, 32, 34, 36, 38, 40, 42, 44 inches.

Price, per dozen, **$9.00**; each.............**75c**
If by mail, postage extra, each, 20 cents.

Lumbermen's Double Breasted Underwear, 90 Cents.

No. 16R6360 Lumbermen's or Farmers' Extra Heavy, Thick, Natural Gray Wool Undershirts, made with double breast and back as shown in the illustration, extra warm and durable. Extra thickness on the chest and back make this underwear particularly desirable in severe climates, affording just that much extra protection to the lungs. Weight, 20 ounces. For lumbermen, farmers, railroad men and others exposed to the severity of the weather. **The same kind as No. 16R6350 but double breasted.** Sizes, breast measure, 36, 38, 40, 42, 44, 46 inches. Price, per dozen, **$10.80**; each........**90c**

If by mail, postage extra, each, 23 cents.

No. 16R6361 Lumbermen's Heavy Wool Drawers to match above shirts. Sizes, waist measure, 32, 34, 36, 38, 40, 42, 44 inches.

Price, per dozen, **$9.00**; each.............**75c**
If by mail, postage extra, each, 20 cents.

MEN'S PLUSH BACK UNDERWEAR.

By plush back we mean underwear that is brushed up soft on the inside, by a machine made especially for this purpose, leaving a plush-like surface.

80 Cents For $1.00 Plush Back Underwear.

No. 16R6370 Men's Heavy Plush Back All Wool Undershirts in light brown or buckskin color, trimmed with pearl buttons, ribbed cuffs and tail. This is a special value we are offering at 80 cents and is seldom retailed at less than $1.00. Sizes, breast measure, 34, 36, 38, 40, 42, 44 inches.

Price, per dozen, **$9.60**; each........**80c**
If by mail, postage extra, each, 20 cents.

No. 16R6371 Men's Heavy Plush Back Drawers, to match above shirts. Made for wear. Sizes, waist measure, 30, 32, 34, 36, 38, 40, 42 inches.

Price, per dozen, **$9.60**; each.............**$0.80**
Two suits of the above underwear......... 3.20

$1.00 for $1.50 Plush Back Underwear.

No. 16R6380 Men's Heavy Plush Back Undershirts of superior quality, trimmed with silk front, pearl buttons and close ribbed cuffs. Is practically non-shrinking, having a single thread of cotton knit into the cloth in such a manner as to reduce shrinkage and increase its durability. An extra soft surface on the inside, extremely warm and we warrant every garment to give satisfaction. Color, mixed golden brown only. We send small samples of this underwear upon receipt of 2 cents in stamps. Sizes, breast measure 34, 36, 38, 40, 42, 44, 46 inches. Average weight, 20 ounces.

Price, per dozen, **$12.00**; each.............**$1.00**

No. 16R6381 Men's Mixed Golden Brown Drawers, to match above shirt, made plush back, pearl buttons, suspender tapes and never rip seams. Sizes, waist measure, 30, 32, 34, 36, 38, 40, 42, 44 inches.

Price, per dozen, **$12.00**; each.............**$1.00**
Two full suits of the above underwear......... 4.00
If by mail, postage extra, each, 23 cents.

$1.30 All Wool Plush Back Underwear.

DONT FAIL TO GIVE SIZE

No. 16R6390 Men's Plush Back Undershirts, made of fine quality lamb's wool, trimmed with silk front and pearl buttons and close fitting ribbed cuffs. Strictly all wool. We especially recommend this quality. Light brown or buckskin color, and **warrant every garment to be perfectly satisfactory.** We will send small sample of this underwear on receipt of 2 cents in stamps. Sizes, breast measure, 36, 38, 40, 42, 44, 46 inches.

Price, per dozen, **$15.60**; each.............**$1.30**
If by mail, postage extra, each, 20 cents.

No. 16R6391 Men's Heavy Plush Back All Wool Drawers, to match above shirts, made with never rip seams and pearl buttons. Sizes, waist measure, 32, 34, 36, 38, 40, 42, 44 inches.

Price, per dozen, **$15.60**; each.............**$1.30**
Two full suits of the above underwear......... 5.20
If by mail, postage extra, each, 20 cents.

LUMBERMEN'S OR FARMERS' UNDERWEAR, $1.00.

Our Special $1.00 Leader, extra heavy, the kind of underwear to wear in the northwest, that will defy the cold and blizzards. Manufactured especially for us and is a special value.

DON'T FAIL TO GIVE SIZE

No. 16R6400 Extra Heavy All Wool Undershirts, with box front as shown in illustration, light fawn color, taped all around neck and front with silk and trimmed with pearl buttons; close fitting ribbed cuffs, excelled in wear and durability only by No. 16R6410, which is the heaviest underwear made. Your local merchant charges you $1.50 for this quality. We especially recommend this grade to men who are exposed or live in extremely severe climates. Made throughout with heavy covered seams that are particularly adapted to the rough wear they are sure to get in the outdoor occupations. Farmers will find this quality especially adapted to their requirements. Average weight, 22 ounces. Sizes, 36, 38, 40, 42, 44, 46 inches breast measure. We will send small sample of this underwear upon receipt of 2 cents in stamps.
Price, per dozen, $12.00; each............$1.00
If by mail, postage extra, 26 cents.

No. 16R6401 Men's Extra Heavy All Wool Drawers, to match above shirts, trimmed with pearl buttons, suspender taped, never rip seams. Sizes, waist measure, 32, 34, 36, 38, 40, 42, 44 inches.
Price, per dozen, $12.00; each............$1.00
Two full suits of the above underwear........ 4.00
If by mail, postage extra, 26 cents.

Alaska Underwear, $1.65.

No. 16R6410 Men's Heavy All Wool Undershirts, made expressly for use in the coldest climates, wind proof and cold proof. Average weight, about 27 ounces. Manufactured expressly for us and is the favorite underwear for the hunter, prospector, surveyor, farmer and miner. Brushed soft on the inside. This is the strongest and most durable underwear made, and is stitched throughout with covered seams, trimmed with silk tape which extends all around the box front and is closed with pearl buttons. Color, dark golden brown. **In this garment is to be found the extreme of warm under garments, and we would recommend them for wear in the coldest climates.** We will send small sample of this underwear upon receipt of 2 cents in stamps. Sizes, breast measure, 36, 38, 40, 42, 44, 46 inches.
Price, per dozen, $19.80; each............$1.65
If by mail, postage extra, 30 cents.

No. 16R6411 Men's Extra Heavy Wool Drawers, plush back, made with the patent covered seams throughout, extra strong and durable. Sizes, waist measure, 32 to 44 inches.
Price, per dozen, $19.80; each............$1.65
Two full suits of the above underwear........ 6.60
If by mail, postage extra, 30 cents.

Our Extra Heavy Lumbermen's Double Breasted Underwear.

DON'T FAIL TO GIVE SIZE

No. 16R6412 Men's Extra Heavy and Thick All Wool Undershirts in a buckskin brown color. Not quite as heavy as the above number, but one of the warmest undergarments made. **Clean, fine all wool, very heavy, double breast and double back. Strong double stitching with Union special sewing machine.** The seam is stronger than cloth itself. Silk binding around neck, ribbed tail and cuffs. Retail value $2.00. We will send small sample of this underwear upon receipt of 2 cents in stamps. Sizes, breast measure, 36, 38, 40, 44, 46 inches.
Price, each............$1.40

No. 16R6413 Men's Heavy All Wool Drawers to match above shirts, made extra strong with double seams, three pearl buttons in front. Sizes, waist, 32, 34, 36, 38, 40, 42, 44.
Price, each............$1.25
If by mail, postage extra, each, 22 cents.

If you forget to give size we cannot fill your order.

Men's Canton Flannel Drawers.

No. 16R6420 Men's Bleached White Canton Flannel Drawers (no shirts), well made throughout, full size in seat, elastic cuffs at ankle. Sizes, 32, 34, 36, 38, 40, 42 inches.
Price, per dozen, $5.40; per pair............45c
Shipping weight, per pair, 15 ounces.

Perforated Buckskin Chamois Underwear for Men and Women.

A superior wind and cold proof garment, made of selected skins, dressed expressly for underwear. Being perforated they give sufficient ventilation to the body which the rules of health require. A secure protection against sudden changes in temperature, and is recommended by leading physicians as an excellent cure and preventive of rheumatism.

For shirt and vest, measure around chest, close up under arms. For drawer measurements give waist and inseam. **Always wear over other underwear.** Should never be worn next to the skin.

Extra Sizes—50 cents extra will be required for each 2 inches larger than sizes quoted below.

No. 16R6422 Men's Perforated Buckskin Undershirts, made of the best quality only. Sizes, 32 to 42. Price, each............$6.00

No. 16R6423 Men's Perforated Buckskin Drawers to match. Sizes, 28 to 40 waist............$6.00

No. 16R6424 Ladies' Perforated Buckskin Undershirts, long sleeves. Sizes, 28 to 40 bust. Price, each...$6.00
Without sleeves............5.00

No. 16R6425 Ladies' Perforated Buckskin Drawers, inseam, 18 to 20 inches; waist, 22 to 36. Price, each.$5.00

No. 16R6426 Men's Perforated Buckskin Vest, buttons close to neck. Weight, 5 ounces. Sizes, 32 to 42 chest. Price, each.....$4.00

LADIES' COMBINATION OR UNION SUITS.

THE GREATLY INCREASED DEMAND for this style of garment is due to its warmth and neatness. Particularly comfortable at the waist, because it allows perfect fitting of the outer garments. Ladies' Union Suits are made to fit busts 32 to 40 inches, except where quoted larger. Always include height and weight in order.

FLEECING: By this we mean that the garment has a soft surface brushed up on the inside, making it soft and non-irritating.

Ladies' Oneita Union Suits, 40 Cents.

No. 16R6430 Ladies' Oneita Style Jersey Ribbed Union Suits, made to button across the bust, made of fine Egyptian cotton and fleeced on the inside. Elastic ribbed cuffs and anklets. Ecru color. Bust, 32 to 40.
Price, each............$0.40
Price, per dozen............4.80

Ladies' Oneita Union Suits, Silver Gray, 40 Cents.

No. 16R6435 Ladies' Oneita Style Cotton Union Suits, made to button across the bust as illustrated, slightly fleeced on the inside. Ribbed cuffs and anklets. Silver gray color. Sizes to fit busts 32 to 40 inches. Price, per dozen, $4.80; each......40c
If by mail, postage extra, 18 cents.

Ladies' Cotton Union Suit, 75 Cents.

No. 16R6437 Ladies' Oneita Style Ribbed Union Suits, made from fine combed Egyptian cotton, ecru color. **A fine, soft cotton suit, perfect fitting,** slightly fleeced on the inside, making a soft, agreeable garment to the skin. Regular winter weight. Sizes to fit busts, 32 to 40. **State height and bust measure in order.** Price, each............$0.75
Per dozen............9.00
If by mail, postage extra, each, 19 cents.

Our S., R. & Co.'s Special Value for 80 Cents.

No. 16R6450 For 80 cents we furnish Ladies' Fine Half Wool Union Suits. Fine Jersey ribbed, full winter weight. Closely ribbed cuffs and anklets, silk trimmed front and soft fleecing on the inside, nonshrinking and thoroughly dependable. Special style front, as shown in the illustration. Elastic, perfect fitting, and easy to put on and off. You cannot buy this quality at retail for less than $1.00, and many dealers ask $1.25 for suits no better. This suit is full size and perfect fitting and we warrant every suit to give entire satisfaction. Light silver gray color. Sizes to fit busts 32 to 40. **State height, and bust measure in your order.** Price, each............$0.80
Per one-half dozen............4.80
If by mail, postage extra, each, 20 cents.

DON'T FAIL TO GIVE SIZE

Our Special Worsted Suit for $1.50.

No. 16R6460 Ladies' Button across the bust style Union Suit, as shown in the illustration; made of three-fourths fine wool worsted yarn, full winter weight. Made with high cut front giving full protection to lungs and neck. Silk trimmed, pearl buttons, close fitting cuffs and anklets. A quality never retailed for less than $2.00 and when you pay our price you are asked only the amount your merchants pay for them. Our suits are always accurately proportioned and sized and we warrant them to fit. Colors, natural gray, white and black. Busts, 32 to 40. **State height, bust measure and color in your order.**
Price, each............$1.50
If by mail, postage extra, each, 20 cents.

DON'T FAIL TO GIVE SIZE

Ladies' Fine Suits, $2.50.

Our Special Quality.

No. 16R6462 Ladies' Fine Union Suits, made from all fine Australian wool yarn. A soft, smooth yarn, that would scarcely irritate the most sensitive skin. The suits are treated with the special process of steam shrinking and cleaning, and are entirely odorless. With proper care in washing, these suits should not shrink enough to be uncomfortable before they are worn out. They are strictly high grade, finished with silk and pearl buttons. We would like your order for two of these suits, as we are sure you will be more than pleased with the quality and fit. Regular winter weight. Colors, natural gray, white and black. Sizes to fit busts 32 to 40. **State height, bust measure and color in your order.**
Price, each............$2.50
Per one-half dozen............15.00
If by mail, postage extra, each, 20 cents.

ALWAYS GIVE BUST MEASURE, HEIGHT AND WEIGHT, WHEN YOU SEND YOUR ORDER FOR LADIES' UNION SUITS.

Ladies' Drop Seat Cotton Union Suit.

No. 16R6465 Ladies' Very Heavy Egyptian Cotton Union Suits, ecru color, with soft fleece lining. Made with drop seat, same as children's. Buttons down front. It will be observed tha the seat buttons below the line of the corset. In this manner a comfortable and practical drop seat suit is made, and is preferred to the other styles by many. Sizes to fit busts 34 to 40. State height and bust measure in order.

Price, each...............$0.70
Per dozen 8.40
If by mail, postage extra, each, 21 cents.

DON'T FAIL TO GIVE SIZE

Ladies' Fine Cotton Union Suit, 85 Cents.

Busts, 32 to 40.

No. 16R6467 Ladies' Princess Style Union Suits; open down front; a practical suit easy to get into and out of. Made from fine combed genuine Egyptian cotton, ecru color that will always remain soft and smooth, silk trimmed neck and front. Pearl buttons. A suit that is not excelled by any of our better qualities for fit and careful manufacture. Regular winter weight. Sizes, 32 to 40 bust measure. State height and measure in your order.

Price, each.............$0.85
Six for.................. 5.10
If by mail, postage extra, each, 20 cents.

OUR SPECIAL VALUES.

Ladies' Fine Wool Union Suits, Open Down Front, $1.50.

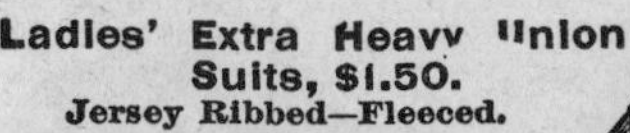

No. 16R6470 Ladies' Princess Jersey Ribbed Union Suits. Opened down the front, fancy silk crocheted neck and front. **Regular winter weight and guaranteed to give entire satisfaction.** They contain enough cotton to keep from shrinking and will wear longer and better than all wool, and are fully as warm. We recommend this suit. Last season we sold an enormous quantity and they proved to be one of the most satisfactory. Colors, **black, white, or natural gray.** Be sure to give height, weight and bust measure in your order. Bust sizes, 32 to 40. State bust and height in order.

Price, each...............$1.50
Per half dozen............ 9.00
If by mail, postage extra, each, 23 cents.

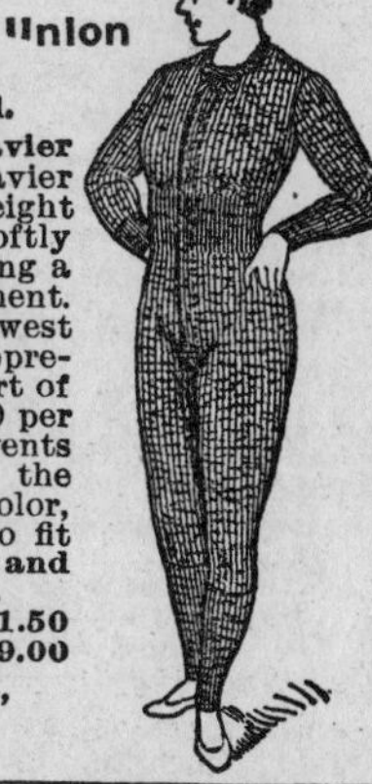

Ladies' Extra Heavy Union Suits, $1.50.

Jersey Ribbed—Fleeced.

No. 16R6471 Ladies' Heavier Wool Union Suits. Knit heavier than the regular standard weight from fine, clean wool, softly fleeced on the inside, making a plump warm winter garment. Women living in the Northwest and coldest sections will appreciate the warmth and comfort of this suit. Contains about 10 per cent of cotton which prevents shrinkage and adds to the strength and durability. Color, natural gray only. Sizes to fit busts 32 to 40. **State height and bust measure in your order.**

Price, each...............$1.50
Per half dozen............ 9.00
If by mail, postage extra, each, 24 cents.

IF YOU WILL REFER TO PAGES 7 TO 10,

you will find full information about freight and express, and will not then need to take the time and trouble to write us.

Sears, Roebuck & Co.'s Special All Worsted Suit, $2.00.

No. 16R6475 Extra Princess Style Union Suits. Buttoned down front; made from fine, clean all worsted yarn; perfect fitting and dependable; fancy crocheted neck and front; shaped waist; extra finely made and finished. Colors, **black, white, and light shade of sanitary gray;** state color in your order. Regular retail price of this suit is $2.75 or $3.00 and we believe that in offering it to our customers at this wholesale price on our small profit plan they are getting the greatest underwear bargain in the country. Be sure to give height, color and bust measure in order. Bust sizes, 32 to 40 inches.

Price, per suit.........$ 2.00
Six suits for........... 12.00
If by mail, postage extra, each, 23 cents.

DON'T FAIL TO GIVE SIZE

Ladies' Australian Worsted Suits, $2.50.

No. 16R6480 Ladies' Princess Style Jersey Ribbed Union Suits, made from select Australian yarns; not too heavy, but the regular winter weight. Union suits are warmer for their weight than old style underwear, as they fit directly against the body, retaining the warmth. Trimmed with crocheted neck and front; shaped waist, and a superior finish throughout. Stitched throughout with the new elastic seam—stronger than the garment itself. Will not irritate the most sensitive skin. Colors, **black or white or blue gray.** Give color, height and bust measure in order. Sizes, bust 32 to 40.

Price, each...............$ 2.50
Six suits for............ 15.00
If by mail, postage extra, each, 23 cents.

DON'T FAIL TO GIVE SIZE

Dr. Wright's Health Union Suits, $1.75.

No. 16R6483 Dr. Wright's Fine Health Union Suits for women. Flat knitted. These suits are made non-shrinking, as the outer surface is of cotton and the inside of fine Australian wool, softly fleeced. The wool only comes in contact with the body. They are heavier and warmer than the usual style form fitting ribbed suits. Ladies who desire extra warm underwear will find these suits cold excluding and very warm. Color, natural gray. Sizes to fit busts 32, 34, 36, 38, 40, 42, 44.

Price, each..........$1.75
If by mail, postage extra, each, 25 cents.

DON'T FAIL TO GIVE SIZE

LADIES' EXTRA SIZE UNION SUITS.

No. 16R6485 Ladies' Extra Size Union Suits, made in natural gray or ecru color; Egyptian cotton, fleece lined, buttoned across bust. Bust sizes, 42, 44, 46. Price, three suits for **$1.95**; each............65c

No. 16R6490 Ladies' Extra Size Natural Gray Wool Union Suits, button across bust; 65 per cent pure wool. A very servicable, warm garment, fleece lined. Bust, 42, 44, 46.

Price, three suits for **$3.00**; each...........**$1.00**

YOU CAN SAVE MONEY

WHEN YOU ORDER SMALL GOODS SHIPPED BY EXPRESS.

YOU CAN SAVE nearly three-fourths of the money you would pay out for express charges, if you anticipate your wants and make up a hundred pound freight shipment of Clothing, Underwear, Household Goods, Hardware, or other goods.

WOMEN'S WINTER UNDERWEAR.

NEVER BEFORE have we been so thoroughly satisfied as we are now with our stock of underwear. We can more surely than ever guarantee entire satisfaction to you.

Compare our prices on the goods with any others.

We will leave it to you if they are not beyond competition.

We would advise careful consideration of our better grades in particular, for they are the cheapest in the end.

Ladies' Ribbed Cotton Underwear, 20 Cents.

DON'T FAIL TO GIVE SIZE

No. 16R6600 Ladies' Fine Jersey Ribbed Cotton Vests, fleece lined, bleached or ecru colors, fancy trimmed neck. Sizes, 3, 4 and 5. Busts, 32 to 40 inches.

Price, each.....$0.20
Per dozen...... 2.40

No. 16R6601 Ladies' Jersey Ribbed Cotton Drawers, ecru color to match above vests. Sizes, 3, 4 and 5.

Price, each.....$0.20
Per dozen...... 2.40
If by mail, postage extra, each, 12 cents.

Ladies' Ribbed Underwear, Silver Gray, 20 Cents.

No. 16R6604 Ladies' Jersey Ribbed Vests, silver gray color, same quality as above. Sizes, 3, 4 and 5. Busts, 32 to 40 inches.

Price, per dozen, **$2.40**; each....................20c

No. 16R6605 Ladies' Jersey Ribbed Drawers, to match above vests. Sizes, 3, 4 and 5.

Price, per dozen, **$2.40**; each....................20c
If by mail, postage extra, each, 12 cents.

Fine Cotton Ribbed Underwear, 30 Cents.

No. 16R6610 Ladies' Fine Jersey Ribbed Egyptian Cotton Vests, slightly heavier than the above, and finer quality. Sizes, 3, 4, 5; busts, 32 to 40. Ecru or bleached colors only.

Price, each.....$0.30
Per dozen...... 3.60

No. 16R6611 Ladies' Fine Ribbed Drawers, to match shirt above. Sizes, 3, 4, 5.

Price, each....$0.30
Per dozen...... 3.60
If by mail, postage extra, each, 13 cents.

Ladies' Fine Combed Egyptian Underwear, 40 Cents.

No. 16R6620 Ladies' Fine Combed Egyptian Cotton Ribbed Vests, ecru or bleached color. Silk crocheted neck and front. A very fine vest, heavy winter weight, soft fleecing on the inside, close ribbed cuffs. Sizes, 3, 4, 5; busts 32 to 40.

Price, per dozen, **$4.80**; each.....................40c

No. 16R6621 Ladies' Fine Combed Egyptian Cotton Drawers, to match above vests. Sizes, 3, 4, 5.

Price, per dozen, **$4.80**; each.....................40c
If by mail, postage extra, each, 15 cents.

Ladies' Seal Lined Fleeced Underwear, 41 Cents.

No. 16R6622 Ladies' Heavy Ribbed Vest, with thick, soft, seal like fleecing on the inside. This is a new kind of fleecing, much thicker and softer than in garments sold heretofore, as they are fleeced by new machines. Heaviest ribbed fleeced undervests made. Silk trimmed neck and pearl buttons. Ecru color only. Sizes, 3, 4, 5 and 6; for busts 32 to 40.

Price, each.................................$0.41
Per half dozen.............................. 2.46

No. 16R6623 Ladies' Heavy Ribbed Drawers, to match above vests, seal lined. Sizes, 3, 4, 5 and 6.

Price, each $0.41
Per half dozen.............................. 2.46
If by mail, postage extra, each, 15 cents.

Nursing Vests, 41 Cents.

Busts, 32, 34, 36, 38, 40.

No. 16R6624 Nursing Vests, made from fine Egyptian cotton, white only. These are fine ribbed vests, silk trimmed neck and front; made with open pockets, as illustrated. A very fine quality cotton yarn is used in this vest. No drawers to match. Sizes, 3, 4, 5 and 6.

Price, each $0.41
Per half dozen 2.46
If by mail, postage extra, each, 13 cents.

Fine White Australian Wool Underwear, $1.00.

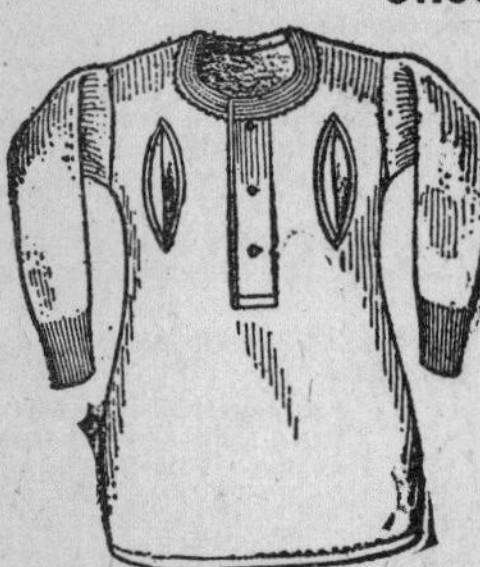

No. 16R6810 Ladies' Fine White Flat Knit Australian Lamb's Wool Undervests, made of 50 per cent pure Australian lamb's wool and fine imported wool; frequently sold for pure Australian. For 40 years the manufacturers of this quality have made goods of this and finer grades, and are excelled by none in skill and workmanship. Strictly high grade. Average weight, 12 ounces. Sizes, 30 to 44 bust.

Price, per dozen, **$12.00**; each **$1.00**

No. 16R6811 Ladies' Fine White Australian Wool Drawers, to match above vests. Sizes, 30 to 44.

Price, per dozen, **$12.00**; each **$1.00**

For two full suits of the above underwear.... **4.00**

Ladies' Scarlet Underwear.

For complete Suits order Vests and Pants the same size.

No. 16R6820 Ladies' Fine All Wool Scarlet Flat Knit Undervests. An excellent value fine all wool garment with silk taped front and neck, pearl buttons. Retail price, $1.00. Average weight, 12 ounces. Sizes, 30 to 44 bust.

Price, each..... **$0.75**
Per dozen...... **9.00**

No. 16R6821 Ladies' Fine All Wool Scarlet Drawers, to match above vests.

Price, each **$0.75**
Per dozen...... **9.00**

Two full suits of the above underwear........ **$3.00**

If by mail, postage extra, each, 15 cents.

Australian Wool Scarlet Underwear.

No. 16R6824 Ladies' Fine Australian Wool Scarlet Undervests. This is one of our especially strong values; a quality that frequently retails at $1.50. Made of three-quarters fine Australian wool and one quarter fine domestic, usually sold for pure Australian. We recommend this quality in particular for its firmness and warmth. Ribbed tail and cuffs, silk trimmed neck and pockets. Sizes, 38 to 44.

Price, each **$1.00**

No. 16R6825 Ladies' Fine Scarlet Drawers to match above vests. Sizes, 28 to 44. Order same size drawers as you wear in vests. Price, each..... **$1.00**

Two full suits of the above underwear....... **4.00**

If b mail, postage extra, each, 15 cents.

LADIES' FLEECE LINED WINTER UNDERWEAR.

By fleece lined we mean that the inside is especially knit and fleeced by a machine made for the purpose, which makes a soft, smooth, non-irritating surface. Sizes, 30 to 44 bust measure. The drawers sizes correspond to vest sizes, viz.: size 36 drawers matches 36 vest. **Always give size.**

Ladies' Cotton Fleeced Underwear, 40 Cents.

No. 16R6830 Ladies' Fine Cotton Fleeced Flat Knit Undervests, natural gray color. Thick and warm. Sizes, 30 to 44 bust.

Price, each..... **$0.40**
Per dozen....... **4.80**

No. 16R6831 Ladies' Fine Cotton Fleeced Drawers to match above vests. Sizes, 30 to 44.

Price, each..... **$0.40**
Per dozen....... **4.80**

Dr. Wright's Fleeced Underwear, 85 Cents.

Every garment branded with "Dr. Wright's Health Underwear."

No. 16R6840 Ladies' Fine Natural Gray Underwear, made by the famous "Dr. Wright Mills"; fine, soft, wool fleecing, and bound all around with silk tape. Not extremely heavy, but thick and very warm. A special leader in value. A small sample of this underwear will be sent upon receipt of 2 cents in stamps. Sizes, 30 to 44 bust.

Price, per dozen, **$10.20**; each **85c**

No. 16R6841 Ladies' Fine Natural Gray Drawers, to match above vests. Sizes, 30 to 44.

Price, per dozen, **$10.20**; each **$0.85**

Two full suits of the above underwear **3.40**

If by mail, postage extra, each 15 cents.

Dr. Wright's Australian Wool Fleeced Underwear, $1.25.

No. 16R6850 Dr. Wright's Ladies' Fine Undervests, soft, natural gray color, with fine Australian lamb's wool fleecing. One of the finest fleeced under garments made for ladies. One of the great advantages in Dr. Wright's underwear is that they will not shrink, and therefore always give lasting service. You might spend $2.00 at home for a garment no finer. A small sample of this underwear will be sent upon receipt of 2 cents in stamps. Every one has the Dr. Wright trademark. F. Wright's Union Suits, see No. 16R6483. Sizes, 30 to 44. Average weight, 11 ounces.

Price, per dozen, **$15.00**; each **$1.25**

No. 16R6851 Ladies' Fine Drawers to match above vests. Sizes, 30 to 44.

Price, per dozen, **$15.00**; each **$1.25**

Two full suits of the above underwear........ **5.00**

If by mail, postage extra, each, 13 cents.

Ladies' Extra Size Underwear.

For large women; bust measures, 42 to 48.

No. 16R6860 Ladies' Bleached Cotton, Fleeced Jersey Ribbed Undervests, winter weight. Sizes, 42 to 46 bust. Sizes, 6, 7, 8.

Price, per dozen, **$3.00**; each.................. **25c**

No. 16R6861 Ladies' Bleached Drawers, to match above vests. Sizes, 6, 7, 8.

Price, per dozen, **$3.00**; each **25c**

If by mail, postage extra, each, 15 cents.

Extra Size Egyptian Cotton Vests, 42 Cents.

No. 16R6870 Ladies' Fine Bleached Egyptian Cotton Vests, heavy weight, Jersey ribbed, fine soft fleecing on the inside; silk trimmed neck and front. Sizes, 7, 8, 9. 42 to 48-inch bust.

Price, each..... **$0.42**
Per dozen.... .. **5.04**

No. 16R6871 Ladies' Fine Bleached Egyptian Cotton Drawers, to match above vests. Sizes, 7, 8, 9.

Price, each..... **$0.42**
Per dozen....... **5.04**

If by mail, postage extra, each, 16 cents.

Ladies' Winter Tights.

No. 16R6880 Ladies' Fine Ribbed Egyptian Cotton Tights. Ecru color, ankle length, open seat and draw string tape at waist. Size, 3, 4 and 5, which will fit women who wear vests of same size.

Price, per doz., **$5.04**; each...**42c**

Ladies' Black Tights, 42 Cents.

No. 16R6832 Ladies' Black Cotton Ribbed Tights. Made from fine Egyptian cotton, ankle length, closed seat and draw string tape at waist. Sizes, 3, 4 and 5. Will fit women who wear vests of same size.

Price, each.................. **$0.42**
Per dozen **5.04**

If by mail, postage extra, each, 15 cents.

Ladies' Half Wool Tights.

No. 16R6884 Ladies' Fine Half-Wool Jersey Ribbed Tights. Made with specially ribbed waist and draw tape and closed ribbed ankles. **This is a superior garment and the usual retail price is $1.00.** Colors, natural gray or black. Sizes, 3, 4 and 5.

Price, per dozen, **$8.40**; each **70c**

If by mail, postage extra, each, 10 cents.

Extra Quality All Worsted Ladies' Tights.

No. 16R6886 Extra Quality All Worsted Fine Jersey Ribbed Ladies' Tights. Made with fine close ribbed elastic waist and draw tape, close ribbed anklets, double elastic seams throughout. **This article seldom retails for less than $2.00.** Made fast black only. Sizes, 3, 4, 5 and 6.

Price, each................................ **$1.50**

If by mail, postage extra, 16 cents.

Ladies' Full Fashioned Tights, $2.00.

No. 16R6888 Ladies' Fine Black Tights, knit from all pure Australian worsted yarn, full fashioned throughout, made on hand machines, good weight. As all seams are knitted together they are seamless. These are the best and retail from $2.50 to $3.00 per pair. Closely knitted waist. Sizes, 3, 4, 5, 6. Will fit ladies wearing same sizes in vests.

Price, each **$2.00**

If by mail, postage extra, each, 18 cents.

IF YOU FORGET

TO GIVE SIZES WANTED,

WE CANNOT FILL YOUR ORDER.

INFANTS' AND CHILDREN'S UNDERVESTS

TABLE OF SIZES FOR INFANTS' SHIRTS.

Size 1, length, 10 inches, suitable for...1 to 3 months
Size 2, length, 12 inches, suitable for...3 to 6 months
Size 3, length, 14 inches, suitable for...6 to 9 months
Size 4, length, 16 inches, suitable for...9 to 12 months
Size 5, length, 17 inches, suitable for...1 to 2 years
Size 6, length, 18 inches, suitable for...2 to 3 years

The Ruben's Infant Shirt.

THE RUBEN'S SHIRT

Is simplicity itself. Is made without any buttons whatever, and is so constructed that DOUBLE PROTECTION is given to the vital parts, the chest, lungs and abdomen. This is by all odds the most sensible and practical infants' shirt ever made. The highest medical authorities pronounce it healthful and as being particularly desirable for infants. **If by mail, postage extra, each, 3 cents.**

No. 16R7000 The Ruben's Infant Shirt. Fine Saxony 66⅔ per cent fine wool with finished neck and double stitched edges. The straps fasten at back with small safety pin, and can be adjusted in an instant. **Fine Jersey ribbed and very soft.**

Length, inches	10	12	14	16	17	18	19
Size	1	2	3	4	5	6	7
Price, each	25c	28c	31c	33c	37c	41c	45c

No. 16R7005 The Ruben's Shirt. Same as above, but made of all pure, soft cream white Saxony wool. Fine Derby ribbed.

Length, inches	10	12	14	16	17	18	19
Size	1	2	3	4	5	6	7
Price, each	32c	35c	38c	42c	45c	47c	50c

Ruben's Shirts at 45 Cents to 66 Cents.

No. 16R7010 The Ruben's Infants' Shirt. Made from finest and softest all wool cream white worsted yarn, fine Derby ribbed with fancy silk braid trimming all around, collarette neck, silk stitching all around straps, skirt, sleeves, cuffs, and over all edges.

Length, inches	10	12	14	16	17	18	19
Size	1	2	3	4	5	6	7
Price, each	45c	48c	50c	53c	56c	60c	66c

Ruben's Silk and Wool Vests.

No. 16R7011 Ruben's Fine Vests for Infants made of finest wool worsted yarn and one-fourth silk. A soft, non-irritating vest, silk trimmed neck, straps, skirt, sleeves and over all edges.

Length, in.	10	12	14	16	17	18	19
Size	1	2	3	4	5	6	7
Price	75c	85c	95c	$1.05	$1.15	$1.20	$1.25

Ruben's All Pure Silk Vests.

No. 16R7012 Ruben's Fine All Pure Spun Silk Vests. This is the finest quality that can be made and every detail is given most careful attention. Knitted from pure silk medium heavy weight.

Length, inches	10	12	14	16	17	18	19
Size	1	2	3	4	5	6	7
Price, each	$1.20	$1.35	$1.50	$1.65	$1.75	$1.85	$1.95

If by mail, postage extra, each, 5 cents.

Infants' Cotton Vests.

No. 16R7015 Infants' Fine Cotton Vests or Wrappers, open down the front, light weight, nicely trimmed. Color, white.

Length, inches	10	11	12	13	14
Sizes	1	2	3	4	5
Price, each	11c	12c	13c	14c	15c

No. 16R7020 Infants' Heavy Cotton Vests or Wrappers, full winter weight, soft fleecing on the inside; open down front. Color, cream white.

Length, inches	10	11	12	13	14
Sizes	1	2	3	4	5
Price, each	13c	14c	15c	16c	17c

Infants' Wool Vests.

If by mail, postage extra, each, 3 cents.

No. 16R7025 Infants' Fine Derby Ribbed Cream White Merino Vests, (wool and cotton mixed), buttoned all the way down front with overcast stitching on neck, cuffs and tail. **Soft and comfortable and non-shrinkable.**

Length, inches	10	12	14	16	17
Sizes	1	2	3	4	5
Price, each	20c	22c	24c	27c	29c

No. 16R7035 Infants' Fine Derby Ribbed Cream White Saxony Wool Knit Vests. Button all the way down the front. Very easily put on and taken off. Neck, front and tail all overcast with silk cross-stitch embroidery. Same style as cut of wool vests above.

Length, in.	10	12	14	16	17
Sizes	1	2	3	4	5
Price, each	23c	25c	27c	30c	34c

Infants' Extra Fine Jersey Ribbed Vests.

No. 16R7040 Infants' Extra Fine Quality Jersey Ribbed Cream White Lamb's Wool Vests. Button all the way down the front. Fine white pearl buttons and silk trimming down the front, 90 per cent purest lamb's wool.

Length, inches	10	12	14	16	17
Sizes	1	2	3	4	5
Price, each	33c	36c	40c	45c	50c

Infants' Fine Ribbed Bands.

No. 16R7055 Infants' Fine Jersey Ribbed Cashmere Wool Bands, with shoulder straps silk crocheted. Will fit perfectly and remain in place without the use of pins. This is accomplished by extra fine rib at bottom of garment. 90 per cent pure lamb's wool and very soft.

Length, inches	8	9	10	11	12
Price, each	25c	28c	31c	33c	36c

If by mail, postage extra, each, 3 cents.

Child's Ribbed Seamless Waist and Shirt Combined.

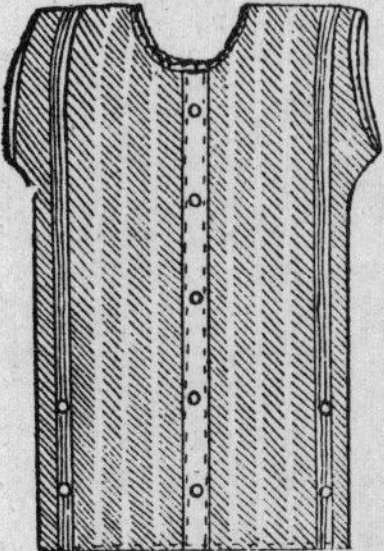

No. 16R7060 This is a Combination Waist and Shirt Combined, for boys and girls, and can be worn either with or without regular undershirt. **It is made of fine Jersey ribbed cotton,** ecru or dark cream color. Made with taped stays running all the way down front and back and over the shoulders and has two rows of waist buttons for fastening on the underclothes. **Strong and durable.** For children from 2 to 12 years of age. Give age of child when ordering.

Price, per dozen, **$1.44**; each 12c

If by mail, postage extra, each, 4 cents.

Dr. Denton's Health Sleeping Garments.

The Genuine Dr. Denton Hygienic Sleeping Garments secure protection from exposure to colds.

FOR CHILDREN—Almost every parent will readily appreciate the value of these garments for their children. They afford such warmth and protection that it makes no difference whether the children kick out of the bed clothing or not. One-half of the ills of children are induced by exposure due to kicking out of the covering at night.

FABRIC—Made of knit merino natural gray cloth, easily washed and will not shrink.

Children's Sleeping Garments.

No. 16R7070 Dr. Denton's Sleeping Garment for Children, with cuffs to roll down over hand and draw cord. Drop seat, moccasin feet, pearl buttons and open down back; made of natural gray knit merino cloth.

Ages	2	3	4	5	6	7	8	9	10
Length, in.	28	30	32	34	36	38	40	42	44
Price, ea.	45c	50c	55c	60c	65c	70c	75c	80c	85c

If by mail, postage extra, each, 15 cents.

CHILDREN'S WINTER UNDERWEAR.

If by mail, postage extra, per suit, 16 cents.

Table of Sizes for Children's and Misses' Undershirts.

Size 16 is suitable for infants under......8 months old
Size 18 is suitable for child..................1 year old
Size 20 is suitable for child..............2 to 3 years old
Size 22 is suitable for child..............4 to 5 years old
Size 24 is suitable for child..............6 to 7 years old
Size 26 is suitable for child..............8 to 9 years old
Size 28 is suitable for child............10 to 11 years old
Size 30 is suitable for child............12 to 13 years old
Size 32 is suitable for child............14 to 15 years old
Size 34 is suitable for child..................16 years old

Children usually require the same size in Vest and Pants.

Children's Ribbed Vests and Pants.

No. 16R7200 Children's Heavy Winter Weight Camel's Hair Color Undervests, with very soft fleece lining, collarette neck and pearl buttons. **Fine Jersey ribbed and perfect fitting. The greatest value ever offered in children's underwear.**

Sizes	16	18	20	22	24
Each	8c	11c	14c	17c	20c
Sizes	26	28	30	32	34
Each	23c	26c	29c	32c	35c

No. 16R7201 Children's Pantalets to match. Open sides.

Sizes	16	18	20	22	24
Each	8c	11c	14c	17c	20c
Sizes	26	28	30	32	34
Each	23c	26c	29c	32c	35c

Children's Ecru Vests and Pants.

No. 16R7210 Children's Winter Weight Jersey Ribbed Undershirts, with soft fleeced lining, same as No. 16R7200, but ecru or bleached color.

Sizes	16	18	20	22	24	26	28	30	32	34
Each	8c	11c	14c	17c	20c	23c	26c	29c	32c	35c

No. 16R7211 Children's Ecru Pantalets. Open sides.

Sizes	16	18	20	22	24	26	28	30	32	34
Each	8c	11c	14c	17c	20c	23c	26c	29c	32c	35c

Children's Merino Vests and Pants.

No. 16R7220 Children's Fine Natural Gray Random Wool Mixed Undershirts. Silk taped front and neck, fine white pearl buttons and elastic ribbed cuffs. **Heavy, soft and warm. Thoroughly well made and will give the best of satisfaction.**

Sizes	16	18	20	22	24
Each	8c	12c	16c	20c	26c
Sizes	26	28	30	32	34
Each	32c	40c	47c	55c	60c

No. 16R7221 Children's Fine Natural Gray Wool Mixed Pantalets, to match above vests. Open sides.

Sizes	16	18	20	22	24
Each	8c	12c	16c	20c	26c
Sizes	26	28	30	32	34
Each	32c	40c	47c	55c	60c

Children's Fleece Lined Vests and Pants.

No. 16R7230 Children's Heavy Flat Fleece Lined Undershirts, all cotton, natural gray, heavy and warm. Special value at our low price.

Sizes	16	18	20	22	24
Each	12c	15c	18c	20c	23c
Sizes	26	28	30	32	34
Each	27c	30c	33c	36c	39c

No. 16R7231 Children's Pantalets, open sides to match.

Sizes	16	18	20	22	24
Each	12c	15c	18c	20c	23c
Sizes	26	28	30	32	34
Each	27c	30c	33c	36c	39c

Children's Finest Australian Wool Underwear.

No. 16R7240 Children's Extra High Grade Pure Australian Lamb's Wool Underwear. The pick of the flock. **Nothing finer made. Handsome light fawn color,** with fine finished neck and white pearl buttons. Soft and fine, and **guaranteed strictly all pure lamb's wool.** No adulteration of any kind.

Sizes	16	18	20	22	24
Each	25c	33c	40c	50c	56c
Sizes	26	28	30	32	34
Each	65c	73c	78c	80c	85c

No. 16R7241 Children's Pantalets to match.

Sizes	16	18	20	22	24
Each	25c	33c	40c	50c	56c
Sizes	26	28	30	32	34
Each	65c	73c	78c	80c	85c

Children's White Wool Underwear.

No. 16R7250 Children's Fine White Australian Lamb's Wool Underwear, same quality and style as No. 16R7240, but white. A beautiful under garment.

Sizes	16	18	20	22	24	26	28	30	32	34
Each	25c	33c	40c	50c	56c	65c	73c	78c	80c	85c

No. 16R7251 Children's Fine White Pantalets, open at sides.

Sizes	16	18	20	22	24	26	28	30	32	34
Each	25c	33c	40c	50c	56c	65c	73c	78c	80c	85c

Boys' and Youths' Winter Underwear.

Boys' sizes are 24, 26, 28, 30, 32 and 34 inches. Always give chest and waist measure in ordering. Usually the drawer size is 2 inches smaller than chest, but some measure the same. **Don't fail to give breast and waist measure.**

If by mail, postage extra, each, 10 cents.

Boys' Ribbed Shirts and Drawers.

No. 16R7260 Boys' Good Weight Ribbed Fleeced Lined Camel's Hair Color Undershirts, with very soft fleece lining, collarette neck, pearl buttons, **Jersey ribbed,** form fitting, **never rip seams** and a durable garment.

Sizes	24	26	28
Price	20c	23c	26c
Sizes	30	32	34
Price	29c	32c	35

No. 16R7261 Boys' Drawers to match, open front.

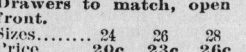

Sizes	24	26	28
Price	20c	23c	26c
Sizes	30	32	34
Price	29c	32c	35c

Boys' Merino Shirts and Drawers.

No. 16R7270 Boys' Natural Gray Merino Wool Mixed Undershirts, with fancy taped neck and front, and cuffs; well made and finished and warranted good.

Sizes	24	26	28
Price	22c	24c	26c
Sizes	30	32	34
Price	28c	30c	32c

No. 16R7271 Boys' Drawers to match; open front.

Sizes	24	26	28
Price	22c	24c	26c
Sizes	30	32	34
Price	28c	30c	32c

Boys' Fleece Lined Underwear, 25 Cents.

Flat Knit.

No. 16R7280 Boys' Fleece Lined Winter Cotton Undershirts, well made and full size. Ribbed cuffs and taped neck. Good, serviceable, warm underwear. Sizes, 24, 26, 28, 30, 32 and 34 breast measure. All sizes same price. Price, half dozen, **$1.50**; each......25c

No. 16R7281 Boys' Fleeced Drawers to match above shirts, button front. Sizes, 24 to 34.

Price, half dozen, **$1.50**; each....................25c

Boys' Warm Wool Fleece Underwear, 42 Cents.

No. 16R7284 Boys' Fine Warm Wool Fleeced Undershirts, made flat knit. These are warm shirts with soft wool fleecing on the inside. Natural gray, Double stitched throughout. Sizes, 24, 26, 28, 30, 32 and 34 breast measure. All sizes same price.

Price, each.................................42c

No. 16R7285 Boys' Wool Fleeced Underdrawers to match above shirts, double stitched never rip seams. Sizes, 24 to 34 waist.

Price, each.................................$0.42
Two full suits of the above underwear.......1.68

Boys' Australian Wool Underwear.

No. 16R7290 Boys' Fine Australian Wool Undershirts, natural gray color. Fine pure all wool of softest quality. **Durable, warm and healthful.** It is well directed economy to buy good woolen underwear for your boy. Made with ribbed cuffs and tail, all seams double stitched by Union special sewing machine and will never rip or tear. Retail price, 75 cents to $1.00.

Sizes	24	26	28
Price	48c	55c	60c
Sizes	30	32	34
Price	65c	70c	75c

No. 16R7291 Drawers to match above, open front, double stitched never rip seams.

Sizes	24	26	28
Price	48c	55c	60c
Sizes	30	32	34
Price	65c	70c	75c

BOYS' UNION SUITS.

Union Suits are in great demand today as they are a practical solution of many vexatious difficulties found in trying to keep drawers in their proper place on active boys. Our Union Suits are carefully proportioned on scientific principles and we warrant them to fit.

Sizes: Measure down back from neck to ankle. Order by length.

Boys' Cotton Union Suits.

No. 16R7295 Boys' Fine Silver Gray Ribbed Cotton Union Suits, full weight, heavy cotton, fleeced on the inside. Collarette neck, button down front and drop seat with long flap extending down below seat. Order by length.

Ages.....	4	5-6	7-8	9-10	11-12	13-14	15
Length..	28	32	36	40	44	48	52
Price, ea.	35c	38c	41c	44c	47c	50c	53c

If by mail, postage extra, each, 18 cents.

Boys' Ribbed Wool Union Suit.

No. 16R7296 Boys' Heavy Warm Ribbed Wool Union Suits. Made from fine clean woolen yarn, natural gray color. They are knitted with 20 per cent cotton yarn, which, however, does not come in contact with the body. The wool only comes next to the skin. Inside softly fleeced. We believe them to be warmer for their weight than any other underwear. Union special covered seams throughout. Drop seat with long flap extending below seat. Button down front. Made especially for us and are unmatched anywhere in value. Order by length.

Ages..........	4	5-6	7-8	9-10	11-12	13-14	15
Length, inches.	28	32	36	40	44	48	52
Price, each....	65c	73c	80c	88c	92c	$1.00	$1.10

If by mail, postage extra, each, 18 cents.

Misses' and Children's Winter Union Suits.

NOTE—Order by length. Measure down back from neck to ankle.

No. 16R7300 Misses' and Children's Natural Gray Jersey Ribbed. Fleece Lined Union Suits. Crocheted neck. Drop seat back.

Ages..........	4	5-6
Length of suit	28	32
Price, each....	23c	25c
Ages..........	7-8	9-10
Length of suit	36	40
Price, each....	27c	29c
Ages..........		11-12
Length of suit		44
Price, each ...		31c

Postage, each, 18 cents.

Misses' Fine Cotton Union Suits.

No. 16R7310 Misses' and Children's Fine Bleached Cotton Union Suits, fine heavy cotton, carefully proportioned and perfect fitting. Soft fleecing throughout. Open down front and drop seat, long flap extending down below seat. Order by length.

Ages..	4	5-6
Length,	28	32
Each,	35c	38c
Ages..	7-8	9-10
Length,	36	40
Each,	41c	44c
Ages..	11-12	13-14
Length,	44	48
Each,	47c	50c

Age, 15; Length, 52; Each.................. 53c

If by mail, postage extra, each, 18 cents.

Merino Wool Back Union Suits.

No. 16R7320 Misses' and Children's Merino Back Lined Union Suit. Made with double back of merino yarn, which gives extra protection to the lungs, where the child needs it most. Heavy weight, natural gray; fine soft fleece lined throughout. Open down front and drop seat, with long flap extending down below the seat. These suits are made especially for us, and we warrant them to fit. Order by length.

Ages...	4	5-6	7-8	9-10	11-12	13-14	15
Length,	28	32	36	40	44	48	52
Each ..	42c	46c	50c	54c	58c	62c	66c

If by mail, postage extra, each, 18 cents.

If you fail to give your size, we cannot fill your order.

Misses' and Children's Heavy Wool Union Suits.

No. 16R7330 Misses' and Children's Fine Ribbed Heavy Warm Wool Union Suits, knitted from fine clean wool and 20 per cent cotton. The cotton does not come in contact with the body, being near the outer surface. Soft fleecing on the inside. **These suits are made especially for us, heavier and warmer than most suits for children, and will be found the best value ever offered near our price.** Fancy trimmed neck, pearl buttons, drop seat, with long flap, extending below seat. Never rip seams throughout. Color, natural gray only. **Order by length.**

Ages........	4	5-6	7-8	9-10	11-12	13-14	15
Length, inch.	28	32	36	40	44	48	52
Price, each...	65c	73c	80c	88c	92c	$1.00	$1.10

If by mail, postage extra, each, 18 cents.

Misses' and Children's Best Australian Union Suits.

Colors: Natural Gray, Black and White.

No. 16R7332 Misses' and Children's Fine Ribbed Australian Wool Worsted Union Suits, the finest suit made for children. The yarn is finest Australian worsted, full winter weight, closely knit, cuffs and anklets. We believe that wool of this quality would not irritate the most sensitive skin, and will prove **the most perfect fitting and healthful union suits made.** You can pay more money but will not get a better suit. Silk trimmed neck and front, fine pearl buttons and silk worked buttonholes. Drop seat with long flap extending below seat. Colors, natural gray, black and white. **State color and length in your order.** Ages 6 to 15 years.

Length, inches,	32	35	38	42	45	48	51
Price....	$1.40	1.48	1.56	1.64	1.70	1.75	1.80

If by mail, postage extra, each, 18 cents.

Misses' Shaped Vests and Pants.

No. 16R7340 Misses, Fine Cotton Vest with Shaped Waist, fleece lined, crocheted neck and front, regular winter weight. **Sizes are by total length of vest.** Ages, 4 to 14 years. Drawers are made to correspond. Order drawers same size as vest for matched suit.

Sizes	Length, inches	Price, each
2	15	20c
3	18	21c
4	21	22c
5	24	24c
6	27	25c
7	30	26c

No. 16R7341 Misses' Open Side Drawers, to match.

Sizes..............	2	3	4	5	6	7
Price, each.......	20c	21c	22c	24c	25c	26c

If by mail, postage extra, each, 11 cents.

Misses' Wool Ribbed Shaped Vests and Pants.

No. 16R7343 Misses' and Children's Half Wool Shaped Undervests; knit from fine clean wool and cotton, softly fleeced on the inside. Every garment carefully proportioned and sized. Follow rules for measurement and you will have no trouble with our sizes. Made with closely knit cuffs, silk trimmed neck and front, with pearl buttons. **The length is the size.** For matched suit order same size drawers as vest. Ages, 4 to 14 years.

Sizes...............	2	3	4	5	6	7
Length, inches...	15	18	21	24	27	30
Price, each......	35c	38c	41c	45c	48c	52c

No. 16R7344 Misses' Woolen Drawers to match above vests. Buttons at sides.

Sizes..............	2	3	4	5	6	7
Price, each.......	35c	38c	41c	45c	48c	52c

If by mail, postage extra, each, 12 cents.

Misses' and Children's Black Tights.

No. 16R7350 Misses' and Childrens' Plain Black Tights, one-half wool, absolutely fast color. Black tights for girls and children are very practical, for the reason that they can be easily slipped on or off over shoes or slippers. When going out into the cold, they can be quickly put on, and easily removed when in doors. These are strictly good value. With closely knitted waist and drawstring.

Sizes,	2	3	4	5	6	7	8
Ages	4	5-6	7-8	9-10	11-12	13-14	15-16
Each	.50	.53	.56	.59	.61	.64	.67

If by mail, postage extra, each, 12 cents.

MEN'S SWEATERS.

WE HAVE NEVER before carried a better line of sweaters, and our sweaters have always been up to the

HIGHEST STANDARD OF EXCELLENCE.

The quality of material is always as good as it is possible to put into them, price considered, and our prices may always be taken as representing the very best garments that can be gotten up or the price. SIZES—Always give breast measure. If you do not state size, we cannot fill your order.

If by mail, postage extra, 17 cents.

Men's Cotton Sweaters, 40 Cents.

No. 16R8000 Men's Heavy Weight Good Cotton Sweaters, roll neck and ribbed cuffs. Fast colors, navy, black or maroon. Always give breast measure. Sizes, 34 to 42.

Price, each. $0.40
Per dozen... 4.80

If by mail, postage extra, each, 20c.

DONT FAIL TO GIVE SIZE

Men's Wool Sweaters, 85 Cents.

No. 16R8004 Men's Heavy Ribbed, Non-shrinkable, three-fourths Wool Sweaters, double neck, ribbed cuffs and tail; a well made, good appearing clean sweater that will give good satisfaction. Colors, black, maroon or navy. Sizes, 34, 36, 38, 40, 42, 44.

Price, each. $0.85
Per dozen 10.20

If by mail, postage extra, each, 16 cents.

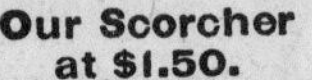

Our Scorcher at $1.50.

No. 16R8008 Extra strong, made from fine domestic wool. Fancy ribbed neck and elastic ribbed cuffs and tail. Perfect fitting. You cannot buy a better sweater at retail for less than $2.00. Colors, black, navy, maroon, or white. Sizes, 34 to 44.

Price, each. $ 1.50
Per dozen... 18.00

If by mail, postage extra, each, 18 cts.

DONT FAIL TO GIVE SIZE

Fine Australian Wool Sweaters, $2.00.

No. 16R8012 Men's Fine Sweaters, made of fine Australian wool yarn, with heavy knitted neck, tail and cuffs. This is a full weight sweater and a special value at our low price, which is about the cost to your home merchant. The following are the colors; Black, maroon, cardinal, navy, gray or royal blue. Sizes, 34, 36, 38, 40, 42, 44. **State size and color in your order.**

Price, each. $2.00.

If by mail, postage extra, 22 cents.

Men's Heavy Weight Australian Wool Sweaters, $3.00.

No. 16R8016 Men's Heavy Weight Australian Wool Sweaters. Knitted very heavy from fine Australian yarn, all wool, with double neck, double ribbed tail and heavy cuffs. A very fine quality that retails at $4.00. If not better than any you could buy at home for $4.00, return and we will refund your money. Full fashioned; all seams knitted together. Average weight, about 20 ounces. Colors, black, navy, maroon, cardinal, royal blue or white. Sizes, 34, 36, 38, 40, 42, 44.

Price, each......$3.00

If by mail, postage extra, each, 25 cents.

Heaviest All Wool Shaker Sweater, $3.75.

No. 16R8020 Men's Heaviest Shaker Fine All Wool Sweater. The heaviest and warmest you can buy. Made from fine clean Shaker yarn with extra heavy neck, tail and cuffs. Average weight, 1¾ lbs. Closely knitted. **A favorite in the Northwest. Just the right kind for hunters, prospectors, stage drivers, cattlemen or any occupation where one is subject to the extreme cold. It is also a favorite with many athletes.** Retail price, $5.00 to $6.00. Colors, only navy blue or buckskin tan. Sizes, 36 to 44 breast measure. Price, each..........$3.75

If by mail, postage extra, each, 34 cents.

Men's New Fancy Sweater, $2.25.

No. 16R8024 Men's Fancy Knitted Sweater, as shown in the illustration. **Made from fine, clean, all wool yarn, in the perpendicular rib effect. Heavy collar, cuffs and tail.** The yarn is a mixture of Australian and domestic wool, and for this quality you would pay from $3.00 to $3.50 at retail. Strictly high grade manufacture. Full weight, average 28 ounces. Colors, black, maroon, royal, navy, white or cardinal. Sizes, 34, 36, 38, 40, 42, 44.

Price, each..$2.25

If by mail, postage extra, each, 34 cents.

Byron Collar Sweaters, $2.50.

No. 16R8028 Men's Fine Worsted Sweaters, made of fine all wool worsted yarn, the best ever put into a sweater for the price. Every detail of finish is carefully carried out and it has no weak points. Made with stripes as shown in cut. Colors, navy, black, maroon, royal blue or green. Sizes, 34 to 44 inches breast measure. Average weight, about 18 ounces.

Price, each.....$ 2.50
Per dozen....... 30.00

If by mail, postage extra, each, 22 cents.

Heavy Honeycomb Knit Sweaters.

No. 16R8032 Men's Honeycomb Knit Sweaters, heavy weight. Something out of the ordinary line of sweaters, new, attractive and durable. The predominating color is on the outer surface which is set off by the background color underneath, there being two colors of yarn in every sweater. Last season we sold hundreds of these sweaters, and we know them to be one of he most satisfactory sweaters ever knitted, and we have improved the quality over last year. Made entirely of worsted yarn, with shaped cuffs, neck and tail. **The finest sweater in the market, and we cheerfully refund your money, if you are not more than pleased.** Regular retail price, $5.00. Colors are navy, black, royal blue or myrtle green. Sizes, 34 to 44 inches breast measure. Price, each....$3.50

If by mail, postage extra, each, 37 cents.

DON'T FAIL TO GIVE SIZE

Men's Fancy Knitted Sweater, $4.25.

No. 16R8036 Under this number we furnish our finest fancy knitted sweater, something entirely new, knitted from the very best Australian worsted. The entire front is knitted, fancy stitch, on hand machines, as illustrated, with a very narrow contrasting horizontal stripe which appears also in the sleeves. Medium weight new style collar, fancy knitted cuffs and tail. **If you want the best sweater, and something new you certainly will not be disappointed in this one.** In the following fancy colors only: Gray, cardinal or royal blue. Sizes, 34, 36, 38, 40, 42 inches breast measure.

Price, each..........$4.25

If by mail, postage extra, each, 28 cents.

Alternating Striped Sweaters.

DON'T FAIL TO GIVE SIZE

No. 16R8040 Men's Alternating Striped Sweaters as shown in illustration. A fine all wool sweater that never fails to give good wear and hold its shape. Colors are black and orange, blue and cardinal, black and cardinal, and green and cardinal. Sizes, 34 to 44 breast measure. Average weight, about 18 ounces.

Price, each.. $1.50

If by mail, postage extra, each, 22 cents.

Honeycomb Knit Fancy Sweater.

No. 16R8044 Men's Fancy Alternating Striped Honeycomb Knitted Sweater, striped about 3 inches wide. **A new and up to date sweater,** as shown in the illustration, made from clean wool. A new popular sweater, meeting approval all over the country. Colors combined as follows: black and cardinal navy and cardinal, green and cardinal, and royal and white. Sizes, 34, 36, 38, 40, 42, 44 breast measure.

Price, each..$2.00

If by mail, postage extra, each, 22 cents.

BOYS' and YOUTHS' SWEATERS.

We call special attention to the four following numbers in boys' sweaters. They are selected stock and at our prices form values that are unapproachable.

Always state breast measure in order.

Sizes, 24, 26, 28, 30, 32, 34 inches breast measure.

Boys' Cotton Sweaters, 39 Cents.

No. 16R8060 Boys' Heavy Cotton Sweater, plain roll collar. Will stand rough wear. Sizes, 24 to 34 breast measure, for boys 8 to 15 years of age. Colors, navy or maroon. Price, per dozen, $4.68; each..............39c

If by mail, postage extra, each, 11 cents.

Boys' Roll Neck Sweaters.

No. 16R8064 Boys' Strong, All Wool, Ribbed Sweater, with fancy ribbed rolled collar; elastic ribbed cuffs and tail; all wool; warranted to give good service. Plain colors, black, maroon or navy. Sizes, 24 to 34 breast measure.

Price, each......$0.75
Per dozen........ 9.00

If by mail, postage extra, each, 10 cents.

Boys' Alternating Stripe Sweaters, $1.00.

No. 16R8072 Boys' Fine All Wool Sweater, made alternating stripes as illustrated. A closely knitted sweater made from fine clean yarn that will not fail to give lasting service. Colors, black and orange, black and red, green and red, royal and white. **A special leader at our low price.** Sizes, 24, 26, 28, 30, 32, 34 breast measure.

Price each...... $1.00

If by mail, postage extra, each, 15 cents.

Boys' Wool Worsted Sweaters, $1.25.

No. 16R8076 Boys' Fine All Wool Worsted Sweaters, made with all worsted neck, cuffs and tail. This is doubtless the best sweater of the season in fine goods. They are made with about ⅛-inch mercerized silk stripe on collar, cuffs and tail. **Usual retail value, $2.00.** Colors, navy, maroon, royal blue, black or cardinal.

Sizes, 24 to 34 breast measure. Suitable for youths up to 15 years of age.

Price, each.......................................$1.25

If by mail, postage extra, each, 16 cents.

ABOUT THE FREIGHT.

ON PAGES 7 TO 10 **you will find complete information regarding freight rates. By noting the weight of the article given in each description, and referring to the point nearest you in the freight rates, you can tell almost exactly what the freight on anything will be to your station. You will find it will amount to next to nothing as compared to the saving in price.**

Boys' Fancy Honeycomb Sweater, $1.20

No. 16R8080 Boys' or Youths' All Wool Honeycomb Knitted Sweaters, alternating stripes as shown in the illustration. A very handsome new style for boys that will not fail to please and give entire satisfaction. The neck, cuffs and tail are closely knitted. Colors, black and cardinal, royal and white, green and cardinal. Sizes, 24 to 34 breast measure. For boys up to 15 years of age.
Price, each.........**$1.20**
If by mail, postage extra, each, 18 cents.

JUNIOR SWEATERS.

For Children 3 to 8 Years. Order by Age.

A Wonderful Sweater for 43 Cents.

No. 16R8084 Children's Junior Sweater, one-half wool, made to button down side, like cut. Close fitting, ribbed cuffs, collar and tail. Made in two colors only, blue with small ½-inch red stripe or red with ½-inch blue stripe. The greatest value ever offered in a child's sweater. Just the thing for play or school. Order by age. Ages, 3, 4, 5, 6 and 7, only.
Price, each............**43c**
If by mail, postage extra, each, 12 cents.

A Favorite Junior Sweater, $1.00.

Ages, 3 to 8 years.

No. 16R8088 Children's Junior Sweaters, made in the popular honeycomb knitted style, of fine, clean all wool yarn; alternating stripes as shown in illustration; stripes about 2 inches wide. Colors, green and cardinal, black and red, royal blue and white. Ages, 3 to 8 years, only.
Price, each.........**$1.00**
If by mail, postage extra, each, 12 cents.

Special Quality Fine All Worsted Sweaters, $1.00.

Ages, 3 to 8 years.

No. 16R8090 Children's Junior All Wool Worsted Sweaters, plain body with stripes on collar, cuffs and tail. We offer this all worsted sweater for ages 3 to 8 years at this unusually low price and if your local merchant could supply this sweater at all he would charge you $1.25 to $1.50. If you want the best plain sweater order this quality. Colors, black, navy, maroon or royal blue. Ages, 3, 4, 5, 6, 7 and 8.
Price, each... ....**$1.00**
If by mail, postage extra, each, 13 cents.

MEN'S CARDIGAN OR KNIT JACKETS.

A close fitting, comfortable, warm jacket, suitable for men of any occupation. The office man, clerk, expressman, the farmer or stockman all find this the best warm jacket. **Each price represents the best value of its kind.** We cannot highly recommend the cheaper grades as they will not hold shape and wear in comparison with better goods. The worsted jackets are always satisfactory and we warrant them to be durable and perfect fitting.

Do not forget to give breast measure.

No. 16R8100 Men's New Style Jacket made without collar, single breasted, double sewed throughout. **Black only.** Absolutely fast color and it is knitted from fine cotton yarn into a firm Jersey cloth. Something new and the best cheap jacket ever offered. Sizes, breast measure 34, 36, 38, 40, 42 only. Price, each...........**85c**
If by mail, postage extra, 23 cents.

MEN'S KNIT JACKETS.

No. 16R8105 Men's Full Weight Knit Jackets, made of cotton worsted, ribbed cuffs, and will fit well. Single breasted. **Black only.** Sizes, 34 to 42 breast measure.
Price, each................**98c**
If by mail, postage extra, 24 cents.

No. 16R8110 Men's Good Quality Worsted Knit Jackets. Made of fine wool worsted yarn with cotton yarn on the back. More durable than an all wool jacket at this price. Single breasted, finished knit front, two pockets, close ribbed cuffs. A reliable article that will give entirely satisfactory wear. Colors, black or brown only. Sizes, 34 to 42 breast measure.
Price, each.......................................**$1.65**
If by mail, postage extra, each, 21 cents.

Men's Knit Jacket, $2.25.

Sizes, 34 to 42.

No. 16R8115 Men's Fine Cardigan or Knit Jacket. Made one-half wool worsted and one-half wool. The wool is on the inside and the worsted the outside. This quality frequently retails at $3.00 each and is a very strong value at our low price. Worsted trimmed front, two pockets, single breasted as illustrated. **A thoroughly good wearing, reliable jacket.** Sizes to fit breast measures 34 to 42. **State breast measure in your order.**
Price, each................**$2.25**
If by mail, postage extra, each, 24 cents.

All Worsted Jackets, $3.00.

No. 16R8120 Men's Single Breasted Fine All Worsted Knit Jackets. A strictly high grade jacket that will fit perfectly, and at our price is the best quality that can be produced. A very finely knitted jacket from high grade all worsted yarn that we warrant to wear as well as any jacket you could buy at retail for $4.00 or $4.50, as this is the amount your local merchant would have to charge you for this quality. Worsted trimmed, two pockets. Regular winter weight. Colors, black or seal brown only. Sizes, 34 to 42 breast measure.
Price, each........... ....**$3.00**
If by mail, postage extra, each, 24 cents.

Men's $2.50 All Wool German Knit Jackets.

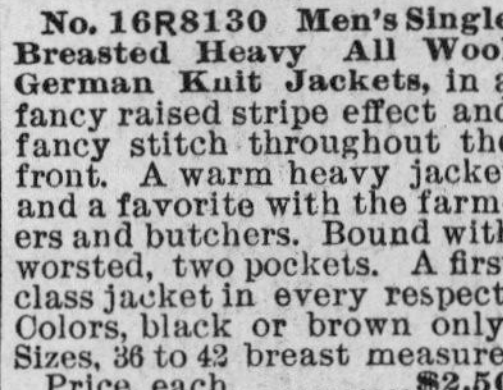

No. 16R8130 Men's Single Breasted Heavy All Wool German Knit Jackets, in a fancy raised stripe effect and fancy stitch throughout the front. A warm heavy jacket and a favorite with the farmers and butchers. Bound with worsted, two pockets. A first class jacket in every respect. Colors, black or brown only. Sizes, 36 to 42 breast measure.
Price, each............**$2.50**
If by mail, postage extra, each, 20 cents.

Men's Double Breasted Cardigan Jackets, $2.25.

No. 16R8135 Men's Double Breasted Knit Jackets, made of fine worsted yarn but part cotton yarn in the inside; a thoroughly good jacket that we warrant to give entire satisfaction and wear well. Dark buttons, two pockets and worsted binding and satin faced lapels. Colors, black or seal brown. A strictly fine value at our low price. Sizes, 34 to 42 breast.
Price, each.................**$2.25**
If by mail, postage extra, 24 cents.

Men's Double Breasted Jacket, $3.00.

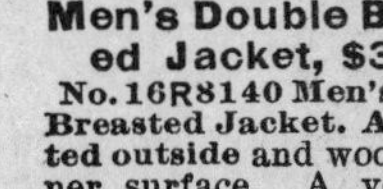

No. 16R8140 Men's Double Breasted Jacket. All worsted outside and wool on inner surface. A very fine high grade jacket, carefully finished, fine worsted cuffs, cloth covered buttons, worsted trimmed, and two pockets. For warmth and durability this quality is the best. Not extremely heavy but above the regular weight by several ounces. Average weight, about 23 ounces. Colors, black or brown. Sizes, 34 to 42 breast measure.
Price, each...........**$3.00**
If by mail, postage extra, each, 26 cents.

Men's Extra Size Cardigan Jackets.

Breast, 44, 46, 48.

No. 16R8145 Men's Extra Large Size Cardigan Jackets. Made especially for big men. Single breasted style with two pockets. **Worsted bound.** These jackets are 80 per cent pure worsted and **will wear much longer than any all wool jacket.** Good heavy weight elastic ribbed and made up in strictly **first class manner. In your search for something really good and dependable do not overlook this** number. Colors, black or brown. Sizes, 44, 46, 48 breast measure. Price, each...................**$2.25**
If by mail, postage extra, 24 cents.

Our Special Quality Extra Size, $3.00.

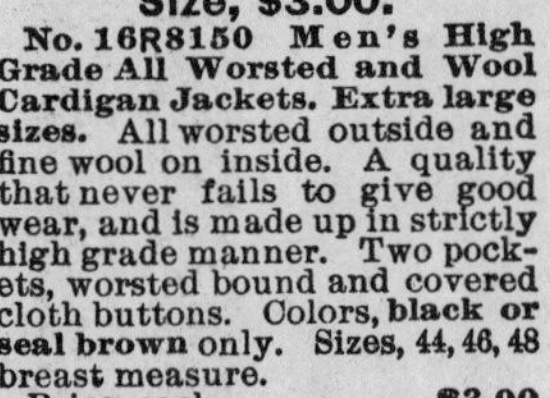

No. 16R8150 Men's High Grade All Worsted and Wool Cardigan Jackets. Extra large sizes. All worsted outside and fine wool on inside. A quality that never fails to give good wear, and is made up in strictly high grade manner. Two pockets, worsted bound and covered cloth buttons. Colors, **black or seal brown** only. Sizes, 44, 46, 48 breast measure.
Price, each..............**$3.00**
If by mail, postage extra, each, 25 cents.

FOR LADIES' CARDIGAN AND KNIT JACKETS

SEE CLOAK DEPARTMENT.

MEN'S STOCKINET OR JERSEY KNIT COATS.

State breast measure or size coat in your order.

No. 16R8160 Men's All Wool, Stockinet Jersey Knit Cloth Coats or Jackets. A very good warm coat for office, home or store; very neat; more dressy than cardigan jacket. In extremely cold weather can be worn under the regular coat. Color, black only. Sizes, 36 to 44 breast measure.
Price, each..........**$3.00**
If by mail, postage extra, each, 38 cents.

Our Special Value for $3.75.

No. 16R8165 Men's Fine, All Wool, Stockinet Knit Cloth Coat, finer quality than the above. These are sometimes called Berlin coats. A perfect fitting coat for home, office or as protection from the cold. Colors, black or dark blue. Sizes, 36 to 44 breast measure. Price, each.....**$3.75**
If by mail, postage extra, 38 cents.

Oxford Gray Fine Coat, $3.75.

No. 16R8170 Men's Fine Stockinet Knitted Cloth Coat, in fine wool, Oxford or dark gray color, double breasted. A very fine coat, carefully cut and tailored and will be found perfect fitting in every respect. A very select coat, out of the usual range in this kind of goods. Trimmed with velvet collar. Full weight. Double breasted style. Sizes, 36 to 44 breast measure.
Price, each.......**$3.75**
If by mail, postage extra, 38 cents.

ALWAYS STATE CORRECT BREAST MEASURE

TAKEN OVER VEST, WHEN ORDERING KNIT JACKETS OR STOCKINET COATS.

Men's Linen Collars and Cuffs

OUR LINEN COLLAR AND CUFF DEPARTMENT IS COMPLETE IN UP TO DATE STYLES. QUALITY GOVERNS ....PRICE.....

Buy Your Collars at Wholesale Prices.
We save you money on Collars and Cuffs.

OUR COLLARS AT 10 CENTS are 4-ply pure linen, and warranted to be such. They are equal to any collars retailing at 15 cents each, and when you buy them from us at 10 cents, or $1.20 per dozen, you buy at the price your merchant pays at wholesale.

OUR CUFFS AT 14 CENTS A PAIR are of pure linen, fine quality 4-ply, the kind that retail for 20 cents a pair, correctly sized and strictly first class workmanship.

Collars are put up one dozen in a box, and cuffs one dozen pairs in a box. The price is the same for one or a dozen, viz.: If price is 10 cents each, the price for one dozen is $1.20.

A WORD ABOUT CHEAP COLLARS: We do not wish to sell cheap collars that are made of cotton or union linen, but for those who wish them we will furnish almost any style for 8 cents each, 96 cents per dozen. We do not recommend them, because we can sell you a pure linen, good quality, for 10 cents, equal to collars retailed everywhere at 15 cents each.

A REMINDER. Do not forget to give size for collars or cuffs. Your order will then have prompt attention.

IF BY MAIL, postage on collars extra, per dozen, 15 cents; each, 2 cents. Cuffs, postage extra, per dozen, 20 cents; per pair, 2 cents.

No. 34R20
Front, 1⅞-in. Back, 1⅝-in.
No. 34R20 Men's Linen Collars. Sizes, 14 to 18.
Each $0.10
Per dozen........ 1.20

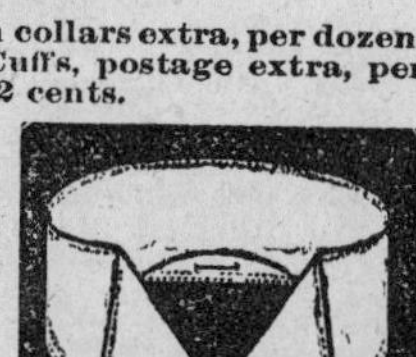
No. 34R23
Front, 2¼-in. Back, 2-in.
No. 34R23 Men's Linen Collars. Sizes, 14 to 17.
Each $0.10
Per dozen........ 1.20

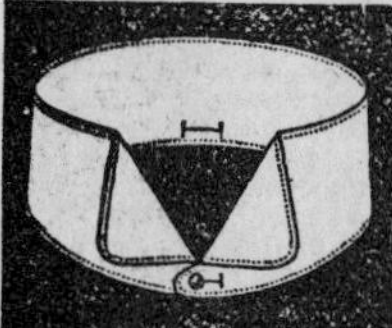
No. 34R28
Front, 2½-in. Back, 2⅜-in.
No. 34R28 Men's Linen Collars. Sizes, 14 to 17.
Each $0.10
Per dozen........ 1.20

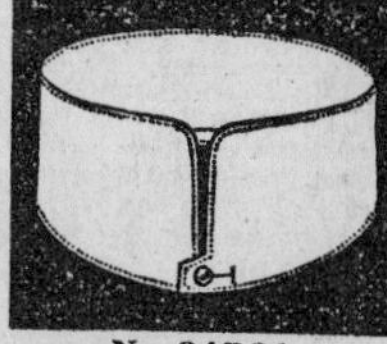
No. 34R31
Front, 2⅛-in. Back, 1⅝-in.
No. 34R31 Men's Linen Collars. Sizes, 14 to 17.
Each $0.10
Per dozen........ 1.20

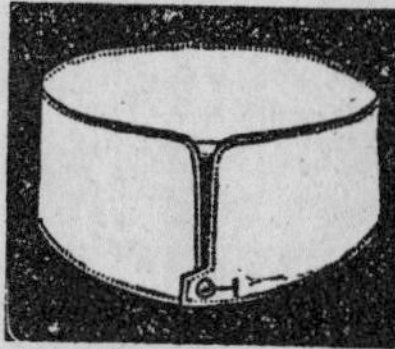
No. 34R35
Front, 2⅝-in. Back, 2¼-in.
No. 34R35 Men's Linen Collars. Sizes, 14 to 17.
Each $0.10
Per dozen........ 1.20

No. 34R40
Front, 3-in. Back, 2½-in.
No. 34R40 Men's Linen Collars. Sizes, 14 to 16½.
Each $0.10
Per dozen........ 1.20

No. 34R44
Front, 3-in. Back, 2¾-in.
No. 34R44 Men's Linen Collars. Sizes, 14 to 16½.
Each $0.10
Per dozen........ 1.20

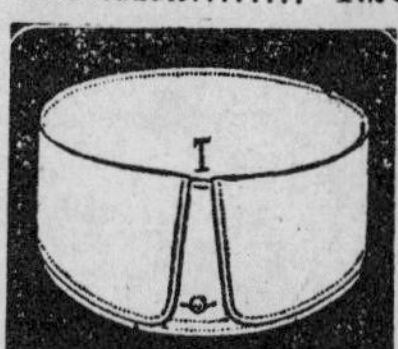
No. 34R46
Front, 2½-in. Back, 2¼-in.
No. 34R46 Men's Linen Collars. Sizes, 14 to 16½. Each......$0.10
Per dozen........ 1.20

No. 34R50
Front, 2-in. Back, 2-in.
No. 34R50 Men's Linen Collars. Sizes, 14 to 17.
Each $0.10
Per dozen........ 1.20

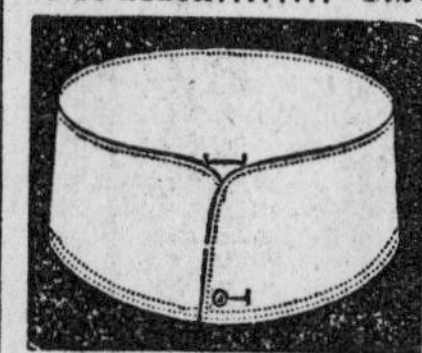
No. 34R58
Front, 2⅝-in. Back, 2⅜-in.
No. 34R58 Men's Linen Collars, 14 to 17.
Each $0.10
Per dozen........ 1.20

No. 34R66
Front, 1⅞-in. Back, 1½-in.
No. 34R66 Men's Linen Collars, 14½ to 19.
Each $0.10
Per dozen........ 1.20

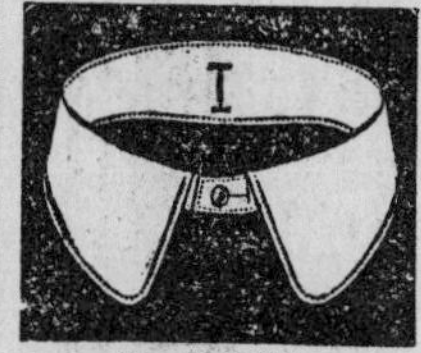
No. 34R74
Points, 2⅜-in. Space, ⅞-in.
No. 34R74 Men's Linen Collars, 14 to 17½.
Price, each......$0.10
Per dozen........ 1.20

No. 34R82
Points, 2⅞-in. Space, ⅝-in.
No. 34R82 Men's Linen Collars, 14 to 18.
Each $0.10
Per dozen........ 1.20

No. 34R54
Front, 3-in. Back, 2¾-in.
No. 34R54 Men's Linen Collars. Sizes, 14 to 16½. Each......$0.10
Per dozen........ 1.20

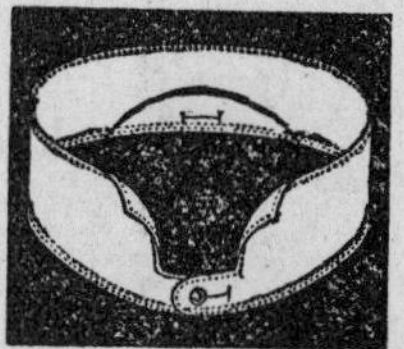
No. 34R64
Front, 1⅝-in. Back, 1½-in.
No. 34R64 Men's Linen Collars, 14½ to 18.
Each $0.10
Per dozen........ 1.20

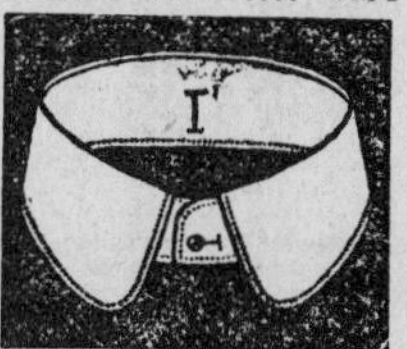
No. 34R70
Points, 2-in. Back, 1⅝-in. Space, 3¾-in.
No. 34R70 Men's Linen Collars, 14 to 17.
Each $0.10
Per dozen........ 1.20

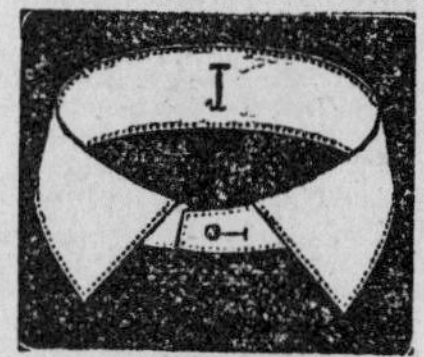
No. 34R78
Points, 2½-in. Space, 1¼-in.
No. 34R78 Men's Linen Collars, 14 to 17½.
Price, each......$0.10
Per dozen........ 1.20

WE can furnish you any of the above styles in our

EXTRA QUALITY LINEN COLLARS

Each.............$0.14
Per dozen......... 1.68

In ordering give regular style number, but allow 14 cents each.

MEN'S LINEN CUFFS AT 14 CENTS PER PAIR.

Sizes, 9½, 10, 10½, 11, 11½ inches.

LET US REMIND YOU AGAIN that cuffs quoted herewith are made 4-ply of pure linen, goods that we warrant to be perfect in workmanship and sizing. We can furnish any styles at 11 cents; per dozen, $1.32; made of cotton, quite frequently sold for linen, but do not recommend them, as we can sell you a regular 20-cent linen cuff at 14 cents per pair. If you buy one pair or one dozen pairs the price per pair is the same.

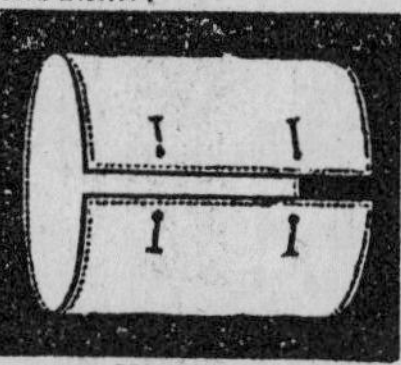
No. 34R200
Width, 3¾-in.
No. 34R200 Men's Linen Cuffs. 9½ to 11½.
Per pair $0.14
Per dozen pairs.. 1.68

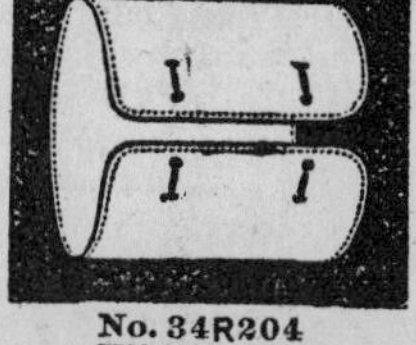
No. 34R204
Width, 4-in.
No. 34R204 Men's Linen Cuffs. 9½ to 11½.
Per pair..........$0.14
Per dozen pairs.. 1.68

No. 34R210
Width, 3¾-in.
No. 34R210 Men's Linen Cuffs. 9½ to 11½.
Per pair..........$0.14
Per dozen pairs.. 1.68

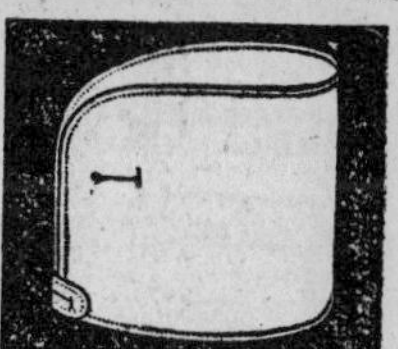
No. 34R214
Width, 4-in.
No. 34R214 Men's Linen Cuffs. 9½ to 11½.
Per pair..........$0.14
Per dozen pairs.. 1.68

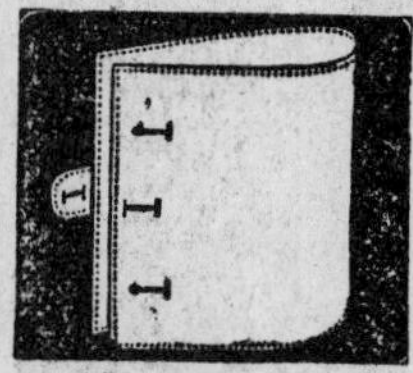
No. 34R218
Width, 4¼-in.
No. 34R218 Men's Linen Cuffs. 9½ to 11½.
Per pair..........$0.14
Per dozen pairs.. 1.68

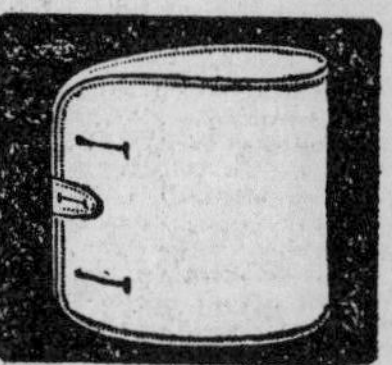
No. 34R222
Width, 4¼-in.
No. 34R222 Men's Linen Cuffs. 9½ to 11½.
Per pair..........$0.14
Per dozen pairs.. 1.68

WE can furnish you any of the above style cuffs in our **FINEST QUALITY LINEN.**
Per pair.............$0.19
Per dozen pairs...... 2.28
In ordering give regular style numbers but allow 19 cents per pair.

BOYS' OR YOUTHS' LINEN COLLARS, 8 CENTS.

Sizes, 12, 12½, 13, 13½, 14 inches.

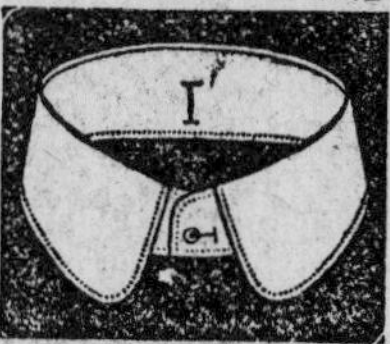
No. 34R250
Back, 1¾-in. Points, 2-in.
No. 34R250 Boys' or Youths' Fine Linen Collars. Sizes, 11 to 14 only.
Price, each........ 8c
Per dozen......... 96c

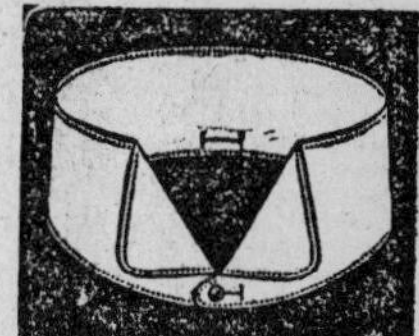
No. 34R252
Back, 2⅛-in. Front, 2⅜-in.
No. 34R252 Boys' or Youths' Fine Linen Collars. Sizes, 12 to 14 only.
Price, each........ 8c
Per dozen......... 96c

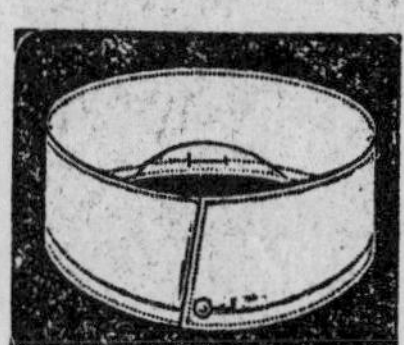
No. 34R254
Front, 1⅝-in. Back, 1½-in.
No. 34R254 Boys' or Youths' Fine Linen Collars. Sizes, 11 to 14 only.
Price, each........ 8c
Per dozen......... 96c

Boys' or Youths' Linen Cuffs.
Sizes, 8, 8½, 9, 9½.

No. 34R260
Width, 3⅝-in.
No. 34R260 Boys' or Youths' Fine Linen Cuffs. Sizes, 8 to 9½.
Price, per pair...$0.14
Per dozen pairs.. 1.68

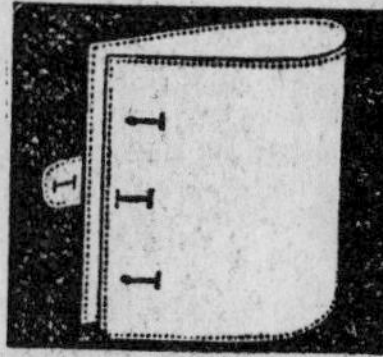
No. 34R261
Width, 3¾-in.
No. 34R261 Boys' or Youths' Fine Linen Cuffs. Sizes, 8 to 9½.
Price, per pair...$0.14
Per dozen pairs... 1.68

No. 34R262
Width, 3¼-in.
No. 34R262 Boys' or Youths' Fine Linen Cuffs. Sizes, 8 to 9½.
Price, per pair...$0.14
Per dozen pairs.. 1.68

IF YOU FAIL TO GIVE SIZES OF COLLARS AND CUFFS WANTED WE CANNOT FILL YOUR ORDER.

Celluloid Waterproof Collars and Cuffs.

The following are the best Waterproof Collars and Cuffs made. Will not break or tear at buttonholes. Order collars half size larger than shirt worn.

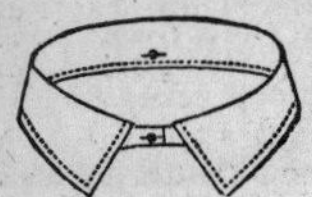

ROYAL.
Front, 1⅞-in.

No. 34R300 Style Royal, Celluloid Collars. Sizes, 12½ to 20 inches.
Each..........$0.11
Per dozen........ 1.32

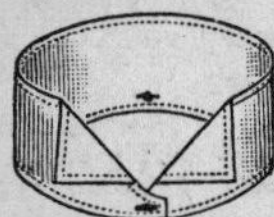

MONARCH.
Front, 2⅛-in. Back, 1⅞-in.

No. 34R304 Style Monarch. Sizes, 12½ to 18½.
Price, each......$0.11
Per dozen......... 1.32

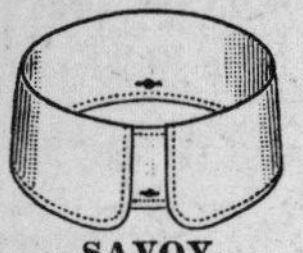

SAVOY.
Front, 2¼-in. Back, 1¾-in.

No. 34R308 Style Savoy. Sizes, 12½ to 18.
Price, each.......$0.11
Per dozen........ 1.32

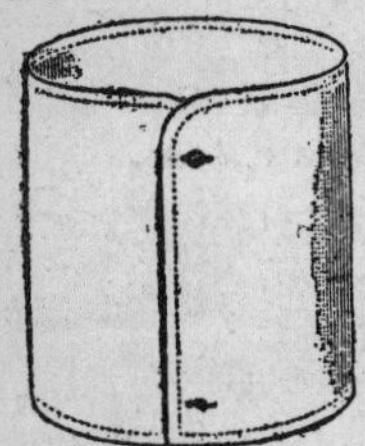

EXCELSIOR.
Width, 3½-in.

No. 34R311 Style Excelsior, Celluloid Cuffs. Sizes, 9 to 11½.
Price, per pair.....23c
Do not forget size when you order collars and cuffs.

Celluloid Shirt Front.

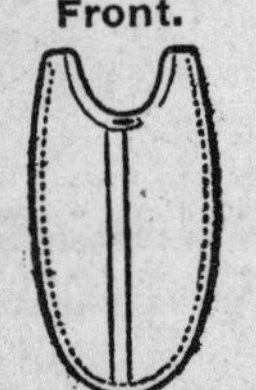

MEDIUM. Front, 9¼ in. Width, 7 in.

No. 34R316 Celluloid Shirt Front, interlined, medium.
Price, each..........35c

When collars and cuffs are ordered sent by mail, always include extra stamps for postage. If by mail, postage on collars, extra, per dozen, 14 cents; each, 1 cent; on cuffs, per dozen pairs, 20 cents; per pair, 2 cents.

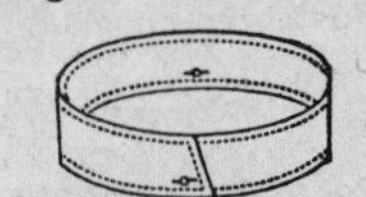

CLERICAL.
Front, 1½-in. Back, 1⅝-in.

No. 34R302 Style Clerical, Celluloid Collars. Sizes, 12 to 19½.
Each............$0.11
Per dozen......... 1.32

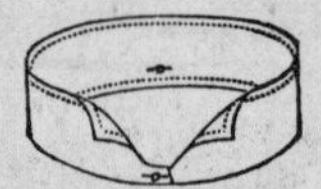

IMPERIAL.
Front, 2-in. Back, 1¾-in.

No. 34R306 Style Imperial, Celluloid Collars. Sizes, 13½ to 18½.
Each............$0.11
Per dozen........ 1.32

Celluloid Cuffs.

FIFTH AVENUE.
Width, 3½-in.

No. 34R310 Style Fifth Avenue, Celluloid Cuffs. Sizes, 9½ to 11½.
Price, per pair......23c

Celluloid Shirt Front.

SHORT. Front, 7 in. Width, 6¾ in.

No. 34R315 Celluloid Shirt Front, interlined, medium length.
Price, each.........27c

Celluloid Shirt Front.

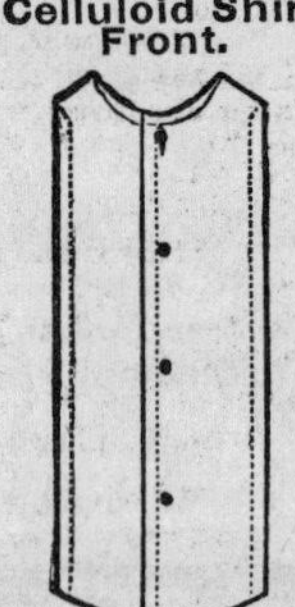

LONG. Front, 13 in. Width, 6⅞ in.

No. 34R318 Long Shirt Front; made of extra quality celluloid, interlined.
Price, each..........42c

Men's Rubber Bosoms.

No. 34R320 Men's Rubber Bosoms, 9¼ inches long, medium length.
Price, each.........55c

WE CAN ONLY FILL ORDERS FOR COLLARS AND CUFFS

WHEN SIZE IS GIVEN

DON'T FORGET SIZE

WHEN YOU WRITE YOUR ORDER

RUBBER COLLARS AND CUFFS FOR MEN AND BOYS.

In polished or dull finish. State kind in your order. Choice of any style, 18 cents each or $2.16 per dozen.

No. 34R330
Front, 2-in. Back, 1¼-in.

No. 34R330 Stylish Turn Down Rubber Collars, polished or dull finish. Sizes, 12 to 18½.
Price, each......$0.18
Per dozen........ 2.16

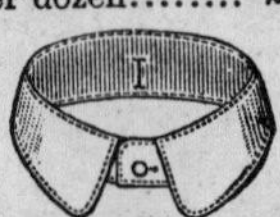

No. 34R331
Front, 2-in. Back, 1⅝-in.

No. 34R331 Stylish Turn Down Rubber Collar, polished or dull finish. Sizes, 12½ to 18½.
Price, each.......$0.18
Per dozen... .... 2.16

No. 34R334
Front, 2-in. Back, 1¾-in.

No. 34R334 A Stylish Wing Rubber Collar in polished or dull finish. Sizes, 12 to 18½.
Price, each......$0.18
Per dozen......... 2.16

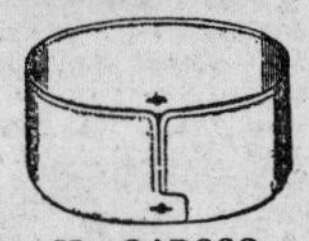

No. 34R338
Front, 2⅝-in. Back, 2¼-in.

No. 34R338 Straight Space Standing Rubber Collar in polished or dull finish. Sizes, 13½ to 17½.
Price, each.......$0.18
Per dozen....... 2.16

No. 34R342
Front, 2-in. Back, 1¾-in.

No. 34R342 A Low Space Rubber Collar in polished or dull finish. Sizes, 12 to 18.
Price, each......$0.18
Per dozen........ 2.16

No. 34R332
Front, 2¼-in. Back, 1¾-in.

No. 34R332 A Stylish High Turned Down Rubber Collar, in polished or dull finish. Sizes, 13½ to 17½.
Price, each......$0.18
Per dozen........ 2.16

No. 34R336
Front, 2⅜-in. Back, 2¼-in.

No. 34R336 A Round Wing Rubber Collar in polished or dull finish. Sizes, 13½ to 17½.
Price, each......$0.18
Per dozen......... 2.16

No. 34R340
Front, 2⅜-in. Back, 2¼-in.

No. 34R340 Straight Band Rubber Collar in polished or dull finish. Sizes, 13½ to 17½.
Price, each......$0.18
Per dozen......... 2.16

No. 34R346

No. 34R346 Men's Rubber Link Cuffs, polished or dull finish. Sizes, 9½, 10, 10½, 11, 11½.
Price, per pair.....37c

No. 34R348

No. 34R348 Men's Rubber Plain Cuffs, in polished or dull finish. Sizes, 9½, 10, 10½, 11, 11½
Price, per pair....37c

Wizard Cuff Holders.

No. 34R368 The Wizard Cuff Holders, improved, nickel plated. Per pair........7c
If by mail, postage extra, 2 cents.

New Derby Link Cuff Holders.

No. 34R369 Men's Derby Link Cuff Holders, make link cuffs out of straight cuffs. A very practical cuff holder. Price, per pair 8c
If by mail, postage extra, 2 cents.

Necktie Holder.

No. 34R370 Men's Necktie Holder, lever clamp, nickel plated. Price, each...........3c
If by mail, postage extra, 1 cent.

Sleeve Protectors.

No. 34R380 Men's Standard Quality Print Oversleeves. Rubber top to hold in place.
Price, per pair..............7c
If by mail, postage extra, 4c.

No. 34R385 Men's Fast Black Sateen Oversleeves. Rubber top.
Price, per pair.........................13c
If by mail, postage extra, each, 4 cents.

OUR NECKWEAR DEPARTMENT.

MEN'S AND BOYS.

OUR IMMENSE and well assorted line of stylish neckwear; every new shape and style represented. Our goods are made up specially for us and are, therefore, made up right. In making your selection pick out the number you want, give color preference, and we will make a careful selection that will please, at a price that will, for the quality you receive, certainly surprise you.

Men's Silk Teck Scarfs, 19 and 25 Cents.

No. 34R400 Men's Silk Teck Scarfs in large assortment of stripes, plaids and floral designs; also plain black silk or satin.
Price, each........................19c
If by mail, postage extra, each, 3 cents.

No. 34R402 Men's Fine Silk Teck Scarfs in large assortment of floral, Persian, plaid and stripe effects. Also all white.
Regular 35c qualities.
Price, each..........25c
If by mail, postage extra, each, 3 cents.

Excellent Value at 35 Cents.

No. 34R404 Fine Brocaded Silk Teck Scarfs of the latest design and shape. Large assortment of light, medium and dark colors in new patterns Also plain black silk or satin. These goods are equal to regular 50-cent neckties.
Price, each... ...35c
If by mail, postage extra, each, 3 cents

No. 34R406 Men's Fine Silk Teck Scarfs. At this price we furnish a scarf which for quality and style is the best. Full width bands, best linings. The latest assortment in grouped stripe, Persian effect and plaids. Strictly reliable high grade goods. Give color preference and we can please you. Remember, you cannot buy better made or more carefully designed scarfs than we offer under this number. Also plain white. Price, each...............45c
If by mail, postage extra, each, 3 cents.

Men's Handsome Silk Teck Scarfs.

No. 34R410 Medium dark and light evening shades, latest new shape, in great variety of designs Persian, floral plaids, etc. In new effects and colorings. All are made in strictly first class manner, wide band and fine linings. An exquisite present. Each scarf put up in beautiful box.
Price, each..............................53c
If by mail, postage extra, each, 10 cents.

No. 34R412 Our new style Teck Scarfs, made to hook in the back. Small knot with wide aprons. A stylish, strictly high grade scarf in large assortment of new silks.
Price, each..................45c
If by mail, postage extra, 3 cents.

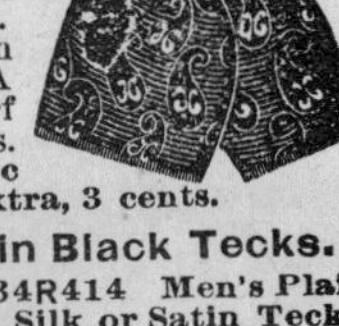

Plain Black Tecks.

No. 34R414 Men's Plain Black Silk or Satin Tecks. 25-cent value.
Price, each...............19c

No. 34R415 Men's Plain Black Silk or Satin Tecks. Superior quality. 35-cent retail values.
Price, each..............25c

No. 34R416 Men's Plain Black Silk or Satin Tecks, finest linings, wide band and wide spreading aprons. Very fine quality. Each, 45c
If by mail, postage extra, 3 cents.

All Black Puff Scarfs.

No. 34R420 Men's Plain Black Silk or Satin Puff Scarfs. Good value. Each..........25c

No. 34R421 Our Special Quality, fine Black Silk or Satin Puffs with wide spreading aprons, wide band, finest workmanship and lining. Strictly first class. Price, each.....45c
If by mail, postage extra, 3c.

Men's Puff Ties, New Colors.

No. 34R422 Men's Fancy Silk and Satin Puff Ties. Fine silk serge lined; latest style patterns in all the new colors.
Price, each..............25c
If by mail, postage extra, 3 cents.

Our Special Quality Puffs at 45 Cents.

No. 34R424 Our line of Puff Scarfs at 45 cents is excelled by none either in quality or careful selection of designs. Every one is carefully made and shaped; full width bands and fine linings. Many new and beautiful effects in Persian combined stripes and figures, plaids and stripes. Give preference and we can please you. Each...45c

If by mail, postage extra, 3 cents.

Highest Quality Teck Scarfs.

No. 34R425 Men's Extra High Quality Fancy Neckwear, made of the finest grades of imported silk and heavy English satins. A beautiful selection of rich and exclusive patterns that cannot be duplicated in the cheaper grades of neckwear; lined with finest quality satin and perfectly made in every way, a scarf that retails everywhere for $1.50. State color you prefer and we will make a selection that will be sure to please you.
Price, each................85c
If by mail, postage extra, 4 cents.

Extra Quality Puffs and Imperials.

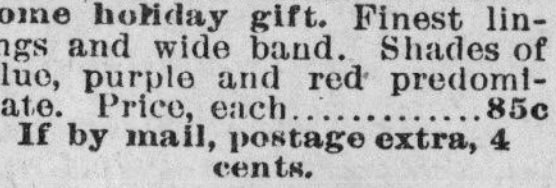

No. 34R426 Men's Extra Quality Fine Silk Puff Scarf. Made of extra quality fine soft imported silk in grand and beautiful designs impossible in the lower price goods. You will pay $1.50 for no finer scarf at retail. A handsome holiday gift. Finest linings and wide band. Shades of blue, purple and red predominate. Price, each............85c
If by mail, postage extra, 4 cents.

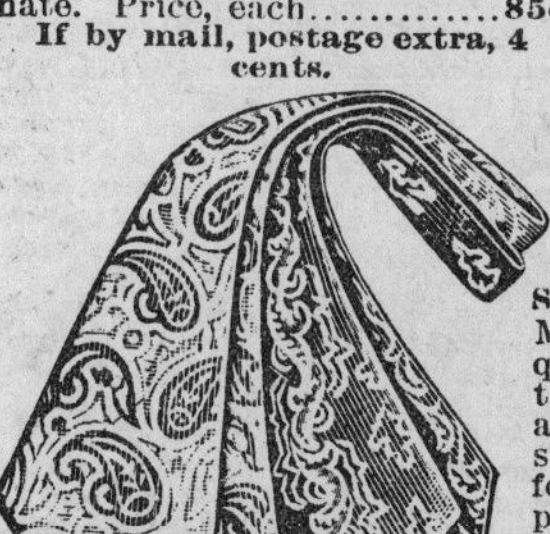

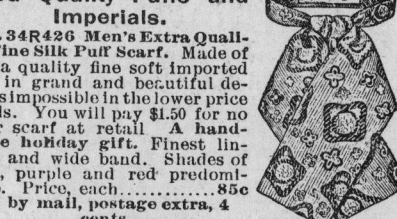

Latest Style and Highest Grade Imperial Scarf at 85 Cents.

No. 34R427 Men's Extra Quality Fine Silk Imperial Scarfs. Made from same quality of silks as the above. Grand and beautiful designs. Can be tied as four in hand or Ascot puff. We can please you with these fine goods. Each.....85c
If by mail, postage extra, 3 cents.

Men's Four in Hand Scarfs.

No. 34R440 Men's Silk Four in Hand Scarfs in large assortment of colors; plaids, stripes and figured designs. 25-cent retail qualities. Also, plain black silk or satin.
Price, each.........19c
If by mail, postage extra, 3 cents.

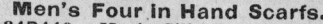

No. 34R441 Men's Silk Four in Hand Scarfs in brocaded effects, floral and Persian designs; also new stripe effects, or plain black or white silk or satin. Retail value, 35 cents.
Price, each..........................25c
If by mail, postage extra, 3 cents.

Fine Silk Four in Hand Scarfs at 45 Cents.

No. 34R443 Men's New Style Silk Four in Hand Scarfs, 1¼ inches in width. They are now in popular favor and tie a small tight knot. Up to date figure effects and stripes.
Price, each..................45c
If by mail, postage extra, 3 cents.

No. 34R444 Men's Staple Shape Silk Four in Hand, graduated slightly. Ties a neat knot of average size. New silks in stripes and new group effects. We want your order for up to date neckwear; we can please you. Strictly high grade. Also, plain black or white silk or satin.
Price, each..................45c
If by mail, postage extra, 3 cents.

Our 45-Cent Imperials.

No. 34R445 Men's Fine Imperials or Wide End Silk Scarfs. Lined, not extreme width, new up to date designs. Strictly high grade goods. Give color preference and we can certainly please you.
Price, each...45c
If by mail, postage extra, 3 cents.

Men's Fine Imperials, Flowing Ends.

No. 34R446 Men's Fine Imperial Silk Scarfs, flowing ends. A very stylish scarf. Large assortment in fine new imported silks. Also plain black silk or satin or plain white.
Price, each.......45c
If by mail, postage extra, 3 cents.

Silk or Satin Full Dress Protectors.

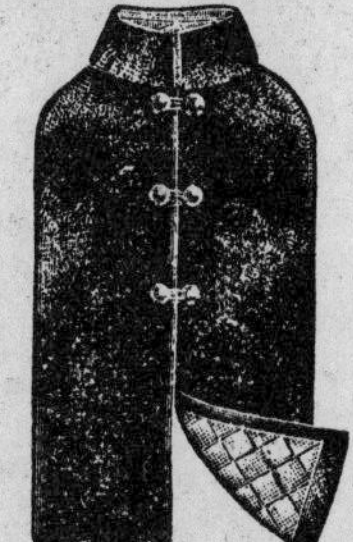

No. 34R448 Fine Silk or Satin Full Dress Protectors with beautiful white quilted silk lining, well padded, made with 2-inch silk collar and buttons with three loops. A handsome protector at a very low price.
Price, each.... ....$1.25
If by mail, postage extra, 8 cents.

The Latest Shield Bow.

No. 34R458 This Handsome Shield Bow so generally worn with the stylish high turn down collar, comes in a beautiful assortment of designs and colors, in rich silks and satins. State your color preference and we will be sure to suit you. It can also be worn with the ordinary turn down collar.
Price, each....................................25c
If by mail, postage extra, 1 cent.

MEN'S FANCY SILK BAND BOWS.

No. 34R460 Men's Fancy Silk Band Bows, with adjustable back fastener. A large assortment, dark and medium colors. Mostly small lots of our 25-cent qualities. Price, each........12c
If by mail, postage extra, 1 cent.

Our Select 25-Cent Bows.

No. 34R464 Men's Fine Silk Bows. Not the ordinary bow you pay 25 cents for, but made with full width bands and from select new silks. Largely in stripes and plaids; also figures and Persian effects. The best bow obtainable for 25 cents. Each...25c
If by mail, postage extra, 1 cent.

GIVE CATALOGUE NUMBER IN FULL WHEN YOU WRITE YOUR ORDER

Extra Quality 50-Cent Bows, 39 Cents.

No. 34R466 Men's Extra Quality Silk Band Bows, made from high grade select silks in a variety of new small effects particularly agreeable to good dressers; wide solid bands and new style knot. The same bow that you pay 50 cents for at home.
Price, each..39c
If by mail, postage extra, 1 cent.

Plain White Bows, 25 Cents.

No. 34R468 Men's Plain White Silk or Satin Bows, same style as No. 34R470. Excellent quality.
Price, each...25c
If by mail, postage extra, 1 cent.

No. 34R469 Fine Black Silk and Satin Bows, full shape, excellent quality, fast black. This is the greatest value ever offered at this price.
Price, each...............15c
If by mail, postage extra, 1 cent.

Black Band Bows.

No. 34R470 Men's Extra Heavy and Fine Black Satin or Silk Band Bows. Latest shapes, square ends, with adjusting clasp at back to fit any size collar. The best quality ever offered at this price. Price, each...............................22c
If by mail, postage extra, 1 cent.

No. 34R472 Men's Extra Quality Fine Black Silk or Satin Band Bows. Newest shape, the kind you pay 50 cents for at home. Wide bands, strictly high grade. Square or pointed ends. Price, each......38c
If by mail, postage extra, 1 cent.

MEN'S SUMMER BAND BOWS.

SPECIAL NOTICE—You can buy one necktie from us at the wholesale price. No reduction for dozen lots.

No. 34R480 They are made of Chelsea cloth or percale; have the adjustable bands to be lengthened or shortened, as desired. It is a pretty tie to wear with negligee or bosom shirts. Price, each...................5c
If by mail, postage extra, 1 cent.

Men's Chelsea Shield Bow.

No. 34R481 Chelsea Cloth Shield Bow to be worn with lay down collar, inexpensive, but very neat and dressy in appearance.
Price, each................5c
If by mail, postage extra, 1 cent.

No. 34R482 Fancy Colored Shield Bows, for turn down collars; made from fancy silks, in a large variety of figures. Price, each...............................8c
If by mail, postage extra, 1 cent.

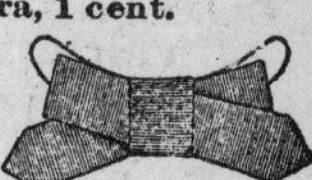

No. 34R483 Fancy colored shield bows for turn down collars, made from fancy colored silks; a large variety of figures in assorted colors.
Price, each...15c
If by mail, postage extra, 1 cent.

No. 34R484 Black Silk or Satin Shield Bows, with elastic loop, for turn down collars. Special value.
Price, each..... ....10c
If by mail, postage extra, 1 cent.

No. 34R485 Men's Very Fine Quality Plain Black Silk Shield Bows for turn down collar. Regular 25c quality at retail. Price, each..........19c
If by mail, postage extra, 1 cent.

White Lawn Dress Bows.

No. 34R490 Men's White Lawn Dress Bows for standing collars. Very neat.
Price, each..................5c
If by mail, postage extra, 1c.

No. 34R491 Fine White Lawn Dress Bows, square or pointed ends, with elastic bands in back, and silk stitched ends. Extra fine finish.
Price, each.....................................10c
If by mail, postage extra, 1 cent.

No. 34R492 These are made in exact imitation of the "tied by wearer" bow. Square ends, elastic in back; adjustable to any size collar. Regular retail price, 25 cents. Price, each..................19c
If by mail, postage extra, 1 cent.

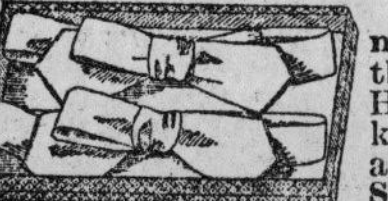

No. 34R493 These are made in exact imitation of those "tied by wearer." Have the natural folds in the knot; pointed ends, elastic, adjustable bands in back. Strictly correct shape.
Regular retail price, 25 cents. Price, each......19c
If by mail, postage extra, 5 cents.

Silk Embroidered Band Bows.

For Standing Collars.

No. 34R495 Men's Fine White Lawn Band Bows, with pointed ends, richly embroidered. Assorted patterns; retail price, 15 cents.
Price, each........10c
If by mail, postage extra, 2 cents.

No. 34R496 White Lawn Bows, large full dress size. Elegantly embroidered ends, with fine silk floss, adjustable band, for standing collar.
Price, each........20c
If by mail, postage extra, 2 cents.

No. 34R497 Men's Fine Lawn Dress Bows, with silk embroidered square ends, in new and rich effects. Price, each.......20c
If by mail, postage extra, 1 cent.

White Lawn Bows.

No. 34R498 White French Lawn Bows, with shield and elastic loop at back; pointed or square ends.
Price, each.....3c
Per dozen.....36c
If by mail, postage extra, each, 1 cent.

No. 34R499 Extra Fine White French Lawn Dress Bows, with shield and elastic loop at back, for turn down collars only. Silk stitched; extra fine high grade finish. Price, each........$0.09
Price, per dozen........1.03
If by mail, postage extra, each, 1 cent.

White Lawn Folded Ties.

These ties are put up in one dozen lots. We do not sell less than one dozen of a kind.

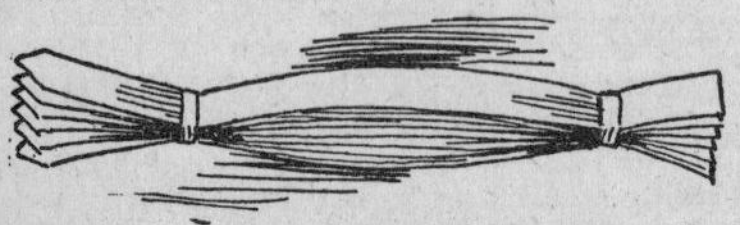

No. 34R500 White Lawn Ties, 1 inch wide, regulation length, good quality. Price, per dozen.....10c
No. 34R501 White Lawn Ties, 1 inch wide, regulation length, fine quality. Price, per dozen.......15c
No. 34R502 Extra Fine Quality White Lawn Ties, with silk stitched square ends, 1 inch wide, full length. Price, per dozen........25c
No. 34R503 Extra Long Fine Quality White Lawn Ties, 39 inches long, 1 inch wide, square ends. Price, per dozen........25c
If by mail, postage extra, per dozen, 5 cents.

Fancy Percale Folded Ties.

No. 34R504 Excellent Quality Fancy Figured Percale Ties, regulation size and length.
Price, per dozen........10c
No. 34R505 Fine French Figured Penang or Chelsea Cloth Ties, fast colors and new and beautiful patterns. Regular 25c quality. Per dozen...18c
If by mail, postage extra, per dozen, 5 cents.

The New Folded Club Tie.

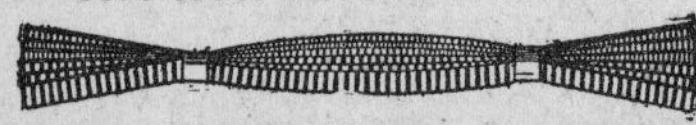

No. 34R506 New String Tie, is made of fine Percales, and comes in stripes and plaids of large assortment. A very suitable tie for general use and for negligee. Price, per dozen........25c
If by mail, postage extra, per dozen, 5 cents.

Men's Fine Washable String Ties.

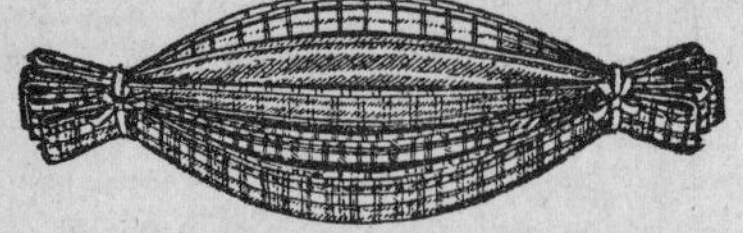

No. 34R507 This New Club Tie is made of very fine Madras cloth; colors woven in, and comes in a large and varied assortment; made with invisible seam, and is reversible; the regular 15-cent style. Our special price, per dozen, 72c; each....6c
If by mail, postage extra, per dozen, 5 cents.

China Silk String Ties.

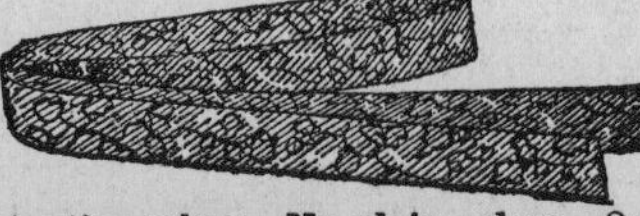

No. 34R508 China Silk String Ties. A large assortment of this popular Club House Tie in fancy combination colors. No plain colors. One inch wide, 36 inches long. Price, each........10c
If by mail, postage extra, each, 1 cent.

INCLUDE YOUR TIES WITH A FREIGHT OR EXPRESS ORDER.

Fancy Silk and Satin Club Ties.

No. 34R509 Fine Quality Silk and Satin Club House String Ties, Assorted Persian, floral, striped, dotted and modest figured patterns. Excellent value. Also plain black silk or satin. Price, each........23c
If by mail, postage extra, 1 cent.

Men's 50-Cent Club Ties, 39 Cents.

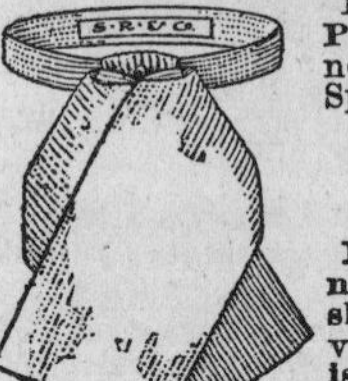

No. 34R510 Men's Fancy Fine Silk Club Tie. Made with wide soft ends and ties with small center and wide ends. A strictly high grade tie; retails at 50 cents. Foulards, Persian and stripe effects. Also plain black and satin or silk. Either pointed or square ends. Price, each........39c
If by mail, postage extra, 1 cent.

Plain Black Club Ties.

No. 34R530 Plain Black or Plain White Silk Club House Ties. Very dressy. 36 inches long, 1 inch wide. Special value. Price, each........25c
If by mail, postage extra, 1 cent.

Men's Fine Black Silk Folded String Ties.

No. 34R531 Men's Fine Black Silk Folded String Ties, all widths from ⅝ to 1⅛ inches.
Price, each........20c
If by mail, postage extra, 1 cent.

All Pure White Neckwear.

No. 34R532 Men's Fine White Pique Puff Scarfs. Handsome new shape, full width band. Special value. Price, each, 45c
If by mail, postage extra, 3 cents.

China Silk Puffs.

No. 34R533 Men's White China Silk Puffs, made similar in shape to above. Pure white, very fine, fashionable and stylish as an evening or party scarf.
Price, each........45c
If by mail, postage extra, 4 cents.

WHITE PIQUE FOUR IN HANDS.

No. 34R545 Pure White Fine French Pique Four in Hand; much finer than the above; more pliable and ties a better knot; reversible. Regular 25-cent value. Price, each........19c
No. 34R546 Extra Quality Finest White French Pique Four in Hand. Positively the highest grade washable scarf made. Remember, there is none better. Reversible, and very durable.
Price, each........25c
If by mail, postage on washable Four in Hands, each, 2 cents.

White Pongee Silk Four in Hand.

No. 34R550 Men's Fine All White Pure Silk Four in Hand Scarfs, very dressy and well made.
Price, each........23c
If by mail, postage extra, 2 cents.
No. 34R551 Men's Fine All White Pure Pongee Silk Four in Hand Scarfs for evening wear.
Price, each........45c
If by mail, postage extra, 2 cents.

Washable Four in Hands.

No. 34R552 Men's Fine Washable Four in Hand Scarfs. Made from imported Scotch Madras cloth; light and medium colors.
Price, each........10c
If by mail, postage extra, 2 cents.

CHILDREN'S WINDSOR TIES.

23-Cent Windsors.

No. 34R560 Fine Imported All Silk Windsor Ties, full length and width. Dark colors. Average width 5 inches. We have a choice assortment of new and beautiful patterns, including Scotch plaids, fancy stripes, dots and neat figures.
Price, each.......23c
If by mail, postage extra, 1 cent.

Plain Silk Windsors.

No. 34R561 Extra Fine All Silk Windsor Ties. Same as above, in plain colors, black, white, navy blue, yellow, red and light blue.
Price, each.......23c
If by mail, postage extra, 1 cent.

Extra Quality All Silk Windsors.

No. 34R562 Finest Extra Quality All Silk Windsor Neckties for boys. The prettiest Windsor tie made. Extra long and 7½ inches wide. A great variety of Scotch plaids, stripes, etc. Drawn stitch ends. State predominating color desired in order.
Price, each........45c
If by mail, postage extra, 2 cents.

Children's Bows.

No. 34R563 Children's Large Fancy Ties in dark and bright colors, made of a soft silk, 5 inches wide, with elastic to go around the collar and fasten with a hook behind the bow. Each, 25c
If by mail, postage extra, 2 cents.

Extra Large All Silk Bows for Children.

No. 34R564 The Largest of Children's Bows, made of pure silk, in a wide, large variety of Scotch and Highland plaids, also swell broad stripe effects. Measures about 13 inches across and the ends are 7¼ inches wide, drawn stitch ends. They are the prettiest, nobby bows for children. Made with elastic band to go around the collar and fasten with a hook bhind the bow. Price, each........45c
If by mail, postage extra, 2 cents.

Junior Neckwear for Boys from 5 to 15 Years of Age.

No. 34R565 To meet a large demand we have made up, specially for boys and youths, a smaller Teck scarf than is worn by men, in a large variety of stripes, plaids, Persian and floral designs. They are new and skillfully made. Look like four in hand tied by wearer.
Price, each........23c
If by mail, postage extra, 4 cents.

Junior Band Bows.

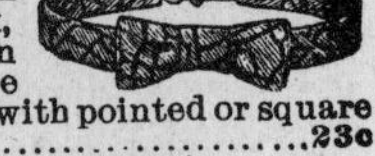

No. 34R566 Boys' Silk Band Bows, with elastic band in back, particularly dressy when worn with Junior shirts. A large variety of new designs, made with pointed or square ends. Price, each........23c
If by mail, postage extra, 4 cents.

The Way Muffler for Men or Women.

This muffler is patented by the Way Manufacturing Company, and is particularly designed for those who are much exposed in all kinds of weather, and gives perfect protection at neck and chest, closing in the back with three snap buttons.

No. 34R600 The Way Muffler, made of knit merino cloth, good quality, in black, navy and maroon.
Price, each........35c
No. 34R602 The Way Muffler, made of fine worsted yarn of excellent quality, in black, navy, myrtle green and maroon. Price, each........45c
No. 34R604 The Way Muffler, made of extra quality worsted yarn, with small stripes running crosswise; stylish and dressy. Colors, black with red stripe, navy with white stripe, and myrtle green with red stripe. Price, each........55c
If by mail, postage extra, each, 5 cents.

DO NOT FORGET
EXTRA POSTAGE WHEN GOODS ARE TO BE SENT BY MAIL.

CASHMERE and SILK MUFFLERS

Very Handsome Designs, All New Goods, Every One a Desirable Style.

If by mail, postage extra, on mufflers, each, 4 cents.

Cashmere Mufflers.

No. 34R610 Soft Cashmere Mufflers, large size, dark and medium colors. Plaids, stripes, checks and fancy figures.
Size, 29 inches square.
Price, each........20c

Imported Worsted Mufflers, 25c.

No. 34R611 Imported Worsted Mufflers, fine soft twill in dark and medium plaids, stripes and checks, in combinations, such as black and white, gray and white, brown mixed, etc.
Size, 29 inches square.
Price, each.......25c

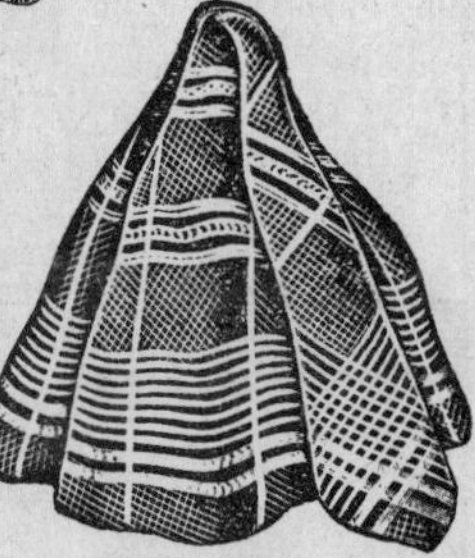

Cream and White Cashmere Mufflers.

No. 34R612 Cream and White Cashmere Mufflers, with dainty interwoven silk stripes of contrasting colors. Will wash and wear well.
Size, 29 inches square.
Price, each.......50c

Wool Cashmere Mufflers, 75 Cents.

No. 34R613 Fine Wool Cashmere Mufflers, soft, warm and comfortable. Will wash and wear well. Handsome medium and dark color plaids, checks and stripes. Particularly large assortment in brown and blue.
Size, 30 inches square.
Price, each.......75c

Silk Mufflers.

No. 34R626 Men's Fancy Figured Silk Mufflers, assorted colors and combinations, blue, pink, green in soft shades, also black and cream white. Size, 25 inches square.
Price, each.....50c
If by mail, postage extra, 4 cents.

Our 50-Cent Good Quality Silk Muffler.

No. 34R628 Good quality Silk Muffler, full size; navy blue, white polka dot.
Size, 28 inches square.
Price, each.......50c
If by mail, postage extra, each, 4 cents.

Our 75-Cent Brocaded Muffler.

No. 34R630 Men's Pure Silk Brocaded Mufflers. Rich floral and scroll designs in beautiful combinations, such as blue, red, green, pink, etc., including all black and cream white. **All pure silk.** Size, 26 inches square. Price, each.75c

A Big Selection of Silk Mufflers at 95 Cents.

No. 34R634 Very Fine Quality Polka Dot Muffler. Made of heavy English twill silk, very soft and a beautiful shade of a dark navy blue.
Size, 30 inches square.
Price, each.....95c
If by mail, postage extra, 4 cents.

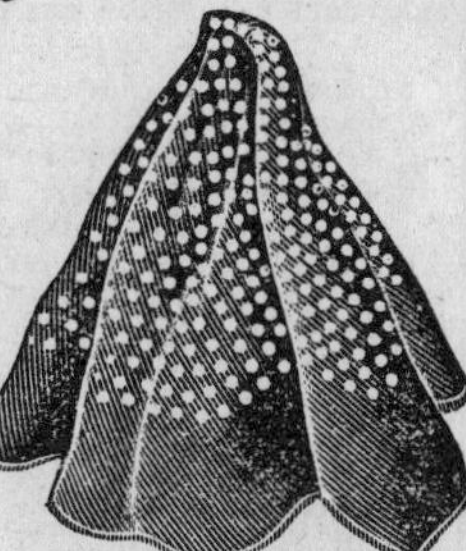

No. 34R638 Ladies' Handsome Silk Mufflers, just a trifle smaller than the men's, heavy brocaded centers in solid black and white with contrasting borders in heavy plain satin, 1½ inches wide, in such colors as crimson, blue, pink, etc.: a beautiful muffler and an elegant quality. Size, 26 inches square. Price, ea..95c
If by mail, postage extra, 4 cents.

Shepherd's Plaids.

No. 34R640 A Very Stylish Muffler in fine twilled silk, black and white Shepherd's plaid patterns, with large broken plaid borders; a handsome and serviceable muffler and always looks well.
Size, 28 inches square.
Price, each.......95c
If by mail, postage extra, 3 cents.

No. 34R642 Extra Fine Large All Silk Brocaded Mufflers, rich Dresden figures in satin relief. Dark and bright colors, such as red, dark blue, light blue, pink, green, etc., also black and cream white.
Size, 30 inches square.
Price, each.....95c

No. 34R644 Extra Heavy All Silk Muffler, woven by new process making it extremely soft, and yet it will not pull out, in heavy irregular stripe effect, giving it a very rich appearance; in dark shades, also cream and black. An elegant muffler at an extremely low price.
Size, 30 inches square.
Price, each.....$1.25
If by mail, postage extra, 4 cents.

No. 34R646 Gentlemen's Richly Brocaded Genuine Swivel Silk Muffler. (Swivel gives the effect of hand embroidery.) Handsome assorted floral designs on colored grounds, such as blue, dark crimson, etc., also black and white. A handsome muffler that will certainly please you.
Size, 28 inches square.
Price, each....$1.25
If by mail, postage extra, 4 cents.

Our $1.50 Muffler.

No. 34R648 This handsome muffler, in extremely rich brocaded patterns, large raised flower effect. The quality is very heavy and gives a rich appearance to the patterns, making them stand out very prominent. Dark, rich colors, also plain cream and black. A quality retailing everywhere for $2.00. Size, 30 in. square. Each..$1.50
If by mail, postage extra, 4 cents.

Full Dress Muffler, $1.50.

No. 34R650 A Full Dress Muffler in pure English twilled silk, plain black with heavy 1-inch black satin border. This muffler can also be used for ordinary wear; very soft finish, giving a very rich effect. It is one of the most popular dress mufflers worn.
Size, 29 inches square.
Price, each...$1.50
If by mail, postage extra, 4 cents.

Imported Muffler, $1.75.

No. 34R652 An Imported Muffler, extra heavy in quality, with rich colored figure designs on black and dark blue grounds. This is a muffler retailed everywhere for $3.00. It will certainly surprise you as to value, as it is sold at less than the ordinary retailer owns them. Mention choice in color of ground and figure when ordering.
Size, 29 inches square.
Price, each....$1.75

If by mail, postage extra, 4 cents.

Oxford Mufflers. A New and Rich Style.

Worn by gentlemen or ladies.

No. 34R654 Fine High Grade Oxford Mufflers, made from new patterns in fine neckwear silks. New Persian effects in most fashionable colors and patterns, fine silk lining or the same on both sides. Special value at our low price.
Price, each..........$1.50
If by mail, postage extra, 5 cents.

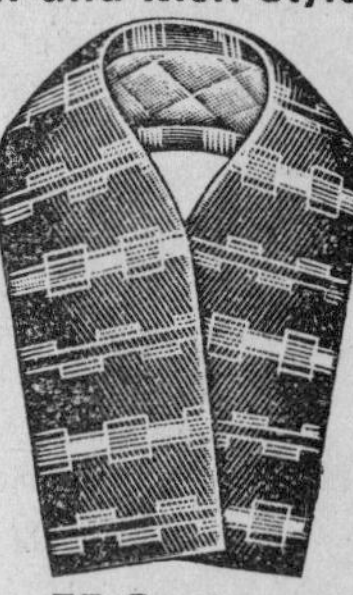

Fine Oxford Muffler, 75 Cents.

No. 34R658 Fine Oxford Mufflers, made of stylish neckwear silks, in large variety of plaids and stripes, with pretty colored silk lining, **very fashionable and up to date.** Give color preference and you will not be disappointed.
Price, each............75c

Silk Oxford Muffler, 45 Cents.

No. 34R660 Good Quality Silk Oxford Mufflers, made with fine satin lining, full size, in large variety of scroll designs, plaids and stripes, or plain black.
Price, each............45c

SEND 5 CENTS
For Sample Book of everything in Men's Custom Tailoring Goods at Lowest Prices.

OUR SUSPENDER DEPARTMENT.

OUR LINE OF SUSPENDERS cannot be excelled for quality and workmanship. Even our cheapest numbers are well made and we warrant every pair to be perfect. We especially recommend the better grades as they invariably give better satisfaction in the long run. You pay but one single small profit to us, and can obtain one pair as cheaply as if you were to buy them in dozen lots from a jobber. WHEN ORDERING SHIPPED BY MAIL, ALWAYS ENCLOSE POSTAGE.

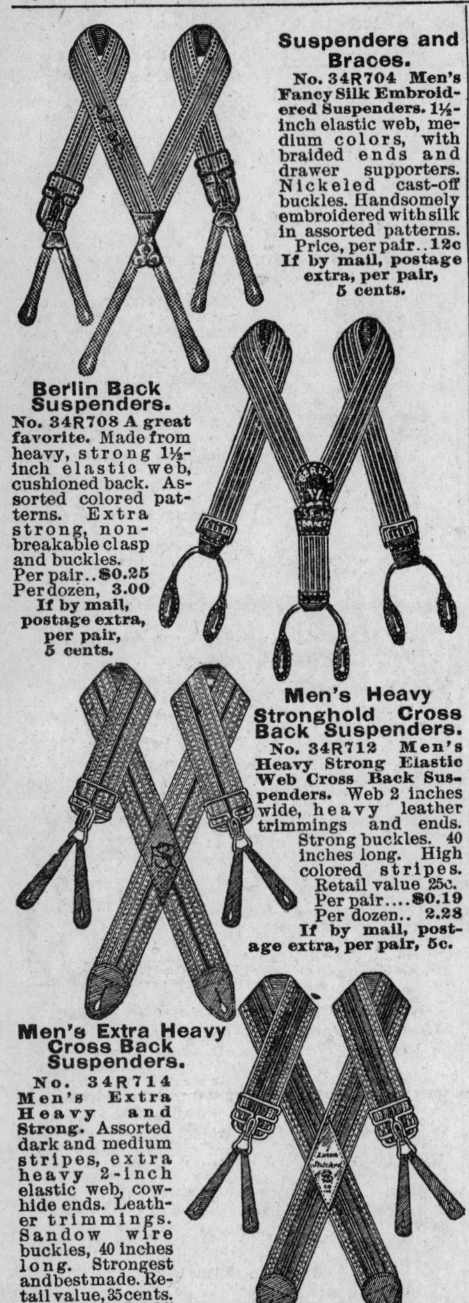

Suspenders and Braces.

No. 34R704 Men's Fancy Silk Embroidered Suspenders. 1½-inch elastic web, medium colors, with braided ends and drawer supporters. Nickeled cast-off buckles. Handsomely embroidered with silk in assorted patterns.
Price, per pair..12c
If by mail, postage extra, per pair, 5 cents.

Berlin Back Suspenders.

No. 34R708 A great favorite. Made from heavy, strong 1½-inch elastic web, cushioned back. Assorted colored patterns. Extra strong, non-breakable clasp and buckles.
Per pair..$0.25
Per dozen, 3.00
If by mail, postage extra, per pair, 5 cents.

Men's Heavy Stronghold Cross Back Suspenders.

No. 34R712 Men's Heavy Strong Elastic Web Cross Back Suspenders. Web 2 inches wide, heavy leather trimmings and ends. Strong buckles. 40 inches long. High colored stripes.
Retail value 25c.
Per pair....$0.19
Per dozen.. 2.28
If by mail, postage extra, per pair, 5c.

Men's Extra Heavy Cross Back Suspenders.

No. 34R714 Men's Extra Heavy and Strong. Assorted dark and medium stripes, extra heavy 2-inch elastic web, cowhide ends. Leather trimmings. Sandow wire buckles, 40 inches long. Strongest and best made. Retail value, 35 cents.
Per pair..$0.25
Per dozen. 3.00
If by mail, postage extra, per pair, 5 cents.

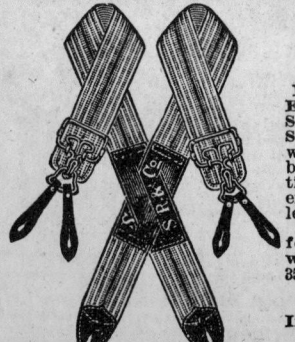

Men's Hercules Suspenders.

No. 34R716 Men's Extra Heavy and Strong Hercules Suspenders. Made with self adjusting back; 2-inch elastic web, cowhide ends, wire buckles, length 40 inches. **Excels all others for strength and wear.** Retail value, 35 cents.
Each........$0.25
Per dozen... 3.00
If by mail, postage extra, per pair, 7 cents.

Plain Black Suspenders.

No. 34R719 Men's Fine Plain Black Suspenders. Close woven 1¼-inch elastic web. Kid trimmings. Ornamental sliding buckles and clasps. Fine black braided mohair ends and drawer supporters, glove snap cast-off. Price, per pair........................23c

Plain White Suspenders.

No. 34R720 Same as above in plain white.
Price, per pair..................................23c
If by mail, postage extra, per pair, 5 cents.

Our New Sears, Roebuck & Co.'s Suspender.

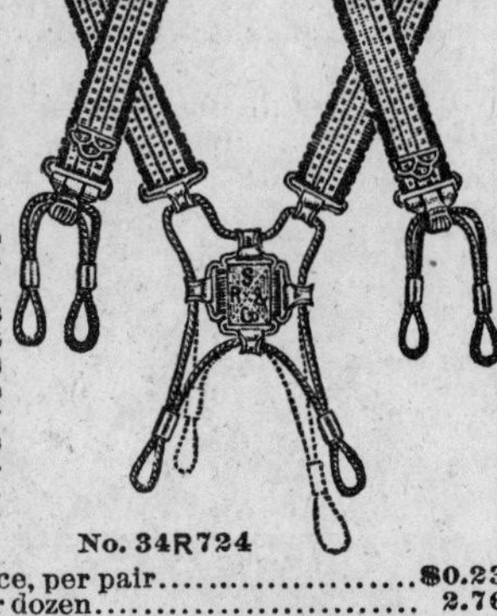

No. 34R724 A New Suspender designed to equalize the extreme movements of the body, relieves the strain on the shoulders and buttons. No matter what position you assume the strain is practically the same on all buttons. Brings ease and comfort and never pulls buttons off. Made in a large variety of strong elastic webs. The running cord is non-elastic, strong and durable.

No. 34R724

Price, per pair.......................$0.23
Per dozen.............................2.76
If by mail, postage extra, per pair, 6 cents.

Floral Design Suspenders.

No. 34R726 Men's Dresden and Floral Pattern Elastic Web Suspenders. New, handsome designs. Ornamental sliding buckles with cast-off. Fancy braided ends and drawer supporters. Leather back and will give lasting satisfaction. Latest novelty. Per pair.......25c
If by mail, postage extra, per pair, 5 cents.

Men's Suspenders, Lisle Web.

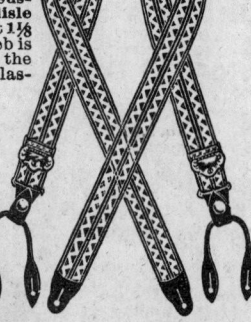

No. 34R727 Men's Suspenders, made from lisle elastic webbing, about 1⅛ inches wide. Lisle web is lighter weight than the usual cotton webs or elastic and is cooler and very comfortable for summer wear. Neat, modest designs, fancy figures and stripes. Nickel plated trimmings, leather ends and cast-off snap buttons. Medium light colors.
Price, each..$0.25
Per dozen... 3.00
If by mail, postage extra, each, 5c.

Fancy Elastic Web Cross Back Kid End Suspenders.

No. 34R728 Handsomely designed, colors woven in web, glove snap fasteners with metal support adding much to durability. Fancy ornamental sliding buckles. Fine kid ends. Medium and light colors.
Per pair.......25c
If by mail, postage extra, per pair, 5 cents.

Extra Long Suspenders.

No. 34R729 Men's Extra Length Plain White or Slate Color Elastic Web Suspenders, made same style as No. 34R728, 40 inches long. Fine and first class in every particular. Price, per pair........45c
If by mail, postage extra, per pair, 5 cents.

Men's Lisle Suspenders, 35 Cents.

No. 34R731 Men's Fancy Suspenders, made from fine quality lisle elastic webbing, 1⅛ inches wide, the same quality that is used in almost all suspenders sold for 50 cents a pair. A smooth surface, light weight suspender, comfortable for summer wear. Fancy design similar to illustration. Fine gilt buckles, kid ends and snap button cast-off. Our low price is made possible by purchasing these goods in quantities from maker for cash. This quality will please and you can save 15 cents. Medium colors.
Per pair......$0.35
Per dozen.... 4.20
If by mail, postage extra, 5c.

Extra Fine Silk Embroidered Suspenders.

No. 34R732 Men's Extra Fine Silk Embroidered Suspenders. Handsome ornamental gold slides and castoff. Braided lisle ends and drawer supporters. **New exclusive patterns.** Light, medium and dark colors. Artistic and elaborate silk embroidery. Charming and effective contrasts. Per pair.40c
If by mail, postage extra, per pair, 5 cents.

The Guyot.

No. 34R740 Bretelle's Universelles. The Famous French Sanitary Suspenders. Light weight, strong, linen web, with elastic in back pieces only. Unexcelled for comfort and durability. Light and dark colors. All colors absolutely fast. Per pair..42c
If by mail, postage extra, per pair, 5 cents.

The Parisian Suspender.

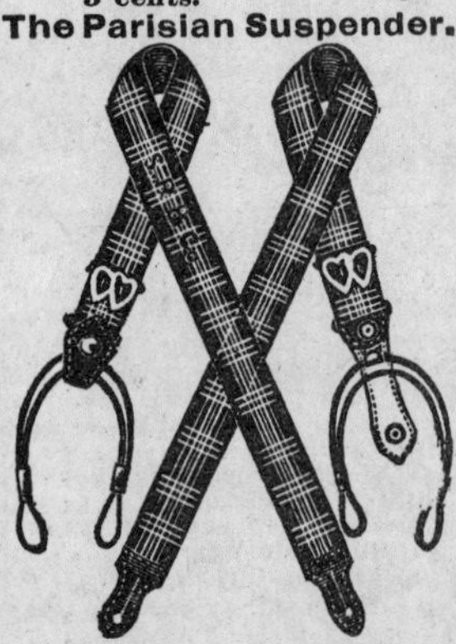

No. 34R744 The New Parisian Suspender. Made of finest imported elastic web in plaids and stripes of medium colors. Full length, cross back, kid trimmed with duplicate rolled and stitched leather ends, one running on the metal, the other on the leather. Thus the strain is equalized, making an unusually attractive and dependable suspender. Regular retail value, 75 cents.
Price, pair....42c
If by mail, postage extra, per pair, 5 cents.

The President Suspender.

No. 34R746 A new style recently patented suspender with improved back which equalizes the strain on all parts with every attitude. Relieves the strain on shoulders and not likely to pull off buttons. Made with strong non-elastic web cord in back and high grade elastic webbing in main parts. Every pair warranted to wear to the entire satisfaction of the purchaser. Made in fancy webs or plain colors.
Price, per pair........$0.45
Per dozen... 5.40

If by mail, postage extra, per pair, 5c.

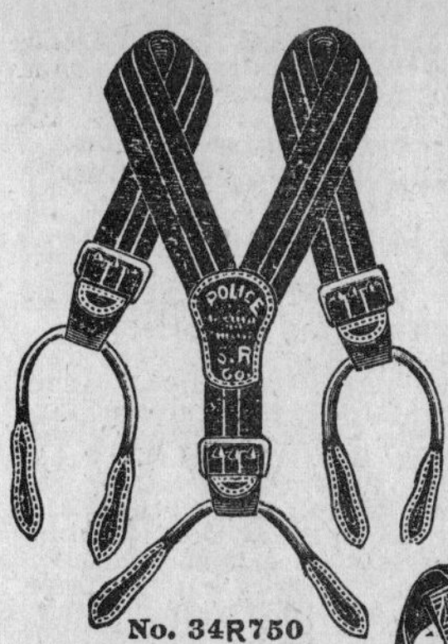

No. 34R750

Extra Strong Police Back Suspenders.

No. 34R750 Firemen's, Policemen's and Mechanics' Extra Super Stout Elastic Web Suspenders. Leather cushioned back and heavy rolled leather ends. Assorted patterns; every pair warranted. Retail value, 50 cents.
Per pair......$0.41
Per dozen.... 4.92
If by mail, postage extra, per pair, 5 cents.

Men's Silk Suspenders, Non-Elastic Web.

No. 34R754 Men's Silk Non Elastic Web Suspenders with entirely new gold and filigree sliding buckles cast-off. Pure silk elastic web ends, tipped with white kid. Fine white embossed kid trimmings, assorted light colors, stripes, fancy figures. Dresden and floral patterns.
Price, per pair. .... .43c
If by mail, postage extra, per pair, 5 cents.

No. 34R754

No. 34R755

Men's Silk Suspenders 43c.

No. 34R755 Men's Fine Suspenders made from fine mercerized silk elastic webing 1½ inches wide. They look like genuine silk but wear much better and are strong and durable. One of the very best new light weight suspenders offered this season. Very comfortable for summer wear. Medium light stripes, gilt buckles, fine leather ends and cast off. Much better than suspenders usually sold for 50 cents. You will appreciate genteel well made suspenders of this kind.
Price, per dozen, $5.16; per pair 43c
If by mail, postage extra, per pair, 5 cents.

Men's Embroidered Suspenders in Covered Boxes.

No. 34R760 Men's Silk Embroidered Suspenders. Imported web, richly embroidered in attractive designs, ornamental sliding buckles, fine braided ends. light or medium colors. No plain colors. Packed one pair in box. Price, per pair..........50c
If by mail, postage extra, per pair, 6 cents.

Men's Embroidered Satin Suspenders.

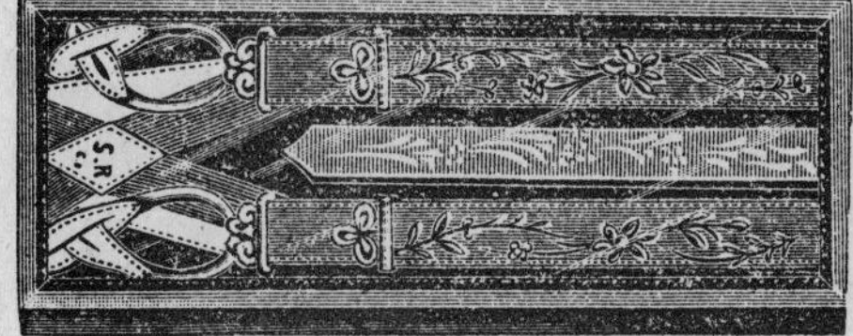

No. 34R764 Fine Quality High Grade Men's Suspenders, made of fine silk or satin, richly embroidered, beautiful floral sprays of contrasting colors embroidered down front. Colors, black, cream, blue, pink, lavender and garnet. Packed one pair in box with perfectly transparent celluloid front. Transparent as glass and will not break. **A very handsome box.** Price, per pair...........................90c
If by mail, postage extra, per pair, 10 cents.

Indianola Leather Suspenders.

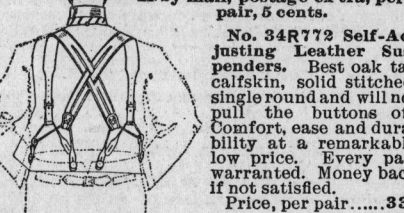

No. 34R770 Self-Adjusting Leather Suspenders. Good quality leather and will give good satisfaction. Price, per pair............23c
If by mail, postage extra, per pair, 5 cents.

No. 34R772 Self-Adjusting Leather Suspenders. Best oak tan calfskin, solid stitched, single round and will not pull the buttons off. Comfort, ease and durability at a remarkably low price. Every pair warranted. Money back if not satisfied.
Price, per pair......33c
If by mail, postage extra, per pair, 5 cents.

Extra Length Leather Suspenders.

No. 34R774 Extra Length, same as above.
Price, per pair...36c
If by mail, postage extra, per pair, 5 cents.

Our Special Leather Suspenders.

No. 34R776 The Latest and Best of all Leather Suspenders. Made of fine quality of grain leather with the new equalizing back which adjusts itself instantly to every movement of the body, giving ease and comfort. The cord mounting is woven especially for this purpose and there is no extra wear on any particular part. Thus the cord will in most cases outwear the other parts. Cast-off snap buttons. Order this suspender and you will never wear any other kind.
Price, per dozen...$5.28
Price, per pair...44c
If by mail, postage extra, per pair, 7 cents.

No. 34R776

Boys' and Youths' Suspenders.

No. 34R780 Boys' Elastic Web Suspenders. Good substantial web, fancy striped patterns, leather trimmings and ends. Per pair.......5c

No. 34R782 Boys' and Youths' Suspenders. Fancy striped patterns, metal grip back, strong elastic web. Woven ends and good strong buckles.
Per pair........10c

No. 34R784 Boys' and Youths' Fancy Silk Embroidered Elastic Web Suspenders. Woven ends and non-breakable wire buckles. New, handsome designs.

No. 34R784

Price, per pair...15c

No. 34R786 Boys' and Youths' Extra Quality Suspenders, elastic web, medium colors, cushion back, cast-off buckles. High grade in every particular. Retail value, 25 cents. Per pair.........19c
If by mail, postage extra, per pair, 5 cents.

Boys' Special Suspender, 19 Cents.

No. 34R787 A new suspender for boys, designed to equalize extreme movements of the body and relieve the strain on shoulders and the buttons. The strain is the same with the body in almost any position. Our low price of 19 cents brings this good suspender within the reach of all, and is the regular wholesale price. Buy this suspender for your boy. They are comfortable strong elastic webs, with strong cord ends.

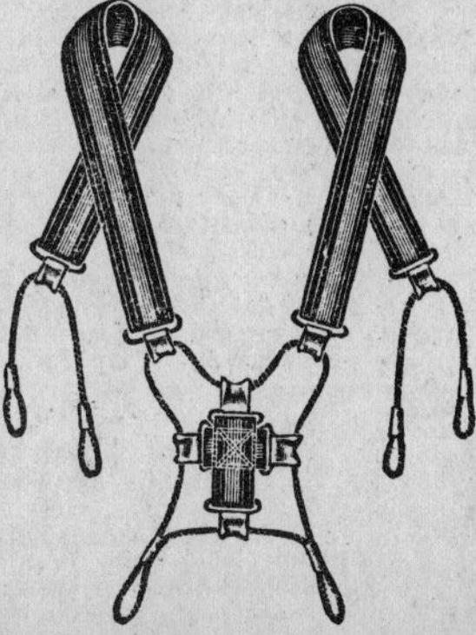

Price, per dozen, $2.28; per pair................19c
If by mail, postage extra, per pair, 5 cents.

Anchor Brace.

No. 34R788 Men's Superior Shoulder Braces. Fancy overshot elastic web.

BRACE UP AND SQUARE YOUR SHOULDERS

Suspender attachment with fine braided lisle ends and drawers supporters. Light and medium colors.
Price, per pair.42c
If by mail, postage extra, per pair, 7 cents.

Gamble Shoulder Brace for Men and Youths.

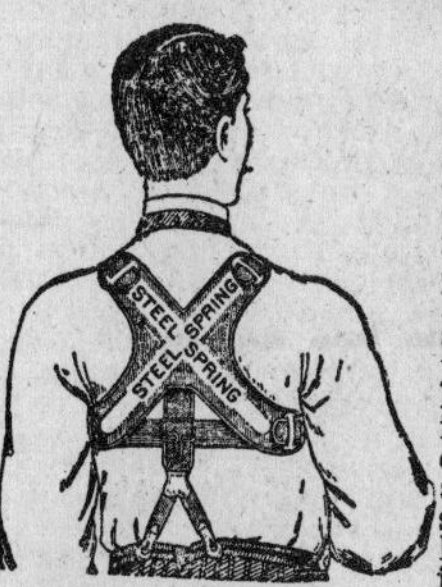

No. 34R790 The special point of merit of this Brace is in two light steel springs which act as if you gently press your thumbs on one's shoulder blades. Only shoulder brace made on the right principle. They are handsomely made, perfectly adjustable, roll leather end, patent cast-off snaps, best hair pads, leather lined in front of arms, most comfortable brace made, and will brace a man up so he will grow strong and healthy. Size, 30 to 40 inches chest measure.
Price, per pair...$1.35
If by mail, postage extra, per pair, 8 cents.

The Gamble Ladies' and Misses' Shoulder Brace.

A Perfect Shoulder Brace and Skirt Supporter Combined.

No. 34R791 The Gamble Shoulder Brace for Ladies. Fine light drab jean web adjustable to any position, finest hair padding, leather lined in front of arms, soft and pliable, will not chafe or irritate the skin. The principle is the same as in the men's brace, No. 34R790. Sizes, 26, 28, 30, 32, 34 and 36-inch bust measure. Measure close under arms and above breasts.
Price, per pair.....$1.00
If by mail, postage extra, per pair, 8 cents.

The Knickerbocker Shoulder Brace.

A Good Shoulder Brace, made of non-elastic web with elastic ends. Easily adjusted by buckles, as shown in cut. One of the most practical and comfortable braces made. Very desirable for children, as they will prevent round or stooped shoulders.

No. 34R794 No. 34R795

No. 34R794 Men's Knickerbocker Shoulder Brace, made of fine web in colors or plain white. Give chest measure. Sizes, 32, 34, 36, 38, 40 inches. Per pair..45c

No. 34R795 Boys' Knickerbocker Shoulder Brace, colored or plain white. Give chest measure. Sizes, 24, 26, 28, 30 inches. Per pair..45c
If by mail, postage extra, per pair, 5 cents.

No. 34R796 Ladies' Knickerbocker Shoulder Brace, non-elastic web, plain white or colored. **Improved Skirt Supporter,** plain white. Sizes, 32, 34, 36, 38 inches. Give bust measure.
Per pair............45c

No. 34R797 Girls' Knickerbocker Shoulder Brace, made same as ladies, in white. Size 24, 26, 28, 30 inches. Give bust measure.
Per pair..............45c

No. 34R797 No. 34R796

If by mail, postage extra, per pair, 5 cents.

HANDKERCHIEF DEPARTMENT.

The growth of our handkerchief department demonstrates to us that our customers are finding out that we can save money for them on small as well as large items. The reason why this department grows so rapidly is because we are offering handkerchiefs, whether cotton, linen or silk, at the lowest possible prices. In domestic cotton handkerchiefs our prices are the lowest, based on the cost to manufacture, for we buy them direct from the manufacturers. Linen, embroidered and silk goods are imported by us, without middlemen's profits. In this manner our position gives the customer advantage over conditions usually prevalent in his home town, where the merchant must pay jobbers' profit before goods can be placed on sale.

We warrant every article to be as represented and satisfactory or we refund your money.

POSTAGE. When ordering by mail, allow postage as given with each number.

PRICES. Some numbers in handkerchiefs are sold by the dozen only. Because of the extremely low price we cannot sell them in smaller quantities.

MEN'S HANDKERCHIEFS.

Men's Turkey Red Handkerchiefs.

Sold by the dozen only.

No. 34R1005 Men's Turkey Red Fancy Printed Handkerchiefs. Size, 18x18 inches.
Price, per dozen.......25c

No. 34R1008 Men's Fine Turkey Red Handkerchiefs, of American manufacture, better than any other Turkey red handkerchiefs and are superior to all others for wear. Owing to our low prices we do not sell these goods in quantities of less than one dozen. Size, 18x17 inches, per dozen.........33c
If by mail, postage extra, per dozen, 10 cents.
Size, 21x20 inches, per dozen......................42c
If by mail, postage extra, per dozen, 14 cents.
Size, 24x23 inches, per dozen..... ....50c
If by mail, postage extra, per dozen, 16 cents.
Size, 28x26 inches, per dozen........ ....68c
If by mail, postage extra, per dozen, 24 cents.

Indigo Blue Handkerchiefs.

No. 34R1110 Men's Genuine Indigo Blue Handkerchiefs, with white figures and dots; fast color. Size, 21 inches, per dozen......52c
If by mail, postage extra, 14c.
Size, 24 inches, per dozen......70c
If by mail, postage extra, 16c.

NOTE—Where handkerchiefs are quoted at dozen rates, it indicates that we do not sell them in less than one dozen lots.

Sateen Handkerchiefs.

No. 34R1112 Imported Sateen Handkerchiefs; full size; fine soft finish, fancy wide navy blue, white dotted and figured borders and figured centers, fast colors.
Price, each 7c
Per dozen.,.................84c
If by mail, postage extra, per dozen, 14 cents.

White Cambric Handkerchiefs.

No. 34R1114 Men's Fine Plain White Linen Finish Cambric Handkerchiefs. Plain hem with rib effect tape border, medium size. Price, each............. 4c
Per dozen.. ....48c

No. 34R1116 Men's Large Size Plain White Cambric Handkerchiefs. Size, 22x22 inches. Ribbed pattern borders. A special value.
Price, per dozen, 96c; each...8c
If by mail, postage extra, per dozen, 14 cents.

Men's Hemstitched Handkerchiefs.

No. 34R1118 Men's White Cambric Handkerchiefs. 1-inch hem, medium size, value exceptionally good. Price, each.....4c
Per dozen:......... ... .48c
If by mail, postage extra, per dozen, 12 cents.

No. 34R1120 Men's Fine White Cambric Cotton Handkerchiefs, made with 1-inch hemstitched border. A very fine quality which usually retails for 15 or 20 cents. Full size.
Price, per dozen, $1.08; each.....................9c
If by mail, postage extra, per dozen, 12 cents.

Men's Extra Large Hemstitched Handkerchiefs.

No. 34R1121 Men's Imported Cambric Handkerchiefs, extra large size, 22 inches square, with 1-inch hemstitched border; one of the most durable handkerchiefs ever brought into the country.
Price, per dozen, $2.40; each.....................20c
If by mail, postage extra, per dozen, 15 cents.

Colored Border Handkerchiefs.

No. 34R1122 Men's Hemmed Colored Border Handkerchiefs. Fine soft finish. White center, with fancy colored borders. Assorted colors and patterns.
Price. per dozen 35c
If by mail, postage extra, per dozen, 12 cents.

No. 34R1124 Men's Hemmed Colored Bordered Handkerchiefs, with woven tape borders. Colors woven in, not printed. White center, soft and fine and excellent for wear. Assorted colors. Full size.
Price, each........ ....4c
Per dozen 48c
If by mail, postage extra, per dozen, 12 cents.

Fancy Plaid Handkerchiefs.

No. 34R1126 Fancy Plaid Center Colors Woven, Handkerchiefs, white, with neat stripes running through entire handkerchief, both ways, forming handsome plaid. Full size, fast colors.
Per dozen, 60c; each... .....5c
If by mail, postage extra, 14c

No. 34R1128 New Design Fancy Colored Border Cambric Handkerchiefs. White center, with 1-inch hemstitched colored border. Assorted patterns and colors. Full size.
Per dozen, 60c; each... .....5c
If by mail, postage extra, 14c.

No. 34R1130 Men's Fine Cambric Handkerchiefs. White center, with new design; colored borders; hemstitched and soft and fine; fast colors; large variety different patterns of the season's newest and best effects; full size.
Per dozen, 96c; each.......8c
If by mail, postage extra, 14c.

All Colored Centers at 9 Cents.

No. 34R1132 Men's Fine Cambric Hemstitched Handkerchiefs. Colored centers and borders, choice assortment of patterns. The centers are of different shades of blue, pink, etc. We always furnish the newest designs.
Per dozen, $1.08; each......9c
If by mail, postage extra, per dozen, 12 cents.

Men's Linen Handkerchiefs, Colored Borders.

No. 34R1134 Pure Linen Hemstitched Handkerchiefs, white centers with handsome and artistic fancy colored borders. Full size. Soft and fine. New effects and combinations. Warranted pure linen and fast colors.
Per dozen., $2.76; each..23c

No. 34R1136 Men's Pure Linen High Grade White Handkerchiefs, made with ½-inch hemstitched colored borders. These are of modest genteel designs that always conform to good taste.
Price, per dozen, $5.40; each.......... ....45c

Men's Japanette Handkerchiefs.

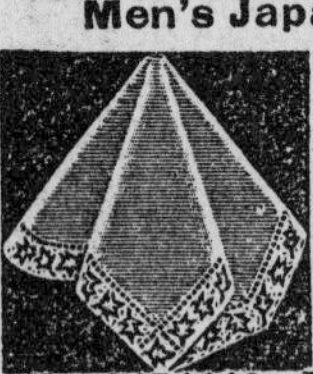

No. 34R1138 Japanette Handkerchiefs are made of soft finished light weight cotton, made to look like silk in color and surface. They are very desirable and wear well. This number is of the new design; colored border; made in large variety, the illustration showing but one. A very satisfactory article.
Price, per dozen, $1.08; each, 9c

No. 34R1140 Men's Cream White Japanette Handkerchiefs, with 1-inch hemstitched border. Size, 18x18 inches. Per dozen, $1.08; each.........9c

Japanette Initial Handkerchiefs.

No. 34R1142 Japanette Initial Handkerchiefs, with 1-inch hem, cream white with handsome silk embroidered initial. Be sure to state what initial is wanted.
Per dozen, $1.44; each.....12c

NOTE—Initial handkerchiefs are made in all initials except I, O, Q, U, V, X, Y, Z.

No. 34R1143 Gentlemen's Fine White Hemstitched Initial Handkerchiefs; an elegant quality, full size and very durable; one that will be sure to give you satisfaction. Per dozen, $1.80; each..15c

Men's Linen Handkerchiefs.

No. 34R1144 Men's Pure Irish Linen Handkerchiefs, plain white with handsomely embroidered initial, full size with ½-inch hem. Put up one-half dozen in box. Be sure to state what initial is wanted.
Price, per dozen, $2.76; per box of ½ dozen, $1.38; each........................23c
If by mail, postage on men's hdkfs., per doz. 14c.

Men's Fine Pure Linen Handkerchiefs.

No. 34R1146 Men's Fine Pure Linen Handkerchiefs, ½-inch hemstitched border and embroidered with small finely worked initial. This quality seldom retails as low as 50 cents. Put up ½ dozen in a box. Do not forget initial wanted in order.
Price, each..................$0.40
Box of ½ dozen............ 2.40

Men's White Linen Handkerchiefs.

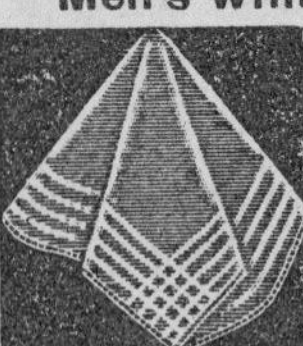

No. 34R1150 Men's Pure Irish Linen Handkerchiefs. Plain white, large size with finished tape borders, the best value possible at this low price. Price, per dozen, $1.56; each........13c

No. 34R1152 Men's Fine White Pure Linen Tape Border Handkerchiefs. Size, 19x19 inches. A very fine cloth at our low price, not too heavy but medium weight, are soft and wear well. Per dozen, $2.76; each..23c

Extra Size Linen Handkerchiefs.

No. 34R1154 Men's Extra Size Pure Irish Linen Handkerchiefs, plain white, tape effect border and hem. Size, 23x23 inches. Never retailed for less than 35 cents. We guarantee them pure linen, and the best value ever offered for 25 cents.
Price, per doz., $3.00; each, 25c

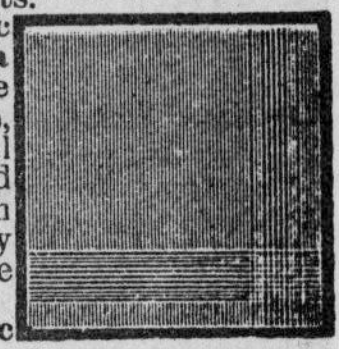

No. 34R1156 Men's Extra Quality White Pure Linen Tape Border Handkerchiefs. Size, 21x21 inches. This is a special grade light weight and fine, and will not fill up the pocket as an ordinary handkerchief. A very fine count. Tape borders are more durable than hemstitched.
Price, per doz., $5.40; each, 45c

If by mail, postage extra, per dozen, on linen handkerchiefs, 14 cents.

Men's Linen Hemstitched Handkerchiefs.

No. 34R1158 Men's Fine Irish Linen White Handkerchiefs, with 1-inch hem. Heavy and strong. Size, 18x18 ins. Warranted extra value, and the same handkerchief that retailers sell at 25 cents. Price, each.........$0.12
Per dozen.......................... 1.44

No. 34R1160 Extra Quality Pure Irish Linen White Handkerchiefs, ½ or 1-inch hem. Size, 19x19 inches, fine hand finish, excellent for wear, and fine and soft to the touch. True merit in these goods. Try them and you will be satisfied.
Price, per dozen, $2.28; each.........................19c

No. 34R1162 This is one of our specialties. Imported direct. Made of selected pure Irish linen. Plain white, with 1-inch hemstitched border; soft hand finish, full size and the equal in wear and finish to any 35-cent handkerchief ever sold.
Price, per dozen, $3.00; each.............................25c

No. 34R1164 Men's Pure Linen White Handkerchiefs; same as above, but with ½-inch hem. These are superior qualities that cannot be excelled.
Price, per dozen, $3.00; each.............................25c

No. 34R1166 Men's Fine Quality White Pure Linen Handkerchiefs; ½-inch hemstitched borders; made of fine Irish linen, hand finished and a value equal to those usually sold at 50 cents. Full size.
Price, each...............$0.35
Per dozen.................. 4.20

No. 34R1168 Men's Extra Quality White Pure Linen Handkerchiefs; made with neat ¼-inch hemstitched borders. Size, 19x19 inches. The finest that can be produced to sell at this price.
Price, per dozen, $5.40; each.............................45c

LADIES' HANDKERCHIEFS.

Ladies' Fancy Cotton Handkerchiefs.

No. 34R1170 Ladies' Hemstitched Handkerchiefs, medium size, fancy colored borders, assorted designs.
Price, each.................... 4c
Per dozen.......................48c
If by mail, postage extra, per dozen, 8 cents.

No. 34R1172 Ladies' Cotton Handkerchiefs with scalloped edges and printed floral design border.
Price, each...................4c
Per dozen 48c
If by mail, postage extra, per dozen, 8 cents.

No. 34R1174 Ladies' Fine Cambric Handkerchiefs with fancy hemstitched colored borders. A fine handkerchief at a low price.
Price, each 6c
Per dozen.........................72c
If by mail, postage extra, per dozen, 8 cents.

Hand Made Irish Linen Handkerchiefs.

Put up one on a card.

No. 34R1238 Ladies' Highest Grade Pure Irish Linen Handkerchiefs with special exquisite and novel designs in real hand made Renaissance lace. This is one of the most beautiful and artistic handkerchiefs ever sold, and being hand work entirely adds much to its strength and durability. Usual retail price, $1.50.
Price, per dozen, $11.40; each.................. 95c
If by mail, postage extra, per dozen, 16 cents.

Children's Handkerchiefs.

If by mail, postage extra, per dozen, 7 cents.

No. 34R1240 Children's Fancy Bordered Cambric Handkerchiefs. Very neat, hemmed borders. A choice assortment of new and novel colorings and pretty designs. Owing to the remarkably low price we make on these goods, we cannot sell them in less than one-half dozen lots.
Price, one-half dozen...8c
Per dozen.................16c

16 Cents Per Dozen for Children's Handkerchiefs.

No. 34R1242 Little Beauties for Little People. Fancy Hemmed Cambric Handkerchiefs in a large assortment of new and beautiful patterns. Handsome pictorial patterns, maps, fancy figures, sketches, etc. Order a dozen assorted patterns; you will be sure to like them and want more of them.

Price, per half dozen,.......8c
Per dozen........................16c

HANDKERCHIEFS

MAKE IDEAL GIFTS.

Our lines are complete with the very best goods at very low prices.

Children's Initial Handkerchiefs.

No. 34R1245 Children's Fancy Bordered Hemstitched Handkerchiefs with fancy embroidered initials. A very pretty and attractive handkerchief and sure to please; they come put up three in a fancy box.
Price, each.........................7c
Per dozen.............................84c

The Fairy Handkerchief.

No. 34R1246 The Fairy Handkerchiefs are the ideal handkerchiefs for little children. Made from extra fine linen-finished cambric, printed in absolutely fast colors, by a patented process which permits washing without injury to the color of the fabric. These handkerchiefs are made in a series of wonderfully colored pictures, from original drawings by some of the finest artists in Europe, each one representing some popular fairy tale, such as Mother Goose, Kris Kringle, Cinderella, Rip Van Winkle, Red Riding Hood and many others equally famous. Order a dozen assorted and make your children happy.
Price, per dozen, 48c; each.............................4c

No. 34R1248 Children's Turkey Red Handkerchiefs; fancy picture figures; a very attractive handkerchief for children, fast colors, hemmed borders.
Price, per dozen..20c

MAKE UP A FREIGHT SHIPMENT

When you order. If you don't need very many goods, surely you can use

GROCERIES.

Refer to pages 14 to 23 for Groceries; if you include enough sugar, coffee, tea, flour or other staples with your order, it can go by freight at a saving in transportation charges over express.

MEN'S SILK HANDKERCHIEFS.

If by mail, postage extra, each, 2c; per dozen, 14c

SPECIAL NOTICE.—Initial handkerchiefs come in all letters of the alphabet except I, O, Q, U, V, X, Y and Z.

No. 34R1260 Pure White Japanese Silk Initial Handkerchiefs. Full size, with neat, hemstitched border and silk embroidered initial.
Price, per dozen, $4.20; six for $2.10; each.....35c

No. 34R1262 Men's Fine Quality White Japanese Silk Initial Handkerchiefs, with wide 1¼-inch hem, full size, 21 inches, richly embroidered silk initial. An acceptable present.
Price, each..........$0.50
Six for.................. 3.00
Per dozen............. 6.00

No. 34R1264 Men's Extra Heavy Pure White Silk Initial Handkerchiefs. Extra large size with very heavy and richly embroidered silk initial. The ideal handkerchief for Christmas and holiday gifts.
Price, each.........$ 0.88
Six for............... 5.28
Per dozen........... 10.56

Men's Fancy Colored Border Silk Handkerchiefs.

No. 34R1266 Men's Japanese silk handkerchiefs, with ½-inch hemstitched colored borders.
Price, each...........$0.24
Per dozen.............. 2.88

No. 34R1268 Men's Japanese silk handkerchiefs, with 1-inch hemstitched fancy colored borders.
Price, each...........$0.35
Per dozen.............. 4.20
If by mail, postage extra, each, 1c; per doz., 14c.

Men's Plain White Japanese Silk Handkerchiefs.

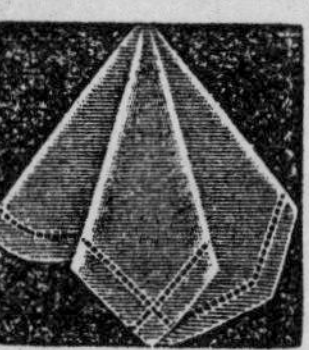

No. 34R1270 Men's Plain White Hemstitched Silk Handkerchiefs. Size, 18, with ½-inch hem. Per doz., $2.76; each.23c

No. 34R1272 Men's Fine Plain White Silk Handkerchiefs. Size, 18½, 1-inch hem; regular 50-cent goods.
Price, each...............$0.34
Per dozen.................. 4.08

No. 34R1274 Men's Fine Japanese Silk Handkerchiefs, size, 20, 1½-inch hem.
Price, per dozen, $8.28; each.......................69c

No. 34R1276 Men's Fine Japanese Handkerchiefs, size, 24, 1½-inch hem.
Price, per dozen, $8.28; each.......................69c

No. 34R1278 Men's Heavy White Silk Handkerchiefs, 20-inch, with 1-inch hemstitched border.
Price, per dozen, $5.16; each 43c

No. 34R1280 Men's Extra Heavy and Extra Fine Japanese Silk Handkerchiefs, with wide hem, large full size, made up expressly for fine trade. Retails at $1.25. Our special price, each......$ 0.88
Per dozen.. 10.56

Men's Plain White Twilled Silk Handkerchiefs.

No. 34R1282 Men's Fine Twilled Silk Handkerchiefs, size, 20 inches, 1-inch hem.
Price, per dozen, $5.40; each.......................45c

No. 34R1284 Men's Fine Twilled Silk Handkerchiefs, in very large size and extra quality. Size, 23½, 1½-inch hem. Per dozen, $10.56; each.....88c

Black Silk Handkerchiefs.

No. 34R1286 Men's Plain Black Silk Handkerchiefs, with hemstitched border.
Price, per dozen, $4.20; each.......................35c

Our Leader at 45 Cents.

No. 34R1288 Men's Fine Japanese Silk Handkerchiefs, in elegant new 1-inch hemstitched fancy colored borders. A beautiful assortment, a few of which are shown in above illustration
Price, per dozen, $5.40; each.......................45c

Solid Center, Colored Border, at 38 Cents

No. 34R1290 Men's Japanese Silk Handkerchiefs, made with solid color center, plum, blue, etc., with hemstitched fancy colored borders. A new, popular handkerchief.

Price, each............$0.38
Per dozen.. .... 4.56

Men's Fancy Silk Handkerchiefs, 45 Cents.

No. 34R1292 Men's Fancy Japanese White Silk Handkerchiefs in beautiful fancy 1½-inch hemstitched colored borders and ring or polka dot effects in center. Color, blue only. New and select designs. Full size.
Price, each............$0.45
Per dozen............. 5.40

All Over Plaid Silk Handkerchiefs, 75 Cents.

No. 34R1294 Men's Fine Japanese Silk Handkerchiefs; large size, in new designs, all over plaid effects and wide hemstitched striped border. A very fine handkerchief. Usual retail price $1.00.
Price, each..........$0.75
Per dozen............ 9.00

Men's Silk Bandana Handkerchiefs.

No. 34R1296 Men's Fine Japanese Silk Bandanas; red only; hemmed tape border in fancy Persian design, and figured centers. Size, 28 inches. A very fine quality at our low price.
Price, each..........$ 0.95
Per dozen.......... 11.40

SEND 5 CENTS for fine Sample Book of Men's Custom Tailoring. Suits, overcoats and pants made to your measure at a big saving over what tailors would usually charge.

FANCY BROCADED SILK HANDKERCHIEFS.

For gentlemen or ladies.

No. 34R1300 Fancy Brocaded Silk Handkerchiefs, small size, assorted colors.
Price, each..........$0.19
Per dozen.......... 2.28

No. 34R1302 Fancy Brocaded Silk Handkerchiefs, in large assortment of colors, blue, red, pink, green, etc.
Price, each $0.23
Per dozen 2.76

No. 34R1304 Fancy Brocaded Silk Handkerchiefs, in pretty new effects, in red, blue, green, pink, etc., and medium dark colors.
Price, each. $0.35
Per dozen...... ..... 4.20
If by mail, postage extra, each, 1 cent; per dozen, 10 cents.

No. 34R1306 Fine Silk Brocaded Handkerchiefs. Large size; richly brocaded in new and beautiful effects in fancy colors; also all black and all cream white.
Price, each..........$0.42
Per dozen.............. 5.04

No. 34R1308 Extra Fine Silk Brocaded Handkerchiefs. Large size, heavy, richly brocaded in new designs, including the combined floral and stripe effects, also plain black or white. Price, per dozen, $8.28; each...69c
If by mail, postage extra, each, 1 cent; per dozen, 10 cents.

LADIES' SILK HANDKERCHIEFS.

SPECIAL NOTICE—The prices on our Handkerchiefs are at the lowest possible point, and no reduction is allowed by the dozen or one hundred lots.
If by mail, postage extra, each, 1 cent.

Ladies' Fancy Silk Embroidered Handkerchiefs.

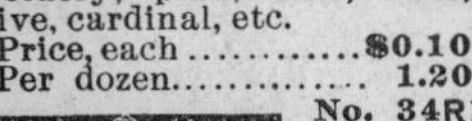

No. 34R1310 Fine Imported White Silk Handkerchiefs. Scalloped edges and contrasting colored silk embroidery, pink, blue, lilac, olive, cardinal, etc.
Price, each............$0.10
Per dozen............ 1.20

No. 34R1312 Ladies' Extra Fine Imported Pure Silk Handkerchiefs. Cream white, scalloped and embroidered borders, delicate colorings, rich floral designs; 11x11 inches; imported direct from Japan; assorted patterns and colors.
Price, each...............$0.15
Per dozen.................. 1.80

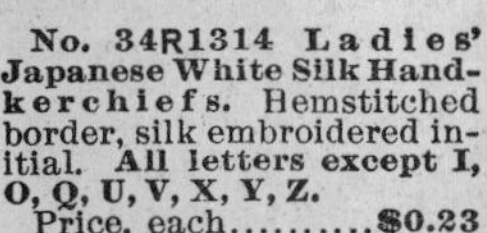

No. 34R1314 Ladies' Japanese White Silk Handkerchiefs. Hemstitched border, silk embroidered initial. **All letters except I, O, Q, U, V, X, Y, Z.**
Price, each..........$0.23
Six for............... 1.38
Per dozen........... 2.76

No. 34R1316 Very Rich and Attractive Pure Silk Handkerchiefs. Cream white, fancy colored silk embroidery, scalloped edges, artistic open work designs.
Price, each...............$0.22
Six for..................... 1.32
Per dozen................. 2.64

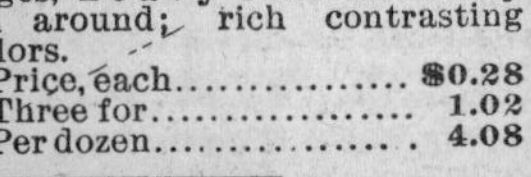

No. 34R1318 New Design Imported Pure White Japanese Silk Handkerchiefs. Scalloped edges, heavy silk embroidery all around; rich contrasting colors.
Price, each...............$0.28
Three for................. 1.02
Per dozen................. 4.08

No. 34R1320 Ladies' Extra Quality, Pure White Japanese Silk Handkerchiefs. Scalloped edge, entirely new design, silk embroidery and open work patterns. All pure white, no colors; dainty and dependable.
Price, each $0.43
Per dozen.................. 5.16

Ladies' Fine Silk Handkerchiefs, Embroidered with Mercerized Silk.

No. 34R1322 Ladies' Fine White Silk Handkerchiefs, scalloped edges, embroidered with mercerized silk.
Price, per doz.. $3.00; ea., 25c

No. 34R1324 Ladies' Fine White Silk Handkerchiefs, scalloped edges, in new and beautiful designs.
Price, per doz., $4.80; ea., 40c

SPECIAL NOTICE—Mercerized silk is very fine Egyptian cotton treated by the new Mercer process, which makes the fiber look like silk, a permanent surface that washes better than pure silk.

No. 34R1326 Ladies' Fine Quality White Silk Handkerchiefs in beautiful floral and scroll designs, with rich and effective outer border. Superior quality. Price, per dozen, $6.00; each.....50c

Very Fine $1.50 Silk Handkerchiefs at $1.00.

No. 34R1328 Ladies' Finest Quality White Silk Handkerchiefs, embroidered in elaborate floral effect around coronet, crowns and other designs. Grand and beautiful effect, to which our illustration does not do justice. If you want the best and prettiest silk handkerchief made, order this one.
Price, per dozen, $12.00; each...............$1.00

MEN'S BELTS.

Always give waist measure when ordering belts. Sizes, waist measure, 30 to 42 inches.

Men's Fine Leather Belts.

No. 34R1900 Leather Belt 1¼ inches wide, mounted with nickel plated harness buckle and side loops. The greatest bargain ever offered in men's belts for the price. Colors, black, orange or tan. Sizes, waist measure, 30 to 42 inches only. Give waist measure in order. Each..20c
If by mail, postage extra, 6 cents.

A Regular 50-Cent Belt for 30 Cents.

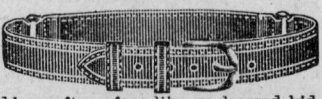

No. 34R1904 Men's Fine Leather Belt, 1¼ inches wide. The leather is called ooze, and has soft surface like undressed kid. Leather lined, nickel plated harness buckle and side loops. Colors, **gray or light brown.** Sizes, waist measure, 30 to 42 inches only. Give waist measure in order. Price, each.................30c
If by mail, postage extra, 6 cents.

A Special Leader for 43 Cents.

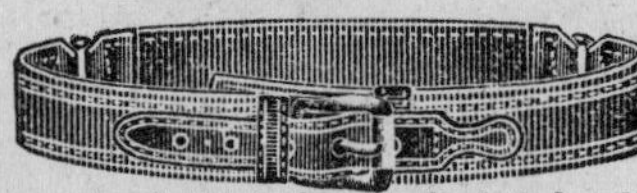

No. 34R1908 Men's Fine English Calf Leather Belt, 1½ inches wide, leather lined and stitched, nickel plated roller buckle, side loops and fancy stitching, and a value seldom to be found for less than 75 cents. Colors, **tan, black** or **orange.** There is no belt that compares with this value at our low prices. Sizes, 30 to 42 inches waist.
Price, each..43c
If by mail, postage extra, 7 cents.

New "Hold Good" Belt, 40 Cents.

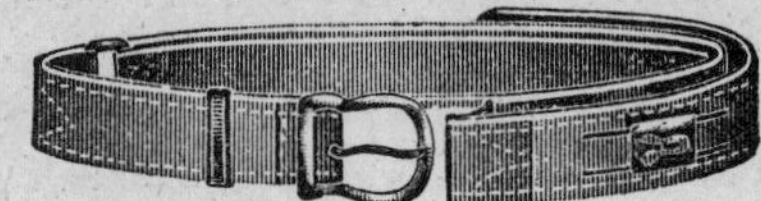

No. 34R1912 Men's New Style Belt, called "Hold Good," as shown in illustration, 1½ inches wide. A practical and useful attachment is placed upon two small steel wires, which fit firmly over the trouser button, holding belt constantly in proper place, and cannot be seen from the outside of belt. Very simple, and will not fail to give entire satisfaction. Retail price, 50 cents; we sell them for 40 cents. Nickel trimmings. Colors, **black, orange or tan.** Sizes, waist measure, 30 to 42 inches.
Price, each.......................................40c
If by mail, postage extra, 7 cents.

Plain Wide Belt, 39 Cents.

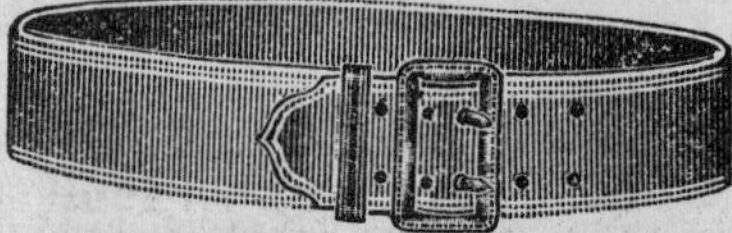

No. 34R1916 Men's Plain Belt, 2⅜ inches wide; made of good leather stock. A good, staple, plain belt, always in good style. Retail price, 50 cents; you buy them from us at your local merchant's cost. Colors, **black, orange or tan.** Sizes, 30 to 42 inches, waist measure. Price, each.............................39c
If by mail, postage extra, 9 cents.

New Braided Belts at 39 Cents.

No. 34R1920 Men's Fine New Style Leather Braided Belts, made of fine ooze leather (like undressed kid), trimmed with fine nickel plated harness buckle. A new and very desirable novelty in belts for this season that will not fail to please. Workmanship the finest. Sizes, waist measure, 30 to 42 inches only. Colors, gray or brown only. Always give waist measure in order. Each.........39c
If by mail, postage extra, 7 cents.

Another 50-Cent Leader.

No. 34R1924 Men's Fine English Calf Leather Belt, 1 inch wide, made with genuine ooze lining (like undressed kid) and three rows of fancy silk stitching. A very handsome and effective straight belt that will be in favor with good dressers this season. Colors, **gray or brown only.** Sizes, waist, 30 to 42 inches.
Price, each.......................................50c
If by mail, postage extra, 7 cents.

GIVE CATALOGUE NUMBER IN FULL WHEN YOU WRITE YOUR ORDER

Men's Patent Leather Belt, 39 Cents.

No. 34R1928 Men's Fine Dash Patent Leather Belt, leather lined, nickel plated harness buckle, fancy side loops, fancy stitched reinforcements, black and white stitching, width 1¼ inches. One of the particularly stylish belts for this season. Sizes, 30 to 42 inches, waist measure.
Price, each.......................................39c
If by mail, postage extra, 7 cents.

Men's Alligator Belts, 50 Cents.

No. 34R1930 Men's Fine Alligator Finish Belts of Fine Leather, firm leather lining, stitched all around, gold plated buckle, equal to any belt retailing at 75 cents. A popular style belt having the approval of good taste. Color, alligator brown only. Sizes, 32 to 40 inches waist.
Price, each..50c
If by mail, postage extra, 7 cents.

Genuine Turkish Morocco Belts, $1.00.

No. 34R1934 Men's Genuine Turkish Morocco Belts made of finest Turkish morocco leather, 1½ inches wide, **fancy braided,** leather lined, silk stitched, morocco tabs, fine nickel plated harness buckle and loops. One of the finest belts obtainable and retails at from $1.50 to $2.00. If you want one of the best buy this number and you will be more than pleased. Colors, brown or tan. Sizes, 30 to 42 inches waist. Price, each.........$1.00
If by mail, postage extra, 7 cents.

Genuine Turkish Morocco Leather Belt.

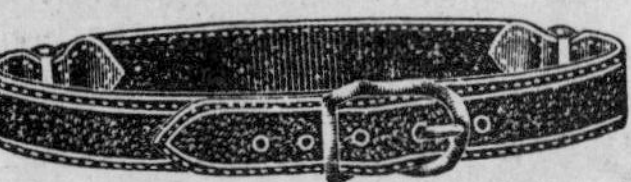

No. 34R1938 Men's Finest Genuine Turkish Morocco Leather Belt. The best leather put into belts. Soft and pliable. Made with fine, soft lining, nickel plated loop buckles, nickel plated side loops of special design and reinforcements of same leather. You may pay $2.00 and not get a handsomer belt for the money. Colors, **black or dark brown.** Sizes, 30 to 42 inches waist.
Price, each..$1.00
If by mail, postage extra, 7 cents.

BOYS' BELTS.

Waist Measure, 24, 26, 28, 30 inches. For larger sizes order men's belts.

No. 34R1950 Boys' Fine Leather Belt, 1¼ inches wide, made of fine, soft leather, trimmed with nickel buckle. This is a special value regular 25-cent belt, which we offer at this low price. Colors, tan or orange. Sizes, waist, 24, 26, 28 and 30 inches. Always give waist measure in ordering. Price, each....15c
If by mail, postage extra, 6 cents.

GETTING 50 CENTS

FOR OUR LARGE CATALOGUE,

GETTING PAY FOR OUR SAMPLES,

HELPS TO MAKE THESE LOW PRICES POSSIBLE.

We do not add the expense of thousands of catalogues and samples to our selling prices and make people who buy pay for thousands of catalogues and samples sent to people who do not buy.

OTHER HOUSES DO THIS. WE DON'T.

AS A RESULT OUR PRICES ARE LOWER THAN ANY OTHER HOUSE.

SEND US 15 CENTS

FOR A YEAR'S SUBSCRIPTION TO OUR

MONEY SAVING GROCERY PRICE LIST,

revised and issued every 60 days to show the lowest possible prices on groceries.

WE CAN SAVE YOU SO MUCH MONEY ON YOUR GROCERIES, IT WILL PAY YOU IMMENSELY TO SEND 15 CENTS FOR THIS PRICE LIST.

GLOVE DEPARTMENT.

OUR GLOVE DEPARTMENT IS ONE OF THE LARGEST IN THIS COUNTRY.

THE ADVANTAGE TO YOU IN BUYING FROM US, is that you have complete lines to select from in each kind of goods, at the lowest possible price. A price made the lowest because we import direct our fine kid gloves, and in domestic gloves, **we purchase direct from the manufacturers.**

DURING THE PAST YEAR the price of glove leather of every kind **has remained strong, with marked advances on some kinds.** Notwithstanding this, we have not advanced a single price, but reduced many. **We can serve you better than any other house and save you money on gloves and mittens.** We sell gloves of almost every kind, including the cheap grades, **but we recommend the better qualities as the cheapest in the end. We warrant every glove to be as represented or we will refund the price paid.**

Always include postage when ordering shipped by mail.

How to Fit a Kid Glove.

In order that satisfactory wear may be had from a kid glove, it is very necessary that it should be put on right the first time. First push the fingers in, leaving out the thumb, and work them into place by rubbing from the tips downward. **Do not press down between the fingers.** Insert the thumb and apply same method as used with fingers; then push the glove on up the hand. **Do not pull by taking hold at wrist, as this destroys the shape. Remember your gloves will give lasting service if fitted right the first time.**

How to Measure Hand for Size of Glove.

Draw a tape around the knuckles, as shown in the illustration. Ladies' kid gloves are not made in sizes larger than size 8, and in fancy colors or the finest qualities do not run larger than 7½.

Ladies' kid glove sizes are as follows: 5½, 5¾, 6, 6¼, 6½, 6¾, 7, 7¼, 7½, 7¾, 8.

Glove Talk.

Ladies' kid gloves are warranted by us only against manufacturers' imperfections. If workmanship is bad or the leather defective, we will exchange for a new pair, provided they are returned to us at once. We cannot exchange gloves that have been worn or make good any ripping or tearing due to carelessness in trying on.

Always give color and size.

Ladies Dressed Kid Gloves.

No. 33R25 Ladies' Dressed Kid Gloves, made with two clasps. An excellent value at our low price. Embroidered backs. This is not a fine glove, but the best that can be sold for this price. **Cable sewn.** Colors, black, white, brown, tan and oxblood. Sizes, 6 to 8. Price, per pair.............................75c
If by mail, postage extra, per pair, 2 cents.

Ladies' Fine French Dressed Kid Gloves.

No. 33R27 Ladies' Fine French Dressed Kid Gloves, made with two clasps, perfect stitching and embroidered backs. This is a superior value and a better glove cannot be bought at our low price. Sizes, 5½ to 8. Colors, black, white, brown, tan, red and slate or gray. **Always give color and size in ordering.** Price, per pair..............**$1.00**
If by mail, postage extra, per pair, 2 cents.

Superfine French Dressed Kid Gloves.

No. 33R30 The Virginia. The best of imported genuine kid gloves. Select light weight kid skins, extremely elastic and pliable, retaining their shape better than any other glove. **Finely stitched and finished;** embroidered backs, **cable sewn.** French gusseted thumbs. Colors, black, white, brown, tan, oxblood, green, slate, gray, blue, primrose, mode and pearl. Sizes, 5½ to 7½ only.
Price, per pair..................................**$1.50**
If by mail, postage extra, per pair, 2 cents.

Genuine Chevrier Kid Gloves for $1.75.

PIQUE SEWN.

No. 33R32 Ladies' Best Dressed Kid Gloves, made by Felix Chevrier of Grenoble, France, from the most select and best kid skins obtainable. Slightly heavier than the regular weight ladies' kid gloves. The best that we can obtain. Embroidered backs and full **pique sewing,** two clasps. A more perfect fitting or better wearing glove is not to be had. **Every pair warranted, and we will replace with new gloves if found defective.** Colors, black, white, brown, tan, slate, gray, mode, pearl, green or blue. Sizes, 5½ to 7¼ only. Price, per pair...........................**$1.75**
If by mail, postage extra, per pair, 2 cents.

Our 95-Cent Foster Hook Lacing Kid Gloves.

No. 33R34 Ladies' Four Hook Lacing Dressed Kid Gloves. Cable sewn. Foster lacing, made of fine quality German dressed stock and will give good satisfaction. Embroidered backs and French gusseted thumb. Colors, black, white, brown, tan, mode, green, blue, and oxblood. Sizes, 5½ to 8. **In mode, green, and blue we cannot furnish larger than 7½.**
Price, per pair.......................................**95c**
If by mail, postage extra, per pair, 2 cents.

Ladies' Four Hook Foster Gloves, $1.25.

No. 33R36 Ladies' Four Hook Foster Lacing Dressed Kid Gloves, cable sewn, finer quality than the above, made with embroidered backs and French gusseted thumbs. Colors, black, white, brown, tan, mode, green, blue and oxblood. Sizes, 5½ to 8. **In mode, green, blue or any fancy colors, size 7½ is the largest we can furnish.** Price, per pair...**$1.25**
If by mail, postage extra, per pair, 2 cents.

Fine Glace Genuine French Kid Gloves for $1.50.

No. 33R38 Ladies' Fine Glace Genuine French Kid Gloves, made four hook Foster lacing, cable sewn. Fine, selected stock. Will retain its shape better than any other glove. Embroidered backs, French gusseted thumbs. Colors, black, white, tan, mode, brown, green, blue, and oxblood. Sizes, 5½ to 7½. Price, per pair.............................**$1.50**
If by mail, postage extra, per pair, 2 cents.

Genuine Kid Suede Gloves.

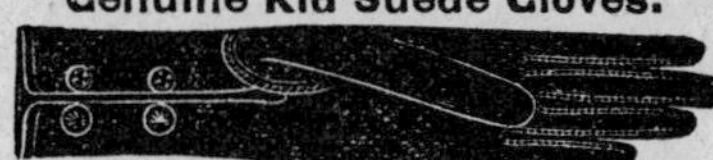

No. 33R40 Ladies' Genuine Kid Suede Gloves, made with embroidered backs, two clasps, **cable sewn.** These are genuine kid suede gloves; we do not handle the cheaper grades for they seldom prove satisfactory. We warrant this glove to be perfect and it will give entire satisfaction. Colors, black, white, brown, gray and pearl. Sizes, 5¾ to 7¼ only. **A fashionable glove for street or evening wear.**
Price, per pair..................................**$1.25**
If by mail, postage extra, per pair, 2 cents.

Mousquetaire Suede Gloves, $1.75, $2.50 and $2.85.

No. 33R42 Finest Imported Undressed Kid or Suede Mousquetaire Gloves. Eight-button length, made with three buttons at wrist and delicately embroidered backs. Colors, black, white, pearl, brown, tan, and gray. Sizes, 5¾ to 7¼ only. Per pair...**$1.75**
If by mail, postage extra, per pair, 2 cents.

No. 33R43 Ladies' Finest Imported Mousquetaire Suede Gloves, same as No. 33R42, in twelve-button or elbow lengths. Colors, black, white, gray, tan, pearl, lilac, primrose, cream, blue, green, and mode. Sizes, 5½ to 7¼ only. Price, per pair..................**$2.50**
If by mail, postage extra, per pair, 2 cents.

No. 33R44 Ladies' Mousquetaire Gloves, same as above, same style and assortment of colors. Sizes, 5½ to 7½; sixteen-button length.
Price, per pair...**$2.85**
If by mail, postage extra, per pair, 2 cents.

Ladies' Genuine Mocha Gloves.

No. 33R46 Ladies' Fine Quality Genuine Mocha Gloves, soft as silk velvet. One of the most satisfactory gloves made. Finest imported Mocha stock, similar to undressed kid, but much superior in quality. Three rows of silk embroidery in back, two snap buttons. Pique sewn, French gusseted thumbs. **Very stylish and dressy.** Colors, black, brown, tan, blue, green, oxblood, red or gray and mode. Sizes, 5½ to 7¾. **Do not forget size.** Price, per pair...**$1.25**
If by mail, postage extra, per pair, 2 cents.

Ladies' Walking or Street Gloves.

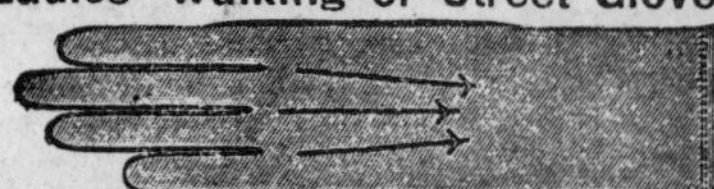

No. 33R48 Ladies' Fashionable Heavy Walking Gloves, made from heavy lamb skins, spear back, two clasps and out seams. Much heavier than kid gloves, stylish, and a good glove for driving. **Perfect fitting, and every pair warranted against manufacturers' imperfections.** Medium color. **English tans only.** Sizes, 6 to 8 only. Price, per pair...**$1.25**
If by mail, postage extra, per pair, 2 cents.

Ladies' Genuine Reindeer Gloves.

OUT SEAMS.

No. 33R50 Ladies' Strictly High Grade Genuine Reindeer Gloves, with surface same as Mocha. Much heavier than Mocha gloves, and a most fashionable glove for street wear or driving; spear back, two clasps, and out seams. English thumb, very soft and pliable. Every pair warranted against manufacturers' imperfections. Grays and English tans only. Sizes, 6 to 8. Price, per pair.....................**$1.50**
If by mail, postage extra, per pair, 2 cents.

Girls' or Misses' Kid Gloves.

No. 33R52 Misses' Fine Glace Kid Gloves, made with two snap buttons and embroidered backs. For misses up to 14 years of age. Colors, black, white, tan, and brown. Sizes, 4½, 4¾, 5, 5¼ and 5½. Take measurement for size same as for ladies' gloves.
Price, per pair.......................................**95c**
If by mail, postage extra, per pair, 2 cents.

Ladies' Chamois Gloves.

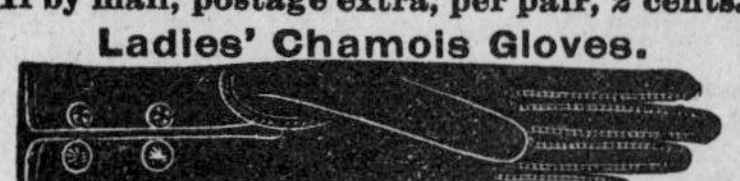

No. 33R54 Ladies' Fine Imported Chamois Gloves, soft and durable, made with two snap buttons and delicate embroidery on backs. Colors, white, pearl and buff. Sizes, 5¾ to 7¾ only.
Price, per pair.......................................**75c**
If by mail, postage extra, per pair, 2 cents.

Ladies' Fine Quality Washable Glove.

No. 33R56 A Castor or Suede Kid Glove, that will wash the same as any fabric glove, with a ticket in each pair explaining how to wash them; with two patent clasps. This is a new process of preparing the kid that will certainly please and prove to be one of the best glove investments you have ever made. Colors in white, pearls and gray only. Sizes, 5¾ to 7½ only. Price, per pair....................**$1.00**
If by mail, postage extra, per pair, 2 cents.

Ladies' Gauntlet Driving Gloves.

No. 33R60 Ladies' Gauntlet Driving Gloves, made of good quality domestic kid. Three point stitched backs and patent snap buttons. Colors, red, tan, brown and black. Sizes, 6 to 8½. One size larger than the regular kid glove, is most satisfactory for a driving glove. Price, per pair........**88c**
If by mail, postage extra, per pair, 4 cents.

Ladies' Kid Gauntlets, $1.20.

No. 33R62 Ladies' Fine Gauntlet Driving Gloves, made of fine imported stock, same style as above. Patent snap buttons and embroidered backs. **We expressly recommend this quality.** Colors, red, tan, brown and black. Sizes, 6 to 8½.
Price, per pair...**$1.20**
If by mail, postage extra, per pair, 4 cents.

Our $1.90 Ladies' Gauntlet Glove.

No. 33R64 Ladies' Fine Gauntlet Glove, made of select light weight Plymouth buckskin. Two snap buttons and embroidered backs. This is the most stylish glove made for ladies' use; a fine fitting glove and one of the most durable kind. Sizes, 6, 6½, 7, 7½, 8 and 8½. Price, per pair..........$1.90
If by mail, postage extra, per pair, 4 cents.

SPECIAL NOTE—As our prices are based on the cost to manufacture, we allow no reductions for quantity purchases. The price for each pair is the same if you buy one pair or 1,000 pairs.

LADIES' SILK AND FABRIC GLOVES.

Sizes, 6, 6½, 7, 7½, 8 and 8½.

Our Special Value at 75 Cents.

No. 33R99 Ladies' Four-Button Pure Silk Glove. Guaranteed all pure Milanese Silk. Genuine double tipped. These gloves are plain black, with three rows of silk stitching on back, or with white stitching in backs, or all white, or white with black embroidered backs, and have two large pearl buttons. Sizes, 6 to 8½. Price, per pair...75c
If by mail, postage extra, per pair, 1 cent.

Our 45-Cent Leader. Special Value.

No. 33R102 Ladies' Pure Silk Glove with Two Patent Clasps, nice quality and **double tipped fingers.** We have them in black with black embroidery, black with white embroidery, white with white embroidery and white with black embroidery. Sizes, 6 to 8½ only. Price, per pair..........45c
If by mail, postage extra, per pair, 1 cent.

Ladies' Lisle Thread Gloves.

No. 33R106 Ladies' Very Fine Lyonnaise Suede Lisle Gloves, with kid glove embroidered backs. An especial quality at this low price. Plain wrists. Colors, black, white, tan and gray. Sizes, 7 to 8½ only. Per pair..........25c
If by mail, postage extra, per pair, 1 cent.

Ladies' Lisle Gloves, 12 Cents.

No. 33R112 Ladies' Lisle Gloves. Plain wrists, three rows stitching in backs. Colors, black, white, tan and gray only. Sizes, 7 to 8½; black, to size 9. Price, per pair..........12c
If by mail, postage extra, per pair, 1 cent.

Girls' or Misses' Lisle Gloves, 14 Cents.

No. 33R114 Girls' or Misses' Lisle Gloves. Plain wrists, three rows silk stitching in back. Colors, tan or white only. State age in order, or glove size measured as for kid gloves. For ages 6 to 14 years. Price, per pair..........14c
If by mail, postage extra, per pair, 1 cent.

Ladies' Silk Mitts.

No. 33R116 Ladies' Pure Silk Mitts, with embroidery back, 10 inches long, in black only. Price, per pair..........11c
If by mail, postage extra, per pair, 1 cent.

Ladies' Silk Mitts at 15 Cents.

No. 33R118 Ladies' Pure Silk Mitts, with hand embroidered back, 11 inches long. In black only. Price, per pair..........15c
If by mail, postage extra, per pair, 1 cent.

Ladies' Silk Mitts, 18 Cents.

No. 33R120 Ladies' Heavy Pure Silk Mitts, with glove embroidery on back, 10 inches long, in black only. Retail value, 25 cents. Price, per pair.....18c
If by mail, postage extra, 1 cent.

Ladies' Silk Mitts.

No. 33R122 Ladies' Semi-Milanese Pure Silk Mitt, 10½ inches long, glove embroidery on back and inserted thumb. Colors, black or cream; an especially strong value. Price, per pair..........23c
If by mail, postage extra, 1 cent.

Ladies' Silk Mitts, 35 Cents.

No. 33R124 Ladies' Heavy Milanese Pure Silk Mitt, 11 inches long, glove embroidery on back and inserted thumb. Color, black only. This quality is equal to the regular 50-cent mitts at retail. Price, per pair..........35c
If by mail, postage extra, 1 cent.

Extra Size Black Silk Mitts.

For Ladies with Large Hands.

No. 33R130 Ladies' Pure Silk Mitt, extra large size for large hands, 10 inches long and glove embroidery on back; in black only. Price, per pair..19c
If by mail, postage extra, 1 cent.

No. 33R132 Ladies' Semi-Milanese Pure Silk Mitts, extra large size for large hands, 10 inches long, glove embroidery backs; heavier than above. Price, per pair..........23c
If by mail, postage extra, 1 cent.

Misses' Pure Silk Mitts.

No. 33R134 Girls' or Misses' Pure Silk Mitts, with silk hand embroidered backs. Colors, black and cream only. Price, per pair..........12c
If by mail, postage extra, per pair, 1 cent.

No. 33R136 Girls' or Misses' Heavy Pure Silk Mitts, with silk hand embroidery. Colors, black and cream only. Price, per pair..........22c
If by mail, postage extra, per pair, 1 cent.

SPECIAL NOTICE. The price per pair is the same if you buy one or 1,000 pairs; no reduction is made for quantity purchases.

Ladies' Black Cashmere Gloves.

No. 33R140 Ladies' Black Cashmere Gloves, inserted thumbs, three rows stitching on back and **double tipped fingers and thumb.** Excellent value. Sizes, 6 to 8½. Price, per pair..........22c

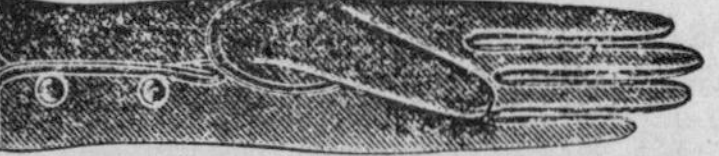

No. 33R141 Ladies' Fine Black Cashmere Gloves, fleece lined, kid glove embroidery with two patent snap buttons. Price, per pair..........25c
If by mail, postage extra, 2 cents.

No. 33R142 Ladies' Extra Heavy Black Cashmere Gloves; fine quality; all wool fleece lining with embroidered backs, and patent snap fastenings; a regular 50-cent quality. Price, per pair..........35c
If by mail, postage extra, 2 cents.

No. 33R144 Ladies' Very Fine Quality Black Cashmere Gloves; fine wool fleece lining; made with long wrists, two patent buttons, kid glove embroidery on backs; an elegant quality; perfect fitting and very durable. Price, per pair..........45c
If by mail, postage extra, 2 cents.

LADIES' AND CHILDREN'S SCOTCH GLOVES.

FALL AND WINTER.

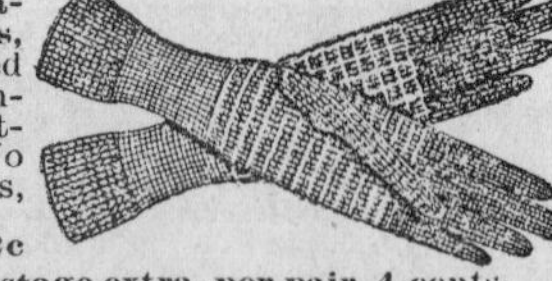

No. 33R150 Ladies' Scotch Gloves, made with shaped ribbed wrists. Fancy backs. Good fitting gloves. No plain colors. Sizes, 6 to 7½. Per pair..........22c
If by mail, postage extra, per pair, 4 cents.

Special Value, 42 Cents.

No. 33R154 Ladies' Fine Scotch Wool Gloves, seamless fingers, perfect fitting, ribbed wrists. Beautiful Scotch plaid backs. Warm and will wear well; no plain colors. Sizes, 6 to 8½. Price, per pair..........42c
If by mail, postage extra, per pair, 4 cents.

Ladies' Plain Colored Scotch Wool Gloves

No. 33R155 Ladies' Plain Colored Fancy Knit Scotch Gloves; made perfectly seamless; an elegant fitting glove; made with long ribbed wrist; very warm and durable. Colors, plain black, red, white, gray and navy blue. Sizes, 6 to 7½. Price, per pair..........35c
If by mail, postage extra, 4 cents.

Ladies' Silk Gloves.

No. 33R156 Ladies' Fancy Pure Silk Golf Gloves, knit from the highest grade silk in blue, cardinal and drab grounds, with fancy colored backs in beautiful colorings; also solid colors, same as above. A handsome and perfect fitting glove, and extremely durable. Price, per pair..........$1.00
If by mail, postage extra, 3 cents.

Children's Fancy Scotch Gloves.

No. 33R158 Children's and Misses' Scotch Wool Gloves, made with fancy backs and palm, elastic wrists, perfect fitting. Ages, 5 to 10 years. Price, per pair..........25c
If by mail, postage extra, per pair, 2 cents.

No. 33R160 Misses' or Boys' All Wool Heavy Scotch Gloves, with fancy honeycomb knit backs, seamless fingers and close ribbed wrists; a warm, perfect fitting glove. Ages, 6 to 14 years. Colors, black, white, gray, blue, brown, cardinal. **The best Scotch gloves for durability, fast color and fit.** Price, per pair..........41c
If by mail, postage extra, per pair, 3 cents.

IF YOU FAIL TO STATE SIZE, we CANNOT fill your order.

LADIES' KNIT WOOL MITTENS.

No. 33R200 Ladies' Fast Black Single Wool Mittens. Price, per pair..........10c

No. 33R202 Ladies' Double Wool Mittens, ribbed, worsted finish, with long elastic ribbed wrists. Black only. Price, per pair..........19c
If by mail, postage extra, per pair, 3 cents.

No. 33R203 Ladies' Fine Mercerized Silk Mittens, with long fancy knit wrists and handsome cord and tassel bows on backs; a very fine mitten and one that will give entire satisfaction. Plain black only. Price, per pair..........24c
If by mail, postage extra, 3 cents.

Ladies' Double Wool Mittens.

No. 33R206 Ladies' Fine All Wool Double Mittens, fast black. Made with long elastic ribbed wrists, satin bow. Special value. Price, per pair..........22c

Ladies' Fancy Wool Knit Mittens.

No. 33R208 Ladies' Fine Fancy Black Saxony Yarn Double Mittens. Fast black. Made with long elastic ribbed wrists. Our leader in value. Price, per pair..........25c

Ladies' Angora Lined Mittens.

No. 33R210 Ladies' Fine Coral Saxony Yarn Double Mittens, with Angora wool lining. Very warm and durable. Black only. Price, per pair.35c

Fancy Back Coral Saxony Mittens.

No. 33R212 Ladies' Double All Wool Black Coral Saxony Mittens, knit from pure yarn. Long elastic wrists. Fancy backs and bows. Price, per pair..40c

Fancy Back Coral Yarn Mittens.

No. 33R214 Ladies' Extra Quality Pure Coral Saxony Yarn Double Mittens, fancy ribbed wrists, black silk bow and open work backs. Price, per pair..........43c
If by mail, postage extra on above, 4 cents per pair.

Coral Yarn Angora Lined Mittens.

No. 33R216 Ladies' Double All Wool Coral Saxony Mittens, knit from finest pure yarn, plain, with satin bow at wrist. Lined with finest **Angora wool,** superior quality. Black only. Price, per pair...45c
If by mail, postage extra, per pair, 2 cents.

Mercerized Silk Mittens.

No. 33R218 Ladies' Fancy Back, Double Mercerized Silk Mittens, pretty patterns, ornamented with silk bow. Black only. Price, per pair..........25c
If by mail, postage extra, per pair, 3 cents.

No. 33R220 Ladies' Lined Jersey Mittens. Ladies' heavy Jersey cloth mittens with heavy lining; a very warm; comfortable mitten; one that fits and looks well. This is a special value and retails for double what we ask for it. Price, per pair..........25c
If by mail, postage extra, 4 cents.

EXTRA SIZE WOOL AND SILK MITTENS.

For Ladies with Large Hands.

No. 33R219 Heavy All Wool Double Mittens, in plain black, with long wrists; a very comfortable and good looking mitten; will wear well. Special value. Price, per pair..........25c
If by mail, postage extra, 4 cents.

No. 33R221 Ladies' Extra Size Double Silk Mittens; for large hands; fancy backs and fine ribbed fancy wrists; in plain black only; an elegant quality and sure to please. Price, per pair..45c
If by mail, postage extra, 4 cents.

LADIES' SILK MITTENS.

Fancy Back Silk Mittens, 45 Cents.

No. 33R222 Ladies' Pure Silk Double Mittens, fancy backs, with wool lining, ornamented at wrists with satin bow. Black only. Price, per pair..........45c
If by mail, postage extra, per pair, 4 cents.

If goods are to go by mail, full cash must be sent with order with extra for postage.

Ladies' Double Silk Mittens, 70 Cents.

No. 33R224 Ladies' Double Silk Mittens, wool lined, long ribbed wrists with satin ribbon bow and handsome open work backs. Price, per pair......70c
If by mail, postage extra, per pair, 4 cents.

Extra Quality Silk Mittens, 95c to $1.25.

No. 33R226 Ladies' Worsted Lined Double Silk Mittens, new design, fancy open work backs and wrists. This is the kind for which your local merchant charges you $1.50 per pair. Trimmed with fine silk bows, heavy and fine. One pair in box. Price, per pair.......95c
If by mail, postage extra, per pair, 4 cents.

No. 33R228 Ladies' Extra High Grade All Silk Double Mittens, raised open work on backs and wrists, satin ribbon bows. You can't buy a prettier mitten at any price. Silk inside and outside. Superior quality. One pair in a box. Regular $1.75 grade.
Price, per pair..............................$1.25
If by mail, postage extra, per pair, 4 cents.

INFANTS' MITTENS.

No. 33R230 Infants' Fancy Knit All Wool Saxony Mittens, with long elastic ribbed wrists. Ages, 1 to 3 years. Colors, black, light blue, cardinal and white. Price, per pair..................10c
If by mail, postage extra, per pair, 1 cent.

Infants' Wool Mittens, 19 Cents.

No. 33R232 Infants' Finest Quality All Wool Saxony Mittens, with silk striped long elastic ribbed wrists. Ages, 1 to 3 years. Colors, cream, white, cardinal, black and light blue. Price, per pair...19c
If by mail, postage extra, per pair, 2 cents.

Infants' Saxony Double Mittens, 23 Cents.

No. 33R233 Infants' Fine Saxony Double Mittens, fancy shell backs, fine wool lining, seamless. Ages, 1 to 4 years. Colors, red, navy and black.
Price, per pair................................23c
If by mail, postage extra, per pair, 2 cents.

Infants' Silk Mittens, 23 Cents.

No. 33R234 Infants' Silk Mittens. Infants' fine mixed silk and wool mittens, long elastic ribbed wrists. Ages, 1 to 3 years. Colors, black, cardinal, light blue and white. Price, per pair..................23c

Infants' Fancy Back Mittens.

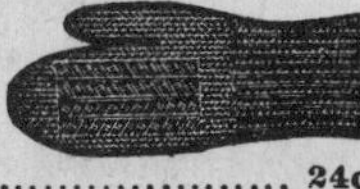

No. 33R238 Infants' Mercerized Silk Mittens, with fine wool lining, fancy open knit backs. Colors, cardinal, sky blue and white. Ages, 1 to 3 years. Price, per pair....................24c
If by mail, postage extra, per pair, 1 cent.

Girls' or Misses' Mittens, Ages 4 to 16.

No. 33R240 Children's Black Single Wool Mittens, with fancy ribbed wrists. Sizes, 3, 4 and 5. Ages, 4 to 16 years. Price, per pair.........................8c

No. 33R242 Children's and Misses' Heavy Ribbed Double Wool Mittens, long seamless wrists, warm and durable, with satin bow at wrists. Sizes, 3, 4 and 5. Ages, 4 to 16 years. Price, per pair..................15c

No. 33R244 Children's and Misses' Heavy Ribbed Double Wool Mittens, knit from fine soft cashmere yarn, with elastic ribbed wrists. Satin bow. Ages, 4 to 16 years. Price, per pair..........................19c
If by mail, postage extra, per pair, 2 cents.

Children's and Misses' Fancy Back Double Mittens.

No. 33R246 Children's and Misses' All Wool Fast Black Mittens, knit from fine coral Saxony yarn, double throughout, with fancy open work backs and long ribbed wrists. Ages, 4 to 16 years.
Price, per pair...................................22c

Children's and Misses' Fancy Back Mittens, 35 Cents.

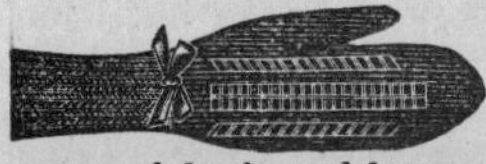

No. 33R248 Children's and Misses' Fine Coral Saxony, Fancy Back Double Mittens, all wool with open work backs and fancy wrists. Ages, 4 to 16 years.
Price, per pair...................................35c
If by mail, postage extra, per pair, 3 cents.

Misses' and Children's Silk Mittens, 43c.

No. 33R250 Misses' and Children's Pure Silk Mittens, wool lined, fancy open knit backs, ornamented at wrists with satin bow. Sizes, 3, 4 and 5. Ages, 4 to 16. Black only. Price, per pair......................43c

Boys' and Youths' Mittens.

If by mail, postage extra, per pair, 2 cents.

No. 33R254 Boys' Heavy Double Wool Mittens, ribbed, with long seamless wrists. Black only. Sizes, 3, 4 and 5. Ages, 4 to 15. Price, per pair..........15c

No. 33R256 Boys' or Youths' Double All Wool Mittens. Heavy mixed yarn and ribbed wrists, seamless. Colors, heather mixture and plain black. Sizes, 4, 5 and 6. Ages, 5 to 15.
Price, per pair.......................................20c

No. 33R258 Boys' or Youths' Double Worsted Yarn Mittens, seamless knit, heavy weight; an extra value. Ages, 4 to 15. Order by age.
Price, per pair......................................25c
If by mail, postage extra, per pair, 4 cents.

LADIES' LINED WINTER GLOVES.

QUALITIES MUCH BETTER THAN YOU WILL FIND IN THE SMALLER STORES.

PRICES THAT ARE LOWER THAN NAMED BY OTHERS.

We pride ourselves on the quality of the following goods. You can order any one of these numbers with every assurance of being well pleased with your purchase.

IN ORDERING DON'T FAIL TO GIVE SIZE, ALSO TO INCLUDE EXTRA MONEY FOR POSTAGE IF THE GOODS ARE TO GO BY MAIL.

No. 33R300 Ladies' Extra Fine Fleece Lined Kid Gloves. Black coney fur tops, stitched backs and snap fasteners. Dark tan and brown. Retails for $1.00 per pair. Sizes, 6 to 8½ only. Price, per pair..75c
If by mail, postage extra, per pair, 4 cents.

No. 33R302 Ladies' Extra Selected Kid Gloves, soft fleece lining, stitched backs and coney fur tops, patent snap fasteners. Tan, brown and red. Sizes, 6 to 8½. Price, per pair.........................$1.00
If by mail, postage extra, per pair, 6 cents.

Ladies' Lined Mocha Gloves.

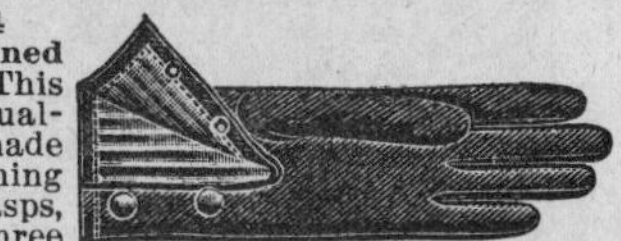

No. 33R304 Ladies' Lined Mocha Gloves. This is an excellent quality of mocha, made with fleece lining and two clasps, cable sewn, three neat rows of stitching on back. For a soft, flexible, warm street glove we especially recommend this one and warrant every pair to be perfect, free from manufacturer's defect. **It is certainly exceptional value at the price we quote, as similar gloves can seldom be had at retail for less than $1.50.** Color, black only. Sizes, 6½ to 8½. Price, per pair..........$1.15
If by mail, postage extra, per pair, 6 cents.

Ladies' Silk Lined Mocha Gloves.

No. 33R306 Ladies' Lined Mocha or Undressed Kid Gloves. An excellent quality of mocha stock that will give good wear. Made with two clasps, pique sewn back, taffeta silk lined. A swell, perfect fitting glove for street wear. Colors, black, gray, brown and tan. Sizes, 5¾ to 8 only.
Price, per pair.................................$1.25
If by mail, postage extra, per pair, 6 cents.

Astrakhan Trimmed Gauntlet Gloves.

No. 33R308 Ladies' Gauntlet Gloves, astrakhan trimmed, mocha palm. Made with a warm fleeced lining. These gloves are finely made, with gussets between fingers. Will fit perfectly, and give entire satisfaction. We especially recommend them as high grade, durable, dressy and very fashionable driving or walking glove. Sizes, 6½ to 8½.
Price, per pair.................................$1.00
If by mail, postage extra, per pair, 8 cents.

Ladies' Lamb Lined Mocha Mittens.

No. 33R310 Ladies' Genuine Lamb Lined Mocha Mittens. The best cold excluders; will keep the hands warm when other kinds of mittens or gloves have failed. **Extremely warm.** A mitten of this quality has never been offered before at our price, and seldom could they be found at $2.50 per pair. We want your order for this mitten. We want our customers to know what we can save them on fine goods. Colors, **medium brown only.** Sizes, 7, 7½, 8, 8½ and 9. Being fur lined, order larger than in regular mittens.
Price, per pair.................................$1.75
If by mail, postage extra, per pair, 8 cents.

Ladies' Plain Top Lined Mittens.

No. 33R314 Ladies' Fine Plain Top Elastic Wrist Kid Mittens, made with soft fleece lining. **Warm,** and will give good satisfaction. Sizes, 6½ to 8.
Price, per pair.................................40c
If by mail, postage extra, per pair, 4 cents.

Ladies' Fur Top Mittens.

No. 33R316 Ladies' Fine Fleece Lined Fur Top Kid Mittens, brown and tan. Sizes, 6 to 8 only.
Per pair.......45c
If by mail, postage extra, per pair, 6 cents.

Ladies' Lined Mocha Mittens.

No. 33R317 Ladies' Mocha Mittens. Extra well lined with striped fleece lining; a very warm and comfortable mitten; patent button fastening. Colors, brown and tan only. Sizes, 6½, 7, 7½, 8, 8½.
Price, per pair.................................50c
If by mail, postage extra, per pair, 4 cents.

No. 33R318 Ladies' Extra Quality Fleece Lined Kid Mittens. Stitched back, and black coney **fur** tops, tan and brown. Sizes, 6 to 8 only. **Special value.**
Price, per pair.................................75c
If by mail, postage extra, per pair, 4 cents.

Our Leader at $1.00.

No. 33R320 Ladies' Imported Kid Mittens. Soft fleece lining, stitched **backs,** patent snap **fasteners,** black **coney** fur tops, **Colors,** dark tan and brown. Sizes, 6 to 8½ only. Price, per pair.....$1.00
If by mail, postage extra, per pair, 4 cents.

Double Silk and Fleece Lined Mocha Mittens.

No. 33R321 Ladies' Genuine Mocha Mittens, with fancy striped silk lining over a wool fleece interlining, making the mitten as warm as if fur lined, yet not having a clumsy appearance. In brown and tan colors **only.** Sizes, 6½, 7, 7½, 8, 8½.
Price, per pair.................................$1.00
If by mail, postage extra, per pair, 4 cents.

Ladies' Genuine Otter Trimmed Mittens.

No. 33R322 Ladies' Genuine Otter Fur Wrist Mittens, fine mocha with warm fleece lining, one clasp at wrist. A very pretty mitten that is sure to give satisfactory wear. Colors, medium dark **tan** only. Sizes, 6 to 8. A rare bargain.
Price, per pair.................................$1.25
If by mail, postage extra, per pair, 4 cents.

Sizes for Boys and Misses, measure hand around knuckles in inches.

Children's Kid Mittens.

No. 33R326 Kid Mittens, for Girls or Boys, heavy fleece lined; ages, 4 to 10 years.
Price, per pair..............42c
If by mail, postage extra, per pair, 4 cents.

No. 33R328 Children's Fancy Back Kid Mittens, elastic wrist, heavy fleece lined; ages, 4 to 10 years.
Price, per pair.................................40c
If by mail, postage extra, per pair, 4 cents.

Misses' Fur Top Mocha Mittens.

No. 33R329 Fine Mocha Mittens, with genuine coney fur top, striped fleece lining, patent button fastener. An excellent wearing mitten. Ages, 3 to 16. Largest size equal to ladies' 6½.
Price, per pair.................................48c
If by mail, postage extra, per pair, 4 cents.

Misses' and Children's Lined Kid Gloves.

No. 33R332 Misses' Kid Gloves, made with warm fleece lining, patent clasps. Cable sewn. Neatly stitched backs. Trimmed with imitation beaver. A very popular glove for misses and children, and one that will give entire satisfaction. Dark colors. Ages 4 to 16. The largest size is equal to 6½ ladies' glove.
Price, per pair.................................75c
If by mail, postage extra, per pair, 4 cents.

DON'T FAIL TO GIVE SIZE.

DON'T FAIL TO SEND EXTRA POSTAGE WHEN GOODS ARE TO GO BY MAIL.

BOYS' WINTER GLOVES AND MITTENS.

Boys' Heavy Wool Mittens.

No. 33R340 Boys' Heavy Knit Wool Mittens, full seamless with heavy tufted wool lining and roll tops. Very thick and warm and will give thoroughly good service. Price, per pair......20c
If by mail, postage extra, per pair, 6 cents.

No. 33R341 Boys' Extra Heavy Scotch Plaid Mittens, woven very close, with heavy tufted wool lining and heavy roll top wrists. Will render great service.
Price, per pair......25c
If by mail, postage extra, per pair, 6 cents.

Boys' Lined Leather Mittens.

For youths with large hands order men's small sizes.

No. 33R342 Boys' Oil Tanned Grain Leather Mittens. Fleece lined, with elastic, close fitting wool knit wrists. Ages, 4 to 10.
Price, per pair......21c
If by mail, postage extra, per pair, 5 cents.

Boys' Horsehide Palm Mittens, Lined.

No. 33R344 Boys' and Youths' Horsehide Fire and Waterproof Tannage Mittens, with green tanned sheep backs. Fleeced lined, welt seams, and close fitting wrists. Never sold before for less than 50 cents per pair. Ages, 5 to 16. State age in order.
Price, per pair......38c
If by mail, postage extra, per pair, 5 cents.

BOYS' OR YOUTHS' WINTER GLOVES AND MITTENS.

NOTE—For large youths, order men's small sizes.

Boys' Scotch Wool Gloves.

No. 33R346 Boys' All Wool Scotch Gloves. Full seamless, good weight, soft and warm. Dark colors, brown, blue, black. State age when ordering. Ages, 5 to 16.
Price, per pair......20c
If by mail, postage extra, per pair, 2 cents.

Boys' Fancy Astrakhan Gloves.

No. 33R347 Fancy Colored Astrakhan Back Gloves with fine all wool Jersey palms, well lined with fine fleece linings. A very dressy glove and one that will give elegant service. Ages, 5 to 12. Price, per pair.25c

If by mail, postage extra, per pair, 5 cents.

Boys' Astrakhan Gloves.

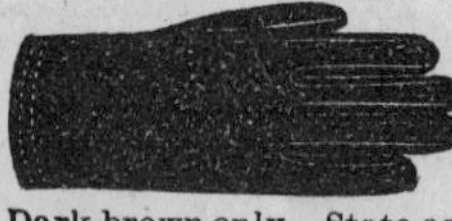

No. 33R348 Boys' or Youths' Astrakhan Back Gloves, made with dogskin palms. Warm, heavy lining. Dressy, neat and warm, and will give good satisfaction. Dark brown only. State age in order. Ages, 5 to 12.
Price, per pair......45c
If by mail, postage extra, per pair, 5 cents.

Boys' or Youths' Kid Gloves.

No. 33R350 Boys' or Youths' Domestic Kid Gloves, made with fleece lining. A good warm glove. Not a working glove; very dressy and neat. Ages, 5 to 16. State age in order. Dark colors only.

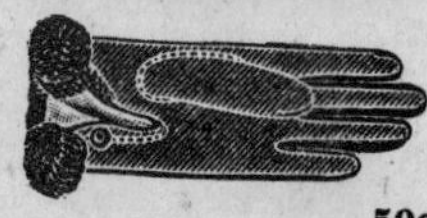

Price, per pair......50c
If by mail, postage extra, per pair, 4 cents.

MEN'S GLOVES.

WE ASK SPECIAL ATTENTION to our very complete assortment of men's gloves for all purposes—dress, driving, working gloves, etc. Our prices, a comparison will show, are extremely low for the qualities described. Bear in mind, our descriptions are accurate and truthful. When we say a glove is made of buckskin, it is buckskin and not an imitation.

IN DRESS GLOVES we show all the leading and popular styles, and you can make no mistake in your selection.

IN DRIVING AND WORKING GLOVES we can recommend every number listed, as we do not catalogue a glove unless it has stood our test for wearing qualities.

OUR PRICES ON GLOVES are uniform with our prices on other goods, and will average 20 to 30 per cent below the prices usually asked.

How to Measure Size of Glove.

Draw a tape line around the knuckles, as shown in the cut.

Men's Gloves are made in these sizes only: 7, 7¼, 7½, 7¾, 8, 8¼, 8½, 8¾, 9, 9½, 10, and 10½.

Men's cheap working gloves are not sized.

☞ **BE SURE TO SEND 4 CENTS PER PAIR EXTRA, FOR POSTAGE ON ALL GLOVES IN THIS COLUMN.**

Men's Domestic Kid Gloves.

Sizes, 8, 8½, 9, 9½, 10, and 10½ only.

No. 33R360 Men's Unlined Domestic Kid Gloves. Smooth, selected stock, stitched backs and patent buttons. Sizes, 8 to 10½ only. Dark brown color only.
Price, per pair......45c

Domestic Kid Gloves, 75 Cents.

No. 33R362 One button, with stitched backs. **Good weight, fit well and will give good service.** Medium and dark brown. Sizes, 7½ to 10½ only.
Price, per pair......75c

Men's Fine Kid Dress Gloves.

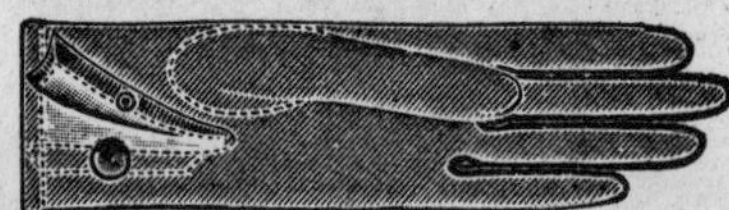

No. 33R364 Men's Imported Stock Kid Gloves, fine dress finish, medium weight, with pique sewn back and patent buttons. Stitched with silk throughout. **All the new shades,** black, brown, tan and English red. Sizes, 7¼ to 10½.
Price, per pair......95c

Men's Fine Kid Gloves, $1.25.

No. 33R366 Men's Fine Kid Gloves, made from select imported stock. One clasp, cable sewn, gusset between fingers, three rows narrow stitching on back. **A staple glove.** Colors, black, brown, tan, oxblood or white. Always state color and size in order. Sizes, 7 to 10½ only.
Price, per pair......$1.25

Men's Fine Pique Sewn Gloves, $1.45.

No. 33R368 Men's Fine Dressed Kid Gloves, made of selected imported kid stock, full pique sewn throughout. A favorite glove with well dressed men. Three rows narrow stitching in back. Colors, brown, English tan, or oxblood. Patent clasps. Sizes, 7 to 10. Price, per pair......$1.45

No. 33R370 Men's Fine Full Dress Gloves, very light in weight and fine quality. Sizes, 7 to 9½. Color, pearl only. Price, per pair......$1.50

Men's Fine Heavy Cape Goat Gloves.

No. 33R372 Men's Fine Heavy Cape Goat Walking Gloves, stitched outseams, a very fashionable glove that will always prove satisfactory for wear. The wear does not come on the thread in the fingers, but is protected by the edge, which extends just beyond the stitching. Very suitable for driving. Spear backs. One clasp and English style thumb. Color, medium dark English tan only. Sizes, 7 to 10.
Price, per pair......$1.50

Men's Extra Quality Cape Coat, $1.90.

No. 33R374 Men's Extra Quality Fine Select Cape Goatskin Gloves, stitched outseams, same style as No. 33R372, but finer quality; the grade which usually retails at $2.25 per pair. Every pair perfect in fit and warranted against manufacturer's defects of any kind. Colors, English tan and oxblood. Sizes, 7 to 10. Price, per pair......$1.90

Men's Undressed Kid or Mocha Gloves

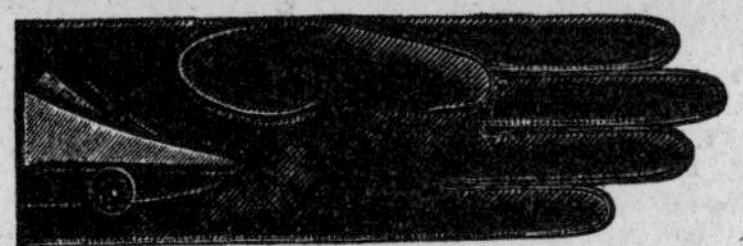

No. 33R376 Men's Mocha or Undressed Kid Gloves of good quality, pique sewn, three rows narrow stitching on back, one clasp. Colors, brown and tan only. Sizes, 7½ to 10 only.
Price, per pair......90c

Men's Genuine Mocha Gloves, $1.35.

No. 33R378 Men's Finest Genuine Mocha Gloves. The best quality Mocha Glove that you can buy. Real Mocha skins remain soft always and have fine velvet like surface. Three narrow rows of stitching on back, **pique sewn,** English thumb, one clasp. We warrant every pair against manufacturer's defects. Colors, brown, tan and gray. Sizes, 7¼ to 10.
Price, per pair......$1.35

Men's Fine Reindeer Gloves, $1.75.

A Fine Glove for Driving.

No. 33R380 Men's Best Quality Reindeer Dress Gloves. Surface is the same as fine Mocha, but skin is much heavier than No. 33R378. **Stitched outseam,** one clasp and spear back. Strictly high grade and every pair warranted against manufacturer's imperfections. A fine walking glove. Many use them for driving. Color, reindeer, which is about the same as a medium dark tan. Sizes, 7¼ to 10 only.
Price, per pair......$1.75
If by mail, postage extra, per pair, 4 cents.

Black Berlin Gloves.

No. 33R384 Men's Black Berlin Cotton Gloves. Good weight; made with plain wrists.
Price, per dozen, $1.20; per pair......10c
If by mail, postage extra, per pair, 1 cent.

White Cotton Military Gloves.

No. 33R386 Men's regular made, set in thumb, White Cotton Military Gloves. Good weight and neat fitting.
Price, per dozen, $1.32; per pair......11c
If by mail, postage extra, per pair, 1 cent.

Men's Driving Gloves.

No. 33R390 Men's Medium Heavy Weight Driving Gloves, with silk stitched backs, patent snap buttons, cut seams and silk sewed throughout. Sizes, 8 to 10½. **Medium dark color.** Price, per pair....50c
If by mail, postage extra, per pair, 3 cents.

New Standwett Driving Gloves.

No. 33R392 A Medium Weight Driving Glove, buckskin color, tanned by a new process. Very soft and pliable. **One of the best ever offered at this price.** Three rows stitching on back; one clasp. Sizes, 7½ to 10. Regular retail price, $1.00.
Price, per pair......75c
If by mail, postage extra, per pair, 4 cents.

Men's Fine Driving Gloves, $1.00.

No. 33R394 Men's Fine Driving Gloves, stitched outseams, choice heavy stock, one clasp and three rows of stitching on back. An excellent driving glove, **but not intended for heavy teaming.** Medium dark colors only in tan and brown. Sizes, 8 to 10½. Price, per pair......$1.00
If by mail, postage extra, per pair, 5 cents.

A WARNING.

BE CAREFUL when buying a pair of gloves to select one that is suitable for the purpose intended, **as the price you pay does not make any difference, if the right kind for your particular wants is not selected by you.**

BUCKSKIN GLOVES.

SPECIAL NOTICE. **We warrant every pair of Saranac, Plymouth and Indian tan buckskin gloves to be genuine deer or buckskin.** All deer skins are more or less scarred. They become scratched while the animal is running wild, or by dragging over the ground after the deer has been killed. The scratch, break or crack is not usually very deep, only the outer grain is broken. The "true skin," or fibrous portion, is not injured, **so the wearing quality of the leather is not materially hurt.** It is, therefore, seldom that buckskin gloves do not bear scratches, either large or small

Genuine Saranac Buckskin Gloves.

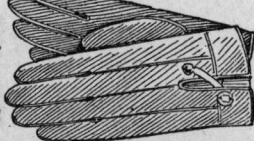

No. 33R400 Ira Parker's Steam and Waterproof Guaranteed Saranac Buckskin Gloves. Regular weight and very strong; unlined. Sewed with waxed linen thread and fitted with Porter string fasteners.
Per pair.... $0.75
Per dozen.... 9.00
If by mail, postage extra, per pair, 16 cents.

Genuine Saranac Buckskin Gloves.

No. 33R402 Heavy Weight, Ira Parker's Genuine Oil Tanned Unlined Saranac Heavy Buckskin Gloves. Stitched backs. **Sewed throughout with waxed linen thread.** The best buckskin gloves ever made anywhere. Patent Porter string fasteners, the **best fasteners known.** Price, per pair......85c
If by mail, postage extra, per pair, 6 cents.

S., R. & Co. Special Horsehide Mittens.

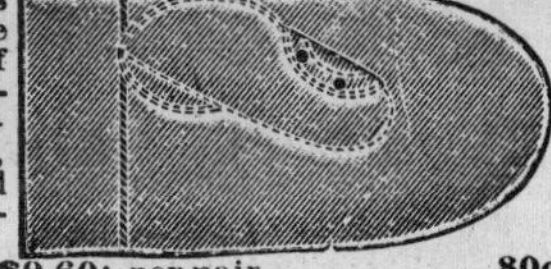

No. 33R486 Men's Genuine Fire and Waterproof Horsehide Mittens, made of genuine horsehide, double stitched and riveted thumb. Unlined.
Price, per dozen $9.60; per pair....80c
If by mail, postage extra, per pair, 8 cents.

Buckskin Choppers' Mittens for 95 Cents.

No. 33R488 Men's Stout, Medium Heavy Weight Indian Tan Buckskin Choppers' Mittens. Heavy welt seams and riveted thumbs. Sewed with waxed thread and warranted real buckskin.
Price, per pair....95c
If by mail, postage extra, per pair, 9 cents.

Fine Jack Buckskin Mittens.

No. 33R490 Genuine Jack Buckskin Mitten. Strictly No. 1 selected stock, light yellow tan, double stitched and double thumb, made out seam and riveted thumb. The best in the world.
Price, per pair....$1.20
If by mail, postage extra, per pair, 6 cents.

Steel Quilted Mittens.

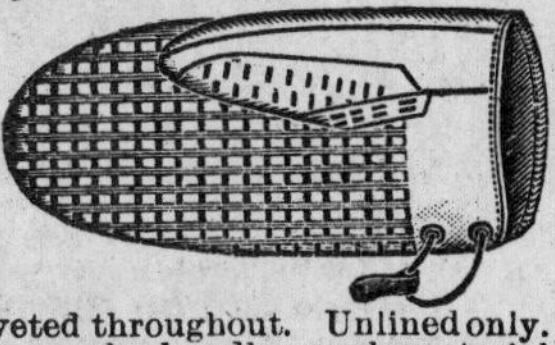

No. 33R492 Men's Steel Quilted Mittens, made from best selected horsehide, fire and water proof tannage, made with flat steel wire clinched all over the palm and thumb, no sewing, but clinched and riveted throughout. Unlined only. The right thing for men who handle rough material of any kind. Price, per dozen, $12.00; per pair, $1.00
If by mail, postage extra, per pair, 11 cents.

MEN'S LINED WORKING GLOVES.

SPECIAL NOTICE. As our price for each pair of gloves is the same as your merchant pays for the same kind when buying by the dozen, we cannot allow any reduction for quantity purchases. One pair or 1,000, the price is the same.

Men's Soft, Oil Tanned Grain Leather Gloves.

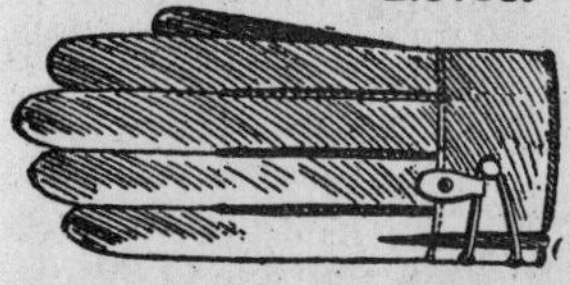

No. 33R502 Heavy stock, soft fleeced lining and stitched backs. extra well made and sewed. Patent string fastener at back. Full size.
Price, per dozen, $3.96; per pair....33c
If by mail, postage extra, per pair, 3 cents.

Men's Oil Tanned Fleece Lined Gloves.

No. 33R504 Men's Fleece Lined Heavy Weight Oil Tanned Grain Leather Gloves, made with welted backs; fancy knit center. Close fitting wrists. Large, full size; regular 50-cent value. Price, per dozen, $4.20; per pair....35c
If by mail, postage extra, per pair, 3 cents.

Heavy Lined Hogskin Gloves.

No. 33R505 Genuine Hogskin Gloves, tanned under a new process, making it an exceptionally good wearing glove. Suitable for very rough work; heavy fleece lining; made with strong welted seams, patent string fasteners, full size.
Price, per dozen, $5.40; per pair....45c
If by mail, postage extra, per pair, 5 cents.

Genuine Oil Tanned Calfskin Gloves.

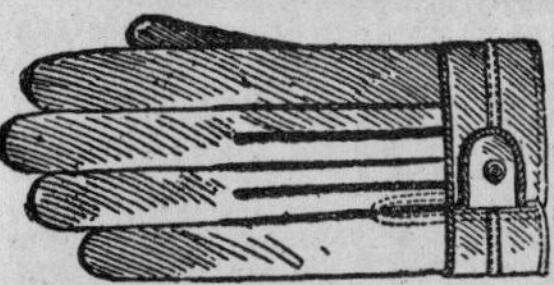

No. 33R508 Men's Very Best Quality Genuine Oil Tanned Calfskin Gloves. Extra heavy weight, with soft wool fleece lining and patent snap button fastener at back; welt seams and banded wrists. Genuine calfskin of the finest quality. No better wearing gloves made.
Price, per dozen, $9.00; per pair....75c
If by mail, postage extra, per pair, 8 cents.

REMEMBER,

OUR ONLY TERMS ARE CASH WITH THE ORDER

WE GUARANTEE ENTIRE SATISFACTION OR REFUND YOUR MONEY.

You Run no Risk in Sending Cash With Your Order.

S., R. & Co. Special Lined Gloves, 82 Cents.

No. 33R512 Men's Lined Gloves, made of best genuine horsehide of selected quality. Fire and waterproof, warranted to remain soft and pliable. Proof against steam, boiling and cold water. Remember we warrant every pair. You will pay $1.00 at retail for gloves not as good. Warm fleece lining, cord fasteners at wrist. Sizes, 9, 9½, 10.
Price, per dozen, $9.84; per pair....82c
If by mail, postage extra, each, 9 cents.

Best Cordovan Horsehide Gloves.

Every pair stamped and warranted genuine.

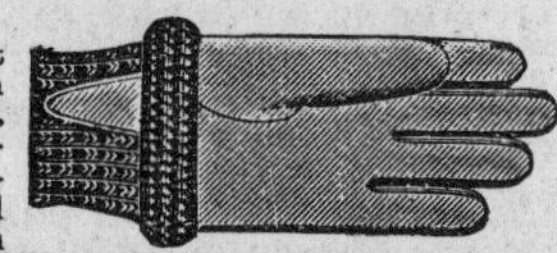

No. 33R516 Men's Kumfort Wrist Cordovan Horsehide Gloves. Fire and waterproof special process tannage and will always remain soft and pliable. Warm fleece lining, long heavy warm Kumfort wrists. Every pair warranted.
Price, per dozen, $10.56; per pair....88c
If by mail, postage extra, per pair, 10 cents.

Men's Extra Size Reindeer Gloves.

No. 33R518 Men's Extra Size Reindeer Gloves. Mammoth in size, for men with extra large hands. Welt seams, waterproof tanned and string backs. Not genuine reindeer, but of tanned reindeer color and surface. An excellent glove that will wear. Warm fleece lining.
Price, per dozen, $9.00; per pair....75c
If by mail, postage extra, per pair, 10 cents.

MEN'S WINTER MITTENS.

Men's Lined Mittens.

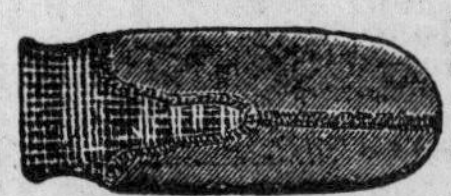

No. 33R522 Men's Oil Tanned Grain Leather Mittens, with soft fleece lining and elastic knit wrists, well sewed, strong and serviceable.
Price, per pair...$0.21
Per dozen....2.52
If by mail, postage extra, per pair, 5 cents.

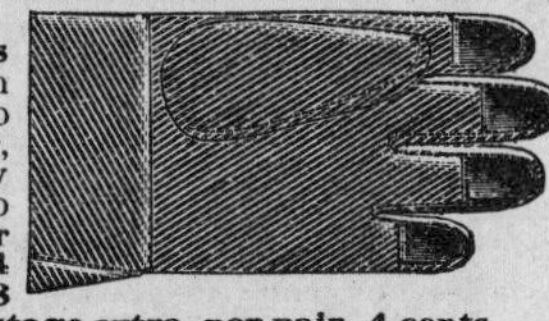

No. 33R523 Heavy Canvas Glove, made with fingers and thumb tipped with leather, making it a very durable glove. No lining. Price, per pair....$0.14
Per dozen..1.68
If by mail, postage extra, per pair, 4 cents.

Men's Canvas Mittens, 8 Cents.

No. 33R524 Men's Canvas Mittens, made with double palms and double thumbs; no lining.
Price, per dozen, 96c; per pair....8c
If by mail, postage extra, per pair, 4 cents.

No. 33R525 Extra Heavy Canvas Mittens, made with two thumbs on each mitten so they can be reversed, when palms are worn out, to the other hand, giving you practically a new mitten. Made with 2-ply canvas on palms. Price, per pair...$0.15
Per dozen....1.80
If by mail, postage extra, per pair, 4 cents.

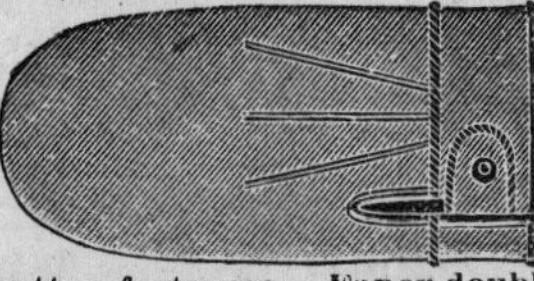

No. 33R528 Men's Heavy Tanned Muleskin Mittens with thick wool fleece lining and heavy ribbed top wool wrists, and the price at which we sell them cannot help but interest economical buyers.
Price, per dozen, $3.48; per pair....29c
If by mail, postage extra, per pair, 6 cents.

No. 33R530 Men's Fire and Waterproof Tanned Heavy Grain Leather Mittens. Extra heavy soft wool fleece lining. Patent back snap button fasteners. Fancy double stitched backs. The equal of any 75-cent mitten sold anywhere.
Price, per dozen, $4.80; per pair....40c
If by mail, postage extra, per pair, 6 cents.

No. 33R532 Men's New Storm King Mittens. Heavy oil tanned grain leather, with close fitting double knit wool wrists, outside of which is an extra wool knit sleeve piece which can be pulled up over the coat sleeve in severe weather. The most comfortable cold weather mitten ever produced.
Price, per dozen, $5.40; per pair....45c
If by mail, postage extra, per pair, 8 cents.

Storm Wrists, String Back Matamora Hogskin Mittens, 45 Cents.

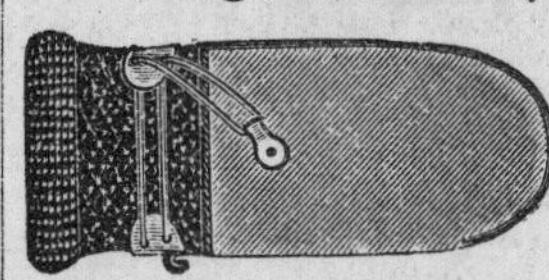

No. 33R534 Men's Heavy Winter Mittens, with palms of Matamora hogskin, welt seams, warm fleece lining, and string and hook on wrists. Regular retail price, 75 cents. Great value.
Price, per dozen, $5.40; per pair....45c
If by mail, postage extra, per pair, 15 cents.

Heavy Horsehide Mittens.

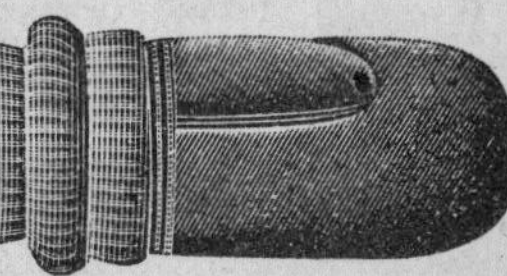

No. 33R535 Men's Extra Heavy Horsehide Mitten, with very heavy knitted wool wrists with over wrists 10 inches long to pull over the coat sleeve, heavy wool lining. This is an exceptionally warm mitten and will give lasting wear and our price is 25 cents per pair less than your home merchants can sell them for.
Price, per pair....75c
If by mail, postage extra, per pair, 15 cents.

Special Lamb Lined Mittens.

No. 33R538 Men's Extra Heavy Mittens, Lamb's Wool Lined Wrists. A regular Klondiker that will keep your hands warm in the coldest weather. Real lamb's wool wrists. Heavy select Cordovan horsehide leather. Reinforced thumbs; welt seams; long, thick wool wrists, thick wool lining in hand and string backs. Order this mitten and you will not suffer with cold hands.
Price, per dozen, $13.80; per pair....$1.15
If by mail, postage extra, per pair, 18 cents.

Lined Horsehide Fireproof Mittens.

Every pair stamped and warranted.

No. 33R540 Men's Genuine Cordovan Horsehide Mittens. Guaranteed to remain soft and pliable in any climate and proof against heat, steam, boiling and cold water. Heavy warm fleece lining, welted seams and very durable.
Price, per dozen, $9.72; per pair....81c
If by mail, postage extra, per pair, 8 cents.

Men's Gauntlet Mittens.

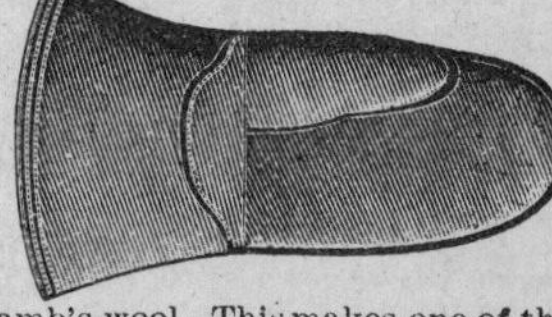

No. 33R541 Men's Extra Heavy Gauntlet Mittens, made with genuine Cordovan horsehide palms and heavy grain leather backs, large deep gauntlets, heavy fleece lined, and wrists of natural lamb's wool. This makes one of the warmest and best wearing mittens for all kinds of rough outside work. Will keep the hands warm in the coldest weather. Price, per pair....$0.85
Per dozen....10.20
If by mail, postage extra, per pair, 15 cents.

Extra Large Oil Tan Calfskin Mittens.

No. 33R542 Men's Extra Heavy and Extra Large Genuine Oil Tanned Calfskin Mittens. Heavy tufted wool lining, welt seams and extra heavy, thick knit wool wrists; warranted genuine calfskin. Full of lasting goodness.
Price, per dozen, $10.20; per pair....85c
If by mail, postage extra, per pair, 8 cents.

Genuine Buckskin Mittens.

No. 33R544 Genuine Buckskin Mittens, heavy weight, lined with heavy all wool fleece, an extra warm mitten, just what you want for very cold weather. Will stand hard wear.
Price, per pair....$1.25
If by mail, postage extra, per pair, 10 cents.

MEN'S FUR GLOVES.

Men's Fur Gauntlet Gloves at 80 Cents.

No. 33R550 A Good Gauntlet Glove, made in imitation brown bear. Gauntlet about 3 inches wide. Dogskin palms and warm fleece lining. Not a cheap appearing glove. Price, per pair........ **$0.80**
Per dozen pairs........ 9.60
If by mail, postage extra, per pair, 9 cents.

Men's Fine Gauntlet Fur Gloves, $1.50.

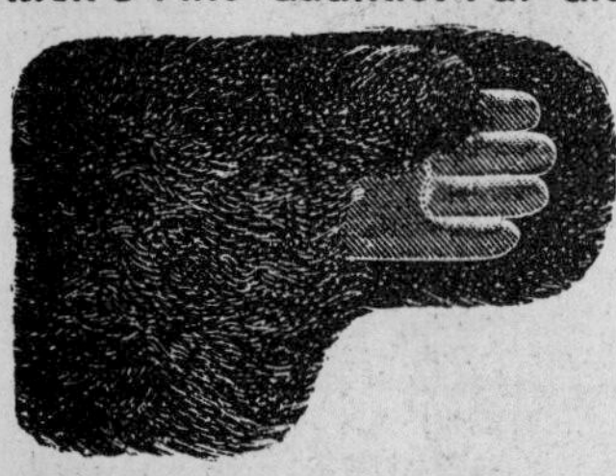

No. 33R552 Men's Extra Quality Baltic Imitation Brown Bear Fur Gauntlet Gloves. Fine and very soft. Close thick fur and unexcelled for wear; finest horsehide palms, corduroy lined, large gauntlets and fine wool fleece lined fingers and thumbs. **A handsome and most serviceable glove.**
Price, per dozen pairs, **$18.00**; per pair...... **$1.50**
If by mail, postage extra, per pair, 20 cents.

Extra Quality Black Fur Gloves, $3.00.

No. 33R556 Men's Extra Quality High Grade Black Fur Gauntlet Gloves. Extra large gauntlet about 10 inches wide, lined with velvet, hand lined with heavy wool lining and reindeer palms. A very fine driving glove that frequently retails at $5.00.
Price, per pair........ **$3.00**
If by mail, postage extra, per pair, 22 cents.

Men's Fur Hunting or Shooting Mittens.

No. 33R560 Men's Fur Hunting or Shooting Mittens; made with one finger. A very useful, all around mitten. Made of imitation brown bear, with horsehide palms, corduroy lined gauntlets, fleece lined hand.
Price, per dozen pairs, **$13.80**; per pair...... **$1.15**
If by mail, postage extra, per pair, 20 cents.

Men's Fur Mittens. $1.50.

No. 33R562 Men's Heavy Imitation Brown Bear Fur Gauntlet Mittens, with best horsehide palms and fine soft wool fleece lining; **thoroughly reliable, warm and comfortable.** They are full of everlasting goodness and you'll like them. **Extra well made throughout.** Price, per pair, **$ 1.50**
Per dozen pairs........ **18.00**
If by mail, postage extra, per pair, 20 cents.

Men's Cashmere Knit Cloth Gloves.

No. 33R570 Men's Cashmere Gloves of good quality, three rows silk cord stitching in back. Full size and fleece lined. Color, black only. Sizes, 8 to 10½.
Price, per dozen pairs, **$2.64**; per pair........ **22c**
If by mail, postage extra, per pair, 2 cents.

Men's Wool Cashmere Gloves, 45 Cents.

No. 33R572 Men's Heavy Warm Wool Cashmere Gloves, three rows stitching in back, warm wool fleece lining and plain wrists. A special leader in value. Sizes, 7½ to 10½. Black only.
Price, per dozen pairs, **$5.40**; per pair........ **45c**
If by mail, postage extra, per pair, 2 cents.

Men's Cashmere Mittens, 45 Cents.

No. 33R574 Men's Heavy and Warm Wool Cashmere Mittens, made with warm wool fleeced lining. A special value. Black only.
Sizes, 8 to 10½. Price, per pair........ **$0.45**
Per dozen pairs........ **5.40**
If by mail, postage extra, per pair, 2 cents.

DO NOT FAIL TO GIVE SIZE OF GLOVES AND MITTENS.

DON'T FAIL TO SEND EXTRA POSTAGE WHERE GOODS ARE TO GO BY MAIL.

MEN'S LINED DRESS GLOVES FOR WINTER.

Men's Lined Kid Gloves, 45 Cents.

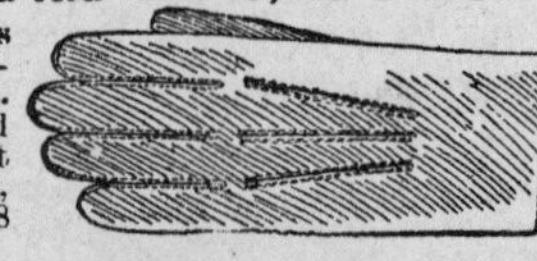

No. 33R580 Men's Fleece Lined Domestic Kid Gloves. Well made and sewed; clear, soft stock, dark colors, no blacks. Sizes, 8 to 10½ only.
Price, per dozen pairs, **$5.40**; per pair. **45c**
If by mail, postage extra, per pair, 4 cents.

Men's Lined Kid Gloves, 75 Cents.

No. 33R582 Men's Fleece Lined Kid Gloves. Fine soft finish, stitched backs; handsome and dressy; dark colors, but no blacks. Sizes, 7½ to 10½ only.
Price, per pair........ **75c**
If by mail, postage extra, per pair, 6 cents.

Men's 98-Cent Kid Gloves.

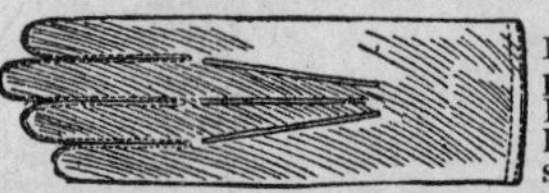

No. 33R584 Men's Extra Quality Imported Kid Gloves. Fine wool fleeced lining. Patent snap button fasteners. Finely made and finished, silk stitched backs. **Very warm and comfortable** as well as handsome and dressy. Dark tan and brown shades only. Sizes, 7½ to 10½.
Price, per dozen pairs, **$11.76**; per pair........ **98c**
If by mail, postage extra, per pair, 3 cents.

$1.50 Men's Silk Lined Gloves, $1.15.

No. 33R586 Men's Fine Quality Kid Gloves, made wtih fine silk lining, very easy to slip on and off, and on the hand looks like an unlined glove. Patent snap buttons, finished backs, pique and outseams. Handsome and dressy. Dark tan, brown and red only. Sizes, 7½ to 10.
Price, per dozen pairs, **$13.80**; per pair.. .. **$1.15**
If by mail, postage extra, per pair, 3 cents.

SPECIAL NOTICE—Lined gloves and mittens are not made in quarter sizes, but in half sizes only; namely, 8, 8½, 9, etc.

Men's Fine Lamb Lined Gloves, $2.90.

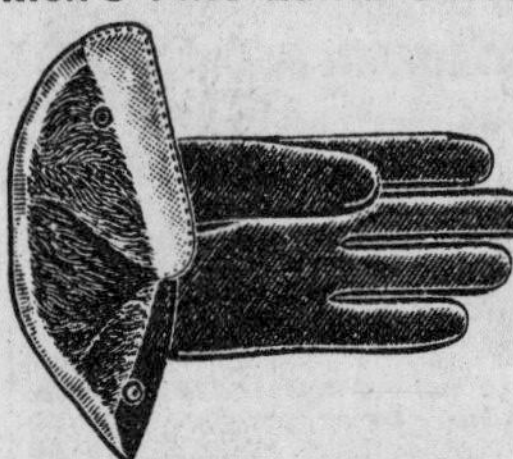

No. 33R590 Men's Extra High Grade Lamb Lined Gloves. These gloves are made of genuine cape goat stock, which is heavier than the usual kid. The stitching is outseam. The advantage in outseam is that the wear comes directly upon the edge and not upon the thread. Hence they seldom rip. **Genuine lamb's wool lining,** skillfully inserted. Extra lap at the wrist to prevent the wind from entering. This is an exceptionally high grade glove in every particular, and usually retails at from $3.50 to $4.00. **Our special price is the lowest that has ever been quoted for a high grade glove of this character.** We guarantee every pair to be perfect and to give entire satisfaction, and should be pleased to receive your order for a glove of this quality. Colors, dark brown and red only. Sizes, 8 to 10½ only.
Price, per pair........ **$2.90**
If by mail, postage extra, per pair, 10 cents.

Our Finest Squirrel Lined Gloves for $3.50. Actually Worth $5.00.

No. 33R593 Squirrel Lined Glove; one of the finest gloves manufactured; made of specially selected imported stock, lined with fine gray squirrel lining, soft as velvet and extremely warm. The fur being so fine does not make the glove have a clumsy appearance on the hand. They are made with the out seam and fine spear back, embroidery on the back, patent clasps and extra long wrists. This glove is retailed everywhere for $5.00 and our price is less than a glove of this quality has ever been sold at. Sizes, 8 to 10½. Color, English tan only, the fashionable color. Price, per pair........ **$3.50**
If by mail, postage extra, per pair, 8 cents.

Men's Fine Lamb Lined Gloves, $1.75.

No. 33R596 Men's Good Quality Lamb Lined Gloves. Not as fine as the above but made of fine domestic kid, elastic wrists, pique sewn back. **We warrant equal to gloves at $2.50 per pair, retail.** Colors, dark brown and red only. Lamb lined gloves are the warmest dress gloves made. Sizes, 8 to 10 only. Price, per pair........ **$1.75**
If by mail, postage extra, per pair, 9 cents.

Men's Lamb Lined Mocha Mittens.

No. 33R598 Men's High Grade Mocha Lamb Lined Mittens. An exceptionally fine quality, something that is not found in every store, and has genuine **lamb lining.** Extremely warm, and we believe a mitten of this quality has never before been offered for less than $2.50. Our price of $1.85 represents little more than the actual cost to us, and is less than the cost to your local merchant. **We should be pleased to receive your order for this quality,** as we especially recommend high grade goods of this character, knowing them to be entirely satisfactory and the most perfect goods of the kind manufactured. Sizes, 8½ to 10. Color, dark brown only. Price, per pair........ **$1.85**
If by mail, postage extra, per pair, 8 cents.

Men's Mocha Gloves, 85 Cents.

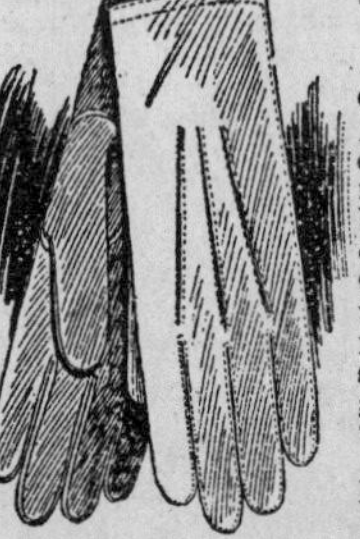

No 33R600 Men's Mocha Gloves, soft undressed kid finish with good wearing qualities, **fine soft wool fleeced lining,** silk stitched backs and snap button fasteners, dark brown and tan. **One of the very best medium weight gloves ever put on the market at our low price. Very stylish and dressy and will give good satisfaction.** Sizes, 7½ to 10½. Per pair... **$ 0.85**
Per dozen pairs........ **10.20**
If by mail, postage extra, per pair, 4 cents.

Men's Silk Lined Mocha Gloves, $1.00.

No. 33R601 Men's Mocha Glove, lined with silk, an elegant looking and perfect fitting glove, in dark brown and tan colors only. The glove is one of the most durable gloves manufactured and always satisfies the wearer. Sizes 7½, 8, 8½, 9, 9½, 10, 10½. Price, per pair........ **$1.00**
If by mail, postage extra, per pair, 4 cents.

Men's Fine Genuine Mocha Gloves, $1.50.

No. 33R602 Men's Finest Quality Genuine Mocha or Undressed Kid Gloves, with fine, warm, fleece lining. A strictly high grade lined glove of best Mocha stock, soft and pliable. Pique sewn, three rows narrow silk stitching in back, and one clasp. Usual retail price, $2.00. **Every pair warranted perfect.** Sizes, 7½ to 10½. Dark brown only.
Price, per dozen pairs, **$18.00**; per pair..... **$1.50**
If by mail, postage extra, per pair, 7 cents.

Men's Fine Fur Top Kid Gloves.

No. 33R606 Men's Fine Fur Top Kid Gloves. Soft fleece lining. Made from **first quality prime stock,** fancy stitched backs; **very warm, comfortable and dressy.** Dark tan and brown, no black. Fine black coney fur tops. Sizes, 7½ to 10½.
Price, per dozen pairs, **$9.00**; per pair........ **75c**
If by mail, postage extra, per pair, 4 cents.

Men's Extra Quality Fur Top Gloves.

No. 33R608 Men's Extra Quality Fine Black Coney Fur Top Gloves; made full size with warm fleece lining, elastic wrists and wide trimmed fur tops, gussets between fingers. Dressy and neat; **a good, warm, reliable glove.** Dark colors only. Sizes, 7½ to 10½. Price, per pair....... **$ 1.00**
Per dozen pairs........ **12.00**
If by mail, postage extra, per pair, 4 cents.

Fine Astrakhan Back Gloves.

No. 33R610 Men's Fine Astrakhan Cloth Glove, with fine dogskin palms and soft fleece lining, with **fine quality astrakhan backs;** new snap button. Very warm and will give excellent wear. Sizes, 7½ to 10½.
Price, per dozen pairs, **$5.40**; per pair........ **45c**
If by mail, postage extra, per pair, 4 cents.

Men's Lined Kid Mittens, Plain Wrists.

No. 33R614 Men's Dark Brown Domestic Kid Mittens. Fleece lined, with elastic wrists and stitched backs. Sizes, 8 to 10½ only.
Price, per dozen pairs, **$5.40**; per pair........ **45c**
If by mail, postage extra, per pair, 4 cents.

Men's Fine Kid Mittens, 75 Cents.

No. 33R616 Men's Fine Kid Mittens. Plain top, soft fleece lining, with elastic wristband, embroidered backs; very soft and warm. Dark brown color. Sizes, 7½ to 10½ only.
Price, per dozen pairs, **$9.00**; per pair........ **75c**
If by mail, postage extra, per pair, 4 cents.

Men's Fine Fur Top Mittens, $1.00.

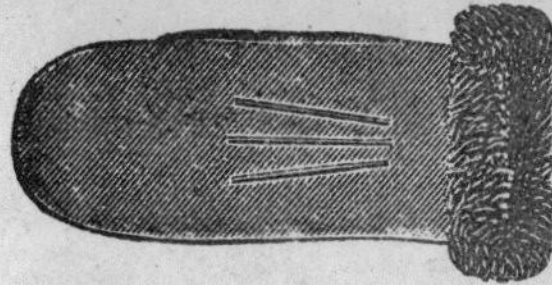

No. 33R618 Men's Extra Fine Fur Top Imported Kid Mittens. Wool fleece lined, with fancy embroidered backs; patent fasteners and black sheared coney fur wrists. Sizes, 7½ to 10½ only. Color, dark brown.
Price, per dozen, $12.00; per pair..........$1.00
If by mail, postage extra, per pair, 4 cents.

Men's Mocha Mittens, Plain Wrists.

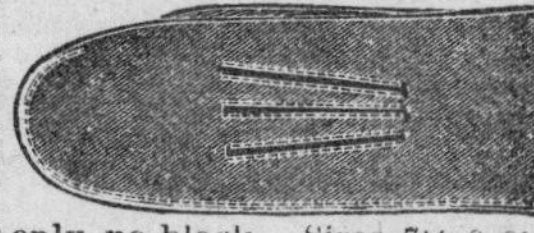

No. 33R620 Men's Fine Quality Mocha Mittens. Full size, soft and warm, made with warm fleece lining, elastic wrists and embroidered backs; dark shades only, no black. Sizes, 7½, 8, 8½, 9, 9½, 10, 10½. Price, per pair..........88c
If by mail, postage extra, per pair, 5 cents.
NOTE—For Men's Lamb Lined Mocha Mittens, see No. 33R598.

WRISTLETS OR PULSE WARMERS.

No. 33R630 Men's Plain Black Double Wool Wristlets. Very elastic and will fit well. Price, per dozen, $1.20; per pair..........10c
No. 33R631 Men's Fancy Colored, Striped, Double Wristlets. Good quality.
Price, per dozen, $2.16; per pair.18c
No. 33R632 Men's Fine Ribbed, Black All Wool Double Wristlets. Medium weight.
Price, per dozen, $2.16; per pair..........18c
No. 33R633 Men's Extra Heavy and Thick Warm All Wool Double Wristlets. Plain black.
Price, per dozen, $2.52; per pair..........21c
If by mail, postage extra, per pair, 2 cents.
No. 33R634 Men's Silk Wristlets. Medium weight. Black and fancy stripes.
Price, per dozen, $3.60; per pair..........30c
If by mail, postage extra, per pair, 1 cent.

Warmpulse Wristlets.

No. 33R640 The best patent wristlet ever made to prevent wind from blowing up sleeve. Made of brown fur with elastic through center; can be worn with any glove and will fit any size wrists.
Price, per pair...$0.25
Per dozen........ 3.00
If by mail, postage extra, per pair, 4 cents.

Men's Saxony Yarn Mittens.

No. 33R646 Men's Plain Black All Wool Double Mittens, made of fine Saxony yarn, seamless and fashioned to shape of hand. Usual retail price, 35 cents.
Price, per dozen, $3.00; per pair..........25c
If by mail postage extra, per pair, 3 cents.

MEN'S SCOTCH WOOL GLOVES.

No. 33R650 Men's All Wool Scotch Gloves. Full seamless, soft and warm, assorted dark and medium colors, heather mixtures or black. Sizes, small, medium and large.
Price, per dozen, $2.52; per pair..........22c
If by mail, postage extra, per pair, 2 cents.

Men's Heavy All Wool Scotch Gloves, 33 Cents.

No. 33R652 Men's Heavy All Wool Scotch Gloves, seamless, durable and warm, double wrists, Oxford gray mixed and brown colors, all dark. Sizes, small, medium and large.
Price, per dozen, $3.96; per pair..........33c
If by mail, postage extra, per pair, 2 cents.

McGeorge Gloves, 45 Cents.

No. 33R654 Men's Extra Quality All Wool Imported genuine McGeorge Scotch Gloves. Full seamless, handsome patterns, assorted colors, dark and medium, soft and comfortable.
Price, per dozen, $5.40; per pair..........45c
If by mail, postage extra, per pair, 2 cents.

GIVE CATALOGUE NUMBER IN FULL WHEN YOU WRITE YOUR ORDER

McGeorge Gloves, 70 Cents.

No. 33R658 Men's Extra High Grade Scotch Gloves, made by J. & D. McGeorge, Dumfries, Scotland, manufacturers of the finest woolen gloves in the world. Handsome plaids in mixed colors, also plain black and white. Seamless and perfect fitting. Give size. Sizes, 7½ to 10.
Price, per dozen, $8.40; per pair..........70c
If by mail, postage extra, per pair, 3 cents.

Men's Extra Heavy Scotch Gloves, 42 Cents.

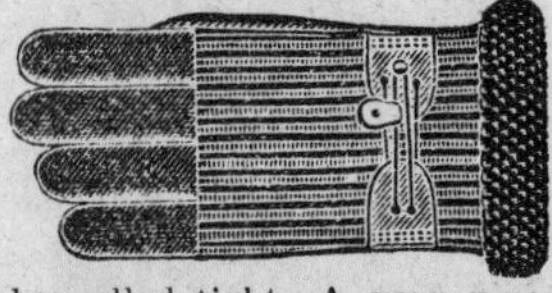

No. 33R664 Men's Extra Heavy Scotch Gloves. These gloves are made extra heavy, with tufted lining, seamless, close fitting, ribbed wrist, storm top, cord at wrist, can be pulled tight. A very warm wool glove that will be found durable and satisfactory in every way. A special value.
Price, per dozen, $5.04; per pair..........42c
If by mail, postage extra, per pair, 10 cents.

Men's Heavy Wool Mittens.

No. 33R666 Men's Heavy Weight Knit Wool Mittens; fancy striped patterns, dark colors, large sizes.
Price, pair..$0.13
Per dozen... 1.56
If by mail, postage extra, per pair, 4 cents.

All Wool Fancy Plaid Mittens.

No. 33R668 Men's Heavy All Wool Fancy Plaid Mittens; close knit, firm and thick; will give excellent service. Price, per doz. $2.28; per pair, 19c
If by mail, postage extra, per pair, 5 cents.

Men's Heavy Knit Wool Mittens, 21 Cents.

No. 33R670 Men's Extra Heavy Knit Wool Mittens, with roll tops and heavy tufted wool lining; assorted dark and medium colors, fancy patterns; very warm and durable. Price, per dozen, $2.52; per pair.21c
If by mail, postage extra, per pair, 5 cents.

Men's Heavy Wool Shooting Mitten.

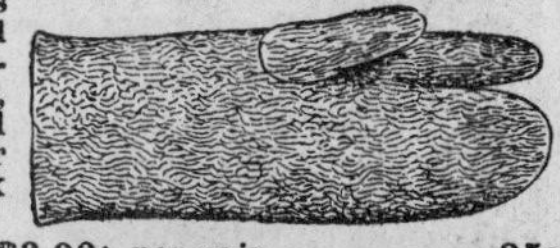

No. 33R672 Men's Heavy All Wool One Finger Shooting Mitten. Fulled, very warm and seamless, will wear like leather. Black or brown.
Price, per dozen, $3.00; per pair..........25c
If by mail, postage extra, per pair, 5 cents.

Thick German Wool Mittens.

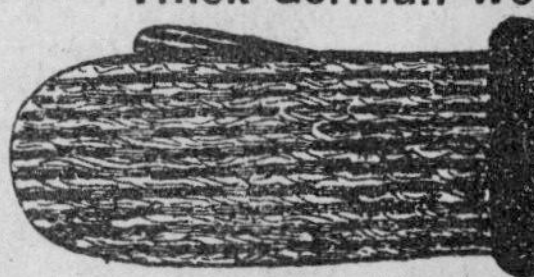

No. 33R674 Men's Extra Heavy and Thick German Wool Mittens, with heavy fringed tops and extra heavy tufted wool lining. Assorted dark and medium fancy mixed colors. Per dozen, $4.20; per pair..........35c
If by mail, postage extra, per pair, 7 cents.

Northwest Heavy Wool Mittens.

No. 33R678 Men's Extra Heavy Thick Mackinaw Wool Mittens. Will wear like leather. Very firm, thick mitten. Dark colors.
Price, per dozen, $4.20; per pair..........35c
If by mail, postage extra, per pair, 9 cents.

A REMINDER: We sell one or one dozen pairs at the same price for each pair. You pay no more for a single pair than the customer who buys one dozen.

Wind and Waterproof Mittens.

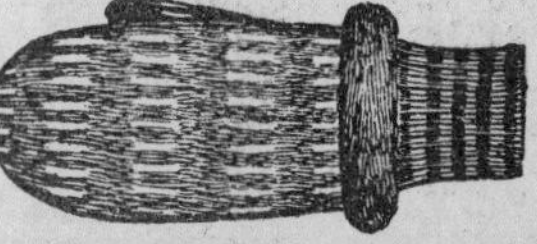

No. 33R680 Men's Wind and Waterproof Heavy Wool Mittens. Heavy thick wool, wool lined, and waterproof interlining. May be wet and cold on outside, but on the inside always warm and dry.
Price, per dozen, $4.80; per pair..........40c
If by mail, postage extra, per pair, 10 cents.

Wind and Waterproof Mittens.

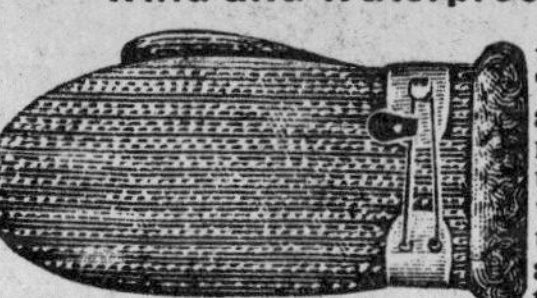

No. 33R681 Extra Heavy Mitten. Thoroughly wind and waterproof; made with heavy tufted wool lining with waterproof interlining, making it an extra warm mitten. Patent string back. Price, per dozen, $4.56; per pair..........38c
If by mail, postage extra, per pair, 10 cents.

Husking Gloves and Pins.

If by mail, postage extra, each, 4 cents.

No. 33R684 Husking Pin, single point, with strap, can adjust to any size hand. Per doz., 36c; each, 3c

Clark's Husking Pin.

No. 33R686 This is the most simple, durable and efficient Husking Pin made, and the strap through which the fingers are placed gives comfort to any size hand, as the adjustment is very simple. Leather shield prevents injury and allows a firm grip.
Price, per dozen, $1.08; each..........9c
If by mail, postage extra, each, 4 cents.

Clark's Improved Husking Pin.

No. 33R688 Clark's New Husking Pin, with curved point. Heavier leather and pin than in the above; to be used in the same manner.
Price, each.......$0.18
Per dozen......... 2.16
If by mail, postage extra, each, 5 cents.

The Ramsey Corn Husker.

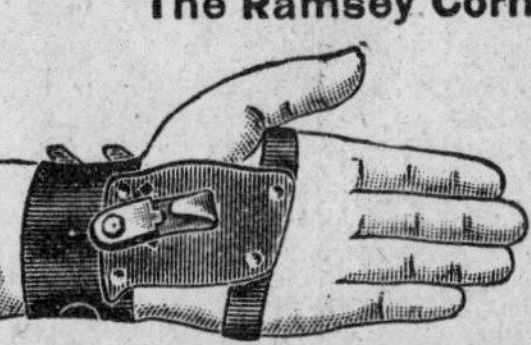

No. 33R690 A new Husker with much to commend, because of its practical points. The hook is very heavy and strong, and adjusts to any angle to suit the user, by loosening the nut with a wrench that goes with each pair. It can be quickly adapted for small or large size corn. Heavy leather wrist strap which divides strain.
Price, per dozen, $3.00; each..........25c
If by mail, postage extra, each, 7 cents.

Wrist Straps.

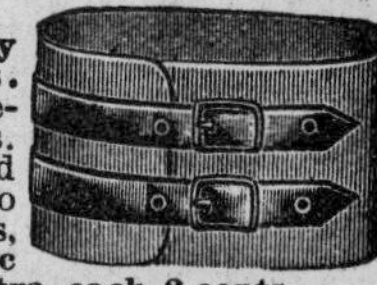

No. 33R692 Men's Heavy Calfskin Wrist Straps. Strengthens the wrist and prevents swelling and soreness. Made 2½ inches wide and buckles around wrist with two small straps. Per dozen pairs, $1.68; per pair, 14c; each, 7c
If by mail, postage extra, each, 2 cents.

Thumb and Finger Husker.

No. 33R694 Husking Pin, with thumb and forefinger attachment and fastened around the wrist with straps and buckle on back; all straps are adjustable. Price, per dozen, $2.16; set, 18c
If by mail, postage extra, 4 cents.

Our 40-Cent Husking Gloves.

No. 33R696 Husking Glove, made of heavy oil tanned grain leather, soft and easy to the hand.
Per pair ..$0.40
Per dozen...4.80
If by mail, postage extra, each, 9 cents.

Heavy Horsehide Husking Gloves, 69 Cents.

No. 33R698 Men's Best Quality Horsehide Husking Gloves, riveted palms and patent husking pin attached. Price, per doz., $8.28; per pair, 69c
If by mail, postage extra, per pair, 9 cents.

Husking Mittens.

No. 33R699 Made of heavy mule skin and palmed with extra tough leather, fingers protected with metal plates, steel husking band and metal plates on thumb piece, fastened with copper rivets, wrist strap and buckle.
Price, per dozen, $4.20; per pair..........35c
If by mail, postage extra, per pair, 8 cents.

---HAT DEPARTMENT---

DO NOT BE SATISFIED WITH ANY STYLE HAT when you can have at no additional expense a hat that will be becoming and at the same time stylish and in good form. Different sections of the country have their styles, due mainly to their difference in occupation and environment. If you live on a ranch and want the proper hat for such a life, we have it. If you wish the fashionable derby or stiff hat, we can supply this.

OUR LINE OF SOFT AND FEDORA SHAPES CANNOT BE EXCELLED.

VALUE. We can sell you a hat at almost any price, but by our manufacturer to the wearer plan we are able to sell to you at almost the same price your home merchant pays for the same quality. We want your order, because we can save you 25 to 40 per cent, and at the same time fill your order with NEW, CLEAN, UP TO DATE GOODS.

HOW TO MEASURE FOR A HAT

Hat size	Inches around head	Hat size	Inches around head	Hat size	Inches around head
5⅞	18¾	6⅝	21	7⅜	23⅜
6	19	6¾	21½	7½	23¾
6⅛	19⅜	6⅞	21⅝	7⅝	24
6¼	19¾	7	22¼	7¾	24½
6⅜	20¼	7⅛	22½	7⅞	25
6½	20¾	7¼	23	8	25¼

Men's Sizes are 6¾, 6⅞, 7, 7⅛, 7¼, 7⅜ and 7½. Extra sizes are: 7⅝ to 8. **Boys' Sizes** are 6½, 6⅝, 6¾, 6⅞ and 7. **Children's Sizes**, 6⅛, 6⅜, 6¼, 6⅝ and 6¾. If you do not have a tape measure at hand, use a strip of paper for measuring and attach same to your order.

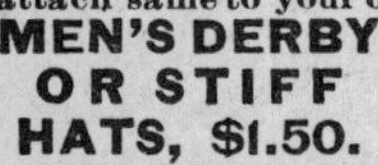

MEN'S DERBY OR STIFF HATS, $1.50.

No. 33R2010 Young Men's Stiff Hat, in fashionable shape. Is a very neat block, not extreme, but stylish. Crown, 4¾ inches; brim, 1⅝ inches. Fine silk band and binding. Colors, black or brown. Sizes, 6¾ to 7½.
Price, each.... **$1.50**
If by mail, postage extra, 34 cents.

A Fashionable Block in Men's Stiff Hats for $2.00.

No. 33R2014 Young Men's Fashionable Stiff Hat. A strictly correct block in a superior quality. A non-breakable hat that will wear like a $3.00 hat. Crown, 4¾ in.; brim, 1⅞ inches. Fine silk band, binding and sweat. We warrant every hat to give satisfactory service. Sizes, 6¾ to 7½. Colors, black or dark brown.
Each.......... **$2.00**
If by mail, postage extra, each, 34 cents.

Late Style and Excellent Value for $2.25.

No. 33R2020 Men's Medium Shape Stiff Hat, a little larger than the above styles. Medium curled brim. Not an extreme in any respect, but a strictly stylish block. Crown, 5 inches; brim, 1⅞ inches. A very fine hat at our low price that we warrant it to give satisfactory wear. Equal to most hats sold at $3.00. Colors, black or dark brown. Sizes, 6¾ to 7⅝.
Price, each....... **$2.25**
Postage extra, 34c.

Men's Fashionable Square Crown Hats $2.00.

No. 33R2026 At this price we have the new style square crown hat. A very fashionable block. Crown, 5½ inches; brim, 2 inches wide. A non-breakable hat that will not fail to please in style and quality. Fine silk band and binding. Imported leather sweatband. Colors, black or dark brown. What size do you wear? Sizes, 6¾ to 7⅝.
Price, each **$2.00**
If by mail, postage extra, 34 cents.

Men's Large or Full Shape Stiff Hats.

No. 33R2040 A style particularly suited to large men. A shapely, staple hat, as shown in illustration. Crown, 5¼ inches; brim, 2¼ inches. Fine silk band and binding. Sizes, 6¾ to 7⅝. Color, black only.
Each..... **$1.50**
If by mail, postage extra, 34 cents.

Our Men's $2.25 Quality Full Shape Hat.

No. 33R2046 Men's Full Shape Hat, same style and dimensions as the above, in the high grade non-breakable stock, with very fine silk band and binding; imported leather sweatband. Color, black only. Sizes, 6¾ to 7¾. Price, each.......................... **$2.25**
If by mail, postage extra, 34 cents.

Dunlap, Knox or Youman Styles.

No. 33R2060 Men's High Grade Stiff Hat, made of very fine quality of fur, with select silk trimmings, in the Dunlap, Knox or Youman styles; small, medium or large shape. We furnish the latest styles or shapes as issued in the spring and fall. The usual retail price of this quality is $3.50 and **combines all the points of merit and non-breakableness of the finest derby hat.** Sizes, 6¾ to 7⅝.
Price, each... **$2.75**
If by mail, postage extra, 34 cents.

Men's Fedora or Alpine Soft Hats.

No. 33R2070 A shapely hat, made to stand the wear. Silk band and binding; good leather sweatband. Colors, black or brown. Made from nutria fur. Weight, 4 ounces. The sizes run from 6¾ to 7½. **What size do you wear?**
Price, each **98c**
If by mail, postage extra, 25 cents.

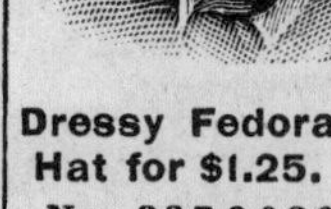

Dressy Fedora Hat for $1.25.

No. 33R2080 Men's Medium Shape Fedora Hat. A quality that is unmatched by any house. Crown, 6 inches; brim, 2⅝ inches. A hat very becoming to men of average build. Colors, black, brown, pearl or gray. Sizes, 6¾ to 7½. **What size do you wear?**
Each........ **$1.25**
If by mail, postage extra, 25 cents.

IF YOU FAIL TO GIVE SIZE, WE CANNOT FILL YOUR ORDER.

Our Trebor Hat, $1.50.

No. 33R2090 We continue to maintain the same grade of fine stock in our Trebor quality as in previous seasons. Made of fine clear nutria fur stock, fine silk band and binding and imported leather sweatband. If not equal to any hat you can buy at home for $2.00, return to us and we refund your money. Crown, 5¾ inches; brim, 2⅛ inches, of shapely medium curl. Colors, black, brown or pearl. Sizes, 6¾ to 7⅝. Price, each.......................... **$1.50**
If by mail, postage extra, 25 cents.

Special Soft Hat for 1902.

No. 33R2092 Men's New Style Soft Fur Hat with high open curled brim similar to the alpine or fedora style. Crown, 5⅝ inches; brim, 2⅛ inches. The stylish and proper hat for young men and at the same time not too extreme. You will pay $2.00 at retail for a hat no better than we send you for $1.50. Fine silk band and binding. Colors, black, steel or pearl. Sizes, 6¾ to 7⅛.
Price, each....... **$1.50**
If by mail, postage extra, 25 cents.

Our Special Soft Hat for 1902.

Full Shape.

No. 33R2094 Men's Full Shape Hats, similar in style to the one above but larger shape. Crown, 6 inches; brim, 2¾ inches. A shape that is particularly desirable for tall or heavy men. The quality we will send you will be found equal to hats retailing for $3.00. Fine nutria fur, fine silk band and binding. High open curled brim, as shown in the illustration. This style will please you. Colors, black or steel. Sizes, 6¾ to 7½.
Price, each...... **$2.25**
If by mail, postage extra, each, 25 cents.

Fine Nutria Fur Fedora Hat for $1.50.

No. 33R2096 The Memphis. Raw Edge Genuine Nutria Fur Fedora. As a late fall and early spring hat this number cannot fail to please. Crown, 5¾ inches; brim, 2⅝ inches. In colors the bands (of gros-grain ribbon), **are** a shade darker than the body of hat, a contrast that lends beauty to this clean cut **hat.** Russia leather sweatband. Colors, fawn, pearl, brown or black. Sizes, 6¾ to 7⅛.
Price, each..... **$1.50**
If by mail, postage extra, each 25 cents.

The Western Fedora.

No. 33R2100 A dress hat for ranchmen, miners, planters, stockmen and farmers. The right style for large men, 6-inch crown, 3½-inch brim. Made from exceptionally fine stock, soft and durable, **and wears like leather.** We warrant every hat to give satisfactory wear. Colors, black, brown, belly beaver or back beaver. The sizes run from 6¾ to 7¾. **What size do you wear?** Weight, 5 ounces.
Price, each ... **$2.00**
If by mail, postage extra, each, 25 cents.

Our Great Leader at $2.40.

No. 33R2106 Men's Extra Quality Fine American Fur Felt. A hat of superior quality that we will warrant to wear equal to any hat you have paid $3.00 or $3.50 for. A pliable, firm stock. If it is not the best hat you have ever seen at such a price and better than your highest expectations, return and we will refund your money. Crown is 5⅝ inches, brim, 2¼ inches. **The curl is just right for a fashionable hat.** Fine silk trimmings and Russia leather sweatband. Colors, black, brown, fawn, pearl or steel gray. Sizes, 6¾ to 7½. Black, the sizes are 6¾ to 7¾.
Price, each $2.40
If by mail, postage extra, each, 25 cents.

Raw Edge Fedora, $2.40.

No. 33R2110 Men's Fine Fedora Hat, same style and quality as above, in black, brown or pearl, but **raw edge,** no binding. Sizes, 6¾ to 7½ only.
Price, each $2.40
If by mail, postage extra, 25 cents.

A Good Hat for Driving.

No. 33R2114 Young Men's New Style Crusher. A comfortable, full shape Crusher to wear instead of a stiff or Fedora hat when driving, traveling or on an outing, etc. A hat in which you will feel well dressed. Made of soft, pliable fur. Raw edge brim, 1-inch grosgrain silk ribbon band, leather sweatband. Colors, black, fawn or steel. Sizes, 6¾ to 7½.
Price, each... $1.50
If by mail, postage extra, each, 25 cents.

The Governor, $2.00.

No. 33R2120 Our Governor, $2.00. A hat made from fine nutria fur stock, beautifully proportioned, boss raw edge. Crown, 6 inches, brim, 3½ inches. Narrow black silk ribbon band and leather sweat. Hats of large proportion must necessarily have the quality in them or they will fail to give satisfaction. **We can positively recommend The Governor to give satisfaction.** Colors, black and belly nutria. Sizes, 6¾ to 7¾.
Price, each $2.00
If by mail, postage extra, each, 34 cents.

$3.50 Governor Hat, $2.75.

No. 33R2122 The Governor Style Hat, made of superior quality fine nutria fur stock, all hand made hat, narrow band, same shape as above. Colors, black or belly nutria. Sizes, 6¾ to 7⅝.
Boss raw edge. Price, each $2.75
If by mail, postage extra, 34 cents.

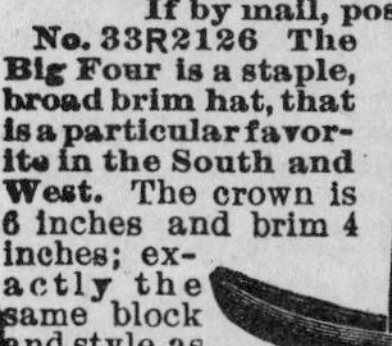

The Big Four.

No. 33R2126 The Big Four is a staple, broad brim hat, that is a particular favorite in the South and West. The crown is 6 inches and brim 4 inches; exactly the same block and style as the famous Stetson hat of this name. Boss raw edge, with narrow silk band. You will pay $3.00 to $3.50 for no better hat if you buy it at home. **We warrant every hat to give entire satisfaction.** Colors, black or belly nutria. Sizes, 6¾ to 7¾. Price, each $2.40
If by mail, postage extra, 34 cents.

Big Four Style for $1.25.

No. 33R2127 Men's Big Four Style Hat. Made of good quality fur; equal to any hat sold at retail for $1.50. Crown, 6 inches; brim, 4 inches. Colors, black or belly nutria. Sizes, 6¾ to 7½.
Price, each $1.25
If by mail, postage extra, each, 34 cents.

GIVE CATALOGUE NUMBER IN FULL WHEN YOU WRITE YOUR ORDER

MEN'S NEW FEDORA HATS.

No. 33R2140 Men's Fine Nutria Fur New Style Fedora Hat, flat brim as shown in the illustration. Fine silk band, medium width. Silk binding on edge extending over the under side to the width of but a single stitching. Fine leather sweatband. Unlined. Crown, 5⅝ inches; brim, 2¾ inches. Colors, black, fawn or pearl. Sizes, 6¾ to 7½ only. This is the quality and style retailing at $3.00.
Price, each $2.25
If by mail, postage extra, 18 cents.

Special Value in Newest Style Fedora Hat for $1.50.

No. 33R2156 Men's New Style Fedora Raw Edge Hat, trimmed with silk band and leather sweatband.

Unlined. This hat is shown with slight indentations in the crown, which is the preferred manner of wearing, but looks equally well with the crown worn up, or creased in the usual manner. Crown, 5 inches; brim, 2⅝ inches. Colors, black or silver gray. Sizes, 6¾ to 7⅝. Retail value, $2.00.
Price, each $1.50
If by mail, postage extra, 18 cents.

Our $1.00 New Style Fedora.

No. 33R2162 Men's Medium Shape New Style Fedora Hat, as shown in the illustration. Raw edge.

Crown, 5¼ inches; brim, 2⅝ inches. Made of good quality fur stock. This is a strong value for a low priced hat, but we recommend better hats as being cheaper in the long run. Colors, black or light gray. Sizes, 6¾ to 7⅜ only.
Price, each $1.00
If by mail, postage extra, 18 cents.

Men's Silk Hats.

No. 33R2180 Men's Silk Hat, well finished, medium, staple style, fine silk ribbon band and binding. Sizes, 6¾ to 7½. Each.... $4.00

No. 33R2182 Men's Very Fine Quality Silk Hat, made in the prevailing style, either Dunlap or Knox blocks. Young men's medium or full shape. A superior quality of silk plush is used in this grade, and finest silk trimmings. **Strictly high grade in every respect.** Sizes, 6¾ to 7½. Price, each......... $6.00

Men's Fur Crusher Hats.

No. 33R2186 We furnish under this number the new Medium Shape Crusher; navy blue, gray, brown and black. Plain narrow silk ribbon band, flexible leather sweatband. Sizes, 6¾ to 7⅝.
Price, each 73c
If by mail, postage extra, 13 cents.

Our 90-Cent Crusher Hat.

No. 33R2192 Men's Finer Grade Crusher, similar in shape to cut No. 33R2186. Narrow silk ribbon band, raw edge, brim, medium curl. Made up from the best grade of crusher stock and without any exception the best value ever offered at this price. Usually is sold by all retailers at $1.25. Colors, navy, black and dark brown. Be sure to state your size and color. When color desired is not stated we send black. Sizes, 6¾ to 7½. Price, each 90c
If by mail, postage extra, 14 cents.

French Pocket or Crusher Hat.

No. 33R2196 The finest, softest, lightest weight pocket hat ever produced. Made from finest French fur felt, with ribbed **silk sweatband.** Roll brim, raw edge and narrow silk ribbon band. **Rolling up a hat of this quality to pack in grip or to put into pocket has very little effect on its shape or appearance.** Colors, black, brown, pearl and navy blue. Sizes, 6¾ to 7⅜ only. **What size do you wear?**
Price, each $1.25
If by mail, postage extra, 15 cents.

Men's Full Shape Crusher Hats.

No. 33R2200 Our $1.25 Special Full Shape Crusher Hat. Made from clear nutria fur. Extra fine soft finish, medium weight. Fine leather sweatband; large full shaped crown that can be creased; full shape brim; made in black, gray or brown only. **A decidedly popular staple hat.** Sizes, 6¾ to 7¾. **What size do you wear?**
Price, each $1.25

No. 33R2204 Men's Crusher, same style as above, in good quality crusher fur stock; a hat that will give good satisfaction. Color, dark blue only. Sizes, 6¾ to 7⅜ only. Price, each 90c
If by mail, postage extra, 18 cents.

Railroad Hats.

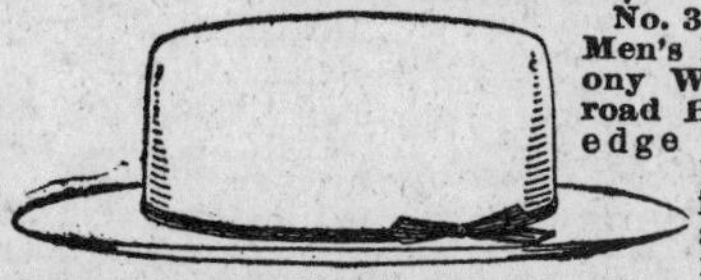

No. 33R2208 Men's Fine Saxony Wool Railroad Hat. Raw edge with cord band, 4-inch crown and 2½-inch brim. Made in black only. Sizes, 6¾ to 7⅜ only. **What size do you wear?** Price, each... .... 45c
If by mail, postage extra, 15 cents.

The Raw Edge Railroad Hat, $1.00.

Cannot be equaled elsewhere under $2.00.

No. 33R2210 Clear Fur Railroad. Narrow silk cord band, raw edge brim. Fine, good leather sweatband. The stock used in the manufacture of this hat is known to the trade as long stock. Long stock is used only in making fine hats. Its use in this hat stamps it a wonder at the price. Colors, black or otter. Sizes, 6¾ to 7½. **What size do you wear?**
Price, each $1.00
If by mail, postage extra, 17 cents.

Our $1.45 Railroad Hat.

No. 33R2212 Men's Clear Fur Railroad Hat, 2½ inch brim, 4-inch crown, silk ribbon band, bound edge and fine leather sweatband. Black or otter. Sizes, 6¾ to 7½. **What size do you wear?** Price, each $1.45
If by mail, postage extra, 15 cents.

Sears, Roebuck & Co.'s Special Railro[ad] Hat, Only $1.85.

A regular $2.75 quality.

No. 33R2214 Clear Nutria Fur. A fine kettle finished hand made hat, fine silk band, raw edge. Russia leather sweatband; 4-inch crown; brim, 2½ inches. Colors, black, brown, and belly nutria. This number we furnish in extra sizes up to 7⅝.
Price, each $1.85
If by mail, postage extra, 17 cents.

Grand Army Hats.

No. 33R2220 Men's Regulation G. A. R. Hat, made from the best Saxony wool with gold cord and G. A. R. wreath. Leather sweat band. Black only. Sizes, 6¾ to 7½ only. **What size do you wear?**
Price, per dozen, $9.00; each 75c
If by mail, postage extra, each, 18 cents.

No. 33R2222 Our best fur G. A. R. Hat. Full regulation shape, with gold cord and G. A. R. wreath; durable, leather sweatband. Great hat for wear; black only. Sizes, 6¾ to 7⅝. Each.... $ 1.25
Supply your post at, per dozen 15.00
If by mail, postage extra, each, 18 cents.

U. S. A. Cavalry Hats.

Adopted by the Government.

No. 33R2224 U. S. A. Regulation Cavalry Hat. The same as used by the government troops and militia. **Made from fine soft fur and intended for hard service.** Narrow silk ribbon band, leather sweat band and raw edge. Back nutria or drab color. Sizes, 6¾ to 7½. **What size do you wear?**
Our price, per dozen, $15.00; each $1.35
If by mail, postage extra, each, 18 cents.

The Roosevelt.

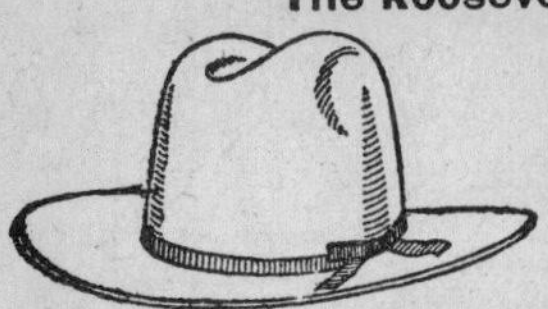

No. 33R2228 **Men's Fur Hat, flat set brim,** in a good quality fur stock, leather sweatband; narrow silk ribbon band. Crown, 6 inches; brim, 3½ inches, flat set. A fuller shape than the Regulation Cavalry Hats. **An excellent hat at our low price.** Colors, black and belly nutria. Sizes, 6¾ to 7½. **What size do you wear?** Price, each..**$1.00**
If by mail, postage extra, 27 cents.

Wool Pasha, 45 Cents.

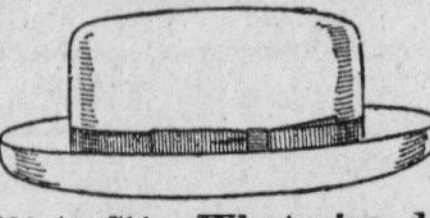

No. 33R2232 **Men's Fine Saxony Wool Soft Hat.** New shape, square crown and soft, curling brim. Silk ribbon band and leather **sweatband.** Colors, black and brown. Sizes, 6¾ to 7½. **What size do you wear?** Price, each..**45c**
If by mail, postage extra, 20 cents.

Young Men's Pasha Hats.

No. 33R2236 **The Pasha Hat**, a new soft nutria fur felt hat made with silk ribbon band, raw edge and curling flange brim. Colors, black or brown. **Very dressy.** Sizes, 6¾ to 7½. **What size do you wear?** Price, each..**$1.25**
If by mail, postage extra, 20 cents.

The Graeco.

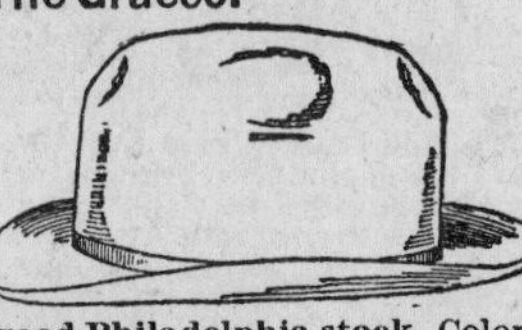

No. 33R2240 **The Graeco. Men's Light Weight Medium Shape Fur Hat.** Slightly curved, raw edge brim. Russia leather sweatband, narrow silk ribbon band. **Made from good Philadelphia stock.** Colors, black, otter and belly nutria. Sizes, 6¾ to 7½. Price, each..**$1.50**
If by mail, postage extra, 20 cents.

JOHN B. STETSON HATS.

This Celebrated Maker's Soft Hats Are Recognized Everywhere as Standard of the World.

Dakota Style.

No. 33R2250 **John B. Stetson Dakota Style.** For many years a most popular shape among those made by Stetson. Crown, 5½ inches; brim, 3½ inches. Raw edge. Colors, **black or belly nutria.** Weight, about 5 ounces. Sizes, 6¾ to 7⅝. **Be sure to state color and size in your order.** Price, each..**$3.90**
If by mail, postage extra, 34 cents.

Columbia Style.

No. 33R2254 **John B. Stetson Columbia Style Soft Hat.** It differs from the Dakota in that the crown is 5¾ inches high and brim 3 inches wide; raw edge. Correctly worn either with or without creasing in crown. **You will always find Stetson's name on the sweatband.** Narrow silk band. Sizes, 6¾ to 7⅝. Colors, **black or belly nutria.** Weight, about 4½ ounces. Price, each..**$3.50**
If by mail, postage extra, 34 cents.

Idaho Style.

No. 33R2256 **John B. Stetson Style Idaho** in finer quality than Columbia or Dakota and the shape is between the two. Crown, 5⅝ inches; brim, 3¼ inches. A boss raw edge that has been popular with many men for years. **Every hat made by Stetson is warranted.** The Idaho is fitted with the "Fray" Russia leather sweatband. Sizes, 6¾ to 7½. Colors, black or belly nutria. Price, each.....**$5.00**
If by mail, postage extra, 34 cents.

Stetson Famous Big Four.

No. 33R2260 **John B. Stetson Style Big Four Hat.** Crown, 6 inches; brim, 4 inches. A large, fine shaped hat much in favor in the South and West. Boss raw edge. Stetson's hats will keep their shape for years. It is well directed economy to purchase a Stetson. Colors, black and belly nutria. Sizes, 6¾ to 7⅝. Price, each..**$5.00**
If by mail, postage extra, 34 cents.

Fedora Style.

No. 33R2264 **J. B. Stetson Fedora or Alpine Style Hat.** Crown, 6 inches; brim, 2⅝ inches wide; or crown, 6¼ inches; brim, 3 inches. Like all other Stetson hats, this one is finished with finest silk trimming and Russia leather sweatband. Colors, black, brown and otter. Sizes, 6¾ to 7½. Price, each..**$3.75**
If by mail, postage extra, 34 cents.

Stetson Railroad Hats.

No. 33R2268 **J. B. Stetson Style Railroad Hat.** Crown, 4½ inches by 2¾ inches brim, raw edge. Every railroad man knows that the Stetson hat is just the right style and shape for his business. Brim is flat, set and trimmed with narrow silk band, and Russia leather sweatband. Colors, black or belly nutria. Sizes, 6¾ to 7½. Price, each..**$3.50**

No. 33R2270 **J. B. Stetson Style Railroad Hat.** Crown, 4½ inches; brim, 2¾ inches. Bound edge, same style as above. Colors, black or belly nutria. Sizes, 6¾ to 7½. Price, each..**$3.50**
If by mail, postage extra, 30 cents.

J. B. Stetson Graeco Style.

No. 33R2274 **J. B. Stetson Style Graeco.** A popular style with many men, particularly for driving. Crown 4¾ inches, brim 2⅝ inches, with slight roll as shown in illustration. Finest Russia leather sweatband. Sizes, 6¾ to 7½. Colors, **black or belly nutria.** Price, each..**$3.50**
If by mail, postage extra, 20 cents.

Stetson Cowboy Hats.

No. 33R2276 **John B. Stetson Cowboy Hat.** Made with stiff brim, 3¾ inches wide, and soft crown, 4⅝ inches high. A great favorite in the west and on the plains among ranchmen and cattlemen. The brim never loses shape. John B. Stetson hats are the best in the world. Fine silk band, as shown in the illustration. Belly nutria color only. Sizes, 6¾ to 7½. Price, each..**$4.50**
If by mail, postage extra, 38 cents.

MEN'S WOOL HATS.

Wool Crusher.

No. 33R2280 **Men's Wool Crusher Hat.** Medium shape, with leather sweatband and narrow silk ribbon band. Sizes, 6¾ to 7⅝ only. Colors, black, blue, gray or brown. **What size do you wear?** Price, each..**45c**
If by mail, postage extra, 13 cents.

Fine Wool Fedora.

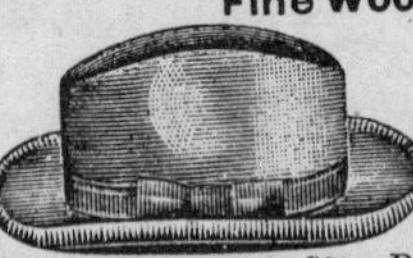

No. 33R2284 **Men's Fine Wool Fedora,** medium shape, leather sweatband. An excellent wearing and fine looking hat. Ribbon band, raw edge brim. Colors, brown, gray or black. Sizes, 6¾ to 7⅝. Price, each..**45c**
If by mail, postage extra, 20 cents.

Genuine Saxony Wool Fedora Hats.

No. 33R2288 **Men's Highest Grade Genuine Saxony Wool Hat.** A shapely hat that will wear in a durable manner, that will please you. **Leather sweatband,** and wide ribbon band of good quality, broad brim. Colors, black, brown or gray. Sizes, 6¾ to 7½. Price, each..**75c**
If by mail, postage extra, 20 cents.

Black Saxony Wool Hats.

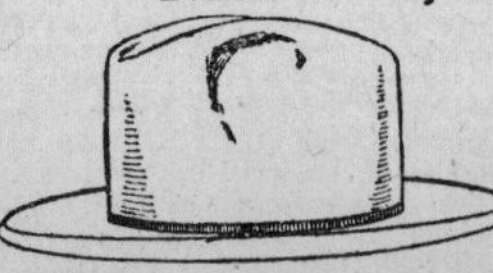

No. 33R2290 **Men's Full Shape Wool Hat.** Silk ribbon band and leather sweatband. Sizes, 6¾ to 7⅝ only. Made in black brown and gray. **What size do you wear?** Price, each..**43c**
If by mail, postage extra, 18 cents.

Planter and Ranch Hats.

No. 33R2294 **Men's Wide Brim Planter Hat.** Made from fine Saxony wool with ribbon band and leather sweatband. Colors, black or drab. Sizes, 6¾ to 7⅝ only. **What size do you wear?** Price, each..**45c**
If by mail, postage extra, 16 cents.

No. 33R2296 **Men's Wide Brim Plain Black Wool Planter Hat. Made** from fine quality Saxony, soft and smooth. Sizes, 6¾ to 7⅝. Price, each....**75c**

No. 33R2298 **Men's Wide Brim Planter Hat.** Same as above, in drab color. Price, each........**75c**
If by mail, postage extra, 20 cents.

The Cuban Shape.

No. 33R2300 **Serviceable Farm Hat for all kinds of weather.** Made of brown duck. Silk cord band, leather sweatband. This is positively best wearing hat at the price. Don't fail to order one for rough wear. You will be more than pleased. Sizes, 6¾ to 7½. **What size do you wear?** Price, each..**45c**
If by mail, postage extra, 20 cents.

Men's Wool Cowboy Hats, 45 Cents.

No. 33R2304 **Men's Wool Cowboy Hat,** like illustration. Light calfskin color only. **Band and binding.** Sizes, 6¾ to 7⅝ only. Price, each......**45c**
If by mail, postage extra, 20 cents.

Fine Wool Ranch Hats, $1.00.

No. 33R2310 **Men's Wide Brim Wool Ranch Hat,** braided, cord bound. Reinforced brim—keeps its shape. A hat that gives satisfaction when subjected to rough usage. Nutria color. **The sizes run from 6¾ to 7½. What size do you wear?** Price..**$1.00**
If by mail, postage extra, 20 cents.

Our $1.00 Saxony Wool Ranch Hat.

No. 33R2314 **Men's Fine Grade Saxony Wool Cowboy Ranch Hat,** with wide brim. Single buckle, embossed leather band and leather binding. Calfskin or nutria color. Sizes, 6¾ to 7⅝. Price, each..**$1.00**
If by mail, postage extra, 20 cents.

COWBOY SOMBREROS.

No 33R2318 **Cowboys' Extra Fine Heavy Weight Saxony Wool Sombrero,** with 4½-inch crown and 4-inch brim, with wide single buckle, embossed leather band and leather binding. Band is embossed in beautiful floral and novelty patterns in variegated colors. Sizes, 6¾ to 7⅝ only. Colors, belly nutria or light calfskin. **What size do you wear?** Price, each..**$1.50**
If by mail, postage extra, 20 cents.

Cow Puncher Sombrero.

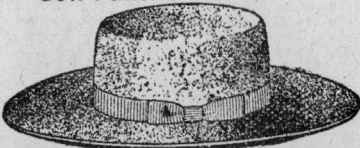

No. 33R2322 **Men's Cow Puncher Sombrero Hat,** made of clear nutria fur stock. Crown, 4½ inches; brim, 4 inches; raw edge; silk braid and fine black satin lining, and black leather sweatband. Weight, 6 ounces; belly nutria color only. Sizes, 6¾ to 7½. **What size do you wear?** Price, each..**$2.50**
If by mail, postage extra, 38 cents.

Pine Ridge Scout.

No. 33R2326 Cowboys' Favorite Sombrero Hat. Belly nutria color; crown, 4 inches; brim, 4 inches; raw edge, flat, stiff, knife blade brim; 1-inch silk ribbon band. Weight, 6 ounces. Sizes, from 6¾ to 7½. **What size do you wear?** Our price, each...**$2.50**

If by mail, postage extra, 38 cents.

The Montana.

No. 33R2328 The Montana. Known throughout the West as a top notcher for appearance, durability and quality, and made from selected nutria fur of a superior grade. Best imported silk band and binding. Crown, 4½ inches; brim, 4½ inches. Weight, 6 ounces. Color, belly nutria. The sizes run from 6¾ to 7½. **What size do you wear?**
Price, each.......................................**$3.00**
If by mail, postage extra, 38 cents.

$3.00 **$3.00**

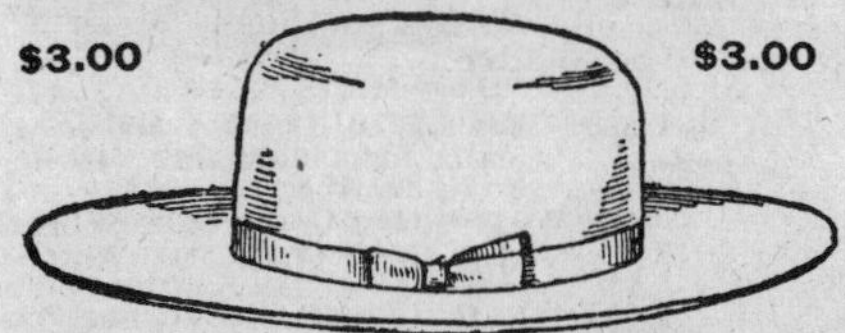

No. 33R2332 This is the Never Flop Hat. There are many so called Never Flop Hats on the market, but there is only one Never Flop that has proven to be all that its name implies, the raw edge, scoop brim, 4 inches wide; 4½-inch crown. Weight, 8 ounces. Color, side nutria. Sizes run from 6¾ to 7½. **What size do you wear?**
Our price, with a guarantee not to flop........**$3.00**
If by mail, postage extra, 38 cents.

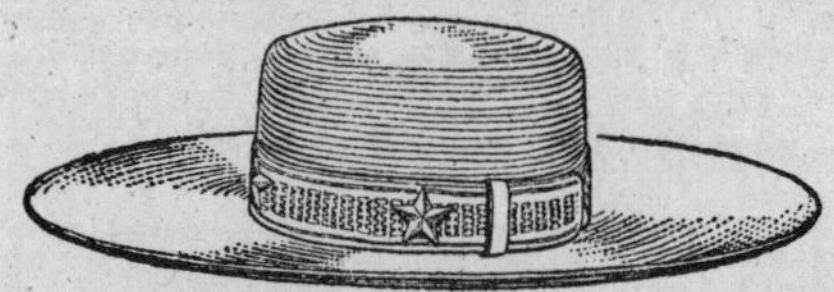

No. 33R2336 The Texas Steer Style Sombrero Hat. Crown, 4½ inches; brim, 5 inches. Fancy leather band with four silver stars. Fine nutria fur, never flop brim. Weight, 8 ounces. Color, side nutria. Sizes, 6¾ to 7½. Price, each. **$3.50**
If by mail, postage extra, 38 cents.

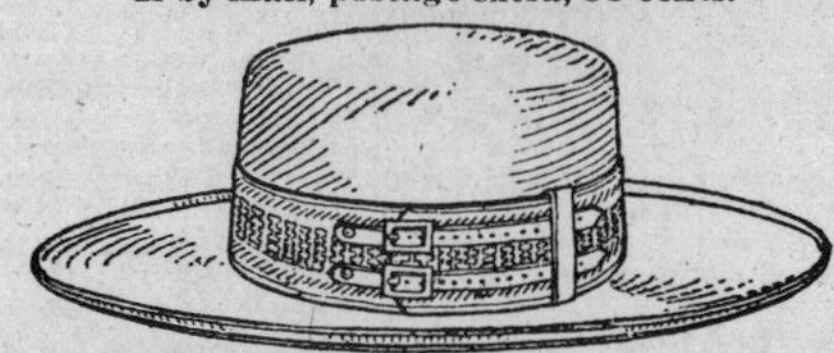

No. 33R2340 The Mountaineer Sombrero. A good friend of the cowboy. A fine fur hat with medium stiff brim; sure to be satisfactory. Crown, 4½ inches; brim, 4 inches, with 2-inch embossed leather band. Calfskin color. Sizes, 6¾ to 7½. Weight, 8 ounces.
Price, each.......................................**$3.00**
If by mail, postage extra, 38 cents.

Mexican Sombrero for $3.00.

No. 33R2344 Mexican Sombrero. Crown, 7 inches; brim, 4 inches; bound with silk. Elaborate fancy trimming. Side nutria color. Sizes, 6¾ to 7½.
Each.......**$3.00**
If by mail, postage extra, 38 cents.

DON'T FAIL TO GIVE SIZE WHEN YOU ORDER A HAT.

The Texan Chief, $4.25.

No. 33R2352 Texan Chief Cowboys' High Crown Mexican Style Sombrero Hat, 5-inch brim and 6½-inch crown; fine leather sweatband; 1-inch silk ribbon band or tassel cord braided band, if desired. Flat, never flop brim with raw edge. One of the very best as well as the most popular sombreros ever made from best quality **clear nutria fur.** Full of real goodness and will give excellent satisfaction. Color, belly nutria. Sizes, 6¾ to 7½. Price, each......**$4.25**
Price, without **fancy cord band**................ 3.50
If by mail, postage extra, 38 cents.

Pride of the West Sombrero.
Our Finest Sombrero, for $6.50.

No. 33R2356 Pride of the West Sombrero. Made with silver tinsel cloth band braided, four silver tinsel stars on crown and four on under side of brim. A very fine cowboy fancy hat that is sure to give satisfaction; crown, 4 inches; brim, 5 inches wide. Color, side nutria. Weight, 12 ounces. Sizes, 6¾ to 7½.
Price, each......................................**$6.50**
If by mail, postage extra, 38 cents.

Leather Hat Bands.

No. 33R2360 Cowboys' 2-inch all leather hat bands. Embossed russet leather, with double straps and two small buckles, will fit any hat. Price, each, **39c**
If by mail, postage extra, 3c.

No. 33R2362 Russet Leather Embossed Hat Bands, 1¼ inches wide, with single strap and buckle. All solid leather, oak tanned. Price, each....... **25c**
If by mail, postage extra, 3 cents.

Imported Silver Tinsel Stars.
For Decorating Cowboys' Hats, Gloves, Etc.

No. 33R2364 Extra Fine Quality Imported Silver Stars. Largely used for decorating sombreros, gauntlet gloves, masquerade costumes, etc. Per gross, **$7.80; dozen......65c**
If by mail, postage extra, per dozen, 4 cents.

BOYS' OR YOUTHS' HATS.

Sizes are 6½, 6⅝, 6¾, 6⅞, 7. Always state size in your order. If you do not know the size, measure as directed on first page of Hat Department.

Boys' Saxony Wool Hats.

No. 33R2370 Boys' and Youths' Saxony Wool Hats, medium shaped crown and brim. Colors, black, blue or brown. Always state size and color wanted. These hats will give excellent service. They are fine in finish and very durable. Made with ribbon band and leather sweatband. Sizes, 6½ to 7 only. **What size do you wear?**
Price, each.......................................**42c**
If by mail, postage extra, 13 cents.

Boys' Wool Fedora, 43 Cents.

No. 33R2374 Boys' Latest Style Fedora Hats. Made from fine Saxony wool, with silk band and leather sweat band. Sizes, 6½ to 7 only. Colors, black, gray or brown. Each... ....**43c**
If by mail, postage extra, 16 cents.

Boys' Wool Golf Style Hat, 43 Cents.

No. 33R2378 Boys' Golf Style Wool Hat, trimmed with narrow band and leather sweatband; raw edge. A good hat at a very low price. Colors, black or light gray. Sizes, 6⅝ to 7 only.
Price, each.......................................**43c**
If by mail, postage extra, 16 cents.

Boys' Telescope Hats.

No. 33R2382 Boys' Wool Hat, Telescope Style. Very popular hat, becoming to most boys. Wide silk band, leather sweat band and raw edge. Colors, black, brown or blue. Sizes, 6½ to 7 only. Price, each...........................**45c**
If by mail, postage extra, 13 cents.

No. 33R2386 Boys' Fine Fur Telescope Style Hat. Made of good quality fur, that will hold color and shape; fine silk band and binding. Equal to any hat at retail for $1.00. Colors, black, brown and fawn. Sizes, 6⅝ to 7 only.
Price, each.......................................**78c**
If by mail, postage extra, 13 cents.

Boys' Fine Fur Golf Style Hat, $1.00.

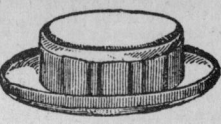

No. 33R2390 Boys' Fine Fur Soft Hat in new golf style. Trimmed with silk band and leather sweatband. Raw edge. **A very popular hat for boys or youths for this season.** A stylish, correct hat, very becoming to most boys. Colors, black or light gray. Sizes, 6⅝ to 7 only. Price, each.................**$1.00**
If by mail postage extra, 16 cents.

Boys' Fine Fedora Hats.

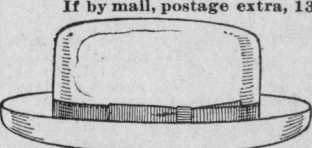

No. 33R2394 Boys' Handsome Fedora Hat. Very latest Fedora style, wide silk ribbon band and binding, fine leather sweatband. **Soft, fine and very dressy.** Made from fine fur felt. Colors, steel and black. Sizes, 6½ to 7⅛ only. A medium shape, suitable for boys up to 16 years of age. Price, each.......**$1.25**
If by mail, postage extra, 15 cents.

The Chester, 78 Cents.

No. 33R2398 Boys' Clear Fur Fedora. Medium wide silk ribbon band and silk binding, leather sweatband. Colors, golden dark brown and black. Sizes, 6½ to 7. Extremely nobby; **regular $1.00 quality. What size do you wear?** Price, each.............**78c**
If by mail, postage extra, 13 cents.

No. 33R2404 Boys' Saxony Wool Pasha. Silk ribbon band; leather sweatband. **A good value.** Colors, brown or black. Sizes 6⅝ to 7. **What size do you wear?** Each..........**45c**
If by mail, postage extra, 13 cents.

Boys' Cowboy Hat, 45 Cents.

No. 33R2408 Rough and Tumble Saxony Wool Hat. Leather band and binding; leather sweat. **Made to stand the rough usage that the school boy's hat is sure to receive.** Colors, belly nutria or gray. Sizes, 6½ to 7. **What size do you wear?**
Price, each.......................................**45c**
If by mail, postage extra, 14 cents.

Conductors' Caps.

Made with patent wire frame. Never get out of shape.

Cut Showing Wire Frame.

No. 33R2420 Conductors' Extra Fine Navy Blue Broadcloth Caps, with patented wire frame and fine leather sweat band. We guarantee them to be the most practical as well as the best wearing caps of this kind made. Money refunded if not exactly as represented. **When lettering is desired we require cash in full with order.** Sizes, 6¾ to 7½.
Price, each.......................................**$1.35**
Price, with Conductor in gold wire block letters.. **2.35**
This price is for plain cap without lettering. Gold wire block embroidered letters will cost 10 cents per letter extra. Allow us one week for delivery. We always put letters like the word Conductor on silk band, detachable.
If by mail, postage extra, 18 cents.

No. 33R2422 Same cap as above in fine black grosgrain silk. Sizes, 6¾ to 7¾. Each...........**$1.45**
Price, with Conductor in gold wire block letters, each.. **2.35**
If by mail, postage extra, 18 cents.

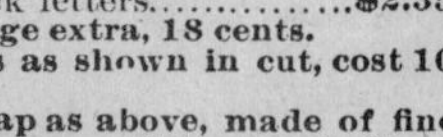

No. 33R2426 Made from finest quality of fine blue broadcloth with wire frame. Sizes, 6¾ to 7¾. Where lettering is desired we require cash in full with order.
Price.........**$1.45**
Price, with Conductor in gold wire block letters..............**$2.35**
If by mail, postage extra, 18 cents.
Gold wire block letters as shown in cut, cost 10 cents extra per letter.

No. 33R2428 Same cap as above, made of fine grosgrain silk, with wire frame. Color, black. Sizes, 6¾ to 7¾. Price, each. **$1.45**
Price, with Conductor in gold wire block letters.....**(If by mail, postage extra, 18c)**.... **2.35**

Nickel Plated Cap Badges.

The following badges are made from German silver, nickel plated.

These badges are made to order with any lettering desired. The full amount of cash must be sent with the order. We do not send these goods C. O. D., and they cannot be returned or exchanged unless we are clearly in error. Always order by catalogue number and state plainly just what lettering you desire and your orders will receive prompt attention and be filled correctly. Allow about five days for making.

No. 33R2438 Official Stars, fourteen letters, such as City Marshal, Deputy, etc. Price..............75c

If by mail, postage extra, 3 cents.

No. 33R2440 Nickel Plated German Silver Badge. Size, ¾x3 inches. Conductor, baggageman, porter, news agent, expressman or any words not exceeding fifteen letters. Made to order. Price, each......50c

If by mail, postage extra, 2 cents.

No. 33R2442 Nickel Plated German Silver Badge, with fancy oval, 1-inch wide by 3 inches long. Suitable for such words as Hotel Porter, A. T. & S. F. R'y Conductor, City Expressman, B. & O. Baggageman and similar words not exceeding twenty-two letters. Always state what letters you want.

Price, each..............................80c

If by mail, postage extra, 2 cents.

NOTE—Larger badges made to order at from $1.25 to $2.50, according to size and lettering. It requires about five days to have these badges made to order.

Black Cotton Shop Caps.

No. 33R2450 Men's Black Cotton Shop Cap; very light, but durable. Sizes, 6¾ to 7½. What size do you wear? Price, per dozen, 96c; each..........8c

If by mail, postage extra, 5 cents.

Engineers' Caps.

No. 33R2454 Engineers' Black Leather Caps. Standard shape, well made and just the cap to wear on the engine. Sizes, 6¾ to 7½.

Price, each.....45c

If by mail, postage extra, each 8 cents.

No. 33R2458 Engineers' Fine Black Silk Caps, with extra wide visor to protect the eyes. Handsomely satin lined. Sizes, 6¾ to 7⅝.

Price, each.........45c

If by mail, postage extra, 5 cents.

Silk Pullman. Special Quality, 50 Cents.

No. 33R2462 Men's Fine Silk Pullman or Skull Cap, with fine silk lining. Black only. Sizes, 6¾ to 7⅝.

Price, each..............50c

If by mail, postage extra, 2 cents.

MEN'S SUMMER CAPS.

Men's sizes, 6¾, 6⅞, 7, 7⅛, 7¼, 7⅜ and 7½.

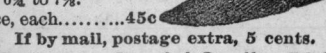

THE SIZE OF A CAP is very important, therefore when you make out your order don't forget to state just what size you want. We can then fill your order promptly and to your entire satisfaction.

Men's Blue Serge Golf Caps, 25 Cents.

No. 33R2500 Men's Light Weight Lined Golf Style Cap, made of fine navy blue wool serge with six-piece top. A regular 35-cent quality. Sizes, 6¾ to 7½ only.

Price, each..............................25c

If by mail, postage extra, each, 4 cents.

Men's Plain Blue Golf Caps, 45 Cents.

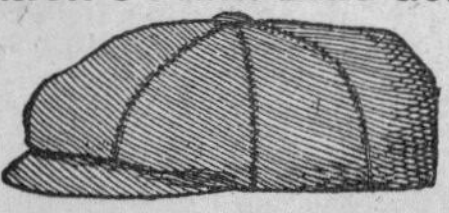

No. 33R2512 Made from a fine quality of navy blue broadcloth, with heavy satin lining and hook down front. Six-piece top with double stitched seams. They would be cheap in large retail stores at 75 cents. Sizes, 6¾ to 7½ only. What size do you wear?

Price, each..............................45c

If by mail, postage extra, 6 cents.

Men's Golf Yacht Caps, 25 Cents.

No. 33R2520 This splendid cap at 25 cents is an exceptional value. Better than anything we have ever been able to offer before at this price. Plaid and checked cassimeres or plain blue. Sizes, 6¾ to 7½ only. What size do you wear? Price, each.....25c

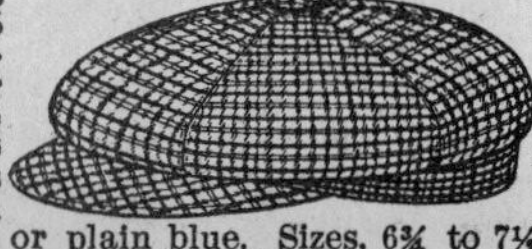

If by mail, postage extra, 8 cents.

Our Special Golf Yacht Cap at 45 Cents.

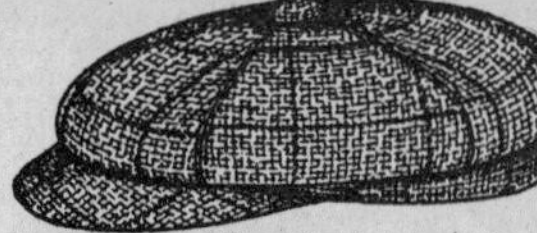

No. 33R2524 Men's Scotch Cheviot Golf Yacht Cap. Handsome broken plaid and nobby checks in brown and gray. Finest Russian leather sweatband, lined with soft rich satin lining. Sizes, 6¾ to 7½ only. Price, each................45c

If by mail, postage extra, 10 cents.

Men's Double Cover Combination Yacht Cap.

No. 33R2530 Men's Double Cover Fine Yacht Cap. The newest and most practical yacht cap made. The cap proper is made with a fine white duck top. The separate cover is made of blue serge and slips over the white top, making a regular style blue cap. When the separate cover is attached, the point of contact is invisible, having exactly the appearance of a regular blue yacht cap. Made in a strictly first class manner throughout, with fine leather sweatband. The band, visor and blue detachable cover are made of fine blue wool serge. The most practical cap introduced for many years. Color, navy blue. Sizes, 6¾ to 7½ only.

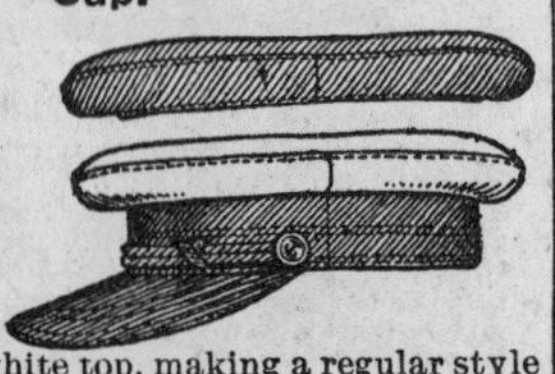

Price, per dozen, $5.40; each..................45c

If by mail, postage extra, each, 12 cents.

Reliable Staple Yacht Caps.

No. 33R2532 Our Special 25-Cent Yacht Cap for Men. Made from fine blue wool cloth, patent leather visor and hercules braid and genuine leather sweatband. A cap usually sold at 50 cents, and a value never offered before at our price. Sizes, 6¾ to 7½ only.

Price, each..................................25c

If by mail, postage extra, 10 cents.

No. 33R2534 The Latest Men's Yacht Cap; made up in imported Scotch cheviot mixtures, plaids and checks of gray and brown; satin lined; patent leather visor with green underlining. Narrow patent leather front band. Trimmed all around with band of 2-inch black French lattice braid. Sizes, 6¾ to 7½ only. What size do you wear?

Price, per dozen, $5.40; each..................45c

If by mail, postage extra, each, 12 cents.

Our 50-Cent Leader.

No. 33R2538 Men's Marine Yacht Caps. Made in blue German broadcloth, heavy hercules braid band, black patent leather visor and ornamental front strap: leather sweatband. Decidedly nobby. Sizes, 6¾ to 7½ only.

Price, per dozen, $6.00; each..................50c

If by mail, postage extra, each, 12 cents.

BOYS' OR YOUTHS' CAPS.

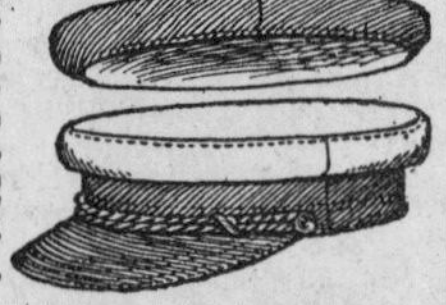

No. 33R2550 Boys' or Youths' Double Cover Fine Yacht Caps. The newest and most practical yacht cap made. The cap proper is made with a fine white duck top. The separate cover is made of blue serge and slips over the white top, making a regular style blue cap. When the separate cover is attached, the point of contact is invisible, having exactly the appearance of a regular blue golf cap. Made in a strictly first class manner throughout with fine leather sweatband. The band, visor and blue detachable cover are made of fine blue wool serge. Navy blue only; an ideal cap for your boy. Sizes, 6⅛ to 7⅛ only.

Price, per dozen, $5.04; each..................42c

If by mail, postage extra, each, 9 cents.

Boys' Navy Blue University Caps.

No. 33R2554 Boys' Finest Navy Blue Broadcloth University Caps. Similar to the golf style, but fuller in the crown, and does not hook down in front; lined with satin. Sizes, 6½ to 7 only. Warranted first class in every way. Price, each..........................45c

If by mail, postage extra, 10 cents.

WE CANNOT FILL YOUR ORDER IF YOU FAIL TO STATE SIZE. BE SURE TO ENCLOSE POSTAGE WHEN ORDERING GOODS TO GO BY MAIL.

Boys' Harvard Golf Caps.

No. 33R2558 The Harvard Golf Cap. Made from fine all wool fancy gray mixed cheviot suitings. Heavy satin lining and patent hook down front, strictly high grade. Sizes, 6⅜ to 7 only.

Price, each.....42c

Postage extra, 6c.

Boys' or Youths' Jockey Caps.

No. 33R2570 Boys' New Style Jockey Cap. A very pretty novelty for this season, made with three rows of black braid on a fine blue serge cloth. Six-piece top cap, with fine, bright silk lining. A strictly high grade cap, and should in no manner be confused with ordinary goods, the workmanship being the very finest. Sizes, 6⅛ to 7 only.

Price, each.......(Postage extra, 6 cents.).....42c

Boys' Golf Yacht Caps.

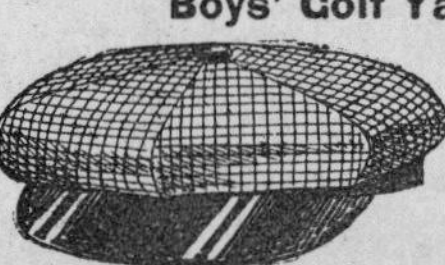

No. 33R2574 Boys' New Style Golf Yacht Cap. Made up in all wool goods in a pretty range of patterns, brown, gray and blue mixtures, patent leather visor, hercules braid trimming. Regular retail value, 50 cents. Sizes, 6¼ to 7 only. What size do you wear? Price, each..........35c

If by mail, postage extra, 8 cents.

Boys' Military Caps.

No. 33R2578 Boys' Fine Navy Blue Cadet or Military Cap. Made from regulation uniform cloth, with gilt cord and buttons. Always a great favorite with the boys. Sizes, 6⅜ to 7⅛ only.

Price, per dozen, $5.16

Price, each.....(Postage extra, each, 10c.).....43c

Our Special Golf Caps at 25 Cents.

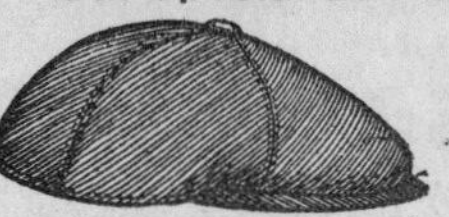

No. 33R2582 Boys', Youths' or Children's Golf Cap, made of fine plain blue wool serge. Six-piece top. Sateen lining. Special quality, equal to caps retailing at 35 cents. Sizes, 6⅛ to 7 only. Price, each........25c

If by mail, postage extra, 6 cents.

Our Special Yacht Caps at 25 Cents.

No. 33R2586 Our Special 25-cent Yacht Cap for Boys or Children. Made from fine blue wool cloth; patent leather visor and hercules braid, with genuine leather sweatband. A cap usually retailing at 50 cents, and a value never offered before at our price. Sizes, 6⅛ to 7⅛ only. Price, each, 25c

If by mail, postage extra, 8 cents.

CHILDREN'S JUNIOR CAPS.

Sizes, 6⅛ to 6¾ only.

These caps are for children from one and one-half to ten years of age and are small shaped and are not in proportion for older children.

Summer Caps for Little People.

No. 33R2592 Children's New Special Design Junior Caps in the popular golf shape. Made from fine all wool cashmere cloth; handsomely designed star top. Gold braid on the red and silver braid on the blue. A new style novelty, one of the most select for the season. Handsome bright color silk lining. Colors, navy blue or red only. Be sure to state color in ordering. Sizes, 6⅛ to 6¾ only.

Price, each....(Postage extra, 6 cents.)... ... 50c

The Princely.

No. 33R2594 Children's Junior Style Cap. Made from fine navy blue serge cloth. Fine bright color satin lining. Eight-piece top, with pretty ornament embroidered on the front. A style of cap becoming to most children, that never fails to please. Special quality and best workmanship throughout. Sizes, 6⅛ to 6¾.

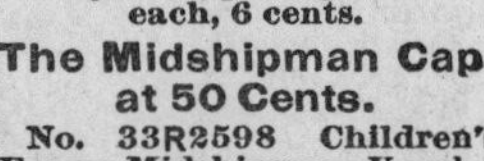

Price, each..............................42c

If by mail, postage extra, each, 6 cents.

The Midshipman Cap at 50 Cents.

No. 33R2598 Children's Fancy Midshipman Yacht Cap. Made from navy blue broadcloth, with leather sweatband, gold band and double gold cord and buttons, ornament on front of crown. Rich and dressy. Nothing but fine materials used in this cap. Sizes, 6⅛ to 6⅞ only.

Price, each...............50c

If by mail, postage extra, each, 11 cents.

BOYS' OR YOUTHS' WINTER CAPS.

Sizes 6½, 6⅝, 6¾, 6⅞ and 7.

As our prices are the lowest possible, quality considered, we allow no reductions for quantity purchases. The price is the same for one or one dozen.

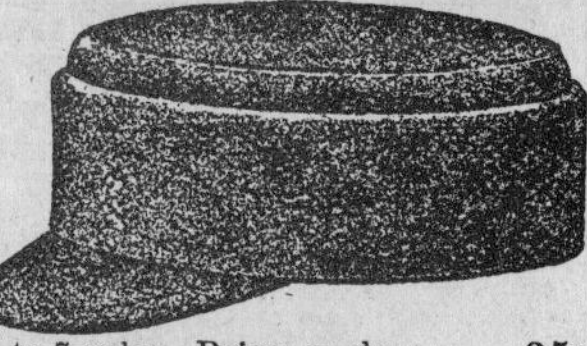

No. 33R2700 Boys' Dark Melton Brighton Caps, with pull down band to protect the ears. Colors, navy blue or dark Oxford gray mixed. Sizes, 6½ to 7 only. Price, each.........25c
If by mail, postage extra, each, 10 cents.

No. 33R2702 Boys' Brighton Caps, made of heavy weight all wool cassimere in dark plaids, brown and gray mixtures; fancy bound with small bow and pull down to protect the ears. Fancy twilled lining. A dressy looking cap. Sizes, 6½ to 7 only. Price, each.......25c
If by mail, postage extra, each, 8 cents.

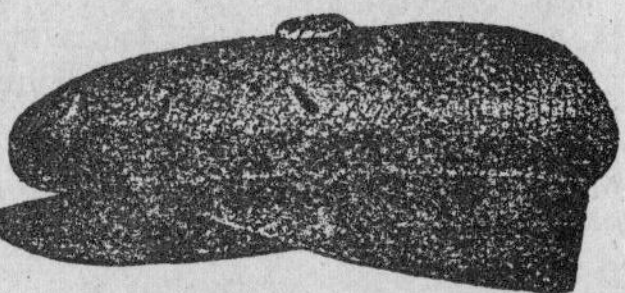

No. 33R2708 Boys' Academy Cap. Made from fine wool yacht cloth, with pull down band to protect the ears. **Nicely lined and well made throughout.** Navy blue, or gray mixed. Sizes, 6½ to 7 only. Price, each...........25c
If by mail, postage extra, each, 9 cents.

No. 33R2714 Boys' Academy Cap. Made from heavy weight cassimere suiting. Fancy plaid and checked patterns, **brown and gray mixtures.** Made with pull down band to protect the ears. Italian cloth lining. Sizes, 6½ to 7 only.
Price, each.......................................39c
If by mail, postage extra, each, 9 cents.

No. 33R2718 Boys' Double Knit Seamless Scotch Wool Knit Turbans. Warm and comfortable and the very best cap for school and knock-about wear. Dark colors, blue and Oxford gray mixed. Sizes, 6½ to 7 only. Price, each..23c
If by mail, postage extra, each, 8 cents.

Our Strong Line of Boys' 50c Winter Caps.

SPECIAL NOTICE—There are caps of all kinds sold at 50 cents, but the line quoted below represents the choice in style and quality, and should not be confused with the grades found in the regular retail stores. Boys' sizes are 6⅜, 6½, 6⅝, 6¾, 6⅞, 7 and 7⅛.

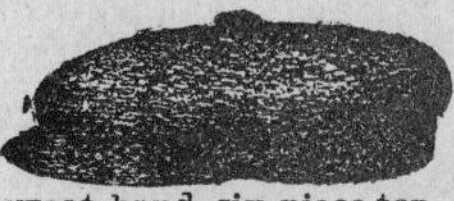

No. 33R2722 Boys' Navy Blue Fine Broadcloth Caps, made in the golf yacht style, with full width **pull down** band. Silk lined, satin sweat-band, six-piece top. Sizes, 6⅜ to 7⅛ only.
Price, each.......................................50c
If by mail, postage extra, each, 10 cents.

Boys' or Youths' Caps for 50 cents.

No. 33R2726 Boys' new style caps, made from oxford gray or oxford brown golf cloth, with wide pull down band, nicely lined with fancy silk lining; 2 silk cord bows in front and bound with silk. A cap you cannot duplicate for less than 75 cents. Sizes, 6⅜ to 7⅛. Price, each...............50c
If by mail, postage extra, each, 10 cents.

Our 50-Cent Boys' Turban.

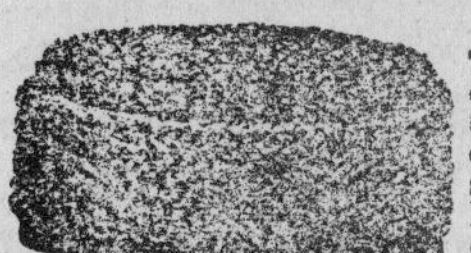

No. 33R2734 Boys' Turban, made of fine quality of heavy chinchilla, with wide pull down band and heavy silk binding. Fancy silk lined. Color, navy blue only. A very dressy looking cap and one that retails for 75 cents. Sizes, 6⅜ to 7⅛ only.
Price, each.......................................50c
If by mail, postage extra, each, 11 cents.

BOYS' OR YOUTHS' PLUSH CAPS.

SPECIAL NOTICE.—We sell no pieced plush caps of any kind, but all are cut from whole cloth. We warrant every one to be perfect in workmanship, and the best value you have seen for the price. Sizes, 6⅜, 6½, 6⅝, 6¾, 6⅞, 7 and 7⅛.

No. 33R2740 Boys' Fine Silk Plush Caps, Brighton style, full width pull down band and silk lined. Sizes, 6⅜ to 7⅛ only.
Price, each.........50c
If by mail, postage extra, each, 10 cents.

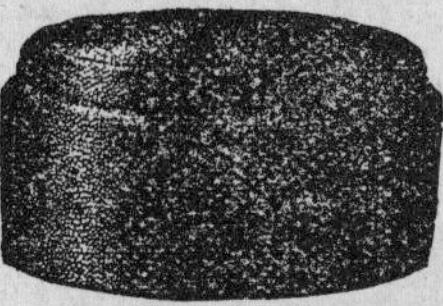

No. 33R2746 Boys' Fine Silk Plush Turban Caps, with handsome satin lining throughout; wide pull down band to protect the ears. **Finely made and finished.** Sizes, 6⅜ to 7⅛ only.
Price, each.......50c
If by mail, postage extra, each, 10 cents.

Boys' Plush Brighton, 75 Cents.

No. 33R2750 Boys' Silk Plush Brighton Style Caps, made of extra quality fine silk plush, with fine satin lining. Regular retail price, $1.00. Sizes, 6⅜ to 7⅛. Price, each..............................75c
If by mail, postage extra, each, 10 cents.

No. 33R2756 Boys' Extra Fine Silk Plush Academy Cap. Latest style, six-piece top with fine heavy satin lining, and pull down band to protect the ears. **This is an exceptionally fine winter cap.** Good, heavy weight; very fine and dressy in appearance. Sizes, 6⅜ to 7⅛ only.
Price, each.......................................75c
If by mail, postage extra, each, 10 cents.

Boys' Silk Plush Cap for 75 Cents.

No. 33R2760 Boys' Extra Quality Fine Silk Plush Caps, in golf style with pull down band. Fine satin lining and it usually retails at $1.00. A very dressy style. Sizes, 6⅜ to 7⅛ only.
Price, each.......................................75c
If by mail, postage extra, each, 10 cents.

Don't forget to give size when you order a cap.

WARM WINTER CAPS FOR LITTLE PEOPLE.

Sizes, 6⅛, 6¼, 6⅜, 6½, 6⅝ and 6¾ only. A line of warm caps made especially for children from two years to about ten years of age. If you do not know size see illustration showing how to measure on first page of this department.

Junior Caps.

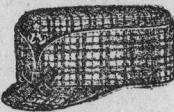

No. 33R2800 Junior Caps made of good quality wool cloth in golf yacht style with silk ornament on front. Navy blue only. Sizes, 6⅛ to 6¾ only. Price, each...............................23c
If by mail, postage extra, each, 6 cents.

No. 33R2804 Junior Caps, made of fancy plaid cassimere cloth, all wool in medium plaid medium dark colors, pretty ornament in front with bow. Wide band to pull down over ears. Sizes, 6⅛ to 6¾ only. Price, each........ 35c
If by mail, postage extra, each, 8 cents.

New Fancy Junior Caps.

No. 33R2810 Junior Caps, made of fine broadcloth, trimmed with fancy plaid velour cloth and white braid; wide pull down band; silk lining; a very pretty, new style that will be popular this season. **Navy blue or bright red.** Sizes, 6⅛ to 6¾ only. Price, each.......................45c
If by mail, postage extra, each, 7 cents.

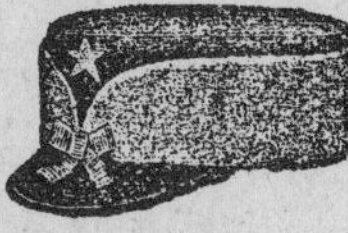

No. 33R2814 Junior Caps in new style and combination. Navy blue broadcloth, with beaver plush band, closed with bow in front and ornamented with star; silk lined. This is another of the new good things for this season. Sizes, 6⅛ to 6¾ only. Price, each.........................45c
If by mail, postage extra, each, 8 cents.

IF YOU FAIL TO STATE SIZE, WE CANNOT FILL YOUR ORDER.

MEN'S FUR CAPS.

No. 33R2830 Men's Fur Cap. Made from **selected muskrat skin;** heavy red flannel lining, wide one-piece turn down band. **Protects** every part of the **neck,** side of the **face** and **head.** Long visor, which, when turned down, affords protection to front of face. Owing to the rush to the northern climates a desirable cap to exclude the cold is a necessity. Sizes, 6¾ to 7½ only. Price, each..............................$2.50
If by mail, postage extra, each, 16 cents.

Genuine Sealskin Caps, for $4.50.

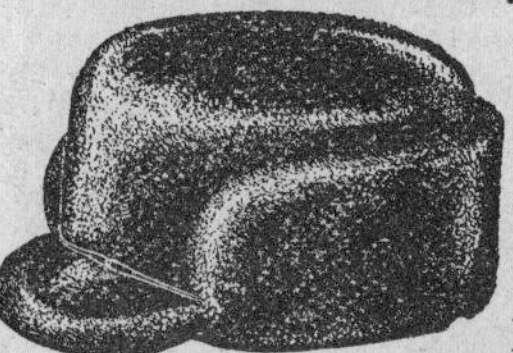

No. 33R2834 Men's Fine Sealskin Caps, elegantly made and lined with heavy rich satin lining; a very stylish cap, and one of the greatest values ever offered at the price. Made with wide, deep turned down band; the visor can be worn up or down. Sizes, 6¾ to 7⅝ only. Price, each, $4.50
If by mail, postage extra, 20 cents.

No. 33R2837 The Driver Style Genuine Sealskin Cap; wide, sliding pull down band lined with fine quality satin. This cap is sold for just one-half what you can buy it for from your home merchants.
Price, each. $4.50
If by mail, postage extra, 20 cents.

No. 33R2840 Men's Turban Style Genuine Sealskin Cap; medium full crown and wide, turned down band; a very warm cap and one of the best values ever offered at our low price.
Price, each. $4.50
If by mail, postage extra, 20 cents.

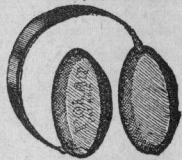

No. 33R2850 Patent Adjustable Polar Ear Muffs. Made from fine black velvet with adjustable spring. Soft fleece lining. Per pair. $0.20
Per dozen pairs........ 2.40

No. 33R2852 Fine Plain Black Velvet Ear Muffs, with elastic cord. Per pair......8c
Per dozen pairs...........96c
If by mail, postage extra, per pair, 2 cents.

Men's Caps, Brighton and Golf Styles.

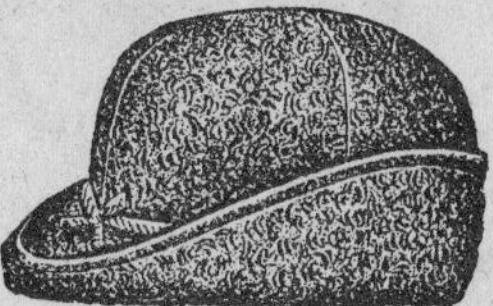

No. 33R2860 Regular 50-cent value; full shape, strong lining, heavy and warm. Black only. Sizes, 6¾ to 7⅜.
Price, each... $0.23
Per dozen..... 2.76
If by mail, postage extra, each, 12 cents.

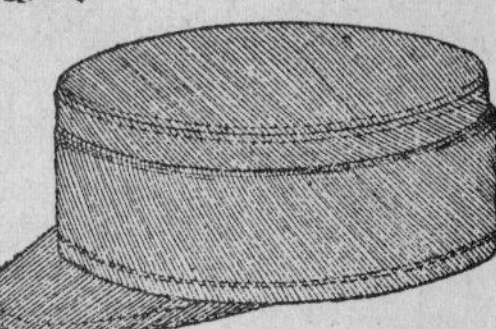

No. 33R2862 The Brighton Cap. Fine navy blue cassimere cloth, with Italian lining and wide pull down band. Sizes, 6¾ to 7½.
Price, each.....25c
If by mail, postage extra, 11 cents.

No. 33R2864 Men's Golf Yacht. Fine navy blue yacht cloth with pull down band and fine sateen lining. Sizes, 6¾ to 7¼ only.
Price, each....25c
If by mail, postage extra each, 14 cents.

Men's Scotch Caps.

No. 33R2868 Navy blue, with extra heavy fine felt lining. These caps are extra heavy and warm, and are full seamless throughout. Made in sizes from 6¾ to 7⅜ only. Double roll band.
Price, each.....43c
If by mail, postage extra, each, 12 cents.

MEN'S WINTER PLUSH CAPS.

SPECIAL NOTICE. All plush caps sold by us are made from real silk plush, cut from whole cloth. We sell no plush caps made from pieces. Such caps never give satisfaction, needing constant repair.

If by mail, postage extra, on plush caps, 14 cents.

Men's Windsor Style Plush Caps.

No. 33R2870 Men's Heavy Silk Plush Windsor. Heavy double roll pull down band, quilted silk lining, double silk cord in front. Made expressly for extreme cold weather. Sizes, 6¾ to 7¾. Price, each....75c

No. 33R2874 Silk Plush Windsor, Satin Lined, $1.00. Heavy durable soft plush used in this cap. Double roll pull down band; serviceable and comfortable. Sizes, 6¾ to 7¾. Price, each.$1.00

No. 33R2878 Men's Genuine Seal Plush Windsor. Money cannot buy a better or higher grade plush cap. Made up with rich imported satin lining, double turn down band, neat silk bow in front. Make an elegant and acceptable Christmas gift. Sizes, 6¾ to 7¾. What size do you wear? Price, each....$1.50

Men's Brighton Style Plush Caps.

No. 33R2882 Men's Heavy Silk Plush Brighton Cap. Good quality, no pieces, strong lining and wide pull down band. The best cap ever offered for this price. Sizes, 6¾ to 7¾. Price, each....45c

No. 33R2886 Men's Fine Silk Plush Brighton Caps, with full width pull down band, silk lining. Regular retail price, $1.00. Sizes, 6¾ to 7¾. Price, each....75c

No. 33R2888 Fine Silk Plush Brighton Cap. Fine satin lined, wide pull down band, a superior quality. We lead all in quality at this price. Sizes, 6¾ to 7¾. Price, each.$1.00

No. 33R2890 Men's French Silk Plush Brighton. Imported satin lining. The quality of plush used in this cap is the finest grade sold to cap makers; caps from which it is made usually sell at from $1.75 to $2.00. Sizes, 6¾ to 7¾. We are quoting them at, each....$1.35

Men's Bismarck Style Cap.

No. 33R2892 Men's Bismarck Style Cap. Made up in good, full shape and of XX silk plush with grosgrain ribbon bow in front; silk lining. Will surely be more than you expect for the reasonable price. Sizes, 6¾ to 7⅝. Price, each....75c

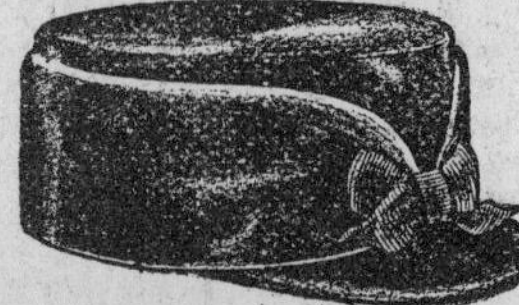

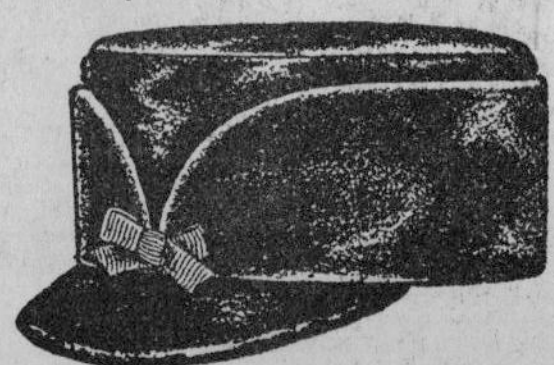

No. 33R2894 Men's Silk Plush Storm King. Satin lining, wide pull down band, thoroughly durable and an excellent value. Sizes, 6¾ to 7¾. Price, each.$1.00

No. 33R2896 Men's Extra Quality Silk Plush Storm King. This superb value is made up regardless of cost for material, as we can afford to sell what others quote at $2.00 for $1.47. Heavy rich satin lining; wide quilted sliding band. **Handsomest cold weather cap in the market.** Always acceptable as a holiday gift. Sizes, 6¾ to 7⅝. Price, each....$1.47

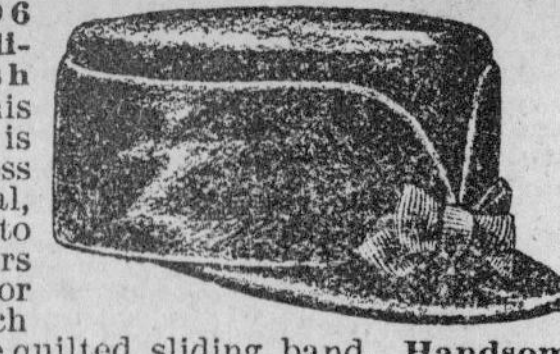

Men's New Storm King Cap.

No. 33R2898 The New Storm King. The latest new style in men's fine silk plush caps, and a success from the start. Full crown, wide pull down band, fine satin lined, heavy satin sweat. Two small bows in front. Regular retail price, $2.00. Sizes, 6¾ to 7¾. Price, each..$1.50

Men's Six-Piece Top Yacht Cap.

No. 33R2902 Men's First Quality Silk Plush Cap. Heavy satin lining; wide turn down band; new six-piece top, double stitched throughout. The plush is extra heavy and will afford warmth and comfort to the wearer. Very stylish and fits closely around the ears. Sizes, 6¾ to 7¾. Price, each....$1.50

Men's Silk Plush Winter Driver.

No. 33R2904 Men's Silk Plush Winter Driver. Silk lining, flat six-piece crown; wide, pull down band. The band can be drawn over the ears without causing crown to lose the shape shown in cut. Sizes, 6¾ to 7¾. Price, each....75c

Men's Plush Yacht Cap.

No. 33R2906 Men's Silk Plush Yacht Style Cap. A new style and extremely popular. Silk lining, neat pull down band that fits closely around the ears. **A great driving cap.** Sizes, 6¾ to 7⅛. **What size do you wear?** Price, each....75c

If by mail, postage extra, 12 cents.

No. 33R2908 Imported Black Kersey Cap, with fine quality imitation mink pull down in a rich shade of seal brown; a very warm and exceedingly handsome cap; very stylish looking. This is one of the very best caps you can buy for driving purposes and one that retails everywhere for $2.50 and $3.00. Sizes, 6¾ to 7⅛. Price, each....$1.75

If by mail, postage extra, 12 cents.

MEN'S WINTER CAPS AT 50 CENTS.

Our line at 50 cents cannot be excelled in quality. All sorts of shapes and kinds are sold at this popular price, but the qualities shown below are as carefully made and sized as our line at double the price, and most of them are equal to those retailing at 75 cents. Every cap warranted perfect in workmanship and as represented.

No. 33R2920 Men's Blue Kersey Cloth Brighton, satin lined, six rows of strong stitching around the band. **A well made, warm cap, that brings 75 cents in your own town.** Sizes, 6¾ to 7⅛. **What size do you wear?** Price, each....50c

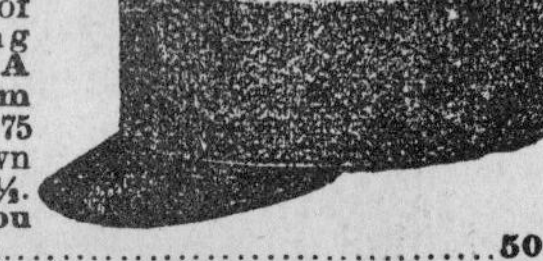

If by mail, postage extra, 12 cents.

Extra Heavy Red Felt Lined Cap.

No. 33R2924 Men's Extra Heavy Brighton Style, Black, All Wool Cheviot Cloth Cap, with heavy red felt lining; extra high crown and wide pull down. A Western favorite. Sizes, 6¾ to 7⅛ only. Price, each....50c

If by mail, postage extra, 12 cents.

Men's Storm King at 50 Cents.

No. 33R2930 Men's Storm King New Style Cap, made of fine Oxford gray cheviot all wool cloth, storm visor, fine lining, wide pull down band joined with two small silk bows, double stitched throughout. A stylish cap. Retail price, 75 cents. Dark Oxford only. Sizes, 6¾ to 7⅛ only. Price, each....50c

If by mail, postage extra, 12 cents.

No. 33R2934 Heavy Winter Golf Style. With turn band; all wool navy blue cheviot; silk lined; made amply full in front to insure comfortable fit in back when pulled down. Navy blue only. Sizes, 6¾ to 7⅛. Price, each....50c

If by mail, postage extra, 11 cents.

No. 33R2938 Men's Fancy Golf Cap. Fine all wool fancy mixed cassimere suiting, assorted checks, plaids and neat mixed patterns, browns, grays, olives, etc. Pull down band. Double stitched and full silk lined. Sizes, 6¾ to 7⅛. Price, each....50c

If by mail, postage extra, 11 cents.

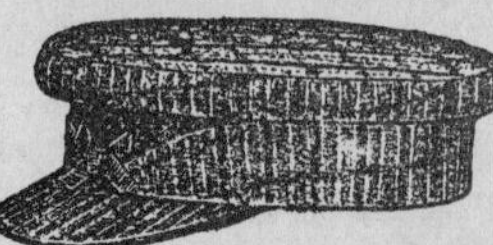

No. 33R2939 Men' New Style Yacb Cap. Made of fine all wool cassimeres in dark plaids and checks, neat patterns in brown and gray effects; a very stylish cap with wide pull down band, silk bow in front. Sizes, 6¾ to 7⅛. Price, each....50c

If by mail, postage extra, 10 cents.

Genuine Golf Cloth Storm King, 75c.

No. 33R2946 Men's Fine Heavy Golf Cloth Oxford gray color. Genuine golf cloth; the reverse side is woven into fancy patterns, which makes a very nobby lining; silk taped seams, fine satin sweatband, wide pull down band bound with silk and closed in front with two small silk bows. Oxford gray only. Sizes, 6¾ to 7⅛. Price...(If by mail, postage extra, 10 cents)...75c

No. 33R2950 Men's Fine Genuine Golf Cloth, Oxford gray color. Fancy self plaid lined. Same cloth as above, silk taped seams, double stitched, heavy satin sweatband, golf style, wide pull down band. **Special value.** Oxford gray only. Sizes, 6¾ to 7⅛. Price, each....75c

If by mail, postage extra, 10 cents.

No. 33R2954 Made from fine quality of navy blue kersey. Each seam is double stitched and sewed in the latest raw edge style; lined with bright satin lining of heaviest quality. An exceptionally genteel and nobby cap that will give excellent satisfaction. Sizes, 6¾ to 7⅛. Price...(If by mail, postage extra, 15 cents)...75c

No. 33R2958 The Ashton Special. High grade imported kersey cap. Finest quality heavy satin lining, wide pull down band, with silk stitching. Adjustable forehead protector inside. Navy blue. Handsome, dressy and thoroughly good. Sizes, 6¾ to 7¾. Price...(If by mail, postage extra, 14 cents)...75c

Men's Heavy Yacht Cap.

No. 33R2960 High Grade Imported Kersey Cap, in black only, heavy silk binding with bow in front, very deep pull down, lined with heavy satin lining, and a very stylish cap. Retail price, $1.25. Sizes, 6¾ to 7½ only. Price, each... 85c

If by mail, postage extra, 10 cents.

Men's Extra Fine Winter Caps.

No. 33R2962 New Havelock style. An ideal cap for cold weather. Handsome and dressy in appearance. Heavy, warm and thoroughly dependable in every way. Made from fine quality imported navy blue kersey cloth, very smooth finish. Heavy satin lining, wide pull down band and adjustable forehead protector inside. Sizes, 6¾ to 7½.
Price...(If by mail, postage extra, 10 cents)...**85c**

No. 33R2963 Men's Havelock Cap, in a very fine quality of dark blue kersey cloth, with small piping of silk velvet and three rows of stitching around the pull down, large silk bow in front, elegantly lined with heavy satin lining. This is an extremely dressy looking cap and exceptional value. Sizes, 6¾ to 7½. Price (If by mail, postage extra, 10 cents) **$1.25**

Northwestern Special, $1.00.

No. 33R2964 Men's Extra Warm Heavy Cap, made of fine all wool kersey cloth. Finely lined and forehead storm protector. The special feature is the heavy pull down genuine sheepskin wool lined band. **Your ears will never get cold if you wear this cap.** Sizes, 6¾ to 7½. Color, black only.
Price (If by mail, postage extra, 10 cents)..**$1.00**

No. 33R2966 Men's Heavy Warm Yacht Cap, made of fine all wool navy blue kersey cloth; pull down band, fancy satin lined, with twilled silk sweatband and adjustable forehead protector. A very dressy and comfortable cap for cold weather. Dark blue only. Price, each......**75c**
If by mail, postage extra, 12 cents.

No. 33R2967 Men's Yacht Cap, in plain black kersey cloth, in a very fine quality, made with a very handsome silk front, as shown in cut, with small silk bow, richly lined with heavy satin and twilled silk sweatband. This is one of the handsomest caps in our line and would retail regularly for $1.50. Sizes, 6¾ to 7½.
Price, each **$1.00**
If by mail, postage extra, 10 cents.

No. 33R2968 Men's Extra Quality Yacht Cap with pull down band. Made from extra quality imported kersey cloth, and double stitched throughout with silk. Heavy satin lining and wide black satin sweatband. **Strictly highest quality.** **Navy blue only.** Sizes, 6¾ to 7½.
Price, each............................**$1.25**
If by mail, postage extra, each, 12 cents.

Extra Fine Havelock Caps.

No. 33R2970 Men's Extra Quality Fine Blue Caps in the new Havelock style, made of fine extra quality imported blue kersey cloth, finest satin lining, deep durable satin sweatband, wide pull down band bound with silk as shown in illustration, stitched with silk thread. You may pay $2.00 but will get no finer cap. Sizes, 6¾ to 7¾. Price, each...............**$1.50**
If by mail, postage extra, each, 14 cents.

MEN'S WARM WEATHER HATS.

The Tycoon.

No. 33R3000 Here is the Tycoon, a practical sunshade. The sweatband is made in such a manner that a free circulation of air keeps the head cool at all times. Made from Yucatan straw. **Ventilated top and exceedingly light.** Sizes, 6¾ to 7½. **What size do you wear?** Price, per dozen, **$5.16**; each.......**43c**
If by mail, postage extra, each, 20 cents.

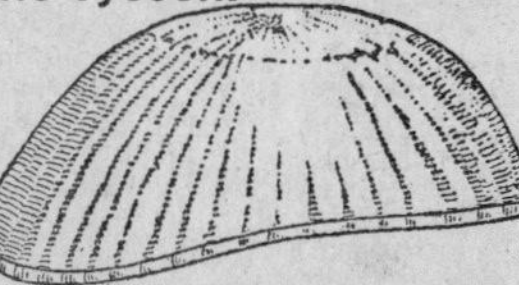

Men's Helmets.

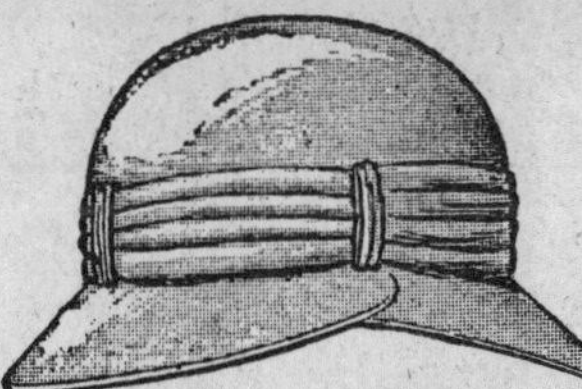

No. 33R3004 They have fine braided straw body, covered with fine slate or dead grass colored silesia, with sash to match. **Patent ventilated sweatband,** allowing perfect ventilation and circulation around entire band. Sizes, 6¾ to 7⅜ only. Price, per doz., **$4.56**; each, **38c**
If by mail, postage extra, each, 22 cents.

The Stanley.

No. 33R3010 This is another of those sensible solid comfort hot weather hats; made with light weight straw crown, covered with colored silesia, trimmed with sash band of same material. Extended sweatband, giving perfect ventilation. Sizes, 6¾ to 7⅜.
Price, per dozen, **$4.56**; each........................**38c**
If by mail, postage extra, 22 cents.

If you forget to give size of hat or cap wanted, we cannot fill your order.

Trunks and Traveling Bags.

WE SELL TRUNKS AT ALL PRICES. We can suit you in style and quality. We want your order, because we can sell you GOOD TRUNKS AND BAGS CHEAPEST. In trunks and bags, as in most other kinds of merchandise, we recommend the medium and better grades, for they are cheapest in the end. **A dollar or two added to the price of a trunk may mean many years of additional usefulness. The particular reasons why we deserve careful consideration and your order, is because we protect you from high prices, from dishonest quality and workmanship.** While we sell the cheaper kinds as well as the better grades, each represents **the best value of that kind at lowest possible prices.** We do not offer one kind of trunk or bag at cost and then ask you to pay too much for another. **THERE IS INTEGRITY in trunks as in other merchandise.** They should be made to stand the wear and tear which they are sure to get from time to time.

OUR TRUNKS AND BAGS are made under careful supervision; every nail, rivet, clamp, hinge and lock is attached with the exactness and skill of thorough workmen. **THIS IS WHY WE WARRANT EVERY TRUNK AND BAG to be as represented and the best of its kind at the lowest possible price.**

If you do not see what you want, write to us for information and get our prices.

WHEN ORDERING duplicate keys, give catalogue number of trunk or bag, also number of letter on key or lock. Duplicate keys furnished at 5 cents each.

Crystallized or Fancy Metal Covered Trunks.

Cross Bar Slats, Iron Bottom.

No. 33R5002 Very substantially made; barrel stave top, iron bound, cross bar slats on top, body slats, set up tray with covered bonnet box, iron bottom.

Length	Width	Height	Weight	Price
26 in.	14½ in.	17½ in.	27 lbs.	$1.65
28 in.	15½ in.	18½ in.	31 lbs.	1.95
30 in.	16½ in.	19½ in.	34 lbs.	2.10
32 in.	17½ in.	20½ in.	37 lbs.	2.40
34 in.	18½ in.	21½ in.	41 lbs.	2.65
36 in.	19½ in.	22½ in.	46 lbs.	2.90

Crystallized Metal Covered Trunks.

Flat Top.

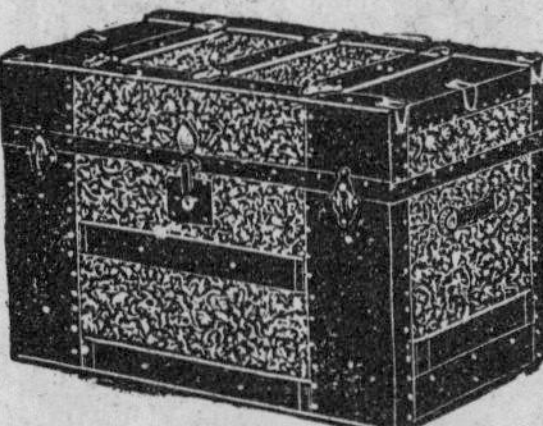

No. 33R5010 Will stand the hard knocks that any trunk is sure to receive. Flat top, large shape, iron bound, cross bar slats on top; long slats on body, set up tray with covered bonnet box. Iron bottom.

Length	Width	Height	Weight	Price
26 in.	14½ in.	17 in.	28 lbs.	$2.25
28 in.	15½ in.	18 in.	32 lbs.	2.50
30 in.	16½ in.	19 in.	35 lbs.	2.75
32 in.	17½ in.	20 in.	39 lbs.	3.00
34 in.	18½ in.	21 in.	43 lbs.	3.25
36 in.	19½ in.	22 in.	46 lbs.	3.50

GIVE CATALOGUE NUMBER IN FULL WHEN YOU WRITE YOUR ORDER

New Shape Up to Date Trunk, Cross Bar Slats, Iron Bottom.

No. 33R5020 Fancy metal covered, flat top, with front and back rounded, hardwood reverse bent slats, metal corner bumpers, clamps, bottom rollers, etc. Monitor lock and patent bar bolts, heavy strap hinges, tray, with bonnet box. Fall-in top and side compartments, all separately covered, and four slats on all sizes. Without a doubt this is the handiest and most substantial trunk ever built for our low price.

Monitor Lock.

Length	Width	Height	Weight	Price
28 in.	16 in.	18½ in.	34 lbs.	$3.20
30 in.	17 in.	19½ in.	39 lbs.	3.45
32 in.	18 in.	20½ in.	44 lbs.	3.90
34 in.	19 in.	21½ in.	51 lbs.	4.15
36 in.	20 in.	22½ in.	55 lbs.	4.40

Crystallized Metal Covered Trunk.

No. 33R5024 Cross bar slats, hinge tray, iron bottom, full finish, with parasol case. Barrel stave top, wide iron bound, five cross bar slats on top and upright on front, end slats, malleable iron corners and shoes, etc., stitched leather handles. Excelsior lock, patent bolts, fancy skeleton work, covered tray with bonnet box, parasol case and side compartment, fall-in top.

Length	Width	Height	Weight	Price
28 in.	16 in.	19½ in.	39 lbs.	$3.65
30 in.	17 in.	20½ in.	42 lbs.	3.95
32 in.	18 in.	21½ in.	47 lbs.	4.30
34 in.	19 in.	22½ in.	51 lbs.	4.70
36 in.	20 in.	23½ in.	58 lbs.	5.10
38 in.	21 in.	24½ in.	64 lbs.	5.60

EXTRA QUALITY CRYSTALLIZED METAL TRUNKS.

GREAT BARGAIN, $2.25 TRUNK.

No. 33R5014 Full finished cross bar slats, iron bottom, barrel stave top, cross bar slats on top, and upright on front, iron clamps, brass Monitor lock, patent bolts, rollers, hinges, etc.; covered tray with bonnet box and side compartments; fall-in top. This is a handsome trunk, very wide and high and extra well made.

Length	Width	Height	Weight	Price
26 in.	14½ in.	17½ in.	30 lbs.	$2.25
28 in.	15½ in.	18½ in.	33 lbs.	2.50
30 in.	16½ in.	19½ in.	37 lbs.	2.75
32 in.	17½ in.	20½ in.	41 lbs.	3.00
34 in.	18½ in.	21½ in.	46 lbs.	3.25
36 in.	19½ in.	22½ in.	50 lbs.	3.50

A $7.50 Crystal Covered Trunk or $4.00.

No. 33R5028 Handsome Silver Crystal Covered Trunk, fitted with parasol case, Excelsior lock, hinge tray **and all of the conveniences to be found in high price trunks.** Large trunk, flat on top with corners rounded, hardwood slats on top and body, heavy bolts, malleable iron, skeleton work, hinges, etc., full finished tray with hat box, side compartment, fall-in top, four slats on all sizes.

Length	Width	Height	Weight	Price
28 in.	17 in.	19½ in.	39 lbs.	$4.00
30 in.	18 in.	20½ in.	43 lbs.	4.30
32 in.	19 in.	21½ in.	47 lbs.	4.60
34 in.	20 in.	22½ in.	52 lbs.	4.90
36 in.	21 in.	23½ in.	59 lbs.	5.30
38 in.	22 in.	24½ in.	64 lbs.	5.70

Our Special for $4.00.

Iron Bottom and Rosewood Finish.

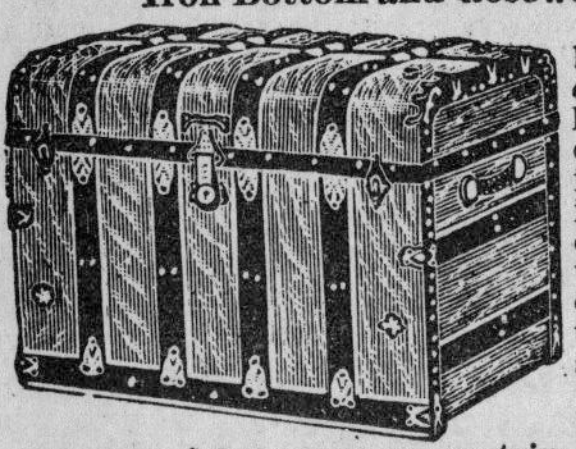

No. 33R5035 High, Wide Trunk covered with heavy iron, enameled, rosewood finished. Flat top, iron bottom, round corners. **Hardwood bent slats over entire top upright on front and end slats.** All protected with heavy metal clamps and bumpers, cross strip clamps and fancy skeleton iron work on ends. **Heavy Excelsior lock and side bolts**, stitched leather handles, heavy hinges, covered tray, with **bonnet and parasol compartments. Handsomely finished and one of the very best values we have ever offered.**

Length	Width	Height	Weight	Price
28 in.	17 in.	19½ in.	39 lbs.	$4.00
30 in.	18 in.	20½ in.	43 lbs.	4.30
32 in.	19 in.	21½ in.	47 lbs.	4.60
34 in.	20 in.	22½ in.	52 lbs.	4.90
36 in.	21 in.	23½ in.	59 lbs.	5.30
38 in.	22 in.	24½ in.	64 lbs.	5.70

Black Enameled Iron Trunk for $4.00.

No. 33R5040 Black Enameled Iron, Round Top Trunk, large size box covered with black enameled iron, flat top **with rounded corners**, hardwood bent slats on top with one extra slat in center full length of trunk, fancy clamps, rollers, leather handles, brass Excelsior lock, **patent bolts**, full covered hinged tray, with bonnet box, fall-in top, **all fancy trimmed. Iron bottom.**

Length	Width	Height	Weight	Price
28 in.	17 in.	20 in.	43 lbs.	$4.00
30 in.	18 in.	21 in.	47 lbs.	4.30
32 in.	19 in.	22 in.	51 lbs.	4.60
34 in.	20 in.	23 in.	57 lbs.	4.90
36 in.	21 in.	24 in.	62 lbs.	5.30
38 in.	22 in.	25 in.	69 lbs.	5.70

Fancy Metal Covered Trunk at $5.75.

Excelsior Lock.

No. 33R5050 Extra High and Wide Trunk, barrel stave top, cross bar slats on top, upright on front, malleable iron bumpers, **Excelsior lock**, fancy chain work, malleable iron bolts, heavy hinges, stitched leather handles, covered tray with bonnet box, **parasol case** and other compartments, fall-in top, **linen faced, crystallized metal**, handsomely trimmed and finished.

Length	Width	Height	Weight	Price
32 in.	19½ in.	24½ in.	54 lbs.	$5.75
34 in.	20½ in.	25½ in.	60 lbs.	6.10
36 in.	21½ in.	26½ in.	65 lbs.	6.50

Canvas Covered Trunk for $2.25.

No. 33R5052 A Good Canvas Covered Trunk at a very low price. Square top, painted canvas cover, hardwood slats on top and body, protected with heavy iron clamps, heavy bottom cleats, Monitor lock and patent bolts and heavy hinges. Set up tray with covered hat compartment. The best low priced canvas covered trunk sold.

Length	Width	Height	Weight	Price
28 in.	16¼ in.	18½ in.	30 lbs.	$2.25
30 in.	17 in.	19¼ in.	35 lbs.	2.50
32 in.	17¾ in.	20 in.	37 lbs.	2.75
34 in.	18½ in.	21 in.	42 lbs.	3.00
36 in.	19½ in.	22 in.	46 lbs.	3.25

Our Square Top Trunk, $2.75.

No. 33R5054 Our Special Low Priced Square Top Trunk, made with leather straps, full covered tray, painted, canvas covered. Hardwood slats on top and body; protected by heavy iron clamps, bottom cleats, brass Monitor lock, buckle bar bolts, heavy hinges, set up tray with hat box and side compartment separately covered. **Remember you can buy trunks from us as cheap as your home merchant.**

Length	Width	Height	Weight	Price
28 in.	16¼ in.	18½ in.	31 lbs.	$2.75
30 in.	17 in.	19¼ in.	36 lbs.	3.00
32 in.	17¾ in.	20 in.	38 lbs.	3.25
34 in.	18½ in.	21 in.	43 lbs.	3.50
36 in.	19½ in.	22 in.	47 lbs.	3.75

Our $3.55 Steel Bound Trunk.

No. 33R5056 Cheapest Steel Bound Trunk in the market, large box, covered with heavy canvas, four heavy hardwood slats on top and two on body running full length of trunk, heavy japanned corners and steel strip clasp, heavy bolts, Monitor lock, hinge tray with hat box and side compartment separately covered, cloth faced. **An honest, strong trunk at a very low price.**

Length	Width	Height	Weight	Price
30 in.	17½ in.	20 in.	41 lbs.	$3.55
32 in.	18½ in.	20¾ in.	45 lbs.	3.85
34 in.	19¼ in.	21½ in.	52 lbs.	4.15
36 in.	20¼ in.	22¼ in.	55 lbs.	4.45
38 in.	21 in.	23 in.	60 lbs.	4.75

Angle Steel Bound Trunk for $4.30 and Up.

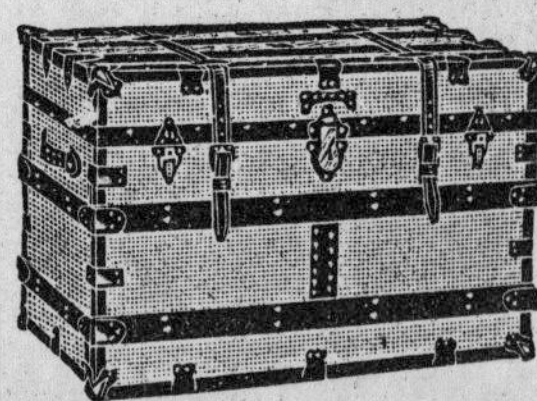

No. 33R5058 Cheapest Steel Bound Trunk, with straps, in the market. Large box, covered with heavy canvas, painted, four heavy hardwood slats on top and two on body running full length of trunk. Front and back of top and bottom and ends protected with our new steel binding, heavy japanned corners and steel strip clamps, with center band, heavy bolts, Monitor lock, hinge tray with hat box and side compartment separately covered, cloth faced. Dress tray.

Length	Width	Height	Weight	Price
30 in.	17½ in.	20 in.	45 lbs.	$4.30
32 in.	18½ in.	20¾ in.	48 lbs.	4.60
34 in.	19¼ in.	21½ in.	53 lbs.	4.90
36 in.	20¼ in.	22¼ in.	56 lbs.	5.20
38 in.	21 in.	23 in.	62 lbs.	5.50

Flat Top Heavy Duck Cover Trunk.

No. 33R5064, Flat Top, Heavy Duck Cover Trunk. Double wide iron bound, two center bands, hardwood slat on top and body, end slats all protected with heavy iron bumpers, corner shoes, etc. Excelsior lock and patent buckle bolts, **heavy hinges, rollers, etc.**, stitched leather handles, high combination **tray, hat box with removable frame, hinged shirt box on side and compartment underneath, all covered, linen finish, iron bottom.**

Length	Width	Height	Weight	Price
30 in.	17¾ in.	20¼ in.	43 lbs.	$5.50
32 in.	18½ in.	21 in.	48 lbs.	5.95
34 in.	19½ in.	22 in.	55 lbs.	6.50

New Steel Bound Trunk.

Special value at $6.00 to $8.00.

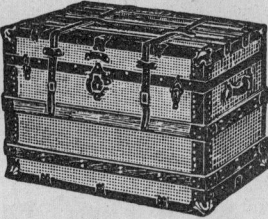

No. 33R5070 Steel bound, brass plated clamps and sole leather straps. Large size box covered with painted canvas, olive colored iron binding, four heavy hardwood slats on top, two slats running full length of trunk on body, with hard wood bottom cleats. Front and back of top and bottom protected with our **new steel binding** running entire length of trunk, heavy brass plated corner shoes and clamps, heavy brass plated bolts and Monitor lock. Sole leather straps, hinge tray with hat box and side compartment separately covered, with cloth facing. Dress tray. Positively the greatest value in a square top trunk ever offered.

Length	Width	Height	Weight	Price
30 in.	18 in.	19½ in.	44 lbs.	$6.00
32 in.	18¾ in.	20¼ in.	48 lbs.	6.50
34 in.	19½ in.	21 in.	53½ lbs.	7.00
36 in.	20¼ in.	22 in.	58½ lbs.	7.50
38 in.	21 in.	22½ in.	64½ lbs.	8.00

Special Canvas Covered Wall Trunk for $4.90.

No. 33R5074 Canvas Covered, Iron Bottom, Cloth Finish, Excelsior Lock, High and Wide Trunk, covered with heavy canvas duck, flat top, with front and back rounded, **hardwood bent slats over entire top, upright on** front, end slats; all protected with tinned clamps, bumpers, cross-strip clamps, fancy skeleton iron work on ends, etc., heavy brass locks, patent side bolts, **stitched leather handles**, heavy hinges, set-up tray, cloth faced.

Length	Width	Height	Weight	Price
30 in.	17½ in.	20½ in.	42½ lbs.	$4.90
32 in.	18½ in.	21½ in.	46 lbs.	4.30
34 in.	19½ in.	22½ in.	50 lbs.	5.70
36 in.	20 in.	23½ in.	55 lbs.	6.10

Canvas Covered Trunks.

No. 33R5078 Large Full Sized Trunk, covered with heavy waterproof canvas, bound with olive enamel iron binding; hardwood slats used entirely on this trunk. **All protected with brazed malleable clamps and corners of the latest pattern.** Heavy valance set buckle, bar bolts, Excelsior lock, stitched leather handles, two heavy sole leather straps. Inside arranged with roomy upper tray, with hat box and side compartments separately covered with folding lids. Extra skirt tray below. Cloth faced. This is one of the best values ever offered to trunk buyers.

Length	Width	Height	Weight	Price
30 in.	18 in.	20½ in.	45½ lbs.	$6.50
32 in.	19 in.	21½ in.	50 lbs.	7.00
34 in.	20 in.	22½ in.	55 lbs.	7.50
36 in.	21 in.	23½ in.	58½ lbs.	8.00
38 in.	22 in.	24½ in.	63 lbs.	8.50
40 in.	22½ in.	25½ in.	70 lbs.	9.00

A $6.00 Canvas Covered Trunk for $4.25.

No. 33R5060 Canvas covered, iron bottom, square top, corners double iron bound, four hardwood slats full length of trunk, **two slats all around body**, japanned steel bumpers and clamps, large brass plated Monitor lock, **heavy bolt locks**, extra wide iron center band on top and body, tray containing hat box and packing compartment, fall-in top, all covered. With dress tray.

Length	Width	Height	Weight	Price
28 in.	17 in.	19½ in.	40 lbs.	$4.25
30 in.	17¾ in.	20¼ in.	44 lbs.	4.55
32 in.	18½ in.	21 in.	46 lbs.	4.95
34 in.	19¼ in.	22 in.	51 lbs.	5.25
36 in.	20 in.	23 in.	56 lbs.	5.75
38 in.	21 in.	24 in.	60 lbs.	6.25

Angle Steel Bound Trunk, $7.50.

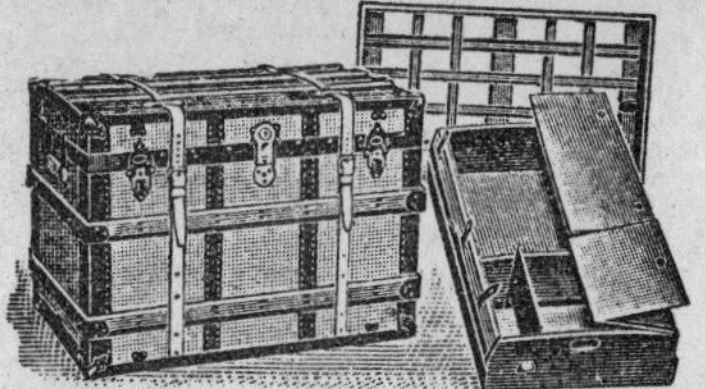

No. 33R5087 One of the best. **Extra large box, slightly rounded top;** made of three-ply veneer wood, heavy painted canvas covered, sole leather straps, four extra hardwood slats on top and two all around body; edges of top and bottom protected with heavy steel binding, heavy steel corner shoes and strip clamps, large tinned buckle bar bolts, strap hinges, heavy hand loops and dowel bolts on ends, large tray, folding lids, sliding partition hat box and dress tray.

Length	Width	Height	Weight	Price
30 in.	19¼ in.	21 in.	60 lbs.	$7.50
32 in.	20 in.	22 in.	62 lbs.	8.00
34 in.	20¼ in.	23 in.	66 lbs.	8.50
36 in.	21¼ in.	24 in.	69 lbs.	9.00
38 in.	22 in.	25 in.	72 lbs.	9.50

Ladies' Dress or Skirt Trunk With Three Dress Trays, All Cloth Lined.

No. 33R5090 **Large, roomy and especially made for ladies' use.** Covered with heavy painted canvas, hardwood slats, all protected with heavy steel clamps, extra heavy corners, bolts and hinges. Heavy sole leather straps, upper tray with sliding partitions, separately covered. About the length of the average skirt. Size, 42 inches outside measurement.

Length	Width	Height	Weight	Price
42 in.	20½ in.	23 in.	80 lbs.	$12.00

Leather Bound, All Riveted, Canvas Covered Trunk for $13.00 to $17.00.

OF STAUNCH CONSTRUCTION.

No. 33R5096 **Strength in every feature.** Covered with heavy canvas, painted, hardwood slats, all protected with heavy brassed clamps, edges bound with leather, heavy sole leather straps. Brass Excelsior lock, tray with hat box and other compartments, separately covered, with folding lids, edge of tray bound with metal binding, dress tray, cloth lined.

Length	Width	Height	Weight	Price
32 in.	19¼ in.	23 in.	58 lbs.	$13.00
34 in.	20¼ in.	24 in.	62 lbs.	14.00
36 in.	21 in.	25 in.	67 lbs.	15.50
38 in.	22 in.	26 in.	75 lbs.	17.00

Our $13.00 Sole Leather Bound Slatless Basswood Trunk.

No. 33R5100 **Slatless Veneer Top Basswood Trunk, sole leather binding and straps, cloth lined,** heavy riveted, large, very light weight and strong, covered with heavy duck, painted, equipped with brassed bumpers, clamps, corner shoes, rollers, extra heavy Excelsior lock, side bolts and heavy hinges, bound with leather all around edges, back and front heavy sole leather straps, high set-up tray; with hat box and side compartment, extra dress tray, cloth finished throughout, a quality seldom found in retail stores.

Length	Width	Height	Weight	Price
32 in.	19 in.	23¾ in.	55 lbs.	$13.00
34 in.	20 in.	24¾ in.	62 lbs.	14.00
36 in.	21 in.	25¾ in.	68 lbs.	15.00
38 in.	22 in.	26¾ in.	73 lbs.	16.00
40 in.	22½ in.	27 in.	78 lbs.	17.00

Wonderful Values in Bureau Trunks.

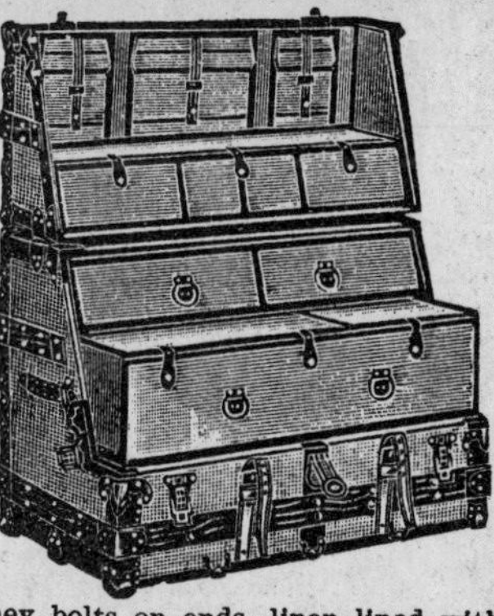

No. 33R5110 **The finest Bureau Trunk made. Steel trimmings, all riveted, Irish linen faced.** Basswood box, canvas covered, olive colored steel binding on edges of top and bottom, trimmed with brass clamps and heavy corner bumpers; all riveted; brass Excelsior lock. Four steel hinges, Hagney bolts on ends, linen lined, with genuine Irish linen facing; all compartments are separately covered and easy of access, and arranged as shown in cut. A veritable traveling chiffonier of great convenience.

Length	Width	Height	Weight	Price
32 in.	20 in.	24 in.	76 lbs.	$16.90
34 in.	20¾ in.	25 in.	82 lbs.	18.25
36 in.	21½ in.	26 in.	88 lbs.	19.60
38 in.	22¼ in.	27 in.	95 lbs.	21.00
40 in.	23 in.	28 in.	102 lbs.	22.50

Our $9.95 Dresser Trunk.

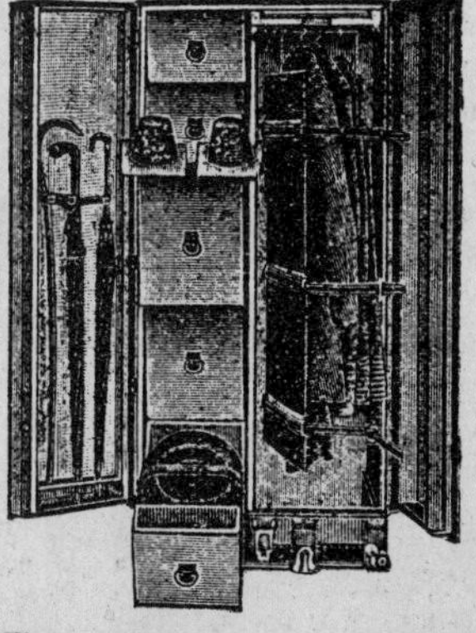

No. 33R5116 **The most durable and cheapest dresser trunk on the market; being well made, will stand rough usage.** Riveted; all space can be utilized, and is accessible at any time; upper part contains three compartments, with three drawers in body. An excellent trunk for skirts and dresses. Covered with heavy painted canvas, hardwood slats on top and around body of trunk; Excelsior lock, heavy steel clamps and corners, patent lever bolts on front and heavy lock bolts on ends. A veritable traveling chiffonier of great convenience.

Length	Width	Height	Weight	Price
32 in.	19¾ in.	22¾ in.	62 lbs.	$ 9.95
34 in.	20¼ in.	23½ in.	69 lbs.	10.75
36 in.	21 in.	24 in.	74 lbs.	11.75
38 in.	22 in.	24½ in.	80 lbs.	12.75

Our New Wardrobe Trunk, $28.00.

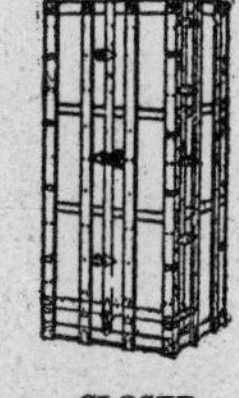

CLOSED.

No. 33R5118 **Something entirely new in wardrobe or dresser trunk style, making one of the most practical trunks of this character on the market.** The trunk is well proportioned, covered with heavy waterproof canvas, painted, edges and center band covered with olive enamel steel binding. We use extra heavy hardwood strips, all protected with brass plated clamps and corner shoes securely riveted. In order to pack the trunk it is placed on end and is made readily accessible by two lids or doors which are well protected with large brass plated bolts and brass Excelsior lock, making it secure while on your journey. Inside arranged with the latest improved coat and skirt hangers, hanging from movable supports so that single garments can be taken from the trunk without disturbing contents; adjustable tapes and clothes frame to keep garments stationary; the trunk is also arranged with numerous drawers on one side for hats, bonnets, shirt waists, underwear, etc. The lid of the trunk has strap loops for carrying parasols and canes. Linen lined throughout. Highest grade workmanship and the best new practical trunk introduced for many years.

Length	Width	Height	Weight	Price
56 in.	26 in.	22 in.	112 lbs.	$28.00

Ladies' Sole Leather Trunk.

No. 33R5120 **Very elegant in style, made of full weight selected leather,** steel ribbed head, new patent roller and clamp combined. Heavy corner clamps, iron frame, heavy dovetailed brass bolts, Excelsior lock, large set-up tray with three pockets in front, separate covered secret parasol case underneath, and linen lined. Separate heavy canvas cover, leather bound edges and capped corners. **This trunk must be seen to be appreciated.** Standard of high grade sole leather ladies' trunk.

Length	Width	Height	Weight	Price
32 in.	19 in.	20½ in.	54 lbs.	$34.00
34 in.	20 in.	21½ in.	58 lbs.	37.00
36 in.	21 in.	22½ in.	62 lbs.	40.00

Gentlemen's Fine Sole Leather Trunk.

No. 33R5126 **Made of heavy leather, copper riveted, strong steel ribs.** Equipped with Excelsior lock, dovetailed side bolts, heavy iron frames, corner clamps and rollers combined, extra good quality sole leather straps and buckles, tray with hat box and other compartments. Separate heavy canvas cover with leather bound edges and capped corners.

Length	Width	Height	Weight	Price
30 in.	17½ in.	19 in.	47 lbs.	$23.00
32 in.	18¾ in.	19¾ in.	50 lbs.	25.50
34 in.	19 in.	20½ in.	53 lbs.	28.00

Canvas Covered Stateroom Trunk.

No. 33R5130 **Iron center band, steel trimmings.** Made to go under berth of any steamship. **This is a very convenient trunk for short journeys.** Japanned iron trimmed; bumpers, clamps, and corner shoes; Monitor lock, side pockets, and setup tray.

Length	Width	Height	Weight	Price
28 in.	17 in.	11½ in.	26 lbs.	$3.50
30 in.	17½ in.	11½ in.	28 lbs.	3.80
32 in.	18¾ in.	11½ in.	31 lbs.	4.10
34 in.	19 in.	11½ in.	34 lbs.	4.40
36 in.	20 in.	11½ in.	37 lbs.	4.80

Special Quality Stateroom Trunk.

No. 33R5136 **Our Special Quality Stateroom or Steamer Trunk.** Covered with heavy canvas, painted; four hardwood slats on top, one on body, with metal tips, all protected with heavy brass clamps and fancy corner bumpers, brass plated Monitor lock and side bolts, fancy metal bound edges and center band, stitched handles, steel hinges, hardwood bottom cleats, protected with two heavy sole leather straps, inside arranged with two compartments separately covered, cloth faced. A reliable trunk.

Length	Width	Height	Weight	Price
32 in.	18¼ in.	11½ in.	34 lbs.	$5.50
34 in.	19 in.	11½ in.	36 lbs.	5.75
36 in.	20 in.	11½ in.	38 lbs.	6.00
38 in.	21 in.	11½ in.	41 lbs.	6.25

Our Highest Grade Steamer Trunk at $9.25 and Upwards.

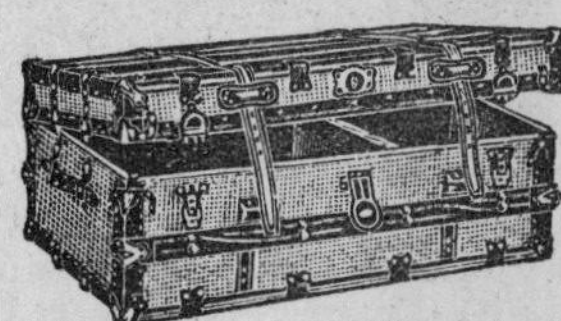

No. 33R5138 **Regular Steamer Trunk, made to go under the berth of any steamship,** canvas covered, edges bound with mottled rawhide, front and back of top and bottom protected with brass plated steel binding, sole leather straps, hardwood slats on top and bottom. All protected with brass plated clamps and corners. Combination dowel bolt and handle, loop, tray with compartments; separately covered movable hat box in body, cloth lined, **Excelsior lock,** corners, hinges, bolt and lock riveted.

Length	Width	Height	Weight	Price
32 in.	18¼ in.	11½ in.	39 lbs.	$ 9.25
34 in.	19 in.	11½ in.	41 lbs.	9.75
36 in.	20 in.	11½ in.	44 lbs.	10.25
38 in.	21 in.	11½ in.	46 lbs.	10.75

GIVE CATALOGUE NUMBER IN FULL WHEN YOU WRITE YOUR ORDER

Imitation Leather Trunks from 55 Cents to $2.10.

No. 33R5150 Imitation Leather; extra well made; iron bands, valance, hinges, hasp lock, long hardwood slats.

Length	Width	Height	Weight	Price
24 in.	14 in.	14 in.	12 lbs.	$0.55
26 in.	14½ in.	14½ in.	14 lbs.	.72
28 in.	15 in.	15 in.	16 lbs.	.85
30 in.	15¾ in.	15¾ in.	18 lbs.	1.00
32 in.	16½ in.	16½ in.	20 lbs.	1.18
34 in.	17½ in.	17½ in.	23 lbs.	1.33
36 in.	18½ in.	18½ in.	25 lbs.	1.60
38 in.	19½ in.	19½ in.	27 lbs.	1.80
40 in.	20½ in.	20½ in.	29 lbs.	2.10

IN ORDERING TRAVELING BAGS GIVE CATALOGUE NUMBER, SIZE AND PRICE.

Rubber Pelissier.

No. 33R5156 Pebble and Alligator finish, japanned frame, flat steel key, lock and tinned iron trimmings, strong iron handle.

Black.

14-inch.....35c 20-inch.....50c
16-inch.....40c 22-inch.....55c
18-inch.....45c 24-inch.....60c

Brown Pebble Finish Rubber Gladstone.

No. 33R5160 Brown Pebble Finish Rubber Gladstone. A splendid imitation of the high grade leather Gladstone. Made on an extra heavy frame, with strong lock, catches and straps, etc., and lined with linen. Will give excellent satisfaction.

Length, 14 inches. Weight, 3 pounds. Price..$0.80
Length, 16 inches. Weight, 3½ pounds. Price. .85
Length, 18 inches. Weight, 4 pounds. Price. .95
Length, 20 inches. Weight, 4½ pounds. Price. 1.10
Length, 22 inches. Weight, 5 pounds. Price. 1.20
Length, 24 inches. Weight, 5½ pounds. Price. 1.30

Alligator Leather Gladstone, $1.50.

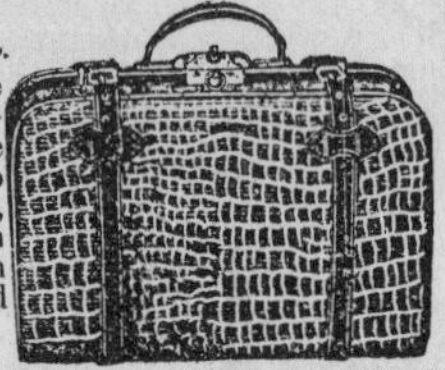

No. 33R5172 Alligator Leather Gladstone. Made of selected goatskin leather, heavy double flange frame, nickel double hasp lock and side catches, heavy English handle, with ring attachment, cloth lined, portfolio. Tan and chestnut.

Length, 14 inches. Weight, 4 pounds. Price..$1.50
Length, 16 inches. Weight, 4¼ pounds. Price. 1.70
Length, 18 inches. Weight, 4½ pounds. Price. 1.90
Length, 20 inches. Weight, 4½ pounds. Price. 2.10
Length, 22 inches. Weight, 5 pounds. Price. 2.30
Length, 24 inches. Weight, 5½ pounds. Price. 2.50

Fine Grain Leather Bag at $2.75 to $4.30

No. 33R5184 One of the most serviceable and best grain leather bags in the market, made of fine selected, full stock grain leather, heavy grain leather straps all around, double flange frame, nickel plated long flat key lock with handle combined, heavy nickel side catches, linen lined. **Brown.**

Length, 14 inches. Weight, 4½ pounds. Price..$2.75
Length, 16 inches. Weight, 5 pounds. Price. 3.05
Length, 18 inches. Weight, 5½ pounds. Price. 3.30
Length, 20 inches. Weight, 6 pounds. Price. 3.60
Length, 22 inches. Weight, 6½ pounds. Price. 3.90
Length, 24 inches. Weight, 7½ pounds. Price. 4.30

Grain Leather Gladstone for $4.50.

No. 33R5188 Grain Leather Gladstone. This bag is made from the very best full stock grain leather, double strong frame, nickel corner protectors, large plate lock, with combination handle, heavy English snap catches, grain leather straps, **full leather lined. Brown.**

Length, 16 inches. Weight, 5½ pounds. Price.$4.50
Length, 18 inches. Weight, 6 pounds. Price. 5.00
Length, 20 inches. Weight, 6½ pounds. Price. 5.50
Length, 22 inches. Weight, 7½ pounds. Price. 6.00

Fitted Grain Leather Gladstone.

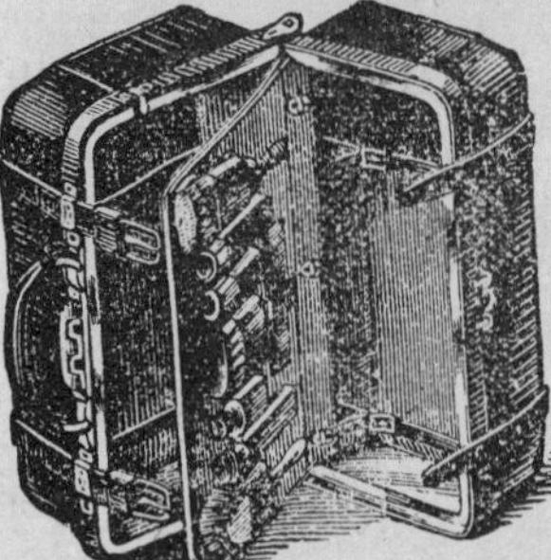

No. 33R5192 Made of best selected grain leather, heavy covered frame with bottom shoes, brass trimmed, English snap catches, partition with pocket on one side and a full set of toilet fittings on the other; leather lined. Dark brown or olive.

Length, 18 inch. Weight, 7½ pounds. Price.$10.50
Length, 20 inch. Weight, 8 pounds. Price. 11.50
Length, 22 inch. Weight, 9 pounds. Price. 12.50

New London Suit Bags.

No. 33R5196 Grain Leather Suit Bag in the New London style. Made from the best selected full stock grain leather, sides and gussets stiffened, heavy frame with bottom shoes, catches and first class lock; leather lined, partition with pocket. Olive and dark brown.

Length, 18 inches. Weight, 6 pounds. Price.$7.00
Length, 20 inches. Weight, 7¼ pounds. Price. 7.50
Length, 22 inches. Weight, 8½ pounds. Price. 8.00
Length, 24 inches. Weight, 9½ pounds. Price. 8.50

London Suit Bags.

No. 33R5200 English Suit Bag, made from finest high grade stock, steel frame, bottom shoes, improved top catches, heavy fine roll handle. Partition with shirt fold on one side and portfolio on the other, leather lined. Distinguished bags of this character are a class of themselves. Extra heavy hand sewed covered frame with latest style trimmings. Colors, olive or dark brown.

Length	Weight	Price	Length	Weight	Price
18 in.	6½ lbs.	$10.75	22 in.	9 lbs.	$12.25
20 in.	7½ lbs.	11.50			

Alligator Cloth Club Bags.

No. 33R5204 Alligator Cloth Club Bag, alligator finish, top push lock, cloth lined, chestnut color.

Length	Weight	Price	Length	Weight	Price
10 in.	1 lb.	35c	14 in.	2 lbs.	55c
11 in.	1¼ lbs.	40c	15 in.	2¼ lbs.	60c
12 in.	1½ lbs.	45c	16 in.	2½ lbs.	65c
13 in.	1¾ lbs.	50c			

Fine Pebble Leather Brown Club Sack at 60c to $1.20, According to Size.

No. 33R5208 Club Sac, selected pebble leather, large plated lock and side catches, leather handles with rings, cloth lined.

Brown.

Length	Weight	Price	Length	Weight	Price
10 in.	1 lb.	60c	14 in.	2 lbs.	$1.00
11 in.	1¼ lbs.	70c	15 in.	2¼ lbs.	1.10
12 in.	1½ lbs.	80c	16 in.	2½ lbs.	1.20
13 in.	1¾ lbs.	90c			

SEND 5 CENTS FOR
CLOTH SAMPLE BOOK, No. 52R,
CONTAINING EVERYTHING IN
MEN'S CUSTOM TAILORING GOODS
AT LOWEST PRICES

Our 75-Cent Alligator Finished Club Bag.

No. 33R5220 Embossed Alligator Finished Club Bag. Made from the best selected stock. Japanned frames, high cut shape, brass plated trimmings, **leatherette lining.** Color, olive only.

A convenient shape, handy to carry, and will hold more than you think.

Length	Weight	Price	Length	Weight	Price
10 in.	1¼ lbs.	$0.75	14 in.	2¼ lbs.	$1.15
11 in.	1½ lbs.	.85	15 in.	2½ lbs.	1.25
12 in.	1¾ lbs.	.95	16 in.	2¾ lbs.	1.35
13 in.	2 lbs.	1.05	17 in.	3 lbs.	1.45

Deep Shape Club Bag, $1.65.

No. 33R5228 One of the best, at a low price. Good genuine grain leather club bag, durably made, heavy japanned frame to match, plated trimmings, cloth lined. Color, brown.

Length	Weight	Price	Length	Weight	Price
10 in.	1½ lbs.	$1.65	14 in.	2½ lbs.	$2.00
11 in.	1¾ lbs.	1.70	15 in.	2¾ lbs.	2.10
12 in.	2 lbs.	1.80	16 in.	3 lbs.	2.20
13 in.	2¼ lbs.	1.90	17 in.	3¼ lbs.	2.30

Leather Lined Deep Club Bag, $3.00.

No. 33R5232 This style of bag is now very popular. They will hold much more and **are but** a few ounces **heavier** than the smaller **shapes.** Full grain leather, **heavy** brass trimmings, **leather** covered steel frame, **full leather lined.** You buy it from us at the wholesale price. Color, **brown.**

Length	Weight	Price	Length	Weight	Price
12 in.	2¼ lbs.	$3.00	16 in.	3¼ lbs.	$4.00
13 in.	2½ lbs.	3.25	17 in.	3½ lbs.	4.25
14 in.	2¾ lbs.	3.50	18 in.	3¾ lbs.	4.50
15 in.	3 lbs.	3.75			

Alligator Club Bag, $4.00.

No. 33R5234 You have perhaps read of such things in irresponsible advertisements, but we doubt if you ever bought a genuine Alligator Bag at this low figure, **$4.00. Leather lined,** hinge stay. Very handsome bag for ladies' use. Amber. **Your highest expectations realized.**

Length	Weight	Price	Length	Weight	Price
12 in.	2¼ lbs.	$4.00	15 in.	3¼ lbs.	$4.90
13 in.	2¾ lbs.	4.30	16 in.	3½ lbs.	5.20
14 in.	3 lbs.	4.60			

A Good Cabinet Bag for $2.50.

No. 33R5236 Cabinet Style Bag, made of genuine grain leather, japanned frame, brass lock and trimmings, heavy handle, cloth lining and inside pockets. This style of bag is roomy and will hold more than club bag styles. Our price is about the cost to your home merchant. Color, brown.

Length	Weight	Price	Length	Weight	Price
12 in.	3¼ lbs.	$2.50	15 in.	4¼ lbs.	$3.25
13 in.	3¾ lbs.	2.75	16 in.	4½ lbs.	3.50
14 in.	4 lbs.	3.00	17 in.	5 lbs.	3.75

Selected Leather Cabinet Bag, $3.50.

No. 33R5238 Best Selected Leather Cabinet Bag, leather covered frame, large brass lock with combination ring handle and top catches, full leather lined, inside pockets. Color, dark brown.

Length	Weight	Price
12 inches	3¾ lbs.	$3.50
13 inches	4 lbs.	3.75
14 inches	4¼ lbs.	4.00
15 inches	4½ lbs.	4.25
16 inches	4¾ lbs.	4.50
17 inches	5 lbs.	4.75
18 inches	5½ lbs.	5.75

GIVE CATALOGUE NUMBER IN FULL WHEN YOU WRITE YOUR ORDER

English Cabinet Bags, $7.50 to $9.00.

No. 33R5244 English Cabinet Bag, hand stitched, steel frame, made of select grain leather, frame leather covered, hand sewed, English sunk lock; new style of spring catches; heavy roll handle on rings, full leather lined pockets on ends. A superbly finished, stylish, durable, first class bag. Colors, olive and dark brown.

Length	Weight	Price	Length	Weight	Price
15 in.	5 lbs.	$7.50	17 in.	6 lbs.	$8.50
16 in.	5½ lbs.	8.00	18 in.	6½ lbs.	9.00

Fine Oxford Bags for $5.90 to $7.10.

No. 33R5254 Full Shape English Oxford Bag, made up in fine grain leather, heavy riveted frame, leather covered, fine brass spring catches and lock, double handles, leather lined, with pocket on sides. Colors, olive or dark brown.

Length	Weight	Price
14 inches	4 lbs.	$5.90
15 inches	4¼ lbs.	6.20
16 inches	4½ lbs.	6.50
17 inches	4¾ lbs.	6.80
18 inches	5 lbs.	7.10

Our High Grade, Leather Lined, English Traveling Bags at $7.50 to $9.00.

No. 33R5260 English Bag, extra high and wide, heavy steel frame, leather covered, hand stitched, best lock and trimmings, English automatic catches and inside stay to hold bag open. English sunk lock. A bag especially adapted for gentlemen's use. Leather lined, with three inside pockets. Color, dark brown.

Length	Weight	Price	Length	Weight	Price
14 in.	4¼ lbs.	$7.50	16 in.	4¾ lbs.	$8.50
15 in.	4½ lbs.	8.00	17 in.	5 lbs.	9.00

DRESS SUIT CASES.

No. 33R5300 Dress Suit Case. Plain canvas, telescope style, heavy collar, leather straps and handles.

Length	Weight	
20 inch	4½ lbs.	$0.90
22 inch	5 lbs.	1.00
24 inch	6 lbs.	1.10

Imitation Leather Suit Case, $1.20.

No. 33R5302 Olive enameled cloth, imitation of leather. Solid leather corners and handle. Brassed lock and bolts. Cloth lined. A good, durable case.

Length	Weight	Price	Length	Weight	Price
20 in.	4½ lbs.	$1.20	24 in.	6 lbs.	$1.50
22 in.	5 lbs.	1.35	26 in.	7 lbs.	1.65

Our Special Dress Suit Case, $2.25.

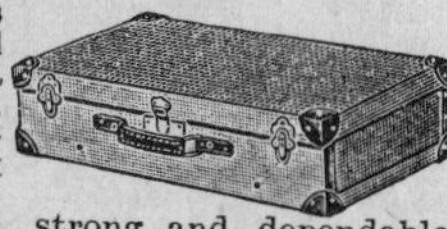

No. 33R5304 Dress Suit Case. Strong wood frame, covered with extra heavy enameled cloth, looks like leather. Leather corners, spring lock and brassed bolts. Inside straps. Very handsome, strong and dependable.
Length, 22 inch. Weight, 5 pounds. Price....$2.25
Length, 24 inch. Weight, 6 pounds. Price.... 2.50

Alligator Keratol Suit Case.

No. 33R5308 The covering used on this case will wear better than the ordinary grade of leather used in suit cases. Heavy sole leather corners and handles, brass plated bolts and lock. Cloth lined and inside straps. Keratol is a new fiber, looks like leather, and is equal to it for wear.
Length, 22 inch. Weight, 6 pounds. Price....$2.85
Length, 24 inch. Weight, 7 pounds. Price.... 3.10
Length, 26 inch. Weight, 8 pounds. Price... 3.35

FINE LEATHER DRESS SUIT CASES.

THERE IS NOTHING MORE CONVENIENT

for a gentleman than a dress suit case. It keeps the clothing in perfect condition, is convenient to pack and unpack, and is easily carried.

Leather Dress Suit Case, $4.10.

No. 33R5312 A most excellent value. Heavy dark brown or olive colored leather. Steel frame, brass spring lock. Cloth lined, with inside straps. Convenient to handle and exceedingly rich in appearance.
Length, 22 inch. Weight, 6 pounds. Price....$4.10
Length, 24 inch. Weight, 7 pounds. Price.... 4.45
Length, 26 inch. Weight, 8 pounds. Price... 4.90

Leather Suit Case, $5.75.

No. 33R5316 Made of heavy fine cowhide case leather. Steel frame, brass plated lock and catches, heavy round handle, duck lined, with strap in body and shirt fold in top. For a sightly and durable case this case cannot be excelled.
Length, 22 inch. Weight, 6½ pounds. Price..$5.75
Length, 24 inch. Weight, 7⅛ pounds. Price.. 6.25
Length, 26 inch. Weight, 8½ pounds. Price.. 6.75

Three-Pocket Suit Case $6.95.

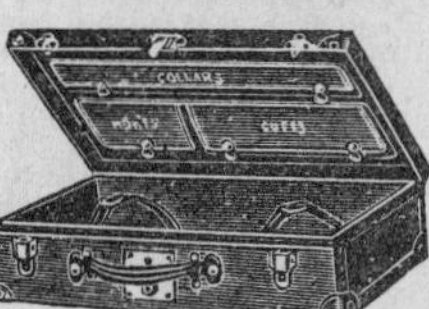

No. 33R5318 A New Suit Case, with three pockets in the lid suitable for holding collars, cuffs and handkerchiefs, etc., where easy accessible. Made from select cowhide case leather, heavy leather corners, newest brass catches and lock and steel frame. Holland linen pockets and lining and inside straps. A most practical case for convenience and durability. Color, brown.
Length, 22 inch. Weight, 6 pounds. Price....$6.95
Length, 24 inch. Weight, 7 pounds. Price.... 7.50

Fine Leather Lined Suit Case, $7.25.

No. 33R5320 Fine Olive or Brown Leather Suit Case, heavy leather covered steel frame, fine rolled handle, etc., fine brass lock and catches. Heavy brass rivets, stitched ends, double corners, leather lined body and shirt fold with fine quilted satin top. If you want the best and finest this is the case you are looking for.
Length, 22 inch. Weight, 6½ pounds. Price..$7 25
Length, 24 inch. Weight, 7½ pounds. Price.. 8.00
Length, 26 inch. Weight, 8½ pounds. Price.. 8.75

English Bellows Case.

No. 33R5322 Up to Date English Bellows Case, made of hand boarded dark brown cowhide leather. Heavy corners, with single accordion bellows side, reinforced with two heavy straps. Heavy roll handle attached to sole leather loops, securely riveted. We use two of the latest style brass combination locks and bolts on this case. Selected Holland linen lined, with movable partition in the center, also portfolio on one side. This is an exceptionally fine case and cannot help but satisfy those looking for a case of this character.
Length, 22 inch. Weight, 9¼ pounds. Price.$12.50
Length, 24 inch. Weight, 10¼ pounds. Price. 13.25
Length, 26 inch. Weight, 11¼ pounds. Price. 14.00

OUR ONLY TERMS ARE

Cash with the Order.

We guarantee safe delivery of the goods, and entire satisfaction or refund your money.

OUR REPUTATION IS ESTABLISHED EVERYWHERE.

READ WHAT OUR BANKERS SAY on pages 12 and 13 of **our large catalogue. You need not hesitate to send us full cash with the order, for we stand ready to immediately return your money for anything not entirely satisfactory, and your money is as safe in our hands as with the largest national bank.**

CANVAS TELESCOPES.

35-Cent to 85-Cent Telescopes.

No. 33R5344 Riveted leather corners and bottom tips, heavy stitched handle; three straps on large sizes, heavy grain leather strap.

Length	Width	Weight	Height	Extended	Price
14 in.	7 in.	1⅛ lbs.	6 in.	12 in.	35c
16 in.	8 in.	2 lbs.	6½ in.	13 in.	45c
18 in.	9 in.	2½ lbs.	7 in.	14 in.	55c
20 in.	10 in.	3 lbs.	7½ in.	15 in.	65c
22 in.	11 in.	3½ lbs.	8 in.	16 in.	75c
24 in.	12 in.	4 lbs.	8½ in.	17 in.	85c

No. 33R5345 Holland linen case, same as above. Dimensions and weight the same.

16-inch, each	60c	22-inch, each	$0.90
18-inch, each	70c	24-inch, each	1.05
20-inch, each	80c	26-inch, each	1.20

Full Leather Bound Canvas Telescope.

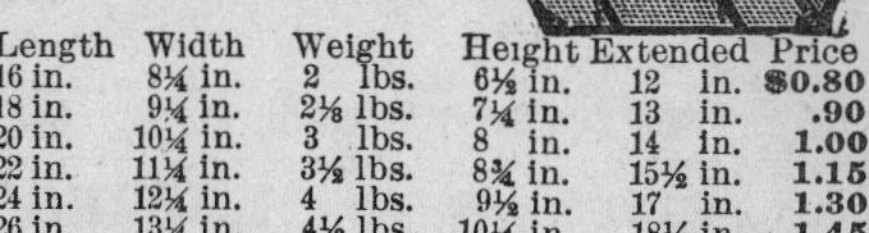

No. 33R5346 Heavy Canvas Leather Bound Telescope, hand sewed, heavy leather tips, grain leather straps all around.

Length	Width	Weight	Height	Extended	Price
16 in.	8¼ in.	2 lbs.	6½ in.	12 in.	$0.80
18 in.	9¼ in.	2⅛ lbs.	7¼ in.	13 in.	.90
20 in.	10¼ in.	3 lbs.	8 in.	14 in.	1.00
22 in.	11¼ in.	3½ lbs.	8¾ in.	15½ in.	1.15
24 in.	12¼ in.	4 lbs.	9½ in.	17 in.	1.30
26 in.	13¼ in.	4½ lbs.	10¼ in.	18½ in.	1.45

With patent lock strap, 50 cents extra.

No. 33R5350 Extra heavy canvas; edges bound all around with wide leather, very heavy corner protectors; two and three sole leather straps; best handle made.

Length	Width	Weight	Height	Extended	Price
16 in.	9¼ in.	4 lbs.	7 in.	13 in.	$2.00
18 in.	10¼ in.	4½ lbs.	7¾ in.	14 in.	2.25
20 in.	11¼ in.	5 lbs.	8½ in.	15 in.	2.50
22 in.	12¼ in.	5½ lbs.	9¼ in.	16 in.	2.75
24 in.	13¼ in.	6½ lbs.	10 in.	17 in.	3.00
26 in.	14¼ in.	8 lbs.	10¾ in.	18 in.	3.40

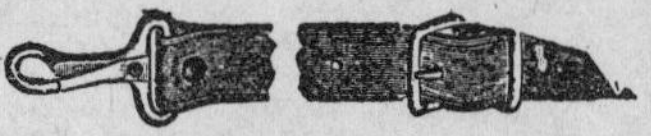

Shoulder or Sling Straps.

No. 33R5354 Solid Grain Leather Shoulder or Sling Straps, for use on club bags, ¾ inch wide with spring snaps. Price, each....18c
No. 33R5354½ Grain leather ½ inch wide spring snaps. Price, each....10c

Shawl Straps.

No. 33R5355 Good, Solid Shawl Straps, with heavy stitched handles and rings, with two straps.
Price, each, 3 feet....25c
Price, each, 4 feet....30c

Trunk or Bag Name Tag.

No. 33R5357 Trunk or Bag Name Tag of brown grain leather. Strap and buckle fastener.
Price, single panel, each....$0.08
Single panel, per dozen.... .96
Price, double panel, each.... .11
Double panel, per dozen.... 1.32
If by mail, postage extra, each, 2 cents.

Package Handles.

No. 33R5359 Handle your packages with a handle. Something new in the way of a handle for satchels. Very convenient for carrying packages. Made exactly the same as a leather handle on a valise with a snap on each end. Price, each....$0.20
Price, per dozen.... 2.40

Trunk Straps.

No. 33R5360 Very Heavy Strong Grain Leather Trunk Strap, made in the following lengths:
1¼ inches wide...... 7 ft., 40c; 8 ft., 50c; 9 ft., 60c
1½ inches wide...... 7 ft., 50c; 8 ft., 60c; 9 ft., 70c

Fiber Lunch Boxes.

No. 33R5361 This is something entirely new, and it is certainly the very best thing in the lunch box line ever produced. These boxes are made from a specially prepared fiber, leather color and thoroughly waterproof. Three sizes, as follows:
Size, 4½x6½x4 inches deep. Price....15c
Size, 5½x7½x4 inches deep. Price....20c
Size, 6 x9x4¾ inches deep. Price....25c

BOOT AND SHOE DEPARTMENT.

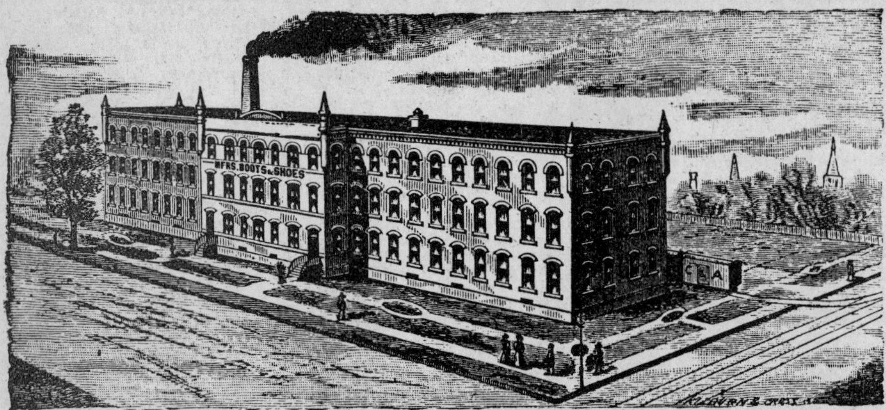

OUR NEW 20th CENTURY SHOE PLANT. Devoted exclusively to the manufacture of fine shoes.

OUR FACTORY was taxed to its fullest capacity last season, and to meet the increased demand for home made shoes we have added more new machinery, thus placing us in a position to make the very best at the lowest prices.

ONE ORDER OF 35,000 PAIRS is now being made for the United States Government, thus demonstrating the high quality of the goods produced. If you appreciate value, the latest styles, foot fitting and shape retaining shoes, send us your order. Tell your friends about us.

HOW TO ORDER. Be sure to state size and width you want.

IT IS CHEAPER to send ladies' shoes, slippers, etc., by mail than by express. The postage rate is 1 cent for each ounce. When you wish goods sent by mail, always send cash in full and include enough extra to pay postage, and we will ship by mail, postpaid. Be sure to enclose enough extra to pay postage. If you send too much, we will promptly return what is over. Weight is given under each description that you may know the amount necessary to send. THE WIDTHS RUN: AA, extremely narrow; A, extra narrow; B, very narrow; C, narrow; D, medium; E, wide; EE, very wide.

WE RECOMMEND good shoes; poor shoes cost less, but do not wear so well, hence the best shoes are cheapest in the end.

LADIES' KID DRESS BOOT, HAND TURNED, $2.75.

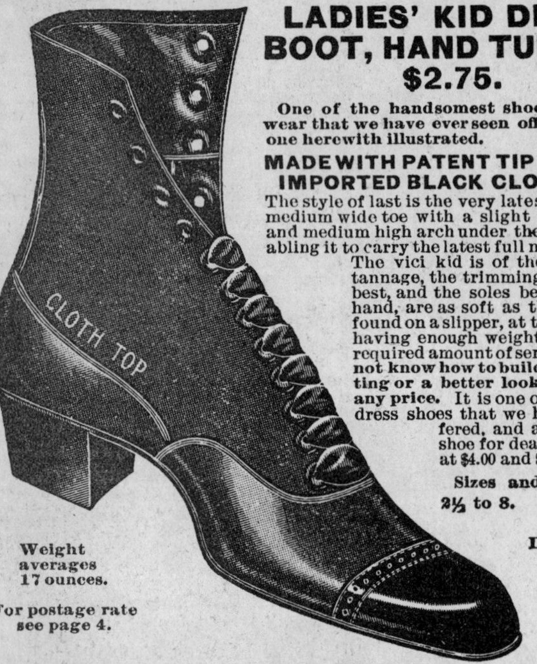

One of the handsomest shoes for dress wear that we have ever seen offered is the one herewith illustrated.

MADE WITH PATENT TIP AND FINE IMPORTED BLACK CLOTH TOP.

The style of last is the very latest, having a medium wide toe with a slight knob effect, and medium high arch under the instep, enabling it to carry the latest full military heel. The vici kid is of the very finest tannage, the trimmings are of the best, and the soles being sewn by hand, are as soft as those usually found on a slipper, at the same time having enough weight to give the required amount of service. **We do not know how to build a better fitting or a better looking shoe at any price.** It is one of the neatest dress shoes that we have ever offered, and a splendid shoe for dealers to retail at $4.00 and $5.00.

Sizes and half sizes, 2½ to 8.

Widths, C, D, E and EE.

Weight averages 17 ounces.

For postage rate see page 4.

No. 15R1 Price, per pair, **$2.75**

LADIES' BEST ENAMEL LACE, $2.85

HAND SEWED DOUBLE STITCHED WELT.

The leather which goes into the vamp of this shoe is known as White Brothers' box enamel, and is the best made of its kind. This leather has a bright finish similar to the patent leather, can be easily polished by simply applying patent leather paste, is very soft and pliable and much more durable than any bright leather heretofore put on the market. **The style of last is the very latest mannish** (not extreme), and is one of the most perfect fitting lasts we have ever seen.

The latest style, shown in the exclusive shops of the large Eastern cities, is the fancy perforated vamp, and we show in this shoe the handsomest effect yet produced. It is exclusive, and therefore will not be found in the ordinary cheap shoes.

This shoe is fitted with the fashionable military heel, fancy perforated tip to match the vamp, a very fine quality of genuine box kid top, custom outside back stay, and fine black silk inside top facing.

This shoe being a genuine double stitched hand sewed welt, and being made of the very best material throughout, is equal to anything ever placed upon the market at any price.

Sizes and half sizes, 2½ to 8.

Widths, A, B, C, D, E and EE.

Weight averages, 32 ounces.

No. 15R3 Price, per pair, **$2.85**

LADIES' DOUBLE STITCHED WELT, $2.85.

A handsomer pattern than the one herewith illustrated we have never seen. It is one of the very latest effects, and at the same time is to be found only in the exclusive custom shops of the largest cities.

We aim to be first in presenting these exclusive effects in shoe building, and we take pleasure in showing this boot to our patrons at the unheard of price of **$2.85** per pair. Made from the very finest kid, over a medium broad toe last, with patent tip. **Carries the full 12-8 Cuban heel, and the genuine Buckeye calf top. The soles are strictly hand welted;** and being stitched double all the way around, produces not only a handsome effect, but a practically indestructible shoe.

NOTHING BETTER CAN BE BOUGHT FOR STREET WEAR AT ANY PRICE.

Those who have not worn a double welt shoe should try a pair, as a shoe with this weight sole is much more comfortable than any other it is possible to secure.

Sizes and half sizes, 2½ to 8. Widths, C, D, E and EE.

Weight averages 25 ounces.

For postage rate see page 4.

No. 15R6 Price, per pair, **$2.85**

WOMEN'S STYLISH PATENT KID WELT, $2.75.

The patent vici upper stock used in this shoe although not guaranteed has been proven to be **the very best patent leather ever used in the manufacture of fine shoes, is as soft as** kid and will not burn the feet as does other patent leathers. The top is **select vici kid, smooth and soft, sewn and finished in silk.** The lace stay is beautifully stitched with a single row of stitching in an artistic design; a perfect shaped shoe as this may well be called, it has a medium round toe with straight tip and the latest heel. This is strictly an up to date shoe for up to date people, a shoe sold by fashionable city merchants for select trade at $5.00 and $6.00 per pair. It requires no polish whatever, as a little rubbing with a soft cloth is sufficient to keep it like new. We name a price, unequaled by any factory or dealer on earth.

Sizes and half sizes, 2½ to 8. Widths, B, C, D, E and EE.

No. 15R13 Per pair **$2.75**

LADIES' LEATHER LINED SHOE, $2.15.

CUSHION SOLE. LACE.

The shoe herewith illustrated has always been one of our most popular styles inasmuch as it is lined throughout with genuine kid, thereby producing a shoe which fits the foot just like a silk stocking. To make this shoe even more popular we have this season at an additional expense, built it with especially prepared **cushion felt inner sole**, making a very comfortable shoe and one which is much more flexible than we have ever been able to offer at this price.

THE STOCK is a soft, plump vici kid, the style of last is a medium coin toe (not extreme), while the heel is a medium military style. The outer sole is cut from the very best of stock, and in fact nothing has been omitted which goes to make up a thoroughly first class shoe.

Weight averages 30 ounces.

Sizes and half sizes, 2½ to 8.

Widths, C, D, E and EE.

For postage rate see page 4.

No. 15R21 Price, per pair, $2.15

LADIES' VELOURS CALF, $2.95.

GOODYEAR WELT. EXTRA HIGH CUT.

One of the most popular shoes shown in large city stores this season is the extra high cut Storm or Skating Boot, illustration of which is herewith shown. This boot is made from a very fine selection of Pfeister & Vogels' velours calf, which is of medium weight, in appearance resembling vici kid and at the same time has the wearing qualities of the box calf or cordovan.

WE BUILD THIS SHOE WITH EXTRA HEAVY DOUBLE SOLES,

fit it with the latest style, large eyelets, long back stay extending from heel to top of shoe, and the very newest Cuban heel. **This shoe is made in our No. 1 Factory**, and, therefore, carries the very best workmanship it is possible to secure.

IT IS A GENUINE GOODYEAR WELT,

insuring a smooth inner sole, no tacks or thread to hurt the foot, and guaranteed to be equal in style, fit and wearing qualities to any shoe sold elsewhere for half as much again.

This boot is especially desirable for mountain wear, skating, and, as stated above is the fad for street wear in all the large cities.

WARRANTED.

Weight averages 32 ounces.

Sizes and half sizes, 2½ to 8.

Widths, C, D, E and EE.

For postage rate see page 4.

No. 15R22 Price, per pair, $2.95

LADIES' CLOTH TOP PATENT VICI, LOUIS XV HEEL. $2.95.

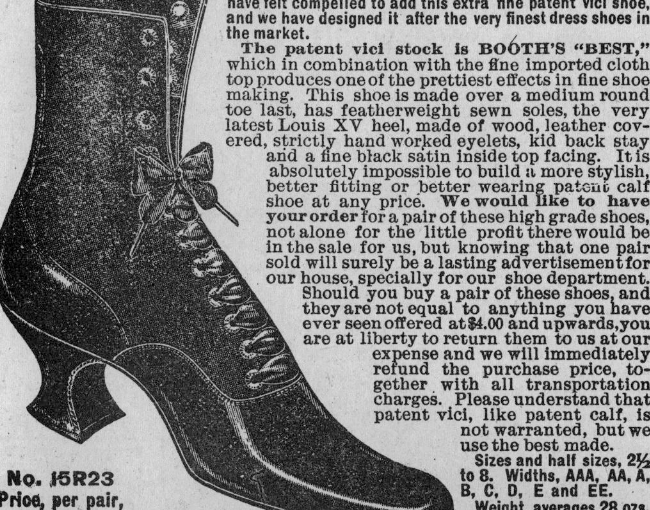

The Louis XV heel is growing in popularity so fast that we have felt compelled to add this extra fine patent vici shoe, and we have designed it after the very finest dress shoes in the market.

The patent vici stock is BOOTH'S "BEST," which in combination with the fine imported cloth top produces one of the prettiest effects in fine shoe making. This shoe is made over a medium round toe last, has featherweight sewn soles, the very latest Louis XV heel, made of wood, leather covered, strictly hand worked eyelets, kid back stay and a fine black satin inside top facing. It is absolutely impossible to build a more stylish, better fitting or better wearing patent calf shoe at any price. **We would like to have your order** for a pair of these high grade shoes, not alone for the little profit there would be in the sale for us, but knowing that one pair sold will surely be a lasting advertisement for our house, specially for our shoe department. Should you buy a pair of these shoes, and they are not equal to anything you have ever seen offered at $4.00 and upwards, you are at liberty to return them to us at our expense and we will immediately refund the purchase price, together with all transportation charges. Please understand that patent vici, like patent calf, is not warranted, but we use the best made.

Sizes and half sizes, 2½ to 8. Widths, AAA, AA, A, B, C, D, E and EE.

Weight averages 28 ozs.

For postage rate, see page 4.

No. 15R23 Price, per pair, $2.95

LATEST STYLE ELASTIC INSTEP LACE, $2.38.

AS ADVERTISED BY US IN THE NEWSPAPERS.

We formerly quoted the Julia Marlowe Lace Boot, with elastic instep, at $2.65, but the manufacturer refused to sell it to us longer unless we would charge our customers at least $3.00 for same. We refused to raise the price to our patrons, hence were compelled to build the shoe herewith illustrated. We have in this shoe combined all of the style usually found in the **$4.00, $5.00 and $6.00 grades**, and at the same time produced a shoe with **elastic goring fitted to the instep in such a manner as to produce a perfectly elastic foot fitting boot. It far excels anything ever attempted in this style of shoe. The most perfect, self adjusting, elastic instep shoe made. This boot will conform to the shape of the foot whether the instep be high or low.**

MADE FROM THE VERY FINEST SELECTION OF VICI KID STOCK

Over our handsome Cincinnati last with plain stitched tip toe.

The style of heel foxing is the very latest and we fit the shoe with a medium concave heel. Nothing enters into the construction of this shoe but strictly high grade materials, including fast color eyelets, black satin inside top band, and to produce the most comfortable shoe possible, we have made it with a medium weight sole, sewn and very flexible. To those wishing a strictly high grade shoe, one combining, style, fit and elastic instep, we recommend it.

THE PRICE is so much lower than all other elastic instep shoes, that there is positively no competition for this shoe, and please understand that there is no better shoe of its kind made at any price.

Sizes and half sizes, 2½ to 8.

Widths, C, D, E and EE.

Weight averages 26 ounces.

For postage rate see page 4.

No. 15R29 Price, per pair..............$2.38

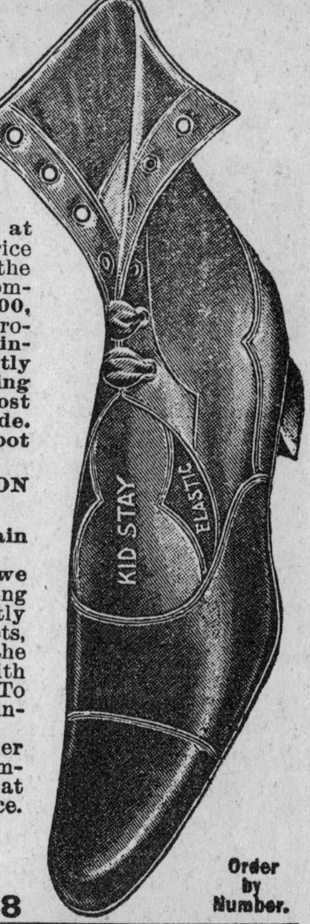

Order by Number.

LADIES' BLACK CLOTH TOP LACE, $1.98.

We change the design of our shoes, keeping up with the very latest styles each season. One of the very latest ones in **Ladies' Dress Shoes is the shoe that we show in the accompanying illustration. This shoe is made of the finest velvet finish vici kid stock**, which is the most dressy and durable stock that can be put in ladies shoes. **The black cloth top is the finest of material**, and we guarantee it to give satisfactory wear and at the same time retain its color and not turn brown. We have perforated the lace stay, vamp and fancy heel foxing in the very latest manner. **You will observe that the lace stay and back stay protect the cloth top**, thus keeping the skirts from coming in contact with the topping. **The sole on this shoe is very flexible, imitation hand turn. We warrant this shoe to give entire satisfaction as to wear and fit,** and assure you that it is one of the most desirable shoes for general wear and service that you would be able to secure at any price.

Sizes and half sizes, 1 to 9.

Widths, C, D, E and EE.

Weight averages 29 ounces.

For postage rate see page 4.

No. 15R37 Price, per pair, $1.98

THE GOODYEAR WELT COLONIAL DAME, $1.95.

One of the latest productions in ladies' fine footwear, suitable for street or party use, is the Colonial Dame, illustration of which we herewith present. This handsome shoe is now all the rage in the large cities and at prices ranging from **$4.00 to $7.00 per pair.** We have in this shoe duplicated the style of one of our foremost custom boot makers and those purchasing the shoe illustrated at **$1.95** may rest assured that they will get just as much style, just as much wear and a fit fully equal to anything ever offered under **$4.00 per pair. The stock from which this shoe is made is Reilley's best patent leather**, the style of toe is medium in width, the last has a slight arch in the instep making it fit snugly, and different from most Colonial shoes, we have fitted a strap under the lap over the instep which holds the shoe in place equally as well as the ordinary lace boot.

Sizes and half sizes 2½ to 8.

Widths, C, D, E and EE.

For postage rate see page 4.

Weight averages 21 ounces.

No. 15R39 Price, per pair, $1.95

Ladies' Sandal Oxford, $1.25.

This Oxford is made of fine vici kid, with open work lace stays, thereby exposing the stocking just enough to produce one of the daintiest effects yet seen in a summer Oxford. The soles are cut from the very best of leather, genuine hand turned, and flexible.

Sizes and half sizes, 2½ to 8.

Widths, D, E and EE.

Weight averages 15 ounces.

For postage rate see page 4.

No. 15R234 Price, per pair............$1.25

Ladies' Patent Leather Oxford, $1.45.

Made from good patent leather stock, medium wide sole, with extension edges, and full perforated vamp, tip and heel foxing. Sizes and half sizes, 2½ to 8.

Widths, D, E and EE.

Weight averages 16 ounces.

For postage rate see page 4.

No. 15R236 Price, per pair............$1.45

Ladies' Vici Mannish Oxford, $1.35

We make this Oxford from fine, soft vici kid stock, which is very durable, and at the same time easy to the foot. The style of last is the medium mannish shape. Sizes and half sizes, 2½ to 8.

Widths, D, E and EE.

Weight averages 16 ounces.

For postage rate see page 4.

No. 15R241 Price, per pair............$1.35

Ladies' Patent Leather Dress Oxfords, $1.25.

A Ladies' All Patent Leather Strictly Hand Turned Oxford, with extra high wood heel. The shoe is of extraordinary value, made with genuine hand turned sole, white kid sock and quarter lining; and it is intended only for dress wear and is not heavy enough to stand rough usage. Sizes and half sizes, 2½ to 8. Widths, D, E and EE.

Weight averages 16 oz.

For postage rate see page 4.

No. 15R244 Price, per pair............$1.25

Ladies' Kid Strap Sandals, $0.95.

Ladies' Kid Strap Sandals hand turned, flexible soles, satin strap at the instep, with metal ornament. Sizes, 2½ to 8. Full widths.

Weight averages about 18 ounces.

For postage rate see page 4.

No. 15R248 Price, per pair............$0.95

Ladies' Serge Buskin Slippers.

Ladies' Serge Buskin Slippers, turn soles, low, flat heels, fine quality. Sizes, 3 to 8. Full width.

Weight averages 18 ounces. For postage rate see page 4.

No. 15R254 Price, per pair............$0.65

Women's Patent Leather Sandals, $0.95.

The extreme popularity of patent leather, especially for dress occasions, has led us to add this sandal. This is not by any means the low grade shoe our price would indicate, but carries just as good leather, as much style and fit, as many sold at double our price. Made with patent leather vamp, kid quarter, high heel and with bow strap Strictly hand turned.

Sizes, 2½ to 8.

Widths, C, D, E and EE.

Weight averages 18 ounces.

For postage rate see page 4.

No. 15R255 Price, per pair............$0.95

Ladies' White Kid Sandals, $1.00.

Ladies' White Kid Strap Sandals, made from a good selection of stock, medium narrow toe, strictly hand turned soles, and fancy bow over instep. Nothing like it ever shown for the money.

Sizes, 2½ to 8.

Widths, D, E and EE.

Weight averages 18 ounces.

For postage rates, see page 4.

No. 15R257 Per pair............$1.00

Ladies' Common Sense Oxfords.

Ladies' Common Sense Oxford, made from good dongola kid stock, with wide, plain toe, low broad heel, and flexible sewed sole.

Sizes, 2½ to 8.

Full widths.

This shoe is very neat and comfortable for house wear.

Weight averages 25 ounces. For postage rate see page 4.

No. 15R258 Price, per pair............$0.95

Ladies' Serge Congress, $0.85.

This Shoe is made from a good quality of serge, leather soles and counters, common sense last, and is not only a very cool and comfortable shoe, but will give excellent service. Sizes, 3 to 8. Width, EE only. Weight averages 28 ounces.

For postage rate see page 4.

No. 15R262 Price, per pair............$0.85

Ladies' Black Kid Oxfords, $1.00.

Made from good, plump dongola kid, medium weight, opera toe, with imitation kid tip, all solid and a very sightly shoe. In this shoe we give extra good value. Sizes, 2½ to 8. Full widths.

Weight averages 22 ounces.

For postage rate see page 4.

No. 15R271 Black. Price, per pair............$1.00

Ladies' Grain Slippers, $0.65

Ladies' Grain Slippers. Damp proof, sewed strong and durable, for out or in-door wear. All solid. Sizes, 3 to 8. Full widths. Weight averages 22 ounces. For postage rate see page 4.

No. 15R272 Price, per pair............$0.65

Ladies' Carpet Slippers, $0.24.

Made from Brussels Carp leather sole and heel, good quality, bound and stayed. Sizes, 3 to 8. Weight averages 18 ounces. For postage rate see page 4.

No. 15R274 Price, per pair...$0.24

Ladies' Red Crocus Slippers, $0.29.

Made from red lamb stock with soft sole, and equal in every way to those ordinarily sold at from $0.50 to $0.65 per pair.

Sizes, 3 to 8. No half sizes.

For postage rate see page 4.

Weight averages 9 ozs.

No. 15R277 Our special price, per pair.....$0.29

WOMEN'S PATENT LEATHER COLONIAL, $1.35.

THE LATEST FAD IN A LADIES' DRESS SHOE IS THE COLONIAL PATTERN,

which we herewith illustrate. This shoe is now all the rage in the large cities, many stores now showing the Colonial shoe almost exclusively in their window displays. We quote on another page a shoe of this pattern made with Goodyear welt sole, which is especially adapted to general and street wear. The shoe herewith illustrated, however,

IS MORE ESPECIALLY ADAPTED TO HOUSE AND PARTY WEAR.

This shoe is made with an entirely new pattern, there being a strap underneath the flap over the instep, which holds the shoe in place perfectly.

This Shoe is Made of Good Patent Leather Stock,

fitted with medium light wood heel, genuine hand turned sole, white kid quarter lined. Equal to anything we have ever seen offered at $2.00 per pair. Those wishing the very latest production in a ladies' low shoe will do well to order this one.

Sizes and half sizes, 2½ to 8.

Widths, D, E and EE.

Weight averages 17 ounces.

For postage rate see page 4.

No. 15R285 Price, per pair............$1.35

Misses' and Child's Fancy Kid Lace, $1.08 and $0.98.

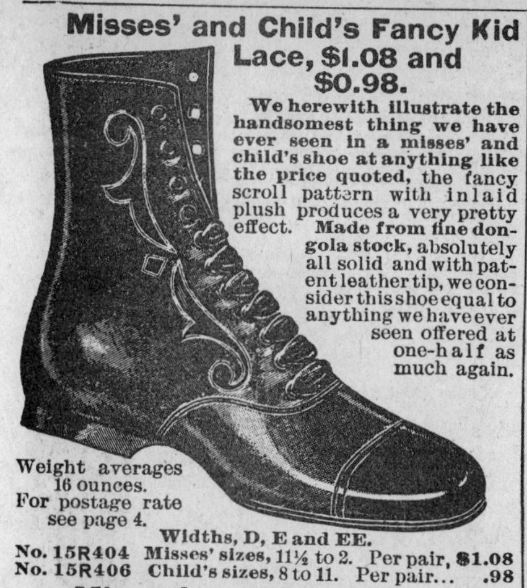

We herewith illustrate the handsomest thing we have ever seen in a misses' and child's shoe at anything like the price quoted, the fancy scroll pattern with inlaid plush produces a very pretty effect. Made from fine dongola stock, absolutely all solid and with patent leather tip, we consider this shoe equal to anything we have ever seen offered at one-half as much again.

Weight averages 16 ounces. For postage rate see page 4.

Widths, D, E and EE.

No. 15R404 Misses' sizes, 11½ to 2. Per pair, **$1.08**
No. 15R406 Child's sizes, 8 to 11. Per pair... **.98**

Misses' and Children's Grain School Shoes, $1.00 and $0.90.

This shoe is made from a genuine kangaroo grain stock over the popular Salem last, with spring heel, medium plump soles and thoroughly reliable inner sole and counters. We realize that a school shoe is subjected to extremely hard wear at times and we have endeavored to build a shoe at this low price which would meet the requirements and give satisfaction.

Widths, full.

Weight averages 28 ounces. For postage rate see page 4.

No. 15R418 Misses' sizes, 11½, 12, 12½, 13, 13½, 1, 1½ and 2. Price, per pair... **$1.00**
No. 15R420 Children's sizes, 8, 8½, 9, 9½, 10, 10½ and 11. Price, per pair... **$0.90**

Misses' and Children's Patent Leather Shoes $0.98 and $0.88.

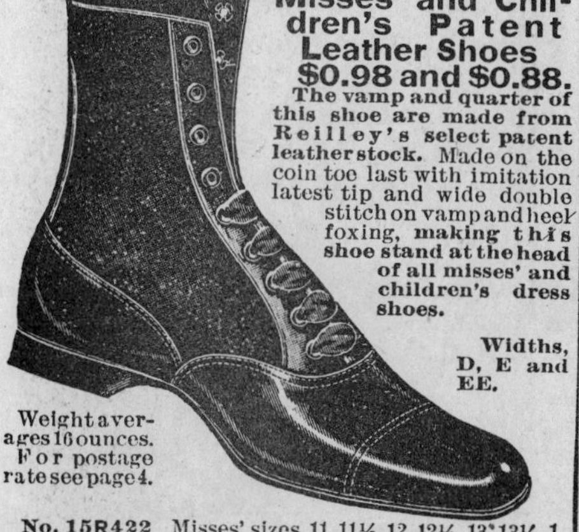

The vamp and quarter of this shoe are made from Reilley's select patent leather stock. Made on the coin toe last with imitation latest tip and wide double stitch on vamp and heel foxing, **making this shoe stand at the head of all misses' and children's dress shoes.**

Widths, D, E and EE.

Weight averages 16 ounces. For postage rate see page 4.

No. 15R422 Misses' sizes, 11, 11½, 12, 12½, 13, 13½, 1, 1½ and 2. Price, per pair... **$0.98**
No. 15R424 Children's sizes, 8, 8½, 9, 9½, 10, 10½ and 11. Price, per pair... **$0.88**

Misses' and Child's Strap Sandals, $0.98 and $0.88.

We herewith illustrate our Misses' and Child's **Dongala Strap Sandal**, made over a medium last, with fancy patent leather tip; suitable for street or dress wear. The shoe, being McKay sewed, has a flexible sole and one which will give a great deal of service.

Weight averages 14 ounces. For postage rate see page 4.

No. 15R460 Misses' sizes, 11½ to 2. Per pair... **$0.98**
No. 15R462 Children's sizes, 8 to 11. Per pair.. **.88**

Little Gents' Box Calf Lace, $1.15.

To furnish a little gents' genuine box calf shoe, which would combine style, fit and wear, at the unheard of price of $1.15, has been a problem, but we are glad to have solved it. **This little gents' shoe is made from a good grade of genuine box calf, over a medium coin toe last, with tip.** It is fitted with medium heavy soles, and so built as to insure good service. **This shoe is made for children, and can be furnished only in sizes quoted below. Not intended for men.**

Sizes and half sizes, 9 to 13½.

Weight averages 24 ounces. For postage rate see page 4.

No. 15R481 Price, per pair... **$1.15**

Shoes for Little Men—Just Like Papa's, $1.00.

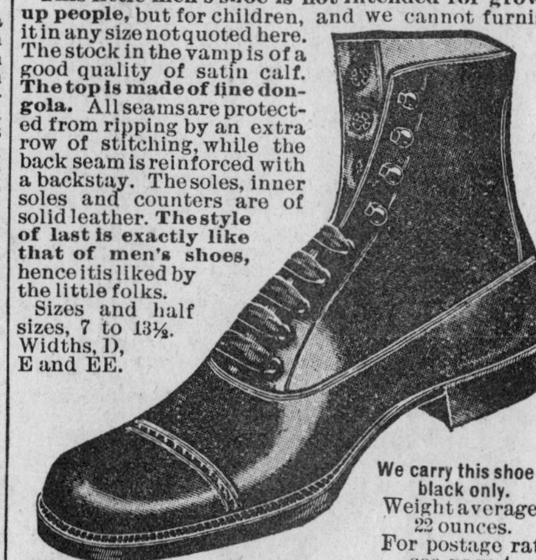

This little men's shoe is not intended for grown up people, but for children, and we cannot furnish it in any size not quoted here. The stock in the vamp is of a good quality of satin calf. **The top is made of fine dongola.** All seams are protected from ripping by an extra row of stitching, while the back seam is reinforced with a backstay. The soles, inner soles and counters are of solid leather. **The style of last is exactly like that of men's shoes,** hence it is liked by the little folks. Sizes and half sizes, 7 to 13½. Widths, D, E and EE.

We carry this shoe in black only. Weight averages 22 ounces. For postage rate see page 4.

No. 15R484 Price, per pair... **$1.00**

Little Gents' Patent Leather Shoes, $1.20.

A Strictly Dress Shoe for little men. The sole, inner sole and counter are made of solid leather, vamp of patent leather, the upper is of bright dongola, the toe and style of the shoe is of the very latest pattern. **This shoe may be polished simply by a little rubbing with a woolen cloth. It always looks neat and dressy. Sizes and half sizes, 9 to 13½. Widths, D, E and EE.**

Weight averages 24 ounces.

For postage rate see page 4

No. 15R486 Price, per pair... **$1.20**

Misses' and Children's Patent Leather Sandals.

The most popular Sandal this season. Made with the latest plain coin toe, flexible sole, vamp of fine patent leather, quarter of bright finish kid, very nicely bound and lined, and ornamented with bow and fancy buckle. Average weight about 10 ounces. For postage rate see page 4. Widths, C, D, E and EE.

No. 15R518 Sizes, 11½, 12, 12½, 13, 13½, 1, 1½ and 2. Price, per pair... **$1.00**
No. 15R520 Sizes, 8, 8½, 9, 9½, 10, 10½ and 11. Price, per pair... **.90**
No. 15R522 Sizes, 5, 5½, 6, 6½, 7 and 7½. Price, per pair... **.80**

Children's Vesting Top Lace, Red, Tan or Black, $0.90.

We herewith illustrate one of our very latest patterns in a child's scroll vesting lace shoe. We make this shoe from a very fine selection of genuine chrome vici kid in bright red, medium chocolate or black, with fancy imported vesting top to match. The soles are strictly hand turned, the shoe is stitched with silk thread and in fact nothing has been omitted to make it strictly high grade in every particular. Sizes, 4, 4½, 5, 5½, 6, 6½, 7, 7½ and 8. Widths, C, D and EE. **Average weight, 12 ounces. For postage rate see page 4.**

No. 15R543 Bright Red. Vesting to match. Per pair... **$0.90**
No. 15R545 Chocolate. Vesting to match. Per pair... **.90**
No. 15R547 Black. Vesting to match. Per pair... **.90**

Children's Patent Leather Leader.

The vamp of this shoe is made of Reilley's selected patent leather stock. Uppers are fine bright finish dongola. Made over a very stylish and dressy coin toe last.

Sizes, 5 to 8 only. Widths, D, E and EE. Average weight about 13 ounces.

No. 15R553

Price, per pair

$0.79

Child's Paris Kid Lace Shoes, Black or Tan, $0.75.

Child's Very Fine Paris Kid Lace Shoes, made over new coin last, with fancy patent leather tip. The shoe is strictly hand turned, flexible soles, has the new heel foxing and for a fine dress shoe is very desirable.

Sizes, 4, 4½, 5, 5½, 6, 6½, 7, 7½ and 8. **Widths, D, E and EE. Weight, about 13 ozs.**

No. 15R555 Black. Per pair... **$0.75**
No. 15R557 Tan, Kid Tip. Per pair... **.75**

Child's Fat Baby Shoes at $0.75.

Child's Fat Baby Shoes, made from fine quality of kid skin, spring heel, patent leather tip and cut with extra wide soles and full ankles. The soles are hand turn, flexible, and it has worked buttonholes. Sizes, 4 to 8.

Width, EE only. Weight, about 13 oz.

No. 15R558 Price, per pair... **$0.75**

Child's Kid Button Shoes, $0.55.

Child's Kid Button, made from soft, glove like stock, spring heel, flexible soles, patent leather tip, **all solid and durable.** Sizes, 5, 5½, 6, 6½, 7, 7½ and 8.

Weight, about 13 ounces.

For postage rate see page 4.

No. 15R568

Price, per pair,

$0.55

Child's Kangaroo Calf Button Shoe.

Child's Kangaroo Calf Button Shoe, cut from good, plump stock; very soft, flexible soles, and **a serviceable, stylish shoe for little money.** Sizes, 5, 6, 7 and 8, no half sizes. **Weight, about 15 ounces.**

No. 15R570

Price, per pair,

$0.75

Infants' Tan or Red Kid Lace, $0.49.

This Infants' Shoe is made from Fine Chrome Lamb, the latest dark chocolate color, or the fashionable red, hand sewed, medium coin toe, with tip, and no heel. Sizes, 2, 2½, 3, 3½, 4, 4½ and 5. Weight, about 10 ounces.

No. 15R574 Tan color, per pair.......... $0.49
No. 15R575 Red, per pair.......... .49

Infants' Shoes, $0.60

Infants' Glazed Dongola Kid Button, very good stock, latest heel foxing, turned soles, no heel, medium toe, with tip and neat tassel at top. A very dressy shoe. Sizes, 2, 2½, 3, 3½, 4, 4½ and 5. Weight, about 10 ounces.

For postage rate see page 4.

No. 15R582 Price, per pair....... $0.60

Infants' Kid Button Shoes, $0.45.

Infants' Kid Button, turned sole, patent leather tip, no heel; a neat and well made shoe. Sizes, 2, 2½, 3, 3½, 4, 4½ and 5. Weight, about 10 ounces. For postage rate see page 4.

No. 15R584 Per pair.... $0.45

Infants' Princess, $0.29.

Made from the finest kid; soft sole, handsomely trimmed with ribbon and has ribbon tie at ankle, which holds it in position. Sizes, 1 to 4. In single carton. Weight about 6 ounces.

No. 15R587 Wine color. Per pair.......... $0.29

Infants' Soft Sole Tan, $0.17.

This shoe is made from a choice selection of genuine kid, fancy stitched, has kid sole. Cut very full so you will have no trouble to put them on. Color, tan. Sizes, 1, 2, 3 and 4.

No. 15R588 Price, per pair.......... $0.17

Infants' Patent Leather Lace, $0.45.

We herewith illustrate our infants' patent leather soft sole lace shoe. Made with fancy red vesting top and patent scroll heel foxing. Sizes, 1, 2, 3 and 4. Full widths only. Weight, 7 ounces.

No. 15R593 Price, per pair.......... $0.45

Infants' Genuine Vici Kid Lace, $0.49.

Infants' Vici Kid Lace, no heel, patent tip, very dressy and serviceable. Sizes, 2, 2½, 3, 3½, 4, 4½ and 5.

Weight, 10 ounces.

For postage rate see page 4.

No. 15R594 Price, per pair...... $0.49

Infants' Soft Sole Lace, $0.16.

Infants' Red Lamb Lace, made with soft sole; equal to those usually sold at double our price. Sizes, 1, 2, 3 and 4. No half sizes. Weight, 6 ounces.

No. 15R597 Price, per pair.......... $0.16

Infants' Moccasins, $0.09.

Infants' Lamb Moccasins, tan color only. We do not exchange these moccasins, as the profit will not admit of it. Sizes 1, 2, 3 and 4. Weight 3 ounces.

No. 15R598 Price, pair.......... $0.09

The Motorman's Best, $2.00.

HIGH CUT.

Men's Best Beaver Felt Shoe, extra high cut, lace, medium toe, solid comfort felt insole. This shoe has a very fine and soft leather foxing, long tip toe, and while it is fully as warm as the all felt shoe, it is more desirable on account of the leather sole and foxing which enables the wearer to go in the snow the same as if he wore a full leather shoe. Sizes, 6 to 12. No half sizes.

Weight about 50 ounces.

For postage rate see page 4.

No. 15R600 Price, per pair.......... $2.00

Ladies' High Cut Felt Lace, $1.25.

A SURE CURE FOR RHEUMATISM

Made of excellent quality of fine serviceable felt. CUT EXTRA HIGH. The sole is solid oak leather. Low, broad, comfortable heel, extra felt lining, and heavy felt cushion insole. Backstay and inside trimmings of leather. We are offering it at a price much below any wholesaler in the country.

WIDTHS, D, E AND EE. SIZES, 2½ TO 8.

Average weight about 27 ounces. For postage rate see page 4.

No. 15R606 Price.......... $1.25

Men's All Felt Shoes, $1.50.

This Shoe is made from the very best beaver felt throughout. The sole is made from one heavy piece of felt, and is very much superior to the two piece soles which are put on the cheaper grades of felt shoes. We guarantee this shoe not only to be warm and comfortable, but to be the best ever offered for the money. Sizes, 6 to 12. No half sizes.

Weight, about 40 ounces.

For postage rate see page 4.

No. 15R610 Price, per pair.......... $1.50

Men's and Women's Hand Sewed Felt Slippers, $0.85 and $0.75.

These slippers we have made especially for our own trade, and we believe them to be superior to anything ever placed upon the market. Made from a fine beaver felt, all wool, with a felt sole sewed on by hand and a leather outer sole made from harness leather. The outer sole is sewed on by hand, making it very flexible and easy. Don't be surprised if they last three winters. We positively guarantee them to outwear any felt slipper ever made.

Order by Number. Weight, about 25 ounces.

For postage rate see page 4.

No. 15R612 Men's sizes, 6 to 12. Per pair..... $0.85
No. 15R614 Ladies' sizes, 3 to 8. Per pair.... .75

Ladies' Felt Button, $1.50.

Made from fine beaver felt and with felt sole from ¼ to ⅜ inch thick. This shoe will wear longer than any felt shoe we have ever seen. If you wear felt shoes do not pass this one, as we warrant it to give entire satisfaction. It is very light, is comfortable and fits as neatly as any dongola shoe. Sizes and half sizes, 2½ to 8.

Weight, about 28 ounces.

For postage rate see page 4.

No. 15R616 Price, per pair.......... $1.50

Ladies' Felt Lace, Leather Sole.

Ladies' Lace Shoe, made from good quality felt, plush trimmed, felt lined throughout and with very flexible leather sole of fair quality. This shoe will give good wear and you will find it very warm and easy. Sizes, 3 to 8. No half sizes. Weight averages 27 ounces.

For postage rate see page 4.

No. 15R620 Price, per pair.......... $0.60

Women's Dongola Foxed Felt Nullifiers, $1.05.

GENUINE HAND TURNED SOLE.

Made of good quality felt. Vamp of dongola, solid leather soles and heels. Fur trimmed and lined throughout with felt. Widths, D, E and EE. Sizes, 2½ to 8. Weight averages about 28 ounces.

For postage rate see page 4.

No. 15R621 Per pair...... $1.05

Women's, Misses' and Children's Felt Nullifiers, $0.85, $0.75 and $0.65.

This line of nullifiers is made of the very best 36-ounce toilet felt, seamless cut, trimmed with fine black fur and black banded vamp. The shoe is made with the very best oak soles which, being sewed on by an entirely new process, are very flexible and easy for the feet.

Weight averages 27 ounces per pair.

For postage rate see page 4.

No. 15R623 Ladies' sizes, 2½ to 8. Widths, D, E and EE. Price, per pair.......... $0.85
No. 15R625 Misses' sizes, 11½ to 2. No heels. Price, per pair.......... .75
No. 15R626 Child's sizes, 8 to 11. No heels. Price, per pair.......... .65

Misses' and Children's Fine Felt Lace, $1.00 and $0.90.

This shoe is made of the most serviceable felt that can be obtained. Vamp and heel foxing are a good grade of dongola. Made over a nobby coin toe last, which gives it the appearance of a fine dress shoe with a cloth top. The sole is sewed by the McKay process. The shoe is lined with felt; has a felt insole. Widths, D, E and EE.

For postage rate see page 4.

No. 15R641 Misses' sizes, 13 to 2. Price..... $1.00
No. 15R643 Children's sizes, 9 to 12½. Price, .90

Infants' Red Felt Lace, $0.65 and $0.55.

Infants' Fine Beaver Red Felt Lace is made up in the very best manner possible, and equal to any infant's felt shoe ever placed upon the market. This shoe is made with an extra felt cushion insole. We carry this shoe in sizes 5 to 8, with a very slight half spring heel, while the smaller sizes 2 to 5 are made with no heel. Average weight about 10 ounces.

No. 15R645 Sizes 5 to 8, with spring heel. Price, $0.65

Sizes, 3 to 5, no heel.

No. 15R646 Price, per pair..........$0.55

For postage rate see page 4.

Ladies' Fine Felt Lace, $1.25.

No. 15R649 This shoe, like the one preceding, is made from a very fine felt, and foxed with a first class dongola kid. You will observe from the illustration that it has a nice kid tip, and being made over the new coin last, looks fully as well as the high priced cloth top shoes. Those who require a felt shoe and at the same time prefer a dressy and good fitting boot will find this one just what they are looking for.

Sizes and half sizes, 2½ to 8. Widths, D, E and EE.

For postage rate see page 4.

Order by Number.

Weight averages 27 ounces.

No. 15R649 Price, per pair..........$1.25

Ladies' Kid Foxed Lace, $1.20.

No. 15R653 Ladies' Fine Felt Lace Shoe, made over a broad toe last, felt lined, and foxed with a fine dongola kid. A shoe which is extremely comfortable, and at the same time will give splendid service.

Sizes, 2½ to 8.

Weight averages 30 ounces.

For postage rate see page 4.

Order by Number.

No. 15R653 Price, per pair..........$1.20

Ladies' Fine Felt Nullifier, $0.69.

No. 15R655 Made of toilet felt, with hand turn leather sole, also leather heel. This shoe is trimmed with a very fine soft fur, flannel lined, and being cut high in front and behind protects the ankles from the cold air; is very soft, light and comfortable and will give good service.

For postage rate see page 4.

Weight averages 27 ounces.

No. 15R655 Price, per pair..........$0.69

Ladies' Plush Bound Felt Slippers, $0.50.

This Slipper is made from a fair quality of felt, is felt lined throughout, has felt inner sole and is made with a genuine hand turned sole. It is a shoe built to meet competition, and, while we can recommend it for a fair and reasonable amount of service, it is not in any way equal to our higher grade slipper quoted above.

Weight averages 18 ounces.

See page 4 for postage rate.

Sizes, 3 to 8. Widths full.

No. 15R657 Price, per pair..........$0.50

MEN'S SPORTING SHOES AT UNHEARD OF PRICES.

TO PLAY GOOD BALL, TO RUN A GOOD RACE, TO PLAY GOOD FOOTBALL, OR TO COMFORTABLY RIDE A BICYCLE, ONE MUST HAVE SHOES ESPECIALLY DESIGNED FOR THE PARTICULAR SPORT INDULGED IN.

OUR PRICES ON SPORTING SHOES ARE LOWER THAN ANY WHOLESALE DEALER ON EARTH.

We earnestly solicit an honest comparison of prices. DEALERS MAY PURCHASE THESE SHOES from us without our name appearing on them at prices quoted. If not cheaper than can be obtained elsewhere we will cheerfully pay transportation charges both ways.

Men's Professional Running Shoes, $1.95.

No. 15R660 This Regulation Running Shoe is made from a strictly first quality of kangaroo calfskin, genuine hand sewed, oak soles, and fitted with six hand forged steel spikes. Dealers, knowing this price to be lower than that which they are paying, may get from one pair to one hundred at this price. Sizes and half sizes, 5 to 10. Widths, C, D, E and EE. Weight averages, packed, 20 ounces.

No. 15R660 Price, per pair..........$1.95

Men's Kangaroo Calf Bicycle Shoe, $1.55.

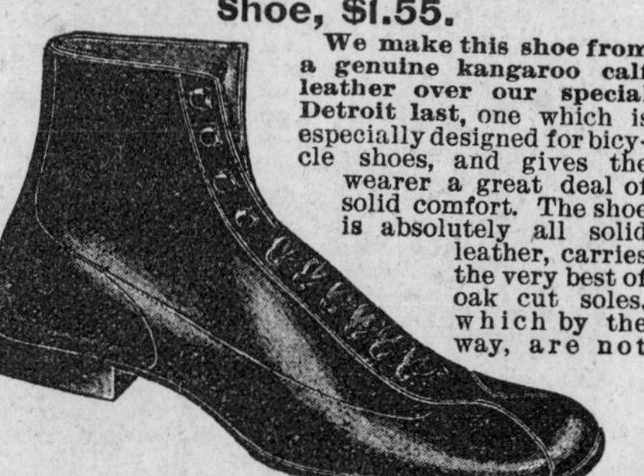

We make this shoe from a genuine kangaroo calf leather over our special Detroit last, one which is especially designed for bicycle shoes, and gives the wearer a great deal of solid comfort. The shoe is absolutely all solid leather, carries the very best of oak cut soles, which by the way, are not ordinarily found on bicycle shoes, and in fact is made strictly on honor. Sizes and half sizes, 5 to 11. Widths full. Weight averages 35 ounces.

No. 15R663 Price, per pair..........$1.55

Men's College Football Shoes, $2.65.

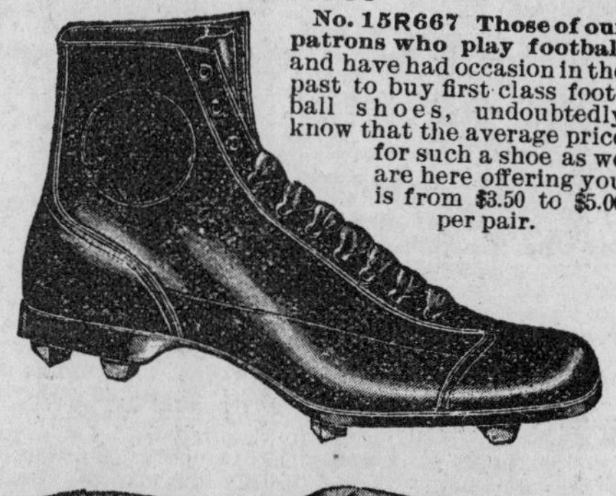

No. 15R667 Those of our patrons who play football and have had occasion in the past to buy first class football shoes, undoubtedly know that the average price for such a shoe as we are here offering you is from $3.50 to $5.00 per pair.

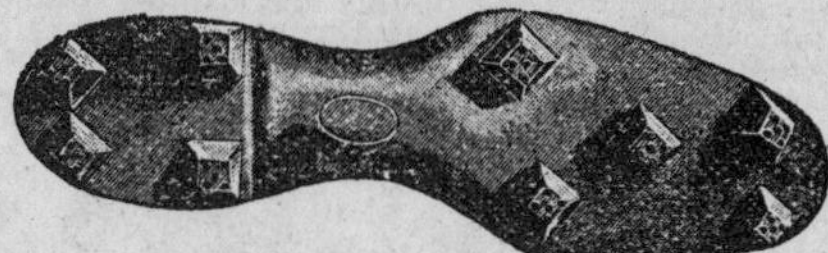

We make this shoe from a fine selection of kangaroo calf over the famous Princeton last, especially designed for football shoes, and fit it with the very best quality of Princeton cleats. Sizes and half sizes, 6 to 11. Full widths only. Weight averages 38 ounces.

No. 15R667 Price, per pair..........$2.65

SHODDY SHOES ARE NOT SOLD BY US. GOOD SHOES MAKE FRIENDS, AND WE DO WANT FRIENDS.

Men's and Boys' Canvas Baseball Shoes, $1.00 and $0.90.

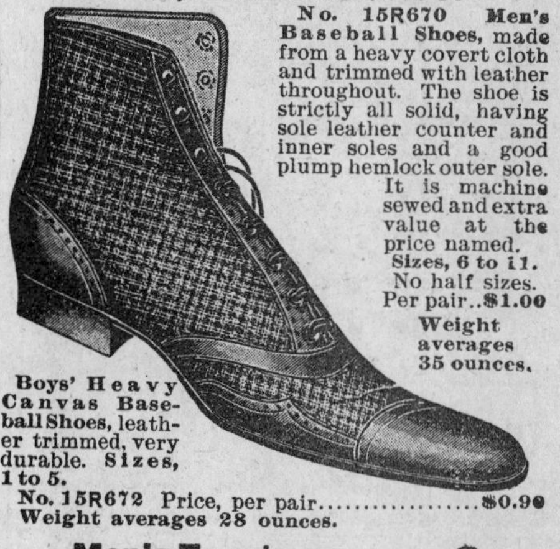

No. 15R670 Men's Baseball Shoes, made from a heavy covert cloth and trimmed with leather throughout. The shoe is strictly all solid, having sole leather counter and inner soles and a good plump hemlock outer sole. It is machine sewed and extra value at the price named. Sizes, 6 to 11. No half sizes. Per pair..$1.00

Weight averages 35 ounces.

Boys' Heavy Canvas Baseball Shoes, leather trimmed, very durable. Sizes, 1 to 5.

No. 15R672 Price, per pair..........$0.90

Weight averages 28 ounces.

Men's Tennis or Outing Oxfords, $0.40

Weight averages 20 ounces.

No. 15R680 This Oxford is made from a good quality of covert cloth, corrugated rubber sole. Sizes, 6 to 11; no half sizes. Price, per pair..........$0.40

Men's Tennis or Outing Shoes.

No. 15R690 This shoe is made from a very good quality of covert cloth, brown kid, lace stays and trimmings; corrugated rubber sole sewed on with waxed thread.

Pair..........$0.50

No. 15R691 Boys' sizes, 1 to 5. Per pair, $0.50

Sizes, 6 to 11; no half sizes. Weight averages 28 ounces.

Men's Baseball Shoes, $2.20.

No. 15R696 Those baseball players who have had occasion to buy these shoes know that the lowest possible price that has ever been offered on such a shoe is $3.00 per pair and that the best price possible last season was $3.50 per pair. Retail dealers who have bought shoes of a similar grade from leading wholesale houses know that the very best price ever quoted on such a shoe is from $2.35 to $2.65 per pair.

For postage rate see page 4.

To play good ball you must have regulation baseball shoes. At this price every club can afford to have them. Made from a good selection of kangaroo calf stock; bottoms made from the very best of oak sole leather, and fitted with genuine league toe and heel plates. Sizes and half sizes, 6 to 11. Full widths only. Weight averages 28 ounces.

No. 15R696 Price, per pair..........$2.20

MEN'S PATENT VICI LACE, $2.85.

YOU WILL UNDOUBTEDLY see patent kid shoes quoted at from $3.50 to $6.00 per pair, but, unlike most concerns, we do not desire to take advantage of this new leather to enlarge our profits. We prefer to furnish this new shoe to you on our **one small profit plan** and still further demonstrate to our patrons our honesty of purpose and our desire to furnish you strictly high grade goods at prices as low or lower than those paid by your local dealer. **We make this** shoe over the popular Brocton last with fancy perforated tips, genuine Goodyear welt soles and good quality kangaroo top. **THE SOLE LEATHER** is of the very best white oak stock. We fit the shoe with fast color eyelets, silk thread, white kid inside top facing and in fact have omitted nothing to make it as dressy as possible.

No. 15R768
Order by Number.

SIZES AND HALF SIZES, 6 TO 11. WIDTHS, B, C, D, E AND EE.
Weight averages about 35 ounces, according to size. For postage rate see page 4.
Price, per pair **$2.85**

MEN'S HEAVY WEIGHT BLUCHER, $2.95

THE ILLUSTRATION herewith shown fairly represents our latest production in a men's strictly high grade blucher shoe, built with full extension edge, and the latest large nickel hooks and eyelets.
THE STOCK from which this shoe is cut is White Brothers' genuine box calf, which is known as the best, high grade oak sole leather, and made with nearly ½-inch extension edge, and the latest style of rope stitching.
THIS SHOE is fitted with large nickel hooks and eyelets, outside backstay extending from heel to top of shoe, fine kid inside lace stay and top band, and stitched throughout with silk thread. Genuine hand sewed welt, and the best we know how to make at any price.

SIZES AND HALF SIZES, 5 TO 11.
WIDTHS, C, D, E AND EE.

No. 15R770
Order by Number.

Average weight, 45 ounces.
For postage rate, see page 4.
Price, per pair **$2.95**

OUR BOX CALF LEADER, $2.95
A $5.00 BENCH MADE SHOE.

THE STOCK IN THIS SHOE is known as White Brothers' Box Calf. The style of last is the very latest, being a medium knob opera with fancy tip, and the shoe being cut with the new circular vamp and new style back stays is one of the nobbiest we have ever seen. The soles are cut from best California oak sole leather, made extra heavy and with full Scotch or extension edges, which protect the uppers and do away with the necessity of wearing rubbers. **The shoe is strictly hand sewed, fitted with best agatine hooks and eyelets** (never turn brassy), and the inside back stay and top facing are of fine bleached calfskin.
GOOD SHOES are the kind we have built our reputation on, and this is one of the best we make.

Sizes and half sizes, 5 to 12.
WIDTHS—C, D, E and EE.

No. 15R771
Order by Number.

WEIGHT, ABOUT 58 OUNCES. FOR POSTAGE RATE SEE PAGE 4.
Price, per pair **$2.95**

MEN'S DRESS VICI KID WELT, $2.85.

WE HAVE IN THIS SHOE used a plump velvet finished vici kid, which is very soft and yet as tough as kangaroo. The style of last is the very latest, and is especially adapted to dress purposes.
THIS SHOE is made in the best possible manner, carrying a flint stone oak sole, with slightly extended edges, stitched throughout with silk and linen, **and with genuine calf inside stays and top band.**
This is one of the handsomest shoes we have ever quoted at any price, and being a genuine hand sewed welt, it will give the wearer a great deal of solid comfort.

Sizes and half sizes, 5 to 11.
Widths, C, D, E and EE.

No. 15R774
ORDER BY NUMBER.

Weight averages 36 ounces.
For postage rate see page 4.
Price, per pair **$2.85**

MEN'S BOX CALF BLUCHERS, $2.85.
TAN OR BLACK. FASHIONABLE BULLDOG LAST. HAND SEWED.

THE STOCK from which these shoes are cut is White Brothers' box calf, and is one of the most serviceable leathers tanned. It has a slightly pebbled surface, is as near waterproof as leather can be made and can be polished by applying the patent leather paste and rubbing with a flannel cloth. Those who have worn box calf shoes will now have nothing else.
THE WORKMANSHIP is the very best that can be had at any price. The shoe is fitted with fast color hooks and eyelets. It is stitched throughout with silk and linen, fitted with the latest outside back stay and carries the **very best California oak soles**, which, being sewed on by hand welt process, are very flexible and more comfortable than a machine sewed shoe can possibly be made.
A BETTER SHOE YOU CANNOT POSSIBLY BUY AT ANY PRICE.
Home Made.

Sizes and half sizes 5 to 12.
Widths, C, D, E and EE.
Weight averages 43 ounces.
For postage rate see page 4.

No. 15R798 Latest tan shade. Per pair $2.85
No. 15R800 Black Box Calf. Per pair 2.85

MEN'S FREAK OXFORDS, $2.55

THE FREAK LAST is now all the rage in the largest cities of the United States, and is also largely worn in London, Paris and all the largest European cities. This last is a broad one and is one of the most comfortable ever made. **The velours calf stock is very soft and pliable**, and retains polish much better than any other leather tanned, and at the same time is very tough and durable.
THIS SHOE is made with the new style of heel foxing, with perforated tip, vamp and lace stay; is the genuine Goodyear welt and carries the best oak leather out sole with full extension edges, and we could not possibly build a better shoe at any price. **It is fully equal to those ordinarily sold at from $3.50 to $5.00 per pair.**

Sizes and half sizes, 5 to 11.
Widths, C, D, E and EE.

No. 15R806
Order by Number.

Weight, about 30 ounces. For postage rate, see page 4.
Price, per pair **$2.55**

MEN'S PATENT LEATHER BUTTON, $2.25.

IMPORTED CLOTH TOP.

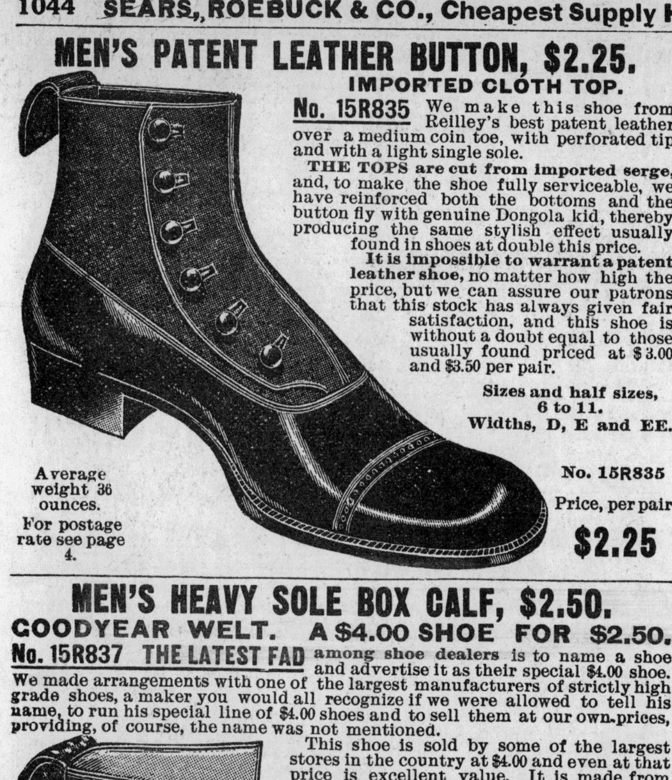

No. 15R835 We make this shoe from Reilley's best patent leather over a medium coin toe, with perforated tip and with a light single sole.

THE TOPS are cut from imported serge, and, to make the shoe fully serviceable, we have reinforced both the bottoms and the button fly with genuine Dongola kid, thereby producing the same stylish effect usually found in shoes at double this price.

It is impossible to warrant a patent leather shoe, no matter how high the price, but we can assure our patrons that this stock has always given fair satisfaction, and this shoe is without a doubt equal to those usually found priced at $3.00 and $3.50 per pair.

Sizes and half sizes, 6 to 11. Widths, D, E and EE.

Average weight 36 ounces. For postage rate see page 4.

No. 15R835 Price, per pair **$2.25**

MEN'S HEAVY SOLE BOX CALF, $2.50.

GOODYEAR WELT. A $4.00 SHOE FOR $2.50.

No. 15R837 THE LATEST FAD among shoe dealers is to name a shoe and advertise it as their special $4.00 shoe. We made arrangements with one of the largest manufacturers of strictly high grade shoes, a maker you would all recognize if we were allowed to tell his name, to run his special line of $4.00 shoes and to sell them at our own prices, providing, of course, the name was not mentioned.

This shoe is sold by some of the largest stores in the country at $4.00 and even at that price is excellent value. It is made from White Bros.' box calf leather over the very latest English last, with fancy perforated tip. The soles are cut from genuine California oak sole leather, made extra heavy and with full extended edges, thereby protecting the uppers and insuring a thoroughly durable shoe. This shoe is genuine Goodyear welt sewn, fitted with bleached calf inside stay and a custom outside back stay. **We want your order** for a pair of these shoes, for we feel that the best advertising we can possibly get is to demonstrate to our patrons the fact that we can and do furnish this strictly high grade $4.00 shoe for little more than half its actual worth.

Sizes and half sizes, 5 to 12. Widths, A, B, C, D, E and EE.

Average weight, 83 ounces. For postage rate see page 4.

No. 15R837 Price, per pair......................................**$2.50**

A MODERN PATENT LEATHER OXFORD FOR MEN.

No. 15R846 A shoe worthy of your consideration. A delightfully easy, stylish and perfect fitting shoe, a standard of real shoe excellence. To produce a genuine Goodyear welt Oxford of such quality as the one we herewith illustrate has never been attempted before by any manufacturer at the price we quote. The stock is excellent quality of patent leather vamp and heel foxing, cut in the very newest style, handsomely perforated and stitched. The top is of genuine pebble calf and the contrast produces an effect seldom found in a man's Oxford at any price. **The inner sole, outer sole, trimmings, etc., are all of select material and highly finished throughout. This is a shoe fitted for swell dressers.** Oxfords were never more in demand than at the present time, we are the leaders in Oxfords and this Oxford is our leader. Owing to the great effort on our part to build this shoe and on account of such a small margin of profit we are able to offer our customers one of the best shoes for the money that has ever been sold by any house in the country.

Sizes and half sizes, 5 to 11. Widths, C, D, E and EE.

Weight averages 30 ounces per pair. For postage rate see page 4.

No. 15R846 Price, per pair......................................**$2.55**

STEEL SHOD LACE, $1.95

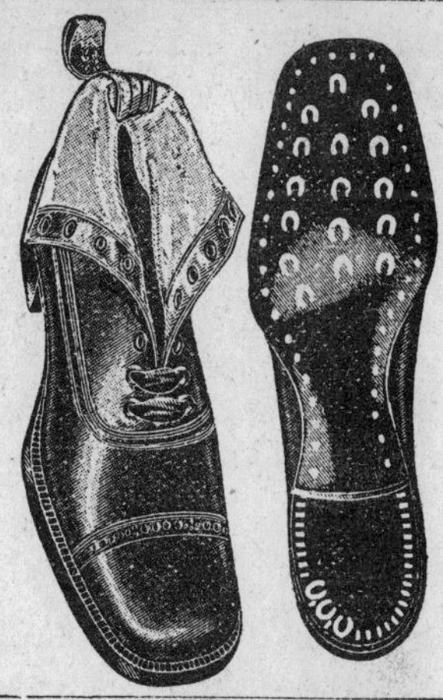

No. 15R854 THIS SHOE is made from a first **quality of Badger calfskin,** over a broad toe last, with tip, and for actual hard wear **excels anything we have ever seen.** Made with double soles, extension edges, and the sole being filled with the famous hardened steel Perfection Circlettes will render twice the service found in any others. We also put circlettes in the heel, thereby preventing it from wearing down on one side.

WE FIT THIS SHOE WITH DONGOLA TOP AND WARRANT IT TO OUTWEAR ANY SHOE EVER OFFERED.........

Especially designed for teamsters, police, railroad men and all those who need a heavy, serviceable shoe.

HOME MADE.

Sizes and half sizes, 5 to 12. Widths, D, E and EE.

Weight averages 48 ounces. For postage rate see page 4.

No. 15R854 Price, per pair......**$1.95**

FEATHERWEIGHT VICI KID LACE, $1.95.

No. 15R858 We illustrate herewith our latest genuine vici kid shoe, made with circle seam, fancy stitched panel and outside back stay from heel to top of shoe. It is especially designed for those wishing a light weight and yet durable shoe. The soles are cut from best of leather, and being made in our **new 20th Century shoe plant,** it has the appearance and in fact is equal to many shoes sold for much more money.

Sizes and half sizes, 6 to 11. Widths, D, E and EE.

Weight averages 35 ounces. For postage rate see page 4.

HOME MADE

No. 15R858 Price, per pair......................................**$1.95**

GOODYEAR WELT LACE, $1.98.

A RECORD BREAKER.

No. 15R863 HOW IT IS MADE. This shoe is made from the Badger calfskin over the fashionable Boston last, with handsomely perforated tip, vamp and lace stay, oak soles and a fine dongola top. The shoe is fitted in the best manner, with fine inside top facing. Fact is, it is made right along side of our best shoes by the same shoemakers, and no matter what the cost to us, you get such a shoe as no one else can offer for the price.

HOME MADE.

Sizes and half sizes, 5 to 11. Widths, D, E and EE.

UNION MADE.

Weight averages 50 ozs. For postage rate see page 4.

No. 15R863 Price, per pair......................................**$1.98**

MEN'S CORK SOLE LACE, $2.00.

No. 15R864 We have it made with a full sheet cork sole placed between the inner sole and the outer sole and extending from sole to heel. The outer sole is cut from the best Union sole leather, and will wear like iron. Stitched throughout with silk thread, fitted with plump dongola top and genuine calfskin inside trimmings. If you are looking for a shoe at this price, you cannot secure the equal of this one in the United States. We think enough of this one to warrant every pair, which means that we will make good any pair that goes wrong.

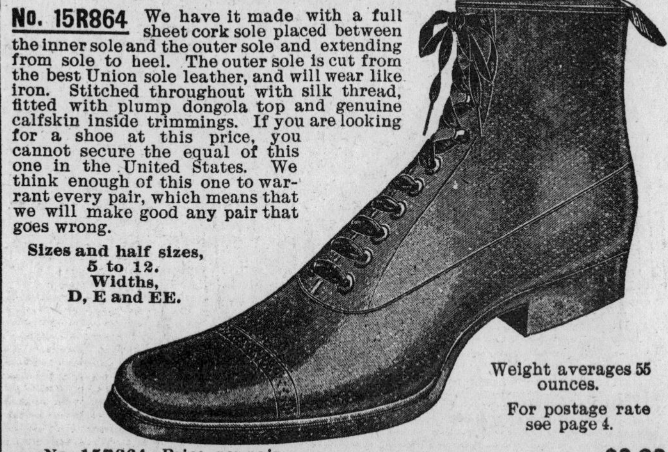

Sizes and half sizes, 5 to 12. Widths, D, E and EE.

Weight averages 55 ounces. For postage rate see page 4.

No. 15R864 Price, per pair......................................**$2.00**

$1.95 HEAVY SOLE RAILROAD SHOE.

LACE OR CONGRESS

MEN'S RAILROAD SHOES, made from first class selection of satin calf stock which is of medium weight and will wear like iron. These shoes are made over a medium broad square toe last, with box toes and fancy imitation tips, are fitted with best dongola tops and genuine calf inside trimmings.

You will observe from illustration that we build them with heavy soles and wide extension edges, which produces a very neat effect, and at the same time fully protects the uppers. Sewed throughout with best linen thread and designed especially for wear, but to get the good wear we have not sacrificed appearance. We make these shoes in the same factory with our higher priced goods, hence you get the same fine workmanship and the same good fitting qualities. There never was a better wearing, better style or better fitting shoe offered for half as much again. Home made and every pair warranted.

Sizes and half sizes, 6 to 12.

Widths, D, E and EE.

Weight, about 60 ounces. For postage rate see page 4.

No. 15R865 Railroad Lace, per pair.............$1.95

No. 15R867 Railroad Congress, per pair......... 1.95

MEN'S VICI LACE, BLACK, $1.95

IMPERIAL CLOTH TOP.

WE HEREWITH ILLUSTRATE our Men's Medium Weight Vici Kid Shoe, made from Foederer's vici kid stock, which is strictly high grade and will outwear any kid stock on the market.

The style is the very latest, being made over the fashionable Arlington last, with neat stitched tip and fitted with the English back stay, best plain Imperial cloth top and large eyelets. The soles are cut from genuine oak sole leather, sewed on by the McKay process, and fair stitched, making the shoe appear like a Goodyear welt.

A better shoe could not possibly be bought elsewhere under $3.00 to $3.50 per pair and being made alongside of our better shoes it receives the same careful attention, thereby giving it the appearance and fitting qualities usually found only in higher grade shoes.

Sizes and half sizes from 5 to 12.
Widths, C, D, E and EE.

Weight averages 43 ounces. For postage rate see page 4.

No. 15R872 Price, per pair..$1.95

MEN'S PATENT LEATHER SHOE, $1.95.

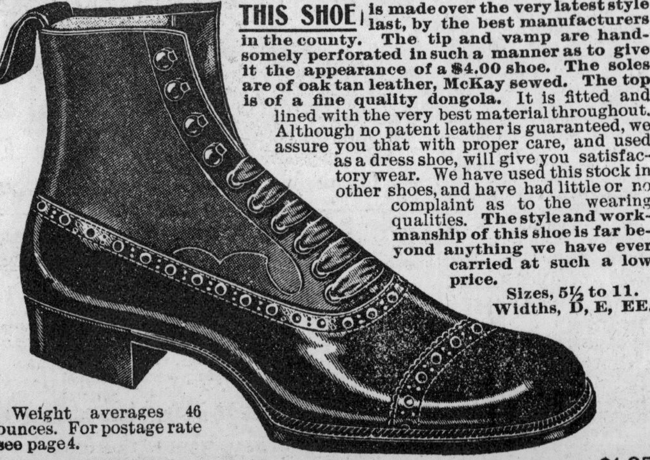

THIS SHOE is made over the very latest style last, by the best manufacturers in the county. The tip and vamp are handsomely perforated in such a manner as to give it the appearance of a $4.00 shoe. The soles are of oak tan leather, McKay sewed. The top is of a fine quality dongola. It is fitted and lined with the very best material throughout. Although no patent leather is guaranteed, we assure you that with proper care, and used as a dress shoe, will give you satisfactory wear. We have used this stock in other shoes, and have had little or no complaint as to the wearing qualities. The style and workmanship of this shoe is far beyond anything we have ever carried at such a low price.

Sizes, 5½ to 11.
Widths, D, E, EE.

Weight averages 46 ounces. For postage rate see page 4.

No. 15R876 Price, per pair..$1.95

MEN'S SATIN CALF LACE, $1.50

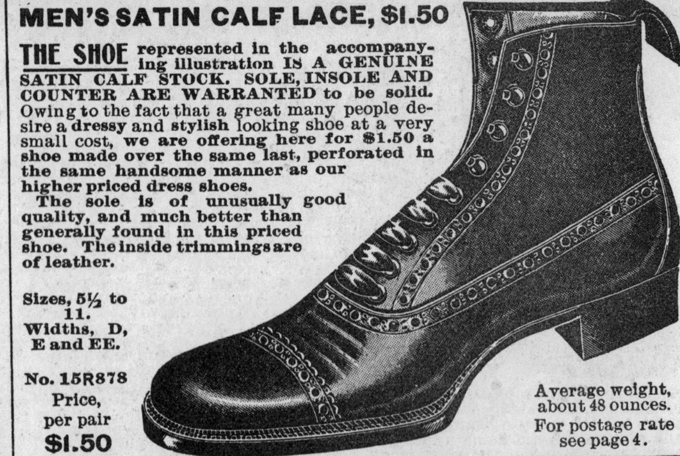

THE SHOE represented in the accompanying illustration IS A GENUINE SATIN CALF STOCK. SOLE, INSOLE AND COUNTER ARE WARRANTED to be solid. Owing to the fact that a great many people desire a dressy and stylish looking shoe at a very small cost, we are offering here for $1.50 a shoe made over the same last, perforated in the same handsome manner as our higher priced dress shoes.

The sole is of unusually good quality, and much better than generally found in this priced shoe. The inside trimmings are of leather.

Sizes, 5½ to 11.
Widths, D, E and EE.

No. 15R878 Price, per pair **$1.50**

Average weight, about 48 ounces. For postage rate see page 4.

MEN'S VELOURS CALF LACE, $1.95.

THE PATTERN of this shoe is our very latest production and one which we have copied from some of our highest grade shoes. The style of last is a medium coin and we have perforated the tip, vamp and lace stay, producing an extraordinary style for this price. The shoe is absolutely all solid leather and will give splendid service. It is not, however, intended for a working shoe, but more especially for dress and street wear.

The velours calf stock is one of the handsomest leathers ever produced.

Sizes and half sizes, 6 to 11.
Widths, D, E and EE.

No. 15R889 Price, per pair **$1.95**

Weight, about 35 ounces. For postage rate see page 4.

MEN'S SEAL CALF, SEAMLESS, $1.55.

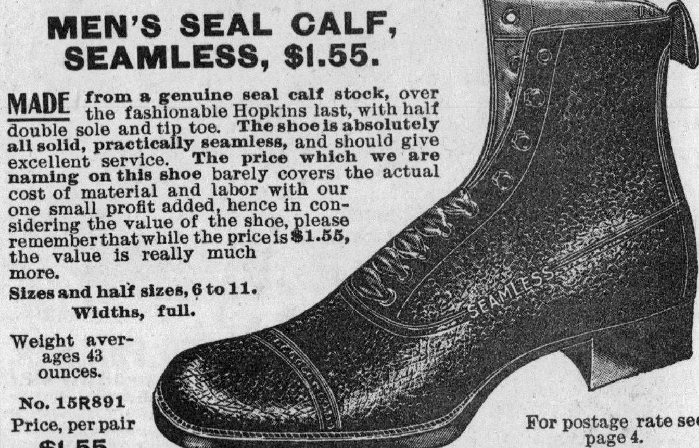

MADE from a genuine seal calf stock, over the fashionable Hopkins last, with half double sole and tip toe. The shoe is absolutely all solid, practically seamless, and should give excellent service. The price which we are naming on this shoe barely covers the actual cost of material and labor with our one small profit added, hence in considering the value of the shoe, please remember that while the price is $1.55, the value is really much more.

Sizes and half sizes, 6 to 11.
Widths, full.

Weight averages 43 ounces.

No. 15R891 Price, per pair **$1.55**

For postage rate see page 4.

MEN'S COMBINED CONGRESS AND LACE, $1.35

WE HAVE never seen a shoe which, to us, seemed so practical. We make it from a good selection of Badger calfskin, medium full coin tip toe and plump soles. It is fitted with glove calf top, absolutely all solid sole leather counter and inner sole, and to those who wish a serviceable shoe at a low price we recommend it. Such a shoe never before was offered at this low price.

Sizes and half sizes, 6 to 11.
Widths, D, E and EE.

Weight averages 38 ounces. For postage rate see page 4.

No. 15R901 Price, per pair..$1.35

Boys' Never Rip Seamless Lace.

This is undoubtedly the most serviceable shoe for boys' wear ever built at any price. Made of very best selection of kangaroo calf, which is very soft, durable and as near waterproof as it is possible to make leather. This shoe is seamless on the sides and back, the only seam being under the tip, which is securely riveted, and the soles being put on with invisible screws, makes a shoe absolutely rip proof. Built especially for those boys who have heretofore found it impossible to get a satisfactory shoe, and absolutely warranted in every particular.

Sizes and half sizes, 1 to 5½. Full widths.

No. 15R892 Price, per pair..................$1.29

Boys' Box Calf Lace, $1.60.

We herewith illustrate one of the handsomest boys' shoes we have ever seen. Made in exact duplicate of our highest grade men's shoes, so far as pattern, style, soles and trimmings go, and equal to any shoe we have ever seen offered at one-half as much again. Box calf stock is today so well known that we need not mention its merits. The shoe is made from the very best of material throughout. Has latest style foxing, perforated vamp, tip and heel piece, has absolutely all solid sole leather counter and inner sole, and the very best of oak out sole.

This is the very best boys' shoe that we make, and one which we consider equal to anything we have ever seen offered up to $2.50 per pair.

Sizes and half sizes, 1 to 5½. Widths, D, E and EE.

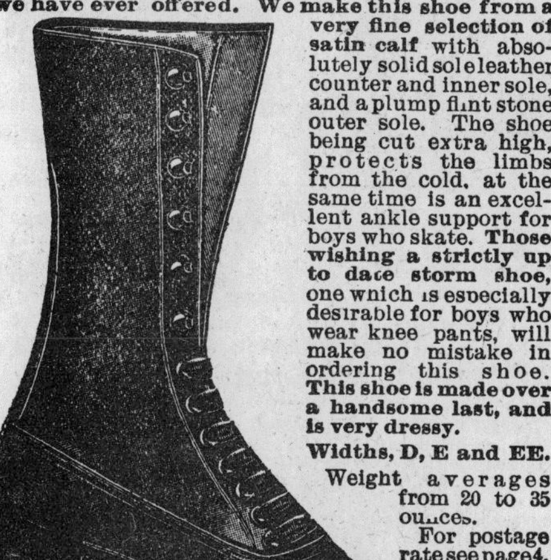

Weight averages 30 ounces. For postage rate see page 4.

No. 15R897 Price, per pair..................$1.60

Boys' and Youths' Storm Shoes.

The sale of our men's extra high cut storm shoe has been so large, that we have felt compelled to add to our line of special high cut shoes for boys and youths and we really feel that it is one of the most appropriate shoes for fall and winter wear that we have ever offered. We make this shoe from a very fine selection of satin calf with absolutely solid sole leather counter and inner sole, and a plump flint stone outer sole. The shoe being cut extra high, protects the limbs from the cold, at the same time is an excellent ankle support for boys who skate. Those wishing a strictly up to date storm shoe, one which is especially desirable for boys who wear knee pants, will make no mistake in ordering this shoe. This shoe is made over a handsome last, and is very dressy.

Widths, D, E and EE.

Weight averages from 20 to 35 ounces. For postage rate see page 4.

No. 15R903 Price, per pair, boys' sizes, 2½ to 5..................$1.65

No. 15R904 Price, per pair, youths' sizes, 11½ to 2..................1.45

MR. CUSTOMER:

EVER SEE SO MANY

UP TO DATE STYLES IN ONE CATALOGUE?

... EVER SEE ...

SUCH RIDICULOUSLY LOW PRICES ON DEPENDABLE MERCHANDISE?

Men's Satin Calf Lace, $1.20.

This is the same fine satin calf shoe that we gave you last season at $1.45, and while we really cannot afford to make the price $1.20, we do so rather than offer those who want a shoe at this price an inferior article. Made over a plain globe last, with plump soles, and absolutely solid one piece sole leather counter and inner sole. The shoe is stitched well, fitted with glove calf top, and on today's market is an exceptional bargain.

Sizes, 6 to 12; no half sizes. Widths, D, E and EE.

Weight averages 40 ounces. For postage rate see page 4

No. 15R908 Price, per pair..................$1.20

Men's Coin Toe Satin Calf Lace, $1.20.

This shoe is made of fine satin calf, made on the latest coin toe last.

Stitched and perforated tip. The sole is made of solid and durable leather. Counter and inner sole also are made solid. This shoe is lined, trimmed and fitted in a manner unusually found in this price shoe.

Sizes and half sizes, 6 to 12.
Widths, D, E and EE.
Average weight, 40 ounces.
For postage rate see page 4.

No. 15R909 Price, per pair..................$1.20

Men's Satin Calf Congress, $1.20.

This shoe we considered excellent value last season at $1.45 per pair, but knowing that all dealers carry a shoe which looks similar, but of much poorer quality, we prefer to stop all competition with one sweeping cut, and make the price $1.20. The stock from which it is made is a good selection of satin calf, and will wear well. Fitted with glove calf top, plump hemlock soles, and genuine sole leather counter and inner sole. No shoddy can enter this shoe. We really believe you would do well to order this shoe if you want something at about this price, as it will fit well and wear well.

Sizes, 6 to 12; no half sizes.
Widths, D, E and EE.
Weight averages 45 ounces.
For postage rate see page 4.

No. 15R910 Price, per pair..................$1.20

Boys' Steel Shod Lace, $1.45 and $1.35.

...FOR DRESS...

We make this shoe from the very best selection of Badger calfskin over a handsome London toe last, with full perforated tip, genuine dongola top, and best white oak sole leather bottoms. The shoe is fitted in the best possible manner, custom back stay, stitched with silk and linen, and the plump outsole filled with brass slugs, heel fitted with hardened steel slugs, and three perfection hardened steel circlettes, making a shoe practically indestructible.

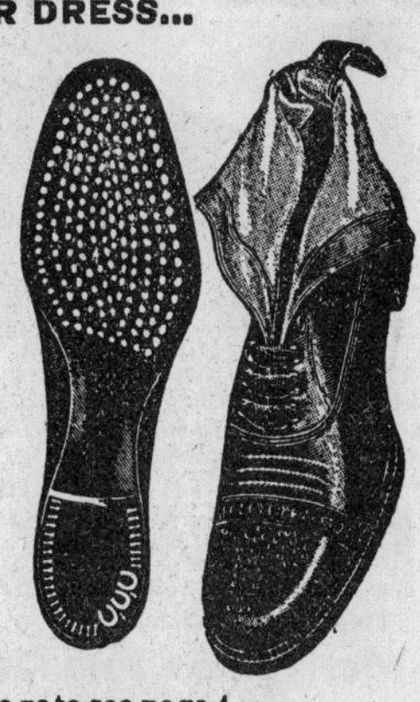

Weight averages 25 to 36 ounces.

For postage rate see page 4.
Widths, D, E and EE.

No. 15R911 Boys' sizes, 2½ to 5½.
Price, per pair..................$1.45

No. 15R913 Youths' sizes, 11½ to 2.
Price, per pair..................1.35

Boys' Satin Calf Lace, $1.15.

A Boys' shoe, made thoroughly solid, one that will stand the hard wear, and still be sold at $1.15, is something we have tried to build for some time. We now have it. Satin calf stock, solid sole leather counter and inner sole, outside back stay. Western made and serviceable.

Sizes, 1 to 5½. No half sizes.
Weight, averages 30 ounces.
For postage rate see page 4.

DON'T FAIL TO GIVE SIZE

No. 15R914 Price, per pair..................$1.15

Men's Seal Calf Seamless, $1.75.

A strictly all solid, heavy sole seal calf shoe, seamless cut and Western made, which insures the best of service, is something we have never before been able to offer at this low price.

This home made shoe is built from best seal calf stock, as near waterproof as it is possible to make leather, and with extra heavy double soles. The soles are cut from best leather fastened on with standard screws, and we fit it with absolutely all solid sole leather insole and counter of best quality. Nothing better can be built at any price.

Sizes and half sizes, 6 to 11. Widths full.

Weight, about 45 ounces.

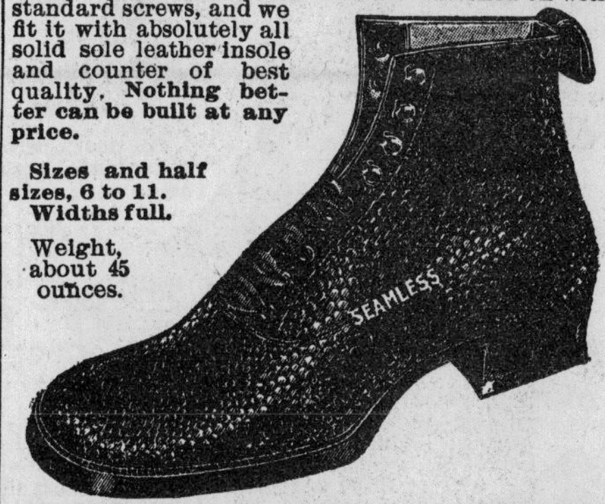

No. 15R925 Price, per pair..................$..75

The German Slipper for Men and Women, $0.78 and $0.73.

Order by Number.

Men's and Women's German Slipper made from heavy embroidered velvet, with leather foxings around the sides, as shown in the illustration, and stout leather soles. Nothing better made for wear and comfort. Wide widths only. No half sizes.

No. 15R978 Women's sizes, 3 to 8.
Price, per pair..............$0.73
No. 15R979 Men's sizes, 6 to 12.
Price, per pair..............$0.78

Men's Dongola Oxfords, $1.35.

DONT FAIL TO GIVE SIZE

Order by Number

This Oxford is made to our order from a fine quality of bright dongola, over the new modified bulldog last, with tip, and when on the foot it has the appearance of a fine shoe. The bottoms are the very best stock, sewed on by the McKay process, and besides being a very neat shoe, it will give the wearer a great deal of wear and solid comfort. Sizes and half sizes, 5 to 12. Widths, D, E and EE. Weight, 28 ounces. For postage rate see page 4.

No. 15R982 Black. Per pair........$1.35

Men's Dongola Nullifiers, $1.30.

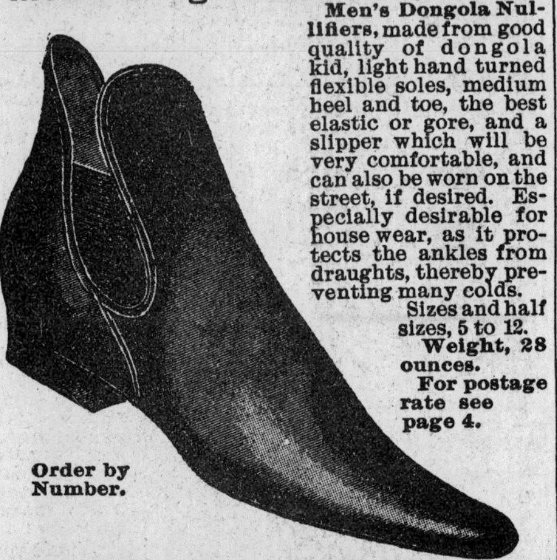

Men's Dongola Nullifiers, made from good quality of dongola kid, light hand turned flexible soles, medium heel and toe, the best elastic or gore, and a slipper which will be very comfortable, and can also be worn on the street, if desired. Especially desirable for house wear, as it protects the ankles from draughts, thereby preventing many colds. Sizes and half sizes, 5 to 12. Weight, 28 ounces. For postage rate see page 4.

Order by Number.

No. 15R984 Black. Per pair........$1.30

Men's Dongola Oxfords, $1.15.

This Shoe is made from a fine dongola kid, light sole, which is very flexible, medium heel, medium common sense toe, and is very durable. Nothing cooler or more comfortable for summer wear. Sizes and half sizes, 5 to 12. Widths, D, E and EE. Weight, 28 oz. For postage rate see page 4.

Order by Number.

No. 15R986 Price, per pair..............$1.15

Patent Leather Oxfords, $1.35.

Cloth Plug.

DONT FAIL TO GIVE SIZE

Order by Number.

Sizes and half sizes, 5 to 12. Widths, C, D, E and EE. Weight, 20 ounces.

Men's Patent Leather Oxford. Made from a good grade of stock over a medium coin plain toe. The bottoms are light hand turn, making them very flexible and especially desirable for dancing. Fitted with silk vesting plug and splendid value at the price.

No. 15R988 Price, per pair..........$1.35
For postage rate see page 4.

Men's Patent Leather Oxfords, $1.45.

Order by Number.

This Oxford is made exactly the same style as those usually offered at $3.00 and $4.00 by the retail shoe dealers. Stock is a good selection of patent leather, style of last is latest English; the soles are of good quality leather with full extension edges and full perforated vamp. Is all the rage in large cities, and is something that cannot ordinarily be obtained in shoes offered at this price. Sizes and half sizes, 5 to 12. Full width. Weight, 30 ounces.

No. 15R989 Price, per pair..........$1.45
For postage rate see page 4.

Men's Oil Grain Slippers, $0.80.

Men's Heavy Slippers, made from good oil grain stock, machine sewed, and all solid. This slipper is damp proof and very serviceable, and should not be compared with the cheap slippers usually sold at this price. Warranted. Sizes, 6 to 12. No half sizes. Full Width. Weight, 28 ounces.

Order by Number.

No. 15R990 Price, per pair..........$0.80
For postage rate see page 4.

Men's Carpet Slippers, $0.29.

Men's Slippers, made from Brussels carpet, bound and stayed, leather sole and counter, and a slipper which will give good wear and lots of comfort. Sizes, 6 to 12. No half sizes. Weight, 20 ounces. For postage rate see page 4.

No. 15R996 Price, per pair..........$0.29

Men's Black Vici Kid Opera Slipper, $1.20.

You will notice by our illustration we have greatly improved the style of this slipper. It is made of genuine vici kid, vamp handsomely inlaid with patent leather under a beautiful new scroll pattern. The soles, insoles and counters are of solid leather. Vamp lined with fine quality canvas, trimmings of leather. A slipper unexcelled for beauty, service and comfort. Sizes, 6 to 11. Widths, C, D, E and EE. Weight, 14 ounces.
For postage rate see page 4.

No. 15R997 Price, per pair..........$1.20

Men's Imitation Alligator Slipper, $0.50.

The vamp of this Slipper is made of imitation alligator skin, as is shown by the accompanying illustration. Quarter made of patent leather. The soles and counter are of solid leather. The shoe is nicely trimmed and bound, giving it a very neat appearance. We quote this slipper at the very low price of 50 cents. Sizes, 6 to 11.

Average weight, 18 ounces.

Order by Number.

No. 15R1010 Price, per pair..........$0.50

Men's and Boys' Velvet Embroidered Slippers, $0.55.

Men's Embroidered Slippers, Everett cut, patent quarter, and a very pretty and serviceable shoe. Sizes, 6 to 11; full widths. Weight, 18 oz.

For postage rate see page 4.

No. 15R1014 Men's sizes, 6 to 11. Price...**$0.55**
No. 15R1015 Boys' sizes, 2 to 5. Price...... **.55**

New Idea Plow Shoe, $1.00.

The accompanying cut illustrates the New Idea Plow Shoe, which we fully believe is destined to become more popular than the Creole or Dom Pedro. It is made from the best Milwaukee oil grain leather, half double sole, absolutely solid sole leather counters and inner soles, and will wear much better than any plow shoe we have ever offered. The principal feature, however, is the crimped tongue, which hugs the instep closely, and the large brass eyelets and strong buckskin laces, which will outwear the shoe. Sizes, 6 to 12; no half sizes.

Weight averages 47 ounces. For postage see page 4.

No. 15R1029 Price, per pair..........$1.00

$0.93 and $0.89 Oil Grain Creole.

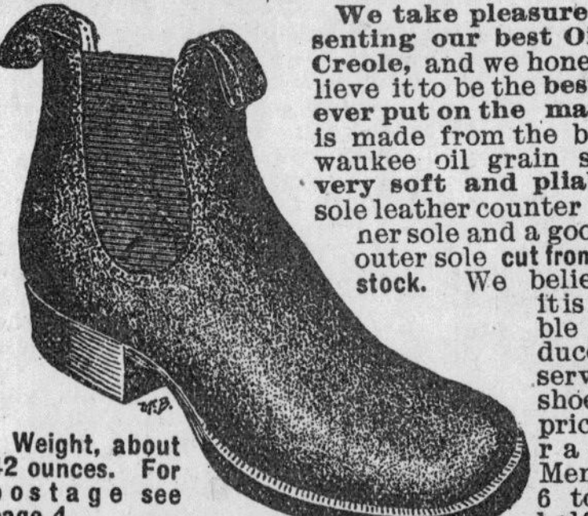

We take pleasure in presenting our best Oil Grain Creole, and we honestly believe it to be the best Creole ever put on the market. It is made from the best Milwaukee oil grain stock, is very soft and pliable, has sole leather counter and inner sole and a good heavy outer sole cut from the best stock. We believe that it is impossible to produce a more serviceable shoe at any price. Warranted. Men's sizes, 6 to 14; no half sizes.

Weight, about 42 ounces. For postage see page 4.

No. 15R1030 Price, per pair..........$0.93
No. 15R1031 Boys' sizes, 2 to 5....... .89

93c and 89c Oil Grain Dom Pedro.

This Shoe is made from best Milwaukee oil grain stock, has sole leather counters and insole, is soft and pliable and will not get hard when wet. It has bellows tongue, which makes it dirt proof. Sizes, 5 to 14; no half sizes. Weight, about 42 ounces.

DONT FAIL TO GIVE SIZE

For postage rate see page 4.

No. 15R1032 Price, per pair..........$0.93
No. 15R1033 Boys' sizes, 2 to 5...... .89

Men's Seal Calf Blucher, $1.75.

No. 15R1037 We herewith illustrate our latest production in a men's neat appearing shoe which at the same time will wear well. Made from a plump seal calf stock, Blucher style cut, broad tip toe, and heavy half-double soles. The Blucher cut shoe having a crimped vamp fits the ankle closely, is dirt excluding and more satisfactory for plowing or general heavy wear than anything we have ever shown at any price. Per pair.......**$1.75**

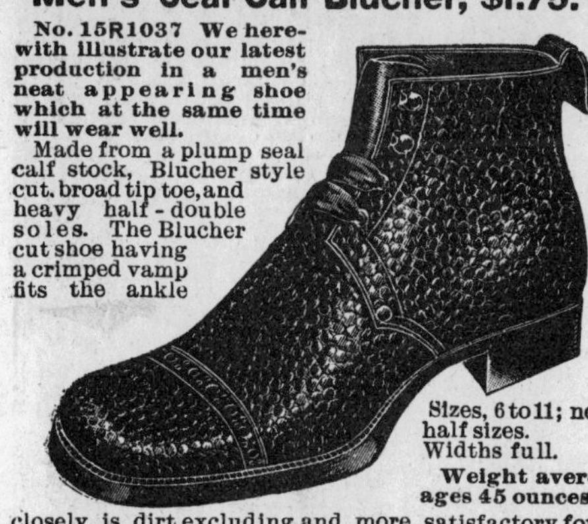

Sizes, 6 to 11; no half sizes. Widths full.
Weight averages 45 ounces.

Men's Spring Heel Plow, $0.98.

No. 15R1040 Men's Two-Buckle Oil Grain Plow Shoe, dirt excluder, spring heel, and a very easy shoe for plowing or harrowing in soft ground; very comfortable on the feet and will give good service. Don't forget that each pair of our plow shoes is fully warranted. Sizes, 6 to 11; no half sizes.
Weight, about 45 ounces.
For postage rate see page 4. Per pair, **$0.98**

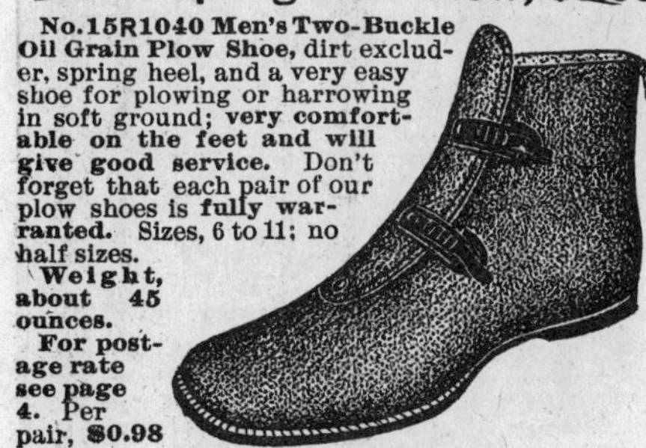

Men's Oil Grain Wood Sole Shoe, $1.09.

No. 15R1047 The Shoe is made from best Milwaukee oil grain leather, and the sole is put on in such a manner as to make it absolutely waterproof. The wood sole being a non-conductor, is much drier, much warmer, than any leather made, besides being lighter. The sole is shaped to the foot, making an easy shoe and one especially desirable for those working in wet places. Sizes, 5 to 12; no half sizes.
Price, per pair...................................**$1.09**
Weight averages 39 ounces. For postage rate see page 4.

Lumbermen's Pacs, $1.98.

No. 15R1062 The accompanying cut represents our best hand sewed Pac with 10-inch leg of oil grain leather and oil tan pac leather uppers; the soles are double sewed and inserted with round, cone-headed Hungarian nails, which add to the wearing qualities. The sole is light and flexible, and very easy to walk in, and does not slip. Sizes, 6 to 12.
Per pair...**$1.98**
Weight, 41 ozs. For postage rate see page 4.

Moccasins, $2.20.

No. 15R1072 This Moccasin is made from the genuine moose skin, smoke tanned by the Indians. The seams, genuine hand stitched, and guaranteed not to rip like the ordinary machine sewed. Nicely embroidered vamp and bellows tongue. A great shoe for hunting or snowshoeing. Sizes, 6 to 12. Per pair....... **$2.20**
Weight, about 18 oz.
Weight averages 25 ounces. See apge 4 for postal rates.

Men's Mining Shoe, $1.50.

No. 15R1076 Men's A Calf Miner. made from a good selection of stock, with full double soles and thoroughly nailed heel and sole. At an additional cost we have fitted this shoe with a heavy iron toe-plate, and also encircled the heel with a heavy iron plate, thereby making it **practically indestructible.** Sizes, 6 to 12; no half sizes. Price, per pair..........................**$1.50**
Weight averages 65 ounces. See page 4 for postage rate.

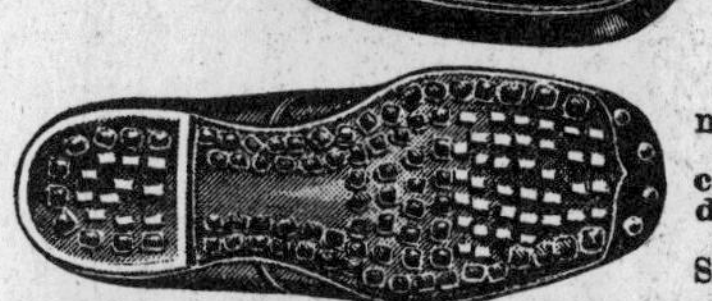

Men's River Boot, $2.95.

No. 15R1080 Strictly Western Made, Oil Grain River Boot, cut from the best Milwaukee grain stock. Made with half double sole and extra heavy tap, which is cut from selected sole leather, guaranteed to hold calks. Heels are low and broad. The boot is made with strap top, is absolutely all solid leather, and is as nearly waterproof as it is possible to make. Sizes, 6 to 11, no half sizes.
Price, per pair... **$2.95**
Weight, about 50 ounces. For postage rate see page 4.

DON'T FAIL TO GIVE SIZE

Our Best River Shoe, $2.95.

No. 15R1082 Since opening our own beautiful daylight factory, we have reduced the cost of manufacturing to such an extent that we are able this season to offer you a much better river shoe at $2.95 than we have ever before sold at any price, and a shoe which we believe equal to any ever placed upon the market. Made from genuine oak tanned calfskin, extra high cut, and with bellows tongue, running to the top of the shoe, thereby making it practically waterproof. This shoe is built with full double sole, and outside tap running nearly to the heel, and securely fastened with standard screws. The grade of sole leather which we use in this shoe is especially fine, from the fact that it is the same as used by the government in all of their army shoes, and, as is well known, the government uses only the best material procurable. Nothing has been omitted to make this the best shoe of its kind ever placed upon the market at any price. Sizes, 6 to 11. No half sizes. Price, per pair...........................**$2.95**

Weight, averages 58 ozs. For postage rate see page 4.

Shoe Pacs, $1.45

No. 15R1090 This Pac is made from an oil tanned pac, leather uppers and soles, with low flat heels, making a very light and serviceable shoe for all kinds of wear. Weight, 29 ounces. Sizes, 6 to 12.
Per pair........**$1.45**

Men's Pacs, $0.98.

No. 15R1091 This Pac is made from good quality leather, well sewed and a bargain. Sizes, 6 to 12.
Price, per pair, **$0.98**
Average weight, 26 ounces.

Men's Kangaroo Calf Logging Shoe, $2.40.

No. 15R1093 This Shoe is made from the genuine kangaroo calf stock, extra high cut, Blucher style, and the tongue being crimped, fits the ankle closely, and the vamp and tongue being one piece produces a shoe which will shed water and is much more practical for loggers use than the ordinary pattern. **This shoe is made with two extra heavy soles and the regulation long outside tap has an extra heavy outside sole leather counter and is fitted with the large Klondike brass eyelets.**
Price, per pair....**$2.40**

Sizes, 6 to 11; no half sizes. Width EE only. Weight, 59 ounces.

Hunting or Prospecting Boot, $4.95.

TAN or BLACK. We have finally succeeded in building a men's hunting or prospecting boot for general wear which we have been striving to produce for years. This boot is made from a genuine Puritan calf stock, which is very soft and as near waterproof as leather can be made. It is made over the latest wide bulldog last, with tip toe, full double sole to heel and extension edges. The boot being a Goodyear welt, is as comfortable as a fine shoe, perfectly smooth insole, no tacks or thread to hurt the foot. **Fitted with four rows of stitching on tip and vamp, and the latest backstay from heel to top of boot.** Where the boot laces at instep it is fitted in such a manner as to make it practically waterproof; and, in fact, we have spared no expense to build the very best boot possible, determined to please our many customers wanting this style of boot. Remember, you have all the comfort of a hand welt fine shoe, just as good fit, and then the advantage of the high cut boot. Sizes and half sizes, 5 to 12; widths, D. E and EE. Shipping weight, 4 pounds.

No. 15R1123 Tan color. Price, per pair...**$4.95**
No. 15R1125 Black. Price, per pair....... **4.95**

ARE YOU A DEALER? DO YOU WANT TO UNDERSELL YOUR COMPETITORS?

BUY OUR SHOES, plain cartons, and without our name. That's what the shrewd merchant is doing. We sell dealers at exactly the same price at which we sell the consumer, but our prices are lower than the dealer can buy elsewhere. Compare our prices with what you are paying.

The Famous, California Kip, $2.65.

No. 15R1128 This Boot is one which we have made specially for our own trade and a great many of our customers will have nothing else. It is made from the best California Kip, medium weight, half double sole, medium toe and heel, and has absolutely solid counters and inner soles. This boot is Chicago made. For hard wear we can recommend it as being first class. Warranted. Sizes, 6 to 12; no half sizes. Weight, 95 ounces.
Price, per pair......$2.65

Men's Kip Boots.

No. 15R1129 Men's Good Whole Stock Kip Boots, half double sole, low flat heel, pegged and serviceable. Sizes, 6 to 12; no half sizes.
Price, per pair.....$2.25

Boys' Kip Boots, $2.15.

No. 15R1131 Boys' Genuine California Whole Stock Kip Boot, made with half double sole, pegged medium toe and heel, and with absolutely solid leather counter and inner sole. This boot is made in exactly the same manner as No. 15R1128, has the same stock and will give the same amount of hard wear. Every pair warranted. Sizes, 1 to 5; no half sizes. Weight, about 54 ounces.
No. 15R1131 Price, per pair..............$2.15
For postage rate see page 4.

Men's Llama Calf Boots, $2.95.

No. 15R1134 The stock from which this Boot is made has a pebbled surface similar to the kangaroo skin, is very soft and pliable and contains enough oil to make it practically waterproof.

THIS BOOT IS MADE WITH FULL DOUBLE SOLE AND OUTSIDE TAP CUT FROM THE VERY BEST OF SOLE LEATHER

And for those who want a thoroughly soft boot which at the same time will outwear anything now on the market, we recommend it.

WARRANTED.

Sizes, 6 to 11. No half sizes. Weight, 50 oz. For postage rate see page 4.
No. 15R1134 Price, per pair..............$2.95

Men's and Boys' Split Boots.

No. 15R1136 Men's Split Boot made from best split stock, half double soles, low broad heels, pegged and serviceable. Sizes, 6 to 12; no half sizes. Weight, about 54 ounces.
Price, per pair.....$1.55

No. 15R1137 Boys' Split Boots, made from good split stock, half double sole, pegged. Sizes, 1 to 5; no half sizes.
Price, per pair.....$1.35
For postage rate see page 4.

Men's Calf Cowboy Boots, $3.75.

No. 15R1152 Made with the new idea Jack Strap. A new and popular boot made of the finest quality of calfskin, soft and durable. Made with medium round box toe and is one of the best fitting boots ever manufactured. Light in weight and very dressy, having a fancy stitched vamp; made with an 18-inch bright grain leg, handsomely stitched; sewn soles of the very best quality of oak tan leather; 1¼-inch solid leather heel, latest ½-inch pull strap; every pair guaranteed. Sizes, 5 to 11. Width, D, E and EE. Average weight, per pair, 45 ounces.
No. 15R1152
Price, per pair..$3.75

Soudan Calf Cowboy Boot, $4.50

No. 15R1155 This Boot is made of the genuine Soudan calf stock, which is very soft and pliable, practically waterproof and is by far the most practical stock we have ever seen for a riding boot. Made with 20-inch leg, fancy stitched and ribbed, hand sewed oak soles, and the 2-inch regulation concave heel. Those wishing the very best cowboy boot to be had at any price will do well to order this one. Our price is below all others. Sizes, 4 to 11. No half sizes. Shipping weight averages 50 ounces.
Price, per pair.....$4.50
For postage rate see page 4.

The Western, $2.25.

No. 15R1156 This Boot is made of genuine calfskin, is all solid and one of the

Most Popular "Cowboy" Boots we have ever sold.

It has extra high heel, medium toe, and is an extremely durable boot for all kinds of wear.

Every Pair Warranted

to be better value than can possibly be obtained elsewhere.

Note reduction. - Size, 5 to 11; no half sizes. Weight, 56 ounces.
No. 15R1156
Price, per pair.....$2.25
For postage rate see page 4.

Our $2.55 Calfskin Boots.

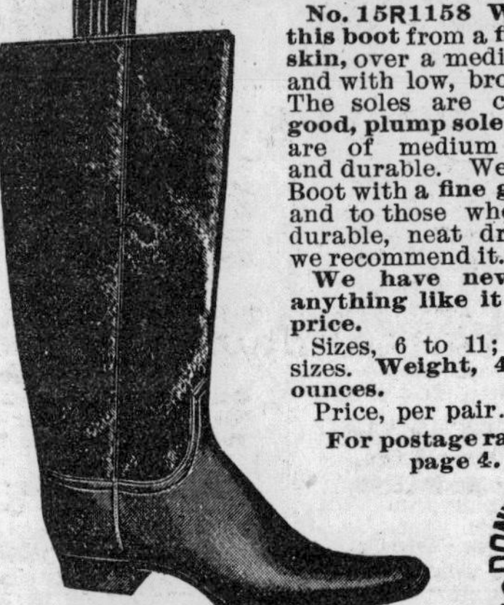

No. 15R1158 We make this boot from a fine calfskin, over a medium last, and with low, broad heel. The soles are cut from good, plump sole leather, are of medium weight, and durable. We fit this Boot with a fine goat leg, and to those who wish a durable, neat dress boot we recommend it.

We have never seen anything like it for the price.

Sizes, 6 to 11; no half sizes. Weight, 45 to 60 ounces.
Price, per pair....$2.55
For postage rate see page 4.

DON'T FAIL TO GIVE SIZE

Oil Grain Plow Boot, $1.75.

No. 15R1163 This Men's Plow Boot is made from the best of Milwaukee oil grain stock, half double sole, solid sole leather counters and inner soles. It is especially designed to give good hard wear, and is sold at a price which will meet the desired wants of a great many. Sizes, 6 to 13; no half sizes. Weight, 48 ounces.
Price, per pair.....$1.75
For postage rate see page 4.

DON'T FAIL TO GIVE SIZE

MENS' CALF PEG BOOT, $2.20

A genuine calf boot at $2.20 is something heretofore unheard of. This boot is made with a nice selection of calfskin vamp, and a good durable split back.

THE BOOT carries a solid sole leather counter, half double sole; is absolutely reliable, and those wishing a calfskin boot not heavy or clumsy will make no mistake in ordering this one.

Sizes, 6 to 11; no half sizes. Weight averages 40 to 55 ounces.
No. 15R1165 Price, per pair..................$2.20

Men's All Wool Knit Boots, $0.75.

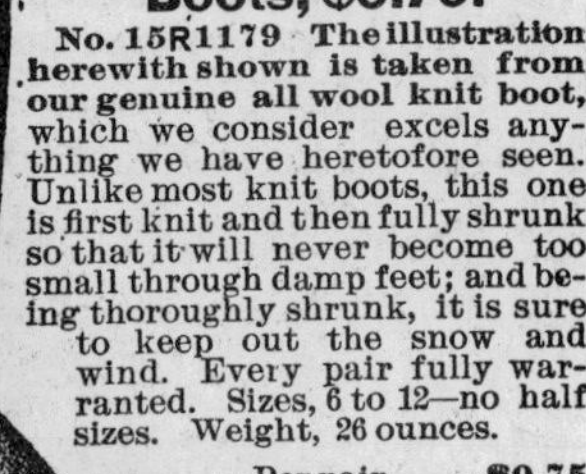

No. 15R1179 The illustration herewith shown is taken from our genuine all wool knit boot, which we consider excels anything we have heretofore seen. Unlike most knit boots, this one is first knit and then fully shrunk so that it will never become too small through damp feet; and being thoroughly shrunk, it is sure to keep out the snow and wind. Every pair fully warranted. Sizes, 6 to 12—no half sizes. Weight, 26 ounces.
Per pair.......$0.75
Per dozen pairs............ 9.00
For postage rate see page 4.

Men's Best Felt Boots, $0.65.

No. 15R1180 This Boot is made from fine quality all wool felt, light color; has genuine calf front, back and side stays, and we guarantee it to be unequaled for the money. Sizes, 6 to 12.
Price, per dozen pairs, $7.80; per pair........$0.65

Boys' Felt Boots, $0.55.

No. 15R1186 Boys' All Wool Felt Boots, extra quality, gray color, calf back and front stays and heel strap for removing. Will give splendid service. Sizes, 1 to 5.
Price, per dozen pairs, $6.60; per pair.......$0.55

Lumbermen's Socks, $0.95.

No. 15R1194 This Lumbermen's Sock is made from the best of pure black wool by one of the best knitting mills in the West. The leg is medium length. It has heavy tufted lining throughout, reinforced feet, and is as good as a sock can possibly be made. It is really worth more than we ask for it. Money back if not satisfactory. Price, per pair...$0.95
Per dozen..............11.40
Weight, 17 ounces.
For postage rate see page 4.

Men's and Boys' Lumbermen's Socks, $0.50 and $0.55.

No. 15R1196 This Lumbermen's Knit Sock is one which we have always sold at 75 cents a pair, but we bought a very large lot this season and shall give our customers the benefit of the price obtained. Made from all wool, heavy tufted foot lining, with long legs and string at tops. The heels and toes are reinforced and being made with a light leg, the sock can be turned inside out if wet and dried almost as easily as a stocking. This is thoroughly reliable and a special bargain for the price named.
No. 15R1196 Men's Sizes.
Price, per pair...........$0.55
Per dozen pairs........... 6.60
Weight, 14 ounces.
No. 15R1197 Boys' Sizes.
Price, per pair...$0.50
Per dozen pairs. 6.00
For postage rate see page 4.

Lumbermen's Combination Sock and Canvas Leggings, $1.00.

No. 15R1199 Probably the most valuable improvement for lumbermen's socks ever thought of is the canvas top, illustration of which we herewith show. **It combines all of the good qualities of the sock and the canvas legging.** The canvas being attached to the sock in such a manner as to **extend down over the rubber overshoe, thereby excluding all snow.** This sock is made **from heavy pure wool,** the foot being tufted and quite heavy, while the canvas top is very heavy; **absolutely waterproof and felt lined to top.** It is fitted with four leather straps and buckles, can be easily adjusted, and is **much more practical than either the old fashioned sock or the felt boot. WARRANTED.**

Price, per dozen pairs, **$12.00;** per pair.....**$1.00**
Weight, 25 ounces. For postage rate see page 4.

Ladies' Jersey Leggings.

No. 15R1201 Ladies' Jersey Leggings, knee length, and with ribbon top. The Jersey cloth legging fits like a stocking, and being all wool, is warm and comfortable. Color, black. Shoe sizes, 1 to 7.

Price, per pair.....................................**$0.65**
Weight, 8 ounces. For postage rate see page 4.

No. 15R1203 Ladies' Fine Black All Wool Melton Leggings, knee length, with 9 buttons and buckle at top. Nothing like it ever offered at this price. Shoe sizes, 1 to 7. Per pair......**$0.48**
Weight, 8 ounces. For postage rate see page 4.

DONT FAIL TO GIVE SIZE

Polar Socks.

For Inside of Rubber Boots.

Fleece lined, for house, chamber, bath room, and especially desirable for inside of rubber boots.

No. 15R1203½ Men's. Sizes, 6 to 11. Price, per dozen, **$1.08;** per pair...........................**$0.09**
If by mail, postage extra, per pair, 4 cents.

Combination Thigh Leggings.

Ladies', Misses' and Children's.

This cut is a very good illustration of our Combination Legging and Overgaiter. It is without a doubt the best fitting, **warmest and most comfortable legging that can be produced.** Being made from a fine black Jersey cloth, it fits as closely as a stocking, and conforms to every movement of the limb. Has 7 buttons up side, and ribbon top.

No. 15R1205 Ladies' sizes, 1 to 7. Per pair.......................**$1.00**
No. 15R1207 Misses' sizes, 12 to 2. Per pair.....................**$0.90**
No. 15R1209 Child's sizes, 8 to 11. Per pair....................**$0.75**
No. 15R1210 Infant's sizes, 4 to 7. Per pair......................**$0.60**
Weight, 9 ounces. For postage rate see page 4.

Ladies' and Men's Overgaiters.

No. 15R1211 Ladies' Fine Overgaiters made heavy for fall and winter wear. Shoe sizes, 1 to 7.
Price, per pair.................................**$0.19**
No. 15R1215 Ladies' 7-button Imported Kersey, Silk Ribbon, Top Facing; the nobbiest and unexcelled.
Price, per pair.................................**$0.59**
No. 15R1219 Men's Heavy 5-button Melton. Price, per pair.....**$0.23**
No. 15R1223 Men's Heavy 5-button imported Kersey shoe. Sizes, 6 to 11.
Price, per pair......**$0.45**
Weight, 8 ounces. For postage rate see page 4.

Men's Extra High Cut Felt Lined Overgaiters, $0.75

No. 15R1226 Men's extra high cut felt lined ten-button overgaiter, made from heavy weight kersey, very warm and comfortable for winter wear. This is the best overgaiter ever placed upon the market.
Weight, 8 to 12 ounces, according to size. Sizes, 6 to 12.
Price, per pair...**$0.75**

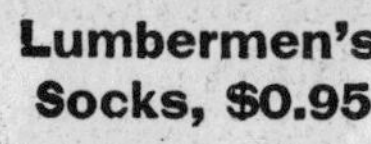

Lumbermen's Socks, $0.95

No. 15R1228 We herewith illustrate our newest lumbermen's knit sock, and while it is a much prettier effect than we have ever before presented it is still just as durable as any ever shown. It is made from pure wool yarn, the color being a mottled brown, with a plain brown rolled top. **This sock has a heavy tufted foot,** lined, reinforced toe and heel, and is made in a thoroughly first class manner throughout. Nothing more durable, and as yet we have to see a sock which will fit and look as well, at any price.

Price, per pair......**$0.95**
Weight, 20 ounces. For postage rate see page 4.

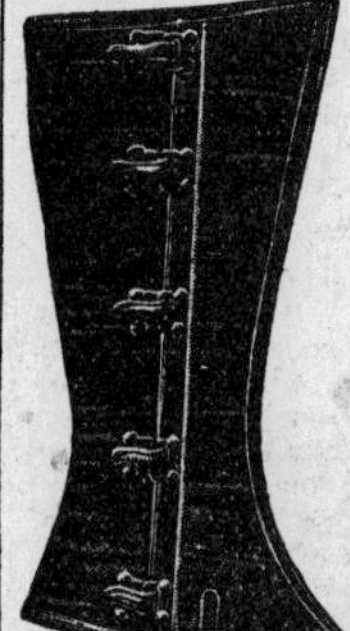

Men's Mackintosh Leggings, $0.70.

No. 15R1231 This legging is known as the army legging. It is made of very strong and durable gray mackintosh cloth, and felt lined throughout. Fastened with automatic snap buckle. Instep strap of fine quality leather, fastened to the legging by means of rivets. It is one of the strongest leggings manufactured, and is absolutely waterproof. Men's sizes only.

Price, per pair.........**$0.70**
Weight, 20 ounces. For postage rate see page 4.

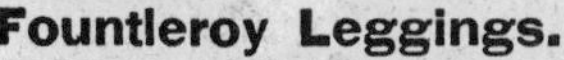

Fountleroy Leggings.

No. 15R1235 Children's Fountleroy Leather Leggings, made of fine russet goat skin, with three buckles at top. Leggings are sewn and made throughout with the best material. A very durable and handsome legging. To fit children from 4 to 10 years of age. When ordering give the age of the child.

Price, per pair..................**$0.98**
Weight, 12 ounces. For postage rate see page 4.

RUBBER BOOTS AND SHOES.

WHEN COMPARING PRICES on Rubber Footwear, we want you to know that **WE HANDLE ONLY FIRST QUALITY RUBBERS.** Many dealers sell second and even third quality rubbers. **OUR PRICES TO DEALERS AND CONSUMERS** are the same. First quality goods cannot be bought cheaper on this earth.

DO NOT BUY RUBBERS which have carried over from last year. They have lost much of their wearing quality. In buying from us you are sure of getting new, fresh goods, since our output is so large that new consignments are constantly arriving from the factory.

BELOW WE QUOTE A LIST OF FIRST, SECOND AND THIRD QUALITY. EVERY RUBBER MADE IS BRANDED ON THE BOTTOM WITH ONE OF THE FOLLOWING NAMES. CONSULT IT BEFORE BUYING.

Following Brands are First Quality.

HOOD RUBBER CO.	Model Rubber Co.	Beacon Falls Rubber Co.
Apsley Rubber Co.	Joseph Bannigan Rubber Co.	Geo. Watkinson & Co.
Sunset Rubber Co.	Concord Rubber Co.	Goodyear India Rubber Glove Co.
American Rubber Co.	Ball Band.	Boston Rubber Shoe Co.
Wales-Goodyear Rubber Co.	Candee Rubber Co.	Woonsocket Rubber Co.

Following Brands are Second Quality.

Connecticut Rubber Co.	Keystone Rubber Co.	Rhode Island Rubber Co.
Wolverine Rubber Co.	Granite Rubber Co.	Woonasquatucket Rubber Co.
Bay State Rubber Co.	Para Rubber Co.	Fairmount Rubber Co.
Union Shoe Co.	Midland Rubber Co.	New Jersey Rubber Co.
Old Colony Rubber Co.	Federal Rubber Co.	Bunker Hill Rubber Co.
Crescent Rubber Co.	Prairie Rubber Co.	
	Hudson Rubber Co.	

Following Brands are Third Quality.

Colonial Rubber Co. — Narragansett Rubber Co.

Men's All Rubber Arctics, $1.17.

DONT FAIL TO GIVE SIZE

Weight, 34 oz. For postage rate see page 4.

No. 15R1298 Men's All Rubber Arctics, made from heavy duck and covered with rubber, making the most durable arctic yet produced and one that can be cleaned with sponge and water. Sizes, 6 to 12. No half sizes. Price per pair............**$1.17**

Heavy Buckle Arctics.

Men's, Boys' and Youths', Women's, Misses' and Children's.

DONT FAIL TO GIVE SIZE

These Arctics are made extra heavy, dull finish, very heavy cloth top, wool fleece lined and are strictly first quality — suitable for heavy wear. Broad toe only.

No. 15R1300 Men's sizes, 6 to 13. Per pair, **$1.00**
No. 15R1302 Boys' sizes, 1 to 5. Per pair.. **.82**
No. 15R1304 Youths' sizes, 10 to 13. Per pair **.64**
No. 15R1306 Women's sizes, 2½ to 8. Per pair **.67**
No. 15R1308 Misses' sizes, spring heel, 11 to 2. Per pair.. **.56**
No. 15R1310 Child's sizes, spring heel, 6 to 10½. Per pair.. **.42**

Men's and Women's Extra Light Buckle Arctics,

For Fine Wear

$1.04, $0.68

Men's Extra Light Buckle Arctics, made from first quality of pure gum rubber, very fine Jersey cloth top and suitable for fine wear. Made over a handsome coin last and which fits splendidly. Weight, 24 ounces.

No. 15R1316 Men's sizes, 6 to 12. Per pair, **$1.04**
No. 15R1318 Women's sizes, 2½ to 8. Round toe only. Price per pair........................ **.68**

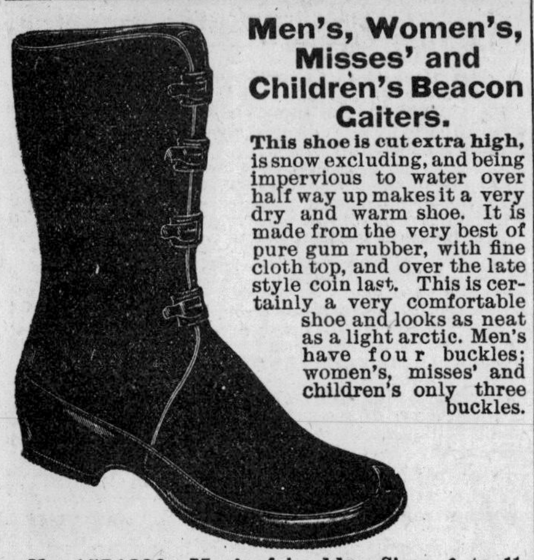

Men's, Women's, Misses' and Children's Beacon Gaiters.

This shoe is cut extra high, is snow excluding, and being impervious to water over half way up makes it a very dry and warm shoe. It is made from the very best of pure gum rubber, with fine cloth top, and over the late style coin last. This is certainly a very comfortable shoe and looks as neat as a light arctic. Men's have four buckles; women's, misses' and children's only three buckles.

No. 15R1320 Men's 4-buckle. Sizes, 6 to 11. Weight, 40 ounces. Per pair....................**$1.55**
No. 15R1319 Women's 3-buckle. Sizes, 2½ to 8. Weight, 24 ounces. Per pair....................**$1.17**
No. 15R1319½ Misses' 3-buckle. Spring heel. Sizes, 11 to 2. Weight, 20 ounces. Per pair.....**$1.02**
No. 15R1320½ Child's 3-buckle. Spring heel. Sizes, 7 to 10½. Weight, 17 ounces. Per pair....**$0.94**

Men's, Ladies' and Misses' Storm Alaskas.

This Storm Alaska differs from the ordinary Alaska, as it is cut high in front and back, and protects the front of the foot more. It is made from first quality rubber, has fine cloth top, wool fleece lined, and makes a very desirable shoe for cold weather.

Made especially to fit the stylish coin toe shoes.

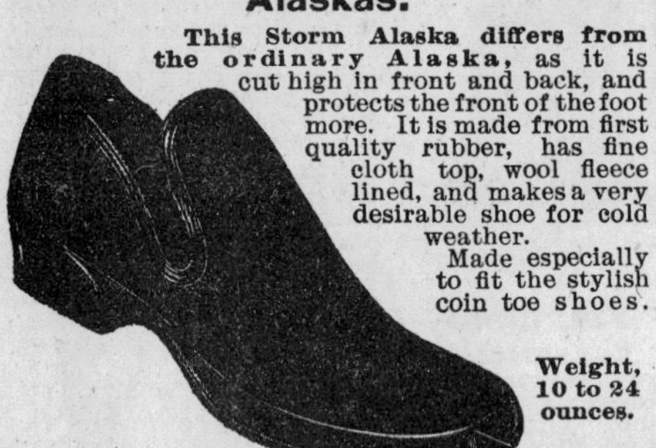

Weight, 10 to 24 ounces.

No. 15R1321½ Men's. Sizes, 6 to 12. Per pair **$0.73**
No. 15R1322 Women's. Sizes, 2½ to 8. Per pair....................**$0.56**
No. 15R1324 Women's. Spring heel. Sizes, 2½ to 8. Per pair....................**$0.56**
No. 15R1325 Misses'. Spring heel. Sizes, 11 to 2. Per pair....................**$0.47**

Men's, Women's, Misses' and Children's Storm Slippers.

Weight, 8 to 18 ounces.

This is one of the most popular rubbers ever sold, as it has a very neat appearance and coming up high in back and front, insures dry feet on stormy days. It is made from light, first quality rubber, net lined and comes in the coin toe last.

No. 15R1336 Men's. Sizes, 6 to 12. Per pair **$0.56**
No. 15R1338 Women's. Sizes, 2½ to 8. Per pair....................**$0.37**
No. 15R1338½ Women's. Spring heel. Sizes, 2½ to 8. Per pair....................**$0.37**
No. 15R1339 Misses'. Spring heel. Sizes, 11 to 2. Per pair....................**$0.32**
No. 15R1339½ Child's. Spring heel. Sizes, 5 to 10½. Per pair....................**$0.26**

Parker's Arctic Socks, 19 Cents.

Fleece lined, unequaled for house, chamber, bath room, and especially desirable for inside of rubber boots.

		Per doz	Per pair
No. 15R1637	Men's sizes, 6 to 11..	**$2.25**	**19c**
No. 15R1639	Ladies' sizes, 3 to 7..	**2.25**	**19c**

Men's and Boys' Self Acting Sandals.

First Quality Self Acting Sandals, put up exclusively for fine trade, and made to fit **the new coin toe** shoes. You can't buy a better fitting rubber or a better quality at any price.

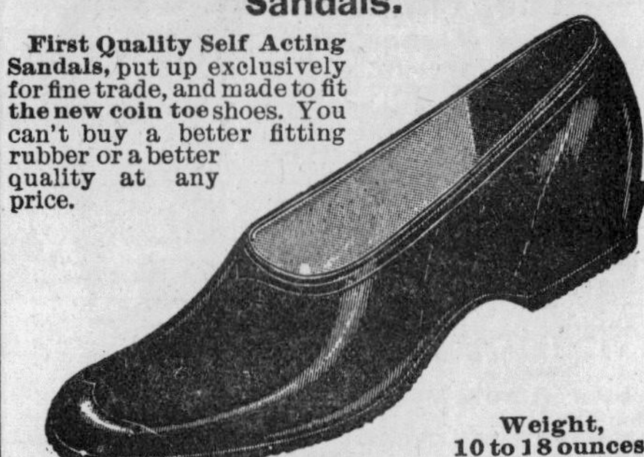

Weight, 10 to 18 ounces.

No. 15R1340 Men's. Sizes, 6 to 12. Per pair **$0.53**
No. 15R1342 Boys'. Sizes, 1 to 5. Per pair **0.43**

Ladies' Imitation Sandals, $0.32.

Ladies' Plain Sandals, medium weight, first quality. Round toe only. Sizes, 2½ to 8. Width, F. Weight, 12 to 15 ounces.
No. 15R1343 Price, per pair....................**$0.32**

Men's and Women's Extra Heavy Rubbers.

Made from first quality pure gum, dull finish, extra heavy, net lined and especially designed for hard wear. **Broad toe only.**

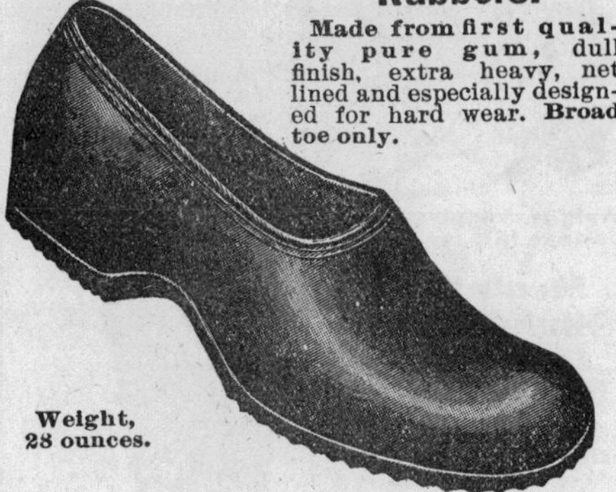

Weight, 28 ounces.

No. 15R1344 Men's. Sizes, 6 to 13. Per pair **$0.70**
No. 15R1345 Women's. Sizes, 2½ to 8. Per pair.. **.35**

Little Gents' Imitation Sandals $0.35.

Little Gents' Sandal, first quality, made to fit our child's shoes quoted for little ones.

Weight, 11 oz.

Sizes and half sizes, 9 to 13½.

No. 15R1357 Price, per pair.................**$0.35**

Men's, Boys' and Youths', Ladies', Misses' and Children's Pebble Leg Boots. $0.82 to $2.45.

First Quality Pebble Leg Short Rubber Boots, bright finish, handsome pebble leg, very light and neat fitting, wool net lined, and will give good service. Nothing better.

Weight, 20 to 50 ounces.

No. 15R1360 Men's. Sizes, 6 to 12. Per pair..**$2.45**
No. 15R1361 Women's. Sizes, 3 to 8. Per pair.................... **1.32**
No. 15R1362 Boys'. Sizes, 1 to 5. Per pair.. **1.80**
No. 15R1363 Misses'. Sizes, 11 to 2. Per pair. **1.02**
No. 15R1364 Youths'. Sizes, 10 to 13½. Per pair.................... **1.32**
No. 15R1364½ Child's. Sizes, 6 to 10½. Per pair.................... **.82**

REMEMBER every rubber we sell is strictly **FIRST QUALITY. NONE BETTER AT ANY PRICE.**

Men's Duck Hip Boots, Rolled Soles, $3.90.

This boot is one which we have made especially for us and is without a doubt the very best and most durable that can be produced at any price. It is made from strictly first quality pure gum rubber over a heavy imported duck, thereby producing a boot which is as nearly puncture and snag proof as it is possible to make it. We build this boot with an extra heavy sole and tap and with rolled edge to heel, thereby protecting the uppers and making the boot much more durable. **Friction lined only.** Should you desire more warmth, we recommend the Arctic Sock, which will produce more warmth than the ordinary felt lined boot and can be taken out at night and dried. Sizes, 6 to 12, no half sizes. Weight, 120 to 130 ounces.
No. 15R1365 Price, per pair....................**$3.90**

Men's and Boys' Hip and Thigh Boots, First Quality.

No. 15R1366 Men's Dull Finish Hip Boots, made from strictly first quality rubber, wool or net lined, and **very** serviceable. Sizes, 6 to 12.
Per pair....................**$3.51**
No. 15R1367 Boys' Dull Finish Storm King Boots, cut just above the knee, strictly first quality, net lined. Sizes, 1 to 5.
Per pair....................**$2.39**
No. 15R1368 Men's Dull Finish Rubber Boots, thigh leg, wool or net lined. Strictly first quality. Sizes, 6 to 12.
Per pair....................**$3.51**
Shipping weight averages 7½ pounds per pair.

Men's Duck Boots, Rolled Soles, $2.60.

We herewith illustrate our men's short boot made over a heavy imported duck cloth and with pure gum rubber, thereby producing a boot which is thoroughly water proof, and by far the most durable that we have ever been able to offer. We make this boot with an extra heavy sole and a heavy rolled edge to the heel. In order to make the heels more solid than those usually found, we have riveted them, thereby making them much more substantial than is usually found on the rubber boot.

We quote the regular dull finish boot and at a price some what lower than we must charge for this one, but we want to call your attention to the fact that this boot is the best that money can make and is much cheaper in the long run than the ordinary common boot. We make it with friction lining only and would suggest that the Arctic Sock be used in case a warmer boot is required. This sock can be removed at night, thoroughly dried and will give, together with this boot, much better satisfaction than the old fashioned felt lined boot. Sizes, 6 to 13. Weight, about 90 ounces.
No. 15R1369 Price, per pair....................**$2.60**

Men's and Boys' Dull Finish Short Rubber Boots, $2.45 and $1.81.

No. 15R1371 Men's Dull Finish Rubber Boots, short 16-inch leg, wool or net lined, first quality. Sizes, 6 to 13. Weight, 81 ounces. Per pair....**$2.45**
No. 15R1372 Boys' Dull Finish Rubber Boots, short 16-inch leg, wool or net lined, first quality Sizes, 1 to 5. Weight, 58 ounces. Per pair....**$1.81**

Lumbermen's Erie, Rolled Sole, $1.90.

This Lumbermen's Erie is made from first quality pure gum, over a heavy imported duck, making it one of the most durable shoes ever sold. It has extra heavy sole, solid heel, front lace, fleece lining, and is snow excluding to the top. To make it doubly strong, we build it with rolled soles.

Width F, for socks only.

No. 15R1382½ Per pair.............$1.90

Weight, 80 Ounces.

Boys' and Men's First Quality Combination Felt Boot and Rubbers.

This combination is composed of a strictly all wool felt boot, made with calf stays and the lumbermen's one buckle rubber ankle boot. Both the felt boot and the rubber ankle boot are strictly first quality, guaranteed to give perfect satisfaction, and by buying them together in this combination you get them considerably cheaper than we could possibly furnish the same articles if bought separately. When ordering state size of shoe worn, and we will send you the same size wool boot with the Perfection to fit which is one size larger than boot. Weight, 90 ounces.

No. 15R1389 Boys' sizes, 1 to 5. Per pair...$1.59
No. 15R1390 Men's sizes, 6 to 12. Per pair.. 1.75

Men's All Wool Knit Boot, Combination, Crack Proof Over, $2.10.

The Knit Boot which we put in this combination is strictly all wool, is made by the latest improved knitting machinery and then thoroughly shrunk, making a very much more shapely and durable knit boot than we have ever seen. The crack proof rolled sole perfection overshoe being made from a heavy duck, covered with first quality pure gum rubber, it is very much superior to those usually sold. The rolled sole is a special feature and one which adds much wear to the outfit, from the fact that it protects the shoe where the upper and the sole join.

We have named an exceedingly close price for this outfit hoping to induce our patrons to buy the best, and should you favor us we guarantee to give you such an outfit as you cannot possibly secure elsewhere for a similar price. When ordering always state size of shoe worn. Sizes, 6 to 12.

No. 15R1391 Per pair.......................$2.10

Weight averages 100 ounces. For postage rate see page 4.

Men's Duck Perfection, Rolled Sole, $1.46.

Men's One Buckle Perfection, made from heavy snag proof duck covered with first quality pure gum rubber with heavy rolled sole which protects the uppers and makes the shoe one of the most durable ever sold. Sizes, 6 to 13. For wool boots only.

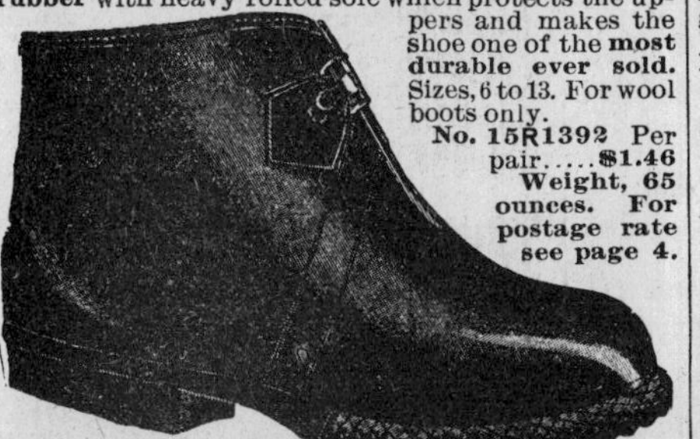

No. 15R1392 Per pair.....$1.46

Weight, 65 ounces. For postage rate see page 4.

Lumbermen's Two-Buckle, Captain, Rolled Edge, $1.55.

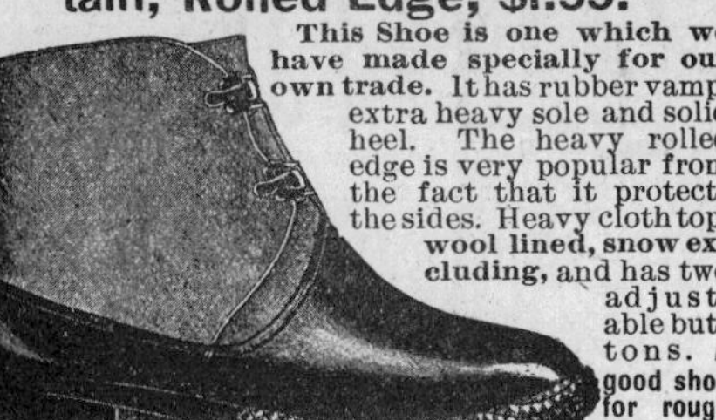

This Shoe is one which we have made specially for our own trade. It has rubber vamp, extra heavy sole and solid heel. The heavy rolled edge is very popular from the fact that it protects the sides. Heavy cloth top, wool lined, snow excluding, and has two adjustable buttons. A good shoe for rough wear.

Width, F, for German socks; W, for wool boots. Sizes, 6 to 12.

No. 15R1394 Per pair.......................$1.55

Shipping weight averages 3 pounds per pair.

Men's Extra Heavy, Rolled Sole.

DON'T FAIL TO GIVE SIZE

Arctics. Men's Extra Heavy Buckle Arctic. Wool lined, with a heavy rolled edge protecting the uppers, and extra heavy sole and heel; first quality only. Sizes, 6 to 13; full widths.

No. 15R1396 Per pair...........$1.14

Weight, 65 ozs. For postage rate, see page 4.

Lumbermen's Perfection.

Men's First Quality Ankle Boot. Made with water tight fold, tap sole and heel, and to buckle closely around the ankle; can be put on or taken off quickly. When ordering be sure to state width—F for German socks; W for wool boots. Sizes, 6 to 13.

No. 15R1398 Per pair...$1.32

Weight, 60 ozs. For postage rate see page 4.

One Buckle.

Lumbermen's Over, Oil Grain Top, $1.98.

This Lumbermen's Over is made of best quality of pure gum rubber. Top of boot oil grain leather, securely stitched and riveted to vamp and fitted with full bellows tongue. Height from heel to top of pac is 10 inches. Large brass eyelets, with strings of rawhide. This shoe is made with a heavy rolled edge sole, ribbed vamp, with seams reinforced throughout by double stitching and rivets. Strictly first quality.

Sizes, 6 to 12.

No. 15R1410 Per pair....$1.98

Weight averages 40 ounces.

Men's Leather Sole Rubber Boots.

Leather sole and insole. Miners', nailed and plain, duck and gum.

No. 15R1418 Men's Duck Hip Boot, nailed. Per pair........$5.15
No. 15R1420 Men's Gum Hip Boot, without nails. Per pair........$4.55
No. 15R1422 Men's Duck Short Boot, nailed. Per pair.... ...$3.90
No. 15R1424 Men's Gum Short Boot, without nails. Per pair........$3.55

Weight, 80 ounces.

A desirable boot for miners, dairymen, etc.

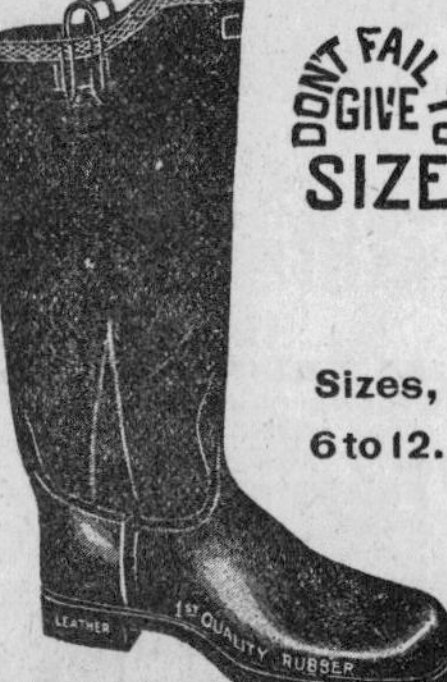

DON'T FAIL TO GIVE SIZE

Sizes, 6 to 12.

Heaton's Patent Button Machine.

No. 15R1450 This is one of the most useful machines ever invented. It is very simple and most any child can fasten the buttons on his own shoes. Every family should have one. Price, each....$0.55

If by mail, postage extra, each, 14 cents.

No. 15R1451 Fasteners for above machine.
Price, per box of 100.................................$0.07
Price, per box of 1000.......................... .70

If by mail, postage extra, per 100, 2 cents.

Black Shoe Buttons.

No. 15R1452 Ordinary Size, first quality black shoe buttons. Price, per great gross, 40c; per gross, $0.04

If by mail, postage extra, per gross, 3 cents.

Seam Fastener.

No. 15R1453 Seam Fastener. For fastening seams of shoes with staples and prevent ripping. Price, each....................$1.00
No. 15R1454 Staples. Price, per box...... .25

The Sears, Roebuck Improved German Repair Machine.

A modern machine with all the latest improvements. The easiest running and most useful shoemakers' repair machine ever manufactured, the arm being the smallest of any machine. It will stitch closer to the toe of a shoe than any other machine made. This machine can be so adjusted as to be used for the very finest of work, as well as the heaviest coarse work. By means of the improved feedbar, you may sew all around in any direction. This machine has no equal in the world, and is fully guaranteed in every part. At the extremely low price we offer this machine parties who have never before been able to own a machine may have the very best at a price below any other machine made. Set up ready for immediate use. with catalogue of parts and complete directions for using. The following extra parts go with every machine: 1 package assorted needles, 1 wrench, 1 pair tweezers, 1 stitch gauge, 1 foot hemmer for fine work, 1 needle plate, 1 cam roller, 4 bobbins, 2 pressure springs, 1 screwdriver, 1 oil can. Weight, 90 pounds.

No. 15R1455 Price, only..............................$35.95

Hammond's Steel Shoe Hammer.

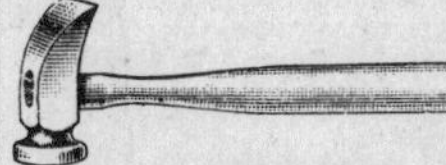

No. 15R1456 Shoemakers' No. 0, 15 ounces Price, each.......$0.30
No. 15R1457 Shoemakers', No. 1, 17 ounces. Price, each.......$0.45
No. 15R1462 Cheap Iron Hammer, medium, .06

Shoemakers' Rasps, Best Quality.

No. 15R1464 8-inch half round; weight, 6 ounces. Price, each......$0.21

Patent Peg Awl Handles, $0.05.

No. 15R1470 Price, each. $0.05
Per dozen..... .60

If by mail, postage extra, each, 4 cents.

Sewing Awl Handles, Doz. $0.12.

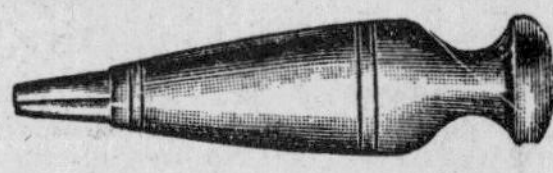

No. 15R1472 Price, doz..$0.12

If by mail, postage extra, each, 2 cents.

Shoemakers' Sewing and Peg Awl Blades.

No. 15R1474 Sewing Awl Blades, assorted. Price, per dozen.......................................$0.11
No. 15R1476 Peg Awl Blades, assorted. Price, per dozen....................................... .05

If by mail, postage extra, per dozen, 1 cent.

Shoemakers' Sewing Needles.

No. 15R1478 Shoemakers' Sewing Needles, assorted. Price, per paper.............................$0.05

If by mail, postage extra, per dozen, 1 cent.

Timmons' Lasting Pincers, $0.50.

No. 15R1482 Timmons' No. 1. Price, each........$0.50

Shipping weight, 1 pound each.

Boot Calks and Calk Sets.

		Per Doz.	Per 100
No. 15R1490	Ball Calks..	$0.06	$0.50
No. 15R1490½	Heel Calks.	.06	0.50
			Each
No. 15R1491	Calk Sets. Weight, 4 oz..		$0.14

Iron Lap Lasts.

Made of iron and very handy to have in the house.
No. 15R1498 Men's large........ $0.14
No. 15R1502 Men's medium........ .13
No. 15R1504 Ladies' medium........ .09
Shipping weight averages 4 pounds each.

Perfection Circlettes. Heel and Toe Protectors.

No. 15R1507 The Perfection Circlettes are made from best steel and broad shoulder, giving double the wear of ordinary circlettes. Especially desirable for children's school shoes.
Price, per gross........ $0.10

No. 15R1507½ Common Circlettes, like illustration, usually sold at 9 or 10 cents. Our price, per gross........ $0.07

Shipping weight averages 5 ounces per gross.

S., R. & Co.'s Safety Cushion Heel, $0.20 and $0.17.

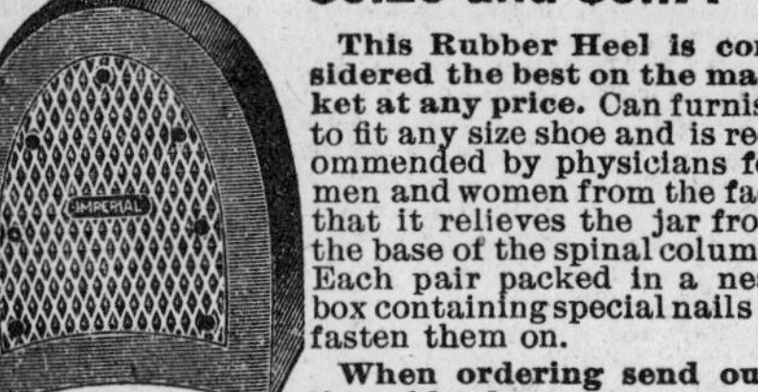

This Rubber Heel is considered the best on the market at any price. Can furnish to fit any size shoe and is recommended by physicians for men and women from the fact that it relieves the jar from the base of the spinal column. Each pair packed in a neat box containing special nails to fasten them on.

When ordering send outline of heel.

No. 15R1509½ Men's sizes, per pair........ $0.20
Per dozen pairs........ 2.40
No. 15R1509¾ Women's sizes, per pair........ .17
Per dozen pairs........ 2.00
If by mail, postage extra, per pair, 5 cents.

Wood Shoe Stretcher, $0.65.

No. 15R1510 Wood Shoe Stretcher, made medium size so it can be used for ladies' or gentlemen's shoes. Has corn and bunion attachments, and is an article which every family should have in the house. Weight, 30 ounces.
Price, each........ $0.65

Patent Shoe Stretcher, $0.55.

CORN AND BUNION CURE.

No. 15R1511 The above illustration shows what this latest shoe stretcher will do. It reaches any part of the shoe without stretching the whole shoe. A sure cure for corns and bunions. Made of japanned iron. Weight, 24 ounces. Price, each........ $0.55

Star Heel Plates, Doz. Pairs, $0.09.

No. 15R1512 Star Heel Plates, to prevent boots and shoes from wearing off at the heels. **No nails or screws required.** No. 1, for child's heels; No. 2, for ladies' heels; No. 3, for boys' heels; No. 4, for men's heels.
Price, per dozen pairs........ $0.09
If by mail, postage extra, per pair, 2 cents.

National Shoe Plates.

No. 15R1513 The National Shoe Plate is the very best on the market; prevents boots and shoes from wearing off at heels, can be used for toe plates or on ball of shoe. No screws or nails required, and one size fits any shoe.
Price, per gross, $0.60; per dozen pairs........ $0.10

Instantaneous Shoe Stretcher, $0.50.

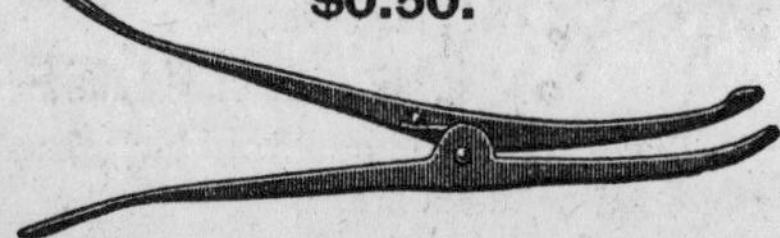

No. 15R1515 Japanned iron. Only stretcher made that will successfully stretch the tip of a shoe as well as any other part. Weight, 20 ounces.
Price, each........ $0.50

Shoe Pegs and Nails.

No. 15R1518 Latest Improved Brass Clinching Nails. Sizes, 3-8, 3½-8, 4-8, 4½-8, 5-8, 5½-8, 6-8, 6½-8 and 7-8.
Price, per pound........ $0.23

No. 15R1520 Baker's Patent Wire Clinch Nails. Sizes, 3-8, 3½-8, and 4-8, 16 wire.
Price, per pound........ $0.12

No. 15R1522 Baker's Patent Wire Clinch Nails, 4½-8, 5-8, 5½-8, 6-8 and 7-8. Price, per pound.. $0.11

No. 15R1524 Iron Clinch Nails, same as used by most cobblers, 3-8, 3½-8, 4-8, 4½-8, 5-8, 5½-8, 6-8.
Price, per pound........ $0.09

No. 15R1526 Common Iron Heel Nails, 3-8, 4-8, 5-8, 6-8. Price, per pound........ $0.05

No. 15R1528 Hungarian Nails, for bottom of miners' boots and shoes. Sizes, 3-8 stout, 3-8 fine.
Price, per pound........ $0.08

No. 15R1530 Shoe Pegs. The famous "Blue Star" peg, made from the best hardwood; nothing better. Sizes, 3-8, 4-8, 5-8, 6-8. Price, per quart........ $0.02

BEST Heel Stiffeners.

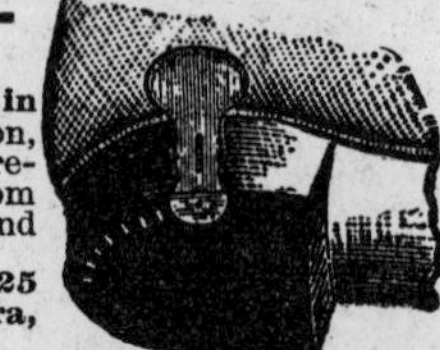

No. 15R1532 The best in the world. Easily put on, and will fit any shoe. Prevents boots and shoes from running over. Nails and screws free.
Price, per doz. pairs, $0.25
If by mail, postage extra, per pair, 2 cents.

Iron Shoe Lasts and Stand, $0.20

No. 15R1540 Reversible Iron Stand, medium height, with three lasts, small, medium and large. Price, per set, complete........ $0.20
Per dozen........ 2.40
Shipping weight, 8 pounds.

No. 15R1541½ 24-inch stand with four lasts.
Per set.. $0.45
Per dozen sets........ 5.40

Bootjack, $0.11.

No. 15R1541 Iron Bootjack, medium size. Price, each........ $0.11
Price, per dozen........ 1.32
Shipping weight, 2 pounds each.

Revolving Eyelet Set and Punch.

No. 15R1542 This Combination is composed of a Revolving Eyelet Set and Punch, used for B long eyelets, **making almost an indispensable tool in any household; will last a lifetime when properly used;** eyelet set and punch combined. Weight, 12 ounces. Price, each........ $0.95

Heel Lifts.

No. 15R1543 Men's heavy.
Price, per dozen pairs........ $0.55
No. 15R1544 Boys' heavy.
Price, per dozen pairs........ $0.45
No. 15R1545 Women's heavy.
Price, per dozen pairs........ $0.45
If by mail, postage extra, per pair, 3 cents.

Men's Jumbo Oak Blocks.

These pieces are cut from best oak sole leather, size 8½x12½ inches, and will cut four different size taps.

	Lbs., per doz.	Price, per doz.	Price, each
No. 15R1546........	9 to 11	$5.16	$0.43
No. 15R1548........	8 to 10	4.56	.38
No. 15R1550........	7 to 8	3.36	.28

Hemlock Tap Soles.

No. 15R1552 Men's Best.
Per dozen pairs........ $1.80
No. 15R1554 Men's Medium. Per dozen pairs... $1.44
No. 15R1555 Boys' Best.
Per dozen pairs........ $1.44
No. 15R1556 Women's Best. Per dozen pairs. $1.44
No. 15R1558 Women's Medium. Per dozen pairs........ $0.96

Sole Leather Strips.

Just the thing for repairs and half soles.

No. 15R1563 Hemlock Strips. 8 inches wide, about 3 feet long. Price, each........ $0.60 to $0.70
No. 15R1565 Oak Strips. 8 inches wide, 1¼ to 2 feet long. Price, each........ $0.50 to $0.60

Rubber Soleing, $0.45.

No. 15R1582 Rubber Soleing, for boots and shoes. Price, per pound, about 8 by 9 inches........ $0.45

Best Calfskin and Kid Patching.

For repairing and patching boots and shoes.
No. 15R1585 Calf Patches. Price, per pound, $0.38
No. 15R1586 Kid Patches. Price, per pound, .23

Sole Leather in Sides.

Hemlock or Red Leather, in sides weighing from 18 to 20 pounds. **This leather is made from slaughter hides,** which will give double the service of the old time dry hide leather. We do not cut sides. If less than a full side is wanted, refer to 15R1563.
No. 15R1587 Per side of 18 pounds........ $5.04
No. 15R1589 Per side of 20 pounds........ 5.60

Elastic Goring.

No. 15R1596 Hub Goring, 5-inch, per yd, $0.50
Hub Wool Goring, 5-inch, per yard........ .60

Shoemakers' Knives and Skivers.

Warranted Theo. Harrington's Best.

Best steel knives on the market. Square point, good for kitchen use. Regardless of where you buy, be sure to get Theo. Harrington's make, which are the best in the world.

		Per doz.	Each
No. 15R1597	Square Point......	$0.72	$0.06
No. 15R1597½	Sharp Point........	.72	.06
No. 15R1598	Curve Point........	.72	.06
No. 15R1599	Thin Kid Skiver....	2.04	.17
No. 15R1599½	Sole Leather Skiver	2.04	.17

If by mail, postage extra, each, 6 cents.

Best Leather Cement.

No. 15R1600 1 ounce. Per bottle, $0.05
Per dozen........ .60
If by mail, postage and tube extra, per bottle, 10 cents.
No. 15R1602 2 ounces. Per bottle, $0.09
Per dozen........ 1.08
If by mail, postage and tube extra, per bottle, 12 cents.

Best Rubber Cement.

Rubber Cement is used for repairing all kinds of rubber boots and shoes, rubber clothing, mackintoshes, etc. Ours is warranted.
No. 15R1604 2 ounces. Per dozen, $0.60
per bottle........ .05
No. 15R1606 4 ounces. Per dozen .96
Per can........ .08

Waterproof Army Shoe Lace.

No. 15R1608 This lace is made from the best of linen, woven very close, is about ⅛-inch wide, 1 yard long, with brass spiral tags. It is without a doubt the best lace ever made for men's shoes, as it has the strength and wearing qualities of the porpoise lace. Used by the U. S. Government.
Price, per dozen pairs........ $0.22
Per gross laces........ 1.32
If by mail, postage extra, per dozen, 2 cents.

Best Porpoise Laces.

Best English Porpoise Laces, with spiral tags, the strongest and best made at any price.
No. 15R1609 36-inch. Price, per dozen pairs. $0.39
No. 15R1609½ 45-inch. Price, per dozen pairs .65
If by mail, postage extra, per dozen, 2 cents.

Men's Flat Tubular Laces.

Very fine.

Black or Tan.		Per gross laces	Per dozen pairs
No. 15R1612	36-inch tan...	$0.84	$0.14
No. 15R1612½	45-inch tan...	.96	.16
No. 15R1613	36-inch black.	.84	.14
No. 15R1613¼	45-inch black.	.96	.16

If by mail, postage extra, per dozen, 2 cents.

Round Cord Laces.

No. 15R1613½ 36-inch Men's Black.
Price, per gross, $0.48; per dozen pairs........ $0.08
No. 15R1614½ 54-inch Ladies' Black.
Price, per gross, $0.60; per dozen pairs........ $0.10
If by mail, postage extra, per dozen, 2 cents.

Ladies' Flat Tubular Laces.

Very fine quality, and all the rage for ladies' shopping bags. Black or Tan.

	Per gross laces	Per dozen pairs
No. 15R1615 27-inch Oxford, Black........	$0.96	$0.16
No. 15R1615½ 27-inch Oxford, Tan........	.96	16
No. 15R1616 54-inch Black.	1.02	.17
No. 15R1617 54-inch Tan....	1.02	.17

If by mail, postage extra, per dozen, 2 cents.

Our Non-Crumpling Hair Insoles.

Made of Genuine Horse Hair, well covered and stitched. Has a patent fine steel stay, running the entire length of sole, causing it to retain its proper shape and to lay perfectly smooth in the shoe, doing away with the great trouble of ruffling or crumpling, making it uncomfortable to the foot, as found in other insoles of this kind that do not have the patent stay. **This sole is considered the healthiest insole ever manufactured.** Is light in weight and recommended by doctors as a cure for rheumatism and other ailments caused directly from cold or damp feet. Unlike other insoles, **these will last longer, and are cleaner and neater insoles than we have ever seen.** They keep the shoe and hoisery clean and pure from the much dreaded effects of perspiring feet. Is a very desirable insole to be worn in rubber boots. **You cannot afford to be without one of our insoles, as our prices are only 8 and 9 cents per pair.**

No. 15R1618 Men's sizes, 6 to 11. Per pair.. $0.09
No. 15R1619 Women's sizes, 3 to 7. Per pair, .08

Peerless Wool Slipper Soles.

The Peerless Slipper Sole is covered by patent and **is by far the best ever placed on the market.** The edges are turned, which does away with all outside stitches. Heavy fleece wool faced. **Used with crocheted uppers.**

No. 15R1620 Men's sizes, 6 to 11, per pair.... $0.25
No. 15R1622 Women's sizes, 3 to 7, per pair. .20
No. 15R1624 Misses' sizes, 13 to 2, per pair. .18
No. 15R1626 Child's sizes, 5 to 12, per pair.. .17
If by mail, postage extra, per pair, 3 cents.

Leather and Cork Insoles.

No. 15R1628 Men's Leather Insoles, sizes 6 to 11. Per dozen pairs, $0.72; per pair.. $0.06
No. 15R1630 Ladies' Leather Insoles, sizes, 3 to 7. Price, per dozen pairs, $0.60; per pair.... $0.05
No. 15R1632 Men's Cork Insoles, sizes 6 to 11. Price, per dozen pairs, $0.60; per pair.... $0.05
No. 15R1634 Ladies' Cork Insoles, sizes 3 to 7. Price, per dozen pairs, $0.48; per pair...... $0.04
If by mail, postage extra, per pair, 2 cents.

Canvas Slippers, $0.10.

For Inside of Rubber Boots.

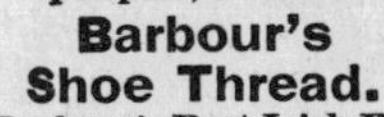

No. 15R1636 Men's First Grade Canvas Slippers, with sheepskin bottoms, used for inside of rubber boots. Sizes, 6 to 11. Per dozen pairs. $1.20; per pair....... $0.10
If by mail, postage extra, per pair, 3 cents.

Barbour's Shoe Thread.

Barbour's Best Irish Flax Shoe Thread, half bleached, is used for hand sewing and is the best on the market at any price.

2-ounce balls.

	No.	Per lb.	Per ball
No. 15R1646	12	$1.44	$0.18
No. 15R1648	3	1.20	.15
No. 15R1650	10	1.04	.13
No. 15R1652	10 (Am. Stan'd)	.72	.09

Rubber Patching, Etc.

No. 15R1656 Medium Patching, dull or luster. Price, per square.... $0.45

Rubber Repair Cloth.

No. 15R1658 Per yard, $2.70; per square ft.. $0.30

Shoemakers' Wax.

No. 15R1660 Price, per dozen.... $0.07
Shipping weight 1 pound per dozen balls.

Shoemakers' Bristles.

No. 15R1662 Price, per ¼ ounce.... $0.20

B Long Eyelets, $0.10.

No. 15R1666 B long. Black, yellow or white. Price, per 1000.... $0.10
If by mail, postage extra, per 1,000, 4 cents.

Eyelet Sets and Punches.

No. 15R1668 Eyelet Set, common. Price.... $0.45
No. 15R1670 Eyelet Set, spring. Price.... $0.55
No. 15R1671 Eyelet Punch. Price.... $0.40
If by mail, postage extra, per set, 10 cents.

Stocking Knee Protectors.

Stocking Knee Protectors are very desirable for boys and girls who wear their stockings out quickly at the knees. We quote below both cloth and leather.

No. 15R1672 Jersey Cloth. Price, per pair.... $0.15
No. 15R1674 Leather. Price, per pair.... .20
If by mail, postage extra, per pair, 2 cents.

Stocking Heel Protectors, $0.09.

Made from a good grade of leather and will save many times its cost every month.

No. 15R1675 Men's. Sizes, 6 to 11. Per pair.... $0.09
No. 15R1676 Women's. Sizes, 3 to 7. Per pair..... .09
No. 15R1677 Boys'. Sizes, 2 to 5. Per pair.... .09
If by mail, postage extra, per pair, 1 cent.

Our Box Calf Combination Dressing.

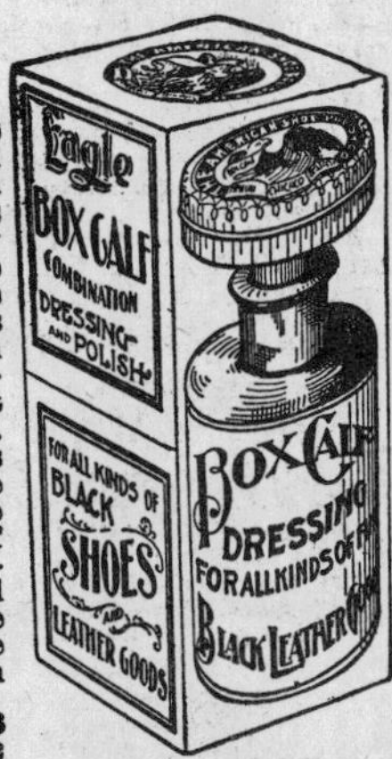

No. 15R1680 Consists of a bottle of cleaner and a box of polish, put up in a handsome carton. This is a polish that not only produces a handsome luster, but at the same time softens and preserves the leather. This polish will keep the shoes in perfect condition with but very little application. May be used on all kinds of leather and will produce a lasting luster. It can be used on the very finest of leather with perfect safety. We highly recommend it to our customers. One bottle of cleaner and one box of polish comes in each carton.

Price, per box...... $0.06
Per dozen...... .72

Frank Miller's Leather Preservative and Waterproof Oil Blacking.

25-Cent Size at 10 Cents.

No. 15R1685 This is the oldest and best leather preservative that was ever manufactured. For over fifty years it has been in use. This blacking is not designed to produce a polish, but renders the leather soft and pliable and makes it absolutely waterproof for farmers, lumbermen, fishermen and sportsmen. We recommend it as the very best leather preservative that can be secured. This blacking is sold everywhere for 25 cents. Price, per box...... $0.10
Per dozen boxes.... 1.20

25c Trilby Polish, $0.12.

No. 15R1701 Trilby Polish has been appropriately termed the 20th century polish. It is the only shoe polish which comes in liquid form that will produce a brilliant polish on **vici kid, enamel, box calf, patent leather, goat, and in fact all dry leathers;** all that is necessary to produce a polish is to apply the liquid with sponge attached to cork, and rub with a cloth free from dirt. Trilby polish preserves the leather, excludes the moisture and when on the shoe will not soil the whitest garment. **Sold everywhere at 25 cents a bottle.**

Price, per dozen, $1.44; per bottle.... $0.12
Unmailable on account of weight.

Gilt Edge Dressing, $0.14

No. 15R1706 Ladies' Gilt Edge Shoe Dressing is very useful for a great many things besides shoes. It will make your old rubbers, **shopping bags and black kid gloves look equal to new. Many use it to dye straw hats and as a stove polish,** thus saving time and labor, dust and brushes, as it requires no rubbing. Weight, 14 oz. **Sold everywhere for 25 cents.** Per dozen, $1.68; per bottle.... $0.14
Unmailable on account of weight.

Patent and Russet Leather Polish, $0.03.

The finest Patent Leather Polish ever sold. It will not injure the leather in any way, and by cleaning the shoes well and applying the polish, then rubbing with a soft woolen cloth, **it quickly produces a brilliant and waterproof luster.** Large 10-cent size.

No. 15R1710 Black. Price, per dozen boxes.... $0.36; per box.... $0.03
No. 15R1712 Russet. Price, per doz. boxes, .36
Per box.... .03
If sent by mail, postage extra, per box 2 cents.

GIVE CATALOGUE NUMBER IN FULL WHEN YOU WRITE YOUR ORDER

Combination Russet, $0.06.

No. 15R1714 Cleaner and Polish, for polishing, cleansing and removing stains from all kinds of russet or tan colored shoes. Also a decorated tin box of polishing paste, for giving russet and tan-colored shoes a brilliant, durable and waterproof polish as follows: First remove the stains and cleanse the leather with our dressing, then apply a thin coating of our **Yellow Polishing Paste** according to directions on box, and you will get an elegant and lasting polish. On new shoes, or those that do not need cleansing, **only the polishing paste need be used. Try them once and you will never be satisfied with any other polish.**

Per dozen, $0.72; per box, $0.06
If by mail, postage and tube extra, per box, 16c.

Waterproof Polish, $0.13.

For Men's and Boys' Shoes.

No. 15R1716 Produces a brilliant jet black polish without brushing, thus saving time, labor and money. It is free from acids and **will not injure leather.** Being waterproof in rain or snow, is largely used in winter **to keep the feet dry, thus preventing cold and rheumatism.** Men or boys who dislike to wear rubbers should use this, **as it sheds water like a rubber.** It is a favorite with gentlemen, as it will not rub off or ruin their pants or soil their hands. Apply with sponge attached to cork.

Price, per bottle.... $0.13
Per dozen.... 1.56
If by mail, postage and tube extra, per bottle, 18 cents.

Bixby's Blackings and Shoe Dressings.

No. 15R1721 Bixby's BBB Blacking, size M, with patent handle. Price, per box... $0.04
Per dozen.... .48
No. 15R1723 Bixby's BBB Blacking, size B, with patent handle. Price, per box... $0.08
Per dozen.... .96

No. 15R1725 Bixby's Royal Polish, a liquid dressing for ladies', misses' and children's shoes, which is equal to many 25-cent dressings. Per case of 1 dozen.... $0.84
Per bottle... .07
No. 15R1727 Pink Label Dressing for ladies', misses' and children's shoes, put up especially for us and guaranteed equal to any 10-cent dressing on the market. Sponge attached to cork. Price, per bottle.... $0.04
Per case of 1 dozen.... .48

Vici Kid Dressing, $0.14.

Regular 25-Cent Size.

Foerderer's Vici Kid is known all over the civilized world, and this dressing is used on every skin before it leaves his factory. **It is the only dressing which produces a lasting and brilliant luster without rubbing, and the fact that Mr. Foerderer uses it on all of his kid stock is sufficient guarantee of its good qualities.** It is applied with a sponge, and **makes kid shoes look like new.** Is suitable for all kid shoes. This dressing is sold everywhere at 25 cents. Each
No. 15R1746 For tan shoes.. $0.14
No. 15R1748 For black shoes. .14
Weight, 13 ounces.

MR. CONSUMER OR MR. DEALER

Where on earth can you buy shoe dressings at these prices?

Every price below wholesalers'. Live dealers appreciate this fact and buy their findings from us.

$1.98 BUYS THE BEST COMBINATION SHOE, HARNESS AND TINNERS' OUTFIT EVER BUILT

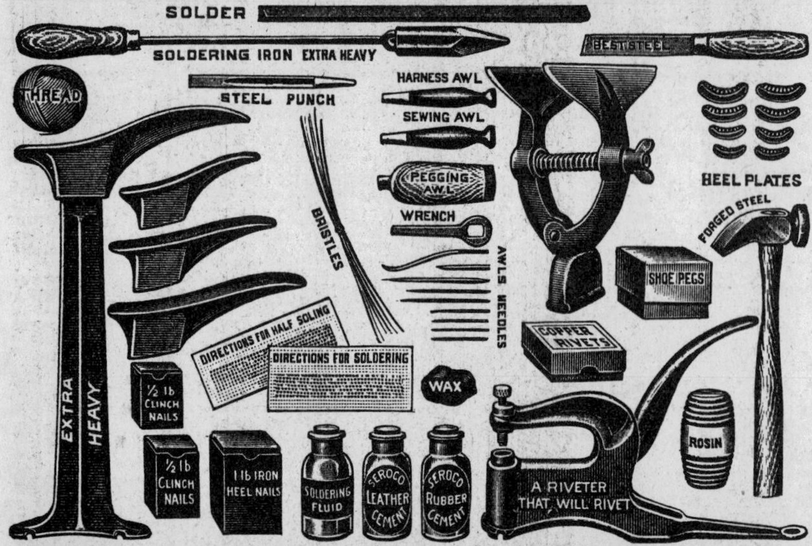

ORDER THIS OUTFIT AT $1.98 and if you do not say it is for all practical uses worth a dozen of any other outfits on the market, you can return it at our expense and we will return your $1.98. Before getting out this big high grade outfit, we purchased the best outfits advertised by other leading houses at $1.60 to $2.50, and we found the best outfit in the lot compared with our big $1.98 outfit about as follows:

OUR HAMMER is made of the best forged steel. The other outfit contained a worthless cast iron hammer, costing 48 cents a dozen.

OUR KNIFE costs as much as two of the other knives.

OUR SOLDERING IRON is extra heavy, the other light and worthless.

OUR RIVETING MACHINE is high grade and practical, the other is almost worthless. We found the same comparison on almost every item that went into the outfit. The best outfit we found put up in a cheap, common box, while ours goes into a handsome stained and varnished hinged tool chest.

Our Big $1.98 Outfit

IS THE ONLY THOROUGHLY RELIABLE AND PRACTICAL OUTFIT ON THE MARKET FOR THE REPAIRING OF BOOTS, SHOES, HARNESS AND TINWARE, ALL HIGH GRADE, STANDARD TOOLS AND FURNISHINGS............

EVERY ARTICLE contained in this outfit is the best money can buy, suitable for the best shoemakers', tinners' and harness makers' use. We guarantee each and every tool to be of the best quality and to give the best of satisfaction. The tools are made by the best manufacturers of the highest grade of tools. The outfit is not composed of worthless cast iron hammers, worthless riveters, knives that will not keep an edge, soldering irons too light to hold the heat and do the work. It is put up on honor, containing only carefully selected tools of the highest standard offered in any combination outfit.

OUR SPECIAL PRICE OF $1.98 barely covers the cost of material and labor, with but our one small percentage of profit added.

OUR CHEAPER OUTFIT AT $1.29 is in every way equal to the best outfit advertised by other houses at $1.60 to $2.50. If any combination outfit you can get from any other house at $1.60 to $2.50 is good enough for you, you will find our $1.29 outfit in every way equal to the best; in fact, it is almost identical to several outfits we got from other houses that sell at $1.60 to $2.50. We, however, urge you to order this, the highest grade outfit made, and when you get it, if you do not say that our forged steel hammer, knife, riveter and soldering iron are worth a dozen of the same tools furnished by others, if you do not say that our outfit at $1.98 is cheaper than any outfit offered by any other house, even at half their present selling price, you can return it to us and we will immediately return your $1.98.

CONTENTS

1 Extra Heavy Iron Stand,
4 Extra Heavy Lasts,
1 Best Riveting Machine,
1 Nickel Plated Steel Shoemakers' Hammer,
1 Patent Peg Awl Handle,
1 Peg Awl,
1 Sewing Awl Handle,
1 Sewing Awl,
1 Harness Awl Handle,
1 Harness Awl,
1 Wrench for Peg Awl Handle,
1 Ounce Best Leather Cement,
1 Bottle Best Rubber Cement,
1 Bunch Bristles,
1 Ball of Thread,
1 Ball of Wax,
1 Package of Shoe Pegs,
1 Pound of Iron Heel Nails,
½ Pound 4/8 Clinch Nails,
½ Pound 5/8 Clinch Nails,
4 Pairs Best Heel Plates,
6 Shoe and Harness Needles,
1 Improved Saw and Harness Clamp,
1 Box Harness and Belt Rivets,
1 Steel Punch,
1 Soldering Iron, Extra Heavy,
1 Bar Solder,
1 Box Rosin,
1 Ounce Soldering Fluid,
1 Copy of Directions for Soldering,
1 Copy of Directions for Shoe Repairing.

This outfit is actually worth four times as much as any outfit ever placed upon the market.

No. 15R1801 Price, each.. **$1.98**

OUR FAMILY BOOT, SHOE, HARNESS AND TINWARE MENDER, $1.29.

ADVERTISED BY MANY CONCERNS AS FIRST QUALITY AT $1.75 AND $1.50.

WE HAVE HAD OUR ATTENTION CALLED TO OUTFITS which, illustrated, look about as our $1.98 article, and at a price which to our customers seemed very low. The usual price of this outfit is anywhere from $1.50 to $1.75. For the benefit of those of our patrons who have seen this outfit advertised at the above mentioned price, we have decided to put in the same outfit, and you will, no doubt, recognize the illustration as the same that you have seen advertised from $1.50 to $1.75. We now offer it to you at the wonderfully low price of $1.29 each. The articles which go to make up this outfit are not to be compared as to quality with our $1.98 outfit shown above. This outfit, at the price named, would necessarily have to be of inferior quality. Please understand, however, that this outfit contains exactly the same tools as those generally sold at a higher price.

CONTENTS

1 Riveting Machine,
1 Box 4/8 Clinch Nails,
1 Box 5/8 Clinch Nails,
1 Box Iron Heel Nails,
1 Iron Stand,
3 Iron Lasts, Nos. 1, 2 and 3,
1 Harness Clamp,
1 Harness Clamp Spring,
1 Pegging Awl Haft,
1 Wrench for Pegging Awl Haft,
1 Sewing Awl Haft,
1 Harness Awl Haft,
1 Hammer,
1 Steel Knife,
12 Pairs Heel Plates, Assorted,
2 Pairs Tap Soles,
2 Pairs Heel Lifts,
2 Sewing Awl Blades,
2 Harness Awl Blades,
2 Pegging Awl Blades,
1 Box Slotted Rivets,
1 Bunch Bristles,
1 Ball Thread,
1 Ball Wax,
1 Bottle of Leather Cement,
1 Bottle Rubber Cement,
1 Copy Instructions,
1 Soldering Set, consisting of Soldering Iron, Scraper, Bar Solder and Box of Rosin.

No. 15R1811 Price, each.... **$1.29**

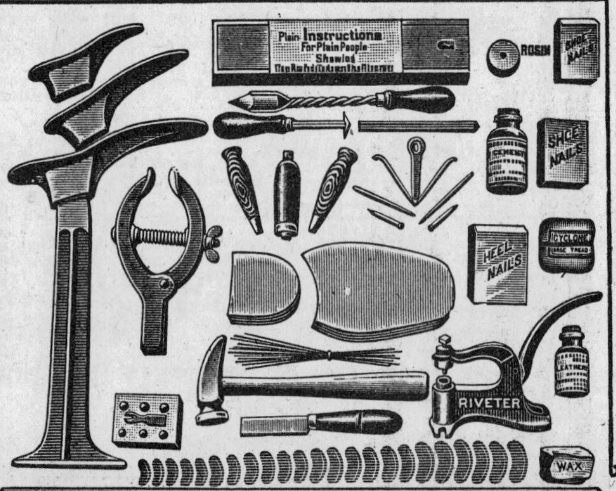

LADIES', MISSES' AND CHILDREN'S WEARING APPAREL.

IN THIS our Department of Wearing Apparel for Ladies', Misses' and Children, we have brought together in one very complete stock the most select patterns and styles, the choicest garments, chosen with care from the most reputable manufacturers and priced at figures that defy any kind of competition.

IN SELECTING OUR STOCK FOR THIS YEAR we have very carefully avoided goods which will not give perfect satisfaction. We have avoided certain manufacturers whose specialty is the low grades of manufactured garments. We believe we are serving our customers' interest better by supplying them with a grade of goods which will please them not only when received, but after long wear. By most advantageous purchases from the most reputable manufacturers we are in a better position to furnish a superior quality at even a lower price than the products of cheap manufacturers are sold by other concerns.

HOW WE MAKE OUR PRICES SO LOW.

WITH A UNIVERSAL TRADE covering the entire country, we are given a purchasing power equalling thousands of retail stores, and are thus able to take entire outputs of certain manufacturers. The manufacturer, in delivering all he makes to one reliable concern, having no expenses of advertising or traveling men, and selling to us on an absolutely spot cash basis, is only too glad to supply us at a very narrow margin above the actual cost to manufacture, and in this manner the goods are procured by us at from 20 to 25 per cent less than the retailer himself can buy at, and selling to our customers on our one narrow margin of profit above the cost to make, it is no wonder that our prices astonish the storekeeper and are a source of great saving to the consumer.

THE GOODS IN THIS CATALOGUE are subject to slight changes in accordance with prevailing styles. We make mention of this fact for the reason that from month to month there may be slight changes in length of jackets, shape of collar or yoke on waists and the style of back or binding on skirts. In all cases we send to our customers the latest prevailing styles.

SIZES OF LADIES' AND CHILDRENS' GARMENTS.

LADIES' CAPES COME IN SIZES from 32 to 44 inches around the bust. When ordering, please give us your bust and neck measure; measure all around; also state height and weight.

LADIES' JACKETS COME IN SIZES from 32 to 42 inches around the bust. No odd sizes, such as 33, 35, 37, etc. Should you have occasion to order any of the above sizes, order 34, 36 38, etc., respectively. When ordering, please give us your bust measure, all around the bust under the arms, and all other measurements as indicated in illustration below.

LADIES' SKIRTS COME IN SIZES from 37 to 44 inches in length, and from 21 to 30 inches around the waist.

LADIES' WRAPPERS AND TEA GOWNS come in sizes from 32 to 44 inches; no odd sizes, and not over 58 to 60 inches in length. When ordering, state bust measure. If a wrapper sent is a few inches longer than ordered, customers will have to shorten it without any allowance from us.

FUR COLLARETTES. Sizes, from 32 to 44 inches around bust. When ordering, please give us your bust and neck measure.

LADIES' SUITS CONSIST OF JACKET AND SKIRT ONLY. Sizes for jacket 32 to 42 inches; no odd sizes. Sizes for skirt from 37 to 44 inches in length and 21 to 30 inches around the waist. When ordering, please state bust and waist measure and length of skirt.

LADIES' SILK AND CLOTH WAISTS Sizes from 32 to 42 inches around the bust; no odd sizes. When ordering, please give us your bust, neck and waist measure.

INFANTS' LONG COATS FOR INFANTS ONLY.

CHILDREN'S AND GIRLS' REEFER JACKETS. SIZES for 4 to 14 year old children and school girls; no odd sizes. When ordering, please state age, number of inches around the bust, height and weight.

CHILDREN'S AND SCHOOL GIRLS' NEWMARKETS, SIZES FOR 4 TO 14 YEARS; no odd sizes. We charge a small advance for each size, as it consumes more material and labor. When ordering, please state age and number of inches around the bust.

MISSES' JACKETS SIZES FOR 14, 16, 18, 20 YEAR OLD Young Ladies; no odd sizes. The size 20 will correspond with 36 to 38 inches around the bust. When ordering, please state age and number of inches around the bust.

LADIES' MUSLIN AND FLANNEL GOWNS SIZES 14, 15, 16 inches, neck measure.

LADIES' MUSLIN AND FLANNEL DRAWERS Sizes 25, 27, 29 inches in length. When ordering, please state open or closed.

LADIES' MUSLIN SKIRTS AND PETTICOATS SIZES 38, 40, 42 inches in length; no longer. When ordering, please state the length you desire.

SPECIAL SIZES. EVERYTHING DIFFERENT THAN THE SIZES mentioned above, are considered as extra sizes, in which case we require 20 per cent above the price quoted in the catalogue. All special orders require about two weeks to make.

ALL STYLES ARE SUBJECT TO SMALL CHANGES, SUCH AS SLEEVES, BUTTONS, LENGTH, ETC. What we mean by this is that in case the style changes with the advance of the season, we shall make these changes before shipping the goods and thus they will be somewhat different from description and illustration, but always the same in value.

IN ORDER TO AVOID DELAY in shipment, please give second choice.

IN ORDERING TAKE MEASURES AS FOLLOWS:

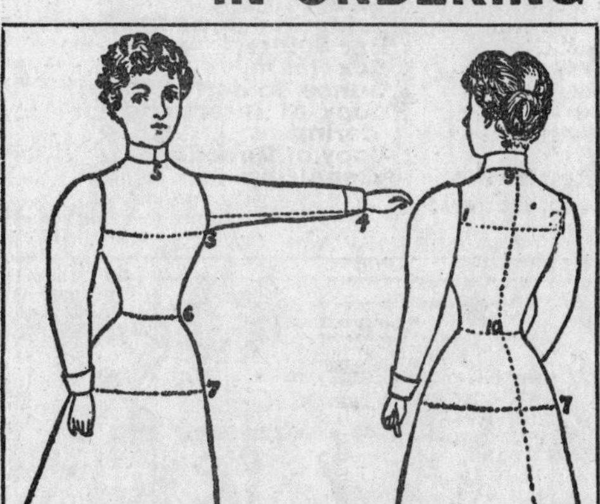

BUST MEASURE—All around under the arms, over fullest part in front and well up over the shoulder blades in back. Your weight....pounds.

6 WAIST—Around smallest part of waist.

7 HIPS—Fullest measure around hips, about 6 inches below the waist line.

1 to 2 ACROSS BACK—From shoulder seam to shoulder seam.

5 NECK—All around neck over dress collar at bottom of collar, not too tight.

3 to 4 SLEEVE LENGTH—Give the exact measure of the inside sleeve seam from armhole (3) to wrist bone (4), with arm extended.

3 ARMHOLES—Around shoulder where the sleeve is sewed in.

9 to 10 LENGTH OF WAIST IN BACK—Measure must be taken from the collar seam (9) to waist line (10) in the back.

NOTE—A correct bust measure will nearly always insure a good fit.

NOTICE CAREFULLY THESE INSTRUCTIONS. While filling out the order blank, taking the measure over your dress, making no allowance whatever, and there will be no trouble about a fit.

FUR CAPES. Bust and neck measure only are necessary. Use the order blanks enclosed, and we will send you others.

FOR MISSES' GARMENTS Take measure same as above, but always state age and weight. These garments come in ages 12 to 18 years only.

FOR CHILDREN. Garments for children from 4 to 12 years of age, state age of child and say whether large or small for age; no further measurement necessary.

IN ORDERING SHIRT WAISTS State your height, your weight, number of inches around the body at bust, taken over dress close up under arms, number of inches around the body at neck, and number of inches around the body at waist.

IN ORDERING A SKIRT State your height and weight, number of inches around body at waist, and length of skirt in front from waist to bottom.

IN ORDERING AN UNDERSKIRT State your height and weight, number of inches around the body at waist, and number of inches from waist to bottom of skirt—desired length.

IN ORDERING A DRESS WRAPPER OR TEA GOWN Take measure exactly the same as for jacket, above explained, and in addition state length of skirt wanted, the number of inches from waist line to bottom of skirt. Where our rules for measurement are carefully followed a perfect fit is insured.

LADIES' MUSLIN, CAMBRIC AND NAINSOOK GOWNS.

SIZES, 14, 15 AND 16 INCHES NECK MEASURE.

Our 39-Cent Leader Gown.

No. 38R502 Ladies' Muslin Gown made Mother Hubbard Style, high neck, yoke trimmed with 8 rows of tucks with lace insertion on each side, lawn collars and cuffs with one row of hemstitching. Extra good value.

Price................39c

If by mail, postage extra, 16 cents.

49 Cents Buys this Muslin Gown.

No. 38R506 Wonderful bargain Ladies' Gown, made of good quality muslin, empire style, bosom trimmed with wide embroidery, reverse with three tucks and hemstitching. Cambric ruffle and cuffs.

Price..............49c

If by mail, postage extra, 15 cents.

A Pretty Style, Only 55 Cents.

No. 38R510 Empire Style Gown, made of good quality of muslin, square front of lawn, and lace edge, lawn collar with lace edging, lawn cuffs with lace edge to match.

Price..................55c

If by mail, postage extra, 17 cents.

No. 38R514 Very neat ladies' gown, made of good quality muslin, empire style; bosom trimmed with three rows lace insertion and embroidery alternating, lace edge to match; tucked revers, lawn collar edged with lace to match, lawn cuffs and matched lace edge. Splendid value.
Price...............75c
If by mail, postage extra, 16 cents.

Price, 75c

Price, 82c

No. 38R518 Ladies' Fine Muslin Gown, empire style; square yoke with open work embroidery insertion; six rows of tucks on each revers, with embroidery insertion and lawn embroidery ruffle; cuffs of lawn embroidery. A very pretty gown.
Price..............82c
If by mail, postage extra, 15 cents.

No. 38R522 Empire Gown, made of good quality muslin; bosom with three rows embroidery and hemstitching, with embroidery edge; reveres with two rows embroidery insertion and hemstitching, medium width embroidery ruffle; cuffs of embroidery. Splendid value.
Price...............89c
If by mail, postage extra, 16 cents.

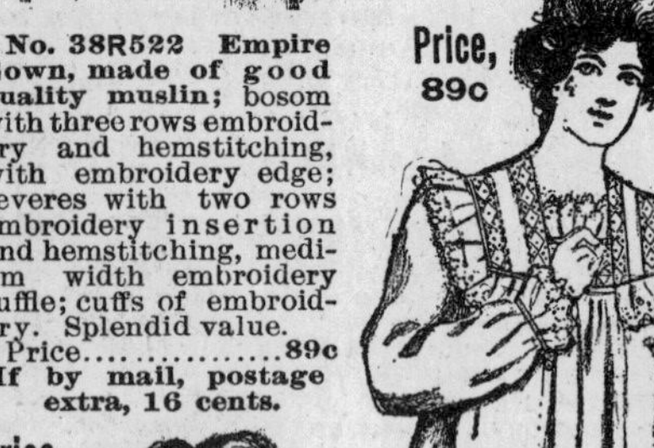

Price, 89c

Price, 98c

No. 38R526 Ladies' Gown, made of cambric, empire style; bosom trimmed with three rows of fine torchon lace insertion and ribbon, large collar with torchon insertion and edge to match; lawn cuffs with torchon lace insertion and matched edge. A very pretty trimmed gown at a very low price.
Price...............98c
If by mail, postage extra, 15 cents.

No. 38R530 A very neat gown, made of good quality muslin; pointed yoke solidly trimmed with fine tucks and insertion of fine embroidery; embroidery edge around neck and front, with cuffs to match.
Price...........$1.10
If by mail, postage extra, 16 cents.

Price, $1.10

Price, $1.15

No. 38R534 Very pretty gown, made of fine cambric, Mother Hubbard style; high round neck bolero effect yoke which is trimmed on each side with three rows of Valenciennes lace insertion alternating with embroidery insertion; narrow lawn ruffle with Valenciennes lace edge to match, herringbone braid; lawn cuffs with lace edge to match and herringbone braid.
Price.............$1.15
If by mail, postage extra, 14 cents.

No. 38R538 A very neat and serviceable gown, made of good quality cambric, Mother Hubbard style; pointed yoke, two wide embroidery insertions each side, ruffle of fine embroidery to match; neck and fly of embroidery, herringbone braid trimming; cuffs of embroidery and herringbone braid trimming. Very good value.
Price..........$1.19
If by mail, postage extra, 15 cents.

Price, $1.25

No. 38R546 A serviceable gown, empire style, made of a soft finish cambric; pointed yoke which is solidly tucked, insertion of embroidery, lawn embroidery collar; revers of two rows of embroidery insertion, lawn embroidery ruffle trimmed with herringbone braid; lawn embroidery cuffs trimmed with herringbone braid.
Price..........$1.39
If by mail, postage extra, 15 cents.

Price, $1.48

No. 38R554 Ladies' Gown, empire style, made of fine nainsook; bosom trimmed with Valenciennes lace insertion with wide edge to match, beading and ribbon insertion with two ribbon bows; revers with one row lace insertion and wide edge to match, edge extending all round back of neck; revers with numerous rows of tucks, beading and ribbon insertion, and cuffs of wide Valenciennes lace edge. A very pretty and attractive gown. Price......$1.59

Price, $1.98

Price, $1.19

No. 38R542 A very pretty gown, Mother Hubbard style, made of soft finish cambric; pointed yoke, four rows of fine Point de Paris lace insertion, alternating with three rows of fine embroidery insertion, three fine tucks on each side, lawn ruffle with lace edge; neck trimmed with Point de Paris lace; lawn cuffs with lace edge to match.
Price..........$1.25
If by mail, postage extra, 16 cents.

Price, $1.39

No. 38R550 A handsome gown, Mother Hubbard style, made of a soft finish cambric; square yoke with two insertions of fine Point de Paris lace, and one row of embroidery insertion; lawn ruffle with Point de Paris edge to match; lawn cuffs with matched lace edge. Price.....$1.48
If by mail, postage extra, 15 cents.

Price, $1.59

No. 38R558 Ladies' Gown, made of a very soft finish cambric; pointed yoke, six rows of fine (three rows on each side) embroidery insertion, plaits alternating; lawn embroidery around neck and front followed with herringbone braid; wide lawn embroidery ruffle, also trimmed with herringbone braid; lawn embroidery cuffs trimmed with herringbone braid.
Price...............$1.98

No. 38R566 A very neat and serviceable gown, made of a very fine grade of nainsook, pointed yoke made of fine embroidered lawn, with numerous rows of hemstitching; has wide lawn embroidered ruffled collar to match and satin ribbon bow; cuffs of lawn embroidery to match. Three plaits in back of yoke. Price.$2.39

Price, $2.39

Price, $2.98

No. 38R570 Beautiful Ladies' Gown, made of high grade nainsook, sailor collar, which is made entirely of Point de Paris lace insertion and a cluster of tucks alternating and trimmed with herringbone braid, ruffle of wide Point de Paris lace to match, satin ribbon bow; similar trimmings on cuffs. A very elaborately trimmed garment. Price. $2.98

SHORT OR ELBOW SLEEVE GOWNS.

Sizes, 14, 15 and 16 inches neck measure.

No. 38R574 Very neat gown, made of soft finish cambric; square neck trimmed with Point de Paris lace insertion and two rows of herringbone braid; ruffle of Point de Paris lace to match and three plaits in back of yoke, ribbon bow, cuffs trimmed to match yoke. Elbow sleeves.
Price...........$1.48

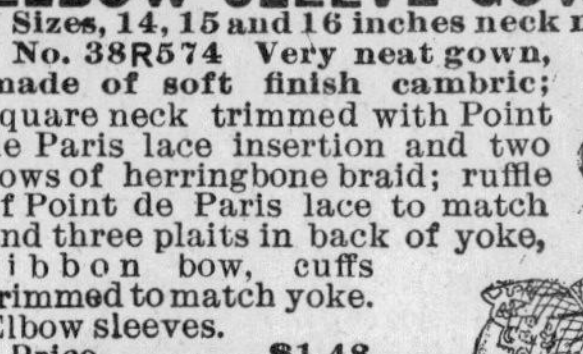

Price, $1.98

No. 38R576 A very attractive gown, made of a high grade nainsook, empire style, square yoke with insertion of Point de Paris lace and edge to match, beading and ribbon insertion. Two rows of lace insertion and edge to match. Point de Paris lace edge at the back of neck. Matched insertion and edge on elbow sleeves. Price...$1.98

No. 38R578 A beautiful Combination Chemise Gown, made of good quality nainsook, round neck, thirteen rows of fine Torchon lace insertion alternating with narrow embroidery insertion edged with fine lace around neck, both front and back, beading and ribbon insertion, embroidery and ribbon insertion at waist forming a bow. elbow sleeves trimmed with two rows lace and embroidery, with lace to match, also beading and ribbon insertion.
Price, each..$2.69

No. 38R582 A very high grade gown made of fine Nainsook, Mother Hubbard style; "V" shape neck, yoke trimmed with four rows of bow knot lace net insertion on each side, with edge to match all around neck, and ribbon insertion with ribbon bow, elbow sleeves with two insertions and wide edge to match. Beading and ribbon insertion and bow. A very pretty gown.
Price, each....$2.98
If by mail, postage extra, on Ladies' Gowns, 15 cents.

LADIES' SKIRTS.

$1.48

No. 38R644 A very neat and serviceable skirt, made of fine muslin, French umbrella style, has a 10-inch lawn flounce, six rows of tucks, a wide ruffle of fine lawn embroidery, dust ruffle and French draw strings. Price..........$1.48
If by mail, postage extra, 19 cents.

$1.69

No. 38R648 A serviceable and pretty skirt, made of fine cambric, has wide, lawn flounces, double ruffle of fine, wide embroidery, has draw strings and dust ruffle. Extra good value. Price..........$1.69
If by mail, postage extra, 17 cents.

$1.85

No. 38R652 A strikingly pretty skirt, made of fine lawn, made with double lawn ruffle, each with an insertion of torchon lace and edge to match; dust ruffle. Very stylish. Price..........$1.85
If by mail, postage extra, 15 cents.

$1.98

No. 38R656 Ladies' Umbrella Style Skirt, made of good quality cambric, has a 10-inch deep lawn flounce with numerous rows of tucks and Valenciennes lace insertion, both tucks and insertion running on the bias. Has a wide lawn ruffle which has six rows of tucks and edged with fine Valenciennes lace to match. Entire flounce is 17 inches deep, making it a very pretty and attractive skirt, has dust ruffle and French draw strings. Price.....$1.98
If by mail, postage extra, 19 cents.

No. 38R660 A Very Pretty Skirt, made of high grade cambric, made with a 17-inch lawn flounce, French style,

$2.19

two wide Point de Paris lace insertions and wide edge to match, numerous rows of hemstitching, dust ruffle and draw strings. Extra good value. Price...$2.19
If by mail, postage extra, 14 cents.

$2.48

No. 38R664 A very stylish skirt, made of fine cambric, made with a wide lawn flounce with numerous rows insertion of wide Duchesse lace all around flounce, alternating with numerous rows of tucks on upper part of flounce, as illustrated; has 4-inch wide lace edging to match; dust ruffle and draw strings. Price..........$2.48
If by mail, postage extra, 16 cents.

$2.98

No. 38R668 A beautiful skirt, made of fine cambric; made with a double wide flounce, upper flounce with two rows of fine Point de Paris lace insertion, above which are four fine tucks, wide edge to match on upper and lower flounce; has dust ruffle, which is also edged with lace to match. Draw strings. A very attractive skirt.
Price..........$2.98
If by mail, postage extra, 19 cents.

No. 38R702

COMBINATION LONG CHEMISE.

Sizes, 32, 34, 36, 38, 40 and 42 inches bust measure. Be sure to give bust measure.

No. 38R702 Ladies' Combination Chemise, made of good quality muslin, low round neck, which is trimmed with Valenciennes lace and around armholes to match, has a 7-inch flounce trimmed with three tucks. Good value. Price..........49c
If by mail, postage extra, 10 cents.

Ladies' Chemise, 98c and $1.48.

No. 38R706 A Fine Cambric Combination Chemise, low round neck, insertion of bowknot lace beading and ribbon insertion with bow knot lace edging to match, trimmed around arm holes with lace to match, has a 6-inch flounce with bow knot lace insertion and edge to match. Exceptionally good value. Price..........98c
If by mail, postage extra, 11 cents.

No. 38R710

No. 38R706

No. 38R710 A very pretty combination chemise, made of a fine grade of lawn; low round neck, insertion of torchon lace and narrow ribbon in front, trimmed all round front and back with one row of feather stitch braid, also edged with torchon lace; has lawn ruffle in front with one row of torchon lace insertion with wide edge to match; arm holes trimmed with feather stitch braid and torchon lace edging, has a wide lawn flounce at bottom with torchon lace insertion and edging to match. Price....$1.48
If by mail, postage extra, 11 cents.

No. 38R714 A beautiful Marguerite combination chemise, made of fine nainsook; trimmed around neck with narrow lawn ruffle which is edged with fine torchon lace, insertion of ribbon; twenty rows of fine torchon lace insertion (ten rows on each side) reaching from neck to waist, and edging on each side to match; fine embroidery insertion at waist with ribbon insertion; eight clusters of fine tucks (three rows in a cluster) in back from neck to waist; has a wide flounce at bottom, three rows of tucks; ruffle with torchon lace edging. Price.......$1.89
If by mail, postage extra, 11c

CORSET COVERS.

Sizes, 32, 34, 36, 38, 40, 42, Bust Measure. Always Give Your Bust Measure.

No. 38R802 Ladies' Plain Muslin Corset Cover; round neck. Perfect fitting. Price, each..........10c
If by mail, postage extra, 4c

No. 38R806 Fine Muslin Corset Cover, "V" shaped neck, trimmed with Hamburg embroidery edge around neck. Very good value. Price, 19c
If by mail, postage extra, 5 cents.

No. 38R810 Good Quality Muslin Corset Cover, has "V" shaped neck with wide insertion of torchon lace, three rows of tucks (each hemstitched) on each side; torchon edging to match in front and around back of neck. Price, each 27c
If by mail, postage extra, 5 cents.

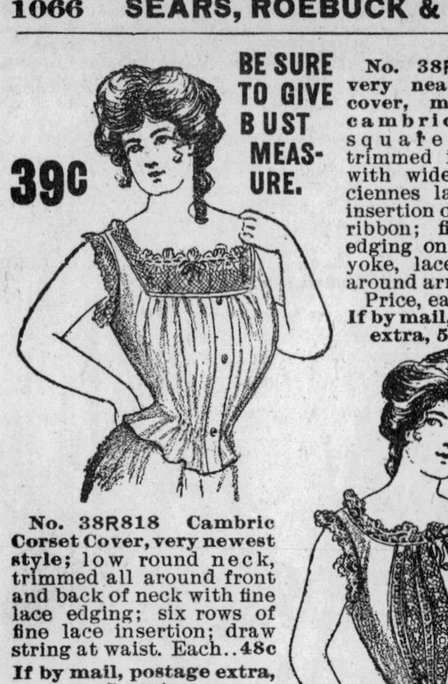

39c

BE SURE TO GIVE BUST MEASURE.

No. 38R814 A very neat corset cover, made of cambric; has a square neck trimmed in front with wide Valenciennes lace with insertion of narrow ribbon; fine lace edging on back of yoke, lace edging around armholes.
Price, each...39c
If by mail, postage extra, 5 cents.

No. 38R818 Cambric Corset Cover, very newest style; low round neck, trimmed all around front and back of neck with fine lace edging; six rows of fine lace insertion; draw string at waist. Each..48c
If by mail, postage extra, 5 cents.

48c

No. 38R822 - Very pretty corset cover, made of fine cambric; low round neck, trimmed both back and front with lawn ruffle which is hemstitched at edge; insertion of narrow ribbon forming a bow in front; has three rows of lace insertion; armholes trimmed with lawn ruffle same as neck. Each.59c
If by mail, postage extra, 5 cents.

59c

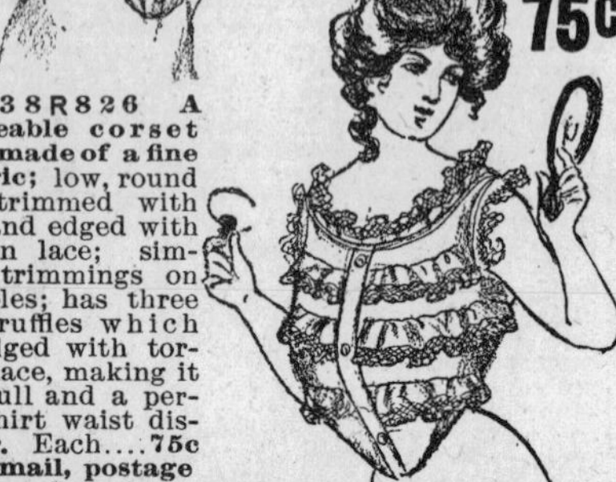

75c

No. 38R826 A serviceable corset cover made of a fine cambric; low, round neck trimmed with lawn and edged with torchon lace; similar trimmings on armholes; has three lawn ruffles which are edged with torchon lace, making it very full and a perfect shirt waist distender. Each....75c
If by mail, postage extra, 5 cents.

98c

BE SURE TO GIVE BUST MEASURE.

No. 38R830 A beautiful corset cover, made of high grade cambric; low, round neck; both front and back trimmed alike around neck with fine Valenciennes lace edging and narrow ribbon insertion; has four rows of embroidery and four rows of lace insertion each alternating. Draw strings at waistband. Price....98c
If by mail, postage extra, 5 cents.

$1.10

No. 38R834 A very handsome Corset Cover made of fine nainsook, low round neck, which is trimmed with fine Valenciennes lace edging and insertion of narrow ribbon, similar trimming on armholes, twenty rows of fine lace (ten rows on each side) insertion reaching from neck to waist. Has twelve rows of fine pin tucks in back reaching from neck to waist. Draw ribbon at waist.
Price...........$1.10
If by mail, postage extra, 5 cents.

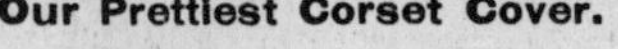

Our Prettiest Corset Cover.

$1.39

No. 38R838 An exceedingly pretty Corset Cover made of very fine nainsook, edged all around the front and back of neck with Valenciennes lace, insertion of narrow ribbon; entire front made with all over lace, cut on the bias; edged down front on each side and around waist with Valenciennes lace, followed with narrow ribbon insertion.
Price..........$1.39
If by mail, postage extra, 5 cents.

LADIES' AND MISSES' DRAWERS.

Lengths 23, 25, 27, 29 inches.

When we quote open and closed style be sure and state style desired; otherwise we will send open style, which are more in demand.

19c

No. 38R850 Very good value muslin drawers, made with wide hem and three rows of tucks. Open or closed styles. Price.......................19c
If by mail, postage extra, 8 cents.

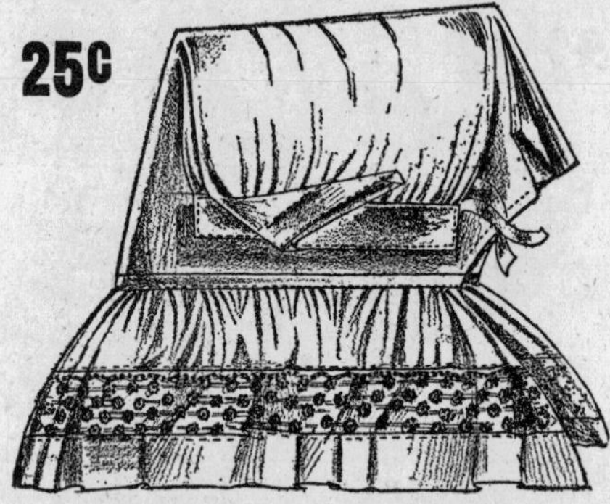

25c

No. 38R854 Extra good value muslin drawers, made with wide flounce, insertion of torchon lace. Open or closed style. A regular 50-cent drawers.
Our price..25c
If by mail, postage extra, 8 cents.

42c

No. 38R858 A fine grade of muslin drawers, with four rows of tucks, 3-inch fine embroidery ruffle. Exceptionally good value. Open style only.
Price..42c
If by mail, postage extra, 8 cents.

39c

No. 38R862 Ladies' Umbrella Style Drawers, made of good quality muslin, wide flounce made of cambric with neat insertion of torchon lace and edging to match. Open or closed style.
Price..39c
If by mail, postage extra, 7 cents.

48c

No. 38R866 Exceptional good value, made of good quality of muslin, three rows of tucks, has lawn ruffle trimmed with three rows of tucks and edged with 3-inch torchon lace. Open style only.
Price..48c
If by mail, postage extra, 8 cents.

55c

No. 38R870 Very good quality muslin drawers, wide flounce with three rows of tucks and hemstitching, insertion of torchon lace and edge to match. Extra good value. Open style only.
Price..55c
If by mail, postage extra, 9 cents.

69c

No. 38R874 Very neat umbrella style drawers, made of good quality of muslin, has a 6-inch deep flounce of lawn open work embroidery, above which is trimmed with eight rows of tucks. Very good value. Open style only. French draw strings.
Price..69c
If by mail, postage extra, 8 cents.

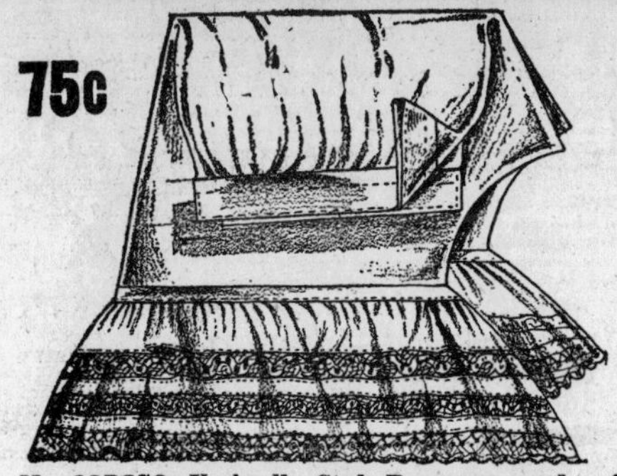

No. 38R878 Umbrella Style Drawers, made of good quality nainsook; wide flounce with two insertions of neat pattern of Valenciennes lace, with edge to match. **Open or closed style.** Price....75c
If by mail, postage extra, 9 cents.

No. 38R882 A very neat and serviceable umbrella style drawers, made of fine nainsook; trimmed with six rows of fine tucks, ruffle (6-inch) of fine embroidery. **Open style only.** Price........98c
If by mail, postage extra, 8 cents.

No. 38R886 Ladies' Umbrella Style Drawers, made of fine cambric; with a very wide lawn flounce, two rows Medici lace insertion in zigzag style, wide Medici lace edging to match. Open or closed style.
Price..$1.10
If by mail, postage extra, 8 cents.

No. 38R890 A very pretty umbrella style drawers, made of fine nainsook; lawn ruffle with three rows of hemstitching, insertion of Cluny lace, beading and ribbon insertion, wide edge to match. **Open style only.** Draw strings. Price........$1.25
If by mail, postage extra, 8 cents.

SHORT CHEMISE.

No. 38R718 Muslin Short Chemise, square yoke, trimmed with torchon lace around yoke and armholes. Price, each....................................24c
If by mail, postage extra, 6 cents.

No. 38R894 A high grade nainsook drawers, made with six rows of fine tucks, beading and ribbon insertion, 5-inch wide ruffle of fine embroidery. **Open or closed style.** Price.....................$1.39
If by mail, postage extra, 9 cents.

No. 38R898 Ladies' Nainsook Drawers, very newest style; has a 6-inch flounce made of lawn; drawer and flounce joined with an insertion of narrow Hamburg embroidery; upper part of flounce has numerous rows of tucks, seven rows of insertion on each flounce of fine Valenciennes lace with edging to match. **Open style only.** French draw strings.
Price..$1.48
If by mail, postage extra, 8 cents.

No. 38R902 A very strikingly pretty umbrella style drawers of high grade nainsook; Vandyke flounce trimmed with bow knot lace, wide insertion to match. **Open style only.** Draw strings.
Price..$1.69
If by mail, postage extra, 9 cents.

No. 38R906 A beautiful style drawers, made of a fine high grade lawn; has ribbon insertion and bow, wide flounce with three ruffles of fine Duchesse lace. Very stylish. **Open style only.** Draw strings.
Price..$1.89
If by mail, postage extra, 8 cents.

LADIES' OR MISSES' SHORT UNDERSKIRTS.

Lengths, 27, 29 and 31 Inches.

ADJUSTABLE WAIST WITH DRAW STRINGS.

No. 38R594 Muslin Short Underskirt, has wide ruffle with three fine tucks, wide hem. Price, each, 32c
If by mail, postage extra, 5 cents.

No. 38R598 Muslin Short Underskirt, has cambric flounce trimmed with torchon lace.
Price, each..43c
If by mail, postage extra, 6 cents.

BRIDAL SETS.

Be sure to give bust measure.

Sizes, 32, 34, 36, 38, 40, 42 inches, bust measure.

Fine Cambric Bridal Set of four pieces, consisting of gown, skirt, drawers and corset cover. **Gown has a yoke with two rows of embroidery,** insertion on each side with three tucks between and insertion down center. Wide Hamburg embroidery trimming around the front and embroidery at neck and sleeves to match. Fine herringbone braid trimming. **Skirt has a double flounce Hamburg embroidery on lawn ruffle.** Has a dust ruffle. **Drawers have a Hamburg embroidery flounce,** with insertion of embroidery with six tucks. Yoke band. (Open) very neat drawers. **Corset cover** has four rows of Hamburg embroidery insertion, with cluster of tucks on each side, trimmed with fine embroidery around neck and armholes. **Do not fail to give bust measure.**
No. 38R908 Price of entire set..............$4.35
If by mail, postage extra, 45 cents.

A trousseau fit for an American queen, made of fine cambric, of four pieces, gown, skirt, drawers and corset cover. **32, 34, 36, 38, 40, 42, bust measure. Gown is made Empire style, fine grade of cambric,** fancy revers, which are trimmed all around with fine point de Paris insertion and lace 4 inches wide. Bosom has one row of insertion and one row of fancy ribbon insertion, also with a 4-inch lace. Sleeves have an insertion of ribbon and 4-inch lace. **Skirt is made of fine cambric,** has a lawn flounce which is made V shape all around and trimmed with 4-inch lace. Above this are two rows of point de Paris lace insertion all around flounce. Has a dust ruffle which is also trimmed with 4-inch lace. **Drawers are made of very fine cambric** (open), has lawn ruffle with one row of point de Paris insertion and trimmed at bottom with lace to match. **Corset cover is made of fine cambric,** with three insertions of point de Paris lace. **Do not fail to give bust measure.**
No. 38R910 Price for entire set..............$5.98
If by mail, postage, extra, 45 cents.

FLANNEL UNDERWEAR FOR LADIES AND MISSES.

We beg to call your attention to the finish of our goods, which is far superior to anything you can get elsewhere. Our goods are all made very full, good length, and as to the fit we have the reputation for having the best on the market. Sizes, 14, 15, 16 inches around neck.

For Muslin Gowns see page 1063.

49 Cents Buys a 75-Cent Flannel Gown.

No. 38R912 Ladies' Flannel Gown, made in plaids and stripes, in blue or pink colors. Turn down collar. Yoke in front and back.
Price....................49c
If by mail, postage extra, 10 cents.

Our 69-Cent Flannel Gowns.

No. 38R914 Ladies' Gown, made of domet flannel, with fancy striped patterns in blue or pink colors. Lay down collar, herringbone braid trimming on yoke and around the flounced cuffs. It is well finished and exceptionally full. Price....69c
If by mail, postage extra, 15 cents.

Ladies' Domet Flannel Gowns for 89 Cents.

Ladies' Fine Gown, made of a high grade domet flannel, lay down collar, pointed yoke in front, collar and cuffs trimmed with herringbone braid to match, double yoke in back.

Can furnish in pink stripes with solid pink yoke or blue stripes with solid blue yoke.

No. 38R918
Price...............89c
If by mail, postage extra, 15 cents.

Our $1.35 Ladies' Gown.

Made of high grade domet flannel, has a wide turn down collar, which is trimmed with satin grosgrain ribbon, bishop sleeves, cuffs trimmed with ribbon to correspond with collar. Colors, pink stripes with pink ribbon or blue stripes with blue ribbon.

No. 38R922 Price, $1.35
If by mail, postage extra, 18 cents.

A Ladies' Beautiful Gown.

Made of daisy cloth (high grade flannel), gathered at yoke in front and back, making it very full; has a wide turn down collar, scalloped and edged with silk stitching, also one row of embroidery all around collar in a fancy design; satin ribbon bow at neck, cuffs trimmed to correspond with collar. Solid colors in pink or light blue.

No. 38R926
Price............$1.48
If by mail, postage extra, 20 cents.

Ladies' or Misses' Flannel Underskirts.

Sizes, 27, 29 and 31 inches in length.

No. 38R930 Ladies' Flannel Underskirts, striped designs in blue or pink colors.
Price, each................25c
If by mail, postage extra, 10 cents.

No. 38R932 Ladies' Underskirt, made of domet flannel. Umbrella shape, trimmed with 6-inch flounce around the bottom. Price. 37c
If by mail, postage extra, 10 cents.

Flounced Underskirt.

No. 38R934 Made of a good quality domet flannel, in striped design in pink or blue colors, umbrella shaped. Trimmed with 6-inch flounce around bottom, which is edged with torchon lace all around. Price...........49c
If by mail, postage extra, 9 cents.

No. 38R934

No. 38R942

No. 38R942 Ladies' Bath Robe with Hood, made of good quality Terry cloth, fancy designs in colors, has draw strings at waist. A very useful garment. Price...(Postage extra, 46 cents)...$3.48

LADIES' BATHING SUITS.

32 to 42 Bust Measure.

No. 38R952 Ladies' Bathing Suit with attached bloomers; made of good quality alpaca; large sailor collar trimmed with three rows of soutache down the front, and detachable skirt trimmed around waistband and bottom with three rows of soutache to match, wide hem. Colors, black or navy blue. Price...$2.98
If by mail, postage extra, 17 cents.
Always give bust measure.

No. 38R956 Ladies' Bathing Suit with attached bloomers; made of fine brilliantine; has large sailor collar and revers which are trimmed with four rows of soutache; has "V" shape yoke, upper part made of same color as sailor collar, which is also trimmed with four rows of soutache; detachable skirt trimmed with four rows of soutache around waistband, down front (both sides) and around bottom, as illustrated. A very nobby bathing suit. Colors, navy blue with red or white collar. Price.............$3.49
If by mail, postage extra, 18 cents.

No. 38R960 Ladies' Bathing Suit with attached bloomers; made of all wool flannel, large sailor collar trimmed with one row of narrow and one row of wide white hercules braid; "V" shape yoke with similar trimmings, two rows of narrow braid on band in front; detachable skirt with two rows of narrow braid around waistband and one round of narrow and wide braid around bottom. Color, navy blue with white trimmings. A wonderful bargain. Price......$3.98
If by mail, postage extra, 24 cents.
Be sure and give bust measure.

For complete line of Stockings see page 971.

No. 38R964 Bathing Cap, made of sateen; pure rubber linings, rubber band in order to make cap fit perfect around head. Keeps the hair dry. Colors, blue or red with white polka dots. Price.................25c
If by mail, postage extra, 4 cents.

No. 38R966 Bathing Cap, made of pure rubber, plaid lining. The correct thing to wear when bathing. Rubber band to make it fit perfect around the head, keeps the hair dry. Color, black only. Price....15c
If by mail, postage extra, 4 cents.

LADIES' DRESSING SACQUES AND KIMONOS.

THE MOST COMFORTABLE and POPULAR HOUSE GARMENTS MADE.

Bust, 32, 34, 36, 38, 40 and 42 inches.

No. 38R972 Ladies' Dressing Sacque, made of good quality percale; yoke both front and back, trimmed with one row of braid; ruffle on collar made of same material as in sacque, bishop sleeves. Colors, fancy patterns, red or blue predominating.
Price.................39c
If by mail, postage extra, 11 cents.

No. 38R976 Ladies' Dressing Sacque, made of good, fancy lawn; collar trimmed with one row of featherstitch braid, ruffle and embroidery edge; cuffs trimmed with braid, ruffle and edge to match collar. Colors, blue, pink or black figures. Price..........48c
If by mail, postage extra, 8 cents.

No. 38R980 Ladies' Dressing Sacque, shirt waist style, made of fine quality fancy lawn; standing collar, shoulder and across bust trimmed with percale, as well as across back; band in front and belt to correspond; bishop sleeves and cuffs to match. Colors, blue, pink or black figures. Exceptionally good value.
Price.....................75c
If by mail, postage extra, 9 cents.
Always give bust measure.

No. 38R984 A Very Pretty Ladies' Dressing Sacque, made of fine quality dimity; has a large yoke (both front and back) made of all over lace, ruffle all around yoke which is edged with lace; ruffle around collar which is trimmed with featherstitch braid and edged with lace, yoke also trimmed with braid to match; bishop sleeves, cuffs made with all over lace. Colors, blue and white or red and white figures. Extra good value.
Price..............89c
If by mail, postage extra, 9 cents.

No. 38R988 Ladies' Dressing Sacque, made of fine dimity; ruffle all around neck and down front of same material as in sacque, featherstitch braid trimmings, bow strings edged with lace; ruffle and featherstitch braid on sleeves; plait in black. Colors, black and white or blue and white figures.
Price..................98c
If by mail, postage extra, 9 cents.

No. 38R992 Ladies' Dressing Sacque, made of high grade fancy striped lawn; wide collar with lawn ruffle to match; featherstitch braid and lace edge; lawn ruffle all around bottom, trimmed with braid and lace to match; sleeves trimmed to correspond. Colors, blue and white or red and white fancy stripes. Price......$1.19
If by mail, postage extra, 8 cents.

No. 38R996 Ladies' Kimono, made of fine figured lawn; trimmed around neck and down front with white lawn; sleeves made to match. Made in pretty combination figures in black and white or pink and white. Price..69c
If by mail, postage extra, 8 cents.

Always Give Bust Measure.

No.38R1002 A very neat Kimono, made of good lawn; yoke (front and back alike) made of pink or blue lawn, revers and cuffs of lawn to correspond. Colors, white only with pink or blue yoke and trimmings. Exceptionally good value.
Price...75c
If by mail, postage extra, 10c.

No. 38R1006 A very pretty Kimono, made of high grade figured dimity; revers made of white lawn; trimming around bottom and cuffs also of white lawn. Colors, very neat figures in gray and white or red and white.
Price.....98c
If by mail, postage extra, 8 cents.

No. 38R1014 Ladies' Dressing Sacque made of wool mixed eiderdown. Collar, front and around bottom crocheted with yarn. Ribbon strings. Sleeves crocheted with yarn. Colors, red, pink, blue or gray. Price, each...........75c
If by mail, postage extra, 11c

No. 38R1016 A very neat and serviceable Ladies' Dressing Sacque, made of good quality eiderdown. Large sailor collar made of white eiderdown, collar, front and around bottom crocheted with yarn to match. Satin ribbon strings. Sleeves crocheted with yarn to match. Colors, cardinal, pink, blue or gray.
Price, each......$1.19
If by mail, postage extra, 14 cents.

Our $1.35 and $1.65 Dressing Sacques.

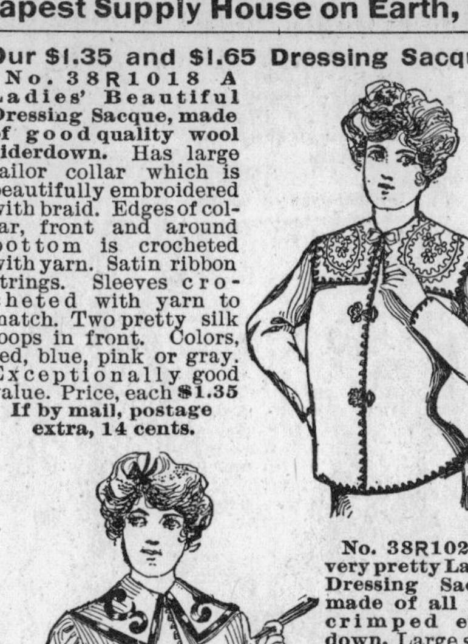

No. 38R1018 A Ladies' Beautiful Dressing Sacque, made of good quality wool eiderdown. Has large sailor collar which is beautifully embroidered with braid. Edges of collar, front and around bottom is crocheted with yarn. Satin ribbon strings. Sleeves crocheted with yarn to match. Two pretty silk loops in front. Colors, red, blue, pink or gray. Exceptionally good value. Price, each $1.35
If by mail, postage extra, 14 cents.

No. 38R1020 A very pretty Ladies' Dressing Sacque, made of all wool crimped eiderdown. Large sailor collar which is neatly appliqued with flannel and bound with satin. Front, around bottom and sleeves crocheted with yarn to match. Colors, red, pink or blue.
Price, each $1.65
If by mail, postage extra, 19 cents.

LADIES' GINGHAM, SATEEN AND WHITE LAWN APRONS.

No. 38R1022 Ladies' Gingham Aprons, good quality, blue and brown checks. Sizes, 36 inches long, 43 inches wide.
Price, each.........................15c
If by mail, postage extra, 5 cents.

No. 38R1026 Ladies' Large Gingham Aprons, made of Amoskeag, the best gingham. Hemmed at bottom, long strings at back, in blue or brown checks; a good, reliable apron. Size, 38 inches long, 54 inches wide.
Price, each.......25c
If by mail, postage extra, 5 cents.

No. 38R1030 Ladies' Fine Quality Black Sateen Aprons. Very desirable as a work apron, does not require frequent washing and always looks neat. Made full and long; hemmed, with one pocket. The quality sold elsewhere at 35 cents. Price, each.......23c
If by mail, postage extra, 5 cents.

No. 38R1034 Ladies' White Lawn Apron. 34 inches long, 39 inches wide. Wide hem at bottom and wide strings. Very good value. Price, each....18c
If by mail, postage extra, 5 cents.

No. 38R1038 Our Leader. Ladies' White Lawn Apron, made with three wide plaits at bottom. Size, 36 inches long, 40 inches wide. Deep hem at bottom and wide strings.
Our price, each......25c
If by mail, postage extra, 6 cents.

No. 38R1042 A very neat Ladies' White Apron, made with six plaits at bottom, wide hem and strings. Size, 35 inches long and 40 inches wide. Exceptionally good value. Price, each 27c
If by mail, postage extra, 6 cents.

No. 38R1046 Ladies' Lawn White Apron, with insertion of open work Swiss embroidery, wide hem at bottom. Size, 35 inches wide, 34 inches long. Wide strings. Well made. Price, each 30c
If by mail, postage extra, 6 cents.

No. 38R1050 A very pretty Ladies' White Lawn Apron. Has three plaits at bottom with wide flounce which has an insertion of embroidery. Size, 34 inches wide, 29 inches long. Widestrings. A very good apron.
Price, each.........37c
If by mail, postage extra, 6 cents.

No. 38R1054 Ladies' White Lawn Apron, has wide flounce with insertion of wide open work embroidery. Size, 35 inches wide and 32 inches long. Widestrings. Extra good value.
Price, each.........40c
If by mail, postage extra, 6 cents.

No. 38R1058 Ladies' beautiful White Lawn Apron, has a wide insertion of fine embroidered lawn, extra wide hem at bottom. Size, 33 inches wide, 36 inches long.
Price, each..........45c
If by mail, postage extra, 6 cents.

No. 38R1062 A very neat Ladies' White Lawn Apron, has insertion all around bottom and sides of fine narrow neat pattern embroidery, wide hem at bottom. Size, 29 inches wide, 32 inches long. Wide strings. Price, each...48c
If by mail, postage extra, 6 cents.

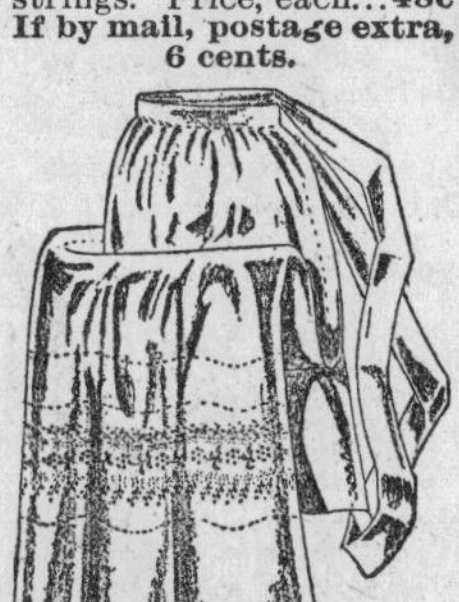

No. 38R1066 A High Grade Ladies' White Lawn Apron, with wide insertion of fine embroidered lawn, has extra wide hem at bottom. Size, 33 inches wide, 36 inches long. Extra wide strings. Well made. Good value.
Price, each........72c
If by mail, postage extra, 6 cents.

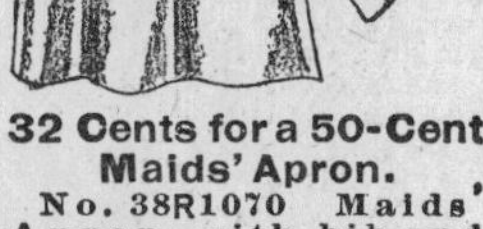

32 Cents for a 50-Cent Maids' Apron.

No. 38R1070 Maids' Apron, with bib and shoulder straps, as per illustration, made of nice white lawn, with wide hem at bottom, long apron ties.
Price, each..............32c
If by mail, postage extra, each, 7 cents.

Hotel or Maids' Apron.

No. 38R1074 Hotel or Maids' Apron, made of good quality and durable lawn, shoulder straps, ruffled and with three tucks, wide hem at side and bottom, and three rows of tucking. Size, 36x50 inches. Price, each........55c
If by mail, postage extra, 8 cents.

CHILDREN'S MUSLIN AND FLANNELETTE GOWNS.

For 2 to 14-year-old children.

No. 38R1102 Child's Gown, made of domet flannel. Yoke in front and back. Striped design in blue or pink colors. For from 2 to 14-year-old children.

Age,	2	4	6	8	10	12	14
Price.	30c	35c	42c	48c	54c	60c	66c

No. 38R1106 Child's Flannel Gown, neatly trimmed with a cream colored pointed yoke in front, cream colored collar, cuffs and band in front. Fancy herringbone trimming to match around collar, yoke and cuffs. Colors, pink or blue striped patterns. Sizes, from 2 to 14-year-old children.

Age	Price
2	45c
4	51c
6	56c
8	61c
10	66c
12	71c
14	78c

If by mail, postage extra, each, 13 cents.

No. 38R1102 No. 38R1106

Cambric Gowns.

If by mail, postage extra, each, 11 cents.

No. 38R1110 No. 38R1114

No. 38R1110 Child's Cambric Gown, yoke in front plaited three times on each side, ruffle collar and cuffs. Sizes, from 2 to 14 years. Price..............37c

No. 38R1114 Child's Cambric Gown, yoke in front, rows of tucking and insertion on either side. Hamburg embroidery around collar, in front and on cuffs. Sizes, from 2 to 14. Price..............49c

Children's Flannel and Cambric Drawers

Sizes, from 2 to 14.

No. 38R1118 Child's Cambric Drawers, nicely trimmed with three tucks around bottom. Sizes, from 2 to 14. Price, each, from 2 to 8, 10c From 10 to 14.....15c If by mail, postage extra, 5 cents.

No. 38R1122 Child's Drawers, made of good quality cambric, nicely trimmed with four rows of tucking around bottom, and edged with Hamburg embroidery very neat. Sizes, from 2 to 14. Price, each, from 2 to 8, 23c; 10 to 14......28c If by mail, postage extra, 5 cents.

No. 38R1118 No. 38R1122

Child's Drawers at 14 and 20 Cents.

No. 38R1126 Child's Drawers, of unbleached canton flannel. Narrow lace trimming all around the bottom. Sizes, from 2 to 14. Price, from 2 to 8, 10c; from 10 to 14....14c If by mail, postage extra, 5 cents.

No. 38R1130 Child's Drawers, made of bleached canton flannel. Hamburg embroidery edge around the bottom, cambric band around waist. Sizes, from 2 to 14.

No. 38R1126

No. 38R1130

Price, from 2 to 8, 15c; from 10 to 14..............20c
If by mail, postage extra, each, 5 cents.

Children's Drawers Suits and Skirts.

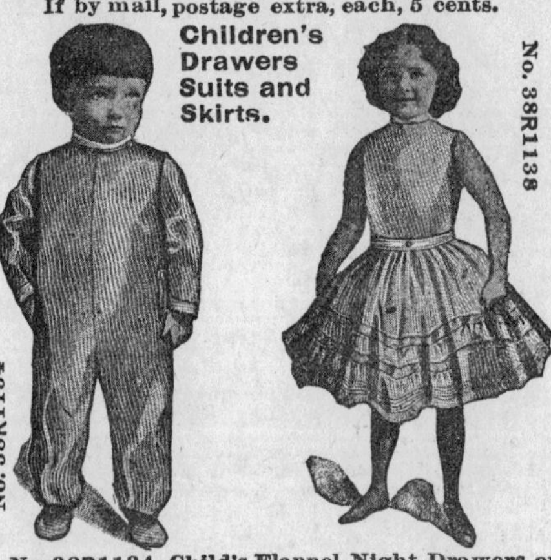

No. 38R1134 No. 38R1138

No. 38R1134 Child's Flannel Night Drawers or Suits, made of unbleached canton flannel, with feet; very comfortable sleeping garment. Sizes, 1 to 8. Price, two for 70c; each...(Postage, 7 cents)...35c

Girl's Underskirts at 40 and 59 Cents.

No. 38R1138 Girls' Underskirts, made of good quality muslin, umbrella shape, double flounce all around the bottom, the lower flounces trimmed with five rows of tucking. Price, from 2 to 8, 35c; from 10 to 14..........40c If by mail, postage extra, 5c.

Girls' Skirts.

No. 38R1142 Made of a very fine quality cambric, trimmed all around bottom, with 3-inch torchon lace, the flounce including lace is 7 inches deep, making it a very pretty skirt. Sizes 2, 4, 6, 8, 10, 12, 14. Price, from 2 to 8, 49c; from 10 to 14..............59c If by mail, postage extra, 7c.

No. 38R1142

See Pages 987 and 988 for Infants' and Children's Wool Underwear.

Child's Flannel Skirts.

Ages 1, 2, 3 Years.

No. 38R1146 Children's Skirt, made of fleece lined canton flannel, with muslin bodice. Price, each.....17c

If by mail, postage extra, each 3 cents.

No. 38R1146

No. 38R1150 Child's Skirt, made of canton flannel, with cambric bodice. Embroidered around the bottom with silk. Price, 39c

No. 38R1150

If by mail, postage extra, each, 5 cents.

Child's Skirt for 55c.

No. 38R1154 Child's Skirt, made of an all wool cream colored flannel with cambric bodice, fancy ruffle of the same material all around the bottom. Very neat and desirable.
Price, each..............55c
If by mail, postage extra, each, 5 cents.

Child's Cambric and Nainsook Skirts.

1, 2 and 3-year-old children.

No. 38R1158 Child's Skirt, with muslin bodice, made of white cambric, three rows of tucking around the bottom.
No. 38R1158 Price, each.18c
If by mail, postage extra, each, 3 cents.

No. 38R1162 Child's Skirt, made of good quality nainsook, with cambric bodice, three rows of narrow tucking around the bottom and one row of embroidered cambric. Pearl buttons in back.
No. 38R1162 Price....49c
If by mail, postage extra, each, 3 cents.

No. 38R1162 No. 38R1158

No. 38R1166 A very pretty Child's Skirt, made of nainsook, with bodice. Has four rows of fine tucks and trimmed with Valenciennes lace around bottom.
Price..................60c
If by mail, postage extra, 6 cents.

For Children 1, 2 and 3 Years of Age.

No. 38R1170 No. 38R1166

No. 38R1170 Child's Shirt with bodice, made of a very high grade nainsook, trimmed with two clusters (four rows in a cluster) of fine tucks, with an insertion of fine Valenciennes lace. Trimmed around bottom with Valenciennes lace to match.
Price.....................75c
If by mail, postage extra, 6 cents.

CHILD'S PRINCESS DRESSES.

Ages 1, 2, 3, 4 years. Scale of measurements giving lengths of dresses in proportion:
Age 1, length 20 inches.
Age 2, length 21 inches.
Age 3, length 22 inches.
Age 4, length 24 inches.

No. 38R1174 A strikingly pretty Child's Dress; made of fine nainsook; has two ruffles of embroidery insertion extending from neck to flounce and twelve rows of tucks; yoke trimmed with herringbone braid and nainsook embroidery, ruffle extending over shoulders; neck and sleeves trimmed with a lawn ruffle and herringbone braid and one row of hemstitching; has a wide nainsook flounce with deep hem. Exceptionally good value. Color, white only.
Price, each..............98c
If by mail, postage extra, 8c.

No. 38R1178 A very pretty Child's Dress, made of fine white lawn; trimmed in front with ten plaits; yoke has embroidery insertion and trimmed with herringbone braid, ruffle all around yoke in front and back; eight plaits in back extending from shoulders to flounce; wide lawn flounce with deep hem, herringbone braid at top of flounce; sleeves and neck trimmed with herringbone braid and embroidery edge.
Price each..............$1.19
If by mail, postage extra, 7c.

No. 38R1182 A beautiful Child's Dress, made of good quality white lawn; panel in front made of open work embroidery with four rows of tucks on each side; yoke trimmed with herringbone braid, embroidery ruffle all around yoke in front and in back; ten rows of tucks in back extending from neck to flounce; has a lawn flounce with open work embroidery, wide hem at bottom; sleeves and neck trimmed with herringbone braid and embroidery edge. A very pretty and attractive dress. Price, each..........$1.69
If by mail, postage extra, 7c.

CHILD'S DRESSES.

Ages, 6 months, 1, 2 and 3-year-old Children.

No. 38R1186 Child's Dress, made of good quality cambric, ruffle around neck and fancy yoke in front with 5-inch cambric embroidery, hemmed with herringbone braid. Price.....25c
Postage extra, 5 cents.

No. 38R1190 Child's Dress, made of white muslin, fancy yoke in front with insertion and tucking and wide ruffle all around yoke over shoulder and ruching in the back, edged with torchon lace, wide hem on bottom. Ages, 6 months, 1, 2 and 3 years. Price.....49c
Postage extra, 6c.

No. 38R1194 Child's Dress, made of good quality white cambric, embroidered cambric around the collar in front and all around the shoulders, fancy insertion in front, with ruffles on sleeves and pearl buttons in back. Ages, 6 months, 1, 2 and 3 years. Price, each.........69c

IF BY MAIL, POSTAGE EXTRA, EACH, 6 CENTS.

No. 38R1198 Child's Dress, made of high grade cambric. Embroidered ruffle around the collar and tucked yoke in front, ending in a point, with embroidered cambric all around the front and back. Embroidered cambric around the sleeves. Very neat and stylish. Ages, 6 months, 1, 2 and 3 years. Price, each..89c
If by mail, postage extra, 6 cents.

No. 38R1202 Child's Dress, made of good quality nainsook, torchon lace trimming around the collar, on yoke and sleeves, and one row of Valenciennes lace insertion on skirt and a wide Valenciennes lace edge to match around bottom. Yoke handsomely trimmed with herringbone braid in front as well as in back. Two rows of triple tucking all around the skirt at bottom. Ages, 6 months, 1, 2 and 3 years. Price......$1.10
If by mail, postage extra, 6 cents.

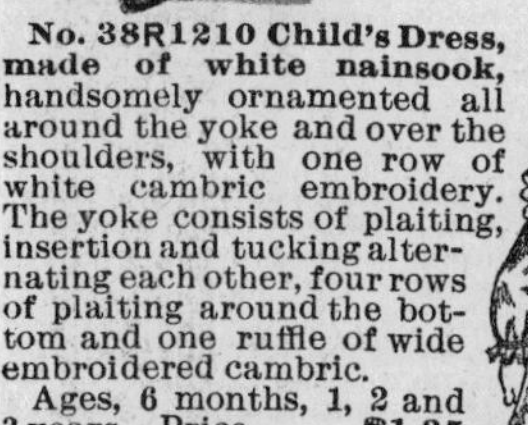

No. 38R1210 Child's Dress, made of white nainsook, handsomely ornamented all around the yoke and over the shoulders, with one row of white cambric embroidery. The yoke consists of plaiting, insertion and tucking alternating each other, four rows of plaiting around the bottom and one ruffle of wide embroidered cambric.
Ages, 6 months, 1, 2 and 3 years. Price........$1.35
If by mail, postage extra, 7 cents.

No. 38R1214 Child's Dress, made of good quality nainsook, fancy yoke in front, made of embroidered cambric all over and herringbone braid around the collar. Two rows of cambric insertion and a white cambric ruffle all around the yoke in front, over the shoulders and around the back. Herringbone braid around the sleeve with ruffle. Wide hem on the bottom. Ages, 6 months, 1, 2 and 3 years. Price, each...$1.48
If by mail, postage extra, 7 cents.

Child's Dress, $1.75.

No. 38R1218 Child's Dress, made of high grade lawn. Swiss embroidery around the collar. Insertion in front, which forms a pleasing effect, and double ruffle of fine Swiss embroidery in front, and one ruffle right from the shoulders to the back, and Swiss insertion around the sleeves as well as ruffles. Two rows of triple tucking in back to the waist. A very desirable style and neat. Ages, 6 months, 1, 2 and 3 years.
Price, each.....$1.75
If by mail, postage extra, 7 cents.

CHILDREN'S APRONS.

For children, ages, 4, 5, 6, 8, 10 and 12 Years.

Gingham Apron, 28 Cents.

No. 38R1226 Girls' Apron, made of good quality gingham in blue or brown and white checks as per illustration. Fancy slashed collar and cuffs trimmed with white braid. Yoke in front and back. Opens in the back and tied with 3-inch strings. Price, each......28c
If by mail, postage extra, 9 cents.

Mention age. Sizes, 4, 5, 6, 8, 10 and 12 years.

No. 38R1230 Girls' Lawn Apron, yoke trimmed with three rows of embroidery, shoulder strap edged with narrow lace. Very good value. **Color, white only.**
Price, each.................32c
If by mail, postage extra, 6 cents.

No. 38R1234 Very neat Girls' Lawn Apron, yoke trimmed with two rows of fine embroidery, flounce over shoulders which is hemstitched, wide hem at bottom. Exceptionally good value. **Color, white only.**
Price, each...............42c
If by mail, postage extra, 7 cents.

48 Cents Buys This Prettily Embroidered Apron.

No. 38R1236 Very pretty Girls' Lawn Apron, yoke made of two rows of fine embroidery, ruffle of fine embroidery, extending from waist to shoulder, wide hem at bottom. **Color, white only.**
Price, each.................48c
If by mail, postage extra, 7 cents.

BE SURE AND GIVE SIZE DESIRED.

No. 38R1240 Girls' Apron, made of good quality of lawn, yoke in front and back, with insertion of embroidery, also insertion over shoulders, with lawn ruffle, which is hemstitched; wide hem at bottom. A regular 75-cent apron. **Color, white only.**
Price, each...................55c
If by mail, postage extra, 7 cents.

Children's White Lawn Aprons.

No. 38R1244 A beautiful Girls' Apron, made of fine white lawn, with insertion of lace all around body with six rows of fine tucks, lace edging around neck and shoulder ruffles, wide hem at bottom. Extra good value.
Price, each.............69c
If by mail, postage extra, 7 cents.

GIVE AGE DESIRED.

No. 38R1248 Very nea Girls' Apron, made of good quality white lawn, eight rows of tucks (each hemstitched), in front, shoulder strap with two wide embroidery insertions and wide lawn ruffle, deep hem at bottom. Exceptionally good value.
Price, each...............82c
If by mail, postage extra, 7 cents.

INFANTS' OUTFIT FOR $6.49.

Infants' Wardrobe Set, consisting of 22 pieces, as follows:

1 **Long Cambric Robe,** embroidery down front and all around bottom	$1.10
1 **Muslin Day Slip,** fancy yoke, made of embroidery, and four rows of tucking	.49
2 **Night Slips,** fancy yoke of embroidery and herringbone braid. Each, 25c	.50
1 **Long Cambric Skirt,** has three rows of tucking around bottom	.33
1 **Short Cambric Skirt,** has three rows of tucking around bottom	.18
1 **Long Flannel Skirt,** with bodice	.35
1 **Short Flannel Skirt,** with bodice	.17
1 **Domet Flannel Wrapper,** with embroidered epaulets over shoulders	.50
1 **Flannel Shawl** (all wool), flower design in one corner, cream color	.49
1 **Pair Knit Bootees**	.09
1 **Pair Knit Bootees**	.15
1 **Knit Sacque**	.23
1 **Knit Sacque,** made of closely knitted zephyr yarn	.49
1 **Elderdown Sacque,** stitched all around collar, front and sleeves with silk	.29
1 **Silk Bonnet**	.25
2 **Rubber Diapers.** Each, 16c	.32
2 **Flannel Bands.** Each, 9c	.18
2 **Pinning Skirts or Barrier Coats.** Each, 19c	.38
No. 38R1260 Price for complete outfit, 22 pieces	$6.49

If by mail, postage extra, 42 cents.

Our $9.99 Infants' Wardrobe Set.

A Very High Grade Infants' Wardrobe Set, consisting of 22 pieces, as follows:

1 **Very Beautiful Cambric Robe,** with cambric embroidery down front, with an insertion of satin ribbon, trimmed with embroidery around bottom	$1.49
1 **Day Slip,** made of good quality of muslin, torchon lace around neck, fancy yoke, two rows of triple tucking, one row of lace insertion and wide lace around bottom	1.10
2 **Night Slips,** fancy yoke in front of cambric embroidery and herringbone braid, ruffle around collar. Each 25c	.50
1 **Long Cambric Skirt,** two rows of triple tucking, also trimmed with embroidery around bottom	.49
1 **Long Canton Flannel Skirt,** scalloped around bottom and stitched with silk	.49
1 **Short Skirt,** made of canton flannel, scalloped, and stitched with silk around bottom, has bodice	.39
1 **Wrapper, Fleece Elderdown,** embroidered around collar	.72
1 **All Wool Flannel Cream Color Shawl,** scalloped and stitched with silk, elaborately embroidered with silk in flower design in corner	.69
1 **Pair Bootees,** very closely knitted	15
1 **Pair Bootees,** very fancy and closely knitted	.30
1 **Knit Sacque,** trimmed with tassels	.35
1 **Knit Sacque,** very fancy border, has imitation yoke	.75
1 **All Wool Flannel Sacque,** neatly stitched all around collar and front with silk	.49
1 **Silk Bonnet**	.25
2 **Rubber Diapers.** Each, 16c	.32
3 **Flannel Bands.** Each, 15c	.45
2 **Pinning Blankets or Barrier Coats,** ea., 48c	.96
No. 38R1264 Price for complete outfit, 22 pieces	$9.99

If by mail, postage extra, 48 cents.

SEND 15 CENTS

for a year's subscription to our money saving

GROCERY PRICE LIST.

Infants' Christening Slips.

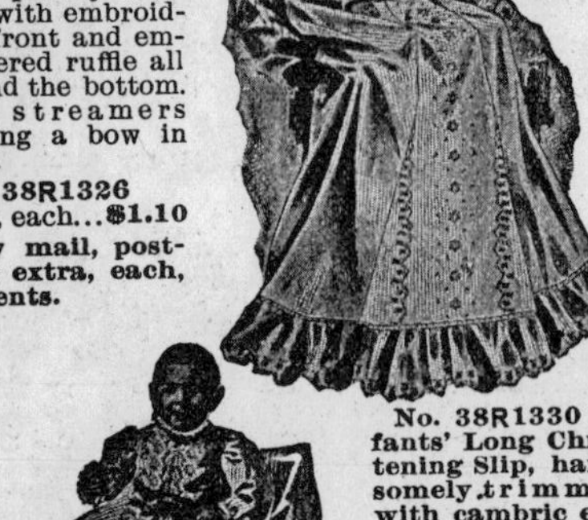

No. 38R1326 Infants' Long Christening Slip, made good quality cambric, with embroidered front and embroidered ruffle all around the bottom. Long streamers forming a bow in front.

No. 38R1326
Price, each...**$1.10**
If by mail, postage extra, each, 5 cents.

No. 38R1330 Infants' Long Christening Slip, handsomely trimmed with cambric embroidery in front. Satin draw string in front, running through the insertion. Wide cambric ruffle on bottom, very stylish and neat.
No. 38R1330
Price, each...**$1.49**
If by mail, postage extra, each, 7 cents.

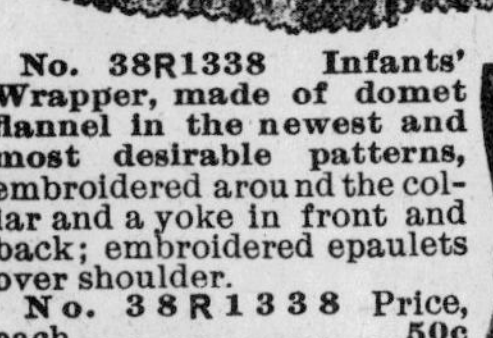

No. 38R1338 Infants' Wrapper, made of domet flannel in the newest and most desirable patterns, embroidered around the collar and a yoke in front and back; embroidered epaulets over shoulder.
No. 38R1338 Price, each....................**50c**
If by mail, postage extra, each, 8 cents.

No. 38R1342 Infants' Wrapper, made of cotton fleece elderdown, honeycomb effect in pinks and blues only, handsomely embroidered around the collar in front and all around the bottom, on yoke and cuffs; satin ribbon in front, forming a nice bow to hold it in place.
No. 38R1342 Price, each....................**72c**
If by mail, postage extra, each, 10 cents.

Infants' Long Cambric and Muslin Skirt.

No. 38R1352 Infants' Long Skirt, made of white cambric, with three rows of tucking around the bottom.
No. 38R1352 Price, each **33c**
If by mail, postage extra, each, 7 cents.

Our 49-Cent Infants' Long Skirt.

No. 38R1356 Infants' Long Skirt, made of cambric, two rows of triple tucking around the bottom and one row of cambric embroidery all around.
No. 38R1356 Price, each.................. **49c**
If by mail, postage extra, each, 7 cents.

Infants' Long Skirt, 75c.

No. 38R1360
Infants' Long Skirt, made of good quality white cambric, two rows of tucking and one row of embroidered cambric all around the bottom.
No.38R1360 Price, each...............**75c**
If by mail, postage extra, each, 7 cents.

No. 38R1364
Infants' Long Skirt, made of fine nainsook, handsomely trimmed with two rows of tucking all around the bottom and one row of Valenciennes insertion and a 4-inch Valenciennes lace trimming all around the bottom.
No.38R1364 Price each...............**98c**
If by mail, postage extra, each, 6 cents.

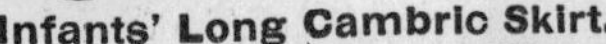

Infants' Long Cambric Skirt.

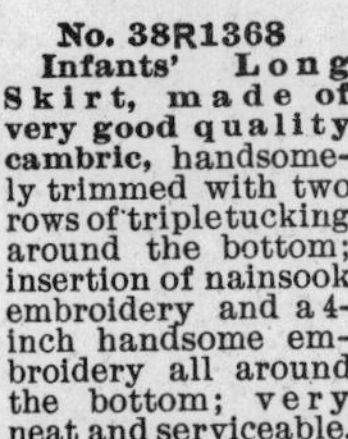

No. 38R1368
Infants' Long Skirt, made of very good quality cambric, handsomely trimmed with two rows of triple tucking around the bottom; insertion of nainsook embroidery and a 4-inch handsome embroidery all around the bottom; very neat and serviceable.
Price, each...**$1.10**
If by mail, postage extra, each, 7 cents.

No. 38R1370 Infants' Long Skirt, made of fine nainsook, trimmed with three clusters (four rows in a cluster) of fine tucks with two rows of Valenciennes insertion. Trimmed around the bottom with wide Valenciennes lace to match. A very pretty and attractive skirt.
Price, each...**$1.48**
If by mail, postage extra, 8 cents.

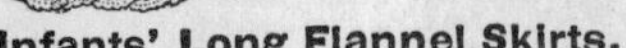

Infants' Long Flannel Skirts.

No. 38R1372 No. 38R1376

No. 38R1372 Infants' Long Skirt, made of fleece lined canton flannel. Price, each **25c**
If by mail, postage extra, each, 7 cents.
No. 38R1376 Infants' Long Skirt, made of good quality fleece lined canton flannel, exceptionally good value. Price, each....................**35c**
If by mail, postage extra, each, 9 cents.

49 Cents Buys a 75-Cent Infants' Long Skirt.

No. 38R1380 Infants' Long Skirt, made of high grade fleece lined canton flannel. Scalloped edge around the bottom, embroidered in silk.
Price, each.....**49c**
If by mail, postage extra, each, 9 cents.

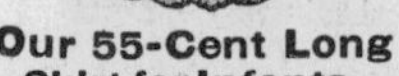

Our 55-Cent Long Skirt for Infants.

No. 38R1384 Infants' Long Skirt, made of an all wool cream colored flannel, very good quality.
Price, each.........**55c**
If by mail, postage extra, each, 6 cents.

No. 38R1388 Infants' Long All Wool Flannel Skirt, with a wide cambric band, beautifully embroidered around the bottom with silk, scalloped and stitched with silk. Crean color only.
Price, each.....**98c**
If by mail, postage extra, 7 cents

Infants' Barrior Coats or Pinning Blankets

No. 38R1392 Infants' Barrior Coats or Pinning Blankets, made of canton flannel. Well made. Cream color. Price, each...........................**18c**
If by mail, postage extra, 6 cents.
No. 38R1396 Infants' Barrior Coats or Pinning Blankets, made of all wool cream color flannel. Good value. Price, each...........................**48c**
If by mail, postage extra, 6 cents.
No. 38R1400 Infants' Bands, made of good canton flannel. Price, each...........................**10c**
If by mail, postage extra, 3 cents.

Infants' Shawls.

No. 38R1404 Infants' Shawl, made of all wool cream colored flannel. Embroidered all around with silk. Flowered design in one of the corners, as shown in illustration. Price, each...........**49c**
If by mail, postage extra, 5c

No. 38R1408 Infants' Shawl, made of all wool cream colored flannel, scalloped edge, elaborately embroidered with silk. Beautiful flowered design, heavily embroidered in silk in corner. Price, each.........**89c**
If by mail, postage extra, 6c.

No.38R1412 Infants' All Wool Flannel Hand Embroidered Shawl, elaborately embroidered with silk in a very pretty flower design, scalloped and stitched with silk. Exceptionally good value.
Price .**$1.19**
If by mail, postage extra, 6 cents.

Children's Bibs.

No. 38R1422 Fancy Figured Bib, Marseilles pattern, fleeced back, with bound edge.
Price, each..........3c
Postage extra, 2 cents.

No. 38R1426 Honey Comb Bib, with bound edge, and trimmed with a wash lace.
Price, each..........4c
Postage extra, 2 cents.

38R1426 38R1422

No. 38R1430 Honey Comb Bib, bound edge, and trimmed with a wide wash lace embroidery, pocket with teething ring.
Price, each.........7c
Postage extra, 2 cents.

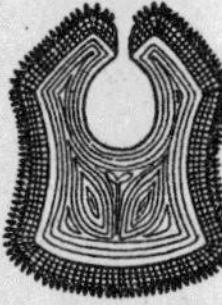

No. 38R1434 Quilted Marseilles Bib, with wash lace edge, very pretty design.
Price, each........ 9c

38R1430 38R1434

If by mail, postage extra, each, 2 cents.

Oilcloth Bibs.

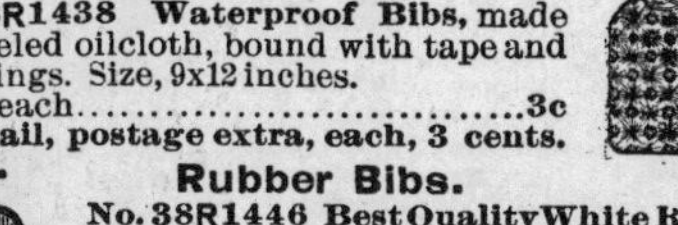

No. 38R1438 Waterproof Bibs, made of enameled oilcloth, bound with tape and neck strings. Size, 9x12 inches.
Price, each..............................3c
If by mail, postage extra, each, 3 cents.

Rubber Bibs.

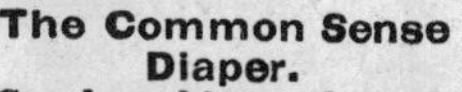

No. 38R1446 Best Quality White Rubber Bibs. Bound with tape all around, positively waterproof. Length, 10, 11 and 12 inches. Measure bibs from chin to lower end.
Each..........7c
If by mail, postage extra, 2c.

The Common Sense Diaper.

Can be adjusted to the baby's hips and limbs so as to fit perfectly, and give absolute ease and comfort. These diapers are made of the best absorbent flannel, which protects the child's clothing, bedding, etc. **Children do not become ruptured or bowlegged when these diapers are used.**

No. 38R1450 Infants' Common Sense Diaper or Absorbent Cloths. Manufactured of the best quality absorbent flannel, hemmed all around; safety pin with each diaper; small, medium and large sizes. Price, 14c
If by mail, postage extra, each, 3 cents.

Rubber Diaper Drawers.

No. 38R1454 White Rubber Diaper Drawers; 3 sizes, large, medium and small.
Price, each....... .....16c
If by mail, postage extra, each, 4 cents.

INFANTS' SILK BONNETS.

No. 38R1462 Japanese Silk Baby Bonnet. Pretty new design silk embroidered with row of Valenciennes lace edging all around cap, and high top ruching, ribbon ties, interlined with wadding and lined with cambric. Cream only. Sizes, 12 to 16.
Price, each...........25c
If by mail, postage extra, 6 cents.

No. 38R1466 Japanese Silk Baby Bonnet. Handsome silk embroidered, graduated ruching with little ribbon bows on top, Valenciennes lace edging around back of cap, lined throughout, wide string bows. In cream only. Sizes, 12 to 17.
Price, each................39c
If by mail, postage extra, 5c.

No. 38R1470 Japanese Silk Baby Bonnet, embroidered with silk very prettily designed. Embroidered in back also, graduated ruche in front with narrow ribbon loops, ruche around neck. A very elaborately trimmed bonnet. Sizes, 13 to 17. Color, cream only.
Price, each........48c
If by mail, postage extra, 4 cents.

No. 38R1474 A very pretty embroidered Japanese Silk Baby Bonnet, edged all around front and neck with lace followed with silk cord. Back beautifully embroidered, pompon on top of ruching and two small ribbon bows. **Bonnet lined with Japanese silk,** wide silk string, very newest design. **Exceptionally good value.** Sizes, 13 to 17. Color, cream only. Price..............53c
If by mail, postage extra, 4 cents.

INFANTS' LAWN BONNETS.

No. 38R1486 A regular 30 cent Bonnet for 19 cents. Made of striped white lawn, trimmed with narrow pink lawn ruffles on side, front, and around neck, and edged with lace. Sizes, 13 to 17. Price..............19c
If by mail, postage extra, 3 cents.

No. 38R1490 A very neat embroidered white lawn Baby Bonnet, very latest design, ruffling of white lawn in front and top edged with lace and narrow ribbon loops on top cap of striped lawn, and edged with lace and embroidered in back. Sizes, 13 to 17. Extra good value. Price.......23c
If by mail, postage extra, 4c

No. 38R1494 A very nice white lawn Baby Bonnet, five rows of tucks, each hemstitched, cording and lace edge in front and around neck, large pompon of ruche on top with narrow ribbon bows, tucks and hemstitching in back. The very latest design. Sizes, 13 to 17. Wide lawn strings. Price...........25c
If by mail, postage extra, 4 cents.

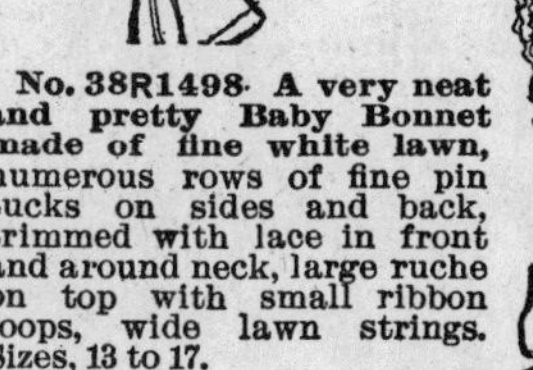

No. 38R1498 A very neat and pretty Baby Bonnet made of fine white lawn, numerous rows of fine pin tucks on sides and back, trimmed with lace in front and around neck, large ruche on top with small ribbon loops, wide lawn strings. Sizes, 13 to 17.
Price.........................39c
If by mail, postage extra, 4 cents.

No. 38R1502 An exceedingly pretty Baby Bonnet made of fine white lawn, fine pin tucks alternating with plaits and hemstitching all around bonnet and back, graduated ruche with narrow ribbon loops on top, lace edging around bottom, wide lawn strings. Sizes, 13 to 17. Very good value.
Price, each.................42c
If by mail, postage extra, each, 4 cents.

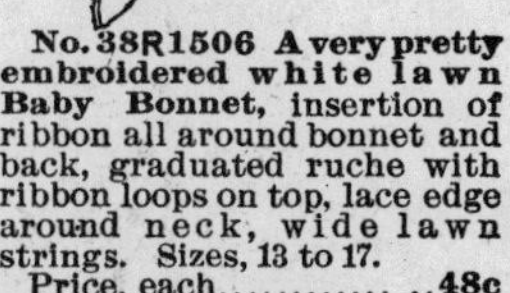

No. 38R1506 A very pretty embroidered white lawn Baby Bonnet, insertion of ribbon all around bonnet and back, graduated ruche with ribbon loops on top, lace edge around neck, wide lawn strings. Sizes, 13 to 17.
Price, each............48c
If by mail, postage extra, each, 4 cents.

No. 38R1510 A beautiful Baby Bonnet, made of fine white lawn, three rows of lace around bonnet, with hemstitching; lace edge to match in front and around neck; embroidery insertion, lace and hemstitching in back to match, wide lawn strings. Sizes, 13 to 17. Exceptionally good value.
Price, each.......53c
If by mail, postage extra, each, 4 cents.

Infants' Eiderdown and Silk Faille Bonnets.

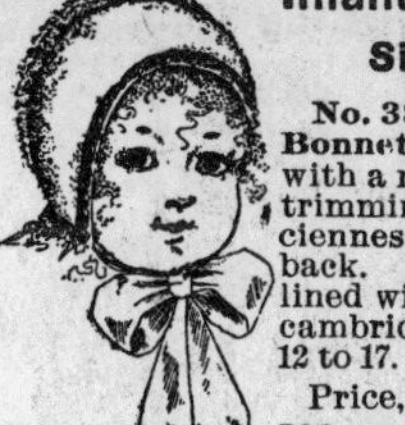

No. 38R1514 Eiderdown Baby Bonnet, round shape as per cut, with a row of plush imitation fur trimming around top and Valenciennes lace edging around top and back. Wide string bows. Interlined with wadding and lined with cambric. Color, cream only. Size, 12 to 17.
Price, each........................25c
If by mail, postage extra, 5 cents.

No. 38R1518 A very pretty bonnet, made of faille silk, in a round shape, with two rows of shirred ribbon around top and finished with silk braid edging, trimmed with French Valenciennes lace in front and neck. Colors, cream, light blue, or cardinal. Sizes, 12 to 17.
Price, each...........55c
If by mail, postage extra, 6 cents.

No. 38R1522 Baby Bonnet, with cape, made of mercerized faille, trimmed with white Point de Paris dark colored lace. Cape trimmed around with same material; trimmed with French Valenciennes lace in front. Two fancy ribbon bows on either side. Interlined with wadding and lined with cambric. Colors, cardinal, navy blue or cream. Sizes, 13 to 17.
Price, each.............57c
If by mail, postage extra, 8 cents.

POKE BONNETS.

Ages, 1 to 5 years.

No. 38R1550 This beautiful puffed Poke Bonnet is made of organdie, in white or blue colors. Has insertion of open work, Swiss embroidery ruffle in front and around neck, which is edged with Valenciennes lace, graduated ruche in front under ruffle, wide organdie strings, lined throughout. Colors, white or light blue.
Price, each.............44c
If by mail, postage extra, 5 cents.

No. 38R1554 A very pretty puffed Poke Bonnet, made of fine white lawn, beading and four rows of narrow insertion, two rows in back, Swiss embroidery ruffle around front and neck, ruching around front under ruffle, wide lawn strings. Sizes, 14 to 17.
Price, each............69c
If by mail, postage extra, 5 cents.

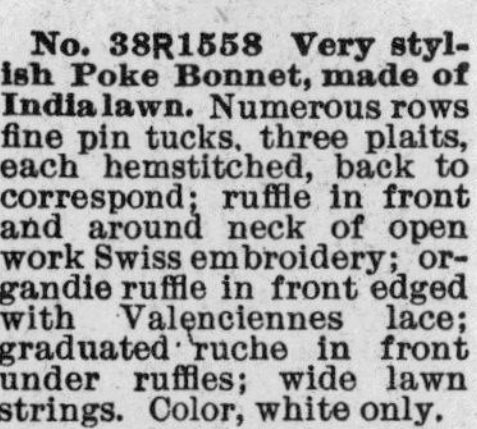

No. 38R1558 Very stylish Poke Bonnet, made of India lawn. Numerous rows fine pin tucks, three plaits, each hemstitched, back to correspond; ruffle in front and around neck of open work Swiss embroidery; organdie ruffle in front edged with Valenciennes lace; graduated ruche in front under ruffles; wide lawn strings. Color, white only.
Price, each.............75c
If by mail, postage extra, 5 cents.

No. 38R1562 Child's Poke Bonnet, made of faille silk. Around the poke in front, and cape it is trimmed with genet fur trimming, and also a row of silk trimming braid which adds to the elegance of this beautiful bonnet. Full ruche at top and around face within the poke. Wide faille strings. Colors, cardinal or navy blue. Sizes, 13 to 17.
Price, each.. ....$1.10
If by mail, postage extra, 10 cents.

No. 38R1566 This is our most elegant design and the best number we have. Poke bonnet, made in faille, Normandy style, with two rows of ½-inch white lamb's wool trimming around top, cape trimmed with same material; between two rows of lamb's wool are two rows of fancy silk braid trimming, while at the top a small fur head and full silk ribbon bow, wide faille strings. We highly recommend this stylish bonnet. Colors, navy blue, light blue, pink, cardinal or cream. Sizes, 13 to 17. Price, each......$1.29
If by mail, postage extra, 8 cents.

No. 38R1570 Poke Bonnet, made of fine quality mercerized faille, with cape of same material. The band on top of cape is wired so as to preserve the shape. Heavy lace ruching at top. Wide faille strings. Lined throughout. A very stylish and serviceable bonnet. Colors, cardinal, navy blue or brown. Sizes, 13 to 17.
Price, each.........74c
If by mail, postage extra, 10 cents.

CHILDREN'S AND MISSES' TAM O'SHANTERS.

No. 38R1594 A very neat and pretty Tam O'Shanter, made of corded lawn, top trimmed with silk cord, good lining. Very nicely made and extra good value. White only.
Price, each...22c
If by mail, postage extra, each, 4 cents.

Round Shape Tam O'Shanter, 25 Cents.

No. 38R1596 Round Shape Tam O'Shanter, made of white pique, trimmed around band with satin ribbon. Always looks neat and dressy.
Price, each 25c
If by mail, postage extra, 4 cents.

No. 38R1610 A Very Pretty Circular Tam O'Shanter, made of all wool flannel; top is braided in the form of small squares of pressed flannel and straw braid, one silk pompon and silk tassel; band trimmed with one row of straw braid. A very neat and pretty design. Colors, blue or red.
Price, each.........53c
If by mail, postage extra, each, 6 cents.

No. 38R1614 Our New College Shape Tam O'Shanter, made of fine quality ribbed flannel. This tam is made of navy blue. Around the brim is a medium wide row of white felt, finished with a row of fancy trimming braid, with a gold thread running through; on top of crown a new, original design, made of white felt; in center of crown is a white felt covered button, over which hangs a silk tassel. The cap is lined, and a very dressy and splendid value. Price, each 39c
If by mail, postage extra, 15 cents.

No. 38R1618 This Pretty College Shape Tam O'Shanter is made of fine quality black velvette; around the curved band are three rows of silk soutache trimming, and over top of crown it is finished with a fancy braided design, and silk tassel; lined throughout; very stylish and one of the prettiest tams made.
Price, each.......48c
If by mail, postage extra, 15c

No. 38R1622 Circular Tam O'Shanter. Trimmed with two rows hercules braid on top and silk pompon; has one row of hercules braid on band; made of pressed flannel, lined throughout; very neat and serviceable. Colors, navy blue or cardinal. Price..25c
If by mail, postage extra, 12 cents.

No. 38R1626 This stylish Circular Tam O'Shanter is made of fine quality black velvette with a row of 1-inch faille silk ribbon around brim, completed with a little bow of same material. For a rich and dressy tam for either a boy or girl, this is an excellent number; lined throughout. Sizes, 6¼ to 6⅞. Price....47c
If by mail, postage extra, 12 cents.

No. 38R1628 Circular Shape Tam O'Shanter. New, original design, making a pretty, elaborate appearance. The top of crown is trimmed with two rows of soutache braid, and is finished with brass buttons as shown in illustration. Two rows of gold soutache around brim; made of fine quality all wool flannel. Can be ordered in cardinal or navy blue. Price..........49c
If by mail, postage extra, 12 cents.

No. 38R1630 Circular Shape Tam O'Shanter. It is a combination tam, made of all good quality flannel; the center design on top of crown is good quality Astrakhan cloth, finished with a covered flannel button in center; the brim is made of the same quality Astrakhan cloth, which can be pulled down over the ears; lined throughout. Can be ordered in combination of colors as follows: Red flannel with black Astrakhan, or navy blue flannel with black Astrakhan. Price..52c
If by mail, postage extra, 12 cents.

MISSES' HATS.

No. 38R1632 Misses' Wash Hat, made of lawn with corded brim and crown corded at top. The brim is edged with a row of white zigzag braid. Nice lawn tie strings. Colors, blue, white or pink. Price........22c
If by mail, postage extra, 6c

No. 38R1634 Misses' Lawn Hat, top made of allover embroidery and trimmed with lace, wide lawn ruffle all around hat which is trimmed with Valenciennes lace, lawn bow in front, wide lawn strings. **Very newest style.** Colors, cream or light blue. Price......42c
If by mail, postage extra, 9c

No. 38R1636 A Beautiful Misses' Hat, made of lawn, entire hat covered with allover lace, large lawn puff in front, the brim is made in very pretty folds and covered with allover lace. An exceedingly pretty misses' hat for very little money. Colors, pink or light blue. Price............53c
If by mail, postage extra, 9c

No. 38R1638 A very pretty Misses' Lawn Hat. The crown is beautifully trimmed with two rows of narrow ribbon, lace and ruffle tucking; has two ruffles all around hat, of which one is trimmed with two rows of narrow ribbon, the other is edged with Valenciennes lace; one row of ribbon under the brim, ruching around front; wide lawn strings; lined with cambric. Colors, blue or red.
Price, each...............82c
If by mail, postage extra, 11c

No. 38R1640 A beautifully trimmed Misses' Lawn Hat. High crown, large bow in front edged with fine Valenciennes lace; brim trimmed with fine straw braid, also edged with straw braid; a very pretty ruffle all around hat edged with Valenciennes lace to match; wide lawn strings. For a stylish and high grade hat we would recommend this number. Colors, pink or light blue. Price, each.........98c
If by mail, postage extra, 11c

BOYS' AND CHILDREN'S CAPS AND TOQUES.

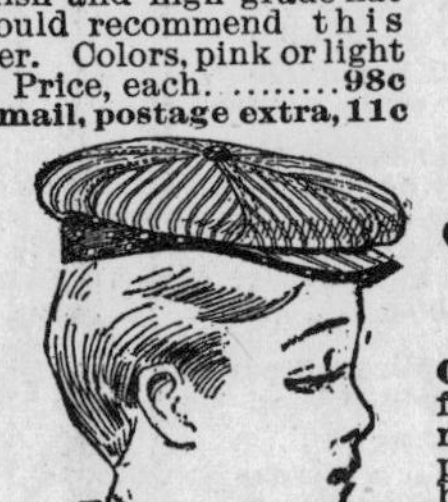

No. 38R1641 Child's Cap, suitable for little boy or girl, made of white cotton pique, with heavy blue polka dot band and shield. A very popular spring and summer cap.
Price.....................25c
If by mail, postage extra, 4c

No. 38R1642 Child's Cap, made of good quality pressed flannel, white fancy band around peak of cap, and fancy design on top of crown of soutache braid; the cap is lined and well made. Colors, cardinal or navy blue. Price........24c
If by mail, postage extra, 10 cents.

No. 38R1643 This is a very neat little cap, made of all wool flannel, fancy ornamental design on crown of silk braid, as shown in illustration. Black velvet rim and peak, black velvet covered button on top of crown, satin lined. A very neat and dressy little cap. Colors, cardinal or navy blue. Price, 41c
If by mail, postage extra, 12c

No. 38R1644 This is a very stylish and dressy little cap for boys. Made of good quality velvette; the rim is made of a fancy mixture of cloth, with a double row of silk cord around front; satin lined. Colors, black only.
Price...............49c
If by mail, postage extra, 12 cents.

No. 38R1645 Child's Toque. Turkish design. Made of nice quality flannel; very ornamental in design; around the crown are two bands of fancy braid, and over the flowing end of the crown seven rows of band trimming as shown in illustration. Silk tassel on end of cap; cap is lined, and a very excellent value. Colors, cardinal or navy.
Price, each (**If by mail, postage extra, 8 cents**) 23c

No. 38R1646 Child's Toque. Oriental design, combination design, made of good quality black velvette and all wool cardinal flannel; with two rows of gold silk soutache braid around brim, while the crown has braided rows of gold soutache braid with gold spikes on ends. (See illustration.) Long silk tassel on end; this is a very original and pretty design.
Price, each.........48c
If by mail, postage extra, 3 cents.

INFANTS' KNIT BOOTEES.

WE SHOW A COMPLETE LINE of these dainty and comfortable articles for infants.

NOTE OUR PRICES AND QUALITIES CAREFULLY.

No. 38R1652 Infants' Bootees' hand crocheted, made of all wool zephyr. Colors, solid white, pink and white, or blue and white. Price, per pair....9c
If by mail, postage extra, per pair, 2c.

No. 38R1656 Infants' Bootees, closely hand crocheted, made of good quality zephyr. Colors, solid white, pink and white, or blue and white. Price, per pair....15c
If by mail, postage extra, per pair, 2 cents.

No. 38R1660 Infants' Bootees, closely hand crocheted, neat design, made of fine zephyr. Colors, solid white, pink and white, or blue and white.
Price, per pair..........20c
If by mail, postage extra, per pair, 2 cents.

No. 38R1664 A very neat all wool Ribbed Bootee, very closely knitted, trimmed with small tassels at ankle. Colors, solid white, pink and white, or blue and white.
Price, per pair..........30c
If by mail, postage extra, per pair, 2 cents.

No. 38R1668 Infants' High Bootees, made of all wool zephyr, closely crocheted, turned over top finished with silk. Colors, solid white, pink and white, or light blue and white.
Price, per pair..........30c
If by mail, postage extra, per pair, 2 cents.

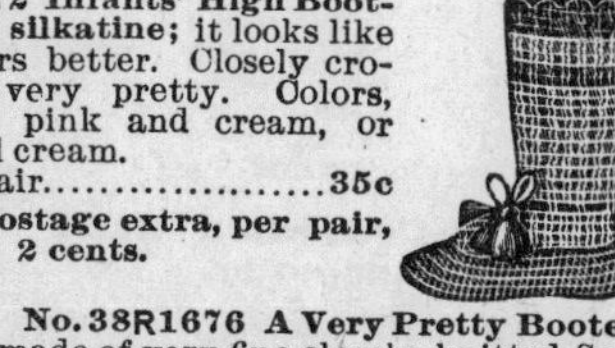

No. 38R1672 Infants' High Bootees, made of silkatine; it looks like silk, but wears better. Closely crocheted and very pretty. Colors, solid cream, pink and cream, or light blue and cream.
Price, per pair..........35c
If by mail, postage extra, per pair, 2 cents.

No. 38R1676 A Very Pretty Bootee, made of very fine closely knitted Saxony yarn; trimmed with baby ribbon, ribbon at ankles; excellent value. Colors, solid white, pink and white, or blue and white.
Price, per pair..........40c
If by mail, postage extra, per pair, 2 cents.

No. 38R1680 Infants' High Bootees, hand crocheted of extra good quality zephyr, with silk fancy work, turned over top; very good quality for the money. Colors, solid white, pink and white, or light blue and white.
Price, per pair..........48c
If by mail, postage extra, per pair, 2 cents.

Infants' Knitted Slippers.

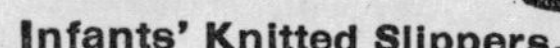

No. 38R1684 Infants' Knitted Slippers, with lamb's wool sole, very pretty, made of all wool yarn. Colors, solid white, white and blue, or white and pink.
Price, per pair..........30c
If by mail, postage extra, per pair, 4 cents.

Infants' Knit Sacques.

No. 38R1696 Infants' Sacque, made of all wool Shetland yarn. Colors, solid cream, pink and cream, or light blue and cream.
Price, each.....23c
If by mail, postage extra, each, 3 cents.

No. 38R1702 Infants' Sacque, closely hand crocheted, made of all wool zephyr, tassels in front, very neat design. Colors, solid white, pink and white, or light blue and white.
Price, each....35c
If by mail, postage extra, each, 4 cents.

Infants' Knit All Wool Sacques.

No. 38R1706 Very Pretty Infants' Sacque, made of a very fine all wool yarn, trimmed around the collar, down the front and bottom with crocheted edging with an insertion of baby ribbon. Colors, solid cream, cream with pink or blue edging. Price, each.....45c
If by mail, postage extra, each, 5 cents.

No. 38R1710 Infants' Sacque, made of an all wool, closely knit domestic zephyr. Very pretty tassel in front. Colors, solid cream, pink and cream, or light blue and cream.
Price, each..55c
If by mail, postage extra, each, 5 cents.

No. 38R1714 An Elegant Infants' Sacque, made of closely knitted zephyr, trimmed around the back extending to front over shoulders (giving it a cape effect) with an insertion of satin ribbon. Crocheted edging also down the front and bottom with an insertion of satin ribbon. Colors, solid cream, or cream with pink or blue edging. Price, each..........72c
If by mail, postage extra, each, 5 cents.

No. 38R1718 Infants' Knitted Sacque, made of an all wool imported zephyr, very closely knit of the newest and best yarn, yoke around shoulders in front and back. Very pretty sleeves. Colors, solid cream, pink and cream, or light blue and cream. Price, each..........79c
If by mail, postage extra, each, 6 cents.

No. 38R1722 A Beautiful Infants' Sacque, made of all wool closely knitted zephyr, very neatly designed around the collar, down the front and bottom, trimmed with tassels at neck. Colors, solid cream, pink and cream, or light blue and cream. Price, each..........95c
If by mail, postage extra, each, 6 cents.

Infants' Flannel and Elderdown Sacques.

No. 38R1726 Infants' Sacque, made of flannel, stitched all around collar, front and sleeves. Colors, cream with blue or pink stripes.
Price, each...19c
If by mail, postage extra, each, 3 cents.

No. 38R1730 Infants' Kimono, made of flannel. has a collar and revers reaching to bottom with cuffs to match. Colors, light blue or pink, cream revers.
Price.... 25c
If by mail, postage extra, each, 6 cents.

No. 38R1734 Infants' Sacque, made of wool elderdown, stitched with silk all around collar in front and around sleeves. Very warm and neat. Colors, solid white, solid pink or solid blue. Price, each..........42c
If by mail, postage extra, each, 5 cents.

Special Value for 49 Cents.

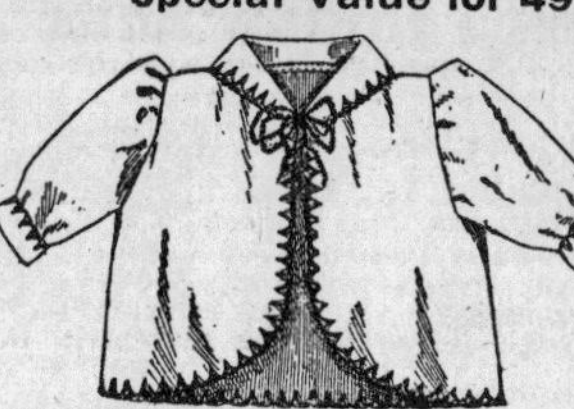

No. 38R1738 Infants' Sacque, made of all wool flannel, neatly stitched around collar and in front, around the cuffs and on the bottom with silk. Cream only. Stitched with either white, pink or blue silk.
Price, each..........49c
If by mail, postage extra, each, 4 cents.

Our 75-Cent Infants' Wool Flannel Sacque.

No. 38R1742 Infants' Sacque, made of all wool flannel, collar, yoke, front, bottom and cuffs are trimmed with silk stitching. A very neat and serviceable sacque. Colors, cream, with blue or pink stitching. Price, each........75c
If by mail, postage extra, each, 5 cents.

INFANTS' AND CHILDREN'S HOODS.

For Infants and Children up to 3 years of age.

20 Cents for This Hood.

No. 38R1750 Infants' Hood with small cape made of Shetland floss, ornamented with silkatine stitching. Colors, cream, pink, or light blue. Price, each........20c
If by mail, postage extra, each, 2 cents.

Real Shetland Yarn.

No. 38R1752 Infants' Hood, made of Shetland yarn, has small cape, with pompon on top, pompon and front trimmed in silk floss. Colors, pink, cream or blue. Each 25c
If by mail, postage extra, 3 cents.

A Neat Hood.

No. 38R1754 Infants' Hood, made of all wool Shetland yarn, white swansdown trimming in front and trimmed with small balls at neck, made of Shetland floss. Colors, blue, pink or cream. Price, each..45c
If by mail, postage extra, 4 cents.

Well Trimmed, 55 Cents.

No. 38R1756 Infants' Hood, made of all wool Shetland yarn, covered with crocheted silkatine, satin ribbon bow on top, trimmed with small pompons, made with Shetland yarn, in front and bottom. Color, cream only. Price, each...55c
If by mail, postage extra, 3 cents.

Split Zephyr.

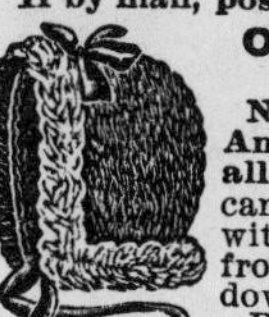

No. 38R1758 Infants' Hood, made of split zephyr crocheted and covered with a knit pattern made of silkatine, four rows of satin ribbon running through the pattern, satin ribbon bow on top, ruffle yarn all around. Colors, pink, cream or light blue. Price, each 69c
If by mail, postage extra, each, 3c.

A Beauty, 92 Cents.

No. 38R1760 Neat Infants' Hood, made of Shetland yarn, entirely covered with silk twist, ribbon bow on top, insertion of ribbon in front with ribbon streamers. Color, cream only.
Price, each..........92c
If by mail, postage extra, 3 cents.

Our Finest Hood, $1.35.

No. 38R1762 Infants' Angora Hood, strictly all wool; for warmth, cannot be excelled; ribbon bow on top with ribbon streamers, trimmed in front and bottom with white swansdown. Colors, white or gray.
Price, each.......... $1.35
If by mail, postage extra, 3 cents.

GET YOUR FRIENDS AND NEIGHBORS to order with you and make up a club order. In this way you can save on freight charges.

CHILDREN'S HOODS, AGES 3 TO 8.

Our 35-Cent Hood.

No. 38R1764 Child's Hood, hand made, trimmed with silk floss and all around with small balls made of Shetland floss. Colors, cream, pink and light blue. Price, each............35c
If by mail, postage extra, each, 3c

With Cape, 48 Censt.

No. 38R1765 Child's Hood, made of Shetland yarn trimmed all over with silk floss, and small balls made of Shetland floss in front, has a cape. Colors, pink, blue or cream. Price, each..48c
If by mail, postage extra, 4 cents.

No. 38R1768 A very pretty child's Hood, made of Shetland floss covered with silk floss, trimmed with a shield on side with a pompon on top, ornamented with small balls made of Shetland floss in front and bottom. Colors, cream, pink or blue. Price, each..........60c
If by mail, postage extra, 3 cents.

With Large Cape, 75 Cents.

No. 38R1770 Child's Hood covered all over with silk floss; large cape reaching over the shoulders, trimmed with white swansdown in front. Color, cream only.
Price, each.................75c
If by mail, postage extra, 5 cents.

No. 38R1772 Child's Stylish Hood, made of Shetland yarn, entirely covered with mercerized silk twist, with an insertion of four rows of baby ribbon, trimmed in front and bottom with swansdown, ribbon streamers. Colors, cream, pink or blue.
Price, each.............................82c
If by mail, postage extra, 4 cents.

No. 38R1774 Child's Hood made of Shetland yarn; ornamented all over with silk floss, has a cape, trimmed in front with white swansdown and ribbon streamers; high in back. Colors, pink, blue or cream. Each......98c
If by mail, postage extra, 4c.

MISSES' HOODS, AGED 8 TO 12.

No. 38R1780 Misses' Hood, made of all wool Shetland yarn, closely hand crocheted. Colors, navy blue, pink, light blue and cardinal.
Price, each.................. 25c
If by mail, postage extra, each, 4 cents.

No. 38R1782 Misses' Hood. For 6 to 12 year old children, made of all wool zephyr yarn, nicely trimmed with fancy ribbon in center of back and on each side, zephyr ruffle in front. Colors, cardinal, light blue or cream.
Price, each.................42c
If by mail, postage extra, each, 5 cents.

Would Retail at $1.00.

No. 38R1784 Misses' Hood, made of Shetland yarn, alternating with one row on each side, and two rows in back with silk twist stitching. Shetland yarn ruffling in back and front stitched with silk twist, lined with knitted Shetland yarn; has large cape. Colors, navy blue, pink or cardinal.
Price, each..................55c
If by mail, postage extra, 6 cents.

A Novelty Toque Style.

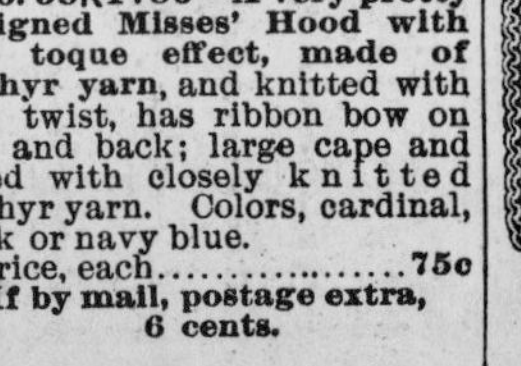

No. 38R1786 A very pretty designed Misses' Hood with the toque effect, made of zephyr yarn, and knitted with silk twist, has ribbon bow on top and back; large cape and lined with closely knitted zephyr yarn. Colors, cardinal, pink or navy blue.
Price, each..................75c
If by mail, postage extra, 6 cents.

LADIES' HOODS.

No. 38R1790 Ladies' Hand Made Hood, closely crocheted, of all wool zephyr, extra large size, large cape to cover neck. Colors, black, cardinal or navy blue. Price, each........ .45c
If by mail, postage extra, 5 cents.

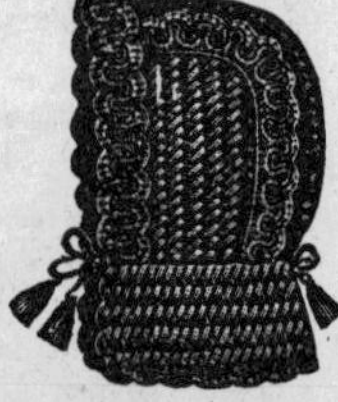

No. 38R1792 Ladies' Hand Made Hood, made of Germantown yarn, with wool lining, flounce in front of same material, large cape to cover neck. Colors, black, cardinal and navy. Price, each.....................70c
If by mail, postage extra, each, 7 cents.

No. 38R1794 Ladies' Fancy Hand Made Hood of all wool zephyr; handsomely trimmed with satin ribbon bow in front; satin ribbon on each side and in back, satin ribbon bow on top and in back of neck, lined throughout with wool yarn, covered with beads and silk floss. Colors, solid black or red, cream with pink or blue trimmings. Price, each, 98c
By mail, postage extra, 1 cent.

No. 38R1796 Ladies' Hand Made Hood, of good quality zephyr, satin bow on top and back of neck, lined with all wool yarn, satin ribbon in front. Black only. Price, each..$1.10
If by mail, postage extra, each, 6 cents.

Ladies' Tab Hoods.

No. 38R1798 Ladies' Hand Made Hood of all wool zephyr, long tab in front and beaded top; lined throughout with wool yarn. Color, black only.
Price, each.................75c
If by mail, postage extra, each, 8 cents.

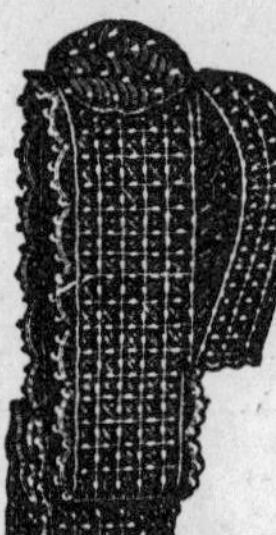

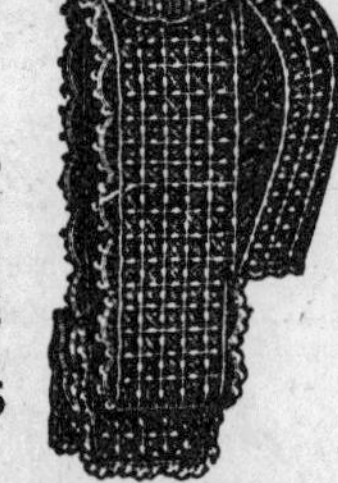

No. 38R1800 Ladies' Tab Hood, made of all wool Shetland yarn, long tab in front, pompon of same material trimmed in beads, bead trimming all over the hood, lined throughout with all wool yarn. Colors, black, cardinal, blue or cream.
Price, each........... ..$1.10
If by mail, postage extra, each, 12 cents.

KNIT FASCINATORS.

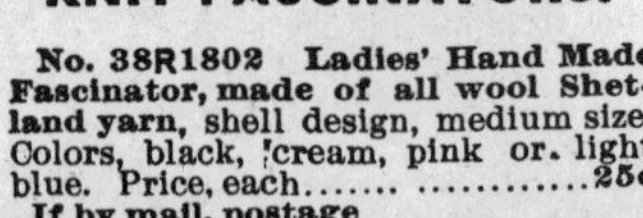

No. 38R1802 Ladies' Hand Made Fascinator, made of all wool Shetland yarn, shell design, medium size. Colors, black, cream, pink or light blue. Price, each...... ....25c
If by mail, postage extra, each, 4 cents.

No. 38R1804 Ladies' Hand Crocheted Fascinator, made of all wool Shetland floss, shell pattern, top ornamented with beads, tassels on ends. Colors, black, cream, pink or light blue. Price, each........ ..40c
If by mail, postage extra, each, 4c

No. 38R1802.

No. 38R1806 Very pretty Hood Fascinator, made of Shetland yarn trimmed with fancy knitted edging, pompon on top, tassels at each end, and lined with fleece wool. Very neat pattern. Colors, black, cardinal, pink or blue.

No. 38R1806.

Price, each.......................45c
If by mail, postage extra, 8 cents.

Knit Fascinators—Continued.

No. 38R1808 Hand Made Fascinator, of loose knitted Shetland Yarn in shell design, ornamented with beads and loops at ends. Colors, cream, black, pink or blue.
Price, each....................... 50c
If by mail, postage extra, 9 cents.

No. 38R1810 Ladies' Large Size Fascinator, hand crocheted, made of all wool Shetland floss in a very new design, loosely knitted loops all around the edges and a satin ribbon bow on top. Very pretty and neat. Colors, black, pink, or light blue. Price, each...................75c
If by mail, postage extra, each, 5 cents.

No. 38R1812 Ladies' Medium Size Fascinator, with loosely knitted loops all over and trimmed with beads. Very good value for the money. This hood is made of all wool Shetland floss. Colors, black, cardinal or cream.
Price, each.........................65c
If by mail, postage extra, each, 10 cents.

No. 38R1814 A Beautiful Ladies' Fascinator, made of Shetland yarn, upper part ornamented with silk floss, sides ornamented with beads, pompon on top of numerous small balls made of Shetland floss, of which edges are trimmed also. Colors, black, pink, cream or blue.
Price, each.......................79c
If by mail, postage extra, 8 cents.

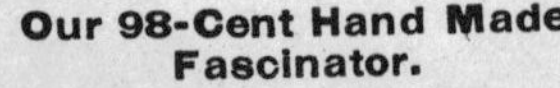

Our 98-Cent Hand Made Fascinator.

No. 38R1816 Ladies' Large Size Fascinator, hand made, of all wool Shetland yarn, loosely knit loops, all over trimmed with beads. Extra heavy and very warm. Colors, black, pink or light blue.
Price, each........................98c
If by mail, postage extra, each, 13 cents.

No. 38R1818 High Class Ladies' Opera Hood Fascinators, made of Shetland yarn, very pretty pattern of small squares, ornamented all over with silk floss, scalloped in back, pompon on top, tassels at each end. Colors, pink, white or light blue.
Price, each $1.15
If by mail, postage extra, 8 cents.

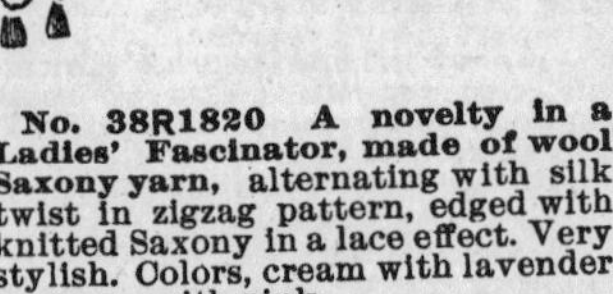

No. 38R1820 A novelty in a Ladies' Fascinator, made of wool Saxony yarn, alternating with silk twist in zigzag pattern, edged with knitted Saxony in a lace effect. Very stylish. Colors, cream with lavender or cream with pink.
Price, each..... ....55c
If by mail, postage extra, 5 cents.

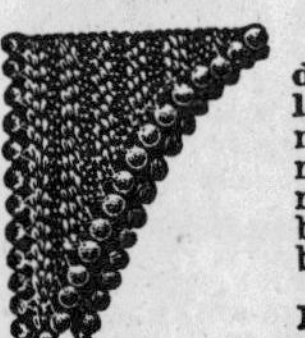

No. 38R1822 Very Pretty Ladies' Fascinator, made of Shetland yarn and chenille, each alternating in the form of loops, trimmed all around with small balls made of Shetland floss. Colors, black and white, black and blue, or black and pink.
Price, each........................85c
If by mail, postage extra, 6 cents.

No. 38R1824 Imported Fascinator, made of very fine Shetland yarn, entirely covered with chenille formed into loops, ornamented with small silk pompons. Colors, black with white pompons, lavender and heliotrope pompons, or light blue with black pompons.
Price, each.........................$1.10
If by mail, postage extra, 5 cents.

Ladies' or Misses' All Wool Knitted Shawls.

No. 38R1830 Ladies' Knitted Shawl, made of all wool Shetland floss, fair size, fancy border. Colors, black, cream, pink or light blue. Price, each.................25c
If by mail, postage extra, each, 4 cents.

No. 38R1832 Ladies' Extra Large Size Wool Shawl, fancy border, hand made. Colors, black, cream, light blue, or cardinal.
Price, each.............................40c
If by mail, postage extra, each, 5 cents.

No. 38R1834 Extra Large Size Ladies' Shawl, made of all wool Shetland yarn, very neat design and pretty border. Colors, black, cream, pink or light blue.
Price, each.........................50c
If by mail, postage extra, each, 6 cents.

No. 38R1836 Ladies' Shawl, made of all wool Shetland yarn, fancy colored design in center and border to match. We furnish this in pink with white or blue with white. Price, each...............55c
If by mail, postage extra, each, 5 cents.

No. 38R1838 A Beautiful Shawl, made of Shetland yarn alternating with rows of mercerized silk twist, has a very pretty border to match. We can highly recommend this shawl as one of the very best values. Colors, solid black, cream with pink or cream with blue.
Price, each.......................75c
If by mail, postage extra, 8 cents.

No. 38R1840 A Very Stylish Shawl, made of imported Shetland yarn, alternating with rows of knitted chenille; has a very pretty border to match, heavy fringe all around to correspond. Colors, black, blue or pink with chenille to correspond.
Price, each.........................98c
If by mail, postage extra, each, 8 cents.

No. 38R1842 A Very Serviceable Shawl, made of imported zephyr, very pretty pattern running on the bias, knotted fringe. Colors, cream or pink.
Price, each.........................$1.48
If by mail, postage extra, each, 13 cents.

Zephyr and Silk Shawls.

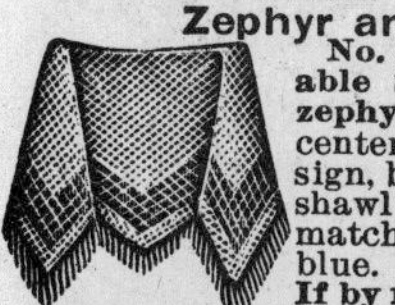

No. 38R1844 Neat and Serviceable Shawl, made of imported zephyr, honeycomb design in center, border also honeycomb design, but larger pattern, giving the shawl a pretty effect, fringe to match. Colors, black, cream or blue. Price, each.............$1.75
If by mail, postage extra, 12 cents.

No. 38R1846 Ladies' High Class Silk Shawl, neat design, pretty border to match, fringe all around shawl to correspond. Size, 50x50 inches. A high grade shawl for little money. Color, black or cream Price, each............$1.98
If by mail, postage extra, each, 6 cents.

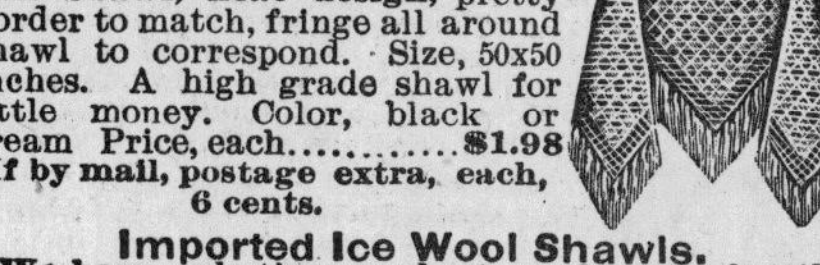

Imported Ice Wool Shawls.

We have only the very best goods and give the best values for the money. A trial order will convince you of this, and you will be more than pleased with the goods you receive. Designs are not always like illustrations.

No. 38R1850 Ladies' Ice Wool Shawl, 28 inches square, plain center, fancy border. Colors, black or cream. Price, each.............50c
If by mail, postage extra, each, 5 cents.

No. 38R1852 Ladies' Ice Wool Shawl, 32 inches square, plain center and fancy border. Colors, black or white. Price, each....75c
If by mail, postage extra, each, 6 cents.

No. 38R1854 Ladies' Extra Fine Ice Wool Shawl, 32 inches square, plain center and a very pretty border. Colors, black or cream. Price, each.............89c
If by mail, postage extra, each, 6 cents.

No. 38R1856 Ladies' Extra Heavy Ice Wool Shawls, 36 inches square, double center and fancy border. Colors, black or cream.
Price, each...................$1.29
If by mail, postage extra, each, 7 cents.

Extra Heavy Ice Wool Shawls.

No. 38R1858 Ladies' Extra Heavy Ice Wool Shawl, very good quality, double center and wide border; one of the prettiest designs shown. Colors, black or cream.
Price, each.........................$1.48
If by mail, postage extra, each, 7 cents.

No. 38R1860 Ladies' Extra Heavy Ice Wool Shawl, double center, closely knit, wide border. It can be seen only in the very highest grade stocks. Exceptional good value for the money. Colors, black or cream. Price, each.........$1.98
If by mail, postage extra, each, 8 cents.

The Latest Fad This Season—Ladies' or Misses' Circular Shawl.

No. 38R1870 Made of all wool Shetland yarn, can be worn over head and shoulders at the same time, or folded double and worn over shoulders. It is shaped at the neck, making it fit perfectly over the shoulders, and giving it a cape effect; a very stylish and serviceable shawl. 36 inches in diameter. Comes in cream with pink or lavender border, or solid cream color.
Price, each....98c
If by mail, postage extra, 8 cents.

No. 38R1872 A Very Pretty Circular Shawl, made same style as No. 38R1870, but 45 inches in diameter. Colors, white with blue or pink borders or solid white. Price, each.........................$1.39
If by mail, postage extra, 10c.

No. 38R1874 A Beautiful Hand Made Circular Shawl. 45 inches in diameter. Made of all wool zephyr, exquisite design interwoven around border with silk twist; very closely knitted. Colors, white trimmed with blue or pink silk twist, or black with black twist. Price each, $2.48
If by mail, postage extra, 14 cents.

LADIES' OR MISSES' KNITTED SHOULDER CAPES.

LATEST CREATION FOR THIS SEASON.
Very stylish and serviceable.

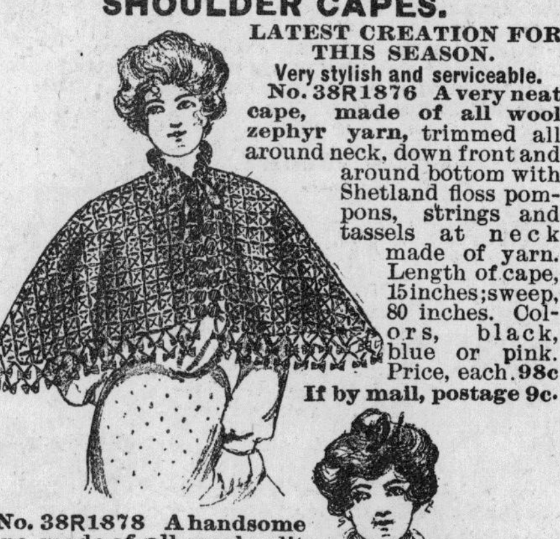

No. 38R1876 A very neat cape, made of all wool zephyr yarn, trimmed all around neck, down front and around bottom with Shetland floss pompons, strings and tassels at neck made of yarn. Length of cape, 15 inches; sweep, 80 inches. Colors, black, blue or pink. Price, each.98c
If by mail, postage 9c.

No. 38R1878 A handsome cape, made of all wool split zephyr yarn, in cream color and trimmed with either blue or pink yarn in the form of squares, trimmed with small pompons around the neck, down front and bottom in colors to correspond, strings and tassels at neck made of yarn. Length of cape, 15 inches; sweep, 80 inches. Colors, cream with blue or pink trimmings. Price, each.............................$1.39
If by mail, postage extra, 9 cents.

Beautiful Double Shoulder Cape, $1.69.

No. 38R1880 A beautiful Double Cape, made of all wool Shetland yarn, lower and upper cape trimmed with Shetland yarn in the form of small squares, upper cape trimmed with silk floss, trimmed around neck, down front and bottom with small pompons made of Shetland floss (front and lower part of both capes trimmed this way), strings and tassels at neck. Length, upper cape, 10 inches; lower cape, 15 inches; sweep, 80 inches. Color, cream with blue or pink trimmings.
Price, each...$1.69
If by mail, postage extra, 11 cents.

LADIES' OR MISSES' KNITTED UNDERSKIRTS.

No. 38R1882 Ladies' Knitted Underskirts; 26 to 28 inches long; tight yoke around the waist. Dark and light colors.
Price, each...40c
If by mail, postage extra, each, 12 cents.

No. 38R1884 Ladies' Knitted Underskirt, made of a cotton mixture, fancy stripe design in dark colors, such as red, blue or gray predominating and other desirable shades. If the selection is left to us, we will always give you the most up to date colors. Average length, 30 inches. Price, each..50c
If by mail, postage extra, each, 17 cents.

No. 38R1886 Ladies' Knitted Underskirt, very pretty and stylish, made in a very pretty design of cotton mixture, and is as good as any wool skirt on the market. Colors, navy blue, tan, light blue or red striped patterns. Average length, 30 inches. Each.............75c
If by mail, postage extra, 15 cents.

No. 38R1888 Ladies' Knitted Underskirt, made of all wool yarn, striped design, closely knitted yoke on top. Average length of skirt, 28 inches. Colors, red or blue predominating, and other desirable shades. Please leave selection to us.
Price, each..............................$1.25
If by mail, postage extra, 15 cents.

No. 38R1890 Ladies' All Wool Knitted Underskirt, striped design, pretty combination in dark colors, closely knitted yoke on top, with draw strings. Blue or red stripes predominating. Average length, 28 inches. Exceptionally heavy and warm colors. Price, each...$1.65
If by mail, postage extra, 13 cents.

No. 38R1892 Ladies' Underskirts, made of fine Egyptian cotton yarn. Length, 30 inches. Draw strings at waist. Colors, blue or pink stripes.
Price...23c
If by mail, postage extra, each, 7 cents.

No. 38R1894 Misses' Underskirts, made same style as No. 38R1892. Length, 18, 20 and 22 inches. Colors, pink or blue stripes. Price.......................18c
If by mail, postage extra, each, 5 cents.

Child's Underskirt.

No. 38R1896 Child's Hand Knit All Wool Underskirt, with waist and shoulder straps, striped pattern. Colors, cardinal, blue or pink stripes predominating, for 2, 3 and 4 year old children.
Price, each.................55c
If by mail, postage extra, 7 cents.

SEND 5 CENTS
FOR CLOTH SAMPLE BOOK
OF
Boy s and Children's Clothing.

Children's and Misses' Tam O'Shanters.

No. 38R1902 Misses' Tam O'Shanter, made of good quality long haired mohair, heavy and warm. Colors, navy, cardinal or gray.
Price, each...(If by mail, postage extra, 12c)...75c

No. 38R1904 Misses' Tam O'Shanter, made of imported camel's hair and lamb's wool. Colors, gray with blue, gray with red, or green with red, also solid colors in gray, blue or red. For 8 to 16 year old girls. Price, each..........79c
If by mail, postage extra, 12 cents.

No. 38R1906 Tam O'Shanter, made of imported camel's hair, 12 inches in diameter, long fuzzy nap made of the best gray material in plain colors, such as navy, cardinal or gray, for 8 to 15 year old girls.
Price, each...(If by mail, postage extra, 12c)...85c

Toboggan Caps or Toques.

No. 38R1908 Woolen Double Toque from 13 to 13½ inches in length, made in combination of colors, such as blue, red, navy or black predominating. Price, each..........25c
If by mail, postage extra, 5 cents.

No. 38R1910 Made of Imported Saxony, light weight, very easy on the head. Colors, navy or cardinal with fancy stripes.
Price, each..........40c
If by mail, postage extra, 3 cents.

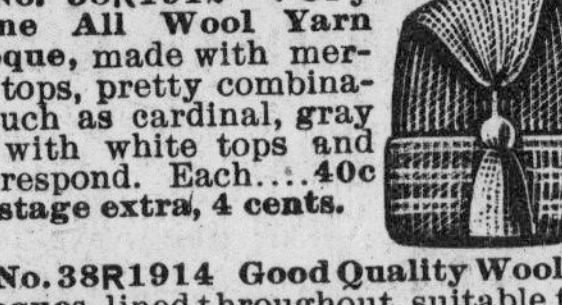

No. 38R1912 Very Fine All Wool Yarn Toque, made with mercerized knitted tops, pretty combination of colors, such as cardinal, gray or navy blue, with white tops and turnovers to correspond. Each....40c
If by mail, postage extra, 4 cents.

No. 38R1914 Good Quality Woolen Toques, lined throughout, suitable for both winter and summer, is 15 inches long. Combination of colors, such as blue, red, navy or black predominating. Price, each..........48c
If by mail, postage extra, 5 cents.

No. 38R1916 Toque, made of imported Saxony worsted. Can furnish in cardinal or navy with fancy stripes. Each 60c
If by mail, postage extra, 6 cents.

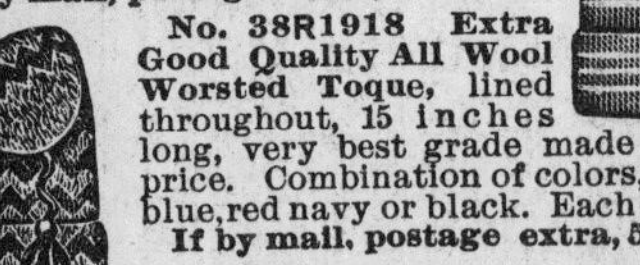

No. 38R1918 Extra Good Quality All Wool Worsted Toque, lined throughout, 15 inches long, very best grade made for the price. Combination of colors, such as blue, red navy or black. Each......50c
If by mail, postage extra, 5 cents.

Children's Drawer Leggings.

No. 38R1920 Child's Drawer Leggings, made of all wool yarn in either white or black. We recommend this as it will not only make the child look neat, but at the same time will keep the body warm, as the drawer legging reaches all around the waist. Sizes for 1, 2 and 3 year old children.
Price, per pair..........35c
If by mail, postage extra, per pair, 6c.

No. 38R1922 Same style as No. 38R1920, made of high grade, closely knitted all wool zephyr. Colors, cream or black, for 1, 2 and 3 year old children. Per pair..50c
If by mail, postage extra, per pair, 7 cents.

No. 38R1924 Black Worsted Leggings for children. Sizes, 16, 18 and 20 inches.
Price, per pair..........25c
If by mail, postage extra, 6 cents.

No. 38R1926 Same, for misses. Sizes, 22, 24 and 26 inches. Price, per pair..........35c
If by mail, postage extra, 8 cents.

No. 38R1928 Same, for ladies. Sizes, 28, 30 and 32 inches. Price, per pair..........45c
If by mail, postage extra, 8 cents.

No. 38R1929 Extra good quality Black Worsted Leggings, for young ladies. Sizes, 22, 24 and 26 inches. Per pair..........45c
If by mail, postage extra, 8 cents.

No. 38R1930 Same style as No. 38R1929 **for ladies.** Sizes, 28, 30 and 32 inches.
Price, per pair..........55c
If by mail, postage extra, per pair, 8cents.

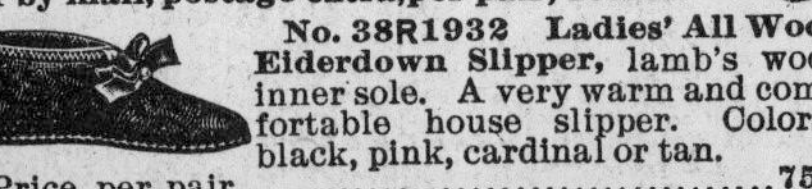

No. 38R1932 Ladies' All Wool Eiderdown Slipper, lamb's wool inner sole. A very warm and comfortable house slipper. Colors, black, pink, cardinal or tan.
Price, per pair..........75c
If by mail, postage extra, 10 cents.

No. 38R1934 Ladies' Knit Slippers, made of all wool zephyr. This yarn is made especially for the purpose and is the best for the money. Fleece lined leather soles, satin bow in front. Colors, black, blue, cardinal and brown. Sizes, from 3 to 7. Price......69c
If by mail, postage extra, 10 cents.

No. 38R1936 Misses' Knit Slippers. Same style as No. 38R1934. Sizes from 11 to 2. Colors, red, blue or pink. Price...(If by mail, postage extra, 8c)....58c

No. 38R1938 Child's Knit Slippers. Same style as No. 38R1934. Sizes from 6 to 10. Colors, red, blue or pink. Price...(If by mail, postage extra, 6c)....49c

LADIES' SHAWLS.

Ladies' Reversible Beaver Shawls.

No. 38R1950 Reversible Beaver Shawl, like illustration; made with knotted fringe in gray or brown, with fancy border. Size, 55x55 inches.
Price, each..........$1.35
If by mail, postage extra, each, 38 cents.

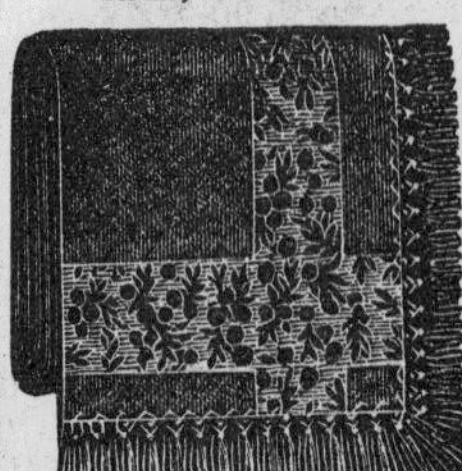

No. 38R1954 Ladies' Reversible Beaver Shawl, weighs about 2 pounds and is about 60 inches square, **good quality for the money and could not be duplicated anywhere for the price.** Colors, gray or brown, with fancy border.
Price, each..........$1.85
If by mail, postage extra, 40 cents.

No. 38R1958 Ladies' Reversible Beaver Shawl, knotted fringe all around, weighs over 2 pounds and is about 60 inches square. Colors, gray or brown, with fancy border.
Price, each..........$2.65
If by mail, postage extra, each, 40 cents.

No. 38R1962 Ladies' Reversible Beaver Shawl, made of fine grade camel's hair. It is very serviceable, as it is a good weight and warm. We furnish these in dark or light solid color, gray or brown. Size, 60x60 in. Weight, 2 pounds.
Price, each..........$3.75
If by mail, postage extra, each, 44 cents.

No. 38R1966 Ladies' All Wool Reversible Beaver Shawl, made with tied knotted fringe all around, exceptionally heavy and very warm. Colors, gray or brown with fancy border. Size, 60x60 inches. Weight, over 2 pounds.
Price, each..........$4.25
If by mail, postage extra, each, 45 cents.

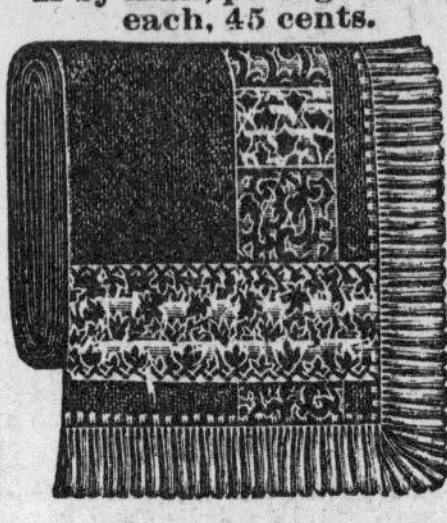

No. 38R1970 Ladies' Reversible High Grade All Wool Beaver Shawl, made with knotted fringe all around, weighs 2½ pounds and is 60 inches square. We furnish this in gray or brown, with fancy border.
Price, each..........$4.95
If by mail, postage extra, each, 45 cents.

Ladies' Double Shawls.

No. 38R1974 Ladies' Double Shawl, weighs about 26 ounces, measures 55x110 inches, made of wool mixture. Colors, gray or brown, with fancy border.
Price, each..........$1.98
If by mail, postage extra, 32 cents.

No. 38R1974

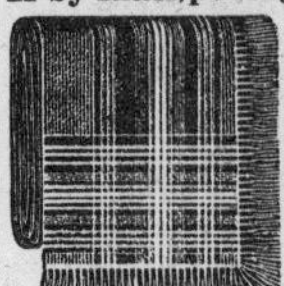

No. 38R1978

No. 38R1978 Ladies' Double Shawl, made of wool mixture, weighs about 30 ounces, measures 55x110 inches with fringe all around. Colors, gray or brown, with fancy border.
Price, each..........$2.35
If by mail, postage extra, 30 cents.

No. 38R1982 Ladies' Double Wool Shawl, weighs about 36 ounces, measures 72x144 inches fancy fringe all around. Colors, gray, brown, or mourning, with fancy border.
Price, each..........$2.98
If by mail, postage extra, 33 cents.

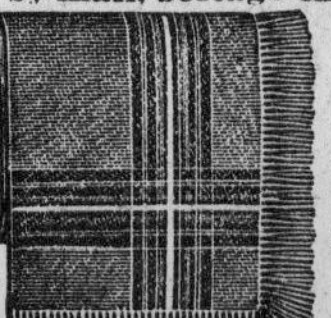

No. 38R1986 Ladies' Double Wool Shawl, made 70x140 inches, fancy fringe all around, good quality wool. Colors, gray, brown or mourning, with fancy border.
Price, each..........$3.98
If by mail, postage extra, 36 cents.

No. 38R1990 Ladies' Double Wool Shawls, extra heavy weight, measures 70x144 inches and has fancy fringe all around, one of the best grades in the market and we can highly recommend this to everybody. Colors, gray, brown or mourning.
Price, each..........$4.95
If by mail, postage extra, 36 cents.

No. 38R1994 Exceptionally Good Value Ladies' All Wool Double Shawl, measures 70 by 140 inches, and weighs about 40 ounces; fancy fringe all around. Furnished in gray, brown or mourning, with neat border.
Price, each..........$6.95
If by mail, postage extra, each, 40 cents.

No. 38R1998 Ladies' Single Shawls, made of wool mixture; weighs about 26 ounces, and is 58 inches square. Colors, gray or brown, with fancy border. Price, each......98c
If by mail, postage extra, each, 30 cents.

No. 38R2002 Ladies' Large Square Shawl, weight, 17 ounces, fancy fringe all around. Shawl comes in gray, brown, or mourning colors, with fancy border. Price, each......$1.35
If by mail, postage extra, each, 25 cents.

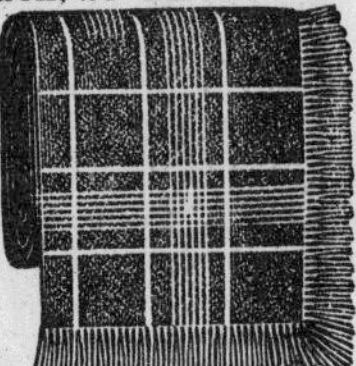

No. 38R2006 Ladies' Large Square Shawl, weight, about 19 ounces, made about 65 inches square, and of all wool material; has fancy fringe all around. Comes in gray, brown, mourning or green plaids, with fancy border. **We can highly recommend this shawl as one of the best articles.** Price, each....$2.35
If by mail, postage extra, each, 25 cents.

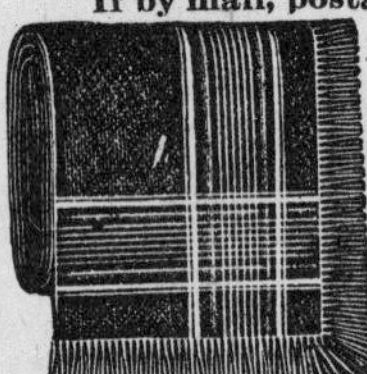

No. 38R2010 Ladies' Large Square Shawl, made of wool material, measures 72 inches square, fancy border all around. Colors, gray, brown or mourning, with fancy borders or plaids.
Price, each..........$2.85
If by mail, postage extra. each, 25 cents.

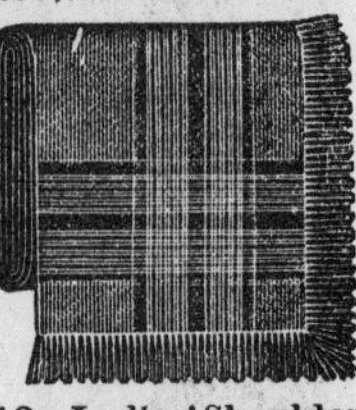

No. 38R2014 Ladies' All Wool Shawl, 72 inches square, weighing about 22 ounces, made of a very fine wool, furnished in brown, gray or mourning colors, with fancy border or solid black.
Price, each..........$3.50
If by mail, postage extra, each, 30 cents.

No. 38R2018 Ladies' Shoulder Shawl, made of merino or wool, comes in gray or brown, with border to match, red and black, or white and black checks. Size, 37x37 inches. Price, each..........20c
If by mail, postage extra, each, 6 cents.

No. 38R2022 Ladies' Merino Shoulder Shawl, 42 inches square, very good grade for the money. Colors, gray or brown with assorted borders, red and black, or black and white checks. Price, each...30c
If by mail, postage extra, each, 8 cents.

No. 38R2026 VeryFine All Wool Shoulder Shawl, 42 inches square, same style as No. 38R2018. Comes in gray or brown, with border to match, or black and white or black and red checks. Price, each......70c
If by mail, postage extra, each, 10 cents.

No. 38R2030 Same style as No. 38R2018, but 47 inches square. Colors, gray or brown, with borders to match, or black and white or black and red checks. Price, each..........85c
If by mail, postage extra, each, 11 cents.

No. 38R2034 Ladies' Fine Cashmere Shawl, measures 57 inches square, made with two-knot silk fringe all around. Black only.
Price, each..........$2.75
If by mail, postage extra, each, 20 cents.

No. 38R2038 Ladies' Fine Cashmere Shawl, 58 inches square, three-knot silk fringe all around; exceptionally good value for the money.
Price, each..........$3.50
If by mail, postage extra, each, 25 cents.

No. 38R2042 Very fine grade of Ladies' Cashmere Shawl, the best for the money. It equals anything that sells for $6.00. We can highly recommend this to be first class in every respect. Measures 58 inches square. It has a four-knot silk fringe all around. Color, black only. Price, each..........$4.95
If by mail, postage extra, each, 25 cents.

Cashmere, Bedford Cord and Silk Infants' Long Cloaks

No. 38R2051 INFANTS' LONG CASHMERE CLOAK. Shoulder cape embroidered nicely with silk; shirred at collar; lined throughout with canton flannel. Colors, cream or tan. Price................**(If by mail, postage extra, 18 cents)**............ **79c**

No. 38R2052 INFANTS' LONG CLOAK. Made of Bedford cord; has flounced shoulder cape, which is trimmed with four rows of silk cord and two rows of satin ribbon; two rows of silk cord on sleeves to match; lined with sateen and interlined with flannel. Exceptionally good value. Color, cream only.
Price....................**(If by mail, postage extra, 19 cents)**..................... **98c**

No. 38R2053 INFANTS' LONG CLOAK. Made of cashmere; large shoulder cape, elaborately embroidered with silk; shirred at neck and embroidered with silk all around bottom; lined throughout with canton flannel. Colors, cream or tan.
Price.....................**(If by mail, postage extra, 21 cents)**...................... **$1.15**

No. 38R2054 INFANTS' LONG CLOAK. Made of good cashmere; shoulder cape beautifully embroidered in a neat floral design; it is embroidered all around with silk; shirring around collar; the bottom is embroidered in a very wide floral design; lined throughout with canton flannel. Color, cream only.
Price.....................**(If by mail, postage extra, 22 cents)**...................... **$1.49**

No. 38R2055 INFANTS' LONG CLOAK. Made of good cashmere; large shoulder cape, neatly embroidered and scalloped with silk; it is shirred at the end of the large collar and neatly trimmed with silk cording; silk embroidery similar to that on the cape ornaments at the bottom; imitation pearl buttons; lined throughout with a good quality sateen. Interlined with flannel; very dressy. Colors, cream or tan.
Price.....................**(If by mail, postage extra, 26 cents)**...................... **$1.69**

No. 38R2056 INFANTS' LONG CLOAK. Made of good quality cashmere; it is very richly embroidered and scalloped with silk on shoulder cape; shirring at neck; the embroidery in itself is the very newest design, and it almost covers the cape; similar embroidery to that on the cape trims the bottom of this cloak and is full 10 inches wide; bishop sleeves; lined throughout with cambric and interlined with shaker flannel. Color, cream only. Price....................**(If by mail, postage extra, 22 cents)**...................... **$1.98**

No. 38R2057 INFANTS' LONG COAT. Made of high grade cashmere; large collar, trimmed ith satin ribbon and silk soutache, alternating with each other; large shoulder cape extends from this collar and is neatly embroidered with small designs, as well as scalloped with silk· similar embroidery around the bottom of coat; lined throughout with a good quality sateen, interlined with shaker flannel; imitation pearl buttons in front. Colors, cream or tan.
Price.....................**(If by mail, postage extra, 26 cents)**...................... **$2.25**

No. 38R2058 A HANDSOME INFANTS' LONG CLOAK. Made of good quality of Bedford cord; a very large shoulder cape which is beautifully trimmed with five rows of silk cord, two narrow and one wide row of fancy ribbon and one row of silk gimp; cloak and cape lined with sateen and cloak interlined with wadding; sleeves trimmed with two rows of silk cord. Color, cream only. Price..**(If by mail, postage extra, 26c)**... **$2.48**

No. 38R2059 INFANTS' LONG CLOAK. Made of good grade of cashmere; large shoulder cape which is beautifully embroidered with silk, scalloped and stitched with silk, very wide; silk embroidery around bottom, in a very beautiful design to match cape; bishop sleeves; cloak interlined with flannel; cloak and shoulder cape lined with sateen. Color, cream only. Price.. ....**(If by mail, postage extra, 26 cents)**.......... **$2.69**

No. 38R2060 AN EXCEEDINGLY PRETTY INFANTS' LONG CLOAK. Made of wool cashmere; has large flannel shoulder cape trimmed with two rows of silk soutache and four rows of narrow ribbon; very neatly embroidered with silk; scalloped and stitched with silk; two rows of narrow ribbon around bottom and embroidered with silk in very pretty design; cloak and cape lined with sateen; cloak interlined with flannel. Color, cream only. Price...............**(If by mail, postage extra, 26 cents)**.............. **$2.75**

No. 38R2061 A HIGH GRADE INFANTS' LONG CLOAK. Made of all wool cashmere; collar trimmed with silk cord and narrow satin ribbon; large shoulder cape beautifully embroidered with silk, edge scalloped and stitched with silk; embroidered around bottom with silk to correspond; interlined with flannel, cloak and shoulder cape lined with sateen; sleeves trimmed with one row of cord and ribbon. Color, cream only.
Price......................**(If by mail, postage extra, 26 cents)**.................... **$2.98**

No. 38R2062 A BEAUTIFUL INFANTS' LONG CLOAK. Made of China silk; has a large silk shoulder cape trimmed with two rows of silk gimp, embroidered with silk in a very pretty design, scalloped and stitched with silk; embroidered around bottom with silk to correspond; interlined with flannel; cloak and shoulder cape lined with fine sateen; sleeves trimmed with two rows of silk gimp. Color, cream only.
Price......................**(If by mail, postage extra, 26 cents)** **$3.89**

CHILD'S WALKING CLOAKS, AGES 1 TO 5.

SCHEDULE OF SIZES ARE AS FOLLOWS:		
	21 inches long for a child 1 year old.	GIVE AGE AND LENGTH DESIRED.
	22 inches long for a child 2 years old.	
	24 inches long for a child 3 years old.	
	26 inches long for a child 4 years old.	
	28 inches long for a child 5 years old.	

No. 38R2075 CHILD'S CLOAK. Made of cashmere; has a wide shoulder cape which is neatly embroidered with silk, scalloped edge and stitched with silk; lined throughout. Colors, cream or tan. Price..............(If by mail, postage extra, 11 cents)............**75c**

No. 38R2076 A VERY PRETTY CHILD'S CLOAK. Made of good quality Bedford cord; has wide shoulder cape which is trimmed with two rows of silk cord and one row of satin ribbon; bishop sleeves; cuffs trimmed with one row of silk cord, satin ribbon strings at neck. lined throughout with canton flannel. Colors, cream, blue or pink. Price ....(If by mail, postage extra, 13 cents)........................**$1.10**

No. 38R2077 CHILD'S CLOAK. Made of fine cashmere; sailor collar beautifully trimmed with two rows of silk gimp and three rows of silk cord; three rows of silk cord on sleeves; we can highly recommend this cloak as one of the best values ever offered; lined throughout with sateen and interlined with wadding. Colors, cream or tan. Price.......................(If by mail, postage extra, 18 cents)........................**$1.89**

CHILD'S COATS OR REEFERS.

AGES, 1, 2, 3, 4 AND 5 YEARS.

No. 38R2078 CHILD'S REEFER. Automobile style, made of Bedford cord; wide collar, trimmed with two rows of silk gimp and edged with wide lace; sleeves trimmed with two rows of silk gimp; lined throughout with sateen; four pearl buttons. Very stylish little coat. Colors, cream or blue. Price..............(If by mail, postage extra, 12 cents)...................**98c**

No. 38R2079 VERY PRETTY CHILD'S REEFER. Automobile style, made of good quality of Bedford cord; wide collar trimmed with silk gimp and satin ribbon edged with wide lace; sleeves trimmed with silk gimp; pearl buttons; entire coat lined with sateen. Colors, cream or pink. Extra good value. Price......(If by mail, postage extra, 12 cents) ..**$1.48**

No. 38R2080 AN EXCEEDINGLY PRETTY CHILD'S COAT. Automobile style, made of fine Bedford cord; collar trimmed with three rows of narrow braid and edged with silk cord; shoulder cape is beautifully trimmed with four rows of narrow silk braid, fancy ribbon and edged with silk cord; two rows of silk braid on sleeves; entire coat lined with sateen; pearl buttons. Colors, cream or blue. Price....(If by mail, postage extra, 15 cents)..... **$1.69**

CHILD'S WASHABLE PIQUE COATS.

AGES 1, 2, 3, 4 AND 5 YEARS.

No. 38R2081 CHILD'S WASHABLE WHITE PIQUE REEFER. Automobile style; large sailor collar trimmed with three rows of herringbone braid and edged with Swiss embroidery; two rows of herringbone braid on sleeves; pearl buttons. Color, white only. Price.. **98c** If by mail, postage extra, 9 cents.

No. 38R2082 CHILD'S WASHABLE WHITE PIQUE REEFER. Made automobile style; large sailor collar made of allover embroidery; two rows of herringbone braid on sleeves; pearl buttons. Color, white only. Price...(If by mail, postage extra, 10 cents)..**$1.39**

CHILD'S EIDERDOWN, FLANNEL AND VELVET CLOAKS

SCHEDULE OF SIZES ARE AS FOLLOWS:		
	22 inches long for child 1 year old.	ALWAYS GIVE AGE AND LENGTH DESIRED.
	24 inches long for child 2 years old.	
	26 inches long for child 3 years old.	
	28 inches long for child 4 years old.	
	30 inches long for child 5 years old.	

No. 38R2083 A VERY NEAT CHILD'S CLOAK. Made of good quality fleeced flannel; has a large sailor collar trimmed with two rows of satin ribbon, edged with narrow braid; lined throughout with canton flannel. Colors, blue and white, or red and white. Price.................. .(If by mail, postage extra, 21 cents)..........................**$1.19**

No. 38R2084 CHILD'S CLOAK. Made of good quality of eiderdown; has wide collar trimmed with four rows of braid and five rows of fancy ribbon and edged with Angora fur; two rows of braid on sleeves; lined throughout with cambric. Colors, pink, light blue or cardinal. Price..... .....(If by mail, postage extra, 18 cents)..........................**$1.48**

No. 38R2085 CHILD'S CLOAK. Made of all wool flannel; collar beautifully embroidered with fancy braid and edged with Angora fur; one row of braid on sleeves; entire cloak lined with sateen. Colors, navy blue or cardinal. Price...................(If by mail, postage extra, 26 cents)........................**$1.89**

No. 38R2086 A VERY NOBBY CHILD'S CLOAK. Automobile style, made of good quality velvet; has large sailor collar which is beautifully trimmed with lace, sleeves trimmed to correspond; has a large detachable neck shield; pearl buttons; lined throughout with sateen. Length, 22, 24, 26, 28 and 30 inches. Colors, blue, green or cardinal. This is positively one of the handsomest child's coats made, very neat and stylish. Price...(If by mail, postage extra, 25 cents).......................................**$3.48**

CHILDREN'S DRESSES. . .

Sizes from 1 to 5 years. When ordering, please state age, height and weight of child. To avoid any misunderstanding, as children vary in size, we show a table giving the relative measurements in proportion to the age:

Age	1	2	3	4	5
Bust	22	22	23	24	25
Length of garment	20	22	24	26	28

No. 38R2101 WONDERFUL BARGAIN IN CHILDREN'S DRESSES. Some are made of percale and lawns in fancy stripes and figures in pink, blue and lavender, all made with fancy yokes. Some trimmed with braid and lace. We do not show a cut of this number, on account of different styles. Leave selection to us, as we know if you will include one or more of these dresses in your order that you will be entirely satisfied with same. The best bargain ever offered by any concern. Ages, 1 to 5 years.
Price............(If by mail, postage extra, 8 cents)............**33c**

No. 38R2102 CHILD'S DRESS, made of gingham in small check pattern, with "V" shape yoke made of chambray, trimmed with four rows of braid to correspond with yoke. Colors, blue or pink. Price...**42c**
If by mail, postage extra, 11 cents.

No. 38R2103 VERY PRETTY CHILD'S DRESS, made of figured lawn, short sleeves, low round neck, collar all around edged with Valenciennes lace, lace trimmings on collar, wide hem at bottom. A very neat and dressy garment. Colors, pink or blue predominating. Price..........**75c**
If by mail, postage extra, 9 cents.

No. 38R2104 CHILD'S DRESS, made of good quality lawn, a very neat pointed yoke made of white fancy openwork lawn, featherstitch braid, ruffles all around front and each trimmed with two rows of torchon lace, collar and cuffs trimmed with lace to match, deep hem at bottom. Colors, pink or blue. Price.... (If by mail, postage extra, 8 cents) **98c**

No. 38R2105 A VERY STYLISH CHILD'S DRESS, made of good quality of madras cloth, yoke made of white pique trimmed with six pearl buttons, straps on each side at waist, trimmed with pearl buttons, has embroidery insertion in front and back over shoulders, followed with a ruffle of wide embroidery. Extra good value. Colors, blue or pink stripes.
Price..............(If by mail, postage extra, 10 cents)............**$1.25**

No. 38R2106 THE VERY NEWEST PRINCESS STYLE CHILD'S DRESS, made of madras, has a very pretty round yoke made with three rows of embroidery insertion and tucks, embroidery and ribbon insertion both front and back, followed with a ruffle of same material as in dress, which is edged with embroidery, large ribbon bow, embroidery and ribbon insertion at flounce, collar and cuffs edged with embroidery, wide hem at bottom. Colors, pink and white or blue and white. Price............**$1.48**
If by mail, postage extra, 12 cents.

GIRLS' TWO-PIECE WASH SAILOR SUITS.

Ages, 4, 6, 8, 10, 12, 14 years.

Always give age, bust, height and weight. See page 1083 for scale of measurements.

No. 38R2107 GIRLS' CRASH TWO-PIECE WASH SAILOR SUIT, wide collar with one row red trimming, similar trimming on inside vest, neck and cuffs, crash tie, wide hem at bottom. Color, red trimming.
Price............(If by mail, postage extra, 17 cents.)............**89c**

No. 38R2108 A VERY PRETTY TWO-PIECE WASH SAILOR SUIT, made of percale, sailor collar trimmed in front and back with white pique and three rows of featherstitch braid, similar trimming on inside vest, three rows of featherstitch braid around neck and cuffs, has matched tie, wide hem at bottom. Colors, blue or red with white polkadots.
Price............(If by mail, postage extra, 16 cents)............**98c**

No. 38R2109 A BEAUTIFUL LINEN CRASH TWO-PIECE WASH SAILOR SUIT, sailor collar trimmed with sateen and four rows of soutache braid, similar trimmings around neck and inside vest, also three pearl buttons, matched tie and trimming on cuffs, sateen trimming around bottom with four rows of soutache. Color, red trimming only. Price........**$1.48**
If by mail, postage extra, 18 cents.

No. 38R2110 A STRIKINGLY PRETTY TWO-PIECE WASH SAILOR SUIT, made of good quality of madras cloth, double sailor collar, under collar made of same material as in dress, upper collar made of white pique, which is trimmed with fancy braid, front of inside vest made of white pique trimmed with a silk ornament, neck made of white pique and trimmed with fancy braid, cuffs and tie to match, wide hem at bottom. Colors, fancy stripes in pink or blue predominating. Price......(If by mail, postage extra, 18 cents) **$1.69**

No. 38R2111 A VERY NOBBY TWO-PIECE WASH SAILOR SUIT, made of chambray, has a large sailor collar made of white sateen trimmed with wide braid to match, front of inside vest made of white sateen with silk ornament, neckband made of sateen and braid trimming, sateen tie to match, wide hem at bottom. Colors, oxblood (red) or blue. Price... (Postage extra, 20c)...**$1.89**

GIRLS' WASH DRESSES.

AGES FROM 4 TO 14 YEARS.

WHEN ORDERING please state Age, Height, Weight and Number of Inches around Bust.

SCALE OF SIZES, SHOWING PROPORTION OF BUST AND LENGTH TO THE AGE OF CHILD

Age	4	6	8	10	12	14
Bust	24	27	28	29	30	31
Skirt length	18	20	22	24	26	28

No. 38R2126 GIRLS' DRESS. Some made of Madras and some made of ginghams in fancy stripes and plaids, round yokes, "V" shape yokes, some trimmed with braid, ruffles and embroidery. **We show no illustration of this number on account of the different styles in this lot.** Colors, pink, blue, red or green effects. Always give second choice. Price........72c

If by mail, postage extra, each, 16 cents.

No. 38R2127 GIRLS' GINGHAM DRESS. Round yoke, three pique straps both front and back, featherstitch braid, three pearl buttons, two ribbon bows, ruffle all around front and back edged with torchon lace; neckband also trimmed with lace to match; waistband and cuffs trimmed with featherstitch braid; wide hem at bottom. Colors, fancy stripes in blue and pink predominating. Price........89c

If by mail, postage extra, each, 14 cents.

No. 38R2128 GIRLS' GINGHAM DRESS. Strap over shoulder with insertion of lace, also strap across yoke with lace insertion, ruffle all around yoke in front and back which is trimmed with narrow braid; wide hem at bottom. Colors, blue and white or red and white checks. Price........98c

If by mail, postage extra, each, 11 cents.

No. 38R2129 GIRLS' DRESS. Made of lawn, yoke trimmed with fancy white lawn, pearl buttons and ribbon bow, ruffle all around yoke in front and back which is edged with embroidery; waistband and cuffs are made of white fancy lawn; wide hem at bottom. Colors, blue and white or pink and white. Price........$1.25

If by mail, postage extra, each, 11 cents.

No. 38R2130 GIRLS' DRESS. Made of fine percale; has "V" shape front made of white pique trimmed with six rows of narrow braid; shoulder cape made of white pique and three rows of narrow braid trimming; neckband with braid trimming; cuffs and waistband made of white pique with narrow braid trimming to match; wide hem at bottom. Colors, blue or red with white figures. Price........$1.39

If by mail, postage extra, each, 16 cents.

No. 38R2131 GIRLS' TRIMMED DRESS. Made of high grade gingham, round yoke made of white pique trimmed with embroidery and small pearl buttons; has double ruffle, upper ruffle made of white pique and lower ruffle made of material as in dress; each ruffle is edged with embroidery; waistband and cuffs of white pique, neck and cuffs trimmed with embroidery to match; wide hem at bottom. Colors, plaids in blue or pink combinations. Price....**(Postage extra, 14c)**......$1.48

No. 38R2132 GIRLS' DRESS, BLOUSE EFFECT. Made of good quality ducking; has triple effect revers, large collar trimmed with white duck and narrow braid; has "V" shape yoke made of white duck; neckband and cuffs trimmed with white duck and narrow braid; one row of white duck and braid around bottom; deep hem. Colors, blue or pink with white polka dots. Price...$1.69

If by mail, postage extra, each, 17 cents.

No. 38R2133 A NOVELTY IN A PINK OR BLUE LAWN DRESS. Made of fine quality lawn, pointed yoke made of white open work lawn trimmed with featherstitch braid, both front and back alike, double ruffle all around point and back, edged with lace; two rows of fine lace in front and one row around waistband; standing collar and sleeves trimmed with lace to match; one row of matched lace around bottom, wide hem. Colors, pink or blue. Price........$1.98

If by mail, postage extra, each, 16 cents.

No. 38R2134 GIRLS' DRESS. Made of good quality of Madras, a very pretty yoke with three insertions of embroidery; wide ruffle with wide embroidery, trimmed with featherstitch braid; embroidery around neck and waist; also on cuffs to match; wide hem at bottom. Colors, blue and white or oxblood (red) and white stripes. Extra good value. Price........$1.75

If by mail, postage extra, each, 14 cents.

No. 38R2135 GIRLS' TRIMMED WASH DRESS. Made of good quality Chambray, with bolero effect; front made of white pique trimmed with six pearl buttons, double ruffle in front extending to back of waist, upper ruffle made of same material as in dress, lower ruffle made of white pique, each edged with embroidery; white pique around waist; neckband and cuffs trimmed with embroidery to match; wide hem at bottom. Colors, blue or oxblood (red). Price........$1.98

If by mail, postage extra, each, 15 cents.

No. 38R2136 GIRLS' DRESS. Made of fine Chambray, has shoulder cape extending around back with three rows of Soutache braid and fine embroidery edge; numerous rows of plaits in front, three rows of embroidery; neck, waistband and cuffs trimmed with three rows of soutache; wide hem at bottom. Colors, oxblood (red) or blue. Price........$1.98

If by mail, postage extra, each, 16 cents.

No. 38R2137 GIRLS' DRESS. Made of high grade gingham, Eton style, edged with embroidery; yoke with three insertions of embroidery; has wide ruffle extending over shoulders with embroidery insertion and edge to match, ribbon bow; neck, waistband and cuffs trimmed with embroidery; wide hem at bottom. Colors, very pretty designs in blue or red predominating. Price......**(If by mail, postage extra, each, 15 cents)**....$2.25

GIRLS' LINED DRESSES.

SIZES 4 TO 14 YEARS. When ordering please state age, height, weight and number of inches around bust. When necessary to make a dress to order, we will charge 20 per cent extra for material and labor. **Special orders must be paid for in advance.**

Scale of sizes, showing proportion of bust and length to the age of child.

Age	4	6	8	10	12	14
Bust	24	27	28	29	30	31
Skirt length	18	20	22	24	26	28

No. 38R2151 EXTRA GOOD VALUE, made of novelty cloth. Girls' dress, has "V" shape yoke made of cashmere, which is trimmed with narrow braid and pearl buttons, ribbon bow; shoulder capes trimmed with narrow ribbon and lined with cambric; waist and cuffs trimmed with cashmere and narrow braid; lined throughout with cambric; wide hem at bottom. Colors, combination plaids in blue or red predominating. Price each.. **$1.19**
If by mail, postage extra, 20 cents.

No. 38R2152 FANCY NOVELTY PLAID GIRLS' DRESS. Round yoke trimmed with velvet to match and ruffle extending over shoulders; velvet trimming on cuffs to correspond; lined throughout with cambric, with wide hem at bottom. Colors, blue or brown predominating. Price. . **$1.25**
If by mail, postage extra, 30 cents.

No. 38R2153 GIRLS' DRESS. Made of fancy novelty cloth; fancy "V" front made of blue or red serge, trimmed with strap made of same material as in dress; braid trimming; large shoulder capes and lined throughout with cambric, wide hem at bottom. Colors, blue or red predominating.
Price, each. .....(If by mail, postage extra, 30 cents)............ **$1.48**

No. 38R2154 GIRLS' DRESS. Made of fancy plaid novelty cloth; very newest shades, large collar extending from front to back, trimmed with lace; pointed yoke in front made of cashmere to match, trimmed with gimp; two rows of gimp on sleeves to match; lined throughout with cambric; wide hem at bottom. Colors, blue or red predominating. Price, each........ **$1.69**
If by mail, postage extra, 30 cents.

No. 38R2155 A SERVICEABLE GIRLS' DRESS. Made of F. F. cashmere; "V" shape yoke trimmed with four clusters of tucks, trimmed with six pearl buttons; ribbon bow; large shoulder capes lined with cambric, trimmed with braid; standing collar; waistband and cuffs trimmed with two rows of braid to match, lined throughout with cambric; wide hem at bottom. Colors, navy blue or brown. Price, each.. .... **$1.98**
If by mail, postage extra, 22 cents.

No. 38R2156 GIRLS' DRESS. Made of novelty plaid, very newest shades; has a "V" shape yoke made of velvet, trimmed with two rows of silk gimp; large shoulder capes trimmed with two rows of silk gimp, velvet tie, standing collar, tie and cuffs trimmed with silk gimp to match; lined throughout with cambric; wide hem at bottom. Colors, combinations in blue or red predominating. Price, each. **$2.25**
If by mail, postage extra, 30 cents.

No. 38R2157 A BEAUTIFULLY TRIMMED GIRLS' DRESS. Made of a fine grade cashmere; Eton effect; tucks in front trimmed with three small and two large pearl buttons; large shoulder capes beautifully trimmed with four rows soutache and one row of silk gimp; standing collar, waistband and cuffs trimmed to match; **gored skirt**; entire dress lined throughout with cambric; wide hem at bottom. Exceptionally good value. Colors blue or brown. Price, each..... (If by mail, postage extra, 20 cents)....... **$2.69**

No. 38R2158 A VERY NOBBY GIRLS' DRESS. Made of all wool cashmere, three plaits made of velvet across yoke; double capes over shoulders, upper cape made of velvet trimmed with three pearl buttons, lower cape made of same material as in dress and trimmed with three rows silk soutache; velvet cuffs to match, **gored skirt**, entire dress lined throughout with cambric, wide hem at bottom. Colors, blue or red. Price, each. **$2.98**
If by mail, postage extra, 19 cents.

GIRLS' LINED TWO-PIECE SAILOR SUITS.

AGES 4 TO 14 YEARS.

No. 38R2159 GIRLS' TWO-PIECE SAILOR SUIT. Made of good quality serge; large sailor collar trimmed four rows soutache; inside vest; standing collar and cuffs trimmed with braid to match; tie made of serge; sailor collar and dress lined throughout with cambric; **skirt made very full with wide hem at bottom.** Very good value. Colors, navy blue or red.
Price, each. . ..(If by mail, postage extra, 26 cents)......... **$2.48**

No. 38R2160 A VERY NEAT TWO-PIECE GIRLS' SAILOR SUIT. Made of good quality Sicilian cloth; has large sailor collar trimmed with four rows of soutache; inside vest; standing collar and sailor collar trimmed with four rows of soutache braid to match; metal buttons; sailor collar and dress lined throughout with cambric; **skirt made very full** with wide hem at bottom. Colors, navy blue or red. Price, each........... ...... **$2.65**
If by mail, postage extra, 28 cents.

No. 38R2161 A VERY NOBBY TWO-PIECE SAILOR SUIT. Made of all wool serge; large sailor collar trimmed with four rows of satouche; taffeta silk bow tie; inside vest with silk ornament; standing collar and cuffs trimmed with four rows of soutache; six pearl buttons. **Gored skirt,** lined throughout with cambric. **Skirt made very full** with wide hem at bottom. Colors, navy blue or brown. Price, each.......................... **$3.48**
If by mail, postage extra, 22 cents.

GIRLS' WHITE LAWN DRESSES. AGES FROM 6 to 14 YEARS.

WHEN ORDERING PLEASE STATE AGE, HEIGHT, WEIGHT AND NUMBER OF INCHES AROUND BUST. Scale of sizes, showing proportion of bust and length to the age of child:

Age	6	8	10	12	14
Bust	27	28	29	30	31
Skirt length	20	22	24	26	28

No. 38R2176 VERY GOOD VALUE GIRLS' WHITE LAWN DRESSES, pointed yoke made of white open work lawn, trimmed with herringbone braid. Wide ruffle all around front and back edged with lace; standing collar trimmed with two rows of herringbone braid; lace to match around cuffs. Color, white only. Price, each...... **98c**
If by mail, postage extra, 11 cents.

No. 38R2177 GIRLS' WHITE LAWN DRESS, very pretty yoke trimmed with plaits and embroidery, also three pearl buttons. Ruffle all round yoke and back edged with embroidery; standing collar and cuffs trimmed with embroidery to match, also around waist; wide hem at bottom; exceptionally good value. Color, white only
Price, each.................**(If by mail, postage extra, 12 cents)**............... **$1.29**

No. 38R2178 A VERY PRETTY GIRLS' DRESS, made of good quality lawn, very neat yoke with three insertions of fine embroidery alternating with numerous rows of fine tucks. Shoulder cape edged with fine embroidery all round front and back. Standing collar, waist and cuffs trimmed with embroidery; wide hem at bottom. Color, white only. Price, each.. ....**(If by mail, postage extra, 12 cents)**.......... **$1.69**

No. 38R2179 A BEAUTIFUL GIRLS' DRESS, made of fine India lawn. Has a very pretty yoke with three rows of fine embroidery insertion alternating with plaits. Ruffle all round front and back with insertion of embroidery and edged with fine fancy embroidery around Eton vest; standing collar, waist and cuffs trimmed with embroidery to match: wide hem at bottom. Color, white only. Price, each **$2.48**
If by mail, postage extra, 15 cents.

MISSES' TWO-PIECE WHITE LAWN DRESSES.

These Dresses Made Only in Regular Sizes as Follows:

Age	14	16	18
Bust	32	34	36
Skirt lengths	32-33	34-35	36-38

BE SURE AND GIVE BUST AND SKIRT LENGTH.

No. 38R2180 A VERY PRETTY MISSES' DRESS, made of good quality of white lawn. Waist is trimmed in front with three rows of fine Valenciennes lace alternating with three rows of satin ribbon ruching. Has shoulder capes trimmed with two rows of lace and ribbon ruching; has six plaits in back extending from neck to waist, satin ribbon around waist band, forming a bow in back; bishop sleeves; standing collar; **skirt made very newest style** with flounce and satin ribbon ruching where flounce is formed. Exceptionally good value.
Price, each..........**(If by mail, postage extra, 17 cents)**........... **$3.75**

No. 38R2181 A BEAUTIFUL MISSES' WHITE LAWN DRESS. Waist is trimmed in front with all over embroidery and narrow ribbon. White lawn folds extending from armholes to center of waist trimmed with ribbon and ornamented ribbon bow; collar and waist band trimmed with two rows of ribbon; sleeves trimmed to match also with three ribbon bows; ten rows of plaits in back extending from neck to waist; cuffs trimmed with ribbon; **skirt beautifully** trimmed around bottom with two lawn ruffles and trimmed with ribbon to match. Color, white only with blue or pink ribbon trimmings. Price, each **$4.98**
If by mail, postage extra, 19 cents.

No. 38R2182 A HANDSOME MISSES' DRESS, made of fine quality white India lawn. Waist made with Eton effect, which is trimmed with embroidery and edged with Valenciennes lace: upper part with numerous rows of plaits; satin ribbon trimming; three rows of plaits extending from shoulder to waist; standing collar and waist band trimmed with embroidery to match; **skirt made very neat** with wide lawn ruffle around bottom: extra good value. Price, each...... **$6.75**
If by mail, postage extra, 21 cents.

MISSES' WASH SKIRTS.

Lengths	32	33	34	35	36	37
Waist	22	23	24	25	26	..

ALWAYS GIVE WAIST AND LENGTH MEASUREMENTS.

No. 38R2183 MISSES' COTTON CRASH SKIRT, with wide flounce. Strap where flounce is formed and numerous rows of stitching around bottom. Price, each........................ **(If by mail, postage extra, 16 cents)**........................ **89c**

No. 38R2184 A VERY PRETTY MISSES' SKIRT, made of blue duck, lap seams with white stitching. Has wide flounce and trimmed with two rows of white duck; numerous rows of white stitching around bottom. Color, blue only with white trimming. Price, each.. **(Postage 17 cents.)** ... **98c**

No. 38R2185 MISSES' SKIRT, made of good quality pique, trimmed with four straps of same material as in skirt. Each strap bound with ducking to match skirt; wide hem at bottom. Colors, solid white or white with blue figures. Price, each .... **(If by mail, postage extra, 17 cents)**...... **$1.48**

CHILDREN'S COATS AND LADIES' WAISTS.

FOR SPRING, FALL AND WINTER.

When ordering give catalogue number, age of child, number of inches around bust, and the color you desire. Sizes are for 4 to 14-year-old children.

No. 17R100 CHILD'S AUTOMOBILE COAT. Made of heavy weight melton; double breasted front, box back; velvet collar and cuffs and velvet flaps several rows of silk cord around the collar and six rows around the turn up cuffs facing in front made of same material. Colors, red or blue.
Price, each..........(If by mail, postage extra, 47 cents)........ ....**$2.95**

No. 17R101 CHILD'S COAT. Made of good quality all wool beaver, shoulder cape bound with satin all around and trimmed with satin straps and gilt cord; similar trimming around storm collar and sleeves; loose back; double breasted front; facing in front made of same material. Colors, red or castor. Price, each..........(If by mail, postage extra, 50 cents).......**$3.25**

No. 17R104 CHILD'S AUTOMOBILE COAT. Made of good quality heavy weight melton; strictly tailor made; large collar and lapels trimmed with white braid; bishop sleeves trimmed with white braid and puff part is made of velvet; double breasted front; facing in front of same material; half tight back. Cadet blue only. Price, each.................................**$4.50**

No. 17R110 CHILD'S REEFER OR BOX COAT. Made of good quality melton; neatly trimmed with cord around the collar, front, back, cuffs; is lined throughout. Color, navy blue with red trimming. Sizes, 4 to 14.
Price, each............(If by mail, postage extra, 34 cents).........**$1.75**

No. 17R113 CHILD'S REEFER JACKET. Made of heavy weight melton; shoulder cape trimmed with several rows of black cord and one row of Baltic seal fur; cape lined with black sateen; black and white cord trimming on collar and similar trimming on the sleeves; double breasted front; box or loose back; facing in front made of same material. Colors, red or navy blue. Sizes, from 4 to 14. Price..(If by mail, postage extra, 49 cents)..**$2.75**

No. 17R115 CHILD'S REEFER JACKET OR BOX COAT. Made of all wool beaver. Shoulder cape embroidered with black and white; cape is lined throughout with black mercerized sateen; double breasted front; box back; facing in front made of same material. Colors, navy or red.
Price, each.............(If by mail, postage extra, 45 cents)..........**$2.95**

No. 17R117 CHILD'S MELTON REEFER JACKET. Double breasted front; trimmed with black velvet around bottom, collar and on cuffs; silk cord trimming all around jacket; has loose back; facing in front made of same material. Colors, red or blue. Price (If by mail, postage extra, 41 cents)**$2.98**

No. 17R118 CHILD'S REEFER JACKET OR AUTOMOBILE COAT. Made of all wool beaver; the jacket is bound around the large storm collar and in front with good quality satin, and trimmed with gilt cord around collar, sleeves and bottom; double breasted front and automobile back; facing in front made of same material. Colors, castor or royal blue.
Price, each.............(If by mail, postage extra, 40 cents)..........**$3.25**

LADIES' FLANNEL WAISTS. For Spring, Fall and Winter.

No. 31R260 LADIES' WAIST. Made of good quality flannelette; high standing detachable collar and attached cuffs; plain back; front gathered at neck and plaited at waist. Can furnish in black, red or blue polkadot patterns. Price, each............(If by mail, postage extra, 10 cents)..........**50c**

No. 31R263 LADIES' STYLISH WAIST. Made of all wool flannel, shirtband in front; plain back; finished with two plaits; soft cuffs, lined half way with cambric. Colors, black, red or blue. Price, each......**98c**
If by mail, postage extra, 16 cents.

No. 31R267 THIS NOBBY LADIES' WAIST is made of all wool flannel; strictly tailor made; finished with straps made of the same material stitched several times; two single plaits in back and several rows of stitching. While the waist is very plain at the same time it is stylish and pretty. Colors, sage green, black or old rose. Price(If by mail, postage extra, 17 cents)**$1.25**

No. 31R268 THIS HANDSOME LADIES' WAIST is made of all wool tricot. The material is fashionable this season and it is one of the new fabrics. This waist is trimmed in front with four straps made of black velvet, finished with three gilt buttons, high standing collar, flaring cuffs, bishop sleeves, plain back, lined throughout with cambric. Colors, old rose, lavender or red.
Price, each..........(If by mail, postage extra, 20 cents)..............**$1.45**

No. 31R270 LADIES' WAIST. Made of all wool French flannel; high standing collar; band in front and lapels made of black velvet trimmed with gilt braid; finished in sailor collar effect; small gilt buttons on band in front; cording in back from neck to waist. Very stylish and pretty garment, is one of the best sellers and also one of the best values. Colors, black, royal blue and old rose. Price, each.....(If by mail, postage extra, 21 cents).......**$1.65**

MISSES' JACKETS OR AUTOMOBILE COATS.

GARMENTS ON THIS PAGE ARE GOOD WEIGHT AND ARE INTENDED FOR EARLY SPRING, ALSO FOR FALL AND WINTER.

WHEN ORDERING always state age, number of inches around bust, and color. The following table shows relative bust measurement to age, on misses' garments.

AGE	12	14	16	18	20
BUST	30	32	34	36	38

A MISSES' GARMENT, while measuring 34 or 36 inches around the bust, will not fit a well developed woman measuring the same, as they are cut on different patterns.

No. 17R121 MISSES' AUTOMOBILE COAT. Made of melton; double breasted front trimmed with pearl buttons; half tight back; collar and lapels are made of black boucle, making it look like fur, and are bound with black mohair braid and trimmed with black and gold tinsel. Very neat and stylish garment for the money. Colors, red or royal blue. Price, each ...... (If by mail, postage extra, 57 cents).............. **$2.95**

No. 17R123 MISSES' BOX COAT. Made of the very best melton; coat shaped collar and lapels; double breasted front trimmed with fancy buttons, half tight back, lined throughout with black mercerized sateen; facing in front made of same material; bound all around the collar, lapels, front, cuffs and pockets with black and gold tinsel. Color, oxford gray only. Price, each.......... (If by mail, postage extra, 62 cents).............. **$3.50**

No. 17R124 MISSES' JACKET. Made of good quality heavy weight melton; double breasted front trimmed with fancy buttons, velvet collar and large lapels trimmed with velvet, same trimming on the pocket flaps and on sleeves; half tight back; facing in front made of same material. Colors, red or blue. Price, each.................. **$3.75**
If by mail, postage extra, 57 cents.

No. 17R125 MISSES' JACKET. Made up in the very latest style, with a yoke in back. This is made of all wool covert cloth; piping of light velvet all around collar, lapels, front, cuffs and pockets; three rows stitching around the jacket; lined throughout with mercerized sateen to match; double breasted front trimmed with white pearl buttons; loose back; three rows stitching on the yoke; facing in front made of same material. Colors, castor or bluish gray. Price, each ....(If by mail, postage extra, 54 cents)................ **$3.95**

No. 17R127 MISSES' JACKET. Made of all wool beaver; velvet collar and coat shape lapels; double breasted front trimmed with six fancy pearl buttons; half tight back trimmed with stitched straps over the seams; facing in front made of same material; lined throughout with mercerized sateen; satin strap trimming around the sleeves. Colors, castor or royal blue. Price, each.......... (If by mail, postage extra, 57 cents)........... **$4.95**

LADIES' JACKETS.

When ordering please state bust measure and length inside of sleeve, measured from under the arm to the wrist. (The average sleeve length is 17 inches.) Also state the color you desire. Regular sizes are 32 to 42 inches around the bust. Shades and sizes different or larger than a regular stock garment will be made to order at 20 per cent above regular price quoted in catalogue. It takes about two weeks to make a special.

No. 17R136 LADIES' JACKET. Made of good quality beaver; velvet collar; coat shape lapels; double breasted front trimmed with fancy buttons; half tight back; 24 inches long; facing in front made of same material; lined throughout with mercerized sateen. Colors, black, blue or brown. Price, each............ (If by mail, postage extra, 58 cents)............ **$3.75**

No. 17R138 NOBBY LADIES' JACKET, STRICTLY TAILOR MADE. Made of good quality all wool melton cloth; high standing collar and lapels stitched several times; strap trimming in front made of same material, also stitched several times; similar trimming on the two seams in back. Entire jacket is bound with black mercerized sateen all around; strap of same material around cuffs and bound with mercerized sateen. Very neat jacket; lined throughout with black mercerized sateen. Color, dark gray only. Price, each .... (If by mail, postage extra, 58 cents).......... **$4.95**

WHEN ORDERING please state bust measure and length of inside sleeves measured from under the arm to the wrist (the average length is 18 inches); also state the color you desire. Regular sizes are from 32 to 42 inches around the bust. Shades or sizes different or larger than a regular stock garment will be made to order at 20 per cent above the regular price quoted. It takes about two weeks to make a special.

When postage is not given, garment cannot be sent by mail.

LADIES' JACKETS AND AUTOMOBILES.

No. 17R131 $3.95

No. 17R147 $10.00

No. 17R148 $12 50

No 17R139 $5.75

No. 17R142 $7 75

No. 17R143 $9.95

No. 17R145 $4.95

No. 17R141 $6.75

No. 17R140 $6.50

No. 17R131 THIS ILLUSTRATION REPRESENTS OUR ENTIRE LOT OF LAST YEAR'S JACKETS. They are not all like picture, but all are of good value. Some of them are fur trimmed, some with coat collars, some like illustration. Materials are kerseys, beavers, boucles and covert cloths. Colors, black, blue, tan and castor. When ordering give general description of what you want and we will send you the best thing for your money as long as they last. Price, each........ **$3.95**

No. 17R139 OUR SPECIAL LEADER. Made of good quality all wool kersey; 24 inches long; high standing collar and lapels stitched with silk four times all around; flaring cuffs, pocket flaps also stitched; double breasted; facing in front made of same material; lined throughout with Romain silk. Best value for the money. Can furnish in black, royal blue or castor. Price, each........ **$5.75**

No. 17R140 LADIES' TAILOR MADE JACKET. Made of all wool pebble cheviot; velvet collar, coat shape lapels, double breasted front; several rows of stitching around the bottom, sleeves and pocket flaps; half tight fitting back; over 24 inches long; lined throughout with Romain silk. Dark gray only. Price, each........ **$6.50**

No. 17R141 LADIES' JACKET. Made of all wool kersey; storm collar, high lapels buttoning at the neck; double breasted front; several rows of stitching, as shown in illustration, on collar and lapels, all around bottom, and on turnover cuffs, as well as on pocket flaps; jacket is 25 inches long, half tight fitting back; facing in front made of same material and lined with Romain silk. Colors, black or castor. Price, each........ **$6.75**

No. 17R142 LADIES' JACKET. Made of all wool kersey, tailor made; l'Aiglon collar, kersey strap yoke effect, with kersey strap trimming all around and several rows of stitching on yoke and all around the bottom and the bell sleeves; three wide straps of same material on seams in back; double breasted front, facing in front made of same material; lined with Romain silk. Colors, black or castor. Price, each........ **$7.75**

No. 17R143 VERY STYLISH AUTOMOBILE COAT. Made of all wool kersey, strictly tailor made; very high collar and large lapels; kersey strap trimming in front, on two seams in back; collar, lapels and bottom are stitched; small straps on the bell sleeves; half tight fitting back; double breasted front trimmed with pearl buttons; facing in front made of same material; lined throughout with very fine satin. Length, 30 inches. Colors, black or castor. Price, each........ **$9.95**

No. 17R145 LADIES' AUTOMOBILE OR OVERCOAT. Made of all wool diagonal cloth; coat shape collar and lapels; turn over cuffs and side pockets bound with velvet piping; double breasted front trimmed with horn buttons; loose back; facing in front made of same material; lined half way with mercerized sateen. Length, 36 inches. Color, dark gray only. Price, each........ **$4.95**

No. 17R147 LADIES' AUTOMOBILE JACKET OR OVERCOAT. Made of all wool rough finished cheviot; l'Aiglon collar, made of velvet, small lapels, yoke effect in front and back as well as the turn over cuffs are bound with velvet; double breasted front trimmed with pearl buttons; half tight back; facing in front made of same material; lined throughout with black Romain silk; 36 inches long. Color, dark gray only. Price, each........ **$10.00**

No. 17R148 LADIES' JACKET. Strictly tailor made of all wool kersey; large collar, lapels and bottom stitched several times with silk; wide kersey strap trimming on seams in back, front and pockets; double breasted front trimmed with pearl buttons; satin trimming on the bell sleeves at the point of the strap; facing front made of same material; lined throughout with fine satin; 36 inches long. Colors, black or tan. Price, each........ **$12.50**

WHEN POSTAGE IS NOT GIVEN, GARMENT CANNOT BE SENT BY MAIL.

LADIES' LONG COATS ...OR AUTOMOBILES.

WHEN ORDERING, please state bust measure and length of sleeves, measured from under the arm to wrist, also the color you desire. Sizes are from 32 to 42 inches around bust. Shades or sizes different or larger than regular stock garment will be made to order at 20 per cent above the regular price quoted in catalogue and cash in full in advance. It takes about two weeks to make a special.

THESE GARMENTS ARE TOO HEAVY TO BE SENT BY MAIL.

No. 17R149 LADIES' AUTOMOBILE JACKET OR OVERCOAT. Made of all wool kersey, strictly tailor made; large collar and lapels made of South American beaver, otherwise called nutria; double breasted front trimmed with fancy buttons; side pockets stitched several times; bell sleeves; half tight fitting back; 36 inches long; facing in front made of same material; lined throughout with satin. Colors, black or castor. Price, each............ **$13.50**

No. 17R151 LADIES' AUTOMOBILE OR OVERCOAT. Made 42 inches long, tailor made; large storm collar and lapels buttoning high at the neck; side pockets; several rows of stitching on collar, lapels, and cuffs; double breasted front; half tight fitting back; trimmed with kersey straps and fancy buttons; facing in front made of the same material; lined throughout with black mercerized sateen. Color, black only. Price, each........... **$7.95**

No. 17R152 LADIES' AUTOMOBILE OR OVERCOAT. Made of all wool kersey; storm collar, lapels buttoning at neck; silk stitching on collar, lapels and around the bottom as well as on the cuffs; double breasted front trimmed with fancy buttons; side pockets; half tight fitting back; facing in front made of same material; lined throughout with fine satin; watch pocket on inside. Made 42 inches long. Colors, black or tan. Price, each................... **$9.50**

LADIES' RAGLANS.

These are all made from 56 to 58 inches in length. If the garment you receive should be longer than you can wear it can easily be altered by cutting off the bottom.

No. 17R303 LADIES' RAGLAN. Made of light weight cotton and wool mixed melton; coat shaped collar and lapels; pointed yoke in front and in back; garment strictly tailor made; side pockets; facing in front of same material. Color, oxford gray. Price, each................ **$5.95**

No. 17R304 LADIES' RAGLAN. Made of good quality melton; coat shaped velvet collar and lapels; strictly tailor made and is stitched several times around the front and on double pointed yoke, which is piped with velvet; wide facing in front of similar material; half tight fitting back; side pockets. Color, oxford gray only. Price, each.................... **$7.50**

No. 17R305 LADIES' RAGLAN. Made of good quality diagonal cloth. We can call it all wool, but there is a little cotton mixed in with it; but for wear it is excellent. Coat shaped collar and lapels; fly front; pointed yoke in front and back; half tight fitting; new cuffs. This garment is strictly tailor made. Color, oxford gray only. Price, each........................ **$8.75**

No. 17R306 LADIES' RAGLAN. Made of good quality kersey; velvet collar, stitched lapels; three rows of stitching in front and on bottom of the garment; pointed yoke in front and back; fly front; wide facing of same material; lined to waist only with black satin; side pockets and cuffs on sleeves. Colors, black or castor. Price, each.. **$12.50**

LADIES' CLOTH CAPES.

THESE ARE SPECIAL VALUES. We offer on this page goods that we can furnish at these prices only as long as our stock on hand lasts. The styles may vary a little, as the garments illustrated hereon are not always exactly like the picture but are made similar to the illustration and description. In every case we guarantee that you will receive exceptional value.

WHEN ORDERING CAPES STATE NUMBER OF GARMENT WANTED, COLOR, BUST MEASURE AND NUMBER OF INCHES AROUND NECK.

No. 17R165 LADIES' DOUBLE CAPE. Made of black or blue beaver, trimmed with braid and fur. 26 inches long. Price, each....................**$1.98**
If by mail, postage extra, 50 cents.

No. 17R166 LADIES' SINGLE CAPES. Made of beaver; 30 inches long; trimmed with fur and braid. Colors, black or blue. Price, each....................**$2.95**
If by mail, postage extra, 60 cents.

No. 17R167 LADIES' SINGLE CAPE. Made of black boucle; 27 to 30 inches long; sateen lining and black Thibet fur trimming. When ordering, give description of style wanted. Price.......**$2.98**

No. 17R168 LADIES' SINGLE CAPES. Made of kersey in black, blue or castor colors; most of them trimmed with kersey straps or embroidery. When ordering, give description of style wanted. Price, each....................**$3.25**
If by mail, postage extra, 62 cents.

No. 17R169 LADIES' GOLF CAPE. Made of all wool material; the hood and flounce around the bottom are made of the plaid side of the cloth; the over collar and the upper part of the cape of the right side in solid colors; trimmed with fringe as shown in illustration. Colors, black, oxford, navy or brown with fancy plaids. Price....**$3.75**
If by mail, postage extra, 48 cents.

No. 17R173 THIS HANDSOME CAPE is made of all wool golf material; over collar and part of the cape from yoke to flounce on bottom made of right side of cloth; the yoke, collar and the flounce are made of the plaid side of the cloth; satin strap trimming stitched with white silk around collar, yoke, above and around the flounce as well as in front; satin strap trimming on yoke and collar. Can furnish in oxford, navy blue or brown with fancy plaid backs. Price, each..........**$5.95**
If by mail, postage extra, 52 cents.

No. 17R177 PLAIN AND TRIMMED KERSEY CAPES. 30 inches long; full sweep. Black only. When ordering state style wanted. Price, each....................**$4.95**

No. 17R179 FUR TRIMMED BOUCLE CAPES. 30 inches long; well lined. Black only. Some of them trimmed with strap trimming. Price, each....................**$4.75**

LADIES' PLUSH CAPES

WHEN ORDERING ALWAYS GIVE US CORRECT MEASUREMENTS. State number of inches around the bust and around the neck, also your height and weight.

SIZES ARE 32, 34, 36, 38, 40, 42 AND 44 INCHES AROUND BUST AND FROM 13 TO 17 INCHES AROUND THE NECK. Sizes different than those mentioned above must be made to order, in which case we require 20 per cent above the price quoted in catalogue.

No. 17R186 LADIES' PLUSH CAPE OR COLLARETTE. Made of good plush; 15 inches long and 70 inches in sweep, neatly embroidered with black soutache and beads all around the cape and trimmed with black Thibet fur around the collar, in front and all around the bottom. The cape is lined throughout with black, blue or red mercerized sateen and interlined with fiber chamois. Price ......(If by mail, postage extra, 30 cents)............ **$1.98**

No. 17R190 LADIES' CRUSHED PLUSH CAPE. The material used in this cape is same grade as the one used in the plain garments. With a special process the plush is crushed, thus giving it a very nice luster and makes it look attractive. The garment we show measures 30 inches in length and 95 inches in sweep. Is lined throughout with a good quality black mercerized sateen and interlined with fiber chamois. Black Thibet fur around the collar and in front. Made with best trimmings and prices cheaper than ever before. Price.........(If by mail, postage extra, 61 cents).......... **$3.98**

No. 17R191 LADIES' CAPE. Is made of a fine seal plush. 20 inches in length, and with the fur added to it it looks as if it was 22 or 23 inches. Beautifully embroidered with black soutache and black beads, giving it a very rich tone and style, black Thibet fur around the large storm collar and all around the bottom. Black soutache embroidery on the storm collar. Lined throughout with black, blue or red mercerized lining and interlined with fiber chamois. Price...(If by mail, postage extra, 51 cent)......... **$3.95**

No. 17R192 LADIES' CAPE. Made of a high grade seal plush. As the demand of last year on this cape exceeded our supply, we have prepared for it in advance and laid in a very large stock of these capes, and are in a position to fill all orders as fast as we get them. This cape measures 30 inches in length and 95 inches in sweep. It is lined throughout with mercerized sateen, and trimmed with black Thibet fur around the collar and front. Price, **$3.98**
If by mail, postage extra, 61 cents.

No. 17R193 LADIES' PLUSH CAPE. Made of a good quality plush, embroidered all over with black soutache and beads. This cape is cut in four pieces. It measures 30 inches in length and 95 inches in sweep. Is trimmed with black Thibet fur around collar and front. The cape is lined throughout with black sateen and interlined with fiber chamois. Price... ..... **$3.98**
If by mail, postage extra, 64 cents.

No. 17R194 LADIES' CAPE. Made of fine seal plush. It measures 30 inches in length and 115 inches in the sweep. Quality of plush used in the cape is as good as we have on the market today. This cape is trimmed with imitation brown bear fur. Has 2½-inch plush facing; lined throughout with black mercerized sateen, and interlined with fiber chamois. Price. ... **$5.75**

No. 17R195 VERY ATTRACTIVE AND STYLISH CAPE. Made of high grade seal plush, embroidered with black soutache and black beads; black Thibet fur around the large storm collar and in front. The cape is lined throughout with black mercerized sateen and interlined with wadding, making it a very heavy and desirable garment. The cape is 30 inches long, and measures 125 inches in the sweep. Inverted plait in back. Price.... **$6.75**

No. 17R196 LADIES' CAPE. 36 inches long, made of fine seal plush. The large storm collar is trimmed with imitation bear fur trimmings. This fur looks like genuine, and you can hardly tell it is an imitation. Cape measures 130 inches in sweep and is lined with black mercerized sateen. Price, **$7.25**

LADIES' FUR AND PLUSH JACKETS AND CAPES.

WHEN ORDERING please state bust measurement and length of inside sleeve (the average sleeve length is 18 inches). Regular sizes are 32 to 42 inches around bust. Sizes different than regular must be made to order, in which case we require 20 per cent above the regular price quoted in catalogue. It takes about two weeks to make a special. If postage is not given garment cannot be sent by mail.

...LADIES' FUR CAPES...

No. 17R206 LADIES' FUR CAPE. Made of black French Coney; 30 inches long and 110 inches in sweep. It is a very serviceable cape, heavy and warm, lined throughout with black satin and interlined with wadding. Price........ **$10.00**

No. 17R211 LADIES' FUR CAPE. Made of XXXX black Astrakhan. The skins used in this cape were all selected by experts. This cape measures 30 inches in length and 110 inches in sweep. The large storm collar is lined throughout with black Skinner satin, and interlined with wadding and canvas. Price........ **$21.50**

...FUR JACKETS...

No. 17R212 THIS OUR SPECIAL LEADER is made of high grade black Baltic seal fur. Perfect fitting, has a large storm collar, large lapels, facing in front; can be worn open or closed, and shows off very pretty both ways. The jacket is 22 inches long, is lined throughout with Skinner satin and interlined with canvas and wadding. Price........ **$14.95**

No. 17R219 LADIES' JACKET OR AUTOMOBILE. 27 inches long. Made of high grade plush, loose back, double breasted front, collar, large lapels and part of bell sleeves are black astrakhan. Facing in front made of same material, lined throughout with romain silk. Price, each........ **$8.95**

No. 17R220 LADIES' PLUSH JACKET. Made of high grade plush; large collar and lapels of South American beaver, otherwise called nutria. Double breasted front, tight back, facing in front made of same material. Lined throughout with romain silk. Length, 22 inches. Price, each........ **$10.00**

LADIES' FUR COLLARETTES.

When ordering please state your bust measure and the number of inches around the neck, also color of lining. Sizes are from 32 to 42 inches around bust and 13 to 17 inches around the neck.

No. 17R224 LADIES' COLLARETTE. Made of Black Baltic Seal Fur, 9 inches long, 65 inches in sweep. It is lined throughout with red, or heliotrope sateen. Very cheap garment for the money. Price........ **$1.35**
If by mail, postage extra, 25 cents.

No. 17R226 LADIES' COLLARETTE. Made of Black Baltic Seal Fur, 9 inches long, 65 inches in sweep. Has a large storm collar, four big tails in front; lined throughout with brown, red or heliotrope high grade satin lining. Price.... (If by mail, postage extra, 26 cents) **$2.50**

No. 17R228 VERY NOBBY COLLARETTE. Made of Black Astrakhan Fur, lined throughout with a guaranteed black satin lining. We want to call your attention to this fur, as there are so many different grades on the market. There are a whole lot of collarettes shown today that sell about the same price as we ask for it, but the difference is that the skins used in our garments are all solid skins and the furs used in garments shown by some are made of small pieces. Price........ **$4.95**
If by mail, postage extra, each, 29 cents.

No. 17R230 THIS NEAT LITTLE COLLARETTE is made of imitation sable around the border and the collar. The color of this fur is on the brownish order. The round yoke and under collar are made of black Baltic seal fur, lined with red or heliotrope color satin lining. Price........ (If by mail, postage extra, 26 cents)........ **$2.95**

No. 17R231 THIS STYLISH COLLARETTE is made with an imitation gray mouflon border and collar, and Baltic seal yoke and under collar. The combination of these two different colors is very striking. It measures 16 inches in length and 70 inches sweep. Lined throughout with red or heliotrope satin lining. Price........ (If by mail, postage extra, 31 cents)........ **$3.95**

LADIES' AND MISSES' FUR COLLARETTES AND STORM COLLARS.

When ordering please give us your bust and neck measurement, and state the color of lining you desire.

No. 17R284 LADIES' STYLISH TAB COLLARETTE Made of Black Baltic Seal Fur. Measures 10 inches in length, two tabs in front, trimmed with eight tails, large storm collar, heavily interlined and lined with red or heliotrope colored satin.
Price.............. ..**(If by mail, postage extra, 88 cents)** $8.25

No. 17R286 NEAT AND NOBBY COLLARETTE. Made of Imitation Gray Chinchilla border, tabs over collar. Round yoke and under collar made of Black Baltic Seal Fur, eight tails to match in front, heavily interlined and lined with red or heliotrope color satin
Price................**(If by mail, postage extra, 82 cents)**.............. .. ..$8 75

No. 17R287 LADIES' STORM COLLAR OR SHORT COLLARETTE Made of Black Baltic Seal Fur, trimmed with six tails in front, interlined and lined with red or heliotrope color satin. Price... ......**(If by mail, postage extra, 81 cents)** $2.85

No. 17R246 LADIES' TAB COLLARETTES. Made of Brown Opossum border, tabs and over collar, Baltic Seal around yoke and under collar. Neatly trimmed with ten tails to match and two small fur heads on each side in front. It is lined thoughout with brown or heliotrope color satin. Price.... ...**(If by mail, postage extra, 88 cents)**....$4.95

FUR SCARFS.

When ordering always mention the number and the name of fur, and this will avoid misunderstanding when filling the order.

No. 17R257 LADIES' CLUSTER SCARF. Made of Black Baltic Seal Fur, neatly trimmed with six imitation bear tails. Price....**(If by mail, postage extra, 20 cents)** ..98c

No. 17R258 VERY ATTRACTIVE SCARF. Made of Genuine Electric Seal, finished with two large tails on both ends and two large heads. It is different than we have shown before and is very pretty. Price, each. ..**(If by mail, postage extra, 24 cents)**. $3.50

No. 17R259 LADIES' CLUSTER SCARF. Made of imitation Stone Marten, looks just like the genuine and wears just as long. Neatly trimmed with six tails to match. Good protection for the neck, and we can recommend it. Price, each.......... ....$2.98
If by mail, postage extra, 17 cents.

No. 17R260 THIS SCARF IS AN IMITATION OF THE GENUINF MARTEN. It is made of Siberian Marten, very fluffy and heavy enough for the neck. Neatly trimmed with six tails. Furnished in black and brown color. Price, each....... ....$2.98
If by mail, postage extra, 21 cents.

No. 17R264 FUR BOA. Made of imitation brown Bear. It is very stylish and attractive. It is very latest thing for the season. Price... ....$8.75
If by mail, postage extra, 27 cents.

No. 17R272 CLEOPATRA SCARF. The latest fad for the season. It is made of Black Baltic Seal Fur, finished with three tabs on each side, each tab finished with imitation bear tails at the end. On the tab is a small fur head with two paws on each side of scarf.
Price..................**(If by mail, postage extra, 28 cents)**....... . . ..$2.75

LADIES' MUFFS.

No. 17R279 ATTRACTIVE MUFF. Made of Black French Coney.
Price.............. ....**(If by mail, postage extra, 19 cents)**........... .. . . .69c

No. 17R280 ATTRACTIVE MUFF. Made in Black Baltic Seal Fur. Lined with satin. Price ....**(If by mail, postage extra, 17 cents)**.. .. . .89c

No. 17R281 ATTRACTIVE MUFF. Made of dyed Muskrat, otherwise called imitation Alaska Seal. Lined throughout with a good satin. Price. $1.48
If by mail, postage extra, 17 cents.

No. 17R282 ATTRACTIVE MUFF. Made of XXXX Grade Black Astrakhan Fur. Large size. Lined throughout with best grade of satin.
Price...............**(If by mail, postage extra, 19 cents)**. $2.75

No. 17R284 ATTRACTIVE MUFF. Made of Electric Seal Fur. Lined throughout with fine satin. Price. ....**(If by mail, postage extra, 19 cents)** $2.50

No. 17R285 ATTRACTIVE MUFF. Made of Imitation Stone Marten, large size down bed. Lined throughout with fine satin. Price......... .. . . $2.98
If by mail, postage extra, 19 cents.

No. 17R286 ATTRACTIVE MUFF. Made of Siberian Marten, in either brown or black colors. Interlined with down bed and lined with fine satin.
Price..................**(If by mail, postage extra, 21 cents)**........................ $2.98

A Handsome Fur Set for $2.25.

No. 17R297 Child's Set, consisting of a white lamb large sailor collar edged all around with Turkish Angora, trimmed with beaver heads in each corner, lined throughout with white satin; a flat muff made of white lamb, trimmed all around with white Angora, small purse on top, beaver trimming in front with bow and satin ribbon streamers to go around neck. Judging from the number of orders we get, it must be very popular throughout the country **We get orders faster than we can fill them.** If you desire one, we would advise you to send in your order as soon as possible and we will give you our prompt attention and see that you get a handsome set, as shown in the illustration. Price, per set.. ... .$2.25
If by mail, postage extra, per set, 20 cents.

Ladies' Cloth and Silk Jackets.

WHEN ORDERING give bust measurements and length of sleeves. The average length of the inside sleeves is 18½ inches. We make these from 32 to 42 inches around bust. Sizes different than specified must be made to order, in which case we charge 20 per cent above the regular price.

No. 17R308 LADIES' JACKET. Made of all wool pebble cheviot, strictly tailor made; coat shaped collar and lapels; lined throughout with silk serge and lapels faced with good quality of satin; double breasted front, tight back. Color black only. Price, each....(If by mail, postage extra, 30 cents)...**$4.25**

No. 17R309 LADIES' JACKET. Made of all wool covert cloth; double breasted loose front and velvet collar; half tight fitting back; patch pocket; pearl buttons; lined throughout with silk serge. Colors, castor or bluish gray. Price, each.......(If by mail, postage extra, 36 cents)...............**$4.75**

LADIES' SILK ETON JACKETS.

No. 17R310 LADIES' ETON JACKET. Tucked all over, neatly finished all around with a border of taffeta silk strap, stitched four times; narrow cuffs stitched; full sleeves; lined throughout with black satin. Color, black only. Price, each.........(If by mail, postage extra, 19 cents).............**$4.95**

No. 17R311 LADIES' SILK ETON JACKET, made of fine taffeta silk, tucked all over, stitched all around the jacket with taffeta silk straps as shown in the illustration. Narrow cuffs, full sleeves, lined throughout with black or white satin. Color, black only. Price, each.......................**$6.75**
If by mail, postage extra, 21 cents.

No. 17R312 LADIES' ETON JACKET. Made of taffeta silk; the jacket is tucked all over; narrow sleeves; border of black taffeta silk stitched and finished with an inch wide strip of white taffeta silk; trimmed with small black buttons. We can furnish this all black or with a white front. Please state which one you desire when ordering. Lined throughout with black satin.
Price, each.............(If by mail, postage extra, 21 cents)..........**$7.25**

No. 17R313 LADIES' ETON JACKET. Made of fine taffeta silk; tucked all over; fancy cuffs trimmed with braid; similar trimming on front and all around the bottom of jacket, with sailor collar stitched several times; trimmed with small buttons; bow in front, made of white or black; lined throughout with black romain silk. Color, black only. Price....................**$7.75**
If by mail, postage extra, 23 cents.

CHILDREN'S COATS AND CAPES.

No. 17R314 CHILD'S REEFER JACKET. Made of wool mixed diagonal cloth; shoulder cape and collar trimmed with white braid; double breasted front, gilt buttons. Colors, navy blue or red.
Price..............(If by mail, postage extra, 22 cents)...............**$1.19**

No. 17R315 VERY NOBBY CHILD'S REEFER. Made of all wool broadcloth; shoulder cape neatly trimmed with flannel to match the jacket, and embroidered with gilt cord; double breasted front, loose back; cape lined with sateen and front faced with same material as jacket is made of. Can furnish in gray with blue applique or red with blue applique.
Price.............(If by mail, postage extra, 25 cents)...................**$2.50**

No. 17R316 CHILD'S LONG AUTOMOBILE COAT. Made of all wool ladies' cloth; double breasted front, loose back, fancy inlaid collar; lined throughout with changeable gloria silk and faced in front of same material as coat is made of. Colors, red or royal blue.
Price.............(If by mail, postage extra, 25 cents)...............**$2.98**

No. 17R317 CHILDREN'S CAPES. Made of all wool sackings in blue, red or royal blue colors; with fancy trimmings. They are not all like cut, but every one is a good style. Sizes, 4 to 12. We will sell only as long as they last. Price...........(If by mail, postage extra, 30 cents)..............**98c**

LADIES' CAPES

FOR

Spring and Summer.

THE CLOTHS USED ARE MEDIUM WEIGHT. THESE CAPES CAN BE WORN IN THE EARLY FALL.

WHEN ORDERING GIVE BUST MEASURE — measured all around the bust under the arms—and the number of inches around the neck. Sizes over 42 inches around bust are specials, and must be made to order, in which case they will cost you 20 per cent above the price quoted in the catalogue. If you fail to allow 20 per cent for extra size, we will make the garment and charge you with the difference.

No. 17R318 LADIES' BLACK CAPE. Made of silk and mohair mixed figured grosgrain; 15 inches long; ruching of satin around the collar, small strip in the front and trimmed with lace and jetting; lined throughout with black mercerized lining. Color, black only. Price..........**(If by mail, postage extra, 17 cents)**..........**$1.49**

No. 17R319 LADIES' CAPE. Made of repellent cloth; 23 inches long; trimmed with lace and two rows of jetting around the shoulders; similar trimming around the collar in addition to silk ruching. Color, black only. Price..........**$1.75**

If by mail, postage extra, 20 cents.

No. 17R320 LADIES' SHOULDER CAPE. Made of black brocaded satin; 15 inches long; trimmed with satin ruching, black jetting and lace around the shoulders; satin ribbon and gauze trimming around the neck; satin ribbon st eamer in front; lined with black mercerized lining. Color, black only. Price..........**$2.98**

If by mail, postage extra, 18 cents.

No. 17R321 LADIES' SHOULDER CAPE. Made of cotton back velvet; 15 inches long; embroidered all around with black soutache, very fancy design; satin ribbon and ruching, also black jet around the collar; satin ribbon streamers in front; lined with black mercerized sateen. Color, black only. Price..........**$2.35**

If by mail, postage extra, 20 cents.

No. 17R322 LADIES' CAPE. Made of cotton mixed worsted; 24 inches long, 100 inches in sweep; embroidered all around with black soutache; collar also embroidered; small satin bow in back and in front; no lining. Color, black only. Price..........**(If by mail, postage extra, 26 cents)**..........**$2.65**

No. 17R323 LADIES' CAPE. Made of good quality all wool repellent cloth; neatly trimmed with a ruffle around the shoulders, which is edged with satin ribbon; one row black jet trimming around the shoulders, lace and satin around the neck finished with a satin bow in front; lined throughout with black mercerized lining. Color, black only. Price..........**(If by mail, postage extra, 33 cents)**..........**$2.98**

No. 17R324 LADIES' CAPE. Made of black grosgrain silk; 23 inches long; has inverted plait in back; trimmed with wide lace, satin ruching, and black jet around the shoulders; similar trimming around the neck; lined throughout with mercerized sateen. Color, black only. Price.....**(If by mail, postage extra, 25 cents)**.....**$3.98**

No. 17R325 STYLISH LADIES' CAPE. Made of black grosgrain silk; 23 inches long; trimmed with wide lace and two rows of satin ribbon ruching around the shoulders; similar trimming all around the neck; lined throughout with black mercerized sateen. Color, black only. Price..........**$4.35**

If by mail, postage extra, 27 cents.

No. 17R326 LADIES' SHOULDER CAPE. Made of black brocaded satin; 18 inches long; inverted plait in back; neatly trimmed in front, reaching to the center of the back with wide lace, and two rows of satin ribbon ruching; finished with two small bows in the back; satin ribbon and lace trimming around neck; bow in front; lined throughout with black mercerized sateen. Color, black only. Price..........**$4.95**

If by mail, postage extra, 29 cents.

No. 17R327 LADIES' CAPE. Made in black brocaded satin; 22 inches long; richly trimmed with satin ribbon ruching and fine gauze on shoulders; similar trimming around the neck. Cape looks very pretty, and is much nicer than illustration shows. Lined throughout with black mercerized sateen. Satin ribbon bow in front. Color, black only. Price..........**(If by mail, postage extra, 31 cents.)**..........**$5.95**

LADIES' TAILOR MADE SUITS

When ordering be sure to give all the measurements required, and say what color you desire.

WE FURNISH THESE in sizes from 32 to 42 inches around the bust and from 38 to 44 inches skirt length. The average length of waist in back is 16 inches and the length of inside seam 18½ to 19 inches. These are regular measurements. Sizes different than these must be made to order, in which case we charge 20 per cent above the regular price. If you fail to enclose 20 per cent for extra size we will make same and charge you with the difference. When postage is not given goods cannot be sent by mail.

If for some reason you have to return the suit to us, never return skirt or jacket alone; return both and we will be pleased to exchange the suit. Parts of suits will not be accepted.

No. 31R315 LADIES' SUIT. Made of a good quality wool mixed repellent cloth, consisting of jacket and skirt. The jacket is made with coat shaped collar and lapels, double breasted front, the back extending to the waist only; dip front, lined throughout with mercerized sateen. The skirt is made with an inverted plait in the back, silk band around the waist, lined throughout with percaline lining, interlined at the bottom and bound with waterproof binding. Colors, black, blue or Oxford gray. Price........................**$5.75**

If by mail, postage extra, 64 cents.

No. 31R316 LADIES' TAILOR MADE SUIT. Consisting of jacket and skirt, made of all wool cheviot serge. The jacket is made with coat shaped collar and lapels, fly front, cuffs on the sleeves, lined throughout with black mercerized lining. The skirt is made with inverted plait in the back and graduated flounce on the bottom; lined throughout with glazed lining and interlined at the flounce; velvet binding on bottom and silk ribbon band around the waist. Colors, black or blue. Price....(Postage extra, 64 cents)....**$6.75**

No. 31R317 LADIES' RAINY DAY OR WALKING SUIT. Made of all wool cloth, consisting of jacket and skirt, coat shaped collar, lapels faced with peau de soie, flaring cuffs. Back of jacket reaches to the waist only, while the front reaches below the waist, three buttons in the front, giving it a very pretty effect; lined throughout with black mercerized sateen lining. The skirt is tailor made with a graduated flounce, stitched all around the bottom, silk ribbon band around the waist and no lining, making it very light and desirable. Color, Oxford gray only. Price........................**$6.75**

No. 31R318 LADIES' TAILOR MADE SUIT. Consisting of skirt and jacket, made of all wool Venetian cloth. Eton jacket, new shaped collar and lapels, double breasted front, reaching just a trifle below the waist in front and to the waist in the back of jacket; lined throughout with romain silk lining. Skirt, tailor made, with flounce around the bottom, lined throughout with glazed percaline, and interlined at the bottom, bound with velvet. Colors, black, castor or bluish gray. Price..(If by mail, postage extra, 64 cents)....**$7.95**

No. 31R319 LADIES' TAILOR MADE SUIT. Consisting of jacket and skirt. Made of all wool Venetian cloth. Jacket is made with the new collar and silk faced lapels; double breasted front, made with yoke which is bound with satin straps; wide plait from yoke to bottom of jacket. The back of jacket is made same as the front and it only reaches to the waist; trimmed cuffs. Jacket is lined with romain silk. The skirt is made with a graduated flounce, trimmed with satin straps; is lined with glazed lining and interlined at the bottom and bound with velvet. Colors, black, blue or red. Price........................**$9.98**

No. 31R320 LADIES' TAILOR MADE SUIT. Consisting of jacket and skirt only. Made of all wool Venetian cloth, coat shaped collar and lapels, double breasted dip front. The jacket extends in back to the waist only, yoke front, stitched and piped with velvet, fancy cuffs with same trimming. The jacket is lined with romain silk; skirt is tailor made with graduated flounce, piped with velvet where the flounce joins the skirt; lined throughout with percaline lining, interlined at the bottom and bound with velvet. A very desirable garment. Colors, black, gray or castor. Price........................**$10.50**

LADIES' TAILOR MADE SUITS.

We furnish these in sizes from 32 to 42 inches around the bust and from 38 to 44 inches in skirt length; the average length of waist in back is 16 inches and the length of inside sleeve 18½ to 19 inches; these are regular measurements; sizes different than these must be made to order, in which case we charge 20 per cent above the regular price. **If for some reason** you have to return a suit to us, never return skirt or jacket alone; return both and we will be pleased to exchange the suit; parts of suits will not be accepted.

No. 31R321 LADIES' TAILOR MADE SUIT. Made of all wool Venetian cloth, coat shaped collar and lapels, fly front, yoke effect, finished with tailor made flaps of the same material; tailor made straps on the back seams; bell sleeves trimmed with straps; jacket lined throughout with romain lining; skirt tailor made with graduated flounce stitched several times, lined with black glazed lining and interlined at the bottom, bound with velvet. An exceptionally pretty suit. Colors, a new shade of gray, or castor. Price........ **$11.00**

No. 31R322 LADIES' TAILOR MADE SUIT. Consisting of a jacket and a rainy day skirt; coat collar and lapels on jacket faced with black peau de soie; double breasted dip front; back reaches only to the waist; velvet collar; bell sleeves; jacket is lined throughout with black satin; tailor made skirt, stitched twelve times around the bottom; silk band around the waist; inverted plait in the back. We can furnish in black or blue wool mixed melton cloth with narrow, invisible white stripes. Price.... **$11.50**

No. 31R323 LADIES' STYLISH BLOUSE SUIT. Consisting of blouse and skirt, made of all wool cheviot serge. The blouse is made with a rolling collar, large lapels and revers, as shown in illustration; trimmed with satin straps; bell sleeves trimmed like the jacket; satin strap trimming in back of jacket, which reaches to the waist only. The jacket is lined throughout with black satin. Tailor made skirt with graduated flounce, trimmed with two rows of satin strap trimmings above the flounce; glazed lining and interlining in the flounce, velvet binding. Colors, black, blue or brown. Price........ **$10.50**

No. 31R324 LADIES' TAILOR MADE SUIT. Consisting of jacket and skirt, made of all wool Venetian cloth. Jacket has coat shaped collar and lapels, single breasted, can be worn as a blouse or buttoned; neatly trimmed with three satin straps reaching from the waist in front all around the shoulders to the waist in back; belt all around the blouse trimmed with satin straps; similar trimmings on the cuffs. The jacket is lined throughout with a good quality of satin lining. The skirt is strictly tailor made, has a graduated flounce, has four rows of satin strap trimmings; glazed lining, interlining at the bottom, velvet binding. Colors, black, royal blue or castor. Price........ **$13.50**

No. 31R325 LADIES' TAILOR MADE SUIT. Consisting of jacket and skirt, made of all wool Venetian cloth. Eton effect jacket, which can be worn open as well; neatly trimmed with satin around the coat shaped collar and lapels and all around the waist; similar trimming on both sides of the front as well as on the back of the jacket, which reaches to the waist only; fancy cuffs, trimmed to match the suit. Jacket lined throughout with black silk lining. The skirt is tailor made, with graduated flounce, trimmed with satin straps stitched around the bottom; has a drop skirt made of black glazed lining. They are the newest things shown for the coming season. Colors, black, castor or blue. Price........ **$13.75**

No. 31R326 LADIES' TAILOR MADE SUIT. Consisting of jacket and skirt. The jacket is made full moire, shaped collar, new shaped lapels, dipped front, yoke effect, stitched and finished with straps of same material from yoke to the bottom of the jacket; strap trimming on the back of the jacket, which reaches to the waist only; several rows of stitching all around the jacket; jacket lined all through with taffeta silk; cuffs made of black moire or watered silk. The skirt is well tailor made, has a graduated flounce, trimmed with strips made of the same material and stitched several times; finished with small, silk covered buttons; is lined throughout with black glazed lining and interlined around the bottom; velvet binding, and silk ribbon around the waist. Colors, black, blue or castor. Price........ **$16.50**

Ladies' Wash Suits and Skirts.

WE FURNISH THESE in sizes from 32 to 42 inches around the bust and from 38 to 44 inches in skirt length. The average length of waist in back is 16 inches and the length of inside seam 18½ to 19 inches. These are regular measurements. Sizes different from these must be made to order, in which case we charge 20 per cent above the regular price.

IF FOR SOME REASON you have to return a suit to us, never return skirt or jacket alone; return both and we will be pleased to exchange the suit. Parts of suits will not be accepted.

No. 31R332 LADIES' WASH SUIT. Consisting of waist and skirt, made of percale and neatly trimmed with white cord and strips of white braid and three rows of white cording around the high standing collar; similar trimming on sleeves and in back; the waist buttons in front, the skirt is also trimmed with white cording and braid in front as shown in illustration and with one row of white cording around the bottom Colors, blue or oxblood. Price..... **(If by mail, postage extra, 27 cents)**. ... **$1.98**

No. 31R333 LADIES' WASH SUIT. Consisting of waist and skirt; is made of duck cloth; high standing collar and detachable yoke in front made of white duck in polkadot patterns, similar trimming bordering the front of waist, and all around the collar of the waist, plain black; this waist buttons in front; the skirt is trimmed with three rows of stripes made of white polkadot ducking and three rows of white cording. A very attractive suit and stylish looking. Color, cadet blue.
Price... .... **(If by mail, postage extra, 28 cents)** **$2.25**

No. 31R334 LADIES' WASH SUIT. Consisting of waist and skirt; it is made of a fast colored, striped pattern gingham; high standing collar and yoke in front made of white pique, large sailor collar bordered with white pique, bow in front of same material; full sleeves and narrow cuffs, the skirt is made with a graduated flounce and is trimmed with white pique; wide hem around the bottom. Colors, blue, pink or gray with white stripes Price........... **(If by mail, postage extra, 20 cents)**........... **$2.50**

No. 31R335 VERY STYLISH LADIES' WASH SUIT. Consisting of waist and skirt; it is made of tan colored grass cloth; the entire front of the waist is tucked and trimmed with open work embroidery, through which satin ribbon is drawn, similar trimmings around high standing collar and cuffs, full sleeves; buttons in back, skirt made with a graduated flounce trimmed in the same way with embroidery as the waist.
Color, tan only. Price..........**(If by mail, postage extra, 26 cents)**.. ..... **$2.98**

No. 31R336 VERY NOBBY WASH SUIT. Consisting of waist and skirt, made of very fine lawn in striped patterns; the waist is trimmed with wide lace in front, on sleeves and on the high standing collar; lace trimming in back forms a pointed yoke; the skirt is made with a graduated flounce trimmed with lace; this flounce is over the skirt, leaving a dust ruffle under the flounce; a very neat and most desirable suit for the summer Colors, black and white, and pink and white, striped pattern.
Price. ... .**(If by mail, postage extra, 26 cents)**................. **$3.50**

No. 31R337 VERY SERVICEABLE LADIES' WASH SUIT Consisting of waist and skirt; it is made of mercerized gingham in solid colors; the upper part of the waist is tucked all over and trimmed with two embroidered straps of the same material in front, embroidered trimming on sleeves, plain back; this waist is made to button in the back only, skirt has a double flounce and is trimmed from the waist down with embroidered straps of the same material. We can furnish in oxblood or light blue colors.
Price. .... **(If by mail, postage extra, 31 cents)**. **$3.98**

No. 31R338 LADIES' SKIRT Made of linen crash, full sweep.
Price .... **(If by mail, postage extra, 16 cents)**. **98c**

No. 31R339 LADIES' SKIRT Made of cotton crash; trimmed with blue pique in front; wide hem around the bottom. Good value for the money
Price.................. **(If by mail, postage extra, 32 cents)**.................. **89c**

No. 31R340 LADIES' WASH SKIRT Made of white pique; flounced bottom, trimmed with open work embroidery between the flounce and the skirt; wide hem around the bottom Color, white only
Price................ **(If by mail, postage extra, 26 cents)**................. **$1.25**

No. 31R341 LADIES' WASH SKIRT. Made of fancy polkadot duck; trimmed with two rows of white pique all around the bottom, forming three squares in the center of the skirt as shown in the picture. Color, blue with white polkadots only.
Price ....**(If by mail, postage extra, 28 cents)**................... **75c**

No. 31R342 LADIES' WASH SKIRT Made of white pique; trimmed with two rows of white open work embroidery; flounced bottom, wide hem; a very pretty design. Color, white only Price.....**(If by mail, postage extra, 26 cents)**.... **$2.95**

LADIES' TAILOR MADE

RAINY DAY OR WALKING SKIRTS.

GOOD FOR EVERY SEASON IN THE YEAR.

WE MAKE THESE SKIRTS from 36 to 43 inches in length and from 23 to 29 inches around the waist. Sizes larger or smaller than specified must be made to order, in which case we require 20 per cent above the price quoted in catalogue. IT TAKES ABOUT TWO WEEKS TO MAKE SPECIAL GARMENTS.

No. 31R346 LADIES' WALKING SKIRT. Made of gray melton cloth; twelve rows of stitching around the bottom; good value for the money; very servicable. Price ... ..(If by mail, postage extra, 52 cents.)...... **$1.98**

No. 31R347 LADIES' SHORT SKIRT. Made of black or blue melton cloth; seven rows of stitching around the bottom and three rows of satin straps; inverted plait in back. Price..(Postage extra, 60 cents)..**$2.35**

No. 31R348 LADIES' SHORT SKIRT. Made of pin striped melton cloth; flounced bottom stitched all around six times; this material is one of the newest things and we know that you will be well pleased with same; exceptionally good value for the money. Colors, black or blue with pin stripes. Price.. .... (If by mail, postage extra, 54 cents.)..............**$2.75**

No. 31R349 VERY GOOD VALUE IN RAINY DAY SKIRT. We make a specialty of this skirt, and we can positively say that it is the best value for the money; it is made of gray diagonal cloth, a cotton and wool mixture; flounced bottom neatly trimmed with hair cording as shown in the illustration; this skirt is well made in every respect with inverted plait in back. Price...........(If by mail, postage extra, 56 cents.)............**$2.98**

No. 31R350 LADIES' RAINY DAY OR WALKING SKIRT. Made of a very good quality of wool mixed diagonal cloth; graduated flounce all around the bottom; stitched twenty times around the bottom; wide facing of same material. Can furnish in dark or light gray. Price...............**$3.25** If by mail, postage extra, 40 cents.

No. 31R351 LADIES' RAINY DAY OR WALKING SKIRT. Made of wool mixed fancy striped cloth; made with a graduated flounce stitched several times around the bottom; these skirts are the very newest for this season and we would advise you to get one of these fancy, short skirts. We can furnish in blue and very dark green with fancy stripes. Price..........**$3.50** If by mail, postage extra, 36 cents.

No 31R352 LADIES' RAINY DAY OR WALKING SKIRT. Made of fancy striped cotton mixed cloth; flounce around the bottom with eight rows of fancy stitching; the top part of the skirt is stitched fifteen times with white stitching, giving this skirt a yoke effect; very stylish. We can furnish this skirt in black or blue with pin stripes. Price..(Postage extra, 53c)..**$3.50**

No. 31R353 LADIES' RAINY DAY OR WALKING SKIRT. Made of good quality melton kersey cloth, in black or blue colors; wide flounce around the bottom stitched fourteen times; trimmed with hair tucking, as shown in illustration; a very neat and plain skirt and serviceable. Colors, black or blue. Price .... (If by mail, postage extra, 52 cents.)... ..**$3.75**

No. 31R354 LADIES' RAINY DAY OR WALKING SKIRT. Made of a good quality of wool mixed melton cloth. Strictly tailor made, wide flounce around the bottom, stitched and trimmed with strips of the same material all around the skirt, finished with silk covered small buttons, inverted plait in back. Color, oxford gray only. Price...(Postage extra, 57c) **$3.98**

No. 31R355 LADIES' RAINY DAY OR WALKING SKIRT. Made with a wide flounce around the bottom, the entire flounce is stitched. Strap trimming cut out of the same material right above the flounce. It is strictly tailor made. Can furnish in oxford gray or brown. Price........**$4.75**

No. 31R356 LADIES' RAINY DAY OR WALKING SKIRT. Made of all wool, invisible checked material, graduated flounce around the bottom, and tucked over the flounce and stitched all around the bottom. The upper part of the skirt extends over the flounce and is stitched five times. Inverted plait in back. Colors, gray mixtures only. Price... ....(If by mail, postage extra, 47 cents.)..........**$4.95**

LADIES' DRESS AND STREET SKIRTS.

WHEN ORDERING please state the length of skirt, measured from waist in front to bottom, and number of inches around the waist, as well as the color you desire. Regular sizes are 23 to 29 inches around the waist and from 38 to 44 inches in length. Sizes different than these must be made to order, in which case we charge 20 per cent above the regular price quoted in catalogue. It takes about two weeks to make a special.

No. 31R360 LADIES' SKIRT. Made of figured Manchester cloth; lined throughout with black percaline and interlined at the bottom with crinoline; measures 100 inches in sweep. Color, black only.
Price, each.........(If by mail, postage extra, 31 cents). **$1.35**

No. 31R361 LADIES' SKIRT. Made of very good quality repellent cloth; flounce bottom, trimmed with one strip of black satin and one row of black satin piping where the flounce joins the skirt; only the flounce of the skirt is lined and interlined; the balance of the skirt has no lining at all, making it a very nice light weight walking skirt; bound with velvet. Colors, black or blue.
Price, each..........(If by mail, postage extra, 39 cents).. .... **$2.75**

No. 31R362 VERY NOBBY SKIRT. Made of good quality repellent cloth; neatly trimmed around the bottom with three rows of satin alternating with three rows of cording; lined throughout with percaline, interlined at the bottom; silk ribbon around the waist and bound with waterproof binding around the bottom. Colors, black or blue.
Price, each........ .(If by mail, postage extra, 42 cents)........... **$3.50**

No. 31R363 LADIES' SKIRT. Made of good quality repellent cloth; flounce around the bottom with three rows of black satin straps; three rows of satin strap trimmings around the hips showing the yoke effect, making a very stylish skirt; lined throughout with black percaline, interlined with crinoline at the bottom; bound with velvet; sweep measures 125 inches. Colors, black, blue or gray.
Price, each..........(If by mail, postage extra, 48 cents) **$3.75**

No. 31R364 VERY NEAT LADIES' SKIRT. Made of good quality all wool cheviot serge, with flounce around the bottom trimmed with black velvet straps as shown in illustration; silk ribbon around the waist; lined throughout with black glazed lining, interlined at the bottom with crinoline; bound with velvet; measures 125 inches around sweep. Colors, black or blue.
Price, each. .. ..(If by mail, postage extra, 47 cents)... .. **$4.35**

No. 31R365 LADIES' SKIRT. Made of good quality Sicilian cloth, strictly tailor made, flounce effect, tailored seams, silk ribbon around waistband, lined throughout with black percaline; flounce interlined with crinoline; bound with velvet; measures 125 inches sweep. Color, black only.
Price, each..... . (If by mail, postage extra, 42 cents). **$3.95**

No. 31R366 VERY ATTRACTIVE LADIES' SKIRT. Made of broadcloth; graduated flounce effect, trimmed with three wide satin straps; each strap is bound with black velvet; lined throughout with black glazed lining, interlined around the bottom with crinoline; silk ribbon around the waist; velvet binding around the bottom; sweep measures a little over 100 inches. Color, black only.
Price, each. ......(If by mail, postage extra, 47 cents). **$4.95**

No. 31R367 LADIES' DRESS SKIRT. Made of all wool cheviot, flare bottom, neatly trimmed with six rows of satin straps; lined throughout with percaline, interlined with canvas around the bottom; velvet binding; silk ribbon around the waist. Colors, black or blue.
Price, each.. .....(If by mail, postage extra, 48 cents).... ... ... **$3.98**

Ladies' Silk Skirts.

WHEN ORDERING, please state the length of skirt desired, measured in front from waist to bottom, and number of inches around the waist. Regular sizes are 38 to 44 inches in length, 23 to 29 inches around the waist. Other sizes than these will be made to order for 20 per cent extra. It takes about two weeks to make a special after we receive the order. If you fail to allow 20 per cent for extra size, we will make the garments and charge you with the difference.

No. 31R376 LADIES' TAFFETA SILK SKIRT. Made with flounce bottom, neatly trimmed with two rows around the bottom and three rows silk ruching on the flounce lined with good quality percaline, interlined with crinoline at the bottom; measures 115 inches around the bottom. Color, black only.
Price............(If by mail, postage extra, 32 cents)................**$7.25**

No. 31R377 VERY STYLISH LADIES' SKIRT. Made of good quality taffeta silk; is well finished and handsomely trimmed around the bottom with five rows of silk ruching and one silk ruffle which is also finished with ruching; the trimmings are the newest serpentine effect; the entire skirt is lined with a good quality percaline interlined around the bottom and bound with velvet; measures 125 inches around the bottom. Color, black only. Price............(If by mail, postage extra, 36 cents)................**$8.95**

No. 31R378 VERY NOBBY SKIRT. Made of fine taffeta silk; the top part of the skirt is tucked all over, as shown in illustration; the lower part is finished with graduated flounce; trimmed with five ruffles in front and eight ruffles in back; each one of the ruffles is finished with silk ruching, lined throughout with percaline, interlined at the bottom and bound with velvet; measures 125 inches sweep. Color, black only.
Price............(If by mail, postage extra, 50 cents)................**$10.50**

No. 31R379 EXTREMELY STYLISH LADIES' SKIRT. Made of a very fine taffeta silk, flounce effect; trimmed around the bottom with one wide strip of moire silk bound on both sides with silk ruching; two knife-plaited ruffles around the bottom, finished with silk ruching; the entire skirt is lined with soft finished percaline and bound with velvet. We can highly recommend this as a very good value for the money. Measures 115 inches sweep. Price............(If by mail, postage extra, 46 cents)............**$11.75**

No. 31R380 VERY NEWEST CREATION IN SKIRTS. Made of very fine taffeta silk, flounce effect; the entire bottom is made of black velvet, with scalloped flounces made of taffeta silk, trimmed with silk ruching; the flounce on the bottom is graduated, is very much narrower in front than in the back; the skirt is lined throughout with black glazed lining and bound with velvet; measures over 125 inches sweep. Color, black only. Price..................(If by mail, postage extra, 50 cents)................**$12.50**

No. 31R381 VERY NEAT LADIES' SKIRT. Made of black silk Peau de Soie; flounce effect, neatly trimmed with three rows of black moire silk, each row finished on both sides with black silk ruching. As you can see from the illustration, the flounce is graduated, as most of the very newest skirts are made. The skirt is made of very good wearing material and we know that you will be pleased with same. Lined throughout with black glazed lining, bound with velvet. Sweep measures 125 inches. Color, black only.
Price..................(If by mail, postage extra, 52 cents)..................**$13.50**

No. 31R382 EXTREMELY STYLISH LADIES' SKIRT. Made of high grade taffeta, finished with graduated flounce, which is trimmed with four double rows of silk ruching in front and eight double rows in the back part of the skirt. In addition to this there are strap trimmings, made of black moire silk running across the flounce, making it a very pretty design; lined throughout with black glazed lining and interlined at the bottom, bound with velvet; sweep measures 125 inches. Color, black only.
Price..................(If by mail, postage extra, 45 cents)................**$14.75**

No. 31R383 WORDS CANNOT DO JUSTICE TO THIS HANDSOME SKIRT Made of very fine grade Peau de Soie silk; this skirt is made in graduated flounce effect, as shown in illustration; it is trimmed all over with silk ruching, alternating with one row of cording made of same material, and also silk insertion which is not brought out well in the illustration; one knife-plaited ruffle all around the bottom, trimmed with two rows silk ruching; the top part of the skirt is trimmed in similar manner, making it a very stylish garment; lined throughout with black glazed lining, interlined at the bottom; bound with velvet; measures 120 inches in sweep around the bottom. Color, black only.
Price............(If by mail, postage extra, 51 cents)................**$17.50**

Ladies' Underskirts.

WHEN ORDERING PLEASE STATE THE LENGTH OF SKIRT, MEASURED IN FRONT FROM WAIST TO BOTTOM. UNDERSKIRT SHOULD BE ABOUT 2 INCHES SHORTER THAN THE OUTSIDE SKIRT. ALSO STATE THE COLOR WANTED

We make these skirts from 38 to 42 inches in length and from 23 to 32 inches waist measure.

No. 31R385 LADIES' UNDERSKIRT. Made of fast colored striped gingham; flounce bottom, finished with ruffle. Colors, gray or blue with white stripes. Price......(**If by mail, postage extra, 12 cents**)........**50c**

No. 31R386 LADIES' UNDERSKIRT. Made of mercerized percaline; flounced bottom; accordion plaited all around and finished with ruching around the bottom, made of same material. Colors, black, blue or cerise. Price............(**If by mail, postage extra, 14 cents**)..............**59c**

No. 31R387 LADIES' UNDERSKIRT. Made of good quality black sateen; flounced bottom, trimmed with two ruffles; very good value for the money. Color, black only. Price (**If by mail, postage extra, 15 cents**) **69c**

No. 31R388 LADIES' UNDERSKIRT. Made of mercerized percaline in black and white stripes; knife plaited flounce, trimmed with black mercerized sateen ruching around bottom. Color, black with white stripes only. Price.................(**If by mail, postage extra, 13 cents**)..............**75c**

No. 31R389 LADIES' UNDERSKIRT. Made of good quality mercerized sateen; large knife plaited flounce, trimmed with ruching of same material around the bottom. This skirt is exceptionally good value. Colors, cadet blue, black or red. Price...**89c**
If by mail, postage extra, 15 cents.

No. 31R390 LADIES' UNDERSKIRT. Made of a very good grade of black mercerized sateen; large flounce around the bottom, finished with three rows of cording and a knife plaited ruffle all around the bottom; the entire flounce is lined with black glazed cloth; this skirt is made of very durable material and we know will give satisfaction. Color, black only. Price.... **98c**
If by mail, postage extra, 20 cents.

No. 31R391 LADIES' UNDERSKIRT. Made of good quality black sateen; flounce around the bottom, finished with ruffle; the flounce is lined throughout with black crinoline; we know that you will be well pleased with the value of this skirt. Color, black only. Price.................. **98c**
If by mail, postage extra, 22 cents.

No. 31R392 VERY ATTRACTIVE LADIES' UNDERSKIRT. Made of black mercerized sateen, with wide flounce around the bottom, finished with a ruffle; the flounce proper is pressed, by a new process, to a fancy shape, making it very pretty and neat; of course, we cannot guarantee the shape of the fancy work if the garment should by accident get wet, but it will last as long as the skirt will if you keep it dry. Colors, black, blue, or cerise. Price...........(**If by mail, postage extra, 16 cents**)..............**98c**

No. 31R393 LADIES' UNDERSKIRT. Made of good quality mercerized sateen; wide flounce on the bottom, trimmed with six ruffles made of the same material. It is an exact imitation of a garment that we used to sell for almost double as much as we ask for this. The flounce is lined throughout with black glazed cloth. You will be surprised at the value when you receive it. Color, black only. Price......(**If by mail, postage extra, 28 cents**).......**$1.25**

No. 31R394 LADIES' UNDERSKIRT. Made of mercerized sateen; wide flounce around the bottom, trimmed with three fluted ruffles, each corded twice. This is a very showy garment and cheap for the money. Color, black only. Price..........(**If by mail, postage extra, 26 cents**)..............**$1.19**

LADIES' SATEEN AND WASH WAISTS.

Sizes from 32 to 42 inches around bust.
No odd sizes, such as 33, 37 or 39 inches.

WHEN ORDERING BE SURE TO STATE SIZE YOU WANT, ALSO COLOR OF THE WAIST. We can please you all. If you wish waists to button in back or in front, we have them. We state under each description how they are made, and that is the only way we can furnish them.

ALWAYS GIVE SECOND CHOICE IN COLOR AND STYLE.

THE MOST EXQUISITE STYLES IN CORSET COVERS ON PAGES 1065 AND 1066.

No. 31R406 LADIES' SATEEN WAIST. Plaited and corded in front; high standing collar of same material; bishop sleeves; six plaits in back. This waist buttons in front. Colors, black, blue and red. Price, each... .(If by mail, postage extra, each, 9 cents)...... **75c**

No. 31R407 LADIES' MERCERIZED SATEEN WAIST. Neatly trimmed with three straps in front and several rows of tucking; high standing collar made of same material; flaring cuffs; twenty plaits in back. Very good value for the money. This waist buttons in front. Colors, black, blue or red.
Price, each....(If by mail, postage extra, each, 8 cents)..... .. **98c**

No. 31R408 LADIES' HIGH GRADE WAIST. Made of good quality mercerized sateen, tucked in front with strap of same material; finished in a bolero effect; neatly trimmed with small buttons; high standing collar made of same material; flaring cuffs; bishop sleeves; plaits in back. This waist buttons in front. Color, black only.
Price, each....(If by mail, postage extra, each, 10 cents).. **$1.25**

No. 31R409 LADIES' STYLISH WAIST. Made of very fine mercerized sateen; yoke effect in front finished with an embroidered strap, as shown, and the yoke proper is tucked; tucking from yoke to waist; high standing collar made of same material; bishop sleeves; tucking in back. This is one of the newest garments shown, and is buttoned in the back. Colors, black or red. Price, each.. **$1.49**
If by mail, postage extra, each, 11 cents.

No. 31R410 LADIES' PERCALE WAIST. Trimmed with three rows of white embroidery; high collar, new cuffs. Colors, pink and white, blue and white and black and white stripe. This waist buttons in front.
Price, each.. ....(If by mail, postage extra, each, 8 cents).................. **49c**

No. 31R411 LADIES' STYLISH WAIST. Made of solid colored percale, tucking and three rows of embroidery in front; high standing collar of same material; newest cuffs; has six plaits in back. Colors, oxblood and blue. This waist buttons in front. Price, each.......(If by mail, postage extra, each, 10 cents)........ **69c**

No. 31R412 LADIES' STYLISH WAIST. Made of good quality gingham; neatly trimmed with white embroidery in front; high standing collar made of same material. This waist buttons in front. Plaits in back. Colors, pink, dark gray, blue and oxblood, with white straps.
Price, each..........(If by mail, postage extra, each, 12 cents).............. **75c**

No. 31R413 LADIES' STYLISH WAIST. Made of solid colored percale; high standing collar and detachable yoke made of white pique; large sailor collar trimmed with three rows of white cord; trimmed cuffs; bishop sleeves tucked all over; bow in front made of same material. Colors, dark or light blue and pink.
Price, each............(If by mail, postage extra, each, 14 cents)................ **89c**

LADIES' STYLISH LAWN WASH WAISTS.

We Furnish These Only as Described and Illustrated. We do not make these to order. Sizes in stock are 32 to 42 in. around the bust.

WHEN ORDERING BE SURE TO STATE THE SIZE AND THE COLOR OF THE WAIST YOU DESIRE.

These goods are subject to small changes in style, but only such that will not change the general appearance of the waist.

See our beautiful styles in Corset Covers on pages 1065 and 1066.

No. 31R433 VERY NEAT WAIST, made of good quality lawn. The yoke is tucked all over and finished, as shown in illustration, with open work embroidery; high standing soft finished collar, trimmed with the same material· new cuffs and sleeves; tucked in back. Buttons in front. Colors, black or white. Price.......................... **$1.35**
If by mail, postage extra, 14 cents.

No. 31R434 VERY ATTRACTIVE LADIES' WAIST, made of imported French lawn. The entire front is embroidered all over; high standing soft finished collar; tucked cuffs; new sleeves; double rows of tucking in back. This waist buttons in back. Color, white only. Price.................. **$1.48**
If by mail, postage extra, 14 cents.

No. 31R435 VERY STYLISH LADIES' WAIST, made of imported French lawn. The entire waist is tucked all over; two rows of lace insertion in front, as shown in illustration; high standing collar, also trimmed with lace; new sleeves. This waist buttons in front. Color, white only. Price...... **$1.48**
If by mail, postage extra, 14 cents.

No. 31R436 VERY NEAT LADIES' WAIST, made of white imported French lawn. The entire front is tucked, trimmed with embroidery, as shown in the illustration; similar trimming on high standing collar and cuffs; tucks in back of waist; new sleeves. This waist buttons in the back only. Color, white only. Price, each.......................... **$1.65**
If by mail, postage extra, 13 cents.

No. 31R437 LADIES' WAIST, made of high grade French lawn. Yoke in front is tucked and finished with embroidery, forming the low yoke effect; high standing soft finished collar, tucked same as cuffs; new sleeves; tucks in back of waist. This waist buttons in back. Color, white only.
Price, each..................(If by mail, postage extra, 14 cents)...................... **$1.75**

No. 31R438 VERY NOBBY WAIST, made of imported French lawn. The entire front is neatly trimmed with open work Swiss embroidery, alternating with tucks; high standing collar, tucked same as cuffs; several rows of tucks on back of waist. This waist is made to button in the back. Color, white only.
Price, each.................. (If by mail, postage extra, 14 cents).................................. **$1.75**

No. 31R439 LADIES' WAIST, made of high grade imported white lawn; very newest effect. The entire front is trimmed with open work embroidery and finished with Valenciennes lace; similar trimming around the cuffs· the front and back part of the waist is tucked; high standing, soft finished collar; newest sleeves. This waist buttons in front. Color, white only. Price, each... (If by mail, postage extra, 15 cents).... **$1.98**

No. 31R440 LADIES' WHITE LAWN WAIST. Fancy yoke in front, tucked several times, finished with hemstitching; yoke is bordered with Swis embroidery, and from yoke to waist it is made of open work Swiss embroidery; similar trimming around the cuffs; high standing soft finished collar with several rows of tucking; back of waist is entirely tucked and finished with hemstitching This waist buttons in the back. Color, white only Price, each......... (If by mail, postage extra, 15 cents)............... **$2.25**

LADIES' SILK WAISTS.

When ordering please state bust measurement, length of waist in back, inside sleeve length and the color you desire.

If you want any other color than listed in catalogue we shall be pleased to make it for 20 per cent above the regular price. If you fail to allow 20 per cent for extra sizes we will make the garment and charge the difference. Sizes measuring over 42 inches bust, 18 inches sleeve and 16½ inches length of waist are considered specials. It takes about two weeks to make specials.

Average postage on silk waists, 18 cents.

FOR VERY STYLISH CORSET COVERS, SEE PAGES 1065 AND 1066.

No. 31R446 STYLISH WAIST. Made of taffeteen silk; the entire front is tucked and trimmed with hemstitched straps, each strap finished with a buckle, nice standing collar, wide cuffs; three rows of tucking in the back; this waist buttons in front. Colors, black, turquoise blue or pink. Price **$2.98**

No. 31R447 EXCEPTIONAL GOOD VALUE IN LADIES' WAIST. Made of black taffeta; the very newest Norfolk style; strap trimmings in front forming a pointed yoke, and finished with tucking from point of yoke to waist; three straps in back from shoulder to waist; high standing collar; wide cuffs; the waist is lined throughout with cambric. Colors, black, pink or turquoise blue; this waist buttons in front. Price **$3.75**

No. 31R448 VERY ATTRACTIVE LADIES' WAIST. Made of taffeteen silk; yoke in front made of white taffeta finished with one strip of lace which is edged with silk cording on both sides; silk embroidery on both sides of the waist; nice standing collar; stitched cuffs; tucks in back from shoulder to waist; lined throughout with cambric; this waist buttons in front. Colors, black with black yoke and black embroidery; pink or lavender with white yoke and white embroidery. Price **$3.95**

No. 31R449 VERY GOOD VALUE LADIES' WAIST. Made of a good quality of taffeta silk; entire front is tucked and trimmed with straps of taffeta silk, each strap stitched several times, high standing collar, trimmed in a similar manner; tucked cuffs and several rows of tucking on the sleeves, five rows of tucking in back of waist; lined throughout with cambric, this waist buttons in front. Colors, black, turquoise blue or old rose. Price **$4.35**

No. 31R450 LADIES' WAIST. Made of fine taffeta silk. The entire front is embroidered in silk, as shown in the illustration. High standing collar with two rows of cording, wide cuffs and full sleeves. This waist is made to button in the back, silk button trimmings in the back of waist; lined throughout with a good quality of cambric. Colors, black with black embroidery, pink or turquoise blue with white embroidery Price **$4.75**

No. 31R451 LADIES' WAIST. Made of very fine peau de soie. This waist is strictly fairly made, five plaits on each side in front, finished with hemstitching and four rows of plaits in back, high standing collar with small flaps and narrow cuffs; full sleeves. This material excels taffeta as far as wear is concerned and we can highly recommend it. Lined throughout with cambric; this waist buttons in front. Colors, black, pink or turquoise blue. Price. **$4.75**

No. 31R452 LADIES' FANCY WAIST. Made of good quality taffeta silk; the yoke in front, which is attached to the high standing fancy collar, is tucked all over; fancy embroidery and gimp trimming around the yoke; the waist from the yoke down and on the side of the yoke is tucked several times; flaring cuffs and fancy tucked sleeves; five rows of tucking in back, the entire waist is lined throughout with a good quality of cambric, this waist buttons in the front. Colors, black, pink or turquoise blue. Price **$4.95**

No. 31R453 LADIES' WAIST. Made of a very fine quality of taffeta silk; yoke in front made of white taffeta tucked all over, fancy embroidery from yoke down all around the waist in front, high standing collar trimmed with two rows of cording; wide cuffs, full sleeves; this waist is made to button in the back; fancy button trimmings in back of waist; lined throughout with a good quality of cambric. Colors, black with black embroidery, red with white or lavender with white embroidery. Price **$4.95**

No. 31R454 LADIES' WAIST. Made of a very fine quality of taffeta silk; yoke in front is tucked all over, revers embroidered with silk; from where the revers meet to the waist instead of buttons we use silk cord lacing, high standing collar flares on both sides; soft rows of tucking in front, on the bishop sleeves and in back; flaring cuffs embroidered; this waist buttons in front. We can furnish in black, turquoise blue or pink. Price. **$6.75**

No. 31R455 LADIES' WAIST. Very fine taffeta silk; the entire front is made of white taffeta silk tucked all over, high standing collar neatly trimmed with taffeta silk strip embroidered on both sides; front of waist is trimmed with pointed silk straps and applique of white, and the collar of waist, fancy sleeves tucked and stitched, four rows of tucks in back from shoulder to the center of the waist; this waist buttons in front. Colors, all black, turquoise blue with white or pink with white front and trimmings. Price **$6.95**

All waists button in front with exception of No. 31R450 and No. 31R453.

...LADIES' WRAPPERS...

WHEN ORDERING please state your bust measure. These goods are made up and are ready for delivery. Bust measuring over 44 inches and sleeve length over 18 inches are considered extra sizes and must be made to order, in which case we require 20 per cent above the regular price. It takes about two weeks to make a special garment.

No. 31R461 LADIES' WRAPPER. Made of calico in striped patterns; neatly trimmed with braid on collar, on yoke, in front and over the shoulder flaps; flounced bottom. Colors, black, blue or red striped patterns. Price.....(If by mail, postage extra, 18 cents)................**75c**

No. 31R462 LADIES' WRAPPER. Made of percale; neatly trimmed with braid on collar and in front as shown in the picture; ruffle in front forming a bolero effect; plaited in back; wide flounce around bottom. Colors black, blue or red striped effects.
Price..........(If by mail, postage extra, 22 cents).............. **89c**

No. 31R463 LADIES' WRAPPER. Made of percale; neatly trimmed with fancy braid around the collar, on yoke, and around the ruffle on shoulder in front and back of wrapper; plaited in back from yoke to waist; wide flounce around the bottom; inside vest of white cambric. Colors, in black gray, blue or red patterns.
Price..............(If by mail, postage extra, 24 cents)............... **98c**

No. 31R464 VERY NEAT LADIES' WRAPPER. Made of good quality percale; trimmed with fancy braid and ruffles as shown in the illustration ruffles extend all around the back, forming a yoke; plaits in back from yoke to waist; wide flounce around the bottom; inside vest made of white cambric Colors, black, gray, blue or red striped patterns.
Price.............(If by mail, postage extra, 18 cents)...................**98c**

No. 31R465 LADIES' WRAPPER. Made of fancy figured lawn; exceptionally nice for summer, being very light weight; richly trimmed with ruffles over the shoulder, extending to the back; ruffles finished with fancy braid; similar trimming on the collar and belt in back and on the flare cuffs wide flounce around the bottom; inside vest made of cambric. Colors, pink, blue, lavender. Price. (If by mail, postage extra, 23 cents). **98c**

No. 31R466 LADIES' WRAPPER. Made of good quality percale; large collar finished with ruffle and trimmed with fancy white braid; similar trimming on front, which is finished with ruffle; same trimming around sleeves and collar; wide flounce around the bottom; plaits in back from neck to waist; inside vest made of cambric. Colors, blue, gray, black or red with fancy figures. Price. . (If by mail, postage extra, 19 cents) **$1.19**

No. 31R467 VERY PRETTY LADIES' WRAPPER. Made of fine percale; yoke in front is made of solid color percale to match the wrapper; is neatly trimmed with white braid on collar, in front and all around the shoulder flaps, which extend to the back; the back of this garment is made similar to the front; the back is plaited from yoke to waist; wide flounce around the bottom; trimmed with white braid; similar trimming on the sleeves and on the belt in the back; white cambric vest. Colors, black, blue or red fancy patterns. Price. ....(If by mail, postage extra, 18 cents)...........**$1.15**

No. 31R468 VERY PRETTY LADIES' WRAPPER. Made of fine percale; yoke in front made of white lawn; collar and yoke as well as the cuffs trimmed with white braid; shoulder ruffles extending all around to the back bordered with white cambric embroidery; plaits in back from yoke to waist; wide flounce around the bottom. Colors, black, gray, blue, pink or lavender. Price......(If by mail, postage extra, 17 cents).....**$1.19**

No. 31R469 LADIES' WRAPPER. Made of fine percale; standing collar trimmed with fancy braid; similar trimming in front, on strap reaching over the shoulders to the back and on shoulder flaps; pointed yoke in back trimmed the same as front; plaits in back from yoke to waist; fancy braid trimming on cuffs and on belt in back; wide flounce around the bottom; inside vest made of white cambric. Colors, black, red or blue with fancy figures. Price ....(If by mail, postage extra, 20 cents)...................**$1.19**

LADIES' WRAPPERS.

WHEN ORDERING please state your bust measure. These goods are made up and are ready for delivery. Bust measuring over 42 inches and sleeve length over 18 inches are considered extra sizes and must be made to order, in which case we require 20 per cent above the regular price. It takes about two weeks to make a special garment. DON'T FAIL TO GIVE BUST MEASURE AND THE COLOR YOU DESIRE.

No. 31R470 LADIES' WRAPPERS. Made of good quality percale, neatly trimmed with plain white cord and fancy braid on collar, on ruffles in front and over the shoulder flaps; collar and vest front are made of solid color percale, to match wrapper; similar trimming on back of the wrapper; plaits in back from neck to waist; wide flounce around the bottom; lined to waist with white cambric. Colors, black, blue or red. Fancy patterns. Price, each........................**$1.25**
If by mail, postage extra, 21 cents.

No. 31R471 LADIES' WRAPPER. Made of good quality percale; neatly trimmed with fancy braid on collar and on shoulder flaps, which extend from front to back; similar trimmings on cuffs, on belt, in front and back; pointed yoke in back with plaits from yoke to waist; wide flounce around the bottom; lined to waist with cambric. Colors, black, blue and red fancy striped patterns.
Price, each..............(If by mail, postage extra, 22 cents).............**$1.25**

No. 31R472 LADIES' WRAPPER. Made of fine percale; collar, ruffles in front and shoulder flaps neatly trimmed with black and white embroidery and fancy braid; similar trimming on the flaring sleeves and belt in back, the ruffles in front giving it the bolero effect; the ruffles extend to the back part of the garment; wide flounce around the bottom; lined to waist with cambric. Colors, black, blue and red fancy striped patterns. Price, each..........(If by mail, postage extra, 21 cents)..........**$1.35**

No. 31R473 LADIES' WRAPPER. Made of good quality percale; collar, yoke in front and back and part of the shoulder flaps embroidered with fancy cord; the embroidered part of the wrapper is made of solid color percale to match wrapper; lace trimming on the ruffle, around the yoke in front and back and shoulder flaps; plaits in back from yoke to waist; wide flounce around the bottom; lined to waist with cambric. Colors, black, gray, red or blue. Price, each...........(If by mail, postage extra, 22 cents).........**$1.48**

No. 31R474 LADIES' WRAPPER. Made of good quality percale, neatly trimmed with strips of duck cloth to match the wrapper, on collar, two rows in front, two around ruffles, which extend from front over the shoulders all around to the back; similar trimming on the back of the wrapper; plaits in back from yoke to waist; double flounce on the bottom trimmed with strap trimmings. Colors, black, dark blue, light blue or red.
Price, each..........(If by mail, postage extra, 26 cents)....................**$1.39**

No. 31R475 LADIES' WRAPPER. Made of fine percale in the newest designs; fancy braid trimming on collar and on yoke in front; two ruffles all around the yoke in front over the shoulders reaching to the back; each ruffle edged with fancy embroidery; fancy braid trimming on sleeves as well as on the back of the belt; wide flounce around the bottom; lined to waist with cambric. Colors, black, blue or red fancy figured stripes. Price, each..............................**$1.65**
If by mail, postage extra, 29 cents.

No. 31R476 LADIES' WRAPPER. Made of fast color sateen; ruffles around the collar and in front; neatly trimmed with satin ribbon around the ruffles and on yoke in front; similar trimming on the back part of belt; lined to waist with cambric. Color, black only, with black, blue, lavender or red color satin ribbon trimming. Please state color you desire in ordering.
Price, each......(If by mail, postage extra, 27 cents)..............**$1.65**

No. 31R477 LADIES' WRAPPER. Made of very fine percale in latest Persian effects; yoke in front made of white lacing; lace trimming around the collar, on the shoulder flaps and in front, as shown in the illustration; back of the wrapper is made the same as the front; similar trimming on the sleeves; wide flounce around the bottom; lined to waist with cambric. Very attractive and stylish looking garment. Colors, Persian patterns, with blue, pink or lavender stripes. Price, each....(If by mail, postage extra, 32c)...**$1.98**

No. 31R478 LADIES' WRAPPER OR TEA GOWN. Made of good quality cashmere; neatly trimmed with velvet ribbon on collar, around the yoke in front and two rows on the shoulder flaps, which extend to back, forming a yoke in back; similar trimming on belt in back; wide flounce around the bottom; lined to waist with cambric. Colors, black, blue, red or brown. Price, each...... (If by mail, postage extra, 31 cents)..........**$2.98**

DEPARTMENT OF MEN'S CUSTOM TAILORING.

The most elegant assortment of fine domestic and foreign suitings, trouserings, silk vestings, etc., ever assembled is what we have to offer our customers for this season, all at prices which defy competition. **We have gone on the theory the last two seasons that our customers want the best goods that can be had. The finest is none too good for our trade.** We are prepared to supply the very best and finest quality of goods that money can purchase. Our sample book this season is filled with fair sized samples of all wool and worsted cassimeres, cheviots, unfinished worsteds, thibets, etc., the best that we have ever been able to offer. We claim to be in a position to supply your clothing wants more satisfactorily than any other house. **We guarantee not only to make you perfect fitting garments**, but we go further and guarantee that you will be pleased with them in every particular. **We want your clothing business. We know that if you will send us but one trial order we can please you so well that you will hereafter send to us for everything you need in the clothing line.** There are people who imagine that it is very difficult to make up perfect fitting goods unless one is right on the ground to try the garments on before they are finished. A great many imagine that it is very difficult to take proper measurements. We know there are thousands of people who have never dealt with us simply because they are afraid that the garments will not fit when they arrive. Possibly you or some of your friends have sent away for clothing and received unsatisfactory garments. You say that one trial of this kind is enough. We know that it is no easy matter to make up satisfactory clothing. **We have been a great many years in learning the business.** We have been continually improving. **We are in a position today to say to anyone wishing a suit or other garments made to special order that we can positively guarantee to make you perfect fitting clothing.** All that we ask is that you follow the instructions given on our order blank. Give us your correct measurements, height and weight and we are sure that we can please you. Our system of detecting incorrect measurements is perfect. It is so simplified that in the thousands of orders that we make up it is seldom that we receive a complaint on account of garments not fitting. **Please bear in mind that in sending us your order we take all the chances. If the garments do not fit or are unsatisfactory, if the quality or color is not just what you expected to get, if for any reason whatsoever, no matter if the fault is yours,** the garment may be returned to us and we will either make new garments or refund your money including the transportation charges you have paid on the shipment. Do not let any excuse about wrong measurements deter you from sending us your order. Do not say that you cannot get your measurement taken. We supply you with all the necessary measuring blanks, instructions for self measurement, order blanks, tape measure, etc. Anyone can take your measure. Anyone who can read and write will take your measure just as accurately as the tailor who has been measuring all his life.

OUR NEW SAMPLE BOOK AND WHY WE ASK 5 CENTS FOR CLOTH SAMPLES.

Our low prices is the only reason. In order to quote you the extremely low prices we do, nearly all sampling expenses must be eliminated. We have learned by experience that thousands of people send for our sample book of custom tailoring merely out of idle curiosity with no intention of ordering. Some order the sample book just for the tape measure, others using the samples for patch work. Tailors all over the United States send for the sample book to find out what prices they must attempt to compete with, and children and other curiosity seekers go to make up the thousands who send for samples without any thought of buying. **If we or any other house furnish these samples free for the asking we must add this cost to the selling price of our goods and we or any other house who sends out broadcast free samples for the asking must add this cost to the selling price of every garment that is sold.** We would have to charge our customers for the sample book that we sent to him to order from as well as several of the sample books that his neighbors and friends might order. It is all added to the selling price and the buyer must pay the expense. We do not believe it is right asking a customer of ours ordering a suit or other garments to pay 25 cents to $1.00 extra to defray an enormous sampling expense for which he is not to blame. We believe that it is right to charge our customers just one small profit. **We make our goods in our own tailoring establishment, make them out of the best material that we can get, use good linings, trimmings, etc., throughout, make and guarantee them to fit and add just one small profit to this actual cost to make.** We believe this is the proper and only way to do business. The 5 cents we ask for our new sample book is all in the interest of the buyer, our customer. It is simply done that we may not be compelled to add many times 5 cents to the goods that you may order. It is simply done to eliminate all of these curiosity seekers and others sending for our sample book with no thought of buying. If you are a customer of ours, or if you intend to order clothing, we know that you will appreciate our position and will not hesitate to send this 5 cents for our sample book. You will save tenfold in the prices that we are able to make. On the other hand, if you do not intend to buy and merely wish to see our samples out of curiosity or for any other reason, we feel, in justice to our customer who does intend to buy, you should pay the 5 cents for this sample book and not compel us to get it from the buyer by adding this extra expense to the selling price of our goods. **For 5 cents, postage stamps taken, we will send our Sample Book No. 52R to any address, postpaid,** with the understanding that if you are not satisfied with the samples shown and prices quoted, that you can buy from us at much lower prices than elsewhere, if you are not satisfied that the book is worth many times the price that we ask, we will be glad to refund the amount that you paid for it.

DESCRIPTION OF THE SAMPLE BOOK.

Our cloth sample book for men's custom tailor suiting for the coming season has the largest, handsomest and most complete custom tailoring line of suitings, trouserings and silk vesting cloths ever presented. It represents fine, high grade custom tailoring at the actual manufacturers' cost for material and labor with but one small profit added. **Along with this sample book is included fashion plates, fashion figures, tape measure, rules for self measurement, complete instructions how to order, full and accurate description of each and every sample in the book,** everything made plain and easy for you to select just the style of garment wanted and insure your getting just what you want at prices way below the usual market value. Send for our sample book and you will get the biggest value for 5 cents you ever received in your life. You will get a book filled with the choicest and most elegant assortments of up to date suitings and other goods you have ever looked at.

DON'T FAIL TO SEND 5 CENTS (stamps accepted) **for our handsome, complete, money saving Men's Custom Tailoring Cloth Sample Book, No. 52R.**

HOW OUR CLOTHING IS MADE.

After the garments are cut, the cloth is passed to the trimmer, who cuts out and assembles the necessary trimmings and sends them with the material to the tailors, where the garments are made up.

Each tailor works only on his particular part of the garments. A vest tailor works on vests only, coat tailors on coats, and pants tailors on pants. They thus become expert in their part of the work.

After the garments are finished, they go to the presser, who presses them thoroughly. They are then sent to another examiner, who remeasures every part carefully, tests the sewing, and certifies that the garments are thoroughly well made, all buttons firmly sewed on and O. K. in every way, according to the customer's order. If correct, the goods go to the packer, who boxes them up ready for shipment. **Every order when received in our custom department is handled with great care and by a perfect system.**

OUR LININGS AND TRIMMINGS.

A good house will not stand wear on a poor foundation, neither will a good cloth, made up into clothing, unless good linings and trimmings are used for a foundation. **All of our coats are lined with a guaranteed quality Armitage or Rampion Mills Italian cloth, in color to match coat.** We guarantee all body linings to give satisfaction, and will replace, free of all expense to our customers, any defective or poor wearing linings.

To Whom It May Concern: New York City.

Messrs. Sears, Roebuck & Co. use very large quantities of our celebrated quality "891" black imported coat linings, dyed and finished by George Armitage, Bradford, England, also our Rampion Mills "New Finish" linings. All of the goods we sell them are fully guaranteed. Our instructions to them are to replace, free of all cost to their customers, any defective or poor wearing linings used in their Tailoring Department.

Yours very truly, D. H. ARNOLD & CO.

ALL OF OUR CUSTOM GARMENTS ARE STITCHED AND SEWED WITH PURE DYE SILK. NO BETTER SEWING SILK CAN BE HAD.

To Whom It May Concern: New York City.

Messrs. Sears, Roebuck & Co. have purchased of us during the past year large quantites of our pure dye machine twist for use in their Custom Tailoring Department. The goods manufactured by us are of one grade, namely, absolutely pure dye, and are made of the very best raw silk obtainable, the result being that while the expense of our goods is greater to them than the cheaper grade, the garments made with this grade of goods are bound to give greater satisfaction. Yours truly, HAMMOND, KNOWLTON & CO.

All coats are satin piped with Skinner guaranteed satin, have fancy sanitary arm shields, hand padded collars, double warp silesia pockets, best ivory or silk soutache buttons, silk tacks on all pockets, silk worked buttonholes. The inside work on our coats is where special pains are taken; a great deal of the work and material used in clothing is where you cannot see it.

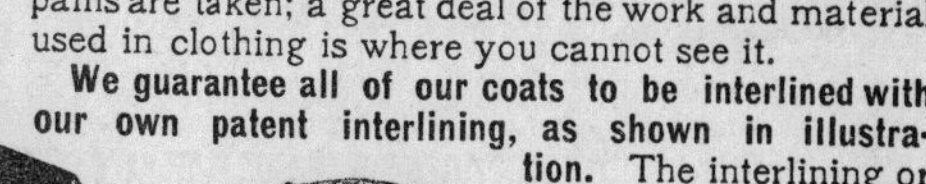

We guarantee all of our coats to be interlined with our own patent interlining, as shown in illustration. The interlining or coat fronts are made from linen canvas, haircloth, padding, wadding, felt and sheeting, all cut and quilted together in a regular coat shape; also taped all around to guard against fraying and insure lasting shape. Pockets are all double stayed with linen holland, also buttons and buttonholes stayed with three-inch strip of holland. A coat made up with our patent interlining will fit better, be more stylish and hold its perfect shape far better than any coat made by your local tailor.

For vests we use nothing but strictly high grade linings and trimmings; they are sewed throughout with silk and linen and we believe from our tailoring department we turn out the best made and best fitting vests in the city. **In our custom pants we use very high grade pants linings, facings and trimmings,** strictly high grade reamed buttons, sateen drill pockets, all sewed throughout with silk and linen, double sewed through crotch, guaranteed never to rip. If they do, send them back and we will replace with new work free of charge.

HOW TO TAKE MEASURES.

You don't know how easy it is until you try. Don't imagine because a tailor makes clothing that no one but a tailor can take your measure. Anyone can do it. **We take all the chances.**

If the garments don't fit you are not out one cent. We guarantee to fit and please you. If we do not, don't take the goods.

Our rules for self measurement are simple. Just follow the instructions given on tailoring order blank, or on back of general merchandise order blank, or, if you have no order blank, on a plain sheet of paper, give your measure, following printed instructions given below.

HEIGHT	WEIGHT	AGE
......ft......in.	............lbs.	..........years.

Stout or Slender ....

In taking measurements, the tape measure should be drawn moderately close, but never tight. To avoid error, take each measurement twice and write it in your order blank, before completing other measurements.

WRITE MEASUREMENTS CAREFULLY.

COAT MEASURE.

(A) All Around at 1 — **BREAST** OVER VEST WITH COAT OFF. .... inches

(B) All Around WAIST at 2 ....inches With Coat Off.

(C) SLEEVE from 3 to 4..........inches

(D) SLEEVE from 3 to 5..........inches

(E) Length rom Collar Seam 6 to Bottom 12........ ....inches

(F) For Coat Styles, 4, 5, or 6, also give length from 6 to 2... ..... inches

VEST MEASURE.

(G) All Around at 1 - - **BREAST** OVER VEST. .... inches

(H) All Around WAIST at 2..........inches

PANTS MEASURE.

(I) All Around at 7 - - **WAIST** WITH VEST OFF. .... inches

(J) All Around SEAT at 8.............inches

(K) From close up in Crotch to 9 - - - **INSEAM** .... inches

(L) From 10 to 11, OUTSIDE SEAM........inches

(M) Width of Pants at KNEE..........inches

(N) BOTTOM......................inches

Prevailing style for pants is 19 inches at the knee and 18 inches at the bottom, or 18 inches at the knee and 17 inches at the bottom.

FOR OVERCOATS.

TAKE SAME MEASURE AS FOR COAT OVER THE VEST ONLY.

EXTRAS.

The prices quoted under each description for men's suits are for suits in sack or cutaway frock styles, in what are termed as average sizes up to and including 42-inch breast measure for coat and 40-inch waist measure for pants. **All other styles and extra sizes we charge extra for as follows:**

For Suits or Overcoats larger than 42 inches and not over 50 inches breast measure - -	**$2.00** extra
Suits—Prince Albert Style, like style 6 or 8 -	**3.50** extra
Suits—Clerical Style, like our style 9 - -	**5.00** extra
Suits—Tuxedo Style, like our style 15 - -	**3.50** extra
Suits—Full Dress Style, like our style 7 - -	**5.00** extra
Silk or Satin Lapels on over or under coat - -	**1.00** extra
Full Silk or Satin Facing all the way down -	**1.50** extra
Silk Braid Binding on coat and vest - - -	**1.50** extra
Worsted Braid Binding on coat and vest - -	**1.00** extra
Silk or Satin Body Lining for overcoat - -	**5.00** extra
Silk or Satin Body Lining for coat and vest back	**5.00** extra
Pants larger than 40 inches waist and not over 50 inches - - - - - - - -	**.50** extra
Pants made broad fall style - - - - -	**.50** extra
Pants one-half or full lined - - - -	**.25** extra
Pants made larger than 22 inches at knee or bottom	**.50** extra

All Suits, unless otherwise ordered, will be made with single breasted 5-button vest, like Style No. A.

Extreme Extra Sizes—For garments larger than 50 inches breast for coat, or 50 inches waist for pants, we will be pleased to quote a special price on receipt of measurements and selection desired.

WE REQUIRE CASH WITH ORDER with the understanding that every garment shall prove satisfactory as to fit, workmanship and material. If for any reason whatsoever you are dissatisfied, the goods may be returned at our expense of transportation charges both ways, and we will either make new garments or refund your money, as desired.

YOU RUN NO RISK in sending cash with your order. Our reputation for honorable dealing is established everywhere. Read what our bankers say about us on pages 12 and 13.

For Men's Ready Made Clothing, take measure same as above, omitting measurements (E), (F), (M) and (N) which are only intended for made to measure garments.

To take measure for Boys' Long Pants Suits, Overcoats and Ulsters, for boys from 12 to 19 years, follow same rules as given above for men's ready made clothing. Remember, 34 inches breast measure is the largest size we can furnish in boys' clothing. For larger sizes make your selections from men's suits.

For Boys' Two-Piece Knee Pants Suits and Vestee Suits, Reefer Overcoats and Ulsters, for boys from 4 to 15 years, state age of boy and say whether large or small of age, and from our long experience we can guarantee a perfect fit.

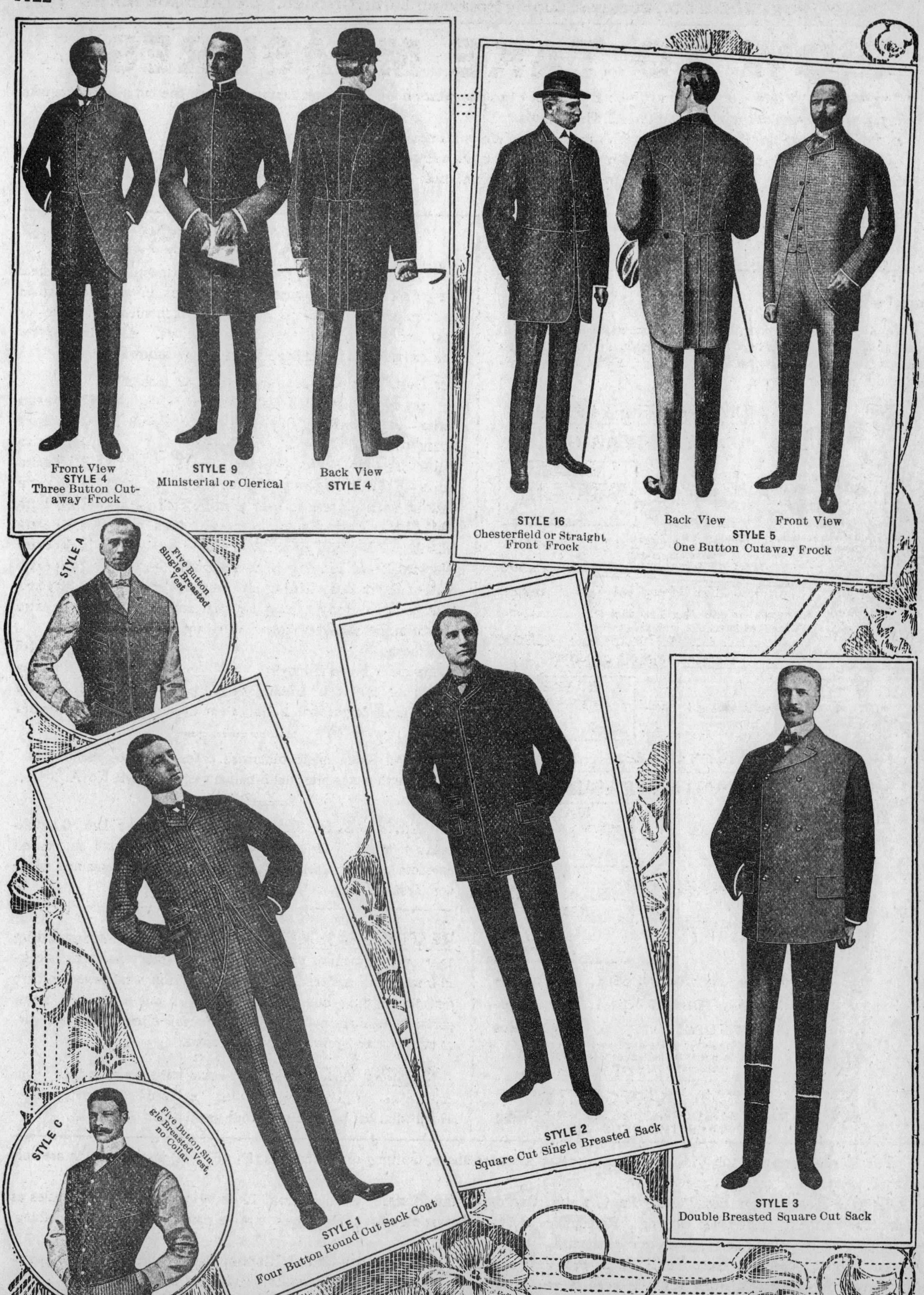
Front View
STYLE 4
Three Button Cut-
away Frock
STYLE 9
Ministerial or Clerical
Back View
STYLE 4
STYLE 16
Chesterfield or Straight
Front Frock
Back View
Front View
STYLE 5
One Button Cutaway Frock
STYLE A
Five Button
Single Breasted
Vest
STYLE 2
Square Cut Single Breasted Sack
STYLE 3
Double Breasted Square Cut Sack
STYLE 1
Four Button Round Cut Sack Coat
STYLE C
Five Button Sin-
gle Breasted Vest,
no Collar

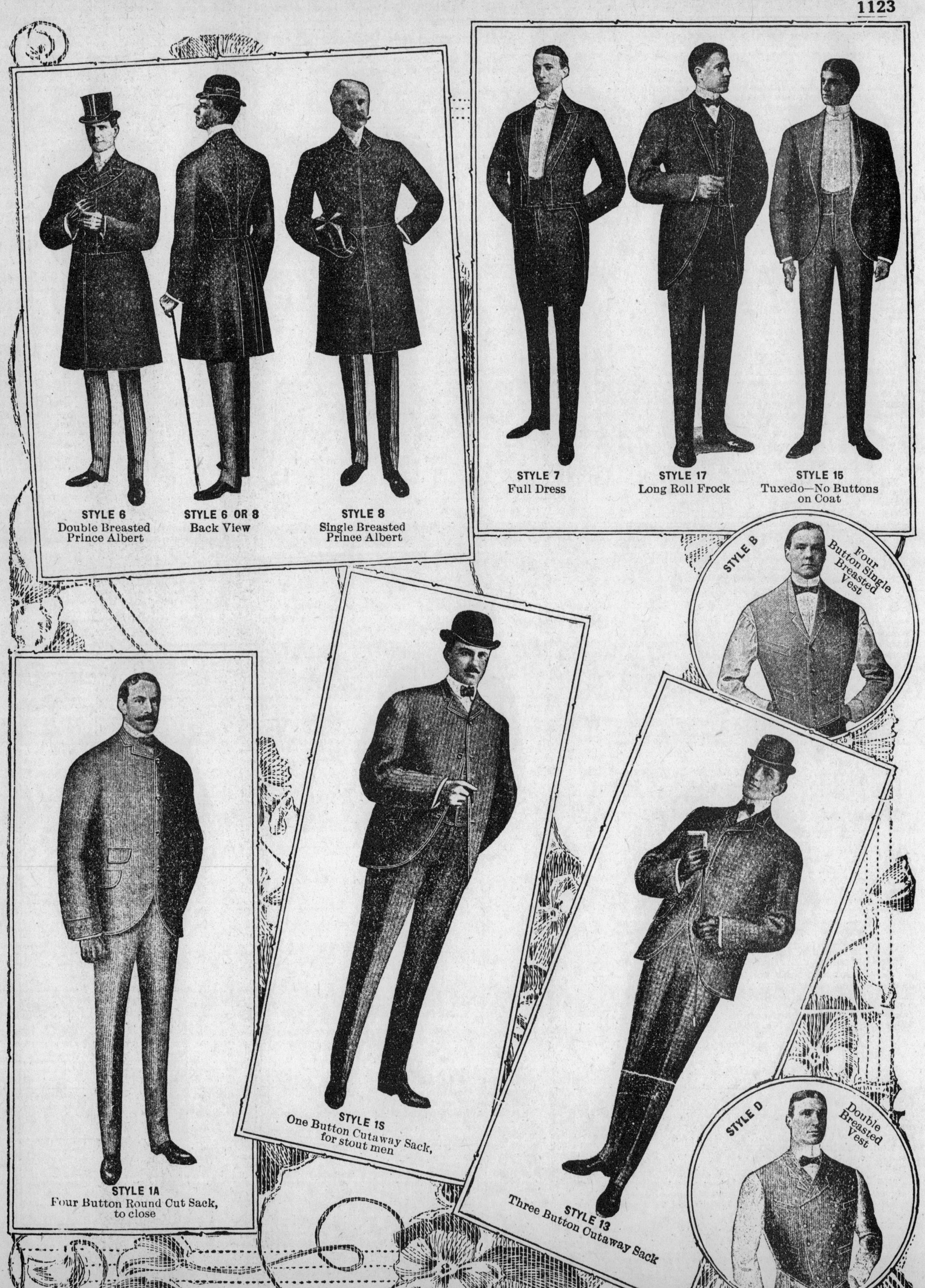
STYLE 6
Double Breasted
Prince Albert
STYLE 6 OR 8
Back View
STYLE 8
Single Breasted
Prince Albert
STYLE 7
Full Dress
STYLE 17
Long Roll Frock
STYLE 15
Tuxedo—No Buttons
on Coat
STYLE B
Four
Button Single
Breasted
Vest
STYLE 1A
Four Button Round Cut Sack,
to close
STYLE 1S
One Button Cutaway Sack,
for stout men
STYLE 13
Three Button Cutaway Sack
STYLE D
Double
Breasted
Vest

Beaver Brook Mills Cheviot, $7.50.

No. 13R2 Good weight all wool cheviot suiting. Dark navy blue background with an almost invisible overplaid effect of dark green; medium weight; will make a splendid dark all wool business suit. **Send today for our big line of custom tailoring suitings and trouserings.**

Price for suit.....................................$7.50
Price for coat and vest............................5.50
Price for pants....................................2.00

Send 5 cents in postage stamps for complete sample book and fashion guide of Tailor Made Clothing, No. 52R. One hundred samples, large fashion plate, tape measure, order blanks, complete instructions for self measurements and how to order. You save $1.00 to $5.00 more by sending 5 cents, as explained on page 1120.

Holmes & Co.'s Fancy Brown Mixed Cheviot, $8.00.

No. 13R4 This all wool fancy cheviot is one of our most desirable spring patterns. The colors are brown and tan with an occasional thread of dark green and light brown. Would be termed a brown mixed cheviot. The cloth is made especially for us out of pure wool stock; we know it to be the best wearing fabric ever made up in a fancy cheviot tailor to order suit at this price.

Price for suit.....................................$8.00
Price for coat and vest............................5.50
Price for pants....................................2.50

Is it not economy to send for our big assortment of samples when we can make to your order and measure the finest fabric ever woven at nearly one-half the price regular tailoring houses are obliged to ask? **Send today for our samples.**

Converse, Stanton & Co.'s Striped Flannel Suiting, $8.00.

No. 13R6 This striped flannel is especially for summer wear. The coat can be made without back lining if preferred; pants made with 2-inch turn-up at bottom, belt straps and suspender buttons on inside of waistband. The cloth is light gray stripe flannel and will make a most handsome summer suit.

Price for suit.....................................$8.00
Price for coat and vest............................5.50
Price for pants....................................2.50

For cloth samples of everything in Men's Custom Tailoring, send 5 cents in postage stamps for Book No. 52R, and by sending 5 cents you can save about $1.00 to $5.00 on a suit, as fully explained on page 1120.

Our sample book will show you a fine line of summer flannels, serges, cassimeres and new unfinished worsteds. You can hardly afford to be without this great money saving clothing book. **Send 5 cents today for sample book No. 52R.**

Converse, Stanton & Co.'s Flannel Suiting.

No. 13R8 This is the same as the above number, only the shade is a dark olive and dark green striped effect, in a medium sized pattern. The material is strictly all wool and will make a most handsome suit.

Price for suit.....................................$8.00
Price for coat and vest............................5.50
Price for pants....................................2.50

Olberman & Co.'s Brown Pin Check Cassimere.

No. 13R10 Dark brown all wool pin check cassimere, a very neat pattern, closely woven, splendid wearing goods. One of the neatest and most desirable shades and materials that we have in our entire line, just such goods as regular tailors use in $15.00 to $20.00 business suits. We could get more but we only ask our customers just one small profit, that is why it pays to get all your clothing from us. You cannot make a mistake.

Price for suit.....................................$9.00
Price for coat and vest............................6.50
Price for pants....................................2.50

You cannot say that you have bought intelligently if you place your order for anything in the clothing line before sending for our new, choice, **up to date samples for 5 cents, postage stamps taken. We send you our complete line of samples. Send for sample book No. 52R.**

Beaver Dam All Wool Gray Tricot Long.

No. 13R12 This number is woven especially for us by the Beaver Dam Woolen Co., of Beaver Dam, Wisconsin. It is the best all wool tricot cassimere in the market, a rich medium gray shade. A suit made from this cloth we guarantee for wear, color, style and workmanship and to equal in every way garments costing double the price elsewhere.

Price for suit.....................................$10.00
Price for coat and vest............................7.25
Price for pants....................................2.75

Extra sizes, larger than 42 inches breast measure, cost extra; also styles 6, 7, 8, 9 and 15; see page 1121.

Send 5 cents for our new sample book of tailor to order suitings, trouserings, vestings, etc. One hundred fair sized samples, tape measure, order blanks, rules for self measurement; everything complete. **Send for sample book No. 52R.**

Stanton 14-Ounce Black Worsted.

No. 13R14 We make to measure this all pure worsted 14-ounce diagonal cloth at a price against which no house can compete. Stanton worsteds are the best wearing black goods in the market; do not get dingy or shine, wears well, retains color and shape; desirable in any style.

Price for suit.....................................$10.00
Price for coat and vest............................7.25
Price for pants....................................2.75

Send 5 cents for our great assortment of samples, the largest line of foreign and domestic fabrics ever offered by any house.

Washington Mills' Gray Diagonal Worsted.

No. 13R16 This medium weight gray diagonal worsted is made by the Washington Mills; especially desirable for spring and summer wear; full 12-ounce goods, and a most excellent wearing fabric for the money.

Price for suit.....................................$10.00
Price for coat and vest............................7.25
Price for pants....................................2.75

Seeing is believing. We cannot expect you to believe that we can save you from $3.00 to $15.00 on a tailor made suit unless you see it. We are sure that our sample book will convince you. **Send today 5 cents for our assortment of nearly 100 choice samples of suitings, trouserings, silk vestings, etc.,** together with order blanks, tape measure, rules for self measurements, how to order, etc.

Ed. T. Steele & Co.'s Fancy Worsted.

No. 13R18 This is a medium weight, all wool worsted fabric, has a raised effect in a basket weave pattern. The color is plain navy blue. One of the handsomest fine worsted cloths we have been able to offer at this popular price. If you send for our samples you will be able to agree with us that this fine, pure worsted goods will make the best $10.00 suit ever shown. **Save time, and more money than time, by sending 5 cents for our big line of samples for made to measure suits. Ask for Book No. 52R.**

Price for suit.....................................$10.00
Price for coat and vest............................7.25
Price for pants....................................2.75

Dudley, Batelle & Co.'s Olive and Blue Plaid Cassimere.

No. 13R20 A medium sized plaid with an olive background and navy blue overplaid. This pattern is especially desirable for young men's wear, and will make a nobby spring and summer suit. One of the new plaid effects.

Price for suit.....................................$10.00
Price for coat and vest............................7.25
Price for pants....................................2.75

The choicest assortment of domestic and foreign suitings, trouserings, vestings, are all assembled in our big book of samples, all at the lowest prices ever quoted for fine, high grade, tailor to order work. **Send 5 cents for Book No. 52R.**

Parker, Wilder & Co.'s All Wool Black Thibet.

No. 13R22 Medium weight all wool very fine black thibet, smooth surface. Resembles broadcloth. Would make a splendid business or dress suit. We get thousands of orders for this particular goods, that is why the price is $10.00. Our customers help us to make low prices. The lower we can make the price and still furnish good goods, the better it suits us.

Price for suit.....................................$10.00
Price for coat and vest............................7.25
Price for pants....................................2.75

We buy cloth direct from the makers in such immense quantities that we get the goods at a very low figure, so low that when the goods are made up in our own tailoring establishment according to our customer's order, with just one small profit added, the customer has saved nearly one-half on his purchase. **Samples of these values can be had by sending 5 cents for our Book No. 52R.**

F. H. Holmes & Co.'s All Wool Gray Vicuna Cloth.

No. 13R24 This dark gray vicuna is very popular cloth for suits for spring and fall overcoats; a medium weight, smooth finished fabric, strictly all wool; one of the best vicuna cloths in the market; guaranteed for wear, color and general satisfaction.

Price for suit.....................................$10.00
Price for coat and vest............................7.25
Price for pants....................................2.75
Price for spring overcoat..........................10.00

For cloth samples of everything in Men's Custom Tailoring, send 5 cents in postage stamps for Book No. 52R, and by sending 5 cents you save $1.00 to $5.00 on a suit as fully explained on page 1120.

Your storekeeper buys where he can get the best goods for the least money, so do we; it's business. If you order your clothing where you can get the best goods by far for the money, you will become one of our many clothing customers.

Meek Bros. & Co.'s All Wool Striped Cassimere Suit.

No. 13R26 The cloth of this number is made by Meek Bros. & Co., one of the best manufacturers of popular priced cassimere cloth. A dark navy blue ground work and an almost invisible stripe effect in dark green, a cloth that we guarantee for wear, and will make a most handsome spring and summer suit.

Price for suit.....................................$10.00
Price for coat and vest............................7.25
Price for pants....................................2.75

When it is cheaper for you to have your clothes made to measure, made just as you want them, made to fit comfortably and shapely, all at less than ready made clothing store prices, is it not a good way to order from our big assortment in our Book No. 52R?

Washington Mills' Heavy Weight Serge.

No. 13R28 All wool navy blue 18-ounce serge. Positively the best all pure worsted goods ever made up at this price. Year around weight. Don't pay $12.00 to $15.00 for a ready made suit. You will be so much better pleased with one made to your measure for less money than the common kind will cost you.

Price for suit.....................................$10.00
Price for coat and vest............................7.25
Price for pants....................................2.75

"I never thought," said one of our regular customers, "that you really did furnish such wonderful value until I sent for your samples and see the same cloth sold in ready made garments by our local storekeepers at more money than you ask for made to measure." **Others who have never seen our sample book should send 5 cents for one at once.**

Hockmeyer & Co.'s Seal Brown Corduroy.

No. 13R30 Heavy weight seal brown fast color corduroy. Excellent quality of pure English dye. **Guaranteed not to break.** Cheap corduroys are poor values at any price. We guarantee this corduroy to wear and give satisfaction. It pays to buy from us, because we warrant everything to be exactly as represented. Any goods purchased from us that is not satisfactory may be returned for exchange or your money.

Price for suit.....................................$10.00
Price for coat and vest............................7.25
Price for pants....................................2.75

There is a deal of satisfaction in getting goods that fit, that feel comfortable the first time on, hold and retain shape, buttons to stay on, has style and finish characteristic only of first class tailoring. **All of this can be had for less money than you pay for ready made garments at your storekeepers. Send 5 cents for our big line of samples. "That tells all."**

Kennebec Mills' Fancy Worsted.

No. 13R32 This olive brown fancy worsted is a medium weight cloth, made by the Kennebec Mills. Olive brown coloring, with almost invisible over plaid effect in dark green. Will make a most handsome spring and summer suit.

Price for suit.....................................$10.00
Price for coat and vest............................7.25
Price for pants....................................2.75

If you could see a sample of the above number you would likely send us your order, if you were in need of a new suit, and when received, you would say positively that you had saved $5.00 on your purchase. **Send 5 cents for sample book today.**

H. Leavett & Co.'s 12-Ounce Serge, $10.00.

No. 13R34 This very fine navy blue 12-ounce serge is one of the best serge goods we have ever offered. At the price we make this material up it is without doubt the best value we have ever been able to give our customers. It is a very fine, diagonal, all worsted navy blue serge, especially suitable for spring and summer wear. Color guaranteed not to fade.

Price for suit.....................................$10.00
Price for coat and vest............................7.25
Price for pants....................................2.75

When you consider that we cut to your measure and make to your order a fine pure worsted serge suit for $10.00, using fine high grade linings, interlinings and trimmings throughout, guarantee to fit and please you, warrant the goods to wear, hold color, shape, not to rip, it seems to us that we should **have your order for at least a sample book showing what wonderful value we can give.**

F. H. Holmes & Co.'s Silk Mixed Cassimere, $10.00.

No. 13R36 This silk mixed cassimere is a medium weight cloth with a black background covered with a mixture of blue silk. It has a striped effect. One of the handsomest cloths for medium priced tailor made suits, we think out for this season.

Price for suit.....................................$10.00
Price for coat and vest............................7.25
Price for pants....................................2.75

It is so much more satisfactory to select the particular pattern and goods you like by getting our sample book and taking your own time and taste in making up your order. When your suit comes it pleases you much better than one from your local storekeeper who may talk you into buying what you do not like.

Riverside Fancy Blue and Green Mixed Worsted, $14.00.

No. 13R78 A decidedly handsome pattern in a dark navy blue and green and red mixture, a broken check pattern. We would like to have you refer to this number in our sample book, as it is positively one of the handsomest new worsted patterns out this season.

Price for suit.......................................$14.00
Price for coat and vest.......................... 10.00
Price for pants.. 4.00

The correct making of men's garments has been a constant study with us for many years; practical, careful, close investigation has placed us beyond the experimental stage in cutting, making and fitting. **You are bound to get satisfaction when ordering from us.**

Lebanon Mills' Fancy Striped Worsted, $14.00.

No. 13R80 In this number we show one of the handsomest late style goods ever woven. It is a dark seal brown color, with a herringbone stripe effect of alternating threads of dark green and seal brown. If you send for our sample book please refer to this number. We are sure that you will agree with us that this cloth is one of the finest and most desirable spring and summer suitings ever offered by us. All pure, fine worsted yarn.

Price for suit.......................................$14.00
Price for coat and vest.......................... 10.00
Price for pants.. 4.00

Puritan Mills' Fancy Shell or Mummie Worsted, $14.00.

No. 13R82 This fancy shell or mummie worsted is in olive and dark brown colors and is one of the newest and most desirable late style fabrics in our line, has an almost invisible over plaid effect in dark red. A hard twisted medium weight cloth, **especially desirable for spring and summer wear.**

Price for suit.......................................$14.00
Price for coat and vest.......................... 10.00
Price for pants.. 4.00

A visit to Chicago and through our departments of pattern making, cutting, trimming, tailoring, examining, sponging, etc., would convince the most skeptical of our ability to furnish just what we claim. The best tailoring possible to produce at lower prices than any other in the United States.

Kunhardt & Co.'s Electric Blue Serge, $15.00.

No. 13R84 This is the best electric or light blue serge we have ever shown; no better cloth can be had no matter what price you pay; will make one of the handsomest spring and summer (plain light blue) suits that you can possibly get. A very fine, thirteen-ounce, closely woven, all worsted serge, guaranteed for color, style and durability.

Price for suit.......................................$15.00
Price coat and vest.......................... 11.00
Price for pants.. 4.00

In our desire to furnish fine tailoring at the lowest possible price, we do not underestimate the fact that nearly everyone nowadays wants good goods and fine workmanship. **The prices we quote are seemingly very low, really one-half the usual prices elsewhere quoted, yet we make our goods up in the very best manner possible.**

Kunhardt & Co.'s Navy Blue Extra Fine Serge, $15.00.

No. 13R86 We have procured this season the very finest navy blue serge fabric made, because we believe that our customers appreciate fine goods. This best, all worsted, very fine, closely woven, guaranteed serge is a material that will give double the satisfaction over the ordinary blue serge materials.

Price for suit.......................................$15.00
Price for coat and vest.......................... 11.00
Price for pants.. 4.00

There is a distinctiveness in style, fit, and finish, a well dressed appearance about the man clothed in one of our made to measure suits, not to be had in ready made garments.

Fitchburg Unfinished Worsted.

No. 13R88 This is a very handsome, fine, unfinished worsted suiting, a dark green pattern with an over plaid effect of navy blue and a single thread of seal brown. Can be termed a dark olive green shade. This is a much finer cloth than is usually to be had except in the best city custom tailoring houses, such a suit that would cost you nearly double our low price. Send for our samples today and you will find, by referring to this number, a most elegant, fine, all worsted material. We know you will appreciate the quality.

Price for suit.......................................$15.00
Price for coat and vest.......................... 11.00
Price for pants.. 4.00

National and Providence Gray Worsted, $15.00.

No. 13R90 This is another very fine all pure worsted cloth. It is a dark gray, almost plain pattern with an inlaid plaid effect of a single thread of blue and green. If you appreciate fine goods, if you are accustomed to paying $35.00 to $40.00 for a suit, send for our samples today and you will find that we can furnish you a suit that you have been in the habit of getting at high prices.

Price for suit.......................................$15.00
Price for coat and vest.......................... 11.00
Price for pants.. 4.00

Greely, Cushman & Record's Black Granite Cloth, $15.00.

No. 13R92 This clear black granite cloth, sometimes called broadcloth, is a smooth surface goods, is good weight for year around wear, makes up in any desirable style and will give splendid satisfaction for wear. It is the best all wool plain granite cloth in the market. We make to your measure and to your order a suit at $15.00 which will compare favorably with garments costing from $25.00 up elsewhere.

Price for suit.......................................$15.00
Price for coat and vest.......................... 11.00
Price for pants.. 4.00

By our perfect system of proving measurements we can positively make you exact fitting garments. All we ask is that you follow the plain instructions given on our order blank and rules for self measurement. If you make a mistake we will detect it. **That's why we can guarantee to fit and please you.** Our expense in misfit clothing is next to nothing.

Puritan Woolen Mills' Fancy Worsted Suitings, $15.00.

No. 13R94 This dark gray Puritan Woolen Mills cloth is acknowledged to be one of the best fabrics woven, universally used by the very best city tailoring establishments. The pattern is a dark gray checked, the colorings are medium and dark gray with an almost invisible over plaid of a single thread of green. A handsome, new, up to date, all worsted fabric.

Price for suit.......................................$15.00
Price for coat and vest.......................... 11.00
Price for pants.. 4.00

We use the best canvas, haircloth, padding, wadding wool shoulder pads for interlining, as fully explained and illustrated on introductory page. All garments are lined with a guaranteed quality of Italian lining. We replace free of charge to our customers any poor wearing lining or material of any kind.

Chase Mills' Fancy Worsted.

No. 13R96 This is a very dark, handsome, hard twisted worsted, one of the finest worsted cloths that we have ever had made up for us. It is made especially for us by the Chase Worsted Mills in a dark, broken check pattern with a dark blue ground work. The small broken check pattern is made up of dark navy blue and green colorings. One of the handsomest high priced suitings in our line. We do not expect to get your order until you see our samples. Send for them today and we are sure that you will then send us your order.

Price for suit.......................................$15.00
Price for coat and vest.......................... 11.00
Price for pants.. 4.00

In fine goods we can give you such extra good value that most of our customers order suits at $15.00 and up. It's really the natural thing to do when one gets nearly double value for the money.

Navy Blue Pullman Cloth, $15.00.

No. 13R98 This is a good weight, year around, all wool, smooth surface, Pullman cloth flannel. This cloth is the same as is used by all first class tailors for blue uniform suits, for railroad employes and others desiring a navy blue suit. The color and wearing qualities of this blue cloth are fully guaranteed.

Price for suit.......................................$15.00
Price for coat and vest.......................... 11.00
Price for pants.. 4.00

Don't you think that you could select a pattern and color from 100 samples of the newest and most desirable late style suitings that would please you? The price will be less than you could buy the same suit for in a clothing store.

Hardt Von Bernuth & Co.'s German Worsted, $18.00.

No. 13R100 This is a clear black 18-ounce German crepe worsted. One of the finest imported suitings, usually to be had only in first class tailoring establishments at double our price. We would like to get your order for a suit of this fine cloth, as we know that you will appreciate the extraordinary value. This cloth is especially desirable in all styles. For full dress or Prince Albert suits it is one of the best numbers in our line.

Price for suit.......................................$18.00
Price for coat and vest.......................... 13.00
Price for pants.. 5.00

Wassell Borrough Extra Fine Imported Gray Worsted, $18.00.

No. 13R102 This plain dark gray fine worsted is the handsomest imported cloth we have ever offered. It is just such goods as you would pay $35.00 a suit, and upwards, from your local tailor. We make the garments to your special order just the way you want them made, using the finest of linings, trimmings, etc., throughout; guarantee a perfect fit at a price that should warrant your sending today for our samples.

Price for suit.......................................$18.00
Price for coat and vest.......................... 13.00
Price for pants.. 5.00

Bushendorff's Imported German Cloth, $20.00.

No. 13R104 Our finest jet black smooth finished worsted fabric is made from the purest Saxony worsted yarn, suitable for all seasons wear. For Prince Albert and all dress styles this is the finest goods you can possibly get, no matter what price you pay. Do not order a suit for forty or sixty dollars before securing our elegant line of samples, as you will save nearly one-half if you want a fine black suit by ordering this number.

Price for suit.......................................$20.00
Price for coat and vest.......................... 14.00
Price for pants.. 6.00

CUSTOM PANTS DEPARTMENT.

IF YOU COMPARE THE QUALITY OF MATERIAL SHOWN IN OUR SAMPLE BOOK FOR CUSTOM PANTS with similar goods offered either by other catalogue houses or your local tailor, you will be convinced that we are the house for you to deal with. Pantaloons cut to your measure, made to your order, fit better, wear longer and are altogether more satisfactory than ready made garments. When you send your order to us you are not only getting better value by far than can be had elsewhere, but the garments will be made to your measurement. No matter what price pants you order, the same care is taken in the making.

SEND 5 CENTS FOR OUR NEW SPECIAL SAMPLE BOOK, showing a fair sized sample of our entire line of suitings, trouserings, vestings, etc. The largest, most complete assortment of fine pure wool and worsted goods ever assembled. **All at prices way below the lowest. One trial order with us for clothing will convince you that our plan is the most economical, the most satisfactory in every way.**

American Woolen Co.'s Tan Worsted, $2.00.

No. 13R110 For $2.00 we make to measure pants from this tan and gray, medium weight, striped worsted, one of the best patterns in our line.
Price for pants.......................................$2.00

Hetzel & Co.'s Fancy Stripe Worsted, $2.25.

No. 13R112 A hard twisted stripe worsted. Dark gray background with alternate stripe effect in dark green and red, a decidedly handsome dark pattern.
Price for pants.......................................$2.25
50 cents extra for pants made larger than 40 inches waist measure.

Riverside Stripe Worsted, $2.50.

No. 13R114 This is a good weight dark drab and black stripe worsted, with single threads of red and green, suitable for year around wear, and will wear the year around.
Price for pants.......................................$2.50

Barrington Mills Worsted.

No. 13R116 A cable cord pattern, in dark brown, tan and drab colorings; a most desirable pattern in a medium weight worsted goods.
Price for pants.......................................$2.50

Washington Mills Stripe Worsted, $3.00.

No. 13R118 Very fine all wool worsted, black ground with stripe effect in light gray, and an occasional thread of red and blue.
Price for pants.......................................$3.00

Granadee Mills Worsted, $3.00.

No. 13R120 All pure worsted, dark stripe pattern in black and dark gray, with single interwoven thread in dark maroon. Price for pants.........$3.00

Light Drab Thornton Worsted, $3.00.

No. 13R122 A stripe effect in drab, with stripes of black, and interwoven single thread of blue. A handsome cloth for an all pure wool spring and summer pants. Price for pants.......................................$3.00

Clifton & Co.'s Fancy Worsted, $3.00.

No. 13R124 A most handsome pattern in hard finished worsted. A stripe effect of olive, dark blue, black and light gray. A dressy, splendid wearing goods.
Price for pants.......................................$3.00

Harrisburg Gray Hairline Cassimere, $3.00.

No. 13R126 Very fine all wool gray hairline cassimere, the same quality of goods that is used in $5.00 retail pants. We make them to your order for $3.00.
Price for pants.......................................$3.00

Black and White Shepherd Check Worsted, $3.00.

No. 13R128 This clear black and white shepherd check worsted is a fine worsted pantaloon cloth for spring and summer wear.
Price for pants.......................................$3.00

Washington Mills' Blue Black Satin Stripe Worsted, $3.50.

No. 13R130 All pure worsted, plain dark blue color, woven in such a manner as to give a satin stripe effect. Makes a well wearing dress pantaloon.
Price for pants.................................$3.50

Wanskuk Mills' Cable Cord Worsted, $3.50.

No. 13R132 Good weight navy blue cord stripe worsted, one of the best numbers in our line, very fine all pure worsted goods. Price for pants...$3.50

Clinton Mills' Fancy Worsted, $3.50.

No. 13R134 This all pure worsted, medium weight cloth is one of the nicest patterns ever woven; a dark stripe effect in dark blue, gray and olive.
Price for pants.................................$3.50

Herncliff & Co.'s Gray and Tan Stripe Worsted.

No. 13R136 A medium shade in gray and tan stripe with single threads of green and blue, medium shade, all worsted goods.
Price for pants.................................$3.50

Chaise & Co.'s Brown Stripe Worsted, $3.50.

No. 13R138 Most handsome shade of seal brown background, with a stripe effect in dark blue and drab, one of the best patterns in our line.
Price for pants.................................$3.50

Fulton Mills' Shepherd Plaid Worsted, $3.50.

No. 13R140 The finest and most desirable thing you can get for a real loud light colored up to date summer dress pant. A broken check effect in white, black and light blue, all pure worsted.
Price for pants.................................$3.50

Doffin & Co.'s English Worsted.

No. 13R142 Very fine quality pure worsted. English goods, black and drab narrow stripe effect, very neat pattern, will make a rich, dressy, splendid wearing pantaloon.
Price for pants.................................$4.00

German Worsted Pants, $4.00.

No. 13R144 The value we offer in this number can be duplicated by first class tailors at from $7.00 to $10.00. A black and white feather stitched pattern in stripe effect. Elegant fine pure worsted goods.
Price for pants.................................$4.00

Fitchburg Dark Stripe Worsted, $4.50.

No. 13R146 The Fitchburg worsteds are considered the best for fine goods by all leading tailors. This is a black and dark blue stripe, with a decided stripe effect of white.
Price for pants.................................$4.50

Fitchburg Gray Stripe Worsted, $4.50.

No. 13R148 This is another most handsome pattern in all pure worsted, a black and gray herringbone stripe effect, one of the best patterns in our line.
Price for pants.................................$4 50

Fancy German Worsted, $5.00.

No. 13R150 If you like fine goods in choice select patterns, you will surely admire this number, made from the finest worsted yarn. Black ground with stripes of white interwoven with red and dark green. The handsomest dark goods we have ever shown.
Price for pants.................................$5.00

Light Colored Fancy German Worsted, $5.00.

No. 13R152 This is a new spring and summer pattern, in a fine imported German worsted, a drab and olive shade with stripe effect of blue, tan and red.
Price for pants.................................$5 00

Our Finest Silk Worsted Pants, $5.50.

No. 13R154 Made from the finest silk and worsted yarn, a medium drab shade with stripe effect in light blue and green; the finest and handsomest pants cloth we think ever woven, usually to be had at the best city tailors at $10.00 and up.
Price for pants.................................$5.50

HOW OUR OVERCOATS AND ULSTERS ARE MADE.

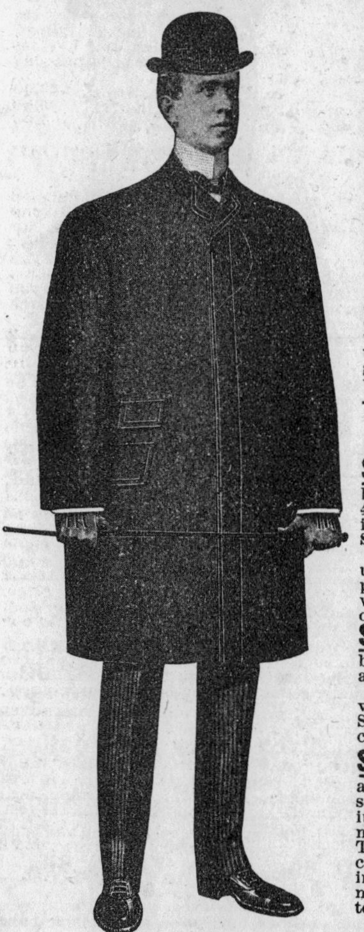

Style 10

OUR HEAVY FALL AND WINTER OVERCOATS are made in our special overcoat department. Our Custom Tailoring Department is divided into sections: One section makes men's coats; another section, vests; another section, men's single pants, and we also have a section for overcoats and ulsters.

OUR OVERCOATS are lined with a heavy double warp overcoat and ulster lining. They are padded, interlined, stiffened and stayed. The garments are all satin piped throughout: they are sewed throughout with silk and linen. We make all garments up in the very latest style. You will find a distinctiveness of fit, style, shape, workmanship and finish in our garments, such as can be had only from the very best city tailoring establishments.

OUR OVERCOATS AND ULSTERS are all made by expert tailors; patterns are all drafted by special mechanics, who draft patterns for overcoats and ulsters only. When your order is received for an overcoat or an ulster, the pattern is first drafted, it is then sent to a cutter along with the material, the garment is cut and trimmed; it is then sent to our tailoring department, and the coat is made up by an expert tailor, who works only on overcoats. We know that this plan produces more satisfactory results, and we are able to turn out a better grade of work, better fitting and more stylish garments than we otherwise could. At the same time, this plan reduces the cost to us, so that we can make the best garments at a lower price than other establishments, whose tailors and cutters work on all sorts of garments.

DESCRIPTION OF STYLES.

STYLE No. 10. Our Style No. 10 Overcoat is a Single Breasted, Fly Front Overcoat. We make these overcoats up as shown by fashion figure. They are made in any length desired up to and including 42 inches. Our price for Style 10 is based on an average length not to exceed 42 inches. If you want a coat longer than 42 inches it will cost you more money See Style 30.

All fly front overcoats in Style 10, unless otherwise ordered, will be made up with silk velvet collar, all seams double stitched, two lower and one cash pockets, two inside breast pockets. The sleeves of all overcoats above $10.00 will be lined with heavy guaranteed quality Skinner satin sleeve lining, body of coat will be lined with extra heavy black double warp Italian cloth lining.

STYLE No. 31. Style No. 31 is a Double Breasted Overcoat, as shown in illustration, on the following page. These coats will be made up in any length up to and including 42 inches. We base our prices on an average length not to exceed 42 inches.

Our Style 31 Overcoat, unless otherwise ordered, will be made with a silk velvet collar, all seams double stitched. Every coat above $10.00 will have Skinner satin sleeve lining, will be satin piped throughout, two lower and one cash pockets, and two inside breast pockets.

STYLE No. 12 ULSTER. Our Style No. 12 Ulster is a long, heavy Winter Overcoat. It is made exactly the same as shown by fashion figure. Has a large storm collar, it is cut double breasted style, all seams are double stitched, **unless otherwise ordered**; has two slanting ulster pockets, two lower outside pockets, two inside breast pockets. We make these ulsters up in any length desired, up to and including 52 inches. The average and proper length of an ulster is governed by the height of the customer who orders the coat. While we will make ulsters, as above stated, in any length desired, not to exceed 52 inches, at the price quoted, we recommend the following schedule of lengths, according to the height of the customers:

From 5 feet to 5 feet 4 inches.................46 inches.
From 5 feet 4½ to 5 feet 7 inches.............48 inches.
From 5 feet 8 to 5 feet 10 inches.............50 inches.
From 5 feet 11 to 6 feet 2 inches.............52 inches.

Style 12

Any ulster ordered longer than 52 inches in length we charge extra for, according to the length desired, at the rate of 50 cents per one inch. If you want a coat 54 inches long, it will cost you $1.00 more than our regular price.

STYLE No. 30. Our Style No. 30 Overcoat is long enough to meet the demand of those who wish an extra long overcoat. This coat can be made in any length from 44 inches and including 50 inches from collar seam to full length desired. It is made the same as our Style No. 10, only it is extra long If you want an extra long coat, longer than the length that we furnish in Style 10, or longer than 42 inches from collar seam to full length desired, order our Style No. 30. It is otherwise made exactly the same as Style No. 10.

Faulkner, Page & Co.'s Navy Blue Chinchilla Overcoating.

No. 13R156 Medium short nap, heavy weight, navy blue chinchilla overcoating. We recommend buying the better class of goods, but if you want an overcoat at $10.00 this is exceptional value and will give you perfect satisfaction Especially desirable in ulsters.
Price for overcoat, style 10.................$10.00
Price for overcoat, style 30 or 31.................11.50
Price for ulster, style 12.................11.50

Frederick Veitor's Heavy Weight Vicuna Overcoating.

No. 13R158 Popular plain gray shade all wool vicuna overcoating. Makes a handsome overcoat or ulster. Why we can supply you with so much better goods than anyone else is fully explained elsewhere.
Price for overcoat, style 10.................$10 00
Price for overcoat, style 30 or 31.................11 50
Price for ulster, style 12.................11.50

Style 30

Washington Mills' All Pure Wool Black Kersey.

No. 13R160 Very smooth finished heavy weight Washington Mills' Jet Black Kersey; regular $15.00 value, and $5.00 is what you will save if you order this number.
Price for overcoat, style 10....................$10.00
Price for overcoat, style 30 or 31....................11.50
Price for ulster, style 12....................11.50

Domerich & Co.'s All Wool Seal Brown Kersey Overcoating.

No. 13R162 Greatest value we have ever offered in seal brown heavy weight smooth finished kersey overcoating. This cloth will cost the average tailor more than we ask you for the garments made up specially to order. You would not hesitate to send us your order and advise your friends to do so if you could but see a sample of this fine material.
Price for overcoat, style 10....................$10.00
Price for overcoat, style 30 or 31....................11.50
Price for ulster, style 12....................11.50

Metcalf Bros. & Co.'s Fine All Wool Navy Blue Kersey Overcoating.

No. 13R164 28-ounce all wool very fine navy blue kersey overcoating, smooth finished, elegant fabric; will make to your special order; all seams double stitched; lined with double warp Italian cloth; is trimmed first class and guaranteed in every way.
Price for overcoat, style 10....................$10.00
Price for overcoat, style 30 or 31....................11.50
Price for ulster, style 12....................11.50
$2.00 extra for overcoat or ulster if breast measure is over 42 inches.

Wendell Fay & Co.'s Extra Fine Black Kersey Overcoating.

No. 13R168 Heavy weight jet black smooth finished kersey overcoating. Considered one of the best fabrics on the market; used extensively in all first class tailoring establishments. To be convinced that you cannot procure similar goods, even in ready made overcoats for less than from $15.00 to $18.00, send for our samples and compare the material with any offered by other houses, and then we know we will get your order.
Price for overcoat, style 10....................$12.00
Price for overcoat, style 30 or 31....................13.50
Price for ulster, style 12....................13.50

Washington Mills' All Wool Tan Kersey Overcoating.

No. 13R170 This is an elegant, handsome, smooth finished, all wool, heavy weight, tan kersey over coating. Never before have we been able to offer such values. That's why we especially desire you to send for our samples, and be fully convinced that we can save you nearly one-half on this fine material.
Price for overcoat, style 10....................$12.00
Price for overcoat, style 30 or 31....................13.50
Price for ulster, style 12....................13.50

Carr & Co.'s Black Kersey Overcoating.

No. 13R172 Nothing better in kersey overcoating than this closely woven, smooth finished, heavy weight black kersey. Ask your local tailor the price of it, and send for our samples and compare the quality of this cloth with what he has offered from $30.00 to $35.00.
Price for overcoat, style 10....................$15.00
Price for overcoat, style 30 or 31....................17.00
Price for ulster, style 12....................17.00

Style 31

Worumbo Oxford Gray Chinchilla.

No. 13R174 We hear a great deal about it, we mean the Worumbo Chinchilla; every one talks about this chinchilla, because they know it is the highest grade chinchilla overcoating made. Your local dealer will tell you the price is high, but the goods is such excellent quality that it will pay to buy the Worumbo in the long run. **How about our price?** You can settle that by sending for our sample book today and be fully convinced that we are offering you the genuine Worumbo chinchilla at about one-half the usual price.
Price for overcoat, style 10....................$15.00
Price for overcoat, style 30 or 31....................17.00
Price for ulster, style 12....................17.00

Carr & Co.'s Seal Brown Kersey Overcoating.

No. 13R176 This Kersey Cloth has a world wide reputation, and if it was not the best kersey woven it could not keep up this reputation. When we receive your order the coat will be made specially fine, lined throughout with excellent quality double warp Italian cloth, heavy satin sleeve lining, made up with the best interlining throughout.
Price for overcoat, style 10....................$15.00
Price for overcoat, style 30 or 31....................17.00
Price for ulster, style 12....................17.00

Wanskuk Dark Gray Oxford Overcoating.

No. 13R180 Plain, dark gray shade, with an almost invisible herringbone stripe effect. If you are in the habit of paying from $35.00 to $50.00 for suits or overcoats, it certainly will pay you to send to us for our sample book; we believe you will like this number. By comparing the quality of the goods with the best to be had elsewhere, we believe that you will send us your order, and you will agree with us that we can save you about one-half on your purchase.
Price for pea jacket and vest, style 32....................$18.00
Price for overcoat, style 10....................18.00
Price for overcoat, style 30 or 31....................20.00
Price for ulster, style 12....................20.00

FANCY IMPORTED WHITE AND FANCY SILK VESTING.

WE DO NOT HAVE FANCY SILK VESTS OR WHITE VESTS READY MADE, but make them to special order in any style that may be desired. It is far more satisfactory to have a fancy or white vest made to your order because the vests will be better made, they will fit you perfectly and give much more general satisfaction than if you bought from ready made stock. We are in a position to furnish fancy silk and white vests made to your own measure at even lower prices than the same grade of goods are usually retailed in the best clothing stores.

Tan and White Figured Imported Dimity Vesting.

No. 13R181 A new wash fabric, very popular for fancy vests. The color is guaranteed absolutely fast. The ground work of this material is of a tan shade covered with white diamond shaped figures; a very neat design.
Price for men's single breasted vest....................$1.25
Price for men's double breasted vest....................1.75

Men's White Basket Weave Washable Vesting.

No. 13R182 This number we make from a nearly plain white heavy basket weave dimity, an all white ground work with raised effect, covered with pin head coloring in dark navy blue. Will make a handsome summer dress vest.
Price for men's single breasted vest....................$1.50
Price for men's double breasted vest....................2.00

Men's Olive Green Basket Weave Vesting.

No. 13R183 This is one of the new spring patterns in an olive green shade covered with small silk figures in black about half an inch apart. If you want one of the newest things out in a nobby, up to date, made to order vest, order this number.
Price for men's single breasted vest....................$1.75
Price for men's double breasted vest....................2.25

Men's Clear White Basket Weave Worsted Vesting.

No. 13R184 This is a heavy basket weave worsted vesting in clear white. It is a handsome fabric, has the appearance of white silk, a cloth that can be washed and will retain finish and shape.
Price for men's single breasted vest....................$2.00
Price for men's double breasted vest....................2.50

Tan Basket Weave Worsted Vesting.

No. 13R186 One of the nobbiest and newest patterns out for spring and summer wear, a tan, basket weave worsted wash cloth with an almost invisible black pin head raised effect.
Price for men's single breasted vest....................$2.00
Price for men's double breasted vest....................2.50

Fancy Silk Vesting.

No. 13R188 This number is a regular fancy silk and worsted vesting. The color is black ground work covered with small raised figures in dark green, red and blue, a decidedly clear and handsome pattern.
Price for men's single breasted vest....................$1.50
Price for men's double breasted vest....................2.00

GIVE CATALOGUE NUMBER IN FULL WHEN YOU WRITE YOUR ORDER

Red and Black Fancy Silk Vesting.

No. 13R190 Made from red and black fancy silk vesting. The ground work is black covered with small pin head dots in red. A desirable, neat pattern, which will make a handsome silk dress vest.
Price for men's single breasted vest....................$1.75
Price for men's double breasted vest....................2.25

Black and Green Fancy Silk Vesting.

No. 13R192 This number is one of the newest spring and summer patterns. It is a black and green ground work covered with small figures in red and olive green, one of the best numbers in our line.
Price for men's single breasted vest....................$2.00
Price for men's double breasted vest....................2.50

Black and Blue Fancy Silk Vesting.

No. 13R194 This is a heavy quality of silk vesting, nearly all black with raised figures of the same color set off with a single coloring in light blue in pin head effect. Vests of this quality are usually retailed at $5.00 and up. We make them to your special order and measure.
Price for men's single breasted vest....................$2.25
Price for men's double breasted vest....................2.75

Men's Fancy Silk Vesting.

No. 13R196 This is one of the finest silk vestings we have. It has a black ground work covered with pure silk figures in black and lavender colorings in satin effect.
Price for men's single breasted vest....................$2.50
Price for men's double breasted vest....................3.00

READY TO WEAR CLOTHING DEPARTMENT.

Men's Ready to Wear Clothing Department

We started a factory two years ago to make ready made clothing. In this factory we make all of our men's and boys' ready made garments. Previous to this time we were in the habit of buying ready made clothing from large manufacturers at the lowest price possible. We found this to be very unsatisfactory and, by starting a factory of our own, **that we could offer to our customers superior made garments at much less price than we were obliged to pay other wholesale houses.** We found that we could take advantage of the market in many instances and procure large quantities of piece goods at way below the market price. When we started our clothing factory we were determined to furnish such value in honest ready made garments as could be had from no other concern. We were determined to make the price so low, consistent with first class workmanship, that our customers could buy from us at very much less price than clothiers or wholesale dealers own their goods. From the very start we have been successful. Our factory has been running to its full capacity, and we are to day turning out a class of goods much superior to anything that we have heretofore been able to furnish. We are to day in a position to furnish you well made ready made garments at about one-half the price similar goods can be obtained for elsewhere. If you send us your order you are sure of getting just what we advertise. You are sure of getting as good value for $5.00 as you would get elsewhere ordinarily for $10.00. Our new present season's line of ready to wear clothing is larger than ever before. We have purchased the goods in immense quantities, and will be able to fill your order promptly, and furnish you just the size that you desire. We solicit your orders with the understanding that the goods will be even better than our representations, or you can return them to us at our expense and we will cheerfully refund your money.

TERMS.

We require cash in full with order. We guarantee to save you money, we guarantee to fit and please you in every way. If the goods prove unsatisfactory when received, return them at our expense and your money will be refunded. We take all the chances.

SIZES AND STYLES.

We make ready to wear clothing only in what are termed as regular sizes. All coats, overcoats and ulsters are made in sizes from 34 to 42 inches breast measure; **no larger or smaller sizes can be had.** Pants are made in sizes from 30 to 40 inches waist measure and from 29 to 36 inches inside seam measure. No larger than 40 inches waist measure, no smaller than 30 inches waist measure, no shorter than 29 inches inseam measure, no longer than 36 inches inseam measure can be had in ready made pants.

All our ready to wear clothing coats are made in round cut sack style, only, as shown by the illustration, opposite each catalogue description. Our ready made overcoats are made in single breasted style, fly front, velvet collar, cut on an average of 40 inches in length. We cannot furnish overcoats longer than 40 inches in our ready made stock. Men's ready made ulsters are cut only in regular sizes from 34 to 42 inches breast measure; they have a large storm collar, two sliding ulster pockets, two lower outside pockets, are cut on an average of 50 inches in length. We cannot furnish ready made ulsters any longer than 50 inches. Do not order any larger or smaller sizes or any other styles than we have described above, as we will have to delay your order. If you desire any different style or size, or if you are very tall or very stout, or particularly hard to fit for any reason whatsoever, it will be better for you to order from our custom tailoring department.

OUR GUARANTEE. If our clothing is not as good or better than you have a right to expect from our samples or descriptions, if it is not better made and a better fit for less money than you can get the same grade elsewhere, if it is not perfectly satisfactory in every respect, we ask you to send it back at our expense of charges both ways and **WE WILL REFUND ALL YOUR MONEY.**

How Our Ready to Wear Clothing is Made.

In making up our ready to wear clothing, we aim to produce the neatest and most substantial garments possible. They are cut, made and trimmed in the latest prevailing style, all coats made in round cut sack style, lined with a good quality of Italian cloth; sateen sleeve lining. All coats are single stitched have broad inside facings, two outside lower pockets, two inside pockets and one change pocket. Vests are made single breasted, five buttons and notched collar. Pants can be furnished with top or side pockets (state kind wanted); they have two hip pockets, one watch pocket, and patent never come off buttons. Pants are cut according to the prevailing style worn this season, which is 18 inches at knee and 17 inches at the bottom for the smaller waists and 19 inches at knee and 18 inches at bottom for the larger sizes. Do not order pants larger at the knee or bottom than as above, as we cannot furnish them. Our overcoats and ulsters are made in the prevailing style. The body and sleeves are lined with good qualtity black Italian cloth; coats are interlined with good quality canvas, well stayed, trimmed and finished first class throughout. All our ready made garments are made over the most perfect fitting patterns, and will fit better and retain their perfect shape longer than the average ready made garments to be had elsewhere.

HOW TO ORDER.

When ordering ready made clothing, our custom tailoring order blank can be used if at hand. If you have no order blank carefully take the following measurements and write them on a sheet of paper:

COAT MEASURE. Number of inches all the way around the breast over the vest and close up under the arms and over the shoulder blades with coat off.......inches. Length of sleeve from center of back and to the elbow and then full length desired to the wrist........inches.

NOTE—Take the sleeve measure with coat on, tracing the arm and bending the elbow.

VEST MEASURE. Same measure as for coat......inches.

PANTS MEASURE. Number of inches around body at waist......inches.

NOTE—Take this measure over the waistband of pants you are wearing.

Length of leg from close up in crotch to heel of shoe....... inches. These are all the measurements necessary to insure a perfect fitting suit, but to further guide us in selecting the proper size be sure to state your correct height and weight.

OVERCOAT OR ULSTER MEASUREMENTS. Number of inches all the way around the breast close up under the arms over the shoulder blades with under coat off............inches. Length of sleeve from center of back to the elbow and then to the wrist with under coat on............inches.

NOTE—Be sure to take overcoat measurements with under coat off, as a 38-inch overcoat is larger than a 38-inch under coat, and we desire your correct measurements all the way around the breast with under coat off.

OUR CLOTH SAMPLE BOOK OF MEN'S READY MADE CLOTHING.

We issue a sample booklet which contains a fair sized cloth sample of everything we handle in Men's Ready Made Clothing, including suits, trousers, overcoats and ulsters.

This sample book contains in addition to cloth samples, tape measure, fashion figures, order blanks, simple rules for self-measurement, instructions how to order, etc.

FOR 5 CENTS (postage stamps taken), this cloth sample book No. 56R will be sent to any address by mail postpaid.

We ask 5 cents in postag stamps fcr this cloth sample book wholly in the interest ol cur customers. By asking 5 cents in postage stamps to defray the expense, we save the cost of the thousands of sample books that are sent out to children, curiosity seekers and others who have no thought of buying, all of which expense other houses are compelled to add to their selling price. In other words, the house that furnishes samples free to everyone must add from 50 cents to $1.00 to the selling price of every suit to cover this cost.

We save you all this, and you pay us only the cost of material and labor with but our one small percentage of profit added, and not one penny figured for sampling expenses.

No. 45R200

Jacob Wendall & Co.'s All Wool Dark Cheviot Ready Made Suit, $4.50.

No. 45R200 This suit is made from a very dark gray almost black mixed all wool cheviot, in round cut sack style only. It is the best suit for $4.50 ever offered by us or any other house. We make all of our ready made suits in our own factory. We purchase all of the material, linings, etc., in very large quantities at the lowest spot cash prices and offer the finished garments to our customers at the actual cost to make, with but one small profit added. This suit is well made and well trimmed. We do not use cheap trimmings or shoddy material. The opposite illustration is an exact reproduction of the suit. You will get positively the best value ever offered. There is a saving to everyone who buys this suit of at least $3.00 per suit.

Price for men's suit, style 1 only........ ....**$4.50**
Price for coat and vest.... **3.00**
Price for pants........... **1.50**

Schaffer & Co.'s All Wool Fancy Cheviot Suit, $5.00.

No. 45R204 This suit is made from a medium weight all wool fancy cheviot. It is an olive and brown mixed shade with an overplaid effect almost invisible. One of the best patterns in our entire line. The coat is made up with good linings, trimmings, etc., throughout, in round cut sack style. The vest is made single breasted, five buttons Pants are made in the regulation style. The opposite cut is a true representation of this suit. We claim this to be the best value for a spring and summer suit ever offered It represents the very best value that we can give. It represents the actual cost of making with no middlemen's profits. You deal direct with first hands, and when you order ready made clothing from us you save from three to ten dollars on your purchase by cutting out all this extra profit Sizes, 34 to 42 only.

Price for men's suit, style 1 only.... .... **$5.00**
Price for coat and vest. **3.50**
Price for pants......... **1.50**

No. 45R204

McIntosh, Greene & Co.'s Brown and Green Mixed Wool Suit, $4.50

No. 45R202 This suit is from a heavy material suitable for year around wear. Made of good quality wool cheviot, dark brown and slightly gray mixed cheviot cloth, made in round cut sack style only, as shown by opposite illustration. A suit that will stand wear, hold its color; and retain its shape. It is such value as you would get at from eight to ten dollars elsewhere. Honest goods at very much lower prices than a similar quality can be had elsewhere has built up for us the largest ready made clothing business in this market. When you order from us you order direct from the makers There is no endless chain of profits attached to the goods that we sell. So confident are we of the value we offer that we ask you to order this suit with the understanding that if it is not entirely satisfactory, you can return it at our expense and we will promptly refund your money

Price for suit, style 1 only ...**$4.50**
Price for coat and vest...... **3.00**
Price for pants............ **1.50**

No. 45R202

Holmes & Long's Black and White Small Checked Cheviot Suit, $5.00.

No. 45R206 This is one of the new black and white cheviot suits so popular for spring and summer wear. It is a very small check pattern in a neat black and white all wool cheviot effect, goods that will wear, hold color, and give universal satisfaction. You will find the same pattern sold by first class retail clothing merchants throughout the country at from nine to twelve dollars per suit. By sending us your order you are saving all of the store keeper's profit, all of the jobber's profit, all of the wholesaler's profit, as we make these suits in our own factory and send them direct to our customers with but one small profit added. Anything that is unsatisfactory in the way of fit, workmanship, quality of goods, style, is our fault; we take all of the chances. We guarantee to please you in every particular, otherwise you can return the garments to us and your money will be cheerfully refunded along with any express charges that you have paid out.

Price of this suit, round cut sack style only.............. **$5.00**
Price for coat and vest...... **3.50**
Price for pants... .... **1.50**

No. 45R206

No 45R208

Men's Navy Blue Mixed Cheviot Suit, $5.50.

No. 45R208 This suit is made from an almost plain navy blue cheviot. It has an invisible green thread, which is interwoven in such a way as to give the cloth an almost plain navy blue effect. It is a medium weight, suitable for all seasons wear, especially for spring and summer use, made in round cut sack style, as shown by opposite illustration Well lined, trimmed and finished, just such a suit as you would imagine would be cheap at $10.00. We are bound to get your clothing business We give such values as no other house can. We give you the opportunity of saving nearly one-half on ready made clothing. Sooner or later you will surely send us a trial order because you cannot afford to pay double our low prices elsewhere If you send us one order we are sure that we will please you so well as to retain your future clothing patronage. This suit is a most excellent one

Price for suit, style No 1 only $5.50
Price for coat and vest.... .. ... 3.75
Price for pants 1.75

IT IS UNNECESSARY TO SEND FOR SAMPLES

of Men's Ready Made Clothing. The description gives you an accurate idea of the goods. We guarantee to please you and in ordering from this catalogue you are sure of satisfaction.

No. 45R210

Converse, Stanton & Co.'s Very Fine Black and White Checked Cassimere Suit.

No. 45R210 This suit is made from a very fine quality of fine all wool black and white checked cassimere, especially for spring and summer wear The handsomest fine all wool light colored summer suit we have ever been able to offer at this figure Made up in round cut sack style Made up with good linings, extra quality of sleeve linings Haircloth and linen canvas interlining A strictly first class, ready made suit, guaranteed to wear, for workmanship and finish

Price for suit, style No. 1 only.. $5.50
Price for coat and vest....... 3.75
Price for pants............... 1.75

YOU SAVE TIME

by ordering direct from this catalogue. You run not the slightest chance, as we always fill your order according to description.

We always guarantee to please and save you money. We prefer to have unsatisfactory goods returned.

You run not the slightest chance by ordering from this catalogue.

No. 45R212

Olberman & Co.'s Dark Brown Mixed Cheviot Suit, $6.00.

No. 45R212 This suit is a dark brown and gold mixed cheviot, strictly all wool, a very good weight. Can be worn most any season of the year. It is, however, intended for a spring and summer suit. A good, honest cloth that will wear well, look well and is one of the best suits in our entire line. Please bear in mind that all of our ready made suits are well made. We use a good quality of linings, trimmings, etc, throughout. We guarantee to fit you, we guarantee to please you in every way. We do not see that you run any risk in sending us your order, because we take all of the chances. In the event of your not being perfectly satisfied with the garments received you can return them to us at our expense and your money will be cheerfully refunded.

Price for suit, style 1 only. $6.00
Price for coat and vest.. 4.00
Price for pants 2.00

WE ADVOCATE

ordering from this catalogue, as we know you will be perfectly satisfied with your purchases.

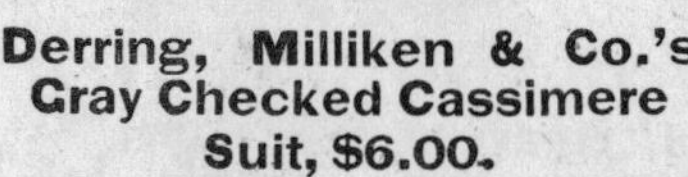

Derring, Milliken & Co.'s Gray Checked Cassimere Suit, $6.00.

No. 45R214 This suit is made from good weight, all wool, very fine quality of cassimere in a medium shade of gray. It is a heavy weight, suitable for all seasons wear, something that will not show the dirt, is positively the best thing for the money in the way of an all wool fine cassimere suit we have ever been able to offer. Made up in round cut sack style, as shown by opposite illustration. The fact that we make these suits only in one style and make them in our own factory in very large quantities, allows us to figure the prices down lower than if we made several styles in one cloth This taken into consideration, and the fact that you pay but one small profit should, we believe, entitle us to at least a trial order You will then find that we can furnish such extraordinary values that we are sure you will continue to favor us with your future patronage

Price for suit, style 1 only... $6.00
Price for coat and vest...... 4.00
Price for pants............. 2.00

IF YOU ORDER FROM THIS CATALOGUE

you will get garments just as we describe.

No. 45R214

All Wool Navy Blue Gilbert Serge Suit, $6.00.

No. 45R216

No. 45R216 There are so **many imitations in navy blue serge,** so many cheap, half-cotton cloths sold as all worsted serge that this particular kind of a suit is condemned by some people because they have never been able to get first class goods. This suit is made from a guaranteed all pure wool worsted serge. We guarantee the color, **we guarantee the cloth to wear and give every satisfaction.** It is a dark, rich navy blue shade. A regular spring and summer weight. Will make one of the handsomest plain suits that can be procured, no matter what price you pay. We cannot afford to offer our customers any goods that will prove unsatisfactory, and we recommend this suit and warrant it to give excellent wear and perfect satisfaction. When you consider that the same quality of goods is sold by regular clothiers at from ten to twelve dollars, **we trust that you will appreciate the extraordinary value by sending us a trial order.**

Price for suit, made in round cut sack only.......**$6.00**
Price for coat and vest... **4.00**
Price for pants......... **2.00**

Dark Seal All Wool Heavy Weight Tricot Long Cassimere, $6.00.

No. 45R218 Many of our customers desire a good weight suit that can be worn at any season of the year. This suit is a heavy weight, is strictly all wool seal brown color, one of the best wearing numbers in our line. You may be able to match this suit for ten dollars, not less. Made in round cut sack style, good quality of linings, trimmings, etc., throughout, warranted in every particular. The fact that this same grade of goods is sold to your local storekeeper at more money than we offer you this suit should entitle us to your consideration in the clothing line. **We want your clothing trade. We are bound to get it if good goods and the lowest prices you ever heard tell of will secure it.**

Price for suit....................**$6.00**
Price for coat and vest.......... **4.00**
Price for pants................. **2.00**

WE ASK YOU to order from this catalogue it you want a ready made suit, for the reason that you can tell from the description just what you are ordering and we will fill your order exactly according to the description

No. 45R218

Men's Black Clay 14-Ounce Worsted Suit, $6.50.

Numbers 45R220 and 45R222

No. 45R220 We offer you in this number a **strictly all wool full 14-ounce black clay worsted suit at a price against which we are positive that no other house will compete.** We offer you a suit that will hold its color and retain its shape, guaranteed not to grow rusty, because it is all pure worsted quality with no cotton mixed threads, such as is used in a great many clay worsted goods. The poorest value on earth is a black suit that is filled with cotton. Please bear in mind that we guarantee to fit and please you in every way no matter what kind of measurements you send us. We take all the chances.

Price for suit...........**$6.50**
Price for coat and vest... **4.25**
Price for pants.......... **2.25**

Medium Weight All Wool Jet Black Thibet Suit.

No. 45R222 This medium weight, all wool, jet black Thibet suit for $6.50 is made from a fine quality of fine black Thibet, a cloth similar to broadcloth or doeskin. It is a smooth surface material, will give excellent wear, and makes a most desirable dress suit. While the price is very low the quality of the goods is the same as is used in $10.00 and $12.00 suits elsewhere. You are really getting this kind of value when you order from us. We make it possible by reason of our making all of our own clothing and offering the finished garments direct to our customers with but one small profit.

Price for suit..............**$6.50**
Price for coat and vest...... **4.25**
Price for pants............. **2.25**

Jacob Wendall & Co.'s Dark Gray Mixed Cassimere, $7.00.

No. 45R224 This suit is made from a dark gray and black mixed cassimere. It has an almost invisible overplaid effect in dark and red and also raised black satin effect, which makes a most desirable up to date pattern. It is good weight and very fine all wool goods, one of the best numbers in our line and one that would surely please the most particular. The suit is made in round cut sack style, as shown by opposite illustration, well lined, trimmed and finished.

Price for suit...............**$7.00**
Price for coat and vest...... **5.00**
Price for pants............. **2.00**

WE SEND a sample book for 5 cents, showing complete line of samples of our ready to wear clothing. Yet we advocate ordering from this catalogue as we know it will be equally as satisfactory.

No. 45R224

No. 45R226

Washington Mills Navy Blue Diagonal Worsted Suit, $7.50.

No. 45R226 **This suit is made from an all pure worsted full eighteen-ounce goods, cloth suitable for all seasons wear.** The color is a dark navy blue with a raised diagonal effect. Makes one of the handsomest dress or business suits you could possibly procure in a plain shade. You will get more wear and satisfaction out of this goods than any suit you ever purchased, we are sure, at anything like this price.

Price for suit..............**$7.50**
Price for coat and vest... **4.50**
Price for pants........... **2.50**

Washington Mills Brown Mixed Fancy Worsted Suit, $8.00.

No. 45R228 **This is an all pure worsted suit. It is full eighteen-ounce goods, suitable for any season of the year; a dark brown checked worsted.** It is a better suit for $8.00 than we believe any other house in the United States can give. It is just the same class of goods as is sold to your local storekeeper by city wholesale houses at more money than we ask for this suit. It is positively the best all pure worsted suit for $8.00 ever offered. Send us a trial order and we are sure that you will be more than pleased.

Price for this handsome suit....**$8.00**
Price for coat and vest........ **5.50**
Price for pants............... **2.50**

Our Finest All Worsted Suit, $10.00.

No. 45R230 **At $10.00 we offer you a very fine all pure worsted suit, the same class of goods as is usually sold at from $18.00 to $20.00 by first class clothing dealers.** There is no better or finer goods to be had in a fancy worsted suit, no matter what price you pay. It is a dark navy blue and green mixed broken checked pattern, a most handsome shade of medium weight cloth. Will make a suit that will give all kinds of wear and at the same time always look neat and dressy. Favor us with an order for this number and you are sure to receive even better value than you expect.

Price for suit made up in round cut sack style only.......**$10.00**
Price for coat and vest...... **7.00**
Price for pants............. **3.00**

No. 45R230

IF YOU ORDER FROM THIS CATALOGUE

YOU GET JUST WHAT WE ADVERTISE.

YOU RUN NO CHANCES WHATEVER.

Men's Genuine All Wool Gray Hair Line Pants, $1.35.

No. 45R232 **These all wool hair line pants are suitable for year around wear.** One of the best wearing and most satisfactory patterns for every day usage that you can possibly procure. The value we offer in this number is only characteristic of our entire line of clothing. We offer the same value in all numbers, all sold at the same one small profit plan, while your local storekeeper will tell you that this is a leader with us because we offer you the pants at a lower price than he can buy them. As ours are made in our own factory they are better made than the usual workmanship in this particular grade of goods

Price for pants, size 30 to 40 inches waist measure, or 30 to 36 inches inseam measure......................**$1.35**

The Best Fine All Wool Gray Striped Pants on Earth for $1.50.

No. 45R234 **Made from a good weight, strictly all wool Brumbach & Co.'s cassimere.** Positively equal in quality and make to many pantaloons advertised at $2.50 by clothing dealers as extra value If you want the best value ever shown for $1.50 in a strictly all wool dark gray, guaranteed for wear, color and fit pantaloons, order this number.

Price for pants, size 30 to 40 inches waist measure, or 30 to 36 inches inseam measure..**$1.50**

Fancy Striped Worsted Pants, $1.75.

No. 45R236 **These pants are made from a hard twisted black and gray striped fancy worsted,** a quality of goods that will give splendid wear. At the same time this is a very handsome, dressy pantaloons, made up in a first class manner; all buttons are well sewed on, good quality curtain lining, double sewed through crotch, warranted not to rip, positively the best pantaloons ever offered for the money

Price for pants, sizes 30 to 40 inches waist measure, or 30 to 36 inches inseam..**$1.75**

Black and Gray Striped Worsted Pants, $2.00.

No. 45R238 **These pants are made from a heavy, all worsted cloth, a high grade smooth finished material suitable for** year around wear, made up over the latest and most perfect fitting patterns, extra heavy pocketing, wide sateen curtain lining. Well made, trimmed and finished throughout, the equal of pants costing double our low price.

Price for pants, sizes 30 to 40 inches waist measure, or 30 to 36 inches inseam..**$2.00**

Washington Mills Blue Black Satin Striped Worsted Pants, $2.50.

No. 45R240 **This handsome pantaloons is made from an all pure worsted medium weight Washington Mills satin striped material.** The same dressy, high grade pantaloons as is sold by your local storekeeper at $5.00. If you order this number we are positive that you will find the value just as we claim, really double value for your money. We claim that no one can match our prices, no one is in a position to furnish the same original style and value. You will claim the same thing if you send us but one trial order. The value received, we are sure, will fully convince you that we are in a position to save you nearly one-half on clothing

The price for this handsome blue black satin striped pants, sizes 30 to 40 inches waist measure, 30 to 36 inches inseam.............. **$2.50**

OVERCOAT

Mackintosh, Greene & Co.'s Dark Frieze Overcoat, $4.50.

No. 45R242 This overcoat is made **from dark Oxford frieze,** the material is especially desirable for winter coats. It is a cloth that will stand wear, give splendid satisfaction, made up as shown by opposite cut. The body is lined with a good quality of Italian lining and a good quality of sleeve lining, and is a well made coat throughout. Soliciting your order for an overcoat, we believe that we are asking you to send us your money for the best value you can possibly get in clothing, better value than can be had anywhere else.

Price for overcoat.....**$4.50**

Mackintosh, Greene & Co.'s Oxford Ulster, $5.00.

No. 45R244 This ulster is made up from the same goods as the above overcoat. It is made of dark Oxford 30-ounce frieze, just such an ulster as will cost double the price elsewhere We can furnish sizes only from 34 to 42 inches breast measure and only one length, 50 inches.

Price for ulster..........**$5.00**

All Wool Blue Black Beaver Overcoat, $5.00.

No. 45R246 This overcoat is made of all wool blue black beaver, heavy weight cloth, goods that will wear and give satisfaction to the one who wears it, made up as shown by above illustration, extra well made, trimmed in a first class manner, single breasted style only. We are offering the coat at our one small margin of profit plan price We purchase all piece goods for ready made clothing for much less than it is actually worth; thus we are enabled to give our customers the value we claim.

Price for overcoat **$5.00**

All Wool Blue Black Beaver Ulster, $6.00.

No. 45R248 This ulster is made from the same material as the above overcoat. It is a dark blue black all wool beaver goods that will give you satisfaction **The price is very low and you may imagine that a good ulster cannot be had for the price we name,** but you can take our word that this coat is an exceptional value and a splendid garment for this money. We guarantee it to be the best coat ever offered for the price, and upon examination, if it is not found satisfactory, your money will be refunded. We take all chances on style, size or quality of goods.

Price for ulster......................................**$6.00**

WE ADVOCATE ORDERING READY MADE CLOTHING FROM OUR CATALOGUE.

It is just as satisfactory, we take the same special care to fill your order exact. You will be always sure of getting garments that will fit and please you. If you desire samples, however, FOR 5 CENTS IN POSTAGE STAMPS we will mail you our cloth sample book of

Mens' Ready to Wear Clothing.

Why we can save you 50 cents to $1.00 more on every overcoat by asking 5 cents for SAMPLE BOOK No. 56R, is explained on page 1129.

Navy Blue Chinchilla Ready Made Overcoat, $6.00.

No. 45R250 This overcoat is made from a dark navy blue heavy weight chinchilla. It is well made and trimmed, sewed throughout with silk and linen; such a coat as you cannot get from your local dealer for less than double our price. Made up as shown by opposite cut. Our cuts are taken from photographs, and will give you a very definite idea as to how the coat will look. Send us your order with the understanding that this coat will fit you, will please you in every way, or it can be returned to us at our expense of express charges both ways.

Price for overcoat..**$6.00**

Navy Blue Chinchilla Ulster, $7.00.

No. 45R252 This ulster is made up of the same material as the above overcoat. It is a heavy weight cloth, especially desirable in men's winter ulsters We would like very much to have you order this navy blue ulster, as we know that you will be well pleased with it, and that you will show it to your friends and neighbors, which will result in many more orders. Please remember, we guarantee to fit you; we guarantee that the coat we send you will be thoroughly satisfactory in every way This coat is made up in the style as shown by ulster fashion figure; made in sizes from 34 to 42 inches breast measure only.

Price for ulster..**$7.00**

WHEN YOU BUY A READY MADE GARMENT FROM US you get a distinctiveness in style, make and fit that you cannot secure elsewhere. The regular ready made clothing you get from the ordinary retail clothing store cannot compare with ours in any particular. We know that if you once buy a ready made suit, overcoat or ulster from us, we will be favored with your future clothing orders. SEND US YOUR ORDER AND BE CONVINCED.

Jet Black All Wool Kersey Overcoat, $7.00.

No. 45R254 We offer this all wool kersey overcoat, made up in the latest style, as shown by opposite illustration. It is thoroughly well sewed, well trimmed and lined throughout and is a garment that is as near perfect as we can make it We quote this coat at a price against which no other house can compete We quote lower prices than local merchants can buy clothing from their regular wholesale house; that's why we think we are entitled to your order and on this basis we solicit a trial order from you.

Price for overcoat........**$7.00**

Men's All Wool Black Kersey Ulster, $8.00.

No. 45R256 This black ulster is made from the same material as the above overcoat. It is a heavy weight, very closely woven black kersey ulster, well made and finished throughout, We use good quality Italian body lining, and an extra heavy sleeve lining, We would like to have your order, as we know we can give you perfect satisfaction, and retain your future patronage in the clothing line. This garment is made up as shown by ulster style 12, fashion figure, and in sizes from 34 to 42 inches breast measure.

Price for ulster style..........**$8.00**

ULSTER

...BOYS' LONG PANTS SUITS...

HOW TO ORDER For measurements follow same rules as laid down for men's clothing and fill out the regular order blank, if possible. If you have no order blank, carefully take the following measures, which are the essential ones in selecting a fit from ready made stock.

1. Chest Measure—All around body close up under arms over vest. Be sure and take this measurement with the coat off and over vest only.
2. Waist Measure—All around over waistband of pants.
3. Length of Pants—From tight up in crotch of pants to heel of shoe.

Do not order larger sizes than 35 inches chest measure or pants over 33 inches long inside seam. The schedule of measurements on preceding page are the only sizes we can furnish If larger sizes are needed, please select from men's garments.

Only such styles as are mentioned under each number can be furnished.

Fleitman & Co.'s Fancy Mixed Cheviot Suit, $3.50.

This, our cheapest round cut sack coat for boys aged 12 to 19 years, is a good wearing cloth. It is made from a medium weight of brown mixed cheviot, a good hard twisted material that will give splendid wear and should not be compared with the common shoddy satinette suits ordinarily retailed by dealers at about this price. We recommend higher priced clothing, yet to anyone ordering this number we guarantee the suit to give perfect satisfaction. The coat is round cut sack style, vest single breasted, pants one hip, two side and one watch pocket.

No. 40R2 Price for boys' long pants suit, style 1 only...**$3.50**

STYLE 1

Jacob Wendall & Co.'s Dark Gray Pin Checked Cassimere Suit, $4.00.

In this number we offer one of the most substantial, desirable gray pin checked, handsome suits we have ever shown. It is a medium weight for spring and summer wear, a color that will not show dirt and a cloth that is guaranteed to give perfect satisfaction. The suit is made in round cut sack style like our style 1. All seams of the coat are double stitched. Good quality of black Italian lining in the coat and vest backs; vest cut single breasted, pants have two side, one hip and one watch pocket. Well made and guaranteed the best value ever offered by us or any other house.

No. 40R4 Price for boys' long pants suit, style 1 only......**$4.00**

Schaffer, Schraum & Co.'s Black and White Cheviot Suit, $4.50.

This all wool, small pattern, black and white checked cheviot suit is a number that we can especially recommend. It is a good color and makes a very neat suit and will compare favorably with garments costing from $6.50 up elsewhere. The suit is made in round cut sack style coat with linings, trimmings, etc., throughout The vest is made single breasted, pants have two hip, two side and one watch pocket, extra buttons inside of coat facing. Extra value is what you will get if you order this number, better value than you would have reason to believe from the description we give.

No. 40R6 Price for boys' long pants suit, style 1 only......**$4.50**

Holmes & Long's All Wool Fancy Cheviot Suit, $4.75.

This is a new, up to date, fancy cheviot suit in an olive mixture with an over plaid effect of dark red. It is a very handsome pattern and strictly all wool, a splendid wearing fabric made up in round cut sack style only. The vest is made single breasted, pants have two side, two hip and one watch pocket Thoroughly well made and satisfactory throughout, guaranteed to fit, to wear and to give better service than garments costing more money elsewhere

No. 40R8 Price for boys' long pants suit, in style 1 only..**$4.75**

This suit is made from the same material as the above number, only we have made it in style 2, which is a single breasted, square cut coat. We simply list it under another number so that there will be no chance of our customers making a mistake in procuring the style suit that they desire. If you wish style 2, single breasted, square cut sack style, order this number.

No. 40R10 Price for boys' long pants suit, style 2 only..............**$4.75**

STYLE 2

Dark Navy Blue All Wool Cheviot Suit, $5.00.

This dark, almost plain, heavy blue cheviot is one of our best numbers. It is an over plaid effect, however, with a single thread of dark green, which is almost invisible. It makes one of the handsomest suits in our line. At the price we especially recommend this number for wear and general appearance. For all around satisfaction we are sure that it will please the most particular. Suit is made in round cut sack style. Vest is cut double breasted, no collar Pants are made with two side, two hip and one watch pocket.

No. 40R12 Price for boys' long pants suit, style 1 only **$5.00**

Fleitman & Co.'s Brown Mixed Cheviot Suit.

This handsome, up to date spring and summer pattern is a brown mixed cheviot. The colorings are dark and medium brown with a mixture of olive, a most desirable pattern The suit is made in round cut sack style, the coat and vest backs are lined with a good quality of black Italian cloth. This handsome dark pattern will make one of the nobbiest suits in our line Pants are made with two side, two hip and one watch pocket.

No. 40R14 Price for boys' long pants suit, style 1 only....**$5.00**

Jet Black Thibet Suit, $5.50.

This all wool jet black thibet suit is a smooth finished cloth. It is good weight and suitable for all seasons wear It is made up in round cut sack only; vest is cut single breasted, notch collar; pants are made with two hip pockets, two side and one watch pocket. Suit is well made throughout, warranted in every particular If you send us one trial order for boys' clothing we are sure that we will be able to sell you boys' garments season after season

No. 40R16 Price for boys' long pants suit, style 1 only............ .... **$5.50**

Our Favorite All Wool Brown Cheviot Suit, $5.50.

In this medium weight all wool brown mixed cheviot suit we offer such value as we are positive you will appreciate. It is a dark brown mixed cheviot goods and makes a most handsome, up to date young man's suit. Is made in round cut sack style; vest is single breasted, with notched collar; pants are made with two hip, two side and one watch pocket. The suit is well lined and well made, warranted in every way

No. 40R18 Price for boys' long pants suit in style 1 only, **$5.50**

STYLE 3

Derring Milliken & Co.'s All Wool Gray Checked Cassimere Suit, $6.00.

This all wool gray checked cassimere suit is one that is desirable for year around wear. It is a smooth finished goods and a color that will stand and not show soil. Guaranteed for wear We call it the best all wool extra fine cassimere suit we have ever offered. Made in round cut sack style; vest cut single breasted; pants have two hip, two side and one watch pocket

No. 40R20 Price for boys' long pants suit, style 1 only.. **$6.00**

Olberman & Co.'s Brown Mixed Cheviot Suit.

This dark brown and gold mixed cheviot makes one of the handsomest and most desirable patterns for year around wear. Heavy enough weight for all seasons purposes Made in round cut sack style. The vest is cut single breasted, five buttons; pants have two side, two hip and one watch pocket We especially recommend this number.

No. 40R22 Price for boys' long pants, round cut suit, style 1 only.. **$6.00**

Very Fine Navy Blue Serge Suit, $6.50.

A poor quality of navy blue serge is poor value at any price. In this number we offer a suit made from a very fine all wool navy blue serge. It is a hard twisted goods, a cloth that will give splendid wear; guaranteed for color. We make it up with good linings, trimmings, etc., throughout. It is made in round cut sack style with double breasted vest. The pants have two side, two hip and one watch pocket If you wish good value and a suit that will give every satisfaction order this number

No. 40R24 Price for boys' long pants suit, style 1 only... **$6.50**

Navy Blue Serge Suit, $6.50.

Made exactly the same as the suit described above, except the coat of this suit is made in square cut single breasted style same as style 2 If you wish a navy blue serge suit in style 2 order this number.

No. 40R26 Price for boys' long pants suit, style 2. ...... **$6.50**

Jet Black All Wool Clay Worsted Suit, $6.50.

A cheap black suit or a suit made from black goods of an inferior quality is poor value at any price. That is why we recommend all wool fine worsted goods in black. That is why we recommend this particular number The cloth is made from a good quality very fine all worsted yarn The coat is made in round sack style. The vest is made single breasted, the pants have two side, two hip and one watch pocket.

No. 40R28 Price for boys' long pants suits, style 1 only... **$6.50**

Black Clay Worsted Suits, $6.50.

Made exactly the same as the above number, only the coat of this suit is made in square cut sack style like our style 2. If you wish a black clay suit in style 2, please order this number

No. 40R30 Price for boys' long pants suit, style 2 only.. **$6.50**

Boys' Double Breasted Black Clay Worsted Suit.

The material is full fourteen-ounce all worsted black clay. If you desire a double breasted square cut coat like style 3 please order this number.

No. 40R32 Price for boys' suit with double breasted square cut coat, style 3... **$7.00**

Stein & Co.'s All Wool Worsted Suit, $7.00.

A dark brown and navy blue mixture formed in a medium sized checked pattern. A handsome, fine, extra quality, hard finished worsted goods, cloth that will wear, hold color and give perfect satisfaction. The coat is made in round cut sack style, vest is cut single breasted with collar Pants have two side, two hip and one watch pocket.

No. 40R34 Price for boys' long pants suit, style 1. ...... **$7.00**

Tallcott & Co.'s Gray Mixed Covert Suit, $7.50.

This is a handsome, light colored gray covert cassimere with a red overplaid, especially for spring and summer wear. If you want a handsome, up to date, very fine suit, we especially recommend this number, as we are sure you will be more than pleased with it. The suit is made with a round cut sack coat well trimmed and lined throughout, vest is double breasted, no collar; pants have two hip, two side and one watch pocket.

No. 40R36 Price for boys' long pants suit, style 1..... **$7.50**

Our Finest All Worsted Fancy Suit, $8.00.

At $8.00 we offer you a suit of a finer quality than is ordinarily kept in the best retail stores. We recommend our $8.00 suit because you can appreciate the extra fine quality of the goods, the fine linings, the well made garments that we can furnish you at this price, value that will guarantee our securing your future patronage. This suit is made of a very fine all worsted cloth in a dark green and navy blue broken checked pattern. The coat is made in round sack style The vest is made single breasted. The pants have two side, two hip and one watch pocket If you order this or any other number in our long pants suits and you are not satisfied that you have gotten the best value you ever had for the money you are at liberty to return it to us and we will cheerfully refund your money

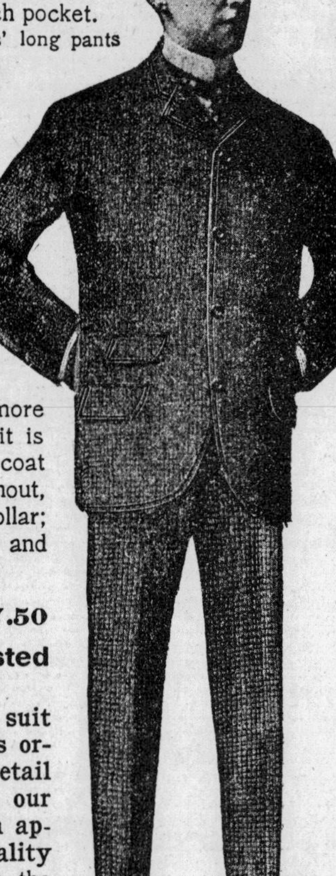

STYLE 1

No. 40R38 Price for boys long pants suits, style 1 only. . **$8.00**

BOYS' TWO-PIECE KNEE PANTS SUITS.

Boys' Two-Piece Cheviot Suit, $1.75.

IN THIS SUIT WE OFFER YOU A GOOD, SUBSTANTIAL BROWN STRIPE CHEVIOT CLOTH, made up like style as shown by opposite illustration, well made and a first class suit in every way if the price is considered. We do not make or advertise cheap, shoddy, or poorly made garments. While we recommend our higher priced numbers, we offer this, our cheapest suit, with the guarantee of its giving perfect and satisfactory wear. The coat is cut double breasted style, as shown by the opposite illustration. Extra set of buttons inside of coat facing. The pants are made double at seat and knees.

No. 40R40 Price for boys' two-piece knee pants suit for boys aged 8 to 15 years......... **$1.75**

Boys' Extra Quality Two-Piece Suit, $2.00.

WE OFFER IN THIS NUMBER EXTRAORDINARY VALUE, such value as you could not obtain from us if it were not for the fact that we use small lots of goods left over from our custom department in making up these suits. We aim to procure only the first cost of the piece goods. We use this number only to dispose of goods left over from our custom department, lines that have been discontinued from last season. In this way we give you dark, neat and desirable patterns at a price which is at least one-third lower than we could ordinarily make the same quality of goods. When you order from this number please state about the shade that you desire and we feel confident that we can please you, at the same time you will receive a better value than you could get from any of our regular lines. The suits are made in double breasted style as shown in illustration. Pants are made double seat and double knees.

No. 40R42 Price for boys' two-piece knee pants suit for boys aged 8 to 15 years........... **$2.00**

While you can order Boys' Clothing direct from this catalogue with every assurance of satisfaction, if you wish first to see samples of our entire line of Boys' and Children's Clothing, **SEND 5 CENTS FOR SAMPLE BOOK No. 64R.**

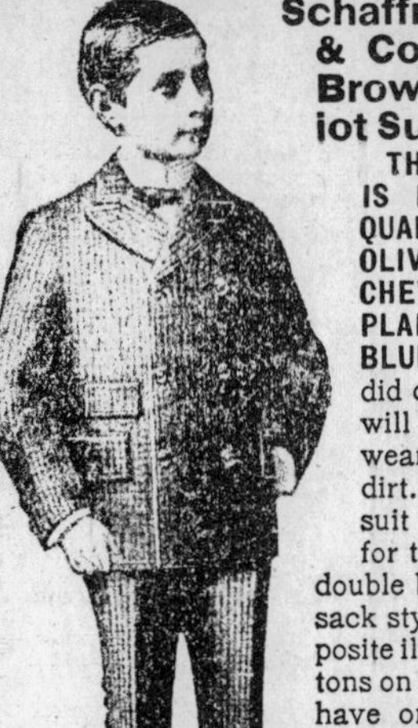

Schaffner, Schraum & Co.'s All Wool Brown Mixed Cheviot Suit, $2.00.

THIS TWO-PIECE SUIT IS MADE FROM A FINE QUALITY OF ALL WOOL OLIVE AND BROWN MIXED CHEVIOT WITH AN OVERPLAID EFFECT IN RED AND BLUE. It is a splendid color, something that will give exceptional wear; will not show the dirt. The best two-piece suit ever offered by us for the money. Made in double breasted, square coat sack style, as shown by opposite illustration. Extra buttons on facing of coat. Pants have one hip and two side pockets, and are made double at the seat and knees. This suit is substantially lined, double sewed and warranted in every way.

No. 40R44 Price for boys' two-piece knee pants suit for boys aged 8 to 15 years.... **$2.00**

Parker, Wilder & Co.'s All Wool Blue Cheviot Suit, $2.50.

AN ALL WOOL GOOD QUALITY OF NAVY BLUE CHEVIOT makes a very nice two-piece suit. In this number we offer a suit which will certainly please our customers, at the same time it is offered to you at a very low price. We know that you will appreciate the fact that we are saving you at least $1.00 on your purchase. This suit is made in double breasted style, as shown by opposite illustration. Pants are made double at the seat and knees and are double sewed throughout the crotch. We make our boys' clothing in our own factory. Made with the idea of securing your future orders. Extra buttons inside of coat facing. Good up to date, all wool, nicely made cheviot suit at $2.50.

No. 40R46 Price for boys' two-piece knee pants suit for boys aged 8 to 15 years...... **$2.50**

Jacob Wendall & Co.'s Fancy Cheviot Suit, $3.00.

THIS TWO-PIECE FANCY CHEVIOT SUIT is made from a dark gray broken check all wool cheviot and has an overplaid effect in a single thread of dark maroon. Made double breasted style, as shown by opposite illustration. Pants have the usual number of pockets, double at seat and knees, double sewed throughout crotch. Well lined and substantially made throughout.

No. 40R48 Price for boys' two-piece knee pants suit for boys aged 8 to 15 years **$3.00**

Boys' Black Clay Worsted Two-Piece Suit, $3.00.

THIS SUIT IS MADE FROM AN ALL PURE 14-OUNCE CLAY WORSTED is well made and lined with a good quality of black Italian cloth. Pants are made with double seat and double knees and double sewed throughout crotch, two side and one hip pockets. Extra buttons inside of coat facing. This is a first class all pure worsted two-piece suit, warranted to wear and give perfect satisfaction.

No. 40R50 Price for boys' two-piece knee pants suit for boys aged 8 to 15 years........... **$3.00**

Boys' Navy Blue Two-Piece Serge Suit, $3.00.

NAVY BLUE SERGE IS VERY POPULAR FOR BOYS' KNEE PANTS SUITS, so popular that a great many dealers use a cheap inferior quality of serge that may look all right when the goods are new, but as the cloth is filled with cotton it will give poor satisfaction when it comes to wear. In this two-piece boys' all worsted navy blue suit we offer you a very fine quality of goods made up in double breasted square coat sack style as shown by opposite illustration; pants have two side and one hip pocket; made with double seat and double knees, extra buttons inside of coat facing; a thoroughly well made up suit, warranted in every way.

No. 40R52 Price for boys' two-piece knee pants suit for boys aged 8 to 15 years................ **$3.00**

Finest Fancy Worsted Cheviot Two-Piece Suit, $3.50.

THIS, OUR FINEST FANCY WORSTED CHEVIOT SUIT AT $3.50, is a better quality of goods than is ordinarily used in boys' clothing, is a very fine, all worsted cloth. The colors are dark brown with blue mixed in a stripe effect. The coat is cut double breasted style, as shown by opposite illustration; pants have two side and one hip pocket, double seat and double knees. Elegantly lined, trimmed and finished. The finest two-piece suit ever offered by us for the money.

No. 40R54 Price for boys' two-piece knee pants suit for boys aged 8 to 15 years.. **$3.50**

BOYS' THREE-PIECE SUITS.

BOYS' THREE-PIECE SUITS ARE MADE FOR BOYS AGED 8 TO 16 YEARS. SEE INTRODUCTORY PAGE FOR FULL INSTRUCTIONS ABOUT MEASUREMENTS, HOW TO ORDER, ETC. BOYS' THREE-PIECE SUITS CONSIST OF ONE ROUND CUT SACK COAT, one double breasted vest with no collar, and one pair of knee pants made with double seat and double knees. Boys' three-piece suits are the most popular style suits worn today for boys aged 8 to 16 years. That is why we show a fine assortment of this particular style of suit. **ALL OF OUR BOYS' CLOTHING IS MADE IN OUR OWN FACTORY, AND MADE OVER THE MOST PERFECT FITTING, LATE STYLE PATTERNS.** Every garment is well sewed and warranted to give perfect satisfaction. You run no chance when ordering boys' clothing from us, as you are bound to get goods that will please you, otherwise it will not cost you one cent, because you can return the goods to us and we will cheerfully refund your money.

Schaffer, Schraum & Co.'s Fancy All Wool Cheviot Three-Piece Suit, $2.75.

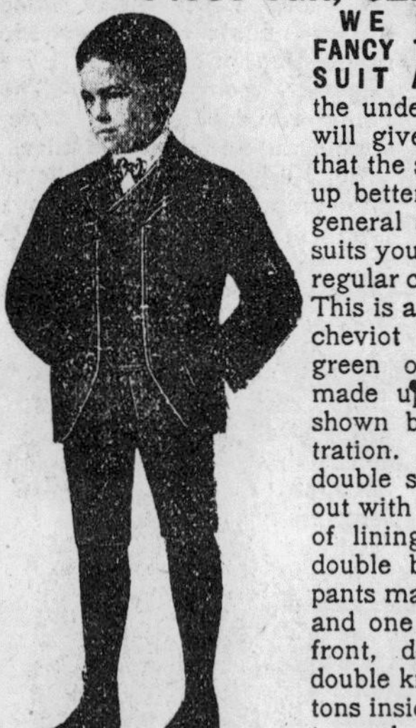

WE OFFER THIS FANCY THREE-PIECE SUIT AT $2.75 with the understanding that it will give splendid wear, that the suit will be made up better and give more general satisfaction than suits you can obtain from regular clothiers at $3.50. This is a dark navy blue cheviot with a red and green overplaid. It is made up in style as shown by opposite illustration. The coat is double stitched throughout with an extra quality of linings, vest is made double breasted style, pants made with two side and one hip pocket, fly front, double seat and double knees. Extra buttons inside of coat facing to replace any that become lost or broken.

No. 40R56 Price for boys' three-piece knee pants suit for boys aged 8 to 16 years...... **$2.75**

Fleitman & Co.'s All Wool Three-Piece Cheviot Suit, $3.00.

THIS IS A SPECIAL PATTERN THAT WE HAVE HAD MADE FOR THREE-PIECE SUITS. It is a brown, broken check, all wool cheviot a splendid wearing cloth and will make a nobby suit for any boy. The coat is made in a round sack style, as shown by opposite illustration; vest double breasted; pants have the usual number of pockets; made double seat and double knees. We specially recommend this suit. It is one of the best values we have ever been able to offer.

No. 40R58 Price for boys' three-piece knee pants suit for boys aged 8 to 16 years....... **$3.00**

YOU CAN ORDER FROM THIS CATALOGUE

WITHOUT SENDING FOR SAMPLES AND ALWAYS BE SURE OF GETTING SATISFACTORY CLOTHING.

Faulkner, Page & Co.'s Navy Blue Worsted Suit, $3.50.

THIS IS A HARD TWISTED, HARD FINISH CLOTH in a medium weight of plain navy blue shade with a raised pattern. You can get a good idea of the size of the pattern from the opposite illustration, which is a true reproduction of this suit. The coat is made in the usual round cut sack style. The vest is made double breasted, no collar. The pants are made with double seat and double knees, fly front, double sewed throughout and guaranteed not to rip.

No. 40R60 Price for boys' three-piece knee pants suit for boys aged 8 to 16 years...... **$3.50**

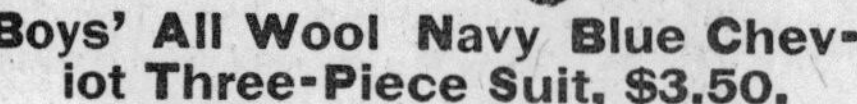

Boys' All Wool Navy Blue Cheviot Three-Piece Suit, $3.50.

THERE IS NOTHING THAT WILL MAKE A MORE DESIRABLE SUIT THAN NAVY BLUE CHEVIOT. This cheviot is an almost plain navy blue. It has an interwoven thread of dark green, which is almost invisible. The material is a good weight, strictly all wool cheviot. Made up in style as shown by opposite illustration. The pants are made with two side and one hip pocket, fly front, double seat and double knees, vest double breasted style. The coat is well lined with black Italian cloth, the entire suit trimmed and finished with first class material throughout.

No. 40R62 Price for boys' three-piece knee pants suit for boys aged 8 to 16 years.. **$3.50**

Brown Mixed All Wool Cheviot Suit, $3.75.

IN THIS NUMBER WE OFFER ONE OF THE BEST VALUES WE HAVE EVER BEEN ABLE TO GIVE, AN ALL WOOL BROWN AND GOLD MIXED CHEVIOT. The suit is made in round cut sack style coat, vest double breasted style, pants have two side and one hip pocket; made double seat and double knees. This is considered one of the best and most desirable suits in our entire line. Will give splendid wear and makes a most handsome suit.

No. 40R64 Price for boys' three-piece knee pants suit for boys aged 8 to 16 years.... **$3.75**

Boys' Three-Piece Navy Blue Serge Suit, $4.00

THIS VERY FINE ALL WOOL, MEDIUM WEIGHT, NAVY BLUE SERGE SUIT at $4.00 is, we believe, the best value ever offered in boys serge suits at this price. You might get equal value at $6.00, but no better. This suit is made in round cut sack style coat, vest is made double breasted, pants have two side and one hip pocket, made double seat and double knees, extra buttons inside of coat facing. A well made, strictly all wool, very fine serge suit is what you will get if you order this number.

No. 40R66 Price for boys' three-piece knee pants suit for boys aged 8 to 16 years.... **$4.00**

Boys' Black Clay Worsted Three-Piece Suit, $4.50

THERE IS NOTHING MORE DESIRABLE FOR A BOYS' THREE-PIECE SUIT THAN BLACK CLAY WORSTED. It makes a handsome dress suit. We use only the best material in our boys' suits and this all wool, black clay worsted is full fourteen-ounce guaranteed strictly pure wool cloth, goods that will wear, hold color, and will not get rusty and dingy like the ordinary cheap grade usually to be had at anywhere near our price. Made up in style as shown by opposite illustration, round cut sack coat, vest double breasted, pants made with double seat and double knees.

No. 40R68 Price for boys' three-piece knee pants suit for boys aged 8 to 16 years......... **$4.50**

Stein & Co.'s Fancy Worsted Three-Piece Suit, $4.75.

THIS MOST HANDSOME SUIT IS MADE FROM AN ALL PURE WORSTED MEDIUM WEIGHT CLOTH, a very closely woven, hard finish fabric, will give exceptional wear. It is a brown and blue mixed coloring formed in a broken checked effect. The suit is made in our regular three-piece style as shown by opposite illustration. The vest is made double breasted, the pants have the usual number of pockets, made double at the seat and knees. Extra well trimmed and finished.

No. 40R70 Price for boys' three-piece knee pants suit for boys aged 8 to 16 years........... **$4.75**

Tallcott & Co.'s Light Checked Worsted Suit, $5.00.

FOR SPRING AND SUMMER WEAR WE ESPECIALLY RECOMMEND THIS NUMBER. It is a light checked all pure worsted suit, a most handsome pattern in medium gray shade with an almost invisible over plaid effect in dark green. Made up in style as shown by opposite illustration. Vest double breasted. Pants made with two side and one hip pocket, cut double at the seat and knees.

No. 40R72 Price for boys' three-piece, knee pants suit for boys aged 8 to 16 years...... **$5.00**

Extra Fine Fancy Worsted Suit, $5.50.

WE OFFER IN THIS NUMBER A SUIT THAT IS OF BETTER MATERIAL and better made than you usually find in the best retail clothing stores. It is a suit that would ordinarily cost double our low price. Made from a very fine extra quality of pure worsted. It is a dark navy blue and green mixed pattern, formed in an over plaid or medium checked effect. If you desire one of the finest all worsted suits that you can possibly secure, order this number. Made in exactly the same style as is shown by the opposite illustration, which is an exact reproduction of this suit. Pants made with double seat and double knees. Extra buttons in facing of coat. Made up with good linings, trimmings, etc., throughout.

No. 40R74 Price for boys' three-piece knee pants suits for boys aged 8 to 16 years.... **$5.50**

Holmes & Long's Fancy Green Mixed Cheviot Suit, $3.00.

THIS IS A DARK GREEN ALL WOOL CHEVIOT, with a faint red and green over plaid. The suit is made in round cut sack style Vest double breasted, without collar. Pants have double knees and double seat and the usual number of pockets. Order this suit, and when received, compare it to what clothing stores usually ask $5.00 for, and if it is not equal to such suits in every way, if you do not feel that you have positively saved $2.00, return the suit to us and get your money back.

No. 40R75 Price for boys' three-piece knee pants suit, for boys aged 8 to 16 years.... **$3.00**

GIVE CATALOGUE NUMBER IN FULL WHEN YOU WRITE YOUR ORDER

BOYS' VESTEE SUITS.

Boys' Vestee Suits are made for Boys from 3 to 8 years of age.

FOR FULL INFORMATION ON STYLES, MEASUREMENTS, ETC., SEE INTRODUCTORY PAGE.

We make a specialty of boys' clothing. We have a factory for the purpose of making boys' clothing only. We are therefore in a position to furnish the latest and most perfect fitting garments at prices which positively defy all competition. When you order from us you save the wholesaler's profit, the jobber's profit and your storekeeper's profit. You save the endless chain of profits that is always attached to boys' clothing when sold over the average retail clothing counter. That is why we earnestly solicit your patronage, because we know that we can furnish you better value, we know that we can furnish you perfect fitting garments, made up better and far more satisfactory, at about one-half the price you are in the habit of paying elsewhere.

Boys' Medium Weight Gray Mixed Cheviot Vestee Suit, $1.50.

THIS SUIT IS MADE OF A MEDIUM WEIGHT OF COTTON AND WOOL MIXED CHEVIOT. It is made in the same style as shown by opposite illustration. It is a good, solid, honest wearing suit. The vest is made double breasted style, the dickey or shield is made from the same material as the suit. Pants are made double seat and double at knees, closed front, buckle at knees, double sewed throughout crotch, elastic waist band. A thoroughly first class suit in every way.

No. 40R76 Price for boys' three-piece vestee suit for boys aged 3 to 8 years........ **$1.50**

Plain Navy Blue Cheviot Vestee Suit, $2.00.

AN ALL WOOL NAVY BLUE CHEVIOT makes a very handsome vestee suit. We think that the suit shown by the opposite illustration is one of the nicest and prettiest vestee suits ever shown by any house. Especially is it a handsome suit when you consider the price. Made with a new style round cut coat; vest is made double breasted style with a red flannel dickey, silk monogram worked in center of dickey. The pants are made double seat and double at knees. The suit is extra well trimmed and finished throughout.

No. 40R78 Price for boys' three-piece vestee suit for boys aged 3 to 8 years......... **$2.00**

All Wool Light Tan and Brown Mixed Cheviot Suit, $2.50.

THIS IS ONE OF THE HANDSOMEST LIGHT COLORED SUITS IN OUR LINE. The suit is made of an all wool cheviot in a tan and light brown coloring. It has an almost invisible over plaid effect in dark green and red. The suit is made the new style imitation double breasted coat. The lapels are faced in satin. The vest is made single breasted style with a tan flannel dickey to match material in suit. The pants are made double seat and double at knees. Garments are well sewed.

No. 40R80 Price for boys' three-piece vestee suit, for boys aged 3 to 8 years............. **$2.50**

Olive Mixed Cassimere Vestee Suit, $2.50.

THIS SUIT IS MADE OF AN ALL WOOL OLIVE AND GREEN MIXED CASSIMERE, a very closely woven and desirable cloth. Coat is made in round cut sack style, as shown by opposite figure. The lapels of coat are satin faced, vest is made single breasted style and has an olive dickey to match material in suit. One of the nicest little vestee suits you could possibly get, no matter what price you pay. We especially recommend it. The pants are made usual style, double seat and double at knees.

No. 40R82 Price for boys' three-piece vestee suit for boys aged 3 to 8 years....... **$2.50**

Olive and Brown Mixed Vestee Suit, $2.50.

THIS SUIT IS MADE FROM A PLAIN SHADE OF OLIVE AND BROWN MIXED ALL WOOL CHEVIOT. It is a medium weight cloth and makes a medium weight desirable spring and summer suit. Suit is made up in a Kitchener yoke style coat, as the opposite illustration will show. Vest is made double breasted style; fancy dickey to match material in suit. This is one of the handsomest, new, up to date, Kitchener vestee suits, strictly all wool and at a price which surely warrants your sending us your order.

No. 40R84 Price for boys' three-piece vestee suit for boys aged 3 to 8 years **$2.50**

Boys' All Wool Green Mixed Cheviot Norfolk Jacket and Pants.

THIS NEW KITCHENER NORFOLK JACKET AND PANTS is made of a green and red mixed cheviot, a very desirable suit that will make a most handsome garment for any boy. The coat is made in style as shown by opposite illustration, with Kitchener yoke front and back, two box plaits down the front of the coat, one box plait in the back. A two and one-half inch belt of the same goods. The pants are made double seat and double knees.

No. 40R86 Price for boys' two-piece Kitchener yoke Norfolk jacket and pants for boys aged 4 to 10 years........ **$2.75**

Light Gray Checked All Worsted Kitchener Vestee Suit, $3.00.

THIS IS ONE OF THE HANDSOMEST KITCHENER VESTEE SUITS WE HAVE EVER MADE UP. It is made of a light colored gray and brown checked all worsted material, with an almost invisible over plaid effect in dark green. The coat is made in a Kitchener yoke style both front and back, the vest double breasted, the dickey is made of gray flannel to match colors in the suit. Pants are double seat and double knees, silver buckle at the knee. To appreciate fully this handsome, light suit, you should send us a trial order.

No. 40R88 Price for Kitchener three-piece vestee suit for boys aged 3 to 8 years...... **$3.00**

Boys' Three-Piece Vestee Navy Blue Serge Suit, $3.00.

OUR LINE WOULD NOT BE COMPLETE WITHOUT THIS HANDSOME NAVY BLUE VESTEE SERGE SUIT. The material is a very fine all wool cloth, warranted to wear and to hold color. Coat is made in single breasted, round cut sack style, with satin faced lapels. Vest is cut double breasted style with dickey of the same material, with silk monogram worked in center of dickey. Pants are made in the usual style, double seat and double knees. We especially recommend this most handsome serge suit because it is excellent value and a suit that we feel sure will please any parent.

No. 40R90 Price for boy's three-piece vestee suit, for boys aged 3 to 8 years. **$3.00**

Boys' Brown Mixed All Wool Cheviot Norfolk Jacket and Pants, $3.00.

THIS NORFOLK JACKET AND PANTS, as shown by opposite illustration, is made from an all wool brown and blue mixed cheviot, is a good weight cloth and makes a handsome up to date new and nobby spring and summer suit. The coat is made Norfolk jacket style with Kitchener yoke both back and front. Double row of box plaits in front, single box plait in back; 2½-inch belt of the same material. Pants are made double seat and double knees. We offer you this new up to date Kitchener Norfolk jacket and pants at $3.00. We know that we are giving you such value as cannot possibly be had elsewhere.

No. 40R92 Price for boys' two-piece Kitchener Norfolk jacket and pants for boys aged 4 to 10 years......... **$3.00**

Our Finest Green and Blue Mixed Fancy Worsted Kitchener Yoke Vestee Suit, $4.00.

THIS SUIT IS MADE FROM FINER MATERIAL THAN IS USUALLY TO BE HAD IN BOYS' CLOTHING. Is a very fine all pure worsted, green and blue mixed cloth, made in a Kitchener yoke round cut sack style, Vest is made double breasted style, dickey of same material as suit with silk monogram in center. Pants are made double seat and double knees. This entire suit is gotten up with good linings and trimmings, etc., throughout. It is really the same kind of a suit that you would get in first class clothing establishments at from $6.00 to $8.00 a suit and upwards.

No. 40R94 Price for boys' three-piece Kitchener vestee suit for boys aged 3 to 8 years........ **$4.00**

BOY'S SINGLE KNEE PANTS.

They are made from remnants left from our custom department; we can, therefore, give much better value than we could if made from regular goods. We also make up a very fine class of goods into boys knee pants, nothing cheap and shoddy. Boys' single knee pants come in sizes ages 4 to 15 years. Give age of boy and if large, average or small of age.

SINGLE KNEE PANTS, made up for boys ages 4 to 15 years, from dark heavy weight cassimeres, cheviots, cotton mixed worsteds, etc.

No. 40R96 Price, per pair.............. **40c**

THE NEXT BEST GRADE is made from a better quality of cassimere goods, in dark patterns, good, honest, wearing cloth.

No. 40R98 Price, per pair............ **50c**

SEAL BROWN CORDUROY KNEE PANTS for boys, ages 6 to 15 years. A good heavy weight splendid corduroy pants, double sewed. Warranted not to rip.

No. 40R100 Price, per pair............ **50c**

BOYS' KNEE PANTS, made from ends of all wool cassimeres, cheviots, etc. They are made from ends left over from our custom department, Made double seat and double knees; patent elastic waistband, two side and two hip pockets.

No. 40R102 Price, per pair............ **75c**

IT PAYS TO BUY BOYS' KNEE PANTS FOR $1.00, when you get them made from ends of the very best worsteds left over from our custom department, made double seat and double knees, patent elastic waistband.

No. 40R104 Price, per pair............ **$1.00**

BOYS' REEFER JACKETS.

Boys' reefer jackets are made in sizes, ages 4 to 8 for small boys, and from 9 to 15 years for large boys. Do not order reefer jacket larger than is stated after each description, as we have only the size mentioned. If your boy wears an age 9 or 10, please be sure and order reefer jacket which is quoted for ages 9 to 15, as we cannot furnish the size desired in goods quoted only for boys ages 4 to 8 years.

If you do not give careful and complete measurements we cannot fill your order.

Gray Frieze Reefer Jacket, $2.00.

THIS REEFER JACKET IS MADE WITH STORM COLLAR, of extra heavy Oxford frieze, cut in double breasted style, two lower pockets with flaps; heavy plaid lining, all seams are double stitched. It is made good and strong for heavy wear, and is a very satisfactory reefer jacket for the price. This jacket is made for boys ages 4 to 15 years.

No. 40R108 Price for boys' reefer jacket, ages 4 to 15 years... **$2.00**

Medium Gray Frieze Reefer, $2.75.

Made from a fancy gray mixture reefer cloth. This is one of the handsomest small boys' reefers we have ever designed. Price is lower for this handsome little coat than you could ordinarily get the plain out of date styles elsewhere. Made up as shown by the opposite illustration; velvet collar, double breasted style, two lower pockets with flaps, all seams double stitched, turnover cuffs. A splendid up to date little man's coat, especially recommended by us.

No. 40R110 Price for boys' fancy reefer, ages 4 to 8 years. Price....... **$2.75**

Boys' Navy Blue Chinchilla Reefer.

MADE UP AS SHOWN IN ILLUSTRATION. This reefer is made for boys 4 to 8 years of age, from good quality of all wool chinchilla. There are a great many imitation chinchilla reefers, made out of material that resembles chinchilla, but when you pull the cloth to pieces it is made out of rags. This kind of chinchilla is a very poor grade of goods to buy at any price. If you want a satisfactory boys' chinchilla reefer, we can recommend this number. If you send us your order we are perfectly willing to guarantee the coat to be all that you would expect.

No. 40R112 Price for boys' chinchilla reefer, ages 4 to 8 years.. **$3.00**

Boys' Navy Blue Chinchilla Reefer, $3.00.

THIS REEFER IS MADE UP IN DOUBLE BREASTED STYLE, just the same as opposite illustration will show. Large storm collar, ulster pockets with flaps, double stitched throughout, good strong sleeve lining. It is a navy blue chinchilla jacket that we can recommend. It pays to buy a good chinchilla reefer. That is why we recommend this number.

No. 40R114 Price for boys' chinchilla reefer, ages 9 to 15 years......... **$3.00**

BOYS' CAPE OVERCOATS.

These cape overcoats are made up in style as shown in fashion figure. They are made up for boys aged from 4 to 12 years. **No larger or smaller sizes can be furnished.** The boy may be aged 12 and wear an age 14 or 15 overcoat. The largest size we have, as above stated, is age 12, which is 28 inches breast measure If your boy wears larger than 28 inches breast measure please do not order cape overcoats quoted below. The largest size we can furnish, as stated above, is age 12, or 28 inches breast measure.

Douel, Miller & Co.'s Cloth Cape Overcoats, $2.00.

THIS COAT IS MADE FROM A HEAVY WEIGHT COTTON AND WOOL MIXED CASSIMERE. It is a good wearing cloth, something that will not show dirt. Dark gray color; is made up in double breasted style, large cape, turn down collar, two outside pockets with flaps; well lined and trimmed throughout.

No. 40R116 Price for boys' cape overcoat, ages 4 to 12 years..**$2.00**

Dark Green and Black Mixed Melton Cape Overcoat, $2.50.

THIS COAT IS MADE FROM A HEAVY WEIGHT DARK GREEN AND BLACK MIXED MELTON CLOTH. Especially desirable, makes one of the handsomest cape overcoats we have ever sent out. Large cape, as shown by the accompanying illustration, made in double breasted style, made perfectly plain, two lower outside pockets, with flaps, turn down collar, well lined, trimmed and finished. It is a warm, durable, fine looking coat, one that we can especially recommend.

No. 40R118 Boys' cape overcoat, 4 to 13 years....**$2.50**

Raritan Beaver Navy Blue Cape Overcoat.

A REGULAR WINTER CLOTH; SMOOTH SURFACE. Nothing more desirable for wear and appearance than this double breasted, extra well made cape overcoat. Made with large detachable cape, double breasted style, large ulster pockets, extra buttons on facing of coat, black Italian body lined.

No. 40R120 Boys' cape overcoat, 8 to 12 years....**$3.50**

BOYS' FLY FRONT, SINGLE BREASTED OVERCOATS AND BOYS' DOUBLE BREASTED ULSTERS.

Styles, as shown below, represent Boys' Fly Front Single Breasted Overcoats and Boys' Double Breasted Ulsters. Boys' fly front overcoats and boys' storm collar double breasted ulsters are made for boys aged 12 to 19 years, or 28 to 35 inches breast measure. If your boy measures more than 35 inches breast measure, he cannot wear a boys' overcoat. He is no longer a boy—that is, in size. You will have to buy men's clothing for him, as 35 is the largest size you can obtain from us or any other house in a boys' overcoat. Please bear this in mind when ordering; it saves delay; it saves correspondence and annoyance.

BOYS' OVERCOAT.

Boys' Gray Fly Front Frieze Overcoat, $3.50.

THIS COAT IS MADE FROM HEAVY WEIGHT DARK GRAY FRIEZE OVERCOAT CLOTH; is made up as shown by illustration, and it comes single breasted style; has velvet collar, all seams are double stitched, two lower and one cash pocket; body is lined with good quality black Italian cloth. Our price is based on the actual cost to manufacture, with but our one small profit added.

No. 40R121 Price for boys' single breasted fly front overcoat, ages 12 to 19 years, 28 to 35 inches breast measure...**$3.50**

Dark Navy Blue Beaver Overcoat, $4.50.

THIS DARK NAVY BLUE BEAVER OVERCOAT is made up in fly front style, velvet collar, two lower pockets with flaps, one cash pocket; all seams are double stitched; extra quality of sleeve lining; body is lined with black Italian cloth. A good smooth finished wool beaver is certainly a good overcoat to buy.

No. 40R122 Price for boys' fly front overcoat, ages 12 to 19 years, 28 to 35 inches breast measure.........**$4.50**

Navy Blue Chinchilla Fly Front Overcoat, $5.00.

THIS OVERCOAT IS MADE FROM A HEAVY, GOOD QUALITY, NAVY BLUE CHINCHILLA. It is made in fly front style, velvet collar, extra well made throughout; all seams are double stitched. It is a coat, at the price, we believe to be far superior to anything offered by any other concern. We recommend it to you with a guarantee that it shall prove satisfactory when received, shall prove satisfactory for wear. Made up in the very latest and most perfect fitting style.

No. 40R124 Price for boys' fly front overcoat, ages 12 to 16 years.......................**$5.00**

Dark Green and Red Mixed Frieze Overcoat, $5.00.

THIS IS A VERY HANDSOME DARK GREEN AND RED MIXED FLY FRONT OVERCOAT; a cloth that will wear like leather; makes a very handsome coat; one that we have heretofore been compelled to ask considerable more money for. It is made up in fly front, single breasted style, as shown by the above illustration; all seams are double stitched, well lined, trimmed and finished throughout For boys ages 12 to 19 years, 28 to 35 breast measure.

No. 40R126 Price for boys' single breasted, fly front overcoat, **$5.00**

All Wool Black Kersey Fly Front Overcoat, $6.00.

THIS COAT IS MADE FROM EXTRA QUALITY, HEAVY WEIGHT, ALL WOOL BLACK KERSEY. For dress wear, for good hard usage, there is nothing more desirable than kersey cloth. We solicit a trial order, with the understanding that the coat will please you in every way. It is made up in fly front, single breasted style, velvet collar, double stitched seams; well lined, trimmed and finished throughout For boys 12 to 19 years, 28 to 35 breast measure.

No 40R128 Price for boys' single breasted overcoat.........**$6.00**

Boys' Extra Gray Frieze Ulster, $4.00.

THIS OXFORD GRAY FRIEZE ULSTER is made from a heavy weight quality dark gray frieze. It is the best low priced ulster we have ever been able to offer. made up as shown by illustration below, large storm collar to ulster, two lower outside pockets with flaps, double breasted style, double stitched throughout, extra set of buttons inside of facing. Average length, 46 inches.

No. 40R131 Price for boys' ulster, ages 12 to 19 years, 28 to 35 inches breast measure..................................**$4.00**

Boys' Navy Blue Beaver Ulster, $5.00.

THIS NAVY BLUE BEAVER ULSTER is made from smooth finished wool beaver ulster cloth, especially adapted for heavy winter ulsters. It is made with a large storm collar, ulster pockets, extra heavy weight, warm and durable. All seams are double stitched; two lower outside pockets with flaps, two ulster pockets; lined throughout body with heavy double warped Italian cloth, extra heavy sleeve linings. The coat is made with an idea of securing your future patronage.

No. 40R133 Price for boys' double breasted storm ulster, ages 12 to 19 years, 28 to 35 inches breast measure........**$5.00**

Boys' Navy Blue Chinchilla Ulsters, $5.50.

THERE IS NOTHING WE KNOW OF THAT WILL MAKE A BETTER OR MORE SATISFACTORY HEAVY STORM WINTER ULSTER than a good quality navy blue chinchilla. It is made up as shown by accompanying illustration, large storm collar, two ulster pockets, two lower outside pockets with flaps; all seams are double stitched; extra buttons inside of coat facing to replace any that become lost or broken. Good quality black Italian body lining, extra strong sleeve lining; well made and finished throughout.

No. 40R135 Price for boys' ulster, ages 12 to 19 years, 28 to 35 inches breast measure..........................**$5.50**

Boys' Dark Red and Green Mixed Frieze Ulster, $5.50.

THIS DARK RED AND GREEN MIXED FRIEZE ULSTER is a material especially adapted for boys' heavy winter ulster overcoats Just the kind of goods that the boys like, because it makes a splendid looking coat. Made as shown by illustration, double breasted style, large storm collar; the seams are double stitched, it is well lined, trimmed and padded, made to fit, look well, to wear equal to ulsters costing a great deal more money elsewhere.

No. 40R136 Price for boys' double breasted storm ulster, ages 12 to 19 years, 28 to 35 inches breast measure **$5.50**

BOYS ULSTER

BOYS' WASH SUITS.

The extraordinary value we offer in Boys' Wash Suits can only be fully appreciated by those who order from this department. A trial order will surely convince you that we are able to furnish new, fresh, up to date, stylish and well made wash suits at much lower prices than similar value can be had from any other house.

NOTE.—Boys' wash suits can be had only in the sizes as mentioned after each description. Always state age of boy and if large or small of age.

Boy's Wash Crash Suit, 35 Cents.

MADE FROM A FAIR QUALITY OF WASH CRASH. Shield and cuffs trimmed with brown duck. Large sailor collar. Anchor monogram in center of shield. Cord and whistle with each suit. A desirable and substantially made wash suit.

No. 40R130 Price for boys' wash suit for boys aged 3 to 10 years......**35c**

Navy Blue and White Percale Wash Suit, 40 Cents.

MADE FROM BLUE AND WHITE PENCIL STRIPE WASH PERCALE, with large sailor collar. Collar and cuffs made from navy blue wash duck. One outside pocket. Cord and whistle attached to each suit. This is a splendid dark wash suit for everyday wear.

No. 40R132 Price for boys' wash suit for boys aged 3 to 10 years..........**40c**

Boys' Crash Wash Suit, 50 Cents.

MADE FROM A GOOD QUALITY OF WASH CRASH. Large sailor collar and cuffs made from navy blue sateen. White monogram worked in center of shield. Cord and whistle with every suit. This is splendid value.

No. 40R134 Price for boys' suit for boys aged 3 to 10 years..........**50c**

Extra Heavy Percale Wash Suit, 65 Cents.

MADE FROM STRIPED WASH PERCALE in a medium shade of tan. Large sailor collar and cuffs of brown duck to match suit. The opposite illustration will give you an accurate idea of the appearance of this most handsome suit. One of the best wearing wash suits we have to offer.

No. 40R138 Price for boys' wash suit for boys aged 3 to 10 years..**65c**

Boy's Pink Chambray Suit, 75 Cents.

MADE FROM AN EXTRA HEAVY QUALITY OF PINK WASH CHAMBRAY. Guaranteed absolutely fast color. Trimmed on collar and shield with white duck. Monogram in center of shield. Large sailor collar. One of the best wash suits you could possibly purchase.

No. 40R140 Price for boys' wash suit for boys aged 3 to 10 years...**75c**

Boys' Brown and White Wash Chambray, 75c.

THIS, ONE OF THE MOST DESIRABLE SUITS IN OUR LINE, is made from a medium brown wash chambray with a raised cord stripe effect; sailor collar trimmed with braid, collar is made of a good quality of brown sateen, white pique shield, monogram in the center. Cord and whistle with each suit. Extra well made and one of the best wash suits we can offer.

No. 40R142 Price for boys' wash suit for boys aged 3 to 10 years..**75c**

Blue and White Pencil Striped Percale Wash Suit, 75 Cents.

THIS SUIT IS MADE FROM AN EXTRA HEAVY NARROW BLUE AND WHITE STRIPED PERCALE. The cuffs and large sailor collar are made from a good quality of dark navy blue sateen, white duck shield and monogram in center. This is a strong, durable suit, and one that we guarantee for color and wear.

No. 40R144 Price for boys' wash suit for boys aged 3 to 10 years.....................**75c**

Extra Fine Wash Suit, 85 Cents.

THIS SUIT IS MADE FROM A VERY FINE LINEN WASH CRASH, most handsomely gotten up and well shaped. Large sailor collar trimmed with four rows of white braid; the back of the collar is made of red sateen shield made of white duck with silk monogram worked in center; the sleeves and cuffs are shaped as shown in illustration; one outside pocket trimmed at top with red sateen. Would cost you double our low price for a similar suit elsewhere.

No. 40R146 Price for boys' wash suit for boys aged 3 to 10 years.**85c**

Extra Fine Blue and White Wash Sateen Suit, $1.00.

THIS MOST HANDSOME WASH SUIT IS MADE OF A VERY FINE QUALITY OF WASH SATEEN in blue and white pencil stripe effect; large sailor collar of same goods trimmed with a neat pattern of insertion; the edge of collar is bound with white duck, cord effect pique shield, with blue and white silk emblem worked in the center; the cuffs of waist and pants at knees are trimmed with white pearl buttons; shaped sleeves. A most handsome summer suit.

No. 40R150 Price for boys' wash suit for boys aged 3 to 10 years..**$1.00**

Very Fine White Pique Wash Suit, $1.25.

VERY FINE BIRD'S-EYE EFFECT WHITE PIQUE WITH LARGE SAILOR COLLAR, made from medium shade of blue wash pique; collar trimmed with four rows of soutache braid, shield is made of blue and white pique with a silk monogram in center. Cord and whistle with each suit. Extra well made throughout and one of the handsomest white suits you could possibly purchase, no matter what price is paid.

No. 40R152 Price for boys' wash suit for boys aged 3 to 10 years..............**$1.25**

Boys' Wash Knee Pants.

MADE FROM A GOOD HEAVY TAN WASH PERCALE, double stitched throughout. A good durable pants.

No. 40R154 Price for boys' knee pants for boys aged 4 to 12 years.....**15c**

Blue and White Striped Percale Knee Pants.

MADE FROM A HEAVY, STONG FABRIC.

No. 40R156 Price for boys' knee pants for boys aged 4 to 12 years......**15c**

All Linen Crash Knee Pants.

MADE FROM A GOOD, STRONG, HEAVY ALL LINEN CRASH that will wash and give splendid wear.

No. 40R158 Price for boys' knee pants for boys aged 6 to 15 years **25c**

Tan Wash Double Breasted Suit, 75 Cents.

THESE SUITS ARE FOR BOYS' WARM WEATHER SUITS, intended for boys aged 9 to 16 years. This number is made from a good quality of brown wash grass cloth, double breasted style as shown by opposite illustration; two outside pockets; double row of pearl buttons; pants trimmed with pearl buttons at knee; extra well made throughout.

No. 40R160 Price for boys' suit for boys aged 9 to 16 years............**75c**

Another Tan Wash Double Breasted Suit.

IN A LITTLE BETTER QUALITY THAN THE ABOVE NUMBER, MADE FROM A WASH DUCK. Cut double breasted style, coat is trimmed with pearl buttons, two outside pockets, double stitched throughout; pants are extra well made, double sewed through seat, one hip pocket, two side pockets, fly front. Just such a suit as as you would pay $1.50 for elsewhere for as good a value.

No. 40R162 Our price for boys' suit for boys aged 9 to 16 years......................**85c**

BOYS' WASH WAISTS.

IN THE BOYS' WAIST DEPARTMENT WE DO NOT ATTEMPT TO COMPETE WITH THE CHEAP, SHODDY, POORLY MADE, ILL FITTING GARMENTS WITH WHICH THE COUNTRY IS ALWAYS FLOODED. We believe that our customers like well made, up to date and at the same time durable garments. We could offer you boys' waists as low as 10 cents that might look well on paper, but this cheap, poorly made trash is poor value at any price. Our waists are guaranteed to fit, to wear and give every satisfaction. We are always ready to refund money on any unsatisfactory goods purchased in this department, or replace the garments even after they have been worn should they at any time prove to be inferior to our customers' expectations.

Boys' Wash Waist 25c

MADE FROM GOOD, HEAVY QUALITY OF WASH PERCALE, in any medium wash colors, plaited front and back. The best 25 cent waist we claim ever offered to the buying public. Come in assorted colors. State your preference and we are sure to please you.

No. 40R164 Price for boys' waist for boys aged 4 to 14 years........**25c**

Boys' Blue and White Wash Percale Waist, 40c.

MADE EXACTLY THE SAME AS OPPOSITE ILLUSTRATION, of heavy guaranteed fast color wash percale, blue and white stripe. Double sewed throughout, double shoulder stay, extension cuffs, collar attached to waist. One of the best numbers in our line.

No. 40R165 Price for boys' waist for boys aged 4 to 12 years..........**40c**

Extra Quality Wash Percale Waist, 45c.

MADE FROM EXTRA QUALITY WASH PERCALE IN DARK NAVY BLUE AND WHITE STRIPE EFFECTS. Mothers' friend. Detachable waistband, three box plaits in front and back, open cuffs, pearl buttons, stationary collar. One of the most desirable and durable boys' waists in our line.

No. 40R166 Price for boys' waist for boys aged 4 to 12 years........**45c**

Blue and White Box Plaited Waists.

FINER QUALITY THAN ABOVE IN MEDIUM BLUE AND WHITE STRIPE FRENCH PERCALE. New shirt waist front, three single box plaits in front and back; made to wear with collar; open cuffs, pearl buttons. Mothers' friend. Patent adjustable waistband.

No. 40R168 Price for boys' waist for boys aged 4 to 12 years.........**50c**

Boys' White Laundered Shirt Waists, 60 Cents.

MADE FROM A FINE QUALITY OF WHITE LAWN MUSLIN. Three box plaits in front and back, trimmed with heavy pearl buttons, open cuffs, collar attached to the waist. A very popular style.

No. 40R170 Price for boys' waist for boys aged 4 to 14 years........**60c**

Boys' White Unlaundered Waist for 50c.

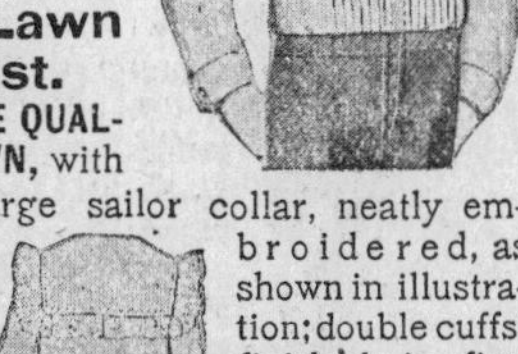

THIS WAIST IS MADE FROM THE SAME MATERIAL AS THE ABOVE NUMBER, only with six rows of narrow box plaits in front and three wide box plaits in back; no collar with waist; shaped shoulders. Extra well made throughout.

No. 40R172 Price for boys' waist for boys aged 4 to 14 years........**50c**

Boys' White Lawn Blouse Waist.

MADE FROM FINE QUALITY OF WHITE LAWN, with large sailor collar, neatly embroidered, as shown in illustration; double cuffs; finished in first class manner.

No. 40R174 Price for boys' waist for boys aged 3 to 10 years..**50c**

ALWAYS SEND CASH WITH YOUR ORDER.

Boys' Laundered Percale Waist, $1.00.

MADE FROM A VERY FINE WASH PERCALE; collars and cuffs attached to the waist; double sewed throughout; extra well stayed at the shoulder; trimmed with pearl buttons. Finest laundered waist we can offer.

No. 40R178 Price for boys' waist for boys aged 4 to 14 years....**$1.00**

Boys' Military Waist, 85 Cents.

MADE IN MILITARY STYLE, as shown in opposite illustration, of a very fine blue and white linen chambray, trimmed in military effect with heavy white pique braid, pearl buttons, double cuffs. One of the newest and handsomest wash waists out this season.

No. 40R180 Price for boys' waist for boys aged 3 to 10 years..........**85c**

Extra Fine White Linen Lawn Waist, $1.00.

ONE OF THE HANDSOMEST WHITE WAISTS YOU CAN POSSIBLY GET, NO MATTER WHAT PRICE YOU PAY. Made from a plain white linon lawn, with a plain and Bedford cord effect, cut in military style; elegantly made and finished: trimmed with heavy ball pearl buttons, double cuffs.

No. 40R182 Price for boys' waist for boys aged 3 to 10 years.....**$1.00**

Boys' Blouse Waist, 75 Cents.

THIS WAIST IS MADE FROM A FINE QUALITY OF LINEN LAWN, with a large sailor collar made from blue and white wash pique, trimmed down the front and on cuffs with the same material. One of the newest and most desirable waists in our line.

No. 40R183 Price for boys' waist for boys aged 3 to 10 years......**75c**

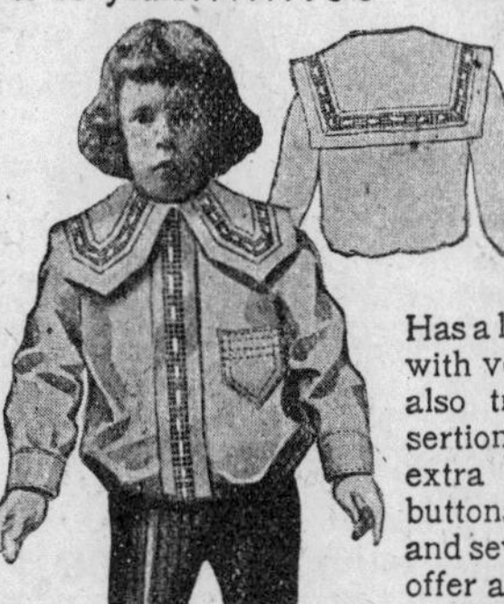

THIS, OUR HIGHEST PRICE WHITE WAIST, IS MADE FROM A VERY FINE QUALITY INDIA LINEN. Has a large collar, inlaid with very fine insertion; also trimmed with insertion down front; extra fine heavy pearl buttons; nicely shaped and sewed. We cannot offer anything better.

No. 40R184 Price for boys' waist for boys aged 3 to 10 years....**$1.00**

Boys' Blue and White Percale Waist, 65 Cents.

MADE OF GOOD QUALITY BLUE AND WHITE PERCALE; laundered front; collar and cuffs attached to waist; trimmed with pearl buttons; double sewed throughout. A most desirable waist.

No. 40R176 Price for boys' waist for boys aged 4 to 14 years....................................**65c**

FUR COAT DEPARTMENT

IF YOU COULD GET $5.00, $10.00, $20.00 OR $50.00 FOR READING OUR FUR COAT TALK, WOULDN'T YOU READ IT?

If you could purchase a coat from us for less money than your local merchant can buy an inferior fur coat, WOULDN'T YOU ORDER FROM US? If you should order one of our $16.00 Natural Brown Galloway Calf Coats, and find it better value than your local dealer can sell for $22.00, your are sure that at least $5.00 has been made on your purchase. We make it possible for you to save from $5.00 to $50.00 on a fur coat. We make it possible for you to purchase at THE ACTUAL COST TO MANUFACTURE WITH BUT ONE SMALL PROFIT ADDED.

WE MAKE IT IMPOSSIBLE FOR YOU TO GET A POOR COAT, by sending you a new one, if by any chance whatsoever, the coat you get should prove unsatisfactory. We started our fur coat factory three years ago to enable us to furnish our customers the very best made goods

AT THE LOWEST POSSIBLE PRICE.

THE VOLUME OF BUSINESS transacted last season was ten times greater than the previous year. We have been guided by our last and previous seasons' business, and are now in a position to furnish our customers better and more perfect made coats than ever before, for less money than they actually cost when we first started our fur coat factory. By making the largest cash purchase on record of raw skins, and all the necessary material used in the construction of fur coats, by tanning, blending, matching, cutting and making this raw material into the very best fur coats that skilled labor can produce, under the personal supervision of an expert fur coat maker, and offering the best guaranteed, perfectly finished coats, direct from our factory to the wearer, with but one small profit added, we claim the right to expect the order of every reader of this catalogue who is in the market for a fur coat. We claim to furnish better coats than can be had elsewhere, and save our customers from $5.00 to $50.00 (according to the price coat purchased) on their purchase. We are the only house who give an absolute guarantee (covering workmanship and wear), for one year from date of purchase.

WE ARE THE ONLY HOUSE who use the waterproof duck interlining, as shown by the opposite skeleton illustration. This extra work and precaution is one feature which makes our coat better than other makes. Our coats are made with 6 inches larger skirt sweep than any other coat that we have ever examined. We use every precaution to make our fur coats the very best that can be produced.

BEFORE ANY SKINS ARE CUT they are tested for strength and durability; any imperfect skins are thrown out and used in cheap coats, such as we do not make or handle. After the skins have been passed by the examiner they are matched and cut into coats. Every coat is double sewed throughout. After this is done it is interlined, as shown in cut, with a 10-ounce waterproof duck. Every seam, with the exception of the seam in the sleeve, is covered with duck and then double sewed through the duck and leather, which makes the sewing so firm that it is utterly impossible for one of our fur coats to rip. The center seam is covered with a 2½-inch strip of duck and single stitched on both sides, also double stitched through the center The front of coat is faced with an 8-inch strip of duck, with three rows of linen sewing on edge of coat. Many of our black coats are also faced down the outside edge with a ⅝-inch worsted tape. Nine-tenths of the work on a fur coat is where you cannot see it; the inside make is just where we take special pains, and on account of this extra work we can give an absolute guarantee against ripping. Having control of the raw material before it is made up, we can also guarantee our fur coats for wear.

WE HOPE THAT OUR ARGUMENT IN BEHALF OF WELL MADE COATS WILL INTEREST YOU ENOUGH TO FAVOR US WITH YOUR ORDER.

SIZES ON MEN'S FUR COATS run from 36 to 46 inches breast measure. Our coats are cut full size and run full 52 inches in length. Fur coats should not be worn tight. When ordering be sure to give your correct height and weight, also the correct measurement around chest under arms, over the coat that you expect to wear the fur coat. Sizes larger than 46 inches chest measure we term as extra sizes, and we make up all extra sizes to special order, for which we charge extra, according to the quality of the goods and size ordered. If you cannot wear a 46-inch breast measure, please let us know the kind of a coat you wish to order, and the size desired, and we will take pleasure in quoting you special prices.

OUR GALLOWAY CALF WINNER COAT FOR $16.00.

We sold hundreds of these coats last season at $18.00, because the price was lower than a good Galloway coat could be gotten for anywhere else. By placing the largest order for skins when the market was low, by controlling and operating our fur coat factory on an economical plan, we can furnish a better coat than our last year's make, at a still lower price. Our winner coat is made from selected Natural Brown Galloway Calf Skins carefully cut and matched. No better or more satisfactory fur coat made for wear than a Galloway. Clean, dressy, light, comfortable, pliable and warm. Plain collar and sleeves, fur wristers, quilted Italian or serge lined, canvas or duck interlined, cable sewed, cut large and roomy Such a coat as would cost you from $22.00 to $28.00 elsewhere. The greatest value ever offered in a guaranteed strictly high grade fur coat.

No. 41R302 Price.............. $16.00

No. 41R302

No. 41R304

OUR $18.00 JET BLACK GALLOWAY CALF COAT

There is nothing more desirable in the fur coat trade than a good, black Galloway calfskin. They are a dressy, light, and an altogether satisfactory coat. To fully appreciate the wonderful value we give in fur coats, before sending us your order, look over the black Galloway coats offered by your local dealer. Send for catalogue and prices from any other mail order house, and then place your order where your better judgment tells you the best value can be had. Our black Galloway coats are made from carefully selected skins, perfectly tanned, cut and matched. This coat is made plain collar and sleeves, as shown by opposite illustration. Quilted Italian lined, waterproof duck interlined, made as good as a fur coat can be made. Warranted for one year, warranted to give you perfect satisfaction, warranted to equal any plain black Galloway coat in the market. Please compare prices.

No. 41R304 Price........ $18.00

THERE IS EVERY REASON WHY WE CAN FURNISH BETTER MADE AND FINER QUALITY IN FUR AND FUR LINED COATS THAN CAN BE HAD ELSEWHERE.

IF YOU CAN SAVE FROM $5.00 TO $50.00 (ACCORDING TO THE GRADE COAT ORDERED) IS IT NOT YOUR DUTY TO DO SO?

MEN'S UNLINED OR SO CALLED SKELETON LINED COATS AND COATS AND VESTS.

Under this heading we quote men's serge coats and coats and vests. They are made up in round cut sack style only as shown below by fashion figure. We make these coats and vests in our own factory. They are better made and are of finer material and will give better satisfaction than any other summer coats and vests that you can procure at this price.

Men's Navy Blue Serge Coat and Vest $3.50.

No. 41R2 Under this number we furnish an all wool, good quality, navy blue serge coat and vest made up in round cut sack style, all seams double stitched, wide facings. The vest is cut in single breasted style with notched collar. Sizes, 34 to 42 only.
Price for men's coat and vest........**$3.50**

Extra Quality Navy Blue Serge Coat and Vest.

No. 41R4 This coat and vest is made of a very fine quality, all wool navy blue serge. It is what is termed skeleton lined or unlined, has wide facings, all seams double stitched, made in style as shown by above fashion figure. It is a better coat and vest than you can procure from any other source, as we make these coats in our own factory and sell them to our customers at the actual cost to make with but one small profit added. Sizes, 34 to 42 only.
Price for men's coat and vest..................**$4.50**

Extra Quality Dark Gray Serge Coat and Vest, $5.00.

No. 41R6 This coat and vest is made without any lining in the coat. It is what is termed a skeleton made coat. The seams are all double sewed, has wide facings; the vest is made up the same as all regular vests, single breasted, five buttons. The cloth is a very fine all wool gray serge. Sizes, 34 to 42 only. Price, for men's coat and vest...........**$5.00**

MEN'S SUMMER CLOTHING.

On this page we list men's summer coats, coats and vests, etc. The goods we sell in this department are not the cheap, ordinarily made garments that are usually sold throughout the country. All of our summer clothing is made especially for us by one of the best manufacturers of summer goods. **The garments are all made in the latest and most perfect fitting styles.** They are well trimmed and finished. You will find by ordering summer clothing from us that you will have a superior quality of goods, better workmanship, and better all round satisfaction than you can possibly procure from any other house at anywhere near the same money.

Style 50

No. 41R8 Men's Black Cotton Summer Coat. Round cut sack style. Sizes, 34 to 42 only. A well made, substantial coat. Style 50 only
Price for men's single coat......................**50c**

No. 41R10 Men's Black and White Striped Cotton Summer Coat. Made from black and white striped wash percale. Size, 34 to 42 only. Style 50 only. Price for men's coat, round cut sack........**75c**

No. 41R12 Men's Black Alpaca Coat. Made from a fair quality of black alpaca, wide facings, round cut sack style 50 only. A splendid coat for the money. Sizes 34 to 44 only.
Price for men's black alpaca coat...............**$1.25**

No. 41R14 Men's Black Alpaca Coats. Made the same as the above number only of a finer quality of black alpaca. Sizes 34 to 42 only, round cut sack style 50 only. Price, each.......................**$1.50**

No. 41R16 Men's Black Alpaca Summer Coats. Made of a good quality of black alpaca, wide facings, extra well made, an excellent coat for the money. Sizes, 34 to 42 only. We have round cut sack style 50 only. Price...**$2.00**

No. 41R18 Extra Quality Black Alpaca Coat. This coat is made from a very fine all worsted alpaca cloth, extra well made throughout, wide facings, all seams double stitched. Sizes, 34 to 44 only. Round cut sack style 50 only. Price, per coat..............**$2.50**

No. 41R20 Finest Silk Finished Alpaca Coat. This coat is made from the finest silk finished alpaca cloth, elegantly made, double sewed throughout and as fine an alpaca coat as you can procure in this style. Sizes, 34 to 44 only. Made in round cut sack style 50 only.
Price, each...**$3.00**

No. 41R22 Men's Black Sicilian Coat and Vest. This coat and vest is made from a fine quality of black Sicilian cloth, with wide French facings and double sewed throughout. The vest is made in regular five button style, single breasted, notched collar. This is a very handsome black summer coat and vest. Sizes, 34 to 44 only. Price for coat and vest, coat in round sack style 50 only..................**$4.50**

Men's Extra Long Black Summer Coats and Coats and Vests, Style 51.

Under this heading we list what is termed as men's extra long summer coats. They are, as is shown by illustration, style 51, a long, **single breasted style of coat.** All of our summer clothing is ready made. We have them only in sizes from 34 to 44 breast measure at the prices quoted.

Style 51

No. 41R26 Men's Extra Long Black Alpaca Summer Coat. Well made, double sewed throughout; a splendid coat for the money. Price for men's coat, style 51 only, sizes 34 to 44 only............**$2.00**

No. 41R28 Men's Extra Long Black Alpaca Summer Coat. Made from a better quality than the above number. Coat made in same style as shown by fashion figure, style 51.
Price, for men's extra long black alpaca coat, style 51 only.........**$2.50**

No. 41R30 Extra Quality of Black Alpaca Coat. This coat is made the same style as is be shown by fashion figure, style 51. It is an extra long black alpaca coat, good quality, well made, double sewed throughout, wide facings, etc. Sizes, 34 to 44.
Price for coat, style 51 only...................**$3.00**

Men's Black Sicilian Coat.

No. 41R32 This is an extra long coat made from an extra fine quality of Sicilian cloth, a material that is a little heavier in weight than alpaca, also has a higher luster. The coat is well made with double facings, well sewed throughout. One of the best black coats you can procure. Price for men's black extra long coat and vest, style 51 only............**$4.00**

Men's Extra Long Black Drap de Ate Coat and Vest.

No. 41R34 This is an extra long coat with vest to match, made of a very fine quality of black Drap de Ate cloth, a material that is similar in weave to cassimere. It is all wool, very fine quality and a most excellent coat and vest, well made, double sewed throughout, wide facings. If you wish a very fine black coat and vest in Style 51 order this number. Sizes, 34 to 44.
Price for men's coat and vest, style 51 only...**$6.00**

MEN'S MINISTERIAL OR SINGLE BREASTED FROCK COATS.

The coats listed under this heading are made up in a ministerial or single breasted frock style, as shown by our illustration or Fashion Figure style No. 52, and are made in sizes from 34 to 44 only, to be had only in style as shown by illustration No. 52.

Style 52

No. 41R36 Men's Black Alpaca Ministerial Coat. Made extra long, ministerial style, like our Style 52.
Price for men's black alpaca ministerial coat, Style 52 only, sizes 34 to 44 only..........**$3.00**

No. 41R38 Extra Quality of Black Alpaca Ministerial Style Coat. This coat is made from a very fine quality of black alpaca. Comes in style 52 only, sizes 34 to 44 only. Price........**$4.00**

Men's Black Drap de Ate Ministerial Coat and Vest.

No. 41R40 This coat and vest is made from a fine quality of black Drap de Ate cloth. The coat is cut in ministerial style like our style 52. The vest is made single breasted, five buttons, notched collar. This is a very fine coat and vest, one that will prove, we are sure, entirely satisfacfory in every respect.
Price for men's black coat and vest like style 52, sizes 34 to 44 only.......................................**$7.50**

BUTCHERS', BARTENDERS', GROCERS', WAITERS' AND COOKS' JACKETS.

No. 41R42 Cooks' or Waiters' Heavy White Drill Jacket, or coat, with one top pocket, single breasted style. Price, each.......................**65c**

No. 41R44 Waiters' Black Sateen Jackets, unlined. Sizes, 34 to 42 only. Price, each..........**65c**

No. 41R46 Heavy White Drill Waiters' Coat, double breasted style, high at the neck, standing collar, three outside pockets. Price, each........**85c**

No. 41R48 Heavy White Duck Coats, double breasted style, rolling collar, three pockets.
Price, each...**$1.00**

No. 41R50 Butchers' White Heavy Cotton Drill Coats, two outside pockets, rolling collar, single breasted coat. Sizes, 36 to 42. Price, each........**70c**

No. 41R52 Butchers' Heavy White Duck Coat, single breasted style, rolling collar, two outside pockets. Price, each.....................................**95c**

No. 41R54 Butchers' Double Breasted Unbleached Cotton Duck Coats, made up with patent riveted buttons. Length, 30 inches. Price, each..**95c**

No. 41R56 Butchers' Aprons, made of good white duck to fit over the head. Lengths, 44, 46, 48 and 50 inches, the measure to be taken from the neck down.
Price, each...**25c**

No. 41R57 Bartenders' or Waiters' Apron. Made of good quality white duck. Size, 38 inches wide by 40 inches long, to fit from waist down.
Price, each...**20c**

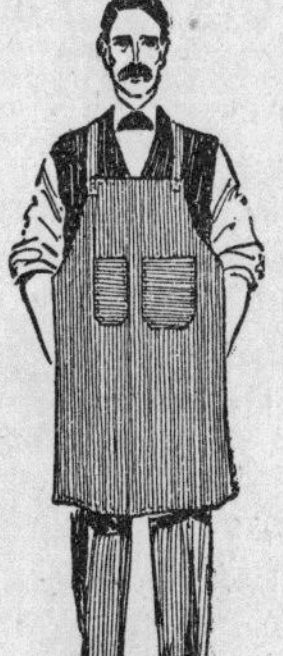

Machinists' Apron.

No. 41R58 Machinists' Apron, made of 8-ounce kaikai duck. (Government standard for uniforms.) Two tool pockets at top as shown. Extra long adjustable strap around waist, patent buckle and riveted button. Length, 35 inches.
Price, each......................**25c**
If by mail, postage extra, each, 8 cents.

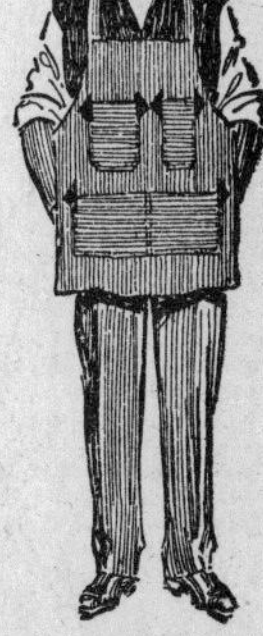

Carpenters' Apron.

No. 41R59 Carpenter's Apron, made of 8-ounce kaikai duck. (Government standard for uniforms.) Two large nail pockets at bottom and two tool pockets at top. Corners of pockets secured by leather. Extra long adjustable strap around waist, patent buckle and riveted button. Length, 24 inches.
Price, each.......................25c
If by mail, postage extra, each, 8 cents.

Men's White Duck Pants.

Men's White Duck Pants are made with suspender buttons on the inside of waistband, belt straps, two side and one hip pocket, and should be ordered full length to allow two and one-half inches turn up at the bottom on account of shrinkage in washing. The white duck pants which we offer are extra well made. They will fit better and give more general satisfaction than the average duck trousers sold by retailers.

No. 41R62 Good Quality White Duck Trousers Extra well made, trimmed and finished. Sizes, 30 to 42 inches waist measure and 30 to 36 inches inseam measure.
Price, per pair...**90c**

No. 41R64 Extra Good Quality White Duck Trousers. Made with belt straps, suspender buttons on inside of waistband, double sewed throughout. Sizes, 30 to 42 inches waist measure, 30 to 36 inches inseam measure. Price, per pair...................**$1.10**

No. 41R66 Extra Fine Quality White Duck Trousers. Well made, trimmed and finished, belt straps, suspender buttons on inside of waistband. Made of an extra quality of fine wash duck. Sizes, 30 to 42 inches waist measure or 30 to 36 inches inseam measure. Price, per pair.................**$1.35**

SEND 5 CENTS
— FOR —
CLOTH SAMPLE BOOK No. 52R
CONTAINING EVERYTHING IN
MEN'S CUSTOM TAILORING.

No. 41R306

Jet Black Curly Dog Coat for $20.00.

We do not recommend the ordinary plain dog coats. While they wear and give satisfaction, we do not like their appearance, as we can furnish coats that will wear as well or better, that will look ten to one more dressy, we advocate buying a fine appearing fur coat. While this coat is a dogskin coat, it does not resemble the ordinary plain black dog coats any closer than our black Galloway coat does a common goatskin. **This coat is made from jet black, glossy curly dogskins, carefully selected, evenly matched, thoroughly deodorized, one of the handsomest and best wearing coats in our line, and the kind of a dog coat that we do recommend.** Made perfectly plain, collar and sleeves, quilted Italian lined, duck interlined, leather arm shields, loops and buttons. Guaranteed for one year from date of sale.

No. 41R306 Price............... **$20.00**

...Good Fur Coats Are Hard to Find...

THERE ARE SO MANY MADE UP TO SELL AND NOT TO WEAR.

That's why it pays to order one of our guaranteed coats.

Our $22.50 Natural Black Bearskin Coat.

This, our most popular coat last season at $24.50, we have reduced to $22.50 because we have saved just $2.00 by making five times the quantity, and therefore give our customers the benefit. This is the same grade of coat which we sold so many of last season, **made from heavy jet black bearskin, very closely furred.** Quilted Italian lined, leather arm shields, sewed throughout with heavy linen, warranted not to rip. Duck interlined. Better this year than ever, and the price is less.

No. 41R308 Price............ **$22.50**

No. 41R308

No. 41R310

A FUR COAT CAN BE A DRESS COAT AS WELL AS A FUR COAT IF YOU GET THE RIGHT KIND. **Our fur coats can be worn at any time or place with every satisfaction to the wearer.**

Jet Black Russian Buffalo Calf Coat for $25.00

No more popular coat in our line than this number. Don't pay $10.00 more for an inferior fur coat. Our price is $3.00 less than last season, but the coat is even better. **The price we make is less than many small manufacturers can produce a similar garment.** Made from jet black, glossy, Russian buffalo calf, best selected stock, southern beaver collar, cuffs and pockets, buttons and loups, quilted Italian lined, duck interlined, guaranteed for wear, appearance, workmanship, warmth, style and finish.

No. 41R310 Price........... **$25.00**

No. 41R312

Our $25.00 Seal Coat.

A VERY HANDSOME JET BLACK COAT. MADE FROM FIRST QUALITY HAIR SEAL.

By importing a large quantity of sealskins

DRESSING, TANNING THE SKINS AND MAKING THEM UP IN OUR OWN FACTORY,

we are able to offer a

GENUINE HAIR SEAL COAT

at about

ONE-HALF THE USUAL PRICE.

Made from jet black first quality hair seal. Very glossy, and presents a fine appearance, as illustration will show. Full southern beaver collar, rolling cuffs and pocket tabs, worsted loops and olives, leather arm shields, quilted Italian lined, duck interlined, edge bound with black worsted. No more sightly or desirable coat in our line than this number.

No. 41R312 Price................ **$25.00**

IF YOU WANT A FUR COAT AT... **$10.00 OR $12.00**

we refer you to our

SHEEP PELT LINED DUCK ULSTERS.....

Just as warm, water and windproof and will wear five times as long.

It will pay you to buy our

Double Extra Sheep Lined Ulster

rather than a cheap all fur coat.

WHY OUR FUR COATS AT OUR PRICES ARE BETTER

Than fur coats sold by other houses at higher prices, is all a question of economy in buying the skins, making the coats, and one small margin of profit above the actual cost of manufacture.

The Fur Coats you buy from Home Storekeepers have passed through at least three hands with three profits, any one of them much larger than our one small profit.

...READ PAGE 1146...

How our Fur Overcoats are made, how we guarantee to satisfy you or refund all your money and pay express charges both ways.

IF EVERY FUR COAT WE SEND OUT WOULDN'T ADVERTISE US WE WOULD WANT TO QUIT THE BUSINESS.....

Our $32.50 First Quality Norway Seal Coat.

This, the handsomest black coat in our entire line, and a coat that we can especially recommend, one which we sold hundreds of last season.

They were all guaranteed for one year from date of sale,

YET WE NEVER RECEIVED A COMPLAINT FROM OUR NORWAY SEAL GOODS.

We claim that this coat, at our last year's price, $32.50, is the finest fur coat ever offered the buying public. We have made it up this season exactly the same as illustration will show. Cut full size, has a large, rolling, genuine otter collar. Also genuine otter cuffs and pocket tabs, worsted loops and olives. Extra quality of black Italian quilted lining, leather arm stays, waterproof duck interlined. While the price of this coat remains the same as last season, **we are using genuine otter collars and cuffs for trimming, which makes it a much finer coat than our last year's garment.** We especially recommend this number for all kinds of wear. It is a favorite with doctors, lawyers, or any one wishing a very handsome, at the same time a splendid wearing coat.

No. 41R314 Price........... **$32.50**

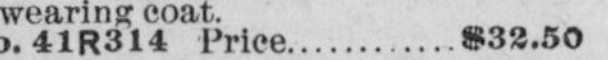

No. 41R314

RACCOONSKIN COATS.

RACCOONSKIN COATS are the most popular high priced fur coats manufactured, always have been and probably always will be. While the price has been steadily advancing year after year, a raccoon coat is still very reasonable in price where the wearing quality of the garment is considered. **They are light, soft and pliable, very heavily furred** and while a cheap Southern, and so called Eastern made raccoonskin coat is as poor a coat as any one could purchase, as they will give no satisfaction whatever, a first class well made Northern coat is still the best fur coat that you can buy. Unless you wish to purchase a good raccoon coat, we would certainly advise you to buy a good article in a Galloway calfskin, or some other standard fur, as a cheap raccoonskin coat is absolutely no good at any price. **We guarantee our raccoonskin coats. Every coat has attached our one year's guarantee, covering wear, workmanship and general finish, so you really take no chances when you send us your order,** as the coat must please you, and if it does not wear satisfactorily, you can return it to us either for a new coat or your money.

Nos. 41R316 41R318 41R328

X Quality Plain Raccoonskin Coat for $30.00.

In offering our customers this coat at our special price of $30.00, we know that we are giving them the best value in a raccoonskin coat that will be sold this year. While we recommend buying our better raccoonskin coats, we guarantee this coat to be all that we claim, a splendid wearing fur coat. **It is made from medium weight skins, perfectly plain collar and sleeves, quilted Italian lined,** buttons and loops, leather arm shields, made up first class in every particular. The skins used are not the best, and the color is consequently light, and the coat is not as desirable as our XX or XXX quality.

No. 41R316 Price.......... $30.00

XX Quality Plain Raccoonskin Coat for $32.00.

This coat is made from carefully selected stock, perfectly plain collar and cuffs, as shown by the opposite fashion figure; Italian or Albert twilled lined, leather arm shields. This is a thoroughly first class coat, and one that will give perfect satisfaction. **We guarantee it for one year.** The coat can be returned to us at any time within one year if it proves unsatisfactory in any way.

No. 41R318 Price.. $32.00

XXXX Quality Northern Raccoonskin Coat for $50.00

Nos. 41R322 41R326

This, our highest priced raccoonskin coat, is one that will please any customer who knows a good thing when he sees it. We have made this coat up from the very choicest skins; they are perfectly matched, as will be seen in illustration No. 41R322. **The general make and finish of this coat is as good as you will be able to get, no matter what price you pay.** It is trimmed with genuine natural otter, both at cuffs and pockets. It also has a large, natural, genuine otter shawl collar. If taken care of, this coat will last a lifetime. We want our customers to have the very best raccoonskin coat that can possibly be made; that is the reason we have taken special pains with this coat. Every part is very carefully examined before it leaves our fur coat factory, and we absolutely guarantee this coat to come up to the expectations of the buyer otherwise it can be returned to us at our expense, and money will be cheerfully refunded along with any expense attached to placing the order with us. **Remember that a fur coat is a high priced garment; you cannot afford to take chances by placing your order with anyone who will not stand back of their goods. You absolutely take no chances by placing your order with us.** Order this number and get the finest, most handsome, and best raccoonskin coat ever seen in your section of the country.

No. 41R322 Price.......... $50.00

XXX Quality Northern Raccoonskin Coat for $42.00.

This coat is made from best northern skins. It is just the same kind of a coat as our plain XXX quality, only this coat is full beaver trimmed. You can get a very good idea as to how it will look in the illustration. You can see that it runs very dark and is a decidedly handsome coat. Lined with extra quality Albert twill quilted lining, trimmed with genuine southern beaver collar and cuffs, also pockets. The sewing throughout all of our coats is the very best. This coat is made with heavy lining, with a cable lock stitch, is guaranteed not to rip. **It is a very handsome first class quality prime raccoonskin coat,** at a price much less than you could get a similar coat anywhere else.

No. 41R326 Price.. $42.00

XXX Quality of Best Plain Raccoonskin Coat for $35.00.

This is the coat that we recommend to our customers. A few dollars added to the price of the raccoon coat is the best investment you can possibly make. There is no economy in buying even a $32.00 coat when you can get the very best coat, of its kind, there is to be had at $3.00 more. It is very hard to compare our raccoon coats with those offered by your local dealer or other catalogue house, as there are certain grades of raccoonskins that we positively will not use in our factory at all; and while it is possible to get up a very cheap coat, sell it for $22.00 or $25.00, as we have said before, they will not give satisfaction, and are therefore unsatisfactory garments to sell, as well as to buy. This, our XXX quality plain raccoonskin coat, is made from prime northern skins, very heavily furred. **The coat runs dark and is nicely matched, just such a coat as you would like to have if you are in the market for a nice raccoonskin coat.** You can choose either the Albert twilled or Italian quilted lining. It has leather arm shields. Order one of these coats with the understanding that it is just what we claim, the best plain raccoonskin coat ever received in your section of the country.

No. 41R328 Price.. $35.00

SHELL OR FUR LINED COATS.

WE MAKE THE MOST COMPLETE ASSORTMENT OF SHELL OR FUR LINED COATS of any house in the country. Our special attention has been given to the fur coat business for the last three years. We now have our fur coat factory running as near right, we believe, as it is possible to run a fur coat plant.

WE CAN OFFER OUR CUSTOMERS SHELL OR FUR LINED COATS FOR LESS MONEY THAN A GREAT MANY MANUFACTURERS CAN MAKE THEM.

We have gotten beyond the experimental stage, and are now in a position to give perfect made, perfect fit, and absolutely guaranteed garments, at ever so much less than your local dealer can buy similar or inferior goods. **Our combination clothing and fur overcoats are very desirable.** They are warm, dressy, and exceptional value.

Our $12.50 Hummer Shell Coat.

There is nothing cheap about this coat except the price. We claim on our introductory page that you can save from $5.00 to $50.00 by placing your order with us for a fur coat. On this our cheapest coat, we certainly claim that you will save at least $5.00 and

WE DOUBT VERY MUCH IF YOU COULD GET A SIMILAR COAT ANYWHERE ELSE FOR LESS THAN $20.00.

No. 41R330

The cloth part of this coat is made from genuine 32-ounce oxford gray melton overcoating. It is made in a regular ulster style, double breasted, has two lower outside pockets, cotton plush lined, all seams are double sewed, has a large ulster collar, made from genuine jet black Norway seal. The outside finish and appearance of this coat is equal to any $20.00 to $35.00 coat on the market. It is lined throughout body with black, or very dark brown, closely furred lambskin, which makes a very handsome lining, not to be compared with the ordinary sheep lined goods, but a really handsome dark curly wool lining. The sleeves are lined throughout with quilted Italian cloth.

RUBBER INTERLINED SLEEVES.

The coat is open at the bottom, and faced with a 2½-inch strip of heavy silesia. This garment is adapted for any kind of wear; it will wear satisfactorily no matter what kind of use you give it. It can be worn at any time or place with perfect comfort to wearer. It is the best and most satisfactory shell fur overcoat ever placed on the market at anything like the price. You cannot appreciate the extraordinary value in the fine make, finish, and general appearance of this coat until you see it. Give us your order with the understanding that it will surpass your expectations, and that you will feel that a saving of at least $5.00 has been made on your purchase. If you do not find upon receipt of the coat that it is all and even more than we claim for it, return it to us at our expense, and your money will be cheerfully refunded.

No. 41R330 Price.. $12.50

FUR COATS SHOULD BE WORN LOOSE.

IN SENDING MEASUREMENTS

Be sure to mention HEIGHT and WEIGHT and give CHEST MEASUREMENT taken close under the arms all around the body over the under coat.

IF YOU ARE LARGER THAN 46-INCH CHEST MEASURE, WRITE US FOR SPECIAL PRICE ON SUCH COAT AS YOU WISH TO BUY.

No. 41R332
$18.00

Astrachan Cloth Shell Overcoat for $18.00.

This coat is made with astrachan cloth lining, as shown in illustration. Our illustrations are accurate, and you can get a very good idea as to how our goods look, as the illustrations are made from photographs taken from the goods themselves. The outside or cloth part of this coat is made from a genuine all wool seal brown kersey. All seams are double stitched. Two lower outside pockets. Large shawl collar, made from seal brown mormat. Worsted loops and olives. The coat is lined throughout body with genuine black astrachan cloth. (Please note that this is astrachan cloth, sometimes called nigger head cloth and not astrachan fur.) This cloth is especially woven for shell coats, and makes a splendid wearing lining. The sleeves are lined with quilted Italian cloth, the bottom of the coat is faced with extra strong silesia, and is **made throughout with the very best material, and in the strongest possible manner.**

No. 41R332 Price..................**$18.00**

Black Hair Seal Shell Overcoat for $25.00.

No. 41R334
$25.00

The cloth part of this coat is made from genuine all wool black kersey. It is made up as shown in illustration. Lined throughout with genuine natural black hair seal. Large rolling shawl collar of the same material, two outside pockets with flaps, double stitched throughout; made up in the very best possible manner, **one of the handsomest shell coats we have ever shown. A coat equal to this one in appearance, style and general workmanship would cost double our price elsewhere.** We will ship this coat with the understanding that it is one of the finest shell coats ever seen in your section of the country, with the understanding that it will wear satisfactory, and that you will be so well pleased with it that you can and will recommend us to your friends and neighbors. If at any time the coat is not all and even better than you expected to receive for the money, you can return it to us and we will either send you a new coat or will refund your money, as desired.

No. 41R334 Price..................**$25.00**

No. 41R336
$35.00

Our $35.00 Genuine Norway Seal Shell Overcoat.

This is one of the finest shell coats ever manufactured. We offer it to our customers at a price which means a positive saving of nearly one half. In fact we doubt if you could get as good a coat for less than double our low price. The shell or cloth part of this coat is made from an extra quality, fine all wool blue black beaver, a cloth that will wear and retain its color and give every satisfaction. All seams are double stitched. It is made with worsted loops and olives, and lined with genuine jet black Norway seal; one of the handsomest furs that we make up into coats. It has a large ulster collar and cuffs from same fur as lining—black Norway seal. **We especially recommend this coat to those who desire something nice, a coat that will not only wear well but look well, one that will please the very best trade.**

No. 41R336 Price.........**$35.00**

Imitation Otter Seal Overcoat for $75.00.

No. 41R338
$75.00

To those who desire a high priced coat, one that would cost from $100.00 to $150.00 elsewhere, we have gotten up this coat. The cloth in this coat is the very finest patent beaver, a very dark blue, almost black color. All seams are double stitched; **has worsted loops and olives,** is lined throughout body and sleeves with very dark imitation otter (blended muskrat.) Trimmed at cuffs with a genuine golden plucked otter; has a large ulster golden otter collar.

THIS IS A DECIDEDLY HANDSOME COAT,

which cannot be had from a regular furrier for less than $150.00.

We claim it to be exactly what it is,

THE FINEST SHELL OR FUR LINED OVERCOAT

ever offered the buying public.

We do not carry these coats in stock, but make them to special order only, consequently require from ten to twelve days to fill orders.

No. 41R338 Price........**$75.00**

Our $50.00 Genuine Astrachan Fur Overcoat.

No. 41R340
$50.00

We sold a great many astrachan fur coats last season at $75.00. We find a great demand for fine fur overcoats, we therefore made our plans this year to furnish a genuine astrachan coat at the lowest price ever quoted, and at the same time furnish a coat that we **can absolutely guarantee to be the best article ever furnished by us or any other house.** If you want a high priced coat and the finest coat there is to be had, we certainly recommend this coat above all others, as it is a coat that would positively cost you $100.00 if it was purchased from any other house.

IT IS MADE FROM

GENUINE ASTRACHAN FUR,

very curly and glossy skins, perfectly matched. Collar, cuffs and pockets are trimmed with genuine natural otter fur. Trimmed with worsted loops and olives. The coat is lined throughout body with a guaranteed first quality Skinner's satin quilted lining. We do not cheapen this coat and sell it to you at a low price by taking anything out of the workmanship or material. The sleeves are lined with very heavy seal brown genuine Skinner guaranteed satin. The coat is 52 inches long, and is made in every way first class, with the very best style, workmanship and finish. **The greatest value in a general astrachan coat ever offered to the buying public.** Last season we were compelled to sell an inferior coat, practically the same class of fur, made up with cotton Italian lining for more money, and when we reduce the price to $50.00, and still furnish better workmanship, **we claim that we have a right to receive your order.**

No. 41R340 Price..........**$50.00**

WHEN YOU ORDER YOUR FUR COAT, you will surely need other clothing as well—underwear, shoes, hose and other winter wear. You will need other things about the house, office or farm. **THIS CATALOGUE IS YOUR GENERAL STORE. If we can serve you well in the purchase of one article, we can serve you just as well on everything you need.**
The express on your fur coat will be as much as the freight on 100 pounds.

YOU WILL SAVE MONEY BY MAKING UP A FREIGHT ORDER.

DUCK CLOTHING.

IN CONNECTION WITH OUR FUR COAT FACTORY we have a department for making duck and sheep lined clothing. There is no one line of staple merchandise on which we can save our customers more money than on duck and sheep lined clothing. We add only one small profit to the actual cost of these goods, and it certainly stands to reason that we can furnish you as good a duck coat for $1.00 as your local dealer can for $1.50. We can furnish a better duck coat we believe for $2.00 than you could get anywhere else for $3.00.

WE MAKE OUR DUCK AND SHEEP LINED CLOTHING through the summer season. We make up thousands of coats and sell them direct to you at little more than the actual cost to make. Does it not seem reasonable to you that when your local storekeeper buys from the wholesale house, the wholesale house from the manufacturer, that you can safely place your order with us, and expect such value for $1.00 as you can get from your local storekeeper for $1.50. It only costs us a few cents to get your order, while it costs the manufacturer a great deal to send out high salaried salesmen to sell goods to your local storekeeper.

WE SOLICIT YOUR PATRONAGE on duck and fur lined coats, with the understanding that we give you better value for your money than you could get anywhere else in the United States. If you do not agree with us when you receive the goods, we would very much like to have you return them at our expense, and your money will be cheerfully refunded. Our duck clothing is better made, better trimmed, than the average coats sold by other dealers. We believe in the very best quality and workmanship. A cheap, skimp made duck coat is a poor article at any price. We depend upon well satisfied customers for advertising, in all departments, and therefore guarantee every coat that we send out.

SIZES. Men's duck coats are made only in the following sizes: Breast measure, 34, 36, 38, 40, 42, 44 and 46 inches. The average length, unless otherwise stated, is 32½ inches. Any coat ordered larger than 46 inches breast measure will cost extra 50 cents per coat. This extra charge is made for the additional expense of making a special order and for the extra material it takes. We do not keep any coats in stock larger than 46 inches breast measure, and charge 50 cents extra for making them up singly, which is the actual cost to us for so doing.

TERMS. Our terms on all duck coats is cash in full with order. Any goods that are unsatisfactory, or do not give full value in wear for the price you pay, may be returned for a new coat, or your money will be refunded.

MEASUREMENTS. Duck clothing should be worn loose. When sending us your size, give correct number of inches around breast, close up under arms, also your height and weight, and we will send you the proper size.

Great Value for $1.00.

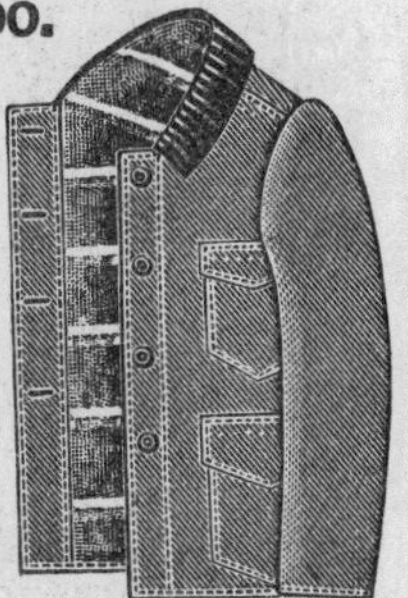

Our $1.00 coat is exceedingly good value. It is a better coat than is generally sold for $1.50 in the best retail stores. This coat is made from a full 8-ounce brown duck. All seams are double stitched, has two outside pockets with flaps, copper riveted, patent never come off buttons; is cut single breasted style. Has a large 4-inch corduroy collar, lined with heavy dark blanketing throughout body and sleeves. Sizes, 34 to 46 inches breast measure. Average length, 32½ inches.

No. 41R360 Price........................$1.00

Our $1.50 Double Breasted Duck Coat.

Extra value is what we give in our special $1.50 coat. We claim this coat equal to the average coat sold at $2.50. It is cut double breasted style, made from full 8½-ounce black duck. All seams are double stitched. Has two outside pockets with flaps; pockets are copper riveted. Two rows of patent never come off buttons; button holes are well worked, guaranteed to stand; has large 5½-inch corduroy collar; lined throughout body and sleeves with fancy heavy blanketing; interlined with waterproof rubber to insure it being water and wind proof. Sizes, 34 to 46 inches breast measure. Average length, 32½ inches.

No. 41R362 Price........................$1.50

Our $2.00 Double Breasted Felt Lined Duck Coat.

A better coat than your local merchant can buy at this price. The coat is made in a double breasted style, as shown by opposite cut. It is made from a full 10-ounce brown duck, double stitched seams throughout, warranted not to rip; has two lower outside pockets with flaps; one upper outside pocket; patent never come off buttons; large 5½-inch extra quality corduroy collar; lined throughout with dark navy blue felt lining. A warm coat, and one that will give perfect satisfaction, and we believe a far better coat than you can buy from any other dealer in the United States for anything like our special price. Sizes, 34 to 46 inches breast measure. Average length, 32½ inches.

No. 41R364 Price........................$2.00

10-Ounce Waterproof Duck Coat.

To those who wish the very best duck coat that can be made, we have gotten up, this year what we think to be the best one ever manufactured. It is made from a full 10-ounce waterproof brown or black duck (state color desired). It is cut in double breasted style; has three outside pockets with flaps, copper riveted. All seams are double sewed, guaranteed not to rip; 6-inch corduroy collar, lined throughout body and sleeves with a warm, heavy mackinaw blanket lining; one inside pocket; faced with duck and double stays; duck arm shields, 2-inch sheep wristers at cuffs. Average length, 33½ inches.

No. 41R366 Price........................$2.50

Our Special Brown Duck Waterproof Coat for $2.00.

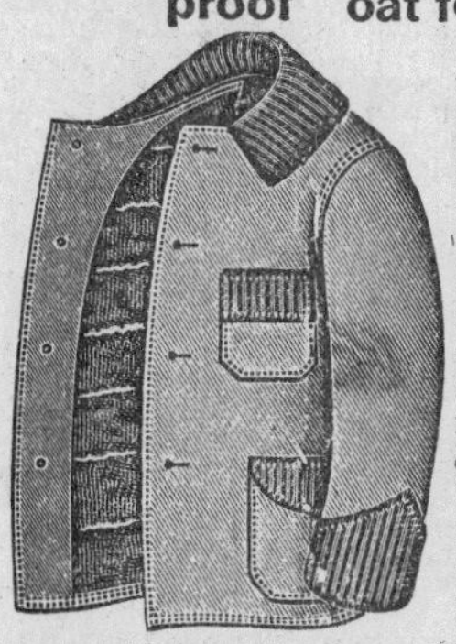

This coat is made from a full 9-ounce brown duck. All seams are double stitched, has three outside pockets, faced with corduroy; large corduroy collar and cuffs, as shown in cut; double stitched throughout; cut single breasted style, patent never come off buttons; it is lined with heavy blanketing, which is fastened to the duck by our special mackintosh process; made just the same as our regular mackintosh coat is made, which makes the coat absolutely wind and waterproof. Sizes, 34 to 46 inches breast measure. Average length, 32½ ins.

No. 41R370 Price........................$2.00

Our $1.75 Dark Gray Oxford Waterproof Coat.

This was one of the most popular coats last season. Is made from a special Oxford gray covert cloth. It is cut in the double breasted style, has two outside pockets, with flaps, large corduroy cemented collar, blanket lined throughout. The blanket lining is fastened to the outside material by a rubberizing process, making the coat absolutely waterproof. You will find these same coats for sale by your local dealer at from $2.50 to $3.50. We believe that our coat is the best there is on the market, and at a price which we know is much less than a similar coat can be had elsewhere. Sizes, 34 to 46 inches breast measure. Average length, 32½ inches.

No. 41R372 Price........................$1.75

Our $3.00 Reversible Corduroy or Duck Coat.

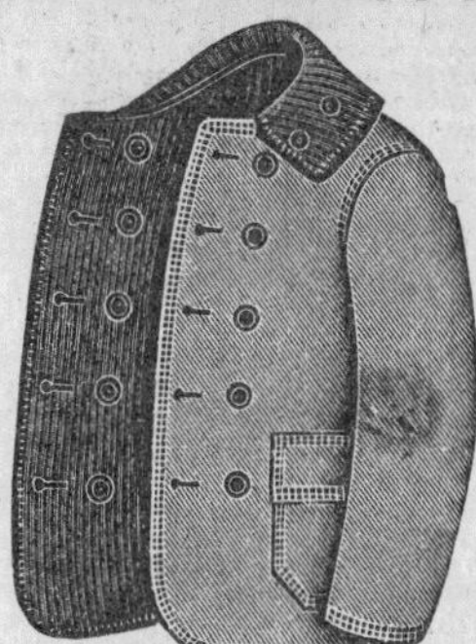

We sold a great many of these coats last season. A splendid garment, and one that will give extraordinary wear and perfect satisfaction. Made to be worn with either corduroy or duck outside, as desired. The duck used is a 9-ounce soft finished brown duck, double sewed throughout with the exception of the sleeves. Two pockets on the outside and two on the corduroy side. This coat can be worn with the corduroy outside or the duck, as preferred. When the corduroy side is exposed, the coat has the appearance of a regular corduroy coat. While the price is less than we sold the coat last season, we have made it even better. Sizes, 34 to 46 inches breast measure. Average length, 33 inches.

No. 41R374 Price........................$3.00

Our $3.50 Brown Duck Ulster.

Our brown duck ulster is an overcoat and duck coat and a mackintosh coat combined. It answers all purposes, keeps out cold or rain. Will outwear any ordinary cloth or fur coat several times over. It is made from 10-ounce duck, has two outside pockets, cut double breasted style, patent buttons, large 5-inch cemented velvet collar, lined throughout body and sleeves with a blue jeans cloth, which is cemented to the duck by our regular mackintosh process, making the coat absolutely waterproof. The armholes are protected with a strap cemented on to the lining. We recommend it for all kinds of hard wear, and guarantee it to give perfect satisfaction. Size, 34 to 46 inches breast measure. The coat is cut full 52 inches long.

No. 41R378 Price........................$3.50

Our Gray Oxford Duck Ulster for $3.00.

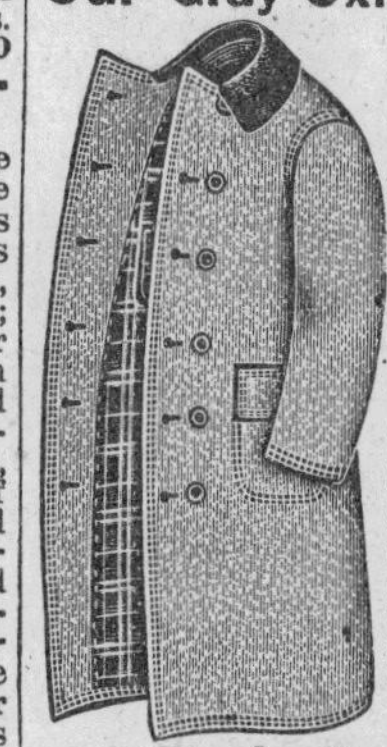

This coat is made in the same style as shown in illustration. It is a regular ulster overcoat, at the same time it is waterproof, windproof and coldproof, one of the best coats that we have ever turned out. The cloth used is a dark gray cotton covert; has two outside pockets with flaps, it is double stitched throughout, has a large cemented velvet collar, lined throughout with heavy plaid blanketing, which is cemented to the outside material by our regular mackintosh process. A coat that will give all kinds of wear. Sizes, 34 to 46 inches breast measure. Average length, 52 inches.

No. 41R380 Price.....$3.00

Boy's Brown Duck Coats.

Made from full 8-ounce brown duck, double stitched throughout, two outside pockets with flaps, lined throughout body and sleeves with a heavy warm blanket lining, 3-inch corduroy collar. A splendid wearing coat; one that will give perfect satisfaction. Sizes, 28 to 34 inches breast measure only. Average length, 30 inches.

No. 41R392 Price........................$1.00

Boy's Black 9-Ounce Duck Coat.

This coat is made from a full 9-ounce black duck, it is double stitched throughout, single breasted style, two outside pockets with flaps, never come off patent buttons, 3-inch corduroy collar, lined throughout body and sleeves with plaid heavy blanket lining; rubber interlined. A first class and serviceable duck coat. Sizes, 28 to 34 inches breast measure.

No. 41R394 Price........................$1.25

Men's Duck Vests.

Men's blanket lined duck vests, made from 8-ounce brown or black duck, as desired. Three outside pockets, cut single breasted style with five buttons. Lined throughout with heavy blanketing. Sizes, 34 to 46 inches breast measure.

No. 41R398 Price in brown or black..........75c

Men's Duck Lined Pants.

Made from brown or black 8-ounce duck. Double stitched seams, one watch pocket, patent never come off buttons, reinforced continuous waistband, swinging pockets, lined throughout with heavy blanketing. In ordering be sure to state shade desired. Sizes, 32 to 42 inches waist measure; 30 to 35 inches inside seam.

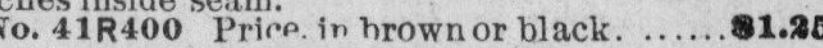

No. 41R400 Price, in brown or black.......$1.25

SHEEP LINED DUCK CLOTHING.

WE CAN FURNISH you sheep lined clothing for less money than you could possibly get from any other house in the United States. We can also furnish you better made coats. In connection with our fur coat factory we have made a specialty of sheep lined clothing, and offer our customers this year the best and most satisfactory line of goods that we have ever gotten out.

THE SAME THING will apply to a sheep lined coat as duck or fur coat, namely, that the very best material, the best workmanship, pays in the long run. While it would be possible for us to offer sheep lined goods, made up with light weight duck, and second, third or fourth quality of lining at a very much less price, we do not deem it advisable. **We guarantee all of our goods to be of the very best quality.** You have everything to gain and nothing to lose by placing your order with us. The average merchant gets only a few dozen coats at a time, pays the wholesaler a good profit and then adds a good profit himself, while we make up hundreds of these coats, and offer them direct at the actual manufacturer's cost with but one small profit added.

TERMS. **We require cash in full with all orders for sheep lined clothing.** We guarantee every garment to be equal, if not better, than the catalogue description. Any coat that is unsatisfactory when received, or proves unsatisfactory, or does not wear well, can be returned to us within any reasonable length of time, and we will replace the defective garment with a new coat, or refund your money, as desired.

SIZES. **Our sheep lined clothing** is made in sizes from 36 to 46 inches, breast measure. Any sizes ordered larger than 46 inches breast measure we will have to make to special order, for which we make an additional charge of 10 per cent.

WHEN ORDERING **sheep pelt lined clothing be sure and give us your exact breast measurement,** to be taken over the garment which you expect to wear the coat ordered. Also give us your accurate height and weight, and we will send you a coat that will fit.

One-Half Sheep Lined Duck Coat for $3.00.

This coat is made from full 10-ounce brown guaranteed duck, has three outside pockets with flaps, double breasted style with large 6-inch corduroy collar. All seams are double sewed, warranted not to rip; is one-half lined with buffed sheep fleece. Sleeves are lined throughout with extra quality stockinet. The lower part of the coat is lined with a very heavy blue felt, 2½-inch sheep wristers at cuffs. For the price we claim this to be one of the best coats ever offered, and guarantee it in every way to give perfect satisfaction to the wearer. Sizes, 36 to 46 inches breast measure. Average length, 32½ inches.

No. 41R408 Price **$3.00**

Full Sheep Lined Duck Coat for $3.50.

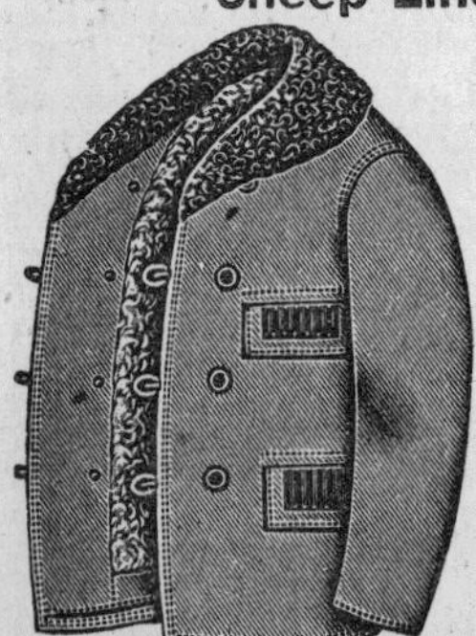

We offer in this coat the greatest value we have ever been able to give in a full sheep lined coat. We sold over a thousand coats last season at $3.75, but we are able to give our customers this year a still better coat at a little lower price. This coat is made from a full 10-ounce waterproof duck. It has three outside pockets with flaps, large 6-inch sheepskin collar, as shown by opposite cut. It is lined throughout body with prime buffed sheep fleece. Patent snap fasteners, as shown in cut. The sleeves are lined with heavy guaranteed stockinet. Sheep fleece wristers at cuffs. This coat is equal to any fur lined duck coat sold at the average retail store at $5.00. Sizes, 34 to 46 inches breast measure. Average length, 33 inches.

No. 41R410 .... **$3.50**

Our $4.50 Lumberman's King Sheep Lined Coat.

We sold hundreds of these coats last season for $5.00. Our customers appreciate a good coat. It shows that our customers want good goods. We believe this to be the best sheep lined coat manufactured today. It is made from a very heavy 10-ounce waterproof duck; has three outside pockets trimmed with brown corduroy; double breasted style; has a large imitation wombat ulster collar; double stitched throughout, open at the bottom, and faced with 2½-inch strip of rubber; lined throughout body with pure white sheep fleece; sleeves are lined with heavy blanketing, tipped at wrists with sheep pelt; patent buttons and leather loops. Strongest and most serviceable sheep lined coat that we can possibly make. Equal in every way to our last season's coat, yet we have been able to reduce the price 50 cents. Sizes, 34 to 46 inches breast measure. Average length, 33 inches.

No. 41R43? Price **$4.50**

Our $6.50 Royal Corduroy Coat.

This coat is made from an extra quality drab corduroy, double breasted style, three outside pockets with flaps; has a large, rolling, genuine wombat collar. The body is lined throughout with fine sheep fleece, sleeves are lined with extra quality, closely woven stockinet, which is fastened with pure rubber to the corduroy, making the slevees water and wind proof. This we believe to be one of the most desirable sheep lined coats ever gotten up. For appearance, comfort, durability, and all kinds of heavy wear, we recommend this, our Royal Corduroy Coat, to give perfect satisfaction. Sizes, 36 to 46 inches breast measure. Average length, 33 inches.

No. 41R424 Price **$6.50**

MEN'S DUCK ULSTERS.

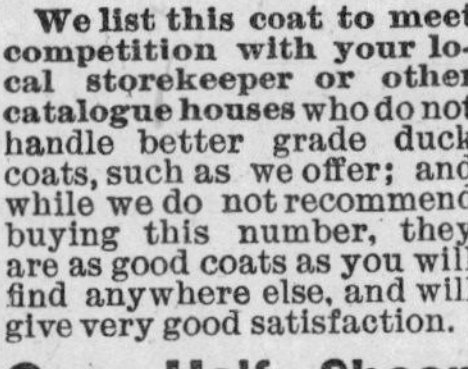

We list this coat to meet competition with your local storekeeper or other catalogue houses who do not handle better grade duck coats, such as we offer; and while we do not recommend buying this number, they are as good coats as you will find anywhere else, and will give very good satisfaction.

One - Half Sheep Lined Ulster, $6.00

This coat is made from a full 8-ounce duck, double stitched seams, patent buttons, three outside pockets, with flaps. It is lined throughout body to hips with buffed sheep pelt fleece. The balance of the lining is a wool blanketing; has a large corduroy storm collar and is a well made coat. Sizes, 34 to 46 inches breast measure. Average length, 54 inches.

No. 41R430 Price, each **$6.00**

Three-Quarter Sheep Lined Ulster for $6.00.

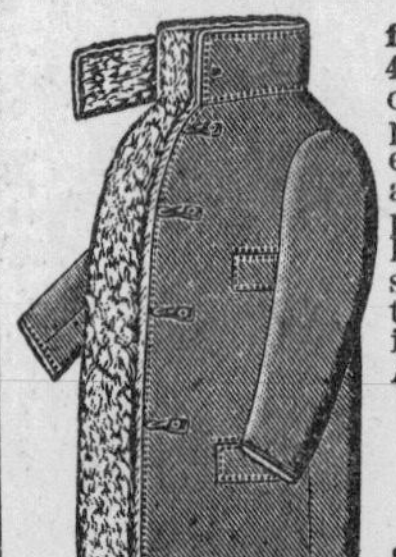

This coat is made from a full 8-ounce duck; it is cut 42 inches long, lined throughout body with buffed sheep pelt fleece, four outside pockets, with flaps; patent snap and ring fasteners, large sheep pelt collar, heavy blanket lined sleeves, and a good, strong, well made coat throughout. Sizes, 34 to 46 inches breast measure. Average length, 42 inches.

No. 41R434 Price... **$6.00**

Our $7.50 Extra Long Ulster.

This coat is made just the same as our 42-inch coat, as described and illustrated above, except it is full 54 inches long. It is lined throughout body with buffed sheep pelt fleece, blanket lined sleeves, patent snap ring fasteners large sheep collar, thoroughly first class coat. Sizes, 36 to 46 breast measure. Average length, 54 inches.

No. 41R438 Price, each **$7.50**

DON'T FAIL TO SEND CAREFUL MEASUREMENTS, and thereby save delay and annoyance.

OUR DOUBLE EXTRA SHEEP PELT LINED DUCK ULSTERS

Our ulster coats quoted below we have gotten up to meet the demands of those who want the very best ulster coats that good material and first class workmanship can produce. We have great faith in good goods. While our cheaper line of duck ulsters are as good as you can get elsewhere, they are not as good as our double extra coats. In this class of goods we have used a heavier grade of duck and the very best and choicest skins. The workmanship and material is first class throughout, and in fact these goods are the result of our efforts to please and furnish our customers the very best goods that skilled workmen can possibly make. One of these coats will cost you a little more money **but it will give more satisfaction and outwear twice over any of the ordinary coats,** such as your local dealer could furnish possibly at about the same price.

Our Double Extra Quality Three-Quarter Sheep Lined Ulsters.

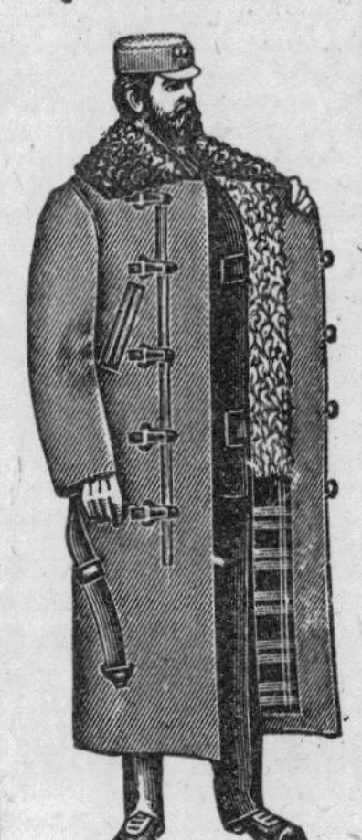

This ulster coat is 54 inches long. Made from best quality 10-ounce waterproof duck. Has a large, Russian lambskin collar. All seams are double stitched; slanting ulster pockets, patent snap and ring fasteners, 2½-inch duck belt, fastened with the celebrated Kootz's patent buckle, which can be unbuckled or fastened with the slightest turn of the wrist. Lined throughout body and above hips, as shown in illustrasion, with a prime white sheep pelt fleece. The balance of the lining is a heavy blanketing. The sleeves are lined with quilted blanket Italian cloth. Back of the quilted lining is rubber lining, which guarantees the coat being absolutely wind and waterproof. Cuffs faced inside with 2 inches of brown corduroy, and above that is a fur wrister for protection from the cold. **If you want the best waterproof coat that will wear for years, one that is guaranteed in every respect, order this number.** Sizes, 36 to 46 inches breast measure. Average length, 54 inches.

No. 41R446 Price **$7.50**

Our Double Extra Full Sheep Lined Duck Ulster for $9.00.

We recommend this coat to our customers in preference to cheap fur goods. It is warmer, will wear longer, and is altogether a more satisfactory coat than the common $10.00 and $12.00 fur coats with which the country is flooded. This coat is made just the same as our three-quarter lined coat, except that it is lined throughout the body with pure white sheep fleece. All seams are double stitched; it has our patent belt and fastener, large brown sheep collar, patent snap and ring fasteners, quilted Italian lined sleeves, backed up with heavy waterproof slicker, making the sleeves wind and waterproof; corduroy facing inside of cuffs, strap and buckle at wrist. Guaranteed for two years; that is, we will replace any coat that is returned to us within this time that has proved unsatisfactory.

No. 41R450 Sizes, 36 to 46. Price **$9.00**

Men's Sheep Pelt Vests, $2.00.

This vest is made from fine sheep pelt. It is to be worn with the sheep pelt next to the body with the tanned side exposed. It is cut single breasted, six buttons, to fit close up to the neck; edge and all seams bound with tape. A very popular vest for doctors, liverymen, or any one exposed to the severe cold. This vest is our own patent, and a much more satisfactory garment than we have heretofore been able to offer. Sizes, 36 to 46 inches breast measure.

No. 41R454 Price **$2.00**

GIVE CATALOGUE NUMBER IN FULL WHEN YOU WRITE YOUR ORDER

Our All Sheepskin Undercoat for $5.00.

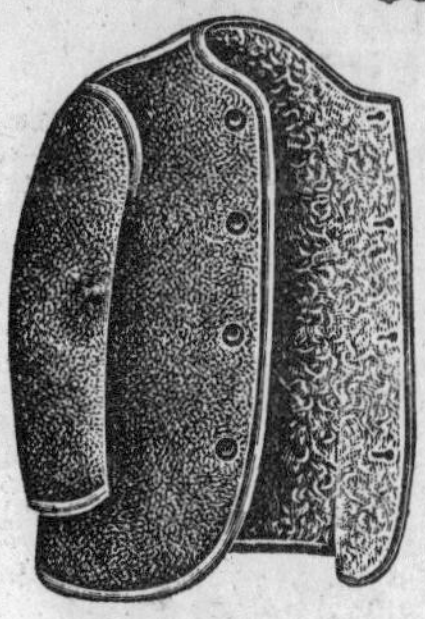

Made from prime sheep skins. Especially adapted for long, cold drives. A splendid coat for anyone to slip on under a cloth overcoat, as it affords absolute protection from the most severe weather. Made up with a tanned sheep pelt exposed, and the reverse side is fine buffed sheep fleece. It is a single breasted style, has four buttons, and made to fit close up to the neck. All seams and edge of garment are taped with braid. Sizes, 36 to 46 inches breast measure.

No. 41R456 Price. $5.00

LEATHER CLOTHING.

Our last season's business on leather clothing was so satisfactory that we have been able to make the largest contract in this class of goods, we believe, ever placed by one house, and are in a position this year to give our customers the very best leather clothing that can be made at a very low price. **If you order a leather coat from us, you can rest assured you will buy it for less money than any merchant throughout the country. We guarantee our leather clothing** to be the very best goods obtainable. We could furnish cheaper goods, as there are second, third and fourth grades of leather clothing, the same as most any other kind of goods. Our leather clothing is reliable; the goods are made for us under contract by the largest and most successful coat manufacturers in the United States. The goods are soft and pliable, no alum, combination or acid tanned leather is used in our goods, we therefore guarantee our leather goods to give satisfaction to the wearer. **You can rest assured that in placing your order with us you are getting the very best grade of goods, and coats that will in every way prove entirely satisfactory.**

SIZES—Sizes on leather goods run from 36 to 46 inches breast measure. Anything larger than 46 inches breast measure will have to be made to special order and will require from ten days to two weeks to fill such orders. **We make an additional charge of 10 per cent for extra sizes.**

We will cheerfully refund your money if the goods when received are not all that we claim, and if the goods do not wear as we claim, they can be returned at our expense, and we will then either refund your money or give you new garments.

Black Blanket Lined Coat, $3.00.

This coat is made from black oiled bark tanned sheepskin; is lined throughout body with heavy blanketing, the sleeves are lined with canvas, has three outside pockets, patent snap buttons, corduroy collar; thoroughly first class coat in every way; one, we believe, you cannot procure elsewhere for less than $4.50. Sizes, 36 to 46 inches breast measure.

No. 41R460 Price..... $3.00

Black Leather Coat. Red Flannel Lined.

This coat is made up as shown in illustration. Has three outside pockets, with flaps, double stitched throughout; patent snap buttons; lined throughout body with all wool red flannel. The leather is soft and pliable, and made from genuine Australian skins. Corduroy collar. **Extra well made throughout; guaranteed for wear.** Sizes, 34 to 46 inches breast measure.

No. 41R462 Price, each.......................$3.50

Reversible Corduroy and Leather Coat, $4.50.

This is the most popular coat that we sell in our leather clothing department. It is the best combination reversible leather and corduroy coat on the market. **No better reversible coat can be had at any price.** It can be worn with leather or corduroy side out as desired. Three pockets on each side, double row patent snap buttons, reversible corduroy or leather collar, the skins are soft and pliable, real Australian bark tanned, finished in the best possible manner. **It is a coat that we can absolutely guarantee to be the equal of the garments you would pay from $6.00 to $7.00 elsewhere.** Our price on this coat to you is less than you could buy them at wholesale. Sizes 36 to 46 inches breast measure.

No. 41R466 Price..............................$4.50

Our $5.50 Sheep Pelt Lined Leather Coat.

This coat is lined throughout body with prime sheep pelt fleece; has a wool blanket sleeve lining, three pockets on outside; patent snap buttons; large sheep pelt storm collar. This coat is absolutely wind and waterproof, and is especially desirable for motormen, lumbermen and teamsters, and all others wishing a warm and splendid wearing coat. **The leather is the best bark tanned Australian skins, guaranteed to keep soft and pliable, to stand wear, and to give perfect satisfaction in every way.** You will find similar goods offered by other mail order concerns at $8.00, and if you will order one from them and one of these coats, and take the one that suits you the best, this will be fair competition. We would advise you to order that way if you have any doubt of our coat being equal to any garments offered by other dealers. Sizes, 36 to 46 inches breast measure.

No. 41R468 Price..............................$5.50

Black Australian Leather Vests.

This vest is made from first quality black Australian leather; has four outside pockets, patent snap buttons; double stitched throughout; lined with all wool red flannel leather. Sizes, 36 to 46 inches breast measure.

No. 41R472 Price..... $2.25

Our $2.75 Corduroy Lined Leather Vests.

This vest is made the same as above number; has four outside pockets, patent snap buttons, and is lined with an extra quality of drab corduroy lining. Sizes, 36 to 46 inches breast measure.

No. 41R474 Price..............................$2.75

Extra Quality Black Leather Pants.

These pants are made from first quality Australian leather; made up with patent buttons, two front pockets; double stitched throughout; [illegible] from plain leather, not [illegible] en ordering, be sure [illegible] he same as for re[illegible]ns. We have sizes [illegible] inches waist meas[illegible] 30 to 35 inches insi[illegible] e larger sizes must b[illegible]cially to order at an ad[illegible]rge of 10 per cent, and requi[illegible] en days to fill special orders.

No. 41R476 Per pair..... $4.00

WE CAN SAVE YOU AS MUCH MONEY

ALMOST ON BOYS' CLOTHING AS ON MEN'S CLOTHING.

IF YOU WOULD LIKE TO SEE SAMPLES OF OUR BOYS' AND CHILDREN'S CLOTHING,

Send 5 Cents for Cloth Sample Book No. 64R.

IF YOU ARE INTERESTED IN FINE MADE TO MEASURE CLOTHING

At about Half the Prices Charged by Tailors Generally,

=DO NOT FAIL TO SEND US 5 CENTS FOR CLOTH SAMPLE BOOK No. 52R.=

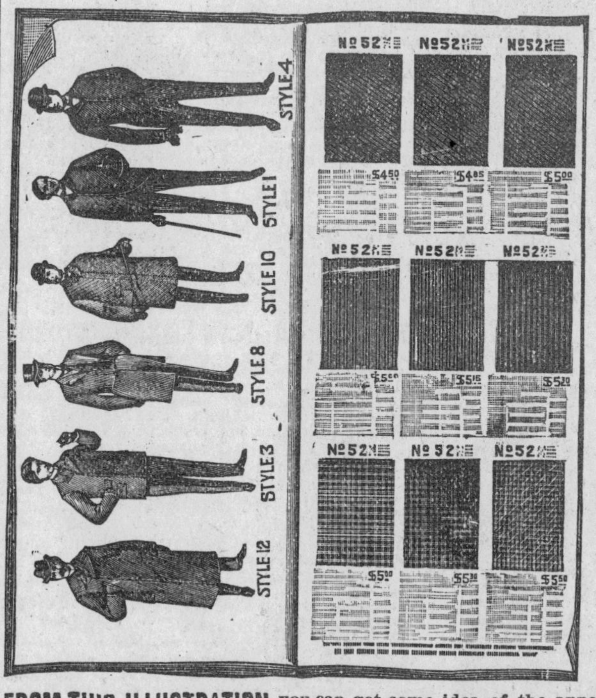

We issue a big cloth sample book, containing cloth samples of our entire line of fabrics for spring and summer, including all the new goods for men's suits, overcoats, coats, vests and pants, the most complete line of foreign and domestic goods shown by any tailoring house, and at prices lower than ever before, prices based on the actual cost of material and labor, prices that will mean a saving to you of fully 50 per cent. **For 5 cent we will mail this handsom cloth sample book No. 52R, post paid, to any address.** This boo will enable you to select just th weight, color, style and pattern of fabric wanted in the very latest style, and will assist you in selecting the style of garment wanted, and will prove to you that you can get from us such garments made to your measure as you could not ge elsewhere at double the price. **The book contains the newest fashion figures, includes tape measure, order blanks, easy rules for self measurement, etc.**

WE ASK 5 CENTS for our cloth sample book **No. 52R for the same reason that we ask 50 cents for our big catalogue, namely, in order that we may quote lower prices than any other house.** If you send us 5 cents for this cloth sample book, you will save the 5 cents fifty times over in the cost of your suit or other goods, and you can feel assured that the prices we quote do not include the cost of thousands of sample books sent to curiosity seekers and to people who never buy.

FROM THIS ILLUSTRATION you can get some idea of the appearance of our cloth sample book **No. 52R. It is a book 6x12 inches in size, in which is pasted a cloth sample of every fabric shown in our tailoring department.** Under the sample is a complete description of the goods, and our special prices at which we make up separate garments, coats, vests, pants and suits. **The book contains fashion plates, fashion figures, rules for self measurements, order blanks and tape measure, explains just how to order, just how anyone without previous experience can take his own measure and have every assurance that the garments ordered will be perfect fitting.**

If you expect to buy anything in the line of clothing, do not fail to send us 5 cents for our handsome, money-saving cloth sample book No. 52R.

MEN'S AND BOYS' OVERALLS, WORKING PANTS AND JACKETS.

IN THIS DEPARTMENT WE CAN SAVE YOU MONEY. We make up all of our overalls, jackets, etc., in connection with our duck coat factory. Every garment is cut full size from the latest and most perfect fitting patterns. We have started our duck coat and overalls factory with a view of serving our customers with the very best class of goods at prices at least 33 per cent lower than the same grade can be gotten elsewhere. Our increase of trade in this department shows that our customers appreciate a venture that affords such a saving on staple merchandise. When ordering other goods you cannot afford to omit at least a year's supply of overalls and jackets; you will save what we gain over other dealers by making our own goods. We will give any assortment of sizes wanted in dozen lots. We furnish all waist measurements, 30, 32, 34, 36, 38, 40, 42, 44, and the following sizes inside seam measure: 30, 31, 32, 33, 34, 35, 36. Any size larger than 44 inches waist measure, or longer than 36 inches inseam will cost extra, as follows: 25 cents on all overalls quoted at 50 cents or more in price, and 10 cents extra on all overalls quoted below 50 cents in price.

MEASUREMENTS. Give waist measure and inseam measure the same as for regular pants; always give waist measure first. Some of our customers order overalls as follows: One pair of overalls, 32x34, and expect to receive 34 waist and 32 inside seam, which they would not get. The order should read: One pair of overalls 34x32; waist measure should always be mentioned first; the best way is to state "waist 34 and inside seam 32" and thus avoid any possibility of mistake.

PLAIN OVERALLS.

Leader Overalls.

Made from 6½-ounce Blue Denim, fine weave, washable goods; double stitched seams; patent buttons; two front and one hip pocket.
No. 41R698 Price, per pair..............................30c

Black Hussar Overalls.

Made from full 8-ounce Black Duck, warranted not to break or rip; made double stitched at all vital parts; taped crotch; extra stayed fly piece; two front and one back pocket.
No. 41R700 Price, per pair..............................40c

Everett Overalls.

This Overalls is made from the Everett Black and Gray Striped Denim, a very neat pattern; double sewed throughout; continuous fly piece; patent buttons; extra well stayed. Two front, one watch, one hip pocket. This is one of our best selling numbers.
No. 41R702 Price, per pair..............................50c

Our 50-Cent Hercules Overalls are 75-Cent Value.

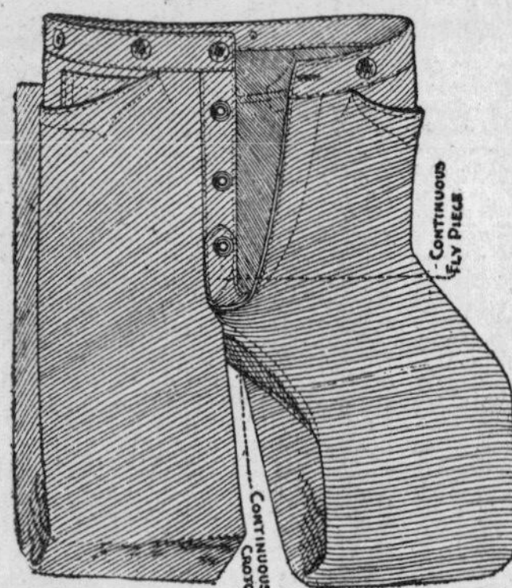

This is really one of the best overalls for 50 cents ever offered; there are none superior and few equal. Made from full 9-ounce York denim; double sewed throughout; reinforced and continuous fly piece; two front, one hip and one watch pocket. Warranted to wear longer and give more general satisfaction than high priced goods usually retailed at 75c and $1.00 per pair.
No. 41R706 Price, per pair..............................50c

Double Wear Overalls for 75 Cents.

This Overalls is made from full 9-ounce Blue York Denim; front is double from waistband to below knee; patent, never rip continuous fly piece; reinforced crotch stay; two front, one hip, one watch pocket; double sewed throughout. No better blue overalls can be had at any price
No. 41R708
Per pair.....75c

Black Texas Ranger Overalls.

The never give out sort. For all kinds of heavy wear this overalls is especially adapted. Made from extra quality fast black 10-ounce duck. Double seat and double from waistband to below knee. Two front, two hip pockets, with safety buttoned flaps over each pocket. Taped and reinforced crotch gusset, double sewed throughout. Fully warranted.
No. 41R710 Price, per pair..............................85c

Cavalry Riding Pants for $1.00.

This pantaloon or riding overalls is especially adapted for Western trade which appreciate a perfectly made up garment. The material is a full 10-ounce, soft finish duck, "mode" or nearly buckskin color. It is made double seat. The entire back half is double, extending between crotch as shown in cut. Continuous never rip fly piece, double stitched crotch piece. Two back, two front pockets, fastened with safety buttoned flaps. Double sewed throughout and warranted in every particular.
No. 41R712 Price, per pair..............................$1.00

Blue Carpenter Apron Overall.

Made from 7-ounce blue washable denim; double sewed throughout at all vital parts; large apron; elastic end suspenders; patent buttons; one rule pocket; one front and one back pocket.
No. 41R716
Per pair.....50c

No. 41R718 Carpenter overalls, same as No. 41R716 above, only the material is 8-ounce black duck. This overalls is warranted in every particular.
Price, per pair..............................50c

Everett Apron Overalls.

Made from the same material as plain overalls, from the Everett gray and black striped denim. This is a very popular overalls; cut full size; large apron, extra rule pocket; double sewed throughout; suspenders of same material with 6-inch elastic ends.
No. 41R720 Price, per pair..............................50c

Plain White Duck Overalls.

No. 41R722 Men's White Duck Overalls, used by painters and paper hangers. Price, per pair....40c
No. 41R724 Same as No. 41R722, only made with apron and suspenders. Price, per pair..............................40c
Miners' Overalls, made from 10-ounce white drill duck, regulation miners' overalls, double sewed, well made throughout.
No. 41R726 Price, per pair..............................70c

Boys' Blue Overalls.

For boys aged 12 to 16 years, or 26 to 32 inches waist measure. When ordering give size the same as for men's overalls.
Made from 7-ounce blue denim; extra well made; double sewed in all vital parts. The kind that is usually sold for 50 cents.
No. 41R728 Price, per pair, 35c

Children's Brownie Overalls.

Made from good quality washable blue denim, with apron and suspenders for boys age 4 to 12 years.
No. 41R730 Per pair.....25c
Best Brownie Overalls in the market. Made from fine, soft finish washable blue denim; double sewed at all vital parts; extra crotch piece; suspenders have 4-inch elastic ends; two front, two hip pockets.
No. 41R732 Per pair.....35c

Railroad Jacket.

This coat is especially gotten up for the use of baggagemen, firemen, brakemen, grocerymen, or anyone employed in a similar class of work. It is a regular coat jacket and made from an extra quality twilled black sateen. Buttons close up to neck, as shown in cut. Watch pocket is cut diagonally so as not to allow timepiece to fall out. Two pencil pockets; three outside pockets; buttons at wrist. This garment is gotten up for a special purpose and we guarantee it to please in every way. All buttons are put on with eyelets and can be removed when coat is washed.
No. 41R734 Price, each..............................85c

Conductors' or Mail Agents' Bib Overalls.

Conductors' or Mail Agents' Bib Overalls, made from same goods as above coat, double stitched throughout, extra large rule pocket, two front, two hip, and watch pockets.
No. 41R736 Price, per pair..............................85c

MEN'S JACKETS.

Our men's working jackets are cut full size, and are extra well made; they are cut over the most perfect fitting patterns; one of our jackets will not only give satisfactory wear, but they are comfortable and will fit as easy as a regular tailor made coat. Sizes 34 to 46 inches chest measure. In ordering, give number of inches around chest close up under arms, or state the size coat usually worn.

Blue and White Check Jackets.

Men's Amoskeag Blue and White Check Jackets; well made and shaped.
No. 41R738
Price, each.....25c
Same color, except made from better material; a most desirable jacket.
No. 41R740
Price, each...40c

This Coat is made from black and white hair line checked denim; a coat specially gotten up for the use of grain elevator men, grocers, lumbermen, etc. Buttons close up to the neck, with neat turn down collar. Double stitched patch pockets. This is a splendid coat for indoor or light outside work.
No. 41R742 Price, each..............................50c

Men's Blue Denim Jacket

This jacket is made from full 8-ounce blue denim. Cut full 28 inches long; buttons close up to collar; patent buttons on sleeves; lower outside pocket. Extra well stayed and sewed.
No. 41R746 Price, each..............................50c

Men's Heavy Working Pants.

Our line of cheap working pants are cut extra large, full sizes, and warranted not to rip or break. They are made in our own factory and cannot be compared with the average cheap made prison goods.
Sizes in pants run from 30 to 42 inches waist, and 30 to 36 inches inside seam measure. Any size larger than 42 inches waist measure or 36 inches inside seam measure will cost extra 25 cents a pair.
Men's Gray Jeans Cloth Pants, well made; double sewed; print curtain lining; patent buttons.
No. 41R750 Price, per pair..............................75c
Very Neat Cotton Worsted Stripe Pants; drab, white and black colors used; blue and white drill curtain lining; swinging pockets; double sewed through seat and crotch; patent never come off buttons.
No. 41R754 Price, per pair..............................$1.00
Extra Fine Quality Jet Black Doeskin Jeans, well made, trimmed and finished; two top, two hip, one watch pockets; double sewed throughout.
No. 41R760 Price, per pair..............................$1.50
Heavy Weight All Wool Dickey Cassimere Pants; dark gray stripe pattern; no better or more satisfactory wearing pants can be had at any price; two side, two hip and watch pockets; good strong linings, double sewed seams, warranted not to rip.
No. 41R764 Price, per pair..............................$1.75

MEN'S RUBBER SURFACE RAIN COATS AND OIL SLICKER CLOTHING.

FOR THIS SEASON we have added several new numbers to the assortment in our surface rubber rain coat department, as the demand last season leads us to believe that the rubber surface coat is the most practical waterproof coat made for very heavy rain storms.

RUBBER COATS ARE MADE UP in the following SIZES FOR MEN:

Size	3	4	5	6	7
Chest measure, inches	36	38	40	42	44

SIZES FOR BOYS: 26 to 34 inches chest measure. Be sure and always give correct height, weight and age of boy when ordering.

A GOOD RUBBER COAT WILL KEEP THE WEARER DRY, which cannot be said of a great many low grade mackintoshes which are sold throughout the country as waterproof. We do not sample rubber coats.

This illustration represents the following coats, which for low priced coats cannot be excelled on the market.

Men's Black Luster Finish Coat, made with lining of woven sheeting, double breasted, two outside pockets with flaps, wide collar and throat latch, split tail in back.
No. 27R100
Price, each............$1.50

Same style coat as above, made in the dull finish and a better grade.
No. 27R101
Price, each............$1.75

Boy's coat, exactly like No. 27R100.
No. 27R102
Price, each............$1.25

Same as No. 27R101, in boys' sizes, 1 to 6, or 26 to 34 chest measure.
No. 27R103
Price, each............$1.50

Men's Medium Weight Rubber Surface Rain Coat.

Men's Dull Finish Rubber Coat, drill lined, made in double breasted style, two outside pockets with flaps, and waterproof throat latch. For a good, serviceable coat at a low price, this number is one of the best obtainable.
No. 27R104 Price, each......................$2.25

Men's Heavy Dull Finish Drill Lined Mountaineer Coat.

This coat has ball and socket fasteners, long slit in back, draw straps and buckle on sleeves, wide collar and throat latch, two large outside pockets with flaps, and extremely long.
No. 27R105 Price, each.................$2.40

Men's Light Weight Rubber Coat.

This coat is a very light rubber surface coat, made with fancy plaid printed lining, black velvet collar, one wide breast pocket, and made 50 inches long with 19-inch slit in back. Comes only in double breasted style, as shown by opposite illustration.
No. 27R106 Price, each.................$2.75

Men's Dull Finish Drill Coat.

Men's Extra Quality Dull Officers' Drill Coat, made with Thompson's automatic buckle, which is one of the best patent clasps on the market. This coat is made average 50 inches long, two large outside pockets, and waterproof throat latch. Sizes 36 to 44 inches breast measure.
No. 27R107 Price for men's dull drill coats............$2.75

USE CARE IN SENDING

COMPLETE MEASUREMENTS

WHEN ORDERING RUBBER CLOTHING.

Men's Heavy Common Sense Rain Coats.

Our common sense rubber coat friction, lined, double back, storm fly front, Thompson's automatic buckle, draw strap on collar and sleeves, and two large outside pockets; average length of these coats, about 54 inches and fully guaranteed. Sizes, 36 to 44 inches.
No. 27R108
Price, each, $3.50

Firemen's Pure Double Gum Rain Coat.

This number represents the best double coated pure gum rubber coat made. Comes 47 inches long, is made with a storm fly front, new patent spear head fasteners, draw buckle on sleeves and collar and two large pockets outside with waterproof flaps. Sizes, 36 to 44 inches breast measure.
No. 27R109 Price for firemen's coat..............$3.75

Policemen's Best Grade Rubber Coat.

Our policemen's coat is the best article on the market. These coats come 53 inches long with a 20-inch slit in back, made with double back and shoulders, which are thoroughly ventilated (see back view below), ball and socket fasteners, draw buckle on sleeves, two pockets inside and extra star holder on left breast. The facings on this coat are very full and it is guaranteed strictly waterproof.
No. 27R110 Price for policemen's coat..................$4.75

Back view showing ventilation under double back.

Sizes are 36 to 44 inches breast measure. All sizes larger than 44 inches will cost 50 cents extra per size. 53 inches long, 20-inch slit.

Long Rubber Leggings.

Average weight, 20 ounces.
Black Rubber Leggings, luster finish, lined with sheeting, adjustable stays and buckles, as shown in illustration.
Size 3, small; 4, medium; 5, large.
No. 27R111 Price, per pair...65c
Black Rubber Leggings, same as above, only finished dull with sheeting lining.
Size 3, small; 4, medium; 5, large.
No. 27R112 Price, per pair...75c

Men's Rubber Cape Caps.

Men's Luster Sheeting Rubber Cape Caps, come in black only, cemented seams. Always mention size. Sizes, 6¾ to 7⅛.
No. 27R113 Price, each.............40c
Men's Rubber Cape Caps, dull finished, sheeting lined same style as above. Sizes, 6¾ to 7⅛.
No. 27R114 Price, each............................50c

Dull Finish Gum Hats.

We only handle one grade in rubber hats and that is the best. Our hat is pure dull finished gum, exact style as shown in illustration, and lined with a fancy plaid print lining and leather sweat band. Sizes, 6¾ to 7⅛. Don't fail to mention size wanted.
No. 27R115 Price, each..........................65c

OIL SLICKER CLOTHING.

There are so many grades of oil slicker clothing, at so many different prices, that unless you deal with a responsible firm, you are liable to get inferior goods, and garments that will only wear one-half as long as good oil slicker clothing should. Second or third grade oil clothing is poor property to buy at any price. **We guarantee our oil slicker clothing to be absolutely waterproof, it will not break or crack**; any oil slicker clothing that is purchased from us that proves unsatisfactory in any way, can be returned at our expense, and we will cheerfully refund money or send new garments, as desired.

Oil clothing should be worn loose. When ordering, please take the number of inches around chest, under arms, over the clothing that you expect to wear the oil clothing over. Also give your correct height and weight.

TERMS—Our terms on oil clothing are cash in full with order. All goods are guaranteed to be first quality, absolutely waterproof, and to wear longer and give more satisfaction than the average goods sold for the best by your local dealer.

Our $2.75 Beatsall Coat.

This coat is adapted for heavy wear. We especially recommend it to motormen, drivers, teamsters, miners and others requiring a reliable and absolutely waterproof coat. This is a new garment, gotten up especially for the class of trade who want a waterproof coat, every part of which must be non-susceptible to leakage. This coat has triple protection, accomplished by an especially constructed storm proof front, back, shoulders and sleeves, etc., made from extra strong, heavy clothing, quadruple oiled, producing a garment that is absolutely waterproof. The patent automatic buttons used on this coat are the best and most convenient fasteners made. **If you want the best, try one of our Beatsall coats.**
No. 27R116 Price, each..........................$2.75

Manhattan Black Cape Coat for $2.75.

The Manhattan Black Oil Cape Coat, as shown in illustration, is made with a large shoulder cape. The coat is especially desirable for all those who are exposed to stormy weather. It is furnished with the cape overlapping and fastened in front, leaving the arms free. Has no binding or girting on any part of the coat; has large fly collar lined with soft flannel; patent snap buckles. **Absolutely waterproof.**
No. 27R117 Price..$2.75

Our $2.65 Pommel Yellow Slicker or Saddle Coat.

This coat is gotten up especially for horseback riders; made from yellow slicker, very heavy cloth, and makes the most perfect rain coat ever manufactured for the use of the horseman. This coat covers the entire saddle, as well as rider, thus insuring a dry seat, while the lower part is wide enough to cover the length of the rider. It is a combination coat, which can be made from a riding to a walking coat by simply adjusting one of the buttons. The best coat obtainable; has patent eyelet fasteners, non-corrosive zinc buttons; all of the latest improvements. **Guaranteed to be strictly waterproof, and the best coat of its kind ever put on the market.** Sizes, 36 to 44 inches breast measure; cut full and large.
No. 27R118 Price, each..........................$2.65

Black Pommel Slicker or Saddle Coat for $2.75.

This coat is made exactly the same as our yellow pommel slicker coat, as described under No. 27R118, except this garment comes in black. Sizes, 36 to 44 inches breast measure.
No. 27R119 Price, each....................$2.75

Empire Express Coat, $2.75.

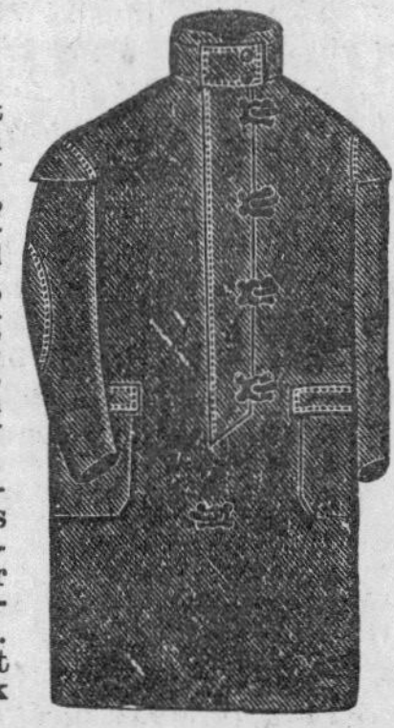

Our Empire Express Coat is the best black oil coat in existence. Especially adapted for car drivers, teamsters, motormen, expressmen, policemen and firemen. Extra heavy, guaranteed strictly waterproof; and in the making of this garment no details, however small, have been overlooked. Has the new patent automatic fasteners, extra high soft flannel collar, large outside pockets with flaps; double throughout. No better material or better made coat can possibly be had at any price. Sizes, 36 to 44 inches breast measure. **Comes in black only.**
No. 27R120 Price, each....................$2.75

Men's Long Black Oil Double Slicker.

This coat is made from extra quality black waterproof oil slicker cloth. It is doubled throughout. You cannot buy a better coat, or one that would give any more service or satisfaction. Second or third quality oil clothing is undesirable, when you can get the best from us at a less or lower price than the inferior goods are sold at elsewhere. Sizes, 34 to 44 inches breast measure.
No. 27R121 Price.... $1.85

Men's Long Yellow Oil Double Slicker.

This coat is made and finished exactly the same as above black oil slicker, only this coat is yellow. Warranted strictly waterproof. Sizes, 36 to 44 inches breast measure.
No. 27R122 Price, each....................$1.85

Men's Heavy Oil Yellow Frocks.

Men's Heavy Oil Frock Coats are worn by miners, fishermen, etc. They reach to the knees and can be worn with apron string or rubber hip boots, as desired. **Warranted strictly waterproof; doubled throughout;** extra stay at shoulders and elbow. Thoroughly reliable in every way. Sizes, 36 to 44 inches breast measure.
No. 27R123 Price...$1.40

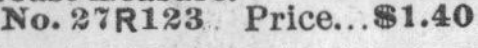

Men's Heavy Oil Black Frocks.

This coat is made just the same as the yellow coat above, except it comes in black. Sizes, 36 to 44 inches breast measure.
No. 27R124 Price, each....................$1.40

Men's Yellow Oil Jackets.

These jackets are made as shown in illustration. Made from heavy yellow oil slicker; double throughout. **Warranted waterproof. The best garment of its kind on the market.** Sizes, 36 to 44 inches breast measure. Average length, 30 inches.
No. 27R125 Price, each...90c

No. 27R126 Men's Black Oil Jackets, same as above, only black. Price, each....................90c

Men's Heavy Double Apron Yellow Oil Pants.

Made as shown in illustration with apron and shoulder straps. Extra well and thoroughly made throughout. Warranted waterproof.
No. 27R127 Price, per pair....................90c

Men's Heavy Double Apron Black Oil Pants.

Made exactly the same as above, except this number is made in black.
No. 27R128 Price, per pair....................90c

Men's Yellow or Black Oil String Pants.

Made double throughout. Reinforced in crotch and waist. Riveted zinc buttons on fly. **Warranted waterproof.**
No. 27R129 Price, per pair, 90c
Men's Black Oil String Pants. Same as above, only black.
No. 27R130 Price, per pair. 90c

GIVE CATALOGUE NUMBER IN FULL WHEN YOU WRITE YOUR ORDER

Squam Sou'westers.

Men's Yellow Oiled Hats Made same as illustration. Cloth lined; warranted waterproof.
No. 27R131 Price, each....25c
Men's Black Oiled Hats. Same as above, only in black.
No. 27R132 Price, each...25c

Manhattan Oil Compound

This compound is used for recoating clothing, and may be applied with a sponge or brush. You can make oil clothing yourself with this compound. It is an excellent thing to have on hand. Every farmer should have a can of this oil compound on hand. It comes in pint cans.
No. 27R133 Price. yellow, per pint can....... 25c
Black Oil Compound. Same as above, only the mixture is black instead of yellow.
No. 27R134 Price, black, per pint can.........25c

LAXETTE WATERPROOF CLOTH GARMENTS.

THE NEW WATERPROOF LAXETTE COATS are fast becoming the popular waterproof garment, which is only natural, as this cloth makes a raincoat for wet weather, a dress spring and fall overcoat for nice weather, a coat that can be worn at any time or place in nearly all climates with perfect comfort and satisfaction to the wearer.

WHAT IS LAXETTE CLOTH. It is an all wool material in a medium weight goods, suitable for a waterproof coat or a spring and fall overcoat. The cloth is treated by a new chemical solution which renders the surface as well as each fiber of the fabric waterproof to the extent that it will withstand any ordinary rain. This treatment in no way affects the appearance, quality or texture of the material. No one would be able to distinguish the difference between two pieces of goods, one waterproofed by this new Laxette treatment, the other untreated, yet the treated cloth would be water repellent. In introducing this new waterproof cloth we wish to say that we have fully investigated its merits. If our customers will order these coats and use them for just the kind of wear for which they are intended, everyone getting a Laxette garment will surely proclaim the merits of this goods as a dress waterproof coat, a spring and fall overcoat, a splendid wearing dressy waterproof garment suitable for all kinds of reasonable wear; not intended or suitable for very heavy, rough usage in such work as teaming, lumbering, heavy farm work, etc., where a slicker or heavy gum or duck coat would be better adapted. With the exception of No. 27R150 coat at $6.00, we make men's Laxette waterproof coats to special order. We make them in our own tailoring department after your order is received, according to the measurements sent us. We thus furnish in this line perfect fitting, up to date garments in either of the two styles illustrated below. To introduce these new Laxette garments we will mail free of expense samples of the fabric. (Ask for samples of Laxette waterproof coats.)

MEASUREMENTS. Use one of our regular tailoring order blanks for mackintosh or overcoat; measurement should be taken exactly the same as for overcoat or mackintosh. We will make garment the proper length according to your height, which should always be given, also weight. Laxette coats should be made from 46 to 52 inches long, depending on the height of the wearer.

STYLE No. 129

Laxette Gray Waterproof Garment.

This waterproof coat is made from a medium weight quality, dark gray wool Laxette cloth. This coat is adapted for any reasonable wear, as a waterproof garment or spring and fall overcoat. This is a ready made coat (the only one we list in Laxette cloth which we carry in stock), can be had only in style No. 129, cut full 48 inches long, slanting raglan pockets, velvet collar, wide facing, turn up cuffs, a well made gray, wool raincoat, to be had only in sizes 34, 36, 38, 40, 42, 44 and 46.
No. 27R150 Price, for coat..........$6.00

Laxette Dark Brown Mixed Waterproof Garment.

This cloth is a medium weight, dark brown and small pin head, gold mixed Laxette waterproof fabric, all wool. Will make a most handsome waterproof or spring and fall overcoat. Can be had in either style, No. 129 or 132. We make this coat to your order with wide facing, double shoulders, iron cloth sleeve lining, a garment for rain or shine. The most comfortable and satisfactory coat you can get for light wear. Sizes, 34 to 42.
No. 27R151 Price for coat....................$8.00

Dark Gray Mixed Covert Laxette Cloth Garment.

This is a very fine all wool closely woven, dark gray mixed Laxette waterproof cloth, a most desirable pattern in dark gray with almost invisible interwoven threads of dark green and red. Will make a most handsome rain or spring overcoat, a dress waterproof coat in either style No. 129 or No. 132. If you wish to see a sample, ask for samples of Laxette waterproof coats. Sizes 34 to 42.
No. 27R152 Price for coat....................$10.00

Dark Gray All Wool Vicuna Laxette Cloth.

This plain dark gray Vicuna cloth will make a rich, fine appearing, waterproof garment, good weight, just the thing for a handsome spring and fall waterproof overcoat. Cut to your measure, made to your order, sleeves lined with Skinner's guaranteed satin, wide facing, double throughout shoulders, a coat to keep you dry in wet weather and a dress overcoat in fine weather. Sizes, 34 to 42.
No. 27R153 Price for coat in style 129 or 132, $12.00

New Olive Green Covert Laxette Cloth.

This olive green Laxette cloth will make one of the handsomest, rainproof, spring overcoats of any number in our line. This same goods is used by the finest city tailors for coats at double our price. We make this coat to your measure, make it with wide facings, double shoulder, satin sleeve lining, turn up cuffs. Made in either style No. 129 or 132. Sizes, 34 to 42 inches breast measure.
No. 27R154 Price for coat....................$12.00

Dark Gray Scotch Cheviot Laxette Cloth.

This cloth is a dark gray cheviot with an almost invisible stripe effect in green and red. A most desirable pattern for a rain or spring overcoat. If you want a stylish rainproof coat, the newest and latest thing, order this or some other number in our rainproof Laxette cloth, cut to your measure, made to your order in either style No. 129 or 132. Sizes, 34 to 42 inches breast measure.
No. 27R155 Price for coat....................$12.00

STYLE No. 132.

Our Finest Dark Plain Gray All Worsted Laxette Cloth.

We cut to your measure a waterproof coat made from this fine pure worsted Laxette cloth fabric for $10.00 less than coats of this same material is sold for by large city retail clothing houses. The usual retail price is from $25.00 to $30.00. To introduce these new waterproof fabrics we are making them to special order for our customers at the actual cost to make with but one small profit added. We use pure satin sleeve lining in this coat, wide facing, velvet or plain collar as desired, a perfect man tailored coat to shed rain, snow, wind or sunshine. Style No. 129 or 132. Sizes, 34 to 42 inches breast measure.
No. 27R156 Price, coat..........$15.00

$2.00 EXTRA FOR SIZES LARGER THAN 42 INCHES CHEST MEASURE.

MACKINTOSHES

QUALITY AND PRICE.

Our prices on mackintoshes are the lowest ever quoted by any house selling direct to the consumer. When you purchase a mackintosh from us you usually pay less than your local merchant can buy them for in quantities, and in no instance do you pay more. **Every mackintosh sold by us represents the best that can possibly be made for the price.** A fine or high grade mackintosh of course will give better and more lasting service than a cheap or ordinary coat. We, therefore, recommend in particular our better grades, but all the low priced mackintoshes quoted by us will give reasonable satisfaction in every instance, and in order to get the best results we append herewith, a few rules or suggestions by which the wearer will invariably obtain entire satisfaction.

HOW TO GET THE BEST RESULTS FROM A MACKINTOSH.

Don't clean with gasoline. Use cold water only.

Don't hang next to a chimney or fireplace. When convenient spread out the coat to dry.

Don't fold up and put under a wagon seat when wet. We warrant our mackintoshes to give entire satisfaction, but cannot warrant against abuse.

Avoid getting oil or grease on your garment, because it will in time separate the two textures, eventually causing garment to leak.

Dampness in Shoulders and Back.

Do not immediately jump at the conclusion that your mackintosh leaks if the lining of the mackintosh should become moist on the inside up about the shoulders and back. This condition almost invariably obtains because the mackintosh cloth is not porous as is other clothing, permitting ventilation, and it therefore causes some condensation of air, which makes the mackintosh lining damp or the coat worn underneath sometimes quite moist.

Loose Fitting Mackintoshes Always Prove More Satisfactory.

Because when tight fitting, the seams are sometimes strained, causing the coat to leak. We, therefore, recommend loose fitting mackintoshes.

WE SELL SATISFACTORY MACKINTOSHES. All mackintoshes sold by us are strictly reliable garments, but too much is sometimes expected of them. (See rules above for preserving mackintoshes.) All cloths made up into mackintoshes are of tested qualities and selected for the making of mackintoshes because of their particular suitability, and will prove a thorough protection from rain under ordinary or severe storms. However, in extraordinary storms or continuous all-day rains, it is possible for the rain to penetrate the best mackintoshes made, in some degree. This is due to the fact that the surface cloth holds some water, namely, it becomes saturated, and if it remains in this condition for many hours, some dampness may be observed on the inside. **For continuous heavy rain storm, an oil slicker or heavy rubber surface coat will be found more satisfactory, but for all general purposes there is no other garment that will be found better than a mackintosh.**

WE ARE RECOGNIZED AS HEADQUARTERS ON MACKINTOSHES. We sell more of these garments than any other house in this city. Our immense volume of business enables us to buy to the very best advantage and our prices, quality considered, will be found below any competition. While we require cash in full with all orders, every garment goes out with our guarantee that it will prove satisfactory in every way or it can be returned to us and your money will be immediately refunded. You are perfectly safe in sending cash with your order. Inquire about us among your own neighbors. Read what our bankers say on pages 12 and 13.

SAMPLES OF MACKINTOSHES.

MACKINTOSH SAMPLES are not considered necessary by most of our customers who prefer to save time by ordering direct from our catalogue, which gives a clear description of the goods and illustration of the style.

HOW TO TAKE MEASURE.

ALL AROUND BREAST. Taken over inside coat, close up under arms.
Correct height......feet. Correct weight......pounds.
Age......years.

SIZES FURNISHED. Our men's mackintoshes come regularly in sizes 34, 36, 38, 40, 42, 44, 46 and 48 inches breast measure. All styles average 52 inches in length.

EXTRA LARGE SIZES, that is above 48 inches breast measure, and all mackintoshes of unusual proportions or styles other than quoted, must be made to order, for which we charge $2.00 extra. Special orders require about two weeks' time in making.

STYLE 120. Men's Single Breasted Mackintosh with detachable cape. This style mackintoshes are all made exactly as shown in illustration.

STYLE 122. Represents our Men's Double Breasted Box Coat Mackintosh. All coats listed under Style 122 are made exactly as the illustration shows.

STYLE 123. Represents our Men's Storm Fly Front Ulster. See illustration.

STYLE 125. Represents a beautiful illustration of a Spring or Fall Top Coat.

HOW THEY ARE MADE. Our mackintoshes are made by the best manufacturers in this country under careful supervision, and cut full size and length, and are not skimped in any part. The proofing and vulcanizing are of the most modern processes, are practically odorless, and we warrant every coat to give **entire satisfaction.**

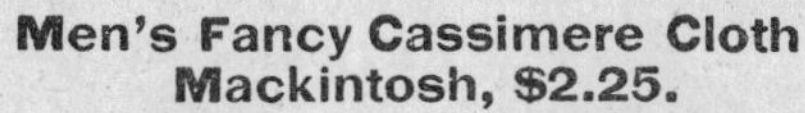

Men's Fancy Cassimere Cloth Mackintosh, $2.25.

Fancy brown cloth, small check, very genteel. Style 122, has fancy woven lining, making a good medium weight coat. **Sizes, 34 to 48 inches breast measure.**

No. 27R200 Price for Men's Double Breasted Box Coat, Style 122. **$2.25**

STYLE 122

Our $1.75 Tan Covert Box Coat.

Made from stylish, heavy weight tan colored covert waterproof cloth. The lining is a modest design, fancy plaid, which makes a serviceable double texture mackintosh. Double breasted style, velvet collar, three pockets, double stitched throughout and ventilations under arms. Full size and length. **Sizes, 34 to 48 inches breast measure.**

No. 27R202 Price for Men's Double Breasted Box Coat, Style 122 ....**$1.75**

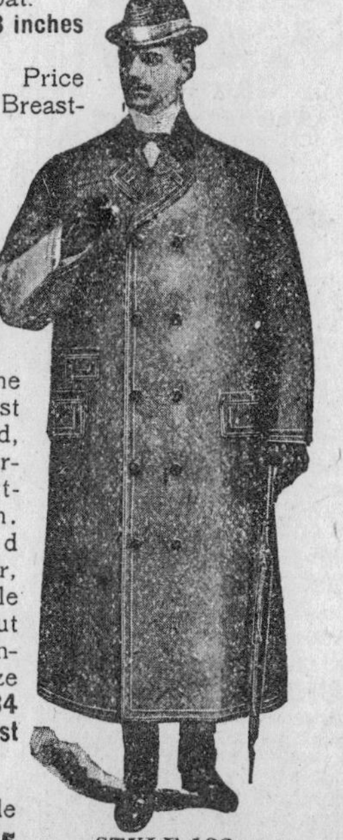

STYLE 122

Men's Special Style Mackintosh, $1.75.

Serviceable as a light weight overcoat. Men's Fine Tan Cotton Covert Mackintosh, double texture, of a style especially suited to spring or fall wear. It is made in the usual box coat style in overcoat length, averaging about 41 inches. The lining is a neat fancy plaid, made with velvet collar and two pockets, wide facing, double sewed throughout, ventilations under arms. **Single breasted fly front, made like a regular light weight top coat. Sizes, 34 to 48 inches breast measure.**

No. 27R204 Price for Men's Single Breasted Fly Front, Style 125 ....**$1.75**

STYLE 125

Heavy Storm Ulster Mackintosh, $3.25.

A heavy Mackintosh for the use of the farmer, stockman, teamster, motorman or any man whose occupation subjects him to extreme exposure. The entire coat is of special construction, designed for rough service, and is strong and durable. Average weight, between 6 and 7 pounds. The surface cloth is of heavy tan covert cloth and the lining of heavy tan color sheeting. The two are cemented together with a special process compound. Made with a large storm collar and wide storm fly front, which closes with ball and socket fasteners, and has draw buckles on the sleeves. Large flaps over pockets, ventilations under arms. Length, 54 inches. **Sizes, 34 to 48 inches breast measure.**

No. 27R206 Price for Men's Ulster Mackintosh, Style 123...**$3.25**

STYLE 123

...n's Fine All Wool Cashmere Mackintoshes, $4.50.

Light weight, suitable for spring and fall. In navy blue, with new design fancy woven plaid lining. A staple, dressy, neat coat, sure to please and give entire satisfaction. The woven lining adds greatly to its durability and appearance; velvet collar and three pockets; made in Styles 120 and 122. **Sizes, 34 to 48 inches breast measure.**

No. 27R208 Price for Men's Detachable Cape Coat, double sewed, Style 120............**$4.50**

No. 27R210 Price for Men's Double Breasted Box Mackintosh, sewed, strapped and cemented seams, Style 122..........................**$4.50**

Black All Wool Tricot Cape Mackintosh, $3.50.

STYLE 120

For $3.50 we furnish Men's Mackintosh Coats in Style 120, Detachable Cape, as shown in illustration, made from one of the finest all wool black tricot mackintosh fabrics on the market. It is lined with a medium dark fancy plaid cloth. The garments are cut full length and full size, trimmed with velvet collar, deep facing, waterproof pockets, sanitary arm ventilators. Thoroughly first class work throughout.

No. 27R212 Price for Men's Detachable Cape Mackintosh, Style 120.............**$3.50**

Navy Blue Double Breasted Tricot Mackintosh, $3.95.

This Mackintosh is made Double Breasted Box Coat, like Style 122. Is cut full length and full size, lined throughout with a special mackintosh lining, and is one of the strongest values ever offered by this or any other house. All seams are sewed, strapped and cemented, sanitary arm ventilators. Two large and one change pocket and velvet collar.

No. 27R214 Price for Men's Double Breasted Box Coat in Navy Blue, Style 122.... ....**$3.95**

Our New Rainproof Overcoat, $5.00

STYLE 115

At $5.00 we offer this, our New Style Raglan Pocket Waterproof Overcoat, as one of the most stylish raincoats of the season. Made of extra heavy Oxford gray melton cloth, with fancy plaid felt lining. Single breasted fly front, large velvet collar, and thoroughly waterproof. The pockets are at the side, as shown in illustration, and are made so the wearer can gain access to the trouser pockets without the necessity of unbuttoning the overcoat, which special feature it has over the old style pockets. Order one of these special waterproof overcoats, and if you don't think we have saved you $5.00, return it to us and we will cheerfully refund your money, together with transportation charges. Color, Oxford gray only. Sizes, 34 to 48 inches breast measure.

No. 27R216 Price for Men's Single Breasted Rainproof Overcoat, Style 115..............**$5.00**

Men's All Wool Brown Covert Mackintosh at $4.50.

STYLE 122

At $4.50 we furnish this reliable All Wool Covert Mackintosh, made with a fancy woven lining, in Style 122 as shown in illustration. The cloth is of a fine texture, all wool, woven especially for the manufacture of mackintoshes, and invariably gives entire satisfaction Average length, 52 inches. Velvet collar, ventilations under arms; sewed, strapped and cemented seams. Sizes, 34 to 48 inches breast measure. Give size, catalogue and style number in order.

No. 27R218 Price for Men's Double Breasted Box Coat, Style 122 .... **$4.50**

Dark Oxford Gray All Wool Mackintosh, $4.50.

STYLE 122

Men's Fine Oxford Gray All Wool Mackintosh, made in Style 122, as described below. The Oxford gray wool cloth is much in favor for outer garments of every kind, particularly mackintoshes. The lining is light weight, making this a particularly suitable garment for spring and fall wear. It is a strictly high grade waterproof mackintosh, very dressy, and would certainly please any well dressed man.

Style 122 is made double breasted box style (see illustration), with velvet collar; three pockets; sewed, strapped and cemented seams; ventilations under arms.

We can please you with a mackintosh of this kind. **Sizes, 34 to 48 inches breast measure.**

No. 27R220 Price for Double Breasted Box Coat, Style 122...................... **$4.50**

Our Handsome Light Color All Wool Tan Kersey Mackintosh, $8.50.

For $8.50 we furnish one of the handsomest coats of the season. Made up equal to coats selling at double this price. It is made of a very light color tan all wool kersey cloth, with fancy plaid lining which harmonizes with the outside cloth; wide velvet collar sanitary arm ventilators; white pearl buttons; two large and one change pocket outside, one inside breast pocket; sewed, strapped and cemented seams throughout. **You will not find a handsomer coat in any establishment.** For men wishing a stylish, swell coat, we cannot recommend this one too highly. Sizes, 34 to 48 inches breast measure.

No. 27R226 Price for Men's Double Breasted Box Coat, Style 122 only................**$8.50**

Men's All Wool Tan Covert Mackintosh, $5.00.

STYLE 122

At $5.00 we furnish this reliable All Wool Covert Mackintosh, made with a fancy woven lining in Style 122, as shown in illustration. The cloth is a fine texture all wool, woven especially for the manufacture of mackintoshes and invariably gives entire satisfaction. Average length, 52 inches. Velvet collar, ventilations under arms; sewed, strapped and cemented seams, two large and one change pockets. Sizes 34 to 48 inches breast measure. Give size, catalogue number and style in order.

No. 27R222 Price for Men's Double Breasted Box Coat, Style 122......**$5.00**

Men's Black Wool Covert Mackintosh, $5.00.

STYLE 122

At $5.00 we furnish Men's Fine All Wool Black Covert Mackintoshes, made with handsome design woven plaid lining. The cloth used in this coat is one of the most reliable known to manufacturers of mackintoshes and invariably gives entire satisfaction. The lining is strong and heavy, adding to the durability and practical value of the garment. Made in Style 122 only. Average length, 52 inches; three pockets, ventilations under arms, large velvet collar, sewed, strapped and cemented seams throughout. Sizes, 34 to 48 inches breast measure.

No. 27R224 Price for Men's Double Breasted Box Coat, Style 122 .... **$5.00**

STYLE 122

DON'T FAIL

To Read Our Descriptions of Our

NEW LAXETTE WATERPROOF COATS

FOR MEN.

MADE WITHOUT RUBBER.

Men's Oxford Gray Golf Lined Heavy Mackintosh, or Waterproof Overcoat, $12.00.

Men's Extra Fine and Extra Heavy Mackintosh, or Waterproof Overcoat. Made of fine smooth surface Oxford gray all wool covert cloth with heavy gray plaid lining of light weight wool golf cloth, which makes up much heavier than a regular mackintosh, and will average 6 to 7 pounds in weight. Velvet collar, arm ventilation, pearl buttons, two large pockets, one change and one inside pocket; sewed, strapped and cemented seams, and fine satin lined sleeves and shoulders. **It takes the place of an overcoat and at the same time proves an efficient protector from rain and wind.** A superior, high grade mackintosh equal to any you can obtain at retail for $20.00. Sizes, 34 to 48 inches breast measure.

No. 27R228 Price for Men's Double Breasted Box Coat, Style 122 only...............**$12.00**

BOYS' MACKINTOSHES.

OUR LITTLE MEN'S MACKINTOSHES are made with the same care and finish as our men's coats, and are sure to give best of satisfaction. Read our instructions on page 1157 about care of mackintoshes In ordering, be sure to give breast measurement, height, weight and age. Remember, mackintoshes should be worn loose.

Boys' Tan Covert Mackintosh, $1.75.

STYLE 122

Boys' or Youths' Fine Tan Covert Cloth Mackintosh, made with fancy lining. A strong, serviceable, double texture mackintosh that will not show soil, will stand rough wear, and is sufficiently heavy to wear as a medium weight overcoat. Made in the double breasted box coat style, two pockets and velvet collar. Sizes, 24, 26, 28, 30, 32 and 34 inches breast measure. **For large youths order men's small sizes.**

No. 27R230 Price for Boys' Double Breasted Box Coat, Style 122....**$1.75**

Boys' Fine All Wool Covert Mackintosh, $3.50.

Boys' or Youths' Fine All Wool Tan Covert Mackintosh. A finer coat than you will find on sale in any retail establishment. A strictly high grade all wool tan covert cloth with fine fancy plaid lining; sewed, strapped and cemented seams, ventilations under arms; velvet collar; three pockets, as shown in illustration. **A coat suitable for your boy to wear instead of a regular overcoat.** A reliable rain coat that will not show soil. Sizes, 24, 26, 28, 30, 32 and 34 inches breast measure. **For large youths over 34 inches breast measure order men's small sizes.**

No. 27R235 Price, Style 122 only....**$3.50**

Boys' Cape Style Mackintoshes, $1.75.

STYLE 120

Boys' or Youths' Mackintosh, made from fancy brown check cassimere cloth. Double texture, print lining. A good, light weight, serviceable boys' rain coat at a very low price; in fact so low in price that you cannot fail to appreciate the value we give. Made of the same cloth as Men's No. 27R200, cape style only. Sizes, 24, 26, 28, 30, 32 and 34 inches breast measure. **For very large youths order men's small sizes.**

No. 27R240 Price for Boys' Detachable Cape Coat, Style 120...**$1.75**

LADIES' MACKINTOSH...

MADE IN THE REGULAR STYLES, CONSISTING OF CAPE WITH BODY BUTTONING FROM THE COLLAR DOWN TO THE BOTTOM.

THE CAPES average 26 inches in length, are always detachable. The sweep of the double breasted style will average 150 inches. **Made with one epaulet in back and velvet collar.**

THE BODY is cut full size, and will average 90 to 92 inches around the bottom.

SIZES. Busts, 32 to 42 inches; lengths, 52, 54, 56, 58, 60, 62. Extreme or disproportionate sizes must be made to order at an extra charge of $2.00, and **full amount of cash must be sent with the order**

How to Order

Give bust measure over fullest part. **MEASUREMENT: Down back to waist and on down to length required. HEIGHT AND WEIGHT. State all four measurements accurately,** and you will be pleased with a correct fit.

Ladies' Waterproof Mackintosh Capes, $1.75. Busts, 34 to 42.

Ladies' Fine Waterproof Mackintosh Capes, made in the fashionable **double breasted** style only from **blue** or **black** all wool cashmere with fancy plaid lining; trimmed with velvet collar. A very useful and serviceable cape that can be worn at any time, but particularly for rainy weather. Sizes, busts 34 to 42. **State bust measure in order.**

No. 27R255 Price, each.......................**$1.75**

Extra Quality Mackintosh Capes, $2.50.

Ladies' Fine Waterproof Mackintosh Capes, made in the fashionable **double breasted** style only, as shown in the illustration. You have your choice of two colors under this number—black fancy brocaded with fancy lining, or plain medium tan color with fancy lining. These are special values at our low price that will not fail to please and give entire satisfaction. Made with velvet collar and pearl buttons; wide facing. Sweep, about 150 inches. Sizes, 34 to 42 bust. **State bust measure in order.**

No. 27R260 Price, each.......................**$2.50**

Ladies' Blue or Black Cashmere Mackintosh, $1.95.

STYLE 176

Ladies' Fine Cotton Cashmere Mackintosh, with fancy plaid lining. **An exceptional value at our low price, which is less than the cost to your local merchant.** A serviceable, satisfactory, low priced over garment, which will not fail to give good wear. Made in double cape style only, as shown in illustration, with velvet collar. Full size in every particular. Colors, black or navy blue. Sizes, bust measure 32 to 42. Lengths, 52 to 62. **Be sure to state color and size correctly, height and weight.**

No. 27R265 Price, each **$1.95**

Ladies' Brown Check Mackintosh, $2.25.

STYLE 178

Ladies' Good Quality Mackintosh, made of fine cotton cashmere, in small brown check and fancy plaid lining. We would recommend the better qualities for durability, but this is a special value at **our low price.** Double breasted style. **Lengths, 52 to 62.**

No. 27R270 Price, each...........**$2.25**

..YOU ARE SURE OF GETTING..
SATISFACTORY GARMENTS
IF YOU ORDER FROM THIS CATALOGUE,
as we guarantee that you will receive satisfactory goods, or you may return the shipment at our expense and your money will be refunded.

Ladies' All Wool Double Cape Mackintosh, $3.25.

STYLE 176

UNDER THIS NUMBER we furnish one of the best of staple mackintoshes. **Made Style 176, from fine all wool cashmere, made especially for use in mackintoshes, with a neatly designed fancy plaid lining.** Absolutely fast in color, and never fails to give entire satisfaction. Like all our mackintoshes, they are carefully waterproofed and vulcanized, which makes them practically odorless, and they will retain their waterproof resisting quality permanently. **Double cape, Style 176,** velvet collar and buttons all the way down front from neck to bottom. Every one is made full size, and we can fit sizes 32 to 42 inches bust measure. Length, 52 to 62 inches. Made in three colors, **black, navy blue and brown. Be sure to state color and measurements correctly in your order.**

No. 27R275 Price, each............**$3.25**

Ladies' Double Breasted Wool Cashmere Mackintosh, $3.25.

THE MATERIAL from which these mackintoshes are made is the same as that in No. 27R275. It is a superior quality that never fails to give entire satisfaction. The only difference between this one and No. 27R275 is in the cape, which is of **a double breasted style 172,** made with wide facing, velvet collar, has a wide, loose fitting back, trimmed with one epaulet at the collar. This is a very fashionable style cape, cut in the same style as our highest priced mackintoshes. The body buttons from the collar down to the bottom in front, and are full size. **We cannot recommend goods of this quality too highly,** as they invariably give entire satisfaction as regards workmanship, serviceableness and appearance. Made in three colors, **black, navy blue and brown.** Sizes, bust measure, 32 to 42 inches; length, 52 to 62 inches. **State color and measurements in your order.**

STYLE 172

No. 27R280 Price, each............**$3.25**

Fine All Wool Tan Covert Mackintosh, $6.00.

STYLE 172

AT THIS EXTREMELY LOW PRICE we furnish Ladies' Fine All Wool Tan Covert Cloth Mackintosh, made with selected fancy plaid lining. This cloth is excelled by none for use in the manufacture of mackintoshes, as the color is absolutely fast, and it has proven more durable than almost any other kind. Made in extremely full size body. The cape is trimmed with pearl buttons, velvet collar, full sweep, wide facings, and has one epaulet in back. Body buttons from collar down to the bottom. **One of the most serviceable of all waterproof mackintoshes, and we guarantee them to give entire satisfaction.** Double breasted style only. Sizes, bust measure, 32 to 42 inches; lengths, 52 to 62 inches. **Color, tan only. See rules for measurement.**

No. 27R285 Price, each............**$6.00**

Ladies' Oxford Gray or Dark Brown Wool Mackintoshes, $5.75.

THESE ARE THE MOST FASHIONABLE of our fine all wool garments, and the colors, Oxford gray or dark brown, are largely in demand this season. A fine all wool cloth of standard quality, made up with fancy woven Scotch plaid lining, of special design that adds greatly to the style of this over garment. **A mackintosh that always looks well and dressy, and for stormy weather cannot be excelled, and we guarantee every one to give entire satisfaction.** Double breasted style, The cape is trimmed with velvet collar, pearl buttons, wide facing, full sweep back, trimmed with one epaulet in back at the collar band. The body buttons from collar down to the bottom. Sizes, bust measure, 32 to 42; lengths, 52 to 62 inches. See rules for measurement.

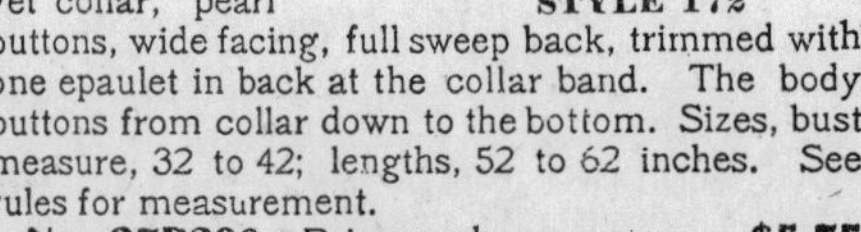

STYLE 172

No. 27R290 Price, each **$5.75**

Fancy Brown Check Mackintoshes, $6.00.

Style 172

Ladies' Fine All Wool Mackintosh, made from fancy English cheviot cloth, dark brown in color. The design is a very small plaid of black and brown mixture, in which brown predominates. It is entirely out of the usual range of mackintosh cloths and is of an unusually pleasing and select design. Lined with medium dark lining, which harmonizes with the surface cloth. **You will make no mistake in ordering this rainproof garment,** and you could not buy its equal of a local merchant for less than $10.00, as we guarantee it to give entire satisfaction. The cape is full sweep, trimmed with velvet collar, pearl buttons, wide facing, and has full, loose back and is made with one epaulet at the collar band. The body buttons from collar down to bottom. Sizes, bust measure 32 to 42 inches; lengths, 52 to 62 inches. **Always state measurements correctly.**

No. 27R293 Price, each............**$6.00**

Our Special Silk Lined Blue Cashmere Mackintosh, $6.50.

Ladies' Fine All Wool Blue Cashmere Mackintosh, made with a new bright red mercerized silk lining. Instead of being a fancy plaid design, it is of solid bright color—red only—of mercerized silk. By mercerized silk we mean a fine cotton texture treated by the Mercer process, which gives it the appearance and many of the properties of silk. It retains this surface permanently, and is much stronger and more durable than silk. **This is one of our very best novelties, which we guarantee to give entire satisfaction.** Made in double breasted style cape as style 172. Trimmed with velvet collar, pearl buttons, wide facing and full sweep back, with one epaulet at the collar. The body is full size and buttons from collar down to bottom. We especially recommend goods of this quality, for they are invariably the cheaper garments in the end. Sizes, busts 32 to 42 inches; lengths, 52 to 62 inches. See rules for measurement.

STYLE 172

No. 27R295 Price, each **$6.50**

GIRLS' OR MISSES' MACKINTOSHES.

Are Sized by Length. Sizes are 34, 36, 38, 40, 42, 44, 46, 48 and 50 inches.

HOW TO ORDER. Four measurements required: Length, age, height and weight. Girls requiring longer than 50 inches should order ladies' size. A very useful rainy weather wrap that will save its price in a short time.

Girls' or Misses' All Wool Cashmere Double Breasted Mackintoshes, $2.75.

Girls' or Misses' Double Breasted Wool Cashmere Mackintoshes. This is the same quality of standard all wool cashmere that is used in the following number and is of the most select quality known to manufacturers of mackintoshes. Fast color, and we warrant every garment to give entire satisfaction. The lining is of a neat plaid design that will not fail to please. Double breasted style is in large demand at the present time and makes a very fashionable garment for girls and misses. Trimmed with velvet collar. Body is made full size in every respect and buttons from collar down to the bottom. **Such qualities as these invariably prove cheap in the long run. Colors, navy blue or brown.** Sizes, by length, 34 to 50 inches. See rules above for measurements.

No. 27R300 Price, each............**$2.75**

Girls' or Misses' Fine All Wool Cashmere Mackintoshes, $2.75.

Girls' or Misses' Fine All Wool Cashmere Mackintoshes. These garments are made from standard wool cashmere, woven especially for making mackintoshes, and strictly fast color. Made up with a select plaid lining in **double cape style,** as shown in illustration. A more satisfactory children's garment is not to be found anywhere, and we especially recommend this quality. **Two colors only, navy blue or brown.** Sizes, lengths 34 to 50 inches. See rules above for measurements.

No. 27R305 Price, each............**$2.75**

Girls' or Misses' Mackintosh, $1.85.

Girls' or Misses' Plain Blue Fine Cotton Cashmere Mackintosh, with fancy plaid lining. Fast color. Made in double cape style only. Trimmed with velvet collar. A staple, reliable, rainproof mackintosh that will not fail to give good wear and entire satisfaction. Sizes, by length, 34 to 50 inches. See rules above for measurements.

No. 27R310 Price, each............**$1.85**

Girls' or Misses' Brown Mackintosh, $1.75.

Girls' or Misses' Fine Cotton Cashmere Mackintosh, made in double cape style, as illustrated. The cloth is a very small dark brown check with fancy plaid lining. **A serviceable girls' or misses' mackintosh at a very low price.** Double cape style only. Trimmed with velvet collar. Buttons from collar down to the bottom. Sizes, 34 to 50 inches in length. See rules above for measurements.

No. 27R315 Price, each............**$1.75**

SPECIAL BARGAINS IN LADIES' MACKINTOSH AND CAPE AND SKIRT SUITS.

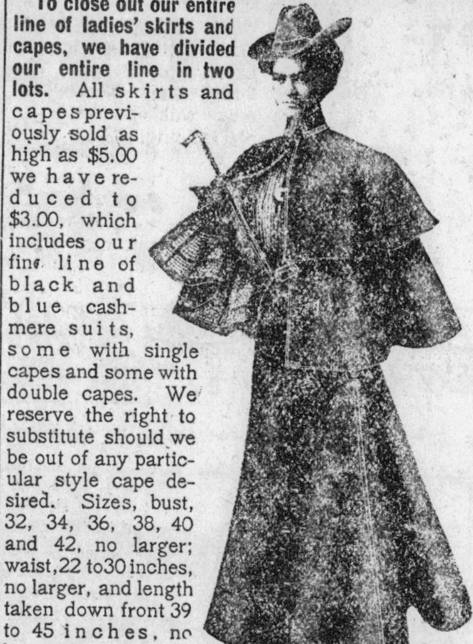

To close out our entire line of ladies' skirts and capes, we have divided our entire line in two lots. All skirts and capes previously sold as high as $5.00 we have reduced to $3.00, which includes our fine line of black and blue cashmere suits, some with single capes and some with double capes. We reserve the right to substitute should we be out of any particular style cape desired. Sizes, bust, 32, 34, 36, 38, 40 and 42, no larger; waist, 22 to 30 inches, no larger, and length taken down front 39 to 45 inches, no longer.

No. 27R320 Price, each, for skirt and cape **$3.00**

Suits of all our high grade capes and skirts that have sold as high as $9.00, and comprises all of the latest shades in black, tan, brown and novelty effects, such suits as you would have to pay your local dealer $15.00 for and you would not do any better. This suit comes only in double breasted cape, as shown in illustration. Sizes same as in lot No. 1. Bust, 32 to 42; waist, 22 to 30; length, 39 to 45.

No. 27R325 Price, each, skirt and cape........**$4.50**

THESE GARMENTS

are the same as are shown by fashionable city stores only.

OUR PRICES

are only half what is usually charged.

Ladies' Regular Fu. Mackintosh.

The success in this special mackintosh was m. we expected, and we again made arrangements with the manufacturer to have made up all ends of 50 to 100 yards into mackintoshes, and we are prepared to furnish our customers with such values as they never had before in the line of mackintoshes. **OUR SPECIAL OF-FER:** If you will leave selection to us, give color preferred and state the measurements correctly according to rules, **we guarant to send you he best b you ever received in clothing of any kind.** Owing to the variety, we cannot warrant sending two of a kind. If our selection does not please you or you do not believe that you bought the mackintosh for less than one-half the price you would have to pay elsewhere, return it to us and we will immediately refund your money. Sizes, bust, 32 to 42 inches; length, 52 to 62 inches. See rules for measurements.

No. 27R330 Price, each............**$4.50**

Ladies' High Grade Automobile Mackintosh.

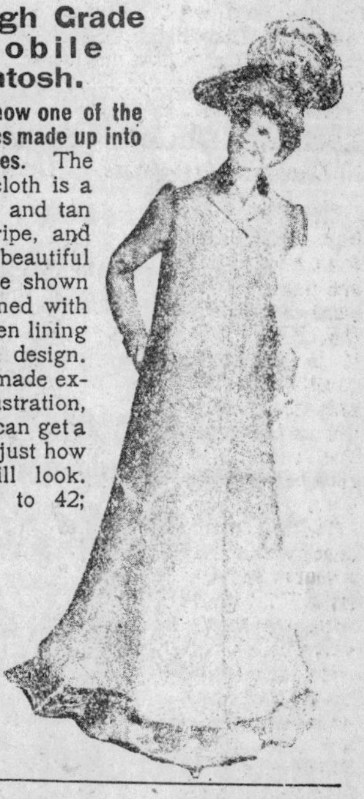

We herewith show one of the handsomest fabrics made up into ladies' automobiles. The design of this cloth is a very fine brown and tan herringbone stripe, and one of the most beautiful patterns we have shown this season. Lined with a very fine woven lining of a pretty plaid design. This garment is made exactly like illustration, from which you can get a decided idea of just how the garment will look. Sizes, bust, 32 to 42; length, 52 to 62. This style garment is generally worn two or three inches shorter than dress skirt.

No. 27R335 Price for ladies' automobile, style 133......**$6.00**

Ladies' and Misses' Automobiles.

This illustration represents our automobile coats for ladies and misses, made up of the genuine standard all wool cashmere ... st colo ... not a cheap cashm ... found their way ... that will give the ... exactly as illustrat ... maroon, with yok ... fail to state color wa

No. 27R340 P. maroon or blue, style

No. 27R345 Pr. maroon only, style 13

FURNACE DEPARTMENT.

HOUSE FURNACES $47.70 AND UPWARDS.

FOR COMPLETE WARMING AND VENTILATING OUR HOT AIR FURNACES ARE UNEXCELLED.

OUR SPECIAL PRICE LIST WILL SECURE US YOUR ORDER IF YOU ARE INTERESTED.

Do not fail to write for price list if you are building a new house, remodeling an old house or desire to put a furnace in your home.

...ACME... Coal Furnace

...AT...

$47.70,

$55.15,

$64.75

and $79.20

According to size, we offer this Acme House Heating Hot Air Furnace delivered on the cars t our factory in Northern Illinois.

sizes, portable form, Nos. 39, 43, 47 and 51.

e pots, 20, 23, 26 and 29 inches.

WO RING FIRE POTS, LARGE ASH PIT, AND ALL PARTS VERY HEAVY.

ROCKING BAR GRATES, AND LARGE DUST FLUE.

WRITE US FOR DIMENSIONS, CAPACITY AND PRICE LIST

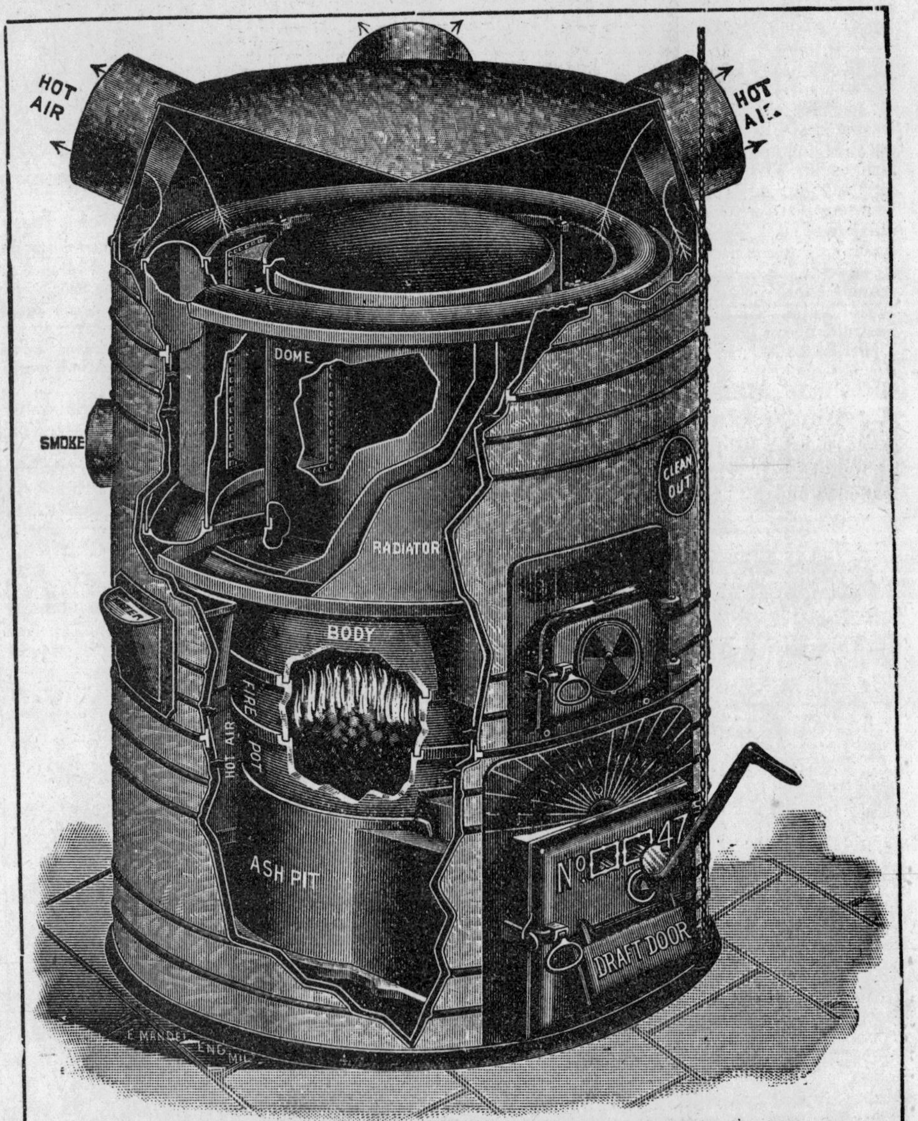

OPEN VIEW SHOWING THE CONSTRUCTION OF THIS CELEBRATED FURNACE FOR COAL.

THIS ACME WARM USE FURNACE

s shown, and at prices unheard of heretofore.

WHILE OUR PRICES OF $47.70 TO $79.20

According to size, is for the furnace as shown, we can furnish at special request any fittings such as wall pipes, round pipes, elbows, floor registers, etc., in fact everything needed to install your furnace in your house, and at prices heretofore unheard of.

P DIRECT DRAFT FURNACES, BUT ARE COMPLETE WITH CIRCULAR FLUE AND LARGE COMBUSTION DOME OVER FIRE POT.

WRITE FOR SPECIAL INFORMATION.